Sports Voice for
the Hobby
Collectors
Digest
The hobby's oldest and
largest publication

23RD EDITION   2009

Baseball
Card

PRICE GUIDE

©2009 Krause Publications, Inc., a subsidiary of F+W Media, Inc.

Published by

kp krause publications

A subsidiary of F+W Media, Inc.

700 East State Street • Iola, WI 54990-0001
715-445-2214 • 888-457-2873
www.krausebooks.com

Our toll-free number to place an order or obtain
a free catalog is (800) 258-0929.

ISSN 1549-6309

ISBN-13: 978-0-89689-722-9
ISBN-10: 0-89689-722-2

Designed by Stacy Bloch
Edited by Joe Clemens

Printed in United States of America

TABLE OF CONTENTS

B

C

L

M

P

T

U

Z

How To Use This Price Guide

This price guide has been uniquely designed to serve the needs of collectors and dealers at all levels from beginning to advanced. It provides a comprehensive guide to more than 26 years of baseball card issues, arranged so that even the most novice hobbyist can consult it with confidence and ease.

The following explanations summarize the general practices used in preparing this price guide's listings. However, because of specialized requirements which may vary from card set to card set, these must not be considered ironclad. Where these standards have been set aside, appropriate notations are usually incorporated.

ARRANGEMENT

The most important feature in identifying and pricing a baseball card is its set of origin. Therefore, the main body of this price guide, covering cards issued from 1981-date, has been alphabetically arranged within specific eras of issue according to the name by which the set is most popularly known to collectors, or by which it can be most easily identified by a person examining a card.

Among those card issuers who produced sets for more than a single year, their sets are then listed chronologically, from earliest to most recent, again within specific eras.

Within each set, the cards are listed by their designated card number, or in the absence of card numbers, alphabetically according to the last name of the player pictured. Listing numbers found in parentheses indicate the number does not appear on the card. Certain cards which fall outside the parameters of the normal card numbering for a specific set may be found at the beginning or end of the listings for that set.

VINTAGE-MODERN ISSUES

The main body of the book details modern major league baseball card issues from 1981-2008, as produced by the major national card companies. In general, prior to about 1990, this will include issues which picture one or more baseball players, usually contemporary with their playing days, printed on paper or cardboard in a variety of shapes and sizes and given away as a premium with the purchase of another product or service. After 1990 or so the definition is broadened to remove the restriction of the card as an ancillary product and to include those printed on plastic, wood, metal, etc.

IDENTIFICATION

While most modern baseball cards are well identified on front, back or both, as to date and is-

sue, such has not always been the case. In general, the back of the card is more useful in identifying the set of origin than the front. The issuer or sponsor's name will usually appear on the back since, after all, baseball cards were first produced as a promotional item to stimulate sales of other products. More often than not, that issuer's name is the name by which the set is known to collectors and under which it will be found listed in this price guide.

In some difficult cases, identifying a baseball card's general age, if not specific year of issue, can usually be accomplished by studying the biological or statistical information on the back of the card. The last year mentioned in either the biography or stats is usually the year which preceded the year of issue.

PHOTOGRAPHS

A photograph of the front of at least one representative card from virtually every set listed in this price guide has been incorporated into the listings to aid in identification.

Photographs have been printed in reduced size. The actual size of cards in each set is given in the introductory text preceding its listing, unless the card is the standard size (2.5" by 3.5").

DATING

The dating of baseball cards by year of issue on the front or back of the card itself is a relatively new phenomenon. In most cases, to accurately determine a date of issue for an unidentified card, it must be studied for clues. As mentioned, the biography, career summary or statistics on the back of the card are the best way to pinpoint a year of issue. In most cases, the year of issue will be the year after the last season mentioned on the card.

NUMBERING

While many baseball card issues as far back as the 1880s have contained card numbers assigned by the issuer to facilitate the collecting of a complete set, the practice has by no means been universal. Even today, not every set bears card numbers.

Logically, those baseball cards which were numbered by their manufacturer are presented in that numerical order within the listings of this catalog whenever possible. In a few cases, complete player checklists were obtained from earlier published sources which did not note card numbers, and so numbers have been arbitrarily assigned. Many other unnumbered issues have been assigned catalog numbers to facilitate their universal

identification within the hobby, especially when buying and selling by mail.

In all cases, numbers which have been assigned, or which otherwise do not appear on the card through error or by design, are shown in this catalog within parentheses. In virtually all cases, unless a more natural system suggested itself by the unique matter of a particular set, the assignment of numbers by the cataloging staff has been done by alphabetical arrangement of the players' last names or the card's principal title.

Significant collectible variations for any particular card are noted within the listings by the application of a suffix letter. In instances of variations, the suffix "a" is assigned to the variation which was created first, when it can be so identified.

NAMES

The identification of a player by full name on the front of his baseball card has been a common practice only since the 1920s. Prior to that, the player's last name and team were the usual information found on the card front.

As a general — though not universally applied — practice, the listings in this volume present the player's name exactly as it appears on the front of the card. If the player's full name only appears on the back, rather than on the front of the card, the listing may correspond to that designation.

Cards which contain misspelled first or last names, or even wrong initials, will have included in their listings the incorrect information, with a correction accompanying in parentheses. This extends, also, to cases where the name on the card does not correspond to the player actually pictured.

In some cases, to facilitate efficient presentations, to maintain ease of use for the reader, or to allow for proper computer sorting of data, a player's name or card title may be listed other than as it appears on the card.

GRADING

It is necessary that some sort of card grading standard be used so that buyer and seller (especially when dealing by mail) may reach an informed agreement on the value of a card.

Modern issues, which have been preserved in top condition in considerable number, are listed only in grade of Near Mint-to-Mint (NM/M), reflective of the fact that there exists in the current market little or no demand for cards of the recent past in lower grades.

Values for lower-grade cards from 1981-date may be generally figured by using a figure of 75 percent of the Mint price for Near Mint specimens, and 40 percent of the Mint price for Excellent cards.

For the benefit of the reader, we present herewith the grading guide which was originally formulated in 1981 by Baseball Cards magazine and Sports Collectors Digest, and has been continually refined since that time.

These grading definitions have been used in the pricing of cards in this book, but they are by no means a universally accepted grading standard.

The potential buyer of a baseball card should keep that in mind when encountering cards of nominally the same grade, but at a price which differs widely from that quoted in this book.

Ultimately, the collector himself must formulate his own personal grading standards in deciding whether cards available for purchase meet the needs of his own collection.

Mint (MT): A perfect card. Well-centered, with parallel borders which appear equal to the naked eye. Four sharp, square corners. No creases, edge dents, surface scratches, paper flaws, loss of luster, yellowing or fading, regardless of age. No imperfectly printed card — out of register, badly cut or ink flawed — or card stained by contact with gum, wax or other substances can be considered truly Mint, even if new out of the pack. Generally, to be considered in Mint condition, a card's borders must exist in a ratio of 60/40 side to side and top to bottom.

Near Mint (NR MT): A nearly perfect card. At first glance, a Near Mint card appears perfect; upon closer examination, however, a minor flaw will be discovered. On well-centered cards, three of the four corners must be perfectly sharp; only one corner shows a minor imperfection upon close inspection. A slightly off-center card with one or more borders being noticeably unequal — but no worse than in a ratio of 70/30 S/S or T/B — would also fit this grade.

Excellent (EX): Corners are still fairly sharp with only moderate wear. Card borders may be off center as much as 80/20. No creases. May have very minor gum, wax or product stains, front or back. Surfaces may show slight loss of luster from rubbing across other cards.

Very Good (VG): Shows obvious handling. Corners rounded and/or perhaps showing minor creases. Other minor creases may be visible. Surfaces may exhibit loss of luster, but all printing is intact. May show major gum, wax or other packaging stains. No major creases, tape marks or extraneous markings or writing. All four borders visible, though the ratio may be as poor as 95/5. Exhibits honest wear.

Good (G): A well-worn card, but exhibits no intentional damage or abuse. May have major or multiple creases. Corners rounded well beyond the border. A good card will generally sell for about 50 percent the value of a card in Very Good condition.

Fair (F or Fr.): Shows excessive wear, along with damage or abuse. Will show all the wear characteristics of a Good card, along with such damage as thumb tack holes in or near margins, evidence of having been taped or pasted, perhaps small tears around the edges, or creases so heavy as to break the cardboard. Backs may

show minor added pen or pencil writing, or be missing small bits of paper. Still, basically a complete card. A Fair card will generally sell for 50 percent the value of a Good specimen.

Poor (P): A card that has been tortured to death. Corners or other areas may be torn off. Card may have been trimmed, show holes from a paper punch or have been used for BB gun practice. Front may have extraneous pen or pencil writing, or other defacement. Major portions of front or back design may be missing. Not a pretty sight.

In addition to these terms, collectors may encounter intermediate grades, such as NM-MT or EX-MT. These cards usually have characteristics of both the lower and higher grades, and are generally priced midway between those two values.

Grading and pricing reflected in this book are for cards which have not been authenticated, graded and encapsulated by one of the third-party certification services. Cards which have been "slabbed" by these services generally sell for a premium above the price which a "raw" card will bring.

ROOKIE CARDS

While the status (and automatic premium value) which a player's rookie card carries has fallen and risen in recent years, and though the hobby still has not reached a universal definition of a rookie card, many significant rookie cards are noted in this price guide's listings by the use of **RC** or **(RC)**. For purposes of this catalog, a player's rookie card is considered to be any card in a licensed set from a major manufacturer in the first year in which that player appears on a card. Beginning with products issued in 2006, cards with a **(RC)** logo indicate the featured player has a rookie card issued prior to that year.

VALUATIONS

Values quoted in this book represent the current retail market at the time of compilation (January, 2008). The quoted values are the result of a unique system of evaluation and verification created by the price guide's editors. Utilizing specialized computer analysis and drawing upon recommendations provided through their daily involvement in the publication of the hobby's leading sports collectors' periodicals, as well as the input of consultants, dealers and collectors, each listing is, in the final analysis, the interpretation of that data by one or more of the editors.

It should be stressed, however, that this book is intended to serve only as an aid in evaluating cards; actual market conditions are constantly changing. This is especially true of the cards of current players, whose on-field performance during the course of a season can greatly affect the value of their cards — upwards or downwards. Because of the extremely volatile nature of new card prices, especially high-end issues, we have chosen not to include the very latest releases such as premium-

price brands from the major companies, feeling it is better to have no listings at all for those cards than to have inaccurate values in print.

Because this volume is intended to reflect the national market, users will find regional price variances caused by demand differences. Cards of Astros slugger Jeff Bagwell will, for instance, often sell at prices greater than quoted herein at shops and shows in the Houston area. Conversely, his cards may be acquired at a discount from these valuations when purchased on the East or West Coast.

Publication of this book is not intended as a solicitation to buy or sell the listed cards by the editors, publishers or contributors.

Again, the values here are retail prices — what a collector can expect to pay when buying a card from a dealer. The wholesale price, that which a collector can expect to receive from a dealer when selling cards, will be significantly lower.

Most dealers operate on a 100 percent mark-up, generally paying about 50 percent of a card's retail value for cards which they are purchasing for inventory. On some high-demand cards, dealers will pay up to 75 percent or even 100 percent or more of retail value, anticipating continued price increases. Conversely, for many low-demand cards, such as common players' cards, dealers may pay as little as 10 percent or even less of retail with many base-brand cards of recent years having no resale value at all.

SETS

Collectors may note that the complete set prices for newer issues quoted in these listings are usually significantly lower than the total of the value of the individual cards which comprise the set. This reflects two factors in the baseball card market. First, a seller is often willing to take a lower composite price for a complete set as a "volume discount" and to avoid carrying in inventory a large number of common player or other lower-demand cards.

Second, to a degree, the value of common cards can be said to be inflated as a result of having a built-in overhead charge to justify the dealer's time in sorting cards, carrying them in stock and filling orders. This accounts for the fact that even new base-brand baseball cards, which cost the dealer around one cent each when bought in bulk, carry individual price tags of five cents or higher.

Some set prices shown, especially for old cards in top condition, are merely theoretical in that it is unlikely that a complete set exists in that condition. In general among older cards the range of conditions found in even the most painstakingly assembled complete set make the set values quoted useful only as a starting point for price negotiations.

ERRORS/VARIATIONS

It is often hard for the beginning collector to understand that an error on a baseball card, in

and of itself, does not usually add premium value to that card. It is usually only when the correcting of an error in the subsequent printing creates a variation that premium value attaches to an error.

Minor errors, such as wrong stats or personal data, misspellings, inconsistencies, etc. — usually affecting the back of the card — are very common, especially in recent years. Unless a corrected variation was also printed, these errors are not noted in the listings of this book because they are not generally perceived by collectors to have premium value.

Many scarce and valuable variations are included in these listings because they are widely collected and often have significant premium value.

Beginning in the early 1990s, some card companies began production of their basic sets at more than one printing facility. This frequently resulted in numerous minor variations. Combined with a general decline in quality control from the mid-1980s through the early 1990s, which allowed unprecedented numbers of uncorrected error cards to be released, this caused a softening of collector interest in errors and variations. Despite the fact most of these modern variations have no premium value, they are listed here as a matter of record.

COUNTERFEITS/REPRINTS

As the value of baseball cards has risen, certain cards and sets have become too expensive for the average collector to obtain. This, along with changes in the technology of color printing, has given rise to increasing numbers of counterfeit and reprint cards.

While both terms describe essentially the same thing — a modern day copy which attempts to duplicate as closely as possible an original baseball card — there are differences which are important to the collector.

Generally, a counterfeit is made with the intention of deceiving somebody into believing it is genuine, thus paying large amounts of money for it. The counterfeiter takes every pain to try to make their fakes look as authentic as possible. In recent years, the 1963 Pete Rose, 1984 Donruss Don Mattingly and more than 100 superstar cards of the late 1960s-early 1990s have been counterfeited — many of which were quickly detected because of the differences in quality of cardboard on which they were printed.

A reprint, on the other hand, while it may have been made to look as close as possible to an original card, is made with the intention of allowing collectors to buy them as substitutes for cards they may never be otherwise able to afford. The big difference is that a reprint is generally marked as such, usually on the back of the card.

In other cases, like the Topps 1952 reprint set and 1953-54 Archives issues, the replicas are printed in a size markedly different from the originals. Collectors should be aware, however, that unscrupulous persons will sometimes cut off or otherwise obliterate the distinguishing word — "Reprint," "Copy," — or modern copyright date on the back of a reprint card in an attempt to pass it as genuine.

A collector's best defense against reprints and counterfeits is to acquire a knowledge of the look and feel of genuine baseball cards of various eras and issues.

Abbreviation Key

OPS: Overprinted "Promotional Sample"

ED: Expansion Draft

AS: All-Star

HL: Hit List or Highlight

RC: Rookie Class

RC or (RC): Rookie Card

SP: Short Print

DT: Double Team

CC: Curtain Calls

GLR: Gold Leaf Rookies

TP: Top Performers

FF: Future Foundation

DK: Diamond King

RR: Rated Rookie

DP: Double Print

IA: In Action

PC: Promo Card

SR: Star Rookie

MODERN MAJOR LEAGUE CARDS
(1981-2008)

The vast majority of cards listed in this section were issued between 1981 and late 2008 and feature major league players only. The term "card" is used rather loosely as in this context it is construed to include virtually any series of cardboard or paper product, of whatever size and/or shape, depicting baseball players. Further, "cards" printed on wood, metal, plastic and other materials are either by their association with other issues or by their compatibility in size with the current 2-1/2" x 3-1/2" card standard also listed here.

Because modern cards are generally not popularly collected in lower grades, cards in this section carry only a Near Mint-to-Mint (NM/M) value quote. In general, post-1980 cards which grade Near Mint (NM) will retail at about 75% of the NM/M price, while Excellent (EX) condition cards bring 40%.

B

1988 Bazooka

	NM/M
Complete Set (22):	3.00
Common Player:	.10
1 George Bell	.10
2 Wade Boggs	.50
3 Jose Canseco	.25
4 Roger Clemens	.60
5 Vince Coleman	.10
6 Eric Davis	.10
7 Tony Fernandez	.10
8 Dwight Gooden	.10
9 Tony Gwynn	.50
10 Wally Joyner	.10
11 Don Mattingly	.60
12 Willie McGee	.10
13 Mark McGwire	.75
14 Kirby Puckett	.50
15 Tim Raines	.10
16 Dave Righetti	.10
17 Cal Ripken, Jr.	1.00
18 Juan Samuel	.10
19 Ryne Sandberg	.50
20 Benny Santiago	.10
21 Darryl Strawberry	.10
22 Todd Worrell	.10

1989 Bazooka

	NM/M
Complete Set (22):	3.00
Common Player:	.10
1 Tim Belcher	.10
2 Damon Berryhill	.10
3 Wade Boggs	.75
4 Jay Buhner	.10

5	Jose Canseco	.25
6	Vince Coleman	.10
7	Cecil Espy	.10
8	Dave Gallagher	.10
9	Ron Gant	.10
10	Kirk Gibson	.10
11	Paul Gibson	.10
12	Mark Grace	.10
13	Tony Gwynn	.75
14	Rickey Henderson	.50
15	Orel Hershiser	.10
16	Gregg Jefferies	.10
17	Ricky Jordan	.10
18	Chris Sabo	.10
19	Gary Sheffield	.40
20	Darryl Strawberry	.10
21	Frank Viola	.10
22	Walt Weiss	.10

1990 Bazooka

	NM/M
Complete Set (22):	3.00
Common Player:	.10
1 Kevin Mitchell	.10
2 Robin Yount	.40
3 Mark Davis	.10
4 Bret Saberhagen	.10
5 Fred McGriff	.10
6 Tony Gwynn	.50
7 Kirby Puckett	.50
8 Vince Coleman	.10
9 Rickey Henderson	.40
10 Ben McDonald	.10
11 Gregg Olson	.10
12 Todd Zeile	.10
13 Carlos Martinez	.10
14 Gregg Jefferies	.10
15 Craig Worthington	.10
16 Gary Sheffield	.25
17 Greg Briley	.10
18 Ken Griffey Jr.	1.50
19 Jerome Walton	.10
20 Bob Geren	.10
21 Tom Gordon	.10
22 Jim Abbott	.10

1991 Bazooka

	NM/M
Complete Set (22):	5.00
Common Player:	.10
1 Barry Bonds	3.50
2 Rickey Henderson	.50
3 Bob Welch	.10
4 Doug Drabek	.10
5 Alex Fernandez	.10
6 Jose Offerman	.10
7 Frank Thomas	.50
8 Cecil Fielder	.10
9 Ryne Sandberg	.75
10 George Brett	1.00
11 Willie McGee	.10

12	Vince Coleman	.10
13	Hal Morris	.10
14	Delino DeShields	.10
15	Robin Ventura	.10
16	Jeff Huson	.10
17	Felix Jose	.10
18	Dave Justice	.10
19	Larry Walker	.10
20	Sandy Alomar, Jr.	.10
21	Kevin Appier	.10
22	Scott Radinsky	.10

1992 Bazooka

	NM/M
Complete Tin-Box Set (22):	16.00
Complete Set (22):	8.00
Common Player:	.25
1 Joe Adcock, Bob Lemon, Willie Mays, Vic Wertz	1.50
2 Carl Furillo, Don Newcombe, Phil Rizzuto, Hank Sauer	.25
3 Ferris Fain, John Logan, Ed Mathews, Bobby Shantz	.25
4 Yogi Berra, Del Crandall, Howie Pollett, Gene Woodling	.25
5 Richie Ashburn, Leo Durocher, Allie Reynolds, Early Wynn	.25
6 Hank Aaron, Ray Boone, Luke Easter, Dick Williams	1.50
7 Ralph Branca, Bob Feller, Rogers Hornsby, Bobby Thomson	.25
8 Jim Gilliam, Billy Martin, Orestes Minoso, Hal Newhouser	.25
9 Smoky Burgess, John Mize, Preacher Roe, Warren Spahn	.25

10	Monte Irvin, Bobo Newsom, Duke Snider, Wes Westrum	.25
11	Carl Erskine, Jackie Jensen, George Kell, Al Schoendienst	.25
12	Bill Bruton, Whitey Ford, Ed Lopat, Mickey Vernon	.25
13	Joe Black, Lew Burdette, Johnny Pesky, Enos Slaughter	.25
14	Gus Bell, Mike Garcia, Mel Parnell, Jackie Robinson	1.25
15	Alvin Dark, Dick Groat, Pee Wee Reese, John Sain	.25
16	Gil Hodges, Sal Maglie, Wilmer Mizell, Billy Pierce	.45
17	Nellie Fox, Ralph Kiner, Ted Kluszewski, Eddie Stanky	.25
18	Ewell Blackwell, Vern Law, Satchell Paige, Jim Wilson	.45
19	Lou Boudreau, Roy Face, Harvey Haddix, Bill Rigney	.25
20	Roy Campanella, Walt Dropo, Harvey Kuenn, Al Rosen	.45
21	Joe Garagiola, Robin Roberts, Casey Stengel, Hoyt Wilhelm	.25
22	John Antonelli, Bob Friend, Dixie Walker, Ted Williams	1.00

1993 Bazooka Team USA

	NM/M
Complete Set (22):	100.00
Complete Tin Set (22):	150.00
Common Player:	.50
1 Terry Harvey	.50
2 Dante Powell	.50
3 Andy Barkett	.50
4 Steve Reich	.50
5 Charlie Nelson	.50
6 Todd Walker	1.00
7 Dustin Hermanson	1.00
8 Pat Clougherty	.50
9 Danny Graves	.50
10 Paul Wilson	.75
11 Todd Helton	90.00
12 Russ Johnson	.50
13 Darren Grass	.50
14 A.J. Hinch	.50
15 Mark Merila	.50
16 John Powell	.50
17 Bob Scafa	.50
18 Matt Beaumont	.50
19 Todd Dunn	.50
20 Mike Martin	.50
21 Carlton Loewer	.50
22 Bret Wagner	.50

1995 Bazooka

		NM/M
Complete Set (132):		3.00
Factory Set (132+5):		5.00
Common Player:		.05
Pack (5):		.30
Wax Box (36):		7.00
1	Greg Maddux	.50
2	Cal Ripken Jr.	1.00
3	Lee Smith	.05
4	Sammy Sosa	.50
5	Jason Bere	.05
6	Dave Justice	.05
7	Kevin Mitchell	.05
8	Ozzie Guillen	.05
9	Roger Clemens	.60
10	Mike Mussina	.30
11	Sandy Alomar	.05
12	Cecil Fielder	.05
13	Dennis Martinez	.05
14	Randy Myers	.05
15	Jay Buhner	.05
16	Ivan Rodriguez	.35
17	Mo Vaughn	.05
18	Ryan Klesko	.05
19	Chuck Finley	.05
20	Barry Bonds	1.00
21	Dennis Eckersley	.35
22	Kenny Lofton	.05
23	Rafael Palmeiro	.35
24	Mike Stanley	.05
25	Gregg Jefferies	.05
26	Robin Ventura	.05
27	Mark McGwire	.75
28	Ozzie Smith	.50
29	Troy Neel	.05
30	Tony Gwynn	.50
31	Ken Griffey Jr.	.65
32	Will Clark	.05
33	Craig Biggio	.05
34	Shawon Dunston	.05
35	Wilson Alvarez	.05
36	Bobby Bonilla	.05
37	Marquis Grissom	.05
38	Ben McDonald	.05
39	Delino DeShields	.05
40	Barry Larkin	.05
41	John Olerud	.05
42	Jose Canseco	.30
43	Greg Vaughn	.05
44	Gary Sheffield	.20
45	Paul O'Neill	.05
46	Bob Hamelin	.05
47	Don Mattingly	.60
48	John Franco	.05
49	Bret Boone	.05
50	Rick Aguilera	.05
51	Tim Wallach	.05
52	Roberto Kelly	.05
53	Danny Tartabull	.05
54	Randy Johnson	.40
55	Greg McMichael	.05
56	Bip Roberts	.05
57	David Cone	.05
58	Raul Mondesi	.05
59	Travis Fryman	.05
60	Jeff Conine	.05
61	Jeff Bagwell	.40
62	Rickey Henderson	.40
63	Fred McGriff	.05
64	Matt Williams	.05
65	Rick Wilkins	.05
66	Eric Karros	.05
67	Mel Rojas	.05
68	Juan Gonzalez	.20
69	Chuck Carr	.05
70	Moises Alou	.05
71	Mark Grace	.05
72	Alex Fernandez	.05
73	Rod Beck	.05
74	Ray Lankford	.05
75	Dean Palmer	.05
76	Joe Carter	.05
77	Mike Piazza	.65
78	Eddie Murray	.40
79	Dave Nilsson	.05
80	Brett Butler	.05
81	Roberto Alomar	.10
82	Jeff Kent	.05
83	Andres Galarraga	.05
84	Brady Anderson	.05

85	Jimmy Key	.05
86	Bret Saberhagen	.05
87	Chili Davis	.05
88	Jose Rijo	.05
89	Wade Boggs	.50
90	Len Dykstra	.05
91	Steve Howe	.05
92	Hal Morris	.05
93	Larry Walker	.05
94	Jeff Montgomery	.05
95	Wil Cordero	.05
96	Jay Bell	.05
97	Tom Glavine	.15
98	Chris Hoiles	.05
99	Steve Avery	.05
100	Ruben Sierra	.05
101	Mickey Tettleton	.05
102	Paul Molitor	.40
103	Carlos Baerga	.05
104	Walt Weiss	.05
105	Darren Daulton	.05
106	Jack McDowell	.05
107	Doug Drabek	.05
108	Mark Langston	.05
109	Manny Ramirez	.40
110	Kevin Appier	.05
111	Andy Benes	.05
112	Chuck Knoblauch	.05
113	Kirby Puckett	.50
114	Dante Bichette	.05
115	Deion Sanders	.10
116	Albert Belle	.05
117	Todd Zeile	.05
118	Devon White	.05
119	Tim Salmon	.05
120	Frank Thomas	.40
121	John Wetteland	.05
122	James Mouton	.05
123	Javy Lopez	.05
124	Carlos Delgado	.25
125	Cliff Floyd	.05
126	Alex Gonzalez	.05
127	Billy Ashley	.05
128	Rondell White	.05
129	Rico Brogna	.05
130	Melvin Nieves	.05
131	Jose Oliva	.05
132	J.R. Phillips	.05

Red Hot Inserts

		NM/M
Complete Set (22):		7.00
Common Player:		.15
1	Greg Maddux	1.00
2	Cal Ripken Jr.	2.00
3	Barry Bonds	2.00
4	Kenny Lofton	.15
5	Mike Stanley	.15
6	Tony Gwynn	1.00
7	Ken Griffey Jr.	1.50
8	Barry Larkin	.15
9	Jose Canseco	.35
10	Paul O'Neill	.15
11	Randy Johnson	.75
12	David Cone	.15
13	Jeff Bagwell	.75
14	Matt Williams	.15
15	Mike Piazza	1.50
16	Roberto Alomar	.25
17	Jimmy Key	.15
18	Wade Boggs	1.00
19	Paul Molitor	.75
20	Carlos Baerga	.15
21	Albert Belle	.15
22	Frank Thomas	.75

1996 Bazooka

		NM/M
Unopened Fact. Set (133):		9.00
Complete Set (132):		6.00
Common Player:		.05
Pack (5):		.40
Wax Box (36):		9.00
1	Ken Griffey Jr.	.75
2	J.T. Snow	.05
3	Rondell White	.05
4	Reggie Sanders	.05
5	Jeff Montgomery	.05
6	Mike Stanley	.05
7	Bernie Williams	.05
8	Mike Piazza	.75
9	Brian Hunter	.05
10	Len Dykstra	.05

11	Ray Lankford	.05
12	Kenny Lofton	.05
13	Robin Ventura	.05
14	Devon White	.05
15	Cal Ripken Jr.	1.50
16	Heathcliff Slocumb	.05
17	Ryan Klesko	.05
18	Terry Steinbach	.05
19	Travis Fryman	.05
20	Sammy Sosa	.50
21	Jim Thome	.35
22	Kenny Rogers	.05
23	Don Mattingly	.60
24	Kirby Puckett	.50
25	Matt Williams	.05
26	Larry Walker	.05
27	Tim Wakefield	.05
28	Greg Vaughn	.05
29	Denny Neagle	.05
30	Ken Caminiti	.05
31	Garret Anderson	.05
32	Brady Anderson	.05
33	Carlos Baerga	.05
34	Wade Boggs	.50
35	Roberto Alomar	.15
36	Eric Karros	.05
37	Jay Buhner	.05
38	Dante Bichette	.05
39	Darren Daulton	.05
40	Jeff Bagwell	.40
41	Jay Bell	.05
42	Dennis Eckersley	.35
43	Will Clark	.05
44	Tom Glavine	.20
45	Rick Aguilera	.05
46	Kevin Seitzer	.05
47	Bret Boone	.05
48	Mark Grace	.05
49	Ray Durham	.05
50	Rico Brogna	.05
51	Kevin Appier	.05
52	Moises Alou	.05
53	Jeff Conine	.05
54	Marty Cordova	.05
55	Jose Mesa	.05
56	Rod Beck	.05
57	Marquis Grissom	.05
58	David Cone	.05
59	Albert Belle	.05
60	Lee Smith	.05
61	Frank Thomas	.40
62	Roger Clemens	.60
63	Bobby Bonilla	.05
64	Paul Molitor	.40
65	Chuck Knoblauch	.05
66	Steve Finley	.05
67	Craig Biggio	.05
68	Ramon Martinez	.05
69	Jason Isringhausen	.05
70	Mark Wohlers	.05
71	Vinny Castilla	.05
72	Ron Gant	.05
73	Juan Gonzalez	.20
74	Mark McGwire	1.00
75	Jeff King	.05
76	Pedro Martinez	.40
77	Chad Curtis	.05
78	John Olerud	.05
79	Greg Maddux	.50
80	Derek Jeter	1.50
81	Mike Mussina	.25
82	Gregg Jefferies	.05
83	Jim Edmonds	.05
84	Carlos Perez	.05
85	Mo Vaughn	.05
86	Todd Hundley	.05
87	Roberto Hernandez	.05
88	Derek Bell	.05
89	Andres Galarraga	.05
90	Brian McRae	.05
91	Joe Carter	.05
92	Orlando Merced	.05
93	Cecil Fielder	.05
94	Dean Palmer	.05
95	Randy Johnson	.40
96	Chipper Jones	.50
97	Barry Larkin	.05
98	Hideo Nomo	.25
99	Gary Gaetti	.05
100	Edgar Martinez	.05
101	John Wetteland	.05
102	Rafael Palmeiro	.35
103	Chuck Finley	.05
104	Ivan Rodriguez	.35

105	Shawn Green	.10
106	Manny Ramirez	.40
107	Lance Johnson	.05
108	Jose Canseco	.20
109	Fred McGriff	.05
110	David Segui	.05
111	Tim Salmon	.05
112	Hal Morris	.05
113	Tino Martinez	.05
114	Bret Saberhagen	.05
115	Brian Jordan	.05
116	David Justice	.05
117	Jack McDowell	.05
118	Barry Bonds	1.50
119	Mark Langston	.05
120	John Valentin	.05
121	Raul Mondesi	.05
122	Quilvio Veras	.05
123	Randy Myers	.05
124	Tony Gwynn	.50
125	Johnny Damon	.20
126	Doug Drabek	.05
127	Bill Pulsipher	.05
128	Paul O'Neill	.05
129	Rickey Henderson	.40
130	Deion Sanders	.10
131	Orel Hershiser	.05
132	Gary Sheffield	.20

Mickey Mantle 1959 Reprint

		NM/M
Mickey Mantle		7.50

1989 Bowman

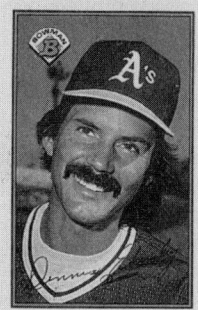

		NM/M
Unopened Fact. Set (484):		20.00
Complete Set (484):		15.00
Common Player:		.05
Wax Pack (12+1):		.75
Wax Box (36):		15.00
Rack Pack (40):		1.00
Rack Box (24):		20.00
1	Oswald Peraza	.05
2	Brian Holton	.05
3	Jose Bautista	.05
4	Pete Harnisch RC	.10
5	Dave Schmidt	.05
6	Gregg Olson	.05
7	Jeff Ballard	.05
8	Bob Melvin	.05
9	Cal Ripken, Jr.	.75
10	Randy Milligan	.05
11	Juan Bell RC	.05
12	Billy Ripken	.05
13	Jim Trabor	.05
14	Pete Stanicek	.05
15	Steve Finley RC	.25
16	Larry Sheets	.05
17	Phil Bradley	.05
18	Brady Anderson	.05
19	Lee Smith	.05
20	Tom Fischer	.05
21	Mike Boddicker	.05
22	Rob Murphy	.05
23	Wes Gardner	.05
24	John Dopson	.05
25	Bob Stanley	.05
26	Roger Clemens	.60

27	Rich Gedman	.05
28	Marty Barrett	.05
29	Luis Rivera	.05
30	Jody Reed	.05
31	Nick Esasky	.05
32	Wade Boggs	.50
33	Jim Rice	.20
34	Mike Greenwell	.05
35	Dwight Evans	.05
36	Ellis Burks	.05
37	Chuck Finley	.05
38	Kirk McCaskill	.05
39	Jim Abbott	.05
40	Bryan Harvey **RC**	.05
41	Bert Blyleven	.05
42	Mike Witt	.05
43	Bob McClure	.05
44	Bill Schroeder	.05
45	Lance Parrish	.05
46	Dick Schofield	.05
47	Wally Joyner	.05
48	Jack Howell	.05
49	Johnny Ray	.05
50	Chili Davis	.05
51	Tony Armas	.05
52	Claudell Washington	.05
53	Brian Downing	.05
54	Devon White	.05
55	Bobby Thigpen	.05
56	Bill Long	.05
57	Jerry Reuss	.05
58	Shawn Hillegas	.05
59	Melido Perez	.05
60	Jeff Bittiger	.05
61	Jack McDowell	.05
62	Carlton Fisk	.40
63	Steve Lyons	.05
64	Ozzie Guillen	.05
65	Robin Ventura	.05
66	Fred Manrique	.05
67	Dan Pasqua	.05
68	Ivan Calderon	.05
69	Ron Kittle	.05
70	Daryl Boston	.05
71	Dave Gallagher	.05
72	Harold Baines	.05
73	Charles Nagy **RC**	.15
74	John Farrell	.05
75	Kevin Wickander	.05
76	Greg Swindell	.05
77	Mike Walker	.05
78	Doug Jones	.05
79	Rich Yett	.05
80	Tom Candiotti	.05
81	Jesse Orosco	.05
82	Bud Black	.05
83	Andy Allanson	.05
84	Pete O'Brien	.05
85	Jerry Browne	.05
86	Brook Jacoby	.05
87	Mark Lewis **RC**	.05
88	Luis Aguayo	.05
89	Cory Snyder	.05
90	Oddibe McDowell	.05
91	Joe Carter	.05
92	Frank Tanana	.05
93	Jack Morris	.05
94	Doyle Alexander	.05
95	Steve Searcy	.05
96	Randy Bockus	.05
97	Jeff Robinson	.05
98	Mike Henneman	.05
99	Paul Gibson	.05
100	Frank Williams	.05
101	Matt Nokes	.05
102	Rico Brogna	.05
103	Lou Whitaker	.05
104	Al Pedrique	.05
105	Alan Trammell	.05
106	Chris Brown	.05
107	Pat Sheridan	.05
108	Gary Pettis	.05
109	Keith Moreland	.05
110	Mel Stottlemyre, Jr.	.05
111	Bret Saberhagen	.05
112	Floyd Bannister	.05
113	Jeff Montgomery	.05
114	Steve Farr	.05
115	Tom Gordon	.05
116	Charlie Leibrandt	.05
117	Mark Gubicza	.05
118	Mike MacFarlane	.05
119	Bob Boone	.05
120	Kurt Stillwell	.05
121	George Brett	.60
122	Frank White	.05
123	Kevin Seitzer	.05
124	Willie Wilson	.05
125	Pat Tabler	.05
126	Bo Jackson	.10
127	Hugh Walker	.05
128	Danny Tartabull	.05
129	Teddy Higuera	.05
130	Don August	.05
131	Juan Nieves	.05
132	Mike Birkbeck	.05
133	Dan Plesac	.05
134	Chris Bosio	.05
135	Bill Wegman	.05
136	Chuck Crim	.05
137	B.J. Surhoff	.05
138	Joey Meyer	.05
139	Dale Sveum	.05
140	Paul Molitor	.40
141	Jim Gantner	.05
142	Gary Sheffield **RC**	.75
143	Greg Brock	.05
144	Robin Yount	.40
145	Glenn Braggs	.05
146	Rob Deer	.05
147	Fred Toliver	.05
148	Jeff Reardon	.05
149	Allan Anderson	.05
150	Frank Viola	.05
151	Shane Rawley	.05
152	Juan Berenguer	.05
153	Johnny Ard	.05
154	Tim Laudner	.05
155	Brian Harper	.05
156	Al Newman	.05
157	Kent Hrbek	.05
158	Gary Gaetti	.05
159	Wally Backman	.05
160	Gene Larkin	.05
161	Greg Gagne	.05
162	Kirby Puckett	.50
163	Danny Gladden	.05
164	Randy Bush	.05
165	Dave LaPoint	.05
166	Andy Hawkins	.05
167	Dave Righetti	.05
168	Lance McCullers	.05
169	Jimmy Jones	.05
170	Al Leiter	.05
171	John Candelaria	.05
172	Don Slaught	.05
173	Jamie Quirk	.05
174	Rafael Santana	.05
175	Mike Pagliarulo	.05
176	Don Mattingly	.60
177	Ken Phelps	.05
178	Steve Sax	.05
179	Dave Winfield	.40
180	Stan Jefferson	.05
181	Rickey Henderson	.40
182	Bob Brower	.05
183	Roberto Kelly	.05
184	Curt Young	.05
185	Gene Nelson	.05
186	Bob Welch	.05
187	Rick Honeycutt	.05
188	Dave Stewart	.05
189	Mike Moore	.05
190	Dennis Eckersley	.35
191	Eric Plunk	.05
192	Storm Davis	.05
193	Terry Steinbach	.05
194	Ron Hassey	.05
195	Stan Royer	.05
196	Walt Weiss	.05
197	Mark McGwire	.65
198	Carney Lansford	.05
199	Glenn Hubbard	.05
200	Dave Henderson	.05
201	Jose Canseco	.30
202	Dave Parker	.05
203	Scott Bankhead	.05
204	Tom Niedenfuer	.05
205	Mark Langston	.05
206	Erik Hanson **RC**	.05
207	Mike Jackson	.05
208	Dave Valle	.05
209	Scott Bradley	.05
210	Harold Reynolds	.05
211	Tino Martinez	.05
212	Rich Renteria	.05
213	Rey Quinones	.05
214	Jim Presley	.05
215	Alvin Davis	.05
216	Edgar Martinez	.05
217	Darnell Coles	.05
218	Jeffrey Leonard	.05
219	Jay Buhner	.05
220	Ken Griffey Jr. **RC**	6.00
221	Drew Hall	.05
222	Bobby Witt	.05
223	Jamie Moyer	.05
224	Charlie Hough	.05
225	Nolan Ryan	.75
226	Jeff Russell	.05
227	Jim Sundberg	.05
228	Julio Franco	.05
229	Buddy Bell	.05
230	Scott Fletcher	.05
231	Jeff Kunkel	.05
232	Steve Buechele	.05
233	Monty Fariss	.05
234	Rick Leach	.05
235	Ruben Sierra	.05
236	Cecil Espy	.05
237	Rafael Palmeiro	.35
238	Pete Incaviglia	.05
239	Dave Steib	.05
240	Jeff Musselman	.05
241	Mike Flanagan	.05
242	Todd Stottlemyre	.05
243	Jimmy Key	.05
244	Tony Castillo	.05
245	Alex Sanchez	.05
246	Tom Henke	.05
247	John Cerutti	.05
248	Ernie Whitt	.05
249	Bob Brenly	.05
250	Rance Mulliniks	.05
251	Kelly Gruber	.05
252	Ed Sprague	.05
253	Fred McGriff	.05
254	Tony Fernandez	.05
255	Tom Lawless	.05
256	George Bell	.05
257	Jesse Barfield	.05
258	Sandy Alomar, Sr.	.05
259	Ken Griffey (With Ken Griffey Jr.)	.30
260	Cal Ripken, Sr.	.05
261	Mel Stottlemyre, Sr.	.05
262	Zane Smith	.05
263	Charlie Puleo	.05
264	Derek Lilliquist	.05
265	Paul Assenmacher	.05
266	John Smoltz	.05
267	Tom Glavine	.25
268	Steve Avery **RC**	.05
269	Pete Smith **RC**	.05
270	Jody Davis	.05
271	Bruce Benedict	.05
272	Andres Thomas	.05
273	Gerald Perry	.05
274	Ron Gant	.05
275	Darrell Evans	.05
276	Dale Murphy	.25
277	Dion James	.05
278	Lonnie Smith	.05
279	Geronimo Berroa	.05
280	Steve Wilson	.05
281	Rick Sutcliffe	.05
282	Kevin Coffman	.05
283	Mitch Williams	.05
284	Greg Maddux	.50
285	Paul Kilgus	.05
286	Mike Harkey	.05
287	Lloyd McClendon	.05
288	Damon Berryhill	.05
289	Ty Griffin	.05
290	Ryne Sandberg	.50
291	Mark Grace	.05
292	Curt Wilkerson	.05
293	Vance Law	.05
294	Shawon Dunston	.05
295	Jerome Walton	.05
296	Mitch Webster	.05
297	Dwight Smith	.05
298	Andre Dawson	.25
299	Jeff Sellers	.05
300	Jose Rijo	.05
301	John Franco	.05
302	Rick Mahler	.05
303	Ron Robinson	.05
304	Danny Jackson	.05
305	Rob Dibble	.05
306	Tom Browning	.05
307	Bo Diaz	.05
308	Manny Trillo	.05
309	Chris Sabo	.05
310	Ron Oester	.05
311	Barry Larkin	.05
312	Todd Benzinger	.05
313	Paul O'Neill	.05
314	Kal Daniels	.05
315	Joel Youngblood	.05
316	Eric Davis	.05
317	Dave Smith	.05
318	Mark Portugal	.05
319	Brian Meyer	.05
320	Jim Deshaies	.05
321	Juan Agosto	.05
322	Mike Scott	.05
323	Rick Rhoden	.05
324	Jim Clancy	.05
325	Larry Andersen	.05
326	Alex Trevino	.05
327	Alan Ashby	.05
328	Craig Reynolds	.05
329	Bill Doran	.05
330	Rafael Ramirez	.05
331	Glenn Davis	.05
332	Willie Ansley **RC**	.05
333	Gerald Young	.05
334	Cameron Drew	.05
335	Jay Howell	.05
336	Tim Belcher	.05
337	Fernando Valenzuela	.05
338	Ricky Horton	.05
339	Tim Leary	.05
340	Bill Bene	.05
341	Orel Hershiser	.05
342	Mike Scioscia	.05
343	Rick Dempsey	.05
344	Willie Randolph	.05
345	Alfredo Griffin	.05
346	Eddie Murray	.40
347	Mickey Hatcher	.05
348	Mike Sharperson	.05
349	John Shelby	.05
350	Mike Marshall	.05
351	Kirk Gibson	.05
352	Mike Davis	.05
353	Bryn Smith	.05
354	Pascual Perez	.05
355	Kevin Gross	.05
356	Andy McGaffigan	.05
357	Brian Holman	.05
358	Dave Wainhouse	.05
359	Denny Martinez	.05
360	Tim Burke	.05
361	Nelson Santovenia	.05
362	Tim Wallach	.05
363	Spike Owen	.05
364	Rex Hudler	.05
365	Andres Galarraga	.05
366	Otis Nixon	.05
367	Hubie Brooks	.05
368	Mike Aldrete	.05
369	Rock Raines	.05
370	Dave Martinez	.05
371	Bob Ojeda	.05
372	Ron Darling	.05
373	Wally Whitehurst	.05
374	Randy Myers	.05
375	David Cone	.05
376	Dwight Gooden	.05
377	Sid Fernandez	.05
378	Dave Proctor	.05
379	Gary Carter	.40
380	Keith Miller	.05
381	Gregg Jefferies	.05
382	Tim Teufel	.05
383	Kevin Elster	.05
384	Dave Magadan	.05
385	Keith Hernandez	.05
386	Mookie Wilson	.05
387	Darryl Strawberry	.05
388	Kevin McReynolds	.05
389	Mark Carreon	.05
390	Jeff Parrett	.05
391	Mike Maddux	.05
392	Don Carman	.05
393	Bruce Ruffin	.05
394	Ken Howell	.05
395	Steve Bedrosian	.05
396	Floyd Youmans	.05
397	Larry McWilliams	.05
398	Pat Combs	.05
399	Steve Lake	.05
400	Dickie Thon	.05
401	Ricky Jordan	.05
402	Mike Schmidt	.60
403	Tom Herr	.05
404	Chris James	.05
405	Juan Samuel	.05
406	Von Hayes	.05
407	Ron Jones	.05
408	Curt Ford	.05
409	Bob Walk	.05
410	Jeff Robinson	.05
411	Jim Gott	.05
412	Scott Medvin	.05
413	John Smiley	.05
414	Bob Kipper	.05
415	Brian Fisher	.05
416	Doug Drabek	.05
417	Mike Lavalliere	.05
418	Ken Oberkfell	.05
419	Sid Bream	.05
420	Austin Manahan	.05
421	Jose Lind	.05
422	Bobby Bonilla	.05
423	Glenn Wilson	.05
424	Andy Van Slyke	.05
425	Gary Redus	.05
426	Barry Bonds	.75
427	Don Heinkel	.05
428	Ken Dayley	.05
429	Todd Worrell	.05
430	Brad DuVall	.05
431	Jose DeLeon	.05
432	Joe Magrane	.05
433	John Ericks	.05
434	Frank DiPino	.05
435	Tony Pena	.05
436	Ozzie Smith	.50
437	Terry Pendleton	.05
438	Jose Oquendo	.05
439	Tim Jones	.05
440	Pedro Guerrero	.05
441	Milt Thompson	.05
442	Willie McGee	.05
443	Vince Coleman	.05
444	Tom Brunansky	.05
445	Walt Terrell	.05
446	Eric Show	.05
447	Mark Davis	.05
448	Andy Benes **RC**	.10
449	Eddie Whitson	.05
450	Dennis Rasmussen	.05
451	Bruce Hurst	.05
452	Pat Clements	.05
453	Benito Santiago	.05
454	Sandy Alomar, Jr.	.05
455	Garry Templeton	.05
456	Jack Clark	.05
457	Tim Flannery	.05
458	Roberto Alomar	.25
459	Camelo Martinez	.05
460	John Kruk	.05
461	Tony Gwynn	.50
462	Jerald Clark	.05
463	Don Robinson	.05
464	Craig Lefferts	.05
465	Kelly Downs	.05
466	Rick Rueschel	.05
467	Scott Garrelts	.05
468	Wil Tejada	.05
469	Kirt Manwaring	.05
470	Terry Kennedy	.05
471	Jose Uribe	.05
472	Royce Clayton **RC**	.10
473	Robby Thompson	.05
474	Kevin Mitchell	.05
475	Ernie Riles	.05
476	Will Clark	.05
477	Donnell Nixon	.05
478	Candy Maldonado	.05
479	Tracy Jones	.05
480	Brett Butler	.05
481	Checklist 1-121	.05
482	Checklist 122-242	.05
483	Checklist 243-363	.05
484	Checklist 364-484	.05

Inserts

BOSTON
Ted Williams

	NM/M
Complete Set (11):	3.50
Common Player:	.10
(1) Richie Ashburn	.10
(2) Yogi Berra	.10
(3) Whitey Ford	.10
(4) Gil Hodges	.10
(5) Mickey Mantle/1951	2.00
(6) Mickey Mantle/1953	1.50
(7) Willie Mays	.50
(8) Satchel Paige	.25
(9) Jackie Robinson	1.00
(10) Duke Snider	.10
(11) Ted Williams	1.00

Tiffany

	NM/M
Unopened Set (495):	165.00
Complete Set (495):	100.00
Common Player:	.25

(Star/rookie cards valued at 4-5X regular-issue 1989 Bowman.)

1990 Bowman

BLUE JAYS • GLENALLEN HILL

	NM/M
Unopened Factory Set (528):	20.00
Complete Set (528):	15.00
Common Player:	.05
Wax Pack (15):	.75
Wax Box (36):	15.00
Jumbo Pack (31):	1.00
Jumbo Box (24):	15.00
Rack Pack (39):	1.50
Rack Box (24):	20.00

1	Tommy Greene **RC**	.05
2	Tom Glavine	.30
3	Andy Nezelek	.05
4	Mike Stanton	.05
5	Rick Lueken	.05
6	Kent Mercker	.05
7	Derek Lilliquist	.05
8	Charlie Liebrandt	.05
9	Steve Avery	.05
10	John Smoltz	.05
11	Mark Lemke	.05
12	Lonnie Smith	.05
13	Oddibe McDowell	.05
14	Tyler Houston **RC**	.05
15	Jeff Blauser	.05
16	Ernie Whitt	.05
17	Alexis Infante	.05
18	Jim Presley	.05
19	Dale Murphy	.25
20	Nick Esasky	.05
21	Rick Sutcliffe	.05
22	Mike Bielecki	.05
23	Steve Wilson	.05
24	Kevin Blankenship	.05
25	Mitch Williams	.05
26	Dean Wilkins	.05
27	Greg Maddux	.50
28	Mike Harkey	.05
29	Mark Grace	.05
30	Ryne Sandberg	.50
31	Greg Smith	.05
32	Dwight Smith	.05
33	Damon Berryhill	.05
34	Earl Cunningham	.05
35	Jerome Walton	.05
36	Lloyd McClendon	.05
37	Ty Griffin	.05
38	Shawon Dunston	.05
39	Andre Dawson	.25
40	Luis Salazar	.05
41	Tim Layana	.05
42	Rob Dibble	.05
43	Tom Browning	.05
44	Danny Jackson	.05
45	Jose Rijo	.05
46	Scott Scudder	.05
47	Randy Myers	.05
48	Brian Lane	.05
49	Paul O'Neill	.05
50	Barry Larkin	.05
51	Reggie Jefferson	.05
52	Jeff Branson	.05
53	Chris Sabo	.05
54	Joe Oliver	.05
55	Todd Benzinger	.05
56	Rolando Roomes	.05
57	Hal Morris	.05
58	Eric Davis	.05
59	Scott Bryant	.05
60	Ken Griffey	.05
61	Darryl Kile **RC**	.05
62	Dave Smith	.05
63	Mark Portugal	.05
64	Jeff Juden **RC**	.05
65	Bill Gullickson	.05
66	Danny Darwin	.05
67	Larry Andersen	.05
68	Jose Cano	.05
69	Dan Schatzeder	.05
70	Jim Deshaies	.05
71	Mike Scott	.05
72	Gerald Young	.05
73	Ken Caminiti	.05
74	Ken Oberkfell	.05
75	Dave Rhode	.05
76	Bill Doran	.05
77	Andujar Cedeno	.05
78	Craig Biggio	.05
79	Karl Rhodes	.05
80	Glenn Davis	.05
81	Eric Anthony **RC**	.05
82	John Wetteland	.05
83	Jay Howell	.05
84	Orel Hershiser	.05
85	Tim Belcher	.05
86	Kiki Jones	.05
87	Mike Hartley	.05
88	Ramon Martinez	.05
89	Mike Scioscia	.05
90	Willie Randolph	.05
91	Juan Samuel	.05
92	Jose Offerman **RC**	.05
93	Dave Hansen	.05
94	Jeff Hamilton	.05
95	Alfredo Griffin	.05
96	Tom Goodwin	.05
97	Kirk Gibson	.05
98	Jose Vizcaino	.05
99	Kal Daniels	.05
100	Hubie Brooks	.05
101	Eddie Murray	.40
102	Dennis Boyd	.05
103	Tim Burke	.05
104	Bill Sampen	.05
105	Brett Gideon	.05
106	Mark Gardner	.05
107	Howard Farmer	.05
108	Mel Rojas	.05
109	Kevin Gross	.05
110	Dave Schmidt	.05
111	Denny Martinez	.05
112	Jerry Goff	.05
113	Andres Galarraga	.05
114	Tim Welch	.05
115	Marquis Grissom **RC**	.25
116	Spike Owen	.05
117	Larry Walker **RC**	1.00
118	Rock Raines	.05
119	Delino DeShields **RC**	.10
120	Tom Foley	.05
121	Dave Martinez	.05
122	Frank Viola	.05
123	Julio Valera	.05
124	Alejandro Pena	.05
125	David Cone	.05
126	Dwight Gooden	.05
127	Kevin Brown	.05
128	John Franco	.05
129	Terry Bross	.05
130	Blaine Beatty	.05
131	Sid Fernandez	.05
132	Mike Marshall	.05
133	Howard Johnson	.05
134	Jaime Roseboro	.05
135	Alan Zinter	.05
136	Keith Miller	.05
137	Kevin Elster	.05
138	Kevin McReynolds	.05
139	Barry Lyons	.05
140	Gregg Jefferies	.05
141	Darryl Strawberry	.05
142	Todd Hundley **RC**	.10
143	Scott Service	.05
144	Chuck Malone	.05
145	Steve Ontiveros	.05
146	Roger McDowell	.05
147	Ken Howell	.05
148	Pat Combs	.05
149	Jeff Parrett	.05
150	Chuck McElroy	.05
151	Jason Grimsley	.05
152	Len Dykstra	.05
153	Mickey Morandini	.05
154	John Kruk	.05
155	Dickie Thon	.05
156	Ricky Jordan	.05
157	Jeff Jackson	.05
158	Darren Daulton	.05
159	Tom Herr	.05
160	Von Hayes	.05
161	Dave Hollins **RC**	.05
162	Carmelo Martinez	.05
163	Bob Walk	.05
164	Doug Drabek	.05
165	Walt Terrell	.05
166	Bill Landrum	.05
167	Scott Ruskin	.05
168	Bob Patterson	.05
169	Bobby Bonilla	.05
170	Jose Lind	.05
171	Andy Van Slyke	.05
172	Mike LaValliere	.05
173	Willie Greene **RC**	.05
174	Jay Bell	.05
175	Sid Bream	.05
176	Tom Prince	.05
177	Wally Backman	.05
178	Moises Alou **RC**	.25
179	Steve Carter	.05
180	Gary Redus	.05
181	Barry Bonds	1.00
182	Don Slaught	.05
183	Joe Magrane	.05
184	Bryn Smith	.05
185	Todd Worrell	.05
186	Jose Deleon	.05
187	Frank DiPino	.05
188	John Tudor	.05
189	Howard Hilton	.05
190	John Ericks	.05
191	Ken Dayley	.05
192	Ray Lankford **RC**	.10
193	Todd Zeile	.05
194	Willie McGee	.05
195	Ozzie Smith	.50
196	Milt Thompson	.05
197	Terry Pendleton	.05
198	Vince Coleman	.05
199	Paul Coleman	.05
200	Jose Oquendo	.05
201	Pedro Guerrero	.05
202	Tom Brunansky	.05
203	Roger Smithberg	.05
204	Eddie Whitson	.05
205	Dennis Rasmussen	.05
206	Craig Lefferts	.05
207	Andy Benes	.05
208	Bruce Hurst	.05
209	Eric Show	.05
210	Rafael Valdez	.05
211	Joey Cora	.05
212	Thomas Howard	.05
213	Rob Nelson	.05
214	Jack Clark	.05
215	Garry Templeton	.05
216	Fred Lynn	.05
217	Tony Gwynn	.50
218	Benny Santiago	.05
219	Mike Pagliarulo	.05
220	Joe Carter	.05
221	Roberto Alomar	.25
222	Bip Roberts	.05
223	Rick Reuschel	.05
224	Russ Swan	.05
225	Eric Gunderson	.05
226	Steve Bedrosian	.05
227	Mike Remlinger	.05
228	Scott Garrelts	.05
229	Ernie Camacho	.05
230	Andres Santana	.05
231	Will Clark	.05
232	Kevin Mitchell	.05
233	Robby Thompson	.05
234	Bill Bathe	.05
235	Tony Perezchica	.05
236	Gary Carter	.40
237	Brett Butler	.05
238	Matt Williams	.05
239	Ernie Riles	.05
240	Kevin Bass	.05
241	Terry Kennedy	.05
242	Steve Hosey **RC**	.05
243	Ben McDonald **RC**	.15
244	Jeff Ballard	.05
245	Joe Price	.05
246	Curt Schilling	.30
247	Pete Harnisch	.05
248	Mark Williamson	.05
249	Gregg Olson	.05
250	Chris Myers	.05
251a	David Segui (No bio. data on back.)	3.50
251b	David Segui (Bio. data on back.)	.05
252	Joe Orsulak	.05
253	Craig Worthington	.05
254	Mickey Tettleton	.05
255	Cal Ripken, Jr.	1.00
256	Billy Ripken	.05
257	Randy Milligan	.05
258	Brady Anderson	.05
259	Chris Hoiles **RC**	.05
260	Mike Devereaux	.05
261	Phil Bradley	.05
262	Leo Gomez **RC**	.05
263	Lee Smith	.05
264	Mike Rochford	.05
265	Jeff Reardon	.05
266	Wes Gardner	.05
267	Mike Boddicker	.05
268	Roger Clemens	.60
269	Rob Murphy	.05
270	Mickey Pina	.05
271	Tony Pena	.05
272	Jody Reed	.05
273	Kevin Romine	.05
274	Mike Greenwell	.05
275	Mo Vaughn **RC**	.60
276	Danny Heep	.05
277	Scott Cooper	.05
278	Greg Blosser **RC**	.05
279	Dwight Evans	.05
280	Ellis Burks	.05
281	Wade Boggs	.50
282	Marty Barrett	.05
283	Kirk McCaskill	.05
284	Mark Langston	.05
285	Bert Blyleven	.05
286	Mike Fetters	.05
287	Kyle Abbott	.05
288	Jim Abbott	.05
289	Chuck Finley	.05
290	Gary DiSarcina	.05
291	Dick Schofield	.05
292	Devon White	.05
293	Bobby Rose	.05
294	Brian Downing	.05
295	Lance Parrish	.05
296	Jack Howell	.05
297	Claudell Washington	.05
298	John Orton	.05
299	Wally Joyner	.05
300	Lee Stevens	.05
301	Chili Davis	.05
302	Johnny Ray	.05
303	Greg Hibbard	.05
304	Eric King	.05
305	Jack McDowell	.05
306	Bobby Thigpen	.05
307	Adam Peterson	.05
308	Scott Radinsky **RC**	.05
309	Wayne Edwards	.05
310	Melido Perez	.05
311	Robin Ventura	.05
312	Sammy Sosa **RC**	2.00
313	Dan Pasqua	.05
314	Carlton Fisk	.40
315	Ozzie Guillen	.05
316	Ivan Calderon	.05
317	Daryl Boston	.05
318	Craig Grebeck	.05
319	Scott Fletcher	.05
320	Frank Thomas **RC**	3.00
321	Steve Lyons	.05
322	Carlos Martinez	.05
323	Joe Skalski	.05
324	Tom Candiotti	.05
325	Greg Swindell	.05
326	Steve Olin	.05
327	Kevin Wickander	.05
328	Doug Jones	.05
329	Jeff Shaw	.05
330	Kevin Bearse	.05
331	Dion James	.05
332	Jerry Browne	.05
333	Albert Belle	.05
334	Felix Fermin	.05
335	Candy Maldonado	.05
336	Cory Snyder	.05
337	Sandy Alomar	.05
338	Mark Lewis	.05
339	Carlos Baerga **RC**	.10
340	Chris James	.05
341	Brook Jacoby	.05
342	Keith Hernandez	.05
343	Frank Tanana	.05
344	Scott Aldred	.05
345	Mike Henneman	.05
346	Steve Wapnick	.05
347	Greg Gohr	.05
348	Eric Stone	.05
349	Brian DuBois	.05
350	Kevin Ritz	.05
351	Rico Brogna	.05
352	Mike Heath	.05
353	Alan Trammell	.05
354	Chet Lemon	.05
355	Dave Bergman	.05
356	Lou Whitaker	.05
357	Cecil Fielder	.05
358	Milt Cuyler	.05
359	Tony Phillips	.05
360	Travis Fryman **RC**	.10
361	Ed Romero	.05
362	Lloyd Moseby	.05
363	Mark Gubicza	.05
364	Bret Saberhagen	.05
365	Tom Gordon	.05
366	Steve Farr	.05
367	Kevin Appier	.05
368	Storm Davis	.05
369	Mark Davis	.05
370	Jeff Montgomery	.05
371	Frank White	.05
372	Brent Mayne	.05

373	Bob Boone	.05
374	Jim Eisenreich	.05
375	Danny Tartabull	.05
376	Kurt Stillwell	.05
377	Bill Pecota	.05
378	Bo Jackson	.10
379	Bob Hamelin **RC**	.05
380	Kevin Seitzer	.05
381	Rey Palacios	.05
382	George Brett	.60
383	Gerald Perry	.05
384	Teddy Higuera	.05
385	Tom Filer	.05
386	Dan Plesac	.05
387	Cal Eldred **RC**	.05
388	Jaime Navarro	.05
389	Chris Bosio	.05
390	Randy Veres	.05
391	Gary Sheffield	.25
392	George Canale	.05
393	B.J. Surhoff	.05
394	Tim McIntosh	.05
395	Greg Brock	.05
396	Greg Vaughn	.05
397	Darryl Hamilton	.05
398	Dave Parker	.05
399	Paul Molitor	.40
400	Jim Gantner	.05
401	Rob Deer	.05
402	Billy Spiers	.05
403	Glenn Braggs	.05
404	Robin Yount	.40
405	Rick Aguilera	.05
406	Johnny Ard	.05
407	Kevin Tapani **RC**	.10
408	Park Pittman	.05
409	Allan Anderson	.05
410	Juan Berenguer	.05
411	Willie Banks	.05
412	Rich Yett	.05
413	Dave West	.05
414	Greg Gagne	.05
415	Chuck Knoblauch **RC**	.50
416	Randy Bush	.05
417	Gary Gaetti	.05
418	Kent Hrbek	.05
419	Al Newman	.05
420	Danny Gladden	.05
421	Paul Sorrento	.05
422	Derek Parks	.05
423	Scott Leius	.05
424	Kirby Puckett	.50
425	Willie Smith	.05
426	Dave Righetti	.05
427	Jeff Robinson	.05
428	Alan Mills	.05
429	Tim Leary	.05
430	Pascual Perez	.05
431	Alvaro Espinoza	.05
432	Dave Winfield	.40
433	Jesse Barfield	.05
434	Randy Velarde	.05
435	Rick Cerone	.05
436	Steve Balboni	.05
437	Mel Hall	.05
438	Bob Geren	.05
439	Bernie Williams **RC**	1.00
440	Kevin Maas **RC**	.05
441	Mike Blowers	.05
442	Steve Sax	.05
443	Don Mattingly	.60
444	Roberto Kelly	.05
445	Mike Moore	.05
446	Reggie Harris	.05
447	Scott Sanderson	.05
448	Dave Otto	.05
449	Dave Stewart	.05
450	Rick Honeycutt	.05
451	Dennis Eckersley	.35
452	Carney Lansford	.05
453	Scott Hemond	.05
454	Mark McGwire	.75
455	Felix Jose	.05
456	Terry Steinbach	.05
457	Rickey Henderson	.40
458	Dave Henderson	.05
459	Mike Gallego	.05
460	Jose Canseco	.30
461	Walt Weiss	.05
462	Ken Phelps	.05
463	Darren Lewis **RC**	.05
464	Ron Hassey	.05
465	Roger Salkeld **RC**	.05
466	Scott Bankhead	.05
467	Keith Comstock	.05
468	Randy Johnson	.40
469	Erik Hanson	.05
470	Mike Schooler	.05
471	Gary Eave	.05
472	Jeffrey Leonard	.05
473	Dave Valle	.05
474	Omar Vizquel	.05
475	Pete O'Brien	.05
476	Henry Cotto	.05
477	Jay Buhner	.05
478	Harold Reynolds	.05
479	Alvin Davis	.05
480	Darnell Coles	.05
481	Ken Griffey Jr.	.65
482	Greg Briley	.05
483	Scott Bradley	.05
484	Tino Martinez	.05
485	Jeff Russell	.05
486	Nolan Ryan	1.00
487	Robb Nen	.05

488	Kevin Brown	.05
489	Brian Bohanon	.05
490	Ruben Sierra	.05
491	Pete Incaviglia	.05
492	Juan Gonzalez **RC**	1.00
493	Steve Buechele	.05
494	Scott Coolbaugh	.05
495	Geno Petralli	.05
496	Rafael Palmeiro	.35
497	Julio Franco	.05
498	Gary Pettis	.05
499	Donald Harris	.05
500	Monty Fariss	.05
501	Harold Baines	.05
502	Cecil Espy	.05
503	Jack Daugherty	.05
504	Willie Blair	.05
505	Dave Steib	.05
506	Tom Henke	.05
507	John Cerutti	.05
508	Paul Kilgus	.05
509	Jimmy Key	.05
510	John Olerud **RC**	.75
511	Ed Sprague	.05
512	Manny Lee	.05
513	Fred McGriff	.05
514	Glenallen Hill	.05
515	George Bell	.05
516	Mookie Wilson	.05
517	Luis Sojo	.05
518	Nelson Liriano	.05
519	Kelly Gruber	.05
520	Greg Myers	.05
521	Pat Borders	.05
522	Junior Felix	.05
523	Eddie Zosky	.05
524	Tony Fernandez	.05
525	Checklist	.05
526	Checklist	.05
527	Checklist	.05
528	Checklist	.05

Tiffany

	NM/M
Unopened Set (539):	200.00
Complete Set (539):	60.00
Common Player:	.25

(Star/rookie cards valued about 4-5X regular-issue 1990 Bowman.)

1991 Bowman

	NM/M
Unopened Factory Set (704):	30.00
Complete Set (704):	20.00
Common Player:	.05
Wax Pack (14):	.75
Wax Box (36):	17.50
Cello Pack (29):	1.50
Cello Box (24):	25.00

1	Rod Carew-I	.10
2	Rod Carew-II	.10
3	Rod Carew-III	.10
4	Rod Carew-IV	.10
5	Rod Carew-V	.10
6	Willie Fraser	.05
7	John Olerud	.05
8	William Suero	.05
9	Roberto Alomar	.20
10	Todd Stottlemyre	.05
11	Joe Carter	.05
12	Steve Karsay **RC**	.10
13	Mark Whiten	.05
14	Pat Borders	.05
15	Mike Timlin	.05
16	Tom Henke	.05
17	Eddie Zosky	.05
18	Kelly Gruber	.05
19	Jimmy Key	.05
20	Jerry Schunk	.05
21	Manny Lee	.05
22	Dave Steib	.05
23	Pat Hentgen	.05
24	Glenallen Hill	.05
25	Rene Gonzales	.05
26	Ed Sprague	.05
27	Ken Dayley	.05
28	Pat Tabler	.05
29	Denis Boucher **RC**	.05
30	Devon White	.05
31	Dante Bichette	.05
32	Paul Molitor	.40
33	Greg Vaughn	.05
34	Dan Plesac	.05
35	Chris George	.05
36	Tim McIntosh	.05
37	Franklin Stubbs	.05
38	Bo Dodson	.05
39	Ron Robinson	.05
40	Ed Nunez	.05
41	Greg Brock	.05
42	Jaime Navarro	.05
43	Chris Bosio	.05
44	B.J. Surhoff	.05
45	Chris Johnson	.05
46	Willie Randolph	.05
47	Narciso Elvira	.05
48	Jim Gantner	.05
49	Kevin Brown	.05
50	Julio Machado	.05
51	Chuck Crim	.05
52	Gary Sheffield	.30
53	Angel Miranda	.05
54	Teddy Higuera	.05
55	Robin Yount	.40
56	Cal Eldred	.05
57	Sandy Alomar	.05
58	Greg Swindell	.05
59	Brook Jacoby	.05
60	Efrain Valdez	.05
61	Ever Magallanes	.05
62	Tom Candiotti	.05
63	Eric King	.05
64	Alex Cole	.05
65	Charles Nagy	.05
66	Mitch Webster	.05
67	Chris James	.05
68	Jim Thome **RC**	3.00
69	Carlos Baerga	.05
70	Mark Lewis	.05
71	Jerry Browne	.05
72	Jesse Orosco	.05
73	Mike Huff	.05
74	Jose Escobar	.05
75	Jeff Manto	.05
76	Turner Ward **RC**	.05
77	Doug Jones	.05
78	Bruce Egloff **RC**	.05
79	Tim Costo	.05
80	Beau Allred	.05
81	Albert Belle	.05
82	John Farrell	.05
83	Glenn Davis	.05
84	Joe Orsulak	.05
85	Mark Williamson	.05
86	Ben McDonald	.05
87	Billy Ripken	.05
88	Leo Gomez	.05
89	Bob Melvin	.05
90	Jeff Robinson	.05
91	Jose Mesa	.05
92	Gregg Olson	.05
93	Mike Devereaux	.05
94	Luis Mercedes	.05
95	Arthur Rhodes **RC**	.10
96	Juan Bell	.05
97	Mike Mussina **RC**	3.00
98	Jeff Ballard	.05
99	Chris Hoiles	.05
100	Brady Anderson	.05
101	Bob Milacki	.05
102	David Segui	.05
103	Dwight Evans	.05
104	Cal Ripken, Jr.	1.00
105	Mike Linskey	.05
106	Jeff Tackett **RC**	.05
107	Jeff Reardon	.05
108	Dana Kiecker	.05
109	Ellis Burks	.05
110	Dave Owen	.05
111	Danny Darwin	.05
112	Mo Vaughn	.05
113	Jeff McNeely	.05
114	Tom Bolton	.05
115	Greg Blosser	.05
116	Mike Greenwell	.05
117	Phil Plantier **RC**	.05
118	Roger Clemens	.60
119	John Marzano	.05
120	Jody Reed	.05
121	Scott Taylor	.05
122	Jack Clark	.05
123	Derek Livernois	.05
124	Tony Pena	.05
125	Tom Brunansky	.05
126	Carlos Quintana	.05
127	Tim Naehring	.05
128	Matt Young	.05
129	Wade Boggs	.50
130	Kevin Morton	.05
131	Pete Incaviglia	.05
132	Rob Deer	.05
133	Bill Gullickson	.05
134	Rico Brogna	.05
135	Lloyd Moseby	.05
136	Cecil Fielder	.05
137	Tony Phillips	.05
138	Mark Leiter	.05
139	John Cerutti	.05
140	Mickey Tettleton	.05
141	Milt Cuyler	.05
142	Greg Gohr	.05
143	Tony Bernazard	.05
144	Dan Gakeler	.05
145	Travis Fryman	.05
146	Dan Petry	.05
147	Scott Aldred	.05
148	John DeSilva	.05
149	Rusty Meacham	.05
150	Lou Whitaker	.05
151	Dave Haas	.05
152	Luis de los Santos	.05
153	Ivan Cruz	.05
154	Alan Trammell	.05
155	Pat Kelly	.05
156	Carl Everett **RC**	.25
157	Greg Cadaret	.05
158	Kevin Maas	.05
159	Jeff Johnson	.05
160	Willie Smith	.05
161	Gerald Williams	.05
162	Mike Humphreys	.05
163	Alvaro Espinoza	.05
164	Matt Nokes	.05
165	Wade Taylor	.05
166	Roberto Kelly	.05
167	John Habyan	.05
168	Steve Farr	.05
169	Jesse Barfield	.05
170	Steve Sax	.05
171	Jim Leyritz	.05
172	Robert Eenhoorn	.05
173	Bernie Williams	.05
174	Scott Lusader	.05
175	Torey Lovullo	.05
176	Chuck Cary	.05
177	Scott Sanderson	.05
178	Don Mattingly	.60
179	Mel Hall	.05
180	Juan Gonzalez	.30
181	Hensley Meulens	.05
182	Jose Offerman	.05
183	Jeff Bagwell **RC**	2.50
184	Jeff Conine **RC**	.25
185	Henry Rodriguez **RC**	.05
186	Jimmie Reese	.05
187	Kyle Abbott	.05
188	Lance Parrish	.05
189	Rafael Montalvo	.05
190	Floyd Bannister	.05
191	Dick Schofield	.05
192	Scott Lewis	.05
193	Jeff Robinson	.05
194	Kent Anderson	.05
195	Wally Joyner	.05
196	Chuck Finley	.05
197	Luis Sojo	.05
198	Jeff Richardson	.05
199	Dave Parker	.05
200	Jim Abbott	.05
201	Junior Felix	.05
202	Mark Langston	.05
203	Tim Salmon **RC**	1.00
204	Cliff Young	.05
205	Scott Bailes	.05
206	Bobby Rose	.05
207	Gary Gaetti	.05
208	Ruben Amaro	.05
209	Luis Polonia	.05
210	Dave Winfield	.40
211	Bryan Harvey	.05
212	Mike Moore	.05
213	Rickey Henderson	.40
214	Steve Chitren	.05
215	Bob Welch	.05
216	Terry Steinbach	.05
217	Ernie Riles	.05
218	Todd Van Poppel **RC**	.10
219	Mike Gallego	.05
220	Curt Young	.05
221	Todd Burns	.05
222	Vance Law	.05
223	Eric Show	.05
224	Don Peters **RC**	.05
225	Dave Stewart	.05
226	Dave Henderson	.05
227	Jose Canseco	.30
228	Walt Weiss	.05
229	Dann Howitt	.05
230	Willie Wilson	.05
231	Harold Baines	.05
232	Scott Hemond	.05
233	Joe Slusarski	.05
234	Mark McGwire	.75
235	Kirk Dressendorfer **RC**	.05
236	Craig Paquette **RC**	.05
237	Dennis Eckersley	.35
238	Dana Allison	.05
239	Scott Bradley	.05
240	Brian Holman	.05
241	Mike Schooler	.05
242	Rich Delucia	.05
243	Edgar Martinez	.05
244	Henry Cotto	.05
245	Omar Vizquel	.05
246a	Ken Griffey Jr.	.65
246b	Ken Griffey Sr. (Should be #255.)	.10
247	Jay Buhner	.05
248	Bill Krueger	.05
249	Dave Fleming **RC**	.05
250	Patrick Lennon **RC**	.05
251	Dave Valle	.05
252	Harold Reynolds	.05
253	Randy Johnson	.40
254	Scott Bankhead	.05
255	(Not issued, see #246b.)	
256	Greg Briley	.05
257	Tino Martinez	.05
258	Alvin Davis	.05
259	Pete O'Brien	.05
260	Erik Hanson	.05

261	Bret Boone **RC**	.50
262	Roger Salkeld	.05
263	Dave Burba	.05
264	Kerry Woodson **RC**	.05
265	Julio Franco	.05
266	Dan Peltier	.05
267	Jeff Russell	.05
268	Steve Buechele	.05
269	Donald Harris	.05
270	Robb Nen	.05
271	Rich Gossage	.05
272	Ivan Rodriguez **RC**	3.00
273	Jeff Huson	.05
274	Kevin Brown	.05
275	Dan Smith **RC**	.05
276	Gary Pettis	.05
277	Jack Daugherty	.05
278	Mike Jeffcoat	.05
279	Brad Arnsberg	.05
280	Nolan Ryan	1.00
281	Eric McCray	.05
282	Scott Chiamparino	.05
283	Ruben Sierra	.05
284	Geno Petralli	.05
285	Monty Fariss	.05
286	Rafael Palmeiro	.35
287	Bobby Witt	.05
288	Dean Palmer	.05
289	Tony Scruggs	.05
290	Kenny Rogers	.05
291	Bret Saberhagen	.05
292	Brian McRae **RC**	.05
293	Storm Davis	.05
294	Danny Tartabull	.05
295	David Howard	.05
296	Mike Boddicker	.05
297	Joel Johnston	.05
298	Tim Spehr	.05
299	Hector Wagner	.05
300	George Brett	.60
301	Mike Macfarlane	.05
302	Kirk Gibson	.05
303	Harvey Pulliam	.05
304	Jim Eisenreich	.05
305	Kevin Seitzer	.05
306	Mark Davis	.05
307	Kurt Stillwell	.05
308	Jeff Montgomery	.05
309	Kevin Appier	.05
310	Bob Hamelin	.05
311	Tom Gordon	.05
312	Kerwin Moore **RC**	.05
313	Hugh Walker	.05
314	Terry Shumpert	.05
315	Warren Cromartie	.05
316	Gary Thurman	.05
317	Steve Bedrosian	.05
318	Danny Gladden	.05
319	Jack Morris	.05
320	Kirby Puckett	.50
321	Kent Hrbek	.05
322	Kevin Tapani	.05
323	Denny Neagle	.05
324	Rich Garces	.05
325	Larry Casian	.05
326	Shane Mack	.05
327	Allan Anderson	.05
328	Junior Ortiz	.05
329	Paul Abbott **RC**	.05
330	Chuck Knoblauch	.05
331	Chili Davis	.05
332	Todd Ritchie **RC**	.05
333	Brian Harper	.05
334	Rick Aguilera	.05
335	Scott Erickson	.05
336	Pedro Munoz	.05
337	Scott Leuis	.05
338	Greg Gagne	.05
339	Mike Pagliarulo	.05
340	Terry Leach	.05
341	Willie Banks	.05
342	Bobby Thigpen	.05
343	Roberto Hernandez **RC**	.10
344	Melido Perez	.05
345	Carlton Fisk	.40
346	Norberto Martin **RC**	.05
347	Johnny Ruffin **RC**	.05
348	Jeff Carter **RC**	.05
349	Lance Johnson	.05
350	Sammy Sosa	.50
351	Alex Fernandez	.05
352	Jack McDowell	.05
353	Bob Wickman	.05
354	Wilson Alvarez	.05
355	Charlie Hough	.05
356	Ozzie Guillen	.05
357	Cory Snyder	.05
358	Robin Ventura	.05
359	Scott Fletcher	.05
360	Cesar Bernhardt	.05
361	Dan Pasqua	.05
362	Tim Raines	.05
363	Brian Drahman	.05
364	Wayne Edwards	.05
365	Scott Radinsky	.05
366	Frank Thomas	.40
367	Cecil Fielder	.05
368	Julio Franco	.05
369	Kelly Gruber	.05
370	Alan Trammell	.05
371	Rickey Henderson	.30
372	Jose Canseco	.15
373	Ellis Burks	.05
374	Lance Parrish	.05
375	Dave Parker	.05
376	Eddie Murray	.30
377	Ryne Sandberg	.35
378	Matt Williams	.05
379	Barry Larkin	.05
380	Barry Bonds	.75
381	Bobby Bonilla	.05
382	Darryl Strawberry	.05
383	Benny Santiago	.05
384	Don Robinson	.05
385	Paul Coleman	.05
386	Milt Thompson	.05
387	Lee Smith	.05
388	Ray Lankford	.05
389	Tom Pagnozzi	.05
390	Ken Hill	.05
391	Jamie Moyer	.05
392	Greg Carmona **RC**	.05
393	John Ericks	.05
394	Bob Tewksbury	.05
395	Jose Oquendo	.05
396	Rheal Cormier	.05
397	Mike Milchin **RC**	.05
398	Ozzie Smith	.50
399	Aaron Holbert **RC**	.05
400	Jose DeLeon	.05
401	Felix Jose	.05
402	Juan Agosto	.05
403	Pedro Guerrero	.05
404	Todd Zeile	.05
405	Gerald Perry	.05
406	Not issued	
407	Bryn Smith	.05
408	Bernard Gilkey	.05
409	Rex Hudler	.05
410a	Ralph Branca, Bobby Thomson	.10
410b	Donovan Osborne	.05
411	Lance Dickson	.05
412	Danny Jackson	.05
413	Jerome Walton	.05
414	Sean Cheetham	.05
415	Joe Girardi	.05
416	Ryne Sandberg	.50
417	Mike Harkey	.05
418	George Bell	.05
419	Rick Wilkins **RC**	.05
420	Earl Cunningham	.05
421	Heathcliff Slocumb	.05
422	Mike Bielecki	.05
423	Jessie Hollins **RC**	.05
424	Shawon Dunston	.05
425	Dave Smith	.05
426	Greg Maddux	.50
427	Jose Vizcaino	.05
428	Luis Salazar	.05
429	Andre Dawson	.25
430	Rick Sutcliffe	.05
431	Paul Assenmacher	.05
432	Erik Pappas	.05
433	Mark Grace	.05
434	Denny Martinez	.05
435	Marquis Grissom	.05
436	Wil Cordero **RC**	.05
437	Tim Wallach	.05
438	Brian Barnes **RC**	.05
439	Barry Jones	.05
440	Ivan Calderon	.05
441	Stan Spencer **RC**	.05
442	Larry Walker	.05
443	Chris Haney **RC**	.05
444	Hector Rivera	.05
445	Delino DeShields	.05
446	Andres Galarraga	.05
447	Gilberto Reyes	.05
448	Willie Greene	.05
449	Greg Colbrunn	.05
450	Rondell White **RC**	.25
451	Steve Frey	.05
452	Shane Andrews **RC**	.10
453	Mike Fitzgerald	.05
454	Spike Owen	.05
455	Dave Martinez	.05
456	Dennis Boyd	.05
457	Eric Bullock	.05
458	Reid Cornelius **RC**	.05
459	Chris Nabholz	.05
460	David Cone	.05
461	Hubie Brooks	.05
462	Sid Fernandez	.05
463	Doug Simons **RC**	.05
464	Howard Johnson	.05
465	Chris Donnels	.05
466	Anthony Young	.05
467	Todd Hundley	.05
468	Rick Cerone	.05
469	Kevin Elster	.05
470	Wally Whitehurst	.05
471	Vince Coleman	.05
472	Dwight Gooden	.05
473	Charlie O'Brien	.05
474	Jeromy Burnitz **RC**	.50
475	John Franco	.05
476	Daryl Boston	.05
477	Frank Viola	.05
478	D.J. Dozier	.05
479	Kevin McReynolds	.05
480	Tom Herr	.05
481	Gregg Jefferies	.05
482	Pete Schourek	.05
483	Ron Darling	.05
484	Dave Magadan	.05
485	Andy Ashby **RC**	.05
486	Dale Murphy	.20
487	Von Hayes	.05
488	Kim Batiste **RC**	.05
489	Tony Longmire **RC**	.05
490	Wally Backman	.05
491	Jeff Jackson	.05
492	Mickey Morandini	.05
493	Darrel Akerfelds	.05
494	Ricky Jordan	.05
495	Randy Ready	.05
496	Darrin Fletcher	.05
497	Chuck Malone	.05
498	Pat Combs	.05
499	Dickie Thon	.05
500	Roger McDowell	.05
501	Len Dykstra	.05
502	Joe Boever	.05
503	John Kruk	.05
504	Terry Mulholland	.05
505	Wes Chamberlain	.05
506	Mike Lieberthal **RC**	.75
507	Darren Daulton	.05
508	Charlie Hayes	.05
509	John Smiley	.05
510	Gary Varsho	.05
511	Curt Wilkerson	.05
512	Orlando Merced **RC**	.05
513	Barry Bonds	1.00
514	Mike Lavalliere	.05
515	Doug Drabek	.05
516	Gary Redus	.05
517	William Pennyfeather **RC**	.05
518	Randy Tomlin	.05
519	Mike Zimmerman **RC**	.05
520	Jeff King	.05
521	Kurt Miller **RC**	.05
522	Jay Bell	.05
523	Bill Landrum	.05
524	Zane Smith	.05
525	Bobby Bonilla	.05
526	Bob Walk	.05
527	Austin Manahan	.05
528	Joe Ausanio **RC**	.05
529	Andy Van Slyke	.05
530	Jose Lind	.05
531	Carlos Garcia **RC**	.05
532	Don Slaught	.05
533	Colin Powell	.25
534	Frank Bolick **RC**	.05
535	Gary Scott **RC**	.05
536	Nikco Riesgo	.05
537	Reggie Sanders **RC**	.25
538	Tim Howard **RC**	.05
539	Ryan Bowen **RC**	.05
540	Eric Anthony	.05
541	Jim Deshaies	.05
542	Tom Nevers	.05
543	Ken Caminiti	.05
544	Karl Rhodes	.05
545	Xavier Hernandez	.05
546	Mike Scott	.05
547	Jeff Juden	.05
548	Darryl Kile	.05
549	Willie Ansley	.05
550	Luis Gonzalez **RC**	1.00
551	Mike Simms **RC**	.05
552	Mark Portugal	.05
553	Jimmy Jones	.05
554	Jim Clancy	.05
555	Pete Harnisch	.05
556	Craig Biggio	.05
557	Eric Yelding	.05
558	Dave Rohde	.05
559	Casey Candaele	.05
560	Curt Schilling	.25
561	Steve Finley	.05
562	Javier Ortiz	.05
563	Andujar Cedeno	.05
564	Rafael Ramirez	.05
565	Kenny Lofton **RC**	.50
566	Steve Avery	.05
567	Lonnie Smith	.05
568	Kent Mercker	.05
569	Chipper Jones **RC**	6.00
570	Terry Pendleton	.05
571	Otis Nixon	.05
572	Juan Berenguer	.05
573	Charlie Leibrandt	.05
574	Dave Justice	.05
575	Keith Mitchell	.05
576	Tom Glavine	.25
577	Greg Olson	.05
578	Rafael Belliard	.05
579	Ben Rivera	.05
580	John Smoltz	.05
581	Tyler Houston	.05
582	Mark Wohlers **RC**	.05
583	Ron Gant	.05
584	Ramon Caraballo	.05
585	Sid Bream	.05
586	Jeff Treadway	.05
587	Javier Lopez **RC**	.75
588	Deion Sanders	.10
589	Mike Heath	.05
590	Ryan Klesko **RC**	.20
591	Bob Ojeda	.05
592	Alfredo Griffin	.05
593	Raul Mondesi **RC**	.25
594	Greg Smith	.05
595	Orel Hershiser	.05
596	Juan Samuel	.05
597	Brett Butler	.05
598	Gary Carter	.40
599	Stan Javier	.05
600	Kal Daniels	.05
601	Jamie McAndrew **RC**	.05
602	Mike Sharperson	.05
603	Jay Howell	.05
604	Eric Karros **RC**	.25
605	Tim Belcher	.05
606	Dan Opperman	.05
607	Lenny Harris	.05
608	Tom Goodwin	.05
609	Darryl Strawberry	.05
610	Ramon Martinez	.05
611	Kevin Gross	.05
612	Zakary Shinall	.05
613	Mike Scioscia	.05
614	Eddie Murray	.40
615	Ronnie Walden	.05
616	Will Clark	.05
617	Adam Hyzdu	.05
618	Matt Williams	.05
619	Don Robinson	.05
620	Jeff Brantley	.05
621	Greg Litton	.05
622	Steve Decker	.05
623	Robby Thompson	.05
624	Mark Leonard **RC**	.05
625	Kevin Bass	.05
626	Scott Garrelts	.05
627	Jose Uribe	.05
628	Eric Gunderson	.05
629	Steve Hosey	.05
630	Trevor Wilson	.05
631	Terry Kennedy	.05
632	Dave Righetti	.05
633	Kelly Downs	.05
634	Johnny Ard	.05
635	Eric Christopherson **RC**	.05
636	Kevin Mitchell	.05
637	John Burkett	.05
638	Kevin Rogers **RC**	.05
639	Bud Black	.05
640	Willie McGee	.05
641	Royce Clayton	.05
642	Tony Fernandez	.05
643	Ricky Bones	.05
644	Thomas Howard	.05
645	Dave Staton	.05
646	Jim Presley	.05
647	Tony Gwynn	.50
648	Marty Barrett	.05
649	Scott Coolbaugh	.05
650	Craig Lefferts	.05
651	Eddie Whitson	.05
652	Oscar Azocar	.05
653	Wes Gardner	.05
654	Bip Roberts	.05
655	Robbie Beckett **RC**	.05
656	Benny Santiago	.05
657	Greg W. Harris	.05
658	Jerald Clark	.05
659	Fred McGriff	.05
660	Larry Andersen	.05
661	Bruce Hurst	.05
662	Steve Martin	.05
663	Rafael Valdez	.05
664	Paul Faries **RC**	.05
665	Andy Benes	.05
666	Randy Myers	.05
667	Rob Dibble	.05
668	Glenn Sutko	.05
669	Glenn Braggs	.05
670	Billy Hatcher	.05
671	Joe Oliver	.05
672	Freddie Benavides	.05
673	Barry Larkin	.05
674	Chris Sabo	.05
675	Mariano Duncan	.05
676	Chris Jones **RC**	.05
677	Gino Minutelli **RC**	.05
678	Reggie Jefferson	.05
679	Jack Armstrong	.05
680	Chris Hammond	.05
681	Jose Rijo	.05
682	Bill Doran	.05
683	Terry Lee	.05
684	Tom Browning	.05
685	Paul O'Neill	.05
686	Eric Davis	.05
687	Dan Wilson **RC**	.05
688	Ted Power	.05
689	Tim Layana	.05
690	Norm Charlton	.05
691	Hal Morris	.05
692	Rickey Henderson	.35
693	Sam Militello **RC**	.05
694	Matt Mieske **RC**	.05
695	Paul Russo **RC**	.05
696	Domingo Mota **RC**	.05
697	Todd Guggiana **RC**	.05
698	Marc Newfield	.05
699	Checklist	.05
700	Checklist	.05
701	Checklist	.05
702	Checklist	.05
703	Checklist	.05
704	Checklist	.05

1992 Bowman

	NM/M
Complete Set (705):	120.00
Common Player:	.10
Pack (15):	6.00
Wax Box (36):	160.00
Jumbo Pack (25):	8.00
Jumbo Box (36):	220.00

1	Ivan Rodriguez	1.25
2	Kirk McCaskill	.10
3	Scott Livingstone	.10
4	Salomon Torres **RC**	.50
5	Carlos Hernandez	.10

6	Dave Hollins	.10
7	Scott Fletcher	.10
8	Jorge Fabregas	.10
9	Andujar Cedeno	.10
10	Howard Johnson	.10
11	Trevor Hoffman **RC**	3.00
12	Roberto Kelly	.10
13	Gregg Jefferies	.10
14	Marquis Grissom	.10
15	Mike Ignasiak	.10
16	Jack Morris	.10
17	William Pennyfeather	.10
18	Todd Stottlemyre	.10
19	Chito Martinez	.10
20	Roberto Alomar	.40
21	Sam Militello	.10
22	Hector Fajardo	.10
23	Paul Quantrill **RC**	.10
24	Chuck Knoblauch	.10
25	Reggie Jefferson	.10
26	Jeremy McGarity	.10
27	Jerome Walton	.10
28	Chipper Jones	15.00
29	Brian Barber **RC**	.10
30	Ron Darling	.10
31	Roberto Petagine **RC**	.10
32	Chuck Finley	.10
33	Edgar Martinez	.10
34	Napolean Robinson	.10
35	Andy Van Slyke	.10
36	Bobby Thigpen	.10
37	Travis Fryman	.10
38	Eric Christopherson	.10
39	Terry Mulholland	.10
40	Darryl Strawberry	.10
41	Manny Alexander **RC**	.10
42	Tracey Sanders **RC**	.10
43	Pete Incaviglia	.10
44	Kim Batiste	.10
45	Frank Rodriguez	.10
46	Greg Swindell	.10
47	Delino DeShields	.10
48	John Ericks	.10
49	Franklin Stubbs	.10
50	Tony Gwynn	2.00
51	Clifton Garrett **RC**	.10
52	Mike Gardella	.10
53	Scott Erickson	.10
54	Gary Caballo	.10
55	Jose Oliva **RC**	.10
56	Brook Fordyce	.10
57	Mark Whiten	.10
58	Joe Slusarski	.10
59	J.R. Phillips **RC**	.10
60	Barry Bonds	4.00
61	Bob Milacki	.10
62	Keith Mitchell	.10
63	Angel Miranda	.10
64	Raul Mondesi	.10
65	Brian Koelling	.10
66	Brian McRae	.10
67	John Patterson	.10
68	John Wetteland	.10
69	Wilson Alvarez	.10
70	Wade Boggs	2.00
71	Darryl Ratliff	.10
72	Jeff Jackson	.10
73	Jeremy Hernandez	.10
74	Darryl Hamilton	.10
75	Rafael Belliard	.10
76	Ricky Trilcek	.10
77	Felipe Crespo **RC**	.10
78	Carney Lansford	.10
79	Ryan Long	.10
80	Kirby Puckett	2.00
81	Earl Cunningham	.10
82	Pedro Martinez	1.50
83	Scott Hatteberg	.10
84	Juan Gonzalez	.75
85	Robert Nutting	.10
86	Calvin Reese **RC**	.50
87	Dave Silvestri	.10
88	Scott Ruffcorn **RC**	.10
89	Rick Aguilera	.10
90	Cecil Fielder	.10
91	Kirk Dressendorfer	.10
92	Jerry DiPoto	.10
93	Mike Felder	.10
94	Craig Paquette	.10
95	Elvin Paulino	.10
96	Donovan Osborne	.10
97	Hubie Brooks	.10
98	Derek Lowe **RC**	4.00
99	David Zancanaro	.10
100	Ken Griffey Jr.	2.75
101	Todd Hundley	.10
102	Mike Trombley	.10
103	Ricky Gutierrez **RC**	.10
104	Braulio Castillo	.10
105	Craig Lefferts	.10
106	Rick Sutcliffe	.10
107	Dean Palmer	.10
108	Henry Rodriguez	.10
109	Mark Clark **RC**	.10
110	Kenny Lofton	.10
111	Mark Carreon	.10
112	J.T. Bruett **RC**	.10
113	Gerald Williams	.10
114	Frank Thomas	1.50
115	Kevin Reimer	.10
116	Sammy Sosa	2.00
117	Mickey Tettleton	.10
118	Reggie Sanders	.10
119	Trevor Wilson	.10
120	Cliff Brantley	.10
121	Spike Owen	.10
122	Jeff Montgomery	.10
123	Alex Sutherland	.10
124	Brien Taylor **RC**	.10
125	Brian Williams	.10
126	Kevin Seitzer	.10
127	Carlos Delgado **RC**	15.00
128	Gary Scott	.10
129	Scott Cooper	.10
130	Domingo Jean **RC**	.10
131	Pat Mahomes **RC**	.10
132	Mike Boddicker	.10
133	Roberto Hernandez	.10
134	Dave Valle	.10
135	Kurt Stillwell	.10
136	Brad Pennington **RC**	.10
137	Jermaine Swifton	.10
138	Ryan Hawblitzel	.10
139	Tito Navarro	.10
140	Sandy Alomar	.10
141	Todd Benzinger	.10
142	Danny Jackson	.10
143	Melvin Nieves **RC**	.25
144	Jim Campanis	.10
145	Luis Gonzalez	.10
146	Dave Doorneweerd	.10
147	Charlie Hayes	.10
148	Greg Maddux	2.00
149	Brian Harper	.10
150	Brent Miller	.10
151	Shawn Estes **RC**	.75
152	Mike Williams	.10
153	Charlie Hough	.10
154	Randy Myers	.10
155	Kevin Young **RC**	.10
156	Rick Wilkins	.10
157	Terry Schumpert	.10
158	Steve Karsay	.10
159	Gary DiSarcina	.10
160	Deion Sanders	.10
161	Tom Browning	.10
162	Dickie Thon	.10
163	Luis Mercedes	.10
164	Ricardo Ingram	.10
165	Tavo Alavarez **RC**	.10
166	Rickey Henderson	1.50
167	Jaime Navarro	.10
168	Billy Ashley **RC**	.10
169	Phil Dauphin	.10
170	Ivan Cruz	.10
171	Harold Baines	.10
172	Bryan Harvey	.10
173	Alex Cole	.10
174	Curtis Shaw	.10
175	Matt Williams	.10
176	Felix Jose	.10
177	Sam Horn	.10
178	Randy Johnson	1.50
179	Ivan Calderon	.10
180	Steve Avery	.10
181	William Suero	.10
182	Bill Swift	.10
183	Howard Battle **RC**	.10
184	Ruben Amaro	.10
185	Jim Abbott	.10
186	Mike Fitzgerald	.10
187	Bruce Hurst	.10
188	Jeff Juden	.10
189	Jeromy Burnitz	.10
190	Dave Burba	.10
191	Kevin Brown	.10
192	Patrick Lennon	.10
193	Jeffrey McNeely	.10
194	Wil Cordero	.10
195	Chili Davis	.10
196	Milt Cuyler	.10
197	Von Hayes	.10
198	Todd Revening **RC**	.10
199	Joel Johnson	.10
200	Jeff Bagwell	1.50
201	Alex Fernandez	.10
202	Todd Jones	.10
203	Charles Nagy	.10
204	Tim Raines	.10
205	Kevin Maas	.10
206	Julio Franco	.10
207	Randy Velarde	.10
208	Lance Johnson	.10
209	Scott Leius	.10
210	Derek Lee	.10
211	Joe Sondrini	.10
212	Royce Clayton	.10
213	Chris George	.10
214	Gary Sheffield	.75
215	Mark Gubicza	.10
216	Mike Moore	.10
217	Rick Huisman	.10
218	Jeff Russell	.10
219	D.J. Dozier	.10
220	Dave Martinez	.10
221	Al Newman	.10
222	Nolan Ryan	4.00
223	Teddy Higuera	.10
224	Damon Buford **RC**	.10
225	Ruben Sierra	.10
226	Tom Nevers	.10
227	Tommy Greene	.10
228	Nigel Wilson **RC**	.10
229	John DeSilva	.10
230	Bobby Witt	.10
231	Greg Cadaret	.10
232	John VanderWal	.10
233	Jack Clark	.10
234	Bill Doran	.10
235	Bobby Bonilla	.10
236	Steve Olin	.10
237	Derek Bell	.10
238	David Cone	.10
239	Victor Cole	.10
240	Rod Bolton	.10
241	Tom Pagnozzi	.10
242	Rob Dibble	.10
243	Michael Carter	.10
244	Don Peters	.10
245	Mike LaValliere	.10
246	Joe Perona	.10
247	Mitch Williams	.10
248	Jay Buhner	.10
249	Andy Benes	.10
250	Alex Ochoa **RC**	.10
251	Greg Blosser	.10
252	Jack Armstrong	.10
253	Juan Samuel	.10
254	Terry Pendleton	.10
255	Ramon Martinez	.10
256	Rico Brogna	.10
257	John Smiley	.10
258	Carl Everett	.10
259	Tim Salmon	.10
260	Will Clark	.10
261	Ugueth Urbina **RC**	.40
262	Jason Wood	.10
263	Dave Magadan	.10
264	Dante Bichette	.10
265	Jose DeLeon	.10
266	Mike Neill **RC**	.10
267	Paul O'Neill	.10
268	Anthony Young	.10
269	Greg Harris	.10
270	Todd Van Poppel	.10
271	Pete Castellano	.10
272	Tony Phillips	.10
273	Mike Gallego	.10
274	Steve Cooke **RC**	.10
275	Robin Ventura	.10
276	Kevin Mitchell	.10
277	Doug Linton	.10
278	Robert Eenhorn	.10
279	Gabe White **RC**	.10
280	Dave Stewart	.10
281	Mo Sanford	.10
282	Greg Perschke	.10
283	Kevin Flora	.10
284	Jeff Williams	.10
285	Keith Miller	.10
286	Andy Ashby	.10
287	Doug Dascenzo	.10
288	Eric Karros	.10
289	Glenn Murray **RC**	.10
290	Troy Percival **RC**	1.00
291	Orlando Merced	.10
292	Peter Hoy	.10
293	Tony Fernandez	.10
294	Juan Guzman	.10
295	Jesse Barfield	.10
296	Sid Fernandez	.10
297	Scott Cepicky	.10
298	Garret Anderson **RC**	6.00
299	Cal Eldred	.10
300	Ryne Sandberg	2.00
301	Jim Gantner	.10
302	Mariano Rivera **RC**	25.00
303	Ron Lockett	.10
304	Jose Offerman	.10
305	Denny Martinez	.10
306	Luis Ortiz **RC**	.10
307	David Howard	.10
308	Russ Springer	.10
309	Chris Howard	.10
310	Kyle Abbott	.10
311	Aaron Sele **RC**	1.00
312	Dave Justice	.10
313	Pete O'Brien	.10
314	Greg Hansell	.10
315	Dave Winfield	1.50
316	Lance Dickson	.10
317	Eric King	.10
318	Vaughn Eshelman	.10
319	Tim Belcher	.10
320	Andres Galarraga	.10
321	Scott Bullett	.10
322	Doug Strange	.10
323	Jerald Clark	.10
324	Dave Righetti	.10
325	Greg Hibbard	.10
326	Eric Dillman	.10
327	Shane Reynolds **RC**	.25
328	Chris Hammond	.10
329	Albert Belle	.10
330	Rich Becker **RC**	.10
331	Eddie Williams	.10
332	Donald Harris	.10
333	Dave Smith	.10
334	Steve Fireovid	.10
335	Steve Buechele	.10
336	Mike Schooler	.10
337	Kevin McReynolds	.10
338	Hensley Meulens	.10
339	Benji Gil **RC**	.10
340	Don Mattingly	2.50
341	Alvin Davis	.10
342	Alan Mills	.10
343	Kelly Downs	.10
344	Leo Gomez	.10
345	Tarrik Brock **RC**	.10
346	Ryan Turner	.10
347	John Smoltz	.10
348	Bill Sampen	.10
349	Paul Byrd	.10
350	Mike Bordick	.10
351	Jose Lind	.10
352	David Wells	.10
353	Barry Larkin	.10
354	Bruce Ruffin	.10
355	Luis Rivera	.10
356	Sid Bream	.10
357	Julian Vasquez	.10
358	Jason Bere **RC**	.10
359	Ben McDonald	.10
360	Scott Stahoviak	.10
361	Kirt Manwaring	.10
362	Jeff Johnson	.10
363	Rob Deer	.10
364	Tony Pena	.10
365	Melido Perez	.10
366	Clay Parker	.10
367	Dale Sveum	.10
368	Mike Scioscia	.10
369	Roger Salkeld	.10
370	Mike Stanley	.10
371	Jack McDowell	.10
372	Tim Wallach	.10
373	Billy Ripken	.10
374	Mike Christopher	.10
375	Paul Molitor	1.50
376	Dave Stieb	.10
377	Pedro Guerrero	.10
378	Russ Swan	.10
379	Bob Ojeda	.10
380	Donn Pall	.10
381	Eddie Zosky	.10
382	Darnell Coles	.10
383	Tom Smith	.10
384	Mark McGwire	3.00
385	Gary Carter	1.50
386	Rich Amaral	.10
387	Alan Embree	.10
388	Jonathan Hurst	.10
389	Bobby Jones **RC**	.10
390	Rico Rossy	.10
391	Dan Smith	.10
392	Terry Steinbach	.10
393	Jon Farrell	.10
394	Dave Anderson	.10
395	Benito Santiago	.10
396	Mark Wohlers	.10
397	Mo Vaughn	.10
398	Randy Kramer	.10
399	John Jaha **RC**	.10
400	Cal Ripken, Jr.	4.00
401	Ryan Bowen	.10
402	Tim McIntosh	.10
403	Bernard Gilkey	.10
404	Junior Felix	.10
405	Cris Colon	.10
406	Marc Newfield	.10
407	Bernie Williams	.10
408	Jay Howell	.10
409	Zane Smith	.10
410	Jeff Shaw	.10
411	Kerry Woodson	.10
412	Wes Chamberlain	.10
413	Dave Mlicki	.10
414	Benny Distefano	.10
415	Kevin Rogers	.10
416	Tim Naehring	.10
417	Clemente Nunez	.10
418	Luis Sojo	.10
419	Kevin Ritz	.10
420	Omar Oliveras	.10
421	Manuel Lee	.10
422	Julio Valera	.10
423	Omar Vizquel	.10
424	Darren Burton	.10
425	Mel Hall	.10
426	Dennis Powell	.10
427	Lee Stevens	.10
428	Glenn Davis	.10
429	Willie Greene	.10
430	Kevin Wickander	.10
431	Dennis Eckersley	1.25
432	Joe Orsulak	.10
433	Eddie Murray	1.50
434	Matt Stairs **RC**	.10
435	Wally Joyner	.10
436	Rondell White	.10
437	Rob Mauer	.10
438	Joe Redfield	.10
439	Mark Lewis	.10
440	Darren Daulton	.10
441	Mike Henneman	.10

442	John Cangelosi	.10
443	Vince Moore **RC**	.10
444	John Wehner	.10
445	Kent Hrbek	.10
446	Mark McLemore	.10
447	Bill Wegman	.10
448	Robby Thompson	.10
449	Mark Anthony	.10
450	Archi Cianfrocco	.10
451	Johnny Ruffin	.10
452	Javier Lopez	.10
453	Greg Gohr	.10
454	Tim Scott	.10
455	Stan Belinda	.10
456	Darrin Jackson	.10
457	Chris Gardner	.10
458	Esteban Beltre	.10
459	Phil Plantier	.10
460	Jim Thome	1.25
461	Mike Piazza **RC**	25.00
462	Matt Sinatro	.10
463	Scott Servais	.10
464	Brian Jordan **RC**	.75
465	Doug Drabek	.10
466	Carl Willis	.10
467	Bret Barbarie	.10
468	Hal Morris	.10
469	Steve Sax	.10
470	Jerry Willard	.10
471	Dan Wilson	.10
472	Chris Hoiles	.10
473	Rheal Cormier	.10
474	John Morris	.10
475	Jeff Reardon	.10
476	Mark Leiter	.10
477	Tom Gordon	.10
478	Kent Bottenfield **RC**	.10
479	Gene Larkin	.10
480	Dwight Gooden	.10
481	B.J. Surhoff	.10
482	Andy Stankiewicz	.10
483	Tino Martinez	.10
484	Craig Biggio	.10
485	Denny Neagle	.10
486	Rusty Meacham	.10
487	Kal Daniels	.10
488	Dave Henderson	.10
489	Tim Costo	.10
490	Doug Davis	.10
491	Frank Viola	.10
492	Cory Snyder	.10
493	Chris Martin	.10
494	Dion James	.10
495	Randy Tomlin	.10
496	Greg Vaughn	.10
497	Dennis Cook	.10
498	Rosario Rodriguez	.10
499	Dave Staton	.10
500	George Brett	2.50
501	Brian Barnes	.10
502	Butch Henry	.10
503	Harold Reynolds	.10
504	David Nied **RC**	.10
505	Lee Smith	.10
506	Steve Chitren	.10
507	Ken Hill	.10
508	Robbie Beckett	.10
509	Troy Afenir	.10
510	Kelly Gruber	.10
511	Bret Boone	.10
512	Jeff Branson	.10
513	Mike Jackson	.10
514	Pete Harnisch	.10
515	Chad Kreuter	.10
516	Joe Vitko	.10
517	Orel Hershiser	.10
518	John Doherty **RC**	.10
519	Jay Bell	.10
520	Mark Langston	.10
521	Dann Howitt	.10
522	Bobby Reed	.10
523	Roberto Munoz	.10
524	Todd Ritchie	.10
525	Bip Roberts	.10
526	Pat Listach **RC**	.10
527	Scott Brosius **RC**	.10
528	John Roper **RC**	.10
529	Phil Hiatt **RC**	.10
530	Denny Walling	.10
531	Carlos Baerga	.10
532	Manny Ramirez **RC**	25.00
533	Pat Clements	.10
534	Ron Gant	.10
535	Pat Kelly	.10
536	Billy Spiers	.10
537	Darren Reed	.10
538	Ken Caminiti	.10
539	Butch Huskey **RC**	.10
540	Matt Nokes	.10
541	John Kruk	.10
542	John Jaha/SP (Foil)	.40
543	Justin Thompson **RC**	.10
544	Steve Hosey	.10
545	Joe Kmak	.10
546	John Franco	.10
547	Devon White	.10
548	Elston Hansen/SP (Foil)	.40
549	Ryan Klesko	.10
550	Danny Tartabull	.10
551	Frank Thomas/SP (Foil)	1.50
552	Kevin Tapani	.10
553a	Willie Banks	.10
553b	Pat Clements	.10
554	B.J. Wallace **RC**/SP (Foil)	.40
555	Orlando Miller **RC**	.10

556	Mark Smith **RC**	.10
557	Tim Wallach (Foil)	.10
558	Bill Gullickson	.10
559	Derek Bell (Foil)	.10
560	Joe Randa (Foil)	.10
561	Frank Seminara	.10
562	Mark Gardner	.10
563	Rick Greene (Foil)	.10
564	Gary Gaetti	.10
565	Ozzie Guillen	.10
566	Charles Nagy (Foil)	.10
567	Mike Milchin	.10
568	Ben Shelton (Foil)	.10
569	Chris Roberts (Foil)	.10
570	Ellis Burks	.10
571	Scott Scudder	.10
572	Jim Abbott (Foil)	.10
573	Joe Carter	.10
574	Steve Finley	.10
575	Jim Olander (Foil)	.10
576	Carlos Garcia	.10
577	Greg Olson	.10
578	Greg Swindell (Foil)	.10
579	Matt Williams (Foil)	.10
580	Mark Grace	.10
581	Howard House (Foil)	.10
582	Luis Polonia	.10
583	Erik Hanson	.10
584	Salomon Torres (Foil)	.10
585	Carlton Fisk	1.50
586	Bret Saberhagen	.10
587	Chad McDonnell **RC** (Foil)	.10
588	Jimmy Key	.10
589	Mike MacFarlane	.10
590	Barry Bonds (Foil)	3.50
591	Jamie McAndrew	.10
592	Shane Mack	.10
593	Kerwin Moore	.10
594	Joe Oliver	.10
595	Chris Sabo	.10
596	Alex Gonzalez **RC**	.50
597	Brett Butler	.10
598	Mark Hutton	.10
599	Andy Benes (Foil)	.10
600	Jose Canseco	.75
601	Darryl Kile	.10
602	Matt Stairs/SP (Foil)	.40
603	Rob Butler (Foil)	.10
604	Willie McGee	.10
605	Jack McDowell	.10
606	Tom Candiotti	.10
607	Ed Martel	.10
608	Matt Mieske (Foil)	.10
609	Darrin Fletcher	.10
610	Rafael Palmeiro	1.25
611	Bill Swift (Foil)	.10
612	Mike Mussina	.75
613	Vince Coleman	.10
614	Scott Cepicky (Foil)	.10
615	Mike Greenwell	.10
616	Kevin McGehee	.10
617	Jeffrey Hammonds (Foil)	.10
618	Scott Taylor	.10
619	Dave Otto	.10
620	Mark McGwire (Foil)	3.00
621	Kevin Tatar	.10
622	Steve Farr	.10
623	Ryan Klesko (Foil)	.10
624	Andre Dawson	.40
626	Tino Martinez/SP (Foil)	.50
627	Chad Curtis **RC**	.50
628	Mickey Morandini	.10
629	Gregg Olson/SP (Foil)	.40
630	Lou Whitaker	.10
631	Arthur Rhodes	.10
632	Brandon Wilson	.10
633	Lance Jennings **RC**	.10
634	Allen Watson **RC**	.10
635	Len Dykstra	.10
636	Joe Girardi	.10
637	Kiki Hernandez/SP (Foil)	.40
638	Mike Hampton **RC**	1.00
639	Al Osuna	.10
640	Kevin Appier	.10
641	Rick Helling/SP (Foil)	.40
642	Jody Reed	.10
643	Ray Lankford	.10
644	John Olerud	.10
645	Paul Molitor/SP (Foil)	1.50
646	Pat Borders	.10
647	Mike Morgan	.10
648	Larry Walker	.10
649	Pete Castellano/SP (Foil)	.40
650	Fred McGriff	.10
651	Walt Weiss	.10
652	Calvin Murray **RC**/SP (Foil)	.40
653	Dave Nilsson	.10
654	Greg Pirkl	.10
655	Robin Ventura/SP (Foil)	.40
656	Mark Portugal	.10
657	Roger McDowell	.10
658	Rick Hirtensteiner/SP (Foil)	.40
659	Glenallen Hill	.10
660	Greg Gagne	.10
661	Charles Johnson/SP (Foil)	.40
662	Brian Hunter	.10
663	Mark Lemke	.10
664	Tim Belcher/SP (Foil)	.40
665	Rich DeLucia	.10
666	Bob Walk	.10
667	Joe Carter/SP (Foil)	.40
668	Jose Guzman	.10
669	Otis Nixon	.10
670	Phil Nevin (Foil)	.10

671	Eric Davis	.10
672	Damion Easley **RC**	.25
673	Will Clark (Foil)	.10
674	Mark Kiefer	.10
675	Ozzie Smith	2.00
676	Manny Ramirez (Foil)	15.00
677	Gregg Olson	.10
678	Cliff Floyd **RC**	1.00
679	Duane Singleton	.10
680	Jose Rijo	.10
681	Willie Randolph	.10
682	Michael Tucker **RC** (Foil)	.25
683	Darren Lewis	.10
684	Dale Murphy	.50
685	Mike Pagliarulo	.10
686	Paul Miller	.10
687	Mike Robertson	.10
688	Mike Devereaux	.10
689	Pedro Astacio	.10
690	Alan Trammell	.10
691	Roger Clemens	2.50
692	Bud Black	.10
693	Turk Wendell	.10
694	Barry Larkin/SP (Foil)	.75
695	Todd Zeile	.10
696	Pat Hentgen	.10
697	Eddie Taubensee **RC**	.10
698	Guillermo Vasquez	.10
699	Tom Glavine	.75
700	Robin Yount	1.50
701	Checklist	.10
702	Checklist	.10
703	Checklist	.10
704	Checklist	.10
705	Checklist	.10

1993 Bowman

		NM/M
Complete Set (708):		35.00
Common Player:		.10
Pack (15):		1.50
Wax Box (24):		35.00
Jumbo Pack (22):		2.50
Jumbo Box (20):		40.00
1	Glenn Davis	.10
2	Hector Roa **RC**	.10
3	Ken Ryan **RC**	.10
4	Derek Wallace **RC**	.10
5	Jorge Fabregas	.10
6	Joe Oliver	.10
7	Brandon Wilson	.10
8	Mark Thompson **RC**	.10
9	Tracy Sanders	.10
10	Rich Renteria	.10
11	Lou Whitaker	.10
12	Brian Hunter **RC**	.10
13	Joe Vitiello	.10
14	Eric Karros	.10
15	Joe Kmak	.10
16	Tavo Alvarez	.10
17	Steve Dunn **RC**	.10
18	Tony Fernandez	.10
19	Melido Perez	.10
20	Mike Lieberthal	.10
21	Terry Steinbach	.10
22	Stan Belinda	.10
23	Jay Buhner	.10
24	Allen Watson	.10
25	Daryl Henderson **RC**	.10
26	Ray McDavid **RC**	.10
27	Shawn Green	.30
28	Bud Black	.10
29	Sherman Obando **RC**	.10
30	Mike Hostetler **RC**	.10
31	Nate Hinchey **RC**	.10
32	Randy Myers	.10
33	Brian Grebeck **RC**	.10
34	John Roper	.10
35	Larry Thomas	.10
36	Alex Cole	.10
37	Tom Kramer **RC**	.10
38	Matt Whisenant **RC**	.10
39	Chris Gomez **RC**	.10
40	Luis Gonzalez	.10
41	Kevin Appier	.10
42	Omar Daal **RC**	.10
43	Duane Singleton	.10
44	Bill Risley	.10
45	Pat Meares **RC**	.10
46	Butch Huskey	.10
47	Bobby Munoz	.10
48	Juan Bell	.10
49	Scott Lydy **RC**	.10
50	Dennis Moeller	.10
51	Marc Newfield	.10
52	Tripp Cromer **RC**	.10
53	Kurt Miller	.10
54	Jim Pena	.10
55	Juan Guzman	.10
56	Matt Williams	.10
57	Harold Reynolds	.10
58	Donnie Elliott **RC**	.10
59	Jon Shave **RC**	.10
60	Kevin Roberson **RC**	.10
61	Hilly Hathaway **RC**	.10
62	Jose Rijo	.10
63	Kerry Taylor **RC**	.10
64	Ryan Hawblitzel	.10
65	Glenallen Hill	.10
66	Ramon D. Martinez **RC**	.10
67	Travis Fryman	.10
68	Tom Nevers	.10
69	Phil Hiatt	.10
70	Tim Wallach	.10
71	B.J. Surhoff	.10
72	Rondell White	.10
73	Denny Hocking **RC**	.10
74	Mike Oquist **RC**	.10
75	Paul O'Neill	.10
76	Willie Banks	.10
77	Bob Welch	.10
78	Jose Sandoval **RC**	.10
79	Bill Haselman	.10
80	Rheal Cormier	.10
81	Dean Palmer	.10
82	Pat Gomez **RC**	.10
83	Steve Karsay	.10
84	Carl Hanselman **RC**	.10
85	T.R. Lewis **RC**	.10
86	Chipper Jones	2.00
87	Scott Hatteberg	.10
88	Greg Hibbard	.10
89	Lance Painter **RC**	.10
90	Chad Mottola **RC**	.10
91	Jason Bere	.10
92	Dante Bichette	.10
93	Sandy Alomar	.10
94	Carl Everett	.10
95	Danny Bautista **RC**	.10
96	Steve Finley	.10
97	David Cone	.10
98	Todd Hollandsworth	.10
99	Matt Mieske	.10
100	Larry Walker	.10
101	Shane Mack	.10
102	Aaron Ledesma **RC**	.10
103	Andy Pettitte **RC**	4.00
104	Kevin Stocker	.10
105	Mike Mobler	.10
106	Tony Menedez	.10
107	Derek Lowe	.10
108	Basil Shabazz	.10
109	Dan Smith	.10
110	Scott Sanders **RC**	.10
111	Todd Stottlemyre	.10
112	Benji Sikonton **RC**	.10
113	Rick Sutcliffe	.10
114	Lee Heath **RC**	.10
115	Jeff Russell	.10
116	Dave Stevens **RC**	.10
117	Mark Holzemer **RC**	.10
118	Tim Belcher	.10
119	Bobby Thigpen	.10
120	Roger Bailey **RC**	.10
121	Tony Mitchell **RC**	.10
122	Junior Felix	.10
123	Rich Robertson **RC**	.10
124	Andy Cook **RC**	.10
125	Brian Bevil **RC**	.10
126	Darryl Strawberry	.10
127	Cal Eldred	.10
128	Cliff Floyd	.10
129	Alan Newman	.10
130	Howard Johnson	.10
131	Jim Abbott	.10
132	Chad McConnell	.10
133	Miguel Jimenez **RC**	.10
134	Brett Backlund **RC**	.10
135	John Cummings **RC**	.10
136	Brian Barber	.10
137	Rafael Palmeiro	1.25
138	Tim Worrell **RC**	.10
139	Jose Pett **RC**	.10
140	Barry Bonds	4.00
141	Damon Buford	.10
142	Jeff Blauser	.10
143	Frankie Rodriguez	.10
144	Mike Morgan	.10
145	Gary DeSarcina	.10
146	Calvin Reese	.10
147	Johnny Ruffin	.10
148	David Nied	.10
149	Charles Nagy	.10
150	Mike Myers **RC**	.10
151	Kenny Carlyle **RC**	.10
152	Eric Anthony	.10
153	Jose Lind	.10
154	Pedro Martinez	1.50
155	Mark Kiefer	.10
156	Tim Laker **RC**	.10
157	Pat Mahomes	.10
158	Bobby Bonilla	.10
159	Domingo Jean	.10
160	Darren Daulton	.10
161	Mark McGwire	3.50
162	Jason Kendall **RC**	1.00

163	Desi Relaford	.10
164	Ozzie Canseco	.10
165	Rick Helling	.10
166	Steve Pegues **RC**	.10
167	Paul Molitor	1.50
168	Larry Carter **RC**	.10
169	Arthur Rhodes	.10
170	Damon Hollins **RC**	.10
171	Frank Viola	.10
172	Steve Trachsel **RC**	.25
173	J.T. Snow **RC**	.50
174	Keith Gordon **RC**	.10
175	Carlton Fisk	1.50
176	Jason Bates **RC**	.10
177	Mike Crosby **RC**	.10
178	Benny Santiago	.10
179	Mike Moore	.10
180	Jeff Juden	.10
181	Darren Burton	.10
182	Todd Williams **RC**	.10
183	John Jaha	.10
184	Mike Lansing **RC**	.50
185	Pedro Grifol **RC**	.10
186	Vince Coleman	.10
187	Pat Kelly	.10
188	Clemente Alvarez **RC**	.10
189	Ron Darling	.10
190	Orlando Merced	.10
191	Chris Bosio	.10
192	Steve Dixon **RC**	.10
193	Doug Dascenzo	.10
194	Ray Holbert **RC**	.10
195	Howard Battle	.10
196	Willie McGee	.10
197	John O'Donoghue **RC**	.10
198	Steve Avery	.10
199	Greg Blosser	.10
200	Ryne Sandberg	2.00
201	Joe Grahe	.10
202	Dan Wilson	.10
203	Domingo Martinez **RC**	.10
204	Andres Galarraga	.10
205	Jamie Taylor **RC**	.10
206	Darrell Whitmore **RC**	.10
207	Ben Blomdahl **RC**	.10
208	Doug Drabek	.10
209	Keith Miller	.10
210	Billy Ashley	.10
211	Mike Farrell **RC**	.10
212	John Wetteland	.10
213	Randy Tomlin	.10
214	Sid Fernandez	.10
215	Quilvio Veras **RC**	.10
216	Dave Hollins	.10
217	Mike Neill	.10
218	Andy Van Slyke	.10
219	Bret Boone	.10
220	Tom Pagnozzi	.10
221	Mike Welch **RC**	.10
222	Frank Seminara	.10
223	Ron Villone	.10
224	D.J. Thielen **RC**	.10
225	Cal Ripken, Jr.	4.00
226	Pedro Borbon **RC**	.10
227	Carlos Quintana	.10
228	Tommy Shields **RC**	.10
229	Tim Salmon	.10
230	John Smiley	.10
231	Ellis Burks	.10
232	Pedro Castellano	.10
233	Paul Byrd	.10
234	Bryan Harvey	.10
235	Scott Livingstone	.10
236	James Mouton **RC**	.10
237	Joe Randa	.10
238	Pedro Astacio	.10
239	Darryl Hamilton	.10
240	Joey Eischen **RC**	.10
241	Edgar Herrera **RC**	.10
242	Dwight Gooden	.10
243	Sam Militello	.10
244	Ron Blazier **RC**	.10
245	Ruben Sierra	.10
246	Al Martin	.10
247	Mike Felder	.10
248	Bob Tewksbury	.10
249	Craig Lefferts	.10
250	Luis Lopez	.10
251	Devon White	.10
252	Will Clark	.10
253	Mark Smith	.10
254	Terry Pendleton	.10
255	Aaron Sele	.10
256	Jose Viera **RC**	.10
257	Damion Easley	.10
258	Rod Lofton **RC**	.10
259	Chris Snopek **RC**	.10
260	Quinton McCracken **RC**	.10
261	Mike Matthews **RC**	.10
262	Hector Carrasco **RC**	.10
263	Rick Greene	.10
264	Chris Bolt **RC**	.10
265	George Brett	2.50
266	Rick Gorecki **RC**	.10
267	Francisco Gamez **RC**	.10
268	Marquis Grissom	.10
269	Kevin Tapani	.10
270	Ryan Thompson	.10
271	Gerald Williams	.10
272	Paul Fletcher **RC**	.10
273	Lance Blankenship	.10
274	Marty Heff **RC**	.10
275	Shawn Estes	.10
276	Rene Arocha **RC**	.10
277	Scott Eyre **RC**	.10
278	Phil Plantier	.10
279	Paul Spoljaric **RC**	.10
280	Chris Gahbs	.10
281	Harold Baines	.10
282	Jose Oliva **RC**	.10
283	Matt Whiteside	.10
284	Brant Brown **RC**	.10
285	Russ Springer	.10
286	Chris Sabo	.10
287	Ozzie Guillen	.10
288	Marcus Moore **RC**	.10
289	Chad Ogea	.10
290	Walt Weiss	.10
291	Brian Edmondson	.10
292	Jimmy Gonzalez	.10
293	Danny Miceli **RC**	.10
294	Jose Offerman	.10
295	Greg Vaughn	.10
296	Frank Bolick	.10
297	Mike Maksudian **RC**	.10
298	John Franco	.10
299	Danny Tartabull	.10
300	Len Dykstra	.10
301	Bobby Witt	.10
302	Trey Beamon **RC**	.10
303	Tino Martinez	.10
304	Aaron Holbert	.10
305	Juan Gonzalez	.75
306	Billy Hall **RC**	.10
307	Duane Ward	.10
308	Rod Beck	.10
309	Jose Mercedes **RC**	.10
310	Otis Nixon	.10
311	Gettys Glaze **RC**	.10
312	Candy Maldonado	.10
313	Chad Curtis	.10
314	Tim Costo	.10
315	Mike Robertson	.10
316	Nigel Wilson	.10
317	Greg McMichael **RC**	.10
318	Scott Pose **RC**	.10
319	Ivan Cruz	.10
320	Greg Swindell	.10
321	Kevin McReynolds	.10
322	Tom Candiotti	.10
323	Bob Wishnevski **RC**	.10
324	Ken Hill	.10
325	Kirby Puckett	2.00
326	Tim Bogar **RC**	.10
327	Mariano Rivera	.30
328	Mitch Williams	.10
329	Craig Paquette	.10
330	Jay Bell	.10
331	Jose Martinez **RC**	.10
332	Rob Deer	.10
333	Brook Fordyce	.10
334	Matt Nokes	.10
335	Derek Lee	.10
336	Paul Ellis **RC**	.10
337	Desi Wilson **RC**	.10
338	Roberto Alomar	.30
339	Jim Tatum (Foil)	.10
340	J.T. Snow (Foil)	.10
341	Tim Salmon (Foil)	.10
342	Russ Davis **RC** (Foil)	.25
343	Javier Lopez (Foil)	.10
344	Troy O'Leary **RC** (Foil)	.10
345	Marty Cordova **RC** (Foil)	.60
346	Bubba Smith **RC** (Foil)	.10
347	Chipper Jones (Foil)	1.50
348	Jessie Hollins (Foil)	.10
349	Willie Greene (Foil)	.10
350	Mark Thompson (Foil)	.10
351	Nigel Wilson (Foil)	.10
352	Todd Jones (Foil)	.10
353	Raul Mondesi (Foil)	.10
354	Cliff Floyd (Foil)	.10
355	Bobby Jones (Foil)	.10
356	Kevin Stocker (Foil)	.10
357	Midre Cummings (Foil)	.10
358	Allen Watson (Foil)	.10
359	Ray McDavid (Foil)	.10
360	Steve Hosey (Foil)	.10
361	Brad Pennington (Foil)	.10
362	Frankie Rodriguez (Foil)	.10
363	Troy Percival (Foil)	.10
364	Jason Bere (Foil)	.10
365	Manny Ramirez (Foil)	.75
366	Justin Thompson (Foil)	.10
367	Joe Vitello (Foil)	.10
368	Tyrone Hill (Foil)	.10
369	David McCarty (Foil)	.10
370	Brien Taylor (Foil)	.10
371	Todd Van Poppel (Foil)	.10
372	Marc Newfield (Foil)	.10
373	Terrell Lowery **RC** (Foil)	.10
374	Alex Gonzalez (Foil)	.10
375	Ken Griffey Jr.	3.00
376	Donovan Osborne	.10
377	Ritchie Moody **RC**	.10
378	Shane Andrews	.10
379	Carlos Delgado	.65
380	Bill Swift	.10
381	Leo Gomez	.10
382	Ron Gant	.10
383	Scott Fletcher	.10
384	Matt Walbeck **RC**	.10
385	Chuck Finley	.10
386	Kevin Mitchell	.10
387	Wilson Alvarez	.10
388	John Burke **RC**	.10
389	Alan Embree	.10
390	Trevor Hoffman	.10
391	Alan Trammell	.10
392	Todd Jones	.10
393	Felix Jose	.10
394	Orel Hershiser	.10
395	Pat Listach	.10
396	Gabe White	.10
397	Dan Serafini **RC**	.10
398	Todd Hundley	.10
399	Wade Boggs	2.00
400	Tyler Green	.10
401	Mike Bordick	.10
402	Scott Bullett	.10
403	Lagrande Russell **RC**	.10
404	Ray Lankford	.10
405	Nolan Ryan	4.00
406	Robbie Beckett	.10
407	Brent Bowers **RC**	.10
408	Adell Davenport **RC**	.10
409	Brady Anderson	.10
410	Tom Glavine	.35
411	Doug Hecker **RC**	.10
412	Jose Guzman	.10
413	Luis Polonia	.10
414	Brian Williams	.10
415	Bo Jackson	.15
416	Eric Young	.10
417	Kenny Lofton	.10
418	Orestes Destrade	.10
419	Tony Phillips	.10
420	Jeff Bagwell	1.50
421	Hark Gardner	.10
422	Brett Butler	.10
423	Graeme Lloyd **RC**	.10
424	Delino DeShields	.10
425	Scott Erickson	.10
426	Jeff Kent	.10
427	Jimmy Key	.10
428	Mickey Morandini	.10
429	Marcos Arkas **RC**	.10
430	Don Slaught	.10
431	Randy Johnson	1.50
432	Omar Olivares	.10
433	Charlie Leibrandt	.10
434	Kurt Stillwell	.10
435	Scott Brow **RC**	.10
436	Robby Thompson	.10
437	Ben McDonald	.10
438	Deion Sanders	.10
439	Tony Pena	.10
440	Mark Grace	.10
441	Eduardo Perez	.10
442	Tim Pugh **RC**	.10
443	Scott Ruffcorn	.10
444	Jay Gainer **RC**	.10
445	Albert Belle	.10
446	Bret Barberie	.10
447	Justin Mashore	.10
448	Pete Harnisch	.10
449	Greg Gagne	.10
450	Eric Davis	.10
451	Dave Mlicki	.10
452	Moises Alou	.10
453	Rick Aguilera	.10
454	Eddie Murray	1.50
455	Bob Wickman	.10
456	Wes Chamberlain	.10
457	Brent Gates	.10
458	Paul Weber	.10
459	Mike Hampton	.10
460	Ozzie Smith	2.00
461	Tom Henke	.10
462	Ricky Gutuerrez	.10
463	Jack Morris	.10
464	Joel Chimelis **RC**	.10
465	Gregg Olson	.10
466	Javier Lopez	.10
467	Scott Cooper	.10
468	Willie Wilson	.10
469	Mark Langston	.10
470	Barry Larkin	.10
471	Rod Bolton	.10
472	Freddie Benavides	.10
473	Ken Ramos **RC**	.10
474	Chuck Carr	.10
475	Cecil Fielder	.10
476	Eddie Taubensee	.10
477	Chris Eddy **RC**	.10
478	Greg Hansell	.10
479	Kevin Reimer	.10
480	Denny Martinez	.10
481	Chuck Knoblauch	.10
482	Mike Draper	.10
483	Spike Owen	.10
484	Terry Mulholland	.10
485	Dennis Eckersley	1.25
486	Blas Minor	.10
487	Dave Fleming	.10
488	Dan Cholonsky	.10
489	Ivan Rodriguez	1.25
490	Gary Sheffield	.45
491	Ed Sprague	.10
492	Steve Hosey	.10
493	Jimmy Haynes **RC**	.10
494	John Smoltz	.10
495	Andre Dawson	.35
496	Rey Sanchez	.10
497	Ty Van Burkleo **RC**	.10
498	Bobby Ayala **RC**	.10
499	Tim Raines	.10
500	Charlie Hayes	.10
501	Paul Sorrento	.10
502	Richie Lewis **RC**	.10
503	Jason Pfaff **RC**	.10
504	Ken Caminiti	.10
505	Mike Macfarlane	.10
506	Jody Reed	.10
507	Bobby Hughes **RC**	.10
508	Wil Cordero	.10
509	George Tsanis **RC**	.10
510	Bret Saberhagen	.10
511	Derek Jeter **RC**	20.00
512	Gene Schall	.10
513	Curtis Shaw	.10
514	Steve Cooke	.10
515	Edgar Martinez	.10
516	Mike Milchin	.10
517	Billy Ripken	.10
518	Andy Benes	.10
519	Juan de la Rosa **RC**	.10
520	John Burkett	.10
521	Alex Ochoa	.10
522	Tony Tarasco **RC**	.10
523	Luis Ortiz	.10
524	Rick Williams	.10
525	Chris Turner **RC**	.10
526	Rob Dibble	.10
527	Jack McDowell	.10
528	Daryl Boston	.10
529	Bill Wertz **RC**	.10
530	Charlie Hough	.10
531	Sean Bergman	.10
532	Doug Jones	.10
533	Jeff Montgomery	.10
534	Roger Cedeno **RC**	.25
535	Robin Yount	1.50
536	Mo Vaughn	.10
537	Brian Harper	.10
538	Juan Castillo	.10
539	Steve Farr	.10
540	John Kruk	.10
541	Troy Neel	.10
542	Danny Clyburn **RC**	.10
543	Jim Converse **RC**	.10
544	Gregg Jefferies	.10
545	Jose Canseco	.40
546	Julio Bruno **RC**	.10
547	Rob Butler	.10
548	Royce Clayton	.10
549	Chris Hoiles	.10
550	Greg Maddux	2.00
551	Joe Ciccarella **RC**	.10
552	Ozzie Timmons	.10
553	Chili Davis	.10
554	Brian Koelling	.10
555	Frank Thomas	1.50
556	Vinny Castilla	.10
557	Reggie Jefferson	.10
558	Rob Natal	.10
559	Mike Henneman	.10
560	Craig Biggio	.10
561	Billy Brewer **RC**	.10
562	Dan Melendez	.10
563	Kenny Felder **RC**	.10
564	Miguel Batista **RC**	.10
565	Dave Winfield	1.50
566	Al Shirley	.10
567	Robert Eenhoorn	.10
568	Mike Williams	.10
569	Tanyon Sturtze **RC**	.10
570	Tim Wakefield	.10
571	Greg Pirkl	.10
572	Sean Lowe **RC**	.25
573	Terry Burows **RC**	.10
574	Kevin Higgins **RC**	.10
575	Joe Carter	.10
576	Kevin Rogers	.10
577	Manny Alexander	.10
578	Dave Justice	.10
579	Brian Conroy **RC**	.10
580	Jessie Hollins **RC**	.10
581	Ron Watson **RC**	.10
582	Bip Roberts	.10
583	Tom Urbani **RC**	.10
584	Jason Hutchins **RC**	.10
585	Carlos Baerga	.10
586	Jeff Mutis	.10
587	Justin Thompson	.10
588	Orlando Miller	.10
589	Brian McRae	.10
590	Ramon Martinez	.10
591	Dave Nilsson	.10
592	Jose Vidro **RC**	1.50
593	Rich Becker	.10
594	Preston Wilson **RC**	1.50
595	Don Mattingly	2.50
596	Tony Longmire	.10
597	Kevin Seitzer	.10
598	Midre Cummings **RC**	.10
599	Omar Vizquel	.10
600	Lee Smith	.10
601	David Hulse **RC**	.10
602	Darrell Sherman **RC**	.10
603	Alex Gonzalez	.10
604	Geronimo Pena	.10
605	Mike Devereaux	.10
606	Sterling Hitchcock **RC**	.25
607	Mike Greenwell	.10
608	Steve Buechele	.10
609	Troy Percival	.10
610	Bobby Kelly	.10
611	James Baldwin **RC**	.10
612	Jerald Clark	.10
613	Albie Lopez **RC**	.10
614	Dave Magadan	.10
615	Mickey Tettleton	.10
616	Sean Runyan **RC**	.10
617	Bob Hamelin	.10
618	Raul Mondesi	.10
619	Tyrone Hill	.10
620	Darrin Fletcher	.10
621	Mike Trombley	.10
622	Jeromy Burnitz	.10

623	Bernie Williams	.10
624	Mike Farmer **RC**	.10
625	Rickey Henderson	1.50
626	Carlos Garcia	.10
627	Jeff Darwin **RC**	.10
628	Todd Zeile	.10
629	Benji Gil	.10
630	Tony Gwynn	2.00
631	Aaron Small **RC**	.10
632	Joe Rosselli **RC**	.10
633	Mike Mussina	1.00
634	Ryan Klesko	.10
635	Roger Clemens	2.50
636	Sammy Sosa	2.00
637	Orlando Palmeiro **RC**	.10
638	Willie Greene	.10
639	George Bell	.10
640	Garvin Alston **RC**	.10
641	Pete Janicki **RC**	.10
642	Chris Sheff **RC**	.10
643	Felipe Lira **RC**	.10
644	Roberto Petagine	.10
645	Wally Joyner	.10
646	Mike Piazza	3.00
647	Jaime Navarro	.10
648	Jeff Hartsock **RC**	.10
649	David McCarty	.10
650	Bobby Jones	.10
651	Mark Hutton	.10
652	Kyle Abbott	.10
653	Steve Cox **RC**	.10
654	Jeff King	.10
655	Norm Charlton	.10
656	Mike Gulan **RC**	.10
657	Julio Franco	.10
658	Cameron Cairncross **RC**	.10
659	John Olerud	.10
660	Salomon Torres	.10
661	Brad Pennington	.10
662	Melvin Nieves	.10
663	Ivan Calderon	.10
664	Turk Wendell	.10
665	Chris Pritchett	.10
666	Reggie Sanders	.10
667	Robin Ventura	.10
668	Joe Girardi	.10
669	Manny Ramirez	1.50
670	Jeff Conine	.10
671	Greg Gohr	.10
672	Andujar Cedeno	.10
673	Les Norman **RC**	.10
674	Mike James **RC**	.10
675	Marshall Boze **RC**	.10
676	B.J. Wallace	.10
677	Kent Hrbek	.10
678	Jack Voight	.10
679	Brien Taylor	.10
680	Curt Schilling	.35
681	Todd Van Poppel	.10
682	Kevin Young	.10
683	Tommy Adams	.10
684	Bernard Gilkey	.10
685	Kevin Brown	.10
686	Fred McGriff	.10
687	Pat Borders	.10
688	Kirt Manwaring	.10
689	Sid Bream	.10
690	John Valentin	.10
691	Steve Olsen **RC**	.10
692	Roberto Mejia **RC**	.10
693	Carlos Delgado (Foil)	.50
694	Steve Gibralter **RC** (Foil)	.10
695	Gary Mota (Foil)	.10
696	Jose Malave **RC** (Foil)	.10
697	Larry Sutton **RC** (Foil)	.10
698	Dan Frye **RC** (Foil)	.10
699	Tim Clark **RC** (Foil)	.10
700	Brian Rupp **RC** (Foil)	.10
701	Felipe Alou, Moises Alou (Foil)	.10
702	Bobby Bonds, Barry Bonds (Foil)	1.00
703	Ken Griffey Sr., Ken Griffey Jr. (Foil)	1.00
704	Hal McRae, Brian McRae (Foil)	.10
705	Checklist 1	.10
706	Checklist 2	.10
707	Checklist 3	.10
708	Checklist 4	.10

1994 Bowman Previews

		NM/M
Complete Set (10):		7.00
Common Player:		.50
1	Frank Thomas	1.50
2	Mike Piazza	3.00
3	Albert Belle	.50
4	Javier Lopez	.50
5	Cliff Floyd	.50
6	Alex Gonzalez	.50
7	Ricky Bottalico	.50
8	Tony Clark	.50
9	Mac Suzuki	.50
10	James Mouton (Foil)	.50

1994 Bowman

		NM/M
Complete Set (682):		40.00
Common Player:		.10
Pack (12):		1.50
Wax Box (24):		30.00
1	Joe Carter	.10
2	Marcus Moore	.10
3	Doug Creek **RC**	.10
4	Pedro Martinez	1.50
5	Ken Griffey Jr.	3.00
6	Greg Swindell	.10
7	J.J. Johnson	.10
8	Homer Bush **RC**	.10
9	Arquimedez Pozo **RC**	.10
10	Bryan Harvey	.10
11	J.T. Snow	.10
12	Alan Benes **RC**	.10
13	Chad Kreuter	.10
14	Eric Karros	.10
15	Frank Thomas	1.50
16	Bret Saberhagen	.10
17	Terrell Lowery	.10
18	Rod Bolton	.10
19	Harold Baines	.10
20	Matt Walbeck	.10
21	Tom Glavine	.30
22	Todd Jones	.10
23	Alberto Castillo	.10
24	Ruben Sierra	.10
25	Don Mattingly	2.50
26	Mike Morgan	.10
27	Jim Musselwhite **RC**	.10
28	Matt Brunson **RC**	.10
29	Adam Meinershagen **RC**	.10
30	Joe Girardi	.10
31	Shane Halter	.10
32	Jose Paniagua **RC**	.10
33	Paul Perkins	.10
34	John Hudek **RC**	.10
35	Frank Viola	.10
36	David Lamb **RC**	.10
37	Marshall Boze	.10
38	Jorge Posada **RC**	6.00
39	Brian Anderson **RC**	.25
40	Mark Whiten	.10
41	Sean Bergman	.10
42	Jose Parra **RC**	.10
43	Mike Robertson	.10
44	Pete Walker **RC**	.10
45	Juan Gonzalez	.75
46	Cleveland Ladell **RC**	.10
47	Mark Smith	.10
48	Kevin Jarvis **RC**	.10
49	Amaury Telemaco **RC**	.10
50	Andy Van Slyke	.10
51	Rikkert Faneyte **RC**	.10
52	Curtis Shaw	.10
53	Matt Drews **RC**	.10
54	Wilson Alvarez	.10
55	Manny Ramirez	1.50
56	Bobby Munoz	.10
57	Ed Sprague	.10
58	Jamey Wright **RC**	.10
59	Jeff Montgomery	.10
60	Kirk Rueter	.10
61	Edgar Martinez	.10
62	Luis Gonzalez	.10
63	Tim Vanegmond **RC**	.10
64	Bip Roberts	.10
65	John Jaha	.10
66	Chuck Carr	.10
67	Chuck Finley	.10
68	Aaron Holbert	.10
69	Cecil Fielder	.10
70	Tom Engle **RC**	.10
71	Ron Karkovice	.10
72	Joe Orsulak	.10
73	Duff Brumley **RC**	.10
74	Craig Clayton **RC**	.10
75	Cal Ripken, Jr.	4.00
76	Brad Fullmer **RC**	.50
77	Tony Tarasco	.10
78	Terry Farrar **RC**	.10
79	Matt Williams	.10
80	Rickey Henderson	1.50
81	Terry Mulholland	.10
82	Sammy Sosa	2.00
83	Paul Sorrento	.10
84	Pete Incaviglia	.10
85	Darren Hall **RC**	.10
86	Scott Klingenbeck	.10
87	Dario Perez **RC**	.10
88	Ugueth Urbina	.10
89	Dave Vanhof **RC**	.10
90	Domingo Jean	.10
91	Otis Nixon	.10
92	Andres Berumen	.10
93	Jose Valentin	.10
94	Edgar Renteria **RC**	5.00
95	Chris Turner	.10
96	Ray Lankford	.10
97	Danny Bautista	.10
98	Chan Ho Park **RC**	1.00
99	Glenn DiSarcina **RC**	.10
100	Butch Huskey	.10
101	Ivan Rodriguez	1.00
102	Johnny Ruffin	.10
103	Alex Ochoa	.10
104	Torii Hunter **RC**	6.00
105	Ryan Klesko	.10
106	Jay Bell	.10
107	Kurt Peltzer **RC**	.10
108	Miguel Jimenez	.10
109	Russ Davis	.10
110	Derek Wallace	.10
111	Keith Lockhart **RC**	.10
112	Mike Lieberthal	.10
113	Dave Stewart	.10
114	Tom Schmidt	.10
115	Brian McRae	.10
116	Moises Alou	.10
117	Dave Fleming	.10
118	Jeff Bagwell	1.50
119	Luis Ortiz	.10
120	Tony Gwynn	2.00
121	Jaime Navarro	.10
122	Benny Santiago	.10
123	Darrel Whitmore	.10
124	John Mabry **RC**	.15
125	Mickey Tettleton	.10
126	Tom Candiotti	.10
127	Tim Raines	.10
128	Bobby Bonilla	.10
129	John Dettmer	.10
130	Hector Carrasco	.10
131	Chris Hoiles	.10
132	Rick Aguilera	.10
133	Dave Justice	.10
134	Esteban Loaiza **RC**	1.50
135	Barry Bonds	4.00
136	Bob Welch	.10
137	Mike Stanley	.10
138	Roberto Hernandez	.10
139	Sandy Alomar	.10
140	Darren Daulton	.10
141	Angel Martinez **RC**	.10
142	Howard Johnson	.10
143	Bob Hamelin	.10
144	J.J. Thobe **RC**	.10
145	Roger Salkeld	.10
146	Orlando Miller	.10
147	Dmitri Young	.10
148	Tim Hyers **RC**	.10
149	Mark Loretta **RC**	3.00
150	Chris Hammond	.10
151	Joel Moore **RC**	.10
152	Todd Zeile	.10
153	Wil Cordero	.10
154	Chris Smith	.10
155	James Baldwin	.10
156	Edgardo Alfonzo **RC**	1.00
157	Kym Ashworth **RC**	.10
158	Paul Bako **RC**	.10
159	Rick Krivda **RC**	.10
160	Pat Mahomes	.10
161	Damon Hollins	.10
162	Felix Martinez **RC**	.10
163	Jason Myers **RC**	.10
164	Izzy Molina **RC**	.10
165	Brien Taylor	.10
166	Kevin Orie **RC**	.10
167	Casey Whitten **RC**	.10
168	Tony Longmire	.10
169	John Olerud	.10
170	Mark Thompson	.10
171	Jorge Fabregas	.10
172	John Wetteland	.10
173	Dan Wilson	.10
174	Doug Drabek	.10
175	Jeffrey McNeely	.10
176	Melvin Nieves	.10
177	Doug Glanville **RC**	.10
178	Javier De La Hoya **RC**	.10
179	Chad Curtis	.10
180	Brian Barber	.10
181	Mike Henneman	.10
182	Jose Offerman	.10
183	Robert Ellis **RC**	.10
184	John Franco	.10
185	Benji Gil	.10
186	Hal Morris	.10
187	Chris Sabo	.10
188	Blaise Ilsley **RC**	.10
189	Steve Avery	.10
190	Rick White **RC**	.10
191	Rod Beck	.10
(192)	Mark McGwire (No card number.)	3.00
193	Jim Abbott	.10
194	Randy Myers	.10
195	Kenny Lofton	.10
196	Mariano Duncan	.10
197	Lee Daniels **RC**	.10
198	Armando Reynoso	.10
199	Joe Randa	.10
200	Cliff Floyd	.10
201	Tim Harkrider **RC**	.10
202	Kevin Gallaher **RC**	.10
203	Scott Cooper	.10
204	Phil Stidham **RC**	.10
205	Jeff D'Amico **RC**	.25
206	Matt Whisenant	.10
207	De Shawn Warren	.10
208	Rene Arocha	.10
209	Tony Clark **RC**	.50
210	Jason Jacome **RC**	.10
211	Scott Christman **RC**	.10
212	Bill Pulsipher	.10
213	Dean Palmer	.10
214	Chad Mottola	.10
215	Manny Alexander	.10
216	Rich Becker	.10
217	Andre King **RC**	.10
218	Carlos Garcia	.10
219	Ron Pezzoni **RC**	.10
220	Steve Karsay	.10
221	Jose Musset **RC**	.10
222	Karl Rhodes	.10
223	Frank Cimorelli **RC**	.10
224	Kevin Jordan **RC**	.10
225	Duane Ward	.10
226	John Burke	.10
227	Mike MacFarlane	.10
228	Mike Lansing	.10
229	Chuck Knoblauch	.10
230	Ken Caminiti	.10
231	Gar Finnvold **RC**	.10
232	Derrek Lee **RC**	12.00
233	Brady Anderson	.10
234	Vic Darensbourg **RC**	.10
235	Mark Langston	.10
236	T.J. Mathews **RC**	.10
237	Lou Whitaker	.10
238	Roger Cedeno	.10
239	Alex Fernandez	.10
240	Ryan Thompson	.10
241	Kerry Lacy **RC**	.10
242	Reggie Sanders	.10
243	Brad Pennington	.10
244	Bryan Eversgerd **RC**	.10
245	Greg Maddux	2.00
246	Jason Kendall	.10
247	J.R. Phillips	.10
248	Bobby Witt	.10
249	Paul O'Neill	.10
250	Ryne Sandberg	2.00
251	Charles Nagy	.10
252	Kevin Stocker	.10
253	Shawn Green	.30
254	Charlie Hayes	.10
255	Donnie Elliott	.10
256	Rob Fitzpatrick **RC**	.10
257	Tim Davis	.10
258	James Mouton	.10
259	Mike Greenwell	.10
260	Ray McDavid	.10
261	Mike Kelly	.10
262	Andy Larkin **RC**	.10
(263)	Marquis Riley (No card number.)	.10
264	Bob Tewksbury	.10
265	Brian Edmondson	.10
266	Eduardo Lantigua **RC**	.10
267	Brandon Wilson	.10
268	Mike Welch	.10
269	Tom Henke	.10
270	Calvin Reese	.10
271	Gregg Zaun **RC**	.10
272	Todd Ritchie	.10
273	Javier Lopez	.10
274	Kevin Young	.10
275	Kirt Manwaring	.10
276	Bill Taylor **RC**	.10
277	Robert Eenhoorn	.10
278	Jessie Hollins	.10
279	Julian Tavarez **RC**	.10
280	Gene Schall	.10
281	Paul Molitor	1.50
282	Neifi Perez **RC**	.10
283	Greg Gagne	.10
284	Marquis Grissom	.10
285	Randy Johnson	1.50
286	Pete Harnisch	.10
287	Joel Bennett **RC**	.10
288	Derek Bell	.10
289	Darryl Hamilton	.10
290	Gary Sheffield	.40
291	Eduardo Perez	.10
292	Basil Shabazz	.10
293	Eric Davis	.10
294	Pedro Astacio	.10
295	Robin Ventura	.10
296	Jeff Kent	.10
297	Rick Helling	.10
298	Joe Oliver	.10
299	Lee Smith	.10
300	Dave Winfield	1.50
301	Deion Sanders	.10
302	Ravelo Manzanillo **RC**	.10
303	Mark Portugal	.10

304	Brent Gates	.10
305	Wade Boggs	2.00
306	Rick Wilkins	.10
307	Carlos Baerga	.10
308	Curt Schilling	.35
309	Shannon Stewart	.10
310	Darren Holmes	.10
311	Robert Toth **RC**	.10
312	Gabe White	.10
313	Mac Suzuki **RC**	.10
314	Alvin Morman **RC**	.10
315	Mo Vaughn	.10
316	Bryce Florie **RC**	.10
317	Gabby Martinez **RC**	.10
318	Carl Everett	.10
319	Kerwin Moore	.10
320	Tom Pagnozzi	.10
321	Chris Gomez	.10
322	Todd Williams	.10
323	Pat Hentgen	.10
324	Kirk Presley **RC**	.10
325	Kevin Brown	.10
326	Jason Isringhausen **RC**	1.50
327	Rick Forney **RC**	.10
328	Carlos Pulido **RC**	.10
329	Terrell Wade **RC**	.10
330	Al Martin	.10
331	Dan Carlson **RC**	.10
332	Mark Acre **RC**	.10
333	Sterling Hitchcock	.10
334	Jon Ratliff **RC**	.10
335	Alex Ramirez **RC**	.10
336	Phil Geisler **RC**	.10
337	Eddie Zambrano **RC** (Foil)	.10
338	Jim Thome (Foil)	.60
339	James Mouton (Foil)	.10
340	Cliff Floyd (Foil)	.10
341	Carlos Delgado (Foil)	.40
342	Roberto Petagine (Foil)	.10
343	Tim Clark (Foil)	.10
344	Bubba Smith (Foil)	.10
345	Randy Curtis **RC** (Foil)	.10
346	Joe Biasucci **RC** (Foil)	.10
347	D.J. Boston **RC** (Foil)	.10
348	Ruben Rivera **RC** (Foil)	.75
349	Bryan Link **RC** (Foil)	.10
350	Mike Bell **RC** (Foil)	.25
351	Marty Watson **RC** (Foil)	.10
352	Jason Myers (Foil)	.10
353	Chipper Jones (Foil)	1.25
354	Brooks Kieschnick (Foil)	.10
355	Calvin Reese (Foil)	.10
356	John Burke (Foil)	.10
357	Kurt Miller (Foil)	.10
358	Orlando Miller (Foil)	.10
359	Todd Hollandsworth (Foil)	.10
360	Rondell White (Foil)	.10
361	Bill Pulsipher (Foil)	.10
362	Tyler Green (Foil)	.10
363	Midre Cummings (Foil)	.10
364	Brian Barber (Foil)	.10
365	Melvin Nieves (Foil)	.10
366	Salomon Torres (Foil)	.10
367	Alex Ochoa (Foil)	.10
368	Frank Rodriguez (Foil)	.10
369	Brian Anderson (Foil)	.10
370	James Baldwin (Foil)	.10
371	Manny Ramirez (Foil)	.75
372	Justin Thompson (Foil)	.10
373	Johnny Damon (Foil)	.50
374	Jeff D'Amico (Foil)	.10
375	Rich Becker (Foil)	.10
376	Derek Jeter (Foil)	3.00
377	Steve Karsay (Foil)	.10
378	Mac Suzuki (Foil)	.10
379	Benji Gil (Foil)	.10
380	Alex Gonzalez (Foil)	.10
381	Jason Bere (Foil)	.10
382	Brett Butler (Foil)	.10
383	Jeff Conine (Foil)	.10
384	Darren Daulton (Foil)	.10
385	Jeff Kent (Foil)	.10
386	Don Mattingly (Foil)	1.50
387	Mike Piazza (Foil)	2.00
388	Ryne Sandberg (Foil)	1.25
389	Rich Amaral	.10
390	Craig Biggio	.10
391	Jeff Suppan **RC**	.35
392	Andy Benes	.10
393	Cal Eldred	.10
394	Jeff Conine	.10
395	Tim Salmon	.10
396	Ray Suplee **RC**	.10
397	Tony Phillips	.10
398	Ramon Martinez	.10
399	Julio Franco	.10
400	Dwight Gooden	.10
401	Kevin Lomon **RC**	.10
402	Jose Rijo	.10
403	Mike Devereaux	.10
404	Mike Zolecki **RC**	.10
405	Fred McGriff	.10
406	Danny Clyburn	.10
407	Robby Thompson	.10
408	Terry Steinbach	.10
409	Luis Polonia	.10
410	Mark Grace	.10
411	Albert Belle	.10
412	John Kruk	.10
413	Scott Spiezio **RC**	.25
414	Ellis Burks	.10
415	Joe Vitiello	.10
416	Tim Costo	.10
417	Marc Newfield	.10
418	Oscar Henriquez **RC**	.10
419	Matt Perisho **RC**	.10
420	Julio Bruno	.10
421	Kenny Felder	.10
422	Tyler Green	.10
423	Jim Edmonds	.10
424	Ozzie Smith	2.00
425	Rick Greene	.10
426	Todd Hollandsworth	.10
427	Eddie Pearson **RC**	.10
428	Quilvio Veras	.10
429	Kenny Rogers	.10
430	Willie Greene	.10
431	Vaughn Eshelman	.10
432	Pat Meares	.10
433	Jermaine Dye **RC**	8.00
434	Steve Cooke	.10
435	Bill Swift	.10
436	Fausto Cruz **RC**	.10
437	Mark Hutton	.10
438	Brooks Kieschnick **RC**	.10
439	Yorkis Perez	.10
440	Len Dykstra	.10
441	Pat Borders	.10
442	Doug Walls **RC**	.10
443	Wally Joyner	.10
444	Ken Hill	.10
445	Eric Anthony	.10
446	Mitch Williams	.10
447	Cory Bailey **RC**	.10
448	Dave Staton	.10
449	Greg Vaughn	.10
450	Dave Magadan	.10
451	Chili Davis	.10
452	Gerald Santos **RC**	.10
453	Joe Perona	.10
454	Delino DeShields	.10
455	Jack McDowell	.10
456	Todd Hundley	.10
457	Ritchie Moody	.10
458	Bret Boone	.10
459	Ben McDonald	.10
460	Kirby Puckett	2.00
461	Gregg Olson	.10
462	Rich Aude **RC**	.10
463	John Burkett	.10
464	Troy Neel	.10
465	Jimmy Key	.10
466	Ozzie Timmons	.10
467	Eddie Murray	1.50
468	Mark Tranberg **RC**	.10
469	Alex Gonzalez	.10
470	David Nied	.10
471	Barry Larkin	.10
472	Brian Looney **RC**	.10
473	Shawn Estes	.10
474	A.J. Sager **RC**	.10
475	Roger Clemens	2.50
476	Vince Moore	.10
477	Scott Karl **RC**	.10
478	Kurt Miller	.10
479	Garret Anderson	.10
480	Allen Watson	.10
481	Jose Lima **RC**	.10
482	Rick Gorecki	.10
483	Jimmy Hurst **RC**	.10
484	Preston Wilson	.10
485	Will Clark	.10
486	Mike Ferry **RC**	.10
487	Curtis Goodwin **RC**	.10
488	Mike Myers	.10
489	Chipper Jones	2.00
490	Jeff King	.10
491	Bill Van Landingham **RC**	.10
492	Carlos Reyes **RC**	.10
493	Andy Pettitte	.30
494	Brant Brown	.10
495	Daron Kirkreit	.10
496	Ricky Bottalico **RC**	.25
497	Devon White	.10
498	Jason Johnson **RC**	.10
499	Vince Coleman	.10
500	Larry Walker	.10
501	Bobby Ayala	.10
502	Steve Finley	.10
503	Scott Fletcher	.10
504	Brad Ausmus	.10
505	Scott Talanoa **RC**	.10
506	Orestes Destrade	.10
507	Gary DiSarcina	.10
508	Willie Smith **RC**	.10
509	Alan Trammell	.10
510	Mike Piazza	3.00
511	Ozzie Guillen	.10
512	Jeromy Burnitz	.10
513	Darren Oliver	.10
514	Kevin Mitchell	.10
515	Rafael Palmeiro	1.00
516	David McCarty	.10
517	Jeff Blauser	.10
518	Trey Beamon	.10
519	Royce Clayton	.10
520	Dennis Eckersley	1.00
521	Bernie Williams	.10
522	Steve Buechele	.10
523	Denny Martinez	.10
524	Dave Hollins	.10
525	Joey Hamilton	.10
526	Andres Galarraga	.10
527	Jeff Granger	.10
528	Joey Eischen	.10
529	Desi Relaford	.10
530	Roberto Petagine	.10
531	Andre Dawson	.30
532	Ray Holbert	.10
533	Duane Singleton	.10
534	Kurt Abbott **RC**	.20
535	Bo Jackson	.20
536	Gregg Jefferies	.10
537	David Mysel	.10
538	Raul Mondesi	.10
539	Chris Snopek	.10
540	Brook Fordyce	.10
541	Ron Frazier **RC**	.10
542	Brian Koelling	.10
543	Jimmy Haynes	.10
544	Marty Cordova	.10
545	Jason Green **RC**	.10
546	Orlando Merced	.10
547	Lou Pote **RC**	.10
548	Todd Van Poppel	.10
549	Pat Kelly	.10
550	Turk Wendell	.10
551	Herb Perry **RC**	.10
552	Ryan Karp **RC**	.10
553	Juan Guzman	.10
554	Bryan Rekar **RC**	.10
555	Kevin Appier	.10
556	Chris Schwab **RC**	.10
557	Jay Buhner	.10
558	Andujar Cedeno	.10
559	Ryan McGuire **RC**	.10
560	Ricky Gutierrez	.10
561	Keith Kimsey **RC**	.10
562	Tim Clark	.10
563	Damion Easley	.10
564	Clint Davis **RC**	.10
565	Mike Moore	.10
566	Orel Hershiser	.10
567	Jason Bere	.10
568	Kevin McReynolds	.10
569	Leland Macon **RC**	.10
570	John Courtright **RC**	.10
571	Sid Fernandez	.10
572	Chad Roper	.10
573	Terry Pendleton	.10
574	Danny Miceli	.10
575	Joe Rosselli	.10
576	Mike Bordick	.10
577	Danny Tartabull	.10
578	Jose Guzman	.10
579	Omar Vizquel	.10
580	Tommy Greene	.10
581	Paul Spoljaric	.10
582	Walt Weiss	.10
583	Oscar Jimenez **RC**	.10
584	Rod Henderson	.10
585	Derek Lowe	.10
586	Richard Hidalgo **RC**	1.00
587	Shayne Bennett **RC**	.10
588	Tim Belk **RC**	.10
589	Matt Mieske	.10
590	Nigel Wilson	.10
591	Jeff Knox **RC**	.10
592	Bernard Gilkey	.10
593	David Cone	.10
594	Paul LoDuca **RC**	5.00
595	Scott Ruffcorn	.10
596	Chris Roberts	.10
597	Oscar Munoz **RC**	.10
598	Scott Sullivan **RC**	.10
599	Matt Jarvis **RC**	.10
600	Jose Canseco	.35
601	Tony Graffanino **RC**	.10
602	Don Slaught	.10
603	Brett King **RC**	.10
604	Jose Herrera **RC**	.10
605	Melido Perez	.10
606	Mike Hubbard **RC**	.10
607	Chad Ogea	.10
608	Wayne Gomes **RC**	.10
609	Roberto Alomar	.25
610	Angel Echevarria **RC**	.10
611	Jose Lind	.10
612	Darrin Fletcher	.10
613	Chris Bosio	.10
614	Darryl Kile	.10
615	Frank Rodriguez	.10
616	Phil Plantier	.10
617	Pat Listach	.10
618	Charlie Hough	.10
619	Ryan Hancock **RC**	.10
620	Darrel Deak **RC**	.10
621	Travis Fryman	.10
622	Brett Butler	.10
623	Lance Johnson	.10
624	Pete Smith	.10
625	James Hurst	.10
626	Roberto Kelly	.10
627	Mike Mussina	.50
628	Kevin Tapani	.10
629	John Smoltz	.10
630	Midre Cummings	.10
631	Salomon Torres	.10
632	Willie Adams	.10
633	Derek Jeter	4.00
634	Steve Trachsel	.10
635	Albie Lopez	.10
636	Jason Moler	.10
637	Carlos Delgado	.50
638	Roberto Mejia	.10
639	Darren Burton	.10
640	B.J. Wallace	.10
641	Brad Clontz **RC**	.10
642	Billy Wagner **RC**	1.00
643	Aaron Sele	.10
644	Cameron Cairncross	.10
645	Brian Harper	.10
(646)	Marc Valdes (No card number.)	.10
647	Mark Ratekin	.10
648	Terry Bradshaw **RC**	.10
649	Justin Thompson	.10
650	Mike Busch **RC**	.10
651	Joe Hall **RC**	.10
652	Bobby Jones	.10
653	Kelly Stinnett **RC**	.10
654	Rod Steph **RC**	.10
655	Jay Powell **RC**	.10
(656)	Keith Garagozzo **RC** (No card number.)	.10
657	Todd Dunn	.10
658	Charles Peterson **RC**	.10
659	Darren Lewis	.10
660	John Wasdin **RC**	.10
661	Tate Seefried **RC**	.10
662	Hector Trinidad **RC**	.10
663	John Carter **RC**	.10
664	Larry Mitchell	.10
665	David Catlett **RC**	.10
666	Dante Bichette	.10
667	Felix Jose	.10
668	Rondell White	.10
669	Tino Martinez	.10
670	Brian Hunter	.10
671	Jose Malave	.10
672	Archi Cianfrocco	.10
673	Mike Matheny **RC**	.15
674	Bret Barberie	.10
675	Andrew Lorraine **RC**	.10
676	Brian Jordan	.10
677	Tim Belcher	.10
678	Antonio Osuna **RC**	.10
679	Checklist I	.10
680	Checklist II	.10
681	Checklist III	.10
682	Checklist IV	.10

1994 Bowman's Best

	NM/M
Complete Set (200):	30.00
Red Set (90):	10.00
Blue Set (90):	20.00
Common Player:	.15
Pack (8):	1.50
Wax Box (24):	30.00

RED SET

1	Paul Molitor	1.50
2	Eddie Murray	1.50
3	Ozzie Smith	2.00
4	Rickey Henderson	1.50
5	Lee Smith	.15
6	Dave Winfield	1.50
7	Roberto Alomar	.30
8	Matt Williams	.15
9	Mark Grace	.15
10	Lance Johnson	.15
11	Darren Daulton	.15
12	Tom Glavine	.35
13	Gary Sheffield	.40
14	Rod Beck	.15
15	Fred McGriff	.15
16	Joe Carter	.15
17	Dante Bichette	.15
18	Danny Tartabull	.15
19	Juan Gonzalez	.75
20	Steve Avery	.15
21	John Wetteland	.15
22	Ben McDonald	.15
23	Jack McDowell	.15
24	Jose Canseco	.65
25	Tim Salmon	.15
26	Wilson Alvarez	.15
27	Gregg Jefferies	.15
28	John Burkett	.15
29	Greg Vaughn	.15
30	Robin Ventura	.15
31	Paul O'Neill	.15
32	Cecil Fielder	.15
33	Kevin Mitchell	.15
34	Jeff Conine	.15
35	Carlos Baerga	.15
36	Greg Maddux	2.00
37	Roger Clemens	2.25
38	Deion Sanders	.15
39	Delino DeShields	.15
40	Ken Griffey Jr.	2.50
41	Albert Belle	1.50
42	Wade Boggs	2.00
43	Andres Galarraga	.15
44	Aaron Sele	.15
45	Don Mattingly	2.25
46	David Cone	.15
47	Lenny Dykstra	.15
48	Brett Butler	.15
49	Bill Swift	.15
50	Bobby Bonilla	.15

51 Rafael Palmeiro 1.25
52 Moises Alou .15
53 Jeff Bagwell 1.50
54 Mike Mussina .50
55 Frank Thomas 1.50
56 Jose Rijo .15
57 Ruben Sierra .15
58 Randy Myers .15
59 Barry Bonds 4.00
60 Jimmy Key .15
61 Travis Fryman .15
62 John Olerud .15
63 David Justice .15
64 Ray Lankford .15
65 Bob Tewksbury .15
66 Chuck Carr .15
67 Jay Buhner .15
68 Kenny Lofton .15
69 Marquis Grissom .15
70 Sammy Sosa 2.00
71 Cal Ripken Jr. 4.00
72 Ellis Burks .15
73 Jeff Montgomery .15
74 Julio Franco .15
75 Kirby Puckett 2.00
76 Larry Walker .15
77 Andy Van Slyke .15
78 Tony Gwynn 2.00
79 Will Clark .15
80 Mo Vaughn .15
81 Mike Piazza 2.50
82 James Mouton .15
83 Carlos Delgado .60
84 Ryan Klesko .15
85 Javy Lopez .15
86 Raul Mondesi .15
87 Cliff Floyd .15
88 Manny Ramirez 1.50
89 Hector Carrasco .15
90 Jeff Granger .15

BLUE SET

1 Chipper Jones 2.00
2 Derek Jeter 4.00
3 Bill Pulsipher .15
4 James Baldwin .15
5 Brooks Kieschnick **RC** .50
6 Justin Thompson .15
7 Midre Cummings .15
8 Joey Hamilton .15
9 Calvin Reese .15
10 Brian Barber .15
11 John Burke .15
12 De Shawn Warren .15
13 Edgardo Alfonzo **RC** .75
14 Eddie Pearson **RC** .15
15 Jimmy Haynes .15
16 Danny Bautista .15
17 Roger Cedeno .15
18 Jon Lieber .15
19 Billy Wagner **RC** .75
20 Tate Seefried **RC** .15
21 Chad Mottola .15
22 Jose Malave .15
23 Terrell Wade **RC** .15
24 Shane Andrews .15
25 Chan Ho Park **RC** .75
26 Kirk Presley **RC** .15
27 Robbie Beckett .15
28 Orlando Miller .15
29 Jorge Posada **RC** 8.00
30 Frank Rodriguez .15
31 Brian Hunter .15
32 Billy Ashley .15
33 Rondell White .15
34 John Roper .15
35 Marc Valdes .15
36 Scott Ruffcorn .15
37 Rod Henderson .15
38 Curt Goodwin .15
39 Russ Davis .15
40 Rick Gorecki .15
41 Johnny Damon .60
42 Roberto Petagine .15
43 Chris Snopek .15
44 Mark Acre .15
45 Todd Hollandsworth .15
46 Shawn Green .35
47 John Carter .15
48 Jim Pittsley .15
49 John Wasdin **RC** .15
50 D.J. Boston .15
51 Tim Clark .15
52 Alex Ochoa .15
53 Chad Roper .15
54 Mike Kelly .15
55 Brad Fullmer **RC** .50
56 Carl Everett .15
57 Tim Belk **RC** .15
58 Jimmy Hurst **RC** .15
59 Mac Suzuki **RC** .15
60 Michael Moore .15
61 Alan Benes **RC** .15
62 Tony Clark **RC** 1.00
63 Edgar Renteria **RC** 8.00
64 Trey Beamon .15
65 LaTroy Hawkins **RC** .15
66 Wayne Gomes **RC** .15
67 Ray McDavid .15
68 John Dettmer .15
69 Willie Greene .15
70 Dave Stevens .15
71 Kevin Orie **RC** .15
72 Chad Ogea .15
73 Ben Van Ryn .15
74 Kym Ashworth .15
75 Dmitri Young .15
76 Herb Perry .15
77 Joey Eischen .15
78 Arquimedez Pozo **RC** .15
79 Ugueth Urbina .15
80 Keith Williams .15
81 John Frascatore **RC** .15
82 Garey Ingram .15
83 Aaron Small .15
84 Olmedo Saenz **RC** .15
85 Jesus Tavarez .15
86 Jose Silva **RC** .15
87 Gerald Witasick Jr. **RC** .15
88 Jay Maldonado .15
89 Keith Heberling .15
90 Rusty Greer **RC** .50

MIRROR IMAGES

91 Frank Thomas, Kevin Young .60
92 Fred McGriff, Brooks Kieschnick **RC** .15
93 Matt Williams, Shane Andrews .15
94 Cal Ripken Jr., Kevin Orie **RC** 1.50
95 Barry Larkin, Derek Jeter 1.50
96 Ken Griffey Jr., Johnny Damon 1.50
97 Barry Bonds, Rondell White 1.50
98 Albert Belle, Jimmy Hurst **RC** .15
99 Raul Mondesi, Ruben Rivera **RC** .15
100 Roger Clemens, Scott Ruffcorn 1.00
101 Greg Maddux, John Wasdin **RC** .75
102 Tim Salmon, Chad Mottola .15
103 Carlos Baerga, Arquimedez Pozo **RC** .15
104 Mike Piazza, Bobby Hughes 1.00
105 Carlos Delgado, Melvin Nieves .50
106 Javy Lopez, Jorge Posada **RC** 2.00
107 Manny Ramirez, Jose Malave .65
108 Travis Fryman, Chipper Jones .75
109 Steve Avery, Bill Pulsipher .15
110 John Olerud, Shawn Green .50

Refractors

Superstars: 8-10X
Stars: 4-8X
(See 1994 Bowman's Best for checklist and base card values.)

1995 Bowman

	NM/M
Complete Set (439):	150.00
Common Player:	.10
Pack (10):	6.00
Wax Box (24):	125.00
Rack Pack (15):	5.00
Rack Box (24):	125.00

1 Billy Wagner .10
2 Chris Widger .10
3 Brent Bowers .10
4 Bob Abreu **RC** 10.00
5 Lou Collier **RC** .10
6 Juan Acevedo **RC** .25
7 Jason Kelley **RC** .10
8 Brian Sackinsky .10
9 Scott Christman .10
10 Damon Hollins .10
11 Willis Otanez **RC** .10
12 Jason Ryan **RC** .10
13 Jason Giambi .75
14 Andy Taulbee **RC** .10
15 Mark Thompson .10
16 Hugo Pivaral **RC** .10
17 Brien Taylor .10
18 Antonio Osuna .10
19 Edgardo Alfonzo .10
20 Carl Everett .10
21 Matt Drews .10
22 Bartolo Colon **RC** 4.00
23 Andruw Jones **RC** 8.00
24 Robert Person **RC** .40
25 Derrek Lee .75
26 John Ambrose **RC** .10
27 Eric Knowles **RC** .10
28 Chris Roberts .10
29 Don Wengert .10
30 Marcus Jensen **RC** .10
31 Brian Barber .10
32 Kevin Brown .10
33 Benji Gil .10
34 Mike Hubbard .10
35 Bart Evans **RC** .10
36 Enrique Wilson **RC** .50
37 Brian Buchanan **RC** .10
38 Ken Ray **RC** .10
39 Micah Franklin **RC** .10
40 Ricky Otero **RC** .10
41 Jason Kendall .10
42 Jimmy Hurst .10
43 Jerry Wolak **RC** .10
44 Jayson Peterson **RC** .10
45 Allen Battle **RC** .10
46 Scott Stahoviak .10
47 Steve Schrenk **RC** .10
48 Travis Miller **RC** .25
49 Eddie Rios **RC** .10
50 Mike Hampton .10
51 Chad Frontera **RC** .10
52 Tom Evans **RC** .10
53 C.J. Nitkowski .10
54 Clay Caruthers **RC** .10
55 Shannon Stewart .10
56 Jorge Posada .50
57 Aaron Holbert .10
58 Harry Berrios **RC** .10
59 Steve Rodriguez .10
60 Shane Andrews .10
61 Will Cunnane **RC** .10
62 Richard Hidalgo .10
63 Bill Selby **RC** .10
64 Jay Cranford **RC** .10
65 Jeff Suppan .10
66 Curtis Goodwin .10
67 John Thomson **RC** .10
68 Justin Thompson .10
69 Troy Percival .10
70 Matt Wagner **RC** .10
71 Terry Bradshaw .10
72 Greg Hansell .10
73 John Burke .10
74 Jeff D'Amico .10
75 Ernie Young .10
76 Jason Bates .10
77 Chris Stynes .10
78 Cade Gaspar **RC** .10
79 Melvin Nieves .10
80 Rick Gorecki .10
81 Felix Rodriguez **RC** .50
82 Ryan Hancock .10
83 Chris Carpenter **RC** 6.00
84 Ray McDavid .10
85 Chris Wimmer .10
86 Doug Glanville .10
87 DeShawn Warren .10
88 Damian Moss **RC** .50
89 Rafael Orellano **RC** .10
90 Vladimir Guerrero **RC** 50.00
91 Raul Casanova **RC** .40
92 Karim Garcia **RC** .75
93 Bryce Florie .10
94 Kevin Orie .10
95 Ryan Nye **RC** .10
96 Matt Sachse **RC** .10
97 Ivan Arteaga **RC** .10
98 Glenn Murray .10
99 Stacy Hollins **RC** .10
100 Jim Pittsley .10
101 Craig Mattson **RC** .10
102 Neifi Perez .10
103 Keith Williams .10
104 Roger Cedeno .10
105 Tony Terry **RC** .10
106 Jose Malave .10
107 Joe Rosselli .10
108 Kevin Jordan .10
109 Sid Roberson **RC** .10
110 Alan Embree .10
111 Terrell Wade .10
112 Bob Wolcott .10
113 Carlos Perez **RC** .10
114 Mike Bovee **RC** .10
115 Tommy Davis **RC** .10
116 Jeremey Kendall **RC** .10
117 Rich Aude .10
118 Rick Huisman .10
119 Tim Belk .10
120 Edgar Renteria .25
121 Calvin Maduro **RC** .10
122 Jerry Martin **RC** .10
123 Ramon Fermin **RC** .10
124 Kimera Bartee **RC** .10
125 Mark Farris .10
126 Frank Rodriguez .10
127 Bobby Higginson **RC** .50
128 Bret Wagner .10
129 Edwin Diaz **RC** .10
130 Jimmy Haynes .10
131 Chris Weinke **RC** .75
132 Damian Jackson **RC** .10
133 Felix Martinez .10
134 Edwin Hurtado **RC** .25
135 Matt Raleigh **RC** .10
136 Paul Wilson .10
137 Ron Villone .10
138 Eric Stuckenschneider **RC** .10
139 Tate Seefried .10
140 Rey Ordonez **RC** .75
141 Eddie Pearson .10
142 Kevin Gallaher .10
143 Torii Hunter .25
144 Daron Kirkreit .10
145 Craig Wilson .10
146 Ugueth Urbina .10
147 Chris Snopek .10
148 Kym Ashworth .10
149 Wayne Gomes .10
150 Mark Loretta .10
151 Ramon Morel **RC** .10
152 Trot Nixon .20
153 Desi Relaford .10
154 Scott Sullivan .10
155 Marc Barcelo .10
156 Willie Adams .10
157 Derrick Gibson **RC** .10
158 Brian Meadows **RC** .10
159 Julian Tavarez .10
160 Bryan Rekar .10
161 Steve Gibralter .10
162 Esteban Loaiza .10
163 John Wasdin .10
164 Kirk Presley .10
165 Mariano Rivera .50
166 Andy Larkin .10
167 Sean Whiteside **RC** .10
168 Matt Apana **RC** .10
169 Shawn Senior **RC** .10
170 Scott Gentile .10
171 Quilvio Veras .10
172 Elieser Marrero **RC** 1.00
173 Mendy Lopez **RC** .10
174 Homer Bush .10
175 Brian Stephenson **RC** .10
176 Jon Nunnally .10
177 Jose Herrera .10
178 Corey Avrard **RC** .10
179 David Bell .10
180 Jason Isringhausen .10
181 Jamey Wright .10
182 Lonell Roberts **RC** .10
183 Marty Cordova .10
185 Amaury Telemaco .10
185 John Mabry .10
186 Andrew Vessel **RC** .10
187 Jim Cole **RC** .10
188 Marquis Riley .10
189 Todd Dunn .10
190 John Carter .10
191 Donnie Sadler **RC** .25
192 Mike Bell .10
193 Chris Cumberland **RC** .10
194 Jason Schmidt .25
195 Matt Brunson .10
196 James Baldwin .10
197 Bill Simas **RC** .10
198 Gus Gandarillas .10
199 Mac Suzuki .10
200 Rick Holifield **RC** .10
201 Fernando Lunar **RC** .10
202 Kevin Jarvis .10
203 Everett Stull **RC** .10
204 Steve Wojciechowski .10
205 Shawn Estes .10
206 Jermaine Dye .10
207 Marc Kroon .10
208 Peter Munro **RC** .10
209 Pat Watkins .10
210 Matt Smith .10
211 Joe Vitiello .10
212 Gerald Witasick Jr. .10
213 Freddy Garcia **RC** .10
214 Glenn Dishman **RC** .10
215 Jay Canizaro **RC** .10
216 Angel Martinez .10
217 Yamil Benitez **RC** .10
218 Fausto Macey **RC** .10
219 Eric Owens .10
220 Checklist .10
221 Dwayne Hosey **RC** .10
222 Brad Woodall **RC** .25
223 Billy Ashley .10
224 Mark Grudzielanek **RC** 2.00
225 Mark Johnson **RC** .10
226 Tim Unroe **RC** .10
227 Todd Greene .10
228 Larry Sutton .10
229 Derek Jeter 3.00
230 Sal Fasano **RC** .10
231 Ruben Rivera .10
232 Chris Truby **RC** .10
233 John Donati .10
234 Decomba Conner **RC** .10
235 Sergio Nunez **RC** .10
236 Ray Brown **RC** .10
237 Juan Melo **RC** .10
238 Hideo Nomo **RC** 4.00
239 Jaime Bluma **RC** .10
240 Jay Payton **RC** 1.50
241 Paul Konerko .75
242 Scott Elarton **RC** .50
243 Jeff Abbott **RC** .25
244 Jim Brower **RC** .10
245 Geoff Blum **RC** .40
246 Aaron Boone **RC** 1.00
247 J.R. Phillips .10
248 Alex Ochoa .10
249 Nomar Garciaparra 5.00
250 Garret Anderson .25
251 Ray Durham .10
252 Paul Shuey .10
253 Tony Clark .10
254 Johnny Damon 1.00
255 Duane Singleton .10
256 LaTroy Hawkins .10

No.	Player	Price
257	Andy Pettitte	.40
258	Ben Grieve	.10
259	Marc Newfield	.10
260	Terrell Lowery	.10
261	Shawn Green	.40
262	Chipper Jones	1.50
263	Brooks Kieschnick	.10
264	Calvin Reese	.10
265	Doug Million	.10
266	Marc Valdes	.10
267	Brian Hunter	.10
268	Todd Hollandsworth	.10
269	Rod Henderson	.10
270	Bill Pulsipher	.10
271	Scott Rolen RC	15.00
272	Trey Beamon	.10
273	Alan Benes	.10
274	Dustin Hermanson	.10
275	Ricky Bottalico	.10
276	Albert Belle	.10
277	Deion Sanders	.25
278	Matt Williams	.10
279	Jeff Bagwell	.75
280	Kirby Puckett	1.50
281	Dave Hollins	.10
282	Don Mattingly	1.50
283	Joey Hamilton	.10
284	Bobby Bonilla	.10
285	Moises Alou	.25
286	Tom Glavine	.25
287	Brett Butler	.10
288	Chris Hoiles	.10
289	Kenny Rogers	.10
290	Larry Walker	.25
291	Tim Raines	.10
292	Kevin Appier	.10
293	Roger Clemens	2.00
294a	Chuck Carr	.10
294b	Cliff Floyd (Should be #394.)	.10
295	Randy Myers	.10
296	Dave Nilsson	.10
297	Joe Carter	.10
298	Chuck Finley	.10
299	Ray Lankford	.10
300	Roberto Kelly	.10
301	Jon Lieber	.10
302	Travis Fryman	.10
303	Mark McGwire	1.50
304	Tony Gwynn	1.00
305	Kenny Lofton	.10
306	Mark Whiten	.10
307	Doug Drabek	.10
308	Terry Steinbach	.10
309	Ryan Klesko	.10
310	Mike Piazza	1.50
311	Ben McDonald	.10
312	Reggie Sanders	.10
313	Alex Fernandez	.10
314	Aaron Sele	.10
315	Gregg Jefferies	.10
316	Rickey Henderson	.75
317	Brian Anderson	.10
318	Jose Valentin	.10
319	Rod Beck	.10
320	Marquis Grissom	.10
321	Ken Griffey Jr.	2.00
322	Bret Saberhagen	.10
323	Juan Gonzalez	.50
324	Paul Molitor	.75
325	Gary Sheffield	.40
326	Darren Daulton	.10
327	Bill Swift	.10
328	Brian McRae	.10
329	Robin Ventura	.10
330	Lee Smith	.10
331	Fred McGriff	.20
332	Delino DeShields	.10
333	Edgar Martinez	.10
334	Mike Mussina	.50
335	Orlando Merced	.10
336	Carlos Baerga	.10
337	Wil Cordero	.10
338	Tom Pagnozzi	.10
339	Pat Hentgen	.10
340	Chad Curtis	.10
341	Darren Lewis	.10
342	Jeff Kent	.20
343	Bip Roberts	.10
344	Ivan Rodriguez	.50
345	Jeff Montgomery	.10
346	Hal Morris	.10
347	Danny Tartabull	.10
348	Raul Mondesi	.10
349	Ken Hill	.10
350	Pedro Martinez	1.00
351	Frank Thomas	.75
352	Manny Ramirez	1.00
353	Tim Salmon	.10
354	William Van Landingham	.10
355	Andres Galarraga	.10
356	Paul O'Neill	.25
357	Brady Anderson	.10
358	Ramon Martinez	.10
359	John Olerud	.10
360	Ruben Sierra	.10
361	Cal Eldred	.10
362	Jay Buhner	.10
363	Jay Bell	.10
364	Wally Joyner	.10
365	Chuck Knoblauch	.10
366	Len Dykstra	.10
367	John Wetteland	.10
368	Roberto Alomar	.25
369	Craig Biggio	.25
370	Ozzie Smith	1.50
371	Terry Pendleton	.10
372	Sammy Sosa	1.00
373	Carlos Garcia	.10
374	Jose Rijo	.10
375	Chris Gomez	.10
376	Barry Bonds	2.00
377	Steve Avery	.10
378	Rick Wilkins	.10
379	Pete Harnisch	.10
380	Dean Palmer	.10
381	Bob Hamelin	.10
382	Jason Bere	.10
383	Jimmy Key	.10
384	Dante Bichette	.10
385	Rafael Palmeiro	.50
386	David Justice	.10
387	Chili Davis	.10
388	Mike Greenwell	.10
389	Todd Zeile	.10
390	Jeff Conine	.10
391	Rick Aguilera	.10
392	Eddie Murray	.50
393	Mike Stanley	.10
394	(Not Issued, see #294.)	
395	Randy Johnson	1.00
396	David Nied	.10
397	Devon White	.10
398	Royce Clayton	.10
399	Andy Benes	.10
400	John Hudek	.10
401	Bobby Jones	.10
402	Eric Karros	.10
403	Will Clark	.25
404	Mark Langston	.10
405	Kevin Brown	.10
406	Greg Maddux	1.50
407	David Cone	.10
408	Wade Boggs	.75
409	Steve Trachsel	.10
410	Greg Vaughn	.10
411	Mo Vaughn	.10
412	Wilson Alvarez	.10
413	Cal Ripken Jr.	3.00
414	Rico Brogna	.10
415	Barry Larkin	.40
416	Cecil Fielder	.10
417	Jose Canseco	.50
418	Jack McDowell	.10
419	Mike Lieberthal	.10
420	Andrew Lorraine	.10
421	Rich Becker	.10
422	Tony Phillips	.10
423	Scott Ruffcorn	.10
424	Jeff Granger	.10
425	Greg Pirkl	.10
426	Dennis Eckersley	.50
427	Jose Lima	.10
428	Russ Davis	.10
429	Armando Benitez	.10
430	Alex Gonzalez	.10
431	Carlos Delgado	.75
432	Chan Ho Park	.10
433	Mickey Tettleton	.10
434	Dave Winfield	.75
435	John Burkett	.10
436	Orlando Miller	.10
437	Rondell White	.10
438	Jose Oliva	.10
439	Checklist	.10

1995 Bowman's Best

	NM/M
Complete Set (195):	200.00
Common Player:	.25
Pack (7):	12.00
Wax Box (24):	275.00
Complete Set Red (90):	45.00
1 Randy Johnson	1.50
2 Joe Carter	.25
3 Russ Davis	.25
4 Moises Alou	.25
5 Gary Sheffield	.40
6 Kevin Appier	.25
7 Denny Neagle	.25
8 Ruben Sierra	.25
9 Darren Daulton	.25
10 Cal Ripken Jr.	4.00
11 Bobby Bonilla	.25
12 Manny Ramirez	1.50
13 Barry Bonds	4.00
14 Eric Karros	.25
15 Greg Maddux	2.00
16 Jeff Bagwell	1.50
17 Paul Molitor	1.50
18 Ray Lankford	.25
19 Mark Grace	.25
20 Kenny Lofton	.25
21 Tony Gwynn	2.00
22 Will Clark	.25
23 Roger Clemens	2.25
24 Dante Bichette	.25
25 Barry Larkin	.25
26 Wade Boggs	2.00
27 Kirby Puckett	2.00
28 Cecil Fielder	.25
29 Jose Canseco	.50
30 Juan Gonzalez	.75
31 David Cone	.25
32 Craig Biggio	.25
33 Tim Salmon	.25
34 David Justice	.25
35 Sammy Sosa	2.00
36 Mike Piazza	2.50
37 Carlos Baerga	.25
38 Jeff Conine	.25
39 Rafael Palmeiro	1.25
40 Bret Saberhagen	.25
41 Len Dykstra	.25
42 Mo Vaughn	.25
43 Wally Joyner	.25
44 Chuck Knoblauch	.25
45 Robin Ventura	.25
46 Don Mattingly	2.25
47 Dave Hollins	.25
48 Andy Benes	.25
49 Ken Griffey Jr.	2.50
50 Albert Belle	.25
51 Matt Williams	.25
52 Rondell White	.25
53 Raul Mondesi	.25
54 Brian Jordan	.25
55 Greg Vaughn	.25
56 Fred McGriff	.25
57 Roberto Alomar	.40
58 Dennis Eckersley	1.25
59 Lee Smith	.25
60 Eddie Murray	1.50
61 Kenny Rogers	.25
62 Ron Gant	.25
63 Larry Walker	.25
64 Chad Curtis	.25
65 Frank Thomas	1.50
66 Paul O'Neill	.25
67 Kevin Seitzer	.25
68 Marquis Grissom	.25
69 Mark McGwire	3.00
70 Travis Fryman	.25
71 Andres Galarraga	.25
72 Carlos Perez RC	.25
73 Tyler Green	.25
74 Marty Cordova	.25
75 Shawn Green	.40
76 Vaughn Eshelman	.25
77 John Mabry	.25
78 Jason Bates	.25
79 Jon Nunnally	.25
80 Ray Durham	.25
81 Edgardo Alfonzo	.25
82 Esteban Loaiza	.25
83 Hideo Nomo RC	10.00
84 Orlando Miller	.25
85 Alex Gonzalez	.25
86 Mark Grudzielanek RC	.65
87 Julian Tavarez	.25
88 Benji Gil	.25
89 Quilvio Veras	.25
90 Ricky Bottalico	.25
Complete Set Blue (90):	150.00
1 Derek Jeter	3.00
2 Vladimir Guerrero RC	80.00
3 Bob Abreu RC	25.00
4 Chan Ho Park	.25
5 Paul Wilson	.25
6 Chad Ogea	.25
7 Andruw Jones RC	10.00
8 Brian Barber	.25
9 Andy Larkin	.25
10 Richie Sexson RC	6.00
11 Everett Stull RC	.25
12 Brooks Kieschnick	.25
13 Matt Murray	.25
14 John Wasdin	.25
15 Shannon Stewart	.25
16 Luis Ortiz	.25
17 Marc Kroon	.25
18 Todd Greene	.25
19 Juan Acevedo	.25
20 Tony Clark	.25
21 Jermaine Dye	.25
22 Derrek Lee	1.00
23 Pat Watkins	.25
24 Calvin Reese	.25
25 Ben Grieve	.25
26 Julio Santana RC	.25
27 Felix Rodriguez RC	.50
28 Paul Konerko	.25
29 Nomar Garciaparra	2.00
30 Pat Ahearne	.25
31 Jason Schmidt	.25
32 Billy Wagner	.25
33 Rey Ordonez RC	1.00
34 Curtis Goodwin	.25
35 Sergio Nunez RC	.25
36 Tim Belk	.25
37 Scott Elarton RC	1.00
38 Jason Isringhausen	.25
39 Trot Nixon	.35
40 Sid Roberson	.25
41 Ron Villone	.25
42 Ruben Rivera	.25
43 Rick Huisman	.25
44 Todd Hollandsworth	.25
45 Johnny Damon	1.00
46 Garret Anderson	.25
47 Jeff D'Amico	.25
48 Dustin Hermanson	.25
49 Juan Encarnacion RC	3.00
50 Andy Pettitte	.50
51 Chris Stynes	.25
52 Troy Percival	.25
53 LaTroy Hawkins	.25
54 Roger Cedeno	.25
55 Alan Benes	.25
56 Karim Garcia RC	1.50
57 Andrew Lorraine	.25
58 Gary Rath RC	.25
59 Bret Wagner	.25
60 Jeff Suppan	.25
61 Bill Pulsipher	.25
62 Jay Payton RC	3.00
63 Alex Ochoa	.25
64 Ugueth Urbina	.25
65 Armando Benitez	.25
66 George Arias	.25
67 Raul Casanova RC	.50
68 Matt Drews	.25
69 Jimmy Haynes	.25
70 Jimmy Hurst	.25
71 C.J. Nitkowski	.25
72 Tommy Davis RC	.25
73 Bartolo Colon RC	5.00
74 Chris Carpenter RC	10.00
75 Trey Beamon	.25
76 Bryan Rekar	.25
77 James Baldwin	.25
78 Marc Valdes	.25
79 Tom Fordham RC	.25
80 Marc Newfield	.25
81 Angel Martinez	.25
82 Brian Hunter	.25
83 Jose Herrera	.25
84 Glenn Dishman RC	.25
85 Jacob Cruz RC	.25
86 Paul Shuey	.25
87 Scott Rolen RC	25.00
88 Doug Million	.25
89 Desi Relaford	.25
90 Michael Tucker	.25
Mirror Image:	.50
1 Ben Davis, Ivan Rodriguez	1.00
2 Mark Redman, Manny Ramirez	1.50
3 Reggie Taylor, Deion Sanders	.50
4 Ryan Jaroncyk, Shawn Green	.50
5 Juan LeBron, Juan Gonzalez	1.00
6 Toby McKnight, Craig Biggio	.50
7 Michael Barrett, Travis Fryman	1.00
8 Corey Jenkins, Mo Vaughn	.50
9 Ruben Rivera, Frank Thomas	1.50
10 Curtis Goodwin, Kenny Lofton	.50
11 Brian Hunter, Tony Gwynn	1.75
12 Todd Greene, Ken Griffey Jr.	2.50
13 Karim Garcia, Matt Williams	.75
14 Billy Wagner, Randy Johnson	1.50
15 Pat Watkins, Jeff Bagwell	1.50

Gold

	NM/M
Complete Set (54):	100.00
Common Player:	.50
Stars/RC's:	2.5X
(See 1995 Bowman #221-274 for checklist and base card values.)	

Refractors

	NM/M
Common Player:	1.00
Stars:	3-6X
Rookies:	2-3X

(See 1995 Bowman's Best for checklist and base card values.)

1996 Bowman

	NM/M
Complete Set (385):	50.00
Common Player:	.10
Foils:	1.5X
Pack (11):	2.00
Wax Box (24):	40.00

1	Cal Ripken Jr.	2.00
2	Ray Durham	.10
3	Ivan Rodriguez	.50
4	Fred McGriff	.20
5	Hideo Nomo	.50
6	Troy Percival	.10
7	Moises Alou	.20
8	Mike Stanley	.10
9	Jay Buhner	.10
10	Shawn Green	.25
11	Ryan Klesko	.10
12	Andres Galarraga	.10
13	Dean Palmer	.10
14	Jeff Conine	.10
15	Brian Hunter	.10
16	J.T. Snow	.10
17	Larry Walker	.25
18	Barry Larkin	.40
19	Alex Gonzalez	.10
20	Edgar Martinez	.10
21	Mo Vaughn	.10
22	Mark McGwire	1.50
23	Jose Canseco	.50
24	Jack McDowell	.10
25	Dante Bichette	.10
26	Wade Boggs	.50
27	Mike Piazza	1.00
28	Ray Lankford	.10
29	Craig Biggio	.25
30	Rafael Palmeiro	.50
31	Ron Gant	.10
32	Javy Lopez	.10
33	Brian Jordan	.10
34	Paul O'Neill	.20
35	Mark Grace	.25
36	Matt Williams	.20
37	Pedro Martinez	.75
38	Rickey Henderson	.50
39	Bobby Bonilla	.10
40	Todd Hollandsworth	.10
41	Jim Thome	.75
42	Gary Sheffield	.40
43	Tim Salmon	.10
44	Gregg Jefferies	.10
45	Roberto Alomar	.25
45p	Roberto Alomar (Unmarked promo card, fielding photo on front.)	3.00
46	Carlos Baerga	.10
47	Mark Grudzielanek	.10
48	Randy Johnson	.75
49	Tino Martinez	.10
50	Robin Ventura	.10
51	Ryne Sandberg	1.50
52	Jay Bell	.10
53	Jason Schmidt	.10
54	Frank Thomas	.75
55	Kenny Lofton	.10
56	Ariel Prieto	.10
57	David Cone	.10
58	Reggie Sanders	.10
59	Michael Tucker	.10
60	Vinny Castilla	.10
61	Lenny Dykstra	.10
62	Todd Hundley	.10
63	Brian McRae	.10
64	Dennis Eckersley	.40
65	Rondell White	.10
66	Eric Karros	.10
67	Greg Maddux	1.50
68	Kevin Appier	.10
69	Eddie Murray	.50
70	John Olerud	.10
71	Tony Gwynn	.75
72	David Justice	.10
73	Ken Caminiti	.10
74	Terry Steinbach	.10
75	Alan Benes	.10
76	Chipper Jones	1.00
77	Jeff Bagwell	.50
77p	Jeff Bagwell (Unmarked promo card, name in gold.)	6.00
78	Barry Bonds	2.00
79	Ken Griffey Jr.	1.50
80	Roger Cedeno	.10
81	Joe Carter	.10
82	Henry Rodriguez	.10
83	Jason Isringhausen	.10
84	Chuck Knoblauch	.10
85	Manny Ramirez	.75
86	Tom Glavine	.30
87	Jeffrey Hammonds	.10
88	Paul Molitor	.75
89	Roger Clemens	2.00
90	Greg Vaughn	.10
91	Marty Cordova	.10
92	Albert Belle	.10
93	Mike Mussina	.40
94	Garret Anderson	.10
95	Juan Gonzalez	.40
96	John Valentin	.10
97	Jason Giambi	.50
98	Kirby Puckett	1.50
99	Jim Edmonds	.25
100	Cecil Fielder	.10
101	Mike Aldrete	.10
102	Marquis Grissom	.10
103	Derek Bell	.10
104	Raul Mondesi	.10
105	Sammy Sosa	1.00
106	Travis Fryman	.10
107	Rico Brogna	.10
108	Will Clark	.25
109	Bernie Williams	.40
110	Brady Anderson	.10
111	Torii Hunter	.10
112	Derek Jeter	2.00
113	Mike Kusiewicz **RC**	.10
114	Scott Rolen	1.00
115	Ramon Castro	.10
116	Jose Guillen **RC**	2.50
117	Wade Walker **RC**	.10
118	Shawn Senior	.10
119	Onan Masaoka **RC**	.10
120	Marlon Anderson **RC**	.75
121	Katsuhiro Maeda **RC**	.25
122	Garrett Stephenson **RC**	.25
123	Butch Huskey	.10
124	D'Angelo Jimenez **RC**	.50
125	Tony Mounce **RC**	.20
126	Jay Canizaro	.10
127	Juan Melo	.10
128	Steve Gibralter	.10
129	Freddy Garcia	.10
130	Julio Santana	.10
131	Richard Hidalgo	.10
132	Jermaine Dye	.10
133	Willie Adams	.10
134	Everett Stull	.10
135	Ramon Morel	.10
136	Chan Ho Park	.10
137	Jamey Wright	.10
138	Luis Garcia **RC**	.10
139	Dan Serafini	.10
140	Ryan Dempster **RC**	.50
141	Tate Seefried	.10
142	Jimmy Hurst	.10
143	Travis Miller	.10
144	Curtis Goodwin	.10
145	Rocky Coppinger **RC**	.10
146	Enrique Wilson	.10
147	Jaime Bluma	.10
148	Andrew Vessel	.10
149	Damian Moss	.10
150	Shawn Gallagher **RC**	.10
151	Pat Watkins	.10
152	Jose Paniagua	.10
153	Danny Graves	.10
154	Bryon Gainey **RC**	.10
155	Steve Soderstrom	.10
156	Cliff Brumbaugh **RC**	.10
157	Eugene Kingsale **RC**	.10
158	Lou Collier	.10
159	Todd Walker	.10
160	Kris Detmers **RC**	.10
161	Josh Booty **RC**	.25
162	Greg Whiteman **RC**	.10
163	Damian Jackson	.10
164	Tony Clark	.10
165	Jeff D'Amico	.10
166	Johnny Damon	.50
167	Rafael Orellano	.10
168	Ruben Rivera	.10
169	Alex Ochoa	.10
170	Jay Powell	.10
171	Tom Evans	.10
172	Ron Villone	.10
173	Shawn Estes	.10
174	John Wasdin	.10
175	Bill Simas	.10
176	Kevin Brown	.10
177	Shannon Stewart	.10
178	Todd Greene	.10
179	Bob Wolcott	.10
180	Chris Snopek	.10
181	Nomar Garciaparra	1.00
182	Cameron Smith **RC**	.10
183	Matt Drews	.10
184	Jimmy Haynes	.10
185	Chris Carpenter	.25
186	Desi Relaford	.10
187	Ben Grieve	.10
188	Mike Bell	.10
189	Luis Castillo **RC**	.75
190	Ugueth Urbina	.10
191	Paul Wilson	.10
191p	Paul Wilson (Unmarked promo card, name in gold.)	1.00
192	Andruw Jones	.75
193	Wayne Gomes	.10
194	Craig Counsell **RC**	.75
195	Jim Cole	.10
196	Brooks Kieshnick	.10
197	Trey Beamon	.10
198	Marino Santana **RC**	.10
199	Bob Abreu	.25
200	Calvin Reese	.10
201	Dante Powell	.10
202	George Arias	.10
202p	George Arias (Unmarked promo card, name in gold.)	1.00
203	Jorge Velandia **RC**	.10
204	George Lombard **RC**	.10
205	Byron Browne **RC**	.10
206	John Frascatore	.10
207	Terry Adams	.10
208	Wilson Delgado **RC**	.10
209	Billy McMillon	.10
210	Jeff Abbott	.10
211	Trot Nixon	.10
212	Amaury Telemaco	.10
213	Scott Sullivan	.10
214	Justin Thompson	.10
215	Decomba Conner	.10
216	Ryan McGuire	.10
217	Matt Luke **RC**	.10
218	Doug Million	.10
219	Jason Dickson **RC**	.25
220	Ramon Hernandez **RC**	.50
221	Mark Bellhorn **RC**	.25
222	Eric Ludwick **RC**	.10
223	Luke Wilcox **RC**	.10
224	Marty Malloy **RC**	.10
225	Gary Coffee **RC**	.10
226	Wendell Magee **RC**	.10
227	Brett Tomko **RC**	.25
228	Derek Lowe	.10
229	Jose Rosado **RC**	.10
230	Steve Bourgeois **RC**	.10
231	Neil Weber **RC**	.10
232	Jeff Ware	.10
233	Edwin Diaz	.10
234	Greg Norton	.10
235	Aaron Boone	.10
236	Jeff Suppan	.10
237	Bret Wagner	.10
238	Elieser Marrero	.10
239	Will Cunnane	.10
240	Brian Barkley **RC**	.10
241	Jay Payton	.10
242	Marcus Jensen	.10
243	Ryan Nye	.10
244	Chad Mottola	.10
245	Scott McClain **RC**	.10
246	Jesse Ibarra **RC**	.10
247	Mike Darr **RC**	.10
248	Bobby Estalella **RC**	.50
249	Michael Barrett	.10
250	Jamie Lopiccolo **RC**	.10
251	Shane Spencer **RC**	.40
252	Ben Petrick **RC**	.50
253	Jason Bell **RC**	.10
254	Arnold Gooch **RC**	.10
255	T.J. Mathews	.10
256	Jason Ryan	.10
257	Pat Cline **RC**	.10
258	Rafael Carmona **RC**	.10
259	Carl Pavano **RC**	1.00
260	Ben Davis	.10
261	Matt Lawton **RC**	1.00
262	Kevin Sefcik **RC**	.10
263	Chris Fussell **RC**	.10
264	Mike Cameron **RC**	1.50
265	Marty Janzen **RC**	.10
266	Livan Hernandez **RC**	1.00
267	Raul Ibanez **RC**	1.50
268	Juan Encarnacion	.10
269	David Yocum **RC**	.10
270	Jonathan Johnson **RC**	.10
271	Reggie Taylor	.10
272	Danny Buxbaum **RC**	.10
273	Jacob Cruz	.10
274	Bobby Morris **RC**	.10
275	Andy Fox **RC**	.10
276	Greg Keagle	.10
277	Charles Peterson	.10
278	Derrek Lee	.50
279	Bryant Nelson **RC**	.10
280	Antone Williamson	.10
281	Scott Elarton	.10
282	Shad Williams **RC**	.10
283	Rich Hunter **RC**	.10
284	Chris Sheff	.10
285	Derrick Gibson	.10
286	Felix Rodriguez	.10
287	Brian Banks **RC**	.10
288	Jason McDonald	.10
289	Glendon Rusch **RC**	.50
290	Gary Rath	.10
291	Peter Munro	.10
292	Tom Fordham	.10
293	Jason Kendall	.10
294	Russ Johnson	.10
295	Joe Long **RC**	.10
296	Robert Smith **RC**	.10
297	Jarrod Washburn **RC**	.75
298	Dave Coggin **RC**	.10
299	Jeff Yoder **RC**	.10
300	Jed Hansen **RC**	.10
301	Matt Morris **RC**	1.00
302	Josh Bishop **RC**	.10
303	Dustin Hermanson	.10
304	Mike Gulan	.10
305	Felipe Crespo	.10
306	Quinton McCracken	.10
307	Jim Bonnici **RC**	.10
308	Sal Fasano	.10
309	Gabe Alvarez **RC**	.10
310	Heath Murray **RC**	.10
311	Jose Valentin **RC**	.10
312	Bartolo Colon	.10
313	Olmedo Saenz	.10
314	Norm Hutchins **RC**	.10
315	Chris Holt **RC**	.10
316	David Doster **RC**	.10
317	Robert Person	.10
318	Donne Wall **RC**	.10
319	Adam Riggs **RC**	.10
320	Homer Bush	.10
321	Brad Rigby **RC**	.10
322	Lou Merloni **RC**	.25
323	Neifi Perez	.10
324	Chris Cumberland	.10
325	Alvie Shepherd **RC**	.10
326	Jarrod Patterson **RC**	.10
327	Ray Ricken **RC**	.10
328	Danny Klassen **RC**	.10
329	David Miller **RC**	.10
330	Chad Alexander **RC**	.10
331	Matt Beaumont	.10
332	Damon Hollins	.10
333	Todd Dunn	.10
334	Mike Sweeney **RC**	1.50
335	Richie Sexson	.40
336	Billy Wagner	.10
337	Ron Wright **RC**	.10
338	Paul Konerko	.25
339	Tommy Phelps **RC**	.10
340	Karim Garcia	.10
341	Mike Grace **RC**	.10
342	Russell Branyan **RC**	.40
343	Randy Winn **RC**	.50
344	A.J. Pierzynski **RC**	1.50
345	Mike Busby **RC**	.10
346	Matt Beech **RC**	.10
347	Jose Cepeda **RC**	.10
348	Brian Stephenson	.10
349	Rey Ordonez	.10
350	Rich Aurilia **RC**	1.00
351	Edgard Velazquez **RC**	.25
352	Raul Casanova	.10
353	Carlos Guillen **RC**	1.00
354	Bruce Aven **RC**	.10
355	Ryan Jones **RC**	.10
356	Derek Aucoin **RC**	.10
357	Brian Rose **RC**	.10
358	Richard Almanzar **RC**	.10
359	Fletcher Bates **RC**	.10
360	Russ Ortiz **RC**	.75
361	Wilton Guerrero **RC**	.10
362	Geoff Jenkins **RC**	1.00
363	Pete Janicki	.10
364	Yamil Benitez	.10
365	Aaron Holbert	.10
366	Tim Belk	.10
367	Terrell Wade	.10
368	Terrence Long	.10
369	Brad Fullmer	.10
370	Matt Wagner	.10
371	Craig Wilson	.10
372	Mark Loretta	.10
373	Eric Owens	.10
374	Vladimir Guerrero	1.00
375	Tommy Davis	.10
376	Donnie Sadler	.10
377	Edgar Renteria	.25
378	Todd Helton	.50
379	Ralph Milliard **RC**	.10
380	Darin Blood **RC**	.10
381	Shayne Bennett	.10
382	Mark Redman	.10
383	Felix Martinez	.10
384	Sean Watkins **RC**	.10
385	Oscar Henriquez	.10

Bowman's Best Preview

NOMAR GARCIAPARRA

		NM/M
Complete Set (30):		18.50
Common Player:		.25
Refractors:		1.5X
Atomic Refractors:		2X
1	Chipper Jones	1.50
2	Alan Benes	.25
3	Brooks Kieshnick	.25
4	Barry Bonds	3.00
5	Rey Ordonez	.25
6	Tim Salmon	.25
7	Mike Piazza	2.00
8	Billy Wagner	.25
9	Andruw Jones	1.00
10	Tony Gwynn	1.50
11	Paul Wilson	.25
12	Calvin Reese	.25
13	Frank Thomas	1.00
14	Greg Maddux	1.50
15	Derek Jeter	3.00
16	Jeff Bagwell	1.00
17	Barry Larkin	.25
18	Todd Greene	.25
19	Ruben Rivera	.25
20	Richard Hidalgo	.25
21	Larry Walker	.25
22	Carlos Baerga	.25
23	Derrick Gibson	.25
24	Richie Sexson	.25
25	Mo Vaughn	.25
26	Hideo Nomo	.50
27	Nomar Garciaparra	1.50
28	Cal Ripken Jr.	3.00
29	Karim Garcia	.25
30	Ken Griffey Jr.	2.00

Minor League Player of the Year

ALEX OCHOA / PLAYER OF THE YEAR CANDIDATE

		NM/M
Complete Set (15):		12.50
Common Player:		.50
1	Andruw Jones	4.00
2	Derrick Gibson	.50
3	Bob Abreu	.75
4	Todd Walker	.50
5	Jamey Wright	.50
6	Wes Helms	.50
7	Karim Garcia	.75
8	Bartolo Colon	2.00
9	Alex Ochoa	.50
10	Mike Sweeney	2.00
11	Ruben Rivera	.50
12	Gabe Alvarez	.50
13	Billy Wagner	.50
14	Vladimir Guerrero	4.00
15	Edgard Velazquez	.50

1952 Mickey Mantle Reprints

		NM/M
Complete Set (4):		20.00
Common Card:		2.50
20	Mickey Mantle/Reprint	2.50
20	Mickey Mantle/Finest	5.00

20	Mickey Mantle/Refractor	7.50
20	Mickey Mantle/ Atomic Refractor	10.00

1996 Bowman's Best

CHUCK KNOBLAUCH

		NM/M
Complete Set (180):		30.00
Common Player:		.25
Refractors:		2X
Atomics:		15X
1952 Mickey Mantle:		2.50
1952 Mantle Finest:		5.00
1952 Mantle Refractor:		7.50
1952 Mantle Atomic:		10.00
Pack (6):		2.50
Wax Box (24):		40.00
1	Hideo Nomo	.75
2	Edgar Martinez	.25
3	Cal Ripken Jr.	4.00
4	Wade Boggs	1.00
5	Cecil Fielder	.25
6	Albert Belle	.50
7	Chipper Jones	1.50
8	Ryne Sandberg	2.00
9	Tim Salmon	.25
10	Barry Bonds	3.00
11	Ken Caminiti	.25
12	Ron Gant	.25
13	Frank Thomas	1.00
14	Dante Bichette	.25
15	Jason Kendall	.25
16	Mo Vaughn	.25
17	Rey Ordonez	.25
18	Henry Rodriguez	.25
19	Ryan Klesko	.25
20	Jeff Bagwell	1.00
21	Randy Johnson	1.50
22	Jim Edmonds	.50
23	Kenny Lofton	.25
24	Andy Pettitte	.50
25	Brady Anderson	.25
26	Mike Piazza	2.50
27	Greg Vaughn	.25
28	Joe Carter	.25
29	Jason Giambi	1.00
30	Ivan Rodriguez	1.00
31	Jeff Conine	.25
32	Rafael Palmeiro	.75
33	Roger Clemens	3.00
34	Chuck Knoblauch	.25
35	Reggie Sanders	.25
36	Andres Galarraga	.25
37	Paul O'Neill	.50
38	Tony Gwynn	2.00
39	Paul Wilson	.25
40	Garret Anderson	.25
41	David Justice	.25
42	Eddie Murray	1.00
43	Mike Grace RC	.25
44	Marty Cordova	.25
45	Kevin Appier	.25
46	Raul Mondesi	.25
47	Jim Thome	1.00
48	Sammy Sosa	2.00
49	Craig Biggio	.50
50	Marquis Grissom	.25
51	Alan Benes	.25

52	Manny Ramirez	1.50
53	Gary Sheffield	.75
54	Mike Mussina	.50
55	Robin Ventura	.25
56	Johnny Damon	1.00
57	Jose Canseco	.75
58	Juan Gonzalez	.75
59	Tino Martinez	.25
60	Brian Hunter	.25
61	Fred McGriff	.25
62	Jay Buhner	.25
63	Carlos Delgado	.75
64	Moises Alou	.50
65	Roberto Alomar	.50
66	Barry Larkin	.50
67	Vinny Castilla	.25
68	Ray Durham	.25
69	Travis Fryman	.25
70	Jason Isringhausen	.25
71	Ken Griffey Jr.	2.50
72	John Smoltz	.25
73	Matt Williams	.25
74	Chan Ho Park	.25
75	Mark McGwire	2.50
76	Jeffrey Hammonds	.25
77	Will Clark	.50
78	Kirby Puckett	2.00
79	Derek Jeter	4.00
80	Derek Bell	.25
81	Eric Karros	.25
82	Lenny Dykstra	.25
83	Larry Walker	.50
84	Mark Grudzielanek	.25
85	Greg Maddux	2.50
86	Carlos Baerga	.25
87	Paul Molitor	1.00
88	John Valentin	.25
89	Mark Grace	.50
90	Ray Lankford	.25
91	Andruw Jones	1.50
92	Nomar Garciaparra	2.00
93	Alex Ochoa	.25
94	Derrick Gibson	.25
95	Jeff D'Amico	.25
96	Ruben Rivera	.25
97	Vladimir Guerrero	1.50
98	Calvin Reese	.25
99	Richard Hidalgo	.25
100	Bartolo Colon	.25
101	Karim Garcia	.25
102	Ben Davis	.25
103	Jay Powell	.25
104	Chris Snopek	.25
105	Glendon Rusch RC	1.00
106	Enrique Wilson	.25
107	Antonio Alfonseca RC	.25
108	Wilton Guerrero RC	.50
109	Jose Guillen RC	3.00
110	Miguel Mejia RC	.25
111	Jay Payton	.25
112	Scott Elarton	.25
113	Brooks Kieschnick	.25
114	Dustin Hermanson	.25
115	Roger Cedeno	.25
116	Matt Wagner	.25
117	Lee Daniels	.25
118	Ben Grieve	.25
119	Ugueth Urbina	.25
120	Danny Graves	.25
121	Dan Donato RC	.25
122	Matt Ruebel RC	.25
123	Mark Sievert RC	.25
124	Chris Stynes	.25
125	Jeff Abbott	.25
126	Rocky Coppinger RC	.25
127	Jermaine Dye	.25
128	Todd Greene	.15
129	Chris Carpenter	1.00
130	Edgar Renteria	.25
131	Matt Drews	.25
132	Edgard Velazquez RC	.50
133	Casey Whitten	.25
134	Ryan Jones RC	.25
135	Todd Walker	.20
136	Geoff Jenkins RC	2.00
137	Matt Morris RC	2.00
138	Richie Sexson	.75
139	Todd Dunwoody RC	.50
140	Gabe Alvarez RC	.50
141	J.J. Johnson	.25
142	Shannon Stewart	.25
143	Brad Fullmer	.25
144	Julio Santana	.25
145	Scott Rolen	1.00
146	Amaury Telemaco	.25
147	Trey Beamon	.25
148	Billy Wagner	.20
149	Todd Hollandsworth	.25
150	Doug Million	.25
151	Jose Valentin RC	.25
152	Wes Helms RC	.50
153	Jeff Suppan	.25
154	Luis Castillo RC	1.50
155	Bob Abreu	.50
156	Paul Konerko	.50
157	Jamey Wright	.25
158	Eddie Pearson	.25
159	Jimmy Haynes	.25
160	Derek Lee	.75
161	Damian Moss	.15
162	Carlos Guillen RC	2.00
163	Chris Fussell RC	.25
164	Mike Sweeney RC	3.00
165	Donnie Sadler	.15
166	Desi Relaford	.25

167	Steve Gibralter	.25
168	Neifi Perez	.25
169	Antone Williamson	.25
170	Marty Janzen RC	.25
171	Todd Helton	1.00
172	Raul Ibanez RC	2.00
173	Bill Selby	.25
174	Shane Monahan RC	.35
175	Robin Jennings RC	.25
176	Bobby Chouinard RC	.25
177	Einar Diaz	.25
178	Jason Thompson	.15
179	Rafael Medina RC	.25
180	Kevin Orie	.25

Mirror Image

ALBERT BELLE

		NM/M
Complete Set (10):		24.00
Common Card:		1.50
Refractors:		1.5X
Atomics:		2X
1	Jeff Bagwell, Todd Helton, Frank Thomas, Richie Sexson	3.00
2	Craig Biggio, Luis Castillo, Roberto Alomar, Desi Relaford	1.50
3	Chipper Jones, Scott Rolen, Wade Boggs, George Arias	3.50
4	Barry Larkin, Neifi Perez, Cal Ripken Jr., Mark Bellhorn	6.00
5	Larry Walker, Karim Garcia, Albert Belle, Ruben Rivera	1.50
6	Barry Bonds, Andruw Jones, Kenny Lofton, Donnie Sadler	6.00
7	Tony Gwynn, Vladimir Guerrero, Ken Griffey Jr., Ben Grieve	4.50
8	Mike Piazza, Ben Davis, Ivan Rodriguez, Jose Valentin	4.50
9	Greg Maddux, Jamey Wright, Mike Mussina, Bartolo Colon	3.50
10	Tom Glavine, Billy Wagner, Randy Johnson, Jarrod Washburn	1.50

Cuts

KEN GRIFFEY JR.

		NM/M
Complete Set (15):		15.00
Common Player:		.25
Refractors:		1.5X
Atomic Refractors:		2X
1	Ken Griffey Jr.	2.50
2	Jason Isringhausen	.25
3	Derek Jeter	4.00
4	Andruw Jones	1.00
5	Chipper Jones	2.00
6	Ryan Klesko	.25
7	Raul Mondesi	.25
8	Hideo Nomo	.50
9	Mike Piazza	2.50

10	Manny Ramirez	1.00
11	Cal Ripken Jr.	4.00
12	Ruben Rivera	.25
13	Tim Salmon	.25
14	Frank Thomas	1.00
15	Jim Thome	.75

1997 Bowman

		NM/M
Complete Set (440):		50.00
Complete Series 1 (221):		25.00
Complete Series 2 (219):		25.00
Common Player:		.10
Series 1 Pack (10):		2.00
Series 1 Wax Box (24):		35.00
Series 2 Pack (10):		2.00
Series 2 Wax Box (24):		35.00
1	Derek Jeter	2.00
2	Edgar Renteria	.10
3	Chipper Jones	1.00
4	Hideo Nomo	.40
5	Tim Salmon	.10
6	Jason Giambi	.50
7	Robin Ventura	.10
8	Tony Clark	.10
9	Barry Larkin	.25
10	Paul Molitor	.75
11	Bernard Gilkey	.10
12	Jack McDowell	.10
13	Andy Benes	.10
14	Ryan Klesko	.10
15	Mark McGwire	1.50
16	Ken Griffey Jr.	1.50
17	Robb Nen	.10
18	Cal Ripken Jr.	2.00
19	John Valentin	.10
20	Ricky Bottalico	.10
21	Mike Lansing	.10
22	Ryne Sandberg	1.00
23	Carlos Delgado	.50
24	Craig Biggio	.25
25	Eric Karros	.10
26	Kevin Appier	.10
27	Mariano Rivera	.50
28	Vinny Castilla	.10
29	Juan Gonzalez	.40
30	Al Martin	.10
31	Jeff Cirillo	.10
32	Eddie Murray	.75
33	Ray Lankford	.10
34	Manny Ramirez	.75
35	Roberto Alomar	.25
36	Will Clark	.25
37	Chuck Knoblauch	.10
38	Harold Baines	.10
39	Trevor Hoffman	.10
40	Edgar Martinez	.10
41	Geronimo Berroa	.10
42	Rey Ordonez	.10
43	Mike Stanley	.10
44	Mike Mussina	.40
45	Kevin Brown	.10
46	Dennis Eckersley	.50
47	Henry Rodriguez	.10
48	Tino Martinez	.10
49	Eric Young	.10
50	Bret Boone	.10
51	Raul Mondesi	.10
52	Sammy Sosa	1.00
53	John Smoltz	.25
54	Billy Wagner	.10
55	Jeff D'Amico	.10
56	Ken Caminiti	.10
57	Jason Kendall	.10
58	Wade Boggs	.75
59	Andres Galarraga	.10
60	Jeff Brantley	.10
61	Mel Rojas	.10
62	Brian Hunter	.10
63	Bobby Bonilla	.10
64	Roger Clemens	1.50
65	Jeff Kent	.20
66	Matt Williams	.10
67	Albert Belle	.10
68	Jeff King	.10
69	John Wetteland	.10
70	Deion Sanders	.25
71	Bubba Trammell **RC**	.25
72	Felix Heredia **RC**	.25
73	Billy Koch **RC**	.25
74	Sidney Ponson **RC**	.25
75	Ricky Ledee **RC**	.25
76	Brett Tomko	.10
77	Braden Looper **RC**	.25
78	Damian Jackson	.10
79	Jason Dickson	.10
80	Chad Green **RC**	.10
81	R.A. Dickey **RC**	.10
82	Jeff Liefer	.10
83	Matt Wagner	.10
84	Richard Hidalgo	.10
85	Adam Riggs	.10
86	Robert Smith	.10
87	Chad Hermansen **RC**	.10
88	Felix Martinez	.10
89	J.J. Johnson	.10
90	Todd Dunwoody	.10
91	Katsuhiro Maeda	.10
92	Darin Erstad	.25
93	Elieser Marrero	.10
94	Bartolo Colon	.10
95	Chris Fussell	.10
96	Ugueth Urbina	.10
97	Josh Paul **RC**	.10
98	Jaime Bluma	.10
99	Seth Greisinger **RC**	.10
100	Jose Cruz **RC**	.25
101	Todd Dunn	.10
102	Joe Young **RC**	.10
103	Jonathan Johnson	.10
104	Justin Towle **RC**	.10
105	Brian Rose	.10
106	Jose Guillen	.10
107	Andruw Jones	.75
108	Mark Kotsay **RC**	1.00
109	Wilton Guerrero	.10
110	Jacob Cruz	.10
111	Mike Sweeney	.10
112	Julio Mosquera	.10
113	Matt Morris	.10
114	Wendell Magee	.10
115	John Thomson	.10
116	Javier Valentin **RC**	.10
117	Tom Fordham	.10
118	Ruben Rivera	.10
119	Mike Drumright **RC**	.10
120	Chris Holt	.10
121	Sean Maloney **RC**	.10
122	Michael Barrett	.10
123	Tony Saunders **RC**	.10
124	Kevin Brown	.10
125	Richard Almanzar	.10
126	Mark Redman	.10
127	Anthony Sanders **RC**	.10
128	Jeff Abbott	.10
129	Eugene Kingsale	.10
130	Paul Konerko	.40
131	Randall Simon **RC**	.25
132	Andy Larkin	.10
133	Rafael Medina	.10
134	Mendy Lopez	.10
135	Freddy Garcia	.10
136	Karim Garcia	.15
137	Larry Rodriguez **RC**	.10
138	Carlos Guillen	.10
139	Aaron Boone	.10
140	Donnie Sadler	.10
141	Brooks Kieschnick	.10
142	Scott Spiezio	.10
143	Everett Stull	.10
144	Enrique Wilson	.10
145	Milton Bradley **RC**	1.50
146	Kevin Orie	.10
147	Derek Wallace	.10
148	Russ Johnson	.10
149	Joe Lagarde **RC**	.10
150	Luis Castillo	.10
151	Jay Payton	.10
152	Joe Long	.10
153	Livan Hernandez	.10
154	Vladimir Nunez **RC**	.15
155	Not issued	
156a	George Arias	.10
156b	Calvin Reese (Should be #155.)	.10
157	Homer Bush	.10
158	Not issued	
159a	Eric Milton **RC**	.50
159b	Chris Carpenter (Should be #158.)	.50
160	Richie Sexson	.40
161	Carl Pavano	.10
162	Chris Gissell **RC**	.10
163	Mac Suzuki	.10
164	Pat Cline	.10
165	Ron Wright	.10
166	Dante Powell	.10
167	Mark Bellhorn	.10
168	George Lombard	.10
169	Pee Wee Lopez **RC**	.10
170	Paul Wilder **RC**	.10
171	Brad Fullmer	.10
172	Willie Martinez **RC**	.10
173	Dario Veras **RC**	.10
174	Dave Coggin	.10
175	Kris Benson **RC**	1.00
176	Torii Hunter	.25
177	D.T. Cromer **RC**	.10
178	Nelson Figueroa **RC**	.10
179	Hiram Bocachica **RC**	.15
180	Shane Monahan	.10
181	Jimmy Anderson **RC**	.10
182	Juan Melo	.10
183	Pablo Ortega **RC**	.10
184	Calvin Pickering **RC**	.50
185	Reggie Taylor	.10
186	Jeff Farnsworth **RC**	.10
187	Terrence Long	.10
188	Geoff Jenkins	.10
189	Steve Rain **RC**	.10
190	Nerio Rodriguez **RC**	.10
191	Derrick Gibson	.10
192	Darin Blood	.10
193	Ben Davis	.10
194	Adrian Beltre **RC**	2.00
195	Damian Sapp **RC**	.10
196	Kerry Wood **RC**	3.00
197	Nate Rolison **RC**	.10
198	Fernando Tatis **RC**	.25
199	Brad Penny **RC**	2.00
200	Jake Westbrook **RC**	.15
201	Edwin Diaz	.10
202	Joe Fontenot **RC**	.10
203	Matt Halloran **RC**	.10
204	Blake Stein **RC**	.10
205	Onan Masaoka	.10
206	Ben Petrick	.10
207	Matt Clement **RC**	1.00
208	Todd Greene	.10
209	Ray Ricken	.10
210	Eric Chavez **RC**	3.00
211	Edgard Velazquez	.10
212	Bruce Chen **RC**	.10
213	Danny Patterson **RC**	.10
214	Jeff Yoder	.10
215	Luis Ordaz **RC**	.10
216	Chris Widger	.10
217	Jason Brester	.10
218	Carlton Loewer	.10
219	Chris Reitsma **RC**	.10
220	Neifi Perez	.10
221	Hideki Irabu **RC**	.25
222	Ellis Burks	.10
223	Pedro Martinez	.75
224	Kenny Lofton	.10
225	Randy Johnson	.75
226	Terry Steinbach	.10
227	Bernie Williams	.25
228	Dean Palmer	.10
229	Alan Benes	.10
230	Marquis Grissom	.10
231	Gary Sheffield	.40
232	Curt Schilling	.40
233	Reggie Sanders	.10
234	Bobby Higginson	.10
235	Moises Alou	.20
236	Tom Glavine	.25
237	Mark Grace	.25
238	Ramon Martinez	.10
239	Rafael Palmeiro	.50
240	John Olerud	.10
241	Dante Bichette	.10
242	Greg Vaughn	.10
243	Jeff Bagwell	.50
244	Barry Bonds	2.00
245	Pat Hentgen	.10
246	Jim Thome	.50
247	Jermaine Allensworth	.10
248	Andy Pettitte	.25
249	Jay Bell	.10
250	John Jaha	.10
251	Jim Edmonds	.25
252	Ron Gant	.10
253	David Cone	.10
254	Jose Canseco	.40
255	Jay Buhner	.10
256	Greg Maddux	1.50
257	Brian McRae	.10
258	Lance Johnson	.10
259	Travis Fryman	.10
260	Paul O'Neill	.20
261	Ivan Rodriguez	.50
262	Gregg Jefferies	.10
263	Fred McGriff	.20
264	Derek Bell	.10
265	Jeff Conine	.10
266	Mike Piazza	1.50
267	Mark Grudzielanek	.10
268	Brady Anderson	.10
269	Marty Cordova	.10
270	Ray Durham	.10
271	Joe Carter	.10
272	Brian Jordan	.10
273	David Justice	.10
274	Tony Gwynn	1.00
275	Larry Walker	.20
276	Cecil Fielder	.10
277	Mo Vaughn	.10
278	Alex Fernandez	.10
279	Michael Tucker	.10
280	Jose Valentin	.10
281	Sandy Alomar	.10
282	Todd Hollandsworth	.10
283	Rico Brogna	.10
284	Rusty Greer	.10
285	Roberto Hernandez	.10
286	Hal Morris	.10
287	Johnny Damon	.75
288	Todd Hundley	.10
289	Rondell White	.10
290	Frank Thomas	.75
291	Don Denbow **RC**	.10
292	Derrek Lee	.50
293	Todd Walker	.10
294	Scott Rolen	.50
295	Wes Helms	.10
296	Bob Abreu	.25
297	John Patterson **RC**	1.50
298	Alex Gonzalez **RC**	.25
299	Grant Roberts **RC**	.25
300	Jeff Suppan	.10
301	Luke Wilcox	.10
302	Marlon Anderson	.10
303	Ray Brown	.10
304	Mike Caruso **RC**	.25
305	Sam Marsonek **RC**	.10
306	Brady Raggio **RC**	.10
307	Kevin McGlinchy **RC**	.25
308	Roy Halladay **RC**	3.00
309	Jeremi Gonzalez **RC**	.25
310	Aramis Ramirez **RC**	4.00
311	Dermal Brown **RC**	.10
312	Justin Thompson	.10
313	Jay Tessmer **RC**	.10
314	Mike Johnson	.10
315	Danny Clyburn	.10
316	Bruce Aven	.10
317	Keith Foulke **RC**	1.50
318	Jimmy Osting **RC**	.10
319	Valerio De Los Santos **RC**	.25
320	Shannon Stewart	.10
321	Willie Adams	.10
322	Larry Barnes	.10
323	Mark Johnson	.10
324	Chris Stowers **RC**	.10
325	Brandon Reed	.10
326	Randy Winn	.10
327	Steven Chavez	.10
328	Nomar Garciaparra	1.00
329	Jacque Jones **RC**	1.00
330	Chris Clemons	.10
331	Todd Helton	.50
332	Ryan Brannan **RC**	.10
333	Alex Sanchez **RC**	.25
334	Arnold Gooch	.10
335	Russell Branyan	.10
336	Daryle Ward	.10
337	John LeRoy **RC**	.10
338	Steve Cox	.10
339	Kevin Witt	.10
340	Norm Hutchins	.10
341	Gabby Martinez	.10
342	Kris Detmers	.10
343	Mike Villano **RC**	.10
344	Preston Wilson	.10
345	Jim Manias **RC**	.10
346	Deivi Cruz **RC**	.25
347	Donzell McDonald **RC**	.10
348	Rod Myers **RC**	.10
349	Shawn Chacon **RC**	.25
350	Elvin Hernandez **RC**	.10
351	Orlando Cabrera **RC**	1.00
352	Brian Banks	.10
353	Robbie Bell	.10
354	Brad Rigby	.10
355	Scott Elarton	.10
356	Kevin Sweeney **RC**	.10
357	Steve Soderstrom	.10
358	Ryan Nye	.10
359	Marlon Allen **RC**	.10
360	Donny Leon **RC**	.10
361	Garrett Neubart **RC**	.10
362	Abraham Nunez **RC**	.25
363	Adam Eaton **RC**	.50
364	Octavio Dotel **RC**	.40
365	Dean Crow **RC**	.10
366	Jason Baker **RC**	.10
367	Sean Casey	.10
368	Joe Lawrence **RC**	.10
369	Adam Johnson **RC**	.10
370	Scott Schoeneweis **RC**	.25
371	Gerald Witasick Jr.	.10
372	Ronnie Belliard **RC**	.25
373	Russ Ortiz	.10
374	Robert Stratton **RC**	.10
375	Bobby Estalella	.10
376	Corey Lee **RC**	.10
377	Carlos Beltran	.50
378	Mike Cameron	.10
379	Scott Randall **RC**	.10
380	Corey Erickson **RC**	.10
381	Jay Canizaro	.10
382	Kerry Robinson **RC**	.10
383	Todd Noel **RC**	.10
384	A.J. Zapp **RC**	.10
385	Jarrod Washburn	.10
386	Ben Grieve	.10
387	Javier Vazquez **RC**	1.50
388	Tony Graffanino	.10
389	Travis Lee **RC**	.50
390	DaRond Stovall	.10
391	Dennis Reyes **RC**	.25
392	Danny Buxbaum	.10
393	Marc Lewis **RC**	.10
394	Kelvim Escobar **RC**	.25
395	Danny Klassen	.10
396	Ken Cloude **RC**	.25
397	Gabe Alvarez	.10
398	Jaret Wright **RC**	.50
399	Raul Casanova	.10
400	Clayton Brunner **RC**	.10
401	Jason Marquis **RC**	.50
402	Marc Kroon	.10
403	Jamey Wright	.10
404	Matt Snyder **RC**	.10
405	Josh Garrett **RC**	.10
406	Juan Encarnacion	.10
407	Heath Murray	.10
408	Brett Herbison **RC**	.10
409	Brent Butler **RC**	.25
410	Danny Peoples **RC**	.25
411	Miguel Tejada **RC**	10.00
412	Damian Moss	.10
413	Jim Pittsley	.10
414	Dmitri Young	.10
415	Glendon Rusch	.10

416	Vladimir Guerrero	.75
417	Cole Liniak RC	.10
418	Ramon Hernandez	.10
419	Cliff Politte RC	.25
420	Mel Rosario RC	.10
421	Jorge Carrion RC	.10
422	John Barnes RC	.10
423	Chris Stowe RC	.10
424	Vernon Wells RC	4.00
425	Brett Caradonna RC	.10
426	Scott Hodges RC	.10
427	Jon Garland RC	1.50
428	Nathan Haynes RC	.25
429	Geoff Goetz RC	.25
430	Adam Kennedy RC	.50
431	T.J. Tucker RC	.10
432	Aaron Akin RC	.10
433	Jayson Werth RC	.50
434	Glenn Davis RC	.10
435	Mark Mangum RC	.10
436	Troy Cameron RC	.10
437	J.J. Davis RC	.10
438	Lance Berkman RC	8.00
439	Jason Standridge RC	.25
440	Jason Dellaero RC	.10
441	Hideki Irabu RC	.25

International

	NM/M
Complete Set (440):	75.00
Complete Series 1 (221):	40.00
Complete Series 2 (219):	40.00
Common Player:	.25
Stars and Rookies:	1.5X

(See 1997 Bowman for checklist and base card values.)

Bowman's Best Preview

		NM/M
Complete Set (20):		30.00
Common Player:		.75
Refractors:		1.5X
Atomic Refractors:		2X
1	Frank Thomas	1.50
2	Ken Griffey Jr.	3.00
3	Barry Bonds	5.00
4	Derek Jeter	5.00
5	Chipper Jones	2.00
6	Mark McGwire	4.00
7	Cal Ripken Jr.	5.00
8	Kenny Lofton	.75
9	Gary Sheffield	.75
10	Jeff Bagwell	1.50
11	Wilton Guerrero	.75
12	Scott Rolen	1.00
13	Todd Walker	.75
14	Ruben Rivera	.75
15	Andruw Jones	1.50
16	Nomar Garciaparra	2.00
17	Vladimir Guerrero	1.50
18	Miguel Tejada	1.00
19	Bartolo Colon	.75
20	Katsuhiro Maeda	.75

International Best

	NM/M
Complete Set (20):	20.00

Common Player:		.60
Refractors:		1.5X
Atomic Refractors:		2X
1	Frank Thomas	1.50
2	Ken Griffey Jr.	2.50
3	Juan Gonzalez	1.50
4	Bernie Williams	.60
5	Hideo Nomo	1.50
6	Sammy Sosa	3.50
7	Larry Walker	.60
8	Vinny Castilla	.60
9	Mariano Rivera	.75
10	Rafael Palmeiro	1.00
11	Nomar Garciaparra	3.50
12	Todd Walker	.60
13	Andruw Jones	1.50
14	Vladimir Guerrero	1.50
15	Ruben Rivera	.60
16	Bob Abreu	.75
17	Karim Garcia	.75
18	Katsuhiro Maeda	.60
19	Jose Cruz Jr.	1.00
20	Damian Moss	.60

Scout's Honor Roll

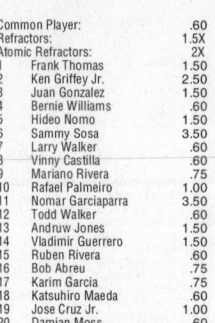

		NM/M
Complete Set (15):		12.50
Common Player:		.50
1	Dmitri Young	.50
2	Bob Abreu	.75
3	Vladimir Guerrero	2.00
4	Paul Konerko	.75
5	Kevin Orie	.50
6	Todd Walker	.50
7	Ben Grieve	.50
8	Darin Erstad	1.00
9	Derek Lee	1.00
10	Jose Cruz	.50
11	Scott Rolen	1.00
12	Travis Lee	.75
13	Andruw Jones	2.00
14	Wilton Guerrero	.50
15	Nomar Garciaparra	2.50

Rookie of the Year Candidates

		NM/M
Complete Set (15):		9.00
Common Player:		.50
1	Jeff Abbott	.50
2	Karim Garcia	.50
3	Todd Helton	2.50
4	Richard Hidalgo	.50
5	Geoff Jenkins	.50
6	Russ Johnson	.50
7	Paul Konerko	.75
8	Mark Kotsay	.50
9	Ricky Ledee	.50
10	Travis Lee	.75
11	Derek Lee	1.50
12	Elieser Marrero	.50
13	Juan Melo	.50
14	Brian Rose	.50
15	Fernando Tatis	.50

Certified Autographs

	NM/M
Common Blue:	2.00
Black:	1.5X

Gold:		4X
Derek Jeter Green:		1.5X
1	Jeff Abbott	2.00
2	Bob Abreu	40.00
3	Willie Adams	2.00
4	Brian Banks	2.00
5	Kris Benson	15.00
6	Darin Blood	2.00
7	Jaime Bluma	2.00
8	Kevin Brown	5.00
9	Ray Brown	2.00
10	Homer Bush	4.00
11	Mike Cameron	8.00
12	Jay Canizaro	3.00
13	Luis Castillo	5.00
14	Dave Coggin	2.00
15	Bartolo Colon	15.00
16	Rocky Coppinger	3.00
17	Jacob Cruz	5.00
18	Jose Cruz	8.00
19	Jeff D'Amico	5.00
20	Ben Davis	5.00
21	Mike Drumbright	5.00
22	Scott Elarton	5.00
23	Darin Erstad	10.00
24	Bobby Estalella	5.00
25	Joe Fontenot	4.00
26	Tom Fordham	2.00
27	Brad Fullmer	5.00
28	Chris Fussell	2.00
29	Karim Garcia	5.00
30	Kris Detmers	2.00
31	Todd Greene	4.00
32	Ben Grieve	5.00
33	Vladimir Guerrero	75.00
34	Jose Guillen	15.00
35	Roy Halladay	65.00
36	Wes Helms	5.00
37	Chad Hermansen	3.00
38	Richard Hidalgo	8.00
39	Todd Hollandsworth	3.00
40	Damian Jackson	3.00
41	Derek Jeter	120.00
42	Andruw Jones	20.00
43	Brooks Kieschnick	3.00
44	Eugene Kingsale	5.00
45	Paul Konerko	15.00
46	Marc Kroon	2.00
47	Derrek Lee	40.00
48	Travis Lee	5.00
49	Terrence Long	4.00
50	Curt Lyons	2.00
51	Elieser Marrero	3.00
52	Rafael Medina	2.00
53	Juan Melo	3.00
54	Shane Monahan	2.00
55	Julio Mosquera	2.00
56	Heath Murray	2.00
57	Ryan Nye	2.00
58	Kevin Orie	4.00
59	Russ Ortiz	5.00
60	Carl Pavano	30.00
61	Jay Payton	5.00
62	Neifi Perez	3.00
63	Sidney Ponson	10.00
64	Calvin Reese	8.00
65	Ray Ricken	3.00
66	Brad Rigby	3.00
67	Adam Riggs	3.00
68	Ruben Rivera	4.00
69	J.J. Johnson	2.00
70	Scott Rolen	40.00
71	Tony Saunders	3.00
72	Donnie Sadler	5.00
73	Richie Sexson	15.00
74	Scott Spiezio	6.00
75	Everett Stull	2.00
76	Mike Sweeney	15.00
77	Fernando Tatis	4.00
78	Miguel Tejada	80.00
79	Justin Thompson	5.00
80	Justin Towle	6.00
81	Billy Wagner	20.00
82	Todd Walker	5.00
83	Luke Wilcox	2.00
84	Paul Wilder	4.00
85	Enrique Wilson	5.00
86	Kerry Wood	60.00
87	Jamey Wright	5.00
88	Ron Wright	5.00
89	Dmitri Young	10.00
90	Nelson Figueroa	2.00

1997 Bowman Chrome

		NM/M
Complete Set (300):		150.00
Common Player:		.25
Pack (3):		5.00
Wax Box (24):		100.00
1	Derek Jeter	4.00
2	Chipper Jones	2.00
3	Hideo Nomo	.75
4	Tim Salmon	.25
5	Robin Ventura	.25
6	Tony Clark	.25
7	Barry Larkin	.50
8	Paul Molitor	1.00
9	Andy Benes	.25
10	Ryan Klesko	.25
11	Mark McGwire	3.00
12	Ken Griffey Jr.	2.50
13	Robb Nen	.25
14	Cal Ripken Jr.	4.00
15	John Valentin	.25
16	Ricky Bottalico	.25
17	Mike Lansing	.25
18	Ryne Sandberg	2.00
19	Carlos Delgado	1.00
20	Craig Biggio	.50
21	Eric Karros	.25
22	Kevin Appier	.25
23	Mariano Rivera	.75
24	Vinny Castilla	.25
25	Juan Gonzalez	.50
26	Al Martin	.25
27	Jeff Cirillo	.25
28	Ray Lankford	.25
29	Manny Ramirez	1.50
30	Roberto Alomar	.40
31	Will Clark	.50
32	Chuck Knoblauch	.25
33	Harold Baines	.25
34	Edgar Martinez	.25
35	Mike Mussina	.50
36	Kevin Brown	.25
37	Dennis Eckersley	.75
38	Tino Martinez	.25
39	Raul Mondesi	.25
40	Sammy Sosa	1.50
41	John Smoltz	.75
42	Billy Wagner	.25
43	Ken Caminiti	.25
44	Wade Boggs	1.50
45	Andres Galarraga	.25
46	Roger Clemens	3.00
47	Matt Williams	.25
48	Albert Belle	.50
49	Jeff King	.25
50	John Wetteland	.25
51	Deion Sanders	.50
52	Ellis Burks	.25
53	Pedro Martinez	1.50
54	Kenny Lofton	.25
55	Randy Johnson	1.50
56	Bernie Williams	.50
57	Marquis Grissom	.25
58	Gary Sheffield	.50
59	Curt Schilling	1.00
60	Reggie Sanders	.25
61	Bobby Higginson	.25
62	Moises Alou	.50
63	Tom Glavine	.50
64	Mark Grace	.50
65	Rafael Palmeiro	1.00
66	John Olerud	.25
67	Dante Bichette	.25
68	Jeff Bagwell	1.00
69	Barry Bonds	3.00
70	Pat Hentgen	.25
71	Jim Thome	1.00
72	Andy Pettitte	.50
73	Jay Bell	.25
74	Jim Edmonds	.50
75	Ron Gant	.25
76	David Cone	.25
77	Jose Canseco	.75
78	Jay Buhner	.25
79	Greg Maddux	2.50
80	Lance Johnson	.25
81	Travis Fryman	.25
82	Paul O'Neill	.50
83	Ivan Rodriguez	1.00
84	Fred McGriff	.25

#	Player	Price
85	Mike Piazza	2.50
86	Brady Anderson	.25
87	Marty Cordova	.25
88	Joe Carter	.25
89	Brian Jordan	.25
90	David Justice	.25
91	Tony Gwynn	2.00
92	Larry Walker	.40
93	Mo Vaughn	.25
94	Sandy Alomar	.25
95	Rusty Greer	.25
96	Roberto Hernandez	.25
97	Hal Morris	.25
98	Todd Hundley	.25
99	Rondell White	.25
100	Frank Thomas	1.50
101	Bubba Trammell RC	.75
102	Sidney Ponson RC	1.50
103	Ricky Ledee RC	.50
104	Brett Tomko	.25
105	Braden Looper RC	.50
106	Jason Dickson	.25
107	Chad Green RC	.25
108	R.A. Dickey RC	.25
109	Jeff Liefer	.25
110	Richard Hidalgo	.25
111	Chad Hermansen RC	.50
112	Felix Martinez	.25
113	J.J. Johnson	.25
114	Todd Dunwoody	.25
115	Katsuhiro Maeda	.25
116	Darin Erstad	.50
117	Elieser Marrero	.25
118	Bartolo Colon	.25
119	Ugueth Urbina	.25
120	Jaime Bluma	.25
121	Seth Greisinger RC	.50
122	Jose Cruz Jr. RC	1.50
123	Todd Dunn	.25
124	Justin Towle RC	.25
125	Brian Rose	.25
126	Jose Guillen	.25
127	Andruw Jones	1.50
128	Mark Kotsay RC	2.50
129	Wilton Guerrero	.25
130	Jacob Cruz	.25
131	Mike Sweeney	.25
132	Matt Morris	.25
133	John Thomson	.25
134	Javier Valentin RC	.25
135	Mike Drumright RC	.25
136	Michael Barrett	.25
137	Tony Saunders RC	.25
138	Kevin Brown	.25
139	Anthony Sanders RC	.25
140	Jeff Abbott	.25
141	Eugene Kingsale	.25
142	Paul Konerko	.25
143	Randall Simon RC	.50
144	Freddy Garcia	.25
145	Karim Garcia	.25
146	Carlos Guillen	.25
147	Aaron Boone	.25
148	Donnie Sadler	.25
149	Brooks Kieschnick	.25
150	Scott Spiezio	.25
151	Kevin Orie	.25
152	Russ Johnson	.25
153	Livan Hernandez	.25
154	Vladimir Nunez RC	.75
155	Calvin Reese	.25
156	Chris Carpenter	.75
157	Eric Milton RC	1.50
158	Richie Sexson	.50
159	Carl Pavano	.25
160	Pat Cline	.25
161	Ron Wright	.25
162	Dante Powell	.25
163	Mark Bellhorn	.25
164	George Lombard	.25
165	Paul Wilder RC	.25
166	Brad Fullmer	.25
167	Kris Benson RC	2.00
168	Torii Hunter	.50
169	D.T. Cromer	.25
170	Nelson Figueroa RC	.50
171	Hiram Bocachica RC	.50
172	Shane Monahan	.25
173	Juan Melo	.25
174	Calvin Pickering RC	1.50
175	Reggie Taylor	.25
176	Geoff Jenkins	.25
177	Steve Rain RC	.25
178	Nerio Rodriguez	.25
179	Derrick Gibson	.25
180	Darin Blood	.25
181	Ben Davis	.25
182	Adrian Beltre RC	8.00
183	Kerry Wood RC	8.00
184	Nate Rolison	.25
185	Fernando Tatis RC	.50
186	Jake Westbrook RC	2.00
187	Edwin Diaz	.25
188	Joe Fontenot RC	.50
189	Matt Halloran RC	.25
190	Matt Clement RC	3.00
191	Todd Greene	.25
192	Eric Chavez RC	10.00
193	Edgard Velazquez	.25
194	Bruce Chen RC	.25
195	Jason Brester	.25
196	Chris Reitsma RC	.50
197	Neifi Perez	.25
198	Hideki Irabu RC	.50
199	Don Denbow RC	.25
200	Derrek Lee	.75
201	Todd Walker	.25
202	Scott Rolen	1.00
203	Wes Helms	.25
204	Bob Abreu	.50
205	John Patterson RC	2.00
206	Alex Gonzalez RC	1.00
207	Grant Roberts RC	.50
208	Jeff Suppan	.25
209	Luke Wilcox	.25
210	Marlon Anderson	.25
211	Mike Caruso RC	.50
212	Roy Halladay RC	8.00
213	Jeremi Gonzalez	.50
214	Aramis Ramirez RC	10.00
215	Dermal Brown RC	.25
216	Justin Thompson	.25
217	Danny Clyburn	.25
218	Bruce Aven	.25
219	Keith Foulke RC	2.00
220	Shannon Stewart	.25
221	Larry Barnes	.25
222	Mark Johnson RC	.25
223	Randy Winn	.25
224	Nomar Garciaparra	2.00
225	Jacque Jones RC	4.00
226	Chris Clemons	.25
227	Todd Helton	1.00
228	Ryan Brannan RC	.25
229	Alex Sanchez RC	.50
230	Russell Branyan	.25
231	Daryle Ward	.25
232	Kevin Witt	.25
233	Gabby Martinez	.25
234	Preston Wilson	.25
235	Donzell McDonald RC	.25
236	Orlando Cabrera RC	5.00
237	Brian Banks	.25
238	Robbie Bell	.25
239	Brad Rigby	.25
240	Scott Elarton	.25
241	Donny Leon RC	.25
242	Abraham Nunez RC	1.00
243	Adam Eaton RC	2.00
244	Octavio Dotel RC	1.00
245	Sean Casey	.35
246	Joe Lawrence RC	.50
247	Adam Johnson RC	.25
248	Ronnie Belliard RC	1.00
249	Bobby Estalella	.25
250	Corey Lee RC	.25
251	Mike Cameron	.25
252	Kerry Robinson RC	.25
253	A.J. Zapp RC	.25
254	Jarrod Washburn	.25
255	Ben Grieve	.25
256	Javier Vazquez RC	3.00
257	Travis Lee RC	1.00
258	Dennis Reyes RC	.50
259	Danny Buxbaum	.25
260	Kelvim Escobar RC	1.00
261	Danny Klassen	.25
262	Ken Cloude RC	.50
263	Gabe Alvarez	.25
264	Clayton Brunner RC	.25
265	Jason Marquis RC	1.50
266	Jamey Wright	.25
267	Matt Snyder RC	.25
268	Josh Garrett RC	.25
269	Juan Encarnacion	.25
270	Heath Murray	.25
271	Brent Butler RC	1.00
272	Danny Peoples RC	.50
273	Miguel Tejada RC	20.00
274	Jim Pittsley	.25
275	Dmitri Young	.25
276	Vladimir Guerrero	1.50
277	Cole Liniak RC	.50
278	Ramon Hernandez	.25
279	Cliff Politte RC	.50
280	Mel Rosario RC	.25
281	Jorge Carrion RC	.25
282	John Barnes RC	.25
283	Chris Stowe RC	.25
284	Vernon Wells RC	15.00
285	Brett Caradonna RC	.25
286	Scott Hodges RC	.25
287	Jon Garland RC	4.00
288	Nathan Haynes RC	.50
289	Geoff Goetz RC	.25
290	Adam Kennedy RC	1.00
291	T.J. Tucker RC	.25
292	Aaron Akin RC	.25
293	Jayson Werth RC	2.50
294	Glenn Davis RC	.25
295	Mark Mangum RC	.25
296	Troy Cameron RC	.25
297	J.J. Davis RC	.25
298	Lance Berkman RC	30.00
299	Jason Standridge RC	.75
300	Jason Dellaero RC	.25

Refractors

NM/M
Common Player: 1.00
Stars: 4X
(See 1997 Bowman Chrome for checklist and base card values.)

International

NM/M
Common Player: 1.00
Stars: 3X
Inserted 1:4
(See 1997 Bowman Chrome for checklist and base card values.)

International Refractors

NM/M
Common Player: 2.00
Stars: 6X
(See 1997 Bowman Chrome for checklist and base card values.)

ROY Candidates

NM/M
Complete Set (15): 9.00
Common Player: .50
Refractors: 1.5X

#	Player	Price
1	Jeff Abbott	.50
2	Karim Garcia	.75
3	Todd Helton	2.50
4	Richard Hidalgo	.50
5	Geoff Jenkins	.50
6	Russ Johnson	.50
7	Paul Konerko	1.00
8	Mark Kotsay	.50
9	Ricky Ledee	.50
10	Travis Lee	.75
11	Derrek Lee	1.50
12	Elieser Marrero	.50
13	Juan Melo	.50
14	Brian Rose	.50
15	Fernando Tatis	.50

Scout's Honor Roll

NM/M
Complete Set (15): 12.00
Common Player: .50
Refractors: 1.5X

#	Player	Price
1	Dmitri Young	.50
2	Bob Abreu	.75
3	Vladimir Guerrero	2.00
4	Paul Konerko	.75
5	Kevin Orie	.50
6	Todd Walker	.50
7	Ben Grieve	.50
8	Darin Erstad	1.00
9	Derrek Lee	1.00
10	Jose Cruz, Jr.	.50
11	Scott Rolen	1.00
12	Travis Lee	.50
13	Andruw Jones	2.00
14	Wilton Guerrero	1.00
15	Nomar Garciaparra	2.50

1997 Bowman's Best

NM/M
Complete Set (200): 25.00
Common Player: .25
Star Refractors: 4X
Star Atomics: 6X
Pack (6): 2.00
Wax Box (24): 40.00

#	Player	Price
1	Ken Griffey Jr.	1.50
2	Cecil Fielder	.25
3	Albert Belle	.25
4	Todd Hundley	.25
5	Mike Piazza	1.00
6	Matt Williams	.25
7	Mo Vaughn	.25
8	Ryne Sandberg	1.50
9	Chipper Jones	1.00
10	Edgar Martinez	.25
11	Kenny Lofton	.25
12	Ron Gant	.25
13	Moises Alou	.25
14	Pat Hentgen	.25
15	Steve Finley	.25
16	Mark Grace	.25
17	Jay Buhner	.25
18	Jeff Conine	.25
19	Jim Edmonds	.25
20	Todd Hollandsworth	.25
21	Andy Pettitte	.50
22	Jim Thome	.75
23	Eric Young	.25
24	Ray Lankford	.25
25	Marquis Grissom	.25
26	Tony Clark	.25
27	Jermaine Allensworth	.25
28	Ellis Burks	.25
29	Tony Gwynn	1.50
30	Barry Larkin	.25
31	John Olerud	.25
32	Mariano Rivera	.40
33	Paul Molitor	1.00
34	Ken Caminiti	.25
35	Gary Sheffield	.45
36	Al Martin	.25
37	John Valentin	.25
38	Frank Thomas	.75
39	John Jaha	.25
40	Greg Maddux	1.50
41	Alex Fernandez	.25
42	Dean Palmer	.25
43	Bernie Williams	.25
44	Deion Sanders	.25
45	Mark McGwire	2.00
46	Brian Jordan	.25
47	Bernard Gilkey	.25
48	Will Clark	.25
49	Kevin Appier	.25
50	Tom Glavine	.40
51	Chuck Knoblauch	.25
52	Rondell White	.25
53	Greg Vaughn	.25
54	Mike Mussina	.50
55	Brian McRae	.25
56	Chili Davis	.25
57	Wade Boggs	1.50
58	Jeff Bagwell	.75
59	Roberto Alomar	.35
60	Dennis Eckersley	.50
61	Ryan Klesko	.25
62	Manny Ramirez	1.00
63	John Wetteland	.25
64	Cal Ripken Jr.	2.00
65	Edgar Renteria	.25
66	Tino Martinez	.25
67	Larry Walker	.25
68	Gregg Jefferies	.25
69	Lance Johnson	.25
70	Carlos Delgado	.50
71	Craig Biggio	.50
72	Jose Canseco	.50
73	Barry Bonds	2.00
74	Juan Gonzalez	.50
75	Eric Karros	.25
76	Reggie Sanders	.25
77	Robin Ventura	.25
78	Hideo Nomo	.50
79	David Justice	.25
80	Vinny Castilla	.25
81	Travis Fryman	.25
82	Derek Jeter	2.00
83	Sammy Sosa	1.50
84	Ivan Rodriguez	.75
85	Rafael Palmeiro	.75
86	Roger Clemens	2.00
87	Jason Giambi	.50
88	Andres Galarraga	.25
89	Jermaine Dye	.25
90	Joe Carter	.25
91	Brady Anderson	.25
92	Derek Bell	.25
93	Randy Johnson	1.00
94	Fred McGriff	.25
95	John Smoltz	.25
96	Harold Baines	.25
97	Raul Mondesi	.25
98	Tim Salmon	.25
99	Carlos Baerga	.25
100	Dante Bichette	.25

101	Vladimir Guerrero	1.00
102	Richard Hidalgo	.25
103	Paul Konerko	.25
104	Alex Gonzalez RC	.50
105	Jason Dickson	.25
106	Jose Rosado	.25
107	Todd Walker	.25
108	Seth Greisinger RC	.40
109	Todd Helton	.75
110	Ben Davis	.25
111	Bartolo Colon	.25
112	Elieser Marrero	.25
113	Jeff D'Amico	.25
114	Miguel Tejada RC	8.00
115	Darin Erstad	.50
116	Kris Benson RC	1.00
117	Adrian Beltre RC	2.00
118	Neifi Perez	.25
119	Calvin Reese	.25
120	Carl Pavano	.25
121	Juan Melo	.25
122	Kevin McGlinchy RC	.50
123	Pat Cline	.25
124	Felix Heredia RC	.40
125	Aaron Boone	.25
126	Glendon Rusch	.25
127	Mike Cameron	.25
128	Justin Thompson	.25
129	Chad Hermansen RC	.25
130	Sidney Ponson RC	1.00
131	Willie Martinez RC	.25
132	Paul Wilder RC	.25
133	Geoff Jenkins	.25
134	Roy Halladay RC	2.00
135	Carlos Guillen	.25
136	Tony Batista	.25
137	Todd Greene	.25
138	Luis Castillo	.25
139	Jimmy Anderson RC	.25
140	Edgard Velazquez	.25
141	Chris Snopek	.25
142	Ruben Rivera	.25
143	Javier Valentin RC	.25
144	Brian Rose	.25
145	Fernando Tatis RC	.50
146	Dean Crow RC	.25
147	Karim Garcia	.25
148	Dante Powell	.25
149	Hideki Irabu RC	.40
150	Matt Morris	.25
151	Wes Helms	.25
152	Russ Johnson	.25
153	Jarrod Washburn	.25
154	Kerry Wood RC	4.00
155	Joe Fontenot RC	.25
156	Eugene Kingsale	.25
157	Terrence Long	.25
158	Calvin Maduro	.25
159	Jeff Suppan	.25
160	DaRond Stovall	.25
161	Mark Redman	.25
162	Ken Cloude RC	.25
163	Bobby Estalella	.25
164	Abraham Nunez RC	.75
165	Derrick Gibson	.25
166	Mike Drumright RC	.25
167	Katsuhiro Maeda	.25
168	Jeff Liefer	.25
169	Ben Grieve	.25
170	Bob Abreu	.25
171	Shannon Stewart	.25
172	Braden Looper RC	.40
173	Brant Brown	.25
174	Marlon Anderson	.25
175	Brad Fullmer	.25
176	Carlos Beltran	.25
177	Nomar Garciaparra	1.50
178	Derek Lee	.75
179	Valerio De Los Santos RC	.25
180	Dmitri Young	.25
181	Jamey Wright	.25
182	Hiram Bocachica RC	.25
183	Wilton Guerrero	.25
184	Chris Carpenter	.25
185	Scott Spiezio	.25
186	Andruw Jones	1.00
187	Travis Lee	.75
188	Jose Cruz Jr. RC	1.00
189	Jose Guillen	.25
190	Jeff Abbott	.25
191	Ricky Ledee RC	.40
192	Mike Sweeney	.25
193	Donnie Sadler	.25
194	Scott Rolen	.75
195	Kevin Orie	.25
196	Jason Conti RC	.25
197	Mark Kotsay RC	.75
198	Eric Milton	1.00
199	Russell Branyan	.25
200	Alex Sanchez RC	.50

Autographs

		NM/M
Complete Set (10):		150.00
Common Player:		5.00
Refractors:		1.5X
Atomics:		2X
29	Tony Gwynn	30.00
33	Paul Molitor	20.00
82	Derek Jeter	100.00
91	Brady Anderson	7.50
98	Tim Salmon	10.00
107	Todd Walker	5.00
183	Wilton Guerrero	5.00
185	Scott Spiezio	5.00

188	Jose Cruz Jr.	6.00
194	Scott Rolen	20.00

Cuts

		NM/M
Complete Set (20):		20.00
Common Player:		.35
Refractors:		1.5X
Atomic Refractors:		2X
1	Derek Jeter	4.00
2	Chipper Jones	1.50
3	Frank Thomas	1.00
4	Cal Ripken Jr.	4.00
5	Mark McGwire	3.00
6	Ken Griffey Jr.	2.00
7	Jeff Bagwell	1.00
8	Mike Piazza	2.00
9	Ken Caminiti	.35
10	Albert Belle	.35
11	Jose Cruz Jr.	.35
12	Wilton Guerrero	.35
13	Darin Erstad	.50
14	Andruw Jones	1.00
15	Scott Rolen	.75
16	Jose Guillen	.35
17	Bob Abreu	.35
18	Vladimir Guerrero	1.00
19	Todd Walker	.35
20	Nomar Garciaparra	1.50

Mirror Image

		NM/M
Complete Set (10):		35.00
Common Card:		2.00
Refractors:		1.5X
Atomic Refractors:		2X
1	Nomar Garciaparra, Derek Jeter, Hiram Bocachica, Barry Larkin	7.50
2	Travis Lee, Frank Thomas, Derrek Lee, Jeff Bagwell	3.50
3	Kerry Wood, Greg Maddux, Kris Benson, John Smoltz	3.50
4	Kevin Brown, Ivan Rodriguez, Elieser Marrero, Mike Piazza	5.00
5	Jose Cruz Jr., Ken Griffey Jr., Andruw Jones, Barry Bonds	7.50
6	Jose Guillen, Juan Gonzalez, Richard Hidalgo, Gary Sheffield	2.00
7	Paul Konerko, Mark McGwire, Todd Helton, Rafael Palmeiro	6.00
8	Wilton Guerrero, Craig Biggio, Donnie Sadler, Chuck Knoblauch	2.00
9	Russell Branyan, Matt Williams, Adrian Beltre, Chipper Jones	3.50
10	Bob Abreu, Kenny Lofton, Vladimir Guerrero, Albert Belle	3.00

1998 Bowman

		NM/M
Complete Set (441):		40.00
Series 1 (221):		20.00
Series 2 (220):		20.00
Common Player:		.10
Internationals:		1.5X
Inserted 1:1		
Series 1 Pack (10):		2.00
Series 1 Wax Box (24):		30.00
Series 2 Pack (10):		1.50
Series 2 Wax Box (24):		25.00
1	Nomar Garciaparra	1.50
2	Scott Rolen	.75
3	Andy Pettitte	.30
4	Ivan Rodriguez	.65
5	Mark McGwire	2.50
6	Jason Dickson	.10
7	Jose Cruz Jr.	.10
8	Jeff Kent	.10
9	Mike Mussina	.30
10	Jason Kendall	.10
11	Brett Tomko	.10
12	Jeff King	.10
13	Brad Radke	.10
14	Robin Ventura	.10
15	Jeff Bagwell	1.00
16	Greg Maddux	1.50
17	John Jaha	.10
18	Mike Piazza	2.00
19	Edgar Martinez	.10
20	David Justice	.10
21	Todd Hundley	.10
22	Tony Gwynn	1.50
23	Larry Walker	.10
24	Bernie Williams	.10
25	Edgar Renteria	.10
26	Rafael Palmeiro	.75
27	Tim Salmon	.10
28	Matt Morris	.10
29	Shawn Estes	.10
30	Vladimir Guerrero	1.00
31	Fernando Tatis	.10
32	Justin Thompson	.10
33	Ken Griffey Jr.	2.00
34	Edgardo Alfonzo	.10
35	Mo Vaughn	.10
36	Marty Cordova	.10
37	Craig Biggio	.10
38	Roger Clemens	1.75
39	Mark Grace	.10
40	Ken Caminiti	.10
41	Tony Womack	.10
42	Albert Belle	.10
43	Tino Martinez	.10
44	Sandy Alomar	.10
45	Jeff Cirillo	.10
46	Jason Giambi	.50
47	Darin Erstad	.25
48	Livan Hernandez	.10
49	Mark Grudzielanek	.10
50	Sammy Sosa	1.50
51	Curt Schilling	.30
52	Brian Hunter	.10
53	Neifi Perez	.10
54	Todd Walker	.10
55	Jose Guillen	.10
56	Jim Thome	.10
57	Tom Glavine	.30
58	Todd Greene	.10
59	Rondell White	.10
60	Roberto Alomar	.25
61	Tony Clark	.10
62	Vinny Castilla	.10
63	Barry Larkin	.10
64	Hideki Irabu	.10
65	Johnny Damon	.35
66	Juan Gonzalez	.50
67	John Olerud	.10
68	Gary Sheffield	.25
69	Raul Mondesi	.10
70	Chipper Jones	1.50
71	David Ortiz	.50
72	Warren Morris RC	.50
73	Alex Gonzalez	.10
74	Nick Bierbrodt	.10
75	Roy Halladay	.10
76	Danny Buxbaum	.10
77	Adam Kennedy	.10
78	Jared Sandberg RC	.75
79	Michael Barrett	.10
80	Gil Meche	.10
81	Jayson Werth	.10
82	Abraham Nunez	.10
83	Ben Petrick	.10
84	Brett Caradonna	.10
85	Mike Lowell RC	3.00
86	Clay Bruner RC	.10
87	John Curtice RC	.10
88	Bobby Estalella	.10
89	Juan Melo	.10
90	Arnold Gooch	.10
91	Kevin Millwood RC	1.00
92	Richie Sexson	.10
93	Orlando Cabrera	.10
94	Pat Cline	.10
95	Anthony Sanders	.10
96	Russ Johnson	.10
97	Ben Grieve	.10
98	Kevin McGlinchy	.10
99	Paul Wilder	.10
100	Russ Ortiz	.10
101	Ryan Jackson RC	.10
102	Heath Murray	.10
103	Brian Rose	.10
104	Ryan Radmanovich RC	.10
105	Ricky Ledee	.10
106	Jeff Wallace RC	.10
107	Ryan Minor RC	.10
108	Dennis Reyes	.10
109	James Manias RC	.10
110	Chris Carpenter	.10
111	Daryle Ward	.10
112	Vernon Wells	.10
113	Chad Green	.10
114	Mike Stoner RC	.10
115	Brad Fullmer	.10
116	Adam Eaton	.10
117	Jeff Liefer	.10
118	Corey Koskie RC	1.00
119	Todd Helton	.75
120	Jaime Jones RC	.10
121	Mel Rosario	.10
122	Geoff Goetz	.10
123	Adrian Beltre	.40
124	Jason Dellaero	.10
125	Gabe Kapler RC	.50
126	Scott Schoeneweis	.10
127	Ryan Brannan	.10
128	Aaron Akin	.10
129	Ryan Anderson RC	.25
130	Brad Penny	.10
131	Bruce Chen	.10
132	Eli Marrero	.10
133	Eric Chavez	.30
134	Troy Glaus RC	3.00
135	Troy Cameron	.10
136	Brian Sikorski RC	.10
137	Mike Kinkade RC	.25
138	Braden Looper	.10
139	Mark Mangum	.10
140	Danny Peoples	.10
141	J.J. Davis	.10
142	Ben Davis	.10
143	Jacque Jones	.10
144	Derrick Gibson	.10
145	Bronson Arroyo	.10
146	Cristian Guzman RC	.50
147	Jeff Abbott	.10
148	Mike Cuddyer RC	1.00
149	Jason Romano	.10
150	Shane Monahan	.10
151	Ntema Ndungidi RC	.10
152	Alex Sanchez	.10
153	Jack Cust RC	1.50
154	Brent Butler	.10
155	Ramon Hernandez	.10
156	Norm Hutchins	.10
157	Jason Marquis	.10
158	Jacob Cruz	.10
159	Rob Burger RC	.10
160	Eric Milton	.10
161	Preston Wilson	.10
162	Jason Fitzgerald RC	.10
163	Dan Serafini	.10
164	Peter Munro	.10
165	Trot Nixon	.10
166	Homer Bush	.10
167	Dermal Brown	.10
168	Chad Hermansen	.10
169	Julio Moreno RC	.10
170	John Roskos RC	.10
171	Grant Roberts	.10
172	Ken Cloude	.10
173	Jason Brester	.10
174	Jason Conti	.10

#	Player	Price
175	Jon Garland	.10
176	Robbie Bell	.10
177	Nathan Haynes	.10
178	Ramon Ortiz RC	.50
179	Shannon Stewart	.10
180	Pablo Ortega	.10
181	Jimmy Rollins RC	4.00
182	Sean Casey	.30
183	Ted Lilly RC	.25
184	Chris Enochs RC	.10
185	Magglio Ordonez RC	3.00
186	Mike Drumright	.10
187	Aaron Boone	.10
188	Matt Clement	.10
189	Todd Dunwoody	.10
190	Larry Rodriguez	.10
191	Todd Noel	.10
192	Geoff Jenkins	.10
193	George Lombard	.10
194	Lance Berkman	.10
195	Marcus McCain RC	.10
196	Ryan McGuire	.10
197	Jhensy Sandoval RC	.10
198	Corey Lee	.10
199	Mario Valdez	.10
200	Robert Fick RC	.20
201	Donnie Sadler	.10
202	Marc Kroon	.10
203	David Miller	.10
204	Jarrod Washburn	.10
205	Miguel Tejada	.30
206	Raul Ibanez	.10
207	John Patterson	.10
208	Calvin Pickering	.10
209	Felix Martinez	.10
210	Mark Redman	.10
211	Scott Elarton	.10
212	Jose Amado RC	.10
213	Kerry Wood	.40
214	Dante Powell	.10
215	Aramis Ramirez	.10
216	A.J. Hinch	.10
217	Dustin Carr RC	.10
218	Mark Kotsay	.10
219	Jason Standridge	.10
220	Luis Ordaz	.10
221	Orlando Hernandez RC	.50
222	Cal Ripken Jr.	3.00
223	Paul Molitor	1.00
224	Derek Jeter	3.00
225	Barry Bonds	3.00
226	Jim Edmonds	.10
227	John Smoltz	.10
228	Eric Karros	.10
229	Ray Lankford	.10
230	Rey Ordonez	.10
231	Kenny Lofton	.10
232	Alex Rodriguez	2.50
233	Dante Bichette	.10
234	Pedro Martinez	1.00
235	Carlos Delgado	.45
236	Rod Beck	.10
237	Matt Williams	.10
238	Charles Johnson	.10
239	Rico Brogna	.10
240	Frank Thomas	1.00
241	Paul O'Neill	.10
242	Jaret Wright	.10
243	Brant Brown	.10
244	Ryan Klesko	.10
245	Chuck Finley	.10
246	Derek Bell	.10
247	Delino DeShields	.10
248	Chan Ho Park	.10
249	Wade Boggs	1.50
250	Jay Buhner	.10
251	Butch Huskey	.10
252	Steve Finley	.10
253	Will Clark	.10
254	John Valentin	.10
255	Bobby Higginson	.10
256	Darryl Strawberry	.10
257	Randy Johnson	1.00
258	Al Martin	.10
259	Travis Fryman	.10
260	Fred McGriff	.10
261	Jose Valentin	.10
262	Andruw Jones	1.00
263	Kenny Rogers	.10
264	Moises Alou	.10
265	Denny Neagle	.10
266	Ugueth Urbina	.10
267	Derek Lee	.45
268	Ellis Burks	.10
269	Mariano Rivera	.30
270	Dean Palmer	.10
271	Eddie Taubensee	.10
272	Brady Anderson	.10
273	Brian Giles	.10
274	Quinton McCracken	.10
275	Henry Rodriguez	.10
276	Andres Galarraga	.10
277	Jose Canseco	.45
278	David Segui	.10
279	Bret Saberhagen	.10
280	Kevin Brown	.10
281	Chuck Knoblauch	.10
282	Jeromy Burnitz	.10
283	Jay Bell	.10
284	Manny Ramirez	1.00
285	Rick Helling	.10
286	Francisco Cordova	.10
287	Bob Abreu	.20
288	J.T. Snow Jr.	.10
289	Hideo Nomo	.50
290	Brian Jordan	.10
291	Javy Lopez	.10
292	Travis Lee	.10
293	Russell Branyan	.10
294	Paul Konerko	.10
295	Masato Yoshii RC	.50
296	Kris Benson	.10
297	Juan Encarnacion	.10
298	Eric Milton	.10
299	Mike Caruso	.10
300	Ricardo Aramboles RC	.10
301	Bobby Smith	.10
302	Billy Koch	.10
303	Richard Hidalgo	.10
304	Justin Baughman RC	.10
305	Chris Gissell	.10
306	Donnie Bridges RC	.10
307	Nelson Lara RC	.10
308	Randy Wolf RC	1.00
309	Jason LaRue RC	.25
310	Jason Gooding RC	.10
311	Edgar Clemente RC	.10
312	Andrew Vessel	.10
313	Chris Reitsma	.10
314	Jesus Sanchez RC	.10
315	Buddy Carlyle RC	.10
316	Randy Winn	.10
317	Luis Rivera	.10
318	Marcus Thames RC	1.50
319	A.J. Pierzynski	.10
320	Scott Randall	.10
321	Damian Sapp	.10
322	Eddie Yarnell RC	.10
323	Luke Allen RC	.10
324	J.D. Smart	.10
325	Willie Martinez	.10
326	Alex Ramirez	.10
327	Eric DuBose RC	.10
328	Kevin Witt	.10
329	Dan McKinley RC	.10
330	Cliff Politte	.10
331	Vladimir Nunez	.10
332	John Halama RC	.25
333	Nerio Rodriguez	.10
334	Desi Relaford	.10
335	Robinson Checo	.10
336	John Nicholson RC	.10
337	Tom LaRosa RC	.10
338	Kevin Nicholson RC	.10
339	Javier Vazquez	.10
340	A.J. Zapp	.10
341	Tom Evans	.10
342	Kerry Robinson	.10
343	Gabe Gonzalez RC	.10
344	Ralph Milliard	.10
345	Enrique Wilson	.10
346	Elvin Hernandez	.10
347	Mike Lincoln RC	.10
348	Cesar King RC	.10
349	Cristian Guzman RC	1.00
350	Donzell McDonald	.10
351	Jim Parque RC	.25
352	Mike Saipe RC	.10
353	Carlos Febles RC	.40
354	Derrell Stenson RC	.25
355	Mark Osborne RC	.10
356	Odalis Perez RC	.40
357	Jason Dewey RC	.10
358	Joe Fontenot	.10
359	Jason Grilli RC	.40
360	Kevin Haverbusch RC	.25
361	Jay Yennaco RC	.10
362	Brian Buchanan	.10
363	John Barnes	.10
364	Chris Fussell	.10
365	Kevin Gibbs RC	.10
366	Joe Lawrence	.10
367	DaRond Stovall	.10
368	Brian Fuentes RC	.10
369	Jimmy Anderson	.10
370	Laril Gonzalez RC	.10
371	Scott Williamson RC	.40
372	Milton Bradley	.10
373	Jason Halper RC	.10
374	Brent Billingsley RC	.10
375	Joe DePastino RC	.10
376	Jake Westbrook	.10
377	Octavio Dotel	.10
378	Jason Williams RC	.10
379	Julio Ramirez RC	.10
380	Seth Greisinger	.10
381	Mike Judd RC	.10
382	Ben Ford RC	.10
383	Tom Bennett	.10
384	Adam Butler RC	.10
385	Wade Miller RC	.75
386	Kyle Peterson RC	.10
387	Kevin Peterman RC	.10
388	Onan Masaoka	.10
389	Jason Rakers RC	.10
390	Rafael Medina	.10
391	Luis Lopez	.10
392	Jeff Yoder	.10
393	Vance Wilson RC	.25
394	Fernando Seguignol RC	.25
395	Ron Wright	.10
396	Ruben Mateo RC	.40
397	Steve Lomasney RC	.25
398	Damian Jackson	.10
399	Mike Jerzembeck RC	.10
400	Luis Rivas RC	.25
401	Kevin Burford RC	.10
402	Glenn Davis	.10
403	Robert Luce RC	.10
404	Cole Liniak	.10
405	Matthew LeCroy RC	.20
406	Jeremy Giambi RC	.40
407	Shawn Chacon	.10
408	Dewayne Wise RC	.10
409	Steve Woodard RC	.25
410	Francisco Cordero RC	.25
411	Damon Minor RC	.20
412	Lou Collier	.10
413	Justin Towle	.10
414	Jan LeBron	.10
415	Michael Coleman	.10
416	Felix Rodriguez	.10
417	Paul Ah Yat RC	.10
418	Kevin Barker RC	.25
419	Brian Meadows	.10
420	Darnell McDonald RC	.20
421	Matt Kinney RC	.25
422	Mike Vavrek RC	.10
423	Courtney Duncan RC	.10
424	Kevin Millar RC	.50
425	Ruben Rivera	.10
426	Steve Shoemaker RC	.10
427	Dan Reichert RC	.10
428	Carlos Lee RC	2.00
429	Rod Barajas	.10
430	Pablo Ozuna RC	.10
431	Todd Belitz RC	.10
432	Sidney Ponson	.10
433	Steve Carver RC	.10
434	Esteban Yan	.10
435	Cedrick Bowers RC	.10
436	Marlon Anderson	.10
437	Carl Pavano	.10
438	Jae Weong Seo RC	.50
439	Jose Taveras RC	.10
440	Matt Anderson RC	.25
441	Darron Ingram RC	.10

International

	NM/M
Common Player:	.25
Stars:	1.5X
Inserted 1:1	

(See 1998 Bowman for check-list and base card values.)

Golden Anniversary

	NM/M
Common Player:	4.00
Veteran Stars:	15-30X
Young Stars:	5-10X
Rookie Cards:	5-10X

(See 1998 Bowman for checklist and base card values.)

Autographs

Nomar Garciaparra

	NM/M
Common Player:	3.00
Inserted 1:149	
Silvers (1:992):	1.5-2.5X

Golds (1:2,976):		2-4X
1	Adrian Beltre	15.00
2	Brad Fullmer	5.00
3	Ricky Ledee	5.00
4	David Ortiz	35.00
5	Fernando Tatis	3.00
6	Kerry Wood	20.00
7	Mel Rosario	3.00
8	Cole Liniak	3.00
9	A.J. Hinch	5.00
10	Jhensy Sandoval	3.00
11	Jose Cruz Jr.	5.00
12	Richard Hidalgo	6.00
13	Geoff Jenkins	8.00
14	Carl Pavano	10.00
15	Richie Sexson	12.00
16	Tony Womack	5.00
17	Scott Rolen	20.00
18	Ryan Minor	5.00
19	Elieser Marrero	3.00
20	Jason Marquis	5.00
21	Mike Lowell	30.00
22	Todd Helton	20.00
23	Chad Green	3.00
24	Scott Elarton	3.00
25	Russell Branyan	3.00
26	Mike Drumright	3.00
27	Ben Grieve	5.00
28	Jacque Jones	8.00
29	Jared Sandberg	5.00
30	Grant Roberts	5.00
31	Mike Stoner	3.00
32	Brian Rose	3.00
33	Randy Winn	5.00
34	Justin Towle	3.00
35	Anthony Sanders	3.00
36	Rafael Medina	3.00
37	Corey Lee	3.00
38	Mike Kinkade	5.00
39	Norm Hutchins	3.00
40	Jason Brester	3.00
41	Ben Davis	5.00
42	Nomar Garciaparra	40.00
43	Jeff Liefer	3.00
44	Eric Milton	6.00
45	Preston Wilson	8.00
46	Miguel Tejada	30.00
47	Luis Ordaz	3.00
48	Travis Lee	5.00
49	Kris Benson	6.00
50	Jacob Cruz	5.00
51	Dermal Brown	3.00
52	Marc Kroon	3.00
53	Chad Hermansen	5.00
54	Roy Halladay	15.00
55	Eric Chavez	10.00
56	Jason Conti	3.00
57	Juan Encarnacion	5.00
58	Paul Wilder	3.00
59	Aramis Ramirez	15.00
60	Cliff Politte	3.00
61	Todd Dunwoody	3.00
62	Paul Konerko	10.00
63	Shane Monahan	3.00
64	Alex Sanchez	3.00
65	Jeff Abbott	3.00
66	John Patterson	3.00
67	Peter Munro	3.00
68	Jarrod Washburn	5.00
69	Derrek Lee	20.00
70	Ramon Hernandez	5.00

Japanese Rookies

Hideo Nomo [P]   11

		NM/M
Complete Set (3):		15.00
Common Player:		5.00
11	Hideo Nomo	10.00
17	Shigetosi Hasegawa	5.00
	Hideki Irabu	5.00

Minor League MVP

		NM/M
Complete Set (11):		9.00
Common Player:		.50
1	Jeff Bagwell	1.00
2	Andres Galarraga	.50
3	Juan Gonzalez	.60
4	Tony Gwynn	1.50
5	Vladimir Guerrero	1.00
6	Derek Jeter	3.00
7	Andruw Jones	1.00
8	Tino Martinez	.50

9	Manny Ramirez	1.00
10	Gary Sheffield	.60
11	Jim Thome	.65

Rookie of the Year Favorites

		NM/M
Complete Set (10):		6.00
Common Player:		.50
1	Adrian Beltre	.75
2	Troy Glaus	3.00
3	Chad Hermansen	.50
4	Matt Clement	.50
5	Eric Chavez	.75
6	Kris Benson	.50
7	Richie Sexson	.50
8	Randy Wolf	.50
9	Ryan Minor	.50
10	Alex Gonzalez	.50

Scout's Choice

		NM/M
Complete Set (21):		8.00
Common Player:		.25
Inserted 1:12		
1	Paul Konerko	.50
2	Richard Hidalgo	.25
3	Mark Kotsay	.25
4	Ben Grieve	.25
5	Chad Hermansen	.25
6	Matt Clement	.25
7	Brad Fullmer	.25
8	Eli Marrero	.25
9	Kerry Wood	1.50
10	Adrian Beltre	1.50
11	Ricky Ledee	.25
12	Travis Lee	.25
13	Abraham Nunez	.25
14	Ryan Anderson	.25
15	Dermal Brown	.25
16	Juan Encarnacion	.25
17	Aramis Ramirez	.25
18	Todd Helton	2.50
19	Kris Benson	.25
20	Russell Branyan	.25
21	Mike Stoner	.25

1998 Bowman Chrome

		NM/M
Complete Set (441):		100.00
Complete Series 1 (221):		60.00
Complete Series 2 (220):		50.00
Common Player:		.20
Series 1 Pack (4):		2.50
Series 2 Pack (4):		2.00
Series 1 Box (24):		45.00
Series 2 Box (24):		35.00
1	Nomar Garciaparra	1.00
2	Scott Rolen	.75
3	Andy Pettitte	.40
4	Ivan Rodriguez	.75
5	Mark McGwire	2.50
6	Jason Dickson	.20
7	Jose Cruz Jr.	.20
8	Jeff Kent	.20
9	Mike Mussina	.50
10	Jason Kendall	.20
11	Brett Tomko	.20
12	Jeff King	.20
13	Brad Radke	.20
14	Robin Ventura	.20
15	Jeff Bagwell	1.00
16	Greg Maddux	1.50
17	John Jaha	.20
18	Mike Piazza	2.00
19	Edgar Martinez	.20
20	David Justice	.20
21	Todd Hundley	.20
22	Tony Gwynn	1.50
23	Larry Walker	.20
24	Bernie Williams	.20
25	Edgar Renteria	.20
26	Rafael Palmeiro	.75
27	Tim Salmon	.20
28	Matt Morris	.20
29	Shawn Estes	.20
30	Vladimir Guerrero	1.00
31	Fernando Tatis	.20
32	Justin Thompson	.20
33	Ken Griffey Jr.	2.00
34	Edgardo Alfonzo	.20
35	Mo Vaughn	.20
36	Marty Cordova	.20
37	Craig Biggio	.20
38	Roger Clemens	2.00
39	Mark Grace	.20
40	Ken Caminiti	.20
41	Tony Womack	.20
42	Albert Belle	.20
43	Tino Martinez	.20
44	Sandy Alomar	.20
45	Jeff Cirillo	.20
46	Jason Giambi	.50
47	Darin Erstad	.45
48	Livan Hernandez	.20
49	Mark Grudzielanek	.20
50	Sammy Sosa	1.50
51	Curt Schilling	.50
52	Brian Hunter	.20
53	Neifi Perez	.20
54	Todd Walker	.20
55	Jose Guillen	.20
56	Jim Thome	.40
57	Tom Glavine	.40
58	Todd Greene	.20
59	Rondell White	.20
60	Roberto Alomar	.35
61	Tony Clark	.20
62	Vinny Castilla	.20
63	Barry Larkin	.20
64	Hideki Irabu	.20
65	Johnny Damon	.60
66	Juan Gonzalez	.50
67	John Olerud	.20
68	Gary Sheffield	.45
69	Raul Mondesi	.20
70	Chipper Jones	1.50
71	David Ortiz	.75
72	Warren Morris RC	.50
73	Alex Gonzalez	.20
74	Nick Bierbrodt	.20
75	Roy Halladay	.20
76	Danny Buxbaum	.20
77	Adam Kennedy	.20
78	Jared Sandberg RC	.50
79	Michael Barrett	.20
80	Gil Meche	.20
81	Jayson Werth	.20
82	Abraham Nunez	.20
83	Ben Petrick	.20
84	Brett Caradonna	.20
85	Mike Lowell RC	6.00
86	Clay Bruner RC	.20
87	John Curtice RC	.20
88	Bobby Estalella	.20
89	Juan Melo	.20
90	Arnold Gooch	.20
91	Kevin Millwood RC	4.00
92	Richie Sexson	.20
93	Orlando Cabrera	.20
94	Pat Cline	.20
95	Anthony Sanders	.20
96	Russ Johnson	.20
97	Ben Grieve	.20
98	Kevin McGlinchy	.20
99	Paul Wilder	.20
100	Russ Ortiz	.20
101	Ryan Jackson RC	.50
102	Heath Murray	.20
103	Brian Rose	.20
104	Ryan Radmanovich RC	.20
105	Ricky Ledee	.20
106	Jeff Wallace RC	.20
107	Ryan Minor RC	.45
108	Dennis Reyes	.20
109	James Manias RC	.20
110	Chris Carpenter	.20
111	Daryle Ward	.20
112	Vernon Wells	.20
113	Chad Green	.20
114	Mike Stoner RC	.20
115	Brad Fullmer	.20
116	Adam Eaton	.20
117	Jeff Liefer	.20
118	Corey Koskie RC	1.50
119	Todd Helton	.75
120	Jaime Jones RC	.20
121	Mel Rosario	.20
122	Geoff Goetz	.20
123	Adrian Beltre	.40
124	Jason Dellaero	.20
125	Gabe Kapler RC	1.00
126	Scott Schoeneweis	.20
127	Ryan Brannan	.20
128	Aaron Akin	.20
129	Ryan Anderson RC	.50
130	Brad Penny	.20
131	Bruce Chen	.20
132	Eli Marrero	.20
133	Eric Chavez	.35
134	Troy Glaus RC	10.00
135	Troy Cameron	.20
136	Brian Sikorski RC	.20
137	Mike Kinkade RC	.50
138	Braden Looper	.20
139	Mark Mangum	.20
140	Danny Peoples	.20
141	J.J. Davis	.20
142	Ben Davis	.20
143	Jacque Jones	.20
144	Derrick Gibson	.20
145	Bronson Arroyo	.20
146	Luis De Los Santos RC	.20
147	Jeff Abbott	.20
148	Mike Cuddyer RC	1.50
149	Jason Romano	.20
150	Shane Monahan	.20
151	Ntema Ndungidi RC	.20
152	Alex Sanchez	.20
153	Jack Cust RC	5.00
154	Brent Butler	.20
155	Ramon Hernandez	.20
156	Norm Hutchins	.20
157	Jason Marquis	.20
158	Jacob Cruz	.20
159	Rob Burger RC	.20
160	Eric Milton	.20
161	Preston Wilson	.20
162	Jason Fitzgerald RC	.20
163	Dan Serafini	.20
164	Peter Munro	.20
165	Trot Nixon	.40
166	Homer Bush	.20
167	Dermal Brown	.20
168	Chad Hermansen	.20
169	Julio Moreno RC	.20
170	John Roskos RC	.20
171	Grant Roberts	.20
172	Ken Cloude	.20
173	Jason Brester	.20
174	Jason Conti	.20
175	Jon Garland	.20
176	Robbie Bell	.20
177	Nathan Haynes	.20
178	Ramon Ortiz RC	.50
179	Shannon Stewart	.20
180	Pablo Ortega	.20
181	Jimmy Rollins RC	10.00
182	Sean Casey	.45
183	Ted Lilly RC	.20
184	Chris Enochs RC	.20
185	Magglio Ordonez RC	3.00
186	Mike Drumright	.20
187	Aaron Boone	.20
188	Matt Clement	.20
189	Todd Dunwoody	.20
190	Larry Rodriguez	.20
191	Todd Noel	.20
192	Geoff Jenkins	.20
193	George Lombard	.20
194	Lance Berkman	.20
195	Marcus McCain RC	.20
196	Ryan McGuire	.20
197	Jhensy Sandoval RC	.20
198	Corey Lee	.20
199	Mario Valdez	.20
200	Robert Fick RC	.20
201	Donnie Sadler	.20
202	Marc Kroon	.20
203	David Miller	.20
204	Jarrod Washburn	.20
205	Miguel Tejada	.40
206	Raul Ibanez	.20
207	John Patterson	.20
208	Calvin Pickering	.20
209	Felix Martinez	.20
210	Mark Redman	.20
211	Scott Elarton	.20
212	Jose Amado RC	.20
213	Kerry Wood	.50
214	Dante Powell	.20
215	Aramis Ramirez	.20
216	A.J. Hinch	.20
217	Dustin Carr RC	.20
218	Mark Kotsay	.20
219	Jason Standridge	.20
220	Luis Ordaz	.20
221	Orlando Hernandez RC	3.00
222	Cal Ripken Jr.	3.00
223	Paul Molitor	1.00
224	Derek Jeter	3.00
225	Barry Bonds	3.00
226	Jim Edmonds	.20
227	John Smoltz	.20
228	Eric Karros	.20
229	Ray Lankford	.20
230	Rey Ordonez	.20
231	Kenny Lofton	.20
232	Alex Rodriguez	2.50
233	Dante Bichette	.20
234	Pedro Martinez	1.00
235	Carlos Delgado	.50
236	Rod Beck	.20
237	Matt Williams	.20
238	Charles Johnson	.20
239	Rico Brogna	.20
240	Frank Thomas	1.00
241	Paul O'Neill	.20
242	Jaret Wright	.20
243	Brant Brown	.20
244	Ryan Klesko	.20
245	Chuck Finley	.20
246	Derek Bell	.20
247	Delino DeShields	.20
248	Chan Ho Park	.20
249	Wade Boggs	1.50
250	Jay Buhner	.20
251	Butch Huskey	.20
252	Steve Finley	.20
253	Will Clark	.20
254	John Valentin	.20
255	Bobby Higginson	.20
256	Darryl Strawberry	.20
257	Randy Johnson	1.00
258	Al Martin	.20
259	Travis Fryman	.20
260	Fred McGriff	.20
261	Jose Valentin	.20
262	Andruw Jones	1.00
263	Kenny Rogers	.20
264	Moises Alou	.20
265	Denny Neagle	.20
266	Ugueth Urbina	.20
267	Derrek Lee	.50
268	Ellis Burks	.20
269	Mariano Rivera	.40
270	Dean Palmer	.20
271	Eddie Taubensee	.20
272	Brady Anderson	.20
273	Brian Giles	.20
274	Quinton McCracken	.20
275	Henry Rodriguez	.20
276	Andres Galarraga	.20
277	Jose Canseco	.40
278	David Segui	.20
279	Bret Saberhagen	.20
280	Kevin Brown	.20
281	Chuck Knoblauch	.20
282	Jeromy Burnitz	.20
283	Jay Bell	.20
284	Manny Ramirez	1.00
285	Rick Helling	.20
286	Francisco Cordova	.20
287	Bob Abreu	.30
288	J.T. Snow Jr.	.20
289	Hideo Nomo	.50
290	Brian Jordan	.20
291	Javy Lopez	.20
292	Aaron Akin RC	.20
293	Russell Branyan	.20
294	Paul Konerko	.20
295	Masato Yoshii RC	1.00
296	Kris Benson	.20
297	Juan Encarnacion	.20
298	Eric Milton	.20
299	Mike Caruso	.20
300	Ricardo Aramboles RC	.20
301	Bobby Smith	.20
302	Billy Koch	.20
303	Richard Hidalgo	.20
304	Justin Baughman RC	.20
305	Chris Gissell	.20
306	Donnie Bridges RC	.20
307	Nelson Lara RC	.20
308	Randy Wolf RC	1.00
309	Jason LaRue RC	.50
310	Jason Gooding RC	.20

311	Edgar Clemente RC	.20
312	Andrew Vessel	.20
313	Chris Reitsma	.20
314	Jesus Sanchez RC	.20
315	Buddy Carlyle RC	.20
316	Randy Winn	.20
317	Luis Rivera	.20
318	Marcus Thames RC	5.00
319	A.J. Pierzynski	.20
320	Scott Randall	.20
321	Damian Sapp	.20
322	Eddie Yarnell RC	.20
323	Luke Allen RC	.20
324	J.D. Smart	.20
325	Willie Martinez	.20
326	Alex Ramirez	.20
327	Eric DuBose RC	.20
328	Kevin Witt	.20
329	Dan McKinley RC	.20
330	Cliff Politte	.20
331	Vladimir Nunez	.20
332	John Halama RC	.50
333	Nerio Rodriguez	.20
334	Desi Relaford	.20
335	Robinson Checo	.20
336	John Nicholson RC	.20
337	Tom LaRosa RC	.20
338	Kevin Nicholson RC	.20
339	Javier Vazquez	.20
340	A.J. Zapp	.20
341	Tom Evans	.20
342	Kerry Robinson	.20
343	Gabe Gonzalez RC	.20
344	Ralph Milliard	.20
345	Enrique Wilson	.20
346	Elvin Hernandez	.20
347	Mike Lincoln RC	.35
348	Cesar King RC	.20
349	Cristian Guzman RC	.50
350	Donzell McDonald	.20
351	Jim Parque RC	.20
352	Mike Saipe RC	.20
353	Carlos Febles RC	.50
354	Dernell Stenson RC	.20
355	Mark Osborne RC	.20
356	Odalis Perez RC	2.00
357	Jason Dewey RC	.20
358	Joe Fontenot	.20
359	Jason Grilli RC	.40
360	Kevin Haverbusch RC	.20
361	Jay Yennaco RC	.20
362	Brian Buchanan	.20
363	John Barnes	.20
364	Chris Fussell	.20
365	Kevin Gibbs RC	.20
366	Joe Lawrence	.20
367	DaRond Stovall	.20
368	Brian Fuentes RC	.20
369	Jimmy Anderson	.20
370	Laril Gonzalez RC	.20
371	Scott Williamson RC	1.00
372	Milton Bradley	.20
373	Jason Halper RC	.20
374	Brent Billingsley RC	.20
375	Joe DePastino RC	.20
376	Jake Westbrook	.20
377	Octavio Dotel	.20
378	Jason Williams RC	.20
379	Julio Ramirez RC	.20
380	Seth Greisinger	.20
381	Mike Judd RC	.20
382	Ben Ford RC	.20
383	Tom Bennett RC	.20
384	Adam Butler RC	.20
385	Wade Miller RC	1.50
386	Kyle Peterson RC	.20
387	Tommy Peterman RC	.20
388	Onan Masaoka	.20
389	Jason Rakers RC	.20
390	Rafael Medina	.20
391	Luis Lopez	.20
392	Jeff Yoder	.20
393	Vance Wilson RC	.20
394	Fernando Seguignol RC	.35
395	Ron Wright	.20
396	Ruben Mateo RC	1.00
397	Steve Lomasney RC	.50
398	Damian Jackson	.20
399	Mike Jerzembeck RC	.20
400	Luis Rivas RC	.50
401	Kevin Burford RC	.20
402	Glenn Davis	.20
403	Robert Luce RC	.20
404	Cole Liniak	.20
405	Matthew LeCroy RC	.50
406	Jeremy Giambi RC	.50
407	Shawn Chacon	.20
408	Dewayne Wise RC	.20
409	Steve Woodard RC	.50
410	Francisco Cordero RC	.20
411	Damon Minor RC	.20
412	Lou Collier	.20
413	Justin Towle	.20
414	Juan LeBron	.20
415	Michael Coleman	.20
416	Felix Rodriguez	.20
417	Paul Ah Yat RC	.20
418	Kevin Barker RC	.20
419	Brian Meadows	.20
420	Darnell McDonald RC	.40
421	Matt Kinney RC	.40
422	Mike Vavrek RC	.20
423	Courtney Duncan RC	.20
424	Kevin Millar RC	1.50
425	Ruben Rivera	.20

426	Steve Shoemaker RC	.20
427	Dan Reichert RC	.20
428	Carlos Lee RC	6.00
429	Rod Barajas RC	.20
430	Pablo Ozuna RC	.50
431	Todd Belitz RC	.20
432	Sidney Ponson	.20
433	Steve Carver RC	.20
434	Esteban Yan RC	.20
435	Cedrick Bowers RC	.20
436	Marlon Anderson	.20
437	Carl Pavano	.20
438	Jae Weong Seo RC	1.00
439	Jose Taveras RC	.20
440	Matt Anderson RC	.50
441	Darron Ingram RC	.20

International

	NM/M
Common Player:	.50
Stars and Rookies:	1.5X

Inserted 1:4
(See 1998 Bowman Chrome for checklist and base card values.)

Refractors

	NM/M
Common Player:	2.00
Stars:	3X

Inserted 1:12
Int'l Refractors: 6X
Inserted 1:24
(See 1998 Bowman Chrome for checklist and base card values.)

Golden Anniversary

JAVY LOPEZ

	NM/M
Common Player:	5.00
Stars:	20X
Common Refractor:	20.00

(See 1998 Bowman Chrome for checklist and base card values.)

Reprints

PAUL KONERKO

1ST IMPRESSIONS

		NM/M
Complete Set (50):		20.00
Common Player:		.25

Inserted 1:12
Refractors: 1.5X
Inserted 1:36

1	Yogi Berra	.75
2	Jackie Robinson	2.00
3	Don Newcombe	.50
4	Satchel Paige	.50
5	Willie Mays	2.00
6	Gil McDougald	.25
7	Don Larsen	.50
8	Elston Howard	.25
9	Robin Ventura	.25
10	Brady Anderson	.25
11	Gary Sheffield	.50
12	Tino Martinez	.50
13	Ken Griffey Jr.	1.50
14	John Smoltz	.50
15	Sandy Alomar Jr.	.25
16	Larry Walker	.50
17	Todd Hundley	.25

18	Mo Vaughn	.25
20	Sammy Sosa	1.00
21	Frank Thomas	.50
21	Chuck Knoblauch	.25
22	Bernie Williams	.25
23	Juan Gonzalez	.25
24	Mike Mussina	.50
25	Jeff Bagwell	.50
26	Tim Salmon	.25
27	Ivan Rodriguez	.50
28	Kenny Lofton	.25
29	Chipper Jones	1.00
30	Javier Lopez	.25
31	Ryan Klesko	.25
32	Raul Mondesi	.25
33	Jim Thome	.50
34	Carlos Delgado	.25
35	Mike Piazza	1.00
36	Manny Ramirez	.50
37	Andy Pettitte	.50
38	Derek Jeter	2.00
39	Brad Fullmer	.25
40	Richard Hidalgo	.25
41	Tony Clark	.25
42	Andruw Jones	.25
43	Vladimir Guerrero	.75
44	Nomar Garciaparra	.75
45	Paul Konerko	.50
46	Ben Grieve	.25
47	Hideo Nomo	.25
48	Scott Rolen	.50
49	Jose Guillen	.25
50	Livan Hernandez	.25

1998 Bowman's Best

Chuck Knoblauch

		NM/M
Complete Set (200):		30.00
Common Player:		.25
Refractors:		8X

Production 400 Sets
Atomic Refractors: 12X
Production 100 Sets
Pack (6): 2.50
Wax Box (24): 35.00

1	Mark McGwire	2.00
2	Hideo Nomo	.50
3	Barry Bonds	3.00
4	Dante Bichette	.25
5	Chipper Jones	1.50
6	Frank Thomas	1.00
7	Kevin Brown	.25
8	Juan Gonzalez	.50
9	Jay Buhner	.25
10	Chuck Knoblauch	.25
11	Cal Ripken Jr.	3.00
12	Matt Williams	.25
13	Jim Edmonds	.25
14	Manny Ramirez	1.00
15	Tony Clark	.25
16	Mo Vaughn	.25
17	Bernie Williams	.25
18	Scott Rolen	.75
19	Gary Sheffield	.40
20	Albert Belle	.25
21	Mike Piazza	2.00
22	John Olerud	.25
23	Tony Gwynn	1.50
24	Jay Bell	.25
25	Jose Cruz Jr.	.25
26	Justin Thompson	.25
27	Ken Griffey Jr.	2.00
28	Sandy Alomar	.25
29	Mark Grudzielanek	.25
30	Mark Grace	.25
31	Ron Gant	.25
32	Javy Lopez	.25
33	Jeff Bagwell	1.00
34	Fred McGriff	.25
35	Rafael Palmeiro	.75
36	Vinny Castilla	.25
37	Andy Benes	.25
38	Pedro Martinez	1.00
39	Andy Pettitte	.40
40	Marty Cordova	.25
41	Rusty Greer	.25
42	Kevin Orie	.25
43	Chan Ho Park	.25
44	Ryan Klesko	.25
45	Alex Rodriguez	2.50
46	Travis Fryman	.25
47	Jeff King	.25

48	Roger Clemens	2.00
49	Darin Erstad	.50
50	Brady Anderson	.25
51	Jason Kendall	.25
52	John Valentin	.25
53	Ellis Burks	.25
54	Brian Hunter	.25
55	Paul O'Neill	.25
56	Ken Caminiti	.25
57	David Justice	.25
58	Eric Karros	.25
59	Pat Hentgen	.25
60	Greg Maddux	1.50
61	Craig Biggio	.25
62	Edgar Martinez	.25
63	Mike Mussina	.50
64	Larry Walker	.25
65	Tino Martinez	.25
66	Jim Thome	.60
67	Tom Glavine	.40
68	Raul Mondesi	.25
69	Marquis Grissom	.25
70	Randy Johnson	1.00
71	Steve Finley	.25
72	Jose Guillen	.25
73	Nomar Garciaparra	1.50
74	Wade Boggs	1.50
75	Bobby Higginson	.25
76	Robin Ventura	.25
77	Derek Jeter	3.00
78	Andruw Jones	1.00
79	Ray Lankford	.25
80	Vladimir Guerrero	1.00
81	Kenny Lofton	.25
82	Ivan Rodriguez	.75
83	Neifi Perez	.25
84	John Smoltz	.25
85	Tim Salmon	.25
86	Carlos Delgado	.25
87	Sammy Sosa	1.50
88	Jaret Wright	.40
89	Roberto Alomar	.25
90	Paul Molitor	1.00
91	Dean Palmer	.25
92	Barry Larkin	.25
93	Jason Giambi	.50
94	Curt Schilling	.40
95	Eric Young	.25
96	Denny Neagle	.25
97	Moises Alou	.25
98	Livan Hernandez	.25
99	Todd Hundley	.25
100	Andres Galarraga	.25
101	Travis Lee	.25
102	Lance Berkman	.25
103	Orlando Cabrera	.25
104	Mike Lowell RC	2.00
105	Ben Grieve	.25
106	Jae Weong Seo RC	.50
107	Richie Sexson	.25
108	Eli Marrero	.25
109	Aramis Ramirez	.25
110	Paul Konerko	.25
111	Carl Pavano	.25
112	Brad Fullmer	.25
113	Matt Clement	.25
114	Donzell McDonald	.25
115	Todd Helton	.75
116	Mike Caruso	.25
117	Donnie Sadler	.25
118	Bruce Chen	.25
119	Jarrod Washburn	.25
120	Adrian Beltre	.40
121	Ryan Jackson RC	.50
122	Kevin Millar RC	1.50
123	Corey Koskie RC	1.00
124	Dermal Brown	.25
125	Kerry Wood	.50
126	Juan Melo	.25
127	Ramon Hernandez	.25
128	Roy Halladay	.25
129	Ron Wright	.25
130	Darnell McDonald RC	.50
131	Odalis Perez RC	.75
132	Alex Cora RC	.25
133	Justin Towle	.25
134	Juan Encarnacion	.25
135	Brian Rose	.25
136	Russell Branyan	.25
137	Cesar King RC	.25
138	Ruben Rivera	.25
139	Ricky Ledee	.25
140	Vernon Wells	.25
141	Luis Rivas RC	.50
142	Brent Butler	.25
143	Karim Garcia	.25
144	George Lombard	.25
145	Masato Yoshii RC	.50
146	Braden Looper	.25
147	Alex Sanchez	.25
148	Kris Benson	.25
149	Mark Kotsay	.25
150	Richard Hidalgo	.25
151	Scott Elarton	.25
152	Ryan Minor RC	.25
153	Troy Glaus RC	5.00
154	Carlos Lee RC	2.00
155	Michael Coleman	.25
156	Jason Grilli RC	.25
157	Julio Ramirez RC	.50
158	Randy Wolf RC	.25
159	Ryan Brannan	.25
160	Edgar Renteria RC	.50
161	Miguel Tejada	.40
162	Chad Hermansen	.25

163	Ryan Anderson RC	.50
164	Ben Petrick	.25
165	Alex Gonzalez	.25
166	Ben Davis	.25
167	John Patterson	.25
168	Cliff Politte	.25
169	Randall Simon	.25
170	Javier Vazquez	.25
171	Kevin Witt	.25
172	Geoff Jenkins	.25
173	David Ortiz	.60
174	Derrick Gibson	.25
175	Abraham Nunez	.25
176	A.J. Hinch	.25
177	Ruben Mateo RC	.75
178	Magglio Ordonez RC	2.50
179	Todd Dunwoody	.25
180	Daryle Ward	.25
181	Mike Kinkade RC	.50
182	Willie Martinez	.25
183	Orlando Hernandez RC	1.50
184	Eric Milton	.25
185	Eric Chavez	.50
186	Damian Jackson	.25
187	Jim Parque RC	.50
188	Dan Reichert RC	.25
189	Mike Drumright	.25
190	Todd Walker	.25
191	Shane Monahan	.25
192	Derrek Lee	.65
193	Jeremy Giambi RC	.50
194	Dan McKinley RC	.25
195	Tony Armas RC	.75
196	Matt Anderson RC	.50
197	Jim Chamblee RC	.25
198	Francisco Cordero RC	.25
199	Calvin Pickering	.25
200	Reggie Taylor	.25

Refractors

	NM/M
Common Player:	4.00
Stars:	8X

Production 400 Sets
(See 1998 Bowman's Best for checklist and base card values.)

Atomic Refractors

	NM/M
Common Player:	6.00
Stars:	12X

Production 100 Sets
(See 1998 Bowman's Best for checklist and base card values.)

Autographs

	NM/M
Complete Set (10):	65.00
Common Player:	5.00
Inserted 1:180	
Refractors:	1.5X
Inserted 1:2,158	
Atomics:	2X
Inserted 1:6,437	
5 Chipper Jones	35.00
10 Chuck Knoblauch	5.00
15 Tony Clark	5.00
20 Albert Belle	8.00
25 Jose Cruz Jr.	5.00
105 Ben Grieve	5.00
110 Paul Konerko	15.00
115 Todd Helton	15.00
120 Adrian Beltre	15.00
125 Kerry Wood	20.00

Mirror Image Fusion

	NM/M
Complete Set (20):	35.00
Common Player (1:12):	.50
Refractor (1:809):	6X
Atomic Refractor (1:3,237):	12X
1	Frank Thomas, David Ortiz	2.00
2	Chuck Knoblauch, Enrique Wilson	.50
3	Nomar Garciaparra, Miguel Tejada	2.50
4	Alex Rodriguez, Mike Caruso	4.50
5	Cal Ripken Jr., Ryan Minor	4.50
6	Ken Griffey Jr., Ben Grieve	3.00
7	Juan Gonzalez, Juan Encarnacion	.75
8	Jose Cruz Jr., Ruben Mateo	.50
9	Randy Johnson, Ryan Anderson	1.50
10	Ivan Rodriguez, A.J. Hinch	1.25
11	Jeff Bagwell, Paul Konerko	1.50
12	Mark McGwire, Travis Lee	3.50
13	Craig Biggio, Chad Hermanson	.50
14	Mark Grudzielanek, Alex Gonzalez	.50
15	Chipper Jones, Adrian Beltre	.50
16	Larry Walker, Mark Kotsay	.50
17	Tony Gwynn, Preston Wilson	2.50
18	Barry Bonds, Richard Hidalgo	4.50
19	Greg Maddux, Kerry Wood	2.50
20	Mike Piazza, Ben Petrick	3.00

Performers

	NM/M
Complete Set (10):	4.00
Common Player:	.35
Refractor (1:309):	3X
Atomic Refractor (1:3,237):	5X
1	Ben Grieve	.35
2	Travis Lee	.35
3	Ryan Minor	.35
4	Todd Helton	2.00
5	Brad Fullmer	.35
6	Paul Konerko	.50
7	Adrian Beltre	.75
8	Richie Sexson	.35
9	Aramis Ramirez	.35
10	Russell Branyan	.35

1999 Bowman

	NM/M
Complete Set (440):	60.00
Complete Series 1 (220):	30.00
Complete Series 2 (220):	35.00
Common Player:	.10
Series 1 Pack (10):	2.00
Series 1 Box (24):	35.00
Series 2 Pack (10):	3.00
Series 2 Box (24):	50.00
1	Ben Grieve	.10
2	Kerry Wood	.40
3	Ruben Rivera	.10
4	Sandy Alomar	.10
5	Cal Ripken Jr.	2.00
6	Mark McGwire	1.75
7	Vladimir Guerrero	.75
8	Moises Alou	.10
9	Jim Edmonds	.10
10	Greg Maddux	1.00
11	Gary Sheffield	.40
12	John Valentin	.10
13	Chuck Knoblauch	.10
14	Tony Clark	.10
15	Rusty Greer	.10
16	Al Leiter	.10
17	Travis Lee	.10
18	Jose Cruz Jr.	.10
19	Pedro Martinez	.75
20	Paul O'Neill	.10
21	Todd Walker	.10
22	Vinny Castilla	.10
23	Barry Larkin	.10
24	Curt Schilling	.40
25	Jason Kendall	.10
26	Scott Erickson	.10
27	Andres Galarraga	.10
28	Jeff Shaw	.10
29	John Olerud	.10
30	Orlando Hernandez	.10
31	Larry Walker	.10
32	Andruw Jones	.75
33	Jeff Cirillo	.10
34	Barry Bonds	2.00
35	Manny Ramirez	.75
36	Mark Kotsay	.10
37	Ivan Rodriguez	.60
38	Jeff King	.10
39	Brian Hunter	.10
40	Ray Durham	.10
41	Bernie Williams	.10
42	Darin Erstad	.30
43	Chipper Jones	1.00
44	Pat Hentgen	.10
45	Eric Young	.10
46	Jaret Wright	.10
47	Juan Guzman	.10
48	Jorge Posada	.10
49	Bobby Higginson	.10
50	Jose Guillen	.10
51	Trevor Hoffman	.10
52	Ken Griffey Jr.	1.50
53	David Justice	.10
54	Matt Williams	.10
55	Eric Karros	.10
56	Derek Bell	.10
57	Ray Lankford	.10
58	Mariano Rivera	.25
59	Brett Tomko	.10
60	Mike Mussina	.40
61	Kenny Lofton	.10
62	Chuck Finley	.10
63	Alex Gonzalez	.10
64	Mark Grace	.10
65	Raul Mondesi	.10
66	David Cone	.10
67	Brad Fullmer	.10
68	Andy Benes	.10
69	John Smoltz	.10
70	Shane Reynolds	.10
71	Bruce Chen	.10
72	Adam Kennedy	.10
73	Jack Cust	.10
74	Matt Clement	.10
75	Derrick Gibson	.10
76	Darnell McDonald	.10
77	Adam Everett RC	.50
78	Ricardo Aramboles	.10
79	Mark Quinn RC	.25
80	Jason Rakers	.10
81	Seth Etherton RC	.35
82	Jeff Urban RC	.25
83	Manny Aybar	.10
84	Mike Nannini RC	.25
85	Onan Masaoka	.10
86	Rod Barajas	.10
87	Mike Frank	.10
88	Scott Randall	.10
89	Justin Bowles RC	.25
90	Chris Haas	.10
91	Arturo McDowell RC	.25
92	Matt Belisle RC	.35
93	Scott Elarton	.10
94	Vernon Wells	.10
95	Pat Cline	.10
96	Ryan Anderson	.10
97	Kevin Barker	.10
98	Ruben Mateo	.10
99	Robert Fick	.10
100	Corey Koskie	.10
101	Ricky Lee	.10
102	Rick Elder RC	.25
103	Jack Cressend RC	.25
104	Joe Lawrence	.10
105	Mike Lincoln	.10
106	Kit Pellow RC	.35
107	Matt Burch RC	.25
108	Brent Fick	.10
109	Jason Dewey	.10
110	Cesar King	.10
111	Julio Ramirez	.10
112	Jake Westbrook	.10
113	Eric Valent RC	.35
114	Roosevelt Brown RC	.35
115	Choo Freeman RC	.25
116	Juan Melo	.10
117	Jason Grilli	.10
118	Jared Sandberg	.10
119	Glenn Davis	.10
120	David Riske RC	.25
121	Jacque Jones	.10
122	Corey Lee	.10
123	Michael Barrett	.10
124	Lariel Gonzalez	.10
125	Mitch Meluskey	.10
126	Freddy Garcia	.10
127	Tony Torcato RC	.25
128	Jeff Liefer	.10
129	Ntema Ndungidi	.10
130	Andy Brown RC	.35
131	Ryan Mills RC	.25
132	Andy Abad RC	.10
133	Carlos Febles	.10
134	Jason Tyner RC	.25
135	Mark Osborne	.10
136	Phil Norton RC	.25
137	Nathan Haynes	.10
138	Roy Halladay	.10
139	Juan Encarnacion	.10
140	Brad Penny	.10
141	Grant Roberts	.10
142	Aramis Ramirez	.10
143	Cristian Guzman	.10
144	Mamon Tucker RC	.25
145	Ryan Bradley	.10
146	Brian Simmons	.10
147	Dan Reichert	.10
148	Russ Branyon	.10
149	Victor Valencia RC	.25
150	Scott Schoeneweis	.10
151	Sean Spencer RC	.25
152	Odalis Perez	.10
153	Joe Fontenot	.10
154	Milton Bradley	.10
155	Josh McKinley RC	.25
156	Terrence Long	.10
157	Danny Klassen	.10
158	Paul Hoover RC	.25
159	Ron Belliard	.10
160	Armando Rios	.10
161	Ramon Hernandez	.10
162	Jason Conti	.10
163	Chad Hermansen	.10
164	Jason Standridge	.10
165	Jason Dellaero	.10
166	John Curtice	.10
167	Clayton Andrews RC	.25
168	Jeremy Giambi	.10
169	Alex Ramirez	.10
170	Gabe Molina RC	.25
171	Mario Encarnacion RC	.25
172	Mike Zywica RC	.25
173	Chip Ambres RC	.25
174	Trot Nixon	.10
175	Pat Burrell RC	2.00
176	Jeff Yoder	.10
177	Chris Jones RC	.10
178	Kevin Witt	.10
179	Keith Luuloa RC	.10
180	Billy Koch	.10
181	Damaso Marte RC	.25
182	Ryan Glynn RC	.10
183	Calvin Pickering	.10
184	Michael Cuddyer	.10
185	Nick Johnson RC	.75
186	Doug Mientkiewicz RC	1.00
187	Nate Cornejo RC	.35
188	Octavio Dotel	.10
189	Wes Helms	.10
190	Nelson Lara	.10
191	Chuck Abbott RC	.10
192	Tony Armas Jr.	.10
193	Gil Meche	.10
194	Ben Petrick	.10
195	Chris George RC	.25
196	Scott Hunter RC	.25
197	Ryan Brannan	.10
198	Amaury Garcia RC	.25
199	Chris Gissell	.10
200	Austin Kearns RC	1.50
201	Alex Gonzalez	.10
202	Wade Miller	.10
203	Scott Williamson	.10
204	Chris Enochs	.10
205	Fernando Seguignol	.10
206	Marlon Anderson	.10
207	Todd Sears RC	.25
208	Nate Bump RC	.25
209	J.M. Gold RC	.25
210	Matt LeCroy	.10
211	Alex Hernandez	.10
212	Luis Rivera	.10
213	Troy Cameron	.10
214	Alex Escobar RC	.50
215	Jason LaRue	.10
216	Kyle Peterson	.10
217	Brent Butler	.10
218	Dernell Stenson	.10
219	Adrian Beltre	.40
220	Daryle Ward	.10
----	Series 1 Checklist Folder	.10
221	Jim Thome	.60
222	Cliff Floyd	.10
223	Rickey Henderson	.75
224	Garret Anderson	.10
225	Ken Caminiti	.10
226	Bret Boone	.10
227	Jeromy Burnitz	.10
228	Steve Finley	.10
229	Miguel Tejada	.40
230	Greg Vaughn	.10
231	Jose Offerman	.10
232	Andy Ashby	.10
233	Albert Belle	.10
234	Fernando Tatis	.10
235	Todd Helton	.65
236	Sean Casey	.25
237	Brian Giles	.10
238	Andy Pettitte	.25
239	Fred McGriff	.25
240	Roberto Alomar	.30
241	Edgar Martinez	.10
242	Lee Stevens	.10
243	Shawn Green	.25
244	Ryan Klesko	.10
245	Sammy Sosa	1.00
246	Todd Hundley	.10
247	Shannon Stewart	.10
248	Randy Johnson	.75
249	Rondell White	.10
250	Mike Piazza	1.50
251	Craig Biggio	.10
252	David Wells	.10
253	Brian Jordan	.10
254	Edgar Renteria	.10
255	Bartolo Colon	.10
256	Frank Thomas	.75

257	Will Clark	.10
258	Dean Palmer	.10
259	Dmitri Young	.10
260	Scott Rolen	.60
261	Jeff Kent	.10
262	Dante Bichette	.10
263	Nomar Garciaparra	1.00
264	Tony Gwynn	1.00
265	Alex Rodriguez	1.75
266	Jose Canseco	.45
267	Jason Giambi	.40
268	Jeff Bagwell	.75
269	Carlos Delgado	.40
270	Tom Glavine	.40
271	Eric Davis	.10
272	Edgardo Alfonzo	.10
273	Tim Salmon	.10
274	Johnny Damon	.35
275	Rafael Palmeiro	.65
276	Denny Neagle	.10
277	Neifi Perez	.10
278	Roger Clemens	1.25
279	Brant Brown	.10
280	Kevin Brown	.10
281	Jay Bell	.10
282	Jay Buhner	.10
283	Matt Lawton	.10
284	Robin Ventura	.10
285	Juan Gonzalez	.35
286	Mo Vaughn	.10
287	Kevin Millwood	.10
288	Tino Martinez	.10
289	Justin Thompson	.10
290	Derek Jeter	2.00
291	Ben Davis	.10
292	Mike Lowell	.10
293	Joe Crede RC	.75
294	Micah Bowie RC	.25
295	Lance Berkman	.10
296	Jason Marquis	.10
297	Chad Green	.10
298	Dee Brown	.10
299	Jerry Hairston Jr.	.10
300	Gabe Kapler	.10
301	Brent Stentz RC	.25
302	Scott Mullen RC	.25
303	Brandon Reed	.10
304	Shea Hillenbrand RC	.50
305	J.D. Closser RC	.25
306	Gary Matthews Jr.	.10
307	Toby Hall RC	.25
308	Jason Phillips RC	.25
309	Jose Macias RC	.25
310	Jung Bong RC	.25
311	Ramon Soler RC	.25
312	Kelly Dransfeldt RC	.25
313	Carlos Hernandez RC	.25
314	Kevin Haverbusch	.10
315	Aaron Myette RC	.25
316	Chad Harville RC	.35
317	Kyle Farnsworth RC	.50
318	Travis Dawkins RC	.50
319	Willie Martinez	.10
320	Carlos Lee	.25
321	Carlos Pena RC	1.00
322	Peter Bergeron RC	.25
323	A.J. Burnett RC	.50
324	Bucky Jacobsen RC	.25
325	Mo Bruce RC	.25
326	Reggie Taylor	.10
327	Jackie Rexrode	.10
328	Alvin Morrow RC	.25
329	Carlos Beltran	.40
330	Eric Chavez	.25
331	John Patterson	.10
332	Jayson Werth	.10
333	Richie Sexson	.10
334	Randy Wolf	.10
335	Eli Marrero	.10
336	Paul LoDuca	.10
337	J.D. Smart	.10
338	Ryan Minor	.10
339	Kris Benson	.10
340	George Lombard	.10
341	Troy Glaus	.75
342	Eddie Yarnell	.10
343	Kip Wells RC	.50
344	C.C. Sabathia RC	2.00
345	Sean Burroughs RC	.50
346	Felipe Lopez RC	1.50
347	Ryan Rupe RC	.25
348	Orber Moreno RC	.25
349	Rafael Roque RC	.25
350	Alfonso Soriano RC	5.00
351	Pablo Ozuna	.10
352	Corey Patterson RC	1.00
353	Braden Looper	.10
354	Robbie Bell	.10
355	Mark Mulder RC	2.00
356	Angel Pena	.10
357	Kevin McGlinchy	.10
358	Michael Restovich RC	.35
359	Eric DuBose	.10
360	Geoff Jenkins	.10
361	Mark Harriger RC	.25
362	Junior Herndon RC	.25
363	Tim Raines Jr. RC	.25
364	Rafael Furcal RC	.75
365	Marcus Giles RC	1.00
366	Ted Lilly	.10
367	Jorge Toca RC	.25
368	David Kelton RC	.35
369	Adam Dunn RC	5.00
370	Guillermo Mota RC	.35
371	Brett Laxton RC	.25
372	Travis Harper RC	.25
373	Tom Davey RC	.25

374	Darren Blakely RC	.25
375	Tim Hudson RC	3.00
376	Jason Romano	.10
377	Dan Reichert	.10
378	Julio Lugo RC	.75
379	Jose Garcia RC	.25
380	Erubiel Durazo RC	.25
381	Jose Jimenez	.10
382	Chris Fussell	.10
383	Steve Lomasney	.25
384	Juan Pena RC	.25
385	Allen Levrault RC	.25
386	Juan Rivera RC	.25
387	Steve Colyer RC	.25
388	Joe Nathan RC	.25
389	Ron Walker RC	.10
390	Nick Bierbrodt	.10
391	Luke Prokopec RC	.25
392	Dave Roberts RC	.40
393	Mike Darr	.10
394	Abraham Nunez RC	.35
395	Giuseppe Chiaramonte RC	.25
396	Jermaine Van Buren RC	.25
397	Mike Kusiewicz	.10
398	Matt Wise RC	.25
399	Joe McEwing RC	.40
400	Matt Holliday RC	5.00
401	Willi Mo Pena RC	1.50
402	Ruben Quevedo RC	.25
403	Rob Ryan RC	.25
404	Freddy Garcia RC	1.00
405	Kevin Eberwein RC	.25
406	Jesus Colome RC	.25
407	Chris Singleton RC	.75
408	Bubba Crosby RC	.50
409	Jesus Cordero RC	.25
410	Donny Leon	.10
411	Goefrey Tomlinson RC	.25
412	Jeff Winchester RC	.25
413	Adam Piatt RC	.50
414	Robert Stratton	.10
415	T.J. Tucker	.10
416	Ryan Langerhans RC	.25
417	Anthony Shumaker RC	.25
418	Matt Miller RC	.25
419	Doug Clark RC	.25
420	Kory DeHaan RC	.25
421	David Eckstein RC	.75
422	Brian Cooper RC	.25
423	Brady Clark RC	.25
424	Chris Magruder RC	.25
425	Bobby Seay RC	.25
426	Aubrey Huff RC	1.00
427	Mike Jerzembeck RC	.10
428	Matt Blank RC	.25
429	Benny Agbayani RC	.25
430	Kevin Beirne RC	.25
431	Josh Hamilton RC	6.00
432	Josh Girdley RC	.25
433	Kyle Snyder RC	.25
434	Mike Paradis RC	.25
435	Jason Jennings RC	.25
436	David Walling RC	.25
437	Omar Ortiz RC	.25
438	Jay Gehrke RC	.25
439	Casey Burns RC	.25
440	Carl Crawford RC	2.50

Gold

		NM/M
Common Player:		3.00
Gold Stars:		10X

(See 1999 Bowman for checklist and base card values.)

International

		NM/M
Common Player:		.25
Int'l Stars:		1.5X

(See 1999 Bowman for checklist and base card values.)

1999 Bowman Pre-Production

		NM/M
Complete Set (6):		4.00
Common Player:		.60
1	Andres Galarraga	.60
2	Raul Mondesi	.60
3	Vinny Castilla	.60
4	Corey Koskie	2.00

DERNELL STENSON

5	Octavio Dotel	.60
6	Dernell Stenson	.60

Autographs

P. Bruce Chen Braves

		NM/M
Common Player:		3.00
Blues inserted 1:162 or 1:85		
Silvers inserted 1:485 or 1:256		
Golds inserted 1:1,954 or 1:1,024		
1	Ruben Mateo/B	5.00
2	Troy Glaus/G	40.00
3	Ben Davis/G	8.00
4	Jayson Werth/B	5.00
5	Jerry Hairston Jr./S	6.00
6	Darnell McDonald/B	4.00
7	Calvin Pickering/B	8.00
8	Ryan Minor/B	4.00
9	Alex Escobar/B	6.00
10	Grant Roberts/B	5.00
11	Carlos Guillen/B	10.00
12	Ryan Anderson/S	6.00
13	Gil Meche/S	5.00
14	Russell Branyan/S	5.00
15	Alex Ramirez/S	5.00
16	Jason Rakers/S	5.00
17	Eddie Yarnall/S	5.00
18	Freddy Garcia/B	15.00
19	Jason Conti/B	3.00
20	Corey Koskie/B	5.00
21	Roosevelt Brown/B	5.00
22	Willie Martinez/B	3.00
23	Mike Jerzembeck/B	3.00
24	Lariel Gonzalez/B	3.00
25	Fernando Seguignol/B	3.00
26	Robert Fick/S	5.00
27	J.D. Smart/B	3.00
28	Ryan Mills/B	3.00
29	Chad Hermansen/G	6.00
30	Jason Grilli/B	5.00
31	Michael Cuddyer/B	5.00
32	Jacque Jones/S	10.00
33	Reggie Taylor/B	3.00
34	Richie Sexson/G	15.00
35	Michael Barrett/B	8.00
36	Paul LoDuca/B	5.00
37	Adrian Beltre/G	30.00
38	Peter Bergeron/B	4.00
39	Joe Fontenot/B	3.00
40	Randy Wolf/B	6.00
41	Nick Johnson/B	12.00
42	Ryan Bradley/B	4.00
43	Mike Lowell/S	15.00
44	Ricky Ledee/B	5.00
45	Mike Lincoln/S	4.00
46	Jeremy Giambi/B	5.00
47	Dermal Brown/B	5.00
48	Derrick Gibson/B	3.00
49	Scott Randall/B	5.00
50	Ben Petrick/S	5.00
51	Jason LaRue/B	3.00
52	Cole Liniak/B	3.00
53	John Curtice/B	3.00
54	Jackie Rexrode/B	3.00
55	John Patterson/B	4.00
56	Brad Penny/S	6.00
57	Jared Sandberg/B	6.00
58	Kerry Wood/G	25.00
59	Eli Marrero/B	5.00
60	Jason Marquis/B	8.00
61	George Lombard/S	5.00
62	Bruce Chen/S	3.00
63	Kevin Witt/S	4.00
64	Vernon Wells/B	15.00
65	Billy Koch/B	3.00
66	Roy Halladay/B	20.00
67	Nathan Haynes/B	3.00
68	Ben Grieve/G	8.00
69	Eric Chavez/G	10.00
70	Lance Berkman/S	50.00

Early Risers

MIKE PIAZZA C

EARLY RISERS

		NM/M
Complete Set (11):		8.00
Common Player:		.25
Inserted 1:12		
1	Mike Piazza	1.00
2	Cal Ripken Jr.	2.00
3	Jeff Bagwell	.50
4	Ben Grieve	.25
5	Kerry Wood	.40
6	Mark McGwire	1.00
7	Nomar Garciaparra	.75
8	Derek Jeter	2.00
9	Scott Rolen	.50
10	Jose Canseco	.45
11	Raul Mondesi	.25

Late Bloomers

LATE BLOOMERS

		NM/M
Complete Set (10):		4.00
Common Player:		.25
Inserted 1:12		
LB1	Mike Piazza	2.00
LB2	Jim Thome	.75
LB3	Larry Walker	.25
LB4	Vinny Castilla	.25
LB5	Andy Pettitte	.50
LB6	Jim Edmonds	.25
LB7	Kenny Lofton	.25
LB8	John Smoltz	.25
LB9	Mark Grace	.25
LB10	Trevor Hoffman	.25

Scout's Choice

		NM/M
Complete Set (21):		12.00
Common Player:		.40
Inserted 1:12		
SC1	Ruben Mateo	.40
SC2	Ryan Anderson	.40
SC3	Pat Burrell	3.00
SC4	Troy Glaus	4.00
SC5	Eric Chavez	1.00
SC6	Adrian Beltre	1.00
SC7	Bruce Chen	.40
SC8	Carlos Beltran	1.00
SC9	Alex Gonzalez	.40
SC10	Carlos Lee	.50
SC11	George Lombard	.40
SC12	Matt Clement	.40
SC13	Calvin Pickering	.40
SC14	Marlon Anderson	.40
SC15	Chad Hermansen	.40
SC16	Russell Branyan	.40

SC17	Jeremy Giambi	.40
SC18	Ricky Ledee	.40
SC19	John Patterson	.40
SC20	Roy Halladay	.75
SC21	Michael Barrett	.40

2000 Rookie of the Year

NM/M

Complete Set (10):		7.00
Common Player:		.50
Inserted 1:12		
1	Ryan Anderson	.50
2	Pat Burrell	2.50
3	A.J. Burnett	.50
4	Ruben Mateo	.50
5	Alex Escobar	.50
6	Pablo Ozuna	.50
7	Mark Mulder	1.00
8	Corey Patterson	1.00
9	George Lombard	.50
10	Nick Johnson	.50

1999 Bowman Chrome

NM/M

Complete Set (440):		175.00
Complete Series 1 (220):		65.00
Complete Series 2 (220):		125.00
Common Player:		.25
Series 1 Pack (4):		3.00
Series 1 Wax Box (24):		50.00
Series 2 Pack (4):		5.00
Series 2 Wax Box (24):		100.00
1	Ben Grieve	.25
2	Kerry Wood	.45
3	Ruben Rivera	.25
4	Sandy Alomar	.25
5	Cal Ripken Jr.	3.00
6	Mark McGwire	1.50
7	Vladimir Guerrero	1.00
8	Moises Alou	.25
9	Jim Edmonds	.25
10	Greg Maddux	1.50
11	Gary Sheffield	.50
12	John Valentin	.25
13	Chuck Knoblauch	.25
14	Tony Clark	.25
15	Rusty Greer	.25
16	Al Leiter	.25
17	Travis Lee	.25
18	Jose Cruz Jr.	.25
19	Pedro Martinez	1.00
20	Paul O'Neill	.25
21	Todd Walker	.25
22	Vinny Castilla	.25
23	Barry Larkin	.25
24	Curt Schilling	.40
25	Jason Kendall	.25
26	Scott Erickson	.25
27	Andres Galarraga	.25
28	Jeff Shaw	.25
29	John Olerud	.25
30	Orlando Hernandez	.40
31	Larry Walker	.25
32	Andruw Jones	.40
33	Jeff Cirillo	.25
34	Barry Bonds	3.00
35	Manny Ramirez	1.00
36	Mark Kotsay	.25
37	Ivan Rodriguez	.50
38	Jeff King	.25
39	Brian Hunter	.25
40	Ray Durham	.25
41	Bernie Williams	.25
42	Darin Erstad	.50
43	Chipper Jones	1.50
44	Pat Hentgen	.25
45	Eric Young	.25
46	Jaret Wright	.25
47	Juan Guzman	.25
48	Jorge Posada	.25
49	Bobby Higginson	.25
50	Jose Guillen	.25
51	Trevor Hoffman	.25
52	Ken Griffey Jr.	2.00
53	David Justice	.25
54	Matt Williams	.25
55	Eric Karros	.25
56	Derek Bell	.25
57	Ray Lankford	.25
58	Mariano Rivera	.40
59	Brett Tomko	.25
60	Mike Mussina	.50
61	Kenny Lofton	.25
62	Chuck Finley	.25
63	Alex Gonzalez	.25
64	Mark Grace	.25
65	Raul Mondesi	.25
66	David Cone	.25
67	Brad Fullmer	.25
68	Andy Benes	.25
69	John Smoltz	.25
70	Shane Reynolds	.25
71	Bruce Chen	.25
72	Adam Kennedy	.25
73	Jack Cust	.25
74	Matt Clement	.25
75	Derrick Gibson	.25
76	Darnell McDonald	.25
77	Adam Everett	.75
78	Ricardo Aramboles	.25
79	Mark Quinn RC	.50
80	Jason Rakers	.25
81	Seth Etherton RC	.50
82	Jeff Urban RC	.35
83	Manny Aybar	.25
84	Mike Nannini RC	.35
85	Onan Masaoka	.25
86	Rod Barajas	.25
87	Mike Frank	.25
88	Scott Randall	.25
89	Justin Bowles RC	.35
90	Chris Haas	.25
91	Arturo McDowell RC	.35
92	Matt Belisle RC	.50
93	Scott Elarton	.25
94	Vernon Wells	.25
95	Pat Cline	.25
96	Ryan Anderson	.25
97	Kevin Barker	.25
98	Ruben Mateo	.25
99	Robert Fick	.25
100	Corey Koskie	.25
101	Ricky Ledee	.25
102	Rick Elder RC	.35
103	Jack Cressend RC	.35
104	Joe Lawrence	.25
105	Mike Lincoln	.25
106	Kit Pellow RC	.50
107	Matt Burch RC	.35
108	Brent Butler	.25
109	Jason Dewey	.25
110	Cesar King	.25
111	Julio Ramirez	.25
112	Jake Westbrook	.25
113	Eric Valent RC	1.00
114	Roosevelt Brown RC	.50
115	Choo Freeman RC	1.50
116	Juan Melo	.25
117	Jason Grilli	.25
118	Jared Sandberg	.25
119	Glenn Davis	.25
120	David Riske RC	.35
121	Jacque Jones	.25
122	Corey Lee	.25
123	Michael Barrett	.25
124	Lariel Gonzalez	.25
125	Mitch Meluskey	.25
126	Freddy Garcia RC	.25
127	Tony Torcato RC	.35
128	Jeff Liefer	.25
129	Ntema Ndungidi	.25
130	Andy Brown RC	.50
131	Ryan Mills RC	.35
132	Andy Abad RC	.50
133	Carlos Febles	.25
134	Jason Tyner RC	.50
135	Mark Osborne	.25
136	Phil Norton RC	.35
137	Nathan Haynes	.25
138	Roy Halladay	.25
139	Juan Encarnacion	.25
140	Brad Penny	.25
141	Grant Roberts	.25
142	Aramis Ramirez	.25
143	Cristian Guzman	.25
144	Mamon Tucker RC	.35
145	Ryan Bradley	.25
146	Brian Simmons	.25
147	Dan Reichert	.25
148	Russ Branyon	.25
149	Victor Valencia RC	.35
150	Scott Schoeneweis	.25
151	Sean Spencer RC	.35
152	Odalis Perez	.25
153	Joe Fontenot	.25
154	Milton Bradley	.25
155	Josh McKinley RC	.35
156	Terrence Long	.25
157	Danny Klassen	.25
158	Paul Hoover RC	.35
159	Ron Belliard	.25
160	Armando Rios	.25
161	Ramon Hernandez	.25
162	Jason Conti	.25
163	Chad Hermansen	.25
164	Jason Standridge	.25
165	Jason Dellaero	.25
166	John Curtice	.25
167	Clayton Andrews RC	.35
168	Jeremy Giambi	.25
169	Alex Ramirez	.25
170	Gabe Molina RC	.35
171	Mario Encarnacion RC	.35
172	Mike Zywica RC	.35
173	Chip Ambres RC	.35
174	Trot Nixon	.25
175	Pat Burrell RC	10.00
176	Jeff Yoder	.25
177	Chris Jones RC	.35
178	Kevin Witt	.25
179	Keith Luuloa RC	.35
180	Billy Koch	.25
181	Damaso Marte RC	.35
182	Ryan Glynn RC	.35
183	Calvin Pickering	.25
184	Michael Cuddyer	.25
185	Nick Johnson RC	2.00
186	Doug Mientkiewicz RC	2.00
187	Nate Cornejo RC	1.00
188	Octavio Dotel	.25
189	Wes Helms	.25
190	Nelson Lara	.25
191	Chuck Abbott RC	.35
192	Tony Armas Jr.	.25
193	Gil Meche	.25
194	Ben Petrick	.25
195	Chris George RC	.35
196	Scott Hunter RC	.35
197	Ryan Brannan	.25
198	Amaury Garcia RC	.35
199	Chris Gissell	.25
200	Austin Kearns RC	2.00
201	Alex Gonzalez	.25
202	Wade Miller	.25
203	Scott Williamson RC	.35
204	Chris Enochs	.25
205	Fernando Seguignol	.25
206	Marlon Anderson	.25
207	Todd Sears RC	.35
208	Nate Bump RC	.35
209	J.M. Gold RC	.50
210	Matt LeCroy RC	.35
211	Alex Hernandez	.25
212	Luis Rivera	.25
213	Troy Cameron	.25
214	Alex Escobar RC	1.00
215	Jason LaRue	.25
216	Kyle Peterson	.25
217	Brent Butler	.25
218	Dernell Stenson	.25
219	Adrian Beltre	.40
220	Daryle Ward	.25
221	Jim Thome	.50
222	Cliff Floyd	.25
223	Rickey Henderson	1.00
224	Garret Anderson	.25
225	Ken Caminiti	.25
226	Bret Boone	.25
227	Jeromy Burnitz	.25
228	Steve Finley	.25
229	Miguel Tejada	.40
230	Greg Vaughn	.25
231	Jose Offerman	.25
232	Andy Ashby	.25
233	Albert Belle	.25
234	Fernando Tatis	.25
235	Todd Helton	.50
236	Sean Casey	.40
237	Brian Giles	.25
238	Andy Pettitte	.40
239	Fred McGriff	.25
240	Roberto Alomar	.40
241	Edgar Martinez	.25
242	Lee Stevens	.25
243	Shawn Green	.40
244	Ryan Klesko	.25
245	Sammy Sosa	1.00
246	Todd Hundley	.25
247	Shannon Stewart	.25
248	Randy Johnson	1.00
249	Rondell White	.25
250	Mike Piazza	2.00
251	Craig Biggio	.25
252	David Wells	.25
253	Brian Jordan	.25
254	Edgar Renteria	.25
255	Bartolo Colon	.25
256	Frank Thomas	1.00
257	Will Clark	.25
258	Dean Palmer	.25
259	Dmitri Young	.25
260	Scott Rolen	.50
261	Jeff Kent	.25
262	Dante Bichette	.25
263	Nomar Garciaparra	.50
264	Tony Gwynn	1.00
265	Alex Rodriguez	2.00
266	Jose Canseco	.50
267	Jason Giambi	.50
268	Jeff Bagwell	.50
269	Carlos Delgado	.50
270	Tom Glavine	.50
271	Eric Davis	.25
272	Edgardo Alfonzo	.25
273	Tim Salmon	.25
274	Johnny Damon	.50
275	Rafael Palmeiro	.50
276	Denny Neagle	.25
277	Neifi Perez	.25
278	Roger Clemens	1.50
279	Brant Brown	.25
280	Kevin Brown	.25
281	Jay Bell	.25
282	Jay Buhner	.25
283	Matt Lawton	.25
284	Robin Ventura	.25
285	Juan Gonzalez	.50
286	Mo Vaughn	.25
287	Kevin Millwood	.25
288	Tino Martinez	.25
289	Justin Thompson	.25
290	Derek Jeter	3.00
291	Ben Davis	.25
292	Mike Lowell	.25
293	Joe Crede RC	3.00
294	Micah Bowie RC	.50
295	Lance Berkman	.25
296	Jason Marquis	.25
297	Chad Green	.25
298	Dee Brown	.25
299	Jerry Hairston Jr.	.25
300	Gabe Kapler	.25
301	Brent Stentz RC	.35
302	Scott Mullen RC	.35
303	Brandon Reed	.25
304	Shea Hillenbrand RC	1.50
305	J.D. Closser RC	.50
306	Gary Matthews Jr.	.25
307	Toby Hall RC	.50
308	Jason Phillips RC	.35
309	Jose Macias RC	.25
310	Jung Bong RC	.35
311	Ramon Soler RC	.35
312	Kelly Dransfeldt RC	.35
313	Carlos Hernandez RC	.50
314	Kevin Haverbusch	.25
315	Aaron Myette RC	.50
316	Chad Harville RC	.50
317	Kyle Farnsworth RC	1.00
318	Travis Dawkins RC	.50
319	Willie Martinez	.25
320	Carlos Lee	.35
321	Carlos Pena RC	4.00
322	Peter Bergeron RC	.50
323	A.J. Burnett RC	4.00
324	Bucky Jacobsen RC	.50
325	Mo Bruce RC	.35
326	Reggie Taylor	.25
327	Jackie Rexrode	.25
328	Alvin Morrow RC	.35
329	Carlos Beltran	.50
330	Eric Chavez	.50
331	John Patterson	.25
332	Jayson Werth	.25
333	Richie Sexson	.25
334	Randy Wolf	.25
335	Eli Marrero	.25
336	Paul LoDuca	.25
337	J.D. Smart	.25
338	Ryan Minor	.25
339	Kris Benson	.25
340	George Lombard	.25
341	Troy Glaus	.50
342	Eddie Yarnell	.25
343	Kip Wells RC	1.00
344	C.C. Sabathia RC	8.00
345	Sean Burroughs RC	1.00
346	Felipe Lopez RC	4.00
347	Ryan Rupe RC	.50
348	Orber Moreno RC	.50
349	Rafael Roque RC	.35
350	Alfonso Soriano RC	20.00
351	Pablo Ozuna	.25
352	Corey Patterson RC	2.00
353	Braden Looper	.25
354	Robbie Bell	.25
355	Mark Mulder RC	2.00
356	Angel Pena	.25

357	Kevin McGlinchy	.25
358	Michael Restovich RC	1.00
359	Eric DuBose	.25
360	Geoff Jenkins	.25
361	Mark Harriger RC	.35
362	Junior Herndon RC	.35
363	Tim Raines Jr. RC	.35
364	Rafael Furcal RC	3.00
365	Marcus Giles RC	1.50
366	Ted Lilly	.25
367	Jorge Toca RC	.35
368	David Kelton RC	1.00
369	Adam Dunn RC	25.00
370	Guillermo Mota RC	.35
371	Brett Laxton RC	.35
372	Travis Harper RC	.35
373	Tom Davey RC	.35
374	Darren Blakely RC	.35
375	Tim Hudson RC	10.00
376	Jason Romano	.25
377	Dan Reichert	.25
378	Julio Lugo RC	.35
379	Jose Garcia RC	.35
380	Erubiel Durazo RC	1.00
381	Jose Jimenez	.25
382	Chris Fussell	.25
383	Steve Lomasney	.25
384	Juan Pena RC	.50
385	Allen Levrault RC	.35
386	Juan Rivera RC	.35
387	Steve Colyer RC	.35
388	Joe Nathan RC	1.50
389	Ron Walker RC	.35
390	Nick Bierbrodt	.25
391	Luke Prokopec RC	.35
392	Dave Roberts RC	.50
393	Mike Darr	.25
394	Abraham Nunez RC	1.00
395	Giuseppe Chiaramonte RC	.35
396	Jermaine Van Buren RC	.35
397	Mike Kusiewicz	.25
398	Matt Wise RC	.35
399	Joe McEwing RC	.50
400	Matt Holliday RC	20.00
401	Willi Mo Pena RC	4.00
402	Ruben Quevedo RC	.35
403	Rob Ryan RC	.35
404	Freddy Garcia RC	2.00
405	Kevin Eberwein RC	.35
406	Jesus Colome RC	.35
407	Chris Singleton RC	.35
408	Bubba Crosby RC	1.00
409	Jesus Cordero RC	.25
410	Donny Leon	.25
411	Goefrey Tomlinson RC	.35
412	Jeff Winchester RC	.35
413	Adam Piatt RC	.50
414	Robert Stratton	.25
415	T.J. Tucker	.25
416	Ryan Langerhans RC	1.00
417	Chris Wakeland	.35
418	Matt Miller RC	.35
419	Doug Clark RC	.35
420	Kory DeHaan RC	.35
421	David Eckstein RC	2.00
422	Brian Cooper RC	.35
423	Brady Clark RC	1.00
424	Chris Magruder RC	.35
425	Bobby Seay RC	.50
426	Aubrey Huff RC	5.00
427	Mike Jerzembeck	.25
428	Matt Blank RC	.35
429	Benny Agbayani RC	.35
430	Kevin Beirne RC	.35
431	Josh Hamilton RC	30.00
432	Josh Girdley RC	.35
433	Kyle Snyder RC	.35
434	Mike Paradis RC	.35
435	Jason Jennings RC	.75
436	David Walling RC	.35
437	Omar Ortiz RC	.35
438	Jay Gehrke RC	.35
439	Casey Burns RC	.35
440	Carl Crawford RC	12.00

Refractors

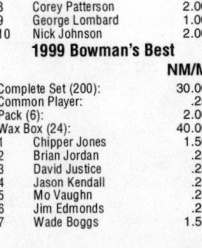

NM/M
Common Player: 1.00
Refractor Stars: 5X
(See 1999 Bowman Chrome for checklist and base card values.)

International

NM/M
Common Player, Series 1: .25
Common Player, Series 2: .50
Stars: 1.5X
Common Refractor: 5.00
Refractors: 12X
(See 1999 Bowman Chrome for checklist and base card values.)

Gold

NM/M
Common Player, Series 1: 1.50
Common Player, Series 2: 2.00
Stars: 3X
Gold Refractors: 30X
(See 1999 Bowman Chrome for checklist and base card values.)

Diamond Aces

NM/M
Complete Set (18): 24.00
Common Player: .50
Inserted 1:21
Refractors: 1.5X
Inserted 1:84

DA1	Troy Glaus	1.50
DA2	Eric Chavez	.75
DA3	Fernando Seguignol	.50
DA4	Ryan Anderson	.50
DA5	Ruben Mateo	.50
DA6	Carlos Beltran	1.00
DA7	Adrian Beltre	.75
DA8	Bruce Chen	.50
DA9	Pat Burrell	2.00
DA10	Mike Piazza	3.00
DA11	Ken Griffey Jr.	3.00
DA12	Chipper Jones	2.00
DA13	Derek Jeter	4.00
DA14	Mark McGwire	3.50
DA15	Nomar Garciaparra	2.00
DA16	Sammy Sosa	2.00
DA17	Juan Gonzalez	.75
DA18	Alex Rodriguez	3.50

Early Impact

NM/M
Complete Set (20): 35.00
Common Player: .75
Inserted 1:15
Refractor: 1.5X
Inserted 1:75

1	Alfonso Soriano	2.00
2	Pat Burrell	2.00
3	Ruben Mateo	.75
4	A.J. Burnett	.75
5	Corey Patterson	1.00
6	Daryle Ward	.75
7	Eric Chavez	1.00
8	Troy Glaus	2.00
9	Sean Casey	1.00
10	Joe McEwing	.75
11	Gabe Kapler	.75
12	Michael Barrett	.75
13	Sammy Sosa	2.50
14	Alex Rodriguez	4.00
15	Mark McGwire	4.00
16	Derek Jeter	5.00
17	Nomar Garciaparra	2.50
18	Mike Piazza	3.00
19	Chipper Jones	2.50
20	Ken Griffey Jr.	3.00

Scout's Choice

NM/M
Complete Set (21): 20.00
Common Player: .75
Inserted 1:12
Refractors: 1.5X
Inserted 1:48

SC1	Ruben Mateo	.75
SC2	Ryan Anderson	.75
SC3	Pat Burrell	3.00
SC4	Troy Glaus	4.00
SC5	Eric Chavez	2.00
SC6	Adrian Beltre	1.50
SC7	Bruce Chen	.75
SC8	Carlos Beltran	2.50
SC9	Alex Gonzalez	.75
SC10	Carlos Lee	1.00
SC11	George Lombard	.75
SC12	Matt Clement	.75
SC13	Calvin Pickering	.75
SC14	Marlon Anderson	.75
SC15	Chad Hermansen	.75
SC16	Russell Branyan	.75
SC17	Jeremy Giambi	.75
SC18	Ricky Ledee	.75
SC19	John Patterson	.75
SC20	Roy Halladay	1.00
SC21	Michael Barrett	.75

2000 Rookie of the Year

NM/M
Complete Set (10): 12.00
Common Player: 1.00
Inserted 1:20
Refractors: 1.5-3X
Inserted 1:100

1	Ryan Anderson	1.00
2	Pat Burrell	4.00
3	A.J. Burnett	1.00
4	Ruben Mateo	1.00
5	Alex Escobar	1.00
6	Pablo Ozuna	1.00
7	Mark Mulder	1.50
8	Corey Patterson	2.00
9	George Lombard	1.00
10	Nick Johnson	2.00

1999 Bowman's Best

NM/M
Complete Set (200): 30.00
Common Player: .25
Pack (6): 2.00
Wax Box (24): 40.00

1	Chipper Jones	1.50
2	Brian Jordan	.25
3	David Justice	.25
4	Jason Kendall	.25
5	Mo Vaughn	.25
6	Jim Edmonds	.25
7	Wade Boggs	1.50
8	Jeromy Burnitz	.25
9	Todd Hundley	.25
10	Rondell White	.25
11	Cliff Floyd	.25
12	Sean Casey	.40
13	Bernie Williams	.25
14	Dante Bichette	.25
15	Greg Vaughn	.25
16	Andres Galarraga	.25
17	Ray Durham	.25
18	Jim Thome	.60
19	Gary Sheffield	.45
20	Frank Thomas	1.00
21	Orlando Hernandez	.35
22	Ivan Rodriguez	.75
23	Jose Cruz Jr.	.25
24	Jason Giambi	.50
25	Craig Biggio	.45
26	Kerry Wood	.45
27	Manny Ramirez	1.00
28	Curt Schilling	.45
29	Mike Mussina	.45
30	Tim Salmon	.25
31	Mike Piazza	2.00
32	Roberto Alomar	.40
33	Larry Walker	.25
34	Barry Larkin	.25
35	Nomar Garciaparra	1.50
36	Paul O'Neill	.25
37	Todd Walker	.25
38	Eric Karros	.25
39	Brad Fullmer	.25
40	John Olerud	.25
41	Todd Helton	.75
42	Raul Mondesi	.25
43	Jose Canseco	.50
44	Matt Williams	.25
45	Ray Lankford	.25
46	Carlos Delgado	.50
47	Darin Erstad	.50
48	Vladimir Guerrero	1.00
49	Robin Ventura	.25
50	Alex Rodriguez	2.50
51	Vinny Castilla	.25
52	Tony Clark	.25
53	Pedro Martinez	1.00
54	Rafael Palmeiro	.65
55	Scott Rolen	.65
56	Tino Martinez	.25
57	Tony Gwynn	1.50
58	Barry Bonds	3.00
59	Kenny Lofton	.25
60	Javy Lopez	.25
61	Mark Grace	.25
62	Travis Lee	.25
63	Kevin Brown	.25
64	Al Leiter	.25
65	Albert Belle	.25
66	Sammy Sosa	1.50
67	Greg Maddux	1.50
68	Mark Kotsay	.25
69	Dmitri Young	.25
70	Mark McGwire	2.50
71	Juan Gonzalez	.50
72	Andruw Jones	1.00
73	Derek Jeter	3.00
74	Randy Johnson	1.00
75	Cal Ripken Jr.	3.00
76	Shawn Green	.35
77	Moises Alou	.25
78	Tom Glavine	.45
79	Sandy Alomar	.25
80	Ken Griffey Jr.	2.00
81	Ryan Klesko	.25
82	Jeff Bagwell	1.00
83	Ben Grieve	.25
84	John Smoltz	.25
85	Roger Clemens	1.75
86	Ken Griffey Jr.	1.00
87	Roger Clemens	.85
88	Derek Jeter	1.50
89	Nomar Garciaparra	.75
90	Mark McGwire	1.25
91	Sammy Sosa	.75
92	Alex Rodriguez	1.25
93	Greg Maddux	.75
94	Vladimir Guerrero	1.00
95	Chipper Jones	.75
96	Kerry Wood	.30
97	Ben Grieve	.25
98	Tony Gwynn	.75

99	Juan Gonzalez		.30
100	Mike Piazza		1.00
101	Eric Chavez		.40
102	Billy Koch		.25
103	Dernell Stenson		.25
104	Marlon Anderson		.25
105	Ron Belliard		.25
106	Bruce Chen		.25
107	Carlos Beltran		.40
108	Chad Hermansen		.25
109	Ryan Anderson		.25
110	Michael Barrett		.25
111	Matt Clement		.25
112	Ben Davis		.25
113	Calvin Pickering		.25
114	Brad Penny		.25
115	Paul Konerko		.35
116	Alex Gonzalez		.25
117	George Lombard		.25
118	John Patterson		.25
119	Rob Bell		.25
120	Ruben Mateo		.25
121	Troy Glaus		.75
122	Ryan Bradley		.25
123	Carlos Lee		.35
124	Gabe Kapler		.25
125	Ramon Hernandez		.25
126	Carlos Febles		.25
127	Mitch Meluskey		.25
128	Michael Cuddyer		.25
129	Pablo Ozuna		.25
130	Jayson Werth		.25
131	Ricky Ledee		.25
132	Jeremy Giambi		.25
133	Danny Klassen		.25
134	Mark DeRosa		.25
135	Randy Wolf		.25
136	Roy Halladay		.35
137	Derrick Gibson		.25
138	Ben Petrick		.25
139	Warren Morris		.25
140	Lance Berkman		.25
141	Russell Branyan		.25
142	Adrian Beltre		.40
143	Juan Encarnacion		.25
144	Fernando Seguignol		.25
145	Corey Koskie		.25
146	Preston Wilson		.25
147	Homer Bush		.25
148	Daryle Ward		.25
149	Joe McEwing RC		.50
150	Peter Bergeron RC		.50
151	Pat Burrell RC		3.00
152	Choo Freeman RC		.50
153	Matt Belisle RC		.50
154	Carlos Pena RC		1.00
155	A.J. Burnett RC		.75
156	Doug Mientkiewicz RC		.75
157	Sean Burroughs RC		.50
158	Mike Zywica RC		.35
159	Corey Patterson RC		1.50
160	Austin Kearns RC		2.00
161	Chip Ambres RC		.35
162	Kelly Dransfeldt RC		.35
163	Mike Nannini RC		.35
164	Mark Mulder RC		2.00
165	Jason Tyner RC		.35
166	Bobby Seay RC		.50
167	Alex Escobar RC		.75
168	Nick Johnson RC		1.00
169	Alfonso Soriano RC		4.00
170	Clayton Andrews RC		.35
171	C.C. Sabathia RC		2.00
172	Matt Holliday RC		5.00
173	Brad Lidge RC		1.00
174	Kit Pellow RC		.50
175	J.M. Gold RC		.50
176	Roosevelt Brown RC		.50
177	Eric Valent RC		.50
178	Adam Everett RC		.75
179	Jorge Toca RC		.35
180	Matt Roney RC		.35
181	Andy Brown RC		.35
182	Phil Norton RC		.35
183	Mickey Lopez RC		.35
184	Chris George RC		.35
185	Arturo McDowell RC		.35
186	Jose Fernandez RC		.35
187	Seth Etherton RC		.50
188	Josh McKinley RC		.50
189	Nate Cornejo RC		.50
190	Giuseppe Chiaramonte RC		.35
191	Mamon Tucker RC		.50
192	Ryan Mills RC		.50
193	Chad Moeller RC		.35
194	Tony Torcato RC		.35
195	Jeff Winchester RC		.35
196	Rick Elder RC		.35
197	Matt Burch RC		.35
198	Jeff Urban RC		.35
199	Chris Jones RC		.35
200	Masao Kida RC		.50

Refractors

	NM/M
Complete Set (200):	250.00
Common Player:	1.00
Stars:	6X

Production 400 Sets
(See 1999 Bowman's Best for
checklist and base card values.)

Atomic Refractors

	NM/M
Common Player:	3.00
Stars:	12X

Production 100 Sets
(See 1999 Bowman's Best for
checklist and base card values.)

Franchise Best

		NM/M
Complete Set (10):		15.00
Common Player:		.75

Production 3,000 Sets

Mach II (1,000):		1.5X
Mach III (500):		2.5X
1	Mark McGwire	2.50
2	Ken Griffey Jr.	1.50
3	Sammy Sosa	1.25
4	Nomar Garciaparra	1.25
5	Alex Rodriguez	2.50
6	Derek Jeter	3.50
7	Mike Piazza	1.50
8	Frank Thomas	1.00
9	Chipper Jones	1.25
10	Juan Gonzalez	.75

Franchise Favorites

	NM/M
Complete Set (6):	12.00

Common Player:		.50
Inserted 1:75		
1A	Derek Jeter	5.00
1B	Don Mattingly	2.00
1C	Derek Jeter,	
	Don Mattingly	5.00
2A	Scott Rolen	.50
2B	Mike Schmidt	1.50
2C	Scott Rolen,	
	Mike Schmidt	1.00

Franchise Favorites Autographs

		NM/M
Common Player:		15.00
Version A & B 1:1,548		
Version C 1:6,191		
1A	Derek Jeter	100.00
1B	Don Mattingly	60.00
1C	Derek Jeter,	
	Don Mattingly	300.00
2A	Scott Rolen	20.00
2B	Mike Schmidt	50.00
2C	Scott Rolen,	
	Mike Schmidt	100.00

Future Foundations

		NM/M
Complete Set (10):		16.00
Common Player:		.75

Production 3,000 Sets

Mach II (1,000):		1.5X
Mach III (500):		2.5X
1	Ruben Mateo	.75
2	Troy Glaus	4.00
3	Eric Chavez	1.50
4	Pat Burrell	4.00
5	Adrian Beltre	1.50
6	Ryan Anderson	.75
7	Alfonso Soriano	3.00
8	Brad Penny	.75
9	Derrick Gibson	.75
10	Bruce Chen	.75

Mirror Image

		NM/M
Complete Set (10):		20.00
Common Player:		1.50
Inserted 1:24		
Refractors (1:96):		1.5X
Atomic Refractors (1:192):		2X
1	Alex Rodriguez,	
	Alex Gonzalez	2.50
2	Ken Griffey Jr., Ruben Mateo	2.00
3	Derek Jeter, Alfonso Soriano	4.00

4	Sammy Sosa,	
	Corey Patterson	1.50
5	Greg Maddux, Bruce Chen	1.50
6	Chipper Jones, Eric Chavez	1.50
7	Vladimir Guerrero,	
	Carlos Beltran	1.50
8	Frank Thomas,	
	Nick Johnson	1.50
9	Nomar Garciaparra,	
	Pablo Ozuna	1.50
10	Mark McGwire, Pat Burrell	3.00

Rookie of the Year

		NM/M
Complete Set (2):		4.00
1	Ben Grieve	2.00
2	Kerry Wood	2.00
A1	Ben Grieve/Auto.	6.00

Rookie Locker Room
Autographs

		NM/M
Common Player:		4.00
Inserted 1:248		
1	Pat Burrell	15.00
2	Michael Barrett	4.00
3	Troy Glaus	10.00
4	Gabe Kapler	4.00
5	Eric Chavez	7.50

Rookie Locker Room
Game-Used Lumber

		NM/M
Complete Set (6):		35.00
Common Player:		4.00
Inserted 1:258		
1	Pat Burrell	10.00
2	Michael Barrett	4.00
3	Troy Glaus	10.00
4	Gabe Kapler	4.00
5	Eric Chavez	7.50
6	Richie Sexson	5.00

Rookie Locker Room
Game-Worn Jerseys

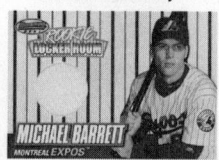

		NM/M
Common Player:		3.00
Inserted 1:270		
1	Richie Sexson	5.00
2	Michael Barrett	3.00
3	Troy Glaus	8.00
4	Eric Chavez	5.00

2000 Bowman

		NM/M
Complete Set (440):		65.00
Common Player:		.15
Common Rookie:		.25
Pack (10):		2.50
Box (24):		40.00
1	Vladimir Guerrero	.75
2	Chipper Jones	.75
3	Todd Walker	.15
4	Barry Larkin	.25
5	Bernie Williams	.40

6	Todd Helton	.75
7	Jermaine Dye	.15
8	Brian Giles	.15
9	Freddy Garcia	.15
10	Greg Vaughn	.15
11	Alex Gonzalez	.15
12	Luis Gonzalez	.25
13	Ron Belliard	.15
14	Ben Grieve	.15
15	Carlos Delgado	.50
16	Brian Jordan	.15
17	Fernando Tatis	.15
18	Ryan Rupe	.15
19	Miguel Tejada	.50
20	Mark Grace	.30
21	Kenny Lofton	.15
22	Eric Karros	.15
23	Cliff Floyd	.15
24	John Halama	.15
25	Cristian Guzman	.15
26	Scott Williamson	.15
27	Mike Lieberthal	.15
28	Tim Hudson	.40
29	Warren Morris	.15
30	Pedro Martinez	1.00
31	John Smoltz	.15
32	Ray Durham	.15
33	Chad Allen	.15
34	Tony Clark	.15
35	Tino Martinez	.15
36	J.T. Snow Jr.	.15
37	Kevin Brown	.25
38	Bartolo Colon	.15
39	Rey Ordonez	.15
40	Jeff Bagwell	.50
41	Ivan Rodriguez	.50
42	Eric Chavez	.25
43	Eric Milton	.15
44	Jose Canseco	.50
45	Shawn Green	.25
46	Rich Aurilia	.15
47	Roberto Alomar	.40
48	Brian Daubach	.15
49	Magglio Ordonez	.25
50	Derek Jeter	2.00
51	Kris Benson	.15
52	Albert Belle	.15
53	Rondell White	.15
54	Justin Thompson	.15
55	Nomar Garciaparra	.75
56	Chuck Finley	.15
57	Omar Vizquel	.15
58	Luis Castillo	.15
59	Richard Hidalgo	.15
60	Barry Bonds	2.00
61	Craig Biggio	.15
62	Doug Glanville	.15
63	Gabe Kapler	.15
64	Johnny Damon	.15
65	Pokey Reese	.15
66	Andy Pettitte	.25
67	B.J. Surhoff	.15
68	Richie Sexson	.40
69	Javy Lopez	.15
70	Raul Mondesi	.15
71	Darin Erstad	.25
72	Kevin Millwood	.15
73	Ricky Ledee	.15
74	John Olerud	.15
75	Sean Casey	.25
76	Carlos Febles	.15
77	Paul O'Neill	.15
78	Bob Abreu	.15
79	Neifi Perez	.15
80	Tony Gwynn	.75
81	Russ Ortiz	.15
82	Matt Williams	.15
83	Chris Carpenter	.15
84	Roger Cedeno	.15
85	Tim Salmon	.30
86	Billy Koch	.15
87	Jeromy Burnitz	.15
88	Edgardo Alfonzo	.15
89	Jay Bell	.15
90	Manny Ramirez	.75
91	Frank Thomas	.75
92	Mike Mussina	.50
93	J.D. Drew	.25
94	Adrian Beltre	.25
95	Alex Rodriguez	2.00
96	Larry Walker	.15
97	Juan Encarnacion	.15
98	Mike Sweeney	.15
99	Rusty Greer	.15
100	Randy Johnson	.75
101	Jose Vidro	.15
102	Preston Wilson	.15
103	Greg Maddux	1.50
104	Jason Giambi	.50
105	Cal Ripken Jr.	2.00
106	Carlos Beltran	.50
107	Vinny Castilla	.15
108	Mariano Rivera	.25
109	Mo Vaughn	.15
110	Rafael Palmeiro	.50
111	Shannon Stewart	.15
112	Mike Hampton	.15
113	Joe Nathan	.15
114	Ben Davis	.15
115	Andruw Jones	.50
116	Robin Ventura	.15
117	Damion Easley	.15
118	Jeff Cirillo	.15
119	Kerry Wood	.25
120	Scott Rolen	.75
121	Sammy Sosa	.75
122	Ken Griffey Jr.	1.50
123	Shane Reynolds	.15
124	Troy Glaus	.40
125	Tom Glavine	.35
126	Michael Barrett	.15
127	Al Leiter	.15
128	Jason Kendall	.15
129	Roger Clemens	2.00
130	Juan Gonzalez	.40
131	Corey Koskie	.15
132	Curt Schilling	.50
133	Mike Piazza	1.00
134	Gary Sheffield	.40
135	Jim Thome	.40
136	Orlando Hernandez	.25
137	Ray Lankford	.15
138	Geoff Jenkins	.15
139	Jose Lima	.15
140	Mark McGwire	1.50
141	Adam Piatt	.15
142	Pat Manning **RC**	.25
143	Marcos Castillo **RC**	.25
144	Lesli Brea **RC**	.25
145	Humberto Cota **RC**	.25
146	Ben Petrick	.15
147	Kip Wells	.15
148	Willi Mo Pena	.25
149	Chris Wakeland	.15
150	Brad Baker **RC**	.25
151	Robbie Morrison **RC**	.25
152	Reggie Taylor	.15
153	Brian Cole **RC**	.25
154	Peter Bergeron	.15
155	Roosevelt Brown	.15
156	Matt Cepicky **RC**	.25
157	Ramon Castro	.15
158	Brad Baisley **RC**	.25
159	Jeff Goldbach **RC**	.25
160	Mitch Meluskey	.15
161	Chad Harville	.15
162	Brian Cooper	.15
163	Marcus Giles	.15
164	Jim Morris	.50
165	Geoff Goetz	.15
166	Bobby Bradley **RC**	.25
167	Rob Bell	.15
168	Joe Crede	.15
169	Michael Restovich	.15
170	Quincy Foster **RC**	.25
171	Enrique Cruz **RC**	.25
172	Mark Quinn	.15
173	Nick Johnson	.15
174	Jeff Liefer	.15
175	Kevin Mench **RC**	.75
176	Steve Lomasney	.15
177	Jayson Werth	.15
178	Tim Drew	.15
179	Chip Ambres	.15
180	Ryan Anderson	.15
181	Matt Blank	.15
182	Giuseppe Chiaramonte	.15
183	Corey Myers **RC**	.25
184	Jeff Yoder	.15
185	Craig Dingman **RC**	.25
186	Jon Hamilton **RC**	.25
187	Toby Hall	.15
188	Russell Branyan	.15
189	Brian Falkenborg **RC**	.25
190	Aaron Harang **RC**	.75
191	Juan Pena	.15
192	Travis Thompson **RC**	.25
193	Alfonso Soriano	.50
194	Alejandro Diaz **RC**	.25
195	Carlos Pena	.15
196	Kevin Nicholson	.15
197	Mo Bruce	.15
198	C.C. Sabathia	.15
199	Carl Crawford	.15
200	Rafael Furcal	.15
201	Andrew Beinbrink **RC**	.25
202	Jimmy Osting	.15
203	Aaron McNeal **RC**	.25
204	Brett Laxton	.15
205	Chris George	.15
206	Felipe Lopez	.15
207	Ben Sheets **RC**	2.00
208	Mike Meyers **RC**	.40
209	Jason Conti	.15
210	Milton Bradley	.15
211	Chris Mears **RC**	.25
212	Carlos Hernandez **RC**	.50
213	Jason Romano	.15
214	Goefrey Tomlinson	.15
215	Jimmy Rollins	.40
216	Pablo Ozuna	.15
217	Steve Cox	.15
218	Terrence Long	.15
219	Jeff DaVanon **RC**	.40
220	Rick Ankiel	.25
221	Jason Standridge	.15
222	Tony Armas	.15
223	Jason Tyner	.15
224	Ramon Ortiz	.15
225	Daryle Ward	.15
226	Enger Veras **RC**	.25
227	Chris Jones **RC**	.25
228	Eric Cammack **RC**	.25
229	Ruben Mateo	.15
230	Ken Harvey **RC**	.50
231	Jake Westbrook	.15
232	Rob Purvis **RC**	.25
233	Choo Freeman	.15
234	Aramis Ramirez	.15
235	A.J. Burnett	.15
236	Kevin Barker	.15
237	Chance Caple **RC**	.25
238	Jarrod Washburn	.15
239	Lance Berkman	.15
240	Michael Wenner **RC**	.25
241	Alex Sanchez	.15
242	Jake Esteves **RC**	.25
243	Grant Roberts	.15
244	Mark Ellis **RC**	.50
245	Donny Leon	.15
246	David Eckstein	.15
247	Dicky Gonzalez **RC**	.25
248	John Patterson	.15
249	Chad Green	.15
250	Scot Shields **RC**	.25
251	Troy Cameron	.15
252	Jose Molina	.15
253	Rob Pugmire **RC**	.25
254	Rick Elder	.15
255	Sean Burroughs	.25
256	Josh Kalinowski **RC**	.25
257	Matt LeCroy	.15
258	Alex Graman **RC**	.50
259	Tomokazu Ohka **RC**	.50
260	Brady Clark	.15
261	Rico Washington **RC**	.25
262	Gary Matthews Jr.	.15
263	Matt Wise	.15
264	Keith Reed **RC**	.50
265	Santiago Ramirez **RC**	.25
266	Ben Broussard **RC**	.50
267	Ryan Langerhans	.15
268	Juan Rivera	.15
269	Shawn Gallagher	.15
270	Jorge Toca	.15
271	Brad Lidge	.15
272	Leo Estrella **RC**	.25
273	Ruben Quevedo	.15
274	Jack Cust	.15
275	T.J. Tucker	.15
276	Mike Colangelo	.15
277	Brian Schneider	.15
278	Calvin Murray	.15
279	Josh Girdley	.15
280	Mike Paradis	.15
281	Chad Hermansen	.15
282	Ty Howington **RC**	.50
283	Aaron Myette	.15
284	D'Angelo Jimenez	.15
285	Dernell Stenson	.15
286	Jerry Hairston Jr.	.15
287	Gary Majewski **RC**	.25
288	Derrin Ebert **RC**	.25
289	Steve Fish **RC**	.25
290	Carlos Hernandez	.15
291	Allen Levrault	.15
292	Sean McNally **RC**	.25
293	Randey Dorame **RC**	.25
294	Wes Anderson **RC**	.50
295	B.J. Ryan	.15
296	Alan Webb **RC**	.25
297	Brandon Inge **RC**	.75
298	David Walling	.15
299	Sun-Woo Kim **RC**	.40
300	Pat Burrell	.25
301	Rick Guttormson **RC**	.25
302	Gil Meche	.15
303	Carlos Zambrano **RC**	3.00
304	Eric Byrnes **RC** (Photo actually Bo Porter.)	1.00
305	Robb Quinlan **RC**	.25
306	Jackie Rexrode	.15
307	Nate Bump	.15
308	Sean DePaula **RC**	.25
309	Matt Riley	.15
310	Ryan Minor	.15
311	J.J. Davis	.15
312	Randy Wolf	.15
313	Jason Jennings	.15
314	Scott Seabol **RC**	.25
315	Doug Davis	.15
316	Todd Moser **RC**	.25
317	Rob Ryan	.15
318	Bubba Crosby	.15
319	Lyle Overbay **RC**	1.00
320	Mario Encarnacion	.15
321	Francisco Rodriguez **RC**	2.00
322	Michael Cuddyer	.15
323	Eddie Yarnall	.15
324	Cesar Saba **RC**	.25
325	Travis Dawkins	.15
326	Alex Escobar	.15
327	Julio Zuleta **RC**	.40
328	Josh Hamilton	.50
329	Nick Neugebauer **RC**	.25
330	Matt Belisle	.15
331	Kurt Ainsworth **RC**	.50
332	Tim Raines Jr.	.15
333	Eric Munson	.15
334	Donzell McDonald	.15
335	Larry Bigbie **RC**	.25
336	Matt Watson	.15
337	Aubrey Huff	.15
338	Julio Ramirez	.15
339	Jason Grabowski **RC**	.25
340	Jon Garland	.15
341	Austin Kearns	.25
342	Josh Pressley	.15
343	Miguel Olivo **RC**	.25
344	Julio Lugo	.15
345	Roberto Vaz	.15
346	Ramon Soler	.15
347	Brandon Phillips **RC**	2.00
348	Vince Faison **RC**	.25
349	Mike Venafro	.15
350	Rick Asadoorian **RC**	.25
351	B.J. Garbe **RC**	.25
352	Dan Reichert	.15
353	Jason Stumm **RC**	.25
354	Ruben Salazar **RC**	.25
355	Francisco Cordero	.15
356	Juan Guzman **RC**	.25
357	Mike Bacsik **RC**	.25
358	Jared Sandberg	.15
359	Rod Barajas	.15
360	Junior Brignac **RC**	.25
361	J.M. Gold	.15
362	Octavio Dotel	.15
363	David Kelton	.15
364	Scott Morgan **RC**	.25
365	Wascar Serrano **RC**	.25
366	Wilton Veras	.15
367	Eugene Kingsale	.15
368	Ted Lilly	.15
369	George Lombard	.15
370	Chris Haas	.15
371	Wilton Pena **RC**	.50
372	Vernon Wells	.15
373	Jason Royer **RC**	.25
374	Jeff Heaverlo **RC**	.25
375	Calvin Pickering	.15
376	Mike Lamb **RC**	.40
377	Kyle Snyder	.15
378	Javier Cardona **RC**	.25
379	Aaron Rowand **RC**	1.00
380	Dee Brown	.15
381	Brett Myers **RC**	1.00
382	Abraham Nunez	.20
383	Eric Valent	.15
384	Jody Gerut **RC**	.25
385	Adam Dunn	.50
386	Jay Gehrke	.15
387	Omar Ortiz	.15
388	Darnell McDonald	.15
389	Chad Alexander	.15
390	J.D. Closser	.15
391	Ben Christensen **RC**	.25
392	Adam Kennedy	.15
393	Nick Green **RC**	.25
394	Ramon Hernandez	.15
395	Roy Oswalt **RC**	4.00
396	Andy Tracy **RC**	.50
397	Eric Gagne	.15
398	Michael Tejera **RC**	.25
399	Adam Everett	.15
400	Corey Patterson	.25
401	Gary Knotts **RC**	.25
402	Ryan Christianson **RC**	.50
403	Eric Ireland **RC**	.25
404	Andrew Good **RC**	.25
405	Brad Penny	.15
406	Jason LaRue	.15
407	Kit Pellow	.15
408	Kevin Beirne	.15
409	Kelly Dransfeldt	.15
410	Jason Grilli	.15
411	Scott Downs **RC**	.25
412	Jesus Colome	.15
413	John Sneed **RC**	.25
414	Tony McKnight **RC**	.25
415	Luis Rivera	.15
416	Adam Eaton	.15
417	Mike MacDougal **RC**	.50
418	Mike Nannini	.15
419	Barry Zito **RC**	2.00
420	Dewayne Wise	.15
421	Jason Dellaero	.15
422	Chad Moeller	.15
423	Jason Marquis	.15
424	Tim Redding **RC**	.50
425	Mark Mulder	.15
426	Josh Paul	.15
427	Chris Enochs	.15
428	Wilfredo Rodriguez **RC**	.50
429	Kevin Witt	.15
430	Scott Sobkowiak **RC**	.25
431	McKay Christensen	.15
432	Jung Bong	.15
433	Keith Evans **RC**	.25
434	Garry Maddox Jr.	.15
435	Ramon Santiago **RC**	.50
436	Alex Cora	.15
437	Carlos Lee	.15
438	Jason Repko **RC**	.25
439	Matt Burch	.15
440	Shawn Sonnier **RC**	.25

Gold

Stars: 10-20X
Rookies: 4-8X
Production 99 Sets
(See 2000 Bowman for checklist and base card values.)

Retro/Future

	NM/M
Common Player:	.25
Stars:	2-3X
Rookies:	.75-2X
Inserted 1:1	

(See 2000 Bowman for checklist and base card values.)

Autographs

Jose Vidro

	NM/M
Common Autograph:	5.00
Blue Inserted 1:144	
Silver 1:312	
Gold 1:1,604	
CA	Chip Ambres/B	5.00
RA	Rick Ankiel/G	25.00
CB	Carlos Beltran/B	40.00
LB	Lance Berkman/S	20.00
DB	Dee Brown/S	8.00
SB	Sean Burroughs/S	8.00
JDC	J.D. Closser/B	5.00
SC	Steve Cox/B	5.00
MC	Michael Cuddyer/S	10.00
JC	Jack Cust/S	15.00
SD	Scott Downs/S	10.00
JDD	J.D. Drew/G	25.00
AD	Adam Dunn/B	25.00
CF	Choo Freeman/B	5.00
RF	Rafael Furcal/S	15.00
AH	Aubrey Huff/B	8.00
JJ	Jason Jennings/B	8.00
NJ	Nick Johnson/S	10.00
AK	Austin Kearns/B	15.00
DK	David Kelton/B	5.00
RM	Ruben Mateo/G	15.00
MM	Mike Meyers/B	5.00
CP	Corey Patterson/S	20.00
BWP	Brad Penny/G	5.00
BP	Ben Petrick/G	10.00
AP	Adam Piatt/S	8.00
MQ	Mark Quinn/S	8.00
MR	Mike Restovich/B	8.00
MR	Matt Riley/S	8.00
JR	Jason Romano/B	5.00
BS	Ben Sheets/B	30.00
AS	Alfonso Soriano/S	40.00
EV	Eric Valent/B	5.00
JV	Jose Vidro/S	10.00
VW	Vernon Wells/B	20.00
SW	Scott Williamson/G	10.00
KJW	Kevin Witt/S	10.00
KLW	Kerry Wood/S	25.00
EY	Eddie Yarnall/S	10.00
JZ	Julio Zuleta/B	5.00

Bowman's Best Previews

		NM/M
Complete Set (10):		15.00
Common Player:		.50
Inserted 1:18		
1	Derek Jeter	4.00
2	Ken Griffey Jr.	3.00
3	Nomar Garciaparra	2.00
4	Mike Piazza	2.00
5	Alex Rodriguez	4.00
6	Sammy Sosa	2.00
7	Mark McGwire	3.00

DEREK JETER

8	Pat Burrell	1.00
9	Josh Hamilton	1.00
10	Adam Piatt	.50

Early Indications

ALEX RODRIGUEZ
SS Seattle Mariners

		NM/M
Complete Set (10):		18.00
Common Player:		1.00
Inserted 1:24		
1	Nomar Garciaparra	1.50
2	Cal Ripken Jr.	4.00
3	Derek Jeter	4.00
4	Mark McGwire	3.00
5	Alex Rodriguez	3.00
6	Chipper Jones	1.50
7	Todd Helton	1.00
8	Vladimir Guerrero	1.00
9	Mike Piazza	1.50
10	Jose Canseco	1.50

Major Power

ALEX RODRIGUEZ

		NM/M
Complete Set (10):		20.00
Common Player:		1.00
Inserted 1:24		
1	Mark McGwire	4.00
2	Chipper Jones	2.50
3	Alex Rodriguez	4.00
4	Sammy Sosa	3.00
5	Rafael Palmeiro	1.00
6	Ken Griffey Jr.	3.00
7	Nomar Garciaparra	3.00
8	Barry Bonds	5.00
9	Derek Jeter	5.00
10	Jeff Bagwell	1.50

Tool Time

		NM/M
Complete Set (20):		8.00
Common Player:		.40
Inserted 1:8		
1	Pat Burrell	1.00
2	Aaron Rowand	.40

RUBEN MATEO

3	Chris Wakeland	.40
4	Ruben Mateo	.40
5	Pat Burrell	1.00
6	Adam Piatt	.50
7	Nick Johnson	1.00
8	Jack Cust	.40
9	Rafael Furcal	.40
10	Julio Ramirez	.40
11	Travis Dawkins	.40
12	Corey Patterson	1.00
13	Ruben Mateo	.40
14	Jason Dellaero	.40
15	Sean Burroughs	.40
16	Ryan Langerhans	.40
17	D'Angelo Jimenez	.40
18	Corey Patterson	1.00
19	Troy Cameron	.40
20	Michael Cuddyer	.50

2000 Bowman Chrome

Mike Mussina

		NM/M
Complete Set (440):		120.00
Common Player:		.25
Common Rookie:		.50
Pack (4):		2.50
Box (24):		50.00
1	Vladimir Guerrero	1.00
2	Chipper Jones	1.00
3	Todd Walker	.25
4	Barry Larkin	.50
5	Bernie Williams	.50
6	Todd Helton	.50
7	Jermaine Dye	.25
8	Brian Giles	.25
9	Freddy Garcia	.25
10	Greg Vaughn	.25
11	Alex Gonzalez	.25
12	Luis Gonzalez	.25
13	Ron Belliard	.25
14	Ben Grieve	.25
15	Carlos Delgado	.75
16	Brian Jordan	.25
17	Fernando Tatis	.25
18	Ryan Rupe	.25
19	Miguel Tejada	.40
20	Mark Grace	.35
21	Kenny Lofton	.25
22	Eric Karros	.25
23	Cliff Floyd	.25
24	John Halama	.25
25	Cristian Guzman	.25
26	Scott Williamson	.25
27	Mike Lieberthal	.25
28	Tim Hudson	.40
29	Warren Morris	.25
30	Pedro Martinez	1.00
31	John Smoltz	.25
32	Ray Durham	.25
33	Chad Allen	.25
34	Tony Clark	.25
35	Tino Martinez	.25
36	J.T. Snow Jr.	.25
37	Kevin Brown	.40
38	Bartolo Colon	.25
39	Rey Ordonez	.25
40	Jeff Bagwell	.50
41	Ivan Rodriguez	.75
42	Eric Chavez	.50

43	Eric Milton	.25
44	Jose Canseco	.50
45	Shawn Green	.50
46	Rich Aurilia	.25
47	Roberto Alomar	.50
48	Brian Daubach	.25
49	Magglio Ordonez	.50
50	Derek Jeter	2.00
51	Kris Benson	.25
52	Albert Belle	.25
53	Rondell White	.25
54	Justin Thompson	.25
55	Nomar Garciaparra	1.00
56	Chuck Finley	.25
57	Omar Vizquel	.25
58	Luis Castillo	.25
59	Richard Hidalgo	.25
60	Barry Bonds	2.00
61	Craig Biggio	.25
62	Doug Glanville	.25
63	Gabe Kapler	.25
64	Johnny Damon	.40
65	Pokey Reese	.25
66	Andy Pettitte	.50
67	B.J. Surhoff	.25
68	Richie Sexson	.50
69	Javy Lopez	.25
70	Raul Mondesi	.25
71	Darin Erstad	.40
72	Kevin Millwood	.25
73	Ricky Ledee	.25
74	John Olerud	.25
75	Sean Casey	.25
76	Carlos Febles	.25
77	Paul O'Neill	.25
78	Bob Abreu	.25
79	Neifi Perez	.25
80	Tony Gwynn	1.00
81	Russ Ortiz	.25
82	Matt Williams	.25
83	Chris Carpenter	.25
84	Roger Cedeno	.25
85	Tim Salmon	.35
86	Billy Koch	.25
87	Jeromy Burnitz	.25
88	Edgardo Alfonzo	.25
89	Jay Bell	.15
90	Manny Ramirez	.75
91	Frank Thomas	.75
92	Mike Mussina	.50
93	J.D. Drew	.40
94	Adrian Beltre	.40
95	Alex Rodriguez	2.00
96	Larry Walker	.25
97	Juan Encarnacion	.25
98	Mike Sweeney	.25
99	Rusty Greer	.25
100	Randy Johnson	.75
101	Jose Vidro	.25
102	Preston Wilson	.25
103	Greg Maddux	1.50
104	Jason Giambi	.75
105	Cal Ripken Jr.	3.00
106	Carlos Beltran	.25
107	Vinny Castilla	.25
108	Mariano Rivera	.35
109	Mo Vaughn	.25
110	Rafael Palmeiro	.50
111	Shannon Stewart	.25
112	Mike Hampton	.25
113	Joe Nathan	.25
114	Ben Davis	.25
115	Andruw Jones	.75
116	Robin Ventura	.25
117	Damion Easley	.25
118	Jeff Cirillo	.25
119	Kerry Wood	.40
120	Scott Rolen	.75
121	Sammy Sosa	1.00
122	Ken Griffey Jr.	2.00
123	Shane Reynolds	.25
124	Troy Glaus	.50
125	Tom Glavine	.40
126	Michael Barrett	.25
127	Al Leiter	.25
128	Jason Kendall	.25
129	Roger Clemens	2.00
130	Juan Gonzalez	.50
131	Corey Koskie	.25
132	Curt Schilling	.75
133	Mike Piazza	1.00
134	Gary Sheffield	.50
135	Jim Thome	.50
136	Orlando Hernandez	.40
137	Ray Lankford	.25
138	Geoff Jenkins	.25
139	Jose Lima	.25
140	Mark McGwire	1.50
141	Adam Piatt	.25
142	Pat Manning RC	.50
143	Marcos Castillo RC	.50
144	Lesli Brea RC	.50
145	Humberto Cota RC	.50
146	Ben Petrick	.25
147	Kip Wells	.25
148	Willi Mo Pena	.40
149	Chris Wakeland	.25
150	Brad Baker RC	.50
151	Robbie Morrison RC	.50
152	Reggie Taylor	.50
153	Matt Ginter RC	.50
154	Peter Bergeron	.25
155	Roosevelt Brown	.50
156	Matt Cepicky RC	.50
157	Ramon Castro	.25

#	Player	Price
158	Brad Baisley RC	.50
159	Jason Hart RC	1.00
160	Mitch Meluskey	.25
161	Chad Harville	.25
162	Brian Cooper	.25
163	Marcus Giles	.25
164	Jim Morris	.50
165	Geoff Goetz	.25
166	Bobby Bradley RC	.50
167	Rob Bell	.25
168	Joe Crede	.25
169	Michael Restovich	.25
170	Quincy Foster RC	.50
171	Enrique Cruz RC	.50
172	Mark Quinn	.25
173	Nick Johnson	.40
174	Jeff Liefer	.25
175	Kevin Mench RC	2.00
176	Steve Lomasney	.25
177	Jayson Werth	.25
178	Tim Drew	.25
179	Chip Ambres	.25
180	Ryan Anderson	.25
181	Matt Blank	.25
182	Giuseppe Chiaramonte	.25
183	Corey Myers RC	.50
184	Jeff Yoder	.25
185	Craig Dingman RC	.50
186	Jon Hamilton RC	.50
187	Toby Hall	.25
188	Russell Branyan	.25
189	Brian Falkenborg RC	.50
190	Aaron Harang RC	3.00
191	Juan Pena	.25
192	Chin-Hui Tsao RC	2.00
193	Alfonso Soriano	.75
194	Alejandro Diaz RC	.50
195	Carlos Pena	.25
196	Kevin Nicholson	.25
197	Mo Bruce	.25
198	C.C. Sabathia	.25
199	Carl Crawford	.25
200	Rafael Furcal	.25
201	Andrew Beinbrink RC	.50
202	Jimmy Osting	.25
203	Aaron McNeal RC	.50
204	Brett Laxton	.25
205	Chris George	.25
206	Felipe Lopez	.25
207	Ben Sheets RC	6.00
208	Mike Meyers RC	.50
209	Jason Conti	.25
210	Milton Bradley	.25
211	Chris Mears RC	.50
212	Carlos Hernandez RC	.50
213	Jason Romano	.25
214	Goefrey Tomlinson	.25
215	Jimmy Rollins	.75
216	Pablo Ozuna	.25
217	Steve Cox	.25
218	Terrence Long	.25
219	Jeff DaVanon	.50
220	Rick Ankiel	.50
221	Jason Standridge	.25
222	Tony Armas	.25
223	Jason Tyner	.25
224	Ramon Ortiz	.25
225	Daryle Ward	.25
226	Enger Veras RC	.50
227	Chris Jones RC	.50
228	Eric Cammack RC	.50
229	Ruben Mateo	.25
230	Ken Harvey RC	1.00
231	Jake Westbrook	.25
232	Rob Purvis RC	.50
233	Choo Freeman	.25
234	Aramis Ramirez	.50
235	A.J. Burnett	.50
236	Kevin Barker	.25
237	Chance Caple RC	.25
238	Jarrod Washburn	.25
239	Lance Berkman	.50
240	Michael Wenner RC	.50
241	Alex Sanchez	.25
242	Jake Esteves RC	.50
243	Grant Roberts	.25
244	Mark Ellis RC	.50
245	Donny Leon	.25
246	David Eckstein	.25
247	Dicky Gonzalez RC	.50
248	John Patterson	.25
249	Chad Green	.25
250	Scot Shields RC	.50
251	Troy Cameron	.25
252	Jose Molina	.25
253	Rob Pugmire RC	.50
254	Rick Elder	.25
255	Sean Burroughs	.50
256	Josh Kalinowski RC	.50
257	Matt LeCroy	.25
258	Alex Graman RC	.50
259	Juan Silvestre RC	.50
260	Brady Clark	.25
261	Rico Washington RC	.50
262	Gary Matthews Jr.	.25
263	Matt Wise	.25
264	Keith Reed RC	.50
265	Santiago Ramirez RC	.50
266	Ben Broussard RC	.50
267	Ryan Langerhans	.25
268	Juan Rivera	.25
269	Shawn Gallagher	.25
270	Jorge Toca	.25
271	Brad Lidge	.25
272	Leo Estrella RC	.50
273	Ruben Quevedo	.25
274	Jack Cust	.25
275	T.J. Tucker	.25
276	Mike Colangelo	.25
277	Brian Schneider	.25
278	Calvin Murray	.25
279	Josh Girdley	.25
280	Mike Paradis	.25
281	Chad Hermansen	.25
282	Ty Howington RC	.50
283	Aaron Myette	.25
284	D'Angelo Jimenez	.25
285	Dernell Stenson	.25
286	Jerry Hairston Jr.	.25
287	Gary Majewski RC	.50
288	Derrin Ebert RC	.50
289	Steve Fish RC	.50
290	Carlos Hernandez	.25
291	Allen Levrault	.25
292	Sean McNally RC	.50
293	Randey Dorame RC	.50
294	Wes Anderson RC	.50
295	B.J. Ryan	.25
296	Alan Webb RC	.50
297	Brandon Inge RC	2.00
298	David Walling	.25
299	Sun-Woo Kim RC	1.00
300	Pat Burrell	.50
301	Rick Guttormson RC	.50
302	Gil Meche	.25
303	Carlos Zambrano RC	10.00
304	Eric Byrnes RC	.50
	(Photo actually Bo Porter.)	4.00
305	Robb Quinlan RC	.50
306	Jackie Rexrode	.25
307	Nate Bump	.25
308	Sean DePaula RC	.50
309	Matt Riley	.25
310	Ryan Minor	.25
311	J.J. Davis	.25
312	Randy Wolf	.25
313	Jason Jennings	.25
314	Scott Seabol RC	.50
315	Doug Davis	.25
316	Todd Moser RC	.50
317	Rob Ryan	.25
318	Bubba Crosby	.25
319	Lyle Overbay RC	2.00
320	Mario Encarnacion	.25
321	Francisco Rodriguez RC	6.00
322	Michael Cuddyer	.25
323	Eddie Yarnall	.25
324	Cesar Saba RC	.50
325	Travis Dawkins	.25
326	Alex Escobar	.25
327	Julio Zuleta RC	.50
328	Josh Hamilton	.75
329	Carlos Urquiola RC	.50
330	Matt Belisle	.25
331	Kurt Ainsworth RC	1.00
332	Tim Raines Jr.	.25
333	Eric Munson	.25
334	Donzell McDonald	.25
335	Larry Bigbie RC	.50
336	Matt Watson	.25
337	Aubrey Huff	.25
338	Julio Ramirez	.25
339	Jason Grabowski RC	.50
340	Jon Garland	.25
341	Austin Kearns	.25
342	Josh Pressley	.25
343	Miguel Olivo RC	.50
344	Julio Lugo	.25
345	Roberto Vaz	.25
346	Ramon Soler	.25
347	Brandon Phillips RC	5.00
348	Vince Faison RC	.50
349	Mike Venafro	.25
350	Rick Asadoorian RC	.50
351	B.J. Garbe RC	.50
352	Dan Reichert	.25
353	Jason Stumm RC	.50
354	Ruben Salazar RC	.50
355	Francisco Cordero	.25
356	Juan Guzman RC	.50
357	Mike Bacsik RC	.50
358	Jared Sandberg	.25
359	Rod Barajas	.25
360	Junior Brignac RC	.50
361	J.M. Gold	.25
362	Octavio Dotel	.25
363	David Kelton	.25
364	Scott Morgan RC	.50
365	Wascar Serrano RC	.50
366	Wilton Veras	.25
367	Eugene Kingsale	.25
368	Ted Lilly	.25
369	George Lombard	.25
370	Chris Haas	.25
371	Wilton Pena RC	.50
372	Vernon Wells	.50
373	Keith Ginter RC	.50
374	Jeff Heaverlo RC	.50
375	Calvin Pickering	.25
376	Mike Lamb RC	.50
377	Kyle Snyder	.25
378	Javier Cardona RC	.50
379	Aaron Rowand RC	3.00
380	Dee Brown	.25
381	Brett Myers RC	2.00
382	Abraham Nunez	.25
383	Eric Valent	.25
384	Jody Gerut RC	.50
385	Adam Dunn	.50
386	Jay Gehrke	.25
387	Omar Ortiz	.25
388	Darnell McDonald	.25
389	Chad Alexander	.25
390	J.D. Closser	.25
391	Ben Christensen RC	.50
392	Adam Kennedy	.25
393	Nick Green RC	.50
394	Ramon Hernandez	.25
395	Roy Oswalt RC	15.00
396	Andy Tracy RC	1.00
397	Eric Gagne	.25
398	Michael Tejera RC	.50
399	Adam Everett	.25
400	Corey Patterson	.50
401	Gary Knotts RC	.50
402	Ryan Christianson RC	.50
403	Eric Ireland RC	.50
404	Andrew Good RC	.50
405	Brad Penny	.25
406	Jason LaRue	.25
407	Kit Pellow	.25
408	Kevin Beirne	.25
409	Kelly Dransfeldt	.25
410	Jason Grilli	.25
411	Scott Downs RC	.50
412	Jesus Colome	.25
413	John Sneed RC	.50
414	Tony McKnight RC	.50
415	Luis Rivera	.25
416	Adam Eaton	.25
417	Mike MacDougal RC	1.00
418	Mike Nannini	.25
419	Barry Zito RC	3.00
420	Dewayne Wise	.25
421	Jason Dellaero	.25
422	Chad Moeller	.25
423	Jason Marquis	.25
424	Tim Redding RC	.50
425	Mark Mulder	.25
426	Josh Paul	.25
427	Chris Enochs	.25
428	Wilfredo Rodriguez RC	.25
429	Kevin Witt	.25
430	Scott Sobkowiak RC	.25
431	McKay Christensen	.25
432	Jung Bong	.25
433	Keith Evans RC	.50
434	Garry Maddox Jr.	.25
435	Ramon Santiago RC	.50
436	Alex Cora	.25
437	Carlos Lee	.25
438	Jason Repko RC	.50
439	Matt Burch	.25
440	Shawn Sonnier RC	1.00

Refractors

Bidding for the Call

Ken Anderson

#	Player	Price
1	Adam Piatt	.50
2	Pat Burrell	1.00
3	Mark Mulder	1.00
4	Nick Johnson	1.00
5	Alfonso Soriano	2.00
6	Chin-Feng Chen	2.50
7	Scott Sobkowiak	.50
8	Corey Patterson	1.00
9	Jack Cust	.50
10	Sean Burroughs	.50
11	Josh Hamilton	2.00
12	Corey Myers	.50
13	Eric Munson	.50
14	Wes Anderson	.50
15	Lyle Overbay	1.00

Meteoric Rise

Mike Piazza

	NM/M
Complete Set (10):	20.00
Common Player:	1.00
Inserted 1:24	
Refractors:	2-4X
Inserted 1:240	
1 Nomar Garciaparra	3.00
2 Mark McGwire	4.00
3 Ken Griffey Jr.	3.00
4 Chipper Jones	2.50
5 Manny Ramirez	2.00
6 Mike Piazza	3.00
7 Cal Ripken Jr.	5.00
8 Ivan Rodriguez	1.00
9 Greg Maddux	3.00
10 Randy Johnson	2.00

Oversize

	NM/M
Complete Set (8):	8.00
Common Player:	.75
Inserted 1:Box	
1 Pat Burrell	2.00
2 Josh Hamilton	2.00
3 Rafael Furcal	1.00
4 Corey Patterson	1.50
5 A.J. Burnett	.75
6 Eric Munson	.75
7 Nick Johnson	1.00
8 Alfonso Soriano	2.00

Rookie Class 2000

	NM/M
Complete Set (10):	8.00
Common Player:	.75
Inserted 1:24	
Refractors:	2-4X
Inserted 1:240	
1 Pat Burrell	2.00
2 Rick Ankiel	.75
3 Ruben Mateo	.75
4 Vernon Wells	1.50
5 Mark Mulder	1.50
6 A.J. Burnett	.75
7 Chad Hermansen	.75

Mariano Rivera

Stars:	4-8X
Rookies:	2-4X
Inserted 1:12	

(See 2000 Bowman Chrome for checklist and base card values.)

Retro/Future

Mike MacDougal

Stars:	1.5-3X
Rookies:	.75X
Inserted 1:6	
Refractors:	6-8X
Rookies:	1-3X
Inserted 1:60	

(See 2000 Bowman Chrome for checklist and base values.)

Bidding for the Call

	NM/M
Complete Set (15):	10.00
Common Player:	.50
Inserted 1:16	
Refractors:	2-4X
Inserted 1:160	

8	Corey Patterson	1.50
9	Rafael Furcal	1.00
10	Mike Lamb	.75

Teen Idols

		NM/M
Complete Set (15):		15.00
Common Player:		.75
Inserted 1:16		
Inserted 1:160		
Refractors:		2-4X
1	Alex Rodriguez	5.00
2	Andruw Jones	1.50
3	Juan Gonzalez	1.00
4	Ivan Rodriguez	1.50
5	Ken Griffey Jr.	3.00
6	Bobby Bradley	.75
7	Brett Myers	.75
8	C.C. Sabathia	.75
9	Ty Howington	.75
10	Brandon Phillips	1.00
11	Rick Asadoorian	.75
12	Wily Pena	1.00
13	Sean Burroughs	.75
14	Josh Hamilton	2.00
15	Rafael Furcal	1.00

2000 Bowman Chrome Draft Picks and Prospects

		NM/M
Complete Set (110):		50.00
Common Player:		.25
1	Pat Burrell	.50
2	Rafael Furcal	.50
3	Grant Roberts	.25
4	Barry Zito	2.00
5	Julio Zuleta	.50
6	Mark Mulder	.50
7	Rob Bell	.50
8	Adam Piatt	.50
9	Mike Lamb	.25
10	Pablo Ozuna	.25
11	Jason Tyner	.25

12	Jason Marquis	.25
13	Eric Munson	.25
14	Seth Etherton	.25
15	Milton Bradley	.25
16	Nick Green	.25
17	Chin-Feng Chen RC	2.00
18	Matt Boone RC	.50
19	Kevin Gregg RC	.50
20	Eddy Garabito RC	.50
21	Aaron Capista RC	.50
22	Esteban German RC	.50
23	Derek Thompson RC	.50
24	Phil Merrell RC	.50
25	Brian O'Connor RC	.50
26	Yamid Haad	.50
27	Hector Mercado RC	.50
28	Jason Woolf RC	.50
29	Eddie Furniss RC	.50
30	Cha Sueng Baek RC	.50
31	Colby Lewis RC	.50
32	Pasqual Coco RC	.50
33	Jorge Cantu RC	2.00
34	Erasmo Ramirez RC	.50
35	Bobby Kielty RC	1.00
36	Joaquin Benoit RC	.50
37	Brian Esposito RC	.50
38	Michael Wenner	.25
39	Juan Rincon RC	.50
40	Yorvit Torrealba RC	.50
41	Chad Durham RC	.50
42	Jim Mann RC	.50
43	Shane Loux RC	.50
44	Luis Rivas	.50
45	Ken Chenard RC	.50
46	Mike Lockwood RC	.50
47	Giovanni Lara RC	.50
48	Bubba Carpenter RC	.50
49	Ryan Dittfurth RC	.50
50	John Stephens RC	.50
51	Pedro Feliz RC	2.00
52	Kenny Kelly RC	.50
53	Neil Jenkins RC	.50
54	Mike Glendenning RC	.50
55	Bo Porter	.25
56	Eric Byrnes	.25
57	Tony Alvarez RC	.50
58	Kazuhiro Sasaki RC	1.00
59	Chad Durbin RC	.50
60	Mike Bynum RC	.50
61	Travis Wilson RC	.50
62	Jose Leon RC	.50
63	Ryan Vogelsong RC	.50
64	Geraldo Guzman RC	.50
65	Craig Anderson RC	.50
66	Carlos Silva RC	1.00
67	Brad Thomas RC	.50
68	Chin-Hui Tsao	1.50
69	Mark Buehrle RC	6.00
70	Juan Salas RC	.50
71	Denny Abreu RC	.50
72	Keith McDonald RC	.50
73	Chris Richard RC	.50
74	Tomas de la Rosa RC	.50
75	Vicente Padilla	1.00
76	Justin Brunette RC	.50
77	Scott Linebrink RC	.50
78	Jeff Sparks RC	.50
79	Tike Redman RC	.50
80	John Lackey RC	3.00
81	Joe Strong RC	.50
82	Brian Tollberg RC	.50
83	Steve Sisco RC	.50
84	Chris Clapinski	.25
85	Augie Ojeda RC	.50
86	Adrian Gonzalez RC	6.00
87	Mike Stodolka RC	.50
88	Adam Johnson RC	.50
89	Matt Wheatland RC	.50
90	Corey Smith RC	.50
91	Rocco Baldelli RC	4.00
92	Keith Bucktrot RC	.50
93	Adam Wainwright RC	4.00
94	Blaine Boyer RC	.50
95	Aaron Herr RC	.50
96	Scott Thorman RC	2.00
97	Brian Digby RC	.50
98	Josh Shortslef RC	.50
99	Sean Smith RC	.50
100	Alex Cruz RC	.50
101	Marc Love RC	.50
102	Kevin Lee RC	.50
103	Timoniel Perez RC	.50
104	Alex Cabrera RC	1.00
105	Shane Hearns RC	.50
106	Tripper Johnson RC	.50
107	Brent Abernathy RC	.50
108	John Cotton RC	.50
109	Brad Wilkerson RC	3.00
110	Jon Rauch RC	.50

2000 Bowman Draft Picks and Prospects

		NM/M
Complete Set (110):		40.00
Common Player:		.15
1	Pat Burrell	.25
2	Rafael Furcal	.15
3	Grant Roberts	.15
4	Barry Zito	.50
5	Julio Zuleta	.15
6	Mark Mulder	.25
7	Rob Bell	.15
8	Adam Piatt	.15
9	Mike Lamb	.15

Pedro Feliz

10	Pablo Ozuna	.15
11	Jason Tyner	.15
12	Jason Marquis	.15
13	Eric Munson	.15
14	Seth Etherton	.15
15	Milton Bradley	.15
16	Nick Green	.15
17	Chin-Feng Chen RC	1.00
18	Matt Boone RC	.25
19	Kevin Gregg RC	.25
20	Eddy Garabito RC	.25
21	Aaron Capista RC	.25
22	Esteban German RC	.25
23	Derek Thompson RC	.25
24	Phil Merrell RC	.25
25	Brian O'Connor RC	.25
26	Yamid Haad	.15
27	Hector Mercado RC	.25
28	Jason Woolf RC	.25
29	Eddie Furniss RC	.25
30	Cha Sueng Baek RC	.25
31	Colby Lewis RC	.25
32	Pasqual Coco RC	.25
33	Jorge Cantu RC	.50
34	Erasmo Ramirez RC	.25
35	Bobby Kielty RC	.50
36	Joaquin Benoit RC	.25
37	Brian Esposito RC	.25
38	Michael Wenner	.15
39	Juan Rincon RC	.25
40	Yorvit Torrealba RC	.25
41	Chad Durham RC	.25
42	Jim Mann RC	.25
43	Shane Loux RC	.25
44	Luis Rivas	.15
45	Ken Chenard RC	.25
46	Mike Lockwood RC	.25
47	Yovanny Lara RC	.25
48	Bubba Carpenter RC	.25
49	Jeremy Griffiths RC	.25
50	John Stephens RC	.25
51	Pedro Feliz RC	.75
52	Kenny Kelly RC	.25
53	Neil Jenkins RC	.25
54	Mike Glendenning RC	.25
55	Bo Porter	.15
56	Eric Byrnes	.15
57	Tony Alvarez RC	.25
58	Kazuhiro Sasaki RC	.50
59	Chad Durbin RC	.25
60	Mike Bynum RC	.25
61	Travis Wilson RC	.25
62	Jose Leon RC	.25
63	Bill Ortega RC	.25
64	Geraldo Guzman RC	.25
65	Craig Anderson RC	.25
66	Carlos Silva RC	.25
67	Brad Thomas RC	.25
68	Chin-Hui Tsao RC	.75
69	Mark Buehrle RC	2.00
70	Juan Salas RC	.25
71	Denny Abreu RC	.25
72	Keith McDonald RC	.25
73	Chris Richard RC	.25
74	Tomas de la Rosa RC	.25
75	Vicente Padilla	.50
76	Justin Brunette RC	.25
77	Scott Linebrink RC	.25
78	Jeff Sparks RC	.25
79	Tike Redman RC	.25
80	John Lackey RC	1.50
81	Joe Strong RC	.25
82	Brian Tollberg RC	.25
83	Steve Sisco RC	.25
84	Chris Clapinski	.15
85	Augie Ojeda RC	.25
86	Adrian Gonzalez RC	2.50
87	Mike Stodolka RC	.25
88	Adam Johnson RC	.25
89	Matt Wheatland RC	.25
90	Corey Smith RC	.25
91	Rocco Baldelli RC	3.00
92	Keith Bucktrot RC	.25
93	Adam Wainwright RC	1.50
94	Blaine Boyer RC	.25
95	Aaron Herr RC	.25
96	Scott Thorman RC	1.00
97	Brian Digby RC	.25
98	Josh Shortslef RC	.25
99	Sean Smith RC	.25
100	Alex Cruz RC	.25

101	Marc Love RC	.25
102	Kevin Lee RC	.25
103	Victor Ramos RC	.25
104	Jason Kanoi RC	.25
105	Luis Escobar RC	.25
106	Tripper Johnson RC	.25
107	Phil Dumatrait RC	.25
108	Bryan Edwards RC	.25
109	Grady Sizemore RC	20.00
110	Thomas Mitchell RC	.25

Autograph

Pat Burrell

		NM/M
Common Autograph:		5.00
Inserted 1:Set		
1	Pat Burrell	20.00
2	Rafael Furcal	20.00
3	Grant Roberts	5.00
4	Barry Zito	20.00
5	Julio Zuleta	5.00
6	Mark Mulder	10.00
7	Bob Bell	5.00
8	Adam Piatt	5.00
9	Mike Lamb	10.00
10	Pablo Ozuna	5.00
11	Jason Tyner	5.00
12	Jason Marquis	10.00
13	Eric Munson	6.00
14	Seth Etherton	5.00
15	Milton Bradley	15.00
16	Not Issued	
17	Michael Wenner	5.00
18	Mike Glendenning	5.00
19	Tony Alvarez	5.00
20	Adrian Gonzalez	70.00
21	Corey Smith	10.00
22	Matt Wheatland	5.00
23	Adam Johnson	5.00
24	Mike Stodolka	5.00
25	Rocco Baldelli	20.00
26	Juan Rincon	5.00
27	Chad Durbin	5.00
28	Yorvit Torrealba	5.00
29	Nick Green	10.00
30	Derek Thompson	5.00
31	John Lackey	50.00
32	Not Issued	
33	Kevin Gregg	8.00
34	Not Issued	
35	Denny Abreu	5.00
36	Brian Tollberg	5.00
37	Yamid Haad	5.00
38	Grady Sizemore	225.00
39	Carlos Silva	10.00
40	Jorge Cantu	25.00
41	Bobby Kielty	5.00
42	Scott Thorman	10.00
43	Juan Salas	10.00
44	Phil Dumatrait	5.00
45	Not Issued	
46	Mike Lockwood	5.00
47	Yovanny Lara	5.00
48	Tripper Johnson	5.00
49	Colby Lewis	5.00
50	Neil Jenkins	5.00
51	Keith Bucktrot	5.00
52	Eric Byrnes	25.00
53	Aaron Herr	5.00
54	Erasmo Ramirez	5.00
55	Chris Richard	5.00
56	Not Issued	
57	Mike Bynum	5.00
58	Brian Esposito	5.00
59	Chris Clapinski	5.00
60	Augie Ojeda	5.00

2000 Bowman's Best

		NM/M
Complete Set (200):		275.00
Common Player:		.20
Common Rookie (151-200):		5.00
Production 2,999 Sets		
Pack (4):		4.00
Box (24):		75.00
1	Nomar Garciaparra	2.00
2	Chipper Jones	1.50
3	Damion Easley	.20
4	Bernie Williams	.40
5	Barry Bonds	3.00
6	Jermaine Dye	.20
7	John Olerud	.20

JUAN GONZALEZ

8	Mike Hampton	.20
9	Cal Ripken Jr.	3.00
10	Jeff Bagwell	1.00
11	Troy Glaus	1.00
12	J.D. Drew	.40
13	Jeromy Burnitz	.20
14	Carlos Delgado	.75
15	Shawn Green	.40
16	Kevin Millwood	.40
17	Rondell White	.20
18	Scott Rolen	.75
19	Jeff Cirillo	.20
20	Barry Larkin	.20
21	Brian Giles	.20
22	Roger Clemens	1.75
23	Manny Ramirez	1.00
24	Alex Gonzalez	.20
25	Mark Grace	.35
26	Fernando Tatis	.20
27	Randy Johnson	1.00
28	Roger Cedeno	.20
29	Brian Jordan	.20
30	Kevin Brown	.40
31	Greg Vaughn	.20
32	Roberto Alomar	.50
33	Larry Walker	.20
34	Rafael Palmeiro	.75
35	Curt Schilling	.50
36	Orlando Hernandez	.20
37	Todd Walker	.20
38	Juan Gonzalez	1.00
39	Sean Casey	.35
40	Tony Gwynn	1.50
41	Albert Belle	.20
42	Gary Sheffield	.40
43	Michael Barrett	.20
44	Preston Wilson	.20
45	Jim Thome	.40
46	Shannon Stewart	.20
47	Mo Vaughn	.20
48	Ben Grieve	.20
49	Adrian Beltre	.35
50	Sammy Sosa	2.00
51	Bob Abreu	.20
52	Edgardo Alfonzo	.20
53	Carlos Febles	.20
54	Frank Thomas	1.00
55	Alex Rodriguez	2.50
56	Cliff Floyd	.20
57	Jose Canseco	.40
58	Erubiel Durazo	.20
59	Tim Hudson	.50
60	Craig Biggio	.20
61	Eric Karros	.20
62	Mike Mussina	.50
63	Robin Ventura	.20
64	Carlos Beltran	.50
65	Pedro Martinez	1.00
66	Gabe Kapler	.20
67	Jason Kendall	.20
68	Derek Jeter	3.00
69	Magglio Ordonez	.50
70	Mike Piazza	2.00
71	Mike Lieberthal	.20
72	Andres Galarraga	.20
73	Raul Mondesi	.20
74	Eric Chavez	.40
75	Greg Maddux	1.50
76	Matt Williams	.30
77	Kris Benson	.20
78	Ivan Rodriguez	.50
79	Pokey Reese	.20
80	Vladimir Guerrero	1.00
81	Mark McGwire	2.50
82	Vinny Castilla	.20
83	Todd Helton	1.00
84	Andruw Jones	.75
85	Ken Griffey Jr.	2.00
86	Mark McGwire	1.25
87	Derek Jeter	1.50
88	Chipper Jones	.75
89	Nomar Garciaparra	1.00
90	Sammy Sosa	.75
91	Cal Ripken Jr.	1.50
92	Juan Gonzalez	.50
93	Alex Rodriguez	1.25
94	Barry Bonds	1.50
95	Sean Casey	.25
96	Vladimir Guerrero	.50
97	Mike Piazza	1.00
98	Shawn Green	.25

99	Jeff Bagwell	.50
100	Ken Griffey Jr.	1.00
101	Rick Ankiel	.50
102	John Patterson	.20
103	David Walling	.20
104	Michael Restovich	.20
105	A.J. Burnett	.20
106	Matt Riley	.20
107	Chad Hermansen	.20
108	Choo Freeman	.20
109	Mark Quinn	.20
110	Corey Patterson	.40
111	Ramon Ortiz	.20
112	Vernon Wells	.40
113	Milton Bradley	.20
114	Travis Dawkins	.20
115	Sean Burroughs	.35
116	Willi Mo Pena	.40
117	Dee Brown	.20
118	C.C. Sabathia	.20
119	Larry Bigbie RC	.20
120	Octavio Dotel	.20
121	Kip Wells	.20
122	Ben Petrick	.20
123	Mark Mulder	.40
124	Jason Standridge	.20
125	Adam Piatt	.20
126	Steve Lomasney	.20
127	Jayson Werth	.20
128	Alex Escobar	.20
129	Ryan Anderson	.20
130	Adam Dunn	.50
131	Omar Ortiz	.20
132	Brad Penny	.20
133	Daryle Ward	.20
134	Eric Munson	.20
135	Nick Johnson	.50
136	Jason Jennings	.20
137	Tim Raines Jr.	.20
138	Ruben Mateo	.20
139	Jack Cust	.20
140	Rafael Furcal	.20
141	Eric Gagne	.35
142	Tony Armas	.20
143	Mike Paradis	.20
144	Chris George	.20
145	Alfonso Soriano	.75
146	Josh Hamilton	.75
147	Michael Cuddyer	.35
148	Jay Gehrke	.20
149	Josh Girdley	.20
150	Pat Burrell	.75
151	Brett Myers RC	10.00
152	Scott Seabol RC	5.00
153	Keith Reed RC	5.00
154	Francisco Rodriguez RC	20.00
155	Barry Zito RC	20.00
156	Pat Manning RC	5.00
157	Ben Christensen RC	5.00
158	Corey Myers RC	5.00
159	Wascar Serrano RC	5.00
160	Wes Anderson RC	5.00
161	Andy Tracy RC	5.00
162	Cesar Saba RC	5.00
163	Mike Lamb RC	5.00
164	Bobby Bradley RC	5.00
165	Vince Faison RC	5.00
166	Ty Howington RC	8.00
167	Ken Harvey RC	8.00
168	Josh Kalinowski RC	5.00
169	Ruben Salazar RC	5.00
170	Aaron Rowand RC	10.00
171	Ramon Santiago RC	5.00
172	Scott Sobkowiak RC	5.00
173	Lyle Overbay RC	10.00
174	Rico Washington RC	5.00
175	Rick Asadoorian RC	5.00
176	Matt Ginter RC	5.00
177	Jason Stumm RC	5.00
178	B.J. Garbe RC	5.00
179	Mike MacDougal RC	5.00
180	Ryan Christianson RC	5.00
181	Kurt Ainsworth RC	5.00
182	Brad Baisley RC	5.00
183	Ben Broussard RC	5.00
184	Aaron McNeal RC	5.00
185	John Sneed RC	5.00
186	Junior Brignac RC	5.00
187	Chance Caple RC	5.00
188	Scott Downs RC	5.00
189	Matt Cepicky RC	5.00
190	Chin-Feng Chen RC	20.00
191	Johan Santana RC	100.00
192	Brad Baker RC	5.00
193	Jason Repko RC	5.00
194	Craig Dingman RC	5.00
195	Chris Wakeland RC	5.00
196	Rogelio Arias RC	5.00
197	Luis Matos RC	8.00
198	Robert Ramsay RC	5.00
199	Willie Bloomquist RC	20.00
200	Tony Pena Jr. RC	5.00

Bets

NM/M

Complete Set (10):		10.00
Common Player:		.75
Inserted 1:15		
1	Pat Burrell	2.00
2	Alfonso Soriano	2.00
3	Corey Patterson	1.50
4	Eric Munson	.75
5	Sean Burroughs	1.00
6	Rafael Furcal	.75
7	Rick Ankiel	1.00
8	Nick Johnson	1.50
9	Ruben Mateo	.75
10	Josh Hamilton	1.00

Franchise 2000

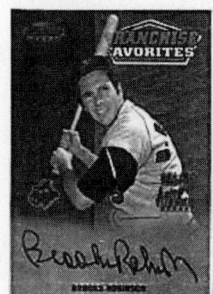

NM/M

Complete Set (25):		60.00
Common Player:		1.00
Inserted 1:18		
1	Cal Ripken Jr.	8.00
2	Nomar Garciaparra	6.00
3	Frank Thomas	2.00
4	Manny Ramirez	2.00
5	Juan Gonzalez	1.50
6	Carlos Beltran	2.00
7	Derek Jeter	8.00
8	Alex Rodriguez	6.00
9	Ben Grieve	1.00
10	Jose Canseco	1.50
11	Ivan Rodriguez	1.50
12	Mo Vaughn	1.00
13	Randy Johnson	3.00
14	Chipper Jones	4.00
15	Sammy Sosa	5.00
16	Ken Griffey Jr.	5.00
17	Larry Walker	1.00
18	Preston Wilson	1.00
19	Jeff Bagwell	2.00
20	Shawn Green	1.00
21	Vladimir Guerrero	2.00
22	Mike Piazza	5.00
23	Scott Rolen	2.00
24	Tony Gwynn	3.50
25	Barry Bonds	8.00

Franchise Favorites Autograph

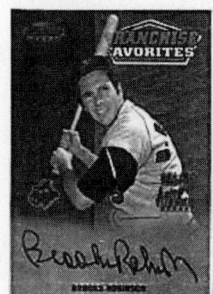

NM/M

Common Player:		20.00
Version A & B 1:1,291		
Version C 1:5,153		
1A	Sean Casey	20.00
1B	Johnny Bench	50.00

1C	Sean Casey, Johnny Bench	100.00
2A	Cal Ripken Jr.	125.00
2B	Brooks Robinson	50.00
2C	Cal Ripken Jr., Brooks Robinson	250.00

Franchise Favorites

NM/M

Complete Set (6):		15.00
Common Player:		1.00
Inserted 1:17		
1A	Sean Casey	1.00
1B	Johnny Bench	3.00
1C	Sean Casey, Johnny Bench	3.00
2A	Cal Ripken Jr.	5.00
2B	Brooks Robinson	2.00
2C	Cal Ripken Jr., Brooks Robinson	5.00

Locker Room Collection Autographs

NM/M

Common Player:		8.00
Inserted 1:57		
1	Carlos Beltran	25.00
2	Rick Ankiel	20.00
3	Vernon Wells	12.00
4	Ruben Mateo	8.00
5	Ben Petrick	8.00
6	Adam Piatt	8.00
7	Eric Munson	8.00
8	Alfonso Soriano	40.00
9	Kerry Wood	25.00
10	Jack Cust	8.00
11	Rafael Furcal	15.00
12	Josh Hamilton	50.00
13	Brad Penny	8.00
14	Dee Brown	8.00
15	Milton Bradley	12.00
16	Ryan Anderson	8.00
17	John Patterson	8.00
18	Nick Johnson	10.00
19	Peter Bergeron	8.00

Locker Room Collection Lumber

NM/M

Common Player:		5.00
Inserted 1:376		
1	Carlos Beltran	15.00
2	Rick Ankiel	5.00
3	Vernon Wells	10.00
4	Adam Kennedy	5.00
5	Ben Petrick	5.00
6	Adam Piatt	5.00
7	Eric Munson	5.00
8	Rafael Furcal	8.00
9	J.D. Drew	8.00
10	Pat Burrell	10.00

Locker Room Collection Jerseys

NM/M

Common Player:		4.00
Inserted 1:206		
1	Carlos Beltran	12.00
2	Rick Ankiel	5.00
3	Adam Kennedy	4.00
4	Ben Petrick	4.00
5	Adam Piatt	4.00

Rookie Signed Baseballs

NM/M

Complete Set (5):		75.00

Best Bets

7	Rick Ankiel	1.00
8	Nick Johnson	1.50
9	Ruben Mateo	.75
10	Josh Hamilton	1.00

Selections

Common Player:	15.00
Inserted 1:688	
1 Josh Hamilton	40.00
2 Rick Ankiel	20.00
3 Alfonso Soriano	50.00
4 Nick Johnson	30.00
5 Corey Patterson	20.00

	NM/M
Complete Set (15):	50.00
Common Player:	1.00
Inserted 1:30	
1 Alex Rodriguez	7.50
2 Ken Griffey Jr.	6.00
3 Pat Burrell	2.00
4 Mark McGwire	7.50
5 Derek Jeter	10.00
6 Nomar Garciaparra	6.00
7 Mike Piazza	6.00
8 Josh Hamilton	1.00
9 Cal Ripken Jr.	10.00
10 Jeff Bagwell	2.50
11 Chipper Jones	5.00
12 Jose Canseco	1.50
13 Carlos Beltran	2.00
14 Kerry Wood	2.00
15 Ben Grieve	1.00

Year By Year

	NM/M
Complete Set (10):	25.00
Common Card:	1.50
Inserted 1:23	
1 Sammy Sosa, Ken Griffey Jr.	4.00
2 Nomar Garciaparra, Vladimir Guerrero	4.00
3 Alex Rodriguez, Jeff Cirillo	5.00
4 Mike Piazza, Pedro Martinez	4.00
5 Derek Jeter, Edgardo Alfonzo	6.00
6 Alfonso Soriano, Rick Ankiel	2.00
7 Mark McGwire, Barry Bonds	6.00
8 Juan Gonzalez, Larry Walker	1.50
9 Ivan Rodriguez, Jeff Bagwell	1.50
10 Shawn Green, Manny Ramirez	1.50

2001 Bowman

LUIS MONTANEZ • SS
CHICAGO CUBS

	NM/M
Complete Set (440):	140.00
Common Player:	.15
Common Rookie:	.25
Golds:	1-2X
Inserted 1:1	

Pack (10):	8.00
Box (24):	160.00
1 Jason Giambi	.40
2 Rafael Furcal	.25
3 Rick Ankiel	.25
4 Freddy Garcia	.15
5 Magglio Ordonez	.50
6 Bernie Williams	.40
7 Kenny Lofton	.15
8 Al Leiter	.15
9 Albert Belle	.15
10 Craig Biggio	.25
11 Mark Mulder	.15
12 Carlos Delgado	.40
13 Darin Erstad	.25
14 Richie Sexson	.15
15 Randy Johnson	.75
16 Greg Maddux	1.50
17 Cliff Floyd	.15
18 Mark Buehrle	.15
19 Chris Singleton	.15
20 Orlando Hernandez	.20
21 Javier Vazquez	.15
22 Jeff Kent	.25
23 Jim Thome	.50
24 John Olerud	.15
25 Jason Kendall	.15
26 Scott Rolen	.50
27 Tony Gwynn	.75
28 Edgardo Alfonzo	.25
29 Pokey Reese	.15
30 Todd Helton	.50
31 Mark Quinn	.15
32 Dan Tosca RC	.25
33 Dean Palmer	.15
34 Jacque Jones	.15
35 Ray Durham	.15
36 Rafael Palmeiro	.50
37 Carl Everett	.15
38 Ryan Dempster	.15
39 Randy Wolf	.15
40 Vladimir Guerrero	.75
41 Livan Hernandez	.15
42 Mo Vaughn	.15
43 Shannon Stewart	.15
44 Preston Wilson	.15
45 Jose Vidro	.15
46 Fred McGriff	.15
47 Kevin Brown	.25
48 Peter Bergeron	.15
49 Miguel Tejada	.50
50 Chipper Jones	.75
51 Edgar Martinez	.15
52 Tony Batista	.15
53 Jorge Posada	.40
54 Ricky Ledee	.15
55 Sammy Sosa	1.00
56 Steve Cox	.15
57 Tony Armas Jr.	.15
58 Gary Sheffield	.40
59 Bartolo Colon	.15
60 Pat Burrell	.40
61 Jay Payton	.15
62 Sean Casey	.25
63 Larry Walker	.25
64 Mike Mussina	.40
65 Nomar Garciaparra	.75
66 Darren Dreifort	.15
67 Richard Hidalgo	.15
68 Troy Glaus	.40
69 Ben Grieve	.15
70 Jim Edmonds	.40
71 Raul Mondesi	.15
72 Andruw Jones	.50
73 Luis Castillo	.15
74 Mike Sweeney	.15
75 Derek Jeter	2.00
76 Ruben Mateo	.15
77 Carlos Lee	.40
78 Cristian Guzman	.15
79 Mike Hampton	.25
80 J.D. Drew	.25
81 Matt Lawton	.15
82 Moises Alou	.25
83 Terrence Long	.15
84 Geoff Jenkins	.15
85 Manny Ramirez	.75
86 Johnny Damon	.50
87 Barry Larkin	.25
88 Pedro Martinez	.75
89 Juan Gonzalez	.40
90 Roger Clemens	2.00
91 Carlos Beltran	.50
92 Brad Radke	.15
93 Orlando Cabrera	.15
94 Roberto Alomar	.50
95 Barry Bonds	2.00
96 Tim Hudson	.25
97 Tom Glavine	.25
98 Jeromy Burnitz	.15
99 Adrian Beltre	.25
100 Mike Piazza	1.00
101 Kerry Wood	.40
102 Steve Finley	.15
103 Alex Cora	.15
104 Bob Abreu	.25
105 Neifi Perez	.15
106 Mark Redman	.15
107 Paul Konerko	.25
108 Jermaine Dye	.25
109 Brian Giles	.25
110 Ivan Rodriguez	.50
111 Vinny Castilla	.15
112 Adam Kennedy	.15
113 Eric Chavez	.25
114 Billy Koch	.15
115 Shawn Green	.25
116 Matt Williams	.15
117 Greg Vaughn	.15
118 Gabe Kapler	.15
119 Jeff Cirillo	.15
120 Frank Thomas	.50
121 David Justice	.15
122 Cal Ripken Jr.	3.00
123 Rich Aurilia	.15
124 Curt Schilling	.40
125 Barry Zito	.25
126 Brian Jordan	.15
127 Chan Ho Park	.15
128 J.T. Snow Jr.	.15
129 Kazuhiro Sasaki	.15
130 Alex Rodriguez	2.00
131 Mariano Rivera	.25
132 Eric Milton	.15
133 Andy Pettitte	.25
134 Scott Elarton	.15
135 Ken Griffey Jr.	1.50
136 Bengie Molina	.15
137 Jeff Bagwell	.50
138 Kevin Millwood	.25
139 Tino Martinez	.25
140 Mark McGwire	1.50
141 Larry Barnes	.15
142 John Buck RC	.25
143 Freddie Bynum RC	.25
144 Abraham Nunez	.15
145 Felix Diaz RC	.25
146 Horatio Estrada RC	.25
147 Ben Diggins	.15
148 Tsuyoshi Shinjo RC	.50
149 Rocco Baldelli	.25
150 Rod Barajas	.15
151 Luis Terrero	.15
152 Milton Bradley	.15
153 Kurt Ainsworth	.15
154 Russell Branyan	.15
155 Ryan Anderson	.15
156 Mitch Jones RC	.25
157 Chip Ambres	.15
158 Steve Bennett RC	.25
159 Ivanon Coffie	.15
160 Sean Burroughs	.25
161 Keith Bucktrot	.15
162 Tony Alvarez	.15
163 Joaquin Benoit	.15
164 Rick Asadoorian	.15
165 Ben Broussard	.25
166 Ryan Madson RC	1.50
167 Dee Brown	.15
168 Sergio Contreras RC	.25
169 John Barnes	.15
170 Ben Washburn RC	.50
171 Erick Almonte RC	.25
172 Shawn Fagan RC	.25
173 Gary Johnson RC	.25
174 Brady Clark	.15
175 Grant Roberts	.15
176 Tony Torcato	.15
177 Ramon Castro	.15
178 Esteban German	.15
179 Joe Hamer RC	.25
180 Nick Neugebauer	.15
181 Dernell Stenson	.15
182 Yhency Brazoban RC	.40
183 Aaron Myette	.15
184 Juan Sosa	.15
185 Brandon Inge	.15
186 Domingo Guante RC	.25
187 Adrian Brown	.15
188 Deivi Mendez RC	.25
189 Luis Matos	.15
190 Pedro Liriano RC	.50
191 Donnie Bridges	.15
192 Alex Cintron	.15
193 Jace Brewer	.15
194 Ron Davenport RC	.50
195 Jason Belcher RC	.25
196 Adrian Hernandez RC	.25
197 Bobby Kielty	.15
198 Reggie Griggs RC	.25
199 Reggie Abercrombie RC	1.00
200 Troy Farnsworth RC	.50
201 Matt Belisle	.15
202 Miguel Villilo RC	.50
203 Adam Everett	.15
204 John Lackey	.25
205 Pasqual Coco	.15
206 Adam Wainwright	.25
207 Matt White RC	.25
208 Chin-Feng Chen	.25
209 Jeff Andra RC	.25
210 Willie Bloomquist	.15
211 Wes Anderson	.15
212 Enrique Cruz	.15
213 Jerry Hairston Jr.	.15
214 Mike Bynum	.15
215 Brian Hitchcox RC	.25
216 Ryan Christianson	.25
217 J.J. Davis	.15
218 Jovanny Cedeno	.15
219 Elvin Nina	.15
220 Alex Graman	.15
221 Arturo McDowell	.15
222 Deivi Santos RC	.25
223 Jody Gerut	.15
224 Sun-Woo Kim	.50
225 Jimmy Rollins	.50
226 Pappy Ndungidi	.15
227 Ruben Salazar	.15
228 Josh Girdley	.15
229 Carl Crawford	.40
230 Luis Montanez RC	.50
231 Ramon Carvajal RC	.25
232 Matt Riley	.15
233 Ben Davis	.15
234 Jason Grabowski	.15
235 Chris George	.15
236 Hank Blalock RC	5.00
237 Roy Oswalt	.25
238 Eric Reynolds RC	.15
239 Brian Cole	.15
240 Denny Bautista RC	.75
241 Hector Garcia RC	.25
242 Joe Thurston RC	.50
243 Brad Cresse	.25
244 Corey Patterson	.25
245 Brett Evert RC	.25
246 Elpidio Guzman RC	.25
247 Vernon Wells	.25
248 Roberto Miniel RC	.25
249 Brian Bass RC	.50
250 Mark Burnett RC	.25
251 Juan Silvestre	.15
252 Pablo Ozuna	.15
253 Jayson Werth	.15
254 Russ Jacobsen RC	.25
255 Chad Hermansen	.15
256 Travis Hafner RC	5.00
257 Bradley Baker	.15
258 Gookie Dawkins	.15
259 Michael Cuddyer	.15
260 Mark Buehrle	.15
261 Ricardo Aramboles	.15
262 Esix Snead RC	.25
263 Wilson Betemit RC	.50
264 Albert Pujols RC	60.00
265 Joe Lawrence	.15
266 Ramon Ortiz	.15
267 Ben Sheets	.50
268 Luke Lockwood RC	.25
269 Toby Hall	.15
270 Jack Cust	.15
271 Pedro Feliz	.15
272 Noel Devarez RC	.25
273 Josh Beckett	.50
274 Alex Escobar	.15
275 Doug Gredvig RC	.15
276 Marcus Giles	.15
277 Jon Rauch	.15
278 Brian Schmitt RC	.25
279 Seung Song RC	.50
280 Kevin Mench	.15
281 Adam Eaton	.15
282 Shawn Sonnier	.15
283 Andy Van Hekken RC	.25
284 Aaron Rowand	.15
285 Tony Blanco RC	.50
286 Ryan Kohlmeier	.15
287 C.C. Sabathia	.40
288 Bubba Crosby	.15
289 Josh Hamilton	.25
290 Dee Haynes RC	.25
291 Jason Marquis	.15
292 Julio Zuleta	.15
293 Carlos Hernandez	.15
294 Matt LeCroy	.15
295 Andy Beal RC	.25
296 Carlos Pena	.25
297 Reggie Taylor	.15
298 Bob Keppel RC	.25
299 Miguel Cabrera (Photo actually Manuel Esquivia.)	.75
300 Ryan Franklin	.15
301 Brandon Phillips	.25
302 Victor Hall RC	.25
303 Tony Pena Jr.	.15
304 Jim Journell RC	.25
305 Cristian Guerrero	.25
306 Miguel Olivo	.15
307 Jin Ho Cho	.15
308 Choo Freeman	.15
309 Danny Borrell RC	.25
310 Doug Mientkiewicz	.15
311 Aaron Herr	.15
312 Keith Ginter	.15
313 Felipe Lopez	.15
314 Jeff Goldbach RC	.15
315 Travis Harper	.15
316 Paul LoDuca	.25
317 Joe Torres	.15
318 Eric Byrnes	.15
319 George Lombard	.15
320 David Krynzel	.15
321 Ben Christensen	.15
322 Aubrey Huff	.15
323 Lyle Overbay	.15
324 Sean McGowan	.15
325 Jeff Heaverlo	.15
326 Timo Perez	.15
327 Octavio Martinez RC	.15
328 Vince Faison	.15
329 David Parrish RC	.15
330 Bobby Bradley	.15
331 Jason Miller RC	.25
332 Corey Spencer RC	.25
333 Craig House	.15
334 Maxim St. Pierre RC	.25
335 Adam Johnson	.15
336 Joe Crede	.15
337 Greg Nash RC	.25
338 Chad Durbin	.15
339 Pat Magness RC	.15
340 Matt Wheatland	.15
341 Julio Lugo	.15

342	Grady Sizemore	.50
343	Adrian Gonzalez	.25
344	Tim Raines Jr.	.15
345	Rainier Olmedo RC	.25
346	Phil Dumatrait	.15
347	Brandon Mims RC	.25
348	Jason Jennings	.15
349	Phil Wilson RC	.25
350	Jason Hart	.15
351	Cesar Izturis	.25
352	Matt Butler RC	.25
353	David Kelton	.15
354	Luke Prokopec	.15
355	Corey Smith	.15
356	Joel Pineiro RC	.75
357	Ken Chenard	.15
358	Keith Reed	.15
359	David Walling	.15
360	Alexis Gomez RC	.50
361	Justin Morneau RC	10.00
362	Josh Fogg RC	.50
363	J.R. House	.15
364	Andy Tracy	.15
365	Kenny Kelly	.15
366	Aaron McNeal	.15
367	Nick Johnson	.15
368	Brian Esposito	.15
369	Charles Frazier RC	.25
370	Scott Heard	.15
371	Patrick Strange	.15
372	Mike Meyers	.15
373	Ryan Ludwick RC	5.00
374	Brad Wilkerson	.15
375	Allen Levrault	.15
376	Seth McClung RC	.40
377	Joe Nathan	.15
378	Rafael Soriano RC	.75
379	Chris Richard	.15
380	Xavier Nady	.15
381	Tike Redman	.15
382	Adam Dunn	.50
383	Jared Abruzzo RC	.25
384	Jason Richardson RC	.25
385	Matt Holliday	.50
386	Darwin Cubillian RC	.25
387	Mike Nannini	.15
388	Blake Williams RC	.15
389	Valentino Pascucci RC	.25
390	Jon Garland	.15
391	Josh Pressley	.15
392	Jose Ortiz	.15
393	Ryan Hannaman RC	.25
394	Steve Smyth RC	.25
395	John Patterson	.15
396	Chad Petty RC	.25
397	Jake Peavy RC	10.00
398	Onix Mercado RC	.25
399	Jason Romano	.15
400	Luis Torres RC	.25
401	Casey Fossum RC	.25
402	Eduardo Figueroa RC	.25
403	Bryan Barnowski RC	.25
404	Tim Redding	.15
405	Jason Standridge	.15
406	Marvin Seale RC	.25
407	Todd Moser	.15
408	Alex Gordon	.15
409	Steve Smitherman RC	.75
410	Ben Petrick	.15
411	Eric Munson	.15
412	Luis Rivas	.15
413	Matt Ginter	.15
414	Alfonso Soriano	.50
415	Rafael Boitel RC	.25
416	Dany Morban RC	.25
417	Justin Woodrowc RC	.25
418	Wilfredo Rodriguez	.15
419	Derrick Van Dusen RC	.25
420	Josh Spoerl RC	.15
421	Juan Pierre	.25
422	J.C. Romero	.15
423	Ed Rogers RC	.25
424	Tomokazu Ohka	.25
425	Ben Hendrickson RC	.25
426	Carlos Zambrano	.25
427	Brett Myers	.15
428	Scott Seabol	.15
429	Thomas Mitchell	.15
430	Jose Reyes RC	25.00
431	Kip Wells	.15
432	Willi Mo Pena	.15
433	Adam Pettyjohn RC	.25
434	Austin Kearns	.15
435	Rico Washington	.15
436	Doug Nickle RC	.25
437	Steve Lomasney	.15
438	Jason Jones RC	.25
439	Bobby Seay	.15
440	Justin Wayne RC	.50

Autographs

JOSH PRESSLEY

		NM/M
Common Autograph:		5.00
Inserted 1:74		
BB	Brian Bannister	5.00
WB	Wilson Betemit	15.00
JB	Jason Botts	5.00
SB	Sean Burroughs	5.00
FB	Freddie Bynum	5.00
ND	Noel Devarez	5.00
JD	Jose Diaz	5.00
BD	Ben Diggins	5.00
AE	Alex Escobar	5.00
RF	Rafael Furcal	15.00
AG	Adrian Gonzalez	15.00

AKG	Alex Gordon	5.00
AJG	Alex Graman	5.00
CG	Cristian Guerrero	5.00
TH	Travis Hafner	30.00
JH	Josh Hamilton	50.00
JWH	Jason Hart	5.00
JRH	J.R. House	5.00
RJ	Russ Jacobson	5.00
AJ	Adam Johnson	5.00
TJ	Tripper Johnson	5.00
DWK	David Kelton	5.00
DK	David Krynzel	5.00
PR	Pedro Liriano	5.00
SM	Sean McGowan	5.00
KM	Kevin Mench	5.00
LM	Luis Montanez	5.00
JM	Justin Morneau	75.00
LO	Lyle Overbay	10.00
ADP	Adam Piatt	5.00
JP	Josh Pressley	5.00
AP	Albert Pujols	500.00
BS	Ben Sheets	20.00
SDS	Steve Smyth	5.00
SS	Shawn Sonnier	5.00
SU	Sixto Urena	5.00
MV	Miguel Villilo	5.00
BW	Brad Wilkerson	10.00
BZ	Barry Zito	15.00

Autoproofs

Common Player:	
Inserted 1:18,259H	
Inserted 1:8,306HTA	
Redemption Expired 4/30/03	
Values Undetermined	

Autographed Rookie Reprints

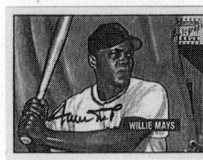

WILLIE MAYS

		NM/M
Common Autograph:		20.00
Inserted 1:2,467		
1	Yogi Berra	70.00
2	Willie Mays	200.00
3	Stan Musial	100.00
4	Duke Snider	35.00
5	Warren Spahn	50.00
6	Ralph Kiner	25.00
7	Don Larsen	30.00
8	Don Zimmer	20.00
10	Minnie Minoso	20.00

Autographed Game-Used Bat Rookie Reprints

Inserted 1:18,259	
No pricing due to scarcity.	

Autographed Three-Piece Game-Used

No pricing due to scarcity.	

Futures Game-Worn Jersey

2000 All-Star Futures Game

		NM/M
Common Player:		5.00
Inserted 1:82		
KA	Kurt Ainsworth	5.00
CA	Craig Anderson	5.00
RA	Ryan Anderson	5.00

BB	Bobby Bradley	5.00
MB	Mike Bynum	5.00
RC	Ramon Castro	5.00
CC	Chin-Feng Chen	25.00
JC	Jack Cust	5.00
TD	Travis Dawkins	5.00
RD	Randey Dorame	5.00
AE	Alex Escobar	5.00
CG	Chris George	5.00
MG	Marcus Giles	5.00
JH	Josh Hamilton	20.00
CH	Carlos Hernandez	5.00
SK	Sun-Woo Kim	5.00
FL	Felipe Lopez	5.00
EM	Eric Munson	5.00
AM	Aaron Myette	5.00
NN	Ntema Ndungidi	5.00
TO	Tomokazu Ohka	5.00
RO	Ramon Ortiz	5.00
DCP	Corey Patterson	5.00
CP	Carlos Pena	5.00
BP	Ben Petrick	5.00
GR	Grant Roberts	5.00
JR	Jason Romano	5.00
BS	Ben Sheets	6.00
CT	Chin-Hui Tsao	15.00
VW	Vernon Wells	8.00
BW	Brad Wilkerson	5.00
TW	Travis Wilson	5.00
BZ	Barry Zito	8.00
JZ	Julio Zuleta	5.00

Futures Game Three-Piece Game-Used

		NM/M
Common Player:		20.00
RC	Ramon Castro	20.00
CC	Chin-Feng Chen	80.00
JC	Jack Cust	20.00
TD	Travis Dawkins	20.00
AE	Alex Escobar	20.00
MG	Marcus Giles	20.00
JH	Josh Hamilton	40.00
FL	Felipe Lopez	20.00
EM	Eric Munson	25.00
NN	Ntema Ndungidi	20.00
DCP	Corey Patterson	25.00
CP	Carlos Pena	25.00
BP	Ben Petrick	20.00
JR	Jason Romano	20.00
VW	Vernon Wells	25.00
BW	Brad Wilkerson	25.00
TW	Travis Wilson	20.00
JZ	Julio Zuleta	20.00

Game-Used Bat Rookie Reprints

	NM/M
Common Player:	10.00
Inserted 1:1,954	
1 Willie Mays	60.00
2 Duke Snider	25.00
3 Minnie Minoso	10.00
4 Hank Bauer	10.00
5 Al Rosen	10.00

Rookie Reprints

WILLIE MAYS

	NM/M
Complete Set (25):	50.00
Common Player:	1.50
Inserted 1:12	
1 Yogi Berra	5.00
2 Ralph Kiner	2.50
3 Stan Musial	8.00
4 Warren Spahn	4.00
5 Roy Campanella	4.00
6 Bob Lemon	1.50

7	Robin Roberts	2.00
8	Duke Snider	4.00
9	Early Wynn	1.50
10	Richie Ashburn	1.50
11	Gil Hodges	2.00
12	Hank Bauer	2.00
13	Don Newcombe	1.50
14	Al Rosen	1.50
15	Willie Mays	8.00
16	Joe Garagiola	2.00
17	Whitey Ford	4.00
18	Lew Burdette	1.50
19	Gil McDougald	1.50
20	Minnie Minoso	1.50
21	Eddie Mathews	4.00
22	Harvey Kuenn	2.00
23	Don Larsen	3.00
24	Elston Howard	2.00
25	Don Zimmer	1.50

Rookie of the Year Dual Jersey

	NM/M
Inserted 1:2,202	
ROYR Kazuhiro Sasaki, Rafael Furcal	20.00

2001 Bowman Chrome

RAFAEL PALMEIRO • 1B
TEXAS RANGERS

	NM/M
Common (1-110, 201-310):	.25
Common Ref. (111-200, 311-330):	4.00
Inserted 1:4	
Common Ref. Auto. (331-350):	25.00
Production 500	
Pack (4):	15.00
Box (24):	350.00
1 Jason Giambi	.60
2 Rafael Furcal	.50
3 Bernie Williams	.50
4 Kenny Lofton	.25
5 Al Leiter	.25
6 Albert Belle	.25
7 Craig Biggio	.50
8 Mark Mulder	.40
9 Carlos Delgado	.75
10 Darin Erstad	.50
11 Richie Sexson	.40
12 Randy Johnson	1.00
13 Greg Maddux	1.50
14 Orlando Hernandez	.25
15 Javier Vazquez	.25
16 Jeff Kent	.25
17 Jim Thome	.50
18 John Olerud	.25
19 Jason Kendall	.25
20 Scott Rolen	.75
21 Tony Gwynn	1.00
22 Edgardo Alfonzo	.25
23 Pokey Reese	.25
24 Todd Helton	.75
25 Mark Quinn	.25
26 Dean Palmer	.25
27 Ray Durham	.25
28 Rafael Palmeiro	.75
29 Carl Everett	.25
30 Vladimir Guerrero	1.00
31 Livan Hernandez	.25
32 Preston Wilson	.25
33 Jose Vidro	.25
34 Fred McGriff	.25
35 Kevin Brown	.25
36 Miguel Tejada	.50
37 Chipper Jones	1.00
38 Edgar Martinez	.25
39 Tony Batista	.25
40 Jorge Posada	.50
41 Sammy Sosa	1.00
42 Gary Sheffield	.50
43 Bartolo Colon	.25
44 Pat Burrell	.50
45 Jay Payton	.25
46 Mike Mussina	.60
47 Nomar Garciaparra	.75
48 Darren Dreifort	.25
49 Richard Hidalgo	.25
50 Troy Glaus	.50
51 Ben Grieve	.25
52 Jim Edmonds	.40
53 Raul Mondesi	.25
54 Andruw Jones	.75
55 Mike Sweeney	.25
56 Derek Jeter	3.00

57 Ruben Mateo .25
58 Cristian Guzman .25
59 Mike Hampton .25
60 J.D. Drew .40
61 Matt Lawton .25
62 Moises Alou .40
63 Terrence Long .25
64 Geoff Jenkins .25
65 Manny Ramirez 1.00
66 Johnny Damon 1.00
67 Pedro Martinez 1.00
68 Juan Gonzalez .50
69 Roger Clemens 2.00
70 Carlos Beltran .75
71 Roberto Alomar .50
72 Barry Bonds 3.00
73 Tim Hudson .50
74 Tom Glavine .50
75 Jeromy Burnitz .25
76 Adrian Beltre .40
77 Mike Piazza 1.00
78 Kerry Wood .40
79 Steve Finley .25
80 Bobby Abreu .40
81 Neifi Perez .25
82 Mark Redman .25
83 Paul Konerko .40
84 Jermaine Dye .25
85 Brian Giles .25
86 Ivan Rodriguez .75
87 Adam Kennedy .25
88 Eric Chavez .40
89 Billy Koch .25
90 Shawn Green .40
91 Matt Williams .25
92 Greg Vaughn .25
93 Jeff Cirillo .25
94 Frank Thomas .75
95 David Justice .25
96 Cal Ripken Jr. 3.00
97 Curt Schilling .75
98 Barry Zito .40
99 Brian Jordan .25
100 Chan Ho Park .25
101 J.T. Snow Jr. .25
102 Kazuhiro Sasaki .25
103 Alex Rodriguez 2.50
104 Mariano Rivera .50
105 Eric Milton .25
106 Andy Pettitte .50
107 Ken Griffey Jr. 2.00
108 Bengie Molina .25
109 Jeff Bagwell .75
110 Mark McGwire 2.00
111 Dan Tosca **RC** 4.00
112 Sergio Contreras **RC** 4.00
113 Mitch Jones **RC** 4.00
114 Ramon Carvajal **RC** 4.00
115 Ryan Madson **RC** 8.00
116 Hank Blalock **RC** 25.00
117 Ben Washburn **RC** 4.00
118 Erick Almonte **RC** 4.00
119 Shawn Fagan **RC** 4.00
120 Gary Johnson **RC** 4.00
121 Brett Evert **RC** 4.00
122 Joe Hamer **RC** 4.00
123 Yhency Brazoban **RC** 4.00
124 Domingo Guante **RC** 4.00
125 Deivi Mendez **RC** 4.00
126 Adrian Hernandez **RC** 4.00
127 Reggie Abercrombie **RC** 6.00
128 Steve Bennett **RC** 4.00
129 Matt White **RC** 4.00
130 Brian Hitchcox **RC** 4.00
131 Deivis Santos **RC** 4.00
132 Luis Montanez **RC** 4.00
133 Eric Reynolds **RC** 4.00
134 Denny Bautista **RC** 8.00
135 Hector Garcia **RC** 4.00
136 Joe Thurston **RC** 6.00
137 Tsuyoshi Shinjo **RC** 6.00
138 Elpidio Guzman **RC** 4.00
139 Brian Bass **RC** 4.00
140 Mark Burnett **RC** 4.00
141 Russ Jacobsen **RC** 4.00
142 Travis Hafner **RC** 25.00
143 Wilson Betemit **RC** 12.00
144 Luke Lockwood **RC** 4.00
145 Noel Devarez **RC** 4.00
146 Doug Gredvig **RC** 4.00
147 Seung Jun Song **RC** 4.00
148 Andy Van Hekken **RC** 4.00
149 Ryan Kohlmeier 4.00
150 Dee Haynes **RC** 4.00
151 Jim Journell **RC** 4.00
152 Chad Petty **RC** 4.00
153 Danny Borrell **RC** 4.00
154 David Krynzel 4.00
155 Octavio Martinez **RC** 4.00
156 David Parrish **RC** 4.00
157 Jason Miller **RC** 4.00
158 Corey Spencer **RC** 4.00
159 Maxim St. Pierre **RC** 4.00
160 Pat Magness **RC** 4.00
161 Rainier Olmedo **RC** 4.00
162 Brandon Mims **RC** 4.00
163 Phil Wilson **RC** 4.00
164 Jose Reyes **RC** 120.00
165 Matt Butler **RC** 4.00
166 Joel Pineiro 4.00
167 Ken Chenard 4.00
168 Alexis Gomez **RC** 4.00
169 Justin Morneau **RC** 60.00
170 Josh Fogg **RC** 4.00
171 Charles Frazier **RC** 4.00
172 Ryan Ludwick **RC** 20.00
173 Seth McClung **RC** 4.00
174 Justin Wayne **RC** 4.00
175 Rafael Soriano **RC** 6.00
176 Jared Abruzzo **RC** 4.00
177 Jason Richardson **RC** 4.00
178 Darwin Cubillan **RC** 4.00
179 Blake Williams **RC** 4.00
180 Valentino Pascucci **RC** 4.00
181 Ryan Hannaman **RC** 4.00
182 Steve Smyth **RC** 4.00
183 Jake Peavy **RC** 65.00
184 Onix Mercado **RC** 4.00
185 Luis Torres **RC** 4.00
186 Casey Fossum **RC** 4.00
187 Eduardo Figueroa **RC** 4.00
188 Bryan Barnowski **RC** 4.00
189 Jason Standridge 4.00
190 Marvin Seale **RC** 4.00
191 Steve Smitherman **RC** 4.00
192 Rafael Boitel **RC** 4.00
193 Dany Morban **RC** 4.00
194 Justin Woodrowc **RC** 4.00
195 Ed Rogers **RC** 4.00
196 Ben Hendrickson **RC** 4.00
197 Thomas Mitchell 4.00
198 Adam Pettyjohn **RC** 4.00
199 Doug Nickle **RC** 4.00
200 Jason Jones **RC** 4.00
201 Larry Barnes .25
202 Ben Diggins .25
203 Dee Brown .25
204 Rocco Baldelli .50
205 Luis Terrero .25
206 Milton Bradley .50
207 Kurt Ainsworth .25
208 Sean Burroughs .25
209 Rick Asadoorian .25
210 Ramon Castro .25
211 Nick Neugebauer .25
212 Aaron Myette .25
213 Luis Matos .25
214 Donnie Bridges .25
215 Alex Cintron .25
216 Bobby Kielty .25
217 Matt Belisle .25
218 Adam Everett .25
219 John Lackey .50
220 Adam Wainwright .75
221 Jerry Hairston Jr. .25
222 Mike Bynum .25
223 Ryan Christianson .25
224 J.J. Davis .25
225 Alex Graman .25
226 Abraham Nunez .25
227 Sun-Woo Kim .25
228 Jimmy Rollins 1.00
229 Ruben Salazar .25
230 Josh Girdley .25
231 Carl Crawford .50
232 Ben Davis .25
233 Jason Grabowski .25
234 Chris George .25
235 Roy Oswalt .75
236 Brian Cole .25
237 Corey Patterson .25
238 Vernon Wells .50
239 Bradley Baker .25
240 Gookie Dawkins .25
241 Michael Cuddyer .25
242 Ricardo Aramboles .25
243 Ben Sheets .50
244 Toby Hall .25
245 Jack Cust .25
246 Pedro Feliz .25
247 Josh Beckett .75
248 Alex Escobar .25
249 Marcus Giles .25
250 Jon Rauch .25
251 Kevin Mench .25
252 Shawn Sonnier .25
253 Aaron Rowand .50
254 C.C. Sabathia .75
255 Bubba Crosby .25
256 Josh Hamilton 1.00
257 Carlos Hernandez .25
258 Carlos Pena .50
259 Miguel Cabrera (Photo actually Manuel Esquivia.) 2.50
260 Brandon Phillips .50
261 Tony Pena Jr. .25
262 Cristian Guerrero .25
263 Jin Ho Cho .25
264 Aaron Herr .25
265 Keith Ginter .25
266 Felipe Lopez .25
267 Travis Harper .25
268 Joe Torres .25
269 Eric Byrnes .50
270 Ben Christensen .25
271 Aubrey Huff .25
272 Lyle Overbay .25
273 Vince Faison .25
274 Bobby Bradley .25
275 Joe Crede .25
276 Matt Wheatland .25
277 Grady Sizemore 1.50
278 Adrian Gonzalez .75
279 Timothy Raines Jr. .25
280 Phil Dumatrait .25
281 Jason Hart .25
282 David Kelton .25
283 David Walling .25
284 J.R. House .25
285 Kenny Kelly .25
286 Aaron McNeal .25
287 Nick Johnson .25
288 Scott Heard .25
289 Brad Wilkerson .25
290 Allen Levrault .25
291 Chris Richard .25
292 Jared Sandberg .25
293 Tike Redman .25
294 Adam Dunn .75
295 Josh Pressley .25
296 Jose Ortiz .25
297 Jason Romano .25
298 Tim Redding .25
299 Alex Gordon .25
300 Ben Petrick .25
301 Eric Munson .25
302 Luis Rivas .25
303 Matt Ginter .25
304 Alfonso Soriano .75
305 Wilfredo Rodriguez .25
306 Brett Myers .25
307 Scott Seabol .25
308 Tony Alvarez .25
309 Donzell McDonald .25
310 Austin Kearns .25
311 Will Ohman **RC** 4.00
312 Ryan Soules **RC** 4.00
313 Cody Ross **RC** 10.00
314 Bill Whitecotton **RC** 4.00
315 Mike Burns **RC** 4.00
316 Manuel Acosta **RC** 4.00
317 Lance Niekro **RC** 6.00
318 Travis Thompson **RC** 4.00
319 Zach Sorensen **RC** 4.00
320 Austin Evans **RC** 4.00
321 Brad Stiles **RC** 4.00
322 Joe Kennedy **RC** 4.00
323 Luke Martin **RC** 4.00
324 Juan Diaz **RC** 4.00
325 Pat Hallmark **RC** 4.00
326 Christian Parker **RC** 4.00
327 Ronny Corona **RC** 4.00
328 Jermaine Clark **RC** 4.00
329 Scott Dunn **RC** 4.00
330 Scott Chiasson **RC** 4.00
331 Greg Nash/Auto. **RC** 25.00
332 Brad Cresse/Auto. 25.00
333 John Buck/Auto. **RC** 50.00
334 Freddie Bynum/Auto. **RC** 25.00
335 Felix Diaz/Auto. **RC** 25.00
336 Jason Belcher/Auto. **RC** 25.00
337 Troy Farnsworth **RC** 25.00
338 Roberto Miniel **RC** 25.00
339 Esix Snead **RC** 25.00
340 Albert Pujols **RC** 2,500
341 Jeff Andra **RC** 25.00
342 Victor Hall **RC** 25.00
343 Pedro Liriano **RC** 25.00
344 Andy Beal **RC** 25.00
345 Bob Keppel **RC** 25.00
346 Brian Schmitt **RC** 25.00
347 Ron Davenport **RC** 100.00
348 Tony Blanco **RC** 25.00
349 Reggie Griggs **RC** 25.00
350 Derrick Van Dusen **RC** 25.00
351a Ichiro Suzuki Eng. **RC** 80.00
351b Ichiro Suzuki Japanese **RC** 80.00

Gold Refractors

Stars: 8-15X
Rookies: 1.5-3X
Production 99 Sets
(See 2001 Bowman Chrome for checklist and base card values.)

X-Fractors

Stars: 4-8X
Rookies: .75-1.5X
Inserted 1:23
(See 2001 Bowman Chrome for checklist and base card values.)

Futures Game Memorabilia

NM/M

Common Player: 5.00
Inserted 1:460
KA Kurt Ainsworth 8.00
CA Craig Anderson 5.00
RA Ryan Anderson 5.00
BB Bobby Bradley 5.00
MB Mike Bynum 5.00
RC Ramon Castro 5.00
CC Chin-Feng Chen 30.00
JC Jack Cust 8.00
RD Randey Dorame 5.00
AE Alex Escobar 5.00
CG Chris George 5.00
MG Marcus Giles 5.00
JH Josh Hamilton 20.00
CH Carlos Hernandez 5.00
SK Sun-Woo Kim 5.00
FL Felipe Lopez 8.00
EM Eric Munson 5.00
AM Aaron Myette 5.00
NN Ntema Ndungidi 5.00
TO Tomokazu Ohka 5.00
DCP Corey Patterson 8.00
CP Carlos Pena 8.00
BP Ben Petrick 5.00
JR Jason Romano 5.00
BS Ben Sheets 8.00
CT Chin-Hui Tsao 40.00
BW Brad Wilkerson 8.00
TW Travis Wilson 5.00
BZ Barry Zito 8.00
JZ Julio Zuleta 5.00

Rookie Reprints

NM/M

Complete Set (25): 50.00
Common Player: 2.00
Inserted 1:12
Refractors: 2-3X
Production 299 Sets
1 Yogi Berra 5.00
2 Ralph Kiner 3.00
3 Stan Musial 6.00
4 Warren Spahn 4.00
5 Roy Campanella 4.00
6 Bob Lemon 2.00
7 Robin Roberts 2.00
8 Duke Snider 4.00
9 Early Wynn 2.00
10 Richie Ashburn 3.00
11 Gil Hodges 3.00
12 Hank Bauer 2.00
13 Don Newcombe 2.00
14 Al Rosen 2.00
15 Willie Mays 8.00
16 Joe Garagiola 3.00
17 Whitey Ford 4.00
18 Lew Burdette 2.00
19 Gil McDougald 2.00
20 Minnie Minoso 2.00
21 Eddie Mathews 4.00
22 Harvey Kuenn 2.00
23 Don Larsen 3.00
24 Elston Howard 2.00
25 Don Zimmer 2.00

Rookie Reprint Relics

NM/M

Common Player: 8.00
Inserted 1:244
1 David Justice 8.00
2 Richie Sexson 8.00
3 Sean Casey 8.00
4 Mike Piazza 40.00

5	Carlos Delgado	8.00
6	Chipper Jones	25.00

2001 Bowman Draft Picks & Prospects

ICHIRO • OF
SEATTLE MARINERS

		NM/M
Complete Set (110):		45.00
Complete Factory Set (112):		50.00
Common Player:		.10
1	Alfredo Amezaga RC	.25
2	Andrew Good	.10
3	Kelly Johnson RC	3.00
4	Larry Bigbie	.10
5	Matt Thompson RC	.40
6	Wilton Chavez RC	.40
7	Joe Borchard RC	.50
8	David Espinosa	.10
9	Zach Day RC	.50
10	Brad Hawpe RC	3.00
11	Nate Cornejo	.10
12	Jim Kavourias RC	.25
13	Brad Lidge	.10
14	Angel Berroa RC	.75
15	Lamont Matthews RC	.25
16	Jose Garcia	.10
17	Grant Balfour RC	.25
18	Ron Chiavacci RC	.25
19	Jae Seo	.10
20	Juan Rivera	.10
21	D'Angelo Jimenez	.10
22	Aaron Harang	.10
23	Marlon Byrd RC	.50
24	Sean Burnett	.25
25	Josh Pearce RC	.25
26	Brandon Duckworth RC	.25
27	Jack Taschner RC	.25
28	Bo Robinson RC	.25
29	Brent Abernathy	.10
30	David Elder RC	.25
31	Scott Cassidy RC	.25
32	Dennis Tankersley RC	.40
33	Denny Stark	.10
34	Dave Williams RC	.25
35	Boof Bonser RC	.50
36	Kris Foster RC	.25
37	Neal Musser RC	.25
38	Shawn Chacon	.10
39	Mike Rivera RC	.25
40	Will Smith RC	.25
41	Morgan Ensberg RC	.50
42	Ken Harvey	.10
43	Ricardo Rodriguez RC	.25
44	Jose Mieses RC	.25
45	Luis Maza RC	.25
46	Julio Perez RC	.25
47	Billy Traber RC	.25
48	David Martinez RC	.25
49	Coco Crisp RC	2.00
50	Mario Ramos RC	.25
51	Matt Thornton RC	.25
52	Xavier Nady	.25
53	Ryan Vogelsong	.10
54	Jim Magrane RC	.25
55	Domingo Valdez RC	.25
56	Brent Butler	.10
57	Brian Tallet RC	.25
58	Brian Reith RC	.25
59	Mario Valenzuela RC	.25
60	Bobby Hill RC	.25
61	Rich Rundles RC	.25
62	Rick Elder	.10
63	J.D. Closser	.10
64	Scot Shields	.10
65	Miguel Olivo	.10
66	Stubby Clapp RC	.25
67	Jerome Williams RC	.25
68	Jason Lane RC	.50
69	Chase Utley RC	35.00
70	Erik Bedard RC	5.00
71	Alex Herrera RC	.20
72	Juan Cruz RC	.20
73	Billy Martin RC	.20
74	Ronnie Merrill RC	.20
75	Jason Kinchen RC	.20
76	Wilken Ruan RC	.20
77	Cody Ransom RC	.20
78	Bud Smith RC	.20
79	Wily Mo Pena	.10
80	Jeff Nettles RC	.20
81	Jamaal Strong RC	.20
82	Bill Ortega	.10
83	Junior Zamora	.10

84	Ichiro Suzuki RC	8.00
85	Fernando Rodney RC	.20
86	Chris Smith RC	.20
87	John Van Benschoten RC	.50
88	Bobby Crosby RC	2.00
89	Kenny Baugh RC	.25
90	Jake Gautreau RC	.25
91	Gabe Gross RC	.50
92	Kris Honel RC	.40
93	Daniel Denham RC	.25
94	Aaron Heilman RC	.50
95	Irvin Guzman RC	1.50
96	Mike Jones RC	.50
97	John-Ford Griffin RC	.25
98	Macay McBride RC	.50
99	John Rheineckar RC	.50
100	Bronson Sardinha RC	.25
101	Jason Weintraub RC	.25
102	J.D. Martin RC	.25
103	Jayson Nix RC	.40
104	Noah Lowry RC	.50
105	Richard Lewis RC	.25
106	Brad Hennessey RC	.25
107	Jeff Mathis RC	.50
108	Jon Skaggs RC	.25
109	Justin Pope RC	.25
110	Josh Burrus RC	.25

Autographs

		NM/M
Common Autograph:		5.00
Inserted 1:Set		
JA	Jared Abruzzo	5.00
AA	Alfredo Amezaga	8.00
GA	Garrett Atkins	40.00
BB	Bobby Bradley	5.00
ANC	Antoine Cameron	5.00
ROC	Ramon Carvajal	5.00
RC	Ryan Church	25.00
AC	Alex Cintron	5.00
RD	Ryan Dittfurth	5.00
AE	Adam Everett	5.00
AF	Alex Fernandez	5.00
AG	Alexis Gomez	5.00
CG	Cristian Guerrero	5.00
BH	Beau Hale	5.00
SH	Scott Heard	5.00
AH	Aaron Herr	5.00
CI	Cesar Izturis	5.00
GJ	Gary Johnson	5.00
NJ	Nick Johnson	8.00
AK	Austin Kearns	10.00
JK	Joe Kennedy	5.00
JL	John Lackey	15.00
FL	Felipe Lopez	8.00
RI	Ryan Ludwick	50.00
RMM	Ryan Madson	10.00
TO	Tomo Ohka	5.00
RO	Roy Oswalt	25.00
CP	Christian Parra	5.00
BP	Brandon Phillips	15.00
JP	Joel Pineiro	10.00
NR	Nick Regilio	5.00
ER	Ed Rogers	5.00
SS	Scott Seabol	5.00
BS	Bud Smith	5.00
BJS	Brian Specht	5.00
JT	Joe Torres	5.00
JMW	Justin Wayne	5.00

Futures Game Relics

		NM/M
Common Player:		4.00
One per factory set.		
AA	Alfredo Amezaga	4.00
AD	Adam Dunn	10.00
AG	Adrian Gonzalez	10.00
AH	Alex Herrera	4.00
BM	Brett Myers	5.00
CD	Cody Ransom	4.00

CG	Chris George	4.00
CH	Carlos Hernandez	5.00
CU	Chase Utley	85.00
EB	Eric Bedard	15.00
GB	Grant Balfour	4.00
HB	Hank Blalock	10.00
JB	Joe Borchard	8.00
JC	Juan Cruz	5.00
JP	Josh Pearce	4.00
JR	Juan Rivera	4.00
LG	Luis Garcia	4.00
MC	Miguel Cabrera	10.00
MR	Mike Rivera	4.00
RR	Ricardo Rodriguez	4.00
SC	Scott Chiasson	4.00
SS	Seung Jun Song	5.00
TB	Toby Hall	4.00
WB	Wilson Betemit	4.00
WP	Wily Mo Pena	5.00
JAP	Juan Pena	4.00

Draft Pick Relics

		NM/M
Common Player:		4.00
One per factory set.		
CI	Cesar Izturis	4.00
GJ	Gary Johnson	4.00
NR	Nick Regilio	4.00
RC	Ryan Church	10.00
BJS	Brian Specht	4.00
JRH	J.R. House	4.00

2001 Bowman Heritage

		NM/M
Complete Set (440):		200.00
Common Player:		.15
Common (331-440):		1.00
Inserted 1:2		
Pack (10):		5.00
Box (24):		100.00
1	Chipper Jones	1.50
2	Pete Harnisch	.15
3	Brian Giles	.15
4	J.T. Snow	.15
5	Bartolo Colon	.15
6	Jorge Posada	.25
7	Shawn Green	.25
8	Derek Jeter	2.50
9	Benito Santiago	.15
10	Ramon Hernandez	.15
11	Bernie Williams	.40
12	Greg Maddux	1.50
13	Barry Bonds	2.00
14	Roger Clemens	1.50
15	Miguel Tejada	.50
16	Pedro Feliz	.15
17	Jim Edmonds	.25
18	Tom Glavine	.40
19	David Justice	.25
20	Rich Aurilia	.15
21	Jason Giambi	.50
22	Orlando Hernandez	.15
23	Shawn Estes	.15
24	Nelson Figueroa	.15
25	Terrence Long	.15
26	Mike Mussina	.50
27	Eric Davis	.15
28	Jimmy Rollins	.75
29	Andy Pettitte	.50
30	Shawon Dunston	.15
31	Tim Hudson	.40
32	Jeff Kent	.25
33	Scott Brosius	.15
34	Livan Hernandez	.15
35	Alfonso Soriano	1.00
36	Mark McGwire	1.50
37	Russ Ortiz	.15
38	Fernando Vina	.15
39	Ken Griffey Jr.	1.50
40	Edgar Renteria	.15

41	Kevin Brown	.15
42	Robb Nen	.15
43	Paul LoDuca	.15
44	Bobby Abreu	.25
45	Adam Dunn	.50
46	Oswaldo Fernandez	.15
47	Marvin Benard	.15
48	Mark Gardner	.15
49	Alex Rodriguez	2.00
50	Preston Wilson	.15
51	Roberto Alomar	.40
52	Ben Davis	.15
53	Derek Bell	.15
54	Ken Caminiti	.15
55	Barry Zito	.25
56	Scott Rolen	.75
57	Geoff Jenkins	.15
58	Mike Cameron	.15
59	Ben Grieve	.15
60	Chuck Knoblauch	.15
61	Matt Lawton	.15
62	Chan Ho Park	.15
63	Lance Berkman	.50
64	Carlos Beltran	.50
65	Dean Palmer	.15
66	Alex Gonzalez	.15
67	Larry Walker	.25
68	Magglio Ordonez	.25
69	Ellis Burks	.15
70	Mark Mulder	.25
71	Randy Johnson	.75
72	John Smoltz	.15
73	Jerry Hairston Jr.	.15
74	Pedro Martinez	.75
75	Fred McGriff	.25
76	Sean Casey	.25
77	C.C. Sabathia	.50
78	Todd Helton	.75
79	Brad Penny	.15
80	Mike Sweeney	.15
81	Billy Wagner	.15
82	Mark Buehrle	.25
83	Cristian Guzman	.15
84	Jose Vidro	.15
85	Pat Burrell	.40
86	Jermaine Dye	.25
87	Brandon Inge	.15
88	David Wells	.15
89	Mike Piazza	1.00
90	Jose Cabrera	.15
91	Cliff Floyd	.15
92	Matt Morris	.15
93	Raul Mondesi	.15
94	Joe Kennedy RC	.50
95	Jack Wilson RC	1.00
96	Andruw Jones	.40
97	Mariano Rivera	.50
98	Mike Hampton	.15
99	Roger Cedeno	.15
100	Jose Cruz	.15
101	Mike Lowell	.40
102	Pedro Astacio	.15
103	Joe Mays	.15
104	John Franco	.15
105	Tim Redding	.15
106	Sandy Alomar	.15
107	Bret Boone	.15
108	Josh Towers RC	.50
109	Matt Stairs	.15
110	Chris Truby	.15
111	Jeff Suppan	.15
112	J.C. Romero	.15
113	Felipe Lopez	.40
114	Ben Sheets	.40
115	Frank Thomas	.75
116	A.J. Burnett	.25
117	Tony Clark	.15
118	Mac Suzuki	.15
119	Brad Radke	.15
120	Jeff Shaw	.15
121	Nick Neugebauer	.15
122	Kenny Lofton	.15
123	Jacque Jones	.15
124	Brent Mayne	.15
125	Carlos Hernandez	.15
126	Shane Spencer	.15
127	John Lackey	.25
128	Sterling Hitchcock	.15
129	Darren Dreifort	.15
130	Rusty Greer	.15
131	Michael Cuddyer	.15
132	Tyler Houston	.15
133	Chin-Feng Chen	.15
134	Ken Harvey	.15
135	Marquis Grissom	.15
136	Russell Branyan	.15
137	Eric Karros	.15
138	Josh Beckett	.50
139	Todd Zeile	.15
140	Corey Koskie	.15
141	Steve Sparks	.15
142	Bobby Seay	.15
143	Tim Raines	.15
144	Julio Zuleta	.15
145	Jose Lima	.15
146	Dante Bichette	.15
147	Randy Keisler	.15
148	Brent Butler	.15
149	Antonio Alfonseca	.15
150	Bryan Rekar	.15
151	Jeffrey Hammonds	.15
152	Larry Bigbie	.15
153	Blake Stein	.15
154	Robin Ventura	.15
155	Rondell White	.15
156	Juan Silvestre	.15
157	Marcus Thames	.15

158	Sidney Ponson	.15
159	Juan Pena	.15
160	Charles Johnson	.15
161	Adam Everett	.15
162	Eric Munson	.15
163	Jason Isringhausen	.15
164	Brad Fullmer	.15
165	Miguel Olivo	.15
166	Fernando Tatis	.15
167	Freddy Garcia	.15
168	Tom Goodwin	.15
169	Armando Benitez	.15
170	Paul Konerko	.40
171	Jeff Cirillo	.15
172	Shane Reynolds	.15
173	Kevin Tapani	.15
174	Joe Crede	.25
175	Omar Infante RC	.50
176	Jake Peavy RC	5.00
177	Corey Patterson	.25
178	Alfredo Amezaga RC	.25
179	Jeromy Burnitz	.15
180	David Segui	.15
181	Marcus Giles	.15
182	Paul O'Neill	.25
183	John Olerud	.15
184	Andy Benes	.15
185	Brad Cresse RC	.25
186	Ricky Ledee	.15
187	Allen Levrault	.15
188	Royce Clayton	.15
189	Kelly Johnson RC	4.00
190	Quilvio Veras	.15
191	Mike Williams	.15
192	Jason Lane RC	1.00
193	Rick Helling	.15
194	Tim Wakefield	.15
195	James Baldwin	.15
196	Cody Ransom RC	.25
197	Bobby Kielty	.15
198	Bobby Jones	.15
199	Steve Cox	.15
200	Jamal Strong RC	.25
201	Steve Lomasney	.15
202	Bill Ortega	.15
203	Mike Matheny	.15
204	Jeff Randazzo RC	.25
205	Aubrey Huff	.15
206	Chuck Finley	.15
207	Denny Bautista RC	.50
208	Terry Mulholland	.15
209	Rey Ordonez	.15
210	Jason Belcher RC	.25
211	Orlando Cabrera	.15
212	Juan Encarnacion	.15
213	Dustin Hermanson	.15
214	Luis Rivas	.15
215	Mark Quinn	.15
216	Randy Velarde	.15
217	Billy Koch	.15
218	Ryan Rupe	.15
219	Keith Ginter	.15
220	Woody Williams	.15
221	Blake Williams RC	.25
222	Aaron Myette	.15
223	Joe Borchard RC	.50
224	Nate Cornejo	.15
225	Julian Tavarez	.15
226	Kevin Millwood	.15
227	Travis Hafner RC	3.00
228	Charles Nagy	.15
229	Mike Lieberthal	.15
230	Jeff Nelson	.15
231	Ryan Dempster	.15
232	Andres Galarraga	.15
233	Chad Durbin	.15
234	Timoniel Perez	.15
235	Troy O'Leary	.15
236	Kevin Young	.15
237	Gabe Kapler	.15
238	Juan Cruz RC	.50
239	Masato Yoshii	.15
240	Aramis Ramirez	.40
241	Matt Cooper RC	.25
242	Randy Flores RC	.25
243	Rafael Furcal	.25
244	David Eckstein	.15
245	Matt Clement	.15
246	Craig Biggio	.40
247	Rick Reed	.15
248	Jose Macias	.15
249	Alex Escobar	.15
250	Roberto Hernandez	.15
251	Andy Ashby	.15
252	Tony Armas	.15
253	Jamie Moyer	.15
254	Jason Tyner	.15
255	Ryan Ludwick RC	4.00
256	Jeff Conine	.15
257	Francisco Cordova	.15
258	Ted Lilly	.15
259	Joe Randa	.15
260	Jeff D'Amico	.15
261	Albie Lopez	.15
262	Kevin Appier	.15
263	Richard Hidalgo	.15
264	Omar Daal	.15
265	Ricky Gutierrez	.15
266	John Rocker	.15
267	Ray Lankford	.15
268	Beau Hale RC	.25
269	Tony Blanco RC	.50
270	Derrek Lee	.75
271	Jamey Wright	.15
272	Alex Gordon	.15
273	Jeff Weaver	.15
274	Jaret Wright	.15
275	Jose Hernandez	.15
276	Bruce Chen	.15
277	Todd Hollandsworth	.15
278	Wade Miller	.15
279	Luke Prokopec	.15
280	Rafael Soriano RC	.75
281	Damion Easley	.15
282	Darren Oliver	.15
283	Brandon Duckworth RC	.25
284	Aaron Herr	.15
285	Ray Durham	.15
286	Adrian Hernandez RC	.25
287	Ugueth Urbina	.15
288	Scott Seabol	.15
289	Lance Niekro RC	.50
290	Trot Nixon	.15
291	Adam Kennedy	.15
292	Brian Schmitt RC	.25
293	Grant Roberts	.15
294	Benny Agbayani	.15
295	Travis Lee	.15
296	Erick Almonte RC	.25
297	Jim Thome	.50
298	Eric Young	.15
299	Daniel Denham RC	.25
300	Boof Bonser RC	.75
301	Denny Neagle	.15
302	Kenny Rogers	.15
303	J.D. Closser	.15
304	Chase Utley RC	20.00
305	Rey Sanchez	.15
306	Sean McGowan	.15
307	Justin Pope RC	.25
308	Torii Hunter	.40
309	B.J. Surhoff	.15
310	Aaron Heilman RC	.50
311	Gabe Gross RC	.50
312	Lee Stevens	.15
313	Todd Hundley	.15
314	Macay McBride RC	.50
315	Edgar Martinez	.15
316	Omar Vizquel	.15
317	Reggie Sanders	.15
318	John-Ford Griffin RC	.50
319	Tim Salmon	.15
	(Photo actually Troy Glaus.)	.50
320	Pokey Reese	.15
321	Jay Payton	.15
322	Doug Glanville	.15
323	Greg Vaughn	.15
324	Ruben Sierra	.15
325	Kip Wells	.15
326	Carl Everett	.15
327	Garret Anderson	.25
328	Jay Bell	.15
329	Barry Larkin	.25
330	Jeff Mathis RC	.50
331	Adrian Gonzalez	2.00
332	Juan Rivera	1.00
333	Tony Alvarez	1.00
334	Xavier Nady	1.00
335	Josh Hamilton	3.00
336	Will Smith RC	1.00
337	Israel Alcantara	1.00
338	Chris George	1.00
339	Sean Burroughs	1.00
340	Jack Cust	1.00
341	Eric Byrnes	1.00
342	Carlos Pena	1.00
343	J.R. House	1.00
344	Carlos Silva	1.00
345	Mike Rivera RC	1.00
346	Adam Johnson	1.00
347	Scott Heard	1.00
348	Alex Cintron	1.00
349	Miguel Cabrera	3.00
350	Nick Johnson	1.00
351	Albert Pujols RC	50.00
352	Ichiro Suzuki RC	20.00
353	Carlos Delgado	1.50
354	Troy Glaus	1.50
355	Sammy Sosa	2.00
356	Ivan Rodriguez	2.00
357	Vladimir Guerrero	2.00
358	Manny Ramirez	2.00
359	Luis Gonzalez	1.00
360	Roy Oswalt	1.50
361	Moises Alou	1.00
362	Juan Gonzalez	1.50
363	Tony Gwynn	2.00
364	Hideo Nomo	1.00
365	Tsuyoshi Shinjo RC	1.00
366	Kazuhiro Sasaki	1.00
367	Cal Ripken Jr.	8.00
368	Rafael Palmeiro	2.00
369	J.D. Drew	1.50
370	Doug Mientkiewicz	1.00
371	Jeff Bagwell	2.00
372	Darin Erstad	1.00
373	Tom Gordon	1.00
374	Ben Petrick	1.00
375	Eric Milton	1.00
376	Nomar Garciaparra	2.00
377	Julio Lugo	1.00
378	Tino Martinez	1.00
379	Javier Vazquez	1.00
380	Jeremy Giambi	1.00
381	Marty Cordova	1.00
382	Adrian Beltre	1.50
383	John Burkett	1.00
384	Aaron Boone	1.00
385	Eric Chavez	1.00
386	Curt Schilling	2.00
387	Cory Lidle	1.00
388	Jason Schmidt	1.00
389	Johnny Damon	3.00
390	Steve Finley	1.00
391	Edgardo Alfonzo	1.00
392	Jose Valentin	1.00
393	Jose Canseco	1.50
394	Ryan Klesko	1.00
395	David Cone	1.00
396	Jason Kendall	1.00
397	Placido Polanco	1.00
398	Glendon Rusch	1.00
399	Aaron Sele	1.00
400	D'Angelo Jimenez	1.00
401	Mark Grace	1.50
402	Al Leiter	1.00
403	Brian Jordan	1.00
404	Phil Nevin	1.00
405	Brent Abernathy	1.00
406	Kerry Wood	1.50
407	Alex Gonzalez	1.00
408	Robert Fick	1.00
409	Dmitri Young	1.00
410	Wes Helms	1.00
411	Trevor Hoffman	1.00
412	Rickey Henderson	2.00
413	Bobby Higginson	1.00
414	Gary Sheffield	1.50
415	Darryl Kile	1.00
416	Richie Sexson	1.00
417	Frank Menechino	1.00
418	Javy Lopez	1.00
419	Carlos Lee	1.00
420	Jon Lieber	1.00
421	Hank Blalock RC	4.00
422	Marlon Byrd RC	1.50
423	Jason Kinchen RC	1.00
424	Morgan Ensberg RC	2.00
425	Greg "Toe" Nash RC	1.00
426	Dennis Tankersley RC	1.00
427	Joel Pineiro	1.00
428	Chris Smith RC	1.00
429	Jake Gautreau RC	1.00
430	John Van Benschoten RC	1.00
431	Travis Thompson	1.00
432	Orlando Hudson RC	3.00
433	Jerome Williams RC	1.00
434	Kevin Reese	1.00
435	Ed Rogers RC	1.00
436	Grant Balfour RC	1.00
437	Adam Pettyjohn RC	1.00
438	Hee Seop Choi RC	1.00
439	Justin Morneau RC	10.00
440	Mitch Jones RC	1.00

Chrome

Stars:	4-8X
SP's:	2-4X

Inserted 1:12
(See 2001 Bowman Heritage for checklist and base card values.)

Autographs

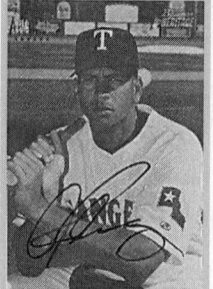

		NM/M
	Common Player:	90.00
BB	Barry Bonds	180.00
RC	Roger Clemens	100.00
AR	Alex Rodriguez	100.00

2001 Bowman Heritage Promos

	NM/M
Complete Set (5):	60.00
Common Player:	6.00

1	Roberto Alomar	6.00
2	Albert Pujols	50.00
3	C.C. Sabathia	6.00
4	Mark McGwire	12.50
5	Juan Gonzalez	6.00

Team Topps Legends Autographs

	NM/M
Common Autograph:	30.00

Inserted 1:332

TT13F	Warren Spahn/1965	40.00
TT21R	Bob Feller/1952	30.00

1948 Bowman Reprints

	NM/M
Complete Set (13):	10.00
Common Player:	.75

Inserted 1:2

1	Ralph Kiner	.75
2	Johnny Mize	.75
3	Bobby Thomson	.75
4	Yogi Berra	1.50
5	Phil Rizzuto	1.00
6	Bob Feller	1.00
7	Enos Slaughter	.75
8	Stan Musial	2.00
9	Hank Sauer	.75
10	Ferris Fain	.75
11	Red Schoendienst	.75
12	Allie Reynolds	.75
13	Johnny Sain	.75

1948 Reprint Relics

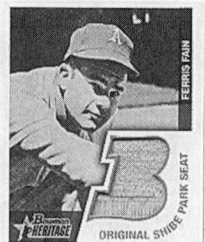

		NM/M
	Common Player:	8.00

Inserted 1:44

YB1	Yogi Berra	20.00
YB2	Yogi Berra	35.00
FF	Ferris Fain	8.00
BF	Bob Feller	12.00
RK	Ralph Kiner	15.00
JM	Johnny Mize	15.00
SM1	Stan Musial	30.00
PR	Phil Rizzuto	15.00
HS	Hank Sauer	8.00
RS	Red Schoendienst	10.00

ES	Enos Slaughter	10.00
BT	Bobby Thomson	8.00

1948 Bowman Reprint Autographs

		NM/M
1	Warren Spahn	40.00
2	Bob Feller	40.00

2001 Bowman's Best

JASON GIAMBI

	NM/M
Complete Set (200):	
Common Player:	.25
Common SP (151-200):	5.00
Production 2,999	
Pack (5):	10.00
Box (24):	200.00
1 Vladimir Guerrero	1.00
2 Miguel Tejada	.50
3 Geoff Jenkins	.25
4 Jeff Bagwell	.75
5 Todd Helton	.75
6 Ken Griffey Jr.	2.00
7 Nomar Garciaparra	.50
8 Chipper Jones	1.00
9 Darin Erstad	.25
10 Frank Thomas	1.00
11 Jim Thome	.50
12 Preston Wison	.25
13 Kevin Brown	.25
14 Derek Jeter	3.00
15 Scott Rolen	.75
16 Ryan Klesko	.25
17 Jeff Kent	.40
18 Raul Mondesi	.25
19 Greg Vaughn	.25
20 Bernie Williams	.40
21 Mike Piazza	1.00
22 Richard Hidalgo	.25
23 Dean Palmer	.25
24 Roberto Alomar	.40
25 Sammy Sosa	.75
26 Randy Johnson	1.00
27 Manny Ramirez	1.00
28 Roger Clemens	2.00
29 Terrence Long	.25
30 Jason Kendall	.25
31 Richie Sexson	.40
32 David Wells	.25
33 Andruw Jones	.50
34 Pokey Reese	.25
35 Juan Gonzalez	.50
36 Carlos Beltran	.75
37 Shawn Green	.40
38 Mariano Rivera	.50
39 John Olerud	.25
40 Jim Edmonds	.40
41 Andres Galarraga	.25
42 Carlos Delgado	.75
43 Kris Benson	.25
44 Andy Pettitte	.40
45 Jeff Cirillo	.25
46 Magglio Ordonez	.50
47 Tom Glavine	.50
48 Garret Anderson	.25
49 Cal Ripken Jr.	3.00
50 Pedro Martinez	1.00
51 Barry Bonds	3.00

52	Alex Rodriguez	2.50
53	Ben Grieve	.25
54	Edgar Martinez	.25
55	Jason Giambi	.50
56	Jeromy Burnitz	.25
57	Mike Mussina	.25
58	Moises Alou	.50
59	Sean Casey	.40
60	Greg Maddux	1.50
61	Tim Hudson	.50
62	Mark McGwire	2.00
63	Rafael Palmeiro	.75
64	Tony Batista	.25
65	Kazuhiro Sasaki	.25
66	Jorge Posada	.50
67	Johnny Damon	1.00
68	Brian Giles	.25
69	Jose Vidro	.25
70	Jermaine Dye	.40
71	Craig Biggio	.40
72	Larry Walker	.40
73	Eric Chavez	.40
74	David Segui	.25
75	Tim Salmon	.40
76	Javy Lopez	.25
77	Paul Konerko	.50
78	Barry Larkin	.50
79	Mike Hampton	.25
80	Bobby Higginson	.25
81	Mark Mulder	.25
82	Pat Burrell	.50
83	Kerry Wood	.50
84	J.T. Snow	.25
85	Ivan Rodriguez	.75
86	Edgardo Alfonzo	.25
87	Orlando Hernandez	.25
88	Gary Sheffield	.50
89	Mike Sweeney	.25
90	Carlos Lee	.50
91	Rafael Furcal	.50
92	Troy Glaus	.50
93	Bartolo Colon	.25
94	Cliff Floyd	.25
95	Barry Zito	.50
96	J.D. Drew	.40
97	Eric Karros	.25
98	Jose Valentin	.25
99	Ellis Burks	.25
100	David Justice	.25
101	Larry Barnes	.25
102	Rod Barajas	.25
103	Tony Pena	.25
104	Jerry Hairston Jr.	.25
105	Keith Ginter	.25
106	Corey Patterson	.40
107	Aaron Rowand	.40
108	Miguel Olivo	.25
109	Gookie Dawkins	.25
110	C.C. Sabathia	.75
111	Ben Petrick	.25
112	Eric Munson	.25
113	Ramon Castro	.25
114	Alex Escobar	.25
115	Josh Hamilton	1.00
116	Jason Marquis	.25
117	Ben Davis	.25
118	Alex Cintron	.25
119	Julio Zuleta	.25
120	Ben Broussard	.25
121	Adam Everett	.25
122	Ramon Carvajal RC	.75
123	Felipe Lopez	.25
124	Alfonso Soriano	1.00
125	Jayson Werth	.25
126	Donzell McDonald	.25
127	Jason Hart	.25
128	Joe Crede	.50
129	Sean Burroughs	.25
130	Jack Cust	.25
131	Corey Smith	.25
132	Adrian Gonzalez	.50
133	J.R. House	.25
134	Steve Lomasney	.25
135	Tim Raines Jr.	.25
136	Tony Alvarez	.25
137	Doug Mientkiewicz	.25
138	Rocco Baldelli	.40
139	Jason Romano	.25
140	Vernon Wells	.50
141	Mike Bynum	.25
142	Xavier Nady	.25
143	Brad Wilkerson	.25
144	Ben Diggins	.25
145	Aubrey Huff	.25
146	Eric Byrnes	.25
147	Alex Gordon	.25
148	Roy Oswalt	.25
149	Brian Esposito	.25
150	Scott Seabol	.25
151	Erick Almonte RC	5.00
152	Gary Johnson RC	5.00
153	Pedro Liriano RC	5.00
154	Matt White RC	5.00
155	Luis Montanez RC	5.00
156	Brad Cresse RC	5.00
157	Wilson Betemit RC	6.00
158	Octavio Dotel RC	5.00
159	Adam Pettyjohn RC	5.00
160	Corey Spencer RC	5.00
161	Mark Burnett RC	5.00
162	Ichiro Suzuki RC	50.00
163	Alexis Gomez RC	5.00
164	Greg "Toe" Nash RC	5.00
165	Roberto Miniel RC	5.00
166	Justin Morneau RC	25.00

167	Ben Washburn RC	5.00
168	Bob Keppel RC	5.00
169	Deivi Mendez RC	5.00
170	Tsuyoshi Shinjo RC	5.00
171	Jared Abruzzo RC	5.00
172	Derrick Van Dusen RC	5.00
173	Hee Seop Choi RC	5.00
174	Albert Pujols RC	150.00
175	Travis Hafner RC	15.00
176	Ron Davenport RC	5.00
177	Luis Torres RC	5.00
178	Jake Peavy RC	30.00
179	Elvis Corporan RC	5.00
180	David Krynzel	5.00
181	Tony Blanco RC	5.00
182	Elpidio Guzman RC	5.00
183	Matt Butler RC	5.00
184	Joe Thurston RC	5.00
185	Andy Beal RC	5.00
186	Kevin Nulton RC	5.00
187	Sneideer Santos RC	5.00
188	Joe Dillon RC	5.00
189	Jeremy Blevins RC	5.00
190	Chris Amador RC	5.00
191	Mark Hendrickson RC	5.00
192	Willy Aybar RC	8.00
193	Antoine Cameron RC	5.00
194	Jonathan Johnson RC	5.00
195	Ryan Ketchner RC	5.00
196	Bjorn Ivy RC	5.00
197	Josh Kroeger RC	5.00
198	Ty Wigginton RC	8.00
199	Stubby Clapp RC	5.00
200	Jerrod Riggan RC	5.00

Autographs

ADRIAN GONZALEZ
FLORIDA MARLINS

		NM/M
Common Player:		8.00
Inserted 1:95		
SB	Sean Burroughs	8.00
BC	Brad Cresse	8.00
AG	Adrian Gonzalez	15.00
JH	Josh Hamilton	35.00
JRH	J.R. House	8.00
TL	Terrence Long	8.00
JR	Jon Rauch	8.00

Exclusive Rookie Autographs

JONATHAN JOHNSON
CHICAGO CUBS

		NM/M
Common Player:		5.00
Inserted 1:50		
WA	Willy Aybar	10.00
SC	Stubby Clapp	5.00
BI	Bjorn Ivy	5.00
JJ	Jonathan Johnson	5.00
TW	Ty Wigginton	10.00
JR	Jerrod Riggan	5.00
SS	Sneideer Santos	5.00
JB	Jeremy Blevins	5.00
MH	Mark Hendrickson	8.00

Franchise Favorites

	NM/M
Complete Set (8):	30.00
Common Player:	1.50
Inserted 1:16	
DM	Don Mattingly	6.00

AR	Alex Rodriguez	6.00
DE	Darin Erstad	1.50
DW	Dave Winfield	1.50
NR	Nolan Ryan	8.00
RJ	Reggie Jackson	2.00
MW	Don Mattingly,	
	Dave Winfield	4.00
RR	Nolan Ryan, Alex Rodriguez	8.00
EJ	Darin Erstad,	
	Reggie Jackson	2.00

Franchise Favorites Autographs

ALEX RODRIGUEZ

		NM/M
Common Player:		20.00
Inserted 1:556		
Combo 1:4,436		
DE	Darin Erstad	10.00
RJ	Reggie Jackson	40.00
EJ	Darin Erstad,	
	Reggie Jackson	65.00
DM	Don Mattingly	60.00
MW	Don Mattingly,	
	Dave Winfield	150.00
AR	Alex Rodriguez	90.00
NR	Nolan Ryan	80.00
RR	Nolan Ryan,	
	Alex Rodriguez	300.00
DW	Dave Winfield	25.00

Franchise Favorites Relics

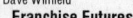

	NM/M
Common Player:	5.00
Jersey 1:139	
Pants 1:307	
Combo Relic 1:1,114	
JB	Jeff Bagwell	10.00
CB	Craig Biggio	6.00
BB	Craig Biggio, Jeff Bagwell	25.00
DE	Darin Erstad	10.00
RJ	Reggie Jackson	10.00
EJ	Reggie Jackson,	
	Darin Erstad	25.00
DM	Don Mattingly	30.00
MW	Don Mattingly,	
	Dave Winfield	65.00
AR	Alex Rodriguez	20.00
NR	Nolan Ryan	40.00
RR	Nolan Ryan,	
	Alex Rodriguez	60.00
DW	Dave Winfield	8.00

Franchise Futures

	NM/M
Complete Set (12):	15.00
Common Player:	1.00
Inserted 1:24	
FF1 Josh Hamilton	2.50
FF2 Wes Helms	1.00
FF3 Alfonso Soriano	4.00
FF4 Nick Johnson	1.00
FF5 Jose Ortiz	1.00
FF6 Ben Sheets	1.50
FF7 Sean Burroughs	1.00
FF8 Ben Petrick	1.00
FF9 Corey Patterson	1.00
FF10 J.R. House	1.00
FF11 Alex Escobar	1.00
FF12 Travis Hafner	1.50

Game-Used Bats

	NM/M
Common Player:	5.00
Inserted 1:267	
PB Pat Burrell	10.00
SB Sean Burroughs	5.00
AG Adrian Gonzalez	10.00
EM Eric Munson	5.00
CP Corey Patterson	5.00

Game-Worn Jerseys

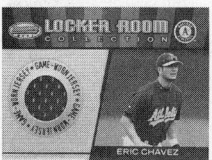

	NM/M
Common Player:	5.00
Inserted 1:133	
EC Eric Chavez	5.00
MM Mark Mulder	5.00
JP Jay Payton	5.00
PR Pokey Reese	5.00
PW Preston Wilson	5.00

Impact Players

	NM/M
Complete Set (20):	15.00
Common Player:	.50
Inserted 1:7	
IP1 Mark McGwire	3.00
IP2 Sammy Sosa	2.00
IP3 Manny Ramirez	1.00
IP4 Troy Glaus	1.00
IP5 Ken Griffey Jr.	2.00
IP6 Gary Sheffield	.75
IP7 Vladimir Guerrero	1.00
IP8 Carlos Delgado	.75
IP9 Jason Giambi	.75
IP10 Frank Thomas	1.50
IP11 Vernon Wells	.60
IP12 Carlos Pena	.50
IP13 Joe Crede	.50
IP14 Keith Ginter	.50
IP15 Aubrey Huff	.50
IP16 Brad Cresse	.50
IP17 Austin Kearns	.75
IP18 Nick Johnson	.50
IP19 Josh Hamilton	.50
IP20 Corey Patterson	.60

Rookie Fever

	NM/M
Complete Set (10):	10.00
Common Player:	.50
Inserted 1:10	
RF1 Chipper Jones	2.00
RF2 Preston Wilson	.50
RF3 Todd Helton	1.00
RF4 Jay Payton	.50
RF5 Ivan Rodriguez	.75
RF6 Manny Ramirez	1.00
RF7 Derek Jeter	4.00
RF8 Orlando Hernandez	.50
RF9 Marcus Quinn	.50
RF10 Terrence Long	.50

Team Topps

	NM/M
Common Player:	10.00
Overall odds 1:71.	
13R Warren Spahn/1952	40.00
37R Tug McGraw/1965	10.00
48R Bobby Richardson/1957	15.00
25R Luis Tiant/1965 + Exchange	10.00
31R Clete Boyer/1957	15.00
23R Gil McDougald/1952	15.00
27R Andy Pafko/1952	15.00
28R Herb Score/1956	15.00
18R Bob Gibson/1959	40.00
29R Moose Skowron/1954	15.00
37F Tug McGraw/1985	10.00
28F Herb Score/1962	15.00

2002 Bowman

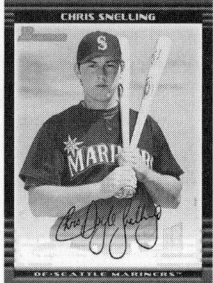

	NM/M
Complete Set (440):	70.00
Common Player:	.15
Common Rookie:	.40
Pack (10):	4.50
Box (24):	90.00
1 Adam Dunn	.50
2 Derek Jeter	2.00
3 Alex Rodriguez	1.50
4 Miguel Tejada	.50
5 Nomar Garciaparra	.75
6 Toby Hall	.15
7 Brandon Duckworth	.15
8 Paul LoDuca	.15
9 Brian Giles	.15
10 C.C. Sabathia	.40
11 Curt Schilling	.75
12 Tsuyoshi Shinjo	.15
13 Ramon Hernandez	.15
14 Jose Cruz Jr.	.15
15 Albert Pujols	2.00
16 Joe Mays	.15
17 Javy Lopez	.15
18 J.T. Snow	.15
19 David Segui	.15
20 Jorge Posada	.40
21 Doug Mientkiewicz	.15
22 Jerry Hairston Jr.	.15
23 Bernie Williams	.40
24 Mike Sweeney	.15
25 Jason Giambi	.50
26 Ryan Dempster	.15
27 Ryan Klesko	.15
28 Mark Quinn	.15
29 Jeff Kent	.25
30 Eric Chavez	.25
31 Adrian Beltre	.25
32 Andruw Jones	.40
33 Alfonso Soriano	1.00
34 Aramis Ramirez	.40
35 Greg Maddux	1.00
36 Andy Pettitte	.50
37 Bartolo Colon	.15
38 Ben Sheets	.40
39 Bobby Higginson	.15
40 Ivan Rodriguez	.50
41 Brad Penny	.15
42 Carlos Lee	.25
43 Damion Easley	.15
44 Preston Wilson	.15
45 Jeff Bagwell	.50
46 Eric Milton	.15
47 Rafael Palmeiro	.50
48 Gary Sheffield	.40
49 J.D. Drew	.25
50 Jim Thome	.50
51 Ichiro Suzuki	1.50
52 Bud Smith	.15
53 Chan Ho Park	.15
54 D'Angelo Jimenez	.15
55 Ken Griffey Jr.	1.50
56 Wade Miller	.15
57 Vladimir Guerrero	.50
58 Troy Glaus	.40
59 Shawn Green	.25
60 Kerry Wood	.40
61 Jack Wilson	.15
62 Kevin Brown	.25
63 Marcus Giles	.15
64 Pat Burrell	.40
65 Larry Walker	.25
66 Sammy Sosa	.75
67 Raul Mondesi	.15
68 Tim Hudson	.25
69 Lance Berkman	.40
70 Mike Mussina	.40
71 Barry Zito	.25
72 Jimmy Rollins	.50
73 Barry Bonds	2.00
74 Craig Biggio	.40
75 Todd Helton	.50
76 Roger Clemens	1.50
77 Frank Catalanotto	.15
78 Josh Towers	.15
79 Roy Oswalt	.40
80 Chipper Jones	1.00
81 Cristian Guzman	.15
82 Darin Erstad	.25
83 Freddy Garcia	.15
84 Jason Tyner	.15
85 Carlos Delgado	.40
86 Jon Lieber	.15
87 Juan Pierre	.15
88 Matt Morris	.15
89 Phil Nevin	.15
90 Jim Edmonds	.25
91 Magglio Ordonez	.25
92 Mike Hampton	.15
93 Rafael Furcal	.25
94 Richie Sexson	.25
95 Luis Gonzalez	.25
96 Scott Rolen	.50
97 Tim Redding	.15
98 Moises Alou	.25
99 Jose Vidro	.15
100 Mike Piazza	1.00
101 Pedro Martinez	.75
102 Geoff Jenkins	.15
103 Johnny Damon	.25
104 Mike Cameron	.15
105 Randy Johnson	.75
106 David Eckstein	.15
107 Javier Vazquez	.15
108 Mark Mulder	.25
109 Robert Fick	.15
110 Roberto Alomar	.40
111 Wilson Betemit	.15
112 Chris Tritle RC	.50
113 Ed Rogers	.15
114 Juan Pena	.15
115 Josh Beckett	.50
116 Juan Cruz	.15
117 Noochie Varner RC	.50
118 Taylor Buchholz RC	.50
119 Mike Rivera	.15
120 Hank Blalock	.40
121 Hansel Izquierdo RC	.50
122 Orlando Hudson	.15
123 Bill Hall	.15
124 Jose Reyes	.75
125 Juan Rivera	.15
126 Eric Valent	.15
127 Scotty Layfield RC	.40
128 Austin Kearns	.25
129 Nic Jackson RC	.25
130 Chris Baker RC	.25
131 Chad Qualls RC	.40
132 Marcus Thames	.15
133 Nathan Haynes	.15
134 Brett Evert	.15
135 Joe Borchard	.15
136 Ryan Christianson	.15
137 Josh Hamilton	.50
138 Corey Patterson	.15
139 Travis Wilson	.15
140 Alex Escobar	.15
141 Alexis Gomez	.15
142 Nick Johnson	.15
143 Kenny Kelly	.15
144 Marlon Byrd	.15
145 Kory DeHaan	.15
146 Matt Belisle	.15
147 Carlos Hernandez	.15
148 Sean Burroughs	.15
149 Angel Berroa	.15
150 Aubrey Huff	.15
151 Travis Hafner	.15
152 Brandon Berger	.15
153 David Krynzel	.15
154 Ruben Salazar	.15
155 J.R. House	.15
156 Juan Silvestre	.15
157 Dewon Brazelton	.15
158 Jayson Werth	.15
159 Larry Barnes	.15
160 Elvis Pena	.15
161 Ruben Gotay RC	.40
162 Tommy Marx RC	.50
163 John Suomi RC	.40
164 Javier Colina	.15
165 Greg Sain RC	.40
166 Robert Cosby RC	.40
167 Angel Pagan RC	1.00
168 Ralph Santana RC	.40
169 Joe Orloski RC	.40
170 Shayne Wright RC	.40
171 Jay Caligiuri RC	.25
172 Greg Montalbano RC	.50
173 Rich Harden RC	4.00
174 Rich Thompson RC	.40
175 Fred Bastardo RC	.40
176 Alejandro Giron RC	.40
177 Jesus Medrano RC	.15
178 Kevin Deaton RC	.40
179 Mike Rosamond RC	.50
180 Jon Guzman RC	.40
181 Gerard Oakes RC	.40
182 Francisco Liriano RC	8.00
183 Matt Allegra RC	.50
184 Mike Snyder RC	.40
185 James Shanks RC	.40
186 Anderson Hernandez RC	.40
187 Dan Trumble RC	.40
188 Luis DePaula RC	.40
189 Randall Shelley RC	.40
190 Richard Lane RC	.40
191 Antwon Rollins RC	.50
192 Ryan Bukvich RC	.40
193 Derrick Lewis	.15
194 Eric Miller RC	.40
195 Justin Schuda RC	.40
196 Brian West RC	.40
197 Adam Roller RC	.40
198 Neal Frendling RC	.40
199 Jeremy Hill RC	.40
200 James Barrett RC	.50
201 Brett Kay RC	.50
202 Ryan Mottl RC	.50
203 Brad Nelson RC	.40
204 Juan Gonzalez	.25
205 Curtis Legendre RC	.40
206 Ronald Acuna RC	.40
207 Chris Flinn RC	.40
208 Nick Alvarez RC	.40
209 Jason Ellison RC	.40
210 Blake McGinley RC	.40
211 Dan Phillips RC	.40
212 Demetrius Heath RC	.40
213 Eric Bruntlett RC	.40
214 Joe Jannetti RC	.40
215 Mike Hill RC	.40
216 Ricardo Cordova RC	.40
217 Mark Hamilton RC	.40
218 David Mattox RC	.50
219 Jose Morgan RC	.50
220 Scott Wiggins RC	.40
221 Steve Green	.15
222 Brian Rogers	.15
223 Chin-Hui Tsao	.40
224 Kenny Baugh RC	.40
225 Nate Teut	.15
226 Josh Wilson RC	.40
227 Christian Parker	.15
228 Tim Raines Jr.	.15
229 Anastacio Martinez RC	.40
230 Richard Lewis	.15
231 Tim Kalita RC	.40
232 Edwin Almonte RC	.40
233 Hee Seop Choi	.25
234 Ty Howington	.15

#	Player	Price
235	Victor Alvarez RC	.40
236	Morgan Ensberg	.15
237	Jeff Austin RC	.40
238	Luis Terrero	.15
239	Adam Wainwright	.25
240	Clint Weibl RC	.40
241	Eric Cyr RC	.40
242	Marlyn Tisdale RC	.40
243	John VanBenschoten	.15
244	Ryan Raburn RC	.40
245	Miguel Cabrera	.75
246	Jung Bong	.15
247	Raul Chavez RC	.40
248	Erik Bedard	.25
249	Chris Snelling RC	.50
250	Joe Rogers RC	.40
251	Nate Field RC	.40
252	Matt Herges	.15
253	Matt Childers RC	.50
254	Erick Almonte	.15
255	Nick Neugebauer	.15
256	Ron Calloway RC	.40
257	Seung Jun Song	.15
258	Brandon Phillips	.50
259	Cole Barthel	.25
260	Jason Lane	.15
261	Jae Weong Seo	.15
262	Randy Flores	.15
263	Scott Chiasson	.15
264	Chase Utley	1.00
265	Tony Alvarez	.15
266	Ben Howard RC	.40
267	Nelson Castro RC	.40
268	Mark Lukasiewicz	.15
269	Eric Glaser RC	.40
270	Rob Henkel RC	.40
271	Jose Valverde RC	.40
272	Ricardo Rodriguez	.15
273	Chris Smith	.15
274	Mark Prior	.50
275	Miguel Olivo	.15
276	Ben Broussard	.15
277	Zach Sorensen	.15
278	Brian Mallette RC	.40
279	Brad Wilkerson	.15
280	Carl Crawford	.25
281	Chone Figgins RC	1.00
282	Jimmy Alvarez RC	.40
283	Gavin Floyd	1.00
284	Josh Bonifay RC	.50
285	Garrett Guzman RC	.50
286	Blake Williams	.15
287	Matt Holliday	.50
288	Ryan Madson	.15
289	Luis Torres	.15
290	Jeff Verplancke RC	.40
291	Nate Espy RC	.50
292	Jeff Lincoln RC	.40
293	Ryan Snare RC	.40
294	Jose Ortiz	.15
295	Eric Munson	.15
296	Denny Bautista	.15
297	Willy Aybar	.15
298	Kelly Johnson	.15
299	Justin Morneau	.50
300	Derrick Van Dusen	.15
301	Chad Petty	.15
302	Mike Restovich	.15
303	Shawn Fagan	.15
304	Yurendell DeCaster RC	.40
305	Justin Wayne	.15
306	Mike Peeples	.40
307	Joel Guzman RC	.75
308	Ryan Vogelsong	.15
309	Jorge Padilla RC	.50
310	Grady Sizemore	.50
311	Joe Jester RC	.40
312	Jim Journell	.15
313	Bobby Seay	.15
314	Ryan Church RC	1.00
315	Grant Balfour	.15
316	Mitch Jones	.15
317	Travis Foley	.50
318	Bobby Crosby	.15
319	Adrian Gonzalez	.25
320	Ronnie Merrill	.15
321	Joel Pineiro	.15
322	John-Ford Griffin	.15
323	Brian Forystek RC	.40
324	Sean Douglass	.15
325	Manny Delcarmen RC	.40
326	Donnie Bridges	.15
327	Jim Kavourias	.15
328	Gabe Gross	.15
329	Greg "Toe" Nash	.15
330	Bill Ortega	.15
331	Joey Hammond RC	.40
332	Ramon Moreta RC	.40
333	Ron Davenport	.15
334	Brett Myers	.15
335	Carlos Pena	.15
336	Ezequiel Astacio RC	.40
337	Ryan Jan RC	.50
338	Josh Girdley	.15
339	Shaun Boyd	.15
340	Juan Rincon	.15
341	Chris Duffy RC	.50
342	Jason Kinchen	.15
343	Brad Thomas	.15
344	David Kelton	.15
345	Rafael Soriano	.15
346	Colin Young RC	.50
347	Eric Byrnes	.15
348	Chris Narveson RC	.50
349	John Rheinecker RC	.40
350	Mike Wilson RC	.40
351	Justin Sherrod RC	.50
352	Deivi Mendez	.15
353	Wily Mo Pena RC	.50
354	Brett Roneberg RC	.50
355	Trey Lunsford RC	.40
356	Jimmy Gobble RC	.50
357	Brent Butler	.15
358	Aaron Heilman	.15
359	Wilkin Ruan	.15
360	Brian Wolfe RC	.40
361	Cody Ransom	.15
362	Koyie Hill	.40
363	Scott Cassidy	.15
364	Tony Fontana RC	.50
365	Mark Teixeira	.50
366	Doug Sessions RC	.40
367	Victor Hall	.15
368	Josh Cisneros RC	.40
369	Kevin Mench	.15
370	Tike Redman	.15
371	Jeff Heaverlo	.15
372	Carlos Brackley RC	.40
373	Brad Hawpe	.50
374	Jesus Colome	.15
375	David Espinosa	.15
376	Jesse Foppert	.75
377	Ross Peeples RC	.40
378	Alexander Requena RC	.40
379	Joe Mauer RC	10.00
380	Carlos Silva	.15
381	David Wright	25.00
382	Craig Kuzmic RC	.50
383	Peter Zamora RC	.40
384	Matt Parker RC	.40
385	Ricardo Rodriguez	.15
386	Gary Cates Jr. RC	.40
387	Justin Reid RC	.50
388	Jake Mauer RC	.50
389	John-Ford Griffin	.15
390	Josh Barfield	.50
391	Luis Maza	.15
392	Henry Pichardo RC	.40
393	Michael Floyd RC	.40
394	Clint Nageotte RC	.50
395	Jim Warden	.15
396	Mauricio Lara RC	.50
397	Alejandro Cadena RC	.40
398	Jonny Gomes RC	1.00
399	Jason Bulger RC	.50
400	Bobby Jenks RC	1.00
401	David Gil RC	.40
402	Joel Crump RC	.40
403	Kazuhisa Ishii RC	.50
404	So Taguchi RC	.50
405	Ryan Doumit RC	1.00
406	Macay McBride	.15
407	Brandon Claussen	.15
408	Chin-Feng Chen	.15
409	Josh Phelps	.25
410	Freddie Money RC	.40
411	Clifford Bartosh RC	.40
412	Josh Pearce	.15
413	Lyle Overbay	.15
414	Ryan Anderson	.15
415	Terrance Hill RC	.40
416	John Rodriguez RC	.40
417	Richard Stahl	.40
418	Brian Specht	.15
419	Chris Latham RC	.50
420	Carlos Cabrera RC	.40
421	Jose Bautista RC	.50
422	Kevin Frederick RC	.40
423	Jerome Williams	.50
424	Napoleon Calzado RC	.50
425	Benito Baez	.15
426	Xavier Nady	.15
427	Jason Botts RC	.40
428	Steve Bechler RC	.50
429	Reed Johnson RC	.40
430	Mark Outlaw RC	.40
431	Billy Sylvester	.15
432	Luke Lockwood	.15
433	Jake Peavy	.25
434	Alfredo Amezaga	.15
435	Aaron Cook RC	.75
436	Josh Shaffer RC	.40
437	Dan Wright	.15
438	Ryan Gripp RC	.50
439	Alex Herrera	.15
440	Jason Bay RC	4.00

Gold

Stars: 1-2.5X
Rookies: 1-2X
Inserted 1:1

Uncirculated

NM/M
Common Player: 4.00
Production 1,000 Sets

#	Player	Price
112	Chris Tritle	6.00
113	Ed Rogers	4.00
114	Juan Pena	4.00
115	Josh Beckett	8.00
116	Juan Cruz	4.00
117	Noochie Varner	6.00
118	Taylor Buchholz	4.00
119	Mike Rivera	4.00
120	Hank Blalock	8.00
121	Hansel Izquierdo	4.00
122	Orlando Hudson	4.00
123	Bill Hall	4.00
124	Jose Reyes	8.00
125	Juan Rivera	4.00
126	Eric Valent	4.00
127	Scotty Layfield	4.00
128	Austin Kearns	8.00
129	Nic Jackson	4.00
130	Chris Baker	4.00
131	Chad Qualls	4.00

Autographs

NM/M
Common Autograph: 5.00
Inserted 1:37

AA	Alfredo Amezaga	5.00
GA	Garrett Atkins	20.00
JB	Josh Beckett	35.00
WB	Wilson Betemit	5.00
LB	Larry Bigbie	5.00
HB	Hank Blalock	15.00
TB	Tony Blanco	5.00
JAB	Jason Botts	5.00
MB	Marlon Byrd	8.00
BDC	Brian Cardwell	5.00
BC	Ben Christensen	5.00
BAC	Brandon Claussen	5.00
JD	Jeff Davanon	5.00
MD	Manny Delcarmen	8.00
RF	Randy Flores	5.00
RF	Ryan Franklin	5.00
KG	Keith Ginter	5.00
TH	Toby Hall	5.00
AH	Aubrey Huff	10.00
GJ	Gary Johnson	5.00
NJ	Nick Johnson	8.00
CK	Charles Kegley	5.00
JL	Jason Lane	8.00
NN	Nick Neugebauer	5.00
RO	Roy Oswalt	15.00
JP	Juan Pena	5.00
MP	Mark Prior	15.00
CR	Cody Ransom	5.00
JS	Juan Silvestre	5.00
TS	Terrmel Sledge	5.00
BS	Bud Smith	5.00
CS	Chris Smith	5.00
WS	Will Smith	5.00
BJS	Brian Specht	5.00
CT	Chris Tritle	5.00
CU	Chase Utley	200.00
DV	Domingo Valdez	5.00
NV	Noochie Varner	5.00
RV	Ryan Vogelsong	5.00
JLW	Jerome Williams	5.00
DW	Dan Wright	5.00

Autographed Futures Game Game-Worn Jersey

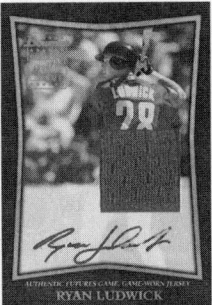

NM/M
Common Player: 15.00
Inserted 1:193

WB	Wilson Betemit	15.00
CH	Carlos Hernandez	15.00
JRH	J.R. House	15.00
NJ	Nick Johnson	20.00
RL	Ryan Ludwick	30.00
CP	Carlos Pena	15.00
DT	Dennis Tankersley	15.00
JW	Jerome Williams	20.00

Autographed Futures Game Game-Used Base

NM/M
Randomly Inserted
TB Toby Hall 15.00

Game-Used Relics

NM/M
Common Player: 4.00
Inserted 1:165

JA1	Jared Abruzzo	4.00
JA2	Jared Abruzzo	4.00
GA	Garrett Atkins	8.00
AB	Angel Berroa	6.00
AC	Antoine Cameron	4.00
RC	Ryan Church	6.00
ALC	Alex Cintron	4.00
NC	Nate Cornejo	4.00
RD	Ryan Dittfurth	4.00
AE	Adam Everett	4.00
AF1	Alex Fernandez	4.00
AF2	Alex Fernandez	4.00
AG	Alexis Gomez	4.00
CG	Cristian Guerrero	4.00
CI	Cesar Izturis	4.00
DJ	D'Angelo Jimenez	4.00
FJ	Forrest Johnson	4.00
AK	Austin Kearns	4.00
JL	Jason Lane	4.00
RM	Ryan Madson	4.00
NN	Nick Neugebauer	4.00
CP	Corey Patterson	4.00
RS	Ruben Salazar	4.00
RST	Richard Stahl	4.00
JS	Jamal Strong	4.00
CY	Colin Young	4.00

2002 Bowman Chrome

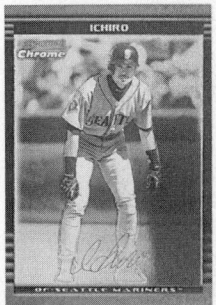

NM/M
Complete Set (405):
Common Player: .25
Common SP: 3.00
Inserted 1:3
Common Auto.(384-402,405) 10.00
Inserted 1:18
Pack (4): 10.00
Box (18): 150.00

#	Player	Price
1	Adam Dunn	.50
2	Derek Jeter	3.00
3	Alex Rodriguez	2.50
4	Miguel Tejada	.50
5	Nomar Garciaparra	.75
6	Toby Hall	.25
7	Brandon Duckworth	.25
8	Paul LoDuca	.25
9	Brian Giles	.25
10	C.C. Sabathia	.50
11	Curt Schilling	.75
12	Tsuyoshi Shinjo	.25
13	Ramon Hernandez	.25
14	Jose Cruz Jr.	.25
15	Albert Pujols	3.00
16	Joe Mays	.25
17	Javy Lopez	.25
18	J.T. Snow	.25
19	David Segui	.25
20	Jorge Posada	.25
21	Doug Mientkiewicz	.25
22	Jerry Hairston Jr.	.25
23	Bernie Williams	.50
24	Mike Sweeney	.25
25	Jason Giambi	.75
26	Ryan Dempster	.25
27	Ryan Klesco	.25
28	Mark Quinn	.25
29	Jeff Kent	.50
30	Eric Chavez	.40
31	Adrian Beltre	.25
32	Andruw Jones	.50
33	Alfonso Soriano	1.00
34	Aramis Ramirez	.50
35	Greg Maddux	2.00
36	Andy Pettitte	.50
37	Bartolo Colon	.25
38	Ben Sheets	.25
39	Bobby Higginson	.25
40	Ivan Rodriguez	.50
41	Brad Penny	.25
42	Carlos Lee	.50

43	Damion Easley	.25
44	Preston Wilson	.25
45	Jeff Bagwell	.50
46	Eric Milton	.25
47	Rafael Palmeiro	.50
48	Gary Sheffield	.50
49	J.D. Drew	.40
50	Jim Thome	.75
51	Ichiro Suzuki	2.00
52	Bud Smith	.25
53	Chan Ho Park	.25
54	D'Angelo Jimenez	.25
55	Ken Griffey Jr.	2.00
56	Wade Miller	.25
57	Vladimir Guerrero	1.00
58	Troy Glaus	.50
59	Shawn Green	.40
60	Kerry Wood	.50
61	Jack Wilson	.25
62	Kevin Brown	.25
63	Marcus Giles	.25
64	Pat Burrell	.50
65	Larry Walker	.40
66	Sammy Sosa	1.00
67	Raul Mondesi	.25
68	Tim Hudson	.40
69	Lance Berkman	.50
70	Mike Mussina	.50
71	Barry Zito	.40
72	Jimmy Rollins	.75
73	Barry Bonds	3.00
74	Craig Biggio	.40
75	Todd Helton	.75
76	Roger Clemens	2.00
77	Frank Catalanotto	.25
78	Josh Towers	.25
79	Roy Oswalt	.40
80	Chipper Jones	1.50
81	Cristian Guzman	.25
82	Darin Erstad	.40
83	Freddy Garcia	.25
84	Jason Tyner	.25
85	Carlos Delgado	.50
86	Jon Lieber	.25
87	Juan Pierre	.25
88	Matt Morris	.25
89	Phil Nevin	.25
90	Jim Edmonds	.40
91	Magglio Ordonez	.40
92	Mike Hampton	.25
93	Rafael Furcal	.50
94	Richie Sexson	.40
95	Luis Gonzalez	.40
96	Scott Rolen	.50
97	Tim Redding	.25
98	Moises Alou	.40
99	Jose Vidro	.25
100	Mike Piazza	1.50
101	Pedro Martinez	1.00
102	Geoff Jenkins	.25
103	Johnny Damon	1.00
104	Mike Cameron	.25
105	Randy Johnson	1.00
106	David Eckstein	.25
107	Javier Vazquez	.25
108	Mark Mulder	.40
109	Robert Fick	.25
110	Roberto Alomar	.40
111	Wilson Betemit	.25
112	Chris Tritle/SP **RC**	4.00
113	Ed Rogers	.25
114	Juan Pena	.25
115	Josh Beckett	.50
116	Juan Cruz	.25
117	Noochie Varner/SP **RC**	5.00
118	Blake Williams	.25
119	Mike Rivera	.25
120	Hank Blalock	.40
121	Hansel Izquierdo/SP **RC**	4.00
122	Orlando Hudson	.25
123	Bill Hall	.25
124	Jose Reyes	1.00
125	Juan Rivera	.25
126	Eric Valent	.25
127	Scotty Layfield/SP **RC**	3.00
128	Austin Kearns	.25
129	Nic Jackson/SP **RC**	5.00
130	Scott Chiasson	.25
131	Chad Qualls/SP **RC**	4.00
132	Marcus Thames	.25
133	Nathan Haynes	.25
134	Joe Borchard	.25
135	Josh Hamilton	1.00
136	Corey Patterson	.25
137	Travis Wilson	.25
138	Alex Escobar	.25
139	Alexis Gomez	.25
140	Nick Johnson	.25
141	Marlon Byrd	.25
142	Kory DeHaan	.25
143	Carlos Hernandez	.25
144	Sean Burroughs	.25
145	Angel Berroa	.25
146	Aubrey Huff	.25
147	Travis Hafner	.50
148	Brandon Berger	.25
149	J.R. House	.25
150	Dewon Brazelton	.25
151	Jayson Werth	.25
152	Larry Barnes	.25
153	Ruben Gotay/SP **RC**	5.00
154	Tommy Marx/SP **RC**	3.00
155	John Suomi/SP **RC**	4.00
156	Javier Colina/SP	3.00
157	Greg Sain/SP **RC**	3.00
158	Robert Cosby/SP **RC**	4.00
159	Angel Pagan/SP **RC**	8.00
160	Ralph Santana **RC**	1.00
161	Joe Orloski **RC**	1.00
162	Shayne Wright/SP **RC**	3.00
163	Jay Caligiuri/SP **RC**	4.00
164	Greg Montalbano/SP **RC**	5.00
165	Rich Harden/SP **RC**	25.00
166	Rich Thompson/SP **RC**	3.00
167	Fred Bastardo/SP **RC**	3.00
168	Alejandro Giron/SP **RC**	3.00
169	Jesus Medrano/SP **RC**	3.00
170	Kevin Deaton/SP **RC**	4.00
171	Mike Rosamond **RC**	1.00
172	Jon Guzman/SP **RC**	3.00
173	Gerard Oakes/SP **RC**	4.00
174	Francisco Liriano/SP **RC**	30.00
175	Matt Allegra/SP **RC**	4.00
176	Mike Snyder/SP **RC**	4.00
177	James Shanks/SP **RC**	3.00
178	Anderson Hernandez/SP **RC**	4.00
179	Dan Trumble/SP **RC**	3.00
180	Luis DePaula/SP **RC**	4.00
181	Randall Shelley/SP **RC**	4.00
182	Richard Lane/SP **RC**	3.00
183	Antwon Rollins/SP **RC**	4.00
184	Ryan Bukvich/SP **RC**	4.00
185	Derrick Lewis/SP	3.00
186	Eric Miller/SP **RC**	3.00
187	Justin Schuda/SP **RC**	3.00
188	Brian West/SP **RC**	4.00
189	Brad Wilkerson	.25
190	Neal Frendling/SP **RC**	3.00
191	Jeremy Hill/SP **RC**	3.00
192	James Barrett/SP **RC**	4.00
193	Brett Kay/SP **RC**	3.00
194	Ryan Mottl/SP **RC**	4.00
195	Brad Nelson/SP **RC**	5.00
196	Juan Gonzalez/SP	3.00
197	Curtis Legendre/SP **RC**	3.00
198	Ronald Acuna/SP **RC**	3.00
199	Chris Flinn/SP **RC**	3.00
200	Nick Alvarez/SP **RC**	3.00
201	Jason Ellison/SP **RC**	4.00
202	Blake McGinley/SP **RC**	3.00
203	Dan Phillips/SP **RC**	3.00
204	Demetrius Heath/SP **RC**	3.00
205	Eric Bruntlett/SP **RC**	3.00
206	Joe Jiannetti/SP **RC**	3.00
207	Mike Hill/SP **RC**	3.00
208	Ricardo Cordova/SP **RC**	3.00
209	Mark Hamilton/SP **RC**	3.00
210	David Mattox/SP **RC**	3.00
211	Jose Morban/SP **RC**	5.00
212	Scott Wiggins/SP **RC**	3.00
213	Steve Green	.25
214	Brian Rogers/SP	3.00
215	Kenny Baugh	.25
216	Anastacio Martinez/SP **RC**	3.00
217	Richard Lewis	.25
218	Tim Kalita/SP **RC**	3.00
219	Edwin Almonte/SP **RC**	3.00
220	Hee Seop Choi	.25
221	Ty Howington	.25
222	Victor Alvarez/SP **RC**	3.00
223	Morgan Ensberg	.25
224	Jeff Austin/SP **RC**	3.00
225	Clint Weibl/SP **RC**	4.00
226	Eric Cyr **RC**	1.00
227	Marlyn Tisdale/SP **RC**	3.00
228	John VanBenschoten	.25
229	Ruben Salazar	.25
230	Raul Chavez/SP **RC**	4.00
231	Brett Evert	.25
232	Joe Rogers/SP **RC**	4.00
233	Adam Wainwright	.50
234	Matt Herges	.25
235	Matt Childers/SP **RC**	4.00
236	Nick Neugebauer	.25
237	Carl Crawford	1.00
238	Seung Jun Song	.25
239	Randy Flores	.25
240	Jason Lane	.25
241	Chase Utley	4.00
242	Ben Howard/SP **RC**	3.00
243	Eric Glaser/SP **RC**	3.00
244	Josh Wilson **RC**	1.00
245	Jose Valverde/SP **RC**	4.00
246	Chris Smith	.25
247	Mark Prior	.50
248	Brian Mallette/SP **RC**	3.00
249	Chone Figgins/SP **RC**	10.00
250	Jimmy Alvarez/SP **RC**	3.00
251	Luis Terrero	.25
252	Josh Bonifay/SP **RC**	4.00
253	Garrett Guzman/SP **RC**	3.00
254	Jeff Verplancke/SP **RC**	3.00
255	Nate Espy/SP **RC**	4.00
256	Jeff Lincoln/SP **RC**	3.00
257	Ryan Snare/SP **RC**	4.00
258	Jose Ortiz	.25
259	Denny Bautista	.25
260	Willy Aybar	.25
261	Kelly Johnson	1.00
262	Shawn Fagan	.25
263	Yurendell DeCaster/SP **RC**	3.00
264	Mike Peeples/SP **RC**	3.00
265	Joel Guzman **RC**	3.00
266	Ryan Vogelsong	.25
267	Jorge Padilla/SP **RC**	3.00
268	Joe Jester/SP **RC**	3.00
269	Ryan Church/SP **RC**	10.00
270	Mitch Jones	.25
271	Travis Foley/SP	3.00
272	Bobby Crosby	.50
273	Adrian Gonzalez	.75
274	Ronnie Merrill	.25
275	Joel Pineiro	.25
276	John-Ford Griffin	.25
277	Brian Forystek/SP **RC**	3.00
278	Sean Douglass	.25
279	Manny Delcarmen/SP **RC**	5.00
280	Jim Kavourias/SP	3.00
281	Gabe Gross	.25
282	Bill Ortega	.25
283	Joey Hammond/SP **RC**	3.00
284	Brett Myers	.50
285	Carlos Pena	.50
286	Ezequiel Astacio/SP **RC**	3.00
287	Edwin Yan/SP **RC**	3.00
288	Chris Duffy/SP **RC**	5.00
289	Jason Kinchen	.25
290	Rafael Soriano	.25
291	Colin Young **RC**	.50
292	Eric Byrnes	.25
293	Chris Narveson/SP **RC**	5.00
294	John Rheinecker **RC**	.50
295	Mike Wilson/SP **RC**	4.00
296	Justin Sherrod/SP **RC**	5.00
297	Deivi Mendez	.25
298	Wily Mo Pena	.25
299	Brett Roneberg/SP **RC**	4.00
300	Trey Lunsford/SP **RC**	3.00
301	Christian Parker	.25
302	Brent Butler	.25
303	Aaron Heilman	.25
304	Wilkin Ruan	.25
305	Kenny Kelly	.25
306	Cody Ransom	.25
307	Koyie Hill/SP	3.00
308	Tony Fontana/SP **RC**	3.00
309	Mark Teixeira	2.00
310	Doug Sessions/SP **RC**	3.00
311	Josh Cisneros/SP **RC**	3.00
312	Carlos Brackley/SP **RC**	3.00
313	Tim Raines Jr.	.25
314	Ross Peeples/SP **RC**	5.00
315	Alexander Requena/SP **RC**	5.00
316	Chin-Hui Tsao	.25
317	Tony Alvarez	.25
318	Craig Kuzmic/SP **RC**	3.00
319	Peter Zamora/SP **RC**	3.00
320	Matt Parker/SP **RC**	3.00
321	Keith Ginter	.25
322	Gary Cates Jr./SP **RC**	3.00
323	Matt Belisle	.25
324	Ben Broussard	.25
324	Jake Mauer/auto **RC**	10.00
325	Dennis Tankersley	.25
326	Juan Silvestre	.25
327	Henry Pichardo/SP **RC**	3.00
328	Michael Floyd/SP **RC**	3.00
329	Clint Nageotte/SP **RC**	5.00
330	Raymond Cabrera/SP **RC**	3.00
331	Mauricio Lara/SP **RC**	4.00
332	Alejandro Cadena/SP **RC**	3.00
333	Jonny Gomes/SP **RC**	8.00
334	Jason Bulger/SP **RC**	4.00
335	Nate Teut	.25
336	David Gil/SP **RC**	3.00
337	Joel Crump/SP **RC**	3.00
338	Brandon Phillips	.50
339	Macay McBride	.50
340	Brandon Claussen	.50
341	Josh Phelps	.25
342	Freddie Money/SP **RC**	4.00
343	Clifford Bartosh/SP **RC**	3.00
344	Terrance Hill/SP **RC**	3.00
345	John Rodriguez/SP **RC**	4.00
346	Chris Latham/SP **RC**	3.00
347	Carlos Cabrera/SP **RC**	3.00
348	Jose Bautista/SP **RC**	5.00
349	Kevin Frederick/SP **RC**	3.00
350	Jerome Williams	.25
351	Napoleon Calzado/SP **RC**	3.00
352	Benito Baez/SP	3.00
353	Xavier Nady	.25
354	Jason Botts/SP **RC**	5.00
355	Steve Bechler/SP **RC**	4.00
356	Reed Johnson/SP **RC**	8.00
357	Mark Outlaw/SP **RC**	3.00
358	Jake Peavy	1.00
359	Josh Shaffer/SP **RC**	3.00
360	Dan Wright/SP	3.00
361	Ryan Gripp/SP **RC**	3.00
362	Nelson Castro/SP **RC**	3.00
363	Jason Bay/SP **RC**	25.00
364	Franklin German/SP **RC**	3.00
365	Corwin Malone/SP	3.00
366	Kelly Ramos/SP **RC**	3.00
367	John Ennis/SP **RC**	3.00
368	George Perez/SP	3.00
369	Rene Reyes/SP **RC**	3.00
370	Rolando Viera/SP **RC**	3.00
371	Earl Snyder/SP **RC**	4.00
372	Kyle Kane/SP **RC**	3.00
373	Mario Ramos/SP **RC**	3.00
374	Tyler Yates/SP **RC**	3.00
375	Jason Young/SP **RC**	5.00
376	Chris Bootcheck/SP **RC**	5.00
377	Jesus Cota/SP **RC**	5.00
378	Corky Miller/SP	3.00
379	Matt Erickson/SP **RC**	3.00
380	Justin Huber/SP **RC**	5.00
381	Felix Escalona/SP **RC**	3.00
382	Kevin Cash/SP **RC**	3.00
383	J.J. Putz/SP **RC**	4.00
384	Chris Snelling **RC**	10.00
385	David Wright	250.00
386	Brian Wolfe **RC**	10.00
387	Justin Reid **RC**	10.00
389	Ryan Raburn **RC**	10.00
390	Josh Barfield	10.00
391	Joe Mauer **RC**	100.00
392	Bobby Jenks **RC**	20.00
393	Rob Henkel **RC**	10.00
394	Jimmy Gobble **RC**	10.00
395	Jesse Foppert	10.00
396	Gavin Floyd	20.00
397	Nate Field **RC**	10.00
398	Ryan Doumit **RC**	25.00
399	Ron Calloway **RC**	10.00
400	Taylor Buchholz **RC**	10.00
401	Adam Roller **RC**	10.00
402	Cole Barthel	10.00
403	Kazuhisa Ishii/SP **RC**	5.00
404	So Taguchi/SP **RC**	4.00
405	Chris Baker **RC**	10.00

Refractors

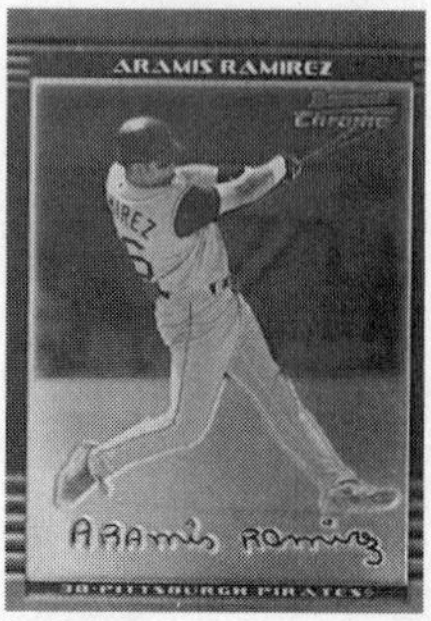

Star Refractors (1-220):	2-3X
SP Refractors:	.5-1.5X
Production 500	
X-Fractors (1-220):	3-5X
SP X-Fractors:	.75-2X
Production 250:	
Gold Refractors (1-220):	8-15X
SP Gold Refractors:	2-4X
Production 50	
Refractor Autos. (384-402,405)	.75-1.5X
Production 500	
X-Fractor Autos.:	.75-2X
Production 250	
Gold Autographs:	2-4X
Production 50	

Uncirculated

Cards:	1-3X
Production 350	
Autos. 10 cards of each player.	
No Pricing	

Rookie Reprints

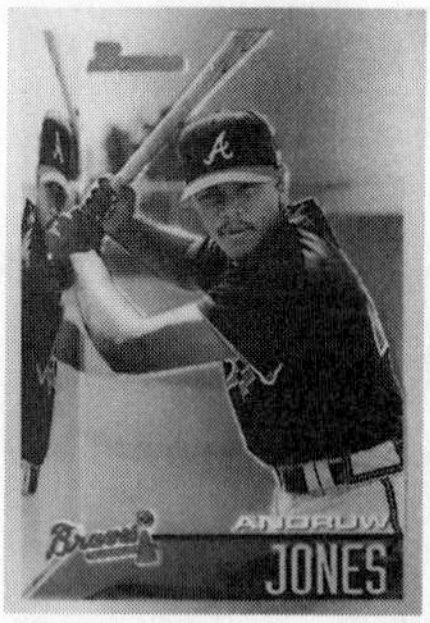

		NM/M
Complete Set (20):		25.00
Common Player:		1.00
Inserted 1:6		
Refractors:		1.5-2X
Inserted 1:18		
JB	Jeff Bagwell	1.50
BC	Bartolo Colon	1.00
CD	Carlos Delgado	1.00
JG	Juan Gonzalez	1.50
LG	Luis Gonzalez	1.00
KG	Ken Griffey Jr.	3.00
VG	Vladimir Guerrero	2.00
DJ	Derek Jeter	5.00
AJ	Andruw Jones	1.50
CJ	Chipper Jones	2.50
JK	Jason Kendall	1.00
MP	Mike Piazza	3.00
JP	Jorge Posada	1.00
IR	Ivan Rodriguez	1.00
SR	Scott Rolen	1.00
GS	Gary Sheffield	1.00
MS	Mike Sweeney	1.00
FT	Frank Thomas	1.50

LW	Larry Walker	1.00
BW	Bernie Williams	1.00

Ishii & Taguchi Autographs

		NM/M
Refractors:		.75-1.5X
Production 100		
X-Fractors:		2-4X
Production 50		
Golds: Production 10		
403	Kazuhisa Ishii	50.00
404	So Taguchi	25.00

2002 Bowman Chrome Draft Picks & Prospects

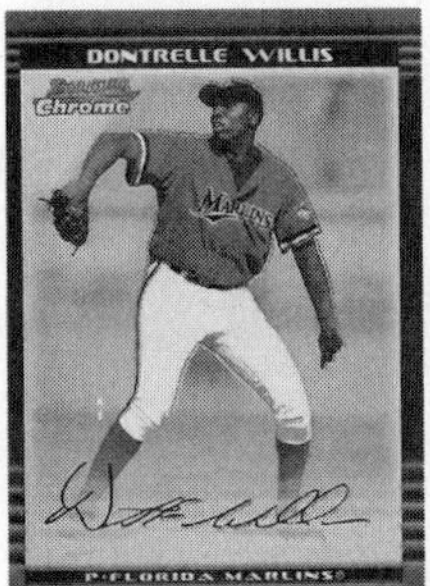

		NM/M
Complete Set (175):		275.00
Common Player:		.25
Common RC:		.75
1-165 Two Per Pack		
Common Auto.(166-175):		10.00
Auto's Inserted 1:45		
BDP1	Clint Everts **RC**	2.00
BDP2	Fred Lewis **RC**	5.00
BDP3	Jonathan Broxton **RC**	2.00
BDP4	Jason Anderson **RC**	.50
BDP5	Mike Eusebio **RC**	.50
BDP6	Zack Greinke **RC**	5.00
BDP7	Joe Blanton **RC**	5.00
BDP8	Sergio Santos **RC**	1.50
BDP9	Jason Cooper **RC**	1.50
BDP10	Delwyn Young **RC**	3.00
BDP11	Jeremy Hermida **RC**	10.00
BDP12	Dan Ortmeyer **RC**	1.50
BDP13	Kevin Jepsen **RC**	2.00
BDP14	Russ Adams **RC**	2.00
BDP15	Mike Nixon **RC**	.50
BDP16	Nick Swisher **RC**	10.00
BDP17	Cole Hamels **RC**	35.00
BDP18	Brian Dopirak **RC**	3.00
BDP19	James Loney **RC**	10.00
BDP20	Denard Span **RC**	3.00
BDP21	Billy Petrick **RC**	.50
BDP22	Jared Doyle **RC**	.50
BDP23	Jeff Francoeur **RC**	15.00
BDP24	Nick Bourgeois **RC**	.50
BDP25	Matt Cain **RC**	15.00
BDP26	John McCurdy **RC**	.50
BDP27	Mark Kiger **RC**	.50
BDP28	Bill Murphy **RC**	1.00
BDP29	Matt Craig **RC**	1.00
BDP30	Mike Megrew **RC**	1.00
BDP31	Ben Crockett **RC**	.50
BDP32	Luke Hagerty **RC**	1.50
BDP33	Matt Whitney **RC**	1.00
BDP34	Dan Meyer **RC**	1.50
BDP35	Jeremy Brown **RC**	1.00
BDP36	Doug Johnson **RC**	.50
BDP37	Steve Obenchain **RC**	.50
BDP38	Matt Clanton **RC**	1.00
BDP39	Mark Teahen **RC**	4.00
BDP40	Thomas Carrow **RC**	.50
BDP41	Micah Schilling **RC**	1.00
BDP42	Blair Johnson **RC**	1.00
BDP43	Jason Pridie **RC**	1.00
BDP44	Joey Votto **RC**	15.00
BDP45	Taber Lee **RC**	.50
BDP46	Adam Peterson **RC**	.50
BDP47	Adam Donachie **RC**	1.00
BDP48	Josh Murray **RC**	1.00
BDP49	Brent Clevlen **RC**	4.00
BDP50	Chad Pleiness **RC**	1.00
BDP51	Zach Hammes **RC**	1.50
BDP52	Chris Snyder **RC**	1.50
BDP53	Chris Smith	.50
BDP54	Justin Maureau **RC**	.50
BDP55	David Bush **RC**	3.00
BDP56	Tim Gilhooly **RC**	.50
BDP57	Blair Barbier **RC**	.50
BDP58	Zach Segovia **RC**	1.00
BDP59	Jeremy Reed **RC**	4.00
BDP60	Matt Pender **RC**	.50
BDP61	Eric Thomas **RC**	.50
BDP62	Justin Jones **RC**	1.50
BDP63	Brian Slocum **RC**	1.00
BDP64	Larry Broadway **RC**	1.50
BDP65	Bo Flowers **RC**	.50
BDP66	Scott White **RC**	1.00
BDP67	Steve Stanley **RC**	.50
BDP68	Alex Merricks **RC**	.50
BDP69	Josh Womack **RC**	.50
BDP70	Dave Jensen **RC**	.50
BDP71	Curtis Granderson **RC**	15.00
BDP72	Pat Osborn **RC**	1.50
BDP73	Nic Carter **RC**	.50
BDP74	Mitch Talbot **RC**	.50
BDP75	Don Murphy **RC**	.50
BDP76	Val Majewski **RC**	1.50
BDP77	Javy Rodriguez **RC**	.50
BDP78	Fernando Pacheco **RC**	1.00
BDP79	Steve Russell **RC**	.50
BDP80	Jon Slack **RC**	.50
BDP81	John Baker **RC**	.50
BDP82	Aaron Coonrod **RC**	.50
BDP83	Josh Johnson **RC**	4.00
BDP84	Jake Blalock **RC**	1.50
BDP85	Alex Hart **RC**	1.50
BDP86	Wes Bankston **RC**	5.00
BDP87	Josh Rupe **RC**	1.00
BDP88	Dan Cevette **RC**	1.00
BDP89	Kiel Fisher **RC**	1.00
BDP90	Alan Rick **RC**	.50
BDP91	Charlie Morton **RC**	1.00
BDP92	Chad Spann **RC**	1.00
BDP93	Kyle Boyer **RC**	1.00
BDP94	Bob Malek **RC**	.50
BDP95	Ryan Rodriguez **RC**	.50
BDP96	Jordan Renz **RC**	.50
BDP97	Randy Frye **RC**	.50
BDP98	Rich Hill **RC**	5.00
BDP99	B.J. Upton **RC**	15.00
BDP100	Dan Christensen **RC**	1.00
BDP101	Casey Kotchman	4.00
BDP102	Eric Good **RC**	.50
BDP103	Mike Fontenot **RC**	2.00
BDP104	John Webb **RC**	.50
BDP105	Jason Dubois **RC**	1.50
BDP106	Ryan Kibler **RC**	.50
BDP107	Jhonny Peralta **RC**	5.00
BDP108	Kirk Saarloos	1.50
BDP109	Rhett Parrott **RC**	.50
BDP110	Jason Grove **RC**	.50
BDP111	Colt Griffin	1.00
BDP112	Dallas McPherson	2.00
BDP113	Oliver Perez **RC**	4.00
BDP114	Marshall McDougall **RC**	.50
BDP115	Mike Wood **RC**	1.00
BDP116	Scott Hairston	1.50
BDP117	Jason Simontacchi **RC**	1.00
BDP118	Taggert Bozied **RC**	1.50
BDP119	Shelley Duncan **RC**	4.00
BDP120	Dontrelle Willis **RC**	4.00
BDP121	Sean Burnett	.25
BDP122	Aaron Cook **RC**	2.50
BPD123	Brett Evert	.25
BDP124	Jimmy Journell	.25
BDP125	Brett Myers	.25
BDP126	Brad Baker	.25
BDP127	Billy Traber	1.50
BDP128	Adam Wainwright	.50
BDP129	Jason Young	1.00
BDP130	John Buck	.25
BDP131	Kevin Cash	.25
BDP132	Jason Stokes **RC**	1.50
BDP133	Drew Henson	.50
BDP134	Chad Tracy **RC**	4.00
BDP135	Orlando Hudson	.50
BDP136	Brandon Phillips	.50
BDP137	Joe Borchard	.25
BDP138	Marlon Byrd	.25
BDP139	Carl Crawford	.50
BDP140	Michael Restovich	.25
BDP141	Corey Hart **RC**	6.00
BDP142	Edwin Almonte	.25
BDP143	Francis Beltran **RC**	1.00
BDP144	Jorge De La Rosa **RC**	.75
BDP145	Gerardo Garcia **RC**	.50
BDP146	Franklyn German **RC**	.50
BDP147	Francisco Liriano	10.00
BDP148	Francisco Rodriguez	.50
BDP149	Ricardo Rodriguez	.25
BDP150	Seung Jun Song	.25
BDP151	John Stephens	.25
BDP152	Justin Huber	2.00
BDP153	Victor Martinez	.50
BDP154	Hee Seop Choi	.25
BDP155	Justin Morneau	.75
BDP156	Miguel Cabrera	2.00
BDP157	Victor Diaz **RC**	2.00
BDP158	Jose Reyes	1.00
BDP159	Omar Infante **RC**	.50
BDP160	Angel Berroa	.25
BDP161	Tony Alvarez	.25
BDP162	Shin-Soo Choo **RC**	4.00
BDP163	Wily Mo Pena	.25
BDP164	Andres Torres	.25
BDP165	Jose Lopez **RC**	4.00
BDP166	Scott Moore/Auto. **RC**	10.00
BDP167	Chris Gruler/Auto. **RC**	10.00
BDP168	Joe Saunders/Auto. **RC**	25.00
BDP169	Jeff Francis/Auto. **RC**	20.00
BDP170	Royce Ring/Auto. **RC**	10.00
BDP171	Greg Miller/Auto.	10.00
BDP172	Brandon Weeden/ Auto. **RC**	10.00
BDP173	Drew Meyer/Auto. **RC**	10.00
BDP174	Khalil Greene/Auto. **RC**	20.00
BDP175	Mark Schramek/ Auto. **RC**	10.00

Refractor

Cards 1-165:	2-4X
Rookies 1-175:	2-3X
1-165 Production 300 Sets	
166-175 Inserted 1:154	

Gold Refractor

Cards 1-165:	8-15X
Rookies 1-165:	5-10X
1-165 Production 50 Sets	
166-175 No Pricing	

X-Fractor

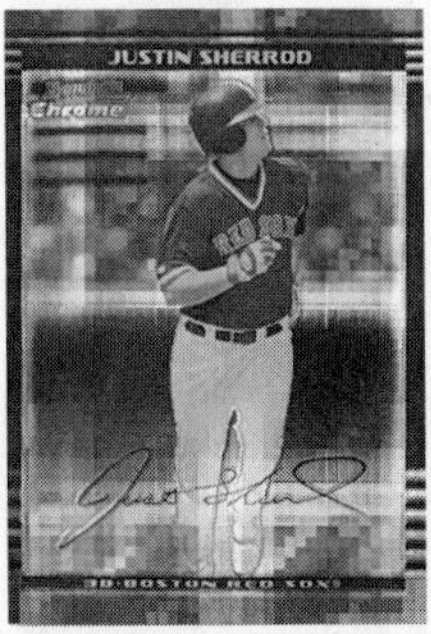

Cards 1-165:	2-5X
Rookies 1-165:	3-4X
Rookies 166-175:	.75-1.5X
1-165 Production 150 Sets	
166-175 Inserted 1:309	

2002 Bowman Draft Picks & Prospects

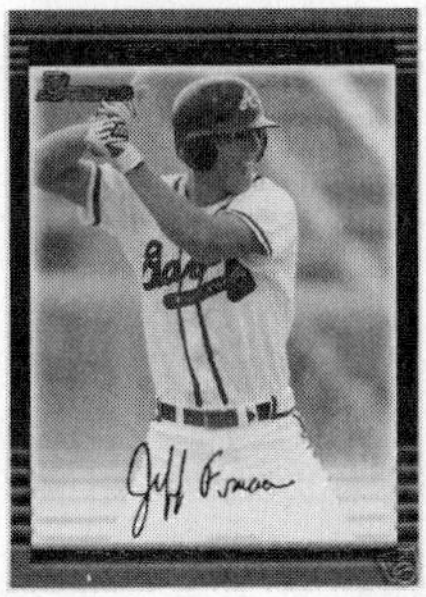

		NM/M
Complete Set (165):		35.00
Common Player:		.15
Common RC:		.25
Pack: (4 + 2 Chrome):		10.00
Box (24):		200.00
BDP1	Clint Everts **RC**	.75
BDP2	Fred Lewis **RC**	1.50
BDP3	Jonathan Broxton **RC**	.75
BDP4	Jason Anderson **RC**	.25
BDP5	Mike Eusebio **RC**	.25
BDP6	Zack Greinke **RC**	2.00
BDP7	Joe Blanton **RC**	2.00
BDP8	Sergio Santos **RC**	.50
BDP9	Jason Cooper **RC**	.50
BDP10	Delwyn Young **RC**	1.00
BDP11	Jeremy Hermida **RC**	3.00
BDP12	Dan Ortmeyer **RC**	.40
BDP13	Kevin Jepsen **RC**	.50
BDP14	Russ Adams **RC**	1.00
BDP15	Mike Nixon **RC**	.40
BDP16	Nick Swisher **RC**	4.00
BDP17	Cole Hamels **RC**	10.00
BDP18	Brian Dopirak **RC**	1.00
BDP19	James Loney **RC**	4.00
BDP20	Denard Span **RC**	1.00
BDP21	Billy Petrick **RC**	.25
BDP22	Jared Doyle **RC**	.25
BDP23	Jeff Francoeur **RC**	5.00
BDP24	Nick Bourgeois **RC**	.25
BDP25	Matt Cain **RC**	5.00
BDP26	John McCurdy **RC**	.40
BDP27	Mark Kiger **RC**	.15
BDP28	Bill Murphy **RC**	.40
BDP29	Matt Craig **RC**	.25
BDP30	Mike Megrew **RC**	.50
BDP31	Ben Crockett **RC**	.25
BDP32	Luke Hagerty **RC**	.50
BDP33	Matt Whitney **RC**	1.00
BDP34	Dan Meyer **RC**	.50
BDP35	Jeremy Brown **RC**	.50
BDP36	Doug Johnson **RC**	.25
BDP37	Steve Obenchain **RC**	.25
BDP38	Matt Clanton **RC**	.40
BDP39	Mark Teahen **RC**	1.50
BDP40	Thomas Carrow **RC**	.25
BDP41	Micah Schilling **RC**	.50
BDP42	Blair Johnson **RC**	.25
BDP43	Jason Pridie **RC**	.75
BDP44	Joey Votto **RC**	4.00
BDP45	Taber Lee **RC**	.25
BDP46	Adam Peterson **RC**	.25
BDP47	Adam Donachie **RC**	.40
BDP48	Josh Murray **RC**	.40
BDP49	Brent Clevlen **RC**	1.00
BDP50	Chad Pleiness **RC**	.40
BDP51	Zach Hammes **RC**	.50
BDP52	Chris Snyder **RC**	.50
BDP53	Chris Smith	.25
BDP54	Justin Maureau **RC**	.25
BDP55	David Bush **RC**	1.00
BDP56	Tim Gilhooly **RC**	.25
BDP57	Blair Barbier **RC**	.25
BDP58	Zach Segovia **RC**	.50
BDP59	Jeremy Reed **RC**	2.00
BDP60	Matt Pender **RC**	.25
BDP61	Eric Thomas **RC**	.25
BDP62	Justin Jones **RC**	1.00
BDP63	Brian Slocum **RC**	.40
BDP64	Larry Broadway **RC**	1.00
BDP65	Bo Flowers **RC**	.25
BDP66	Scott White **RC**	.75
BDP67	Steve Stanley **RC**	.25
BDP68	Alex Merricks **RC**	.25
BDP69	Josh Womack **RC**	.40
BDP70	Dave Jensen **RC**	.25
BDP71	Curtis Granderson **RC**	4.00
BDP72	Pat Osborn **RC**	.40
BDP73	Nic Carter **RC**	.25
BDP74	Mitch Talbot **RC**	.25
BDP75	Don Murphy **RC**	.25
BDP76	Val Majewski **RC**	.50
BDP77	Javy Rodriguez **RC**	.25
BDP78	Fernando Pacheco **RC**	.40
BDP79	Steve Russell **RC**	.25
BDP80	Jon Slack **RC**	.25
BDP81	John Baker **RC**	.25
BDP82	Aaron Coonrod **RC**	.25
BDP83	Josh Johnson **RC**	2.00
BDP84	Jake Blalock **RC**	.75
BDP85	Alex Hart **RC**	.50
BDP86	Wes Bankston **RC**	1.00
BDP87	Josh Rupe **RC**	.40
BDP88	Dan Cevette **RC**	.75
BDP89	Kiel Fisher **RC**	.50
BDP90	Alan Rick **RC**	.25
BDP91	Charlie Morton **RC**	.50
BDP92	Chad Spann **RC**	.50
BDP93	Kyle Boyer **RC**	.25
BDP94	Bob Malek **RC**	.25
BDP95	Ryan Rodriguez **RC**	.25
BDP96	Jordan Renz **RC**	.25
BDP97	Randy Frye **RC**	.25
BDP98	Rich Hill **RC**	2.00
BDP99	B.J. Upton **RC**	5.00
BDP100	Dan Christensen **RC**	.50
BDP101	Casey Kotchman	1.00
BDP102	Eric Good **RC**	.25
BDP103	Mike Fontenot **RC**	.75
BDP104	John Webb **RC**	.25
BDP105	Jason Dubois **RC**	.75
BDP106	Ryan Kibler **RC**	.25
BDP107	Jhonny Peralta **RC**	2.50
BDP108	Kirk Saarloos	.75
BDP109	Rhett Parrott **RC**	.25
BDP110	Jason Grove **RC**	.25
BDP111	Colt Griffin	.50
BDP112	Dallas McPherson	1.00
BDP113	Oliver Perez **RC**	1.50
BDP114	Marshall McDougall **RC**	.25
BDP115	Mike Wood **RC**	.40
BDP116	Scott Hairston	1.00
BDP117	Jason Simontacchi **RC**	.50
BDP118	Taggert Bozied **RC**	1.00
BDP119	Shelley Duncan **RC**	2.00
BDP120	Dontrelle Willis **RC**	2.00
BDP121	Sean Burnett	.15
BDP122	Aaron Cook **RC**	.50
BPD123	Brett Evert	.15
BDP124	Jimmy Journell	.15
BDP125	Brett Myers	.15
BDP126	Brad Baker	.15
BDP127	Billy Traber	.50
BDP128	Adam Wainwright	.15
BDP129	Jason Young **RC**	.40
BDP130	John Buck	.15
BDP131	Kevin Cash **RC**	.25
BDP132	Jason Stokes **RC**	.50
BDP133	Drew Henson	.25
BDP134	Chad Tracy **RC**	1.50
BDP135	Orlando Hudson	.15
BDP136	Brandon Phillips	.15
BDP137	Joe Borchard	.15
BDP138	Marlon Byrd	.15
BDP139	Carl Crawford	.25
BDP140	Michael Restovich	.15
BDP141	Corey Hart **RC**	2.00
BDP142	Edwin Almonte	.15
BDP143	Francis Beltran **RC**	.25
BDP144	Jorge De La Rosa **RC**	.50
BDP145	Gerardo Garcia **RC**	.25
BDP146	Franklyn German **RC**	.25
BDP147	Francisco Liriano	4.00
BDP148	Francisco Rodriguez	.50
BDP149	Ricardo Rodriguez	.15
BDP150	Seung Jun Song	.15
BDP151	John Stephens	.15
BDP152	Justin Huber **RC**	1.00
BDP153	Victor Martinez	.50
BDP154	Hee Seop Choi	.15
BDP155	Justin Morneau	.50
BDP156	Miguel Cabrera	.75
BDP157	Victor Diaz **RC**	1.00
BDP158	Jose Reyes	.50
BDP159	Omar Infante **RC**	.25
BDP160	Angel Berroa	.15
BDP161	Tony Alvarez	.15

BDP162	Shin-Soo Choo **RC**	1.00
BDP163	Wily Mo Pena	.15
BDP164	Andres Torres	.15
BDP165	Jose Lopez **RC**	2.00

Gold

Rookies: .75-1.5X
Inserted 1:1

Fabric of Future

		NM/M
Common Player:		4.00
Inserted 1:55		
EA	Edwin Almonte	4.00
TA	Tony Alvarez	4.00
FB	Francis Beltran	4.00
AB	Angel Berroa	4.00
SB	Sean Burnett	4.00
KC	Kevin Cash	4.00
HC	Hee Seop Choi	4.00
SC	Shin-Soo Choo	8.00
CC	Carl Crawford	8.00
JR	Jorge de la Rosa	4.00
VD	Victor Diaz	4.00
GG	Gerardo Garcia	4.00
FG	Franklyn German	4.00
CH	Corey Hart	10.00
DH	Drew Henson	5.00
JH	Justin Huber	4.00
JK	Josh Karp	4.00
FL	Francisco Liriano	10.00
JL	Jose Lopez	8.00
BM	Brett Meyers	4.00
WP	Wily Mo Pena	4.00
MR	Michael Restovich	4.00
JS	John Stephens	4.00
JS	Jason Stokes	4.00
AT	Andres Torres	4.00
BT	Billy Traber	4.00
CT	Chad Tracy	8.00
AW	Adam Wainwright	10.00

Freshman Fiber

		NM/M
Common Player:		4.00
Bat inserted 1:605		
Jersey 1:45		
BA	Brent Abernathy	4.00
DB	Dewon Brazelton	4.00
MB	Marlon Byrd/Bat	4.00
TH	Toby Hall	4.00
JH	Josh Hamilton	10.00
AH	Aubrey Huff	6.00
AK	Austin Kearns/Bat	4.00
JK	Joe Kennedy	4.00
JS	Jared Sandberg	4.00
JWS	Jason Standridge	4.00
MT	Mark Teixeira/Bat	10.00
JV	John Van Benschoten	4.00

Signs of the Future

		NM/M
Common Autograph:		5.00
EB	Erik Bedard	15.00
LB	Larry Bigbie	5.00
TB	Taylor Buchholz	5.00
DD	Daniel Denham	5.00
ME	Morgan Ensberg	8.00
MF	Mike Fontenot	8.00
KH	Kris Honel	5.00
BI	Brandon Inge	10.00
NJ	Nic Jackson	5.00
MJ	Mitch Jones	5.00
BK	Bob Keppel	5.00
TL	Todd Linden	8.00
JM	Jake Mauer	5.00
JEM	Justin Morneau	25.00
LN	Lance Niekro	5.00
CP	Christian Parra	5.00
BP	Brandon Phillips	15.00
JR	Juan Rivera	5.00
BS	Bud Smith	5.00
AT	Chad Tracy	10.00
JW	Jerome Williams	5.00

2002 Bowman Heritage

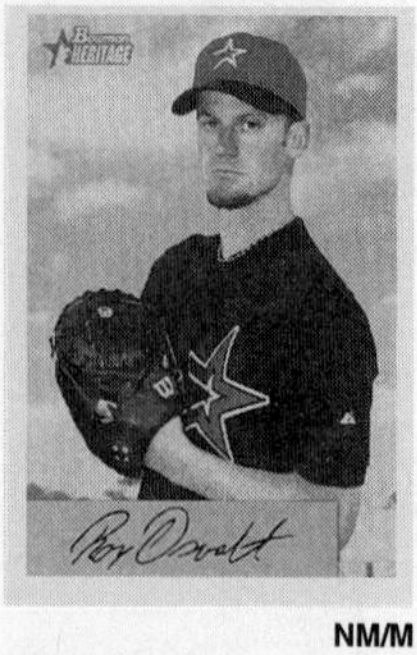

		NM/M
Complete Set (440):		190.00
Common Player:		.25
Common SP:		1.00
Inserted 1:2		
Black Box Variations:		2-3X
Inserted 1:2		
Pack (10):		3.00
Box (24):		60.00
1	Brent Abernathy	.25
2	Jermaine Dye	.25
3	James Shanks **RC**	.40
4	Chris Flinn **RC**	.40
5	Mike Peeples/SP **RC**	1.50
6	Gary Sheffield	.50
7	Livan Hernandez/SP	1.00
8	Jeff Austin **RC**	.40
9	Jeremy Giambi	.25
10	Adam Roller **RC**	.50
11	Sandy Alomar Jr./SP	1.00
12	Matt Williams/SP	1.00
13	Hee Seop Choi	.25
14	Jose Offerman	.25
15	Robin Ventura	.25
16	Craig Biggio	.50
17	David Wells	.40
18	Rob Henkel **RC**	.40
19	Edgar Martinez	.25
20	Matt Morris/SP	2.00
21	Jose Valentin	.25
22	Barry Bonds	2.50
23	Justin Schuda **RC**	.50
24	Josh Phelps	.25
25	John Rodriguez **RC**	.50
26	Angel Pagan **RC**	1.50
27	Aramis Ramirez	.50
28	Jack Wilson	.25
29	Roger Clemens	2.00
30	Kazuhisa Ishii **RC**	.50
31	Carlos Beltran	.75
32	Drew Henson/SP	1.50
33	Kevin Young/SP	1.00
34	Juan Cruz	.25
35	Curtis Legendre **RC**	.40
36	Jose Morban **RC**	.50
37	Ricardo Cordova/SP **RC**	1.50
38	Adam Everett	.25
39	Mark Prior	.40
40	Jose Bautista **RC**	.75
41	Travis Foley	.25
42	Kerry Wood	.50
43	B.J. Surhoff	.25
44	Moises Alou	.40
45	Joey Hammond **RC**	.50
46	Eric Bruntlett **RC**	.50
47	Carlos Guillen	.25
48	Joe Crede	.40
49	Dan Phillips **RC**	.50
50	Jason LaRue	.25
51	Javy Lopez	.25
52	Larry Bigbie/SP	1.00
53	Chris Baker **RC**	.75
54	Marty Cordova	.25
55	C.C. Sabathia	.25
56	Mike Piazza	1.00
57	Brian Giles	.25
58	Mike Bordick/SP	1.00
59	Tyler Houston/SP	1.00
60	Gabe Kapler	.25
61	Ben Broussard	.25
62	Steve Finley/SP	1.50
63	Koyie Hill	.25
64	Jeff D'Amico	.25
65	Edwin Almonte **RC**	.50
66a	Pedro J. Martinez	1.00
66b	Nomar Garciaparra (Same front and back as his #289 card.)	1.00
67	Travis Fryman/SP	1.50
68	Brady Clark	.25
69	Reed Johnson/SP **RC**	2.00
70	Mark Grace/SP	4.00
71	Tony Batista/SP	1.00
72	Roy Oswalt	.50
73	Pat Burrell	.50
74	Dennis Tankersley	.25
75	Ramon Ortiz	.25
76	Neal Frendling/SP **RC**	1.50
77	Omar Vizquel/SP	2.00
78	Hideo Nomo	.25
79	Orlando Hernandez/SP	1.50
80	Andy Pettitte	.50
81	Cole Barthel	.25
82	Bret Boone	.25
83	Alfonso Soriano	1.00
84	Brandon Duckworth	.25
85	Ben Grieve	.25
86	Mike Rosamond/SP **RC**	1.50
87	Luke Prokopec	.25
88	Chone Figgins **RC**	2.00
89	Rick Ankiel/SP	2.00
90	David Eckstein	.25
91	Corey Koskie	.25
92	David Justice	.25
93	Jimmy Alvarez **RC**	.40
94	Jason Schmidt	.40
95	Reggie Sanders	.25
96	Victor Alvarez **RC**	.40
97	Brett Roneberg **RC**	.40
98	D'Angelo Jimenez	.25
99	Hank Blalock	.40
100	Juan Rivera	.25
101	Mark Buehrle/SP	1.50
102	Juan Uribe	.25
103	Royce Clayton/SP	1.00
104	Brett Kay **RC**	.50
105	John Olerud	.25
106	Richie Sexson	.40
107	Chipper Jones	1.00
108	Adam Dunn	.50
109	Tim Salmon/SP	1.50
110	Eric Karros	.25
111	Jose Vidro	.25
112	Jerry Hairston Jr.	.25
113	Anastacio Martinez **RC**	.50
114	Robert Fick/SP	1.50
115	Randy Johnson	1.00
116	Trot Nixon/SP	2.00
117	Nick Bierbrodt/SP	1.00
118	Jim Edmonds	.40
119	Rafael Palmeiro	.50
120	Jose Macias	.25
121	Josh Beckett	.50
122	Sean Douglass	.25
123	Jeff Kent	.40
124	Tim Redding	.25
125	Xavier Nady	.25
126	Carl Everett	.25
127	Joe Randa	.25
128	Luke Hudson/SP	1.00
129	Eric Miller **RC**	.40
130	Melvin Mora	.25
131	Adrian Gonzalez	.25
132	Larry Walker/SP	1.50
133	Nic Jackson/SP **RC**	2.00
134	Mike Lowell/SP	1.50
135	Jim Thome	.50
136	Eric Milton	.25
137	Rich Thompson/SP **RC**	1.50
138	Placido Polanco/SP	1.00
139	Juan Pierre	.25
140	David Segui	.25
141	Chuck Finley	.25
142	Felipe Lopez	.25
143	Toby Hall	.25
144	Fred Bastardo **RC**	.50
145	Troy Glaus	.50
146	Todd Helton	.75
147	Ruben Gotay/SP **RC**	1.50
148	Darin Erstad	.40
149	Ryan Gripp/SP **RC**	1.50
150	Orlando Cabrera	.25
151	Jason Young **RC**	.50
152	Sterling Hitchcock/SP	1.00
153	Miguel Tejada	.75
154	Al Leiter	.25
155	Taylor Buchholz **RC**	.40
156	Juan Gonzalez	.40
157	Damion Easley	.25
158	Jimmy Gobble **RC**	1.00
159	Dennis Ulacia/SP	1.00
160	Shane Reynolds/SP	1.00
161	Javier Colina	.25
162	Frank Thomas	1.00
163	Chuck Knoblauch	.25
164	Sean Burroughs	.25
165	Greg Maddux	1.50
166	Jason Ellison **RC**	.50
167	Tony Womack	.25
168	Randall Shelley/SP **RC**	1.50
169	Jason Marquis	.25
170	Brian Jordan	.25
171	Darryl Kile	.25
172	Barry Zito	.40
173	Matt Allegra/SP **RC**	1.50
174	Ralph Santana/SP **RC**	1.50
175	Carlos Lee	.40
176	Richard Hidalgo/SP	1.00
177	Kevin Deaton **RC**	.50
178	Juan Encarnacion	.25
179	Mark Quinn	.25
180	Rafael Furcal	.40
181	Garret Anderson	.50
182	David Wright	15.00
183	Jose Reyes	.50
184	Mario Ramos/SP	1.00
185	J.D. Drew	.50
186	Juan Gonzalez	.50
187	Nick Neugebauer	.25
188	Alejandro Giron **RC**	.50
189	John Burkett	.25
190	Ben Sheets	.50
191	Vinny Castilla/SP	1.00
192	Cory Lidle	.25
193	Fernando Vina	.25
194	Russell Branyan/SP	1.00
195	Ben Davis	.25
196	Angel Berroa	.25
197	Alex Gonzalez	.25
198	Jared Sandberg	.25
199	Travis Lee/SP	1.00
200	Luis DePaula/SP **RC**	1.50
201	Ramon Hernandez/SP	1.00
202	Brandon Inge	.25
203	Aubrey Huff	.25
204	Mike Rivera	.25
205	Brad Nelson **RC**	.50
206	Colt Griffin/SP	2.00
207	Joel Pineiro	.25
208	Adam Pettyjohn	.25
209	Mark Redman	.25
210	Roberto Alomar/SP	3.00
211	Denny Neagle	.25
212	Adam Kennedy	.25
213	Jason Arnold/SP	2.00
214	Jamie Moyer	.25
215	Aaron Boone	.25
216	Doug Glanville	.25
217	Nick Johnson/SP	1.00
218	Mike Cameron/SP	1.50
219	Tim Wakefield/SP	1.50
220	Todd Stottlemyre/SP	1.00
221	Mo Vaughn	.25
222	Vladimir Guerrero	1.00
223	Bill Ortega	.25
224	Kevin Brown	.25
225	Peter Bergeron/SP	1.00
226	Shannon Stewart/SP	1.50
227	Eric Chavez	.50
228	Clint Weibl **RC**	.40
229	Todd Hollandsworth/SP	1.00
230	Jeff Bagwell	.50
231	Chad Qualls **RC**	.40
232	Ben Howard **RC**	1.00
233	Rondell White/SP	1.50
234	Fred McGriff	.20
235	Steve Cox/SP	1.00
236	Chris Tritle **RC**	1.50
237	Eric Valent	.25
238	Joe Mauer **RC**	5.00
239	Shawn Green	.40
240	Jimmy Rollins	.75
241	Edgar Renteria	.25
242	Edwin Yan **RC**	.40
243	Noochie Varner **RC**	.40
244	Kris Benson/SP	1.50
245	Mike Hampton	.25
246	So Taguchi **RC**	1.00
247	Sammy Sosa	.75
248	Terrence Long	.25
249	Jason Bay **RC**	4.00
250	Kevin Millar/SP	1.00
251	Albert Pujols	2.50
252	Chris Latham **RC**	.40
253	Eric Byrnes	.25
254	Napoleon Calzado/SP **RC**	1.50
255	Bobby Higginson	.25
256	Ben Molina	.25
257	Torii Hunter/SP	3.00
258	Jason Giambi	.50
259	Bartolo Colon	.25
260	Benito Baez	.25
261	Ichiro Suzuki	2.00
262	Mike Sweeney	.25
263	Brian West **RC**	.40
264	Brad Penny	.25
265	Kevin Millwood/SP	2.00
266	Orlando Hudson	.25
267	Doug Mientkiewicz	.25
268	Luis Gonzalez/SP	1.50
269	Jay Caligiuri **RC**	.40
270	Nate Cornejo/SP	1.00
271	Lee Stevens	.25
272	Eric Hinske	.25
273	Antwon Rollins **RC**	.50
274	Bobby Jenks **RC**	1.00
275	Joe Mays	.25
276	Josh Shaffer **RC**	.40
277	Jonny Gomes **RC**	3.00
278	Bernie Williams	.50
279	Ed Rogers	.25
280	Carlos Delgado	.50
281	Raul Mondesi/SP	1.50
282	Jose Ortiz	.25
283	Cesar Izturis	.25
284	Ryan Dempster/SP	1.00
285	Brian Daubach	.25
286	Hansel Izquierdo **RC**	.40
287	Mike Lieberthal/SP	1.00
288	Marcus Thames	.25
289	Nomar Garciaparra	.50
290	Brad Fullmer	.25
291	Tino Martinez	.25
292	James Barrett **RC**	.40
293	Jacque Jones	.25
294	Nick Alvarez/SP **RC**	1.50
295	Jason Grove/SP **RC**	1.50
296	Mike Wilson/SP **RC**	1.50
297	J.T. Snow	.25
298	Cliff Floyd	.25
299	Todd Hundley/SP	1.00
300	Tony Clark/SP	1.00
301	Demetrius Heath **RC**	.40
302	Morgan Ensberg	.25
303	Cristian Guzman	.25
304	Frank Catalanotto	.25
305	Jeff Weaver	.25
306	Tim Hudson	.50
307	Scott Wiggins/SP **RC**	1.50
308	Shea Hillenbrand/SP	2.00
309	Todd Walker/SP	1.00
310	Tsuyoshi Shinjo	.25
311	Adrian Beltre	.40
312	Craig Kuzmic **RC**	.40
313	Paul Konerko	.40
314	Scott Hairston	1.50
315	Chan Ho Park	.25
316	Jorge Posada	.40
317	Chris Snelling **RC**	.75
318	Keith Foulke	.25
319	John Smoltz	.50
320	Ryan Church/SP **RC**	3.00
321	Mike Mussina	.75
322	Tony Armas Jr/SP	1.00
323	Craig Counsell	.25
324	Marcus Giles	.25
325	Greg Vaughn	.25
326	Curt Schilling	.75
327	Jeromy Burnitz	.25
328	Eric Byrnes	.25
329	Johnny Damon	.75
330	Michael Floyd/SP **RC**	1.50
331	Edgardo Alfonzo	.25
332	Jeremy Hill **RC**	.40
333	Josh Bonifay **RC**	.40
334	Byung-Hyun Kim	.25
335	Keith Ginter	.25
336	Ronald Acuna/SP **RC**	1.50
337	Mike Hill/SP **RC**	1.50
338	Sean Casey	.25

339	Matt Anderson/SP	1.00
340	Dan Wright	.25
341	Ben Petrick	.25
342	Mike Sirotka/SP	1.00
343	Alex Rodriguez	2.50
344	Einar Diaz	.25
345	Derek Jeter	2.50
346	Jeff Conine	.25
347	Ray Durham/SP	1.00
348	Wilson Betemit/SP	1.00
349	Jeffrey Hammonds	.25
350	Dan Trumble RC	.40
351	Phil Nevin/SP	1.50
352	A.J. Burnett	.25
353	Bill Mueller	.25
354	Charles Nagy	.25
355	Rusty Greer/SP	1.00
356	Jason Botts RC	.25
357	Magglio Ordonez	.50
358	Kevin Appier	.25
359	Brad Radke	.25
360	Chris George	.25
361	Chris Piersoll RC	.25
362	Ivan Rodriguez	.50
363	Jim Kavourias	.25
364	Rick Helling/SP	1.00
365	Dean Palmer	.25
366	Rich Aurilia/SP	1.00
367	Ryan Vogelsong	.25
368	Matt Lawton	.25
369	Wade Miller	.25
370	Dustin Hermanson	.25
371	Craig Wilson	.25
372	Todd Zeile/SP	1.00
373	Jon Guzman RC	.40
374	Ellis Burks	.25
375	Robert Cosby/SP RC	1.50
376	Jason Kendall	.25
377	Scott Rolen/SP	4.00
378	Andruw Jones	.50
379	Greg Sain RC	.40
380	Paul LoDuca	.25
381	Scotty Layfield RC	.40
382	Drew Henson	.50
383	Garrett Guzman RC	.40
384	Jack Cust	.25
385	Shayne Wright RC	.40
386	Derrek Lee	.75
387	Jesus Medrano RC	.40
388	Javier Vazquez	.25
389	Preston Wilson/SP	1.50
390	Gavin Floyd	1.50
391	Sidney Ponson/SP	1.00
392	Jose Hernandez	.25
393	Scott Erickson/SP	1.00
394	Jose Valverde RC	.40
395	Mark Hamilton/SP RC	1.50
396	Brad Cresse	.25
397	Danny Bautista	.25
398	Ray Lankford/SP	1.00
399	Miguel Batista/SP	1.00
400	Brent Butler	.25
401	Manny Delcarmen/SP RC	1.50
402	Kyle Farnsworth/SP	1.00
403	Freddy Garcia	.25
404	Joe Jiannetti RC	.40
405	Josh Barfield	.40
406	Corey Patterson	.25
407	Josh Towers	.25
408	Carlos Pena	.25
409	Jeff Cirillo	.25
410	Jon Lieber	.25
411	Woody Williams/SP	1.00
412	Richard Lane/SP RC	1.50
413	Alex Gonzalez	.25
414	Wilkin Ruan	.25
415	Geoff Jenkins	.25
416	Carlos Hernandez	.25
417	Matt Clement/SP	1.50
418	Jose Cruz Jr.	.25
419	Jake Mauer RC	.50
420	Matt Childers RC	.50
421	Tom Glavine/SP	2.50
422	Ken Griffey Jr.	2.00
423	Anderson Hernandez RC	.40
424	John Suomi RC	.40
425	Doug Sessions RC	.40
426	Jaret Wright	.25
427	Rolando Viera/SP RC	1.50
428	Aaron Sele	.25
429	Dmitri Young	.25
430	Ryan Klesko	.25
431	Kevin Tapani/SP	1.00
432	Joe Kennedy	.25
433	Austin Kearns	.40
434	Roger Cedeno	.25
435	Lance Berkman	.50
436	Frank Menechino	.25
437	Brett Myers	.25
438	Bobby Abreu	.50
439	Shawn Estes	.25

Chrome Refractor

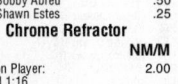

	NM/M
Common Player:	2.00
Inserted 1:16	
Production 350 Sets	
Gold Refractors:	2-4X
Inserted 1:32	
Production 175 Sets	

1	Edwin Almonte	.75
2	Moises Alou	4.00
3	Benito Baez	2.00
4	Lance Berkman	5.00
5	Bret Boone	2.00
6	Taylor Buchholz	2.00
7	Pat Burrell	5.00
8	Sean Burroughs	2.00
9	Orlando Cabrera	4.00
10	Sean Casey	3.00
11	Matt Childers	2.00
12	Brady Clark	2.00
13	Roger Clemens	10.00
14	Marty Cordova	2.00
15	Craig Counsell	2.00
16	Juan Cruz	2.00
17	Jack Cust	3.00
18	Ben Davis	2.00
19	Sean Douglass	2.00
20	Brandon Duckworth	2.00
21	David Eckstein	3.00
22	Morgan Ensberg	2.00
23	Darin Erstad	3.00
24	Carl Everett	2.00
25	Nomar Garciaparra	5.00
26	Marcus Giles	2.00
27	Alex Gonzalez	2.00
28	Juan Gonzalez	4.00
29	Shawn Green	3.00
30	Cristian Guzman	2.00
31	Mike Hampton	3.00
32	Rob Henkel	2.00
33	Dave Wells	2.00
34	Brad Fullmer	2.00
35	Jeremy Giambi	2.00
36	Koyie Hill	2.00
37	Tim Hudson	4.00
38	Hansel Izquierdo	2.00
39	Geoff Jenkins	2.00
40	D'Angelo Jimenez	2.00
41	Andruw Jones	5.00
42	Brian Jordan	2.00
43	Jason Kendall	2.00
44	Ryan Klesko	2.00
45	Paul Konerko	4.00
46	Matt Lawton	2.00
47	Scotty Layfield	2.00
48	Paul LoDuca	2.00
49	Terrence Long	2.00
50	Pedro Martinez	8.00
51	Tino Martinez	4.00
52	Jake Mauer	2.00
53	Fred McGriff	4.00
54	Doug Mientkiewicz	2.00
55	Wade Miller	2.00
56	Melvin Mora	3.00
57	Mike Mussina	5.00
58	Hideo Nomo	4.00
59	Tomokazu Ohka	2.00
60	Magglio Ordonez	4.00
61	Rafael Palmeiro	5.00
62	Corey Patterson	3.00
63	Carlos Pena	5.00
64	Josh Phelps	2.00
65	Joel Pineiro	2.00
66	Luke Prokopec	2.00
67	Mark Quinn	2.00
68	Joe Randa	2.00
69	Tim Redding	2.00
70	Mark Redman	2.00
71	Jose Reyes	10.00
72	Juan Rivera	2.00
73	John Rodriguez	2.00
74	Antwon Rollins	2.00
75	C.C. Sabathia	5.00
76	Reggie Sanders	2.00
77	Curt Schilling	6.00
78	Jason Schmidt	3.00
79	David Segui	3.00
80	Richie Sexson	4.00
81	Doug Sessions	2.00
82	John Smoltz	5.00
83	Alfonso Soriano	6.00
84	Lee Stevens	2.00
85	Mike Sweeney	2.00
86	Dennis Tankersley	2.00
87	Marcus Thames	2.00
88	Frank Thomas	8.00
89	Josh Towers	2.00
90	Brent Abernathy	2.00
91	Eric Valent	2.00
92	Jose Valverde	2.00
93	Mo Vaughn	2.00
94	Robin Ventura	2.00
95	Jack Wilson	2.00
96	Dan Wright	2.00
97	Dmitri Young	2.00
98	Barry Zito	3.00
99	Shayne Wright	2.00
100	Ryan Vogelsong	2.00
101	Noochie Varner	2.00
102	Ben Sheets	4.00
103	Ed Rogers	2.00
104	Mike Rivera	2.00
105	Edgar Renteria	4.00
106	Brad Penny	2.00
107	Ramon Ortiz	2.00
108	Nick Neugebauer	4.00
109	Xavier Nady	2.00
110	Randy Johnson	8.00

Autographs

	NM/M
Common Player:	8.00
Inserted 1:45	
LB	Lance Berkman	30.00
HB	Hank Blalock	10.00
KG	Keith Ginter	8.00
TH	Toby Hall	2.00
DH	Drew Henson	10.00
KI	Kazuhisa Ishii	10.00
CI	Cesar Izturis	10.00
PL	Paul LoDuca	2.00
JM	Joe Mauer	60.00
RO	Roy Oswalt	15.00
MP	Mark Prior	15.00
AP	Albert Pujols	200.00
JR	Juan Rivera	8.00

Relics

DARIN ERSTAD

	NM/M
Common Player:	4.00
Inserted 1:47	
EA	Edgardo Alfonzo	4.00
JB	Josh Beckett	10.00
BB	Barry Bonds	20.00
EC	Eric Chavez	4.00
CD	Carlos Delgado	5.00
JE	Jim Edmonds	4.00
DE	Darin Erstad	4.00
NG	Nomar Garciaparra	8.00
TG	Tony Gwynn	10.00
TH	Todd Helton	8.00
CJ	Chipper Jones	8.00
PK	Paul Konerko	8.00
GM	Greg Maddux	15.00
EM	Edgar Martinez	4.00
MP	Mike Piazza	10.00
AP	Albert Pujols	20.00
MR	Mariano Rivera	8.00
IR	Ivan Rodriguez	5.00
SR	Scott Rolen	10.00
TS	Tim Salmon	4.00
KS	Kazuhiro Sasaki	4.00
JS	John Smoltz	8.00
FT	Frank Thomas	8.00
JT	Jim Thome	8.00
LW	Larry Walker	4.00
PW	Preston Wilson	2.00

Team Topps Legends
Autographs

	NM/M
Common Player:	8.00
Gil McDougald	10.00
Joe Pepitone	10.00
Bobby Richardson	10.00
Robin Roberts	15.00
Warren Spahn	40.00
Luis Tiant	10.00
Carl Yastrzemski	40.00

1954 Bowman Reprints

	NM/M
Complete Set (20):	40.00
Common Player:	2.00
Inserted 1:12	
RA	Richie Ashburn	2.00
YB	Yogi Berra	4.00
DC	Del Crandell	2.00
BF	Bob Feller	2.50
WF	Whitey Ford	4.00
NF	Nellie Fox	2.00
CL	Clem Labine	2.00
DL	Don Larsen	3.00
JL	Johnny Logan	2.00
WM	Willie Mays	6.00
GM	Gil McDougald	2.00
DM	Don Mueller	2.00
JP	Jimmy Piersall	2.00
AR	Allie Reynolds	2.00
PR	Phil Rizzuto	3.00
ES	Enos Slaughter	2.00
DS	Duke Snider	4.00
WW	Wes Westrum	2.00
HW	Hoyt Wilhelm	2.00
DW	Davey Williams	2.00

1954 Bowman Reprint
Autographs

	NM/M
Common Player:	10.00
Inserted 1:118	
YB	Yogi Berra	50.00
DC	Del Crandell	15.00
CL	Clem Labine	15.00
JL	Johnny Logan	15.00
DM	Don Mueller	10.00
DW	Davey Williams	10.00

2002 Bowman's Best

	NM/M
Complete Set (181):	
Common Player:	.25
Common (91-181):	4.00
Inserted 1:Pack	
Blue (1-90):	1-2X
Production 300	
Red (1-90):	1-2X
Production 200	
Gold (1-90):	3-6X
Production 50	
Blue (91-181):	.75-1X
Production 500	
Red (91-181):	1-1.5X
Production 150	
Gold (91-181):	1-2X
Production 50	
Pack (5):	18.00
Box (10):	150.00

1	Josh Beckett	.75
2	Derek Jeter	3.00
3	Alex Rodriguez	3.00
4	Miguel Tejada	.50
5	Nomar Garciaparra	.75
6	Aramis Ramirez	.75
7	Jeremy Giambi	.25
8	Bernie Williams	.50
9	Juan Pierre	.25
10	Chipper Jones	2.00
11	Jimmy Rollins	.75
12	Alfonso Soriano	1.00
13	Daryle Ward	.25
14	Paul Konerko	.50
15	Tim Hudson	.50
16	Doug Mientkiewicz	.25
17	Todd Helton	.75
18	Moises Alou	.40
19	Juan Gonzalez	.50

20 Jorge Posada .50
21 Jeff Kent .50
22 Roger Clemens 2.00
23 Phil Nevin .25
24 Brian Giles .40
25 Carlos Delgado .50
26 Jason Giambi .50
27 Vladimir Guerrero 1.00
28 Cliff Floyd .25
29 Shea Hillenbrand .25
30 Ken Griffey Jr. 2.50
31 Mike Piazza 1.50
32 Carlos Pena .40
33 Larry Walker .50
34 Magglio Ordonez .50
35 Mike Mussina .50
36 Andruw Jones .50
37 Mark Teixeira .50
38 Curt Schilling .50
39 Eric Chavez .40
40 Bartolo Colon .40
41 Eric Hinske .25
42 Sean Burroughs .25
43 Randy Johnson 1.00
44 Adam Dunn .50
45 Pedro Martinez 1.50
46 Garret Anderson .25
47 Jim Thome .50
48 Gary Sheffield .75
49 Tsuyoshi Shinjo .25
50 Albert Pujols 3.00
51 Ichiro Suzuki 2.00
52 C.C. Sabathia .75
53 Bobby Abreu .50
54 Ivan Rodriguez .50
55 J.D. Drew .50
56 Jacque Jones .25
57 Jason Kendall .25
58 Javier Vazquez .25
59 Jeff Bagwell .50
60 Greg Maddux 2.50
61 Jim Edmonds .40
62 Austin Kearns .25
63 Jose Vidro .25
64 Kevin Brown .25
65 Preston Wilson .25
66 Sammy Sosa .75
67 Lance Berkman .75
68 Mark Mulder .40
69 Marty Cordova .25
70 Frank Thomas .75
71 Mike Cameron .25
72 Mike Sweeney .25
73 Barry Bonds 3.00
74 Troy Glaus .40
75 Barry Zito .40
76 Pat Burrell .50
77 Paul LoDuca .25
78 Rafael Palmeiro .50
79 Mark Prior .40
80 Darin Erstad .25
81 Richie Sexson .40
82 Roberto Alomar .50
83 Roy Oswalt .50
84 Ryan Klesko .25
85 Luis Gonzalez .25
86 Scott Rolen .50
87 Shannon Stewart .25
88 Shawn Green .40
89 Toby Hall .25
90 Bret Boone .40
91 Casey Kotchman/Bat 8.00
92 Jose Valverde/Auto. **RC** 8.00
93 Cole Barthel/Bat 4.00
94 Brad Nelson/Auto. **RC** 8.00
95 Mauricio Lara/Auto. **RC** 8.00
96 Ryan Gripp/Bat **RC** 4.00
97 Brian West/Auto. **RC** 8.00
98 Chris Piersoll/Auto. **RC** 8.00
99 Ryan Church/Auto. **RC** 20.00
100 Javier Colina/Auto. 8.00
101 Juan Gonzalez/Auto. 8.00
102 Benito Baez/Auto. 8.00
103 Mike Hill/Bat **RC** 4.00
104 Jason Grove/Auto. **RC** 8.00
105 Koyie Hill/Auto. 8.00
106 Mark Outlaw/Auto. **RC** 8.00
107 Jason Bay/Bat **RC** 15.00
108 Jorge Padilla/Auto. **RC** 8.00
109 Peter Zamora/Auto. **RC** 8.00
110 Joe Mauer/Auto. **RC** 60.00
111 Franklyn German/Auto. **RC** 8.00
112 Chris Flinn/Auto. **RC** 8.00
113 David Wright/Bat 40.00
114 Anastacio Martinez/Auto. **RC** 8.00
115 Nic Jackson/Bat **RC** 8.00
116 Rene Reyes/Auto. **RC** 8.00
117 Colin Young/Auto. **RC** 8.00
118 Joe Orloski/Auto. **RC** 8.00
119 Mike Wilson/Auto. **RC** 8.00
120 Rich Thompson/Auto. **RC** 8.00
121 Jake Mauer/Auto. **RC** 8.00
122 Mario Ramos/Auto. 8.00
123 Doug Sessions/Auto. **RC** 8.00
124 Doug DeVore/Bat **RC** 4.00
125 Travis Foley/Auto. 10.00
126 Chris Baker/Auto. **RC** 8.00
127 Michael Floyd/Auto. **RC** 8.00
128 Josh Barfield/Bat 5.00
129 Jose Bautista/Bat **RC** 5.00
130 Gavin Floyd/Auto. 15.00
131 Jason Botts/Bat **RC** 4.00
132 Clint Nageotte/Auto. **RC** 10.00
133 Jesus Cota/Auto. **RC** 10.00
134 Ron Calloway/Bat **RC** 4.00
135 Kevin Cash/Bat **RC** 4.00
136 Jonny Gomes/Auto. **RC** 15.00
137 Dennis Ulacia/Auto. 8.00
138 Ryan Snare/Auto. **RC** 8.00
139 Kevin Deaton/Auto. **RC** 8.00
140 Bobby Jenks/Auto. **RC** 15.00
141 Casey Kotchman/Auto. 20.00
142 Adam Walker/Auto. **RC** 8.00
143 Mike Gonzalez/Auto. **RC** 8.00
144 Ruben Gotay/Bat **RC** 5.00
145 Jason Grove/Bat **RC** 4.00
146 Freddy Sanchez/Auto. **RC** 15.00
147 Jason Arnold/Auto. 10.00
148 Scott Hairston/Auto. 10.00
149 Jason St. Clair/Auto. **RC** 8.00
150 Chris Tritle/Bat **RC** 4.00
151 Edwin Yan/Bat **RC** 4.00
152 Freddy Sanchez/Bat **RC** 10.00
153 Greg Sain/Bat **RC** 4.00
154 Yurendell DeCaster/Bat **RC** 5.00
155 Noochie Varner/Bat **RC** 5.00
156 Nelson Castro/Auto. **RC** 8.00
157 Randall Shelley/Bat **RC** 5.00
158 Reed Johnson/Bat **RC** 10.00
159 Ryan Raburn/Auto. **RC** 8.00
160 Jose Morban/Bat **RC** 5.00
161 Justin Schuda/Auto. **RC** 8.00
162 Henry Pichardo/Auto. **RC** 8.00
163 Josh Bard/Auto. **RC** 10.00
164 Josh Bonifay/Auto. **RC** 8.00
165 Brandon League/Auto. 8.00
166 Julio DePaula/Auto. **RC** 10.00
167 Todd Linden/Auto. **RC** 10.00
168 Francisco Liriano/Auto. **RC** 75.00
169 Chris Snelling/Auto. **RC** 10.00
170 Blake McGinley/Auto. **RC** 8.00
171 Cody McKay/Auto. **RC** 8.00
172 Jason Stanford/Auto. **RC** 8.00
173 Lenny Dinardo/Auto. **RC** 8.00
174 Greg Montalbano/Auto. **RC** 8.00
175 Earl Snyder/Auto. **RC** 8.00
176 Justin Huber/Auto. **RC** 10.00
177 Chris Narveson/Auto. **RC** 8.00
178 Jon Switzer/Auto. 8.00
179 Ronald Acuna/Auto. **RC** 8.00
180 Chris Duffy/Bat **RC** 8.00
181 Kazuhisa Ishii/Bat **RC** 8.00

2003 Bowman

	NM/M
Complete Set (330):	75.00
Common Player:	.15
Common Rookie:	.40
Pack (10):	3.00
Box (24):	60.00

1 Garret Anderson .15
2 Derek Jeter 2.00
3 Gary Sheffield .40
4 Matt Morris .25
5 Derek Lowe .15
6 Andy Van Hekken .15
7 Sammy Sosa .75
8 Ken Griffey Jr. 1.50
9 Omar Vizquel .15
10 Jorge Posada .40
11 Lance Berkman .40
12 Mike Sweeney .15
13 Adrian Beltre .25
14 Richie Sexson .25
15 A.J. Pierzynski .15
16 Bartolo Colon .15
17 Mike Mussina .40
18 Paul Byrd .15
19 Bobby Abreu .40
20 Miguel Tejada .50
21 Aramis Ramirez .40
22 Edgardo Alfonzo .15
23 Edgar Martinez .25
24 Albert Pujols 2.00
25 Carl Crawford .25
26 Eric Hinske .15
27 Tim Salmon .25
28 Luis Gonzalez .25
29 Jay Gibbons .15
30 John Smoltz .40
31 Tim Wakefield .15
32 Mark Prior .50
33 Magglio Ordonez .25
34 Adam Dunn .50
35 Larry Walker .25
36 Luis Castillo .15
37 Wade Miller .15
38 Carlos Beltran .50
39 Odalis Perez .15
40 Alex Sanchez .15
41 Torii Hunter .25
42 Cliff Floyd .15
43 Andy Pettitte .25
44 Francisco Rodriguez .15
45 Eric Chavez .40
46 Kevin Millwood .25
47 Dennis Tankersley .15
48 Hideo Nomo .25
49 Freddy Garcia .15
50 Randy Johnson .75
51 Aubrey Huff .15
52 Carlos Delgado .40
53 Troy Glaus .50
54 Junior Spivey .15
55 Mike Hampton .15
56 Sidney Ponson .15
57 Aaron Boone .15
58 Kerry Wood .40
59 Willie Harris .15
60 Nomar Garciaparra .50
61 Todd Helton .50
62 Mike Lowell .15
63 Roy Oswalt .40
64 Raul Ibanez .15
65 Brian Jordan .15
66 Geoff Jenkins .15
67 Jermaine Dye .15
68 Tom Glavine .25
69 Bernie Williams .40
70 Vladimir Guerrero .75
71 Mark Mulder .25
72 Jimmy Rollins .40
73 Oliver Perez .15
74 Rich Aurilia .15
75 Joel Pineiro .15
76 J.D. Drew .25
77 Ivan Rodriguez .50
78 Josh Phelps .15
79 Darin Erstad .40
80 Curt Schilling .75
81 Paul LoDuca .15
82 Marty Cordova .15
83 Manny Ramirez .75
84 Bobby Hill .15
85 Paul Konerko .40
86 Austin Kearns .25
87 Jason Jennings .15
88 Brad Penny .15
89 Jeff Bagwell .75
90 Shawn Green .40
91 Jason Schmidt .40
92 Doug Mientkiewicz .15
93 Jose Vidro .15
94 Bret Boone .15
95 Jason Giambi .50
96 Barry Zito .40
97 Roy Halliday .40
98 Pat Burrell .40
99 Sean Burroughs .15
100 Barry Bonds 2.00
101 Kazuhiro Sasaki .15
102 Fernando Vina .15
103 Chan Ho Park .15
104 Andruw Jones .75
105 Adam Kennedy .15
106 Shea Hillenbrand .15
107 Greg Maddux 1.50
108 Jim Edmonds .40
109 Pedro J. Martinez 1.00
110 Moises Alou .25
111 Jeff Weaver .15
112 C.C. Sabathia .15
113 Robert Fick .15
114 A.J. Burnett .15
115 Jeff Kent .25
116 Kevin Brown .25
117 Rafael Furcal .25
118 Cristian Guzman .15
119 Brad Wilkerson .15
120 Mike Piazza 1.00
121 Alfonso Soriano .75
122 Mark Ellis .15
123 Vicente Padilla .15
124 Eric Gagne .15
125 Ryan Klesko .15
126 Ichiro Suzuki 1.50
127 Tony Batista .15
128 Roberto Alomar .40
129 Alex Rodriguez 2.00
130 Jim Thome .75
131 Jarrod Washburn .15
132 Orlando Hudson .15
133 Chipper Jones 1.50
134 Rodrigo Lopez .15
135 Johnny Damon .75
136 Matt Clement .15
137 Frank Thomas .75
138 Ellis Burks .15
139 Carlos Pena .15
140 Josh Beckett .25
141 Joe Randa .15
142 Brian Giles .25
143 Kazuhisa Ishii .15
144 Corey Koskie .15
145 Orlando Cabrera .15
146 Mark Buehrle .25
147 Roger Clemens 2.00
148 Tim Hudson .40
149 Randy Wolf .15
150 Josh Fogg .15
151 Phil Nevin .15
152 John Olerud .15
153 Scott Rolen .75
154 Joe Kennedy .15
155 Rafael Palmeiro .75
156 Chad Hutchinson .40
157 Quincy Carter .15
158 Hee Seop Choi .15
159 Joe Borchard .15
160 Brandon Phillips .15
161 Wily Mo Pena .15
162 Victor Martinez .25
163 Jason Stokes .15
164 Ken Harvey .15
165 Juan Rivera .15
166 Jose Contreras **RC** 1.00
167 Dan Haren 1.00
168 Michel Hernandez **RC** .50
169 Eider Torres **RC** .40
170 Chris De La Cruz **RC** .50
171 Ramon A. Martinez **RC** .50
172 Mike Adams **RC** .40
173 Justin Arneson **RC** .50
174 Jamie Athas **RC** .40
175 Dwaine Bacon **RC** .40
176 Clint Barmes **RC** .50
177 B.J. Barns **RC** .40
178 Tyler Johnson **RC** .40
179 Bobby Basham **RC** .50
180 T.J. Bohn **RC** .50
181 J.D. Durbin **RC** .50
182 Brandon Bowe **RC** .40
183 Craig Brazell **RC** .50
184 Dusty Brown **RC** .50
185 Brian Bruney **RC** .50
186 Greg Bruso **RC** .40
187 Jaime Bubela **RC** .50
188 Bryan Bullington **RC** .50
189 Brian Burgamy **RC** .40
190 Eny Cabreja **RC** .50
191 Daniel Cabrera **RC** 1.00
192 Ryan Cameron **RC** .40
193 Lance Caraccioli **RC** .50
194 David Cash **RC** .40
195 Bernie Castro **RC** .40
196 Ismael Castro **RC** .40
197 Daryl Clark **RC** .50
198 Jeff Clark **RC** .50
199 Chris Colton **RC** .40
200 Dexter Cooper **RC** .40
201 Callix Crabbe **RC** .40
202 Chien-Ming Wang **RC** 5.00
203 Eric Crozier **RC** .50
204 Nook Logan **RC** .40
205 David DeJesus **RC** .75
206 Matt DeMarco **RC** .40
207 Chris Duncan **RC** 2.00
208 Eric Eckenstahler .40
209 Willie Eyre **RC** .40
210 Evel Bastida-Martinez **RC** .40
211 Chris Fallon **RC** .75
212 Mike Flannery **RC** .40
213 Mike O'Keefe **RC** .40
214 Ben Francisco **RC** 1.00
215 Kason Gabbard **RC** 1.00
216 Mike Gallo **RC** .40
217 Jairo Garcia **RC** .40
218 Angel Garcia **RC** .40
219 Michael Garciaparra .50
220 Joey Gomes .40
221 Dusty Gomon **RC** .40
222 Bryan Grace **RC** .40
223 Tyson Graham **RC** .40
224 Henry Guerrero **RC** .40
225 Franklin Gutierrez **RC** .50
226 Carlos Guzman **RC** .50
227 Matthew Hagen **RC** .40
228 Josh Hall **RC** .50
229 Rob Hammock **RC** .50
230 Brendan Harris **RC** .75
231 Gary Harris **RC** .40
232 Clay Hensley **RC** .75
233 Michael Hinckley **RC** .40
234 Luis Hodge **RC** .40
235 Donnie Hood **RC** .50
236 Travis Ishikawa **RC** .50
237 Edwin Jackson **RC** .50
238 Ardley Jansen **RC** .50
239 Ferenc Jongejan **RC** .40
240 Matt Kata **RC** .50
241 Kazuhiro Takeoka **RC** .40
242 Beau Kemp **RC** .40
243 Il Kim **RC** .50
244 Brennan King **RC** .40
245 Cris Kroski **RC** .40
246 Jason Kubel **RC** 1.50
247 Pete LaForest **RC** .40
248 Wilfredo Ledezma **RC** .40
249 Jeremy Bonderman 3.00
250 Gonzalo Lopez **RC** .40
251 Brian Luderer **RC** .50
252 Ruddy Lugo **RC** .40
253 Wayne Lydon **RC** .40
254 Mark Malaska **RC** .40
255 Andy Marte **RC** 1.00
256 Tyler Martin **RC** .40
257 Branden Florence **RC** .40
258 Aneudis Mateo **RC** .40
259 Derell McCall **RC** .40
260 Brian McCann 5.00
261 Mike McNutt **RC** .40
262 Jacabo Meque **RC** .40
263 Derek Michaelis **RC** .50
264 Aaron Miles **RC** 1.00
265 Jose Morales .40

266	Dustin Moseley RC	.40
267	Adrian Myers RC	.40
268	Dan Neil RC	.40
269	Jon Nelson RC	.50
270	Mike Neu RC	.40
271	Leigh Neuage RC	.40
272	Weston O'Brien RC	.50
273	Trent Oeltjen RC	.50
274	Tim Olson RC	.50
275	David Pahucki RC	.40
276	Nathan Panther RC	.50
277	Arnie Munoz RC	.40
278	David Pember RC	.40
279	Jason Perry RC	.50
280	Matthew Peterson RC	.40
281	Ryan Shealy RC	1.00
282	Jorge Piedra RC	.40
283	Simon Pond RC	.40
284	Aaron Rakers RC	.40
285	Hanley Ramirez RC	5.00
286	Manuel Ramirez RC	.40
287	Kevin Randel RC	.50
288	Darrell Rasner RC	.40
289	Prentice Redman RC	.50
290	Eric Reed RC	.50
291	Wilton Reynolds RC	.40
292	Eric Riggs RC	.40
293	Carlos Rijo RC	.40
294	Rajai Davis RC	.50
295	Aron Weston RC	.40
296	Arturo Rivas RC	.50
297	Kyle Roat RC	.40
298	Bubba Nelson RC	.50
299	Levi Robinson RC	.40
300	Ray Sadler RC	.40
301	Gary Schneidmiller RC	.50
302	Jon Schuerholz RC	.75
303	Corey Shafer RC	.50
304	Brian Shackelford RC	.40
305	Bill Simon RC	.40
306	Haj Turay RC	.40
307	Sean Smith	.40
308	Ryan Spataro RC	.40
309	Jemel Spearman RC	.40
310	Keith Stamler RC	.40
311	Luke Steidlmayer RC	.50
312	Adam Stern	.50
313	Jay Sitzman RC	.50
314	Thomari Story-Harden RC	.50
315	Terry Tiffee RC	.50
316	Nick Trzesniak RC	.50
317	Denny Tussen RC	.40
318	Scott Tyler	.40
319	Shane Victorino RC	.40
320	Doug Waechter RC	.50
321	Brandon Watson RC	.40
322	Todd Wellemeyer RC	.50
323	Eli Whiteside RC	.40
324	Josh Willingham RC	1.00
325	Travis Wong RC	.40
326	Brian Wright RC	.40
327	Kevin Youkilis RC	3.00
328	Andy Sisco	.50
329	Dustin Yount RC	.50
330	Andrew Dominique RC	.40

Gold

Stars (1-165):	1-2X
Rookies (166-330):	1-2X
Inserted 1:1	

Uncirculated

Stars (1-165):	3-5X
Rookies (166-330):	2-4X
Production 250 Sets	

Future Fiber Relics

		NM/M
	Common Player:	4.00
RB	Rocco Baldelli	4.00
WB	Wilson Betemit	4.00
HB	Hank Blalock	6.00
JB	Jason Botts	4.00
SB	Sean Burroughs	4.00
KC	Kevin Cash	4.00
KD	Kory DeHaan	4.00
CD	Chris Duffy	4.00
PF	Pedro Feliz	5.00
AG	Adrian Gonzalez	4.00
JG	Jason Grove	4.00
JH	Josh Hamilton	10.00
NH	Nathan Haynes	4.00
DH	Drew Henson	4.00
AH	Aubrey Huff	5.00
RJ	Reed Johnson	4.00
AK	Austin Kearns	4.00
CK	Casey Kotchman	6.00
RK	Ryan Langerhans	4.00
JDM	Jake Mauer	4.00
JM	Joe Mauer	8.00
XN	Xavier Nady	6.00
MR	Michael Restovich	4.00
WR	Wilkin Ruan	4.00
FS	Freddy Sanchez	6.00
RS	Randall Shelley	4.00
BS	Bud Smith	4.00
ES	Esix Snead	4.00
ST	So Taguchi	4.00
JW	Justin Wayne	4.00
TW	Travis Wilson	4.00
DW	David Wright	15.00
EY	Edwin Yan	4.00

Futures Game Gear Relics

		NM/M
	Common Player:	4.00
	Inserted 1:26	
EA	Edwin Almonte	4.00
TA	Tony Alvarez	4.00
BB	Brad Baker	4.00
FB	Francis Beltran	4.00
JEB	Joe Borchard	4.00
JB	John Buck	4.00
SB	Sean Burnett	4.00
MB	Marlon Byrd	4.00
MC	Miguel Cabrera	10.00
KC	Kevin Cash	4.00
HC	Hee Seop Choi	4.00
SC	Shin-Soo Choo	4.00
AC	Aaron Cook	5.00
CC	Carl Crawford	6.00
JDR	Jorge De La Rosa	4.00
VD	Victor Diaz	4.00
RD	Ryan Dittfurth	4.00
BE	Brett Evert	4.00
GG	Gerardo Garcia	4.00
BH	Bill Hall	4.00
CH	Corey Hart	6.00
DH	Drew Henson	4.00
JH	Justin Huber	4.00
OH	Orlando Hudson	4.00
OI	Omar Infante	4.00
JJ	Jimmy Journell	4.00
JK	Josh Karp	4.00
FL	Francisco Liriano	6.00
JL	Jose Lopez	4.00
VM	Victor Martinez	6.00
JM	Justin Morneau	10.00
BM	Brett Myers	5.00
LO	Lyle Overbay	5.00
WP	Wily Mo Pena	4.00
BP	Brandon Phillips	6.00
MR	Mike Restovich	4.00
JR	Jose Reyes	10.00
FR	Francisco Rodriguez	5.00
RR	Rodrigo Rodriguez	4.00
SS	Seung Jun Song	4.00
JMS	John Stephens	4.00
JS	Jason Stokes	4.00
BT	Billy Traber	4.00
CT	Chad Tracey	4.00
AW	Adam Wainwright	10.00
JY	Jason Young	4.00

Futures Game MVP Autograph

		NM/M
	Complete Set (1):	
JR	Jose Reyes	40.00

ROY Dual Relic

		NM/M
	Inserted 1:765	
JH	Eric Hinske,	
	Jason Jennings	10.00

Signs of the Future

		NM/M
	Common Autograph:	5.00
	Red Autographs:	1-2.5X
	Production 50 Sets	
JA	Jason Arnold	5.00
JB	John Buck	10.00
BB	Bryan Bullington	8.00
QC	Quincy Carter	8.00
NC	Nelson Castro	5.00
RC	Ryan Church	20.00
JC	Jesus Cota	5.00
JOG	Jonny Gomes	8.00
DG	Doug Gredvig	5.00
KG	Khalil Greene	20.00
ZG	Zack Greinke	20.00

JG	Jason Grove	5.00
JGU	Jeremy Guthrie	10.00
CH	Cole Hamels	80.00
JRH	Joel Hanrahan	5.00
CJH	Corey Hart	30.00
KH	Koyie Hill	5.00
CMH	Chad Hutchinson	10.00
BJ	Bobby Jenks	15.00
BK	Ben Kozlowski	5.00
BL	Brandon League	5.00
DL	Donald Levinski	5.00
FL	Fred Lewis	20.00
TL	Todd Linden	5.00
JL	James Loney	25.00
VM	Val Majewski	5.00
DHM	Dustin McGowan	15.00
CP	Chris Piersoll	5.00
HR	Hanley Ramirez	75.00
PR	Prentice Redman	5.00
JR	Jose Reyes	40.00
JSC	Jason St. Clair	5.00
FS	Freddy Sanchez	10.00
ZS	Zach Segovia	5.00
DS	Doug Sessions	5.00
BS	Brian Slocum	5.00
RS	Ryan Snare	5.00
MT	Mitch Talbot	5.00
AT	Andres Torres	5.00
AV	Andy Van Hekken	5.00
OV	Oscar Villarreal	5.00

Dual Signs of the Future Autograph

		NM/M
	Inserted 1:9,220	
CH	Quincy Carter,	
	Chad Hutchinson	15.00

2003 Bowman Chrome

CRAIG BRAZELL

	NM/M
Complete Set (351):	400.00
Common Player:	.25
Common Rookie:	1.00
Common RC Auto. (331-350):	10.00
Pack (4):	7.00
Box (18):	100.00

1	Garret Anderson	.25
2	Derek Jeter	3.00
3	Gary Sheffield	.50
4	Matt Morris	.35
5	Derek Lowe	.25
6	Andy Van Hekken	.25
7	Sammy Sosa	.75
8	Ken Griffey Jr.	2.00
9	Omar Vizquel	.40
10	Jorge Posada	.50
11	Lance Berkman	.50
12	Mike Sweeney	.25
13	Adrian Beltre	.50
14	Richie Sexson	.40
15	A.J. Pierzynski	.25
16	Bartolo Colon	.25
17	Mike Mussina	.75
18	Paul Byrd	.25
19	Bobby Abreu	.50
20	Miguel Tejada	.50
21	Aramis Ramirez	.50
22	Edgardo Alfonzo	.25
23	Edgar Martinez	.40
24	Albert Pujols	3.00
25	Carl Crawford	.40
26	Eric Hinske	.25
27	Tim Salmon	.40
28	Luis Gonzalez	.40
29	Jay Gibbons	.25
30	John Smoltz	.50
31	Tim Wakefield	.25
32	Mark Prior	.50
33	Magglio Ordonez	.40
34	Adam Dunn	.75
35	Larry Walker	.40
36	Luis Castillo	.25
37	Wade Miller	.25
38	Carlos Beltran	.75
39	Odalis Perez	.25
40	Alex Sanchez	.25
41	Torii Hunter	.50
42	Cliff Floyd	.25
43	Andy Pettitte	.50
44	Francisco Rodriguez	.25

45	Eric Chavez	.50
46	Kevin Millwood	.40
47	Dennis Tankersley	.25
48	Hideo Nomo	.50
49	Freddy Garcia	.25
50	Randy Johnson	.75
51	Aubrey Huff	.25
52	Carlos Delgado	.50
53	Troy Glaus	.50
54	Junior Spivey	.25
55	Mike Hampton	.25
56	Sidney Ponson	.25
57	Aaron Boone	.25
58	Kerry Wood	.50
59	Willie Harris	.25
60	Nomar Garciaparra	.50
61	Todd Helton	.75
62	Mike Lowell	.25
63	Roy Oswalt	.50
64	Raul Ibanez	.25
65	Brian Jordan	.25
66	Geoff Jenkins	.25
67	Jermaine Dye	.25
68	Tom Glavine	.50
69	Bernie Williams	.50
70	Vladimir Guerrero	1.00
71	Mark Mulder	.50
72	Jimmy Rollins	.50
73	Oliver Perez	.25
74	Rich Aurilia	.25
75	Joel Pineiro	.25
76	J.D. Drew	.40
77	Ivan Rodriguez	.40
78	Josh Phelps	.25
79	Darin Erstad	.40
80	Curt Schilling	1.00
81	Paul LoDuca	.25
82	Marty Cordova	.25
83	Manny Ramirez	1.00
84	Bobby Hill	.25
85	Paul Konerko	.25
86	Austin Kearns	.40
87	Jason Jennings	.25
88	Brad Penny	.25
89	Jeff Bagwell	.50
90	Shawn Green	.40
91	Jason Schmidt	.40
92	Doug Mientkiewicz	.25
93	Jose Vidro	.25
94	Bret Boone	.25
95	Jason Giambi	.50
96	Barry Zito	.50
97	Roy Halladay	.50
98	Pat Burrell	.50
99	Sean Burroughs	.25
100	Barry Bonds	3.00
101	Kazuhiro Sasaki	.25
102	Fernando Vina	.25
103	Chan Ho Park	.25
104	Andruw Jones	.50
105	Adam Kennedy	.25
106	Shea Hillenbrand	.25
107	Greg Maddux	2.00
108	Jim Edmonds	.40
109	Pedro J. Martinez	1.00
110	Moises Alou	.40
111	Jeff Weaver	.25
112	C.C. Sabathia	.25
113	Robert Fick	.25
114	A.J. Burnett	.25
115	Jeff Kent	.40
116	Kevin Brown	.25
117	Rafael Furcal	.40
118	Cristian Guzman	.25
119	Brad Wilkerson	.25
120	Mike Piazza	1.00
121	Alfonso Soriano	1.00
122	Mark Ellis	.25
123	Vicente Padilla	.25
124	Eric Gagne	.25
125	Ryan Klesko	.25
126	Ichiro Suzuki	2.00
127	Tony Batista	.25
128	Roberto Alomar	.50
129	Alex Rodriguez	2.50
130	Jim Thome	.50
131	Jarrod Washburn	.25
132	Orlando Hudson	.25
133	Chipper Jones	1.50
134	Rodrigo Lopez	.25
135	Johnny Damon	1.00
136	Matt Clement	.25
137	Frank Thomas	1.00
138	Ellis Burks	.25
139	Carlos Pena	.25
140	Josh Beckett	.50
141	Joe Randa	.25
142	Brian Giles	.25
143	Kazuhisa Ishii	.25
144	Corey Koskie	.25
145	Orlando Cabrera	.25
146	Mark Buehrle	.40
147	Roger Clemens	2.00
148	Tim Hudson	.50
149	Randy Wolf	.25
150	Josh Fogg	.25
151	Phil Nevin	.25
152	John Olerud	.25
153	Scott Rolen	.50
154	Joe Kennedy	.25
155	Rafael Palmeiro	.50
156	Chad Hutchinson	.50
157	Quincy Carter	.25
158	Hee Seop Choi	.40
159	Joe Borchard	.25

160	Brandon Phillips	.25
161	Wily Mo Pena	.25
162	Victor Martinez	.50
163	Jason Stokes	.25
164	Ken Harvey	.25
165	Juan Rivera	.25
166	Joe Valentine **RC**	1.00
167	Dan Haren	4.00
168	Michel Hernandez **RC**	1.00
169	Eider Torres **RC**	1.00
170	Chris De La Cruz **RC**	1.00
171	Ramon A. Martinez **RC**	1.00
172	Mike Adams **RC**	1.00
173	Justin Arneson **RC**	1.00
174	Jamie Athas **RC**	1.00
175	Dwaine Bacon **RC**	1.00
176	Clint Barmes **RC**	1.50
177	B.J. Barns **RC**	1.00
178	Tyler Johnson **RC**	1.00
179	Brandon Webb **RC**	15.00
180	T.J. Bohn **RC**	1.00
181	Ozzie Chavez **RC**	1.00
182	Brandon Bowe **RC**	1.00
183	Craig Brazell **RC**	1.00
184	Dusty Brown **RC**	1.00
185	Brian Bruney **RC**	1.00
186	Greg Bruso **RC**	1.00
187	Jaime Bubela **RC**	1.00
188	Matt Diaz **RC**	2.00
189	Brian Burgamy **RC**	1.00
190	Eny Cabreja **RC**	1.00
191	Daniel Cabrera **RC**	3.00
192	Ryan Cameron **RC**	1.00
193	Lance Caraccioli **RC**	1.00
194	David Cash **RC**	1.00
195	Bernie Castro **RC**	1.00
196	Ismael Castro **RC**	1.00
197	Cory Doyne **RC**	1.00
198	Jeff Clark **RC**	1.00
199	Chris Colton **RC**	1.00
200	Dexter Cooper **RC**	1.00
201	Callix Crabbe **RC**	1.00
202	Chien-Ming Wang **RC**	15.00
203	Eric Crozier **RC**	1.00
204	Nook Logan **RC**	1.00
205	David DeJesus **RC**	4.00
206	Matt DeMarco **RC**	1.00
207	Chris Duncan **RC**	4.00
208	Eric Eckenstahler	1.00
209	Willie Eyre **RC**	1.00
210	Evel Bastida-Martinez **RC**	1.00
211	Chris Fallon **RC**	1.00
212	Mike Flannery **RC**	1.00
213	Mike O'Keefe **RC**	1.00
214	Lew Ford **RC**	1.00
215	Kason Gabbard **RC**	3.00
216	Mike Gallo **RC**	1.00
217	Jairo Garcia **RC**	1.00
218	Angel Garcia **RC**	1.00
219	Michael Garciaparra	1.00
220	Jeremy Griffiths	1.00
221	Dusty Gomon **RC**	1.00
222	Bryan Grace **RC**	1.00
223	Tyson Graham **RC**	1.00
224	Henry Guerrero **RC**	1.00
225	Franklin Gutierrez **RC**	4.00
226	Carlos Guzman **RC**	1.00
227	Matthew Hagen **RC**	1.00
228	Josh Hall **RC**	1.00
229	Rob Hammock **RC**	1.00
230	Brendan Harris **RC**	1.50
231	Gary Harris **RC**	1.00
232	Clay Hensley **RC**	1.00
233	Michael Hinckley **RC**	1.00
234	Luis Hodge **RC**	1.00
235	Donnie Hood **RC**	1.00
236	Matt Hensley **RC**	1.00
237	Edwin Jackson **RC**	1.50
238	Ardley Jansen **RC**	1.00
239	Ferenc Jongejan **RC**	1.00
240	Matt Kata **RC**	1.00
241	Kazuhiro Takeoka **RC**	1.00
242	Charlie Manning **RC**	1.00
243	Il Kim **RC**	1.00
244	Brennan King **RC**	1.00
245	Cris Kroski **RC**	1.00
246	David Martinez	1.00
247	Pete LaForest **RC**	1.00
248	Wilfredo Ledezma **RC**	1.00
249	Jeremy Bonderman	4.00
250	Gonzalo Lopez **RC**	1.00
251	Brian Luderer **RC**	1.00
252	Ruddy Lugo **RC**	1.00
253	Wayne Lydon **RC**	1.00
254	Mark Malaska **RC**	1.00
255	Andy Marte **RC**	1.00
256	Tyler Martin **RC**	1.00
257	Branden Florence **RC**	1.00
258	Aneudis Mateo **RC**	1.00
259	Derell McCall **RC**	1.00
260	Elizardo Ramirez **RC**	1.00
261	Mike McNutt **RC**	1.00
262	Jacabo Meque **RC**	1.00
263	Derek Michaelis **RC**	1.00
264	Aaron Miles **RC**	2.00
265	Jose Morales	1.00
266	Dustin Moseley **RC**	1.00
267	Adrian Myers **RC**	1.00
268	Dan Neil **RC**	1.00
269	Jon Nelson **RC**	1.00
270	Mike Neu **RC**	1.00
271	Leigh Neuage **RC**	1.00
272	Weston O'Brien **RC**	1.00
273	Trent Oeltjen **RC**	1.00
274	Tim Olson **RC**	1.00
275	David Pahucki **RC**	1.00
276	Nathan Panther **RC**	1.00
277	Arnie Munoz **RC**	1.00
278	David Pember **RC**	1.00
279	Jason Perry **RC**	1.00
280	Matthew Peterson **RC**	1.00
281	Greg Aquino **RC**	1.00
282	Jorge Piedra **RC**	1.00
283	Simon Pond **RC**	1.00
284	Aaron Rakers **RC**	1.00
285	Felix Sanchez **RC**	1.00
286	Manuel Ramirez **RC**	1.00
287	Kevin Randel **RC**	1.00
288	Kelly Shoppach **RC**	3.00
289	Prentice Redman **RC**	1.00
290	Eric Reed **RC**	1.00
291	Wilton Reynolds **RC**	1.00
292	Eric Riggs **RC**	1.00
293	Carlos Rijo **RC**	1.00
294	Tyler Adamczyk **RC**	1.00
295	Jon-Mark Sprowl **RC**	1.00
296	Arturo Rivas **RC**	1.00
297	Kyle Roat **RC**	1.00
298	Bubba Nelson **RC**	1.00
299	Levi Robinson **RC**	1.00
300	Ray Sadler **RC**	1.00
301	Rylan Reed **RC**	1.00
302	Jon Schuerholz **RC**	1.00
303	Nobuaki Yoshida **RC**	1.00
304	Brian Shackelford **RC**	1.00
305	Bill Simon **RC**	1.00
306	Haj Turay **RC**	1.00
307	Sean Smith	1.00
308	Ryan Spataro **RC**	1.00
309	Jemel Spearman **RC**	1.00
310	Keith Stamler **RC**	1.00
311	Luke Steidlmayer **RC**	1.00
312	Adam Stern	1.00
313	Jay Sitzman **RC**	1.00
314	Mike Wodnicki **RC**	1.00
315	Terry Tiffee **RC**	1.00
316	Nick Trzesniak **RC**	1.00
317	Denny Tussen **RC**	1.00
318	Scott Tyler	1.00
319	Shane Victorino **RC**	5.00
320	Doug Waechter **RC**	1.00
321	Brandon Watson **RC**	1.00
322	Todd Wellemeyer **RC**	2.00
323	Eli Whiteside **RC**	1.00
324	Josh Willingham **RC**	4.00
325	Travis Wong **RC**	1.00
326	Brian Wright **RC**	1.00
327	Felix Pie **RC**	5.00
328	Andy Sisco	1.00
329	Dustin Yount **RC**	1.00
330	Andrew Dominique **RC**	1.00
331	Brian McCann	80.00
332	Jose Contreras **RC**	50.00
333	Corey Shafer **RC**	10.00
334	Hanley Ramirez **RC**	200.00
335	Ryan Shealy **RC**	15.00
336	Kevin Youkilis **RC**	45.00
337	Jason Kubel **RC**	20.00
338	Aron Weston **RC**	10.00
339	J.D. Durbin **RC**	10.00
340	Gary Schneidmiller **RC**	10.00
341	Travis Ishikawa **RC**	10.00
342	Ben Francisco **RC**	20.00
343	Bobby Basham **RC**	10.00
344	Joey Gomes	10.00
345	Beau Kemp **RC**	10.00
346	Thomari Story-Harden **RC**	10.00
347	Daryl Clark **RC**	10.00
348	Bryan Bullington **RC**	10.00
349	Rajai Davis **RC**	10.00
350	Darrell Rasner	10.00
351	Willie Mays	3.00

Refractors

Stars (1-165, 351):	2-4X
Rookies (166-350):	.5-1.5X
X-Fractors (1-165, 351):	3-6X
X-Fractors (166-350):	1-2X
Uncirc.Gold Refractors(1-165):	5-10X
Gold Refractors (166-350):	2-3X
Production 170 Sets	
Gold Refractors (331-350):	1-3X

Willie Mays Autograph

		NM/M
Production 150		
351AU	Willie Mays	225.00

2003 Bowman Chrome Draft Picks & Prospects

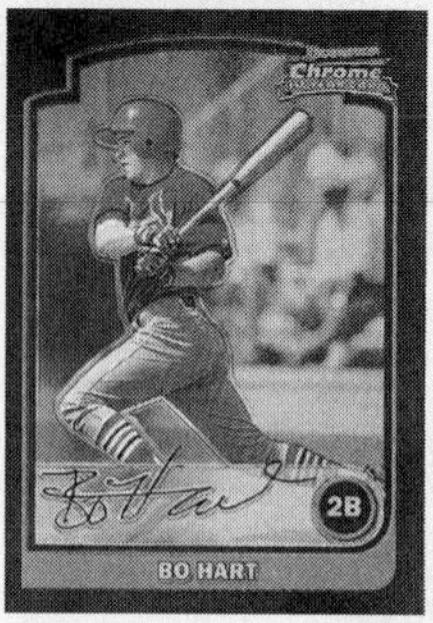

		NM/M
Complete Set (176):		500.00
Common Player:		.25
Common Rookie:		1.00
Common Rk Autograph (166-176):		10.00
BDP1	Dontrelle Willis	.50
BDP2	Freddy Sanchez	.25
BDP3	Miguel Cabrera	.75
BDP4	Ryan Ludwick	.75
BDP5	Ty Wigginton	.25
BDP6	Mark Teixeira	.75
BDP7	Trey Hodges	.25
BDP8	Laynce Nix	.25
BDP9	Antonio Perez	.25
BDP10	Jody Gerut	.25
BDP11	Jae Weong Seo	.25
BDP12	Erick Almonte	.25
BDP13	Lyle Overbay	.25
BDP14	Billy Traber	.25
BDP15	Andres Torres	.25
BDP16	Jose Valverde	.25
BDP17	Aaron Heilman	.25
BDP18	Brandon Larson	.25
BDP19	Jung Bong	.25
BDP20	Jesse Foppert	.25
BDP21	Angel Berroa	.25
BDP22	Jeff DaVanon	.25
BDP23	Kurt Ainsworth	.25
BDP24	Brandon Claussen	.25
BDP25	Xavier Nady	.25
BDP26	Travis Hafner	.50
BDP27	Jerome Williams	.25
BDP28	Jose Reyes	.75
BDP29	Sergio Mitre **RC**	1.00
BDP30	Bo Hart **RC**	1.00
BDP31	Adam Miller **RC**	5.00
BDP32	Brian Finch **RC**	1.00
BDP33	Taylor Mattingly **RC**	2.00
BDP34	Daric Barton **RC**	4.00
BDP35	Chris Ray **RC**	2.00
BDP36	Jarrod Saltalamacchia **RC**	8.00
BDP37	Dennis Dove **RC**	1.00
BDP38	James Houser **RC**	1.50
BDP39	Clinton King **RC**	2.00
BDP40	Lou Palmisano **RC**	2.00
BDP41	Dan Moore **RC**	1.00
BDP42	Craig Stansberry **RC**	1.50
BDP43	Jo Jo Reyes **RC**	3.00
BDP44	Jake Stevens **RC**	1.00
BDP45	Tom Gorzelanny **RC**	1.50
BDP46	Brian Marshall **RC**	1.50
BDP47	Scott Beerer **RC**	1.00
BDP48	Javi Herrera **RC**	1.50
BDP49	Steve Lerud **RC**	1.50
BDP50	Josh Banks **RC**	2.00
BDP51	Jonathan Papelbon **RC**	20.00
BDP52	Juan Valdes **RC**	1.50
BDP53	Beau Vaghan	1.50
BDP54	Matt Chico **RC**	1.50
BDP55	Todd Jennings **RC**	1.50
BDP56	Tony Gwynn Jr. **RC**	3.00
BDP57	Matt Harrison **RC**	1.50
BDP58	Aaron Marsden	1.00
BDP59	Casey Abrams **RC**	1.00
BDP60	Cory Stuart **RC**	1.00
BDP61	Mike Wagner **RC**	1.00
BDP62	Jordan Pratt **RC**	1.50
BDP63	Andre Randolph **RC**	1.00
BDP64	Blake Balkcom **RC**	1.00
BDP65	Josh Muecke **RC**	1.00
BDP66	Jamie D'Antona **RC**	1.50
BDP67	Cole Seifrig **RC**	1.50
BDP68	Josh Anderson **RC**	1.00
BDP69	Matt Lorenzo **RC**	1.00
BDP70	Nate Spears **RC**	1.50
BDP71	Chris Goodman **RC**	1.50
BDP72	Brian McFall **RC**	1.50
BDP73	Billy Hogan **RC**	1.50
BDP74	Jamie Romak **RC**	1.50
BDP75	Jeff Cook **RC**	1.50
BDP76	Brooks McNiven **RC**	1.00
BDP77	Xavier Paul **RC**	1.50
BDP78	Bob Zimmerman **RC**	1.00
BDP79	Mickey Hall **RC**	1.00
BDP80	Shaun Marcum **RC**	3.00
BDP81	Matt Nachreiner **RC**	1.00
BDP82	Chris Kinsey **RC**	1.00
BDP83	Jonathan Fulton **RC**	1.50
BDP84	Edgardo Baez **RC**	1.50
BDP85	Robert Valido **RC**	1.50
BDP86	Kenny Lewis **RC**	1.50
BDP87	Trent Peterson **RC**	1.00
BDP88	Johnny Woodard **RC**	1.00
BDP89	Wes Littleton **RC**	1.50
BDP90	Sean Rodriguez **RC**	3.00
BDP91	Kyle Pearson **RC**	1.00
BDP92	Josh Rainwater **RC**	1.50
BDP93	Travis Schlichting **RC**	1.50
BDP94	Tim Battle **RC**	1.50
BDP95	Aaron Hill **RC**	2.00
BDP96	Bob McCrory **RC**	1.00
BDP97	Rick Guarno **RC**	1.00
BDP98	Brandon Yarbrough **RC**	1.00
BDP99	Peter Stonard **RC**	1.50
BDP100	Darin Downs **RC**	1.50
BDP101	Matt Bruback **RC**	1.00
BDP102	Danny Garcia **RC**	1.00
BDP103	Cory Stewart **RC**	1.00
BDP104	Ferdin Tejeda **RC**	1.50
BDP105	Kade Johnson **RC**	1.00
BDP106	Andrew Brown **RC**	1.50
BDP107	Aquilino Lopez **RC**	1.00
BDP108	Stephen Randolph **RC**	1.00
BDP109	Dave Matranga **RC**	1.00
BDP110	Dustin McGowan **RC**	3.00
BDP111	Juan Camacho **RC**	1.50
BDP112	Cliff Lee	1.00
BDP113	Jeff Duncan **RC**	1.00
BDP114	C.J. Wilson	.50
BDP115	Brandon Roberson **RC**	1.00
BDP116	David Corrente **RC**	1.00
BDP117	Kevin Beavers **RC**	1.00
BDP118	Anthony Webster **RC**	1.50
BDP119	Oscar Villarreal **RC**	1.00
BDP120	Hong-Chih Kuo **RC**	5.00
BDP121	Josh Barfield	.15
BDP122	Denny Bautista	.15
BDP123	Chris Burke	1.50
BDP124	Robinson Cano **RC**	10.00
BDP125	Jose Castillo	.15
BDP126	Neal Cotts	.15
BDP127	Jorge De La Rosa	.15
BDP128	J.D. Durbin	.15
BDP129	Edwin Encarnacion	2.00
BDP130	Gavin Floyd	.15
BDP131	Alexis Gomez	.15
BDP132	Edgar Gonzalez **RC**	1.00
BDP133	Khalil Greene	.50
BDP134	Zack Greinke	.15
BDP135	Franklin Gutierrez	1.50
BDP136	Rich Harden	.15
BDP137	J.J. Hardy	3.00
BDP138	Ryan Howard	35.00
BDP139	Justin Huber	.15
BDP140	David Kelton	.15
BDP141	David Krynzel	.15
BDP142	Pete LaForest	.15
BDP143	Adam LaRoche	.15
BDP144	Preston Larrison	1.00
BDP145	John Maine **RC**	5.00
BDP146	Andy Marte	1.00
BDP147	Jeff Mathis	.15
BDP148	Joe Mauer	1.00
BDP149	Clint Nageotte	.15
BDP150	Chris Narveson	.15
BDP151	Ramon Nivar **RC**	1.00
BDP152	Felix Pie	3.00
BDP153	Guillermo Quiroz **RC**	1.00
BDP154	Rene Reyes	.15
BDP155	Royce Ring	.15
BDP156	Alexis Rios	2.50
BDP157	Grady Sizemore	1.00
BDP158	Stephen Smitherman	.15
BDP159	Seung Jun Song	.15
BDP160	Scott Thorman	.15
BDP161	Chad Tracy	.15
BDP162	Chin-Hui Tsao	.15
BDP163	John Van Benschoten **RC**	1.00
BDP164	Kevin Youkilis	5.00
BDP165	Chien-Ming Wang	6.00
BDP166	Chris Lubanski/ Auto. **RC**	20.00
BDP167	Ryan Harvey/Auto. **RC**	15.00
BDP168	Matt Murton/Auto. **RC**	15.00
BDP169	Jay Sborz/Auto. **RC**	10.00
BDP170	Brandon Wood/ Auto. **RC**	50.00
BDP171	Nicholas Markakis/ Auto. **RC**	65.00
BDP172	Rickie Weeks/Auto. **RC**	20.00
BDP173	Eric Duncan/Auto. **RC**	15.00
BDP174	Chad Billingsley/ Auto. **RC**	50.00
BDP175	Ryan Wagner/Auto. **RC**	10.00
BDP176	Delmon Young/ Auto. **RC**	60.00

Refractor

JOHN MAINE

Rookies (29-165):		2-4X
Inserted 1:11		
Autos. (166-176):		.75-1.5X
Inserted 1:196		

X-Fractor

BROOKS McNIVEN

Rookies (29-165):		2-4X
Production 130 Sets		
Autos. (166-176):		.75-2X
Inserted 1:393		

Gold Refractor

Rookies (29-165):		3-5X
Production 50 Sets		
Autos. (166-176):		No Pricing
Inserted 1:1,479		

2003 Bowman Draft Picks & Prospects

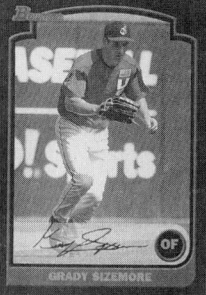

GRADY SIZEMORE

		NM/M
Complete Set (165):		35.00
Common Player:		.15
Common Rookie:		.25
Pack (5 + 2 Chrome):		8.00
Box (24):		180.00
BDP1	Dontrelle Willis	.40
BDP2	Freddy Sanchez	.15
BDP3	Miguel Cabrera	.50
BDP4	Ryan Ludwick	.40
BDP5	Ty Wigginton	.15
BDP6	Mark Teixeira	.50
BDP7	Trey Hodges	.15
BDP8	Laynce Nix	.15
BDP9	Antonio Perez	.15
BDP10	Jody Gerut	.15
BDP11	Jae Seong Seo	.15
BDP12	Erick Almonte	.15
BDP13	Lyle Overbay	.15
BDP14	Billy Traber	.15
BDP15	Andres Torres	.15
BDP16	Jose Valverde	.15
BDP17	Aaron Heilman	.15
BDP18	Brandon Larson	.15
BDP19	Jung Bong	.15
BDP20	Jesse Foppert	.15
BDP21	Angel Berroa	.15
BDP22	Jeff DaVanon	.15
BDP23	Kurt Ainsworth	.15
BDP24	Brandon Claussen	.15
BDP25	Xavier Nady	.15
BDP26	Travis Hafner	.40
BDP27	Jerome Williams	.15
BDP28	Jose Reyes	.40
BDP29	Sergio Mitre RC	.25
BDP30	Bo Hart RC	.50
BDP31	Adam Miller RC	2.00
BDP32	Brian Finch RC	.25
BDP33	Taylor Mattingly RC	.75
BDP34	Daric Barton RC	2.00
BDP35	Chris Ray RC	.25
BDP36	Jarrod Saltalamacchia RC	2.00
BDP37	Dennis Dove RC	.50
BDP38	James Houser RC	.50
BDP39	Clinton King RC	.50
BDP40	Lou Palmisano RC	.50
BDP41	Dan Moore RC	.50
BDP42	Craig Stansberry RC	.50
BDP43	Jo Jo Reyes RC	.75
BDP44	Jake Stevens RC	.50
BDP45	Tom Gorzelanny RC	1.00
BDP46	Brian Marshall RC	.50
BDP47	Scott Beerer RC	.25
BDP48	Javi Herrera RC	.50
BDP49	Steve Lerud RC	.75
BDP50	Josh Banks RC	.75
BDP51	Jonathan Papelbon RC	10.00
BDP52	Juan Valdes RC	.50
BDP53	Beau Vaghan	.50
BDP54	Matt Chico RC	.50
BDP55	Todd Jennings RC	.50
BDP56	Tony Gwynn Jr. RC	1.00
BDP57	Matt Harrison RC	.25
BDP58	Aaron Mardsen	.25
BDP59	Casey Abrams RC	.25
BDP60	Cory Stuart RC	.25
BDP61	Mike Wagner RC	.25
BDP62	Jordan Pratt RC	.50
BDP63	Andre Randolph RC	.25
BDP64	Blake Balkcom RC	.50
BDP65	Josh Muecke RC	.25
BDP66	Jamie D'Antona RC	1.00
BDP67	Cole Seifrig RC	.50
BDP68	Josh Anderson RC	.50
BDP69	Matt Lorenzo RC	.50
BDP70	Nate Spears RC	.50
BDP71	Chris Goodman RC	.50
BDP72	Brian McFall RC	.50
BDP73	Billy Hogan RC	.50
BDP74	Jamie Romak RC	.50
BDP75	Jeff Cook RC	.50
BDP76	Brooks McNiven RC	.25
BDP77	Xavier Paul RC	1.00
BDP78	Bob Zimmerman RC	.25
BDP79	Mickey Hall RC	.50
BDP80	Shaun Marcum RC	.75
BDP81	Matt Nachreiner RC	.25
BDP82	Chris Kinsey RC	.25
BDP83	Jonathan Fulton RC	.50
BDP84	Edgardo Baez RC	.50
BDP85	Robert Valido RC	.75
BDP86	Kenny Lewis RC	.50
BDP87	Trent Peterson RC	.50
BDP88	Johnny Woodard RC	.25
BDP89	Wes Littleton RC	.50
BDP90	Sean Rodriguez RC	1.00
BDP91	Kyle Pearson RC	.25
BDP92	Josh Rainwater RC	.75
BDP93	Travis Schlichting RC	.75
BDP94	Tim Battle RC	.75
BDP95	Aaron Hill RC	.75
BDP96	Bob McCrory RC	.25
BDP97	Rick Guarno RC	.25
BDP98	Brandon Yarbrough RC	.25
BDP99	Peter Stonard RC	.50
BDP100	Darin Downs RC	.50
BDP101	Matt Bruback RC	.25
BDP102	Danny Garcia RC	.25
BDP103	Cory Stewart RC	.25
BDP104	Ferdin Tejeda RC	.50
BDP105	Kade Johnson RC	.25
BDP106	Andrew Brown RC	.25
BDP107	Aquilino Lopez RC	.25
BDP108	Stephen Randolph RC	.25
BDP109	Dave Matranga RC	.25
BDP110	Dustin McGowan RC	1.50
BDP111	Juan Camacho RC	.50
BDP112	Cliff Lee	.25
BDP113	Jeff Duncan RC	.50
BDP114	C.J. Wilson	.25
BDP115	Brandon Roberson RC	.25
BDP116	David Corrente RC	.25
BDP117	Kevin Beavers RC	.25
BDP118	Anthony Webster RC	.50
BDP119	Oscar Villarreal RC	.25
BDP120	Hong-Chih Kuo RC	2.00
BDP121	Josh Barfield	.15
BDP122	Denny Bautista RC	.25
BDP123	Chris Burke	.75
BDP124	Robinson Cano RC	8.00
BDP125	Jose Castillo	.15
BDP126	Neal Cotts	.15
BDP127	Jorge De La Rosa	.15
BDP128	J.D. Durbin	.25
BDP129	Edwin Encarnacion	.50
BDP130	Gavin Floyd	.15
BDP131	Alexis Gomez	.15
BDP132	Edgar Gonzalez RC	.25
BDP133	Khalil Greene	.25
BDP134	Zack Greinke	.15
BDP135	Franklin Gutierrez	.15
BDP136	Rich Harden	.15
BDP137	J.J. Hardy	2.00
BDP138	Ryan Howard	20.00
BDP139	Justin Huber	.15
BDP140	David Kelton	.15
BDP141	David Krynzel	.15
BDP142	Pete LaForest	.15
BDP143	Adam LaRoche	.15
BDP144	Preston Larrison	.15
BDP145	John Maine RC	3.00
BDP146	Andy Marte	1.00
BDP147	Jeff Mathis	.25
BDP148	Joe Mauer	.50
BDP149	Clint Nageotte	.15
BDP150	Chris Narveson	.15
BDP151	Ramon Nivar RC	.25
BDP152	Felix Pie RC	4.00
BDP153	Guillermo Quiroz RC	.15
BDP154	Rene Reyes	.15
BDP155	Royce Ring	.15
BDP156	Alexis Rios	.75
BDP157	Grady Sizemore	.75
BDP158	Stephen Smitherman	.15
BDP159	Seung Jun Song	.15
BDP160	Scott Thorman	.15
BDP161	Chad Tracy	.15
BDP162	Chin-Hui Tsao	.15
BDP163	John Van Benschoten RC	.25
BDP164	Kevin Youkilis	1.00
BDP165	Chien-Ming Wang	3.00

Gold

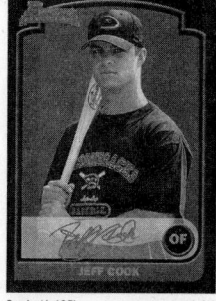

JEFF COOK

Cards (1-165):		1-2X
Inserted 1:1		

Fabric of Future

Adam LaRoche

		NM/M
Common Player:		4.00
JB	Josh Barfield	6.00
RC	Robinson Cano	20.00
JD	J.D. Durbin	4.00
GF	Gavin Floyd	6.00
EG	Edgar Gonzalez	4.00
KG	Khalil Greene	8.00
ZG	Zack Greinke	6.00
FG	Franklin Gutierrez	6.00
RH	Rich Harden	6.00
RJH	Ryan Howard	30.00
JH	Justin Huber	5.00
AL	Adam LaRoche	8.00
AM	Andy Marte	8.00
JSM	Jeff Mathis	6.00
JM	Joe Mauer	10.00
CN	Chris Narveson	4.00
FP	Felix Pie	6.00
RR	Rene Reyes	4.00
RRR	Royce Ring	4.00
GS	Grady Sizemore	10.00

Prospect Premiums

		NM/M
Common Player:		4.00
RB	Rocco Baldelli	6.00
HB	Hank Blalock	6.00
CC	Carl Crawford	5.00
TH	Travis Hafner	8.00
BH	Brendan Harris	4.00
NH	Nathan Haynes	4.00
JM	Justin Morneau	8.00
CS	Chris Snelling	4.00
JT	Joe Thurston	4.00
CU	Chase Utley	10.00

Signs of the Future

		NM/M
Common Player:		5.00
JA	Jason Arnold	5.00
ZG	Zack Greinke	15.00
CS	Cory Stewart	5.00
DT	Dennis Tankersley	5.00
AT	Andres Torres	8.00

2003 Bowman Heritage

MIGUEL CABRERA • Third Base • MARLINS

		NM/M
Complete Set (280):		60.00
Common Player:		.25
Cards 171-180 have three versions.		
Pack (8):		3.00
Box (24):		65.00
1	Jorge Posada	.50
2	Todd Helton	.75
3	Marcus Giles	.25
4	Eric Chavez	.25
5	Edgar Martinez	.25
6	Luis Gonzalez	.25
7	Corey Patterson	.25
8	Preston Wilson	.25
9	Ryan Klesko	.25
10	Randy Johnson	1.00
11	Eric Byrnes	.25
12	Carlos Lee	.40
13	Steve Finley	.25
14	A.J. Pierzynski	.25
15	Troy Glaus	.40
16	Darin Erstad	.25
17	Moises Alou	.40
18	Torii Hunter	.50
19	Marlon Byrd	.25
20	Mark Prior	.40
21	Shannon Stewart	.25
22	Craig Biggio	.40
23	Johnny Damon	.75
24	Robert Fick	.25
25	Jason Giambi	.75
26	Fernando Vina	.25
27	Aubrey Huff	.25
28	Benito Santiago	.25
29	Jay Gibbons	.25
30	Ken Griffey Jr.	2.00
31	Rocco Baldelli	.40
32	Pat Burrell	.50
33	A.J. Burnett	.25
34	Omar Vizquel	.25
35	Greg Maddux	1.50
36	Jae Weong Seo	.25
37	C.C. Sabathia	.25
38	Geoff Jenkins	.25
39	Ty Wigginton	.25
40	Jeff Kent	.40
41	Orlando Hudson	.25
42	Edgardo Alfonzo	.25
43	Greg Myers	.25
44	Melvin Mora	.25
45	Sammy Sosa	.75
46	Russ Ortiz	.25
47	Josh Beckett	.50
48	David Wells	.25
49	Woody Williams	.25
50	Alex Rodriguez	2.00
51	Randy Wolf	.25
52	Carlos Beltran	.75
53	Austin Kearns	.25
54	Trot Nixon	.25
55	Ivan Rodriguez	.50
56	Shea Hillenbrand	.25
57	Roberto Alomar	.40
58	John Olerud	.25
59	Michael Young	.25
60	Garret Anderson	.25
61	Mike Lieberthal	.25
62	Adam Dunn	.50
63	Raul Ibanez	.25
64	Kenny Lofton	.25
65	Ichiro Suzuki	1.50
66	Jarrod Washburn	.25
67	Shawn Chacon	.25
68	Alex Gonzalez	.25
69	Roy Halladay	.40
70	Vladimir Guerrero	1.00
71	Hee Seop Choi	.25
72	Brandon Phillips	.25
73	Ray Durham	.25
74	Mark Teixeira	.75
75	Hank Blalock	.40
76	Jerry Hairston Jr.	.25
77	Erubiel Durazo	.25
78	Frank Catalanotto	.25
79	Jacque Jones	.25
80	Bobby Abreu	.50
81	Mike Hampton	.25
82	Zach Day	.25
83	Jimmy Rollins	.75
84	Joel Pineiro	.25
85	Brett Myers	.25
86	Frank Thomas	.75
87	Aramis Ramirez	.40
88	Paul LoDuca	.25
89	Bobby Higginson	.25
90	Brian Giles	.25
91	Jose Cruz Jr.	.25

92	Derek Lowe	.25
93	Mark Buehrle	.25
94	Wade Miller	.25
95	Derek Jeter	2.00
96	Bret Boone	.25
97	Tony Batista	.25
98	Sean Casey	.25
99	Eric Hinske	.25
100	Albert Pujols	2.00
101	Runelvys Hernandez	.25
102	Vernon Wells	.40
103	Kerry Wood	.40
104	Lance Berkman	.50
105	Alfonso Soriano	1.00
106	Ken Harvey	.25
107	Bartolo Colon	.25
108	Andy Pettitte	.40
109	Rafael Furcal	.40
110	Dontrelle Willis	.25
111	Carl Crawford	.40
112	Scott Rolen	.50
113	Chipper Jones	1.00
114	Magglio Ordonez	.50
115	Bernie Williams	.50
116	Roy Oswalt	.50
117	Kevin Brown	.25
118	Cristian Guzman	.25
119	Kazuhisa Ishii	.25
120	Larry Walker	.40
121	Miguel Tejada	.50
122	Manny Ramirez	1.00
123	Mike Mussina	.50
124	Mike Lowell	.25
125	Barry Bonds	2.00
126	Aaron Boone	.25
127	Carlos Delgado	.50
128	Jose Vidro	.25
129	Brad Radke	.25
130	Rafael Palmeiro	.50
131	Mark Mulder	.25
132	Jason Schmidt	.25
133	Gary Sheffield	.50
134	Richie Sexson	.25
135	Barry Zito	.25
136	Tom Glavine	.40
137	Jim Edmonds	.40
138	Andruw Jones	.40
139	Pedro J. Martinez	1.00
140	Curt Schilling	.75
141	Joe Kennedy	.25
142	Nomar Garciaparra	.50
143	Vicente Padilla	.25
144	Kevin Millwood	.40
145	Shawn Green	.40
146	Jeff Bagwell	.50
147	Hideo Nomo	.50
148	Fred McGriff	.25
149	Matt Morris	.25
150	Roger Clemens	1.50
151	Damian Moss	.25
152	Orlando Cabrera	.25
153	Tim Hudson	.40
154	Mike Sweeney	.25
155	Jim Thome	.75
156	Rich Aurilia	.25
157	Mike Piazza	1.00
158	Edgar Renteria	.25
159	Javy Lopez	.25
160	Jamie Moyer	.25
161	Miguel Cabrera	.75
162	Adam Loewen **RC**	1.00
163	Jose Reyes	.75
164	Zack Greinke	.25
165	Cole Hamels	.25
166	Jeremy Guthrie	.25
167	Victor Martinez	.40
168	Rich Harden	.25
169	Joe Mauer	.50
170	Khalil Greene	.25
171	Willie Mays	2.00
172	Phil Rizzuto	.50
173	Al Kaline	1.00
174	Warren Spahn	1.00
175	Jimmy Piersall	.50
176	Luis Aparicio	.50
177	Whitey Ford	1.00
178	Harmon Killebrew	1.00
179	Duke Snider	1.00
180	Bobby Richardson	.50
181	David Martinez	.25
182	Felix Pie **RC**	3.00
183	Kevin Correia **RC**	.50
184	Brandon Webb **RC**	4.00
185	Matt Diaz **RC**	.50
186	Lew Ford **RC**	.50
187	Jeremy Griffiths	.25
188	Matt Hensley **RC**	.75
189	Danny Garcia **RC**	.50
190	Elizardo Ramirez **RC**	.50
191	Greg Aquino **RC**	.50
192	Felix Sanchez **RC**	.50
193	Kelly Shoppach **RC**	.75
194	Bubba Nelson **RC**	.50
195	Mike O'Keefe **RC**	.50
196	Hanley Ramirez **RC**	8.00
197	Todd Wellemeyer **RC**	.75
198	Dustin Moseley **RC**	.75
199	Eric Crozier **RC**	.50
200	Ryan Shealy **RC**	1.00
201	Jeremy Bonderman	2.00
202	Bo Hart **RC**	.50
203	Dusty Brown **RC**	.50
204	Rob Hammock **RC**	.50
205	Jorge Piedra **RC**	.50
206	Jason Kubel **RC**	1.50
207	Stephen Randolph **RC**	.50
208	Andy Sisco	.50
209	Matt Kata **RC**	.50
210	Robinson Cano **RC**	6.00
211	Ben Francisco **RC**	1.00
212	Arnie Munoz **RC**	.50
213	Ozzie Chavez **RC**	.50
214	Beau Kemp **RC**	.50
215	Travis Wong **RC**	.50
216	Brian McCann	5.00
217	Aquilino Lopez **RC**	.50
218	Bobby Basham **RC**	.50
219	Tim Olson **RC**	.50
220	Nathan Panther **RC**	.50
221	Wilfredo Ledezma **RC**	.50
222	Josh Willingham **RC**	1.00
223	David Cash **RC**	.50
224	Oscar Villarreal **RC**	.50
225	Jeff Duncan **RC**	.75
226	Dan Haren	2.00
227	Michel Hernandez **RC**	.50
228	Matt Murton **RC**	1.00
229	Clay Hensley **RC**	.75
230	Tyler Johnson **RC**	.50
231	Tyler Martin **RC**	.50
232	J.D. Durbin **RC**	.75
233	Shane Victorino **RC**	2.00
234	Rajai Davis **RC**	1.00
235	Chien-Ming Wang **RC**	6.00
236	Travis Ishikawa **RC**	.50
237	Eric Eckenstahler	.25
238	Dustin McGowan **RC**	2.00
239	Prentice Redman **RC**	.50
240	Haj Turay **RC**	.50
241	Matt DeMarco **RC**	.50
242	Lou Palmisano **RC**	.50
243	Eric Reed **RC**	.50
244	Willie Eyre **RC**	.50
245	Ferdin Tejeda **RC**	.75
246	Michael Garciaparra	.25
247	Michael Hinckley **RC**	.50
248	Branden Florence **RC**	.50
249	Trent Oeltjen **RC**	.50
250	Mike Neu **RC**	.75
251	Chris Lubanski **RC**	1.00
252	Brandon Wood **RC**	4.00
253	Delmon Young **RC**	4.00
253	Delmon Young/Auto. **RC**	40.00
254	Matt Harrison **RC**	.50
255	Chad Billingsley **RC**	3.00
256	Josh Anderson **RC**	.50
257	Brian McFall	.75
258	Ryan Wagner **RC**	.50
259	Billy Hogan **RC**	.50
260	Nate Spears **RC**	.50
261	Ryan Harvey **RC**	1.00
262	Wes Littleton **RC**	.50
263	Xavier Paul **RC**	.75
264	Sean Rodriguez **RC**	1.00
265	Brian Finch **RC**	.50
266	Josh Rainwater **RC**	.50
267	Brian Snyder **RC**	.75
268	Eric Duncan **RC**	1.50
269	Rickie Weeks **RC**	3.00
270	Tim Battle **RC**	.50
271	Scott Beerer **RC**	.50
272	Aaron Hill **RC**	.75
273	Casey Abrams **RC**	.50
274	Jonathan Fulton **RC**	.50
275	Todd Jennings **RC**	.50
276	Jordan Pratt **RC**	.50
277	Tom Gorzelanny **RC**	1.00
278	Matt Lorenzo **RC**	.75
279	Jarrod Saltalamacchia **RC**	3.00
280	Mike Wagner **RC**	.50

Diamond Cuts

DIAMOND CUTS
SCOTT ROLEN • Third Base • ST. LOUIS CARDINALS

		NM/M
Common Player:		4.00
Red:		1-2X
Production 56 Sets		
JA	Jeremy Affeldt	4.00
MA	Moises Alou	5.00
TA	Tony Armas Jr.	4.00
JB	Jeff Bagwell	6.00
CB	Craig Biggio	6.00
HB	Hank Blalock	6.00
BB	Bret Boone	4.00
EC	Eric Chavez	4.00
JE	Jim Edmonds	6.00
JG	Jason Giambi	8.00
TG	Troy Glaus	6.00
MG	Mark Grace	6.00
VG	Vladimir Guerrero	8.00
CG	Cristian Guzman	4.00
TH	Todd Helton	6.00
RH	Rickey Henderson	12.00
JJ	Jason Jennings	4.00
AJ	Andruw Jones	6.00
CJ1	Chipper Jones/Jsy	8.00
CJ2	Chipper Jones/Bat	8.00
AK	Austin Kearns	6.00
PL	Paul LoDuca	4.00
JL	Javy Lopez	4.00
PM	Pedro J. Martinez	8.00
KM	Kevin Millwood	4.00
MM	Mark Mulder	4.00
BM	Brett Myers	4.00
HN	Hideo Nomo	8.00
RP1	Rafael Palmeiro/Jsy	8.00
RP2	Rafael Palmeiro/Bat	8.00
JLP	Josh Phelps	4.00
AP	Albert Pujols	15.00
JR	Jose Reyes	6.00
AR1	Alex Rodriguez/Jsy	10.00
AR2	Alex Rodriguez/Bat	10.00
SR1	Scott Rolen/Jsy	8.00
SR2	Scott Rolen/Bat	10.00
KI	Kazuhiro Sasaki	4.00
GS	Gary Sheffield	6.00
AS	Alfonso Soriano	8.00
SS1	Sammy Sosa/Jsy	10.00
SS2	Sammy Sosa/Bat	10.00
MS	Mike Sweeney	4.00
MT	Miguel Tejada	6.00
JV	Javier Vazquez	4.00
JW	Jarrod Washburn	4.00
VW	Vernon Wells	4.00
BW	Bernie Williams	6.00
KW	Kerry Wood	5.00
BZ	Barry Zito	6.00

Keith Olbermann Autograph

KEITH OLBERMANN

		NM/M
Inserted 1:1,421		
KO	Keith Olbermann	50.00

Signs of Greatness

		NM/M
Common Player:		6.00
Inserted 1:30		
Red Ink:		No Pricing
Production One Set		
CB	Chad Billingsley	25.00
RC	Robinson Cano	75.00
JD	Jeff Duncan	8.00
BF	Brian Finch	8.00
TG	Tom Gorzelanny	10.00
RH	Rich Harden	15.00
MM	Matt Murton	15.00
FP	Felix Pie	15.00
BS	Brian Snyder	8.00
RW	Rickie Weeks	15.00
DW	Dontrelle Willis	15.00
KY	Kevin Youkilis	25.00

2003 Bowman's Best

DAN HAREN

		NM/M
Complete Set:		
Common Player:		.50
Pack (5):		40.00
Box (10):		350.00
Veterans		
GJA	Garret Anderson	.50
LB	Lance Berkman	.75
BLB	Barry Bonds	4.00
PB	Pat Burrell	.50
WRC	Roger Clemens	3.00
NG	Nomar Garciaparra	1.50
JGG	Jason Giambi	1.00
BSG	Brian Giles	.50
SG	Shawn Green	.50
KG	Ken Griffey Jr.	2.50
VG	Vladimir Guerrero	1.50
TH	Todd Helton	1.00
TKH	Torii Hunter	.75
DJ	Derek Jeter	4.00
RJ	Randy Johnson	1.50
CJ	Chipper Jones	1.50
AK	Austin Kearns	.50
JFK	Jeff Kent	.50
GM	Greg Maddux	2.50
PM	Pedro J. Martinez	1.50
MOR	Magglio Ordonez	.50
MJP	Mike Piazza	1.50
MP	Mark Prior	1.00
AP	Albert Pujols	4.00
MR	Manny Ramirez	1.50
AR	Alex Rodriguez	3.00
CMS	Curt Schilling	1.50
AS	Alfonso Soriano	1.50
SS	Sammy Sosa	2.50
IS	Ichiro Suzuki	2.50
MS	Mike Sweeney	.50
MT	Miguel Tejada	1.00
JT	Jim Thome	1.00
LW	Larry Walker	.50
BZ	Barry Zito	.75
First-Year Players		
JB	Jeremy Bonderman	4.00
TJB	T.J. Bohn	1.00
MB	Matt Bruback **RC**	1.00
BC	Bernie Castro **RC**	1.00
JC	Jose Contreras **RC**	2.00
MD	Matt Diaz **RC**	2.00
BJH	Bo Hart **RC**	1.00
RM	Ramon Martinez	1.00
MO	Mike O'Keefe **RC**	1.00
JMS	Jon-Mark Sprowl **RC**	1.00
TT	Terry Tiffee	1.00
HT	Haj Turay **RC**	2.00
SV	Shane Victorino **RC**	3.00
CW	Chien-Ming Wang **RC**	15.00
DY	Dustin Yount **RC**	1.00
First-Year Player Autographs		
Common Auto:		8.00
Inserted 1:1		
TA	Tyler Adamczyk **RC**	8.00
GA	Greg Aquino **RC**	8.00
BWB	Bobby Basham **RC**	10.00
GB	Gregor Blanco **RC**	10.00
AB	Andrew Brown **RC**	8.00
BB	Bryan Bullington **RC**	10.00
RC	Ryan Cameron **RC**	8.00
DC	David Cash **RC**	8.00
OC	Ozzie Chavez **RC**	8.00
RD	Rajai Davis **RC**	15.00
CDC	Chris De La Cruz **RC**	10.00
MD	Matt Diaz **RC**	10.00
CAD	Carlos Duran **RC**	10.00
JDD	J.D. Durbin **RC**	10.00
WE	Willie Eyre **RC**	8.00
BF	Branden Florence **RC**	8.00
LF	Lew Ford **RC**	10.00
BLF	Ben Francisco **RC**	20.00
JG	Joey Gomes	10.00
JRG	Jeremy Griffiths	10.00
MNH	Matt Hagen **RC**	10.00
RWH	Robby Hammock **RC**	10.00
DH	Dan Haren	30.00
BH	Brendan Harris **RC**	15.00
MDH	Matt Hensley **RC**	8.00
MH	Michel Hernandez **RC**	10.00
MHI	Michael Hinckley **RC**	10.00
RH	Ryan Howard	250.00
TI	Travis Ishikawa **RC**	10.00
KJ	Kade Johnson **RC**	8.00
TJ	Tyler Johnson **RC**	8.00
MK	Matt Kata **RC**	10.00
BK	Beau Kemp **RC**	8.00
JK	Jason Kubel **RC**	15.00
PL	Pete LaForest **RC**	10.00
WL	Wilfredo Ledezma **RC**	10.00
NL	Nook Logan **RC**	10.00
MDM	Mark Malaska **RC**	8.00
CM	Charlie Manning **RC**	8.00
DM	David Martinez	10.00
AM	Aneudis Mateo **RC**	8.00
BM	Brian McCann	50.00
DMM	Dustin McGowan **RC**	20.00
JM	Jose Morales	10.00
DAM	Dustin Moseley **RC**	10.00
TO	Tim Olson **RC**	10.00
FP	Felix Pie **RC**	30.00
ER	Elizardo Ramirez **RC**	10.00

HR Hanley Ramirez **RC** 125.00
DR Darrell Rasner 15.00
PR Prentice Redman **RC** 8.00
FS Felix Sanchez **RC** 10.00
GS Gary Schneidmiller **RC** 8.00
CSS Corey Shafer **RC** 10.00
RS Ryan Shealy **RC** 10.00
KS Kelly Shoppach **RC** 10.00
CS Cory Stewart **RC** 10.00
TSH Thomari Story-Harden **RC** 8.00
FT Ferdin Tejeda **RC** 10.00
ET Eider Torres **RC** 10.00
ST Scott Tyler 10.00
JV Joe Valentine **RC** 8.00
OV Oscar Villarreal **RC**
DW Doug Waechter **RC** 10.00
AW Aron Weston **RC** 8.00
JW Josh Willingham **RC** 20.00
CJW C.J. Wilson 8.00
KY Kevin Youkilis **RC** 40.00
CW Chien-Ming Wang **RC** 150.00

Red

Red Autographs: 2-4X
Inserted 1:63
Red Base Card: 4-8X
Red Rookies: 2-3X
Production 50

Blue

Blue Autographs: 1-1.5X
Inserted 1:32
Blue Base Card: 3-5X
Blue Rookies: 1-2X
Production 100

Double Play

NM/M

Common Card: 20.00
Inserted 1:55
EB Elizardo Ramirez, Bryan Bullington 25.00
GK Joey Gomes, Jason Kubel 50.00
SR Felix Sanchez, Darrell Rasner 20.00
YS Kevin Youkilis, Kelly Shoppach 40.00
HV Dan Haren, Joe Valentine 25.00
GM Jeremy Griffiths, David Martinez 20.00
HM Michael Hinckley, Brian McCann 20.00
RS Prentice Redman, Gary Schneidmiller 20.00
LL Nook Logan, Wilfredo Ledezma 25.00
SB Corey Shafer, Gregor Blanco 25.00

First-Year Player Relics

NM/M

Common Player: 5.00
RLD Rajai Davis 10.00
JLF Lew Ford 5.00
JGG Joey Gomes 5.00
RJH Ryan Howard 50.00
JJK Jason Kubel 8.00
HRB Hanley Ramirez 30.00
RNS Ryan Shealy 5.00
KBS Kelly Shoppach 8.00
KEY Kevin Youkilis 10.00

Triple Play

NM/M

Inserted 1:219
DRS Rajai Davis, Hanley Ramirez, Ryan Shealy 85.00
BCS Andrew Brown, David Cash, Cory Stewart 30.00

2004 Bowman

ROGER CLEMENS

NM/M

Complete Set (330): 70.00
Common Player: .15
Common Rookie: .50
Pack (10): 2.50
Box (24): 50.00
1 Garret Anderson .15
2 Larry Walker .25
3 Derek Jeter 2.00
4 Curt Schilling .75
5 Carlos Zambrano .40
6 Shawn Green .25
7 Manny Ramirez .75
8 Randy Johnson .75
9 Jeremy Bonderman .25
10 Alfonso Soriano .75
11 Scott Rolen .50
12 Kerry Wood .25
13 Eric Gagne .25
14 Ryan Klesko .15
15 Kevin Millar .15
16 Ty Wigginton .15
17 David Ortiz .75
18 Luis Castillo .15
19 Bernie Williams .40
20 Edgar Renteria .25
21 Matt Kata .15
22 Bartolo Colon .25
23 Derrek Lee .50
24 Gary Sheffield .40
25 Nomar Garciaparra .50
26 Kevin Millwood .25
27 Corey Patterson .25
28 Carlos Beltran .50
29 Mike Lieberthal .15
30 Troy Glaus .40
31 Preston Wilson .15
32 Jorge Posada .50
33 Bo Hart .15
34 Mark Prior .40
35 Hideo Nomo .25
36 Jason Kendall .15
37 Shea Hillenbrand .15
38 Dmitri Young .15
39 Aaron Boone .15
40 Jim Edmonds .40
41 Ryan Ludwick .15
42 Brandon Webb .25
43 Todd Helton .50
44 Jacque Jones .15
45 Xavier Nady .15
46 Tim Salmon .25
47 Kelvim Escobar .15
48 Tony Batista .15
49 Nick Johnson .15
50 Jim Thome .50
51 Casey Blake .15
52 Trot Nixon .25
53 Luis Gonzalez .25
54 Dontrelle Willis .25
55 Mike Mussina .40
56 Carl Crawford .25
57 Mark Buehrle .25
58 Scott Podsednik .25
59 Brian Giles .15
60 Rafael Furcal .25
61 Miguel Cabrera .75
62 Rich Harden .15
63 Mark Teixeira .50
64 Frank Thomas .75
65 Johan Santana .50
66 Jason Schmidt .25
67 Aramis Ramirez .40
68 Jose Reyes .75
69 Magglio Ordonez .25
70 Mike Sweeney .15
71 Eric Chavez .25
72 Rocco Baldelli .25
73 Sammy Sosa .50
74 Javy Lopez .15
75 Roy Oswalt .25
76 Raul Ibanez .15
77 Ivan Rodriguez .50
78 Jerome Williams .15
79 Carlos Lee .25
80 Geoff Jenkins .15
81 Sean Burroughs .15
82 Marcus Giles .15
83 Mike Lowell .15
84 Barry Zito .40
85 Aubrey Huff .15
86 Esteban Loaiza .15
87 Torii Hunter .25
88 Phil Nevin .15
89 Andruw Jones .50
90 Josh Beckett .40
91 Mark Mulder .25
92 Hank Blalock .25
93 Jason Phillips .15
94 Russ Ortiz .15
95 Juan Pierre .15
96 Tom Glavine .25
97 Gil Meche .15
98 Ramon Ortiz .15
99 Richie Sexson .40
100 Albert Pujols 2.00
101 Javier Vazquez .15
102 Johnny Damon .75
103 Alex Rodriguez 1.50
104 Omar Vizquel .25
105 Chipper Jones .75
106 Lance Berkman .40
107 Tim Hudson .40
108 Carlos Delgado .40
109 Austin Kearns .25
110 Orlando Cabrera .25
111 Edgar Martinez .25
112 Melvin Mora .15
113 Jeff Bagwell .50
114 Marlon Byrd .15
115 Vernon Wells .25
116 C.C. Sabathia .25
117 Cliff Floyd .15
118 Ichiro Suzuki 1.00
119 Miguel Olivo .15
120 Mike Piazza .75
121 Adam Dunn .40
122 Paul Lo Duca .15
123 Brett Myers .25
124 Michael Young .25
125 Larry Bigbie .15
126 Greg Maddux 1.00
127 Vladimir Guerrero .75
128 Miguel Tejada .40
129 Andy Pettitte .40
130 Jose Cruz .15
131 Ken Griffey Jr. 1.50
132 Shannon Stewart .15
133 Joel Pineiro .15
134 Luis Matos .15
135 Jeff Kent .25
136 Randy Wolf .15
137 Chris Woodward .15
138 Jody Gerut .15
139 Jose Vidro .15
140 Bret Boone .15
141 Bill Mueller .15
142 Angel Berroa .15
143 Bobby Abreu .25
144 Roy Halladay .25
145 Delmon Young .50
146 Jonny Gomes .15
147 Rickie Weeks .40
148 Edwin Jackson .15
149 Neal Cotts .15
150 Jason Bay .40
151 Khalil Greene .25
152 Joe Mauer .40
153 Bobby Jenks .15
154 Chin-Feng Chen .15
154 Chin-Feng Chen/Jsy 10.00
155 Chien-Ming Wang .75
155 Chien-Ming Wang/Jsy 20.00
156 Mickey Hall .15
156 Mickey Hall/Jsy 5.00
157 James Houser .15
157 James Houser/Jsy 5.00
158 Jay Sborz .15
158 Jay Sborz/Jsy 5.00
159 Jonathan Fulton .15
159 Jonathan Fulton/Jsy 5.00
160 Steve Lerud .15
160 Steve Lerud/Jsy 5.00
161 Grady Sizemore .50
161 Grady Sizemore/Auto. 40.00
162 Felix Pie .50
162 Felix Pie/Auto. 15.00
163 Dustin McGowan .15
163 Dustin McGowan/Auto. 10.00
164 Chris Lubanski .15
164 Chris Lubanski/Auto. 10.00
164 Chris Lubanski/Jsy 5.00
165 Tom Gorzelanny .15
165 Tom Gorzelanny/Auto. 10.00
166 Rudy Guillen **RC** 1.00
166 Rudy Guillen/Auto. **RC** 10.00
167 Bobby Brownlie **RC** 1.00
167 Bobby Brownlie/Auto. **RC** 10.00
168 Conor Jackson 1.50
168 Conor Jackson/Auto. 25.00
169 Matt Moses 1.00
169 Matt Moses/Auto. 10.00
170 Ervin Santana **RC** 1.50
170 Ervin Santana/Auto. **RC** 20.00
171 Merkin Valdez **RC** .50
171 Merkin Valdez/Auto. **RC** 10.00
172 Erick Aybar **RC** 1.00
172 Erick Aybar/Auto. **RC** 10.00
173 Brad Sullivan .50
173 Brad Sullivan/Auto. 10.00
174 David Aardsma .50
174 David Aardsma/Auto. 10.00
175 Brad Snyder .75
175 Brad Snyder/Auto. 10.00
176 Alberto Callaspo **RC** .75
177 Brandon Medders **RC** .50
178 Zach Miner **RC** 1.00
179 Charlie Zink **RC** .40
180 Adam Greenberg .75
181 Kevin Howard **RC** .50
182 Wanell Severino **RC** .50
183 Kevin Kouzmanoff 2.00
184 Joel Zumaya **RC** 2.00
185 Skip Schumaker **RC** .50
186 Nic Ungs **RC** .50
187 Todd Self **RC** .50
188 Brian Steffek **RC** .50
189 Brock Peterson **RC** .50
190 Greg Thissen **RC** .50
191 Frank Brooks **RC** .50
192 Estee Harris **RC** .50
192 Estee Harris/Jsy **RC** 5.00
193 Chris Mabeus **RC** .50
194 Daniel Giese **RC** .50
195 Jared Wells **RC** .50
196 Carlos Sosa **RC** .50
197 Bobby Madritsch .50
198 Calvin Hayes **RC** .50
199 Omar Quintanilla .50
200 Chris O'Riordan **RC** .50
201 Tim Hutting **RC** .50
202 Carlos Quentin 4.00
203 Brayan Pena **RC** .50
204 Jeff Salazar **RC** 1.00
205 David Murphy 1.50
206 Alberto Garcia **RC** .50
207 Ramon Ramirez **RC** .50
208 Luis Bolivar **RC** .50
209 Rodney Choy Foo **RC** .50
210 Kyle Sleeth .50
211 Anthony Acevedo **RC** .50
212 Chad Santos **RC** .50
213 Jason Frasor **RC** .75
214 Jesse Roman **RC** .50
215 James Tomlin **RC** .50
216 Josh Labandeira **RC** .75
217 Joaquin Arias **RC** .50
218 Don Sutton **RC** (Photo actually Nick Swisher.) 1.00
219 Danny Gonzalez **RC** .50
220 Javier Guzman **RC** .50
221 Anthony Lerew **RC** .50
221 Anthony Lerew/Jsy **RC** 5.00
222 Jon Knott **RC** .50
223 Jesse English **RC** .50
224 Felix Hernandez **RC** 5.00
225 Travis Hanson .50
226 Jesse Floyd **RC** .50
227 Nick Gorneault **RC** .50
228 Craig Ansman **RC** .50
229 Wardell Starling **RC** .50
230 Carl Loadenthal **RC** .50
231 David Crouthers .50
232 Harvey Garcia **RC** .50
233 Casey Kopitzke **RC** .50
234 Ricky Nolasco 1.00
235 Miguel Perez **RC** .50
236 Ryan Mulhern **RC** .50
237 Chris Aguila **RC** .50
238 Brooks Conrad **RC** .50
239 Damaso Espino **RC** .50
240 Jereme Milons **RC** .50
241 Luke Hughes **RC** .50
242 Kory Casto .50
243 Jose Valdez **RC** .50
244 J.T. Stotts .50
245 Lee Gwaltney **RC** .50
246 Yoann Torrealba **RC** .50
247 Omar Falcon **RC** .50
248 Jon Coutlangus **RC** .50
249 George Sherrill **RC** .50
250 John Santor **RC** .50
251 Tony Richie **RC** .50
252 Kevin Richardson **RC** .50
253 Tim Bittner **RC** .50
254 Dustin Nippert **RC** 1.00
255 Jose Capellan **RC** .50
256 Donald Levinski .50
257 Jerome Gamble **RC** .50
258 Jeff Keppinger **RC** 1.00
259 Jason Szuminski **RC** .50
260 Akinori Otsuka **RC** .75
261 Ryan Budde .50
262 Shingo Takatsu **RC** .75
263 Jeffrey Allison .40
264 Hector Gimenez **RC** .50
265 Tim Frend **RC** .50
266 Tom Farmer **RC** .50
267 Shawn Hill **RC** .50
268 Lastings Milledge 3.00
269 Scott Proctor **RC** .75
270 Jorge Mejia **RC** .50
271 Terry Jones **RC** .50
272 Zach Duke **RC** 1.00
273 Tim Stauffer .75
274 Luke Anderson **RC** .50
275 Hunter Brown **RC** .50
276 Matt Lemanczyk **RC** .50
277 Fernando Cortez **RC** .50
278 Vince Perkins **RC** .50
279 Tommy Murphy **RC** .50
280 Mike Gosling .50
281 Paul Bacot .50
282 Matt Capps **RC** .75
283 Juan Gutierrez **RC** .50
284 Teodoro Encarnacion **RC** .50
285 Juan Cedeno **RC** .50
286 Matt Creighton **RC** .50
287 Ryan Hankins **RC** .50
288 Leo Nunez **RC** .50
289 Dave Wallace **RC** .50
290 Rob Tejeda **RC** .75
291 Lincoln Holdzkom **RC** .50
292 Jason Hirsh 1.50
293 Tydus Meadows **RC** .50
294 Khalid Ballouli **RC** .50
295 Benji DeQuin **RC** .50
296 Tyler Davidson 1.00
297 Brent Colamarino **RC** .50
298 Marcus McBeth **RC** .50
299 Brad Eldred **RC** .75
300 David Pauley **RC** .50
301 Yadier Molina **RC** 1.00
302 Chris Shelton **RC** 1.00
303 Travis Blackley **RC** .50
304 Jon DeVries .50
305 Sheldon Fulse **RC** .50
306 Vito Chiaravalloti **RC** .50
307 Warner Madrigal **RC** .50
308 Reid Gorecki **RC** .50
309 Sung Jung **RC** .50
310 Peter Shier **RC** .50
311 Michael Mooney **RC** .50
312 Kenny Perez **RC** .50
313 Mike Mallory **RC** .50
314 Ben Himes **RC** .50
315 Ivan Ochoa **RC** .50
316 Donald Kelly **RC** .50
317 Logan Kensing **RC** .50
318 Kevin Davidson **RC** .50
319 Brian Pilkington .50
320 Alex Romero **RC** .50
321 Chad Chop **RC** .50
322 Dioner Navarro **RC** .75
323 Casey Myers **RC** .50
324 Mike Rouse .50
325 Sergio Silva **RC** .50
326 J.J. Furmaniak **RC** .50
327 Brad Vericker **RC** .50
328 Blake Hawksworth **RC** 1.00
329 Brock Jacobsen **RC** .50
330 Alec Zumwalt **RC** .50

Gold

Stars: 1-2X
Rookies: 1-2X
Inserted 1:1

1st Edition

	NM/M
Stars:	3-5X
Rookies:	1-2X
HTA Exclusive	
Pack (10):	4.00
Box (20):	75.00

Uncirculated

Stars: 4-8X
Rookies: 3-5X
Production 245 Sets

Base of the Future Auto. Relic

	NM/M
HTA Exclusive	
GS Grady Sizemore	40.00

Futures Game Gear

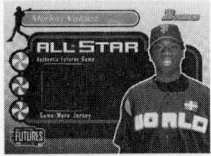

	NM/M
Common Player:	4.00
DB Denny Bautista	6.00
CB Chris Burke	6.00
JC Jose Castillo	4.00
NC Neal Cotts	5.00
JD Jorge De La Rosa	4.00
EE Edwin Encarnacion	8.00
SH Shawn Hill	4.00
EJ Edwin Jackson	4.00
DK David Kelton	4.00
DBK David Krynzel	4.00
PL Pete LaForest	4.00
JM John Maine	10.00
CN Clint Nageotte	6.00
RN Ramon Nivar	4.00
GQ Guillermo Quiroz	4.00
AR Alexis Rios	8.00
ES Ervin Santana	8.00
SS Stephen Smitherman	4.00
SJS Seung Jun Song	4.00
CT Chad Tracy	8.00
ST Scott Thorman	8.00
MV Merkin Valdez	4.00
JV John VanBenschoten	6.00
CW Chien-Ming Wang	40.00
KY Kevin Youkilis	4.00

Rookie of the Year Dual Relic

	NM/M
Inserted 1:829	
BW Angel Berroa, Dontrelle Willis	15.00

Signs of Future

	NM/M
Common Autograph:	8.00
Red Ink:	No Pricing
Production 25 Sets	
JB Justin Backsmeyer	10.00
IC Ismael Castro	8.00
BC Brent Clevelen	10.00
ED Eric Duncan	15.00
BF Brian Finch	8.00
RH Ryan Harvey	10.00
AH Aaron Hill	10.00
JH James Houser	8.00
TJ Tyler Johnson	8.00
TL Todd Linden	8.00
NM Nicholas Markakis	25.00
BM Brandon Medders	8.00
MM Matt Murton	10.00
CS Corey Shafer	8.00
GS Grady Sizemore	40.00
BS Brian Snyder	8.00
DS Denard Span	20.00
JV Joey Votto	30.00
BW Brandon Wood	15.00

2004 Bowman Chrome

	NM/M
Complete Set (350):	
Common Player:	.25
Common Rookie:	1.00
Common Rookie Auto. (331-350):	10.00
Inserted 1:18	
Pack (4):	5.00
Box (18):	80.00
1 Garret Anderson	.50
2 Larry Walker	.50
3 Derek Jeter	2.50
4 Curt Schilling	.75
5 Carlos Zambrano	.50
6 Shawn Green	.50
7 Manny Ramirez	1.00
8 Randy Johnson	1.00
9 Jeremy Bonderman	1.00
10 Alfonso Soriano	1.00
11 Scott Rolen	.50
12 Kerry Wood	.50
13 Eric Gagne	.50
14 Ryan Klesko	.25
15 Kevin Millar	.25
16 Ty Wigginton	.25
17 David Ortiz	1.50
18 Luis Castillo	.25
19 Bernie Williams	.50
20 Edgar Renteria	.50
21 Matt Kata	.25
22 Bartolo Colon	.50
23 Derrek Lee	.50
24 Gary Sheffield	.75
25 Nomar Garciaparra	.50
26 Kevin Millwood	.50
27 Corey Patterson	.50
28 Carlos Beltran	.75
29 Mike Lieberthal	.25
30 Troy Glaus	.25
31 Preston Wilson	.25
32 Jorge Posada	.50
33 Bo Hart	.25
34 Mark Prior	.50
35 Hideo Nomo	.50
36 Jason Kendall	.25
37 Roger Clemens	2.50
38 Dmitri Young	.25
39 Jason Giambi	.75
40 Jim Edmonds	.25
41 Ryan Ludwick	.25
42 Brandon Webb	.25
43 Todd Helton	.75
44 Jacque Jones	.25
45 Jamie Moyer	.25
46 Tim Salmon	.50
47 Kelvim Escobar	.25
48 Tony Batista	.25
49 Nick Johnson	.25
50 Jim Thome	1.00
51 Casey Blake	.50
52 Trot Nixon	.50
53 Luis Gonzalez	.50
54 Dontrelle Willis	.50
55 Mike Mussina	.50
56 Carl Crawford	.50
57 Mark Buehrle	.50
58 Scott Podsednik	.50

59 Brian Giles	.50
60 Rafael Furcal	.50
61 Miguel Cabrera	1.00
62 Rich Harden	.50
63 Mark Teixeira	.75
64 Frank Thomas	.75
65 Johan Santana	.75
66 Jason Schmidt	.50
67 Aramis Ramirez	.50
68 Jose Reyes	.75
69 Magglio Ordonez	.50
70 Mike Sweeney	.25
71 Eric Chavez	.50
72 Rocco Baldelli	.50
73 Sammy Sosa	.75
74 Javy Lopez	.25
75 Roy Oswalt	.50
76 Raul Ibanez	.25
77 Ivan Rodriguez	.75
78 Jerome Williams	.25
79 Carlos Lee	.50
80 Geoff Jenkins	.25
81 Sean Burroughs	.25
82 Marcus Giles	.25
83 Mike Lowell	.50
84 Barry Zito	.50
85 Aubrey Huff	.25
86 Esteban Loaiza	.25
87 Torii Hunter	.50
88 Phil Nevin	.25
89 Andruw Jones	.75
90 Josh Beckett	.50
91 Mark Mulder	.50
92 Hank Blalock	.50
93 Jason Phillips	.25
94 Russ Ortiz	.25
95 Juan Pierre	.25
96 Tom Glavine	.50
97 Gil Meche	.25
98 Ramon Ortiz	.25
99 Richie Sexson	.50
100 Albert Pujols	2.50
101 Javier Vazquez	.25
102 Johnny Damon	1.00
103 Alex Rodriguez	2.50
104 Omar Vizquel	.50
105 Chipper Jones	1.00
106 Lance Berkman	.50
107 Tim Hudson	.50
108 Carlos Delgado	.50
109 Austin Kearns	.40
110 Orlando Cabrera	.25
111 Edgar Martinez	.50
112 Melvin Mora	.25
113 Jeff Bagwell	.75
114 Marlon Byrd	.25
115 Vernon Wells	.50
116 C.C. Sabathia	.50
117 Cliff Floyd	.25
118 Ichiro Suzuki	2.00
119 Miguel Olivo	.25
120 Mike Piazza	1.00
121 Adam Dunn	.75
122 Paul Lo Duca	.25
123 Brett Myers	.50
124 Michael Young	.50
125 Sidney Ponson	.25
126 Greg Maddux	2.00
127 Vladimir Guerrero	1.00
128 Miguel Tejada	.50
129 Andy Pettitte	.50
130 Rafael Palmeiro	.75
131 Ken Griffey Jr.	2.00
132 Shannon Stewart	.25
133 Joel Pineiro	.25
134 Luis Matos	.25
135 Jeff Kent	.50
136 Randy Wolf	.25
137 Chris Woodward	.25
138 Jody Gerut	.25
139 Jose Vidro	.25
140 Bret Boone	.25
141 Bill Mueller	.25
142 Angel Berroa	.25
143 Bobby Abreu	.50
144 Roy Halladay	.50
145 Delmon Young	.50
146 Jonny Gomes	.25
147 Rickie Weeks	.50
148 Edwin Jackson	.25
149 Neal Cotts	.25
150 Jason Bay	.50
151 Khalil Greene	.50
152 Joe Mauer	.50
153 Bobby Jenks	.25
154 Chin-Feng Chen	.25
155 Chien-Ming Wang	.75
156 Mickey Hall	.25
157 James Houser	.25
158 Jay Sborz	.25
159 Jonathan Fulton	.25
160 Steve Lerud	.25
161 Grady Sizemore	.75
162 Felix Pie	.50
163 Dustin McGowan	.25
164 Chris Lubanski	.25
165 Tom Gorzelanny	.50
166 Rudy Guillen RC	2.00
167 Aarom Baldiris RC	2.00
168 Conor Jackson	8.00
169 Matt Moses	2.00
170 Ervin Santana RC	4.00
171 Merkin Valdez RC	2.00
172 Erick Aybar RC	3.00
173 Brad Sullivan	1.00
174 Joey Gathright RC	2.00
175 Brad Snyder	.50

176 Alberto Callaspo RC	3.00
177 Brandon Medders RC	1.00
178 Zach Miner RC	3.00
179 Charlie Zink RC	1.00
180 Adam Greenberg	2.50
181 Kevin Howard RC	1.00
182 Wanell Severino RC	1.00
183 Chin-Lung Hu RC	3.00
184 Joel Zumaya RC	5.00
185 Skip Schumaker RC	1.00
186 Nic Ungs RC	1.00
187 Todd Self RC	1.00
188 Brian Steffek RC	1.00
189 Brock Peterson RC	1.00
190 Greg Thissen RC	1.00
191 Frank Brooks RC	1.00
192 Scott Olsen RC	3.00
193 Chris Mabeus RC	1.00
194 Daniel Giese RC	1.00
195 Jared Wells RC	1.00
196 Carlos Sosa RC	1.00
197 Bobby Madritsch	1.00
198 Calvin Hayes RC	1.00
199 Omar Quintanilla	1.00
200 Chris O'Riordan RC	1.00
201 Tim Hutting RC	1.00
202 Carlos Quentin	12.00
203 Brayan Pena RC	1.00
204 Jeff Salazar RC	1.00
205 David Murphy	4.00
206 Alberto Garcia RC	1.00
207 Ramon Ramirez RC	2.00
208 Luis Bolivar RC	1.00
209 Rodney Choy Foo RC	1.00
210 Fausto Carmona RC	5.00
211 Anthony Acevedo RC	2.00
212 Chad Santos RC	1.00
213 Jason Frasor RC	1.00
214 Jesse Roman RC	1.00
215 James Tomlin RC	1.00
216 Josh Labandeira RC	1.00
217 Ryan Meaux RC	1.00
218 Don Sutton RC	2.00
219 Danny Gonzalez RC	1.00
220 Javier Guzman RC	2.00
221 Anthony Lerew RC	2.00
222 Jon Connolly RC	2.00
223 Jesse English RC	1.00
224 Hector Made RC	2.00
225 Travis Hanson	1.00
226 Jesse Floyd RC	1.00
227 Nick Gorneault RC	1.00
228 Craig Ansman RC	1.00
229 Paul McAnulty RC	2.00
230 Carl Loadenthal RC	1.00
231 David Crouthers	1.00
232 Harvey Garcia RC	1.00
233 Casey Kopitzke RC	1.00
234 Ricky Nolasco	3.00
235 Miguel Perez RC	1.00
236 Ryan Mulhern RC	1.00
237 Chris Aguila RC	1.00
238 Brooks Conrad RC	1.00
239 Damaso Espino RC	1.00
240 Jereme Milons RC	1.00
241 Luke Hughes RC	1.50
242 Kory Casto RC	1.00
243 Jose Valdez RC	1.00
244 J.T. Stotts	1.00
245 Lee Gwaltney RC	1.00
246 Yoann Torrealba RC	1.00
247 Omar Falcon RC	1.00
248 Jon Coutlangus RC	1.00
249 George Sherrill RC	2.00
250 John Santor RC	1.00
251 Tony Richie RC	1.00
252 Kevin Richardson RC	1.00
253 Tim Bittner RC	1.00
254 Chris Saenz RC	1.00
255 Jose Capellan RC	1.00
256 Donald Levinski	1.00
257 Jerome Gamble RC	1.00
258 Jeff Keppinger RC	4.00
259 Jason Szuminski RC	1.00
260 Akinori Otsuka RC	.50
261 Ryan Budde	1.00
262 Marland Williams RC	1.00
263 Jeffrey Allison	1.00
264 Hector Gimenez RC	1.00
265 Tim Frend RC	1.00
266 Tom Farmer RC	1.00
267 Shawn Hill RC	1.00
268 Mike Huggins RC	1.00
269 Scott Proctor RC	1.50
270 Jorge Mejia RC	1.00
271 Terry Jones RC	1.00
272 Zach Duke RC	2.00
273 Jesse Crain	1.00
274 Luke Anderson RC	1.00
275 Hunter Brown RC	1.00
276 Matt Lemanczyk RC	1.00
277 Fernando Cortez RC	1.00
278 Vince Perkins RC	1.00
279 Tommy Murphy RC	1.00
280 Mike Gosling	1.00
281 Paul Bacot	1.00
282 Matt Capps RC	2.00
283 Juan Gutierrez RC	1.00
284 Teodoro Encarnacion RC	1.00
285 Chad Bentz RC	1.00
286 Kazuo Matsui RC	1.50
287 Ryan Hankins RC	1.00
288 Leo Nunez RC	1.00
289 Dave Wallace RC	1.00
290 Rob Tejeda RC	1.00
291 Paul Maholm RC	1.00
292 Casey Daigle RC	1.00

293 Tydus Meadows **RC** 1.00
294 Khalid Ballouli **RC** 1.00
295 Benji DeQuin **RC** 1.00
296 Tyler Davidson 1.00
297 Brent Colamarino **RC** 1.00
298 Marcus McBeth **RC** 1.00
299 Brad Eldred **RC** 1.50
300 David Pauley **RC** 2.00
301 Yadier Molina **RC** 4.00
302 Chris Shelton **RC** 2.00
303 Nyjer Morgan **RC** 1.00
304 Jon DeVries 1.00
305 Sheldon Fulse **RC** 1.00
306 Vito Chiaravalloti **RC** 1.00
307 Warner Madrigal **RC** 2.00
308 Reid Gorecki **RC** 1.00
309 Sung Jung **RC** 1.00
310 Peter Shier **RC** 1.00
311 Michael Mooney **RC** 1.00
312 Kenny Perez **RC** 1.00
313 Mike Mallory **RC** 1.00
314 Ben Himes **RC** 1.00
315 Ivan Ochoa **RC** 1.00
316 Donald Kelly **RC** 1.00
317 Tom Mastny **RC** 1.00
318 Kevin Davidson **RC** 1.00
319 Brian Pilkington 1.00
320 Alex Romero **RC** 1.00
321 Chad Chop **RC** 1.00
322 Kody Kirkland **RC** 1.00
323 Casey Myers **RC** 1.00
324 Mike Rouse 1.00
325 Sergio Silva **RC** 1.00
326 J.J. Furmaniak **RC** 2.00
327 Brad Vericker **RC** 1.00
328 Blake Hawksworth **RC** 2.00
329 Brock Jacobsen **RC** 1.00
330 Alec Zumwalt **RC** 1.00
331 Wardell Starling **RC** 10.00
332 Estee Harris **RC** 10.00
333 Kyle Sleeth 10.00
334 Dioner Navarro **RC** 15.00
335 Logan Kensing **RC** 10.00
336 Travis Blackley **RC** 10.00
337 Lincoln Holdzkom **RC** 10.00
338 Jason Hirsh 10.00
339 Juan Cedeno **RC** 10.00
340 Matt Creighton **RC** 10.00
341 Tim Stauffer 10.00
342 Shingo Takatsu **RC** 10.00
343 Lastings Milledge 30.00
344 Dustin Nippert **RC** 10.00
345 Felix Hernandez **RC** 100.00
346 Joaquin Arias **RC** 10.00
347 Kevin Kouzmanoff 20.00
348 Bobby Brownlie **RC** 10.00
349 David Aardsma 10.00
350 Jon Knott **RC** 10.00

Refractor

Stars (1-165): 2-4X
Rookies (166-330): 1-2X
Inserted 1:4
Autograph (331-350): 1-2X
Inserted 1:100

Gold Refractor

Stars (1-165): 4-8X
Rookies (166-330): 3-5X
Production 50
Autograph (331-350): No Pricing
Inserted 1:1,003

X-Fractor

Stars (1-165): 3-5X
Rookies (166-330): 2-4X
Production 173
Autograph (331-350): No Pricing
Inserted 1:200

Stars Of The Future

NM/M

Inserted 1:600
YSS Delmon Young, Kyle Sleeth, Tim Stauffer 60.00
LHC Chris Lubanski, Ryan Harvey, Chad Cordero 40.00
MHD Nicholas Markakis, Aaron Hill, Eric Duncan 50.00

2004 Bowman Chrome Draft Picks & Prospects

NM/M

Complete Set (175):
Common Player: .25
Common Rookie: 1.00
Common RC Auto. (166-175): 15.00
Inserted 1:60
BDP1 Lyle Overbay .50
BDP2 David Newhan .25
BDP3 J.R. House .25
BDP4 Chad Tracy .25
BDP5 Humberto Quintero .25
BDP6 David Bush .25
BDP7 Scott Hairston .25
BDP8 Mike Wood .25
BDP9 Alexis Rios .50
BDP10 Sean Burnett .25
BDP11 Wilson Valdez .25
BDP12 Lew Ford .25
BDP13 Freddie Thon **RC** 1.00
BDP14 Zack Greinke .25
BDP15 Bucky Jacobsen .25
BDP16 Kevin Youkilis .50
BDP17 Grady Sizemore .75
BDP18 Denny Bautista .25
BDP19 David DeJesus .25
BDP20 Casey Kotchman .25
BDP21 David Kelton .25
BDP22 Charles Thomas **RC** 1.00
BDP23 Kazuhito Tadano **RC** 1.50
BDP24 Justin Leone **RC** 1.00
BDP25 Eduardo Villacis **RC** 1.00
BDP26 Brian Dallimore **RC** 1.00
BDP27 Nick Green **RC** 1.00
BDP28 Sam McConnell **RC** 1.00
BDP29 Brad Halsey **RC** 1.00
BDP30 Roman Colon **RC** 1.00
BDP31 Josh Fields **RC** 5.00
BDP32 Cody Bunkelman **RC** 1.00
BDP33 Jay Rainville **RC** 3.00
BDP34 Richie Robnett **RC** 3.00
BDP35 Jon Poterson **RC** 2.50
BDP36 Huston Street **RC** 5.00
BDP37 Erick San Pedro **RC** 1.00
BDP38 Cory Dunlap **RC** 3.00
BDP39 Kurt Suzuki **RC** 3.00
BDP40 Anthony Swarzak **RC** 2.00
BDP41 Ian Desmond **RC** 3.00
BDP42 Chris Covington **RC** 1.50
BDP43 Christian Garcia **RC** 1.50
BDP44 Gaby Hernandez **RC** 5.00
BDP45 Steven Register **RC** 1.00
BDP46 Eduardo Morlan **RC** 2.50
BDP47 Collin Balester **RC** 2.00
BDP48 Nathan Phillips **RC** 1.00
BDP49 Dan Schwartzbauer **RC** 1.00
BDP50 Rafael Gonzalez **RC** 1.00
BDP51 K.C. Herren **RC** 2.00
BDP52 William Susdorf **RC** 1.00
BDP53 Rob Johnson **RC** 1.00
BDP54 Louis Marson **RC** 2.00
BDP55 Joe Koshansky **RC** 5.00
BDP56 Jamar Walton **RC** 3.00
BDP57 Mark Lowe **RC** 2.50
BDP58 Matt Macri **RC** 3.00
BDP59 Donny Lucy **RC** 1.00
BDP60 Mike Ferris **RC** 2.00
BDP61 Mike Nickeas **RC** 1.50
BDP62 Eric Hurley **RC** 3.00
BDP63 Scott Elbert **RC** 3.00
BDP64 Blake DeWitt **RC** 5.00
BDP65 Danny Putnam **RC** 2.00
BDP66 J.P. Howell **RC** 3.00
BDP67 John Wiggins **RC** 1.00
BDP68 Justin Orenduff **RC** 2.00
BDP69 Ray Liotta **RC** 2.00
BDP70 Billy Buckner **RC** 1.00
BDP71 Eric Campbell **RC** 3.00
BDP72 Olin Wick **RC** 2.00
BDP73 Sean Gamble **RC** 1.50
BDP74 Seth Smith **RC** 3.00
BDP75 Wade Davis **RC** 4.00
BDP76 Joe Jacobitz **RC** 1.00
BDP77 J.A. Happ **RC** 2.00
BDP78 Eric Ridener **RC** 1.00
BDP79 Matt Tuiasosopo **RC** 3.00
BDP80 Bradley Bergesen **RC** 1.00
BDP81 Javy Guerra **RC** 1.50
BDP82 Buck Shaw **RC** 2.00
BDP83 Paul Janish **RC** 2.00
BDP84 Sean Kazmar **RC** 1.00
BDP85 Josh Johnson **RC** 1.50
BDP86 Angel Salome **RC** 2.00
BDP87 Jordan Parraz **RC** 1.00
BDP88 Kelvin Vazquez **RC** 1.00
BDP89 Grant Hansen **RC** 1.00
BDP90 Matt Fox **RC** 2.00
BDP91 Trevor Plouffe **RC** 2.00
BDP92 Wes Whisler **RC** 1.00
BDP93 Curtis Thigpen **RC** 2.00
BDP94 Donnie Smith **RC** 1.00
BDP95 Luis Rivera **RC** 1.50
BDP96 Jesse Hoover **RC** 1.00
BDP97 Jason Vargas **RC** 1.00
BDP98 Clary Carlsen **RC** 1.00
BDP99 Mark Robinson **RC** 1.00
BDP100 J.C. Holt **RC** 1.50
BDP101 Chad Blackwell **RC** 1.00
BDP102 Daryl Jones **RC** 2.00
BDP103 Jonathan Tierce **RC** 1.00
BDP104 Patrick Bryant **RC** 1.00
BDP105 Eddie Prasch **RC** 1.50
BDP106 Mitch Einertson **RC** 2.00
BDP107 Kyle Waldrop **RC** 2.00
BDP108 Jeff Marquez **RC** 2.00
BDP109 Zach Jackson **RC** 1.00
BDP110 Josh Wahpepah **RC** 1.00
BDP111 Adam Lind **RC** 3.00
BDP112 Kyle Bloom **RC** 1.00
BDP113 Ben Harrison **RC** 1.00
BDP114 Taylor Tankersley **RC** 2.00
BDP115 Steven Jackson **RC** 1.00
BDP116 David Purcey **RC** 1.50
BDP117 Jacob McGee **RC** 4.00
BDP118 Lucas Harrell **RC** 1.00
BDP119 Brandon Allen **RC** 2.50
BDP120 Van Pope **RC** 1.50
BDP121 Jeff Francis .25
BDP122 Joe Blanton .25
BDP123 Wilfredo Ledezma .25
BDP124 Bryan Bullington .25
BDP125 Jairo Garcia .25
BDP126 Matt Cain .75
BDP127 Arnie Munoz .25
BDP128 Clint Everts .25
BDP129 Jesus Cota .25
BDP130 Gavin Floyd .25
BDP131 Edwin Encarnacion .25
BDP132 Koyie Hill .25
BDP133 Ruben Gotay .25
BDP134 Jeff Mathis .25
BDP135 Andy Marte .50
BDP136 Dallas McPherson .25
BDP137 Justin Morneau .50
BDP138 Rickie Weeks .40
BDP139 Joel Guzman .25
BDP140 Shin-Soo Choo .25
BDP141 Yusmeiro Petit **RC** 5.00
BDP142 Jorge Cortes **RC** 1.00
BDP143 Val Majewski .25
BDP144 Felix Pie .50
BDP145 Aaron Hill .25
BDP146 Jose Capellan .25
BDP147 Dioner Navarro **RC** 2.00
BDP148 Fausto Carmona 1.00
BDP149 Robinzon Diaz **RC** 1.00
BDP150 Felix Hernandez 5.00
BDP151 Andres Blanco **RC** 1.00
BDP152 Jason Kubel .25
BDP153 Willy Taveras **RC** 2.50
BDP154 Merkin Valdez 1.00
BDP155 Robinson Cano 1.00
BDP156 Bill Murphy **RC** .50
BDP157 Chris Burke .25
BDP158 Kyle Sleeth .75
BDP159 B.J. Upton .75
BDP160 Tim Stauffer 1.00
BDP161 David Wright 2.50
BDP162 Conor Jackson 3.00
BDP163 Brad Thompson **RC** 2.00
BDP164 Delmon Young .50
BDP165 Jeremy Reed .25
BDP166 Matt Bush **RC** 15.00
BDP167 Mark Rogers **RC** 15.00
BDP168 Thomas Diamond **RC** 15.00
BDP169 Greg Golson **RC** 20.00
BDP170 Homer Bailey **RC** 40.00
BDP171 Chris Lambert **RC** 10.00
BDP172 Neil Walker **RC** 20.00
BDP173 Bill Bray **RC** 10.00
BDP174 Phillip Hughes **RC** 85.00
BDP175 Gio Gonzalez **RC** 35.00

Refractor

Rookies: 2-4X
Inserted 1:11
Rookie Autos. (166-175): .75-1.5X
Inserted 1:204

Gold Refractor

Rookies: 10-20X
Production 50
Rookie Autos. (166-175): 3-5X
Inserted 1:2,045

X-Fractor

Rookies: 3-6X
Production 125
Rookie Autos. (166-175): 1-2X
Inserted 1:407

2004 Bowman Chrome Draft Picks AFLAC

NM/M

Complete Set (12): 35.00
One redemption per box.
1 C.J. Henry 4.00
2 John Drennen 2.00
3 Beau Jones 2.00
4 Jeff Lyman 1.00
5 Andrew McCutchen 8.00
6 Chris Volstad 2.00
7 Jonathan Egan 1.00
8 P.J. Phillips 2.00
9 Steve Johnson 1.00
10 Ryan Tucker 1.00
11 Cameron Maybin 25.00
12 Shane Funk 1.00

Gold Refractor

No Pricing
Production 50 Sets

Refractor

Refractors: 4-6X
Production 550 Sets

X-Fractor

X-Refractors: 10-15X
Production 125 Sets

Red Refractor

No Pricing
Production One Set

2004 Bowman Draft Picks & Prospects

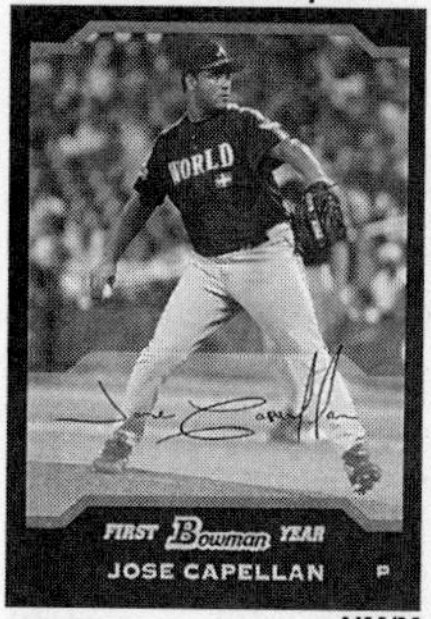

NM/M

Complete Set (1-165): 30.00
Common Player: .15
Common Rookie: .25
Pack (5 Bowman + 2 Chrome): 5.00
Box (24): 100.00
BDP1 Lyle Overbay .25
BDP2 David Newhan .15
BDP3 J.R. House .15
BDP4 Chad Tracy .15
BDP5 Humberto Quintero .15
BDP6 David Bush .15
BDP7 Scott Hairston .15
BDP8 Mike Wood .15
BDP9 Alexis Rios .25
BDP10 Sean Burnett .15
BDP11 Wilson Valdez .15
BDP12 Lew Ford .15
BDP13 Freddy Thon **RC** .25
BDP14 Zack Greinke .15
BDP15 Bucky Jacobsen .15
BDP16 Kevin Youkilis .25
BDP17 Grady Sizemore .25
BDP18 Denny Bautista .15
BDP19 David DeJesus .15
BDP20 Casey Kotchman .15
BDP21 David Kelton .15
BDP22 Charles Thomas **RC** .25
BDP23 Kazuhito Tadano **RC** .50
BDP24 Justin Leone **RC** .25
BDP25 Eduardo Villacis .25
BDP26 Brian Dallimore **RC** .25
BDP27 Nick Green .25
BDP28 Sam McConnell .25
BDP29 Brad Halsey **RC** .25
BDP30 Roman Colon **RC** .25
BDP31 Josh Fields **RC** 2.00
BDP32 Cody Bunkelman .50
BDP33 Jay Rainville **RC** 1.00
BDP34 Richie Robnett **RC** 1.00
BDP35 Jon Poterson **RC** .75
BDP36 Huston Street **RC** 1.00
BDP37 Erick San Pedro **RC** .25
BDP38 Cory Dunlap 1.00
BDP39 Kurt Suzuki **RC** .75
BDP40 Anthony Swarzak .50
BDP41 Ian Desmond 1.00
BDP42 Chris Covington .40
BDP43 Christian Garcia .40
BDP44 Gaby Hernandez **RC** 1.00
BDP45 Steven Register .25
BDP46 Eduardo Morlan .25
BDP47 Collin Balester .50
48 Nathan Phillips .25
49 Dan Schwartzbauer .25
50 Rafael Gonzalez .25
51 K.C. Herren **RC** .50
52 William Susdorf .25
53 Rob Johnson .25
54 Louis Marson .50
55 Joe Koshansky **RC** 1.00
56 Jamar Walton 1.00
57 Mark Lowe .75
58 Matt Macri **RC** .75
59 Donny Lucy .25
60 Mike Ferris .50
61 Mike Nickeas .50

62 Eric Hurley RC .75
63 Scott Elbert RC 1.00
64 Blake DeWitt RC 1.50
65 Danny Putnam RC .50
66 J.P. Howell RC .75
67 John Wiggins .25
68 Justin Orenduff RC .50
69 Ray Liotta RC .75
70 Billy Buckner RC .25
71 Eric Campbell RC 1.00
72 Olin Wick .25
73 Sean Gamble .40
74 Seth Smith 1.00
75 Wade Davis RC 1.00
76 Joe Jacobitz .25
77 J.A. Happ .50
78 Eric Riedner .25
79 Matt Tuiasosopo RC 1.00
80 Bradley Bergesen .25
81 Javy Guerra .40
82 Buck Shaw .50
83 Paul Janish .50
84 Sean Kazmar .25
85 Josh Johnson RC .50
86 Angel Salome .50
87 Jordan Parraz RC .50
88 Kelvin Vazquez .25
89 Grant Hansen .25
90 Matt Fox RC .50
91 Trevor Plouffe RC 1.00
92 Wes Whisler .50
93 Curtis Thigpen .50
94 Donnie Smith RC .25
95 Luis Rivera .40
96 Jesse Hoover .25
97 Jason Vargas RC 1.00
98 Clary Carlsen .25
99 Mark Robinson .25
100 J.C. Holt RC .40
101 Chad Blackwell .25
102 Daryl Jones RC .75
103 Jonathan Tierce .25
104 Patrick Bryant .25
105 Eddie Prasch .40
106 Mitch Einertson RC .75
107 Kyle Waldrop RC .75
108 Jeff Marquez RC .50
109 Zach Jackson RC .50
110 Josh Wahpepah .25
111 Adam Lind RC 1.00
112 Kyle Bloom .25
113 Ben Harrison .25
114 Taylor Tankersley RC .75
115 Steven Jackson .25
116 David Purcey RC .50
117 Jacob McGee 1.50
118 Lucas Harrell RC .25
119 Brandon Allen .75
120 Van Pope .25
121 Jeff Francis .15
122 Joe Blanton .15
123 Wilfredo Ledezma .15
124 Bryan Bullington .15
125 Jairo Garcia .15
126 Matt Cain .40
127 Arnie Munoz .15
128 Clint Everts .15
129 Jesus Cota .15
130 Gavin Floyd .15
131 Edwin Encarnacion .15
132 Koyie Hill .15
133 Ruben Gotay .15
134 Jeff Mathis .15
135 Andy Marte .25
136 Dallas McPherson .15
137 Justin Morneau .40
138 Rickie Weeks .25
139 Joel Guzman .15
140 Shin-Soo Choo .15
141 Yusmeiro Petit RC 2.00
142 Jorge Cortes .25
143 Val Majewski .15
144 Felix Pie .15
145 Aaron Hill .15
146 Jose Capellan .25
147 Dioner Navarro RC .25
148 Fausto Carmona RC .50
149 Robinzon Diaz .25
150 Felix Hernandez 2.00
151 Andres Blanco .25
152 Jason Kubel .15
153 Willy Taveras RC 1.00
154 Merkin Valdez .40
155 Robinson Cano .50
156 Bill Murphy .25
157 Chris Burke .15
158 Kyle Sleeth .25
159 B.J. Upton .25
160 Tim Stauffer 1.00
161 David Wright 1.00
162 Conor Jackson .25
163 Brad Thompson RC .25
164 Delmon Young .40
165 Jeremy Reed .15

Gold
Rookies: .75-1.5X
Inserted 1:1

Red
No Pricing
Production One Set

Printing Plates
No Pricing
Production one for each color.

AFLAC All-Americans
Complete Set (40)
No Pricing

Prospect Premiums
NM/M
Common Player: 4.00
AB Angel Berroa 4.00
KC Kevin Cash 4.00
RH Ryan Harvey 6.00
CJ Conor Jackson 10.00
EJ Edwin Jackson 4.00
LM Lastings Milledge 15.00
DN Dioner Navarro 4.00
CQ Carlos Quentin 8.00
JR Jeremy Reed 6.00
NS Nick Swisher 8.00
BU B.J. Upton 8.00
DY Delmon Young 8.00

Signs of the Future
NM/M
Common Player: 8.00
CC Chad Cordero 8.00
JH James Houser 8.00
AL Adam Loewen 10.00
PM Paul Maholm 8.00
TP Tyler Pelland 8.00
TT Terry Tiffee 8.00

AFLAC
NM/M
Complete Set (12): 10.00
One redemption per box.
Red: No Pricing
Production One Set
1 C.J. Henry 1.00
2 John Drennen .75
3 Beau Jones .75
4 Jeff Lyman .50
5 Andrew McCutchen 2.50
6 Chris Volstad 1.00
7 Jonathan Egan .50
8 P.J. Phillips 1.00
9 Steve Johnson .50
10 Ryan Tucker .50
11 Cameron Maybin 8.00
12 Shane Funk .50

2004 Bowman Heritage

NM/M
Complete Set (347):
Common Player: .15
Common SP: 4.00
Common SP Rookie: 4.00
SP's inserted 1:3
Pack (8): 4.00
Box (24): 80.00
1 Tom Glavine .40
2 Mike Piazza/SP 8.00
3 Sidney Ponson .15
4 Jerry Hairston Jr. .15
5 Jermaine Dye .25
6 Bobby Crosby .15
7 Carlos Zambrano .25
8 Moises Alou .15
9 Alex Rodriguez/SP 10.00
10 Derek Jeter 2.00
11 Rafael Furcal .25
12 J.D. Drew .25
13 Joe Mauer/SP 4.00
14 Brad Radke .15
15 Johnny Damon .75
16 Derek Lowe .25
17 Pat Burrell .25
18 Mike Lieberthal .15
19 Cliff Lee .15
20 Ronnie Belliard .15
21 Eric Gagne/SP 4.00
22 Brad Penny .15
23 Al Kaline .50
24 Mike Maroth .15
25 Magglio Ordonez/SP 4.00
26 Mark Buehrle .25
27 Jack Wilson .15
28 Oliver Perez .15
29 Al "Red" Schoendienst .15
30 Yadier Molina RC 1.50
31 Ryan Freel .15
32 Adam Dunn .50
33 Paul Konerko .40
34 Esteban Loaiza .15
35 Ivan Rodriguez .50
36 Carlos Guillen .15
37 Adrian Beltre .25
38 C.C. Sabathia .25
39 Hideo Nomo .40
40 Victor Martinez/SP 4.00
41 Bobby Abreu .25
42 Randy Wolf .15
43 Johnny Estrada .15
44 Russ Ortiz .15
45 Kenny Rogers .15
46 Hank Blalock/SP 4.00
47 David Ortiz 1.00
48 Pedro Martinez/SP 6.00
49 Austin Kearns .25
50 Ken Griffey Jr./SP 6.00
51 Mark Prior .50
52 Kerry Wood .40
53 Eric Chavez .25
54 Tim Hudson .25
55 Rafael Palmeiro/SP 4.00
56 Javy Lopez .15
57 Jason Bay .40
58 Craig Wilson .15
59 Ed "Whitey" Ford .50
60 Jason Giambi .50
61 Scott Rolen/SP 4.00
62 Matt Morris .15
63 Javier Vazquez .15
64 Jim Thome .50
65 Don Zimmer .25
66 Shawn Green .25
67 Don Larsen .15
68 Gary Sheffield .40
69 Jorge Posada .50
70 Bernie Williams .40
71 Chipper Jones .75
72 Andruw Jones .50
73 Jim Thomson .15
74 Jim Edmonds .40
75 Albert Pujols 2.00
76 Chris Carpenter .50
77 Aubrey Huff/SP 4.00
78 Carl Crawford .40
79 Victor Zambrano .15
80 Alfonso Soriano/SP 5.00
81 Lance Berkman .40
82 Mike Sweeney .15
83 Ken Harvey .15
84 Angel Berroa .15
85 A.J. Burnett .15
86 Mike Lowell .15
87 Miguel Cabrera/SP 5.00
88 Preston Wilson .15
89 Todd Helton/SP 4.00
90 Larry Walker .25
91 Vladimir Guerrero .75
92 Garret Anderson .15
93 Bartolo Colon .15
94 Scott Hairston .15
95 Richie Sexson/SP 4.00
96 Sean Casey .25
97 Johnny Podres .40
98 Andy Pettitte .40
99 Roy Oswalt .25
100 Roger Clemens/SP 8.00
101 Scott Podsednik .25
102 Ben Sheets .25
103 Lyle Overbay .15
104 Nick Johnson/SP 4.00
105 Zach Day .15
106 Jose Reyes .75
107 Khalil Greene .25
108 Sean Burroughs .15
109 David Wells/SP 4.00
110 Jason Schmidt .25
111 Neifi Perez .15
112 Edgar Renteria .25
113 Rich Aurilia .15
114 Edgar Martinez .25
115 Joel Pineiro .15
116 Mark Teixeira .40
117 Michael Young .25
118 Ricardo Rodriguez .15
119 Carlos Delgado .50
120 Roy Halladay .25
121 Jose Guillen .15
122 Troy Glaus .40
123 Shea Hillenbrand .15
124 Luis Gonzalez .25
125 Horacio Ramirez .15
126 Melvin Mora .15
127 Miguel Tejada/SP 4.00
128 Manny Ramirez .75
129 Tim Wakefield .25
130 Curt Schilling/SP 5.00
131 Aramis Ramirez .40
132 Sammy Sosa/SP 4.00
133 Matt Clement .15
134 Juan Uribe .15
135 Dontrelle Willis .25
136 Paul LoDuca .15
137 Juan Pierre .15
138 Kevin Brown .15
139 Brian Giles, Marcus Giles .15
140 Brian Giles .15
141 Nomar Garciaparra/SP 4.00
142 Cesar Izturis .15
143 Don Newcombe .15
144 Craig Biggio .25
145 Carlos Beltran .50
146 Torii Hunter .25
147 Livan Hernandez .15
148 Cliff Floyd .15
149 Barry Zito .40
150 Mark Mulder .25
151 Rocco Baldelli .25
152 Bret Boone .15
153 Jamie Moyer .15
154 Ichiro Suzuki 1.50
155 Brett Myers .25
156 Carl Pavano .15
157 Josh Beckett .25
158 Randy Johnson .75
159 Trot Nixon .15
160 Dmitri Young .15
161 Jacque Jones .15
162 Lew Ford .15
163 Jose Vidro .15
164 Mark Kotsay .15
165 A.J. Pierzynski .15
166 Dewon Brazelton .15
167 Jeromy Burnitz .15
168 Johan Santana .50
169 Greg Maddux 1.00
170 Carl Erskine .15
171 Robin Roberts .15
172 Freddy Garcia .15
173 Carlos Lee .25
174 Jeff Bagwell .40
175 Jeff Kent .25
176 Kazuhisa Ishii .15
177 Orlando Cabrera .25
178 Shannon Stewart .15
179 Mike Cameron .15
180 Mike Mussina .40
181 Frank Thomas .75
182 Jaret Wright .15
183 Alex Gonzalez/SP 4.00
184 Matt Lawton .15
185 Derrek Lee .50
186 Omar Vizquel .25
187 Jeremy Bonderman .25
188 Jake Westbrook .15
189 Zack Greinke/SP 4.00
190 Chad Tracy .15
191 Rondell White .15
192 Alex Gonzalez .15
193 Geoff Jenkins .15
194 Ralph Kiner .40
195 Al Leiter .15
196 Kevin Millwood .25
197 Jason Kendall .15
198 Kris Benson .15
199 Ryan Klesko .15
200 Mark Loretta .15
201 Richard Hidalgo .15
202 Reed Johnson .15
203 Luis Castillo .15
204 Jon Zeringue/SP RC 4.00
205 Matt Bush RC 2.00
206 Kurt Suzuki/SP RC 4.00
207 Mark Rogers RC 2.00
208 Jason Vargas/SP RC 4.00
209 Homer Bailey RC 4.00
210 Ray Liotta/SP RC 4.00
211 Eric Campbell RC 2.00
212 Thomas Diamond RC 2.00
213 Gaby Hernandez/SP RC 8.00
214 Neil Walker RC 2.00
215 Bill Bray RC 1.00
216 Wade Davis/SP RC 5.00
217 David Purcey RC 2.00
218 Scott Elbert RC 2.00
219 Josh Fields RC 3.00
220 Josh Johnson/SP 4.00
221 Chris Lambert RC 2.00
222 Trevor Plouffe RC 3.00
223 Bruce Froemming .15
224 Matt Macri/SP RC 4.00
225 Greg Golson RC 2.00
226 Phillip Hughes RC 6.00
227 Kyle Waldrop RC 2.00
228 Matt Tuiasosopo/SP RC 4.00
229 Richie Robnett RC 2.00
230 Taylor Tankersley RC 1.50
231 Blake DeWitt RC 3.00
232 Charlie Reliford .15
233 Eric Hurley RC 1.00
234 Jordan Parraz/SP RC 4.00
235 J.P. Howell RC 2.00
236 Dana DeMuth .15
237 Zach Jackson RC 1.00
238 Justin Orenduff RC 1.00
239 Brad Thompson RC 1.00
240 J.C. Holt/SP RC 4.00
241 Matt Fox RC 1.00
242 Danny Putnam RC 1.00
243 Daryl Jones/SP RC 4.00
244 Jon Poterson RC 1.00
245 Gio Gonzalez RC 2.00
246 Lucas Harrell/SP RC 4.00
247 Jerry Crawford .15
248 Jay Rainville RC 2.00
249 Donnie Smith/SP RC 4.00
250 Huston Street RC 2.00
251 Jeff Marquez RC 1.00
252 Reid Brignac RC 3.00
253 Yusmeiro Petit RC 2.00
254 K.C. Herren RC 1.00
255 Dale Scott .15
256 Erick San Pedro RC 1.00
257 Ed Montague .15
258 Billy Buckner RC 1.00
259 Mitch Einertson RC 4.00
260 Aarom Baldiris RC 1.00
261 Conor Jackson 2.00
262 Rick Reed .15
263 Ervin Santana RC 3.00
264 Gerry Davis .15
265 Merkin Valdez RC 1.00
266 Joey Gathright RC 1.00
267 Alberto Callaspo RC .75
268 Carlos Quentin/SP 8.00
269 Gary Darling .15
270 Jeff Salazar/SP RC 4.00
271 Akinori Otsuka/SP RC 4.00
272 Joe Brinkman .15
273 Omar Quintanilla .50

274 Brian Runge .15
275 Tom Mastny **RC** .50
276 John Hirschbeck .15
277 Warner Madrigal **RC** .50
278 Joe West .15
279 Paul Maholm **RC** 1.00
280 Larry Young .15
281 Mike Reilly .15
282 Kazuo Matsui/SP **RC** 4.00
283 Randy Marsh .15
284 Frank Francisco **RC** .50
285 Zach Duke **RC** 2.00
286 Tim McClelland .15
287 Jesse Crain .75
288 Hector Gimenez **RC** .50
289 Marland Williams **RC** .50
290 Brian Gorman .15
291 Jose Capellan/SP **RC** 4.00
292 Tim Welke .15
293 Javier Guzman **RC** .50
294 Paul McAnulty **RC** .50
295 Hector Made **RC** .50
296 Jon Connolly **RC** .50
297 Don Sutton **RC** 1.00
298 Fausto Carmona **RC** 2.00
299 Ramon Ramirez **RC** .50
300 Brad Snyder 1.00
301 Chin-Lung Hu **RC** 1.00
302 Rudy Guillen **RC** .50
303 Matt Moses 1.00
304 Brad Halsey/SP **RC** 4.00
305 Erick Aybar **RC** 1.50
306 Brad Sullivan 1.00
307 Nick Gorneault **RC** 1.00
308 Craig Ansman **RC** 1.00
309 Ricky Nolasco 2.00
310 Luke Hughes **RC** 1.00
311 Danny Gonzalez **RC** 1.00
312 Josh Labandeira **RC** .50
313 Donald Levinski .50
314 Vince Perkins **RC** .50
315 Tommy Murphy **RC** .50
316 Chad Bentz **RC** .50
317 Chris Shelton **RC** 2.00
318 Nyjer Morgan/SP **RC** 4.00
319 Kody Kirkland **RC** 1.00
320 Blake Hawksworth **RC** .50
321 Alex Romero **RC** .50
322 Mike Gosling .50
323 Ryan Budde .50
324 Kevin Howard **RC** .50
325 Wanell Macia **RC** .50
326 Travis Blackley **RC** 1.00
327 Kazuhito Tadano/SP **RC** 4.00
328 Shingo Takatsu **RC** 1.00
329 Joaquin Arias **RC** 1.00
330 Juan Cedeno **RC** .75
331 Bobby Brownlie **RC** 1.00
332 Lastings Milledge 4.00
333 Estee Harris **RC** .75
334 Tim Stauffer/SP 4.00
335 Jon Knott .50
336 David Aardsma .50
337 Wardell Starling **RC** .50
338 Dioner Navarro **RC** 1.50
339 Logan Kensing **RC** .50
340 Jason Hirsh 1.50
341 Matt Creighton **RC** .50
342 Felix Hernandez/SP **RC** 10.00
343 Kyle Sleeth .50
344 Dustin Nippert **RC** .50
345 Anthony Lerew **RC** .50
346 Chris Saenz **RC** .50
347 Steve Palermo .15
348 Barry Bonds 20.00

Black & White

Stars: 2X
SP Stars: .5-1X
Rookies: 1-2X
SP Rookies: .5-.75X
Inserted 1:1

Mohagany

Stars: 15-25X
SP Stars: 3-4X
Rookies: 4-8X
SP Rookies: 3-5X
Production 25 Sets

Printing Plates

No Pricing
Production One Set

Commissioner's Cut

Production One
No Pricing

Signs of Authority

NM/M
Common Autograph: 15.00
Inserted 1:49
Red Ink: 1.5-2X
Production 55 Sets
JB Joe Brinkman 15.00
JC Jerry Crawford 15.00
GDA Gary Darling 15.00
GD Gerry Davis 15.00
DD Dana DeMuth 15.00
BF Bruce Froemming 20.00
BG Brian Gorman 15.00
JH John Hirschbeck 15.00
RM Randy Marsh 15.00
TM Tim McClelland 15.00
EM Ed Montague 15.00
SP Steve Palermo 15.00
ER Rick Reed 15.00
MR Mike Reilly 15.00
CM Charlie Reliford 15.00
BR Brian Runge 15.00
DS Dale Scott 20.00
TW Tim Welke 15.00
JW Joe West 20.00
LY Larry Young 15.00

Signs of Glory

NM/M
Common Autograph: 25.00
Inserted 1:246
Red Ink: 2X
Production 55 Sets
GK George Kell 25.00
BK Bob Kuzava 25.00
PR Elwin "Preacher Roe 30.00
BS Bobby Shantz 25.00
MS Bill "Moose" Skowron 30.00

Signs of Greatness

NM/M
Common Autograph: 10.00
Inserted 1:57
Red Ink: 2-4X
Production 55 Sets
BB Bill Bray
MB Matt Bush 15.00
TD Thomas Diamond 15.00
GG Greg Golson 20.00
PH Phillip Hughes 40.00
CL Chris Lambert 10.00
JM Jeff Marquez 10.00
TP Trevor Plouffe 10.00
JR Jay Rainville 15.00
MR Mark Rogers 15.00
NW Neil Walker 20.00

Threads of Greatness

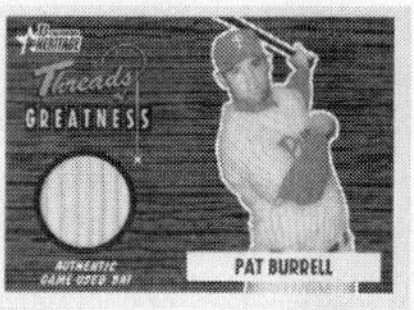

NM/M
Common Player: 4.00
Inserted 1:12
Gold: 2-3X
Production 55 Sets
MA Moises Alou 5.00
JB Jeff Bagwell 8.00
JB2 Jeff Bagwell 8.00
RB Rocco Baldelli 4.00
TB Tony Batista 4.00
JB Josh Beckett 4.00
JB2 Josh Beckett 4.00
AB Adrian Beltre 5.00
AGB Armando Benitez 4.00
LB Lance Berkman 8.00
LB2 Lance Berkman 8.00
AMB Angel Berroa 4.00
HB Hank Blalock 5.00
HB2 Hank Blalock 5.00
WB3 Wade Boggs 8.00
BB Bret Boone 4.00
BB2 Bret Boone 4.00
PB Pat Burrell 4.00
MC Miguel Cabrera 8.00
EC Eric Chavez 4.00
EC2 Eric Chavez 4.00
RC Roger Clemens 10.00
BC Bobby Cox 4.00
JD Johnny Damon 10.00
CE Carl Everett 4.00
NG Nomar Garciaparra 8.00
JG Jason Giambi 5.00
JG2 Jason Giambi 5.00
JAG Juan Gonzalez 5.00
RH Roy Halladay 5.00
TH Todd Helton 6.00
AJ Andruw Jones 5.00
DJ David Justice 4.00
PL Paul LoDuca 4.00
JL Javy Lopez 4.00
ML Mike Lowell 4.00
JM Joe Mauer 8.00
MCD Mike McDougal 4.00
KM Kevin Millwood 4.00
MM Mark Mulder 4.00
MM2 Mark Mulder 4.00
HN Hideo Nomo 8.00
JO John Olerud 4.00
JO2 John Olerud 4.00
AEP Andy Pettitte 4.00
MP Mike Piazza 10.00
MP2 Mike Piazza 10.00
AP Albert Pujols 15.00
AP2 Albert Pujols 15.00
MR Manny Ramirez 8.00
MR2 Manny Ramirez 8.00
JR Jose Reyes 10.00
AR Alex Rodriguez 15.00
CS C.C. Sabathia 6.00
JDS Jason Schmidt 5.00
GS Gary Sheffield 5.00
RS Ruben Sierra 4.00
JS John Smoltz 5.00
JS2 John Smoltz 6.00
AS Alfonso Soriano 8.00
SS Sammy Sosa 8.00
SS2 Sammy Sosa 8.00
SS3 Sammy Sosa 8.00
MS Mike Sweeney 4.00
MCT Mark Teixeira 5.00
MT Miguel Tejada 5.00
MT2 Miguel Tejada 5.00
MT3 Miguel Tejada 5.00
FT Frank Thomas 8.00
JT Jim Thome 8.00
JT2 Jim Thome 8.00
OV Omar Vizquel 4.00
JW Jarrod Washburn 4.00
VW Vernon Wells 5.00
BW Bernie Williams 5.00
DW Dontrelle Willis 5.00
KW Kerry Wood 4.00
KW2 Kerry Wood 4.00
MY Michael Young 4.00
BZ Barry Zito 4.00

2004 Bowman Sterling

NM/M
Common Rookie: 5.00
Pack (5): 60.00
Box (6): 325.00
ABA Aarom Baldiris **RC** 5.00
BBR Bill Bray **RC** 5.00
RBR Reid Brignac **RC** 15.00
BBU Billy Buckner **RC** 5.00
JC Jose Capellan **RC** 5.00
FC Fausto Carmona **RC** 8.00
JCR Jesse Crain **RC** 5.00
TD Thomas Diamond **RC** 5.00
'D Zach Duke **RC** 5.00
ME Mitch Einertson **RC** 5.00
BE Brad Eldred **RC** 5.00
MF Mike Ferris **RC** 5.00
JFI Josh Fields **RC** 8.00
MFO Matt Fox **RC** 5.00
JG Joey Gathright **RC** 5.00
GG Greg Golson **RC** 8.00
GIG Gio Gonzalez **RC** 8.00
FG Freddy Guzman **RC** 5.00
GH Gaby Hernandez **RC** 8.00
FH Felix Hernandez **RC** 20.00
KCH K.C. Herren **RC** 5.00
JH Jesse Hoover **RC** 5.00
JPH J.P. Howell **RC** 5.00
PH Phillip Hughes **RC** 15.00
EH Eric Hurley **RC** 5.00
CJ Conor Jackson 10.00
ZJ Zach Jackson **RC** 5.00
CLA Chris Lambert **RC** 5.00
CH Chin-Lung Hu **RC** 8.00
MMC Matt Macri **RC** 5.00
HM Hector Made **RC** 5.00
PGM Paul Maholm **RC** 5.00
NM Nyjer Morgan **RC** 5.00
CN Chris Nelson **RC** 8.00
JO Justin Orenduff **RC** 5.00
YP Yusmeiro Petit **RC** 8.00
DPU David Purcey **RC** 5.00
OQ Omar Quintanilla **RC** 5.00
MRO Mark Rogers **RC** 5.00
ESP Erick San Pedro **RC** 5.00
NS Nate Schierholtz **RC** 5.00
SSM Seth Smith **RC** 8.00
KS Kurt Suzuki **RC** 6.00
KT Kazuhito Tadano **RC** 5.00
CT Curtis Thigpen **RC** 5.00
BT Brad Thompson **RC** 5.00
NW Neil Walker **RC** 8.00
AWH Anthony Whittington **RC** 5.00
MW Marland Williams **RC** 5.00
JZ Jon Zeringue **RC** 5.00

Rookie Relic Autographs
HB Homer Bailey **RC** 40.00
BB Brian Bixler **RC** 10.00
MB Matt Bush **RC** 15.00
BD Blake DeWitt **RC** 25.00
CG Christian Garcia **RC** 10.00
SK Scott Kazmir 40.00
JM Jeff Marquez **RC** 10.00
SO Scott Olsen **RC** 15.00
TP Trevor Plouffe **RC** 15.00
DP Danny Putnam **RC** 10.00
HS Huston Street **RC** 15.00
TT Taylor Tankersley **RC** 10.00
MT Matt Tuiasosopo **RC** 10.00
KWA Kyle Waldrop **RC** 10.00

Prospect Relic Autographs
RC Robinson Cano 30.00
CC Chad Cordero 10.00
DD David DeJesus 15.00
RH Ryan Harvey 15.00
CL Chris Lubanski 15.00
FP Felix Pie 20.00
BU B.J. Upton 25.00
AW Adam Wainwright 20.00
DW David Wright 50.00
DY Delmon Young 15.00

Rookie Autographs:
CA Chris Aguila **RC** 8.00
AC Alberto Callaspo **RC** 15.00
HG Hector Gimenez **RC** 10.00
BH Blake Hawksworth **RC** 10.00
LH Lincoln Holdzkom **RC** 10.00
RM Ryan Meaux **RC** 8.00
MM Matt Moses **RC** 10.00
VP Vince Perkins **RC** 8.00
CQ Carlos Quentin 30.00
JR Jay Rainville **RC** 10.00
AR Alex Romero **RC** 8.00
MR Mike Rouse 8.00
JS Jeremy Sowers **RC** 15.00
AZ Alec Zumwalt **RC** 8.00

Relics: 5.00
MA Moises Alou 5.00
JB Jeff Bagwell 8.00
RB Rocco Baldelli 5.00
CIB Carlos Beltran 10.00
LB Lance Berkman 5.00
AB Angel Berroa 5.00
CB Craig Biggio 5.00
HJB Hank Blalock 5.00
MC Miguel Cabrera 8.00
LC Luis Castillo 5.00
HC Hee Seop Choi 5.00
BC2 Bobby Crosby 5.00
JD Johnny Damon 10.00
AD Adam Dunn 8.00
JE Johnny Estrada 5.00
EG Eric Gagne 5.00
TG Troy Glaus 5.00
TMG Tom Glavine 8.00
VG Vladimir Guerrero 10.00
TLH Todd Helton 8.00
RJH Richard Hidalgo 5.00
NJ Nick Johnson 5.00
AJ Andruw Jones 8.00
AK Austin Kearns 5.00
JK Jason Kendall 5.00
PL Paul LoDuca 5.00
TM Tino Martinez 5.00
MAM Mark Mulder 5.00
LN Laynce Nix 5.00
RO Russ Ortiz 5.00
RP Rafael Palmeiro 6.00
MJP Mike Piazza 10.00
JP Juan Pierre 5.00
MP Mark Prior 8.00
AP Albert Pujols 20.00
ANR Aramis Ramirez 8.00
MAR Manny Ramirez 8.00
PR Pokey Reese 5.00
AER Alex Rodriguez 15.00
IR Ivan Rodriguez 8.00
GS Gary Sheffield 8.00
SS Sammy Sosa 10.00
MCT Mark Teixeira 6.00
MT1 Miguel Tejada/bat 8.00
MT2 Miguel Tejada/jsy 8.00
FT Frank Thomas 10.00
BW Bernie Williams 8.00
DWW Dontrelle Willis 5.00
KW Kerry Wood 5.00
MY Michael Young 5.00

Refractors

Regular Rookies: 1.5-2X
Rookie Relic Autos.: 1-2X
Rookie Autos.: 1-2X
Prospect Relic Autos.: 1-2X
Relics: 1-2X
Production 199 Sets

Black Refractors

No Pricing
Production 25 Sets

Red Refractor

No Pricing
Production One Set

Uncirculated

No Pricing
Production 16 Sets

Autographed Originals

No Pricing

2004 Bowman's Best

		NM/M
Complete Set:		
Common Player:		.25
Pack (5):		15.00
Box (10):		125.00

Veterans

GA	Garret Anderson	.25
CB	Carlos Beltran	.75
HB	Hank Blalock	.50
MTC	Miguel Cabrera	1.00
EC	Eric Chavez	.50
RC	Roger Clemens	2.50
CD	Carlos Delgado	.50
NAG	Nomar Garciaparra	1.00
JG	Jason Giambi	.75
BG	Brian Giles	.25
VG	Vladimir Guerrero	1.00
TLH	Todd Helton	.75
RJ	Randy Johnson	1.00
LWJ	Chipper Jones	1.00
JLO	Javy Lopez	.25
MO	Magglio Ordonez	.25
LO	Lyle Overbay	.25
MJP	Mike Piazza	1.50
JP	Jorge Posada	.50
MWP	Mark Prior	.75
AP	Albert Pujols	3.00
MAR	Manny Ramirez	1.00
AER	Alex Rodriguez	2.50
IR	Ivan Rodriguez	.75
SR	Scott Rolen	1.00
CMS	Curt Schilling	.50
JDS	Jason Schmidt	.50
RS	Richie Sexson	.50
AS	Alfonso Soriano	1.00
SS	Sammy Sosa	1.00
IS	Ichiro Suzuki	2.00
MT	Miguel Tejada	.50
JT	Jim Thome	.75
JAV	Jose Vidro	.25
MY	Michael Young	1.00

First-Year Players

	Common Rookie	1.00
JJC	Jon Connolly RC	2.00
JRG	Joey Gathright RC	2.00
DG	Danny Gonzalez RC	1.00
NG	Nick Gorneault RC	1.00
MG	Mike Gosling	1.00
CH	Chin-Lung Hu RC	2.00
TJ	Terry Jones	1.00
AL	Anthony Lerew RC	1.00
HM	Hector Made RC	2.00
WM	Warner Madrigal RC	2.00
PMM	Paul McAnulty RC	2.00
AO	Akinori Otsuka RC	1.00
TS	Todd Self RC	1.00
KS	Kyle Sleeth	1.00
DS	Don Sutton RC	1.00

First-Year Player Autographs

	Common Autograph:	8.00
DA	David Aardsma	10.00
CMA	Craig Ansman RC	10.00
JA	Joaquin Arias RC	10.00
EA	Erick Aybar RC	15.00
BB	Bobby Brownlie RC	10.00
RB	Ryan Budde	10.00
KC	Kory Casto	10.00
JC	Juan Cedeno RC	10.00
VC	Vito Chiaravalloti RC	10.00
MDC	Matt Creighton RC	8.00
DC	David Crouthers	10.00
TD	Tyler Davidson	10.00
ZD	Zach Duke RC	10.00
JE	Jesse English RC	10.00
AG	Adam Greenberg	10.00
RG	Rudy Guillen RC	10.00
TOH	Travis Hanson	10.00
EH	Estee Harris RC	10.00
FH	Felix Hernandez RC	75.00
SH	Shawn Hill	10.00
JH	Jason Hirsh	15.00
LTH	Luke Hughes RC	15.00
CJ	Conor Jackson	25.00
LK	Logan Kensing RC	10.00
JK	Jon Knott RC	10.00
KK	Kevin Kouzmanoff	20.00
JL	Josh Labandeira RC	8.00
DL	Donald Levinski	10.00
PM	Paul Maholm RC	15.00
TRM	Tom Mastny RC	10.00
BEM	Brandon Medders RC	8.00
LM	Lastings Milledge	25.00
YM	Yadier Molina RC	10.00
DM	David Murphy	30.00
DN	Dioner Navarro RC	15.00
DDN	Dustin Nippert RC	10.00
RN	Ricky Nolasco	20.00
BP	Brayan Pena RC	8.00
QQ	Omar Quintanilla	10.00
RR	Ramon Ramirez RC	10.00
JS	Jeff Salazar RC	10.00
ES	Ervin Santana RC	20.00
BMS	Brad Snyder	15.00
WS	Wardell Starling RC	10.00
TJS	Tim Stauffer RC	10.00
BS	Brad Sullivan	10.00
JSZ	Jason Szuminski RC	10.00
RT	Rob Tejeda RC	10.00
NU	Nic Ungs RC	10.00
MV	Merkin Valdez RC	10.00
CZ	Charlie Zink RC	10.00

First-Year Player Relics

TB	Travis Blackley RC	5.00
KRK	Kody Kirkland RC	6.00
KM	Kazuo Matsui RC	6.00
KT	Kazuhito Tadano RC	6.00
ST	Shingo Takatsu RC	8.00

Green

Green Stars:	4-8X
Green Non-auto. RC's:	1.5-3X
Production 100	
Green RC Autos.:	1-2X

Red

Red Stars:	No Pricing
Production 20	
Red Non-Auto. RC's:	No Pricing
Red RC Autos.:	No Pricing

Double Play Autographs

	NM/M
Common Duo:	20.00
Inserted 1:33	

MH	Lastings Milledge, Estee Harris	40.00
QS	Omar Quintanilla, Brad Snyder	20.00
SC	Tim Stauffer, Vito Chiaravalloti	20.00
HJ	Travis Hanson, Conor Jackson	25.00
MN	Brandon Medders, Dustin Nippert	20.00
UK	Nic Ungs, Kevin Kouzmanoff	25.00
CC	Matt Creighton, David Crouthers	20.00
EN	Jesse English, Ricky Nolasco	20.00
SV	Ervin Santana, Merkin Valdez	30.00
SK	Jeff Salazar, Jon Knott	20.00

Triple Play Autographs

	NM/M
Common Trio:	30.00
Inserted 1:109	

CBA	Juan Cedeno, Bobby Brownlie, Joaquin Arias	30.00
ALS	David Aardsma, Donald Levinski, Brad Sullivan	25.00
SSV	Tim Stauffer, Ervin Santana, Merkin Valdez	50.00

2005 Bowman

		NM/M
Complete Set (330):		60.00
Common Player:		.15
Common Rookie:		.50
Pack (10):		3.00
Box (24):		60.00

1	Gavin Floyd	.15
2	Eric Chavez	.25
3	Miguel Tejada	.50

4	Dmitri Young	.15
5	Hank Blalock	.25
6	Kerry Wood	.25
7	Andy Pettitte	.40
8	Pat Burrell	.25
9	Johnny Estrada	.15
10	Frank Thomas	.50
11	Juan Pierre	.25
12	Tom Glavine	.40
13	Lyle Overbay	.25
14	Jim Edmonds	.40
15	Steve Finley	.15
16	Jermaine Dye	.25
17	Omar Vizquel	.15
18	Nick Johnson	.15
19	Brian Giles	.15
20	Justin Morneau	.50
21	Preston Wilson	.15
22	Wily Mo Pena	.15
23	Rafael Palmeiro	.50
24	Scott Kazmir	.25
25	Derek Jeter	2.00
26	Barry Zito	.25
27	Mike Lowell	.15
28	Jason Bay	.25
29	Ken Harvey	.15
30	Nomar Garciaparra	.75
31	Roy Halladay	.25
32	Todd Helton	.50
33	Mark Kotsay	.15
34	Jake Peavy	.25
35	David Wright	1.00
36	Dontrelle Willis	.40
37	Marcus Giles	.15
38	Chone Figgins	.15
39	Sidney Ponson	.15
40	Randy Johnson	.75
41	John Smoltz	.25
42	Kevin Millar	.15
43	Mark Teixeira	.50
44	Alex Rios	.25
45	Mike Piazza	1.00
46	Victor Martinez	.25
47	Jeff Bagwell	.25
48	Shawn Green	.25
49	Ivan Rodriguez	.50
50	Alex Rodriguez	1.50
51	Kazuo Matsui	.15
52	Mark Mulder	.40
53	Michael Young	.25
54	Javy Lopez	.15
55	Johnny Damon	.75
56	Jeff Francis	.15
57	Rich Harden	.25
58	Bobby Abreu	.40
59	Mark Loretta	.15
60	Gary Sheffield	.40
61	Jamie Moyer	.15
62	Garret Anderson	.25
63	Vernon Wells	.25
64	Orlando Cabrera	.25
65	Magglio Ordonez	.15
66	Ronnie Belliard	.15
67	Carlos Lee	.25
68	Carl Pavano	.15
69	Jon Lieber	.15
70	Aubrey Huff	.15
71	Rocco Baldelli	.25
72	Jason Schmidt	.25
73	Bernie Williams	.40
74	Hideki Matsui	1.50
75	Ken Griffey Jr.	1.50
76	Josh Beckett	.25
77	Mark Buehrle	.25
78	David Ortiz	.75
79	Luis Gonzalez	.25
80	Scott Rolen	.75
81	Joe Mauer	.50
82	Jose Reyes	.75
83	Adam Dunn	.50
84	Greg Maddux	1.00
85	Bartolo Colon	.25
86	Bret Boone	.15
87	Mike Mussina	.50
88	Ben Sheets	.40
89	Lance Berkman	.40
90	Miguel Cabrera	.75
91	C.C. Sabathia	.25
92*	Mike Maroth	.15
93	Andruw Jones	.50
94	Jack Wilson	.15
95	Ichiro Suzuki	1.50
96	Geoff Jenkins	.15
97	Zack Greinke	.15
98	Jorge Posada	.40
99	Travis Hafner	.40
100	Barry Bonds	2.00
101	Aaron Rowand	.15
102	Aramis Ramirez	.40
103	Curt Schilling	.75
104	Melvin Mora	.15
105	Albert Pujols	2.00
106	Austin Kearns	.25
107	Shannon Stewart	.15
108	Carl Crawford	.40
109	Carlos Zambrano	.40
110	Roger Clemens	2.00
111	Javier Vazquez	.15
112	Randy Wolf	.15
113	Chipper Jones	.75
114	Larry Walker	.25
115	Alfonso Soriano	.75
116	Brad Wilkerson	.15
117	Bobby Crosby	.15
118	Jim Thome	.75
119	Oliver Perez	.25
120	Vladimir Guerrero	.75
121	Roy Oswalt	.40
122	Torii Hunter	.25
123	Rafael Furcal	.25
124	Luis Castillo	.15
125	Carlos Beltran	.50
126	Mike Sweeney	.15
127	Johan Santana	.50
128	Tim Hudson	.40
129	Troy Glaus	.40
130	Manny Ramirez	.75
131	Jeff Kent	.25
132	Jose Vidro	.15
133	Edgar Renteria	.25
134	Russ Ortiz	.15
135	Sammy Sosa	.75
136	Carlos Delgado	.40
137	Richie Sexson	.25
138	Pedro Martinez	.75
139	Adrian Beltre	.25
140	Mark Prior	.40
141	Omar Quintanilla	.15
142	Carlos Quentin	.15
143	Dan Johnson	.15
144	Jake Stevens	.15
145	Nate Schierholtz	.15
146	Neil Walker	.15
147	Bill Bray	.15
148	Taylor Tankersley	.15
149	Trevor Plouffe	.15
150	Felix Hernandez	.50
151	Phillip Hughes	.50
152	James Houser	.15
153	David Murphy	.15
154	Ervin Santana	.15
155	Anthony Whittington	.15
156	Chris Lambert	.15
157	Jeremy Sowers	.15
158	Gio Gonzalez	.15
159	Blake DeWitt	.25
160	Thomas Diamond	.15
161	Greg Golson	.15
162	David Aardsma	.15
163	Paul Maholm	.15
164	Mark Rogers	.15
165	Homer Bailey	.50
166	Chip Cannon RC	1.00
167	Tony Giarratano RC	.15
168	Darren Fenster RC	.50
169	Elvys Quezada RC	.75
170	Glen Perkins RC	1.00
171	Ian Kinsler RC	4.00
172	Michael Bourn	1.00
173	Jeremy West RC	.75
174	Justin Verlander RC	3.00
175	Kevin West RC	.50
176	Luis Hernandez RC	1.00
177	Matt Campbell RC	.75
178	Nate McLouth RC	1.00
179	Ryan Goleski RC	.50
180	Matt Lindstrom RC	.50
181	Matt DeSalvo RC	1.00
182	Kole Strayhorn	.50
183	Jose Vaquedano RC	.50
184	James Jurries RC	.50
185	Ian Bladergroen RC	.50
186	Eric Nielsen RC	.75
187	Chris Vines RC	1.00
188	Chris Denorfia RC	.50
189	Kevin Melillo RC	.50
190	Melky Cabrera RC	2.00
191	Ryan Sweeney	1.50
192	Sean Marshall RC	1.00
193	Andy LaRoche RC	3.00
194	Tyler Pelland RC	1.50
195	Mike Morse RC	.75
196	Wes Swackhamer RC	.50
197	Wade Robinson RC	.50
198	Dan Santin RC	.50
199	Steven Doetsch RC	.50
200	Shane Costa	.50
201	Scott Mathieson RC	.75
202	Ben Jones RC	.50
203	Michael Rogers RC	.50
204	Matt Rogelstad RC	.50
205	Luis Ramirez RC	1.00
206	Landon Powell RC	.75
207	Erik Cordier RC	1.00
208	Chris Seddon RC	.50
209	Chris Roberson RC	.75

210	Tom Oldham RC	.50
211	Dana Eveland RC	1.00
212	Cody Haerther RC	.75
213	Danny Core RC	.50
214	Craig Tatum RC	.75
215	Elliot Johnson RC	.75
216	Ender Chavez RC	.75
217	Errol Simonitsch RC	.75
218	Matt Van Der Bosch RC	.75
219	Eulogio de la Cruz RC	.50
220	C.J. Smith RC	.50
221	Adam Boeve RC	.75
222	Adam Harben RC	.75
223	Baltazar Lopez RC	.75
224	Russ Martin RC	2.50
225	Brian Bannister RC	1.00
226	Brian Miller RC	.50
227	Casey McGehee RC	.50
228	Humberto Sanchez RC	1.50
229	Javon Moran RC	.50
230	Brandon McCarthy RC	1.50
231	Danny Zell RC	.50
232	Jake Postlewait RC	.50
233	Juan Tejeda RC	.50
234	Keith Ramsey RC	.50
235	Lorenzo Scott RC	.75
236	Wladimir Balentien RC	1.00
237	Martin Prado RC	.50
238	Matt Albers RC	1.00
239	Brian Schweiger RC	.50
240	Brian Stavisky RC	.50
241	Pat Misch RC	.50
242	Pat Osborn RC	.50
243	Ryan Feierabend RC	1.00
244	Shaun Marcum	.50
245	Kevin Collins RC	.50
246	Stuart Pomeranz RC	.50
247	Tetsu Yofu RC	.75
248	Hernan Iribarren RC	1.00
249	Mike Spiegel RC	.50
250	Tony Arnerich RC	.50
251	Manny Parra RC	1.00
252	Drew Anderson RC	.75
253	T.J. Beam RC	1.00
254	Pedro Lopez RC	.75
255	Andy Sides RC	.75
256	Bear Bay RC	.50
257	Bill McCarthy RC	1.00
258	Daniel Haigwood RC	1.50
259	Brian Sprout RC	.75
260	Bryan Triplett	.75
261	Steve Bondurant	.50
262	Darwinson Salazar RC	.75
263	David Shepard RC	.50
264	Johan Silva RC	.75
265	J.B. Thurmond RC	.50
266	Brandon Moorhead RC	.50
267	Kyle Nichols RC	.50
268	Jonathan Sanchez RC	1.00
269	Mike Esposito RC	.50
270	Erik Schindewolf RC	.75
271	Peeter Ramos RC	.75
272	Juan Senreiso RC	.50
273	Matthew Kemp RC	3.00
274	Vinny Rottino RC	.50
275	Micah Furtado RC	.50
276	George Kottaras RC	1.00
277	Billy Butler RC	4.00
278	Buck Coats RC	.50
279	Ken Durost RC	.50
280	Nic Touchstone RC	.50
281	Jerry Owens RC	1.00
282	Stefan Bailie	.50
283	Jesse Gutierrez RC	.50
284	Chuck Tiffany RC	1.00
285	Brendan Ryan RC	.50
286	Hayden Penn RC	2.00
287	Shawn Bowman RC	.50
288	Alexander Smit RC	.50
289	Micah Schnurstein RC	.75
290	Jared Gothreaux RC	.50
291	Jair Jurrjens RC	1.50
292	Bobby Livingston RC	.75
293	Ryan Speier RC	.50
294	Zachary Parker RC	.50
295	Christian Colonel RC	.75
296	Scott Mitchinson RC	.50
297	Neil Wilson RC	.50
298	Chuck James RC	2.00
299	Heath Totten RC	.50
300	Sean Tracey RC	.75
301	Ismael Ramirez RC	.50
302	Matt Brown RC	.50
303	Franklin Morales RC	1.00
304	Brandon Sing RC	1.00
305	D.J. Houlton RC	.50
306	Jayce Tingler RC	.50
307	Mitchell Arnold RC	.50
308	Jim Burt RC	.75
309	Jason Motte RC	.50
310	David Gassner RC	.75
311	Andy Santana RC	.50
312	Kelvin Pichardo RC	.50
313	Carlos Carrasco RC	1.50
314	Willy Mota RC	.50
315	Frank Mata RC	.50
316	Carlos Gonzalez RC	2.50
317	Jeff Niemann RC	1.00
318	Chris Young RC	3.00
319	Billy Sadler	.50
320	Ricky Barrett	.50
321	Benjamin Harrison	.50
322	Steve Nelson RC	.50
323	Daryl Thompson RC	1.50
324	Philip Humber RC	1.50

325	Jeremy Harts RC	.50
326	Nick Masset RC	.50
327	Mike Rodriguez RC	.50
328	Mike Garber RC	.50
329	Kennard Bibbs RC	.50
330	Ryan Garko RC	1.50

Gold

Stars:	1-2X
Rookies:	1-2X
Inserted 1:1	

White

Stars:	3-6X
Rookies:	3-6X
Production 240 Sets	

Printing Plates

No Pricing
Production One Set

1st Edition

NM/M

Stars:	3-5X
Rookies:	1-2X
HTA Exclusive	
Pack (10):	3.50
Box (20):	60.00

A-Rod Throwbacks

NM/M

Complete Set (4):	6.00
Common A-Rod:	2.00
94-AR-97-AR Alex Rodriguez	2.00

A-Rod Throwbacks Autographs

NM/M

Production 1-225

96A-AR	Alex Rodriguez/99	150.00
97A-AR	Alex Rodriguez/225	150.00

A-Rod Throwbacks Relic

NM/M

Quantity produced listed

96R-AR	Alex Rodriguez/99	20.00
97R-AR	Alex Rodriguez/800	15.00

Autographed Base Card Variations

NM/M

Inserted 1:1,599

141	Omar Quintanilla	8.00
142	Carlos Quentin	20.00
143	Dan Johnson	10.00
144	Jake Stevens	10.00
145	Nate Schierholtz	10.00
146	Neil Walker	15.00
147	Bill Bray	8.00
148	Taylor Tankersley	10.00
149	Trevor Plouffe	12.00
150	Felix Hernandez	30.00
151	Phillip Hughes	40.00
152	James Houser	10.00
153	David Murphy	15.00
154	Ervin Santana	15.00
155	Anthony Whittington	8.00
156	Chris Lambert	12.00

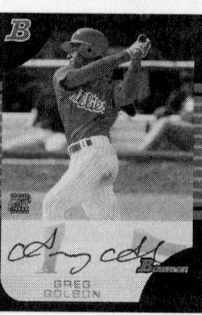

157	Jeremy Sowers	15.00
158	Gio Gonzalez	15.00
159	Blake DeWitt	20.00
160	Thomas Diamond	15.00
161	Greg Golson	12.00
162	David Aardsma	10.00
163	Paul Maholm	12.00
164	Mark Rogers	15.00
165	Homer Bailey	25.00

Dual Rookie of the Year Relic

NM/M

Inserted 1:668

ROY-BC	Jason Bay, Bobby Crosby	15.00

Futures Game Gear

NM/M

JB	Joe Blanton	5.00
BB	Bryan Bullington	5.00
MC	Matt Cain	5.00
SC	Shin-Soo Choo	6.00
JCO	Jorge Cortes	5.00
JC	Jesus Cota	5.00
EE	Edwin Encarnacion	5.00
CE	Clint Everts	5.00
GF	Gavin Floyd	5.00
JF	Jeff Francis	5.00
JG	Jairo Garcia	5.00
RG	Ruben Gotay	5.00
JGU	Joel Guzman	5.00
AH	Aaron Hill	5.00
KH	Koyie Hill	5.00
WL	Wilfredo Ledezma	5.00
VM	Val Majewski	5.00
AMA	Andy Marte	8.00
JM	Jeff Mathis	5.00
DM	Dallas McPherson	8.00
JMO	Justin Morneau	8.00
AM	Arnie Munoz	5.00
YP	Yusmeiro Petit	8.00
FP	Felix Pie	8.00
RW	Rickie Weeks	8.00

Relic Base Card Variations

NM/M

Inserted 1:50

2	Eric Chavez	5.00
5	Hank Blalock	8.00
23	Rafael Palmeiro	8.00
43	Mark Teixeira	8.00
49	Ivan Rodriguez	8.00
50	Alex Rodriguez	15.00
60	Gary Sheffield	8.00
65	Magglio Ordonez	8.00
78	David Ortiz	10.00
83	Adam Dunn	8.00
90	Miguel Cabrera	8.00
93	Andruw Jones	8.00
100	Barry Bonds	25.00
104	Melvin Mora	5.00
105	Albert Pujols	20.00
115	Alfonso Soriano	8.00
120	Vladimir Guerrero	8.00
125	Carlos Beltran	10.00
130	Manny Ramirez	8.00
135	Sammy Sosa	12.00

Signs of the Future

NM/M

Common Auto:		8.00
BB	Brian Bixler	10.00
MC	Melky Cabrera	25.00
RC	Robinson Cano	45.00
CC	Chad Cordero	10.00
BC	Bobby Crosby	15.00
BD	Blake DeWitt	20.00
CG	Christian Garcia	10.00
TG	Tom Gorzelanny	10.00
PH	Phillip Hughes	40.00
TH	Tim Hutting	10.00
SK	Scott Kazmir	15.00
AL	Adam Loewen	10.00
PM	Paul Maholm	10.00
DM	Dallas McPherson	10.00
SO	Scott Olson	10.00
TP	Trevor Plouffe	15.00
DP	Dan Putnam	10.00
JR	Jay Rainville	15.00
RR	Rickie Robnett	8.00
ES	Ervin Santana	15.00
JS	Jay Sborz	10.00
BMS	Brad Snyder	10.00
HS	Huston Street	25.00
BS	Brad Sullivan	10.00
TT	Taylor Tankersley	12.00
RW	Ryan Wagner	10.00
KW	Kyle Waldrop	10.00
AW	Anthony Whittington	10.00
DW	David Wright	70.00

Two of a Kind Autograph

No Pricing
Production 13

2005 Bowman Chrome

NM/M

Complete Set (352):		
Common Player:		.25
Common Rookie:		1.00
Common RC Auto. (331-352):		10.00
Pack (24):		8.00
Box (18):		125.00
1	Gavin Floyd	.25
2	Eric Chavez	.50
3	Miguel Tejada	.75
4	Dmitri Young	.25
5	Hank Blalock	.50
6	Kerry Wood	.50
7	Andy Pettitte	.50
8	Pat Burrell	.50
9	Johnny Estrada	.25
10	Frank Thomas	.75
11	Juan Pierre	.25
12	Tom Glavine	.50
13	Lyle Overbay	.25
14	Jim Edmonds	.50
15	Steve Finley	.25
16	Jermaine Dye	.25
17	Omar Vizquel	.25
18	Nick Johnson	.25
19	Brian Giles	.25
20	Justin Morneau	.50
21	Preston Wilson	.25
22	Wily Mo Pena	.25
23	Rafael Palmeiro	.75
24	Scott Kazmir	.50
25	Derek Jeter	3.00
26	Barry Zito	.50
27	Mike Lowell	.25
28	Jason Bay	.50
29	Ken Harvey	.25
30	Nomar Garciaparra	1.00
31	Roy Halladay	.50
32	Todd Helton	.75
33	Mark Kotsay	.25
34	Jake Peavy	.25
35	David Wright	1.00
36	Dontrelle Willis	.50
37	Marcus Giles	.25
38	Chone Figgins	.25
39	Sidney Ponson	.25
40	Randy Johnson	1.00
41	John Smoltz	.50
42	Kevin Millar	.25
43	Mark Teixeira	.75
44	Alex Rios	.25
45	Mike Piazza	1.00

46	Victor Martinez	.50
47	Jeff Bagwell	.75
48	Shawn Green	.50
49	Ivan Rodriguez	.75
50	Alex Rodriguez	2.50
51	Kazuo Matsui	.25
52	Mark Mulder	.50
53	Michael Young	.50
54	Javy Lopez	.25
55	Johnny Damon	1.00
56	Jeff Francis	.25
57	Rich Harden	.50
58	Bobby Abreu	.50
59	Mark Loretta	.25
60	Gary Sheffield	.50
61	Jamie Moyer	.25
62	Garret Anderson	.50
63	Vernon Wells	.50
64	Orlando Cabrera	.25
65	Magglio Ordonez	.25
66	Ronnie Belliard	.25
67	Carlos Lee	.50
68	Carl Pavano	.25
69	Jon Lieber	.25
70	Aubrey Huff	.25
71	Rocco Baldelli	.25
72	Jason Schmidt	.50
73	Bernie Williams	.50
74	Hideki Matsui	2.00
75	Ken Griffey Jr.	2.00
76	Josh Beckett	.50
77	Mark Buehrle	.40
78	David Ortiz	1.00
79	Luis Gonzalez	.25
80	Scott Rolen	1.00
81	Joe Mauer	.75
82	Jose Reyes	.75
83	Adam Dunn	.75
84	Greg Maddux	2.00
85	Bartolo Colon	.40
86	Bret Boone	.25
87	Mike Mussina	.50
88	Ben Sheets	.50
89	Lance Berkman	.50
90	Miguel Cabrera	1.00
91	C.C. Sabathia	.25
92	Mike Maroth	.25
93	Andruw Jones	.50
94	Jack Wilson	.25
95	Ichiro Suzuki	2.00
96	Geoff Jenkins	.25
97	Zack Greinke	.25
98	Jorge Posada	.50
99	Travis Hafner	.50
100	Barry Bonds	3.00
101	Aaron Rowand	.25
102	Aramis Ramirez	.50
103	Curt Schilling	1.00
104	Melvin Mora	.25
105	Albert Pujols	3.00
106	Austin Kearns	.40
107	Shannon Stewart	.25
108	Carl Crawford	.50
109	Carlos Zambrano	.50
110	Roger Clemens	3.00
111	Javier Vazquez	.25
112	Randy Wolf	.25
113	Chipper Jones	1.00
114	Larry Walker	.50
115	Alfonso Soriano	1.00
116	Brad Wilkerson	.25
117	Bobby Crosby	.25
118	Jim Thome	.75
119	Oliver Perez	.25
120	Vladimir Guerrero	1.00
121	Roy Oswalt	.50
122	Torii Hunter	.40
123	Rafael Furcal	.25
124	Luis Castillo	.25
125	Carlos Beltran	.75
126	Mike Sweeney	.25
127	Johan Santana	.75
128	Tim Hudson	.50
129	Troy Glaus	.50
130	Manny Ramirez	1.00
131	Jeff Kent	.40
132	Jose Vidro	.25
133	Edgar Renteria	.40
134	Russ Ortiz	.25
135	Sammy Sosa	1.00
136	Carlos Delgado	.50
137	Richie Sexson	.50
138	Pedro Martinez	1.00
139	Adrian Beltre	.50
140	Mark Prior	.75
141	Omar Quintanilla	.25
142	Carlos Quentin	.25
143	Dan Johnson	.25
144	Jake Stevens	.25
145	Nate Schierholtz	.25
146	Neil Walker	.25
147	Bill Bray	.25
148	Taylor Tankersley	.25
149	Trevor Plouffe	.25
150	Felix Hernandez	1.00
151	Phillip Hughes	.50
152	James Houser	.25
153	David Murphy	.25
154	Ervin Santana	.25
155	Anthony Whittington	.25
156	Chris Lambert	.25
157	Jeremy Sowers	.25
158	Gio Gonzalez	.25
159	Blake DeWitt	.25
160	Thomas Diamond	.25
161	Greg Golson	.25
162	David Aardsma	.25
163	Paul Maholm	.25
164	Mark Rogers	.25
165	Homer Bailey	.50
166	Elvin Puello **RC**	1.00
167	Tony Giarratano **RC**	1.50
168	Darren Fenster **RC**	1.00
169	Elvys Quezada **RC**	1.00
170	Glen Perkins **RC**	2.50
171	Ian Kinsler **RC**	12.00
172	Adam Bostick **RC**	1.00
173	Jeremy West **RC**	2.00
174	Brett Harper **RC**	2.00
175	Kevin West **RC**	1.00
176	Luis Hernandez **RC**	1.00
177	Matt Campbell **RC**	1.00
178	Nate McLouth **RC**	3.00
179	Ryan Goleski **RC**	2.00
180	Matt Lindstrom **RC**	1.00
181	Matt DeSalvo **RC**	3.00
182	Kole Strayhorn **RC**	1.00
183	Jose Vaquedano **RC**	1.00
184	James Jurries **RC**	2.00
185	Ian Bladergroen **RC**	2.50
186	Kila Kaaihue **RC**	4.00
187	Luke Scott **RC**	4.00
188	Chris Denorfia **RC**	3.00
189	Jai Miller **RC**	1.50
190	Melky Cabrera **RC**	6.00
191	Ryan Sweeney	4.00
192	Sean Marshall **RC**	2.00
193	Eric Abreu **RC**	2.00
194	Tyler Pelland **RC**	1.50
195	Cole Armstrong **RC**	1.50
196	John Hudgins **RC**	1.00
197	Wade Robinson **RC**	1.00
198	Dan Santin **RC**	1.50
199	Steven Doetsch **RC**	1.50
200	Shane Costa **RC**	1.00
201	Scott Mathieson **RC**	2.00
202	Ben Jones **RC**	2.00
203	Michael Rogers **RC**	1.00
204	Matt Rogelstad **RC**	1.50
205	Luis Ramirez **RC**	1.00
206	Landon Powell **RC**	2.00
207	Erik Cordier **RC**	1.50
208	Chris Seddon **RC**	1.00
209	Chris Roberson **RC**	1.50
210	Tom Oldham **RC**	1.00
211	Dana Eveland **RC**	2.50
212	Cody Haerther **RC**	1.00
213	Danny Core **RC**	1.00
214	Craig Tatum **RC**	1.00
215	Elliot Johnson **RC**	2.50
216	Ender Chavez **RC**	1.00
217	Errol Simonitsch **RC**	1.50
218	Matt Van Der Bosch **RC**	1.00
219	Eulogio de la Cruz **RC**	1.00
220	Drew Toussaint **RC**	1.50
221	Adam Boeve **RC**	2.00
222	Adam Harben **RC**	1.50
223	Baltazar Lopez **RC**	2.00
224	Russell Martin **RC**	8.00
225	Brian Bannister **RC**	2.00
226	Chris Walker **RC**	1.00
227	Casey McGehee **RC**	1.50
228	Humberto Sanchez **RC**	6.00
229	Javon Moran **RC**	1.00
230	Brandon McCarthy **RC**	2.00
231	Danny Zell **RC**	1.00
232	Kevin Barry **RC**	1.00
233	Juan Tejeda **RC**	1.50
234	Keith Ramsey **RC**	1.00
235	Lorenzo Scott **RC**	1.00
236	Jonathan Barratt **RC**	1.00
237	Martin Prado **RC**	2.00
238	Matt Albers **RC**	3.00
239	Brian Schweiger **RC**	1.00
240	Raul Tablado **RC**	1.00
241	Pat Misch **RC**	1.00
242	Pat Osborn **RC**	1.00
243	Ryan Feierabend **RC**	1.00
244	Shaun Marcum	1.00
245	Kevin Collins **RC**	1.00
246	Stuart Pomeranz **RC**	1.00
247	Tetsu Yofu **RC**	1.00
248	Hernan Iribarren **RC**	3.00
249	Michael Spidale **RC**	1.00
250	Tony Americh **RC**	1.00
251	Manny Parra **RC**	3.00
252	Drew Anderson **RC**	1.00
253	T.J. Beam **RC**	3.00
254	Claudio Arias **RC**	2.00
255	Andy Sides **RC**	1.00
256	Bear Bay **RC**	2.00
257	Bill McCarthy **RC**	1.00
258	Daniel Haigwood **RC**	2.00
259	Brian Sprout **RC**	1.00
260	Bryan Triplett **RC**	1.00
261	Steve Bondurant **RC**	1.00
262	Darwinson Salazar **RC**	1.00
263	David Shepard **RC**	1.00
264	Johan Silva **RC**	1.50
265	J.B. Thurmond **RC**	1.00
266	Brandon Moorhead **RC**	1.00
267	Kyle Nichols **RC**	2.00
268	Jonathan Sanchez **RC**	4.00
269	Mike Esposito **RC**	1.00
270	Erik Schindewolf **RC**	2.00
271	Peeter Ramos **RC**	1.00
272	Juan Senreiso **RC**	1.00
273	Travis Chick **RC**	2.00
274	Vinny Rottino **RC**	1.00
275	Micah Furtado **RC**	1.00
276	George Kottaras **RC**	2.00
277	Abel Gomez **RC**	1.50
278	Buck Coats **RC**	1.00
279	Ken Durost **RC**	1.00
280	Nick Touchstone **RC**	1.00
281	Jerry Owens **RC**	2.00
282	Stefan Bailie **RC**	1.00
283	Jesse Gutierrez **RC**	1.00
284	Chuck Tiffany **RC**	3.00
285	Brendan Ryan **RC**	1.00
286	Julio Pimentel **RC**	1.50
287	Shawn Bowman **RC**	1.50
288	Alexander Smit **RC**	1.50
289	Micah Schnurstein **RC**	1.50
290	Jared Gothreaux **RC**	1.00
291	Jair Jurrjens **RC**	4.00
292	Bobby Livingston **RC**	1.00
293	Ryan Speier **RC**	1.00
294	Zachary Parker **RC**	1.00
295	Christian Colonel **RC**	1.00
296	Scott Mitchinson **RC**	1.00
297	Neil Wilson **RC**	1.00
298	Chuck James **RC**	5.00
299	Heath Totten **RC**	1.00
300	Sean Tracey **RC**	1.00
301	Tadahito Iguchi **RC**	2.50
302	Matt Brown **RC**	1.00
303	Franklin Morales **RC**	3.00
304	Brandon Sing **RC**	3.00
305	D.J. Houlton **RC**	1.50
306	Jayce Tingler **RC**	1.00
307	Mitchell Arnold **RC**	1.00
308	Jim Burt **RC**	1.00
309	Jason Motte **RC**	1.00
310	David Gassner **RC**	1.00
311	Andy Santana **RC**	1.00
312	Kelvin Pichardo **RC**	1.00
313	Carlos Carrasco **RC**	5.00
314	Willy Mota **RC**	2.00
315	Frank Mata **RC**	1.00
316	Carlos Gonzalez **RC**	10.00
317	Jesse Floyd **RC**	1.00
318	Chris Young **RC**	6.00
319	Billy Sadler	1.00
320	Ricky Barrett **RC**	1.00
321	Benjamin Harrison **RC**	2.00
322	Steve Nelson **RC**	1.00
323	Daryl Thompson **RC**	5.00
324	Davis Romero **RC**	1.00
325	Jeremy Harts **RC**	1.00
326	Nick Masset **RC**	1.00
327	Thomas Pauly **RC**	1.00
328	Mike Garber **RC**	1.00
329	Kennard Bibbs **RC**	1.00
330	Colter Bean **RC**	1.00
331	Justin Verlander **RC**	50.00
332	Chip Cannon **RC**	25.00
333	Kevin Melillo **RC**	20.00
334	Jake Postlewait **RC**	10.00
335	Wes Swackhamer **RC**	15.00
336	Mike Rodriguez **RC**	15.00
337	Philip Humber **RC**	30.00
338	Jeff Niemann **RC**	30.00
339	Brian Miller **RC**	10.00
340	Chris Vines **RC**	10.00
341	Andy LaRoche **RC**	40.00
342	Michael Bourn	30.00
343	Eric Nielsen **RC**	15.00
344	Wladimir Balentien **RC**	25.00
345	Ismael Ramirez **RC**	15.00
346	Pedro Lopez **RC**	10.00
347	Shawn Bowman **RC**	15.00
348	Hayden Penn **RC**	20.00
349	Matthew Kemp **RC**	90.00
350	Brian Stavisky **RC**	10.00
351	C.J. Smith **RC**	10.00
352	Mike Morse **RC**	15.00
353	Billy Butler **RC**	60.00

Refractor

Stars (1-165): 2-4X
Rookies (166-330): 1-2X
Inserted 1:4
Autograph (331-353): 1-2X
Production 500

X-Fractor

Stars (1-165): 3-5X
Rookies (166-330): 2-5X
Autograph (331-353): 1-2.5X
Production 225 Sets

Blue Refractor

Stars (1-165): 3-5X
Rookies (166-330): 3-5X
Autograph (331-353): 1-2.5X
Production 150 Sets

Gold Refractor

Stars (1-165): 8-15X
Rookies (166-330): 15-25X
Autograph (331-353): 3-6X
Production 50 Sets

Red Refractor

No Pricing
Production 5 Sets

Superfractor

No Pricing
Production One Set

Printing Plates

No Pricing
Production one set per color.

A-Rod Throwback

NM/M

Complete Set (4): 6.00
Common A-Rod: 2.00
Inserted 1:9
Refractor: 2-3X
Production 499 Sets
X-Fractor: 3-5X
Production 99 Sets
Superfractor: No Pricing
Production One Set
94AR-97AR Alex Rodriguez 2.00

A-Rod Throwback Autograph

NM/M

Quantity produced listed
96AR Alex Rodriguez/50 160.00
97AR Alex Rodriguez/99 150.00

One Of A Kind Autograph

No Pricing
Production 13

2005 Bowman Chrome Draft Picks & Prospects

NM/M

Complete Set (180):
Common Player: .25
Common Rookie: 1.00
Common Rk Auto. (166-180): 15.00

BDP1	Rickie Weeks	.40
BDP2	Kyle Davies	.25
BDP3	Garrett Atkins	.25
BDP4	Chien-Ming Wang	.75
BDP5	Dallas McPherson	.25
BDP6	Dan Johnson	.25
BDP7	Andy Sisco	.25
BDP8	Ryan Doumit	.25
BDP9	J.P. Howell	.25
BDP10	Tim Stauffer	.25
BDP11	Willy Taveras	.25
BDP12	Aaron Hill	.25
BDP13	Victor Diaz	.25
BDP14	Wilson Betemit	.25
BDP15	Ervin Santana	.25
BDP16	Mike Morse	.25
BDP17	Yadier Molina	.25
BDP18	Kelly Johnson	.25
BDP19	Clint Barmes	.25
BDP20	Robinson Cano	.75
BDP21	Brad Thompson	.25
BDP22	Jorge Cantu	.25
BDP23	Brad Halsey	.25
BDP24	Lance Niekro	.25
BDP25	D.J. Houlton	.25
BDP26	Ryan Church	.25
BDP27	Hayden Penn	.25
BDP28	Chris Young	1.00
BDP29	Chad Orvella	.50
BDP30	Mark Teahen	.25
BDP31	Mark McCormick **RC**	1.00
BDP32	Jay Bruce **RC**	20.00
BDP33	Beau Jones **RC**	2.50
BDP34	Tyler Greene **RC**	1.50
BDP35	Zach Ward **RC**	2.50
BDP36	Josh Bell **RC**	4.00
BDP37	Josh Wall **RC**	2.00

BDP38 Nick Webber **RC** 1.00
BDP39 Travis Buck **RC** 3.00
BDP40 Kyle Winters **RC** 1.00
BDP41 Mitch Boggs **RC** 1.00
BDP42 Tommy Mendoza **RC** 2.00
BDP43 Brad Corley **RC** 1.50
BDP44 Drew Butera **RC** 1.00
BDP45 Ryan Mount **RC** 1.50
BDP46 Tyler Herron **RC** 1.50
BDP47 Nick Weglarz **RC** 4.00
BDP48 Brandon Erbe **RC** 5.00
BDP49 Cody Allen **RC** 1.00
BDP50 Eric Fowler **RC** 1.00
BDP51 James Boone **RC** 1.50
BDP52 Josh Flores **RC** 3.00
BDP53 Brandon Monk **RC** 2.00
BDP54 Kieron Pope **RC** 2.50
BDP55 Kyle Cofield **RC** 1.50
BDP56 Brent Lillibridge **RC** 2.50
BDP57 Daryl Jones **RC** 1.50
BDP58 Eli Iorg **RC** 2.00
BDP59 Brett Hayes **RC** 1.00
BDP60 Mike Durant **RC** 3.00
BDP61 Michael Bowden **RC** 5.00
BDP62 Paul Kelly **RC** 2.00
BDP63 Andrew McCutchen **RC** 8.00
BDP64 Travis Wood **RC** 3.00
BDP65 Cesar Ramos **RC** 1.00
BDP66 Chaz Roe **RC** 1.50
BDP67 Matt Torra **RC** 2.00
BDP68 Kevin Slowey **RC** 6.00
BDP69 Trayvon Robinson **RC** 1.50
BDP70 Reid Engel **RC** 1.50
BDP71 Kris Harvey **RC** 2.00
BDP72 Craig Italiano **RC** 2.50
BDP73 Matt Maloney **RC** 3.00
BDP74 Sean West **RC** 4.00
BDP75 Henry Sanchez **RC** 2.50
BDP76 Scott Blue **RC** 1.00
BDP77 Jordan Schafer **RC** 4.00
BDP78 Chris Robinson **RC** 1.00
BDP79 Chris Hobdy **RC** 1.00
BDP80 Brandon Durden **RC** 1.00
BDP81 Clay Buchholz **RC** 20.00
BDP82 Josh Geer **RC** 1.00
BDP83 Sam LeCure **RC** 1.00
BDP84 Justin Thomas **RC** 1.00
BDP85 Brett Gardner **RC** 2.50
BDP86 Tommy Manzella **RC** 1.00
BDP87 Matt Green **RC** 1.00
BDP88 Yunel Escobar **RC** 3.00
BDP89 Mike Costanzo **RC** 3.00
BDP90 Nick Hundley **RC** 1.00
BDP91 Zach Simons **RC** 1.00
BDP92 Jacob Marceaux **RC** 1.00
BDP93 Jed Lowrie **RC** 4.00
BDP94 Brandon Snyder **RC** 4.00
BDP95 Matt Goyen **RC** 1.00
BDP96 Jon Egan **RC** 1.50
BDP97 Drew Thompson **RC** 1.50
BDP98 Bryan Anderson **RC** 4.00
BDP99 Clayton Richard **RC** 1.00
BDP100 Jimmy Shull **RC** 1.00
BDP101 Mark Pawelek **RC** 5.00
BDP102 P.J. Phillips **RC** 1.50
BDP103 John Drennen **RC** 3.00
BDP104 Nolan Reimold **RC** 4.00
BDP105 Troy Tulowitzki **RC** 8.00
BDP106 Kevin Whelan **RC** 1.00
BDP107 Wade Townsend **RC** 2.00
BDP108 Micah Owings **RC** 4.00
BDP109 Ryan Tucker **RC** 1.50
BDP110 Jeff Clement **RC** 5.00
BDP111 Josh Sullivan **RC** 1.00
BDP112 Jeff Lyman **RC** 1.00
BDP113 Brian Bogusevic **RC** 2.00
BDP114 Trevor Bell **RC** 2.00
BDP115 Brent Cox **RC** 1.50
BDP116 Michael Billek **RC** 1.00
BDP117 Garrett Olson **RC** 4.00
BDP118 Steven Johnson **RC** 1.00
BDP119 Chase Headley **RC** 6.00
BDP120 Daniel Carte **RC** 2.00
BDP121 Francisco Liriano 1.50
BDP122 Fausto Carmona .25
BDP123 Zach Jackson .25
BDP124 Adam Loewen .25
BDP125 Chris Lambert .25
BDP126 Scott Mathieson **RC** 1.00
BDP127 Paul Maholm .25
BDP128 Fernando Nieve .25
BDP129 Justin Verlander 3.00
BDP130 Yusmeiro Petit .25
BDP131 Joel Zumaya 1.00
BDP132 Merkin Valdez .25
BDP133 Ryan Garko **RC** 4.00
BDP134 Edinson Volquez **RC** 15.00
BDP135 Russell Martin 3.00
BDP136 Conor Jackson .25
BDP137 Miguel Montero **RC** 3.00
BDP138 Josh Barfield .25
BDP139 Delmon Young .50
BDP140 Andy LaRoche 2.00
BDP141 William Bergolla .25
BDP142 B.J. Upton .25
BDP143 Hernan Iribarren 1.00
BDP144 Brandon Wood 1.00
BDP145 Jose Bautista .25
BDP146 Edwin Encarnacion .25
BDP147 Javier Herrera **RC** 4.00
BDP148 Jeremy Hermida .25
BDP149 Frank Diaz **RC** 1.00
BDP150 Chris Young 2.00
BDP151 Shin-Soo Choo .25
BDP152 Kevin Thompson .25
BDP153 Hanley Ramirez 1.00
BDP154 Lastings Milledge .50
BDP155 Luis Montanez .25
BDP156 Justin Huber .25
BDP157 Zachary Duke .25
BDP158 Jeff Francoeur .50
BDP159 Melky Cabrera 3.00
BDP160 Bobby Jenks .25
BDP161 Ian Snell .25
BDP162 Fernando Cabrera .25
BDP163 Troy Patton 2.00
BDP164 Anthony Lerew .25
BDP165 Nelson Cruz **RC** 3.00
BDP166 Stephen Drew **RC** 75.00
BDP167 Jered Weaver **RC** 60.00
BDP168 Ryan Braun **RC** 200.00
BDP169 John Mayberry Jr. **RC** 25.00
BDP170 Aaron Thompson **RC** 20.00
BDP171 Cesar Carrillo **RC** 25.00
BDP172 Jacoby Ellsbury **RC** 125.00
BDP173 Matt Garza **RC** 40.00
BDP174 Cliff Pennington **RC** 15.00
BDP175 Colby Rasmus **RC** 100.00
BDP176 Chris Volstad **RC** 30.00
BDP177 Ricky Romero **RC** 15.00
BDP178 Ryan Zimmerman **RC** 75.00
BDP179 C.J. Henry **RC** 30.00
BDP180 Eddy Martinez **RC** 25.00

Refractor

Rookies: 2-4X
Inserted 1:11
Rk Autos. (166-180): 1-1.5X
Production 500

Blue Refractor

Rookies: 4-6X
Rk Autos. (166-180): 1.5-3X
Production 150 Sets

Gold Refractor

Rookies: 8-15X
Rk Autos. (166-180): 4-6X
Production 50 Sets

Red Refractor

No Pricing
Production One Set

X-Fractor

Rookies: 4-6X
Rk Autos. (166-180): 1-2X
Production 250 Sets

SuperFractor

No Pricing
Production One Set

2005 Bowman Draft Picks & Prospects

NM/M

Complete Set (165): 30.00
Commmon Player: .15
Common Rookie .25
Pack (5 + 2 Chrome): 7.00
Box (24): 140.00
BDP1 Rickie Weeks .15
BDP2 Kyle Davies .15
BDP3 Garrett Atkins .15
BDP4 Chien-Ming Wang .50
BDP5 Dallas McPherson .15
BDP6 Dan Johnson .15
BDP7 Andy Sisco .15
BDP8 Ryan Doumit .15
BDP9 J.P. Howell .15
BDP10 Tim Stauffer .15
BDP11 Willy Taveras .15
BDP12 Aaron Hill .15
BDP13 Victor Diaz .15
BDP14 Wilson Betemit .15
BDP15 Ervin Santana .15
BDP16 Mike Morse .15
BDP17 Yadier Molina .15
BDP18 Kelly Johnson .15
BDP19 Clint Barmes .15
BDP20 Robinson Cano .40
BDP21 Brad Thompson .15
BDP22 Jorge Cantu .15
BDP23 Brad Halsey .15
BDP24 Lance Niekro .15
BDP25 D.J. Houlton .15
BDP26 Ryan Church .15
BDP27 Hayden Penn .15
BDP28 Chris Young .50
BDP29 Chad Orvella .15
BDP30 Mark Teahen .15
BDP31 Mark McCormick **RC** .25
BDP32 Jay Bruce **RC** 10.00
BDP33 Beau Jones **RC** .75
BDP34 Tyler Greene **RC** .40
BDP35 Zach Ward **RC** .75
BDP36 Josh Bell **RC** 1.00
BDP37 Josh Wall **RC** .50
BDP38 Nick Webber **RC** .25
BDP39 Travis Buck **RC** 1.00
BDP40 Kyle Winters **RC** .25
BDP41 Mitch Boggs **RC** .25
BDP42 Tommy Mendoza **RC** .50
BDP43 Brad Corley **RC** .40
BDP44 Drew Butera **RC** .25
BDP45 Ryan Mount **RC** .40
BDP46 Tyler Herron **RC** .50
BDP47 Nick Weglarz **RC** 1.50
BDP48 Brandon Erbe **RC** 1.50
BDP49 Cody Allen **RC** .25
BDP50 Eric Fowler **RC** .25
BDP51 James Boone **RC** .50
BDP52 Josh Flores **RC** .75
BDP53 Brandon Monk **RC** .50
BDP54 Kieron Pope **RC** .75
BDP55 Kyle Cofield **RC** .40
BDP56 Brent Lillibridge **RC** .75
BDP57 Daryl Jones **RC** .40
BDP58 Eli Iorg **RC** .50
BDP59 Brett Hayes **RC** .25
BDP60 Mike Durant **RC** .75
BDP61 Michael Bowden **RC** 1.50
BDP62 Paul Kelly **RC** .50
BDP63 Andrew McCutchen **RC** 1.50
BDP64 Travis Wood **RC** .75
BDP65 Cesar Ramos **RC** .25
BDP66 Chaz Roe **RC** .40
BDP67 Matt Torra **RC** .50
BDP68 Kevin Slowey **RC** 2.00
BDP69 Trayvon Robinson **RC** .40
BDP70 Reid Engel **RC** .40
BDP71 Kris Harvey **RC** .50
BDP72 Craig Italiano **RC** .50
BDP73 Matt Maloney **RC** 1.00
BDP74 Sean West **RC** 1.00
BDP75 Henry Sanchez **RC** .50
BDP76 Scott Blue **RC** .25
BDP77 Jordan Schafer **RC** 1.50
BDP78 Chris Robinson **RC** .25
BDP79 Chris Hobdy **RC** .25
BDP80 Brandon Durden **RC** .25
BDP81 Clay Buchholz **RC** 5.00
BDP82 Josh Geer **RC** .25
BDP83 Sam LeCure **RC** .25
BDP84 Justin Thomas **RC** .25
BDP85 Brett Gardner **RC** 1.00
BDP86 Tommy Manzella **RC** .25
BDP87 Matt Green **RC** .25
BDP88 Yunel Escobar **RC** .75
BDP89 Mike Costanzo **RC** .75
BDP90 Nick Hundley **RC** .25
BDP91 Zach Simons **RC** .25
BDP92 Jacob Marceaux **RC** .25
BDP93 Jed Lowrie **RC** 1.00
BDP94 Brandon Snyder **RC** 1.00
BDP95 Matt Goyen **RC** .25
BDP96 Jon Egan **RC** .40
BDP97 Drew Thompson **RC** .40
BDP98 Bryan Anderson **RC** 1.00
BDP99 Clayton Richard **RC** .25
BDP100 Jimmy Shull **RC** .25
BDP101 Mark Pawelek **RC** 1.00
BDP102 P.J. Phillips **RC** .40
BDP103 John Drennen **RC** .75
BDP104 Nolan Reimold **RC** 1.50
BDP105 Troy Tulowitzki **RC** 3.00
BDP106 Kevin Whelan **RC** .25
BDP107 Wade Townsend **RC** .50
BDP108 Micah Owings **RC** 1.50
BDP109 Ryan Tucker **RC** .40
BDP110 Jeff Clement **RC** 1.50
BDP111 Josh Sullivan **RC** .25
BDP112 Jeff Lyman **RC** .25
BDP113 Brian Bogusevic **RC** .75
BDP114 Trevor Bell **RC** .50
BDP115 Brent Cox **RC** .75
BDP116 Michael Billek **RC** .25
BDP117 Garrett Olson **RC** 1.00
BDP118 Steven Johnson **RC** .25
BDP119 Chase Headley **RC** 1.50
BDP120 Daniel Carte **RC** .50
BDP121 Francisco Liriano .75
BDP122 Fausto Carmona .15
BDP123 Zach Jackson .15
BDP124 Adam Loewen .15
BDP125 Chris Lambert .15
BDP126 Scott Mathieson **RC** .25
BDP127 Paul Maholm .15
BDP128 Fernando Nieve .15
BDP129 Justin Verlander .75
BDP130 Yusmeiro Petit .40
BDP131 Joel Zumaya .25
BDP132 Merkin Valdez .15
BDP133 Ryan Garko **RC** .75
BDP134 Edinson Volquez **RC** 4.00
BDP135 Russell Martin .50
BDP136 Conor Jackson .15
BDP137 Miguel Montero **RC** .50
BDP138 Josh Barfield .15
BDP139 Delmon Young .25
BDP140 Andy LaRoche .75
BDP141 William Bergolla .15
BDP142 B.J. Upton .15
BDP143 Hernan Iribarren **RC** .25
BDP144 Brandon Wood .40
BDP145 Jose Bautista .15
BDP146 Edwin Encarnacion .15
BDP147 Javier Herrera **RC** 1.00
BDP148 Jeremy Hermida .25
BDP149 Frank Diaz **RC** .25
BDP150 Chris Young .50
BDP151 Shin-Soo Choo .15
BDP152 Kevin Thompson .15
BDP153 Hanley Ramirez .50
BDP154 Lastings Milledge .25
BDP155 Luis Montanez .15
BDP156 Justin Huber .15
BDP157 Zachary Duke .15
BDP158 Jeff Francoeur .25
BDP159 Melky Cabrera 1.00
BDP160 Bobby Jenks .15
BDP161 Ian Snell .15
BDP162 Fernando Cabrera .15
BDP163 Troy Patton .50
BDP164 Anthony Lerew .15
BDP165 Nelson Cruz **RC** .75

White

Rookies: 3-5X
Production 225 Sets

Red

No Pricing
Production One Set

Base Relic Variations

NM/M

Common Player: 4.00
BDP121 Francisco Liriano 8.00
BDP122 Fausto Carmona 4.00
BDP123 Zach Jackson 4.00
BDP124 Adam Loewen 4.00
BDP125 Chris Lambert 4.00
BDP126 Scott Mathieson 4.00
BDP127 Paul Maholm 4.00
BDP128 Fernando Nieve 4.00
BDP129 Justin Verlander 8.00
BDP130 Yusmeiro Petit 6.00
BDP131 Joel Zumaya 10.00
BDP132 Merkin Valdez 4.00
BDP133 Ryan Garko 6.00
BDP134 Edinson Volquez 20.00
BDP135 Russell Martin 6.00
BDP136 Conor Jackson 6.00
BDP137 Miguel Montero 6.00
BDP138 Josh Barfield 4.00
BDP139 Delmon Young 6.00
BDP140 Andy LaRoche 6.00
BDP141 William Bergolla 4.00
BDP142 B.J. Upton 4.00
BDP143 Hernan Iribarren 4.00
BDP144 Brandon Wood 10.00
BDP145 Jose Bautista 4.00
BDP146 Edwin Encarnacion 4.00
BDP147 Javier Herrera 6.00
BDP148 Jeremy Hermida 6.00
BDP149 Frank Diaz 4.00
BDP150 Chris Young 6.00

Signs of the Future

NM/M

Common Player: 8.00
HB Homer Bailey 25.00
BB Bill Bray 8.00
JF Jeff Frazier 8.00
GG Greg Golson 8.00
AG Angel Guzman 10.00
JH Justin Hoyman 8.00
JJ Justin Jones 8.00
DL Donald Lucey 8.00
TL Tyler Lumsden 8.00
DM David Murphy 15.00
JP Jonathan Poterson 8.00
DP David Purcey 8.00
RR Richie Robnett 8.00
JS Jeremy Sowers 10.00

2005 Bowman Heritage

NM/M

Complete Set (349):
Common Player (1-300): .15
Common SP (301-349): 3.00
Inserted 1:3
Draft Pick Variations (325-349): 1-1.5X

One DPV pack per hobby box.
Pack (8): 4.00
Box (24): 85.00
1 Steven White **RC** .75
2 Jorge Posada .25
3 Brett Myers .15
4 Pat Burrell .25
5 Grady Sizemore .50
6 Jeff Weaver .15
7 Jeff Kent .25
8 Mark Kotsay .15
9 Nick Swisher .15
10 Scott Rolen .50
11 Matt Morris .25
12 Luis Castillo .15
13 Pedro Feliz .15
14 Omar Vizquel .15
15 Edgar Renteria .25
16 David Wells .15
17 Chad Cordero .15
18 Brad Wilkerson .15
19 Kelly Johnson .15
20 Johnny Estrada .15
21 Brian Roberts .25
22 Jeromy Burnitz .15
23 Magglio Ordonez .15
24 Adam Dunn .50
25 Randy Johnson .75
26 Derek Jeter 2.00
27 Jon Lieber .15
28 Jim Thome .50
29 Ronnie Belliard .15
30 Jake Westbrook .15
31 Bengie Molina .15
32 J.D. Drew .25
33 Rich Harden .25
34 David Eckstein .15
35 Scott Podsednik .25
36 Mark Buehrle .25
37 Barry Bonds 2.00
38 Brian Schneider .15
39 Tim Wakefield .15
40 Craig Wilson .15
41 Jose Vidro .15
42 Jacque Jones .15
43 Felix Hernandez .50
44 Nomar Garciaparra .75
45 Neifi Perez .15
46 Brandon Inge .15
47 Felipe Lopez .15
48 Ken Griffey Jr. 1.50
49 Robinson Cano .40
50 Jason Giambi .50
51 Mike Lieberthal .15
52 Bobby Abreu .25
53 C.C. Sabathia .15
54 Aaron Boone .15
55 Milton Bradley .15
56 Derek Lowe .15
57 Barry Zito .25
58 Jim Edmonds .40
59 Jon Garland .15
60 Tadahito Iguchi **RC** 1.50
61 Jason Schmidt .25
62 David Ortiz .75
63 Matt Lawton .15
64 Zachary Duke .25
65 Gary Sheffield .40
66 Chipper Jones .75
67 Sammy Sosa .75
68 Rafael Palmeiro .50
69 Carlos Zambrano .25
70 Aramis Ramirez .25
71 Chris Shelton .15
72 Wily Mo Pena .15
73 Mike Mussina .25
74 Chien-Ming Wang .50
75 Randy Wolf .15
76 Jimmy Rollins .25
77 Chase Utley .50
78 Kevin Millwood .15
79 Victor Martinez .25
80 Morgan Ensberg .25
81 Bartolo Colon .25
82 Bobby Crosby .15
83 Dan Johnson .15
84 Danny Haren .15
85 Yadier Molina .15
86 Mark Mulder .25
87 Russell Branyan .15
88 Lyle Overbay .15
89 Edgardo Alfonzo .15
90 Mike Matheny .15
91 J.T. Snow .15
92 Curt Schilling .75
93 Oliver Perez .15
94 Mark Redman .15
95 Esteban Loaiza .15
96 Livan Hernandez .15
97 Ryan Church .15
98 Kyle Davies .15
99 Mike Hampton .15
100 Jeff Francoeur .25
101 Javy Lopez .15
102 Mark Prior .75
103 Kerry Wood .25
104 Carlos Guillen .15
105 Dmitri Young .15
106 David Wright 1.00
107 Cliff Floyd .15
108 Carlos Beltran .50
109 Melky Cabrera **RC** 2.00
110 Carl Pavano .15
111 Jamie Moyer .15
112 Joel Pineiro .15
113 Adrian Beltre .25
114 Jhonny Peralta .15
115 Travis Hafner .40
116 Cesar Izturis .15
117 Brad Penny .15
118 Garret Anderson .25
119 Scott Kazmir .15
120 Aubrey Huff .15
121 Larry Walker .25
122 Albert Pujols 2.00
123 Paul Konerko .25
124 Frank Thomas .50
125 Phil Nevin .15
126 Brian Giles .15
127 Ramon Hernandez .15
128 Johnny Damon .75
129 Trot Nixon .15
130 Rocco Baldelli .15
131 Carl Crawford .25
132 Alfonso Soriano .50
133 Mark Teixeira .50
134 Gustavo Chacin .15
135 Vernon Wells .25
136 Erik Bedard .15
137 Daniel Cabrera .15
138 Michael Barrett .15
139 Greg Maddux 1.00
140 Javier Vazquez .15
141 Chad Tracy .15
142 Michael Young .15
143 Kenny Rogers .15
144 Mike Piazza .75
145 Jose Reyes .40
146 Geoff Jenkins .15
147 Carlos Lee .25
148 Brady Clark .15
149 Torii Hunter .25
150 Johan Santana .75
151 Steve Finley .15
152 Darin Erstad .25
153 Jake Peavy .25
154 Xavier Nady .15
155 Ryan Klesko .15
156 Ichiro Suzuki 1.50
157 Richie Sexson .40
158 Raul Ibanez .15
159 Freddy Garcia .15
160 Brad Hawpe .15
161 Jeff Francis .15
162 Todd Helton .40
163 Clint Barmes .15
164 Rodrigo Lopez .15
165 Melvin Mora .15
166 Brandon Webb .15
167 Shawn Green .25
168 Moises Alou .25
169 Matt Clement .25
170 John Smoltz .40
171 Rafael Furcal .25
172 Jeff Bagwell .25
173 Roger Clemens 2.00
174 Dontrelle Willis .40
175 Paul LoDuca .15
176 Zack Greinke .15
177 David DeJesus .15
178 Mike Sweeney .15
179 Ben Sheets .25
180 Doug Davis .15
181 Mike Cameron .15
182 Lance Berkman .40
183 Craig Biggio .25
184 Shannon Stewart .15
185 Joe Mauer .50
186 Justin Morneau .25
187 Mike Maroth .15
188 Ivan Rodriguez .50
189 Luis Gonzalez .15
190 Troy Glaus .25
191 Adam Eaton .15
192 Khalil Greene .25
193 Mike Lowell .15
194 Miguel Cabrera .75
195 Roy Halladay .25
196 Ted Lilly .15
197 Alex Rios .15
198 Josh Beckett .25
199 A.J. Burnett .15
200 Juan Pierre .15
201 Marcus Giles .15
202 Craig Tatum **RC** .50
203 Hayden Penn **RC** .50
204 C.J. Smith **RC** .25
205 Matt Albers **RC** 1.00
206 Jared Gothreaux **RC** .25
207 Mike Rodriguez **RC** .25
208 Hernan Iribarren **RC** .25
209 Manny Parra **RC** 2.00
210 Kevin Collins **RC** .25
211 Buck Coats **RC** .50
212 Jeremy West **RC** .50
213 Ian Bladergroen **RC** .25
214 Chuck Tiffany **RC** 1.50
215 Andy LaRoche **RC** 2.00
216 Frank Diaz **RC** .25
217 Jai Miller **RC** .25
218 Tony Giarratano **RC** .50
219 Danny Zell **RC** .25
220 Justin Verlander **RC** 5.00
221 Ryan Sweeney 1.00
222 Brandon McCarthy **RC** 1.00
223 Jerry Owens **RC** .25
224 Glen Perkins **RC** .50
225 Kevin West **RC** .25
226 Billy Butler **RC** 4.00
227 Shane Costa **RC** .50
228 Erik Schindewolf **RC** .50
229 Miguel Montero **RC** .75
230 Stephen Drew **RC** 4.00
231 Matt DeSalvo **RC** 1.00
232 Ben Jones **RC** .75
233 Bill McCarthy **RC** .25
234 Chuck James **RC** 2.00
235 Brandon Sing **RC** .75
236 Andy Santana **RC** .75
237 Brendan Ryan **RC** .50
238 Wes Swackhamer **RC** .50
239 Jeff Niemann **RC** 1.00
240 Ian Kinsler **RC** 4.00
241 Micah Furtado **RC** .50
242 Ryan Mount **RC** 1.00
243 P.J. Phillips **RC** .50
244 Trevor Bell **RC** 1.00
245 Jered Weaver **RC** 4.00
246 Eddy Martinez-Esteve **RC** .75
247 Brian Bannister **RC** 1.00
248 Philip Humber **RC** 1.00
249 Michael Rogers **RC** .50
250 Landon Powell **RC** .50
251 Kennard Bibbs **RC** .50
252 Nelson Cruz **RC** 1.00
253 Paul Kelly **RC** .75
254 Kevin Slowey **RC** 2.00
255 Brandon Snyder **RC** 1.00
256 Nolan Reimold **RC** 1.50
257 Brian Stavisky **RC** .25
258 Javier Herrera **RC** 1.50
259 Russell Martin **RC** 3.00
260 Matthew Kemp **RC** 3.00
261 Wade Townsend **RC** .75
262 Nick Touchstone **RC** .50
263 Ryan Feierabend **RC** .50
264 Bobby Livingston **RC** .50
265 Wladimir Balentien **RC** .75
266 Keiichi Yabu **RC** 1.00
267 Craig Italiano **RC** .50
268 Ryan Goleski **RC** .50
269 Ryan Garko **RC** 1.50
270 Michael Bourn .50
271 Scott Mathieson **RC** .75
272 Scott Mitchinson **RC** .75
273 Tyler Greene **RC** 1.00
274 Mark McCormick **RC** .50
275 Daryl Jones **RC** .50
276 Travis Chick **RC** .50
277 Luis Hernandez **RC** .25
278 Steven Doetsch **RC** .25
279 Chris Vines **RC** .50
280 Mike Costanzo **RC** 1.00
281 Matt Maloney **RC** 1.00
282 Matt Goyen **RC** .25
283 Jacob Marceaux **RC** .25
284 David Gassner **RC** .25
285 Ricky Barrett **RC** .50
286 Jon Egan **RC** .50
287 Scott Blue **RC** .50
288 Steve Bondurant **RC** .50
289 Kevin Melillo **RC** .50
290 Brad Corley **RC** .50
291 Brent Lillibridge **RC** 1.00
292 Mike Morse **RC** .25
293 Justin Thomas **RC** .50
294 Nick Webber **RC** .25
295 Mitch Boggs **RC** .25
296 Jeff Lyman **RC** .50
297 Jordan Schafer **RC** 2.00
298 Ismael Ramirez **RC** .25
299 Chris Young **RC** 2.50
300 Brian Miller **RC** .50
301 Jason Bay 4.00
302 Tim Hudson 3.00
303 Miguel Tejada 4.00
304 Jeremy Bonderman 3.00
305 Alex Rodriguez 8.00
306 Rickie Weeks 3.00
307 Manny Ramirez 6.00
308 Nick Johnson 3.00
309 Andruw Jones 4.00
310 Hideki Matsui 6.00
311 Jeremy Reed 5.00
312 Dallas McPherson 3.00
313 Vladimir Guerrero 5.00
314 Eric Chavez 3.00
315 Chris Carpenter 4.00
316 Aaron Hill 3.00
317 Derrek Lee 5.00
318 Mark Loretta 3.00
319 Garrett Atkins 3.00
320 Hank Blalock 3.00
321 Chris Young 5.00
322 Roy Oswalt 3.00
323 Carlos Delgado 4.00
324 Pedro Martinez 5.00
325 Jeff Clement **RC** 4.00
326 Jimmy Shull **RC** 4.00
327 Daniel Carte **RC** 4.00
328 Travis Buck **RC** 4.00
329 Chris Volstad **RC** 3.00
330 Andrew McCutchen **RC** 8.00
331 Cliff Pennington **RC** 4.00
332 John Mayberry Jr. **RC** 4.00
333 C.J. Henry **RC** 4.00
334 Ricky Romero **RC** 5.00
335 Aaron Thompson **RC** 5.00
336 Cesar Carrillo **RC** 4.00
337 Jacoby Ellsbury **RC** 15.00
338 Matt Garza **RC** 8.00
339 Colby Rasmus **RC** 8.00
340 Ryan Zimmerman **RC** 8.00
341 Ryan Braun **RC** 20.00
342 Brent Lillibridge **RC** 3.00
343 Jay Bruce **RC** 10.00
344 Matt Green **RC** 4.00
345 Brent Cox **RC** 6.00
346 Jed Lowrie **RC** 4.00
347 Beau Jones **RC** 3.00
348 Eli Iorg **RC** 4.00
349 Chaz Roe **RC** 4.00

Mahogany

Stars (1-300): 1-2X
SP's (301-349): .5-1X
Inserted 1:1

Red

No Pricing
Production One Set

Printing Plates

No Pricing
Production one set per color.

Mini

Stars (1-300): 1-2X
SP's (301-349): .5-1X
Inserted 1:1

Draft Pick Variation

NM/M

Variations (325-349): 1-1.5X base
One DPV pack per hobby box.
325 Jeff Clement 10.00
326 Jimmy Shull 6.00
327 Daniel Carte 6.00
328 Travis Buck 5.00
329 Chris Volstad 5.00
330 Andrew McCutchen 12.00
331 Cliff Pennington 6.00
332 John Mayberry Jr. 6.00
333 C.J. Henry 8.00
334 Ricky Romero 6.00
335 Aaron Thompson 6.00
336 Cesar Carrillo 6.00
337 Jacoby Ellsbury 20.00
338 Matt Garza 10.00
339 Colby Rasmus 15.00
340 Ryan Zimmerman 10.00
341 Ryan Braun 30.00
342 Brent Lillibridge 6.00
343 Jay Bruce 15.00
344 Matt Green 6.00
345 Brent Cox 6.00
346 Jed Lowrie 6.00
347 Beau Jones 5.00
348 Eli Iorg 6.00
349 Chaz Roe 6.00

Future Greatness

NM/M

Common Player: 4.00
TB Tony Blanco 4.00
JB Joe Blanton 4.00
BB Bryan Bullington 4.00
MC Matt Cain 8.00
FC Fausto Carmona 4.00
SC Shin-Soo Choo 4.00
JC Jorge Cortes 4.00
JCO Jesus Cota 4.00
EE Edwin Encarnacion 4.00
CE Clint Everts 4.00
GF Gavin Floyd 4.00
JF Jeff Francis 4.00
JGA Jairo Garcia 4.00
RG Ruben Gotay 6.00
JG Joel Guzman 4.00
AH Aaron Hill 4.00
KH Koyie Hill 4.00
JK Jason Kubel 4.00
WL Wilfredo Ledezma 4.00
VM Val Majewski 4.00
AMA Andy Marte 8.00
JMA Jeff Mathis 8.00
DM Dallas McPherson 4.00
JM Justin Morneau 8.00
AM Arnie Munoz 4.00
JP Juan Perez 4.00
YP Yusmeiro Petit 4.00
FP Felix Pie 6.00
BT Brad Thompson 15.00
RW Rickie Weeks 6.00
DY Delmon Young 8.00

Pieces of Greatness

NM/M

Common Player: 4.00
JB Josh Beckett 4.00
CB Carlos Beltran 6.00
BB Barry Bonds 20.00
MC Miguel Cabrera 8.00
EC Eric Chavez 4.00
RC Roger Clemens 10.00
BC Bobby Crosby 4.00
JD Johnny Damon 8.00
CD Carlos Delgado 6.00
AD Adam Dunn 8.00
JG Josh Gibson 15.00
TG Troy Glaus 4.00
RH Rich Harden 4.00
TH Todd Helton 6.00
JK Jeff Kent 4.00
PK Paul Konerko 6.00
PM Pedro Martinez 8.00
MMO Melvin Mora 4.00
MM Mark Mulder 4.00
BM Brett Myers 4.00
AP Albert Pujols 20.00
MR Manny Ramirez 8.00

BR	Brian Roberts	4.00
AR	Alex Rodriguez	15.00
JS	John Smoltz	8.00
IS	Ichiro Suzuki	15.00
MT	Miguel Tejada	6.00
JT	Jim Thome	6.00
DW	Dontrelle Willis	6.00
DWR	David Wright	15.00
BZ	Barry Zito	4.00

Signs of Greatness

		NM/M
Common Player:		6.00
RB	Ryan Braun	75.00
JB	Jay Bruce	80.00
PB	Patrick Bryant	10.00
MB	Matt Bush	15.00
TC	Travis Chick	6.00
TD	Thomas Diamond	10.00
SE	Scott Elbert	15.00
MG	Matt Green	8.00
AG	Angel Guzman	8.00
JH	J.P. Howell	8.00
PH	Philip Humber	20.00
ZJ	Zach Jackson	8.00
JJ	Jason Jaramillo	10.00
DJ	Dan Johnson	8.00
BL	Brent Lillibridge	10.00
DL	Donald Lucey	8.00
EM	Eddy Martinez-Esteve	8.00
JM	John Mayberry Jr.	20.00
AM	Andrew McCutchen	35.00
JP	Jonathan Papelbon	40.00
DP	David Purcey	8.00
RR	Ricky Romero	10.00
HS	Huston Street	20.00
CT	Curtis Thigpen	10.00
WW	Wes Whisler	10.00
JZ	Jon Zeringue	8.00
RZ	Ryan Zimmerman	25.00

51 Topps Heritage Blue Back

		NM/M
Common Player:		1.00
1	Adam Dunn	3.00
2	Zachary Duke	1.50
3	Alex Rodriguez	8.00
4	Vladimir Guerrero	3.00
5	Andruw Jones	2.00
6	Travis Chick	2.00
7	Alfonso Soriano	2.00
8	Scott Rolen	3.00
9	Brian Bannister	2.00
10	Randy Johnson	3.00
11	Barry Bonds	8.00
12	Pat Burrell	1.50
13	Barry Zito	1.50
14	Nomar Garciaparra	3.00
15	C.C. Sabathia	1.00
16	Miguel Tejada	2.00
17	Hideki Matsui	6.00
18	John Smoltz	2.00
19	Ken Griffey Jr.	5.00
20	Chris Carpenter	1.50
21	Ian Kinsler	3.00
22	Chuck Tiffany	1.50
23	Gary Sheffield	2.00
24	Mark Mulder	1.50
25	Ichiro Suzuki	5.00
26	Kerry Wood	1.50
27	Jose Reyes	1.00
28	Derrek Lee	2.00
29	Justin Verlander	2.00
30	Johnny Damon	3.00
31	Chris Volstad	1.00
32	Jeremy Bonderman	1.00
33	David Ortiz	3.00
34	Morgan Ensberg	1.00
35	Mark Buehrle	1.00
36	Chuck James	2.00
37	Miguel Cabrera	3.00
38	Magglio Ordonez	1.00
39	Michael Young	1.00
40	Carlos Beltran	2.00
41	Nick Johnson	1.00
42	Billy Butler	2.00
43	Brian Giles	1.00
44	Paul Konerko	1.50
45	Roy Oswalt	1.50
46	Bobby Abreu	1.50
47	Sammy Sosa	3.00
48	Aramis Ramirez	1.50
49	Torii Hunter	1.00
50	Aubrey Huff	1.00
51	Vernon Wells	1.00
52	Joe Mauer	1.50

51 Topps Heritage Red Back

		NM/M
Common Player:		1.00
1	Andy LaRoche	3.00
2	Mike Piazza	4.00
3	Pedro Martinez	3.00
4	Wladimir Balentien	1.00
5	Tim Hudson	1.50
6	Richie Sexson	1.50
7	Carlos Delgado	1.00
8	Derek Jeter	8.00
9	Ryan Zimmerman	6.00
10	Mark Teixeira	2.00
11	David Wright	3.00
12	Jake Peavy	1.50
13	Jose Vidro	1.00
14	Jim Thome	2.00

15	Carlos Zambrano	1.50
16	Hank Blalock	1.50
17	Johan Santana	2.00
18	Cliff Pennington	1.00
19	Rafael Palmeiro	1.50
20	Curt Schilling	2.00
21	Brandon McCarthy	2.00
22	Stephen Drew	8.00
23	Jeff Niemann	2.00
24	Eric Chavez	1.00
25	Hernan Iribarren	1.00
26	Jered Weaver	2.00
27	Edgar Renteria	1.00
28	Travis Hafner	1.00
29	Frank Thomas	1.50
30	Brian Roberts	1.00
31	Anthony Reyes	1.00
32	Scott Kazmir	1.00
33	Carlos Lee	1.00
34	Jimmy Rollins	1.00
35	Garret Anderson	1.00
36	Jason Schmidt	1.00
37	Jon Garland	1.00
38	Dontrelle Willis	1.50
39	C.J. Henry	3.00
40	Greg Maddux	4.00
41	Todd Helton	2.00
42	Ivan Rodriguez	2.00
43	Chipper Jones	3.00
44	Rich Harden	1.50
45	Mark Prior	3.00
46	Roy Halladay	1.50
47	Albert Pujols	8.00
48	Roger Clemens	8.00
49	Andrew McCutchen	4.00
50	Scott Podsednik	1.50
51	Manny Ramirez	3.00
52	Carl Crawford	1.00
53	Jim Edmonds	1.50
54	Wily Mo Pena	1.00

2005 Bowman Sterling

		NM/M
Pack (5):		60.00
Box (6):		325.00
First Year Autographs		
MA	Matt Albers **RC**	20.00
RB	Ryan Braun **RC**	125.00
TC	Travis Chick **RC**	10.00
MG	Matt Green **RC**	10.00
CH	C.J. Henry **RC**	15.00
GK	George Kottaras **RC**	20.00
EM	Eddy Martinez-Esteve **RC**	15.00
JM	John Mayberry Jr. **RC**	20.00
GO	Garrett Olson **RC**	20.00
CP	Cliff Pennington **RC**	15.00
HS	Humberto Sanchez **RC**	25.00
BS	Brandon Sing **RC**	15.00
AT	Aaron Thompson **RC**	15.00
CV	Chris Volstad **RC**	20.00
SW	Steven White **RC**	10.00
Autographed First Year Relics		
TB	Trevor Bell **RC**	15.00
MB	Michael Bowden **RC**	40.00
JB	Jay Bruce **RC**	100.00
MC	Mike Conroy **RC**	15.00
BC	J. Brent Cox **RC**	15.00
JE	Jacoby Ellsbury **RC**	100.00
JG	Josh Geer **RC**	15.00
PH	Philip Humber **RC**	25.00
EI	Eli Iorg **RC**	15.00
BJ	Beau Jones **RC**	15.00
BL	Bobby Livingston **RC**	15.00
JL	Jed Lowrie **RC**	40.00
SM	Steve Marek **RC**	15.00
RM	Russell Martin **RC**	40.00
BM	Brandon McCarthy **RC**	15.00
AM	Andrew McCutchen **RC**	50.00
TM	Tyler Minges **RC**	15.00
JCN	John Nelson **RC**	15.00
JN	Jeff Niemann **RC**	20.00
JO	Justin Olson **RC**	10.00
CPP	Carmen Pignatiello **RC**	15.00
CR	Colby Rasmus **RC**	80.00
CRO	Chaz Roe **RC**	15.00
CS	C.J. Smith **RC**	10.00
RT	Raul Tablado **RC**	15.00
JV	Justin Verlander **RC**	40.00
Autographed Prospect Base Relics		
BB	Billy Buckner	15.00
SE	Scott Elbert	15.00
BE	Brad Eldred	15.00
JF	Josh Fields	20.00
AL	Adam Lind	15.00
CN	Chris Nelson	15.00
DP	Dustin Pedroia	85.00
CT	Curtis Thigpen	10.00
First Year Base Cards		
BA	Brian Anderson	4.00
BRB	Brian Bogusevic **RC**	5.00
CBU	Clay Buchholz **RC**	30.00
TBU	Travis Buck **RC**	6.00
BBU	Billy Butler **RC**	10.00
CC	Cesar Carrillo **RC**	6.00
DC	Daniel Carte **RC**	4.00
JC	Jeff Clement **RC**	15.00
MCO	Mike Constanzo **RC**	6.00
BCR	Brad Corley **RC**	4.00
JDR	John Drennen **RC**	8.00
SD	Stephen Drew **RC**	10.00
JEG	Jon Egan **RC**	6.00
YE	Yunel Escobar **RC**	6.00
MGA	Matt Garza **RC**	10.00
TG	Tyler Greene **RC**	6.00
BH	Brett Hayes **RC**	4.00
CHE	Chase Headley **RC**	6.00
THE	Tyler Herron **RC**	5.00
NH	Nick Hundley **RC**	4.00
TI	Tadahito Iguchi **RC**	6.00
HI	Hernan Iribarren **RC**	4.00
CI	Craig Italiano **RC**	6.00
CJ	Chuck James **RC**	8.00
PK	Paul Kelly **RC**	8.00
ACL	Andy LaRoche **RC**	10.00
JLY	Jeff Lyman **RC**	6.00
MAM	Matt Maloney **RC**	8.00
JMA	Jacob Marceaux **RC**	4.00
MMC	Mark McCormick **RC**	4.00
RMO	Ryan Mount **RC**	6.00
PP	P.J. Phillips **RC**	4.00
CRA	Cesar Ramos **RC**	4.00
NR	Nolan Reimold **RC**	8.00
RR	Ricky Romero **RC**	6.00
HAS	Henry Sanchez **RC**	6.00
ZS	Zach Simons **RC**	4.00
KS	Kevin Slowey **RC**	15.00
BSN	Brandon Snyder **RC**	8.00
DT	Drew Thompson **RC**	4.00
CLT	Chuck Tiffany **RC**	6.00
MTO	Matt Torra **RC**	6.00
WT	Wade Townsend **RC**	4.00
TT	Troy Tulowitzki **RC**	10.00
JW	Josh Wall **RC**	6.00
JWE	Jered Weaver **RC**	15.00
NW	Nick Webber **RC**	4.00
KW	Kevin Whelan **RC**	4.00
TW	Travis Wood **RC**	4.00
RZ	Ryan Zimmerman **RC**	20.00

Refractors

Rookies:	1.5-2X
Rookie Auto.:	1-2X
Rookie Relic Auto.:	1-2X
Production 199 Sets	

Black Refractors

No Pricing
Production 25 Sets

Red Refractor

No Pricing
Production One Set

MLB Logo Patch

No Pricing
Production One Set

Original Autographs

		NM/M
Production 1-160		
AJ4	Andruw Jones 02 B/122	25.00
AJ6	Andruw Jones 03 B/112	25.00
AJ8	Andruw Jones 04 B/71	25.00
DL1	Derrek Lee 95 B/27	25.00
DL2	Derrek Lee 96 B/29	25.00
DL5	Derrek Lee 98 B/22	25.00
DL6	Derrek Lee 04 B/92	20.00
DL7	Derrek Lee 04 BC/26	25.00
DW1	David Wright 04 BD/98	85.00
DW3	David Wright 05 B/139	85.00
GA1	Garret Anderson 04 BC/36	20.00
GA2	Garret Anderson 05 B/48	20.00
JR1	Jeremy Reed 04 BD/82	15.00
JR2	Jeremy Reed 04 BCD/48	20.00
MC2	Miguel Cabrera 02 BD/26	50.00
MC4	Miguel Cabrera 03 BD/27	50.00
MC5	Miguel Cabrera 03 BCD/25	50.00
MC6	Miguel Cabrera 04 B/127	25.00
MC7	Miguel Cabrera 04 BC/25	50.00
MC8	Miguel Cabrera 05 B/154	25.00
MC9	Miguel Cabrera 05 BC/25	50.00
MK3	Mark Kotsay 99 B/56	15.00
MK5	Mark Kotsay 99 B/75	15.00
MK7	Mark Kotsay 05 B/160	10.00
MK8	Mark Kotsay 05 BC/46	15.00
MY1	Michael Young 04 B/148	15.00
MY2	Michael Young 04 BC/64	15.00
MY3	Michael Young 05 B/92	15.00

Relics

	NM/M
Common Player:	4.00
Refractor:	1-1.5X
Production 199 Sets	
Black Refractor:	2-4X
Production 25 Sets	

JBE	Josh Beckett	4.00
RBE	Ronnie Belliard	4.00
CB	Carlos Beltran	6.00
HB	Hank Blalock	4.00
BLB	Barry Bonds	20.00
MCA	Miguel Cabrera	8.00
EC	Eric Chavez	4.00
JD	Johnny Damon	8.00
CD	Carlos Delgado	4.00
JPE	Jim Edmonds	6.00
RF	Rafael Furcal	4.00
JGI	Josh Gibson	15.00
MGI	Marcus Giles	4.00
KG	Khalil Greene	6.00
VG	Vladimir Guerrero	8.00
TLH	Todd Helton	6.00
THU	Tim Hudson	4.00
TH	Torii Hunter	4.00
LWJ	Chipper Jones	8.00
DL	Derrek Lee	6.00
PL	Paul LoDuca	4.00
GM	Greg Maddux	10.00
PM	Pedro Martinez	8.00
TM	Tino Martinez	4.00
VM	Victor Martinez	4.00
HM	Hideki Matsui	15.00
KM	Kevin Millar	4.00
BMU	Bill Mueller	4.00
MM	Mark Mulder	4.00
TN	Trot Nixon	4.00
DO	David Ortiz	10.00
MP	Mike Piazza	8.00
JP	Jorge Posada	6.00
MPR	Mark Prior	6.00
AP	Albert Pujols	20.00
ARA	Aramis Ramirez	4.00
MR	Manny Ramirez	8.00
AR	Alex Rodriguez	20.00
IR	Ivan Rodriguez	6.00
SR	Scott Rolen	8.00
CSU	Curt Schilling	6.00
GS	Gary Sheffield	6.00
JS	John Smoltz	6.00
AS	Alfonso Soriano	6.00
SS	Sammy Sosa	8.00
MTE	Mark Teixeira	8.00
MT	Miguel Tejada	6.00
DW	Dontrelle Willis	6.00
MY	Michael Young	4.00
BZ	Barry Zito	4.00

2005 Bowman's Best

		NM/M
Common Player:		.25
Common Rookie:		1.00
Common Rookie Auto. (101-143):		10.00
Production 974		
Pack (5):		14.00
Box (10):		120.00
1	Jose Vidro	.25
2	Adam Dunn	.50
3	Manny Ramirez	.75
4	Miguel Tejada	.50
5	Ken Griffey Jr.	1.00
6	Pedro Martinez	1.00
7	Alex Rodriguez	1.50
8	Ichiro Suzuki	1.50

9 Alfonso Soriano .75
10 Brian Giles .25
11 Roger Clemens 2.00
12 Todd Helton .50
13 Ivan Rodriguez .50
14 David Ortiz .75
15 Sammy Sosa 1.00
16 Chipper Jones .75
17 Mark Buehrle .50
18 Miguel Cabrera .75
19 Johan Santana .75
20 Randy Johnson .75
21 Jim Thome .50
22 Vladimir Guerrero .75
23 Dontrelle Willis .50
24 Nomar Garciaparra .75
25 Barry Bonds 2.00
26 Curt Schilling .75
27 Carlos Beltran .50
28 Albert Pujols 2.00
29 Mark Prior .75
30 Derek Jeter 2.00
31 Ryan Garko RC 4.00
32 Eulogio de la Cruz RC 1.00
33 Luke Scott RC 3.00
34 Shane Costa RC 1.00
35 Casey McGehee RC 1.00
36 Jered Weaver RC 8.00
37 Kevin Melillo RC 2.00
38 D.J. Houlton RC 2.00
39 Brandon Moorhead RC 1.00
40 Jerry Owens RC 1.00
41 Elliot Johnson RC 1.50
42 Kevin West RC 2.00
43 Hernan Iribarren RC 1.00
44 Miguel Montero RC 6.00
45 Craig Tatum RC 1.00
46 Ryan Sweeney 2.00
47 Micah Furtado RC 4.00
48 Cody Haerther RC 1.00
49 Erik Abreu RC 1.00
50 Chuck Tiffany RC 2.00
51 Tadahito Iguchi RC 4.00
52 Frank Diaz RC 3.00
53 Errol Simonitsch RC 1.00
54 Wade Robinson RC 2.00
55 Adam Boeve RC 1.00
56 Steve Bondurant RC 1.00
57 Jason Motte RC 1.00
58 Juan Senreiso RC 1.00
59 Vinny Rottino RC 1.00
60 Jai Miller RC 1.00
61 Thomas Pauly RC 1.00
62 Tony Giarratano RC 1.00
63 Alexander Smit RC 1.00
64 Keiichi Yabu RC 2.50
65 Brian Bannister RC 2.50
66 Kennard Bibbs RC 1.00
67 Anthony Reyes RC 4.00
68 Tom Oldham RC 1.00
69 Benjamin Harrison RC 2.00
70 Daryl Thompson RC 4.00
71 Kevin Collins RC 1.00
72 Wes Swackhamer RC 1.50
73 Landon Powell RC 1.50
74 Matt Brown RC 1.00
75 Russell Martin RC 6.00
76 Nick Touchstone RC 1.00
77 Steven White RC 1.00
78 Ian Bladergroen RC 1.00
79 Sean Marshall RC 2.00
80 Nick Masset RC 1.00
81 Ryan Goleski RC 1.50
82 Matt Campbell RC 1.00
83 Manny Parra RC 5.00
84 Melky Cabrera RC 5.00
85 Ryan Feierabend RC 1.50
86 Nate McLouth RC 1.50
87 Glen Perkins RC 2.50
88 Kila Kaaihue RC 1.50
89 Dana Eveland RC 1.50
90 Tyler Pelland RC 1.00
91 Matt Van Der Bosch RC 1.00
92 Andy Santana RC 1.00
93 Eric Nielsen RC 1.00
94 Brendan Ryan RC 1.00
95 Ian Kinsler RC 5.00
96 Matthew Kemp RC 8.00
97 Stephen Drew RC 10.00
98 Peeter Ramos RC 2.00
99 Chris Seddon RC 2.00
100 Chuck James RC 6.00
101 Travis Chick RC 1.00
102 Justin Verlander RC 40.00
103 Billy Butler RC 30.00
104 Chris Young RC 80.00
105 Jake Postlewait RC 1.00
106 C.J. Smith RC 1.00
107 Mike Rodriguez RC 12.00
108 Philip Humber RC 25.00
109 Jeff Niemann RC 20.00
110 Brian Miller RC 5.00
111 Chris Vines RC 12.00
112 Andy LaRoche RC 15.00
113 Mike Bourn RC 15.00
114 Wladimir Balentien RC 20.00
115 Ismael Ramirez RC 10.00
116 Hayden Penn RC 15.00
117 Pedro Lopez RC 10.00
118 Shawn Bowman RC 15.00
119 Chad Orvella RC 10.00
120 Sean Tracey RC 10.00
121 Bobby Livingston RC 10.00
122 Michael Rogers RC 10.00
123 Willy Mota RC 15.00

124 Brandon McCarthy RC 15.00
125 Mike Morse RC 10.00
126 Matt Lindstrom RC 10.00
127 Brian Stavisky RC 10.00
128 Rich Gardner RC 10.00
129 Scott Mitchinson RC 10.00
130 Billy McCarthy RC 10.00
131 Brandon Sing RC 15.00
132 Matt Albers RC 12.00
133 George Kottaras RC 15.00
134 Luis Hernandez RC 10.00
135 Humberto Sanchez RC 20.00
136 Buck Coats RC 10.00
137 Jonathan Barratt RC 10.00
138 Raul Tablado RC 12.00
139 Jake Mullinax RC 15.00
140 Edgar Varela RC 12.00
141 Ryan Garko RC 25.00
142 Nate McLouth RC 15.00
143 Shane Costa RC 10.00

Blue Refractor

Stars:	2-4X
Rookies:	1-2X
Production 499	
Rookie Autos.	1-1.5X
Production 299	

Gold Refractor

No Pricing
Production 25 Sets

Green Refractor

Stars:	2-3X
Rookies:	1-2X
Production 899	
Rookie Autos.	1-1.5X
Production 399	

Red Refractor

Stars:	3-5X
Rookies:	2-3X
Rookie Autos.	1.5-2X
Production 199 Sets	

Silver Refractor

Stars:	4-6X
Rookies:	2-3X
Rookie Autos.	1.5-3X
Production 99 Sets	

Printing Plates

No Pricing
Production one set for each color.

Printing Plates Autograph

No Pricing
Production one set for each color.

A-Rod Throwback Autograph

NM/M
Production 100
AR   Alex Rodriguez   150.00

Bowman's Best Shortstops

Production 25
No Pricing

Mirror Image Spokesmen

Production 10
No Pricing

Mirror Image Throwback

NM/M
Production 50
RR   Cal Ripken Jr.,
       Alex Rodriguez   450.00

2006 Bowman

NM/M
Complete Set (231):

Common Player (1-200): .15
Common RC (201-220): .25
Common Auto. (219-231): 10.00
Pack (10): 3.00
Box (24): 60.00
1 Nick Swisher .25
2 Ted Lilly .15
3 John Smoltz .25
4 Lyle Overbay .15
5 Alfonso Soriano .50
6 Javier Vazquez .15
7 Ronnie Belliard .15
8 Jose Reyes .75
9 Brian Roberts .25
10 Curt Schilling .75
11 Adam Dunn .50
12 Zack Greinke .25
13 Carlos Guillen .25
14 Jon Garland .25
15 Robinson Cano .25
16 Chris Burke .15
17 Barry Zito .25
18 Russ Adams .15
19 Chris Capuano .15
20 Scott Rolen .50
21 Kerry Wood .25
22 Scott Kazmir .25
23 Brandon Webb .25
24 Jeff Kent .25
25 Albert Pujols 2.00
26 C.C. Sabathia .25
27 Adrian Beltre .25
28 Brad Wilkerson .15
29 Randy Wolf .15
30 Jason Bay .25
31 Austin Kearns .15
32 Clint Barmes .15
33 Mike Sweeney .15
34 Justin Verlander (RC) .25
35 Justin Morneau .25
36 Scott Podsednik .15
37 Jason Giambi .50
38 Steve Finley .15
39 Morgan Ensberg .15
40 Eric Chavez .25
41 Roy Halladay .25
42 Horacio Ramirez .15
43 Ben Sheets .25
44 Chris Carpenter .40
45 Andruw Jones .50
46 Carlos Zambrano .25
47 Jonny Gomes .15
48 Shawn Green .15
49 Moises Alou .25
50 Ichiro Suzuki 1.50
51 Juan Pierre .15
52 Grady Sizemore .40
53 Kazuo Matsui .15
54 Jose Vidro .15
55 Jake Peavy .25
56 Dallas McPherson .15
57 Ryan Howard 1.00
58 Zachary Duke .15
59 Michael Young .25
60 Todd Helton .50
61 David DeJesus .15
62 Ivan Rodriguez .50
63 Johan Santana .50
64 Danny Haren .25
65 Derek Jeter 2.00
66 Greg Maddux 1.00
67 Jorge Cantu .15
68 Conor Jackson (RC) .40
69 Victor Martinez .25
70 David Wright 1.00
71 Ryan Church .15
72 Khalil Greene .15
73 Jimmy Rollins .50
74 Hank Blalock .25
75 Pedro Martinez .75
76 Jonathan Papelbon (RC) 2.00
77 Felipe Lopez .15
78 Jeff Francis .15
79 Andrew Sisco .15
80 Hideki Matsui 1.50
81 Ken Griffey Jr. 1.50
82 Nomar Garciaparra .50
83 Kevin Millwood .25
84 Paul Konerko .25
85 A.J. Burnett .15
86 Mike Piazza .75
87 Brian Giles .25
88 Johnny Damon .50
89 Jim Thome .50
90 Roger Clemens 1.50
91 Aaron Rowand .15
92 Rafael Furcal .25
93 Gary Sheffield .50
94 Mike Cameron .15
95 Carlos Delgado .50
96 Jorge Posada .40
97 Denny Bautista .15
98 Mike Maroth .15
99 Brad Radke .15
100 Alex Rodriguez 2.00
101 Freddy Garcia .15
102 Oliver Perez .15
103 Jon Lieber .15
104 Melvin Mora .25
105 Travis Hafner .40
106 Matt Cain (RC) .25
107 Derek Lowe .15
108 Luis Castillo .15
109 Livan Hernandez .15
110 Tadahito Iguchi .15

111 Shawn Chacon .15
112 Frank Thomas .40
113 Josh Beckett .40
114 Aubrey Huff .15
115 Derek Lee .15
116 Chien-Ming Wang .50
117 Joe Crede .15
118 Torii Hunter .25
119 J.D. Drew .25
120 Troy Glaus .40
121 Sean Casey .15
122 Edgar Renteria .25
123 Craig Wilson .15
124 Adam Eaton .15
125 Jeff Francoeur .40
126 Bruce Chen .15
127 Cliff Floyd .15
128 Jeremy Reed .15
129 Jake Westbrook .15
130 Wily Mo Pena .15
131 Toby Hall .15
132 David Ortiz .75
133 David Eckstein .15
134 Brady Clark .15
135 Marcus Giles .15
136 Aaron Hill .25
137 Mark Kotsay .15
138 Carlos Lee .40
139 Roy Oswalt .40
140 Chone Figgins .25
141 Mike Mussina .50
142 Orlando Hernandez .25
143 Maggio Ordonez .25
144 Jim Edmonds .40
145 Bobby Abreu .40
146 Nick Johnson .15
147 Carlos Beltran .50
148 Jhonny Peralta .25
149 Pedro Feliz .15
150 Miguel Tejada .25
151 Luis Gonzalez .15
152 Carl Crawford .25
153 Yadier Molina .15
154 Rich Harden .25
155 Tim Wakefield .15
156 Rickie Weeks .25
157 Johnny Estrada .15
158 Gustavo Chacin .15
159 Dan Johnson .15
160 Willy Taveras .15
161 Garret Anderson .25
162 Randy Johnson .75
163 Jermaine Dye .25
164 Joe Mauer .50
165 Ervin Santana .25
166 Jeremy Bonderman .15
167 Garrett Atkins .25
168 Manny Ramirez .75
169 Brad Eldred .15
170 Chase Utley .75
171 Mark Loretta .15
172 John Patterson .15
173 Tom Glavine .25
174 Dontrelle Willis .50
175 Mark Teixeira .50
176 Felix Hernandez .40
177 Cliff Lee .15
178 Jason Schmidt .25
179 Chad Tracy .15
180 Rocco Baldelli .15
181 Aramis Ramirez .25
182 Andy Pettitte .25
183 Mark Mulder .25
184 Geoff Jenkins .15
185 Chipper Jones .75
186 Vernon Wells .25
187 Bobby Crosby .15
188 Lance Berkman .40
189 Vladimir Guerrero .75
190 Jose Capellan (RC) .15
191 Brad Penny .15
192 Jose Guillen .15
193 Brett Myers .25
194 Miguel Cabrera .75
195 Bartolo Colon .15
196 Craig Biggio .25
197 Tim Hudson .25
198 Mark Prior .25
199 Mark Buehrle .25
200 Barry Bonds 2.00
201 Anderson Hernandez (RC) .25
202 Charlton Jimerson (RC) .25
203 Jeremy Accardo RC .50
204 Hanley Ramirez (RC) 1.00
205 Matt Capps (RC) .25
206 John-Ford Griffin (RC) .25
207 Chuck James (RC) .25
208 Jaime Bubela (RC) .25
209 Mark Woodyard (RC) .25
210 Jason Botts (RC) .25
211 Chris Demaria RC .25
212 Miguel Perez (RC) .25
213 Tom Gorzelanny (RC) .25
214 Adam Wainwright (RC) .50
215 Ryan Garko (RC) .50
216 Jason Bergmann RC .50
217 J.J. Furmaniak (RC) .25
218 Francisco Liriano (RC) 1.00
219 Kenji Johjima RC 2.00
219 Kenji Johjima/Auto. RC 50.00
220 Craig Hansen RC 1.50
220 Craig Hansen/Auto. RC 15.00
221 Ryan Zimmerman/ Auto. (RC) 25.00
222 Joey Devine/Auto. RC 10.00
223 Scott Olsen/Auto (RC) 10.00

224	Darrell Rasner/Auto (RC)	10.00
225	Craig Breslow/Auto. RC	10.00
226	Reggie Abercrombie/ Auto. (RC)	10.00
227	Dan Uggla/Auto. (RC)	35.00
228	Willie Eyre/Auto. (RC)	10.00
229	Joel Zumaya/Auto. (RC)	20.00
230	Ricky Nolasco/Auto. (RC)	10.00
231	Ian Kinsler/Auto. (RC)	25.00

Blue
Stars: 2-4X
Rookies (201-220): 2-4X
RC Auto. (219-231): 1-1.5X
Production 500 Sets

Red
No Pricing
Production One Set

White
Stars: 3-6X
Rookies (201-220): 3-6X
RC Auto. (219-231): 1-2X
Production 120 Sets

Base of the Future
NM/M
JH Justin Huber 10.00

Chrome Prospects

NM/M

	Common Prospect:	.50
BC1	Alex Gordon	20.00
BC2	Jonathan George	.50
BC3	Scott Walter	.50
BC4	Brian Holliday	.50
BC5	Ben Copeland	1.00
BC6	Bobby Wilson	1.50
BC7	Mayker Sandoval	1.50
BC8	Alejandro de Aza	2.00
BC9	David Munoz	.75
BC10	Josh LeBlanc	1.00
BC11	Philippe Valiquette	1.00
BC12	Edwin Bellorin	1.00
BC13	Jason Quarles	1.00
BC14	Mark Trumbo	2.00
BC15	Steve Kelly	.75
BC16	Jamie Hoffman	.75
BC17	Joseph Bauserman	1.00
BC18	Nick Adenhart	5.00
BC19	Mike Butia	.75
BC20	Jon Weber	.75
BC21	Luis Valdez	1.00
BC22	Rafael Rodriguez	1.00
BC23	Wyatt Toregas	1.00
BC24	John Vanden Berg	.75
BC25	Mike Connolly	.75
BC26	Mike O'Connor	1.50
BC27	Garrett Mock	.75
BC28	Bill Layman	.75
BC29	Luis Pena	.75
BC30	Billy Killian	1.00
BC31	Ross Ohlendorf	.50
BC32	Mark Kaiser	.75
BC33	Ryan Costello	.75
BC34	Dale Thayer	.50
BC35	Steve Garrabrants	.75
BC36	Samuel Deduno	.75
BC37	Juan Portes	3.00
BC38	Javier Martinez	.75
BC39	Clint Sammons	1.00
BC40	Andrew Kown	1.50
BC41	Matt Tolbert	.75
BC42	Michael Ekstrom	.75
BC43	Shawn Norris	.75
BC44	Diory Hernandez	.75
BC45	Chris Maples	.75
BC46	Aaron Hathaway	1.00
BC47	Steven Baker	.75
BC48	Greg Creek	1.00
BC49	Collin Mahoney	.75
BC50	Corey Ragsdale	1.50
BC51	Ariel Nunez	.50
BC52	Max Ramirez	4.00
BC53	Eric Rodland	1.00
BC54	Dante Brinkley	1.00
BC55	Casey Craig	1.00
BC56	Ryan Spilborghs	2.50
BC57	Fredy Deza	.75
BC58	Jeff Frazier	.50
BC59	Vince Cordova	.50
BC60	Oswaldo Navarro	1.00
BC61	Jarod Rine	.75
BC62	Jordan Tata	1.50
BC63	Ben Julianel	1.00
BC64	Yung-Chi Chen	5.00
BC65	Carlos Torres	1.50
BC66	Juan Francia	1.50
BC67	Brett Smith	1.00
BC68	Francisco Leandro	1.00
BC69	Chris Turner	3.00
BC70	Matt Joyce	3.00
BC71	Jason Jones	1.00
BC72	Jose Diaz	.50
BC73	Kevin Ool	.75
BC74	Nate Bumstead	1.00
BC75	Omir Santos	1.00
BC76	Shawn Riggans	1.00
BC77	Ofilio Castro	.50
BC78	Mike Rozier	1.50
BC79	Wilkin Ramirez	2.00
BC80	Yobal Duenas	1.00
BC81	Adam Bourassa	1.00
BC82	Tony Granadillo	1.00
BC83	Brad McCann	4.00
BC84	Dustin Majewski	1.00
BC85	Kelvin Jimenez	.50
BC86	Mark Reed	2.00
BC87	Asdrubal Cabrera	3.00
BC88	James Barthmaier	1.00
BC89	Brandon Boggs	1.00
BC90	Raul Valdez	1.00
BC91	Jose Campusano	1.50
BC92	Henry Owens	1.00
BC93	Tug Hulett	1.00
BC94	Nate Gold	1.00
BC95	Lee Mitchell	1.00
BC96	John Hardy	.75
BC97	Aaron Wideman	.75
BC98	Brandon Roberts	1.50
BC99	Lou Santangelo	.50
BC100	Kyle Kendrick	2.50
BC101	Michael Collins	2.00
BC102	Camilo Vazquez	.75
BC103	Mark McLemore	.50
BC104	Alexander Peralta	.50
BC105	Josh Whitesell	1.00
BC106	Carlos Guevara	.50
BC107	Michael Aubrey	1.50
BC108	Brandon Chaves	1.00
BC109	Leonard Davis	1.00
BC110	Kendry Morales	1.50

Chrome Prospects Refractor
Refractor (1-110): 2-4X
Production 500 Sets

Chrome Prospects Blue Refractor
Blue Refractor (1-110): 4-6X
Production 150 Sets

Chrome Prospects Gold Refractor
Gold Refractor (1-110): 8-15X
Production 50 Sets

Chrome Prospects Orange Refractor
No Pricing
Production 25 Sets

Chrome Prospects Red Refractor
No Pricing
Production Five Sets

Chrome Prospects X-Fractor
X-Fractor (1-110): 3-6X
Production 250 Sets

Prospects

NM/M

	Common Player:	.25
B1	Alex Gordon	8.00
B2	Jonathan George	.25
B3	Scott Walter	.25
B4	Brian Holliday	.25
B5	Ben Copeland	.50
B6	Bobby Wilson	.50
B7	Mayker Sandoval	.50
B8	Alejandro de Aza	.75
B9	David Munoz	.25
B10	Josh LeBlanc	.50
B11	Philippe Valiquette	.50
B12	Edwin Bellorin	.50
B13	Jason Quarles	.50
B14	Mark Trumbo	.75
B15	Steve Kelly	.25
B16	Jamie Hoffman	.25
B17	Joseph Bauserman	.50
B18	Nick Adenhart	2.00
B19	Mike Butia	.25
B20	Jon Weber	.25
B21	Luis Valdez	.25
B22	Rafael Rodriguez	.75
B23	Wyatt Toregas	.75
B24	John Vanden Berg	.25
B25	Mike Connolly	.25
B26	Mike O'Connor	1.00
B27	Garrett Mock	.25
B28	Bill Layman	.25
B29	Luis Pena	.25
B30	Billy Killian	.50
B31	Ross Ohlendorf	.25
B32	Mark Kaiser	.25
B33	Ryan Costello	.25
B34	Dale Thayer	.25
B35	Steve Garrabrants	.25
B36	Samuel Deduno	.25
B37	Juan Portes	1.00
B38	Javier Martinez	.25
B39	Clint Sammons	.25
B40	Andrew Kown	.75
B41	Matt Tolbert	.25
B42	Michael Ekstrom	.25
B43	Shawn Norris	.25
B44	Diory Hernandez	.25
B45	Chris Maples	.25
B46	Aaron Hathaway	.25
B47	Steven Baker	.25
B48	Greg Creek	.25
B49	Collin Mahoney	.25
B50	Corey Ragsdale	.25
B51	Ariel Nunez	.25
B52	Max Ramirez	1.50
B53	Eric Rodland	.50
B54	Dante Brinkley	.50
B55	Casey Craig	.50
B56	Ryan Spilborghs	1.00
B57	Fredy Deza	.25
B58	Jeff Frazier	.25
B59	Vince Cordova	.25
B60	Oswaldo Navarro	.75
B61	Jarod Rine	.25
B62	Jordan Tata	.75
B63	Ben Julianel	.50
B64	Yung-Chi Chen	1.50
B65	Carlos Torres	.50
B66	Juan Francia	.50
B67	Brett Smith	.50
B68	Francisco Leandro	.50
B69	Chris Turner	1.00
B70	Matt Joyce	1.00
B71	Jason Jones	.25
B72	Jose Diaz	.25
B73	Kevin Ool	.25
B74	Nate Bumstead	.25
B75	Omir Santos	.25
B76	Shawn Riggans	.25
B77	Ofilio Castro	.25
B78	Mike Rozier	.75
B79	Wilkin Ramirez	.75
B80	Yobal Duenas	.25
B81	Adam Bourassa	.50
B82	Tony Granadillo	.25
B83	Brad McCann	1.50
B84	Dustin Majewski	.50
B85	Kelvin Jimenez	.25
B86	Mark Reed	1.00
B87	Asdrubal Cabrera	1.00
B88	James Barthmaier	.50
B89	Brandon Boggs	.50
B90	Raul Valdez	.25
B91	Jose Campusano	.50
B92	Henry Owens	.25
B93	Tug Hulett	.50
B94	Nate Gold	.25
B95	Lee Mitchell	.25
B96	John Hardy	.25
B97	Aaron Wideman	.25
B98	Brandon Roberts	.50
B99	Lou Santangelo	.25
B100	Kyle Kendrick	.75
B101	Michael Collins	.75
B102	Camilo Vazquez	.25
B103	Mark McLemore	.25
B104	Alexander Peralta	.25
B105	Josh Whitesell	.50
B106	Carlos Guevara	.25
B107	Michael Aubrey	.50
B108	Brandon Chaves	.25
B109	Leonard Davis	.25
B110	Kendry Morales	.75
B111	Koby Clemens	15.00
B112	Lance Broadway	15.00
B113	Cameron Maybin	75.00
B114	Mike Aviles	25.00
B115	Kyle Blanks	35.00
B116	Chris Dickerson	10.00
B117	Sean Gallagher	20.00
B118	Jamar Hill	10.00
B119	Garrett Mock	10.00
B120	Kendry Morales	15.00
B121	Russel Rohlicek	15.00
B122	Clete Thomas	15.00
B123	Josh Kinney	15.00
B124	Justin Huber	10.00

Prospects Blue
Blue: 2-3X
Blue Autos.: 1.5X
Production 500 Sets

Prospects Gold
Gold: 1-1.5X
Inserted 1:1

Prospects White
White: 4-6X
White Autos.: 1.5-2X
Production 120 Sets

Signs of the Future
NM/M

	Common Auto.:	10.00
BB	Brian Bogusevic	10.00
MB	Michael Bowden	20.00
RB	Ryan Braun	40.00
TB	Travis Buck	15.00
JC	Jeff Clement	20.00
BC	Ben Copeland	10.00
MC	Mike Costanzo	10.00
TC	Trevor Crowe	10.00
JD	John Drennen	10.00
JE	Jacoby Ellsbury	70.00
YE	Yunel Escobar	10.00
JM	John Mayberry Jr.	15.00
GO	Garrett Olson	15.00
CR	Cesar Ramos	.75
RR	Ricky Romero	10.00
HS	Henry Sanchez	10.00
DS	Denard Span	20.00
AT	Aaron Thompson	15.00
RT	Ryan Tucker	10.00
TT	Troy Tulowitzki	25.00
SW	Sean West	10.00

2006 Bowman Chrome

NM/M
Complete Set (224):
Common Player: .25
Common Rookie (201-220): .50
Pack (4): 9.00
Box (18): 150.00

1	Nick Swisher	.25
2	Ted Lilly	.25
3	John Smoltz	.50
4	Lyle Overbay	.25
5	Alfonso Soriano	.75
6	Javier Vazquez	.25
7	Ronnie Belliard	.25
8	Jose Reyes	.75
9	Brian Roberts	.50
10	Curt Schilling	.75
11	Adam Dunn	.75
12	Zack Greinke	.50
13	Carlos Guillen	.50
14	Jon Garland	.25
15	Robinson Cano	.50
16	Chris Burke	.25
17	Barry Zito	.25
18	Russ Adams	.25
19	Chris Capuano	.25
20	Scott Rolen	.75
21	Kerry Wood	.25
22	Scott Kazmir	.50
23	Brandon Webb	.75
24	Jeff Kent	.40
25	Albert Pujols	2.50
26	C.C. Sabathia	.50
27	Adrian Beltre	.25
28	Brad Wilkerson	.25
29	Randy Wolf	.25
30	Jason Bay	.50
31	Austin Kearns	.25
32	Clint Barmes	.25
33	Mike Sweeney	.25
34	Kevin Youkilis	.50
35	Justin Morneau	.50
36	Scott Podsednik	.25
37	Jason Giambi	.25
38	Steve Finley	.25
39	Morgan Ensberg	.25
40	Eric Chavez	.25
41	Roy Halladay	.25
42	Horacio Ramirez	.25
43	Ben Sheets	.40
44	Chris Carpenter	.50

45	Andruw Jones	.75
46	Carlos Zambrano	.50
47	Jonny Gomes	.40
48	Shawn Green	.40
49	Moises Alou	.40
50	Ichiro Suzuki	1.50
51	Juan Pierre	.25
52	Grady Sizemore	.75
53	Kazuo Matsui	.25
54	Jose Vidro	.25
55	Jake Peavy	.50
56	Dallas McPherson	.25
57	Ryan Howard	2.00
58	Zachary Duke	.25
59	Michael Young	.50
60	Todd Helton	.75
61	David DeJesus	.25
62	Ivan Rodriguez	.75
63	Johan Santana	.75
64	Danny Haren	.50
65	Derek Jeter	2.50
66	Greg Maddux	1.50
67	Jorge Cantu	.25
68	J.J. Hardy	.25
69	Victor Martinez	.50
70	David Wright	1.50
71	Ryan Church	.50
72	Khalil Greene	.25
73	Jimmy Rollins	.75
74	Hank Blalock	.40
75	Pedro Martinez	1.00
76	Chris Shelton	.25
77	Felipe Lopez	.25
78	Jeff Francis	.25
79	Andrew Sisco	.25
80	Hideki Matsui	1.50
81	Ken Griffey Jr.	1.50
82	Nomar Garciaparra	.50
83	Kevin Millwood	.25
84	Paul Konerko	.50
85	A.J. Burnett	.25
86	Mike Piazza	1.00
87	Brian Giles	.40
88	Johnny Damon	1.00
89	Jim Thome	.75
90	Roger Clemens	2.50
91	Aaron Rowand	.25
92	Rafael Furcal	.50
93	Gary Sheffield	.50
94	Mike Cameron	.25
95	Carlos Delgado	.50
96	Jorge Posada	.50
97	Denny Bautista	.25
98	Mike Maroth	.25
99	Brad Radke	.25
100	Alex Rodriguez	2.50
101	Freddy Garcia	.25
102	Oliver Perez	.25
103	Jon Lieber	.25
104	Melvin Mora	.25
105	Travis Hafner	.50
106	Alex Rios	.50
107	Derek Lowe	.25
108	Luis Castillo	.25
109	Livan Hernandez	.25
110	Tadahito Iguchi	.25
111	Shawn Chacon	.25
112	Frank Thomas	.75
113	Josh Beckett	.75
114	Aubrey Huff	.25
115	Derrek Lee	.75
116	Chien-Ming Wang	.75
117	Joe Crede	.50
118	Torii Hunter	.50
119	J.D. Drew	.50
120	Troy Glaus	.50
121	Sean Casey	.40
122	Edgar Renteria	.50
123	Craig Wilson	.25
124	Adam Eaton	.25
125	Jeff Francoeur	.75
126	Bruce Chen	.25
127	Cliff Floyd	.25
128	Jeremy Reed	.25
129	Jake Westbrook	.25
130	Wily Mo Pena	.25
131	Toby Hall	.25
132	David Ortiz	1.00
133	David Eckstein	.25
134	Brady Clark	.25
135	Marcus Giles	.25
136	Aaron Hill	.25
137	Mark Kotsay	.25
138	Carlos Lee	.50
139	Roy Oswalt	.50
140	Chone Figgins	.50
141	Mike Mussina	.75
142	Orlando Hernandez	.25
143	Magglio Ordonez	.50
144	Jim Edmonds	.50
145	Bobby Abreu	.50
146	Nick Johnson	.25
147	Carlos Beltran	.75
148	Jhonny Peralta	.25
149	Pedro Feliz	.25
150	Miguel Tejada	.75
151	Luis Gonzalez	.40
152	Carl Crawford	.50
153	Yadier Molina	.25
154	Rich Harden	.50
155	Tim Wakefield	.25
156	Rickie Weeks	.50
157	Johnny Estrada	.25
158	Gustavo Chacin	.25
159	Dan Johnson	.25
160	Willy Taveras	.25
161	Garret Anderson	.40
162	Randy Johnson	1.00
163	Jermaine Dye	.50
164	Joe Mauer	.75
165	Ervin Santana	.50
166	Jeremy Bonderman	.50
167	Garrett Atkins	.50
168	Manny Ramirez	1.00
169	Brad Eldred	.25
170	Chase Utley	.75
171	Mark Loretta	.25
172	John Patterson	.25
173	Tom Glavine	.50
174	Dontrelle Willis	.50
175	Mark Teixeira	.50
176	Felix Hernandez	.50
177	Cliff Lee	.25
178	Jason Schmidt	.40
179	Chad Tracy	.25
180	Rocco Baldelli	.25
181	Aramis Ramirez	.50
182	Andy Pettitte	.50
183	Mark Mulder	.25
184	Geoff Jenkins	.25
185	Chipper Jones	.75
186	Vernon Wells	.50
187	Bobby Crosby	.25
188	Lance Berkman	.50
189	Vladimir Guerrero	.75
190	Coco Crisp	.25
191	Brad Penny	.25
192	Jose Guillen	.25
193	Brett Myers	.25
194	Miguel Cabrera	.75
195	Bartolo Colon	.25
196	Craig Biggio	.40
197	Tim Hudson	.50
198	Mark Prior	.50
199	Mark Buehrle	.40
200	Barry Bonds	2.50
201	Anderson Hernandez **(RC)**	.50
202	Jose Capellan **(RC)**	.50
203	Jeremy Accardo **RC**	1.00
204	Hanley Ramirez **(RC)**	1.50
205	Matt Capps **(RC)**	.50
206	Jonathan Papelbon **(RC)**	4.00
207	Chuck James **(RC)**	.50
208	Matt Cain **(RC)**	1.00
209	Cole Hamels **(RC)**	1.00
210	Jason Botts **(RC)**	.50
211	Lastings Milledge **(RC)**	.50
212	Conor Jackson **(RC)**	.75
213	Yusmeiro Petit **(RC)**	.50
214	Alay Soler **RC**	.50
215	Willy Aybar **(RC)**	.50
216	Adam Loewen **(RC)**	.50
217	Justin Verlander **(RC)**	1.00
218	Francisco Liriano **(RC)**	3.00
219	Kenji Johjima **RC**	3.00
219	Kenji Johjima/Auto. **RC**	75.00
220	Craig Hansen **RC**	2.00
221	Prince Fielder/Auto. **(RC)**	65.00
222	Josh Barfield/Auto. **(RC)**	10.00
223	Fausto Carmona/ Auto. **(RC)**	30.00
224	James Loney/Auto. **(RC)**	50.00

Refractor

Refractor (1-200): 2-4X
Refractor (201-220): 2-3X
Inserted 1:4
Autograph (219, 221-224): 1-1.5X
Production 500

Blue Refractor

Blue Refractor (1-200): 3-6X
Blue Refractor (201-220): 4-6X
Production 150
Blue Ref. Auto. (219, 221-224): 1-2.5X
Production 150

Gold Refractor

Gold Refractor (1-200): 8-15X
Gold Refractor (201-220): 8-15X
Production 50
Gold Ref Auto. (219, 221-224): 3-5X
Production 50

Orange Refractor

Orange Refractor (1-200): 15-25X
Orange Refractor (201-220): 15-25X
Production 25
Orange Ref Auto. (221-224): No Pricing
Production 25

Red Refractor

No Pricing
Production Five Sets

Super Fractor

No Pricing
Production One Set

X-Fractor

X-Refractor (1-200): 3-5X
X-Refractor (201-220): 3-5X
Production 250
X-Fractor Auto. (219, 221-224): 1-2X
Production 225

Printing Plates

No Pricing
Production One Set

Bowman Chrome Prospects

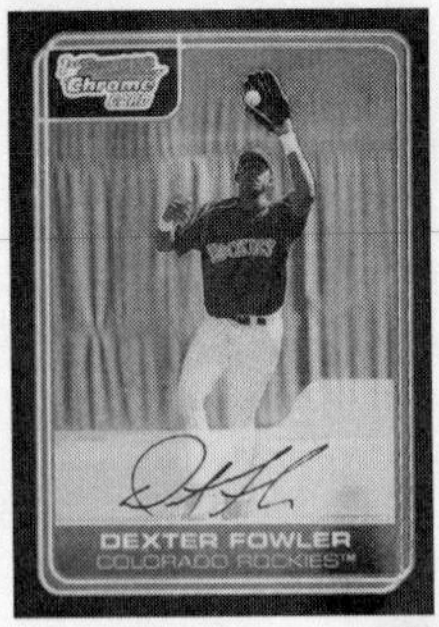
DEXTER FOWLER
COLORADO ROCKIES

		NM/M
Common Prospect:		.50
BC111	Koby Clemens	2.00
BC112	Lance Broadway	1.50
BC113	Cameron Maybin	10.00
BC114	Mike Aviles	2.50
BC115	Kyle Blanks	3.00
BC116	Chris Dickerson	1.00
BC117	Sean Gallagher	3.00
BC118	Jamar Hill	.50
BC119	Garrett Mock	.75
BC120	Russel Rohlicek	.50
BC121	Clete Thomas	1.00
BC122	Elvis Andrus	5.00
BC123	Brandon Moss	.75
BC124	Mark Holliman	1.50
BC125	Jose Tabata	8.00
BC126	Corey Wimberly	2.00
BC127	Bobby Wilson	1.00
BC128	Edward Mujica	1.50
BC129	Hunter Pence	8.00
BC130	Adam Heether	.50
BC131	Andy Wilson	.50
BC132	Radhames Liz	3.00
BC133	Garrett Patterson	.50
BC134	Carlos Gomez	10.00
BC135	Jared Lansford	1.00
BC136	Jose Arredondo	2.00
BC137	Renee Cortez	1.00
BC138	Francisco Rosario	.50
BC139	Brian Stokes	.50
BC140	Will Thompson	.50
BC141	Ernesto Frieri	1.00
BC142	Jose Mijares	1.00
BC143	Jeremy Slayden	2.00
BC144	Brandon Fahey	1.00
BC145	Jason Windsor	1.50
BC146	Shawn Nottingham	1.00
BC147	Dallas Trahern	1.00
BC148	Jon Niese	3.00
BC149	A.J. Shappi	.50
BC150	Jordan Pals	.50
BC151	Tim Moss	.50
BC152	Stephen Marek	1.00
BC153	Mat Gamel	8.00
BC154	Sean Henn	.50
BC155	Matt Guillory	.50
BC156	Brandon Jones	4.00
BC157	Gary Galvez	1.00
BC158	Shane Lindsay	1.50
BC159	Jesus Reina	.50
BC160	Lorenzo Cain	4.00
BC161	Chris Britton	1.00
BC162	Yovani Gallardo	4.00
BC163	Matt Walker	1.00
BC164	Shaun Cumberland	1.00
BC165	Ryan Patterson	2.00
BC166	Michael Hollimon	2.00
BC167	Eude Brito	.50
BC168	John Bowker	1.50
BC169	James Avery	.50
BC170	John Bannister	.50
BC171	Juan Ciriaco	.50
BC172	Manuel Corpas	1.00
BC173	Leo Rosales	.50
BC174	Tim Kennelly	.50
BC175	Adam Russell	.50
BC176	Jeremy Hellickson	5.00
BC177	Ryan Klosterman	.50
BC178	Evan Meek	1.00
BC179	Steve Murphy	2.00
BC180	Scott Feldman	.50
BC181	Pablo Sandoval	1.50
BC182	Dexter Fowler	2.00
BC183	Jairo Cuevas	1.50
BC184	Andrew Pinckney	1.00
BC185	Marino Salas	.50
BC186	Justin Christian	.50
BC187	Ching-Lung Lo	3.00
BC188	Randy Roth	2.00
BC189	Andrew Sonnanstine	3.00
BC190	Josh Outman	3.00
BC191	Yuber A. Rodriguez	1.00
BC192	Hainley Statia	2.00
BC193	Kevin Estrada	1.50
BC194	Jeff Karstens	1.50
BC195	Corey Coles	.50
BC196	Gustavo Espinoza	1.00
BC197	Brian Horwitz	.50
BC198	Landon Jacobsen	.50
BC199	Ben Krosschell	1.00
BC200	Jason Jaramillo	1.00
BC201	Josh Wilson	.50
BC202	Jason Ray	.50
BC203	Brent Dlugach	1.00
BC204	Cesar Jimenez	1.00
BC205	Eric Haberer	.50
BC206	Felipe Paulino	.50
BC207	Alcides Escobar	4.00
BC208	Jose Ascanio	1.00
BC209	Yoel Hernandez	1.00
BC210	Geoff Vandel	1.00
BC211	Travis Denker	1.50
BC212	Ramon Alvarado	1.00
BC213	Welinson Baez	1.50
BC214	Chris Kolkhorst	.50
BC215	Emiliano Fruto	1.00
BC216	Luis Cota	1.00
BC217	Mark Worrell	.50
BC218	Cla Meredith	1.50
BC219	Emmanuel Garcia	1.50
BC220	B.J. Szymanski	1.00
BC221	Alex Gordon/Auto.	125.00
BC222	Mark Pawelek/Auto.	25.00
BC223	Justin Upton/Auto.	140.00
BC224	Sean West/Auto.	15.00
BC225	Tyler Greene/Auto.	15.00
BC226	Josh Kinney/Auto.	15.00
BC227	Pedro Lopez/Auto.	10.00
BC228	Troy Patton/Auto.	20.00
BC229	Chris Iannetta/Auto.	20.00
BC230	Jared Wells/Auto.	10.00
BC231	Brandon Wood/Auto.	20.00
BC232	Josh Geer/Auto.	15.00
BC233	Cesar Carrillo/Auto.	10.00
BC234	Franklin Gutierrez/Auto.	15.00
BC235	Matt Garza/Auto.	20.00
BC236	Eli Iorg/Auto.	15.00
BC237	Trevor Bell/Auto.	10.00
BC238	Jeff Lyman/Auto.	15.00
BC239	Jon Lester/Auto.	40.00
BC240	Kendry Morales/Auto.	15.00
BC241	J. Brent Cox/Auto.	15.00
BC242	Jose Bautista/Auto.	15.00
BC243	Josh Sullivan/Auto.	15.00
BC244	Brandon Snyder/Auto.	15.00
BC245	Elvin Puello/Auto.	10.00
BC246	Henry Sanchez/Auto.	15.00
BC247	Jacob Marceaux/Auto.	10.00

Prospects Refractors

Refractor (111-220): 2-4X
Refractor Auto. (221-247): 1-1.5X
Production 500 Sets

Prospects Blue Refractors

NM/M

Blue Refractor (111-220): 4-6X
Blue Refractor Auto. (221-247): 1-2.5X
Production 150 Sets

Prospects Gold Refractors

Gold Refractor (111-220): 8-15X
Gold Refractor Auto. (221-247): 3-5X
Production 50 Sets

Prospects Orange Refractors

Orange Refractor (111-220): 15-25X
Orange Refractor Auto. (221-247): 4-6X
Production 25 Sets

Prospects Red Refractors

No Pricing
Production Five Sets

Prospects Super Fractors

No Pricing
Production One Set

Prospects X-Fractors

X-Refractor (111-220): 3-5X
Production 250
X-Refractor Auto. (221-247): 1-2X
Production 225

2006 Bowman Chrome Draft

		NM/M
Complete Set (55):		25.00
Common Player:		.50
1	Matt Kemp **(RC)**	1.50
2	Taylor Tankersley **(RC)**	.50
3	Michael Napoli **RC**	1.50
4	Brian Bannister **(RC)**	.50
5	Melky Cabrera **(RC)**	.50
6	Bill Bray **(RC)**	.50
7	Brian Anderson **(RC)**	.50
8	Jered Weaver **(RC)**	2.00
9	Chris Duncan **(RC)**	.50
10	Boof Bonser **(RC)**	1.00
11	Mike Rouse **(RC)**	.50
12	David Pauley **(RC)**	.50
13	Russell Martin **(RC)**	1.50
14	Jeremy Sowers **(RC)**	.50
15	Kevin Reese **(RC)**	.50
16	John Rheinecker **(RC)**	.50
17	Tommy Murphy **(RC)**	.50
18	Sean Marshall **(RC)**	.50
19	Jason Kubel **(RC)**	.50
20	Chad Billingsley **(RC)**	1.50
21	Kendry Morales **(RC)**	1.00
22	Jon Lester **(RC)**	3.00
23	Brandon Fahey **RC**	.50
24	Josh Johnson **(RC)**	.50
25	Kevin Frandsen **(RC)**	.50
26	Casey Janssen **RC**	.50

27	Scott Thorman (RC)	1.00
28	Scott Mathieson (RC)	.50
29	Jeremy Hermida (RC)	.50
30	Dustin Nippert (RC)	.50
31	Kevin Thompson (RC)	.50
32	Bobby Livingston (RC)	.50
33	Travis Ishikawa (RC)	.50
34	Jeff Mathis (RC)	.50
35	Charlie Haeger RC	1.00
36	Josh Willingham (RC)	.50
37	Taylor Buchholz (RC)	.50
38	Joel Guzman (RC)	.50
39	Zach Jackson (RC)	.50
40	Howie Kendrick (RC)	1.00
41	T.J. Beam (RC)	1.00
42	Ty Taubenheim RC	1.00
43	Erick Aybar (RC)	.50
44	Anibal Sanchez (RC)	1.00
45	Mike Pelfrey RC	5.00
46	Shawn Hill (RC)	.50
47	Chris Roberson (RC)	.50
48	Carlos Villanueva RC	.50
49	Andre Ethier (RC)	1.50
50	Anthony Reyes (RC)	1.00
51	Franklin Gutierrez (RC)	.50
52	Angel Guzman (RC)	.50
53	Michael O'Connor RC	.50
54	James Shields RC	3.00
55	Nate McLouth (RC)	.50

Refractor
Refractor (1-55): 2-4X

Gold Refractor
Gold Refractor (1-55): 8-15X
Production 50 Sets

Orange Refractor
Orange Refractor (1-55): 15-25X
Production 25 Sets

Red Refractor
No Pricing
Production Five Sets

X-Fractor
X-Fractor (1-55): 3-6X
Production 299 Sets

SuperFractor
No Pricing
Production One Set

Draft Picks
NM/M

Complete Set (90):
Common Draft Pick (1-65): 1.00
Common (66-90): 20.00

1	Tyler Colvin	3.00
2	Chris Marrero	5.00
3	Hank Conger	3.00
4	Chris Parmelee	5.00
5	Jason Place	5.00
6	Billy Rowell	6.00
7	Travis Snider	10.00
8	Colton Willems	3.00
9	Chase Fontaine	2.00
10	Jon Jay	2.00
11	Wade Leblanc	1.50
12	Justin Masterson	8.00
13	Gary Daley	1.50
14	Justin Edwards	1.00
15	Charlie Yarbrough	1.50
16	Cyle Hankerd	4.00
17	Zach McAllister	2.00
18	Tyler Robertson	1.00
19	Joe Smith	1.00
20	Nate Culp	1.00
21	John Holdzkom	1.00
22	Patrick Bresnehan	1.00
23	Chad Lee	1.00
24	Ryan Morris	1.00
25	D'Arby Myers	1.50
26	Garrett Olson	2.00
27	Jon Still	1.50
28	Brandon Rice	1.00
29	Chris Davis	8.00
30	Zack Daeges	1.50
31	Bobby Henson	1.50
32	George Kontos	1.50
33	Jermaine Mitchell	1.50
34	Adam Coe	1.50
35	Dustin Richardson	1.50
36	Allen Craig	2.00
37	Austin McClune	1.50
38	Doug Fister	1.00
39	Corey Madden	1.00
40	Justin Jacobs	1.50
41	Jim Negrych	1.00
42	Tyler Norrick	1.50
43	Adam Davis	1.00
44	Brett Logan	1.00
45	Brian Omogrosso	1.00
46	Kyle Drabek	4.00
47	Jamie Ortiz	2.00
48	Alex Presley	1.00
49	Terrance Warren	1.50
50	David Christensen	2.00
51	Helder Velazquez	2.00
52	Matt McBride	1.50
53	Quintin Berry	2.00
54	Michael Eisenberg	1.00
55	Dan Garcia	1.00
56	Scott Cousins	1.00
57	Sean Land	1.00
58	Kristopher Medlen	1.50
59	Tyler Reves	1.00
60	John Shelby	1.50
61	Jordan Newton	1.50
62	Ricky Orta	1.00
63	Jason Donald	1.50
64	David Huff	1.50
65	Brett Sinkbeil	1.00
66	Evan Longoria/Auto.	180.00
67	Cody Johnson/Auto.	40.00
68	Kris Johnson/Auto.	20.00
69	Kasey Kiker/Auto.	20.00
70	Ronny Bourquin/Auto.	10.00
71	Adrian Cardenas/Auto.	40.00
72	Matt Antonelli/Auto.	40.00
73	Brooks Brown/Auto.	15.00
74	Steven Evarts/Auto.	20.00
75	Joshua Butler/Auto.	15.00
76	Chad Huffman/Auto.	20.00
77	Steven Wright/Auto.	10.00
78	Cory Rasmus/Auto.	20.00
79	Brad Furnish/Auto.	10.00
80	Andrew Carpenter/Auto.	20.00
81	Dustin Evans/Auto.	10.00
82	Tommy Hickman/Auto.	20.00
83	Matt Long/Auto.	15.00
84	Clayton Kershaw/Auto.	100.00
85	Kyle McCulloch/Auto.	15.00
86	Pedro Beato/Auto.	20.00
87	Kyler Burke/Auto.	20.00
88	Stephen Englund/Auto.	15.00
89	Michael Felix/Auto.	15.00
90	Sean Watson/Auto.	15.00

Draft Picks Refractor

EVAN LONGORIA
TAMPA BAY DEVIL RAYS*

Refractor (1-65): 2-4X
Refractor Auto. (66-90): 1-1.5X
Production 500 for #'s 66-90

Draft Picks Blue Refractor
Blue Refractor (1-65): 4-8X
Production 199 Sets
Blue Auto. (66-90): 1-2.5X
Production 150 Sets

Draft Picks Gold Refractor
Gold Refractor (1-65): 8-15X
Production 50 Sets
Gold Auto. (66-90): 3-5X
Production 50 Sets

Draft Picks Orange Refractor
Orange Refractor (1-65): 15-25X
Production 25 Sets
Orange Auto. (66-90): No Pricing
Production 25 Sets

Draft Picks Red Refractor
No Pricing
Production Five Sets

Draft Picks SuperFractor
No Pricing
Production One Set

Draft Picks X-Fractor
X-Fractor (1-65): 3-6X
Production 299 Sets
X-Fractor Auto. (66-90): 1-2X
Production 225 Sets

Future's Game Prospects
NM/M

Complete Set (45): 20.00
Common Player: .50

1	Nick Adenhart	1.00
2	Joel Guzman	.50
3	Ryan Braun	.50
4	Carlos Carrasco	.50
5	Neil Walker	.50
6	Pablo Sandoval	.50
7	Gio Gonzalez	.50
8	Joey Votto	.50
9	Luis Cruz	.50
10	Nolan Reimold	.50
11	Juan Salas	.50
12	Josh Fields	1.00
13	Yovani Gallardo	1.00
14	Radhames Liz	.50
15	Eric Patterson	.50
16	Cameron Maybin	2.50
17	Edgar Martinez	.50
18	Hunter Pence	1.50
19	Phillip Hughes	2.00
20	Trent Oeltjen	.50
21	Nick Pereira	.50
22	Wladimir Balentien	.50
23	Stephen Drew	1.50
24	Davis Romero	.50
25	Joe Koshansky	.50
26	Chin-Lung Hu	2.00
27	Jason Hirsh	.50
28	Jose Tabata	2.00
29	Eric Hurley	.50
30	Yung-Chi Chen	2.50
31	Howie Kendrick	1.00
32	Humberto Sanchez	1.00
33	Alex Gordon	4.00
34	Yunel Escobar	.50
35	Travis Buck	.50
36	Billy Butler	1.00
37	Homer Bailey	1.00
38	George Kottaras	.50
39	Kurt Suzuki	.50
40	Joaquin Arias	.50
41	Matt Lindstrom	.50
42	Sean Smith	.50
43	Carlos Gonzalez	.50
44	Jaime Garcia	2.00
45	Jose Garcia	1.00

Future's Game Refractor
Refractor (1-45): 2-4X

Future's Game Blue Refractor
Blue (1-45): 4-8X
Production 199 Sets

Future's Game Gold Refractor
Gold (1-45): 8-15X
Production 50 Sets

Future's Game Orange Refractor
Orange (1-45): 15-30X
Production 25 Sets

Future's Game Red Refractor
No Pricing
Production Five Sets

Future's Game X-Fractor
X-Fractor (1-45): 3-6X
Production 299 Sets

Head of the Class Dual Auto.
NM/M

Production 174
Refractor: 1-1.5X
Production 50
Gold Refractor: No Pricing
Production 25
RU Alex Rodriguez,
Justin Upton 150.00

2006 Bowman Draft
NM/M

Complete Set (55): 10.00
Common Player: .25
Pack (5 + 2 Chrome): 5.00
Box (24): 100.00

1	Matthew Kemp (RC)	.50
2	Taylor Tankersley (RC)	.25
3	Michael Napoli RC	.50
4	Brian Bannister (RC)	.50
5	Melky Cabrera (RC)	.50
6	Bill Bray (RC)	.25
7	Brian Anderson (RC)	.25
8	Jered Weaver (RC)	.75
9	Chris Duncan (RC)	.25
10	Boof Bonser (RC)	.50
11	Mike Rouse (RC)	.25
12	David Pauley (RC)	.25
13	Russell Martin (RC)	.25
14	Jeremy Sowers (RC)	.25
15	Kevin Reese (RC)	.25
16	John Rheinecker (RC)	.25
17	Tommy Murphy (RC)	.25
18	Sean Marshall (RC)	.25
19	Jason Kubel (RC)	.25
20	Chad Billingsley (RC)	.75
21	Kendry Morales (RC)	.50
22	Jon Lester (RC)	1.00
23	Brandon Fahey RC	.25
24	Josh Johnson (RC)	.25
25	Kevin Frandsen (RC)	.25
26	Casey Janssen RC	.25
27	Scott Thorman (RC)	.25
28	Scott Mathieson (RC)	.25
29	Jeremy Hermida (RC)	.25
30	Dustin Nippert (RC)	.25
31	Kevin Thompson (RC)	.25
32	Bobby Livingston (RC)	.25
33	Travis Ishikawa (RC)	.25
34	Jeff Mathis (RC)	.25
35	Charlie Haeger RC	.50
36	Josh Willingham (RC)	.25
37	Taylor Buchholz (RC)	.25
38	Joel Guzman (RC)	.25
39	Zach Jackson (RC)	.50
40	Howie Kendrick (RC)	.50
41	T.J. Beam (RC)	.25
42	Ty Taubenheim RC	.25
43	Erick Aybar (RC)	.25
44	Anibal Sanchez (RC)	.25
45	Mike Pelfrey RC	2.00
46	Shawn Hill (RC)	.25
47	Chris Roberson (RC)	.25
48	Carlos Villanueva RC	.25
49	Andre Ethier (RC)	.50
50	Anthony Reyes (RC)	.25
51	Franklin Gutierrez (RC)	.25
52	Angel Guzman (RC)	.25
53	Michael O'Connor RC	.25
54	James Shields RC	.50
55	Nate McLouth (RC)	.25

Gold
Gold (1-55): 1-2X
Inserted 1:1

Red
No Pricing
Production One Set

White
White (1-55): 2-5X
Production 225 Sets

Printing Plates
No Pricing
Production one set per color.

Draft Picks
NM/M

Complete Set (65): 20.00
Common Draft Pick (1-65): .50

1	Tyler Colvin	1.00
2	Chris Marrero	1.50
3	Hank Conger	1.00
4	Chris Parmelee	1.00
5	Jason Place	1.00
6	Billy Rowell	1.00
7	Travis Snider	3.00
8	Colton Willems	.75
9	Chase Fontaine	.50
10	Jon Jay	.50
11	Wade Leblanc	1.00
12	Justin Masterson	2.50
13	Gary Daley	.50
14	Justin Edwards	.50
15	Charlie Yarbrough	.50
16	Cyle Hankerd	1.00
17	Zach McAllister	.50
18	Tyler Robertson	.50
19	Joe Smith	.50
20	Nate Culp	.50
21	John Holdzkom	.50
22	Patrick Bresnehan	.50
23	Chad Lee	.50
24	Ryan Morris	.50
25	D'Arby Myers	.75
26	Garrett Olson	.75
27	Jon Still	.50
28	Brandon Rice	.50
29	Chris Davis	2.50
30	Zack Daeges	.50
31	Bobby Henson	.50
32	George Kontos	.50
33	Jermaine Mitchell	.75
34	Adam Coe	.50
35	Dustin Richardson	.50
36	Allen Craig	.50
37	Austin McClune	.50
38	Doug Fister	.50
39	Corey Madden	.50
40	Justin Jacobs	.50
41	Jim Negrych	.50
42	Tyler Norrick	.50
43	Adam Davis	.50
44	Brett Logan	.50
45	Brian Omogrosso	.50
46	Kyle Drabek	1.00
47	Jamie Ortiz	.50
48	Alex Presley	.50
49	Terrance Warren	.50
50	David Christensen	.50
51	Helder Velazquez	.50
52	Matt McBride	.50
53	Quintin Berry	.50
54	Michael Eisenberg	.50
55	Dan Garcia	.50
56	Scott Cousins	.50
57	Sean Land	.50
58	Kristopher Medlen	.50
59	Tyler Reves	.50
60	John Shelby	.50
61	Jordan Newton	.50
62	Ricky Orta	.50
63	Jason Donald	.50
64	David Huff	.50
65	Brett Sinkbeil	.50

Future's Game Prospects
NM/M

Complete Set (45): 10.00
Common player: .25

1	Nick Adenhart	.50
2	Joel Guzman	.25
3	Ryan Braun	.25
4	Carlos Carrasco	.25
5	Neil Walker	.25
6	Pablo Sandoval	.25
7	Gio Gonzalez	.25
8	Joey Votto	.25
9	Luis Cruz	.25
10	Nolan Reimold	.25
11	Juan Salas	.25
12	Josh Fields	.50
13	Yovani Gallardo	.50
14	Radhames Liz	.25
15	Eric Patterson	.25
16	Cameron Maybin	1.00
17	Edgar Martinez	.25
18	Hunter Pence	.75
19	Phillip Hughes	.75

20	Trent Oeltjen	.25
21	Nick Pereira	.25
22	Wladimir Balentien	.25
23	Stephen Drew	.50
24	Davis Romero	.25
25	Joe Koshansky	.25
26	Chin-Lung Hu	.50
27	Jason Hirsh	.25
28	Jose Tabata	.75
29	Eric Hurley	.25
30	Yung-Chi Chen	.75
31	Howie Kendrick	.50
32	Humberto Sanchez	.50
33	Alex Gordon	1.50
34	Yunel Escobar	.25
35	Travis Buck	.25
36	Billy Butler	.50
37	Homer Bailey	.50
38	George Kottaras	.25
39	Kurt Suzuki	.25
40	Joaquin Arias	.25
41	Matt Lindstrom	.25
42	Sean Smith	.25
43	Carlos Gonzalez	.25
44	Jaime Garcia	.50
45	Jose Garcia	.50

Future's Game Prospects Relics

		NM/M
Common Player:		4.00
1	Nick Adenhart	8.00
2	Joel Guzman	4.00
3	Ryan Braun	15.00
4	Carlos Carrasco	4.00
5	Neil Walker	4.00
6	Pablo Sandoval	4.00
7	Gio Gonzalez	4.00
8	Joey Votto	8.00
9	Luis Cruz	4.00
10	Nolan Reimold	4.00
11	Juan Salas	4.00
12	Josh Fields	6.00
13	Yovani Gallardo	8.00
14	Radhames Liz	4.00
15	Eric Patterson	6.00
16	Cameron Maybin	10.00
17	Edgar Martinez	4.00
18	Hunter Pence	10.00
19	Phillip Hughes	10.00
20	Trent Oeltjen	4.00
21	Nick Pereira	4.00
22	Wladimir Balentien	5.00
23	Stephen Drew	8.00
24	Davis Romero	4.00
25	Joe Koshansky	4.00
26	Chin-Lung Hu	15.00
27	Jason Hirsh	4.00
28	Jose Tabata	8.00
29	Eric Hurley	4.00
30	Yung-Chi Chen	50.00
31	Howie Kendrick	8.00
32	Humberto Sanchez	6.00
33	Alex Gordon	15.00
34	Yunel Escobar	8.00
35	Travis Buck	6.00
36	Billy Butler	8.00
37	Homer Bailey	8.00
38	George Kottaras	4.00
39	Kurt Suzuki	4.00
40	Joaquin Arias	4.00
41	Matt Lindstrom	4.00
42	Sean Smith	4.00
43	Carlos Gonzalez	4.00
44	Jaime Garcia	6.00
45	Jose Garcia	4.00

Signs of the Future

		NM/M
Common Autograph:		6.00
BS	Brandon Snyder	8.00
KC	Koby Clemens	15.00
AG	Alex Gordon	50.00
CI	Chris Iannetta	15.00
MO	Micah Owings	20.00
JC	Jeff Clement	20.00
CR	Clayton Richard	8.00
TB	Travis Buck	15.00
BJ	Beau Jones	15.00
DJ	Daryl Jones	8.00
CDR	Chaz Roe	8.00
JM	Jacob Marceaux	8.00
CTI	Craig Italiano	10.00
JB	Jay Bruce	40.00
WT	Wade Townsend	8.00
MM	Mark McCormick	8.00
HS	Henry Sanchez	6.00
MC	Mike Costanzo	8.00
CRA	Cesar Ramos	8.00

2006 Bowman Heritage

		NM/M
Complete Set (300):		
Common Player (1-200):		.15
Common SP (even #'s 202-300):		3.00
Inserted 1:3		
Pack (8):		3.00
Box (24):		60.00
1	David Wright	1.00
2	Andruw Jones	.25
3	Ryan Howard	1.50
4	Jason Bay	.40
5	Paul Konerko	.40
6	Jake Peavy	.25
7	Todd Jones	.15
8	Troy Glaus	.25
9	Rocco Baldelli	.15
10	Rafael Furcal	.25
11	Freddy Sanchez	.15
12	Jermaine Dye	.25
13	A.J. Burnett	.15
14	Michael Cuddyer	.15
15	Barry Zito	.25
16	Chipper Jones	.75
17	Paul LoDuca	.15
18	Mark Mulder	.15
19	Raul Ibanez	.15
20	Carlos Delgado	.40
21	Marcus Giles	.15
22	Danny Haren	.25
23	Justin Morneau	.40
24	Livan Hernandez	.15
25	Ken Griffey Jr.	1.50
26	Aaron Hill	.15
27	Tadahito Iguchi	.15
28	Nate Robertson	.15
29	Kevin Millwood	.15
30	Jim Thome	.50
31	Aubrey Huff	.15
32	Dontrelle Willis	.25
33	Khalil Greene	.25
34	Doug Davis	.15
35	Ivan Rodriguez	.50
36	Rickie Weeks	.25
37	Jhonny Peralta	.25
38	Yadier Molina	.15
39	Eric Chavez	.25
40	Alfonso Soriano	.75
41	Pat Burrell	.25
42	B.J. Ryan	.15
43	Carl Crawford	.25
44	Preston Wilson	.15
45	Jorge Posada	.40
46	Carlos Zambrano	.25
47	Mark Teahen	.15
48	Nick Johnson	.15
49	Mark Kotsay	.15
50	Derek Jeter	2.00
51	Moises Alou	.25
52	Ryan Freel	.15
53	Shannon Stewart	.15
54	Casey Blake	.15
55	Edgar Renteria	.25
56	Frank Thomas	.50
57	Ty Wigginton	.15
58	Jeff Kent	.25
59	Chien-Ming Wang	.50
60	Josh Beckett	.50
61	Chase Utley	.75
62	Gary Matthews	.15
63	Torii Hunter	.25
64	Bobby Jenks	.15
65	Wilson Betemit	.15
66	Jeremy Bonderman	.25
67	Scott Rolen	.75
68	Brad Penny	.15
69	Jacque Jones	.15
70	Jose Reyes	.75
71	Brian Roberts	.25
72	John Smoltz	.25
73	Johnny Estrada	.15
74	Ronnie Belliard	.15
75	Vladimir Guerrero	.75
76	A.J. Pierzynski	.15
77	Garrett Atkins	.40
78	Adam LaRoche	.15
79	Mark Loretta	.15
80	Todd Helton	.50
81	Jose Vidro	.15
82	Carlos Guillen	.25
83	Michael Barrett	.15
84	Lyle Overbay	.15
85	Travis Hafner	.25
86	Shea Hillenbrand	.15
87	Julio Lugo	.15
88	Tim Hudson	.25
89	Scott Podsednik	.15
90	Roy Halladay	.25
91	Bartolo Colon	.15
92	Ryan Langerhans	.15
93	Tom Glavine	.40
94	Ken Rogers	.15
95	Robinson Cano	.50
96	Mark Prior	.25
97	Jason Schmidt	.25
98	Bengie Molina	.15
99	Jon Lieber	.15
100	Alex Rodriguez	2.00
101	Scott Kazmir	.25
102	Jeff Francoeur	.50
103	Chris Carpenter	.40
104	Juan Uribe	.15
105	Mariano Rivera	.40
106	Rich Harden	.25
107	Jack Wilson	.15
108	Austin Kearns	.15
109	Marcus Thames	.15
110	Miguel Tejada	.25
111	Chone Figgins	.25
112	Bronson Arroyo	.15
113	Chad Cordero	.15
114	Bill Hall	.15
115	Curt Schilling	.50
116	David Eckstein	.15
117	Ramon Hernandez	.15
118	Eric Byrnes	.25
119	Clint Barmes	.15
120	Bobby Abreu	.25
121	Joe Crede	.25
122	Derek Lowe	.15
123	Jason Marquis	.15
124	Erik Bedard	.25
125	Derrek Lee	.50
126	Brian McCann	.40
127	Magglio Ordonez	.25
128	Ben Sheets	.25
129	Brandon Inge	.15
130	Miguel Cabrera	.75
131	Jim Edmonds	.25
132	John Lackey	.40
133	Kevin Mench	.15
134	Adrian Beltre	.25
135	Curtis Granderson	.50
136	Shawn Green	.25
137	Jose Contreras	.15
138	Joe Nathan	.15
139	Bobby Crosby	.15
140	Johnny Damon	.50
141	Brad Hawpe	.15
142	Brandon Phillips	.40
143	Victor Martinez	.40
144	Jimmy Rollins	.75
145	Corey Patterson	.15
146	Grady Sizemore	.50
147	Placido Polanco	.15
148	Mike Lowell	.25
149	Francisco Rodriguez	.15
150	Ichiro Suzuki	1.50
151	Kris Benson	.15
152	Scott Hatteberg	.15
153	Akinori Otsuka	.15
154	Cesar Izturis	.15
155	Roger Clemens	2.00
156	Kerry Wood	.25
157	Tom Gordon	.15
158	Sean Casey	.15
159	Jose Lopez	.15
160	Orlando Hernandez	.15
161	Aramis Ramirez	.40
162	J.D. Drew	.25
163	David DeJesus	.15
164	Craig Biggio	.25
165	Brad Myers	.15
166	C.C. Sabathia	.40
167	Zachary Duke	.15
168	Luis Castillo	.15
169	Hideki Matsui	1.00
170	Brian Giles	.15
171	Coco Crisp	.15
172	Richie Sexson	.25
173	Nomar Garciaparra	.75
174	Roy Oswalt	.25
175	David Ortiz	.75
176	Matt Morris	.15
177	Felipe Lopez	.15
178	Garret Anderson	.15
179	Kevin Youkilis	.25
180	Alex Rios	.40
181	John Garland	.15
182	Luis Gonzalez	.15
183	Cliff Floyd	.15
184	Juan Encarnacion	.15
185	Nick Swisher	.25
186	Mike Cameron	.15
187	Jose Castillo	.15
188	Ray Durham	.15
189	Jorge Cantu	.15
190	Andy Pettitte	.25
191	Chad Tracy	.15
192	Adrian Gonzalez	.40
193	Jose Valentin	.15
194	Mark Buehrle	.25
195	Huston Street	.15
196	Chris Capuano	.15
197	Aaron Rowand	.15
198	Billy Wagner	.15
199	Orlando Cabrera	.25
200	Albert Pujols	2.00
201	Dan Uggla **(RC)**	1.00
202	Alay Soler **RC**	1.00
203	Matt Kemp **(RC)**	1.50
204	Michael Napoli **RC**	3.00
205	Joel Zumaya **(RC)**	1.00
206	Mike Pelfrey **RC**	5.00
207	Ian Kinsler **(RC)**	.50
208	Josh Willingham **(RC)**	3.00
209	Erick Aybar **(RC)**	.50
210	Willie Eyre **(RC)**	3.00
211	Kendry Morales **(RC)**	.50
212	Scott Thorman **(RC)**	3.00
213	Hanley Ramirez **(RC)**	1.00
214	Boof Bonser **(RC)**	4.00
215	Anthony Reyes **(RC)**	.50
216	Justin Huber **(RC)**	3.00
217	Yusmeiro Petit **(RC)**	.50
218	Jason Bartlett **(RC)**	3.00
219	Shin-Soo Choo **(RC)**	1.00
220	Francisco Liriano **(RC)**	5.00
221	Craig Hansen **RC**	2.00
222	Ricky Nolasco **(RC)**	3.00
223	Adam Loewen **(RC)**	.50
224	Scott Olsen **(RC)**	3.00
225	Cole Hamels **(RC)**	1.50
226	Martin Prado **(RC)**	3.00
227	James Loney **(RC)**	1.00
228	Kevin Thompson **(RC)**	3.00
229	Adam Jones **(RC)**	1.00
230	Josh Johnson **(RC)**	3.00
231	Anderson Hernandez **(RC)**	.40
232	Tony Gwynn Jr. **(RC)**	3.00
233	Casey Janssen **RC**	.50
234	Taylor Tankersley **(RC)**	3.00
235	Mike Thompson **RC**	.50
236	Jeremy Sowers **(RC)**	3.00
237	Anibal Sanchez **(RC)**	.50
238	Adam Wainwright **(RC)**	4.00
239	Rich Hill **(RC)**	.50
240	Russell Martin **(RC)**	4.00
241	Joe Inglett **RC**	.50
242	Tony Pena **(RC)**	3.00
243	Joshua Sharpless **RC**	.50
244	Darrell Rasner **(RC)**	3.00
245	Joe Saunders **(RC)**	.50
246	Jon Lester **(RC)**	6.00
247	Jeremy Hermida **(RC)**	.50
248	Chad Billingsley **(RC)**	4.00
249	Bobby Livingston **(RC)**	.50
250	Justin Verlander **(RC)**	5.00
251	Mickey Mantle	10.00
252	Hank Blalock	3.00
253	Manny Ramirez	1.00
254	Mike Mussina	5.00
255	Greg Maddux	2.00
256	Jason Giambi	4.00
257	Mark Teixeira	.75
258	Carlos Beltran	4.00
259	Matt Holliday	1.00
260	Pedro Martinez	5.00
261	Joe Mauer	1.00
262	Melvin Mora	3.00
263	Mike Piazza	1.50
264	B.J. Upton	4.00
265	Vernon Wells	.75
266	Gary Sheffield	4.00
267	Randy Johnson	1.00
268	Ryan Zimmerman	4.00
269	Lance Berkman	.75
270	Johan Santana	5.00
271	Carlos Lee	.50
272	Brandon Webb	4.00
273	Adam Dunn	.75
274	Michael Young	3.00
275	Barry Bonds	2.00
276	Jonathan Papelbon **(RC)**	5.00
277	Howie Kendrick **(RC)**	1.00
278	Melky Cabrera **(RC)**	3.00
279	Jered Weaver **(RC)**	1.00
280	Josh Barfield **(RC)**	3.00
281	Chuck James **(RC)**	1.00
282	Lastings Milledge **(RC)**	5.00
283	Nicholas Markakis **(RC)**	1.00
284	Jose Capellan **(RC)**	3.00
285	Prince Fielder **(RC)**	3.00
286	Jason Botts **(RC)**	3.00
287	Eliezer Alfonzo **RC**	.50
288	Sean Marshall **(RC)**	3.00
289	Ryan Garko **(RC)**	.75
290	Stephen Drew **(RC)**	5.00
291	Joel Guzman **(RC)**	.50
292	Hong-Chih Kuo **(RC)**	3.00
293	Zach Miner **(RC)**	.50
294	Angel Guzman **(RC)**	3.00
295	Andre Ethier **(RC)**	1.00
296	Fausto Carmona **(RC)**	3.00
297	Ronny Paulino **(RC)**	.75
298	Matt Cain **(RC)**	5.00
299	Carlos Quentin **(RC)**	.75
300	Kenji Johjima **RC**	5.00

Foil

Foil (1-300): 1-2X
Foil (301-350): .5-1X
Inserted 1:1

Black

No Pricing
Production One Set

Printing Plates

No Pricing
Production One Set

Mini

Mini (1-300): 1-2X
Inserted 1:1

Draft Pick Variations

NM/M

One five card pack per box.

		NM/M
BHP76	Evan Longoria	8.00
BHP77	Adrian Cardenas	1.00
BHP78	Steven Wright	1.00
BHP79	Andrew Carpenter	2.00
BHP80	Dustin Evans	2.00
BHP81	Chad Tracy	1.00
BHP82	Matthew Sulentic	4.00
BHP83	Adam Ottavino	2.00
BHP84	Matt Long	1.00
BHP85	Clayton Kershaw	5.00
BHP86	Matt Antonelli	3.00
BHP87	Chris Parmelee	2.00
BHP88	Billy Rowell	3.00
BHP89	Chase Fontaine	1.00
BHP90	Chris Murrero	2.00
BHP91	Jamie Ortiz	2.00
BHP92	Sean Watson	1.00
BHP93	Brooks Brown	1.00
BHP94	Brad Furnish	2.00
BHP95	Chad Huffman	2.00
BHP96	Pedro Beato	1.00
BHP97	Kyler Burke	1.00
BHP98	Stephen Englund	1.00
BHP99	Tyler Norrick	1.00
BHP100	Brent Sinkbeil	1.00

Pieces of Greatness

PIECES OF GREATNESS
AUTHENTIC GAME-WORN JERSEY

		NM/M
Common Player:		5.00

Inserted 1:12

White:		1.5-3X

Production 49 Sets

Black: No Pricing
Production One Set

LB	Lance Berkman	6.00
CB	Craig Biggio	8.00
HB	Hank Blalock	5.00
BB	Barry Bonds	25.00
MB	Milton Bradley	5.00
RC	Robinson Cano	20.00
AD	Adam Dunn	5.00
JD	Jermaine Dye	5.00
DE	David Eckstein	15.00
EE	Edwin Encarnacion	5.00
ME	Morgan Ensberg	5.00
CF	Cliff Floyd	5.00
JF	Jeff Francoeur	10.00
RF	Rafael Furcal	5.00
VG	Vladimir Guerrero	10.00
THE	Todd Helton	8.00
RH	Ryan Howard	25.00
TH	Torii Hunter	5.00
AJ	Andruw Jones	8.00
AJ2	Andruw Jones	8.00
CJ	Chipper Jones	8.00
CJ2	Chipper Jones	8.00
NJ	Nick Johnson	5.00
JK	Jeff Kent	5.00
AL	Adam LaRoche	5.00
DL	Derrek Lee	5.00
JL	Javy Lopez	5.00
ML	Mike Lowell	5.00
GM	Greg Maddux	10.00
VM	Victor Martinez	5.00
XN	Xavier Nady	5.00
MO	Magglio Ordonez	5.00
DO	David Ortiz	15.00
AJP	A.J. Pierzynski	5.00
SP	Scott Podsednik	10.00
AP	Albert Pujols	25.00
AP2	Albert Pujols	25.00
ARA	Aramis Ramirez	5.00
MR	Manny Ramirez	8.00
BR	Brian Roberts	5.00
AR	Alex Rodriguez	20.00
CS	Curt Schilling	8.00
GS	Gary Sheffield	8.00
NS	Nick Swisher	8.00
JT	Jim Thome	8.00
CU	Chase Utley	8.00
BW	Brad Wilkerson	5.00
DW	Dontrelle Willis	5.00
MY	Michael Young	5.00
BZ	Barry Zito	5.00

Prospects

NM/M

Common Prospect: .50
Inserted 2:Pack
Black: No Pricing
Production One Set

BHP1	Justin Upton	6.00
BHP2	Koby Clemens	1.00
BHP3	Lance Broadway	1.00
BHP4	Cameron Maybin	3.00
BHP5	Garrett Mock	1.00
BHP6	Alex Gordon	6.00
BHP7	Ben Copeland	1.00
BHP8	Nick Adenhart	2.00
BHP9	Yung-Chi Chen	3.00
BHP10	Tim Moss	.50
BHP11	Francisco Leandro	.50
BHP12	Brad McCann	1.00
BHP13	Dallas Trahern	1.00
BHP14	Dustin Majewski	1.00
BHP15	James Barthmaier	1.00
BHP16	Nate Gold	1.00
BHP17	John Hardy	.50
BHP18	Mark McLemore	.50
BHP19	Michael Aubrey	1.00
BHP20	Mark Holliman	2.00
BHP21	Bobby Wilson	.50
BHP22	Radhames Liz	1.00
BHP23	Jose Tabata	2.00
BHP24	Jared Lansford	.50
BHP25	Brent Dlugach	1.00
BHP26	Steve Garrabrants	.50
BHP27	Eric Haberer	.50
BHP28	Chris Dickerson	.50
BHP29	Welinson Baez	.50
BHP30	Chris Kolkhorst	.50
BHP31	Brandon Moss	.50
BHP32	Corey Wimberly	.50
BHP33	Ryan Patterson	1.00
BHP34	Michael Hollimon	.50
BHP35	John Bannister	.50
BHP36	Pablo Sandoval	.50
BHP37	Dexter Fowler	.50
BHP38	Elvis Andrus	2.00
BHP39	Jason Windsor	1.00
BHP40	B.J. Szymanski	1.00
BHP41	Yovani Gallardo	2.00
BHP42	John Bowker	1.50
BHP43	Justin Christian	1.00
BHP44	Andrew Sonnanstine	2.00
BHP45	Jeremy Slayden	.50
BHP46	Brandon Jones	.50
BHP47	Travis Denker	1.00
BHP48	Emmanuel Garcia	1.00
BHP49	Landon Jacobsen	2.00
BHP50	Kevin Estrada	1.00
BHP51	Ross Ohlendorf	.50
BHP52	Wyatt Toregas	.50
BHP53	Andrew Kown	1.00
BHP54	Steve Kelly	.50
BHP55	Mike Butia	.50
BHP56	Mike Connolly	.50
BHP57	Brian Horwitz	.50
BHP58	Dale Thayer	.50
BHP59	Diory Hernandez	1.00
BHP60	Samuel Deduno	1.00
BHP61	Jamie Hoffman	1.00
BHP62	Matt Tolbert	1.00
BHP63	Michael Ekstrom	.50
BHP64	Chris Maples	1.00
BHP65	Adam Coe	1.00
BHP66	Max Ramirez	.50
BHP67	Evan MacLane	.50
BHP68	Jose Campusano	.50
BHP69	Lou Santangelo	1.00
BHP70	Shawn Riggans	1.00
BHP71	Kyle Kendrick	.75
BHP72	Oswaldo Navarro	.50
BHP73	Eric Rodland	1.00
BHP74	Omir Santos	1.00
BHP75	Kyle McCulloch	.50
BHP76	Evan Longoria	6.00
BHP77	Adrian Cardenas	1.00
BHP78	Steven Wright	.50
BHP79	Andrew Carpenter	1.00
BHP80	Dustin Evans	1.50
BHP81	Chad Tracy	.50
BHP82	Matthew Sulentic	3.00
BHP83	Adam Ottavino	1.50
BHP84	Matt Long	.50
BHP85	Clayton Kershaw	6.00
BHP86	Matt Antonelli	1.00
BHP87	Chris Parmelee	2.00
BHP88	Billy Rowell	1.00
BHP89	Chase Fontaine	1.00
BHP90	Chris Murrero	2.00
BHP91	Jamie Ortiz	1.00
BHP92	Sean Watson	1.00
BHP93	Brooks Brown	1.00
BHP94	Brad Furnish	1.00
BHP95	Chad Huffman	1.00
BHP96	Pedro Beato	1.50
BHP97	Kyler Burke	1.00
BHP98	Stephen Englund	1.00
BHP99	Tyler Norrick	.50
BHP100	Brent Sinkbeil	.50

Signs of Greatness

	NM/M
Common Autograph:	8.00

White: No Pricing
Production Five Sets
Black: No Pricing
Production One Set

BB	Brian Bogusevic	10.00
LB	Lance Broadway	15.00
KC	Koby Clemens	15.00
JCL	Jeff Clement	15.00
JC	Jesus Cota	8.00
TC	Trevor Crowe	15.00
JD	John Drennen	8.00
SG	Sean Gallagher	15.00
AG	Alex Gordon	50.00
JH	Justin Huber	8.00
CI	Craig Italiano	8.00
SL	Sam LeCure	8.00
MM	Matt Maloney	8.00
CM	Cameron Maybin	40.00
JS	Jarrod Saltalamacchia	15.00
BS	Brandon Snyder	10.00
ST	Steve Tolleson	8.00
WT	Wade Townsend	8.00
RT	Ryan Tucker	8.00
JU	Justin Upton	90.00
KW	Kevin Whelan	10.00
BW	Brandon Wood	15.00

2006 Bowman Originals

		NM/M
Complete Set (55):		50.00
Common Player (1-35):		1.00
Common Player (36-55):		2.00
Pack (7):		50.00
Box (6):		250.00
1	David Wright	3.00
2	Derek Jeter	5.00
3	Eric Chavez	1.00
4	Ken Griffey Jr.	4.00
5	Albert Pujols	5.00
6	Ryan Howard	5.00
7	Joe Mauer	1.50
8	Andruw Jones	1.50
9	Nomar Garciaparra	2.00
10	Michael Young	1.00
11	Miguel Tejada	1.50
12	Alfonso Soriano	2.00
13	Alex Rodriguez	5.00
14	Paul Konerko	1.50
15	Carl Crawford	1.00
16	Nick Johnson	1.00
17	Jim Thome	1.50
18	Ivan Rodriguez	1.50
19	Chipper Jones	2.00
20	Pedro Martinez	1.00
21	Carlos Delgado	1.50
22	Roger Clemens	3.00
23	Mark Teixeira	1.50
24	Manny Ramirez	2.00
25	Barry Bonds	5.00
26	Vernon Wells	1.00
27	Vladimir Guerrero	2.00
28	Miguel Cabrera	2.00
29	Victor Martinez	1.00
30	Derrek Lee	1.50
31	Carlos Lee	1.00
32	Ichiro Suzuki	3.00
33	Johan Santana	1.50
34	David Ortiz	2.00
35	Jason Bay	1.50
36	Kendry Morales (RC)	3.00
37	Nicholas Markakis (RC)	5.00
38	Conor Jackson (RC)	2.00
39	Justin Verlander (RC)	5.00
40	Ryan Zimmerman (RC)	5.00
41	Jeremy Hermida (RC)	2.00
42	Dan Uggla (RC)	4.00
43	Matthew Kemp (RC)	3.00
44	Lastings Milledge (RC)	5.00
45	Kenji Johjima RC	5.00
46	Ian Kinsler (RC)	3.00
47	Hanley Ramirez (RC)	5.00
48	Melky Cabrera (RC)	3.00
49	Willy Aybar (RC)	3.00
50	Jonathan Papelbon (RC)	6.00
51	Prince Fielder (RC)	5.00
52	Cole Hamels (RC)	5.00
53	Josh Barfield (RC)	2.00
54	Alay Soler RC	5.00
55	Russell Martin (RC)	3.00

Blue

Blue (1-55): 2-3X
Production 249 Sets

Black

Black (1-55): 3-5X
Production 99 Sets

Red

No Pricing
Production One Set

Printing Plates

No Pricing
Production one set per color.

Buyback Autographs

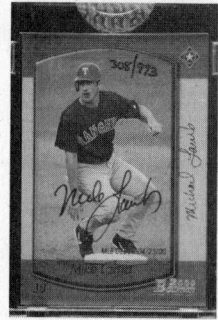

	NM/M
Adam Loewen/68	15.00
Adam Loewen/719	10.00
Adam Loewen/198	15.00
Adrian Gonzalez/976	20.00
Albert Pujols/44	250.00
Albert Pujols/50	250.00
Alex Gordon/49	250.00
Alex Gordon/32	280.00
Andrew McCutchen/391	40.00
Andrew McCutchen/33	60.00
Andrew McCutchen/561	35.00
Andruw Jones/34	30.00
Andruw Jones/22	40.00
Andruw Jones/24	40.00
Andruw Jones/28	30.00
Andruw Jones/48	20.00
Andy LaRoche/109	40.00
Andy LaRoche/60	40.00
Andy LaRoche/60	40.00
Andy LaRoche/734	25.00
Alex Rodriguez/21	150.00
Alex Rodriguez/22	150.00
B.J. Upton/58	30.00

B.J. Upton/136	25.00
B.J. Upton/667	20.00
B.J. Upton/120	25.00
Beau Jones/576	15.00
Beau Jones/63	30.00
Beau Jones/329	20.00
Beau Jones/33	30.00
Billy Buckner/99	25.00
Billy Buckner/432	20.00
Billy Buckner/182	20.00
Billy Buckner/33	30.00
Billy Wagner/56	30.00
Billy Wagner/47	30.00
Billy Wagner/64	25.00
Billy Wagner/90	20.00
Billy Wagner/99	20.00
Billy Wagner/37	30.00
Billy Wagner/38	30.00
Brandon Phillips/46	15.00
Brandon Phillips/26	20.00
Brandon Phillips/67	10.00
Brandon Phillips/28	20.00
Brandon Phillips/32	15.00
Brandon Phillips/140	10.00
Brandon Phillips/35	15.00
Brandon Phillips/335	10.00
Brandon Phillips/257	10.00
Brandon Snyder/461	15.00
Brandon Wood/70	30.00
Brandon Wood/100	30.00
Brandon Wood/627	20.00
Brandon Wood/239	30.00
Brent Cox/240	15.00
Brent Cox/66	20.00
Brent Cox/688	15.00
Carl Crawford/37	25.00
Carl Crawford/40	25.00
Carl Crawford/20	30.00
Carl Crawford/30	25.00
Carl Crawford/71	20.00
Carl Crawford/71	20.00
Carl Crawford/334	15.00
Carl Crawford/279	15.00
Carlos Silva/996	10.00
Cesar Ramos/25	25.00
Cesar Ramos/76	25.00
Cesar Ramos/161	15.00
Cesar Ramos/732	10.00
Chase Utley/23	100.00
Chase Utley/150	75.00
Chase Utley/303	75.00
Chase Utley/23	80.00
Chaz Roe/73	15.00
Chaz Roe/774	10.00
Chaz Roe/132	10.00
Chien-Ming Wang/25	500.00
Chien-Ming Wang/25	600.00
Chien-Ming Wang/25	500.00
Chien-Ming Wang/25	600.00
Chipper Jones/20	85.00
Chipper Jones/20	85.00
Chipper Jones/20	85.00
Chipper Jones/20	85.00
Chipper Jones/20	85.00
Chris Young/70	20.00
Chris Young/772	20.00
Chris Young/146	20.00
Chris Young/211	20.00
Chris Young/44	75.00
Chris Young/88	40.00
Chris Young/81	40.00
Chris Young/558	25.00
Clint Barmes/61	20.00
Clint Barmes/113	15.00
Clint Barmes/375	10.00
Clint Barmes/430	10.00
Conor Jackson/70	30.00
Conor Jackson/78	50.00
Conor Jackson/457	20.00
Conor Jackson/360	20.00
Craig Italiano/160	15.00
Craig Italiano/658	10.00
Craig Italiano/163	15.00
Dan Johnson/276	15.00
Dan Johnson/575	15.00
Dan Johnson/101	15.00
Dan Johnson/29	20.00
David Wright/543	60.00
David Wright/264	150.00
David Wright/45	80.00
David Wright/64	80.00
Derrek Lee/61	25.00
Dontrelle Willis/147	15.00
Dontrelle Willis/55	20.00
Dontrelle Willis/525	15.00
Dontrelle Willis/79	20.00
Dontrelle Willis/78	20.00
Dontrelle Willis/24	20.00
Dontrelle Willis/36	20.00
Eli Iorg/167	15.00
Eli Iorg/151	15.00
Eli Iorg/672	15.00
Eric Chavez/34	20.00
Eric Chavez/301	15.00
Eric Chavez/25	20.00
Eric Chavez/70	15.00
Eric Chavez/62	15.00
Ervin Santana/369	15.00
Ervin Santana/544	15.00
Ervin Santana/51	20.00
Ervin Santana/109	20.00
Ervin Santana/76	20.00
Ervin Santana/67	20.00
Ervin Santana/62	50.00
Fausto Carmona/131	10.00
Fausto Carmona/56	15.00
Fausto Carmona/263	10.00
Francisco Cordero/64	10.00
Francisco Cordero/87	10.00
Francisco Cordero/49	10.00
Francisco Cordero/138	10.00
Francisco Cordero/140	10.00
Francisco Liriano/142	35.00
Francisco Liriano/63	40.00
Francisco Liriano/47	35.00
Francisco Liriano/222	30.00
Francisco Liriano/350	25.00
Francisco Liriano/212	65.00
Garrett Atkins/121	15.00
Garrett Atkins/27	20.00
Garrett Atkins/209	15.00
Garrett Atkins/581	15.00
Garrett Atkins/38	15.00
Hanley Ramirez/435	30.00
Hanley Ramirez/98	35.00
Hanley Ramirez/466	30.00
Jason Bay/24	30.00
Jason Bay/298	20.00
Jason Bay/50	25.00
Jason Bay/58	25.00
Jason Bay/70	25.00
Jason Botts/29	15.00
Jason Botts/31	15.00
Jason Botts/269	10.00
Jason Botts/46	15.00
Jason Botts/59	15.00
Jason Botts/577	10.00
Jason Kubel/232	15.00
Jason Kubel/127	15.00
Jason Kubel/25	25.00
Jason Kubel/77	20.00
Jason Marquis/944	8.00
Jason Marquis/26	20.00
Jay Bruce/66	125.00
Jay Bruce/434	60.00
Jed Lowrie/123	25.00
Jed Lowrie/141	25.00
Jed Lowrie/716	25.00
Jeff Mathis/127	15.00
Jeff Mathis/185	15.00
Jeff Mathis/97	15.00
Jerome Williams/292	8.00
Jerome Williams/48	10.00
Jerome Williams/45	10.00
Jerome Williams/97	8.00
Joel Guzman/274	15.00
Joel Guzman/54	20.00
Joel Guzman/53	20.00
Joel Zumaya/233	50.00
Joel Zumaya/57	50.00
Joel Zumaya/96	80.00
Joel Zumaya/582	40.00
Joel Zumaya/163	50.00
John Drennen/78	30.00
John Drennen/387	15.00
John Van Benschoten/51	15.00
John Van Benschoten/24	20.00
John Van Benschoten/130	15.00
John Van Benschoten/272	10.00
Jonny Gomes/341	15.00
Jonny Gomes/27	50.00
Jonny Gomes/175	15.00
Jonny Gomes/363	10.00
Josh Barfield/158	15.00
Josh Barfield/557	10.00
Josh Barfield/178	20.00
Josh Geer/343	10.00
Josh Geer/138	10.00
Justin Huber/32	15.00
Justin Huber/99	15.00
Justin Huber/572	10.00
Justin Huber/212	10.00
Justin Huber/26	20.00
Justin Huber/37	15.00
Justin Upton/1000	80.00
Kevin Gregg/988	10.00
Lastings Milledge/166	30.00
Lastings Milledge/166	30.00
Lastings Milledge/632	20.00
Mark Mulder/20	20.00
Mark Mulder/20	20.00
Mark Mulder/20	20.00
Mark Mulder/20	20.00
Mark Mulder/20	20.00
Matt Cain/36	30.00
Matt Cain/389	20.00
Matt Maloney/350	20.00
Matt Maloney/50	60.00
Matt Maloney/20	75.00
Matt Maloney/60	60.00
Matt Torra/456	15.00
Matt Torra/37	30.00
Melky Cabrera/606	25.00
Melky Cabrera/191	30.00
Melky Cabrera/60	40.00
Melky Cabrera/24	60.00
Melky Cabrera/95	30.00
Merkin Valdez/41	15.00
Merkin Valdez/325	8.00
Merkin Valdez/70	15.00
Merkin Valdez/66	15.00
Micah Owings/138	30.00
Micah Owings/648	20.00
Michael Bowden/27	50.00
Michael Bowden/24	50.00
Michael Bowden/449	25.00
Miguel Cabrera/70	30.00
Miguel Cabrera/70	30.00
Miguel Cabrera/69	30.00
Miguel Cabrera/98	30.00
Miguel Cabrera/63	30.00
Miguel Cabrera/130	40.00
Mike Costanzo/466	15.00
Mike Lamb/993	10.00
Morgan Ensberg/74	15.00
Morgan Ensberg/334	10.00
Morgan Ensberg/64	15.00
Nick Swisher/342	15.00
Nick Swisher/73	25.00
Nick Swisher/31	30.00
Nolan Reimold/41	60.00
Nolan Reimold/419	20.00
Nolan Reimold/30	60.00
Rich Harden/87	20.00
Rich Harden/82	20.00
Rich Harden/70	20.00
Rich Harden/68	20.00
Rich Harden/68	30.00
Ricky Nolasco/52	15.00
Ricky Nolasco/256	10.00
Ricky Nolasco/148	15.00
Robinson Cano/90	50.00
Robinson Cano/72	50.00
Robinson Cano/101	50.00
Robinson Cano/222	40.00
Roy Oswalt/96	25.00
Roy Oswalt/42	30.00
Roy Oswalt/61	30.00
Roy Oswalt/63	40.00
Roy Oswalt/25	50.00
Roy Oswalt/199	25.00
Russell Martin/33	40.00
Russell Martin/96	30.00
Russell Martin/577	25.00
Russell Martin/252	25.00
Ryan Howard/50	350.00
Scott Elbert/79	50.00
Scott Elbert/330	35.00
Scott Elbert/60	50.00
Scott Kazmir/99	25.00
Scott Kazmir/36	30.00
Scott Kazmir/153	20.00
Scott Kazmir/26	30.00
Scott Kazmir/661	20.00
Scott Mathieson/472	8.00
Scott Mathieson/108	20.00
Scott Mathieson/72	25.00
Scott Thorman/980	10.00
Sean West/394	20.00
Sean West/70	30.00
Shaun Marcum/133	15.00
Shaun Marcum/26	20.00
Shaun Marcum/138	20.00
Shaun Marcum/153	20.00
Shaun Marcum/33	25.00
Travis Buck/60	40.00
Travis Buck/44	60.00
Travis Buck/747	20.00
Travis Hafner/114	20.00
Travis Hafner/96	20.00
Travis Hafner/386	20.00
Travis Hafner/45	25.00
Travis Hafner/280	20.00
Trevor Bell/146	15.00
Trevor Bell/28	15.00
Trevor Bell/689	15.00
Troy Patton/211	15.00
Troy Patton/50	30.00
Troy Patton/736	15.00
Vernon Wells/52	25.00
Vernon Wells/100	25.00
Vernon Wells/25	40.00
Vernon Wells/96	25.00
Vernon Wells/68	25.00
Vernon Wells/56	25.00
Vernon Wells/40	40.00
Vernon Wells/29	40.00
Vernon Wells/426	20.00
Vladimir Guerrero/21	80.00
Vladimir Guerrero/45	60.00
Vladimir Guerrero/20	80.00
Wade Townsend/423	15.00
Wade Townsend/53	20.00
Wily Mo Pena/79	20.00
Wily Mo Pena/70	20.00
Wily Mo Pena/69	20.00
Wily Mo Pena/134	20.00
Wily Mo Pena/62	20.00
Xavier Nady/105	20.00
Xavier Nady/72	20.00
Xavier Nady/192	15.00
Xavier Nady/213	15.00
Xavier Nady/294	15.00
Xavier Nady/41	20.00
Yunel Escobar/69	30.00
Yunel Escobar/395	20.00
Yusmeiro Petit/68	20.00
Yusmeiro Petit/102	20.00
Yusmeiro Petit/160	15.00
Yusmeiro Petit/630	15.00

Prospects

NM/M

Common Player:		2.00
Blue:		1.5-2X
Production 249 Sets		
Black:		2-4X
Production 99 Sets		
Red:		No Pricing
Production One Set		
1	Cameron Maybin	10.00
2	Koby Clemens	2.00
3	Lance Broadway	2.00
4	Chris Dickerson	2.00

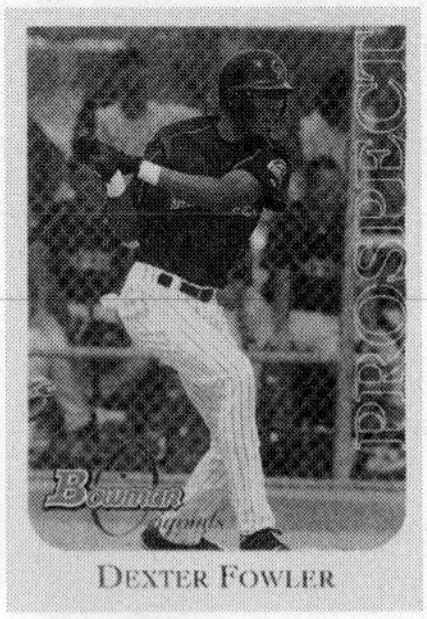

5	Garrett Mock	2.00
6	Ben Copeland	2.00
7	Nick Adenhart	4.00
8	Brad McCann	3.00
9	Dustin Majewski	2.00
10	Jimmy Barthmaier	2.00
11	Michael Aubrey	2.00
12	Evan Longoria	12.00
13	Clayton Kershaw	12.00
14	Juan Francia	2.00
15	Elvis Andrus	6.00
16	Mark Trumbo	2.00
17	Shawn Riggans	2.00
18	Asdrubal Cabrera	2.00
19	Mark McLemore	2.00
20	Radhames Liz	3.00
21	Mat Gamel	5.00
22	Wilkin Ramirez	2.00
23	Jared Lansford	2.00
24	Hunter Pence	6.00
25	Justin Upton	10.00
26	Brent Dlugach	2.00
27	B.J. Szymanski	2.00
28	Stephen Marek	2.00
29	Shaun Cumberland	2.00
30	Yovani Gallardo	4.00
31	Will Venable	2.00
32	A.J. Shappi	2.00
33	Dallas Trahern	2.00
34	Jason Jaramillo	2.00
35	Jose Tabata	5.00
36	Jose Campusano	2.00
37	Ryan Patterson	3.00
38	Andrew Pinckney	2.00
39	Dexter Fowler	2.00
40	Cody Johnson	3.00
41	Steve Murphy	2.00
42	Mark Reed	2.00
43	Chris Iannetta	2.00
44	Michael Hollimon	2.00
45	Omir Santos	2.00
46	Diory Hernandez	2.00
47	Matt Tolbert	2.00
48	Jeff Frazier	2.00
49	Max Ramirez	3.00
50	Alex Gordon	10.00
51	Steve Garrabrants	2.00
52	Steven Baker	2.00
53	Ryan Klosterman	2.00
54	Michael Collins	2.00
55	Corey Wimberly	2.00

2006 Bowman Sterling

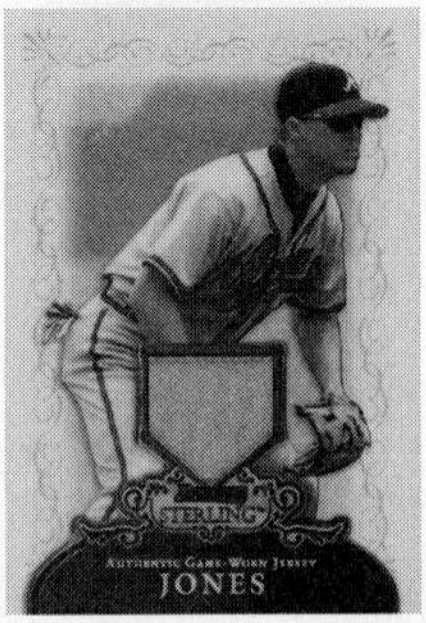

NM/M

Common Relic:		5.00
Pack (5):		60.00
Box (6):		300.00
CB	Carlos Beltran	8.00
CB2	Carlos Beltran	8.00
LB	Lance Berkman	5.00
HB	Hank Blalock	5.00
BLB	Barry Bonds	20.00
MC	Miguel Cabrera	10.00
MC2	Miguel Cabrera	10.00
RC	Robinson Cano	15.00
CC	Chris Carpenter	8.00
EC	Eric Chavez	5.00

JDD	Johnny Damon	8.00
AD	Adam Dunn	5.00
ME	Morgan Ensberg	5.00
VG	Vladimir Guerrero	10.00
JRH	Rich Harden	5.00
TH	Todd Helton	8.00
RH	Ryan Howard	25.00
AJ	Andruw Jones	8.00
LWJ	Chipper Jones	8.00
PK	Paul Konerko	8.00
MCM	Mickey Mantle	80.00
PM	Pedro Martinez	8.00
HM	Hideki Matsui	20.00
MM	Mark Mulder	5.00
DO	David Ortiz	10.00
MJP	Mike Piazza	10.00
AP	Albert Pujols	25.00
AP2	Albert Pujols	25.00
AR	Aramis Ramirez	8.00
MR	Manny Ramirez	10.00
MR2	Manny Ramirez	10.00
BR	Brian Roberts	5.00
AER	Alex Rodriguez	20.00
IR	Ivan Rodriguez	8.00
SR	Scott Rolen	8.00
JAS	Johan Santana	8.00
CS	Curt Schilling	8.00
GS	Grady Sizemore	8.00
APS	Alfonso Soriano	10.00
IS	Ichiro Suzuki	25.00
MCT	Mark Teixeira	8.00
MT	Miguel Tejada	8.00
JHT	Jim Thome	8.00
DWW	Dontrelle Willis	5.00
DW	David Wright	20.00
Common Rookie:		4.00
BA	Brian Anderson **(RC)**	4.00
WA	Willy Aybar **(RC)**	4.00
BB	Brian Bannister **(RC)**	4.00
CRB	Chad Billingsley **(RC)**	10.00
BON	Boof Bonser **(RC)**	6.00
MCC	Melky Cabrera **(RC)**	6.00
JD	Joey Devine **RC**	4.00
SD	Stephen Drew **(RC)**	10.00
KF	Kevin Frandsen **(RC)**	4.00
RK	Ryan Garko **(RC)**	6.00
DG	David Gassner **(RC)**	4.00
EG	Enrique Gonzalez **(RC)**	4.00
FG	Franklin Gutierrez **(RC)**	4.00
TGJ	Tony Gwynn Jr. **(RC)**	6.00
CRH	Craig Hansen **RC**	8.00
CJ	Conor Jackson **(RC)**	4.00
CHJ	Chuck James **(RC)**	6.00
CJJ	Casey Janssen **RC**	4.00
KJ	Kenji Johjima **RC**	10.00
JJ	Josh Johnson **(RC)**	6.00
JK	Jeff Karstens **RC**	6.00
MK	Matthew Kemp **(RC)**	6.00
HK	Howie Kendrick **(RC)**	6.00
FL	Francisco Liriano **(RC)**	10.00
JL	James Loney **(RC)**	6.00
NM	Nicholas Markakis **(RC)**	8.00
RM	Russell Martin **(RC)**	6.00
SM	Scott Mathieson **(RC)**	6.00
JM	Jeff Mathis **(RC)**	6.00
KM	Kendry Morales **(RC)**	4.00
SO	Scott Olsen **(RC)**	4.00
JP	Jonathan Papelbon **(RC)**	10.00
DP	David Pauley **(RC)**	6.00
MPP	Mike Pelfrey **RC**	10.00
HP	Hayden Penn **(RC)**	4.00
CQ	Carlos Quentin **(RC)**	4.00
HR	Hanley Ramirez **(RC)**	8.00
AS	Anibal Sanchez **(RC)**	4.00
JS	James Shields **RC**	10.00
MS	Matt Smith **(RC)**	4.00
ALS	Alay Soler **RC**	4.00
JBS	Jeremy Sowers **(RC)**	4.00
TT	Taylor Tankersley **(RC)**	4.00
JTA	Jordan Tata **RC**	6.00
DU	Dan Uggla **(RC)**	6.00
JV	Justin Verlander **(RC)**	10.00
JW	Jered Weaver **(RC)**	8.00
RZ	Ryan Zimmerman **(RC)**	10.00
BZ	Benjamin Zobrist **(RC)**	6.00
JZ	Joel Zumaya **(RC)**	4.00
Common Rookie Autograph:		
JLB	Josh Barfield **(RC)**	10.00
JCB	Jason Botts **(RC)**	10.00
AE	Andre Ethier **(RC)**	15.00
JI	Joe Inglett **RC**	15.00
IK	Ian Kinsler **(RC)**	25.00
LM	Lastings Milledge **(RC)**	15.00
ZM	Zach Miner **(RC)**	10.00
RN	Ricky Nolasco **(RC)**	10.00
Common Rookie Relic Auto.:		
JB	Jason Bulger **(RC)**	10.00
PF	Prince Fielder **(RC)**	50.00
CI	Chris Iannetta **RC**	15.00
CH	Cole Hamels **(RC)**	40.00
HK	Howie Kendrick **(RC)**	15.00
JTL	Jon Lester **(RC)**	40.00
BL	Bobby Livingston **(RC)**	10.00
MN	Erik Naposki **RC**	15.00
RP	Ronny Paulino **(RC)**	10.00
YP	Yusmeiro Petit **(RC)**	15.00
MP	Martin Prado **(RC)**	15.00
ALR	Anthony Reyes **(RC)**	15.00
JT	Jack Taschner **(RC)**	10.00
ST	Scott Thorman **(RC)**	10.00

Refractors

Rookies:	1.5-2X
Rookie Auto.:	1-2X
Rookie Relic Auto.:	1-2X

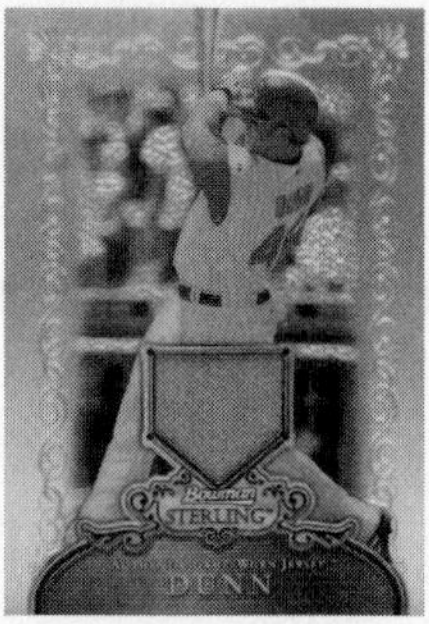

Relics:	1-2X
Prospects:	1.5-2X
Prospect Auto.:	1-2X

Production 199 Sets

Black Refractors

No Pricing
Production 25 Sets

Gold Refractors

No Pricing
Production 10 Sets

Red Refractors

No Pricing
Production One Set

Printing Plates

No Pricing
Production One Set

Prospect

		NM/M
NA	Nick Adenhart	6.00
EA	Elvis Andrus	10.00
MRA	Michael Aubrey	5.00
JRB	Jimmy Barthmaier	5.00
AJC	Asdrubal Cabrera	6.00
JAC	Jose Campusano	5.00
YC	Yung-Chi Chen	15.00
ADC	Adam Coe	5.00
MC	Michael Collins	5.00
BC	Ben Copeland	5.00
SC	Shaun Cumberland	5.00
CD	Chris Dickerson	5.00
BD	Brent Dlugach	5.00
DF	Dexter Fowler	6.00
JF	Juan Francia	5.00
JKF	Jeff Frazier	5.00
YG	Yovani Gallardo	8.00
MG	Mat Gamel	15.00
SGG	Steve Garrabrants	5.00
DIH	Diory Hernandez	5.00
MH	Michael Hollimon	5.00
JJ	Jason Jaramillo	5.00
BJ	Brandon Jones	5.00
RK	Ryan Klosterman	5.00
JTL	Jared Lansford	5.00
RL	Radhames Liz	5.00
EM	Evan MacLane	5.00
DM	Dustin Majewski	6.00
SM	Stephen Marek	5.00
BWM	Brad McCann	5.00
MSM	Mark McLemore	5.00
GLM	Garrett Mock	5.00
SMM	Steve Murphy	5.00
ON	Oswaldo Navarro	5.00
RP	Ryan Patterson	6.00
HP	Hunter Pence	6.00
AP	Andrew Pinckney	5.00
MRR	Max Ramirez	6.00
WR	Wilkin Ramirez	5.00
MR	Mark Reed	5.00
SR	Shawn Riggans	5.00
OS	Omir Santos	5.00
AS	A.J. Shappi	5.00
BJS	B.J. Szymanski	5.00
JT	Jose Tabata	10.00
CMT	Matt Tolbert	8.00
DT	Dallas Trahern	5.00
MT	Mark Trumbo	6.00
WV	Will Venable	5.00
CW	Corey Wimberly	5.00

Prospect Autographs

		NM/M
BA	Brandon Allen	8.00
MAA	Matt Antonelli	20.00
MA	Mike Aviles	25.00
PB	Pedro Beato	10.00
RB	Ronny Bourquin	10.00
BB	Brooks Brown	10.00
TB	Travis Buck	15.00
KB	Kyler Burke	10.00
JBU	Joshua Butler	10.00
AC	Adrian Cardenas	25.00
KC	Koby Clemens	15.00
JC	Jeff Clement	20.00
TC	Tyler Colvin	20.00
HC	Hank Conger	20.00
TC	Trevor Crowe	10.00
CD	Chris Dickerson	10.00
KD	Kyle Drabek	15.00
DE	Dustin Evans	10.00
SE	Steven Evarts	15.00
MF	Michael Felix	10.00
BF	Brad Furnish	10.00
AG	Alex Gordon	50.00
DH	Daniel Haigwood	10.00
BH	Brett Hayes	10.00
CH	Chase Headley	25.00
LH	Luke Hochevar	25.00
DHU	David Huff	20.00
CHH	Chad Huffman	15.00
JJ	Jeremy Jeffress	20.00
CJ	Cody Johnson	20.00
KJ	Kris Johnson	15.00
CK	Clayton Kershaw	60.00
KK	Kasey Kiker	10.00
EL	Evan Longoria	100.00
PL	Pedro Lopez	8.00
CM	Cameron Maybin	50.00
MM	Mark McCormick	10.00
KM	Kyle McCulloch	10.00
GM	Garrett Mock	10.00
BM	Brandon Moss	15.00
JN	Jason Neighborgall	10.00
AO	Adam Ottavino	10.00
MO	Micah Owings	20.00
CP	Chris Parmelee	20.00
TP	Troy Patton	20.00
EP	Elvin Puello	10.00
CR	Cory Rasmus	10.00
JR	Joshua Rodriguez	10.00
BR	Billy Rowell	25.00
JS	Jarrod Saltalamacchia	20.00
BSI	Brett Sinkbeil	10.00
BS	Brandon Snyder	10.00
WT	Wade Townsend	10.00
CT	Chad Tracy	10.00
JU	Justin Upton	75.00
SWA	Sean Watson	10.00
JW	Johnny Whittleman	15.00
CW	Colten Willems	15.00
BW	Brandon Wood	20.00
SW	Steven Wright	10.00

2007 Bowman

		NM/M
Complete Set (237):		
Common Player:		.15
Common RC (201-220):		.25
Common RC Auto.:		10.00
Pack (10):		3.00
Box (24):		55.00
1	Hanley Ramirez	.50
2	Justin Verlander	.50
3	Ryan Zimmerman	.40
4	Jered Weaver	.50
5	Stephen Drew	.50
6	Jonathan Papelbon	.50
7	Melky Cabrera	.25
8	Francisco Liriano	.25
9	Prince Fielder	.75
10	Dan Uggla	.25
11	Jeremy Sowers	.15
12	Carlos Quentin	.15
13	Chuck James	.15
14	Andre Ethier	.25
15	Cole Hamels	.50
16	Kenji Johjima	.25
17	Chad Bilingsley	.25
18	Ian Kinsler	.25
19	Jason Hirsh	.15
20	Nicholas Markakis	.25
21	Jeremy Hermida	.15
22	Ryan Shealy	.15
23	Scott Olsen	.15
24	Russell Martin	.40
25	Conor Jackson	.25
26	Erik Bedard	.40
27	Brian McCann	.25
28	Michael Barrett	.25
29	Brandon Phillips	.40
30	Garrett Atkins	.25
31	Freddy Garcia	.15
32	Mark Loretta	.15
33	Craig Biggio	.25
34	Jeremy Bonderman	.25
35	Johan Santana	.75
36	Jorge Posada	.40
37	Brian Bannister	.15
38	Carlos Delgado	.50
39	Gary Mathews Jr.	.15
40	Mike Cameron	.15
41	Adrian Beltre	.25
42	Freddy Sanchez	.15
43	Austin Kearns	.15
44	Mark Buehrle	.15
45	Miguel Cabrera	.75
46	Josh Beckett	.50
47	Chone Figgins	.25
48	Edgar Renteria	.25
49	Derek Lowe	.25
50	Ryan Howard	1.50
51	Shawn Green	.15
52	Jason Giambi	.50
53	Ervin Santana	.15
54	Jack Wilson	.15
55	Roy Oswalt	.50
56	Danny Haren	.25
57	Jose Vidro	.15
58	Kevin Millwood	.15
59	Jim Edmonds	.25
60	Carl Crawford	.50
61	Randy Wolf	.15
62	Paul LoDuca	.15
63	Johnny Estrada	.15
64	Brian Roberts	.25
65	Manny Ramirez	.75
66	Jose Contreras	.15
67	Josh Barfield	.15
68	Juan Pierre	.15
69	David DeJesus	.15
70	Gary Sheffield	.40
71	Jon Lieber	.15
72	Randy Johnson	.75
73	Rickie Weeks	.25
74	Brian Giles	.15
75	Ichiro Suzuki	1.00
76	Nick Swisher	.25
77	Justin Morneau	.50
78	Scott Kazmir	.25
79	Lyle Overbay	.15
80	Alfonso Soriano	.75
81	Brandon Webb	.25
82	Joe Crede	.15
83	Corey Patterson	.15
84	Kenny Rogers	.15
85	Ken Griffey Jr.	1.50
86	Cliff Lee	.15
87	Mike Lowell	.25
88	Marcus Giles	.15
89	Orlando Cabrera	.25
90	Derek Jeter	2.00
91	Josh Johnson	.15
92	Carlos Guillen	.15
93	Bill Hall	.25
94	Michael Cuddyer	.15
95	Miguel Tejada	.50
96	Todd Helton	.50
97	C.C. Sabathia	.25
98	Tadahito Iguchi	.15
99	Jose Reyes	.75
100	David Wright	1.00
101	Barry Zito	.25
102	Jake Peavy	.25
103	Richie Sexson	.40
104	A.J. Burnett	.15
105	Eric Chavez	.25
106	Jorge Cantu	.15
107	Grady Sizemore	.50
108	Bronson Arroyo	.15
109	Mike Mussina	.40
110	Maggilo Ordonez	.25
111	Anibal Sanchez	.15
112	Jeff Francoeur	.40
113	Kevin Youkilis	.40
114	Aubrey Huff	.15
115	Carlos Zambrano	.25
116	Mark Teahen	.15
117	Carlos Silva	.15
118	Pedro Martinez	.50
119	Hideki Matsui	.75
120	Mike Piazza	.75
121	Jason Schmidt	.25
122	Greg Maddux	1.50
123	Joe Blanton	.15
124	Chris Carpenter	.75
125	David Ortiz	.75
126	Alex Rios	.25
127	Nick Johnson	.15
128	Carlos Lee	.25
129	Pat Burrell	.25
130	Ben Sheets	.25
131	Kazuo Matsui	.15
132	Adam Dunn	.50
133	Jermaine Dye	.25
134	Curt Schilling	.75
135	Chad Tracy	.15
136	Vladimir Guerrero	.75
137	Melvin Mora	.15
138	John Smoltz	.25
139	Craig Monroe	.15
140	Dontrelle Willis	.25
141	Jeff Francis	.15
142	Chipper Jones	.75
143	Frank Thomas	.50
144	Brett Myers	.25
145	Xavier Nady	.15
146	Robinson Cano	.40
147	Jeff Kent	.15
148	Scott Rolen	.50
149	Roy Halladay	.25
150	Joe Mauer	.25
151	Bobby Abreu	.25
152	Matt Cain	.25
153	Hank Blalock	.15
154	Chris Capuano	.15
155	Jake Westbrook	.15
156	Javier Vazquez	.15
157	Garret Anderson	.15
158	Aramis Ramirez	.40
159	Mark Kotsay	.15
160	Matthew Kemp	.40
161	Adrian Gonzalez	.25
162	Felix Hernandez	.25
163	David Eckstein	.15
164	Curtis Granderson	.40
165	Paul Konerko	.25
166	Orlando Hudson	.15
167	Tim Hudson	.25
168	J.D. Drew	.25
169	Chien-Ming Wang	.50
170	Jimmy Rollins	.50
171	Matt Morris	.15
172	Raul Ibanez	.15
173	Mark Teixeira	.40
174	Ted Lilly	.15
175	Albert Pujols	2.00
176	Carlos Beltran	.50
177	Lance Berkman	.40
178	Ivan Rodriguez	.50
179	Torii Hunter	.25
180	Johnny Damon	.50

181 Chase Utley .75
182 Jason Bay .40
183 Jeff Weaver .15
184 Troy Glaus .25
185 Rocco Baldelli .15
186 Rafael Furcal .25
187 Jim Thome .50
188 Travis Hafner .40
189 Matt Holliday .50
190 Andruw Jones .50
191 Ramon Hernandez .15
192 Victor Martinez .25
193 Aaron Hill .15
194 Michael Young .25
195 Vernon Wells .25
196 Mark Mulder .15
197 Derrek Lee .50
198 Tom Glavine .40
199 Chris Young .25
200 Alex Rodriguez 2.00
201 Delmon Young **(RC)** .50
202 Alexi Casilla **RC** .25
203 Shawn Riggans **(RC)** .25
204 Jeff Baker **(RC)** .50
205 Hector Gimenez **(RC)** .25
206 Ubaldo Jimenez **(RC)** .50
207 Adam Lind **(RC)** .50
208 Joaquin Arias **(RC)** .25
209 David Murphy **(RC)** .25
210 Daisuke Matsuzaka **RC** 6.00
211 Jerry Owens **(RC)** .25
212 Ryan Sweeney **(RC)** .25
213 Kei Igawa **RC** 1.00
214 Fred Lewis **(RC)** .25
215 Philip Humber **(RC)** .25
216 Kevin Hooper **(RC)** .25
217 Jeff Fiorentino **(RC)** .25
218 Michael Bourn **(RC)** .50
219 Hideki Okajima **RC** 3.00
219 Hideki Okajima/Auto. **RC** 40.00
220 Josh Fields **(RC)** .50
221 Andrew Miller/Auto. **RC** 30.00
222 Troy Tulowitzki/Auto. **(RC)** 20.00
223 Ryan Braun/Auto. **RC** 15.00
224 Oswaldo Navarro/Auto. **RC** 10.00
225 Philip Humber/Auto. **(RC)** 15.00
226 Mitch Maier/Auto. **(RC)** 15.00
227 Jerry Owens/Auto. **(RC)** 15.00
228 Mike Rabelo/Auto. **RC** 20.00
229 Delwyn Young/Auto. **(RC)** 10.00
230 Miguel Montero/Auto. **(RC)** 15.00
231 Akinori Iwamura/Auto. **RC** 25.00
232 Matt Lindstrom/Auto. **(RC)** 10.00
233 Josh Hamilton/Auto. **(RC)** 40.00
235 Elijah Dukes/Auto. **RC** 10.00
236 Sean Henn/Auto. **(RC)** 10.00
237 Barry Bonds 2.00

Blue

Blue: 2-4X
Blue RC Auto.: 1X
Production 500 Sets

Gold

Gold (1-220): 1-2X
Inserted 1:1

Orange

Orange: 3-6X
Orange RC Auto.: 1-1.5X
Production 250 Sets

Red

No Pricing
Production One Set

Printing Plates

No Pricing
Production one set per color.

Alex Rodriguez Road to 500

NM/M

Common Rodriguez: 2.00
Inserted 2:Box
Autograph: No Pricing
Production One Set

Chrome Prospects

NM/M

Complete Set (110): 50.00
Common Player: .50
Inserted 2:Hobby Pack
1 Cooper Brannon 1.00
2 Jason Taylor 2.50
3 Shawn O'Malley 1.00
4 Robert Alcombrack 1.00
5 Dellin Betances 4.00
6 Jeremy Papelbon 2.00
7 Adam Carr 1.00
8 Matthew Clarkson .50
9 Darin McDonald 1.00
10 Brandon Rice 1.00
11 Matthew Sweeney 2.50
12 Scott Deal .50
13 Brennan Boesch 1.00
14 Scott Taylor 1.00
15 Michael Brantley 2.00
16 Yahmed Yema 1.00
17 Brandon Morrow 5.00
18 Cole Garner 1.00
19 Erik Lis 1.50
20 Lucas French 1.00
21 Aaron Cunningham 3.00
22 Ryan Schreppel .50
23 Kevin Russo 1.00
24 Yohan Pino 1.00
25 Michael Sullivan .50
26 Trey Shields .50
27 Danny Matienzo .50
28 Chuck Lofgren 2.00
29 Gerrit Simpson .50
30 David Haehnel .50
31 Marvin Lowrance 1.00
32 Kevin Ardoin .50
33 Edwin Maysonet .50
34 Derek Griffith .50
35 Sam Fuld 1.00
36 Chase Wright 1.50
37 Brandon Roberts .50
38 Kyle Aselton .50
39 Steven Sollmann 1.00
40 Michael Devaney 1.00
41 Charlie Fermaint .50
42 Jesse Litsch 1.50
43 Bryan Hansen 1.00
44 Ramon Garcia .50
45 John Otness 1.50
46 Trey Hearne .50
47 Habelito Hernandez .50
48 Edgar Garcia 1.50
49 Seth Fortenberry 1.00
50 Reid Brignac 2.00
51 Derek Rodriguez .50
52 Ervin Alcantara 1.00
53 Tom Hottovy 1.00
54 Jesus Flores 1.00
55 Matt Palmer .50
56 Brian Henderson .50
57 John Gragg .50
58 Jay Garthwaite 1.00
59 Esmerling Vasquez .50
60 Gilberto Mejia .50
61 Aaron Jensen .50
62 Cedric Brooks .50
63 Brandon Mann .50
64 Myron Leslie 1.00
65 Ray Aguilar .50
66 Jesus Guzman 2.00
67 Sean Thompson .50
68 Jarrett Hoffpauir 1.00
69 Matt Goodson .50
70 Neal Musser .50
71 Tony Abreu 4.00
72 Tony Peguero .50
73 Michael Bertram 1.00
74 Randy Wells 1.00
75 Bradley Davis .50
76 Jay Sawatski 1.00
77 Vic Buttler .50
78 Jose Oyervidez .50
79 Doug Deeds 1.00
80 Daniel Dement 1.00
81 Spike Lundberg .50
82 Ricardo Nanita .50
83 Brad Knox 1.00
84 Will Venable 1.00
85 Greg Smith 1.50
86 Pedro Powell 1.00
87 Gabriel Medina 1.00
88 Duke Sardinha .50
89 Mike Madsen 1.50
90 Rayner Bautista .50
91 T.J. Nall .50
92 Neil Sellers 1.00
93 Andrew Dobies 1.00
94 Leo Daigle .50
95 Brian Duensing 1.50
96 Vincent Blue 1.00
97 Fernando Rodriguez 1.00
98 Derin McMains .50
99 Adam Bass 1.00
100 Justin Ruggiano 1.50
101 Jared Burton 1.00
102 Mike Parisi 1.00
103 Aaron Peel 1.00
104 Evan Englebrook 1.00
105 Sendy Vasquez .50
106 Desmond Jennings 3.00
107 Clay Harris 1.00
108 Cody Strait 1.00
109 Ryan Mullins 1.00
110 Ryan Webb 1.00

Chrome Prospects Refractor

Refractor (1-110): 2-4X
Production 500 Sets

Chrome Prospects Blue Refractor

Blue Refractor (1-110): 4-8X
Production 150 Sets

Chrome Prospects Gold Refractor

Gold Refractor (1-110): 10-20X
Production 50 Sets

Chrome Prospects Orange Refractor

Orange Refractor (1-110): No Pricing
Production 25 Sets

Chrome Prospects Red Refractor

Red Refractor (1-110): No Pricing
Production Five Sets

Chrome Prospects SuperFractor

Superfractor (1-110): No Pricing
Production One Set

Chrome Prospects X-Fractor

X-Fractor (1-110): 3-6X
Production 275 Sets

Prospects

NM/M

Complete Set (135):
Common Player (1-110): .25
Common Auto. (111-135): 10.00
1 Cooper Brannon .25
2 Jason Taylor .75
3 Shawn O'Malley .25
4 Robert Alcombrack .25
5 Dellin Betances 1.00
6 Jeremy Papelbon .50
7 Adam Carr .25
8 Matthew Clarkson .25
9 Darin McDonald .25
10 Brandon Rice .25
11 Matthew Sweeney .50
12 Scott Deal .25
13 Brennan Boesch .25
14 Scott Taylor .25
15 Michael Brantley .50
16 Yahmed Yema .25
17 Brandon Morrow 1.50
18 Cole Garner .25
19 Erik Lis .50
20 Lucas French .25
21 Aaron Cunningham 1.00
22 Ryan Schreppel .25
23 Kevin Russo .25
24 Yohan Pino .25
25 Michael Sullivan .25
26 Trey Shields .25
27 Danny Matienzo .25
28 Chuck Lofgren .50
29 Gerrit Simpson .25
30 David Haehnel .25
31 Marvin Lowrance .25
32 Kevin Ardoin .25
33 Edwin Maysonet .25
34 Derek Griffith .25
35 Sam Fuld .25
36 Chase Wright .50
37 Brandon Roberts .25
38 Kyle Aselton .25
39 Steven Sollmann .25
40 Michael Devaney .25
41 Charlie Fermaint .25
42 Jesse Litsch .50
43 Bryan Hansen .25
44 Ramon Garcia .25
45 John Otness .50
46 Trey Hearne .25
47 Habelito Hernandez .25
48 Edgar Garcia .50
49 Seth Fortenberry .25
50 Reid Brignac .50
51 Derek Rodriguez .25
52 Ervin Alcantara .25
53 Tom Hottovy .25
54 Jesus Flores .25
55 Matt Palmer .25
56 Brian Henderson .25
57 John Gragg .25
58 Jay Garthwaite .25
59 Esmerling Vasquez .25
60 Gilberto Mejia .25
61 Aaron Jensen .25
62 Cedric Brooks .25
63 Brandon Mann .25
64 Myron Leslie .25
65 Ray Aguilar .25
66 Jesus Guzman .50
67 Sean Thompson .25
68 Jarrett Hoffpauir .25
69 Matt Goodson .25
70 Neal Musser .25
71 Tony Abreu 1.50
72 Tony Peguero .25
73 Michael Bertram .25
74 Randy Wells .25
75 Bradley Davis .25
76 Jay Sawatski .25
77 Vic Buttler .25
78 Jose Oyervidez .25
79 Doug Deeds .25
80 Daniel Dement .25
81 Spike Lundberg .25
82 Ricardo Nanita .25
83 Brad Knox .25
84 Will Venable .25
85 Greg Smith .50
86 Pedro Powell .25
87 Gabriel Medina .25
88 Duke Sardinha .25
89 Mike Madsen .50
90 Rayner Bautista .25
91 T.J. Nall .25
92 Neil Sellers .25
93 Andrew Dobies .25
94 Leo Daigle .25
95 Brian Duensing .50
96 Vincent Blue .25
97 Fernando Rodriguez .25
98 Derin McMains .25
99 Adam Bass .25
100 Justin Ruggiano .50
101 Jared Burton .25
102 Mike Parisi .25
103 Aaron Peel .25
104 Evan Englebrook .25
105 Sendy Vasquez .25
106 Desmond Jennings .75
107 Clay Harris .25
108 Cody Strait .25
109 Ryan Mullins .25
110 Ryan Webb .25
111 Kyle Drabek 15.00
112 Evan Longoria 50.00
113 Tyler Colvin 15.00
114 Matt Long 10.00
115 Jeremy Jeffress 15.00
116 Kasey Kiker 15.00
117 Hank Conger 15.00
118 Cody Johnson 15.00
119 David Huff 15.00
120 Tommy Hickman 10.00
121 Chris Parmelee 15.00
122 Dustin Evans 10.00
123 Brett Sinkbeil 10.00
124 Andrew Carpenter 15.00
125 Colton Willems 10.00
126 Matt Antonelli 15.00
127 Marcus Sanders 15.00
128 Joshua Rodriguez 15.00
129 Keith Weiser 10.00
130 Chad Tracy 15.00
131 Matthew Sulentic 15.00
132 Adam Ottavino 15.00
133 Jarrod Saltalamacchia 25.00
134 Kyle Blanks 15.00
135 Brad Eldred 10.00

Prospects Blue

Blue (1-110): 2-4X
Blue RC Auto. (111-135): 1X
Production 500 Sets

Prospects Gold

Gold (1-110): 1-2X
Inserted 1:1

Prospects Orange

Orange (1-110): 3-6X
Orange RC Auto. (111-135): 1-1.5X
Production 250 Sets

Prospects Red

No Pricing
Production One Set

Signs of the Future

NM/M

Common Auto: 10.00
KD Kyle Drabek 15.00
DB Dellin Betances 60.00
JBC J. Brent Cox 15.00
JD John Drennen 10.00
DS Denard Span 15.00
KC Koby Clemens 15.00
EH Estee Harris 10.00
MN Mike Neu 10.00
RO Ross Ohlendorf 15.00
CG Chris Getz 10.00
AR Adam Russell 15.00
JC Jesus Cota 10.00
JB John Baker 10.00
BM Brandon Moss 10.00
CS Chad Santos 10.00
KS Kurt Suzuki 15.00
JJ Jair Jurrjens 30.00
MA Mike Aviles 10.00
TT Taylor Teagarden 10.00
SK Shane Komine 10.00
ME Mike Edwards 10.00
MM Matthew Merricks 10.00
JDA Jamie D'Antona 10.00
JBB John Bowker 15.00
CR Chris Robinson 10.00
JW Jared Wells 10.00
BF Ben Fritz 10.00
BB Brian Bixler 10.00
CM Christopher McConnell 10.00
JCB Jordan Brown 15.00
FP Felix Pie 20.00
ER Eric Reed 10.00
AM Andrew McCutchen 20.00
MR Michael Rogers 10.00
RB Reid Brignac 20.00
RG Rich Gardner 10.00
SG Sean Gallagher 10.00
CJS Chris Seddon 10.00

2007 Bowman Chrome

NM/M

Common Player: .25
Common RC: .50
Pack (4): 6.00
Box (18): 95.00
1 Hanley Ramirez .75
2 Justin Verlander .75
3 Ryan Zimmerman .50
4 Jered Weaver .50
5 Stephen Drew .40
6 Jonathan Papelbon .50
7 Melky Cabrera .50
8 Francisco Liriano .25
9 Prince Fielder 1.00
10 Dan Uggla .50
11 Jeremy Sowers .25
12 Carlos Quentin .25
13 Chuck James .25
14 Andre Ethier .50
15 Cole Hamels .50
16 Kenji Johjima .25
17 Chad Billingsley .50
18 Ian Kinsler .50
19 Jason Hirsh .25

20 Nicholas Markakis .50
21 Jeremy Hermida .25
22 Ryan Shealy .25
23 Scott Olsen .25
24 Russell Martin .50
25 Conor Jackson .25
26 Erik Bedard .50
27 Brian McCann .50
28 Michael Barrett .25
29 Brandon Phillips .50
30 Garrett Atkins .50
31 Freddy Garcia .25
32 Mark Loretta .25
33 Craig Biggio .50
34 Jeremy Bonderman .50
35 Johan Santana .75
36 Jorge Posada .75
37 Victor Martinez .50
38 Carlos Delgado .75
39 Gary Matthews .50
40 Mike Cameron .25
41 Adrian Beltre .50
42 Freddy Sanchez .25
43 Austin Kearns .25
44 Mark Buehrle .25
45 Miguel Cabrera 1.00
46 Josh Beckett .75
47 Chone Figgins .50
48 Edgar Renteria .50
49 Derek Lowe .25
50 Ryan Howard 2.00
51 Shawn Green .25
52 Jason Giambi .50
53 Ervin Santana .25
54 Aaron Hill .25
55 Roy Oswalt .50
56 Danny Haren .40
57 Jose Vidro .25
58 Kevin Millwood .25
59 Jim Edmonds .50
60 Carl Crawford .50
61 Randy Wolf .25
62 Paul LoDuca .25
63 Johnny Estrada .25
64 Brian Roberts .50
65 Manny Ramirez 1.00
66 Jose Contreras .25
67 Josh Barfield .25
68 Juan Pierre .25
69 David DeJesus .25
70 Gary Sheffield .75
71 Michael Young .50
72 Randy Johnson .75
73 Rickie Weeks .40
74 Brian Giles .25
75 Ichiro Suzuki 1.50
76 Nick Swisher .50
77 Justin Morneau .75
78 Scott Kazmir .50
79 Lyle Overbay .25
80 Alfonso Soriano 1.00
81 Brandon Webb .50
82 Joe Crede .25
83 Corey Patterson .25
84 Kenny Rogers .25
85 Ken Griffey Jr. 2.00
86 Cliff Lee .25
87 Mike Lowell .50
88 Marcus Giles .25
89 Orlando Cabrera .50
90 Derek Jeter 2.50
91 Ramon Hernandez .25
92 Carlos Guillen .25
93 Bill Hall .25
94 Michael Cuddyer .25
95 Miguel Tejada .75
96 Todd Helton .75
97 C.C. Sabathia .50
98 Tadahito Iguchi .25
99 Jose Reyes 1.00
100 David Wright 1.00
101 Barry Zito .50
102 Jake Peavy .50
103 Richie Sexson .50
104 A.J. Burnett .25
105 Eric Chavez .25
106 Vernon Wells .50
107 Grady Sizemore .75
108 Bronson Arroyo .25
109 Mike Mussina .50
110 Magglio Ordonez .50
111 Anibal Sanchez .25
112 Jeff Francoeur .50
113 Kevin Youkilis .50
114 Aubrey Huff .25
115 Carlos Zambrano .50
116 Mark Teahen .25
117 Mark Mulder .50
118 Pedro Martinez 1.00
119 Hideki Matsui 1.50
120 Mike Piazza 1.00
121 Jason Schmidt .25
122 Greg Maddux 2.00
123 Joe Blanton .25
124 Chris Carpenter .75
125 David Ortiz 1.00
126 Alex Rios .40
127 Nick Johnson .25
128 Carlos Lee .50
129 Pat Burrell .50
130 Ben Sheets .50
131 Derrek Lee .50
132 Adam Dunn .50
133 Jermaine Dye .40
134 Curt Schilling .75
135 Chad Tracy .25
136 Vladimir Guerrero 1.00
137 Melvin Mora .25
138 John Smoltz .50
139 Craig Monroe .25
140 Dontrelle Willis .25
141 Jeff Francis .25
142 Chipper Jones 1.00
143 Frank Thomas 1.00
144 Brett Myers .25
145 Tom Glavine .75
146 Robinson Cano .75
147 Jeff Kent .50
148 Scott Rolen .75
149 Roy Halladay .50
150 Joe Mauer .50
151 Bobby Abreu .50
152 Matt Cain .50
153 Hank Blalock .50
154 Chris Young .50
155 Jake Westbrook .25
156 Javier Vazquez .25
157 Garret Anderson .25
158 Aramis Ramirez .50
159 Mark Kotsay .25
160 Matthew Kemp .50
161 Adrian Gonzalez .50
162 Felix Hernandez .50
163 David Eckstein .25
164 Curtis Granderson .50
165 Paul Konerko .50
166 Alex Rodriguez 2.50
167 Tim Hudson .50
168 J.D. Drew .25
169 Chien-Ming Wang 1.00
170 Jimmy Rollins .75
171 Matt Morris .25
172 Raul Ibanez .25
173 Mark Teixeira .75
174 Ted Lilly .25
175 Albert Pujols 2.50
176 Carlos Beltran 1.00
177 Lance Berkman .50
178 Ivan Rodriguez .75
179 Torii Hunter .50
180 Johnny Damon .75
181 Chase Utley 1.00
182 Jason Bay .50
183 Jeff Weaver .25
184 Troy Glaus .50
185 Rocco Baldelli .25
186 Rafael Furcal .50
187 Jim Thome .75
188 Travis Hafner .50
189 Matt Holliday .50
190 Andruw Jones .50
191 Andrew Miller **RC** 4.00
192 Ryan Braun **RC** .50
193 Oswaldo Navarro **RC** .50
194 Mike Rabelo **RC** .50
195 Delwyn Young **(RC)** .50
196 Miguel Montero **(RC)** .50
197 Matt Lindstrom **(RC)** .50
198 Josh Hamilton **(RC)** 2.00
199 Elijah Dukes **RC** 1.00
200 Sean Henn **(RC)** .50
201 Delmon Young **(RC)** 1.00
202 Alexi Casilla **RC** 1.00
203 Hunter Pence **(RC)** 8.00
204 Jeff Baker **(RC)** .50
205 Hector Gimenez **(RC)** .50
206 Ubaldo Jimenez **(RC)** .75
207 Adam Lind **(RC)** 1.00
208 Joaquin Arias **(RC)** 1.00
209 David Murphy **(RC)** .50
210 Daisuke Matsuzaka **RC** 8.00
211 Jerry Owens **(RC)** .50
212 Ryan Sweeney **(RC)** .50
213 Kei Igawa **RC** 1.00
214 Mitch Maier **RC** .50
215 Philip Humber **(RC)** 1.00
216 Troy Tulowitzki **(RC)** 2.00
217 Tim Lincecum **RC** 8.00
218 Michael Bourn **(RC)** 1.00
219 Hideki Okajima **RC** 2.00
220 Josh Fields **(RC)** 1.00

Refractors

Refractor (1-190): 2-4X
Refractor RC (191-220): 1.5-2X
Inserted 4:Box

Blue Refractor

Blue Refractor (1-190): 4-6X
Blue Refractor RC (191-220): 3-5X
Production 150 Sets

Gold Refractor

Gold Refractor (1-190): 10-15X
Gold Refractor RC (191-220): 8-15X
Production 50 Sets

Orange Refractor

Orange Refractor (1-190): 10-20X
Orange Refractor RC(191-220): 10-20X
Production 25 Sets

Red Refractor

Production Five Sets

Super-Fractor

Production One Set

X-Fractor

X-Fractor (1-190): 3-5X
X-Fractor RC (191-220): 2-4X
Production 250 Sets

Printing Plates

Production One Set

Chrome Prospects

NM/M
Common Player: .50
Common Auto. (221-256): 10.00
BC1 Cooper Brannon 1.00
BC2 Jason Taylor 1.00
BC3 Shawn O'Malley .50
BC4 Robert Alcombrack .50
BC5 Dellin Betances 4.00
BC6 Jeremy Papelbon 1.00
BC7 Adam Carr .50
BC8 Matthew Clarkson .50
BC9 Darin McDonald .50
BC10 Brandon Rice .50
BC11 Matthew Sweeney 3.00
BC12 Scott Deal .50
BC13 Brennan Boesch .50
BC14 Scott Taylor .50
BC15 Michael Brantley 1.00
BC16 Yahmed Yema .50
BC17 Brandon Morrow 1.00
BC18 Cole Garner .50
BC19 Erik Lis 1.00
BC20 Lucas French .50
BC21 Aaron Cunningham 3.00
BC22 Ryan Schreppel .50
BC23 Kevin Russo .50
BC24 Yohan Pino 1.00
BC25 Michael Sullivan 1.00
BC26 Trey Shields 1.00
BC27 Danny Matienzo .50
BC28 Chuck Lofgren .50
BC29 Gerrit Simpson .50
BC30 David Haehnel .50
BC31 Marvin Lowrance .50
BC32 Kevin Ardoin .50
BC33 Edwin Maysonet .50
BC34 Derek Griffith .50
BC35 Sam Fuld 1.00
BC36 Chase Wright 2.00
BC37 Brandon Roberts .50
BC38 Kyle Aselton .50
BC39 Steven Sollmann .50
BC40 Michael Devaney .50
BC41 Charlie Fermaint .50
BC42 Jesse Litsch 1.00
BC43 Bryan Hansen .50
BC44 Ramon Garcia 1.00
BC45 John Otness .50
BC46 Trey Hearne .50
BC47 Habelito Hernandez .50
BC48 Edgar Garcia .50
BC49 Seth Fortenberry .50
BC50 Reid Brignac 1.00
BC51 Derek Rodriguez .50
BC52 Ervin Alcantara .50
BC53 Tom Hottovy .50
BC54 Jesus Flores 1.00
BC55 Matt Palmer .50
BC56 Brian Henderson .50
BC57 John Gragg .50
BC58 Jay Garthwaite .50
BC59 Esmerling Vasquez .50
BC60 Gilberto Mejia 1.00
BC61 Aaron Jensen .50
BC62 Cedric Brooks 1.00
BC63 Brandon Mann .50
BC64 Myron Leslie 1.00
BC65 Ray Aguilar .50
BC66 Jesus Guzman 2.00
BC67 Sean Thompson .50
BC68 Jarrett Hoffpauir 1.00
BC69 Matt Goodson .50
BC70 Neal Musser .50
BC71 Tony Abreu 1.50
BC72 Tony Peguero 1.00
BC73 Michael Bertram .50
BC74 Randy Wells .50
BC75 Bradley Davis .50
BC76 Jay Sawatski .50
BC77 Vic Buttler 1.00
BC78 Jose Oyervidez 1.00
BC79 Doug Deeds 1.00
BC80 Daniel Dement .50
BC81 Spike Lundberg .50
BC82 Ricardo Nanita 1.00
BC83 Brad Knox 1.00
BC84 Will Venable 1.00
BC85 Greg Smith .50
BC86 Pedro Powell .50
BC87 Gabriel Medina .50
BC88 Duke Sardinha .50
BC89 Mike Madsen .50
BC90 Rayner Bautista .50
BC91 T.J. Nall .50
BC92 Neil Sellers .50
BC93 Andrew Dobies .50
BC94 Leo Daigle .50
BC95 Brian Duensing 2.00
BC96 Vincent Blue .50
BC97 Fernando Rodriguez .50
BC98 Derin McMains .50
BC99 Adam Bass .50
BC100 Justin Ruggiano 1.00
BC101 Jared Burton 1.00
BC102 Mike Parisi .50
BC103 Aaron Peel 1.00
BC104 Evan Englebrook .50
BC105 Sendy Vasquez .50
BC106 Desmond Jennings 1.50
BC107 Clay Harris 1.00
BC108 Cody Strait .50
BC109 Ryan Mullins .50
BC110 Ryan Webb .50
BC111 Mike Carp 1.00
BC112 Greg Porter .50
BC113 Joe Ness .50
BC114 Matt Camp .50
BC115 Carlos Fisher .50
BC116 Bryan Bass .50
BC117 Jeff Baisley 1.00
BC118 Burke Badenhop 1.00
BC119 Grant Psomas .50
BC120 Eric Young Jr. 1.00
BC121 Henry Rodriguez 1.00
BC122 Carlos Fernandez 1.00
BC123 Chris Errecart 1.00
BC124 Brandon Hynick 1.50
BC125 Jose Constanza .50
BC126 Steve Delabar .50
BC127 Raul Barron .50
BC128 Nick DeBarr .50
BC129 Reegie Corona 1.00
BC130 Thomas Fairchild .50
BC131 Bryan Byrne .50
BC132 Kurt Mertins .50
BC133 Erik Averill .50
BC134 Matt Young .50
BC135 Ryan Rogowski .50
BC136 Andrew Bailey 2.00
BC137 Jonathan Van Every .50
BC138 Scott Shoemaker .50
BC139 Steve Singleton .50
BC140 Mitch Atkins .50
BC141 Robert Rohrbaugh 1.00
BC142 Ole Sheldon .50
BC143 Adam Ricks .50
BC144 Daniel Mayora 1.50
BC145 Johnny Cueto 10.00
BC146 Jim Fasano .50
BC147 Jared Goedert 1.50
BC148 Jonathan Ash .50
BC149 Derek Miller .50
BC150 Juan Miranda 1.50
BC151 J.R. Mathes .50
BC152 Craig Cooper .50
BC153 Drew Locke .50
BC154 Michael MacDonald .50
BC155 Ryan Norwood .50
BC156 Tony Butler 1.50
BC157 Pat Dobson .50
BC158 Cody Ehlers .50
BC159 Dan Fournier .50
BC160 Joe Gaetti .50
BC161 Mark Wagner 1.50
BC162 Tommy Hanson 3.00
BC163 Sharlon Schoop .50
BC164 Woods Fines .50
BC165 Chad Boyd .50
BC166 Kala Kaaihu 3.00
BC167 Chris Salamida 1.00
BC168 Brendan Katin 1.00
BC169 Terrance Blunt .50
BC170 Tobi Stoner 1.00
BC171 Phil Coke .50
BC172 O.D. Gonzalez .50
BC173 Christopher Cody .50
BC174 Cedric Hunter 2.00
BC175 Whit Robbins .50
BC176 Chris Begg .50
BC177 Nathan Southard .50
BC178 Dan Brauer .50
BC179 Jared Keel .50
BC180 Chance Douglass 1.00
BC181 Daniel Murphy 1.00
BC182 Anthony Hatch .50
BC183 Justin Byler 1.00
BC184 Scott Lewis .50
BC185 Andrew Fie 1.00
BC186 Chorye Spoone 1.00
BC187 Cole Bruce .50
BC188 Adam Cowart 1.00
BC189 Chris Nowak .50
BC190 Gorkys Hernandez 4.00
BC191 Devin Ivany .50
BC192 Jordan Smith .50
BC193 Philip Britton .50
BC194 Cole Gillespie 1.00
BC195 Brett Anderson 2.50
BC196 Joe Mather 1.00
BC197 Eddie Degerman .50
BC198 Ronald Prettyman .50
BC199 Patrick Reilly .50
BC200 Tyler Clippard 1.00
BC201 Nick Van Stratten .50
BC202 Todd Redmond .50
BC203 Michael Martinez .50
BC204 Alberto Bastardo .75
BC205 Vasili Spanos .50
BC206 Shane Benson .50
BC207 Brent Johnson .50
BC208 Brett Campbell .50
BC209 Dustin Martin .50
BC210 Chris Carter 2.00
BC211 Alfred Joseph .50
BC212 Carlos Leon .50
BC213 Gabriel Sanchez 1.00
BC214 Carlos Corporan .50
BC215 Emerson Frostad .50
BC216 Karl Gelinas .50
BC217 Ryan Finan .50
BC218 Noe Rodriguez .50
BC219 Archie Gilbert .50
BC220 Jeff Locke 3.00
BC221 Fernando Martinez/ Auto. 100.00

BC222 Jeremy Papelbon/Auto. 20.00
BC223 Ryan Adams/Auto. 10.00
BC224 Chris Perez/Auto. 10.00
BC225 J.R. Towles/Auto. 30.00
BC226 Tommy Mendoza/Auto. 10.00
BC227 Jeff Samardzija/Auto. 40.00
BC228 Sergio Perez/Auto. 15.00
BC229 Justin Reed/Auto. 20.00
BC230 Luke Hochevar/Auto. 30.00
BC231 Ivan DeJesus/Auto. 25.00
'C232 Kevin Mulvey/Auto. 30.00
BC233 Chris Coghlan/Auto. 20.00
BC234 Trevor Cahill/Auto. 45.00
BC235 Peter Bourjos/Auto. 20.00
BC236 Joba Chamberlain/Auto. 160.00
BC237 Josh Rodriguez/Auto. 15.00
BC238 Tim Lincecum/Auto. 120.00
BC239 Josh Papelbon/Auto. 20.00
BC240 Greg Reynolds/Auto. 20.00
BC241 Wes Hodges/Auto. 25.00
BC242 Chad Reineke/Auto. 20.00
BC243 Emmanuel Burriss/Auto. 20.00
BC244 Henry Sosa/Auto. 20.00
BC245 Cesar Nicolas/Auto. 15.00
BC246 Young Il Jung/Auto. 20.00
BC247 Eric Patterson/Auto. 15.00
BC248 Hunter Pence/Auto. 35.00
BC249 Dellin Betances/Auto. 60.00
BC250 Will Venable/Auto. 20.00
BC251 Zach McAllister/Auto. 20.00
BC252 Mark Hamilton/Auto 20.00
BC253 Paul Estrada/Auto. 15.00
BC254 Brad Lincoln/Auto. 15.00
BC255 Cedric Hunter/Auto. 35.00
BC256 Chad Rodgers/Auto. 15.00

Chrome Prospects Refractor

Refractor (1-200): 3-5X
Refractor Auto.(201-256): 1-1.5X
Production 500 Sets

Chrome Prospects Blue Refractor

Blue Refractor (1-200): 5-10X
Blue Refractor Auto.(201-256): 1.5-2.5X
Production 150 Sets

Chrome Prospects Gold Refractor

Gold Refractor (1-200): 15-25X
Gold Refractor Auto.(201-256): 3-5X
Production 50 Sets

Chrome Prospects Orange Refractor

Orange Refractor (1-200): No Pricing
Orange Refract Auto. (201-256): No Pricing
Production 25 Sets

Chrome Prospects Red Refractor

No Pricing
Production Five Sets

Chrome Prospects X-Fractor

X-Fractor (1-200): 4-8X
Production 250 Sets
X-Fractor/Auto. (201-256): 1-2X
Production 225 Sets

2007 Bowman Chrome Draft

NM/M

Complete Set (54): 25.00
Common RC: .50
1 Travis Buck **(RC)** .50
2 Matt Chico **(RC)** .50
3 Justin Upton **RC** 2.50
4 Chase Wright **RC** 1.00
5 Kevin Kouzmanoff **(RC)** .50
6 John Danks **(RC)** 1.00
7 Alejandro De Aza **RC** .50
8 Jamie Vermilyea **RC** .50
9 Jesus Flores **RC** .50
10 Glen Perkins **(RC)** .50
11 Tim Lincecum **RC** 2.50
12 Cameron Maybin **RC** 2.00
13 Brandon Morrow **RC** .50
14 Mike Rabelo **RC** .50
15 Alex Gordon **RC** 2.00
16 Zack Segovia **(RC)** .50
17 Jon Knott **(RC)** .50
18 Joba Chamberlain **RC** 5.00
19 Danny Putnam **(RC)** .50
20 Matt DeSalvo **(RC)** .50
21 Fred Lewis **(RC)** .50
22 Sean Gallagher **(RC)** .50
23 Brandon Wood **(RC)** .50
24 Dennis Dove **(RC)** .50
25 Hunter Pence **(RC)** 2.00
26 Jarrod Saltalamacchia **(RC)** .50
27 Ben Francisco **(RC)** .50
28 Doug Slaten **RC** .50
29 Tony Abreu **RC** .50
30 Billy Butler **(RC)** 1.00
31 Jesse Litsch **RC** .50
32 Nate Schierholtz **(RC)** .50
33 Jared Burton **RC** .50
34 Matt Brown **RC** .50
35 Dallas Braden **RC** .50
36 Carlos Gomez **RC** 1.00
37 Brian Stokes **(RC)** .50
38 Kory Casto **(RC)** .50
39 Mark McLemore **(RC)** .50
40 Andy LaRoche **(RC)** 1.00
41 Tyler Clippard **(RC)** .50
42 Curtis Thigpen **(RC)** .50
43 Yunel Escobar **(RC)** .50
44 Andrew Sonnanstine **RC** .50
45 Felix Pie **(RC)** .50
46 Homer Bailey **(RC)** 1.00
47 Kyle Kendrick **RC** .50
48 Angel Sanchez **RC** .50
49 Phil Hughes **(RC)** 2.00
50 Ryan Braun **(RC)** 2.00
51 Kevin Slowey **(RC)** .50
52 Brendan Ryan **(RC)** .50
53 Yovani Gallardo **(RC)** 1.00
54 Mark Reynolds **RC** .50
237 Barry Bonds 2.00

Refractor

Refractor: 2-3X
Inserted 1:11

Blue Refractor

Blue Refractor: 3-5X
Production 199 Sets

Gold Refractor

Gold Refractor: 8-15X
Production 50 Sets

Orange Refractor

Orange Refractor: No Pricing
Production 25 Sets

Red Refractor

No Pricing
Production Five Sets

SuperFractor

No Pricing
Production One Set

X-Fractor

X-Fractor: 3-4X
Production 299 Sets

Draft Picks

NM/M

Common Draft Pick (1-65): .50
Common DP Auto. (111-140): 15.00
1 Cody Crowell .75
2 Karl Bolt .50
3 Corey Brown .50
4 Tyler Mach .50
5 Trevor Pippin .50
6 Ed Easley .50
7 Cory Luebke .50
8 Darin Mastroianni .50
9 Ryan Zink .75
10 Brandon Hamilton 1.00
11 Kyle Lotzkar 1.00
12 Freddie Freeman 4.00
13 Nicholas Barnese 1.50
14 Travis d'Arnaud .75
15 Eric Eiland 1.00
16 John Ely .50
17 Oliver Marmol .50
18 Eric Sogard .50
19 Lars Davis .50
20 Sam Runion 1.50
21 Austin Gallagher 1.50
22 Matt West 1.50
23 Derek Norris .75
24 Taylor Holiday .50
25 Dustin Biell .50
26 Julio Borbon 1.00
27 Brant Rustich .50
28 Andrew Lambo 3.00
29 Corey Kluber .50
30 Justin Jackson 1.50
31 Scott Carroll .50
32 Danny Rams .75
33 Thomas Eager .50
34 Matt Dominguez 3.00
35 Steven Souza 1.00
36 Craig Heyer .50
37 Michael Taylor 3.00
38 Drew Bowman .50
39 Frank Gailey .50
40 Jeremy Hefner .50
41 Reynaldo Navarro .75
42 Daniel Descalso 1.00
43 Leroy Hunt .50
44 Jason Kiley .50
45 Ryan Pope 1.50
46 Josh Horton .75
47 Jason Monti .50
48 Richard Lucas .50
49 Jonathan Lucroy 1.50
50 Sean Doolittle 2.50
51 Mike McDade .50
52 Charlie Culberson 1.50
53 Michael Moustakas 5.00
54 Jason Heyward 6.00
55 David Price 6.00
56 Brad Mills .50
57 John Tolisano 1.00
58 Jarrod Parker 2.00
59 Wendell Fairley 3.00
60 Gary Gattis 1.00
61 Madison Bumgarner 4.00
62 Danny Payne .50
63 Jake Smolinski 1.50
64 Matt LaPorta 8.00
65 Jackson Williams .50
111 Daniel Moskos 15.00
112 Ross Detwiler 25.00
113 Tim Alderson 30.00
114 Beau Mills 35.00
115 Devin Mesoraco 25.00
116 Kyle Lotzkar 20.00
117 Blake Beavan 30.00
118 Peter Kozma 20.00
119 Chris Withrow 25.00
120 Cory Luebke 20.00
121 Nick Schmidt 20.00
122 Michael Main 25.00
123 Aaron Poreda 20.00
124 James Simmons 15.00
125 Ben Revere 30.00
126 Joe Savery 20.00
127 Jonathan Gilmore 25.00
128 Todd Frazier 25.00
129 Matt Mangini 20.00
130 Casey Weathers 20.00
131 Nick Noonan 35.00
132 Kellen Kulbacki 30.00
133 Michael Burgess 40.00
134 Nick Hagadone 30.00
135 Clayton Mortensen 20.00
136 Justin Jackson 20.00
137 Ed Easley 15.00
138 Corey Brown 25.00
139 Danny Payne 20.00
140 Travis d'Arnaud 15.00

Draft Picks Refractor

Refractor (1-65): 2-4X
Inserted 1:11
Refractor Auto. (111-140): 1-1.5X
Production 500 for autos.

Draft Picks Blue Refractor

Blue Refract.(1-65): 6-12X
Production 199
Blue Refr. Auto. (111-140): 2-3X
Production 150 Sets

Draft Picks Gold Refractor

Gold Refract.(1-65): 20-30X
Gold Refr. Auto. (111-140): 4-8X
Production 50 Sets

Draft Picks Orange Refractor

No Pricing
Production 25 Sets

Draft Picks Red Refractor

No Pricing
Production Five Sets

Draft Picks X-Fractor

X-Fractor (1-65): 4-8X
Production 299
X-Fractor Auto. (111-140): 1-2X
Production 225

Draft Picks SuperFractor

No Pricing
Production One Set

Draft Picks Printing Plate

No Pricing
Production one set per color.

Future's Game Prospects

NM/M

Complete Set (66-110): 15.00
Common Prospect: .50
66 Pedro Beato .50
67 Collin Balester .50
68 Carlos Carrasco .50
69 Clay Buchholz 1.00
70 Emiliano Fruto .50
71 Joba Chamberlain 5.00
72 Deolis Guerra .50
73 Kevin Mulvey .50
74 Franklin Morales .50
75 Luke Hochevar 1.00
76 Henry Sosa .50
77 Clayton Kershaw 1.00
78 Rich Thompson .50
79 Chuck Lofgren .50
80 Rick Vanden Hurk .50
81 Mike Madsen .50
82 Robinzon Diaz .50
83 Jeff Niemann .50
84 Max Ramirez .50
85 Geovany Soto .50
86 Elvis Andrus 1.00
87 Bryan Anderson .50
88 German Duran .50
89 J.R. Towles .50
90 Alcides Escobar .50
91 Brian Bocock .50
92 Chin-Lung Hu .50
93 Adrian Cardenas .50
94 Freddy Sandoval .50
95 Chris Coghlan .50
96 Craig Stansberry .50
97 Brent Lillibridge .50
98 Joey Votto .50
99 Evan Longoria 3.00
100 Wladimir Balentien .50
101 Johnny Whittleman .50
102 Gorkys Hernandez .50
103 Jay Bruce 2.00
104 Matt Tolbert .50
105 Jacoby Ellsbury 2.50
106 Mike Saunders 2.50
107 Cameron Maybin 2.00
108 Carlos Gonzalez .50
109 Colby Rasmus 1.00
110 Justin Upton 2.00

Future's Game Refractor

Refractor: 2-3X
Inserted 1:11

Future's Game Blue Refractor

Blue Refractor: 3-5X
Production 199 Sets

Future's Game Gold Refractor

Gold Refractor: 8-15X
Production 50 Sets

Future's Game Orange Refractor

No Pricing
Production 25 Sets

Future's Game Red Refractor

No Pricing
Production Five Sets

Future's Game Superfractor

No Pricing
Production One Set

Future's Game X-Fractor

X-Fractor: 3-4X
Production 299 Sets

Future's Game Prospects Patch

NM/M

Common Player: 15.00
Production 99 Sets
66 Pedro Beato 25.00
67 Collin Balester 15.00
68 Carlos Carrasco 15.00
69 Clay Buchholz 35.00
70 Emiliano Fruto 15.00
71 Joba Chamberlain 75.00
72 Deolis Guerra 30.00
73 Kevin Mulvey 15.00
74 Franklin Morales 15.00
75 Luke Hochevar 30.00
76 Henry Sosa 20.00
77 Clayton Kershaw 20.00
78 Rich Thompson 15.00
79 Chuck Lofgren 20.00
80 Rick Vanden Hurk 20.00
81 Mike Madsen 15.00
82 Robinzon Diaz 15.00
83 Jeff Niemann 15.00
84 Max Ramirez 15.00
85 Geovany Soto 25.00
86 Elvis Andrus 25.00
87 Bryan Anderson 20.00
88 German Duran 25.00
89 J.R. Towles 25.00
90 Alcides Escobar 15.00
91 Brian Bocock 15.00
92 Chin-Lung Hu 60.00
93 Adrian Cardenas 20.00
94 Freddy Sandoval 15.00
95 Chris Coghlan 15.00
96 Craig Stansberry 15.00
97 Brent Lillibridge 15.00
98 Joey Votto 20.00
99 Evan Longoria 30.00
100 Wladimir Balentien 10.00
101 Johnny Whittleman 20.00
102 Gorkys Hernandez 15.00
103 Jay Bruce 40.00
104 Matt Tolbert 20.00
105 Jacoby Ellsbury 65.00
106 Mike Saunders 25.00
107 Cameron Maybin 25.00
108 Carlos Gonzalez 20.00
109 Colby Rasmus 30.00
110 Justin Upton 40.00

Future's Game Prospects Base

NM/M

Common Player: 8.00
Production 135 Sets .50
86 Elvis Andrus 8.00
87 Bryan Anderson 8.00
88 German Duran 8.00
89 J.R. Towles 10.00
91 Brian Bocock 8.00
92 Chin-Lung Hu 25.00
93 Adrian Cardenas 10.00
94 Freddy Sandoval 8.00
95 Chris Coghlan 8.00
97 Brent Lillibridge 8.00
98 Joey Votto 10.00
99 Evan Longoria 20.00
101 Johnny Whittleman 8.00
102 Gorkys Hernandez 8.00
103 Jay Bruce 20.00
105 Jacoby Ellsbury 25.00
106 Mike Saunders 10.00
108 Carlos Gonzalez 8.00
109 Colby Rasmus 20.00
110 Justin Upton 20.00

2007 Bowman Draft

NM/M

Complete Set (54): 15.00
Common RC: .25
Hobby Pack (7): 4.00
Hobby Box (24): 80.00
1 Travis Buck **(RC)** .25
2 Matt Chico **(RC)** .25
3 Justin Upton **RC** 1.00
4 Chase Wright **RC** .50

5	Kevin Kouzmanoff **(RC)**	.25
6	John Danks **(RC)**	.50
7	Alejandro De Aza **RC**	.25
8	Jamie Vermilyea **RC**	.25
9	Jesus Flores **RC**	.25
10	Glen Perkins **(RC)**	.25
11	Tim Lincecum **RC**	1.00
12	Cameron Maybin **RC**	1.00
13	Brandon Morrow **RC**	.25
14	Mike Rabelo **RC**	.25
15	Alex Gordon **RC**	1.00
16	Zack Segovia **(RC)**	.25
17	Jon Knott **(RC)**	.25
18	Joba Chamberlain **RC**	2.50
19	Danny Putnam **(RC)**	.25
20	Matt DeSalvo **(RC)**	.25
21	Fred Lewis **(RC)**	.25
22	Sean Gallagher **(RC)**	.25
23	Brandon Wood **(RC)**	.25
24	Dennis Dove **(RC)**	.25
25	Hunter Pence **(RC)**	1.00
26	Jarrod Saltalamacchia **(RC)**	.25
27	Ben Francisco **(RC)**	.25
28	Doug Slaten **RC**	.25
29	Tony Abreu **RC**	.25
30	Billy Butler **(RC)**	.50
31	Jesse Litsch **RC**	.25
32	Nate Schierholtz **(RC)**	.25
33	Jared Burton **RC**	.25
34	Matt Brown **RC**	.25
35	Dallas Braden **RC**	.25
36	Carlos Gomez **RC**	.50
37	Brian Stokes **(RC)**	.25
38	Kory Casto **(RC)**	.25
39	Mark McLemore **(RC)**	.25
40	Andy LaRoche **(RC)**	.50
41	Tyler Clippard **(RC)**	.25
42	Curtis Thigpen **(RC)**	.25
43	Yunel Escobar **(RC)**	.25
44	Andrew Sonnanstine **RC**	.25
45	Felix Pie **(RC)**	.25
46	Homer Bailey **(RC)**	.50
47	Kyle Kendrick **RC**	.25
48	Angel Sanchez **RC**	.25
49	Phil Hughes **(RC)**	1.00
50	Ryan Braun **(RC)**	1.00
51	Kevin Slowey **(RC)**	.25
52	Brendan Ryan **(RC)**	.25
53	Yovani Gallardo **(RC)**	.50
54	Mark Reynolds **RC**	.25
237	Barry Bonds	1.00

Blue

Blue: 2-4X
Production 399 Sets

Gold

Gold: 1-2X
Inserted 1:1

Red

Production One Set

Printing Plates

No Pricing
Production one set per color.

A-Rod Road to 500

NM/M

Common A-Rod (426-450): 2.00
Inserted 2:Box
Autographs: No Pricing
Production One Set

Draft Picks

NM/M

Complete Set (65): 15.00
Common Draft Pick: .25

1	Cody Crowell	.25
2	Karl Bolt	.25
3	Corey Brown	.25
4	Tyler Mach	.25
5	Trevor Pippin	.25
6	Ed Easley	.25
7	Cory Luebke	.25
8	Darin Mastroianni	.25
9	Ryan Zink	.25
10	Brandon Hamilton	.50
11	Kyle Lotzkar	.50
12	Freddie Freeman	1.50
13	Nicholas Barnese	.50
14	Travis d'Arnaud	.25
15	Eric Eiland	.50
16	John Ely	.25
17	Oliver Marmol	.25
18	Eric Sogard	.25
19	Lars Davis	.25
20	Sam Runion	.50
21	Austin Gallagher	.50
22	Matt West	.50
23	Derek Norris	.25
24	Taylor Holiday	.25
25	Dustin Biell	.25
26	Julio Borbon	.50
27	Brant Rustich	.25
28	Andrew Lambo	1.00
29	Corey Kluber	.25
30	Justin Jackson	.50
31	Scott Carroll	.25
32	Danny Rams	.25
33	Thomas Eager	.25
34	Matt Dominguez	1.00
35	Steven Souza	.50
36	Craig Heyer	.25
37	Michael Taylor	1.00
38	Drew Bowman	.25
39	Frank Gailey	.25
40	Jeremy Hefner	.25
41	Reynaldo Navarro	.25
42	Daniel Descalso	.50
43	Leroy Hunt	.25
44	Jason Kiley	.25
45	Ryan Pope	.50
46	Josh Horton	.25
47	Jason Monti	.25
48	Richard Lucas	.25
49	Jonathan Lucroy	.50
50	Sean Doolittle	.75
51	Mike McDade	.25
52	Charlie Culberson	.50
53	Michael Moustakas	1.50
54	Jason Heyward	2.00
55	David Price	2.00
56	Brad Mills	.25
57	John Tolisano	.50
58	Jarrod Parker	.75
59	Wendell Fairley	1.00
60	Gary Gattis	.50
61	Madison Bumgarner	1.50
62	Danny Payne	.25
63	Jake Smolinski	.50
64	Matt LaPorta	2.50
65	Jackson Williams	.25

Draft Picks Blue

Blue: 2-4X
Production 399 Sets

Draft Picks Gold

Gold: 1-2X
Inserted 1:1

Draft Picks Red

No Pricing
Production One Set

Draft Picks Printing Plates

Production one set per color.

Future's Game Prospects

NM/M

Complete Set (66-110): 8.00
Common Prospect: .25

66	Pedro Beato	.25
67	Collin Balester	.25
68	Carlos Carrasco	.25
69	Clay Buchholz	.50
70	Emiliano Fruto	.25
71	Joba Chamberlain	2.00
72	Deolis Guerra	.25
73	Kevin Mulvey	.25
74	Franklin Morales	.25
75	Luke Hochevar	.50
76	Henry Sosa	.25
77	Clayton Kershaw	.50
78	Rich Thompson	.25
79	Chuck Lofgren	.25
80	Rick Vanden Hurk	.25
81	Mike Madsen	.25
82	Robinzon Diaz	.25
83	Jeff Niemann	.25
84	Max Ramirez	.25
85	Geovany Soto	.50
86	Elvis Andrus	.50
87	Bryan Anderson	.25
88	German Duran	.25
89	J.R. Towles	.50
90	Alcides Escobar	.25
91	Brian Bocock	.25
92	Chin-Lung Hu	.25
93	Adrian Cardenas	.25
94	Freddy Sandoval	.25
95	Chris Coghlan	.25
96	Craig Stansberry	.25
97	Brent Lillibridge	.25
98	Joey Votto	.25
99	Evan Longoria	1.00
100	Wladimir Balentien	.25
101	Johnny Whittleman	.25
102	Gorkys Hernandez	.25
103	Jay Bruce	1.00
104	Matt Tolbert	.25
105	Jacoby Ellsbury	1.00
106	Mike Saunders	1.00
107	Cameron Maybin	1.00
108	Carlos Gonzalez	.25
109	Colby Rasmus	.50
110	Justin Upton	1.00

Future's Game Prospects Blue

Blue: 2-4X
Production 399 Sets

Future's Game Prospects Gold

Gold: 1-2X
Inserted 1:1

Future's Game Prospects Red

No Pricing
Production One Set

Future's Game Prospect Printing Plate

Production one set per color.

Future's Game Prospects Jersey

NM/M

Complete Player: 5.00

68	Carlos Carrasco	5.00
69	Clay Buchholz	15.00
71	Joba Chamberlain	30.00
73	Kevin Mulvey	5.00
74	Franklin Morales	5.00
75	Luke Hochevar	8.00
78	Rich Thompson	5.00
83	Jeff Niemann	8.00
84	Max Ramirez	5.00
89	J.R. Towles	8.00
95	Chris Coghlan	5.00
96	Craig Stansberry	5.00
97	Brent Lillibridge	5.00
98	Joey Votto	10.00
102	Gorkys Hernandez	8.00
105	Jacoby Ellsbury	25.00
106	Mike Saunders	10.00
107	Cameron Maybin	10.00
108	Carlos Gonzalez	8.00
110	Justin Upton	15.00

Head of the Class Dual Autograph

NM/M

Production 174 Sets
Refractor: 1-1.5X
Production 50 Sets
Gold Refractor: No Pricing
Production 25 Sets
SuperFractor: No Pricing
Production One Set

GH	Jonathan Gilmore, Jason Heyward	75.00
HP	Luke Hochevar, David Price	50.00

Signs of the Future

NM/M

Common Auto.: 10.00

HC	Hank Conger	15.00
AL	Anthony Lerew	10.00
BA	Brandon Allen	10.00
CM	Casey McGehee	10.00
PH	Philip Humber	10.00
CMM	Carlos Marmol	20.00
RD	Ryan Delaughter	10.00
AM	Adam Miller	15.00
CD	Chris Dickerson	10.00
CMC	Chris McConnell	15.00
JK	John Koronka	10.00
JR	John Rheinecker	10.00
JV	Jonathan Van Every	15.00
TC	Trevor Crowe	15.00
FM	Fernando Martinez	30.00
JGA	Jaime Garcia	15.00
JG	Jose Garcia	

2007 Bowman Heritage

NM/M

Complete Set (251):
Common player (1-200): .25
Common RC (201-251): .50
Common SP: 3.00
Inserted 1:3
SP's don't have auto on front.
Pack (8): 3.00
Box (24): 60.00

1	Jeff Francoeur	.50
2	Jered Weaver	.40
3	Derrek Lee	.50
4	Todd Helton	.50
5	Shawn Hill	.25
6	Ivan Rodriguez	.50
7	Mickey Mantle	5.00
8	Ramon Hernandez	.25
9	Randy Johnson	.75
10	Jermaine Dye	.25
11	Brian Roberts	.40
12	Hank Blalock	.40
13	Chien-Ming Wang	.75
14	Mike Lowell	.50
15	Brandon Webb	.50
16	Kelly Johnson	.25
17	Nick Johnson	.25
18	Zach Duke	.25
19	Aaron Hill	.25
20	Miguel Tejada	.50
21	Mark Buehrle	.40
22	Michael Young	.40
23	Carlos Delgado	.50
24	Anibal Sanchez	.25
25	Vladimir Guerrero	.75
26	Russell Martin	.40
27	Lance Berkman	.40
28	Bobby Crosby	.25
29	Javier Vazquez	.25
30	Manny Ramirez	.75
31	Rich Hill	.25
32	Mike Sweeney	.25
33	Jeff Kent	.40
34	Noah Lowry	.25
35	Alfonso Soriano	.75
36	Paul LoDuca	.25
37	J.D. Drew	.25
38	C.C. Sabathia	.50
39	Craig Biggio	.40
40	Adam Dunn	.50
41	Josh Beckett	.50
42	Carlos Guillen	.25
43	Jeff Francis	.25
44	Orlando Hudson	.25
45	Grady Sizemore	.75
46	Jason Jennings	.25
47	Mark Teixeira	.50
48	Freddy Garcia	.25
49	Adrian Gonzalez	.40
50	Albert Pujols	2.00
51	Tom Glavine	.50
52	J.J. Hardy	.40
53	Bobby Abreu	.40
54	Bartolo Colon	.25
55	Garrett Atkins	.40
56	Moises Alou	.40
57	Cliff Lee	.25
58	Mike Cuddyer	.25
59	Brandon Phillips	.40
60	Jeremy Bonderman	.40
61	Rickie Weeks	.40
62	Chris Carpenter	.50
63	Frank Thomas	.75
64	Victor Martinez	.50
65	Dontrelle Willis	.40
66	Jim Thome	.50
67	Aaron Rowand	.40
68	Andy Pettitte	.50
69	Brian McCann	.40
70	Roger Clemens	2.00
71	Gary Matthews	.25
72	Bronson Arroyo	.25
73	Jeremy Hermida	.25
74	Eric Chavez	.40
75	David Ortiz	.75
76	Stephen Drew	.50
77	Ronnie Belliard	.25
78	James Shields	.25
79	Richie Sexson	.40
80	Johan Santana	.75
81	Orlando Cabrera	.25
82	Aramis Ramirez	.50
83	Greg Maddux	1.00
84	Reggie Sanders	.25
85	Carlos Zambrano	.50
86	Bengie Molina	.25
87	David DeJesus	.25
88	Adam Wainwright	.40
89	Conor Jackson	.25
90	David Wright	1.00
91	Ryan Garko	.25
92	Bill Hall	.25
93	Marcus Giles	.25
94	Kenny Rogers	.25
95	Joe Mauer	.40
96	Hanley Ramirez	.75
97	Brian Giles	.25
98	Danny Haren	.25
99	Robinson Cano	.50
100	Ryan Howard	1.00
101	Andruw Jones	.40
102	Aaron Harang	.25
103	Hideki Matsui	1.50
104	Nick Swisher	.40
105	Pedro Martinez	.75
106	Felipe Lopez	.25
107	Erik Bedard	.50
108	Rafael Furcal	.40
109	Curt Schilling	.50
110	Jose Reyes	.75
111	Adam LaRoche	.40
112	Mike Mussina	.50
113	Melvin Mora	.25
114	Zack Greinke	.25
115	Justin Morneau	.75
116	Ervin Santana	.25
117	Ken Griffey Jr.	1.50
118	David Eckstein	.25
119	Jamie Moyer	.25
120	Jorge Posada	.50
121	Justin Verlander	.50
122	Sammy Sosa	.75
123	Jason Schmidt	.25
124	Josh Willingham	.25
125	Roy Oswalt	.50
126	Travis Hafner	.40
127	John Maine	.40
128	Willy Taveras	.25
129	Magglio Ordonez	.50
130	Barry Zito	.40
131	Prince Fielder	1.00
132	Michael Barrett	.25
133	Livan Hernandez	.25
134	Troy Glaus	.40
135	Rocco Baldelli	.40
136	Jason Giambi	.50
137	Austin Kearns	.25
138	Dan Uggla	.40
139	Pat Burrell	.40
140	Carlos Beltran	.50
141	Carlos Quentin	.25
142	Johnny Estrada	.25
143	Torii Hunter	.40
144	Carlos Lee	.50
145	Mike Piazza	.75
146	Mark Teahen	.25
147	Juan Pierre	.40
148	Paul Konerko	.50
149	Freddy Sanchez	.25
150	Derek Jeter	2.00
151	Orlando Hernandez	.25
152	Raul Ibanez	.25
153	John Smoltz	.50
154	Scott Rolen	.50
155	Jimmy Rollins	.50
156	A.J. Burnett	.25
157	Jason Varitek	.50
158	Ben Sheets	.40
159	Matt Cain	.40
160	Carl Crawford	.40
161	Jeff Suppan	.25
162	Tadahito Iguchi	.25
163	Kevin Millwood	.25
164	Chris Duncan	.25
165	Rich Harden	.25
166	Joe Crede	.25

167 Chipper Jones .75
168 Gary Sheffield .50
169 Cole Hamels .50
170 Jason Bay .40
171 Jhonny Peralta .40
172 Aubrey Huff .25
173 Xavier Nady .25
174 Kazuo Matsui .25
175 Vernon Wells .40
176 Johnny Damon .50
177 Jim Edmonds .40
178 Jose Vidro .25
179 Garret Anderson .25
180 Alex Rios .40
181 Ichiro Suzuki 1.50
181 Ichiro Suzuki/SP 6.00
182 Jake Peavy .50
182 Jake Peavy/SP 4.00
183 Ian Kinsler .50
183 Ian Kinsler/SP 3.00
184 Tom Gorzelanny .25
184 Tom Gorzelanny/SP 3.00
185 Miguel Cabrera .75
185 Miguel Cabrera/SP 5.00
186 Scott Kazmir .40
186 Scott Kazmir/SP 3.00
187 Matt Holliday .50
187 Matt Holliday/SP 5.00
188 Roy Halladay .50
188 Roy Halladay/SP 4.00
189 Ryan Zimmerman .50
189 Ryan Zimmerman/SP 4.00
190 Alex Rodriguez 2.00
190 Alex Rodriguez/SP 8.00
191 Kenji Johjima .25
191 Kenji Johjima/SP 3.00
192 Gil Meche .25
192 Gil Meche/SP 3.00
193 Chase Utley .75
193 Chase Utley/SP 5.00
194 Jeremy Sowers .25
194 Jeremy Sowers/SP 3.00
195 John Lackey .25
195 John Lackey/SP 3.00
196 Nick Markakis .50
196 Nick Markakis/SP 4.00
197 Tim Hudson .40
197 Tim Hudson/SP 3.00
198 B.J. Upton .50
198 B.J. Upton/SP 4.00
199 Felix Hernandez .50
199 Felix Hernandez/SP 4.00
200 Barry Bonds 2.00
200 Barry Bonds/SP 8.00
201 Jarrod Saltalamacchia **(RC)** .50
202 Tim Lincecum **RC** 5.00
203 Kory Casto **(RC)** .50
204 Sean Henn **(RC)** .50
205 Hector Gimenez **(RC)** .50
206 Homer Bailey **(RC)** 1.00
207 Yunel Escobar **(RC)** .50
208 Matt Lindstrom **(RC)** .50
209 Tyler Clippard **(RC)** .50
210 Joe Smith **RC** .50
211 Tony Abreu **RC** .50
212 Billy Butler **(RC)** 1.00
213 Gustavo Molina **RC** .50
214 Brian Stokes **(RC)** .50
215 Kevin Slowey **(RC)** .50
216 Curtis Thigpen **(RC)** .50
217 Carlos Gomez **RC** 2.00
218 Rick Vanden Hurk **RC** .50
219 Michael Bourn **(RC)** .50
220 Jeff Baker **(RC)** .50
221 Andy LaRoche **(RC)** 1.00
222 Andrew Sonnanstine **RC** .50
223 Chase Wright **RC** .50
224 Mark Reynolds **RC** 2.00
225 Matt Chico **(RC)** .50
226 Hunter Pence **(RC)** 2.00
226 Hunter Pence/SP 6.00
227 John Danks **(RC)** .50
227 John Danks/SP 3.00
228 Elijah Dukes **RC** .50
228 Elijah Dukes/SP 3.00
229 Kei Igawa **RC** 1.00
229 Kei Igawa/SP 4.00
230 Felix Pie **(RC)** .75
230 Felix Pie/SP 3.00
231 Jesus Flores **RC** .50
231 Jesus Flores/SP 3.00
232 Dallas Braden **RC** .50
232 Dallas Braden/SP 3.00
233 Akinori Iwamura **RC** 1.00
233 Akinori Iwamura/SP 4.00
234 Ryan Braun **(RC)** 2.50
234 Ryan Braun/SP 8.00
235 Alex Gordon **RC** 2.00
235 Alex Gordon/SP 6.00
236 Micah Owings **(RC)** .50
236 Micah Owings/SP 3.00
237 Kevin Kouzmanoff **(RC)** .75
237 Kevin Kouzmanoff/SP 3.00
238 Glen Perkins **(RC)** .50
238 Glen Perkins/SP 3.00
239 Danny Putnam **(RC)** .50
239 Danny Putnam/SP 3.00
240 Phil Hughes **(RC)** 2.00
240 Phil Hughes/SP 6.00
241 Ryan Sweeney **(RC)** .50
241 Ryan Sweeney/SP 3.00
242 Josh Hamilton **(RC)** 1.00
242 Josh Hamilton/SP 4.00
243 Hideki Okajima **RC** 1.00
243 Hideki Okajima/SP 4.00
244 Adam Lind **(RC)** .50
244 Adam Lind/SP 3.00
245 Travis Buck **(RC)** .50
245 Travis Buck/SP 3.00
246 Miguel Montero **(RC)** .50
246 Miguel Montero/SP 3.00
247 Brandon Morrow **RC** 1.00
247 Brandon Morrow/SP 4.00
248 Troy Tulowitzki **(RC)** 2.00
248 Troy Tulowitzki/SP 6.00
249 Delmon Young **(RC)** 1.00
249 Delmon Young/SP 4.00
250 Daisuke Matsuzaka **RC** 5.00
250 Daisuke Matsuzaka/SP 15.00
251 Joba Chamberlain **RC** 10.00

Red

Production One Set

Black

Black: 10-15X
Black SP's: 3-5X
Production 52 Sets

Rainbow

Rainbow: 1-2X
Rainbow SP's: .5-1X
Inserted 1:1

Printing Plates

Production one set per color.

A-Rod Road to 500

NM/M
Common A-Rod (351-375): 2.00
Inserted 2:Box
Autograph: No Pricing
Production One Set

Box Topper

NM/M
Common Player: 3.00
Inserted 1:Box
1 Alex Rodriguez 10.00
2 Barry Bonds 10.00
3 Ryan Howard 6.00
4 David Wright 6.00
5 Ichiro Suzuki 6.00
6 Hideki Matsui 6.00
7 Mickey Mantle 15.00
8 Manny Ramirez 3.00
9 David Ortiz 4.00
10 Vladimir Guerrero 3.00
11 Jose Reyes 5.00
12 Albert Pujols 10.00
13 Alfonso Soriano 3.00
14 Matt Holliday 3.00
15 Miguel Cabrera 3.00
16 Phil Hughes 8.00
17 Daisuke Matsuzaka 10.00
18 Delmon Young 3.00
19 Troy Tulowitzki 5.00
20 Felix Pie 3.00
21 Alex Gordon 8.00
22 Hunter Pence 5.00
23 Akinori Iwamura 3.00
24 Josh Hamilton 3.00
25 Kei Igawa 3.00

Mickey Mantle Shortprints

NM/M
Complete Set (5): 40.00
Common Mantle: 10.00
Black: 3-6X
Production 52 Sets
Red: No Pricing
Production One Set
1-5 Mickey Mantle 10.00

Pieces of Greatness

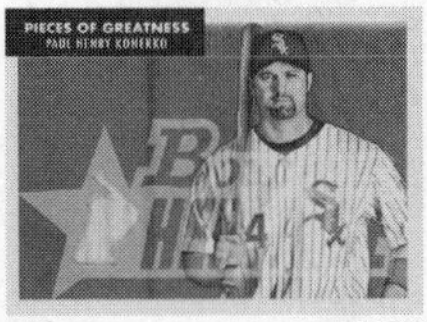

NM/M
Common Player: 4.00
Black: 2-3X
Production 52 Sets
Red: No Pricing
RB Rocco Baldelli 4.00
LB Lance Berkman 6.00
CB Craig Biggio 6.00
JB Jeremy Bonderman 4.00
BB Barry Bonds 20.00
MC Miguel Cabrera 8.00
RC Robinson Cano 8.00
RC2 Robinson Cano 8.00
EC Eric Chavez 4.00
BC Bobby Crosby 4.00
JD Johnny Damon 8.00
JDD J.D. Drew 4.00
AD Adam Dunn 6.00
JE Juan Encarnacion 4.00
DE Darin Erstad 4.00
AE Andre Ethier 4.00
JF Jeff Francoeur 10.00
JFR Jeff Francis 4.00
RF Rafael Furcal 4.00
BG Brian Giles 4.00
AG Alex Gonzalez 4.00
LG Luis Gonzalez 4.00
SG Shawn Green 4.00
VG Vladimir Guerrero 8.00
CH Cole Hamels 10.00
RH Rich Harden 4.00
TH Todd Helton 8.00
TH2 Todd Helton 8.00
THU Tim Hudson 6.00
TI Tadahito Iguchi 4.00
AJ Andruw Jones 6.00
JK Jeff Kent 4.00
PK Paul Konerko 6.00
PK2 Paul Konerko 6.00
CK Corey Koskie 4.00
AL Adam LaRoche 4.00
BL Brad Lidge 4.00
ML Mike Lowell 6.00
GM Greg Maddux 10.00
HM Hideki Matsui 15.00
JM Joe Mauer 6.00
YM Yadier Molina 4.00
MM Mark Mulder 4.00
TN Trot Nixon 4.00
MO Magglio Ordonez 4.00
DO David Ortiz 8.00
DO2 David Ortiz 8.00
CP Corey Patterson 4.00
MP Mike Piazza 8.00
AR Aramis Ramirez 8.00
MR Manny Ramirez 8.00
MR2 Manny Ramirez 8.00
JR Jose Reyes 10.00
ARO Alex Rodriguez 15.00
IR Ivan Rodriguez 6.00
CS Curt Schilling 8.00
GS Gary Sheffield 6.00
GSI Grady Sizemore 10.00
NS Nick Swisher 4.00
MT Mark Teixeira 8.00
MTE Miguel Tejada 6.00
FT Frank Thomas 8.00
CU Chase Utley 8.00
TW Tim Wakefield 4.00
DW Dontrelle Willis 4.00
DWR David Wright 10.00
BZBarry Zito 4.00
CBE Carlos Beltran 8.00
CT Chad Tracy 4.00

Prospects

NM/M
Common Prospect: .50
Inserted 2:Pack
Black: 10-15X
Production 52 Sets
Red: No Pricing
Production One Set
1 Thomas Fairchild .50
2 Peter Bourjos 1.00
3 Brett Campbell .50
4 Cesar Nicolas .50
5 Kala Kaaihu 1.00
6 Zach McAllister 1.00
7 Chad Reineke .50
8 Anthony Hatch .50
9 Cedric Hunter 1.00
10 Chris Carter 1.50
11 Tommy Hanson 2.00
12 Dellin Betances 2.00
13 John Otness .50
14 Derin McMains .50
15 Greg Reynolds .50
16 Jonathan Van Every .50
17 Eddie Degerman .50
18 Cody Strait .50
19 Noe Rodriguez .50
20 Young-Il Jung .50
21 Reegie Corona 1.00
22 Carlos Corporan .50
23 Chance Douglass .50
24 Leo Daigle .50
25 Jeff Samardzija 2.00
26 Mark Wagner .50
27 Chuck Lofgren 1.00
28 Bryan Byrne 1.00
29 Daniel Mayora 1.00
30 Gorkys Hernandez 2.00
31 Joshua Rodriguez .50
32 Brad Knox .50
33 Scott Lewis .50
34 Joe Gaetti .50
35 Mike Saunders 1.00
36 Brendan Katin .50
37 Brennan Boesch .50
38 Jay Garthwaite .50
39 Michael Devaney .50
40 J.R. Towles 1.50
41 Joe Ness 1.00
42 Michael Martinez 1.00
43 Justin Byler 1.00
44 Chris Coghlan 1.00
45 Eric Young Jr. 1.00
46 J.R. Mathes 1.00
47 Ivan DeJesus Jr. .50
48 Woods Fines .50
49 Andrew Fie .50
50 Luke Hochevar 2.00
51 Will Venable .50
52 Todd Redmond .50
53 Matthew Sweeney .50
54 Trevor Cahill 3.00
55 Mike Carp .50
56 Henry Sosa .50
57 Emerson Frostad .50
58 Jeremy Jeffress 1.00
59 Whit Robbins .50
60 Joba Chamberlain 10.00
61 Raul Barron .50
62 Aaron Cunningham 1.00
63 Greg Smith 1.00
64 Jeff Baisley .50
65 Vic Buttler .50
66 Steve Singleton .50
67 Josh Papelbon 1.00
68 Ryan Finan .50
69 Deolis Guerra 1.50
70 Vasili Spanos 1.00
71 Patrick Reilly .50
72 Tom Hottovy 1.00
73 Daniel Murphy .50
74 Matt Young 1.00
75 Brian Bocock 1.00
76 Chris Salamida .50
77 Nathan Southard .50
78 Brandon Hynick 1.50
79 Chris Nowak .50
80 Reid Brignac 1.00
81 Cole Garner .50
82 Nick Van Stratten 1.00
83 Jeremy Papelbon 1.00
84 Jarrett Hoffpauir .50
85 Kevin Mulvey 1.00
86 Matt Miller .50
87 Devin Ivany 1.00
88 Marcus Sanders .50
89 Michael MacDonald .50
90 Gabriel Sanchez .50
91 Ryan Norwood .50
92 Jim Fasano .50
93 Ryan Adams .50
94 Evan Englebrook .50
95 Juan Miranda 2.00
96 Greg Porter .50
97 Shane Benson .50
98 Sam Fuld 1.00
99 Cooper Brannon .50
100 Fernando Martinez 4.00

Signs of Greatness

NM/M
Common Autograph: 8.00
Black: 1.5-2X
Production 52 Sets
Red: No Pricing
Production One Set
DW David Wright 75.00
CJ Chipper Jones 60.00
CC Carl Crawford 15.00
CH Cole Hamels 30.00
JH J.P. Howell 8.00
BJ Blake Johnson 15.00
JP Jorge Posada 35.00
NR Nolan Reimold 15.00
CA Carlos Arroyo 15.00
JB John Buck 15.00
JC Jorge Cantu 8.00
GM Garrett Mock 10.00
AO Adam Ottavino 15.00
RD Rajai Davis 10.00
MM Matt Maloney 10.00
WJB Joe Benson 15.00
JCB Jordan Brown 15.00
TG Tony Giarratano 8.00
GG Glenn Gibson 15.00
EJ Elliot Johnson 10.00
JM Jeff Manship 15.00
SS Scott Sizemore 15.00
MT Mike Thompson 8.00
SE Stephen Englund 10.00
AF Andrew Fie 15.00
SJ Seth Johnston 10.00
SK Sean Kazmar 10.00
JL Jeff Locke 20.00
SP Steve Pearce 20.00
CS Chorye Spoone 15.00
WCS Cody Strait 10.00
JT J.R. Towles 15.00
JW Johnny Whittleman 10.00

2007 Bowman Sterling

NM/M
Common RC: 3.00
Common RC Auto.: 10.00
Pack (5): 55.00
Box (6): 300.00
AAL Adam Lind **(RC)** 3.00
AG Alex Gordon **RC** 8.00
AI Akinori Iwamura **RC** 4.00
AL Andy LaRoche **(RC)** 4.00
AM Andrew Miller **RC** 8.00
AS Andrew Sonnanstine **RC** 5.00
BB Billy Butler **(RC)** 5.00
BF Ben Francisco **(RC)** 3.00
BS Brian Stokes **(RC)** 6.00
BW Brandon Wood **(RC)** 4.00
CG Carlos Gomez **RC** 5.00
CH Chase Headley/Auto. **(RC)** 15.00
CM Cameron Maybin/Auto. **RC** 20.00
CT Curtis Thigpen **(RC)** 3.00
DM Daisuke Matsuzaka **RC** 10.00
DMM David Murphy **(RC)** 3.00
DP Danny Putnam **(RC)** 3.00
DY Delmon Young **(RC)** 4.00
FL Fred Lewis **(RC)** 3.00
FP Felix Pie/Auto. **(RC)** 15.00
GO Garrett Olson **(RC)** 3.00
GP Glen Perkins/Auto. **(RC)** 10.00

HB	Homer Bailey/Auto. **(RC)**	15.00
HG	Hector Gimenez **(RC)**	3.00
HO	Hideki Okajima **RC**	5.00
HP	Hunter Pence **(RC)**	8.00
JB	Jeff Baker **(RC)**	3.00
JC1	Joba Chamberlain **RC**	15.00
JC2	Joba Chamberlain/ Auto. **RC**	100.00
JD	John Danks/Auto. **(RC)**	15.00
JDF	Josh Fields **(RC)**	3.00
JE	Jacoby Ellsbury **(RC)**	10.00
JF	Jesus Flores **RC**	4.00
JH	Josh Hamilton/Auto. **(RC)**	60.00
JL	Jesse Litsch/Auto. **RC**	10.00
JQF	Jake Fox **RC**	4.00
JR	Jo Jo Reyes **(RC)**	4.00
JS	Jarrod Saltalamacchia/ Auto. **(RC)**	15.00
JU	Justin Upton **RC**	8.00
KI	Kei Igawa **RC**	3.00
KK	Kevin Kouzmanoff **(RC)**	3.00
KKS	Kurt Suzuki/Auto. **(RC)**	10.00
KRK	Kyle Kendrick/Auto. **RC**	15.00
KS	Kevin Slowey/Auto. **(RC)**	15.00
MB	Michael Bourn **(RC)**	3.00
MC	Matt Chico/Auto. **(RC)**	10.00
MF	Mike Fontenot **(RC)**	4.00
MK	Masumi Kuwata **RC**	8.00
MM	Miguel Montero **(RC)**	3.00
MO	Micah Owings **(RC)**	3.00
MP	Manny Parra **(RC)**	4.00
MR	Mark Reynolds **RC**	5.00
MSM	Mark McLemore **(RC)**	3.00
NG	Nick Gorneault/Auto. **(RC)**	10.00
NS	Nate Schierholtz/ Auto. **(RC)**	10.00
PH	Phil Hughes **(RC)**	5.00
PH	Phil Hughes/Auto. **(RC)**	25.00
RB	Ryan Braun/Auto. **(RC)**	40.00
RS	Ryan Sweeney **(RC)**	3.00
RV	Rick Vanden Hurk **RC**	4.00
SD	Shelley Duncan **(RC)**	4.00
SG	Sean Gallagher **(RC)**	3.00
TA	Tony Abreu **RC**	3.00
TB	Travis Buck **(RC)**	3.00
TC	Tyler Clippard **(RC)**	3.00
TL	Tim Lincecum/Auto. **RC**	65.00
TM	Travis Metcalf **RC**	4.00
UJ	Ubaldo Jimenez **(RC)**	3.00
YE	Yunel Escobar **(RC)**	3.00
YG	Yovani Gallardo/Auto. **(RC)**	20.00
	Common Memorabilia:	4.00
AER	Alex Rodriguez	20.00
AJ	Andruw Jones	6.00
AP	Albert Pujols	15.00
AR	Alex Rios	8.00
AS	Alfonso Soriano	8.00
BLB	Barry Bonds	15.00
BP	Brad Penny	4.00
BR	Brian Roberts	6.00
BU	B.J. Upton	6.00
BW	Brandon Webb	6.00
CAB	Craig Biggio	6.00
CAG	Carlos Guillen	6.00
CH	Cole Hamels	8.00
CL	Carlos Lee	6.00
CMS	Curt Schilling	6.00
DDY	Dmitri Young	4.00
DO	David Ortiz	8.00
DW	David Wright	10.00
DWW	Dontrelle Willis	4.00
EC	Eric Chavez	4.00
IS	Ichiro Suzuki	20.00
JAV	Jason Varitek	10.00
JBR	Jose Reyes	10.00
JE	Jim Edmonds	4.00
JS	Johan Santana	8.00
JV	Justin Verlander	10.00
LB	Lance Berkman	6.00
MAR	Manny Ramirez	8.00
MC	Melky Cabrera	8.00
MCT	Mark Teixeira	8.00
MH	Matt Holliday	8.00
MJO	Magglio Ordonez	6.00
MM	Mickey Mantle	80.00
MT	Miguel Tejada	6.00
MY	Michael Young	6.00
OC	Orlando Cabrera	4.00
PF	Prince Fielder	10.00
RB	Rocco Baldelli	4.00
RC	Roger Clemens	15.00
RJC	Robinson Cano	10.00
RJH	Ryan Howard	15.00
RZ	Ryan Zimmerman	8.00
SK	Scott Kazmir	6.00
TH	Tim Hudson	6.00
TLH	Todd Helton	6.00
TW	Tim Wakefield	6.00
VG	Vladimir Guerrero	8.00

Refractors

RC's: 1-2X
RC Auto.: 1-2X
Relics: 1-2X

Black Refractors

No Pricing
Production 25 Sets

Red Refractors

Production One Set

Printing Plates

Production one set per color.

Dual Autographs

NM/M

Common Dual Auto.: 20.00
Refractors: 1-1.5X
Production 199 Sets
Black Refractor: No pricing
Production 25 Sets
Red Refractors: No pricing
Production One Set

BV	Jay Bruce, Joey Votto	75.00
CH	Shin-Soo Choo, Chin-Lung Hu	30.00
GM	Deolis Guerra, Fernando Martinez	50.00
HC	Phil Hughes, Joba Chamberlain	140.00
HP	Luke Hochevar, David Price	40.00
LC	Evan Longoria, Carl Crawford	30.00
MM	John Maine, Lastings Milledge	20.00
PB	Hunter Pence, Ryan Braun	60.00
PP	Jeremy Papelbon, Josh Papelbon	25.00
PS	Felix Pie, Jeff Samardzija	30.00

Prospects

NM/M

Common Prospect: 3.00
Common Prospect Auto.: 8.00

AC	Adrian Cardenas/Jsy/Auto.	10.00
AF	Andrew Fie	3.00
ALC	Aaron Cunningham	5.00
AP	Aaron Poreda/Auto.	15.00
BB	Brian Bocock/Jsy/Auto.	15.00
BB	Blake Beavan/Auto.	15.00
BEL	Brad Lincoln	3.00
BH	Brandon Hamilton	3.00
BHB	Burke Badenhop	3.00
BL	Bryan LaHair/Auto.	8.00
BM	Brandon MaGee/Auto.	8.00
BMI	Beau Mills/Auto.	20.00
BR	Ben Revere/Auto.	20.00
BWH	Brandon Hynick	5.00
CB	Collin Balester/Jsy/Auto.	10.00
CC	Chris Carter	8.00
CD	Chance Douglass	3.00
CG	Cole Gillespie/Auto.	15.00
CH	Chin-Lung Hu/Jsy/Auto.	50.00
CH	Cedric Hunter	3.00
CK	Clayton Kershaw/Jsy/Auto.	35.00
CL	Chuck Lofgren/Jsy/Auto.	15.00
CM	Clayton Mortensen/Auto.	10.00
CN	Chris Nowak	3.00
CR	Colby Rasmus/Jsy/Auto.	35.00
CS	Cody Strait	3.00
CW	Chris Withrow/Auto.	20.00
CWW	Casey Weathers/Auto.	10.00
DB	Daniel Bard/Auto.	20.00
DBE	Dellin Betances	8.00
DG	Deolis Guerra/Jsy/Auto.	30.00
DI	Devin Ivany	3.00
DJ	Desmond Jennings	5.00
DL	Drew Locke	3.00
DM	Daniel Moskos/Auto.	15.00
DME	Devin Mesoraco/Auto.	15.00
DMM	Derek Miller	5.00
DPP	David Price/Auto.	75.00
DS	James Simmons/Auto.	10.00
EE	Ed Easley	3.00
EL	Evan Longoria/Jsy/Auto.	60.00
EL	Erik Lis/Auto.	10.00
EM	Emerson Frostad	3.00
EY	Eric Young Jr.	3.00
FF	Freddie Freeman	6.00
GD	German Duran/Jsy/Auto.	15.00
GH	Gorkys Hernandez	6.00
GP	Greg Porter	3.00
GR	Greg Reynolds	3.00
GS	Greg Smith	3.00
HS	Henry Sosa/Jsy/Auto.	20.00
ID	Ivan DeJesus	4.00
IS	Ian Stewart/Jsy/Auto.	25.00
JA	J.P. Arencibia/Auto.	20.00
JAA	James Avery/Auto.	8.00
JB	Jay Bruce Jersey/Auto.	50.00
JB	Joe Benson/Auto.	15.00
JBO	Julio Borbon/Auto.	15.00
JG	Jonathan Gilmore/Auto.	15.00
JGA	Joe Gaetti	3.00
JGO	Jared Goedert	3.00
JH	Jason Heyward/Auto.	65.00
JJ	Justin Jackson	3.00
JL	Jeff Locke	8.00
JM	Joe Mather	5.00
JO	Josh Outman/Auto.	10.00
JP	Jason Place	3.00
JPA	Jeremy Papelbon	5.00
JPP	Josh Papelbon	5.00
JS	Joe Savery/Auto.	15.00
JS	Jeff Samardzija	5.00
JSM	Jake Smolinski	5.00
JT	J.R. Towles	6.00
JV	Joey Votto/Jsy/Auto.	25.00
JV	Josh Vitters/Auto.	40.00
JVE	Jonathan Van Every	3.00
JW	Johnny Whittleman/ Jsy/Auto.	10.00
KA	Kevin Ahrens/Auto.	20.00
KK	Kellen Kulbacki/Auto.	15.00
KK	Kala Kaaihu	6.00
MB	Michael Burgess/Auto.	25.00
MBB	Madison Bumgarner/Auto.	40.00
MC	Mike Carp	3.00
MCA	Mitch Canham/Auto.	10.00
MD	Mike Daniel/Auto.	10.00
MDE	Michael Devaney	3.00
MDO	Matt Dominguez/Auto.	25.00
MH	Mark Hamilton	3.00
MIM	Michael Main/Auto.	15.00
MLP	Matt LaPorta/Auto.	65.00
MM	Mike Madsen/Jsy/Auto.	10.00
MM	Matt McBride/Auto.	10.00
MMG	Matt Mangini/Auto.	15.00
MP	Mike Parisi/Auto.	10.00
MS	Mike Saunders	6.00
MY	Matt Young	3.00
NH	Nick Hagadone/Auto.	20.00
NN	Nick Noonan/Auto.	20.00
NS	Nick Schmidt/Auto.	10.00
OS	Ole Sheldon	3.00
PB	Pedro Beato/Jsy/Auto.	10.00
PK	Peter Kozma/Auto.	15.00
RD	Ross Detwiler/Auto.	20.00
RM	Ryan Mount/Auto.	8.00
RT	Rich Thompson	3.00
SF	Sam Fuld	6.00
SP	Steve Pearce/Jsy/Auto.	30.00
TA	Tim Alderson/Auto.	25.00
TF	Todd Frazier/Auto.	20.00
TF	Thomas Fairchild	3.00
TM	Tommy Manzella/Auto.	8.00
TS	Travis Snider/Auto.	35.00
TW	Ty Weeden/Auto.	15.00
VB	Vic Buttler	3.00
VS	Vasili Spanos	3.00
WF	Wendell Fairley/Auto.	25.00
WT	Wade Townsend/Auto.	8.00
ZM	Zach McAllister	3.00

Prospects Refractors

Prospects: 1-2X
Autos.: 1-2X
Production 199 Sets

Prospects Black Refractors

No Pricing
Production 25 Sets

Prospects Red Refractors

Production One Set

A-Rod Road to 500

NM/M

Common A-Rod (450-475): 10.00
Autographs: No Pricing
Production One Set

2007 Bowman's Best

NM/M

Common Player (1-33): .75
Common Auto. (23-51): 15.00
Common RC (52-81): 4.00
Production 799
Common RC Auto. (71-99): 10.00
Pack (5): 20.00
Box (15): 240.00

1	Jose Reyes	2.00
2	Derek Jeter	4.00
3	Vladimir Guerrero	1.50
4	Ichiro Suzuki	3.00
5	Jason Bay	.75
6	Joe Mauer	.75
7	Alfonso Soriano	1.50
8	David Ortiz	1.50
9	Andruw Jones	.75
10	Roger Clemens	3.00
11	Grady Sizemore	1.50
12	Magglio Ordonez	.75
13	Carl Crawford	.75
14	Chase Utley	1.50
15	Mark Teixeira	1.00
16	Ryan Zimmerman	1.00
17	Ken Griffey Jr.	3.00
18	Derrek Lee	1.00
19	Barry Bonds	4.00
20	Chipper Jones	1.50
21	Vernon Wells	.75
22	Manny Ramirez	1.50
23	Alex Rodriguez	4.00
23	Alex Rodriguez/Auto.	150.00
24	Ryan Howard	2.50
24	Ryan Howard/Auto.	65.00
25	Tom Glavine	1.00
25	Tom Glavine/Auto.	60.00
26	Gary Sheffield	1.00
26	Gary Sheffield/Auto.	25.00
27	Miguel Cabrera	1.50
27	Miguel Cabrera/Auto.	25.00
28	Robinson Cano	1.00
28	Robinson Cano/Auto.	30.00
29	David Wright	2.00
29	David Wright/Auto.	40.00
30	Jim Thome	1.00
30	Jim Thome/Auto.	35.00
31	Albert Pujols	4.00
31	Albert Pujols/Auto.	160.00
32	Jorge Posada	.75
33	Brian McCann	.75
33	Brian McCann/Auto.	35.00
34	Josh Barfield/Auto.	10.00
35	Melky Cabrera/Auto.	25.00
36	Bill Hall/Auto.	15.00
37	Cole Hamels/Auto.	30.00
38	Adam LaRoche/Auto.	15.00
39	Matt Holliday/Auto.	25.00
40	Jeremy Hermida/Auto.	10.00
41	Jonathan Papelbon/ Auto.	25.00
42	Hanley Ramirez/Auto.	25.00
43	Justin Verlander/Auto.	25.00
44	Andre Ethier/Auto.	15.00
46	Erik Bedard/Auto.	20.00
47	Freddy Sanchez/Auto.	15.00
48	Adrian Gonzalez/Auto.	15.00
49	Russell Martin/Auto.	20.00
50	B.J. Upton/Auto.	15.00
51	Prince Fielder/Auto.	30.00
52	Tony Abreu **RC**	4.00
53	Ben Francisco **(RC)**	4.00
54	Billy Butler **(RC)**	8.00
55	Phil Hughes **(RC)**	15.00
56	Josh Fields **(RC)**	4.00
57	Carlos Gomez **RC**	6.00
58	Akinori Iwamura **RC**	4.00
59	Matt Brown **RC**	4.00
60	Jesus Flores **RC**	4.00
61	Mike Fontenot **(RC)**	4.00
62	Ryan Feierabend **(RC)**	4.00
63	Miguel Montero **(RC)**	4.00
64	Daisuke Matsuzaka **RC**	15.00
64	Daisuke Matsuzaka/Jsy **RC**	25.00
65	Kei Igawa **RC**	4.00
66	Shawn Riggans **(RC)**	4.00
67	Masumi Kuwata **RC**	10.00
68	Kevin Slowey **(RC)**	4.00
69	Josh Hamilton **(RC)**	6.00
70	Curtis Thigpen **(RC)**	6.00
71	Justin Upton **RC**	12.00
71	Justin Upton/Auto. **RC**	75.00
72	Delmon Young **(RC)**	6.00
72	Delmon Young/Auto. **(RC)**	20.00
73	Brandon Wood **(RC)**	6.00
73	Brandon Wood/ Auto. **(RC)**	15.00
74	Felix Pie **(RC)**	6.00
74	Felix Pie/Auto. **(RC)**	15.00
75	Alex Gordon **RC**	10.00
75	Alex Gordon/Auto. **RC**	40.00
76	Mark Reynolds **RC**	6.00
76	Mark Reynolds/Auto. **RC**	30.00
77	Tyler Clippard **(RC)**	6.00
77	Tyler Clippard/Auto.	20.00
78	Adam Lind **(RC)**	4.00
78	Adam Lind/Auto. **(RC)**	15.00
79	Hunter Pence **(RC)**	10.00
79	Hunter Pence/Auto. **(RC)**	25.00
81	Jarrod Saltalamacchia **(RC)**	6.00
81	Jarrod Saltalamacchia/ Auto. **(RC)**	15.00
82	Kevin Kouzmanoff/ Auto. **(RC)**	15.00
83	Glen Perkins/Auto. **(RC)**	10.00
84	Michael Bourn/Auto. **(RC)**	10.00
85	Andrew Miller/Auto. **RC**	20.00
86	Fred Lewis/Auto. **(RC)**	15.00
88	Joba Chamberlain/ Auto. **RC**	100.00
89	Hideki Okajima/Auto. **RC**	30.00
90	Troy Tulowitzki/Auto. **(RC)**	25.00
91	Ryan Sweeney/ Auto. **(RC)**	10.00
92	Matt Lindstrom/Auto. **(RC)**	10.00
93	Tim Lincecum/Auto. **RC**	65.00
94	Homer Bailey/Auto. **(RC)**	20.00
95	Matt DeSalvo/Auto. **(RC)**	15.00
96	Alejandro De Aza/Auto. **RC**	10.00
97	Ryan Braun/Auto. **(RC)**	50.00
99	Andy LaRoche **(RC)**	15.00

Green

Green (1-33): 2-4X
Green RC (52-99): 1-2X
Production 249

Blue

NM/M

Blue (1-33): 3-5X
Blue Auto.(23-51): 1-1.5X
Blue RC (52-81): 1-2X
Blue RC Auto.(71-99): 1-1.5X
Matsuzaka Blue Jersey 40.00
Production 99 Sets

Gold

NM/M

Gold (1-33): 4-6X
Gold Auto.(23-51): 1-2X
Gold RC (52-81): 2-4X
Gold RC Auto.(71-99): 1-2X
Matsuzaka Gold Jersey 60.00
Production 50 Sets

Red

No Pricing
Production One Set

Printing Plates

Production one set per color.

AROD 500

NM/M

Inserted 1:20
AR500 Alex Rodriguez 8.00

A-Rod Road to 500

NM/M

Common A-Rod (401-425): 15.00
Autographs: No Pricing
Production One Set

Barry Bonds 756

NM/M

Inserted 1:20
BB756 Barry Bonds 8.00

Prospects

		NM/M
Common player (1-40):		4.00
Production 499		
Common Auto. (37-60):		10.00
1	Greg Smith	15.00
2	J.R. Towles	6.00
3	Jeff Locke	15.00
4	Henry Sosa	6.00
5	Ivan DeJesus Jr.	8.00
6	Brad Lincoln	6.00
7	Josh Papelbon	8.00
8	Mark Hamilton	6.00
9	Sam Fuld	10.00
10	Thomas Fairchild	4.00
11	Chris Carter	6.00
12	Chuck Lofgren	4.00
13	Joe Gaetti	4.00
14	Zach McAllister	4.00
15	Cole Gillespie	10.00
16	Jeremy Papelbon	6.00
17	Mike Carp	4.00
18	Cody Strait	4.00
19	Gorkys Hernandez	8.00
20	Andrew Fie	4.00
21	Erik Lis	4.00
22	Chance Douglass	4.00
23	Vasili Spanos	4.00
24	Desmond Jennings	4.00
25	Vic Buttler	4.00
26	Cedric Hunter	4.00
27	Emerson Frostad	4.00
28	Michael Devaney	6.00
29	Eric Young Jr.	4.00
30	Evan Englebrook	4.00
31	Aaron Cunningham	8.00
32	Dellin Betances	10.00
33	Mike Saunders	6.00
34	Deolis Guerra	10.00
35	Brian Bocock	8.00
36	Rich Thompson	6.00
37	Greg Reynolds	4.00
37	Greg Reynolds/Auto.	10.00
38	Jeff Samardzija	8.00
38	Jeff Samardzija/Auto.	25.00
39	Evan Longoria	10.00
39	Evan Longoria/Auto.	50.00
40	Luke Hochevar	8.00
40	Luke Hochevar/Auto.	25.00
41	James Avery/Auto.	8.00
42	Joe Mather/Auto.	15.00
43	Hank Conger/Auto.	15.00
44	Adam Miller/Auto.	15.00
45	Clayton Kershaw/Auto.	35.00
46	Adam Ottavino/Auto.	15.00
47	Jason Place/Auto.	20.00
48	Billy Rowell/Auto.	20.00
49	Brett Sinkbeil/Auto.	10.00
50	Colton Willems/Auto.	15.00
51	Cameron Maybin/Auto.	25.00
52	Jeremy Jeffress/Auto.	15.00
53	Fernando Martinez/Auto.	40.00
54	Chris Marrero/Auto.	40.00
55	Kyle McCulloch/Auto.	15.00
56	Chris Parmelee/Auto.	15.00
57	Emmanuel Burris/Auto.	15.00
58	Chris Coghlan/Auto.	15.00
59	Chris Perez/Auto.	15.00
60	David Huff/Auto.	10.00

Prospects Blue

Blue (1-40): 1-2X
Blue Auto.(37-60): 1-1.5X
Production 99 Sets

Prospects Green

Green (1-40): 1-1.5X
Production 249 Sets

Prospects Gold

Gold (1-40): 2-3X
Gold Auto. (37-60): 1.5-3X
Production 50 Sets

Prospects Red

Production One Set

2008 Bowman

		NM/M
Common Player (1-200):		.15
Common RC (201-220):		.25
Common RC Auto. (221-230):		10.00
Pack (10):		3.00
Box (24):		65.00
1	Ryan Braun	.75
2	David DeJesus	.15
3	Brandon Phillips	.40
4	Mark Teixeira	.40
5	Daisuke Matsuzaka	.75
6	Justin Upton	.50
7	Jered Weaver	.25
8	Todd Helton	.50
9	Cameron Maybin	.25
10	Erik Bedard	.25
11	Jason Bay	.25
12	Cole Hamels	.40
13	Bobby Abreu	.40
14	Carlos Zambrano	.40
15	Vladimir Guerrero	.75
16	Joe Blanton	.15
17	Bengie Molina	.15
18	Paul Maholm	.15
19	Adrian Gonzalez	.25
20	Brandon Webb	.50
21	Carl Crawford	.25
22	A.J. Burnett	.25
23	Dmitri Young	.15
24	Jeremy Hermida	.15
25	C.C. Sabathia	.50
26	Adam Dunn	.50
27	Matt Garza	.15
28	Adrian Beltre	.25
29	Kevin Millwood	.15
30	Manny Ramirez	.75
31	Javier Vazquez	.15
32	Carlos Delgado	.40
33	Jason Schmidt	.15
34	Torii Hunter	.40
35	Ivan Rodriguez	.50
36	Nick Markakis	.40
37	Gil Meche	.15
38	Garrett Atkins	.25
39	Fausto Carmona	.25
40	Joe Mauer	.25
41	Tom Glavine	.50
42	Hideki Matsui	1.00
43	Scott Rolen	.50
44	Tim Lincecum	.40
45	Prince Fielder	.75
46	Ted Lilly	.15
47	Frank Thomas	.50
48	Tom Gorzelanny	.15
49	Lance Berkman	.50
50	David Ortiz	.75
51	Dontrelle Willis	.15
52	Travis Hafner	.25
53	Aaron Harang	.25
54	Chris Young	.25
55	Vernon Wells	.25
56	Francisco Liriano	.25
57	Eric Chavez	.15
58	Phil Hughes	.40
59	Melvin Mora	.15
60	Johan Santana	.75
61	Brian McCann	.25
62	Pat Burrell	.25
63	Chris Carpenter	.25
64	Brian Giles	.15
65	Jose Reyes	.75
66	Hanley Ramirez	.75
67	Ubaldo Jimenez	.15
68	Felix Pie	.15
69	Jeremy Bonderman	.25
70	Jimmy Rollins	.50
71	Miguel Tejada	.50
72	Derek Lowe	.25
73	Alex Gordon	.40
74	John Maine	.25
75	Alfonso Soriano	.50
76	Richie Sexson	.25
77	Ben Sheets	.25
78	Hunter Pence	.40
79	Magglio Ordonez	.25
80	Josh Beckett	.50
81	Victor Martinez	.25
82	Mark Buehrle	.25
83	Jason Varitek	.40
84	Chien-Ming Wang	.50
85	Ken Griffey Jr.	1.50
86	Billy Butler	.15
87	Brad Penny	.15
88	Carlos Beltran	.50
89	Curt Schilling	.50
90	Jorge Posada	.40
91	Andruw Jones	.25
92	Bobby Crosby	.15
93	Freddy Sanchez	.15
94	Barry Zito	.15
95	Miguel Cabrera	.75
96	B.J. Upton	.25
97	Matt Cain	.25
98	Lyle Overbay	.15
99	Austin Kearns	.15
100	Alex Rodriguez	2.00
101	Rich Harden	.15
102	Justin Morneau	.40
103	Oliver Perez	.15
104	Gary Matthews	.15
105	Matt Holliday	.40
106	Justin Verlander	.40
107	Orlando Cabrera	.25
108	Rich Hill	.25
109	Tim Hudson	.25
110	Ryan Zimmerman	.25
111	Roy Oswalt	.40
112	Nick Swisher	.25
113	Raul Ibanez	.15
114	Kelly Johnson	.15
115	Alex Rios	.25
116	John Lackey	.25
117	Robinson Cano	.25
118	Michael Young	.25
119	Jeff Francis	.15
120	Grady Sizemore	.50
121	Mike Lowell	.25
122	Aramis Ramirez	.40
123	Stephen Drew	.25
124	Yovani Gallardo	.25
125	Chase Utley	.75
126	Dan Haren	.25
127	Jose Vidro	.15
128	Ronnie Belliard	.15
129	Yunel Escobar	.25
130	Greg Maddux	1.50
131	Garret Anderson	.15
132	Aubrey Huff	.15
133	Paul Konerko	.25
134	Dan Uggla	.25
135	Roy Halladay	.25
136	Andre Ethier	.15
137	Orlando Hernandez	.15
138	Troy Tulowitzki	.40
139	Carlos Guillen	.25
140	Scott Kazmir	.25
141	Aaron Rowand	.25
142	Jim Edmonds	.15
143	Jermaine Dye	.25
144	Orlando Hudson	.15
145	Derrek Lee	.50
146	Travis Buck	.15
147	Zack Greinke	.25
148	Jeff Kent	.25
149	John Smoltz	.50
150	David Wright	1.00
151	Joba Chamberlain	1.00
152	Adam LaRoche	.15
153	Kevin Youkilis	.25
154	Troy Glaus	.25
155	Nick Johnson	.15
156	J.J. Hardy	.15
157	Felix Hernandez	.40
158	Khalil Greene	.15
159	Gary Sheffield	.40
160	Albert Pujols	2.00
161	Chuck James	.15
162	Rocco Baldelli	.15
163	Eric Byrnes	.25
164	Brad Hawpe	.25
165	Delmon Young	.25
166	Chris Young	.25
167	Brian Roberts	.25
168	Russell Martin	.40
169	Hank Blalock	.25
170	Yadier Molina	.15
171	Jeremy Guthrie	.15
172	Chipper Jones	.75
173	Johnny Damon	.50
174	Ryan Garko	.15
175	Jake Peavy	.50
176	Chone Figgins	.25
177	Edgar Renteria	.25
178	Jim Thome	.50
179	Carlos Pena	.25
180	Corey Patterson	.15
181	Dustin Pedroia	.25
182	Brett Myers	.25
183	Josh Hamilton	.50
184	Randy Johnson	.50
185	Ichiro Suzuki	1.50
186	Aaron Hill	.15
187	Jarrod Saltalamacchia	.15
188	Mike Cuddyer	.15
189	Jeff Francoeur	.40
190	Derek Jeter	2.00
191	Curtis Granderson	.50
192	James Loney	.25
193	Brian Bannister	.15
194	Carlos Lee	.40
195	Pedro Martinez	.50
196	Asdrubal Cabrera	.15
197	Kenji Johjima	.25
198	Bartolo Colon	.15
199	Jacoby Ellsbury	.50
200	Ryan Howard	.75
201	Radhames Liz **RC**	.50
202	Justin Ruggiano **RC**	.50
203	Lance Broadway **RC**	.50
204	Joey Votto **(RC)**	.50
205	Billy Buckner **(RC)**	.25
206	Joe Koshansky **(RC)**	.25
207	Ross Detwiler **RC**	.50
208	Chin-Lung Hu **(RC)**	.50
209	Luke Hochevar **RC**	1.50
210	Jeff Clement **(RC)**	.50
211	Troy Patton **(RC)**	.50
212	Hiroki Kuroda **RC**	1.00
213	Emilio Bonifacio **RC**	.50
214	Andres Galarraga **RC**	1.00
215	Josh Anderson **(RC)**	.50
216	Nick Blackburn **RC**	2.50
217	Seth Smith **(RC)**	.50
218	Jonathan Meloan **RC**	.50
219	Alberto Gonzalez **(RC)**	.50
220	Josh Banks **(RC)**	.50
221	Clay Buchholz/Auto. **(RC)**	25.00
222	Nyjer Morgan/Auto. **(RC)**	10.00
223	Brandon Jones/Auto. **RC**	10.00
224	Sam Fuld/Auto. **RC**	10.00
225	Daric Barton/Auto. **(RC)**	10.00
226	Chris Seddon/Auto. **(RC)**	10.00
227	J.R. Towles/Auto. **RC**	10.00
228	Steve Pearce/Auto. **RC**	15.00
229	Ross Ohlendorf/Auto. **RC**	10.00
230	Clint Sammons/Auto. **(RC)**	10.00

Red

Production One Set

Orange

Orange (1-220): 3-6X
Orange Auto. (221-230): 1-1.5X
Production 250 Sets

Blue

Blue (1-220): 2-4X
Blue Auto. (221-230): 1X
Production 500 Sets

Gold

Gold (1-220): 1-2X
Inserted 1:1

Chrome Prospects

		NM/M
Common Prospect (1-110):		.50
Inserted 2:Pack		
Common Auto.(111-130):		10.00
BCP1	Max Sapp	1.00
BCP2	Jamie Richmond	1.00
BCP3	Darren Ford	.50
BCP4	Sergio Romo	.50
BCP5	Jacob Butler	.50
BCP6	Glenn Gibson	.50
BCP7	Tom Hagan	1.00
BCP8	Michael McCormick	.50
BCP9	Gregorio Petit	1.00
BCP10	Bobby Parnell	1.00
BCP11	Jeff Kindel	.50
BCP12	Anthony Claggett	1.00
BCP13	Chris Frey	.50
BCP14	Jonah Nickerson	.50
BCP15	Anthony Martinez	.50
BCP16	Rusty Ryal	.50
BCP17	Justin Berg	.50
BCP18	Gerardo Parra	1.50
BCP19	Wesley Wright	.50
BCP20	Stephen Chapman	.50
BCP21	Chance Chapman	.50
BCP22	Brett Pill	.50
BCP23	Zach Phillips	.50
BCP24	John Raynor	1.50
BCP25	Danny Duffy	2.00
BCP26	Brian Finegan	.50
BCP27	Jonathan Venters	1.00
BCP28	Steve Tolleson	1.00
BCP29	Ben Jukich	.50
BCP30	Matt Weston	.50
BCP31	Kyle Mura	.50
BCP32	Luke Hetherington	.50
BCP33	Michael Daniel	1.00
BCP34	Jake Renshaw	1.00
BCP35	Greg Halman	2.50
BCP36	Ryan Khoury	1.00
BCP37	Ryan Ouellette	1.00
BCP38	Mike Brantley	.50
BCP39	Eric Brown	.50
BCP40	Jose Duarte	.50
BCP41	Eli Tintor	1.00
BCP42	Kent Sakamoto	.50
BCP43	Luke Montz	1.50
BCP44	Alex Cobb	.50
BCP45	Mike McKenry	.50
BCP46	Javier Castillo	.50
BCP47	Jeff Stevens	.50
BCP48	Greg Burns	.50
BCP49	Blake Johnson	.50
BCP50	Austin Jackson	4.00
BCP51	Anthony Recker	.50
BCP52	Luis Durango	.50
BCP53	Engel Beltre	3.00
BCP54	Seth Bynum	.50
BCP55	Ryan Strieby	.50
BCP56	Iggy Suarez	1.00
BCP57	Ryan Morris	.50
BCP58	Scott Van Slyke	.50
BCP59	Tyler Kolodny	1.50
BCP60	Joseph Martinez	.50
BCP61	Aaron Mathews	.50
BCP62	Phillip Cuadrado	.50
BCP63	Alex Liddi	.50
BCP64	Alex Burnett	.50
BCP65	Brian Barton	1.00
BCP66	David Welch	.50
BCP67	Kyle Reynolds	.50
BCP68	Francisco Hernandez	.50
BCP69	Logan Morrison	3.00
BCP70	Ronald Ramirez	.50
BCP71	Brad Miller	.50
BCP72	Braedyn Pruitt	1.00
BCP73	Jason Fernandez	.50
BCP74	Joseph Mahoney	1.00
BCP75	Quentin Davis	.50
BCP76	P.J. Walters	1.50
BCP77	Jordan Czarniecki	.50
BCP78	Jonathan Mota	1.00
BCP79	Michael Hernandez	.50
BCP80	James Guerrero	.50
BCP81	Chris Johnson	.50
BCP82	Daniel Cortes	1.50
BCP83	Sal Sanchez	.50
BCP84	Sean Henry	.50
BCP85	Caleb Gindl	1.50
BCP86	Tommy Everidge	.50
BCP87	Matt Rizzotti	.50
BCP88	Luis Munoz	.50
BCP89	Matt Klimas	.50
BCP90	Angel Reyes	1.00
BCP91	Sean Danielson	.50
BCP92	Omar Poveda	.50
BCP93	Mario Lisson	.50
BCP94	Brian Mathews	.50
BCP95	Matt Buschmann	.50
BCP96	Greg Thomson	.50
BCP97	Matt Inouye	.50
BCP98	Aneury Rodriguez	.50
BCP99	Bradley Harman	.50
BCP100	Aaron Bates	1.00
BCP101	Graham Taylor	.50
BCP102	Kenny Holmberg	.50
BCP103	Greg Dowling	.50
BCP104	Ronnie Ray	.50
BCP105	Mike Wlodarczyk	.50
BCP106	Jose Martinez	.50
BCP107	Jason Stephens	1.00
BCP108	Will Rhymes	.50
BCP109	Joey Side	.50
BCP110	Brandon Waring	5.00
BCP111	David Price/Auto.	60.00
BCP112	Michael Moustakas/ Auto.	50.00
BCP113	Matt LaPorta/Auto.	65.00
BCP114	Wendell Fairley/Auto.	20.00

BCP115 Josh Vitters/Auto. 40.00
BCP116 Jonathan Bachanov/ Auto. 20.00
BCP117 Edward Kunz/Auto. 15.00
BCP118 Matt Dominguez/Auto. 20.00
BCP119 Kyle Lotzkar/Auto. 15.00
BCP120 Madison Bumgarner/ Auto. 30.00
BCP121 Jason Heyward/Auto. 50.00
BCP122 Julio Borbon/Auto. 15.00
BCP123 Josh Smoker/Auto. 20.00
BCP124 Jarrod Parker/Auto. 20.00
BCP125 Kevin Ahrens/Auto. 15.00
BCP126 J.P. Arencibia/Auto. 15.00
BCP127 Josh Bell/Auto. 15.00
BCP128 Scott Cousins/Auto. 15.00
BCP129 Brandon Hynick/Auto. 15.00
BCP130 Alan Johnson/Auto. 10.00

Chrome Prospects Refractor

Refractor (1-110): 3-5X
Production 599
Refractor Autos. (111-130): 1-1.5X
Auto. Production 500

Chrome Prospects Blue Refractor

Blue (1-110): 5-10X
Blue Autos. (111-130): 2-3X
Production 150 Sets

Chrome Prospects Gold Refractor

Gold (1-110): 15-25X
Gold Autos. (111-130): 4-6X
Production 50 Sets

Chrome Prospects X-Fractor

X-Fractor (1-110): 4-8X
Production 275
X-Fractor Autos. (111-130): 1-2X
Auto. Production 250

Chrome Prospects Orange Refractor

No Pricing
Production 25 Sets

Chrome Prospects Red Refractor

No Pricing
Production Five Sets

Chrome Prospects SuperFractor

Production One Set

Prospects

NM/M

Complete Set (110): 25.00
Common Prospect: .25
Inserted 2:Pack
BP1 Max Sapp .50
BP2 Jamie Richmond .50
BP3 Darren Ford .25
BP4 Sergio Romo .25
BP5 Jacob Butler .25
BP6 Glenn Gibson .25
BP7 Tom Hagan .50
BP8 Michael McCormick .25
BP9 Gregorio Petit .50
BP10 Bobby Parnell .50
BP11 Jeff Kindel .25
BP12 Anthony Claggett .50
BP13 Chris Frey .25
BP14 Jonah Nickerson .25
BP15 Anthony Martinez .25
BP16 Rusty Ryal .25
BP17 Justin Berg .25
BP18 Gerardo Parra .50
BP19 Wesley Wright .25
BP20 Stephen Chapman .25
BP21 Chance Chapman .25
BP22 Brett Pill .25
BP23 Zach Phillips .25
BP24 John Raynor .50
BP25 Danny Duffy .50
BP26 Brian Finegan .25
BP27 Jonathan Venters .50
BP28 Steve Tolleson .50
BP29 Ben Jukich .25
BP30 Matt Weston .25
BP31 Kyle Mura .25
BP32 Luke Hetherington .25
BP33 Michael Daniel .50
BP34 Jake Renshaw .50
BP35 Greg Halman 1.00
BP36 Ryan Khoury .50
BP37 Ryan Ouellette .50
BP38 Mike Brantley .25
BP39 Eric Brown .25
BP40 Jose Duarte .25
BP41 Eli Tintor .50
BP42 Kent Sakamoto .25
BP43 Luke Montz .50
BP44 Alex Cobb .25
BP45 Mike McKenry .25
BP46 Javier Castillo .25
BP47 Jeff Stevens .25
BP48 Greg Burns .25
BP49 Blake Johnson .25
BP50 Austin Jackson 1.50
BP51 Anthony Recker .25
BP52 Luis Durango .25
BP53 Engel Beltre 1.00
BP54 Seth Bynum .25
BP55 Ryan Strieby .25
BP56 Iggy Suarez .50
BP57 Ryan Morris .25
BP58 Scott Van Slyke .25
BP59 Tyler Kolodny .50
BP60 Joseph Martinez .25
BP61 Aaron Mathews .25
BP62 Phillip Cuadrado .25
BP63 Alex Liddi .25
BP64 Alex Burnett .25
BP65 Brian Barton .50
BP66 David Welch .25
BP67 Kyle Reynolds .25
BP68 Francisco Hernandez .25
BP69 Logan Morrison 1.00
BP70 Ronald Ramirez .25
BP71 Brad Miller .25
BP72 Braedyn Pruitt .50
BP73 Jason Fernandez .25
BP74 Joseph Mahoney .50
BP75 Quentin Davis .25
BP76 P.J. Walters .75
BP77 Jordan Czarniecki .25
BP78 Jonathan Mota .50
BP79 Michael Hernandez .25
BP80 James Guerrero .25
BP81 Chris Johnson .25
BP82 Daniel Cortes .50
BP83 Sal Sanchez .25
BP84 Sean Henry .25
BP85 Caleb Gindl .75
BP86 Tommy Everidge .25
BP87 Matt Rizzotti .25
BP88 Luis Munoz .25
BP89 Matt Klimas .25
BP90 Angel Reyes .50
BP91 Sean Danielson .25
BP92 Omar Poveda .25
BP93 Mario Lisson .25
BP94 Brian Mathews .25
BP95 Matt Buschmann .25
BP96 Greg Thomson .25
BP97 Matt Inouye .25
BP98 Aneury Rodriguez .25
BP99 Bradley Harman .25
BP100 Aaron Bates .50
BP101 Graham Taylor .25
BP102 Kenny Holmberg .25
BP103 Greg Dowling .25
BP104 Ronnie Ray .25
BP105 Mike Wlodarczyk .25
BP106 Jose Martinez .25
BP107 Jason Stephens .50
BP108 Will Rhymes .25
BP109 Joey Side .25
BP110 Brandon Waring 1.50

Prospects Blue

Blue (1-110): 2-4X
Production 500 Sets

Prospects Gold

Gold (1-110): 1-2X
Inserted 1:3

Prospects Orange

Orange (1-110): 3-5X
Production 250 Sets

Prospects Red

Production One Set

Scouts Autographs

NM/M

Common Auto.: 5.00
BF Bob Fontaine Jr. 5.00
TD Tony DeMacio 5.00
MR Mike Rizzo 5.00
JD Jon Deeble 5.00
TC Ty Coslow 5.00
TCU Tom Couston 5.00
RA Ralph Avila 5.00
LW Leon Wurth 5.00
JL Jerry Lafferty 5.00
CB Chris Bourjos 5.00
BS Bowman Scout 10.00
AS Alex Smith 5.00
TK Tim Kelly 5.00
DJ Dave Jennings 5.00
JC Jerome Cochran 5.00
DO Dan Ontiveros 5.00
DL Don Lyle 5.00
JH Josue Herrera 5.00
JM Joe Mason 5.00
BB Bill Buck 5.00
BE Bob Engle 5.00

2008 Bowman Chrome

NM/M

Common Player (1-190): .25
Common RC (191-220): .50
Pack (4): 4.00
Box (18): 60.00
1 Ryan Braun .75
2 David DeJesus .25
3 Brandon Phillips .50
4 Mark Teixeira .50
5 Daisuke Matsuzaka .75
6 Justin Upton .50
7 Jered Weaver .25
8 Todd Helton .50
9 Adam Jones .40
10 Erik Bedard .40
11 Jason Bay .40
12 Cole Hamels .50
13 Bobby Abreu .50
14 Carlos Zambrano .50
15 Vladimir Guerrero .75
16 Joe Blanton .25
17 Paul Maholm .25
18 Adrian Gonzalez .40
19 Brandon Webb .50
20 Carl Crawford .50
21 A.J. Burnett .25
22 Dmitri Young .25
23 Jeremy Hermida .25
24 C.C. Sabathia .50
25 Adam Dunn .50
26 Matt Garza .25
27 Adrian Beltre .40
28 Kevin Millwood .25
29 Manny Ramirez .75
30 Javier Vazquez .25
31 Carlos Delgado .50
32 Torii Hunter .50
33 Ivan Rodriguez .50
34 Nick Markakis .50
35 Gil Meche .25
36 Garrett Atkins .40
37 Fausto Carmona .25
38 Joe Mauer .50
39 Tom Glavine .50
40 Hideki Matsui .75
41 Scott Rolen .40
42 Tim Lincecum .50
43 Prince Fielder .50
44 Kazuo Matsui .25
45 Tom Gorzelanny .25
46 Lance Berkman .50
47 David Ortiz .75
48 Dontrelle Willis .25
49 Travis Hafner .25
50 Aaron Harang .25
51 Chris Young .40
52 Vernon Wells .40
53 Francisco Liriano .40
54 Eric Chavez .25
55 Phil Hughes .50
56 Melvin Mora .25
57 Johan Santana .75
58 Brian McCann .40
59 Pat Burrell .50
60 Chris Carpenter .25
61 Brian Giles .25
62 Jose Reyes .75
63 Hanley Ramirez .75
64 Ubaldo Jimenez .25
65 Felix Pie .25
66 Jeremy Bonderman .25
67 Jimmy Rollins .50
68 Miguel Tejada .40
69 Derek Lowe .25
70 Alex Gordon .40
71 John Maine .25
72 Alfonso Soriano .75
73 Ben Sheets .40
74 Hunter Pence .50
75 Magglio Ordonez .40
76 Josh Beckett .50
77 Victor Martinez .40
78 Mark Buehrle .25
79 Jason Varitek .40
80 Chien-Ming Wang .50
81 Ken Griffey Jr. 1.50
82 Billy Butler .25
83 Brad Penny .25
84 Carlos Beltran .50
85 Curt Schilling .50
86 Jorge Posada .50
87 Andruw Jones .40
88 Bobby Crosby .25
89 Freddy Sanchez .25
90 Barry Zito .25
91 Miguel Cabrera .75
92 B.J. Upton .40
93 Matt Cain .40
94 Lyle Overbay .25
95 Austin Kearns .25
96 Alex Rodriguez 2.50
97 Rich Harden .40
98 Justin Morneau .50
99 Oliver Perez .25
100 Gary Matthews Jr. .25
101 Matt Holliday .50
102 Justin Verlander .40
103 Orlando Cabrera .25
104 Rich Hill .25
105 Tim Hudson .40
106 Ryan Zimmerman .40
107 Roy Oswalt .40
108 Nick Swisher .40
109 Raul Ibanez .25
110 Kelly Johnson .25
111 Alex Rios .50
112 John Lackey .40
113 Robinson Cano .50
114 Michael Young .40
115 Jeff Francis .25
116 Grady Sizemore .75
117 Mike Lowell .50
118 Aramis Ramirez .50
119 Stephen Drew .25
120 Yovani Gallardo .40
121 Chase Utley .75
122 Dan Haren .40
123 Yunel Escobar .25
124 Greg Maddux 1.50
125 Garret Anderson .25
126 Aubrey Huff .25
127 Paul Konerko .40
128 Dan Uggla .40
129 Roy Halladay .40
130 Andre Ethier .25
131 Orlando Hernandez .25
132 Troy Tulowitzki .40
133 Carlos Guillen .40
134 Scott Kazmir .40
135 Aaron Rowand .40
136 Jim Edmonds .25
137 Jermaine Dye .40
138 Orlando Hudson .25
139 Derrek Lee .50
140 Travis Buck .25
141 Zack Greinke .25
142 Jeff Kent .40
143 John Smoltz .50
144 David Wright 1.00
145 Joba Chamberlain 1.00
146 Adam LaRoche .25
147 Kevin Youkilis .50
148 Troy Glaus .40
149 Nick Johnson .25
150 J.J. Hardy .25
151 Felix Hernandez .40
152 Gary Sheffield .40
153 Albert Pujols 2.50
154 Chuck James .25
155 Kosuke Fukudome **RC** 5.00
156 Eric Byrnes .25
157 Brad Hawpe .25
158 Delmon Young .25
159 Brian Roberts .25
160 Russell Martin .40
161 Hank Blalock .25
162 Yadier Molina .25
163 Jeremy Guthrie .25
164 Chipper Jones 1.00
165 Johnny Damon .50
166 Ryan Garko .25
167 Jake Peavy .50
168 Chone Figgins .40
169 Edgar Renteria .40
170 Jim Thome .50
171 Carlos Pena .40
172 Dustin Pedroia .50
173 Brett Myers .25
174 Josh Hamilton .75
175 Randy Johnson .75
176 Ichiro Suzuki 1.50
177 Aaron Hill .25
178 Corey Hart .40
179 Jarrod Saltalamacchia .25
180 Jeff Francoeur .25
181 Derek Jeter 2.50
182 Curtis Granderson .50
183 James Loney .25
184 Brian Bannister .25
185 Carlos Lee .50
186 Pedro Martinez .50
187 Asdrubal Cabrera .25
188 Kenji Johjima .25
189 Jacoby Ellsbury .50
190 Ryan Howard .75
191 Sean Rodriguez **(RC)** .50
192 Justin Ruggiano **RC** 1.00
193 Jed Lowrie **(RC)** 1.00
194 Joey Votto **(RC)** 1.50
195 Denard Span **(RC)** 2.00
196 Bradley Harman **RC** 1.00
197 Jeff Niemann **(RC)** .50
198 Chin-Lung Hu **(RC)** 1.00
199 Luke Hochevar **RC** 1.00
200 German Duran **RC** .50
201 Troy Patton **(RC)** .50
202 Hiroki Kuroda **RC** 1.00
203 David Purcey **(RC)** .50
204 Armando Galarraga **RC** 3.00
205 John Bowker **(RC)** .50
206 Nick Blackburn **RC** 2.00
207 Hernan Iribarren **(RC)** .50
208 Greg Smith **RC** .50
209 Alberto Gonzalez **(RC)** 1.00
210 Justin Masterson **RC** 1.00
211 Brian Barton **RC** 1.00
212 Robinzon Diaz **(RC)** .50
213 Clete Thomas **RC** 1.00
214 Kazuo Fukumori **RC** 1.00
215 Jayson Nix **(RC)** .50
216 Evan Longoria **RC** 5.00
217 Johnny Cueto **RC** 1.50
218 Matt Tolbert **RC** 1.00
219 Masahide Kobayashi **RC** 1.50
220 Callix Crabbe **(RC)** .50

Refractor

Refractor (1-190): 2-4X
RC (191-220): 1.5-2X

X-Fractor

X-Fractor (1-190): 3-5X
RC (191-220): 2-4X
Production 250 Sets

Blue Refractor

Blue Refractor (1-190): 4-6X
RC (191-220): 3-5X
Production 150 Sets

Gold Refractor

Gold Refractor (1-190): 10-15X
RC (191-220): 8-15X
Production 50 Sets

Orange Refractor

Orange Refractor (1-190): 10-20X
RC (191-220): 10-20X
Production 25 Sets

Red Refractor

No Pricing
Production 5 Sets

Super-Fractor

Production One Set

Chrome Prospects

		NM/M
Common Prospect (131-240):		.50
Common Prospect/ Auto. (241-285):		10.00
131	Zhenwang Zhang	1.00
132	Chris Nash	.50
133	Sergio Morales	.50
134	Carlos Santana	2.00
135	Carlos Monasterios	.50
136	Quincy Latimore	1.00
137	Yamaico Navarro	1.50
138	Ryan Mullins	.50
139	Collin DeLome	.50
140	Hector Correa	.50
141	Mitch Canham	1.00
142	Robert Fish	.50
143	Ryan Royster	.50
144	Eric Barrett	1.00
145	Deibinson Romero	.50
146	Jeff Gerbe	.50
147	Lucas Duda	.50
148	Bryan Morris	1.00
149	Andrew Romine	1.00
150	Glenn Gibson	.50
151	Dan Brezeale	.50
152	Shairon Martis	1.00
153	Helder Velazquez	.50
154	Alan Farina	.50
155	Brandon Barnes	.50
156	Waldis Joaquin	.50
157	Luis De La Cruz	.50
158	Yunesky Sanchez	.50
159	Mitch Hilligoss	1.00
160	Vin Mazzaro	1.00
161	Marcus Davis	.50
162	Tony Barnette	.50
163	Joe Benson	1.00
164	Jake Arrieta	1.50
165	Alfredo Silverio	.50
166	Duane Below	.50
167	Kai Liu	1.00
168	Zach Britton	.50
169	Jaime Pedroza	.50
170	Frank Herrmann	.50
171	Justin Turner	1.00
172	Jeff Manship	.50
173	Paul Winterling	.50
174	Nathan Vineyard	1.00
175	Jason Delaney	.50
176	Ivan Nova	.50
177	Esmailyn Gonzalez	1.00
178	Brett Cecil	1.00
179	Jose Martinez	1.50
180	Brad Peacock	1.00
181	Justin Snyder	1.00
182	Steve Garrison	1.00
183	Joe Mahoney	.50
184	Graham Godfrey	.50
185	Larry Williams	.50
186	Jeremy Haynes	.50
187	Brent Brewer	.50
188	Jhoulys Chacin	3.00
189	Nevin Ashley	.50
190	Justin Cassel	.50
191	Jon Jay	.50
192	Chris Huseby	1.00
193	D.J. Jones	1.00
194	David Bromberg	1.00
195	Juan Francisco	2.50
196	Zach Jevne	.50
197	Darwin Barney	.50
198	Jose Ortegano	1.00
199	Dominic Brown	1.50
200	Kyle Ginley	.50
201	David Wood	.50
202	Jhonny Nunez	.50
203	Carlos Rivero	1.50
204	Anthony Varvaro	.50
205	Christian Lopez	.50
206	Travis Banwart	.50
207	Rhyne Hughes	1.00
208	Heath Rollins	1.00
209	Zack Cozart	1.00
210	Mike Dunn	1.00
211	Chris Pettit	.50
212	Dan Berlind	.50
213	Ernesto Mejia	1.50
214	Hector Rondon	1.00
215	Jose Vallejo	.50
216	Kyle Schmidt	.50
217	Bubba Bell	1.00
218	Charlie Furbush	.50
219	Pedro Baez	1.50
220	Brandon MaGee	.50
221	Clint Robinson	.50
222	Fabio Castillo	1.00
223	Brad Emaus	.50
224	Mike DeJesus	.50
225	Brandon Laird	1.00
226	R.J. Seidel	1.00
227	Agustin Murillo	.50
228	Trevor Reckling	2.00
229	Hector Gomez	1.50
230	Jordan Norberto	.50
231	Steve Hill	.50
232	Hassan Pena	.50
233	Justin Henry	1.00
234	Chase Lirette	.50
235	Christian Marrero	.50
236	Will Kline	.50
237	Johan Limonta	.50
238	Duke Welker	.50
239	Jeudy Valdez	.50
240	Elvin Ramirez	.50
241	Josh Kreuzer/Auto.	15.00
242	Ryan Zink/Auto.	20.00
243	Matt Harrison/Auto.	20.00
244	Dustin Richardson/Auto.	15.00
245	Faustino de los Santos/Auto.	15.00
246	Austin Jackson/Auto.	50.00
247	Jordan Schafer/Auto.	25.00
248	Daryl Thompson/Auto.	15.00
249	Lars Anderson/Auto.	90.00
250	Tim Bascom/Auto.	15.00
251	Brandon Hicks/Auto.	20.00
252	David Kopp/Auto.	10.00
253	Dan Lehmann/Auto.	10.00
254	Jordan Zimmerman/Auto.	20.00
255	Cale Iorg/Auto.	15.00
256	Austin Romine/Auto.	20.00
257	Chaz Roe/Auto.	10.00
258	Danny Rams/Auto.	15.00
259	Daniel Bard/Auto	20.00
260	Engel Beltre/Auto.	50.00
261	Michael Watt/Auto.	15.00
262	Brennan Boesch/Auto.	15.00
263	Matt Latos/Auto.	20.00
264	John Jaso/Auto.	15.00
265	Adrian Alaniz/Auto.	20.00
266	Matt Green/Auto.	15.00
267	Andrew Lambo/Auto	20.00
268	Michael McCardell Auto.	20.00
269	Chris Valaika/Auto.	20.00
270	Cole Rohrbough/Auto.	20.00
271	Andrew Brackman/Auto.	30.00
272	Bud Norris/Auto.	15.00
273	Ryan Kalish/Auto.	35.00
274	Jake McGee/Auto.	15.00
275	Aaron Cunningham/Auto.	20.00
276	Mitch Boggs/Auto.	15.00
277	Bradley Suttle/Auto.	15.00
278	Henry Rodriguez/Auto.	15.00
279	Mario Lisson/Auto.	15.00
280	Ludovicus Van Mil/Auto.	15.00
281	Angel Villalona/Auto.	75.00
282	Mark Melancon/Auto.	20.00
283	Brian Dinkelman/Auto.	15.00
284	Daniel McCutchen/Auto.	15.00
285	Rene Tosoni/Auto.	15.00

Chrome Prospects Refractor

Refractor (131-240): 3-5X
Refractor Auto. (241-285): 1-1.5X
Production 500 Sets

Chrome Prospects X-Fractor

X-fractor (131-240): 4-8X
X-fractor Auto. (241-285): 1-1.5X
Production 250 Sets

Chrome Prospects Blue Refractor

Blue (131-240): 6-12X
Blue Auto. (241-285): 1-2X
Production 150 Sets

Chrome Prospects Gold Refractor

Gold (131-240): 15-25X
Gold Auto. (241-285): 3-5X
Production 50 Sets

Chrome Prospects Orange Refractor

Orange (131-240): No Pricing
Orange Auto. (241-285): No Pricing
Production 25 Sets

Chrome Prospects Red Refractor

Red (131-240): No Pricing
Red Auto. (241-285): No Pricing
Production 5 Sets

Chrome Prospects Super-Fractor

Production One Set

Head of the Class

Refractor: 1-1.5X
Production 99 Sets
Gold Refactor: 2-2.5X
Production 50 Sets

FL	Prince Fielder, Matt LaPorta	75.00
LP	Evan Longoria, David Price/350	100.00
CH	Joba Chamberlain, Phil Hughes/350	75.00

C

1996 Circa

	NM/M
Complete Set (200):	15.00
Common Player:	.10
Raves:	30X
Pack (8):	1.50
Wax Box (24):	25.00

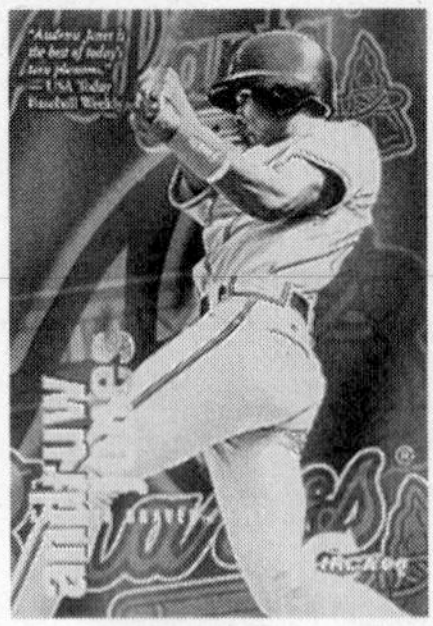

1	Roberto Alomar	.25
2	Brady Anderson	.10
3	Rocky Coppinger **RC**	.10
4	Eddie Murray	.75
5	Mike Mussina	.35
6	Randy Myers	.10
7	Rafael Palmeiro	.65
8	Cal Ripken Jr.	2.00
9	Jose Canseco	.50
10	Roger Clemens	1.00
11	Mike Greenwell	.10
12	Tim Naehring	.10
13	John Valentin	.10
14	Mo Vaughn	.10
15	Tim Wakefield	.10
16	Jim Abbott	.10
17	Garret Anderson	.10
18	Jim Edmonds	.10
19	Darin Erstad **RC**	2.00
20	Chuck Finley	.10
21	Troy Percival	.10
22	Tim Salmon	.10
23	J.T. Snow	.10
24	Wilson Alvarez	.10
25	Harold Baines	.10
26	Ray Durham	.10
27	Alex Fernandez	.10
28	Tony Phillips	.10
29	Frank Thomas	.75
30	Robin Ventura	.10
31	Sandy Alomar Jr.	.10
32	Albert Belle	.10
33	Kenny Lofton	.10
34	Dennis Martinez	.10
35	Jose Mesa	.10
36	Charles Nagy	.10
37	Manny Ramirez	.75
37p	Manny Ramirez/OPS	2.00
38	Jim Thome	.60
39	Travis Fryman	.10
40	Bob Higginson	.10
41	Melvin Nieves	.10
42	Alan Trammell	.10
43	Kevin Appier	.10
44	Johnny Damon	.30
45	Keith Lockhart	.10
46	Jeff Montgomery	.10
47	Joe Randa	.10
48	Bip Roberts	.10
49	Ricky Bones	.10
50	Jeff Cirillo	.10
51	Marc Newfield	.10
52	Dave Nilsson	.10
53	Kevin Seitzer	.10
54	Ron Coomer	.10
55	Marty Cordova	.10
56	Roberto Kelly	.10
57	Chuck Knoblauch	.10
58	Paul Molitor	.75
59	Kirby Puckett	1.00
60	Scott Stahoviak	.10
61	Wade Boggs	1.00
62	David Cone	.10
63	Cecil Fielder	.10
64	Dwight Gooden	.10
65	Derek Jeter	2.00
66	Tino Martinez	.10
67	Paul O'Neill	.10
68	Andy Pettitte	.35
69	Ruben Rivera	.10
70	Bernie Williams	.10
71	Geronimo Berroa	.10
72	Jason Giambi	.45
73	Mark McGwire	1.50
74	Terry Steinbach	.10
75	Todd Van Poppel	.10
76	Jay Buhner	.10
77	Norm Charlton	.10
78	Ken Griffey Jr.	1.25
79	Randy Johnson	.75
80	Edgar Martinez	.10
81	Alex Rodriguez	1.50
82	Paul Sorrento	.10
83	Dan Wilson	.10
84	Will Clark	.10
85	Kevin Elster	.10
86	Juan Gonzalez	.40
87	Rusty Greer	.10
88	Ken Hill	.10
89	Mark McLemore	.10
90	Dean Palmer	.10
91	Roger Pavlik	.10
92	Ivan Rodriguez	.65
93	Joe Carter	.10
94	Carlos Delgado	.35
95	Juan Guzman	.10
96	John Olerud	.10
97	Ed Sprague	.10
98	Jermaine Dye	.10
99	Tom Glavine	.30
100	Marquis Grissom	.10
101	Andruw Jones	.75
102	Chipper Jones	1.00
103	David Justice	.10
104	Ryan Klesko	.10
105	Greg Maddux	1.00
106	Fred McGriff	.10
107	John Smoltz	.10
108	Brant Brown	.10
109	Mark Grace	.10
110	Brian McRae	.10
111	Ryne Sandberg	1.00
112	Sammy Sosa	1.00
113	Steve Trachsel	.10
114	Bret Boone	.10
115	Eric Davis	.10
116	Steve Gibralter	.10
117	Barry Larkin	.10
118	Reggie Sanders	.10
119	John Smiley	.10
120	Dante Bichette	.10
121	Ellis Burks	.10
122	Vinny Castilla	.10
123	Andres Galarraga	.10
124	Larry Walker	.10
125	Eric Young	.10
126	Kevin Brown	.10
127	Greg Colbrunn	.10
128	Jeff Conine	.10
129	Charles Johnson	.10
130	Al Leiter	.10
131	Gary Sheffield	.50
132	Devon White	.10
133	Jeff Bagwell	.75
134	Derek Bell	.10
135	Craig Biggio	.10
136	Doug Drabek	.10
137	Brian Hunter	.10
138	Darryl Kile	.10
139	Shane Reynolds	.10
140	Brett Butler	.10
141	Eric Karros	.10
142	Ramon Martinez	.10
143	Raul Mondesi	.10
144	Hideo Nomo	.40
145	Chan Ho Park	.10
146	Mike Piazza	1.25
147	Moises Alou	.10
148	Yamil Benitez	.10
149	Mark Grudzielanek	.10
150	Pedro Martinez	.75
151	Henry Rodriguez	.10
152	David Segui	.10
153	Rondell White	.10
154	Carlos Baerga	.10
155	John Franco	.10
156	Bernard Gilkey	.10
157	Todd Hundley	.10
158	Jason Isringhausen	.10
159	Lance Johnson	.10
160	Alex Ochoa	.10
161	Rey Ordonez	.10
162	Paul Wilson	.10
163	Ron Blazier	.10
164	Ricky Bottalico	.10
165	Jim Eisenreich	.10
166	Pete Incaviglia	.10
167	Mickey Morandini	.10
168	Ricky Otero	.10
169	Curt Schilling	.25
170	Jay Bell	.10
171	Charlie Hayes	.10
172	Jason Kendall	.10
173	Jeff King	.10
174	Al Martin	.10
175	Alan Benes	.10
176	Royce Clayton	.10
177	Brian Jordan	.10
178	Ray Lankford	.10
179	John Mabry	.10
180	Willie McGee	.10
181	Ozzie Smith	1.00
182	Todd Stottlemyre	.10
183	Andy Ashby	.10
184	Ken Caminiti	.10
185	Steve Finley	.10
186	Tony Gwynn	1.00
187	Rickey Henderson	.75
188	Wally Joyner	.10
189	Fernando Valenzuela	.10
190	Greg Vaughn	.10
191	Rod Beck	.10
192	Barry Bonds	2.00
193	Shawon Dunston	.10
194	Chris Singleton	.10
195	Robby Thompson	.10
196	Matt Williams	.10
197	Barry Bonds Checklist	.75
198	Ken Griffey Jr. Checklist	.65
199	Cal Ripken Jr. Checklist	.75
200	Frank Thomas Checklist	.40

Rave

		NM/M
Common Player:		2.00
Stars:		30X

(See 1996 Circa for checklist and base card values.)

Access

		NM/M
Complete Set (30):		50.00
Common Player:		.60
1	Cal Ripken Jr.	6.00
2	Mo Vaughn	.60
3	Tim Salmon	.75
4	Frank Thomas	2.00
5	Albert Belle	.75
6	Kenny Lofton	.60
7	Manny Ramirez	2.00
8	Paul Molitor	2.00
9	Kirby Puckett	3.00
10	Paul O'Neill	.60
11	Mark McGwire	5.00
12	Ken Griffey Jr.	4.00
13	Randy Johnson	2.00
14	Greg Maddux	3.00
15	John Smoltz	.60
16	Sammy Sosa	4.00
17	Barry Larkin	.60
18	Gary Sheffield	1.00
19	Jeff Bagwell	2.00
20	Hideo Nomo	2.00
21	Mike Piazza	4.00
22	Moises Alou	.60
23	Henry Rodriguez	.60
24	Rey Ordonez	.60
25	Jay Bell	.60
26	Ozzie Smith	3.00
27	Tony Gwynn	3.00
28	Rickey Henderson	2.00
29	Barry Bonds	6.00
30	Matt Williams	.60
30p	Matt Williams/OPS	1.00

Boss

		NM/M
Complete Set (50):		50.00
Common Player:		.45
1	Roberto Alomar	1.00
2	Cal Ripken Jr.	5.00
2p	Cal Ripken Jr./OPS	3.00
3	Jose Canseco	1.50
4	Mo Vaughn	.45
5	Tim Salmon	.60
6	Frank Thomas	2.00
7	Robin Ventura	.45
8	Albert Belle	.60
9	Kenny Lofton	.45
10	Manny Ramirez	2.00
11	Dave Nilsson	.45
12	Chuck Knoblauch	.45
13	Paul Molitor	2.00
14	Kirby Puckett	3.00
15	Wade Boggs	3.00
16	Dwight Gooden	.45
17	Paul O'Neill	.45
18	Mark McGwire	4.00

REGGIE SANDERS

19	Jay Buhner	.45
20	Ken Griffey Jr.	3.50
21	Randy Johnson	2.00
22	Will Clark	.60
23	Juan Gonzalez	2.00
24	Joe Carter	.45
25	Tom Glavine	.45
26	Ryan Klesko	.45
27	Greg Maddux	3.00
28	John Smoltz	.45
29	Ryne Sandberg	3.00
30	Sammy Sosa	3.50
31	Barry Larkin	.45
32	Reggie Sanders	.45
33	Dante Bichette	.45
34	Andres Galarraga	.45
35	Charles Johnson	.45
36	Gary Sheffield	1.50
37	Jeff Bagwell	2.00
38	Hideo Nomo	2.00
39	Mike Piazza	3.50
40	Moises Alou	.45
41	Henry Rodriguez	.45
42	Rey Ordonez	.45
43	Ricky Otero	.45
44	Jay Bell	.45
45	Royce Clayton	.45
46	Ozzie Smith	3.00
47	Tony Gwynn	3.00
48	Rickey Henderson	2.00
49	Barry Bonds	5.00
50	Matt Williams	.45

1997 Circa

		NM/M
Complete Set (400):		15.00
Common Player:		.10
Pack (8):		1.00
Retail Wax Box (18):		15.00
Hobby Wax Box (36):		30.00
1	Kenny Lofton	.10
2	Ray Durham	.10
3	Mariano Rivera	.20
4	Jon Lieber	.10
5	Tim Salmon	.10
6	Mark Grudzielanek	.10
7	Neifi Perez	.10
8	Cal Ripken Jr.	3.00
9	John Olerud	.10
10	Edgar Renteria	.10
11	Jose Rosado	.10
12	Mickey Morandini	.10
13	Orlando Miller	.10
14	Ben McDonald	.10
15	Hideo Nomo	.40
16	Fred McGriff	.10
17	Sean Berry	.10
18	Roger Pavlik	.10
19	Aaron Sele	.10
20	Joey Hamilton	.10
21	Roger Clemens	1.25
22	Jose Herrera	.10
23	Ryne Sandberg	1.00
24	Ken Griffey Jr.	1.50
25	Barry Bonds	3.00
26	Dan Naulty	.10
27	Wade Boggs	1.00

28	Ray Lankford	.10
29	Rico Brogna	.10
30	Wally Joyner	.10
31	F.P. Santangelo	.10
32	Vinny Castilla	.10
33	Eddie Murray	.75
34	Kevin Elster	.10
35	Mike Macfarlane	.10
36	Jeff Kent	.10
37	Orlando Merced	.10
38	Jason Isringhausen	.10
39	Chad Ogea	.10
40	Greg Gagne	.10
41	Curt Lyons	.10
42	Mo Vaughn	.10
43	Rusty Greer	.10
44	Shane Reynolds	.10
45	Frank Thomas	.75
46	Chris Hoiles	.10
47	Scott Sanders	.10
48	Mark Lemke	.10
49	Fernando Vina	.10
50	Mark McGwire	2.00
51	Bernie Williams	.10
52	Bobby Higginson	.10
53	Kevin Tapani	.10
54	Rich Becker	.10
55	Felix Heredia **RC**	.30
56	Delino DeShields	.10
57	Rick Wilkins	.10
58	Edgardo Alfonzo	.10
59	Brett Butler	.10
60	Ed Sprague	.10
61	Joe Randa	.10
62	Ugueth Urbina	.10
63	Todd Greene	.10
64	Devon White	.10
65	Bruce Ruffin	.10
66	Mark Gardner	.10
67	Omar Vizquel	.10
68	Luis Gonzalez	.10
69	Tom Glavine	.25
70	Cal Eldred	.10
71	William Van Landingham	.10
72	Jay Buhner	.10
73	James Baldwin	.10
74	Robin Jennings	.10
75	Terry Steinbach	.10
76	Billy Taylor	.10
77	Armando Benitez	.10
78	Joe Girardi	.10
79	Jay Bell	.10
80	Damon Buford	.10
81	Deion Sanders	.15
82	Bill Haselman	.10
83	John Flaherty	.10
84	Todd Stottlemyre	.10
85	J.T. Snow	.10
86	Felipe Lira	.10
87	Steve Avery	.10
88	Trey Beamon	.10
89	Alex Gonzalez	.10
90	Mark Clark	.10
91	Shane Andrews	.10
92	Randy Myers	.10
93	Gary Gaetti	.10
94	Jeff Blauser	.10
95	Tony Batista	.10
96	Todd Worrell	.10
97	Jim Edmonds	.10
98	Eric Young	.10
99	Roberto Kelly	.10
100	Alex Rodriguez	2.00
100p	Alex Rodriguez/OPS	2.00
101	Julio Franco	.10
102	Jeff Bagwell	.75
103	Bobby Witt	.10
104	Tino Martinez	.10
105	Shannon Stewart	.10
106	Brian Banks	.10
107	Eddie Taubensee	.10
108	Terry Mulholland	.10
109	Lyle Mouton	.10
110	Jeff Conine	.10
111	Johnny Damon	.30
112	Quivilo Veras	.10
113	Wilton Guerrero	.10
114	Dmitri Young	.10
115	Garret Anderson	.10
116	Bill Pulsipher	.10
117	Jacob Brumfield	.10
118	Mike Lansing	.10
119	Jose Canseco	.50
120	Mike Bordick	.10
121	Kevin Stocker	.10
122	Frank Rodriguez	.10
123	Mike Cameron	.10
124	Tony Womack **RC**	.25
125	Bret Boone	.10
126	Moises Alou	.10
127	Tim Naehring	.10
128	Brant Brown	.10
129	Todd Zeile	.10
130	Dave Nilsson	.10
131	Donne Wall	.10
132	Jose Mesa	.10
133	Mark McLemore	.10
134	Mike Stanton	.10
135	Dan Wilson	.10
136	Jose Offerman	.10
137	David Justice	.10
138	Kirt Manwaring	.10
139	Raul Casanova	.10
140	Ron Coomer	.10
141	Dave Hollins	.10

142	Shawn Estes	.10
143	Darren Daulton	.10
144	Turk Wendell	.10
145	Darrin Fletcher	.10
146	Marquis Grissom	.10
147	Andy Benes	.10
148	Nomar Garciaparra	1.00
149	Andy Pettitte	.30
150	Tony Gwynn	1.00
151	Robb Nen	.10
152	Kevin Seitzer	.10
153	Ariel Prieto	.10
154	Scott Karl	.10
155	Carlos Baerga	.10
156	Wilson Alvarez	.10
157	Thomas Howard	.10
158	Kevin Appier	.10
159	Russ Davis	.10
160	Justin Thompson	.10
161	Pete Schourek	.10
162	John Burkett	.10
163	Roberto Alomar	.25
164	Darren Holmes	.10
165	Travis Miller	.10
166	Mark Langston	.10
167	Juan Guzman	.10
168	Pedro Astacio	.10
169	Mark Johnson	.10
170	Mark Leiter	.10
171	Heathcliff Slocumb	.10
172	Dante Bichette	.10
173	Brian Giles **RC**	1.00
174	Paul Wilson	.10
175	Eric Davis	.10
176	Charles Johnson	.10
177	Willie Greene	.10
178	Geronimo Berroa	.10
179	Mariano Duncan	.10
180	Robert Person	.10
181	David Segui	.10
182	Ozzie Guillen	.10
183	Osvaldo Fernandez	.10
184	Dean Palmer	.10
185	Bob Wickman	.10
186	Eric Karros	.10
187	Travis Fryman	.10
188	Andy Ashby	.10
189	Scott Stahoviak	.10
190	Norm Charlton	.10
191	Craig Paquette	.10
192	John Smoltz	.10
193	Orel Hershiser	.10
194	Glenallen Hill	.10
195	George Arias	.10
196	Brian Jordan	.10
197	Greg Vaughn	.10
198	Rafael Palmeiro	.60
199	Darryl Kile	.10
200	Derek Jeter	3.00
201	Jose Vizcaino	.10
202	Rick Aguilera	.10
203	Jason Schmidt	.10
204	Trot Nixon	.10
205	Tom Pagnozzi	.10
206	Mark Wohlers	.10
207	Lance Johnson	.10
208	Carlos Delgado	.40
209	Cliff Floyd	.10
210	Kent Mercker	.10
211	Matt Mieske	.10
212	Ismael Valdes	.10
213	Shawon Dunston	.10
214	Melvin Nieves	.10
215	Tony Phillips	.10
216	Scott Spiezio	.10
217	Michael Tucker	.10
218	Matt Williams	.10
219	Ricky Otero	.10
220	Kevin Ritz	.10
221	Darryl Strawberry	.10
222	Troy Percival	.10
223	Eugene Kingsale	.10
224	Julian Tavarez	.10
225	Jermaine Dye	.10
226	Jason Kendall	.10
227	Sterling Hitchcock	.10
228	Jeff Cirillo	.10
229	Roberto Hernandez	.10
230	Ricky Bottalico	.10
231	Bobby Bonilla	.10
232	Edgar Martinez	.10
233	John Valentin	.10
234	Ellis Burks	.10
235	Benito Santiago	.10
236	Terrell Wade	.10
237	Armando Reynoso	.10
238	Danny Graves	.10
239	Ken Hill	.10
240	Dennis Eckersley	.65
241	Darin Erstad	.25
242	Lee Smith	.10
243	Cecil Fielder	.10
244	Tony Clark	.10
245	Scott Erickson	.10
246	Bob Abreu	.10
247	Ruben Sierra	.10
248	Chili Davis	.10
249	Darryl Hamilton	.10
250	Albert Belle	.10
251	Todd Hollandsworth	.10
252	Terry Adams	.10
253	Rey Ordonez	.10
254	Steve Finley	.10
255	Jose Valentin	.10
256	Royce Clayton	.10

257	Sandy Alomar	.10
258	Mike Lieberthal	.10
259	Ivan Rodriguez	.65
260	Rod Beck	.10
261	Ron Karkovice	.10
262	Mark Gubicza	.10
263	Chris Holt	.10
264	Jaime Bluma	.10
265	Francisco Cordova	.10
266	Javy Lopez	.10
267	Reggie Jefferson	.10
268	Kevin Brown	.10
269	Scott Brosius	.10
270	Dwight Gooden	.10
271	Marty Cordova	.10
272	Jeff Brantley	.10
273	Joe Carter	.10
274	Todd Jones	.10
275	Sammy Sosa	1.00
276	Randy Johnson	.75
277	B.J. Surhoff	.10
278	Chan Ho Park	.10
279	Jamey Wright	.10
280	Manny Ramirez	.75
281	John Franco	.10
282	Tim Worrell	.10
283	Scott Rolen	.60
284	Reggie Sanders	.10
285	Mike Fetters	.10
286	Tim Wakefield	.10
287	Trevor Hoffman	.10
288	Donovan Osborne	.10
289	Phil Nevin	.10
290	Jermaine Allensworth	.10
291	Rocky Coppinger	.10
292	Tim Raines	.10
293	Henry Rodriguez	.10
294	Paul Sorrento	.10
295	Tom Goodwin	.10
296	Raul Mondesi	.10
297	Allen Watson	.10
298	Derek Bell	.10
299	Gary Sheffield	.45
300	Paul Molitor	.75
301	Shawn Green	.15
302	Darren Oliver	.10
303	Jack McDowell	.10
304	Denny Neagle	.10
305	Doug Drabek	.10
306	Mel Rojas	.10
307	Andres Galarraga	.10
308	Alex Ochoa	.10
309	Gary DiSarcina	.10
310	Ron Gant	.10
311	Gregg Jefferies	.10
312	Ruben Rivera	.10
313	Vladimir Guerrero	.75
314	Willie Adams	.10
315	Bip Roberts	.10
326	Mark Grace	.10
317	Bernard Gilkey	.10
318	Marc Newfield	.10
319	Al Leiter	.10
320	Otis Nixon	.10
321	Tom Candiotti	.10
322	Mike Stanley	.10
323	Jeff Fassero	.10
324	Billy Wagner	.10
325	Todd Walker	.10
326	Chad Curtis	.10
327	Quinton McCracken	.10
328	Will Clark	.10
329	Andruw Jones	.75
330	Robin Ventura	.10
331	Curtis Pride	.10
332	Barry Larkin	.10
333	Jimmy Key	.10
334	David Wells	.10
335	Mike Holtz	.10
336	Paul Wagner	.10
337	Greg Maddux	1.00
338	Curt Schilling	.35
339	Steve Trachsel	.10
340	John Wetteland	.10
341	Rickey Henderson	.75
342	Ernie Young	.10
343	Harold Baines	.10
344	Bobby Jones	.10
345	Jeff D'Amico	.10
346	John Mabry	.10
347	Pedro Martinez	.75
348	Mark Lewis	.10
349	Dan Miceli	.10
350	Chuck Knoblauch	.10
351	John Smiley	.10
352	Brady Anderson	.10
353	Jim Leyritz	.10
354	Al Martin	.10
355	Pat Hentgen	.10
356	Mike Piazza	1.50
357	Charles Nagy	.10
358	Luis Castillo	.10
359	Paul O'Neill	.10
360	Steve Reed	.10
361	Tom Gordon	.10
362	Craig Biggio	.10
363	Jeff Montgomery	.10
364	Jamie Moyer	.10
365	Ryan Klesko	.10
366	Todd Hundley	.10
367	Bobby Estalella	.10
368	Jason Giambi	.50
369	Brian Hunter	.10
370	Ramon Martinez	.10
371	Carlos Garcia	.10

372	Hal Morris	.10
373	Juan Gonzalez	.40
374	Brian McRae	.10
375	Mike Mussina	.40
376	John Ericks	.10
377	Larry Walker	.10
378	Chris Gomez	.10
379	John Jaha	.10
380	Rondell White	.10
381	Chipper Jones	1.00
382	David Cone	.10
383	Alan Benes	.10
384	Troy O'Leary	.10
385	Ken Caminiti	.10
386	Jeff King	.10
387	Mike Hampton	.10
388	Jaime Navarro	.10
389	Brad Radke	.10
390	Joey Cora	.10
391	Jim Thome	.60
392	Alex Fernandez	.10
393	Chuck Finley	.10
394	Andruw Jones Checklist	.35
395	Ken Griffey Jr. Checklist	.60
396	Frank Thomas Checklist	.35
397	Alex Rodriguez Checklist	.75
398	Cal Ripken Jr. Checklist	1.00
399	Mike Piazza Checklist	.60
400	Greg Maddux Checklist	.45

Rave

Common Player:	3.00
Stars/Rookies:	10-15X

(See 1997 Circa for checklist and base card values.)

Boss

	NM/M	
Complete Set (20):		10.00
Common Player:		.15
Super Boss:		2X
1	Jeff Bagwell	.60
2	Albert Belle	.15
3	Barry Bonds	2.00
4	Ken Caminiti	.15
5	Juan Gonzalez	.30
6	Ken Griffey Jr.	1.00
7	Tony Gwynn	.75
8	Derek Jeter	2.00
9	Andruw Jones	.60
10	Chipper Jones	.75
11	Greg Maddux	.75
12	Mark McGwire	1.50
13	Mike Piazza	1.00
14	Manny Ramirez	.60
15	Cal Ripken Jr.	2.00
16	Alex Rodriguez	1.50
17	John Smoltz	.15
18	Frank Thomas	.60
19	Mo Vaughn	.15
20	Bernie Williams	.15

Emerald Autographs

	NM/M
Complete Set (6):	100.00
Common Player:	6.00

100	Alex Rodriguez	75.00
241	Darin Erstad	9.00
251	Todd Hollandsworth	6.00
283	Scott Rolen	12.00
308	Alex Ochoa	6.00
325	Todd Walker	6.00

Fast Track

	NM/M	
Complete Set (10):		12.00
Common Player:		.50
1	Vladimir Guerrero	1.50
2	Todd Hollandsworth	.50
3	Derek Jeter	4.00
4	Andruw Jones	1.50
5	Chipper Jones	2.50
6	Andy Pettitte	1.00
7	Mariano Rivera	.75
8	Alex Rodriguez	3.00
9	Scott Rolen	1.25
10	Todd Walker	.50

Icons

	NM/M	
Complete Set (12):		25.00
Common Player:		.50
1	Juan Gonzalez	.75
2	Ken Griffey Jr.	3.00
3	Tony Gwynn	2.00
4	Derek Jeter	5.00
5	Chipper Jones	2.00
6	Greg Maddux	2.00
7	Mark McGwire	4.00
8	Mike Piazza	3.00
9	Cal Ripken Jr.	5.00
10	Alex Rodriguez	4.00
11	Frank Thomas	1.50
12	Matt Williams	.50

Limited Access

	NM/M
Complete Set (15):	30.00
Common Player:	1.25

1	Jeff Bagwell	2.00
2	Albert Belle	1.25
3	Barry Bonds	5.00
4	Juan Gonzalez	1.50
5	Ken Griffey Jr.	3.25
6	Tony Gwynn	2.50
7	Derek Jeter	5.00
8	Chipper Jones	2.50
9	Greg Maddux	2.50
10	Mark McGwire	4.00
11	Mike Piazza	3.50
12	Cal Ripken Jr.	5.00
13	Alex Rodriguez	4.00
14	Frank Thomas	2.00
15	Mo Vaughn	1.25

Rave Reviews

	NM/M	
Complete Set (12):		75.00
Common Player:		3.00
1	Albert Belle	3.00
2	Barry Bonds	12.00
3	Juan Gonzalez	3.00
4	Ken Griffey Jr.	7.50
5	Tony Gwynn	6.00
6	Greg Maddux	6.00
7	Mark McGwire	9.00
8	Eddie Murray	4.00
9	Mike Piazza	7.50
10	Cal Ripken Jr.	12.00
11	Alex Rodriguez	9.00
12	Frank Thomas	4.50

1998 Circa Thunder

	NM/M	
Complete Set (300):		10.00
Common Player:		.10
Pack (8):		1.00
Wax Box (36):		20.00
1	Ben Grieve	.10
2	Derek Jeter	2.50
3	Alex Rodriguez	2.00
4	Paul Molitor	.75

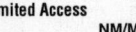

5	Nomar Garciaparra	1.00
6	Fred McGriff	.10
7	Kenny Lofton	.10
8a	Cal Ripken Jr.	2.50
8b	Marquis Grissom	
	(Should be #280.)	.10
8s	Cal Ripken Jr. ("PROMOTIONAL	
	SAMPLE" on back.)	2.50
9	Matt Williams	.10
10	Chipper Jones	1.00
11	Barry Larkin	.10
12	Steve Finley	.10
13	Billy Wagner	.10
14	Rico Brogna	.10
15	Tim Salmon	.10
16	Hideo Nomo	.40
17	Tony Clark	.10
18	Jason Kendall	.10
19	Juan Gonzalez	.40
20	Jeromy Burnitz	.10
21	Roger Clemens	1.25
22	Mark Grace	.10
23	Robin Ventura	.10
24	Manny Ramirez	.75
25	Mark McGwire	2.00
26	Gary Sheffield	.50
27	Vladimir Guerrero	.75
28	Butch Huskey	.10
29	Cecil Fielder	.10
30	Roderick Myers	.10
31	Greg Maddux	1.00
32	Bill Mueller	.10
33	Larry Walker	.10
34	Henry Rodriguez	.10
35	Mike Mussina	.35
36	Ricky Ledee	.10
37	Bobby Bonilla	.10
38	Curt Schilling	.35
39	Luis Gonzalez	.10
40	Troy Percival	.10
41	Eric Milton	.10
42	Mo Vaughn	.10
43	Raul Mondesi	.10
44	Kenny Rogers	.10
45	Frank Thomas	.75
46	Jose Canseco	.50
47	Tom Glavine	.35
48	Rich Butler RC	.10
49	Jay Buhner	.10
50	Jose Cruz Jr.	.10
51	Bernie Williams	.10
52	Doug Glanville	.10
53	Travis Fryman	.10
54	Rey Ordonez	.10
55	Jeff Conine	.10
56	Trevor Hoffman	.10
57	Kirk Rueter	.10
58	Ron Gant	.10
59	Carl Everett	.10
60	Joe Carter	.10
61	Livan Hernandez	.10
62	John Jaha	.10
63	Ivan Rodriguez	.65
64	Willie Blair	.10
65	Todd Helton	.65
66	Kevin Young	.10
67	Mike Caruso	.10
68	Steve Trachsel	.10
69	Marty Cordova	.10
70	Alex Fernandez	.10
71	Eric Karros	.10
72	Reggie Sanders	.10
73	Russ Davis	.10
74	Roberto Hernandez	.10
75	Barry Bonds	2.50
76	Alex Gonzalez	.10
77	Roberto Alomar	.25
78	Troy O'Leary	.10
79	Bernard Gilkey	.10
80	Ismael Valdes	.10
81	Travis Lee	.10
82	Brant Brown	.10
83	Gary DiSarcina	.10
84	Joe Randa	.10
85	Jaret Wright	.10
86	Quilvio Veras	.10
87	Rickey Henderson	.75
88	Randall Simon	.10
89	Mariano Rivera	.25
90	Ugueth Urbina	.10
91	Fernando Vina	.10
92	Alan Benes	.10
93	Dante Bichette	.10
94	Karim Garcia	.10
95	A.J. Hinch	.10
96	Shane Reynolds	.10
97	Kevin Stocker	.10
98	John Wetteland	.10
99	Terry Steinbach	.10
100	Ken Griffey Jr.	1.50
101	Mike Cameron	.10
102	Damion Easley	.10
103	Randy Myers	.10
104	Jason Schmidt	.10
105	Jeff King	.10
106	Gregg Jefferies	.10
107	Sean Casey	.15
108	Mark Kotsay	.10
109	Brad Fullmer	.10
110	Wilson Alvarez	.10
111	Sandy Alomar Jr.	.10
112	Walt Weiss	.10
113	Doug Jones	.10
114	Andy Benes	.10
115	Paul O'Neill	.10

116	Dennis Eckersley	.65
117	Todd Greene	.10
118	Bobby Jones	.10
119	Darrin Fletcher	.10
120	Eric Young	.10
121	Jeffrey Hammonds	.10
122	Mickey Morandini	.10
123	Chuck Knoblauch	.10
124	Moises Alou	.10
125	Miguel Tejada	.15
126	Brian Anderson	.10
127	Edgar Renteria	.10
128	Mike Lansing	.10
129	Quinton McCracken	.10
130	Ray Lankford	.10
131	Andy Ashby	.10
132	Kelvim Escobar	.10
133	Mike Lowell RC	.75
134	Randy Johnson	.75
135	Andres Galarraga	.10
136	Armando Benitez	.10
137	Rusty Greer	.10
138	Jose Guillen	.10
139	Paul Konerko	.15
140	Edgardo Alfonzo	.10
141	Jim Leyritz	.10
142	Mark Clark	.10
143	Brian Johnson	.10
144	Scott Rolen	.60
145	David Cone	.10
146	Jeff Shaw	.10
147	Shannon Stewart	.10
148	Brian Hunter	.10
149	Garret Anderson	.10
150	Jeff Bagwell	.75
151	James Baldwin	.10
152	Devon White	.10
153	Jim Thome	.60
154	Wally Joyner	.10
155	Mark Wohlers	.10
156	Jeff Cirillo	.10
157	Jason Giambi	.60
158	Royce Clayton	.10
159	Dennis Reyes	.10
160	Raul Casanova	.10
161	Pedro Astacio	.10
162	Todd Dunwoody	.10
163	Sammy Sosa	1.00
164	Todd Hundley	.10
165	Wade Boggs	1.00
166	Robb Nen	.10
167	Dan Wilson	.10
168	Hideki Irabu	.10
169	B.J. Surhoff	.10
170	Carlos Delgado	.40
171	Fernando Tatis	.10
172	Bob Abreu	.15
173	David Ortiz	.50
174	Tony Womack	.10
175	Magglio Ordonez RC	1.00
176	Aaron Boone	.10
177	Brian Giles	.10
178	Kevin Appier	.10
179	Chuck Finley	.10
180	Brian Rose	.10
181	Ryan Klesko	.10
182	Mike Stanley	.10
183	Dave Nilsson	.10
184	Carlos Perez	.10
185	Jeff Blauser	.10
186	Richard Hidalgo	.10
187	Charles Johnson	.10
188	Vinny Castilla	.10
189	Joey Hamilton	.10
190	Bubba Trammell	.10
191	Eli Marrero	.10
192	Scott Erickson	.10
193	Pat Hentgen	.10
194	Jorge Fabregas	.10
195	Tino Martinez	.10
196	Bobby Higginson	.10
197	Dave Hollins	.10
198	Rolando Arrojo RC	.25
199	Joey Cora	.10
200	Mike Piazza	1.50
201	Reggie Jefferson	.10
202	John Smoltz	.10
203	Bobby Smith	.10
204	Tom Goodwin	.10
205	Omar Vizquel	.10
206	John Olerud	.10
207	Matt Stairs	.10
208	Bobby Estalella	.10
209	Miguel Cairo	.10
210	Shawn Green	.20
211	Jon Nunnally	.10
212	Al Leiter	.10
213	Matt Lawton	.10
214	Brady Anderson	.10
215	Jeff Kent	.10
216	Ray Durham	.10
217	Al Martin	.10
218	Jeff D'Amico	.10
219	Kevin Tapani	.10
220	Jim Edmonds	.10
221	Jose Vizcaino	.10
222	Jay Bell	.10
223	Ken Caminiti	.10
224	Craig Biggio	.10
225	Bartolo Colon	.10
226	Neifi Perez	.10
227	Delino DeShields	.10
228	Javier Lopez	.10
229	David Wells	.10
230	Brad Rigby	.10

231	John Franco	.10
232	Michael Coleman	.10
233	Edgar Martinez	.10
234	Francisco Cordova	.10
235	Johnny Damon	.30
236	Deivi Cruz	.10
237	J.T. Snow	.10
238	Enrique Wilson	.10
239	Rondell White	.10
240	Aaron Sele	.10
241	Tony Saunders	.10
242	Ricky Bottalico	.10
243	Cliff Floyd	.10
244	Chili Davis	.10
245	Brian McRae	.10
246	Brad Radke	.10
247	Chan Ho Park	.10
248	Lance Johnson	.10
249	Rafael Palmeiro	.65
250	Tony Gwynn	1.00
251	Denny Neagle	.10
252	Dean Palmer	.10
253	Jose Valentin	.10
254	Matt Morris	.10
255	Ellis Burks	.10
256	Jeff Suppan	.10
257	Jimmy Key	.10
258	Justin Thompson	.10
259	Brett Tomko	.10
260	Mark Grudzielanek	.10
261	Mike Hampton	.10
262	Jeff Fassero	.10
263	Charles Nagy	.10
264	Pedro Martinez	.75
265	Todd Zeile	.10
266	Will Clark	.10
267	Abraham Nunez	.10
268	Dave Martinez	.10
269	Jason Dickson	.10
270	Eric Davis	.10
271	Kevin Orie	.10
272	Derrek Lee	.50
273	Andruw Jones	.75
274	Juan Encarnacion	.10
275	Carlos Baerga	.10
276	Andy Pettitte	.35
277	Brent Brede	.10
278	Paul Sorrento	.10
279	Mike Lieberthal	.10
280	(Not issued, see #8)	
281	Darin Erstad	.25
282	Willie Greene	.10
283	Derek Bell	.10
284	Scott Spiezio	.10
285	David Segui	.10
286	Albert Belle	.10
287	Ramon Martinez	.10
288	Jeremi Gonzalez	.10
289	Shawn Estes	.10
290	Ron Coomer	.10
291	John Valentin	.10
292	Kevin Brown	.10
293	Michael Tucker	.10
294	Brian Jordan	.10
295	Darryl Kile	.10
296	David Justice	.10
297	Jose Cruz Jr. Checklist	.10
298	Alex Rodriguez Checklist	1.00
299	Ken Griffey Jr. Checklist	.75
300	Frank Thomas Checklist	.65

2B	Barry Bonds	2.00
3B	Roger Clemens	1.00
4B	Jose Cruz Jr.	.25
5B	Nomar Garciaparra	1.00
6B	Juan Gonzalez	.40
7B	Ken Griffey Jr.	1.25
8B	Tony Gwynn	1.00
9B	Derek Jeter	2.00
10B	Chipper Jones	1.00
11B	Travis Lee	.25
12B	Greg Maddux	1.00
13B	Pedro Martinez	.75
14B	Mark McGwire	1.50
15B	Mike Piazza	1.25
16B	Cal Ripken Jr.	2.00
17B	Alex Rodriguez	1.50
18B	Scott Rolen	.65
19B	Frank Thomas	.75
20B	Larry Walker	.25

Fast Track

	NM/M
Complete Set (10):	8.00
Common Player:	.25
Inserted 1:24	
1FT Jose Cruz Jr.	.25
2FT Juan Encarnacion	.25
3FT Brad Fullmer	.25
4FT Nomar Garciaparra	4.00
5FT Todd Helton	2.50
6FT Livan Hernandez	.25
7FT Travis Lee	.25
8FT Neifi Perez	.25
9FT Scott Rolen	1.50
10FT Jaret Wright	.25

Limited Access

	NM/M
Complete Set (15):	17.50
Common Player:	.50
Inserted 1:18	
1LA Jeff Bagwell	1.25
2LA Roger Clemens	1.75

Rave

	NM/M
Common Player:	2.00
Stars:	15X

(See 1998 Circa Thunder for checklist and base card values.)

Super Rave

	NM/M
Common Player:	6.00
Stars:	40X

(See 1998 Circa Thunder for checklist and base card values.)

Boss

	NM/M
Complete Set (20):	10.00
Common Player:	.25
Inserted 1:6	
1B Jeff Bagwell	.75

3LA	Jose Cruz Jr.	.50
4LA	Nomar Garciaparra	1.50
5LA	Juan Gonzalez	1.00
6LA	Ken Griffey Jr.	2.00
7LA	Tony Gwynn	1.50
8LA	Derek Jeter	3.00
9LA	Greg Maddux	1.50
10LA	Pedro Martinez	1.25
11LA	Mark McGwire	2.50
12LA	Mike Piazza	2.00
13LA	Alex Rodriguez	2.50
14LA	Frank Thomas	1.25
15LA	Larry Walker	.50

Quick Strike

NM/M

Complete Set (12):		20.00
Common Player:		.50
Inserted 1:36		
1QS	Jeff Bagwell	2.00
2QS	Roger Clemens	2.75
3QS	Jose Cruz Jr.	.50
4QS	Nomar Garciaparra	2.50
5QS	Ken Griffey Jr.	3.00
6QS	Greg Maddux	2.50
7QS	Pedro Martinez	2.00
8QS	Mark McGwire	4.00
9QS	Mike Piazza	3.00
10QS	Alex Rodriguez	4.00
11QS	Frank Thomas	2.00
12QS	Larry Walker	.50

Rave Reviews

NM/M

Complete Set (15):		100.00
Common Player:		2.00
Inserted 1:288		
1RR	Jeff Bagwell	5.00
2RR	Barry Bonds	15.00
3RR	Roger Clemens	7.50
4RR	Jose Cruz Jr.	2.00
5RR	Nomar Garciaparra	6.00
6RR	Juan Gonzalez	3.50
7RR	Ken Griffey Jr.	15.00
8RR	Tony Gwynn	6.00
9RR	Derek Jeter	15.00
10RR	Greg Maddux	6.00
11RR	Mark McGwire	12.50
12RR	Mike Piazza	10.00
13RR	Alex Rodriguez	12.50
14RR	Frank Thomas	5.00
15RR	Larry Walker	2.00

Thunder Boomers

NM/M

Complete Set (12): 50.00

Common Player:		1.50
Inserted 1:96		
1TB	Jeff Bagwell	6.00
2TB	Barry Bonds	10.00
3TB	Jay Buhner	1.50
4TB	Andres Galarraga	1.50
5TB	Juan Gonzalez	3.00
6TB	Ken Griffey Jr.	7.50
7TB	Tino Martinez	1.50
8TB	Mark McGwire	9.00
9TB	Mike Piazza	7.50
10TB	Frank Thomas	6.00
11TB	Jim Thome	4.50
12TB	Larry Walker	3.00

1994 Collector's Choice

NM/M

Unopened Fact. Set (675):		25.00
Complete Set (670):		20.00
Common Player:		.05
Silver Signature:		2.5X
Gold Signature:		15X
Series 1 Pack (12):		.35
Series 1 Box (36):		8.00
Series 2 Pack (12):		.75
Series 2 Box (36):		17.50
1	Rich Becker RC	.05
2	Greg Blosser	.05
3	Midre Cummings	.05
4	Carlos Delgado	.30
5	Steve Dreyer RC	.05
6	Carl Everett RC	.50
7	Cliff Floyd	.05
8	Alex Gonzalez	.05
9	Shawn Green	.10
10	Butch Huskey	.05
11	Mark Hutton	.05
12	Miguel Jimenez	.05
13	Steve Karsay	.05
14	Marc Newfield	.05
15	Luis Ortiz	.05
16	Manny Ramirez	.60
17	Johnny Ruffin	.05
18	Scott Stahoviak RC	.05
19	Salomon Torres	.05
20	Gabe White RC	.10
21	Brian Anderson RC	.05
22	Wayne Gomes RC	.05
23	Jeff Granger	.05
24	Steve Soderstrom RC	.05
25	Trot Nixon RC	.50
26	Kirk Presley RC	.05
27	Matt Brunson RC	.05
28	Brooks Kieschnick RC	.05
29	Billy Wagner RC	.50
30	Matt Drews RC	.05
31	Kurt Abbott RC	.05
32	Luis Alicea	.05
33	Roberto Alomar	.20
34	Sandy Alomar Jr.	.05
35	Moises Alou	.05
36	Wilson Alvarez	.05
37	Rich Amaral	.05
38	Eric Anthony	.05
39	Luis Aquino	.05
40	Jack Armstrong	.05
41	Rene Arocha	.05
42	Rich Aude RC	.05
43	Brad Ausmus	.05
44	Steve Avery	.05
45	Bob Ayrault	.05
46	Willie Banks	.05
47	Bret Barberie	.05
48	Kim Batiste	.05
49	Rod Beck	.05
50	Jason Bere	.05
51	Sean Berry	.05
52	Dante Bichette	.05
53	Jeff Blauser	.05
54	Mike Blowers	.05
55	Tim Bogar	.05
56	Tom Bolton	.05
57	Ricky Bones	.05
58	Bobby Bonilla	.05
59	Bret Boone	.05
60	Pat Borders	.05
61	Mike Bordick	.05
62	Daryl Boston	.05
63	Ryan Bowen	.05
64	Jeff Branson	.05
65	George Brett	.85
66	Steve Buechele	.05
67	Dave Burba	.05
68	John Burkett	.05
69	Jeromy Burnitz	.05
70	Brett Butler	.05
71	Rob Butler	.05
72	Ken Caminiti	.05
73	Cris Carpenter	.05
74	Vinny Castilla	.05
75	Andujar Cedeno	.05
76	Wes Chamberlain	.05
77	Archi Cianfrocco	.05
78	Dave Clark	.05
79	Jerald Clark	.05
80	Royce Clayton	.05
81	David Cone	.05
82	Jeff Conine	.05
83	Steve Cooke	.05
84	Scott Cooper	.05
85	Joey Cora	.05
86	Tim Costa	.05
87	Chad Curtis	.05
88	Ron Darling	.05
89	Danny Darwin	.05
90	Rob Deer	.05
91	Jim Deshaies	.05
92	Delino DeShields	.05
93	Rob Dibble	.05
94	Gary DiSarcina	.05
95	Doug Drabek	.05
96	Scott Erickson	.05
97	Rikkert Faneyte RC	.05
98	Jeff Fassero	.05
99	Alex Fernandez	.05
100	Cecil Fielder	.05
101	Dave Fleming	.05
102	Darrin Fletcher	.05
103	Scott Fletcher	.05
104	Mike Gallego	.05
105	Carlos Garcia	.05
106	Jeff Gardner	.05
107	Brent Gates	.05
108	Benji Gil	.05
109	Bernard Gilkey	.05
110	Chris Gomez	.05
111	Luis Gonzalez	.05
112	Tom Gordon	.05
113	Jim Gott	.05
114	Mark Grace	.05
115	Tommy Greene	.05
116	Willie Greene	.05
117	Ken Griffey Jr.	1.00
118	Bill Gullickson	.05
119	Ricky Gutierrez	.05
120	Juan Guzman	.05
121	Chris Gwynn	.05
122	Tony Gwynn	.75
123	Jeffrey Hammonds	.05
124	Erik Hanson	.05
125	Gene Harris	.05
126	Greg Harris	.05
127	Bryan Harvey	.05
128	Billy Hatcher	.05
129	Hilly Hathaway	.05
130	Charlie Hayes	.05
131	Rickey Henderson	.60
132	Mike Henneman	.05
133	Pat Hentgen	.05
134	Roberto Hernandez	.05
135	Orel Hershiser	.05
136	Phil Hiatt	.05
137	Glenallen Hill	.05
138	Ken Hill	.05
139	Eric Hillman	.05
140	Chris Hoiles	.05
141	Dave Hollins	.05
142	David Hulse	.05
143	Todd Hundley	.05
144	Pete Incaviglia	.05
145	Danny Jackson	.05
146	John Jaha	.05
147	Domingo Jean	.05
148	Gregg Jefferies	.05
149	Reggie Jefferson	.05
150	Lance Johnson	.05
151	Bobby Jones	.05
152	Chipper Jones	.75
153	Todd Jones	.05
154	Brian Jordan	.05
155	Wally Joyner	.05
156	Dave Justice	.05
157	Ron Karkovice	.05
158	Eric Karros	.05
159	Jeff Kent	.05
160	Jimmy Key	.05
161	Mark Kiefer	.05
162	Darryl Kile	.05
163	Jeff King	.05
164	Wayne Kirby	.05
165	Ryan Klesko	.05
166	Chuck Knoblauch	.05
167	Chad Kreuter	.05
168	John Kruk	.05
169	Mark Langston	.05
170	Mike Lansing	.05
171	Barry Larkin	.05
172	Manuel Lee	.05
173	Phil Leftwich RC	.05
174	Darren Lewis	.05
175	Derek Lilliquist	.05
176	Jose Lind	.05
177	Albie Lopez	.05
178	Javier Lopez	.05
179	Torey Lovullo	.05
180	Scott Lydy	.05
181	Mike Macfarlane	.05
182	Shane Mack	.05
183	Greg Maddux	.75
184	Dave Magadan	.05
185	Joe Magrane	.05
186	Kirt Manwaring	.05
187	Al Martin	.05
188	Pedro A. Martinez RC	.05
189	Pedro Martinez	.60
190	Ramon Martinez	.05
191	Tino Martinez	.05
192	Don Mattingly	.85
193	Derrick May	.05
194	David McCarty	.05
195	Ben McDonald	.05
196	Roger McDowell	.05
197	Fred McGriff	.05
198	Mark McLemore	.05
199	Greg McMichael	.05
200	Jeff McNeely	.05
201	Brian McRae	.05
202	Pat Meares	.05
203	Roberto Mejia	.05
204	Orlando Merced	.05
205	Jose Mesa	.05
206	Blas Minor	.05
207	Angel Miranda	.05
208	Paul Molitor	.60
209	Raul Mondesi	.05
210	Jeff Montgomery	.05
211	Mickey Morandini	.05
212	Mike Morgan	.05
213	Jamie Moyer	.05
214	Bobby Munoz	.05
215	Troy Neel	.05
216	Dave Nilsson	.05
217	John O'Donoghue	.05
218	Paul O'Neill	.05
219	Jose Offerman	.05
220	Joe Oliver	.05
221	Greg Olson	.05
222	Donovan Osborne	.05
223	Jayhawk Owens	.05
224	Mike Pagliarulo	.05
225	Craig Paquette	.05
226	Roger Pavlik	.05
227	Brad Pennington	.05
228	Eduardo Perez	.05
229	Mike Perez	.05
230	Tony Phillips	.05
231	Hipolito Pichardo	.05
232	Phil Plantier	.05
233	Curtis Pride RC	.05
234	Tim Pugh	.05
235	Scott Radinsky	.05
236	Pat Rapp	.05
237	Kevin Reimer	.05
238	Armando Reynoso	.05
239	Jose Rijo	.05
240	Cal Ripken, Jr.	2.00
241	Kevin Roberson	.05
242	Kenny Rogers	.05
243	Kevin Rogers	.05
244	Mel Rojas	.05
245	John Roper	.05
246	Kirk Rueter	.05
247	Scott Ruffcorn	.05
248	Ken Ryan	.05
249	Nolan Ryan	2.00
250	Bret Saberhagen	.05
251	Tim Salmon	.05
252	Reggie Sanders	.05
253	Curt Schilling	.20
254	David Segui	.05
255	Aaron Sele	.05
256	Scott Servais	.05
257	Gary Sheffield	.30
258	Ruben Sierra	.05
259	Don Slaught	.05
260	Lee Smith	.05
261	Cory Snyder	.05
262	Paul Sorrento	.05
263	Sammy Sosa	.75
264	Bill Spiers	.05
265	Mike Stanley	.05
266	Dave Staton	.05
267	Terry Steinbach	.05
268	Kevin Stocker	.05
269	Todd Stottlemyre	.05
270	Doug Strange	.05
271	Bill Swift	.05
272	Kevin Tapani	.05
273	Tony Tarasco	.05
274	Julian Tavarez RC	.05
275	Mickey Tettleton	.05
276	Ryan Thompson	.05
277	Chris Turner	.05
278	John Valentin	.05
279	Todd Van Poppel	.05
280	Andy Van Slyke	.05
281	Mo Vaughn	.05
282	Robin Ventura	.05
283	Frank Viola	.05
284	Jose Vizcaino	.05
285	Omar Vizquel	.05
286	Larry Walker	.05
287	Duane Ware	.05
288	Allen Watson	.05
289	Bill Wegman	.05
290	Turk Wendell	.05
291	Lou Whitaker	.05
292	Devon White	.05
293	Rondell White	.05
294	Mark Whiten	.05
295	Darrell Whitmore	.05

296 Bob Wickman .05
297 Rick Wilkins .05
298 Bernie Williams .05
299 Matt Williams .05
300 Woody Williams .05
301 Nigel Wilson .05
302 Dave Winfield .60
303 Anthony Young .05
304 Eric Young .05
305 Todd Zeile .05
306 Jack McDowell, John Burkett, Tom Glavine/TP .05
307 Randy Johnson/TP .25
308 Randy Myers/TP .05
309 Jack McDowell/TP .05
310 Mike Piazza/TP .40
311 Barry Bonds/TP .60
312 Andres Galarraga/TP .05
313 Juan Gonzalez, Barry Bonds/TP .45
314 Albert Belle/TP .05
315 Kenny Lofton/TP .05
316 Barry Bonds Checklist 1-64 .50
317 Ken Griffey Jr. Checklist 65-128 .35
318 Mike Piazza Checklist 129-192 .35
319 Kirby Puckett Checklist 193-256 .25
320 Nolan Ryan Checklist 257-320 .50
321 Roberto Alomar Checklist 321-370 .10
322 Roger Clemens Checklist 371-420 .30
323 Juan Gonzalez Checklist 421-470 .10
324 Ken Griffey Jr. Checklist 471-520 .35
325 David Justice Checklist 521-570 .05
32 John Kruk Checklist 571-620 .05
327 Frank Thomas Checklist 621-670 .20
328 Tim Salmon Angels Checklist .05
329 Jeff Bagwell Astros Checklist .20
330 Mark McGwire Athletics Checklist .45
331 Roberto Alomar Blue Jays Checklist .10
332 David Justice Braves Checklist .05
333 Pat Listach Brewers Checklist .05
334 Ozzie Smith Cardinals Checklist .25
335 Ryne Sandberg Cubs Checklist .25
336 Mike Piazza Dodgers Checklist .35
337 Cliff Floyd Expos Checklist .05
338 Barry Bonds Giants Checklist .50
339 Albert Belle Indians Checklist .05
340 Ken Griffey Jr. Mariners Checklist .35
341 Gary Sheffield Marlins Checklist .10
342 Dwight Gooden Mets Checklist .05
343 Cal Ripken, Jr. Orioles Checklist .50
344 Tony Gwynn Padres Checklist .25
345 Lenny Dykstra Phillies Checklist .05
346 Andy Van Slyke Pirates Checklists .05
347 Juan Gonzalez Rangers Checklist .10
348 Roger Clemens Red Sox Checklist .30
349 Barry Larkin Reds Checklist .05
350 Andres Galarraga Rockies Checklist .05
351 Kevin Appier Royals Checklist .05
352 Cecil Fielder Tigers Checklist .05
353 Kirby Puckett Twins Checklist .25
354 Frank Thomas White Sox Checklist .20
355 Don Mattingly Yankees Checklist .30
356 Bo Jackson .10
357 Randy Johnson .60
358 Darren Daulton .05
359 Charlie Hough .05
360 Andres Galarraga .05
361 Mike Felder .05
362 Chris Hammond .05
363 Shawon Dunston .05
364 Junior Felix .05
365 Ray Lankford .05
366 Darryl Strawberry .05
367 Dave Magadan .05
368 Gregg Olson .05
369 Len Dykstra .05
370 Darrin Jackson .05
371 Dave Stewart .05
372 Terry Pendleton .05
373 Arthur Rhodes .05
374 Benito Santiago .05
375 Travis Fryman .05
376 Scott Brosius .05
377 Stan Belinda .05
378 Derek Parks .05
379 Kevin Seitzer .05
380 Wade Boggs .75
381 Wally Whitehurst .05
382 Scott Leius .05
383 Danny Tartabull .05
384 Harold Reynolds .05
385 Tim Raines .05
386 Darryl Hamilton .05
387 Felix Fermin .05
388 Jim Eisenreich .05
389 Kurt Abbott .05
390 Kevin Appier .05
391 Chris Bosio .05
392 Randy Tomlin .05
393 Bob Hamelin .05
394 Kevin Gross .05
395 Wil Cordero .05
396 Joe Girardi .05
397 Orestes Destrade .05
398 Chris Haney .05
399 Xavier Hernandez .05
400 Mike Piazza 1.00
401 Alex Arias .05
402 Tom Candiotti .05
403 Kirk Gibson .05
404 Chuck Carr .05
405 Brady Anderson .05
406 Greg Gagne .05
407 Bruce Ruffin .05
408 Scott Hemond .05
409 Keith Miller .05
410 John Wetteland .05
411 Eric Anthony .05
412 Andre Dawson .25
413 Doug Henry .05
414 John Franco .05
415 Julio Franco .05
416 Dave Hansen .05
417 Mike Harkey .05
418 Jack Armstrong .05
419 Joe Orsulak .05
420 John Smoltz .05
421 Scott Livingstone .05
422 Darren Holmes .05
423 Ed Sprague .05
424 Jay Buhner .05
425 Kirby Puckett .75
426 Phil Clark .05
427 Anthony Young .05
428 Reggie Jefferson .05
429 Mariano Duncan .05
430 Tom Glavine .20
431 Dave Henderson .05
432 Melido Perez .05
433 Paul Wagner .05
434 Tim Worrell .05
435 Ozzie Guillen .05
436 Mike Butcher .05
437 Jim Deshaies .05
438 Kevin Young .05
439 Tom Browning .05
440 Mike Greenwell .05
441 Mike Stanton .05
442 John Doherty .05
443 John Dopson .05
444 Carlos Baerga .05
445 Jack McDowell .05
446 Kent Mercker .05
447 Ricky Jordan .05
448 Jerry Browne .05
449 Fernando Vina .05
450 Jim Abbott .05
451 Teddy Higuera .05
452 Tim Naehring .05
453 Jim Leyritz .05
454 Frank Castillo .05
455 Joe Carter .05
456 Craig Biggio .05
457 Geronimo Pena .05
458 Alejandro Pena .05
459 Mike Moore .05
460 Randy Myers .05
461 Greg Myers .05
462 Greg Hibbard .05
463 Jose Guzman .05
464 Tom Pagnozzi .05
465 Marquis Grissom .05
466 Tim Wallach .05
467 Joe Grahe .05
468 Bob Tewksbury .05
469 B.J. Surhoff .05
470 Kevin Mitchell .05
471 Bobby Witt .05
472 Milt Thompson .05
473 John Smiley .05
474 Alan Trammell .05
475 Mike Mussina .30
476 Rick Aguilera .05
477 Jose Valentin .05
478 Harold Baines .05
479 Bip Roberts .05
480 Edgar Martinez .05
481 Rheal Cormier .05
482 Hal Morris .05
483 Pat Kelly .05
484 Roberto Kelly .05
485 Chris Sabo .05
486 Kent Hrbek .05
487 Scott Kamieniecki .05
488 Walt Weiss .05
489 Karl Rhodes .05
490 Derek Bell .05
491 Chili Davis .05
492 Brian Harper .05
493 Felix Jose .05
494 Trevor Hoffman .05
495 Dennis Eckersley .50
496 Pedro Astacio .05
497 Jay Bell .05
498 Randy Velarde .05
499 David Wells .05
500 Frank Thomas .60
501 Mark Lemke .05
502 Mike Devereaux .05
503 Chuck McElroy .05
504 Luis Polonia .05
505 Damion Easley .05
506 Greg A. Harris .05
507 Chris James .05
508 Terry Mulholland .05
509 Pete Smith .05
510 Rickey Henderson .60
511 Sid Fernandez .05
512 Al Leiter .05
513 Doug Jones .05
514 Steve Farr .05
515 Chuck Finley .05
516 Bobby Thigpen .05
517 Jim Edmonds .05
518 Graeme Lloyd .05
519 Dwight Gooden .05
520 Pat Listach .05
521 Kevin Bass .05
522 Willie Banks .05
523 Steve Finley .05
524 Delino DeShields .05
525 Mark McGwire 1.50
526 Greg Swindell .05
527 Chris Nabholz .05
528 Scott Sanders .05
529 David Segui .05
530 Howard Johnson .05
531 Jaime Navarro .05
532 Jose Vizcaino .05
533 Mark Lewis .05
534 Pete Harnisch .05
535 Robby Thompson .05
536 Marcus Moore .05
537 Kevin Brown .05
538 Mark Clark .05
539 Sterling Hitchcock .05
540 Will Clark .05
541 Denis Boucher .05
542 Jack Morris .05
543 Pedro Munoz .05
544 Bret Boone .05
545 Ozzie Smith .75
546 Dennis Martinez .05
547 Dan Wilson .05
548 Rick Sutcliffe .05
549 Kevin McReynolds .05
550 Roger Clemens .85
551 Todd Benzinger .05
552 Bill Haselman .05
553 Bobby Munoz .05
554 Ellis Burks .05
555 Ryne Sandberg .75
556 Lee Smith .05
557 Danny Bautista .05
558 Rey Sanchez .05
559 Norm Charlton .05
560 Jose Canseco .35
561 Tim Belcher .05
562 Denny Neagle .05
563 Eric Davis .05
564 Jody Reed .05
565 Kenny Lofton .05
566 Gary Gaetti .05
567 Todd Worrell .05
568 Mark Portugal .05
569 Dick Schofield .05
570 Andy Benes .05
571 Zane Smith .05
572 Bobby Ayala .05
573 Chip Hale .05
574 Bob Welch .05
575 Deion Sanders .10
576 Dave Nied .05
577 Pat Mahomes .05
578 Charles Nagy .05
579 Otis Nixon .05
580 Dean Palmer .05
581 Roberto Petagine .05
582 Dwight Smith .05
583 Jeff Russell .05
584 Mark Dewey .05
585 Greg Vaughn .05
586 Brian Hunter .05
587 Willie McGee .05
588 Pedro J. Martinez .60
589 Roger Salkeld .05
590 Jeff Bagwell .60
591 Spike Owen .05
592 Jeff Reardon .05
593 Erik Pappas .05
594 Brian Williams .05
595 Eddie Murray .60
596 Henry Rodriguez .05
597 Erik Hanson .05
598 Stan Javier .05
599 Mitch Williams .05
600 John Olerud .05
601 Vince Coleman .05
602 Damon Berryhill .05
603 Tom Brunansky .05
604 Robb Nen .05
605 Rafael Palmeiro .50
606 Cal Eldred .05
607 Jeff Brantley .05
608 Alan Mills .05
609 Jeff Nelson .05
610 Barry Bonds 2.00
611 Carlos Pulido **RC** .05
612 Tim Hyers **RC** .05
613 Steve Howe .05
614 Brian Turang **RC** .05
615 Leo Gomez .05
616 Jesse Orosco .05
617 Dan Pasqua .05
618 Marvin Freeman .05
619 Tony Fernandez .05
620 Albert Belle .05
621 Eddie Taubensee .05
622 Mike Jackson .05
623 Jose Bautista .05
624 Jim Thome .40
625 Ivan Rodriguez .50
626 Ben Rivera .05
627 Dave Valle .05
628 Tom Henke .05
629 Omar Vizquel .05
630 Juan Gonzalez .30
631 Roberto Alomar .10
632 Barry Bonds .60
633 Juan Gonzalez .15
634 Ken Griffey Jr. .50
635 Michael Jordan 1.50
636 Dave Justice .05
637 Mike Piazza .50
638 Kirby Puckett .25
639 Tim Salmon .05
640 Frank Thomas .35
641 Alan Benes/FF **RC** .05
642 Johnny Damon/FF .35
643 Brad Fullmer/FF **RC** .25
644 Derek Jeter/FF 2.00
645 Derrek Lee/FF **RC** .75
646 Alex Ochoa/FF .05
647 Alex Rodriguez/FF **RC** 6.00
648 Jose Silva/FF **RC** .05
649 Terrell Wade/FF **RC** .05
650 Preston Wilson/FF .05
651 Shane Andrews .05
652 James Baldwin .05
653 Ricky Bottalico **RC** .10
654 Tavo Alvarez .05
655 Donnie Elliott .05
656 Joey Eischen .05
657 Jason Giambi .50
658 Todd Hollandsworth .05
659 Brian Hunter .05
660 Charles Johnson .05
661 Michael Jordan **RC** 3.00
662 Jeff Juden .05
663 Mike Kelly .05
664 James Mouton .05
665 Ray Holbert .05
666 Pokey Reese .05
667 Ruben Santana **RC** .05
668 Paul Spoljaric .05
669 Luis Lopez .05
670 Matt Walbeck .05

Gold Signature

NM/M

Common Player: 2.00
Stars: 15X

(See 1994 Collector's Choice for checklist and base card values.)

Silver Signature

NM/M

Common Player: .15
Stars: 2.5X

(See 1994 Collector's Choice for checklist and base card values.)

647 Alex Rodriguez (White Letters. Some A-Rod Silver Signature parallels were mistakenly printed on base cards with his name and

other details on front and back printed in white, rather than gray.) 100.00

Home Run All-Stars

		NM/M
Complete Set (8):		4.00
Common Player:		.25
1HA	Juan Gonzalez	.50
2HA	Ken Griffey Jr.	1.50
3HA	Barry Bonds	2.50
4HAa	Bobby Bonilla	.25
4HAb	Cecil Fielder	.25
6HA	Albert Belle	.25
7HA	David Justice	.25
8HA	Mike Piazza	1.50

1995 Collector's Choice

		NM/M
Unopened Fact. Set (545):		17.50
Complete Set (530):		12.50
Common Player:		.05
Silver Stars:		2X
Gold Stars:		6X
Pack (12):		1.00
Wax Box (36):		20.00
1	Charles Johnson	.05
2	Scott Ruffcorn	.05
3	Ray Durham	.05
4	Armando Benitez	.05
5	Alex Rodriguez	1.25
6	Julian Tavarez	.05
7	Chad Ogea	.05
8	Quilvio Veras	.05
9	Phil Nevin	.05
10	Michael Tucker	.05
11	Mark Thompson	.05
12	Rod Henderson	.05
13	Andrew Lorraine	.05
14	Joe Randa	.05
15	Derek Jeter	1.50
16	Tony Clark	.05
17	Juan Castillo	.05
18	Mark Acre	.05
19	Orlando Miller	.05
20	Paul Wilson	.05
21	John Mabry	.05
22	Garey Ingram	.05
23	Garret Anderson	.05
24	Dave Stevens	.05
25	Dustin Hermanson	.05
26	Paul Shuey	.05
27	J.R. Phillips	.05
28	Ruben Rivera/FF	.05
29	Nomar Garciaparra/FF	.75
30	John Wasdin/FF	.05
31	Jim Pittsley/FF	.05
32	Scott Elarton/FF **RC**	.15
33	Raul Casanova/FF **RC**	.05
34	Todd Greene/FF	.05
35	Bill Pulsipher/FF	.05
36	Trey Beamon/FF	.05
37	Curtis Goodwin/FF	.05
38	Doug Million/FF	.05
39	Karim Garcia/FF **RC**	1.00
40	Ben Grieve/FF	.05
41	Mark Farris/FF	.05
42	Juan Acevedo/FF **RC**	.05
43	C.J. Nitkowski/FF	.05
44	Travis Miller/FF **RC**	.10
45	Reid Ryan/FF	.10
46	Nolan Ryan	1.50
47	Robin Yount	.50
48	Ryne Sandberg	.75
49	George Brett	.85
50	Mike Schmidt	.85
51	Cecil Fielder	.05
52	Nolan Ryan	.75
53	Rickey Henderson	.20
54	George Brett, Robin Yount, Dave Winfield	.25
55	Sid Bream	.05
56	Carlos Baerga	.05
57	Lee Smith	.05
58	Mark Whiten	.05
59	Joe Carter	.05
60	Barry Bonds	.75
61	Tony Gwynn	.40
62	Ken Griffey Jr.	.50
63	Greg Maddux	.40
64	Frank Thomas	.35
65	Dennis Martinez, Kenny Rogers	.05
66	David Cone (Cy Young)	.05
67	Greg Maddux (Cy Young)	.75
68	Jimmy Key (Most Victories)	.05
69	Fred McGriff (All-Star MVP)	.05
70	Ken Griffey Jr. (HR Champ)	1.00
71	Matt Williams (HR Champ)	.05
72	Paul O'Neill (Btg Title)	.05
73	Tony Gwynn (Batting Title)	.40
74	Randy Johnson (Ks Leader)	.60
75	Frank Thomas (MVP)	.60
76	Jeff Bagwell (MVP)	.60
77	Kirby Puckett (RBI leader)	.75
78	Bob Hamelin (ROY)	.05
79	Raul Mondesi (ROY)	.05
80	Mike Piazza/AS	1.00
81	Kenny Lofton (SB Leader)	.05
82	Barry Bonds (Gold Glove)	1.50
83	Albert Belle/AS	.05
84	Juan Gonzalez (HR Champ)	.30
85	Cal Ripken Jr. (2,000 Straight Games)	1.50
86	Barry Bonds (What's the Call?)	.75
87	Mike Piazza	.60
88	Ken Griffey Jr.	.50
89	Frank Thomas	.35
90	Juan Gonzalez	.10
91	Jorge Fabregas	.05
92	J.T. Snow	.05
93	Spike Owen	.05
94	Eduardo Perez	.05
95	Bo Jackson	.10
96	Damion Easley	.05
97	Gary DiSarcina	.05
98	Jim Edmonds	.05
99	Chad Curtis	.05
100	Tim Salmon	.05
101	Chili Davis	.05
102	Chuck Finley	.05
103	Mark Langston	.05
104	Brian Anderson	.05
105	Lee Smith	.05
106	Phil Leftwich	.05
107	Chris Donnels	.05
108	John Hudek	.05
109	Craig Biggio	.05
110	Luis Gonzalez	.05
111	Brian L. Hunter	.05
112	James Mouton	.05
113	Scott Servais	.05
114	Tony Eusebio	.05
115	Derek Bell	.05
116	Doug Drabek	.05
117	Shane Reynolds	.05
118	Darryl Kile	.05
119	Greg Swindell	.05
120	Phil Plantier	.05
121	Todd Jones	.05
122	Steve Ontiveros	.05
123	Bobby Witt	.05
124	Brent Gates	.05
125	Rickey Henderson	.60
126	Scott Brosius	.05
127	Mike Bordick	.05
128	Fausto Cruz	.05
129	Stan Javier	.05
130	Mark McGwire	1.25
131	Geronimo Berroa	.05
132	Terry Steinbach	.05
133	Steve Karsay	.05
134	Dennis Eckersley	.50
135	Ruben Sierra	.05
136	Ron Darling	.05
137	Todd Van Poppel	.05
138	Alex Gonzalez	.05
139	John Olerud	.05
140	Roberto Alomar	.20
141	Darren Hall	.05
142	Ed Sprague	.05
143	Devon White	.05
144	Shawn Green	.20
145	Paul Molitor	.60
146	Pat Borders	.05
147	Carlos Delgado	.35
148	Juan Guzman	.05
149	Pat Hentgen	.05
150	Joe Carter	.05
151	Dave Stewart	.05
152	Todd Stottlemyre	.05
153	Dick Schofield	.05
154	Chipper Jones	.75
155	Ryan Klesko	.05
156	Dave Justice	.05
157	Mike Kelly	.05
158	Roberto Kelly	.05
159	Tony Tarasco	.05
160	Javier Lopez	.05
161	Steve Avery	.05
162	Greg McMichael	.05
163	Kent Mercker	.05
164	Mark Lemke	.05
165	Tom Glavine	.20
166	Jose Oliva	.05
167	John Smoltz	.05
168	Jeff Blauser	.05
169	Troy O'Leary	.05
170	Greg Vaughn	.05
171	Jody Reed	.05
172	Kevin Seitzer	.05
173	Jeff Cirillo	.05
174	B.J. Surhoff	.05
175	Cal Eldred	.05
176	Jose Valentin	.05
177	Turner Ward	.05
178	Darryl Hamilton	.05
179	Pat Listach	.05
180	Matt Mieske	.05
181	Brian Harper	.05
182	Dave Nilsson	.05
183	Mike Fetters	.05
184	John Jaha	.05
185	Ricky Bones	.05
186	Geronimo Pena	.05
187	Bob Tewksbury	.05
188	Todd Zeile	.05
189	Danny Jackson	.05
190	Ray Lankford	.05
191	Bernard Gilkey	.05
192	Brian Jordan	.05
193	Tom Pagnozzi	.05
194	Rick Sutcliffe	.05
195	Mark Whiten	.05
196	Tom Henke	.05
197	Rene Arocha	.05
198	Allen Watson	.05
199	Mike Perez	.05
200	Ozzie Smith	.75
201	Anthony Young	.05
202	Rey Sanchez	.05
203	Steve Buechele	.05
204	Shawon Dunston	.05
205	Mark Grace	.05
206	Glenallen Hill	.05
207	Eddie Zambrano	.05
208	Rick Wilkins	.05
209	Derrick May	.05
210	Sammy Sosa	.75
211	Kevin Roberson	.05
212	Steve Trachsel	.05
213	Willie Banks	.05
214	Kevin Foster	.05
215	Randy Myers	.05
216	Mike Morgan	.05
217	Rafael Bournigal	.05
218	Delino DeShields	.05
219	Tim Wallach	.05
220	Eric Karros	.05
221	Jose Offerman	.05
222	Tom Candiotti	.05
223	Ismael Valdes	.05
224	Henry Rodriguez	.05
225	Billy Ashley	.05
226	Darren Dreifort	.05
227	Ramon Martinez	.05
228	Pedro Astacio	.05
229	Orel Hershiser	.05
230	Brett Butler	.05
231	Todd Hollandsworth	.05
232	Chan Ho Park	.05
233	Mike Lansing	.05
234	Sean Berry	.05
235	Rondell White	.05
236	Ken Hill	.05
237	Marquis Grissom	.05
238	Larry Walker	.05
239	John Wetteland	.05
240	Cliff Floyd	.05
241	Joey Eischen	.05
242	Lou Frazier	.05
243	Darrin Fletcher	.05
244	Pedro J. Martinez	.60
245	Wil Cordero	.05
246	Jeff Fassero	.05
247	Butch Henry	.05
248	Mel Rojas	.05
249	Kirk Rueter	.05
250	Moises Alou	.05
251	Rod Beck	.05
252	John Patterson	.05
253	Robby Thompson	.05
254	Royce Clayton	.05
255	William Van Landingham	.05
256	Darren Lewis	.05
257	Kirt Manwaring	.05
258	Mark Portugal	.05
259	Bill Swift	.05
260	Rikkert Faneyte	.05
261	Mike Jackson	.05
262	Todd Benzinger	.05
263	Bud Black	.05
264	Salomon Torres	.05
265	Eddie Murray	.60
266	Mark Clark	.05
267	Paul Sorrento	.05
268	Jim Thome	.45
269	Omar Vizquel	.05
270	Carlos Baerga	.05
271	Jeff Russell	.05
272	Herbert Perry	.05
273	Sandy Alomar Jr.	.05
274	Dennis Martinez	.05
275	Manny Ramirez	.60
276	Wayne Kirby	.05
277	Charles Nagy	.05
278	Albie Lopez	.05
279	Jeromy Burnitz	.05
280	Dave Winfield	.60
281	Tim Davis	.05
282	Marc Newfield	.05
283	Tino Martinez	.05
284	Mike Blowers	.05
285	Goose Gossage	.05
286	Luis Sojo	.05
287	Edgar Martinez	.05
288	Rich Amaral	.05
289	Felix Fermin	.05
290	Jay Buhner	.05
291	Dan Wilson	.05
292	Bobby Ayala	.05
293	Dave Fleming	.05
294	Greg Pirkl	.05
295	Reggie Jefferson	.05
296	Greg Hibbard	.05
297	Yorkis Perez	.05
298	Kurt Miller	.05
299	Chuck Carr	.05
300	Gary Sheffield	.30
301	Jerry Browne	.05
302	Dave Magadan	.05
303	Kurt Abbott	.05
304	Pat Rapp	.05
305	Jeff Conine	.05
306	Benito Santiago	.05
307	Dave Weathers	.05
308	Robb Nen	.05
309	Chris Hammond	.05
310	Bryan Harvey	.05
311	Charlie Hough	.05
312	Greg Colbrunn	.05
313	David Segui	.05
314	Rico Brogna	.05
315	Jeff Kent	.05
316	Jose Vizcaino	.05
317	Jim Lindeman	.05
318	Carl Everett	.05
319	Ryan Thompson	.05
320	Bobby Bonilla	.05
321	Joe Orsulak	.05
322	Pete Harnisch	.05
323	Doug Linton	.05
324	Todd Hundley	.05
325	Bret Saberhagen	.05
326	Kelly Stinnett	.05
327	Jason Jacome	.05
328	Bobby Jones	.05
329	John Franco	.05
330	Rafael Palmeiro	.50
331	Chris Hoiles	.05
332	Leo Gomez	.05
333	Chris Sabo	.05
334	Brady Anderson	.05
335	Jeffrey Hammonds	.05
336	Dwight Smith	.05
337	Jack Voigt	.05
338	Harold Baines	.05
339	Ben McDonald	.05
340	Mike Mussina	.30
341	Bret Barberie	.05
342	Jamie Moyer	.05
343	Mike Oquist	.05
344	Sid Fernandez	.05
345	Eddie Williams	.05
346	Joey Hamilton	.05
347	Brian Williams	.05
348	Luis Lopez	.05
349	Steve Finley	.05
350	Andy Benes	.05
351	Andujar Cedeno	.05
352	Bip Roberts	.05
353	Ray McDavid	.05
354	Ken Caminiti	.05
355	Trevor Hoffman	.05
356	Mel Nieves	.05
357	Brad Ausmus	.05
358	Andy Ashby	.05
359	Scott Sanders	.05
360	Gregg Jefferies	.05
361	Mariano Duncan	.05
362	Dave Hollins	.05
363	Kevin Stocker	.05
364	Fernando Valenzuela	.05
365	Lenny Dykstra	.05
366	Jim Eisenreich	.05
367	Ricky Bottalico	.05
368	Doug Jones	.05
369	Ricky Jordan	.05
370	Darren Daulton	.05
371	Mike Lieberthal	.05
372	Bobby Munoz	.05
373	John Kruk	.05
374	Curt Schilling	.20
375	Orlando Merced	.05
376	Carlos Garcia	.05
377	Lance Parrish	.05
378	Steve Cooke	.05
379	Jeff King	.05
380	Jay Bell	.05
381	Al Martin	.05
382	Paul Wagner	.05
383	Rick White	.05
384	Midre Cummings	.05
385	Jon Lieber	.05
386	Dave Clark	.05
387	Don Slaught	.05
388	Denny Neagle	.05
389	Zane Smith	.05
390	Andy Van Slyke	.05
391	Ivan Rodriguez	.50
392	David Hulse	.05
393	John Burkett	.05

394	Kevin Brown	.05
395	Dean Palmer	.05
396	Otis Nixon	.05
397	Rick Helling	.05
398	Kenny Rogers	.05
399	Darren Oliver	.05
400	Will Clark	.05
401	Jeff Frye	.05
402	Kevin Gross	.05
403	John Dettmer	.05
404	Manny Lee	.05
405	Rusty Greer	.05
406	Aaron Sele	.05
407	Carlos Rodriguez	.05
408	Scott Cooper	.05
409	John Valentin	.05
410	Roger Clemens	.85
411	Mike Greenwell	.05
412	Tim Vanegmond	.05
413	Tom Brunansky	.05
414	Steve Farr	.05
415	Jose Canseco	.35
416	Joe Hesketh	.05
417	Ken Ryan	.05
418	Tim Naehring	.05
419	Frank Viola	.05
420	Andre Dawson	.25
421	Mo Vaughn	.05
422	Jeff Brantley	.05
423	Pete Schourek	.05
424	Hal Morris	.05
425	Deion Sanders	.10
426	Brian L. Hunter	.05
427	Bret Boone	.05
428	Willie Greene	.05
429	Ron Gant	.05
430	Barry Larkin	.05
431	Reggie Sanders	.05
432	Eddie Taubensee	.05
433	Jack Morris	.05
434	Jose Rijo	.05
435	Johnny Ruffin	.05
436	John Smiley	.05
437	John Roper	.05
438	David Nied	.05
439	Roberto Mejia	.05
440	Andres Galarraga	.05
441	Mike Kingery	.05
442	Curt Leskanic	.05
443	Walt Weiss	.05
444	Marvin Freeman	.05
445	Charlie Hayes	.05
446	Eric Young	.05
447	Ellis Burks	.05
448	Joe Girardi	.05
449	Lance Painter	.05
450	Dante Bichette	.05
451	Bruce Ruffin	.05
452	Jeff Granger	.05
453	Wally Joyner	.05
454	Jose Lind	.05
455	Jeff Montgomery	.05
456	Gary Gaetti	.05
457	Greg Gagne	.05
458	Vince Coleman	.05
459	Mike Macfarlane	.05
460	Brian McRae	.05
461	Tom Gordon	.05
462	Kevin Appier	.05
463	Billy Brewer	.05
464	Mark Gubicza	.05
465	Travis Fryman	.05
466	Danny Bautista	.05
467	Sean Bergman	.05
468	Mike Henneman	.05
469	Mike Moore	.05
470	Cecil Fielder	.05
471	Alan Trammell	.05
472	Kirk Gibson	.05
473	Tony Phillips	.05
474	Mickey Tettleton	.05
475	Lou Whitaker	.05
476	Chris Gomez	.05
477	John Doherty	.05
478	Greg Gohr	.05
479	Bill Gullickson	.05
480	Rick Aguilera	.05
481	Matt Walbeck	.05
482	Kevin Tapani	.05
483	Scott Erickson	.05
484	Steve Dunn	.05
485	David McCarty	.05
486	Scott Leius	.05
487	Pat Meares	.05
488	Jeff Reboulet	.05
489	Pedro Munoz	.05
490	Chuck Knoblauch	.05
491	Rich Becker	.05
492	Alex Cole	.05
493	Pat Mahomes	.05
494	Ozzie Guillen	.05
495	Tim Raines	.05
496	Kirk McCaskill	.05
497	Olmedo Saenz	.05
498	Scott Sanderson	.05
499	Lance Johnson	.05
500	Michael Jordan	1.50
501	Warren Newson	.05
502	Ron Karkovice	.05
503	Wilson Alvarez	.05
504	Jason Bere	.05
505	Robin Ventura	.05
506	Alex Fernandez	.05
507	Roberto Hernandez	.05
508	Norberto Martin	.05
509	Bob Wickman	.05
510	Don Mattingly	.85

511	Melido Perez	.05
512	Pat Kelly	.05
513	Randy Velarde	.05
514	Tony Fernandez	.05
515	Jack McDowell	.05
516	Luis Polonia	.05
517	Bernie Williams	.05
518	Danny Tartabull	.05
519	Mike Stanley	.05
520	Wade Boggs	.75
521	Jim Leyritz	.05
522	Steve Howe	.05
523	Scott Kamieniecki	.05
524	Russ Davis	.05
525	Jim Abbott	.05
526	Eddie Murray Checklist 1-106	.20
527	Alex Rodriguez Checklist 107-212	.40
528	Jeff Bagwell Checklist 213-318	.20
529	Joe Carter Checklist 319-424	.05
530	Fred McGriff Checklist 425-530	.05
---	National Packtime Offer Card	.05

Gold Signature

NM/M	
Common Player:	.50
Stars:	6X

(See 1995 Collector's Choice for checklist and base card values.)

Silver Signature

NM/M	
Common Player:	.10
Stars:	2X

(See 1995 Collector's Choice for checklist and base card values.)

Michael Jordan Jumbo

	NM/M	
661	Michael Jordan	15.00

1995 Collector's Choice/SE

	NM/M	
Complete Set (265):		17.50
Common Player:		.05
Silver Stars:		1.5X
Gold Stars:		8X
Pack (12):		1.25
Wax Box (36):		25.00
1	Alex Rodriguez	1.50
2	Derek Jeter	2.00
3	Dustin Hermanson	.05
4	Bill Pulsipher	.05
5	Terrell Wade	.05
6	Darren Dreifort	.05
7	LaTroy Hawkins	.05
8	Alex Ochoa	.05
9	Paul Wilson	.05
10	Ernie Young	.05
11	Alan Benes	.05
12	Garret Anderson	.05
13	Armando Benitez	.05
14	Robert Perez	.05
15	Herbert Perry	.05
16	Jose Silva	.05
17	Orlando Miller	.05
18	Russ Davis	.05
19	Jason Isringhausen	.05
20	Ray McDavid	.05
21	Duane Singleton	.05
22	Paul Shuey	.05
23	Steve Dunn	.05
24	Mike Lieberthal	.05
25	Chan Ho Park	.05
26	Ken Griffey Jr.	.65
27	Tony Gwynn	.40
28	Chuck Knoblauch	.05
29	Frank Thomas	.35
30	Matt Williams	.05
31	Chili Davis	.05
32	Chad Curtis	.05
33	Brian Anderson	.05
34	Chuck Finley	.05
35	Tim Salmon	.05
36	Bo Jackson	.10
37	Doug Drabek	.05
38	Craig Biggio	.05
39	Ken Caminiti	.05
40	Jeff Bagwell	.65
41	Darryl Kile	.05
42	John Hudek	.05
43	Brian L. Hunter	.05
44	Dennis Eckersley	.60
45	Mark McGwire	1.50
46	Brent Gates	.05
47	Steve Karsay	.05
48	Rickey Henderson	.65
49	Terry Steinbach	.05
50	Ruben Sierra	.05
51	Roberto Alomar	.25
52	Carlos Delgado	.05
53	Alex Gonzalez	.05
54	Joe Carter	.25
55	Paul Molitor	.65
56	Juan Guzman	.05
57	John Olerud	.25
58	Shawn Green	.25
59	Tom Glavine	.25
60	Greg Maddux	.75
61	Roberto Kelly	.05
62	Ryan Klesko	.05
63	Javier Lopez	.05
64	Jose Oliva	.05
65	Fred McGriff	.25
66	Steve Avery	.05
67	Dave Justice	.25
68	Ricky Bones	.05
69	Cal Eldred	.05
70	Greg Vaughn	.05
71	Dave Nilsson	.05
72	Jose Valentin	.05
73	Matt Mieske	.05
74	Todd Zeile	.05
75	Ozzie Smith	.75
76	Bernard Gilkey	.05
77	Ray Lankford	.05
78	Bob Tewksbury	.05
79	Mark Whiten	.05
80	Gregg Jefferies	.05

	NM/M	
81	Randy Myers	.05
82	Shawon Dunston	.05
83	Mark Grace	.05
84	Derrick May	.05
85	Sammy Sosa	.75
86	Steve Trachsel	.05
87	Brett Butler	.05
88	Delino DeShields	.05
89	Orel Hershiser	.05
90	Mike Piazza	1.00
91	Todd Hollandsworth	.05
92	Eric Karros	.05
93	Ramon Martinez	.05
94	Tim Wallach	.05
95	Raul Mondesi	.05
96	Larry Walker	.05
97	Wil Cordero	.05
98	Marquis Grissom	.05
99	Ken Hill	.05
100	Cliff Floyd	.05
101	Pedro J. Martinez	.65
102	John Wetteland	.05
103	Rondell White	.05
104	Moises Alou	.05
105	Barry Bonds	2.00
106	Darren Lewis	.05
107	Mark Portugal	.05
108	Matt Williams	.05
109	William Van Landingham	.05
110	Bill Swift	.05
111	Robby Thompson	.05
112	Rod Beck	.05
113	Darryl Strawberry	.05
114	Jim Thome	.50
115	Dave Winfield	.65
116	Eddie Murray	.75
117	Manny Ramirez	.75
118	Carlos Baerga	.05
119	Kenny Lofton	.05
120	Albert Belle	.05
121	Mark Clark	.05
122	Dennis Martinez	.05
123	Randy Johnson	.65
124	Jay Buhner	.05
125	Ken Griffey Jr.	1.00
125a	Ken Griffey Jr./OPS	1.50
126	Rich Gossage	.05
127	Tino Martinez	.05
128	Reggie Jefferson	.05
129	Edgar Martinez	.05
130	Gary Sheffield	.30
131	Pat Rapp	.05
132	Bret Barberie	.05
133	Chuck Carr	.05
134	Jeff Conine	.05
135	Charles Johnson	.05
136	Benito Santiago	.05
137	Matt Williams	.05
138	Jeff Bagwell	.35
139	Kenny Lofton	.05
140	Tony Gwynn	.40
141	Jimmy Key	.05
142	Greg Maddux	.40
143	Randy Johnson	.25
144	Lee Smith	.05
145	Bobby Bonilla	.05
146	Jason Jacome	.05
147	Jeff Kent	.05
148	Ryan Thompson	.05
149	Bobby Jones	.05
150	Bret Saberhagen	.05
151	John Franco	.05
152	Lee Smith	.05
153	Rafael Palmeiro	.60
154	Brady Anderson	.05
155	Cal Ripken Jr.	2.00
156	Jeffrey Hammonds	.05
157	Mike Mussina	.35
158	Chris Hoiles	.05
159	Ben McDonald	.05
160	Tony Gwynn	.75
161	Joey Hamilton	.05
162	Andy Benes	.05
163	Trevor Hoffman	.05
164	Phil Plantier	.05
165	Derek Bell	.05
166	Bip Roberts	.05
167	Eddie Williams	.05
168	Fernando Valenzuela	.05
169	Mariano Duncan	.05
170	Lenny Dykstra	.05
171	Darren Daulton	.05
172	Danny Jackson	.05
173	Bobby Munoz	.05
174	Doug Jones	.05
175	Jay Bell	.05
176	Zane Smith	.05
177	Jon Lieber	.05
178	Carlos Garcia	.05
179	Orlando Merced	.05
180	Andy Van Slyke	.05
181	Rick Helling	.05
182	Rusty Greer	.05
183	Kenny Rogers	.05
184	Will Clark	.05
185	Jose Canseco	.40
186	Juan Gonzalez	.35
187	Dean Palmer	.05
188	Ivan Rodriguez	.60
189	John Valentin	.05
190	Roger Clemens	.85
191	Aaron Sele	.05
192	Scott Cooper	.05
193	Mike Greenwell	.05
194	Mo Vaughn	.05
195	Andre Dawson	.25
196	Ron Gant	.05

197	Jose Rijo	.05
198	Bret Boone	.05
199	Deion Sanders	.10
200	Barry Larkin	.05
201	Hal Morris	.05
202	Reggie Sanders	.05
203	Kevin Mitchell	.05
204	Marvin Freeman	.05
205	Andres Galarraga	.05
206	Walt Weiss	.05
207	Charlie Hayes	.05
208	David Nied	.05
209	Dante Bichette	.05
210	David Cone	.05
211	Jeff Montgomery	.05
212	Felix Jose	.05
213	Mike Macfarlane	.05
214	Wally Joyner	.05
215	Bob Hamelin	.05
216	Brian McRae	.05
217	Kirk Gibson	.05
218	Lou Whitaker	.05
219	Chris Gomez	.05
220	Cecil Fielder	.05
221	Mickey Tettleton	.05
222	Travis Fryman	.05
223	Tony Phillips	.05
224	Rick Aguilera	.05
225	Scott Erickson	.05
226	Chuck Knoblauch	.05
227	Kent Hrbek	.05
228	Shane Mack	.05
229	Kevin Tapani	.05
230	Kirby Puckett	.75
231	Julio Franco	.05
232	Jack McDowell	.05
233	Jason Bere	.05
234	Alex Fernandez	.05
235	Frank Thomas	.65
236	Ozzie Guillen	.05
237	Robin Ventura	.05
238	Michael Jordan	2.00
239	Wilson Alvarez	.05
240	Don Mattingly	.85
241	Jim Abbott	.05
242	Jim Leyritz	.05
243	Paul O'Neill	.05
244	Melido Perez	.05
245	Wade Boggs	.75
246	Mike Stanley	.05
247	Danny Tartabull	.05
248	Jimmy Key	.05
249	Greg Maddux	.40
250	Randy Johnson	.20
251	Bret Saberhagen	.05
252	John Wetteland	.05
253	Mike Piazza	.50
254	Jeff Bagwell	.35
255	Craig Biggio	.05
256	Matt Williams	.05
257	Wil Cordero	.05
258	Kenny Lofton	.05
259	Barry Bonds	.75
260	Dante Bichette	.05
261	Ken Griffey Jr. Checklist 1-53	.35
262	Goose Gossage Checklist 54-106	.05
263	Cal Ripken Jr. Checklist 107-159	.45
264	Kenny Rogers Checklist 160-212	.05
265	John Valentin Checklist 213-265	.05

Gold

NM/M		
Common Player:		1.00
Stars:		8X

(For checklist and base card values,
see 1995 Collector's Choice SE.)

Silver

NM/M		
Common Player:		.15
Stars:		1.5X

(For checklist and base card values,
see 1995 Collector's Choice SE.)

Ichiro Suzuki

NM/M		
59	Ichiro Suzuki	1,000

1996 Collector's Choice

NM/M		
Unopened Fact. Set (790):		17.50
Complete Set: (760):		12.50
Traded Set (366T-395T):		3.00
Common Player:		.05
Series 1 Pack (12):		.75
Series 1 Wax Box (36):		22.50
Series 2 Pack (14):		1.00
Series 2 Wax Box (40):		25.00
1	Cal Ripken Jr.	2.00
2	Edgar Martinez, Tony Gwynn	.05
3	Albert Belle, Dante Bichette	.05
4	Albert Belle, Mo Vaughn, Dante Bichette	.05
5	Kenny Lofton, Quilvio Veras	.05
6	Mike Mussina, Greg Maddux	.40
7	Randy Johnson, Hideo Nomo	.25
8	Randy Johnson, Greg Maddux	.40
9	Jose Mesa, Randy Myers	.05
10	Johnny Damon	.35
11	Rick Krivda	.05
12	Roger Cedeno	.05
13	Angel Martinez	.05
14	Ariel Prieto	.05
15	John Wasdin	.05
16	Edwin Hurtado	.05
17	Lyle Mouton	.05

18	Chris Snopek	.05
19	Mariano Rivera	.15
20	Ruben Rivera	.05
21	Juan Castro **RC**	.05
22	Jimmy Haynes	.05
23	Bob Wolcott	.05
24	Brian Barber	.05
25	Frank Rodriguez	.05
26	Jesus Tavarez	.05
27	Glenn Dishman	.05
28	Jose Herrera	.05
29	Chan Ho Park	.05
30	Jason Isringhausen	.05
31	Doug Johns	.05
32	Gene Schall	.05
33	Kevin Jordan	.05
34	Matt Lawton **RC**	.10
35	Karim Garcia	.05
36	George Williams	.05
37	Orlando Palmeiro	.05
38	Jamie Brewington	.05
39	Robert Person	.05
40	Greg Maddux	.75
41	Marquis Grissom	.05
42	Chipper Jones	.75
43	David Justice	.05
44	Mark Lemke	.05
45	Fred McGriff	.05
46	Javy Lopez	.05
47	Mark Wohlers	.05
48	Jason Schmidt	.05
49	John Smoltz	.05
50	Curtis Goodwin	.05
51	Gregg Zaun	.05
52	Armando Benitez	.05
53	Manny Alexander	.05
54	Chris Hoiles	.05
55	Harold Baines	.05
56	Ben McDonald	.05
57	Scott Erickson	.05
58	Jeff Manto	.05
59	Luis Alicea	.05
60	Roger Clemens	.85
61	Rheal Cormier	.05
62	Vaughn Eshelman	.05
63	Zane Smith	.05
64	Mike Macfarlane	.05
65	Erik Hanson	.05
66	Tim Naehring	.05
67	Lee Tinsley	.05
68	Troy O'Leary	.05
69	Garret Anderson	.05
70	Chili Davis	.05
71	Jim Edmonds	.05
72	Troy Percival	.05
73	Mark Langston	.05
74	Spike Owen	.05
75	Tim Salmon	.05
76	Brian Anderson	.05
77	Lee Smith	.05
78	Jim Abbott	.05
79	Jim Bullinger	.05
80	Mark Grace	.05
81	Todd Zeile	.05
82	Kevin Foster	.05
83	Howard Johnson	.05
84	Brian McRae	.05
85	Randy Myers	.05
86	Jaime Navarro	.05
87	Luis Gonzalez	.05
88	Ozzie Timmons	.05
89	Wilson Alvarez	.05
90	Frank Thomas	.60
91	James Baldwin	.05
92	Ray Durham	.05
93	Alex Fernandez	.05
94	Ozzie Guillen	.05
95	Tim Raines	.05
96	Roberto Hernandez	.05
97	Lance Johnson	.05
98	John Kruk	.05
99	Mark Portugal	.05
100	Don Mattingly (Traditional Threads)	.65
101	Jose Canseco	.15
102	Raul Mondesi	.05
103	Cecil Fielder	.05
104	Ozzie Smith	.40
105	Frank Thomas	.45
106	Sammy Sosa	.50
107	Fred McGriff	.05
108	Barry Bonds	1.00
109	Thomas Howard	.05
110	Ron Gant	.05
111	Eddie Taubensee	.05
112	Hal Morris	.05
113	Jose Rijo	.05
114	Pete Schourek	.05
115	Reggie Sanders	.05
116	Benito Santiago	.05
117	Jeff Brantley	.05
118	Julian Tavarez	.05
119	Carlos Baerga	.05
120	Jim Thome	.40
121	Jose Mesa	.05
122	Dennis Martinez	.05
123	Dave Winfield	.60
124	Eddie Murray	.60
125	Manny Ramirez	.60
126	Paul Sorrento	.05
127	Kenny Lofton	.05
128	Eric Young	.05
129	Jason Bates	.05
130	Bret Saberhagen	.05
131	Andres Galarraga	.05

132	Joe Girardi	.05
133	John Vander Wal	.05
134	David Nied	.05
135	Dante Bichette	.05
136	Vinny Castilla	.05
137	Kevin Ritz	.05
138	Felipe Lira	.05
139	Joe Boever	.05
140	Cecil Fielder	.05
141	John Flaherty	.05
142	Kirk Gibson	.05
143	Brian Maxcy	.05
144	Lou Whitaker	.05
145	Alan Trammell	.05
146	Bobby Higginson	.05
147	Chad Curtis	.05
148	Quilvio Veras	.05
149	Jerry Browne	.05
150	Andre Dawson	.25
151	Robb Nen	.05
152	Greg Colbrunn	.05
153	Chris Hammond	.05
154	Kurt Abbott	.05
155	Charles Johnson	.05
156	Terry Pendleton	.05
157	Dave Weathers	.05
158	Mike Hampton	.05
159	Craig Biggio	.05
160	Jeff Bagwell	.60
161	Brian L. Hunter	.05
162	Mike Henneman	.05
163	Dave Magadan	.05
164	Shane Reynolds	.05
165	Derek Bell	.05
166	Orlando Miller	.05
167	James Mouton	.05
168	Melvin Bunch	.05
169	Tom Gordon	.05
170	Kevin Appier	.05
171	Tom Goodwin	.05
172	Greg Gagne	.05
173	Gary Gaetti	.05
174	Jeff Montgomery	.05
175	Jon Nunnally	.05
176	Michael Tucker	.05
177	Joe Vitiello	.05
178	Billy Ashley	.05
179	Tom Candiotti	.05
180	Hideo Nomo	.30
181	Chad Fonville	.05
182	Todd Hollandsworth	.05
183	Eric Karros	.05
184	Roberto Kelly	.05
185	Mike Piazza	1.00
186	Ramon Martinez	.05
187	Tim Wallach	.05
188	Jeff Cirillo	.05
189	Sid Roberson	.05
190	Kevin Seitzer	.05
191	Mike Fetters	.05
192	Steve Sparks	.05
193	Matt Mieske	.05
194	Joe Oliver	.05
195	B.J. Surhoff	.05
196	Alberto Reyes	.05
197	Fernando Vina	.05
198	LaTroy Hawkins	.05
199	Marty Cordova	.05
200	Kirby Puckett	.75
201	Brad Radke	.05
202	Pedro Munoz	.05
203	Scott Klingenbeck	.05
204	Pat Meares	.05
205	Chuck Knoblauch	.05
206	Scott Stahoviak	.05
207	Dave Stevens	.05
208	Shane Andrews	.05
209	Moises Alou	.05
210	David Segui	.05
211	Cliff Floyd	.05
212	Carlos Perez	.05
213	Mark Grudzielanek	.05
214	Butch Henry	.05
215	Rondell White	.05
216	Mel Rojas	.05
217	Ugueth Urbina	.05
218	Edgardo Alfonzo	.05
219	Carl Everett	.05
220	John Franco	.05
221	Todd Hundley	.05
222	Bobby Jones	.05
223	Bill Pulsipher	.05
224	Rico Brogna	.05
225	Jeff Kent	.05
226	Chris Jones	.05
227	Butch Huskey	.05
228	Robert Eenhoorn	.05
229	Sterling Hitchcock	.05
230	Wade Boggs	.75
231	Derek Jeter	2.00
232	Tony Fernandez	.05
233	Jack McDowell	.05
234	Andy Pettitte	.35
235	David Cone	.05
236	Mike Stanley	.05
237	Don Mattingly	.85
238	Geronimo Berroa	.05
239	Scott Brosius	.05
240	Rickey Henderson	.60
241	Terry Steinbach	.05
242	Mike Gallego	.05
243	Jason Giambi	.40
244	Steve Ontiveros	.05
245	Dennis Eckersley	.50
246	Dave Stewart	.05

247	Don Wengert	.05
248	Paul Quantrill	.05
249	Ricky Bottalico	.05
250	Kevin Stocker	.05
251	Lenny Dykstra	.05
252	Tony Longmire	.05
253	Tyler Green	.05
254	Mike Mimbs	.05
255	Charlie Hayes	.05
256	Mickey Morandini	.05
257	Heathcliff Slocumb	.05
258	Jeff King	.05
259	Midre Cummings	.05
260	Mark Johnson	.05
261	Freddy Garcia	.05
262	Jon Lieber	.05
263	Esteban Loaiza	.05
264	Danny Miceli	.05
265	Orlando Merced	.05
266	Denny Neagle	.05
267	Steve Parris	.05
268	Greg Maddux Fantasy Team '95	.35
269	Randy Johnson Fantasy Team '95	.20
270	Hideo Nomo Fantasy Team '95	.15
271	Jose Mesa Fantasy Team '95	.05
272	Mike Piazza Fantasy Team '95	.60
273	Mo Vaughn Fantasy Team '95	.05
274	Craig Biggio Fantasy Team '95	.05
275	Edgar Martinez Fantasy Team '95	.05
276	Barry Larkin Fantasy Team '95	.05
277	Sammy Sosa F antasy Team '95	.50
278	Dante Bichette Fantasy Team '95	.05
279	Albert Belle Fantasy Team '95	.05
280	Ozzie Smith	.75
281	Mark Sweeney	.05
282	Terry Bradshaw	.05
283	Allen Battle	.05
284	Danny Jackson	.05
285	Tom Henke	.05
286	Scott Cooper	.05
287	Tripp Cromer	.05
288	Bernard Gilkey	.05
289	Brian Jordan	.05
290	Tony Gwynn	.75
291	Brad Ausmus	.05
292	Bryce Florie	.05
293	Andres Berumen	.05
294	Ken Caminiti	.05
295	Bip Roberts	.05
296	Trevor Hoffman	.05
297	Roberto Petagine	.05
298	Jody Reed	.05
299	Fernando Valenzuela	.05
300	Barry Bonds	2.00
301	Mark Leiter	.05
302	Mark Carreon	.05
303	Royce Clayton	.05
304	Kirt Manwaring	.05
305	Glenallen Hill	.05
306	Deion Sanders	.10
307	Joe Rosselli	.05
308	Robby Thompson	.05
309	William Van Landingham	.05
310	Ken Griffey Jr.	1.00
311	Bobby Ayala	.05
312	Joey Cora	.05
313	Mike Blowers	.05
314	Darren Bragg	.05
315	Randy Johnson	.60
316	Alex Rodriguez	1.50
317	Andy Benes	.05
318	Tino Martinez	.05
319	Dan Wilson	.05
320	Will Clark	.05
321	Jeff Frye	.05
322	Benji Gil	.05
323	Rick Helling	.05
324	Mark McLemore	.05
325	Dave Nilsson	.05
326	Larry Walker	.05
327	Jose Canseco	.15
328	Raul Mondesi	.05
329	Manny Ramirez	.30
330	Robert Eenhoorn	.05
331	Chili Davis	.05
332	Hideo Nomo	.15
333	Benji Gil	.05
334	Fernando Valenzuela	.05
335	Dennis Martinez	.05
336	Roberto Kelly	.05
337	Carlos Baerga	.05
338	Juan Gonzalez	.15
339	Roberto Alomar	.10
340	Chan Ho Park	.05
341	Andres Galarraga	.05
342	Midre Cummings	.05
343	Otis Nixon	.05
344	Jeff Russell	.05
345	Ivan Rodriguez	.50
346	Mickey Tettleton	.05
347	Bob Tewksbury	.05
348	Domingo Cedeno	.05
349	Lance Parrish	.05
350	Joe Carter	.05
351	Devon White	.05
352	Carlos Delgado	.35
353	Alex Gonzalez	.05
354	Darren Hall	.05
355	Paul Molitor	.60
356	Al Leiter	.05
357	Randy Knorr	.05
358	Checklist 1-46(12-player Astros-Padres trade)	.05
359	Hideo Nomo Checklist 47-92	.15
360	Ramon Martinez Checklist 93-138	.05
361	Robin Ventura Checklist 139-184	.05
362	Cal Ripken Jr. Checklist 185-230	.30
363	Ken Caminiti Checklist 231-275	.05
364	Eddie Murray Checklist 276-320	.20
365	Randy Johnson Checklist 321-365	.15
366	Tony Pena A.L. Divisional Series	.10
367	Jim Thome A.L. Divisional Series	.25
368	Don Mattingly A.L. Divisional Series	.60
369	Jim Leyritz A.L. Divisional Series	.10
370	Ken Griffey Jr. A.L. Divisional Series	.60
371	Edgar Martinez A.L. Divisional Series	.10
372	Pete Schourek N.L. Divisional Series	.10
373	Mark Lewis N.L. Divisional Series	.10
374	Chipper Jones N.L. Divisonal Series	.50
375	Fred McGriff N.L. Divisonal Series	.10
376	Javy Lopez N.L. Championship Series	.10
377	Fred McGriff N.L. Championship Series	.10
378	Charlie O'Brien N.L. Championship Series	.10
379	Mike Devereaux N.L. Championship Series	.10
380	Mark Wohlers N.L. Championship Series	.10
381	Bob Wolcott A.L. Championship Series	.10
382	Manny Ramirez A.L. Championship Series	.25
383	Jay Buhner A.L. Championship Series	.10
384	Orel Hershiser A.L. Championship Series	.10
385	Kenny Lofton A.L. Championship Series	.10
386	Greg Maddux World Series	.50
387	Javy Lopez World Series	.10
388	Kenny Lofton World Series	.10
389	Eddie Murray World Series	.10
390	Luis Polonia World Series	.10
391	Pedro Borbon World Series	.10
392	Jim Thome World Series	.25
393	Orel Hershiser World Series	.10
394	David Justice World Series	.10
395	Tom Glavine World Series	.10
396	Greg Maddux Braves Team Checklist	.25
397	Brett Butler Mets Team Checklist	.05
398	Darren Daulton Phillies Team Checklist	.05
399	Gary Sheffield Marlins Team Checklist	.05
400	Moises Alou Expos Team Checklist	.05
401	Barry Larkin Reds Team Checklist	.05
402	Jeff Bagwell Astros Team Checklist	.20
403	Sammy Sosa Cubs Team Checklist	.35
404	Ozzie Smith Cardinals Team Checklist	.25
405	Jeff King Pirates Team Checklist	.05
406	Mike Piazza Dodgers Team Checklist	.50
407	Dante Bichette Rockies Team Checklist	.05
408	Tony Gwynn Padres Team Checklist	.25
409	Barry Bonds Giants Team Checklist	.45
410	Kenny Lofton Indians Team Checklist	.05
411	Jon Nunnally Royals Team Checklist	.05
412	Frank Thomas White Sox Team Checklist	.20
413	Greg Vaughn Brewers Team Checklist	.05
414	Paul Molitor Twins Team Checklist	.20
415	Ken Griffey Jr. Mariners Team Checklist	.35
416	Jim Edmonds Angels Team Checklist	.05
417	Juan Gonzalez Rangers Team Checklist	.15
418	Mark McGwire Athletics Team Checklist	.75
419	Roger Clemens Red Sox Team Checklist	.30
420	Wade Boggs Yankees Team Checklist	.35
421	Cal Ripken Jr. Orioles Team Checklist	.40
422	Cecil Fielder Tigers Team Checklist	.05
423	Joe Carter Blue Jays Team Checklist	.05
424	Osvaldo Fernandez **RC**	.15
425	Billy Wagner	.05
426	George Arias	.05
427	Mendy Lopez	.05
428	Jeff Suppan	.05
429	Rey Ordonez	.05
430	Brooks Kieschnick	.05
431	Raul Ibanez **RC**	.05
432	Livan Hernandez **RC**	.20
433	Shannon Stewart	.05
434	Steve Cox	.05
435	Trey Beamon	.05
436	Sergio Nunez	.05
437	Jermaine Dye	.05
438	Mike Sweeney **RC**	.45
439	Richard Hidalgo	.05
440	Todd Greene	.05
441	Robert Smith **RC**	.05
442	Rafael Orellano	.05
443	Wilton Guerrero **RC**	.05
444	David Doster **RC**	.05
445	Jason Kendall	.05
446	Edgar Renteria	.05
447	Scott Spiezio	.05
448	Jay Canizaro	.05
449	Enrique Wilson	.05
450	Bob Abreu	.10
451	Dwight Smith	.05
452	Jeff Blauser	.05
453	Steve Avery	.05
454	Brad Clontz	.05
455	Tom Glavine	.20
456	Mike Mordecai	.05
457	Rafael Belliard	.05
458	Greg McMichael	.05
459	Pedro Borbon	.05
460	Ryan Klesko	.05
461	Terrell Wade	.05
462	Brady Anderson	.05
463	Roberto Alomar	.20
464	Bobby Bonilla	.05
465	Mike Mussina	.40
466	Cesar Devarez **RC**	.05
467	Jeffrey Hammonds	.05
468	Mike Devereaux	.05
469	B.J. Surhoff	.05
470	Rafael Palmeiro	.50
471	John Valentin	.05
472	Mike Greenwell	.05
473	Dwayne Hosey	.05
474	Tim Wakefield	.05
475	Jose Canseco	.35
476	Aaron Sele	.05
477	Stan Belinda	.05
478	Mike Stanley	.05
479	Jamie Moyer	.05
480	Mo Vaughn	.05
481	Randy Velarde	.05
482	Gary DiSarcina	.05
483	Jorge Fabregas	.05
484	Rex Hudler	.05
485	Chuck Finley	.05
486	Tim Wallach	.05
487	Eduardo Perez	.05
488	Scott Sanderson	.05
489	J.T. Snow	.05
490	Sammy Sosa	.75
491	Terry Adams	.05
492	Matt Franco	.05
493	Scott Servais	.05
494	Frank Castillo	.05
495	Ryne Sandberg	.75
496	Rey Sanchez	.05
497	Steve Trachsel	.05
498	Jose Hernandez	.05
499	Dave Martinez	.05
500	Babe Ruth	1.00
501	Ty Cobb	.50
502	Walter Johnson	.10
503	Christy Mathewson	.10
504	Honus Wagner	.25
505	Robin Ventura	.05
506	Jason Bere	.05
507	Mike Cameron **RC**	.25
508	Ron Karkovice	.05
509	Matt Karchner	.05
510	Harold Baines	.05
511	Kirk McCaskill	.05
512	Larry Thomas	.05
513	Danny Tartabull	.05
514	Steve Gibralter	.05
515	Bret Boone	.05
516	Jeff Branson	.05
517	Kevin Jarvis	.05
518	Xavier Hernandez	.05
519	Eric Owens	.05
520	Barry Larkin	.05
521	Dave Burba	.05
522	John Smiley	.05
523	Paul Assenmacher	.05
524	Chad Ogea	.05
525	Orel Hershiser	.05
526	Alan Embree	.05
527	Tony Pena	.05
528	Omar Vizquel	.05
529	Mark Clark	.05
530	Albert Belle	.05
531	Charles Nagy	.05
532	Herbert Perry	.05
533	Darren Holmes	.05
534	Ellis Burks	.05
535	Bill Swift	.05
536	Armando Reynoso	.05
537	Curtis Leskanic	.05
538	Quinton McCracken	.05
539	Steve Reed	.05
540	Larry Walker	.05
541	Walt Weiss	.05
542	Bryan Rekar	.05
543	Tony Clark	.05
544	Steve Rodriguez	.05
545	C.J. Nitkowski	.05
546	Todd Steverson	.05
547	Jose Lima	.05
548	Phil Nevin	.05
549	Chris Gomez	.05
550	Travis Fryman	.05
551	Mark Lewis	.05
552	Alex Arias	.05
553	Marc Valdes	.05
554	Kevin Brown	.05
555	Jeff Conine	.05
556	John Burkett	.05
557	Devon White	.05
558	Pat Rapp	.05
559	Jay Powell	.05
560	Gary Sheffield	.30
561	Jim Dougherty	.05
562	Todd Jones	.05
563	Tony Eusebio	.05
564	Darryl Kile	.05
565	Doug Drabek	.05
566	Mike Simms	.05
567	Derrick May	.05
568	Donne Wall **RC**	.05
569	Greg Swindell	.05
570	Jim Pittsley	.05
571	Bob Hamelin	.05
572	Mark Gubicza	.05
573	Chris Haney	.05
574	Keith Lockhart	.05
575	Mike Macfarlane	.05
576	Les Norman	.05
577	Joe Randa	.05
578	Chris Stynes	.05
579	Greg Gagne	.05
580	Raul Mondesi	.05
581	Delino DeShields	.05
582	Pedro Astacio	.05
583	Antonio Osuna	.05
584	Brett Butler	.05
585	Todd Worrell	.05
586	Mike Blowers	.05
587	Felix Rodriguez	.05
588	Ismael Valdes	.05
589	Ricky Bones	.05
590	Greg Vaughn	.05
591	Mark Loretta	.05
592	Cal Eldred	.05
593	Chuck Carr	.05
594	Dave Nilsson	.05
595	John Jaha	.05
596	Scott Karl	.05
597	Pat Listach	.05
598	Jose Valentin **RC**	.05
599	Mike Trombley	.05
600	Paul Molitor	.60
601	Dave Hollins	.05
602	Ron Coomer	.05
603	Matt Walbeck	.05
604	Roberto Kelly	.05
605	Rick Aguilera	.05
606	Pat Mahomes	.05
607	Jeff Reboulet	.05
608	Rich Becker	.05
609	Tim Scott	.05
610	Pedro J. Martinez	.60
611	Kirk Rueter	.05
612	Tavo Alvarez	.05
613	Yamil Benitez	.05
614	Darrin Fletcher	.05
615	Mike Lansing	.05
616	Henry Rodriguez	.05
617	Tony Tarasco	.05
618	Alex Ochoa	.05
619	Tim Bogar	.05
620	Bernard Gilkey	.05
621	Dave Mlicki	.05
622	Brent Mayne	.05
623	Ryan Thompson	.05
624	Pete Harnisch	.05
625	Lance Johnson	.05
626	Jose Vizcaino	.05
627	Doug Henry	.05
628	Scott Kamieniecki	.05
629	Jim Leyritz	.05
630	Ruben Sierra	.05
631	Pat Kelly	.05
632	Joe Girardi	.05
633	John Wetteland	.05
634	Melido Perez	.05
635	Paul O'Neill	.05
636	Jorge Posada	.05
637	Bernie Williams	.05
638	Mark Acre	.05
639	Mike Bordick	.05
640	Mark McGwire	1.50

641	Fausto Cruz	.05
642	Ernie Young	.05
643	Todd Van Poppel	.05
644	Craig Paquette	.05
645	Brent Gates	.05
646	Pedro Munoz	.05
647	Andrew Lorraine	.05
648	Sid Fernandez	.05
649	Jim Eisenreich	.05
650	Johnny Damon	.30
651	Dustin Hermanson	.05
652	Joe Randa	.05
653	Michael Tucker	.05
654	Alan Benes	.05
655	Chad Fonville	.05
656	David Bell	.05
657	Jon Nunnally	.05
658	Chan Ho Park	.05
659	LaTroy Hawkins	.05
660	Jamie Brewington	.05
661	Quinton McCracken	.05
662	Tim Unroe	.05
663	Jeff Ware	.05
664	Todd Greene	.05
665	Andrew Lorraine	.05
666	Ernie Young	.05
667	Toby Borland	.05
668	Lenny Webster	.05
669	Benito Santiago	.05
670	Gregg Jefferies	.05
671	Darren Daulton	.05
672	Curt Schilling	.25
673	Mark Whiten	.05
674	Todd Zeile	.05
675	Jay Bell	.05
676	Paul Wagner	.05
677	Dave Clark	.05
678	Nelson Liriano	.05
679	Ramon Morel	.05
680	Charlie Hayes	.05
681	Angelo Encaracion	.05
682	Al Martin	.05
683	Jacob Brumfield	.05
684	Mike Kingery	.05
685	Carlos Garcia	.05
686	Tom Pagnozzi	.05
687	David Bell	.05
688	Todd Stottlemyre	.05
689	Jose Oliva	.05
690	Ray Lankford	.05
691	Mike Morgan	.05
692	John Frascatore	.05
693	John Mabry	.05
694	Mark Petkovsek	.05
695	Alan Benes	.05
696	Steve Finley	.05
697	Marc Newfield	.05
698	Andy Ashby	.05
699	Marc Kroon	.05
700	Wally Joyner	.05
701	Joey Hamilton	.05
702	Dustin Hermanson	.05
703	Scott Sanders	.05
704	Marty Cordova	.05
705	Hideo Nomo	.15
706	Mo Vaughn	.05
707	Barry Larkin	.05
708	Randy Johnson	.20
709	Greg Maddux	.35
710	Mark McGwire	.75
711	Ron Gant	.05
712	Andujar Cedeno	.05
713	Brian Johnson	.05
714	J.R. Phillips	.05
715	Rod Beck	.05
716	Sergio Valdez	.05
717	Marvin Benard **RC**	.25
718	Steve Scarsone	.05
719	Rich Aurilia **RC**	.10
720	Matt Williams	.05
721	John Patterson	.05
722	Shawn Estes	.05
723	Russ Davis	.05
724	Rich Amaral	.05
725	Edgar Martinez	.05
726	Norm Charlton	.05
727	Paul Sorrento	.05
728	Luis Sojo	.05
729	Arquimedez Pozo	.05
730	Jay Buhner	.05
731	Chris Bosio	.05
732	Chris Widger	.05
733	Kevin Gross	.05
734	Darren Oliver	.05
735	Dean Palmer	.05
736	Matt Whiteside	.05
737	Luis Ortiz	.05
738	Roger Pavlik	.05
739	Damon Buford	.05
740	Juan Gonzalez	.30
741	Rusty Greer	.05
742	Lou Frazier	.05
743	Pat Hentgen	.05
744	Tomas Perez	.05
745	Juan Guzman	.05
746	Otis Nixon	.05
747	Robert Perez	.05
748	Ed Sprague	.05
749	Tony Castillo	.05
750	John Olerud	.05
751	Shawn Green	.10
752	Jeff Ware	.05
753	Dante Bichette, Larry Walker, Andres Galarraga, Vinny Castilla Checklist 396-441/ Blake St. Bombers	.05
754	Greg Maddux Checklist 442-487	.25

755	Marty Cordova Checklist 488-533	.05
756	Ozzie Smith Checklist 534-579	.35
757	John Vander Wal Checklist 580-625	.05
758	Andres Galarraga Checklist 626-670	.05
759	Frank Thomas Checklist 671-715	.20
760	Tony Gwynn Checklist 716-760	.25
761	Randy Myers	.10
762	Kent Mercker	.10
763	David Wells	.05
764	Tom Gordon	.10
765	Wil Cordero	.10
766	Dave Magadan	.10
767	Doug Jones	.10
768	Kevin Tapani	.10
769	Curtis Goodwin	.10
770	Julio Franco	.10
771	Jack McDowell	.10
772	Al Leiter	.10
773	Sean Berry	.10
774	Bip Roberts	.10
775	Jose Offerman	.10
776	Ben McDonald	.10
777	Dan Serafini	.10
778	Ryan McGuire	.10
779	Tim Raines	.10
780	Tino Martinez	.10
781	Kenny Rogers	.10
782	Bob Tewksbury	.10
783	Rickey Henderson	.60
784	Ron Gant	.10
785	Gary Gaetti	.10
786	Andy Benes	.10
787	Royce Clayton	.10
788	Darryl Hamilton	.10
789	Ken Hill	.10
790	Erik Hanson	.10

Gold Signature

	NM/M
Common Player:	1.00
Stars:	10X

(See 1996 Collector's Choice for checklist and base card values.)

Silver Signature

	NM/M
Common Player:	.10
Stars:	1.5X

(See 1996 Collector's Choice for checklist and base card values.)

A Cut Above

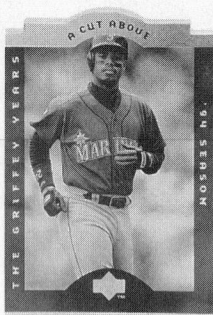

	NM/M
Complete Set (10):	8.00
Common Card:	1.00
CA1	Ken Griffey Jr. (Teenage Rookie)	1.00
CA2	Ken Griffey Jr. (Great Defense)	1.00
CA3	Ken Griffey Jr. (Fun-Loving)	1.00
CA4	Ken Griffey Jr. (All-Star Games)	1.00
CA5	Ken Griffey Jr. ('93 Season)	1.00
CA6	Ken Griffey Jr. ('94 HR Records)	1.00
CA7	Ken Griffey Jr. ('94 Season)	1.00
CA8	Ken Griffey Jr. ('95 Season)	1.00
CA9	Ken Griffey Jr. ('95 Postseason)	1.00
CA10	Ken Griffey Jr. ('96: A Look Ahead)	1.00

Cal Ripken Jr. Jumbo

	NM/M
1	Cal Ripken Jr.	5.00

Nomo Scrapbook

	NM/M
Complete Set (5):	10.00
Common Card:	2.00
Japanese:	3X
1-5	Hideo Nomo	2.00

Ripken Collection

	NM/M
Complete Set (1-4, 9-12)	15.00
Common Card:	2.50
Header Card:	2.00

(See also Upper Deck Series 1 and 2, and Upper Deck/SP)

1997 Collector's Choice

	NM/M
Factory Set (516):	16.00
Complete Set (506):	12.00
Common Player:	.05
Pack (12):	1.00

Wax Box (36):		20.00
1	Andruw Jones	1.00
2	Rocky Coppinger	.05
3	Jeff D'Amico	.05
4	Dmitri Young	.05
5	Darin Erstad	.75
6	Jermaine Allensworth	.05
7	Damian Jackson	.05
8	Bill Mueller	.05
9	Jacob Cruz	.05
10	Vladimir Guerrero	1.00
11	Marty Janzen	.05
12	Kevin L. Brown	.05
13	Willie Adams	.05
14	Wendell Magee	.05
15	Scott Rolen	.65
16	Matt Beech	.05
17	Neifi Perez	.05
18	Jamey Wright	.05
19	Jose Paniagua	.05
20	Todd Walker	.05
21	Justin Thompson	.05
22	Robin Jennings	.05
23	Dario Veras **RC**	.05
24	Brian Lesher	.05
25	Nomar Garciaparra	1.25
26	Luis Castillo	.05
27	Brian Giles **RC**	.75
28	Jermaine Dye	.05
29	Terrell Wade	.05
30	Fred McGriff	.05
31	Marquis Grissom	.05
32	Ryan Klesko	.05
33	Javier Lopez	.05
34	Mark Wohlers	.05
35	Tom Glavine	.25
36	Denny Neagle	.05
37	Scott Erickson	.05
38	Chris Hoiles	.05
39	Roberto Alomar	.25
40	Eddie Murray	.75
41	Cal Ripken Jr.	2.00
42	Randy Myers	.05
43	B.J. Surhoff	.05
44	Rick Krivda	.05
45	Jose Canseco	.50
46	Heathcliff Slocumb	.05
47	Jeff Suppan	.05
48	Tom Gordon	.05
49	Aaron Sele	.05
50	Mo Vaughn	.05
51	Darren Bragg	.05
52	Wil Cordero	.05
53	Scott Bullett	.05
54	Terry Adams	.05
55	Jackie Robinson	.35
56	Tony Gwynn, Alex Rodriguez (Batting Leaders)	.35
57	Andres Galarraga, Mark McGwire (Homer Leaders)	.50
58	Andres Galarraga, Albert Belle (RBI Leaders)	.05
59	Eric Young, Kenny Lofton (SB Leaders)	.05
60	John Smoltz, Andy Pettitte (Victory Leaders)	.05
61	John Smoltz, Roger Clemens (Strikout Leaders)	.20
62	Kevin Brown, Juan Guzman (ERA Leaders)	.05
63	John Wetteland, Todd Worrell, Jeff Brantley (Save Leaders)	.05
64	Scott Servais	.05
65	Sammy Sosa	1.00
66	Ryne Sandberg	1.00
67	Frank Castillo	.05
68	Rey Sanchez	.05
69	Steve Trachsel	.05
70	Robin Ventura	.05
71	Wilson Alvarez	.05
72	Tony Phillips	.05
73	Lyle Mouton	.05
74	Mike Cameron	.05
75	Harold Baines	.05
76	Albert Belle	.05
77	Chris Snopek	.05
78	Reggie Sanders	.05
79	Jeff Brantley	.05
80	Barry Larkin	.05
81	Kevin Jarvis	.05
82	John Smiley	.05

83	Pete Schourek	.05
84	Thomas Howard	.05
85	Lee Smith	.05
86	Omar Vizquel	.05
87	Julio Franco	.05
88	Orel Hershiser	.05
89	Charles Nagy	.05
90	Matt Williams	.05
91	Dennis Martinez	.05
92	Jose Mesa	.05
93	Sandy Alomar Jr.	.05
94	Jim Thome	.50
95	Vinny Castilla	.05
96	Armando Reynoso	.05
97	Kevin Ritz	.05
98	Larry Walker	.05
99	Eric Young	.05
100	Dante Bichette	.05
101	Quinton McCracken	.05
102	John Vander Wal	.05
103	Phil Nevin	.05
104	Tony Clark	.05
105	Alan Trammell	.05
106	Felipe Lira	.05
107	Curtis Pride	.05
108	Bobby Higginson	.05
109	Mark Lewis	.05
110	Travis Fryman	.05
111	Al Leiter	.05
112	Devon White	.05
113	Jeff Conine	.05
114	Charles Johnson	.05
115	Andre Dawson	.25
116	Edgar Renteria	.05
117	Robb Nen	.05
118	Kevin Brown	.05
119	Derek Bell	.05
120	Bob Abreu	.10
121	Mike Hampton	.05
122	Todd Jones	.05
123	Billy Wagner	.05
124	Shane Reynolds	.05
125	Jeff Bagwell	.75
126	Brian L. Hunter	.05
127	Jeff Montgomery	.05
128	Rod Myers **RC**	.05
129	Tim Belcher	.05
130	Kevin Appier	.05
131	Mike Sweeney	.05
132	Craig Paquette	.05
133	Joe Randa	.05
134	Michael Tucker	.05
135	Raul Mondesi	.05
136	Tim Wallach	.05
137	Brett Butler	.05
138	Karim Garcia	.10
139	Todd Hollandsworth	.05
140	Eric Karros	.05
141	Hideo Nomo	.40
142	Ismael Valdes	.05
143	Cal Eldred	.05
144	Scott Karl	.05
145	Matt Mieske	.05
146	Mike Fetters	.05
147	Mark Loretta	.05
148	Fernando Vina	.05
149	Jeff Cirillo	.05
150	Dave Nilsson	.05
151	Kirby Puckett	1.00
152	Rich Becker	.05
153	Chuck Knoblauch	.05
154	Marty Cordova	.05
155	Paul Molitor	.75
156	Rick Aguilera	.05
157	Pat Meares	.05
158	Frank Rodriguez	.05
159	David Segui	.05
160	Henry Rodriguez	.05
161	Shane Andrews	.05
162	Pedro J. Martinez	.75
163	Mark Grudzielanek	.05
164	Mike Lansing	.05
165	Rondell White	.05
166	Ugueth Urbina	.05
167	Rey Ordonez	.05
168	Robert Person	.05
169	Carlos Baerga	.05
170	Bernard Gilkey	.05
171	John Franco	.05
172	Pete Harnisch	.05
173	Butch Huskey	.05
174	Paul Wilson	.05
175	Bernie Williams	.05
176	Dwight Gooden	.05
177	Wade Boggs	1.00
178	Ruben Rivera	.05
179	Jim Leyritz	.05
180	Derek Jeter	2.00
181	Tino Martinez	.05
182	Tim Raines	.05
183	Scott Brosius	.05
184	Jason Giambi	.60
185	Geronimo Berroa	.05
186	Ariel Prieto	.05
187	Scott Spiezio	.05
188	John Wasdin	.05
189	Ernie Young	.05
190	Mark McGwire	1.50
191	Jim Eisenreich	.05
192	Ricky Bottalico	.05
193	Darren Daulton	.05
194	David Doster	.05
195	Gregg Jefferies	.05
196	Lenny Dykstra	.05
197	Curt Schilling	.20
198	Todd Stottlemyre	.05
199	Willie McGee	.05
200	Ozzie Smith	1.00
201	Dennis Eckersley	.65
202	Ray Lankford	.05
203	John Mabry	.05
204	Alan Benes	.05
205	Ron Gant	.05
206	Archi Cianfrocco	.05
207	Fernando Valenzuela	.05
208	Greg Vaughn	.05
209	Steve Finley	.05
210	Tony Gwynn	1.00
211	Rickey Henderson	.75
212	Trevor Hoffman	.05
213	Jason Thompson	.05
214	Osvaldo Fernandez	.05
215	Glenallen Hill	.05
216	William Van Landingham	.05
217	Marvin Benard	.05
218	Juan Gonzalez	.10
219	Roberto Alomar	.05
220	Brian Jordan	.05
221	John Smoltz	.05
222	Javy Lopez	.05
223	Bernie Williams	.05
224	Jim Leyritz, John Wetteland	.05
225	Barry Bonds	2.00
226	Rich Aurilia	.05
227	Jay Canizaro	.05
228	Dan Wilson	.05
229	Bob Wolcott	.05
230	Ken Griffey Jr.	1.25
231	Sterling Hitchcock	.05
232	Edgar Martinez	.05
233	Joey Cora	.05
234	Norm Charlton	.05
235	Alex Rodriguez	1.50
236	Bobby Witt	.05
237	Darren Oliver	.05
238	Kevin Elster	.05
239	Rusty Greer	.05
240	Juan Gonzalez	.40
241	Will Clark	.05
242	Dean Palmer	.05
243	Ivan Rodriguez	.65
244	Ken Griffey Jr. Checklist	.25
245	Ken Griffey Jr. Checklist	.25
246	Ken Griffey Jr. Checklist	.25
247	Ken Griffey Jr. Checklist	.25
248	Ken Griffey Jr. Checklist	.25
249	Ken Griffey Jr. Checklist	.25
250	Eddie Murray	.75
251	Troy Percival	.05
252	Garret Anderson	.05
253	Allen Watson	.05
254	Jason Dickson	.05
255	Jim Edmonds	.05
256	Chuck Finley	.05
257	Randy Velarde	.05
258	Shigetosi Hasegawa	.05
259	Todd Greene	.05
260	Tim Salmon	.05
261	Mark Langston	.05
262	Dave Hollins	.05
263	Gary DiSarcina	.05
264	Kenny Lofton	.05
265	John Smoltz	.05
266	Greg Maddux	1.00
267	Jeff Blauser	.05
268	Alan Embree	.05
269	Mark Lemke	.05
270	Chipper Jones	1.00
271	Mike Mussina	.65
272	Rafael Palmeiro	.65
273	Jimmy Key	.05
274	Mike Bordick	.05
275	Brady Anderson	.05
276	Eric Davis	.05
277	Jeffrey Hammonds	.05
278	Reggie Jefferson	.05
279	Tim Naehring	.05
280	John Valentin	.05
281	Troy O'Leary	.05
282	Shane Mack	.05
283	Mike Stanley	.05
284	Tim Wakefield	.05
285	Brian McRae	.05
286	Brooks Kieschnick	.05
287	Shawon Dunston	.05
288	Kevin Foster	.05
289	Mel Rojas	.05
290	Mark Grace	.05
291	Brant Brown	.05
292	Amaury Telemaco	.05
293	Dave Martinez	.05
294	Jaime Navarro	.05
295	Ray Durham	.05
296	Ozzie Guillen	.05
297	Roberto Hernandez	.05
298	Ron Karkovice	.05
299	James Baldwin	.05
300	Frank Thomas	.75
301	Eddie Taubensee	.05
302	Bret Boone	.05
303	Willie Greene	.05
304	Dave Burba	.05
305	Deion Sanders	.10
306	Reggie Sanders	.05
307	Hal Morris	.05
308	Pokey Reese	.05
309	Tony Fernandez	.05
310	Manny Ramirez	.75
311	Chad Ogea	.05
312	Jack McDowell	.05
313	Kevin Mitchell	.05
314	Chad Curtis	.05
315	Steve Kline	.05
316	Kevin Seitzer	.05
317	Kirt Manwaring	.05
318	Bill Swift	.05
319	Ellis Burks	.05
320	Andres Galarraga	.05
321	Bruce Ruffin	.05
322	Mark Thompson	.05
323	Walt Weiss	.05
324	Todd Jones	.05
325	Andruw Jones	.50
326	Chipper Jones	.75
327	Mo Vaughn	.05
328	Frank Thomas	.50
329	Albert Belle	.10
330	Mark McGwire	1.00
331	Derek Jeter	1.50
332	Alex Rodriguez	1.00
333	Jay Buhner	.05
334	Ken Griffey Jr.	.75
335	Brian L. Hunter	.05
336	Brian Johnson	.05
337	Omar Olivares	.05
338	Deivi Cruz **RC**	.05
339	Damion Easley	.05
340	Melvin Nieves	.05
341	Moises Alou	.05
342	Jim Eisenreich	.05
343	Mark Hutton	.05
344	Alex Fernandez	.05
345	Gary Sheffield	.35
346	Pat Rapp	.05
347	Brad Ausmus	.05
348	Sean Berry	.05
349	Darryl Kile	.05
350	Craig Biggio	.05
351	Chris Holt	.05
352	Luis Gonzalez	.05
353	Pat Listach	.05
354	Jose Rosado	.05
355	Mike Macfarlane	.05
356	Tom Goodwin	.05
357	Chris Haney	.05
358	Chili Davis	.05
359	Jose Offerman	.05
360	Johnny Damon	.30
361	Bip Roberts	.05
362	Ramon Martinez	.05
363	Pedro Astacio	.05
364	Todd Zeile	.05
365	Mike Piazza	1.25
366	Greg Gagne	.05
367	Chan Ho Park	.05
368	Wilton Guerrero	.05
369	Todd Worrell	.05
370	John Jaha	.05
371	Steve Sparks	.05
372	Mike Matheny	.05
373	Marc Newfield	.05
374	Jeromy Burnitz	.05
375	Jose Valentin	.05
376	Ben McDonald	.05
377	Roberto Kelly	.05
378	Bob Tewksbury	.05
379	Ron Coomer	.05
380	Brad Radke	.05
381	Matt Lawton	.05
382	Dan Naulty	.05
383	Scott Stahoviak	.05
384	Matt Wagner	.05
385	Jim Bullinger	.05
386	Carlos Perez	.05
387	Darrin Fletcher	.05
388	Chris Widger	.05
389	F.P. Santangelo	.05
390	Lee Smith	.05
391	Bobby Jones	.05
392	John Olerud	.05
393	Mark Clark	.05
394	Jason Isringhausen	.05
395	Todd Hundley	.05
396	Lance Johnson	.05
397	Edgardo Alfonzo	.05
398	Alex Ochoa	.05
399	Darryl Strawberry	.05
400	David Cone	.05
401	Paul O'Neill	.05
402	Joe Girardi	.05
403	Charlie Hayes	.05
404	Andy Pettitte	.25
405	Mariano Rivera	.25
406	Mariano Duncan	.05
407	Kenny Rogers	.05
408	Cecil Fielder	.05
409	George Williams	.05
410	Jose Canseco	.35
411	Tony Batista	.05
412	Steve Karsay	.05
413	Dave Telgheder	.05
414	Billy Taylor	.05
415	Mickey Morandini	.05
416	Calvin Maduro	.05
417	Mark Leiter	.05
418	Kevin Stocker	.05
419	Mike Lieberthal	.05
420	Rico Brogna	.05
421	Mark Portugal	.05
422	Rex Hudler	.05
423	Mark Johnson	.05
424	Esteban Loiaza	.05
425	Lou Collier	.05
426	Kevin Elster	.05
427	Francisco Cordova	.05
428	Marc Wilkins	.05
429	Joe Randa	.05
430	Jason Kendall	.05
431	Jon Lieber	.05
432	Steve Cooke	.05
433	Emil Brown **RC**	.05
434	Tony Womack **RC**	.25
435	Al Martin	.05
436	Jason Schmidt	.05
437	Andy Benes	.05
438	Delino DeShields	.05
439	Royce Clayton	.05
440	Brian Jordan	.05
441	Donovan Osborne	.05
442	Gary Gaetti	.05
443	Tom Pagnozzi	.05
444	Joey Hamilton	.05
445	Wally Joyner	.05
446	John Flaherty	.05
447	Chris Gomez	.05
448	Sterling Hitchcock	.05
449	Andy Ashby	.05
450	Ken Caminiti	.05
451	Tim Worrell	.05
452	Jose Vizcaino	.05
453	Rod Beck	.05
454	Wilson Delgado	.05
455	Darryl Hamilton	.05
456	Mark Lewis	.05
457	Mark Gardner	.05
458	Rick Wilkins	.05
459	Scott Sanders	.05
460	Kevin Orie	.05
461	Glendon Rusch	.05
462	Juan Melo	.05
463	Richie Sexson	.05
464	Bartolo Colon	.05
465	Jose Guillen	.05
466	Heath Murray	.05
467	Aaron Boone	.05
468	Bubba Trammell **RC**	.05
469	Jeff Abbott	.05
470	Derrick Gibson	.05
471	Matt Morris	.05
472	Ryan Jones	.05
473	Pat Cline	.05
474	Adam Riggs	.05
475	Jay Payton	.05
476	Derrek Lee	.50
477	Elieser Marrero	.05
478	Lee Tinsley	.05
479	Jamie Moyer	.05
480	Jay Buhner	.05
481	Bob Wells	.05
482	Jeff Fassero	.05
483	Paul Sorrento	.05
484	Russ Davis	.05
485	Randy Johnson	.75
486	Roger Pavlik	.05
487	Damon Buford	.05
488	Julio Santana	.05
489	Mark McLemore	.05
490	Mickey Tettleton	.05
491	Ken Hill	.05
492	Benji Gil	.05
493	Ed Sprague	.05
494	Mike Timlin	.05
495	Pat Hentgen	.05
496	Orlando Merced	.05
497	Carlos Garcia	.05
498	Carlos Delgado	.35
499	Juan Guzman	.05
500	Roger Clemens	1.00
501	Erik Hanson	.05
502	Otis Nixon	.05
503	Shawn Green	.10
504	Charlie O'Brien	.05
505	Joe Carter	.05
506	Alex Gonzalez	.05

All-Star Connection

		NM/M
Complete Set (45):		10.00
Common Player:		.10
1	Mark McGwire	1.00
2	Chuck Knoblauch	.10
3	Jim Thome	.35
4	Alex Rodriguez	1.00
5	Ken Griffey Jr.	.75
6	Brady Anderson	.10
7	Albert Belle	.10

8	Ivan Rodriguez	.40
9	Pat Hentgen	.10
10	Frank Thomas	.50
11	Roberto Alomar	.25
12	Robin Ventura	.10
13	Cal Ripken Jr.	1.50
14	Juan Gonzalez	.25
15	Manny Ramirez	.50
16	Bernie Williams	.10
17	Terry Steinbach	.10
18	Andy Pettitte	.25
19	Jeff Bagwell	.50
20	Craig Biggio	.10
21	Ken Caminiti	.10
22	Barry Larkin	.10
23	Tony Gwynn	.60
24	Barry Bonds	1.50
25	Kenny Lofton	.10
26	Mike Piazza	.75
27	John Smoltz	.10
28	Andres Galarraga	.10
29	Ryne Sandberg	.60
30	Chipper Jones	.75
31	Mark Grudzielanek	.10
32	Sammy Sosa	.60
33	Steve Finley	.10
34	Gary Sheffield	.25
35	Todd Hundley	.10
36	Greg Maddux	.60
37	Mo Vaughn	.10
38	Eric Young	.10
39	Vinny Castilla	.10
40	Derek Jeter	1.50
41	Lance Johnson	.10
42	Ellis Burks	.10
43	Dante Bichette	.10
44	Javy Lopez	.10
45	Hideo Nomo	.25

Big Shots

		NM/M
Complete Set (19):		15.00
Common Player:		.25
Gold Signature Edition:		2X
1	Ken Griffey Jr.	2.00
2	Nomar Garciaparra	1.50
3	Brian Jordan	.25
4	Scott Rolen	.75
5	Alex Rodriguez	2.50
6	Larry Walker	.25
7	Mariano Rivera	.35
8	Cal Ripken Jr.	3.00
9	Deion Sanders	.25
10	Frank Thomas	1.00
11	Dean Palmer	.25
12	Ken Caminiti	.25
13	Derek Jeter	3.00
14	Barry Bonds	3.00
15	Chipper Jones	1.50
16	Mo Vaughn	.25
17	Jay Buhner	.25
18	Mike Piazza	2.00
19	Tony Gwynn	1.50

Big Show

		NM/M
Complete Set (45):		7.00
Common Player:		.10
World Headquarters:		8X
1	Greg Maddux	.50
2	Chipper Jones	.50
3	Andruw Jones	.40
4	John Smoltz	.10
5	Cal Ripken Jr.	1.00
6	Roberto Alomar	.25
7	Rafael Palmeiro	.35
8	Eddie Murray	.40
9	Jose Canseco	.30
10	Roger Clemens	.55

11	Mo Vaughn	.10
12	Jim Edmonds	.10
13	Tim Salmon	.10
14	Sammy Sosa	.50
15	Albert Belle	.10
16	Frank Thomas	.40
17	Barry Larkin	.10
18	Kenny Lofton	.10
19	Manny Ramirez	.40
20	Matt Williams	.10
21	Dante Bichette	.10
22	Gary Sheffield	.30
23	Craig Biggio	.10
24	Jeff Bagwell	.40
25	Todd Hollandsworth	.10
26	Raul Mondesi	.10
27	Hideo Nomo	.25
28	Mike Piazza	.60
29	Paul Molitor	.40
30	Kirby Puckett	.50
31	Rondell White	.10
32	Rey Ordonez	.10
33	Paul Wilson	.10
34	Derek Jeter	1.00
35	Andy Pettitte	.25
36	Mark McGwire	.75
37	Jason Kendall	.10
38	Ozzie Smith	.50
39	Tony Gwynn	.50
40	Barry Bonds	1.00
41	Alex Rodriguez	.75
42	Jay Buhner	.10
43	Ken Griffey Jr.	.60
44	Randy Johnson	.40
45	Juan Gonzalez	.25

Big Show World Headquarters

	NM/M
Complete Set (45):	50.00
Common Player:	1.50
Stars:	8X

(See 1997 Collector's Choice Big Show for checklist and base card values.)

Clearly Dominant

	NM/M
Complete Set (5):	16.00
Common Card:	4.00
CD1-CD5 Ken Griffey Jr.	4.00

Clearly Dominant Jumbos

	NM/M
Complete Set (5):	10.00
Common Card:	2.00
1-5 Ken Griffey Jr.	2.00

Hot List Jumbos

		NM/M
Complete Set (10):		15.00
Common Player:		.50
325	Andruw Jones	1.50
326	Chipper Jones	2.00
327	Mo Vaughn	.50
328	Frank Thomas	1.50
329	Albert Belle	.50
330	Mark McGwire	3.00
331	Derek Jeter	4.00
332	Alex Rodriguez	3.00

333	Jay Buhner	.50
334	Ken Griffey Jr.	2.50

New Frontier

		NM/M
Complete Set (40):		75.00
Common Player:		1.00
1	Alex Rodriguez	5.00
2	Tony Gwynn	3.00
3	Jose Canseco	1.25
4	Hideo Nomo	1.25
5	Mark McGwire	5.00
6	Barry Bonds	6.00
7	Juan Gonzalez	1.25
8	Ken Caminiti	1.00
9	Tim Salmon	1.00
10	Mike Piazza	4.00
11	Ken Griffey Jr.	4.00
12	Andres Galarraga	1.00
13	Jay Buhner	1.00
14	Dante Bichette	1.00
15	Frank Thomas	2.00
16	Ryne Sandberg	3.00
17	Roger Clemens	3.50
18	Andruw Jones	2.00
19	Jim Thome	1.50
20	Sammy Sosa	3.00
21	David Justice	1.00
22	Deion Sanders	1.00
23	Todd Walker	1.00
24	Kevin Orie	1.00
25	Albert Belle	1.00
26	Jeff Bagwell	2.00
27	Manny Ramirez	2.00
28	Brian Jordan	1.00
29	Derek Jeter	6.00
30	Chipper Jones	3.00
31	Mo Vaughn	1.00
32	Gary Sheffield	1.50
33	Carlos Delgado	1.50
34	Vladimir Guerrero	2.00
35	Cal Ripken Jr.	6.00
36	Greg Maddux	3.00
37	Cecil Fielder	1.00
38	Todd Hundley	1.00
39	Mike Mussina	1.25
40	Scott Rolen	1.50

Premier Power

		NM/M
Complete Set (20):		20.00
Common Player:		.40
Gold:		2X
1	Mark McGwire	3.00
2	Brady Anderson	.40
3	Ken Griffey Jr.	2.50
4	Albert Belle	.40
5	Juan Gonzalez	.60
6	Andres Galarraga	.40
7	Jay Buhner	.40
8	Mo Vaughn	.40
9	Barry Bonds	3.50
10	Gary Sheffield	.75
11	Todd Hundley	.40
12	Frank Thomas	1.50
13	Sammy Sosa	2.00
14	Ken Caminiti	.40
15	Vinny Castilla	.40
16	Ellis Burks	.40
17	Rafael Palmeiro	1.00
18	Alex Rodriguez	3.00
19	Mike Piazza	2.50
20	Eddie Murray	1.50

Premier Power Jumbo

		NM/M
Complete Set (20):		15.00
Common Player:		.50
1	Mark McGwire	2.50
2	Brady Anderson	.50
3	Ken Griffey Jr.	2.00
4	Albert Belle	.50
5	Juan Gonzalez	.75
6	Andres Galarraga	.50
7	Jay Buhner	.50
8	Mo Vaughn	.50
9	Barry Bonds	3.00
10	Gary Sheffield	.65
11	Todd Hundley	.50
12	Frank Thomas	1.00
13	Sammy Sosa	1.50
14	Ken Caminiti	.50
15	Vinny Castilla	.50
16	Ellis Burks	.50
17	Rafael Palmeiro	.75
18	Alex Rodriguez	2.50
19	Mike Piazza	2.00
20	Eddie Murray	1.00

Stick'Ums

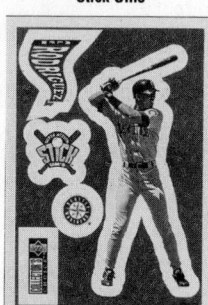

		NM/M
Complete Set (30):		5.00
Common Player:		.05
1	Ozzie Smith	.50
2	Andruw Jones	.40
3	Alex Rodriguez	.75
4	Paul Molitor	.40
5	Jeff Bagwell	.40
6	Manny Ramirez	.40
7	Kenny Lofton	.05
8	Albert Belle	.05
9	Jay Buhner	.05
10	Chipper Jones	.50
11	Barry Larkin	.05
12	Dante Bichette	.05
13	Mike Piazza	.60
14	Andres Galarraga	.05
15	Barry Bonds	1.00
16	Brady Anderson	.05
17	Gary Sheffield	.20
18	Jim Thome	.35
19	Tony Gwynn	.50
20	Cal Ripken Jr.	1.00
21	Sammy Sosa	.50
22	Juan Gonzalez	.20
23	Greg Maddux	.50
24	Ken Griffey Jr.	.60
25	Mark McGwire	.75
26	Kirby Puckett	.50
27	Mo Vaughn	.05
28	Vladimir Guerrero	.40
29	Ken Caminiti	.05
30	Frank Thomas	.40

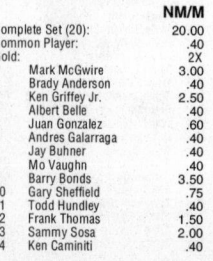

Toast of the Town

	NM/M
Complete Set (30):	40.00
Common Player:	.30
1 Andruw Jones	2.00
2 Chipper Jones	2.50
3 Greg Maddux	2.50
4 John Smoltz	.30
5 Kenny Lofton	.30
6 Brady Anderson	.30
7 Cal Ripken Jr.	6.00
8 Mo Vaughn	.30
9 Sammy Sosa	2.50
10 Albert Belle	.30
11 Frank Thomas	2.00
12 Barry Larkin	.30
13 Manny Ramirez	2.00
14 Jeff Bagwell	2.00
15 Mike Piazza	4.00
16 Paul Molitor	2.00
17 Vladimir Guerrero	2.00
18 Todd Hundley	.30
19 Derek Jeter	6.00
20 Andy Pettitte	.45
21 Bernie Williams	.30
22 Mark McGwire	5.00
23 Scott Rolen	1.00
24 Ken Caminiti	.30
25 Tony Gwynn	2.50
26 Barry Bonds	6.00
27 Ken Griffey Jr.	4.00
28 Alex Rodriguez	5.00
29 Juan Gonzalez	.75
30 Roger Clemens	3.00

1997 Collector's Choice Update

	NM/M
Complete Set (30):	2.00
Common Player:	.10
1 Jim Leyritz	.10
2 Matt Perisho	.10
3 Michael Tucker	.10
4 Mike Johnson	.10
5 Jaime Navarro	.10
6 Doug Drabek	.10
7 Terry Mulholland	.10
8 Brett Tomko	.10
9 Marquis Grissom	.10
10 David Justice	.10
11 Brian Moehler	.10
12 Bobby Bonilla	.10
13 Todd Dunwoody	.10
14 Tony Saunders	.10
15 Jay Bell	.10
16 Jeff King	.10
17 Terry Steinbach	.10
18 Steve Bieser	.10
19 Takashi Kashiwada RC	.10
20 Hideki Irabu	.10
21 Damon Mashore	.10
22 Quilvio Veras	.10
23 Will Cunnane	.10
24 Jeff Kent	.50
25 J.T. Snow	.10
26 Dante Powell	.10

17 Jose Cruz Jr.	.10
28 John Burkett	.10
29 John Wetteland	.10
30 Benito Santiago	.10

1998 Collector's Choice

	NM/M
Unopened Fact. Set (540):	15.00
Complete Set (530):	10.00
Common Player:	.05
Pack (14):	1.00
Wax Box (36):	15.00
1 Nomar Garciaparra	.50
2 Roger Clemens	.50
3 Larry Walker	.05
4 Mike Piazza	.60
5 Mark McGwire	.75
6 Tony Gwynn	.45
7 Jose Cruz Jr.	.05
8 Frank Thomas	.40
9 Tino Martinez	.05
10 Ken Griffey Jr.	.60
11 Barry Bonds	.85
12 Scott Rolen	.30
13 Randy Johnson	.15
14 Ryne Sandberg	.15
15 Eddie Murray	.15
16 Kevin Brown	.05
17 Greg Maddux	.35
18 Sandy Alomar Jr.	.05
19 Ken Griffey Jr., Adam Riggs Checklist	.40
20 Nomar Garciaparra, Charlie O'Brien Checklist	.05
21 Ben Grieve, Ken Griffey Jr., Larry Walker, Mark McGwire Checklist	.50
22 Mark McGwire, Cal Ripken Jr. Checklist	.50
23 Tino Martinez Checklist	.05
24 Jason Dickson	.05
25 Darin Erstad	.25
26 Todd Greene	.05
27 Chuck Finley	.05
28 Garret Anderson	.05
29 Dave Hollins	.05
30 Rickey Henderson	.60
31 John Smoltz	.05
32 Michael Tucker	.05
33 Jeff Blauser	.05
34 Javier Lopez	.60
35 Andruw Jones	.60
36 Denny Neagle	.05
37 Randall Simon	.05
38 Mark Wohlers	.05
39 Harold Baines	.05
40 Cal Ripken Jr.	1.50
41 Mike Bordick	.05
42 Jimmy Key	.05
43 Armando Benitez	.05
44 Scott Erickson	.05
45 Eric Davis	.05
46 Bret Saberhagen	.05
47 Darren Bragg	.05
48 Steve Avery	.05
49 Jeff Frye	.05
50 Aaron Sele	.05
51 Scott Hatteberg	.05
52 Tom Gordon	.05
53 Kevin Orie	.05
54 Kevin Foster	.05
55 Ryne Sandberg	.75
56 Doug Glanville	.05
57 Tyler Houston	.05
58 Steve Trachsel	.05
59 Mark Grace	.05
60 Frank Thomas	.60
61 Scott Eyre RC	.05
62 Jeff Abbott	.05
63 Chris Clemons	.05
64 Jorge Fabregas	.05
65 Robin Ventura	.05
66 Matt Karchner	.05
67 Jon Nunnally	.05
68 Aaron Boone	.05
69 Pokey Reese	.05
70 Deion Sanders	.10
71 Jeff Shaw	.05
72 Eduardo Perez	.05
73 Brett Tomko	.05
74 Bartolo Colon	.05
75 Manny Ramirez	.60

76 Jose Mesa	.05
77 Brian Giles	.05
78 Richie Sexson	.05
79 Orel Hershiser	.05
80 Matt Williams	.05
81 Walt Weiss	.05
82 Jerry DiPoto	.05
83 Quinton McCracken	.05
84 Neifi Perez	.05
85 Vinny Castilla	.05
86 Ellis Burks	.05
87 John Thomson	.05
88 Willie Blair	.05
89 Bob Hamelin	.05
90 Tony Clark	.05
91 Todd Jones	.05
92 Deivi Cruz	.05
93 Frank Catalanotto RC	.15
94 Justin Thompson	.05
95 Gary Sheffield	.25
96 Kevin Brown	.05
97 Charles Johnson	.05
98 Bobby Bonilla	.05
99 Livan Hernandez	.05
100 Paul Konerko	.10
101 Craig Counsell	.05
102 Magglio Ordonez RC	1.00
103 Garrett Stephenson	.05
104 Ken Cloude	.05
105 Miguel Tejada	.25
106 Juan Encarnacion	.05
107 Dennis Reyes	.05
108 Orlando Cabrera	.05
109 Kelvim Escobar (Rookie Class)	.05
110 Ben Grieve	.05
111 Brian Rose	.05
112 Fernando Tatis	.05
113 Tom Evans	.05
114 Tom Fordham	.05
115 Mark Kotsay	.05
116 Mario Valdez	.05
117 Jeremi Gonzalez	.05
118 Todd Dunwoody	.05
119 Javier Valentin	.05
120 Todd Helton	.50
121 Jason Varitek	.10
122 Chris Carpenter	.05
123 Kevin Millwood RC	.75
124 Brad Fullmer	.05
125 Jaret Wright	.05
126 Brad Rigby	.05
127 Edgar Renteria	.05
128 Robb Nen	.05
129 Tony Pena	.05
130 Craig Biggio	.05
131 Brad Ausmus	.05
132 Shane Reynolds	.05
133 Mike Hampton	.05
134 Billy Wagner	.05
135 Richard Hidalgo	.05
136 Jose Rosado	.05
137 Yamil Benitez	.05
138 Felix Martinez	.05
139 Jeff King	.05
140 Jose Offerman	.05
141 Joe Vitiello	.05
142 Tim Belcher	.05
143 Brett Butler	.05
144 Greg Gagne	.05
145 Mike Piazza	1.00
146 Ramon Martinez	.05
147 Raul Mondesi	.05
148 Adam Riggs	.05
149 Eddie Murray	.50
150 Jeff Cirillo	.05
151 Scott Karl	.05
152 Mike Fetters	.05
153 Dave Nilsson	.05
154 Antone Williamson	.05
155 Jeff D'Amico	.05
156 Jose Valentin	.05
157 Brad Radke	.05
158 Torii Hunter	.05
159 Chuck Knoblauch	.05
160 Paul Molitor	.60
161 Travis Miller	.05
162 Rich Robertson	.05
163 Ron Coomer	.05
164 Mark Grudzielanek	.05
165 Lee Smith	.05
166 Vladimir Guerrero	.60
167 Dustin Hermanson	.05
168 Ugueth Urbina	.05
169 F.P. Santangelo	.05
170 Rondell White	.05
171 Bobby Jones	.05
172 Edgardo Alfonzo	.05
173 John Franco	.05
174 Carlos Baerga	.05
175 Butch Huskey	.05
176 Rey Ordonez	.05
177 Matt Franco	.05
178 Dwight Gooden	.05
179 Chad Curtis	.05
180 Tino Martinez	.05
181 Charlie O'Brien	.05
182 Sandy Alomar Jr.	.05
183 Raul Casanova	.05
184 Jim Leyritz	.05
185 Mike Piazza	.60
186 Ivan Rodriguez	.20
187 Charles Johnson	.05
188 Brad Ausmus	.05
189 Brian Johnson	.05

190 Wade Boggs	.75
191 David Wells	.05
192 Tim Raines	.05
193 Ramiro Mendoza	.05
194 Willie Adams	.05
195 Matt Stairs	.05
196 Jason McDonald	.05
197 Dave Magadan	.05
198 Mark Bellhorn	.05
199 Ariel Prieto	.05
200 Jose Canseco	.35
201 Bobby Estalella	.05
202 Tony Barron RC	.05
203 Midre Cummings	.05
204 Ricky Bottalico	.05
205 Mike Grace	.05
206 Rico Brogna	.05
207 Mickey Morandini	.05
208 Lou Collier	.05
209 Kevin Polcovich RC	.05
210 Kevin Young	.05
211 Jose Guillen	.05
212 Esteban Loaiza	.05
213 Marc Wilkins	.05
214 Jason Schmidt	.05
215 Gary Gaetti	.05
216 Fernando Valenzuela	.05
217 Willie McGee	.05
218 Alan Benes	.05
219 Eli Marrero	.05
220 Mark McGwire	1.25
221 Matt Morris	.05
222 Trevor Hoffman	.05
223 Will Cunnane	.05
224 Joey Hamilton	.05
225 Ken Caminiti	.05
226 Derrek Lee	.35
227 Mark Sweeney	.05
228 Carlos Hernandez	.05
229 Brian Johnson	.05
230 Jeff Kent	.05
231 Kirk Rueter	.05
232 Bill Mueller	.05
233 Dante Powell	.05
234 J.T. Snow	.05
235 Shawn Estes	.05
236 Dennis Martinez	.05
237 Jamie Moyer	.05
238 Dan Wilson	.05
239 Joey Cora	.05
240 Ken Griffey Jr.	1.00
241 Paul Sorrento	.05
242 Jay Buhner	.05
243 Hanley Frias RC	.05
244 John Burkett	.05
245 Juan Gonzalez	.30
246 Rick Helling	.05
247 Darren Oliver	.05
248 Mickey Tettleton	.05
249 Ivan Rodriguez	.45
250 Joe Carter	.05
251 Pat Hentgen	.05
252 Marty Janzen	.05
253 Frank Thomas, Tony Gwynn	.25
254 Mark McGwire, Ken Griffey Jr., Larry Walker	.50
255 Ken Griffey Jr., Andres Galarraga	.40
256 Brian Hunter, Tony Womack	.05
257 Roger Clemens, Denny Neagle	.10
258 Roger Clemens, Curt Schilling	.30
259 Roger Clemens, Pedro J. Martinez	.25
260 Randy Myers, Jeff Shaw	.05
261 Nomar Garciaparra, Scott Rolen	.25
262 Charlie O'Brien	.05
263 Shannon Stewart	.05
264 Robert Person	.05
265 Carlos Delgado	.25
266 Matt Williams, Travis Lee Checklist	.05
267 Nomar Garciaparra, Cal Ripken Jr. Checklist	.50
268 Mark McGwire, Mike Piazza Checklist	.50
269 Tony Gwynn, Ken Griffey Jr. Checklist	.40
270 Fred McGriff, Jose Cruz Jr. Checklist	.05
271 Andruw Jones	.25
272 Alex Rodriguez	.65
273 Juan Gonzalez	.15
274 Nomar Garciaparra	.50
275 Ken Griffey Jr.	.60
276 Tino Martinez	.05
277 Roger Clemens	.40
278 Barry Bonds	.85
279 Mike Piazza	.60
280 Tim Salmon	.05
281 Gary DiSarcina	.05
282 Cecil Fielder	.05
283 Ken Hill	.05
284 Troy Percival	.05
285 Jim Edmonds	.05
286 Allen Watson	.05
287 Brian Anderson	.05
288 Jay Bell	.05
289 Jorge Fabregas	.05
290 Devon White	.05
291 Yamil Benitez	.05

No.	Player	Price
292	Jeff Suppan	.05
293	Tony Batista	.05
294	Brent Brede	.05
295	Andy Benes	.05
296	Felix Rodriguez	.05
297	Karim Garcia	.05
298	Omar Daal	.05
299	Andy Stankiewicz	.05
300	Matt Williams	.05
301	Willie Blair	.05
302	Ryan Klesko	.05
303	Tom Glavine	.25
304	Walt Weiss	.05
305	Greg Maddux	.75
306	Chipper Jones	.75
307	Keith Lockhart	.05
308	Andres Galarraga	.05
309	Chris Hoiles	.05
310	Roberto Alomar	.25
311	Joe Carter	.05
312	Doug Drabek	.05
313	Jeffrey Hammonds	.05
314	Rafael Palmeiro	.40
315	Mike Mussina	.40
316	Brady Anderson	.05
317	B.J. Surhoff	.05
318	Dennis Eckersley	.45
319	Jim Leyritz	.05
320	Mo Vaughn	.05
321	Nomar Garciaparra	.75
322	Reggie Jefferson	.05
323	Tim Naehring	.05
324	Troy O'Leary	.05
325	Pedro J. Martinez	.50
326	John Valentin	.05
327	Mark Clark	.05
328	Rod Beck	.05
329	Mickey Morandini	.05
330	Sammy Sosa	.75
331	Jeff Blauser	.05
332	Lance Johnson	.05
333	Scott Servais	.05
334	Kevin Tapani	.05
335	Henry Rodriguez	.05
336	Jaime Navarro	.05
337	Benji Gil	.05
338	James Baldwin	.05
339	Mike Cameron	.05
340	Ray Durham	.05
341	Chris Snopek	.05
342	Eddie Taubensee	.05
343	Bret Boone	.05
344	Willie Greene	.05
345	Barry Larkin	.05
346	Chris Stynes	.05
347	Pete Harnisch	.05
348	Dave Burba	.05
349	Sandy Alomar Jr.	.05
350	Kenny Lofton	.05
351	Geronimo Berroa	.05
352	Omar Vizquel	.05
353	Travis Fryman	.05
354	Dwight Gooden	.05
355	Jim Thome	.40
356	David Justice	.05
357	Charles Nagy	.05
358	Chad Ogea	.05
359	Pedro Astacio	.05
360	Larry Walker	.05
361	Mike Lansing	.05
362	Kirt Manwaring	.05
363	Dante Bichette	.05
364	Jamey Wright	.05
365	Darryl Kile	.05
366	Luis Gonzalez	.05
367	Joe Randa	.05
368	Raul Casanova	.05
369	Damion Easley	.05
370	Brian L. Hunter	.05
371	Bobby Higginson	.05
372	Brian Moehler	.05
373	Scott Sanders	.05
374	Jim Eisenreich	.05
375	Derrek Lee	.35
376	Jay Powell	.05
377	Cliff Floyd	.05
378	Alex Fernandez	.05
379	Felix Heredia	.05
380	Jeff Bagwell	.60
381	Bill Spiers	.05
382	Chris Holt	.05
383	Carl Everett	.05
384	Derek Bell	.05
385	Moises Alou	.05
386	Ramon Garcia	.05
387	Mike Sweeney	.05
388	Glendon Rusch	.05
389	Kevin Appier	.05
390	Dean Palmer	.05
391	Jeff Conine	.05
392	Johnny Damon	.25
393	Jose Vizcaino	.05
394	Todd Hollandsworth	.05
395	Eric Karros	.05
396	Todd Zeile	.05
397	Chan Ho Park	.05
398	Ismael Valdes	.05
399	Eric Young	.05
400	Hideo Nomo	.25
401	Mark Loretta	.05
402	Doug Jones	.05
403	Jeromy Burnitz	.05
404	John Jaha	.05
405	Marquis Grissom	.05
406	Mike Matheny	.05
407	Todd Walker	.05
408	Marty Cordova	.05
409	Matt Lawton	.05
410	Terry Steinbach	.05
411	Pat Meares	.05
412	Rick Aguilera	.05
413	Otis Nixon	.05
414	Derrick May	.05
415	Carl Pavano	.05
416	A.J. Hinch	.05
417	David Dellucci RC	.10
418	Bruce Chen	.05
419	Darron Ingram RC	.05
420	Sean Casey	.20
421	Mark L. Johnson	.05
422	Gabe Alvarez	.05
423	Alex Gonzalez	.05
424	Daryle Ward	.05
425	Russell Branyan	.05
426	Mike Caruso	.05
427	Mike Kinkade RC	.20
428	Ramon Hernandez	.05
429	Matt Clement	.05
430	Travis Lee	.05
431	Shane Monahan	.05
432	Rich Butler RC	.05
433	Chris Widger	.05
434	Jose Vidro	.05
435	Carlos Perez	.05
436	Ryan McGuire	.05
437	Brian McRae	.05
438	Al Leiter	.05
439	Rich Becker	.05
440	Todd Hundley	.05
441	Dave Mlicki	.05
442	Bernard Gilkey	.05
443	John Olerud	.05
444	Paul O'Neill	.05
445	Andy Pettitte	.30
446	David Cone	.05
447	Chili Davis	.05
448	Bernie Williams	.05
449	Joe Girardi	.05
450	Derek Jeter	1.50
451	Mariano Rivera	.20
452	George Williams	.05
453	Kenny Rogers	.05
454	Tom Candiotti	.05
455	Rickey Henderson	.60
456	Jason Giambi	.40
457	Scott Spiezio	.05
458	Doug Glanville	.05
459	Desi Relaford	.05
460	Curt Schilling	.20
461	Bob Abreu	.10
462	Gregg Jefferies	.05
463	Scott Rolen	.40
464	Mike Lieberthal	.05
465	Tony Womack	.05
466	Jermaine Allensworth	.05
467	Francisco Cordova	.05
468	Jon Lieber	.05
469	Al Martin	.05
470	Jason Kendall	.05
471	Todd Stottlemyre	.05
472	Royce Clayton	.05
473	Brian Jordan	.05
474	John Mabry	.05
475	Ray Lankford	.05
476	Delino DeShields	.05
477	Ron Gant	.05
478	Mark Langston	.05
479	Steve Finley	.05
480	Tony Gwynn	.75
481	Andy Ashby	.05
482	Wally Joyner	.05
483	Greg Vaughn	.05
484	Sterling Hitchcock	.05
485	J. Kevin Brown	.05
486	Orel Hershiser	.05
487	Charlie Hayes	.05
488	Darryl Hamilton	.05
489	Mark Gardner	.05
490	Robb Nen	1.50
491	Robb Nen	.05
492	Kirk Rueter	.05
493	Randy Johnson	.50
494	Jeff Fassero	.05
495	Alex Rodriguez	1.25
496	David Segui	.05
497	Rich Amaral	.05
498	Russ Davis	.05
499	Bubba Trammell	.05
500	Wade Boggs	.75
501	Roberto Hernandez	.05
502	Dave Martinez	.05
503	Dennis Springer	.05
504	Paul Sorrento	.05
505	Wilson Alvarez	.05
506	Mike Kelly	.05
507	Albie Lopez	.05
508	Tony Saunders	.05
509	John Flaherty	.05
510	Fred McGriff	.05
511	Quinton McCracken	.05
512	Terrell Wade	.05
513	Kevin Stocker	.05
514	Kevin Elster	.05
515	Will Clark	.05
516	Bobby Witt	.05
517	Tom Goodwin	.05
518	Aaron Sele	.05
519	Lee Stevens	.05
520	Rusty Greer	.05
521	John Wetteland	.05
522	Darrin Fletcher	.05
523	Jose Canseco	.35
524	Randy Myers	.05
525	Jose Cruz Jr.	.05
526	Shawn Green	.15
527	Tony Fernandez	.05
528	Alex Gonzalez	.05
529	Ed Sprague	.05
530	Roger Clemens	.85

Cover Glory 5x7

		NM/M
Complete Set (10):		10.00
Common Player:		1.00
1	Nomar Garciaparra	1.50
2	Roger Clemens	2.00
3	Larry Walker	1.00
4	Mike Piazza	2.50
5	Mark McGwire	3.00
6	Tony Gwynn	1.50
7	Jose Cruz Jr.	1.00
8	Frank Thomas	1.25
9	Tino Martinez	1.00
10	Ken Griffey Jr.	2.50

Evolution Revolution

		NM/M
Complete Set (28):		36.00
Common Player:		.40
Inserted 1:13		
1	Tim Salmon	.40
2	Greg Maddux	2.50
3	Cal Ripken Jr.	6.00
4	Mo Vaughn	.40
5	Sammy Sosa	2.50
6	Frank Thomas	1.50
7	Barry Larkin	.40
8	Jim Thome	.65
9	Larry Walker	.40
10	Travis Fryman	.40
11	Gary Sheffield	.65
12	Jeff Bagwell	1.50
13	Johnny Damon	.65
14	Mike Piazza	4.00
15	Jeff Cirillo	.40
16	Paul Molitor	1.50
17	Vladimir Guerrero	1.50
18	Todd Hundley	.40
19	Tino Martinez	.40
20	Jose Canseco	.65
21	Scott Rolen	.75
22	Al Martin	.40
23	Mark McGwire	5.00
24	Tony Gwynn	2.50
25	Barry Bonds	6.00
26	Ken Griffey Jr.	4.00
27	Juan Gonzalez	.75
28	Roger Clemens	3.00

Mini Bobbing Heads

		NM/M
Complete Set (30):		20.00
Common Player:		.25
Inserted 1:3		
1	Tim Salmon	.25
2	Travis Lee	.25

No.	Player	Price
3	Matt Williams	.25
4	Chipper Jones	1.00
5	Greg Maddux	1.00
6	Cal Ripken Jr.	2.50
7	Nomar Garciaparra	1.00
8	Mo Vaughn	.25
9	Sammy Sosa	1.00
10	Frank Thomas	.75
11	Kenny Lofton	.25
12	Jaret Wright	.25
13	Larry Walker	.25
14	Tony Clark	.25
15	Edgar Renteria	.25
16	Jeff Bagwell	.75
17	Mike Piazza	1.50
18	Vladimir Guerrero	.75
19	Derek Jeter	2.50
20	Ben Grieve	.25
21	Scott Rolen	.50
22	Mark McGwire	2.00
23	Tony Gwynn	1.00
24	Barry Bonds	2.50
25	Ken Griffey Jr.	1.50
26	Alex Rodriguez	2.00
27	Fred McGriff	.25
28	Juan Gonzalez	.40
29	Roger Clemens	1.25
30	Jose Cruz Jr.	.25

Rookie Class: Prime Choice

		NM/M
Complete Set (18):		30.00
Common Player:		2.00
415	Carl Pavano	2.00
416	A.J. Hinch	2.00
417	David Dellucci	2.00
418	Bruce Chen	2.00
419	Darron Ingram	2.00
420	Sean Casey	5.00
421	Mark L. Johnson	2.00
422	Gabe Alvarez	2.00
423	Alex Gonzalez	2.00
424	Daryle Ward	2.00
425	Russell Branyan	2.00
426	Mike Caruso	2.00
427	Mike Kinkade	2.00
428	Ramon Hernandez	2.00
429	Matt Clement	2.00
430	Travis Lee	2.50
431	Shane Monahan	2.00
432	Rich Butler	2.00

StarQuest - Series 1

	NM/M
Complete Set (90):	185.00

Common Special Delivery (1-45):		.25
Inserted 1:1		
Common Student of the Game		
(46-65):		.75
Inserted 1:21		
Common Super Power (66-80):		2.00
Inserted 1:71		
Common Superstar Domain		
(81-90):		3.00
Inserted 1:145		
1	Nomar Garciaparra	1.50
2	Scott Rolen	.75
3	Jason Dickson	.25
4	Jaret Wright	.25
5	Kevin Orie	.25
6	Jose Guillen	.25
7	Matt Morris	.25
8	Mike Cameron	.25
9	Kevin Polcovich	.25
10	Jose Cruz Jr.	.25
11	Miguel Tejada	.40
12	Fernando Tatis	.25
13	Todd Helton	.65
14	Ken Cloude	.25
15	Ben Grieve	.25
16	Dante Powell	.25
17	Bubba Trammell	.25
18	Juan Encarnacion	.25
19	Derrek Lee	.50
20	Paul Konerko	.35
21	Richard Hidalgo	.25
22	Denny Neagle	.25
23	David Justice	.25
24	Pedro J. Martinez	1.00
25	Greg Maddux	1.50
26	Edgar Martinez	.25
27	Cal Ripken Jr.	2.50
28	Tim Salmon	.25
29	Shawn Estes	.25
30	Ken Griffey Jr.	2.00
31	Brad Radke	.25
32	Andy Pettitte	.40
33	Curt Schilling	.50
34	Raul Mondesi	.25
35	Alex Rodriguez	2.25
36	Jeff Kent	.25
37	Jeff Bagwell	1.00
38	Juan Gonzalez	.50
39	Barry Bonds	2.50
40	Mark McGwire	2.00
41	Frank Thomas	1.00
42	Ray Lankford	.25
43	Tony Gwynn	1.50
44	Mike Piazza	1.75
45	Tino Martinez	.25
46	Nomar Garciaparra	3.00
47	Paul Molitor	1.50
48	Chuck Knoblauch	.75
49	Rusty Greer	.75
50	Cal Ripken Jr.	6.00
51	Roberto Alomar	1.00
52	Scott Rolen	1.00
53	Derek Jeter	6.00
54	Mark Grace	.75
55	Randy Johnson	1.50
56	Craig Biggio	.75
57	Kenny Lofton	.75
58	Eddie Murray	1.50
59	Ryne Sandberg	2.00
60	Rickey Henderson	1.50
61	Darin Erstad	1.00
62	Jim Edmonds	.75
63	Ken Caminiti	.75
64	Ivan Rodriguez	1.25
65	Tony Gwynn	2.00
66	Tony Clark	2.00
67	Andres Galarraga	2.00
68	Rafael Palmeiro	3.00
69	Manny Ramirez	6.00
70	Albert Belle	2.00
71	Jay Buhner	2.00
72	Mo Vaughn	2.00
73	Barry Bonds	15.00
74	Chipper Jones	7.50
75	Jeff Bagwell	6.00
76	Jim Thome	3.00
77	Sammy Sosa	7.50
78	Todd Hundley	2.00
79	Matt Williams	2.00
80	Vinny Castilla	2.00
81	Jose Cruz Jr.	3.00
82	Frank Thomas	7.50
83	Juan Gonzalez	4.00
84	Mike Piazza	15.00
85	Alex Rodriguez	20.00
86	Larry Walker	3.00
87	Tino Martinez	3.00
88	Greg Maddux	12.50
89	Mark McGwire	20.00
90	Ken Griffey Jr.	15.00

StarQuest - Series 2

		NM/M
Complete Set (30):		17.50
Common Player:		.25
Singles 1:1		
Doubles 1:21		2X
Triples 1:71		6X
Home Runs:		15X
1	Ken Griffey Jr.	1.25
2	Jose Cruz Jr.	.25
3	Cal Ripken Jr.	2.00
4	Roger Clemens	1.00
5	Frank Thomas	.75
6	Derek Jeter	2.00

7	Alex Rodriguez	1.50
8	Andruw Jones	.75
9	Vladimir Guerrero	.75
10	Mark McGwire	1.50
11	Kenny Lofton	.25
12	Pedro J. Martinez	.75
13	Greg Maddux	1.00
14	Larry Walker	.25
15	Barry Bonds	2.00
16	Chipper Jones	1.00
17	Jeff Bagwell	.75
18	Juan Gonzalez	.50
19	Tony Gwynn	1.00
20	Mike Piazza	1.25
21	Tino Martinez	.25
22	Mo Vaughn	.20
23	Ben Grieve	.25
24	Scott Rolen	.60
25	Nomar Garciaparra	1.00
26	Paul Konerko	.35
27	Jaret Wright	.25
28	Gary Sheffield	.50
29	Travis Lee	.25
30	Todd Helton	.65

Stickums

		NM/M
Complete Set (30):		7.00
Common Player:		.10
Inserted 1:3		
1	Andruw Jones	.35
2	Chipper Jones	.50
3	Cal Ripken Jr.	1.00
4	Nomar Garciaparra	.45
5	Mo Vaughn	.10
6	Ryne Sandberg	.45
7	Sammy Sosa	.45
8	Frank Thomas	.35
9	Albert Belle	.10
10	Jim Thome	.30
11	Manny Ramirez	.30
12	Larry Walker	.10
13	Gary Sheffield	.20
14	Jeff Bagwell	.35
15	Mike Piazza	.60
16	Paul Molitor	.35
17	Pedro J. Martinez	.35
18	Todd Hundley	.10
19	Derek Jeter	1.00
20	Tino Martinez	.10
21	Curt Schilling	.25
22	Mark McGwire	.75
23	Tony Gwynn	.45
24	Barry Bonds	1.00
25	Ken Griffey Jr.	.60
26	Alex Rodriguez	.75
27	Juan Gonzalez	.20
28	Ivan Rodriguez	.30
29	Roger Clemens	.50
30	Jose Cruz Jr.	.10

D

1981 Donruss

	NM/M
Complete Set (605):	

TOM SEAVER PITCHER

Uncut Sheet Set (5):		
Common Player:		.06
Wax Pack (18):		
Wax Box (36):		
1	Ozzie Smith	1.50
2	Rollie Fingers	.70
3	Rick Wise	.06
4	Gene Richards	.06
5	Alan Trammell	.08
6	Tom Brookens	.06
7a	Duffy Dyer (1980 Avg. .185)	.20
7b	Duffy Dyer (1980 Avg. 185)	.06
8	Mark Fidrych	.11
9	Dave Rozema	.06
10	Ricky Peters	.06
11	Mike Schmidt	2.25
12	Willie Stargell	.90
13	Tim Foli	.06
14	Manny Sanguillen	.06
15	Grant Jackson	.06
16	Eddie Solomon	.06
17	Omar Moreno	.06
18	Joe Morgan	.90
19	Rafael Landestoy	.06
20	Bruce Bochy	.06
21	Joe Sambito	.06
22	Manny Trillo	.06
23a	Dave Smith RC (Incomplete box around stats.)	.08
23b	Dave Smith RC (Complete box around stats.)	.11
24	Terry Puhl	.06
25	Bump Wills	.06
26a	John Ellis (Danny Walton photo - with bat.)	.25
26b	John Ellis (John Ellis photo - with glove.)	.06
27	Jim Kern	.06
28	Richie Zisk	.06
29	John Mayberry	.06
30	Bob Davis	.06
31	Jackson Todd	.06
32	Al Woods	.06
33	Steve Carlton	1.25
34	Lee Mazzilli	.06
35	John Stearns	.06
36	Roy Jackson	.06
37	Mike Scott	.06
38	Lamar Johnson	.06
39	Kevin Bell	.06
40	Ed Farmer	.06
41	Ross Baumgarten	.06
42	Leo Sutherland	.06
43	Dan Meyer	.06
44	Ron Reed	.06
45	Mario Mendoza	.06
46	Rick Honeycutt	.06
47	Glenn Abbott	.06
48	Leon Roberts	.06
49	Rod Carew	1.25
50	Bert Campaneris	.06
51a	Tom Donahue (Incorrect spelling.)	.20
51b	Tom Donohue (Donohue on front.)	.06
52	Dave Frost	.06
53	Ed Halicki	.06
54	Dan Ford	.06
55	Garry Maddox	.06
56a	Steve Garvey (Surpassed 25 HR..)	.90
56b	Steve Garvey (Surpassed 21 HR..)	.45
57	Bill Russell	.06
58	Don Sutton	.70
59	Reggie Smith	.06
60	Rick Monday	.06
61	Ray Knight	.08
62	Johnny Bench	1.25
63	Mario Soto	.06
64	Doug Bair	.06
65	George Foster	.08
66	Jeff Burroughs	.06
67	Keith Hernandez	.08
68	Tom Herr	.06
69	Bob Forsch	.06
70	John Fulgham	.06
71a	Bobby Bonds (Lifetime HR 986.)	.25
71b	Bobby Bonds (Lifetime HR 326.)	.11

72a	Rennie Stennett ("...breaking broke leg..." on back)	.20
72b	Rennie Stennett ("...breaking leg..." on back)	.06
73	Joe Strain	.06
74	Ed Whitson	.06
75	Tom Griffin	.06
76	Bill North	.06
77	Gene Garber	.06
78	Mike Hargrove	.06
79	Dave Rosello	.06
80	Ron Hassey	.06
81	Sid Monge	.06
82a	Joe Charboneau RC ("For some reason, Phillies..." on back.)	1.50
82b	Joe Charboneau RC ("Phillies..." on back.)	.20
83	Cecil Cooper	.06
84	Sal Bando	.06
85	Moose Haas	.06
86	Mike Caldwell	.06
87a	Larry Hisle ("...Twins with 28 RBI." on back.)	.20
87b	Larry Hisle ("...Twins with 28 HR" on back.)	.06
88	Luis Gomez	.06
89	Larry Parrish	.06
90	Gary Carter	.90
91	Bill Gullickson RC	.11
92	Fred Norman	.06
93	Tommy Hutton	.06
94	Carl Yastrzemski	1.25
95	Glenn Hoffman	.06
96	Dennis Eckersley	.90
97a	Tom Burgmeier (Throws: Right)	.20
97b	Tom Burgmeier (Throws: Left)	.06
98	Win Remmerswaal	.06
99	Bob Horner	.08
100	George Brett	2.25
101	Dave Chalk	.06
102	Dennis Leonard	.06
103	Renie Martin	.06
104	Amos Otis	.06
105	Graig Nettles	.11
106	Eric Soderholm	.06
107	Tommy John	.08
108	Tom Underwood	.06
109	Lou Piniella	.11
110	Mickey Klutts	.06
111	Bobby Murcer	.06
112	Eddie Murray	1.25
113	Rick Dempsey	.06
114	Scott McGregor	.06
115	Ken Singleton	.06
116	Gary Roenicke	.06
117	Dave Revering	.06
118	Mike Norris	.06
119	Rickey Henderson	1.50
120	Mike Heath	.06
121	Dave Cash	.06
122	Randy Jones	.06
123	Eric Rasmussen	.06
124	Jerry Mumphrey	.06
125	Richie Hebner	.06
126	Mark Wagner	.06
127	Jack Morris	.08
128	Dan Petry	.06
129	Bruce Robbins	.06
130	Champ Summers	.06
131a	Pete Rose ("See card 251" on back.)	1.50
131b	Pete Rose ("See card 371" on back.)	1.50
132	Willie Stargell	.90
133	Ed Ott	.06
134	Jim Bibby	.06
135	Bert Blyleven	.08
136	Dave Parker	.08
137	Bill Robinson	.06
138	Enos Cabell	.06
139	Dave Bergman	.06
140	J.R. Richard	.08
141	Ken Forsch	.06
142	Larry Bowa	.08
143	Frank LaCorte (Photo actually Randy Niemann.)	.06
144	Dennis Walling	.06
145	Buddy Bell	.08
146	Fergie Jenkins	.70
147	Danny Darwin	.06
148	John Grubb	.06
149	Alfredo Griffin	.06
150	Jerry Garvin	.06
151	Paul Mirabella RC	.06
152	Rick Bosetti	.06
153	Dick Ruthven	.06
154	Frank Taveras	.06
155	Craig Swan	.06
156	Jeff Reardon RC	.70
157	Steve Henderson	.06
158	Jim Morrison	.06
159	Glenn Borgmann	.06
160	Lamarr Hoyt (LaMarr) RC	.08
161	Rich Wortham	.06
162	Thad Bosley	.06
163	Julio Cruz	.06
164a	Del Unser (No 3B in stat heads.)	.20
164b	Del Unser (3B in stat heads)	.06
165	Jim Anderson	.06
166	Jim Beattie	.06
167	Shane Rawley	.06
168	Joe Simpson	.06
169	Rod Carew	1.25

170	Fred Patek	.06
171	Frank Tanana	.06
172	Alfredo Martinez	.06
173	Chris Knapp	.06
174	Joe Rudi	.06
175	Greg Luzinski	.06
176	Steve Garvey	.45
177	Joe Ferguson	.06
178	Bob Welch	.08
179	Dusty Baker	.08
180	Rudy Law	.06
181	Dave Concepcion	.06
182	Johnny Bench	1.25
183	Mike LaCoss	.06
184	Ken Griffey	.08
185	Dave Collins	.06
186	Brian Asselstine	.06
187	Garry Templeton	.06
188	Mike Phillips	.06
189	Pete Vukovich	.06
190	John Urrea	.06
191	Tony Scott	.06
192	Darrell Evans	.08
193	Milt May	.06
194	Bob Knepper	.06
195	Randy Moffitt	.06
196	Larry Herndon	.06
197	Rick Camp	.06
198	Andre Thornton	.06
199	Tom Veryzer	.06
200	Gary Alexander	.06
201	Rick Waits	.06
202	Rick Manning	.06
203	Paul Molitor	.90
204	Jim Gantner	.06
205	Paul Mitchell	.06
206	Reggie Cleveland	.06
207	Sixto Lezcano	.06
208	Bruce Benedict	.06
209	Rodney Scott	.06
210	John Tamargo	.06
211	Bill Lee	.06
212	Andre Dawson	.60
213	Rowland Office	.06
214	Carl Yastrzemski	1.25
215	Jerry Remy	.06
216	Mike Torrez	.06
217	Skip Lockwood	.06
218	Fred Lynn	.08
219	Chris Chambliss	.06
220	Willie Aikens	.06
221	John Wathan	.06
222	Dan Quisenberry	.06
223	Willie Wilson	.08
224	Clint Hurdle	.06
225	Bob Watson	.06
226	Jim Spencer	.06
227	Ron Guidry	.11
228	Reggie Jackson	1.50
229	Oscar Gamble	.06
230	Jeff Cox	.06
231	Luis Tiant	.08
232	Rich Dauer	.06
233	Dan Graham	.06
234	Mike Flanagan	.06
235	John Lowenstein	.06
236	Benny Ayala	.06
237	Wayne Gross	.06
238	Rick Langford	.06
239	Tony Armas	.06
240a	Bob Lacy (Incorrect spelling.)	.20
240b	Bob Lacey (Correct spelling.)	.06
241	Gene Tenace	.06
242	Bob Shirley	.06
243	Gary Lucas	.06
244	Jerry Turner	.06
245	John Wockenfuss	.06
246	Stan Papi	.06
247	Milt Wilcox	.06
248	Dan Schatzeder	.06
249	Steve Kemp	.06
250	Jim Lentine	.06
251	Pete Rose	1.50
252	Bill Madlock	.08
253	Dale Berra	.06
254	Kent Tekulve	.06
255	Enrique Romo	.06
256	Mike Easler	.06
257	Chuck Tanner	.06
258	Art Howe	.08
259	Alan Ashby	.06
260	Nolan Ryan	3.75
261a	Vern Ruhle (Ken Forsch photo - head shot.)	.20
261b	Vern Ruhle (Vern Ruhle photo - waist to head shot.)	.08
262	Bob Boone	.08
263	Cesar Cedeno	.08
264	Jeff Leonard	.06
265	Pat Putnam	.06
266	Jon Matlack	.06
267	Dave Rajsich	.06
268	Billy Sample	.06
269	Damaso Garcia **RC**	.08
270	Tom Buskey	.06
271	Joey McLaughlin	.06
272	Barry Bonnell	.06
273	Tug McGraw	.08
274	Mike Jorgensen	.06
275	Pat Zachry	.06
276	Neil Allen	.06
277	Joel Youngblood	.06
278	Greg Pryor	.06
279	Britt Burns **RC**	.08
280	Rich Dotson **RC**	.20
281	Chet Lemon	.06
282	Rusty Kuntz	.06
283	Ted Cox	.06
284	Sparky Lyle	.06
285	Larry Cox	.06
286	Floyd Bannister	.06
287	Byron McLaughlin	.06
288	Rodney Craig	.06
289	Bobby Grich	.06
290	Dickie Thon	.06
291	Mark Clear	.06
292	Dave Lemanczyk	.06
293	Jason Thompson	.06
294	Rick Miller	.06
295	Lonnie Smith	.06
296	Ron Cey	.06
297	Steve Yeager	.06
298	Bobby Castillo	.06
299	Manny Mota	.06
300	Jay Johnstone	.06
301	Dan Driessen	.06
302	Joe Nolan	.06
303	Paul Householder	.06
304	Harry Spilman	.06
305	Cesar Geronimo	.06
306a	Gary Mathews (Mathews on front.)	.25
306b	Gary Matthews (Matthews on front.)	.06
307	Ken Reitz	.06
308	Ted Simmons	.06
309	John Littlefield	.06
310	George Frazier	.06
311	Dane Iorg	.06
312	Mike Ivie	.06
313	Dennis Littlejohn	.06
314	Gary LaVelle (Lavelle)	.06
315	Jack Clark	.08
316	Jim Wohlford	.06
317	Rick Matula	.06
318	Toby Harrah	.06
319a	Dwane Kuiper (Dwane on front.)	.20
319b	Duane Kuiper (Duane on front.)	.06
320	Len Barker	.06
321	Victor Cruz	.06
322	Dell Alston	.06
323	Robin Yount	.90
324	Charlie Moore	.06
325	Lary Sorensen	.06
326a	Gorman Thomas ("...30-HR mark 4th..." on back)	.20
326b	Gorman Thomas ("...30-HR mark 3rd..." on back)	.06
327	Bob Rodgers	.06
328	Phil Niekro	.70
329	Chris Speier	.06
330a	Steve Rodgers (Rodgers on front.)	.20
330b	Steve Rogers (Rogers on front.)	.06
331	Woodie Fryman	.06
332	Warren Cromartie	.06
333	Jerry White	.06
334	Tony Perez	.90
335	Carlton Fisk	.90
336	Dick Drago	.06
337	Steve Renko	.06
338	Jim Rice	.60
339	Jerry Royster	.06
340	Frank White	.06
341	Jamie Quirk	.06
342a	Paul Spittorff (Spittorff on front.)	.20
342b	Paul Splittorff (Splittorff on front.)	.06
343	Marty Pattin	.06
344	Pete LaCock	.06
345	Willie Randolph	.06
346	Rick Cerone	.06
347	Rich Gossage	.08
348	Reggie Jackson	1.50
349	Ruppert Jones	.06
350	Dave McKay	.06
351	Yogi Berra	.40
352	Doug Decinces (DeCinces)	.08
353	Jim Palmer	.90
354	Tippy Martinez	.06
355	Al Bumbry	.06
356	Earl Weaver	.40
357a	Bob Picciolo (Bob on front.)	.20
357b	Rob Picciolo (Rob on front.)	.06
358	Matt Keough	.06
359	Dwayne Murphy	.06
360	Brian Kingman	.06
361	Bill Fahey	.06
362	Steve Mura	.06
363	Dennis Kinney	.06
364	Dave Winfield	.90
365	Lou Whitaker	.08
366	Lance Parrish	.08
367	Tim Corcoran	.06
368	Pat Underwood	.06
369	Al Cowens	.06
370	Sparky Anderson	.40
371	Pete Rose	2.25
372	Phil Garner	.06
373	Steve Nicosia	.06
374	John Candelaria	.06
375	Don Robinson	.06
376	Lee Lacy	.06
377	John Milner	.06
378	Craig Reynolds	.06
379a	Luis Pujois (Pujois on front.)	.20
379b	Luis Pujols (Pujols on front.)	.06
380	Joe Niekro	.06
381	Joaquin Andujar	.06
382	Keith Moreland **RC**	.11
383	Jose Cruz	.06
384	Bill Virdon	.06
385	Jim Sundberg	.06
386	Doc Medich	.06
387	Al Oliver	.08
388	Jim Norris	.06
389	Bob Bailor	.06
390	Ernie Whitt	.06
391	Otto Velez	.06
392	Roy Howell	.06
393	Bob Walk **RC**	.08
394	Doug Flynn	.06
395	Pete Falcone	.06
396	Tom Hausman	.06
397	Elliott Maddox	.06
398	Mike Squires	.06
399	Marvis Foley	.06
400	Steve Trout	.06
401	Wayne Nordhagen	.06
402	Tony Larussa (LaRussa)	.08
403	Bruce Bochte	.06
404	Bake McBride	.06
405	Jerry Narron	.06
406	Rob Dressler	.06
407	Dave Heaverlo	.06
408	Tom Paciorek	.06
409	Carney Lansford	.06
410	Brian Downing	.06
411	Don Aase	.06
412	Jim Barr	.06
413	Don Baylor	.08
414	Jim Fregosi	.06
415	Dallas Green	.06
416	Dave Lopes	.06
417	Jerry Reuss	.06
418	Rick Sutcliffe	.08
419	Derrel Thomas	.06
420	Tommy LaSorda (Lasorda)	.40
421	Charlie Leibrandt **RC**	.20
422	Tom Seaver	1.25
423	Ron Oester	.06
424	Junior Kennedy	.06
425	Tom Seaver	1.25
426	Bobby Cox	.08
427	Leon Durham **RC**	.15
428	Terry Kennedy	.06
429	Silvio Martinez	.06
430	George Hendrick	.06
431	Red Schoendienst	.40
432	John LeMaster	.06
433	Vida Blue	.08
434	John Montefusco	.06
435	Terry Whitfield	.06
436	Dave Bristol	.06
437	Dale Murphy	.60
438	Jerry Dybzinski	.06
439	Jorge Orta	.06
440	Wayne Garland	.06
441	Miguel Dilone	.06
442	Dave Garcia	.06
443	Don Money	.06
444a	Buck Martinez (Photo reversed.)	.25
444b	Buck Martinez (Photo correct.)	.08
445	Jerry Augustine	.06
446	Ben Oglivie	.06
447	Jim Slaton	.06
448	Doyle Alexander	.06
449	Tony Bernazard	.06
450	Scott Sanderson	.06
451	Dave Palmer	.06
452	Stan Bahnsen	.06
453	Dick Williams	.06
454	Rick Burleson	.06
455	Gary Allenson	.06
456	Bob Stanley	.06
457a	John Tudor **RC** (Lifetime W/L 9.7.)	.30
457b	John Tudor **RC** (Lifetime W/L 9-7.)	.15
458	Dwight Evans	.08
459	Glenn Hubbard	.06
460	U L Washington	.06
461	Larry Gura	.06
462	Rich Gale	.06
463	Hal McRae	.08
464	Jim Frey	.06
465	Bucky Dent	.08
466	Dennis Werth	.06
467	Ron Davis	.06
468	Reggie Jackson	2.00
469	Bobby Brown	.06
470	Mike Davis **RC**	.08
471	Gaylord Perry	.90
472	Mark Belanger	.06
473	Jim Palmer	.90
474	Sammy Stewart	.06
475	Tim Stoddard	.06
476	Steve Stone	.08
477	Jeff Newman	.06
478	Steve McCatty	.06
479	Billy Martin	.08
480	Mitchell Page	.06
481	Steve Carlton (CY)	.30
482	Bill Buckner	.08
483a	Ivan DeJesus (Lifetime hits 702.)	.20
483b	Ivan DeJesus (Lifetime hits 642.)	.06
484	Cliff Johnson	.06
485	Lenny Randle	.06
486	Larry Milbourne	.06
487	Roy Smalley	.06
488	John Castino	.06
489	Ron Jackson	.06
490a	Dave Roberts (1980 highlights begins "Showed pop...")	.20
490b	Dave Roberts (1980 highlights begins "Declared himself...")	.06
491	George Brett (MVP)	1.25
492	Mike Cubbage	.06
493	Rob Wilfong	.06
494	Danny Goodwin	.06
495	Jose Morales	.06
496	Mickey Rivers	.06
497	Mike Edwards	.06
498	Mike Sadek	.06
499	Lenn Sakata	.06
500	Gene Michael	.06
501	Dave Roberts	.06
502	Steve Dillard	.06
503	Jim Essian	.06
504	Rance Mulliniks	.06
505	Darrell Porter	.06
506	Joe Torre	.40
507	Terry Crowley	.06
508	Bill Travers	.06
509	Nelson Norman	.06
510	Bob McClure	.06
511	Steve Howe **RC**	.11
512	Dave Rader	.06
513	Mick Kelleher	.06
514	Kiko Garcia	.06
515	Larry Biittner	.06
516a	Willie Norwood (1980 highlights begins "Spent most...")	.20
516b	Willie Norwood (1980 highlights begins "Traded to...")	.06
517	Bo Diaz	.06
518	Juan Beniquez	.06
519	Scot Thompson	.06
520	Jim Tracy	.06
521	Carlos Lezcano	.06
522	Joe Amalfitano	.06
523	Preston Hanna	.06
524a	Ray Burris (1980 highlights begins "Went on...")	.20
524b	Ray Burris (1980 highlights begins "Drafted by...")	.06
525	Broderick Perkins	.06
526	Mickey Hatcher	.06
527	John Goryl	.06
528	Dick Davis	.06
529	Butch Wynegar	.06
530	Sal Butera	.06
531	Jerry Koosman	.06
532a	Jeff (Geoff) Zahn (1980 highlights begins "Was 2nd in...")	.20
532b	Jeff (Geoff) Zahn (1980 highlights begins "Signed a 3 year ...")	.06
533	Dennis Martinez	.06
534	Gary Thomasson	.06
535	Steve Macko	.06
536	Jim Kaat	.11
537	George Brett, Rod Carew Best Hitters	1.25
538	Tim Raines **RC**	2.25
539	Keith Smith	.06
540	Ken Macha	.06
541	Burt Hooton	.06
542	Butch Hobson	.06
543	Bill Stein	.06
544	Dave Stapleton	.06
545	Bob Pate	.06
546	Doug Corbett	.06
547	Darrell Jackson	.06
548	Pete Redfern	.06
549	Roger Erickson	.06
550	Al Hrabosky	.06
551	Dick Tidrow	.06
552	Dave Ford	.06
553	Dave Kingman	.08
554a	Mike Vail (1980 highlights begins "After...")	.20
554b	Mike Vail (1980 highlights begins "Traded...")	.06
555a	Jerry Martin (1980 highlights begins "Overcame...")	.20
555b	Jerry Martin (1980 highlights begins "Traded...")	.06
556a	Jesus Figueroa (1980 highlights begins "Had...")	.20
556b	Jesus Figueroa (1980 highlights begins "Traded...")	.06
557	Don Stanhouse	.06
558	Barry Foote	.06
559	Tim Blackwell	.06
560	Bruce Sutter	.90
561	Rick Reuschel	.06
562	Lynn McGlothen	.06
563a	Bob Owchinko (1980 highlights begins "Traded...")	.20
563b	Bob Owchinko (1980 highlights begins "Involved...")	.06
564	John Verhoeven	.06
565	Ken Landreaux	.06
566a	Glen Adams (Glen on front.)	.20
566b	Glenn Adams (Glenn on front.)	.06
567	Hosken Powell	.06

568 Dick Noles .06
569 Danny Ainge **RC** 1.50
570 Bobby Mattick .06
571 Joe LeFebvre (Lefebvre) .06
572 Bobby Clark .06
573 Dennis Lamp .06
574 Randy Lerch .06
575 Mookie Wilson **RC** .25
576 Ron LeFlore .06
577 Jim Dwyer .06
578 Bill Castro .06
579 Greg Minton .06
580 Mark Littell .06
581 Andy Hassler .06
582 Dave Stieb .06
583 Ken Oberkfell .06
584 Larry Bradford .06
585 Fred Stanley .06
586 Bill Caudill .06
587 Doug Capilla .06
588 George Riley .06
589 Willie Hernandez .06
590 Mike Schmidt (MVP) 1.25
591 Steve Stone (Cy Young 1980) .08
592 Rick Sofield .06
593 Bombo Rivera .06
594 Gary Ward .06
595a Dave Edwards (1980 highlights begins "Sidelined...") .20
595b Dave Edwards (1980 highlights begins "Traded...") .06
596 Mike Proly .06
597 Tommy Boggs .06
598 Greg Gross .06
599 Elias Sosa .06
600 Pat Kelly .06
---- Checklist 1-120 (51 Tom Donohue) .20
---- Checklist 1-120 (51 Tom Donahue) .08
---- Checklist 121-240 .08
---- Checklist 241-360 (306 Gary Mathews) .20
---- Checklist 241-360 (306 Gary Matthews) .08
---- Checklist 361-480 (379 Luis Pujois) .20
---- Checklist 361-480 (379 Luis Pujols) .08
---- Checklist 481-600 (566 Glen Adams) .20
---- Checklist 481-600 (566 Glenn Adams) .08

1982 Donruss

	NM/M
Unopened Fact. Set (660):	50.00
Complete Set (660):	45.00
Complete Set, Uncut Sheets (5):	175.00
Common Player:	.10
Babe Ruth Puzzle:	1.00
Wax Pack (15):	2.50
Wax Box (36):	80.00

1 Pete Rose/DK 4.00
2 Gary Carter/DK 1.25
3 Steve Garvey/DK .45
4 Vida Blue/DK .10
5a Alan Trammel/DK (Last name incorrect.) 1.00
5b Alan Trammell/DK (Corrected) .30
6 Len Barker/DK .10
7 Dwight Evans/DK .15
8 Rod Carew/DK 1.25
9 George Hendrick/DK .10
10 Phil Niekro/DK 1.00
11 Richie Zisk/DK .10
12 Dave Parker/DK .10
13 Nolan Ryan/DK 5.00
14 Ivan DeJesus/DK .10
15 George Brett/DK 2.00
16 Tom Seaver/DK 1.25
17 Dave Kingman/DK .15
18 Dave Winfield/DK 1.25
19 Mike Norris/DK .10
20 Carlton Fisk/DK 1.25
21 Ozzie Smith/DK 1.50
22 Roy Smalley/DK .10
23 Buddy Bell/DK .10
24 Ken Singleton/DK .10
25 John Mayberry/DK .10
26 Gorman Thomas/DK .10
27 Earl Weaver .50
28 Rollie Fingers 1.00
29 Sparky Anderson .50
30 Dennis Eckersley 1.25
31 Dave Winfield 1.25
32 Burt Hooton .10
33 Rick Waits .10
34 George Brett 2.00
35 Steve McCatty .10
36 Steve Rogers .10
37 Bill Stein .10
38 Steve Renko .10
39 Mike Squires .10
40 George Hendrick .10
41 Bob Knepper .10
42 Steve Carlton 1.25
43 Larry Biittner .10
44 Chris Welsh .10
45 Steve Nicosia .10
46 Jack Clark .10
47 Chris Chambliss .10
48 Ivan DeJesus .10
49 Lee Mazzilli .10
50 Julio Cruz .10
51 Pete Redfern .10
52 Dave Stieb .10
53 Doug Corbett .10
54 George Bell **RC** .50
55 Joe Simpson .10
56 Rusty Staub .10
57 Hector Cruz .10
58 Claudell Washington .10
59 Enrique Romo .10
60 Gary Lavelle .10
61 Tim Flannery .10
62 Joe Nolan .10
63 Larry Bowa .10
64 Sixto Lezcano .10
65 Joe Sambito .10
66 Bruce Kison .10
67 Wayne Nordhagen .10
68 Woodie Fryman .10
69 Billy Sample .10
70 Amos Otis .10
71 Matt Keough .10
72 Toby Harrah .10
73 Dave Righetti **RC** .30
74 Carl Yastrzemski 1.50
75 Bob Welch .10
76a Alan Trammel (Last name misspelled.) 1.00
76b Alan Trammell (Corrected) .10
77 Rick Dempsey .10
78 Paul Molitor 1.25
79 Dennis Martinez .10
80 Jim Slaton .10
81 Champ Summers .10
82 Carney Lansford .10
83 Barry Foote .10
84 Steve Garvey .45
85 Rick Manning .10
86 John Wathan .10
87 Brian Kingman .10
88 Andre Dawson .50
89 Jim Kern .10
90 Bobby Grich .10
91 Bob Forsch .10
92 Art Howe .10
93 Marty Bystrom .10
94 Ozzie Smith 1.50
95 Dave Parker .10
96 Doyle Alexander .10
97 Al Hrabosky .10
98 Frank Taveras .10
99 Tim Blackwell .10
100 Floyd Bannister .10
101 Alfredo Griffin .10
102 Dave Engle .10
103 Mario Soto .10
104 Ross Baumgarten .10
105 Ken Singleton .10
106 Ted Simmons .10
107 Jack Morris .10
108 Bob Watson .10
109 Dwight Evans .10
110 Tom Lasorda .50
111 Bert Blyleven .10
112 Dan Quisenberry .10
113 Rickey Henderson 1.25
114 Gary Carter 1.25
115 Brian Downing .10
116 Al Oliver .10
117 LaMarr Hoyt .10
118 Cesar Cedeno .10
119 Keith Moreland .10
120 Bob Shirley .10
121 Terry Kennedy .10
122 Frank Pastore .10
123 Gene Garber .10
124 Tony Pena .10
125 Allen Ripley .10
126 Randy Martz .10
127 Richie Zisk .10
128 Mike Scott .10
129 Lloyd Moseby .10
130 Rob Wilfong .10
131 Tim Stoddard .10
132 Gorman Thomas .10
133 Dan Petry .10
134 Bob Stanley .10
135 Lou Piniella .15
136 Pedro Guerrero .10
137 Len Barker .10
138 Richard Gale .10
139 Wayne Gross .10
140 Tim Wallach **RC** .50
141 Gene Mauch .10
142 Doc Medich .10
143 Tony Bernazard .10
144 Bill Virdon .10
145 John Littlefield .10
146 Dave Bergman .10
147 Dick Davis .10
148 Tom Seaver 1.50
149 Matt Sinatro .10
150 Chuck Tanner .10
151 Leon Durham .10
152 Gene Tenace .10
153 Al Bumbry .10
154 Mark Brouhard .10
155 Rick Peters .10
156 Jerry Remy .10
157 Rick Reuschel .10
158 Steve Howe .10
159 Alan Bannister .10
160 U L Washington .10
161 Rick Langford .10
162 Bill Gullickson .10
163 Mark Wagner .10
164 Geoff Zahn .10
165 Ron LeFlore .10
166 Dane Iorg .10
167 Joe Niekro .10
168 Pete Rose 3.00
169 Dave Collins .10
170 Rick Wise .10
171 Jim Bibby .10
172 Larry Herndon .10
173 Bob Horner .10
174 Steve Dillard .10
175 Mookie Wilson .10
176 Dan Meyer .10
177 Fernando Arroyo .10
178 Jackson Todd .10
179 Darrell Jackson .10
180 Al Woods .10
181 Jim Anderson .10
182 Dave Kingman .10
183 Steve Henderson .10
184 Brian Asselstine .10
185 Rod Scurry .10
186 Fred Breining .10
187 Danny Boone .10
188 Junior Kennedy .10
189 Sparky Lyle .10
190 Whitey Herzog .10
191 Dave Smith .10
192 Ed Ott .10
193 Greg Luzinski .10
194 Bill Lee .10
195 Don Zimmer .10
196 Hal McRae .10
197 Mike Norris .10
198 Duane Kuiper .10
199 Rick Cerone .10
200 Jim Rice .45
201 Steve Yeager .10
202 Tom Brookens .10
203 Jose Morales .10
204 Roy Howell .10
205 Tippy Martinez .10
206 Moose Haas .10
207 Al Cowens .10
208 Dave Stapleton .10
209 Bucky Dent .10
210 Ron Cey .10
211 Jorge Orta .10
212 Jamie Quirk .10
213 Jeff Jones .10
214 Tim Raines .25
215 Jon Matlack .10
216 Rod Carew 1.50
217 Jim Kaat .15
218 Joe Pittman .10
219 Larry Christenson .10
220 Juan Bonilla .10
221 Mike Easler .10
222 Vida Blue .10
223 Rick Camp .10
224 Mike Jorgensen .10
225 Jody Davis **RC** .15
226 Mike Parrott .10
227 Jim Clancy .10
228 Hosken Powell .10
229 Tom Hume .10
230 Britt Burns .10
231 Jim Palmer 1.25
232 Bob Rodgers .10
233 Milt Wilcox .10
234 Dave Revering .10
235 Mike Torrez .10
236 Robert Castillo .10
237 Von Hayes **RC** .25
238 Renie Martin .10
239 Dwayne Murphy .10
240 Rodney Scott .10
241 Fred Patek .10
242 Mickey Rivers .10
243 Steve Trout .10
244 Jose Cruz .10
245 Manny Trillo .10
246 Lary Sorensen .10
247 Dave Edwards .10
248 Dan Driessen .10
249 Tommy Boggs .10
250 Dale Berra .10
251 Ed Whitson .10
252 Lee Smith **RC** 4.00
253 Tom Paciorek .10
254 Pat Zachry .10
255 Luis Leal .10
256 John Castino .10
257 Rich Dauer .10
258 Cecil Cooper .10
259 Dave Rozema .10
260 John Tudor .10
261 Jerry Mumphrey .10
262 Jay Johnstone .10
263 Bo Diaz .10
264 Dennis Leonard .10
265 Jim Spencer .10
266 John Milner .10
267 Don Aase .10
268 Jim Sundberg .10
269 Lamar Johnson .10
270 Frank LaCorte .10
271 Barry Evans .10
272 Enos Cabell .10
273 Del Unser .10
274 George Foster .10
275 Brett Butler **RC** .50
276 Lee Lacy .10
277 Ken Reitz .10
278 Keith Hernandez .10
279 Doug DeCinces .10
280 Charlie Moore .10
281 Lance Parrish .10
282 Ralph Houk .10
283 Rich Gossage .10
284 Jerry Reuss .10
285 Mike Stanton .10
286 Frank White .10
287 Bob Owchinko .10
288 Scott Sanderson .10
289 Bump Wills .10
290 Dave Frost .10
291 Chet Lemon .10
292 Tito Landrum .10
293 Vern Ruhle .10
294 Mike Schmidt 2.00
295 Sam Mejias .10
296 Gary Lucas .10
297 John Candelaria .10
298 Jerry Martin .10
299 Dale Murphy .50
300 Mike Lum .10
301 Tom Hausman .10
302 Glenn Abbott .10
303 Roger Erickson .10
304 Otto Velez .10
305 Danny Goodwin .10
306 John Mayberry .10
307 Lenny Randle .10
308 Bob Bailor .10
309 Jerry Morales .10
310 Rufino Linares .10
311 Kent Tekulve .10
312 Joe Morgan 1.25
313 John Urrea .10
314 Paul Householder .10
315 Garry Maddox .10
316 Mike Ramsey .10
317 Alan Ashby .10
318 Bob Clark .10
319 Tony LaRussa .15
320 Charlie Lea .10
321 Danny Darwin .10
322 Cesar Geronimo .10
323 Tom Underwood .10
324 Andre Thornton .10
325 Rudy May .10
326 Frank Tanana .10
327 Davey Lopes .10
328 Richie Hebner .10
329 Mike Flanagan .10
330 Mike Caldwell .10
331 Scott McGregor .10
332 Jerry Augustine .10
333 Stan Papi .10
334 Rick Miller .10
335 Graig Nettles .15
336 Dusty Baker .10
337 Dave Garcia .10
338 Larry Gura .10
339 Cliff Johnson .10
340 Warren Cromartie .10
341 Steve Comer .10
342 Rick Burleson .10
343 John Martin .10
344 Craig Reynolds .10
345 Mike Proly .10
346 Ruppert Jones .10
347 Omar Moreno .10
348 Greg Minton .10
349 Rick Mahler **RC** .10
350 Alex Trevino .10
351 Mike Krukow .10
352a Shane Rawley (Jim Anderson photo - shaking hands.) .50
352b Shane Rawley (Correct photo - kneeling.) .15
353 Garth Iorg .10
354 Pete Mackanin .10
355 Paul Moskau .10
356 Richard Dotson .10
357 Steve Stone .10
358 Larry Hisle .10
359 Aurelio Lopez .10
360 Oscar Gamble .10
361 Tom Burgmeier .10
362 Terry Forster .10
363 Joe Charboneau .25
364 Ken Brett .10

365	Tony Armas	.10
366	Chris Speier	.10
367	Fred Lynn	.10
368	Buddy Bell	.10
369	Jim Essian	.10
370	Terry Puhl	.10
371	Greg Gross	.10
372	Bruce Sutter	1.25
373	Joe Lefebvre	.10
374	Ray Knight	.10
375	Bruce Benedict	.10
376	Tim Foli	.10
377	Al Holland	.10
378	Ken Kravec	.10
379	Jeff Burroughs	.10
380	Pete Falcone	.10
381	Ernie Whitt	.10
382	Brad Havens	.10
383	Terry Crowley	.10
384	Don Money	.10
385	Dan Schatzeder	.10
386	Gary Allenson	.10
387	Yogi Berra	.50
388	Ken Landreaux	.10
389	Mike Hargrove	.10
390	Darryl Motley	.10
391	Dave McKay	.10
392	Stan Bahnsen	.10
393	Ken Forsch	.10
394	Mario Mendoza	.10
395	Jim Morrison	.10
396	Mike Ivie	.10
397	Broderick Perkins	.10
398	Darrell Evans	.10
399	Ron Reed	.10
400	Johnny Bench	1.50
401	Steve Bedrosian **RC**	.20
402	Bill Robinson	.10
403	Bill Buckner	.10
404	Ken Oberkfell	.10
405	Cal Ripken, Jr. **RC**	40.00
406	Jim Gantner	.10
407	Kirk Gibson	.10
408	Tony Perez	1.00
409	Tommy John	.10
410	Dave Stewart **RC**	2.50
411	Dan Spillner	.10
412	Willie Aikens	.10
413	Mike Heath	.10
414	Ray Burris	.10
415	Leon Roberts	.10
416	Mike Witt **RC**	.15
417	Bobby Molinaro	.10
418	Steve Braun	.10
419	Nolan Ryan	4.00
420	Tug McGraw	.10
421	Dave Concepcion	.10
422a	Juan Eichelberger (Gary Lucas photo - white player.)	.50
422b	Juan Eichelberger (Correct photo - black player.)	.10
423	Rick Rhoden	.10
424	Frank Robinson	.50
425	Eddie Miller	.10
426	Bill Caudill	.10
427	Doug Flynn	.10
428	Larry Anderson (Andersen)	.10
429	Al Williams	.10
430	Jerry Garvin	.10
431	Glenn Adams	.10
432	Barry Bonnell	.10
433	Jerry Narron	.10
434	John Stearns	.10
435	Mike Tyson	.10
436	Glenn Hubbard	.10
437	Eddie Solomon	.10
438	Jeff Leonard	.10
439	Randy Bass	.10
440	Mike LaCoss	.10
441	Gary Matthews	.10
442	Mark Littell	.10
443	Don Sutton	1.00
444	John Harris	.10
445	Vada Pinson	.10
446	Elias Sosa	.10
447	Charlie Hough	.10
448	Willie Wilson	.10
449	Fred Stanley	.10
450	Tom Veryzer	.10
451	Ron Davis	.10
452	Mark Clear	.10
453	Bill Russell	.10
454	Lou Whitaker	.10
455	Dan Graham	.10
456	Reggie Cleveland	.10
457	Sammy Stewart	.10
458	Pete Vuckovich	.10
459	John Wockenfuss	.10
460	Glenn Hoffman	.10
461	Willie Randolph	.10
462	Fernando Valenzuela	.10
463	Ron Hassey	.10
464	Paul Splittorff	.10
465	Rob Picciolo	.10
466	Larry Parrish	.10
467	Johnny Grubb	.10
468	Dan Ford	.10
469	Silvio Martinez	.10
470	Kiko Garcia	.10
471	Bob Boone	.10
472	Luis Salazar	.10
473	Randy Niemann	.10
474	Tom Griffin	.10
475	Phil Niekro	1.00
476	Hubie Brooks	.10
477	Dick Tidrow	.10
478	Jim Beattie	.10
479	Damaso Garcia	.10
480	Mickey Hatcher	.10
481	Joe Price	.10
482	Ed Farmer	.10
483	Eddie Murray	1.25
484	Ben Oglivie	.10
485	Kevin Saucier	.10
486	Bobby Murcer	.10
487	Bill Campbell	.10
488	Reggie Smith	.10
489	Wayne Garland	.10
490	Jim Wright	.10
491	Billy Martin	.10
492	Jim Fanning	.10
493	Don Baylor	.10
494	Rick Honeycutt	.10
495	Carlton Fisk	1.25
496	Denny Walling	.10
497	Bake McBride	.10
498	Darrell Porter	.10
499	Gene Richards	.10
500	Ron Oester	.10
501	Ken Dayley **RC**	.10
502	Jason Thompson	.10
503	Milt May	.10
504	Doug Bird	.10
505	Bruce Bochte	.10
506	Neil Allen	.10
507	Joey McLaughlin	.10
508	Butch Wynegar	.10
509	Gary Roenicke	.10
510	Robin Yount	1.25
511	Dave Tobik	.10
512	Rich Gedman **RC**	.15
513	Gene Nelson **RC**	.10
514	Rick Monday	.10
515	Miguel Dilone	.10
516	Clint Hurdle	.10
517	Jeff Newman	.10
518	Grant Jackson	.10
519	Andy Hassler	.10
520	Pat Putnam	.10
521	Greg Pryor	.10
522	Tony Scott	.10
523	Steve Mura	.10
524	Johnnie LeMaster	.10
525	Dick Ruthven	.10
526	John McNamara	.10
527	Larry McWilliams	.10
528	Johnny Ray **RC**	.15
529	Pat Tabler **RC**	.15
530	Tom Herr	.10
531a	San Diego Chicken (W/trademark symbol.)	.75
531b	San Diego Chicken (No trademark symbol.)	.50
532	Sal Butera	.10
533	Mike Griffin	.10
534	Kelvin Moore	.10
535	Reggie Jackson	2.00
536	Ed Romero	.10
537	Derrel Thomas	.10
538	Mike O'Berry	.10
539	Jack O'Connor	.10
540	Bob Ojeda **RC**	.25
541	Roy Lee Jackson	.10
542	Lynn Jones	.10
543	Gaylord Perry	1.00
544a	Phil Garner (Photo reversed.)	.50
544b	Phil Garner (Photo correct.)	.10
545	Garry Templeton	.10
546	Rafael Ramirez	.10
547	Jeff Reardon	.10
548	Ron Guidry	.10
549	Tim Laudner **RC**	.15
550	John Henry Johnson	.10
551	Chris Bando	.10
552	Bobby Brown	.10
553	Larry Bradford	.10
554	Scott Fletcher **RC**	.20
555	Jerry Royster	.10
556	Shooty Babbitt	.10
557	Kent Hrbek **RC**	2.00
558	Ron Guidry, Tommy John Yankee Winners	.15
559	Mark Bomback	.10
560	Julio Valdez	.10
561	Buck Martinez	.10
562	Mike Marshall **RC**	.15
563	Rennie Stennett	.10
564	Steve Crawford	.10
565	Bob Babcock	.10
566	Johnny Podres	.10
567	Paul Serna	.10
568	Harold Baines	1.00
569	Dave LaRoche	.10
570	Lee May	.10
571	Gary Ward	.10
572	John Denny	.10
573	Roy Smalley	.10
574	Bob Brenly **RC**	.20
575	Reggie Jackson, Dave Winfield Bronx Bombers	1.50
576	Luis Pujols	.10
577	Butch Hobson	.10
578	Harvey Kuenn	.10
579	Cal Ripken, Sr.	.10
580	Juan Berenguer	.10
581	Benny Ayala	.10
582	Vance Law	.10
583	Rick Leach **RC**	.15
584	George Frazier	.10
585	Pete Rose, Mike Schmidt Phillies Finest	1.00
586	Joe Rudi	.10
587	Juan Beniquez	.10
588	Luis DeLeon **RC**	.10
589	Craig Swan	.10
590	Dave Chalk	.10
591	Billy Gardner	.10
592	Sal Bando	.10
593	Bert Campaneris	.10
594	Steve Kemp	.10
595a	Randy Lerch (Braves)	.25
595b	Randy Lerch (Brewers)	.10
596	Bryan Clark	.10
597	Dave Ford	.10
598	Mike Scioscia	.10
599	John Lowenstein	.10
600	Rene Lachmann (Lachemann)	.10
601	Mick Kelleher	.10
602	Ron Jackson	.10
603	Jerry Koosman	.10
604	Dave Goltz	.10
605	Ellis Valentine	.10
606	Lonnie Smith	.10
607	Joaquin Andujar	.10
608	Garry Hancock	.10
609	Jerry Turner	.10
610	Bob Bonner	.10
611	Jim Dwyer	.10
612	Terry Bulling	.10
613	Joel Youngblood	.10
614	Larry Milbourne	.10
615	Phil Roof (Photo actually Gene Roof.)	.10
616	Keith Drumright	.10
617	Dave Rosello	.10
618	Rickey Keeton	.10
619	Dennis Lamp	.10
620	Sid Monge	.10
621	Jerry White	.10
622	Luis Aguayo **RC**	.10
623	Jamie Easterly	.10
624	Steve Sax **RC**	.50
625	Dave Roberts	.10
626	Rick Bosetti	.10
627	Terry Francona **RC**	.15
628	Johnny Bench, Tom Seaver Pride of the Reds	1.00
629	Paul Mirabella	.10
630	Rance Mulliniks	.10
631	Kevin Hickey	.10
632	Reid Nichols	.10
633	Dave Geisel	.10
634	Ken Griffey	.10
635	Bob Lemon	.15
636	Orlando Sanchez	.10
637	Bill Almon	.10
638	Danny Ainge	1.00
639	Willie Stargell	1.25
640	Bob Sykes	.10
641	Ed Lynch	.10
642	John Ellis	.10
643	Fergie Jenkins	1.00
644	Lenn Sakata	.10
645	Julio Gonzales	.10
646	Jesse Orosco	.10
647	Jerry Dybzinski	.10
648	Tommy Davis	.10
649	Ron Gardenhire	.10
650	Felipe Alou	.10
651	Harvey Haddix	.10
652	Willie Upshaw	.10
653	Bill Madlock	.10
----	Checklist 1-26 DK (5 Trammel)	.25
----	Checklist 1-26 DK (5 Trammell)	.10
----	Checklist 27-130	.10
----	Checklist 131-234	.10
----	Checklist 235-338	.10
----	Checklist 339-442	.10
----	Checklist 443-544	.10
----	Checklist 545-653	.10

1983 Donruss

	NM/M
Unopened Fact. Set (660):	50.00
Complete Set (660):	40.00
Common Player:	.10
Ty Cobb Puzzle:	2.50
Wax Pack (15):	2.50
Wax Box (36):	80.00

1	Fernando Valenzuela/DK	.15
2	Rollie Fingers/DK	.75
3	Reggie Jackson/DK	2.50
4	Jim Palmer/DK	1.00
5	Jack Morris/DK	.15
6	George Foster/DK	.15
7	Jim Sundberg/DK	.10
8	Willie Stargell/DK	1.00
9	Dave Stieb/DK	.15
10	Joe Niekro/DK	.15
11	Rickey Henderson/DK	1.25
12	Dale Murphy/DK	.50
13	Toby Harrah/DK	.10
14	Bill Buckner/DK	.15
15	Willie Wilson/DK	.10
16	Steve Carlton/DK	1.25
17	Ron Guidry/DK	.15
18	Steve Rogers/DK	.10
19	Kent Hrbek/DK	.10
20	Keith Hernandez/DK	.10
21	Floyd Bannister/DK	.10
22	Johnny Bench/DK	2.00
23	Britt Burns/DK	.10
24	Joe Morgan/DK	1.25
25	Carl Yastrzemski/DK	2.00
26	Terry Kennedy/DK	.10
27	Gary Roenicke	.10
28	Dwight Bernard	.10
29	Pat Underwood	.10
30	Gary Allenson	.10
31	Ron Guidry	.10
32	Burt Hooton	.10
33	Chris Bando	.10
34	Vida Blue	.10
35	Rickey Henderson	1.25
36	Ray Burris	.10
37	John Butcher	.10
38	Don Aase	.10
39	Jerry Koosman	.10
40	Bruce Sutter	1.00
41	Jose Cruz	.10
42	Pete Rose	3.00
43	Cesar Cedeno	.10
44	Floyd Chiffer	.10
45	Larry McWilliams	.10
46	Alan Fowlkes	.10
47	Dale Murphy	.50
48	Doug Bird	.10
49	Hubie Brooks	.10
50	Floyd Bannister	.10
51	Jack O'Connor	.10
52	Steve Senteney	.10
53	Gary Gaetti **RC**	1.00
54	Damaso Garcia	.10
55	Gene Nelson	.10
56	Mookie Wilson	.10
57	Allen Ripley	.10
58	Bob Horner	.10
59	Tony Pena	.10
60	Gary Lavelle	.10
61	Tim Lollar	.10
62	Frank Pastore	.10
63	Garry Maddox	.10
64	Bob Forsch	.10
65	Harry Spilman	.10
66	Geoff Zahn	.10
67	Salome Barojas	.10
68	David Palmer	.10
69	Charlie Hough	.10
70	Dan Quisenberry	.10
71	Tony Armas	.10
72	Rick Sutcliffe	.10
73	Steve Balboni	.10
74	Jerry Remy	.10
75	Mike Scioscia	.10
76	John Wockenfuss	.10
77	Jim Palmer	1.00
78	Rollie Fingers	.75
79	Joe Nolan	.10
80	Pete Vuckovich	.10
81	Rick Leach	.10
82	Rick Miller	.10
83	Graig Nettles	.15
84	Ron Cey	.10
85	Miguel Dilone	.10
86	John Wathan	.10
87	Kelvin Moore	.10
88a	Byrn Smith (First name incorrect.)	.35
88b	Bryn Smith (First name correct.)	.10
89	Dave Hostetler	.10
90	Rod Carew	1.50
91	Lonnie Smith	.10
92	Bob Knepper	.10
93	Marty Bystrom	.10
94	Chris Welsh	.10
95	Jason Thompson	.10
96	Tom O'Malley	.10
97	Phil Niekro	.75
98	Neil Allen	.10
99	Bill Buckner	.10
100	Ed Vande Berg **RC**	.10
101	Jim Clancy	.10
102	Robert Castillo	.10
103	Bruce Berenyi	.10
104	Carlton Fisk	1.25
105	Mike Flanagan	.10
106	Cecil Cooper	.10
107	Jack Morris	.10
108	Mike Morgan	.10
109	Luis Aponte	.10
110	Pedro Guerrero	.10

111	Len Barker	.10
112	Willie Wilson	.10
113	Dave Beard	.10
114	Mike Gates	.10
115	Reggie Jackson	2.50
116	George Wright	.10
117	Vance Law	.10
118	Nolan Ryan	4.00
119	Mike Krukow	.10
120	Ozzie Smith	2.00
121	Broderick Perkins	.10
122	Tom Seaver	1.50
123	Chris Chambliss	.10
124	Chuck Tanner	.10
125	Johnnie LeMaster	.10
126	Mel Hall **RC**	.15
127	Bruce Bochte	.10
128	Charlie Puleo **RC**	.10
129	Luis Leal	.10
130	John Pacella	.10
131	Glenn Gulliver	.10
132	Don Money	.10
133	Dave Rozema	.10
134	Bruce Hurst	.10
135	Rudy May	.10
136	Tom LaSorda (Lasorda)	.40
137	Dan Spillner (Photo actually Ed Whitson.)	.10
138	Jerry Martin	.10
139	Mike Norris	.10
140	Al Oliver	.10
141	Daryl Sconiers	.10
142	Lamar Johnson	.10
143	Harold Baines	.10
144	Alan Ashby	.10
145	Garry Templeton	.10
146	Al Holland	.10
147	Bo Diaz	.10
148	Dave Concepcion	.10
149	Rick Camp	.10
150	Jim Morrison	.10
151	Randy Martz	.10
152	Keith Hernandez	.10
153	John Lowenstein	.10
154	Mike Caldwell	.10
155	Milt Wilcox	.10
156	Rich Gedman	.10
157	Rich Gossage	.20
158	Jerry Reuss	.10
159	Ron Hassey	.10
160	Larry Gura	.10
161	Dwayne Murphy	.10
162	Woodie Fryman	.10
163	Steve Comer	.10
164	Ken Forsch	.10
165	Dennis Lamp	.10
166	David Green	.10
167	Terry Puhl	.10
168	Mike Schmidt	2.50
169	Eddie Milner **RC**	.10
170	John Curtis	.10
171	Don Robinson	.10
172	Richard Gale	.10
173	Steve Bedrosian	.10
174	Willie Hernandez	.10
175	Ron Gardenhire	.10
176	Jim Beattie	.10
177	Tim Laudner	.10
178	Buck Martinez	.10
179	Kent Hrbek	.10
180	Alfredo Griffin	.10
181	Larry Andersen	.10
182	Pete Falcone	.10
183	Jody Davis	.10
184	Glenn Hubbard	.10
185	Dale Berra	.10
186	Greg Minton	.10
187	Gary Lucas	.10
188	Dave Van Gorder	.10
189	Bob Dernier	.10
190	Willie McGee **RC**	1.50
191	Dickie Thon	.10
192	Bob Boone	.10
193	Britt Burns	.10
194	Jeff Reardon	.10
195	Jon Matlack	.10
196	Don Slaught **RC**	.15
197	Fred Stanley	.10
198	Rick Manning	.10
199	Dave Righetti	.10
200	Dave Stapleton	.10
201	Steve Yeager	.10
202	Enos Cabell	.10
203	Sammy Stewart	.10
204	Moose Haas	.10
205	Lenn Sakata	.10
206	Charlie Moore	.10
207	Alan Trammell	.10
208	Jim Rice	.40
209	Roy Smalley	.10
210	Bill Russell	.10
211	Andre Thornton	.10
212	Willie Aikens	.10
213	Dave McKay	.10
214	Tim Blackwell	.10
215	Buddy Bell	.10
216	Doug DeCinces	.10
217	Tom Herr	.10
218	Frank LaCorte	.10
219	Steve Carlton	1.25
220	Terry Kennedy	.10
221	Mike Easler	.10
222	Jack Clark	.10
223	Gene Garber	.10
224	Scott Holman	.10
225	Mike Proly	.10
226	Terry Bulling	.10
227	Jerry Garvin	.10
228	Ron Davis	.10
229	Tom Hume	.10
230	Marc Hill	.10
231	Dennis Martinez	.10
232	Jim Gantner	.10
233	Larry Pashnick	.10
234	Dave Collins	.10
235	Tom Burgmeier	.10
236	Ken Landreaux	.10
237	John Denny	.10
238	Hal McRae	.10
239	Matt Keough	.10
240	Doug Flynn	.10
241	Fred Lynn	.10
242	Billy Sample	.10
243	Tom Paciorek	.10
244	Joe Sambito	.10
245	Sid Monge	.10
246	Ken Oberkfell	.10
247	Joe Pittman (Photo actually Juan Eichelberger.)	.10
248	Mario Soto	.10
249	Claudell Washington	.10
250	Rick Rhoden	.10
251	Darrell Evans	.10
252	Steve Henderson	.10
253	Manny Castillo	.10
254	Craig Swan	.10
255	Joey McLaughlin	.10
256	Pete Redfern	.10
257	Ken Singleton	.10
258	Robin Yount	1.25
259	Elias Sosa	.10
260	Bob Ojeda	.10
261	Bobby Murcer	.10
262	Candy Maldonado **RC**	.10
263	Rick Waits	.10
264	Greg Pryor	.10
265	Bob Owchinko	.10
266	Chris Speier	.10
267	Bruce Kison	.10
268	Mark Wagner	.10
269	Steve Kemp	.10
270	Phil Garner	.10
271	Gene Richards	.10
272	Renie Martin	.10
273	Dave Roberts	.10
274	Dan Driessen	.10
275	Rufino Linares	.10
276	Lee Lacy	.10
277	Ryne Sandberg **RC**	12.00
278	Darrell Porter	.10
279	Cal Ripken, Jr.	4.00
280	Jamie Easterly	.10
281	Bill Fahey	.10
282	Glenn Hoffman	.10
283	Willie Randolph	.10
284	Fernando Valenzuela	.10
285	Alan Bannister	.10
286	Paul Splittorff	.10
287	Joe Rudi	.10
288	Bill Gullickson	.10
289	Danny Darwin	.10
290	Andy Hassler	.10
291	Ernesto Escarrega	.10
292	Steve Mura	.10
293	Tony Scott	.10
294	Manny Trillo	.10
295	Greg Harris	.10
296	Luis DeLeon	.10
297	Kent Tekulve	.10
298	Atlee Hammaker	.10
299	Bruce Benedict	.10
300	Fergie Jenkins	.75
301	Dave Kingman	.10
302	Bill Caudill	.10
303	John Castino	.10
304	Ernie Whitt	.10
305	Randy S. Johnson	.10
306	Garth Iorg	.10
307	Gaylord Perry	.75
308	Ed Lynch	.10
309	Keith Moreland	.10
310	Rafael Ramirez	.10
311	Bill Madlock	.10
312	Milt May	.10
313	John Montefusco	.10
314	Wayne Krenchicki	.10
315	George Vukovich	.10
316	Joaquin Andujar	.10
317	Craig Reynolds	.10
318	Rick Burleson	.10
319	Richard Dotson	.10
320	Steve Rogers	.10
321	Dave Schmidt	.10
322	Bud Black **RC**	.15
323	Jeff Burroughs	.10
324	Von Hayes	.10
325	Butch Wynegar	.10
326	Carl Yastrzemski	1.50
327	Ron Roenicke	.10
328	Howard Johnson **RC**	1.00
329	Rick Dempsey	.10
330a	Jim Slaton (One yellow box on back.)	.25
330b	Jim Slaton (Two yellow boxes on back.)	.10
331	Benny Ayala	.10
332	Ted Simmons	.10
333	Lou Whitaker	.10
334	Chuck Rainey	.10
335	Lou Piniella	.15
336	Steve Sax	.10
337	Toby Harrah	.10
338	George Brett	2.50
339	Davey Lopes	.10
340	Gary Carter	1.25
341	John Grubb	.10
342	Tim Foli	.10
343	Jim Kaat	.15
344	Mike LaCoss	.10
345	Larry Christenson	.10
346	Juan Bonilla	.10
347	Omar Moreno	.10
348	Chili Davis	.10
349	Tommy Boggs	.10
350	Rusty Staub	.15
351	Bump Wills	.10
352	Rick Sweet	.10
353	Jim Gott **RC**	.15
354	Terry Felton	.10
355	Jim Kern	.10
356	Bill Almon	.10
357	Tippy Martinez	.10
358	Roy Howell	.10
359	Dan Petry	.10
360	Jerry Mumphrey	.10
361	Mark Clear	.10
362	Mike Marshall	.10
363	Lary Sorensen	.10
364	Amos Otis	.10
365	Rick Langford	.10
366	Brad Mills	.10
367	Brian Downing	.10
368	Mike Richardt	.10
369	Aurelio Rodriguez	.10
370	Dave Smith	.10
371	Tug McGraw	.10
372	Doug Bair	.10
373	Ruppert Jones	.10
374	Alex Trevino	.10
375	Ken Dayley	.10
376	Rod Scurry	.10
377	Bob Brenly	.10
378	Scot Thompson	.10
379	Julio Cruz	.10
380	John Stearns	.10
381	Dale Murray	.10
382	Frank Viola **RC**	1.50
383	Al Bumbry	.10
384	Ben Oglivie	.10
385	Dave Tobik	.10
386	Bob Stanley	.10
387	Andre Robertson	.10
388	Jorge Orta	.10
389	Ed Whitson	.10
390	Don Hood	.10
391	Tom Underwood	.10
392	Tim Wallach	.10
393	Steve Renko	.10
394	Mickey Rivers	.10
395	Greg Luzinski	.10
396	Art Howe	.10
397	Alan Wiggins	.10
398	Jim Barr	.10
399	Ivan DeJesus	.10
400	Tom Lawless **RC**	.10
401	Bob Walk	.10
402	Jimmy Smith	.10
403	Lee Smith	.20
404	George Hendrick	.10
405	Eddie Murray	1.25
406	Marshall Edwards	.10
407	Lance Parrish	.10
408	Carney Lansford	.10
409	Dave Winfield	1.25
410	Bob Welch	.10
411	Larry Milbourne	.10
412	Dennis Leonard	.10
413	Dan Meyer	.10
414	Charlie Lea	.10
415	Rick Honeycutt	.10
416	Mike Witt	.10
417	Steve Trout	.10
418	Glenn Brummer	.10
419	Denny Walling	.10
420	Gary Matthews	.10
421	Charlie Liebrandt (Leibrandt)	.10
422	Juan Eichelberger	.10
423	Matt Guante (Cecilio) **RC**	.10
424	Bill Laskey	.10
425	Jerry Royster	.10
426	Dickie Noles	.10
427	George Foster	.10
428	Mike Moore **RC**	.25
429	Gary Ward	.10
430	Barry Bonnell	.10
431	Ron Washington	.10
432	Rance Mulliniks	.10
433	Mike Stanton	.10
434	Jesse Orosco	.10
435	Larry Bowa	.10
436	Biff Pocoroba	.10
437	Johnny Ray	.10
438	Joe Morgan	1.25
439	Eric Show **RC**	.15
440	Larry Biittner	.10
441	Greg Gross	.10
442	Gene Tenace	.10
443	Danny Heep	.10
444	Bobby Clark	.10
445	Kevin Hickey	.10
446	Scott Sanderson	.10
447	Frank Tanana	.10
448	Cesar Geronimo	.10
449	Jimmy Sexton	.10
450	Mike Hargrove	.10
451	Doyle Alexander	.10
452	Dwight Evans	.10
453	Terry Forster	.10
454	Tom Brookens	.10
455	Rich Dauer	.10
456	Rob Picciolo	.10
457	Terry Crowley	.10
458	Ned Yost	.10
459	Kirk Gibson	.10
460	Reid Nichols	.10
461	Oscar Gamble	.10
462	Dusty Baker	.10
463	Jack Perconte	.10
464	Frank White	.10
465	Mickey Klutts	.10
466	Warren Cromartie	.10
467	Larry Parrish	.10
468	Bobby Grich	.10
469	Dane Iorg	.10
470	Joe Niekro	.10
471	Ed Farmer	.10
472	Tim Flannery	.10
473	Dave Parker	.10
474	Jeff Leonard	.10
475	Al Hrabosky	.10
476	Ron Hodges	.10
477	Leon Durham	.10
478	Jim Essian	.10
479	Roy Lee Jackson	.10
480	Brad Havens	.10
481	Joe Price	.10
482	Tony Bernazard	.10
483	Scott McGregor	.10
484	Paul Molitor	1.25
485	Mike Ivie	.10
486	Ken Griffey	.10
487	Dennis Eckersley	1.00
488	Steve Garvey	.40
489	Mike Fischlin	.10
490	U.L. Washington	.10
491	Steve McCatty	.10
492	Roy Johnson	.10
493	Don Baylor	.10
494	Bobby Johnson	.10
495	Mike Squires	.10
496	Bert Roberge	.10
497	Dick Ruthven	.10
498	Tito Landrum	.10
499	Sixto Lezcano	.10
500	Johnny Bench	1.50
501	Larry Whisenton	.10
502	Manny Sarmiento	.10
503	Fred Breining	.10
504	Bill Campbell	.10
505	Todd Cruz	.10
506	Bob Bailor	.10
507	Dave Stieb	.10
508	Al Williams	.10
509	Dan Ford	.10
510	Gorman Thomas	.10
511	Chet Lemon	.10
512	Mike Torrez	.10
513	Shane Rawley	.10
514	Mark Belanger	.10
515	Rodney Craig	.10
516	Onix Concepcion	.10
517	Mike Heath	.10
518	Andre Dawson	.50
519	Luis Sanchez	.10
520	Terry Bogener	.10
521	Rudy Law	.10
522	Ray Knight	.10
523	Joe Lefebvre	.10
524	Jim Wohlford	.10
525	Julio Franco **RC**	2.00
526	Ron Oester	.10
527	Rick Mahler	.10
528	Steve Nicosia	.10
529	Junior Kennedy	.10
530a	Whitey Herzog (One yellow box on back.)	.25
530b	Whitey Herzog (Two yellow boxes on back.)	.15
531a	Don Sutton (Blue frame.)	.75
531b	Don Sutton (Green frame.)	.75
532	Mark Brouhard	.10
533a	Sparky Anderson (One yellow box on back.)	.50
533b	Sparky Anderson (Two yellow boxes on back.)	.50
534	Roger LaFrancois	.10
535	George Frazier	.10
536	Tom Niedenfuer	.10
537	Ed Glynn	.10
538	Lee May	.10
539	Bob Kearney	.10
540	Tim Raines	.10
541	Paul Mirabella	.10
542	Luis Tiant	.10
543	Ron LeFlore	.10
544	Dave LaPoint **RC**	.15
545	Randy Moffitt	.10
546	Luis Aguayo	.10
547	Brad Lesley	.10
548	Luis Salazar	.10
549	John Candelaria	.10
550	Dave Bergman	.10
551	Bob Watson	.10
552	Pat Tabler	.10
553	Brent Gaff	.10
554	Al Cowens	.10
555	Tom Brunansky	.10
556	Lloyd Moseby	.10
557a	Pascual Perez (Twins)	.25
557b	Pascual Perez (Braves)	.10

558	Willie Upshaw	.10
559	Richie Zisk	.10
560	Pat Zachry	.10
561	Jay Johnstone	.10
562	Carlos Diaz	.10
563	John Tudor	.10
564	Frank Robinson	.50
565	Dave Edwards	.10
566	Paul Householder	.10
567	Ron Reed	.10
568	Mike Ramsey	.10
569	Kiko Garcia	.10
570	Tommy John	.10
571	Tony LaRussa	.10
572	Joel Youngblood	.10
573	Wayne Tolleson **RC**	.10
574	Keith Creel	.10
575	Billy Martin	.10
576	Jerry Dybzinski	.10
577	Rick Cerone	.10
578	Tony Perez	1.00
579	Greg Brock **RC**	.10
580	Glen Wilson (Glenn)	.10
581	Tim Stoddard	.10
582	Bob McClure	.10
583	Jim Dwyer	.10
584	Ed Romero	.10
585	Larry Herndon	.10
586	Wade Boggs **RC**	10.00
587	Jay Howell	.10
588	Dave Stewart	.10
589	Bert Blyleven	.10
590	Dick Howser	.10
591	Wayne Gross	.10
592	Terry Francona	.10
593	Don Werner	.10
594	Bill Stein	.10
595	Jesse Barfield	.10
596	Bobby Molinaro	.10
597	Mike Vail	.10
598	Tony Gwynn **RC**	12.00
599	Gary Rajsich	.10
600	Jerry Ujdur	.10
601	Cliff Johnson	.10
602	Jerry White	.10
603	Bryan Clark	.10
604	Joe Ferguson	.10
605	Guy Sularz	.10
606a	Ozzie Virgil (Green frame around photo.)	.25
606b	Ozzie Virgil (Orange frame around photo.)	.10
607	Terry Harper	.10
608	Harvey Kuenn	.10
609	Jim Sundberg	.10
610	Willie Stargell	1.25
611	Reggie Smith	.10
612	Rob Wilfong	.10
613	Joe Niekro, Phil Niekro Niekro Brothers	.25
614	Lee Elia	.10
615	Mickey Hatcher	.10
616	Jerry Hairston Sr.	.10
617	John Martin	.10
618	Wally Backman	.10
619	Storm Davis **RC**	.15
620	Alan Knicely	.10
621	John Stuper	.10
622	Matt Sinatro	.10
623	Gene Petralli **RC**	.10
624	Duane Walker	.10
625	Dick Williams	.10
626	Pat Corrales	.10
627	Vern Ruhle	.10
628	Joe Torre	.10
629	Anthony Johnson	.10
630	Steve Howe	.10
631	Gary Woods	.10
632	Lamarr Hoyt (LaMarr)	.10
633	Steve Swisher	.10
634	Terry Leach	.10
635	Jeff Newman	.10
636	Brett Butler	.10
637	Gary Gray	.10
638	Lee Mazzilli	.10
639a	Ron Jackson (A's)	2.50
639b	Ron Jackson (Angels - green frame around photo.)	.25
639c	Ron Jackson (Angels - red frame around photo.)	.15
640	Juan Beniquez	.10
641	Dave Rucker	.10
642	Luis Pujols	.10
643	Rick Monday	.10
644	Hosken Powell	.10
645	San Diego Chicken	.20
646	Dave Engle	.10
647	Dick Davis	.10
648	Vida Blue, Joe Morgan, Frank Robinson MVP's	.15
649	Al Chambers	.10
650	Jesus Vega	.10
651	Jeff Jones	.10
652	Marvis Foley	.10
653	Ty Cobb (puzzle)	.10
----	Dick Perez DK checklist (No word "Checklist" on back.)	.25
----	Dick Perez DK Checklist (Word "Checklist"on back.)	.10
----	Checklist 27-130	.10
----	Checklist 131-234	.10
----	Checklist 235-338	.10
----	Checklist 339-442	.10
----	Checklist 443-546	.10
----	Checklist 547-653	.10

1984 Donruss

	NM/M
Unopened Fact. Set (658):	150.00
Complete Set (660):	75.00
Common Player:	.15
Duke Snider Puzzle:	2.00
Wax Pack (15):	4.50
Wax Box (36):	150.00
Rack Pack (45):	15.00

A	Rollie Fingers, Gaylord Perry Living Legends	1.50
B	Johnny Bench, Carl Yastrzemski Living Legends	4.00
1a	Robin Yount/DK (Steel)	2.50
1b	Robin Yount/DK (Steele)	3.00
2a	Dave Concepcion/DK (Steel)	.25
2b	Dave Concepcion/DK (Steele)	.35
3a	Dwayne Murphy/DK (Steel)	.25
3b	Dwayne Murphy/DK (Steele)	.35
4a	John Castino/DK (Steel)	.25
4b	John Castino/DK (Steele)	.35
5a	Leon Durham/DK (Steel)	.25
5b	Leon Durham/DK (Steele)	.35
6a	Rusty Staub/DK (Steel)	.30
6b	Rusty Staub/DK (Steele)	.45
7a	Jack Clark/DK (Steel)	.25
7b	Jack Clark/DK (Steele)	.35
8a	Dave Dravecky/DK (Steel)	.25
8b	Dave Draveck/DK (Steele)	.35
9a	Al Oliver/DK (Steel)	.35
9b	Al Oliver/DK (Steele)	.50
10a	Dave Righetti/DK (Steel)	.25
10b	Dave Righetti/DK (Steele)	.35
11a	Hal McRae/DK (Steel)	.25
11b	Hal McRae/DK (Steele)	.35
12a	Ray Knight/DK (Steel)	.25
12b	Ray Knight/DK (Steele)	.35
13a	Bruce Sutter/DK (Steel)	2.50
13b	Bruce Sutter/DK (Steele)	3.00
14a	Bob Horner/DK (Steel)	.25
14b	Bob Horner/DK(Steele)	.35
15a	Lance Parrish/DK (Steel)	.25
15b	Lance Parrish/DK (Steele)	.35
16a	Matt Young/DK (Steel)	.25
16b	Matt Young/DK (Steele)	.35
17a	Fred Lynn/DK (Steel)	.35
17b	Fred Lynn/DK (Steele)	.50
18a	Ron Kittle/DK (Steel)	.25
18b	Ron Kittle/DK (Steele)	.35
19a	Jim Clancy/DK (Steel)	.25
19b	Jim Clancy/DK (Steele)	.35
20a	Bill Madlock/DK (Steel)	.25
20b	Bill Madlock/DK (Steele)	.35
21a	Larry Parrish/DK (Steel)	.25
21b	Larry Parrish/DK (Steele)	.35
22a	Eddie Murray/DK (Steel)	2.50
22b	Eddie Murray/DK (Steele)	3.00
23a	Mike Schmidt/DK (Steel)	3.00
23b	Mike Schmidt/DK (Steele)	4.00
24a	Pedro Guerrero/DK (Steel)	.25
24b	Pedro Guerrero/DK (Steele)	.35
25a	Andre Thornton/DK (Steel)	.25
25b	Andre Thornton/DK (Steele)	.35
26a	Wade Boggs/DK (Steel)	3.00
26b	Wade Boggs/DK (Steele)	3.00
27	Joel Skinner **RC** (RR)	.15
28	Tom Dunbar (RR)	.15
29a	Mike Stenhouse (RR) (no number on back)	.15
29b	Mike Stenhouse (RR) (29 on back)	1.00
30a	Ron Darling **RC** (RR) (no number on back)	1.50
30b	Ron Darling **RC** (RR) (30 on back)	2.50
31	Dion James **RC** (RR)	.15
32	Tony Fernandez **RC** (RR)	3.00
33	Angel Salazar (RR)	.15
34	Kevin McReynolds **RC** (RR)	1.50
35	Dick Schofield **RC** (RR)	.20
36	Brad Komminsk **RC** (RR)	.15
37	Tim Teufel **RC** (RR)	.25
38	Doug Frobel (RR)	.15
39	Greg Gagne **RC** (RR)	1.00
40	Mike Fuentes (RR)	.15
41	Joe Carter **RC** (RR)	8.00
42	Mike Brown (RR)	.15
43	Mike Jeffcoat (RR)	.15
44	Sid Fernandez **RC** (RR)	2.00
45	Brian Dayett (RR)	.15
46	Chris Smith (RR)	.15
47	Eddie Murray	3.00
48	Robin Yount	3.00
49	Lance Parrish	.15
50	Jim Rice	1.00
51	Dave Winfield	3.00
52	Fernando Valenzuela	.15
53	George Brett	5.00
54	Rickey Henderson	3.00
55	Gary Carter	3.00
56	Buddy Bell	.15
57	Reggie Jackson	5.00
58	Harold Baines	.15
59	Ozzie Smith	4.00
60	Nolan Ryan	8.00
61	Pete Rose	7.50
62	Ron Oester	.15
63	Steve Garvey	.75
64	Jason Thompson	.15
65	Jack Clark	.15
66	Dale Murphy	1.50
67	Leon Durham	.15
68	Darryl Strawberry	2.00
69	Richie Zisk	.15
70	Kent Hrbek	.15
71	Dave Stieb	.15
72	Ken Schrom	.15
73	George Bell	.15
74	John Moses	.15
75	Ed Lynch	.15
76	Chuck Rainey	.15
77	Biff Pocoroba	.15
78	Cecilio Guante	.15
79	Jim Barr	.15
80	Kurt Bevacqua	.15
81	Tom Foley	.15
82	Joe Lefebvre	.15
83	Andy Van Slyke **RC**	2.00
84	Bob Lillis	.15
85	Rick Adams	.15
86	Jerry Hairston Sr.	.15
87	Bob James	.15
88	Joe Altobelli	.15
89	Ed Romero	.15
90	John Grubb	.15
91	John Henry Johnson	.15
92	Juan Espino	.15
93	Candy Maldonado	.15
94	Andre Thornton	.15
95	Onix Concepcion	.15
96	Don Hill **RC**	.15
97	Andre Dawson	1.50
98	Frank Tanana	.15
99	Curt Wilkerson **RC**	.15
100	Larry Gura	.15
101	Dwayne Murphy	.15
102	Tom Brennan	.15
103	Dave Righetti	.15
104	Steve Sax	.15
105	Dan Petry	.15
106	Cal Ripken, Jr.	8.00
107	Paul Molitor	3.00
108	Fred Lynn	.15
109	Neil Allen	.15
110	Joe Niekro	.15
111	Steve Carlton	3.00
112	Terry Kennedy	.15
113	Bill Madlock	.15
114	Chili Davis	.15
115	Jim Gantner	.15
116	Tom Seaver	4.00
117	Bill Buckner	.15
118	Bill Caudill	.15
119	Jim Clancy	.15
120	John Castino	.15
121	Dave Concepcion	.15
122	Greg Luzinski	.15
123	Mike Boddicker	.15
124	Pete Ladd	.15
125	Juan Berenguer	.15
126	John Montefusco	.15
127	Ed Jurak	.15
128	Tom Niedenfuer	.15
129	Bert Blyleven	.25
130	Bud Black	.15
131	Gorman Heimueller	.15
132	Dan Schatzeder	.15
133	Ron Jackson	.15
134	Tom Henke **RC**	1.00
135	Kevin Hickey	.15
136	Mike Scott	.15
137	Bo Diaz	.15
138	Glenn Brummer	.15
139	Sid Monge	.15
140	Rich Gale	.15
141	Brett Butler	.15
142	Brian Harper	.15
143	John Rabb	.15
144	Gary Woods	.15
145	Pat Putnam	.15
146	Jim Acker **RC**	.15
147	Mickey Hatcher	.15
148	Todd Cruz	.15
149	Tom Tellmann	.15
150	John Wockenfuss	.15
151	Wade Boggs	5.00
152	Don Baylor	.15
153	Bob Welch	.15
154	Alan Bannister	.15
155	Willie Aikens	.15
156	Jeff Burroughs	.15
157	Bryan Little	.15
158	Bob Boone	.15
159	Dave Hostetler	.15
160	Jerry Dybzinski	.15
161	Mike Madden	.15
162	Luis DeLeon	.15
163	Willie Hernandez	.15
164	Frank Pastore	.15
165	Rick Camp	.15
166	Lee Mazzilli	.15
167	Scot Thompson	.15
168	Bob Forsch	.15
169	Mike Flanagan	.15
170	Rick Manning	.15
171	Chet Lemon	.15
172	Jerry Remy	.15
173	Ron Guidry	.20
174	Pedro Guerrero	.15
175	Willie Wilson	.15
176	Carney Lansford	.15
177	Al Oliver	.15
178	Jim Sundberg	.15
179	Bobby Grich	.15
180	Richard Dotson	.15
181	Joaquin Andujar	.15
182	Jose Cruz	.15
183	Mike Schmidt	5.00
184	Gary Redus **RC**	.25
185	Garry Templeton	.15
186	Tony Pena	.15
187	Greg Minton	.15
188	Phil Niekro	1.50
189	Fergie Jenkins	1.50
190	Mookie Wilson	.15
191	Jim Beattie	.15
192	Gary Ward	.15
193	Jesse Barfield	.15
194	Pete Filson	.15
195	Roy Lee Jackson	.15
196	Rick Sweet	.15
197	Jesse Orosco	.15
198	Steve Lake **RC**	.15
199	Ken Dayley	.15
200	Manny Sarmiento	.15
201	Mark Davis	.15
202	Tim Flannery	.15
203	Bill Scherrer	.15
204	Al Holland	.15
205	David Von Ohlen	.15
206	Mike LaCoss	.15
207	Juan Beniquez	.15
208	Juan Agosto **RC**	.15
209	Bobby Ramos	.15
210	Al Bumbry	.15
211	Mark Brouhard	.15
212	Howard Bailey	.15
213	Bruce Hurst	.15
214	Bob Shirley	.15
215	Pat Zachry	.15
216	Julio Franco	.15
217	Mike Armstrong	.15
218	Dave Beard	.15
219	Steve Rogers	.15
220	John Butcher	.15
221	Mike Smithson **RC**	.15
222	Frank White	.15
223	Mike Heath	.15
224	Chris Bando	.15
225	Roy Smalley	.15
226	Dusty Baker	.15
227	Lou Whitaker	.15
228	John Lowenstein	.15
229	Ben Oglivie	.15
230	Doug DeCinces	.15
231	Lonnie Smith	.15
232	Ray Knight	.15
233	Gary Matthews	.15
234	Juan Bonilla	.15
235	Rod Scurry	.15
236	Atlee Hammaker	.15
237	Mike Caldwell	.15
238	Keith Hernandez	.15
239	Larry Bowa	.15
240	Tony Bernazard	.15
241	Damaso Garcia	.15
242	Tom Brunansky	.15
243	Dan Driessen	.15
244	Ron Kittle	.15
245	Tim Stoddard	.15
246	Bob L. Gibson	.15
247	Marty Castillo	.15
248	Don Mattingly **RC**	25.00
249	Jeff Newman	.15
250	Alejandro Pena **RC**	.15
251	Toby Harrah	.15
252	Cesar Geronimo	.15
253	Tom Underwood	.15
254	Doug Flynn	.15
255	Andy Hassler	.15
256	Odell Jones	.15
257	Rudy Law	.15
258	Harry Spilman	.15
259	Marty Bystrom	.15
260	Dave Rucker	.15
261	Ruppert Jones	.15
262	Jeff Jones	.15
263	Gerald Perry **RC**	.15
264	Gene Tenace	.15
265	Brad Wellman	.15
266	Dickie Noles	.15
267	Jamie Allen	.15
268	Jim Gott	.15
269	Ron Davis	.15
270	Benny Ayala	.15
271	Ned Yost	.15
272	Dave Rozema	.15
273	Dave Stapleton	.15
274	Lou Piniella	.25
275	Jose Morales	.15

276 Brod Perkins .15
277 Butch Davis .15
278 Tony Phillips .15
279 Jeff Reardon .15
280 Ken Forsch .15
281 Pete O'Brien **RC** .15
282 Tom Paciorek .15
283 Frank LaCorte .15
284 Tim Lollar .15
285 Greg Gross .15
286 Alex Trevino .15
287 Gene Garber .15
288 Dave Parker .15
289 Lee Smith .25
290 Dave LaPoint .15
291 John Shelby **RC** .15
292 Charlie Moore .15
293 Alan Trammell .15
294 Tony Armas .15
295 Shane Rawley .15
296 Greg Brock .15
297 Hal McRae .15
298 Mike Davis .15
299 Tim Raines .15
300 Bucky Dent .15
301 Tommy John .25
302 Carlton Fisk 3.00
303 Darrell Porter .15
304 Dickie Thon .15
305 Garry Maddox .15
306 Cesar Cedeno .15
307 Gary Lucas .15
308 Johnny Ray .15
309 Andy McGaffigan .15
310 Claudell Washington .15
311 Ryne Sandberg 5.00
312 George Foster .15
313 Spike Owen **RC** .25
314 Gary Gaetti .15
315 Willie Upshaw .15
316 Al Williams .15
317 Jorge Orta .15
318 Orlando Mercado .15
319 Junior Ortiz **RC** .15
320 Mike Proly .15
321 Randy S. Johnson .15
322 Jim Morrison .15
323 Max Venable .15
324 Tony Gwynn 5.00
325 Duane Walker .15
326 Ozzie Virgil .15
327 Jeff Lahti .15
328 Bill Dawley **RC** .15
329 Rob Wilfong .15
330 Marc Hill .15
331 Ray Burris .15
332 Allan Ramirez .15
333 Chuck Porter .15
334 Wayne Krenchicki .15
335 Gary Allenson .15
336 Bob Meacham **RC** .15
337 Joe Beckwith .15
338 Rick Sutcliffe .15
339 Mark Huismann **RC** .15
340 Tim Conroy **RC** .15
341 Scott Sanderson .15
342 Larry Biittner .15
343 Dave Stewart .15
344 Darryl Motley .15
345 Chris Codiroli **RC** .15
346 Rick Behenna .15
347 Andre Robertson .15
348 Mike Marshall .15
349 Larry Herndon .15
350 Rich Dauer .15
351 Cecil Cooper .15
352 Rod Carew 3.00
353 Willie McGee .15
354 Phil Garner .15
355 Joe Morgan 3.00
356 Luis Salazar .15
357 John Candelaria .15
358 Bill Laskey .15
359 Bob McClure .15
360 Dave Kingman .15
361 Ron Cey .15
362 Matt Young **RC** .15
363 Lloyd Moseby .15
364 Frank Viola .15
365 Eddie Milner .15
366 Floyd Bannister .15
367 Dan Ford .15
368 Moose Haas .15
369 Doug Bair .15
370 Ray Fontenot **RC** .15
371 Luis Aponte .15
372 Jack Fimple .15
373 Neal Heaton **RC** .15
374 Greg Pryor .15
375 Wayne Gross .15
376 Charlie Lea .15
377 Steve Lubratich .15
378 Jon Matlack .15
379 Julio Cruz .15
380 John Mizerock .15
381 Kevin Gross **RC** .15
382 Mike Ramsey .15
383 Doug Gwosdz .15
384 Kelly Paris .15
385 Pete Falcone .15
386 Milt May .15
387 Fred Breining .15
388 Craig Lefferts **RC** .25
389 Steve Henderson .15
390 Randy Moffitt .15
391 Ron Washington .15
392 Gary Roenicke .15
393 Tom Candiotti **RC** .75
394 Larry Pashnick .15
395 Dwight Evans .15
396 Goose Gossage .25
397 Derrel Thomas .15
398 Juan Eichelberger .15
399 Leon Roberts .15
400 Davey Lopes .15
401 Bill Gullickson .15
402 Geoff Zahn .15
403 Billy Sample .15
404 Mike Squires .15
405 Craig Reynolds .15
406 Eric Show .15
407 John Denny .15
408 Dann Bilardello .15
409 Bruce Benedict .15
410 Kent Tekulve .15
411 Mel Hall .15
412 John Stuper .15
413 Rick Dempsey .15
414 Don Sutton 1.50
415 Jack Morris .15
416 John Tudor .15
417 Willie Randolph .15
418 Jerry Reuss .15
419 Don Slaught .15
420 Steve McCatty .15
421 Tim Wallach .15
422 Larry Parrish .15
423 Brian Downing .15
424 Britt Burns .15
425 David Green .15
426 Jerry Mumphrey .15
427 Ivan DeJesus .15
428 Mario Soto .15
429 Gene Richards .15
430 Dale Berra .15
431 Darrell Evans .15
432 Glenn Hubbard .15
433 Jody Davis .15
434 Danny Heep .15
435 Ed Nunez **RC** .15
436 Bobby Castillo .15
437 Ernie Whitt .15
438 Scott Ullger .15
439 Doyle Alexander .15
440 Domingo Ramos .15
441 Craig Swan .15
442 Warren Brusstar .15
443 Len Barker .15
444 Mike Easler .15
445 Renie Martin .15
446 Dennis Rasmussen **RC** .25
447 Ted Power .15
448 Charlie Hudson **RC** .15
449 Danny Cox **RC** .15
450 Kevin Bass .15
451 Daryl Sconiers .15
452 Scott Fletcher .15
453 Bryn Smith .15
454 Jim Dwyer .15
455 Rob Picciolo .15
456 Enos Cabell .15
457 Dennis Boyd **RC** .20
458 Butch Wynegar .15
459 Burt Hooton .15
460 Ron Hassey .15
461 Danny Jackson **RC** .15
462 Bob Kearney .15
463 Terry Francona .15
464 Wayne Tolleson .15
465 Mickey Rivers .15
466 John Wathan .15
467 Bill Almon .15
468 George Vukovich .15
469 Steve Kemp .15
470 Ken Landreaux .15
471 Milt Wilcox .15
472 Tippy Martinez .15
473 Ted Simmons .15
474 Tim Foli .15
475 George Hendrick .15
476 Terry Puhl .15
477 Von Hayes .15
478 Bobby Brown .15
479 Lee Lacy .15
480 Joel Youngblood .15
481 Jim Slaton .15
482 Mike Fitzgerald **RC** .15
483 Keith Moreland .15
484 Ron Roenicke .15
485 Luis Leal .15
486 Bryan Oelkers .15
487 Bruce Berenyi .15
488 LaMarr Hoyt .15
489 Joe Nolan .15
490 Marshall Edwards .15
491 Mike Laga **RC** .15
492 Rick Cerone .15
493 Mike Miller (Rick) .15
494 Rick Honeycutt .15
495 Mike Hargrove .15
496 Joe Simpson .15
497 Keith Atherton **RC** .15
498 Chris Welsh .15
499 Bruce Kison .15
500 Bob Johnson .15
501 Jerry Koosman .15
502 Frank DiPino .15
503 Tony Perez 2.00
504 Ken Oberkfell .15
505 Mark Thurmond **RC** .15
506 Joe Price .15
507 Pascual Perez .15
508 Marvell Wynne **RC** .15
509 Mike Krukow .15
510 Dick Ruthven .15
511 Al Cowens .15
512 Cliff Johnson .15
513 Randy Bush **RC** .15
514 Sammy Stewart .15
515 Bill Schroeder **RC** .15
516 Aurelio Lopez .15
517 Mike Brown .15
518 Graig Nettles .25
519 Dave Sax .15
520 Gerry Willard .15
521 Paul Splittorff .15
522 Tom Burgmeier .15
523 Chris Speier .15
524 Bobby Clark .15
525 George Wright .15
526 Dennis Lamp .15
527 Tony Scott .15
528 Ed Whitson .15
529 Ron Reed .15
530 Charlie Puleo .15
531 Jerry Royster .15
532 Don Robinson .15
533 Steve Trout .15
534 Bruce Sutter 2.50
535 Bob Horner .15
536 Pat Tabler .15
537 Chris Chambliss .15
538 Bob Ojeda .15
539 Alan Ashby .15
540 Jay Johnstone .15
541 Bob Dernier .15
542 Brook Jacoby **RC** .15
543 U.L. Washington .15
544 Danny Darwin .15
545 Kiko Garcia .15
546 Vance Law .15
547 Tug McGraw .15
548 Dave Smith .15
549 Len Matuszek .15
550 Tom Hume .15
551 Dave Dravecky .15
552 Rick Rhoden .15
553 Duane Kuiper .15
554 Rusty Staub .20
555 Bill Campbell .15
556 Mike Torrez .15
557 Dave Henderson .15
558 Len Whitehouse .15
559 Barry Bonnell .15
560 Rick Lysander .15
561 Garth Iorg .15
562 Bryan Clark .15
563 Brian Giles .15
564 Vern Ruhle .15
565 Steve Bedrosian .15
566 Larry McWilliams .15
567 Jeff Leonard .15
568 Alan Wiggins .15
569 Jeff Russell **RC** .15
570 Salome Barojas .15
571 Dane Iorg .15
572 Bob Knepper .15
573 Gary Lavelle .15
574 Gorman Thomas .15
575 Manny Trillo .15
576 Jim Palmer 3.00
577 Dale Murray .15
578 Tom Brookens .15
579 Rich Gedman .15
580 Bill Doran **RC** .25
581 Steve Yeager .15
582 Dan Spillner .15
583 Dan Quisenberry .15
584 Rance Mulliniks .15
585 Storm Davis .15
586 Dave Schmidt .15
587 Bill Russell .15
588 Pat Sheridan **RC** .15
589 Rafael Ramirez .15
590 Bud Anderson .15
591 George Frazier .15
592 Lee Tunnell **RC** .15
593 Kirk Gibson .15
594 Scott McGregor .15
595 Bob Bailor .15
596 Tom Herr .15
597 Luis Sanchez .15
598 Dave Engle .15
599 Craig McMurtry **RC** .15
600 Carlos Diaz .15
601 Tom O'Malley .15
602 Nick Esasky **RC** .15
603 Ron Hodges .15
604 Ed Vande Berg .15
605 Alfredo Griffin .15
606 Glenn Hoffman .15
607 Hubie Brooks .15
608 Richard Barnes (Photo actually Neal Heaton.) .15
609 Greg Walker **RC** .15
610 Ken Singleton .15
611 Mark Clear .15
612 Buck Martinez .15
613 Ken Griffey .20
614 Reid Nichols .15
615 Doug Sisk **RC** .15
616 Bob Brenly .15
617 Joey McLaughlin .15
618 Glenn Wilson .15
619 Bob Stoddard .15
620 Len Sakata (Lenn) .15
621 Mike Young **RC** .15
622 John Stefero .15
623 Carmelo Martinez **RC** .15
624 Dave Bergman .15
625 David Green, Willie McGee, Lonnie Smith, Ozzie Smith Runnin' Reds .75
626 Rudy May .15
627 Matt Keough .15
628 Jose DeLeon **RC** .15
629 Jim Essian .15
630 Darnell Coles **RC** .15
631 Mike Warren .15
632 Del Crandall .15
633 Dennis Martinez .15
634 Mike Moore .15
635 Lary Sorensen .15
636 Ricky Nelson .15
637 Omar Moreno .15
638 Charlie Hough .15
639 Dennis Eckersley 2.50
640 Walt Terrell **RC** .15
641 Denny Walling .15
642 Dave Anderson **RC** .15
643 Jose Oquendo **RC** .15
644 Bob Stanley .15
645 Dave Geisel .15
646 Scott Garrelts **RC** .15
647 Gary Pettis **RC** .15
648 Duke Snider Puzzle Card .15
649 Johnnie LeMaster .15
650 Dave Collins .15
651 San Diego Chicken .25
---- Checklist 1-26 DK (Perez-Steel on back.) .15
---- Checklist 1-26 DK (Perez-Steele on back.) .15
---- Checklist 27-130 .15
---- Checklist 131-234 .15
---- Checklist 235-338 .15
---- Checklist 339-442 .15
---- Checklist 443-546 .15
---- Checklist 547-651 .15

1985 Donruss

	NM/M
Unopened Fact. Set (660):	75.00
Complete Set (660):	50.00
Common Player:	.10
Lou Gehrig Puzzle:	3.00
Wax Pack (15):	4.00
Wax Box (36):	120.00
Rack Pack (45):	7.00

1 Ryne Sandberg/DK 2.50
2 Doug DeCinces/DK .10
3 Rich Dotson/DK .10
4 Bert Blyleven/DK .25
5 Lou Whitaker/DK .10
6 Dan Quisenberry/DK .10
7 Don Mattingly/DK 4.00
8 Carney Lansford/DK .10
9 Frank Tanana/DK .10
10 Willie Upshaw/DK .10
11 Claudell Washington/DK .10
12 Mike Marshall/DK .10
13 Joaquin Andujar/DK .10
14 Cal Ripken, Jr./DK 6.00
15 Jim Rice/DK .75
16 Don Sutton/DK 1.00
17 Frank Viola/DK .10
18 Alvin Davis/DK .10
19 Mario Soto/DK .10
20 Jose Cruz/DK .10
21 Charlie Lea/DK .10
22 Jesse Orosco/DK .10
23 Juan Samuel/DK .10
24 Tony Pena/DK .10
25 Tony Gwynn/DK 2.50
26 Bob Brenly/DK .10
27 Danny Tartabull **RC** (RR) 1.50
28 Mike Bielecki **RC** (RR). .10
29 Steve Lyons **RC** (RR). .25
30 Jeff Reed **RC** (RR) .10
31 Tony Brewer (RR) .10
32 John Morris **RC** (RR) .10
33 Daryl Boston **RC** (RR) .15
34 Alfonso Pulido (RR) .10
35 Steve Kiefer **RC** (RR) .10
36 Larry Sheets **RC** (RR) .10
37 Scott Bradley **RC** (RR) .10

38	Calvin Schiraldi **RC** (RR)	.10
39	Shawon Dunston **RC** (RR)	1.50
40	Charlie Mitchell (RR)	.10
41	Billy Hatcher **RC** (RR)	.15
42	Russ Stephans (RR)	.10
43	Alejandro Sanchez (RR)	.10
44	Steve Jeltz **RC** (RR)	.10
45	Jim Traber **RC** (RR)	.10
46	Doug Loman (RR)	.10
47	Eddie Murray	2.00
48	Robin Yount	2.00
49	Lance Parrish	.10
50	Jim Rice	.75
51	Dave Winfield	2.00
52	Fernando Valenzuela	.10
53	George Brett	3.00
54	Dave Kingman	.10
55	Gary Carter	2.00
56	Buddy Bell	.10
57	Reggie Jackson	3.00
58	Harold Baines	.10
59	Ozzie Smith	2.00
60	Nolan Ryan	6.00
61	Mike Schmidt	3.00
62	Dave Parker	.10
63	Tony Gwynn	2.50
64	Tony Pena	.10
65	Jack Clark	.10
66	Dale Murphy	.60
67	Ryne Sandberg	2.50
68	Keith Hernandez	.10
69	Alvin Davis	.10
70	Kent Hrbek	.10
71	Willie Upshaw	.10
72	Dave Engle	.10
73	Alfredo Griffin	.10
74a	Jack Perconte (Last line of highlights begins "Batted .346...")	.10
74b	Jack Perconte (Last line of highlights begins "Led the ...")	.15
75	Jesse Orosco	.10
76	Jody Davis	.10
77	Bob Horner	.10
78	Larry McWilliams	.10
79	Joel Youngblood	.10
80	Alan Wiggins	.10
81	Ron Oester	.10
82	Ozzie Virgil	.10
83	Ricky Horton **RC**	.10
84	Bill Doran	.10
85	Rod Carew	2.00
86	LaMarr Hoyt	.10
87	Tim Wallach	.10
88	Mike Flanagan	.10
89	Jim Sundberg	.10
90	Chet Lemon	.10
91	Bob Stanley	.10
92	Willie Randolph	.10
93	Bill Russell	.10
94	Julio Franco	.10
95	Dan Quisenberry	.10
96	Bill Caudill	.10
97	Bill Gullickson	.10
98	Danny Darwin	.10
99	Curtis Wilkerson	.10
100	Bud Black	.10
101	Tony Phillips	.10
102	Tony Bernazard	.10
103	Jay Howell	.10
104	Burt Hooton	.10
105	Milt Wilcox	.10
106	Rich Dauer	.10
107	Don Sutton	1.00
108	Mike Witt	.10
109	Bruce Sutter	1.50
110	Enos Cabell	.10
111	John Denny	.10
112	Dave Dravecky	.10
113	Marvell Wynne	.10
114	Johnnie LeMaster	.10
115	Chuck Porter	.10
116	John Gibbons	.10
117	Keith Moreland	.10
118	Darnell Coles	.10
119	Dennis Lamp	.10
120	Ron Davis	.10
121	Nick Esasky	.10
122	Vance Law	.10
123	Gary Roenicke	.10
124	Bill Schroeder	.10
125	Dave Rozema	.10
126	Bobby Meacham	.10
127	Marty Barrett	.10
128	R.J. Reynolds **RC**	.15
129	Ernie Camacho	.10
130	Jorge Orta	.10
131	Lary Sorensen	.10
132	Terry Francona	.10
133	Fred Lynn	.10
134	Bobby Jones	.10
135	Jerry Hairston Sr.	.10
136	Kevin Bass	.10
137	Garry Maddox	.10
138	Dave LaPoint	.10
139	Kevin McReynolds	.10
140	Wayne Krenchicki	.10
141	Rafael Ramirez	.10
142	Rod Scurry	.10
143	Greg Minton	.10
144	Tim Stoddard	.10
145	Steve Henderson	.10
146	George Bell	.10
147	Dave Meier	.10
148	Sammy Stewart	.10
149	Mark Brouhard	.10
150	Larry Herndon	.10
151	Oil Can Boyd	.10
152	Brian Dayett	.10
153	Tom Niedenfuer	.10
154	Brook Jacoby	.10
155	Onix Concepcion	.10
156	Tim Conroy	.10
157	Joe Hesketh **RC**	.15
158	Brian Downing	.10
159	Tommy Dunbar	.10
160	Marc Hill	.10
161	Phil Garner	.10
162	Jerry Davis	.10
163	Bill Campbell	.10
164	John Franco **RC**	1.50
165	Len Barker	.10
166	Benny Distefano **RC**	.10
167	George Frazier	.10
168	Tito Landrum	.10
169	Cal Ripken, Jr.	6.00
170	Cecil Cooper	.10
171	Alan Trammell	.10
172	Wade Boggs	2.50
173	Don Baylor	.10
174	Pedro Guerrero	.10
175	Frank White	.10
176	Rickey Henderson	2.00
177	Charlie Lea	.10
178	Pete O'Brien	.10
179	Doug DeCinces	.10
180	Ron Kittle	.10
181	George Hendrick	.10
182	Joe Niekro	.10
183	Juan Samuel	.10
184	Mario Soto	.10
185	Goose Gossage	.15
186	Johnny Ray	.10
187	Bob Brenly	.10
188	Craig McMurtry	.10
189	Leon Durham	.10
190	Dwight Gooden	.25
191	Barry Bonnell	.10
192	Tim Teufel	.10
193	Dave Stieb	.10
194	Mickey Hatcher	.10
195	Jesse Barfield	.10
196	Al Cowens	.10
197	Hubie Brooks	.10
198	Steve Trout	.10
199	Glenn Hubbard	.10
200	Bill Madlock	.10
201	Jeff Robinson **RC**	.10
202	Eric Show	.10
203	Dave Concepcion	.10
204	Ivan DeJesus	.10
205	Neil Allen	.10
206	Jerry Mumphrey	.10
207	Mike Brown	.10
208	Carlton Fisk	2.00
209	Bryn Smith	.10
210	Tippy Martinez	.10
211	Dion James	.10
212	Willie Hernandez	.10
213	Mike Easler	.10
214	Ron Guidry	.10
215	Rick Honeycutt	.10
216	Brett Butler	.10
217	Larry Gura	.10
218	Ray Burris	.10
219	Steve Rogers	.10
220	Frank Tanana	.10
221	Ned Yost	.10
222	Bret Saberhagen	.25
223	Mike Davis	.10
224	Bert Blyleven	.15
225	Steve Kemp	.10
226	Jerry Reuss	.10
227	Darrell Evans	.10
228	Wayne Gross	.10
229	Jim Gantner	.10
230	Bob Boone	.10
231	Lonnie Smith	.10
232	Frank DiPino	.10
233	Jerry Koosman	.10
234	Graig Nettles	.15
235	John Tudor	.10
236	John Rabb	.10
237	Rick Manning	.10
238	Mike Fitzgerald	.10
239	Gary Matthews	.10
240	Jim Presley **RC**	.10
241	Dave Collins	.10
242	Gary Gaetti	.10
243	Dann Bilardello	.10
244	Rudy Law	.10
245	John Lowenstein	.10
246	Tom Tellmann	.10
247	Howard Johnson	.10
248	Ray Fontenot	.10
249	Tony Armas	.10
250	Candy Maldonado	.10
251	Mike Jeffcoat **RC**	.10
252	Dane Iorg	.10
253	Bruce Bochte	.10
254	Pete Rose	5.00
255	Don Aase	.10
256	George Wright	.10
257	Britt Burns	.10
258	Mike Scott	.10
259	Len Matuszek	.10
260	Dave Rucker	.10
261	Craig Lefferts	.10
262	Jay Tibbs **RC**	.10
263	Bruce Benedict	.10
264	Don Robinson	.10
265	Gary Lavelle	.10
266	Scott Sanderson	.10
267	Matt Young	.10
268	Ernie Whitt	.10
269	Houston Jimenez	.10
270	Ken Dixon **RC**	.10
271	Peter Ladd	.10
272	Juan Berenguer	.10
273	Roger Clemens	25.00
274	Rick Cerone	.10
275	Dave Anderson	.10
276	George Vukovich	.10
277	Greg Pryor	.10
278	Mike Warren	.10
279	Bob James	.10
280	Bobby Grich	.10
281	Mike Mason **RC**	.10
282	Ron Reed	.10
283	Alan Ashby	.10
284	Mark Thurmond	.10
285	Joe Lefebvre	.10
286	Ted Power	.10
287	Chris Chambliss	.10
288	Lee Tunnell	.10
289	Rich Bordi	.10
290	Glenn Brummer	.10
291	Mike Boddicker	.10
292	Rollie Fingers	1.00
293	Lou Whitaker	.10
294	Dwight Evans	.10
295	Don Mattingly	5.00
296	Mike Marshall	.10
297	Willie Wilson	.10
298	Mike Heath	.10
299	Tim Raines	.10
300	Larry Parrish	.10
301	Geoff Zahn	.10
302	Rich Dotson	.10
303	David Green	.10
304	Jose Cruz	.10
305	Steve Carlton	2.00
306	Gary Redus	.10
307	Steve Garvey	.40
308	Jose DeLeon	.10
309	Randy Lerch	.10
310	Claudell Washington	.10
311	Lee Smith	.25
312	Darryl Strawberry	.10
313	Jim Beattie	.10
314	John Butcher	.10
315	Damaso Garcia	.10
316	Mike Smithson	.10
317	Luis Leal	.10
318	Ken Phelps	.10
319	Wally Backman	.10
320	Ron Cey	.10
321	Brad Komminsk	.10
322	Jason Thompson	.10
323	Frank Williams **RC**	.10
324	Tim Lollar	.10
325	Eric Davis **RC**	1.50
326	Von Hayes	.10
327	Andy Van Slyke	.10
328	Craig Reynolds	.10
329	Dick Schofield	.10
330	Scott Fletcher	.10
331	Jeff Reardon	.10
332	Rick Dempsey	.10
333	Ben Oglivie	.10
334	Dan Petry	.10
335	Jackie Gutierrez	.10
336	Dave Righetti	.10
337	Alejandro Pena	.10
338	Mel Hall	.10
339	Pat Sheridan	.10
340	Keith Atherton	.10
341	David Palmer	.10
342	Gary Ward	.10
343	Dave Stewart	.10
344	Mark Gubicza **RC**	.50
345	Carney Lansford	.10
346	Jerry Willard	.10
347	Ken Griffey	.10
348	Franklin Stubbs **RC**	.10
349	Aurelio Lopez	.10
350	Al Bumbry	.10
351	Charlie Moore	.10
352	Luis Sanchez	.10
353	Darrell Porter	.10
354	Bill Dawley	.10
355	Charlie Hudson	.10
356	Garry Templeton	.10
357	Cecilio Guante	.10
358	Jeff Leonard	.10
359	Paul Molitor	2.00
360	Ron Gardenhire	.10
361	Larry Bowa	.10
362	Bob Kearney	.10
363	Garth Iorg	.10
364	Tom Brunansky	.10
365	Brad Gulden	.10
366	Greg Walker	.10
367	Mike Young	.10
368	Rick Waits	.10
369	Doug Bair	.10
370	Bob Shirley	.10
371	Bob Ojeda	.10
372	Bob Welch	.10
373	Neal Heaton	.10
374	Danny Jackson (Photo actually Steve Farr.)	.10
375	Donnie Hill	.10
376	Mike Stenhouse	.10
377	Bruce Kison	.10
378	Wayne Tolleson	.10
379	Floyd Bannister	.10
380	Vern Ruhle	.10
381	Tim Corcoran	.10
382	Kurt Kepshire	.10
383	Bobby Brown	.10
384	Dave Van Gorder	.10
385	Rick Mahler	.10
386	Lee Mazzilli	.10
387	Bill Laskey	.10
388	Thad Bosley	.10
389	Al Chambers	.10
390	Tony Fernandez	.10
391	Ron Washington	.10
392	Bill Swaggerty	.10
393	Bob L. Gibson	.10
394	Marty Castillo	.10
395	Steve Crawford	.10
396	Clay Christiansen	.10
397	Bob Bailor	.10
398	Mike Hargrove	.10
399	Charlie Leibrandt	.10
400	Tom Burgmeier	.10
401	Razor Shines	.10
402	Rob Wilfong	.10
403	Tom Henke	.10
404	Al Jones	.10
405	Mike LaCoss	.10
406	Luis DeLeon	.10
407	Greg Gross	.10
408	Tom Hume	.10
409	Rick Camp	.10
410	Milt May	.10
411	Henry Cotto **RC**	.10
412	Dave Von Ohlen	.10
413	Scott McGregor	.10
414	Ted Simmons	.10
415	Jack Morris	.10
416	Bill Buckner	.10
417	Butch Wynegar	.10
418	Steve Sax	.10
419	Steve Balboni	.10
420	Dwayne Murphy	.10
421	Andre Dawson	.65
422	Charlie Hough	.10
423	Tommy John	.15
424a	Tom Seaver (Floyd Bannister photo, left-hander.)	2.00
424b	Tom Seaver (Correct photo.)	7.50
425	Tom Herr	.10
426	Terry Puhl	.10
427	Al Holland	.10
428	Eddie Milner	.10
429	Terry Kennedy	.10
430	John Candelaria	.10
431	Manny Trillo	.10
432	Ken Oberkfell	.10
433	Rick Sutcliffe	.10
434	Ron Darling	.10
435	Spike Owen	.10
436	Frank Viola	.10
437	Lloyd Moseby	.10
438	Kirby Puckett	8.00
439	Jim Clancy	.10
440	Mike Moore	.10
441	Doug Sisk	.10
442	Dennis Eckersley	1.50
443	Gerald Perry	.10
444	Dale Berra	.10
445	Dusty Baker	.10
446	Ed Whitson	.10
447	Cesar Cedeno	.10
448	Rick Schu **RC**	.10
449	Joaquin Andujar	.10
450	Mark Bailey **RC**	.10
451	Ron Romanick **RC**	.10
452	Julio Cruz	.10
453	Miguel Dilone	.10
454	Storm Davis	.10
455	Jaime Cocanower	.10
456	Barbaro Garbey	.10
457	Rich Gedman	.10
458	Phil Niekro	1.00
459	Mike Scioscia	.10
460	Pat Tabler	.10
461	Darryl Motley	.10
462	Chris Codoroli (Codiroli)	.10
463	Doug Flynn	.10
464	Billy Sample	.10
465	Mickey Rivers	.10
466	John Wathan	.10
467	Bill Krueger	.10
468	Andre Thornton	.10
469	Rex Hudler	.10
470	Sid Bream **RC**	.25
471	Kirk Gibson	.10
472	John Shelby	.10
473	Moose Haas	.10
474	Doug Corbett	.10
475	Willie McGee	.10
476	Bob Knepper	.10
477	Kevin Gross	.10
478	Carmelo Martinez	.10
479	Kent Tekulve	.10
480	Chili Davis	.10
481	Bobby Clark	.10
482	Mookie Wilson	.10
483	Dave Owen	.10
484	Ed Nunez	.10
485	Rance Mulliniks	.10
486	Ken Schrom	.10
487	Jeff Russell	.10
488	Tom Paciorek	.10

489 Dan Ford .10
490 Mike Caldwell .10
491 Scottie Earl .10
492 Jose Rijo .10
493 Bruce Hurst .10
494 Ken Landreaux .10
495 Mike Fischlin .10
496 Don Slaught .10
497 Steve McCatty .10
498 Gary Lucas .10
499 Gary Pettis .10
500 Marvis Foley .10
501 Mike Squires .10
502 Jim Pankovitz **RC** .10
503 Luis Aguayo .10
504 Ralph Citarella .10
505 Bruce Bochy .10
506 Bob Owchinko .10
507 Pascual Perez .10
508 Lee Lacy .10
509 Atlee Hammaker .10
510 Bob Dernier .10
511 Ed Vande Berg .10
512 Cliff Johnson .10
513 Len Whitehouse .10
514 Dennis Martinez .10
515 Ed Romero .10
516 Rusty Kuntz .10
517 Rick Miller .10
518 Dennis Rasmussen .10
519 Steve Yeager .10
520 Chris Bando .10
521 U.L. Washington .10
522 Curt Young **RC** .10
523 Angel Salazar .10
524 Curt Kaufman .10
525 Odell Jones .10
526 Juan Agosto .10
527 Denny Walling .10
528 Andy Hawkins .10
529 Sixto Lezcano .10
530 Skeeter Barnes .10
531 Randy S. Johnson .10
532 Jim Morrison .10
533 Warren Brusstar .10
534a Jeff Pendleton **RC** (Error) 1.00
534b Terry Pendleton **RC** (Correct) 4.50
535 Vic Rodriguez .10
536 Bob McClure .10
537 Dave Bergman .10
538 Mark Clear .10
539 Mike Pagliarulo **RC** .25
540 Terry Whitfield .10
541 Joe Beckwith .10
542 Jeff Burroughs .10
543 Dan Schatzeder .10
544 Donnie Scott .10
545 Jim Slaton .10
546 Greg Luzinski .10
547 Mark Salas **RC** .10
548 Dave Smith .10
549 John Wockenfuss .10
550 Frank Pastore .10
551 Tim Flannery .10
552 Rick Rhoden .10
553 Mark Davis .10
554 Jeff Dedmon **RC** .15
555 Gary Woods .10
556 Danny Heep .10
557 Mark Langston .10
558 Darrell Brown .10
559 Jimmy Key .10
560 Rick Lysander .10
561 Doyle Alexander .10
562 Mike Stanton .10
563 Sid Fernandez .10
564 Richie Hebner .10
565 Alex Trevino .10
566 Brian Harper .10
567 Dan Gladden **RC** .25
568 Luis Salazar .10
569 Tom Foley .10
570 Larry Andersen .10
571 Danny Cox .10
572 Joe Sambito .10
573 Juan Beniquez .10
574 Joel Skinner .10
575 Randy St. Claire **RC** .10
576 Floyd Rayford .10
577 Roy Howell .10
578 John Grubb .10
579 Ed Jurak .10
580 John Montefusco .10
581 Orel Hershiser **RC** 3.00
582 Tom Waddell **RC** .10
583 Mark Huismann .10
584 Joe Morgan 2.00
585 Jim Wohlford .10
586 Dave Schmidt .10
587 Jeff Kunkel **RC** .10
588 Hal McRae .10
589 Bill Almon .10
590 Carmen Castillo .10
591 Omar Moreno .10
592 Ken Howell **RC** .10
593 Tom Brookens .10
594 Joe Nolan .10
595 Willie Lozado .10
596 Tom Nieto **RC** .10
597 Walt Terrell .10
598 Al Oliver .10
599 Shane Rawley .10
600 Denny Gonzalez **RC** .10
601 Mark Grant **RC** .10
602 Mike Armstrong .10
603 George Foster .10
604 Davey Lopes .10
605 Salome Barojas .10
606 Roy Lee Jackson .10
607 Pete Filson .10
608 Duane Walker .10
609 Glenn Wilson .10
610 Rafael Santana **RC** .10
611 Roy Smith .10
612 Ruppert Jones .10
613 Joe Cowley .10
614 Al Nipper **RC** (Photo actually Mike Brown.) .15
615 Gene Nelson .10
616 Joe Carter .10
617 Ray Knight .10
618 Chuck Rainey .10
619 Dan Driessen .10
620 Daryl Sconiers .10
621 Bill Stein .10
622 Roy Smalley .10
623 Ed Lynch .10
624 Jeff Stone **RC** .10
625 Bruce Berenyi .10
626 Kelvin Chapman .10
627 Joe Price .10
628 Steve Bedrosian .10
629 Vic Mata .10
630 Mike Krukow .10
631 Phil Bradley **RC** .15
632 Jim Gott .10
633 Randy Bush .10
634 Tom Browning **RC** .25
635 Lou Gehrig Puzzle Card .10
636 Reid Nichols .10
637 Dan Pasqua **RC** .25
638 German Rivera .10
639 Don Schulze **RC** .10
640a Mike Jones (Last line of highlights begins "Was 11- 7...") .10
640b Mike Jones (Last line of highlights begins "Spent some ...") .15
641 Pete Rose 4.00
642 Wade Rowdon **RC** .10
643 Jerry Narron .10
644 Darrell Miller **RC** .10
645 Tim Hulett **RC** .10
646 Andy McGaffigan .10
647 Kurt Bevacqua .10
648 John Russell **RC** .10
649 Ron Robinson **RC** .10
650 Donnie Moore .10
651a Don Mattingly, Dave Winfield Two for the Title (Yellow letters.) 3.00
651b Don Mattingly, Dave Winfield Two for the Title (White letters.) 4.50
652 Tim Laudner .10
653 Steve Farr **RC** .10
---- Checklist 1-26 DK .10
---- Checklist 27-130 .10
---- Checklist 131-234 .10
---- Checklist 235-338 .10
---- Checklist 339-442 .10
---- Checklist 443-546 .10
---- Checklist 547-653 .10

1986 Donruss

	NM/M
Unopened Factory Set (660):	35.00
Complete Set (660):	30.00
Common Player:	.05
Hank Aaron Puzzle:	3.00
Wax Pack (15):	1.25
Wax Box (36):	35.00
Rack Pack (45):	2.50

1 Kirk Gibson/DK .15
2 Goose Gossage/DK .15
3 Willie McGee/DK .10
4 George Bell/DK .05
5 Tony Armas/DK .05
6 Chili Davis/DK .05
7 Cecil Cooper/DK .05
8 Mike Boddicker/DK .05
9 Davey Lopes/DK .05
10 Bill Doran/DK .05
11 Bret Saberhagen/DK .10
12 Brett Butler/DK .10
13 Harold Baines/DK .15
14 Mike Davis/DK .05
15 Tony Perez/DK 1.00
16 Willie Randolph/DK .05
17 Bob Boone/DK .10
18 Orel Hershiser/DK .10
19 Johnny Ray/DK .05
20 Gary Ward/DK .05
21 Rick Mahler/DK .05
22 Phil Bradley/DK .05
23 Jerry Koosman/DK .10
24 Tom Brunansky/DK .05
25 Andre Dawson/DK .50
26 Dwight Gooden (DK) .10
27 Kal Daniels **RC** (RR) .15
28 Fred McGriff **RC** (RR) 4.00
29 Cory Snyder **RC** (RR) .10
30 Jose Guzman **RC** (RR) .05
31 Ty Gainey **RC** (RR) .05
32 Johnny Abrego **RC** (RR) .05
33a Andres Galarraga **RC** (RR) (Accent mark over e of Andres on back.) 2.00
33b Andres Galarraga **RC** (RR) (No accent mark.) 2.00
34 Dave Shipanoff **RC** (RR) .05
35 Mark McLemore **RC** (RR) .50
36 Marty Clary **RC** (RR) .05
37 Paul O'Neill **RC** (RR) 2.00
38 Danny Tartabull (RR) .05
39 Jose Canseco **RC** (RR) 6.00
40 Juan Nieves **RC** (RR) .05
41 Lance McCullers **RC** (RR) .05
42 Rick Surhoff **RC** (RR) .05
43 Todd Worrell **RC** (RR) .25
44 Bob Kipper (RR) .05
45 John Habyan **RC** (RR) .05
46 Mike Woodard **RC** (RR) .05
47 Mike Boddicker .05
48 Robin Yount 1.50
49 Lou Whitaker .05
50 Dennis Boyd .05
51 Rickey Henderson 1.50
52 Mike Marshall .05
53 George Brett 2.50
54 Dave Kingman .05
55 Hubie Brooks .05
56 Oddibe McDowell **RC** .15
57 Doug DeCinces .05
58 Britt Burns .05
59 Ozzie Smith 2.00
60 Jose Cruz .05
61 Mike Schmidt 2.50
62 Pete Rose 3.00
63 Steve Garvey .40
64 Tony Pena .05
65 Chili Davis .05
66 Dale Murphy .40
67 Ryne Sandberg 2.00
68 Gary Carter 1.50
69 Alvin Davis .05
70 Kent Hrbek .05
71 George Bell .05
72 Kirby Puckett 2.00
73 Lloyd Moseby .05
74 Bob Kearney .05
75 Dwight Gooden .05
76 Gary Matthews .05
77 Rick Mahler .05
78 Benny Distefano .05
79 Jeff Leonard .05
80 Kevin McReynolds .05
81 Ron Oester .05
82 John Russell .05
83 Tommy Herr .05
84 Jerry Mumphrey .05
85 Ron Romanick .05
86 Daryl Boston .05
87 Andre Dawson .50
88 Eddie Murray 1.50
89 Dion James .05
90 Chet Lemon .05
91 Bob Stanley .05
92 Willie Randolph .05
93 Mike Scioscia .05
94 Tom Waddell .05
95 Danny Jackson .05
96 Mike Davis .05
97 Mike Fitzgerald .05
98 Gary Ward .05
99 Pete O'Brien .05
100 Bret Saberhagen .05
101 Alfredo Griffin .05
102 Brett Butler .05
103 Ron Guidry .15
104 Jerry Reuss .05
105 Jack Morris .05
106 Rick Dempsey .05
107 Ray Burris .05
108 Brian Downing .05
109 Willie McGee .05
110 Bill Doran .05
111 Kent Tekulve .05
112 Tony Gwynn 2.00
113 Marvell Wynne .05
114 David Green .05
115 Jim Gantner .05
116 George Foster .05
117 Steve Trout .05
118 Mark Langston .05
119 Tony Fernandez .05
120 John Butcher .05
121 Ron Robinson .05
122 Dan Spillner .05
123 Mike Young .05
124 Paul Molitor 1.50
125 Kirk Gibson .05
126 Ken Griffey .05
127 Tony Armas .05
128 Mariano Duncan **RC** .15
129 Pat Tabler (Mr. Clutch) .05
130 Frank White .05
131 Carney Lansford .05
132 Vance Law .05
133 Dick Schofield .05
134 Wayne Tolleson .05
135 Greg Walker .05
136 Denny Walling .05
137 Ozzie Virgil .05
138 Ricky Horton .05
139 LaMarr Hoyt .05
140 Wayne Krenchicki .05
141 Glenn Hubbard .05
142 Cecilio Guante .05
143 Mike Krukow .05
144 Lee Smith .15
145 Edwin Nunez .05
146 Dave Stieb .05
147 Mike Smithson .05
148 Ken Dixon .05
149 Danny Darwin .05
150 Chris Pittaro .05
151 Bill Buckner .05
152 Mike Pagliarulo .05
153 Bill Russell .05
154 Brook Jacoby .05
155 Pat Sheridan .05
156 Mike Gallego **RC** .05
157 Jim Wohlford .05
158 Gary Pettis .05
159 Toby Harrah .05
160 Richard Dotson .05
161 Bob Knepper .05
162 Dave Dravecky .05
163 Greg Gross .05
164 Eric Davis .05
165 Gerald Perry .05
166 Rick Rhoden .05
167 Keith Moreland .05
168 Jack Clark .05
169 Storm Davis .05
170 Cecil Cooper .05
171 Alan Trammell .05
172 Roger Clemens 2.50
173 Don Mattingly 2.50
174 Pedro Guerrero .05
175 Willie Wilson .05
176 Dwayne Murphy .05
177 Tim Raines .05
178 Larry Parrish .05
179 Mike Witt .05
180 Harold Baines .05
181 Vince Coleman **RC** .35
182 Jeff Heathcock **RC** .05
183 Steve Carlton 1.50
184 Mario Soto .05
185 Goose Gossage .10
186 Johnny Ray .05
187 Dan Gladden .05
188 Bob Horner .05
189 Rick Sutcliffe .05
190 Keith Hernandez .05
191 Phil Bradley .05
192 Tom Brunansky .05
193 Jesse Barfield .05
194 Frank Viola .05
195 Willie Upshaw .05
196 Jim Beattie .05
197 Darryl Strawberry .05
198 Ron Cey .05
199 Steve Bedrosian .05
200 Steve Kemp .05
201 Manny Trillo .05
202 Garry Templeton .05
203 Dave Parker .05
204 John Denny .05
205 Terry Pendleton .05
206 Terry Puhl .05
207 Bobby Grich .05
208 Ozzie Guillen **RC** 2.00
209 Jeff Reardon .05
210 Cal Ripken, Jr. 3.00
211 Bill Schroeder .05
212 Dan Petry .05
213 Jim Rice .50
214 Dave Righetti .05
215 Fernando Valenzuela .05
216 Julio Franco .05
217 Darryl Motley .05
218 Dave Collins .05
219 Tim Wallach .05
220 George Wright .05
221 Tommy Dunbar .05
222 Steve Balboni .05
223 Jay Howell .05
224 Joe Carter .05
225 Ed Whitson .05
226 Orel Hershiser .05
227 Willie Hernandez .05
228 Lee Lacy .05
229 Rollie Fingers 1.00
230 Bob Boone .05
231 Joaquin Andujar .05
232 Craig Reynolds .05
233 Shane Rawley .05
234 Eric Show .05
235 Jose DeLeon .05
236 Jose Uribe **RC** .05
237 Moose Haas .05
238 Wally Backman .05
239 Dennis Eckersley 1.25

240	Mike Moore	.05
241	Damaso Garcia	.05
242	Tim Teufel	.05
243	Dave Concepcion	.05
244	Floyd Bannister	.05
245	Fred Lynn	.05
246	Charlie Moore	.05
247	Walt Terrell	.05
248	Dave Winfield	1.50
249	Dwight Evans	.05
250	Dennis Powell **RC**	.05
251	Andre Thornton	.05
252	Onix Concepcion	.05
253	Mike Heath	.05
254a	David Palmer (2B on front)	.05
254b	David Palmer (P on front)	.15
255	Donnie Moore	.05
256	Curtis Wilkerson	.05
257	Julio Cruz	.05
258	Nolan Ryan	3.00
259	Jeff Stone	.05
260a	John Tudor (1981 Games is .18)	.05
260b	John Tudor (1981 Games is 18)	.15
261	Mark Thurmond	.05
262	Jay Tibbs	.05
263	Rafael Ramirez	.05
264	Larry McWilliams	.05
265	Mark Davis	.05
266	Bob Dernier	.05
267	Matt Young	.05
268	Jim Clancy	.05
269	Mickey Hatcher	.05
270	Sammy Stewart	.05
271	Bob L. Gibson	.05
272	Nelson Simmons	.05
273	Rich Gedman	.05
274	Butch Wynegar	.05
275	Ken Howell	.05
276	Mel Hall	.05
277	Jim Sundberg	.05
278	Chris Codiroli	.05
279	Herman Winningham **RC**	.05
280	Rod Carew	1.50
281	Don Slaught	.05
282	Scott Fletcher	.05
283	Bill Dawley	.05
284	Andy Hawkins	.05
285	Glenn Wilson	.05
286	Nick Esasky	.05
287	Claudell Washington	.05
288	Lee Mazzilli	.05
289	Jody Davis	.05
290	Darrell Porter	.05
291	Scott McGregor	.05
292	Ted Simmons	.05
293	Aurelio Lopez	.05
294	Marty Barrett	.05
295	Dale Berra	.05
296	Greg Brock	.05
297	Charlie Leibrandt	.05
298	Bill Krueger	.05
299	Bryn Smith	.05
300	Burt Hooton	.05
301	Stu Cliburn **RC**	.05
302	Luis Salazar	.05
303	Ken Dayley	.05
304	Frank DiPino	.05
305	Von Hayes	.05
306a	Gary Redus (1983 2B is .20)	.05
306b	Gary Redus (1983 2B is 20)	.15
307	Craig Lefferts	.05
308	Sam Khalifa	.05
309	Scott Garrelts	.05
310	Rick Cerone	.05
311	Shawon Dunston	.05
312	Howard Johnson	.05
313	Jim Presley	.05
314	Gary Gaetti	.05
315	Luis Leal	.05
316	Mark Salas	.05
317	Bill Caudill	.05
318	Dave Henderson	.05
319	Rafael Santana	.05
320	Leon Durham	.05
321	Bruce Sutter	1.25
322	Jason Thompson	.05
323	Bob Brenly	.05
324	Carmelo Martinez	.05
325	Eddie Milner	.05
326	Juan Samuel	.05
327	Tom Nieto	.05
328	Dave Smith	.05
329	Urbano Lugo **RC**	.05
330	Joel Skinner	.05
331	Bill Gullickson	.05
332	Floyd Rayford	.05
333	Ben Oglivie	.05
334	Lance Parrish	.05
335	Jackie Gutierrez	.05
336	Dennis Rasmussen	.05
337	Terry Whitfield	.05
338	Neal Heaton	.05
339	Jorge Orta	.05
340	Donnie Hill	.05
341	Joe Hesketh	.05
342	Charlie Hough	.05
343	Dave Rozema	.05
344	Greg Pryor	.05
345	Mickey Tettleton	.05
346	George Vukovich	.05
347	Don Baylor	.05
348	Carlos Diaz	.05
349	Barbaro Garbey	.05
350	Larry Sheets	.05
351	Ted Higuera **RC**	.10
352	Juan Beniquez	.05
353	Bob Forsch	.05
354	Mark Bailey	.05
355	Larry Andersen	.05
356	Terry Kennedy	.05
357	Don Robinson	.05
358	Jim Gott	.05
359	Earnest Riles **RC**	.05
360	John Christensen **RC**	.05
361	Ray Fontenot	.05
362	Spike Owen	.05
363	Jim Acker	.05
364a	Ron Davis (Last line in highlights ends with "...inMay.")	.05
364b	Ron Davis (Last line in highlights ends with "...relievers (9).")	.15
365	Tom Hume	.05
366	Carlton Fisk	1.50
367	Nate Snell	.05
368	Rick Manning	.05
369	Darrell Evans	.05
370	Ron Hassey	.05
371	Wade Boggs	2.00
372	Rick Honeycutt	.05
373	Chris Bando	.05
374	Bud Black	.05
375	Steve Henderson	.05
376	Charlie Lea	.05
377	Reggie Jackson	2.50
378	Dave Schmidt	.05
379	Bob James	.05
380	Glenn Davis	.05
381	Tim Corcoran	.05
382	Danny Cox	.05
383	Tim Flannery	.05
384	Tom Browning	.05
385	Rick Camp	.05
386	Jim Morrison	.05
387	Dave LaPoint	.05
388	Davey Lopes	.05
389	Al Cowens	.05
390	Doyle Alexander	.05
391	Tim Laudner	.05
392	Don Aase	.05
393	Jaime Cocanower	.05
394	Randy O'Neal	.05
395	Mike Easler	.05
396	Scott Bradley	.05
397	Tom Niedenfuer	.05
398	Jerry Willard	.05
399	Lonnie Smith	.05
400	Bruce Bochte	.05
401	Terry Francona	.05
402	Jim Slaton	.05
403	Bill Stein	.05
404	Tim Hulett	.05
405	Alan Ashby	.05
406	Tim Stoddard	.05
407	Garry Maddox	.05
408	Ted Power	.05
409	Len Barker	.05
410	Denny Gonzalez	.05
411	George Frazier	.05
412	Andy Van Slyke	.05
413	Jim Dwyer	.05
414	Paul Householder	.05
415	Alejandro Sanchez	.05
416	Steve Crawford	.05
417	Dan Pasqua	.05
418	Enos Cabell	.05
419	Mike Jones	.05
420	Steve Kiefer	.05
421	Tim Burke **RC**	.05
422	Mike Mason	.05
423	Ruppert Jones	.05
424	Jerry Hairston Sr.	.05
425	Tito Landrum	.05
426	Jeff Calhoun	.05
427	Don Carman **RC**	.05
428	Tony Perez	1.00
429	Jerry Davis	.05
430	Bob Walk	.05
431	Brad Wellman	.05
432	Terry Forster	.05
433	Billy Hatcher	.05
434	Clint Hurdle	.05
435	Ivan Calderon **RC**	.05
436	Pete Filson	.05
437	Tom Henke	.05
438	Dave Engle	.05
439	Tom Filer	.05
440	Gorman Thomas	.05
441	Rick Aguilera **RC**	.25
442	Scott Sanderson	.05
443	Jeff Dedmon	.05
444	Joe Orsulak **RC**	.10
445	Atlee Hammaker	.05
446	Jerry Royster	.05
447	Buddy Bell	.05
448	Dave Rucker	.05
449	Ivan DeJesus	.05
450	Jim Pankovits	.05
451	Jerry Narron	.05
452	Bryan Little	.05
453	Gary Lucas	.05
454	Dennis Martinez	.05
455	Ed Romero	.05
456	Bob Melvin **RC**	.05
457	Glenn Hoffman	.05
458	Bob Shirley	.05
459	Bob Welch	.05
460	Carmen Castillo	.05
461	Dave Leeper	.05
462	Tim Birtsas **RC**	.05
463	Randy St. Claire	.05
464	Chris Welsh	.05
465	Greg Harris	.05
466	Lynn Jones	.05
467	Dusty Baker	.05
468	Roy Smith	.05
469	Andre Robertson	.05
470	Ken Landreaux	.05
471	Dave Bergman	.05
472	Gary Roenicke	.05
473	Pete Vuckovich	.05
474	Kirk McCaskill **RC**	.10
475	Jeff Lahti	.05
476	Mike Scott	.05
477	Darren Daulton **RC**	1.50
478	Graig Nettles	.15
479	Bill Almon	.05
480	Greg Minton	.05
481	Randy Ready	.05
482	Len Dykstra **RC**	1.50
483	Thad Bosley	.05
484	Harold Reynolds **RC**	1.00
485	Al Oliver	.05
486	Roy Smalley	.05
487	John Franco	.05
488	Juan Agosto	.05
489	Al Pardo	.05
490	Bill Wegman **RC**	.05
491	Frank Tanana	.05
492	Brian Fisher **RC**	.05
493	Mark Clear	.05
494	Len Matuszek	.05
495	Ramon Romero	.05
496	John Wathan	.05
497	Rob Picciolo	.05
498	U.L. Washington	.05
499	John Candelaria	.05
500	Duane Walker	.05
501	Gene Nelson	.05
502	John Mizerock	.05
503	Luis Aguayo	.05
504	Kurt Kepshire	.05
505	Ed Wojna	.05
506	Joe Price	.05
507	Milt Thompson **RC**	.05
508	Junior Ortiz	.05
509	Vida Blue	.05
510	Steve Engel	.05
511	Karl Best	.05
512	Cecil Fielder **RC**	2.00
513	Frank Eufemia	.05
514	Tippy Martinez	.05
515	Billy Robidoux **RC**	.05
516	Bill Scherrer	.05
517	Bruce Hurst	.05
518	Rich Bordi	.05
519	Steve Yeager	.05
520	Tony Bernazard	.05
521	Hal McRae	.05
522	Jose Rijo	.05
523	Mitch Webster **RC**	.05
524	Jack Howell **RC**	.05
525	Alan Bannister	.05
526	Ron Kittle	.05
527	Phil Garner	.05
528	Kurt Bevacqua	.05
529	Kevin Gross	.05
530	Bo Diaz	.05
531	Ken Oberkfell	.05
532	Rick Reuschel	.05
533	Ron Meridith	.05
534	Steve Braun	.05
535	Wayne Gross	.05
536	Ray Searage	.05
537	Tom Brookens	.05
538	Al Nipper	.05
539	Billy Sample	.05
540	Steve Sax	.05
541	Dan Quisenberry	.05
542	Tony Phillips	.05
543	Floyd Youmans **RC**	.05
544	Steve Buechele **RC**	.05
545	Craig Gerber	.05
546	Joe DeSa	.05
547	Brian Harper	.05
548	Kevin Bass	.05
549	Tom Foley	.05
550	Dave Van Gorder	.05
551	Bruce Bochy	.05
552	R.J. Reynolds	.05
553	Chris Brown **RC**	.05
554	Bruce Benedict	.05
555	Warren Brusstar	.05
556	Danny Heep	.05
557	Darnell Coles	.05
558	Greg Gagne	.05
559	Ernie Whitt	.05
560	Ron Washington	.05
561	Jimmy Key	.05
562	Billy Swift	.05
563	Ron Darling	.05
564	Dick Ruthven	.05
565	Zane Smith	.05
566	Sid Bream	.05
567a	Joel Youngblood (P on front)	.05
567b	Joel Youngblood (IF on front)	.15
568	Mario Ramirez	.05
569	Tom Runnells	.05
570	Rick Schu	.05
571	Bill Campbell	.05
572	Dickie Thon	.05
573	Al Holland	.05
574	Reid Nichols	.05
575	Bert Roberge	.05
576	Mike Flanagan	.05
577	Tim Leary	.05
578	Mike Laga	.05
579	Steve Lyons	.05
580	Phil Niekro	1.00
581	Gilberto Reyes	.05
582	Jamie Easterly	.05
583	Mark Gubicza	.05
584	Stan Javier **RC**	.15
585	Bill Laskey	.05
586	Jeff Russell	.05
587	Dickie Noles	.05
588	Steve Farr	.05
589	Steve Ontiveros **RC**	.05
590	Mike Hargrove	.05
591	Marty Bystrom	.05
592	Franklin Stubbs	.05
593	Larry Herndon	.05
594	Bill Swaggerty	.05
595	Carlos Ponce	.05
596	Pat Perry **RC**	.05
597	Ray Knight	.05
598	Steve Lombardozzi **RC**	.05
599	Brad Havens	.05
600	Pat Clements **RC**	.05
601	Joe Niekro	.05
602	Hank Aaron Puzzle Card	.05
603	Dwayne Henry **RC**	.05
604	Mookie Wilson	.05
605	Buddy Biancalana	.05
606	Rance Mulliniks	.05
607	Alan Wiggins	.05
608	Joe Cowley	.05
609a	Tom Seaver (Green stripes around name.)	1.50
609b	Tom Seaver (Yellow stripes around name.)	2.00
610	Neil Allen	.05
611	Don Sutton	1.00
612	Fred Toliver **RC**	.05
613	Jay Baller	.05
614	Marc Sullivan	.05
615	John Grubb	.05
616	Bruce Kison	.05
617	Bill Madlock	.05
618	Chris Chambliss	.05
619	Dave Stewart	.05
620	Tim Lollar	.05
621	Gary Lavelle	.05
622	Charles Hudson	.05
623	Joel Davis **RC**	.05
624	Joe Johnson **RC**	.05
625	Sid Fernandez	.05
626	Dennis Lamp	.05
627	Terry Harper	.05
628	Jack Lazorko	.05
629	Roger McDowell **RC**	.25
630	Mark Funderburk	.05
631	Ed Lynch	.05
632	Rudy Law	.05
633	Roger Mason **RC**	.05
634	Mike Felder **RC**	.05
635	Ken Schrom	.05
636	Bob Ojeda	.05
637	Ed Vande Berg	.05
638	Bobby Meacham	.05
639	Cliff Johnson	.05
640	Garth Iorg	.05
641	Dan Driessen	.05
642	Mike Brown	.05
643	John Shelby	.05
644	Pete Rose (RB)	.50
645	Joe Niekro, Phil Niekro Knuckle Brothers	.25
646	Jesse Orosco	.05
647	Billy Beane **RC**	.05
648	Cesar Cedeno	.05
649	Bert Blyleven	.15
650	Max Venable	.05
651	Vince Coleman, Willie McGee Fleet Feet	.25
652	Calvin Schiraldi	.05
653	Pete Rose King of Kings	3.00
----	Checklist 1-26 DK	.05
----	Checklist 27-130 (45 is Beane)	.05
----	Checklist 27-130 (45 is Habyan)	.05
----	Checklist 131-234	.05
----	Checklist 235-338	.05
----	Checklist 339-442	.05
----	Checklist 443-546	.05
----	Checklist 547-653	.05

Rookies

		NM/M
Unopened Set (56):		35.00
Opened Set (56):		30.00
Common Player:		.05
1	Wally Joyner **RC**	.50
2	Tracy Jones	.05
3	Allan Anderson	.05
4	Ed Correa	.05
5	Reggie Williams	.05
6	Charlie Kerfeld	.05
7	Andres Galarraga	.15
8	Bob Tewksbury	.05
9	Al Newman	.05
10	Andres Thomas	.05
11	Barry Bonds **RC**	25.00
12	Juan Nieves	.05
13	Mark Eichhorn	.05
14	Dan Plesac	.05
15	Cory Snyder	.05
16	Kelly Gruber	.05

17 Kevin Mitchell **RC** .25
18 Steve Lombardozzi .05
19 Mitch Williams .05
20 John Cerutti .05
21 Todd Worrell .05
22 Jose Canseco 2.00
23 Pete Incaviglia **RC** .15
24 Jose Guzman .05
25 Scott Bailes .05
26 Greg Mathews .05
27 Eric King .05
28 Paul Assenmacher .05
29 Jeff Sellers .05
30 Bobby Bonilla **RC** .25
31 Doug Drabek **RC** .25
32 Will Clark **RC** 1.00
33 Bip Roberts .05
34 Jim Deshaies .05
35 Mike LaValliere .05
36 Scott Bankhead .05
37 Dale Sveum .05
38 Bo Jackson **RC** 2.00
39 Rob Thompson .05
40 Eric Plunk .05
41 Bill Bathe .05
42 John Kruk **RC** .25
43 Andy Allanson .05
44 Mark Portugal .05
45 Danny Tartabull .05
46 Bob Kipper .05
47 Gene Walter .05
48 Rey Quinonez .05
49 Bobby Witt .05
50 Bill Mooneyham .05
51 John Cangelosi .05
52 Ruben Sierra **RC** .25
53 Rob Woodward .05
54 Ed Hearn .05
55 Joel McKeon .05
56 Checklist 1-56 .05

1987 Donruss

	NM/M
Unopened Fact. Set (660):	40.00
Complete Set (660):	30.00
Common Player:	.05
Roberto Clemente Puzzle:	2.50
Wax Pack (15):	1.25
Wax Box (36):	35.00
Rack Pack (45):	3.00
Jumbo Rack (75):	4.00

1 Wally Joyner/DK .25
2 Roger Clemens/DK 1.00
3 Dale Murphy/DK .25
4 Darryl Strawberry/DK .10
5 Ozzie Smith/DK .75
6 Jose Canseco/DK .40
7 Charlie Hough/DK .05
8 Brook Jacoby/DK .05
9 Fred Lynn/DK .10
10 Rick Rhoden/DK .05
11 Chris Brown/DK .05
12 Von Hayes/DK .05
13 Jack Morris/DK .10
14a Kevin McReynolds/DK (No yellow stripe on back.) .25
14b Kevin McReynolds/DK (Yellow stripe on back.) .25
15 George Brett/DK 1.00
16 Ted Higuera/DK .05
17 Hubie Brooks/DK .05
18 Mike Scott (DK) .05
19 Kirby Puckett (DK) .75
20 Dave Winfield (DK) .60
21 Lloyd Moseby (DK) .05
22a Eric Davis/DK (No yellow stripe on back.) .25
22b Eric Davis/DK (Yellow stripe on back.) .15
23 Jim Presley/DK .05
24 Keith Moreland/DK .05
25a Greg Walker/DK (No yellow stripe on back.) .25
25b Greg Walker/DK (Yellow stripe on back.) .10
26 Steve Sax/DK .10
27 Checklist 1-27 .05
28 B.J. Surhoff **RC** (RR) .30
29 Randy Myers **RC** (RR) .50
30 Ken Gerhart **RC** (RR) .05
31 Benito Santiago (RR) .15
32 Greg Swindell **RC** (RR) .15
33 Mike Birkbeck **RC** (RR) .05
34 Terry Steinbach **RC** (RR) .25
35 Bo Jackson (RR) 1.50
36 Greg Maddux **RC** (RR) 8.00
37 Jim Lindeman **RC** (RR) .05
38 Devon White **RC** (RR) .75
39 Eric Bell **RC** (RR) .05
40 Will Fraser **RC** (RR) .05
41 Jerry Browne **RC** (RR) .05
42 Chris James **RC** (RR) .05
43 Rafael Palmeiro **RC** (RR) 4.00
44 Pat Dodson **RC** (RR) .05
45 Duane Ward **RC** (RR) .10
46 Mark McGwire (RR) 6.00
47 Bruce Fields **RC** (RR) (Photo actually Darnell Coles.) .10
48 Eddie Murray .60
49 Ted Higuera .05
50 Kirk Gibson .05
51 Oil Can Boyd .05
52 Don Mattingly 1.00
53 Pedro Guerrero .05
54 George Brett 1.00
55 Jose Rijo .05
56 Tim Raines .05
57 Ed Correa **RC** .05
58 Mike Witt .05
59 Greg Walker .05
60 Ozzie Smith .75
61 Glenn Davis .05
62 Glenn Wilson .05
63 Tom Browning .05
64 Tony Gwynn .75
65 R.J. Reynolds .05
66 Will Clark .25
67 Ozzie Virgil .05
68 Rick Sutcliffe .05
69 Gary Carter .60
70 Mike Moore .05
71 Bert Blyleven .10
72 Tony Fernandez .05
73 Kent Hrbek .05
74 Lloyd Moseby .05
75 Alvin Davis .05
76 Keith Hernandez .05
77 Ryne Sandberg .75
78 Dale Murphy .40
79 Sid Bream .05
80 Chris Brown .05
81 Steve Garvey .25
82 Mario Soto .05
83 Shane Rawley .05
84 Willie McGee .05
85 Jose Cruz .05
86 Brian Downing .05
87 Ozzie Guillen .05
88 Hubie Brooks .05
89 Cal Ripken, Jr. 2.50
90 Juan Nieves .05
91 Lance Parrish .05
92 Jim Rice .25
93 Ron Guidry .10
94 Fernando Valenzuela .05
95 Andy Allanson **RC** .05
96 Willie Wilson .05
97 Jose Canseco .40
98 Jeff Reardon .05
99 Bobby Witt **RC** .20
100 Checklist 28-133 .05
101 Jose Guzman .05
102 Steve Balboni .05
103 Tony Phillips .05
104 Brook Jacoby .05
105 Dave Winfield .60
106 Orel Hershiser .05
107 Lou Whitaker .05
108 Fred Lynn .05
109 Bill Wegman .05
110 Donnie Moore .05
111 Jack Clark .05
112 Bob Knepper .05
113 Von Hayes .05
114 Bip Roberts **RC** .25
115 Tony Pena .05
116 Scott Garrelts .05
117 Paul Molitor .60
118 Darryl Strawberry .05
119 Shawon Dunston .05
120 Jim Presley .05
121 Jesse Barfield .05
122 Gary Gaetti .05
123 Kurt Stillwell **RC** .10
124 Joel Davis .05
125 Mike Boddicker .05
126 Robin Yount .60
127 Alan Trammell .05
128 Dave Righetti .05
129 Dwight Evans .05
130 Mike Scioscia .05
131 Julio Franco .05
132 Bret Saberhagen .05
133 Mike Davis .05
134 Joe Hesketh .05
135 Wally Joyner .05
136 Don Slaught .05
137 Daryl Boston .05
138 Nolan Ryan 2.50
139 Mike Schmidt 1.00
140 Tommy Herr .05
141 Garry Templeton .05
142 Kal Daniels .05
143 Billy Sample .05
144 Johnny Ray .05
145 Rob Thompson **RC** .10
146 Bob Dernier .05
147 Danny Tartabull .05
148 Ernie Whitt .05
149 Kirby Puckett .75
150 Mike Young .05
151 Ernest Riles .05
152 Frank Tanana .05
153 Rich Gedman .05
154 Willie Randolph .05
155a Bill Madlock (Name in brown band.) .10
155b Bill Madlock (Name in red band.) .25
156a Joe Carter (Name in brown band.) .10
156b Joe Carter (Name in red band.) .25
157 Danny Jackson .05
158 Carney Lansford .05
159 Bryn Smith .05
160 Gary Pettis .05
161 Oddibe McDowell .05
162 John Cangelosi **RC** .10
163 Mike Scott .05
164 Eric Show .05
165 Juan Samuel .05
166 Nick Esasky .05
167 Zane Smith .05
168 Mike Brown .05
169 Keith Moreland .05
170 John Tudor .05
171 Ken Dixon .05
172 Jim Gantner .05
173 Jack Morris .05
174 Bruce Hurst .05
175 Dennis Rasmussen .05
176 Mike Marshall .05
177 Dan Quisenberry .05
178 Eric Plunk .05
179 Tim Wallach .05
180 Steve Buechele .05
181 Don Sutton .50
182 Dave Schmidt .05
183 Terry Pendleton .05
184 Jim Deshaies **RC** .05
185 Steve Bedrosian .05
186 Pete Rose 2.00
187 Dave Dravecky .05
188 Rick Reuschel .05
189 Dan Gladden .05
190 Rick Mahler .05
191 Thad Bosley .05
192 Ron Darling .05
193 Matt Young .05
194 Tom Brunansky .05
195 Dave Stieb .05
196 Frank Viola .05
197 Tom Henke .05
198 Karl Best .05
199 Dwight Gooden .05
200 Checklist 134-239 .05
201 Steve Trout .05
202 Rafael Ramirez .05
203 Bob Walk .05
204 Roger Mason .05
205 Terry Kennedy .05
206 Ron Oester .05
207 John Russell .05
208 Greg Mathews **RC** .05
209 Charlie Kerfeld .05
210 Reggie Jackson 1.00
211 Floyd Bannister .05
212 Vance Law .05
213 Rich Bordi .05
214 Dan Plesac **RC** .10
215 Dave Collins .05
216 Bob Stanley .05
217 Joe Niekro .05
218 Tom Niedenfuer .05
219 Brett Butler .05
220 Charlie Leibrandt .05
221 Steve Ontiveros .05
222 Tim Burke .05
223 Curtis Wilkerson .05
224 Pete Incaviglia **RC** .10
225 Lonnie Smith .05
226 Chris Codiroli .05
227 Scott Bailes **RC** .05
228 Rickey Henderson .60
229 Ken Howell .05
230 Darnell Coles .05
231 Don Aase .05
232 Tim Leary .05
233 Bob Boone .05
234 Ricky Horton .05
235 Mark Bailey .05
236 Kevin Gross .05
237 Lance McCullers .05
238 Cecilio Guante .05
239 Bob Melvin .05
240 Billy Jo Robidoux .05
241 Roger McDowell .05
242 Leon Durham .05
243 Ed Nunez .05
244 Jimmy Key .05
245 Mike Smithson .05
246 Bo Diaz .05
247 Carlton Fisk .60
248 Larry Sheets .05
249 Juan Castillo **RC** .05
250 Eric King **RC** .05
251 Doug Drabek .05
252 Wade Boggs .75
253 Mariano Duncan .05
254 Pat Tabler .05
255 Frank White .05
256 Alfredo Griffin .05
257 Floyd Youmans .05
258 Rob Wilfong .05
259 Pete O'Brien .05
260 Tim Hulett .05
261 Dickie Thon .05
262 Darren Daulton .05
263 Vince Coleman .05
264 Andy Hawkins .05
265 Eric Davis .05
266 Andres Thomas **RC** .05
267 Mike Diaz **RC** .05
268 Chili Davis .05
269 Jody Davis .05
270 Phil Bradley .05
271 George Bell .05
272 Keith Atherton .05
273 Storm Davis .05
274 Rob Deer .05
275 Walt Terrell .05
276 Roger Clemens 1.00
277 Mike Easler .05
278 Steve Sax .05
279 Andre Thornton .05
280 Jim Sundberg .05
281 Bill Bathe .05
282 Jay Tibbs .05
283 Dick Schofield .05
284 Mike Mason .05
285 Jerry Hairston Sr. .05
286 Bill Doran .05
287 Tim Flannery .05
288 Gary Redus .05
289 John Franco .05
290 Paul Assenmacher **RC** .10
291 Joe Orsulak .05
292 Lee Smith .10
293 Mike Laga .05
294 Rick Dempsey .05
295 Mike Felder .05
296 Tom Brookens .05
297 Al Nipper .05
298 Mike Pagliarulo .05
299 Franklin Stubbs .05
300 Checklist 240-345 .05
301 Steve Farr .05
302 Bill Mooneyham **RC** .05
303 Andres Galarraga .05
304 Scott Fletcher .05
305 Jack Howell .05
306 Russ Morman **RC** .05
307 Todd Worrell .05
308 Dave Smith .05
309 Jeff Stone .05
310 Ron Robinson .05
311 Bruce Bochy .05
312 Jim Winn .05
313 Mark Davis .05
314 Jeff Dedmon .05
315 Jamie Moyer **RC** .10
316 Wally Backman .05
317 Ken Phelps .05
318 Steve Lombardozzi .05
319 Rance Mulliniks .05
320 Tim Laudner .05
321 Mark Eichhorn **RC** .10
322 Lee Guetterman **RC** .05
323 Sid Fernandez .05
324 Jerry Mumphrey .05
325 David Palmer .05
326 Bill Almon .05
327 Candy Maldonado .05
328 John Kruk .05
329 John Denny .05
330 Milt Thompson .05
331 Mike LaValliere **RC** .10
332 Alan Ashby .05
333 Doug Corbett .05
334 Ron Karkovice **RC** .05
335 Mitch Webster .05
336 Lee Lacy .05
337 Glenn Braggs **RC** .05
338 Dwight Lowry .05
339 Don Baylor .05
340 Brian Fisher .05
341 Reggie Williams **RC** .05
342 Tom Candiotti .05
343 Rudy Law .05
344 Curt Young .05
345 Mike Fitzgerald .05

346	Ruben Sierra	.05
347	Mitch Williams **RC**	.25
348	Jorge Orta	.05
349	Mickey Tettleton	.05
350	Ernie Camacho	.05
351	Ron Kittle	.05
352	Ken Landreaux	.05
353	Chet Lemon	.05
354	John Shelby	.05
355	Mark Clear	.05
356	Doug DeCinces	.05
357	Ken Dayley	.05
358	Phil Garner	.05
359	Steve Jeltz	.05
360	Ed Whitson	.05
361	Barry Bonds	10.00
362	Vida Blue	.05
363	Cecil Cooper	.05
364	Bob Ojeda	.05
365	Dennis Eckersley	.50
366	Mike Morgan	.05
367	Willie Upshaw	.05
368	Allan Anderson **RC**	.05
369	Bill Gullickson	.05
370	Bobby Thigpen **RC**	.10
371	Juan Beniquez	.05
372	Charlie Moore	.05
373	Dan Petry	.05
374	Rod Scurry	.05
375	Tom Seaver	.75
376	Ed Vande Berg	.05
377	Tony Bernazard	.05
378	Greg Pryor	.05
379	Dwayne Murphy	.05
380	Andy McGaffigan	.05
381	Kirk McCaskill	.05
382	Greg Harris	.05
383	Rich Dotson	.05
384	Craig Reynolds	.05
385	Greg Gross	.05
386	Tito Landrum	.05
387	Craig Lefferts	.05
388	Dave Parker	.05
389	Bob Horner	.05
390	Pat Clements	.05
391	Jeff Leonard	.05
392	Chris Speier	.05
393	John Moses	.05
394	Garth Iorg	.05
395	Greg Gagne	.05
396	Nate Snell	.05
397	Bryan Clutterbuck **RC**	.05
398	Darrell Evans	.05
399	Steve Crawford	.05
400	Checklist 346-451	.05
401	Phil Lombardi **RC**	.05
402	Rick Honeycutt	.05
403	Ken Schrom	.05
404	Bud Black	.05
405	Donnie Hill	.05
406	Wayne Krenchicki	.05
407	Chuck Finley **RC**	.35
408	Toby Harrah	.05
409	Steve Lyons	.05
410	Kevin Bass	.05
411	Marvell Wynne	.05
412	Ron Roenicke	.05
413	Tracy Jones **RC**	.05
414	Gene Garber	.05
415	Mike Bielecki	.05
416	Frank DiPino	.05
417	Andy Van Slyke	.05
418	Jim Dwyer	.05
419	Ben Oglivie	.05
420	Dave Bergman	.05
421	Joe Sambito	.05
422	Bob Tewksbury **RC**	.30
423	Len Matuszek	.05
424	Mike Kingery **RC**	.05
425	Dave Kingman	.05
426	Al Newman **RC**	.05
427	Gary Ward	.05
428	Ruppert Jones	.05
429	Harold Baines	.05
430	Pat Perry	.05
431	Terry Puhl	.05
432	Don Carman	.05
433	Eddie Milner	.05
434	LaMarr Hoyt	.05
435	Rick Rhoden	.05
436	Jose Uribe	.05
437	Ken Oberkfell	.05
438	Ron Davis	.05
439	Jesse Orosco	.05
440	Scott Bradley	.05
441	Randy Bush	.05
442	John Cerutti **RC**	.05
443	Roy Smalley	.05
444	Kelly Gruber	.05
445	Bob Kearney	.05
446	Ed Hearn **RC**	.05
447	Scott Sanderson	.05
448	Bruce Benedict	.05
449	Junior Ortiz	.05
450	Mike Aldrete **RC**	.05
451	Kevin McReynolds	.05
452	Rob Murphy **RC**	.05
453	Kent Tekulve	.05
454	Curt Ford	.05
455	Davey Lopes	.05
456	Bobby Grich	.05
457	Jose DeLeon	.05
458	Andre Dawson	.35
459	Mike Flanagan	.05
460	Joey Meyer **RC**	.05
461	Chuck Cary **RC**	.05
462	Bill Buckner	.05
463	Bob Shirley	.05
464	Jeff Hamilton **RC**	.05
465	Phil Niekro	.50
466	Mark Gubicza	.05
467	Jerry Willard	.05
468	Bob Sebra **RC**	.05
469	Larry Parrish	.05
470	Charlie Hough	.05
471	Hal McRae	.05
472	Dave Leiper **RC**	.05
473	Mel Hall	.05
474	Dan Pasqua	.05
475	Bob Welch	.05
476	Johnny Grubb	.05
477	Jim Traber	.05
478	Chris Bosio **RC**	.05
479	Mark McLemore	.05
480	John Morris	.05
481	Billy Hatcher	.05
482	Dan Schatzeder	.05
483	Rich Gossage	.10
484	Jim Morrison	.05
485	Bob Brenly	.05
486	Bill Schroeder	.05
487	Mookie Wilson	.05
488	Dave Martinez **RC**	.10
489	Harold Reynolds	.05
490	Jeff Hearron	.05
491	Mickey Hatcher	.05
492	Barry Larkin **RC**	2.00
493	Bob James	.05
494	John Habyan	.05
495	Jim Adduci **RC**	.05
496	Mike Heath	.05
497	Tim Stoddard	.05
498	Tony Armas	.05
499	Dennis Powell	.05
500	Checklist 452-557	.05
501	Chris Bando	.05
502	David Cone **RC**	2.00
503	Jay Howell	.05
504	Tom Foley	.05
505	Ray Chadwick **RC**	.05
506	Mike Loynd **RC**	.05
507	Neil Allen	.05
508	Danny Darwin	.05
509	Rick Schu	.05
510	Jose Oquendo	.05
511	Gene Walter	.05
512	Terry McGriff **RC**	.05
513	Ken Griffey	.05
514	Benny Distefano	.05
515	Terry Mulholland **RC**	.25
516	Ed Lynch	.05
517	Bill Swift	.05
518	Manny Lee	.05
519	Andre David	.05
520	Scott McGregor	.05
521	Rick Manning	.05
522	Willie Hernandez	.05
523	Marty Barrett	.05
524	Wayne Tolleson	.05
525	Jose Gonzalez **RC**	.05
526	Cory Snyder	.05
527	Buddy Biancalana	.05
528	Moose Haas	.05
529	Wilfredo Tejada **RC**	.05
530	Stu Cliburn	.05
531	Dale Mohorcic **RC**	.05
532	Ron Hassey	.05
533	Ty Gainey	.05
534	Jerry Royster	.05
535	Mike Maddux **RC**	.05
536	Ted Power	.05
537	Ted Simmons	.05
538	Rafael Belliard **RC**	.05
539	Chico Walker	.05
540	Bob Forsch	.05
541	John Stefero	.05
542	Dale Sveum **RC**	.05
543	Mark Thurmond	.05
544	Jeff Sellers **RC**	.05
545	Joel Skinner	.05
546	Alex Trevino	.05
547	Randy Kutcher **RC**	.05
548	Joaquin Andujar	.05
549	Casey Candaele **RC**	.10
550	Jeff Russell	.05
551	John Candelaria	.05
552	Joe Cowley	.05
553	Danny Cox	.05
554	Denny Walling	.05
555	Bruce Ruffin **RC**	.10
556	Buddy Bell	.05
557	Jimmy Jones **RC**	.05
558	Bobby Bonilla	.05
559	Jeff Robinson	.05
560	Ed Olwine	.05
561	Glenallen Hill **RC**	.25
562	Lee Mazzilli	.05
563	Mike Brown	.05
564	George Frazier	.05
565	Mike Sharperson **RC**	.10
566	Mark Portugal **RC**	.05
567	Rick Leach	.05
568	Mark Langston	.05
569	Rafael Santana	.05
570	Manny Trillo	.05
571	Cliff Speck	.05
572	Bob Kipper	.05
573	Kelly Downs **RC**	.05
574	Randy Asadoor **RC**	.05
575	Dave Magadan **RC**	.25
576	Marvin Freeman **RC**	.05
577	Jeff Lahti	.05
578	Jeff Calhoun	.05
579	Gus Polidor	.05
580	Gene Nelson	.05
581	Tim Teufel	.05
582	Odell Jones	.05
583	Mark Ryal	.05
584	Randy O'Neal	.05
585	Mike Greenwell **RC**	.50
586	Ray Knight	.05
587	Ralph Bryant **RC**	.05
588	Carmen Castillo	.05
589	Ed Wojna	.05
590	Stan Javier	.05
591	Jeff Musselman **RC**	.05
592	Mike Stanley **RC**	.05
593	Darrell Porter	.05
594	Drew Hall **RC**	.05
595	Rob Nelson **RC**	.05
596	Bryan Oelkers	.05
597	Scott Nielsen **RC**	.05
598	Brian Holton **RC**	.05
599	Kevin Mitchell	.05
600	Checklist 558-660	.05
601	Jackie Gutierrez	.05
602	Barry Jones **RC**	.05
603	Jerry Narron	.05
604	Steve Lake	.05
605	Jim Pankovits	.05
606	Ed Romero	.05
607	Dave LaPoint	.05
608	Don Robinson	.05
609	Mike Krukow	.05
610	Dave Valle **RC**	.05
611	Len Dykstra	.05
612	Roberto Clemente Puzzle Card	.25
613	Mike Trujillo	.05
614	Damaso Garcia	.05
615	Neal Heaton	.05
616	Juan Berenguer	.05
617	Steve Carlton	.75
618	Gary Lucas	.05
619	Geno Petralli	.05
620	Rick Aguilera	.05
621	Fred McGriff	.05
622	Dave Henderson	.05
623	Dave Clark **RC**	.05
624	Angel Salazar	.05
625	Randy Hunt	.05
626	John Gibbons	.05
627	Kevin Brown **RC**	2.00
628	Bill Dawley	.05
629	Aurelio Lopez	.05
630	Charlie Hudson	.05
631	Ray Soff	.05
632	Ray Hayward **RC**	.05
633	Spike Owen	.05
634	Glenn Hubbard	.05
635	Kevin Elster **RC**	.10
636	Mike LaCoss	.05
637	Dwayne Henry	.05
638	Rey Quinones **RC**	.05
639	Jim Clancy	.05
640	Larry Andersen	.05
641	Calvin Schiraldi	.05
642	Stan Jefferson **RC**	.05
643	Marc Sullivan	.05
644	Mark Grant	.05
645	Cliff Johnson	.05
646	Howard Johnson	.05
647	Dave Sax	.05
648	Dave Stewart	.05
649	Danny Heep	.05
650	Joe Johnson	.05
651	Bob Brower **RC**	.05
652	Rob Woodward	.05
653	John Mizerock	.05
654	Tim Pyznarski **RC**	.05
655	Luis Aquino **RC**	.05
656	Mickey Brantley	.05
657	Doyle Alexander	.05
658	Sammy Stewart	.05
659	Jim Acker	.05
660	Pete Ladd	.05

Rookies

	NM/M
Unopened Fact. Set (56):	15.00
Complete Set (56):	10.00
Common Player:	.05

1	Mark McGwire	6.00
2	Eric Bell	.05
3	Mark Williamson	.05
4	Mike Greenwell	.05
5	Ellis Burks	.05
6	DeWayne Buice	.05
7	Mark Mclemore (McLemore)	.05
8	Devon White	.05
9	Willie Fraser	.05
10	Lester Lancaster	.05
11	Ken Williams	.05
12	Matt Nokes	.05
13	Jeff Robinson	.05
14	Bo Jackson	.25
15	Kevin Seitzer	.05
16	Billy Ripken	.05
17	B.J. Surhoff	.05
18	Chuck Crim	.05
19	Mike Birbeck	.05
20	Chris Bosio	.05
21	Les Straker	.05
22	Mark Davidson	.05
23	Gene Larkin	.05
24	Ken Gerhart	.05
25	Luis Polonia	.05
26	Terry Steinbach	.05
27	Mickey Brantley	.05
28	Mike Stanley	.05
29	Jerry Browne	.05
30	Todd Benzinger	.05
31	Fred McGriff	.25
32	Mike Henneman	.05
33	Casey Candaele	.05
34	Dave Magadan	.05
35	David Cone	.05
36	Mike Jackson	.05
37	John Mitchell	.05
38	Mike Dunne	.05
39	John Smiley	.05
40	Joe Magrane	.05
41	Jim Lindeman	.05
42	Shane Mack	.05
43	Stan Jefferson	.05
44	Benito Santiago	.05
45	Matt Williams **RC**	1.50
46	Dave Meads	.05
47	Rafael Palmeiro	4.00
48	Bill Long	.05
49	Bob Brower	.05
50	James Steels	.05
51	Paul Noce	.05
52	Greg Maddux	5.00
53	Jeff Musselman	.05
54	Brian Holton	.05
55	Chuck Jackson	.05
56	Checklist 1-56	.03

1988 Donruss

	NM/M
Unopened Fact. Set (660):	10.00
Complete Set (660):	8.00
Common Player:	.05
Stan Musial Puzzle:	1.00
Wax Pack (15):	.40
Wax Box (36):	10.00
Cello Pack (36):	.75
Cello Box (24):	12.00
Rack Pack (45):	.75

1	Mark McGwire/DK	.75
2	Tim Raines/DK	.05
3	Benito Santiago/DK	.05
4	Alan Trammell/DK	.05
5	Danny Tartabull/DK	.05
6	Ron Darling/DK	.05
7	Paul Molitor/DK	.40
8	Devon White/DK	.05
9	Andre Dawson/DK	.25
10	Julio Franco/DK	.05
11	Scott Fletcher/DK	.05
12	Tony Fernandez/DK	.05
13	Shane Rawley/DK	.05
14	Kal Daniels/DK	.05
15	Jack Clark/DK	.05
16	Dwight Evans/DK	.05
17	Tommy John/DK	.05
18	Andy Van Slyke/DK	.05
19	Gary Gaetti/DK	.05
20	Mark Langston/DK	.05
21	Will Clark/DK	.05
22	Glenn Hubbard/DK	.05
23	Billy Hatcher/DK	.05

24	Bob Welch/DK	.05
25	Ivan Calderon/DK	.05
26	Cal Ripken, Jr./DK	1.00
27	Checklist 1-27	.05
28	Mackey Sasser **RC** (RR)	.05
29	Jeff Treadway **RC** (RR)	.05
30	Mike Campbell **RC** (RR)	.05
31	Lance Johnson **RC** (RR)	.15
32	Nelson Liriano **RC** (RR)	.05
33	Shawn Abner (RR)	.05
34	Roberto Alomar **RC** (RR)	1.00
35	Shawn Hillegas **RC** (RR)	.05
36	Joey Meyer (RR)	.05
37	Kevin Elster (RR)	.05
38	Jose Lind **RC** (RR)	.05
39	Kirt Manwaring **RC** (RR)	.05
40	Mark Grace **RC** (RR)	.50
41	Jody Reed **RC** (RR)	.10
42	John Farrell **RC** (RR)	.05
43	Al Leiter **RC** (RR)	.20
44	Gary Thurman **RC** (RR)	.05
45	Vicente Palacios **RC** (RR)	.05
46	Eddie Williams **RC** (RR)	.05
47	Jack McDowell **RC** (RR)	.20
48	Ken Dixon	.05
49	Mike Birkbeck	.05
50	Eric King	.05
51	Roger Clemens	.60
52	Pat Clements	.05
53	Fernando Valenzuela	.05
54	Mark Gubicza	.05
55	Jay Howell	.05
56	Floyd Youmans	.05
57	Ed Correa	.05
58	DeWayne Buice **RC**	.05
59	Jose DeLeon	.05
60	Danny Cox	.05
61	Nolan Ryan	1.00
62	Steve Bedrosian	.05
63	Tom Browning	.05
64	Mark Davis	.05
65	R.J. Reynolds	.05
66	Kevin Mitchell	.05
67	Ken Oberkfell	.05
68	Rick Sutcliffe	.05
69	Dwight Gooden	.05
70	Scott Bankhead	.05
71	Bert Blyleven	.10
72	Jimmy Key	.05
73	Les Straker **RC**	.05
74	Jim Clancy	.05
75	Mike Moore	.05
76	Ron Darling	.05
77	Ed Lynch	.05
78	Dale Murphy	.20
79	Doug Drabek	.05
80	Scott Garrelts	.05
81	Ed Whitson	.05
82	Rob Murphy	.05
83	Shane Rawley	.05
84	Greg Mathews	.05
85	Jim Deshaies	.05
86	Mike Witt	.05
87	Donnie Hill	.05
88	Jeff Reed	.05
89	Mike Boddicker	.05
90	Ted Higuera	.05
91	Walt Terrell	.05
92	Bob Stanley	.05
93	Dave Righetti	.05
94	Orel Hershiser	.05
95	Chris Bando	.05
96	Bret Saberhagen	.05
97	Curt Young	.05
98	Tim Burke	.05
99	Charlie Hough	.05
100a	Checklist 28-137	.05
100b	Checklist 28-133	.05
101	Bobby Witt	.05
102	George Brett	.60
103	Mickey Tettleton	.05
104	Scott Bailes	.05
105	Mike Pagliarulo	.05
106	Mike Scioscia	.05
107	Tom Brookens	.05
108	Ray Knight	.05
109	Dan Plesac	.05
110	Wally Joyner	.05
111	Bob Forsch	.05
112	Mike Scott	.05
113	Kevin Gross	.05
114	Benito Santiago	.05
115	Bob Kipper	.05
116	Mike Krukow	.05
117	Chris Bosio	.05
118	Sid Fernandez	.05
119	Jody Davis	.05
120	Mike Morgan	.05
121	Mark Eichhorn	.05
122	Jeff Reardon	.05
123	John Franco	.05
124	Richard Dotson	.05
125	Eric Bell	.05
126	Juan Nieves	.05
127	Jack Morris	.05
128	Rick Rhoden	.05
129	Rich Gedman	.05
130	Ken Howell	.05
131	Brook Jacoby	.05
132	Danny Jackson	.05
133	Gene Nelson	.05
134	Neal Heaton	.05
135	Willie Fraser	.05
136	Jose Guzman	.05
137	Ozzie Guillen	.05
138	Bob Knepper	.05
139	Mike Jackson **RC**	.05
140	Joe Magrane **RC**	.05
141	Jimmy Jones	.05
142	Ted Power	.05
143	Ozzie Virgil	.05
144	Felix Fermin **RC**	.05
145	Kelly Downs	.05
146	Shawon Dunston	.05
147	Scott Bradley	.05
148	Dave Stieb	.05
149	Frank Viola	.05
150	Terry Kennedy	.05
151	Bill Wegman	.05
152	Matt Nokes **RC**	.10
153	Wade Boggs	.50
154	Wayne Tolleson	.05
155	Mariano Duncan	.05
156	Julio Franco	.05
157	Charlie Leibrandt	.05
158	Terry Steinbach	.05
159	Mike Fitzgerald	.05
160	Jack Lazorko	.05
161	Mitch Williams	.05
162	Greg Walker	.05
163	Alan Ashby	.05
164	Tony Gwynn	.50
165	Bruce Ruffin	.05
166	Ron Robinson	.05
167	Zane Smith	.05
168	Junior Ortiz	.05
169	Jamie Moyer	.05
170	Tony Pena	.05
171	Cal Ripken, Jr.	1.00
172	B.J. Surhoff	.05
173	Lou Whitaker	.05
174	Ellis Burks **RC**	.20
175	Ron Guidry	.10
176	Steve Sax	.05
177	Danny Tartabull	.05
178	Carney Lansford	.05
179	Casey Candaele	.05
180	Scott Fletcher	.05
181	Mark McLemore	.05
182	Ivan Calderon	.05
183	Jack Clark	.05
184	Glenn Davis	.05
185	Luis Aguayo	.05
186	Bo Diaz	.05
187	Stan Jefferson	.05
188	Sid Bream	.05
189	Bob Brenly	.05
190	Dion James	.05
191	Leon Durham	.05
192	Jesse Orosco	.05
193	Alvin Davis	.05
194	Gary Gaetti	.05
195	Fred McGriff	.05
196	Steve Lombardozzi	.05
197	Rance Mulliniks	.05
198	Rey Quinones	.05
199	Gary Carter	.40
200a	Checklist 138-247	.05
200b	Checklist 134-239	.05
201	Keith Moreland	.05
202	Ken Griffey	.05
203	Tommy Gregg **RC**	.05
204	Will Clark	.05
205	John Kruk	.05
206	Buddy Bell	.05
207	Von Hayes	.05
208	Tommy Herr	.05
209	Craig Reynolds	.05
210	Gary Pettis	.05
211	Harold Baines	.05
212	Vance Law	.05
213	Ken Gerhart	.05
214	Jim Gantner	.05
215	Chet Lemon	.05
216	Dwight Evans	.05
217	Don Mattingly	.60
218	Franklin Stubbs	.05
219	Pat Tabler	.05
220	Bo Jackson	.10
221	Tony Phillips	.05
222	Tim Wallach	.05
223	Ruben Sierra	.05
224	Steve Buechele	.05
225	Frank White	.05
226	Alfredo Griffin	.05
227	Greg Swindell	.05
228	Willie Randolph	.05
229	Mike Marshall	.05
230	Alan Trammell	.05
231	Eddie Murray	.40
232	Dale Sveum	.05
233	Dick Schofield	.05
234	Jose Oquendo	.05
235	Bill Doran	.05
236	Milt Thompson	.05
237	Marvell Wynne	.05
238	Bobby Bonilla	.05
239	Chris Speier	.05
240	Glenn Braggs	.05
241	Wally Backman	.05
242	Ryne Sandberg	.50
243	Phil Bradley	.05
244	Kelly Gruber	.05
245	Tom Brunansky	.05
246	Ron Oester	.05
247	Bobby Thigpen	.05
248	Fred Lynn	.05
249	Paul Molitor	.40
250	Darrell Evans	.05
251	Gary Ward	.05
252	Bruce Hurst	.05
253	Bob Welch	.05
254	Joe Carter	.05
255	Willie Wilson	.05
256	Mark McGwire	.75
257	Mitch Webster	.05
258	Brian Downing	.05
259	Mike Stanley	.05
260	Carlton Fisk	.40
261	Billy Hatcher	.05
262	Glenn Wilson	.05
263	Ozzie Smith	.50
264	Randy Ready	.05
265	Kurt Stillwell	.05
266	David Palmer	.05
267	Mike Diaz	.05
268	Rob Thompson	.05
269	Andre Dawson	.25
270	Lee Guetterman	.05
271	Willie Upshaw	.05
272	Randy Bush	.05
273	Larry Sheets	.05
274	Rob Deer	.05
275	Kirk Gibson	.05
276	Marty Barrett	.05
277	Rickey Henderson	.40
278	Pedro Guerrero	.05
279	Brett Butler	.05
280	Kevin Seitzer	.05
281	Mike Davis	.05
282	Andres Galarraga	.05
283	Devon White	.05
284	Pete O'Brien	.05
285	Jerry Hairston Sr.	.05
286	Kevin Bass	.05
287	Carmelo Martinez	.05
288	Juan Samuel	.05
289	Kal Daniels	.05
290	Albert Hall	.05
291	Andy Van Slyke	.05
292	Lee Smith	.10
293	Vince Coleman	.05
294	Tom Niedenfuer	.05
295	Robin Yount	.40
296	Jeff Robinson **RC**	.05
297	Todd Benzinger **RC**	.10
298	Dave Winfield	.40
299	Mickey Hatcher	.05
300a	Checklist 248-357	.05
300b	Checklist 240-345	.05
301	Bud Black	.05
302	Jose Canseco	.25
303	Tom Foley	.05
304	Pete Incaviglia	.05
305	Bob Boone	.05
306	Bill Long **RC**	.05
307	Willie McGee	.05
308	Ken Caminiti **RC**	.20
309	Darren Daulton	.05
310	Tracy Jones	.05
311	Greg Booker	.05
312	Mike LaValliere	.05
313	Chili Davis	.05
314	Glenn Hubbard	.05
315	Paul Noce **RC**	.05
316	Keith Hernandez	.05
317	Mark Langston	.05
318	Keith Atherton	.05
319	Tony Fernandez	.05
320	Kent Hrbek	.05
321	John Cerutti	.05
322	Mike Kingery	.05
323	Dave Magadan	.05
324	Rafael Palmeiro	.35
325	Jeff Dedmon	.05
326	Barry Bonds	1.00
327	Jeffrey Leonard	.05
328	Tim Flannery	.05
329	Dave Concepcion	.05
330	Mike Schmidt	.60
331	Bill Dawley	.05
332	Larry Andersen	.05
333	Jack Howell	.05
334	Ken Williams **RC**	.05
335	Bryn Smith	.05
336	Billy Ripken **RC**	.10
337	Greg Brock	.05
338	Mike Heath	.05
339	Mike Greenwell	.05
340	Claudell Washington	.05
341	Jose Gonzalez	.05
342	Mel Hall	.05
343	Jim Eisenreich	.05
344	Tony Bernazard	.05
345	Tim Raines	.05
346	Bob Brower	.05
347	Larry Parrish	.05
348	Thad Bosley	.05
349	Dennis Eckersley	.35
350	Cory Snyder	.05
351	Rick Cerone	.05
352	John Shelby	.05
353	Larry Herndon	.05
354	John Habyan	.05
355	Chuck Crim **RC**	.05
356	Gus Polidor	.05
357	Ken Dayley	.05
358	Danny Darwin	.05
359	Lance Parrish	.05
360	James Steels **RC**	.05
361	Al Pedrique **RC**	.05
362	Mike Aldrete	.05
363	Juan Castillo	.05
364	Len Dykstra	.05
365	Luis Quinones	.05
366	Jim Presley	.05
367	Lloyd Moseby	.05
368	Kirby Puckett	.50
369	Eric Davis	.05
370	Gary Redus	.05
371	Dave Schmidt	.05
372	Mark Clear	.05
373	Dave Bergman	.05
374	Charles Hudson	.05
375	Calvin Schiraldi	.05
376	Alex Trevino	.05
377	Tom Candiotti	.05
378	Steve Farr	.05
379	Mike Gallego	.05
380	Andy McGaffigan	.05
381	Kirk McCaskill	.05
382	Oddibe McDowell	.05
383	Floyd Bannister	.05
384	Denny Walling	.05
385	Don Carman	.05
386	Todd Worrell	.05
387	Eric Show	.05
388	Dave Parker	.05
389	Rick Mahler	.05
390	Mike Dunne **RC**	.10
391	Candy Maldonado	.05
392	Bob Dernier	.05
393	Dave Valle	.05
394	Ernie Whitt	.05
395	Juan Berenguer	.05
396	Mike Young	.05
397	Mike Felder	.05
398	Willie Hernandez	.05
399	Jim Rice	.25
400a	Checklist 358-467	.05
400b	Checklist 346-451	.05
401	Tommy John	.10
402	Brian Holton	.05
403	Carmen Castillo	.05
404	Jamie Quirk	.05
405	Dwayne Murphy	.05
406	Jeff Parrett **RC**	.05
407	Don Sutton	.35
408	Jerry Browne	.05
409	Jim Winn	.05
410	Dave Smith	.05
411	Shane Mack **RC**	.05
412	Greg Gross	.05
413	Nick Esasky	.05
414	Damaso Garcia	.05
415	Brian Fisher	.05
416	Brian Dayett	.05
417	Curt Ford	.05
418	Mark Williamson **RC**	.05
419	Bill Schroeder	.05
420	Mike Henneman **RC**	.10
421	John Marzano **RC**	.05
422	Ron Kittle	.05
423	Matt Young	.05
424	Steve Balboni	.05
425	Luis Polonia **RC**	.05
426	Randy St. Claire	.05
427	Greg Harris	.05
428	Johnny Ray	.05
429	Ray Searage	.05
430	Ricky Horton	.05
431	Gerald Young **RC**	.05
432	Rick Schu	.05
433	Paul O'Neill	.05
434	Rich Gossage	.10
435	John Cangelosi	.05
436	Mike LaCoss	.05
437	Gerald Perry	.05
438	Dave Martinez	.05
439	Darryl Strawberry	.05
440	John Moses	.05
441	Greg Gagne	.05
442	Jesse Barfield	.05
443	George Frazier	.05
444	Garth Iorg	.05
445	Ed Nunez	.05
446	Rick Aguilera	.05
447	Jerry Mumphrey	.05
448	Rafael Ramirez	.05
449	John Smiley **RC**	.10
450	Atlee Hammaker	.05
451	Lance McCullers	.05
452	Guy Hoffman	.05
453	Chris James	.05
454	Terry Pendleton	.05
455	Dave Meads **RC**	.05
456	Bill Buckner	.05
457	John Pawlowski **RC**	.05
458	Bob Sebra	.05
459	Jim Dwyer	.05
460	Jay Aldrich **RC**	.05
461	Frank Tanana	.05
462	Oil Can Boyd	.05
463	Dan Pasqua	.05
464	Tim Crews **RC**	.10
465	Andy Allanson	.05
466	Bill Pecota **RC**	.05
467	Steve Ontiveros	.05
468	Hubie Brooks	.05
469	Paul Kilgus **RC**	.05
470	Dale Mohorcic	.05
471	Dan Quisenberry	.05
472	Dave Stewart	.05
473	Dave Clark	.05
474	Joel Skinner	.05
475	Dave Anderson	.05
476	Dan Petry	.05
477	Carl Nichols **RC**	.05
478	Ernest Riles	.05
479	George Hendrick	.05

480 John Morris .05
481 Manny Hernandez **RC** .05
482 Jeff Stone .05
483 Chris Brown .05
484 Mike Bielecki .05
485 Dave Dravecky .05
486 Rick Manning .05
487 Bill Almon .05
488 Jim Sundberg .05
489 Ken Phelps .05
490 Tom Henke .05
491 Dan Gladden .05
492 Barry Larkin .05
493 Fred Manrique **RC** .05
494 Mike Griffin .05
495 Mark Knudson **RC** .05
496 Bill Madlock .05
497 Tim Stoddard .05
498 Sam Horn **RC** .05
499 Tracy Woodson **RC** .05
500a Checklist 468-577 .05
500b Checklist 452-557 .05
501 Ken Schrom .05
502 Angel Salazar .05
503 Eric Plunk .05
504 Joe Hesketh .05
505 Greg Minton .05
506 Geno Petralli .05
507 Bob James .05
508 Robbie Wine **RC** .05
509 Jeff Calhoun .05
510 Steve Lake .05
511 Mark Grant .05
512 Frank Williams .05
513 Jeff Blauser **RC** .10
514 Bob Walk .05
515 Craig Lefferts .05
516 Manny Trillo .05
517 Jerry Reed .05
518 Rick Leach .05
519 Mark Davidson **RC** .05
520 Jeff Ballard **RC** .05
521 Dave Stapleton **RC** .05
522 Pat Sheridan .05
523 Al Nipper .05
524 Steve Trout .05
525 Jeff Hamilton .05
526 Tommy Hinzo **RC** .05
527 Lonnie Smith .05
528 Greg Cadaret **RC** .05
529 Rob McClure (Bob) .05
530 Chuck Finley .05
531 Jeff Russell .05
532 Steve Lyons .05
533 Terry Puhl .05
534 Eric Nolte **RC** .05
535 Kent Tekulve .05
536 Pat Pacillo **RC** .05
537 Charlie Puleo .05
538 Tom Prince **RC** .05
539 Greg Maddux .50
540 Jim Lindeman .05
541 Pete Stanicek **RC** .05
542 Steve Kiefer .05
543 Jim Morrison .05
544 Spike Owen .05
545 Jay Buhner **RC** .50
546 Mike Devereaux **RC** .10
547 Jerry Don Gleaton .05
548 Jose Rijo .05
549 Dennis Martinez .05
550 Mike Loynd .05
551 Darrell Miller .05
552 Dave LaPoint .05
553 John Tudor .05
554 Rocky Childress **RC** .05
555 Wally Ritchie **RC** .05
556 Terry McGriff .05
557 Dave Leiper .05
558 Jeff Robinson .05
559 Jose Uribe .05
560 Ted Simmons .05
561 Lester Lancaster **RC** .10
562 Keith Miller **RC** .05
563 Harold Reynolds .05
564 Gene Larkin **RC** .05
565 Cecil Fielder .05
566 Roy Smalley .05
567 Duane Ward .05
568 Bill Wilkinson **RC** .05
569 Howard Johnson .05
570 Frank DiPino .05
571 Pete Smith **RC** .05
572 Darnell Coles .05
573 Don Robinson .05
574 Rob Nelson .05
575 Dennis Rasmussen .05
576 Steve Jeltz (Photo actually Juan Samuel.) .05
577 Tom Pagnozzi **RC** .05
578 Ty Gainey .05
579 Gary Lucas .05
580 Ron Hassey .05
581 Herm Winningham .05
582 Rene Gonzales **RC** .05
583 Brad Komminsk .05
584 Doyle Alexander .05
585 Jeff Sellers .05
586 Bill Gullickson .05
587 Tim Belcher .05
588 Doug Jones **RC** .05
589 Melido Perez **RC** .05
590 Rick Honeycutt .05
591 Pascual Perez .05
592 Curt Wilkerson .05
593 Steve Howe .05
594 John Davis **RC** .05
595 Storm Davis .05
596 Sammy Stewart .05
597 Neil Allen .05
598 Alejandro Pena .05
599 Mark Thurmond .05
600a Checklist 578-BC26 .05
600b Checklist 558-660 .05
601 Jose Mesa **RC** .10
602 Don August **RC** .05
603 Terry Leach/SP .10
604 Tom Newell **RC** .05
605 Randall Byers/SP **RC** .10
606 Jim Gott .05
607 Harry Spilman .05
608 John Candelaria .05
609 Mike Brumley **RC** .05
610 Mickey Brantley .05
611 Jose Nunez/SP **RC** .10
612 Tom Nieto .05
613 Rick Reuschel .05
614 Lee Mazzilli/SP .10
615 Scott Lusader **RC** .05
616 Bobby Meacham .05
617 Kevin McReynolds/SP .10
618 Gene Garber .05
619 Barry Lyons/SP **RC** .10
620 Randy Myers .05
621 Donnie Moore .05
622 Domingo Ramos .05
623 Ed Romero .05
624 Greg Myers **RC** .10
625 Billy Ripken, Cal Ripken, Jr., Cal Ripken, Sr. Ripken Baseball Family .40
626 Pat Perry .05
627 Andres Thomas/SP .10
628 Matt Williams/SP .15
629 Dave Hengel **RC** .05
630 Jeff Musselman/SP .10
631 Tim Laudner .05
632 Bob Ojeda/SP .10
633 Rafael Santana .05
634 Wes Gardner **RC** .05
635 Roberto Kelly/SP **RC** .15
636 Mike Flanagan/SP .10
637 Jay Bell **RC** .35
638 Bob Melvin .05
639 Damon Berryhill **RC** .05
640 David Wells/SP **RC** .40
641 Stan Musial Puzzle Card .05
642 Doug Sisk .05
643 Keith Hughes **RC** .05
644 Tom Glavine **RC** 1.00
645 Al Newman .05
646 Scott Sanderson .05
647 Scott Terry .05
648 Tim Teufel/SP .10
649 Garry Templeton/SP .10
650 Manny Lee/SP .10
651 Roger McDowell/SP .10
652 Mookie Wilson/SP .10
653 David Cone/SP .10
654 Ron Gant/SP **RC** .20
655 Joe Price/SP .10
656 George Bell/SP .10
657 Gregg Jefferies/SP **RC** .25
658 Todd Stottlemyre/SP **RC** .25
659 Geronimo Berroa/SP **RC** .20
660 Jerry Royster/SP .10

Rookies

	NM/M
Complete Set (56):	4.00
Common Player:	.05

1 Mark Grace .25
2 Mike Campbell .05
3 Todd Frowirth .05
4 Dave Stapleton .05
5 Shawn Abner .05
6 Jose Cecena .05
7 Dave Gallagher .05
8 Mark Parent .05
9 Cecil Espy .05
10 Pete Smith .05
11 Jay Buhner .25
12 Pat Borders .05
13 Doug Jennings .05
14 Brady Anderson **RC** 1.00
15 Pete Stanicek .05
16 Roberto Kelly .05
17 Jeff Treadway .05
18 Walt Weiss .05
19 Paul Gibson .05
20 Tim Crews .05
21 Melido Perez .05
22 Steve Peters .05
23 Craig Worthington .05
24 John Trautwein .05
25 DeWayne Vaughn .05
26 David Wells .15
27 Al Leiter .15
28 Tim Belcher .05
29 Johnny Paredes .05
30 Chris Sabo .05
31 Damon Berryhill .05
32 Randy Milligan .05
33 Gary Thurman .05
34 Kevin Elster .05
35 Roberto Alomar 1.50
36 Edgar Martinez **RC** (Photo actually Edwin Nunez.) 1.50
37 Todd Stottlemyre .15
38 Joey Meyer .05
39 Carl Nichols .05
40 Jack McDowell .05
41 Jose Bautista .05
42 Sil Campusano .05
43 John Dopson .05
44 Jody Reed .05
45 Darrin Jackson .05
46 Mike Capel .05
47 Ron Gant .05
48 John Davis .05
49 Kevin Coffman .05
50 Cris Carpenter .05
51 Mackey Sasser .05
52 Luis Alicea .05
53 Bryan Harvey .05
54 Steve Ellsworth .05
55 Mike Macfarlane .05
56 Checklist 1-56 .05

1989 Donruss

	NM/M
Unopened Fact. Set (660):	17.50
Complete Set (660):	15.00
Common Player:	.05
Warren Spahn Puzzle:	.50
Wax Pack (15):	.75
Wax Box (36):	15.00
Cello Pack (32):	1.00
Cello Box (24):	15.00
Rack Pack (45):	.75

1 Mike Greenwell/DK .05
2 Bobby Bonilla/DK .05
3 Pete Incaviglia/DK .05
4 Chris Sabo/DK .05
5 Robin Yount/DK .40
6 Tony Gwynn/DK .50
7 Carlton Fisk/DK .40
8 Cory Snyder/DK .05
9 David Cone/DK .05
10 Kevin Seitzer/DK .05
11 Rick Reuschel/DK .05
12 Johnny Ray/DK .05
13 Dave Schmidt/DK .05
14 Andres Galarraga/DK .05
15 Kirk Gibson/DK .05
16 Fred McGriff/DK .05
17 Mark Grace/DK .15
18 Jeff Robinson/DK .05
19 Vince Coleman/DK .05
20 Dave Henderson/DK .05
21 Harold Reynolds/DK .05
22 Gerald Perry/DK .05
23 Frank Viola/DK .05
24 Steve Bedrosian/DK .05
25 Glenn Davis/DK .05
26 Don Mattingly/DK .60
27 Checklist 1-27 .05
28 Sandy Alomar, Jr. **RC** (RR) .35
29 Steve Searcy **RC** (RR) .05
30 Cameron Drew **RC** (RR) .05
31 Gary Sheffield **RC** (RR) 1.00
32 Erik Hanson **RC** (RR) .05
33 Ken Griffey Jr. **RC** (RR) 6.00
34 Greg Harris **RC** (RR) .05
35 Gregg Jefferies (RR) .05
36 Luis Medina **RC** (RR) .05
37 Carlos Quintana **RC** (RR) .05
38 Felix Jose **RC** (RR) .05
39 Cris Carpenter **RC** (RR) .05
40 Ron Jones **RC** (RR) .05
41 Dave West **RC** (RR) .05
42 Randy Johnson **RC** (RR) 3.00
43 Mike Harkey **RC** (RR) .05
44 Pete Harnisch **RC** (RR) .10
45 Tom Gordon **RC** (RR) .25
46 Gregg Olson **RC** (RR) .10
47 Alex Sanchez **RC** (RR) .05
48 Ruben Sierra .05
49 Rafael Palmeiro .35
50 Ron Gant .05
51 Cal Ripken, Jr. 1.00
52 Wally Joyner .05
53 Gary Carter .40
54 Andy Van Slyke .05
55 Robin Yount .40
56 Pete Incaviglia .05
57 Greg Brock .05
58 Melido Perez .05
59 Craig Lefferts .05
60 Gary Pettis .05
61 Danny Tartabull .05
62 Guillermo Hernandez .05
63 Ozzie Smith .50
64 Gary Gaetti .05
65 Mark Davis .05
66 Lee Smith .05
67 Dennis Eckersley .35
68 Wade Boggs .50
69 Mike Scott .05
70 Fred McGriff .05
71 Tom Browning .05
72 Claudell Washington .05
73 Mel Hall .05
74 Don Mattingly .60
75 Steve Bedrosian .05
76 Juan Samuel .05
77 Mike Scioscia .05
78 Dave Righetti .05
79 Alfredo Griffin .05
80 Eric Davis .05
81 Juan Berenguer .05
82 Todd Worrell .05
83 Joe Carter .05
84 Steve Sax .05
85 Frank White .05
86 John Kruk .05
87 Rance Mulliniks .05
88 Alan Ashby .05
89 Charlie Leibrandt .05
90 Frank Tanana .05
91 Jose Canseco .25
92 Barry Bonds 1.00
93 Harold Reynolds .05
94 Mark McLemore .05
95 Mark McGwire .75
96 Eddie Murray .40
97 Tim Raines .05
98 Rob Thompson .05
99 Kevin McReynolds .05
100 Checklist 28-137 .05
101 Carlton Fisk .40
102 Dave Martinez .05
103 Glenn Braggs .05
104 Dale Murphy .15
105 Ryne Sandberg .50
106 Dennis Martinez .05
107 Pete O'Brien .05
108 Dick Schofield .05
109 Henry Cotto .05
110 Mike Marshall .05
111 Keith Moreland .05
112 Tom Brunansky .05
113 Kelly Gruber .05
114 Brook Jacoby .05
115 Keith Brown **RC** .05
116 Matt Nokes .05
117 Keith Hernandez .05
118 Bob Forsch .05
119 Bert Blyleven .10
120 Willie Wilson .05
121 Tommy Gregg .05
122 Jim Rice .25
123 Bob Knepper .05
124 Danny Jackson .05
125 Eric Plunk .05
126 Brian Fisher .05
127 Mike Pagliarulo .05
128 Tony Gwynn .50
129 Lance McCullers .05
130 Andres Galarraga .05
131 Jose Uribe .05
132 Kirk Gibson .05
133 David Palmer .05
134 R.J. Reynolds .05
135 Greg Walker .05
136 Kirk McCaskill .05
137 Shawon Dunston .05
138 Andy Allanson .05
139 Rob Murphy .05
140 Mike Aldrete .05
141 Terry Kennedy .05
142 Scott Fletcher .05
143 Steve Balboni .05
144 Bret Saberhagen .05
145 Ozzie Virgil .05
146 Dale Sveum .05
147 Darryl Strawberry .05
148 Harold Baines .10
149 George Bell .05
150 Dave Parker .05
151 Bobby Bonilla .05
152 Mookie Wilson .05

153	Ted Power	.05
154	Nolan Ryan	1.00
155	Jeff Reardon	.05
156	Tim Wallach	.05
157	Jamie Moyer	.05
158	Rich Gossage	.10
159	Dave Winfield	.40
160	Von Hayes	.05
161	Willie McGee	.05
162	Rich Gedman	.05
163	Tony Pena	.05
164	Mike Morgan	.05
165	Charlie Hough	.05
166	Mike Stanley	.05
167	Andre Dawson	.20
168	Joe Boever	.05
169	Pete Stanicek	.05
170	Bob Boone	.05
171	Ron Darling	.05
172	Bob Walk	.05
173	Rob Deer	.05
174	Steve Buechele	.05
175	Ted Higuera	.05
176	Ozzie Guillen	.05
177	Candy Maldonado	.05
178	Doyle Alexander	.05
179	Mark Gubicza	.05
180	Alan Trammell	.05
181	Vince Coleman	.05
182	Kirby Puckett	.50
183	Chris Brown	.05
184	Marty Barrett	.05
185	Stan Javier	.05
186	Mike Greenwell	.05
187	Billy Hatcher	.05
188	Jimmy Key	.05
189	Nick Esasky	.05
190	Don Slaught	.05
191	Cory Snyder	.05
192	John Candelaria	.05
193	Mike Schmidt	.60
194	Kevin Gross	.05
195	John Tudor	.05
196	Neil Allen	.05
197	Orel Hershiser	.05
198	Kal Daniels	.05
199	Kent Hrbek	.05
200	Checklist 138-247	.05
201	Joe Magrane	.05
202	Scott Bailes	.05
203	Tim Belcher	.05
204	George Brett	.60
205	Benito Santiago	.05
206	Tony Fernandez	.05
207	Gerald Young	.05
208	Bo Jackson	.10
209	Chet Lemon	.05
210	Storm Davis	.05
211	Doug Drabek	.05
212	Mickey Brantley (Photo actually Nelson Simmons.)	.05
213	Devon White	.05
214	Dave Stewart	.05
215	Dave Schmidt	.05
216	Bryn Smith	.05
217	Brett Butler	.05
218	Bob Ojeda	.05
219	Steve Rosenberg **RC**	.05
220	Hubie Brooks	.05
221	B.J. Surhoff	.05
222	Rick Mahler	.05
223	Rick Sutcliffe	.05
224	Neal Heaton	.05
225	Mitch Williams	.05
226	Chuck Finley	.05
227	Mark Langston	.05
228	Jesse Orosco	.05
229	Ed Whitson	.05
230	Terry Pendleton	.05
231	Lloyd Moseby	.05
232	Greg Swindell	.05
233	John Franco	.05
234	Jack Morris	.05
235	Howard Johnson	.05
236	Glenn Davis	.05
237	Frank Viola	.05
238	Kevin Seitzer	.05
239	Gerald Perry	.05
240	Dwight Evans	.05
241	Jim Deshaies	.05
242	Bo Diaz	.05
243	Carney Lansford	.05
244	Mike LaValliere	.05
245	Rickey Henderson	.40
246	Roberto Alomar	.20
247	Jimmy Jones	.05
248	Pascual Perez	.05
249	Will Clark	.05
250	Fernando Valenzuela	.05
251	Shane Rawley	.05
252	Sid Bream	.05
253	Steve Lyons	.05
254	Brian Downing	.05
255	Mark Grace	.05
256	Tom Candiotti	.05
257	Barry Larkin	.05
258	Mike Krukow	.05
259	Billy Ripken	.05
260	Cecilio Guante	.05
261	Scott Bradley	.05
262	Floyd Bannister	.05
263	Pete Smith	.05
264	Jim Gantner	.05
265	Roger McDowell	.05
266	Bobby Thigpen	.05
267	Jim Clancy	.05
268	Terry Steinbach	.05
269	Mike Dunne	.05
270	Dwight Gooden	.05
271	Mike Heath	.05
272	Dave Smith	.05
273	Keith Atherton	.05
274	Tim Burke	.05
275	Damon Berryhill	.05
276	Vance Law	.05
277	Rich Dotson	.05
278	Lance Parrish	.05
279	Dennis Walling	.05
280	Roger Clemens	.60
281	Greg Mathews	.05
282	Tom Niedenfuer	.05
283	Paul Kilgus	.05
284	Jose Guzman	.05
285	Calvin Schiraldi	.05
286	Charlie Puleo	.05
287	Joe Orsulak	.05
288	Jack Howell	.05
289	Kevin Elster	.05
290	Jose Lind	.05
291	Paul Molitor	.40
292	Cecil Espy	.05
293	Bill Wegman	.05
294	Dan Pasqua	.05
295	Scott Garrelts	.05
296	Walt Terrell	.05
297	Ed Hearn	.05
298	Lou Whitaker	.05
299	Ken Dayley	.05
300	Checklist 248-357	.05
301	Tommy Herr	.05
302	Mike Brumley	.05
303	Ellis Burks	.05
304	Curt Young	.05
305	Jody Reed	.05
306	Bill Doran	.05
307	David Wells	.05
308	Ron Robinson	.05
309	Rafael Santana	.05
310	Julio Franco	.05
311	Jack Clark	.05
312	Chris James	.05
313	Milt Thompson	.05
314	John Shelby	.05
315	Al Leiter	.05
316	Mike Davis	.05
317	Chris Sabo **RC**	.15
318	Greg Gagne	.05
319	Jose Oquendo	.05
320	John Farrell	.05
321	Franklin Stubbs	.05
322	Kurt Stillwell	.05
323	Shawn Abner	.05
324	Mike Flanagan	.05
325	Kevin Bass	.05
326	Pat Tabler	.05
327	Mike Henneman	.05
328	Rick Honeycutt	.05
329	John Smiley	.05
330	Rey Quinones	.05
331	Johnny Ray	.05
332	Bob Welch	.05
333	Larry Sheets	.05
334	Jeff Parrett	.05
335	Rick Reuschel	.05
336	Randy Myers	.05
337	Ken Williams	.05
338	Andy McGaffigan	.05
339	Joey Meyer	.05
340	Dion James	.05
341	Les Lancaster	.05
342	Tom Foley	.05
343	Geno Petralli	.05
344	Dan Petry	.05
345	Alvin Davis	.05
346	Mickey Hatcher	.05
347	Marvell Wynne	.05
348	Danny Cox	.05
349	Dave Stieb	.05
350	Jay Bell	.05
351	Jeff Treadway	.05
352	Luis Salazar	.05
353	Len Dykstra	.05
354	Juan Agosto	.05
355	Gene Larkin	.05
356	Steve Farr	.05
357	Paul Assenmacher	.05
358	Todd Benzinger	.05
359	Larry Andersen	.05
360	Paul O'Neill	.05
361	Ron Hassey	.05
362	Jim Gott	.05
363	Ken Phelps	.05
364	Tim Flannery	.05
365	Randy Ready	.05
366	Nelson Santovenia **RC**	.05
367	Kelly Downs	.05
368	Danny Heep	.05
369	Phil Bradley	.05
370	Jeff Robinson	.05
371	Ivan Calderon	.05
372	Mike Witt	.05
373	Greg Maddux	.50
374	Carmen Castillo	.05
375	Jose Rijo	.05
376	Joe Price	.05
377	R.C. Gonzalez	.05
378	Oddibe McDowell	.05
379	Jim Presley	.05
380	Brad Wellman	.05
381	Tom Glavine	.20
382	Dan Plesac	.05
383	Wally Backman	.05
384	Dave Gallagher **RC**	.05
385	Tom Henke	.05
386	Luis Polonia	.05
387	Junior Ortiz	.05
388	David Cone	.05
389	Dave Bergman	.05
390	Danny Darwin	.05
391	Dan Gladden	.05
392	John Dopson **RC**	.05
393	Frank DiPino	.05
394	Al Nipper	.05
395	Willie Randolph	.05
396	Don Carman	.05
397	Scott Terry	.05
398	Rick Cerone	.05
399	Tom Pagnozzi	.05
400	Checklist 358-467	.05
401	Mickey Tettleton	.05
402	Curtis Wilkerson	.05
403	Jeff Russell	.05
404	Pat Perry	.05
405	Jose Alvarez **RC**	.05
406	Rick Schu	.05
407	Sherman Corbett **RC**	.05
408	Dave Magadan	.05
409	Bob Kipper	.05
410	Don August	.05
411	Bob Brower	.05
412	Chris Bosio	.05
413	Jerry Reuss	.05
414	Atlee Hammaker	.05
415	Jim Walewander	.05
416	Mike Macfarlane **RC**	.10
417	Pat Sheridan	.05
418	Pedro Guerrero	.05
419	Allan Anderson	.05
420	Mark Parent **RC**	.05
421	Bob Stanley	.05
422	Mike Gallego	.05
423	Bruce Hurst	.05
424	Dave Meads	.05
425	Jesse Barfield	.05
426	Rob Dibble **RC**	.15
427	Joel Skinner	.05
428	Ron Kittle	.05
429	Rick Rhoden	.05
430	Bob Dernier	.05
431	Steve Jeltz	.05
432	Rick Dempsey	.05
433	Roberto Kelly	.05
434	Dave Anderson	.05
435	Herm Winningham	.05
436	Al Newman	.05
437	Jose DeLeon	.05
438	Doug Jones	.05
439	Brian Holton	.05
440	Jeff Montgomery	.05
441	Dickie Thon	.05
442	Cecil Fielder	.05
443	John Fishel **RC**	.05
444	Jerry Don Gleaton	.05
445	Paul Gibson **RC**	.05
446	Walt Weiss	.05
447	Glenn Wilson	.05
448	Mike Moore	.05
449	Chili Davis	.05
450	Dave Henderson	.05
451	Jose Bautista **RC**	.05
452	Rex Hudler	.05
453	Bob Brenly	.05
454	Mackey Sasser	.05
455	Daryl Boston	.05
456	Mike Fitzgerald	.05
457	Jeffery Leonard	.05
458	Bruce Sutter	.35
459	Mitch Webster	.05
460	Joe Hesketh	.05
461	Bobby Witt	.05
462	Stew Cliburn	.05
463	Scott Bankhead	.05
464	Ramon Martinez **RC**	.25
465	Dave Leiper	.05
466	Luis Alicea **RC**	.05
467	John Cerutti	.05
468	Ron Washington	.05
469	Jeff Reed	.05
470	Jeff Robinson	.05
471	Sid Fernandez	.05
472	Terry Puhl	.05
473	Charlie Lea	.05
474	Israel Sanchez **RC**	.05
475	Bruce Benedict	.05
476	Oil Can Boyd	.05
477	Craig Reynolds	.05
478	Frank Williams	.05
479	Greg Cadaret	.05
480	Randy Kramer **RC**	.05
481	Dave Eiland **RC**	.05
482	Eric Show	.05
483	Garry Templeton	.05
484	Wallace Johnson	.05
485	Kevin Mitchell	.05
486	Tim Crews	.05
487	Mike Maddux	.05
488	Dave LaPoint	.05
489	Fred Manrique	.05
490	Greg Minton	.05
491	Doug Dascenzo **RC**	.05
492	Willie Upshaw	.05
493	Jack Armstrong **RC**	.05
494	Kirt Manwaring	.05
495	Jeff Ballard	.05
496	Jeff Kunkel	.05
497	Mike Campbell	.05
498	Gary Thurman	.05
499	Zane Smith	.05
500	Checklist 468-577	.05
501	Mike Birkbeck	.05
502	Terry Leach	.05
503	Shawn Hillegas	.05
504	Manny Lee	.05
505	Doug Jennings **RC**	.05
506	Ken Oberkfell	.05
507	Tim Teufel	.05
508	Tom Brookens	.05
509	Rafael Ramirez	.05
510	Fred Toliver	.05
511	Brian Holman **RC**	.05
512	Mike Bielecki	.05
513	Jeff Pico **RC**	.05
514	Charles Hudson	.05
515	Bruce Ruffin	.05
516	Larry McWilliams	.05
517	Jeff Sellers	.05
518	John Costello **RC**	.05
519	Brady Anderson	.05
520	Craig McMurtry	.05
521	Ray Hayward	.05
522	Drew Hall	.05
523	Mark Lemke **RC**	.05
524	Oswald Peraza **RC**	.05
525	Bryan Harvey **RC**	.05
526	Rick Aguilera	.05
527	Tom Prince	.05
528	Mark Clear	.05
529	Jerry Browne	.05
530	Juan Castillo	.05
531	Jack McDowell	.05
532	Chris Speier	.05
533	Darrell Evans	.05
534	Luis Aquino	.05
535	Eric King	.05
536	Ken Hill **RC**	.05
537	Randy Bush	.05
538	Shane Mack	.05
539	Tom Bolton	.05
540	Gene Nelson	.05
541	Wes Gardner	.05
542	Ken Caminiti	.05
543	Duane Ward	.05
544	Norm Charlton **RC**	.10
545	Hal Morris **RC**	.25
546	Rich Yett	.05
547	Hensley Meulens **RC**	.10
548	Greg Harris	.05
549	Darren Daulton	.05
550	Jeff Hamilton	.05
551	Luis Aguayo	.05
552	Tim Leary	.05
553	Ron Oester	.05
554	Steve Lombardozzi	.05
555	Tim Jones **RC**	.05
556	Bud Black	.05
557	Alejandro Pena	.05
558	Jose DeJesus **RC**	.05
559	Dennis Rasmussen	.05
560	Pat Borders **RC**	.25
561	Craig Biggio	.05
562	Luis de los Santos **RC**	.05
563	Fred Lynn	.05
564	Todd Burns **RC**	.05
565	Felix Fermin	.05
566	Darnell Coles	.05
567	Willie Fraser	.05
568	Glenn Hubbard	.05
569	Craig Worthington **RC**	.05
570	Johnny Paredes **RC**	.05
571	Don Robinson	.05
572	Barry Lyons	.05
573	Bill Long	.05
574	Tracy Jones	.05
575	Juan Nieves	.05
576	Andres Thomas	.05
577	Rolando Roomes **RC**	.05
578	Luis Rivera	.05
579	Chad Kreuter **RC**	.10
580	Tony Armas	.05
581	Jay Buhner	.05
582	Ricky Horton	.05
583	Andy Hawkins	.05
584	Sil Campusano **RC**	.05
585	Dave Clark	.05
586	Van Snider **RC**	.05
587	Todd Frohwirth	.05
588	Warren Spahn Puzzle Card	.05
589	William Brennan **RC**	.05
590	German Gonzalez **RC**	.05
591	Ernie Whitt	.05
592	Jeff Blauser	.05
593	Spike Owen	.05
594	Matt Williams	.05
595	Lloyd McClendon	.05
596	Steve Ontiveros	.05
597	Scott Medvin **RC**	.05
598	Hipolito Pena **RC**	.05
599	Jerald Clark **RC**	.05
600a	Checklist 578-BC26 (#635 is Kurt Schilling)	.10
600b	Checklist 578-BC26 (#635 is Curt Schilling)	.05
601	Carmelo Martinez	.05
602	Mike LaCoss	.05
603	Mike Devereaux	.05
604	Alex Madrid **RC**	.05
605	Gary Redus	.05
606	Lance Johnson	.05
607	Terry Clark **RC**	.05
608	Manny Trillo	.05
609	Scott Jordan **RC**	.05

610 Jay Howell .05
611 Francisco Melendez RC .05
612 Mike Boddicker .05
613 Kevin Brown .05
614 Dave Valle .05
615 Tim Laudner .05
616 Andy Nezelek RC .05
617 Chuck Crim .05
618 Jack Savage .05
619 Adam Peterson .05
620 Todd Stottlemyre .05
621 Lance Blankenship RC .05
622 Miguel Garcia RC .05
623 Keith Miller .05
624 Ricky Jordan RC .05
625 Ernest Riles .05
626 John Moses .05
627 Nelson Liriano .05
628 Mike Smithson .05
629 Scott Sanderson .05
630 Dale Mohorcic .05
631 Marvin Freeman .05
632 Mike Young .05
633 Dennis Lamp .05
634 Dante Bichette RC .25
635 Curt Schilling RC 3.00
636 Scott May RC .05
637 Mike Schooler RC .05
638 Rick Leach .05
639 Tom Lampkin RC .05
640 Brian Meyer RC .05
641 Brian Harper .05
642 John Smoltz .05
643 Jose Canseco (40/40) .15
644 Bill Schroeder .05
645 Edgar Martinez .10
646 Dennis Cook RC .05
647 Barry Jones .05
648 Orel Hershiser (59 and Counting) .05
649 Rod Nichols RC .05
650 Jody Davis .05
651 Bob Milacki RC .05
652 Mike Jackson .05
653 Derek Lilliquist RC .05
654 Paul Mirabella .05
655 Mike Diaz .05
656 Jeff Musselman .05
657 Jerry Reed .05
658 Kevin Blankenship RC .05
659 Wayne Tolleson .05
660 Eric Hetzel RC .05

Rookies

Ramon Martinez

	NM/M
Complete Set (56):	8.00
Common Player:	.05
1 Gary Sheffield	.75
2 Gregg Jefferies	.05
3 Ken Griffey Jr.	5.00
4 Tom Gordon	.05
5 Billy Spiers	.05
6 Deion Sanders RC	.50
7 Donn Pall	.05
8 Steve Carter	.05
9 Francisco Oliveras	.05
10 Steve Wilson	.05
11 Bob Geren	.05
12 Tony Castillo	.05
13 Kenny Rogers	.05
14 Carlos Martinez	.05
15 Edgar Martinez	.05
16 Jim Abbott	.05
17 Torey Lovullo	.05
18 Mark Carreon	.05
19 Geronimo Berroa	.05
20 Luis Medina	.05
21 Sandy Alomar, Jr.	.05
22 Bob Milacki	.05
23 Joe Girardi RC	.10
24 German Gonzalez	.05
25 Craig Worthington	.05
26 Jerome Walton	.05
27 Gary Wayne	.05
28 Tim Jones	.05
29 Dante Bichette	.05
30 Alexis Infante	.05
31 Ken Hill	.05
32 Dwight Smith	.05
33 Luis de los Santos	.05
34 Eric Yelding	.05
35 Gregg Olson	.05
36 Phil Stephenson	.05

37 Ken Patterson .05
38 Rick Wrona .05
39 Mike Brumley .05
40 Cris Carpenter .05
41 Jeff Brantley .05
42 Ron Jones .05
43 Randy Johnson 2.00
44 Kevin Brown .05
45 Ramon Martinez .05
46 Greg Harris .05
47 Steve Finley .05
48 Randy Kramer .05
49 Erik Hanson .05
50 Matt Merullo .05
51 Mike Devereaux .05
52 Clay Parker .05
53 Omar Vizquel .05
54 Derek Lilliquist .05
55 Junior Felix .05
56 Checklist .05

1989 Donruss Traded

Rafael Palmeiro OF

	NM/M
Complete Set (56):	2.00
Common Player:	.05
1 Jeffrey Leonard	.05
2 Jack Clark	.05
3 Kevin Gross	.05
4 Tommy Herr	.05
5 Bob Boone	.05
6 Rafael Palmeiro	.30
7 John Dopson	.05
8 Willie Randolph	.05
9 Chris Brown	.05
10 Wally Backman	.05
11 Steve Ontiveros	.05
12 Eddie Murray	.45
13 Lance McCullers	.05
14 Spike Owen	.05
15 Rob Murphy	.05
16 Pete O'Brien	.05
17 Ken Williams	.05
18 Nick Esasky	.05
19 Nolan Ryan	1.50
20 Brian Holton	.05
21 Mike Moore	.05
22 Joel Skinner	.05
23 Steve Sax	.05
24 Rick Mahler	.05
25 Mike Aldrete	.05
26 Jesse Orosco	.05
27 Dave LaPoint	.05
28 Walt Terrell	.05
29 Eddie Williams	.05
30 Mike Devereaux	.05
31 Julio Franco	.05
32 Jim Clancy	.05
33 Felix Fermin	.05
34 Curtis Wilkerson	.05
35 Bert Blyleven	.05
36 Mel Hall	.05
37 Eric King	.05
38 Mitch Williams	.05
39 Jamie Moyer	.05
40 Rick Rhoden	.05
41 Phil Bradley	.05
42 Paul Kilgus	.05
43 Milt Thompson	.05
44 Jerry Browne	.05
45 Bruce Hurst	.05
46 Claudell Washington	.05
47 Todd Benzinger	.05
48 Steve Balboni	.05
49 Oddibe McDowell	.05
50 Charles Hudson	.05
51 Ron Kittle	.05
52 Andy Hawkins	.05
53 Tom Brookens	.05
54 Tom Niedenfuer	.05
55 Jeff Parrett	.05
56 Checklist	.05

1990 Donruss Previews

	NM/M
Complete Set (12):	85.00
Common Player:	3.00
1 Todd Zeile	3.00
2 Ben McDonald	3.00
3 Bo Jackson	7.50
4 Will Clark	3.00

1990 PREVIEW CARDS

No. 10 of 12

JEROME WALTON

OUTFIELDER

CAREER HIGHLIGHTS

5 Dave Stewart	3.00
6 Kevin Mitchell	3.00
7 Nolan Ryan	50.00
8 Howard Johnson	3.00
9 Tony Gwynn	25.00
10 Jerome Walton	3.00
11 Wade Boggs	25.00
12 Kirby Puckett	25.00

1990 Donruss

Kirby Puckett OF TWINS

	NM/M
Unopened Factory Set (716):	10.00
Complete Set (716):	7.50
Common Player:	.05
Carl Yastrzemski Puzzle:	1.00
Wax Pack (16):	.50
Wax Box (36):	10.00
Rack Pack (48):	1.00
Blister Rack (78):	1.50
1 Bo Jackson/DK	.15
2 Steve Sax/DK	.05
3a Ruben Sierra/DK (No vertical black line at top-right on back.)	.25
3b Ruben Sierra/DK (Vertical line at top-right on back.)	.10
4 Ken Griffey Jr./DK	.65
5 Mickey Tettleton/DK	.05
6 Dave Stewart/DK	.05
7 Jim Deshaies/DK	.05
8 John Smoltz/DK	.05
9 Mike Bielecki/DK	.05
10a Brian Downing/DK (Reversed negative.)	.25
10b Brian Downing/DK (Corrected)	.05
11 Kevin Mitchell/DK	.05
12 Kelly Gruber/DK	.05
13 Joe Magrane/DK	.05
14 John Franco/DK	.05
15 Ozzie Guillen/DK	.05
16 Lou Whitaker/DK	.05
17 John Smiley/DK	.05
18 Howard Johnson/DK	.05
19 Willie Randolph/DK	.05
20 Chris Bosio/DK	.05
21 Tommy Herr/DK	.05
22 Dan Gladden/DK	.05
23 Ellis Burks/DK	.05
24 Pete O'Brien/DK	.05
25 Bryn Smith/DK	.05
26 Ed Whitson/DK	.05
27 Checklist 1-27	.05
28 Robin Ventura (Rated Rookie)	.05
29 Todd Zeile RC (RR)	.15
30 Sandy Alomar, Jr. (RR)	.05
31 Kent Mercker RC (RR)	.10
32 Ben McDonald RC (RR)	.25
33a Juan Gonzalez (Reversed negative.) RC (RR)	2.00
33b Juan Gonzalez RC (RR) (Corrected)	1.50
34 Eric Anthony RC (RR)	.05
35 Mike Fetters RC (RR)	.05
36 Marquis Grissom RC (RR)	.50
37 Greg Vaughn RC (RR)	.25
38 Brian DuBois RC (RR)	.05
39 Steve Avery RC (RR)	.10
40 Mark Gardner RC (RR)	.05
41 Andy Benes (RR)	.05
42 Delino DeShields RC (RR)	.15
43 Scott Coolbaugh RC (RR)	.05
44 Pat Combs RC (RR)	.10
45 Alex Sanchez RC (RR)	.05
46 Kelly Mann RC (RR)	.05
47 Julio Machado RC (RR)	.05
48 Pete Incaviglia	.05
49 Shawon Dunston	.05

50 Jeff Treadway .05
51 Jeff Ballard .05
52 Claudell Washington .05
53 Juan Samuel .05
54 John Smiley .05
55 Rob Deer .05
56 Geno Petralli .05
57 Chris Bosio .05
58 Carlton Fisk .40
59 Kirt Manwaring .05
60 Chet Lemon .05
61 Bo Jackson .10
62 Doyle Alexander .05
63 Pedro Guerrero .05
64 Allan Anderson .05
65 Greg Harris .05
66 Mike Greenwell .05
67 Walt Weiss .05
68 Wade Boggs .50
69 Jim Clancy .05
70 Junior Felix RC .05
71 Barry Larkin .05
72 Dave LaPoint .05
73 Joel Skinner .05
74 Jesse Barfield .05
75 Tommy Herr .05
76 Ricky Jordan .05
77 Eddie Murray .40
78 Steve Sax .05
79 Tim Belcher .05
80 Danny Jackson .05
81 Kent Hrbek .05
82 Milt Thompson .05
83 Brook Jacoby .05
84 Mike Marshall .05
85 Kevin Seitzer .05
86 Tony Gwynn .50
87 Dave Steib .05
88 Dave Smith .05
89 Bret Saberhagen .05
90 Alan Trammell .05
91 Tony Phillips .05
92 Doug Drabek .05
93 Jeffrey Leonard .05
94 Wally Joyner .05
95 Carney Lansford .05
96 Cal Ripken, Jr. 1.00
97 Andres Galarraga .05
98 Kevin Mitchell .05
99 Howard Johnson .05
100a Checklist 28-129 .05
100b Checklist 28-125 .05
101 Melido Perez .05
102 Spike Owen .05
103 Paul Molitor .40
104 Geronimo Berroa .05
105 Ryne Sandberg .50
106 Bryn Smith .05
107 Steve Buechele .05
108 Jim Abbott .05
109 Alvin Davis .05
110 Lee Smith .05
111 Roberto Alomar .20
112 Rick Reuschel .05
113a Kelly Gruber (Born 2/22.) .05
113b Kelly Gruber (Born 2/26.) .20
114 Joe Carter .05
115 Jose Rijo .05
116 Greg Minton .05
117 Bob Ojeda .05
118 Glenn Davis .05
119 Jeff Reardon .05
120 Kurt Stillwell .05
121 John Smoltz .05
122 Dwight Evans .05
123 Eric Yelding .05
124 John Franco .05
125 Jose Canseco .20
126 Barry Bonds 1.00
127 Lee Guetterman .05
128 Jack Clark .05
129 Dave Valle .05
130 Hubie Brooks .05
131 Ernest Riles .05
132 Mike Morgan .05
133 Steve Jeltz .05
134 Jeff Robinson .05
135 Ozzie Guillen .05
136 Chili Davis .05
137 Mitch Webster .05
138 Jerry Browne .05
139 Bo Diaz .05
140 Robby Thompson .05
141 Craig Worthington .05
142 Julio Franco .05
143 Brian Holman .05
144 George Brett .60
145 Tom Glavine .20
146 Robin Yount .40
147 Gary Carter .40
148 Ron Kittle .05
149 Tony Fernandez .05
150 Dave Stewart .05
151 Gary Gaetti .05
152 Kevin Elster .05
153 Gerald Perry .05
154 Jesse Orosco .05
155 Wally Backman .05
156 Dennis Martinez .05
157 Rick Sutcliffe .05
158 Greg Maddux .50
159 Andy Hawkins .05
160 John Kruk .05
161 Jose Oquendo .05
162 John Dopson .05

163	Joe Magrane	.05
164	Billy Ripken	.05
165	Fred Manrique	.05
166	Nolan Ryan	1.00
167	Damon Berryhill	.05
168	Dale Murphy	.20
169	Mickey Tettleton	.05
170a	Kirk McCaskill (Born 4/19.)	.05
170b	Kirk McCaskill (Born 4/9.)	.10
171	Dwight Gooden	.05
172	Jose Lind	.05
173	B.J. Surhoff	.05
174	Ruben Sierra	.05
175	Dan Plesac	.05
176	Dan Pasqua	.05
177	Kelly Downs	.05
178	Matt Nokes	.05
179	Luis Aquino	.05
180	Frank Tanana	.05
181	Tony Pena	.05
182	Dan Gladden	.05
183	Bruce Hurst	.05
184	Roger Clemens	.60
185	Mark McGwire	.75
186	Rob Murphy	.05
187	Jim Deshaies	.05
188	Fred McGriff	.05
189	Rob Dibble	.05
190	Don Mattingly	.60
191	Felix Fermin	.05
192	Roberto Kelly	.05
193	Dennis Cook	.05
194	Darren Daulton	.05
195	Alfredo Griffin	.05
196	Eric Plunk	.05
197	Orel Hershiser	.05
198	Paul O'Neill	.05
199	Randy Bush	.05
200a	Checklist 130-231	.05
200b	Checklist 126-223	.05
201	Ozzie Smith	.50
202	Pete O'Brien	.05
203	Jay Howell	.05
204	Mark Gubicza	.05
205	Ed Whitson	.05
206	George Bell	.05
207	Mike Scott	.05
208	Charlie Leibrandt	.05
209	Mike Heath	.05
210	Dennis Eckersley	.35
211	Mike LaValliere	.05
212	Darnell Coles	.05
213	Lance Parrish	.05
214	Mike Moore	.05
215	Steve Finley **RC**	.20
216	Tim Raines	.05
217a	Scott Garrelts (Born 10/20.)	.05
217b	Scott Garrelts (Born 10/30.)	.10
218	Kevin McReynolds	.05
219	Dave Gallagher	.05
220	Tim Wallach	.05
221	Chuck Crim	.05
222	Lonnie Smith	.05
223	Andre Dawson	.20
224	Nelson Santovenia	.05
225	Rafael Palmeiro	.35
226	Devon White	.05
227	Harold Reynolds	.05
228	Ellis Burks	.05
229	Mark Parent	.05
230	Will Clark	.05
231	Jimmy Key	.05
232	John Farrell	.05
233	Eric Davis	.05
234	Johnny Ray	.05
235	Darryl Strawberry	.05
236	Bill Doran	.05
237	Greg Gagne	.05
238	Jim Eisenreich	.05
239	Tommy Gregg	.05
240	Marty Barrett	.05
241	Rafael Ramirez	.05
242	Chris Sabo	.05
243	Dave Henderson	.05
244	Andy Van Slyke	.05
245	Alvaro Espinoza	.05
246	Garry Templeton	.05
247	Gene Harris	.05
248	Kevin Gross	.05
249	Brett Butler	.05
250	Willie Randolph	.05
251	Roger McDowell	.05
252	Rafael Belliard	.05
253	Steve Rosenberg	.05
254	Jack Howell	.05
255	Marvell Wynne	.05
256	Tom Candiotti	.05
257	Todd Benzinger	.05
258	Don Robinson	.05
259	Phil Bradley	.05
260	Cecil Espy	.05
261	Scott Bankhead	.05
262	Frank White	.05
263	Andres Thomas	.05
264	Glenn Braggs	.05
265	David Cone	.05
266	Bobby Thigpen	.05
267	Nelson Liriano	.05
268	Terry Steinbach	.05
269	Kirby Puckett	.50
270	Gregg Jefferies	.05
271	Jeff Blauser	.05
272	Cory Snyder	.05
273	Roy Smith	.05
274	Tom Foley	.05
275	Mitch Williams	.05
276	Paul Kilgus	.05
277	Don Slaught	.05
278	Von Hayes	.05
279	Vince Coleman	.05
280	Mike Boddicker	.05
281	Ken Dayley	.05
282	Mike Devereaux	.05
283	Kenny Rogers **RC**	.05
284	Jeff Russell	.05
285	Jerome Walton **RC**	.10
286	Derek Lilliquist	.05
287	Joe Orsulak	.05
288	Dick Schofield	.05
289	Ron Darling	.05
290	Bobby Bonilla	.05
291	Jim Gantner	.05
292	Bobby Witt	.05
293	Greg Brock	.05
294	Ivan Calderon	.05
295	Steve Bedrosian	.05
296	Mike Henneman	.05
297	Tom Gordon	.05
298	Lou Whitaker	.05
299	Terry Pendleton	.05
300a	Checklist 232-333	.05
300b	Checklist 224-321	.05
301	Juan Berenguer	.05
302	Mark Davis	.05
303	Nick Esasky	.05
304	Rickey Henderson	.40
305	Rick Cerone	.05
306	Craig Biggio	.05
307	Duane Ward	.05
308	Tom Browning	.05
309	Walt Terrell	.05
310	Greg Swindell	.05
311	Dave Righetti	.05
312	Mike Maddux	.05
313	Len Dykstra	.05
314	Jose Gonzalez	.05
315	Steve Balboni	.05
316	Mike Scioscia	.05
317	Ron Oester	.05
318	Gary Wayne **RC**	.05
319	Todd Worrell	.05
320	Doug Jones	.05
321	Jeff Hamilton	.05
322	Danny Tartabull	.05
323	Chris James	.05
324	Mike Flanagan	.05
325	Gerald Young	.05
326	Bob Boone	.05
327	Frank Williams	.05
328	Dave Parker	.05
329	Sid Bream	.05
330	Mike Schooler	.05
331	Bert Blyleven	.10
332	Bob Welch	.05
333	Bob Milacki	.05
334	Tim Burke	.05
335	Jose Uribe	.05
336	Randy Myers	.05
337	Eric King	.05
338	Mark Langston	.05
339	Ted Higuera	.05
340	Oddibe McDowell	.05
341	Lloyd McClendon	.05
342	Pascual Perez	.05
343	Kevin Brown	.05
344	Chuck Finley	.05
345	Erik Hanson	.05
346	Rich Gedman	.05
347	Bip Roberts	.05
348	Matt Williams	.05
349	Tom Henke	.05
350	Brad Komminsk	.05
351	Jeff Reed	.05
352	Brian Downing	.05
353	Frank Viola	.05
354	Terry Puhl	.05
355	Brian Harper	.05
356	Steve Farr	.05
357	Joe Boever	.05
358	Danny Heep	.05
359	Larry Andersen	.05
360	Rolando Roomes	.05
361	Mike Gallego	.05
362	Bob Kipper	.05
363	Clay Parker	.05
364	Mike Pagliarulo	.05
365	Ken Griffey Jr.	.65
366	Rex Hudler	.05
367	Pat Sheridan	.05
368a	Kirk Gibson (May 25 birthdate.)	.05
368b	Kirk Gibson (May 28 birthdate.)	.05
369	Jeff Parrett	.05
370	Bob Walk	.05
371	Ken Patterson	.05
372	Bryan Harvey	.05
373	Mike Bielecki	.05
374	Tom Magrann **RC**	.05
375	Rick Mahler	.05
376	Craig Lefferts	.05
377	Gregg Olson	.05
378	Jamie Moyer	.05
379	Randy Johnson	.40
380	Jeff Montgomery	.05
381	Marty Clary	.05
382	Bill Spiers **RC**	.05
383	Dave Magadan	.05
384	Greg Hibbard **RC**	.05
385	Ernie Whitt	.05
386	Rick Honeycutt	.05
387	Dave West	.05
388	Keith Hernandez	.05
389	Jose Alvarez	.05
390	Albert Belle	.05
391	Rick Aguilera	.05
392	Mike Fitzgerald	.05
393	Dwight Smith **RC**	.05
394	Steve Wilson **RC**	.05
395	Bob Geren **RC**	.05
396	Randy Ready	.05
397	Ken Hill	.05
398	Jody Reed	.05
399	Tom Brunansky	.05
400a	Checklist 334-435	.05
400b	Checklist 322-419	.05
401	Rene Gonzales	.05
402	Harold Baines	.05
403	Cecilio Guante	.05
404	Joe Girardi	.05
405a	Sergio Valdez **RC** (Black line crosses S in Sergio.)	.10
405b	Sergio Valdez (Corrected)	.05
406	Mark Williamson	.05
407	Glenn Hoffman	.05
408	Jeff Innis **RC**	.05
409	Randy Kramer	.05
410	Charlie O'Brien	.05
411	Charlie Hough	.05
412	Gus Polidor	.05
413	Ron Karkovice	.05
414	Trevor Wilson	.05
415	Kevin Ritz **RC**	.05
416	Gary Thurman	.05
417	Jeff Robinson	.05
418	Scott Terry	.05
419	Tim Laudner	.05
420	Dennis Rasmussen	.05
421	Luis Rivera	.05
422	Jim Corsi	.05
423	Dennis Lamp	.05
424	Ken Caminiti	.05
425	David Wells	.05
426	Norm Charlton	.05
427	Deion Sanders	.05
428	Dion James	.05
429	Chuck Cary	.05
430	Ken Howell	.05
431	Steve Lake	.05
432	Kal Daniels	.05
433	Lance McCullers	.05
434	Lenny Harris	.05
435	Scott Scudder **RC**	.05
436	Gene Larkin	.05
437	Dan Quisenberry	.05
438	Steve Olin **RC**	.05
439	Mickey Hatcher	.05
440	Willie Wilson	.05
441	Mark Grant	.05
442	Mookie Wilson	.05
443	Alex Trevino	.05
444	Pat Tabler	.05
445	Dave Bergman	.05
446	Todd Burns	.05
447	R.J. Reynolds	.05
448	Jay Buhner	.05
449	Lee Stevens **RC**	.05
450	Ron Hassey	.05
451	Bob Melvin	.05
452	Dave Martinez	.05
453	Greg Litton **RC**	.05
454	Mark Carreon	.05
455	Scott Fletcher	.05
456	Otis Nixon	.05
457	Tony Fossas **RC**	.05
458	John Russell	.05
459	Paul Assenmacher	.05
460	Zane Smith	.05
461	Jack Daugherty **RC**	.05
462	Rich Monteleone **RC**	.05
463	Greg Briley	.05
464	Mike Smithson	.05
465	Benito Santiago	.05
466	Jeff Brantley **RC**	.05
467	Jose Nunez	.05
468	Scott Bailes	.05
469	Ken Griffey	.05
470	Bob McClure	.05
471	Mackey Sasser	.05
472	Glenn Wilson	.05
473	Kevin Tapani **RC**	.10
474	Bill Buckner	.05
475	Ron Gant	.05
476	Kevin Romine	.05
477	Juan Agosto	.05
478	Herm Winningham	.05
479	Storm Davis	.05
480	Jeff King	.05
481	Kevin Mmahat **RC**	.05
482	Carmelo Martinez	.05
483	Omar Vizquel	.05
484	Jim Dwyer	.05
485	Bob Knepper	.05
486	Dave Anderson	.05
487	Ron Jones	.05
488	Jay Bell	.05
489	Sammy Sosa **RC**	3.00
490	Kent Anderson **RC**	.05
491	Domingo Ramos	.05
492	Dave Clark	.05
493	Tim Birtsas	.05
494	Ken Oberkfell	.05
495	Larry Sheets	.05
496	Jeff Kunkel	.05
497	Jim Presley	.05
498	Mike Macfarlane	.05
499	Pete Smith	.05
500a	Checklist 436-537	.05
500b	Checklist 420-517	.05
501	Gary Sheffield	.20
502	Terry Bross **RC**	.05
503	Jerry Kutzler **RC**	.05
504	Lloyd Moseby	.05
505	Curt Young	.05
506	Al Newman	.05
507	Keith Miller	.05
508	Mike Stanton **RC**	.20
509	Rich Yett	.05
510	Tim Drummond **RC**	.05
511	Joe Hesketh	.05
512	Rick Wrona **RC**	.05
513	Luis Salazar	.05
514	Hal Morris	.05
515	Terry Mullholland	.05
516	John Morris	.05
517	Carlos Quintana	.05
518	Frank DiPino	.05
519	Randy Milligan	.05
520	Chad Kreuter	.05
521	Mike Jeffcoat	.05
522	Mike Harkey	.05
523a	Andy Nezelek (Born 1985.)	.05
523b	Andy Nezelek (Born 1965.)	.05
524	Dave Schmidt	.05
525	Tony Armas	.05
526	Barry Lyons	.05
527	Rick Reed **RC**	.05
528	Jerry Reuss	.05
529	Dean Palmer **RC**	.10
530	Jeff Peterek **RC**	.05
531	Carlos Martinez **RC**	.05
532	Atlee Hammaker	.05
533	Mike Brumley	.05
534	Terry Leach	.05
535	Doug Strange **RC**	.05
536	Jose DeLeon	.05
537	Shane Rawley	.05
538	Joey Cora	.05
539	Eric Hetzel	.05
540	Gene Nelson	.05
541	Wes Gardner	.05
542	Mark Portugal	.05
543	Al Leiter	.05
544	Jack Armstrong	.05
545	Greg Cadaret	.05
546	Rod Nichols	.05
547	Luis Polonia	.05
548	Charlie Hayes	.05
549	Dickie Thon	.05
550	Tim Crews	.05
551	Dave Winfield	.40
552	Mike Davis	.05
553	Ron Robinson	.05
554	Carmen Castillo	.05
555	John Costello	.05
556	Bud Black	.05
557	Rick Dempsey	.05
558	Jim Acker	.05
559	Eric Show	.05
560	Pat Borders	.05
561	Danny Darwin	.05
562	Rick Luecken **RC**	.05
563	Edwin Nunez	.05
564	Felix Jose	.05
565	John Cangelosi	.05
566	Billy Swift	.05
567	Bill Schroeder	.05
568	Stan Javier	.05
569	Jim Traber	.05
570	Wallace Johnson	.05
571	Donell Nixon	.05
572	Sid Fernandez	.05
573	Lance Johnson	.05
574	Andy McGaffigan	.05
575	Mark Knudson	.05
576	Tommy Greene **RC**	.05
577	Mark Grace	.05
578	Larry Walker **RC**	1.00
579	Mike Stanley	.05
580	Mike Witt	.05
581	Scott Bradley	.05
582	Greg Harris	.05
583a	Kevin Hickey (Black stripe over top of "K" vertical stroke.)	.05
583b	Kevin Hickey (Black stripe under "K.")	.05
584	Lee Mazzilli	.05
585	Jeff Pico	.05
586	Joe Oliver **RC**	.05
587	Willie Fraser	.05
588	Carl Yastrzemski Puzzle Card	.05
589	Kevin Bass	.05
590	John Moses	.05
591	Tom Pagnozzi	.05
592	Tony Castillo **RC**	.05
593	Jerald Clark	.05
594	Dan Schatzeder	.05
595	Luis Quinones	.05
596	Pete Harnisch	.05
597	Gary Redus	.05
598	Mel Hall	.05
599	Rick Schu	.05
600a	Checklist 538-639	.05
600b	Checklist 518-617	.05
601	Mike Kingery	.05
602	Terry Kennedy	.05
603	Mike Sharperson	.05
604	Don Carman	.05
605	Jim Gott	.05

606 Donn Pall .05
607 Rance Mulliniks .05
608 Curt Wilkerson .05
609 Mike Felder .05
610 Guillermo Hernandez .05
611 Candy Maldonado .05
612 Mark Thurmond .05
613 Rick Leach .05
614 Jerry Reed .05
615 Franklin Stubbs .05
616 Billy Hatcher .05
617 Don August .05
618 Tim Teufel .05
619 Shawn Hillegas .05
620 Manny Lee .05
621 Gary Ward .05
622 Mark Guthrie **RC** .05
623 Jeff Musselman .05
624 Mark Lemke .05
625 Fernando Valenzuela .05
626 Paul Sorrento **RC** .05
627 Glenallen Hill .05
628 Les Lancaster .05
629 Vance Law .05
630 Randy Velarde .05
631 Todd Frohwirth .05
632 Willie McGee .05
633 Oil Can Boyd .05
634 Cris Carpenter .05
635 Brian Holton .05
636 Tracy Jones .05
637 Terry Steinbach/AS .05
638 Brady Anderson .05
639a Jack Morris (Black line crosses J of Jack.) .10
639b Jack Morris (Corrected) .05
640 Jaime Navarro **RC** .05
641 Darrin Jackson .05
642 Mike Dyer **RC** .05
643 Mike Schmidt .60
644 Henry Cotto .05
645 John Cerutti .05
646 Francisco Cabrera **RC** .05
647 Scott Sanderson .05
648 Brian Meyer .05
649 Ray Searage .05
650 Bo Jackson/AS .25
651 Steve Lyons .05
652 Mike LaCoss .05
653 Ted Power .05
654 Howard Johnson/AS .05
655 Mauro Gozzo **RC** .05
656 Mike Blowers **RC** .05
657 Paul Gibson .05
658 Neal Heaton .05
659a Nolan Ryan 5,000 K's (King of Kings (#665) back.) 1.50
659b Nolan Ryan 5,000 K's (Correct back.) .60
660a Harold Baines/AS (Black line through star on front, Recent Major League Performance on back.) .25
660b Harold Baines/AS (Black line through star on front, All-Star Game Performance on back.) .25
660c Harold Baines/AS (Black line behind star on front, Recent Major League Performance on back.) .25
660d Harold Baines/AS (Black line behind star on front, All-Star Game Performance on back.) .10
661 Gary Pettis .05
662 Clint Zavaras **RC** .05
663 Rick Reuschel/AS .05
664 Alejandro Pena .05
665a Nolan Ryan (King of Kings) (5,000 K's (#659) back.) 1.50
665b Nolan Ryan (King of Kings) (Correct back.) 1.00
665c Nolan Ryan (King of Kings) (No number on back.) 1.00
666 Ricky Horton .05
667 Curt Schilling .05
668 Bill Landrum .05
669 Todd Stottlemyre .05
670 Tim Leary .05
671 John Wetteland **RC** .25
672 Calvin Schiraldi .05
673 Ruben Sierra/AS .05
674 Pedro Guerrero/AS .05
675 Ken Phelps .05
676 Cal Ripken/AS .50
677 Denny Walling .05
678 Goose Gossage .05
679 Gary Mielke **RC** .05
680 Bill Bathe .05
681 Tom Lawless .05
682 Xavier Hernandez **RC** .05
683 Kirby Puckett/AS .25
684 Mariano Duncan .05
685 Ramon Martinez .05
686 Tim Jones .05
687 Tom Filer .05
688 Steve Lombardozzi .05
689 Bernie Williams **RC** 1.00
690 Chip Hale **RC** .05
691 Beau Allred **RC** .05
692 Ryne Sandberg/AS .25
693 Jeff Huson **RC** .05
694 Curt Ford .05
695 Eric Davis/AS .05
696 Scott Lusader .05
697 Mark McGwire/AS .40
698 Steve Cummings **RC** .05
699 George Canale **RC** .05
700a Checklist 640-715/BC1-BC26 .05
700b Checklist 640-716/BC1-BC26 .05
700c Checklist 618-716 .05
701 Julio Franco/AS .05
702 Dave Johnson **RC** .05
703 Dave Stewart/AS .05
704 Dave Justice **RC** .50
705 Tony Gwynn/AS .25
706 Greg Myers .05
707 Will Clark/AS .05
708 Benito Santiago/AS .05
709 Larry McWilliams .05
710 Ozzie Smith/AS .25
711 John Olerud **RC** .50
712 Wade Boggs/AS .25
713 Gary Eave **RC** .05
714 Bob Tewksbury .05
715 Kevin Mitchell/AS .05
716 A. Bartlett Giamatti .25

Rookies

NM/M

Complete Set (56): 1.00
Common Player: .05
1 Sandy Alomar .05
2 John Olerud .40
3 Pat Combs .05
4 Brian Dubois .05
5 Felix Jose .05
6 Delino DeShields .05
7 Mike Stanton .05
8 Mike Munoz .05
9 Craig Grebeck .05
10 Joe Kraemer .05
11 Jeff Huson .05
12 Bill Sampen .05
13 Brian Bohanon .05
14 Dave Justice .40
15 Robin Ventura .05
16 Greg Vaughn .05
17 Wayne Edwards .05
18 Shawn Boskie .05
19 Carlos Baerga **RC** .20
20 Mark Gardner .05
21 Kevin Appier .05
22 Mike Harkey .05
23 Tim Layana .05
24 Glenallen Hill .05
25 Jerry Kutzler .05
26 Mike Blowers .05
27 Scott Ruskin .05
28 Dana Kiecker .05
29 Willie Blair .05
30 Ben McDonald .05
31 Todd Zeile .05
32 Scott Coolbaugh .05
33 Xavier Hernandez .05
34 Mike Hartley .05
35 Kevin Tapani .05
36 Kevin Wickander .05
37 Carlos Hernandez .05
38 Brian Traxler .05
39 Marty Brown .05
40 Scott Radinsky .05
41 Julio Machado .05
42 Steve Avery .05
43 Mark Lemke .05
44 Alan Mills .05
45 Marquis Grissom .05
46 Greg Olson .05
47 Dave Hollins .05
48 Jerald Clark .05
49 Eric Anthony .05
50 Tim Drummond .05
51 John Burkett .05
52 Brent Knackert .05
53 Jeff Shaw .05
54 John Orton .05
55 Terry Shumpert .05
56 Checklist .05

1991 Donruss

NM/M

Factory Set w/Previews (788): 12.00
Factory Collector's Set (792): 12.00
Complete Set (770): 8.00
Common Player: .05

Willie Stargell Puzzle: .50
Series 1 or 2 Pack (15): .50
Series 1 or 2 Wax Box (36): 12.50
1 Dave Steib/DK .05
2 Craig Biggio/DK .05
3 Cecil Fielder/DK .05
4 Barry Bonds/DK 1.00
5 Barry Larkin/DK .05
6 Dave Parker/DK .05
7 Len Dykstra/DK .05
8 Bobby Thigpen/DK .05
9 Roger Clemens/DK .60
10 Ron Gant/DK .05
11 Delino DeShields/DK .05
12 Roberto Alomar/DK .20
13 Sandy Alomar/DK .05
14 Ryne Sandberg/DK .50
15 Ramon Martinez/DK .05
16 Edgar Martinez/DK .05
17 Dave Magadan/DK .05
18 Matt Williams/DK .05
19 Rafael Palmeiro/DK .40
20 Bob Welch/DK .05
21 Dave Righetti/DK .05
22 Brian Harper/DK .05
23 Gregg Olson/DK .05
24 Kurt Stillwell/DK .05
25 Pedro Guerrero/DK .05
26 Chuck Finley/DK .05
27 Diamond King checklist .05
28 Tino Martinez (Rated Rookie) .05
29 Mark Lewis (RR) .05
30 Bernard Gilkey **RC** (RR) .10
31 Hensley Meulens (RR) .05
32 Derek Bell **RC** (RR) .30
33 Jose Offerman (RR) .05
34 Terry Bross (RR) .05
35 Leo Gomez **RC** (RR) .05
36 Derrick May (RR) .05
37 Kevin Morton **RC** (RR) .05
38 Moises Alou (RR) .05
39 Julio Valera **RC** (RR) .05
40 Milt Cuyler (RR) .05
41 Phil Plantier **RC** (RR) .10
42 Scott Chiamparino **RC** (RR) .05
43 Ray Lankford **RC** (RR) .20
44 Mickey Morandini **RC** (RR) .10
45 Dave Hansen (RR) .05
46 Kevin Belcher **RC** (RR) .05
47 Darrin Fletcher (RR) .05
48 Steve Sax/AS .05
49 Ken Griffey Jr./AS .30
50a Jose Canseco/AS (A's in stat line on back.) .10
50b Jose Canseco/AS (AL in stat line on back.) .25
51 Sandy Alomar/AS .05
52 Cal Ripken, Jr./AS .50
53 Rickey Henderson/AS .20
54 Bob Welch/AS .05
55 Wade Boggs/AS .25
56 Mark McGwire/AS .50
57a Jack McDowell (Career Games 30) .05
57b Jack McDowell (Career Games 63) .25
58 Jose Lind .05
59 Alex Fernandez .05
60 Pat Combs .05
61 Mike Walker **RC** .05
62 Juan Samuel .05
63 Mike Blowers .05
64 Mark Guthrie .05
65 Mark Salas .05
66 Tim Jones .05
67 Tim Leary .05
68 Andres Galarraga .05
69 Bob Milacki .05
70 Tim Belcher .05
71 Todd Zeile .05
72 Jerome Walton .05
73 Kevin Seitzer .05
74 Jerald Clark .05
75 John Smoltz .05
76 Mike Henneman .05
77 Ken Griffey Jr. .65
78 Jim Abbott .05
79 Gregg Jefferies .05
80 Kevin Reimer .05
81 Roger Clemens .60
82 Mike Fitzgerald .05
83 Bruce Hurst .05
84 Eric Davis .05
85 Paul Molitor .40
86 Will Clark .05
87 Mike Bielecki .05
88 Bret Saberhagen .05
89 Nolan Ryan 1.00
90 Bobby Thigpen .05
91 Dickie Thon .05
92 Duane Ward .05
93 Luis Polonia .05
94 Terry Kennedy .05
95 Kent Hrbek .05
96 Danny Jackson .05
97 Sid Fernandez .05
98 Jimmy Key .05
99 Franklin Stubbs .05
100 Checklist 28-103 .05
101 R.J. Reynolds .05
102 Dave Stewart .05
103 Dan Pasqua .05
104 Dan Plesac .05
105 Mark McGwire .75
106 John Farrell .05
107 Don Mattingly .60
108 Carlton Fisk .40
109 Ken Oberkfell .05
110 Darrel Akerfelds .05
111 Gregg Olson .05
112 Mike Scioscia .05
113 Bryn Smith .05
114 Bob Geren .05
115 Tom Candiotti .05
116 Kevin Tapani .05
117 Jeff Treadway .05
118 Alan Trammell .05
119 Pete O'Brien .05
120 Joel Skinner .05
121 Mike LaValliere .05
122 Dwight Evans .05
123 Jody Reed .05
124 Lee Guetterman .05
125 Tim Burke .05
126 Dave Johnson .05
127 Fernando Valenzuela .05
128 Jose DeLeon .05
129 Andre Dawson .20
130 Gerald Perry .05
131 Greg Harris .05
132 Tom Glavine .25
133 Lance McCullers .05
134 Randy Johnson .40
135 Lance Parrish .05
136 Mackey Sasser .05
137 Geno Petralli .05
138 Dennis Lamp .05
139 Dennis Martinez .05
140 Mike Pagliarulo .05
141 Hal Morris .05
142 Dave Parker .05
143 Brett Butler .05
144 Paul Assenmacher .05
145 Mark Gubicza .05
146 Charlie Hough .05
147 Sammy Sosa .50
148 Randy Ready .05
149 Kelly Gruber .05
150 Devon White .05
151 Gary Carter .40
152 Gene Larkin .05
153 Chris Sabo .05
154 David Cone .05
155 Todd Stottlemyre .05
156 Glenn Wilson .05
157 Bob Walk .05
158 Mike Gallego .05
159 Greg Hibbard .05
160 Chris Bosio .05
161 Mike Moore .05
162 Jerry Browne .05
163 Steve Sax .05
164 Melido Perez .05
165 Danny Darwin .05
166 Roger McDowell .05
167 Bill Ripken .05
168 Mike Sharperson .05
169 Lee Smith .05
170 Matt Nokes .05
171 Jesse Orosco .05
172 Rick Aguilera .05
173 Jim Presley .05
174 Lou Whitaker .05
175 Harold Reynolds .05
176 Brook Jacoby .05
177 Wally Backman .05
178 Wade Boggs .50
179 Chuck Cary .05
180 Tom Foley .05
181 Pete Harnisch .05
182 Mike Morgan .05
183 Bob Tewksbury .05
184 Joe Girardi .05
185 Storm Davis .05
186 Ed Whitson .05
187 Steve Avery .05
188 Lloyd Moseby .05
189 Scott Bankhead .05
190 Mark Langston .05
191 Kevin McReynolds .05
192 Julio Franco .05
193 John Dopson .05
194 Oil Can Boyd .05
195 Bip Roberts .05
196 Billy Hatcher .05

197	Edgar Diaz	.05
198	Greg Litton	.05
199	Mark Grace	.05
200	Checklist 104-179	.05
201	George Brett	.60
202	Jeff Russell	.05
203	Ivan Calderon	.05
204	Ken Howell	.05
205	Tom Henke	.05
206	Bryan Harvey	.05
207	Steve Bedrosian	.05
208	Al Newman	.05
209	Randy Myers	.05
210	Daryl Boston	.05
211	Manny Lee	.05
212	Dave Smith	.05
213	Don Slaught	.05
214	Walt Weiss	.05
215	Donn Pall	.05
216	Jamie Navarro	.05
217	Willie Randolph	.05
218	Rudy Seanez	.05
219	Jim Leyritz **RC**	.15
220	Ron Karkovice	.05
221	Ken Caminiti	.05
222a	Von Hayes (Traded players' first names included in How Acquired on back.)	.05
222b	Von Hayes (No first names.)	.05
223	Cal Ripken, Jr.	1.00
224	Lenny Harris	.05
225	Milt Thompson	.05
226	Alvaro Espinoza	.05
227	Chris James	.05
228	Dan Gladden	.05
229	Jeff Blauser	.05
230	Mike Heath	.05
231	Omar Vizquel	.05
232	Doug Jones	.05
233	Jeff King	.05
234	Luis Rivera	.05
235	Ellis Burks	.05
236	Greg Cadaret	.05
237	Dave Martinez	.05
238	Mark Williamson	.05
239	Stan Javier	.05
240	Ozzie Smith	.50
241	Shawn Boskie **RC**	.05
242	Tom Gordon	.05
243	Tony Gwynn	.50
244	Tommy Gregg	.05
245	Jeff Robinson	.05
246	Keith Comstock	.05
247	Jack Howell	.05
248	Keith Miller	.05
249	Bobby Witt	.05
250	Rob Murphy	.05
251	Spike Owen	.05
252	Garry Templeton	.05
253	Glenn Braggs	.05
254	Ron Robinson	.05
255	Kevin Mitchell	.05
256	Les Lancaster	.05
257	Mel Stottlemyre **RC**	.10
258	Kenny Rogers	.05
259	Lance Johnson	.05
260	John Kruk	.05
261	Fred McGriff	.05
262	Dick Schofield	.05
263	Trevor Wilson	.05
264	David West	.05
265	Scott Scudder	.05
266	Dwight Gooden	.05
267	Willie Blair **RC**	.05
268	Mark Portugal	.05
269	Doug Drabek	.05
270	Dennis Eckersley	.35
271	Eric King	.05
272	Robin Yount	.40
273	Carney Lansford	.05
274	Carlos Baerga	.05
275	Dave Righetti	.05
276	Scott Fletcher	.05
277	Eric Yelding	.05
278	Charlie Hayes	.05
279	Jeff Ballard	.05
280	Orel Hershiser	.05
281	Jose Oquendo	.05
282	Mike Witt	.05
283	Mitch Webster	.05
284	Greg Gagne	.05
285	Greg Olson **RC**	.05
286	Tony Phillips	.05
287	Scott Bradley	.05
288	Cory Snyder	.05
289	Jay Bell	.05
290	Kevin Romine	.05
291	Jeff Robinson	.05
292	Steve Frey	.05
293	Craig Worthington	.05
294	Tim Crews	.05
295	Joe Magrane	.05
296	Hector Villanueva **RC**	.05
297	Terry Shumpert **RC**	.05
298	Joe Carter	.05
299	Kent Mercker	.05
300	Checklist 180-255	.05
301	Chet Lemon	.05
302	Mike Schooler	.05
303	Dante Bichette	.05
304	Kevin Elster	.05
305	Jeff Huson	.05
306	Greg Harris	.05
307	Marquis Grissom	.05
308	Calvin Schiraldi	.05
309	Mariano Duncan	.05
310	Bill Spiers	.05
311	Scott Garrelts	.05
312	Mitch Williams	.05
313	Mike Macfarlane	.05
314	Kevin Brown	.05
315	Robin Ventura	.05
316	Darren Daulton	.05
317	Pat Borders	.05
318	Mark Eichhorn	.05
319	Jeff Brantley	.05
320	Shane Mack	.05
321	Rob Dibble	.05
322	John Franco	.05
323	Junior Felix	.05
324	Casey Candaele	.05
325	Bobby Bonilla	.05
326	Dave Henderson	.05
327	Wayne Edwards	.05
328	Mark Knudson	.05
329	Terry Steinbach	.05
330	Colby Ward **RC**	.05
331	Oscar Azocar **RC**	.05
332	Scott Radinsky **RC**	.10
333	Eric Anthony	.05
334	Steve Lake	.05
335	Bob Melvin	.05
336	Kal Daniels	.05
337	Tom Pagnozzi	.05
338	Alan Mills **RC**	.05
339	Steve Olin	.05
340	Juan Berenguer	.05
341	Francisco Cabrera	.05
342	Dave Bergman	.05
343	Henry Cotto	.05
344	Sergio Valdez	.05
345	Bob Patterson	.05
346	John Marzano	.05
347	Dana Kiecker **RC**	.05
348	Dion James	.05
349	Hubie Brooks	.05
350	Bill Landrum	.05
351	Bill Sampen **RC**	.05
352	Greg Briley	.05
353	Paul Gibson	.05
354	Dave Eiland	.05
355	Steve Finley	.05
356	Bob Boone	.05
357	Steve Buechele	.05
358	Chris Hoiles	.05
359	Larry Walker	.05
360	Frank DiPino	.05
361	Mark Grant	.05
362	Dave Magadan	.05
363	Robby Thompson	.05
364	Lonnie Smith	.05
365	Steve Farr	.05
366	Dave Valle	.05
367	Tim Naehring **RC**	.05
368	Jim Acker	.05
369	Jeff Reardon	.05
370	Tim Teufel	.05
371	Juan Gonzalez	.20
372	Luis Salazar	.05
373	Rick Honeycutt	.05
374	Greg Maddux	.50
375	Jose Uribe	.05
376	Donnie Hill	.05
377	Don Carman	.05
378	Craig Grebeck **RC**	.05
379	Willie Fraser	.05
380	Glenallen Hill	.05
381	Joe Oliver	.05
382	Randy Bush	.05
383	Alex Cole	.05
384	Norm Charlton	.05
385	Gene Nelson	.05
386a	Checklist 256-331 (Blue Borders)	.05
386b	Checklist 256-331 (Green Borders)	.05
387	Rickey Henderson/MVP	.20
388	Lance Parrish/MVP	.05
389	Fred McGriff/MVP	.05
390	Dave Parker/MVP	.05
391	Candy Maldonado/MVP	.05
392	Ken Griffey Jr./MVP	.50
393	Gregg Olson/MVP	.05
394	Rafael Palmeiro/MVP	.20
395	Roger Clemens/MVP	.30
396	George Brett/MVP	.30
397	Cecil Fielder/MVP	.05
398	Brian Harper/MVP	.05
399	Bobby Thigpen/MVP	.05
400	Roberto Kelly/MVP	.05
401	Danny Darwin/MVP	.05
402	Dave Justice/MVP	.05
403	Lee Smith/MVP	.05
404	Ryne Sandberg/MVP	.25
405	Eddie Murray/MVP	.05
406	Tim Wallach/MVP	.05
407	Kevin Mitchell/MVP	.05
408	Darryl Strawberry/MVP	.05
409	Joe Carter/MVP	.05
410	Len Dykstra/MVP	.05
411	Doug Drabek/MVP	.05
412	Chris Sabo/MVP	.05
413	Paul Marak **RC** (RR)	.05
414	Tim McIntosh (RR)	.05
415	Brian Barnes **RC** (RR)	.05
416	Eric Gunderson **RC** (RR)	.05
417	Mike Gardiner **RC** (RR)	.05
418	Steve Carter (RR)	.05
419	Gerald Alexander **RC** (RR)	.05
420	Rich Garces **RC** (RR)	.05
421	Chuck Knoblauch **RC** (RR)	.50
422	Scott Aldred **RC** (RR)	.05
423	Wes Chamberlain **RC** (RR)	.05
424	Lance Dickson **RC** (RR)	.05
425	Greg Colbrunn **RC** (RR)	.10
426	Rich Delucia **RC** (RR)	.05
427	Jeff Conine **RC** (RR)	.50
428	Steve Decker **RC** (RR)	.05
429	Turner Ward **RC** (RR)	.05
430	Mo Vaughn (RR)	.05
431	Steve Chitren **RC** (RR)	.05
432	Mike Benjamin (RR)	.05
433	Ryne Sandberg/AS	.25
434	Len Dykstra/AS	.05
435	Andre Dawson/AS	.15
436	Mike Scioscia/AS	.05
437	Ozzie Smith/AS	.25
438	Kevin Mitchell/AS	.05
439	Jack Armstrong/AS	.05
440	Chris Sabo/AS	.05
441	Will Clark/AS	.05
442	Mel Hall	.05
443	Mark Gardner	.05
444	Mike Devereaux	.05
445	Kirk Gibson	.05
446	Terry Pendleton	.05
447	Mike Harkey	.05
448	Jim Eisenreich	.05
449	Benito Santiago	.05
450	Oddibe McDowell	.05
451	Cecil Fielder	.05
452	Ken Griffey Sr.	.05
453	Bert Blyleven	.10
454	Howard Johnson	.05
455	Monty Farris	.05
456	Tony Pena	.05
457	Tim Raines	.05
458	Dennis Rasmussen	.05
459	Luis Quinones	.05
460	B.J. Surhoff	.05
461	Ernest Riles	.05
462	Rick Sutcliffe	.05
463	Danny Tartabull	.05
464	Pete Incaviglia	.05
465	Carlos Martinez	.05
466	Ricky Jordan	.05
467	John Cerutti	.05
468	Dave Winfield	.40
469	Francisco Oliveras	.05
470	Roy Smith	.05
471	Barry Larkin	.05
472	Ron Darling	.05
473	David Wells	.05
474	Glenn Davis	.05
475	Neal Heaton	.05
476	Ron Hassey	.05
477	Frank Thomas	.40
478	Greg Vaughn	.05
479	Todd Burns	.05
480	Candy Maldonado	.05
481	Dave LaPoint	.05
482	Alvin Davis	.05
483	Mike Scott	.05
484	Dale Murphy	.20
485	Ben McDonald	.05
486	Jay Howell	.05
487	Vince Coleman	.05
488	Alfredo Griffin	.05
489	Sandy Alomar	.05
490	Kirby Puckett	.50
491	Andres Thomas	.05
492	Jack Morris	.05
493	Matt Young	.05
494	Greg Myers	.05
495	Barry Bonds	1.00
496	Scott Cooper	.05
497	Dan Schatzeder	.05
498	Jesse Barfield	.05
499	Jerry Goff	.05
500	Checklist 332-408	.05
501	Anthony Telford **RC**	.05
502	Eddie Murray	.40
503	Omar Olivares **RC**	.05
504	Ryne Sandberg	.50
505	Jeff Montgomery	.05
506	Mark Parent	.05
507	Ron Gant	.05
508	Frank Tanana	.05
509	Jay Buhner	.05
510	Max Venable	.05
511	Wally Whitehurst	.05
512	Gary Pettis	.05
513	Tom Brunansky	.05
514	Tim Wallach	.05
515	Craig Lefferts	.05
516	Tim Layana **RC**	.05
517	Darryl Hamilton	.05
518	Rick Reuschel	.05
519	Steve Wilson	.05
520	Kurt Stillwell	.05
521	Rafael Palmeiro	.30
522	Ken Patterson	.05
523	Len Dykstra	.05
524	Tony Fernandez	.05
525	Kent Anderson	.05
526	Mark Leonard **RC**	.05
527	Allan Anderson	.05
528	Tom Browning	.05
529	Frank Viola	.05
530	John Olerud	.05
531	Juan Agosto	.05
532	Zane Smith	.05
533	Scott Sanderson	.05
534	Barry Jones	.05
535	Mike Felder	.05
536	Jose Canseco	.20
537	Felix Fermin	.05
538	Roberto Kelly	.05
539	Brian Holman	.05
540	Mark Davidson	.05
541	Terry Mulholland	.05
542	Randy Milligan	.05
543	Jose Gonzalez	.05
544	Craig Wilson **RC**	.05
545	Mike Hartley	.05
546	Greg Swindell	.05
547	Gary Gaetti	.05
548	Dave Justice	.05
549	Steve Searcy	.05
550	Erik Hanson	.05
551	Dave Stieb	.05
552	Andy Van Slyke	.05
553	Mike Greenwell	.05
554	Kevin Maas	.05
555	Delino Deshields	.05
556	Curt Schilling	.20
557	Ramon Martinez	.05
558	Pedro Guerrero	.05
559	Dwight Smith	.05
560	Mark Davis	.05
561	Shawn Abner	.05
562	Charlie Leibrandt	.05
563	John Shelby	.05
564	Bill Swift	.05
565	Mike Fetters	.05
566	Alejandro Pena	.05
567	Ruben Sierra	.05
568	Carlos Quintana	.05
569	Kevin Gross	.05
570	Derek Lilliquist	.05
571	Jack Armstrong	.05
572	Greg Brock	.05
573	Mike Kingery	.05
574	Greg Smith	.05
575	Brian McRae **RC**	.10
576	Jack Daugherty	.05
577	Ozzie Guillen	.05
578	Joe Boever	.05
579	Luis Sojo	.05
580	Chili Davis	.05
581	Don Robinson	.05
582	Brian Harper	.05
583	Paul O'Neill	.05
584	Bob Ojeda	.05
585	Mookie Wilson	.05
586	Rafael Ramirez	.05
587	Gary Redus	.05
588	Jamie Quirk	.05
589	Shawn Hilligas	.05
590	Tom Edens **RC**	.05
591	Joe Klink	.05
592	Charles Nagy	.05
593	Eric Plunk	.05
594	Tracy Jones	.05
595	Craig Biggio	.05
596	Jose DeJesus	.05
597	Mickey Tettleton	.05
598	Chris Gwynn	.05
599	Rex Hudler	.05
600	Checklist 409-506	.05
601	Jim Gott	.05
602	Jeff Manto	.05
603	Nelson Liriano	.05
604	Mark Lemke	.05
605	Clay Parker	.05
606	Edgar Martinez	.05
607	Mark Whiten **RC**	.10
608	Ted Power	.05
609	Tom Bolton	.05
610	Tom Herr	.05
611	Andy Hawkins	.05
612	Scott Ruskin	.05
613	Ron Kittle	.05
614	John Wetteland	.05
615	Mike Perez **RC**	.05
616	Dave Clark	.05
617	Brent Mayne	.05
618	Jack Clark	.05
619	Marvin Freeman	.05
620	Edwin Nunez	.05
621	Russ Swan	.05
622	Johnny Ray	.05
623	Charlie O'Brien	.05
624	Joe Bitker **RC**	.05
625	Mike Marshall	.05
626	Otis Nixon	.05
627	Andy Benes	.05
628	Ron Oester	.05
629	Ted Higuera	.05
630	Kevin Bass	.05
631	Damon Berryhill	.05
632	Bo Jackson	.10
633	Brad Arnsberg	.05
634	Jerry Willard	.05
635	Tommy Greene	.05
636	Bob MacDonald **RC**	.05
637	Kirk McCaskill	.05
638	John Burkett	.05
639	Paul Abbott **RC**	.05
640	Todd Benzinger	.05
641	Todd Hundley	.05
642	George Bell	.05
643	Javier Ortiz **RC**	.05
644	Sid Bream	.05
645	Bob Welch	.05
646	Phil Bradley	.05
647	Bill Krueger	.05
648	Rickey Henderson	.40
649	Kevin Wickander	.05

650	Steve Balboni	.05
651	Gene Harris	.05
652	Jim Deshaies	.05
653	Jason Grimsley	.05
654	Joe Orsulak	.05
655	Jimmy Poole RC	.05
656	Felix Jose	.05
657	Dennis Cook	.05
658	Tom Brookens	.05
659	Junior Ortiz	.05
660	Jeff Parrett	.05
661	Jerry Don Gleaton	.05
662	Brent Knackert	.05
663	Rance Mulliniks	.05
664	John Smiley	.05
665	Larry Andersen	.05
666	Willie McGee	.05
667	Chris Nabholz RC	.05
668	Brady Anderson	.05
669	Darren Holmes RC	.10
670	Ken Hill	.05
671	Gary Varsho	.05
672	Bill Pecota	.05
673	Fred Lynn	.05
674	Kevin D. Brown	.05
675	Dan Petry	.05
676	Mike Jackson	.05
677	Wally Joyner	.05
678	Danny Jackson	.05
679	Bill Haselman RC	.05
680	Mike Boddicker	.05
681	Mel Rojas RC	.05
682	Roberto Alomar	.20
683	Dave Justice (R.O.Y.)	.05
684	Chuck Crim	.05
685a	Matt Williams (Last line of Career Highlights ends, "most DP's in.")	.10
685b	Matt Williams (Last line ends "8/24-27/87.")	.25
686	Shawon Dunston	.05
687	Jeff Schulz RC	.05
688	John Barfield RC	.05
689	Gerald Young	.05
690	Luis Gonzalez RC	.75
691	Frank Wills	.05
692	Chuck Finley	.05
693	Sandy Alomar (R.O.Y.)	.05
694	Tim Drummond	.05
695	Herm Winningham	.05
696	Darryl Strawberry	.05
697	Al Leiter	.05
698	Karl Rhodes RC	.05
699	Stan Belinda	.05
700	Checklist 507-604	.05
701	Lance Blankenship	.05
702	Willie Stargell (Puzzle Card)	.05
703	Jim Gantner	.05
704	Reggie Harris RC	.05
705	Rob Ducey	.05
706	Tim Hulett	.05
707	Atlee Hammaker	.05
708	Xavier Hernandez	.05
709	Chuck McElroy	.05
710	John Mitchell	.05
711	Carlos Hernandez	.05
712	Geronimo Pena	.05
713	Jim Neidlinger RC	.05
714	John Orton	.05
715	Terry Leach	.05
716	Mike Stanton	.05
717	Walt Terrell	.05
718	Luis Aquino	.05
719	Bud Black	.05
720	Bob Kipper	.05
721	Jeff Gray RC	.05
722	Jose Rijo	.05
723	Curt Young	.05
724	Jose Vizcaino	.05
725	Junior Tomlin RC	.05
726	Junior Noboa	.05
727	Bob Welch (Award Winner)	.05
728	Gary Ward	.05
729	Rob Deer	.05
730	David Segui RC	.05
731	Mark Carreon	.05
732	Vicente Palacios	.05
733	Sam Horn	.05
734	Howard Farmer RC	.05
735	Ken Dayley	.05
736	Kelly Mann	.05
737	Joe Grahe RC	.05
738	Kelly Downs	.05
739	Jimmy Kremers RC	.05
740	Kevin Appier	.05
741	Jeff Reed	.05
742	Jose Rijo (World Series)	.05
743	Dave Rohde RC	.05
744	Len Dykstra, Dale Murphy Dr. Dirt/Mr. Clean	.10
745	Paul Sorrento	.05
746	Thomas Howard	.05
747	Matt Stark RC	.05
748	Harold Baines	.05
749	Doug Dascenzo	.05
750	Doug Drabek (Award Winner)	.05
751	Gary Sheffield	.20
752	Terry Lee RC	.05
753	Jim Vatcher RC	.05
754	Lee Stevens	.05
755	Randy Veres	.05
756	Bill Doran	.05
757	Gary Wayne	.05
758	Pedro Munoz RC	.05

759	Chris Hammond	.05
760	Checklist 605-702	.05
761	Rickey Henderson (MVP)	.20
762	Barry Bonds (MVP)	.50
763	Billy Hatcher (World Series)	.05
764	Julio Machado	.05
765	Jose Mesa	.05
766	Willie Randolph (World Series)	.05
767	Scott Erickson RC	.10
768	Travis Fryman	.05
769	Rich Rodriguez RC	.05
770	Checklist 703-770; BC1-BC22	.05

Elite

	NM/M
Complete Set (10):	250.00
Common Player:	15.00
1 Barry Bonds	60.00
2 George Brett	40.00
3 Jose Canseco	25.00
4 Andre Dawson	15.00
5 Doug Drabek	7.50
6 Cecil Fielder	7.50
7 Rickey Henderson	25.00
8 Matt Williams	7.50
--- Nolan Ryan (Legend)	65.00
--- Ryne Sandberg (Signature)	100.00

Rookies

	NM/M
Complete Set (56):	4.00
Common Player:	.05
1 Pat Kelly	.05
2 Rich DeLucia	.05
3 Wes Chamberlain	.05
4 Scott Leius	.05
5 Darryl Kile	.05
6 Milt Cuyler	.05
7 Todd Van Poppel	.05
8 Ray Lankford	.05
9 Brian Hunter	.05
10 Tony Perezchica	.05
11 Ced Landrum	.05
12 Dave Burba	.05
13 Ramon Garcia	.05
14 Ed Sprague	.05
15 Warren Newson	.05
16 Paul Faries	.05
17 Luis Gonzalez	.15
18 Charles Nagy	.05
19 Chris Hammond	.05
20 Frank Castillo	.05
21 Pedro Munoz	.05
22 Orlando Merced	.05
23 Jose Melendez	.05
24 Kirk Dressendorfer	.05
25 Heathcliff Slocumb	.05
26 Doug Simons	.05
27 Mike Timlin	.05
28 Jeff Fassero	.05
29 Mark Leiter	.05
30 Jeff Bagwell RC	2.50
31 Brian McRae	.05
32 Mark Whiten	.05

33	Ivan Rodriguez RC	1.50
34	Wade Taylor	.05
35	Darren Lewis	.05
36	Mo Vaughn	.25
37	Mike Remlinger	.05
38	Rick Wilkins	.05
39	Chuck Knoblauch	.05
40	Kevin Morton	.05
41	Carlos Rodriguez	.05
42	Mark Lewis	.05
43	Brent Mayne	.05
44	Chris Haney	.05
45	Denis Boucher	.05
46	Mike Gardiner	.05
47	Jeff Johnson	.05
48	Dean Palmer	.05
49	Chuck McElroy	.05
50	Chris Jones	.05
51	Scott Kamieniecki	.05
52	Al Osuna	.05
53	Rusty Meacham	.05
54	Chito Martinez	.05
55	Reggie Jefferson	.05
56	Checklist	.05

1992 Donruss

	NM/M
Unopened Retail Set (788):	15.00
Unopened Hobby Set (784):	12.50
Unopened "Coca-Cola" Set (784):	25.00
Complete Set (784):	12.00
Common Player:	.05
Rod Carew Puzzle:	.50
Series 1 or 2 Pack (15):	.50
Series 1 or 2 Wax Box (36):	15.00
Blister Rack (92):	1.50
1 Mark Wohlers RC	.05
2 Wil Cordero	.05
3 Kyle Abbott	.05
4 Dave Nilsson RC	.05
5 Kenny Lofton	.15
6 Luis Mercedes RC	.05
7 Roger Salkeld RC	.05
8 Eddie Zosky	.05
9 Todd Van Poppel RC	.10
10 Frank Seminara RC	.05
11 Andy Ashby RC	.10
12 Reggie Jefferson	.05
13 Ryan Klesko	.05
14 Carlos Garcia RC	.10
15 John Ramos RC	.05
16 Eric Karros	.05
17 Pat Lennon RC	.05
18 Eddie Taubensee RC	.05
19 Roberto Hernandez RC	.05
20 D.J. Dozier	.05
21 Dave Henderson/AS	.05
22 Cal Ripken, Jr./AS	.50
23 Wade Boggs/AS	.25
24 Ken Griffey Jr./AS	.50
25 Jack Morris/AS	.05
26 Danny Tartabull/AS	.05
27 Cecil Fielder/AS	.05
28 Roberto Alomar/AS	.10
29 Sandy Alomar/AS	.05
30 Rickey Henderson/AS	.25
31 Ken Hill	.05
32 John Habyan	.05
33 Otis Nixon	.05
34 Tim Wallach	.05
35 Cal Ripken, Jr.	1.00
36 Gary Carter	.35
37 Juan Agosto	.05
38 Doug Dascenzo	.05
39 Kirk Gibson	.05
40 Benito Santiago	.05
41 Otis Nixon	.05
42 Andy Allanson	.05
43 Brian Holman	.05
44 Dick Schofield	.05
45 Dave Magadan	.05
46 Rafael Palmeiro	.35
47 Jody Reed	.05
48 Ivan Calderon	.05
49 Greg Harris	.05
50 Chris Sabo	.05
51 Paul Molitor	.35
52 Robby Thompson	.05
53 Dave Smith	.05
54 Mark Davis	.05

55	Kevin Brown	.05
56	Donn Pall	.05
57	Len Dykstra	.05
58	Roberto Alomar	.15
59	Jeff Robinson	.05
60	Willie McGee	.05
61	Jay Buhner	.05
62	Mike Pagliarulo	.05
63	Paul O'Neill	.05
64	Hubie Brooks	.05
65	Kelly Gruber	.05
66	Ken Caminiti	.05
67	Gary Redus	.05
68	Harold Baines	.05
69	Charlie Hough	.05
70	B.J. Surhoff	.05
71	Walt Weiss	.05
72	Shawn Hillegas	.05
73	Roberto Kelly	.05
74	Jeff Ballard	.05
75	Craig Biggio	.05
76	Pat Combs	.05
77	Jeff Robinson	.05
78	Tim Belcher	.05
79	Cris Carpenter	.05
80	Checklist 1-79	.05
81	Steve Avery	.05
82	Chris James	.05
83	Brian Harper	.05
84	Charlie Leibrandt	.05
85	Mickey Tettleton	.05
86	Pete O'Brien	.05
87	Danny Darwin	.05
88	Bob Walk	.05
89	Jeff Reardon	.05
90	Bobby Rose	.05
91	Danny Jackson	.05
92	John Morris	.05
93	Bud Black	.05
94	Tommy Greene	.05
95	Rick Aguilera	.05
96	Gary Gaetti	.05
97	David Cone	.05
98	John Olerud	.05
99	Joel Skinner	.05
100	Jay Bell	.05
101	Bob Milacki	.05
102	Norm Charlton	.05
103	Chuck Crim	.05
104	Terry Steinbach	.05
105	Juan Samuel	.05
106	Steve Howe	.05
107	Rafael Belliard	.05
108	Joey Cora	.05
109	Tommy Greene	.05
110	Gregg Olson	.05
111	Frank Tanana	.05
112	Lee Smith	.05
113	Greg Harris	.05
114	Dwayne Henry	.05
115	Chili Davis	.05
116	Kent Mercker	.05
117	Brian Barnes	.05
118	Rich DeLucia	.05
119	Andre Dawson	.20
120	Carlos Baerga	.05
121	Mike LaValliere	.05
122	Jeff Gray	.05
123	Bruce Hurst	.05
124	Alvin Davis	.05
125	John Candelaria	.05
126	Matt Nokes	.05
127	George Bell	.05
128	Bret Saberhagen	.05
129	Jeff Russell	.05
130	Jim Abbott	.05
131	Bill Gullickson	.05
132	Todd Zeile	.05
133	Dave Winfield	.35
134	Wally Whitehurst	.05
135	Matt Williams	.05
136	Tom Browning	.05
137	Marquis Grissom	.05
138	Erik Hanson	.05
139	Rob Dibble	.05
140	Don August	.05
141	Tom Henke	.05
142	Dan Pasqua	.05
143	George Brett	.60
144	Jerald Clark	.05
145	Robin Ventura	.05
146	Dale Murphy	.20
147	Dennis Eckersley	.30
148	Eric Yelding	.05
149	Mario Diaz	.05
150	Casey Candaele	.05
151	Steve Olin	.05
152	Luis Salazar	.05
153	Kevin Maas	.05
154	Nolan Ryan	.50
155	Barry Jones	.05
156	Chris Hoiles	.05
157	Bobby Ojeda	.05
158	Pedro Guerrero	.05
159	Paul Assenmacher	.05
160	Checklist 80-157	.05
161	Mike Macfarlane	.05
162	Craig Lefferts	.05
163	Brian Hunter RC	.05
164	Alan Trammell	.05
165	Ken Griffey Jr.	.65
166	Lance Parrish	.05
167	Brian Downing	.05
168	John Barfield	.05
169	Jack Clark	.05

170	Chris Nabholz	.05
171	Tim Teufel	.05
172	Chris Hammond	.05
173	Robin Yount	.35
174	Dave Righetti	.05
175	Joe Girardi	.05
176	Mike Boddicker	.05
177	Dean Palmer	.05
178	Greg Hibbard	.05
179	Randy Ready	.05
180	Devon White	.05
181	Mark Eichhorn	.05
182	Mike Felder	.05
183	Joe Klink	.05
184	Steve Bedrosian	.05
185	Barry Larkin	.05
186	John Franco	.05
187	Ed Sprague **RC**	.05
188	Mark Portugal	.05
189	Jose Lind	.05
190	Bob Welch	.05
191	Alex Fernandez	.05
192	Gary Sheffield	.20
193	Rickey Henderson	.35
194	Rod Nichols	.05
195	Scott Kamieniecki **RC**	.05
196	Mike Flanagan	.05
197	Steve Finley	.05
198	Darren Daulton	.05
199	Leo Gomez	.05
200	Mike Morgan	.05
201	Bob Tewksbury	.05
202	Sid Bream	.05
203	Sandy Alomar	.05
204	Greg Gagne	.05
205	Juan Berenguer	.05
206	Cecil Fielder	.05
207	Randy Johnson	.35
208	Tony Pena	.05
209	Doug Drabek	.05
210	Wade Boggs	.45
211	Bryan Harvey	.05
212	Jose Vizcaino	.05
213	Alonzo Powell **RC**	.05
214	Will Clark	.05
215	Rickey Henderson	.20
216	Jack Morris	.05
217	Junior Felix	.05
218	Vince Coleman	.05
219	Jimmy Key	.05
220	Alex Cole	.05
221	Bill Landrum	.05
222	Randy Milligan	.05
223	Jose Rijo	.05
224	Greg Vaughn	.05
225	Dave Stewart	.05
226	Lenny Harris	.05
227	Scott Sanderson	.05
228	Jeff Blauser	.05
229	Ozzie Guillen	.05
230	John Kruk	.05
231	Bob Melvin	.05
232	Milt Cuyler	.05
233	Felix Jose	.05
234	Ellis Burks	.05
235	Pete Harnisch	.05
236	Kevin Tapani	.05
237	Terry Pendleton	.05
238	Mark Gardner	.05
239	Harold Reynolds	.05
240	Checklist 158-237	.05
241	Mike Harkey	.05
242	Felix Fermin	.05
243	Barry Bonds	1.00
244	Roger Clemens	.60
245	Dennis Rasmussen	.05
246	Jose DeLeon	.05
247	Orel Hershiser	.05
248	Mel Hall	.05
249	Rick Wilkins **RC**	.05
250	Tom Gordon	.05
251	Kevin Reimer	.05
252	Luis Polonia	.05
253	Mike Henneman	.05
254	Tom Pagnozzi	.05
255	Chuck Finley	.05
256	Mackey Sasser	.05
257	John Burkett	.05
258	Hal Morris	.05
259	Larry Walker	.05
260	Billy Swift	.05
261	Joe Oliver	.05
262	Julio Machado	.05
263	Todd Stottlemyre	.05
264	Matt Merullo	.05
265	Brent Mayne	.05
266	Thomas Howard	.05
267	Lance Johnson	.05
268	Terry Mulholland	.05
269	Rick Honeycutt	.05
270	Luis Gonzalez	.05
271	Jose Guzman	.05
272	Jimmy Jones	.05
273	Mark Lewis	.05
274	Rene Gonzales	.05
275	Jeff Johnson **RC**	.05
276	Dennis Martinez	.05
277	Delino DeShields	.05
278	Sam Horn	.05
279	Kevin Gross	.05
280	Jose Oquendo	.05
281	Mark Grace	.05
282	Mark Gubicza	.05
283	Fred McGriff	.05
284	Ron Gant	.05
285	Lou Whitaker	.05
286	Edgar Martinez	.05
287	Ron Tingley	.05
288	Kevin McReynolds	.05
289	Ivan Rodriguez	.30
290	Mike Gardiner	.05
291	Chris Haney **RC**	.05
292	Darrin Jackson	.05
293	Bill Doran	.05
294	Ted Higuera	.05
295	Jeff Brantley	.05
296	Les Lancaster	.05
297	Jim Eisenreich	.05
298	Ruben Sierra	.05
299	Scott Radinsky	.05
300	Jose DeJesus	.05
301	Mike Timlin **RC**	.05
302	Luis Sojo	.05
303	Kelly Downs	.05
304	Scott Bankhead	.05
305	Pedro Munoz	.05
306	Scott Scudder	.05
307	Kevin Elster	.05
308	Duane Ward	.05
309	Darryl Kile **RC**	.10
310	Orlando Merced	.05
311	Dave Henderson	.05
312	Tim Raines	.05
313	Mark Lee	.05
314	Mike Gallego	.05
315	Charles Nagy	.05
316	Jesse Barfield	.05
317	Todd Frohwirth	.05
318	Al Osuna	.05
319	Darrin Fletcher	.05
320	Checklist 238-316	.05
321	David Segui	.05
322	Stan Javier	.05
323	Bryn Smith	.05
324	Jeff Treadway	.05
325	Mark Whiten	.05
326	Kent Hrbek	.05
327	Dave Justice	.05
328	Tony Phillips	.05
329	Rob Murphy	.05
330	Kevin Morton	.05
331	John Smiley	.05
332	Luis Rivera	.05
333	Wally Joyner	.05
334	Heathcliff Slocumb **RC**	.05
335	Rick Cerone	.05
336	Mike Remlinger **RC**	.05
337	Mike Moore	.05
338	Lloyd McClendon	.05
339	Al Newman	.05
340	Kirk McCaskill	.05
341	Howard Johnson	.05
342	Greg Myers	.05
343	Kal Daniels	.05
344	Bernie Williams	.05
345	Shane Mack	.05
346	Gary Thurman	.05
347	Dante Bichette	.05
348	Mark McGwire	.75
349	Travis Fryman	.05
350	Ray Lankford	.05
351	Mike Jeffcoat	.05
352	Jack McDowell	.05
353	Mitch Williams	.05
354	Mike Devereaux	.05
355	Andres Galarraga	.05
356	Henry Cotto	.05
357	Scott Bailes	.05
358	Jeff Bagwell	.35
359	Scott Leius	.05
360	Zane Smith	.05
361	Bill Pecota	.05
362	Tony Fernandez	.05
363	Glenn Braggs	.05
364	Bill Spiers	.05
365	Vicente Palacios	.05
366	Tim Burke	.05
367	Randy Tomlin	.05
368	Kenny Rogers	.05
369	Brett Butler	.05
370	Pat Kelly	.05
371	Bip Roberts	.05
372	Gregg Jefferies	.05
373	Kevin Bass	.05
374	Ron Karkovice	.05
375	Paul Gibson	.05
376	Bernard Gilkey	.05
377	Dave Gallagher	.05
378	Bill Wegman	.05
379	Pat Borders	.05
380	Ed Whitson	.05
381	Gilberto Reyes	.05
382	Russ Swan	.05
383	Andy Van Slyke	.05
384	Wes Chamberlain	.05
385	Steve Chitren	.05
386	Greg Olson	.05
387	Brian McRae	.05
388	Rich Rodriguez	.05
389	Steve Decker	.05
390	Chuck Knoblauch	.05
391	Bobby Witt	.05
392	Eddie Murray	.35
393	Juan Gonzalez	.20
394	Scott Ruskin	.05
395	Jay Howell	.05
396	Checklist 317-396	.05
397	Royce Clayton	.05
398	John Jaha **RC**	.05
399	Dan Wilson	.05
400	Archie Corbin **RC**	.05
401	Barry Manuel **RC**	.05
402	Kim Batiste	.05
403	Pat Mahomes **RC**	.05
404	Dave Fleming	.05
405	Jeff Juden	.05
406	Jim Thome	.40
407	Sam Militello	.05
408	Jeff Nelson **RC**	.05
409	Anthony Young	.05
410	Tino Martinez	.05
411	Jeff Mutis **RC**	.05
412	Rey Sanchez **RC**	.05
413	Chris Gardner **RC**	.05
414	John Vander Wal **RC**	.10
415	Reggie Sanders	.05
416	Brian Williams **RC**	.05
417	Mo Sanford	.05
418	David Weathers **RC**	.05
419	Hector Fajardo **RC**	.05
420	Steve Foster **RC**	.05
421	Lance Dickson	.05
422	Andre Dawson/AS	.15
423	Ozzie Smith/AS	.25
424	Chris Sabo/AS	.05
425	Tony Gwynn/AS	.25
426	Tom Glavine/AS	.05
427	Bobby Bonilla/AS	.05
428	Will Clark/AS	.05
429	Ryne Sandberg/AS	.25
430	Benito Santiago/AS	.05
431	Ivan Calderon/AS	.05
432	Ozzie Smith	.45
433	Tim Leary	.05
434	Bret Saberhagen	.05
435	Mel Rojas	.05
436	Ben McDonald	.05
437	Tim Crews	.05
438	Rex Hudler	.05
439	Chico Walker	.05
440	Kurt Stillwell	.05
441	Tony Gwynn	.45
442	John Smoltz	.05
443	Lloyd Moseby	.05
444	Mike Schooler	.05
445	Joe Grahe	.05
446	Dwight Gooden	.05
447	Oil Can Boyd	.05
448	John Marzano	.05
449	Bret Barberie	.05
450	Mike Maddux	.05
451	Jeff Reed	.05
452	Dale Sveum	.05
453	Jose Uribe	.05
454	Bob Scanlan	.05
455	Kevin Appier	.05
456	Jeff Huson	.05
457	Ken Patterson	.05
458	Ricky Jordan	.05
459	Tom Candiotti	.05
460	Lee Stevens	.05
461	Rod Beck **RC**	.10
462	Dave Valle	.05
463	Scott Erickson	.05
464	Chris Jones	.05
465	Mark Carreon	.05
466	Rob Ducey	.05
467	Jim Corsi	.05
468	Jeff King	.05
469	Curt Young	.05
470	Bo Jackson	.15
471	Chris Bosio	.05
472	Jamie Quirk	.05
473	Jesse Orosco	.05
474	Alvaro Espinoza	.05
475	Joe Orsulak	.05
476	Checklist 397-477	.05
477	Gerald Young	.05
478	Wally Backman	.05
479	Juan Bell	.05
480	Mike Scioscia	.05
481	Omar Olivares	.05
482	Francisco Cabrera	.05
483	Greg Swindell	.05
484	Terry Leach	.05
485	Tommy Gregg	.05
486	Scott Aldred	.05
487	Greg Briley	.05
488	Phil Plantier	.05
489	Curtis Wilkerson	.05
490	Tom Brunansky	.05
491	Mike Fetters	.05
492	Frank Castillo	.05
493	Joe Boever	.05
494	Kirt Manwaring	.05
495	Wilson Alvarez	.05
496	Gene Larkin	.05
497	Gary DiSarcina	.05
498	Frank Viola	.05
499	Manuel Lee	.05
500	Albert Belle	.05
501	Stan Belinda	.05
502	Dwight Evans	.05
503	Eric Davis	.05
504	Darren Holmes	.05
505	Mike Bordick	.05
506	Dave Hansen	.05
507	Lee Guetterman	.05
508	Keith Mitchell **RC**	.05
509	Melido Perez	.05
510	Dickie Thon	.05
511	Mark Williamson	.05
512	Mark Salas	.05
513	Milt Thompson	.05
514	Mo Vaughn	.05
515	Jim Deshaies	.05
516	Rich Garces	.05
517	Lonnie Smith	.05
518	Spike Owen	.05
519	Tracy Jones	.05
520	Greg Maddux	.45
521	Carlos Martinez	.05
522	Neal Heaton	.05
523	Mike Greenwell	.05
524	Andy Benes	.05
525	Jeff Schaefer	.05
526	Mike Sharperson	.05
527	Wade Taylor	.05
528	Jerome Walton	.05
529	Storm Davis	.05
530	Jose Hernandez **RC**	.05
531	Mark Langston	.05
532	Rob Deer	.05
533	Geronimo Pena	.05
534	Juan Guzman **RC**	.10
535	Pete Schourek	.05
536	Todd Benzinger	.05
537	Billy Hatcher	.05
538	Tom Foley	.05
539	Dave Cochrane	.05
540	Mariano Duncan	.05
541	Edwin Nunez	.05
542	Rance Mulliniks	.05
543	Carlton Fisk	.35
544	Luis Aquino	.05
545	Ricky Bones	.05
546	Craig Grebeck	.05
547	Charlie Hayes	.05
548	Jose Canseco	.25
549	Andujar Cedeno	.05
550	Geno Petralli	.05
551	Javier Ortiz	.05
552	Rudy Seanez	.05
553	Rich Gedman	.05
554	Eric Plunk	.05
555	Nolan Ryan, Rich Gossage	.25
556	Checklist 478-555	.05
557	Greg Colbrunn	.05
558	Chito Martinez **RC**	.05
559	Darryl Strawberry	.05
560	Luis Alicea	.05
561	Dwight Smith	.05
562	Terry Shumpert	.05
563	Jim Vatcher	.05
564	Deion Sanders	.10
565	Walt Terrell	.05
566	Dave Burba	.05
567	Dave Howard	.05
568	Todd Hundley	.05
569	Jack Daugherty	.05
570	Scott Cooper	.05
571	Bill Sampen	.05
572	Jose Melendez	.05
573	Freddie Benavides	.05
574	Jim Gantner	.05
575	Trevor Wilson	.05
576	Ryne Sandberg	.45
577	Kevin Seitzer	.05
578	Gerald Alexander	.05
579	Mike Huff	.05
580	Von Hayes	.05
581	Derek Bell	.05
582	Mike Stanley	.05
583	Kevin Mitchell	.05
584	Mike Jackson	.05
585	Dan Gladden	.05
586	Ted Power	.05
587	Jeff Innis	.05
588	Bob MacDonald	.05
589	Jose Tolentino **RC**	.05
590	Bob Patterson	.05
591	Scott Brosius **RC**	.10
592	Frank Thomas	.35
593	Darryl Hamilton	.05
594	Kirk Dressendorfer	.05
595	Jeff Shaw	.05
596	Don Mattingly	.60
597	Glenn Davis	.05
598	Andy Mota	.05
599	Jason Grimsley	.05
600	Jimmy Poole	.05
601	Jim Gott	.05
602	Stan Royer	.05
603	Marvin Freeman	.05
604	Denis Boucher	.05
605	Denny Neagle	.05
606	Mark Lemke	.05
607	Jerry Don Gleaton	.05
608	Brent Knackert	.05
609	Carlos Quintana	.05
610	Bobby Bonilla	.05
611	Joe Hesketh	.05
612	Daryl Boston	.05
613	Shawon Dunston	.05
614	Danny Cox	.05
615	Darren Lewis	.05
616	Alejandro Pena, Kent Mercker, Mark Wohlers	.05
617	Kirby Puckett	.45
618	Franklin Stubbs	.05
619	Chris Donnels	.05
620	David Wells	.05
621	Mike Aldrete	.05
622	Bob Kipper	.05
623	Anthony Telford	.05
624	Randy Myers	.05
625	Willie Randolph	.05
626	Joe Slusarski	.05
627	John Wetteland	.05
628	Greg Cadaret	.05
629	Tom Glavine	.20
630	Wilson Alvarez	.05

No.	Player	Price
631	Wally Ritchie	.05
632	Mike Mussina	.25
633	Mark Leiter	.05
634	Gerald Perry	.05
635	Matt Young	.05
636	Checklist 556-635	.05
637	Scott Hemond	.05
638	David West	.05
639	Jim Clancy	.05
640	Doug Piatt	.05
641	Omar Vizquel	.05
642	Rick Sutcliffe	.05
643	Glenallen Hill	.05
644	Gary Varsho	.05
645	Tony Fossas	.05
646	Jack Howell	.05
647	Jim Campanis RC	.05
648	Chris Gwynn	.05
649	Jim Leyritz	.05
650	Chuck McElroy	.05
651	Sean Berry	.05
652	Donald Harris	.05
653	Don Slaught	.05
654	Rusty Meacham RC	.05
655	Scott Terry	.05
656	Ramon Martinez	.05
657	Keith Miller	.05
658	Ramon Garcia	.05
659	Milt Hill RC	.05
660	Steve Frey	.05
661	Bob McClure	.05
662	Ced Landrum RC	.05
663	Doug Henry RC	.05
664	Candy Maldonado	.05
665	Carl Willis	.05
666	Jeff Montgomery	.05
667	Craig Shipley RC	.05
668	Warren Newson RC	.05
669	Mickey Morandini	.05
670	Brook Jacoby	.05
671	Ryan Bowen RC	.05
672	Bill Krueger	.05
673	Rob Mallicoat	.05
674	Doug Jones	.05
675	Scott Livingstone	.05
676	Danny Tartabull	.05
677	Joe Carter	.05
678	Cecil Espy	.05
679	Randy Velarde	.05
680	Bruce Ruffin	.05
681	Ted Wood RC	.05
682	Dan Plesac	.05
683	Eric Bullock	.05
684	Junior Ortiz	.05
685	Dave Hollins	.05
686	Dennis Martinez	.05
687	Larry Andersen	.05
688	Doug Simons	.05
689	Tim Spehr RC	.05
690	Calvin Jones RC	.05
691	Mark Guthrie	.05
692	Alfredo Griffin	.05
693	Joe Carter	.05
694	Terry Mathews RC	.05
695	Pascual Perez	.05
696	Gene Nelson	.05
697	Gerald Williams	.05
698	Chris Cron RC	.05
699	Steve Buechele	.05
700	Paul McClellan	.05
701	Jim Lindeman	.05
702	Francisco Oliveras	.05
703	Rob Maurer RC	.05
704	Pat Hentgen RC	.15
705	Jaime Navarro	.05
706	Mike Magnante RC	.05
707	Nolan Ryan	1.00
708	Bobby Thigpen	.05
709	John Cerutti	.05
710	Steve Wilson	.05
711	Hensley Meulens	.05
712	Rheal Cormier RC	.05
713	Scott Bradley	.05
714	Mitch Webster	.05
715	Roger Mason	.05
716	Checklist 636-716	.05
717	Jeff Fassero RC	.05
718	Cal Eldred	.05
719	Sid Fernandez	.05
720	Bob Zupcic RC	.05
721	Jose Offerman	.05
722	Cliff Brantley RC	.05
723	Ron Darling	.05
724	Dave Stieb	.05
725	Hector Villanueva	.05
726	Mike Hartley	.05
727	Arthur Rhodes RC	.05
728	Randy Bush	.05
729	Steve Sax	.05
730	Dave Otto	.05
731	John Wehner RC	.05
732	Dave Martinez	.05
733	Ruben Amaro RC	.05
734	Billy Ripken	.05
735	Steve Farr	.05
736	Shawn Abner	.05
737	Gil Heredia RC	.05
738	Ron Jones	.05
739	Tony Castillo	.05
740	Sammy Sosa	.45
741	Julio Franco	.05
742	Tim Naehring	.05
743	Steve Wapnick RC	.05
744	Craig Wilson	.05
745	Darrin Chapin RC	.05
746	Chris George RC	.05
747	Mike Simms	.05
748	Rosario Rodriguez	.05
749	Skeeter Barnes	.05
750	Roger McDowell	.05
751	Dann Howitt	.05
752	Paul Sorrento	.05
753	Braulio Castillo RC	.05
754	Yorkis Perez RC	.05
755	Willie Fraser	.05
756	Jeremy Hernandez RC	.05
757	Curt Schilling	.20
758	Steve Lyons	.05
759	Dave Anderson	.05
760	Willie Banks	.05
761	Mark Leonard	.05
762	Jack Armstrong	.05
763	Scott Servais	.05
764	Ray Stephens	.05
765	Junior Noboa	.05
766	Jim Olander RC	.05
767	Joe Magrane	.05
768	Lance Blankenship	.05
769	Mike Humphreys RC	.05
770	Jarvis Brown RC	.05
771	Damon Berryhill	.05
772	Alejandro Pena	.05
773	Jose Mesa	.05
774	Gary Cooper RC	.05
775	Carney Lansford	.05
776	Mike Bielecki	.05
777	Charlie O'Brien	.05
778	Carlos Hernandez	.05
779	Howard Farmer	.05
780	Mike Stanton	.05
781	Reggie Harris	.05
782	Xavier Hernandez	.05
783	Bryan Hickerson RC	.05
784	Checklist 717-BC8	.05

Diamond Kings

FRED McGRIFF

		NM/M
Complete Set (27):		17.50
Common Player:		.40
1	Paul Molitor	2.00
2	Will Clark	.50
3	Joe Carter	.50
4	Julio Franco	.50
5	Cal Ripken, Jr.	6.00
6	Dave Justice	.50
7	George Bell	.50
8	Frank Thomas	2.00
9	Wade Boggs	4.00
10	Scott Sanderson	.50
11	Jeff Bagwell	2.00
12	John Kruk	.50
13	Felix Jose	.50
14	Harold Baines	.50
15	Dwight Gooden	.50
16	Brian McRae	.50
17	Jay Bell	.50
18	Brett Butler	.50
19	Hal Morris	.50
20	Mark Langston	.50
21	Scott Erickson	.50
22	Randy Johnson	2.00
23	Greg Swindell	.50
24	Dennis Martinez	.50
25	Tony Phillips	.50
26	Fred McGriff	.50
27	Checklist	.10

Elite

		NM/M
Complete Set (12):		300.00
Common Player:		7.50
9	Wade Boggs	15.00
10	Joe Carter	7.50
11	Will Clark	7.50
12	Dwight Gooden	7.50
13	Ken Griffey Jr.	30.00
14	Tony Gwynn	15.00
15	Howard Johnson	7.50
16	Terry Pendleton	7.50
17	Kirby Puckett	15.00
18	Frank Thomas	15.00

KEN GRIFFEY, JR.

The ELITE Series

---	Rickey Henderson (Legend)	20.00
---	Cal Ripken, Jr. (Signature)	250.00

1992 Donruss Previews

RYAN KLESKO — BRAVES • FIRST BASE

		NM/M
Complete Set (12):		25.00
Common Player:		.50
1	Wade Boggs	2.50
2	Barry Bonds	7.50
3	Will Clark	.50
4	Andre Dawson	.75
5	Dennis Eckersley	1.50
6	Robin Ventura	.50
7	Ken Griffey Jr.	4.00
8	Kelly Gruber	.50
9	Ryan Klesko	.50
10	Cal Ripken, Jr.	7.50
11	Nolan Ryan	7.50
12	Todd Van Poppel	.50

Rookies

HARVEY PULLIAM — ROYALS • OUTFIELD

		NM/M
Complete Set (132):		6.00
Common Player:		.05
Pack (12):		.50
Wax Box (36):		10.00
1	Kyle Abbott	.05
2	Troy Afenir	.05
3	Rich Amaral	.05
4	Ruben Amaro	.05
5	Billy Ashley	.05
6	Pedro Astacio	.05
7	Jim Austin	.05
8	Robert Ayrault	.05
9	Kevin Baez	.05
10	Esteban Beltre	.05
11	Brian Bohanon	.05
12	Kent Bottenfield	.05
13	Jeff Branson	.05
14	Brad Brink	.05
15	John Briscoe	.05
16	Doug Brocail	.05
17	Rico Brogna	.05
18	J.T. Bruett	.05
19	Jacob Brumfield	.05
20	Jim Bullinger	.05
21	Kevin Campbell	.05
22	Pedro Castellano	.05
23	Mike Christopher	.05
24	Archi Cianfrocco	.05
25	Mark Clark	.05
26	Craig Colbert	.05
27	Victor Cole	.05
28	Steve Cooke	.05
29	Tim Costo	.05
30	Chad Curtis	.05
31	Doug Davis	.05
32	Gary DiSarcina	.05
33	John Doherty	.05
34	Mike Draper	.05
35	Monty Fariss	.05
36	Bien Figueroa	.05
37	John Flaherty	.05
38	Tim Fortugno	.05
39	Eric Fox	.05
40	Jeff Frye RC	.05
41	Ramon Garcia	.05
42	Brent Gates	.05
43	Tom Goodwin	.05
44	Buddy Groom	.05
45	Jeff Grotewold	.05
46	Juan Guerrero	.05
47	Johnny Guzman	.05
48	Shawn Hare	.05
49	Ryan Hawblitzel	.05
50	Bert Heffernan	.05
51	Butch Henry	.05
52	Cesar Hernandez	.05
53	Vince Horsman	.05
54	Steve Hosey	.05
55	Pat Howell	.05
56	Peter Hoy	.05
57	Jon Hurst	.05
58	Mark Hutton	.05
59	Shawn Jeter	.05
60	Joel Johnston	.05
61	Jeff Kent	1.00
62	Kurt Knudsen	.05
63	Kevin Koslofski	.05
64	Danny Leon	.05
65	Jesse Levis	.05
66	Tom Marsh	.05
67	Ed Martel	.05
68	Al Martin	.05
69	Pedro Martinez	2.00
70	Derrick May	.05
71	Matt Maysey	.05
72	Russ McGinnis	.05
73	Tim McIntosh	.05
74	Jim McNamara	.05
75	Jeff McNeely	.05
76	Rusty Meacham	.05
77	Tony Melendez	.05
78	Henry Mercedes	.05
79	Paul Miller	.05
80	Joe Millette	.05
81	Blas Minor	.05
82	Dennis Moeller	.05
83	Raul Mondesi	.25
84	Rob Natal	.05
85	Troy Neel	.05
86	David Nied	.05
87	Jerry Nielsen	.05
88	Donovan Osborne	.05
89	John Patterson	.05
90	Roger Pavlik	.05
91	Dan Peltier	.05
92	Jim Pena	.05
93	William Pennyfeather	.05
94	Mike Perez	.05
95	Hipolito Pichardo	.05
96	Greg Pirkl	.05
97	Harvey Pulliam	.05
98	Manny Ramirez RC	3.00
99	Pat Rapp	.05
100	Jeff Reboulet	.05
101	Darren Reed	.05
102	Shane Reynolds	.05
103	Bill Risley	.05
104	Ben Rivera	.05
105	Henry Rodriguez	.05
106	Rico Rossy	.05
107	Johnny Ruffin	.05
108	Steve Scarsone	.05
109	Tim Scott	.05
110	Steve Shifflett	.05
111	Dave Silvestri	.05
112	Matt Stairs	.05
113	William Suero	.05
114	Jeff Tackett	.05
115	Eddie Taubensee	.05
116	Rick Trlicek	.05
117	Scooter Tucker	.05
118	Shane Turner	.05
119	Julio Valera	.05
120	Paul Wagner	.05
121	Tim Wakefield	.05
122	Mike Walker	.05
123	Bruce Walton	.05
124	Lenny Webster	.05
125	Bob Wickman	.05
126	Mike Williams	.05
127	Kerry Woodson	.05
128	Eric Young	.05
129	Kevin Young	.05
130	Pete Young	.05
131	Checklist	.05
132	Checklist	.05

Rookie Phenoms

BRET BOONE
SEATTLE MARINERS • SS/2B

		NM/M
Complete Set (20):		12.50
Common Player:		.25
1	Moises Alou	.25
2	Bret Boone	.50
3	Jeff Conine	.25
4	Dave Fleming	.25
5	Tyler Green	.25
6	Eric Karros	.25
7	Pat Listach	.25
8	Kenny Lofton	.25
9	Mike Piazza	10.00
10	Tim Salmon	.50
11	Andy Stankiewicz	.25
12	Dan Walters	.25
13	Ramon Caraballo	.25
14	Brian Jordan	.25
15	Ryan Klesko	.25
16	Sam Militello	.25
17	Frank Seminara	.25
18	Salomon Torres	.25
19	John Valentin	.25
20	Wil Cordero	.25

Update

RICK SUTCLIFFE
ORIOLES • PITCHER

		NM/M
Complete Set (22):		15.00
Common Player:		.50
1	Pat Listach	.50
2	Andy Stankiewicz	.50
3	Brian Jordan	.50
4	Dan Walters	.50
5	Chad Curtis	.50
6	Kenny Lofton	1.50
7	Mark McGwire	8.00
8	Eddie Murray	1.00
9	Jeff Reardon	.50
10	Frank Viola	.50
11	Gary Sheffield	.75
12	George Bell	.50
13	Rick Sutcliffe	.50
14	Wally Joyner	.50
15	Kevin Seitzer	.50
16	Bill Krueger	.50
17	Danny Tartabull	.50
18	Dave Winfield	2.00
19	Gary Carter	1.50
20	Bobby Bonilla	.50
21	Cory Snyder	.50
22	Bill Swift	.50

1993 Donruss

		NM/M
Complete Set (792):		10.00
Common Player:		.05
Series 1 or 2 Pack (14):		.50
Series 1 or 2 Box (36):		10.00
1	Craig Lefferts	.05
2	Kent Mercker	.05
3	Phil Plantier	.05
4	Alex Arias RC	.05
5	Julio Valera	.05
6	Dan Wilson	.05
7	Frank Thomas	.50
8	Eric Anthony	.05

ROBERTO ALOMAR 2B

9	Derek Lilliquist	.05
10	Rafael Bournigal RC	.05
11	Manny Alexander RC	.05
12	Bret Barberie	.05
13	Mickey Tettleton	.05
14	Anthony Young	.05
15	Tim Spehr	.05
16	Bob Ayrault RC	.05
17	Bill Wegman	.05
18	Jay Bell	.05
19	Rick Aguilera	.05
20	Todd Zeile	.05
21	Steve Farr	.05
22	Andy Benes	.05
23	Lance Blankenship	.05
24	Ted Wood	.05
25	Omar Vizquel	.05
26	Steve Avery	.05
27	Brian Bohanon	.05
28	Rick Wilkins	.05
29	Devon White	.05
30	Bobby Ayala RC	.05
31	Leo Gomez	.05
32	Mike Simms	.05
33	Ellis Burks	.05
34	Steve Wilson	.05
35	Jim Abbott	.05
36	Tim Wallach	.05
37	Wilson Alvarez	.05
38	Daryl Boston	.05
39	Sandy Alomar, Jr.	.05
40	Mitch Williams	.05
41	Rico Brogna	.05
42	Gary Varsho	.05
43	Kevin Appier	.05
44	Eric Wedge	.05
45	Dante Bichette	.05
46	Jose Oquendo	.05
47	Mike Trombley RC	.05
48	Dan Walters	.05
49	Gerald Williams	.05
50	Bud Black	.05
51	Bobby Witt	.05
52	Mark Davis	.05
53	Shawn Barton RC	.05
54	Paul Assenmacher	.05
55	Kevin Reimer	.05
56	Billy Ashley RC	.05
57	Eddie Zosky	.05
58	Chris Sabo	.05
59	Billy Ripken	.05
60	Scooter Tucker RC	.05
61	Tim Wakefield RC	.10
62	Mitch Webster	.05
63	Jack Clark	.05
64	Mark Gardner	.05
65	Lee Stevens	.05
66	Todd Hundley	.05
67	Bobby Thigpen	.05
68	Dave Hollins	.05
69	Jack Armstrong	.05
70	Alex Cole	.05
71	Mark Carreon	.05
72	Todd Worrell	.05
73	Steve Shifflett RC	.05
74	Jerald Clark	.05
75	Paul Molitor	.50
76	Larry Carter RC	.05
77	Rich Rowland	.05
78	Damon Berryhill	.05
79	Willie Banks	.05
80	Hector Villanueva	.05
81	Mike Gallego	.05
82	Tim Belcher	.05
83	Mike Bordick	.05
84	Craig Biggio	.05
85	Lance Parrish	.05
86	Brett Butler	.05
87	Mike Timlin	.05
88	Brian Barnes	.05
89	Brady Anderson	.05
90	D.J. Dozier	.05
91	Frank Viola	.05
92	Darren Daulton	.05
93	Chad Curtis	.05
94	Zane Smith	.05
95	George Bell	.05
96	Rex Hudler	.05
97	Mark Whiten	.05
98	Tim Teufel	.05
99	Kevin Ritz	.05

100	Jeff Brantley	.05
101	Jeff Conine	.05
102	Vinny Castilla	.05
103	Greg Vaughn	.05
104	Steve Buechele	.05
105	Darren Reed	.05
106	Bip Roberts	.05
107	John Habyan	.05
108	Scott Servais	.05
109	Walt Weiss	.05
110	J.T. Snow RC	.50
111	Jay Buhner	.05
112	Darryl Strawberry	.05
113	Roger Pavlik RC	.05
114	Chris Nabholz	.05
115	Pat Borders	.05
116	Pat Howell RC	.05
117	Gregg Olson	.05
118	Curt Schilling	.25
119	Roger Clemens	.65
120	Victor Cole RC	.05
121	Gary DiSarcina	.05
122	Checklist 1-80	.05
123	Steve Sax	.05
124	Chuck Carr	.05
125	Mark Lewis	.05
126	Tony Gwynn	.60
127	Travis Fryman	.05
128	Dave Burba	.05
129	Wally Joyner	.05
130	John Smoltz	.05
131	Cal Eldred	.05
132	Checklist 81-159	.05
133	Arthur Rhodes	.05
134	Jeff Blauser	.05
135	Scott Cooper	.05
136	Doug Strange	.05
137	Luis Sojo	.05
138	Jeff Branson RC	.05
139	Alex Fernandez	.05
140	Ken Caminiti	.05
141	Charles Nagy	.05
142	Tom Candiotti	.05
143	Willie Green	.05
144	John Vander Wal	.05
145	Kurt Knudsen RC	.05
146	John Franco	.05
147	Eddie Pierce RC	.05
148	Kim Batiste	.05
149	Darren Holmes	.05
150	Steve Cooke RC	.05
151	Terry Jorgensen	.05
152	Mark Clark RC	.05
153	Randy Velarde	.05
154	Greg Harris	.05
155	Kevin Campbell RC	.05
156	John Burkett	.05
157	Kevin Mitchell	.05
158	Deion Sanders	.05
159	Jose Canseco	.25
160	Jeff Hartsock RC	.05
161	Tom Quinlan RC	.05
162	Tim Pugh RC	.05
163	Glenn Davis	.05
164	Shane Reynolds RC	.10
165	Jody Reed	.05
166	Mike Sharperson	.05
167	Scott Lewis	.05
168	Dennis Martinez	.05
169	Scott Radinsky	.05
170	Dave Gallagher	.05
171	Jim Thome	.45
172	Terry Mulholland	.05
173	Milt Cuyler	.05
174	Bob Patterson	.05
175	Jeff Montgomery	.05
176	Tim Salmon	.25
177	Franklin Stubbs	.05
178	Donovan Osborne	.05
179	Jeff Reboulet RC	.05
180	Jeremy Hernandez	.05
181	Charlie Hayes	.05
182	Matt Williams	.05
183	Mike Raczka	.05
184	Francisco Cabrera	.05
185	Rich DeLucia	.05
186	Sammy Sosa	.60
187	Ivan Rodriguez	.45
188	Bret Boone	.15
189	Juan Guzman	.05
190	Tom Browning	.05
191	Randy Milligan	.05
192	Steve Finley	.05
193	John Patterson	.05
194	Kip Gross	.05
195	Tony Fossas	.05
196	Ivan Calderon	.05
197	Junior Felix	.05
198	Pete Schourek	.05
199	Craig Grebeck	.05
200	Juan Bell	.05
201	Glenallen Hill	.05
202	Danny Jackson	.05
203	John Kiely	.05
204	Bob Tewksbury	.05
205	Kevin Koslofski RC	.05
206	Craig Shipley	.05
207	John Jaha	.05
208	Royce Clayton	.05
209	Mike Piazza	2.00
210	Ron Gant	.05
211	Scott Erickson	.05
212	Doug Dascenzo	.05
213	Andy Stankiewicz	.05
214	Geronimo Berroa	.05

215	Dennis Eckersley	.45
216	Al Osuna	.05
217	Tino Martinez	.05
218	Henry Rodriguez RC	.05
219	Ed Sprague	.05
220	Ken Hill	.05
221	Chito Martinez	.05
222	Bret Saberhagen	.05
223	Mike Greenwell	.05
224	Mickey Morandini	.05
225	Chuck Finley	.05
226	Denny Neagle	.05
227	Kirk McCaskill	.05
228	Rheal Cormier	.05
229	Paul Sorrento	.05
230	Darrin Jackson	.05
231	Rob Deer	.05
232	Bill Swift	.05
233	Kevin McReynolds	.05
234	Terry Pendleton	.05
235	Dave Nilsson	.05
236	Chuck McElroy	.05
237	Derek Parks	.05
238	Norm Charlton	.05
239	Matt Nokes	.05
240	Juan Guerrero RC	.05
241	Jeff Parrett	.05
242	Ryan Thompson	.05
243	Dave Fleming	.05
244	Dave Hansen	.05
245	Monty Fariss	.05
246	Archi Cianfrocco RC	.05
247	Pat Hentgen	.05
248	Bill Pecota	.05
249	Ben McDonald	.05
250	Cliff Brantley	.05
251	John Valentin RC	.05
252	Jeff King	.05
253	Reggie Williams RC	.05
254	Checklist 160-238	.05
255	Ozzie Guillen	.05
256	Mike Perez	.05
257	Thomas Howard	.05
258	Kurt Stillwell	.05
259	Mike Henneman	.05
260	Steve Decker	.05
261	Brent Mayne	.05
262	Otis Nixon	.05
263	Mark Keifer RC	.05
264	Checklist 239-317	.05
265	Richie Lewis RC	.05
266	Pat Gomez RC	.05
267	Scott Taylor RC	.05
268	Shawon Dunston	.05
269	Greg Myers	.05
270	Tim Costo	.05
271	Greg Hibbard	.05
272	Pete Harnisch	.05
273	Dave Milcki RC	.05
274	Orel Hershiser	.05
275	Sean Berry	.05
276	Doug Simons	.05
277	John Doherty RC	.05
278	Eddie Murray	.50
279	Chris Haney	.05
280	Stan Javier	.05
281	Jaime Navarro	.05
282	Orlando Merced	.05
283	Kent Hrbek	.05
284	Bernard Gilkey	.05
285	Russ Springer	.05
286	Mike Maddux	.05
287	Eric Fox RC	.05
288	Mark Leonard	.05
289	Tim Leary	.05
290	Brian Hunter	.05
291	Donald Harris	.05
292	Bob Scanlan	.05
293	Turner Ward	.05
294	Hal Morris	.05
295	Jimmy Poole	.05
296	Doug Jones	.05
297	Tony Pena	.05
298	Ramon Martinez	.05
299	Tim Fortugno RC	.05
300	Marquis Grissom	.05
301	Lance Johnson	.05
302	Jeff Kent RC	1.00
303	Reggie Jefferson	.05
304	Wes Chamberlain	.05
305	Shawn Hare RC	.05
306	Mike LaValliere	.05
307	Gregg Jefferies	.05
308	Troy Neel RC	.05
309	Pat Listach	.05
310	Geronimo Pena	.05
311	Pedro Munoz	.05
312	Guillermo Velasquez RC	.05
313	Roberto Kelly	.05
314	Mike Jackson	.05
315	Rickey Henderson	.05
316	Mark Lemke	.05
317	Erik Hanson	.05
318	Derrick May	.05
319	Geno Petralli	.05
320	Melvin Nieves (Rated Rookie)	.05
321	Doug Linton RC	.05
322	Rob Dibble	.05
323	Chris Hoiles	.05
324	Jimmy Jones	.05
325	Dave Staton	.05
326	Pedro Martinez	.05
327	Paul Quantrill RC	.05
328	Greg Colbrunn	.05
329	Hilly Hathaway RC	.05

330	Jeff Innis	.05
331	Ron Karkovice	.05
332	Keith Shepherd **RC**	.05
333	Alan Embree **RC**	.05
334	Paul Wagner **RC**	.05
335	Dave Haas **RC**	.05
336	Ozzie Canseco	.05
337	Bill Sampen	.05
338	Rich Rodriguez	.05
339	Dean Palmer	.05
340	Greg Litton	.05
341	Jim Tatum	.05
342	Todd Haney **RC**	.05
343	Larry Casian	.05
344	Ryne Sandberg	.60
345	Sterling Hitchcock **RC**	.10
346	Chris Hammond	.05
347	Vince Horsman **RC**	.05
348	Butch Henry **RC**	.05
349	Dann Howitt	.05
350	Roger McDowell	.05
351	Jack Morris	.05
352	Bill Krueger	.05
353	Cris Colon **RC**	.05
354	Joe Vitko **RC**	.05
355	Willie McGee	.05
356	Jay Baller	.05
357	Pat Mahomes	.05
358	Roger Mason	.05
359	Jerry Nielsen **RC**	.05
360	Tom Pagnozzi	.05
361	Kevin Baez **RC**	.05
362	Tim Scott **RC**	.05
363	Domingo Martinez **RC**	.05
364	Kirt Manwaring	.05
365	Rafael Palmeiro	.45
366	Ray Lankford	.05
367	Tim McIntosh	.05
368	Jessie Hollins **RC**	.05
369	Scott Leius	.05
370	Bill Doran	.05
371	Sam Militello **RC**	.05
372	Ryan Bowen	.05
373	Dave Henderson	.05
374	Dan Smith	.05
375	Steve Reed **RC**	.05
376	Jose Offerman	.05
377	Kevin Brown	.05
378	Darrin Fletcher	.05
379	Duane Ward	.05
380	Wayne Kirby (Rated Rookie)	.05
381	Steve Scarsone **RC**	.05
382	Mariano Duncan	.05
383	Ken Ryan **RC**	.05
384	Lloyd McClendon	.05
385	Brian Holman	.05
386	Braulio Castillo	.05
387	Danny Leon **RC**	.05
388	Omar Olivares	.05
389	Kevin Wickander	.05
390	Fred McGriff	.05
391	Phil Clark	.05
392	Darren Lewis	.05
393	Phil Hiatt **RC**	.10
394	Mike Morgan	.05
395	Shane Mack	.05
396	Checklist 318-396	.05
397	David Segui	.05
398	Rafael Belliard	.05
399	Tim Naehring	.05
400	Frank Castillo	.05
401	Joe Grahe	.05
402	Reggie Sanders	.05
403	Roberto Hernandez	.05
404	Luis Gonzalez	.05
405	Carlos Baerga	.05
406	Carlos Hernandez	.05
407	Pedro Astacio	.05
408	Mel Rojas	.05
409	Scott Livingstone	.05
410	Chico Walker	.05
411	Brian McRae	.05
412	Ben Rivera	.05
413	Ricky Bones	.05
414	Andy Van Slyke	.05
415	Chuck Knoblauch	.05
416	Luis Alicea	.05
417	Bob Wickman	.05
418	Doug Brocail	.05
419	Scott Brosius	.05
420	Rod Beck	.05
421	Edgar Martinez	.05
422	Ryan Klesko	.05
423	Nolan Ryan	1.50
424	Rey Sanchez	.05
425	Roberto Alomar	.20
426	Barry Larkin	.05
427	Mike Mussina	.30
428	Jeff Bagwell	.50
429	Mo Vaughn	.05
430	Eric Karros	.05
431	John Orton	.05
432	Wil Cordero	.05
433	Jack McDowell	.05
434	Howard Johnson	.05
435	Albert Belle	.05
436	John Kruk	.05
437	Skeeter Barnes	.05
438	Don Slaught	.05
439	Rusty Meacham	.05
440	Tim Laker	.05
441	Robin Yount	.50
442	Brian Jordan	.05
443	Kevin Tapani	.05
444	Gary Sheffield	.25
445	Rich Monteleone	.05
446	Will Clark	.05
447	Jerry Browne	.05
448	Jeff Treadway	.05
449	Mike Schooler	.05
450	Mike Harkey	.05
451	Julio Franco	.05
452	Kevin Young	.05
453	Kelly Gruber	.05
454	Jose Rijo	.05
455	Mike Devereaux	.05
456	Andujar Cedeno	.05
457	Damion Easley	.05
458	Kevin Gross	.05
459	Matt Young	.05
460	Matt Stairs	.05
461	Luis Polonia	.05
462	Dwight Gooden	.05
463	Warren Newson	.05
464	Jose DeLeon	.05
465	Jose Mesa	.05
466	Danny Cox	.05
467	Dan Gladden	.05
468	Gerald Perry	.05
469	Mike Boddicker	.05
470	Jeff Gardner	.05
471	Doug Henry	.05
472	Mike Benajmin	.05
473	Dan Peltier	.05
474	Mike Stanton	.05
475	John Smiley	.05
476	Dwight Smith	.05
477	Jim Leyritz	.05
478	Dwayne Henry	.05
479	Mark McGwire	1.00
480	Pete Incaviglia	.05
481	Dave Cochrane	.05
482	Eric Davis	.05
483	John Olerud	.05
484	Ken Bottenfield	.05
485	Mark McLemore	.05
486	Dave Magadan	.05
487	John Marzano	.05
488	Ruben Amaro	.05
489	Rob Ducey	.05
490	Stan Belinda	.05
491	Dan Pasqua	.05
492	Joe Magrane	.05
493	Brook Jacoby	.05
494	Gene Harris	.05
495	Mark Leiter	.05
496	Bryan Hickerson	.05
497	Tom Gordon	.05
498	Pete Smith	.05
499	Chris Bosio	.05
500	Shawn Boskie	.05
501	Dave West	.05
502	Milt Hill	.05
503	Pat Kelly	.05
504	Joe Boever	.05
505	Terry Steinbach	.05
506	Butch Huskey	.05
507	David Valle	.05
508	Mike Scioscia	.05
509	Kenny Rogers	.05
510	Moises Alou	.05
511	David Wells	.05
512	Mackey Sasser	.05
513	Todd Frohwirth	.05
514	Ricky Jordan	.05
515	Mike Gardiner	.05
516	Gary Redus	.05
517	Gary Gaetti	.05
518	Checklist 397-476	.05
519	Carlton Fisk	.50
520	Ozzie Smith	.60
521	Rod Nichols	.05
522	Benito Santiago	.05
523	Bill Gullickson	.05
524	Robby Thompson	.05
525	Mike Macfarlane	.05
526	Sid Bream	.05
527	Darryl Hamilton	.05
528	Checklist 477-555	.05
529	Jeff Tackett	.05
530	Greg Olson	.05
531	Bob Zupcic	.05
532	Mark Grace	.05
533	Steve Frey	.05
534	Dave Martinez	.05
535	Robin Ventura	.05
536	Casey Candaele	.05
537	Kenny Lofton	.05
538	Jay Howell	.05
539	Fernando Ramsey	.05
540	Larry Walker	.05
541	Cecil Fielder	.05
542	Lee Guetterman	.05
543	Keith Miller	.05
544	Len Dykstra	.05
545	B.J. Surhoff	.05
546	Bob Walk	.05
547	Brian Harper	.05
548	Lee Smith	.05
549	Danny Tartabull	.05
550	Frank Seminara	.05
551	Henry Mercedes	.05
552	Dave Righetti	.05
553	Ken Griffey Jr.	.75
554	Tom Glavine	.25
555	Juan Gonzalez	.25
556	Jim Bullinger	.05
557	Derek Bell	.05
558	Cesar Hernandez	.05
559	Cal Ripken, Jr.	1.50
560	Eddie Taubensee	.05
561	John Flaherty	.05
562	Todd Benzinger	.05
563	Hubie Brooks	.05
564	Delino DeShields	.05
565	Tim Raines	.05
566	Sid Fernandez	.05
567	Steve Olin	.05
568	Tommy Greene	.05
569	Buddy Groom	.05
570	Randy Tomlin	.05
571	Hipolito Pichardo	.05
572	Rene Arocha (Rated Rookie)	.05
573	Mike Fetters	.05
574	Felix Jose	.05
575	Gene Larkin	.05
576	Bruce Hurst	.05
577	Bernie Williams	.05
578	Trevor Wilson	.05
579	Bob Welch	.05
580	Dave Justice	.05
581	Randy Johnson	.50
582	Jose Vizcaino	.05
583	Jeff Huson	.05
584	Rob Maurer	.05
585	Todd Stottlemyre	.05
586	Joe Oliver	.05
587	Bob Milacki	.05
588	Rob Murphy	.05
589	Greg Pirkl	.05
590	Lenny Harris	.05
591	Luis Rivera	.05
592	John Wetteland	.05
593	Mark Langston	.05
594	Bobby Bonilla	.05
595	Esteban Beltre	.05
596	Mike Hartley	.05
597	Felix Fermin	.05
598	Carlos Garcia	.05
599	Frank Tanana	.05
600	Pedro Guerrero	.05
601	Terry Shumpert	.05
602	Wally Whitehurst	.05
603	Kevin Seitzer	.05
604	Chris James	.05
605	Greg Gohr	.05
606	Mark Wohlers	.05
607	Kirby Puckett	.60
608	Greg Maddux	.60
609	Don Mattingly	.65
610	Greg Cadaret	.05
611	Dave Stewart	.05
612	Mark Portugal	.05
613	Pete O'Brien	.05
614	Bobby Ojeda	.05
615	Joe Carter	.05
616	Pete Young	.05
617	Sam Horn	.05
618	Vince Coleman	.05
619	Wade Boggs	.60
620	Todd Pratt **RC**	.05
621	Ron Tingley	.05
622	Doug Drabek	.05
623	Scott Hemond	.05
624	Tim Jones	.05
625	Dennis Cook	.05
626	Jose Melendez	.05
627	Mike Munoz	.05
628	Jim Pena	.05
629	Gary Thurman	.05
630	Charlie Leibrandt	.05
631	Scott Fletcher	.05
632	Andre Dawson	.25
633	Greg Gagne	.05
634	Greg Swindell	.05
635	Kevin Maas	.05
636	Xavier Hernandez	.05
637	Ruben Sierra	.05
638	Dimitri Young	.05
639	Harold Reynolds	.05
640	Tom Goodwin	.05
641	Todd Burns	.05
642	Jeff Fassero	.05
643	Dave Winfield	.50
644	Willie Randolph	.05
645	Luis Mercedes	.05
646	Dale Murphy	.20
647	Danny Darwin	.05
648	Dennis Moeller	.05
649	Chuck Crim	.05
650	Checklist 556-634	.05
651	Shawn Abner	.05
652	Tracy Woodson	.05
653	Scott Scudder	.05
654	Tom Lampkin	.05
655	Alan Trammell	.05
656	Cory Snyder	.05
657	Chris Gwynn	.05
658	Lonnie Smith	.05
659	Jim Austin	.05
660	Checklist 635-713	.05
661	Tim Hulett	.05
662	Marvin Freeman	.05
663	Greg Harris	.05
664	Heathcliff Slocumb	.05
665	Mike Butcher	.05
666	Steve Foster	.05
667	Donn Pall	.05
668	Darryl Kile	.05
669	Jesse Levis	.05
670	Jim Gott	.05
671	Mark Hutton **RC**	.05
672	Brian Drahman	.05
673	Chad Kreuter	.05
674	Tony Fernandez	.05
675	Jose Lind	.05
676	Kyle Abbott	.05
677	Dan Plesac	.05
678	Barry Bonds	1.50
679	Chili Davis	.05
680	Stan Royer	.05
681	Scott Kamienlecki	.05
682	Carlos Martinez	.05
683	Mike Moore	.05
684	Candy Maldanado	.05
685	Jeff Nelson	.05
686	Lou Whitaker	.05
687	Jose Guzman	.05
688	Manuel Lee	.05
689	Bob MacDonald	.05
690	Scott Bankhead	.05
691	Alan Mills	.05
692	Brian Williams	.05
693	Tom Brunansky	.05
694	Lenny Webster	.05
695	Greg Briley	.05
696	Paul O'Neill	.05
697	Joey Cora	.05
698	Charlie O'Brien	.05
699	Junior Ortiz	.05
700	Ron Darling	.05
701	Tony Phillips	.05
702	William Pennyfeather	.05
703	Mark Gubicza	.05
704	Steve Hosey	.05
705	Henry Cotto	.05
706	David Hulse **RC**	.05
707	Mike Pagliarulo	.05
708	Dave Stieb	.05
709	Melido Perez	.05
710	Jimmy Key	.05
711	Jeff Russell	.05
712	David Cone	.05
713	Russ Swan	.05
714	Mark Guthrie	.05
715	Checklist 714-792	.05
716	Al Martin	.05
717	Randy Knorr	.05
718	Mike Stanley	.05
719	Rick Sutcliffe	.05
720	Terry Leach	.05
721	Chipper Jones	1.00
722	Jim Eisenreich	.05
723	Tom Henke	.05
724	Jeff Frye	.05
725	Harold Baines	.05
726	Scott Sanderson	.05
727	Tom Foley	.05
728	Bryan Harvey/ED	.05
729	Tom Edens	.05
730	Eric Young/ED	.05
731	Dave Weathers/ED	.05
732	Spike Owen	.05
733	Scott Aldred/ED	.05
734	Cris Carpenter/ED	.05
735	Dion James	.05
736	Joe Girardi/ED	.05
737	Nigel Wilson/ED	.05
738	Scott Chiamparino/ED	.05
739	Jeff Reardon	.05
740	Willie Blair/ED	.05
741	Jim Corsi/ED	.05
742	Ken Patterson	.05
743	Andy Ashby/ED	.05
744	Rob Natal/ED	.05
745	Kevin Bass	.05
746	Freddie Benavides/ED	.05
747	Chris Donnels/ED	.05
748	Kerry Woodson **RC**	.05
749	Calvin Jones/ED	.05
750	Gary Scott	.05
751	Joe Orsulak	.05
752	Armando Reynoso/ED	.05
753	Monty Farriss/ED	.05
754	Billy Hatcher	.05
755	Denis Boucher/ED	.05
756	Walt Weiss	.05
757	Mike Fitzgerald	.05
758	Rudy Seanez	.05
759	Bret Barberie/ED	.05
760	Mo Sanford/ED	.05
761	Pedro Castellano/ED **RC**	.05
762	Chuck Carr/ED	.05
763	Steve Howe	.05
764	Andres Galarraga	.05
765	Jeff Conine/ED	.05
766	Ted Power	.05
767	Butch Henry/ED	.05
768	Steve Decker/ED	.05
769	Storm Davis	.05
770	Vinny Castilla/ED	.05
771	Junior Felix/ED	.05
772	Walt Terrell	.05
773	Brad Ausmus/ED	.05
774	Jamie McAndrewv	.05
775	Milt Thompson	.05
776	Charlie Hayes/ED	.05
777	Jack Armstrong/ED	.05
778	Dennis Rasmussen	.05
779	Darren Holmes/ED	.05
780	Alex Arias **RC**	.05
781	Randy Bush	.05
782	Javier Lopez (Rated Rookie)	.05
783	Dante Bichette	.05
784	John Johnstone/ED	.05
785	Rene Gonzales	.05
786	Alex Cole/ED	.05
787	Jeromy Burnitz (Rated Rookie)	.05
788	Michael Huff	.05
789	Anthony Telford	.05

790	Jerald Clark/ED	.05
791	Joel Johnston	.05
792	David Nied	.05

Diamond Kings

		NM/M
Complete Set (31):		17.50
Common Player:		.25
1	Ken Griffey Jr.	4.00
2	Ryne Sandberg	3.00
3	Roger Clemens	3.50
4	Kirby Puckett	3.00
5	Bill Swift	.25
6	Larry Walker	.25
7	Juan Gonzalez	.75
8	Wally Joyner	.25
9	Andy Van Slyke	.25
10	Robin Ventura	.25
11	Bip Roberts	.25
12	Roberto Kelly	.25
13	Carlos Baerga	.25
14	Orel Hershiser	.25
16	Cecil Fielder	.25
16	Robin Yount	1.50
17	Darren Daulton	.25
18	Mark McGwire	4.00
19	Tom Glavine	.75
20	Roberto Alomar	.50
21	Gary Sheffield	.75
22	Bob Tewksbury	.25
23	Brady Anderson	.25
24	Craig Biggio	.25
25	Eddie Murray	1.50
26	Luis Polonia	.25
27	Nigel Wilson	.25
28	David Nied	.25
29	Pat Listach	.25
30	Eric Karros	.25
31	Checklist	.05

Elite

		NM/M
Complete Set (20):		150.00
Common Player:		10.00
19	Fred McGriff	10.00
20	Ryne Sandberg	20.00
21	Eddie Murray	15.00
22	Paul Molitor	15.00
23	Barry Larkin	10.00
24	Don Mattingly	25.00
25	Dennis Eckersley	15.00
26	Roberto Alomar	12.50
27	Edgar Martinez	10.00
28	Gary Sheffield	12.50
29	Darren Daulton	10.00
30	Larry Walker	10.00
31	Barry Bonds	30.00
32	Andy Van Slyke	10.00
33	Mark McGwire	25.00
34	Cecil Fielder	10.00
35	Dave Winfield	15.00
36	Juan Gonzalez	12.50
---	Robin Yount (Legend)	17.50
---	Will Clark (Signature)	40.00

1993 Donruss Elite Dominators

		NM/M
Complete Set (20):		135.00
Common Player:		3.00
1	Ryne Sandberg	10.00
2	Fred McGriff	3.00
3	Greg Maddux	10.00
4	Ron Gant	3.00
5	Dave Justice	3.00
6	Don Mattingly	12.00
7	Tim Salmon	3.00
8	Mike Piazza	12.00
9	John Olerud	3.00
10	Nolan Ryan	20.00
11	Juan Gonzalez	5.00
12	Ken Griffey Jr.	12.00
13	Frank Thomas	7.50
14	Tom Glavine	4.50
15	George Brett	12.00
16	Barry Bonds	20.00
17	Albert Belle	3.00
18	Paul Molitor	7.50
19	Cal Ripken, Jr.	20.00
20	Roberto Alomar	5.00
Autographed Cards:		
6	Don Mattingly	35.00
10	Nolan Ryan	65.00
11	Juan Gonzalez	20.00
18	Paul Molitor	20.00

Long Ball Leaders

		NM/M
Complete Set (18):		5.00
Common Player:		.10
1	Rob Deer	.10
2	Fred McGriff	.10
3	Albert Belle	.10
4	Mark McGwire	2.00
5	Dave Justice	.10
6	Jose Canseco	.25
7	Kent Hrbek	.10
8	Roberto Alomar	.20
9	Ken Griffey Jr.	1.50
10	Frank Thomas	.50
11	Darryl Strawberry	.10
12	Felix Jose	.10
13	Cecil Fielder	.10
14	Juan Gonzalez	.20
15	Ryne Sandberg	.75
16	Gary Sheffield	.20
17	Jeff Bagwell	.50
18	Larry Walker	.10

1993 Donruss Masters of the Game

		NM/M
Complete Set (16):		15.00
Common Player:		1.00
1	Frank Thomas	1.50
2	Nolan Ryan	3.00
3	Gary Sheffield	1.25
4	Fred McGriff	1.00
5	Ryne Sandberg	1.75
6	Cal Ripken, Jr.	3.00
7	Jose Canseco	1.25

8	Ken Griffey Jr.	2.50
9	Will Clark	1.00
10	Roberto Alomar	1.00
11	Juan Gonzalez	1.25
12	David Justice	1.00
13	Kirby Puckett	1.75
14	Barry Bonds	3.00
15	Robin Yount	1.50
16	Deion Sanders	1.00

MVPs

		NM/M
Complete Set (26):		10.00
Common Player:		.10
1	Luis Polonia	.10
2	Frank Thomas	.60
3	George Brett	.75
4	Paul Molitor	.60
5	Don Mattingly	.75
6	Roberto Alomar	.25
7	Terry Pendleton	.10
8	Eric Karros	.10
9	Larry Walker	.10
10	Eddie Murray	.60
11	Darren Daulton	.10
12	Ray Lankford	.10
13	Will Clark	.10
14	Cal Ripken, Jr.	2.00
15	Roger Clemens	.75
16	Carlos Baerga	.10
17	Cecil Fielder	.10
18	Kirby Puckett	.65
19	Mark McGwire	1.50
20	Ken Griffey Jr.	1.25
21	Juan Gonzalez	.30
22	Ryne Sandberg	.65
23	Bip Roberts	.10
24	Jeff Bagwell	.75
25	Barry Bonds	2.00
26	Gary Sheffield	.25

Spirit of the Game

		NM/M
Complete Set (20):		5.00
Common Player:		.25
1	Dave Winfield, Mike Bordick Turning Two	.35
2	David Justice Play at the Plate	.25
3	Roberto Alomar In There	.30
4	Dennis Eckersley Pumped	.60
5	Juan Gonzalez, Jose Canseco Dynamic Duo	.50
6	Frank Thomas, George Bell Gone	.60
7	Wade Boggs Safe or Out?	.75
8	Will Clark The Thrill	.30
9	Damon Berryhill, Bip Roberts, Glenn Braggs Safe at Home	.25
10	Cecil Fielder, Mickey Tettleton, Rob Deer Thirty X 31	.25
11	Kenny Lofton Bag Bandit	.25
12	Fred McGriff, Gary Sheffield Back to Back	.30
13	Greg Gagne, Barry Larkin Range Rovers	.25
14	Ryne Sandberg The Ball Stops Here	.75
15	Carlos Baerga, Gary Gaetti Over the Top	.25
16	Danny Tartabull At the Wall	.25
17	Brady Anderson Head First	.25
18	Frank Thomas Big Hurt	.65
19	Kevin Gross No-Hitter	.25
20	Robin Yount 3,000	.65

1993 Donruss Previews

		NM/M
Complete Set (22):		60.00
Common Player:		1.50
1	Tom Glavine	2.00
2	Ryne Sandberg	5.00
3	Barry Larkin	1.50
4	Jeff Bagwell	4.00
5	Eric Karros	1.50
6	Larry Walker	1.50
7	Eddie Murray	4.00
8	Darren Daulton	1.50
9	Andy Van Slyke	1.50
10	Gary Sheffield	2.00
11	Will Clark	1.50
12	Cal Ripken Jr.	9.00
13	Roger Clemens	6.00
14	Frank Thomas	4.00
15	Cecil Fielder	1.50
16	George Brett	6.00
17	Robin Yount	4.00
18	Don Mattingly	6.00
19	Dennis Eckersley	3.50
20	Ken Griffey Jr.	7.50
21	Jose Canseco	2.50
22	Roberto Alomar	2.00

1994 Donruss

		NM/M
Complete Set (660):		15.00
Common Player:		.05
Series 1 or 2 Pack (13):		.50
Series 1 or 2 Box (36):		12.50
1	Nolan Ryan (Career Salute 27 Years.)	2.00

2	Mike Piazza	1.00
3	Moises Alou	.05
4	Ken Griffey Jr.	1.00
5	Gary Sheffield	.25
6	Roberto Alomar	.20
7	John Kruk	.05
8	Gregg Olson	.05
9	Gregg Jefferies	.05
10	Tony Gwynn	.65
11	Chad Curtis	.05
12	Craig Biggio	.05
13	John Burkett	.05
14	Carlos Baerga	.05
15	Robin Yount	.60
16	Dennis Eckersley	.50
17	Dwight Gooden	.05
18	Ryne Sandberg	.65
19	Rickey Henderson	.60
20	Jack McDowell	.05
21	Jay Bell	.05
22	Kevin Brown	.05
23	Robin Ventura	.05
24	Paul Molitor	.60
25	Dave Justice	.05
26	Rafael Palmeiro	.50
27	Cecil Fielder	.05
28	Chuck Knoblauch	.05
29	Dave Hollins	.05
30	Jimmy Key	.05
31	Mark Langston	.05
32	Darryl Kile	.05
33	Ruben Sierra	.05
34	Ron Gant	.05
35	Ozzie Smith	.65
36	Wade Boggs	.65
37	Marquis Grissom	.05
38	Will Clark	.05
39	Kenny Lofton	.05
40	Cal Ripken, Jr.	2.00
41	Steve Avery	.05
42	Mo Vaughn	.05
43	Brian McRae	.05
44	Mickey Tettleton	.05
45	Barry Larkin	.05
46	Charlie Hayes	.05
47	Kevin Appier	.05
48	Robby Thompson	.05
49	Juan Gonzalez	.30
50	Paul O'Neill	.05
51	Marcos Armas	.05
52	Mike Butcher	.05
53	Ken Caminiti	.05
54	Pat Borders	.05
55	Pedro Munoz	.05
56	Tim Belcher	.05
57	Paul Assenmacher	.05
58	Damon Berryhill	.05
59	Ricky Bones	.05
60	Rene Arocha	.05
61	Shawn Boskie	.05
62	Pedro Astacio	.05
63	Frank Bolick	.05
64	Bud Black	.05
65	Sandy Alomar, Jr.	.05
66	Rich Amaral	.05
67	Luis Aquino	.05
68	Kevin Baez	.05
69	Mike Devereaux	.05
70	Andy Ashby	.05
71	Larry Andersen	.05
72	Steve Cooke	.05
73	Mario Daiz	.05
74	Rob Deer	.05
75	Bobby Ayala	.05
76	Freddie Benavides	.05
77	Stan Belinda	.05
78	John Doherty	.05
79	Willie Banks	.05
80	Spike Owen	.05
81	Mike Bordick	.05
82	Chili Davis	.05
83	Luis Gonzalez	.05
84	Ed Sprague	.05
85	Jeff Reboulet	.05
86	Jason Bere	.05
87	Mark Hutton	.05
88	Jeff Blauser	.05
89	Cal Eldred	.05
90	Bernard Gilkey	.05
91	Frank Castillo	.05
92	Jim Gott	.05
93	Greg Colbrunn	.05
94	Jeff Brantley	.05
95	Jeremy Hernandez	.05
96	Norm Charlton	.05
97	Alex Arias	.05
98	John Franco	.05
99	Chris Hoiles	.05
100	Brad Ausmus	.05
101	Wes Chamberlain	.05
102	Mark Dewey	.05
103	Benji Gil	.05
104	John Dopson	.05
105	John Smiley	.05
106	David Nied	.05
107	George Brett (Career Salute 21 Years.)	.75
108	Kirk Gibson	.05
109	Larry Casian	.05
110	Ryne Sandberg 2,000 Hits Checklist	.25
111	Brent Gates	.05
112	Damion Easley	.05
113	Pete Harnisch	.05
114	Danny Cox	.05
115	Kevin Tapani	.05
116	Roberto Hernandez	.05
117	Domingo Jean	.05
118	Sid Bream	.05
119	Doug Henry	.05
120	Omar Olivares	.05
121	Mike Harkey	.05
122	Carlos Hernandez	.05
123	Jeff Fassero	.05
124	Dave Burba	.05
125	Wayne Kirby	.05
126	John Cummings	.05
127	Bret Barberie	.05
128	Todd Hundley	.05
129	Tim Hulett	.05
130	Phil Clark	.05
131	Danny Jackson	.05
132	Tom Foley	.05
133	Donald Harris	.05
134	Scott Fletcher	.05
135	Johnny Ruffin	.05
136	Jerald Clark	.05
137	Billy Brewer	.05
138	Dan Gladden	.05
139	Eddie Guardado	.05
140	Cal Ripken, Jr. 2,000 Hits Checklist	.35
141	Scott Hemond	.05
142	Steve Frey	.05
143	Xavier Hernandez	.05
144	Mark Eichhorn	.05
145	Ellis Burks	.05
146	Jim Leyritz	.05
147	Mark Lemke	.05
148	Pat Listach	.05
149	Donovan Osborne	.05
150	Glenallen Hill	.05
151	Orel Hershiser	.05
152	Darrin Fletcher	.05
153	Royce Clayton	.05
154	Derek Lilliquist	.05
155	Mike Felder	.05
156	Jeff Conine	.05
157	Ryan Thompson	.05
158	Ben McDonald	.05
159	Ricky Gutierrez	.05
160	Terry Mulholland	.05
161	Carlos Garcia	.05
162	Tom Henke	.05
163	Mike Greenwell	.05
164	Thomas Howard	.05
165	Joe Girardi	.05
166	Hubie Brooks	.05
167	Greg Gohr	.05
168	Chip Hale	.05
169	Rick Honeycutt	.05
170	Hilly Hathaway	.05
171	Todd Jones	.05
172	Tony Fernandez	.05
173	Bo Jackson	.10
174	Bobby Munoz	.05
175	Greg McMichael	.05
176	Graeme Lloyd	.05
177	Tom Pagnozzi	.05
178	Derrick May	.05
179	Pedro Martinez	.60
180	Ken Hill	.05
181	Bryan Hickerson	.05
182	Jose Mesa	.05
183	Dave Fleming	.05
184	Henry Cotto	.05
185	Jeff Kent	.05
186	Mark McLemore	.05
187	Trevor Hoffman	.05
188	Todd Pratt	.05
189	Blas Minor	.05
190	Charlie Leibrandt	.05
191	Tony Pena	.05
192	Larry Luebbers **RC**	.05
193	Greg Harris	.05
194	David Cone	.05
195	Bill Gullickson	.05
196	Brian Harper	.05
197	Steve Karsay	.05
198	Greg Myers	.05
199	Mark Portugal	.05
200	Pat Hentgen	.05
201	Mike La Valliere	.05
202	Mike Stanley	.05
203	Kent Mercker	.05
204	Dave Nilsson	.05
205	Erik Pappas	.05
206	Mike Morgan	.05
207	Roger McDowell	.05
208	Mike Lansing	.05
209	Kirt Manwaring	.05
210	Randy Milligan	.05
211	Erik Hanson	.05
212	Orestes Destrade	.05
213	Mike Maddux	.05
214	Alan Mills	.05
215	Tim Mauser	.05
216	Ben Rivera	.05
217	Don Slaught	.05
218	Bob Patterson	.05
219	Carlos Quintana	.05
220	Tim Raines 2,000 Hits Checklist	.05
221	Hal Morris	.05
222	Darren Holmes	.05
223	Chris Gwynn	.05
224	Chad Kreuter	.05
225	Mike Hartley	.05
226	Scott Lydy	.05
227	Eduardo Perez	.05
228	Greg Swindell	.05
229	Al Leiter	.05
230	Scott Radinsky	.05
231	Bob Wickman	.05
232	Otis Nixon	.05
233	Kevin Reimer	.05
234	Geronimo Pena	.05
235	Kevin Roberson	.05
236	Jody Reed	.05
237	Kirk Rueter	.05
238	Willie McGee	.05
239	Charles Nagy	.05
240	Tim Leary	.05
241	Carl Everett	.05
242	Charlie O'Brien	.05
243	Mike Pagliarulo	.05
244	Kerry Taylor	.05
245	Kevin Stocker	.05
246	Joel Johnston	.05
247	Geno Petralli	.05
248	Jeff Russell	.05
249	Joe Oliver	.05
250	Robert Mejia	.05
251	Chris Haney	.05
252	Bill Krueger	.05
253	Shane Mack	.05
254	Terry Steinbach	.05
255	Luis Polonia	.05
256	Eddie Taubensee	.05
257	Dave Stewart	.05
258	Tim Raines	.05
259	Bernie Williams	.05
260	John Smoltz	.05
261	Kevin Seitzer	.05
262	Bob Tewksbury	.05
263	Bob Scanlan	.05
264	Henry Rodriguez	.05
265	Tim Scott	.05
266	Scott Sanderson	.05
267	Eric Plunk	.05
268	Edgar Martinez	.05
269	Charlie Hough	.05
270	Joe Orsulak	.05
271	Harold Reynolds	.05
272	Tim Teufel	.05
273	Bobby Thigpen	.05
274	Randy Tomlin	.05
275	Gary Redus	.05
276	Ken Ryan	.05
277	Tim Pugh	.05
278	Jayhawk Owens	.05
279	Phil Hiatt	.05
280	Alan Trammell	.05
281	Dave McCarty	.05
282	Bob Welch	.05
283	J.T. Snow	.05
284	Brian Williams	.05
285	Devon White	.05
286	Steve Sax	.05
287	Tony Tarasco	.05
288	Bill Spiers	.05
289	Allen Watson	.05
290	Rickey Henderson 2,000 Hits Checklist	.05
291	Joe Vizcaino	.05
292	Darryl Strawberry	.05
293	John Wetteland	.05
294	Bill Swift	.05
295	Jeff Treadway	.05
296	Tino Martinez	.05
297	Richie Lewis	.05
298	Bret Saberhagen	.05
299	Arthur Rhodes	.05
300	Guillermo Velasquez	.05
301	Milt Thompson	.05
302	Doug Strange	.05
303	Aaron Sele	.05
304	Bip Roberts	.05
305	Bruce Ruffin	.05
306	Jose Lind	.05
307	David Wells	.05
308	Bobby Witt	.05
309	Mark Wohlers	.05
310	B.J. Surhoff	.05
311	Mark Whiten	.05
312	Turk Wendell	.05
313	Raul Mondesi	.05
314	Brian Turang **RC**	.05
315	Chris Hammond	.05
316	Tim Bogar	.05
317	Brad Pennington	.05
318	Tim Worrell	.05
319	Mitch Williams	.05
320	Rondell White	.05
321	Frank Viola	.05
322	Manny Ramirez	.75
323	Gary Wayne	.05
324	Mike Macfarlane	.05
325	Russ Springer	.05
326	Tim Wallach	.05
327	Salomon Torres (Rated Rookie)	.05
328	Omar Vizquel	.05
329	Andy Tomberlin **RC**	.05
330	Chris Sabo	.05
331	Mike Mussina	.30
332	Andy Benes	.05
333	Darren Daulton	.05
334	Orlando Merced	.05
335	Mark McGwire	1.50
336	Dave Winfield	.60
337	Sammy Sosa	.65
338	Eric Karros	.05
339	Greg Vaughn	.05
340	Don Mattingly	.75
341	Frank Thomas	.60
342	Fred McGriff	.05
343	Kirby Puckett	.65
344	Roberto Kelly	.05
345	Wally Joyner	.05
346	Andres Galarraga	.05
347	Bobby Bonilla	.05
348	Benito Santiago	.05
349	Barry Bonds	2.00
350	Delino DeShields	.05
351	Albert Belle	.05
352	Randy Johnson	.60
353	Tim Salmon	.05
354	John Olerud	.05
355	Dean Palmer	.05
356	Roger Clemens	.75
357	Jim Abbott	.05
358	Mark Grace	.05
359	Ozzie Guillen	.05
360	Lou Whitaker	.05
361	Jose Rijo	.05
362	Jeff Montgomery	.05
363	Chuck Finley	.05
364	Tom Glavine	.25
365	Jeff Bagwell	.60
366	Joe Carter	.05
367	Ray Lankford	.05
368	Ramon Martinez	.05
369	Jay Buhner	.05
370	Matt Williams	.05
371	Larry Walker	.05
372	Jose Canseco	.30
373	Len Dykstra	.05
374	Bryan Harvey	.05
375	Andy Van Slyke	.05
376	Ivan Rodriguez	.50
377	Kevin Mitchell	.05
378	Travis Fryman	.05
379	Duane Ward	.05
380	Greg Maddux	.65
381	Scott Servais	.05
382	Greg Olson	.05
383	Rey Sanchez	.05
384	Tom Kramer	.05
385	David Valle	.05
386	Eddie Murray	.60
387	Kevin Higgins	.05
388	Dan Wilson	.05
389	Todd Frohwirth	.05
390	Gerald Williams	.05
391	Hipolito Pichardo	.05
392	Pat Meares	.05
393	Luis Lopez	.05
394	Ricky Jordan	.05
395	Bob Walk	.05
396	Sid Fernandez	.05
397	Todd Worrell	.05
398	Darryl Hamilton	.05
399	Randy Myers	.05
400	Rod Brewer	.05
401	Lance Blankenship	.05
402	Steve Finley	.05
403	Phil Leftwich **RC**	.05
404	Juan Guzman	.05
405	Anthony Young	.05
406	Jeff Gardner	.05
407	Ryan Bowen	.05
408	Fernando Valenzuela	.05
409	David West	.05
410	Kenny Rogers	.05
411	Bob Zupcic	.05
412	Eric Young	.05
413	Bret Boone	.05
414	Danny Tartabull	.05
415	Bob MacDonald	.05
416	Ron Karkovice	.05
417	Scott Cooper	.05
418	Dante Bichette	.05
419	Tripp Cromer	.05
420	Billy Ashley	.05
421	Roger Smithberg	.05
422	Dennis Martinez	.05
423	Mike Blowers	.05
424	Darren Lewis	.05
425	Junior Ortiz	.05
426	Butch Huskey	.05
427	Jimmy Poole	.05
428	Walt Weiss	.05
429	Scott Bankhead	.05
430	Deion Sanders	.05
431	Scott Bullett	.05
432	Jeff Huson	.05
433	Tyler Green	.05
434	Billy Hatcher	.05
435	Bob Hamelin	.05
436	Reggie Sanders	.05
437	Scott Erickson	.05
438	Steve Reed	.05
439	Randy Velarde	.05
440	Checklist (Tony Gwynn 2,000 Hits)	.15
441	Terry Leach	.05
442	Danny Bautista	.05
443	Kent Hrbek	.05
444	Rick Wilkins	.05
445	Tony Phillips	.05
446	Dion James	.05
447	Joey Cora	.05
448	Andre Dawson	.15
449	Pedro Castellano	.05
450	Tom Gordon	.05
451	Rob Dibble	.05
452	Ron Darling	.05
453	Chipper Jones	.65
454	Joe Grahe	.05

No.	Player	Price
455	Domingo Cedeno	.05
456	Tom Edens	.05
457	Mitch Webster	.05
458	Jose Bautista	.05
459	Troy O'Leary	.05
460	Todd Zeile	.05
461	Sean Berry	.05
462	Brad Holman **RC**	.05
463	Dave Martinez	.05
464	Mark Lewis	.05
465	Paul Carey	.05
466	Jack Armstrong	.05
467	David Telgheder	.05
468	Gene Harris	.05
469	Danny Darwin	.05
470	Kim Batiste	.05
471	Tim Wakefield	.05
472	Craig Lefferts	.05
473	Jacob Brumfield	.05
474	Lance Painter	.05
475	Milt Cuyler	.05
476	Melido Perez	.05
477	Derek Parks	.05
478	Gary DiSarcina	.05
479	Steve Bedrosian	.05
480	Eric Anthony	.05
481	Julio Franco	.05
482	Tommy Greene	.05
483	Pat Kelly	.05
484	Nate Minchey	.05
485	William Pennyfeather	.05
486	Harold Baines	.05
487	Howard Johnson	.05
488	Angel Miranda	.05
489	Scott Sanders	.05
490	Shawon Dunston	.05
491	Mel Rojas	.05
492	Jeff Nelson	.05
493	Archi Cianfrocco	.05
494	Al Martin	.05
495	Mike Gallego	.05
496	Mike Henneman	.05
497	Armando Reynoso	.05
498	Mickey Morandini	.05
499	Rick Renteria	.05
500	Rick Sutcliffe	.05
501	Bobby Jones	.05
502	Gary Gaetti	.05
503	Rick Aguilera	.05
504	Todd Stottlemyre	.05
505	Mike Mohler	.05
506	Mike Stanton	.05
507	Jose Guzman	.05
508	Kevin Rogers	.05
509	Chuck Carr	.05
510	Chris Jones	.05
511	Brent Mayne	.05
512	Greg Harris	.05
513	Dave Henderson	.05
514	Eric Hillman	.05
515	Dan Peltier	.05
516	Craig Shipley	.05
517	John Valentin	.05
518	Wilson Alvarez	.05
519	Andujar Cedeno	.05
520	Troy Neel	.05
521	Tom Candiotti	.05
522	Matt Mieske	.05
523	Jim Thome	.50
524	Lou Frazier	.05
525	Mike Jackson	.05
526	Pedro Martinez	.05
527	Roger Pavlik	.05
528	Kent Bottenfield	.05
529	Felix Jose	.05
530	Mark Guthrie	.05
531	Steve Farr	.05
532	Craig Paquette	.05
533	Doug Jones	.05
534	Luis Alicea	.05
535	Cory Snyder	.05
536	Paul Sorrento	.05
537	Nigel Wilson	.05
538	Jeff King	.05
539	Willie Green	.05
540	Kirk McCaskill	.05
541	Al Osuna	.05
542	Greg Hibbard	.05
543	Brett Butler	.05
544	Jose Valentin	.05
545	Wil Cordero	.05
546	Chris Bosio	.05
547	Jamie Moyer	.05
548	Jim Eisenreich	.05
549	Vinny Castilla	.05
550	Checklist (Dave Winfield 3,000 Hits)	.05
551	John Roper	.05
552	Lance Johnson	.05
553	Scott Kamieniecki	.05
554	Mike Moore	.05
555	Steve Buechele	.05
556	Terry Pendleton	.05
557	Todd Van Poppel	.05
558	Rob Butler	.05
559	Zane Smith	.05
560	David Hulse	.05
561	Tim Costo	.05
562	John Habyan	.05
563	Terry Jorgensen	.05
564	Matt Nokes	.05
565	Kevin McReynolds	.05
566	Phil Plantier	.05
567	Chris Turner	.05
568	Carlos Delgado	.40
569	John Jaha	.05
570	Dwight Smith	.05
571	John Vander Wal	.05
572	Trevor Wilson	.05
573	Felix Fermin	.05
574	Marc Newfield	.05
575	Jeromy Burnitz	.05
576	Leo Gomez	.05
577	Curt Schilling	.25
578	Kevin Young	.05
579	Jerry Spradlin **RC**	.05
580	Curt Leskanic	.05
581	Carl Willis	.05
582	Alex Fernandez	.05
583	Mark Holzemer	.05
584	Domingo Martinez	.05
585	Pete Smith	.05
586	Brian Jordan	.05
587	Kevin Gross	.05
588	J.R. Phillips	.05
589	Chris Nabholz	.05
590	Bill Wertz	.05
591	Derek Bell	.05
592	Brady Anderson	.05
593	Matt Turner	.05
594	Pete Incaviglia	.05
595	Greg Gagne	.05
596	John Flaherty	.05
597	Scott Livingstone	.05
598	Rod Bolton	.05
599	Mike Perez	.05
600	Checklist (Roger Clemens 2,000 Strikeouts)	.25
601	Tony Castillo	.05
602	Henry Mercedes	.05
603	Mike Fetters	.05
604	Rod Beck	.05
605	Damon Buford	.05
606	Matt Whiteside	.05
607	Shawn Green	.25
608	Midre Cummings	.05
609	Jeff McMeeley	.05
610	Danny Sheaffer	.05
611	Paul Wagner	.05
612	Torey Lovullo	.05
613	Javier Lopez	.05
614	Mariano Duncan	.05
615	Doug Brocail	.05
616	Dave Hansen	.05
617	Ryan Klesko	.05
618	Eric Davis	.05
619	Scott Ruffcorn	.05
620	Mike Trombley	.05
621	Jaime Navarro	.05
622	Rheal Cormier	.05
623	Jose Offerman	.05
624	David Segui	.05
625	Robb Nen (Rated Rookie)	.05
626	Dave Gallagher	.05
627	Julian Tavarez **RC**	.05
628	Chris Gomez	.05
629	Jeffrey Hammonds	.05
630	Scott Brosius	.05
631	Willie Blair	.05
632	Doug Drabek	.05
633	Bill Wegman	.05
634	Jeff McKnight	.05
635	Rich Rodriguez	.05
636	Steve Trachsel	.05
637	Buddy Groom	.05
638	Sterling Hitchcock	.05
639	Chuck McElroy	.05
640	Rene Gonzales	.05
641	Dan Plesac	.05
642	Jeff Branson	.05
643	Darrell Whitmore	.05
644	Paul Quantrill	.05
645	Rich Rowland	.05
646	Curtis Pride **RC**	.05
647	Erik Plantenberg	.05
648	Albie Lopez	.05
649	Rich Batchelor **RC**	.05
650	Lee Smith	.05
651	Cliff Floyd	.05
652	Pete Schourek	.05
653	Reggie Jefferson	.05
654	Bill Haselman	.05
655	Steve Hosey	.05
656	Mark Clark	.05
657	Mark Davis	.05
658	Dave Magadan	.05
659	Candy Maldonado	.05
660	Checklist (Mark Langston 2,000 Strikeouts)	.05

Special Edition - Gold

		NM/M
Complete Set (100):		7.50
Common Player:		.10
1	Nolan Ryan	1.50
2	Mike Piazza	1.00
3	Moises Alou	.10
4	Ken Griffey Jr.	1.00
5	Gary Sheffield	.25
6	Roberto Alomar	.20
7	John Kruk	.10
8	Gregg Olson	.10
9	Gregg Jefferies	.10
10	Tony Gwynn	.65
11	Chad Curtis	.10
12	Craig Biggio	.10
13	John Burkett	.10
14	Gary Baerga	.10
15	Robin Yount	.60
16	Dennis Eckersley	.50
17	Dwight Gooden	.10

18	Ryne Sandberg	.65
19	Rickey Henderson	.60
20	Jack McDowell	.10
21	Jay Bell	.10
22	Kevin Brown	.10
23	Robin Ventura	.10
24	Paul Molitor	.60
25	David Justice	.10
26	Rafael Palmeiro	.50
27	Cecil Fielder	.10
28	Chuck Knoblauch	.10
29	Dave Hollins	.10
30	Jimmy Key	.10
31	Mark Langston	.10
32	Darryl Kile	.10
33	Ruben Sierra	.10
34	Ron Gant	.10
35	Ozzie Smith	.65
36	Wade Boggs	.65
37	Marquis Grissom	.10
38	Will Clark	.10
39	Kenny Lofton	.10
40	Cal Ripken, Jr.	1.50
41	Steve Avery	.10
42	Mo Vaughn	.10
43	Brian McRae	.10
44	Mickey Tettleton	.10
45	Barry Larkin	.10
46	Charlie Hayes	.10
47	Kevin Appier	.10
48	Robby Thompson	.10
49	Juan Gonzalez	.30
50	Paul O'Neill	.10
51	Mike Mussina	.40
52	Andy Benes	.10
53	Darren Daulton	.10
54	Orlando Merced	.10
55	Mark McGwire	1.25
56	Dave Winfield	.60
57	Sammy Sosa	.65
58	Eric Karros	.10
59	Greg Vaughn	.10
60	Don Mattingly	.75
61	Frank Thomas	.60
62	Fred McGriff	.10
63	Kirby Puckett	.65
64	Roberto Kelly	.10
65	Wally Joyner	.10
66	Andres Galarraga	.10
67	Bobby Bonilla	.10
68	Benito Santiago	.10
69	Jeff Bagwell	1.50
70	Delino DeShields	.10
71	Albert Belle	.10
72	Randy Johnson	.60
73	Tim Salmon	.10
74	John Olerud	.10
75	Dean Palmer	.10
76	Roger Clemens	.75
77	Jim Abbott	.10
78	Mark Grace	.10
79	Ozzie Guillen	.10
80	Lou Whitaker	.10
81	Jose Rijo	.10
82	Jeff Montgomery	.10
83	Chuck Finley	.10
84	Tom Glavine	.25
85	Jeff Bagwell	.60
86	Joe Carter	.10
87	Ray Lankford	.10
88	Ramon Martinez	.10
89	Doc Gooden	.10
90	Matt Williams	.10
91	Larry Walker	.10
92	Jose Canseco	.25
93	Len Dykstra	.10
94	Bryan Harvey	.10
95	Andy Van Slyke	.10
96	Ivan Rodriguez	.50
97	Kevin Mitchell	.10
98	Travis Fryman	.10
99	Duane Ward	.10
100	Greg Maddux	.65

Anniversary-1984

		NM/M
Complete Set (10):		20.00
Common Player:		1.00
1	Joe Carter	1.00
2	Robin Yount	1.50
3	George Brett	2.50
4	Rickey Henderson	1.50
5	Nolan Ryan	6.00

RICKEY HENDERSON OF

6	Cal Ripken, Jr.	6.00
7	Wade Boggs	2.00
8	Don Mattingly	2.50
9	Ryne Sandberg	2.00
10	Tony Gwynn	2.00

Decade Dominators

DOMINATORS
CECIL FIELDER
HOMERUNS

		NM/M
Complete Set (20):		15.00
Common Player:		.35
Series 1		
1	Cecil Fielder	.35
2	Barry Bonds	2.50
3	Fred McGriff	.35
4	Matt Williams	.35
5	Joe Carter	.35
6	Juan Gonzalez	.40
7	Jose Canseco	.50
8	Ron Gant	.35
9	Ken Griffey Jr.	1.50
10	Mark McGwire	2.00
Series 2		
1	Tony Gwynn	1.00
2	Frank Thomas	.75
3	Paul Molitor	.75
4	Edgar Martinez	.35
5	Kirby Puckett	1.00
6	Ken Griffey, Jr.	1.50
7	Barry Bonds	2.50
8	Willie McGee	.35
9	Len Dykstra	1.50
10	John Kruk	.35

Diamond Kings

DIAMOND KINGS
Bobby Bonilla

		NM/M
Complete Set (30):		12.00
Common Player:		.25
1	Barry Bonds	2.50
2	Mo Vaughn	.25
3	Steve Avery	.25
4	Tim Salmon	.25
5	Rick Wilkins	.25
6	Brian Harper	.25

#	Player	Price
7	Andres Galarraga	.25
8	Albert Belle	.25
9	John Kruk	.25
10	Ivan Rodriguez	.75
11	Tony Gwynn	1.25
12	Brian McRae	.25
13	Bobby Bonilla	.25
14	Ken Griffey Jr.	2.00
15	Mike Piazza	2.00
16	Don Mattingly	1.50
17	Barry Larkin	.25
18	Ruben Sierra	.25
19	Orlando Merced	.25
20	Greg Vaughn	.25
21	Gregg Jefferies	.25
22	Cecil Fielder	.25
23	Moises Alou	.25
24	John McRae	.25
25	Gary Sheffield	.25
26	Mike Mussina	.60
27	Jeff Bagwell	1.00
28	Frank Thomas	1.00
29	Dave Winfield	1.00
30	Dick Perez (Checklist)	.25

Elite

TIM SALMON

		NM/M
Complete Set (12):		50.00
Common Player:		4.00
37	Frank Thomas	6.00
38	Tony Gwynn	7.50
39	Tim Salmon	4.00
40	Albert Belle	4.00
41	John Kruk	4.00
42	Juan Gonzalez	5.00
43	John Olerud	4.00
44	Barry Bonds	12.00
45	Ken Griffey Jr.	9.00
46	Mike Piazza	9.00
47	Jack McDowell	4.00
48	Andres Galarraga	4.00

Long Ball Leaders

		NM/M
Complete Set (10):		6.00
Common Player:		.30
1	Cecil Fielder	.30
2	Dean Palmer	.30
3	Andres Galarraga	.30
4	Bo Jackson	.40
5	Ken Griffey Jr.	1.50
6	Dave Justice	.30
7	Mike Piazza	1.50
8	Frank Thomas	1.00
9	Barry Bonds	3.00
10	Juan Gonzalez	.50

MVPs

		NM/M
Complete Set (28):		20.00
Common Player:		.25
1	Dave Justice	.25
2	Mark Grace	.25
3	Jose Rijo	.25
4	Andres Galarraga	.25
5	Bryan Harvey	.25
6	Jeff Bagwell	1.00

ANDRES GALARRAGA-1B

#	Player	Price
7	Mike Piazza	2.50
8	Moises Alou	.25
9	Bobby Bonilla	.25
10	Len Dykstra	.25
11	Jeff King	.25
12	Gregg Jefferies	.25
13	Tony Gwynn	1.50
14	Barry Bonds	4.00
15	Cal Ripken, Jr.	4.00
16	Mo Vaughn	.25
17	Tim Salmon	.25
18	Frank Thomas	1.00
19	Albert Belle	.25
20	Cecil Fielder	.25
21	Wally Joyner	.25
22	Greg Vaughn	.25
23	Kirby Puckett	1.50
24	Don Mattingly	2.00
25	Ruben Sierra	.25
26	Ken Griffey Jr.	2.50
27	Juan Gonzalez	.50
28	John Olerud	.25

Spirit of the Game

Spirit of the Game

		NM/M
Complete Set (10):		10.00
Common Player:		.70
1	John Olerud	.50
2	Barry Bonds	2.50
3	Ken Griffey Jr.	2.00
4	Mike Piazza	2.00
5	Juan Gonzalez	.60
6	Frank Thomas	1.00
7	Tim Salmon	.50
8	Dave Justice	.50
9	Don Mattingly	1.50
10	Len Dykstra	.50

1995 Donruss

		NM/M
Complete Set (550):		20.00
Common Player:		.05
Press Proofs:		15X
Series 1 or 2 Pack (12):		.75
Series 1 or 2 Wax Box (36):		20.00
1	Dave Justice	.05
2	Rene Arocha	.05
3	Sandy Alomar Jr.	.05
4	Luis Lopez	.05
5	Mike Piazza	1.50
6	Bobby Jones	.05
7	Damion Easley	.05
8	Barry Bonds	2.50
9	Mike Mussina	.40
10	Kevin Seitzer	.05
11	John Smiley	.05
12	W. Van Landingham	.05
13	Ron Darling	.05
14	Walt Weiss	.05
15	Mike Lansing	.05
16	Allen Watson	.05
17	Aaron Sele	.05
18	Randy Johnson	.65
19	Dean Palmer	.05
20	Jeff Bagwell	.65
21	Curt Schilling	.25
22	Darrell Whitmore	.05
23	Steve Trachsel	.05
24	Dan Wilson	.05
25	Steve Finley	.05
26	Bret Boone	.05
27	Charles Johnson	.05
28	Mike Stanton	.05
29	Ismael Valdes	.05
30	Salomon Torres	.05
31	Eric Anthony	.05
32	Spike Owen	.05
33	Joey Cora	.05
34	Robert Eenhoorn	.05
35	Rick White	.05
36	Omar Vizquel	.05
37	Carlos Delgado	.45
38	Eddie Williams	.05
39	Shawon Dunston	.05
40	Darrin Fletcher	.05
41	Leo Gomez	.05
42	Juan Gonzalez	.40
43	Luis Alicea	.05
44	Ken Ryan	.05
45	Lou Whitaker	.05
46	Mike Blowers	.05
47	Willie Blair	.05
48	Todd Van Poppel	.05
49	Roberto Alomar	.25
50	Ozzie Smith	.75
51	Sterling Hitchcock	.05
52	Mo Vaughn	.05
53	Rick Aguilera	.05
54	Kent Mercker	.05
55	Don Mattingly	1.00
56	Bob Scanlan	.05
57	Wilson Alvarez	.05
58	Jose Mesa	.05
59	Scott Kamieniecki	.05
60	Todd Jones	.05
61	John Kruk	.05
62	Mike Stanley	.05
63	Tino Martinez	.05
64	Eddie Zambrano	.05
65	Todd Hundley	.05
66	Jamie Moyer	.05
67	Rich Amaral	.05
68	Jose Valentin	.05
69	Alex Gonzalez	.05
70	Kurt Abbott	.05
71	Delino DeShields	.05
72	Brian Anderson	.05
73	John Vander Wal	.05
74	Turner Ward	.05
75	Tim Raines	.05
76	Mark Acre	.05
77	Jose Offerman	.05
78	Jimmy Key	.05
79	Mark Whiten	.05
80	Mark Gubicza	.05
81	Darren Hall	.05
82	Travis Fryman	.05
83	Cal Ripken, Jr.	2.50
84	Geronimo Berroa	.05
85	Bret Barberie	.05
86	Andy Ashby	.05
87	Steve Avery	.05
88	Rich Becker	.05
89	John Valentin	.05
90	Glenallen Hill	.05
91	Carlos Garcia	.05
92	Dennis Martinez	.05
93	Pat Kelly	.05
94	Orlando Miller	.05
95	Felix Jose	.05
96	Mike Kingery	.05
97	Jeff Kent	.05
98	Pete Incaviglia	.05
99	Chad Curtis	.05
100	Thomas Howard	.05
101	Hector Carrasco	.05
102	Tom Pagnozzi	.05
103	Danny Tartabull	.05
104	Donnie Elliott	.05
105	Danny Jackson	.05
106	Steve Dunn	.05
107	Roger Salkeld	.05
108	Jeff King	.05
109	Cecil Fielder	.05
110	Checklist	.05
111	Denny Neagle	.05
112	Troy Neel	.05
113	Rod Beck	.05
114	Alex Rodriguez	2.00
115	Joey Eischen	.05
116	Tom Candiotti	.05
117	Ray McDavid	.05
118	Vince Coleman	.05
119	Pete Harnisch	.05
120	David Nied	.05
121	Pat Rapp	.05
122	Sammy Sosa	.75
123	Steve Reed	.05
124	Jose Oliva	.05
125	Rick Bottalico	.05
126	Jose DeLeon	.05
127	Pat Hentgen	.05
128	Will Clark	.05
129	Mark Dewey	.05
130	Greg Vaughn	.05
131	Darren Dreifort	.05
132	Ed Sprague	.05
133	Lee Smith	.05
134	Charles Nagy	.05
135	Phil Plantier	.05
136	Jason Jacome	.05
137	Jose Lima	.05
138	J.R. Phillips	.05
139	J.T. Snow	.05
140	Mike Huff	.05
141	Billy Brewer	.05
142	Jeromy Burnitz	.05
143	Ricky Bones	.05
144	Carlos Rodriguez	.05
145	Luis Gonzalez	.05
146	Mark Lemke	.05
147	Al Martin	.05
148	Mike Bordick	.05
149	Robb Nen	.05
150	Wil Cordero	.05
151	Edgar Martinez	.05
152	Gerald Williams	.05
153	Esteban Beltre	.05
154	Mike Moore	.05
155	Mark Langston	.05
156	Mark Clark	.05
157	Bobby Ayala	.05
158	Rick Wilkins	.05
159	Bobby Munoz	.05
160	Checklist	.05
161	Scott Erickson	.05
162	Paul Molitor	.65
163	Jon Lieber	.05
164	Jason Grimsley	.05
165	Norberto Martin	.05
166	Javier Lopez	.05
167	Brian McRae	.05
168	Gary Sheffield	.40
169	Marcus Moore	.05
170	John Hudek	.05
171	Kelly Stinett	.05
172	Chris Gomez	.05
173	Rey Sanchez	.05
174	Juan Guzman	.05
175	Chan Ho Park	.05
176	Terry Shumpert	.05
177	Steve Ontiveros	.05
178	Brad Ausmus	.05
179	Tim Davis	.05
180	Billy Ashley	.05
181	Vinny Castilla	.05
182	Bill Spiers	.05
183	Randy Knorr	.05
184	Brian Hunter	.05
185	Pat Meares	.05
186	Steve Buechele	.05
187	Kirt Manwaring	.05
188	Tim Naehring	.05
189	Matt Mieske	.05
190	Josias Manzanillo	.05
191	Greg McMichael	.05
192	Chuck Carr	.05
193	Midre Cummings	.05
194	Darryl Strawberry	.05
195	Greg Gagne	.05
196	Steve Cooke	.05
197	Woody Williams	.05
198	Ron Karkovice	.05
199	Phil Leftwich	.05
200	Jim Thome	.50
201	Brady Anderson	.05
202	Pedro Martinez	.65
203	Steve Karsay	.05
204	Reggie Sanders	.05
205	Bill Risley	.05
206	Jay Bell	.05
207	Kevin Brown	.05
208	Tim Scott	.05
209	Len Dykstra	.05
210	Willie Greene	.05
211	Jim Eisenreich	.05
212	Cliff Floyd	.05
213	Otis Nixon	.05
214	Eduardo Perez	.05
215	Manuel Lee	.05
216	Armando Benitez RC	.10
217	Dave McCarty	.05
218	Scott Livingstone	.05
219	Chad Kreuter	.05
220	Checklist	.05
221	Brian Jordan	.05
222	Matt Whiteside	.05
223	Jim Edmonds	.05
224	Tony Gwynn	.75
225	Jose Lind	.05
226	Marvin Freeman	.05
227	Ken Hill	.05
228	David Hulse	.05
229	Joe Hesketh	.05
230	Roberto Petagine	.05
231	Jeffrey Hammonds	.05
232	John Jaha	.05
233	John Burkett	.05
234	Hal Morris	.05
235	Tony Castillo	.05
236	Ryan Bowen	.05
237	Wayne Kirby	.05
238	Brent Mayne	.05
239	Jim Bullinger	.05

#	Player	Value
240	Mike Lieberthal	.05
241	Barry Larkin	.05
242	David Segui	.05
243	Jose Bautista	.05
244	Hector Fajardo	.05
245	Orel Hershiser	.05
246	James Mouton	.05
247	Scott Leius	.05
248	Tom Glavine	.25
249	Danny Bautista	.05
250	Jose Mercedes	.05
251	Marquis Grissom	.05
252	Charlie Hayes	.05
253	Ryan Klesko	.05
254	Vicente Palacios	.05
255	Matias Carillo	.05
256	Gary DiSarcina	.05
257	Kirk Gibson	.05
258	Garey Ingram	.05
259	Alex Fernandez	.05
260	John Mabry	.05
261	Chris Howard	.05
262	Miguel Jimenez	.05
263	Heath Slocumb	.05
264	Albert Belle	.05
265	Dave Clark	.05
266	Joe Orsulak	.05
267	Joey Hamilton	.05
268	Mark Portugal	.05
269	Kevin Tapani	.05
270	Sid Fernandez	.05
271	Steve Dreyer	.05
272	Denny Hocking	.05
273	Troy O'Leary	.05
274	Milt Cuyler	.05
275	Frank Thomas	.65
276	Jorge Fabregas	.05
277	Mike Gallego	.05
278	Mickey Morandini	.05
279	Roberto Hernandez	.05
280	Henry Rodriguez	.05
281	Garret Anderson	.05
282	Bob Wickman	.05
283	Gar Finnvold	.05
284	Paul O'Neill	.05
285	Royce Clayton	.05
286	Chuck Knoblauch	.05
287	Johnny Ruffin	.05
288	Dave Nilsson	.05
289	David Cone	.05
290	Chuck McElroy	.05
291	Kevin Stocker	.05
292	Jose Rijo	.05
293	Sean Berry	.05
294	Ozzie Guillen	.05
295	Chris Hoiles	.05
296	Kevin Foster	.05
297	Jeff Frye	.05
298	Lance Johnson	.05
299	Mike Kelly	.05
300	Ellis Burks	.05
301	Roberto Kelly	.05
302	Dante Bichette	.05
303	Alvaro Espinoza	.05
304	Alex Cole	.05
305	Rickey Henderson	.65
306	Dave Weathers	.05
307	Shane Reynolds	.05
308	Bobby Bonilla	.05
309	Junior Felix	.05
310	Jeff Fassero	.05
311	Darren Lewis	.05
312	John Doherty	.05
313	Scott Servais	.05
314	Rick Helling	.05
315	Pedro Martinez	.65
316	Wes Chamberlain	.05
317	Bryan Eversgerd	.05
318	Trevor Hoffman	.05
319	John Patterson	.05
320	Matt Walbeck	.05
321	Jeff Montgomery	.05
322	Mel Rojas	.05
323	Eddie Taubensee	.05
324	Ray Lankford	.05
325	Jose Vizcaino	.05
326	Carlos Baerga	.05
327	Jack Voigt	.05
328	Julio Franco	.05
329	Brent Gates	.05
330	Checklist	.05
331	Greg Maddux	.75
332	Jason Bere	.05
333	Bill Wegman	.05
334	Tuffy Rhodes	.05
335	Kevin Young	.05
336	Andy Benes	.05
337	Pedro Astacio	.05
338	Reggie Jefferson	.05
339	Tim Belcher	.05
340	Ken Griffey Jr.	1.50
341	Mariano Duncan	.05
342	Andres Galarraga	.05
343	Rondell White	.05
344	Cory Bailey	.05
345	Bryan Harvey	.05
346	John Franco	.05
347	Greg Swindell	.05
348	David West	.05
349	Fred McGriff	.05
350	Jose Canseco	.35
351	Orlando Merced	.05
352	Rheal Cormier	.05
353	Carlos Pulido	.05
354	Terry Steinbach	.05
355	Wade Boggs	.75
356	B.J. Surhoff	.05
357	Rafael Palmeiro	.60
358	Anthony Young	.05
359	Tom Brunansky	.05
360	Todd Stottlemyre	.05
361	Chris Turner	.05
362	Joe Boever	.05
363	Jeff Blauser	.05
364	Derek Bell	.05
365	Matt Williams	.05
366	Jeremy Hernandez	.05
367	Joe Girardi	.05
368	Mike Devereaux	.05
369	Jim Abbott	.05
370	Manny Ramirez	.65
371	Kenny Lofton	.05
372	Mark Smith	.05
373	Dave Fleming	.05
374	Dave Stewart	.05
375	Roger Pavlik	.05
376	Hipolito Pichardo	.05
377	Bill Taylor	.05
378	Robin Ventura	.05
379	Bernard Gilkey	.05
380	Kirby Puckett	.75
381	Steve Howe	.05
382	Devon White	.05
383	Roberto Mejia	.05
384	Darrin Jackson	.05
385	Mike Morgan	.05
386	Rusty Meacham	.05
387	Bill Swift	.05
388	Lou Frazier	.05
389	Andy Van Slyke	.05
390	Brett Butler	.05
391	Bobby Witt	.05
392	Jeff Conine	.05
393	Tim Hyers	.05
394	Terry Pendleton	.05
395	Ricky Jordan	.05
396	Eric Plunk	.05
397	Melido Perez	.05
398	Darryl Kile	.05
399	Mark McLemore	.05
400	Greg Harris	.05
401	Jim Leyritz	.05
402	Doug Strange	.05
403	Tim Salmon	.05
404	Terry Mulholland	.05
405	Robby Thompson	.05
406	Ruben Sierra	.05
407	Tony Phillips	.05
408	Moises Alou	.05
409	Felix Fermin	.05
410	Pat Listach	.05
411	Kevin Bass	.05
412	Ben McDonald	.05
413	Scott Cooper	.05
414	Jody Reed	.05
415	Deion Sanders	.05
416	Ricky Gutierrez	.05
417	Gregg Jefferies	.05
418	Jack McDowell	.05
419	Al Leiter	.05
420	Tony Longmire	.05
421	Paul Wagner	.05
422	Geronimo Pena	.05
423	Ivan Rodriguez	.60
424	Kevin Gross	.05
425	Kirk McCaskill	.05
426	Greg Myers	.05
427	Roger Clemens	1.00
428	Chris Hammond	.05
429	Randy Myers	.05
430	Roger Mason	.05
431	Bret Saberhagen	.05
432	Jeff Reboulet	.05
433	John Olerud	.05
434	Bill Gullickson	.05
435	Eddie Murray	.65
436	Pedro Munoz	.05
437	Charlie O'Brien	.05
438	Jeff Nelson	.05
439	Mike Macfarlane	.05
440	Checklist	.05
441	Derrick May	.05
442	John Roper	.05
443	Darryl Hamilton	.05
444	Dan Miceli	.05
445	Tony Eusebio	.05
446	Jerry Browne	.05
447	Wally Joyner	.05
448	Brian Harper	.05
449	Scott Fletcher	.05
450	Bip Roberts	.05
451	Pete Smith	.05
452	Chili Davis	.05
453	Dave Hollins	.05
454	Tony Pena	.05
455	Butch Henry	.05
456	Craig Biggio	.05
457	Zane Smith	.05
458	Ryan Thompson	.05
459	Mike Jackson	.05
460	Mark McGwire	2.00
461	John Smoltz	.05
462	Steve Scarsone	.05
463	Greg Colbrunn	.05
464	Shawn Green	.25
465	David Wells	.05
466	Jose Hernandez	.05
467	Chip Hale	.05
468	Tony Tarasco	.05
469	Kevin Mitchell	.05
470	Billy Hatcher	.05
471	Jay Buhner	.05
472	Ken Caminiti	.05
473	Tom Henke	.05
474	Todd Worrell	.05
475	Mark Eichhorn	.05
476	Bruce Ruffin	.05
477	Chuck Finley	.05
478	Marc Newfield	.05
479	Paul Shuey	.05
480	Bob Tewksbury	.05
481	Ramon Martinez	.05
482	Melvin Nieves	.05
483	Todd Zeile	.05
484	Benito Santiago	.05
485	Stan Javier	.05
486	Kirk Rueter	.05
487	Andre Dawson	.25
488	Eric Karros	.05
489	Dave Magadan	.05
490	Checklist	.05
491	Randy Velarde	.05
492	Larry Walker	.05
493	Cris Carpenter	.05
494	Tom Gordon	.05
495	Dave Burba	.05
496	Darren Bragg	.05
497	Darren Daulton	.05
498	Don Slaught	.05
499	Pat Borders	.05
500	Lenny Harris	.05
501	Joe Ausanio	.05
502	Alan Trammell	.05
503	Mike Fetters	.05
504	Scott Ruffcorn	.05
505	Rich Rowland	.05
506	Juan Samuel	.05
507	Bo Jackson	.10
508	Jeff Branson	.05
509	Bernie Williams	.05
510	Paul Sorrento	.05
511	Dennis Eckersley	.60
512	Pat Mahomes	.05
513	Rusty Greer	.05
514	Luis Polonia	.05
515	Willie Banks	.05
516	John Wetteland	.05
517	Mike LaValliere	.05
518	Tommy Greene	.05
519	Mark Grace	.05
520	Bob Hamelin	.05
521	Scott Sanderson	.05
522	Joe Carter	.05
523	Jeff Brantley	.05
524	Andrew Lorraine	.05
525	Rico Brogna	.05
526	Shane Mack	.05
527	Mark Wohlers	.05
528	Scott Sanders	.05
529	Chris Bosio	.05
530	Andujar Cedeno	.05
531	Kenny Rogers	.05
532	Doug Drabek	.05
533	Curt Leskanic	.05
534	Craig Shipley	.05
535	Craig Grebeck	.05
536	Cal Eldred	.05
537	Mickey Tettleton	.05
538	Harold Baines	.05
539	Tim Wallach	.05
540	Damon Buford	.05
541	Lenny Webster	.05
542	Kevin Appier	.05
543	Raul Mondesi	.05
544	Eric Young	.05
545	Russ Davis	.05
546	Mike Benjamin	.05
547	Mike Greenwell	.05
548	Scott Brosius	.05
549	Brian Dorsett	.05
550	Checklist	.05

All-Stars

		NM/M
Complete Set (18):		26.00
Common Player:		.40
AL1	Jimmy Key	.40
AL2	Ivan Rodriguez	1.25
AL3	Frank Thomas	1.50
AL4	Roberto Alomar	.60
AL5	Wade Boggs	2.00
AL6	Cal Ripken, Jr.	4.50
AL7	Joe Carter	.40
AL8	Ken Griffey Jr.	3.00
AL9	Kirby Puckett	2.00
NL1	Greg Maddux	2.00
NL2	Mike Piazza	3.00
NL3	Gregg Jefferies	.40
NL4	Mariano Duncan	.40
NL5	Matt Williams	.40
NL6	Ozzie Smith	2.00
NL7	Barry Bonds	4.50
NL8	Tony Gwynn	2.00
NL9	Dave Justice	.40

Bomb Squad

		NM/M
Complete Set (6):		3.00
Common Player:		.50
1	Ken Griffey Jr., Matt Williams	1.00
2	Frank Thomas, Jeff Bagwell	.75
3	Albert Belle, Barry Bonds	1.50
4	Jose Canseco, Fred McGriff	.60
5	Cecil Fielder, Andres Galarraga	.50
6	Joe Carter, Kevin Mitchell	.50

Diamond Kings

		NM/M
Complete Set (29):		35.00
Common Player:		.75
1	Frank Thomas	3.00
2	Jeff Bagwell	3.00
3	Chili Davis	.75
4	Dante Bichette	.75
5	Ruben Sierra	.75
6	Jeff Conine	.75
7	Paul O'Neill	.75
8	Bobby Bonilla	.75
9	Joe Carter	.75
10	Moises Alou	.75
11	Kenny Lofton	.75
12	Matt Williams	.75
13	Kevin Seitzer	.75
14	Sammy Sosa	3.50
15	Scott Cooper	.75
16	Raul Mondesi	.75
17	Will Clark	.75

Press Proofs

	NM/M
Complete Set (550):	150.00
Common Player:	1.00
Stars:	15X

(See 1995 Donruss for checklist and base card values.)

18	Lenny Dykstra	.75
19	Kirby Puckett	3.50
20	Hal Morris	.75
21	Travis Fryman	.75
22	Greg Maddux	3.50
23	Rafael Palmeiro	2.50
24	Tony Gwynn	3.50
25	David Cone	.75
26	Al Martin	.75
27	Ken Griffey Jr.	5.00
28	Gregg Jefferies	.75
29	Checklist	.10

Dominators

		NM/M
Complete Set (9):		7.50
Common Player:		.50
1	David Cone, Mike Mussina, Greg Maddux	1.00
2	Ivan Rodriguez, Mike Piazza, Darren Daulton	2.00
3	Fred McGriff, Frank Thomas, Jeff Bagwell	1.50
4	Roberto Alomar, Carlos Baerga, Craig Biggio	.75
5	Robin Ventura, Travis Fryman, Matt Williams	.50
6	Cal Ripken Jr., Barry Larkin, Wil Cordero	2.50
7	Albert Belle, Barry Bonds, Moises Alou	2.50
8	Ken Griffey Jr., Kenny Lofton, Marquis Grissom	2.00
9	Kirby Puckett, Paul O'Neill, Tony Gwynn	2.00

Elite

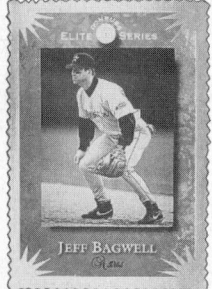

		NM/M
Complete Set (12):		100.00
Common Player:		6.00
49	Jeff Bagwell	12.00
50	Paul O'Neill	6.00
51	Greg Maddux	15.00
52	Mike Piazza	17.50
53	Matt Williams	6.00
54	Ken Griffey Jr.	17.50
55	Frank Thomas	12.00
56	Barry Bonds	20.00
57	Kirby Puckett	15.00
58	Fred McGriff	6.00
59	Jose Canseco	9.00
60	Albert Belle	6.00

Long Ball Leaders

		NM/M
Complete Set (8):		7.50
Common Player:		.50
1	Frank Thomas	1.50
2	Fred McGriff	.50
3	Ken Griffey Jr.	2.00
4	Matt Williams	.50
5	Mike Piazza	2.00
6	Jose Canseco	.75
7	Barry Bonds	2.50
8	Jeff Bagwell	1.50

Mound Marvels

		NM/M
Complete Set (8):		7.50
Common Player:		1.00
1	Greg Maddux	4.00
2	David Cone	1.00
3	Mike Mussina	2.00
4	Bret Saberhagen	1.00
5	Jimmy Key	1.00
6	Doug Drabek	1.00
7	Randy Johnson	3.00
8	Jason Bere	1.00

1996 Donruss

		NM/M
Complete Set (550):		20.00
Complete Series 1 (330):		12.00
Complete Series 2 (220):		10.00
Common Player:		.05
Press Proofs:		7X
Series 1 Pack (12):		1.00
Series 1 Wax Box (36):		20.00
Series 2 Pack (12):		1.00
Series 2 Wax Box (18):		12.50
1	Frank Thomas	1.00
2	Jason Bates	.05
3	Steve Sparks	.05
4	Scott Servais	.05
5	Angelo Encarnacion	.05
6	Scott Sanders	.05
7	Billy Ashley	.05
8	Alex Rodriguez	2.00
9	Sean Bergman	.05
10	Brad Radke	.05
11	Andy Van Slyke	.05
12	Joe Girardi	.05
13	Mark Grudzielanek	.05
14	Rick Aguilera	.05
15	Randy Veres	.05
16	Tim Bogar	.05
17	Dave Veres	.05
18	Kevin Stocker	.05
19	Marquis Grissom	.05
20	Will Clark	.05
21	Jay Bell	.05
22	Allen Battle	.05
23	Frank Rodriguez	.05
24	Terry Steinbach	.05
25	Gerald Williams	.05
26	Sid Roberson	.05
27	Gregg Zaun	.05
28	Ozzie Timmons	.05
29	Vaughn Eshelman	.05
30	Ed Sprague	.05
31	Gary DiSarcina	.05
32	Joe Boever	.05
33	Steve Avery	.05
34	Brad Ausmus	.05
35	Kirt Manwaring	.05
36	Gary Sheffield	.25
37	Jason Bere	.05
38	Jeff Manto	.05
39	David Cone	.05
40	Manny Ramirez	1.00
41	Sandy Alomar	.05
42	Curtis Goodwin	.05
43	Tino Martinez	.05
44	Woody Williams	.05
45	Dean Palmer	.05
46	Hipolito Pichardo	.05
47	Jason Giambi	.60
48	Lance Johnson	.05
49	Bernard Gilkey	.05
50	Kirby Puckett	1.25
51	Tony Fernandez	.05
52	Alex Gonzalez	.05
53	Bret Saberhagen	.05
54	Lyle Mouton	.05
55	Brian McRae	.05
56	Mark Gubicza	.05
57	Sergio Valdez	.05
58	Darrin Fletcher	.05
59	Steve Parris	.05
60	Johnny Damon	.35
61	Rickey Henderson	1.00
62	Darrell Whitmore	.05
63	Roberto Petagine	.05
64	Trenidad Hubbard	.05
65	Heathcliff Slocumb	.05
66	Steve Finley	.05
67	Mariano Rivera	.25
68	Brian Hunter	.05
69	Jamie Moyer	.05
70	Ellis Burks	.05
71	Pat Kelly	.05
72	Mickey Tettleton	.05
73	Garret Anderson	.05
74	Andy Pettitte	.75
75	Glenallen Hill	.05
76	Brent Gates	.05
77	Lou Whitaker	.05
78	David Segui	.05
79	Dan Wilson	.05
80	Pat Listach	.05
81	Jeff Bagwell	1.00
82	Ben McDonald	.05
83	John Valentin	.05
84	John Jaha	.05
85	Pete Schourek	.05
86	Bryce Florie	.05
87	Brian Jordan	.05
88	Ron Karkovice	.05
89	Al Leiter	.05
90	Tony Longmire	.05
91	Nelson Liriano	.05
92	David Bell	.05
93	Kevin Gross	.05
94	Tom Candiotti	.05
95	Dave Martinez	.05
96	Greg Myers	.05
97	Rheal Cormier	.05
98	Chris Hammond	.05
99	Randy Myers	.05
100	Bill Pulsipher	.05
101	Jason Isringhausen	.05
102	Dave Stevens	.05
103	Roberto Alomar	.20
104	Bob Higginson	.05
105	Eddie Murray	1.00
106	Matt Walbeck	.05
107	Mark Wohlers	.05
108	Jeff Nelson	.05
109	Tom Goodwin	.05
110	Cal Ripken Jr. Checklist 1-83 (2,131 Consecutive Games)	1.25
111	Rey Sanchez	.05
112	Hector Carrasco	.05
113	B.J. Surhoff	.05
114	Dan Miceli	.05
115	Dean Hartgraves	.05
116	John Burkett	.05
117	Gary Gaetti	.05
118	Ricky Bones	.05
119	Mike Macfarlane	.05
120	Bip Roberts	.05
121	Dave Mlicki	.05
122	Chili Davis	.05
123	Mark Whiten	.05
124	Herbert Perry	.05
125	Butch Henry	.05
126	Derek Bell	.05
127	Al Martin	.05
128	John Franco	.05
129	William Van Landingham	.05
130	Mike Bordick	.05
131	Mike Mordecai	.05
132	Robby Thompson	.05
133	Greg Colbrunn	.05
134	Domingo Cedeno	.05
135	Chad Curtis	.05
136	Jose Hernandez	.05
137	Scott Klingenbeck	.05
138	Ryan Klesko	.05
139	John Smiley	.05
140	Charlie Hayes	.05
141	Jay Buhner	.05
142	Doug Drabek	.05
143	Roger Pavlik	.05
144	Todd Worrell	.05
145	Cal Ripken Jr.	2.50
146	Steve Reed	.05
147	Chuck Finley	.05
148	Mike Blowers	.05
149	Orel Hershiser	.05
150	Allen Watson	.05
151	Ramon Martinez	.05
152	Melvin Nieves	.05
153	Tripp Cromer	.05
154	Yorkis Perez	.05
155	Stan Javier	.05
156	Mel Rojas	.05
157	Aaron Sele	.05
158	Eric Karros	.05
159	Robb Nen	.05
160	Raul Mondesi	.05
161	John Wetteland	.05
162	Tim Scott	.05
163	Kenny Rogers	.05
164	Melvin Bunch	.05
165	Rod Beck	.05
166	Andy Benes	.05
167	Lenny Dykstra	.05
168	Orlando Merced	.05
169	Tomas Perez	.05
170	Xavier Hernandez	.05
171	Ruben Sierra	.05
172	Alan Trammell	.05
173	Mike Fetters	.05
174	Wilson Alvarez	.05
175	Erik Hanson	.05
176	Travis Fryman	.05
177	Jim Abbott	.05
178	Bret Boone	.05
179	Sterling Hitchcock	.05
180	Pat Mahomes	.05
181	Mark Acre	.05
182	Charles Nagy	.05
183	Rusty Greer	.05
184	Mike Stanley	.05
185	Jim Bullinger	.05
186	Shane Andrews	.05
187	Brian Keyser	.05
188	Tyler Green	.05
189	Mark Grace	.05
190	Bob Hamelin	.05
191	Luis Ortiz	.05
192	Joe Carter	.05
193	Eddie Taubensee	.05
194	Brian Anderson	.05
195	Edgardo Alfonzo	.05
196	Pedro Munoz	.05
197	David Justice	.05
198	Trevor Hoffman	.05
199	Bobby Ayala	.05
200	Tony Eusebio	.05
201	Jeff Russell	.05
202	Mike Hampton	.05
203	Walt Weiss	.05
204	Joey Hamilton	.05
205	Roberto Hernandez	.05
206	Greg Vaughn	.05
207	Felipe Lira	.05
208	Harold Baines	.05
209	Tim Wallach	.05
210	Manny Alexander	.05
211	Tim Laker	.05
212	Chris Haney	.05
213	Brian Maxcy	.05
214	Eric Young	.05
215	Darryl Strawberry	.05
216	Barry Bonds	2.50
217	Tim Naehring	.05
218	Scott Brosius	.05
219	Reggie Sanders	.05
220	Eddie Murray Checklist 84-166 (3,000 Career Hits)	.35
221	Luis Alicea	.05
222	Albert Belle	.05
223	Benji Gil	.05
224	Dante Bichette	.05
225	Bobby Bonilla	.05
226	Todd Stottlemyre	.05
227	Jim Edmonds	.05
228	Todd Jones	.05
229	Shawn Green	.25
230	Javy Lopez	.05
231	Ariel Prieto	.05
232	Tony Phillips	.05
233	James Mouton	.05
234	Jose Oquendo	.05
235	Royce Clayton	.05
236	Chuck Carr	.05
237	Doug Jones	.05
238	Mark Mclemore (Mclemore)	.05
239	Bill Swift	.05
240	Scott Leius	.05
241	Russ Davis	.05
242	Ray Durham	.05
243	Matt Mieske	.05
244	Brent Mayne	.05
245	Thomas Howard	.05
246	Troy O'Leary	.05
247	Jacob Brumfield	.05
248	Mickey Morandini	.05
249	Todd Hundley	.05
250	Chris Bosio	.05
251	Omar Vizquel	.05
252	Mike Lansing	.05
253	John Mabry	.05
254	Mike Perez	.05
255	Delino DeShields	.05
256	Wil Cordero	.05
257	Mike James	.05
258	Todd Van Poppel	.05
259	Joey Cora	.05
260	Andre Dawson	.25
261	Jerry DiPoto	.05
262	Rick Krivda	.05
263	Glenn Dishman	.05
264	Mike Mimbs	.05
265	John Ericks	.05
266	Jose Canseco	.35
267	Jeff Branson	.05
268	Curt Leskanic	.05
269	Jon Nunnally	.05

No.	Player	Price
270	Scott Stahoviak	.05
271	Jeff Montgomery	.05
272	Hal Morris	.05
273	Esteban Loaiza	.05
274	Rico Brogna	.05
275	Dave Winfield	1.00
276	J.R. Phillips	.05
277	Todd Zeile	.05
278	Tom Pagnozzi	.05
279	Mark Lemke	.05
280	Dave Magadan	.05
281	Greg McMichael	.05
282	Mike Morgan	.05
283	Moises Alou	.05
284	Dennis Martinez	.05
285	Jeff Kent	.05
286	Mark Johnson	.05
287	Darren Lewis	.05
288	Brad Clontz	.05
289	Chad Fonville	.05
290	Paul Sorrento	.05
291	Lee Smith	.05
292	Tom Glavine	.25
293	Antonio Osuna	.05
294	Kevin Foster	.05
295	Sandy Martinez RC	.05
296	Mark Leiter	.05
297	Julian Tavarez	.05
298	Mike Kelly	.05
299	Joe Oliver	.05
300	John Flaherty	.05
301	Don Mattingly	1.50
302	Pat Meares	.05
303	John Doherty	.05
304	Joe Vitiello	.05
305	Vinny Castilla	.05
306	Jeff Brantley	.05
307	Mike Greenwell	.05
308	Midre Cummings	.05
309	Curt Schilling	.25
310	Ken Caminiti	.05
311	Scott Erickson	.05
312	Carl Everett	.05
313	Charles Johnson	.05
314	Alex Diaz	.05
315	Jose Mesa	.05
316	Mark Carreon	.05
317	Carlos Perez	.05
318	Ismael Valdes	.05
319	Frank Castillo	.05
320	Tom Henke	.05
321	Spike Owen	.05
322	Joe Orsulak	.05
323	Paul Menhart	.05
324	Pedro Borbon	.05
325	Paul Molitor Checklist 167-249 (1,000 Career RBI)	.35
326	Jeff Cirillo	.05
327	Edwin Hurtado	.05
328	Orlando Miller	.05
329	Steve Ontiveros	.05
330	Kirby Puckett Checklist 250-330 (1,000 Career RBI)	.75
331	Scott Bullett	.05
332	Andres Galarraga	.05
333	Cal Eldred	.05
334	Sammy Sosa	1.25
335	Don Slaught	.05
336	Jody Reed	.05
337	Roger Cedeno	.05
338	Ken Griffey Jr.	1.75
339	Todd Hollandsworth	.05
340	Mike Trombley	.05
341	Gregg Jefferies	.05
342	Larry Walker	.05
343	Pedro Martinez	.05
344	Dwayne Hosey	.05
345	Terry Pendleton	.05
346	Pete Harnisch	.05
347	Tony Castillo	.05
348	Paul Quantrill	.05
349	Fred McGriff	.05
350	Ivan Rodriguez	.65
351	Butch Huskey	.05
352	Ozzie Smith	1.25
353	Marty Cordova	.05
354	John Wasdin	.05
355	Wade Boggs	1.25
356	Dave Nilsson	.05
357	Rafael Palmeiro	.65
358	Luis Gonzalez	.05
359	Reggie Jefferson	.05
360	Carlos Delgado	.60
361	Orlando Palmeiro	.05
362	Chris Gomez	.05
363	John Smoltz	.05
364	Marc Newfield	.05
365	Matt Williams	.05
366	Jesus Tavarez	.05
367	Bruce Ruffin	.05
368	Sean Berry	.05
369	Randy Velarde	.05
370	Tony Pena	.05
371	Jim Thome	.60
372	Jeffrey Hammonds	.05
373	Bob Wolcott	.05
374	Juan Guzman	.05
375	Juan Gonzalez	.50
376	Michael Tucker	.05
377	Doug Johns	.05
378	Mike Cameron RC	.75
379	Ray Lankford	.05
380	Jose Parra	.05
381	Jimmy Key	.05
382	John Olerud	.05

No.	Player	Price
383	Kevin Ritz	.05
384	Tim Raines	.05
385	Rich Amaral	.05
386	Keith Lockhart	.05
387	Steve Scarsone	.05
388	Cliff Floyd	.05
389	Rich Aude	.05
390	Hideo Nomo	.50
391	Geronimo Berroa	.05
392	Pat Rapp	.05
393	Dustin Hermanson	.05
394	Greg Maddux	1.25
395	Darren Daulton	.05
396	Kenny Lofton	.05
397	Ruben Rivera	.05
398	Billy Wagner	.05
399	Kevin Brown	.05
400	Mike Kingery	.05
401	Bernie Williams	.05
402	Otis Nixon	.05
403	Damion Easley	.05
404	Paul O'Neill	.05
405	Deion Sanders	.05
406	Dennis Eckersley	1.00
407	Tony Clark	.05
408	Rondell White	.05
409	Luis Sojo	.05
410	David Hulse	.05
411	Shane Reynolds	.05
412	Chris Hoiles	.05
413	Lee Tinsley	.05
414	Scott Karl	.05
415	Ron Gant	.05
416	Brian Johnson	.05
417	Jose Oliva	.05
418	Jack McDowell	.05
419	Paul Molitor	1.00
420	Ricky Bottalico	.05
421	Paul Wagner	.05
422	Terry Bradshaw	.05
423	Bob Tewksbury	.05
424	Mike Piazza	1.75
425	Luis Andujar RC	.05
426	Mark Langston	.05
427	Stan Belinda	.05
428	Kurt Abbott	.05
429	Shawon Dunston	.05
430	Bobby Jones	.05
431	Jose Vizcaino	.05
432	Matt Lawton RC	.05
433	Pat Hentgen	.05
434	Cecil Fielder	.05
435	Carlos Baerga	.05
436	Rich Becker	.05
437	Chipper Jones	1.25
438	Bill Risley	.05
439	Kevin Appier	.05
440	Checklist	.05
441	Jaime Navarro	.05
442	Barry Larkin	.05
443	Jose Valentin RC	.05
444	Bryan Rekar	.05
445	Rick Wilkins	.05
446	Quilvio Veras	.05
447	Greg Gagne	.05
448	Mark Kiefer	.05
449	Bobby Witt	.05
450	Andy Ashby	.05
451	Alex Ochoa	.05
452	Jorge Fabregas	.05
453	Gene Schall	.05
454	Ken Hill	.05
455	Tony Tarasco	.05
456	Donnie Wall	.05
457	Carlos Garcia	.05
458	Ryan Thompson	.05
459	Marvin Benard RC	.05
460	Jose Herrera	.05
461	Jeff Blauser	.05
462	Chris Hook	.05
463	Jeff Conine	.05
464	Devon White	.05
465	Danny Bautista	.05
466	Steve Trachsel	.05
467	C.J. Nitkowski	.05
468	Mike Devereaux	.05
469	David Wells	.05
470	Jim Eisenreich	.05
471	Edgar Martinez	.05
472	Craig Biggio	.05
473	Jeff Frye	.05
474	Karim Garcia	.05
475	Jimmy Haynes	.05
476	Darren Holmes	.05
477	Tim Salmon	.05
478	Randy Johnson	1.00
479	Eric Plunk	.05
480	Scott Cooper	.05
481	Chan Ho Park	.05
482	Ray McDavid	.05
483	Mark Petkovsek	.05
484	Greg Swindell	.05
485	George Williams	.05
486	Yamil Benitez	.05
487	Tim Wakefield	.05
488	Kevin Tapani	.05
489	Derrick May	.05
490	Ken Griffey Jr. Checklist	1.00
491	Derek Jeter	2.50
492	Jeff Fassero	.05
493	Benito Santiago	.05
494	Tom Gordon	.05
495	Jamie Brewington	.05
496	Vince Coleman	.05
497	Kevin Jordan	.05

No.	Player	Price
498	Jeff King	.05
499	Mike Simms	.05
500	Jose Rijo	.05
501	Denny Neagle	.05
502	Jose Lima	.05
503	Kevin Seitzer	.05
504	Alex Fernandez	.05
505	Mo Vaughn	.05
506	Phil Nevin	.05
507	J.T. Snow	.05
508	Andujar Cedeno	.05
509	Ozzie Guillen	.05
510	Mark Clark	.05
511	Mark McGwire	2.00
512	Jeff Reboulet	.05
513	Armando Benitez	.05
514	LaTroy Hawkins	.05
515	Brett Butler	.05
516	Tavo Alvarez	.05
517	Chris Snopek	.05
518	Mike Mussina	.50
519	Darryl Kile	.05
520	Wally Joyner	.05
521	Willie McGee	.05
522	Kent Mercker	.05
523	Mike Jackson	.05
524	Troy Percival	.05
525	Tony Gwynn	1.25
526	Ron Coomer	.05
527	Darryl Hamilton	.05
528	Phil Plantier	.05
529	Norm Charlton	.05
530	Craig Paquette	.05
531	Dave Burba	.05
532	Mike Henneman	.05
533	Terrell Wade	.05
534	Eddie Williams	.05
535	Robin Ventura	.05
536	Chuck Knoblauch	.05
537	Les Norman	.05
538	Brady Anderson	.05
539	Roger Clemens	1.50
540	Mark Portugal	.05
541	Mike Matheny	.05
542	Jeff Parrett	.05
543	Roberto Kelly	.05
544	Damon Buford	.05
545	Chad Ogea	.05
546	Jose Offerman	.05
547	Brian Barber	.05
548	Danny Tartabull	.05
549	Duane Singleton	.05
550	Tony Gwynn Checklist	.75

Press Proofs

MARK LEMKE

	NM/M
Complete Set (550):	150.00
Common Player:	.50

(Star cards valued 7X corresponding regular-issue cards.)

Diamond Kings

DONRUSS DIAMOND KINGS

Frank Thomas

	NM/M
Complete Set (31):	160.00
Common Player:	2.25
1	Frank Thomas	7.50
2	Mo Vaughn	2.50

No.	Player	Price
3	Manny Ramirez	7.50
4	Mark McGwire	13.50
5	Juan Gonzalez	4.00
6	Roberto Alomar	3.00
7	Tim Salmon	2.50
8	Barry Bonds	15.00
9	Tony Gwynn	10.00
10	Reggie Sanders	2.50
11	Larry Walker	2.50
12	Pedro Martinez	7.50
13	Jeff King	2.50
14	Mark Grace	2.50
15	Greg Maddux	10.00
16	Don Mattingly	12.50
17	Gregg Jefferies	2.50
18	Chad Curtis	2.50
19	Jason Isringhausen	2.50
20	B.J. Surhoff	2.50
21	Jeff Conine	2.50
22	Kirby Puckett	10.00
23	Derek Bell	2.50
24	Wally Joyner	2.50
25	Brian Jordan	2.50
26	Edgar Martinez	2.50
27	Hideo Nomo	4.00
28	Mike Mussina	5.00
29	Eddie Murray	7.50
30	Cal Ripken Jr.	15.00
31	Checklist	.25

Elite

ELITE SERIES

	NM/M
Complete Set (12):	55.00
Complete Series 1 (61-66):	25.00
Complete Series 2 (67-72):	30.00
Common Player Series 1:	2.50
Common Player Series 2:	2.00
61	Cal Ripken Jr.	12.00
63	Hideo Nomo	3.00
63	Reggie Sanders	2.00
64	Mo Vaughn	2.00
65	Tim Salmon	2.50
66	Chipper Jones	8.00
67	Manny Ramirez	6.00
68	Greg Maddux	10.00
69	Frank Thomas	6.00
70	Ken Griffey Jr.	10.00
71	Dante Bichette	2.00
72	Tony Gwynn	8.00

Freeze Frame

FREEZE FRAME

	NM/M
Complete Set (8):	16.00
Common Player:	1.00
1	Frank Thomas	2.00
2	Ken Griffey Jr.	3.00
3	Cal Ripken Jr.	4.00
4	Hideo Nomo	1.50
5	Greg Maddux	2.50
6	Albert Belle	1.00
7	Chipper Jones	2.50
8	Mike Piazza	3.00

Hit List

	NM/M
Complete Set (16):	30.00
Common Player:	.60
1	Tony Gwynn	3.00
2	Ken Griffey Jr.	5.00
3	Will Clark	.60
4	Mike Piazza	.60
5	Carlos Baerga	.60
6	Mo Vaughn	.60
7	Mark Grace	.60
8	Kirby Puckett	3.00
9	Frank Thomas	2.00
10	Barry Bonds	6.00
11	Jeff Bagwell	2.00

12	Edgar Martinez	.60
13	Tim Salmon	.60
14	Wade Boggs	3.00
15	Don Mattingly	4.00
16	Eddie Murray	2.00

Long Ball Leaders

		NM/M
Complete Set (8):		45.00
Common Player:		1.50
1	Barry Bonds	15.00
2	Ryan Klesko	1.50
3	Mark McGwire	15.00
4	Raul Mondesi	1.50
5	Cecil Fielder	1.50
6	Ken Griffey Jr.	12.00
7	Larry Walker	1.50
8	Frank Thomas	6.00

Power Alley

		NM/M
Complete Set (10):		30.00
Common Player		2.00
Die-cuts 2X		
1	Frank Thomas	4.00
2	Barry Bonds	7.50
3	Reggie Sanders	2.00
4	Albert Belle	2.00
5	Tim Salmon	2.00
6	Dante Bichette	2.00
7	Mo Vaughn	2.00
8	Jim Edmonds	2.00
9	Manny Ramirez	4.00
10	Ken Griffey Jr.	6.00

Pure Power

		NM/M
Complete Set (8):		25.00
Common Player:		2.25
1	Raul Mondesi	2.25
2	Barry Bonds	10.00
3	Albert Belle	2.25
4	Frank Thomas	4.50
5	Mike Piazza	7.50

6	Dante Bichette	2.25
7	Manny Ramirez	4.50
8	Mo Vaughn	2.25

Round Trippers

		NM/M
Complete Set (10):		35.00
Common Player:		2.50
1	Albert Belle	2.50
2	Barry Bonds	7.50
3	Jeff Bagwell	4.00
4	Tim Salmon	2.50
5	Mo Vaughn	2.50
6	Ken Griffey Jr.	5.00
7	Mike Piazza	5.00
8	Cal Ripken Jr.	7.50
9	Frank Thomas	4.00
9p	Frank Thomas (Promo)	2.50
10	Dante Bichette	2.50

Showdown

		NM/M
Complete Set (8):		22.50
Common Player:		.75
1	Frank Thomas, Hideo Nomo	3.00
2	Barry Bonds, Randy Johnson	6.00
3	Greg Maddux, Ken Griffey Jr.	5.00
4	Roger Clemens, Tony Gwynn	4.50
5	Mike Piazza, Mike Mussina	5.00
6	Cal Ripken Jr., Pedro Martinez	6.00
7	Tim Wakefield, Matt Williams	.75
8	Manny Ramirez, Carlos Perez	2.50

1997 Donruss

	NM/M
Complete Set (450):	20.00
Series 1 Set (270):	10.00
Update Set (180):	10.00
Common Player:	.05
Common Press Proof:	.50
Press Proof Stars:	5X
Common Press Proof Gold:	2.00
Press Proof Gold Stars:	10X
Wax Pack (10):	1.50
Hobby Wax Box (18):	25.00
Retail Wax Box (36):	40.00
Magazine Pack (13):	1.50

Magazine Box (24):		20.00
Update Pack (10):		1.50
Update Wax Box (24):		30.00
1	Juan Gonzalez	.40
2	Jim Edmonds	.05
3	Tony Gwynn	1.00
4	Andres Galarraga	.05
5	Joe Carter	.05
6	Raul Mondesi	.05
7	Greg Maddux	1.00
8	Travis Fryman	.05
9	Brian Jordan	.05
10	Henry Rodriguez	.05
11	Manny Ramirez	.75
12	Mark McGwire	1.75
13	Marc Newfield	.05
14	Craig Biggio	.05
15	Sammy Sosa	1.00
16	Brady Anderson	.05
17	Wade Boggs	1.00
18	Charles Johnson	.05
19	Matt Williams	.05
20	Denny Neagle	.05
21	Ken Griffey Jr.	1.50
22	Robin Ventura	.05
23	Barry Larkin	.05
24	Todd Zeile	.05
25	Chuck Knoblauch	.05
26	Todd Hundley	.05
27	Roger Clemens	1.25
28	Michael Tucker	.05
29	Rondell White	.05
30	Osvaldo Fernandez	.05
31	Ivan Rodriguez	.65
32	Alex Fernandez	.05
33	Jason Isringhausen	.05
34	Chipper Jones	1.00
35	Paul O'Neill	.05
36	Hideo Nomo	.40
37	Roberto Alomar	.20
38	Derek Bell	.05
39	Paul Molitor	.75
40	Andy Benes	.05
41	Steve Trachsel	.05
42	J.T. Snow	.05
43	Jason Kendall	.05
44	Alex Rodriguez	1.75
45	Joey Hamilton	.05
46	Carlos Delgado	.50
47	Jason Giambi	.50
48	Larry Walker	.05
49	Derek Jeter	2.00
50	Kenny Lofton	.05
51	Devon White	.05
52	Matt Mieske	.05
53	Melvin Nieves	.05
54	Jose Canseco	.40
55	Tino Martinez	.05
56	Rafael Palmeiro	.65
57	Edgardo Alfonzo	.05
58	Jay Buhner	.05
59	Shane Reynolds	.05
60	Steve Finley	.05
61	Bobby Higginson	.05
62	Dean Palmer	.05
63	Terry Pendleton	.05
64	Marquis Grissom	.05
65	Mike Stanley	.05
66	Moises Alou	.05
67	Ray Lankford	.05
68	Marty Cordova	.05
69	John Olerud	.05
70	David Cone	.05
71	Benito Santiago	.05
72	Ryne Sandberg	1.00
73	Rickey Henderson	.75
74	Roger Cedeno	.05
75	Wilson Alvarez	.05
76	Tim Salmon	.05
77	Orlando Merced	.05
78	Vinny Castilla	.05
79	Ismael Valdes	.05
80	Dante Bichette	.05
81	Kevin Brown	.05
82	Andy Pettitte	.40
83	Scott Stahoviak	.05
84	Mickey Tettleton	.05
85	Jack McDowell	.05
86	Tom Glavine	.30
87	Gregg Jefferies	.05
88	Chili Davis	.05
89	Randy Johnson	.75
90	John Mabry	.05
91	Billy Wagner	.05
92	Jeff Cirillo	.05
93	Trevor Hoffman	.05
94	Juan Guzman	.05
95	Geronimo Berroa	.05
96	Bernard Gilkey	.05
97	Danny Tartabull	.05
98	Johnny Damon	.35
99	Charlie Hayes	.05
100	Reggie Sanders	.05
101	Robby Thompson	.05
102	Bobby Bonilla	.05
103	Reggie Jefferson	.05
104	John Smoltz	.05
105	Jim Thome	.60
106	Ruben Rivera	.05
107	Darren Oliver	.05
108	Mo Vaughn	.05
109	Roger Pavlik	.05
110	Terry Steinbach	.05
111	Jermaine Dye	.05
112	Mark Grudzielanek	.05
113	Rick Aguilera	.05
114	Jamey Wright	.05
115	Eddie Murray	.75
116	Brian Hunter	.05
117	Hal Morris	.05
118	Tom Pagnozzi	.05
119	Mike Mussina	.40
120	Mark Grace	.05
121	Cal Ripken Jr.	2.00
122	Tom Goodwin	.05
123	Paul Sorrento	.05
124	Jay Bell	.05
125	Todd Hollandsworth	.05
126	Edgar Martinez	.05
127	George Arias	.05
128	Greg Vaughn	.05
129	Roberto Hernandez	.05
130	Delino DeShields	.05
131	Bill Pulsipher	.05
132	Joey Cora	.05
133	Mariano Rivera	.15
134	Mike Piazza	1.50
135	Carlos Baerga	.05
136	Jose Mesa	.05
137	Will Clark	.05
138	Frank Thomas	.75
139	John Wetteland	.05
140	Shawn Estes	.05
141	Garret Anderson	.05
142	Andre Dawson	.25
143	Eddie Taubensee	.05
144	Ryan Klesko	.05
145	Rocky Coppinger	.05
146	Jeff Bagwell	.75
147	Donovan Osborne	.05
148	Greg Myers	.05
149	Brant Brown	.05
150	Kevin Elster	.05
151	Bob Wells	.05
152	Wally Joyner	.05
153	Rico Brogna	.05
154	Dwight Gooden	.05
155	Jermaine Allensworth	.05
156	Ray Durham	.05
157	Cecil Fielder	.05
158	Ryan Hancock	.05
159	Gary Sheffield	.30
160	Albert Belle	.05
161	Tomas Perez	.05
162	David Doster	.05
163	John Valentin	.05
164	Danny Graves	.05
165	Jose Paniagua	.05
166	Brian Giles RC	.50
167	Barry Bonds	2.00
168	Sterling Hitchcock	.05
169	Bernie Williams	.05
170	Fred McGriff	.05
171	George Williams	.05
172	Amaury Telemaco	.05
173	Ken Caminiti	.05
174	Ron Gant	.05
175	David Justice	.05
176	James Baldwin	.05
177	Pat Hentgen	.05
178	Ben McDonald	.05
179	Tim Naehring	.05
180	Jim Eisenreich	.05
181	Ken Hill	.05
182	Paul Wilson	.05
183	Marvin Benard	.05
184	Alan Benes	.05
185	Ellis Burks	.05
186	Scott Servais	.05
187	David Segui	.05
188	Scott Brosius	.05
189	Jose Offerman	.05
190	Eric Davis	.05
191	Brett Butler	.05
192	Curtis Pride	.05
193	Yamil Benitez	.05
194	Chan Ho Park	.05
195	Bret Boone	.05
196	Omar Vizquel	.05
197	Orlando Miller	.05
198	Ramon Martinez	.05
199	Harold Baines	.05
200	Eric Young	.05
201	Fernando Vina	.05
202	Alex Gonzalez	.05
203	Fernando Valenzuela	.05
204	Steve Avery	.05
205	Ernie Young	.05
206	Kevin Appier	.05

#	Player	Price
207	Randy Myers	.05
208	Jeff Suppan	.05
209	James Mouton	.05
210	Russ Davis	.05
211	Al Martin	.05
212	Troy Percival	.05
213	Al Leiter	.05
214	Dennis Eckersley	.65
215	Mark Johnson	.05
216	Eric Karros	.05
217	Royce Clayton	.05
218	Tony Phillips	.05
219	Tim Wakefield	.05
220	Alan Trammell	.05
221	Eduardo Perez	.05
222	Butch Huskey	.05
223	Tim Belcher	.05
224	Jamie Moyer	.05
225	F.P. Santangelo	.05
226	Rusty Greer	.05
227	Jeff Brantley	.05
228	Mark Langston	.05
229	Ray Montgomery	.05
230	Rich Becker	.05
231	Ozzie Smith	1.00
232	Rey Ordonez	.05
233	Ricky Otero	.05
234	Mike Cameron	.05
235	Mike Sweeney	.05
236	Mark Lewis	.05
237	Luis Gonzalez	.05
238	Marcus Jensen	.05
239	Ed Sprague	.05
240	Jose Valentin	.05
241	Jeff Frye	.05
242	Charles Nagy	.05
243	Carlos Garcia	.05
244	Mike Hampton	.05
245	B.J. Surhoff	.05
246	Wilton Guerrero	.05
247	Frank Rodriguez	.05
248	Gary Gaetti	.05
249	Lance Johnson	.05
250	Darren Bragg	.05
251	Darryl Hamilton	.05
252	John Jaha	.05
253	Craig Paquette	.05
254	Jaime Navarro	.05
255	Shawon Dunston	.05
256	Ron Wright	.05
257	Tim Belk	.05
258	Jeff Darwin	.05
259	Ruben Sierra	.05
260	Chuck Finley	.05
261	Darryl Strawberry	.05
262	Shannon Stewart	.05
263	Pedro Martinez	.05
264	Neifi Perez	.05
265	Jeff Conine	.05
266	Orel Hershiser	.05
267	Eddie Murray Checklist 1-90 (500 Career HR)	.05
268	Paul Molitor Checklist 91-180 (3,000 Career Hits)	.05
269	Barry Bonds Checklist 181-270 (300 Career HR)	.90
270	Mark McGwire Checklist - inserts (300 Career HR)	.75
271	Matt Williams	.05
272	Todd Zeile	.05
273	Roger Clemens	1.25
274	Michael Tucker	.05
275	J.T. Snow	.05
276	Kenny Lofton	.05
277	Jose Canseco	.40
278	Marquis Grissom	.05
279	Moises Alou	.05
280	Benito Santiago	.05
281	Willie McGee	.05
282	Chili Davis	.05
283	Ron Coomer	.05
284	Orlando Merced	.05
285	Delino DeShields	.05
286	John Wetteland	.05
287	Darren Daulton	.05
288	Lee Stevens	.05
289	Albert Belle	.05
290	Sterling Hitchcock	.05
291	David Justice	.05
292	Eric Davis	.05
293	Brian Hunter	.05
294	Darryl Hamilton	.05
295	Steve Avery	.05
296	Joe Vitiello	.05
297	Jaime Navarro	.05
298	Eddie Murray	.75
299	Randy Myers	.05
300	Francisco Cordova	.05
301	Javier Lopez	.05
302	Geronimo Berroa	.05
303	Jeffrey Hammonds	.05
304	Deion Sanders	.05
305	Jeff Fassero	.05
306	Curt Schilling	.25
307	Robb Nen	.05
308	Mark McLemore	.05
309	Jimmy Key	.05
310	Quilvio Veras	.05
311	Bip Roberts	.05
312	Esteban Loaiza	.05
313	Andy Ashby	.05
314	Sandy Alomar Jr.	.05
315	Shawn Green	.20
316	Luis Castillo	.05
317	Benji Gil	.05
318	Otis Nixon	.05
319	Aaron Sele	.05
320	Brad Ausmus	.05
321	Troy O'Leary	.05
322	Terrell Wade	.05
323	Jeff King	.05
324	Kevin Seitzer	.05
325	Mark Wohlers	.05
326	Edgar Renteria	.05
327	Dan Wilson	.05
328	Brian McRae	.05
329	Rod Beck	.05
330	Julio Franco	.05
331	Dave Nilsson	.05
332	Glenallen Hill	.05
333	Kevin Elster	.05
334	Joe Girardi	.05
335	David Wells	.05
336	Jeff Blauser	.05
337	Darryl Kile	.05
338	Jeff Kent	.05
339	Jim Leyritz	.05
340	Todd Stottlemyre	.05
341	Tony Clark	.05
342	Chris Hoiles	.05
343	Mike Lieberthal	.05
344	Matt Lawton	.05
345	Alex Ochoa	.05
346	Chris Snopek	.05
347	Rudy Pemberton	.05
348	Eric Owens	.05
349	Joe Randa	.05
350	John Olerud	.05
351	Steve Karsay	.05
352	Mark Whiten	.05
353	Bob Abreu	.10
354	Bartolo Colon	.05
355	Vladimir Guerrero	.75
356	Darin Erstad	.30
357	Scott Rolen	.60
358	Andruw Jones	.75
359	Scott Spiezio	.05
360	Karim Garcia	.05
361	Hideki Irabu RC	.25
362	Nomar Garciaparra	1.00
363	Dmitri Young	.05
364	Bubba Trammell RC	.25
365	Kevin Orie	.05
366	Jose Rosado	.05
367	Jose Guillen	.05
368	Brooks Kieschnick	.05
369	Pokey Reese	.05
370	Glendon Rusch	.05
371	Jason Dickson	.05
372	Todd Walker	.05
373	Justin Thompson	.05
374	Todd Greene	.05
375	Jeff Suppan	.05
376	Trey Beamon	.05
377	Damon Mashore	.05
378	Wendell Magee	.05
379	Shigetosi Hasegawa	.05
380	Bill Mueller	.05
381	Chris Widger	.05
382	Tony Grafanino	.05
383	Derrek Lee	.50
384	Brian Moehler	.05
385	Quinton McCracken	.05
386	Matt Morris	.05
387	Marvin Benard	.05
388	Deivi Cruz RC	.25
389	Javier Valentin RC	.05
390	Todd Dunwoody	.05
391	Derrick Gibson	.05
392	Raul Casanova	.05
393	George Arias	.05
394	Tony Womack RC	.25
395	Antone Williamson	.05
396	Jose Cruz Jr. RC	.50
397	Desi Relaford	.05
398	Frank Thomas/HL	.40
399	Ken Griffey Jr./HL	.65
400	Cal Ripken Jr./HL	1.00
401	Chipper Jones/HL	.50
402	Mike Piazza/HL	.65
403	Gary Sheffield/HL	.15
404	Alex Rodriguez/HL	.75
405	Wade Boggs/HL	.50
406	Juan Gonzalez /HL	.20
407	Tony Gwynn/HL	.50
408	Edgar Martinez /HL	.05
409	Jeff Bagwell/HL	.40
410	Larry Walker/HL	.05
411	Kenny Lofton/HL	.40
412	Manny Ramirez/HL	.75
413	Mark McGwire/HL	.75
414	Roberto Alomar/HL	.10
415	Derek Jeter/HL	1.00
416	Brady Anderson/HL	.05
417	Paul Molitor/HL	.35
418	Dante Bichette/HL	.05
419	Jim Edmonds/HL	.05
420	Mo Vaughn/HL	.05
421	Barry Bonds/HL	.90
422	Rusty Greer/HL	.05
423	Greg Maddux	.50
424	Andy Pettitte	.15
425	John Smoltz	.05
426	Randy Johnson	.40
427	Hideo Nomo	.20
428	Roger Clemens	.60
429	Tom Glavine	.15
430	Pat Hentgen	.05
431	Kevin Brown	.05
432	Mike Mussina	.20
433	Alex Fernandez	.05
434	Kevin Appier	.05
435	David Cone	.05
436	Jeff Fassero	.05
437	John Wetteland	.05
438	Barry Bonds, Ivan Rodriguez/IS	.90
439	Ken Griffey Jr., Andres Galarraga/IS	.65
440	Fred McGriff, Rafael Palmeiro/IS	.05
441	Barry Larkin, Jim Thome/IS	.05
442	Sammy Sosa, Albert Belle/IS	.50
443	Bernie Williams, Todd Hundley/IS	.05
444	Chuck Knoblauch, Brian Jordan/IS	.05
445	Mo Vaughn, Jeff Conine/IS	.05
446	Ken Caminiti, Jason Giambi/IS	.25
447	Raul Mondesi, Tim Salmon/IS	.05
448	Cal Ripken Jr. Checklist	.75
449	Greg Maddux Checklist	.60
450	Ken Griffey Jr. Checklist	.50

Press Proofs

	NM/M
Common Player:	.50
Stars/Rookies:	5X
Common Gold Player:	2.00
Gold Stars/Rookies:	10X

See 1997 Donruss for checklist and base card values.)

Armed and Dangerous

		NM/M
Complete Set (15):		35.00
Common Player:		1.00
1	Ken Griffey Jr.	4.00
2	Raul Mondesi	1.00
3	Chipper Jones	3.00
4	Ivan Rodriguez	1.50
5	Randy Johnson	2.00
6	Alex Rodriguez	5.00
7	Larry Walker	1.00
8	Cal Ripken Jr.	6.00
9	Kenny Lofton	1.00
10	Barry Bonds	6.00
11	Derek Jeter	6.00
12	Charles Johnson	1.00
13	Greg Maddux	3.00
14	Roberto Alomar	1.00
15	Barry Larkin	1.00

Diamond Kings

		NM/M
Complete Set (10):		30.00
Common Player:		1.00
Canvas (1st 500):		2X
1	Ken Griffey Jr.	6.00
2	Cal Ripken Jr.	10.00
3	Mo Vaughn	1.00
4	Chuck Knoblauch	1.00
5	Jeff Bagwell	2.50
6	Henry Rodriguez	1.00
7	Mike Piazza	6.00
8	Ivan Rodriguez	2.50

9	Frank Thomas	3.00
10	Chipper Jones	5.00

Elite Inserts

Elite Series

		NM/M
Complete Set (12):		100.00
Common Player:		3.00
Promos:		50 Percent
1	Frank Thomas	7.50
2	Paul Molitor	7.50
3	Sammy Sosa	10.00
4	Barry Bonds	20.00
5	Chipper Jones	10.00
6	Alex Rodriguez	15.00
7	Ken Griffey Jr.	12.50
8	Jeff Bagwell	7.50
9	Cal Ripken Jr.	20.00
10	Mo Vaughn	3.00
11	Mike Piazza	12.50
12	Juan Gonzalez	4.50

Frank Thomas The Big Heart

		NM/M
Complete Set (4):		20.00
Common Card:		5.00
1	Frank Thomas, Rod Carew	5.00
2-4	Frank Thomas	5.00

Jackie Robinson Rookie Reprint

		NM/M
79	Jackie Robinson	10.00

Longball Leaders

		NM/M
Complete Set (15):		20.00
Common Player:		.50
1	Frank Thomas	2.00
2	Albert Belle	.50
3	Mo Vaughn	.50
4	Brady Anderson	.50
5	Greg Vaughn	.50
6	Ken Griffey Jr.	3.00

7	Jay Buhner	.50
8	Juan Gonzalez	.75
9	Mike Piazza	3.00
10	Jeff Bagwell	2.00
11	Sammy Sosa	2.50
12	Mark McGwire	4.00
13	Cecil Fielder	.50
14	Ryan Klesko	.50
15	Jose Canseco	.85

Rated Rookies

		NM/M
Complete Set (30):		10.00
Common Player:		.50
1	Jason Thompson	.50
2	LaTroy Hawkins	.50
3	Scott Rolen	1.50
4	Trey Beamon	.50
5	Kimera Bartee	.50
6	Nerio Rodriguez	.50
7	Jeff D'Amico	.50
8	Quinton McCracken	.50
9	John Wasdin	.50
10	Robin Jennings	.50
11	Steve Gibralter	.50
12	Tyler Houston	.50
13	Tony Clark	.50
14	Ugueth Urbina	.50
15	Billy McMillon	.50
16	Raul Casanova	.50
17	Brooks Kieschnick	.50
18	Luis Castillo	.50
19	Edgar Renteria	.50
20	Andruw Jones	2.00
21	Chad Mottola	.50
22	Makoto Suzuki	.50
23	Justin Thompson	.50
24	Darin Erstad	1.00
25	Todd Walker	.50
26	Todd Greene	.50
27	Vladimir Guerrero	2.00
28	Darren Dreifort	.50
29	John Burke	.50
30	Damon Mashore	.50

Rocket Launchers

		NM/M
Complete Set (15):		25.00
Common Player:		.75
1	Frank Thomas	2.50
2	Albert Belle	.75
3	Chipper Jones	3.00
4	Mike Piazza	4.00
5	Mo Vaughn	.75
6	Juan Gonzalez	1.00
7	Fred McGriff	.75
8	Jeff Bagwell	2.50
9	Matt Williams	.75
10	Gary Sheffield	1.00
11	Barry Bonds	5.00
12	Manny Ramirez	2.00
13	Henry Rodriguez	.75

14	Jason Giambi	1.50
15	Cal Ripken Jr.	5.00

Update Press Proofs

	NM/M
Common Player:	.50
Stars:	7X
Common Player, Gold:	2.00
Gold Stars:	15X
(See 1997 Donruss (#271-450) for checklist, base card values.)	

Update Cal Ripken

		NM/M
Complete Set (10):		75.00
Common Card:		10.00
1-9	Cal Ripken Jr.	10.00
10	Cal Ripken Jr.	
	(Book insert.)	10.00

Update Dominators

		NM/M
Complete Set (20):		22.50
Common Player:		.50
1	Frank Thomas	1.25
2	Ken Griffey Jr.	2.25
3	Greg Maddux	1.50
4	Cal Ripken Jr.	3.00
5	Alex Rodriguez	2.50
6	Albert Belle	.50

7	Mark McGwire	2.50
8	Juan Gonzalez	.65
9	Chipper Jones	1.50
10	Hideo Nomo	.65
11	Roger Clemens	2.00
12	John Smoltz	.50
13	Mike Piazza	2.25
14	Sammy Sosa	1.50
15	Matt Williams	.50
16	Kenny Lofton	.50
17	Barry Larkin	.50
18	Rafael Palmeiro	1.00
19	Ken Caminiti	.50
20	Gary Sheffield	.75

Update Franchise Features

		NM/M
Complete Set (15):		45.00
Common Player:		2.00
1	Ken Griffey Jr., Andruw Jones	4.00
2	Frank Thomas, Darin Erstad	2.50
3	Alex Rodriguez, Nomar Garciaparra	5.00
4	Chuck Knoblauch, Wilton Guerrero	2.00
5	Juan Gonzalez, Bubba Trammell	2.00
6	Chipper Jones, Todd Walker	3.00
7	Barry Bonds, Vladimir Guerrero	6.00
8	Mark McGwire, Dmitri Young	5.00
9	Mike Piazza, Mike Sweeney	4.00
10	Mo Vaughn, Tony Clark	2.00
11	Gary Sheffield, Jose Guillen	2.00
12	Kenny Lofton, Shannon Stewart	2.00
13	Cal Ripken Jr., Scott Rolen	6.00
14	Derek Jeter, Pokey Reese	6.00
15	Tony Gwynn, Bob Abreu	3.00

Update Power Alley

		NM/M
Complete Set (24):		100.00
Common Gold:		7.50
Common Blue:		3.00
Common Green:		1.50
Die-Cuts:		3X
1	Frank Thomas/G	7.50
2	Ken Griffey Jr./G	10.00
3	Cal Ripken Jr./G	15.00
4	Jeff Bagwell/B	5.00
5	Mike Piazza/B	7.50
6	Andruw Jones/GR	3.50
7	Alex Rodriguez/G	12.50
8	Albert Belle/GR	1.50
9	Mo Vaughn/GR	1.50
10	Chipper Jones/B	6.00
11	Juan Gonzalez/B	3.00
12	Ken Caminiti/GR	1.50
13	Manny Ramirez/GR	3.50
14	Mark McGwire/GR	6.00
15	Kenny Lofton/B	3.00

16	Barry Bonds/GR	7.50
17	Gary Sheffield/GR	1.50
18	Tony Gwynn/GR	4.50
19	Vladimir Guerrero/B	5.00
20	Ivan Rodriguez/B	3.50
21	Paul Molitor/B	5.00
22	Sammy Sosa/GR	4.50
23	Matt Williams/GR	1.50
24	Derek Jeter/GR	7.50

Update Rookie Diamond Kings

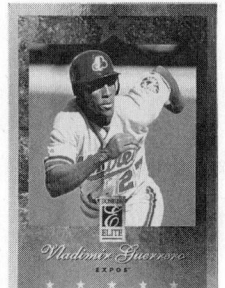

		NM/M
Complete Set (10):		20.00
Common Player:		1.50
Canvas:		1.5X
1	Andruw Jones	4.00
2	Vladimir Guerrero	10.00
3	Scott Rolen	2.00
4	Todd Walker	1.50
5	Bartolo Colon	2.00
6	Jose Guillen	1.50
7	Nomar Garciaparra	6.00
8	Darin Erstad	2.00
9	Dmitri Young	1.50
10	Wilton Guerrero	1.50

1997 Donruss Elite

		NM/M
Complete Set (150):		10.00
Common Player:		.10
Common Elite Star:		.50
Elite Stars Stars/RC's:		4X
Pack (6):		2.50
Wax Box (18):		35.00
1	Juan Gonzalez	.40
2	Alex Rodriguez	2.00
3	Frank Thomas	.75
4	Greg Maddux	1.00
5	Ken Griffey Jr.	1.50
6	Cal Ripken Jr.	2.50
7	Mike Piazza	1.50
8	Chipper Jones	1.00
9	Albert Belle	.10
10	Andruw Jones	.75
11	Vladimir Guerrero	.75
12	Mo Vaughn	.10
13	Ivan Rodriguez	.65
14	Andy Pettitte	.40
15	Tony Gwynn	1.00
16	Barry Bonds	2.50
17	Jeff Bagwell	.75
18	Manny Ramirez	.75
19	Kenny Lofton	.10
20	Roberto Alomar	.20
21	Mark McGwire	2.00
22	Ryan Klesko	.10
23	Tim Salmon	.10
24	Derek Jeter	2.50
25	Eddie Murray	.75
26	Jermaine Dye	.10
27	Ruben Rivera	.10
28	Jim Edmonds	.10
29	Mike Mussina	.40
30	Randy Johnson	.75
31	Sammy Sosa	1.00
32	Hideo Nomo	.40
33	Chuck Knoblauch	.10

34	Paul Molitor	.75
35	Rafael Palmeiro	.75
36	Brady Anderson	.10
37	Will Clark	.10
38	Craig Biggio	.10
39	Jason Giambi	.50
40	Roger Clemens	1.25
41	Jay Buhner	.10
42	Edgar Martinez	.10
43	Gary Sheffield	.35
44	Fred McGriff	.10
45	Bobby Bonilla	.10
46	Tom Glavine	.25
47	Wade Boggs	1.00
48	Jeff Conine	.10
49	John Smoltz	.10
50	Jim Thome	.60
51	Billy Wagner	.10
52	Jose Canseco	.40
53	Javy Lopez	.10
54	Cecil Fielder	.10
55	Garret Anderson	.10
56	Alex Ochoa	.10
57	Scott Rolen	.60
58	Darin Erstad	.30
59	Rey Ordonez	.10
60	Dante Bichette	.10
61	Joe Carter	.10
62	Moises Alou	.10
63	Jason Isringhausen	.10
64	Karim Garcia	.10
65	Brian Jordan	.10
66	Ruben Sierra	.10
67	Todd Hollandsworth	.10
68	Paul Wilson	.10
69	Ernie Young	.10
70	Ryne Sandberg	1.00
71	Raul Mondesi	.10
72	George Arias	.10
73	Ray Durham	.10
74	Dean Palmer	.10
75	Shawn Green	.30
76	Eric Young	.10
77	Jason Kendall	.10
78	Greg Vaughn	.10
79	Terrell Wade	.10
80	Bill Pulsipher	.10
81	Bobby Higginson	.10
82	Mark Grudzielanek	.10
83	Ken Caminiti	.10
84	Todd Greene	.10
85	Carlos Delgado	.50
86	Mark Grace	.10
87	Rondell White	.10
88	Barry Larkin	.10
89	J.T. Snow	.10
90	Alex Gonzalez	.10
91	Raul Casanova	.10
92	Marc Newfield	.10
93	Jermaine Allensworth	.10
94	John Mabry	.10
95	Kirby Puckett	1.00
96	Travis Fryman	.10
97	Kevin Brown	.15
98	Andres Galarraga	.10
99	Marty Cordova	.10
100	Henry Rodriguez	.10
101	Sterling Hitchcock	.10
102	Trey Beamon	.10
103	Brett Butler	.10
104	Rickey Henderson	.75
105	Tino Martinez	.10
106	Kevin Appier	.10
107	Brian Hunter	.10
108	Eric Karros	.10
109	Andre Dawson	.10
110	Darryl Strawberry	.10
111	James Baldwin	.10
112	Chad Mottola	.10
113	Dave Nilsson	.10
114	Carlos Baerga	.10
115	Chan Ho Park	.10
116	John Jaha	.10
117	Alan Benes	.10
118	Mariano Rivera	.20
119	Ellis Burks	.10
120	Tony Clark	.10
121	Todd Walker	.10
122	Dwight Gooden	.10
123	Ugueth Urbina	.10
124	David Cone	.10
125	Ozzie Smith	1.00
126	Kimera Bartee	.10
127	Rusty Greer	.10
128	Pat Hentgen	.10
129	Charles Johnson	.10
130	Quinton McCracken	.10
131	Troy Percival	.10
132	Shane Reynolds	.10
133	Charles Nagy	.10
134	Tom Goodwin	.10
135	Ron Gant	.10
136	Dan Wilson	.10
137	Matt Williams	.10
138	LaTroy Hawkins	.10
139	Kevin Seitzer	.10
140	Michael Tucker	.10
141	Todd Hundley	.10
142	Alex Fernandez	.10
143	Marquis Grissom	.10
144	Steve Finley	.10
145	Curtis Pride	.10
146	Derek Bell	.10
147	Butch Huskey	.10
148	Dwight Gooden	.10
149	Al Leiter	.10
150	Hideo Nomo	.40

Stars

	NM/M
Common Player:	1.00

(Star players in the Elite Star parallel issue valued at 4X regular Elites.)

Leather & Lumber

		NM/M
Complete Set (10):		140.00
Common Player:		4.00
1	Ken Griffey Jr.	20.00
2	Alex Rodriguez	25.00
3	Frank Thomas	9.00
4	Chipper Jones	12.50
5	Ivan Rodriguez	7.50
6	Cal Ripken Jr.	35.00
7	Barry Bonds	35.00
8	Chuck Knoblauch	4.00
9	Manna Ramirez	9.00
10	Mark McGwire	25.00

Passing the Torch

		NM/M
Complete Set (12):		110.00
Common Player:		4.50
1	Cal Ripken Jr.	20.00
2	Alex Rodriguez	15.00
3	Cal Ripken Jr., Alex Rodriguez	17.50
4	Kirby Puckett	10.00
5	Andruw Jones	7.50
6	Kirby Puckett, Andruw Jones	7.50
7	Cecil Fielder	4.50
8	Frank Thomas	7.50
9	Cecil Fielder, Frank Thomas	6.00
10	Ozzie Smith	10.00
11	Derek Jeter	20.00
12	Ozzie Smith, Derek Jeter	12.00

Passing the Torch Autographs

		NM/M
Common Card:		15.00
1	Cal Ripken Jr.	200.00
2	Alex Rodriguez	275.00
3	Cal Ripken Jr., Alex Rodriguez	750.00
4	Kirby Puckett	80.00
5	Andruw Jones	40.00
6	Kirby Puckett, Andruw Jones	140.00
7	Cecil Fielder	45.00
8	Frank Thomas	75.00
9	Cecil Fielder, Frank Thomas	125.00
10	Ozzie Smith	120.00
11	Derek Jeter	160.00
12	Ozzie Smith, Derek Jeter	325.00

Turn of the Century

		NM/M
Complete Set (20):		55.00
Common Player:		1.00
Die-Cuts:		3X
Samples:		1X
1	Alex Rodriguez	10.00
2	Andruw Jones	6.00
3	Chipper Jones	7.50
4	Todd Walker	1.00
5	Scott Rolen	4.00
6	Trey Beamon	1.00
7	Derek Jeter	12.50
8	Darin Erstad	3.00
9	Tony Clark	1.00
10	Todd Greene	1.00
11	Jason Giambi	3.00
12	Justin Thompson	1.00
13	Ernie Young	1.00
14	Jason Kendall	1.00
15	Alex Ochoa	1.00
16	Brooks Kieschnick	1.00
17	Bobby Higginson	1.00
18	Ruben Rivera	1.00
19	Chan Ho Park	1.00
20	Chad Mottola	1.00

1997 Donruss Limited

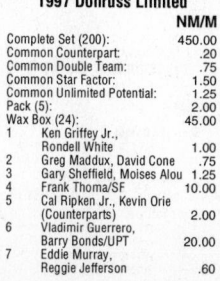

		NM/M
Complete Set (200):		450.00
Common Counterpart:		.20
Common Double Team:		.75
Common Star Factor:		1.50
Common Unlimited Potential:		1.25
Pack (5):		2.00
Wax Box (24):		45.00
1	Ken Griffey Jr., Rondell White	
2	Greg Maddux, David Cone	.75
3	Gary Sheffield, Moises Alou	1.25
4	Frank Thomas/SF	10.00
5	Cal Ripken Jr., Kevin Orie (Counterparts)	2.00
6	Vladimir Guerrero, Barry Bonds/UPT	20.00
7	Eddie Murray, Reggie Jefferson	.60

8	Manny Ramirez, Marquis Grissom/DT	2.50
9	Mike Piazza/SF	15.00
10	Barry Larkin, Rey Ordonez	.20
11	Jeff Bagwell, Eric Karros	.60
12	Chuck Knoblauch, Ray Durham	.20
13	Alex Rodriguez, Edgar Renteria	1.50
14	Matt Williams, Vinny Castilla	.20
15	Todd Hollandsworth, Bob Abreu	.20
16	John Smoltz, Pedro Martinez	.60
17	Jose Canseco, Chili Davis	.40
18	Jose Cruz, Jr., Ken Griffey Jr./UPT	15.00
19	Ken Griffey Jr./SF	15.00
20	Paul Molitor, John Olerud	.60
21	Roberto Alomar, Luis Castillo	.35
22	Derek Jeter, Lou Collier	2.00
23	Chipper Jones, Robin Ventura	.75
24	Gary Sheffield, Ron Gant	.25
25	Ramon Martinez, Bobby Jones	.20
26	Mike Piazza, Raul Mondesi/DT	7.50
27	Darin Erstad, Jeff Bagwell/UPT	7.50
28	Ivan Rodriguez/SF	7.50
29	J.T. Snow, Kevin Young	.20
30	Ryne Sandberg, Julio Franco	.75
31	Travis Fryman, Chris Snopek	.20
32	Wade Boggs, Russ Davis	.75
33	Brooks Kieschnick, Marty Cordova	
34	Andy Pettitte, Denny Neagle	.35
35	Paul Molitor, Matt Lawton/DT	2.50
36	Scott Rolen, Cal Ripken Jr./UPT	20.00
37	Cal Ripken Jr./SF	20.00
38	Jim Thome, Dave Nilsson	.50
39	Tony Womack, Carlos Baerga	.20
40	Nomar Garciaparra, Mark Grudzielanek	
41	Todd Greene, Chris Widger	.20
42	Deion Sanders, Bernard Gilkey	.20
43	Hideo Nomo, Charles Nagy	.50
44	Ivan Rodriguez, Rusty Greer/DT	2.00
45	Todd Walker, Chipper Jones/UPT	10.00
46	Greg Maddux/SF	12.00
47	Mo Vaughn, Cecil Fielder	.20
48	Craig Biggio, Scott Spiezio	.20
49	Pokey Reese, Jeff Blauser	.20
50	Ken Caminiti, Joe Randa	.20
51	Albert Belle, Shawn Green	.20
52	Randy Johnson, Jason Dickson	.60
53	Hideo Nomo, Chan Ho Park/DT	2.00
54	Scott Spiezio, Chuck Knoblauch/UPT	1.25
55	Chipper Jones/F	12.00
56	Tino Martinez, Ryan McGuire	.20
57	Eric Young, Wilton Guerrero	.20
58	Ron Coomer, Dave Hollins	.20
59	Sammy Sosa, Angel Echevarria	.75
60	Dennis Reyes, Jimmy Key	.20
61	Barry Larkin, Deion Sanders/DT	.75
62	Wilton Guerrero, Roberto Alomar/UPT	2.00
63	Albert Belle/SF	1.50
64	Mark McGwire, Andres Galarraga	1.50
65	Edgar Martinez, Todd Walker	.20
66	Steve Finley, Rich Becker	.20
67	Tom Glavine, Andy Ashby	.30
68	Sammy Sosa, Ryne Sandberg/DT	5.00
69	Nomar Garciaparra, Alex Rodriguez/UPT	15.00
70	Jeff Bagwell/SF	10.00
71	Darin Erstad, Mark Grace	.40
72	Scott Rolen, Edgardo Alfonzo	.50

73 Kenny Lofton, Lance Johnson .20
74 Joey Hamilton, Brett Tomko .20
75 Eddie Murray,
  Tim Salmon/DT 2.50
76 Dmitri Young,
  Mo Vaughn/UPT 1.25
77 Juan Gonzalez/SF 3.00
78 Frank Thomas, Tony Clark .60
79 Shannon Stewart, Bip Roberts .20
80 Shawn Estes, Alex Fernandez .20
81 John Smoltz, Javier Lopez/DT .75
82 Todd Greene,
  Mike Piazza/UPT 15.00
83 Derek Jeter/SF 20.00
84 Dmitri Young,
  Antone Williamson .20
85 Rickey Henderson,
  Darryl Hamilton .60
86 Billy Wagner,
  Dennis Eckersley .60
87 Larry Walker,
  Eric Young/DT .75
88 Mark Kotsay,
  Juan Gonzalez/UPT 3.00
89 Barry Bonds/SF 20.00
90 Will Clark, Jeff Conine .20
91 Tony Gwynn, Brett Butler .75
92 John Wetteland, Rod Beck .20
93 Bernie Williams,
  Tino Martinez/DT 1.25
94 Andruw Jones,
  Kenny Lofton/UPT 7.50
95 Mo Vaughn/SF 1.50
96 Joe Carter, Derrek Lee .50
97 John Mabry,
  F.P. Santangelo .20
98 Esteban Loaiza,
  Wilson Alvarez .20
99 Matt Williams,
  David Justice/DT .75
100 Derrek Lee,
  Frank Thomas/UPT 7.50
101 Mark McGwire/SF 17.50
102 Fred McGriff, Paul Sorrento .20
103 Jermaine Allensworth,
  Bernie Williams .20
104 Ismael Valdes, Chris Holt .20
105 Fred McGriff, Ryan Klesko/DT .75
106 Tony Clark,
  Mark McGwire/UPT 17.50
107 Tony Gwynn/SF 12.00
108 Jeffrey Hammonds, Ellis Burks .20
109 Shane Reynolds, Andy Benes .20
110 Roger Clemens,
  Carlos Delgado/DT 10.00
111 Karim Garcia,
  Albert Belle/UPT 1.25
112 Paul Molitor/SF 10.00
113 Trey Beamon, Eric Owens .20
114 Curt Schilling, Darryl Kile
  (Counterparts) .30
115 Tom Glavine,
  Michael Tucker/DT .75
116 Pokey Reese,
  Derek Jeter/UPT 20.00
117 Manny Ramirez/SF 10.00
118 Juan Gonzalez, Brant Brown .40
119 Juan Guzman,
  Francisco Cordova .20
120 Randy Johnson,
  Edgar Martinez/DT 2.50
121 Hideki Irabu,
  Greg Maddux/UPT 10.00
122 Alex Rodriguez/SF 17.50
123 Barry Bonds,
  Quinton McCracken 2.00
124 Roger Clemens, Alan Benes .85
125 Wade Boggs, Paul O'Neill/DT 1.75
126 Mike Cameron,
  Larry Walker/UPT 1.25
127 Gary Sheffield/SF 2.50
128 Andruw Jones, Raul Mondesi .60
129 Brian Anderson, Terrell Wade .20
130 Brady Anderson,
  Rafael Palmeiro/DT .75
131 Neifi Perez, Barry Larkin/UPT 1.25
132 Ken Caminiti/SF 1.50
133 Larry Walker, Rusty Greer .20
134 Mariano Rivera, Mark Wohlers .30
135 Hideki Irabu,
  Andy Pettitte/DT 1.50
136 Jose Guillen,
  Tony Gwynn/UPT 10.00
137 Hideo Nomo/SF 3.00
138 Vladimir Guerrero,
  Jim Edmonds .60
139 Justin Thompson,
  Dwight Gooden .20
140 Andres Galarraga,
  Dante Bichette/DT .75
141 Kenny Lofton/SF 1.50
142 Tim Salmon,
  Manny Ramirez .60
143 Kevin Brown, Matt Morris .20
144 Craig Biggio, Bob Abreu .75
145 Roberto Alomar/SF 2.00
146 Jose Guillen, Brian Jordan .20
147 Bartolo Colon, Kevin Appier .20
148 Ray Lankford,
  Brian Jordan/DT .75
149 Chuck Knoblauch/SF 1.50
150 Henry Rodriguez,
  Ray Lankford .20
151 Jaret Wright, Ben McDonald .20

152 Bobby Bonilla,
  Kevin Brown/DT .75
153 Barry Larkin/SF 1.50
154 David Justice, Reggie Sanders .20
155 Mike Mussina, Ken Hill .40
156 Mark Grace,
  Brooks Kieschnick .75
157 Jim Thome/SF 2.50
158 Michael Tucker,
  Curtis Goodwin .20
159 Jeff Suppan, Jeff Fassero .20
160 Mike Mussina,
  Jeffrey Hammonds/DT 1.00
161 John Smoltz 1.50
162 Moises Alou, Eric Davis .20
163 Sandy Alomar Jr., Dan Wilson .20
164 Rondell White,
  Henry Rodriguez/DT .75
165 Roger Clemens/SF 12.50
166 Brady Anderson, Al Martin .20
167 Jason Kendall,
  Charles Johnson .20
168 Jason Giambi,
  Jose Canseco/DT 2.00
169 Larry Walker/SF 1.50
170 Jay Buhner, Geronimo Berroa .20
171 Ivan Rodriguez,
  Mike Sweeney .50
172 Kevin Appier,
  Jose Rosado/DT .75
173 Bernie Williams/SF 1.50
174 Todd Dunwoody,
  Brian Giles RC .40
175 Javier Lopez, Scott Hatteberg .20
176 John Jaha, Jeff Cirillo/DT .75
177 Andy Pettitte/SF 2.00
178 Dante Bichette, Butch Huskey .20
179 Raul Casanova, Todd Hundley .20
180 Jim Edmonds,
  Garret Anderson/DT .75
181 Deion Sanders/SF 1.50
182 Ryan Klesko, Paul O'Neill .20
183 Joe Carter, Pat Hentgen/DT .75
184 Brady Anderson/SF 1.50
185 Carlos Delgado, Wally Joyner .50
186 Jermaine Dye,
  Johnny Damon/DT 1.00
187 Randy Johnson/SF 7.50
188 Todd Hundley,
  Carlos Baerga/DT .75
189 Tom Glavine/SF 2.50
190 Damon Mashore,
  Jason McDonald/DT .75
191 Wade Boggs/SF 12.00
192 Al Martin, Jason Kendall/DT .75
193 Matt Williams/SF .75
194 Will Clark, Dean Palmer/DT .75
195 Sammy Sosa/SF 12.00
196 Jose Cruz, Jr., Jay Buhner/DT .75
197 Eddie Murray/SF 10.00
198 Darin Erstad,
  Jason Dickson/DT 1.00
199 Fred McGriff/SF 1.50
200 Bubba Trammell,
  Bobby Higginson/DT .75

Exposure

	NM/M
Common Counterparts:	.75
Common Double Team:	3.00
Common Star Factor:	6.50
Common Unlimited:	4.50
Stars:	4X

(See 1997 Donruss Limited for checklist and base card values.)

Exposure Non-Glossy

	NM/M
Common Non-Glossy:	.50
Stars:	25 Percent

(See 1997 Donruss Limited and Limited Exposure to calculate base card values.)

Fabric of the Game

	NM/M
Complete Set: (69):	275.00
Common Player:	1.50
Complete Canvas Set (23):	80.00
Rickey Henderson/100	12.00
Barry Bonds/250	15.00

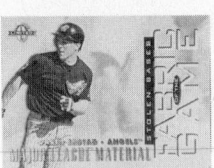

Kenny Lofton/250 2.50
Roberto Alomar/250 4.50
Ryne Sandberg/250 12.00
Tony Gwynn/500 7.50
Barry Larkin/500 2.00
Brady Anderson/500 2.00
Chuck Knoblauch/500 2.00
Craig Biggio/500 2.00
Sammy Sosa/750 7.50
Gary Sheffield/750 2.00
Eric Young/750 1.50
Larry Walker/v 1.50
Ken Griffey Jr./750 10.00
Deion Sanders/750 1.50
Raul Mondes/1,000 1.50
Rondell White/1,000 1.50
Derek Jeter/1,000 10.00
Nomar Garciaparra/1,000 6.00
Wilton Guerrero/1,000 1.50
Pokey Reese/1,000 1.50
Darin Erstad/1,000 2.00
Complete Leather Set (23): 90.00
Paul Molitor/100 15.00
Wade Boggs/250 12.00
Cal Ripken Jr./250 20.00
Tony Gwynn/250 12.00
Joe Carter/250 2.50
Rafael Palmeiro/500 5.00
Mark Grace/500 1.50
Bobby Bonilla/500 1.50
Andres Galarraga/500 1.50
Edgar Martinez/500 1.50
Ken Caminiti/500 1.50
Ivan Rodriguez/750 4.50
Frank Thomas/750 6.00
Jeff Bagwell/750 6.00
Albert Belle/750 1.50
Bernie Williams/750 1.50
Chipper Jones/1,000 7.50
Rusty Greer/1,000 1.50
Todd Walker/1,000 1.50
Scott Rolen/1,000 3.00
Bob Abreu/1,000 1.50
Jose Guillen/1,000 1.50
Jose Cruz, Jr./1,000 1.50
Complete Wood Set (23): 110.00
Eddie Murray/100 12.00
Cal Ripken Jr./250 20.00
Barry Bonds/250 20.00
Mark McGwire/250 17.50
Fred McGriff/250 3.50
Ken Griffey Jr./500 7.50
Albert Belle/500 2.00
Frank Thomas/500 6.50
Juan Gonzalez /500 5.00
Matt Williams/500 2.00
Mike Piazza/750 7.50
Jeff Bagwell/750 6.00
Mo Vaughn/750 1.50
Gary Sheffield/750 2.00
Tim Salmon/750 1.50
David Justice/750 1.50
Manny Ramirez/1,000 5.00
Jim Thome/1,000 2.50
Tino Martinez/1,000 1.50
Andruw Jones/1,000 3.50
Vladimir Guerrero/1,000 5.00
Tony Clark/1,000 1.50
Dmitri Young/1,000 1.50

1997 Donruss Preferred

	NM/M
Complete Set (200):	225.00
Common Bronze:	.10
Common Silver:	.60
Common Gold:	1.25
Common Platinum:	6.00
Cut to the Chase:	1.5X

Tin Pack (5): 2.50
Tin Box (24): 40.00
1 Frank Thomas/P 7.50
2 Ken Griffey Jr./P 12.50
3 Cecil Fielder/B .10
4 Chuck Knoblauch/B 1.25
5 Garret Anderson/B .10
6 Greg Maddux/P 10.00
7 Matt Williams/S .60
8 Marquis Grissom/S .60
9 Jason Isringhausen/B .10
10 Larry Walker/S .60
11 Charles Nagy/B .10
12 Dan Wilson/B .10
13 Albert Belle/G 1.25
14 Javier Lopez/B .10
15 David Cone/B .10
16 Bernard Gilkey/B .10
17 Andres Galarraga/S .60
18 Bill Pulsipher/B .10
19 Alex Fernandez/B .10
20 Andy Pettitte/S 1.25
21 Mark Grudzielanek/B .10
22 Juan Gonzalez/P 6.00
23 Reggie Sanders/B .10
24 Kenny Lofton/G 1.25
25 Andy Ashby/B .10
26 John Wetteland/B .10
27 Bobby Bonilla/B .10
28 Hideo Nomo/B 2.50
29 Joe Carter/B .10
30 Jose Canseco/B .40
31 Ellis Burks/B .10
32 Edgar Martinez/B .60
33 Chan Ho Park/B .10
34 David Justice/B .10
35 Carlos Delgado/B .50
36 Jeff Cirillo/B .60
37 Charles Johnson/B .10
38 Manny Ramirez/G 4.50
39 Greg Vaughn/B .10
40 Henry Rodriguez/B .10
41 Darryl Strawberry/B .10
42 Jim Thome/G 2.50
43 Ryan Klesko/B .60
44 Jermaine Allensworth/B .10
45 Brian Jordan/B 1.25
46 Tony Gwynn/P 10.00
47 Rafael Palmeiro/G 3.50
48 Dante Bichette/S .60
49 Ivan Rodriguez/G 3.50
50 Mark McGwire/G 8.00
51 Tim Salmon/S .60
52 Roger Clemens/S 1.50
53 Matt Lawton/B .10
54 Wade Boggs/S 3.50
55 Travis Fryman/B .10
56 Bobby Higginson/B .60
57 John Jaha/S .60
58 Rondell White/S .60
59 Tom Glavine/S 1.25
60 Eddie Murray/S 2.50
61 Vinny Castilla/B .10
62 Todd Hundley/B .10
63 Jay Buhner/S .60
64 Paul O'Neill/B .10
65 Steve Finley/B .10
66 Kevin Appier/B .10
67 Ray Durham/B .10
68 Dave Nilsson/B .10
69 Jeff Bagwell/G 4.50
70 Al Martin/S .60
71 Paul Molitor/S 4.50
72 Kevin Brown/B .60
73 Ron Gant/B .10
74 Dwight Gooden/B .10
75 Quinton McCracken/B .10
76 Rusty Greer/B .10
77 Juan Guzman/B .10
78 Fred McGriff/S .60
79 Tino Martinez/B .10
80 Ray Lankford/B .10
81 Ken Caminiti/G 1.25
82 James Baldwin/B .10
83 Jermaine Dye/G 1.25
84 Mark Grace/S .60
85 Pat Hentgen/S .60
86 Jason Giambi/S 1.50
87 Brian Hunter/S .60
88 Andy Benes/B .10
89 Jose Rosado/B .10
90 Shawn Green/B .25
91 Jason Kendall/B .10
92 Alex Rodriguez/P 15.00
93 Chipper Jones/P 10.00
94 Barry Bonds/G 10.00
95 Brady Anderson/G 1.25
96 Ryne Sandberg/S 3.50
97 Lance Johnson/S .10
98 Cal Ripken Jr./P 17.50
99 Craig Biggio/S .60
100 Dean Palmer/B .10
101 Gary Sheffield/G 1.50
102 Johnny Damon/S .35
103 Mo Vaughn/S 1.25
104 Randy Johnson/S 2.50
105 Raul Mondesi/S .60
106 Roberto Alomar/S 2.00
107 Mike Piazza/P 12.50
108 Rey Ordonez/B .10
109 Barry Larkin/S 1.25
110 Tony Clark/S .60
111 Bernie Williams/S .60
112 John Smoltz/G 1.25
113 Moises Alou/B .10

114	Will Clark/B	.10
115	Sammy Sosa/B	6.00
116	Jim Edmonds/S	.60
117	Jeff Conine/B	.10
118	Joey Hamilton/B	.10
119	Todd Hollandsworth/B	.10
120	Troy Percival/B	.10
121	Paul Wilson/B	.10
122	Ken Hill/B	.10
123	Mariano Rivera/S	.75
124	Eric Karros/B	.10
125	Derek Jeter/G	10.00
126	Eric Young/S	.60
127	John Mabry/B	.10
128	Gregg Jefferies/B	.10
129	Ismael Valdes/S	.60
130	Marty Cordova/B	.10
131	Omar Vizquel/B	.10
132	Mike Mussina/S	1.25
133	Darin Erstad/S	.30
134	Edgar Renteria/S	.60
135	Billy Wagner/B	.10
136	Alex Ochoa/B	.10
137	Luis Castillo/B	.10
138	Rocky Coppinger/B	.10
139	Mike Sweeney/B	.10
140	Michael Tucker/B	.10
141	Chris Snopek/B	.10
142	Dmitri Young/S	.60
143	Andruw Jones/P	7.50
144	Mike Cameron/S	.60
145	Brant Brown/B	.10
146	Todd Walker/G	1.25
147	Nomar Garciaparra/G	6.00
148	Glendon Rusch/B	.10
149	Karim Garcia/S	.60
150	Bubba Trammell/S RC	.60
151	Todd Greene/B	.10
152	Wilton Guerrero/G	1.25
153	Scott Spiezio/B	.10
154	Brooks Kieschnick/B	.10
155	Vladimir Guerrero/G	4.50
156	Brian Giles/S RC	1.50
157	Pokey Reese/B	.10
158	Jason Dickson/G	1.25
159	Kevin Orie/S	.60
160	Scott Rolen/S	3.00
161	Bartolo Colon/S	.60
162	Shannon Stewart/G	1.25
163	Wendell Magee/B	.10
164	Jose Guillen/S	.60
165	Bob Abreu/S	.60
166	Deivi Cruz/B RC	.25
167	Alex Rodriguez/B	3.00
168	Frank Thomas/B	.75
169	Cal Ripken Jr./B	4.00
170	Chipper Jones/B	1.50
171	Mike Piazza/B	2.50
172	Tony Gwynn/S	3.50
173	Juan Gonzalez/B	.40
174	Kenny Lofton/S	.60
175	Ken Griffey Jr./B	2.50
176	Mark McGwire/S	3.00
177	Jeff Bagwell/B	.75
178	Paul Molitor/S	2.50
179	Andruw Jones/B	.75
180	Manny Ramirez/S	2.50
181	Ken Caminiti/S	.60
182	Barry Bonds/B	4.00
183	Mo Vaughn/B	.10
184	Derek Jeter/B	4.00
185	Barry Larkin/S)	.60
186	Ivan Rodriguez/B	.65
187	Albert Belle/S	.60
188	John Smoltz/S	.60
189	Chuck Knoblauch/S	.60
190	Brian Jordan/S	.60
191	Gary Sheffield/S	1.00
192	Jim Thome/B	2.00
193	Brady Anderson/S	.60
194	Hideo Nomo/S	1.50
195	Sammy Sosa/S	3.50
196	Greg Maddux/B	1.25
197	Vladimir Guerrero/B Checklist	.40
198	Scott Rolen/B Checklist	.15
199	Todd Walker/B Checklist	.10
200	Nomar Garciaparra/B Checklist	.60

Cut To The Chase

Precious Metals

Typical Value:		1.5X

(See 1997 Donruss Preferred for checklist and base card values.)

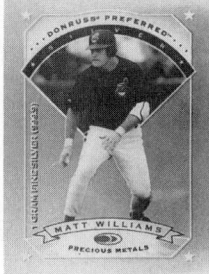

		NM/M
Common Player:		7.50
1	Frank Thomas/P	45.00
2	Ken Griffey Jr./P	75.00
3	Greg Maddux/P	60.00
4	Albert Belle/G	7.50
5	Juan Gonzalez/P	25.00
6	Kenny Lofton/G	7.50
7	Tony Gwynn/P	60.00
8	Ivan Rodriguez/G	30.00
9	Mark McGwire/G	90.00
10	Matt Williams/S	7.50
11	Wade Boggs/S	60.00
12	Eddie Murrayv	45.00
13	Jeff Bagwell/G	45.00
14	Ken Caminiti/G	7.50
15	Alex Rodriguez/P	90.00
16	Chipper Jones/P	60.00
17	Barry Bonds/P	125.00
18	Cal Ripken Jr./P	125.00
19	Mo Vaughn/G	7.50
20	Mike Piazza/G	75.00
21	Derek Jeter/G	125.00
22	Bernie Williams/S	7.50
23	Andruw Jones/P	45.00
24	Vladimir Guerrero/G	45.00
25	Jose Guillen/S	7.50

Staremasters

		NM/M
Complete Set (20):		55.00
Common Player:		1.00
Samples:		50 Percent
1	Alex Rodriguez	6.00
2	Frank Thomas	3.00
3	Chipper Jones	4.00
4	Cal Ripken Jr.	7.50
5	Mike Piazza	4.50
6	Juan Gonzalez	2.25
7	Derek Jeter	7.50
8	Jeff Bagwell	3.00
9	Ken Griffey Jr.	4.50
10	Tony Gwynn	4.00
11	Barry Bonds	7.50
12	Albert Belle	1.00
13	Greg Maddux	4.00
14	Mark McGwire	6.00
15	Ken Caminiti	1.00
16	Hideo Nomo	2.25
17	Gary Sheffield	1.50
18	Andruw Jones	3.00
19	Mo Vaughn	1.00
20	Ivan Rodriguez	2.25

X-Ponential Power

		NM/M
Complete Set (20):		50.00
Common Player:		1.00
1A	Manny Ramirez	3.50
1B	Jim Thome	2.00
2A	Paul Molitor	3.50
2B	Chuck Knoblauch	1.00

3A	Ivan Rodriguez	2.50
3B	Juan Gonzalez	2.00
4A	Albert Belle	1.00
4B	Frank Thomas	3.50
5A	Roberto Alomar	1.25
5B	Cal Ripken Jr.	9.00
6A	Tim Salmon	1.00
6B	Jim Edmonds	1.00
7A	Ken Griffey Jr.	6.00
7B	Alex Rodriguez	7.50
8A	Chipper Jones	5.00
8B	Andruw Jones	3.50
9A	Mike Piazza	6.00
9B	Raul Mondesi	1.00
10A	Tony Gwynn	4.50
10B	Ken Caminiti	1.00

1997 Donruss Signature

Michael Tucker - Braves

		NM/M
Complete Set (100):		15.00
Common Player:		.10
Platinum Stars/RC's:		12X
Pack (5):		7.50
Wax Box (12):		80.00
1	Mark McGwire	1.25
2	Kenny Lofton	.10
3	Tony Gwynn	.75
4	Tony Clark	.10
5	Tim Salmon	.10
6	Ken Griffey Jr.	1.00
7	Mike Piazza	1.00
8	Greg Maddux	.75
9	Roberto Alomar	.20
10	Andres Galarraga	.10
11	Roger Clemens	.90
12	Bernie Williams	.10
13	Rondell White	.10
14	Kevin Appler	.10
15	Ray Lankford	.10
16	Frank Thomas	.65
17	Will Clark	.10
18	Chipper Jones	.75
19	Jeff Bagwell	.65
20	Manny Ramirez	.65
21	Ryne Sandberg	.75
22	Paul Molitor	.65
23	Gary Sheffield	.10
24	Jim Edmonds	.10
25	Barry Larkin	.10
26	Rafael Palmeiro	.60
27	Alan Benes	.10
28	David Justice	.10
29	Randy Johnson	.65
30	Barry Bonds	1.50
31	Mo Vaughn	.10
32	Michael Tucker	.10
33	Larry Walker	.10
34	Tino Martinez	.10
35	Jose Guillen	.10
36	Carlos Delgado	.40
37	Jason Dickson	.10
38	Tom Glavine	.25
39	Raul Mondesi	.10
40	Jose Cruz Jr. RC	.50
41	Johnny Damon	.20
42	Mark Grace	.10
43	Juan Gonzalez	.35

44	Vladimir Guerrero	.65
45	Kevin Brown	.10
46	Justin Thompson	.10
47	Eric Young	.10
48	Ron Coomer	.10
49	Mark Kotsay	.10
50	Scott Rolen	.60
51	Derek Jeter	1.50
52	Jim Thome	.50
53	Fred McGriff	.10
54	Albert Belle	.10
55	Garret Anderson	.10
56	Wilton Guerrero	.10
57	Jose Canseco	.40
58	Cal Ripken Jr.	1.50
59	Sammy Sosa	.75
60	Dmitri Young	.10
61	Alex Rodriguez	1.25
62	Javier Lopez	.10
63	Sandy Alomar Jr.	.10
64	Joe Carter	.10
65	Dante Bichette	.10
66	Al Martin	.10
67	Darin Erstad	.30
68	Pokey Reese	.10
69	Brady Anderson	.10
70	Andruw Jones	.65
71	Ivan Rodriguez	.50
72	Nomar Garciaparra	.75
73	Moises Alou	.10
74	Andy Pettitte	.35
75	Jay Buhner	.10
76	Craig Biggio	.10
77	Wade Boggs	.75
78	Shawn Estes	.10
79	Neifi Perez	.10
80	Rusty Greer	.10
81	Pedro Martinez	.60
82	Mike Mussina	.40
83	Jason Giambi	.40
84	Hideo Nomo	.35
85	Todd Hundley	.10
86	Deion Sanders	.10
87	Mike Cameron	.10
88	Bobby Bonilla	.10
89	Todd Greene	.10
90	Kevin Orie	.10
91	Ken Caminiti	.10
92	Chuck Knoblauch	.10
93	Matt Morris	.10
94	Matt Williams	.10
95	Pat Hentgen	.10
96	John Smoltz	.10
97	Edgar Martinez	.10
98	Jason Kendall	.10
99	Ken Griffey Jr. Checklist	.50
100	Frank Thomas Checklist	.30

Press Proofs

	NM/M
Common Player:	2.00
Stars:	12X

(See 1997 Donruss Signature for checklist and base card prices.)

Autographs (Red)

	NM/M
Complete Set (116):	700.00

Common Player: 2.00
(1) Jeff Abbott/3,900 2.00
(2) Bob Abreu/3,900 8.00
(3) Edgardo Alfonzo/3,900 3.00
(4) Roberto Alomar/150 50.00
(5) Sandy Alomar Jr./1,400 6.00
(6) Moises Alou/900 10.00
(7) Garret Anderson/3,900 7.00
(8) Andy Ashby/3,900 3.00
(10) Trey Beamon/3,900 2.00
(12) Alan Benes/3,900 2.00
(13) Geronimo Berroa/3,900 2.00
(14) Wade Boggs/150 175.00
(18) Kevin L. Brown/3,900 2.00
(20) Brett Butler/1,400 3.50
(21) Mike Cameron/3,900 7.00
(22) Giovanni Carrara/2,900 2.00
(23) Luis Castillo/3,900 4.00
(24) Tony Clark/3,900 3.00
(25) Will Clark/1,400 12.00
(27) Lou Collier/3,900 2.00
(28) Bartolo Colon/3,900 12.50
(29) Ron Coomer/3,900 2.00
(30) Marty Cordova/3,900 3.00
(31) Jacob Cruz /3,900 2.00
(32) Jose Cruz Jr./900 8.00
(33) Russ Davis/3,900 3.00
(34) Jason Dickson/3,900 2.00
(35) Todd Dunwoody/3,900 2.00
(36) Jermaine Dye/3,900 3.00
(37) Jim Edmonds/3,900 12.00
(38) Darin Erstad/900 8.00
(39) Bobby Estalella/3,900 3.00
(40) Shawn Estes/3,900 3.00
(41) Jeff Fassero/3,900 2.00
(42) Andres Galarraga/900 6.00
(43) Karim Garcia/3,900 3.00
(45) Derrick Gibson/3,900 2.00
(46) Brian Giles/3,900 8.00
(47) Tom Glavine/150 50.00
(49) Rick Gorecki/900 4.50
(50) Shawn Green/1,900 15.00
(51) Todd Greene/3,900 3.00
(52) Rusty Greer/3,900 3.00
(53) Ben Grieve/3,900 3.00
(54) Mark Grudzielanek/3,900 3.00
(55) Vladimir Guerrero/1,900 20.00
(56) Wilton Guerrero/2,150 3.00
(57) Jose Guillen/2,900 8.00
(59) Jeffrey Hammonds/2,150 3.50
(60) Todd Helton/1,400 16.00
(61) Todd Hollandsworth/2,900 3.00
(62) Trenidad Hubbard/900 4.00
(63) Todd Hundley/1,400 3.00
(66) Bobby Jones/3,900 2.00
(68) Brian Jordan/1,400 4.00
(69) David Justice/900 10.00
(70) Eric Karros/650 4.50
(71) Jason Kendall/3,900 6.00
(72) Jimmy Key/3,900 5.00
(73) Brooks Kieschnick/3,900 2.00
(74) Ryan Klesko/225 10.00
(76) Paul Konerko/3,900 10.00
(77) Mark Kotsay/2,400 3.00
(78) Ray Lankford/3,900 4.00
(79) Barry Larkin/150 35.00
(80) Derrek Lee/3,900 10.00
(81) Esteban Loaiza/3,900 3.00
(82) Javier Lopez/1,400 10.00
(84) Edgar Martinez/150 50.00
(85) Pedro Martinez/900 35.00
(87) Rafael Medina/3,900 2.00
(88) Raul Mondesi (May not exist.)
(88) Raul Mondesi (Exchange Card) 3.00
(89) Matt Morris/3,900 10.00
(92) Paul O'Neill/900 15.00
(93) Kevin Orie/3,900 2.00
(94) David Ortiz/3,900 50.00
(95) Rafael Palmeiro/900 30.00
(96) Jay Payton/3,900 2.50
(97) Neifi Perez/3,900 2.00
(99) Manny Ramirez/900 40.00
(100) Joe Randa/3,900 2.00
(101) Calvin Reese/3,900 3.00
(102) Edgar Renteria (?) 20.00
(102) Edgar Renteria (Exchange Card) 3.00
(103) Dennis Reyes/3,900 2.00
(106) Henry Rodriguez/3,900 2.00
(108) Scott Rolen/1,900 25.00
(109) Kirk Rueter/2,900 3.00
(110) Ryne Sandberg/400 60.00
(112) Dwight Smith/2,900 3.00
(113) J.T. Snow (900) 4.00
(114) Scott Spiezio/3,900 2.00
(115) Shannon Stewart/2,900 3.00
(116) Jeff Suppan/1,900 3.00
(117) Mike Sweeney/3,900 6.00
(118) Miguel Tejada/3,900 25.00
(121) Justin Thompson/2,400 3.00
(122) Brett Tomko/3,900 3.00
(123) Bubba Trammell/3,900 2.50
(124) Michael Tucker/3,900 2.00
(125) Javier Valentin/3,900 2.00
(126) Mo Vaughn/150 12.00
(127) Robin Ventura/1,400 8.00
(128) Terrell Wade/3,900 2.00
(129) Billy Wagner/3,900 12.00
(130) Larry Walker (900) 25.00
(131) Todd Walker (2,400) 3.00
(132) Rondell White/3,900 6.00
(133) Kevin Wickander/900 4.00
(134) Chris Widger/3,900 2.00
(136) Matt Williams/150 25.00
(137) Antone Williamson/3,900 2.00
(138) Dan Wilson/3,900 2.00
(139) Tony Womack/3,900 5.00
(140) Jaret Wright/3,900 12.00
(141) Dmitri Young/3,900 8.00
(142) Eric Young/3,900 2.50
(143) Kevin Young/3,900 2.50

Autographs Promo

NM/M

Frank Thomas 6.00

Century Marks (Blue)

NM/M

Common Player: 20.00
(1) Jeff Abbott 20.00
(2) Bob Abreu 30.00
(3) Edgardo Alfonzo 20.00
(4) Roberto Alomar 75.00
(5) Sandy Alomar Jr. 25.00
(6) Moises Alou 35.00
(7) Garret Anderson 60.00
(8) Andy Ashby 20.00
(9) Jeff Bagwell 80.00
(10) Trey Beamon 20.00
(11) Albert Belle 30.00
(12) Alan Benes 20.00
(13) Geronimo Berroa 20.00
(14) Wade Boggs 100.00
(15) Barry Bonds 300.00
(16) Bobby Bonilla 20.00
(17) Kevin Brown 75.00
(18) Kevin L. Brown 20.00
(19) Jay Buhner 30.00
(20) Brett Butler 30.00
(21) Mike Cameron 25.00
(22) Giovanni Carrara 20.00
(23) Luis Castillo 20.00
(24) Tony Clark 20.00
(25) Will Clark 100.00
(26) Roger Clemens 200.00
(27) Lou Collier 20.00
(28) Bartolo Colon 30.00
(29) Ron Coomer 20.00
(30) Marty Cordova 20.00
(31) Jacob Cruz 20.00
(32) Jose Cruz Jr. 30.00
(33) Russ Davis 20.00
(34) Jason Dickson 25.00
(35) Todd Dunwoody 25.00
(36) Jermaine Dye 20.00
(37) Jim Edmonds 60.00
(38) Darin Erstad 40.00
(39) Bobby Estalella 20.00
(40) Shawn Estes 20.00
(41) Jeff Fassero 20.00
(42) Andres Galarraga 30.00
(43) Karim Garcia 20.00
(44) Nomar Garciaparra/SP/62 225.00
(45) Derrick Gibson 20.00
(46) Brian Giles 30.00
(47) Tom Glavine 100.00
(48) Juan Gonzalez 55.00
(49) Rick Gorecki 20.00
(50) Shawn Green 90.00
(51) Todd Greene 20.00
(52) Rusty Greer 20.00
(53) Ben Grieve 20.00
(54) Mark Grudzielanek 20.00
(55) Vladimir Guerrero 100.00
(56) Wilton Guerrero 20.00
(57) Jose Guillen 30.00
(58) Tony Gwynn 95.00
(59) Jeffrey Hammonds 20.00
(60) Todd Helton 60.00
(61) Todd Hollandsworth 20.00
(62) Trenidad Hubbard 20.00
(63) Todd Hundley 25.00
(64) Derek Jeter 200.00
(65) Andruw Jones 50.00
(66) Bobby Jones 20.00
(67) Chipper Jones 100.00
(68) Brian Jordan 35.00
(69) David Justice 30.00
(70) Eric Karros 25.00
(71) Jason Kendall 30.00
(72) Jimmy Key 50.00
(73) Brooks Kieschnick 20.00
(74) Ryan Klesko 25.00
(75) Chuck Knoblauch 20.00
(76) Paul Konerko 25.00
(77) Mark Kotsay 25.00
(78) Ray Lankford 20.00
(79) Barry Larkin 60.00
(80) Derrek Lee 40.00
(81) Esteban Loaiza 20.00
(82) Javy Lopez 45.00
(83) Greg Maddux 175.00
(84) Edgar Martinez 50.00
(85) Pedro Martinez 100.00
(86) Tino Martinez 50.00
(87) Rafael Medina 20.00
(88) Raul Mondesi 35.00
(88) Raul Mondesi (Exchange card.) 5.00
(89) Matt Morris 40.00
(90) Eddie Murray 75.00
(91) Mike Mussina 80.00
(92) Paul O'Neill 40.00
(93) Kevin Orie 20.00
(94) David Ortiz 100.00
(95) Rafael Palmeiro 80.00
(96) Jay Payton 20.00
(97) Neifi Perez 20.00
(98) Andy Petitte 50.00
(99) Manny Ramirez 100.00
(100) Joe Randa 20.00
(101) Calvin Reese 20.00
(102) Edgar Renteria 50.00
(102) Edgar Renteria (Exchange card.) 5.00
(103) Dennis Reyes 20.00
(104) Cal Ripken Jr. 225.00
(105) Alex Rodriguez 180.00
(106) Henry Rodriguez 20.00
(107) Ivan Rodriguez 75.00
(108) Scott Rolen 75.00
(109) Kirk Rueter 20.00
(110) Ryne Sandberg 125.00
(111) Gary Sheffield 50.00
(112) Dwight Smith 20.00
(113) J.T. Snow 25.00
(114) Scott Spiezio 20.00
(115) Shannon Stewart 25.00
(116) Jeff Suppan 20.00
(117) Mike Sweeney 25.00
(118) Miguel Tejada 120.00
(119) Frank Thomas 80.00
(120) Jim Thome 75.00
(120) Jim Thome (Exchange card.) 5.00
(121) Justin Thompson 20.00
(122) Brett Tomko 20.00
(123) Bubba Trammell 20.00
(124) Michael Tucker 20.00
(125) Javier Valentin 20.00
(126) Mo Vaughn 25.00
(127) Robin Ventura 30.00
(128) Terrell Wade 20.00
(129) Billy Wagner 40.00
(130) Larry Walker 80.00
(131) Todd Walker 25.00
(132) Rondell White 25.00
(133) Kevin Wickander 20.00
(134) Chris Widger 20.00
(135) Bernie Williams 75.00
(136) Matt Williams 30.00
(137) Antone Williamson 20.00
(138) Dan Wilson 20.00
(139) Tony Womack 25.00
(140) Jaret Wright 35.00
(141) Dmitri Young 30.00
(142) Eric Young 30.00
(143) Kevin Young 20.00

Millennium Marks (Green)

NM/M

Complete Set (143): 1,450
Common Player: 2.00
(1) Jeff Abbott 2.00
(2) Bob Abreu 8.00
(3) Edgardo Alfonzo 5.00
(4) Roberto Alomar 20.00
(5) Sandy Alomar Jr. 8.00
(6) Moises Alou 15.00
(7) Garret Anderson 10.00
(8) Andy Ashby 5.00
(9) Jeff Bagwell/400 75.00
(10) Trey Beamon 2.00
(11) Albert Belle/400 12.50
(12) Alan Benes 2.00
(13) Geronimo Berroa 2.00
(14) Wade Boggs 30.00
(15) Barry Bonds/400 200.00

(16) Bobby Bonilla/900 7.50
(17) Kevin Brown/900 20.00
(18) Kevin L. Brown 10.00
(19) Jay Buhner/900 10.00
(20) Brett Butler 6.00
(21) Mike Cameron 4.00
(22) Giovanni Carrara 2.00
(23) Luis Castillo 5.00
(24) Tony Clark 5.00
(25) Will Clark 12.00
(26) Roger Clemens/400 120.00
(27) Lou Collier 2.00
(28) Bartolo Colon 8.00
(29) Ron Coomer 2.00
(30) Marty Cordova 2.00
(31) Jacob Cruz 2.00
(32) Jose Cruz Jr. 6.00
(33) Russ Davis 2.00
(34) Jason Dickson 5.00
(35) Todd Dunwoody 5.00
(36) Jermaine Dye 5.00
(37) Jim Edmonds 30.00
(38) Darin Erstad 10.00
(39) Bobby Estalella 3.00
(40) Shawn Estes 2.00
(41) Jeff Fassero 4.00
(42) Andres Galarraga 10.00
(43) Karim Garcia 3.50
(44) Nomar Garciaparra/650 75.00
(45) Derrick Gibson 4.00
(46) Brian Giles 8.00
(47) Tom Glavine 25.00
(48) Juan Gonzalez /900 25.00
(49) Rick Gorecki 2.00
(50) Shawn Green 20.00
(51) Todd Greene 7.50
(52) Rusty Greer 7.50
(53) Ben Grieve 5.00
(54) Mark Grudzielanek 2.00
(55) Vladimir Guerrero 25.00
(56) Wilton Guerrero 2.00
(57) Jose Guillen 6.00
(58) Tony Gwynn/900 30.00
(59) Jeffrey Hammonds 2.00
(60) Todd Helton 30.00
(61) Todd Hollandsworth 2.00
(62) Trenidad Hubbard 2.00
(63) Todd Hundley 6.00
(64) Derek Jeter/400 100.00
(65) Andruw Jones/900 15.00
(66) Bobby Jones 2.00
(67) Chipper Jones 30.00
(68) Brian Jordan 7.50
(69) David Justice 10.00
(70) Eric Karros 6.00
(71) Jason Kendall 8.00
(72) Jimmy Key 2.00
(73) Brooks Kieschnick 4.00
(74) Ryan Klesko 5.00
(75) Chuck Knoblauch/900 5.00
(76) Paul Konerko 5.00
(77) Mark Kotsay 6.00
(78) Ray Lankford 2.00
(79) Barry Larkin 30.00
(80) Derrek Lee 20.00
(81) Esteban Loaiza 2.00
(82) Javy Lopez 8.00
(83) Greg Maddux/400 80.00
(84) Edgar Martinez 25.00
(85) Pedro Martinez 40.00
(86) Tino Martinez/900 15.00
(87) Rafael Medina 2.00
(88) Raul Mondesi 10.00
(88) Raul Mondesi (Exchange card.) 2.00
(89) Matt Morris 15.00
(90) Eddie Murray/900 27.50
(91) Mike Mussina/900 20.00
(92) Paul O'Neill 12.50
(93) Kevin Orie 2.00
(94) David Ortiz 40.00
(95) Rafael Palmeiro 30.00
(96) Jay Payton 5.00
(97) Neifi Perez 2.00
(98) Andy Petitte/900 25.00
(99) Manny Ramirez 30.00
(100) Joe Randa 2.00
(101) Calvin Reese 2.00
(102) Edgar Renteria 30.00
(102) Edgar Renteria (Exchange card.) 2.00

(103)	Dennis Reyes	3.00
(104)	Cal Ripken Jr./400	135.00
(105)	Alex Rodriguez/400	100.00
(106)	Henry Rodriguez	3.00
(107)	Ivan Rodriguez/900	20.00
(108)	Scott Rolen	25.00
(109)	Kirk Rueter	2.00
(110)	Ryne Sandberg	40.00
(111)	Gary Sheffield/400	25.00
(112)	Dwight Smith	2.00
(113)	J.T. Snow	7.50
(114)	Scott Spiezio	5.00
(115)	Shannon Stewart	2.00
(116)	Jeff Suppan	2.00
(117)	Mike Sweeney	5.00
(118)	Miguel Tejada	40.00
(119)	Frank Thomas/400	50.00
(120)	Jim Thome/900	30.00
(120)	Jim Thome (Exchange card.)	2.00
(121)	Justin Thompson	2.00
(122)	Brett Tomko	2.00
(123)	Bubba Trammell	4.00
(124)	Michael Tucker	2.00
(125)	Javier Valentin	2.00
(126)	Mo Vaughn	8.00
(127)	Robin Ventura	8.00
(128)	Terrell Wade	2.00
(129)	Billy Wagner	10.00
(130)	Larry Walker	20.00
(131)	Todd Walker	6.00
(132)	Rondell White	6.00
(133)	Kevin Wickander	2.00
(134)	Chris Widger	2.00
(135)	Bernie Williams/400	60.00
(136)	Matt Williams	10.00
(137)	Antone Williamson	2.00
(138)	Dan Wilson	2.00
(139)	Tony Womack	2.00
(140)	Jaret Wright	15.00
(141)	Dmitri Young	5.00
(142)	Eric Young	2.00
(143)	Kevin Young	2.00

Notable Nicknames

		NM/M
	Common Player:	20.00
(1)	Ernie Banks (Mr. Cub)	150.00
(2)	Tony Clark (The Tiger)	20.00
(3)	Roger Clemens (The Rocket)	300.00
(4)	Reggie Jackson (Mr. October)	125.00
(5)	Randy Johnson (Big Unit)	300.00
(6)	Stan Musial (The Man)	180.00
(7)	Ivan Rodriguez (Pudge)	100.00
(8)	Frank Thomas (The Big Hurt)	125.00
(9)	Mo Vaughn (Hit Dog)	20.00
(10)	Billy Wagner (The Kid)	40.00

Significant Signatures

		NM/M
	Common Player:	15.00
(1)	Ernie Banks	25.00
(2)	Johnny Bench	30.00
(3)	Yogi Berra	30.00
(4)	George Brett	40.00
(5)	Lou Brock	25.00
(6)	Rod Carew	25.00
(7)	Steve Carlton	20.00
(8)	Larry Doby	35.00
(9)	Carlton Fisk	30.00
(10)	Bob Gibson	25.00
(11)	Reggie Jackson	25.00
(12)	Al Kaline	25.00
(13)	Harmon Killebrew	30.00
(14)	Don Mattingly	40.00
(15)	Stan Musial	45.00
(16)	Jim Palmer	15.00
(17)	Brooks Robinson	30.00
(18)	Frank Robinson	15.00
(19)	Mike Schmidt	35.00
(20)	Tom Seaver	30.00
(21)	Duke Snider	20.00
(22)	Carl Yastrzemski	40.00

1997 Donruss Team Sets

		NM/M
Comp. Angels Set (1-15):		1.25
Comp. Braves Set (16-30):		3.00
Comp. Orioles Set (31-45):		2.50
Comp. Red Sox Set (46-60):		1.50
Comp. White Sox Set (61-75):		2.00
Comp. Indians Set (76-90):		1.50
Comp. Rockies Set (91-105):		1.50
Comp. Dodgers Set (106-120):		2.25
Comp. Yankees Set (121-135):		4.50
Comp. Mariners Set (136-150):		4.50
Comp. Cardinals Set (151-165):		2.00
Common Player:		.05
Pennant Edition Stars:		3X
1	Jim Edmonds	.05
2	Tim Salmon	.05
3	Tony Phillips	.05
4	Garret Anderson	.05
5	Troy Percival	.05
6	Mark Langston	.05
7	Chuck Finley	.05
8	Eddie Murray	.75
9	Jim Leyritz	.05
10	Darin Erstad	.30
11	Jason Dickson	.05
12	Allen Watson	.05
13	Shigetosi Hasegawa	.05
14	Dave Hollins	.05
15	Gary DiSarcina	.05
16	Greg Maddux	1.00
17	Denny Neagle	.05
18	Chipper Jones	1.00
19	Tom Glavine	.25
20	John Smoltz	.05
21	Ryan Klesko	.05
22	Fred McGriff	.05
23	Michael Tucker	.05
24	Kenny Lofton	.05
25	Javier Lopez	.05
26	Mark Wohlers	.05
27	Jeff Blauser	.05
28	Andruw Jones	.75
29	Tony Graffanino	.05
30	Terrell Wade	.05
31	Brady Anderson	.05
32	Roberto Alomar	.15
33	Rafael Palmeiro	.65
34	Mike Mussina	.35
35	Cal Ripken Jr.	2.00
36	Rocky Coppinger	.05
37	Randy Myers	.05
38	B.J. Surhoff	.05
39	Eric Davis	.05
40	Armando Benitez	.05
41	Jeffrey Hammonds	.05
42	Jimmy Key	.05
43	Chris Hoiles	.05
44	Mike Bordick	.05
45	Pete Incaviglia	.05
46	Mike Stanley	.05
47	Reggie Jefferson	.05
48	Mo Vaughn	.05
49	John Valentin	.05
50	Tim Naehring	.05
51	Jeff Suppan	.05
52	Tim Wakefield	.05
53	Jeff Frye	.05
54	Darren Bragg	.05
55	Steve Avery	.05
56	Shane Mack	.05
57	Aaron Sele	.05
58	Troy O'Leary	.05
59	Rudy Pemberton	.05
60	Nomar Garciaparra	1.00
61	Robin Ventura	.05
62	Wilson Alvarez	.05
63	Roberto Hernandez	.05
64	Frank Thomas	.75
65	Ray Durham	.05
66	James Baldwin	.05
67	Harold Baines	.05
68	Doug Drabek	.05
69	Mike Cameron	.05
70	Albert Belle	.05
71	Jaime Navarro	.05
72	Chris Snopek	.05
73	Lyle Mouton	.05
74	Dave Martinez	.05
75	Ozzie Guillen	.05
76	Manny Ramirez	.75
77	Jack McDowell	.05
78	Jim Thome	.50
79	Jose Mesa	.05
80	Brian Giles	.05
81	Omar Vizquel	.05
82	Charles Nagy	.05
83	Orel Hershiser	.05
84	Matt Williams	.05
85	Marquis Grissom	.05
86	David Justice	.05
87	Sandy Alomar	.05
88	Kevin Seitzer	.05
89	Julio Franco	.05
90	Bartolo Colon	.05
91	Andres Galarraga	.05
92	Larry Walker	.05
93	Vinny Castilla	.05
94	Dante Bichette	.05
95	Jamey Wright	.05
96	Ellis Burks	.05
97	Eric Young	.05
98	Neifi Perez	.05
99	Quinton McCracken	.05
100	Bruce Ruffin	.05
101	Walt Weiss	.05
102	Roger Bailey	.05
103	Jeff Reed	.05
104	Bill Swift	.05
105	Kirt Manwaring	.05
106	Raul Mondesi	.05
107	Hideo Nomo	.35
108	Roger Cedeno	.05
109	Ismael Valdes	.05
110	Todd Hollandsworth	.05
111	Mike Piazza	1.50
112	Brett Butler	.05
113	Chan Ho Park	.05
114	Ramon Martinez	.05
115	Eric Karros	.05
116	Wilton Guerrero	.05
117	Todd Zeile	.05
118	Karim Garcia	.05
119	Greg Gagne	.05
120	Darren Dreifort	.05
121	Wade Boggs	1.00
122	Paul O'Neill	.05
123	Derek Jeter	2.00
124	Tino Martinez	.05
125	David Cone	.05
126	Andy Pettitte	.25
127	Charlie Hayes	.05
128	Mariano Rivera	.15
129	Dwight Gooden	.05
130	Cecil Fielder	.05
131	Not Issued	
132	Darryl Strawberry	.05
133	Joe Girardi	.05
134	David Wells	.05
135	Hideki Irabu	.05
136	Ken Griffey Jr.	1.25
137	Alex Rodriguez	1.50
138	Jay Buhner	.05
139	Randy Johnson	.75
140	Paul Sorrento	.05
141	Edgar Martinez	.05
142	Joey Cora	.05
143	Bob Wells	.05
144	Not Issued	
145	Jamie Moyer	.05
146	Jeff Fassero	.05
147	Dan Wilson	.05
148	Jose Cruz, Jr.	.05
149	Scott Sanders	.05
150	Rich Amaral	.05
151	Brian Jordan	.05
152	Andy Benes	.05
153	Ray Lankford	.05
154	John Mabry	.05
155	Tom Pagnozzi	.05
156	Ron Gant	.05
157	Alan Benes	.05
158	Dennis Eckersley	.65
159	Royce Clayton	.05
160	Todd Stottlemyre	.05
161	Gary Gaetti	.05
162	Willie McGee	.05
163	Delino DeShields	.05
164	Dmitri Young	.05
165	Matt Morris	.05

MVP

		NM/M
Complete Set (18):		45.00
Common Player:		.50
1	Ivan Rodriguez	1.50
2	Mike Piazza	5.50
3	Frank Thomas	2.50
4	Jeff Bagwell	2.50
5	Chuck Knoblauch	.50
6	Eric Young	.50
7	Alex Rodriguez	6.00
8	Barry Larkin	.50
9	Cal Ripken Jr.	6.00
10	Chipper Jones	4.00
11	Albert Belle	.50
12	Barry Bonds	7.50
13	Ken Griffey Jr.	5.50
14	Kenny Lofton	.50
15	Juan Gonzalez	1.00
16	Larry Walker	.50
17	Roger Clemens	5.00
18	Greg Maddux	4.00

1997 Donruss VXP 1.0

		NM/M
Complete Set (50):		17.50
Common Player:		.25
1	Darin Erstad	.40
2	Jim Thome	.50
3	Alex Rodriguez	1.50
4	Greg Maddux	1.00
5	Scott Rolen	.65
6	Roberto Alomar	.30
7	Tony Clark	.25
8	Randy Johnson	.75
9	Sammy Sosa	1.00
10	Ozzie Guillen	.25
11	Cal Ripken Jr.	2.00
12	Paul Molitor	.75
13	Jose Cruz Jr.	.20
14	Barry Larkin	.25
15	Ken Caminiti	.25
16	Rafael Palmeiro	.65
17	Chuck Knoblauch	.25
18	Juan Gonzalez	.40
19	Larry Walker	.25
20	Tony Gwynn	1.00
21	Brady Anderson	.25
22	Derek Jeter	2.00
23	Rusty Greer	.25
24	Gary Sheffield	.35
25	Barry Bonds	2.00
26	Mo Vaughn	.20
27	Tino Martinez	.25
28	Ivan Rodriguez	.65
29	Jeff Bagwell	.75
30	Tim Salmon	.25
31	Nomar Garciaparra	1.00
32	Bernie Williams	.25
33	Kenny Lofton	.25
34	Mike Piazza	1.25
35	Jim Edmonds	.25
36	Frank Thomas	.75
37	Andy Pettitte	.35
38	Andruw Jones	.75
39	Raul Mondesi	.25
40	John Smoltz	.25
41	Albert Belle	.25
42	Mark McGwire	1.50
43	Chipper Jones	1.00
44	Hideo Nomo	.40
45	David Justice	.25
46	Manny Ramirez	.75
47	Ken Griffey Jr.	1.25
48	Roger Clemens	1.00
49	Vladimir Guerrero	.75
50	Ryne Sandberg	1.00

1997 Donruss VXP 1.0 CDs

		NM/M
Complete Set (6):		12.00
Common Player:		2.00
(1)	Ken Griffey Jr.	2.25
(2)	Greg Maddux	2.00
(3)	Mike Piazza	2.25

(4) Cal Ripken Jr. 3.00
(5) Alex Rodriguez 2.50
(6) Frank Thomas 2.00

1998 Donruss

	NM/M
Complete Set (420):	30.00
Complete Series 1 (170):	10.00
Complete Update 2 (250):	15.00
Common Player:	.05
Silver Press Proofs:	3X
Production 1,500 Sets	
Gold Press Proofs:	8X
Production 500 Sets	
Pack (10):	1.00
Wax Box (24):	16.00

1 Paul Molitor .75
2 Juan Gonzalez .40
3 Darryl Kile .05
4 Randy Johnson .75
5 Tom Glavine .25
6 Pat Hentgen .05
7 David Justice .05
8 Kevin Brown .05
9 Mike Mussina .45
10 Ken Caminiti .05
11 Todd Hundley .05
12 Frank Thomas .75
13 Ray Lankford .05
14 Justin Thompson .05
15 Jason Dickson .05
16 Kenny Lofton .05
17 Ivan Rodriguez .65
18 Pedro Martinez .75
19 Brady Anderson .05
20 Barry Larkin .05
21 Chipper Jones 1.50
22 Tony Gwynn 1.50
23 Roger Clemens 1.50
24 Sandy Alomar Jr. .05
25 Tino Martinez .05
26 Jeff Bagwell .75
27 Shawn Estes .05
28 Ken Griffey Jr. 1.75
29 Javier Lopez .05
30 Denny Neagle .05
31 Mike Piazza 1.75
32 Andres Galarraga .05
33 Larry Walker .05
34 Alex Rodriguez 2.00
35 Greg Maddux 1.50
36 Albert Belle .05
37 Barry Bonds 2.50
38 Mo Vaughn .05
39 Kevin Appier .05
40 Wade Boggs 1.50
41 Garret Anderson .05
42 Jeffrey Hammonds .05
43 Marquis Grissom .05
44 Jim Edmonds .05
45 Brian Jordan .05
46 Raul Mondesi .05
47 John Valentin .05
48 Brad Radke .05
49 Ismael Valdes .05
50 Matt Stairs .05
51 Matt Williams .05
52 Reggie Jefferson .05
53 Alan Benes .05
54 Charles Johnson .05
55 Chuck Knoblauch .05
56 Edgar Martinez .05
57 Nomar Garciaparra 1.50
58 Craig Biggio .05
59 Bernie Williams .05
60 David Cone .05
61 Cal Ripken Jr. 2.50
62 Mark McGwire 2.00
63 Roberto Alomar .20
64 Fred McGriff .05
65 Eric Karros .05
66 Robin Ventura .05
67 Darin Erstad .30
68 Michael Tucker .05
69 Jim Thome .60
70 Mark Grace .05
71 Lou Collier .05
72 Karim Garcia .05
73 Alex Fernandez .05
74 J.T. Snow .05
75 Reggie Sanders .05
76 John Smoltz .05
77 Tim Salmon .05
78 Paul O'Neill .05
79 Vinny Castilla .05
80 Rafael Palmeiro .65
81 Jaret Wright .05
82 Jay Buhner .05
83 Brett Butler .05
84 Todd Greene .05
85 Scott Rolen .65
86 Sammy Sosa 1.50
87 Jason Giambi .50
88 Carlos Delgado .50
89 Deion Sanders .05
90 Wilton Guerrero .05
91 Andy Pettitte .30
92 Brian Giles .05
93 Dmitri Young .05
94 Ron Coomer .05
95 Mike Cameron .05
96 Edgardo Alfonzo .05
97 Jimmy Key .05
98 Ryan Klesko .05
99 Andy Benes .05
100 Derek Jeter 2.50
101 Jeff Fassero .05
102 Neifi Perez .05
103 Hideo Nomo .40
104 Andruw Jones .75
105 Todd Helton .50
106 Livan Hernandez .05
107 Brett Tomko .05
108 Shannon Stewart .05
109 Bartolo Colon .05
110 Matt Morris .05
111 Miguel Tejada .20
112 Pokey Reese .05
113 Fernando Tatis .05
114 Todd Dunwoody .05
115 Jose Cruz Jr. .05
116 Chan Ho Park .05
117 Kevin Young .05
118 Rickey Henderson .75
119 Hideki Irabu .05
120 Francisco Cordova .05
121 Al Martin .05
122 Tony Clark .05
123 Curt Schilling .25
124 Rusty Greer .05
125 Jose Canseco .40
126 Edgar Renteria .05
127 Todd Walker .05
128 Wally Joyner .05
129 Bill Mueller .05
130 Jose Guillen .05
131 Manny Ramirez .75
132 Bobby Higginson .05
133 Kevin Orie .05
134 Will Clark .05
135 Dave Nilsson .05
136 Jason Kendall .05
137 Ivan Cruz .05
138 Gary Sheffield .25
139 Bubba Trammell .05
140 Vladimir Guerrero .75
141 Dennis Reyes .05
142 Bobby Bonilla .05
143 Ruben Rivera .05
144 Ben Grieve .05
145 Moises Alou .05
146 Tony Womack .05
147 Eric Young .05
148 Paul Konerko .10
149 Dante Bichette .05
150 Joe Carter .05
151 Rondell White .05
152 Chris Holt .05
153 Shawn Green .20
154 Mark Grudzielanek .05
155 Jermaine Dye .05
156 Ken Griffey Jr. .90
157 Frank Thomas .50
158 Chipper Jones .75
159 Mike Piazza .90
160 Cal Ripken Jr. 1.25
161 Greg Maddux .75
162 Juan Gonzalez .20
163 Alex Rodriguez 1.00
164 Mark McGwire 1.00
165 Derek Jeter 1.25
166 Larry Walker Checklist .05
167 Tony Gwynn Checklist .60
168 Tino Martinez Checklist .05
169 Scott Rolen Checklist .15
170 Nomar Garciaparra Checklist .60
171 Mike Sweeney .05
172 Dustin Hermanson .05
173 Darren Dreifort .05
174 Ron Gant .05
175 Todd Hollandsworth .05
176 John Jaha .05
177 Kerry Wood .30
178 Chris Stynes .05
179 Kevin Elster .05
180 Derek Bell .05
181 Darryl Strawberry .05
182 Damion Easley .05
183 Jeff Cirillo .05
184 John Thomson .05
185 Dan Wilson .05
186 Jay Bell .05
187 Bernard Gilkey .05
188 Marc Valdes .05
189 Ramon Martinez .05
190 Charles Nagy .05
191 Derek Lowe .05
192 Andy Benes .05
193 Delino DeShields .05
194 Ryan Jackson **RC** .05
195 Kenny Lofton .05
196 Chuck Knoblauch .05
197 Andres Galarraga .05
198 Jose Canseco .50
199 John Olerud .05
200 Lance Johnson .05
201 Darryl Kile .05
202 Luis Castillo .05
203 Joe Carter .05
204 Dennis Eckersley .65
205 Steve Finley .05
206 Esteban Loaiza .05
207 Ryan Christenson **RC** .05
208 Deivi Cruz .05
209 Mariano Rivera .15
210 Mike Judd **RC** .05
211 Billy Wagner .05
212 Scott Spiezio .05
213 Russ Davis .05
214 Jeff Suppan .05
215 Doug Glanville .05
216 Dmitri Young .05
217 Rey Ordonez .05
218 Cecil Fielder .05
219 Masato Yoshii **RC** .10
220 Raul Casanova .05
221 Rolando Arrojo **RC** .20
222 Ellis Burks .05
223 Butch Huskey .05
224 Brian Hunter .05
225 Marquis Grissom .05
226 Kevin Brown .05
227 Joe Randa .05
228 Henry Rodriguez .05
229 Omar Vizquel .05
230 Fred McGriff .05
231 Matt Williams .05
232 Moises Alou .05
233 Travis Fryman .05
234 Wade Boggs 1.50
235 Pedro Martinez .75
236 Rickey Henderson .75
237 Bubba Trammell .05
238 Mike Caruso .05
239 Wilson Alvarez .05
240 Geronimo Berroa .05
241 Eric Milton .05
242 Scott Erickson .05
243 Todd Erdos **RC** .05
244 Bobby Hughes .05
245 Dave Hollins .05
246 Dean Palmer .05
247 Carlos Baerga .05
248 Jose Silva .05
249 Jose Cabrera **RC** .05
250 Tom Evans .05
251 Marty Cordova .05
252 Hanley Frias **RC** .05
253 Javier Valentin .05
254 Mario Valdez .05
255 Joey Cora .05
256 Mike Lansing .05
257 Jeff Kent .05
258 David Dellucci **RC** .10
259 Curtis King **RC** .05
260 David Segui .05
261 Royce Clayton .05
262 Jeff Blauser .05
263 Manny Aybar **RC** .05
264 Mike Cather **RC** .05
265 Todd Zeile .05
266 Richard Hidalgo .05
267 Dante Powell .05
268 Mike DeJean **RC** .05
269 Ken Cloude .05
270 Danny Klassen .05
271 Sean Casey .15
272 A.J. Hinch .05
273 Rich Butler **RC** .05
274 Ben Ford **RC** .05
275 Billy McMillon .05
276 Wilson Delgado .05
277 Orlando Cabrera .05
278 Geoff Jenkins .05
279 Enrique Wilson .05
280 Derrek Lee .60
281 Marc Pisciotta **RC** .05
282 Abraham Nunez .05
283 Aaron Boone .05
284 Brad Fullmer .05
285 Rob Stanifer **RC** .05
286 Preston Wilson .05
287 Greg Norton .05
288 Bobby Smith .05
289 Josh Booty .05
290 Russell Branyan .05
291 Jeremi Gonzalez .05
292 Michael Coleman .05
293 Cliff Politte .05
294 Eric Ludwick .05
295 Rafael Medina .05
296 Jason Varitek .05
297 Ron Wright .05
298 Mark Kotsay .05
299 David Ortiz .50
300 Frank Catalanotto **RC** .20
301 Robinson Checo .05
302 Kevin Millwood **RC** .75
303 Jacob Cruz .05
304 Javier Vazquez .05
305 Magglio Ordonez **RC** 1.50
306 Kevin Witt .05
307 Derrick Gibson .05
308 Shane Monahan .05
309 Brian Rose .05
310 Bobby Estalella .05
311 Felix Heredia .05
312 Desi Relaford .05
313 Esteban Yan **RC** .05
314 Ricky Ledee .05
315 Steve Woodard **RC** .05
316 Pat Watkins .05
317 Damian Moss .05
318 Bob Abreu .05
319 Jeff Abbott .05
320 Miguel Cairo .05
321 Rigo Beltran **RC** .05
322 Tony Saunders .05
323 Randall Simon .05
324 Hiram Bocachica .05
325 Richie Sexson .05
326 Karim Garcia .05
327 Mike Lowell **RC** 1.00
328 Pat Cline .05
329 Matt Clement .05
330 Scott Elarton .05
331 Manuel Barrios **RC** .05
332 Bruce Chen .05
333 Juan Encarnacion .05
334 Travis Lee .05
335 Wes Helms .05
336 Chad Fox **RC** .05
337 Donnie Sadler .05
338 Carlos Mendoza **RC** .05
339 Damian Jackson .05
340 Julio Ramirez **RC** .05
341 John Halama **RC** .05
342 Edwin Diaz .05
343 Felix Martinez .05
344 Eli Marrero .05
345 Carl Pavano .05
346 Vladimir Guerrero/HL .40
347 Barry Bonds/HL 1.25
348 Darin Erstad/HL .10
349 Albert Belle/HL .05
350 Kenny Lofton/HL .05
351 Mo Vaughn/HL .05
352 Jose Cruz Jr./HL .05
353 Tony Clark/HL .05
354 Roberto Alomar/HL .10
355 Manny Ramirez/HL .40
356 Paul Molitor/HL .40
357 Jim Thome/HL .05
358 Tino Martinez/HL .05
359 Tim Salmon/HL .05
360 David Justice/HL .05
361 Raul Mondesi/HL .05
362 Mark Grace/HL .05
363 Craig Biggio/HL .05
364 Larry Walker/HL .05
365 Mark McGwire/HL 1.00
366 Juan Gonzalez/HL .20
367 Derek Jeter/HL 1.25
368 Chipper Jones/HL .75
369 Frank Thomas/HL .50
370 Alex Rodriguez/HL 1.00
371 Mike Piazza/HL .90
372 Tony Gwynn/HL .75
373 Jeff Bagwell/HL .40
374 Nomar Garciaparra/HL .75
375 Ken Griffey Jr./HL .90
376 Livan Hernandez .05
377 Chan Ho Park .05
378 Mike Mussina .20
379 Andy Pettitte .05
380 Greg Maddux .75
381 Hideo Nomo .20
382 Roger Clemens .80
383 Randy Johnson .40
384 Pedro Martinez .40
385 Jaret Wright .05
386 Ken Griffey Jr. .90
387 Todd Helton .05
388 Paul Konerko .05
389 Cal Ripken Jr. 1.25
390 Larry Walker .05
391 Ken Caminiti .05
392 Jose Guillen .05
393 Jim Edmonds .05
394 Barry Larkin .05
395 Bernie Williams .05
396 Tony Clark .05
397 Jose Cruz Jr. .05
398 Ivan Rodriguez .30
399 Darin Erstad .10
400 Scott Rolen .15
401 Mark McGwire 1.00
402 Andruw Jones .40
403 Juan Gonzalez .20
404 Derek Jeter 1.25
405 Chipper Jones .75
406 Greg Maddux .75
407 Frank Thomas .50
408 Alex Rodriguez 1.00

409	Mike Piazza	.90
410	Tony Gwynn	.75
411	Jeff Bagwell	.40
412	Nomar Garciaparra	.75
413	Hideo Nomo	.20
414	Barry Bonds	1.25
415	Ben Grieve	.05
416	Barry Bonds Checklist	1.25
417	Mark McGwire Checklist	1.00
418	Roger Clemens Checklist	.65
419	Livan Hernandez Checklist	.05
420	Ken Griffey Jr. Checklist	.75

Gold Press Proofs

	NM/M
Common Player:	1.00
Stars/RC's:	6X
Production 500 Sets	

(See 1998 Donruss for checklist and base card values.)

Silver Press Proofs

	NM/M
Complete Set (420):	150.00
Common Player:	.50
Stars/RC's:	2X
Production 1,500 Sets	

(See 1998 Donruss for checklist and base card values.)

Crusade

		NM/M
Common Player:		4.00
Production 250 Sets		
Purples (100 Sets):		1X
Reds (25 Sets):		4X
5	Jason Dickson	4.00
6	Todd Greene	4.00
7	Roberto Alomar	5.00
8	Cal Ripken Jr.	40.00
12	Mo Vaughn	4.00
13	Nomar Garciaparra	15.00

16	Mike Cameron	4.00
20	Sandy Alomar Jr.	4.00
21	David Justice	4.00
25	Justin Thompson	4.00
27	Kevin Appier	4.00
33	Tino Martinez	4.00
36	Hideki Irabu	4.00
37	Jose Canseco	8.00
39	Ken Griffey Jr.	30.00
42	Edgar Martinez	5.00
45	Will Clark	6.00
47	Rusty Greer	4.00
50	Shawn Green	5.00
51	Jose Cruz Jr.	4.00
52	Kenny Lofton	4.00
53	Chipper Jones	15.00
62	Kevin Orie	4.00
65	Deion Sanders	6.00
67	Larry Walker	6.00
68	Dante Bichette	4.00
71	Todd Helton	10.00
74	Bobby Bonilla	4.00
75	Kevin Brown	4.00
78	Craig Biggio	6.00
82	Wilton Guerrero	4.00
85	Pedro Martinez	15.00
86	Edgardo Alfonzo	4.00
88	Scott Rolen	10.00
89	Francisco Cordova	4.00
90	Jose Guillen	4.00
92	Ray Lankford	4.00
93	Mark McGwire	20.00
94	Matt Morris	4.00
100	Shawn Estes	4.00

1998 Donruss Days

		NM/M
Complete Set (14):		16.00
Common Player:		.50
1	Frank Thomas	1.00
2	Tony Clark	.50
3	Ivan Rodriguez	.65
4	David Justice	.50
5	Nomar Garciaparra	1.50
6	Mark McGwire	2.50
7	Travis Lee	.50
8	Cal Ripken Jr.	3.00
9	Jeff Bagwell	1.00
10	Barry Bonds	3.00
11	Ken Griffey Jr.	2.00
12	Derek Jeter	3.00
13	Raul Mondesi	.50
14	Greg Maddux	1.50

Diamond Kings

		NM/M
Complete Set (20):		65.00
Common Player:		2.00
Production 9,500 Sets		
Canvas (1st 500 Sets):		2X
1	Cal Ripken Jr.	9.00
2	Greg Maddux	4.50
3	Ivan Rodriguez	2.50
4	Tony Gwynn	4.50
5	Paul Molitor	3.00
6	Kenny Lofton	2.00
7	Andy Pettitte	2.00
8	Darin Erstad	2.00

9	Randy Johnson	3.00
10	Derek Jeter	9.00
11	Hideo Nomo	2.50
12	David Justice	2.00
13	Bernie Williams	2.00
14	Roger Clemens	5.00
15	Barry Larkin	2.00
16	Andruw Jones	3.00
17	Mike Piazza	6.50
18	Frank Thomas	3.00
18s	Frank Thomas (Sample)	3.00
19	Alex Rodriguez	7.50
20	Ken Griffey Jr.	6.50

Longball Leaders

		NM/M
Complete Set (24):		50.00
Common Player:		1.00
Production 5,000 Sets		
1	Ken Griffey Jr.	5.00
2	Mark McGwire	6.00
3	Tino Martinez	1.00
4	Barry Bonds	7.50
5	Frank Thomas	3.00
6	Albert Belle	1.00
7	Mike Piazza	5.00
8	Chipper Jones	4.00
9	Vladimir Guerrero	3.00
10	Matt Williams	1.00
11	Sammy Sosa	4.00
12	Tim Salmon	1.00
13	Raul Mondesi	1.00
14	Jeff Bagwell	3.00
15	Mo Vaughn	1.00
16	Manny Ramirez	3.00
17	Jim Thome	2.00
18	Jim Edmonds	1.00
19	Tony Clark	1.00
20	Nomar Garciaparra	4.00
21	Juan Gonzalez	1.50
22	Scott Rolen	2.00
23	Larry Walker	1.00
24	Andres Galarraga	1.00

Production Line-ob

		NM/M
Complete Set (20):		85.00
Common Player:		1.50
1	Frank Thomas/456	6.00
2	Edgar Martinez/456	1.50
3	Roberto Alomar/390	2.00
4	Chuck Knoblauch/390	1.50
5	Mike Piazza/431	10.00
6	Barry Larkin/440	1.50
7	Kenny Lofton/409	1.50
8	Jeff Bagwell/425	6.00
9	Barry Bonds/446	15.00
10	Rusty Greer/405	1.50
11	Gary Sheffield/424	2.00
12	Mark McGwire/393	12.00
13	Chipper Jones/371	8.00
14	Tony Gwynn/409	8.00
15	Craig Biggio/415	1.50
16	Mo Vaughn/420	1.50
17	Bernie Williams/408	1.50
18	Ken Griffey Jr./382	6.00
19	Brady Anderson/393	1.50
20	Derek Jeter/370	15.00

Production Line-pi

		NM/M
Complete Set (20):		85.00
Common Player:		1.50
1	Frank Thomas/1,067	5.00
2	Mark McGwire/1,039	12.00
3	Barry Bonds/1.031	12.50
4	Jeff Bagwell/1,017	5.00
5	Ken Griffey Jr./1,028	10.00
6	Alex Rodriguez/846	12.00
7	Chipper Jones/850	7.00
8	Mike Piazza/1,070	10.00
9	Mo Vaughn/980	1.50
10	Brady Anderson/863	1.50
11	Manny Ramirez/963	5.00
12	Albert Belle/823	1.50
13	Jim Thome/1,001	2.50
14	Bernie Williams/952	1.50
15	Scott Rolen/846	2.00
16	Vladimir Guerrero/833	5.00
17	Larry Walker/1,172	1.50
18	David Justice/1,013	1.50
19	Tino Martinez/948	1.50
20	Tony Gwynn/957	7.00

Production Line-sg

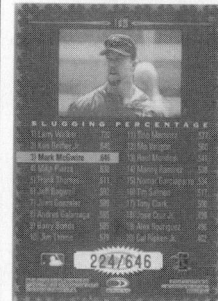

		NM/M
Complete Set (20):		135.00
Common Player:		3.00
1	Mark McGwire/646	20.00
2	Ken Griffey Jr./646	12.50
3	Andres Galarraga/585	3.00
4	Barry Bonds/585	22.50
5	Juan Gonzalez/589	4.50
6	Mike Piazza/638	12.50
7	Jeff Bagwell/592	7.50
8	Manny Ramirez/538	7.50
9	Jim Thome/579	4.50
10	Mo Vaughn/560	3.00
11	Larry Walker/720	3.00
12	Tino Martinez/577	3.00
13	Frank Thomas/611	7.50
14	Tim Salmon/517	3.00
15	Raul Mondesi/541	3.00
16	Alex Rodriguez/496	15.00
17	Nomar Garciaparra/534	10.00
18	Jose Cruz Jr./499	3.00
19	Tony Clark/500	3.00
20	Cal Ripken Jr./402	25.00

Rated Rookies

		NM/M
Complete Set (30):		32.50
Common Player:		1.00
Medalists (250 Sets):		6X
1	Mark Kotsay	1.00
2	Neifi Perez	1.00
3	Paul Konerko	1.50
4	Jose Cruz Jr.	1.00
5	Hideki Irabu	1.00
6	Mike Cameron	1.00
7	Jeff Suppan	1.00
8	Kevin Orie	1.00
9	Pokey Reese	1.00
10	Todd Dunwoody	1.00
11	Miguel Tejada	1.50
12	Jose Guillen	1.00

13	Bartolo Colon	1.50
14	Derek Lee	2.50
15	Antone Williamson	1.00
16	Wilton Guerrero	1.00
17	Jaret Wright	1.00
18	Todd Helton	4.00
19	Shannon Stewart	1.00
20	Nomar Garciaparra	6.00
21	Brett Tomko	1.00
22	Fernando Tatis	1.00
23	Raul Ibanez	1.00
24	Dennis Reyes	1.00
25	Bobby Estalella	1.00
26	Lou Collier	1.00
27	Bubba Trammell	1.00
28	Ben Grieve	1.00
29	Ivan Cruz	1.00
30	Karim Garcia	1.00

Update Crusade

NM/M

Complete Set, Green (30):		325.00
Common Player:		6.00
Production 250 Sets		
Purples (100 Sets):		3X
Reds (25 Sets):		10X
1	Tim Salmon	6.00
2	Garret Anderson	6.00
7	Rafael Palmeiro	15.00
10	Brady Anderson	6.00
14	Frank Thomas	15.00
17	Robin Ventura	6.00
22	Matt Williams	6.00
23	Tony Clark	6.00
29	Chuck Knoblauch	6.00
31	Bernie Williams	6.00
32	Derek Jeter	50.00
38	Jason Giambi	10.00
43	Jay Buhner	6.00
44	Juan Gonzalez	7.50
49	Carlos Delgado	9.00
55	Greg Maddux	20.00
57	Tom Glavine	9.00
60	Mark Grace	6.00
61	Sammy Sosa	20.00
63	Barry Larkin	6.00
69	Neifi Perez	6.00
72	Gary Sheffield	7.50
77	Jeff Bagwell	15.00
80	Raul Mondesi	6.00
81	Hideo Nomo	7.50
83	Rondell White	6.00
84	Vladimir Guerrero	15.00
87	Todd Hundley	6.00
96	Brian Jordan	6.00
99	Barry Bonds	50.00

Update Dominators

NM/M

Complete Set (30):		25.00
Common Player:		.25
Approx:		
1	Roger Clemens	1.50
2	Tony Clark	.25
3	Darin Erstad	.50
4	Jeff Bagwell	1.00
5	Ken Griffey Jr.	1.75

6	Andruw Jones	1.00
7	Juan Gonzalez	.50
8	Ivan Rodriguez	.75
9	Randy Johnson	1.00
10	Tino Martinez	.25
11	Mark McGwire	2.00
12	Chuck Knoblauch	.25
13	Jim Thome	.65
14	Alex Rodriguez	2.00
15	Hideo Nomo	.50
16	Jose Cruz Jr.	.25
17	Chipper Jones	1.50
18	Tony Gwynn	1.50
19	Barry Bonds	2.50
20	Mo Vaughn	.25
21	Cal Ripken Jr.	2.50
22	Greg Maddux	1.50
23	Manny Ramirez	1.00
24	Andres Galarraga	1.00
25	Vladimir Guerrero	1.00
26	Albert Belle	.25
27	Nomar Garciaparra	1.50
28	Kenny Lofton	.25
29	Mike Piazza	1.75
30	Frank Thomas	1.00

Update Elite

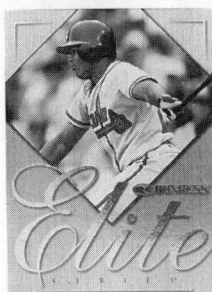

NM/M

Complete Set (20):		115.00
Common Player:		3.00
Production 2,500 Sets		
1	Jeff Bagwell	4.50
2	Andruw Jones	4.50
3	Ken Griffey Jr.	7.50
4	Derek Jeter	15.00
5	Juan Gonzalez	3.50
6	Mark McGwire	10.00
7	Ivan Rodriguez	3.50
8	Paul Molitor	4.50
9	Hideo Nomo	3.50
10	Mo Vaughn	3.00
11	Chipper Jones	6.00
12	Nomar Garciaparra	6.00
13	Mike Piazza	7.50
14	Frank Thomas	4.50
15	Greg Maddux	6.00
16	Cal Ripken Jr.	15.00
17	Alex Rodriguez	10.00
18	Scott Rolen	3.50
19	Barry Bonds	15.00
20	Tony Gwynn	6.00

Update FANtasy Team

NM/M

Complete Set (20):		35.00
Common Player (1-10)		
(1,750 Sets):		1.50
Common Player (11-20)		
(3,750 Sets):		1.00
Die-Cuts (250 Each):		2X
1	Frank Thomas	2.00
2	Ken Griffey Jr.	3.50
3	Cal Ripken Jr.	5.00
4	Jose Cruz Jr.	1.00
5	Travis Lee	1.00
6	Greg Maddux	2.50
7	Alex Rodriguez	4.00

8	Mark McGwire	4.00
9	Chipper Jones	2.50
10	Andruw Jones	2.00
11	Mike Piazza	3.50
12	Tony Gwynn	2.50
13	Larry Walker	1.00
14	Nomar Garciaparra	3.00
15	Jaret Wright	1.00
16	Livan Hernandez	1.00
17	Roger Clemens	2.75
18	Derek Jeter	5.00
19	Scott Rolen	1.25
20	Jeff Bagwell	1.50

Update Rookie Diamond Kings

NM/M

Complete Set (12):		20.00
Common Player:		2.00
Production 9,500 Sets		
Canvas (500 Sets):		2X
1	Travis Lee	2.00
2	Fernando Tatis	2.00
3	Livan Hernandez	2.00
4	Todd Helton	5.00
5	Derek Lee	3.50
6	Jaret Wright	2.00
7	Ben Grieve	2.00
8	Paul Konerko	2.50
9	Jose Cruz Jr.	2.00
10	Mark Kotsay	2.00
11	Todd Greene	2.00
12	Brad Fullmer	2.00

Update Sony MLB 99

NM/M

Complete Set (20):		3.00
Common Player:		.05
1	Cal Ripken Jr.	.75
2	Nomar Garciaparra	.40
3	Barry Bonds	.75
4	Mike Mussina	.20
5	Pedro Martinez	.25
6	Derek Jeter	.75
7	Andruw Jones	.25
8	Kenny Lofton	.05
9	Gary Sheffield	.15
10	Raul Mondesi	.05
11	Jeff Bagwell	.25
12	Tim Salmon	.05
13	Tom Glavine	.15
14	Ben Grieve	.05
15	Matt Williams	.05
16	Juan Gonzalez	.25
17	Mark McGwire	.50
18	Bernie Williams	.05
19	Andres Galarraga	.05
20	Jose Cruz Jr.	.05

1998 Donruss Collections

NM/M

Complete Donruss Set (200):	100.00
Complete Leaf Set (200):	125.00
Complete Elite Set (150):	125.00
Complete Preferred Set (200):	300.00
Prized Collections Parallel:	2X
Pack (5):	4.00
Wax Box (20):	75.00

Samples:		6X
	DONRUSS	
1	Paul Molitor	2.00
2	Juan Gonzalez	1.00
3	Darryl Kile	.25
4	Randy Johnson	2.00
5	Tom Glavine	.50
6	Pat Hentgen	.25
7	David Justice	.25
8	Kevin Brown	.25
9	Mike Mussina	.50
10	Ken Caminiti	.25
11	Todd Hundley	.25
12	Frank Thomas	2.00
13	Ray Lankford	.25
14	Justin Thompson	.25
15	Jason Dickson	.25
16	Kenny Lofton	.25
17	Ivan Rodriguez	1.50
18	Pedro Martinez	2.00
19	Brady Anderson	.25
20	Barry Larkin	.25
21	Chipper Jones	3.00
22	Tony Gwynn	3.00
23	Roger Clemens	3.25
24	Sandy Alomar Jr.	.25
25	Tino Martinez	.25
26	Jeff Bagwell	2.00
27	Shawn Estes	.25
28	Ken Griffey Jr.	3.50
29	Javier Lopez	.25
30	Denny Neagle	.25
31	Mike Piazza	3.50
32	Andres Galarraga	.25
33	Larry Walker	.25
34	Alex Rodriguez	4.50
35	Greg Maddux	3.00
36	Albert Belle	.25
37	Barry Bonds	6.00
38	Mo Vaughn	.25
39	Kevin Appier	.25
40	Wade Boggs	3.00
41	Garret Anderson	.25
42	Jeffrey Hammonds	.25
43	Marquis Grissom	.25
44	Jim Edmonds	.25
45	Brian Jordan	.25
46	Raul Mondesi	.25
47	John Valentin	.25
48	Brad Radke	.25
49	Ismael Valdes	.25
50	Matt Stairs	.25
51	Matt Williams	.25
52	Reggie Jefferson	.25
53	Alan Benes	.25
54	Charles Johnson	.25
55	Chuck Knoblauch	.25
56	Edgar Martinez	.25
57	Nomar Garciaparra	3.00
58	Craig Biggio	.25
59	Bernie Williams	.50
60	David Cone	.25
61	Cal Ripken Jr.	6.00
62	Mark McGwire	4.50
63	Roberto Alomar	.50
64	Fred McGriff	.25
65	Eric Karros	.25
66	Robin Ventura	.25
67	Darin Erstad	.50
68	Michael Tucker	.25
69	Jim Thome	1.00
70	Mark Grace	.25
71	Lou Collier	.25
72	Karim Garcia	.25
73	Alex Fernandez	.25
74	J.T. Snow	.25
75	Reggie Sanders	.25
76	John Smoltz	.25
77	Tim Salmon	.25
78	Paul O'Neill	.25
79	Vinny Castilla	.25
80	Rafael Palmeiro	1.50
81	Jaret Wright	.25
82	Jay Buhner	.25
83	Brett Butler	.25
84	Todd Greene	.25
85	Scott Rolen	1.50
86	Sammy Sosa	3.00
87	Jason Giambi	1.00
88	Carlos Delgado	.75
89	Deion Sanders	.25
90	Wilton Guerrero	.25

91 Andy Pettitte .45
92 Brian Giles .25
93 Dmitri Young .25
94 Ron Coomer .25
95 Mike Cameron .25
96 Edgardo Alfonzo .25
97 Jimmy Key .25
98 Ryan Klesko .25
99 Andy Benes .25
100 Derek Jeter 6.00
101 Jeff Fassero .25
102 Neifi Perez .25
103 Hideo Nomo 1.00
104 Andruw Jones 2.00
105 Todd Helton 1.50
106 Livan Hernandez .25
107 Brett Tomko .25
108 Shannon Stewart .25
109 Bartolo Colon .25
110 Matt Morris .25
111 Miguel Tejada .40
112 Pokey Reese .25
113 Fernando Tatis .25
114 Todd Dunwoody .25
115 Jose Cruz Jr. .25
116 Chan Ho Park .25
117 Kevin Young .25
118 Rickey Henderson 2.00
119 Hideki Irabu .25
120 Francisco Cordova .25
121 Al Martin .25
122 Tony Clark .25
123 Curt Schilling .40
124 Rusty Greer .25
125 Jose Canseco .60
126 Edgar Renteria .25
127 Todd Walker .25
128 Wally Joyner .25
129 Bill Mueller .25
130 Jose Guillen .25
131 Manny Ramirez 2.00
132 Bobby Higginson .25
133 Kevin Orie .25
134 Will Clark .25
135 Dave Nilsson .25
136 Jason Kendall .25
137 Ivan Cruz .25
138 Gary Sheffield .40
139 Bubba Trammell .25
140 Vladimir Guerrero 2.00
141 Dennis Reyes .25
142 Bobby Bonilla .25
143 Ruben Rivera .25
144 Ben Grieve .25
145 Moises Alou .25
146 Tony Womack .25
147 Eric Young .25
148 Paul Konerko .35
149 Dante Bichette .25
150 Joe Carter .25
151 Rondell White .25
152 Chris Holt .25
153 Shawn Green .40
154 Mark Grudzielanek .25
155 Jermaine Dye .25
156 Ken Griffey Jr. 1.75
157 Frank Thomas 1.00
158 Chipper Jones 1.50
159 Mike Piazza 1.75
160 Cal Ripken Jr. 3.00
161 Greg Maddux 1.50
162 Juan Gonzalez .50
163 Alex Rodriguez 2.25
164 Mark McGwire 2.25
165 Derek Jeter 3.00
166 Larry Walker (Checklist) .25
167 Tony Gwynn (Checklist) .75
168 Tino Martinez (Checklist) .25
169 Scott Rolen (Checklist) .40
170 Nomar Garciaparra (Checklist) .75

DONRUSS RATED ROOKIES

1 Mark Kotsay .50
2 Neifi Perez .50
3 Paul Konerko 1.00
4 Jose Cruz Jr. .50
5 Hideki Irabu .50
6 Mike Cameron .50
7 Jeff Suppan .50
8 Kevin Orie .50
9 Pokey Reese .50
10 Todd Dunwoody .50
11 Miguel Tejada 1.00
12 Jose Guillen .50
13 Bartolo Colon .50
14 Derrek Lee .75
15 Antone Williamson .50
16 Wilton Guerrero .50
17 Jaret Wright .50
18 Todd Helton 2.00
19 Shannon Stewart .50
20 Nomar Garciaparra 3.00
21 Brett Tomko .50
22 Fernando Tatis .50
23 Raul Ibanez .50
24 Dennis Reyes .50
25 Bobby Estalella .50
26 Lou Collier .50
27 Bubba Trammell .50
28 Ben Grieve .50
29 Ivan Cruz .50
30 Karim Garcia .50

LEAF

1 Rusty Greer .25
2 Tino Martinez .25
3 Bobby Bonilla .25
4 Jason Giambi .65
5 Matt Morris .25
6 Craig Counsell .25
7 Reggie Jefferson .25
8 Brian Rose .25
9 Ruben Rivera .25
10 Shawn Estes .25
11 Tony Gwynn 3.00
12 Jeff Abbott .25
13 Jose Cruz Jr. .25
14 Francisco Cordova .25
15 Ryan Klesko .25
16 Tim Salmon .25
17 Brett Tomko .25
18 Matt Williams .25
19 Joe Carter .25
20 Harold Baines .25
21 Gary Sheffield .40
22 Charles Johnson .25
23 Aaron Boone .35
24 Eddie Murray 2.00
25 Matt Stairs .25
26 David Cone .25
27 Jon Nunnally .25
28 Chris Stynes .25
29 Enrique Wilson .25
30 Randy Johnson 2.00
31 Garret Anderson .25
32 Manny Ramirez 2.00
33 Jeff Suppan .25
34 Rickey Henderson 2.00
35 Scott Spiezio .25
36 Rondell White .25
37 Todd Greene .25
38 Delino DeShields .25
39 Kevin Brown .25
40 Chili Davis .25
41 Jimmy Key .25
42 Not Issued
43 Mike Mussina 1.00
44 Joe Randa .25
45 Chan Ho Park .25
46 Brad Radke .25
47 Geronimo Berroa .25
48 Wade Boggs 3.00
49 Kevin Appier .25
50 Moises Alou .25
51 David Justice .25
52 Ivan Rodriguez 1.50
53 J.T. Snow .25
54 Brian Giles .25
55 Will Clark .25
56 Justin Thompson .25
57 Javier Lopez .25
58 Hideki Irabu .25
59 Mark Grudzielanek .25
60 Abraham Nunez .25
61 Todd Hollandsworth .25
62 Jay Bell .25
63 Nomar Garciaparra 3.00
64 Vinny Castilla .25
65 Lou Collier .25
66 Kevin Orie .25
67 John Valentin .25
68 Robin Ventura .25
69 Denny Neagle .25
70 Tony Womack .25
71 Dennis Reyes .25
72 Wally Joyner .25
73 Kevin Brown .35
74 Ray Durham .25
75 Mike Cameron .25
76 Dante Bichette .25
77 Jose Guillen .25
78 Carlos Delgado .60
79 Paul Molitor 2.00
80 Jason Kendall .25
81 Mark Belhorn .25
82 Damian Jackson .25
83 Bill Mueller .25
84 Kevin Young .25
85 Curt Schilling .50
86 Jeffrey Hammonds .25
87 Sandy Alomar Jr. .25
88 Bartolo Colon .25
89 Wilton Guerrero .25
90 Bernie Williams .25
91 Deion Sanders .25
92 Mike Piazza 3.50
93 Butch Huskey .25
94 Edgardo Alfonzo .25
95 Alan Benes .25
96 Craig Biggio .25
97 Mark Grace .25
98 Shawn Green .40
99 Derrek Lee 1.00
100 Ken Griffey Jr. 3.50
101 Tim Raines .25
102 Pokey Reese .25
103 Lee Stevens .25
104 Shannon Stewart .25
105 John Smoltz .25
106 Frank Thomas 2.00
107 Jeff Fassero .25
108 Jay Buhner .25
109 Jose Canseco .45
110 Omar Vizquel .25
111 Travis Fryman .25
112 Dave Nilsson .25
113 John Olerud .25
114 Larry Walker .25
115 Jim Edmonds .25
116 Bobby Higginson .25
117 Todd Hundley .25
118 Paul O'Neill .25
119 Bip Roberts .25
120 Ismael Valdes .25
121 Pedro Martinez 2.00
122 Jeff Cirillo .25
123 Andy Benes .25
124 Bobby Jones .25
125 Brian Hunter .25
126 Darryl Kile .25
127 Pat Hentgen .25
128 Marquis Grissom .25
129 Eric Davis .25
130 Chipper Jones 3.00
131 Edgar Martinez .25
132 Andy Pettitte .50
133 Cal Ripken Jr. 6.00
134 Scott Rolen 1.50
135 Ron Coomer .25
136 Luis Castillo .25
137 Fred McGriff .25
138 Neifi Perez .25
139 Eric Karros .25
140 Alex Fernandez .25
141 Jason Dickson .25
142 Lance Johnson .25
143 Ray Lankford .25
144 Sammy Sosa 3.00
145 Eric Young .25
146 Bubba Trammell .25
147 Todd Walker .25
148 Mo Vaughn/CC .25
149 Jeff Bagwell/CC 2.00
150 Kenny Lofton/CC .25
151 Raul Mondesi/CC .25
152 Mike Piazza/CC 3.50
153 Chipper Jones/CC 3.00
154 Larry Walker/CC .25
155 Greg Maddux/CC 3.00
156 Ken Griffey Jr./CC 3.50
157 Frank Thomas/CC 2.00
158 Darin Erstad/GLS 2.00
159 Roberto Alomar/GLS 1.50
160 Albert Belle/GLS 1.00
161 Jim Thome/GLS 2.00
162 Tony Clark/GLS 1.00
163 Chuck Knoblauch/GLS 1.00
164 Derek Jeter/GLS 12.00
165 Alex Rodriguez/GLS 8.00
166 Tony Gwynn/GLS 6.00
167 Roger Clemens/GLS 7.00
168 Barry Larkin/GLS 1.00
169 Andres Galarraga/GLS 1.00
170 Vladimir Guerrero/GLS 4.50
171 Mark McGwire/GLS 8.00
172 Barry Bonds/GLS 12.00
173 Juan Gonzalez/GLS 2.50
174 Andruw Jones/GLS 4.50
175 Paul Molitor/GLS 4.50
176 Hideo Nomo/GLS 2.50
177 Cal Ripken Jr./GLS 12.50
178 Brad Fullmer/GLR 1.00
179 Jaret Wright/GLR 1.00
180 Bobby Estalella/GLR 1.00
181 Ben Grieve/GLR 1.00
182 Paul Konerko/GLR 1.50
183 David Ortiz /GLR 3.00
184 Todd Helton/GLR 3.00
185 Juan Encarnacion/GLR 1.00
186 Miguel Tejada/GLR 1.50
187 Jacob Cruz/GLR 1.00
188 Mark Kotsay/GLR 1.00
189 Fernando Tatis/GLR 1.00
190 Ricky Ledee/GLR 1.00
191 Richard Hidalgo/GLR 1.00
192 Richie Sexson/GLR 1.00
193 Luis Ordaz/GLR 1.00
194 Eli Marrero/GLR 1.00
195 Livan Hernandez/GLR 1.00
196 Homer Bush/GLR 1.00
197 Raul Ibanez/GLR 1.00
198 Nomar Garciaparra Checklist 1.00
199 Scott Rolen Checklist .75
200 Jose Cruz Jr. Checklist .25
201 Al Martin .25

ELITE

1 Ken Griffey Jr. 4.00
2 Frank Thomas 2.50
3 Alex Rodriguez 6.00
4 Mike Piazza 4.00
5 Greg Maddux 3.00
6 Cal Ripken Jr. 7.00
7 Chipper Jones 3.00
8 Derek Jeter 7.00
9 Tony Gwynn 3.00
10 Andruw Jones 2.50
11 Juan Gonzalez 1.25
12 Jeff Bagwell 2.50
13 Mark McGwire 6.00
14 Roger Clemens 3.00
15 Albert Belle .50
16 Barry Bonds 7.00
17 Kenny Lofton .50
18 Ivan Rodriguez 2.00
19 Manny Ramirez 2.50
20 Jim Thome 1.50
21 Chuck Knoblauch .50
22 Paul Molitor 2.50
23 Barry Larkin .50
24 Andy Pettitte 1.00
25 John Smoltz .50
26 Randy Johnson 2.50
27 Bernie Williams .50
28 Larry Walker .50
29 Mo Vaughn .50
30 Bobby Higginson .50
31 Edgardo Alfonzo .50
32 Justin Thompson .50
33 Jeff Suppan .50
34 Roberto Alomar 1.00
35 Hideo Nomo 1.25
36 Rusty Greer .50
37 Tim Salmon .50
38 Jim Edmonds .50
39 Gary Sheffield .75
40 Ken Caminiti .50
41 Sammy Sosa 3.00
42 Tony Womack .50
43 Matt Williams .50
44 Andres Galarraga .50
45 Garret Anderson .50
46 Rafael Palmeiro 2.00
47 Mike Mussina 1.00
48 Craig Biggio .50
49 Wade Boggs 3.00
50 Tom Glavine .75
51 Jason Giambi 1.00
52 Will Clark .50
53 David Justice .50
54 Sandy Alomar Jr. .50
55 Edgar Martinez .50
56 Brady Anderson .50
57 Eric Young .50
58 Ray Lankford .50
59 Kevin Brown .60
60 Raul Mondesi .50
61 Bobby Bonilla .50
62 Javier Lopez .50
63 Fred McGriff .50
64 Rondell White .50
65 Todd Hundley .50
66 Mark Grace .50
67 Alan Benes .50
68 Jeff Abbott .50
69 Bob Abreu .50
70 Deion Sanders .50
71 Tino Martinez .50
72 Shannon Stewart .50
73 Homer Bush .50
74 Carlos Delgado 1.50
75 Raul Ibanez .50
76 Hideki Irabu .50
77 Jose Cruz Jr. .50
78 Tony Clark .50
79 Wilton Guerrero .50
80 Vladimir Guerrero 2.50
81 Scott Rolen 2.25
82 Nomar Garciaparra 3.00
83 Darin Erstad 1.00
84 Chan Ho Park .50
85 Mike Cameron .50
86 Todd Walker .50
87 Todd Dunwoody .50
88 Neifi Perez .50
89 Brett Tomko .50
90 Jose Guillen .50
91 Matt Morris .50
92 Bartolo Colon .50
93 Jaret Wright .50
94 Shawn Estes .50
95 Livan Hernandez .50
96 Bobby Estalella .50
97 Ben Grieve .50
98 Paul Konerko .75
99 David Ortiz 1.00
100 Todd Helton 2.00
101 Juan Encarnacion .50
102 Bubba Trammell .50
103 Miguel Tejada 1.00
104 Jacob Cruz .50
105 Todd Greene .50
106 Kevin Orie .50
107 Mark Kotsay .50
108 Fernando Tatis .50
109 Jay Payton .50
110 Pokey Reese .50
111 Derrek Lee 1.50
112 Richard Hidalgo .50
113 Ricky Ledee .50
114 Lou Collier .50
115 Ruben Rivera .50
116 Shawn Green 1.00
117 Moises Alou .50
118 Ken Griffey Jr. 2.00
119 Frank Thomas 1.25
120 Alex Rodriguez 3.00
121 Mike Piazza 2.00
122 Greg Maddux 1.75
123 Cal Ripken Jr. 3.50
124 Chipper Jones 2.00
125 Derek Jeter 3.50
126 Tony Gwynn 1.75
127 Andruw Jones 1.25
128 Juan Gonzalez .75
129 Jeff Bagwell 1.25
130 Mark McGwire 3.00
131 Roger Clemens 1.75
132 Albert Belle .50
133 Barry Bonds 3.50
134 Kenny Lofton .50
135 Ivan Rodriguez 1.00
136 Manny Ramirez 1.25
137 Jim Thome 1.00
138 Chuck Knoblauch .50
139 Paul Molitor 1.25
140 Barry Larkin .50
141 Mo Vaughn .50
142 Hideki Irabu .50
143 Jose Cruz Jr. .50
144 Tony Clark .50
145 Vladimir Guerrero 1.25
146 Scott Rolen 1.00

147	Nomar Garciaparra	2.00
148	Nomar Garciaparra Checklist	1.00
149	Larry Walker Checklist	.50
150	Tino Martinez Checklist	.50

PREFERRED

1	Ken Griffey Jr./EX	12.00
2	Frank Thomas/EX	7.50
3	Cal Ripken Jr./EX	17.50
4	Alex Rodriguez/EX	15.00
5	Greg Maddux/EX	10.00
6	Mike Piazza/EX	12.00
7	Chipper Jones/EX	10.00
8	Tony Gwynn/FB	10.00
9	Derek Jeter/FB	17.50
10	Jeff Bagwell/EX	7.50
11	Juan Gonzalez/EX	4.00
12	Nomar Garciaparra/EX	10.00
13	Andruw Jones/FB	7.50
14	Hideo Nomo/FB	4.00
15	Roger Clemens/FB	13.50
16	Mark McGwire/FB	15.00
17	Scott Rolen/FB	6.00
18	Vladimir Guerrero/FB	7.50
19	Barry Bonds/FB	17.50
20	Darin Erstad/FB	4.00
21	Albert Belle/FB	2.00
22	Kenny Lofton/FB	2.00
23	Mo Vaughn/FB	2.00
24	Tony Clark/FB	2.00
25	Ivan Rodriguez/FB	6.00
26	Larry Walker/CL	2.00
27	Eddie Murray/CL	7.50
28	Andy Pettitte/CL	4.00
29	Roberto Alomar/CL	2.00
30	Randy Johnson/CL	7.50
31	Manny Ramirez/CL	7.50
32	Paul Molitor/FB	7.50
33	Mike Mussina/CL	4.00
34	Jim Thome/FB	2.00
35	Tino Martinez/CL	2.00
36	Gary Sheffield/CL	3.00
37	Chuck Knoblauch/CL	2.00
38	Bernie Williams/CL	2.00
39	Tim Salmon/CL	2.00
40	Sammy Sosa/CL	10.00
41	Wade Boggs/MZ	10.00
42	Will Clark/GS	2.00
43	Andres Galarraga/CL	2.00
44	Raul Mondesi/CL	2.00
45	Rickey Henderson/GS	6.50
46	Jose Canseco/GS	4.00
47	Pedro Martinez/GS	6.50
48	Jay Buhner/GS	2.00
49	Ryan Klesko/GS	2.00
50	Barry Larkin/CL	2.00
51	Charles Johnson/GS	2.00
52	Tom Glavine/GS	3.00
53	Edgar Martinez/CL	2.00
54	Fred McGriff/GS	2.00
55	Moises Alou/MZ	2.00
56	Dante Bichette/GS	2.00
57	Jim Edmonds/CL	2.00
58	Mark Grace/MZ	2.00
59	Chan Ho Park/MZ	2.00
60	Justin Thompson/MZ	2.00
61	John Smoltz/MZ	2.00
62	Craig Biggio/CL	2.00
63	Ken Caminiti/MZ	2.00
64	Deion Sanders/MZ	2.00
65	Carlos Delgado/GS	4.00
66	David Justice/CL	2.00
67	J.T. Snow/GS	2.00
68	Jason Giambi/CL	4.00
69	Garret Anderson/MZ	2.00
70	Rondell White/MZ	2.00
71	Matt Williams/MZ	2.00
72	Brady Anderson/MZ	2.00
73	Eric Karros/GS	2.00
74	Javier Lopez/GS	2.00
75	Pat Hentgen/GS	2.00
76	Todd Hundley/GS	2.00
77	Ray Lankford/GS	2.00
78	Denny Neagle/GS	2.00
79	Henry Rodriguez/GS	2.00
80	Sandy Alomar Jr./MZ	2.00
81	Rafael Palmeiro/MZ	5.00
82	Robin Ventura/GS	2.00
83	John Olerud/GS	2.00
84	Omar Vizquel/GS	2.00
85	Joe Randa/GS	2.00
86	Lance Johnson/GS	2.00
87	Kevin Brown/GS	2.00
88	Curt Schilling/GS	4.00
89	Ismael Valdes/GS	2.00
90	Francisco Cordova/GS	2.00
91	David Cone/GS	2.00
92	Paul O'Neill/GS	2.00
93	Jimmy Key/GS	2.00
94	Brad Radke/GS	2.00
95	Kevin Appier/GS	2.00
96	Al Martin/GS	2.00
97	Rusty Greer/MZ	2.00
98	Reggie Jefferson/GS	2.00
99	Ron Coomer/GS	2.00
100	Vinny Castilla/GS	2.00
101	Bobby Bonilla/MZ	2.00
102	Eric Young/GS	2.00
103	Tony Womack/GS	2.00
104	Jason Kendall/GS	2.00
105	Jeff Suppan/GS	2.00
106	Shawn Estes/MZ	2.00
107	Shawn Green/GS	2.00
108	Edgardo Alfonzo/MZ	2.00
109	Alan Benes/MZ	2.00
110	Bobby Higginson/GS	2.00
111	Mark Grudzielanek/GS	2.00
112	Wilton Guerrero/GS	2.00
113	Todd Greene/MZ	2.00
114	Pokey Reese/GS	2.00
115	Jose Guillen/CL	2.00
116	Neifi Perez/MZ	2.00
117	Luis Castillo/GS	2.00
118	Edgar Renteria/GS	2.00
119	Karim Garcia/GS	2.00
120	Butch Huskey/GS	2.00
121	Michael Tucker/GS	2.00
122	Jason Dickson/GS	2.00
123	Todd Walker/MZ	2.00
124	Brian Jordan/GS	2.00
125	Joe Carter/GS	2.00
126	Matt Morris/MZ	2.00
127	Brett Tomko/MZ	2.00
128	Mike Cameron/CL	2.00
129	Russ Davis/GS	2.00
130	Shannon Stewart/MZ	2.00
131	Kevin Orie/GS	2.00
132	Scott Spiezio/GS	2.00
133	Brian Giles/GS	2.00
134	Raul Casanova/GS	2.00
135	Jose Cruz Jr./CL	2.00
136	Hideki Irabu/GS	2.00
137	Bubba Trammell/GS	2.00
138	Richard Hidalgo/CL	2.00
139	Paul Konerko/CL	2.50
140	Todd Helton/FB	5.00
141	Miguel Tejada/CL	3.00
142	Fernando Tatis/MZ	2.00
143	Ben Grieve/FB	2.00
144	Travis Lee/FB	2.00
145	Mark Kotsay/CL	2.00
146	Eli Marrero/MZ	2.00
147	David Ortiz/CL	4.00
148	Juan Encarnacion/MZ	2.00
149	Jaret Wright/MZ	2.00
150	Livan Hernandez/CL	2.00
151	Ruben Rivera/GS	2.00
152	Brad Fullmer/MZ	2.00
153	Dennis Reyes/GS	2.00
154	Enrique Wilson/MZ	2.00
155	Todd Dunwoody/MZ	2.00
156	Derrick Gibson/MZ	2.00
157	Aaron Boone/MZ	2.00
158	Ron Wright/MZ	2.00
159	Preston Wilson/MZ	2.00
160	Abraham Nunez/GS	2.00
161	Shane Monahan/GS	2.00
162	Carl Pavano/GS	2.00
163	Derrek Lee/GS	4.00
164	Jeff Abbott/GS	2.00
165	Wes Helms/MZ	2.00
166	Brian Rose/GS	2.00
167	Bobby Estalella/GS	2.00
168	Ken Griffey Jr./GS	9.00
169	Frank Thomas/GS	6.00
170	Cal Ripken Jr./GS	15.00
171	Alex Rodriguez/GS	12.00
172	Greg Maddux/GS	7.50
173	Mike Piazza/GS	9.00
174	Chipper Jones/GS	8.00
175	Tony Gwynn/GS	7.50
176	Derek Jeter/GS	15.00
177	Jeff Bagwell/GS	6.00
178	Juan Gonzalez/GS	3.00
179	Nomar Garciaparra/GS	7.50
180	Andruw Jones/GS	6.00
181	Hideo Nomo/GS	3.00
182	Roger Clemens/GS	8.00
183	Mark McGwire/GS	12.00
184	Scott Rolen/GS	3.00
185	Barry Bonds/GS	15.00
186	Darin Erstad/GS	3.00
187	Mo Vaughn/GS	2.00
188	Ivan Rodriguez/GS	5.00
189	Larry Walker/MZ	2.00
190	Andy Pettitte/GS	3.00
191	Randy Johnson/MZ	6.00
192	Paul Molitor/GS	6.00
193	Jim Thome/GS	4.00
194	Tino Martinez/MZ	2.00
195	Gary Sheffield/GS	3.00
196	Albert Belle/GS	2.00
197	Jose Cruz Jr./GS	2.00
198	Todd Helton/GS	5.00
199	Ben Grieve/GS	2.00
200	Paul Konerko/GS	2.50

1998 Donruss Elite

	NM/M
Complete Set (150):	15.00
Common Player:	.10
Aspirations (750 Sets):	2.5X
Status (100 Sets):	15X
Pack (5):	2.50
Wax Box (18):	40.00

1	Ken Griffey Jr.	1.50
2	Frank Thomas	.75
3	Alex Rodriguez	2.00
4	Mike Piazza	1.50
5	Greg Maddux	1.00
6	Cal Ripken Jr.	2.50
7	Chipper Jones	1.00
8	Derek Jeter	2.50
9	Tony Gwynn	1.00
10	Andruw Jones	.75
11	Juan Gonzalez	.40
12	Jeff Bagwell	.75
13	Mark McGwire	2.00
14	Roger Clemens	1.25
15	Albert Belle	.10
16	Barry Bonds	2.50
17	Kenny Lofton	.10
18	Ivan Rodriguez	.65
19	Manny Ramirez	.75
20	Jim Thome	.50
21	Chuck Knoblauch	.10
22	Paul Molitor	.75
23	Barry Larkin	.10
24	Andy Pettitte	.40
25	John Smoltz	.10
26	Randy Johnson	.75
27	Bernie Williams	.10
28	Larry Walker	.10
29	Mo Vaughn	.10
30	Bobby Higginson	.10
31	Edgardo Alfonzo	.10
32	Justin Thompson	.10
33	Jeff Suppan	.10
34	Roberto Alomar	.30
35	Hideo Nomo	.40
36	Rusty Greer	.10
37	Tim Salmon	.10
38	Jim Edmonds	.10
39	Gary Sheffield	.25
40	Ken Caminiti	.10
41	Sammy Sosa	1.00
42	Tony Womack	.10
43	Matt Williams	.10
44	Andres Galarraga	.10
45	Garret Anderson	.10
46	Rafael Palmeiro	.65
47	Mike Mussina	.40
48	Craig Biggio	.10
49	Wade Boggs	1.00
50	Tom Glavine	.25
51	Jason Giambi	.50
52	Will Clark	.10
53	David Justice	.10
54	Sandy Alomar Jr.	.10
55	Edgar Martinez	.10
56	Brady Anderson	.10
57	Eric Young	.10
58	Ray Lankford	.10
59	Kevin Brown	.10
60	Raul Mondesi	.10
61	Bobby Bonilla	.10
62	Javier Lopez	.10
63	Fred McGriff	.10
64	Rondell White	.10
65	Todd Hundley	.10
66	Mark Grace	.10
67	Alan Benes	.10
68	Jeff Abbott	.10
69	Bob Abreu	.10
70	Deion Sanders	.10
71	Tino Martinez	.10
72	Shannon Stewart	.10
73	Homer Bush	.10
74	Carlos Delgado	.50
75	Raul Ibanez	.10
76	Hideki Irabu	.10
77	Jose Cruz Jr.	.10
78	Tony Clark	.10
79	Wilton Guerrero	.10
80	Vladimir Guerrero	.75
81	Scott Rolen	.60
82	Nomar Garciaparra	1.00
83	Darin Erstad	.30
84	Chan Ho Park	.10
85	Mike Cameron	.10
86	Todd Walker	.10
87	Todd Dunwoody	.10
88	Neifi Perez	.10
89	Brett Tomko	.10
90	Jose Guillen	.10
91	Matt Morris	.10
92	Bartolo Colon	.10
93	Jaret Wright	.10
94	Shawn Estes	.10
95	Livan Hernandez	.10
96	Bobby Estalella	.10
97	Ben Grieve	.10
98	Paul Konerko	.15
99	David Ortiz	.40
100	Todd Helton	.65
101	Juan Encarnacion	.10
102	Bubba Trammell	.10
103	Miguel Tejada	.25
104	Jacob Cruz	.10
105	Todd Greene	.10
106	Kevin Orie	.10
107	Mark Kotsay	.10
108	Fernando Tatis	.10
109	Jay Payton	.10
110	Pokey Reese	.10
111	Derrek Lee	.10
112	Richard Hidalgo	.10
113	Ricky Ledee	.10
114	Lou Collier	.10
115	Ruben Rivera	.10
116	Shawn Green	.20
117	Moises Alou	.10
118	Ken Griffey Jr.	.65
119	Frank Thomas	.40
120	Alex Rodriguez	.75
121	Mike Piazza	.65
122	Greg Maddux	.50
123	Cal Ripken Jr.	1.00
124	Chipper Jones (Generations)	.50
125	Derek Jeter	1.00
126	Tony Gwynn	.50
127	Andruw Jones	.40
128	Juan Gonzalez	.20
129	Jeff Bagwell	.40
130	Mark McGwire	.75
131	Roger Clemens	.65
132	Albert Belle	.10
133	Barry Bonds	1.00
134	Kenny Lofton	.10
135	Ivan Rodriguez	.25
136	Manny Ramirez	.40
137	Jim Thome	.25
138	Chuck Knoblauch	.10
139	Paul Molitor	.40
140	Barry Larkin	.10
141	Mo Vaughn	.10
142	Hideki Irabu	.10
143	Jose Cruz Jr.	.10
144	Tony Clark	.10
145	Vladimir Guerrero	.40
146	Scott Rolen	.20
147	Nomar Garciaparra	.50
148	Nomar Garciaparra Checklist	.40
149	Larry Walker Checklist	.10
150	Tino Martinez Checklist	.10

Aspirations

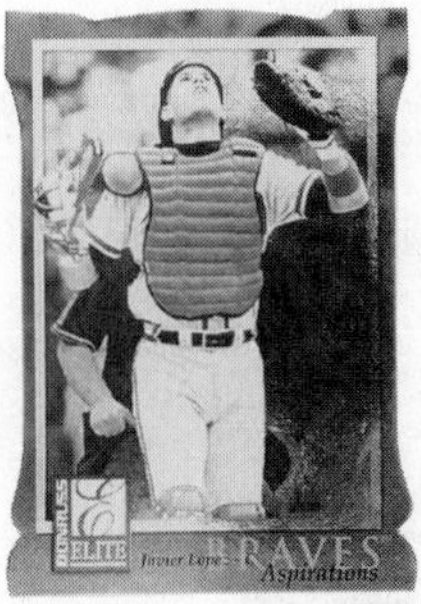

	NM/M
Common Player:	.50
Stars/Rookies:	2.5X

(See 1998 Donruss Elite for checklist and base card values.)

Status

	NM/M
Common Player:	1.50
Stars/Rookies:	15X

(See 1998 Donruss Elite for checklist and base card values.)

Back to the Future

		NM/M
Complete Set (8):		40.00
Common Player:		2.50
Production 1,400 Sets		
1	Cal Ripken Jr., Paul Konerko	9.00
2	Jeff Bagwell, Todd Helton	4.50
3	Eddie Mathews, Chipper Jones	5.00
4	Juan Gonzalez, Ben Grieve	2.50

5	Hank Aaron, Jose Cruz Jr.	10.00
6	Frank Thomas, David Ortiz	4.50
7	Nolan Ryan, Greg Maddux	9.00
8	Alex Rodriguez, Nomar Garciaparra	9.00

Back to the Future Autographs

		NM/M
	Production 100 Sets	
1a	Paul Konerko	30.00
1b	Cal Ripken Jr.	150.00
2	Jeff Bagwell, Todd Helton	120.00
3	Eddie Mathews, Chipper Jones	200.00
4	Juan Gonzalez, Ben Grieve	30.00
5	Hank Aaron, Jose Cruz Jr.	250.00
6	Not Issued In Augraphed Form7	
	Nolan Ryan, Greg Maddux	850.00
8	Alex Rodriguez, Nomar Garciaparra	450.00
2	Frank Thomas (Specially autographed Elite)	45.00

Craftsmen

		NM/M
Complete Set (30):		40.00
Common Player:		.50
Production 3,500 Sets		
Master Craftsman (100 Sets):		10X
1	Ken Griffey Jr.	3.00
2	Frank Thomas	1.50
3	Alex Rodriguez	4.00
4	Cal Ripken Jr.	5.00
5	Greg Maddux	2.00
6	Mike Piazza	3.00
7	Chipper Jones	2.00
8	Derek Jeter	5.00
9	Tony Gwynn	2.00
10	Nomar Garciaparra	2.00
11	Scott Rolen	1.25
12	Jose Cruz Jr.	.50
13	Tony Clark	.50
14	Vladimir Guerrero	1.50
15	Todd Helton	1.25
16	Ben Grieve	.50
17	Andruw Jones	1.50
18	Jeff Bagwell	1.50
19	Mark McGwire	4.00
20	Juan Gonzalez	.75
21	Roger Clemens	2.50
22	Albert Belle	.50
23	Barry Bonds	5.00
24	Kenny Lofton	.50
25	Ivan Rodriguez	1.25
26	Paul Molitor	1.50
27	Barry Larkin (Incorrect "CARDINALS" on front.)	.50
28	Mo Vaughn	.50
29	Larry Walker	.50
30	Tino Martinez	.50

Prime Numbers

		NM/M
Common Card:		5.00
Samples: 50 Percent Player's Common		
1A	Ken Griffey Jr. 2/94	25.00
1B	Ken Griffey Jr. 9/204	20.00
1C	Ken Griffey Jr. 4/290	17.50
2A	Frank Thomas 4/56	25.00
2B	Frank Thomas 5/406	7.50
2C	Frank Thomas 6/450	7.50
3A	Mark McGwire 3/87	30.00
3B	Mark McGwire 8/307	20.00
3C	Mark McGwire 7/380	20.00
4A	Cal Ripken Jr. 5/17	135.00
4B	Cal Ripken Jr. 1/507	13.50
4C	Cal Ripken Jr. 7/510	13.50
5A	Mike Piazza 5/76	30.00
5B	Mike Piazza 7/506	12.00
5C	Mike Piazza 6/570	12.00
6A	Chipper Jones 4/89	25.00
6B	Chipper Jones 8/409	10.00
6C	Chipper Jones 9/480	10.00
7A	Tony Gwynn 3/72	25.00
7B	Tony Gwynn 7/302	9.00
7C	Tony Gwynn 2/370	9.00
8A	Barry Bonds 3/74	45.00
8B	Barry Bonds 7/304	12.00
8C	Barry Bonds 4/370	12.00
9A	Jeff Bagwell 4/25	25.00
9B	Jeff Bagwell 2/405	7.50
9C	Jeff Bagwell 5/420	7.50
10A	Juan Gonzalez 5/89	9.00
10B	Juan Gonzalez 8/509	6.00
10C	Juan Gonzalez 9/580	6.00
11A	Alex Rodriguez 5/34	55.00
11B	Alex Rodriguez 3/504	12.00
11C	Alex Rodriguez 4/530	12.00
12A	Kenny Lofton 3/54	15.00
12B	Kenny Lofton 5/304	5.00
12C	Kenny Lofton 4/350	5.00

1998 Donruss Preferred

		NM/M
Complete Set (200):		90.00
Common Grand Stand (5:1):		.10
Common Mezzanine (1:6):		.20
Common Club Level (1:12):		.30
Common Field Box (1:23):		.40
Common Executive Suite (1:65):		1.50
Tin Pack (5):		3.00
Tin Box (24):		40.00
1	Ken Griffey Jr./EX	4.00
2	Frank Thomas/EX	2.50
3	Cal Ripken Jr./EX	7.50
4	Alex Rodriguez/EX	5.00
5	Greg Maddux/EX	3.00
6	Mike Piazza/EX	4.00
7	Chipper Jones/EX	3.00
8	Tony Gwynn/EX	2.50
9	Derek Jeter/FB	6.00
10	Jeff Bagwell/EX	2.50
11	Juan Gonzalez/EX	1.50
12	Nomar Garciaparra/EX	3.00
13	Andruw Jones/FB	2.00
14	Hideo Nomo/FB	.65
15	Roger Clemens/FB	3.00
16	Mark McGwire/FB	5.00
17	Scott Rolen/FB	.75
18	Vladimir Guerrero/FB	2.00
19	Barry Bonds/FB	6.00
20	Darin Erstad/FB	.40
21	Albert Belle/FB	.40
22	Kenny Lofton/FB	.40
23	Mo Vaughn/FB	.40
24	Tony Clark/FB	.40
25	Ivan Rodriguez/FB	1.50
26	Larry Walker/CL	.30
27	Eddie Murray/CL	1.00
28	Andy Pettitte/CL	.45
29	Roberto Alomar/CL	.40
30	Randy Johnson/CL	1.00
31	Manny Ramirez/CL	1.00
32	Paul Molitor/FB	2.00
33	Mike Mussina/CL	.50
34	Jim Thome/FB	.75
35	Tino Martinez/CL	.30
36	Gary Sheffield/CL	.45
37	Chuck Knoblauch/CL	.30
38	Bernie Williams/CL	.30
39	Tim Salmon/CL	.30
40	Sammy Sosa/CL	1.50
41	Wade Boggs/MZ	.75
42	Will Clark/GS	.50
43	Andres Galarraga/CL	.30
44	Raul Mondesi/CL	.30
45	Rickey Henderson/GS	.50
46	Jose Canseco/GS	.35
47	Pedro Martinez/GS	.50
48	Jay Buhner/GS	.10
49	Ryan Klesko/GS	.10
50	Barry Larkin/CL	.30
51	Charles Johnson/GS	.10
52	Tom Glavine/GS	.25
53	Edgar Martinez/CL	.30
54	Fred McGriff/GS	.10
55	Moises Alou/MZ	.20
56	Dante Bichette/GS	.10
57	Jim Edmonds/CL	.30
58	Mark Grace/MZ	.20
59	Chan Ho Park/MZ	.20
60	Justin Thompson/MZ	.20
61	John Smoltz/MZ	.20
62	Craig Biggio/CL	.30
63	Ken Caminiti/MZ	.20
64	Deion Sanders/CL	.20
65	Carlos Delgado/GS	.10
66	David Justice/CL	.30
67	J.T. Snow/GS	.10
68	Jason Giambi/CL	.50
69	Garret Anderson/MZ	.20
70	Rondell White/MZ	.20
71	Matt Williams/MZ	.20
72	Brady Anderson/MZ	.20
73	Eric Karros/GS	.10
74	Javier Lopez/GS	.10
75	Pat Hentgen/GS	.10
76	Todd Hundley/GS	.10
77	Ray Lankford/GS	.10
78	Denny Neagle/GS	.10
79	Henry Rodriguez/GS	.10
80	Sandy Alomar Jr./MZ	.20
81	Rafael Palmeiro/MZ	.50
82	Robin Ventura/GS	.10
83	John Olerud/GS	.10
84	Omar Vizquel/GS	.10
85	Joe Randa/GS	.10
86	Lance Johnson/GS	.10
87	Kevin Brown/GS	.20
88	Curt Schilling/GS	.25
89	Ismael Valdes/GS	.10
90	Francisco Cordova/GS	.10
91	David Cone/GS	.10
92	Paul O'Neill/GS	.10
93	Jimmy Key/GS	.10
94	Brad Radke/GS	.10
95	Kevin Appier/GS	.10
96	Al Martin/GS	.10
97	Rusty Greer/MZ	.20
98	Reggie Jefferson/GS	.10
99	Ron Coomer/GS	.10
100	Vinny Castilla/GS	.10
101	Bobby Bonilla/MZ	.20
102	Eric Young/GS	.10
103	Tony Womack/GS	.10
104	Jason Kendall/GS	.10
105	Jeff Suppan/GS	.10
106	Shawn Estes/MZ	.20
107	Shawn Green/GS	.25
108	Edgardo Alfonzo/MZ	.20
109	Alan Benes/MZ	.20
110	Bobby Higginson/MZ	.10
111	Mark Grudzielanek/GS	.10
112	Wilton Guerrero/GS	.10
113	Todd Greene/MZ	.20
114	Pokey Reese/GS	.10
115	Jose Guillen/CL	.30
116	Neifi Perez/MZ	.10
117	Luis Castillo/GS	.10
118	Edgar Renteria/GS	.10
119	Karim Garcia/GS	.10
120	Butch Huskey/GS	.10
121	Michael Tucker/GS	.10
122	Jason Dickson/GS	.10
123	Todd Walker/MZ	.10
124	Brian Jordan/GS	.10
125	Joe Carter/GS	.10
126	Matt Morris/MZ	.20
127	Brett Tomko/MZ	.20
128	Mike Cameron/MZ	.30
129	Russ Davis/GS	.10
130	Shannon Stewart/MZ	.20
131	Kevin Orie/GS	.10
132	Scott Spiezio/GS	.10
133	Brian Giles/GS	.10
134	Raul Casanova/GS	.10
135	Jose Cruz Jr./CL	.30
136	Hideki Irabu/GS	.10
137	Bubba Trammell/GS	.10
138	Richard Hidalgo/CL	.30
139	Paul Konerko/GS	.35
140	Todd Helton/FB	1.00
141	Miguel Tejada/CL	.40
142	Fernando Tatis/MZ	.20
143	Ben Grieve/FB	.40
144	Travis Lee/FB	.65
145	Mark Kotsay/CL	.20
146	Eli Marrero/MZ	.20
147	David Ortiz/CL	.50
148	Juan Encarnacion/MZ	.20
149	Jaret Wright/MZ	.20
150	Livan Hernandez/CL	.30
151	Ruben Rivera/GS	.10
152	Brad Fullmer/MZ	.20
153	Dennis Reyes/GS	.10
154	Enrique Wilson/MZ	.20
155	Todd Dunwoody/MZ	.20
156	Derrick Gibson/MZ	.20
157	Aaron Boone/MZ	.20
158	Ron Wright/MZ	.20
159	Preston Wilson/MZ	.20
160	Abraham Nunez/GS	.10
161	Shane Monahan/GS	.10
162	Carl Pavano/GS	.10
163	Derrek Lee/GS	.35
164	Jeff Abbott/GS	.10
165	Wes Helms/MZ	.20
166	Brian Rose/GS	.10
167	Bobby Estalella/GS	.10
168	Ken Griffey Jr./GS	.75
169	Frank Thomas/GS	.50
170	Cal Ripken Jr./GS	1.50
171	Alex Rodriguez/GS	1.00
172	Greg Maddux/GS	.60
173	Mike Piazza/GS	.75
174	Chipper Jones/GS	.60
175	Tony Gwynn/GS	.60
176	Derek Jeter/GS	1.50
177	Jeff Bagwell/GS	.50
178	Juan Gonzalez/GS	.30
179	Nomar Garciaparra/GS	.60
180	Andruw Jones/GS	.50
181	Hideo Nomo/GS	.30
182	Roger Clemens/GS	.65
183	Mark McGwire/GS	1.00
184	Scott Rolen/GS	.35
185	Barry Bonds/GS	1.50
186	Darin Erstad/GS	.25
187	Mo Vaughn/GS	.10
188	Ivan Rodriguez/GS	.40
189	Larry Walker/MZ	.20
190	Andy Pettitte/GS	.30
191	Randy Johnson/MZ	.60
192	Paul Molitor/GS	.50
193	Jim Thome/GS	.35
194	Tino Martinez/MZ	.20
195	Gary Sheffield/GS	.20
196	Albert Belle/GS	.10
197	Jose Cruz Jr./GS	.10
198	Todd Helton/GS	.40
199	Ben Grieve/GS	.10
200	Paul Konerko/GS	.20

Seating

	NM/M
Common Grand Stand:	.50
Stars and Rookies:	4X
Common Mezzanine:	.50
Stars and Rookies:	2X
Common Club Level:	.50
Stars and Rookies:	2X
Common Field Box:	1.00
Stars and Rookies:	1.5X
Common Executive Suite:	2.50
Stars and Rookies:	1X

(See 1998 Donruss Preferred for checklistand base card values.)

Great X-pectations

		NM/M
Complete Set (26):		35.00
Common Player:		.75
Die-Cuts:		3X
Samples:		1X
1	Jeff Bagwell, Travis Lee	1.25
2	Jose Cruz Jr., Ken Griffey Jr.	2.00
3	Larry Walker, Ben Grieve	.75
4	Frank Thomas, Todd Helton	1.25
5	Jim Thome, Paul Konerko	1.00
6	Alex Rodriguez, Miguel Tejada	2.50
7	Greg Maddux, Livan Hernandez	1.75
8	Roger Clemens, Jaret Wright	1.75

9	Albert Belle, Juan Encarnacion	.75
10	Mo Vaughn, David Ortiz	1.00
11	Manny Ramirez, Mark Kotsay	1.25
12	Tim Salmon, Brad Fullmer	.75
13	Cal Ripken Jr., Fernando Tatis	3.50
14	Hideo Nomo, Hideki Irabu	1.50
15	Mike Piazza, Todd Greene	2.00
16	Gary Sheffield, Richard Hidalgo	.75
17	Paul Molitor, Darin Erstad	1.25
18	Ivan Rodriguez, Eli Marrero	1.00
19	Ken Caminiti, Todd Walker	.75
20	Tony Gwynn, Jose Guillen	1.75
21	Derek Jeter, Nomar Garciaparra	1.75
22	Chipper Jones, Scott Rolen	1.75
23	Juan Gonzalez, Andruw Jones	1.25
24	Barry Bonds, Vladimir Guerrero	3.50
25	Mark McGwire, Tony Clark	2.50
26	Bernie Williams, Mike Cameron	.75

Precious Metals

		NM/M
Complete Set (30):		850.00
Common Player:		7.50
1	Ken Griffey Jr.	50.00
2	Frank Thomas	35.00
3	Cal Ripken Jr.	75.00
4	Alex Rodriguez	60.00
5	Greg Maddux	45.00
6	Mike Piazza	50.00
7	Chipper Jones	45.00
8	Tony Gwynn	45.00
9	Derek Jeter	75.00
10	Jeff Bagwell	35.00
11	Juan Gonzalez	15.00
12	Nomar Garciaparra	45.00
13	Andruw Jones	35.00
14	Hideo Nomo	15.00
15	Roger Clemens	45.00
16	Mark McGwire	60.00
17	Scott Rolen	25.00
18	Barry Bonds	75.00
19	Darin Erstad	15.00
20	Kenny Lofton	7.50
21	Mo Vaughn	7.50
22	Ivan Rodriguez	25.00
23	Randy Johnson	35.00
24	Paul Molitor	35.00
25	Jose Cruz Jr.	7.50
26	Paul Konerko	7.50
27	Todd Helton	25.00
28	Ben Grieve	7.50
29	Travis Lee	7.50
30	Mark Kotsay	7.50

Title Waves

		NM/M
Complete Set (30):		100.00
Common Player:		1.00
1	Nomar Garciaparra	5.00
2	Scott Rolen	2.50

3	Roger Clemens	5.50
4	Gary Sheffield	1.50
5	Jeff Bagwell	3.50
6	Cal Ripken Jr.	10.00
7	Frank Thomas	3.50
8	Ken Griffey Jr.	6.00
9	Larry Walker	1.00
10	Derek Jeter	10.00
11	Juan Gonzalez	2.00
12	Bernie Williams	1.00
13	Andruw Jones	3.50
14	Andy Pettitte	1.50
15	Ivan Rodriguez	2.50
16	Alex Rodriguez	8.00
17	Mark McGwire	8.00
18	Andres Galarraga	1.00
19	Hideo Nomo	2.00
20	Mo Vaughn	1.00
21	Randy Johnson	3.50
22	Chipper Jones	5.00
23	Greg Maddux	5.00
24	Manny Ramirez	3.50
25	Tony Gwynn	5.00
26	Albert Belle	1.00
27	Kenny Lofton	1.00
28	Mike Piazza	6.00
29	Paul Molitor	3.50
30	Barry Bonds	10.00

1998 Donruss Signature Series

		NM/M
Complete Set (140):		30.00
Common Player:		.10
Signature Proofs:		12X
Pack (5):		12.50
Wax Box (12):		150.00
1	David Justice	.10
2	Derek Jeter	2.50
3	Nomar Garciaparra	1.00
4	Ryan Klesko	.75
5	Jeff Bagwell	1.00
6	Dante Bichette	.10
7	Ivan Rodriguez	.65
8	Albert Belle	.10
9	Cal Ripken Jr.	2.50
10	Craig Biggio	.10
11	Barry Larkin	.10
12	Jose Guillen	.10
13	Will Clark	.10
14	J.T. Snow	.10
15	Chuck Knoblauch	.10
16	Todd Walker	.10
17	Scott Rolen	.60
18	Rickey Henderson	.75
19	Juan Gonzalez	.40
20	Justin Thompson	.10
21	Roger Clemens	1.25
22	Ray Lankford	.10
23	Jose Cruz Jr.	.10
24	Ken Griffey Jr.	1.50
25	Andruw Jones	.75
26	Darin Erstad	.30
27	Jim Thome	.50
28	Wade Boggs	1.00
29	Ken Caminiti	.10
30	Todd Hundley	.10
31	Mike Piazza	1.50
32	Sammy Sosa	1.00
33	Larry Walker	.10
34	Matt Williams	.10
35	Frank Thomas	.75
36	Gary Sheffield	.30
37	Alex Rodriguez	2.00
38	Hideo Nomo	.40
39	Kenny Lofton	.10
40	John Smoltz	.10
41	Mo Vaughn	.10
42	Edgar Martinez	.10
43	Paul Molitor	.75
44	Rafael Palmeiro	.65
45	Barry Bonds	2.50
46	Vladimir Guerrero	.75
47	Carlos Delgado	.50
48	Bobby Higginson	.10
49	Greg Maddux	1.00
50	Jim Edmonds	.10
51	Randy Johnson	.75
52	Mark McGwire	2.00
53	Rondell White	.10
54	Raul Mondesi	.10
55	Manny Ramirez	.75
56	Pedro Martinez	.75
57	Tim Salmon	.10
58	Moises Alou	.10
59	Fred McGriff	.10
60	Garret Anderson	.10
61	Sandy Alomar Jr.	.10
62	Chan Ho Park	.10
63	Mark Kotsay	.10
64	Mike Mussina	.50
65	Tom Glavine	.25
66	Tony Clark	.10
67	Mark Grace	.10
68	Tony Gwynn	1.00
69	Tino Martinez	.10
70	Kevin Brown	.10
71	Todd Greene	.10
72	Andy Pettitte	.30
73	Livan Hernandez	.10
74	Curt Schilling	.25
75	Andres Galarraga	.10
76	Rusty Greer	.10
77	Jay Buhner	.10
78	Bobby Bonilla	.10
79	Chipper Jones	1.00
80	Eric Young	.10
81	Jason Giambi	.50
82	Javy Lopez	.10
83	Roberto Alomar	.25
84	Bernie Williams	.10
85	A.J. Hinch	.10
86	Kerry Wood	.40
87	Juan Encarnacion	.10
88	Brad Fullmer	.10
89	Ben Grieve	.10
90	Magglio Ordonez RC	2.00
91	Todd Helton	.65
92	Richard Hidalgo	.10
93	Paul Konerko	.15
94	Aramis Ramirez	.10
95	Ricky Ledee	.10
96	Derek Lee	.50
97	Travis Lee	.15
98	Matt Anderson RC	.25
99	Jaret Wright	.10
100	David Ortiz	.35
101	Carl Pavano	.10
102	Orlando Hernandez RC	.50
103	Fernando Tatis	.10
104	Miguel Tejada	.30
105	Rolando Arrojo RC	.50
106	Kevin Millwood RC	1.00
107	Ken Griffey Jr. (Checklist)	.50
108	Frank Thomas (Checklist)	.30
109	Cal Ripken Jr. (Checklist)	.75
110	Greg Maddux (Checklist)	.40
111	John Olerud	.10
112	David Cone	.10
113	Vinny Castilla	.10
114	Jason Kendall	.10
115	Brian Jordan	.10
116	Hideki Irabu	.10
117	Bartolo Colon	.10
118	Greg Vaughn	.10
119	David Segui	.10
120	Bruce Chen	.10
121	Julio Ramirez RC	.10
122	Troy Glaus RC	4.00
123	Jeremy Giambi RC	.50
124	Ryan Minor RC	.15
125	Richie Sexson	.10
126	Dermal Brown	.10
127	Adrian Beltre	.15
128	Eric Chavez	.30
129	J.D. Drew RC	4.00
130	Gabe Kapler RC	.30
131	Masato Yoshii RC	.25
132	Mike Lowell RC	2.00
133	Jim Parque RC	.25
134	Roy Halladay	.10
135	Carlos Lee RC	1.00
136	Jin Ho Cho RC	.25
137	Michael Barrett	.10
138	Fernando Seguignol RC	.40
139	Odalis Perez RC	.50
140	Mark McGwire (Checklist)	.65

Proofs

	NM/M
Complete Set (140):	450.00
Common Player:	1.00

Stars/Rookies: 12X
(See 1998 Donruss Signature Series for checklist and base card values.)

Autographs (Red)

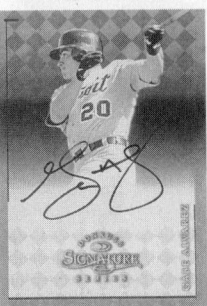

		NM/M
Common Player:		2.50
(1)	Roberto Alomar/150	35.00
(2)	Sandy Alomar Jr./700	10.00
(3)	Moises Alou/900	15.00
(4)	Gabe Alvarez/2,900	2.50
(5)	Wilson Alvarez/1,600	4.00
(6)	Jay Bell/1,500	4.00
(7)	Adrian Beltre/1,900	25.00
(8)	Andy Benes/2,600	4.00
(9)	Aaron Boone/3,400	8.00
(10)	Russell Branyan/1,650	4.00
(11)	Orlando Cabrera/3,100	8.00
(12)	Mike Cameron/1,150	8.00
(13)	Joe Carter/400	10.00
(14)	Sean Casey/2,275	8.00
(15)	Bruce Chen/150	5.00
(16)	Tony Clark/2,275	5.00
(17)	Will Clark/1,400	15.00
(18)	Matt Clement/1,400	4.00
(19)	Pat Cline/400	5.00
(20)	Ken Cloude/3,400	2.50
(21)	Michael Coleman/2,800	2.50
(22)	David Cone/25	50.00
(23)	Jeff Conine/1,400	5.00
(24)	Jacob Cruz (3,200)	2.50
(25)	Russ Davis/3,500	2.50
(26)	Jason Dickson/1,400	4.00
(27)	Todd Dunwoody/3,500	2.50
(28)	Juan Encarnacion/3,400	5.00
(29)	Darin Erstad/700	10.00
(30)	Bobby Estalella/3,400	4.00
(31)	Jeff Fassero/3,400	2.50
(32)	John Franco/1,800	2.50
(33)	Brad Fullmer/3,100	5.00
(34)	Jason Giambi/3,100	15.00
(35)	Derrick Gibson/1,200	5.00
(36)	Todd Greene/1,400	5.00
(37)	Ben Grieve/1,400	5.00
(38)	Mark Grudzielanek/3,200	4.00
(39)	Vladimir Guerrero/2,100	25.00
(40)	Wilton Guerrero/1,900	4.00
(41)	Jose Guillen/2,400	5.00
(42)	Todd Helton/1,300	20.00
(43)	Richard Hidalgo/3,400	4.00
(44)	A.J. Hinch/2,900	4.00
(45)	Butch Huskey/1,900	4.00
(46)	Raul Ibanez/3,300	2.50
(47)	Damian Jackson/900	2.50
(48)	Geoff Jenkins/3,100	6.00
(49)	Eric Karros/650	8.00
(50)	Ryan Klesko/400	8.00
(51)	Mark Kotsay/3,600	5.00
(52)	Ricky Ledee/2,200	5.00
(53)	Derrek Lee/3,400	10.00
(54)	Travis Lee/150	10.00
(54s)	Travis Lee (Facsimile autograph, "SAMPLE" on back.)	3.00
(55)	Javier Lopez/650	8.00
(56)	Mike Lowell/3,500	10.00
(57)	Greg Maddux/12	625.00
(58)	Eli Marrero/3,400	5.00

(59)	Al Martin/1,300	4.00
(60)	Rafael Medina/1,400	2.50
(61)	Scott Morgan/900	4.50
(62)	Abraham Nunez/3,500	2.50
(63)	Paul O'Neill/1,000	20.00
(64)	Luis Ordaz/2,700	2.50
(65)	Magglio Ordonez/3,200	15.00
(66)	Kevin Orie/1,350	5.00
(67)	David Ortiz/3,400	25.00
(68)	Rafael Palmeiro/1,000	25.00
(69)	Carl Pavano/2,600	5.00
(70)	Neifi Perez/3,300	2.50
(71)	Dante Powell/3,050	2.50
(72)	Aramis Ramirez/2,800	10.00
(73)	Mariano Rivera/900	35.00
(74)	Felix Rodriguez/1,400	3.00
(75)	Henry Rodriguez/3,400	3.00
(76)	Scott Rolen/1,900	30.00
(77)	Brian Rose/1,400	3.00
(78)	Curt Schilling/900	30.00
(79)	Richie Sexson/3,500	8.00
(80)	Randall Simon/3,500	3.00
(81)	J.T. Snow/400	10.00
(82)	Jeff Suppan/1,400	5.00
(83)	Fernando Tatis/3,900	3.00
(84)	Miguel Tejada/3,800	15.00
(85)	Brett Tomko/3,400	2.50
(86)	Bubba Trammell/3,900	2.50
(87)	Ismael Valdez/1,900	5.00
(88)	Robin Ventura/1,400	5.00
(89)	Billy Wagner/3,900	10.00
(90)	Todd Walker/1,900	5.00
(91)	Daryle Ward/400	4.00
(92)	Rondell White/3,400	5.00
(93)	Antone Williamson/3,350	2.50
(94)	Dan Wilson/2,400)	4.00
(95)	Enrique Wilson/3,400	2.50
(96)	Preston Wilson/2,100	5.00
(97)	Tony Womack/3,500	2.50
(98)	Kerry Wood/3,400	10.00

Century Marks (Blue)

		NM/M
	Common Player:	10.00
(1)	Roberto Alomar	60.00
(2)	Sandy Alomar Jr.	15.00
(3)	Moises Alou	40.00
(4)	Gabe Alvarez	10.00
(5)	Wilson Alvarez	10.00
(6)	Brady Anderson	15.00
(7)	Jay Bell	15.00
(8)	Albert Belle	20.00
(9)	Adrian Beltre	25.00
(10)	Andy Benes	10.00
(11)	Wade Boggs	60.00
(12)	Barry Bonds	250.00
(13)	Aaron Boone	25.00
(14)	Russell Branyan	10.00
(15)	Jay Buhner	10.00
(16)	Ellis Burks	10.00
(17)	Orlando Cabrera	25.00
(18)	Mike Cameron	10.00
(19)	Ken Caminiti	25.00
(20)	Joe Carter	20.00
(21)	Sean Casey	15.00
(22)	Bruce Chen	10.00
(23)	Tony Clark	10.00
(24)	Will Clark	40.00
(25)	Roger Clemens	200.00
(26)	Matt Clement	20.00
(27)	Pat Cline	10.00
(28)	Ken Cloude	10.00
(29)	Michael Coleman	10.00
(30)	David Cone	25.00
(31)	Jeff Conine	10.00
(32)	Jacob Cruz	10.00
(33)	Jose Cruz Jr.	15.00
(34)	Russ Davis	10.00
(35)	Jason Dickson	10.00
(36)	Todd Dunwoody	10.00
(37)	Scott Elarton	10.00
(38)	Darin Erstad	25.00
(39)	Bobby Estalella	10.00
(40)	Jeff Fassero	10.00
(41)	John Franco	10.00
(42)	Brad Fullmer	10.00
(43)	Andres Galarraga	15.00
(44)	Nomar Garciaparra	80.00
(45)	Jason Giambi	40.00
(46)	Derrick Gibson	10.00
(47)	Tom Glavine	75.00
(48)	Juan Gonzalez	50.00
(49)	Todd Greene	10.00
(50)	Ben Grieve	10.00
(51)	Mark Grudzielanek	10.00
(52)	Vladimir Guerrero	75.00
(53)	Wilton Guerrero	10.00
(54)	Jose Guillen	10.00
(55)	Tony Gwynn	80.00
(56)	Todd Helton	60.00
(57)	Richard Hidalgo	10.00
(58)	A.J. Hinch	10.00
(59)	Butch Huskey	10.00
(60)	Raul Ibanez	10.00
(61)	Damian Jackson	10.00
(62)	Geoff Jenkins	10.00
(63)	Derek Jeter	200.00
(64)	Randy Johnson	150.00
(65)	Chipper Jones	120.00
(66)	Eric Karros/50	15.00
(67)	Jason Kendall (Unsigned)	20.00
(68)	Ryan Klesko	10.00
(69)	Chuck Knoblauch	10.00
(70)	Mark Kotsay	10.00
(71)	Ricky Ledee	10.00
(72)	Derrek Lee	25.00
(73)	Travis Lee	15.00
(74)	Javier Lopez	25.00
(75)	Mike Lowell	30.00
(76)	Greg Maddux	150.00
(77)	Eli Marrero	10.00
(78)	Al Martin	10.00
(79)	Rafael Medina	10.00
(80)	Paul Molitor	50.00
(81)	Scott Morgan	10.00
(82)	Mike Mussina	75.00
(83)	Abraham Nunez	15.00
(84)	Paul O'Neill	40.00
(85)	Luis Ordaz	10.00
(86)	Magglio Ordonez	30.00
(87)	Kevin Orie	10.00
(88)	David Ortiz	75.00
(89)	Rafael Palmeiro	75.00
(90)	Carl Pavano	25.00
(91)	Neifi Perez	10.00
(92)	Andy Pettitte	50.00
(93)	Aramis Ramirez	25.00
(94)	Cal Ripken Jr.	200.00
(95)	Mariano Rivera	75.00
(96)	Alex Rodriguez	200.00
(97)	Felix Rodriguez	10.00
(98)	Henry Rodriguez	10.00
(99)	Scott Rolen	70.00
(100)	Brian Rose	10.00
(101)	Curt Schilling	50.00
(102)	Richie Sexson	20.00
(103)	Randall Simon	10.00
(104)	J.T. Snow	10.00
(105)	Darryl Strawberry	40.00
(106)	Jeff Suppan	10.00
(107)	Fernando Tatis	10.00
(108)	Brett Tomko	10.00
(109)	Bubba Trammell	10.00
(110)	Ismael Valdez	10.00
(111)	Robin Ventura	20.00
(112)	Billy Wagner	40.00
(113)	Todd Walker	15.00
(114)	Daryle Ward	10.00
(115)	Rondell White	20.00
(116)	Matt Williams/80	35.00
(117)	Antone Williamson	10.00
(118)	Dan Wilson	15.00
(119)	Enrique Wilson	10.00
(120)	Preston Wilson	15.00
(121)	Tony Womack	10.00
(122)	Kerry Wood	40.00

Millennium Marks (Green)

		NM/M
	Common Player:	3.00
(1)	Roberto Alomar	25.00
(2)	Sandy Alomar Jr.	5.00
(3)	Moises Alou	10.00
(4)	Gabe Alvarez	3.00
(5)	Wilson Alvarez	3.00
(6)	Brady Anderson/800	8.00
(7)	Jay Bell	3.00
(8)	Albert Belle/400	10.00
(9)	Adrian Beltre	15.00
(10)	Andy Benes	3.00
(11)	Wade Boggs/900	20.00
(12)	Barry Bonds/400	150.00
(13)	Aaron Boone	4.00
(14)	Russell Branyan	3.00
(15)	Jay Buhner/400	10.00
(16)	Ellis Burks/900	5.00
(17)	Orlando Cabrera	6.00
(18)	Mike Cameron	5.00
(19)	Ken Caminiti/900	20.00
(20)	Joe Carter	8.00
(21)	Sean Casey	8.00
(22)	Bruce Chen	3.00
(23)	Tony Clark	5.00
(24)	Will Clark	25.00
(25)	Roger Clemens/400	75.00
(26)	Matt Clement/900	8.00
(27)	Pat Cline	3.00
(28)	Ken Cloude	3.00
(29)	Michael Coleman	3.00
(30)	David Cone	10.00
(31)	Jeff Conine	3.00
(32)	Jacob Cruz	3.00
(33)	Jose Cruz Jr./850	5.00
(34)	Russ Davis/950	3.00
(35)	Jason Dickson/950	3.00
(36)	Todd Dunwoody	3.00
(37)	Scott Elarton/900	3.00
(38)	Juan Encarnacion	5.00
(39)	Darin Erstad	5.00
(40)	Bobby Estalella	3.00
(41)	Jeff Fassero	3.00
(42)	John Franco/950	5.00
(43)	Brad Fullmer	3.00
(44)	Andres Galarraga/900	10.00
(45)	Nomar Garciaparra/400	60.00
(46)	Jason Giambi	20.00
(47)	Derrick Gibson	3.00
(48)	Tom Glavine/700	25.00
(49)	Juan Gonzalez	20.00
(50)	Todd Greene	3.00
(51)	Ben Grieve	4.00
(52)	Mark Grudzielanek	3.00
(53)	Vladimir Guerrero	30.00
(54)	Wilton Guerrero	3.00
(55)	Jose Guillen	3.00
(56)	Tony Gwynn/900	30.00
(57)	Todd Helton	20.00
(58)	Richard Hidalgo	3.00
(59)	A.J. Hinch	3.00
(60)	Butch Huskey	3.00
(61)	Raul Ibanez	3.00
(62)	Damian Jackson	3.00
(63)	Geoff Jenkins	3.00
(64)	Derek Jeter/400	100.00
(65)	Randy Johnson/800	50.00
(66)	Chipper Jones/900	30.00
(67)	Eric Karros	5.00
(68)	Ryan Klesko	5.00
(69)	Chuck Knoblauch/900	10.00
(70)	Mark Kotsay	5.00
(71)	Ricky Ledee	3.00
(72)	Derrek Lee	20.00
(73)	Travis Lee	5.00
(74)	Javier Lopez/800	10.00
(75)	Mike Lowell	10.00
(76)	Greg Maddux/400	85.00
(77)	Eli Marrero	3.00
(78)	Al Martin/950	3.00
(79)	Rafael Medina/850	3.00
(80)	Paul Molitor/900	20.00
(81)	Scott Morgan	3.00
(82)	Mike Mussina/900	15.00
(83)	Abraham Nunez	3.00
(84)	Paul O'Neill/900	20.00
(85)	Luis Ordaz	3.00
(86)	Magglio Ordonez	15.00
(87)	Kevin Orie	3.00
(88)	David Ortiz	40.00
(89)	Rafael Palmeiro/900	30.00
(90)	Carl Pavano	10.00
(91)	Neifi Perez	3.00
(92)	Andy Pettitte/900	20.00
(93)	Dante Powell/950	3.00
(94)	Aramis Ramirez	10.00
(95)	Cal Ripken Jr./375	100.00
(96)	Mariano Rivera	30.00
(97)	Alex Rodriguez/350	75.00
(98)	Felix Rodriguez	5.00
(99)	Henry Rodriguez	3.00
(100)	Scott Rolen	20.00
(101)	Brian Rose	3.00
(102)	Curt Schilling	20.00
(103)	Richie Sexson	8.00
(104)	Randall Simon	3.00
(105)	J.T. Snow	4.00
(106)	Darryl Strawberry/900	40.00
(107)	Jeff Suppan	3.00
(108)	Fernando Tatis	5.00
(109)	Miguel Tejada	40.00
(110)	Brett Tomko	3.00
(111)	Bubba Trammell	3.00
(112)	Ismael Valdes	3.00
(113)	Robin Ventura	5.00
(114)	Billy Wagner/900	10.00
(115)	Todd Walker	4.00
(116)	Daryle Ward	3.00
(117)	Rondell White	5.00
(118)	Matt Williams/820	8.00
(119)	Antone Williamson	3.00
(120)	Dan Wilson	3.00
(121)	Enrique Wilson	3.00
(122)	Preston Wilson/400	10.00
(123)	Tony Womack	3.00
(124)	Kerry Wood	20.00

Signature Series Preview Autographs

		NM/M
	Common Player:	10.00
(1)	Sandy Alomar Jr./96	30.00
(2)	Moises Alou	50.00
(3)	Andy Benes/135	15.00
(4)	Russell Branyan/188	15.00
(5)	Sean Casey	85.00
(6)	Tony Clark/188	20.00
(7)	Juan Encarnacion /193	15.00
(8)	Brad Fullmer/396	10.00
(9)	Juan Gonzalez/108	115.00
(10)	Ben Grieve/100	35.00
(11)	Todd Helton/101	50.00
(12)	Richard Hidalgo/380	10.00
(13)	A.J. Hinch/400	10.00
(14)	Damian Jackson/15	65.00
(15)	Geoff Jenkins	185.00
(16)	Derek Jeter	1,225
(17)	Chipper Jones/112	125.00
(18)	Chuck Knoblauch/98	50.00
(19)	Travis Lee/101	20.00
(20)	Mike Lowell/450	15.00
(21)	Greg Maddux/92	165.00
(22)	Kevin Millwood/395	30.00
(23)	Magglio Ordonez/420	50.00
(24)	David Ortiz/393	75.00
(25)	Rafael Palmeiro/107	50.00
(26)	Cal Ripken Jr./22	850.00
(27)	Alex Rodriguez/23	1,150
(28)	Curt Schilling/100	100.00
(29)	Randall Simon/380	10.00
(30)	Fernando Tatis/400	10.00
(31)	Miguel Tejada/375	40.00
(32)	Robin Ventura/95	30.00
(33)	Dan Wilson	85.00
(34)	Kerry Wood/373	40.00

Redemption Baseballs

		NM/M
	Common Autographed Ball:	15.00
	Redemption Card:	10 Percent
(1)	Roberto Alomar/60	35.00
(2)	Sandy Alomar Jr./60	20.00
(3)	Ernie Banks/12	85.00
(4)	Ken Caminiti/60	20.00
(5)	Tony Clark/60	20.00
(6)	Jacob Cruz /12	20.00
(7)	Russ Davis/60	15.00
(8)	Juan Encarnacion/60	20.00
(9)	Bobby Estalella/60	15.00
(10)	Jeff Fassero/60	15.00
(11)	Mark Grudzielanek/60	15.00
(12)	Ben Grieve/30	20.00
(13)	Jose Guillen/120	20.00
(14)	Tony Gwynn /60	100.00
(15)	Al Kaline/12	75.00
(16)	Paul Konerko/100	15.00
(17)	Travis Lee/100	20.00
(18)	Mike Lowell/60	15.00
(19)	Eli Marrero/60	15.00
(20)	Eddie Mathews/12	80.00
(21)	Paul Molitor/60	65.00
(22)	Stan Musial/12	125.00
(23)	Abraham Nunez /12	20.00
(24)	Luis Ordaz/12	20.00
(25)	Maggio Ordonez/12	50.00
(26)	Scott Rolen/60	45.00
(27)	Bubba Trammell/24	25.00
(28)	Robin Ventura/60	20.00
(29)	Billy Wagner/60	20.00
(30)	Rondell White/60	20.00
(31)	Antone Williamson/12	15.00
(32)	Tony Womack/60	15.00

Significant Signatures

	NM/M
Complete Set (18):	425.00
Common Player:	10.00
Ernie Banks	25.00
Yogi Berra	25.00
George Brett	40.00
Catfish Hunter	35.00
Al Kaline	25.00
Harmon Killebrew	25.00
Ralph Kiner	10.00
Sandy Koufax	100.00
Eddie Mathews	25.00
Don Mattingly	50.00

Willie McCovey	25.00
Stan Musial	40.00
Phil Rizzuto	
(Edition of 1,000.)	20.00
Nolan Ryan	60.00
Nolan Ryan	
(Exchange card.)	5.00
Ozzie Smith	20.00
Ozzie Smith	
(Exchange card.)	5.00
Duke Snider	25.00
Don Sutton	12.00
Billy Williams	12.00

2001 Donruss

NM/M

Complete Set (220):	
Common Player:	.15
Common Rated Rookie (151-200):	4.00
Production 2001	
Hobby Pack (5):	6.00
Hobby Box (24):	120.00
The Rookies Coupon:	1.00
Inserted 1:72	
Baseball's Best Coupon:	1.00
Inserted 1:720	
Exchange Deadline 11/01/01	
1	Alex Rodriguez	2.00
2	Barry Bonds	2.50
3	Cal Ripken Jr.	2.50
4	Chipper Jones	1.00
5	Derek Jeter	2.50
6	Troy Glaus	.50
7	Frank Thomas	.75
8	Greg Maddux	1.00
9	Ivan Rodriguez	.50
10	Jeff Bagwell	.50
11	Jose Canseco	.40
12	Todd Helton	.50
13	Ken Griffey Jr.	1.50
14	Manny Ramirez	.75
15	Mark McGwire	2.00
16	Mike Piazza	1.50
17	Nomar Garciaparra	.75
18	Pedro Martinez	1.00
19	Randy Johnson	.75
20	Rick Ankiel	.40
21	Ricky Henderson	.75
22	Roger Clemens	1.50
23	Sammy Sosa	.75
24	Tony Gwynn	1.00
25	Vladimir Guerrero	.75
26	Eric Davis	.15
27	Roberto Alomar	.25
28	Mark Mulder	.25
29	Pat Burrell	.40
30	Harold Baines	.15
31	Carlos Delgado	.40
32	J.D. Drew	.25
33	Jim Edmonds	.40
34	Darin Erstad	.25
35	Jason Giambi	.50
36	Tom Glavine	.50
37	Juan Gonzalez	.40
38	Mark Grace	.25
39	Shawn Green	.25
40	Tim Hudson	.25
41	Andruw Jones	.50

42	David Justice	.25
43	Jeff Kent	.25
44	Barry Larkin	.25
45	Pokey Reese	.15
46	Mike Mussina	.40
47	Hideo Nomo	.25
48	Rafael Palmeiro	.50
49	Adam Piatt	.15
50	Scott Rolen	.75
51	Gary Sheffield	.40
52	Bernie Williams	.25
53	Bob Abreu	.40
54	Edgardo Alfonzo	.15
55	Jermaine Clark **RC**	.15
56	Albert Belle	.15
57	Craig Biggio	.25
58	Andres Galarraga	.15
59	Edgar Martinez	.15
60	Fred McGriff	.15
61	Magglio Ordonez	.40
62	Jim Thome	.50
63	Matt Williams	.15
64	Kerry Wood	.25
65	Moises Alou	.25
66	Brady Anderson	.15
67	Garret Anderson	.25
68	Tony Armas Jr.	.15
69	Tony Batista	.15
70	Jose Cruz Jr.	.15
71	Carlos Beltran	.50
72	Adrian Beltre	.25
73	Kris Benson	.15
74	Lance Berkman	.50
75	Kevin Brown	.15
76	Jay Buhner	.15
77	Jeromy Burnitz	.15
78	Ken Caminiti	.15
79	Sean Casey	.25
80	Luis Castillo	.15
81	Eric Chavez	.25
82	Jeff Cirillo	.15
83	Bartolo Colon	.15
84	David Cone	.15
85	Freddy Garcia	.15
86	Johnny Damon	.50
87	Ray Durham	.15
88	Jermaine Dye	.15
89	Juan Encarnacion	.15
90	Terrence Long	.15
91	Carl Everett	.15
92	Steve Finley	.15
93	Cliff Floyd	.15
94	Brad Fullmer	.15
95	Brian Giles	.15
96	Luis Gonzalez	.15
97	Rusty Greer	.15
98	Jeffrey Hammonds	.15
99	Mike Hampton	.15
100	Orlando Hernandez	.15
101	Richard Hidalgo	.15
102	Geoff Jenkins	.15
103	Jacque Jones	.15
104	Brian Jordan	.15
105	Gabe Kapler	.15
106	Eric Karros	.15
107	Jason Kendall	.15
108	Adam Kennedy	.15
109	Byung-Hyun Kim	.15
110	Ryan Klesko	.15
111	Chuck Knoblauch	.15
112	Paul Konerko	.40
113	Carlos Lee	.40
114	Kenny Lofton	.15
115	Javy Lopez	.15
116	Tino Martinez	.25
117	Ruben Mateo	.15
118	Kevin Millwood	.15
119	Ben Molina	.15
120	Raul Mondesi	.15
121	Trot Nixon	.15
122	John Olerud	.15
123	Paul O'Neill	.25
124	Chan Ho Park	.25
125	Andy Pettitte	.25
126	Jorge Posada	.25
127	Mark Quinn	.15
128	Aramis Ramirez	.40
129	Mariano Rivera	.40
130	Tim Salmon	.15
131	Curt Schilling	.75
132	Richie Sexson	.25
133	John Smoltz	.40
134	J.T. Snow	.15
135	Jay Payton	.15
136	Shannon Stewart	.15
137	B.J. Surhoff	.15
138	Mike Sweeney	.15
139	Fernando Tatis	.15
140	Miguel Tejada	.40
141	Jason Varitek	.40
142	Greg Vaughn	.15
143	Mo Vaughn	.25
144	Robin Ventura	.15
145	Jose Vidro	.15
146	Omar Vizquel	.15
147	Larry Walker	.25
148	David Wells	.15
149	Rondell White	.15
150	Preston Wilson	.15
151	Brent Abernathy	4.00
152	Cory Aldridge **RC**	4.00
153	Gene Altman **RC**	4.00
154	Josh Beckett	8.00
155	Wilson Betemit **RC**	8.00
156	Albert Pujols/500 **RC**	250.00

157	Joe Crede	8.00
158	Jack Cust	4.00
159	Ben Sheets/500	40.00
160	Alex Escobar	4.00
161	Adrian Hernandez **RC**	4.00
162	Pedro Feliz	4.00
163	Nate Frese **RC**	4.00
164	Carlos Garcia **RC**	4.00
165	Marcus Giles	4.00
166	Alexis Gomez **RC**	4.00
167	Jason Hart	4.00
168	Eric Hinske **RC**	8.00
169	Cesar Izturis	4.00
170	Nick Johnson	4.00
171	Mike Young	4.00
172	Brian Lawrence **RC**	4.00
173	Steve Lomasney	4.00
174	Nick Maness **RC**	4.00
175	Jose Mieses **RC**	4.00
176	Greg Miller **RC**	4.00
177	Eric Munson	4.00
178	Xavier Nady	4.00
179	Blaine Neal **RC**	4.00
180	Abraham Nunez	4.00
181	Jose Ortiz	4.00
182	Jeremy Owens **RC**	4.00
183	Pablo Ozuna	4.00
184	Corey Patterson	4.00
185	Carlos Pena	6.00
186	Wily Mo Pena	4.00
187	Timo Perez	4.00
188	Adam Pettyjohn **RC**	4.00
189	Luis Rivas	4.00
190	Jackson Melian **RC**	4.00
191	Wilken Ruan **RC**	4.00
192	Duaner Sanchez **RC**	4.00
193	Alfonso Soriano	8.00
194	Rafael Soriano **RC**	6.00
195	Ichiro Suzuki **RC**	60.00
196	Billy Sylvester **RC**	4.00
197	Juan Uribe **RC**	4.00
198	Eric Valent	4.00
199	Carlos Valderrama **RC**	4.00
200	Matt White **RC**	4.00
201	Alex Rodriguez	2.50
202	Barry Bonds	3.00
203	Cal Ripken Jr.	3.00
204	Chipper Jones	1.00
205	Derek Jeter	2.50
206	Troy Glaus	.50
207	Frank Thomas	.75
208	Greg Maddux	1.50
209	Ivan Rodriguez	.50
210	Jeff Bagwell	.50
211	Todd Helton	.50
212	Ken Griffey Jr.	1.50
213	Manny Ramirez	.75
214	Mark McGwire	1.50
215	Mike Piazza	1.50
216	Pedro Martinez	.75
217	Sammy Sosa	1.00
218	Tony Gwynn	1.00
219	Vladimir Guerrero	.75
220	Nomar Garciaparra	.75

Stat Line Career

NM/M

Cards #1-150 print run 251-400:	3-6X
1-150 p/r 201-250:	4-8X
1-150 p/r 151-200:	4-8X
1-150 p/r 101-150:	5-10X
1-150 p/r 61-100:	10-20X
1-150 p/r 41-60:	20-30X
1-150 p/r 21-40:	25-40X
1-150 p/r 15-20:	30-60X
Common (151-200) p/r 251-400:	1.00
Common (151-200) p/r 151-250:	1.00
Common (151-200) p/r 101-150:	2.00
Common (151-200) p/r 76-100:	2.00
Common (151-200) p/r 31-75:	4.00
Common (151-200) p/r 20-30:	6.00
cards 201-220 p/r 201-400:	1-2X
201-220 p/r 101-200:	2-4X
201-220 p/r 75-100:	3-5X
201-220 p/r 40-74:	4-8X
156	Albert Pujols/154	150.00
190	Jackson Melian/26	50.00
195	Ichiro Suzuki/106	200.00

Stat Line Season

NM/M

Cards #1-150 print run 151-200:	4-8X

1-150 p/r 101-150:	4-8X
1-150 p/r 76-100:	10-20X
1-150 p/r 51-75:	10-20X
1-150 p/r 36-50:	15-25X
1-150 p/r 21-35:	20-40X
Common (151-200) p/r 151-200:	1.00
Common (151-200) p/r 101-150:	1.00
Common (151-200) p/r 101-150:	1.00
Common (151-200) p/r 76-100:	2.00
Common (151-200) p/r 31-75:	3.00
Common (151-200) p/r 20-30	6.00
cards 201-220 p/r 151-200:	1-3X
201-220 p/r 101-150:	2-4X
201-220 p/r 75-100:	3-5X
201-220 p/r 40-74:	4-8X
156	Albert Pujols/17	400.00
190	Jackson Melian/73	40.00
195	Ichiro Suzuki/153	150.00

All-Time Diamond Kings

NM/M

Complete Set (10):	150.00
Common Player:	8.00
Production 2,500 Sets	
Studio Series:	2-3X
Production 250	
#9 Undetermined Redemp.	
1a	Frank Robinson	8.00
1b	Willie Mays (Should have	
	been ATDK-9.)	25.00
2	Harmon Killebrew	8.00
3	Mike Schmidt	20.00
5	Reggie Jackson	8.00
5	Nolan Ryan	35.00
7	George Brett	20.00
7	Tom Seaver	10.00
9	Hank Aaron	25.00
9	Redemption, Willie Mays	
	(See #1b.)	
10	Stan Musial	20.00

All-Time Diamond Kings
Autograph

NM/M

Production 50 Sets	
1	Frank Robinson	75.00
1	Willie Mays	200.00
2	Harmon Killebrew	80.00
3	Mike Schmidt	150.00
5	Reggie Jackson	80.00
5	Nolan Ryan	250.00
6	George Brett	200.00
7	Tom Seaver	85.00
8	Hank Aaron	275.00
10	Stan Musial	120.00

Bat Kings

NM/M

Common Card:	10.00
Production 250 Sets	
1	Ivan Rodriguez	10.00
2	Tony Gwynn	25.00
3	Barry Bonds	50.00
4	Todd Helton	10.00
5	Troy Glaus	10.00
6	Mike Schmidt	40.00

7	Reggie Jackson	15.00
8	Harmon Killebrew	15.00
9	Frank Robinson	15.00
10	Hank Aaron	75.00

Bat Kings Autograph

NM/M

Production 50 Sets
1	Ivan Rodriguez	75.00
2	Tony Gwynn	120.00
3	Barry Bonds/No Auto.	50.00
3	Barry Bonds/ Auto.	200.00
4	Todd Helton	65.00
5	Troy Glaus	65.00
6	Mike Schmidt	150.00
7	Reggie Jackson	100.00
8	Harmon Killebrew	100.00
9	Frank Robinson	100.00
10	Hank Aaron	300.00

2001 Donruss Baseball's Best

NM/M

Complete Set, Bronze (330): 100.00
999 produced
Stars: 2-3X
Complete Set, Silver (330): 300.00
499 produced
Stars: 2-4X
Complete Set, Gold (330): 550.00
99 produced
Stars: 4-8X
(See 2001 Donruss, The Rookies, Rookies DK for checklists and base values.)

Diamond Kings Reprints

NM/M

Complete Set (20): 160.00
Common Player: 5.00
#'d to yr. produced
1	Rod Carew	5.00
2	Nolan Ryan	25.00
3	Tom Seaver	10.00
4	Carlton Fisk	10.00
5	Reggie Jackson	12.00
6	Steve Carlton	5.00
7	Johnny Bench	10.00
8	Joe Morgan	5.00
9	Mike Schmidt	20.00
10	Wade Boggs	15.00
11	Cal Ripken Jr.	25.00
12	Tony Gwynn	15.00
13	Andre Dawson	5.00
14	Ozzie Smith	15.00
15	George Brett	20.00
16	Dave Winfield	5.00
17	Paul Molitor	10.00
18	Will Clark	5.00
19	Robin Yount	10.00
20	Ken Griffey Jr.	17.50

Diamond Kings Reprints Autograph

NM/M

Common Player:

PAUL MOLITOR

DKR1	Rod Carew/82	40.00
DKR2	Nolan Ryan/82	150.00
DKR3	Tom SeaveR/82	75.00
DKR4	Carlton Fisk/82	65.00
DKR5	Reggie Jackson/83	60.00
DKR6	Steve Carlton/83	40.00
DKR7	Johnny Bench/83	80.00
DKR8	Joe Morgan/83	30.00
DKR9	Mike Schmidt/84	120.00
DKR10	Wade Boggs/84	60.00
DKR11	Cal Ripken Jr./85	180.00
DKR12	Tony Gwynn/86	80.00
DKR13	Andre Dawson/86	35.00
DKR14	Ozzie Smith/87	80.00
DKR15	George Brett/87	120.00
DKR16	Dave Winfield/87	40.00
DKR17	Paul Molitor/88	60.00
DKR18	Will Clark/88	75.00
DKR19	Robin Yount/89	80.00
DKR20	Ken Griffey Jr./89/No Auto.	25.00

Elite Series

NM/M

Complete Set (20): 75.00
Common Player: 2.00
Production 2,500 Sets
Dominators: 5-8X
Production 25 Sets
1	Vladimir Guerrero	4.00
2	Cal Ripken Jr.	10.00
3	Greg Maddux	5.00
4	Alex Rodriguez	8.00
5	Barry Bonds	10.00
6	Chipper Jones	5.00
7	Derek Jeter	10.00
8	Ivan Rodriguez	2.50
9	Ken Griffey Jr.	7.00
10	Mark McGwire	8.00
11	Mike Piazza	7.00
12	Nomar Garciaparra	7.00
13	Pedro Martinez	4.00
14	Randy Johnson	4.00
15	Roger Clemens	6.00
16	Sammy Sosa	7.00
17	Tony Gwynn	5.00
18	Darin Erstad	3.00
19	Andruw Jones	4.00
20	Bernie Williams	2.00

Jersey Kings

NM/M

Common Card: 25.00
Production 250 Sets

1	Vladimir Guerrero	15.00
2	Cal Ripken Jr.	50.00
3	Greg Maddux	25.00
4	Chipper Jones	15.00
5	Roger Clemens	25.00
6	George Brett	30.00
7	Tom Seaver	15.00
8	Nolan Ryan	50.00
9	Stan Musial	30.00
10	Willie Mays	30.00

Jersey Kings Autographs

NM/M

Production 50 Sets
1	Vladimir Guerrero	90.00
2	Cal Ripken Jr.	225.00
3	Greg Maddux	150.00
4	Chipper Jones	100.00
5	Roger Clemens	150.00
6	George Brett	200.00
7	Tom Seaver	75.00
8	Nolan Ryan	200.00
9	Stan Musial	120.00
10	Ozzie Smith	100.00

Longball Leaders

NM/M

Complete Set (20): 50.00
Common Player: 1.00
Production 1,000 Sets
Die-Cut Parallel: 3-5X
#'d to '00 HR Total
1	Vladimir Guerrero	4.00
2	Alex Rodriguez	8.00
3	Barry Bonds	10.00
4	Troy Glaus	4.00
5	Frank Thomas	4.00
6	Jeff Bagwell	4.00
7	Todd Helton	4.00
8	Ken Griffey Jr.	6.00
9	Manny Ramirez	4.00
10	Mike Piazza	6.00
11	Sammy Sosa	6.00
12	Carlos Delgado	2.00
13	Jim Edmonds	1.00
14	Jason Giambi	3.00
15	David Justice	1.00
16	Rafael Palmeiro	3.00
17	Gary Sheffield	2.00
18	Jim Thome	1.00
19	Tony Batista	1.00
20	Richard Hidalgo	1.00

Production Line

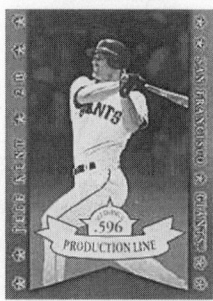

NM/M

Complete Set (60): 150.00

Common Player: .50
Die-Cut OBP (1-20): 1-2X
Die-Cut SLG (21-40): 1-2.5X
Die-Cut PI (41-60): 1.5-3X
Production 100 Sets
1	Jason Giambi/476	3.00
2	Carlos Delgado/470	2.00
3	Todd Helton/463	3.00
4	Manny Ramirez/457	3.00
5	Barry Bonds/440	15.00
6	Gary Sheffield/438	2.00
7	Frank Thomas/436	3.00
8	Nomar Garciaparra/434	10.00
9	Brian Giles/432	1.00
10	Edgardo Alfonzo/425	.50
11	Jeff Kent/424	.75
12	Jeff Bagwell/424	3.00
13	Edgar Martinez/423	.75
14	Alex Rodriguez/420	10.00
15	Luis Castillo/418	.50
16	Will Clark/418	2.50
17	Jorge Posada/417	2.00
18	Derek Jeter/416	12.00
19	Bob Abreu/416	1.00
20	Moises Alou/416	.75
21	Todd Helton/698	3.00
22	Manny Ramirez/697	3.00
23	Barry Bonds/688	15.00
24	Carlos Delgado/664	2.00
25	Vladimir Guerrero/664	3.00
26	Jason Giambi/647	3.00
27	Gary Sheffield/643	2.00
28	Richard Hidalgo/636	.50
29	Sammy Sosa/634	8.00
30	Frank Thomas/625	3.00
31	Moises Alou/623	.75
32	Jeff Bagwell/615	3.00
33	Mike Piazza/614	8.00
34	Alex Rodriguez/606	10.00
35	Troy Glaus/604	3.00
36	Nomar Garciaparra/599	10.00
37	Jeff Kent/596	3.00
38	Brian Giles/594	.75
39	Geoff Jenkins/588	.50
40	Carl Everett/587	.50
41	Todd Helton/1161	3.00
42	Manny Ramirez/1154	3.00
43	Carlos Delgado/1134	2.00
44	Barry Bonds/1128	12.00
45	Jason Giambi/1123	3.00
46	Gary Sheffield/1081	2.00
47	Vladimir Guerrero/1074	3.00
48	Frank Thomas/1061	3.00
49	Sammy Sosa/1040	8.00
50	Moises Alou/1039	1.00
51	Jeff Bagwell/1039	3.00
52	Nomar Garciaparra/1033	10.00
53	Richard Hidalgo/1027	.50
54	Alex Rodriguez/1026	10.00
55	Brian Giles/1026	1.00
56	Jeff Kent/1020	1.00
57	Mike Piazza/1012	8.00
58	Troy Glaus/1008	3.00
59	Edgar Martinez/1002	1.00
60	Jim Edmonds/994	1.00

Rookie Reprints

NM/M

Complete Set (40): 200.00
Common Player: 3.00
#'d to Original Yr. issued
1	Cal Ripken Jr.	20.00
2	Wade Boggs	10.00
3	Tony Gwynn	10.00
4	Ryne Sandberg	10.00
5	Don Mattingly	12.00
6	Joe Carter	3.00
7	Roger Clemens	15.00
8	Kirby Puckett	10.00
9	Orel Hershiser	3.00
10	Andres Galarraga	3.00
11	Jose Canseco	5.00
12	Fred McGriff	3.00
13	Paul O'Neill	3.00
14	Mark McGwire	15.00
15	Barry Bonds	20.00
16	Kevin Brown	3.00
17	David Cone	3.00
18	Rafael Palmeiro	8.00
19	Barry Larkin	3.00
20	Bo Jackson	5.00

21 Greg Maddux 10.00
22 Roberto Alomar 4.00
23 Mark Grace 3.00
24 David Wells 3.00
25 Tom Glavine 4.00
26 Matt Williams 3.00
27 Ken Griffey Jr. 12.00
28 Randy Johnson 8.00
29 Gary Sheffield 5.00
30 Craig Biggio 3.00
31 Curt Schilling 5.00
32 Larry Walker 3.00
33 Bernie Williams 4.00
34 Sammy Sosa 12.00
35 Juan Gonzalez 8.00
36 David Justice 3.00
37 Ivan Rodriguez 6.00
38 Jeff Bagwell 8.00
39 Jeff Kent 3.00
40 Manny Ramirez 8.00

Rookie Reprints Autographs

NM/M
Common Player:
#'d to last 2 digits of yr. issued
1 Cal Ripken/82 150.00
2 Wade Boggs/83 40.00
3 Tony Gwynn/83 75.00
4 Ryne Sandberg/83 100.00
5 Don Mattingly/84 100.00
6 Joe Carter/84 20.00
7 Roger Clemens/85 200.00
8 Kirby Puckett/85 60.00
9 Orel Hershiser/85 25.00
10 Andres Galarraga/86 30.00
15 Barry Bonds/87 200.00
16 Kevin Brown/87 30.00
17 David Cone/87 30.00
18 Rafael Palmeiro/87 50.00
20 Bo Jackson/87 85.00
21 Greg Maddux/87 150.00
22 Roberto Alomar/88 40.00
24 David Wells/88 25.00
25 Tom Glavine/88 40.00
28 Randy Johnson/89 100.00
29 Gary Sheffield/89 50.00
31 Curt Schilling/89 75.00
35 Juan Gonzalez/90 40.00
36 David Justice/90 25.00
37 Ivan Rodriguez/91 40.00
39 Manny Ramirez/91 100.00

1999 Diamond Kings

NM/M
Complete Set (5): 40.00
Common Player: 8.00
Production 2,500 Sets
1 Scott Rolen 8.00
2 Sammy Sosa 10.00
3 Juan Gonzalez 8.00
4 Ken Griffey Jr. 10.00
5 Derek Jeter 20.00

1999 Retro

NM/M
Complete Set (100): 200.00
Common Player: .25

Inserted 1:Hobby Pack
Common (81-100): 3.00
Production 1:1999
1 Ken Griffey Jr. 2.00
2 Nomar Garciaparra 2.00
3 Alex Rodriguez 3.00
4 Mark McGwire 2.50
5 Sammy Sosa 2.00
6 Chipper Jones 1.50
7 Mike Piazza 2.00
8 Barry Larkin .50
9 Andruw Jones 1.00
10 Albert Belle .25
11 Jeff Bagwell 1.00
12 Tony Gwynn 1.50
13 Manny Ramirez 1.00
14 Mo Vaughn .25
15 Barry Bonds 4.00
16 Frank Thomas 1.00
17 Vladimir Guerrero 1.00
18 Derek Jeter 3.00
19 Randy Johnson 1.00
20 Greg Maddux 1.50
21 Pedro Martinez 1.00
22 Cal Ripken Jr. 3.00
23 Ivan Rodriguez .75
24 Matt Williams .25
25 Javy Lopez .25
26 Tim Salmon .25
27 Raul Mondesi .25
28 Todd Helton 1.00
29 Magglio Ordonez .75
30 Sean Casey .25
31 Jeromy Burnitz .25
32 Jeff Kent .25
33 Jim Edmonds .25
34 Jim Thome .25
35 Dante Bichette .25
36 Larry Walker .25
37 Will Clark .50
38 Omar Vizquel .50
39 Mike Mussina .50
40 Eric Karros .25
41 Kenny Lofton .25
42 David Justice .25
43 Craig Biggio .50
44 J.D. Drew .25
45 Rickey Henderson 1.00
46 Bernie Williams .50
47 Brian Giles .25
48 Paul O'Neill .50
49 Orlando Hernandez .50
50 Jason Giambi .50
51 Curt Schilling 1.00
52 Scott Rolen 1.00
53 Mark Grace .50
54 Moises Alou .50
55 Jason Kendall .25
56 Ray Lankford .25
57 Kerry Wood .50
58 Gary Sheffield .75
59 Ruben Mateo .25
60 Darin Erstad .25
61 Troy Glaus 1.00
62 Jose Canseco .50
63 Wade Boggs 1.50
64 Tom Glavine .50
65 Gabe Kapler .25
66 Juan Gonzalez 1.00
67 Rafael Palmeiro .75
68 Richie Sexson .25
69 Carl Everett .25
70 David Wells .25
71 Carlos Delgado .75
72 Eric Davis .50
73 Shawn Green .50
74 Andres Galarraga .25
75 Edgar Martinez .25
76 Roberto Alomar .50
77 John Olerud .25
78 Luis Gonzalez .25
79 Kevin Brown .25
80 Roger Clemens 2.00
81 Josh Beckett 5.00
82 Alfonso Soriano 8.00
83 Alex Escobar .50
84 Pat Burrell .50
85 Eric Chavez .50
86 Erubiel Durazo .50
87 Abraham Nunez .50
88 Carlos Pena 2.00
89 Nick Johnson .50
90 Eric Munson .50
91 Corey Patterson .50
92 Wily Mo Pena .50
93 Rafael Furcal 1.00
94 Eric Valent .50
95 Mark Mulder 1.00
96 Chad Hutchinson 1.00
97 Freddy Garcia .50
98 Tim Hudson 1.00
99 Rick Ankiel 1.00
100 Kip Wells .50

1999 Retro Stat Line Career

NM/M
Cards #1-80 print run 251-400: 2-3X
(1-80) p/r 151-250: 2-4X
(1-80) p/r 101-150: 3-6X
(1-80) p/r 76-100: 4-8X
(1-80) p/r 51-75: 5-10X
(1-80) p/r 30-50: 8-15X
1 Ken Griffey Jr./350 20.00
2 Nomar Garciaparra/309 20.00
3 Alex Rodriguez/313 20.00

4 Mark McGwire/219 25.00
5 Sammy Sosa/273 12.00
6 Chipper Jones/297 15.00
7 Mike Piazza/333 20.00
8 Barry Larkin/305 5.00
9 Andruw Jones/273 6.00
10 Albert Belle/321 2.50
11 Jeff Bagwell/304 8.00
12 Tony Gwynn/339 12.00
13 Manny Ramirez/154 15.00
14 Mo Vaughn/304 2.50
15 Barry Bonds/290 12.00
16 Frank Thomas/286 10.00
17 Vladimir Guerrero/305 10.00
18 Derek Jeter/308 25.00
19 Randy Johnson/336 8.00
20 Greg Maddux/202 20.00
21 Pedro Martinez/298 10.00
22 Cal Ripken Jr./276 25.00
23 Ivan Rodriguez/232 8.00
24 Matt Williams/299 4.00
25 Javy Lopez/333 2.50
26 Tim Salmon/179 4.00
27 Raul Mondesi/295 2.50
28 Todd Helton/310 8.00
29 Magglio Ordonez/173 4.00
30 Sean Casey/269 2.50
31 Jeromy Burnitz/294 2.50
32 Jeff Kent/193 5.00
33 Jim Edmonds/294 5.00
34 Jim Thome/163 4.00
35 Dante Bichette/300 2.50
36 Larry Walker/225 8.00
37 Will Clark/302 6.00
38 Omar Vizquel/196 4.00
39 Mike Mussina/118 10.00
40 Eric Karros/177 4.00
41 Kenny Lofton/311 2.50
42 David Justice/214 5.00
43 Craig Biggio/218 2.50
44 J.D. Drew/35 25.00
45 Rickey Henderson/283 6.00
46 Bernie Williams/213 6.00
47 Brian Giles/157 4.00
48 Paul O'Neill/223 5.00
49 Orlando Hernandez/313 2.50
50 Jason Giambi/73 15.00
51 Curt Schilling/336 2.50
52 Scott Rolen/220 5.00
53 Mark Grace/310 2.50
54 Moises Alou/201 3.00
55 Jason Kendall/308 2.50
56 Ray Lankford/225 3.00
57 Kerry Wood/233 3.00
58 Gary Sheffield/202 5.00
59 Ruben Mateo/384 2.50
60 Darin Erstad/179 3.00
61 Troy Glaus/218 10.00
62 Jose Canseco/296 6.00
63 Wade Boggs/329 4.00
64 Tom Glavine/331 5.00
66 Juan Gonzalez/301 5.00
67 Rafael Palmeiro/314 5.00
68 Richie Sexson/308 2.50
69 Carl Everett/209 3.00
70 David Wells/124 5.00
71 Carlos Delgado/333 6.00
72 Eric Davis/342 2.50
73 Shawn Green/77 15.00
74 Andres Galarraga/364 4.00
75 Edgar Martinez/318 4.00
76 Roberto Alomar/302 6.00
77 John Olerud/301 2.50
78 Luis Gonzalez/237 3.00
79 Kevin Brown/330 2.50
80 Roger Clemens/295 12.00
82 Alfonso Soriano/113 15.00
83 Alex Escobar/181 10.00
84 Pat Burrell/303 12.00
85 Eric Chavez/314 2.50
86 Erubiel Durazo/147 5.00
87 Abraham Nunez/106 15.00
88 Carlos Pena/46 25.00
89 Nick Johnson/259 6.00
90 Eric Munson/392 6.00
91 Corey Patterson/117 15.00
92 Wily Mo Pena/247 8.00
93 Rafael Furcal/137 20.00
94 Eric Valent/53 10.00
97 Freddy Garcia/397 6.00
98 Tim Hudson/17 50.00

99 Rick Ankiel/222 10.00
100 Kip Wells/371 2.50

1999 Retro Stat Line Season

NM/M
Cards #1-80 print run 251-400: 2-3X
(1-80) p/r 151-250: 2-4X
(1-80) p/r 101-150: 3-6X
(1-80) p/r 76-100: 4-8X
(1-80) p/r 51-75: 5-10X
(1-80) p/r 30-50: 8-15X
1 Ken Griffey Jr./56 70.00
2 Nomar Garciaparra/35 100.00
3 Alex Rodriguez/42 100.00
4 Mark McGwire/70 80.00
5 Sammy Sosa/66 40.00
6 Chipper Jones/123 30.00
7 Mike Piazza/111 50.00
8 Barry Larkin/166 8.00
9 Andruw Jones/31 30.00
10 Albert Belle/49 8.00
11 Jeff Bagwell/164 12.00
12 Tony Gwynn/148 25.00
13 Manny Ramirez/145 20.00
14 Mo Vaughn/40 10.00
15 Barry Bonds/120 25.00
16 Frank Thomas/155 15.00
17 Vladimir Guerrero/38 40.00
18 Derek Jeter/127 60.00
19 Randy Johnson/19 75.00
20 Pedro Martinez/19 80.00
21 Cal Ripken Jr./163 40.00
22 Ivan Rodriguez/186 12.00
23 Matt Williams/136 8.00
24 Javy Lopez/106 6.00
25 Tim Salmon/139 5.00
26 Raul Mondesi/162 4.00
27 Todd Helton/25 60.00
28 Magglio Ordonez/151 4.00
29 Sean Casey/82 8.00
30 Jeromy Burnitz/125 5.00
31 Jeff Kent/128 8.00
32 Jim Edmonds/115 12.00
33 Jim Thome/129 6.00
34 Dante Bichette/122 5.00
35 Larry Walker/113 15.00
36 Will Clark/169 10.00
37 Omar Vizquel/166 4.00
38 Mike Mussina/175 10.00
39 Eric Karros/150 5.00
40 Kenny Lofton/54 10.00
41 David Justice/151 6.00
42 Craig Biggio/51 10.00
43 Rickey Henderson/66 25.00
44 Bernie Williams/26 30.00
45 Brian Giles/94 6.00
46 Paul O'Neill/116 4.00
47 Orlando Hernandez/12 35.00
48 Jason Giambi/166 10.00
49 Curt Schilling/15 40.00
50 Scott Rolen/31 30.00
51 Mark Grace/92 15.00
52 Moises Alou/124 5.00
53 Jason Kendall/175 4.00
54 Ray Lankford/156 4.00
55 Kerry Wood/13 50.00
56 Gary Sheffield/132 10.00
57 Ruben Mateo/134 5.00
58 Darin Erstad/159 10.00
59 Jose Canseco/46 30.00
60 Wade Boggs/122 15.00
61 Tom Glavine/29 50.00
62 Gabe Kapler/25 20.00
63 Juan Gonzalez/50 30.00
64 Rafael Palmeiro/121 10.00
65 Carl Everett/138 5.00
66 David Wells/163 4.00
67 Carlos Delgado/155 10.00
68 Eric Davis/148 5.00
69 Shawn Green/100 12.00
70 Andres Galarraga/44 20.00
71 Edgar Martinez/102 10.00
72 Roberto Alomar/166 15.00
73 John Olerud/22 20.00
74 Luis Gonzalez/146 5.00
75 Kevin Brown/19 18.00
76 Roger Clemens/20 120.00
77 Josh Beckett/178 10.00
78 Alex Escobar/27 40.00
85 Eric Chavez/33 15.00
86 Erubiel Durazo/19 20.00

87	Abraham Nunez/95	10.00
88	Carlos Pena/319	6.00
89	Nick Johnson/17	50.00
90	Eric Munson/16	40.00
91	Corey Patterson/22	40.00
93	Rafael Furcal/88	20.00
95	Mark Mulder/113	6.00
96	Chad Hutchinson/51	6.00
98	Tim Hudson/152	15.00
99	Rick Ankiel/12	40.00
100	Kip Wells/135	2.50

2000 Diamond Kings

		NM/M
Complete Set (5):		35.00
Common Player:		8.00
Production 2,500 Sets		
Studio:		1-2X
Production 250 Sets		
1	Frank Thomas	8.00
2	Greg Maddux	9.00
3	Alex Rodriguez	10.00
4	Jeff Bagwell	8.00
5	Manny Ramirez	8.00

2000 Retro

		NM/M
Complete Set (100):		90.00
Common Player:		.25
Common (81-100):		3.00
Production 2,000		
1	Vladimir Guerrero	1.00
2	Alex Rodriguez	4.00
3	Ken Griffey Jr.	2.50
4	Nomar Garciaparra	1.00
5	Mike Piazza	1.50
6	Mark McGwire	2.00
7	Sammy Sosa	1.50
8	Chipper Jones	1.00
9	Jim Edmonds	.50
10	Tony Gwynn	1.00
11	Andruw Jones	.75
12	Albert Belle	.25
13	Jeff Bagwell	.75
14	Manny Ramirez	1.00
15	Mo Vaughn	.25
16	Barry Bonds	4.00
17	Frank Thomas	1.00
18	Ivan Rodriguez	.75
19	Derek Jeter	4.00
20	Randy Johnson	1.00
21	Greg Maddux	1.00
22	Pedro Martinez	1.00
23	Cal Ripken Jr.	4.00
24	Mark Grace	.50
25	Javy Lopez	.25
26	Ray Durham	.25
27	Todd Helton	1.00
28	Magglio Ordonez	.75
29	Sean Casey	.25
30	Darin Erstad	.50
31	Barry Larkin	.50
32	Will Clark	.50
33	Jim Thome	.75
34	Dante Bichette	.25
35	Larry Walker	.50
36	Ken Caminiti	.25
37	Omar Vizquel	.25
38	Miguel Tejada	.50
39	Eric Karros	.25
40	Gary Sheffield	.75
41	Jeff Cirillo	.25
42	Rondell White	.25
43	Rickey Henderson	.75
44	Bernie Williams	.50
45	Brian Giles	.25
46	Paul O'Neill	.50
47	Orlando Hernandez	.25
48	Ben Grieve	.25
49	Jason Giambi	.50
50	Curt Schilling	1.00
51	Scott Rolen	1.00
52	Bobby Abreu	.50
53	Jason Kendall	.25
54	Fernando Tatis	.25
55	Jeff Kent	.25
56	Mike Mussina	.50
57	Troy Glaus	.75
58	Jose Canseco	.50
59	Wade Boggs	1.00
60	Fred McGriff	.25
61	Juan Gonzalez	.75
62	Rafael Palmeiro	.75
63	Rusty Greer	.25
64	Carl Everett	.25
65	David Wells	.25
66	Carlos Delgado	.50
67	Shawn Green	.40
68	David Justice	.25
69	Edgar Martinez	.25
70	Andres Galarraga	.25
71	Roberto Alomar	.50
72	Jermaine Dye	.25
73	John Olerud	.25
74	Luis Gonzalez	.25
75	Craig Biggio	.50
76	Kevin Millwood	.25
77	Kevin Brown	.25
78	John Smoltz	.50
79	Roger Clemens	3.00
80	Mike Hampton	.25
81	Tomas De La Rosa	.25
82	C.C. Sabathia	1.00
83	Ryan Christenson	.25
84	Pedro Feliz	.50
85	Jose Ortiz	.25
86	Xavier Nady	.50
87	Julio Zuleta	.25
88	Jason Hart	.25
89	Keith Ginter	.25
90	Brent Abernathy	.25
91	Timo Perez	.50
92	Juan Pierre	.50
93	Tike Redman	.50
94	Mike Lamb	.50
95	Ben Sheets	1.00
96	Kazuhiro Sasaki	.50
97	Barry Zito	1.00
98	Adam Bernero	.25
99	Chad Durbin	.25
100	Matt Ginter	.25

2000 Retro Stat Line Career

	NM/M
Cards #1-80 print run 251-400:	2-3X
1-80 p/r 151-250:	2-4X
1-80 p/r 101-150:	3-6X
1-80 p/r 76-100:	4-8X
1-80 p/r 51-75:	5-10X
1-80 p/r 31-50:	8-15X
1-80 p/r 21-30:	15-25X
Common (81-100) p/r 251-400:	1.00
Common (81-100) p/r 151-250:	1.00
Common (81-100) p/r 101-150:	2.00
Common (81-100) p/r 76-100:	2.00
Common (81-100) p/r 31-75:	3.00

2000 Retro Stat Line Season

	NM/M
Cards #1-80 print run 251-400:	2-3X
1-80 p/r 151-250:	2-4X
1-80 p/r 101-150:	3-6X
1-80 p/r 76-100:	4-8X
1-80 p/r 51-75:	5-10X
1-80 p/r 21-30:	15-25X
Common (81-100) p/r 151-200:	1.00
Common (81-100) p/r 81-150:	2.00
Common (81-100) p/r 51-80:	2.00

2001 Diamond Kings

		NM/M
Complete Set (20):		150.00
Common Player:		5.00
Production 2,500 Sets		
Studio Canvas Parallel:		1-2X
Production 250		
1	Alex Rodriguez	12.50
2	Cal Ripken Jr.	15.00
3	Mark McGwire	12.50
4	Ken Griffey Jr.	10.00
5	Derek Jeter	15.00
6	Nomar Garciaparra	10.00
7	Mike Piazza	10.00
8	Roger Clemens	9.00
9	Greg Maddux	8.00
10	Chipper Jones	8.00
11	Tony Gwynn	8.00
12	Barry Bonds	15.00
13	Sammy Sosa	10.00
14	Vladimir Guerrero	6.00
15	Frank Thomas	6.00
16	Troy Glaus	6.00
17	Todd Helton	6.00
18	Ivan Rodriguez	5.00
19	Pedro Martinez	6.00
20	Carlos Delgado	5.00

2001 Diamond Kings Studio Series Autograph

		NM/M
Common Autograph:		50.00
Production 50 Sets		
1	Alex Rodriguez	180.00
2	Cal Ripken Jr.	250.00
8	Roger Clemens	150.00
9	Greg Maddux	150.00
10	Chipper Jones	100.00
11	Tony Gwynn	80.00
14	Vladimir Guerrero	100.00
16	Troy Glaus	50.00
17	Todd Helton	60.00
18	Ivan Rodriguez	60.00

2001 Donruss Class of 2001

RAMON VAZQUEZ

		NM/M
Complete Set (300):		
Common Player:		.20
Common (101-200):		3.00
Production 1,875		
Common (201-300):		3.00
Production 625		
Pack (3):		6.00
Box (24 + Bobble Head):		125.00
1	Alex Rodriguez	2.00
2	Barry Bonds	2.50
3	Vladimir Guerrero	.75
4	Jim Edmonds	.20
5	Derek Jeter	2.50
6	Jose Canseco	.40
7	Rafael Furcal	.20
8	Cal Ripken Jr.	2.50
9	Brad Radke	.20
10	Miguel Tejada	.40
11	Pat Burrell	.50
12	Ken Griffey Jr.	1.50
13	Cliff Floyd	.20
14	Luis Gonzalez	.20
15	Frank Thomas	.75
16	Mike Sweeney	.20
17	Paul LoDuca	.20
18	Lance Berkman	.20
19	Tony Gwynn	1.00
20	Chipper Jones	1.00
21	Eric Chavez	.40
22	Kerry Wood	.35
23	Jorge Posada	.40
24	J.D. Drew	.50
25	Garret Anderson	.20
26	Mike Piazza	1.50
27	Kenny Lofton	.20
28	Mike Mussina	.40
29	Paul Konerko	.20
30	Bernie Williams	.20
31	Eric Milton	.20
32	Shawn Green	.40
33	Paul O'Neill	.20
34	Juan Gonzalez	.35
35	Andres Galarraga	.20
36	Gary Sheffield	.40
37	Ben Grieve	.20
38	Scott Rolen	.60
39	Mark Grace	.20
40	Hideo Nomo	.35
41	Barry Zito	.50
42	Edgar Martinez	.20
43	Jarrod Washburn	.20
44	Greg Maddux	1.00
45	Mark Buehrle	.20
46	Larry Walker	.20
47	Trot Nixon	.20
48	Nomar Garciaparra	1.50
49	Robert Fick	.20
50	Sean Casey	.40
51	Joe Mays	.20
52	Roger Clemens	1.50
53	Chan Ho Park	.20
54	Carlos Delgado	.50
55	Phil Nevin	.20
56	Jason Giambi	.50
57	Raul Mondesi	.20
58	Roberto Alomar	.35
59	Ryan Klesko	.20
60	Andruw Jones	.75
61	Gabe Kapler	.20
62	Darin Erstad	.35
63	Cristian Guzman	.20
64	Kazuhiro Sasaki	.20
65	Doug Mientkiewicz	.20
66	Sammy Sosa	1.50
67	Mike Hampton	.20
68	Rickey Henderson	.75
69	Mark Mulder	.30
70	Mark McGwire	2.00
71	Freddy Garcia	.20
72	Ivan Rodriguez	.60
73	Terrence Long	.20
74	Jeff Bagwell	.75
75	Moises Alou	.20
76	Todd Helton	.65
77	Preston Wilson	.20
78	Pedro Martinez	.75
79	Bobby Abreu	.20
80	Manny Ramirez	.75
81	Jose Vidro	.20
82	Randy Johnson	.75
83	Richie Sexson	.20
84	Troy Glaus	.65
85	Kevin Brown	.20
86	Carlos Lee	.20
87	Adrian Beltre	.30
88	Brian Giles	.20
89	Jermaine Dye	.20
90	Craig Biggio	.20
91	Richard Hidalgo	.20
92	Magglio Ordonez	.20
93	Aramis Ramirez	.20
94	Jeff Kent	.20
95	Curt Schilling	.50
96	Tim Hudson	.40
97	Fred McGriff	.20
98	Barry Larkin	.20
99	Jim Thome	.60
100	Tom Glavine	.40
101	Sean Douglass RC	3.00
102	Rob Mackowiak RC	3.00
103	Jeremy Fikac RC	3.00
104	Henry Mateo RC	3.00
105	Geronimo Gil RC	3.00
106	Ramon Vazquez RC	5.00
107	Pedro Santana RC	3.00
108	Ryan Jensen RC	3.00
109	Paul Phillips RC	3.00
110	Saul Rivera RC	3.00
111	Larry Bigbie	3.00
112	Josh Phelps	3.00
113	Justin Kaye RC	3.00
114	Kris Keller RC	3.00
115	Adam Bernero	3.00
116	Victor Zambrano RC	3.00
117	Felipe Lopez	3.00
118	Brian Roberts RC	10.00
119	Kurt Ainsworth	3.00
120	George Perez RC	3.00
121	Wilson Guzman RC	3.00
122	Derrick Lewis RC	3.00
123	Nate Teut RC	3.00
124	Martin Vargas RC	3.00
125	Brandon Inge	3.00
126	Travis Phelps RC	3.00
127	Les Walrond RC	3.00
128	Justin Atchley RC	3.00
129	Studby Clapp RC	3.00
130	Bret Prinz RC	3.00
131	Bert Snow RC	3.00
132	Joe Crede	3.00
133	Nick Punto RC	3.00
134	Carlos Hernandez RC	3.00
135	Ken Vining RC	3.00
136	Luis Pineda RC	3.00
137	Winston Abreu RC	3.00
138	Matt Ginter	3.00
139	Jason Smith RC	3.00
140	Gene Altman RC	3.00
141	Brian Rogers RC	3.00
142	Michael Cuddyer	3.00
143	Mike Penney RC	3.00
144	Scott Podsednik RC	10.00
145	Esix Snead RC	3.00
146	Steve Watkins RC	3.00
147	Orlando Woodards RC	3.00
148	Mike Young	3.00
149	Chris George	3.00
150	Blaine Neal RC	3.00
151	Ben Sheets	3.00
152	Scott Stewart RC	3.00
153	Mike Koplove RC	3.00
154	Kyle Lohse RC	8.00
155	Dee Brown	3.00
156	Aubrey Huff	3.00
157	Pablo Ozuna	3.00
158	Bill Ortega	3.00
159	Toby Hall	3.00
160	Kevin Olsen RC	3.00
161	Will Ohman RC	3.00
162	Nate Cornejo	3.00
163	Jack Cust	3.00
164	Juan Rivera	3.00
165	Jerrod Riggan RC	3.00
166	Dustan Mohr RC	3.00
167	Doug Nickle RC	3.00
168	Craig Monroe RC	3.00
169	Jason Jennings	3.00
170	Bart Miadich RC	3.00
171	Luis Rivas	3.00
172	Tim Christman RC	3.00
173	Luke Hudson RC	3.00
174	Brett Jodie RC	3.00
175	Jorge Julio RC	4.00
176	David Espinosa	3.00
177	Mike Maroth RC	3.00

178	Keith Ginter RC	3.00
179	Juan Moreno RC	3.00
180	Brandon Knight RC	3.00
181	Steve Lomasney	3.00
182	John Grabow RC	3.00
183	Steve Green RC	3.00
184	Jason Karnuth RC	3.00
185	Bob File RC	3.00
186	Brent Abernathy	3.00
187	Morgan Ensberg RC	5.00
188	Wily Mo Pena RC	3.00
189	Ken Harvey	3.00
190	Josh Pearce RC	3.00
191	Cesar Izturis	3.00
192	Eric Hinske RC	5.00
193	Joe Beimel RC	3.00
194	Timo Perez	3.00
195	Troy Mattes RC	3.00
196	Eric Valent	3.00
197	Ed Rogers RC	3.00
198	Grant Balfour RC	3.00
199	Benito Baez RC	3.00
200	Vernon Wells	3.00
201	Joe Kennedy RC	4.00
202	Wilson Betemit RC	8.00
203	Christian Parker RC	3.00
204	Jay Gibbons RC	5.00
205	Carlos Garcia RC	4.00
206	Jack Wilson RC	3.00
207	Johnny Estrada RC	5.00
208	Wilkin Ruan RC	3.00
209	Brandon Duckworth RC	5.00
210	Willie Harris RC	5.00
211	Marlon Byrd RC	8.00
212	C.C. Sabathia	8.00
213	Dennis Tankersley RC	3.00
214	Brandon Larson RC	5.00
215	Alexis Gomez RC	4.00
216	Bill Hall RC	8.00
217	Antonio Perez RC	3.00
218	Jeremy Affeldt RC	4.00
219	Junior Spivey RC	5.00
220	Casey Fossum RC	5.00
221	Brandon Lyon RC	4.00
222	Angel Santos RC	4.00
223	Lance Davis RC	3.00
224	Zach Day RC	4.00
225	David Williams RC	3.00
226	Cesar Crespo RC	3.00
227	Jose Acevedo RC	3.00
228	Travis Hafner RC	20.00
229	Orlando Hudson RC	10.00
230	Jose Mieses RC	3.00
231	Ricardo Rodriguez RC	3.00
232	Alfonso Soriano	3.00
233	Jason Hart	3.00
234	Endy Chavez RC	3.00
235	Delvin James RC	3.00
236	Ryan Drese RC	3.00
237	Jeremy Owens RC	3.00
238	Brad Voyles RC	3.00
239	Nate Frese	3.00
240	Josh Beckett	3.00
241	Roy Oswalt	3.00
242	Juan Uribe RC	5.00
243	Cory Aldridge RC	3.00
244	Adam Dunn	3.00
245	Bud Smith RC	3.00
246	Adrian Hernandez RC	3.00
247	Matt Guerrier RC	3.00
248	Jimmy Rollins	3.00
249	Wilmy Caceres RC	3.00
250	Jason Michaels RC	3.00
251	Ichiro Suzuki RC	50.00
252	John Buck RC	3.00
253	Andres Torres RC	3.00
254	Alfredo Amezaga RC	3.00
255	Corky Miller RC	3.00
256	Rafael Soriano RC	10.00
257	Donaldo Mendez RC	3.00
258	Victor Martinez RC	40.00
259	Corey Patterson	3.00
260	Horacio Ramirez RC	8.00
261	Elpidio Guzman RC	3.00
262	Juan Diaz RC	3.00
263	Mike Rivera RC	3.00
264	Brian Lawrence RC	3.00
265	Josue Perez RC	3.00
266	Jose Nunez	3.00
267	Erik Bedard RC	20.00
268	Albert Pujols RC	150.00
269	Duaner Sanchez RC	3.00
270	Cody Ransom RC	3.00
271	Greg Miller RC	3.00
272	Adam Pettyjohn RC	3.00
273	Tsuyoshi Shinjo RC	3.00
274	Claudio Vargas RC	3.00
275	Justin Duchscherer RC	8.00
276	Tim Spooneybarger RC	3.00
277	Rick Bauer RC	3.00
278	Josh Fogg RC	3.00
279	Brian Reith RC	3.00
280	Scott MacRae RC	3.00
281	Ryan Ludwick RC	15.00
282	Erick Almonte RC	3.00
283	Josh Towers RC	5.00
284	Juan Pena	3.00
285	David Brous RC	3.00
286	Erik Hiljus RC	3.00
287	Nick Neugebauer RC	3.00
288	Jackson Melian RC	3.00
289	Billy Sylvester RC	3.00
290	Carlos Valderrama RC	3.00
291	Jose Cueto RC	3.00
292	Matt White RC	3.00
293	Nick Maness RC	3.00
294	Jason Lane RC	5.00

295	Brandon Berger RC	3.00
296	Angel Berroa RC	5.00
297	Juan Cruz RC	4.00
298	Dewon Brazelton RC	3.00
299	Mark Prior RC	10.00
300	Mark Teixeira RC	40.00

First Class

Stars (1-100):		5-10X
Production 100		
SP's (101-300):		1-3X
Production 50		

Aces

			NM/M
Complete Set (20):			70.00
Common Player:			3.00
Inserted 1:30			
1	Roger Clemens		12.00
2	Randy Johnson		7.50
3	Freddy Garcia		3.00
4	Greg Maddux		10.00
5	Tim Hudson		5.00
6	Curt Schilling		5.00
7	Mark Buehrle		3.00
8	Matt Morris		3.00
9	Joe Mays		3.00
10	Javier Vazquez		3.00
11	Mark Mulder		4.00
12	Wade Miller		3.00
13	Barry Zito		5.00
14	Pedro Martinez		7.50
15	Al Leiter		3.00
16	Chan Ho Park		3.00
17	John Burkett		3.00
18	C.C. Sabathia		3.00
19	Jamie Moyer		3.00
20	Mike Mussina		5.00

Bobblehead

		NM/M
Common Bobblehead:		10.00
One per box.		
1	Ichiro Suzuki	40.00
2	Cal Ripken Jr.	40.00
3	Derek Jeter	35.00
4	Mark McGwire	35.00
5	Albert Pujols	40.00
6	Ken Griffey Jr.	20.00
7	Nomar Garciaparra	20.00
8	Mike Piazza	20.00
9	Alex Rodriguez	20.00
10	Manny Ramirez	10.00
11	Tsuyoshi Shinjo	10.00
12	Hideo Nomo	10.00
13	Chipper Jones	15.00
14	Sammy Sosa	20.00
15	Roger Clemens	17.50
16	Tony Gwynn	15.00
17	Barry Bonds	35.00
18	Kazuhiro Sasaki	10.00
19	Pedro Martinez	10.00
20	Jeff Bagwell	10.00
21	Ichiro Suzuki ROY	40.00
22	Albert Pujols ROY	40.00

Bobblehead Cards

		NM/M
Common Player:		4.00
1-20 2,000 Produced		
21-22 1,000 Produced		
1	Ichiro Suzuki	15.00
2	Cal Ripken Jr.	12.00
3	Derek Jeter	12.00
4	Mark McGwire	10.00
5	Albert Pujols	10.00
6	Ken Griffey Jr.	8.00
7	Nomar Garciaparra	8.00
8	Mike Piazza	8.00
9	Alex Rodriguez	8.00
10	Manny Ramirez	5.00
11	Tsuyoshi Shinjo	4.00
12	Hideo Nomo	5.00
13	Chipper Jones	6.00
14	Sammy Sosa	8.00
15	Roger Clemens	7.00
16	Tony Gwynn	6.00
17	Barry Bonds	15.00
18	Kazuhiro Sasaki	4.00
19	Pedro Martinez	5.00
20	Jeff Bagwell	5.00
21	Ichiro Suzuki	15.00
22	Albert Pujols	15.00

Crusade

		NM/M
Complete Set (25):		125.00
Common Player:		3.00
1	Roger Clemens/275	15.00
2	Luis Gonzalez/275	3.00
3	Troy Glaus/275	6.00
4	Freddy Garcia/300	3.00
5	Sean Casey/285	5.00
6	Bobby Abreu/300	5.00
7	Matt Morris/300	5.00
8	Cal Ripken Jr./275	25.00
9	Miguel Tejada/275	5.00
10	Vladimir Guerrero/275	10.00
11	Mark Buehrle/100	5.00
12	Mike Sweeney/300	3.00
13	Ivan Rodriguez /275	8.00
14	Jeff Bagwell/275	8.00
15	Joe Mays/250	3.00
16	Cliff Floyd/300	3.00
17	Lance Berkman/300	3.00
18	Aramis Ramirez/100	5.00
19	Tony Gwynn/300	10.00
20	Shannon Stewart/100	5.00
21	Todd Helton/275	5.00
22	Chipper Jones/275	12.00
23	Javier Vazquez/100	5.00
24	Shawn Green/275	5.00
25	Barry Bonds/300	25.00

Crusade Autographs

		NM/M
Common Player:		
11	Mark Buehrle/200	10.00
15	Joe Mays/50	10.00
18	Aramis Ramirez/200	8.00
20	Shannon Stewart/200	8.00
23	Javier Vazquez /200	10.00

26	Albert Pujols/50	750.00
27	Wilson Betemit/200	10.00
29	Roy Oswalt/200	12.00
30	Johnny Estrada/200	8.00
31	Nick Johnson/200	12.00
32	Aubrey Huff/200	8.00
33	Corey Patterson/200	10.00
34	Jay Gibbons/200	20.00
35	Marcus Giles/200	8.00
36	Juan Cruz /200	8.00
39	Bud Smith/200	8.00
40	Alex Escobar/200	8.00
41	Joe Kennedy/200	8.00
42	Alexis Gomez/200	10.00
44	Josh Towers/200	8.00
45	Joe Crede/200	10.00
46	Brandon Duckworth/200	12.00
48	Jose Ortiz/200	8.00
49	Casey Fossum/200	12.00
50	Adam Dunn/100	30.00

Diamond Aces

		NM/M
Common Player:		5.00
Varying quantities produced		
1	Roger Clemens/200	30.00
2	Randy Johnson/750	10.00
3	Freddy Garcia/350	5.00
4	Greg Maddux/750	20.00
5	Tim Hudson/750	8.00
6	Curt Schilling/525	8.00
7	Mark Buehrle/750	5.00
9	Joe Mays/750	5.00
10	Javier Vazquez/500	5.00
11	Mark Mulder/300	6.00
12	Wade Miller/525	5.00
13	Barry Zito/550	8.00
14	Pedro Martinez/550	15.00
15	Al Leiter/525	5.00
16	Chan Ho Park/400	5.00
17	John Burkett/700	5.00
18	C.C. Sabathia/550	5.00
19	Jamie Moyer/700	5.00

Diamond Dominators

		NM/M
Common Player:		4.00
Varying quantities produced		
1	Manny Ramirez/725	8.00
2	Lance Berkman/725	4.00
3	Juan Gonzalez/500	6.00
4	Albert Pujols/125	65.00
5	Jason Giambi/250	8.00
6	Mike Sweeney/325	4.00
7	Rafael Palmeiro/550	8.00
8	Luis Gonzalez/725	4.00
10	Cliff Floyd/725	4.00
11	Roberto Alomar/200	8.00
12	Paul LoDuca/600	4.00
13	Shannon Stewart/725	6.00
14	Barry Bonds/250	30.00
15	Larry Walker/725	6.00
16	Shawn Green/500	6.00
17	Moises Alou/550	4.00
18	Cal Ripken/250	50.00
19	Brian Giles/725	5.00
20	Magglio Ordonez/725	5.00
21	Jose Vidro/725	4.00
22	Edgar Martinez/200	6.00
23	Aramis Ramirez/200	5.00
24	Tony Gwynn/500	10.00
25	Richie Sexson/725	6.00
26	Todd Helton/725	8.00
27	Garret Anderson/725	6.00
28	Chipper Jones/725	12.00
29	Troy Glaus/200	8.00
30	Jeff Bagwell/325	8.00

Dominators

		NM/M
Complete Set (30):		90.00
Common Player:		2.00
Inserted 1:20		
1	Manny Ramirez	4.00
2	Lance Berkman	2.00
3	Juan Gonzalez	4.00
4	Albert Pujols	10.00
5	Jason Giambi	3.00
6	Mike Sweeney	2.00
7	Rafael Palmeiro	4.00
8	Luis Gonzalez	2.00
9	Ichiro Suzuki	10.00
10	Cliff Floyd	2.00
11	Roberto Alomar	4.00
12	Paul LoDuca	2.00
13	Shannon Stewart	2.00
14	Barry Bonds	10.00
15	Larry Walker	2.00
16	Shawn Green	3.00
17	Moises Alou	2.00
18	Cal Ripken Jr.	10.00
19	Brian Giles	2.00
20	Magglio Ordonez	3.00
21	Jose Vidro	2.00
22	Edgar Martinez	2.00
23	Aramis Ramirez	2.00
24	Tony Gwynn	5.00
25	Richie Sexson	2.00
26	Todd Helton	4.00
27	Garret Anderson	2.00
28	Chipper Jones	5.00
29	Troy Glaus	4.00
30	Jeff Bagwell	4.00

Final Rewards

		NM/M
Common Player:		5.00
Varying quantities produced		
1	Jason Giambi/250	10.00
2	Ichiro Suzuki/50	120.00
3	Roger Clemens/200	30.00
4	Freddy Garcia/250	5.00
5	Ichiro Suzuki/50	120.00
6	Albert Pujols/125	60.00

7	Barry Bonds/200	40.00
8	Albert Pujols/125	60.00
9	Randy Johnson/250	15.00

First Class Autographs

		NM/M
Common Player:		
10	Miguel Tejada/75	30.00
17	Paul LoDuca/250	20.00
21	Eric Chavez/100	15.00
41	Barry Zito/100	10.00
45	Mark Buehrle/100	20.00
49	Robert Fick/100	10.00
50	Sean Casey/100	10.00
51	Joe Mays/100	10.00
59	Ryan Klesko/50	10.00
69	Mark Mulder/100	10.00
73	Terrence Long/100	10.00
81	Jose Vidro/100	10.00
83	Richie Sexson/100	15.00
84	Troy Glaus/100	20.00
89	Jermaine Dye/100	15.00
91	Richard Hidalgo/100	8.00
93	Aramis Ramirez/100	25.00
96	Tim Hudson/100	25.00

Rewards

		NM/M
Common Player:		5.00
Inserted 1:212		
1	Jason Giambi	7.50
2	Ichiro Suzuki	40.00
3	Roger Clemens	20.00
4	Freddy Garcia	5.00
5	Ichiro Suzuki	40.00
6	Albert Pujols	30.00
7	Barry Bonds	30.00
8	Albert Pujols	30.00
9	Randy Johnson	10.00
10	Matt Morris	5.00

Rookie Autographs

		NM/M
Common Autograph:		8.00
109	Paul Phillips/250	8.00

ROOKIE PHENOMS

114	Kris Keller/250	8.00
115	Adam Bernero/250	8.00
120	George Perez/250	8.00
123	Nate Teut/250	8.00
124	Martin Vargas/250	8.00
127	Les Walrond/250	8.00
132	Joe Crede/250	10.00
137	Winston Abreu/250	8.00
138	Matt Ginter/250	8.00
140	Gene Altman/250	8.00
142	Michael Cuddyer/250	8.00
143	Mike Penney/250	8.00
145	Esix Snead/250	8.00
147	Orlando Woodards/250	8.00
148	Jeff Deardorff/100	8.00
150	Blaine Neal/250	8.00
156	Aubrey Huff/250	10.00
157	Pablo Ozuna/250	8.00
158	Bill Ortega/250	8.00
160	Kevin Olsen/250	8.00
161	Will Ohman/250	8.00
163	Jack Cust/250	10.00
168	Craig Monroe/250	8.00
169	Jason Jennings/250	8.00
171	Luis Rivas/250	8.00
173	Luke Hudson/250	12.00
176	David Espinosa/250	8.00
177	Mike Maroth/250	8.00
178	Keith Ginter/250	8.00
181	Steve Lomasney/250	8.00
182	John Grabow/250	8.00
184	Jason Karnuth/250	8.00
186	Brent Abernathy/250	8.00
188	Wily Mo Pena/250	15.00
191	Cesar Izturis/250	8.00
192	Eric Hinske/250	10.00
194	Timo Perez/100	8.00
196	Eric Valent/250	8.00
201	Joe Kennedy/100	8.00
202	Wilson Betemit/100	15.00
203	Christian Parker/100	8.00
204	Jay Gibbons/100	20.00
205	Carlos Garcia/200	8.00
206	Jack Wilson/100	15.00
207	Johnny Estrada/200	20.00
208	Wilkin Ruan/200	8.00
209	Brandon Duckworth/100	8.00
211	Marlon Byrd/100	20.00
213	Dennis Tankersley/100	10.00
214	Brandon Larson/200	8.00
215	Alexis Gomez/200	10.00
216	Bill Hall/100	20.00
217	Antonio Perez/100	8.00
218	Jeremy Affeldt/200	10.00
220	Casey Fossum/200	8.00
224	Zach Day/200	8.00
225	David Williams/200	8.00
227	Jose Acevedo/200	8.00
229	Orlando Hudson/200	25.00
230	Jose Mieses/200	8.00
231	Ric Rodriguez/200	8.00
232	Alfonso Soriano/100	40.00
233	Jason Hart/100	8.00
234	Endy Chavez/200	8.00
235	Delvin James/100	8.00
237	Jeremy Owens/200	8.00
238	Brad Voyles/200	8.00
239	Nate Frese/200	8.00
240	Josh Beckett/25	80.00
241	Roy Oswalt/100	25.00
242	Juan Uribe/150	10.00
243	Cory Aldridge/200	8.00
244	Adam Dunn/100	30.00
245	Bud Smith/100	8.00
246	Adrian Hernandez/100	8.00
249	Wilmy Caceres/200	8.00
250	Jason Michaels/200	8.00
252	John Buck/100	15.00
253	Andres Torres/100	8.00
255	Corky Miller/100	8.00
256	Rafael Soriano/200	10.00
257	Donaldo Mendez/200	8.00
259	Corey Patterson/100	15.00
260	Horacio Ramirez/200	10.00
261	Elpidio Guzman/200	8.00
262	Juan Diaz/200	8.00
264	Brian Lawrence/200	10.00
265	Josue Perez/200	8.00
266	Jose Nunez/200	8.00
268	Albert Pujols/100	500.00
269	Duaner Sanchez/200	8.00

271	Greg Miller/200	8.00
272	Adam Pettyjohn/200	8.00
274	Claudio Vargas/200	8.00
279	Brian Reith/200	8.00
283	Josh Towers/100	8.00
285	David Brous/200	8.00
287	Nick Neugebauer/100	8.00
289	Billy Sylvester/200	8.00
290	Carlos Valderrama/200	8.00
292	Matt White/200	8.00
293	Nick Maness/200	8.00
296	Angel Berroa/100	15.00
297	Juan Cruz/100	8.00
298	Dewon Brazelton/100	8.00
299	Mark Prior/100	40.00
300	Mark Teixeira/100	250.00

Rookie Crusade

		NM/M
Complete Set (25):		110.00
Common Player:		3.00
26	Albert Pujols/250	30.00
27	Wilson Betemit/100	3.00
28	C.C. Sabathia/290	3.00
29	Roy Oswalt/100	4.00
30	Johnny Estrada/100	3.00
31	Nick Johnson/100	4.00
32	Aubrey Huff/100	3.00
33	Corey Patterson/200	4.00
34	Jay Gibbons/100	3.00
35	Marcus Giles/100	4.00
36	Juan Cruz/100	3.00
37	Tsuyoshi Shinjo/300	3.00
38	Ben Sheets/285	3.00
39	Bud Smith/100	3.00
40	Alex Escobar/100	3.00
41	Joe Kennedy/100	3.00
42	Alexis Gomez/100	3.00
43	Jimmy Rollins (300)	3.00
44	Josh Towers/100	3.00
45	Joe Crede/100	3.00
46	Brandon Duckworth/100	3.00
47	Ichiro Suzuki/300	40.00
48	Jose Ortiz/100	3.00
49	Casey Fossum/100	3.00
50	Adam Dunn/200	5.00

Rookie Team

		NM/M
Complete Set (15):		65.00
Common Player:		3.00
Inserted 1:83		
1	Jay Gibbons	5.00
2	Alfonso Soriano	6.00
3	Jimmy Rollins	3.00
4	Wilson Betemit	3.00
5	Albert Pujols	20.00
6	Johnny Estrada	3.00
7	Ichiro Suzuki	15.00
8	Tsuyoshi Shinjo	4.00
9	Adam Dunn	5.00
10	C.C. Sabathia	3.00
11	Ben Sheets	3.00
12	Roy Oswalt	4.00
13	Bud Smith	3.00
14	Josh Towers	3.00
15	Juan Cruz	3.00

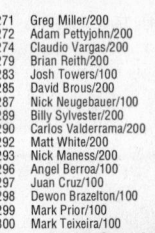

Rookie Team Materials

	NM/M
Common Player:	5.00
Varying quantities produced	
1 Jay Gibbons/100	8.00
2 Alfonso Soriano/100	15.00
3 Jimmy Rollins/200	5.00
5 Albert Pujols/100	65.00
6 Johnny Estrada/100	5.00
7 Ichiro Suzuki/50	120.00
8 Tsuyoshi Shinjo/200	10.00
9 Adam Dunn/200	8.00
10 C.C. Sabathia/200	5.00
11 Ben Sheets/200	5.00
13 Bud Smith/250	5.00
14 Josh Towers/200	5.00
15 Juan Cruz/200	5.00

Yearbook

	NM/M
Complete Set (25):	85.00
Common Player:	2.00
Inserted 1:24	
1 Barry Bonds	12.00
2 Mark Mulder	3.00
3 Luis Gonzalez	2.00
4 Lance Berkman	2.00
5 Matt Morris	2.00
6 Roy Oswalt	2.50
7 Todd Helton	3.00
8 Tsuyoshi Shinjo	2.00
9 C.C. Sabathia	2.00
10 Curt Schilling	3.00
11 Rickey Henderson	3.00
12 Jamie Moyer	2.00
13 Shawn Green	2.00
14 Randy Johnson	4.00
15 Jim Thome	2.00
16 Larry Walker	2.00
17 Jimmy Rollins	2.00
18 Kazuhiro Sasaki	2.00
19 Hideo Nomo	3.00
20 Roger Clemens	7.50
21 Bud Smith	2.00
22 Ichiro Suzuki	10.00
23 Albert Pujols	15.00
24 Cal Ripken Jr.	15.00
25 Tony Gwynn	5.00

Yearbook Scrapbook

	NM/M
Common Player:	4.00
Varying quantities produced	
1 Barry Bonds/525	30.00
2 Mark Mulder/500	6.00
3 Luis Gonzalez/500	4.00
4 Lance Berkman/525	4.00
5 Roy Oswalt/150	6.00
7 Todd Helton/525	6.00
8 Tsuyoshi Shinjo/75	15.00
9 C.C. Sabathia/500	4.00
10 Curt Schilling/525	6.00
11 Rickey Henderson/200	15.00
12 Jamie Moyer/500	4.00
13 Shawn Green/525	5.00
14 Randy Johnson/500	8.00

15 Jim Thome/400	4.00
16 Larry Walker/500	4.00
18 Kazuhiro Sasaki/500	4.00
19 Hideo Nomo/150	50.00
20 Roger Clemens/475	20.00
21 Bud Smith/525	4.00
22 Ichiro Suzuki/75	80.00
23 Albert Pujols/150	50.00
24 Cal Ripken/525	30.00
25 Tony Gwynn/500	10.00

2001 Donruss Classics

	NM/M
Common Player:	.50
Common SP (101-150):	5.00
Production 585	
Common SP (151-200):	3.00
Production 1,755	
Pack (6):	12.00
Box (18):	180.00
1 Alex Rodriguez	3.00
2 Barry Bonds	3.00
3 Cal Ripken Jr.	4.00
4 Chipper Jones	2.00
5 Derek Jeter	3.00
6 Troy Glaus	.75
7 Frank Thomas	1.00
8 Greg Maddux	2.00
9 Ivan Rodriguez	1.00
10 Jeff Bagwell	1.00
11 Cliff Floyd	.50
12 Todd Helton	1.00
13 Ken Griffey Jr.	2.00
14 Manny Ramirez	1.00
15 Mark McGwire	3.00
16 Mike Piazza	2.00
17 Nomar Garciaparra	3.00
18 Pedro Martinez	1.50
19 Randy Johnson	1.50
20 Rick Ankiel	.50
21 Rickey Henderson	.75
22 Roger Clemens	3.00
23 Sammy Sosa	2.50
24 Tony Gwynn	1.50
25 Vladimir Guerrero	1.50
26 Kazuhiro Sasaki	.50
27 Roberto Alomar	.75
28 Barry Zito	.75
29 Pat Burrell	.75
30 Harold Baines	.75
31 Carlos Delgado	.75
32 J.D. Drew	.50
33 Jim Edmonds	.75
34 Darin Erstad	.75
35 Jason Giambi	1.00
36 Tom Glavine	.75
37 Juan Gonzalez	1.00
38 Mark Grace	.75
39 Shawn Green	.75
40 Tim Hudson	.75
41 Andruw Jones	.75
42 Jeff Kent	.50
43 Barry Larkin	.75
44 Rafael Furcal	.50
45 Mike Mussina	.75
46 Hideo Nomo	.75
47 Rafael Palmeiro	1.00
48 Scott Rolen	1.00
49 Gary Sheffield	.75
50 Bernie Williams	.75
51 Bob Abreu	.50
52 Edgardo Alfonso	.50
53 Edgar Martinez	.50
54 Magglio Ordonez	.75
55 Kerry Wood	.75
56 Adrian Beltre	.50
57 Lance Berkman	.75
58 Kevin Brown	.75
59 Sean Casey	.50
60 Eric Chavez	.75
61 Bartolo Colon	.50
62 Johnny Damon	.50
63 Jermaine Dye	.50
64 Juan Encarnacion	.50
65 Carl Everett	.50
66 Brian Giles	.75
67 Mike Hampton	.50
68 Richard Hidalgo	.50
69 Geoff Jenkins	.75
70 Jacque Jones	.50
71 Jason Kendall	.75
72 Ryan Klesko	.75
73 Chan Ho Park	.50
74 Richie Sexson	.75
75 Mike Sweeney	.50
76 Fernando Tatis	.50
77 Miguel Tejada	.75
78 Jose Vidro	.50
79 Larry Walker	.75
80 Preston Wilson	.50
81 Craig Biggio	.75
82 Fred McGriff	.75
83 Jim Thome	1.00
84 Garret Anderson	.75
85 Russell Branyan	.50
86 Tony Batista	.50
87 Terrence Long	.50
88 Brad Fullmer	.50
89 Rusty Greer	.50
90 Orlando Hernandez	.50
91 Gabe Kapler	.50
92 Paul Konerko	.50
93 Carlos Lee	.50
94 Kenny Lofton	.75
95 Raul Mondesi	.50
96 Jorge Posada	.75
97 Tim Salmon	.75
98 Greg Vaughn	.50
99 Mo Vaughn	.50
100 Omar Vizquel	.50
101 Jimmy Rollins	5.00
102 Cory Aldridge RC	5.00
103 Wilmy Caceres RC	5.00
104 Josh Beckett	6.00
105 Wilson Betemit RC	5.00
106 Timo Perez	5.00
107 Albert Pujols	240.00
108 Bud Smith RC	5.00
109 Jack Wilson RC	10.00
110 Alex Escobar	5.00
111 Johnny Estrada RC	10.00
112 Pedro Feliz	5.00
113 Nate Frese RC	5.00
114 Carlos Garcia RC	5.00
115 Brandon Larson RC	5.00
116 Alexis Gomez RC	5.00
117 Jason Hart	5.00
118 Adam Dunn	5.00
119 Marcus Giles	5.00
120 Christian Parker RC	5.00
121 Jackson Melian RC	5.00
122 Eric Chavez	5.00
123 Adrian Hernandez RC	5.00
124 Joe Kennedy RC	5.00
125 Jose Mieses RC	5.00
126 C.C. Sabathia	5.00
127 Eric Munson	5.00
128 Xavier Nady	5.00
129 Horacio Ramirez RC	10.00
130 Abraham Nunez	5.00
131 Jose Ortiz	5.00
132 Jeremy Owens RC	5.00
133 Claudio Vargas RC	5.00
134 Corey Patterson	5.00
135 Audres Torres	5.00
136 Ben Sheets	5.00
137 Joe Crede	5.00
138 Adam Pettyjohn RC	5.00
139 Elpidio Guzman RC	5.00
140 Jay Gibbons RC	10.00
141 Wilkin Ruan RC	5.00
142 Tsuyoshi Shinjo RC	10.00
143 Alfonso Soriano	5.00
144 Nick Johnson	5.00
145 Ichiro Suzuki RC	80.00
146 Juan Uribe RC	8.00
147 Jack Cust	5.00
148 Carlos Valderrama RC	5.00
149 Matt White RC	5.00
150 Hank Aaron	10.00
151 Ernie Banks	4.00
152 Johnny Bench	6.00
153 George Brett	10.00
154 Lou Brock	3.00
155 Rod Carew	3.00
156 Steve Carlton	4.00
157 Bob Feller	3.00
158 Bob Gibson	5.00
159 Reggie Jackson	5.00
160 Al Kaline	6.00
161 Sandy Koufax	600.00
162 Don Mattingly	10.00
164 Willie Mays	10.00
165 Willie McCovey	3.00
166 Joe Morgan	3.00
167 Stan Musial	8.00
168 Jim Palmer	3.00
169 Brooks Robinson	5.00
170 Frank Robinson	3.00
171 Nolan Ryan	15.00
172 Mike Schmidt	10.00
173 Tom Seaver	5.00
174 Warren Spahn	4.00
175 Robin Yount	5.00
176 Wade Boggs	4.00
177 Ty Cobb	10.00
178 Lou Gehrig	10.00
179 Luis Aparicio	3.00
180 Babe Ruth	15.00
181 Ryne Sandberg	10.00
182 Yogi Berra	5.00
183 Roberto Clemente	10.00
184 Eddie Murray	5.00
185 Robin Roberts	5.00
186 Duke Snider	5.00
187 Orlando Cepeda	3.00
188 Billy Williams	3.00
189 Juan Marichal	3.00
190 Harmon Killebrew	5.00
191 Kirby Puckett	8.00
192 Carlton Fisk	4.00
193 Dave Winfield	3.00
194 Whitey Ford	4.00
195 Paul Molitor	4.00
196 Tony Perez	3.00
197 Ozzie Smith	6.00
198 Ralph Kiner	3.00
199 Fergie Jenkins	4.00
200 Phil Rizzuto	4.00

Benchmarks

	NM/M
Common Player:	5.00
Inserted 1:18	
1 Todd Helton	5.00
2 Roberto Clemente	40.00
3 Mark McGwire	30.00
4 Barry Bonds	40.00
5 Bob Gibson	10.00
6 Ken Griffey Jr.	20.00
7 Frank Robinson	8.00
8 Greg Maddux	15.00
9 Reggie Jackson	10.00
10 Sammy Sosa	20.00
11 Willie Stargell	8.00
12 Vladimir Guerrero	8.00
13 Johnny Bench	15.00
14 Tony Gwynn	15.00
15 Mike Schmidt	17.50
16 Ivan Rodriguez	6.00
17 Jeff Bagwell	10.00
18 Cal Ripken Jr.	40.00
20 Kirby Puckett	15.00
21 Frank Thomas	8.00
22 Joe Morgan	5.00
23 Mike Piazza	20.00
25 Andruw Jones	5.00

Benchmarks Autographs

	NM/M
5 Bob Gibson	60.00
7 Frank Robinson	50.00
9 Reggie Jackson	100.00
15 Mike Schmidt	100.00
22 Joe Morgan	50.00
25 Andruw Jones	60.00

Classic Combos

	NM/M
Common Card:	20.00
1 Roberto Clemente	125.00
2 Willie Stargell	25.00
3 Babe Ruth	450.00
4 Lou Gehrig	300.00
5 Hank Aaron	100.00
6 Eddie Mathews	30.00
7 Johnny Bench	40.00
8 Joe Morgan	20.00
9 Robin Yount	40.00
10 Paul Molitor	35.00
11 Steve Carlton	25.00
12 Mike Schmidt	75.00

13	Stan Musial	75.00
14	Lou Brock	20.00
15	Yogi Berra	30.00
16	Phil Rizzuto	25.00
17	Ernie Banks	40.00
18	Billy Williams	20.00
19	Don Mattingly	70.00
21	Jackie Robinson	100.00
22	Duke Snider	30.00
23	Frank Robinson	25.00
26	Brooks Robinson	40.00
26	Willie McCovey	30.00
27	Ryne Sandberg	60.00
29	Harmon Killebrew	40.00
30	Rod Carew	40.00
31	Roberto Clemente, Willie Stargell	200.00
32	Babe Ruth, Lou Gehrig	1,000
33	Hank Aaron, Eddie Mathews	200.00
34	Johnny Bench, Joe Morgan	80.00
35	Robin Yount, Paul Molitor	100.00
36	Steve Carlton, Mike Schmidt	200.00
37	Stan Musial, Lou Brock	150.00
38	Phil Rizzuto, Yogi Berra	100.00
39	Ernie Banks, Billy Williams	
41	Jackie Robinson, Duke Snider	150.00
42	Brooks Robinson, Frank Robinson	75.00
43	Willie McCovey, Orlando Cepeda	60.00
45	Harmon Killebrew, Rod Carew	100.00

Classic Combos Autographs
No pricing due to scarcity.

Legendary Lumberjacks

		NM/M
Common Player:		5.00
Inserted 1:18		
1	Hack Wilson/244	75.00
2	Chipper Jones	10.00
3	Rogers Hornsby/SP/301	85.00
4	Nellie Fox	75.00
5	Ivan Rodriguez	10.00
6	Jimmie Foxx/300	120.00
7	Hank Aaron	50.00
8	Yogi Berra	15.00
9	Ernie Banks/SP/300	50.00
10	George Brett	25.00
11	Ty Cobb/SP/100	150.00
12	Roberto Clemente	125.00
13	Carlton Fisk	5.00
14	Reggie Jackson	10.00
15	Al Kaline	15.00
16	Harmon Killebrew	15.00
17	Ralph Kiner	5.00
18	Roger Maris/SP/275	120.00
19	Eddie Mathews	25.00
20	Ted Williams/SP/300	125.00
21	Willie McCovey	5.00
22	Eddie Murray	10.00
23	Joe Morgan/SP/268	20.00
24	Frank Robinson	10.00
25	Tony Perez	5.00
26	Mike Schmidt	20.00
27	Ryne Sandberg	25.00
28	Duke Snider/SP/300	25.00
30	Billy Williams	5.00
31	Dave Winfield	8.00
32	Robin Yount	10.00
33	Barry Bonds	30.00
34	Stan Musial/SP/300	35.00
35	Johnny Bench/SP/300	20.00
36	Orlando Cepeda	8.00
37	Jeff Bagwell	8.00
38	Frank Thomas	8.00
39	Juan Gonzalez	8.00
40	Cal Ripken Jr.	40.00
41	Rafael Palmeiro	8.00
42	Troy Glaus/SP/100	15.00
43	Manny Ramirez	8.00
44	Paul Molitor	15.00
45	Tony Gwynn	8.00
46	Rod Carew	8.00
47	Lou Brock	8.00
48	Wade Boggs	8.00
49	Babe Ruth/SP	225.00
50	Lou Gehrig/SP	150.00

Legendary Lumberjacks Autographs
		NM/M
No pricing due to scarcity.

LL24 Frank Robinson 200.00

Significant Signatures
	NM/M
Common Autograph:	5.00

Inserted 1:18		
101	Aubrey Huff	6.00
103	Cory Aldridge	5.00
105	Josh Beckett/SP	30.00
106	Wilson Betemit	5.00
107	Timo Perez	5.00
108	Albert Pujols	600.00
110	Jack Wilson	10.00
111	Alex Escobar	5.00
112	Johnny Estrada	20.00
113	Pedro Feliz	5.00
114	Nate Frese	5.00
115	Carlos Garcia	5.00
116	Brandon Larson	8.00
118	Jason Hart	5.00
119	Adam Dunn/SP	25.00
120	Marcus Giles	8.00
121	Christian Parker	5.00
126	Jose Mieses	5.00
127	C.C. Sabathia	25.00
129	Xavier Nady	8.00
130	Horacio Ramirez	10.00
131	Abraham Nunez	5.00
132	Jose Ortiz	5.00
133	Jeremy Owens	5.00
134	Claudio Vargas	5.00
135	Corey Patterson/SP	20.00
136	Andres Torres	5.00
137	Ben Sheets/SP	25.00
138	Joe Crede	8.00
139	Adam Pettyjohn	5.00
140	Elpidio Guzman	5.00
141	Jay Gibbons	15.00
142	Wilkin Ruan	5.00
144	Alfonso Soriano/SP	40.00
145	Nick Johnson	10.00
147	Juan Uribe	10.00
149	Carlos Valderrama	5.00
151	Hank Aaron/SP	400.00
152	Ernie Banks	35.00
153	Johnny Bench/SP	100.00
154	George Brett/SP	75.00
155	Lou Brock	15.00
156	Rod Carew	25.00
157	Steve Carlton	25.00
158	Bob Feller	15.00
159	Bob Gibson	25.00
160	Reggie Jackson/SP	65.00
161	Al Kaline	40.00
162	Nolan Ryan/SP	150.00
163	Don Mattingly	80.00
164	Willie Mays/SP	160.00
165	Willie McCovey	20.00
166	Joe Morgan	10.00
167	Stan Musial/SP	85.00
168	Jim Palmer	15.00
169	Brooks Robinson	40.00
170	Frank Robinson	20.00
171	Nolan Ryan/SP	150.00
172	Mike Schmidt	75.00
173	Tom Seaver	30.00
174	Warren Spahn	40.00
175	Aubrey Huff/SP	100.00
176	Wade Boggs/SP	50.00
179	Luis Aparicio	10.00
181	Ryne Sandberg	75.00
182	Yogi Berra	30.00
184	Eddie Murray	50.00
185	Ron Santo	25.00
186	Duke Snider	25.00
187	Orlando Cepeda	10.00
188	Billy Williams	10.00
189	Juan Marichal	15.00
190	Harmon Killebrew	40.00
191	Kirby Puckett/SP	60.00
192	Carlton Fisk	20.00
193	Dave Winfield/SP	50.00
194	Whitey Ford	25.00
195	Paul Molitor/SP	50.00
196	Tony Perez	15.00
197	Ozzie Smith/SP	80.00
198	Ralph Kiner	25.00
199	Fergie Jenkins	10.00
200	Phil Rizzuto	40.00

Stadium Stars
		NM/M
Common Player:		4.00
Inserted 1:18		
1	Babe Ruth	40.00
2	Cal Ripken Jr.	20.00

3	Brooks Robinson	8.00
4	Tony Gwynn	10.00
5	Ty Cobb	25.00
6	Vladimir Guerrero	8.00
7	Lou Gehrig	35.00
8	Nomar Garciaparra	12.00
9	Sammy Sosa	12.00
10	Reggie Jackson	8.00
11	Alex Rodriguez	12.00
12	Derek Jeter	20.00
13	Willie McCovey	4.00
14	Mark McGwire	15.00
15	Chipper Jones	10.00
16	Honus Wagner	10.00
17	Ken Griffey Jr.	12.00
18	Frank Robinson	8.00
19	Barry Bonds	20.00
20	Yogi Berra	8.00
21	Mike Piazza	12.00
22	Roger Clemens	10.00
23	Duke Snider	8.00
24	Frank Thomas	8.00
25	Andruw Jones	8.00

Stadium Stars Autographs
No pricing due to scarcity.

Timeless Treasures

		NM/M
Inserted 1:420		
1	Mark McGwire/Ball	200.00
2	Babe Ruth/Seat	60.00
3	Harmon Killebrew/Bat	30.00
4	Derek Jeter/Base	25.00
5	Barry Bonds/Ball	85.00

Timeless Tributes

Stars (1-100):	4-8X
SP's (101-150):	1-1.5X
SP's (151-200):	1-2.5X
Production 100 Sets	

(See 2001 Donruss Classics for checklist and base cards values.)

2001 Donruss Elite
	NM/M
Complete Set (200):	
Common Player:	.25
Common (151-200):	5.00
Production 900	
Common 201-250:	4.00
(#201-250 available by redemption)	
Pack (5):	12.00
Box (18):	200.00
1 Alex Rodriguez	2.00
2 Barry Bonds	2.50
3 Cal Ripken Jr.	2.50
4 Chipper Jones	1.50
5 Derek Jeter	2.50
6 Troy Glaus	.75
7 Frank Thomas	1.00
8 Greg Maddux	1.50
9 Ivan Rodriguez	.75
10 Jeff Bagwell	1.00
11 Jose Canseco	.50
12 Todd Helton	.75

13	Ken Griffey Jr.	1.75
14	Manny Ramirez	1.00
15	Mark McGwire	2.00
16	Mike Piazza	1.75
17	Nomar Garciaparra	1.50
18	Pedro Martinez	1.00
19	Randy Johnson	1.00
20	Rick Ankiel	.25
21	Ricky Henderson	1.00
22	Roger Clemens	1.75
23	Sammy Sosa	1.50
24	Tony Gwynn	1.50
25	Vladimir Guerrero	.50
26	Eric Davis	.35
27	Roberto Alomar	.35
28	Mark Mulder	.50
29	Pat Burrell	.35
30	Harold Baines	.60
31	Carlos Delgado	.60
32	J.D. Drew	.40
33	Jim Edmonds	.25
34	Darin Erstad	.35
35	Jason Giambi	.50
36	Tom Glavine	.50
37	Juan Gonzalez	.50
38	Mark Grace	.40
39	Shawn Green	.40
40	Tim Hudson	.40
41	Andruw Jones	1.00
42	David Justice	.25
43	Jeff Kent	.25
44	Barry Larkin	.25
45	Pokey Reese	.25
46	Mike Mussina	.50
47	Hideo Nomo	.50
48	Rafael Palmeiro	.65
49	Adam Piatt	.25
50	Scott Rolen	.65
51	Gary Sheffield	.40
52	Bernie Williams	.25
53	Bob Abreu	.25
54	Edgardo Alfonzo	.25
55	Jermaine Clark RC	.25
56	Albert Belle	.25
57	Craig Biggio	.25
58	Andres Galarraga	.25
59	Edgar Martinez	.25
60	Fred McGriff	.25
61	Magglio Ordonez	.25
62	Jim Thome	.65
63	Matt Williams	.25
64	Kerry Wood	.50
65	Moises Alou	.25
66	Brady Anderson	.25
67	Garret Anderson	.25
68	Tony Armas Jr.	.25
69	Tony Batista	.25
70	Jose Cruz Jr.	.25
71	Carlos Beltran	.50
72	Adrian Beltre	.40
73	Kris Benson	.25
74	Lance Berkman	.25
75	Kevin Brown	.25
76	Jay Buhner	.25
77	Jeromy Burnitz	.25
78	Ken Caminiti	.25
79	Sean Casey	.40
80	Luis Castillo	.25
81	Eric Chavez	.40
82	Jeff Cirillo	.25
83	Bartolo Colon	.25
84	David Cone	.25
85	Freddy Garcia	.25
86	Johnny Damon	.50
87	Ray Durham	.25
88	Jermaine Dye	.25
89	Juan Encarnacion	.25
90	Terrence Long	.25
91	Carl Everett	.25
92	Steve Finley	.25
93	Cliff Floyd	.25
94	Brad Fulmer	.25
95	Brian Giles	.25
96	Luis Gonzalez	.25
97	Rusty Greer	.25
98	Jeffrey Hammonds	.25
99	Mike Hampton	.25
100	Orlando Hernandez	.35
101	Richard Hidalgo	.25
102	Geoff Jenkins	.25
103	Jacque Jones	.25

104	Brian Jordan	.25
105	Gabe Kapler	.25
106	Eric Karros	.25
107	Jason Kendall	.25
108	Adam Kennedy	.25
109	Byung-Hyun Kim	.25
110	Ryan Klesko	.25
111	Chuck Knoblauch	.25
112	Paul Konerko	.25
113	Carlos Lee	.25
114	Kenny Lofton	.25
115	Javy Lopez	.25
116	Tino Martinez	.25
117	Ruben Mateo	.25
118	Kevin Millwood	.25
119	Ben Molina	.25
120	Raul Mondesi	.25
121	Trot Nixon	.25
122	John Olerud	.25
123	Paul O'Neill	.25
124	Chan Ho Park	.25
125	Andy Pettitte	.40
126	Jorge Posada	.35
127	Mark Quinn	.25
128	Aramis Ramirez	.25
129	Mariano Rivera	.35
130	Tim Salmon	.25
131	Curt Schilling	.40
132	Richie Sexson	.25
133	John Smoltz	.25
134	J.T. Snow	.25
135	Jay Payton	.25
136	Shannon Stewart	.25
137	B.J. Surhoff	.25
138	Mike Sweeney	.25
139	Fernando Tatis	.25
140	Miguel Tejada	.40
141	Jason Varitek	.25
142	Greg Vaughn	.25
143	Mo Vaughn	.25
144	Robin Ventura	.25
145	Jose Vidro	.25
146	Omar Vizquel	.25
147	Larry Walker	.25
148	David Wells	.25
149	Rondell White	.25
150	Preston Wilson	.25
151	Brent Abernathy	5.00
152	Cory Aldridge RC	5.00
153	Gene Altman RC	5.00
154	Josh Beckett	6.00
155	Wilson Betemit RC	5.00
156	Albert Pujols RC	400.00
157	Joe Crede	5.00
158	Jack Cust	5.00
159	Ben Sheets	5.00
160	Alex Escobar	5.00
161	Adrian Hernandez RC	5.00
162	Pedro Feliz	5.00
163	Nate Frese RC	5.00
164	Carlos Garcia RC	5.00
165	Marcus Giles	5.00
166	Alexis Gomez RC	5.00
167	Jason Hart	5.00
168	Aubrey Huff	5.00
169	Cesar Izturis	5.00
170	Nick Johnson	5.00
171	Jack Wilson RC	10.00
172	Brian Lawrence RC	5.00
173	Christian Parker RC	5.00
174	Nick Maness RC	5.00
175	Jose Mieses RC	5.00
176	Greg Miller RC	5.00
177	Eric Munson	5.00
178	Xavier Nady	5.00
179	Blaine Neal RC	5.00
180	Abraham Nunez	5.00
181	Jose Ortiz	5.00
182	Jeremy Owens RC	5.00
183	Jay Gibbons RC	10.00
184	Corey Patterson	5.00
185	Carlos Pena	5.00
186	C.C. Sabathia	5.00
187	Timo Perez	5.00
188	Adam Pettyjohn RC	5.00
189	Donaldo Mendez RC	5.00
190	Jackson Melian RC	5.00
191	Wilken Ruan RC	5.00
192	Duaner Sanchez RC	5.00
193	Alfonso Soriano	5.00
194	Rafael Soriano RC	10.00
195	Ichiro Suzuki RC	150.00
196	Billy Sylvester RC	5.00
197	Juan Uribe RC	5.00
198	Tsuyoshi Shinjo RC	10.00
199	Carlos Valderrama RC	5.00
200	Matt White RC	5.00
201	Adam Dunn	4.00
202	Joe Kennedy	4.00
203	Mike Rivera	4.00
204	Erick Almonte	4.00
205	Brandon Duckworth	4.00
206	Victor Martinez RC	100.00
207	Rick Bauer	4.00
208	Jeff Deardorff	4.00
209	Antonio Perez	4.00
210	Bill Hall	30.00
211	Dennis Tankersley	6.00
212	Jeremy Affeldt	8.00
213	Junior Spivey	4.00
214	Casey Fossum	6.00
215	Brandon Lyon	4.00
216	Angel Santos	8.00
217	Cody Ransom	4.00
218	Jason Lane	35.00

219	David Williams	4.00
220	Alex Herrera	4.00
221	Ryan Drese	4.00
222	Travis Hafner	40.00
223	Bud Smith	4.00
224	Johnny Estrada	25.00
225	Ricardo Rodriguez	4.00
226	Brandon Berger	4.00
227	Claudio Vargas	4.00
228	Luis Garcia	4.00
229	Marlon Byrd	20.00
230	Hee Seop Choi	20.00
231	Corky Miller	4.00
232	Justin Duchscherer	6.00
233	Tim Spooneybarger	4.00
234	Roy Oswalt	4.00
235	Willie Harris	4.00
236	Josh Towers	4.00
237	Juan Pena	4.00
238	Alfredo Amezaga	4.00
239	Geronimo Gil	4.00
240	Juan Cruz	4.00
241	Ed Rogers	4.00
242	Joe Thurston	4.00
243	Orlando Hudson RC	10.00
244	John Buck RC	8.00
245	Martin Vargas	4.00
246	David Brous	4.00
247	Dewon Brazelton	4.00
248	Mark Prior	50.00
249	Angel Berroa	10.00
250	Mark Teixeira	100.00

Aspirations

Cards 1-150 print run 76-100:	5-10X
1-150 p/r 51-75:	8-15X
1-150 p/r 26-50:	10-25X
Cards 151-200 print run 76-100:	1X
151-200 p/r 51-75:	1.5X
151-200 p/r 26-50:	1.5-2X
Varying quantities produced	

Status

Cards 1-150 print run 76-100:	5-10X
1-150 p/r 51-75:	8-15X
1-150 p/r 26-50:	10-25X
Cards 151-200 print run 76-100:	1X
151-200 p/r 51-75:	1.5X
151-200 p/r 26-50:	1.5-2X
Varying quantities produced	

Back 2 Back Jacks

		NM/M
Common Player:		15.00
Singles production 100.		
Doubles production 50.		
SP print runs listed.		
1	Ernie Banks/75	20.00
2	Ryne Sandberg/75	40.00
3	Babe Ruth	200.00
4	Lou Gehrig	150.00
5	Eddie Matthews	25.00
6	Troy Glaus	15.00
7	Don Mattingly/50	50.00
8	Todd Helton	20.00
9	Wade Boggs	15.00
10	Tony Gwynn	25.00
11	Robin Yount	25.00
12	Paul Molitor/50	25.00
13	Mike Schmidt/50	40.00
14	Scott Rolen/75	20.00
15	Reggie Jackson	20.00
16	Dave Winfield	15.00
17	Johnny Bench/50	40.00
18	Joe Morgan	15.00
19	Brooks Robinson/50	40.00
20	Cal Ripken Jr.	50.00
21	Ty Cobb	100.00
22	Al Kaline/50	40.00
23	Frank Robinson/50	25.00
24	Frank Thomas	20.00
25	Roberto Clemente	80.00
26	Vladimir Guerrero/50	25.00
27	Harmon Killebrew/50	25.00
28	Kirby Puckett	20.00
29	Yogi Berra/75	35.00
30	Phil Rizzuto/75	30.00
31	Ernie Banks, Ryne Sandberg	80.00
32	Babe Ruth, Lou Gehrig	350.00
33	Troy Glaus, Eddie Matthews	40.00
34	Don Mattingly, Todd Helton	50.00
35	Tony Gwynn, Wade Boggs	75.00
36	Paul Molitor, Robin Yount	50.00
37	Mike Schmidt, Scott Rolen	80.00
38	Dave Winfield, Reggie Jackson	40.00
39	Joe Morgan, Johnny Bench	50.00
40	Brooks Robinson, Cal Ripken Jr.	100.00

41	Al Kaline, Ty Cobb	175.00
42	Frank Robinson, Frank Thomas	40.00
43	Roberto Clemente, Vladimir Guerrero	100.00
44	Harmon Killebrew, Kirby Puckett	50.00
45	Phil Rizzuto, Yogi Berra/25	100.00

Back 2 Back Jacks Auto.

DON MATTINGLY • 1B

		NM/M
Common Autograph:		60.00
Print runs listed.		
1	Ernie Banks/25	200.00
2	Ryne Sandberg/25	250.00
6	Troy Glaus/50	50.00
7	Don Mattingly/50	200.00
12	Paul Molitor/50	75.00
13	Mike Schmidt/50	150.00
14	Scott Rolen/25	60.00
17	Johnny Bench/50	100.00
19	Brooks Robinson/50	75.00
22	Al Kaline/50	100.00
23	Frank Robinson/50	50.00
26	Vladimir Guerrero/50	100.00
27	Harmon Killebrew/50	100.00
29	Yogi Berra/25	125.00
30	Phil Rizzuto/25	125.00
45	Phil Rizzuto, Yogi Berra/25	200.00

Passing the Torch

		NM/M
Common Player:		4.00
Singles production 1,000.		
Doubles production 500.		
1	Stan Musial	8.00
2	Tony Gwynn	6.00
3	Willie Mays	10.00
4	Barry Bonds	15.00
5	Mike Schmidt	10.00
6	Scott Rolen	4.00
7	Cal Ripken Jr.	15.00
8	Alex Rodriguez	10.00
9	Hank Aaron	10.00
10	Andruw Jones	4.00
11	Nolan Ryan	15.00
12	Pedro Martinez	5.00
13	Wade Boggs	6.00
14	Nomar Garciaparra	8.00
15	Don Mattingly	10.00
16	Todd Helton	5.00
17	Stan Musial, Tony Gwynn	10.00
18	Barry Bonds, Willie Mays	20.00
19	Mike Schmidt, Scott Rolen	15.00
20	Alex Rodriguez, Cal Ripken Jr.	25.00
21	Andruw Jones, Hank Aaron	15.00
22	Nolan Ryan, Pedro Martinez	25.00
23	Nomar Garciaparra, Wade Boggs	15.00
24	Don Mattingly, Todd Helton	15.00

Passing the Torch Autos.

STAN MUSIAL
ST. LOUIS CARDINALS

		NM/M
Common Player:		30.00
Singles production 100.		
Doubles production 50.		
1	Stan Musial	100.00
2	Tony Gwynn	75.00
3	Willie Mays	200.00
4	Barry Bonds	275.00
5	Mike Schmidt	100.00
6	Scott Rolen	50.00
7	Cal Ripken Jr.	150.00
8	Alex Rodriguez	120.00

9	Hank Aaron	275.00
10	Andruw Jones	30.00
11	Nolan Ryan	125.00
12	Pedro Martinez	75.00
13	Wade Boggs	30.00
14	Nomar Garciaparra	50.00
15	Don Mattingly	100.00
16	Todd Helton	40.00
17	Stan Musial, Tony Gwynn	175.00
18	Barry Bonds, Willie Mays	900.00
19	Mike Schmidt, Scott Rolen	150.00
20	Alex Rodriguez, Cal Ripken Jr.	400.00
21	Andruw Jones, Hank Aaron	350.00
22	Nolan Ryan, Pedro Martinez	300.00
22	Nolan Ryan, Roger Clemens FB redemp.	375.00
23	Wade Boggs FB Redemp.	25.00
24	Don Mattingly, Todd Helton	200.00

Prime Numbers

CAL RIPKEN JR

		NM/M
Print runs listed.		
1a	Alex Rodriguez/300	8.00
1b	Alex Rodriguez/308	8.00
1c	Alex Rodriguez/350	8.00
2a	Ken Griffey Jr./400	6.00
2b	Ken Griffey Jr./408	6.00
2c	Ken Griffey Jr./430	6.00
3a	Mark McGwire/500	8.00
3b	Mark McGwire/504	8.00
3c	Mark McGwire/550	8.00
4a	Cal Ripken Jr./400	10.00
4b	Cal Ripken Jr./407	10.00
4c	Cal Ripken Jr./410	10.00
5a	Derek Jeter/300	10.00
5b	Derek Jeter/302	10.00
5c	Derek Jeter/320	10.00
6a	Mike Piazza/300	6.00
6b	Mike Piazza/302	6.00
6c	Mike Piazza/360	6.00
7a	Nomar Garciaparra/300	6.00
7b	Nomar Garciaparra/302	6.00
7c	Nomar Garciaparra/370	6.00
8a	Sammy Sosa/300	6.00
8b	Sammy Sosa/306	6.00
8c	Sammy Sosa/380	6.00
9a	Vladimir Guerrero/300	4.00
9b	Vladimir Guerrero/305	4.00
9c	Vladimir Guerrero/340	4.00
10a	Tony Gwynn/300	4.00
10b	Tony Gwynn/304	4.00
10c	Tony Gwynn/390	4.00

Primary Colors

Delgado blue jays • 1B

		NM/M
Complete Set (40):		100.00
Common Player:		1.00
Production 975 Sets		
Red Die-Cut:		3-5X
Production 25		
Blues:		1-1.5X
Production 200		

Blue Die-Cut: 1.5-3X
Production 50
Yellows: 3-5X
Production 25
Yellow Die-Cut: 1.5-2X
Production 75

1	Alex Rodriguez	8.00
2	Barry Bonds	10.00
3	Cal Ripken Jr.	10.00
4	Chipper Jones	5.00
5	Derek Jeter	10.00
6	Troy Glaus	4.00
7	Frank Thomas	4.00
8	Greg Maddux	5.00
9	Ivan Rodriguez	2.50
10	Jeff Bagwell	4.00
11	Todd Helton	4.00
12	Ken Griffey Jr.	6.00
13	Manny Ramirez	4.00
14	Mark McGwire	8.00
15	Mike Piazza	6.00
16	Nomar Garciaparra	6.00
17	Pedro Martinez	4.00
18	Randy Johnson	4.00
19	Rick Ankiel	1.25
20	Roger Clemens	5.50
21	Sammy Sosa	6.00
22	Tony Gwynn	5.00
23	Vladimir Guerrero	4.00
24	Carlos Delgado	2.00
25	Jason Giambi	2.50
26	Andruw Jones	4.00
27	Bernie Williams	1.50
28	Roberto Alomar	1.50
29	Shawn Green	1.50
30	Barry Larkin	1.00
31	Scott Rolen	3.00
32	Gary Sheffield	2.00
33	Rafael Palmeiro	3.00
34	Albert Belle	1.00
35	Magglio Ordonez	1.50
36	Jim Thome	1.00
37	Jim Edmonds	1.00
38	Darin Erstad	2.00
39	Kris Benson	1.00
40	Sean Casey	1.50

Throwback Threads

NM/M

Common Player: 15.00
Singles production 100.
Doubles production 50.
SP production listed.

1	Stan Musial/75	50.00
2	Tony Gwynn/75	25.00
3	Willie McCovey	15.00
4	Barry Bonds	50.00
5	Babe Ruth	250.00
6	Lou Gehrig	200.00
7	Mike Schmidt/75	40.00
8	Scott Rolen	20.00
9	Harmon Killebrew/75	30.00
10	Kirby Puckett	20.00
11	Al Kaline/75	40.00
12	Eddie Matthews	25.00
13	Hank Aaron/75	60.00
14	Andruw Jones/50	15.00
15	Lou Brock	15.00
16	Ozzie Smith	25.00
17	Ernie Banks/75	35.00
18	Ryne Sandberg	50.00
19	Roberto Clemente	100.00
20	Vladimir Guerrero/50	30.00
21	Frank Robinson/50	25.00
22	Frank Thomas	15.00
23	Brooks Robinson/50	25.00
24	Cal Ripken Jr.	50.00
25	Roger Clemens	30.00
26	Pedro Martinez	20.00
27	Reggie Jackson	15.00
28	Dave Winfield	15.00
29	Don Mattingly/50	60.00
30	Todd Helton	15.00
31	Stan Musial, Tony Gwynn/25	120.00
32	Barry Bonds, Willie McCovey	85.00
33	Babe Ruth, Lou Gehrig	500.00
34	Mike Schmidt, Scott Rolen/25	150.00
35	Harmon Killebrew, Kirby Puckett	50.00
36	Al Kaline, Eddie Matthews	50.00
37	Andruw Jones, Hank Aaron	85.00
38	Lou Brock, Ozzie Smith	50.00
39	Ernie Banks, Ryne Sandberg/25	125.00
40	Roberto Clemente, Vladimir Guerrero	90.00
41	Frank Robinson, Frank Thomas	40.00
42	Brooks Robinson, Cal Ripken Jr.	85.00
43	Pedro Martinez, Roger Clemens	60.00
44	Dave Winfield, Reggie Jackson	30.00
45	Don Mattingly, Todd Helton	75.00

Throwback Threads Autograph

NM/M

Production Listed
Football Exchange for 21 & 22 will be redeemed for #'s listed for 21 & 22.

1	Stan Musial/25	150.00
2	Tony Gwynn/25	100.00
7	Mike Schmidt/25	200.00
9	Harmon Killebrew/25	125.00
11	Al Kaline/25	120.00
13	Hank Aaron/25	250.00
14	Andruw Jones/50	50.00
17	Ernie Banks/25	150.00
20	Vladimir Guerrero/50	75.00
21	Frank Robinson/ 50 FB Redemp	40.00
22	Frank Thomas/ 50 FB redemp	50.00
23	Brooks Robinson/50	100.00
29	Don Mattingly/50	150.00
31	Stan Musial, Tony Gwynn/25	225.00
34	Mike Schmidt, Scott Rolen/25	225.00
39	Ernie Banks, Ryne Sandberg/25	250.00

Title Waves

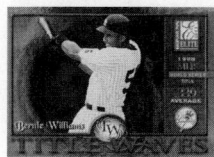

NM/M

Common Player: 1.00
Numbered to title year.
Holofoil: 2-3X
Production 100 Sets

1	Tony Gwynn/1994	5.00
2	Todd Helton/2000	4.00
3	Nomar Garciaparra/2000	6.00
4	Frank Thomas/1997	4.00
5	Alex Rodriguez/1996	8.00
6	Jeff Bagwell/1994	4.00
7	Mark McGwire/1998	8.00
8	Sammy Sosa/2000	6.00
9	Ken Griffey Jr./1997	6.00
10	Albert Belle/1995	1.00
11	Barry Bonds/1993	10.00
12	Jose Canseco/1991	2.00
13	Manny Ramirez/1999	4.00
14	Sammy Sosa/1998	6.00
15	Andres Galarraga/1996	1.00
16	Todd Helton/2000	4.00
17	Ken Griffey Jr./1997	6.00
18	Jeff Bagwell/1994	4.00
19	Mike Piazza/1995	6.00
20	Alex Rodriguez/1995	8.00
21	Jason Giambi/2000	2.00
22	Ivan Rodriguez/1999	2.50
23	Greg Maddux/1997	5.00
24	Pedro Martinez/1994	4.00
25	Derek Jeter/2000	10.00
26	Bernie Williams/1998	1.50
27	Roger Clemens/1999	8.00
28	Chipper Jones/1995	4.00
29	Mark McGwire/1990	8.00
30	Cal Ripken Jr./1983	10.00

Turn of the Century Auto.

NM/M

Common Autograph: 8.00
Production 100 Sets
Redemp. deadline 5/01/03.

151	Brent Abernathy	8.00
152	Cory Aldridge	8.00
153	Gene Altman	8.00
154	Josh Beckett	80.00
155	Wilson Betemit	25.00
156	Albert Pujols	900.00
157	Joe Crede	30.00
158	Jack Cust	10.00
159	Ben Sheets	30.00
160	Alex Escobar	8.00
161	Adrian Hernandez	8.00
162	Pedro Feliz	8.00
163	Nate Frese	8.00
164	Carlos Garcia	8.00
165	Marcus Giles	20.00
166	Alexis Gomez	10.00
167	Jason Hart	8.00
168	Aubrey Huff	10.00
169	Cesar Izturis	20.00
170	Nick Johnson	20.00
171	Jack Wilson	15.00
172	Brian Lawrence	10.00
173	Christian Parker	8.00
174	Nick Maness	8.00
175	Jose Mieses	10.00
176	Greg Miller	8.00
177	Eric Munson	10.00
178	Xavier Nady	15.00
179	Blaine Neal	8.00
180	Abraham Nunez	10.00
181	Jose Ortiz	10.00
182	Jeremy Owens	8.00
183	Jay Gibbons	25.00
184	Corey Patterson	20.00
185	Carlos Pena	25.00
186	C.C. Sabathia	40.00
187	Timoniel Perez	8.00
188	Adam Pettyjohn	8.00
189	Donaldo Mendez	8.00
190	Jackson Melian	8.00
191	Wilken Ruan	8.00
192	Duaner Sanchez	8.00
193	Alfonso Soriano	60.00
194	Rafael Soriano	10.00
196	Billy Sylvester	8.00
197	Juan Uribe	20.00
199	Carlos Valderrama	10.00
200	Matt White	10.00

2001 Donruss Signature Series

NM/M

Complete Set (311):
Common Player: .50
Common (111-165): 8.00
Auto. print run 330
Common (166-311): 4.00
Production 800
Box: 100.00

1	Alex Rodriguez	3.00
2	Barry Bonds	4.00
3	Cal Ripken Jr.	4.00
4	Chipper Jones	2.00
5	Derek Jeter	1.50
6	Troy Glaus	1.50
7	Frank Thomas	1.50
8	Greg Maddux	2.00
9	Ivan Rodriguez	1.00
10	Jeff Bagwell	1.50
11	John Olerud	.50
12	Todd Helton	1.50
13	Ken Griffey Jr.	2.50
14	Manny Ramirez	1.50
15	Mark McGwire	2.50
16	Mike Piazza	2.50
17	Nomar Garciaparra	2.50
18	Moises Alou	.50
19	Aramis Ramirez	.50
20	Curt Schilling	.75
21	Pat Burrell	.75
22	Doug Mientkiewicz	.50
23	Carlos Delgado	.75
24	J.D. Drew	.75
25	Cliff Floyd	.50
26	Freddy Garcia	.50
27	Roberto Alomar	.75
28	Barry Zito	.50
29	Juan Encarnacion	.50
30	Paul Konerko	.75
31	Mark Mulder	.75
32	Andy Pettitte	.75
33	Jim Edmonds	.50
34	Darin Erstad	1.00
35	Jason Giambi	1.00
36	Tom Glavine	.75
37	Juan Gonzalez	1.50
38	Fred McGriff	.50
39	Shawn Green	.75
40	Tim Hudson	.50
41	Andruw Jones	1.50
42	Jeff Kent	.50
43	Barry Larkin	.50
44	Brad Radke	.50
45	Mike Mussina	.75
46	Hideo Nomo	.75
47	Rafael Palmeiro	1.50
48	Scott Rolen	1.50
49	Gary Sheffield	.75
50	Bernie Williams	.75
51	Bobby Abreu	.50
52	Edgardo Alfonzo	.50
53	Edgar Martinez	.50
54	Magglio Ordonez	.75
55	Kerry Wood	.75
56	Adrian Beltre	.75
57	Lance Berkman	.50
58	Kevin Brown	.65
59	Sean Casey	.50
60	Eric Chavez	.75
61	Bartolo Colon	.50
62	Sammy Sosa	2.50
63	Jermaine Dye	.50
64	Tony Gwynn	2.00
65	Carl Everett	.50
66	Brian Giles	.50
67	Mike Hampton	.50
68	Richard Hidalgo	.50
69	Geoff Jenkins	.50
70	Tony Clark	.50
71	Roger Clemens	2.25
72	Ryan Klesko	.50
73	Chan Ho Park	.50
74	Richie Sexson	.50
75	Mike Sweeney	.50
76	Kazuhiro Sasaki	.50
77	Miguel Tejada	.75
78	Jose Vidro	.50
79	Larry Walker	.50
80	Preston Wilson	.50
81	Craig Biggio	.50
82	Andres Galarraga	.50
83	Jim Thome	.50
84	Vladimir Guerrero	1.50
85	Rafael Furcal	.50
86	Cristian Guzman	.50
87	Terrence Long	.50
88	Bret Boone	.50
89	Wade Miller	.50
90	Eric Milton	.50
91	Gabe Kapler	.50
92	Johnny Damon	.75
93	Carlos Lee	.50
94	Kenny Lofton	.50
95	Raul Mondesi	.50
96	Jorge Posada	.65
97	Mark Grace	.50
98	Robert Fick	.50
99	Joe Mays	.50
100	Aaron Sele	.50
101	Ben Grieve	.50
102	Luis Gonzalez	.65
103	Ray Durham	.50
104	Mark Quinn	.50
105	Jose Canseco	1.00
106	David Justice	.50
107	Pedro Martinez	1.50
108	Randy Johnson	1.50
109	Phil Nevin	.50
110	Rickey Henderson	.75
111	Alex Escobar/Auto.	8.00
112	Johnny Estrada/Auto. **RC**	15.00
113	Pedro Feliz/Auto.	8.00
114	Nate Frese/Auto.	8.00
115	Ricardo Rodriguez/Auto. **RC**	8.00
116	Brandon Larson/Auto. **RC**	8.00
117	Alexis Gomez/Auto. **RC**	8.00
118	Jason Hart/Auto.	8.00
119	C.C. Sabathia/Auto.	20.00
120	Endy Chavez/Auto. **RC**	8.00
121	Christian Parker/Auto. **RC**	8.00
122	Jackson Melian **RC**	8.00
123	Joe Kennedy/Auto. **RC**	10.00
124	Adrian Hernandez/Auto. **RC**	8.00
125	Cesar Izturis/Auto.	10.00
126	Jose Mieses/Auto. **RC**	8.00
127	Roy Oswalt/Auto.	30.00
128	Eric Munson/Auto.	8.00
129	Xavier Nady/Auto.	8.00
130	Horacio Ramirez/Auto. **RC**	15.00
131	Abraham Nunez/Auto.	8.00
132	Jose Ortiz/Auto.	8.00
133	Jeremy Owens/Auto. **RC**	8.00
134	Claudio Vargas/Auto. **RC**	8.00
135	Corey Patterson/Auto.	15.00

136	Carlos Pena	15.00
137	Bud Smith/Auto. RC	8.00
138	Adam Dunn/Auto.	25.00
139	Adam Pettyjohn/Auto.	8.00
140	Elpidio Guzman/Auto. RC	8.00
141	Jay Gibbons/Auto. RC	15.00
142	Wilken Ruan/Auto. RC	8.00
143	Tsuyoshi Shinjo RC	8.00
144	Alfonso Soriano/Auto.	30.00
145	Marcus Giles/Auto.	10.00
146	Ichiro Suzuki RC	75.00
147	Juan Uribe/Auto.	10.00
148	David Williams/Auto. RC	8.00
149	Carlos Valderrama/Auto. RC	8.00
150	Matt White/Auto. RC	8.00
151	Albert Pujols/Auto. RC	700.00
152	Donaldo Mendez/Auto. RC	8.00
153	Cory Aldridge/Auto. RC	8.00
154	Brandon Duckworth/Auto. RC	8.00
155	Josh Beckett/Auto.	30.00
156	Wilson Betemit/Auto. RC	15.00
157	Ben Sheets/Auto.	25.00
158	Andres Torres/Auto. RC	8.00
159	Aubrey Huff/Auto.	15.00
160	Jack Wilson/Auto. RC	15.00
161	Rafael Soriano/Auto. RC	8.00
162	Nick Johnson/Auto.	12.00
163	Carlos Garcia/Auto. RC	8.00
164	Josh Towers/Auto. RC	10.00
165	Jason Michaels/Auto. RC	8.00
166	Ryan Drese RC	4.00
167	Dewon Brazelton RC	4.00
168	Kevin Olsen RC	4.00
169	Benito Baez RC	4.00
170	Mark Prior RC	20.00
171	Wilmy Caceres RC	4.00
172	Mark Teixeira RC	35.00
173	Willie Harris RC	4.00
174	Mike Koplove RC	4.00
175	Brandon Knight RC	4.00
176	John Grabow RC	4.00
177	Jeremy Affeldt RC	4.00
178	Brandon Inge	4.00
179	Casey Fossum RC	6.00
180	Scott Stewart RC	4.00
181	Luke Hudson RC	4.00
182	Ken Vining RC	4.00
183	Toby Hall	4.00
184	Eric Knott RC	4.00
185	Kris Foster RC	4.00
186	David Brous RC	4.00
187	Roy Smith RC	4.00
188	Grant Balfour RC	4.00
189	Jeremy Fikac RC	4.00
190	Morgan Ensberg RC	10.00
191	Ryan Freel RC	6.00
192	Ryan Jensen RC	4.00
193	Lance Davis RC	4.00
194	Delvin James RC	4.00
195	Timo Perez	4.00
196	Michael Cuddyer	4.00
197	Bob File RC	4.00
198	Martin Vargas RC	4.00
199	Kris Keller RC	4.00
200	Tim Spooneybarger RC	4.00
201	Adam Everett	4.00
202	Josh Fogg RC	6.00
203	Kip Wells	4.00
204	Rick Bauer RC	4.00
205	Brent Abernathy	4.00
206	Erick Almonte RC	4.00
207	Pedro Santana RC	4.00
208	Ken Harvey	4.00
209	Jerrod Riggan RC	4.00
210	Nick Punto RC	4.00
211	Steve Green RC	4.00
212	Nick Neugebauer	4.00
213	Chris George	4.00
214	Mike Penny	4.00
215	Bret Prinz RC	4.00
216	Tim Christman RC	4.00
217	Sean Douglass RC	4.00
218	Brett Jodie RC	4.00
219	Juan Diaz RC	4.00
220	Carlos Hernandez RC	4.00
221	Alex Cintron	4.00
222	Juan Cruz RC	4.00
223	Larry Bigbie	4.00
224	Junior Spivey RC	8.00
225	Luis Rivas	4.00
226	Brandon Lyon RC	4.00
227	Tony Cogan RC	4.00
228	Justin Duchscherer RC	6.00
229	Tike Redman	4.00
230	Jimmy Rollins	5.00
231	Scott Podsednik RC	15.00
232	Jose Acevedo RC	4.00
233	Luis Pineda RC	4.00
234	Josh Phelps	4.00
235	Paul Phillips RC	4.00
236	Brian Roberts RC	10.00
237	Orlando Woodwards	4.00
238	Bart Miadich RC	4.00
239	Les Walrond RC	4.00
240	Brad Voyles RC	4.00
241	Joe Crede	8.00
242	Juan Moreno RC	4.00
243	Matt Ginter	4.00
244	Brian Rogers RC	4.00
245	Pablo Ozuna	4.00
246	Geronimo Gil RC	4.00
247	Mike Maroth RC	4.00
248	Josue Perez RC	4.00
249	Dee Brown	4.00
250	Victor Zambrano RC	4.00
251	Nick Maness RC	4.00
252	Kyle Lohse RC	6.00
253	Greg Miller RC	4.00
254	Henry Mateo RC	4.00
255	Duaner Sanchez RC	4.00
256	Rob Mackowiak RC	6.00
257	Steve Lomasney	4.00
258	Angel Santos RC	4.00
259	Winston Abreu RC	4.00
260	Brandon Berger RC	4.00
261	Tomas De La Rosa	4.00
262	Ramon Vazquez RC	4.00
263	Mickey Callaway	4.00
264	Corky Miller RC	4.00
265	Keith Ginter	4.00
266	Cody Ransom RC	4.00
267	Doug Nickle RC	4.00
268	Derrick Lewis RC	4.00
269	Eric Hinske RC	6.00
270	Travis Phelps RC	4.00
271	Eric Valent	4.00
272	Michael Rivera RC	4.00
273	Esix Snead RC	4.00
274	Troy Mattes RC	4.00
275	Jermaine Clark	4.00
276	Nate Cornejo	4.00
277	George Perez RC	4.00
278	Juan Rivera	4.00
279	Justin Atchley RC	4.00
280	Adam Johnson	4.00
281	Gene Altman RC	4.00
282	Jason Jennings	4.00
283	Scott MacRae RC	4.00
284	Craig Monroe RC	6.00
285	Bert Snow RC	4.00
286	Stubby Clapp RC	4.00
287	Jack Cust	4.00
288	Will Ohman RC	4.00
289	Wily Mo Pena RC	4.00
290	Joe Beimel RC	4.00
291	Jason Karnuth RC	4.00
292	Bill Ortega	4.00
293	Nate Teut RC	4.00
294	Erik Hiljus RC	4.00
295	Jason Smith RC	4.00
296	Juan Pena	4.00
297	David Espinosa	4.00
298	Tim Redding	4.00
299	Brian Lawrence RC	4.00
300	Brian Reith RC	4.00
301	Chad Durbin	4.00
302	Kurt Ainsworth RC	4.00
303	Blaine Neal RC	4.00
304	Jorge Julio RC	4.00
305	Adam Bernero	4.00
306	Travis Hafner RC	20.00
307	Dustan Mohr RC	4.00
308	Cesar Crespo RC	4.00
309	Billy Sylvester RC	4.00
310	Zach Day RC	6.00
311	Angel Berroa RC	8.00

Signature Stats

	NM/M
Quantity produced listed	
Roberto Alomar/120	40.00
Moises Alou/124	6.00
Luis Aparicio/313	10.00
Lance Berkman/297	15.00
Wade Boggs/51	75.00
Lou Brock/118	15.00
Gary Carter/32	50.00
Joe Carter/121	10.00
Sean Casey/103	10.00
Darin Erstad/100	15.00
Bob Feller/26	50.00
Cliff Floyd/45	15.00
Whitey Ford/72	40.00
Andres Galarraga/150	8.00
Bob Gibson/112	25.00
Brian Giles/123	10.00
Troy Glaus/102	20.00
Luis Gonzalez/114	10.00
Vladimir Guerrero/131	30.00
Richard Hidalgo/314	6.00
Bo Jackson/32	85.00
Al Kaline/128	45.00
Gabe Kapler/302	6.00
Ralph Kiner/54	30.00
Carlos Lee/261	10.00
Kenny Lofton/210	6.00
Edgar Martinez/145	20.00
Joe Mays/115	6.00
Paul Molitor/41	50.00
Mark Mulder/145	25.00
Magglio Ordonez/126	10.00
Rafael Palmeiro/47	40.00
Kirby Puckett/31	100.00
Manny Ramirez/45	60.00
Alex Rodriguez/132	85.00
Ivan Rodriguez/113	30.00

Shannon Stewart/319	6.00
Mike Sweeney/144	6.00
Miguel Tejada/115	35.00
Joe Torre/230	25.00
Javier Vazquez/405	6.00
Jose Vidro/330	6.00
Hoyt Wilhelm/243	6.00

Signature Proofs

Stars (1-110):	2-3X
Production 175	
Cards (111-311) Production 25	

Award Winning Signatures

	NM/M
Common Player:	20.00
Jeff Bagwell/94	65.00
Carlos Beltran/99	40.00
Johnny Bench/68	75.00
Yogi Berra/55	50.00
Craig Biggio/97	25.00
Barry Bonds/93	200.00
Rod Carew/77	50.00
Orlando Cepeda/67	20.00
Andre Dawson/77	20.00
Dennis Eckersley/92	25.00
Dennis Eckersley/92	25.00
Whitey Ford/61	50.00
Jason Giambi/100	20.00
Bob Gibson/68	40.00
Juan Gonzalez/96	35.00
Orel Hershiser/88	25.00
Al Kaline/67	75.00
Fred Lynn/75	15.00
Fred Lynn/75	15.00
Jim Palmer/76	25.00
Cal Ripken/83	150.00
Phil Rizzuto/50	40.00
Brooks Robinson/64	40.00
Scott Rolen/97	30.00
Ryne Sandberg/84	90.00
Warren Spahn/57	50.00
Frank Thomas/94	35.00
Billy Williams/61	20.00
Kerry Wood/98	40.00
Robin Yount/89	60.00

Century Marks

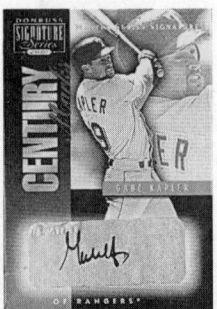

	NM/M
Common Autograph:	5.00
Brent Abernathy/184	5.00
Roberto Alomar/120	40.00
Rick Ankiel/119	15.00
Lance Berkman/121	15.00

Mark Buehrle/224	10.00
Wilmy Caceres/194	5.00
Eric Chavez/170	10.00
Joe Crede/154	5.00
Jack Cust/178	10.00
Brandon Duckworth/183	5.00
David Espinosa/199	5.00
Johnny Estrada/198	5.00
Pedro Feliz/180	5.00
Robert Fick/232	5.00
Cliff Floyd/146	8.00
Casey Fossum/100	10.00
Jay Gibbons/175	15.00
Keith Ginter/163	5.00
Troy Glaus/144	20.00
Luis Gonzalez/101	10.00
Vladimir Guerrero/187	30.00
Richard Hidalgo/173	5.00
Tim Hudson/145	25.00
Adam Johnson/130	5.00
Gabe Kapler/150	8.00
Joe Kennedy/219	5.00
Ryan Klesko/176	10.00
Carlos Lee/179	8.00
Terrence Long/180	5.00
Edgar Martinez/110	20.00
Joe Mays/209	5.00
Greg Miller/194	5.00
Wade Miller/180	5.00
Mark Mulder/203	20.00
Xavier Nady/180	5.00
Magglio Ordonez/104	10.00
Jose Ortiz/187	5.00
Roy Oswalt/192	10.00
Wily Mo Pena/203	10.00
Brad Penny/198	5.00
Aramis Ramirez/241	20.00
Luis Rivas/163	5.00
Alex Rodriguez/110	120.00
Scott Rolen/106	30.00
Mike Sweeney/99	10.00
Eric Valent/163	5.00
Kip Wells/223	5.00
Kerry Wood/109	25.00

Milestone Marks

	NM/M
Common Player:	10.00
Ernie Banks/285	35.00
Yogi Berra/120	50.00
Wade Boggs/98	60.00
Barry Bonds/55	200.00
George Brett/27	150.00
George Brett/23	150.00
Lou Brock/83	25.00
Rod Carew/110	30.00
Steve Carlton/75	35.00
Gary Carter/213	20.00
Bobby Doerr/192	15.00
Bob Feller/202	15.00
Whitey Ford/186	25.00
Steve Garvey/175	10.00
Tony Gwynn/99	50.00
Fergie Jenkins/149	15.00
Al Kaline/149	40.00
Harmon Killebrew/127	40.00
Ralph Kiner/105	20.00
Willie McCovey/20	75.00
Paul Molitor/96	40.00
Eddie Murray/46	70.00
Stan Musial/109	75.00
Phil Niekro/300	10.00
Tony Perez/146	15.00
Cal Ripken/25	200.00
Frank Robinson/136	20.00
Mike Schmidt/40	125.00
Mike Schmidt/23	150.00
Enos Slaughter/117	20.00
Warren Spahn/300	40.00
Alan Trammell/154	25.00
Hoyt Wilhelm/227	10.00
Dave Winfield/31	50.00
Dave Winfield/80	80.00

Notable Nicknames

	NM/M
Common Player:	30.00
Production 100	
Ernie Banks	75.00
Orlando Cepeda	40.00
Will Clark	80.00

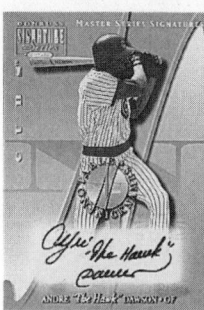

Roger Clemens/50	250.00
Andre Dawson	30.00
Bob Feller	50.00
Carlton Fisk	70.00
Andres Galarraga	40.00
Luis Gonzalez	30.00
Reggie Jackson	75.00
Harmon Killebrew	80.00
Stan Musial	120.00
Brooks Robinson	80.00
Nolan Ryan	250.00
Ryne Sandberg	150.00
Enos Slaughter	60.00
Duke Snider	75.00
Frank Thomas	100.00

Team Trademarks

	NM/M
Rick Ankiel/179	10.00
Ernie Banks/180	50.00
Johnny Bench/20	75.00
Yogi Berra/124	40.00
Wade Boggs/89	75.00
Barry Bonds/77	200.00
Lou Brock/29	35.00
Steve Carlton/174	25.00
Sean Casey/123	15.00
Orlando Cepeda/100	20.00
Roger Clemens/30 (Red Sox)	125.00
Roger Clemens/21 (Yankees)	150.00
Andre Dawson/176	15.00
Bobby Doerr/193	20.00
Whitey Ford/94	40.00
Steve Garvey/182	20.00
Bob Gibson/98	30.00
Juan Gonzalez/70	40.00
Shawn Green/109	20.00
Orel Hershiser/210	15.00
Reggie Jackson/73	50.00
Fergie Jenkins/213	15.00
Chipper Jones/74	50.00
Pedro Martinez/27	85.00
Don Mattingly/72	125.00
Willie Mays/197	125.00
Willie McCovey/26	70.00
Joe Morgan/33	80.00
Eddie Murray/45	35.00
Stan Musial/65	90.00
Mike Mussina/85 (Orioles)	40.00
Mike Mussina/95 (Yankees)	50.00
Phil Niekro/187	10.00
Rafael Palmeiro/99	30.00
Jim Palmer/142	15.00
Tony Perez/73	15.00
Manny Ramirez/57	50.00
Cal Ripken Jr./47	200.00
Phil Rizzuto/98	40.00
Brooks Robinson/146	25.00
Frank Robinson/118 (Orioles)	25.00
Frank Robinson/116 (Reds)	25.00
Alex Rodriguez/100	100.00
Ivan Rodriguez/62	50.00
Scott Rolen/39	40.00

Nolan Ryan/153	100.00
Ryne Sandberg/52	100.00
Curt Schilling/163	40.00
Mike Schmidt/107	75.00
Tom Seaver/25	125.00
Gary Sheffield/194	20.00
Enos Slaughter/215	20.00
Duke Snider/47	50.00
Warren Spahn/140	40.00
Joe Torre/90	40.00
Billy Williams/194	10.00
Kerry Wood/52	40.00

2001 Donruss Studio

Jason Giambi • 1B
OAKLAND ATHLETICS

	NM/M
Complete Set (200):	
Common Player:	.25
Common SP (151-200):	4.00
Production 700	
Pack (6):	8.00
Box (18) + 5x7 Auto.	140.00
1 Alex Rodriguez	2.00
2 Barry Bonds	2.50
3 Cal Ripken Jr.	2.50
4 Chipper Jones	1.00
5 Derek Jeter	2.50
6 Troy Glaus	.65
7 Frank Thomas	.75
8 Greg Maddux	1.00
9 Ivan Rodriguez	.65
10 Jeff Bagwell	.75
11 Mark Quinn	.25
12 Todd Helton	.65
13 Ken Griffey Jr.	1.50
14 Manny Ramirez	.75
15 Mark McGwire	2.00
16 Mike Piazza	1.50
17 Nomar Garciaparra	1.00
18 Robin Ventura	.25
19 Aramis Ramirez	.25
20 J.T. Snow	.25
21 Pat Burrell	.60
22 Curt Schilling	.50
23 Carlos Delgado	.50
24 J.D. Drew	.40
25 Cliff Floyd	.25
26 Brian Jordan	.25
27 Roberto Alomar	.35
28 Barry Zito	.40
29 Harold Baines	.25
30 Brad Penny	.25
31 Jose Cruz	.25
32 Andy Pettitte	.40
33 Jim Edmonds	.25
34 Darin Erstad	.35
35 Jason Giambi	.60
36 Tom Glavine	.50
37 Juan Gonzalez	.35
38 Mark Grace	.25
39 Shawn Green	.50
40 Tim Hudson	.25
41 Andruw Jones	.75
42 Jeff Kent	.25
43 Barry Larkin	.25
44 Rafael Furcal	.25
45 Mike Mussina	.50
46 Hideo Nomo	.50
47 Rafael Palmeiro	.65
48 Scott Rolen	.60
49 Gary Sheffield	.50
50 Bernie Williams	.25
51 Bobby Abreu	.25
52 Edgardo Alfonzo	.25
53 Edgar Martinez	.25
54 Magglio Ordonez	.25
55 Kerry Wood	.50
56 Matt Morris	.25
57 Lance Berkman	.25
58 Kevin Brown	.25
59 Sean Casey	.40
60 Eric Chavez	.25
61 Bartolo Colon	.25
62 Johnny Damon	.50
63 Jermaine Dye	.25
64 Juan Encarnacion	.25
65 Carl Everett	.25
66 Brian Giles	.25
67 Mike Hampton	.25
68 Richard Hidalgo	.25
69 Geoff Jenkins	.25
70 Jacque Jones	.25
71 Jason Kendall	.25
72 Ryan Klesko	.25
73 Chan Ho Park	.25
74 Richie Sexson	.25
75 Mike Sweeney	.25
76 Fernando Tatis	.25
77 Miguel Tejada	.50
78 Jose Vidro	.25
79 Larry Walker	.25
80 Preston Wilson	.25
81 Craig Biggio	.25
82 Fred McGriff	.25
83 Jim Thome	.65
84 Garret Anderson	.25
85 Mark Mulder	.40
86 Tony Batista	.25
87 Terrence Long	.25
88 Brad Fullmer	.25
89 Rusty Greer	.25
90 Orlando Hernandez	.25
91 Gabe Kapler	.25
92 Paul Konerko	.25
93 Carlos Lee	.25
94 Kenny Lofton	.25
95 Raul Mondesi	.25
96 Jorge Posada	.40
97 Tim Salmon	.25
98 Greg Vaughn	.25
99 Mo Vaughn	.25
100 Omar Vizquel	.25
101 Ben Grieve	.25
102 Luis Gonzalez	.25
103 Ray Durham	.25
104 Ryan Dempster	.25
105 Eric Karros	.25
106 David Justice	.25
107 Pedro Martinez	.75
108 Randy Johnson	.75
109 Rick Ankiel	.25
110 Rickey Henderson	.75
111 Roger Clemens	1.25
112 Sammy Sosa	1.00
113 Tony Gwynn	1.00
114 Vladimir Guerrero	.75
115 Kazuhiro Sasaki	.25
116 Phil Nevin	.25
117 Ruben Mateo	.25
118 Shannon Stewart	.25
119 Matt Williams	.25
120 Tino Martinez	.25
121 Ken Caminiti	.25
122 Edgar Renteria	.25
123 Charles Johnson	.25
124 Aaron Sele	.25
125 Javy Lopez	.25
126 Mariano Rivera	.35
127 Shea Hillenbrand	.25
128 Jeff D'Amico	.25
129 Brady Anderson	.25
130 Kevin Millwood	.25
131 Trot Nixon	.25
132 Mike Lieberthal	.25
133 Juan Pierre	.25
134 Russ Ortiz	.25
135 Jose Macias	.25
136 John Smoltz	.25
137 Jason Varitek	.25
138 Dean Palmer	.25
139 Jeff Cirillo	.25
140 Paul O'Neill	.25
141 Andres Galarraga	.25
142 David Wells	.25
143 Brad Radke	.25
144 Wade Miller	.25
145 John Olerud	.25
146 Moises Alou	.25
147 Carlos Beltran	.50
148 Jeromy Burnitz	.25
149 Steve Finley	.25
150 Joe Mays	.25
151 Alex Escobar	4.00
152 Johnny Estrada RC	8.00
153 Pedro Feliz	4.00
154 Nate Frese RC	4.00
155 Dee Brown	4.00
156 Brandon Larson RC	5.00
157 Alexis Gomez RC	4.00
158 Jason Hart	4.00
159 C.C. Sabathia	4.00
160 Josh Towers RC	6.00
161 Christian Parker RC	4.00
162 Jackson Melian RC	4.00
163 Joe Kennedy RC	4.00
164 Adrian Hernandez RC	4.00
165 Jimmy Rollins	4.00
166 Jose Mieses RC	4.00
167 Roy Oswalt	5.00
168 Eric Munson	4.00
169 Xavier Nady	4.00
170 Horacio Ramirez RC	8.00
171 Abraham Nunez	4.00
172 Jose Ortiz	4.00
173 Jeremy Owens RC	4.00
174 Claudio Vargas RC	4.00
175 Corey Patterson	4.00
176 Carlos Pena	4.00
177 Bud Smith RC	5.00
178 Adam Dunn	4.00
179 Adam Pettyjohn RC	4.00
180 Elpidio Guzman RC	4.00
181 Jay Gibbons RC	10.00
182 Wilkin Ruan RC	4.00
183 Tsuyoshi Shinjo RC	4.00
184 Alfonso Soriano	6.00
185 Marcus Giles	4.00
186 Ichiro Suzuki RC	85.00
187 Juan Uribe RC	6.00
188 David Williams RC	4.00
189 Carlos Valderrama RC	4.00
190 Matt White RC	4.00
191 Albert Pujols RC	240.00
192 Donaldo Mendez RC	4.00
193 Cory Aldridge RC	4.00
194 Endy Chavez RC	4.00
195 Josh Beckett	4.00
196 Wilson Betemit RC	4.00
197 Ben Sheets	4.00
198 Andres Torres RC	4.00
199 Aubrey Huff	4.00
200 Jack Wilson RC	8.00

Proofs

Chipper Jones • 3B
ATLANTA BRAVES

Values Undetermined
Production 25 Sets
(See 2001 Studio for checklist.)

Diamond Collection

	NM/M
Common Player:	5.00
1 Vladimir Guerrero	10.00
2 Barry Bonds	30.00
3 Cal Ripken Jr.	30.00
4 Nomar Garciaparra	20.00
5 Greg Maddux	15.00
6 Frank Thomas	10.00
7 Roger Clemens	20.00
8 Luis Gonzalez/SP	6.00
9 Tony Gwynn	15.00
10 Carlos Lee/SP	6.00
11 Troy Glaus	8.00
12 Randy Johnson	10.00
13 Manny Ramirez/SP	15.00
14 Pedro Martinez	10.00
15 Todd Helton	10.00
16 Jeff Bagwell	10.00
17 Rickey Henderson	10.00
18 Kazuhiro Sasaki	5.00
19 Albert Pujols/SP	50.00
20 Ivan Rodriguez	8.00
21 Darin Erstad	6.00
22 Andruw Jones	8.00
23 Roberto Alomar	8.00
25 Juan Gonzalez	10.00
26 Shawn Green	7.50
27 Lance Berkman	5.00
28 Scott Rolen	9.00
29 Rafael Palmeiro	8.00
30 J.D. Drew	8.00
31 Kerry Wood	8.00
32 Jim Edmonds	5.00
33 Tom Glavine/SP	8.00
34 Hideo Nomo/SP	50.00
36 Tim Hudson	8.00
37 Miguel Tejada	5.00
38 Chipper Jones	15.00
39 Edgar Martinez/SP	8.00
40 Chan Ho Park	5.00
41 Magglio Ordonez	5.00
42 Sean Casey	5.00
43 Larry Walker	5.00
45 Cliff Floyd	5.00
46 Mike Sweeney	5.00
47 Kevin Brown	5.00
48 Richie Sexson	5.00
49 Jermaine Dye	5.00
50 Craig Biggio	5.00

Leather & Lumber

	NM/M
Common Player:	5.00
Combos:	No Pricing
Production 25 Sets	
1 Barry Bonds	25.00

2	Cal Ripken Jr.	25.00
3	Miguel Tejada	5.00
5	Frank Thomas	8.00
6	Greg Maddux	10.00
7	Ivan Rodriguez	8.00
8	Jeff Bagwell/SP	10.00
9	Sean Casey/SP	6.00
10	Todd Helton	8.00
11	Cliff Floyd	5.00
12	Hideo Nomo	40.00
13	Chipper Jones	10.00
14	Rickey Henderson	8.00
15	Richard Hidalgo	5.00
16	Mike Piazza	15.00
17	Larry Walker	5.00
18	Tony Gwynn	10.00
19	Vladimir Guerrero	8.00
20	Rafael Furcal	5.00
21	Roberto Alomar/SP	8.00
23	Albert Pujols	60.00
24	Raul Mondesi	5.00
25	J.D. Drew	5.00
26	Jim Edmonds	5.00
27	Darin Erstad/SP	6.00
28	Craig Biggio	5.00
29	Kenny Lofton	5.00
30	Juan Gonzalez	5.00
31	John Olerud	5.00
32	Shawn Green	5.00
33	Andruw Jones/SP	8.00
34	Moises Alou	5.00
35	Jeff Kent	5.00
36	Ryan Klesko	5.00
37	Luis Gonzalez	5.00
38	Rafael Palmeiro	5.00
40	Scott Rolen	8.00
41	Carlos Lee	5.00
42	Bobby Abreu	5.00
43	Edgardo Alfonzo	5.00
44	Bernie Williams	5.00
45	Brian Giles	5.00
46	Jermaine Dye	5.00
47	Lance Berkman	5.00
48	Edgar Martinez	5.00
49	Richie Sexson	5.00
50	Magglio Ordonez	5.00

Masterstokes

		NM/M
Common Player:		8.00
Production 200 Sets		
1	Tony Gwynn	25.00
2	Ivan Rodriguez	10.00
3	J.D. Drew	8.00
4	Cal Ripken Jr.	60.00
5	Hideo Nomo	50.00
6	Darin Erstad	8.00
7	Frank Thomas	12.00
8	Andruw Jones	12.00
9	Roberto Alomar	8.00
10	Larry Walker	8.00
11	Vladimir Guerrero	12.00
12	Barry Bonds	65.00
14	Luis Gonzalez	8.00
16	Juan Gonzalez	12.00
17	Todd Helton	8.00
18	Jeff Bagwell	12.00
19	Albert Pujols	75.00
20	Shawn Green	8.00
21	Magglio Ordonez	8.00
22	Scott Rolen	12.00
23	Rafael Palmeiro	10.00
24	Sean Casey	8.00
25	Jim Edmonds	8.00
26	Chipper Jones	20.00
27	Cliff Floyd	8.00
28	Carlos Lee	8.00
29	Edgar Martinez	8.00
30	Lance Berkman	8.00

Private Signings

Rick Ankiel • P
ST. LOUIS CARDINALS

		NM/M
Common Player:		8.00
Inserted 1:Hobby Box		
1	Alex Rodriguez	80.00
2	Miguel Tejada	25.00
3	Ben Sheets	15.00
4	Tony Gwynn/SP/190	60.00
5	Wilson Betemit	8.00
6	Rick Ankiel	25.00
7	Ivan Rodriguez/SP/150	30.00
8	Ryan Klesko	8.00
9	Jason Giambi/SP/250	15.00
10	Brad Penny	8.00
11	Gabe Kapler	8.00
12	Vladimir Guerrero	30.00
13	Alex Escobar	8.00
14	Edgar Martinez	15.00
15	Cal Ripken/SP/50	200.00
16	Brian Giles	8.00
17	Todd Helton/SP/125	25.00
18	Mike Sweeney	8.00
19	Cliff Floyd	8.00
20	Corey Patterson	12.00
21	Alfonso Soriano	40.00
22	Bobby Abreu	8.00
23	Shawn Green/SP/190	20.00
24	C.C. Sabathia	25.00
25	Luis Gonzalez	8.00
26	Barry Bonds/SP/95	200.00
27	Rafael Palmeiro/SP/250	30.00
28	Mike Mussina/SP/144	40.00
29	Roger Clemens/SP/200	100.00
30	Greg Maddux/SP/200	80.00
31	Troy Glaus	20.00
32	Kerry Wood	15.00
33	Roberto Alomar/SP/200	30.00
34	Tom Glavine	40.00
35	Frank Thomas	20.00
36	Carlos Lee	8.00
37	Scott Rolen	20.00
38	Andruw Jones/SP/250	20.00
39	Manny Ramirez/SP/115	40.00
40	Magglio Ordonez	12.00
41	Lance Berkman	8.00
42	Josh Beckett	30.00
43	Adam Dunn	15.00
44	Albert Pujols/SP/50	600.00
45	Darin Erstad	12.00
46	Curt Schilling	40.00
47	Barry Zito	12.00
48	Sean Casey	8.00

Round Trip Tickets

No Pricing
Production 25 Sets

Warning Track

		NM/M
Common Player:		4.00
1	Andruw Jones	8.00
2	Rafael Palmeiro	7.00
3	Gary Sheffield	5.00
4	Larry Walker	4.00
5	Shawn Green	4.00

6	Mike Piazza	12.00
7	Barry Bonds	20.00
8	J.D. Drew	4.00
9	Magglio Ordonez	4.00
10	Todd Helton	8.00
11	Juan Gonzalez	8.00
12	Pat Burrell	5.00
13	Mark McGwire	15.00
14	Frank Robinson	4.00
15	Manny Ramirez	8.00
16	Lance Berkman	4.00
18	Johnny Bench	10.00
19	Chipper Jones	10.00
20	Mike Schmidt	15.00
21	Vladimir Guerrero	8.00
22	Sammy Sosa	12.00
23	Cal Ripken Jr.	20.00
24	Roberto Alomar	4.00
25	Willie Stargell	4.00
27	Scott Rolen	7.00
28	Roberto Clemente/SP	50.00
29	Tony Gwynn	10.00
30	Ivan Rodriguez	5.00
31	Sean Casey	4.00
32	Frank Thomas	8.00
33	Jeff Bagwell	8.00
34	Jeff Kent	4.00
35	Reggie Jackson	8.00

2001 Donruss The Rookies

MARK TEIXEIRA
TEXAS RANGERS • 3B

		NM/M
Complete Set (105):		80.00
Complete Factory Set (106):		100.00
Common Player:		.25
1	Adam Dunn	.50
2	Ryan Drese RC	.40
3	Bud Smith RC	.25
4	Tsuyoshi Shinjo	.50
5	Roy Oswalt	.50
6	Wilmy Caceres RC	.25
7	Willie Harris RC	.25
8	Andres Torres RC	.25
9	Brandon Knight RC	.25
10	Horacio Ramirez RC	.75
11	Benito Baez RC	.25
12	Jeremy Affeldt RC	.25
13	Ryan Jensen RC	.25
14	Casey Fossum RC	.50
15	Ramon Vazquez RC	.50
16	Dustan Mohr RC	.25
17	Saul Rivera RC	.25
18	Zach Day RC	.50
19	Erik Hiljus RC	.25
20	Cesar Crespo RC	.25
21	Wilson Guzman RC	.25
22	Travis Hafner RC	6.00
23	Grant Balfour RC	.25
24	Johnny Estrada RC	1.50
25	Morgan Ensberg RC	1.00
26	Jack Wilson RC	1.50
27	Aubrey Huff	.25
28	Endy Chavez RC	.50
29	Delvin James RC	.25
30	Michael Cuddyer	.25
31	Jason Michaels RC	.25
32	Martin Vargas RC	.25
33	Donaldo Mendez RC	.25
34	Jorge Julio RC	.25
35	Tim Spooneybarger RC	.25
36	Kurt Ainsworth RC	.25
37	Josh Fogg RC	.50
38	Brian Reith RC	.25
39	Rick Baurer RC	.25
40	Tim Redding	.25
41	Erick Almonte RC	.50
42	Juan Pena	.25
43	Ken Harvey	.25
44	David Brous RC	.25
45	Kevin Olsen RC	.25
46	Henry Mateo RC	.25
47	Nick Neugebauer RC	.25
48	Mike Penney RC	.25
49	Jay Gibbons RC	1.00
50	Tim Christman RC	.25
51	Brandon Duckworth RC	.50
52	Brett Jodie RC	.25
53	Christian Parker RC	.25
54	Carlos Hernandez RC	.25
55	Brandon Larson RC	.50
56	Nick Punto RC	.25
57	Elpidio Guzman RC	.25

58	Joe Beimel RC	.25
59	Junior Spivey RC	.50
60	Will Ohman RC	.25
61	Brandon Lyon RC	.25
62	Stubby Clapp RC	.25
63	Justin Duchscherer RC	1.50
64	Jimmy Rollins	.40
65	David Williams RC	.40
66	Craig Monroe RC	.40
67	Jose Acevedo RC	.25
68	Jason Jennings	.25
69	Josh Phelps	.25
70	Brian Roberts RC	2.00
71	Claudio Vargas RC	.25
72	Adam Johnson	.25
73	Bart Miadich RC	.25
74	Juan Rivera	.25
75	Brad Voyles RC	.25
76	Nate Cornejo	.25
77	Juan Moreno RC	.25
78	Brian Rogers RC	.25
79	Ricardo Rodriguez RC	.40
80	Geronimo Gil	.25
81	Joe Kennedy RC	.40
82	Kevin Joseph RC	.25
83	Josue Perez RC	.25
84	Victor Zambrano RC	.40
85	Josh Towers RC	.25
86	Mike Rivera RC	.25
87	Mark Prior RC	6.00
88	Juan Cruz RC	.40
89	Dewon Brazelton RC	.40
90	Angel Berroa RC	1.00
91	Mark Teixeira RC	15.00
92	Cody Ransom RC	.25
93	Angel Santos RC	.25
94	Corky Miller RC	.40
95	Brandon Berger RC	.40
96	Corey Patterson	.25
97	Albert Pujols RC	60.00
98	Josh Beckett	.50
99	C.C. Sabathia	.25
100	Alfonso Soriano	.75
101	Ben Sheets	.25
102	Rafael Soriano RC	.50
103	Wilson Betemit RC	.50
104	Ichiro Suzuki RC	10.00
105	Jose Ortiz	.25

Rookie Diamond Kings

		NM/M
Complete Set (5):		40.00
Inserted 1:Rookies Set		
106	C.C. Sabathia	5.00
107	Tsuyoshi Shinjo	8.00
108	Albert Pujols	25.00
109	Roy Oswalt	8.00
110	Ichiro Suzuki	12.00

2002 Donruss

	NM/M
Complete Set (220):	100.00
Common Player:	.15
Common (151-200):	1.00
Inserted 1:4	
Common (201-220):	1.00
Inserted 1:8	

#	Player	Price
	Pack (5):	2.00
	Box (24):	40.00
1	Alex Rodriguez	1.50
2	Barry Bonds	2.00
3	Derek Jeter	2.00
4	Robert Fick	.15
5	Juan Pierre	.20
6	Torii Hunter	.25
7	Todd Helton	.75
8	Cal Ripken Jr.	2.00
9	Manny Ramirez	.75
10	Johnny Damon	.25
11	Mike Piazza	1.25
12	Nomar Garciaparra	1.25
13	Pedro Martinez	.75
14	Brian Giles	.15
15	Albert Pujols	1.50
16	Roger Clemens	1.00
17	Sammy Sosa	1.25
18	Vladimir Guerrero	.75
19	Tony Gwynn	1.00
20	Pat Burrell	.35
21	Carlos Delgado	.50
22	Tino Martinez	.15
23	Jim Edmonds	.15
24	Jason Giambi	.50
25	Tom Glavine	.30
26	Mark Grace	.20
27	Tony Armas Jr.	.15
28	Andruw Jones	.75
29	Ben Sheets	.15
30	Jeff Kent	.15
31	Barry Larkin	.15
32	Joe Mays	.15
33	Mike Mussina	.40
34	Hideo Nomo	.60
35	Rafael Palmeiro	.65
36	Scott Brosius	.15
37	Scott Rolen	.65
38	Gary Sheffield	.35
39	Bernie Williams	.35
40	Bobby Abreu	.15
41	Edgardo Alfonzo	.15
42	C.C. Sabathia	.15
43	Jeremy Giambi	.15
44	Craig Biggio	.15
45	Andres Galarraga	.15
46	Edgar Martinez	.30
47	Fred McGriff	.25
48	Magglio Ordonez	.25
49	Jim Thome	.15
50	Matt Williams	.15
51	Kerry Wood	.50
52	Moises Alou	.15
53	Brady Anderson	.15
54	Garret Anderson	.15
55	Juan Gonzalez	.75
56	Bret Boone	.15
57	Jose Cruz Jr.	.15
58	Carlos Beltran	.50
59	Adrian Beltre	.25
60	Joe Kennedy	.15
61	Lance Berkman	.15
62	Kevin Brown	.25
63	Tim Hudson	.35
64	Jeromy Burnitz	.15
65	Jarrod Washburn	.15
66	Sean Casey	.20
67	Eric Chavez	.25
68	Bartolo Colon	.15
69	Freddy Garcia	.15
70	Jermaine Dye	.15
71	Terrence Long	.15
72	Cliff Floyd	.15
73	Luis Gonzalez	.25
74	Ichiro Suzuki	1.50
75	Mike Hampton	.15
76	Richard Hidalgo	.15
77	Geoff Jenkins	.15
78	Gabe Kapler	.15
79	Ken Griffey Jr.	1.25
80	Jason Kendall	.15
81	Josh Towers	.15
82	Ryan Klesko	.15
83	Paul Konerko	.15
84	Carlos Lee	.15
85	Kenny Lofton	.15
86	Josh Beckett	.40
87	Raul Mondesi	.15
88	Trot Nixon	.15
89	John Olerud	.15
90	Paul O'Neill	.15
91	Chan Ho Park	.15
92	Andy Pettitte	.35
93	Jorge Posada	.30
94	Mark Quinn	.15
95	Aramis Ramirez	.15
96	Curt Schilling	.40
97	Richie Sexson	.15
98	John Smoltz	.15
99	Wilson Betemit	.15
100	Shannon Stewart	.15
101	Alfonso Soriano	.75
102	Mike Sweeney	.15
103	Miguel Tejada	.40
104	Greg Vaughn	.15
105	Robin Ventura	.15
106	Jose Vidro	.15
107	Larry Walker	.15
108	Preston Wilson	.15
109	Corey Patterson	.20
110	Mark Mulder	.25
111	Tony Clark	.15
112	Roy Oswalt	.15
113	Jimmy Rollins	.40
114	Kazuhiro Sasaki	.15
115	Barry Zito	.40
116	Javier Vazquez	.15
117	Mike Cameron	.15
118	Phil Nevin	.15
119	Bud Smith	.15
120	Cristian Guzman	.15
121	Al Leiter	.15
122	Brad Radke	.15
123	Bobby Higginson	.15
124	Robert Person	.15
125	Adam Dunn	.50
126	Ben Grieve	.15
127	Rafael Furcal	.15
128	Jay Gibbons	.15
129	Paul LoDuca	.15
130	Wade Miller	.15
131	Tsuyoshi Shinjo	.15
132	Eric Milton	.15
133	Rickey Henderson	.75
134	Roberto Alomar	.40
135	Darin Erstad	.50
136	J.D. Drew	.35
137	Shawn Green	.25
138	Randy Johnson	.75
139	Mark McGwire	1.50
140	Jose Canseco	.40
141	Jeff Bagwell	.75
142	Greg Maddux	1.00
143	Mark Buehrle	.15
144	Ivan Rodriguez	.65
145	Frank Thomas	.75
146	Rich Aurilia	.15
147	Troy Glaus	.75
148	Ryan Dempster	.15
149	Chipper Jones	1.00
150	Matt Morris	.15
151	Marlon Byrd	2.00
152	Ben Howard RC	4.00
153	Brandon Backe RC	2.00
154	Jorge De La Rosa RC	2.00
155	Corky Miller	1.00
156	Dennis Tankersley	1.00
157	Kyle Kane RC	3.00
158	Justin Duchscherer	1.00
159	Brian Mallette RC	3.00
160	Chris Baker RC	3.00
161	Jason Lane	1.00
162	Hee Seop Choi	1.50
163	Juan Cruz	1.00
164	Rodrigo Rosario RC	2.00
165	Matt Guerrier	1.00
166	Anderson Machado RC	3.00
167	Geronimo Gil	1.00
168	Dewon Brazelton	1.00
169	Mark Prior	5.00
170	Bill Hall	1.00
171	Jorge Padilla RC	4.00
172	Jose Cueto	1.00
173	Allan Simpson RC	3.00
174	Doug DeVore RC	1.00
175	Josh Pearce	1.00
176	Angel Berroa	1.00
177	Steve Bechler RC	3.00
178	Antonio Perez	1.00
179	Mark Teixeira	3.00
180	Erick Almonte	1.00
181	Orlando Hudson	1.00
182	Mike Rivera	1.00
183	Raul Chavez RC	2.00
184	Juan Pena	1.00
185	Travis Hughes RC	2.00
186	Ryan Ludwick	1.00
187	Ed Rogers	1.00
188	Andy Pratt RC	2.00
189	Nick Neugebauer	1.00
190	Tom Shearn RC	3.00
191	Eric Cyr RC	3.00
192	Victor Martinez	1.00
193	Brandon Berger	1.00
194	Erik Bedard	1.00
195	Fernando Rodney	1.00
196	Joe Thurston	1.00
197	John Buck	1.00
198	Jeff Deardorff RC	2.00
199	Ryan Jamison RC	2.00
200	Alfredo Amezaga	1.00
201	Luis Gonzalez	1.00
202	Roger Clemens	4.00
203	Barry Zito	1.25
204	Bud Smith	1.00
205	Magglio Ordonez	1.25
206	Kerry Wood	1.50
207	Freddy Garcia	1.00
208	Adam Dunn	1.50
209	Curt Schilling	2.00
210	Lance Berkman	1.50
211	Rafael Palmeiro	2.00
212	Ichiro Suzuki	4.00
213	Bobby Abreu	1.00
214	Mark Mulder	1.00
215	Roy Oswalt	1.50
216	Mike Sweeney	1.00
217	Paul LoDuca	1.00
218	Aramis Ramirez	1.00
219	Randy Johnson	2.00
220	Albert Pujols	5.00

Stat Line Career

	NM/M
Cards 1-150 print run 251-400:	2-4X
1-150 p/r 151-250:	3-6X
1-150 p/r 101-150:	4-8X
1-150 p/r 61-100:	5-10X
1-150 p/r 31-60:	8-20X
1-150 p/r 15-30:	15-30X

Common 151-200 p/r 251-400:	1.00
Common 151-200 p/r 151-250:	1.00
Common 151-200 p/r 76-150:	2.00
Common 151-200 p/r 30-75:	4.00

Stat Line Season

	NM/M
cards 1-150 print run 151-200:	3-6X
1-150 p/r 101-150:	4-8X
1-150 p/r 76-100:	5-10X
1-150 p/r 51-75:	6-12X
1-150 p/r 31-50:	8-20X
1-150 p/r 15-30:	15-30X
Comm. 151-200 p/r 151-200:	1.00
Comm. 151-200 p/r 101-150:	1.50
Comm. 151-200 p/r 76-100:	2.00
Comm. 151-200 p/r 30-75:	4.00

All-Time Diamond Kings

	NM/M
Complete Set (10):	80.00
Common Player:	5.00
Production 2,500 Sets	
Studio Series:	2-3X
Production 250 Sets	
1 Ted Williams	15.00
2 Cal Ripken Jr.	15.00
3 Lou Gehrig	10.00
4 Babe Ruth	15.00
5 Roberto Clemente	10.00
6 Don Mattingly	10.00
7 Kirby Puckett	8.00
8 Stan Musial	8.00
9 Yogi Berra	5.00
10 Ernie Banks	5.00

Autographs

	NM/M
Common Autograph:	15.00
Varying quantities produced	
203 Barry Zito/200	20.00
204 Bud Smith/200	10.00
205 Magglio Ordonez/200	20.00
206 Kerry Wood/200	30.00
207 Freddy Garcia/200	10.00
208 Adam Dunn/200	25.00
210 Lance Berkman/175	20.00
211 Rafael Palmeiro/25	20.00
213 Bobby Abreu/200	15.00
214 Mark Mulder/200	15.00
215 Roy Oswalt/200	15.00
216 Mike Sweeney/200	15.00
217 Paul LoDuca/200	15.00
218 Aramis Ramirez/200	20.00
220 Albert Pujols/200	150.00

Bat Kings

	NM/M
Quantities produced listed	
Studio Series:	1.5-3X
Production 25 or 50	
1 Jason Giambi/250	15.00
2 Alex Rodriguez/250	25.00
3 Mike Piazza/250	20.00
4 Roberto Clemente/125	100.00
5 Babe Ruth/125	220.00

Diamond Kings

(Base Set)

	NM/M
Complete Set (20):	80.00
Common Player:	2.00
Production 2,500 Sets	
Studio Series:	2-3X
Production 250 Sets	
1 Nomar Garciaparra	6.00
2 Shawn Green	2.00
3 Randy Johnson	4.00
4 Derek Jeter	7.50
5 Carlos Delgado	3.00
6 Roger Clemens	5.00
7 Jeff Bagwell	4.00
8 Vladimir Guerrero	4.00
9 Luis Gonzalez	2.00
10 Mike Piazza	6.00
11 Ichiro Suzuki	6.00
12 Pedro Martinez	4.00
13 Todd Helton	4.00
14 Sammy Sosa	6.00
15 Ivan Rodriguez	3.50
16 Barry Bonds	7.50
17 Albert Pujols	6.00
18 Jim Thome	2.00
19 Alex Rodriguez	6.00
20 Jason Giambi	3.00

Elite Series

	NM/M
Complete Set (15):	30.00
Common Player:	2.00
Production 2,500 Sets	
Autographs:	No Pricing
Production 25	
1 Barry Bonds	8.00
2 Lance Berkman	2.00
3 Jason Giambi	2.50
4 Nomar Garciaparra	6.00
5 Curt Schilling	2.50
6 Vladimir Guerrero	3.00
7 Shawn Green	2.00
8 Troy Glaus	3.00
9 Jeff Bagwell	3.00
10 Manny Ramirez	3.00
11 Eric Chavez	2.00
12 Carlos Delgado	2.50
13 Mike Sweeney	2.00
14 Todd Helton	3.00
15 Luis Gonzalez	2.00

Elite Series Legends

	NM/M
Complete Set (5):	15.00
Common Player:	3.00
Production 2,500	
16 Enos Slaughter	3.00
17 Frank Robinson	4.00
18 Bob Gibson	4.00
19 Warren Spahn	4.00
20 Whitey Ford	4.00

Elite Series Legends Autographs

	NM/M
Production 250 Sets	
16 Enos Slaughter	30.00
17 Frank Robinson	30.00
18 Bob Gibson	35.00
19 Warren Spahn	40.00
20 Whitey Ford	40.00

Jersey Kings

	NM/M
Quantity produced listed	
Studio Series:	1.5-3X
Production 25 or 50	
1 Alex Rodriguez/250	15.00
2 Jason Giambi/250	10.00
3 Carlos Delgado/250	8.00
4 Barry Bonds/250	25.00
5 Randy Johnson/250	10.00
6 Jim Thome/250	8.00
7 Shawn Green/250	8.00
8 Pedro Martinez/250	10.00
9 Jeff Bagwell/250	10.00
10 Vladimir Guerrero/250	10.00
11 Ivan Rodriguez/250	10.00
12 Nomar Garciaparra/250	15.00
13 Don Mattingly/125	80.00
14 Ted Williams/125	125.00
15 Lou Gehrig/125	200.00

Longball Leaders

	NM/M
Complete Set (20):	40.00
Common Player:	1.00
Production 1,000 Sets	
Seasonal Sum Parallel:	2-4X
Parallel #'d to 2001 HR Total.	
1 Barry Bonds	8.00
2 Sammy Sosa	6.00

3	Luis Gonzalez	1.00
4	Alex Rodriguez	6.00
5	Shawn Green	1.50
6	Todd Helton	3.00
7	Jim Thome	1.00
8	Rafael Palmeiro	2.50
9	Richie Sexson	1.00
10	Troy Glaus	3.00
11	Manny Ramirez	3.00
12	Phil Nevin	1.00
13	Jeff Bagwell	3.00
14	Carlos Delgado	2.00
15	Jason Giambi	2.00
16	Chipper Jones	4.00
17	Larry Walker	1.00
18	Albert Pujols	6.00
19	Brian Giles	1.00
20	Bret Boone	1.00

Production Line

NM/M

Common Card: 2.00
Numbered to category stat.

1	Barry Bonds/515	8.00
2	Jason Giambi/477	4.50
3	Larry Walker/449	2.00
4	Sammy Sosa/437	6.00
5	Todd Helton/432	2.00
6	Lance Berkman/430	2.00
7	Luis Gonzalez/429	2.00
8	Chipper Jones/427	6.00
9	Edgar Martinez/423	2.00
10	Gary Sheffield/417	2.00
11	Jim Thome/416	3.00
12	Roberto Alomar/415	3.00
13	J.D. Drew/414	2.00
14	Jim Edmonds/410	2.00
15	Carlos Delgado/408	3.00
16	Manny Ramirez/405	4.00
17	Brian Giles/404	2.00
18	Albert Pujols/403	8.00
19	John Olerud/401	2.00
20	Alex Rodriguez/399	8.00
21	Barry Bonds/863	6.00
22	Sammy Sosa/737	5.00
23	Luis Gonzalez/688	1.50
24	Todd Helton/685	2.00
25	Larry Walker/662	1.50
26	Jason Giambi/660	2.00
27	Jim Thome/624	2.00
28	Alex Rodriguez/620	5.00
29	Lance Berkman/620	1.50
30	J.D. Drew/613	1.50
31	Albert Pujols/610	5.00
32	Manny Ramirez/609	2.00
33	Chipper Jones/605	3.00
34	Shawn Green/598	1.50
35	Brian Giles/590	1.50
36	Juan Gonzalez/590	2.00
37	Phil Nevin/588	1.50
38	Gary Sheffield/583	1.50
39	Bret Boone/578	1.50
40	Cliff Floyd/578	1.50
41	Barry Bonds/1,378	5.00
42	Sammy Sosa/1,174	4.00
43	Jason Giambi/1,137	1.50
44	Todd Helton/1,117	1.50
45	Luis Gonzalez/1,117	1.00
46	Larry Walker/1,111	1.00
47	Lance Berkman/1,050	1.00
48	Jim Thome/1,040	1.50
49	Chipper Jones/1,032	2.50
50	J.D. Drew/1,027	1.00
51	Alex Rodriguez/1,021	1.00
52	Manny Ramirez/1,014	1.50
53	Albert Pujols/1,013	4.00
54	Gary Sheffield/1,000	1.50
55	Brian Giles/994	1.00
56	Phil Nevin/976	1.00
57	Jim Edmonds/974	1.50
58	Shawn Green/970	1.00
59	Cliff Floyd/968	1.00
60	Edgar Martinez/966	1.00

Recollection Collection

NM/M

Complete Set (47):
Common Player:

6	Steve Carlton 83/30	40.00
7	Steve Carlton 87/30	40.00
8	Gary Carter 87/100	25.00
9	Gary Carter 89/100	25.00
11	Joe Carter 87/45	25.00
13	Andre Dawson 81/50	20.00
14	Andre Dawson 83/50	20.00
16	Andre Dawson 87/45	20.00
17	Dennis Eckersley 81/45	20.00
24	Steve Garvey 87/75	20.00
26	Fergie Jenkins 81/40	25.00
46	Tom Seaver 87/60	60.00
47	Don Sutton 87/200	15.00

Rookie Year Materials - Bats

NM/M

Production 250 Sets

1	Barry Bonds	40.00
2	Cal Ripken Jr.	40.00
3	Kirby Puckett	15.00
4	Johnny Bench	15.00

Rookie Year Materials - Jerseys

NM/M

Quantity produced listed
Parallel #'d to 25 or 50.

1	Nomar Garciaparra/250	20.00
2	Randy Johnson/250	10.00
3	Ivan Rodriguez/250	10.00
4	Vladimir Guerrero/250	15.00
5	Stan Musial/50	80.00
6	Yogi Berra/50	50.00

Rookie Year Materials - Bats Autographs

NM/M

Numbered to debut year.

1	Barry Bonds/86	125.00
2	Cal Ripken Jr./81	140.00
3	Kirby Puckett/84	120.00
4	Johnny Bench/68	75.00

2002 Donruss Classics

NM/M

Complete Set (200):
Common Player: .50
Common (101-150): 3.00
Common (151-200): 2.00
Production 1,500
Pack (6): 5.00
Box (18): 70.00

1	Alex Rodriguez	3.00
2	Barry Bonds	4.00
3	C.C. Sabathia	.50
4	Chipper Jones	2.00
5	Derek Jeter	4.00
6	Troy Glaus	1.50
7	Frank Thomas	1.50
8	Greg Maddux	2.00
9	Ivan Rodriguez	1.25
10	Jeff Bagwell	1.50
11	Mark Buehrle	.50
12	Todd Helton	1.50
13	Ken Griffey Jr.	2.50
14	Manny Ramirez	1.50
15	Brad Penny	.50
16	Mike Piazza	2.50
17	Nomar Garciaparra	2.50
18	Pedro J. Martinez	1.50
19	Randy Johnson	1.50
20	Bud Smith	.50
21	Rickey Henderson	1.50
22	Roger Clemens	2.25
23	Sammy Sosa	2.50
24	Brandon Duckworth	.50
25	Vladimir Guerrero	1.50
26	Kazuhiro Sasaki	.50
27	Roberto Alomar	.65
28	Barry Zito	.75
29	Rich Aurilia	.50
30	Ben Sheets	.50
31	Carlos Delgado	.50
32	J.D. Drew	.75
33	Jermaine Dye	.50
34	Darin Erstad	.75
35	Jason Giambi	1.00
36	Tom Glavine	.60
37	Juan Gonzalez	1.50
38	Luis Gonzalez	.35
39	Shawn Green	.75
40	Tim Hudson	.65
41	Andruw Jones	1.50
42	Shannon Stewart	.50
43	Barry Larkin	.50
44	Wade Miller	.50
45	Mike Mussina	.65
46	Hideo Nomo	1.00
47	Rafael Palmeiro	1.25
48	Scott Rolen	1.00
49	Gary Sheffield	.75
50	Bernie Williams	.65
51	Bobby Abreu	.50
52	Javier Vazquez	.50
53	Edgar Martinez	.50
54	Magglio Ordonez	.75
55	Kerry Wood	1.00
56	Adrian Beltre	.65
57	Lance Berkman	.50
58	Kevin Brown	.50
59	Sean Casey	.50
60	Eric Chavez	.75
61	Robert Person	.50
62	Jeremy Giambi	.50
63	Freddy Garcia	.50
64	Alfonso Soriano	1.50
65	Doug Davis	.50
66	Brian Giles	.50
67	Moises Alou	.50
68	Richard Hidalgo	.50
69	Paul LoDuca	.50
70	Aramis Ramirez	.50
71	Andres Galarraga	.50
72	Ryan Klesko	.50
73	Chan Ho Park	.50
74	Richie Sexson	.50
75	Mike Sweeney	.50
76	Aubrey Huff	.75
77	Miguel Tejada	.75
78	Jose Vidro	.50
79	Larry Walker	.50
80	Roy Oswalt	.75
81	Craig Biggio	.50
82	Juan Pierre	.50
83	Jim Thome	.50
84	Josh Towers	.50
85	Alex Escobar	.50
86	Cliff Floyd	.50
87	Terrence Long	.50
88	Curt Schilling	.75
89	Carlos Beltran	1.00
90	Albert Pujols	2.50
91	Gabe Kapler	.50
92	Mark Mulder	.50
93	Carlos Lee	.50
94	Robert Fick	.50
95	Raul Mondesi	.50
96	Ichiro Suzuki	2.50
97	Adam Dunn	.75
98	Corey Patterson	.50
99	Tsuyoshi Shinjo	.50
100	Joe Mays	.50
101	Juan Cruz	3.00
102	Marlon Byrd	5.00
103	Luis Garcia	3.00
104	Jorge Padilla RC	6.00
105	Dennis Tankersley	3.00
106	Josh Pearce	3.00
107	Ramon Vazquez	3.00
108	Chris Baker RC	3.00
109	Eric Cyr RC	3.00
110	Reed Johnson RC	3.00
111	Ryan Jamison RC	3.00
112	Antonio Perez	3.00
113	Satoru Komiyama RC	3.00
114	Austin Kearns	3.00
115	Juan Pena	3.00
116	Orlando Hudson	3.00
117	Kazuhisa Ishii	6.00
118	Eric Bedard	3.00
119	Luis Ugueto RC	3.00
120	Ben Howard RC	4.00
121	Morgan Ensberg	3.00
122	Doug DeVore RC	4.00
123	Josh Phelps	4.00
124	Angel Berroa	4.00
125	Ed Rogers	3.00
126	Takahito Nomura RC	3.00
127	John Ennis RC	3.00
128	Bill Hall	3.00
129	Dewon Brazelton	3.00
130	Hank Blalock	5.00
131	So Taguchi RC	5.00
132	Jorge De La Rosa RC	3.00
133	Matt Thornton	3.00
134	Brandon Backe RC	3.00
135	Jeff Deardorff RC	3.00
136	Steve Smyth	3.00
137	Anderson Machado RC	5.00
138	John Buck	3.00
139	Mark Prior	15.00
140	Sean Burroughs	3.00
141	Alex Herrera	3.00
142	Francis Beltran RC	3.00
143	Jason Romano	3.00
144	Michael Cuddyer	3.00
145	Steve Bechler RC	3.00
146	Alfredo Amezaga	3.00
147	Ryan Ludwick	3.00
148	Martin Vargas	3.00
149	Allan Simpson RC	3.00
150	Mark Teixeira	4.00
151	Hank Aaron	8.00
152	Ernie Banks	6.00
153	Johnny Bench	6.00
154	George Brett	10.00
155	Lou Brock	3.00
156	Rod Carew	3.00
157	Steve Carlton	4.00
158	Joe Torre	3.00
159	Dennis Eckersley	2.50
160	Reggie Jackson	5.00
161	Al Kaline	6.00
162	Dave Parker	2.00
163	Don Mattingly	10.00
164	Tony Gwynn	6.00
165	Willie McCovey	3.00
166	Joe Morgan	3.00
167	Stan Musial	8.00
168	Jim Palmer	3.00
169	Brooks Robinson	5.00
170	Bo Jackson	6.00
171	Nolan Ryan	15.00
172	Mike Schmidt	8.00
173	Tom Seaver	5.00
174	Cal Ripken Jr.	15.00
175	Robin Yount	6.00
176	Wade Boggs	5.00
177	Gary Carter	3.00
178	Ron Santo	2.00
179	Luis Aparicio	2.00
180	Bobby Doerr	3.00
181	Ryne Sandberg	6.00
182	Yogi Berra	5.00
183	Will Clark	5.00
184	Eddie Murray	4.00
185	Andre Dawson	3.00
186	Duke Snider	5.00
187	Orlando Cepeda	3.00
188	Billy Williams	2.00
189	Juan Marichal	4.00
190	Harmon Killebrew	5.00
191	Kirby Puckett	6.00
192	Carlton Fisk	4.00
193	Dave Winfield	3.00
194	Alan Trammell	3.00
195	Paul Molitor	3.00
196	Tony Perez	3.00
197	Ozzie Smith	3.00
198	Ralph Kiner	3.00
199	Fergie Jenkins	2.00
200	Phil Rizzuto	3.00

Timeless Tributes

Stars (1-100): 2-4X
SP's (101-150): 1-2X
SP's (151-200): 2-3X
Production 100 Sets

Classic Combos

Too scarce to price.

Classic Singles

NM/M

Common Player: 10.00
Some too scarce to price.

1	Cal Ripken Jr./Jsy/50	40.00
2	Eddie Murray/Jsy/50	15.00
3	George Brett/Jsy/100	35.00
4	Bo Jackson/Jsy/100	20.00
5	Ted Williams/Bat/50	200.00
6	Jimmie Foxx/Bat/50	60.00
7	Reggie Jackson/Jsy/50	15.00
8	Steve Carlton/Jsy/50	30.00
9	Mel Ott/Jsy/50	70.00
10	"Catfish" Hunter/Jsy/100	10.00
11	Nolan Ryan/Jsy/100	40.00
12	Rickey Henderson/Jsy/100	25.00
13	Robin Yount/Jsy/100	25.00
14	Orlando Cepeda/Jsy/100	10.00
15	Ty Cobb/Bat/50	150.00
16	Babe Ruth/Bat/50	275.00
17	Dave Parker/Jsy/100	10.00
18	Willie Stargell/Jsy/100	10.00
19	Ernie Banks/Bat/100	25.00
20	Mike Schmidt/Jsy/100	35.00
21	Duke Snider/Jsy/50	25.00
22	Jackie Robinson/Jsy/50	75.00
23	Rickey Henderson/Bat/100	25.00
24	TBD	
25	Lou Gehrig/Bat/50	175.00
26	Jimmie Foxx/Bat/50	65.00
27	Tony Gwynn/Bat/100	20.00
28	Bobby Doerr/Jsy/100	15.00
29	Joe Torre/Jsy/100	10.00

Legendary Hats

NM/M

50 Sets Produced

1	Don Mattingly/50	150.00
2	George Brett	150.00

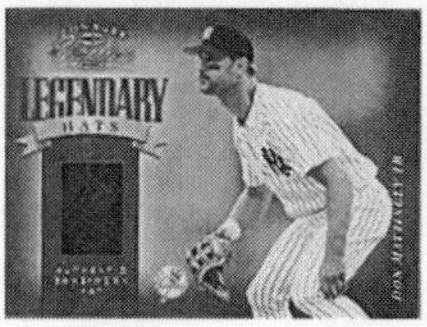

3	Wade Boggs	30.00
5	Ryne Sandberg	120.00

Legendary Spikes

NM/M

50 Sets Produced

1	Don Mattingly	125.00
2	Eddie Murray	30.00
3	Paul Molitor	50.00
4	Harmon Killebrew	40.00
5	Mike Schmidt	100.00

Legendary Leather

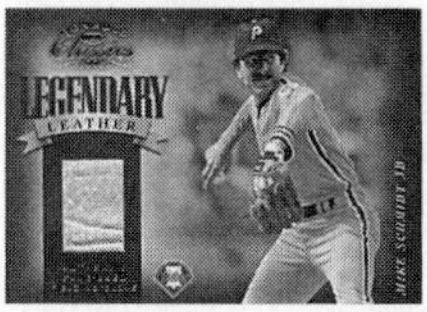

NM/M

50 Sets Produced

1	Don Mattingly	125.00
2	Wade Boggs	30.00
4	Kirby Puckett	50.00
5	Mike Schmidt	80.00

Legendary Lumberjacks

NM/M

Varying quantities produced

1	Don Mattingly/500	20.00
2	George Brett/400	20.00
3	Stan Musial/100	35.00
4	Lou Gehrig/50	175.00
5	Mike Piazza/500	10.00
6	Mel Ott/50	75.00
7	Ted Williams/50	150.00
8	Bo Jackson/500	8.00
9	Kirby Puckett/500	15.00
10	Rafael Palmeiro/500	10.00
11	Andre Dawson/500	5.00
12	Ozzie Smith/500	15.00
13	Paul Molitor/500	15.00
14	Babe Ruth/50	220.00
15	Carlton Fisk/500	8.00
16	Rickey Henderson/500	10.00
17	Gary Carter/500	5.00
18	Cal Ripken Jr/100	40.00
19	Eddie Matthews/100	20.00
20	Luis Aparicio/500	5.00
21	Al Kaline/100	25.00
22	Eddie Murray/500	8.00
23	Yogi Berra/100	25.00
24	Alex Rodriguez/500	10.00
25	Tony Gwynn/500	10.00
26	Roberto Clemente/100	80.00
27	Mike Schmidt/400	20.00
28	Reggie Jackson/500	10.00
29	Ryne Sandberg/500	20.00
30	Joe Morgan/400	5.00
31	Joe Torre/500	5.00
32	Gary Sheffield/500	5.00
33	Nomar Garciaparra/500	10.00
34	Jeff Bagwell/500	8.00
35	Manny Ramirez/500	8.00

New Millennium Classics

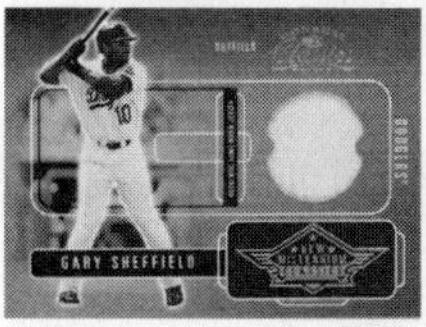

NM/M

Common Player: 4.00
Varying quantities produced
All jerseys unless noted.

1	Curt Schilling/500	6.00
2	Vladimir Guerrero/100	15.00
3	Jim Thome/500	8.00
4	Troy Glaus/400	6.00
5	Ivan Rodriguez/200	6.00
6	Todd Helton/400	8.00
7	Sean Casey/500	4.00
8	Scott Rolen/475	8.00
9	Ken Griffey Jr./150/Base	10.00
10	Hideo Nomo/100	25.00
11	Tom Glavine/350	5.00
12	Pedro Martinez/100	15.00
13	Cliff Floyd/500	4.00
14	Shawn Green/125	8.00
15	Rafael Palmeiro/250	8.00
16	Luis Gonzalez/100	5.00
17	Lance Berkman/100	6.00
18	Frank Thomas/500	8.00
19	Randy Johnson/400	8.00
20	Moises Alou/500	4.00
21	Chipper Jones/500	8.00
22	Larry Walker/300	4.00
23	Mike Sweeney/500	4.00
24	Juan Gonzalez/300	6.00
25	Roger Clemens/100	20.00
26	Albert Pujols/300/Base	15.00
27	Magglio Ordonez/500	5.00
28	Alex Rodriguez/400	10.00
29	Jeff Bagwell/125	10.00
30	Kazuhiro Sasaki/500	4.00
31	Barry Larkin/300	6.00
32	Andruw Jones/350	8.00
33	Kerry Wood/200	8.00
34	Rickey Henderson/100	10.00
35	Greg Maddux/100	15.00
36	Brian Giles/400	4.00
37	Craig Biggio/100	5.00
38	Roberto Alomar/400	6.00
39	Mike Piazza/400	10.00
40	Bernie Williams/100	10.00
41	Ichiro Suzuki/150/Ball	30.00
42	Kenny Lofton/450	4.00
43	Mark Mulder/500	4.00
44	Kazuhisa Ishii/100	15.00
45	Darin Erstad/500	4.00
46	Jose Vidro/500	4.00
47	Miguel Tejada/475	6.00
48	Roy Oswalt/500	5.00
50	Barry Zito/500	6.00
51	Manny Ramirez/400	8.00
52	Nomar Garciaparra/400	10.00
53	C.C. Sabathia/500	4.00
54	Carlos Delgado/500	8.00
55	Gary Sheffield/500	6.00
56	J.D. Drew/500	5.00
57	Barry Bonds/150/Ball	25.00
58	Derek Jeter/150/Ball	25.00
59	Edgar Martinez/400	5.00
60	Sammy Sosa/150/Ball	15.00

Significant Signatures

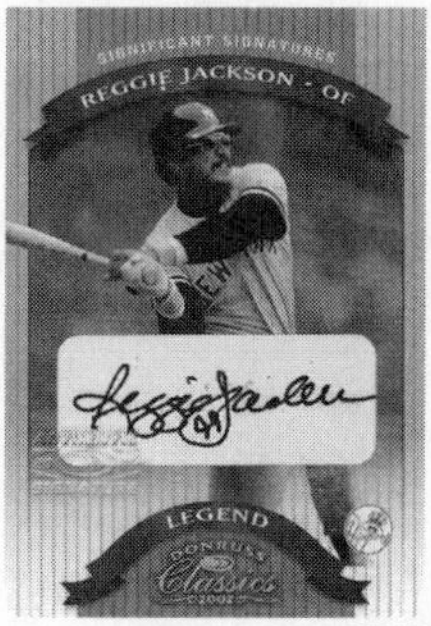

NM/M

Common Prospect Autograph: 5.00
Varying quantities produced, many not priced due to scarcity.

101	Juan Cruz/400	6.00
102	Marlon Byrd/500	10.00
103	Luis Garcia/500	6.00
104	Jorge Padilla/500	10.00
105	Dennis Tankersley/250	10.00
106	Josh Pearce/500	8.00
107	Ramon Vazquez/500	5.00
108	Chris Baker/500 **RC**	8.00
109	Eric Cyr/500	6.00
110	Reed Johnson/500	10.00
111	Ryan Jamison/500	5.00
112	Antonio Perez/500	5.00
113	Satoru Komiyama/50	40.00
114	Austin Kearns/500	15.00
115	Juan Pena/500	5.00
116	Orlando Hudson/400	10.00
117	Kazuhisa Ishii/50	40.00
118	Eric Bedard/500	15.00
119	Luis Ugueto/250	10.00
120	Ben Howard/500	8.00
121	Morgan Ensberg/500	10.00
122	Doug DeVore/500	8.00
123	Josh Phelps/500	8.00
124	Angel Berroa/500	10.00
125	Ed Rogers/500	5.00
127	John Ennis/500	5.00
128	Bill Hall/400	10.00
129	Dewon Brazelton/400	8.00
130	Hank Blalock/100	20.00
131	So Taguchi/150	30.00
132	Jorge De La Rosa/500	5.00
133	Matt Thornton/500	5.00
134	Brandon Backe/500	5.00
135	Jeff Deardorff/500	5.00
136	Steve Smyth/400	5.00
137	Anderson Machado/500	10.00
138	John Buck/500	5.00
139	Mark Prior/250	25.00
140	Sean Burroughs/50	10.00
141	Alex Herrera/500	5.00
142	Francis Beltran/500	5.00
143	Jason Romano/500	5.00
144	Michael Cuddyer/400	8.00
145	Steve Bechler/500	8.00
146	Alfredo Amezaga/500	5.00
147	Ryan Ludwick/500	15.00
148	Martin Vargas/500	5.00
149	Allan Simpson/500	5.00
150	Mark Teixeira/200	30.00
152	Ernie Banks/25	100.00
153	Johnny Bench/25	125.00
154	George Brett/25	260.00
155	Lou Brock/100	30.00
157	Steve Carlton/125	35.00
159	Dennis Eckersley/500	15.00
161	Al Kaline/125	35.00
162	Dave Parker/500	10.00
163	Don Mattingly/50	75.00
168	Jim Palmer/125	25.00
169	Brooks Robinson/125	40.00
177	Gary Carter/150	25.00
178	Ron Santo/500	20.00
179	Luis Aparicio/400	10.00
180	Bobby Doerr/500	15.00
182	Yogi Berra/25	80.00
184	Eddie Murray/25	60.00
185	Andre Dawson/200	20.00
186	Duke Snider/25	70.00
187	Orlando Cepeda/125	25.00
188	Billy Williams/200	15.00
189	Juan Marichal/500	15.00
190	Harmon Killebrew/100	50.00
194	Alan Trammell/200	25.00
195	Paul Molitor/25	60.00
196	Tony Perez/150	15.00
198	Ralph Kiner/125	20.00
199	Fergie Jenkins/200	15.00
200	Phil Rizzuto/125	40.00

Timeless Treasures

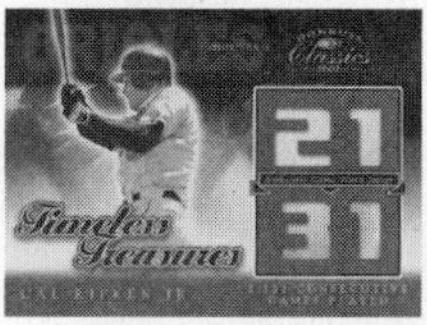

NM/M

Some not priced.

5	Ted Williams/Bat/42	140.00
6	Ted Williams/Bat/47	140.00
7	Ted Williams/Bat/46	140.00
8	Ted Williams/Bat/49	140.00
10	Cal Ripken Jr./Jsy/98	50.00
11	Cal Ripken Jr./Jsy/82	50.00
12	Cal Ripken Jr./Jsy/83	50.00
13	Cal Ripken Jr./Jsy/91	50.00

2002 Donruss Diamond Kings

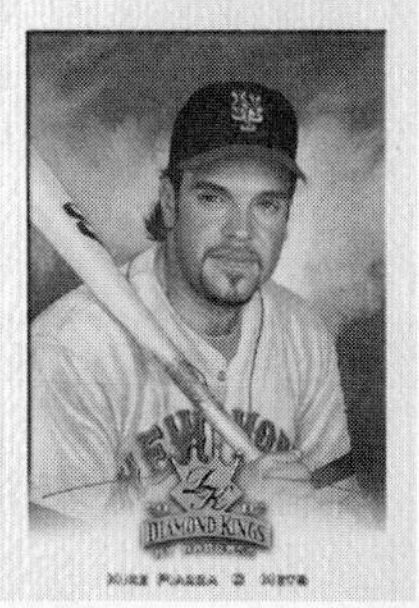

NM/M

Complete Set (150):	150.00
Common Player:	.40
Common SP (101-150):	2.00
Inserted 1:3	
Pack (4):	4.50
Box (24):	80.00

1	Vladimir Guerrero	1.00
2	Adam Dunn	.75
3	Tsuyoshi Shinjo	.40
4	Adrian Beltre	.60
5	Troy Glaus	1.00
6	Albert Pujols	2.00
7	Trot Nixon	.40
8	Alex Rodriguez	2.50
9	Tom Glavine	.50
10	Alfonso Soriano	1.00
11	Todd Helton	1.00
12	Joe Torre	.40
13	Tim Hudson	.50
14	Andruw Jones	1.00
15	Shawn Green	.50
16	Aramis Ramirez	.40
17	Shannon Stewart	.40
18	Barry Bonds	3.00
19	Sean Casey	.40
20	Barry Larkin	.40
21	Scott Rolen	.75
22	Barry Zito	.50
23	Sammy Sosa	2.00
24	Bartolo Colon	.40
25	Ryan Klesko	.40
26	Ben Grieve	.40
27	Roy Oswalt	.50
28	Kazuhiro Sasaki	.40
29	Roger Clemens	1.75
30	Bernie Williams	.50
31	Roberto Alomar	.50
32	Bobby Abreu	.40
33	Robert Fick	.40
34	Bret Boone	.40
35	Rickey Henderson	1.00
36	Brian Giles	.40
37	Richie Sexson	.40
38	Bud Smith	.40
39	Richard Hidalgo	.40
40	C.C. Sabathia	.40
41	Rich Aurilia	.40
42	Carlos Beltran	.75
43	Raul Mondesi	.40
44	Carlos Delgado	.50
45	Randy Johnson	1.00
46	Chan Ho Park	.40
47	Rafael Palmeiro	.75
48	Chipper Jones	1.50
49	Phil Nevin	.40
50	Cliff Floyd	.40
51	Pedro Martinez	1.00
52	Craig Biggio	.40
53	Paul LoDuca	.40
54	Cristian Guzman	.40
55	Pat Burrell	.50
56	Curt Schilling	.50
57	Orlando Cabrera	.40
58	Darin Erstad	.65
59	Omar Vizquel	.40
60	Derek Jeter	3.00
61	Nomar Garciaparra	2.00
62	Edgar Martinez	.40
63	Moises Alou	.40
64	Eric Chavez	.50
65	Mike Sweeney	.40
66	Frank Thomas	1.00
67	Mike Piazza	2.00
68	Gary Sheffield	.50
69	Mike Mussina	.50
70	Greg Maddux	1.50
71	Juan Gonzalez	1.00
72	Hideo Nomo	.65
73	Miguel Tejada	.50
74	Ichiro Suzuki	2.00
75	Matt Morris	.40
76	Ivan Rodriguez	.75
77	Mark Mulder	.40
78	J.D. Drew	.40
79	Mark Grace	.50
80	Jason Giambi	.50
81	Mark Buehrle	.40
82	Jose Vidro	.40
83	Manny Ramirez	1.00
84	Jeff Bagwell	1.00
85	Magglio Ordonez	.50
86	Ken Griffey Jr.	2.00
87	Luis Gonzalez	.40
88	Jim Edmonds	.40
89	Larry Walker	.40
90	Jim Thome	.40
91	Lance Berkman	.40
92	Jorge Posada	.50
93	Kevin Brown	.40
94	Joe Mays	.40
95	Kerry Wood	.75
96	Mark Ellis	.40
97	Austin Kearns	.75
98	Jorge De La Rosa **RC**	.50
99	Brandon Berger	.40
100	Ryan Ludwick	.40
101	Marlon Byrd	2.00
102	Brandon Backe **RC**	2.00
103	Juan Cruz	2.00
104	Anderson Machado **RC**	3.00
105	So Taguchi **RC**	4.00
106	Dewon Brazelton	2.00
107	Josh Beckett	3.00
108	John Buck	2.00
109	Jorge Padilla **RC**	3.00
110	Hee Seop Choi	2.00
111	Angel Berroa	2.00
112	Mark Teixeira	3.00
113	Victor Martinez	2.00
114	Kazuhisa Ishii **RC**	6.00
115	Dennis Tankersley	2.00
116	Wilson Valdez **RC**	2.00
117	Antonio Perez	2.00
118	Ed Rogers	2.00
119	Wilson Betemit	2.00
120	Mike Rivera	2.00
121	Mark Prior	6.00
122	Roberto Clemente	6.00
123	Roberto Clemente	6.00
124	Roberto Clemente	6.00
125	Roberto Clemente	6.00
126	Roberto Clemente	6.00
127	Babe Ruth	10.00
128	Ted Williams	8.00
129	Andre Dawson	2.00
130	Eddie Murray	3.00
131	Juan Marichal	3.00
132	Kirby Puckett	5.00
133	Alan Trammell	2.00

134	Bobby Doerr	2.00
135	Carlton Fisk	3.00
136	Eddie Mathews	4.00
137	Mike Schmidt	6.00
138	Jim "Catfish" Hunter	2.00
139	Nolan Ryan	10.00
140	George Brett	6.00
141	Gary Carter	2.00
142	Paul Molitor	4.00
143	Lou Gehrig	8.00
144	Ryne Sandberg	5.00
145	Tony Gwynn	5.00
146	Ron Santo	2.00
147	Cal Ripken Jr.	10.00
148	Al Kaline	4.00
149	Bo Jackson	3.00
150	Don Mattingly	8.00

Bronze Foil

Cards 1-100:	1-2X
Cards 101-150:	.5X
Inserted 1:6	
Gold Foil (1-100):	4-8X
Gold Foil (101-150):	2-3X
Production 100 Sets	
Silver Foil (1-100):	3-4X
Silver Foil (101-150):	1-2X
Production 400 Sets	

Diamond Cut

		NM/M
Common Signature (1-30):		5.00
1	Vladimir Guerrero/400	30.00
2	Mark Prior/400	30.00
3	Victor Martinez/500	10.00
4	Marlon Byrd/500	15.00
5	Bud Smith/500	10.00
6	Joe Mays/500	10.00
7	Troy Glaus/500	20.00
8	Ron Santo/500	15.00
9	Roy Oswalt/500	20.00
10	Angel Berroa/500	10.00
11	Mark Buehrle/500	15.00
12	John Buck/500	10.00
13	Barry Larkin/250	40.00
14	Gary Carter/300	30.00
15	Mark Teixeira/300	25.00
16	Alan Trammell/500	20.00
17	Kazuhisa Ishii/100	40.00
18	Rafael Palmeiro/125	50.00
19	Austin Kearns/500	25.00
20	Joe Torre/125	40.00
21	J.D. Drew/400	20.00
22	So Taguchi/500	20.00
23	Juan Marichal/500	15.00
24	Bobby Doerr/500	20.00
25	Carlos Beltran/500	10.00
26	Robert Fick/500	10.00
27	Albert Pujols/200	180.00
28	Shannon Stewart/500	10.00
29	Antonio Perez/500	10.00
30	Wilson Betemit/500	10.00
Jerseys (31-80):		
31	Alex Rodriguez/500	15.00
32	Curt Schilling/500	8.00
33	George Brett/300	30.00
34	Hideo Nomo/100	40.00
35	Ivan Rodriguez/500	8.00
36	Don Mattingly/200	40.00
37	Joe Mays/500	5.00
38	Lance Berkman/400	5.00
39	Tony Gwynn/500	10.00
40	Darin Erstad/500	5.00
41	Adrian Beltre/400	5.00
42	Frank Thomas/500	8.00
43	Cal Ripken Jr./300	30.00
44	Jose Vidro/500	5.00
45	Randy Johnson/300	8.00
46	Carlos Delgado/500	6.00
47	Roger Clemens/400	20.00
48	Luis Gonzalez/500	5.00
49	Marlon Byrd/500	5.00
50	Carlton Fisk/500	8.00
51	Manny Ramirez/500	8.00
52	Vladimir Guerrero/500	8.00
53	Barry Larkin/500	8.00
54	Aramis Ramirez/500	5.00
55	Todd Helton/500	8.00
56	Carlos Beltran/250	5.00
57	Jeff Bagwell/250	8.00
58	Larry Walker/500	5.00
59	Al Kaline/200	25.00
60	Chipper Jones/500	8.00
61	Bernie Williams/500	6.00
62	Bud Smith/500	5.00
63	Edgar Martinez/500	5.00
64	Pedro Martinez/500	8.00
65	Andre Dawson/200	10.00
66	Mike Piazza/100	40.00
67	Barry Zito/500	6.00
68	Bo Jackson/300	8.00
69	Nolan Ryan/400	50.00

70	Troy Glaus/500	6.00
71	Jorge Posada/500	8.00
72	Ted Williams/100	200.00
73	Nomar Garciaparra/500	15.00
74	"Catfish" Hunter/100	25.00
75	Gary Carter/500	8.00
76	Craig Biggio/500	5.00
77	Andruw Jones/500	8.00
78	Rickey Henderson/250	30.00
79	Greg Maddux/400	15.00
80	Kerry Wood/500	10.00
Bats (81-100):		
81	Alex Rodriguez/500	20.00
82	Don Mattingly/425	30.00
83	Craig Biggio/500	5.00
84	Kazuhisa Ishii/375	8.00
85	Eddie Murray/500	8.00
86	Carlton Fisk/500	8.00
87	Tsuyoshi Shinjo/500	5.00
88	Bo Jackson/500	10.00
89	Eddie Mathews/100	30.00
90	Chipper Jones/500	8.00
91	Adam Dunn/375	6.00
92	Tony Gwynn/200	10.00
93	Kirby Puckett/500	15.00
94	Andre Dawson/500	5.00
95	Bernie Williams/500	6.00
96	Roberto Clemente/300	70.00
97	Babe Ruth/500	250.00
98	Roberto Alomar/500	8.00
99	Frank Thomas/500	8.00
100	So Taguchi/500	6.00

DK Originals

		NM/M
Complete Set (15):		50.00
Common Player:		2.00
Production 1,000 Sets		
1	Alex Rodriguez	7.00
2	Kazuhisa Ishii	2.00
3	Pedro Martinez	3.00
4	Nomar Garciaparra	6.00
5	Albert Pujols	6.00
6	Chipper Jones	5.00
7	So Taguchi	2.00
8	Jeff Bagwell	3.00
9	Vladimir Guerrero	3.00
10	Derek Jeter	8.00
11	Sammy Sosa	6.00
12	Ichiro Suzuki	6.00
13	Barry Bonds	8.00
14	Jason Giambi	3.00
15	Mike Piazza	6.00

Heritage Collection

		NM/M
Complete Set (25):		100.00
Common Player:		2.00
Inserted 1:23		
1	Lou Gehrig	8.00
2	Nolan Ryan	10.00
3	Ryne Sandberg	4.00
4	Ted Williams	8.00
5	Roberto Clemente	8.00
6	Mike Schmidt	6.00
7	Roger Clemens	5.00
8	Kirby Puckett	4.00

9	Andre Dawson	2.00
10	Carlton Fisk	2.00
11	Don Mattingly	8.00
12	Juan Marichal	2.00
13	George Brett	8.00
14	Bo Jackson	3.00
15	Eddie Mathews	3.00
16	Randy Johnson	3.00
17	Alan Trammell	2.00
18	Tony Gwynn	4.00
19	Paul Molitor	3.00
20	Barry Bonds	10.00
21	Eddie Murray	3.00
22	Jim "Catfish" Hunter	2.00
23	Rickey Henderson	3.00
24	Cal Ripken Jr.	10.00
25	Babe Ruth	10.00

2002 Donruss Diamond Kings - LCS Programs

		NM/M
Complete Sheet Set (2):		20.00
Common Player:		.50
ALCS SHEET		10.00
1	Cal Ripken Jr.	3.00
2	Nomar Garciaparra	1.50
3	Roger Clemens	1.25
4	Alex Rodriguez	2.00
5	Troy Glaus	1.00
6	Miguel Tejada	.50
7	Alfonso Soriano	1.00
8	Ted Williams	2.50
—	Header Card	.10
NLCS SHEET		10.00
1	Randy Johnson	1.00
2	Josh Beckett	.75
3	Mike Piazza	1.50
4	Greg Maddux	1.25
5	Lance Berkman	.50
6	Mark Prior	2.00
7	Adam Dunn	1.00
8	Tony Gwynn	1.25
—	Header Card	.10

2002 Donruss Diamond Kings Original Paintings

(See 2002 Donruss Diamond Kings for checklist.)

Recollection Collection

		NM/M
Common Player:		
22	Fred Lynn 87 DK/28	15.00
30	Roy Oswalt 01 RDK Black/48	20.00
47	Alan Trammell 88 DK/110	30.00

Ramly T204

		NM/M
Complete Set (25):		120.00
Common Player:		3.00
Production 1,000 Sets		
1	Vladimir Guerrero	4.00
2	Jeff Bagwell	4.00
3	Barry Bonds	15.00
4	Rickey Henderson	4.00
5	Mike Piazza	8.00
6	Derek Jeter	15.00
7	Kazuhisa Ishii	3.00
8	Ichiro Suzuki	10.00
9	Chipper Jones	5.00
10	Sammy Sosa	8.00
11	Don Mattingly	10.00
12	Shawn Green	3.00
13	Nomar Garciaparra	6.00
14	Luis Gonzalez	3.00
15	Albert Pujols	8.00

16	Cal Ripken Jr.	15.00
17	Todd Helton	4.00
18	Hideo Nomo	3.00
19	Alex Rodriguez	10.00
20	So Taguchi	3.00
21	Lance Berkman	3.00
22	Tony Gwynn	5.00
23	Roger Clemens	6.00
24	Jason Giambi	4.00
25	Ken Griffey Jr.	8.00

Timeline

		NM/M
Complete Set (10):		60.00
Common Card:		3.00
Inserted 1:60		
1	Lou Gehrig, Don Mattingly	10.00
2	Hideo Nomo, Ichiro Suzuki	6.00
3	Cal Ripken Jr., Alex Rodriguez	10.00
4	Mike Schmidt, Scott Rolen	8.00
5	Ichiro Suzuki, Albert Pujols	8.00
6	Curt Schilling, Randy Johnson	5.00
7	Chipper Jones, Eddie Mathews	5.00
8	Lou Gehrig, Cal Ripken Jr.	10.00
9	Derek Jeter, Roger Clemens	10.00
10	Kazuhiko Ishimine, So Taguchi	3.00

2002 Donruss Diamond Kings Samples

	NM/M
Common Player:	.25
Stars:	1.5-2X
Gold:	10X
(See 2002 Donruss Diamond Kings for checklist and base card values.)	

2002 Donruss Elite

	NM/M
Complete Set (200):	
Common Player:	.25
Common (101-150):	2.00
Inserted 1:10	
Common (151-200):	3.00
Production 1,500	

#	Player	Price
	Pack (5):	3.00
	Box (20):	50.00
1	Vladimir Guerrero	.75
2	Bernie Williams	.35
3	Ichiro Suzuki	1.50
4	Roger Clemens	1.25
5	Greg Maddux	1.00
6	Fred McGriff	.25
7	Jermaine Dye	.25
8	Ken Griffey Jr.	1.50
9	Todd Helton	.75
10	Torii Hunter	.40
11	Pat Burrell	.40
12	Chipper Jones	1.00
13	Ivan Rodriguez	.50
14	Roy Oswalt	.40
15	Shannon Stewart	.25
16	Magglio Ordonez	.40
17	Lance Berkman	.25
18	Mark Mulder	.25
19	Al Leiter	.25
20	Sammy Sosa	1.50
21	Scott Rolen	.75
22	Aramis Ramirez	.25
23	Alfonso Soriano	.75
24	Phil Nevin	.25
25	Barry Bonds	2.50
26	Joe Mays	.25
27	Jeff Kent	.25
28	Mark Quinn	.25
29	Adrian Beltre	.35
30	Freddy Garcia	.25
31	Pedro J. Martinez	.75
32	Darryl Kile	.25
33	Mike Cameron	.25
34	Frank Catalanotto	.25
35	Jose Vidro	.25
36	Jim Thome	.25
37	Javy Lopez	.25
38	Paul Konerko	.25
39	Jeff Bagwell	.75
40	Curt Schilling	.40
41	Miguel Tejada	.40
42	Jim Edmonds	.25
43	Ellis Burks	.25
44	Mark Grace	.35
45	Robb Nen	.25
46	Jeff Conine	.25
47	Derek Jeter	2.50
48	Mike Lowell	.25
49	Javier Vazquez	.25
50	Manny Ramirez	.75
51	Bartolo Colon	.25
52	Carlos Beltran	.50
53	Tim Hudson	.40
54	Rafael Palmeiro	.65
55	Jimmy Rollins	.50
56	Andruw Jones	.75
57	Orlando Cabrera	.25
58	Dean Palmer	.25
59	Bret Boone	.25
60	Carlos Febles	.25
61	Ben Grieve	.25
62	Richie Sexson	.25
63	Alex Rodriguez	2.00
64	Juan Pierre	.25
65	Bobby Higginson	.25
66	Barry Zito	.40
67	Raul Mondesi	.25
68	Albert Pujols	2.00
69	Omar Vizquel	.25
70	Bobby Abreu	.25
71	Corey Koskie	.25
72	Tom Glavine	.40
73	Paul LoDuca	.25
74	Terrence Long	.25
75	Matt Morris	.25
76	Andy Pettitte	.40
77	Rich Aurilia	.25
78	Todd Walker	.25
79	John Olerud	.25
80	Mike Sweeney	.25
81	Ray Durham	.25
82	Fernando Vina	.25
83	Nomar Garciaparra	1.50
84	Mariano Rivera	.35
85	Mike Piazza	1.50
86	Mark Buehrle	.25
87	Adam Dunn	.50
88	Luis Gonzalez	.35
89	Richard Hidalgo	.25
90	Brad Radke	.25
91	Russ Ortiz	.25
92	Brian Giles	.25
93	Billy Wagner	.25
94	Cliff Floyd	.25
95	Eric Milton	.25
96	Bud Smith	.25
97	Wade Miller	.25
98	Jon Lieber	.25
99	Derrek Lee	.25
100	Jose Cruz Jr.	.25
101	Dmitri Young	2.00
102	Mo Vaughn	2.00
103	Tino Martinez	2.00
104	Larry Walker	2.50
105	Chuck Knoblauch	2.00
106	Troy Glaus	3.00
107	Jason Giambi	4.00
108	Travis Fryman	2.00
109	Josh Beckett	4.00
110	Edgar Martinez	2.00
111	Tim Salmon	2.00
112	C.C. Sabathia	2.00
113	Randy Johnson	5.00
114	Juan Gonzalez	4.00
115	Carlos Delgado	4.00
116	Hideo Nomo	4.00
117	Kerry Wood	4.00
118	Brian Jordan	2.00
119	Carlos Pena	2.00
120	Roger Cedeno	2.00
121	Chan Ho Park	2.00
122	Rafael Furcal	2.00
123	Frank Thomas	4.00
124	Mike Mussina	4.00
125	Rickey Henderson	5.00
126	Sean Casey	2.00
127	Barry Larkin	2.00
128	Kazuhiro Sasaki	2.00
129	Moises Alou	2.00
130	Jeff Cirillo	2.00
131	Jason Kendall	2.00
132	Gary Sheffield	3.00
133	Ryan Klesko	2.00
134	Kevin Brown	2.00
135	Darin Erstad	2.00
136	Roberto Alomar	3.00
137	Brad Fullmer	2.00
138	Eric Chavez	2.00
139	Ben Sheets	2.00
140	Trot Nixon	2.00
141	Garret Anderson	2.00
142	Shawn Green	2.50
143	Troy Percival	2.00
144	Craig Biggio	2.50
145	Jorge Posada	2.50
146	J.D. Drew	3.00
147	Johnny Damon	2.00
148	Jeromy Burnitz	2.00
149	Robin Ventura	2.00
150	Aaron Sele	2.00
151	Cam Esslinger RC	3.00
152	Ben Howard RC	4.00
153	Brandon Backe RC	3.00
154	Jorge De La Rosa RC	3.00
155	Austin Kearns	5.00
156	Carlos Zambrano	3.00
157	Kyle Kane RC	3.00
158	So Taguchi RC	5.00
159	Brian Mallette RC	3.00
160	Brett Jodie	3.00
161	Elio Serrano RC	3.00
162	Joe Thurston	3.00
163	Kevin Olsen	3.00
164	Rodrigo Rosario RC	4.00
165	Matt Guerrier	3.00
166	Anderson Machado RC	5.00
167	Bert Snow	3.00
168	Franklyn German RC	3.00
169	Brandon Claussen	3.00
170	Jason Romano	3.00
171	Jorge Padilla RC	3.00
172	Jose Cueto	3.00
173	Allan Simpson RC	3.00
174	Doug DeVore RC	3.00
175	Justin Duchscherer	3.00
176	Josh Pearce	3.00
177	Steve Bechler RC	3.00
178	Josh Phelps	3.00
179	Juan Diaz	3.00
180	Victor Alvarez RC	3.00
181	Ramon Vazquez	3.00
182	Mike Rivera	3.00
183	Kazuhisa Ishii RC	6.00
184	Henry Mateo	3.00
185	Travis Hughes RC	5.00
186	Zach Day	3.00
187	Brad Voyles	3.00
188	Sean Douglass	3.00
189	Nick Neugebauer	3.00
190	Tom Shearn RC	3.00
191	Eric Cyr RC	3.00
192	Adam Johnson	3.00
193	Michael Cuddyer	3.00
194	Erik Bedard	3.00
195	Mark Ellis	3.00
196	Carlos Hernandez	3.00
197	Deivi Santos	3.00
198	Morgan Ensberg	3.00
199	Ryan Jamison RC	3.00
200	Cody Ransom	3.00

Aspirations

1-100 print run 26-50:	15-30X
1-100 p/r 51-80:	8-15X
101-150 p/r 26-50:	1.5-3X
101-150 p/r 51-99:	1-2X

Status

1-100 print run 36-70:	10-20X
1-100 p/r 71-100:	5-10X
101-150 p/r 36-70:	1-2X
101-150 p/r 71-100:	1X

All-Star Salutes

NM/M

#	Player	Price
	Common Player:	1.00
	Century:	1-2X
	Production 100	
1	Ichiro Suzuki	5.00
2	Tony Gwynn	4.00
3	Magglio Ordonez	1.50
4	Cal Ripken Jr.	8.00
5	Tony Gwynn	4.00
6	Kazuhiro Sasaki	1.00
7	Freddy Garcia	1.00
8	Luis Gonzalez	1.00
9	Lance Berkman	1.00
10	Derek Jeter	8.00
11	Chipper Jones	4.00
12	Randy Johnson	3.00
13	Andruw Jones	3.00
14	Pedro J. Martinez	3.00
15	Jim Thome	1.00
16	Rafael Palmeiro	2.50
17	Barry Larkin	1.00
18	Ivan Rodriguez	2.50
19	Omar Vizquel	1.00
20	Edgar Martinez	1.00
21	Larry Walker	1.00
22	Javy Lopez	1.00
23	Mariano Rivera	1.25
24	Frank Thomas	3.00
25	Greg Maddux	4.00

Back to the Future

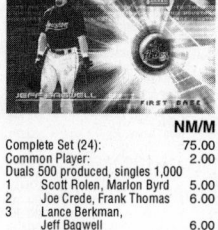

NM/M

#	Player	Price
	Complete Set (24):	75.00
	Common Player:	2.00
	Duals 500 produced, singles 1,000	
1	Scott Rolen, Marlon Byrd	5.00
2	Joe Crede, Frank Thomas	6.00
3	Lance Berkman, Jeff Bagwell	6.00
4	Marcus Giles, Chipper Jones	10.00
5	Shawn Green, Paul LoDuca	4.00
7	Kerry Wood, Juan Cruz	4.00
8	Vladimir Guerrero, Orlando Cabrera	6.00
9	Scott Rolen	3.00
10	Marlon Byrd	2.00
11	Frank Thomas	4.00
12	Joe Crede	4.00
13	Jeff Bagwell	4.00
14	Lance Berkman	2.00
15	Chipper Jones	6.00
16	Marcus Giles	2.50
17	Shawn Green	2.00
18	Paul LoDuca	2.00
19	Jim Edmonds	2.00
20	Kerry Wood	3.00
21	Juan Cruz	2.00
22	Vladimir Guerrero	4.00
23	Orlando Cabrera	2.00

Back to the Future Threads

NM/M

#	Player	Price
	Common Card:	10.00
	Duals 50 produced, singles 100	
1	Scott Rolen, Marlon Byrd	30.00
2	Joe Crede, Frank Thomas	40.00
3	Lance Berkman, Jeff Bagwell	30.00
4	Marcus Giles, Chipper Jones	50.00
5	Shawn Green, Paul LoDuca	30.00
7	Kerry Wood, Juan Cruz	35.00
8	Vladimir Guerrero, Orlando Cabrera	10.00
9	Scott Rolen	15.00
10	Marlon Byrd	10.00
11	Frank Thomas	25.00
12	Joe Crede	10.00
13	Jeff Bagwell	25.00
14	Lance Berkman	15.00
15	Chipper Jones	25.00
16	Marcus Giles	15.00
17	Shawn Green	15.00
18	Paul LoDuca	10.00
19	Jim Edmonds	10.00
20	So Taguchi	15.00
21	Kerry Wood	15.00
22	Juan Cruz	10.00
23	Vladimir Guerrero	25.00
24	Orlando Cabrera	10.00

Back 2 Back Jacks

NM/M

#	Player	Price
	Common Card:	10.00
	Dual Production 75	
	Single Production 150	
1	Ivan Rodriguez, Alex Rodriguez	40.00
2	Kirby Puckett, Dave Winfield	50.00
3	Ted Williams, Nomar Garciaparra	150.00
4	Jeff Bagwell, Craig Biggio	25.00
5	Eddie Murray, Cal Ripken Jr.	125.00
6	Andruw Jones, Chipper Jones	25.00
7	Roberto Clemente, Willie Stargell	120.00
8	Lou Gehrig, Don Mattingly	180.00
9	Larry Walker, Todd Helton	20.00
10	Manny Ramirez, Trot Nixon	25.00
11	Alex Rodriguez	30.00
12	Ivan Rodriguez	15.00
13	Kirby Puckett	40.00
14	Dave Winfield	15.00
15	Ted Williams	100.00
16	Nomar Garciaparra	40.00
17	Jeff Bagwell	15.00
18	Craig Biggio	10.00
19	Eddie Murray	20.00
20	Cal Ripken Jr.	60.00
21	Andruw Jones	10.00
22	Chipper Jones	20.00
23	Roberto Clemente	80.00
25	Lou Gehrig	160.00
26	Don Mattingly	65.00
27	Larry Walker	10.00
28	Todd Helton	15.00
29	Manny Ramirez	20.00
30	Trot Nixon	10.00

Career Bests

NM/M

#	Player	Price
	Common Player:	2.00
1	Albert Pujols/1,013	8.00
2	Alex Rodriguez/52	20.00
3	Alex Rodriguez/135	15.00
4	Andruw Jones/104	6.00
5	Barry Bonds/73	25.00
6	Barry Bonds/1,379	10.00
7	Barry Bonds/177	20.00
8	C.C. Sabathia/171	4.00
9	Carlos Beltran/876	2.00
10	Chipper Jones/330	6.00
11	Derek Jeter/900	15.00
12	Eric Chavez/114	4.00
13	Frank Catalanotto/330	2.00
14	Ichiro Suzuki/838	15.00
15	Ichiro Suzuki/127	15.00
16	J.D. Drew/27	20.00
17	J.D. Drew/1,027	2.00
18	Jason Giambi/660	5.00
19	Jim Thome/49	25.00
20	Jim Thome/624	4.00
21	Jorge Posada/95	8.00
22	Jose Cruz Jr/856	2.00
23	Kazuhiro Sasaki/45	15.00
24	Kerry Wood/336	5.00
25	Lance Berkman/1,050	3.00
26	Magglio Ordonez/382	3.00
27	Mark Mulder/345	2.00
28	Pat Burrell/27	20.00
29	Pat Burrell/469	3.00
30	Randy Johnson/372	6.00
31	Richie Sexson/547	3.00

34	Roberto Alomar/956	3.00
35	Sammy Sosa/160	12.00
36	Sammy Sosa/1,174	6.00
37	Shawn Green/125	4.00
39	Trot Nixon/150	3.00
40	Troy Glaus/108	5.00

Passing the Torch

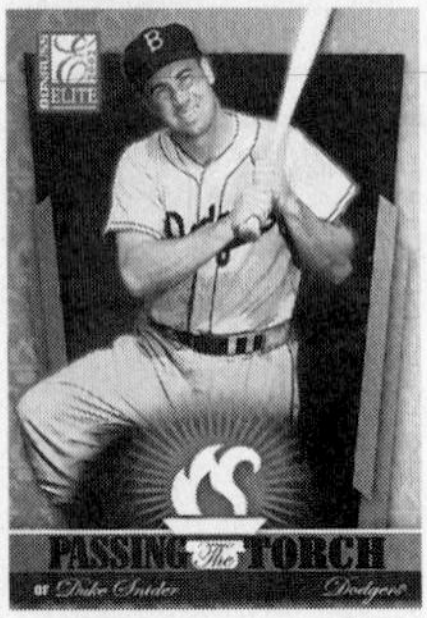

		NM/M
Common Card:		4.00
Dual 500, single 1,000 produced.		
1	Fergie Jenkins, Mark Prior	10.00
2	Nolan Ryan, Roy Oswalt	25.00
3	Ozzie Smith, J.D. Drew	8.00
4	George Brett, Carlos Beltran	15.00
5	Kirby Puckett, Michael Cuddyer	10.00
6	Johnny Bench, Adam Dunn	8.00
7	Duke Snider, Paul LoDuca	6.00
8	Tony Gwynn, Xavier Nady	10.00
9	Fergie Jenkins	4.00
10	Mark Prior	8.00
11	Nolan Ryan	15.00
12	Roy Oswalt	5.00
13	Ozzie Smith	6.00
14	J.D. Drew	4.00
15	George Brett	10.00
16	Carlos Beltran	6.00
17	Kirby Puckett	6.00
18	Michael Cuddyer	4.00
19	Johnny Bench	6.00
20	Adam Dunn	6.00
21	Duke Snider	6.00
22	Paul LoDuca	4.00
23	Tony Gwynn	6.00
24	Xavier Nady	4.00

Passing the Torch Autos.

		NM/M
Common Autograph:		15.00
1	Ferguson Jenkins, Mark Prior/50	100.00
2	Nolan Ryan, Roy Oswalt/50	180.00
3	Ozzie Smith, J.D. Drew/50	125.00
4	George Brett, Carlos Beltran/25	300.00
5	Kirby Puckett, Michael Cuddyer/50	100.00
6	Johnny Bench, Adam Dunn/50	100.00
7	Duke Snider, Paul LoDuca/50	80.00
8	Tony Gwynn, Xavier Nady/50	120.00
9	Fergie Jenkins/50	40.00
10	Mark Prior/100	20.00
11	Nolan Ryan/100	125.00
12	Roy Oswalt/100	25.00
13	Ozzie Smith/25	160.00
14	J.D. Drew/100	30.00
15	George Brett/25	300.00
16	Carlos Beltran/100	40.00
17	Kirby Puckett/25	150.00
18	Michael Cuddyer/100	15.00
19	Johnny Bench/100	50.00
20	Adam Dunn/50	40.00
21	Duke Snider/100	30.00
22	Paul LoDuca/100	15.00
23	Tony Gwynn/100	50.00
24	Xavier Nady/100	15.00

Recollection Collection

		NM/M
Common Player:		
2	Alfredo Amezaga 01/50	15.00
13	Orlando Hudson 01/50	20.00
18	Antonio Perez 01/50	15.00
20	Mike Rivera 01/50	15.00
22	Claudio Vargas 01/50	15.00
23	Martin Vargas 01/50	15.00

Throwback Threads

		NM/M
Common Card:		15.00
Dual 50, single 100 Produced.		
1	Manny Ramirez, Ted Williams	125.00
2	Mike Piazza, Carlton Fisk	50.00
3	George Brett, Bo Jackson	125.00
4	Randy Johnson, Curt Schilling	40.00
5	Don Mattingly, Lou Gehrig	250.00
6	Bernie Williams, Dave Winfield	25.00
7	Rickey Henderson	75.00
8	Paul Molitor, Robin Yount	75.00
9	J.D. Drew, Stan Musial	100.00
10	Andre Dawson, Ryne Sandberg	100.00
11	Babe Ruth, Reggie Jackson	325.00
12	Brooks Robinson, Cal Ripken Jr.	120.00
13	Ted Williams, Nomar Garciaparra	125.00
14	Shawn Green, Jackie Robinson	80.00
15	Tony Gwynn, Cal Ripken Jr.	120.00
16	Ted Williams	75.00
17	Manny Ramirez	20.00
18	Carlton Fisk	25.00
19	Mike Piazza	20.00
20	Bo Jackson	20.00
21	George Brett	50.00
22	Curt Schilling	20.00
23	Randy Johnson	20.00
24	Don Mattingly	50.00
25	Lou Gehrig	200.00
26	Bernie Williams	15.00
27	Dave Winfield	15.00
29	Rickey Henderson	40.00
30	Robin Yount	30.00
31	Paul Molitor	25.00
32	Stan Musial	65.00
33	J.D. Drew	15.00
34	Andre Dawson	15.00
35	Ryne Sandberg	50.00
36	Babe Ruth	250.00
37	Reggie Jackson	25.00
38	Brooks Robinson	25.00
39	Cal Ripken Jr.	75.00
40	Nomar Garciaparra	40.00
41	Jackie Robinson	80.00
42	Shawn Green	15.00
43	Pedro J. Martinez	20.00
44	Nolan Ryan	80.00
45	Kazuhiro Sasaki	15.00
46	Tony Gwynn	25.00
47	Carlton Fisk	20.00
48	Cal Ripken Jr.	75.00
49	Rod Carew	20.00
50	Nolan Ryan	80.00
51	Alex Rodriguez	25.00
52	Greg Maddux	25.00
53	Pedro J. Martinez	20.00
54	Rickey Henderson	30.00
55	Rod Carew	20.00
56	Roberto Clemente	100.00
57	Hideo Nomo	40.00
58	Rickey Henderson	40.00
59	Dave Parker	15.00
60	Eddie Mathews	25.00
61	Eddie Murray	20.00
62	Nolan Ryan	80.00
63	Tom Seaver	25.00
64	Roger Clemens	40.00
65	Rickey Henderson	40.00

Throwback Threads Auto.

No Pricing
Production 5-25

Turn of the Century

		NM/M
Common Player:		8.00
154	Jorge De La Rosa/50	8.00
156	Carlos Zambrano/50	8.00
157	Kyle Kane/50	8.00
158	So Taguchi/25	15.00
159	Brian Mallette/50	8.00
160	Brett Jodie/50	8.00
165	Matt Guerrier/50	8.00
168	Franklyn German/50	8.00
169	Brandon Claussen/50	15.00
171	Jorge Padilla/50	10.00
172	Jose Cueto/50	8.00
176	Josh Pearce/50	8.00
177	Steve Bechler/50	8.00
178	Josh Phelps/50	8.00
180	Victor Alvarez/50	8.00
182	Michael Rivera/50	8.00
183	Kazuhisa Ishii/125	20.00
184	Henry Mateo/50	8.00
186	Zach Day/50	8.00
189	Nick Neugebauer/100	8.00
192	Adam Johnson/125	8.00
193	Michael Cuddyer/50	8.00
195	Mark Ellis/25	10.00
196	Carlos Hernandez/150	8.00
198	Morgan Ensberg/50	8.00
200	Cody Ransom/150	8.00

Turn of the Century Autographs

		NM/M
Common Autograph:		10.00
151	Cam Esslinger/150	10.00
152	Ben Howard/150	10.00
153	Brandon Backe/150	15.00
154	Jorge De La Rosa/100	10.00
155	Austin Kearns/150	15.00
156	Carlos Zambrano/100	20.00
157	Kyle Kane/100	10.00
158	So Taguchi/125	20.00
159	Brian Mallette/100	10.00
160	Brett Jodie/100	10.00
161	Elio Serrano/150	10.00
162	Joe Thurston/150	10.00
163	Kevin Olsen/150	10.00
164	Rodrigo Rosario/150	10.00
165	Matt Guerrier/100	10.00
166	Anderson Machado/150	10.00
167	Bert Snow/150	10.00
168	Franklyn German/100	10.00
169	Brandon Claussen/100	15.00
170	Jason Romano/150	10.00
171	Jorge Padilla/100	15.00
172	Jose Cueto/100	10.00
173	Allan Simpson/150	10.00
174	Doug DeVore/150	15.00
175	Justin Duchscherer/150	10.00
176	Josh Pearce/100	10.00
177	Steve Bechler/100	10.00
178	Josh Phelps/100	15.00
179	Juan Diaz/150	10.00
180	Victor Alvarez/100	10.00
181	Ramon Vazquez/150	10.00
182	Michael Rivera/100	10.00
183	Kazuhisa Ishii/25	150.00
184	Henry Mateo/100	10.00
185	Travis Hughes/150	10.00
186	Zach Day/100	10.00
187	Brad Voyles/150	10.00
188	Sean Douglass/150	10.00
189	Nick Neugebauer/50	10.00
190	Tom Shearn/150	10.00
191	Eric Cyr/150	10.00
192	Adam Johnson/25	10.00
193	Michael Cuddyer/100	10.00
194	Erik Bedard/150	20.00
195	Mark Ellis/125	10.00
197	Deivis Santos/150	10.00
198	Morgan Ensberg/100	10.00
199	Ryan Jamison/150	10.00

2002 Donruss Fan Club

		NM/M
Complete Set (300):		
Common Player:		.25
Common (201-260):		3.00
Production 1,350		
Common (261-300):		2.00
Production 2,025		
Pack (5):		3.50
Box (20):		60.00
1	Alex Rodriguez	2.00
2	Pedro Martinez	.75
3	Vladimir Guerrero	.75
4	Jim Edmonds	.25
5	Derek Jeter	2.50
6	Johnny Damon	.40
7	Rafael Furcal	.25
8	Cal Ripken Jr.	2.50
9	Brad Radke	.25
10	Bret Boone	.25
11	Pat Burrell	.50
12	Roy Oswalt	.50
13	Cliff Floyd	.25
14	Robin Ventura	.25
15	Frank Thomas	.75
16	Mariano Rivera	.35
17	Paul LoDuca	.25
18	Geoff Jenkins	.25
19	Tony Gwynn	1.00
20	Chipper Jones	1.00
21	Eric Chavez	.40
22	Kerry Wood	.60
23	Jorge Posada	.35
24	J.D. Drew	.40
25	Garret Anderson	.25
26	Javier Vazquez	.25
27	Kenny Lofton	.25
28	Mike Mussina	.45
29	Paul Konerko	.25
30	Bernie Williams	.45
31	Eric Milton	.25
32	Craig Wilson	.25
33	Paul O'Neill	.25
34	Dmitri Young	.25
35	Andres Galarraga	.25
36	Gary Sheffield	.40
37	Ben Grieve	.25
38	Scott Rolen	.75
39	Mark Grace	.35
40	Albert Pujols	2.00
41	Barry Zito	.40
42	Edgar Martinez	.25
43	Jarrod Washburn	.25
44	Juan Pierre	.25
45	Mark Buehrle	.25
46	Larry Walker	.25
47	Trot Nixon	.25
48	Wade Miller	.25
49	Robert Fick	.25
50	Sean Casey	.40
51	Joe Mays	.25
52	Brad Fullmer	.25
53	Chan Ho Park	.25
54	Carlos Delgado	.50
55	Phil Nevin	.25
56	Mike Cameron	.25
57	Raul Mondesi	.25
58	Roberto Alomar	.40
59	Ryan Klesko	.25
60	Andruw Jones	.75
61	Gabe Kapler	.25
62	Darin Erstad	.65
63	Cristian Guzman	.25
64	Kazuhiro Sasaki	.25
65	Doug Mientkiewicz	.25
66	Sammy Sosa	1.50
67	Mike Hampton	.25
68	Rickey Henderson	.75
69	Mark Mulder	.35
70	Jeff Conine	.25
71	Freddy Garcia	.25
72	Ivan Rodriguez	.65
73	Terrence Long	.25
74	Adam Dunn	.50
75	Moises Alou	.25
76	Todd Helton	.75
77	Preston Wilson	.25
78	Roger Cedeno	.25
79	Tony Armas Jr.	.25
80	Manny Ramirez	.75
81	Jose Vidro	.25
82	Randy Johnson	.75
83	Richie Sexson	.25
84	Troy Glaus	.75
85	Kevin Brown	.35
86	Woody Williams	.25
87	Adrian Beltre	.40
88	Brian Giles	.25
89	Jermaine Dye	.25
90	Craig Biggio	.25
91	Richard Hidalgo	.25
92	Magglio Ordonez	.40
93	Al Leiter	.25
94	Jeff Kent	.25
95	Curt Schilling	.50
96	Tim Hudson	.50
97	Fred McGriff	.25
98	Barry Larkin	.25
99	Jim Thome	.25
100	Tom Glavine	.40
101	Alfonso Soriano	.75
102	Jamie Moyer	.25
103	Vinny Castilla	.25
104	Rich Aurilia	.25
105	Matt Morris	.25
106	Rafael Palmeiro	.65
107	Joe Crede	.25
108	Barry Bonds	2.50
109	Robert Person	.25
110	Nomar Garciaparra	1.50
111	Brandon Duckworth	.25
112	Russ Ortiz	.25
113	Jeff Weaver	.25
114	Carlos Beltran	.50
115	Ellis Burks	.25
116	Jeremy Giambi	.25
117	Carlos Lee	.25
118	Ken Griffey Jr.	1.50
119	Torii Hunter	.40
120	Andy Petitte	.40
121	Jose Canseco	.40
122	Charles Johnson	.25
123	Nick Johnson	.25
124	Luis Gonzalez	.35
125	Rondell White	.25
126	Miguel Tejada	.50
127	Jose Cruz Jr.	.25
128	Brent Abernathy	.25
129	Scott Brosius	.25
130	Jon Lieber	.25
131	John Smoltz	.25
132	Mike Sweeney	.25
133	Shannon Stewart	.25
134	Derrek Lee	.25
135	Brian Jordan	.25
136	Rusty Greer	.25
137	Mike Piazza	1.50
138	Billy Wagner	.25
139	Shawn Green	.35
140	Orlando Cabrera	.25
141	Jeff Bagwell	.75
142	Aaron Sele	.25
143	Hideo Nomo	.75
144	Marlon Anderson	.25
145	Todd Walker	.25
146	Bobby Higginson	.25
147	Ichiro Suzuki	2.00
148	Juan Uribe	.25
149	Jason Kendall	.25
150	Mark Quinn	.25
151	Ben Sheets	.25
152	Paul Abbott	.25
153	Aubrey Huff	.25
154	Greg Maddux	1.00
155	Darryl Kile	.25
156	John Burkett	.25
157	Juan Gonzalez	.75
158	Javy Lopez	.25
159	Aramis Ramirez	.25
160	Lance Berkman	.25
161	David Cone	.25
162	Edgar Renteria	.25
163	Roger Clemens	1.25
164	Frank Catalanotto	.25
165	Bartolo Colon	.25
166	Mark McGwire	2.00
167	Jay Gibbons	.25
168	Tony Clark	.25
169	Tsuyoshi Shinjo	.25
170	Brad Penny	.25
171	Marcus Giles	.25
172	Matt Williams	.25
173	Bud Smith	.25
174	Tino Martinez	.25
175	Ryan Dempster	.25
176	Jimmy Rollins	.40
177	Edgardo Alfonzo	.25
178	Jason Giambi	.50

179	Aaron Boone	.25
180	Matt Dunigan	.25
181	Mike Lowell	.25
182	Jose Ortiz	.25
183	Johnny Estrada	.25
184	Shane Reynolds	.25
185	Joe Kennedy	.25
186	Corey Patterson	.25
187	Jeromy Burnitz	.25
188	C.C. Sabathia	.25
189	Doug Davis	.25
190	Omar Vizquel	.25
191	John Olerud	.25
192	Dee Brown	.25
193	Kip Wells	.25
194	A.J. Burnett	.25
195	Josh Towers	.25
196	Jason Varitek	.25
197	Jason Isringhausen	.25
198	Fernando Vina	.25
199	Ramon Ortiz	.25
200	Bobby Abreu	.25
201	Willie Harris	3.00
202	Angel Santos	3.00
203	Corky Miller	3.00
204	Mike Rivera	3.00
205	Justin Duchscherer	3.00
206	Rick Bauer	3.00
207	Angel Berroa	3.00
208	Juan Cruz	3.00
209	Dewon Brazelton	3.00
210	Mark Prior	10.00
211	Mark Teixeira	8.00
212	Geronimo Gil	3.00
213	Casey Fossum	3.00
214	Ken Harvey	3.00
215	Michael Cuddyer	3.00
216	Wilson Betemit	3.00
217	David Brous	3.00
218	Juan Pena	3.00
219	Travis Hafner	4.00
220	Erick Almonte	3.00
221	Morgan Ensberg	3.00
222	Martin Vargas	3.00
223	Brandon Berger	3.00
224	Zach Day	3.00
225	Brad Voyles	3.00
226	Jeremy Affeldt	3.00
227	Nick Neugebauer	3.00
228	Tim Redding	3.00
229	Adam Johnson	3.00
230	Doug DeVore RC	4.00
231	Cody Ransom	3.00
232	Marlon Byrd	3.00
233	Delvin James	3.00
234	Eric Munson	3.00
235	Dennis Tankersley	3.00
236	Josh Beckett	8.00
237	Bill Hall	3.00
238	Kevin Olsen	3.00
239	Francis Beltran RC	5.00
240	Antonio Perez	3.00
241	Orlando Hudson	3.00
242	Anderson Machado RC	6.00
243	Tom Shearn RC	5.00
244	Brian Mallette RC	4.00
245	Raul Chavez RC	4.00
246	Andy Pratt RC	4.00
247	Jorge De La Rosa RC	4.00
248	Jeff Deardorff RC	4.00
249	Ben Howard RC	4.00
250	Brandon Backe RC	4.00
251	Ed Rogers	3.00
252	Travis Hughes RC	5.00
253	Rodrigo Rosario RC	5.00
254	Alfredo Amezaga	3.00
255	Jorge Padilla RC	5.00
256	Victor Martinez	4.00
257	Steve Bechler RC	4.00
258	Chris Baker RC	4.00
259	Ryan Freel	3.00
260	Allan Simpson RC	3.00
261	Alex Rodriguez	6.00
262	Vladimir Guerrero	3.00
263	Bud Smith	2.00
264	Miguel Tejada	2.00
265	Craig Biggio	2.00
266	Luis Gonzalez	2.00
267	Ivan Rodriguez	3.00
268	C.C. Sabathia	2.00
269	Jeff Bagwell	2.00
270	Aramis Ramirez	2.00
271	Bobby Abreu	2.00
272	Rich Aurilia	2.00
273	Jason Giambi	3.00
274	Rickey Henderson	3.00
275	Wade Miller	2.00
276	Andruw Jones	3.00
277	Troy Glaus	3.00
278	Roy Oswalt	2.00
279	Tony Gwynn	3.00
280	Adam Dunn	3.00
281	Larry Walker	2.00
282	Jose Canseco	3.00
283	Todd Helton	3.00
284	Lance Berkman	2.00
285	Cal Ripken Jr.	10.00
286	Albert Pujols	8.00
287	Alfonso Soriano	3.00
288	Mark Mulder	2.00
289	Mike Hampton	2.00
290	Andres Galarraga	2.00
291	Barry Bonds	8.00
292	Ben Sheets	2.00
293	Ichiro Suzuki	6.00
294	J.D. Drew	2.00
295	Jose Ortiz	2.00
296	Kerry Wood	3.00
297	Mark McGwire	8.00
298	Mike Sweeney	2.00
299	Pat Burrell	3.00
300	Tim Hudson	3.00

Artist

		NM/M
Complete Set (14):		60.00
Common Player:		3.00
Production 300 Sets		
1	Pedro Martinez	8.00
2	Curt Schilling	6.00
3	Kevin Brown	3.00
4	Tim Hudson	5.00
5	Kerry Wood	7.50
6	Barry Zito	4.00
7	Hideo Nomo	6.00
8	Randy Johnson	8.00
9	Greg Maddux	10.00
10	Roger Clemens	15.00
11	Kazuhiro Sasaki	3.00
12	Joe Mays	3.00
13	Mark Mulder	3.00
14	Javier Vazquez	3.00

Artist Autographs

		NM/M
Production 15-100		
6	Barry Zito/100	35.00

Autographs

		NM/M
Common Player:		5.00
Varying quantities produced		
201	Willie Harris/500	5.00
203	Corky Miller/500	5.00
205	Justin Duchscherer/500	10.00
207	Angel Berroa/500	15.00
208	Juan Cruz/175	8.00
209	Dewon Brazelton/52	15.00
210	Mark Prior/425	40.00
211	Mark Teixeira/425	25.00
213	Casey Fossum/100	15.00
215	Michael Cuddyer/52	15.00
216	Wilson Betemit/500	5.00
217	David Brous/500	5.00
218	Juan A. Pena/188	8.00
219	Travis Hafner/375	10.00
221	Morgan Ensberg/52	15.00
222	Martin Vargas/500	5.00
223	Brandon Berger/500	5.00
224	Zach Day/500	5.00
225	Brad Voyles/500	5.00
226	Jeremy Affeldt/250	5.00
227	Nick Neugebauer/225	8.00
228	Tim Redding/500	5.00
229	Adam Johnson/425	5.00
230	Doug DeVore/300	8.00
231	Cody Ransom/500	5.00
232	Marlon Byrd/475	15.00
233	Delvin James/375	5.00
234	Eric Munson/325	8.00
235	Dennis Tankersley/500	5.00
238	Kevin Olsen/325	5.00
240	Antonio Perez/525	5.00
241	Orlando Hudson/525	10.00
248	Jeff Deardorff/475	5.00
251	Ed Rogers/400	5.00
255	Jorge Padilla/450	15.00
260	Allan Simpson/475	8.00
278	Roy Oswalt/75	35.00

Craftsmen

		NM/M
Complete Set (18):		80.00
Common Player:		3.00
Production 300 Sets		
1	Ichiro Suzuki	10.00
2	Todd Helton	5.00
3	Manny Ramirez	5.00
4	Luis Gonzalez	3.00
5	Roberto Alomar	3.50
6	Moises Alou	3.00
7	Darin Erstad	3.00
8	Mike Piazza	10.00
9	Edgar Martinez	3.00
10	Vladimir Guerrero	6.00
11	Juan Gonzalez	5.00
12	Nomar Garciaparra	8.00
13	Tony Gwynn	6.00
14	Jeff Bagwell	5.00
15	Albert Pujols	15.00
16	Larry Walker	3.00
17	Paul LoDuca	3.00
18	Lance Berkman	3.00

Craftsmen Autographs

		NM/M
Common Player:		
17	Paul LoDuca/100	20.00

Master Craftsmen

		NM/M
Common Player:		5.00
Production 150 Sets/H		
1	Ichiro Suzuki/Ball/51	75.00
2	Todd Helton	10.00
3	Manny Ramirez	10.00
4	Luis Gonzalez	8.00
5	Roberto Alomar	8.00
6	Moises Alou	8.00
7	Darin Erstad	8.00
8	Mike Piazza	15.00
9	Edgar Martinez	8.00
10	Vladimir Guerrero	15.00
11	Juan Gonzalez	8.00
12	Nomar Garciaparra	20.00
13	Tony Gwynn/175	20.00
14	Jeff Bagwell	10.00
15	Albert Pujols/175	25.00
16	Larry Walker/175	5.00
17	Paul LoDuca/175	5.00
18	Lance Berkman	8.00

Double Features

		NM/M
Complete Set (10):		80.00
Common Card:		8.00
Production 125 Sets		
1	Larry Walker, Todd Helton	10.00
2	Jose Vidro, Vladimir Guerrero	10.00
3	Jason Giambi, Jeremy Giambi	8.00
4	Nomar Garciaparra, Manny Ramirez	15.00
5	Troy Glaus, Darin Erstad	8.00
6	Shawn Green, Paul LoDuca	8.00
7	Jeff Bagwell, Craig Biggio	10.00
8	Pedro Martinez, Hideo Nomo	12.00
9	Curt Schilling, Randy Johnson	10.00
10	Andruw Jones, Chipper Jones	12.00

Double Features Game-Used

		NM/M
Common Card:		10.00
Production 50 Sets		
1	Larry Walker, Todd Helton	15.00
2	Jose Vidro, Vladimir Guerrero	20.00
3	Jason Giambi, Jeremy Giambi	15.00
4	Nomar Garciaparra, Manny Ramirez	30.00
5	Troy Glaus, Darin Erstad	15.00
6	Shawn Green, Paul LoDuca	10.00
7	Jeff Bagwell, Craig Biggio	15.00
8	Pedro Martinez, Hideo Nomo	30.00
9	Curt Schilling, Randy Johnson	15.00
10	Andruw Jones, Chipper Jones	20.00

Franchise Features

		NM/M
Complete Set (40):		180.00
Common Player:		3.00
Production 300 Sets		
1	Cliff Floyd	3.00
2	Mike Piazza	12.00
3	Cal Ripken Jr.	25.00
4	Mike Sweeney	3.00
5	Curt Schilling	5.00
6	Aramis Ramirez	3.00
7	Vladimir Guerrero	8.00
8	Andruw Jones	8.00
9	Tim Hudson	3.00
10	Bernie Williams	3.00
11	Pedro Martinez	8.00
12	Roberto Alomar	3.00
13	Joe Mays	3.00
14	Jason Giambi	5.00
15	Kazuhiro Sasaki	3.00
16	Magglio Ordonez	3.00
17	Nomar Garciaparra	12.00
18	Juan Gonzalez	8.00
19	Carlos Beltran	3.00
20	Javier Vazquez	3.00
21	Miguel Tejada	3.00
22	Luis Gonzalez	3.00
23	Greg Maddux	10.00
24	Rafael Palmeiro	6.00
25	Freddy Garcia	3.00
26	Barry Zito	4.00
27	Paul LoDuca	3.00
28	Robert Fick	3.00
29	Roger Clemens	10.00
30	Eric Chavez	3.00
31	Ivan Rodriguez	5.00
32	Chipper Jones	10.00
33	Kerry Wood	6.00
34	Randy Johnson	8.00
35	Alex Rodriguez	12.00
36	Manny Ramirez	8.00
37	Mark Buehrle	3.00
38	Mark Mulder	3.00
39	Ichiro Suzuki	15.00
40	Troy Glaus	4.00

Franchise Features Game-Used

		NM/M
Common Player:		4.00
Production 150 Sets		
All Jerseys unless noted.		
1	Cliff Floyd	4.00
2	Mike Piazza	15.00
3	Cal Ripken Jr.	30.00
4	Mike Sweeney	4.00
5	Curt Schilling	8.00
6	Aramis Ramirez	6.00
7	Vladimir Guerrero	8.00
8	Andruw Jones	8.00
9	Tim Hudson	6.00
10	Bernie Williams	6.00
11	Pedro Martinez	10.00
12	Roberto Alomar	6.00
13	Joe Mays	4.00
14	Jason Giambi	8.00
15	Kazuhiro Sasaki	5.00
16	Magglio Ordonez	6.00
17	Nomar Garciaparra	20.00
18	Juan Gonzalez	8.00
19	Carlos Beltran	8.00
20	Javier Vazquez	4.00
21	Miguel Tejada	8.00
22	Luis Gonzalez	5.00
23	Greg Maddux	15.00
24	Rafael Palmeiro	10.00
25	Freddy Garcia	4.00
26	Barry Zito	8.00
27	Paul LoDuca	4.00
28	Robert Fick	4.00
29	Roger Clemens	20.00
30	Eric Chavez/bat	4.00
31	Ivan Rodriguez	8.00
32	Chipper Jones	15.00
33	Kerry Wood	10.00
34	Randy Johnson	15.00
35	Alex Rodriguez	15.00
36	Manny Ramirez	8.00
37	Mark Buehrle	4.00
38	Mark Mulder	6.00
39	Ichiro Suzuki/Ball	80.00
40	Troy Glaus	6.00

Franchise Features Autos.

		NM/M
Production 15-100		
6	Aramis Ramirez/100	20.00
9	Tim Hudson/50	25.00
13	Joe Mays/75	10.00
19	Carlos Beltran/100	20.00

25	Freddy Garcia/100	20.00
26	Barry Zito/100	30.00
27	Paul LoDuca/100	15.00
28	Robert Fick/100	15.00
30	Eric Chavez/50	20.00
37	Mark Buehrle/100	15.00

League Leaders

NM/M

Common Player: 3.00
Production 300 Sets

1	Roger Clemens	12.00
2	Curt Schilling	5.00
3	Matt Morris	3.00
4	Randy Johnson	6.00
5	Mark Mulder	4.00
6	Curt Schilling	5.00
7	Mike Mussina	4.00
8	Joe Mays	3.00
9	Matt Morris	3.00
10	Tim Hudson	4.00
11	Mark Buehrle	3.00
12	Greg Maddux	10.00
13	Freddy Garcia	3.00
14	Randy Johnson	6.00
15	Curt Schilling	5.00
16	Chan Ho Park	3.00
17	Roger Clemens	12.00
18	Mike Mussina	4.00
19	Javier Vazquez	3.00
20	Kerry Wood	8.00
21	Randy Johnson	6.00
22	Barry Zito	4.00
23	Hideo Nomo	8.00
24	Ichiro Suzuki	10.00
25	Todd Helton	6.00
26	Albert Pujols	20.00
27	Alex Rodriguez	12.00
28	Shannon Stewart	3.00
29	Luis Gonzalez	3.00
30	Alex Rodriguez	12.00
31	Barry Bonds	20.00
32	Sammy Sosa	15.00
33	Luis Gonzalez	3.00
34	Todd Helton	6.00
35	Jim Thome	3.00
36	Shawn Green	4.00
37	Jeff Bagwell	7.50
38	Todd Helton	5.00
39	Luis Gonzalez	3.00
40	Lance Berkman	3.00
41	Juan Gonzalez	6.00
42	Larry Walker	3.00
43	Ichiro Suzuki	10.00
44	Lance Berkman	3.00
45	Todd Helton	5.00

League Leaders Autographs

NM/M

Production 15-100

5	Mark Mulder/100	20.00
11	Mark Buehrle/100	15.00
13	Freddy Garcia/100	15.00
19	Javier Vazquez/100	15.00
26	Albert Pujols/100	150.00
28	Shannon Stewart/100	15.00

League Leaders Game-Used

NM/M

Common Player: 4.00
Production 150 or 175

1	Roger Clemens	20.00
2	Curt Schilling	10.00
4	Randy Johnson	8.00
5	Mark Mulder	6.00
6	Curt Schilling	5.00
7	Mike Mussina/Shoe/50	25.00
8	Joe Mays	4.00
10	Tim Hudson	6.00
11	Mark Buehrle	4.00
12	Greg Maddux	15.00
13	Freddy Garcia	4.00
14	Randy Johnson	8.00
15	Curt Schilling	10.00
16	Chan Ho Park	4.00
17	Roger Clemens	20.00
18	Mike Mussina/Shoe/50	25.00
19	Javier Vazquez	4.00
20	Kerry Wood	10.00
21	Randy Johnson	8.00
22	Barry Zito	6.00
23	Hideo Nomo	15.00
24	Ichiro Suzuki/Ball/51	75.00
25	Todd Helton	8.00
26	Albert Pujols	20.00
27	Alex Rodriguez	15.00
28	Shannon Stewart	4.00
29	Luis Gonzalez	5.00
30	Alex Rodriguez	15.00
31	Barry Bonds	25.00
32	Sammy Sosa	15.00
33	Luis Gonzalez	4.00
34	Todd Helton	8.00
35	Jim Thome	10.00
36	Shawn Green	5.00
37	Jeff Bagwell	8.00
38	Todd Helton	8.00
39	Luis Gonzalez	4.00
40	Lance Berkman	4.00
41	Juan Gonzalez	6.00
42	Larry Walker	4.00
43	Ichiro Suzuki/Ball/51	75.00
44	Lance Berkman	4.00
45	Todd Helton	8.00

Master Artists

NM/M

Common Player: 5.00
Production 150 Sets

1	Pedro Martinez	15.00
2	Curt Schilling	10.00
3	Kevin Brown	5.00
4	Tim Hudson	6.00
5	Kerry Wood	5.00
6	Barry Zito	8.00
7	Hideo Nomo	15.00
8	Randy Johnson	15.00
9	Greg Maddux	15.00
10	Roger Clemens	20.00
11	Kazuhiro Sasaki	5.00
12	Joe Mays	5.00
13	Mark Mulder	5.00
14	Javier Vazquez	5.00

Pure Power

NM/M

Complete Set (18): 65.00
Common Player: 2.00
Production 300 Sets

1	Sammy Sosa	8.00
2	Lance Berkman	2.00
3	Chipper Jones	6.00
4	Troy Glaus	4.00
5	Barry Bonds	12.00
6	Todd Helton	4.00
7	Manny Ramirez	4.00
8	Jason Giambi	3.00
9	Juan Gonzalez	4.00
10	Albert Pujols	10.00
11	Jim Thome	4.00
12	Mike Piazza	8.00
13	Frank Thomas	4.00
14	Richie Sexson	2.00
15	Jeff Bagwell	4.00
16	Rafael Palmeiro	3.00
17	Luis Gonzalez	2.00
18	Shawn Green	2.50

Pure Power Autographs

NM/M

Varying quantities produced

14	Richie Sexson/100	20.00

Pure Power Masters

NM/M

Complete Set (18) 125.00
Common Player: 5.00
Production 150

1	Sammy Sosa	15.00
2	Lance Berkman	5.00
3	Chipper Jones	10.00
4	Troy Glaus	8.00
5	Barry Bonds	25.00
6	Todd Helton	8.00
7	Manny Ramirez	8.00
8	Jason Giambi	6.00
9	Juan Gonzalez	8.00
10	Albert Pujols	20.00
11	Jim Thome	5.00
12	Mike Piazza	15.00
13	Frank Thomas	8.00
14	Richie Sexson	5.00
15	Jeff Bagwell	8.00
16	Rafael Palmeiro	5.00
17	Luis Gonzalez	5.00
18	Shawn Green	5.00

Records

NM/M

Complete Set (5): 50.00
Common Player: 8.00
Production 300

1-3	Barry Bonds	15.00
4-5	Rickey Henderson	8.00

Records Game-Used

NM/M

Production 150

1	Barry Bonds	40.00
2	Barry Bonds	40.00
3	Barry Bonds	40.00
4	Rickey Henderson	20.00
5	Rickey Henderson	20.00

2002 Donruss Originals

NM/M

Complete Set (400): 75.00
Common Player: .10
Common Rated Rookie: .50
Pack (5): 2.00
Hobby Box (24): 40.00

1	So Taguchi RC	.75
2	Allan Simpson RC	.50
3	Brian Mallette RC	.50
4	Ben Howard RC	.50
5	Kazuhisa Ishii RC	.50
6	Francis Beltran RC	.50
7	Jorge Padilla RC	.50
8	Brandon Puffer RC	.50
9	Oliver Perez RC	1.00
10	Kirk Saarloos	.50
11	Travis Driskill RC	.50
12	Jeremy Lambert RC	.50
13	John Foster RC	.50
14	Steve Kent RC	.50
15	Shawn Sedlacek RC	.50
16	Alex Rodriguez	1.25
17	Lance Berkman	.10
18	Kevin Brown	.10
19	Garret Anderson	.10
20	Bobby Abreu	.10
21	Richard Hidalgo	.10
22	Matt Morris	.10
23	Manny Ramirez	.60
24	Derek Jeter	1.50
25	Kerry Wood	.30
26	Mark Grace	.15
27	Edgar Martinez	.10
28	Nomar Garciaparra	1.00
29	Roberto Alomar	.25
30	Jason Giambi	.50
31	Juan Gonzalez	.60
32	Albert Pujols	1.00
33	Juan Cruz	.10
34	Troy Glaus	.60
35	Greg Maddux	.75
36	Adam Dunn	.40
37	J.D. Drew	.25
38	Tsuyoshi Shinjo	.10
39	Vladimir Guerrero	.60
40	Barry Bonds	1.50
41	Carlos Delgado	.40
42	Ken Griffey Jr.	1.00
43	Carlos Pena	.10
44	Jeff Kent	.10
45	Roger Clemens	.75
46	Frank Thomas	.60
47	Larry Walker	.10
48	Pedro J. Martinez	.60
49	Moises Alou	.10
50	Andruw Jones	.60
51	Luis Gonzalez	.25
52	Adrian Beltre	.10
53	Bobby Hill	.10
54	Roy Oswalt	.20
55	Tim Hudson	.20
56	Trot Nixon	.10
57	Jeff Bagwell	.60
58	Bernie Williams	.30
59	Magglio Ordonez	.25
60	Bartolo Colon	.10
61	Shawn Green	.20
62	Mark Buehrle	.10
63	Sean Casey	.10
64	Rickey Henderson	.60
65	Aramis Ramirez	.10
66	Ichiro Suzuki	1.00
67	Cliff Floyd	.10
68	Darin Erstad	.40
69	Paul LoDuca	.10
70	Ivan Rodriguez	.50
71	Mo Vaughn	.10
72	Todd Helton	.60
73	Raul Mondesi	.10
74	Sammy Sosa	1.00
75	Cristian Guzman	.10
76	Jimmy Rollins	.25
77	Hideo Nomo	.50
78	C.C. Sabathia	.10
79	Wade Miller	.10
80	Drew Henson	.20
81	Chipper Jones	.75
82	Miguel Tejada	.25
83	Freddy Garcia	.10
84	Richie Sexson	.10
85	Robin Ventura	.10
86	Jose Vidro	.10
87	Rich Aurilia	.10
88	Scott Rolen	.60
89	Carlos Beltran	.40
90	Austin Kearns	.25
91	Kazuhisa Sasaki	.10
92	Carlos Hernandez	.10
93	Randy Johnson	.60
94	Jim Thome	.10
95	Curt Schilling	.40
96	Alfonso Soriano	.50
97	Barry Larkin	.10
98	Rafael Palmeiro	.50
99	Tom Glavine	.25
100	Barry Zito	.20
101	Craig Biggio	.20
102	Mike Piazza	1.00
103	Ben Sheets	.20
104	Mark Mulder	.20
105	Mike Mussina	.25
106	Jim Edmonds	.10
107	Paul Konerko	.10
108	Pat Burrell	.25
109	Chan Ho Park	.10
110	Mike Sweeney	.10
111	Phil Nevin	.10
112	Brian Giles	.10
113	Eric Chavez	.20
114	Corey Patterson	.20
115	Gary Sheffield	.25
116	Kazuhisa Ishii	2.00
117	Kyle Kane RC	.50
118	Eric Junge RC	.50
119	Luis Ugueto RC	.50
120	Cam Esslinger RC	.50
121	Earl Snyder RC	.50
122	Oliver Perez	1.00
123	Victor Alvarez RC	.50
124	Tom Shearn RC	.50
125	Corey Thurman RC	.50
126	Satoru Komiyama RC	.50
127	Hansel Izquierdo RC	.50
128	Elio Serrano RC	.50
129	Michael Crudale RC	.50
130	Chris Snelling RC	1.50
131	Nomar Garciaparra	1.00
132	Roger Clemens	.75
133	Hank Blalock	.25
134	Eric Chavez	.20
135	Corey Patterson	.20
136	Richie Sexson	.10
137	Freddy Garcia	.10
138	Miguel Tejada	.25
139	Alex Rodriguez/SP	1.50
140	Adrian Beltre	.10
141	Bobby Abreu	.10
142	Bret Boone	.10
143	Tim Hudson	.20
144	Roy Oswalt	.20
145	Derek Jeter	1.50
146	Rich Aurilia	.15
147	Mark Grace	.15
148	Kerry Wood/SP	1.00
149	Geronimo Gil	.10
150	Mark Buehrle	.10
151	Jim Edmonds	.10
152	Ichiro Suzuki	1.00
153	Juan Gonzalez	.60
154	Darin Erstad	.10
155	Barry Bonds/SP	2.50
156	Greg Maddux	.75
157	Adam Dunn	.40
158	Todd Helton	.60
159	Roberto Alomar	.25
160	Sammy Sosa	1.00
161	Sean Burroughs	.10
162	Albert Pujols	1.00
163	Carlos Delgado	.25
164	Frank Thomas	.60
165	Ken Griffey Jr.	1.00
166	Jason Giambi/SP	1.00
167	Chipper Jones	.75
168	Ivan Rodriguez	.50
169	Pedro Martinez/SP	1.00
170	Gary Sheffield	.25
171	Andruw Jones	.60
172	Luis Gonzalez	.25
173	Raul Mondesi	.10
174	Jose Vidro	.10
175	Garret Anderson/SP	.50
176	Scott Rolen	.60
177	Kazuhiro Sasaki	.10
178	Jeff Bagwell	.60
179	Manny Ramirez	.60
180	Jim Thome	.10
181	Ben Sheets	.20
182	Randy Johnson	.60
183	Lance Berkman	.10
184	Shawn Green	.20
185	Rickey Henderson	.60
186	Edgar Martinez	.10
187	Barry Larkin	.10
188	Bernie Williams	.30
189	Luis Aparicio	.10
190	Troy Glaus/SP	.50
191	Mike Mussina	.30
192	Pee Wee Reese	.10
193	Craig Biggio	.10
194	Vladimir Guerrero	.60
195	J.D. Drew	.20
196	Jeff Kent	.10
197	Dewon Brazelton	.10
198	Tsuyoshi Shinjo/SP	.40
199	Sean Casey	.10
200	Hideo Nomo	.50
201	C.C. Sabathia	.10
202	Larry Walker	.10
203	Mark Teixeira	.20
204	Mike Sweeney	.10
205	Moises Alou	.10
206	Mark Prior	.75
207	Javier Vazquez	.10
208	Phil Nevin	.10
209	Harmon Killebrew	.50
210	Brian Giles	.10
211	Carlos Beltran	.40

212	Don Drysdale	.40
213	Matt Morris	.10
214	Trot Nixon	.10
215	Magglio Ordonez	.25
216	Curt Schilling/SP	.75
217	Mark Mulder	.20
218	Alfonso Soriano	1.00
219	Rafael Palmeiro/SP	.75
220	Tom Glavine	.25
221	Barry Zito	.25
222	Mike Piazza	1.00
223	Bartolo Colon	.10
224	Cliff Floyd	.10
225	Paul LoDuca	.10
226	Cristian Guzman	.10
227	Mo Vaughn	.10
228	Aramis Ramirez	.10
229	Pat Burrell	.25
230	Chan Ho Park	.10
231	Satoru Komiyama	.50
232	Brandon Backe RC	.50
233	Anderson Machado RC	.50
234	Doug DeVore RC	.50
235	Steve Bechler RC	.50
236	John Ennis RC	.50
237	Rodrigo Rosario RC	.50
238	Jorge Sosa RC	.50
239	Ken Huckaby RC	.50
240	Mike Moriarty RC	.50
241	Kirk Saarloos	1.00
242	Kevin Frederick RC	.50
243	Aaron Guiel RC	.50
244	Jose Rodriguez	.50
245	So Taguchi	1.00
246	Albert Pujols	1.00
247	Derek Jeter	1.50
248	Brian Giles	.10
249	Mike Cameron	.10
250	Josh Beckett	.25
251	Ken Griffey Jr./SP	1.50
252	Aramis Ramirez	.10
253	Miguel Tejada	.25
254	Carlos Delgado	.25
255	Pedro J. Martinez	.60
256	Raul Mondesi	.10
257	Roger Clemens	.75
258	Gary Sheffield	.25
259	Jose Vidro	.10
260	Alex Rodriguez	1.25
261	Larry Walker	.10
262	Mark Mulder	.20
263	Scott Rolen	.60
264	Tim Hudson	.20
265	Manny Ramirez	.60
266	Rich Aurilia	.10
267	Roy Oswalt	.10
268	Mark Grace	.15
269	Lance Berkman	.30
270	Nomar Garciaparra	1.00
271	Barry Bonds	1.50
272	Ryan Klesko	.10
273	Ichiro Suzuki	1.00
274	Shawn Green	.20
275	Darin Erstad	.40
276	Bernie Williams	.30
277	Greg Maddux/SP	1.00
278	Eric Hinske	.10
279	Randy Johnson	.60
280	Todd Helton	.60
281	Sammy Sosa/SP	1.50
282	Nick Johnson	.10
283	Jose Cruz Jr.	.10
284	Frank Thomas	.60
285	Tsuyoshi Shinjo	.10
286	Troy Glaus	.60
287	Jason Giambi	.50
288	Chipper Jones/SP	1.00
289	Roberto Alomar	.30
290	Bobby Hill	.10
291	Garret Anderson	.10
292	Andruw Jones	.60
293	Luis Gonzalez	.15
294	Mike Mussina	.30
295	Ivan Rodriguez/SP	.75
296	Barry Larkin	.10
297	Kazuhiro Sasaki	.10
298	Alfonso Soriano	.50
299	Jeff Bagwell/SP	.75
300	Bobby Abreu	.10
301	Ben Sheets	.20
302	Curt Schilling	.40
303	Jim Thome	.10
304	Kerry Wood	.10
305	Mark Buehrle	.10
306	Rickey Henderson	.60
307	Rafael Palmeiro	.50
308	Jim Edmonds	.10
309	Mike Piazza	.50
310	Edgar Martinez	.10
311	Tom Glavine	.25
312	Adrian Beltre	.10
313	Adam Dunn	.40
314	Craig Biggio	.10
315	Vladimir Guerrero/SP	1.00
316	Bret Boone	.10
317	Hideo Nomo/SP	.75
318	Jeff Kent	.10
319	Juan Gonzalez	.60
320	Sean Casey	.10
321	C.C. Sabathia	.10
322	J.D. Drew	.20
323	Torii Hunter/SP	.40
324	Chan Ho Park	.10
325	Mike Sweeney	.10
326	Javier Vazquez	.10

327	Jorge Posada	.25
328	Barry Zito	.25
329	Willie McCovey	.10
330	Kevin Brown	.20
331	Mo Vaughn	.10
332	Carlos Beltran	.40
333	Bobby Doerr	.10
334	Matt Morris	.10
335	Trot Nixon	.10
336	Magglio Ordonez	.25
337	Paul LoDuca	.10
338	Phil Nevin	.10
339	Eric Chavez	.20
340	Corey Patterson	.20
341	Richie Sexson	.10
342	Pat Burrell	.25
343	Freddy Garcia	.10
344	Bartolo Colon	.10
345	Cliff Floyd	.10
346	Deivis Santos	.50
347	Felix Escalona RC	.50
348	Miguel Asencio RC	.50
349	Takahito Nomura RC	.50
350	Jorge Padilla	.50
351	Vladimir Guerrero	.60
352	Ichiro Suzuki	1.00
353	Jay Gibbons	.10
354	Alfonso Soriano	.50
355	Mark Buehrle	.10
356	Shawn Green	.20
357	Barry Larkin	.10
358	Josh Fogg	.10
359	Shannon Stewart	.10
360	Andruw Jones	.60
361	Juan Gonzalez	.60
362	Ken Griffey Jr.	1.00
363	Tim Hudson	.20
364	Roy Oswalt/SP	.50
365	Carlos Delgado	.40
366	Albert Pujols/SP	2.00
367	Willie Stargell	.25
368	Roger Clemens	.75
369	Luis Gonzalez	.25
370	Barry Zito	.25
371	Alex Rodriguez	1.25
372	Troy Glaus	.60
373	Vladimir Guerrero	.60
374	Jeff Bagwell	.60
375	Randy Johnson	.60
376	Manny Ramirez	.60
377	Derek Jeter/SP	2.00
378	C.C. Sabathia	.10
379	Rickey Henderson	.60
380	J.D. Drew	.20
381	Nomar Garciaparra	1.00
382	Darin Erstad	.40
383	Ben Sheets	.20
384	Frank Thomas	.60
385	Barry Bonds	1.50
386	Pedro J. Martinez	.60
387	Mark Mulder	.20
388	Greg Maddux	.75
389	Todd Helton	.60
390	Lance Berkman	.10
391	Sammy Sosa	1.00
392	Mike Piazza	1.00
393	Chipper Jones	.75
394	Adam Dunn	.40
395	Jason Giambi	.50
396	Eric Chavez	.20
397	Bobby Abreu	.10
398	Aramis Ramirez	.10
399	Paul LoDuca	.10
400	Miguel Tejada	.25

Aqueous Glossy

Stars (1-400): 3-5X
Average of 1:Box

All-Stars

9	Cal Ripken Jr.	8.00
10	Carlton Fisk	2.00
11	Roger Clemens	5.00
12	Jeff Bagwell	3.00
13	Kirby Puckett	8.00
14	Nolan Ryan	10.00
15	Ryne Sandberg	5.00
16	Ivan Rodriguez	2.00
17	Sammy Sosa	5.00
18	Greg Maddux	5.00
19	Alex Rodriguez	8.00
20	Todd Helton	3.00
21	Randy Johnson	3.00
22	Troy Glaus	5.00
23	Ichiro Suzuki	6.00
24	Barry Bonds	8.00
25	Derek Jeter	10.00

Champions

		NM/M
Complete Set (25):		75.00
Common Player:		2.00
Production 800 Sets		
1	Nolan Ryan	10.00
2	George Brett	6.00
3	Edgar Martinez	2.00
4	Mike Schmidt	6.00
5	Randy Johnson	3.00
6	Tony Gwynn	4.00
7	John Smoltz	2.00
8	Roger Clemens	4.00
9	Mel Ott	2.00
10	Todd Helton	3.00
11	Bernie Williams	2.00
12	Troy Glaus	3.00
13	Steve Carlton	2.00
14	Ryne Sandberg	2.00
15	Ted Williams	8.00
16	Alex Rodriguez	8.00
17	Lou Boudreau	2.00
18	Luis Gonzalez	2.00
19	Rickey Henderson	2.00
20	Jose Canseco	2.00
21	Stan Musial	5.00
22	Randy Johnson	3.00
23	Don Mattingly	6.00
24	Nomar Garciaparra	4.00
25	Wade Boggs	4.00

Champions Materials

		NM/M
Common Player:		8.00
Varying quantities produced		
1	Nolan Ryan/78	65.00
2	George Brett/80	30.00
3	Edgar Martinez/92	10.00
4	Mike Schmidt/80	40.00
5	Randy Johnson/94	15.00
6	Tony Gwynn/84	20.00
7	John Smoltz/96	8.00
8	Roger Clemens/88	20.00
9	Todd Helton/100	10.00
10	Bernie Williams/98	10.00
11	Troy Glaus/100	10.00
12	Steve Carlton/80	15.00
13	Ryne Sandberg/90	40.00
14	Ted Williams/42	200.00
15	Alex Rodriguez/96	20.00
16	Lou Boudreau/44	15.00
17	Luis Gonzalez/99	8.00
18	Rickey Henderson/82	20.00
19	Stan Musial/50	60.00
20	Randy Johnson/88	15.00
21	Don Mattingly/84	60.00
22	Nomar Garciaparra/100	30.00
23	Wade Boggs/88	15.00

Gamers

		NM/M
Common Player:		3.00
Varying quantities produced		
1	Alfonso Soriano/400	8.00
2	Shawn Green/500	5.00
3	Curt Schilling/250	8.00
4	Hideo Nomo/100	20.00
5	Toby Hall/500	4.00
6	Andruw Jones/500	4.00
7	Cliff Floyd/500	3.00
8	Mark Ellis/500	4.00
9	Gabe Kapler/500	4.00
10	Andres Galarraga/500	3.00

		NM/M
Complete Set (25):		90.00
Common Player:		2.00
Inserted 1:30		
1	George Brett	8.00
2	Rickey Henderson	4.00
3	Mike Schmidt	6.00
4	Vladimir Guerrero	3.00
5	Tony Gwynn	3.00
6	Curt Schilling	2.00
7	Don Mattingly	8.00
8	Roberto Alomar	2.00

11	Freddy Garcia/500	3.00
12	Tsuyoshi Shinjo/200	4.00
13	Robin Ventura/500	3.00
14	Paul LoDuca/500	3.00
15	Manny Ramirez/500	8.00
16	Garret Anderson/250	5.00
17	Joe Kennedy/500	3.00
18	Roger Clemens/500	15.00
19	Gary Sheffield/500	6.00
20	Vernon Wells/500	4.00
22	Hideo Nomo/100	40.00
23	Tim Hudson/500	6.00
24	Larry Bigbie/500	4.00
25	Larry Walker/500	4.00
27	John Olerud/500	3.00
28	Chipper Jones/500	8.00
29	Tony Gwynn/500	10.00
30	Juan Gonzalez/500	8.00
31	Jacque Jones/500	8.00
32	Frank Thomas/500	8.00
33	Luis Gonzalez/500	4.00
34	Geoff Jenkins/500	6.00
35	J.D. Drew/500	3.00
36	Edgardo Alfonzo/500	3.00
37	Todd Helton/500	8.00
38	Brad Penny/500	4.00
39	Robert Fick/500	3.00
40	Will Clark/500	15.00
41	Tony Armas Jr./500	3.00
42	Nick Johnson/400	3.00
43	Ben Grieve/500	3.00
44	Vladimir Guerrero/500	8.00
45	Jason Jennings/500	3.00
46	Carlos Lee/500	3.00
47	Carlos Delgado/500	6.00
48	Chan Ho Park/500	3.00
49	Juan Diaz/500	3.00
50	Alex Rodriguez/400	15.00

Hit List

		NM/M
Complete Set (20):		40.00
Common Player:		1.00
Production 1,500 Sets		
1	Ichiro Suzuki	4.00
2	Shawn Green	1.00
3	Alex Rodriguez	5.00
4	Nomar Garciaparra	4.00
5	Derek Jeter	6.00
6	Barry Bonds	6.00
7	Mike Piazza	4.00
8	Albert Pujols	4.00
9	Chipper Jones	3.00
10	Sammy Sosa	4.00
11	Rickey Henderson	2.00
12	Frank Thomas	2.00
13	Jeff Bagwell	2.00
14	Vladimir Guerrero	2.00
15	Todd Helton	2.00
16	Adam Dunn	1.00
17	Rafael Palmeiro	1.00
18	Manny Ramirez	2.00
19	Lance Berkman	1.00
20	Jason Giambi	1.50

Hit List Total Bases

		NM/M
Common Player:		5.00
Numbered to career high total bases.		
1	Ichiro Suzuki/Base/316	15.00
2	Shawn Green/Bat/370	6.00
3	Alex Rodriguez/Bat/393	15.00
4	Nomar Garciaparra/Bat/365	10.00
5	Derek Jeter/346/Base	20.00
6	Barry Bonds/Base/411	20.00
7	Mike Piazza/Bat/355	10.00
8	Albert Pujols/Base/360	10.00
9	Chipper Jones/Bat/359	8.00
10	Sammy Sosa/Base/425	10.00
11	Rickey Henderson/Bat/285	10.00
12	Frank Thomas/Bat/364	8.00
13	Jeff Bagwell/Bat/363	8.00
14	Vladimir Guerrero/Bat/379	8.00
15	Todd Helton/Bat/405	8.00
16	Adam Dunn/Bat/141	8.00
17	Rafael Palmeiro/Bat/356	8.00
18	Manny Ramirez/Bat/346	8.00
19	Lance Berkman/Bat/358	5.00
20	Jason Giambi/Base/343	6.00

2002 Donruss Originals - LCS Programs

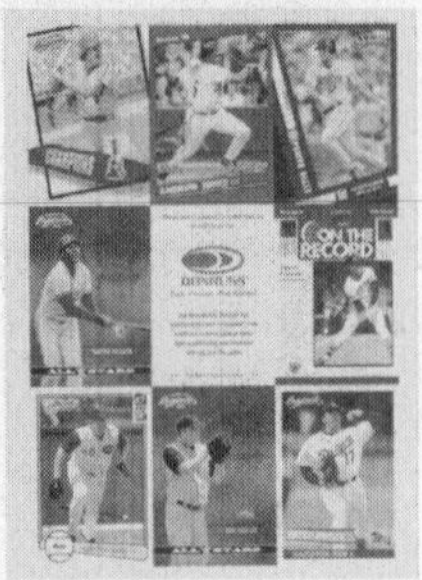

		NM/M
Complete Sheet Set (2):		16.00
Common Player:		.50
	ALCS SHEET	8.00
9	Manny Ramirez (1986 style)	1.00
10	Nolan Ryan/AS	2.50
11	Roger Clemens (Champions)	1.50
12	Alex Rodriguez/AS	2.00
13	Paul Konerko (1982 style)	.50
14	Don Mattingly/AS	1.50
15	Miguel Tejada (1984 style)	.50
16	Rickey Henderson (Making History)	.50
---	Header Card	.10
	NLCS SHEET	8.00
25	Mike Schmidt (Champions)	2.00
26	Andruw Jones (1986 style)	1.00
27	Lance Berkman (Power Alley)	.50
28	Vladimir Guerrero/AS	1.00
29	Roberto Clemente (On The Record)	3.00
30	Austin Kearns (1982 style)	.50
31	Curt Schilling/AS	.50
32	Kazuhisa Ishii (1984 style)	1.00
---	Header Card	.10

Making History

		NM/M
Complete Set (10):		30.00
Common Player:		2.00
Production 800 Sets		
1	Rafael Palmeiro	2.00
2	Roger Clemens	5.00
3	Greg Maddux	4.00
4	Randy Johnson	3.00
5	Barry Bonds	8.00
6	Mike Piazza	6.00
7	Roberto Alomar	2.00
8	Rickey Henderson	2.00
9	Sammy Sosa	6.00
10	Tom Glavine	2.00

Making History Materials

		NM/M
Production 100 Sets		
1	Rafael Palmeiro	15.00
2	Roger Clemens	20.00
3	Greg Maddux	15.00
4	Randy Johnson	10.00
5	Barry Bonds/Base	20.00
6	Mike Piazza	15.00
7	Roberto Alomar	8.00
8	Rickey Henderson	25.00
9	Sammy Sosa/base	15.00
10	Tom Glavine	10.00

Mound Marvels

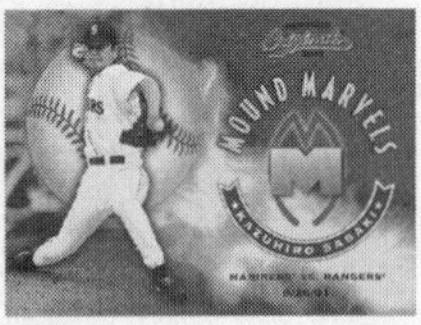

		NM/M
Complete Set (15):		30.00
Common Player:		1.00
Inserted 1:40		
1	Roger Clemens	6.00
2	Matt Morris	1.00
3	Pedro J. Martinez	5.00
4	Randy Johnson	5.00
5	Wade Miller	1.00
6	Tim Hudson	1.50
7	Mike Mussina	3.00
8	C.C. Sabathia	1.00
9	Kazuhiro Sasaki	1.00
10	Curt Schilling	4.00
11	Hideo Nomo	2.50
12	Roger Clemens	6.00
13	Mark Buehrle	1.00
14	Barry Zito	1.50
15	Roy Oswalt	1.50

Mound Marvels High Heat

		NM/M
Production 100 Sets		
1	Roger Clemens	25.00
2	Matt Morris	10.00
3	Pedro J. Martinez	20.00
4	Randy Johnson	15.00
5	Wade Miller	8.00
6	Tim Hudson	10.00
7	Mike Mussina	15.00
8	C.C. Sabathia	10.00
9	Kazuhiro Sasaki	10.00
10	Curt Schilling	15.00
11	Hideo Nomo	40.00
12	Roger Clemens	25.00
13	Mark Buehrle	8.00
14	Barry Zito	15.00
15	Roy Oswalt	8.00

Nifty Fifty Bats

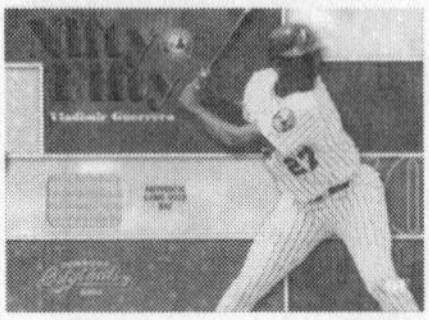

		NM/M
Common Player:		5.00
Production 50 Sets		
1	Alex Rodriguez	20.00
2	Kerry Wood	15.00
3	Ivan Rodriguez	15.00
4	Geronimo Gil	5.00
5	Vladimir Guerrero	15.00
6	Corky Miller	5.00
7	Todd Helton	12.00
8	Rickey Henderson	15.00
9	Andruw Jones	10.00
10	Barry Bonds/Ball	30.00
11	Tom Glavine	10.00
12	Mark Teixeira	10.00
13	Mike Piazza	15.00
14	Austin Kearns	8.00
15	Rickey Henderson	15.00
16	Derek Jeter/Ball	20.00
17	Barry Larkin	8.00
18	Jeff Bagwell	10.00
19	Bernie Williams	10.00
20	Frank Thomas	10.00
21	Lance Berkman	8.00
22	Marlon Byrd	6.00
23	Randy Johnson	15.00
24	Ichiro Suzuki/Ball	40.00
25	Darin Erstad	8.00
26	Jason Lane	5.00
27	Roberto Alomar	10.00
28	Ken Griffey Jr./Ball	20.00
29	Tsuyoshi Shinjo	8.00
30	Pedro Martinez	15.00
31	Rickey Henderson	15.00
32	Albert Pujols/Ball	20.00
33	Nomar Garciaparra	15.00
34	Troy Glaus	10.00
35	Chipper Jones	15.00
36	Adam Dunn	8.00
37	Jason Giambi/Ball	10.00
38	Greg Maddux	20.00
39	Mike Piazza	15.00
40	So Taguchi	8.00
41	Manny Ramirez	10.00
42	Scott Rolen	15.00
43	Sammy Sosa/Ball	15.00
44	Shawn Green	8.00
45	Rickey Henderson	15.00
46	Alex Rodriguez	20.00
47	Hideo Nomo	30.00
48	Kazuhisa Ishii	8.00
49	Luis Gonzalez	8.00
50	Jim Thome	15.00

Nifty Fifty Combos

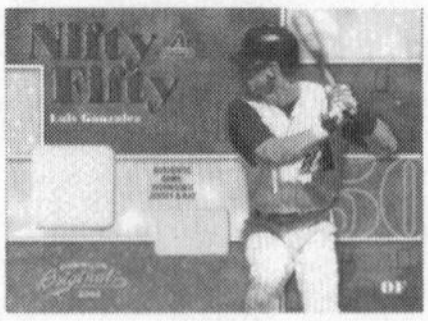

		NM/M
Production 50 Sets		
All bat & jerseys unless noted.		
1	Alex Rodriguez	30.00
2	Kerry Wood	20.00
3	Ivan Rodriguez	20.00
4	Geronimo Gil	10.00
5	Vladimir Guerrero	20.00
6	Corky Miller	10.00
7	Todd Helton	20.00
8	Rickey Henderson	25.00
9	Andruw Jones	15.00
10	Barry Bonds/Base/Ball	40.00
11	Tom Glavine	20.00
12	Mark Teixeira	20.00
13	Mike Piazza	25.00
14	Austin Kearns	15.00
15	Rickey Henderson	25.00
16	Derek Jeter/Base/Ball	30.00
17	Barry Larkin	15.00
18	Jeff Bagwell	20.00
19	Bernie Williams	20.00
20	Frank Thomas	20.00
21	Lance Berkman	15.00
22	Marlon Byrd	15.00
23	Randy Johnson	20.00
24	Ichiro Suzuki/Base/Ball	60.00
25	Darin Erstad	15.00
26	Jason Lane	10.00
27	Roberto Alomar	15.00
28	Ken Griffey Jr./Base/Ball	25.00
29	Tsuyoshi Shinjo	10.00
30	Pedro Martinez	20.00
31	Rickey Henderson	25.00
32	Albert Pujols/Base/Ball	50.00
33	Nomar Garciaparra	30.00
34	Troy Glaus	15.00
35	Chipper Jones	20.00
36	Adam Dunn	15.00
37	Jason Giambi	20.00
38	Greg Maddux	25.00
39	Mike Piazza	25.00
40	So Taguchi	15.00
41	Manny Ramirez	20.00
42	Scott Rolen	20.00
43	Sammy Sosa/Base/Ball	25.00
44	Shawn Green	10.00
45	Rickey Henderson	25.00
46	Alex Rodriguez	30.00
47	Hideo Nomo	30.00
48	Kazuhisa Ishii	15.00
49	Luis Gonzalez	10.00
50	Jim Thome	20.00

Nifty Fifty Jersey

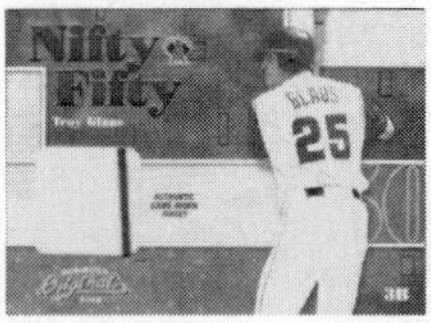

		NM/M
Common Player:		5.00
Production 50 Sets		
2	Kerry Wood	15.00
3	Ivan Rodriguez	15.00
4	Geronimo Gil	5.00
5	Vladimir Guerrero	15.00
6	Corky Miller	5.00
7	Todd Helton	12.00
8	Rickey Henderson	15.00
9	Andruw Jones	10.00
11	Tom Glavine	10.00
12	Mark Teixeira	10.00
13	Mike Piazza	15.00
14	Austin Kearns	8.00
15	Rickey Henderson	15.00
16	Derek Jeter/Base	20.00
17	Barry Larkin	8.00
18	Jeff Bagwell	10.00
19	Bernie Williams	10.00
20	Frank Thomas	10.00
21	Lance Berkman	8.00
22	Marlon Byrd	8.00
23	Randy Johnson	15.00
24	Ichiro Suzuki/Base	40.00
25	Darin Erstad	8.00
26	Jason Lane	5.00
27	Roberto Alomar	10.00
28	Ken Griffey Jr./Base	20.00
29	Tsuyoshi Shinjo	8.00
30	Pedro Martinez	15.00
31	Rickey Henderson	15.00
32	Albert Pujols/Base	20.00
33	Nomar Garciaparra	20.00
34	Troy Glaus	10.00
35	Chipper Jones	15.00
36	Adam Dunn	8.00
37	Jason Giambi/Base	10.00
38	Greg Maddux	20.00
39	Mike Piazza	15.00
40	So Taguchi	8.00
41	Manny Ramirez	10.00
42	Scott Rolen	15.00
43	Sammy Sosa/Base	15.00
44	Shawn Green	8.00
45	Rickey Henderson	15.00
46	Alex Rodriguez	20.00
47	Hideo Nomo	30.00
48	Kazuhisa Ishii	8.00
49	Luis Gonzalez	8.00
50	Jim Thome	15.00

On The Record

		NM/M
Complete Set (15):		60.00
Common Player:		3.00
Production 800 Sets		
1	Ty Cobb	6.00
2	Jimmie Foxx	4.00
3	Lou Gehrig	10.00
4	Dale Murphy	5.00
5	Steve Carlton	3.00
6	Randy Johnson	4.00
7	Greg Maddux	6.00
8	Roger Clemens	8.00
9	Yogi Berra	5.00
10	Don Mattingly	8.00
11	Rickey Henderson	4.00
12	Stan Musial	6.00
13	Jackie Robinson	6.00
14	Roberto Clemente	10.00
15	Mike Schmidt	6.00

On the Record Materials

		NM/M
Varying quantities produced		
3	Lou Gehrig/34	220.00
4	Dale Murphy/83	10.00
5	Steve Carlton/72	10.00
6	Randy Johnson/100	10.00
7	Greg Maddux/93	15.00
8	Roger Clemens/87	20.00
9	Yogi Berra/51	12.00
10	Don Mattingly/85	25.00
11	Rickey Henderson/90	15.00
13	Jackie Robinson/49	50.00
14	Roberto Clemente/66	75.00
15	Mike Schmidt/80	25.00

Power Alley

		NM/M
Complete Set (15):		30.00
Common Player:		1.00
Production 1,500 Sets		
Die-Cut Parallel:		1.5-2X
Production 100 Sets		
1	Barry Bonds	6.00
2	Sammy Sosa	3.00
3	Lance Berkman	1.00
4	Luis Gonzalez	1.00
5	Alex Rodriguez	5.00
6	Troy Glaus	2.00
7	Vladimir Guerrero	2.00
8	Jason Giambi	1.50
9	Mike Piazza	3.00
10	Todd Helton	2.00
11	Mike Schmidt	4.00
12	Don Mattingly	4.00
13	Andre Dawson	1.50
14	Reggie Jackson	2.00
15	Dale Murphy	1.50

Signature Marks

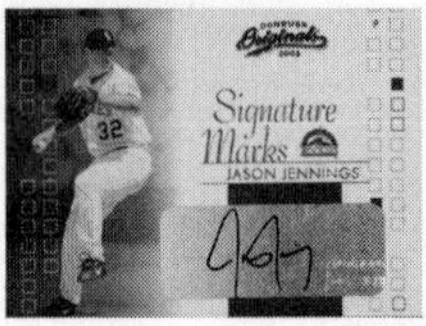

		NM/M
Common Autograph:		5.00
Varying quantities produced		
Many not priced, lack of market info.		
1	Kazuhisa Ishii/50	
2	Eric Hinske/200	8.00
3	Cesar Izturis/200	5.00
4	Roy Oswalt/100	20.00
5	Jack Cust/200	8.00
6	Nick Johnson/200	8.00
7	Jason Hart/200	6.00
8	Mark Prior/100	30.00
9	Luis Garcia/200	5.00
10	Jay Gibbons/200	10.00
11	Corky Miller/200	8.00
12	Antonio Perez/100	8.00
13	Andres Torres/200	5.00
14	Brandon Claussen/200	8.00
15	Ed Rogers/200	5.00
16	Jorge Padilla/200	10.00
17	Francis Beltran/200	5.00
18	Kip Wells/200	6.00
19	Ryan Ludwick/200	10.00
20	Juan Cruz/100	8.00
21	Juan Diaz/200	5.00
22	Marcus Giles/200	10.00
23	Joe Kennedy/200	10.00
24	Wade Miller/100	10.00
25	Corey Patterson/100	10.00
26	Angel Berroa/200	10.00
27	Ricardo Rodriguez/200	5.00
28	Toby Hall/200	8.00
29	Carlos Pena/50	10.00
30	Jason Jennings/200	8.00
31	Rafael Soriano/200	10.00
32	Marlon Byrd/100	10.00
33	Rodrigo Rosario/200	5.00
35	Brent Abernathy/200	5.00
36	Bill Hall/200	15.00
37	Fernando Rodney/200	10.00
38	Josh Pearce/200	8.00
39	Brian Lawrence/200	8.00
40	Tim Redding/200	5.00
42	Jeremy Giambi/200	5.00
43	Victor Martinez/200	25.00
44	Hank Blalock/50	25.00
46	Geronimo Gil/200	5.00
47	So Taguchi/50	25.00
48	Austin Kearns/200	15.00
49	Alfonso Soriano/50	40.00

What If - Rookies

		NM/M
Complete Set (23):		75.00
Common Player:		1.50
Inserted 1:12		
1	Wade Boggs	6.00
2	Ryne Sandberg	6.00
3	Cal Ripken Jr.	12.50
4	Tony Gwynn	6.00
5	Don Mattingly	10.00
6	Wade Boggs	6.00
7	Roger Clemens	7.50
8	Kirby Puckett	6.00
9	Eric Davis	1.50
10	Dwight Gooden	1.50
11	Eric Davis	1.50
12	Roger Clemens	7.50
13	Kirby Puckett	6.00
14	Dwight Gooden	1.50
15	Barry Bonds	12.50
16	Will Clark	1.50
17	Barry Larkin	1.50
18	Greg Maddux	6.00
19	Rafael Palmeiro	4.00
20	Craig Biggio	1.50
21	Gary Sheffield	1.50
22	Randy Johnson	5.00
23	Curt Schilling	3.00

What If - '78

		NM/M
Complete Set (27):		75.00
Common Player:		1.50
Inserted 1:12		
1	Paul Molitor	4.00
2	Alan Trammell	1.50
3	Ozzie Smith	6.00
4	George Brett	10.00
5	Johnny Bench	6.00
6	Rod Carew	4.00
7	Carlton Fisk	1.50
8	Reggie Jackson	5.00
9	Dale Murphy	2.00
10	Joe Morgan	1.50
11	Eddie Murray	4.00
12	Jim Palmer	2.00
13	Tom Seaver	4.00
14	Willie Stargell	2.00
15	Dave Winfield	2.00
16	Dave Parker	1.50
17	Mike Schmidt	8.00
18	Eddie Mathews	4.00
19	Lou Brock	1.50
20	Willie McCovey	1.50
21	Andre Dawson	1.50
22	Dennis Eckersley	4.00
23	Robin Yount	4.00
24	Nolan Ryan	15.00
25	Steve Carlton	1.50
26	Paul Molitor	4.00
27	Ozzie Smith	6.00

What If - '80

		NM/M
Complete Set (25):		75.00
Common Player:		1.50
Inserted 1:12		
1	Rickey Henderson	3.00
2	Johnny Bench	6.00
3	George Brett	10.00
4	Steve Carlton	2.50
5	Rod Carew	2.00
6	Gary Carter	1.50
7	Carlton Fisk	1.50
8	Reggie Jackson	5.00
9	Dave Parker	1.50
10	Dale Murphy	3.00
11	Paul Molitor	4.00
12	Mike Schmidt	8.00
13	Alan Trammell	1.50
14	Dave Winfield	1.50
15	Robin Yount	4.00
16	Joe Morgan	1.50
17	Jim Palmer	4.00
18	Nolan Ryan	15.00
19	Tom Seaver	4.00
20	Ozzie Smith	6.00
21	Willie McCovey	1.50
22	Andre Dawson	1.50
23	Eddie Murray	2.00
24	Al Kaline	1.50
25	Duke Snider	4.00

2002 Donruss Studio

BRIAN GILES / OF

		NM/M
Complete Set (250):		150.00
Common Player:		.25
Common (201-250):		3.00
Production 1,500		
Pack (5):		3.00
Box (18):		45.00
1	Vladimir Guerrero	.75
2	Chipper Jones	1.00
3	Bobby Abreu	.25
4	Barry Zito	.40
5	Larry Walker	.25
6	Miguel Tejada	.40
7	Mike Sweeney	.25
8	Shannon Stewart	.25
9	Sammy Sosa	1.50
10	Bud Smith	.25
11	Wilson Betemit	.25
12	Kevin Brown	.35
13	Ellis Burks	.25
14	Pat Burrell	.40
15	Cliff Floyd	.25
16	Marcus Giles	.25
17	Troy Glaus	.75
18	Barry Larkin	.25
19	Carlos Lee	.25
20	Brian Lawrence	.25
21	Paul LoDuca	.25
22	Ben Grieve	.25
23	Shawn Green	.40
24	Mike Cameron	.25
25	Roger Clemens	1.25
26	Joe Crede	.25
27	Jose Cruz	.25
28	Jeremy Affeldt	.25
29	Adrian Beltre	.25
30	Josh Beckett	.50
31	Roberto Alomar	.40
32	Toby Hall	.25
33	Mike Hampton	.25
34	Eric Milton	.25
35	Eric Munson	.25
36	Trot Nixon	.25
37	Roy Oswalt	.40
38	Chan Ho Park	.25
39	Charles Johnson	.25
40	Nick Johnson	.25
41	Tim Hudson	.40
42	Cristian Guzman	.25
43	Drew Henson	.25
44	Mark Grace	.35
45	Luis Gonzalez	.35
46	Pedro J. Martinez	.75
47	Joe Mays	.25
48	Jorge Posada	.40
49	Aramis Ramirez	.25
50	Kip Wells	.25
51	Moises Alou	.25
52	Omar Vizquel	.25
53	Ichiro Suzuki	1.50
54	Jimmy Rollins	.40
55	Freddy Garcia	.25
56	Steve Green	.25
57	Brian Jordan	.25
58	Paul Konerko	.35
59	Jack Cust	.25
60	Sean Casey	.25
61	Bret Boone	.25
62	Hideo Nomo	.60
63	Magglio Ordonez	.40
64	Frank Thomas	.75
65	Josh Towers	.25
66	Javier Vazquez	.25
67	Robin Ventura	.25
68	Aubrey Huff	.25
69	Richard Hidalgo	.25
70	Brandon Claussen	.25
71	Bartolo Colon	.25
72	John Buck	.25
73	Dee Brown	.25
74	Barry Bonds	2.00
75	Jason Giambi	.50
76	Erick Almonte	.25
77	Ryan Dempster	.25
78	Jim Edmonds	.25
79	Jay Gibbons	.25
80	Shigetoshi Hasegawa	.25
81	Todd Helton	.75
82	Erik Bedard	.25
83	Carlos Beltran	.50
84	Rafael Soriano	.25
85	Gary Sheffield	.25
86	Richie Sexson	.25
87	Mike Rivera	.25
88	Jose Ortiz	.25
89	Abraham Nunez	.25
90	Dave Williams	.25
91	Preston Wilson	.25
92	Jason Jennings	.25
93	Juan Diaz	.25
94	Steve Smyth	.25
95	Phil Nevin	.25
96	John Olerud	.25
97	Brad Penny	.25
98	Andy Pettitte	.25
99	Juan Pierre	.25
100	Manny Ramirez	.75
101	Edgardo Alfonzo	.25
102	Michael Cuddyer	.25
103	Johnny Damon	.40
104	Carlos Zambrano	.35
105	Jose Vidro	.25
106	Tsuyoshi Shinjo	.25
107	Ed Rogers	.25
108	Scott Rolen	.75
109	Mariano Rivera	.35
110	Tim Redding	.25
111	Josh Phelps	.25
112	Gabe Kapler	.25
113	Edgar Martinez	.25
114	Fred McGriff	.25
115	Raul Mondesi	.25
116	Wade Miller	.25
117	Mike Mussina	.40
118	Rafael Palmeiro	.65
119	Adam Johnson	.25
120	Rickey Henderson	.75
121	Bill Hall	.25
122	Ken Griffey Jr.	1.50
123	Geronimo Gil	.25
124	Robert Fick	.25
125	Darin Erstad	.50
126	Brandon Duckworth	.25
127	Garret Anderson	.25
128	Pedro Feliz	.25
129	Jeff Cirillo	.25
130	Brian Giles	.25
131	Craig Biggio	.25
132	Willie Harris	.25
133	Doug Davis	.25
134	Jeff Kent	.25
135	Terrence Long	.25
136	Carlos Delgado	.50
137	Tino Martinez	.25
138	Donaldo Mendez	.25
139	Sean Douglass	.25
140	Eric Chavez	.40
141	Rick Ankiel	.25
142	Jeremy Giambi	.25
143	Juan Pena	.25
144	Bernie Williams	.40
145	Craig Wilson	.25
146	Ricardo Rodriguez	.25
147	Albert Pujols	1.50
148	Antonio Perez	.25
149	Russ Ortiz	.25
150	Corky Miller	.25
151	Rich Aurilia	.25
152	Kerry Wood	.50
153	Joe Thurston	.25
154	Jeff Deardorff RC	.25
155	Jermaine Dye	.25
156	Andruw Jones	.75
157	Victor Martinez	.25
158	Nick Neugebauer	.25
159	Matt Morris	.25
160	Casey Fossum	.25
161	J.D. Drew	.40
162	Matt Childers RC	.50
163	Mark Buehrle	.25
164	Jeff Bagwell	.75
165	Kazuhiro Sasaki	.25
166	Ben Sheets	.40
167	Alex Rodriguez	1.50
168	Adam Pettyjohn	.25
169	Chris Snelling RC	.50
170	Robert Person	.25
171	Juan Uribe	.25
172	Mo Vaughn	.25
173	Alfredo Amezaga	.25
174	Ryan Drese	.25
175	Corey Thurman RC	.25
176	Jim Thome	.50
177	Orlando Cabrera	.25
178	Eric Cyr RC	.50
179	Greg Maddux	1.00
180	Earl Snyder RC	.25
181	C.C. Sabathia	.25
182	Mark Mulder	.40
183	Jose Mieses	.25
184	Joe Kennedy	.25
185	Randy Johnson	.75
186	Tom Glavine	.40
187	Eric Junge RC	.25
188	Mike Piazza	1.50
189	Corey Patterson	.40
190	Carlos Pena	.25
191	Curt Schilling	.40
192	Nomar Garciaparra	1.50
193	Lance Berkman	.25
194	Ryan Klesko	.25
195	Ivan Rodriguez	.65
196	Alfonso Soriano	.75
197	Derek Jeter	2.00
198	David Justice	.25
199	Juan Gonzalez	.75
200	Adam Dunn	.50
201	Victor Alvarez RC	3.00
202	Miguel Asencio RC	3.00
203	Brandon Backe RC	3.00
204	Chris Baker RC	4.00
205	Steve Bechler RC	4.00
206	Francis Beltran RC	4.00
207	Angel Berroa	3.00
208	Hank Blalock	4.00
209	Dewon Brazelton	3.00
210	Sean Burroughs	3.00
211	Marlon Byrd	3.00
212	Raul Chavez RC	3.00
213	Juan Cruz	3.00
214	Jorge De La Rosa RC	3.00
215	Doug DeVore RC	3.00
216	John Ennis RC	3.00
217	Felix Escalona RC	3.00
218	Morgan Ensberg	3.00
219	Cam Esslinger RC	3.00
220	Kevin Frederick RC	3.00
221	Franklyn German RC	3.00
222	Eric Hinske RC	4.00
223	Ben Howard RC	3.00
224	Orlando Hudson RC	3.00
225	Travis Hughes RC	5.00
226	Kazuhisa Ishii RC	6.00
227	Ryan Jamison RC	3.00
228	Reed Johnson RC	4.00
229	Kyle Kane RC	3.00
230	Austin Kearns	3.00
231	Satoru Komiyama RC	4.00
232	Jason Lane	3.00
233	Jeremy Lambert RC	3.00
234	Anderson Machado RC	4.00
235	Brian Mallette RC	3.00
236	Takahito Nomura RC	3.00
237	Jorge Padilla RC	4.00
238	Luis Ugueto RC	3.00
239	Mark Prior	10.00
240	Rene Reyes RC	3.00
241	Deivis Santos	3.00
242	Elio Serrano RC	3.00
243	Tom Shearn RC	3.00
244	Allan Simpson RC	3.00
245	So Taguchi RC	5.00
246	Dennis Tankersley	3.00
247	Mark Teixeira	6.00
248	Matt Thornton	3.00
249	Bobby Hill	3.00
250	Ramon Vazquez	3.00

Proof

Proofs (1-200):	4-8X
Proofs (201-250):	1-2X
Production 100 Sets	

Classic Studio

WILLIE McCOVEY • 1B SAN FRANCISCO GIANTS

		NM/M
Complete Set (25):		90.00
Common Player:		3.00
Production 1,000 Sets		
First Ballot:		3-4X
Print run based on HOF year.		
1	Kirby Puckett	5.00
2	George Brett	8.00
3	Nolan Ryan	10.00
4	Mike Schmidt	8.00
5	Steve Carlton	3.00
6	Reggie Jackson	5.00
7	Tom Seaver	3.00
8	Joe Morgan	3.00
9	Jim Palmer	3.00
10	Johnny Bench	5.00
11	Willie McCovey	3.00
12	Brooks Robinson	4.00
13	Al Kaline	5.00
14	Stan Musial	6.00
15	Ozzie Smith	6.00
16	Dave Winfield	3.00
17	Robin Yount	5.00
18	Rod Carew	3.00
19	Willie Stargell	3.00
20	Lou Brock	3.00
21	Ernie Banks	5.00
22	Ted Williams	10.00
23	Jackie Robinson	8.00
24	Roberto Clemente	10.00
25	Lou Gehrig	10.00

Classic Studio Autograph

No Pricing	
Production 15-20	

Diamond Collection

JASON GIAMBI • 1B

		NM/M
Complete Set (25):		65.00
Common Player:		1.50
Inserted 1:17		

1 Todd Helton 3.00
2 Chipper Jones 4.00
3 Lance Berkman 1.50
4 Derek Jeter 8.00
5 Hideo Nomo 3.00
6 Kazuhisa Ishii 1.50
7 Barry Bonds 8.00
8 Alex Rodriguez 6.00
9 Ichiro Suzuki 5.00
10 Mike Piazza 5.00
11 Jim Thome 1.50
12 Greg Maddux 4.00
13 Jeff Bagwell 3.00
14 Vladimir Guerrero 3.00
15 Ken Griffey Jr. 5.00
16 Jason Giambi 2.50
17 Nomar Garciaparra 5.00
18 Albert Pujols 6.00
19 Manny Ramirez 3.00
20 Pedro J. Martinez 3.00
21 Roger Clemens 4.50
22 Randy Johnson 3.00
23 Mark Prior 2.00
24 So Taguchi 1.70
25 Sammy Sosa 5.00

Diamond Collection
Artist's Proof

NM/M
Common Jersey Card: 4.00
Varying quantities produced
1 Todd Helton/200 8.00
2 Chipper Jones/150 10.00
3 Lance Berkman/200 6.00
4 Derek Jeter/200/Base 20.00
5 Hideo Nomo/150 25.00
6 Kazuhisa Ishii/150 8.00
7 Barry Bonds/200/Base 25.00
8 Alex Rodriguez/150 15.00
9 Ichiro Suzuki/200/Base 25.00
10 Mike Piazza/150 15.00
11 Jim Thome/150 10.00
12 Greg Maddux/150 15.00
13 Jeff Bagwell/150 8.00
14 Vladimir Guerrero/200 8.00
15 Ken Griffey Jr./200/Base 10.00
16 Jason Giambi/200/Base 6.00
17 Nomar Garciaparra/150 10.00
18 Albert Pujols/Base/200 10.00
19 Manny Ramirez/150 8.00
20 Pedro Martinez/150 8.00
21 Roger Clemens/150 15.00
22 Randy Johnson/150 8.00
23 So Taguchi/150 8.00
24 Sammy Sosa/200/Base 15.00

Hats Off

NM/M
Common Player: 8.00
Production 100
MLB Logo: No Pricing
Production One Set
10 Carlos Lee 10.00
14 Mark Buehrle 10.00
16 Paul LoDuca 10.00
22 Brandon Duckworth 10.00
26 J.D. Drew 12.00
28 Wade Miller 10.00
30 Brian Giles 10.00
31 Lance Berkman 10.00
32 Shannon Stewart 10.00
33 Kazuhisa Ishii 20.00
35 Rafael Palmeiro 20.00
36 Roy Oswalt 15.00
37 Jason Lane 10.00
38 Andruw Jones 15.00
39 Brad Penny 10.00
40 Bud Smith 8.00
41 Carlos Beltran 15.00
42 Magglio Ordonez 20.00
43 Craig Biggio 10.00
45 Jeff Bagwell 25.00
47 Juan Cruz 8.00
48 Kerry Wood 25.00
49 Brandon Berger 8.00
50 Juan Pierre 8.00

Leather & Lumber

NM/M
Common Player: 5.00
Production 200 unless noted.
Artist's Proofs: 1.5-2X
Production 50
1 Nomar Garciaparra 15.00
2 Jeff Bagwell/150 8.00
3 Alex Rodriguez 15.00
4 Vladimir Guerrero/100 10.00
5 Luis Gonzalez 8.00
6 Chipper Jones 10.00
7 Shawn Green 5.00
8 Kirby Puckett/100 15.00
9 Juan Gonzalez 8.00
10 Troy Glaus 8.00
11 Don Mattingly/100 30.00
12 Todd Helton 8.00
13 Jim Thome 10.00
14 Rickey Henderson 15.00
15 Mike Schmidt/100 35.00
16 Adam Dunn/100 15.00
17 Ivan Rodriguez 10.00
18 Manny Ramirez/150 8.00
19 Tsuyoshi Shinjo 8.00
20 Andruw Jones/150 15.00
21 Roberto Alomar 8.00
22 Lance Berkman 5.00
23 Derek Jeter/50/Ball 30.00
24 Ichiro Suzuki/50/Ball 60.00
25 Mike Piazza 15.00

Masterstrokes

NM/M
Complete Set (25): 50.00
Common Player: 1.50
Inserted 1:17
1 Vladimir Guerrero 3.00
2 Frank Thomas 3.00
3 Alex Rodriguez 6.00
4 Manny Ramirez 3.00
5 Jeff Bagwell 3.00
6 Jim Thome 1.50
7 Ichiro Suzuki 5.00
8 Andruw Jones 3.00
9 Troy Glaus 3.00
10 Chipper Jones 3.00
11 Juan Gonzalez 3.00
12 Lance Berkman 1.50
13 Mike Piazza 5.00
14 Darin Erstad 2.00
15 Albert Pujols 6.00
16 Kazuhisa Ishii 1.50
17 Shawn Green 1.50
18 Rafael Palmeiro 2.00
19 Todd Helton 3.00
20 Carlos Delgado 1.50
21 Ivan Rodriguez 2.00
22 Luis Gonzalez 1.50
23 Derek Jeter 8.00
24 Nomar Garciaparra 5.00
15 J.D. Drew 5.00

Masterstrokes Artist's Proof

NM/M
All Jersey/bat unless noted.
Varying quantities produced
1 Vladimir Guerrero/200 15.00
2 Frank Thomas/200 15.00
3 Alex Rodriguez/100 25.00
4 Manny Ramirez/200 10.00
5 Jeff Bagwell/150 10.00
6 Jim Thome/200 15.00
7 Ichiro Suzuki/100/Ball/Base 50.00
8 Andruw Jones/200 10.00
9 Troy Glaus/200 10.00
10 Chipper Jones/200 15.00
11 Juan Gonzalez/200 10.00
12 Lance Berkman/200 8.00
13 Mike Piazza/200 25.00
14 Darin Erstad/200 10.00
15 Albert Pujols/100/Ball/Base 30.00
16 Kazuhisa Ishii/150 15.00
17 Shawn Green/200 10.00
18 Rafael Palmeiro/200 20.00
19 Todd Helton/200 15.00
20 Carlos Delgado/200 10.00
21 Ivan Rodriguez/200 15.00
22 Luis Gonzalez/200 10.00
23 Derek Jeter/100/Ball/Base 35.00
24 Nomar Garciaparra/150 25.00
25 J.D. Drew/150 8.00

Private Signings

NM/M
Common Autograph: 5.00
Varying quantities produced
1 Vladimir Guerrero/25 75.00
2 Chipper Jones/15 150.00
3 Bobby Abreu/50 20.00
4 Barry Zito/25 25.00
5 Miguel Tejada/50 25.00
6 Mike Sweeney/50 15.00
7 Shannon Stewart/100 10.00
8 Bud Smith/100 5.00
10 Wilson Betemit/250 8.00
12 Kevin Brown/25 25.00
15 Cliff Floyd/50 15.00
16 Marcus Giles/250 10.00
17 Troy Glaus/50 25.00
18 Barry Larkin/25 50.00
19 Carlos Lee/25 20.00
20 Brian Lawrence/250 8.00
21 Paul LoDuca/50 15.00
24 Roger Clemens/15 175.00
26 Joe Crede/250 5.00
28 Jeremy Affeldt/250 8.00
29 Adrian Beltre/25 20.00
30 Josh Beckett/25 40.00
31 Roberto Alomar/25 50.00
32 Toby Hall/250 8.00
37 Roy Oswalt/50 20.00
40 Nick Johnson/250 8.00
43 Drew Henson/250 15.00
45 Luis Gonzalez/15 25.00
47 Joe Mays/100 8.00
49 Aramis Ramirez/50 20.00
50 Kip Wells/250 8.00
51 Moises Alou/15 25.00
55 Freddy Garcia/50 10.00
56 Steve Green/250 5.00
59 Jack Cust/250 10.00
60 Sean Casey/50 10.00
62 Magglio Ordonez/15 40.00
65 Josh Towers/250 8.00
66 Javier Vazquez/100 15.00
68 Aubrey Huff/250 8.00
69 Richard Hidalgo/250 15.00
70 Brandon Claussen/250 10.00
72 John Buck/250 5.00
73 Dee Brown/250 5.00
76 Erick Almonte/250 5.00
79 Jay Gibbons/250 15.00
81 Todd Helton/15 85.00
82 Erik Bedard/250 5.00
84 Rafael Soriano/250 10.00
85 Gary Sheffield/15 40.00
86 Richie Sexson/50 20.00
87 Mike Rivera/250 5.00
88 Jose Ortiz/250 5.00
89 Abraham Nunez/250 5.00
90 Dave Williams/250 5.00
92 Jason Jennings/250 8.00
93 Juan Diaz/250 5.00
94 Steve Smyth/250 5.00
97 Brad Penny/80 10.00
99 Juan Pierre/100 15.00
100 Manny Ramirez/15 75.00
102 Michael Cuddyer/250 5.00
104 Carlos Zambrano/250 15.00
105 Jose Vidro/100 10.00
107 Ed Rogers/250 8.00
110 Tim Redding/250 5.00
111 Josh Phelps/250 8.00
112 Gabe Kapler/100 10.00
113 Edgar Martinez/250 40.00
116 Wade Miller/250 8.00
118 Rafael Palmeiro/25 40.00
121 Bill Hall/250 5.00
123 Geronimo Gil/250 5.00
124 Robert Fick/150 10.00
126 Brandon Duckworth/250 8.00
128 Pedro Feliz/250 8.00
130 Brian Giles/15 25.00
131 Craig Biggio/15 40.00
132 Willie Harris/250 5.00
133 Doug Davis/250 8.00
135 Terrence Long/150 10.00
138 Donaldo Mendez/250 5.00
139 Sean Douglass/250 5.00
140 Eric Chavez/15 25.00
141 Rick Ankiel/250 20.00
142 Jeremy Giambi/100 6.00
143 Juan Pena/250 8.00
144 Bernie Williams/15 75.00
145 Craig Wilson/250 5.00
146 Ricardo Rodriguez/250 10.00
147 Albert Pujols/25 200.00
148 Antonio Perez/250 5.00
150 Corky Miller/250 8.00
151 Rich Aurilia/25 5.00
152 Kerry Wood/25 30.00
153 Joe Thurston/250 5.00
154 Jeff Deardorff/250 5.00
157 Victor Martinez/250 15.00
158 Nick Neugebauer/150 5.00
160 Casey Fossum/250 8.00
161 J.D. Drew/25 25.00
162 Matt Childers/250 5.00
163 Mark Buehrle/150 10.00
166 Ben Sheets/100 5.00
167 Alex Rodriguez/15 165.00
168 Adam Pettyjohn/250 5.00
169 Chris Snelling/250 10.00
170 Robert Person/250 5.00
171 Juan Uribe/250 10.00
173 Alfredo Amezaga/250 5.00
175 Corey Thurman/250 5.00
178 Eric Cyr/250 5.00
179 Greg Maddux/15 200.00
180 Earl Snyder/250 5.00
181 C.C. Sabathia/50 20.00
182 Mark Mulder/50 15.00
183 Jose Mieses/250 5.00
184 Joe Kennedy/250 5.00
187 Eric Junge/250 5.00
189 Corey Patterson/205 20.00
190 Carlos Pena/250 10.00
191 Curt Schilling/15 80.00
195 Ivan Rodriguez/15 50.00
196 Alfonso Soriano/40 40.00
201 Victor Alvarez/250 5.00
203 Brandon Backe/250 5.00
204 Chris Baker/250 5.00
205 Steve Bechler/250 8.00
206 Francis Beltran/250 5.00
207 Angel Berroa/250 10.00
208 Hank Blalock/100 20.00
209 Dewon Brazelton/200 5.00
210 Sean Burroughs/50 20.00
211 Marlon Byrd/200 10.00
212 Raul Chavez/250 5.00
213 Juan Cruz/50 15.00
214 Jorge De La Rosa/250 5.00
215 Doug DeVore/250 5.00
216 John Ennis/250 5.00
217 Felix Escalona/250 5.00
218 Morgan Ensberg/250 10.00
219 Cam Esslinger/250 5.00
220 Kevin Frederick/250 5.00
221 Franklyn German/250 5.00
222 Eric Hinske/250 8.00
223 Ben Howard/250 5.00
224 Orlando Hudson/250 10.00
225 Travis Hughes/250 10.00
226 Kazuhisa Ishii/50 25.00
227 Ryan Jamison/250 5.00
228 Reed Johnson/250 10.00
229 Kyle Kane/250 5.00
230 Austin Kearns/250 20.00
231 Satoru Komiyama/50 10.00
232 Jason Lane/250 5.00
233 Jeremy Lambert/250 5.00
234 Anderson Machado/200 10.00
235 Brian Mallette/250 5.00
236 Takahito Nomura/100 20.00
237 Jorge Padilla/200 10.00
238 Luis Ugueto/250 5.00
239 Mark Prior/100 30.00
240 Rene Reyes/250 5.00
241 Deivis Santos/250 5.00
242 Elio Serrano/250 5.00
243 Tom Shearn/250 5.00
244 Allan Simpson/250 5.00
245 So Taguchi/100 5.00
246 Dennis Tankersley/100 10.00
247 Mark Teixeira/50 40.00
248 Matt Thornton/250 5.00
249 Bobby Hill/100 10.00
250 Ramon Vazquez/250 5.00

Spirit of the Game

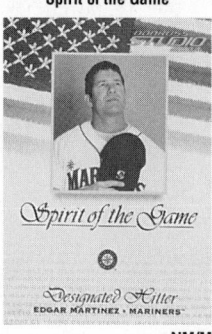

Spirit of the Game
Designated Hitter
EDGAR MARTINEZ • MARINERS

NM/M
Complete Set (50): 60.00
Common Player: 1.00
Inserted 1:9
1 Alex Rodriguez 5.00
2 Curt Schilling 1.50
3 Hideo Nomo 2.00
4 Derek Jeter 6.00
5 Mike Sweeney 1.00
6 Mike Piazza 4.00
7 Roger Clemens 3.00
8 Shawn Green 1.50
9 Vladimir Guerrero 2.00
10 Carlos Lee 1.00
11 Edgar Martinez 1.00
12 Albert Pujols 5.00
13 Mark Prior 2.00
14 Mark Buehrle 1.00
15 Chipper Jones 3.00
16 Paul LoDuca 1.00
17 Frank Thomas 2.00
18 Randy Johnson 1.00
19 Cliff Floyd 1.00
20 Todd Helton 1.00
21 Luis Gonzalez 1.00
22 Brandon Duckworth 1.00
23 Jason Giambi 1.50
24 Juan Uribe 1.00
25 Dewon Brazelton 1.00
26 J.D. Drew 1.50
27 Troy Glaus 2.00
28 Wade Miller 1.00
29 Darin Erstad 1.50
30 Brian Giles 1.00
31 Lance Berkman 1.00
32 Shannon Stewart 1.00
33 Kazuhisa Ishii 1.00
34 Corey Patterson 1.00
35 Rafael Palmeiro 1.50
36 Roy Oswalt 1.00
37 Jason Lane 1.00
38 Andruw Jones 2.00
39 Brad Penny 1.00
40 Bud Smith 1.00
41 Carlos Beltran 1.00
42 Magglio Ordonez 1.50
43 Craig Biggio 2.00
44 Hank Blalock 1.50
45 Jeff Bagwell 2.00

46 Josh Beckett 1.50
47 Juan Cruz 1.00
48 Kerry Wood 1.50
49 Brandon Berger 1.00
50 Juan Pierre 1.00

Studio Stars

	NM/M
Complete Set (50):	60.00
Common Player:	1.00
Production 700 Sets	
Golds:	1.5-2X
Production 250 Sets	
Platinums:	3-5X
Production 50 Sets	
1 Mike Piazza	3.00
2 Ivan Rodriguez	1.50
3 Albert Pujols	4.00
4 Scott Rolen	2.00
5 Alex Rodriguez	4.00
6 Curt Schilling	1.50
7 Vladimir Guerrero	2.00
8 Jim Thome	1.00
9 Derek Jeter	5.00
10 C.C. Sabathia	1.00
11 Sammy Sosa	3.00
12 Adam Dunn	1.50
13 Bernie Williams	1.00
14 Ichiro Suzuki	4.00
15 Barry Bonds	5.00
16 Rickey Henderson	2.00
17 Ken Griffey Jr.	3.00
18 Kazuhisa Ishii	1.00
19 Kerry Wood	1.50
20 Todd Helton	1.50
21 Hideo Nomo	2.00
22 Frank Thomas	2.00
23 Manny Ramirez	2.00
24 Luis Gonzalez	1.00
25 Rafael Palmeiro	1.50
26 Mike Mussina	1.50
27 Roy Oswalt	1.00
28 Darin Erstad	1.00
29 Barry Larkin	1.00
30 Randy Johnson	2.00
31 Tom Glavine	1.00
32 Lance Berkman	1.00
33 Juan Gonzalez	2.00
34 Shawn Green	1.00
35 Nomar Garciaparra	3.00
36 Troy Glaus	2.00
37 Tim Hudson	1.00
38 Carlos Delgado	1.50
39 Jason Giambi	1.50
40 Andruw Jones	2.00
41 Roberto Alomar	1.00
42 Greg Maddux	2.50
43 Pedro J. Martinez	2.00
44 Tony Gwynn	3.00
45 Alfonso Soriano	1.50
46 Chipper Jones	2.50
47 J.D. Drew	1.00
48 Roger Clemens	2.75
49 Barry Zito	1.00
50 Jeff Bagwell	1.50

2002 Donruss The Rookies

	NM/M
Complete Set (110):	20.00
Common Player:	.15
Common Rookie:	.25
Pack (5):	2.00
Box (24):	40.00
1 Kazuhisa Ishii RC	1.00
2 P.J. Bevis RC	.25
3 Jason Simontacchi RC	.50
4 John Lackey	.15
5 Travis Driskill RC	.25

6 Carl Sadler RC .25
7 Tim Kalita RC .25
8 Nelson Castro RC .25
9 Francis Beltran RC .25
10 So Taguchi RC .50
11 Ryan Bukvich RC .25
12 Brian Fitzgerald .15
13 Kevin Frederick RC .25
14 Chone Figgins RC .75
15 Marlon Byrd .15
16 Ron Calloway RC .25
17 Jason Lane .15
18 Satoru Komiyama RC .25
19 John Ennis RC .25
20 Juan Brito RC .25
21 Gustavo Chacin RC .50
22 Josh Bard RC .50
23 Brett Myers .15
24 Mike Smith RC .25
25 Eric Hinske .15
26 Jake Peavy .15
27 Todd Donovan RC .25
28 Luis Ugueto RC .25
29 Corey Thurman RC .25
30 Takahito Nomura RC .25
31 Andy Shibilo RC .25
32 Mike Crudale RC .25
33 Earl Snyder RC .25
34 Brian Tallet .50
35 Miguel Asencio RC .25
36 Felix Escalona RC .25
37 Drew Henson .40
38 Steve Kent RC .25
39 Rene Reyes RC .25
40 Edwin Almonte RC .25
41 Chris Snelling RC .75
42 Franklyn German RC .25
43 Jeriome Robertson RC .25
44 Colin Young RC .25
45 Jeremy Lambert RC .25
46 Kirk Saarloos RC .75
47 Matt Childers RC .25
48 Justin Wayne .15
49 Jose Valverde RC .25
50 Wily Mo Pena .15
51 Victor Alvarez RC .25
52 Julius Matos RC .25
53 Aaron Cook RC .40
54 Jeff Austin RC .25
55 Adrian Burnside RC .25
56 Brandon Puffer RC .25
57 Jeremy Hill RC .25
58 Jaime Cerda RC .25
59 Aaron Guiel RC .25
60 Ron Chiavacci .15
61 Kevin Cash RC .25
62 Elio Serrano .15
63 Julio Mateo RC .25
64 Cam Esslinger RC .25
65 Ken Huckaby RC .25
66 Wiki Nieves RC .25
67 Luis Martinez RC .25
68 Scotty Layfield RC .25
69 Jeremy Guthrie RC .75
70 Hansel Izquierdo RC .25
71 Shane Nance RC .25
72 Jeff Baker RC .50
73 Clifford Bartosh RC .25
74 Mitch Wylie RC .25
75 Oliver Perez RC .75
76 Matt Thornton .15
77 John Foster RC .25
78 Joe Borchard .15
79 Eric Junge RC .25
80 Jorge Sosa RC .25
81 Runelvys Hernandez RC .25
82 Kevin Mench .15
83 Ben Kozlowski RC .50
84 Trey Hodges RC .40
85 Reed Johnson RC .25
86 Eric Eckenstahler RC .25
87 Franklin Nunez RC .25
88 Victor Martinez .50
89 Kevin Gryboski RC .25
90 Jason Jennings .15
91 Jim Rushford RC .25
92 Jeremy Ward RC .25
93 Adam Walker RC .25
94 Freddy Sanchez RC .50
95 Wilson Valdez RC .25
96 Lee Gardner .15
97 Eric Good RC .25
98 Hank Blalock .50
99 Mark Corey .15
100 Jason Davis RC .40
101 Mike Gonzalez RC .25
102 David Ross RC .25
103 Tyler Yates RC .25
104 Cliff Lee RC 1.00
105 Mike Moriarty RC .25
106 Josh Hancock RC .25
107 Jason Beverlin RC .25
108 Clay Condrey RC .25
109 Shawn Sedlacek RC .25
110 Sean Burroughs .15

Donruss Originals
401 Runelvys Hernandez RC .50
402 Wilson Valdez RC .25
403 Brian Tallet 1.00
404 Chone Figgins RC .25
405 Jeriome Robertson RC .50
406 Shane Nance RC .25
407 Aaron Cook RC .75
408 Trey Hodges RC .75
409 Matt Childers RC .40
410 Mitch Wylie RC .25
411 Rene Reyes RC .25
412 Mike Smith .25
413 Jason Simontacchi RC .75
414 Luis Martinez .40
415 Kevin Cash RC .40
416 Todd Donovan .25
417 Scotty Layfield .25
418 Joe Borchard .25
419 Adrian Burnside .25
420 Ben Kozlowski .25
421 Clay Condrey .25
422 Cliff Lee 1.00
423 Josh Bard .25
424 Freddy Sanchez 1.00
425 Ron Calloway .25

Donruss Studio
Common Studio RC:	3.00
Production 1,500	
251 Freddy Sanchez RC	5.00
252 Josh Bard RC	3.00
253 Trey Hodges RC	5.00
254 Jorge Sosa RC	3.00
255 Ben Kozlowski RC	3.00
256 Eric Good RC	3.00
257 Brian Tallet	5.00
258 P.J. Bevis RC	3.00
259 Rodrigo Rosario RC	3.00
260 Kirk Saarloos	3.00
261 Runelvys Hernandez RC	4.00
262 Josh Hancock RC	3.00
263 Tim Kalita RC	3.00
264 Jason Simontacchi RC	3.00
265 Clay Condrey RC	3.00
266 Cliff Lee RC	10.00
267 Aaron Guiel RC	4.00
268 Andy Pratt RC	4.00
269 Wilson Valdez RC	4.00
270 Oliver Perez RC	4.00
271 Joe Borchard	3.00
272 Jeriome Robertson RC	4.00
273 Aaron Cook RC	5.00
274 Kevin Cash RC	3.00
275 Chone Figgins RC	3.00

Best of Fan Club
Common Best of Fan Club RC:	3.00
Production 1,350	
Best of Fan Club Spotlights:	1.5-3X
Production 100 Sets	
201 Kirk Saarloos	3.00
202 Oliver Perez RC	4.00
203 So Taguchi RC	6.00
204 Runelvys Hernandez RC	5.00
205 Freddy Sanchez RC	5.00
206 Cliff Lee RC	10.00
207 Kazuhisa Ishii RC	8.00
208 Kevin Cash RC	5.00
209 Trey Hodges RC	6.00
210 Wilson Valdez RC	4.00
211 Satoru Komiyama RC	3.00
212 Luis Ugueto RC	3.00
213 Joe Borchard	3.00
214 Brian Tallet	3.00
215 Jeriome Robertson RC	5.00
216 Eric Junge RC	4.00
217 Aaron Cook RC	4.00
218 Jason Simontacchi RC	4.00
219 Miguel Asencio RC	3.00
220 Josh Bard RC	3.00
221 Earl Snyder RC	3.00
222 Felix Escalona RC	3.00
223 Rene Reyes RC	3.00
224 Chone Figgins RC	3.00
225 Chris Snelling RC	5.00

Fan Club
Inserted 1:4 Retail	
201 Kirk Saarloos	1.50
202 Oliver Perez RC	2.00
203 So Taguchi RC	1.50
204 Runelvys Hernandez RC	1.50
205 Freddy Sanchez RC	1.50
206 Cliff Lee	3.00
207 Kazuhisa Ishii RC	4.00
208 Kevin Cash	1.50
209 Trey Hodges	1.50
210 Wilson Valdez	1.00
211 Satoru Komiyama RC	1.00
212 Luis Ugueto RC	1.50
213 Joe Borchard	2.00
214 Brian Tallet	3.00
215 Jeriome Robertson RC	1.50
216 Eric Junge	1.50
217 Aaron Cook	1.50
218 Jason Simontacchi	1.50
219 Miguel Asencio	1.50
220 Josh Bard	1.50
221 Earl Snyder RC	1.50
222 Felix Escalona	1.00
223 Rene Reyes	1.00
224 Chone Figgins	1.00
225 Chris Snelling RC	1.50

Elite
Common Elite RC:	4.00
Production 1,000	
Elite Turn of the Century:	1-2.5X
Production 100 Sets	
201 Chris Snelling RC	5.00
202 Satoru Komiyama RC	5.00
203 Jason Simontacchi RC	8.00
204 Tim Kalita RC	5.00
205 Runelvys Hernandez RC	5.00
206 Kirk Saarloos	5.00
207 Aaron Guiel RC	6.00
208 Luis Ugueto RC	5.00
209 Gustavo Chacin RC	5.00
210 Francis Beltran RC	5.00
211 Takahito Nomura RC	5.00
212 Oliver Perez RC	6.00
213 Miguel Asencio RC	4.00
214 Rene Reyes RC	5.00
215 Jeff Baker RC	15.00
216 Jon Adkins RC	5.00
217 Carlos Rivera RC	5.00
218 Corey Thurman RC	5.00
219 Earl Snyder RC	5.00
220 Felix Escalona RC	5.00
221 Jeremy Guthrie RC	15.00
222 Josh Hancock RC	5.00
223 Ben Kozlowski RC	5.00
224 Eric Good RC	5.00
225 Eric Junge RC	5.00
226 Andy Pratt RC	5.00
227 Matt Thornton RC	5.00
228 Jorge Sosa RC	5.00
229 Mike Smith RC	5.00
230 Mitch Wylie RC	5.00
231 John Ennis RC	5.00
232 Reed Johnson RC	5.00
233 Joe Borchard	8.00
234 Ron Calloway RC	5.00
235 Brian Tallet	5.00
236 Chris Baker RC	5.00
237 Cliff Lee RC	20.00
238 Matt Childers RC	5.00
239 Freddy Sanchez RC	5.00
240 Chone Figgins RC	8.00
241 Kevin Cash RC	5.00
242 Josh Bard RC	5.00
243 Jeriome Robertson RC	5.00
244 Jeremy Hill RC	5.00
245 Shane Nance RC	5.00
246 Wes Obermueller RC	5.00
247 Trey Hodges RC	5.00
248 Eric Eckenstahler RC	5.00
249 Jim Rushford RC	5.00
250 Jose Castillo RC	10.00
251 Garrett Atkins RC	20.00
252 Alexis Rios RC	100.00
253 Ryan Church RC	10.00
254 Jimmy Gobble RC	8.00
255 Corwin Malone	6.00
257 Nic Jackson RC	6.00
258 Tommy Whiteman RC	8.00
259 Mario Ramos	5.00
260 Rob Bowen RC	8.00
261 Josh Wilson RC	5.00
262 Tim Hummel RC	5.00
264 Gerald Laird RC	15.00
265 Vinnie Chulk RC	5.00
266 Jesus Medrano RC	5.00
272 Adam LaRoche RC	20.00
273 Adam Morrissey RC	5.00
274 Henri Stanley RC	5.00
275 Walter Young RC	10.00

Donruss Classics
Common Classics RC:	3.00
Production 1,500	
Classics Timeless Tributes:	1.5-3X
Production 100 Sets	
201 Oliver Perez RC	4.00
202 Aaron Cook RC	5.00
203 Eric Junge RC	3.00
204 Freddy Sanchez RC	5.00
205 Cliff Lee RC	10.00
206 Runelvys Hernandez RC	5.00
207 Chone Figgins RC	5.00
208 Rodrigo Rosario RC	3.00
209 Kevin Cash RC	3.00
210 Josh Bard RC	3.00
211 Felix Escalona RC	3.00
212 Jeriome Robertson RC	5.00
213 Jason Simontacchi RC	5.00
214 Shane Nance RC	3.00
215 Ben Kozlowski RC	3.00
216 Brian Tallet	5.00
217 Earl Snyder RC	3.00
218 Andy Pratt RC	3.00
219 Trey Hodges RC	5.00
220 Kirk Saarloos RC	5.00
221 Rene Reyes RC	3.00
222 Joe Borchard RC	3.00
223 Wilson Valdez RC	3.00
224 Miguel Asencio RC	3.00
225 Chris Snelling RC	5.00

Diamond Kings
Common DK RC:	3.00
Inserted 1:10	
151 Chris Snelling RC	4.00
152 Satoru Komiyama RC	3.00
153 Oliver Perez RC	33.00
154 Kirk Saarloos	3.00
155 Rene Reyes RC	3.00
156 Runelvys Hernandez RC	3.00
157 Rodrigo Rosario RC	3.00
158 Jason Simontacchi RC	3.00
159 Miguel Asencio RC	3.00
160 Aaron Cook RC	3.00

Autographs
	NM/M
Production 15-100	5.00
Print runs listed.	
2 P.J. Bevis/50	20.00
9 Francis Beltran/100	5.00
13 Kevin Frederick/100	5.00
14 Chone Figgins/100	20.00
15 Marlon Byrd/100	10.00
17 Jason Lane/100	8.00
19 John Ennis/100	10.00
22 Josh Bard/100	10.00

25	Eric Hinske/100	10.00
28	Luis Ugueto/100	5.00
29	Corey Thurman/100	5.00
30	Takahito Nomura/100	20.00
33	Earl Snyder/100	10.00
34	Brian Tallet/100	15.00
37	Drew Henson/50	20.00
39	Rene Reyes/50	15.00
40	Edwin Almonte/50	15.00
41	Chris Snelling/50	20.00
42	Franklyn German/100	5.00
45	Jeremy Lambert/100	5.00
46	Kirk Saarloos/100	10.00
47	Matt Childers/100	5.00
50	Wily Mo Pena/100	15.00
51	Victor Alvarez/100	5.00
61	Kevin Cash/100	8.00
62	Elio Serrano/100	5.00
64	Cam Esslinger/100	5.00
69	Jeremy Guthrie/100	15.00
71	Shane Nance/100	8.00
72	Jeff Baker/100	20.00
76	Matt Thornton/100	10.00
78	Joe Borchard/100	10.00
82	Kevin Mench/100	10.00
83	Ben Kozlowski/100	8.00
84	Trey Hodges/100	5.00
85	Reed Johnson/100	15.00
88	Victor Martinez/100	25.00
90	Jason Jennings/100	8.00
95	Wilson Valdez/100	5.00
97	Eric Good/100	10.00
98	Hank Blalock/100	30.00
104	Cliff Lee/100	20.00
110	Sean Burroughs/50	10.00

Best of Fan Club Autograph

		NM/M
Production 10-100		
Print runs listed.		
201	Kirk Saarloos/100	10.00
208	Kevin Cash/50	10.00
209	Trey Hodges/100	10.00
210	Wilson Valdez/50	10.00
212	Luis Ugueto/75	10.00
213	Joe Borchard/50	15.00
214	Brian Tallet/50	15.00
220	Josh Bard/50	8.00
221	Earl Snyder/100	8.00
223	Rene Reyes/50	8.00
224	Chone Figgins/100	8.00
225	Chris Snelling/100	10.00

Donruss Classics Signatures

		NM/M
Print runs listed.		
203	Eric Junge/50	10.00
205	Cliff Lee/100	40.00
207	Chone Figgins/100	10.00
208	Rodrigo Rosario/250	10.00
209	Kevin Cash/100	10.00
210	Josh Bard/100	10.00
214	Shane Nance/200	10.00
215	Ben Kozlowski/200	10.00
216	Brian Tallet/100	15.00
217	Earl Snyder/100	10.00
218	Andy Pratt/250	10.00
219	Trey Hodges/250	15.00

220	Kirk Saarloos/100	20.00
221	Rene Reyes/50	10.00
222	Joe Borchard/100	10.00
223	Wilson Valdez/100	10.00
225	Chris Snelling/100	25.00

Donruss Studio Private Signing

		NM/M
Print runs listed.		
252	Josh Bard/100	10.00
253	Trey Hodges/100	10.00
255	Ben Kozlowski/200	5.00
257	Brian Tallet/100	15.00
258	P.J. Bevis/50	15.00
259	Rodrigo Rosario/250	5.00
260	Kirk Saarloos/100	10.00
263	Tim Kalita/50	8.00
266	Cliff Lee/100	30.00
268	Andy Pratt/250	8.00
269	Wilson Valdez/200	5.00
271	Joe Borchard/100	15.00
274	Kevin Cash/100	8.00
275	Chone Figgins/100	8.00

Elite Turn of the Cent. Auto.

		NM/M
Common Autograph:		
Print runs listed.		
201	Chris Snelling/50	20.00
206	Kirk Saarloos/50	20.00
215	Jeff Baker/100	20.00
216	Jon Adkins/100	10.00
217	Carlos Rivera/100	15.00
221	Jeremy Guthrie/100	25.00
223	Ben Kozlowski/100	10.00
224	Eric Good/100	10.00
240	Chone Figgins/100	30.00
241	Kevin Cash/100	10.00
247	Trey Hodges/100	15.00
251	Garrett Atkins/100	50.00
253	Ryan Church/100	35.00
254	Jimmy Gobble/100	10.00
255	Corwin Malone/100	15.00
258	Tom Whiteman/100	10.00
259	Mario Ramos/100	10.00
260	Rob Bowen/100	10.00
261	Josh Wilson/100	10.00
262	Tim Hummel/100	10.00
264	Gerald Laird/100	25.00
266	Jesus Medrano/100	10.00
272	Adam LaRoche/100	30.00
273	Adam Morrissey/100	10.00
274	Henri Stanley/100	10.00

Fan Club Autograph

		NM/M
Common Autograph:		
Print runs listed.		
201	Kirk Saarloos/100	10.00
208	Kevin Cash/50	8.00
209	Trey Hodges/50	10.00
210	Wilson Valdez/50	10.00
212	Luis Ugueto/75	10.00
213	Joe Borchard/50	15.00
214	Brian Tallet/50	15.00
220	Josh Bard/50	8.00
221	Earl Snyder/100	8.00
223	Rene Reyes/50	8.00
224	Chone Figgins/100	8.00

Phenoms

		NM/M
Common Player:		3.00
Production 1,000 Sets		
1	Kazuhisa Ishii	5.00
2	Eric Hinske	3.00
3	Jason Lane	3.00
4	Victor Martinez	5.00
5	Mark Prior	6.00
6	Antonio Perez	3.00
7	John Buck	3.00
8	Joe Borchard	3.00
9	Alexis Gomez	3.00
10	Sean Burroughs	3.00
11	Carlos Pena	3.00
12	Bill Hall	3.00
13	Alfredo Amezaga	3.00
14	Ed Rogers	3.00
15	Mark Teixeira	5.00

16	Chris Snelling	4.00
17	Nick Johnson	3.00
18	Angel Berroa	3.00
19	Orlando Hudson	3.00
20	Drew Henson	3.00
21	Austin Kearns	3.00
22	Dewon Brazelton	3.00
23	Dennis Tankersley	3.00
24	Josh Beckett	4.00
25	Marlon Byrd	4.00

Phenoms Autographs

		NM/M
Common Autograph:		5.00
Print runs listed.		
2	Eric Hinske/500	10.00
3	Jason Lane/500	5.00
4	Victor Martinez/225	10.00
5	Mark Prior/100	15.00
6	Antonio Perez/500	5.00
7	John Buck/100	8.00
8	Joe Borchard/100	10.00
9	Alexis Gomez/400	5.00
10	Sean Burroughs/150	5.00
11	Carlos Pena/150	8.00
12	Bill Hall/200	8.00
13	Alfredo Amezaga/500	5.00
14	Ed Rogers/500	5.00
15	Mark Teixeira/100	20.00
16	Chris Snelling/100	10.00
17	Nick Johnson/250	8.00
18	Angel Berroa/500	5.00
19	Orlando Hudson/400	15.00
20	Drew Henson/500	25.00
21	Austin Kearns/75	10.00
22	Dewon Brazelton/350	5.00
23	Dennis Tankersley/100	8.00
24	Josh Beckett/125	30.00
25	Marlon Byrd/500	10.00

Rookie Crusade

		NM/M
Common Player:		3.00
Production 1,500 Sets		
1	Corky Miller	3.00
2	Jack Cust	3.00
3	Erik Bedard	3.00
4	Andres Torres	3.00
5	Geronimo Gil	3.00
6	Rafael Soriano	3.00
7	Johnny Estrada	3.00
8	Steve Bechler	3.00
9	Adam Johnson	3.00
10	So Taguchi	3.00
11	Dee Brown	3.00
12	Kevin Frederick	3.00
13	Allan Simpson	3.00
14	Ricardo Rodriguez	3.00
15	Jason Hart	3.00
16	Matt Childers	3.00
17	Jason Jennings	3.00
18	Anderson Machado	3.00
19	Fernando Rodney	3.00
20	Brandon Larson	3.00
21	Satoru Komiyama	3.00
22	Francis Beltran	3.00
23	Joe Thurston	3.00
24	Josh Pearce	3.00
25	Carlos Hernandez	3.00
26	Ben Howard	3.00
27	Wilson Valdez	3.00
28	Victor Alvarez	3.00
29	Cesar Izturis	3.00
30	Endy Chavez	3.00
31	Michael Cuddyer	4.00
32	Bobby Hill	3.00
33	Willie Harris	3.00
34	Joe Crede	3.00
35	Jorge Padilla	3.00
36	Brandon Backe	3.00
37	Franklyn German	3.00
38	Xavier Nady	3.00
39	Raul Chavez	3.00
40	Shane Nance	3.00
41	Brandon Claussen	4.00
42	Tom Shearn	3.00
43	Freddy Sanchez	3.00
44	Chone Figgins	3.00
45	Cliff Lee	4.00
46	Brian Mallette	3.00
47	Mike Rivera	3.00

48	Elio Serrano	3.00
49	Rodrigo Rosario	3.00
50	Earl Snyder	3.00

Rookie Crusade Autograph

		NM/M
Common Autograph:		5.00
Print runs listed.		
1	Corky Miller/500	5.00
2	Jack Cust/500	6.00
3	Erik Bedard/100	10.00
4	Andres Torres/500	5.00
5	Geronimo Gil/500	5.00
6	Rafael Soriano/500	8.00
7	Johnny Estrada/400	5.00
8	Steve Bechler/500	6.00
9	Adam Johnson/500	5.00
11	Dee Brown/500	5.00
12	Kevin Frederick/150	5.00
13	Allan Simpson/150	5.00
14	Ricardo Rodriguez/500	5.00
15	Jason Hart/500	5.00
16	Matt Childers/150	5.00
17	Jason Jennings/500	5.00
18	Anderson Machado/500	5.00
19	Fernando Rodney/500	5.00
20	Brandon Larson/400	5.00
22	Francis Beltran/500	5.00
23	Joe Thurston/500	5.00
24	Josh Pearce/500	5.00
25	Carlos Hernandez/500	5.00
26	Ben Howard/500	6.00
27	Wilson Valdez/500	5.00
28	Victor Alvarez/500	5.00
29	Cesar Izturis/500	8.00
30	Endy Chavez/500	5.00
31	Michael Cuddyer/375	10.00
32	Bobby Hill/250	5.00
33	Willie Harris/500	5.00
34	Joe Crede/100	8.00
35	Jorge Padilla/475	10.00
36	Brandon Backe/350	5.00
37	Franklyn German/500	5.00
38	Xavier Nady/500	8.00
39	Raul Chavez/500	5.00
40	Shane Nance/500	5.00
41	Brandon Claussen/150	10.00
42	Tom Shearn/500	5.00
44	Chone Figgins/500	5.00
45	Cliff Lee/500	20.00
46	Brian Mallette/150	5.00
47	Mike Rivera/400	5.00
48	Elio Serrano/500	5.00
49	Rodrigo Rosario/500	10.00
50	Earl Snyder/100	10.00

2003 Donruss

		NM/M
Complete Set (400):		40.00
Common Player:		.15
Pack (13):		1.50
Box (24):		30.00
1	Vladimir Guerrero	.75
2	Derek Jeter	2.00
3	Adam Dunn	.50
4	Greg Maddux	1.00
5	Lance Berkman	.40
6	Ichiro Suzuki	2.00
7	Mike Piazza	1.00
8	Alex Rodriguez	2.00
9	Tom Glavine	.25
10	Randy Johnson	.75
11	Nomar Garciaparra	1.00
12	Jason Giambi	.50
13	Sammy Sosa	1.00
14	Barry Zito	.25
15	Chipper Jones	1.00
16	Magglio Ordonez	.25
17	Larry Walker	.25
18	Alfonso Soriano	.75
19	Curt Schilling	.50
20	Barry Bonds	2.00
21	Joe Borchard	.15
22	Chris Snelling	.15
23	Brian Tallet	.15
24	Cliff Lee	.15
25	Freddy Sanchez	.15
26	Chone Figgins	.15
27	Kevin Cash	.15
28	Josh Bard	.15
29	Jeriome Robertson	.15

#	Player	Price
30	Jeremy Hill	.15
31	Shane Nance	.15
32	Jake Peavy Padres	.15
33	Trey Hodges	.15
34	Eric Eckenstahler	.15
35	Jim Rushford	.15
36	Oliver Perez	.15
37	Kirk Saarloos	.15
38	Hank Blalock	.50
39	Francisco Rodriguez	.25
40	Runelvys Hernandez	.15
41	Aaron Cook	.15
42	Josh Hancock	.15
43	P.J. Bevis	.15
44	Jon Adkins	.15
45	Tim Kalita	.15
46	Nelson Castro	.15
47	Colin Young	.15
48	Adrian Burnside	.15
49	Luis Martinez	.15
50	Peter Zamora	.15
51	Todd Donovan	.15
52	Jeremy Ward	.15
53	Wilson Valdez	.15
54	Eric Good	.15
55	Jeff Baker	.15
56	Mitch Wylie	.15
57	Ron Calloway	.15
58	Jose Valverde	.15
59	Jason Davis	.15
60	Scotty Layfield	.15
61	Matt Thornton	.15
62	Adam Walker	.15
63	Gustavo Chacin	.15
64	Ron Chiavacci	.15
65	Wiki Nieves	.15
66	Clifford Bartosh	.15
67	Mike Gonzalez	.15
68	Justin Wayne	.15
69	Eric Junge	.15
70	Ben Kozlowski	.15
71	Darin Erstad	.25
72	Garret Anderson	.40
73	Troy Glaus	.40
74	David Eckstein	.15
75	Adam Kennedy	.15
76	Kevin Appier	.15
77	Jarrod Washburn	.15
78	Scott Spiezio	.15
79	Tim Salmon	.25
80	Ramon Ortiz	.15
81	Bengie Molina	.15
82	Brad Fullmer	.15
83	Troy Percival	.15
84	David Segui	.15
85	Jay Gibbons	.15
86	Tony Batista	.15
87	Scott Erickson	.15
88	Jeff Conine	.15
89	Melvin Mora	.15
90	Buddy Groom	.15
91	Rodrigo Lopez	.15
92	Marty Cordova	.15
93	Geronimo Gil	.15
94	Kenny Lofton	.15
95	Shea Hillenbrand	.15
96	Manny Ramirez	.50
97	Pedro Martinez	.75
98	Nomar Garciaparra	1.00
99	Rickey Henderson	.40
100	Johnny Damon	.25
101	Trot Nixon	.15
102	Derek Lowe	.15
103	Hee Seop Choi	.15
104	Mark Teixeira	.40
105	Tim Wakefield	.15
106	Jason Varitek	.25
107	Frank Thomas	.50
108	Joe Crede	.15
109	Magglio Ordonez	.25
110	Ray Durham	.15
111	Mark Buehrle	.15
112	Paul Konerko	.25
113	Jose Valentin	.15
114	Carlos Lee	.15
115	Royce Clayton	.15
116	C.C. Sabathia	.15
117	Ellis Burks	.15
118	Omar Vizquel	.25
119	Jim Thome	.75
120	Matt Lawton	.15
121	Travis Fryman	.15
122	Earl Snyder	.15
123	Ricky Gutierrez	.15
124	Einar Diaz	.15
125	Danys Baez	.15
126	Robert Fick	.15
127	Bobby Higginson	.15
128	Steve Sparks	.15
129	Mike Rivera	.15
130	Wendell Magee	.15
131	Randall Simon	.15
132	Carlos Pena	.15
133	Mark Redman	.15
134	Juan Acevedo	.15
135	Mike Sweeney	.15
136	Aaron Guiel	.15
137	Carlos Beltran	.40
138	Joe Randa	.15
139	Paul Byrd	.15
140	Shawn Sedlacek	.15
141	Raul Ibanez	.15
142	Michael Tucker	.15
143	Torii Hunter	.40
144	Jacque Jones	.15
145	David Ortiz	.40
146	Corey Koskie	.15
147	Brad Radke	.15
148	Doug Mientkiewicz	.15
149	A.J. Pierzynski	.15
150	Dustan Mohr	.15
151	Michael Cuddyer	.15
152	Eddie Guardado	.15
153	Cristian Guzman	.15
154	Derek Jeter	2.00
155	Bernie Williams	.50
156	Roger Clemens	1.50
157	Mike Mussina	.50
158	Jorge Posada	.40
159	Alfonso Soriano	.75
160	Jason Giambi	.50
161	Robin Ventura	.25
162	Andy Pettitte	.25
163	David Wells	.15
164	Nick Johnson	.15
165	Jeff Weaver	.15
166	Raul Mondesi	.15
167	Rondell White	.15
168	Tim Hudson	.25
169	Barry Zito	.40
170	Mark Mulder	.25
171	Miguel Tejada	.40
172	Eric Chavez	.25
173	Billy Koch	.15
174	Jermaine Dye	.15
175	Scott Hatteberg	.15
176	Terrence Long	.15
177	David Justice	.25
178	Ramon Hernandez	.15
179	Ted Lilly	.15
180	Ichiro Suzuki	1.50
181	Edgar Martinez	.25
182	Mike Cameron	.15
183	John Olerud	.15
184	Bret Boone	.25
185	Dan Wilson	.15
186	Freddy Garcia	.15
187	Jamie Moyer	.15
188	Carlos Guillen	.15
189	Ruben Sierra	.15
190	Kazuhiro Sasaki	.15
191	Mark McLemore	.15
192	Chris Snelling	.15
193	Joel Pineiro	.15
194	Jeff Cirillo	.15
195	Rafael Soriano	.15
196	Ben Grieve	.15
197	Aubrey Huff	.15
198	Steve Cox	.15
199	Toby Hall	.15
200	Randy Winn	.15
201	Brent Abernathy	.15
202	Chris Gomez	.15
203	John Flaherty	.15
204	Paul Wilson	.15
205	Chan Ho Park	.15
206	Alex Rodriguez	2.00
207	Juan Gonzalez	.50
208	Rafael Palmeiro	.50
209	Ivan Rodriguez	.50
210	Rusty Greer	.15
211	Kenny Rogers	.15
212	Ismael Valdes	.15
213	Frank Catalanotto	.15
214	Hank Blalock	.50
215	Michael Young	.15
216	Kevin Mench	.15
217	Herbert Perry	.15
218	Gabe Kapler	.25
219	Carlos Delgado	.25
220	Shannon Stewart	.15
221	Eric Hinske	.15
222	Roy Halladay	.25
223	Felipe Lopez	.15
224	Vernon Wells	.25
225	Josh Phelps	.15
226	Jose Cruz	.15
227	Curt Schilling	.50
228	Randy Johnson	.75
229	Luis Gonzalez	.25
230	Mark Grace	.40
231	Junior Spivey	.15
232	Tony Womack	.15
233	Matt Williams	.25
234	Steve Finley	.15
235	Byung-Hyun Kim	.15
236	Craig Counsell	.15
237	Greg Maddux	1.00
238	Tom Glavine	.40
239	John Smoltz	.25
240	Chipper Jones	1.00
241	Gary Sheffield	.25
242	Andruw Jones	.40
243	Vinny Castilla	.15
244	Damian Moss	.15
245	Rafael Furcal	.15
246	Javy Lopez	.25
247	Kevin Millwood	.15
248	Kerry Wood	.75
249	Fred McGriff	.25
250	Sammy Sosa	1.00
251	Alex Gonzalez	.15
252	Corey Patterson	.25
253	Moises Alou	.15
254	Juan Cruz	.15
255	Jon Lieber	.15
256	Matt Clement	.15
257	Mark Prior	.75
258	Ken Griffey Jr.	1.00
259	Barry Larkin	.25
260	Adam Dunn	.50
261	Sean Casey	.15
262	Jose Rijo	.15
263	Elmer Dessens	.15
264	Austin Kearns	.25
265	Corky Miller	.15
266	Todd Walker	.15
267	Chris Reitsma	.15
268	Ryan Dempster	.15
269	Aaron Boone	.15
270	Danny Graves	.15
271	Brandon Larson	.15
272	Larry Walker	.25
273	Todd Helton	.50
274	Juan Uribe	.15
275	Juan Pierre	.15
276	Mike Hampton	.15
277	Todd Zeile	.15
278	Todd Hollandsworth	.15
279	Jason Jennings	.15
280	Josh Beckett	.40
281	Mike Lowell	.15
282	Derrek Lee	.25
283	A.J. Burnett	.15
284	Luis Castillo	.15
285	Tim Raines	.15
286	Preston Wilson	.15
287	Juan Encarnacion	.15
288	Charles Johnson	.15
289	Jeff Bagwell	.50
290	Craig Biggio	.25
291	Lance Berkman	.40
292	Daryle Ward	.15
293	Roy Oswalt	.40
294	Richard Hidalgo	.15
295	Octavio Dotel	.15
296	Wade Miller	.15
297	Julio Lugo	.15
298	Billy Wagner	.15
299	Shawn Green	.40
300	Adrian Beltre	.25
301	Paul LoDuca	.15
302	Eric Karros	.15
303	Kevin Brown	.15
304	Hideo Nomo	.40
305	Odalis Perez	.15
306	Eric Gagne	.40
307	Brian Jordan	.15
308	Cesar Izturis	.15
309	Mark Grudzielanek	.15
310	Kazuhisa Ishii	.15
311	Geoff Jenkins	.15
312	Richie Sexson	.40
313	Jose Hernandez	.15
314	Ben Sheets	.25
315	Ruben Quevedo	.15
316	Jeffrey Hammonds	.15
317	Alex Sanchez	.15
318	Eric Young	.15
319	Takahito Nomura	.15
320	Vladimir Guerrero	.75
321	Jose Vidro	.15
322	Orlando Cabrera	.15
323	Michael Barrett	.15
324	Javier Vazquez	.15
325	Tony Armas Jr.	.15
326	Andres Galarraga	.15
327	Tomokazu Ohka	.15
328	Bartolo Colon	.15
329	Fernando Tatis	.15
330	Brad Wilkerson	.15
331	Masato Yoshii	.15
332	Mike Piazza	1.00
333	Jeromy Burnitz	.15
334	Roberto Alomar	.50
335	Mo Vaughn	.15
336	Al Leiter	.25
337	Pedro Astacio	.15
338	Edgardo Alfonzo	.15
339	Armando Benitez	.15
340	Timoniel Perez	.15
341	Jay Payton	.15
342	Roger Cedeno	.15
343	Rey Ordonez	.15
344	Steve Trachsel	.15
345	Satoru Komiyama	.15
346	Scott Rolen	.75
347	Pat Burrell	.40
348	Bobby Abreu	.25
349	Mike Lieberthal	.15
350	Brandon Duckworth	.15
351	Jimmy Rollins	.25
352	Marlon Anderson	.15
353	Travis Lee	.15
354	Vicente Padilla	.15
355	Randy Wolf	.15
356	Jason Kendall	.15
357	Brian Giles	.25
358	Aramis Ramirez	.40
359	Pokey Reese	.15
360	Kip Wells	.15
361	Josh Fogg	.15
362	Mike Williams	.15
363	Jack Wilson	.15
364	Craig Wilson	.15
365	Kevin Young	.15
366	Ryan Klesko	.15
367	Phil Nevin	.15
368	Brian Lawrence	.15
369	Mark Kotsay	.15
370	Brett Tomko	.15
371	Trevor Hoffman	.15
372	Deivi Cruz	.15
373	Bubba Trammell	.15
374	Sean Burroughs	.15
375	Barry Bonds	2.00
376	Jeff Kent	.25
377	Rich Aurilia	.15
378	Tsuyoshi Shinjo	.15
379	Benito Santiago	.15
380	Kirk Rueter	.15
381	Livan Hernandez	.15
382	Russ Ortiz	.15
383	David Bell	.15
384	Jason Schmidt	.40
385	Reggie Sanders	.15
386	J.T. Snow	.15
387	Robb Nen	.15
388	Ryan Jensen	.15
389	Jim Edmonds	.40
390	J.D. Drew	.25
391	Albert Pujols	1.50
392	Fernando Vina	.15
393	Tino Martinez	.25
394	Edgar Renteria	.40
395	Matt Morris	.15
396	Woody Williams	.15
397	Jason Isringhausen	.15
398	Placido Polanco	.15
399	Eli Marrero	.15
400	Jason Simontacchi	.15

Stat Line Career

Cards serial numbered 251-400:	3-6X
Print run 151-250:	4-8X
Print run 101-150:	5-10X
Print run 61-100:	8-15X
Print run 31-60:	10-20X
Numbered to career stat.	

Stat Line Season

Cards serial numbered 151-200:	4-8X
Print run 101-150:	5-10X
Print run 61-100:	8-15X
Print run 31-60:	10-20X
Numbered to 2002 stat.	

All-Stars

	NM/M
Complete Set (10):	25.00
Common Player:	1.50
Retail only.	
1 Ichiro Suzuki	5.00
2 Alex Rodriguez	6.00
3 Nomar Garciaparra	3.00
4 Derek Jeter	6.00
5 Manny Ramirez	2.00
6 Barry Bonds	6.00
7 Adam Dunn	1.50
8 Mike Piazza	3.00
9 Sammy Sosa	4.00
10 Todd Helton	1.50

Anniversary 1983

	NM/M
Complete Set (20):	50.00
Common Player:	1.50
Inserted 1:12	
1 Dale Murphy	2.00
2 Jim Palmer	2.00
3 Nolan Ryan	6.00
4 Ozzie Smith	4.00
5 Tom Seaver	4.00
6 Mike Schmidt	5.00

7	Steve Carlton	2.00
8	Robin Yount	3.00
9	Ryne Sandberg	4.00
10	Cal Ripken Jr.	8.00
11	Fernando Valenzuela	1.50
12	Andre Dawson	2.00
13	George Brett	6.00
14	Eddie Murray	3.00
15	Dave Winfield	2.00
16	Johnny Bench	4.00
17	Wade Boggs	2.00
18	Tony Gwynn	4.00
19	San Diego Chicken	1.50
20	Ty Cobb	5.00

Bat Kings

		NM/M
Common Player:		10.00
Studio Series:		1.5-3X
Production 25 or 50		
1	Scott Rolen/250	20.00
2	Frank Thomas/250	15.00
3	Chipper Jones/250	20.00
4	Ivan Rodriguez/250	15.00
5	Stan Musial/100	40.00
6	Nomar Garciaparra/250	25.00
7	Vladimir Guerrero/250	15.00
8	Adam Dunn/250	15.00
9	Lance Berkman/250	10.00
10	Magglio Ordonez/250	10.00
11	Ernie Banks/50	40.00
12	Manny Ramirez/100	25.00
13	Mike Piazza/100	40.00
14	Alex Rodriguez/100	25.00
15	Todd Helton/100	20.00
16	Andre Dawson/100	20.00
17	Cal Ripken Jr/100	60.00
18	Tony Gwynn/100	25.00
19	Don Mattingly/100	60.00
20	Ryne Sandberg/100	45.00

Diamond Kings

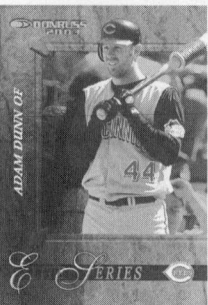

		NM/M
Complete Set (20):		120.00
Common Player:		2.00
Production 2,500 Sets		
Studio Series:		1.5-3X
Production 250 Sets		
1	Vladimir Guerrero	5.00
2	Derek Jeter	15.00
3	Adam Dunn	5.00
4	Greg Maddux	8.00
5	Lance Berkman	3.00
6	Ichiro Suzuki	10.00
7	Mike Piazza	8.00
8	Alex Rodriguez	10.00
9	Tom Glavine	3.00
10	Randy Johnson	8.00
11	Nomar Garciaparra	10.00
12	Jason Giambi	5.00
13	Sammy Sosa	8.00
14	Barry Zito	3.00
15	Chipper Jones	5.00
16	Magglio Ordonez	2.00
17	Larry Walker	2.00
18	Alfonso Soriano	8.00
19	Curt Schilling	4.00
20	Barry Bonds	15.00

Elite Series

		NM/M
Complete Set (15):		50.00
Common Player:		2.00
Production 2,500 Sets		
Dominators:		No Pricing
Production 25 Sets		
1	Alex Rodriguez	8.00
2	Barry Bonds	10.00
3	Ichiro Suzuki	8.00
4	Vladimir Guerrero	4.00
5	Randy Johnson	4.00
6	Pedro Martinez	4.00
7	Adam Dunn	3.00
8	Sammy Sosa	6.00
9	Jim Edmonds	2.00
10	Greg Maddux	6.00
11	Kazuhisa Ishii	2.00
12	Jason Giambi	3.00
13	Nomar Garciaparra	6.00
14	Tom Glavine	2.00
15	Todd Helton	3.00

Jersey Kings

		NM/M
Common Player:		10.00
Studio Series:		1.5-3X
Production 25 or 50		
1	Juan Gonzalez/250	15.00
2	Greg Maddux/250	20.00
3	Nomar Garciaparra/250	20.00
4	Troy Glaus/250	15.00
5	Reggie Jackson/100	20.00
6	Alex Rodriguez/250	25.00
7	Alfonso Soriano/250	15.00
8	Curt Schilling/250	12.00
9	Vladimir Guerrero/250	15.00
10	Adam Dunn/250	15.00
11	Mark Grace/100	25.00
12	Roger Clemens/100	30.00
13	Jeff Bagwell/100	25.00
14	Tom Glavine/100	20.00
15	Mike Piazza/100	25.00
16	Rod Carew/100	25.00
17	Rickey Henderson/100	25.00
18	Mike Schmidt/100	40.00
19	Cal Ripken Jr/100	60.00
20	Dale Murphy/100	15.00

Longball Leaders

		NM/M
Complete Set (10):		30.00
Common Player:		1.50
Production 1,000 Sets		
Seasonal Sum:		4-6X
Numbered to 2002 HR total.		
1	Alex Rodriguez	6.00
2	Alfonso Soriano	4.00
3	Rafael Palmeiro	2.00
4	Jim Thome	3.00
5	Jason Giambi	3.00
6	Sammy Sosa	5.00
7	Barry Bonds	8.00
8	Lance Berkman	2.00
9	Shawn Green	1.50
10	Vladimir Guerrero	4.00

Production Line

		NM/M
Complete Set (30):		120.00
Common Player:		2.00
Numbered to selected stat		
Die-Cuts:		1-3X
Production 100 Sets		
1	Alex Rodriguez/1,015	6.00
2	Jim Thome/1,122	3.00
3	Lance Berkman/982	2.00
4	Barry Bonds/1,381	8.00
5	Sammy Sosa/993	5.00
6	Vladimir Guerrero/1,010	3.00
7	Barry Bonds/582	10.00
8	Jason Giambi/435	6.00
9	Vladimir Guerrero/417	4.00
10	Adam Dunn/400	3.00
11	Troy Glaus/435	6.00
12	Todd Helton/429	3.00
13	Rafael Palmeiro/571	2.00
14	Sammy Sosa/594	6.00
15	Alex Rodriguez/623	6.00
16	Larry Walker/602	2.00
17	Lance Berkman/578	2.00
18	Alfonso Soriano/547	5.00
19	Ichiro Suzuki/321	8.00
20	Mike Sweeney/340	2.00
21	Manny Ramirez/349	4.00
22	Larry Walker/338	2.00
23	Barry Bonds/370	12.00
24	Jim Edmonds/311	2.00
25	Alfonso Soriano/300	6.00
26	Jason Giambi/335	6.00
27	Miguel Tejada/336	4.00
28	Brian Giles/309	3.00
29	Vladimir Guerrero/364	5.00
30	Pat Burrell/319	2.00

Timber and Threads

		NM/M
Common Player:		6.00
1	Al Kaline/Bat/125	25.00
2	Alex Rodriguez/Bat/350	20.00
3	Carlos Delgado/Bat/250	8.00
4	Cliff Floyd/Bat/250	8.00
5	Eddie Mathews/Bat/125	25.00
6	Edgar Martinez/Bat/125	10.00
7	Ernie Banks/Bat/50	40.00
8	Ivan Rodriguez/Bat/125	15.00
9	J.D. Drew/Bat/125	8.00
10	Jorge Posada/Bat/300	10.00
11	Lou Brock/Bat/125	20.00
12	Mike Piazza/Bat/125	25.00
13	Mike Schmidt/Bat/125	50.00
14	Reggie Jackson/Bat/125	20.00
15	Rickey Henderson/Bat/125	25.00
16	Robin Yount/Bat/125	35.00
17	Rod Carew/Bat/125	25.00
18	Scott Rolen/Bat/125	20.00
19	Shawn Green/Bat/200	8.00
20	Willie Stargell/Bat/125	15.00
21	Alex Rodriguez/Jsy/175	20.00
22	Andruw Jones/Jsy/275	8.00
23	Brooks Robinson/Jsy/150	25.00
24	Chipper Jones/Jsy/150	20.00
25	Greg Maddux/Jsy/175	20.00
26	Hideo Nomo/Jsy/300	40.00
27	Ivan Rodriguez/Jsy/225	10.00
28	Jack Morris/Jsy/150	8.00
29	J.D. Drew/Jsy/150	8.00
30	Jeff Bagwell/Jsy/500	15.00
31	Jim Thome/Jsy/200	15.00
32	John Smoltz/Jsy/175	8.00
33	John Olerud/Jsy/450	8.00
34	Kerry Wood/Jsy/200	15.00
35	Harmon Killebrew/Jsy/50	60.00
36	Larry Walker/Jsy/500	8.00
37	Magglio Ordonez/Jsy/150	10.00
38	Manny Ramirez/Jsy/500	15.00
39	Mike Piazza/Jsy/300	15.00
40	Mike Sweeney/Jsy/300	8.00
41	Nomar Garciaparra/Jsy/200	25.00
42	Paul Konerko/Jsy/500	10.00
43	Pedro Martinez/Jsy/175	15.00
44	Randy Johnson/Jsy/175	15.00
45	Roger Clemens/Jsy/350	20.00
46	Shawn Green/Jsy/250	8.00
47	Todd Helton/Jsy/175	8.00
48	Tom Glavine/Jsy/225	12.00
49	Tony Gwynn/Jsy/150	12.00
50	Vladimir Guerrero/Jsy/450	15.00

2003 Donruss Champions

		NM/M
Complete Set (300):		40.00
Common Player:		.15
Pack (8):		2.00
Box (24):		40.00
1	Adam Kennedy	.15
2	Alfredo Amezaga	.15
3	Chone Figgins	.15
4	Darin Erstad	.25
5	David Eckstein	.15
6	Garret Anderson	.40
7	Jarrod Washburn	.15
8	Nolan Ryan	2.00
9	Tim Salmon	.25
10	Troy Glaus	.40
11	Troy Percival	.15
12	Curt Schilling	.50
13	Junior Spivey	.15
14	Luis Gonzalez	.15
15	Mark Grace	.50
16	Randy Johnson	1.00
17	Steve Finley	.15
18	Andruw Jones	.40
19	Chipper Jones	.75
20	Dale Murphy	.50
21	Gary Sheffield	.40
22	Greg Maddux	1.00
23	John Smoltz	.25
24	Andy Pratt	.15
25	Adam LaRoche	.15
26	Trey Hodges	.15
27	Warren Spahn	.75
28	Cal Ripken Jr.	3.00
29	Ed Rogers	.15
30	Brian Roberts	.15
31	Geronimo Gil	.15
32	Jay Gibbons	.15
33	Josh Towers	.15
34	Casey Fossum	.15
35	Cliff Floyd	.15
36	Derek Lowe	.15
37	Fred Lynn	.15
38	Freddy Sanchez	.15
39	Manny Ramirez	.50
40	Nomar Garciaparra	1.00
41	Pedro J. Martinez	.75
42	Rickey Henderson	.50
43	Shea Hillenbrand	.15
44	Trot Nixon	.15
45	Bobby Hill	.15
46	Corey Patterson	.25
47	Fred McGriff	.25
48	Hee Seop Choi	.15
49	Juan Cruz	.15
50	Kerry Wood	.75
51	Mark Prior	1.00
52	Moises Alou	.25
53	Nic Jackson	.15
54	Ryne Sandberg	1.00
55	Sammy Sosa	1.50
56	Carlos Lee	.15
57	Corwin Malone	.15
58	Frank Thomas	.50
59	Joe Borchard	.15
60	Joe Crede	.15
61	Magglio Ordonez	.25
62	Mark Buehrle	.15
63	Paul Konerko	.25
64	Tim Hummel	.15
65	Jon Adkins	.15
66	Adam Dunn	.50
67	Austin Kearns	.25
68	Barry Larkin	.40
69	Jose Acevedo	.15
70	Corky Miller	.15
71	Eric Davis	.15
72	Ken Griffey Jr.	1.00
73	Sean Casey	.15
74	Wily Mo Pena	.25
75	Bob Feller	.50
76	Brian Tallet	.15
77	C.C. Sabathia	.15
78	Cliff Lee	.15
79	Earl Snyder	.15
80	Ellis Burks	.15
81	Jeremy Guthrie	.15
82	Travis Hafner	.25
83	Luis Garcia	.15
84	Omar Vizquel	.25
85	Ricardo Rodriguez	.15
86	Ryan Church	.15
87	Victor Martinez	.15
88	Brandon Phillips	.15
89	Jack Cust	.15
90	Jason Jennings	.15
91	Jeff Baker	.15
92	Garrett Atkins	.15
93	Juan Uribe	.15
94	Larry Walker	.25
95	Rene Reyes	.15
96	Todd Helton	.50
97	Alan Trammell	.25
98	Fernando Rodney	.15
99	Carlos Pena	.15
100	Jack Morris	.15
101	Bobby Higginson	.15
102	Mike Maroth	.15
103	Robert Fick	.15
104	Jesus Medrano	.15
105	Josh Beckett	.40
106	Luis Castillo	.25
107	Mike Lowell	.25
108	Juan Pierre	.15
109	Josh Wilson	.15
110	Tim Redding	.15
111	Carlos Hernandez	.15
112	Craig Biggio	.25
113	Henri Stanley	.15
114	Jason Lane	.15
115	Jeff Bagwell	.50
116	John Buck	.15
117	Kirk Saarloos	.15
118	Lance Berkman	.75
119	Nolan Ryan	2.00
120	Richard Hidalgo	.15
121	Rodrigo Rosario	.15
122	Roy Oswalt	.25
123	Tommy Whiteman RC	.15
124	Wade Miller	.15
125	Alexis Gomez	.15
126	Angel Berroa	.15
127	Brandon Berger	.15
128	Carlos Beltran	.40
129	George Brett	2.00
130	Jimmy Gobble	.15
131	Dee Brown	.15

132 Mike Sweeney .15
133 Raul Ibanez .15
134 Runelvys Hernandez .15
135 Adrian Beltre .40
136 Brian Jordan .15
137 Cesar Izturis .15
138 Victor Alvarez .15
139 Hideo Nomo .50
140 Joe Thurston .15
141 Kazuhisa Ishii .15
142 Kevin Brown .25
143 Odalis Perez .15
144 Paul LoDuca .15
145 Shawn Green .25
146 Ben Sheets .25
147 Bill Hall .15
148 Nick Neugebauer .15
149 Richie Sexson .40
150 Robin Yount 1.00
151 Shane Nance .15
152 Takahito Nomura .15
153 A.J. Pierzynski .15
154 Joe Mays .15
155 Kirby Puckett 1.00
156 Adam Johnson .15
157 Rob Bowen .15
158 Torii Hunter .40
159 Andres Galarraga .15
160 Endy Chavez .15
161 Javier Vazquez .15
162 Jose Vidro .15
163 Vladimir Guerrero .75
164 Dwight Gooden .15
165 Mike Piazza 1.00
166 Roberto Alomar .40
167 Tom Glavine .40
168 Alfonso Soriano .75
169 Bernie Williams .40
170 Brandon Claussen .15
171 Derek Jeter 2.00
172 Don Mattingly 1.50
173 Drew Henson .15
174 Jason Giambi .50
175 Joe Torre .25
176 Jorge Posada .40
177 Mike Mussina .50
178 Nick Johnson .15
179 Roger Clemens 1.50
180 Whitey Ford .75
181 Adam Morrissey .15
182 Barry Zito .40
183 David Justice .15
184 Eric Chavez .40
185 Jermaine Dye .15
186 Mark Mulder .25
187 Miguel Tejada .40
188 Reggie Jackson .75
189 Terrence Long .15
190 Tim Hudson .25
191 Anderson Machado .15
192 Bobby Abreu .40
193 Brandon Duckworth .15
194 Jim Thome .75
195 Eric Junge .15
196 Jeremy Giambi .15
197 Johnny Estrada .15
198 Jorge Padilla .15
199 Marlon Byrd .15
200 Mike Schmidt 1.50
201 Pat Burrell .50
202 Steve Carlton .25
203 Aramis Ramirez .25
204 Brian Giles .25
205 Carlos Rivera .15
206 Craig Wilson .15
207 Dave Williams .15
208 Jack Wilson .15
209 Jose Castillo .15
210 Kip Wells .15
211 Roberto Clemente 1.50
212 Walter Young .15
213 Ben Howard .15
214 Brian Lawrence .15
215 Clifford Bartosh .15
216 Dennis Tankersley .15
217 Oliver Perez .15
218 Phil Nevin .15
219 Ryan Klesko .25
220 Sean Burroughs .15
221 Tony Gwynn .75
222 Xavier Nady .15
223 Mike Rivera .15
224 Barry Bonds 2.00
225 Benito Santiago .15
226 Jason Schmidt .40
227 Jeff Kent .25
228 Kenny Lofton .15
229 Rich Aurilia .15
230 Robb Nen .15
231 Tsuyoshi Shinjo .15
232 Bret Boone .15
233 Chris Snelling .15
234 Edgar Martinez .25
235 Freddy Garcia .15
236 Ichiro Suzuki 1.50
237 John Olerud .25
238 Kazuhiro Sasaki .15
239 Mike Cameron .15
240 Rafael Soriano .15
241 Albert Pujols 1.50
242 J.D. Drew .40
243 Jim Edmonds .40
244 Ozzie Smith 1.00
245 Scott Rolen .75
246 So Taguchi .15
247 Stan Musial 1.00
248 Antonio Perez .15
249 Aubrey Huff .15
250 Dewon Brazelton .15
251 Delvin James .15
252 Joe Kennedy .15
253 Toby Hall .15
254 Alex Rodriguez 2.00
255 Ben Kozlowski .15
256 Gerald Laird .15
257 Hank Blalock .50
258 Ivan Rodriguez .50
259 Juan Gonzalez .50
260 Kevin Mench .15
261 Mario Ramos .15
262 Mark Teixeira .25
263 Nolan Ryan 2.00
264 Rafael Palmeiro .50
265 Alexis Rios .15
266 Carlos Delgado .40
267 Eric Hinske .15
268 Josh Phelps .15
269 Kevin Cash .15
270 Orlando Hudson .15
271 Roy Halladay .15
272 Shannon Stewart .15
273 Vernon Wells .15
274 Vinnie Chulk .15
275 Jason Anderson .15
276 Craig Brazell **RC** .50
277 Terrmel Sledge **RC** .50
278 Ryan Cameron **RC** .50
279 Clint Barmes **RC** .50
280 Jhonny Peralta .50
281 Todd Wellemeyer **RC** .50
282 Jon Leicester **RC** .40
283 Brandon Webb **RC** 2.00
284 Tim Olson **RC** .50
285 Matt Kata **RC** .75
286 Rob Hammock **RC** .50
287 Pete LaForest **RC** .50
288 Nook Logan **RC** .50
289 Prentice Redman **RC** .40
290 Joe Valentine **RC** .40
291 Jose Contreras **RC** 1.00
292 Josh Stewart **RC** .40
293 Mike Nicolas **RC** .40
294 Marshall McDougall .15
295 Travis Chapman .15
296 Jose Morban .15
297 Michael Hessman **RC** .40
298 Buddy Hernandez **RC** .40
299 Shane Victorino **RC** .40
300 Jason Dubois .15
301 Hideki Matsui **RC** 3.00

Metalized

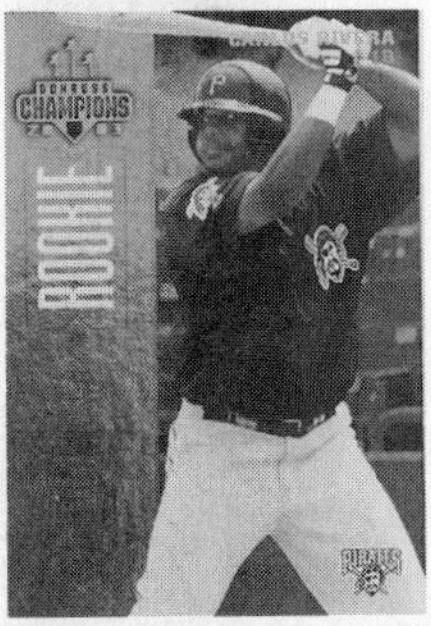

Stars: 4-8X
RC's: 1-3X
Production 100 Sets
Holofoils: No Pricing
Production 25 Sets

Autographs

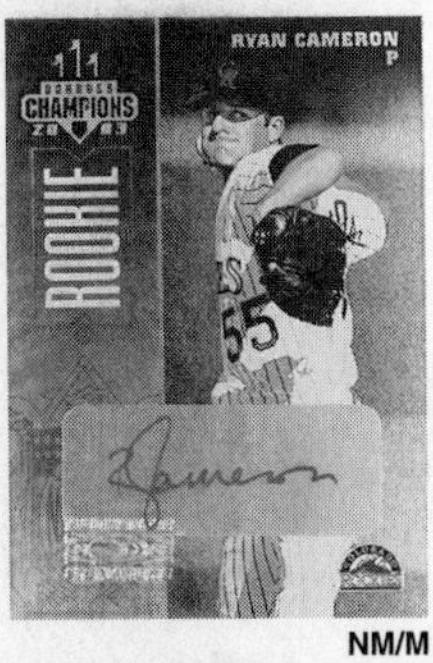

NM/M

Common Autograph: 5.00
2 Alfredo Amezaga/325 8.00
3 Chone Figgins/375 10.00
13 Junior Spivey/45 10.00
24 Andy Pratt/475 8.00
25 Adam LaRoche/400 10.00
26 Trey Hodges/305 5.00
29 Ed Rogers/305 5.00
30 Brian Roberts/500 35.00
31 Geronimo Gil/150 8.00
32 Jay Gibbons/475 8.00
33 Josh Towers/500 10.00
34 Casey Fossum/160 5.00
35 Cliff Floyd/70 20.00
37 Fred Lynn/80 20.00
38 Freddy Sanchez/400 15.00
46 Corey Patterson/100 15.00
49 Juan Cruz/250 8.00
51 Mark Prior/50 30.00
53 Nic Jackson/100 10.00
57 Corwin Malone/400 8.00
59 Joe Borchard/215 8.00
64 Tim Hummel/400 5.00
65 Jon Adkins/400 5.00
66 Adam Dunn/100 30.00
67 Austin Kearns/50 20.00
69 Jose Acevedo/315 5.00
70 Corky Miller/295 5.00
71 Eric Davis/45 25.00
74 Wily Mo Pena/450 15.00
76 Brian Tallet/250 8.00
78 Cliff Lee/330 15.00
79 Earl Snyder/225 8.00
81 Jeremy Guthrie/400 8.00
83 Luis Garcia/395 5.00
86 Ryan Church/395 10.00
87 Victor Martinez/250 25.00
88 Brandon Phillips/375 10.00
89 Jack Cust/498 10.00
90 Jason Jennings/375 8.00
91 Jeff Baker/400 8.00
92 Garrett Atkins/400 8.00
95 Rene Reyes/350 8.00
98 Fernando Rodney/500 8.00
100 Jack Morris/50 20.00
102 Mike Maroth/400 8.00
104 Jesus Medrano/500 8.00
109 Josh Wilson/400 8.00
110 Tim Redding/375 8.00
111 Carlos Hernandez/250 8.00
113 Henri Stanley/390 5.00
114 Jason Lane/250 10.00
117 Kirk Saarloos/149 8.00
120 Richard Hidalgo/120 10.00
121 Rodrigo Rosario/500 10.00
122 Roy Oswalt/100 20.00
124 Wade Miller/125 10.00
126 Angel Berroa/400 10.00
127 Brandon Berger/325 8.00
130 Jimmy Gobble/400 8.00
131 Dee Brown/500 8.00
132 Mike Sweeney/45 20.00
134 Runelvys Hernandez/400 5.00
138 Victor Alvarez/308 8.00
144 Paul LoDuca/45 20.00
146 Ben Sheets/50 20.00
147 Bill Hall/450 10.00
148 Nick Neugebauer/375 5.00
151 Shane Nance/150 8.00
152 Takahito Nomura/50 20.00
153 A.J. Pierzynski/250 10.00
156 Adam Johnson/500 8.00
157 Rob Bowen/375 8.00
158 Torii Hunter/45 20.00
160 Endy Chavez/280 10.00
161 Javier Vazquez/50 15.00
162 Jose Vidro/45 15.00
164 Dwight Gooden/45 30.00
170 Brandon Claussen/475 10.00
178 Nick Johnson/500 8.00
181 Adam Morrissey/395 8.00
185 Jermaine Dye/125 15.00
189 Terrence Long/250 10.00
191 Anderson Machado/500 8.00
193 Brandon Duckworth/100 10.00
195 Eric Junge/279 8.00
196 Jeremy Giambi/195 8.00
205 Carlos Rivera/400 8.00
206 Craig Wilson/245 10.00
207 Dave Williams/265 8.00
208 Jack Wilson/500 15.00
212 Walter Young/400 8.00
213 Ben Howard/500 8.00
214 Brian Lawrence/500 8.00
215 Clifford Bartosh/400 8.00
222 Xavier Nady/250 8.00
223 Mike Rivera/90 8.00
233 Chris Snelling/200 8.00
240 Rafael Soriano/500 8.00
248 Antonio Perez/500 8.00
249 Aubrey Huff/475 15.00
250 Dewon Brazelton/50 15.00
251 Delvin James/400 8.00
252 Joe Kennedy/250 8.00
253 Toby Hall/500 8.00
255 Ben Kozlowski/400 8.00
256 Gerald Laird/450 8.00
257 Hank Blalock/50 25.00
260 Kevin Mench/475 10.00
261 Mario Ramos/475 5.00
262 Mark Teixeira/40 40.00
265 Alexis Rios/50 20.00
267 Eric Hinske/390 10.00
269 Kevin Cash/375 8.00
274 Vinnie Chulk/100 10.00
275 Jason Anderson/493 15.00
276 Craig Brazell/500 15.00
277 Terrmel Sledge/500 10.00
278 Ryan Cameron/475 8.00
279 Clint Barmes/475 15.00
280 Jhonny Peralta/500 15.00
281 Todd Wellemeyer/477 10.00
282 Jon Leicester/480 8.00
283 Brandon Webb/500 50.00
284 Tim Olson/500 10.00
285 Matt Kata/487 10.00
286 Rob Hammock/486 10.00
287 Pete LaForest/500 10.00
288 Nook Logan/500 10.00
289 Prentice Redman/488 10.00
290 Joe Valentine/475 8.00
291 Jose Contreras/100 25.00
292 Josh Stewart/485 10.00
293 Mike Nicolas/500 10.00
295 Travis Chapman/100 15.00
296 Jose Morban/475 8.00
297 Michael Hessman/500 8.00
298 Buddy Hernandez/500 8.00
299 Shane Victorino/480 8.00
300 Jason Dubois/480 10.00
302 Ryan Wagner/100 15.00
303 Adam Loewen/100 10.00
304 Chien-Ming Wang/100 200.00
305 Hong-Chih Kuo/100 80.00
307 Dan Haren/100 25.00
309 Ramon Nivar/100 15.00

Call to the Hall

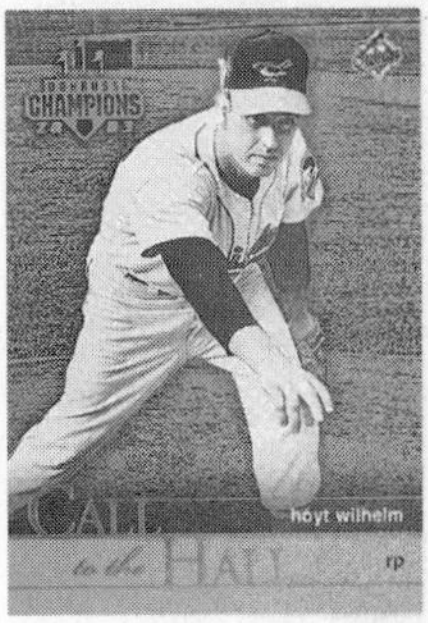

NM/M

Complete Set (10): 30.00
Common Player: 2.00
Metalized: 2-4X
Production 100 Sets
Holofoils: No Pricing
Production 25 Sets
1 Nolan Ryan/2,490 10.00
2 Tom Seaver/2,490 4.00
3 Phil Rizzuto/2,500 4.00
4 Orlando Cepeda/2,500 2.00
5 Al Kaline/2,500 5.00
6 Hoyt Wilhelm/2,500 2.00
7 Luis Aparicio/2,500 2.00
8 Billy Williams/2,500 2.00
9 Jim Palmer/2,500 2.00
10 Mike Schmidt/2,500 6.00

Call to the Hall Autographs

No Pricing
Quantity produced listed

Grand Champions

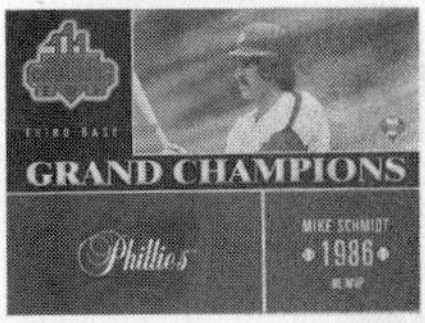

NM/M

Complete Set (25): 80.00
Common Player: 2.00
Inserted 1:18
Metalized: 2-4X
Production 100 Sets
Holo Foils: No Pricing
Production 25 Sets
1 Stan Musial 6.00
2 Bob Feller 2.00
3 Reggie Jackson 3.00
4 George Brett 8.00
5 Jim Palmer 2.00
6 Harmon Killebrew 4.00
7 Ernie Banks 4.00
8 Frank Robinson 2.00
9 Greg Maddux 4.00
10 Whitey Ford 4.00
11 Bob Gibson 4.00
12 Mike Schmidt 6.00
13 Nolan Ryan 10.00
14 Warren Spahn 4.00
15 Rod Carew 3.00
16 Hoyt Wilhelm 2.00
17 Duke Snider 4.00
18 Tom Seaver 4.00

19	Steve Carlton	3.00
20	Yogi Berra	4.00
21	Cal Ripken Jr.	10.00
22	Tony Gwynn	4.00
23	Wade Boggs	2.00
24	Rickey Henderson	3.00
25	Roger Clemens	8.00

Grand Champions Autos.

No Pricing

Numbers Game

NM/M

Quantity produced listed

1	Vladimir Guerrero/Jsy/200	10.00
2	Nomar Garciaparra/Jsy/200	20.00
3	Magglio Ordonez/Jsy/100	8.00
4	Garret Anderson/Jsy/50	15.00
5	Derek Jeter/Base/200	20.00
6	Jim Thome/Jsy/200	8.00
7	Torii Hunter/Jsy/200	10.00
8	Todd Helton/Jsy/200	10.00
9	Andruw Jones/Jsy/200	6.00
11	Luis Gonzalez/Jsy/200	5.00
12	Manny Ramirez/Jsy/200	12.00
13	Paul Konerko/Jsy/200	6.00
14	Alex Rodriguez/Jsy/200	20.00
15	Carlos Beltran/Jsy/200	4.00
16	Bernie Williams/Jsy/200	8.00
17	Barry Bonds/Base/200	20.00
18	Miguel Tejada/Jsy/50	15.00
19	Jason Giambi/Base/200	8.00
20	Ichiro Suzuki/Base/200	25.00
21	Ivan Rodriguez/Jsy/100	15.00
22	Rafael Palmeiro/Jsy/200	10.00
23	Carlos Delgado/Jsy/200	5.00
24	Vernon Wells/Jsy/200	4.00
25	Sammy Sosa/Jsy/200	20.00
26	Chipper Jones/Jsy/200	12.00
27	Adam Dunn/Jsy/44	25.00
28	Larry Walker/Jsy/200	8.00
29	Shawn Green/Jsy/100	10.00
30	Richie Sexson/Jsy/200	6.00
31	Jose Vidro/Jsy/200	4.00
32	Mike Piazza/Jsy/50	40.00
33	Roberto Alomar/Jsy/100	15.00
34	Bobby Abreu/Jsy/200	5.00
35	Pat Burrell/Jsy/200	8.00
36	Brian Giles/Jsy/200	6.00
37	Albert Pujols/Base/200	15.00
38	Lance Berkman/Jsy/50	15.00
39	Ryan Klesko/Jsy/200	6.00
40	Jeff Kent/Jsy/200	4.00

Team Colors

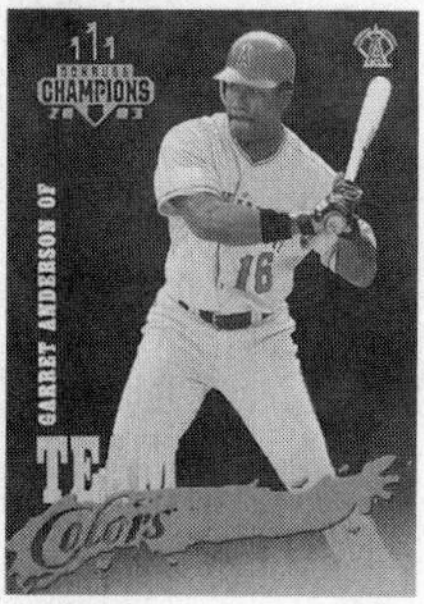

NM/M

Complete Set (30):		60.00
Common Player:		1.00
Inserted 1:10		
1	Miguel Tejada	1.50
2	Mike Schmidt	5.00
3	George Brett	6.00
4	Magglio Ordonez	1.00
5	Ryne Sandberg	4.00
6	Adam Dunn	1.50
7	Mark Prior	2.00
8	Tony Gwynn	2.00
9	Troy Glaus	1.50
10	Stan Musial	4.00
11	Kirby Puckett	3.00
12	Don Mattingly	5.00
13	Bobby Abreu	1.00
14	Ichiro Suzuki	4.00
15	Cal Ripken Jr.	8.00
16	Chipper Jones	3.00
17	Carlos Beltran	1.50
18	Alfonso Soriano	2.00
19	Albert Pujols	5.00
20	Andruw Jones	1.50
21	Bernie Williams	1.50
22	Todd Helton	1.50
23	Roberto Clemente	6.00
24	Jim Thome	1.50
25	Carlos Delgado	1.00
26	Derek Jeter	6.00
27	Garret Anderson	1.00
28	Nomar Garciaparra	4.00
29	Torii Hunter	1.00
30	Vladimir Guerrero	2.00

Team Colors Materials

NM/M

Quantity produced listed

1	Miguel Tejada/Jsy/50	15.00
2	Mike Schmidt/Jsy/200	35.00
3	George Brett/Jsy/200	35.00
4	Magglio Ordonez/Jsy/100	8.00
5	Ryne Sandberg/Jsy/200	30.00
6	Adam Dunn/Jsy/44	20.00
7	Mark Prior/Jsy/200	8.00
8	Tony Gwynn/Jsy/200	15.00
9	Troy Glaus/Jsy/200	8.00
10	Stan Musial/Jsy/200	35.00
11	Kirby Puckett/Jsy/200	15.00
12	Don Mattingly/Jsy/200	40.00
13	Bobby Abreu/Jsy/200	5.00
14	Ichiro Suzuki/Base/200	25.00
15	Cal Ripken Jr./Jsy/200	40.00
16	Chipper Jones/Jsy/200	12.00
17	Carlos Beltran/Jsy/200	8.00
19	Albert Pujols/Base/200	15.00
20	Andruw Jones/Jsy/200	6.00
21	Bernie Williams/Jsy/200	8.00
22	Todd Helton/Jsy/200	10.00
23	Roberto Clemente/Jsy/200	80.00
24	Jim Thome/Jsy/200	8.00
25	Carlos Delgado/Jsy/200	5.00
26	Derek Jeter/Base/200	20.00
27	Garret Anderson/Jsy/50	12.00
28	Nomar Garciaparra/Jsy/200	20.00
29	Torii Hunter/Jsy/200	10.00
30	Vladimir Guerrero/ Jsy/200	10.00

Total Game

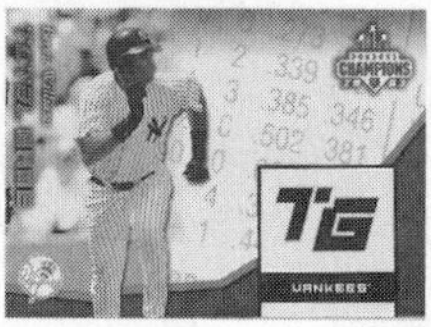

NM/M

Complete Set (40):		60.00
Common Player:		1.00
Inserted 1:9		
1	Vladimir Guerrero	2.00
2	Nomar Garciaparra	4.00
3	Magglio Ordonez	1.00
4	Garret Anderson	1.00
5	Derek Jeter	6.00
6	Jim Thome	1.50
7	Torii Hunter	1.50
8	Todd Helton	1.50
9	Andruw Jones	1.50
10	Alfonso Soriano	2.00
11	Luis Gonzalez	1.00
12	Manny Ramirez	1.50
13	Paul Konerko	1.00
14	Alex Rodriguez	5.00
15	Carlos Beltran	1.00
16	Bernie Williams	1.50
17	Barry Bonds	6.00
18	Miguel Tejada	1.00
19	Jason Giambi	1.00
20	Ichiro Suzuki	4.00
21	Ivan Rodriguez	1.50
22	Rafael Palmeiro	1.50
23	Carlos Delgado	1.00
24	Vernon Wells	1.00
25	Sammy Sosa	4.00
26	Chipper Jones	2.00
27	Adam Dunn	1.50
28	Larry Walker	1.00
29	Shawn Green	1.00
30	Richie Sexson	1.00
31	Jose Vidro	1.00
32	Mike Piazza	3.00
33	Roberto Alomar	1.50
34	Bobby Abreu	1.00
35	Pat Burrell	1.00
36	Brian Giles	1.00
37	Albert Pujols	5.00
38	Lance Berkman	1.00
39	Ryan Klesko	1.00
40	Jeff Kent	1.00

Statistical Champs

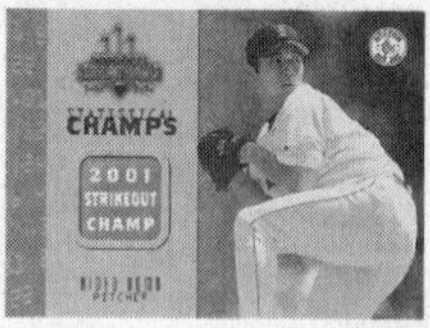

NM/M

Complete Set (30):		40.00
Common Player:		1.00
Inserted 1:10		
1	Alex Rodriguez	5.00
2	Alfonso Soriano	2.00
3	Curt Schilling	1.50
4	Eddie Mathews	2.00
5	Fred Lynn	1.00
6	Harmon Killebrew	2.00
7	Hideo Nomo	1.00
8	Jim Thome	1.50
9	Kirby Puckett	3.00
10	Luis Gonzalez	1.00
11	Manny Ramirez	1.50
12	Jason Giambi	1.00
13	Mike Schmidt	4.00
14	Nomar Garciaparra	4.00
15	Lou Brock	1.50
16	Randy Johnson	2.00
17	Reggie Jackson	2.00
18	Rickey Henderson	1.50
19	Roberto Clemente	5.00
20	Barry Zito	1.50
21	Todd Helton	1.50
22	Tom Seaver	3.00
23	Tony Gwynn	2.00
24	Torii Hunter	1.00
25	Troy Glaus	1.00
26	Wade Boggs	1.50
27	Rod Carew	1.50
28	Juan Gonzalez	1.50
29	Sammy Sosa	3.00
30	Warren Spahn	2.00

Statistical Champs Materials

NM/M

Quantity produced listed

1	Alex Rodriguez/Jsy/250	20.00
3	Curt Schilling/Jsy/225	8.00
4	Eddie Mathews/Jsy/200	20.00
6	Harmon Killebrew/Jsy/250	20.00
7	Hideo Nomo/Jsy/110	50.00
8	Jim Thome/Jsy/250	8.00
9	Kirby Puckett/Jsy/250	20.00
10	Luis Gonzalez/Jsy/250	5.00
11	Manny Ramirez/Jsy/155	10.00
12	Jason Giambi/Jsy/250	10.00
13	Mike Schmidt/Jsy/250	35.00
14	Nomar Garciaparra/Jsy/99	30.00
15	Lou Brock/Jsy/250	15.00
16	Randy Johnson/Jsy/100	15.00
17	Reggie Jackson/Jsy/200	15.00
18	Rickey Henderson/Jsy/184	15.00
20	Barry Zito/Jsy/100	10.00
21	Todd Helton/Jsy/250	10.00
22	Tom Seaver/Jsy/100	30.00
23	Tony Gwynn/Jsy/200	15.00
24	Torii Hunter/Jsy/250	10.00
25	Troy Glaus/Jsy/125	10.00
26	Wade Boggs/Jsy/250	15.00
27	Rod Carew/Hat/150	15.00
28	Juan Gonzalez/Jsy/250	8.00
29	Sammy Sosa/Jsy/250	20.00
30	Warren Spahn/Jsy/150	30.00

World Series Champions

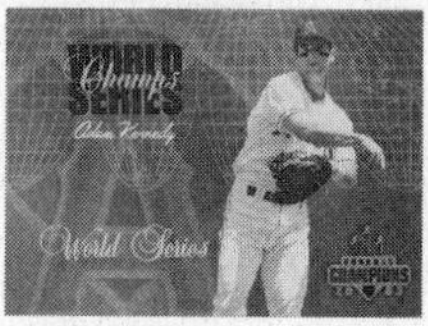

NM/M

Complete Set (15):		20.00
Common Player:		1.50
Production 2,002 Sets		
Metalized:		2-3X
Production 100 Sets		
Holo Foil:		No Pricing
Production 25 Sets		
1	Troy Glaus	3.00
2	Jarrod Washburn	1.50
3	Darin Erstad	2.50
4	Troy Percival	1.50
5	David Eckstein	1.50
6	Francisco Rodriguez	2.00
7	Garret Anderson	2.50
8	John Lackey	1.50
9	Tim Salmon	2.00
10	Chone Figgins	1.50
11	Adam Kennedy	1.50
12	Scott Spiezio	1.50
13	Ben Molina	1.50
14	Brad Fullmer	1.50
15	Troy Glaus MVP	3.00

World Series Champions Autograph

No Pricing

2003 Donruss Classics

NM/M

Complete Set (200):		
Common Player:		.40
Common Legends (101-150):		3.00
Production 1,500		
Common Prospect (151-200):		3.00
Production 1,500		
Pack (7):		4.50
Box (18):		70.00
1	Troy Glaus	.50
2	Barry Bonds	3.00
3	Miguel Tejada	.50
4	Randy Johnson	1.00
5	Eric Hinske	.40
6	Barry Zito	.50
7	Jason Jennings	.40
8	Derek Jeter	3.00
9	Vladimir Guerrero	1.00
10	Corey Patterson	.50

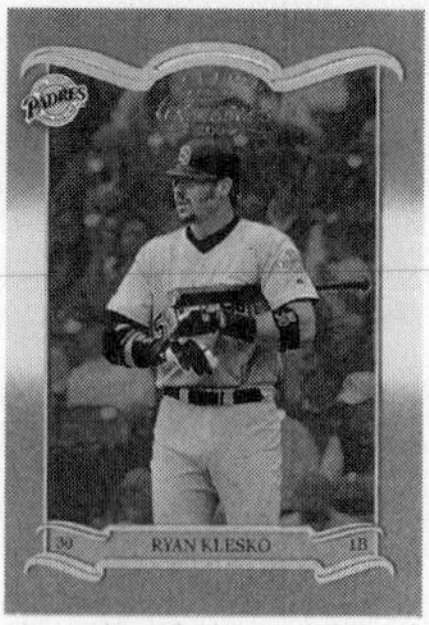

11	Manny Ramirez	.75
12	Edgar Martinez	.50
13	Roy Oswalt	.50
14	Andruw Jones	.75
15	Alex Rodriguez	3.00
16	Mark Mulder	.50
17	Kazuhisa Ishii	.40
18	Gary Sheffield	.50
19	Jay Gibbons	.40
20	Roberto Alomar	.50
21	A.J. Pierzynski	.40
22	Eric Chavez	.50
23	Roger Clemens	2.00
24	C.C. Sabathia	.40
25	Jose Vidro	.40
26	Shannon Stewart	.40
27	Mark Teixeira	.50
28	Joe Thurston	.40
29	Josh Beckett	.75
30	Jeff Bagwell	.75
31	Geronimo Gil	.40
32	Curt Schilling	.75
33	Frank Thomas	.75
34	Lance Berkman	.50
35	Adam Dunn	.75
36	Christian Parker	.40
37	Jim Thome	1.00
38	Shawn Green	.50
39	Drew Henson	.40
40	Chipper Jones	1.00
41	Kevin Mench	.40
42	Hideo Nomo	.50
43	Andres Galarraga	.40
44	Doug Davis	.40
45	Mark Prior	1.00
46	Sean Casey	.40
47	Magglio Ordonez	.50
48	Tom Glavine	.50
49	Marlon Byrd	.40
50	Albert Pujols	2.00
51	Mark Buehrle	.40
52	Aramis Ramirez	.50
53	Pat Burrell	.50
54	Craig Biggio	.50
55	Alfonso Soriano	1.00
56	Kerry Wood	1.00
57	Wade Miller	.40
58	Hank Blalock	.75
59	Cliff Floyd	.40
60	Jason Giambi	.50
61	Carlos Beltran	.50
62	Brian Roberts	.40
63	Paul LoDuca	.40
64	Tim Redding	.40
65	Sammy Sosa	2.00
66	Joe Borchard	.40
67	Ryan Klesko	.40
68	Richie Sexson	.50
69	Carlos Lee	.40
70	Rickey Henderson	.75
71	Brian Tallet	.40
72	Luis Gonzalez	.50
73	Satoru Komiyama	.40
74	Tim Hudson	.50
75	Ken Griffey Jr.	1.50
76	Adam Johnson	.40
77	Bobby Abreu	.60
78	Adrian Beltre	.40
79	Rafael Palmeiro	.75
80	Ichiro Suzuki	2.00
81	Kenny Lofton	.40
82	Brian Giles	.50
83	Barry Larkin	.50
84	Robert Fick	.40
85	Ben Sheets	.50
86	Scott Rolen	1.00
87	Nomar Garciaparra	1.50
88	Brandon Phillips	.40
89	Ben Kozlowski	.40
90	Bernie Williams	.75
91	Pedro J. Martinez	1.00
92	Todd Helton	.75
93	Jermaine Dye	.40
94	Carlos Delgado	.50
95	Mike Piazza	1.50
96	Junior Spivey	.40
97	Torii Hunter	.50
98	Mike Sweeney	.40
99	Ivan Rodriguez	.75
100	Greg Maddux	1.50
101	Ernie Banks	5.00

102 Steve Garvey 3.00
103 George Brett 8.00
104 Lou Brock 3.00
105 Hoyt Wilhelm 3.00
106 Steve Carlton 4.00
107 Joe Torre 3.00
108 Dennis Eckersley 4.00
109 Reggie Jackson 5.00
110 Al Kaline 8.00
111 Harold Reynolds 3.00
112 Don Mattingly 8.00
113 Tony Gwynn 5.00
114 Willie McCovey 4.00
115 Joe Morgan 3.00
116 Stan Musial 8.00
117 Jim Palmer 3.00
118 Brooks Robinson 5.00
119 Don Sutton 3.00
120 Nolan Ryan 10.00
121 Mike Schmidt 6.00
122 Tom Seaver 5.00
123 Cal Ripken Jr. 8.00
124 Robin Yount 5.00
125 Bob Feller 3.00
126 Joe Carter 3.00
127 Jack Morris 3.00
128 Luis Aparicio 3.00
129 Bobby Doerr 3.00
130 Dave Parker 3.00
131 Yogi Berra 5.00
132 Will Clark 3.00
133 Fred Lynn 3.00
134 Andre Dawson 3.00
135 Duke Snider 4.00
136 Orlando Cepeda 3.00
137 Billy Williams 3.00
138 Dale Murphy 4.00
139 Harmon Killebrew 5.00
140 Kirby Puckett 6.00
141 Carlton Fisk 3.00
142 Eric Davis 3.00
143 Alan Trammell 3.00
144 Paul Molitor 5.00
145 Jose Canseco 3.00
146 Ozzie Smith 5.00
147 Ralph Kiner 3.00
148 Dwight Gooden 3.00
149 Phil Rizzuto 5.00
150 Lenny Dykstra 3.00
151 Adam LaRoche 4.00
152 Tim Hummel 3.00
153 Matt Kata **RC** 4.00
154 Jeff Baker 3.00
155 Josh Stewart **RC** 3.00
156 Marshall McDougall 4.00
157 Jhonny Peralta 4.00
158 Mike Nicolas **RC** 3.00
159 Jeremy Guthrie 3.00
160 Craig Brazell **RC** 4.00
161 Joe Valentine **RC** 4.00
162 Buddy Hernandez 3.00
163 Freddy Sanchez 4.00
164 Shane Victorino **RC** 4.00
165 Corwin Malone 4.00
166 Jason Dubois 3.00
167 Josh Wilson 3.00
168 Tim Olson **RC** 3.00
169 Clifford Bartosh 3.00
170 Michael Hessman **RC** 4.00
171 Ryan Church 5.00
172 Garrett Atkins 4.00
173 Jose Morban 3.00
174 Ryan Cameron **RC** 4.00
175 Todd Wellemeyer **RC** 4.00
176 Travis Chapman 3.00
177 Jason Anderson 4.00
178 Adam Morrissey 3.00
179 Jose Contreras **RC** 5.00
180 Nic Jackson 3.00
181 Rob Hammock **RC** 4.00
182 Carlos Rivera 3.00
183 Vinnie Chulk 3.00
184 Pete LaForest **RC** 3.00
185 Jon Leicester **RC** 4.00
186 Termel Sledge **RC** 3.00
187 Jose Castillo 3.00
188 Gerald Laird 3.00
189 Nook Logan **RC** 4.00
190 Clint Barmes **RC** 5.00
191 Jesus Medrano 3.00
192 Henri Stanley 4.00
193 Hideki Matsui **RC** 10.00
194 Walter Young 3.00
195 Jon Adkins 3.00
196 Tommy Whiteman **RC** 4.00
197 Rob Bowen 3.00
198 Brandon Webb **RC** 8.00
199 Prentice Redman **RC** 4.00
200 Jimmy Gobble 3.00

Combos

NM/M

Varying quantities produced
CC1 Babe Ruth, Lou Gehrig/50 475.00
CC2 Jackie Robinson, Pee Wee Reese/50 80.00
CC3 Bobby Doerr, Fred Lynn/25 65.00
CC4 Honus Wagner, Roberto Clemente/50 150.00
CC5 Kirby Puckett, Torii Hunter/25 75.00
CC6 Sammy Sosa, Ryne Sandberg/25 100.00
CC7 Hideo Nomo, Kazuhisa Ishii/25 75.00
CC8 Mike Schmidt, Steve Carlton/25 150.00
CC9 Robin Yount, Paul Molitor/25 100.00
CC12 Don Mattingly, Jason Giambi/25 150.00
CC13 Stan Musial, Ozzie Smith/25 100.00

Dress Code

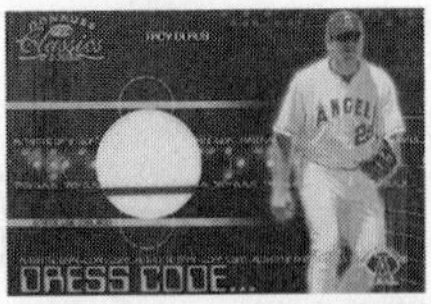

NM/M

Common Player: 4.00
Quantity produced listed
1 Roger Clemens/Jsy/500 15.00
2 M. Tejada/Jsy/Hat/Bat/250 20.00
3 V. Guerrero/Jsy/425 8.00
4 Kazuhisa Ishii/Jsy/250 10.00
5 Chipper Jones/Jsy/425 10.00
6 Troy Glaus/Jsy/425 8.00
7 Rafael Palmeiro/Jsy/425 8.00
8 Rickey Henderson/Jsy/250 10.00
9 Pedro Martinez/Jsy/425 8.00
10 Andruw Jones/Jsy/425 6.00
11 Nomar Garciaparra/Jsy/500 12.00
12 Carlos Delgado/Jsy/500 5.00
13 R.Henderson/Jsy/Hat/250 20.00
14 K. Wood/Jsy/Hat/250 20.00
15 L. Berkman/Jsy/Hat/50 20.00
16 Tony Gwynn/Quad/100 65.00
17 Mark Mulder/Jsy/425 8.00
18 Jim Thome/Jsy/500 8.00
19 Mike Piazza/Jsy/500 15.00
20 Mike Mussina/Jsy/500 10.00
21 Luis Gonzalez/Jsy/500 5.00
22 Ryan Klesko/Jsy/500 5.00
23 Richie Sexson/Jsy/500 6.00
24 Curt Schilling/Jsy/200 10.00
25 A. Rodriguez/Jsy/500 12.00
26 B. Williams/Jsy/425 8.00
27 Cal Ripken Jr/Jsy/500 35.00
28 C.C. Sabathia/Jsy/500 4.00
29 M. Piazza/Bat/Jsy/200 30.00
30 Rickey Henderson/Hat/Jsy/250 15.00
31 Torii Hunter/Jsy/425 8.00
32 Mark Teixeira/Jsy/425 8.00
33 D. Murphy/Jsy/Bat/300 15.00
34 Todd Helton/Jsy/425 8.00
35 Eric Chavez/Jsy/425 8.00
36 Vernon Wells/Jsy/425 5.00
37 J. Bagwell/Jsy/Hat/100 25.00
38 Nick Johnson/Jsy/425 5.00
39 Tim Hudson/Jsy/Hat/250 10.00
40 Shawn Green/Jsy/425 5.00
41 Mark Buehrle/Jsy/500 5.00
42 Garret Anderson/Jsy/100 5.00
43 Alex Rodriguez/Jsy/500 12.00
44 Jason Giambi/Jsy/500 8.00
45 Carlos Beltran/Jsy/500 5.00
46 Adam Dunn/Jsy/Hat/100 30.00
47 Jorge Posada/Jsy/425 8.00
48 Roy Oswalt/Jsy/Hat/200 15.00
49 Rich Aurilia/Jsy/500 5.00
50 Jason Jennings/Quad/250 15.00
51 Mark Prior/Quad/250 40.00
52 Jim Edmonds/Jsy/500 8.00
53 Fred McGriff/Jsy/500 8.00
54 A. Soriano/Jsy/Shoe/100 15.00
55 Jeff Kent/Jsy/425 5.00
56 Hideo Nomo/Jsy/200 30.00
57 Manny Ramirez/Jsy/425 8.00
58 J. Canseco/Jsy/Bat/350 15.00
59 M. Ordonez/Jsy/500 6.00
60 A. Trammell/Jsy/Bat/250 10.00
61 Bobby Abreu/Jsy/500 6.00
62 R.Henderson/Dual Jsy/200 20.00
63 Josh Beckett/Jsy/500 6.00
64 Barry Larkin/Jsy/500 8.00
65 Randy Johnson/Jsy/200 10.00
66 Juan Gonzalez/Jsy/500 8.00
67 Barry Zito/Jsy/Hat/125 15.00
68 Roger Clemens/Jsy/500 15.00
69 Rickey Henderson/Hat/Jsy/100 25.00
70 Hideo Nomo/Jsy/100 50.00
71 Paul Konerko/Jsy/400 6.00
72 Pat Burrell/Jsy/400 8.00
73 F.Thomas/Jsy/Pan ts/250 15.00
74 Sammy Sosa/Jsy/500 15.00
75 G. Maddux/Glove/Jsy/50 60.00

Legendary Hats

NM/M

Varying quantities produced
1 Roberto Clemente/80 100.00
2 Kirby Puckett/50 50.00
3 Mike Schmidt/50 75.00
4 Tony Gwynn/50 50.00
5 Rickey Henderson/50 60.00

Legendary Spikes

NM/M

Production 50 Sets
1 Kirby Puckett 60.00
2 Tony Gwynn 50.00
3 Don Mattingly 125.00
4 Frank Robinson 35.00
5 Gary Carter 30.00

Legendary Leather

NM/M

Varying quantities produced
1 Nolan Ryan/80 110.00

Legendary Lumberjacks

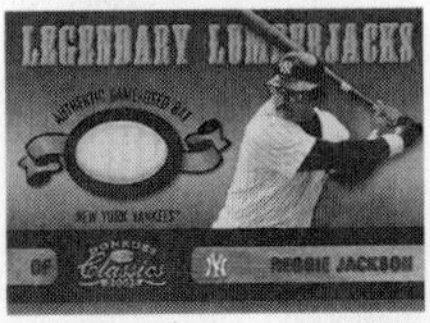

NM/M

Common Player: 10.00
Varying quantities produced
1 Babe Ruth/100 180.00
2 Lou Gehrig/80 125.00
3 George Brett/250 25.00
4 Duke Snider/250 20.00
5 Roberto Clemente/25 165.00
6 Ryne Sandberg/400 35.00
7 Robin Yount/300 25.00
8 Harmon Killebrew/250 25.00
9 Al Kaline/250 25.00
10 Eddie Mathews/225 20.00
11 Brooks Robinson/400 15.00
13 Kirby Puckett/375 20.00
14 Jose Canseco/400 15.00
15 Nellie Fox/325 20.00
16 Don Mattingly/400 35.00
17 Joe Torre/250 10.00
18 Cal Ripken Jr/250 40.00
19 Richie Ashburn/250 20.00
20 Mike Schmidt/250 30.00
21 Dale Murphy/250 25.00
22 Thurman Munson/400 15.00
23 Tony Gwynn/400 10.00
24 Orlando Cepeda/225 10.00
25 Ty Cobb/25 225.00
26 Paul Molitor/325 10.00
27 Ralph Kiner/200 10.00
28 Frank Robinson/225 20.00
29 Yogi Berra/50 50.00
30 Reggie Jackson/375 15.00
31 Rod Carew/325 15.00
32 Carlton Fisk/325 15.00
33 Rogers Hornsby/50 60.00
34 Mel Ott/125 30.00
35 Jimmie Foxx/50 60.00

Legends of the Fall

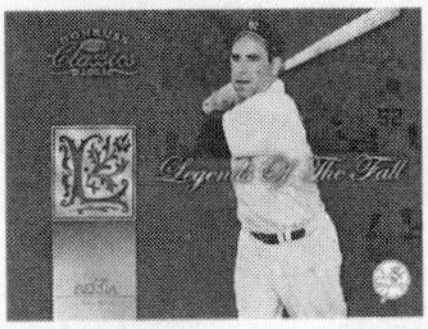

NM/M

Complete Set (10): 40.00
Common Player: 3.00
Production 2,500 Sets
1 Reggie Jackson 4.00
2 Duke Snider 4.00
3 Roberto Clemente 8.00
4 Mel Ott 5.00
5 Yogi Berra 5.00
6 Jackie Robinson 6.00
7 Enos Slaughter 3.00
8 Willie Stargell 4.00
9 Bobby Doerr 3.00
10 Thurman Munson 5.00

Legends of the Fall Fabrics

NM/M

Quantity produced listed 3.00
1 Reggie Jackson/100 20.00
3 Roberto Clemente/50 120.00
6 Jackie Robinson/50 80.00
8 Willie Stargell/100 20.00
9 Bobby Doerr/100 20.00

Membership

NM/M

Complete Set (15): 65.00
Common Player: 3.00
Production 2,500 Sets
1 Babe Ruth 10.00
2 Steve Carlton 3.00
3 Honus Wagner 6.00
4 Warren Spahn 5.00
5 Eddie Mathews 5.00
6 Nolan Ryan 10.00
7 Rogers Hornsby 5.00
8 Ernie Banks 5.00
9 Harmon Killebrew 5.00

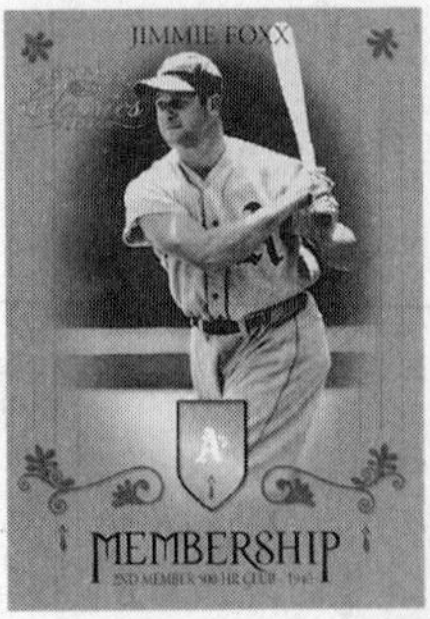

10 Tom Seaver 5.00
11 Jimmie Foxx 6.00
12 Ty Cobb 6.00
13 Frank Robinson 4.00
14 Mel Ott 5.00
15 Lou Gehrig 8.00

Membership VIP Memorabilia

NM/M

Varying quantities produced
1 Babe Ruth/Bat/29 325.00
2 Steve Carlton/Jsy/81 25.00
4 Warren Spahn/Jsy/61 50.00
5 Eddie Mathews/Bat/67 60.00
6 Nolan Ryan/Jsy/80 75.00
7 R. Hornsby/Bat/31 75.00
8 Ernie Banks/Jsy/70 35.00
9 H. Killebrew/Jsy/71 60.00
10 Tom Seaver/Jsy/81 30.00
11 Jimmie Foxx/Bat/40 60.00
13 F. Robinson/Jsy/71 25.00
14 Mel Ott/Jsy/45 50.00

Significant Signatures

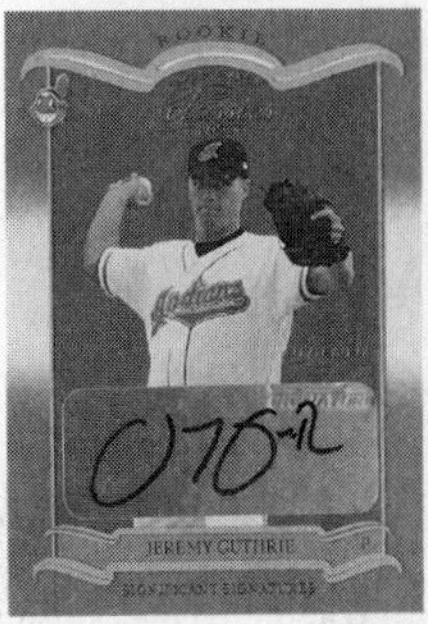

NM/M

Common Autograph: 8.00
#'s 201-211 exclusive to Donruss Rookies
5 Eric Hinske/250 15.00
6 Barry Zito/25 40.00
7 Jason Jennings/250 10.00
10 Corey Patterson/100 15.00
13 Roy Oswalt/100 20.00
16 Mark Mulder/100 25.00
19 Jay Gibbons/250 10.00
21 A.J. Pierzynski/75 20.00
22 Eric Chavez/20 40.00
25 Jose Vidro/75 15.00
27 Mark Teixeira/50 40.00
31 Geronimo Gil/50 10.00
35 Adam Dunn/100 40.00
36 Christian Parker/250 10.00
39 Drew Henson/100 20.00
41 Kevin Mench/250 10.00
45 Mark Prior/50 30.00
56 Kerry Wood/15 60.00
57 Wade Miller/200 10.00
58 Hank Blalock/50 25.00
62 Brian Roberts/250 25.00
63 Paul LoDuca/100 15.00
64 Tim Redding/250 8.00
66 Joe Borchard/100 15.00
68 Richie Sexson/20 40.00
69 Carlos Lee/25 20.00
73 Satoru Komiyama/124 20.00
76 Adam Johnson/200 8.00
84 Robert Fick/50 10.00
88 Brandon Phillips/250 10.00
89 Ben Kozlowski/150 8.00
93 Jermaine Dye/100 20.00
96 Junior Spivey/100 15.00
97 Torii Hunter/50 25.00
102 Steve Garvey/100 20.00
108 Dennis Eckersley/50 30.00
111 Harold Reynolds/50 25.00
119 Don Sutton/100 20.00
120 Nolan Ryan/50 200.00

123 Cal Ripken Jr/50 220.00
126 Joe Carter/100 25.00
127 Jack Morris/100 20.00
128 Luis Aparicio/50 20.00
132 Will Clark/20 125.00
133 Fred Lynn/50 15.00
134 Andre Dawson/50 30.00
136 Orlando Cepeda/100 20.00
137 Billy Williams/100 15.00
142 Eric Davis/50 25.00
143 Alan Trammell/50 35.00
148 Dwight Gooden/50 40.00
149 Phil Rizzuto/20 75.00
150 Lenny Dykstra/50 25.00
151 Adam LaRoche/250 15.00
152 Tim Hummel/500 8.00
153 Matt Kata/500 15.00
154 Jeff Baker/500 10.00
155 Josh Stewart/177 10.00
156 Marshall McDougall/500 10.00
157 Jhonny Peralta/500 20.00
158 Mike Nicolas/500 8.00
159 Jeremy Guthrie/500 10.00
160 Craig Brazell/500 15.00
161 Joe Valentine/172 10.00
162 Buddy Hernandez/500 8.00
163 Freddy Sanchez/500 10.00
164 Shane Victorino/351 8.00
165 Corwin Malone/500 8.00
166 Jason Dubois/500 12.00
167 Josh Wilson/500 8.00
168 Tim Olson/500 8.00
169 Clifford Bartosh/500 8.00
170 Michael Hessman/427 8.00
171 Ryan Church/500 10.00
172 Garrett Atkins/500 8.00
173 Jose Morban/500 8.00
174 Ryan Cameron/500 10.00
175 Todd Wellemeyer/500 10.00
176 Travis Chapman/477 10.00
177 Jason Anderson/500 15.00
178 Adam Morrissey/500 8.00
179 Jose Contreras/100 20.00
180 Nic Jackson/500 8.00
181 Rob Hammock/500 10.00
182 Carlos Rivera/500 8.00
183 Vinnie Chulk/500 8.00
184 Pete LaForest/177 10.00
185 Jon Leicester/500 8.00
186 Termel Sledge/500 8.00
187 Jose Castillo/500 10.00
188 Gerald Laird/500 8.00
189 Nook Logan/427 8.00
190 Clint Barmes/100 20.00
191 Jesus Medrano/500 8.00
192 Henri Stanley/500 8.00
194 Walter Young/500 10.00
195 Jon Adkins/500 8.00
196 Tommy Whiteman/500 8.00
197 Rob Bowen/500 8.00
198 Brandon Webb/500 40.00
199 Prentice Redman/127 10.00
200 Jimmy Gobble/500 10.00
201 Jeremy Bonderman/100 50.00
202 Adam Loewen/100 10.00
203 Chien-Ming Wang/50 220.00
205 Ryan Wagner/100 10.00
206 Dan Haren/100 40.00
209 Ramon Nivar/100 15.00

Singles

NM/M

Common Player: 10.00
Varying quantities produced
1 Babe Ruth/Jsy/100 275.00
2 Lou Gehrig/Jsy/80 200.00
3 Jackie Robinson/Jsy/80 75.00
5 Bobby Doerr/Jsy/100 15.00
6 Fred Lynn/Jsy/100 12.00
7 Honus Wagner/Seat/100 35.00
8 Roberto Clemente/Jsy/80 100.00
9 Kirby Puckett/Jsy/100 40.00
10 Torii Hunter/Jsy/100 10.00
11 Sammy Sosa/Jsy/100 25.00
12 Ryne Sandberg/Jsy/100 40.00
13 Hideo Nomo/Jsy/50 90.00
14 Kazuhisa Ishii/Jsy/50 15.00
15 Mike Schmidt/Jsy/100 45.00
16 Steve Carlton/Jsy/100 15.00
17 Robin Yount/Jsy/100 30.00
18 Paul Molitor/Jsy/100 20.00
19 Mike Piazza/Jsy/100 25.00
20 Duke Snider/Jsy/50 35.00
21 Al Kaline/Jsy/50 50.00
23 Don Mattingly/Jsy/100 60.00
24 Jason Giambi/Jsy/100 10.00
26 Ozzie Smith/Jsy/100 40.00
27 Roger Clemens/Jsy/100 25.00
28 Pedro Martinez/Jsy/100 20.00
29 Thurman Munson/Jsy/50 50.00
30 Yogi Berra/Jsy/25 70.00

Timeless Treasures

NM/M

Varying quantities produced
1 Tony Gwynn, Stan Musial/50 100.00
3 Vladimir Guerrero, Roberto Clemente/50 125.00
5 Jason Giambi, Don Mattingly/50 100.00

2003 Donruss Diamond Kings

NM/M

Complete Set (176): 90.00

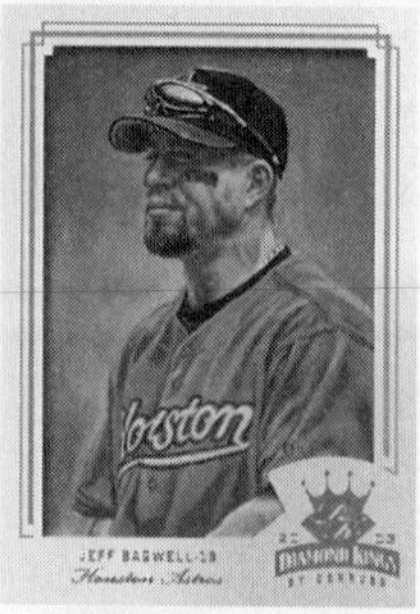
JEFF BAGWELL
Houston Astros
DIAMOND KINGS
BY DONRUSS

Common Player: .40
Common (151-176): 1.00
Pack (5): 4.00
Box (24): 75.00
1 Darin Erstad .50
2 Garret Anderson .50
3 Troy Glaus .50
4 David Eckstein .40
5 Jarrod Washburn .40
6 Adam Kennedy .40
7 Jay Gibbons .40
8 Tony Batista .40
9 Melvin Mora .40
10 Rodrigo Lopez .40
11 Manny Ramirez .75
12 Pedro J. Martinez 1.00
13 Nomar Garciaparra 1.50
14 Rickey Henderson .60
15 Johnny Damon .50
16 Derek Lowe .40
17 Cliff Floyd .40
18 Frank Thomas .75
19 Magglio Ordonez .50
20 Paul Konerko .40
21 Mark Buehrle .40
22 C.C. Sabathia .40
23 Omar Vizquel .40
24 Jim Thome .75
25 Ellis Burks .40
26 Robert Fick .40
27 Bobby Higginson .40
28 Randall Simon .40
29 Carlos Pena .40
30 Carlos Beltran .75
31 Paul Byrd .40
32 Raul Ibanez .40
33 Mike Sweeney .40
34 Torii Hunter .50
35 Corey Koskie .40
36 A.J. Pierzynski .40
37 Cristian Guzman .40
38 Jacque Jones .40
39 Derek Jeter 3.00
40 Bernie Williams .60
41 Roger Clemens 2.00
42 Mike Mussina .60
43 Jorge Posada .50
44 Alfonso Soriano 1.00
45 Jason Giambi .50
46 Robin Ventura .40
47 David Wells .40
48 Tim Hudson .50
49 Barry Zito .50
50 Mark Mulder .50
51 Miguel Tejada .50
52 Eric Chavez .50
53 Jermaine Dye .40
54 Ichiro Suzuki 2.00
55 Edgar Martinez .50
56 John Olerud .40
57 Dan Wilson .40
58 Joel Pineiro .40
59 Kazuhiro Sasaki .40
60 Freddy Garcia .40
61 Aubrey Huff .40
62 Steve Cox .40
63 Randy Winn .40
64 Alex Rodriguez 2.50
65 Juan Gonzalez .50
66 Rafael Palmeiro .75
67 Ivan Rodriguez .75
68 Kenny Rogers .40
69 Carlos Delgado .50
70 Eric Hinske .40
71 Roy Halladay .40
72 Vernon Wells .40
73 Shannon Stewart .40
74 Curt Schilling .75
75 Randy Johnson 1.00
76 Luis Gonzalez .40
77 Mark Grace .50
78 Junior Spivey .40
79 Greg Maddux 1.50
80 Tom Glavine .50
81 John Smoltz .40
82 Chipper Jones 1.00
83 Gary Sheffield .40
84 Andruw Jones .50
85 Kerry Wood 1.00
86 Fred McGriff .40
87 Sammy Sosa 1.50
88 Mark Prior 1.00
89 Ken Griffey Jr. 1.50
90 Barry Larkin .50
91 Adam Dunn .75
92 Sean Casey .40
93 Austin Kearns .50
94 Aaron Boone .40
95 Larry Walker .40
96 Todd Helton .75
97 Jason Jennings .40
98 Jay Payton .40
99 Josh Beckett .50
100 Mike Lowell .40
101 A.J. Burnett .40
102 Jeff Bagwell .75
103 Craig da Luz .40
104 Lance Berkman .50
105 Roy Oswalt .40
106 Wade Miller .40
107 Shawn Green .50
108 Adrian Beltre .50
109 Hideo Nomo .50
110 Kazuhisa Ishii .40
111 Odalis Perez .40
112 Paul LoDuca .40
113 Ben Sheets .40
114 Richie Sexson .50
115 Jose Hernandez .40
116 Vladimir Guerrero 1.00
117 Jose Vidro .40
118 Tomokazu Ohka .40
119 Andres Galarraga .40
120 Bartolo Colon .40
121 Mike Piazza 1.50
122 Roberto Alomar .50
123 Mo Vaughn .40
124 Al Leiter .40
125 Edgardo Alfonzo .40
126 Pat Burrell .75
127 Bobby Abreu .50
128 Mike Lieberthal .40
129 Vicente Padilla .40
130 Marlon Byrd .40
131 Jason Kendall .40
132 Brian Giles .40
133 Aramis Ramirez .50
134 Kip Wells .40
135 Ryan Klesko .40
136 Phil Nevin .40
137 Brian Lawrence .40
138 Sean Burroughs .40
139 Mark Kotsay .40
140 Barry Bonds 3.00
141 Jeff Kent .40
142 Benito Santiago .40
143 Kirk Reuter .40
144 Jason Schmidt .50
145 Jim Edmonds .50
146 J.D. Drew .50
147 Albert Pujols 2.00
148 Tino Martinez .40
149 Matt Morris .40
150 Scott Rolen 1.00
151 Joe Borchard 2.00
152 Cliff Lee 1.00
153 Brian Tallet 1.00
154 Freddy Sanchez 1.00
155 Chone Figgins 1.00
156 Kevin Cash 1.00
157 Justin Wayne 1.00
158 Ben Kozlowski 1.00
159 Babe Ruth 6.00
160 Jackie Robinson 4.00
161 Ozzie Smith 4.00
162 Lou Gehrig 5.00
163 Stan Musial 4.00
164 Mike Schmidt 5.00
165 Carlton Fisk 2.00
166 George Brett 6.00
167 Dale Murphy 4.00
168 Cal Ripken Jr. 8.00
169 Tony Gwynn 3.00
170 Don Mattingly 6.00
171 Jack Morris 2.00
172 Ty Cobb 5.00
173 Nolan Ryan 6.00
174 Ryne Sandberg 5.00
175 Thurman Munson 4.00
176 Jose Contreras **RC** 8.00
Common Signature (1-25): 10.00
Quantity produced listed
1 Barry Zito/75 50.00
2 Edgar Martinez/125 50.00
3 Jay Gibbons/150 25.00
4 Joe Borchard/150 20.00
5 Marlon Byrd/150 20.00
6 Adam Dunn/150 40.00
7 Torii Hunter/150 40.00
8 Vladimir Guerrero/25 150.00
9 Wade Miller/150 25.00
10 Alfonso Soriano/100 60.00
11 Brian Lawrence/150 10.00
12 Cliff Floyd/100 25.00
13 Dale Murphy/75 75.00
14 Jack Morris/150 25.00
15 Eric Hinske/150 25.00
16 Jason Jennings/150 20.00
17 Mark Buehrle/150 30.00
18 Mark Prior/150 40.00
19 Mark Mulder/150 30.00
20 Mike Sweeney/150 25.00
21 Nolan Ryan/50 200.00
22 Don Mattingly/75 100.00
23 Andruw Jones/75 40.00
24 Aubrey Huff/150 20.00

Common Jerseys (26-75): 5.00
26 Nolan Ryan/250 50.00
27 Ozzie Smith/400 15.00
28 Rickey Henderson/300 10.00
29 Jack Morris/500 5.00
30 George Brett/350 25.00
31 Cal Ripken Jr./300 40.00
32 Ryne Sandberg/450 20.00
33 Don Mattingly/400 25.00
34 Tony Gwynn/400 15.00
35 Dale Murphy/350 10.00
36 Carlton Fisk/400 10.00
38 Lou Gehrig/50 240.00
39 Garret Anderson/450 8.00
40 Pedro J. Martinez/400 10.00
41 Nomar Garciaparra/350 15.00
42 Maggio Ordonez/450 8.00
43 C.C. Sabathia/500 5.00
44 Omar Vizquel/250 8.00
45 Jim Thome/500 10.00
46 Torii Hunter/500 8.00
47 Roger Clemens/500 15.00
48 Alfonso Soriano/400 10.00
49 Tim Hudson/500 8.00
50 Barry Zito/350 6.00
51 Mark Mulder/500 6.00
52 Miguel Tejada/400 8.00
53 John Olerud/350 5.00
54 Alex Rodriguez/500 15.00
55 Rafael Palmeiro/500 8.00
56 Curt Schilling/500 8.00
57 Randy Johnson/400 10.00
58 Greg Maddux/350 12.00
59 John Smoltz/400 6.00
60 Chipper Jones/450 10.00
61 Andruw Jones/500 8.00
62 Kerry Wood/500 10.00
63 Mark Prior/500 10.00
64 Adam Dunn/350 10.00
65 Larry Walker/500 5.00
66 Todd Helton/500 8.00
67 Jeff Bagwell/500 10.00
68 Roy Oswalt/500 8.00
69 Hideo Nomo/150 15.00
70 Kazuhisa Ishii/250 5.00
71 Vladimir Guerrero/500 10.00
72 Mike Piazza/500 15.00
73 Joe Borchard/500 5.00
74 Ryan Klesko/500 5.00
75 Shawn Green/500 6.00
Common Bat (76-105): 5.00
76 George Brett/350 25.00
77 Ozzie Smith/450 15.00
78 Cal Ripken Jr/150 50.00
79 Don Mattingly/400 25.00
80 Babe Ruth/50 200.00
81 Dale Murphy/350 10.00
82 Rickey Henderson/500 10.00
83 Ivan Rodriguez/500 8.00
84 Marlon Byrd/500 5.00
85 Eric Chavez/500 8.00
86 Nomar Garciaparra/500 15.00
87 Alex Rodriguez/500 15.00
88 Vladimir Guerrero/500 10.00
89 Paul LoDuca/500 5.00
90 Richie Sexson/500 6.00
91 Mike Piazza/350 15.00
92 J.D. Drew/500 8.00
93 Juan Gonzalez/500 8.00
94 Pat Burrell/500 8.00
95 Adam Dunn/250 15.00
96 Mike Schmidt/500 20.00
97 Ryne Sandberg/500 20.00
98 Edgardo Alfonzo/500 5.00
99 Andruw Jones/500 8.00
100 Carlos Beltran/500 6.00
101 Jeff Bagwell/500 10.00
102 Lance Berkman/500 8.00
103 Luis Gonzalez/500 5.00
104 Carlos Delgado/500 6.00
105 Jim Edmonds/250 8.00
Combos (106-110):
Some Combos & Autos. not priced
106 Alfonso Soriano/75 40.00
107 Greg Maddux/ Jsy/Auto./50 140.00
109 Adam Dunn/Bat/Auto./50 60.00
110 Rickey Henderson/ Jsy/Bat/50 20.00

DK Evolution

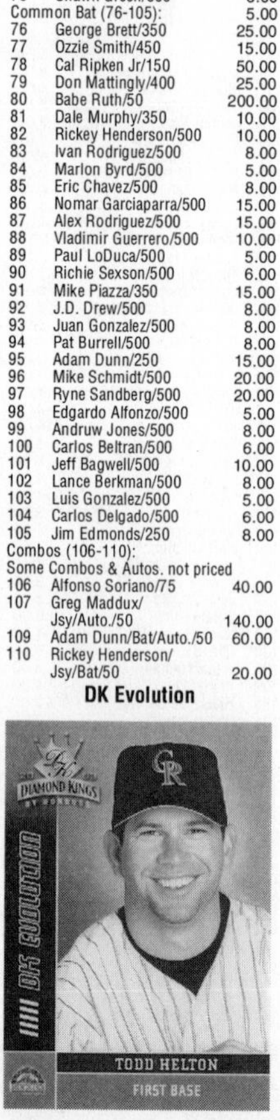
DIAMOND KINGS
DK EVOLUTION
TODD HELTON
FIRST BASE

	NM/M
Complete Set (25):	85.00
Common Player:	2.00
Inserted 1:18	
1 Cal Ripken Jr.	10.00
2 Ichiro Suzuki	6.00
3 Randy Johnson	4.00
4 Pedro J. Martinez	4.00
5 Nolan Ryan	10.00
6 Derek Jeter	10.00
7 Kerry Wood	4.00
8 Alex Rodriguez	8.00
9 Magglio Ordonez	2.00
10 Greg Maddux	5.00
11 Todd Helton	3.00
12 Sammy Sosa	5.00
13 Lou Gehrig	8.00
14 Lance Berkman	2.00
15 Barry Zito	2.00
16 Barry Bonds	10.00
17 Tom Glavine	2.00
18 Shawn Green	2.00
19 Roger Clemens	8.00
20 Nomar Garciaparra	6.00
21 Tony Gwynn	4.00
22 Vladimir Guerrero	3.00
23 Albert Pujols	8.00
24 Chipper Jones	4.00
25 Alfonso Soriano	4.00

Framed Portraits Bronze

Cards (1-150):	1-2.5X
Cards (151-176):	.75-1.5X
Silvers (1-150):	3-5X
Silvers (151-176):	2-3X
Production 400 Sets	
Golds (1-150):	5-10X
Golds (151-176):	3-6X
Production 100 Sets	

Hall of Fame Heroes

	NM/M
Complete Set (10):	40.00
Common Player:	3.00
Inserted 1:43	
1 Bob Feller	3.00
2 Al Kaline	6.00
3 Lou Boudreau	3.00
4 Duke Snider	4.00
5 Jackie Robinson	6.00
6 Early Wynn	3.00
7 Yogi Berra	4.00
8 Stan Musial	6.00
9 Ty Cobb	6.00
10 Ted Williams	8.00

HOF Heroes Materials

	NM/M
Common Player:	30.00
Production 50 Sets	
1 Bob Feller/Jsy	70.00
2 Al Kaline/Bat	45.00
3 Lou Boudreau/Jsy	40.00
4 Duke Snider/Bat	30.00
7 Yogi Berra/Bat	40.00
8 Stan Musial/Bat	100.00
9 Ty Cobb/Bat	110.00
10 Ted Williams/Jsy	175.00

Heritage Collection

	NM/M
Complete Set (25):	100.00
Common Player:	2.00
Inserted 1:23	
1 Ozzie Smith	5.00
2 Lou Gehrig	8.00
3 Stan Musial	6.00
4 Mike Schmidt	6.00
5 Carlton Fisk	2.00
6 George Brett	10.00
7 Dale Murphy	4.00
8 Cal Ripken Jr.	10.00
9 Tony Gwynn	4.00
10 Don Mattingly	8.00
11 Jack Morris	2.00
12 Ty Cobb	8.00
13 Nolan Ryan	12.00
14 Ryne Sandberg	6.00
15 Thurman Munson	4.00
16 Ichiro Suzuki	6.00
17 Derek Jeter	10.00

18 Greg Maddux	5.00
19 Sammy Sosa	5.00
20 Pedro J. Martinez	4.00
21 Alex Rodriguez	8.00
22 Roger Clemens	5.00
23 Barry Bonds	10.00
24 Lance Berkman	2.00
25 Vladimir Guerrero	3.00

2003 Donruss Diamond Kings
Inserts Hawaii

	NM/M
Common Player:	4.00

HERITAGE COLLECTION

1 Ozzie Smith	25.00
2 Lou Gehrig	35.00
3 Stan Musial	25.00
4 Mike Schmidt	35.00
5 Carlton Fisk	20.00
6 George Brett	60.00
7 Dale Murphy	15.00
8 Cal Ripken Jr.	75.00
9 Tony Gwynn	45.00
10 Don Mattingly	45.00
11 Jack Morris	6.00
12 Ty Cobb	35.00
13 Nolan Ryan	75.00
14 Ryne Sandberg	55.00
15 Thurman Munson	15.00
16 Ichiro Suzuki	75.00
17 Derek Jeter	75.00
18 Greg Maddux	25.00
19 Sammy Sosa	45.00
20 Pedro Martinez	9.00
21 Alex Rodriguez	60.00
22 Roger Clemens	25.00
23 Barry Bonds	75.00
24 Lance Berkman	6.00
25 Vladimir Guerrero	9.00

HALL OF FAME HEROES

1 Bob Feller	6.00
2 Al Kaline	15.00
3 Lou Boudreau	4.00
4 Duke Snider	10.00
5 Jackie Robinson	15.00
6 Early Wynn	4.00
7 Yogi Berra	15.00
8 Stan Musial	15.00
9 Ty Cobb	9.00
10 Ted Williams	15.00

TEAM TIMELINE

1 Nolan Ryan, Roy Oswalt	35.00
2 Dale Murphy, Chipper Jones	15.00
3 Stan Musial, Jim Edmonds	10.00
4 George Brett, Mike Sweeney	30.00
5 Tony Gwynn, Ryan Klesko	15.00
6 Carlton Fisk, Magglio Ordonez	10.00
7 Mike Schmidt, Pat Burrell	20.00
8 Don Mattingly, Bernie Williams	25.00
9 Ryne Sandberg, Kerry Wood	25.00
10 Lou Gehrig, Alfonso Soriano	20.00

Team Timelines

	NM/M
Complete Set (10):	85.00
Common Card:	4.00
Production 1,000 Sets	
1 Nolan Ryan, Roy Oswalt	15.00
2 Dale Murphy, Chipper Jones	8.00
3 Stan Musial, Jim Edmonds	10.00
4 George Brett, Mike Sweeney	12.00
5 Tony Gwynn, Ryan Klesko	6.00
6 Carlton Fisk, Magglio Ordonez	4.00
7 Mike Schmidt, Pat Burrell	12.00
8 Don Mattingly, Bernie Williams	12.00
9 Ryne Sandberg, Kerry Wood	10.00
10 Lou Gehrig, Alfonso Soriano	10.00

Team Timelines Materials

	NM/M
Common Card:	30.00
Production 100 unless noted.	
1 Nolan Ryan, Roy Oswalt	120.00
2 Dale Murphy, Chipper Jones	40.00
3 Stan Musial, Jim Edmonds	45.00
4 George Brett, Mike Sweeney	65.00
5 Tony Gwynn, Ryan Klesko	40.00
6 Carlton Fisk, Magglio Ordonez	30.00
7 Mike Schmidt, Pat Burrell	90.00
8 Don Mattingly, Bernie Williams	70.00
9 Ryne Sandberg, Kerry Wood	60.00
10 Lou Gehrig, Alfonso Soriano/50	200.00

Recollection

No Pricing	
Production 2-15	

Recollection Autographs

	NM/M
Common Player:	
1 Adrian Beltre/40	15.00
2 Brandon Berger/99	10.00
9 Mark Buehrle/73	10.00
15 Andre Dawson/24	25.00
16 Andre Dawson/50	20.00
17 Andre Dawson/28	25.00
19 Jorge De La Rosa/148	5.00
24 Rob Fick/150	8.00
37 Tim Hudson/50	15.00
42 Ryan Ludwick/130	8.00
55 Roy Oswalt/65	15.00
56 Roy Oswalt/100	15.00
70 Bud Smith/114	5.00
72 Shannon Stewart/50	8.00

2003 Donruss Elite

	NM/M
Complete Set (200):	
Common Player:	.25
Common Rookie (181-200):	3.00
Production 1,750	
Pack (5):	3.50
Box (20):	60.00
1 Darin Erstad	.40
2 David Eckstein	.25
3 Garret Anderson	.40
4 Jarrod Washburn	.25
5 Tim Salmon	.40
6 Troy Glaus	.25
7 Marty Cordova	.25
8 Melvin Mora	.25
9 Rodrigo Lopez	.25
10 Tony Batista	.25
11 Derek Lowe	.40
12 Johnny Damon	.25
13 Manny Ramirez	.50
14 Nomar Garciaparra	1.50
15 Pedro J. Martinez	.75

16 Shea Hillenbrand	.25
17 Carlos Lee	.25
18 Joe Crede	.25
19 Frank Thomas	.50
20 Magglio Ordonez	.40
21 Mark Buehrle	.25
22 Paul Konerko	.25
23 C.C. Sabathia	.25
24 Ellis Burks	.25
25 Omar Vizquel	.40
26 Brian Tallet	.25
27 Bobby Higginson	.25
28 Carlos Pena	.25
29 Mark Redman	.25
30 Steve Sparks	.25
31 Carlos Beltran	.50
32 Joe Randa	.25
33 Mike Sweeney	.25
34 Raul Ibanez	.25
35 Runelvys Hernandez	.25
36 Brad Radke	.25
37 Corey Koskie	.25
38 Cristian Guzman	.25
39 David Ortiz	.50
40 Doug Mientkiewicz	.25
41 Jacque Jones	.25
42 Torii Hunter	.40
43 Alfonso Soriano	.75
44 Andy Pettitte	.40
45 Bernie Williams	.50
46 David Wells	.25
47 Derek Jeter	2.00
48 Jason Giambi	.40
49 Jeff Weaver	.25
50 Jorge Posada	.40
51 Mike Mussina	.40
52 Roger Clemens	1.50
53 Barry Zito	.40
54 Eric Chavez	.40
55 Jermaine Dye	.25
56 Mark Mulder	.40
57 Miguel Tejada	.40
58 Tim Hudson	.40
59 Bret Boone	.25
60 Chris Snelling	.25
61 Edgar Martinez	.40
62 Freddy Garcia	.25
63 Ichiro Suzuki	1.50
64 Jamie Moyer	.25
65 John Olerud	.25
66 Kazuhiro Sasaki	.25
67 Aubrey Huff	.25
68 Joe Kennedy	.25
69 Paul Wilson	.25
70 Alex Rodriguez	1.50
71 Chan Ho Park	.25
72 Hank Blalock	.50
73 Juan Gonzalez	.50
74 Kevin Mench	.25
75 Rafael Palmeiro	.50
76 Carlos Delgado	.40
77 Eric Hinske	.25
78 Josh Phelps	.25
79 Roy Halladay	.40
80 Shannon Stewart	.25
81 Vernon Wells	.25
82 Curt Schilling	.50
83 Junior Spivey	.25
84 Luis Gonzalez	.40
85 Mark Grace	.50
86 Randy Johnson	.75
87 Steve Finley	.25
88 Andruw Jones	.50
89 Chipper Jones	.75
90 Gary Sheffield	.50
91 Greg Maddux	1.00
92 John Smoltz	.40
93 Corey Patterson	.40
94 Kerry Wood	.75
95 Mark Prior	1.00
96 Moises Alou	.40
97 Sammy Sosa	1.50
98 Adam Dunn	.50
99 Austin Kearns	.40
100 Barry Larkin	.40
101 Ken Griffey Jr.	1.00
102 Sean Casey	.25
103 Jason Jennings	.25
104 Jay Payton	.25
105 Larry Walker	.40
106 Todd Helton	.50
107 A.J. Burnett	.25
108 Josh Beckett	.25
109 Juan Encarnacion	.25
110 Mike Lowell	.25
111 Craig Biggio	.40
112 Daryle Ward	.25
113 Jeff Bagwell	.50
114 Lance Berkman	.40
115 Roy Oswalt	.40
116 Jason Lane	.25
117 Adrian Beltre	.50
118 Hideo Nomo	.50
119 Kazuhisa Ishii	.25
120 Kevin Brown	.40
121 Odalis Perez	.25
122 Paul LoDuca	.25
123 Shawn Green	.40
124 Ben Sheets	.25
125 Jeffrey Hammonds	.25
126 Jose Hernandez	.25
127 Richie Sexson	.50
128 Bartolo Colon	.25
129 Brad Wilkerson	.25
130 Javier Vazquez	.25

131	Jose Vidro	.25
132	Michael Barrett	.25
133	Vladimir Guerrero	.75
134	Al Leiter	.25
135	Mike Piazza	1.00
136	Mo Vaughn	.25
137	Pedro Astacio	.25
138	Roberto Alomar	.40
139	Pat Burrell	.40
140	Vicente Padilla	.25
141	Jimmy Rollins	.40
142	Bobby Abreu	.40
143	Marlon Byrd	.25
144	Brian Giles	.40
145	Jason Kendall	.40
146	Aramis Ramirez	.40
147	Josh Fogg	.25
148	Ryan Klesko	.40
149	Phil Nevin	.25
150	Sean Burroughs	.25
151	Mark Kotsay	.25
152	Barry Bonds	2.00
153	Damian Moss	.25
154	Jason Schmidt	.50
155	Benito Santiago	.25
156	Rich Aurilia	.25
157	Scott Rolen	.75
158	J.D. Drew	.40
159	Jim Edmonds	.40
160	Matt Morris	.40
161	Tino Martinez	.25
162	Albert Pujols	1.50
163	Russ Ortiz	.25
164	Rey Ordonez	.25
165	Paul Byrd	.25
166	Kenny Lofton	.25
167	Kenny Rogers	.25
168	Rickey Henderson	.50
169	Fred McGriff	.40
170	Charles Johnson	.25
171	Mike Hampton	.25
172	Jim Thome	.75
173	Travis Hafner	.25
174	Ivan Rodriguez	.50
175	Ray Durham	.25
176	Jeremy Giambi	.25
177	Jeff Kent	.40
178	Cliff Floyd	.25
179	Kevin Millwood	.25
180	Tom Glavine	.50
181	Hideki Matsui **RC**	10.00
182	Jose Contreras **RC**	5.00
183	Termel Sledge **RC**	3.00
184	Lew Ford **RC**	6.00
185	Jhonny Peralta	4.00
186	Alexis Rios	4.00
187	Jeff Baker	3.00
188	Jeremy Guthrie	3.00
189	Jose Castillo	3.00
190	Garrett Atkins	3.00
191	Jeremy Bonderman	8.00
192	Adam LaRoche	3.00
193	Vinnie Chulk	3.00
194	Walter Young	3.00
195	Jimmy Gobble	3.00
196	Prentice Redman **RC**	4.00
197	Jason Anderson	3.00
198	Nic Jackson	3.00
199	Travis Chapman	3.00
200	Shane Victorino **RC**	3.00

Aspirations

		NM/M
Stars print run 25-50:		10-15X
Rookies (181-200) p/r 25-50:		1-3X
Stars p/r 51-99:		5-10X
Serial numbered to jersey number.		
Gold One-of-One's exist.		
181	Hideki Matsui/45	125.00

Status

		NM/M
Stars print run 25-50:		10-15X
Rookies (181-200) p/r 25-50:		1-3X
Stars p/r 51-99:		5-10X
Gold Status:		No Pricing
Production 24 Sets		
181	Hideki Matsui/55	120.00

All-Time Career Best

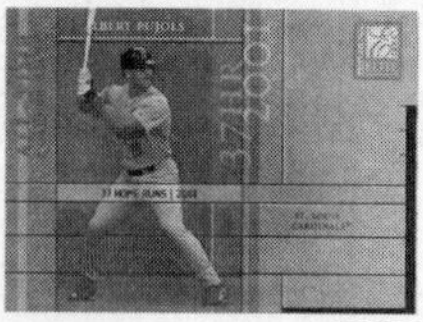

		NM/M
Complete Set (45):		120.00
Common Player:		2.00
Inserted 1:9		
Gold print run 25-50:		4-8X
Gold print run 51-100:		3-5X
Gold p/r 101-239:		1.5-3X
Numbered to career stat.		
1	Babe Ruth	6.00
2	Ty Cobb	4.00
3	Jackie Robinson	4.00
4	Lou Gehrig	5.00
5	Thurman Munson	2.00
6	Nolan Ryan	8.00
7	Mike Schmidt	4.00
8	Don Mattingly	5.00
9	Yogi Berra	3.00
10	Rod Carew	2.00
11	Reggie Jackson	3.00
12	Al Kaline	4.00
13	Harmon Killebrew	4.00
14	Eddie Mathews	3.00
15	Stan Musial	4.00
16	Jim Palmer	2.00
17	Phil Rizzuto	2.00
18	Brooks Robinson	3.00
19	Tom Seaver	3.00
20	Robin Yount	4.00
21	Carlton Fisk	3.00
22	Dale Murphy	4.00
23	Cal Ripken Jr.	8.00
24	Tony Gwynn	4.00
25	Andre Dawson	2.00
26	Derek Jeter	6.00
27	Ken Griffey Jr.	4.00
28	Albert Pujols	4.00
29	Sammy Sosa	4.00
30	Jason Giambi	3.00
31	Randy Johnson	3.00
32	Greg Maddux	4.00
33	Rickey Henderson	3.00
34	Pedro Martinez	3.00
35	Jeff Bagwell	3.00
36	Alex Rodriguez	5.00
37	Vladimir Guerrero	3.00
38	Chipper Jones	3.00
39	Shawn Green	2.00
40	Tom Glavine	2.00
41	Curt Schilling	2.00
42	Todd Helton	2.00
43	Roger Clemens	4.00
44	Lance Berkman	2.00
45	Nomar Garciaparra	5.00

All-Time Career Best Materials

		NM/M
Common Player:		5.00
Varying quantities produced		
1	Babe Ruth/Bat/25	250.00
2	Ty Cobb/Bat/25	150.00
3	Jackie Robinson/Jsy/50	50.00
4	Lou Gehrig/Bat/100	100.00
5	Thurman Munson/Bat/200	15.00
6	Nolan Ryan/Jsy/400	40.00
7	Mike Schmidt/Jsy/400	30.00
8	Don Mattingly/Jsy/250	40.00
9	Yogi Berra/Bat/100	25.00
10	Rod Carew/Bat/400	10.00
11	Reggie Jackson/Bat/400	10.00
12	Al Kaline/Bat/400	20.00
13	Harmon Killebrew/Jsy/400	15.00
14	Eddie Mathews/Bat/200	25.00
15	Stan Musial/Bat/100	40.00
16	Jim Palmer/Jsy/200	10.00
17	Phil Rizzuto/Bat/400	10.00
18	Brooks Robinson/Bat/400	15.00
19	Tom Seaver/Jsy/400	15.00
20	Robin Yount/Bat/400	15.00
21	Carlton Fisk/Bat/400	10.00
22	Dale Murphy/Bat/400	10.00
23	Cal Ripken Jr/Bat/400	35.00
24	Tony Gwynn/Jsy/400	12.00
25	Andre Dawson/Bat/400	5.00
26	Derek Jeter/Base/400	15.00
27	Ken Griffey Jr./Base/400	10.00
28	Albert Pujols/Base/400	15.00
29	Sammy Sosa/Bat/400	12.00
30	Jason Giambi/Bat/400	8.00
31	Randy Johnson/Jsy/400	8.00
32	Greg Maddux/Jsy/400	10.00
33	Rickey Henderson/Bat/400	10.00
34	Pedro Martinez/Jsy/400	10.00
35	Jeff Bagwell/Jsy/400	8.00
36	Alex Rodriguez/Bat/400	12.00
37	Vladimir Guerrero/Bat/400	8.00
38	Chipper Jones/Bat/400	10.00
39	Shawn Green/Bat/400	5.00
40	Tom Glavine/Jsy/400	5.00
41	Curt Schilling/Jsy/400	8.00
42	Todd Helton/Bat/400	8.00
43	Roger Clemens/Jsy/400	20.00
44	Lance Berkman/Bat/400	5.00
45	Nomar Garciaparra/Bat/400	15.00

All-Time Career Best Materials Gold

		NM/M
Numbered to career stat.		
Some not priced yet.		
1	Babe Ruth/60	125.00
4	Lou Gehrig/49	125.00
5	Thurman Munson/105	25.00
7	Mike Schmidt/48	50.00
8	Don Mattingly/53	60.00
9	Yogi Berra/30	50.00
10	Rod Carew/239	10.00
11	Reggie Jackson/39	25.00
12	Al Kaline/29	50.00
13	Harmon Killebrew/140	20.00
14	Eddie Mathews/31	50.00
18	Brooks Robinson/118	20.00
20	Robin Yount/49	40.00
21	Carlton Fisk/107	15.00
22	Dale Murphy/44	40.00
23	Cal Ripken Jr./211	40.00
24	Tony Gwynn/220	10.00
25	Andre Dawson/49	15.00
27	Ken Griffey Jr./56	25.00
28	Albert Pujols/37	30.00
29	Sammy Sosa/66	35.00
30	Jason Giambi/137	10.00
33	Rickey Henderson/130	20.00
35	Jeff Bagwell/47	15.00
36	Alex Rodriguez/393	10.00
37	Vladimir Guerrero/44	25.00
38	Chipper Jones/45	20.00
39	Shawn Green/49	15.00
41	Curt Schilling/35	20.00
42	Todd Helton/59	15.00
44	Lance Berkman/55	15.00
45	Nomar Garciaparra/35	50.00

Back to the Future

		NM/M
Complete Set (15):		35.00
Common Card:		2.00
#'s 1-10 production 1,000:		
#'s 11-15 production 500		
1	Kerry Wood	4.00
2	Mark Prior	4.00
3	Magglio Ordonez	2.50
4	Joe Borchard	2.00
5	Lance Berkman	3.00
6	Jason Lane	2.00
7	Rafael Palmeiro	3.00
8	Mark Teixeira	3.00
9	Carlos Delgado	3.00
10	Josh Phelps	2.00
11	Kerry Wood, Mark Prior	4.00
12	Joe Borchard, Magglio Ordonez	2.50
13	Jason Lane, Lance Berkman	3.00
14	Mark Teixeira, Rafael Palmeiro	3.00
15	Carlos Delgado, Josh Phelps	3.00

Back to the Future Threads

		NM/M
Common Card:		4.00
Singles production 250:		
Doubles production 125:		
1	Kerry Wood	10.00
2	Mark Prior	12.00
3	Magglio Ordonez	5.00
4	Joe Borchard	5.00
5	Lance Berkman	6.00
6	Jason Lane	4.00
7	Rafael Palmeiro	8.00
8	Mark Teixeira	10.00
9	Carlos Delgado	8.00
10	Josh Phelps	6.00
11	Kerry Wood, Mark Prior	20.00
12	Joe Borchard, Magglio Ordonez	8.00
13	Jason Lane, Lance Berkman	8.00
14	Mark Teixeira, Rafael Palmeiro	15.00
15	Carlos Delgado, Josh Phelps	8.00

Back 2 Back Jacks

		NM/M
Common Player:		
1	Adam Dunn/250	10.00
2	Alex Rodriguez/250	15.00
3	Alfonso Soriano/250	10.00
4	Andruw Jones/250	8.00
5	Chipper Jones/250	10.00
6	Jason Giambi/250	8.00
7	Jeff Bagwell/250	8.00
8	Jim Thome/250	8.00
9	Juan Gonzalez/250	8.00
10	Lance Berkman/250	6.00
11	Magglio Ordonez/250	4.00
12	Manny Ramirez/250	8.00
13	Miguel Tejada/250	6.00
14	Mike Piazza/250	15.00
15	Nomar Garciaparra/250	15.00
16	Rafael Palmeiro/250	8.00
17	Rickey Henderson/250	10.00
18	Sammy Sosa/250	15.00
19	Scott Rolen/250	8.00
20	Shawn Green/250	6.00
21	Todd Helton/250	8.00
22	Vladimir Guerrero/250	8.00
23	Ivan Rodriguez/250	8.00
24	Eric Chavez/250	6.00
25	Larry Walker/250	6.00
26	Troy Glaus/250, Garret Anderson	8.00
27	Adam Dunn, Austin Kearns/125	20.00
28	Alex Rodriguez, Rafael Palmeiro/125	20.00
29	Eric Chavez, Miguel Tejada/125	10.00
30	Frank Thomas, Magglio Ordonez/125	15.00
31	Jeff Bagwell, Lance Berkman/125	15.00
32	Manny Ramirez, Nomar Garciaparra/125	30.00
33	Jose Vidro, Vladimir Guerrero/125	15.00
34	Mike Piazza, Roberto Alomar/125	20.00
35	Larry Walker, Todd Helton/125	15.00
36	Babe Ruth/100	150.00
37	Cal Ripken Jr./100	65.00
38	Don Mattingly/100	50.00
39	Kirby Puckett/100	20.00
40	Roberto Clemente/100	75.00
41	Alfonso Soriano, Phil Rizzuto/75	25.00
42	Andre Dawson, Sammy Sosa/75	40.00
43	Ozzie Smith, Scott Rolen/75	60.00
44	Don Mattingly, Jason Giambi/75	75.00
45	Rickey Henderson, Ty Cobb/75	125.00
46	Joe Morgan, Johnny Bench/50	35.00
47	Brooks Robinson, Cal Ripken Jr./50	100.00
48	Bo Jackson, George Brett/50	100.00
49	Babe Ruth, Lou Gehrig/50	375.00
50	Thurman Munson, Yogi Berra/50	60.00

Career Best

		NM/M
Common Player:		3.00
Numbered to statistic.		
3	Garret Anderson/56	6.00
4	Andruw Jones/83	6.00
6	Magglio Ordonez/38	6.00
7	Magglio Ordonez/135	4.00
8	Adam Dunn/26	15.00
10	Lance Berkman/42	6.00
11	Lance Berkman/128	3.00
12	Shawn Green/385	3.00
13	Alfonso Soriano/39	12.00
14	Alfonso Soriano/300	5.00
15	Jason Giambi/120	5.00
16	Derek Jeter/32	30.00
17	Vladimir Guerrero/40	12.00
18	Vladimir Guerrero/417	5.00
19	Barry Zito/23	8.00
20	Miguel Tejada/34	8.00
21	Barry Bonds/198	15.00
22	Barry Bonds/370	15.00
23	Ichiro Suzuki/388	8.00
24	Alex Rodriguez/57	15.00
25	Alex Rodriguez/142	10.00

Career Best Materials

		NM/M
Common Player:		4.00
Production 500 Sets		
1	Randy Johnson/Jsy	8.00
2	Curt Schilling/Jsy	8.00
3	Garret Anderson/Bat	4.00
4	Andruw Jones/Bat	6.00
5	Kerry Wood/Shoe	10.00
6	Magglio Ordonez/Bat	4.00
7	Magglio Ordonez/Bat	4.00
8	Adam Dunn/Bat	6.00
9	Roy Oswalt/Jsy	5.00
10	Lance Berkman/Bat	5.00
11	Lance Berkman/Bat	5.00
12	Shawn Green/Bat	4.00
13	Alfonso Soriano/Bat	10.00
14	Alfonso Soriano/Bat	10.00
15	Jason Giambi/Bat	8.00
16	Derek Jeter/Base	15.00
17	Vladimir Guerrero/Bat	8.00
18	Vladimir Guerrero/Bat	8.00
19	Barry Zito/Jsy	6.00
20	Miguel Tejada/Bat	6.00
21	Barry Bonds/Base	15.00
22	Barry Bonds/Base	15.00
23	Ichiro Suzuki/Base	15.00
24	Alex Rodriguez/Jsy	10.00
25	Alex Rodriguez/Jsy	10.00

Career Best Materials Auto.

		NM/M
Quantity produced listed		
3	Garret Anderson/Bat/75	35.00
8	Adam Dunn/Bat/100	50.00
9	Roy Oswalt/Jsy/250	30.00
17	Vladimir Guerrero/Bat/50	75.00
18	Vladimir Guerrero/Bat/50	75.00
19	Barry Zito/Jsy/75	40.00

Elite Dominators

No Pricing, 25 Sets Produced

Highlights

		NM/M
Production 500 Sets		
1	Sammy Sosa	10.00
2	Rafael Palmeiro	8.00
3	Hideki Matsui	10.00
4	Jose Contreras	4.00
5	Kevin Millwood	4.00

Highlights Autographs

		NM/M
Production 50 Sets		
2	Rafael Palmeiro	75.00
4	Jose Contreras	25.00

Passing the Torch

		NM/M
Complete Set (15):		50.00
Common Player:		1.50
1	Stan Musial	6.00
2	Jim Edmonds	2.00

3	Dale Murphy	3.00
4	Andruw Jones	3.00
5	Roger Clemens	8.00
6	Mark Prior	3.00
7	Tom Seaver	3.00
8	Tom Glavine	1.50
9	Mike Schmidt	8.00
10	Pat Burrell	2.00
11	Jim Edmonds, Stan Musial	8.00
12	Andruw Jones, Dale Murphy	5.00
13	Mark Prior, Roger Clemens	8.00
14	Tom Glavine, Tom Seaver	5.00
15	Mike Schmidt, Pat Burrell	10.00

Passing the Torch Autograph

NM/M

Common Auto (1-10): 30.00
#'s 1-10 Production 50
#'s 11-15 Production 25
No pricing for #'s 11-15.

1	Stan Musial	80.00
2	Jim Edmonds	40.00
3	Dale Murphy	50.00
4	Andruw Jones	30.00
5	Roger Clemens	125.00
6	Mark Prior	40.00
7	Tom Seaver	60.00
8	Tom Glavine	50.00
9	Mike Schmidt	100.00
10	Pat Burrell	40.00

Recollection Autographs

NM/M

Some not priced due to scarcity.

1	Jeremy Affeldt/75	15.00
2	Erick Almonte/75	8.00
4	Adrian Beltre/36	30.00
7	Brandon Berger/83	8.00
8	Angel Berroa/28	25.00
13	Jeff Deardorff/53	8.00
14	Ryan Drese/100	25.00
21	Luis Garcia/28	15.00
22	Geronimo Gil/75	8.00
28	Travis Hafner Black/52	30.00
30	Bill Hall/27	15.00
35	Gerald Laird/46	30.00
36	Jason Lane/27	15.00
44	Victor Martinez/52	100.00
46	Roy Oswalt Black/61	20.00
51	Ricardo Rodriguez/75	8.00
55	Bud Smith/50	10.00
56	Bud Smith/28	10.00
58	Junior Spivey/45	20.00
59	Tim Spooneybarger/100	8.00
61	Shannon Stewart/35	20.00
64	Claudio Vargas/51	8.00

Throwback Threads

NM/M

	Common Player:	4.00
1	Randy Johnson/Jsy	8.00
2	Randy Johnson/Hat	10.00
3	Roger Clemens/Jsy	20.00
4	Roger Clemens/Jsy	20.00
5	Manny Ramirez/Jsy	8.00
6	Greg Maddux/Jsy	15.00
7	Jason Giambi/Jsy	6.00
8	Jason Giambi/Jsy	6.00
9	Alex Rodriguez/Jsy	10.00
10	Alex Rodriguez/Jsy	10.00
11	Miguel Tejada/Jsy	6.00
12	Alfonso Soriano/Jsy	8.00
13	Nomar Garciaparra/Jsy	15.00
14	Pedro J. Martinez/Jsy	8.00
15	Pedro J. Martinez/Jsy	8.00
16	Andruw Jones/Jsy	6.00
17	Chipper Jones/Jsy	8.00
18	Barry Zito/Jsy	8.00
19	Mark Mulder/Jsy	4.00
20	Lance Berkman/Jsy	6.00
21	Magglio Ordonez/Jsy	4.00
22	Mike Piazza/Jsy	15.00
23	Mike Piazza/Jsy	15.00
24	Rickey Henderson/Jsy	8.00
25	Rickey Henderson/Jsy	8.00
26	Rickey Henderson/Jsy	8.00
27	Sammy Sosa/Jsy	15.00
28	Shawn Green/Jsy	5.00
29	Troy Glaus/Jsy	6.00
30	Vladimir Guerrero/Jsy	8.00
31	Adam Dunn/Jsy	8.00
32	Jeff Bagwell/Jsy	8.00
33	Curt Schilling/Jsy	8.00
34	Hideo Nomo/Jsy	20.00
35	Hideo Nomo/Jsy	20.00
36	Hideo Nomo/Jsy	20.00
37	Kerry Wood/Jsy	10.00
38	Mark Prior/Jsy	8.00
39	Roberto Alomar/Jsy	6.00
40	Todd Helton/Jsy	8.00
41	Jim Thome/Jsy	8.00
42	Rafael Palmeiro/Jsy	8.00
43	Juan Gonzalez/Jsy	8.00
44	Vernon Wells/Jsy	4.00
45	Torii Hunter/Jsy	6.00
46	Randi Johnson/Jsy	15.00
47	Roger Clemens/Jsy	30.00
48	Jason Giambi/Jsy	10.00
49	Alex Rodriguez/Jsy	25.00
50	Pedro J. Martinez/Jsy	20.00
51	Mike Piazza/Jsy	25.00
52	Rickey Henderson/Jsy	20.00
53	Rickey Henderson	20.00
54	Rickey Henderson/Hat, Rickey Henderson/Jsy	20.00
55	Hideo Nomo/Jsy	40.00
56	Randy Johnson/Jsy	15.00
57	Curt Schilling, Randy Johnson/Jsy	15.00
58	Alfonso Soriano, Jason Giambi	25.00
59	Barry Zito, Mark Mulder	15.00
60	Andruw Jones, Chipper Jones/Jsy	20.00
61	Greg Maddux, Tom Glavine	40.00
62	Jeff Bagwell, Lance Berkman/Jsy	15.00
63	Mark Prior, Roger Clemens/Jsy	20.00
64	Alex Rodriguez, Rafael Palmeiro/Jsy	20.00
65	Jim Thome, Roberto Alomar/Jsy	20.00
66	Mike Piazza, Roberto Alomar/Jsy	20.00
67	Mark Grace, Sammy Sosa/Jsy	25.00
68	Larry Walker, Todd Helton/Jsy	20.00
69	Adam Dunn, Austin Kearns/Jsy	20.00
70	Alex Rodriguez, Ivan Rodriguez/Jsy	20.00
71	Bobby Abreu, Marlon Byrd/Jsy	15.00
72	Eric Chavez, Miguel Tejada/Jsy	15.00
73	Greg Maddux, John Smoltz/Jsy	30.00
74	Kerry Wood, Mark Prior/Jsy	10.00
75	Barry Zito, Tim Hudson/Jsy	10.00
76	Babe Ruth	250.00
77	Ty Cobb	100.00
78	Jackie Robinson	75.00
79	Lou Gehrig	125.00
80	Thurman Munson	30.00
81	Nolan Ryan	40.00
82	Don Mattingly	50.00
83	Mike Schmidt	40.00
84	Reggie Jackson	20.00
85	George Brett	40.00
86	Cal Ripken Jr.	50.00
87	Tony Gwynn	15.00
88	Yogi Berra	25.00
89	Stan Musial	40.00
90	Jim Palmer	10.00
91	Thurman Munson	50.00
92	Chipper Jones, Dale Murphy	50.00
93	Don Mattingly, Jason Giambi	80.00
94	Andre Dawson, Sammy Sosa	40.00
95	Mark Prior, Nolan Ryan	50.00
96	Babe Ruth, Lou Gehrig	475.00
97	Joe Morgan, Tom Seaver	40.00
98	Harmon Killebrew, Rod Carew	40.00
99	Nolan Ryan	90.00
100	Reggie Jackson	35.00

Throwback Threads Auto.

NM/M

	Production 5-75	4.00
30	Vladimir Guerrero/50	75.00
31	Adam Dunn/50	75.00
37	Kerry Wood/50	75.00
38	Mark Prior/75	50.00
39	Roberto Alomar/50	75.00

Turn of the Century Autos.

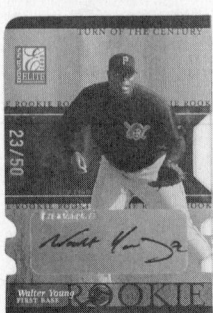

NM/M

Common Autograph: 10.00
Production 50 Sets

182	Jose Contreras	40.00
183	Terrmel Sledge	15.00
184	Lew Ford	20.00
185	Jhonny Peralta	35.00
186	Alexis Rios	40.00
187	Jeff Baker	15.00
188	Jeremy Guthrie	15.00
189	Jose Castillo	15.00
190	Garrett Atkins	25.00
191	Jeremy Bonderman	40.00
192	Adam LaRoche	15.00
193	Vinnie Chulk	15.00
194	Walter Young	15.00
195	Jimmy Gobble	15.00
196	Prentice Redman	15.00
197	Jason Anderson	15.00
198	Nic Jackson	15.00
199	Travis Chapman	10.00
200	Shane Victorino	25.00

2003 Donruss Rookie & Traded

ADAM LOEWEN

NM/M

	Complete Set (65):	8.00
	Common Player:	.25
	Pack (8):	8.00
	Box (24):	150.00
1	Jeremy Bonderman	.50
2	Adam Loewen	.50
3	Dan Haren	.50
4	Jose Contreras RC	.50
5	Hideki Matsui RC	2.00
6	Arnie Munoz	.25
7	Miguel Cabrera	.25
8	Andrew Brown RC	.25
9	Josh Hall RC	.25
10	Josh Stewart RC	.25
11	Clint Barmes RC	.25
12	Luis Ayala RC	.25
13	Brandon Webb RC	1.50
14	Greg Aquino	.25
15	Chien-Ming Wang RC	2.00
16	Rickie Weeks RC	1.00
17	Edgar Gonzalez RC	.25
18	Dontrelle Willis	.25
19	Bo Hart RC	.25
20	Rosman Garcia RC	.25
21	Jeremy Griffiths	.25
22	Craig Brazell RC	.25
23	Daniel Cabrera RC	.50
24	Fernando Cabrera RC	.25
25	Terrmel Sledge RC	.25
26	Ramon Nivar	.25
27	Rob Hammock RC	.25
28	Francisco Rosario RC	.25
29	Cory Stewart	.25
30	Felix Sanchez	.25
31	Jorge Cordova	.25
32	Rocco Baldelli	.50
33	Beau Kemp RC	.25
34	Micheal Nakamura RC	.25
35	Rett Johnson RC	.25
36	Guillermo Quiroz RC	.25
37	Hong-Chih Kuo RC	1.00
38	Ian Ferguson RC	.25
39	Franklin Perez	.25
40	Tim Olson RC	.25
41	Jerome Williams	.25
42	Rich Fischer	.25
43	Phil Seibel RC	.25
44	Aaron Looper RC	.25
45	Jae Weong Seo	.25
46	Chad Gaudin RC	.25
47	Matt Kata RC	.25
48	Ryan Wagner RC	.25
49	Michel Hernandez RC	.25
50	Diegomar Markwell	.25
51	Doug Waechter	.25
52	Mike Nicolas	.25
53	Prentice Redman RC	.25
54	Shane Bazzell	.25
55	Delmon Young RC	1.00
56	Brian Stokes	.25
57	Matt Bruback	.25
58	Nook Logan RC	.25
59	Oscar Villarreal RC	.25
60	Pete LaForest RC	.25
61	Shea Hillenbrand	.25
62	Aramis Ramirez	.40
63	Aaron Boone	.25
64	Roberto Alomar	.50
65	Rickey Henderson	.50

Team Heroes

	Common Player (541-548):	.25
	Team Heroes Glossy:	1-2X
541	Rickie Weeks RC	.75
542	Hideki Matsui RC	1.50
543	Ramon Nivar	.25
544	Adam Loewen RC	.25
545	Brandon Webb RC	1.50
546	Dan Haren	.25
547	Delmon Young RC	1.00
548	Ryan Wagner RC	.25

Champions

Common Player (302-309): .25
Metalized: 4-8X
Production 100

302	Ryan Wagner RC	.25
303	Adam Loewen RC	.25
304	Chien-Ming Wang RC	2.50
305	Hong-Chih Kuo RC	1.00
306	Delmon Young RC	1.50
307	Dan Haren	.50
308	Rickie Weeks RC	1.00
309	Ramon Nivar	.25

Leaf

Common Player (321-329): .25
Leaf Red Press Proofs: 4-8X
Production 100
Leaf Blue Press Proofs: 5-10X
Production 50

321	Hideki Matsui RC	1.50
322	Ramon Nivar	.25
323	Adam Loewen RC	.25
324	Brandon Webb RC	2.00
325	Chien-Ming Wang RC	2.50
326	Delmon Young RC	1.50
327	Ryan Wagner RC	.25
328	Dan Haren	.50
329	Rickie Weeks RC	1.00

Playoff Prestige

Common Player (201-210): .25
Prestige X-Tra Points: 5-10X
Production 50

201	Jeremy Bonderman	.50
202	Brandon Webb RC	2.00
203	Adam Loewen RC	.25
204	Chien-Ming Wang RC	2.50
205	Hong-Chih Kuo RC	1.00
206	Delmon Young RC	1.50
207	Ryan Wagner RC	.25
208	Dan Haren	.50
209	Rickie Weeks RC	1.00
210	Ramon Nivar	.25

Classics

Common Player (201-211): 4.00
Production 100
Classics Timeless Tributes: .75-1.5X
Production 100

201	Jeremy Bonderman	5.00
202	Adam Loewen RC	4.00
203	Chien-Ming Wang RC	20.00
204	Hong-Chih Kuo RC	8.00
205	Ryan Wagner RC	4.00
206	Dan Haren	6.00
207	Dontrelle Willis	4.00
208	Rickie Weeks RC	6.00
209	Ramon Nivar	4.00
210	Chad Gaudin RC	4.00
211	Delmon Young RC	8.00

Studio

Common Player (201-211): 3.00
Production 1,500
Studio Proof: 1-1.5X
Production 100

201	Adam Loewen RC	3.00
202	Jeremy Bonderman	5.00
203	Brandon Webb RC	10.00
204	Chien-Ming Wang RC	8.00
205	Chad Gaudin RC	3.00
206	Ryan Wagner RC	3.00
207	Hong-Chih Kuo RC	8.00
208	Dan Haren	3.00
209	Rickie Weeks RC	6.00
210	Ramon Nivar	3.00
211	Delmon Young RC	8.00

Diamond Kings
Common Player (177-201): 3.00
Inserted 1:30
DK Portraits Bronze: .5-1X
DK Portraits Silver: 1-1.5X
Production 100
DK Portraits Gold: 1-2X
Production 50
177 Hideki Matsui **RC** 10.00
178 Jeremy Bonderman 5.00
179 Brandon Webb **RC** 10.00
180 Adam Loewen **RC** 4.00
181 Chien-Ming Wang **RC** 15.00
182 Hong-Chih Kuo **RC** 6.00
183 Clint Barmes **RC** 3.00
184 Guillermo Quiroz **RC** 4.00
185 Edgar Gonzalez **RC** 3.00
186 Todd Wellemeyer **RC** 4.00
187 Dan Haren 4.00
188 Dustin McGowan 5.00
189 Preston Larrison 3.00
191 Kevin Youkilis 8.00
192 Bubba Nelson 3.00
193 Chris Burke 3.00
194 J.D. Durbin 4.00
195 Ryan Howard 20.00
196 Jason Kubel **RC** 5.00
197 Brendan Harris 5.00
198 Brian Bruney 3.00
199 Ramon Nivar 3.00
200 Rickie Weeks **RC** 5.00
201 Delmon Young **RC** 8.00

Leaf Certified Materials
Mirror Red Signature: .75-1.5X
Production 100 or 50
Mirror Blue Signature: 1-1.5X
Mirror Gold Signature: No Pricing
Mirror Emerald Signature: No Pricing
Mirror Reds: .2-.4X
Production 100
Mirror Blues: .4-.6X
Production 50
Mirror Golds: No Pricing
Production 25
251 Adam Loewen/Auto./250 **RC** 15.00
252 Dan Haren/Auto./250 30.00
253 Dontrelle Willis/Auto./250 20.00
254 Ramon Nivar/Auto./250 10.00
255 Chad Gaudin/Auto./250 20.00
256 Kevin Correia/Auto./250 **RC** 10.00
257 Rickie Weeks/Auto./100 **RC** 60.00
258 Ryan Wagner/Auto./250 **RC** 10.00
259 Delmon Young/Auto./100 **RC** 125.00

Playoff Absolute
Common Player (201-208): 4.00
Production 1,000
Spectrum: 1-2X
Production 100
201 Adam Loewen **RC** 4.00
202 Ramon Nivar 4.00
203 Dan Haren 6.00
204 Dontrelle Willis 4.00
205 Chad Gaudin 4.00
206 Rickie Weeks **RC** 6.00
207 Ryan Wagner **RC** 4.00
208 Delmon Young **RC** 8.00

Elite Extra Edition
Common Player (1-58): 4.00
Production 900
Elite Status: 1-3X
Numbered to Jersey Number
Elite Aspirations: 1-2X
Varying quantities produced
Turn of Century non-Auto: 1-2X
Production 100
Elite Gold Status: No Pricing
Production 24
1 Adam Loewen **RC** 4.00
2 Brandon Webb **RC** 15.00
3 Chien-Ming Wang **RC** 25.00
4 Hong-Chih Kuo **RC** 15.00
5 Clint Barmes **RC** 4.00
6 Guillermo Quiroz **RC** 3.00
7 Edgar Gonzalez **RC** 3.00
8 Todd Wellemeyer **RC** 6.00
9 Alfredo Gonzalez **RC** 3.00
10 Craig Brazell **RC** 3.00
11 Tim Olson **RC** 3.00
12 Rich Fischer 3.00
13 Daniel Cabrera **RC** 5.00
14 Francisco Rosario **RC** 4.00
15 Francisco Cruceta **RC** 4.00
16 Alejandro Machado 4.00
17 Andrew Brown **RC** 4.00
18 Rob Hammock **RC** 4.00
19 Arnie Munoz 4.00
20 Felix Sanchez 4.00
21 Nook Logan **RC** 4.00
22 Cory Stewart 4.00
23 Michel Hernandez **RC** 4.00
24 Rett Johnson **RC** 4.00
25 Josh Hall **RC** 4.00
26 Doug Waechter 4.00
27 Matt Kata **RC** 4.00
28 Dan Haren 8.00
29 Dontrelle Willis 4.00
30 Ramon Nivar 4.00
31 Chad Gaudin **RC** 5.00
32 Rickie Weeks **RC** 8.00
33 Ryan Wagner **RC** 4.00
34 Kevin Correia **RC** 4.00
35 Bo Hart **RC** 4.00
36 Oscar Villarreal **RC** 4.00
37 Josh Willingham **RC** 5.00
38 Jeff Duncan **RC** 5.00
39 David DeJesus **RC** 6.00
40 Dustin McGowan **RC** 8.00
41 Preston Larrison 4.00
43 Kevin Youkilis 8.00
44 Bubba Nelson 4.00
45 Chris Burke 6.00
46 J.D. Durbin 4.00
47 Ryan Howard 50.00
48 Jason Kubel **RC** 6.00
49 Brendan Harris 6.00
50 Brian Bruney 4.00
52 Byron Gettis 4.00
53 Edwin Jackson **RC** 4.00
55 Daniel Garcia 4.00
57 Chad Cordero **RC** 4.00
58 Delmon Young **RC** 15.00

Common Leaf Limited Phenom:
Silver Spotlights: 1X
Production 50
Gold Spotlights: No Pricing
Production 10 or 25
201 Delmon Young/Auto./99 **RC** 125.00
202 Rickie Weeks/Auto./99 **RC** 60.00
203 Edwin Jackson/Auto./99 **RC** 25.00
204 Dan Haren/Auto./99 40.00

Signature Series:
151 Delmon Young/Auto./200 **RC** 80.00
152 Rickie Weeks/Auto./200 **RC** 30.00
153 Edwin Jackson/Auto./200 15.00

Stat Line Season/Career

Cards serial #'d from 101-150: 1-2X
Cards serial #'d from 50-100: 2-3X
Cards serial #'d under 26-49: 3-4X
Cards numbered under 25 not priced.

Autographs

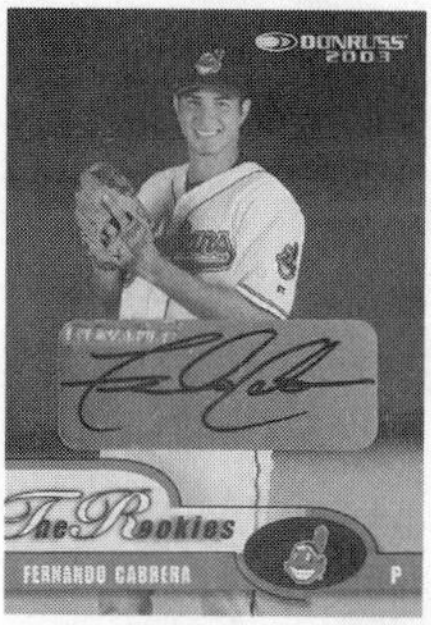

NM/M
Common Autograph: 5.00
1 Jeremy Bonderman/50 40.00
2 Adam Loewen/500 10.00
3 Dan Haren/100 30.00
4 Jose Contreras/100 25.00
6 Arnie Munoz/584 5.00
7 Miguel Cabrera/50 50.00
8 Andrew Brown/584 5.00
9 Josh Hall/1000 10.00
10 Josh Stewart/300 5.00
11 Clint Barmes/129 15.00
12 Luis Ayala/1000 5.00
13 Brandon Webb/100 50.00
14 Greg Aquino/1000 5.00
15 Chien-Ming Wang/100 200.00
17 Edgar Gonzalez/400 5.00
19 Bo Hart/150 5.00
20 Rosman Garcia/250 5.00
21 Jeremy Griffiths/812 5.00
22 Craig Brazell/205 5.00
23 Daniel Cabrera/383 15.00
24 Fernando Cabrera/1000 5.00
25 Termel Sledge/250 5.00
26 Ramon Nivar/100 5.00
27 Rob Hammock/201 10.00
29 Cory Stewart/1000 5.00
30 Felix Sanchez/1000 5.00
31 Jorge Cordova/1000 5.00
33 Beau Kemp/1000 5.00
34 Micheal Nakamura/1000 5.00
35 Rett Johnson/1000 8.00
36 Guillermo Quiroz/90 15.00
37 Hong-Chih Kuo/50 150.00
38 Ian Ferguson/1000 5.00
39 Franklin Perez/1000 5.00
40 Tim Olson/150 5.00
41 Jerome Williams/50 10.00
42 Rich Fischer/734 5.00
43 Phil Seibel/1000 5.00
44 Aaron Looper/513 5.00
45 Jae Weong Seo/50 30.00
47 Matt Kata/203 10.00
48 Ryan Wagner/100 10.00
50 Diegomar Markwell/1000 5.00
51 Doug Waechter/583 5.00
52 Mike Nicolas/1000 5.00
53 Prentice Redman/425 5.00
54 Shane Bazell/1000 5.00
55 Delmon Young/75 100.00
56 Brian Stokes/1000 5.00
57 Matt Bruback/513 5.00
58 Nook Logan/150 5.00
59 Oscar Villarreal/150 5.00
60 Pete LaForest/250 5.00

Gamers

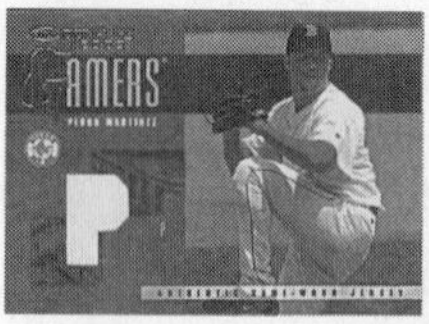

NM/M
Common Player: 4.00
Production 500
Position: 1-2X
Production 100
Number: 1-2X
Production 100
Patch: No Pricing
Production 25
Rewards: No Pricing
Production 10
1 Nomar Garciaparra 8.00
2 Alex Rodriguez 8.00
3 Mike Piazza 8.00
4 Greg Maddux 8.00
5 Roger Clemens 10.00
6 Sammy Sosa 8.00
7 Randy Johnson 8.00
8 Albert Pujols 15.00
9 Alfonso Soriano 8.00
10 Chipper Jones 8.00
11 Mark Prior 6.00
12 Hideo Nomo 6.00
13 Adam Dunn 6.00
14 Juan Gonzalez 5.00
15 Vladimir Guerrero 8.00
16 Pedro J. Martinez 8.00
17 Jim Thome 6.00
18 Brandon Webb/200 6.00
19 Mike Mussina 6.00
20 Mark Teixeira 5.00
21 Barry Larkin 5.00
22 Ivan Rodriguez 6.00
23 Hank Blalock 6.00
24 Rafael Palmeiro 6.00
25 Curt Schilling 6.00
26 Troy Glaus 5.00
27 Bernie Williams 6.00
28 Scott Rolen 6.00
29 Torii Hunter 5.00
30 Nick Johnson 4.00
31 Kazuhisa Ishii 4.00
32 Shawn Green 5.00
33 Jeff Bagwell 6.00
34 Lance Berkman 4.00
35 Roy Oswalt 4.00
36 Kerry Wood 4.00
37 Todd Helton 6.00
38 Manny Ramirez 8.00
39 Andruw Jones 5.00
40 Frank Thomas 8.00
41 Gary Sheffield 5.00
42 Magglio Ordonez 5.00
43 Mike Sweeney 4.00
44 Carlos Beltran 6.00
45 Richie Sexson 5.00
46 Jeff Kent 5.00
47 Carlos Delgado 5.00
48 Vernon Wells 4.00
49 Dontrelle Willis 8.00
50 Jae Weong Seo 4.00

Gamers Autograph

NM/M
Production 5-50 4.00
Many not priced due to scarcity.
20 Mark Teixeira/50 30.00
23 Hank Blalock/50 20.00
29 Torii Hunter/50 20.00
35 Roy Oswalt/50 20.00
43 Mike Sweeney/50 15.00
48 Vernon Wells/30 20.00
49 Dontrelle Willis/50 20.00

Leaf Autographs

NM/M
Common Autograph:
304 Jose Contreras/100 25.00
322 Ramon Nivar/100 10.00
323 Adam Loewen/100 10.00
324 Brandon Webb/100 50.00
325 Chien-Ming Wang/50 250.00
327 Ryan Wagner/100 10.00
328 Dan Haren/100 30.00

Playoff Prestige Autograph

NM/M
Quantity produced listed
201 Jeremy Bonderman/100 40.00
202 Brandon Webb/100 50.00
203 Adam Loewen/100 10.00
204 Chien-Ming Wang/50 250.00
205 Hong-Chih Kuo/100 150.00
207 Ryan Wagner/100 10.00
208 Dan Haren/100 25.00
210 Ramon Nivar/100 15.00

Recollection Autographs

NM/M
Common Player:
7 Jack McDowell 88/75 20.00

Turn of the Century Autograph

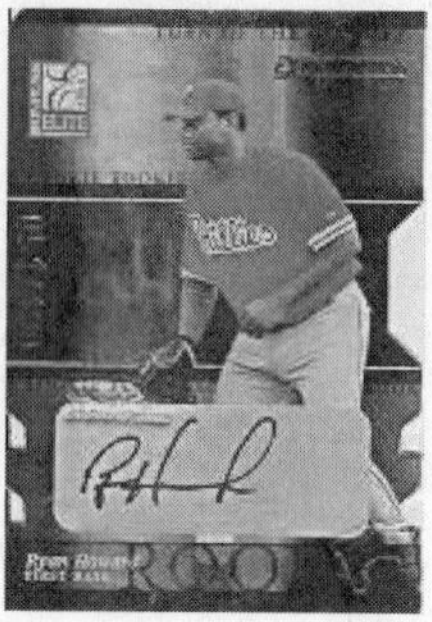

NM/M
Common Player: 10.00
Production 100
Aspirations: .75-1.5X
Varying quantities produced
1 Adam Loewen 15.00
2 Brandon Webb 125.00
3 Chien-Ming Wang 250.00
4 Hong-Chih Kuo 150.00
5 Clint Barmes 15.00
6 Guillermo Quiroz 20.00
7 Edgar Gonzalez 10.00
8 Todd Wellemeyer 20.00
9 Alfredo Gonzalez 10.00
10 Craig Brazell 10.00
11 Tim Olson 10.00
12 Rich Fischer 10.00
13 Daniel Cabrera 30.00
14 Francisco Rosario 10.00
15 Francisco Cruceta 10.00
16 Alejandro Machado 10.00
17 Andrew Brown 10.00
18 Rob Hammock 10.00
19 Arnie Munoz 10.00
20 Felix Sanchez 10.00
21 Nook Logan 10.00
22 Cory Stewart 10.00
23 Michel Hernandez 10.00
24 Rett Johnson 10.00
25 Josh Hall 15.00
26 Doug Waechter 10.00
27 Matt Kata 10.00
28 Dan Haren 75.00
29 Dontrelle Willis/25 40.00
30 Ramon Nivar 10.00
31 Chad Gaudin 20.00
32 Rickie Weeks/25 60.00
33 Ryan Wagner 10.00
35 Bo Hart 10.00
36 Oscar Villarreal 10.00
37 Josh Willingham 30.00
38 Jeff Duncan 15.00
40 Dustin McGowan 30.00
41 Preston Larrison 10.00
43 Kevin Youkilis 60.00
44 Bubba Nelson 15.00
45 Chris Burke 25.00
46 J.D. Durbin 15.00
47 Ryan Howard 500.00
48 Jason Kubel 30.00
49 Brendan Harris 20.00
50 Brian Bruney 10.00
52 Byron Gettis 10.00
53 Edwin Jackson 25.00
55 Daniel Garcia 10.00
58 Delmon Young 125.00

2003 Donruss Signature Series

NM/M
Complete Set (150): 150.00
Common Player: .50
Common Rk (101-150): 1.00
Inserted 1:Tin
Tin: 35.00
1 Garret Anderson .75
2 Tim Salmon .75
3 Troy Glaus .75
4 Curt Schilling 1.00
5 Luis Gonzalez .75
6 Mark Grace .75
7 Matt Williams .50
8 Randy Johnson 1.50
9 Andruw Jones 1.00
10 Chipper Jones 1.50
11 Gary Sheffield .75
12 Greg Maddux 2.00
13 Johnny Damon .75

14	Manny Ramirez	1.00
15	Nomar Garciaparra	2.50
16	Pedro J. Martinez	1.50
17	Corey Patterson	.75
18	Kerry Wood	1.50
19	Mark Prior	2.00
20	Sammy Sosa	2.50
21	Bartolo Colon	.50
22	Frank Thomas	1.00
23	Magglio Ordonez	.50
24	Paul Konerko	.50
25	Adam Dunn	1.00
26	Austin Kearns	.75
27	Barry Larkin	.75
28	Ken Griffey Jr.	2.00
29	C.C. Sabathia	.50
30	Omar Vizquel	.50
31	Larry Walker	.50
32	Todd Helton	1.00
33	Ivan Rodriguez	1.00
34	Josh Beckett	.75
35	Craig Biggio	.75
36	Jeff Bagwell	1.00
37	Jeff Kent	.50
38	Lance Berkman	.75
39	Richard Hidalgo	.50
40	Roy Oswalt	.75
41	Carlos Beltran	1.00
42	Mike Sweeney	.50
43	Runelvys Hernandez	.50
44	Hideo Nomo	.75
45	Kazuhisa Ishii	.50
46	Paul LoDuca	.50
47	Shawn Green	.75
48	Ben Sheets	.75
49	Richie Sexson	.75
50	A.J. Pierzynski	.50
51	Torii Hunter	.75
52	Javier Vazquez	.50
53	Jose Vidro	.50
54	Vladimir Guerrero	1.50
55	Cliff Floyd	.50
56	David Cone	.50
57	Mike Piazza	2.00
58	Roberto Alomar	.75
59	Tom Glavine	.75
60	Alfonso Soriano	1.50
61	Derek Jeter	4.00
62	Drew Henson	.50
63	Jason Giambi	.75
64	Mike Mussina	1.00
65	Nick Johnson	.50
66	Roger Clemens	3.00
67	Barry Zito	.75
68	Eric Chavez	.75
69	Mark Mulder	.75
70	Miguel Tejada	.75
71	Tim Hudson	.75
72	Bobby Abreu	.75
73	Jim Thome	1.00
74	Kevin Millwood	.50
75	Pat Burrell	.50
76	Brian Giles	.50
77	Jason Kendall	.50
78	Kenny Lofton	.50
79	Phil Nevin	.50
80	Ryan Klesko	.50
81	Andres Galarraga	.50
82	Barry Bonds	4.00
83	Rich Aurilia	.50
84	Edgar Martinez	.50
85	Freddy Garcia	.50
86	Ichiro Suzuki	2.50
87	Albert Pujols	3.00
88	Jim Edmonds	.75
89	Scott Rolen	1.50
90	So Taguchi	.50
91	Rocco Baldelli	.50
92	Alex Rodriguez	3.00
93	Hank Blalock	1.00
94	Juan Gonzalez	1.00
95	Mark Teixeira	.75
96	Rafael Palmeiro	1.00
97	Carlos Delgado	1.00
98	Eric Hinske	.50
99	Roy Halladay	.75
100	Vernon Wells	.50
101	Hideki Matsui **RC**	10.00
102	Jose Contreras **RC**	3.00
103	Jeremy Bonderman	4.00
104	Bernie Castro **RC**	1.00
105	Alfredo Gonzalez **RC**	1.00
106	Arnie Munoz **RC**	1.00
107	Andrew Brown **RC**	1.50
108	Josh Hall **RC**	1.50
109	Josh Stewart **RC**	1.50
110	Clint Barmes **RC**	1.50
111	Brandon Webb **RC**	8.00
112	Chien-Ming Wang **RC**	15.00
113	Edgar Gonzalez **RC**	1.00
114	Alejandro Machado **RC**	1.00
115	Jeremy Griffiths	1.00
116	Craig Brazell **RC**	1.50
117	Shane Bazell **RC**	1.50
118	Fernando Cabrera **RC**	1.50
119	Termel Sledge **RC**	1.50
120	Rob Hammock **RC**	1.50
121	Francisco Rosario **RC**	1.50
122	Francisco Cruceta **RC**	1.50
123	Rett Johnson **RC**	1.50
124	Guillermo Quiroz **RC**	2.00
125	Hong-Chih Kuo **RC**	3.00
126	Ian Ferguson **RC**	1.50
127	Tim Olson **RC**	1.00
128	Todd Wellemeyer **RC**	2.50
129	Richard Fischer **RC**	1.00
130	Phil Seibel **RC**	1.00
131	Joe Valentine **RC**	1.00
132	Matt Kata **RC**	1.50
133	Michael Hessman **RC**	1.00
134	Michel Hernandez **RC**	1.00
135	Doug Waechter **RC**	1.50
136	Prentice Redman **RC**	1.50
137	Nook Logan **RC**	1.00
138	Oscar Villarreal **RC**	1.00
139	Pete LaForest **RC**	1.00
140	Matt Bruback **RC**	1.00
141	Dontrelle Willis	1.50
142	Greg Aquino **RC**	1.00
143	Lew Ford **RC**	2.00
144	Jeff Duncan **RC**	2.00
145	Dan Haren	2.00
146	Miguel Ojeda **RC**	1.00
147	Rosman Garcia **RC**	1.00
148	Felix Sanchez **RC**	1.00
149	Jon Leicester **RC**	1.00
150	Roger Deago **RC**	1.00

Authentic Cuts

No Pricing
Quantity produced listed

Autographs

NM/M

Common Auto.: 8.00
Some not priced due to scarcity.

1	Garret Anderson	15.00
6	Mark Grace/141	40.00
7	Matt Williams	10.00
8	Randy Johnson/50	60.00
10	Chipper Jones/50	50.00
14	Manny Ramirez/50	40.00
17	Barry Larkin/159	25.00
33	Ivan Rodriguez/50	35.00
38	Lance Berkman/75	20.00
39	Richard Hidalgo	8.00
40	Roy Oswalt/150	15.00
42	Mike Sweeney	8.00
50	A.J. Pierzynski	8.00
51	Torii Hunter	15.00
53	Jose Vidro	6.00
54	Vladimir Guerrero	20.00
55	Cliff Floyd	8.00
56	David Cone/35	15.00
58	Roberto Alomar/50	30.00
65	Nick Johnson	10.00
67	Barry Zito/150	10.00
68	Eric Chavez	10.00
69	Mark Mulder/50	15.00
72	Bobby Abreu	15.00
78	Kenny Lofton/229	10.00
80	Ryan Klesko/150	10.00
81	Andres Galarraga	8.00
83	Rich Aurilia/122	8.00
84	Edgar Martinez	15.00
89	Scott Rolen/200	20.00
90	So Taguchi/220	10.00
95	Mark Teixeira/150	20.00
100	Vernon Wells	10.00
102	Jose Contreras	20.00
141	Dontrelle Willis/150	20.00

Century

NM/M

Common Auto.: 15.00
Production 100 Sets
Decades: No Pricing
Production 10 Sets

1	Garret Anderson	15.00
7	Matt Williams	15.00
27	Barry Larkin	30.00
39	Richard Hidalgo	15.00
42	Mike Sweeney	15.00
50	A.J. Pierzynski	15.00
51	Torii Hunter	20.00
53	Jose Vidro	15.00
54	Vladimir Guerrero	30.00
55	Cliff Floyd	15.00
62	Drew Henson	15.00
65	Nick Johnson	15.00
69	Mark Mulder	25.00
72	Bobby Abreu	20.00
78	Kenny Lofton	15.00
81	Andres Galarraga	15.00
84	Edgar Martinez	25.00
89	Scott Rolen	30.00
90	So Taguchi	15.00
100	Vernon Wells	15.00
102	Jose Contreras	25.00

Century Notations

NM/M

Production 100 Sets
Decade Notations: No Pricing
Production 10 Sets

1	Garret Anderson	20.00
7	Matt Williams	15.00
50	A.J. Pierzynski	15.00
68	Eric Chavez	15.00
78	Kenny Lofton	15.00
84	Edgar Martinez	25.00

Century Proofs

Stars (1-100): 2-4X
Century (101-150): 1-2X
Production 100 Sets

Decade Proofs

Production 10 Sets
No pricing due to scarcity.

INKredible - Three

NM/M

Production 50 Sets

1	Barry Zito, Mark Mulder, Tim Hudson	300.00
2	Andruw Jones, Chipper Jones, Greg Maddux	325.00
3	Ernie Banks, Kerry Wood, Mark Prior	300.00
4	Harmon Killebrew, Kirby Puckett, Torii Hunter	175.00
5	Javier Vazquez, Jose Vidro, Vladimir Guerrero	90.00

INKredible - Four

NM/M

Production 25 Sets
Limited pricing due to scarcity.

4	Brooks Robinson, Cal Ripken Jr., Frank Robinson, Jim Palmer	500.00
6	Bo Jackson, Carlos Beltran, George Brett, Mike Sweeney	225.00
7	Curt Schilling, Junior Spivey, Mark Grace, Randy Johnson	475.00
10	Joe Carter, Roberto Alomar, Ryan Klesko, Tony Gwynn	200.00

INKredible - Six

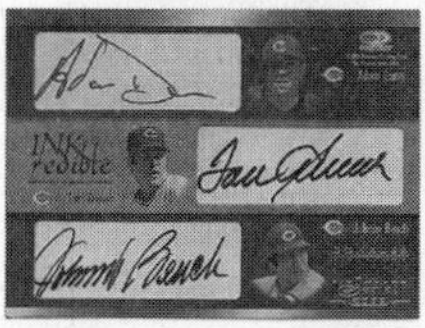

NM/M

Production 10 Sets
Limited pricing due to scarcity.

3	Andre Dawson, Ernie Banks, Kerry Wood, Mark Grace, Mark Prior, Ryne Sandberg	1,500
5	Alex Rodriguez, Don Mattingly, George Brett, Hideo Nomo, Nolan Ryan, Roger Clemens	3,100

Legends of Summer

NM/M

Complete Set (40): 125.00
Common Player: 3.00
Production 250 Sets
Century: 1X
Production 100 Sets
Decades: No Pricing
Production 10 Sets

1	Al Kaline	5.00
2	Alan Trammell	3.00
3	Andre Dawson	3.00
4	Babe Ruth	10.00
5	Billy Williams	3.00
6	Bo Jackson	4.00
7	Bob Feller	3.00
8	Bobby Doerr	3.00
9	Brooks Robinson	5.00
10	Dale Murphy	5.00
11	Dennis Eckersley	3.00
12	Don Mattingly	8.00
13	Duke Snider	3.00
14	Eric Davis	3.00
15	Frank Robinson	3.00
16	Fred Lynn	3.00
17	Gary Carter	3.00
18	Harmon Killebrew	5.00
19	Jack Morris	3.00
20	Jim Palmer	3.00
21	Jim Abbott	3.00
22	Joe Morgan	3.00
23	Joe Torre	3.00
24	Johnny Bench	5.00
25	Jose Canseco	3.00
26	Kirby Puckett	5.00
27	Lenny Dykstra	3.00
28	Lou Brock	3.00
29	Ralph Kiner	3.00
30	Mike Schmidt	6.00
31	Nolan Ryan	10.00
32	Nolan Ryan	10.00
33	Orel Hershiser	3.00
34	Phil Rizzuto	3.00
35	Orlando Cepeda	3.00
36	Ryne Sandberg	8.00
37	Stan Musial	6.00
38	Steve Garvey	3.00
39	Tony Perez	3.00
40	Ty Cobb	6.00

Legends of Summer Auto.

NM/M

Common Autograph: 8.00

1	Al Kaline	20.00
2	Alan Trammell	10.00
3	Andre Dawson	10.00
5	Billy Williams	8.00
6	Bo Jackson/100	50.00
7	Bob Feller	15.00
8	Bobby Doerr	15.00
9	Brooks Robinson	25.00
10	Dale Murphy/75	40.00
11	Dennis Eckersley	10.00
12	Don Mattingly/50	75.00
13	Duke Snider/225	20.00
14	Eric Davis	8.00
15	Frank Robinson	10.00
16	Fred Lynn	8.00
17	Gary Carter	10.00
18	Harmon Killebrew/171	20.00
19	Jack Morris	8.00
20	Jim Palmer	10.00
21	Jim Abbott	8.00
22	Joe Morgan/125	15.00
23	Joe Torre	10.00
24	Johnny Bench/75	30.00
25	Jose Canseco/75	30.00
26	Kirby Puckett/75	35.00
27	Lenny Dykstra	10.00
28	Lou Brock	15.00
29	Ralph Kiner	10.00
30	Mike Schmidt/75	60.00
31	Nolan Ryan/75	110.00
33	Orel Hershiser	20.00
34	Phil Rizzuto	15.00
35	Orlando Cepeda	15.00
36	Ryne Sandberg/75	60.00
37	Stan Musial/200	40.00
38	Steve Garvey	10.00
39	Tony Perez	10.00

Legends of Summer Century

NM/M

Production 100 Sets
Decades: No Pricing
Production 10 Sets

1	Al Kaline	25.00
2	Alan Trammell	20.00
3	Andre Dawson	15.00
5	Billy Williams	15.00
6	Bo Jackson	50.00
7	Bob Feller	25.00
8	Bobby Doerr	20.00
9	Brooks Robinson	30.00
11	Dennis Eckersley	15.00
12	Don Mattingly	65.00
14	Eric Davis	15.00
15	Frank Robinson	15.00
16	Fred Lynn	15.00
17	Gary Carter	20.00
19	Jack Morris	15.00
20	Jim Palmer	20.00
21	Jim Abbott	15.00
23	Joe Torre	15.00
27	Lenny Dykstra	15.00
28	Lou Brock	25.00
29	Ralph Kiner	15.00
33	Orel Hershiser	60.00
34	Phil Rizzuto	30.00
35	Orlando Cepeda	20.00
36	Ryne Sandberg	65.00
37	Stan Musial	60.00
38	Steve Garvey	15.00
39	Tony Perez	15.00

Notations

NM/M

Varying quantities produced
Many not priced due to scarcity.

1	Garret Anderson/75	20.00
7	Matt Williams/250	10.00
7	Matt Williams/50	20.00
45	Kazuhisa Ishii/35	35.00
50	A.J. Pierzynski/200	10.00
53	Jose Vidro/40	15.00
62	Drew Henson/73	20.00
68	Eric Chavez/50	20.00
78	Kenny Lofton/150	10.00
80	Ryan Klesko/75	20.00
83	Rich Aurilia/61	15.00
84	Edgar Martinez/250	10.00
84	Edgar Martinez/60	20.00
100	Vernon Wells/75	15.00

Notable Nicknames

NM/M

Complete Set (20): 75.00
Common Player: 3.00
Production 750 Sets
Century: 1-1.5X
Production 100 Sets
Decade: No Pricing
Production 10 Sets

1	Andre Dawson	3.00
2	Torii Hunter	3.00
3	Brooks Robinson	5.00
4	Carlton Fisk	3.00
5	Mike Mussina	4.00
6	Don Mattingly	8.00
7	Duke Snider	4.00
8	Eric Davis	3.00
9	Frank Thomas	4.00
10	Randy Johnson	5.00
11	Lenny Dykstra	3.00
12	Ivan Rodriguez	3.00
13	Nolan Ryan	10.00
14	Phil Rizzuto	3.00
15	Reggie Jackson	4.00
16	Roger Clemens	8.00
17	Ryne Sandberg	8.00
18	Stan Musial	6.00
19	Luis Gonzalez	3.00
20	Will Clark	4.00

Notable Nicknames Auto.

NM/M

Quantity produced listed
Decades: No Pricing
Production 10 Sets

		NM/M
1	Andre "The Hawk" Dawson/100	30.00
2	Torii "Spiderman" Hunter/100	30.00
3	Brooks "Hoover" Robinson	60.00
4	Carlton "Pudge" Fisk/100	50.00
5	Mike "Moose" Mussina/100	80.00
6	Don "Donnie Baseball" Mattingly/100	100.00
7	Duke "Duke of Flatbush" Snider/100	60.00
8	Eric "The Red" Davis/40	50.00
9	Frank "The Big Hurt" Thomas/100	60.00
10	Randy "Big Unit" Johnson/100	100.00
11	Lenny "Nails" Dykstra/100	20.00
12	Ivan "Pudge" Rodriguez/75	50.00
14	Phil "Scooter" Rizzuto/100	50.00
15	Reggie "Mr. October" Jackson/100	60.00
16	Roger "The Rocket" Clemens/100	150.00
17	Ryne "Ryno" Sandberg/100	75.00
18	Stan "The Man" Musial/100	85.00
19	Luis "Gonzo" Gonzalez/100	25.00
20	Will "The Thrill" Clark/100	60.00

Players Collection Auto.

NM/M

Quantity produced listed

		NM/M
	Roberto Alomar/75	30.00
	Adrian Beltre/104	30.00
	Lance Berkman/50	20.00
	Craig Biggio/26	35.00
	Joe Borchard/53	10.00
	J.D. Drew/52	20.00
	Jim Edmonds/52	25.00
	Todd Helton/50	40.00
	Jason Jennings/49	10.00
	Chipper Jones/51	50.00
	Paul LoDuca/227	8.00
	Magglio Ordonez/102	20.00
	Mark Prior/27	100.00
	Ivan Rodriguez/52	35.00
	Richie Sexson/50	20.00
	Matt Williams/482	8.00

Signature Cuts

NM/M

Some not priced due to scarcity.
Decades: No Pricing
Production 10 Sets

		NM/M
8	Randy Johnson/40	60.00
33	Ivan Rodriguez/122	30.00
54	Vladimir Guerrero/34	35.00
58	Roberto Alomar/100	30.00
64	Mike Mussina/82	40.00
73	Jim Thome/127	30.00
80	Ryan Klesko/35	20.00
81	Andres Galarraga/51	20.00
89	Scott Rolen/36	40.00

Team Trademarks

NM/M

Complete Set (40): 150.00
Common Player: 3.00
Production 100 Sets
Century: 1X
Production 100 Sets
Decade: No Pricing
Production 10 Sets

		NM/M
1	Adam Dunn	3.00
2	Andre Dawson	3.00
3	Babe Ruth	10.00
4	Barry Bonds	10.00
5	Brooks Robinson	4.00
6	Cal Ripken Jr.	10.00
7	Derek Jeter	8.00
8	Don Mattingly	8.00
9	Frank Robinson	3.00
10	Fred Lynn	3.00
11	Gary Carter	3.00
12	George Brett	6.00
13	Greg Maddux	5.00
14	Ichiro Suzuki	6.00
15	Jim Palmer	3.00
16	Jose Contreras	3.00
17	Kerry Wood	4.00
18	Lou Gehrig	8.00
19	Magglio Ordonez	3.00
20	Mark Grace	3.00
21	Mike Schmidt	8.00
22	Nolan Ryan	10.00
23	Nolan Ryan	10.00
24	Reggie Jackson	4.00
25	Rickey Henderson	3.00
26	Roberto Clemente	6.00
27	Roger Clemens	6.00
28	Roger Clemens	6.00
29	Ryne Sandberg	6.00
30	Sammy Sosa	6.00
31	Stan Musial	6.00
32	Steve Carlton	3.00
33	Tim Hudson	3.00
34	Tom Glavine	3.00
35	Tom Seaver	4.00
36	Tony Gwynn	4.00
37	Torii Hunter	3.00
38	Ty Cobb	6.00
39	Vladimir Guerrero	4.00
40	Will Clark	4.00

Team Trademarks Autograph

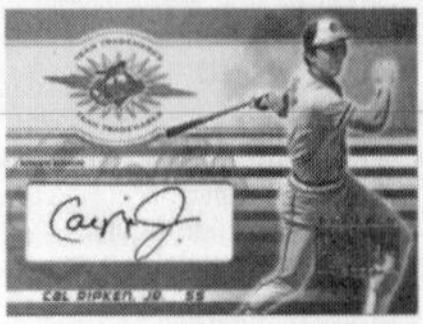

NM/M

Quantity produced listed

		NM/M
1	Adam Dunn/50	35.00
2	Andre Dawson/250	10.00
5	Brooks Robinson/250	20.00
6	Cal Ripken Jr./50	200.00
8	Don Mattingly/75	85.00
10	Fred Lynn/250	8.00
11	Gary Carter/250	10.00
12	George Brett/50	100.00
13	Greg Maddux/50	85.00
16	Jose Contreras/250	15.00
17	Kerry Wood/50	40.00
19	Magglio Ordonez/75	15.00
20	Mark Grace/25	90.00
23	Nolan Ryan/50	110.00
24	Reggie Jackson/75	25.00
25	Rickey Henderson/50	100.00
27	Roger Clemens/50	110.00
28	Roger Clemens/50	110.00
29	Ryne Sandberg/100	60.00
31	Stan Musial/200	50.00
32	Steve Carlton/150	20.00
33	Tim Hudson/100	35.00
34	Tom Glavine/50	35.00
35	Tom Seaver/50	35.00
36	Tony Gwynn/50	60.00
37	Torii Hunter/250	10.00
39	Vladimir Guerrero/250	20.00
40	Will Clark/125	30.00

Team Trademarks Century

NM/M

Production 100 Sets
Decade: No Pricing
Production 10 Sets

		NM/M
2	Andre Dawson	15.00
5	Brooks Robinson	30.00
9	Frank Robinson	15.00
10	Fred Lynn	15.00
11	Gary Carter	20.00
15	Jim Palmer	15.00
16	Jose Contreras	25.00
20	Mark Grace	60.00
29	Ryne Sandberg	65.00
31	Stan Musial	65.00
32	Steve Carlton	25.00
34	Tom Glavine	25.00
37	Steve Hunter	15.00
39	Vladimir Guerrero	25.00

Team Trademarks Notations

NM/M

Quantity produced listed

		NM/M
2	Andre Dawson/250	10.00
2	Andre Dawson/150	10.00
5	Brooks Robinson/75	35.00
5	Brooks Robinson/125	30.00
10	Fred Lynn/50	20.00
15	Jim Palmer/32	25.00
15	Jim Palmer/128	15.00
15	Jim Palmer/150	15.00
29	Ryne Sandberg/40	80.00
29	Ryne Sandberg/55	75.00
32	Steve Carlton/50	35.00
33	Tim Hudson/50	45.00
40	Will Clark/52	60.00

2003 Donruss Studio

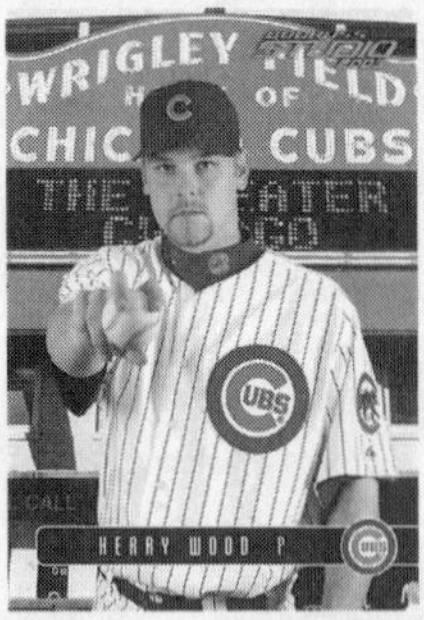

NM/M

Complete Set (200): 35.00
Common Player: .25
Pack (6): 4.00
Box (20): 60.00

		NM/M
1	Darin Erstad	.40
2	David Eckstein	.25
3	Garret Anderson	.50
4	Jarrod Washburn	.25
5	Tim Salmon	.50
6	Troy Glaus	.50
7	Jay Gibbons	.25
8	Melvin Mora	.25
9	Rodrigo Lopez	.25
10	Tony Batista	.25
11	Freddy Sanchez	.25
12	Derek Lowe	.25
13	Johnny Damon	.40
14	Manny Ramirez	.75
15	Nomar Garciaparra	1.50
16	Pedro J. Martinez	1.00
17	Rickey Henderson	.50
18	Shea Hillenbrand	.25
19	Carlos Lee	.25
20	Frank Thomas	.75
21	Magglio Ordonez	.40
22	Bartolo Colon	.25
23	Paul Konerko	.25
24	Josh Stewart **RC**	.50
25	C.C. Sabathia	.25
26	Jeremy Guthrie	.25
27	Ellis Burks	.25
28	Omar Vizquel	.40
29	Victor Martinez	.25
30	Cliff Lee	.25
31	Jhonny Peralta	.50
32	Brian Tallet	.25
33	Bobby Higginson	.25
34	Carlos Pena	.25
35	Nook Logan **RC**	.25
36	Steve Sparks	.25
37	Travis Chapman	.25
38	Carlos Beltran	.75
39	Joe Randa	.25
40	Mike Sweeney	.25
41	Jimmy Gobble	.25
42	Michael Tucker	.25
43	Runelvys Hernandez	.25
44	Brad Radke	.25
45	Corey Koskie	.25
46	Cristian Guzman	.25
47	J.C. Romero	.25
48	Doug Mientkiewicz	.25
49	Lew Ford **RC**	1.50
50	Jacque Jones	.40
51	Torii Hunter	.50
52	Alfonso Soriano	.75
53	Nick Johnson	.25
54	Bernie Williams	.50
55	Jose Contreras **RC**	1.50
56	Derek Jeter	3.00
57	Jason Giambi	.50
58	Brandon Claussen	.25
59	Jorge Posada	.50
60	Mike Mussina	.50
61	Roger Clemens	2.00
62	Hideki Matsui **RC**	5.00
63	Barry Zito	.50
64	Adam Morrissey	.25
65	Eric Chavez	.40
66	Jermaine Dye	.25
67	Mark Mulder	.40
68	Miguel Tejada	.50
69	Joe Valentine **RC**	.25
70	Tim Hudson	.50
71	Bret Boone	.40
72	Chris Snelling	.25
73	Edgar Martinez	.25
74	Freddy Garcia	.25
75	Ichiro Suzuki	2.00
76	Jamie Moyer	.25
77	John Olerud	.40
78	Kazuhiro Sasaki	.25
79	Aubrey Huff	.25
80	Joe Kennedy	.25
81	Dewon Brazelton	.25
82	Pete LaForest **RC**	.25
83	Alex Rodriguez	2.50
84	Chan Ho Park	.25
85	Hank Blalock	.75
86	Juan Gonzalez	.75
87	Kevin Mench	.25
88	Rafael Palmeiro	.75
89	Carlos Delgado	.50
90	Eric Hinske	.25
91	Josh Phelps	.25
92	Roy Halladay	.40
93	Shannon Stewart	.25
94	Vernon Wells	.40
95	Vinnie Chulk	.25
96	Curt Schilling	.75
97	Junior Spivey	.25
98	Luis Gonzalez	.50
99	Mark Grace	.50
100	Randy Johnson	1.00
101	Andruw Jones	.75
102	Chipper Jones	1.00
103	Gary Sheffield	.50
104	Greg Maddux	1.50
105	John Smoltz	.50
106	Mike Hampton	.25
107	Adam LaRoche	.25
108	Michael Hessman **RC**	.50
109	Corey Patterson	.40
110	Kerry Wood	1.00
111	Mark Prior	1.00
112	Moises Alou	.50
113	Sammy Sosa	1.50
114	Adam Dunn	.75
115	Austin Kearns	.40
116	Barry Larkin	.40
117	Ken Griffey Jr.	1.50
118	Sean Casey	.25
119	Jason Jennings	.25
120	Jay Payton	.25
121	Larry Walker	.40
122	Todd Helton	.75
123	Jeff Baker	.25
124	Clint Barmes **RC**	1.00
125	Ivan Rodriguez	.75
126	Josh Beckett	.50
127	Juan Encarnacion	.25
128	Mike Lowell	.25
129	Craig Biggio	.40
130	Jason Lane	.25
131	Jeff Bagwell	.75
132	Lance Berkman	.50
133	Roy Oswalt	.40
134	Jeff Kent	.40
135	Hideo Nomo	.50
136	Kazuhisa Ishii	.25
137	Kevin Brown	.40
138	Odalis Perez	.25
139	Paul LoDuca	.25
140	Shawn Green	.50
141	Adrian Beltre	.50
142	Ben Sheets	.40
143	Bill Hall	.25
144	Jeffrey Hammonds	.25
145	Richie Sexson	.50
146	Termel Sledge **RC**	.75
147	Brad Wilkerson	.25
148	Javier Vazquez	.25
149	Jose Vidro	.25
150	Michael Barrett	.25
151	Vladimir Guerrero	.75
152	Al Leiter	.25
153	Mike Piazza	2.00
154	Mo Vaughn	.25
155	Cliff Floyd	.25
156	Roberto Alomar	.50
157	Roger Cedeno	.25
158	Tom Glavine	.50
159	Prentice Redman **RC**	.50
160	Bobby Abreu	.50
161	Jimmy Rollins	.40
162	Mike Lieberthal	.25
163	Pat Burrell	.50
164	Vicente Padilla	.25
165	Jim Thome	.75
166	Kevin Millwood	.40
167	Aramis Ramirez	.50
168	Brian Giles	.40
169	Jason Kendall	.40
170	Josh Fogg	.25
171	Kip Wells	.25
172	Jose Castillo	.25
173	Mark Kotsay	.25
174	Oliver Perez	.25
175	Phil Nevin	.25
176	Ryan Klesko	.40
177	Sean Burroughs	.25
178	Brian Lawrence	.25
179	Shane Victorino **RC**	.25
180	Barry Bonds	3.00
181	Benito Santiago	.25
182	Ray Durham	.25
183	Rich Aurilia	.25
184	Damian Moss	.25
185	Albert Pujols	2.00
186	J.D. Drew	.25
187	Jim Edmonds	.50
188	Matt Morris	.40
189	Tino Martinez	.25
190	Scott Rolen	.75
191	Troy Glaus, Tim Salmon	.50
192	Sean Casey, Corky Miller	.25
193	Carlos Lee, Frank Thomas	.50
194	Lance Berkman, Jeff Kent	.25
195	Jose Contreras, Mariano Rivera	1.00
196	Alex Rodriguez, Juan Gonzalez	1.00
197	Andy Pettitte, David Wells	.25
198	Shawn Green, Dave Roberts	.25
199	Mike Lieberthal, Jimmy Rollins	.40
200	Mike Mussina, Hideki Matsui	2.00

Proofs

Stars (1-200): 4-8X
Rookies (1-200): 2-3X
Production 100 Sets

Big League Challenge

NM/M

Complete Set (50): 125.00
Common Player: 1.50
Production 400 Sets
Proofs 4-8X
Production 25 Sets

		NM/M
1	Jose Canseco	2.00
2	Magglio Ordonez	1.50
3	Alex Rodriguez	5.00
4	Lance Berkman	1.50
5	Rafael Palmeiro	3.00
6	Nomar Garciaparra	5.00
7	Nomar Garciaparra	5.00
8	Nomar Garciaparra	5.00
9	Troy Glaus	2.00
10	Mark McGwire	6.00
11	Mark McGwire	6.00

12 Mark McGwire 6.00
13 Jim Thome 3.00
14 Chipper Jones 3.00
15 Shawn Green 1.50
16 Alex Rodriguez 5.00
17 Alex Rodriguez 5.00
18 Alex Rodriguez 5.00
19 Alex Rodriguez 5.00
20 Jason Giambi 2.00
21 Pat Burrell 1.50
22 Mike Piazza 4.00
23 Mike Piazza 4.00
24 Mike Piazza 4.00
25 Frank Thomas 2.00
26 Rafael Palmeiro 2.00
27 Todd Helton 2.00
28 Jose Canseco 2.00
29 Albert Pujols 5.00
30 Troy Glaus 2.00
31 Barry Bonds 6.00
32 Barry Bonds 6.00
33 Barry Bonds 6.00
34 Todd Helton 3.00
35 Rafael Palmeiro 3.00
36 Jim Thome 3.00
37 Ozzie Smith 3.00
38 Troy Glaus 2.00
39 Shawn Green 1.50
40 Barry Bonds 6.00
41 Barry Bonds 6.00
42 Barry Bonds 6.00
43 Magglio Ordonez 1.50
44 Alex Rodriguez 5.00
45 Alex Rodriguez 5.00
46 Alex Rodriguez 5.00
47 Lance Berkman 1.50
48 Rafael Palmeiro 3.00
49 Pat Burrell 1.50
50 Albert Pujols 5.00

Big League Challenge Materials

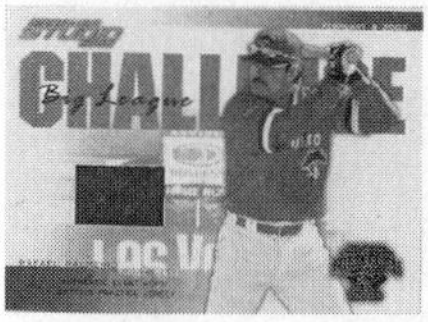

NM/M
Common Player: 4.00
Inserted 1:20
2 Magglio Ordonez/Jsy 4.00
3 Alex Rodriguez/Jsy 10.00
4 Lance Berkman/Jsy 4.00
15 Shawn Green/Jsy 4.00
29 Albert Pujols/Jsy 15.00
36 Jim Thome/Jsy 6.00
39 Shawn Green/Pants 4.00
40 Barry Bonds/Base 10.00
41 Barry Bonds/Base 10.00
42 Barry Bonds/Base 10.00
43 Magglio Ordonez/Jsy 4.00
45 Alex Rodriguez/Jsy 10.00
46 Alex Rodriguez/Pants 10.00
47 Lance Berkman/Jsy 4.00
48 Rafael Palmeiro/Jsy 6.00
50 Albert Pujols/Pants 10.00

Big League Challenge Prime Material

NM/M
Common Player: 10.00
2 Magglio Ordonez/100 10.00
3 Alex Rodriguez/100 25.00
15 Shawn Green/50 15.00
29 Albert Pujols/100 25.00
36 Jim Thome/50 20.00
45 Alex Rodriguez/100 25.00
48 Rafael Palmeiro/100 15.00

Enshrinement

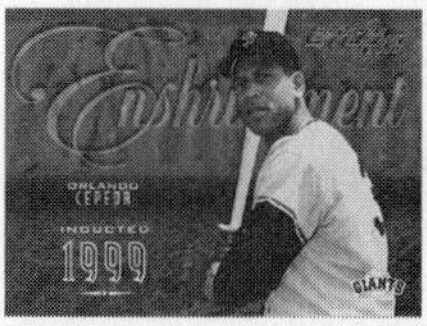

NM/M
Complete Set (50): 180.00
Common Player: 3.00
Production 750 Sets
Proofs: 5-10X
Production 20 or 21
1 Gary Carter 4.00
2 Ozzie Smith 10.00
3 Kirby Puckett 6.00
4 Carlton Fisk 4.00
5 Tony Perez 3.00
6 Nolan Ryan 15.00
7 George Brett 12.00
8 Robin Yount 10.00
9 Orlando Cepeda 3.00
10 Phil Niekro 3.00
11 Mike Schmidt 10.00
12 Richie Ashburn 6.00
13 Steve Carlton 4.00
14 Phil Rizzuto 4.00
15 Reggie Jackson 6.00
16 Tom Seaver 5.00
17 Rollie Fingers 3.00
18 Rod Carew 5.00
19 Gaylord Perry 3.00
20 Fergie Jenkins 3.00
21 Jim Palmer 3.00
22 Joe Morgan 3.00
23 Johnny Bench 6.00
24 Willie Stargell 4.00
25 Billy Williams 3.00
26 Jim "Catfish" Hunter 3.00
27 Willie McCovey 3.00
28 Bobby Doerr 3.00
29 Lou Brock 4.00
30 Enos Slaughter 3.00
31 Hoyt Wilhelm 3.00
32 Harmon Killebrew 6.00
33 Pee Wee Reese 3.00
34 Luis Aparicio 3.00
35 Brooks Robinson 6.00
36 Juan Marichal 4.00
37 Frank Robinson 5.00
38 Bob Gibson 4.00
39 Al Kaline 6.00
40 Duke Snider 6.00
41 Eddie Mathews 5.00
42 Robin Roberts 3.00
43 Ralph Kiner 3.00
44 Whitey Ford 5.00
45 Roberto Clemente 10.00
46 Warren Spahn 4.00
47 Yogi Berra 5.00
48 Early Wynn 3.00
49 Stan Musial 6.00
50 Bob Feller 4.00

Enshrinement Autographs

NM/M
Varying quantities produced
1 Gary Carter/50 30.00
5 Tony Perez/50 50.00
9 Orlando Cepeda/50 25.00
10 Phil Niekro/50 20.00
13 Steve Carlton/50 40.00
14 Phil Rizzuto/15 50.00
20 Fergie Jenkins/50 20.00
21 Jim Palmer/25 35.00
22 Joe Morgan/10 50.00
28 Bobby Doerr/100 20.00
31 Hoyt Wilhelm/50 25.00
34 Luis Aparicio/100 15.00
35 Brooks Robinson/25 65.00
37 Frank Robinson/25 50.00
43 Ralph Kiner/25 40.00
50 Bob Feller/100 25.00

Leather & Lumber

NM/M
Common Player: 5.00
1 Adam Dunn/400 10.00
2 Alex Rodriguez/250 12.00
3 Alfonso Soriano/250 10.00
4 Andruw Jones/400 8.00
5 Austin Kearns/400 8.00
6 Chipper Jones/400 10.00
7 Derek Jeter/100 35.00
8 Don Mattingly/100 40.00
9 Edgar Martinez 10.00
10 Frank Thomas/400 8.00
11 Fred McGriff/400 8.00
13 Greg Maddux/150 15.00
14 Hideki Matsui/Ball/100 40.00
15 Hideo Nomo/150 15.00
16 Ichiro Suzuki/Ball/100 40.00
17 Ivan Rodriguez/250 8.00
18 Jason Giambi/400 8.00
19 Jeff Bagwell/400 8.00
20 Jim Edmonds/150 8.00
21 Jim Thome/400 10.00
22 Juan Gonzalez/400 8.00
23 Kerry Wood/250 10.00
24 Kirby Puckett/100 25.00
25 Lance Berkman/400 5.00
26 Magglio Ordonez/400 5.00
27 Manny Ramirez/250 10.00
28 Mark Prior/400 8.00
29 Miguel Tejada/200 5.00
30 Mike Piazza/400 10.00
31 Mike Schmidt/200 25.00
32 Nomar Garciaparra/400 15.00
33 Pat Burrell/400 8.00
34 Pedro Martinez/150 10.00
36 Randy Johnson/250 10.00
37 Rickey Henderson/175 10.00
38 Sammy Sosa/300 10.00
39 Shawn Green/400 5.00
40 Vladimir Guerrero/400 8.00

Leather & Lumber Dual

NM/M
Common Player:
Those without bat & ball are noted.
1 Adam Dunn/50 25.00
2 Alex Rodriguez/50 30.00
4 Andruw Jones/50 25.00
5 Austin Kearns/Shoe/50 25.00
6 Chipper Jones/25 45.00
8 Don Mattingly/25 80.00
10 Frank Thomas/50 30.00
13 Greg Maddux/Shoe/50 35.00
17 Ivan Rodriguez/50 25.00
19 Jeff Bagwell/25 35.00
23 Kerry Wood/50 35.00
24 Kirby Puckett/25 50.00
25 Lance Berkman/50 12.00
28 Mark Prior/Shoe/25 50.00
29 Miguel Tejada/25 15.00
33 Pat Burrell/25 20.00
36 Randy Johnson/25 40.00
38 Sammy Sosa/Shoe/25 60.00

Masterstrokes

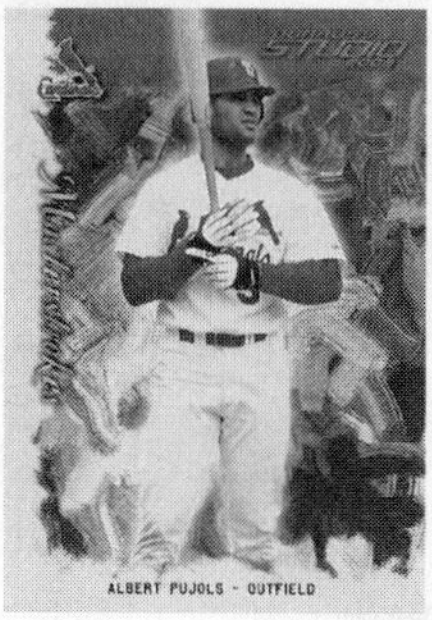

NM/M
Complete Set (25): 50.00
Common Player: 1.00
Production 1,000 Sets
1 Adam Dunn 2.00
2 Albert Pujols 3.00
3 Alex Rodriguez 5.00
4 Alfonso Soriano 3.00
5 Andruw Jones 1.50
6 Chipper Jones 3.00
7 Derek Jeter 6.00
8 Greg Maddux 3.00
9 Hideki Matsui 8.00
10 Hideo Nomo 1.50
11 Ivan Rodriguez 2.00
12 Jason Giambi 1.50
13 Jeff Bagwell 2.00
14 Juan Gonzalez 1.50
15 Ken Griffey Jr. 3.00
16 Lance Berkman 1.00
17 Magglio Ordonez 1.00
18 Manny Ramirez 2.00
19 Mark Prior 2.00
20 Miguel Tejada 1.00
21 Mike Piazza 4.00
22 Nomar Garciaparra 4.00
23 Pat Burrell 1.50
24 Sammy Sosa 4.00
25 Vladimir Guerrero 1.50

Masterstrokes Artist's Proof

NM/M
Common Player: 15.00
Production 50 Sets
1 Adam Dunn 25.00
2 Albert Pujols 50.00
3 Alex Rodriguez 50.00
4 Alfonso Soriano 25.00
5 Andruw Jones 20.00
6 Chipper Jones 30.00
7 Derek Jeter 50.00
8 Greg Maddux 25.00
9 Hideki Matsui 75.00
10 Hideo Nomo 100.00
11 Ivan Rodriguez 20.00
12 Jason Giambi 15.00
13 Jeff Bagwell 25.00
14 Juan Gonzalez 25.00
15 Ken Griffey Jr. 30.00
16 Lance Berkman 15.00
17 Magglio Ordonez 15.00
18 Manny Ramirez 20.00
19 Mark Prior 20.00
20 Miguel Tejada 15.00
21 Mike Piazza 35.00
22 Nomar Garciaparra 40.00
23 Pat Burrell 15.00
24 Sammy Sosa 40.00
25 Vladimir Guerrero 25.00

Players Collection

NM/M
Common Player: 4.00
Production 300 Sets
1 Adam Dunn 8.00
2 Adrian Beltre 6.00
3 Alex Rodriguez 10.00
4 Alfonso Soriano 8.00
5 Andruw Jones 6.00
6 Andy Pettitte 4.00
7 Barry Larkin 6.00
8 Barry Zito 4.00
9 Ben Grieve 4.00
10 Bernie Williams 8.00
11 Cal Ripken Jr. 30.00

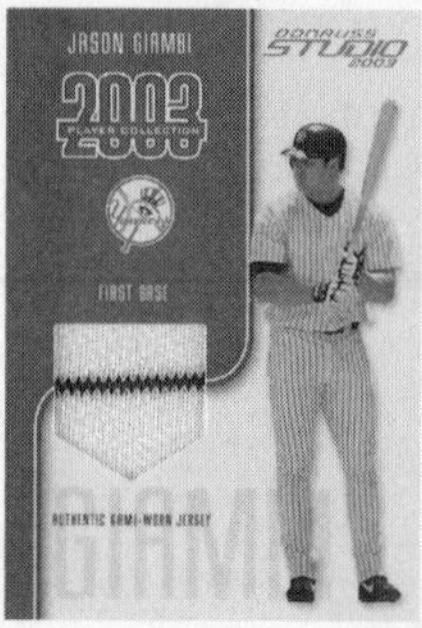

12 Carlos Delgado 5.00
13 C.C. Sabathia 4.00
14 Chipper Jones 10.00
15 Craig Biggio 4.00
16 Curt Schilling 6.00
17 Alex Rodriguez 10.00
18 Frank Thomas 8.00
19 Freddy Garcia 4.00
20 Jay Bell 4.00
21 Roger Clemens 12.00
22 Tony Gwynn 10.00
23 Ivan Rodriguez 6.00
24 Jason Giambi 6.00
25 Jason Jennings 4.00
26 Jay Payton 4.00
27 J.D. Drew 4.00
28 Jeff Bagwell 8.00
29 Jeromy Burnitz 4.00
30 Jim Edmonds 6.00
31 Jim Thome 8.00
32 Joe Borchard 4.00
33 Joe Mays 4.00
34 John Olerud 4.00
35 David Wells 4.00
36 Juan Gonzalez 6.00
37 Kazuhiro Sasaki 4.00
38 Chan Ho Park 4.00
39 Kerry Wood 8.00
40 Kevin Brown 5.00
41 Lance Berkman 4.00
42 Larry Walker 4.00
43 Bret Boone 4.00
44 Magglio Ordonez 4.00
45 Manny Ramirez 6.00
46 Mark Mulder 4.00
47 Mark Prior 8.00
48 Matt Williams 4.00
49 Miguel Tejada 6.00
50 Mike Piazza 10.00
51 Nomar Garciaparra 10.00
52 Doug Davis 4.00
53 Paul Konerko 4.00
54 Paul LoDuca 4.00
55 Pedro J. Martinez 8.00
56 Preston Wilson 4.00
57 Rafael Palmeiro 8.00
58 Marlon Byrd 4.00
59 Reggie Sanders 4.00
60 Richie Sexson 5.00
61 Rickey Henderson 10.00
62 Rickey Henderson 10.00
63 Robert Person 4.00
64 Jeff Bagwell 8.00
65 Roger Clemens 12.00
66 Roy Oswalt 4.00
67 Ryan Klesko 4.00
68 Sammy Sosa 12.00
69 Shawn Green 5.00
70 Steve Finley 4.00
71 Terrence Long 4.00
72 Tim Hudson 5.00
73 Toby Hall 4.00
74 Todd Helton 8.00
75 Travis Lee 4.00
76 Troy Glaus 6.00
77 Tsuyoshi Shinjo 4.00
78 Vernon Wells 4.00
79 Vladimir Guerrero 8.00
80 Wes Helms 4.00
81 Alex Rodriguez 10.00
82 Alfonso Soriano 8.00
83 Barry Larkin 6.00
84 Roberto Alomar 6.00
85 Ivan Rodriguez 6.00
86 Jason Giambi 6.00
87 Jeff Bagwell 8.00
88 Juan Gonzalez 6.00
89 Larry Walker 4.00
90 Luis Gonzalez 4.00
91 Magglio Ordonez 4.00
92 Manny Ramirez 8.00
93 Marlon Byrd 4.00
94 Mike Piazza 10.00
95 Pat Burrell 8.00
96 Todd Helton 8.00
97 Rickey Henderson 10.00
98 Andruw Jones 6.00
99 Craig Biggio 4.00
100 Mark Prior 8.00

Private Signings

		NM/M
7	Jay Gibbons/100	10.00
11	Freddy Sanchez/150	25.00
24	Josh Stewart/200	8.00
26	Jeremy Guthrie/125	8.00
29	Victor Martinez/200	20.00
30	Cliff Lee/150	15.00
31	Jhonny Peralta/200	20.00
35	Nook Logan/100	8.00
37	Travis Chapman/150	8.00
41	Jimmy Gobble/200	8.00
47	J.C. Romero/200	8.00
49	Lew Ford/200	15.00
51	Torii Hunter/50	20.00
53	Nick Johnson/100	10.00
55	Jose Contreras/100	25.00
58	Brandon Claussen/200	10.00
69	Joe Valentine/200	8.00
79	Aubrey Huff/50	20.00
81	Dewon Brazelton/75	10.00
82	Pete LaForest/200	10.00
85	Hank Blalock/50	20.00
87	Kevin Mench/200	8.00
90	Eric Hinske/125	8.00
95	Vinnie Chulk/100	8.00
97	Junior Spivey/50	10.00
107	Adam LaRoche/200	15.00
108	Michael Hessman/200	8.00
111	Mark Prior/50	20.00
119	Jason Jennings/50	10.00
123	Jeff Baker/75	10.00
124	Clint Barmes/200	10.00
130	Jason Lane/100	10.00
139	Paul LoDuca/75	15.00
143	Bill Hall/50	20.00
146	Termel Sledge/125	10.00
149	Jose Vidro/50	15.00
159	Prentice Redman/200	10.00
160	Bobby Abreu/50	20.00
171	Kip Wells/100	10.00
172	Jose Castillo/175	8.00
178	Brian Lawrence/100	10.00
179	Shane Victorino/200	10.00
201	Adam Loewen/100	20.00
202	Jeremy Bonderman/50	30.00
203	Brandon Webb/100	50.00
204	Chien-Ming Wang/50	250.00
206	Ryan Wagner/100	10.00
207	Hong-Chih Kuo/25	175.00
208	Dan Haren/100	25.00
210	Ramon Nivar/100	15.00

Recollection Autographs 5x7

		NM/M
3	Sean Casey/125	15.00
5	Troy Glaus/82	20.00
8	Vladimir Guerrero/125	35.00
10	Todd Helton/55	35.00
12	Ryan Klesko/75	15.00
18	Ivan Rodriguez/50	40.00
19	C.C. Sabathia/50	20.00
20	Curt Schilling/75	30.00
23	Mike Sweeney/42	15.00
24	Miguel Tejada/44	30.00
26	Kerry Wood/200	25.00
27	Barry Zito/200	15.00

Spirit of the Game

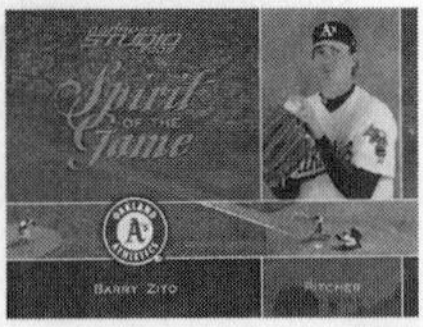

		NM/M
Complete Set (35):		60.00
Common Player:		1.00
Production 1,250 Sets		
1	Garret Anderson	1.00
2	Nomar Garciaparra	3.00
3	Pedro J. Martinez	2.00
4	Rickey Henderson	1.50
5	Magglio Ordonez	1.00
6	Torii Hunter	1.50
7	Alfonso Soriano	2.00
8	Jose Contreras	1.00
9	Derek Jeter	5.00
10	Jason Giambi	1.50
11	Roger Clemens	4.00
12	Hideki Matsui	6.00
13	Barry Zito	1.50
14	Ichiro Suzuki	3.00
15	Alex Rodriguez	4.00
16	Curt Schilling	2.00
17	Randy Johnson	2.00
18	Andruw Jones	1.50
19	Chipper Jones	2.00
20	Greg Maddux	3.00
21	Sammy Sosa	3.00
22	Adam Dunn	2.00
23	Ken Griffey Jr.	3.00
24	Todd Helton	2.00
25	Ivan Rodriguez	2.00
26	Lance Berkman	1.00
27	Hideo Nomo	1.50
28	Shawn Green	1.00
29	Vladimir Guerrero	2.00
30	Mike Piazza	3.00
31	Roberto Alomar	1.50
32	Jim Thome	2.00
33	Barry Bonds	5.00
34	Albert Pujols	3.00
35	Scott Rolen	2.00

Stars

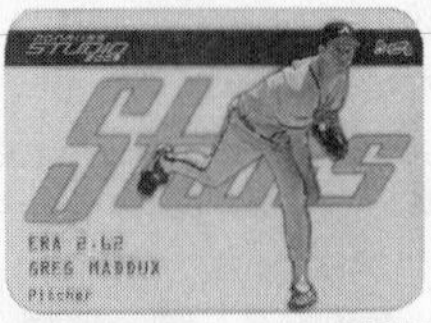

		NM/M
Complete Set (50):		65.00
Common Player:		1.00
Inserted 1:5		
Golds:		3-5X
Production 100 Sets		
1	Troy Glaus	1.50
2	Manny Ramirez	2.00
3	Nomar Garciaparra	3.00
4	Pedro J. Martinez	2.00
5	Rickey Henderson	1.50
6	Torii Hunter	1.50
7	Frank Thomas	1.50
8	Magglio Ordonez	1.00
9	Alfonso Soriano	2.00
10	Jose Contreras	1.00
11	Derek Jeter	5.00
12	Jason Giambi	1.50
13	Roger Clemens	4.00
14	Mike Mussina	1.50
15	Barry Zito	1.50
16	Miguel Tejada	1.00
17	Ichiro Suzuki	4.00
18	Alex Rodriguez	1.00
19	Juan Gonzalez	1.00
20	Rafael Palmeiro	2.00
21	Hank Blalock	2.00
22	Curt Schilling	2.00
23	Randy Johnson	2.00
24	Junior Spivey	1.00
25	Andruw Jones	1.50
26	Chipper Jones	2.00
27	Greg Maddux	3.00
28	Kerry Wood	2.00
29	Mark Prior	1.50
30	Sammy Sosa	3.00
31	Adam Dunn	2.00
32	Ken Griffey Jr.	3.00
33	Austin Kearns	1.50
34	Larry Walker	1.00
35	Todd Helton	2.00
36	Ivan Rodriguez	2.00
37	Jeff Bagwell	2.00
38	Lance Berkman	1.00
39	Craig Biggio	1.00
40	Hideo Nomo	1.50
41	Shawn Green	1.00
42	Vladimir Guerrero	2.00
43	Mike Piazza	3.00
44	Tom Glavine	1.50
45	Roberto Alomar	1.50
46	Pat Burrell	1.50
47	Jim Thome	2.00
48	Barry Bonds	5.00
49	Albert Pujols	4.00
50	Scott Rolen	2.00

2003 Donruss Team Heroes

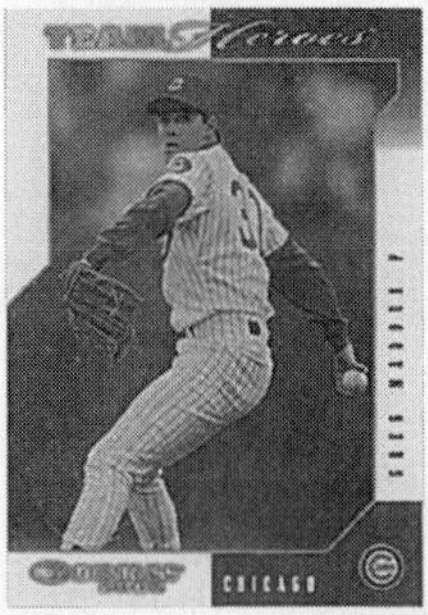

		NM/M
Complete Set (540):		55.00
Common Player:		.15
Pack (13):		1.50
Box (24):		25.00
1	Adam Kennedy	.15
2	Steve Green	.15
3	Rod Carew	.40
4	Alfredo Amezaga	.15
5	Reggie Jackson	.50
6	Jarrod Washburn	.15
7	Nolan Ryan	3.00
8	Tim Salmon	.25
9	Garret Anderson	.25
10	Darin Erstad	.25
11	Elpidio Guzman	.15
12	David Eckstein	.15
13	Troy Percival	.15
14	Troy Glaus	.75
15	Doug DeVore	.15
16	Tony Womack	.15
17	Matt Williams	.25
18	Junior Spivey	.15
19	Mark Grace	.50
20	Curt Schilling	.75
21	Erubiel Durazo	.15
22	Craig Counsell	.15
23	Byung-Hyun Kim	.15
24	Randy Johnson	1.00
25	Luis Gonzalez	.40
26	John Smoltz	.15
27	Tim Spooneybarger	.15
28	Dale Murphy	.50
29	Warren Spahn	.50
30	Jason Marquis	.15
31	Kevin Millwood	.15
32	Javy Lopez	.15
33	Vinny Castilla	.15
34	Julio Franco	.15
35	Trey Hodges	.15
36	Chipper Jones	1.50
37	Gary Sheffield	.25
38	Billy Sylvester	.15
39	Tom Glavine	.40
40	Rafael Furcal	.15
41	Cory Aldridge	.15
42	Greg Maddux	1.50
43	John Ennis	.15
44	Wes Helms	.15
45	Horacio Ramirez	.15
46	Derrick Lewis	.15
47	Marcus Giles	.15
48	Eddie Mathews	.75
49	Wilson Betemit	.15
50	Andruw Jones	.50
51	Josh Towers	.15
52	Ed Rogers	.15
53	Kris Foster	.15
54	Brooks Robinson	.75
55	Cal Ripken Jr.	3.00
56	Brian Roberts	.15
57	Luis Rivera	.15
58	Rodrigo Lopez	.15
59	Geronimo Gil	.15
60	Erik Bedard	.15
61	Jim Palmer	.40
62	Jay Gibbons	.15
63	Travis Driskill	.15
64	Larry Bigbie	.15
65	Eddie Murray	.40
66	Hoyt Wilhelm	.15
67	Bobby Doerr	.15
68	Pedro J. Martinez	1.00
69	Roger Clemens	1.50
70	Nomar Garciaparra	2.00
71	Trot Nixon	.15
72	Dennis Eckersley	.40
73	John Burkett	.15
74	Tim Wakefield	.15
75	Wade Boggs	.40
76	Cliff Floyd	.15
77	Casey Fossum	.15
78	Johnny Damon	.15
79	Fred Lynn	.15
80	Rickey Henderson	.40
81	Juan Diaz	.15
82	Manny Ramirez	.75
83	Carlton Fisk	.50
84	Jorge De La Rosa	.15
85	Shea Hillenbrand	.15
86	Derek Lowe	.15
87	Jason Varitek	.15
88	Carlos Baerga	.15
89	Freddy Sanchez	.15
90	Ugueth Urbina	.15
91	Rey Sanchez	.15
92	Josh Hancock	.15
93	Tony Clark	.15
94	Dustin Hermanson	.15
95	Ryne Sandberg	1.50
96	Fred McGriff	.25
97	Alex Gonzalez	.15
98	Mark Belhorn	.15
99	Fergie Jenkins	.25
100	Jon Lieber	.15
101	Francis Beltran	.15
102	Greg Maddux	1.50
103	Nate Frese	.15
104	Andre Dawson	.25
105	Carlos Zambrano	.15
106	Steve Smyth	.15
107	Ernie Banks	1.00
108	Will Ohman	.15
109	Kerry Wood	.50
110	Bobby Hill	.15
111	Moises Alou	.15
112	Hee Seop Choi	.15
113	Corey Patterson	.15
114	Sammy Sosa	1.50
115	Mark Prior	.50
116	Juan Cruz	.15
117	Ron Santo	.15
118	Billy Williams	.15
119	Antonio Alfonseca	.15
120	Matt Clement	.15
121	Carlton Fisk	.50
122	Joe Crede	.15
123	Magglio Ordonez	.40
124	Frank Thomas	.75
125	Joe Borchard	.15
126	Royce Clayton	.15
127	Luis Aparicio	.15
128	Willie Harris	.15
129	Kyle Kane	.15
130	Paul Konerko	.25
131	Matt Ginter	.15
132	Carlos Lee	.15
133	Mark Buehrle	.15
134	Adam Dunn	.75
135	Eric Davis	.15
136	Johnny Bench	1.00
137	Joe Morgan	.25
138	Austin Kearns	.40
139	Barry Larkin	.40
140	Ken Griffey Jr.	2.00
141	Luis Pineda	.15
142	Corky Miller	.15
143	Brandon Larson	.15
144	Wily Mo Pena	.15
145	Lance Davis	.15
146	Tom Seaver	1.00
147	Luke Hudson	.15
148	Sean Casey	.15
149	Tony Perez	.15
150	Todd Walker	.15
151	Aaron Boone	.15
152	Jose Rijo	.15
153	Ryan Dempster	.15
154	Danny Graves	.15
155	Matt Lawton	.15
156	Cliff Lee	.15
157	Ryan Drese	.15
158	Danys Baez	.15
159	Einar Diaz	.15
160	Milton Bradley	.15
161	Earl Snyder	.15
162	Ellis Burks	.15
163	Lou Boudreau	.15
164	Bob Feller	.15
165	Ricardo Rodriguez	.15
166	Victor Martinez	.15
167	Alex Herrera	.15
168	Omar Vizquel	.15
169	David Elder	.15
170	C.C. Sabathia	.15
171	Alex Escobar	.15
172	Brian Tallet	.15
173	Jim Thome	.75
174	Rene Reyes	.15
175	Juan Uribe	.15
176	Jason Romano	.15
177	Juan Pierre	.15
178	Jason Jennings	.15
179	Jose Ortiz	.15
180	Larry Walker	.25
181	Cam Esslinger	.15
182	Todd Helton	.50
183	Aaron Cook	.15
184	Jack Cust	.15
185	Jack Morris	.15
186	Mike Rivera	.15
187	Bobby Higginson	.15
188	Fernando Rodney	.15
189	Al Kaline	1.00
190	Carlos Pena	.15
191	Alan Trammell	.15
192	Mike Maroth	.15
193	Adam Pettyjohn	.15
194	David Espinosa	.15
195	Adam Bernero	.15
196	Franklyn German	.15
197	Robert Fick	.15
198	Andres Torres	.15
199	Luis Castillo	.15
200	Preston Wilson	.15
201	Pablo Ozuna	.15
202	Brad Penny	.15
203	Josh Beckett	.15
204	Charles Johnson	.15
205	Wilson Valdez	.15
206	A.J. Burnett	.15
207	Abraham Nunez	.15
208	Mike Lowell	.15
209	Jose Cueto	.15
210	Jeriome Robertson	.15
211	Jeff Bagwell	.75
212	Kirk Saarloos	.15
213	Craig Biggio	.25
214	Rodrigo Rosario	.15
215	Roy Oswalt	.25
216	John Buck	.15
217	Tim Redding	.15
218	Morgan Ensberg	.15
219	Richard Hidalgo	.15
220	Wade Miller	.15
221	Lance Berkman	.50
222	Raul Chavez	.15
223	Carlos Hernandez	.15
224	Greg Miller	.15
225	Tom Shearn	.15
226	Jason Lane	.15
227	Nolan Ryan	3.00
228	Billy Wagner	.15
229	Octavio Dotel	.15
230	Shane Reynolds	.15
231	Julio Lugo	.15
232	Daryle Ward	.15
233	Mike Sweeney	.15
234	Angel Berroa	.15
235	George Brett	1.50
236	Brad Voyles	.15
237	Brandon Berger	.15

238 Chad Durbin .15
239 Alexis Gomez .15
240 Jeremy Affeldt .15
241 Bo Jackson .75
242 Dee Brown .15
243 Tony Cogan .15
244 Carlos Beltran .15
245 Joe Randa .15
246 Pee Wee Reese .25
247 Andy Ashby .15
248 Cesar Izturis .15
249 Duke Snider .50
250 Mark Grudzielanek .15
251 Chin-Feng Chen .15
252 Brian Jordan .15
253 Steve Garvey .15
254 Odalis Perez .15
255 Hideo Nomo .50
256 Kevin Brown .15
257 Eric Karros .15
258 Joe Thurston .15
259 Carlos Garcia .15
260 Shawn Green .40
261 Paul LoDuca .15
262 Kazuhisa Ishii .15
263 Victor Alvarez .15
264 Eric Gagne .15
265 Don Sutton .15
266 Orel Hershiser .15
267 Dave Roberts .15
268 Adrian Beltre .15
269 Don Drysdale .50
270 Jackie Robinson 1.50
271 Tyler Houston .15
272 Omar Daal .15
273 Marquis Grissom .15
274 Paul Quantrill .15
275 Paul Molitor .50
276 Jose Hernandez .15
277 Takahito Nomura .15
278 Nick Neugebauer .15
279 Jose Mieses .15
280 Richie Sexson .40
281 Matt Childers .15
282 Bill Hall .15
283 Ben Sheets .15
284 Brian Mallette .15
285 Geoff Jenkins .15
286 Robin Yount .75
287 Jeff Deardorff .15
288 Luis Rivas .15
289 Harmon Killebrew .50
290 Michael Cuddyer .15
291 Torii Hunter .15
292 Kevin Frederick .15
293 Adam Johnson .15
294 Jack Morris .15
295 Rod Carew .40
296 Kirby Puckett 1.50
297 Joe Mays .15
298 Jacque Jones .15
299 Cristian Guzman .15
300 Kyle Lohse .15
301 Eric Milton .15
302 Brad Radke .15
303 Doug Mientkiewicz .15
304 Corey Koskie .15
305 Jose Vidro .15
306 Claudio Vargas .15
307 Gary Carter .15
308 Andre Dawson .25
309 Henry Mateo .15
310 Andres Galarraga .15
311 Zach Day .15
312 Bartolo Colon .15
313 Endy Chavez .15
314 Javier Vazquez .15
315 Michael Barrett .15
316 Vladimir Guerrero 1.00
317 Orlando Cabrera .15
318 Al Leiter .15
319 Timoniel Perez .15
320 Rey Ordonez .15
321 Gary Carter .15
322 Armando Benitez .15
323 Dwight Gooden .15
324 Pedro Astacio .15
325 Roberto Alomar .50
326 Edgardo Alfonzo .15
327 Nolan Ryan 3.00
328 Mo Vaughn .25
329 Ryan Jamison .15
330 Satoru Komiyama .15
331 Mike Piazza 2.50
332 Tom Seaver 1.00
333 Jorge Posada .40
334 Derek Jeter 2.50
335 Babe Ruth 3.00
336 Lou Gehrig 2.50
337 Andy Pettitte .40
338 Mariano Rivera .25
339 Robin Ventura .15
340 Yogi Berra 1.00
341 Phil Rizzuto .50
342 Bernie Williams .50
343 Alfonso Soriano 1.50
344 Drew Henson .15
345 Erick Almonte .15
346 Rondell White .15
347 Christian Parker .15
348 Joe Torre .25
349 Nick Johnson .15
350 Raul Mondesi .15
351 Brandon Claussen .15
352 Reggie Jackson .50
353 Roger Clemens 1.50
354 Don Mattingly 2.00
355 Jason Giambi 1.50
356 Adrian Hernandez .15
357 Jeff Weaver .15
358 Mike Mussina .50
359 Brett Jodie .15
360 David Wells .15
361 Enos Slaughter .15
362 Whitey Ford .50
363 Eric Chavez .25
364 Miguel Tejada .40
365 Barry Zito .25
366 Bert Snow .15
367 Rickey Henderson .50
368 Juan A. Pena .15
369 Terrence Long .15
370 Dennis Eckersley .40
371 Mark Ellis .15
372 Tim Hudson .25
373 Jose Canseco .50
374 Reggie Jackson .50
375 Mark Mulder .15
376 David Justice .25
377 Jermaine Dye .15
378 Brett Myers .15
379 Lenny Dykstra .15
380 Vicente Padilla .15
381 Bobby Abreu .15
382 Pat Burrell .50
383 Jorge Padilla .15
384 Jeremy Giambi .15
385 Mike Lieberthal .15
386 Anderson Machado .15
387 Marlon Byrd .15
388 Bud Smith .15
389 Eric Valent .15
390 Elio Serrano .15
391 Jimmy Rollins .25
392 Brandon Duckworth .15
393 Robin Roberts .15
394 Marlon Anderson .15
395 Robert Person .15
396 Johnny Estrada .15
397 Mike Schmidt 1.00
398 Eric Junge .15
399 Jason Michaels .15
400 Steve Carlton .40
401 Placido Polanco .15
402 John Grabow .15
403 Tomas De La Rosa .15
404 Tike Redman .15
405 Willie Stargell .40
406 Dave Williams .15
407 John Candelaria .15
408 Jack Wilson .15
409 Matt Guerrier .15
410 Jason Kendall .15
411 Josh Fogg .15
412 Aramis Ramirez .15
413 Dave Parker .15
414 Roberto Clemente 2.00
415 Kip Wells .15
416 Brian Giles .25
417 Honus Wagner 1.50
418 Ramon Vazquez .15
419 Oliver Perez .15
420 Ryan Klesko .15
421 Brian Lawrence .15
422 Ben Howard .15
423 Ozzie Smith 1.00
424 Dennis Tankersley .15
425 Tony Gwynn 1.00
426 Sean Burroughs .15
427 Xavier Nady .15
428 Phil Nevin .15
429 Trevor Hoffman .15
430 Jake Peavy .15
431 Cody Ransom .15
432 Kenny Lofton .15
433 Mel Ott .50
434 Tsuyoshi Shinjo .15
435 Deivis Santos .15
436 Rich Aurilia .15
437 Will Clark .50
438 Pedro Feliz .15
439 J.T. Snow .15
440 Robb Nen .15
441 Carlos Valderrama .15
442 Willie McCovey .15
443 Jeff Kent .25
444 Orlando Cepeda .15
445 Barry Bonds 2.50
446 Alex Rodriguez 2.50
447 Allan Simpson .15
448 Antonio Perez .15
449 Edgar Martinez .15
450 Freddy Garcia .15
451 Chris Snelling .15
452 Matt Thornton .15
453 Kazuhiro Sasaki .15
454 Harold Reynolds .15
455 Randy Johnson 1.00
456 Bret Boone .15
457 Rafael Soriano .15
458 Luis Ugueto .15
459 Ken Griffey Jr. 2.00
460 Ichiro Suzuki 2.00
461 Jamie Moyer .15
462 Joel Pineiro .15
463 Jeff Cirillo .15
464 John Olerud .15
465 Mike Cameron .15
466 Ruben Sierra .15
467 Mark McLemore .15
468 Carlos Guillen .15
469 Dan Wilson .15
470 Shigetoshi Hasegawa .15
471 Ben Davis .15
472 Ozzie Smith 1.00
473 Matt Morris .15
474 Edgar Renteria .15
475 Les Walrond .15
476 Albert Pujols 1.00
477 Stan Musial 1.50
478 J.D. Drew .15
479 Josh Pearce .15
480 Enos Slaughter .15
481 Jason Simontacchi .15
482 Jeremy Lambert .15
483 Tino Martinez .15
484 Rogers Hornsby .50
485 Rick Ankiel .25
486 Jim Edmonds .25
487 Scott Rolen .50
488 Kevin Joseph .15
489 Fernando Vina .15
490 Jason Isringhausen .15
491 Lou Brock .40
492 Joe Torre .25
493 Bob Gibson .50
494 Chuck Finley .15
495 So Taguchi .15
496 Ben Grieve .15
497 Toby Hall .15
498 Brent Abernathy .15
499 Brandon Backe .15
500 Felix Escalona .15
501 Matt White .15
502 Randy Winn .15
503 Carl Crawford .15
504 Dewon Brazelton .15
505 Joe Kennedy .15
506 Wade Boggs .50
507 Aubrey Huff .15
508 Alex Rodriguez 2.50
509 Ivan Rodriguez .50
510 Will Clark .75
511 Hank Blalock .15
512 Travis Hughes .15
513 Travis Hafner .15
514 Ryan Ludwick .15
515 Doug Davis .15
516 Juan Gonzalez .50
517 Jason Hart .15
518 Mark Teixeira .40
519 Nolan Ryan 3.00
520 Rafael Palmeiro .50
521 Kevin Mench .15
522 Chan Ho Park .15
523 Kenny Rogers .15
524 Rusty Greer .15
525 Michael Young .15
526 Carlos Delgado .40
527 Vernon Wells .15
528 Orlando Hudson .15
529 Shannon Stewart .15
530 Joe Carter .15
531 Chris Baker .15
532 Eric Hinske .15
533 Corey Thurman .15
534 Josh Phelps .15
535 Reed Johnson .15
536 Brian Bowles .15
537 Roy Halladay .15
538 Jose Cruz Jr. .15
539 Kelvim Escobar .15
540 Chris Carpenter .15

Glossy

Stars: 1-2.5X
Inserted 1:1

Stat Line

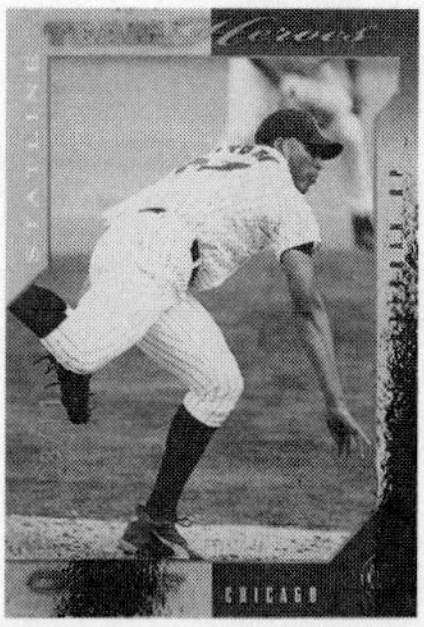

Cards serial numbered 151-250: 4-8X
Print run 101-150: 5-10X
Print run 51-100: 8-15X
Print run 26-50: 10-20X

Autographs

NM/M

Common Player: 6.00
Some not priced due to scarcity.

4 Alfredo Amezaga/250 6.00
5 Reggie Jackson/5
11 Elpidio Guzman/100 10.00
15 Doug DeVore/122 10.00
38 Billy Sylvester/250 6.00
41 Cory Aldridge/250 8.00
45 Horacio Ramirez/200 8.00
46 Derrick Lewis/250 6.00
47 Marcus Giles/200 8.00
49 Wilson Betemit/75 10.00
51 Josh Towers/110 10.00
52 Ed Rogers/250 6.00
53 Kris Foster/250 6.00
56 Brian Roberts/250 35.00
59 Geronimo Gil/60 10.00
60 Erik Bedard/250 8.00
62 Jay Gibbons/181 10.00
64 Larry Bigbie/100 10.00
77 Casey Fossum/250 6.00
79 Fred Lynn/50 20.00
81 Juan Diaz/250 6.00
84 Jorge De La Rosa/250 6.00
99 Fergie Jenkins/50 25.00
101 Francis Beltran/250 8.00
103 Nate Frese/250 6.00
105 Carlos Zambrano/150 20.00
108 Will Ohman/50 10.00
110 Bobby Hill/150 8.00
115 Mark Prior/50 40.00
116 Juan Cruz/50 10.00
122 Joe Crede/250 10.00
125 Joe Borchard/250 10.00
127 Luis Aparicio/50 20.00
128 Willie Harris/129 8.00
129 Kyle Kane/100 10.00
131 Matt Ginter/250 6.00
132 Carlos Lee/50 15.00
133 Mark Buehrle/50 20.00
135 Eric Davis/75 20.00
138 Austin Kearns/71 20.00
142 Corky Miller/250 6.00
143 Brandon Larson/143 10.00
144 Wily Mo Pena/250 15.00
147 Luke Hudson/50 12.00
149 Tony Perez/50 20.00
156 Cliff Lee/250 20.00
161 Earl Snyder/250 8.00
165 Ricardo Rodriguez/250 8.00
166 Victor Martinez/200 25.00
167 Alex Herrera/250 6.00
171 Alex Escobar/125 10.00
172 Brian Tallet/250 10.00
174 Rene Reyes/250 6.00
176 Jason Romano/50 15.00
177 Juan Pierre/66 15.00
178 Jason Jennings/250 10.00
179 Jose Ortiz/250 8.00
181 Cam Esslinger/250 6.00
184 Jack Cust/250 10.00
185 Jack Morris/50 20.00
186 Mike Rivera/250 6.00
188 Fernando Rodney/250 6.00
190 Carlos Pena/96 12.00
192 Mike Maroth/250 6.00
193 Adam Pettyjohn/250 6.00
194 David Espinosa/250 6.00
195 Adam Bernero/250 6.00
196 Franklyn German/250 8.00
197 Robert Fick/50 10.00
198 Andres Torres/250 6.00
201 Pablo Ozuna/250 6.00
205 Wilson Valdez/250 6.00
207 Abraham Nunez/250 8.00
212 Kirk Saarloos/250 8.00
214 Rodrigo Rosario/250 6.00
215 Roy Oswalt/50 20.00
217 Tim Redding/250 6.00
218 Morgan Ensberg/250 6.00
219 Richard Hidalgo/100 10.00
220 Wade Miller/200 10.00
222 Raul Chavez/125 15.00
223 Carlos Hernandez/250 10.00
224 Greg Miller/90 10.00
226 Jason Lane/250 10.00
234 Angel Berroa/200 10.00
236 Brad Voyles/200 10.00
237 Brandon Berger/250 8.00
238 Chad Durbin/250 8.00
239 Alexis Gomez/165 10.00
240 Jeremy Affeldt/250 6.00
242 Dee Brown/50 12.00
243 Tony Cogan/250 6.00
248 Cesar Izturis/200 10.00
253 Steve Garvey/75 30.00
258 Joe Thurston/108 10.00
259 Carlos Garcia/100 8.00
261 Paul LoDuca/50 20.00
263 Victor Alvarez/250 6.00
265 Don Sutton/50 20.00
277 Takahito Nomura/100 20.00
279 Jose Mieses/50 15.00
281 Matt Childers/50 12.00
283 Ben Sheets/100 20.00
284 Brian Mallette/250 6.00
287 Jeff Deardorff/100 6.00
288 Luis Rivas/200 8.00
290 Michael Cuddyer/250 10.00
291 Torii Hunter/100 25.00
294 Jack Morris/50 20.00
305 Jose Vidro/50 15.00
306 Claudio Vargas/150 6.00
309 Henry Mateo/250 6.00
311 Zach Day/250 6.00
313 Endy Chavez/250 6.00
314 Javier Vazquez/50 15.00
323 Dwight Gooden/75 25.00
344 Drew Henson/50 25.00
345 Erick Almonte/250 6.00

347	Christian Parker/200	6.00
351	Brandon Claussen/250	6.00
356	Adrian Hernandez/200	6.00
359	Brett Jodie/250	8.00
366	Bert Snow/250	6.00
368	Juan Pena/250	8.00
371	Mark Ellis/150	6.00
379	Lenny Dykstra/75	25.00
383	Jorge Padilla/250	8.00
384	Jeremy Giambi/100	10.00
386	Anderson Machado/250	6.00
387	Marlon Byrd/200	10.00
388	Bud Smith/125	10.00
389	Eric Valent/100	8.00
390	Elio Serrano/250	8.00
392	Brandon Duckworth/100	10.00
395	Robert Person/100	10.00
396	Johnny Estrada/209	15.00
398	Eric Junge/250	8.00
399	Jason Michaels/221	6.00
402	John Grabow/250	6.00
406	Dave Williams/250	6.00
407	John Candelaria/100	10.00
408	Jack Wilson/250	6.00
409	Matt Guerrier/200	6.00
412	Aramis Ramirez/50	30.00
413	Dave Parker/50	20.00
415	Kip Wells/250	8.00
418	Ramon Vazquez/200	6.00
419	Oliver Perez/150	10.00
421	Brian Lawrence/250	8.00
422	Ben Howard/250	6.00
427	Xavier Nady/50	15.00
431	Cody Ransom/100	10.00
435	Deivis Santos/100	10.00
438	Pedro Feliz/50	15.00
441	Carlos Valderrama/250	6.00
447	Allan Simpson/250	6.00
448	Antonio Perez/250	6.00
451	Chris Snelling/100	10.00
452	Matt Thornton/200	6.00
454	Harold Reynolds/100	15.00
457	Rafael Soriano/250	6.00
458	Luis Ugueto/50	10.00
475	Les Walrond/50	12.00
479	Josh Pearce/200	6.00
497	Toby Hall/200	8.00
498	Brent Abernathy/250	6.00
499	Brandon Backe/250	8.00
500	Felix Escalona/50	10.00
504	Dewon Brazelton/100	10.00
505	Joe Kennedy/200	6.00
507	Aubrey Huff/100	15.00
512	Travis Hughes/200	6.00
514	Ryan Ludwick/250	10.00
515	Doug Davis/250	6.00
517	Jason Hart/123	10.00
518	Mark Teixeira/50	40.00
521	Kevin Mench/250	10.00
528	Orlando Hudson/120	10.00
531	Chris Baker/200	6.00
532	Eric Hinske/250	10.00
533	Corey Thurman/250	8.00
534	Josh Phelps/150	10.00
535	Reed Johnson/250	6.00
536	Brian Bowles/250	6.00
543	Ramon Nivar/100	15.00
544	Adam Loewen/100	10.00
545	Brandon Webb/100	30.00
546	Dan Haren/100	25.00
548	Ryan Wagner/100	15.00

Timeline Threads

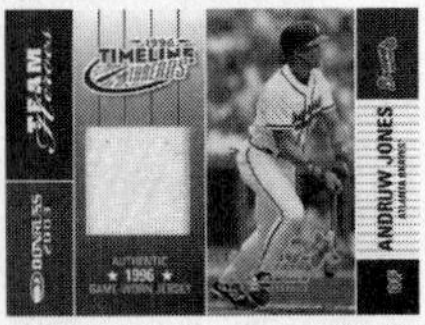

NM/M

Common Player:
Quantity produced listed

1	Bobby Doerr/39	20.00
2	Phil Rizzuto/47	30.00
3	Yogi Berra/47	35.00
4	Pee Wee Reese/58	15.00
6	Al Kaline/64	40.00
7	Orlando Cepeda/65	15.00
8	Eddie Mathews/66	40.00
9	Lou Brock/66	15.00
10	Juan Marichal/67	15.00
11	Ernie Banks/68	40.00
12	Willie Stargell/68	15.00
13	Jim Palmer/69	15.00
14	Luis Aparicio/69	15.00
15	Tom Seaver/69	30.00
16	Harmon Killebrew/71	50.00
17	Joe Morgan/74	15.00
18	Brooks Robinson/76	30.00
19	Mike Schmidt/81	65.00
20	Willie McCovey/77	15.00
21	Robin Yount/78	40.00
22	Reggie Jackson/79	20.00
23	Rod Carew/85	25.00
24	Nolan Ryan/91	80.00
25	Tony Gwynn/98	25.00
26	Alex Rodriguez/100	25.00
27	Carlos Delgado/101	10.00
28	Lance Berkman/102	10.00
29	Randy Johnson/100	20.00
30	Josh Beckett/101	15.00
31	Eric Davis/89	10.00
32	Todd Helton/100	15.00
33	Jose Canseco/89	25.00
34	Mike Piazza/101	25.00
35	Fred Lynn/75	10.00
36	Mike Sweeney/101	10.00
37	Miguel Tejada/101	15.00
38	Curt Schilling/101	15.00
39	Dale Murphy/87	40.00
40	Jim Thome/101	20.00
41	Adam Dunn/102	15.00
42	Nomar Garciaparra/100	25.00
43	Vladimir Guerrero/100	15.00
44	Alfonso Soriano/102	20.00
45	Wade Boggs/90	15.00
46	Randy Johnson/89	20.00
47	Hal Newhouser/55	15.00
48	Chipper Jones/93	20.00
49	Andruw Jones/96	15.00
50	Frank Thomas/94	15.00

2003 Donruss Timeless Treasures

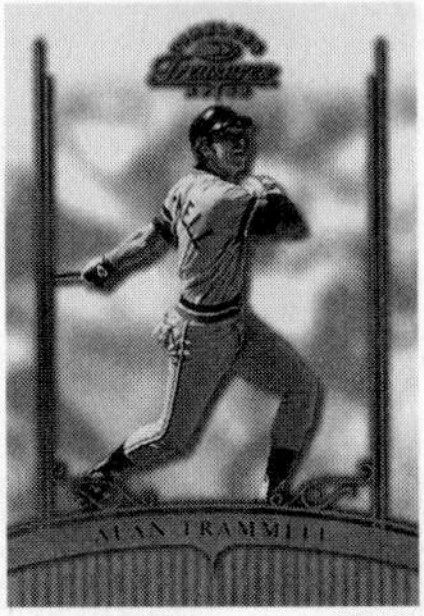

NM/M

Complete Set (100):
Common Player: 2.00
Production 900 Sets
Tin (4): 100.00

1	Adam Dunn	3.00
2	Al Kaline	5.00
3	Alan Trammell	2.00
4	Albert Pujols	8.00
5	Alex Rodriguez	8.00
6	Alfonso Soriano	4.00
7	Andre Dawson	2.00
8	Andruw Jones	3.00
9	Austin Kearns	2.00
10	Babe Ruth	10.00
11	Barry Bonds	10.00
12	Barry Larkin	2.00
13	Barry Zito	3.00
14	Bernie Williams	4.00
15	Bo Jackson	4.00
16	Brooks Robinson	4.00
17	Cal Ripken Jr.	10.00
18	Carlton Fisk	2.00
19	Chipper Jones	4.00
20	Curt Schilling	3.00
21	Dale Murphy	2.00
22	Derek Jeter	10.00
23	Don Mattingly	10.00
24	Duke Snider	3.00
25	Eddie Mathews	4.00
26	Frank Robinson	2.00
27	Frank Thomas	4.00
28	Garret Anderson	2.00
29	Gary Carter	2.00
30	George Brett	8.00
31	Greg Maddux	6.00
32	Harmon Killebrew	4.00
33	Hideki Matsui **RC**	10.00
34	Hideo Nomo	3.00
35	Ichiro Suzuki	6.00
36	Ivan Rodriguez	4.00
37	Jackie Robinson	6.00
38	Jason Giambi	3.00
39	Jeff Bagwell	4.00
40	Jim Edmonds	3.00
41	Jim Palmer	3.00
42	Jim Thome	4.00
43	Joe Morgan	2.00
44	Jorge Posada	3.00
45	Jose Contreras **RC**	5.00
46	Juan Gonzalez	3.00
47	Kazuhisa Ishii	2.00
48	Ken Griffey Jr.	5.00
49	Kerry Wood	4.00
50	Kirby Puckett	5.00
51	Lance Berkman	2.00
52	Larry Walker	2.00
53	Lou Brock	3.00
54	Lou Gehrig	8.00
55	Magglio Ordonez	2.00
56	Mark Prior	4.00
57	Miguel Tejada	3.00
58	Mike Mussina	3.00
59	Mike Piazza	6.00
60	Mike Schmidt	8.00
61	Nolan Ryan	10.00
62	Nomar Garciaparra	6.00
63	Ozzie Smith	5.00
64	Pat Burrell	2.00
65	Pedro J. Martinez	4.00
66	Pee Wee Reese	2.00
67	Phil Rizzuto	4.00
68	Rafael Palmeiro	3.00
69	Randy Johnson	5.00
70	Reggie Jackson	4.00
71	Richie Ashburn	2.00
72	Rickey Henderson	3.00
73	Roberto Alomar	3.00
74	Roberto Clemente	8.00
75	Robin Yount	4.00
76	Rod Carew	3.00
77	Roger Clemens	8.00
78	Rogers Hornsby	4.00
79	Roy Oswalt	2.00
80	Ryan Klesko	2.00
81	Ryne Sandberg	6.00
82	Sammy Sosa	6.00
83	Scott Rolen	4.00
84	Shawn Green	3.00
85	Stan Musial	6.00
86	Steve Carlton	3.00
87	Thurman Munson	5.00
88	Todd Helton	4.00
89	Tom Glavine	2.00
90	Tom Seaver	4.00
91	Tony Gwynn	4.00
92	Tony Perez	2.00
93	Torii Hunter	2.00
94	Troy Glaus	3.00
95	Ty Cobb	6.00
96	Vernon Wells	2.00
97	Vladimir Guerrero	4.00
98	Warren Spahn	4.00
99	Willie McCovey	3.00
100	Yogi Berra	5.00

Silver

Stars (1-100): 3-5X
Production 50 Sets
Golds: No Pricing
Production 10 Sets
Platinum 1-of-1's exist.

Award Materials

NM/M

Quantity produced listed

1	Ivan Rodriguez/100	10.00
2	Mike Schmidt/50	60.00
3	Roberto Clemente/50	80.00
4	Roger Clemens/50	25.00
5	Randy Johnson/100	15.00
6	Pedro J. Martinez/100	15.00
7	Ivan Rodriguez/100	10.00
8	Jeff Bagwell/100	15.00
9	Frank Thomas/100	15.00
10	Cal Ripken Jr./75	50.00
11	Tom Seaver/50	25.00

Award Materials Auto.

No Pricing

Award Prime Materials

NM/M

Quantity produced listed

6	Pedro J. Martinez/50	30.00
9	Frank Thomas/50	25.00

Award Winning MLB Logos

No Pricing

Classic Combos

NM/M

Quantity produced listed

1	Jason Giambi/100	15.00
2	Adrian Beltre/100	10.00
3	Alex Rodriguez/100	25.00
4	Alfonso Soriano/100	30.00
5	Andruw Jones/100	15.00
6	Andre Dawson/100	15.00
7	Barry Larkin/100	10.00
8	Barry Zito/100	15.00
9	Cal Ripken Jr./100	60.00
10	Chipper Jones/100	20.00
11	Don Mattingly/10	50.00
12	Eric Chavez/100	10.00
13	Frank Thomas/100	15.00
14	Greg Maddux/100	25.00
15	Ivan Rodriguez/100	15.00
16	Jeff Bagwell/100	15.00
17	Jim Thome/100	15.00
18	Juan Gonzalez/100	15.00
19	Kazuhisa Ishii/100	10.00
20	Kerry Wood/100	15.00
21	Lance Berkman/100	10.00
22	Magglio Ordonez/100	10.00
23	Manny Ramirez/100	15.00
24	Miguel Tejada/100	10.00
25	Mike Piazza/100	20.00
26	Nomar Garciaparra/100	20.00
27	Pedro J. Martinez/100	20.00
28	Randy Johnson/100	15.00
29	Rickey Henderson/100	20.00
30	Ryne Sandberg/100	30.00
32	Shawn Green/100	10.00
33	Todd Helton/100	10.00
34	Tony Gwynn/100	20.00
35	Vladimir Guerrero/100	15.00

Classic Combos Auto.

NM/M

Quantity produced listed

8	Barry Zito/25	100.00
22	Maggilo Ordonez/25	65.00
34	Tony Gwynn/25	100.00

Classic Prime Combos

NM/M

Quantity produced listed

6	Andre Dawson/25	40.00
11	Don Mattingly/25	75.00
16	Jeff Bagwell/25	50.00

Game Day Materials

NM/M

Quantity produced listed

1	Tony Gwynn/100	15.00
2	Maggilo Ordonez/100	8.00
3	George Brett/100	40.00
4	Rickey Henderson/100	15.00
5	Billy Williams/100	10.00
6	Frank Thomas/100	10.00
7	Tony Gwynn/75	20.00
10	Ryne Sandberg/100	30.00
11	Miguel Tejada/100	10.00

Game Day Materials Autograph

No Pricing

HOF Materials

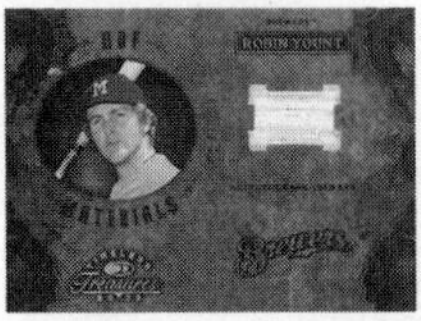

NM/M

Quantity produced listed

1	Al Kaline	25.00
2	Babe Ruth/75	140.00
3	Carlton Fisk/100	15.00
4	Eddie Mathews/100	20.00
5	Gary Carter/100	15.00
6	George Brett/100	35.00
7	Harmon Killebrew/100	25.00
8	Joe Morgan/100	10.00
9	Kirby Puckett/100	20.00
10	Lou Gehrig/100	110.00
11	Luis Aparicio/100	10.00
12	Mike Schmidt/100	25.00
13	Ozzie Smith/100	25.00
14	Phil Rizzuto/100	10.00
15	Reggie Jackson/100	15.00
16	Richie Ashburn/100	15.00
17	Roberto Clemente/100	60.00
18	Robin Yount/100	20.00
19	Rod Carew/100	15.00
20	Rogers Hornsby/100	45.00
21	Stan Musial/100	35.00
22	Ty Cobb/100	120.00
23	Willie McCovey/100	10.00
24	Yogi Berra/100	30.00
25	Al Kaline/100	25.00
26	Babe Ruth/50	300.00
27	Bobby Doerr/100	15.00
28	Brooks Robinson/100	15.00
29	Eddie Mathews/100	20.00
30	Harmon Killebrew/100	25.00
31	Ty Cobb/50	150.00
32	Joe Morgan/100	10.00
33	Lou Brock/100	10.00
34	Lou Gehrig/50	225.00
35	Mike Schmidt/100	25.00
36	Nolan Ryan/100	40.00
37	Nolan Ryan/100	40.00
38	Nolan Ryan/100	40.00
39	Phil Rizzuto/100	10.00
40	Reggie Jackson/25	25.00
41	Reggie Jackson/100	15.00
42	Roberto Clemente/50	90.00
43	Robin Yount/100	20.00
44	Rod Carew/100	15.00
45	Stan Musial/100	35.00
46	Tom Seaver/100	20.00
47	Steve Carlton/100	15.00
48	Carlton Fisk/100	15.00
49	Pee Wee Reese/100	15.00
50	Jackie Robinson/50	85.00

HOF Materials Autographs

NM/M

Quantity produced listed

7	Harmon Killebrew/25	80.00
12	Mike Schmidt/15	180.00
24	Yogi Berra/15	150.00
28	Brooks Robinson/25	75.00
30	Harmon Killebrew/50	75.00
39	Phil Rizzuto/25	65.00
43	Robin Yount/25	175.00

HOF Cuts

NM/M

Production One Set
Ty Cobb (8/03 Auction) — 6,500

HOF Combos

NM/M

Quantity produced listed
1 Al Kaline/50 — 50.00
4 Kirby Puckett/75 — 40.00
6 Mike Schmidt/100 — 50.00
7 Nolan Ryan/50 — 100.00
8 Phil Rizzuto/50 — 30.00
9 Reggie Jackson/25 — 40.00
11 Rod Carew/100 — 25.00
14 George Brett/85 — 85.00
15 Carlton Fisk/100 — 20.00

HOF Combos Autographs
No Pricing

HOF Letters
No Pricing

HOF Induction Year Combos

NM/M

Production 25 Sets
6 Enos Slaughter, Lou Brock/25 — 60.00
8 Phil Rizzuto, Steve Carlton/25 — 45.00
10 George Brett, Robin Yount/25 — 185.00

HOF Logos

NM/M

Quantity produced listed
29 Eddie Mathews/35 — 65.00
36 Nolan Ryan/35 — 100.00
37 Nolan Ryan/35 — 100.00
38 Nolan Ryan/35 — 100.00
43 Robin Yount/35 — 50.00

HOF Numbers

NM/M

Quantity produced listed
35 Mike Schmidt/50 — 40.00
36 Nolan Ryan/35 — 100.00
43 Robin Yount/35 — 50.00
47 Steve Carlton/40 — 20.00
48 Carlton Fisk/35 — 45.00

HOF Prime Combos

Quantity produced listed
No Pricing

Home Run Materials

NM/M

Quantity produced listed
1 Harmon Killebrew/100 — 20.00
2 Harmon Killebrew/100 — 20.00
3 Jose Canseco/100 — 15.00
4 Magglio Ordonez/100 — 8.00
5 Rafael Palmeiro/100 — 15.00
6 Rafael Palmeiro/100 — 15.00
7 Rafael Palmeiro/100 — 15.00
8 Alex Rodriguez/100 — 15.00
9 Alex Rodriguez/100 — 15.00
10 Alex Rodriguez/100 — 15.00
11 Alex Rodriguez/20 — 75.00
12 Adam Dunn/100 — 15.00

Home Run Materials Auto.

NM/M

Quantity produced listed
1 Harmon Killebrew/25 — 80.00
3 Jose Canseco/25 — 100.00

Material Ink

NM/M

Quantity produced listed
1 Adam Dunn/50 — 45.00
2 Alan Trammell/100 — 30.00
3 Alex Rodriguez/25 — 150.00
5 Andre Dawson/100 — 30.00
6 Barry Zito/100 — 45.00
7 Bo Jackson/100 — 60.00
8 Bob Feller/25 — 70.00
9 Bobby Doerr/50 — 45.00
11 Cal Ripken Jr./50 — 200.00
12 Cal Ripken Jr./50 — 200.00
13 Cal Ripken Jr./25 — 225.00
14 Dale Murphy/50 — 45.00
15 Dave Parker/75 — 35.00
16 David Cone/100 — 30.00
17 Don Mattingly/100 — 85.00
18 Duke Snider/25 — 75.00
19 Edgar Martinez/50 — 50.00
20 Gary Carter/100 — 25.00
21 Harmon Killebrew/75 — 70.00
22 Jim Edmonds/25 — 55.00
23 Jim Thome/50 — 50.00
24 Joe Carter/100 — 30.00
25 Jose Canseco/50 — 50.00
26 Jose Vidro/100 — 20.00
27 Kazuhisa Ishii/100 — 40.00
28 Kerry Wood/50 — 60.00
29 Lance Berkman/50 — 40.00
30 Mark Mulder/25 — 65.00
32 Mike Schmidt/50 — 90.00
33 Nick Johnson/100 — 25.00
34 Nolan Ryan/25 — 225.00
35 Nolan Ryan/25 — 225.00
36 Nolan Ryan/25 — 225.00
37 Paul LoDuca/100 — 25.00
38 Paul Molitor/50 — 45.00
40 Reggie Jackson/40 — 85.00
41 Roberto Alomar/50 — 50.00
42 Roberto Alomar/100 — 40.00
43 Robin Yount/50 — 75.00
47 Ryan Klesko/75 — 25.00
48 Ryne Sandberg/25 — 140.00
50 Stan Musial/25 — 150.00
51 Steve Carlton/100 — 35.00
52 Steve Carlton/100 — 35.00
53 Todd Helton/50 — 60.00
54 Tom Seaver/50 — 50.00
55 Tony Gwynn/25 — 100.00
56 Torii Hunter/100 — 40.00
57 Vladimir Guerrero/100 — 40.00
58 Will Clark/50 — 85.00

Material MLB Logo Ink
No Pricing

Milestone Materials

NM/M

Quantity produced listed
3 Rickey Henderson/100 — 15.00

Past and Present

NM/M

Production 100 Sets
1 Alex Rodriguez/100 — 20.00
2 Hideo Nomo/100 — 25.00
3 Jason Giambi/100 — 20.00
4 Juan Gonzalez/100 — 15.00
5 Mike Piazza/100 — 20.00
6 Pedro J. Martinez/100 — 15.00
7 Randy Johnson/100 — 15.00
8 Rickey Henderson/100 — 20.00
9 Roberto Alomar/100 — 15.00
10 Roger Clemens/100 — 20.00
11 Sammy Sosa/100 — 35.00

Past & Present Letters

NM/M

Quantity produced listed
1 Alex Rodriguez/75 — 30.00
2 Hideo Nomo/25 — 90.00
4 Juan Gonzalez/50 — 25.00
6 Pedro J. Martinez/50 — 35.00
7 Randy Johnson/75 — 40.00

Past and Present Logos

NM/M

Quantity produced listed
1 Hideo Nomo/25 — 90.00
3 Jason Giambi/75 — 40.00
5 Mike Piazza/75 — 40.00

Past & Present Numbers

NM/M

Quantity produced listed
2 Hideo Nomo/25 — 75.00
3 Jason Giambi/25 — 40.00
6 Pedro J. Martinez/50 — 40.00
7 Randy Johnson/50 — 40.00

Past & Present Patches
No Pricing

Post Season Materials
No Pricing

Post Season Materials Auto.

NM/M

Quantity produced listed
1 Ozzie Smith/15 — 125.00

Post Season Prime Material

NM/M

No Pricing
1 Ozzie Smith/75 — 50.00

Prime Materials

NM/M

Quantity produced listed
1 Tony Gwynn/100 — 15.00
2 Magglio Ordonez/100 — 8.00
4 Rickey Henderson/100 — 15.00
6 Frank Thomas/100 — 10.00
7 Tony Gwynn/75 — 20.00
10 Ryne Sandberg/100 — 30.00
11 Miguel Tejada/100 — 10.00

Prime Material Ink

NM/M

Quantity produced listed
2 Alan Trammell/50 — 50.00
5 Andre Dawson/25 — 60.00
7 Bo Jackson/50 — 100.00
20 Gary Carter/50 — 50.00
24 Joe Carter/50 — 50.00
26 Jose Vidro/25 — 40.00
27 Kazuhisa Ishii/50 — 50.00
33 Nick Johnson/50 — 45.00
53 Steve Carlton/50 — 50.00
58 Torii Hunter/50 — 50.00
59 Vladimir Guerrero/50 — 70.00
60 Will Clark/25 — 180.00

Rookie Year Materials

NM/M

Common Player: — 8.00
1 Cal Ripken Jr./100 — 50.00
2 Mike Schmidt/50 — 40.00
3 Rafael Palmeiro/100 — 15.00
4 Nomar Garciaparra/100 — 20.00
6 Stan Musial/42 — 70.00
7 Yogi Berra/99 — 30.00
9 Ivan Rodriguez/100 — 10.00
12 Vladimir Guerrero/100 — 15.00
14 Ivan Rodriguez/91 — 10.00
15 Andruw Jones/96 — 15.00
16 Andruw Jones/100 — 15.00
17 Fred Lynn/100 — 10.00
18 Jeff Kent/100 — 8.00
19 Gary Sheffield/100 — 10.00
20 Ron Santo/100 — 15.00
21 Juan Gonzalez/100 — 15.00
22 Alfonso Soriano/100 — 25.00
23 Ryan Klesko/92 — 10.00
24 Adam Dunn/100 — 12.00
25 Hideo Nomo/100 — 25.00
26 Mark Prior/99 — 15.00
27 Pat Burrell/99 — 10.00
28 Magglio Ordonez/100 — 8.00
29 Kirby Puckett/84 — 25.00
30 Albert Pujols/100 — 30.00
31 Albert Pujols/100 — 30.00

R.Y. Materials Autograph

NM/M

Quantity produced listed
7 Yogi Berra/25 — 150.00
26 Mark Prior/25 — 150.00
28 Magglio Ordonez/25 — 50.00

Rookie Year Combos

NM/M

Quantity produced listed
6 Mark Prior/50 — 40.00
7 Albert Pujols/50 — 80.00

Rookie Year Materials Letter

NM/M

Quantity produced listed
4 Nomar Garciaparra/35 — 40.00
9 Ivan Rodriguez/35 — 20.00
12 Vladimir Guerrero/35 — 25.00
15 Andruw Jones/25 — 35.00
30 Albert Pujols/25 — 90.00

R.Y. Materials Logos

NM/M

Quantity produced listed
12 Vladimir Guerrero/50 — 25.00
15 Andruw Jones/50 — 25.00
17 Fred Lynn/25 — 25.00
18 Jeff Kent/50 — 20.00
19 Gary Sheffield/50 — 15.00
22 Alfonso Soriano/20 — 60.00
23 Ryan Klesko/50 — 15.00
30 Albert Pujols/50 — 75.00

R.Y. Materials Numbers

NM/M

Quantity produced listed
12 Vladimir Guerrero/50 — 25.00
15 Andruw Jones/15 — 25.00
17 Fred Lynn/30 — 25.00
18 Jeff Kent/25 — 20.00
19 Gary Sheffield/25 — 30.00
21 Juan Gonzalez/30 — 30.00
22 Alfonso Soriano/35 — 50.00
23 Ryan Klesko/35 — 20.00
26 Mark Prior/35 — 40.00
30 Albert Pujols/25 — 90.00

R.Y. Materials Patches
No Pricing

2004 Donruss

NM/M

Complete Set (400): — 75.00
Common Player: — .10
Pack (10): — 3.50
Box (24): — 65.00
1 Derek Jeter — 2.00
2 Greg Maddux — 1.00
3 Albert Pujols — 1.50
4 Ichiro Suzuki — 1.00
5 Alex Rodriguez — 1.50
6 Roger Clemens — 1.50
7 Andruw Jones — .50
8 Barry Bonds — 2.00
9 Jeff Bagwell — .50
10 Randy Johnson — .75
12 Scott Rolen — .50
13 Lance Berkman — .40
14 Barry Zito — .25
15 Manny Ramirez — .50
16 Carlos Delgado — .50
17 Alfonso Soriano — .75
18 Todd Helton — .50
19 Mike Mussina — .50
20 Nomar Garciaparra — 1.50
21 Chipper Jones — 1.00
22 Mark Prior — 2.00
23 Jim Thome — .50
24 Vladimir Guerrero — .75
25 Pedro Martinez — .75
26 Sergio Mitre — .10
27 Adam Loewen — .10
28 Alfredo Gonzalez — .10
29 Miguel Ojeda — .10
30 Rosman Garcia — .10
32 Arnie Munoz — .10
33 Andrew Brown — .10
34 Josh Hall — .10
34 Josh Stewart — .10
35 Clint Barmes — .10
36 Brandon Webb — .10
37 Chien-Ming Wang — .40
38 Edgar Gonzalez — .10
39 Alejandro Machado — .10
40 Jeremy Griffiths — .10
41 Craig Brazell — .10
42 Daniel Cabrera — .10
43 Fernando Cabrera — .10
44 Terrmel Sledge — .10
45 Rob Hammock — .10
46 Francisco Rosario — .10
47 Francisco Cruceta — .10
48 Rett Johnson — .10
49 Guillermo Quiroz — .10
50 Hong-Chih Kuo — .10
51 Ian Ferguson — .10
52 Tim Olson — .10
53 Todd Wellemeyer — .10
54 Rich Fischer — .10
55 Phil Seibel — .10
56 Joe Valentine — .10
57 Matt Kata — .10
58 Michael Hessman — .10
59 Michel Hernandez — .10
60 Doug Waechter — .10
61 Prentice Redman — .10
62 Nook Logan — .10
63 Oscar Villarreal — .10
64 Pete LaForest — .10
65 Matt Bruback — .10
66 Dan Haren — .10

264 • 2004 Donruss

67	Greg Aquino	.10
68	Lew Ford	.10
69	Jeff Duncan	.10
70	Ryan Wagner	.10
71	Bengie Molina	.10
72	Brad Fullmer	.10
73	Darin Erstad	.25
74	David Eckstein	.10
75	Garret Anderson	.25
76	Jarrod Washburn	.10
77	Kevin Appier	.10
78	Scott Spiezio	.10
79	Tim Salmon	.25
80	Troy Glaus	.40
81	Troy Percival	.10
82	Jason Johnson	.10
83	Jay Gibbons	.25
84	Melvin Mora	.10
85	Sidney Ponson	.10
86	Tony Batista	.10
87	Bill Mueller	.10
88	Byung-Hyun Kim	.10
89	David Ortiz	.25
90	Derek Lowe	.25
91	Johnny Damon	.25
92	Casey Fossum	.10
93	Manny Ramirez	.50
94	Nomar Garciaparra	1.50
95	Pedro J. Martinez	.75
96	Todd Walker	.10
97	Trot Nixon	.10
98	Bartolo Colon	.25
99	Carlos Lee	.10
100	D'Angelo Jimenez	.10
101	Esteban Loaiza	.10
102	Frank Thomas	.50
103	Joe Crede	.10
104	Jose Valentin	.10
105	Magglio Ordonez	.25
106	Mark Buehrle	.10
107	Paul Konerko	.10
108	Brandon Phillips	.10
109	C.C. Sabathia	.10
110	Ellis Burks	.10
111	Jeremy Guthrie	.10
112	Josh Bard	.10
113	Matt Lawton	.10
114	Milton Bradley	.10
115	Omar Vizquel	.20
116	Travis Hafner	.10
117	Bobby Higginson	.10
118	Carlos Pena	.10
119	Dmitri Young	.20
120	Eric Munson	.10
121	Jeremy Bonderman	.10
122	Nate Cornejo	.10
123	Omar Infante	.10
124	Ramon Santiago	.10
125	Angel Berroa	.10
126	Carlos Beltran	.25
127	Desi Relaford	.10
128	Jeremy Affeldt	.10
129	Joe Randa	.10
130	Ken Harvey	.10
131	Mike MacDougal	.10
132	Michael Tucker	.10
133	Mike Sweeney	.20
134	Raul Ibanez	.20
135	Runelvys Hernandez	.10
136	A.J. Pierzynski	.10
137	Brad Radke	.10
138	Corey Koskie	.10
139	Cristian Guzman	.10
140	Doug Mientkiewicz	.10
141	Dustan Mohr	.10
142	Jacque Jones	.10
143	Kenny Rogers	.10
144	Bobby Kielty	.10
145	Kyle Lohse	.10
146	Luis Rivas	.10
147	Torii Hunter	.25
148	Alfonso Soriano	.75
149	Andy Pettitte	.40
150	Bernie Williams	.40
151	David Wells	.10
152	Derek Jeter	2.00
153	Hideki Matsui	2.00
154	Jason Giambi	.75
155	Jorge Posada	.50
156	Jose Contreras	.40
157	Mike Mussina	.50
158	Nick Johnson	.10
159	Robin Ventura	.20
160	Roger Clemens	1.50
161	Barry Zito	.25
162	Chris Singleton	.10
163	Eric Byrnes	.10
164	Eric Chavez	.25
165	Erubiel Durazo	.10
166	Keith Foulke	.10
167	Mark Ellis	.10
168	Miguel Tejada	.40
169	Mark Mulder	.25
170	Ramon Hernandez	.10
171	Ted Lilly	.10
172	Terrence Long	.10
173	Tim Hudson	.25
174	Bret Boone	.25
175	Carlos Guillen	.10
176	Dan Wilson	.10
177	Edgar Martinez	.25
178	Freddy Garcia	.10
179	Gil Meche	.10
180	Ichiro Suzuki	1.00
181	Jamie Moyer	.10
182	Joel Pineiro	.10
183	John Olerud	.20
184	Mike Cameron	.10
185	Randy Winn	.10
186	Ryan Franklin	.10
187	Kazuhiro Sasaki	.10
188	Aubrey Huff	.10
189	Carl Crawford	.10
190	Joe Kennedy	.10
191	Marlon Anderson	.10
192	Rey Ordonez	.10
193	Rocco Baldelli	.25
194	Toby Hall	.10
195	Travis Lee	.10
196	Alex Rodriguez	1.50
197	Carl Everett	.10
198	Chan Ho Park	.10
199	Einar Diaz	.10
200	Hank Blalock	.50
201	Ismael Valdes	.10
202	Juan Gonzalez	.50
203	Mark Teixeira	.40
204	Mike Young	.10
205	Rafael Palmeiro	.50
206	Carlos Delgado	.50
207	Kelvim Escobar	.10
208	Eric Hinske	.10
209	Frank Catalanotto	.10
210	Josh Phelps	.10
211	Orlando Hudson	.10
212	Roy Halladay	.25
213	Shannon Stewart	.10
214	Vernon Wells	.25
215	Carlos Baerga	.10
216	Curt Schilling	.40
217	Junior Spivey	.10
218	Luis Gonzalez	.25
219	Lyle Overbay	.10
220	Mark Grace	.25
221	Matt Williams	.20
222	Randy Johnson	.75
223	Shea Hillenbrand	.10
224	Steve Finley	.10
225	Andruw Jones	.50
226	Chipper Jones	1.00
227	Gary Sheffield	.40
228	Greg Maddux	1.00
229	Javy Lopez	.25
230	John Smoltz	.25
231	Marcus Giles	.20
232	Mike Hampton	.10
233	Rafael Furcal	.25
234	Robert Fick	.10
235	Russ Ortiz	.10
236	Alex Gonzalez	.10
237	Carlos Zambrano	.10
238	Corey Patterson	.10
239	Hee Seop Choi	.10
240	Kerry Wood	.50
241	Mark Belhorn	.10
242	Mark Prior	1.50
243	Moises Alou	.25
244	Sammy Sosa	1.50
245	Aaron Boone	.10
246	Adam Dunn	.40
247	Austin Kearns	.40
248	Barry Larkin	.25
249	Felipe Lopez	.10
250	Jose Guillen	.10
251	Ken Griffey Jr.	1.00
252	Jason LaRue	.10
253	Scott Williamson	.10
254	Sean Casey	.20
255	Shawn Chacon	.10
256	Chris Stynes	.10
257	Jason Jennings	.10
258	Jay Payton	.20
259	Jose Hernandez	.10
260	Larry Walker	.25
261	Preston Wilson	.20
262	Ronnie Belliard	.10
263	Todd Helton	.50
264	A.J. Burnett	.10
265	Alex Gonzalez	.10
266	Brad Penny	.10
267	Derrek Lee	.10
268	Ivan Rodriguez	.50
269	Josh Beckett	.50
270	Juan Encarnacion	.10
271	Juan Pierre	.10
272	Luis Castillo	.10
273	Mike Lowell	.10
274	Todd Hollandsworth	.10
275	Billy Wagner	.25
276	Brad Ausmus	.10
277	Craig Biggio	.25
278	Jeff Bagwell	.50
279	Jeff Kent	.25
280	Lance Berkman	.25
281	Richard Hidalgo	.10
282	Roy Oswalt	.25
283	Wade Miller	.10
284	Adrian Beltre	.10
285	Brian Jordan	.10
286	Cesar Izturis	.10
287	Dave Roberts	.10
288	Eric Gagne	.25
289	Fred McGriff	.25
290	Hideo Nomo	.40
291	Kazuhisa Ishii	.10
292	Kevin Brown	.25
293	Paul LoDuca	.10
294	Shawn Green	.40
295	Ben Sheets	.25
296	Geoff Jenkins	.25
297	Rey Sanchez	.10
298	Richie Sexson	.40
299	Wes Helms	.10
300	Brad Wilkerson	.10
301	Claudio Vargas	.10
302	Endy Chavez	.10
303	Fernando Tatis	.10
304	Javier Vazquez	.25
305	Jose Vidro	.10
306	Michael Barrett	.10
307	Orlando Cabrera	.20
308	Tony Armas Jr.	.10
309	Vladimir Guerrero	.75
310	Zach Day	.10
311	Al Leiter	.10
312	Cliff Floyd	.10
313	Jae Weong Seo	.10
314	Jeromy Burnitz	.10
315	Mike Piazza	1.00
316	Mo Vaughn	.10
317	Roberto Alomar	.40
318	Roger Cedeno	.10
319	Tom Glavine	.25
320	Jose Reyes	.40
321	Bobby Abreu	.20
322	Brett Myers	.10
323	David Bell	.10
324	Jim Thome	.50
325	Jimmy Rollins	.25
326	Kevin Millwood	.25
327	Marlon Byrd	.10
328	Mike Lieberthal	.10
329	Pat Burrell	.40
330	Randy Wolf	.10
331	Aramis Ramirez	.10
332	Brian Giles	.25
333	Jason Kendall	.20
334	Kenny Lofton	.20
335	Kip Wells	.10
336	Kris Benson	.10
337	Randall Simon	.10
338	Reggie Sanders	.10
339	Albert Pujols	2.00
340	Edgar Renteria	.10
341	Fernando Vina	.10
342	J.D. Drew	.10
343	Jim Edmonds	.25
344	Matt Morris	.10
345	Mike Matheny	.10
346	Scott Rolen	.50
347	Tino Martinez	.10
348	Woody Williams	.10
349	Brian Lawrence	.10
350	Mark Kotsay	.10
351	Mark Loretta	.10
352	Ramon Vazquez	.10
353	Rondell White	.10
354	Ryan Klesko	.25
355	Sean Burroughs	.10
356	Trevor Hoffman	.10
357	Xavier Nady	.10
358	Andres Galarraga	.10
359	Barry Bonds	2.00
360	Benito Santiago	.10
361	Deivi Cruz	.10
362	Edgardo Alfonzo	.10
363	J.T. Snow	.10
364	Jason Schmidt	.10
365	Kirk Rueter	.10
366	Kurt Ainsworth	.10
367	Marquis Grissom	.10
368	Ray Durham	.10
369	Rich Aurilia	.10
370	Tim Worrell	.10
371	Troy Glaus	.20
372	Melvin Mora	.10
373	Nomar Garciaparra	.75
374	Magglio Ordonez	.20
375	Omar Vizquel	.10
376	Dmitri Young	.10
377	Mike Sweeney	.10
378	Torii Hunter	.20
379	Derek Jeter	1.00
380	Barry Zito	.20
381	Ichiro Suzuki	.50
382	Rocco Baldelli	.20
383	Alex Rodriguez	.75
384	Carlos Delgado	.25
385	Randy Johnson	.40
386	Greg Maddux	.50
387	Sammy Sosa	.75
388	Ken Griffey Jr.	.50
389	Todd Helton	.25
390	Ivan Rodriguez	.25
391	Jeff Bagwell	.25
392	Hideo Nomo	.20
393	Richie Sexson	.20
394	Vladimir Guerrero	.40
395	Mike Piazza	.50
396	Jim Thome	.25
397	Jason Kendall	.10
398	Albert Pujols	1.00
399	Ryan Klesko	.10
400	Barry Bonds	1.00

Black Press Proofs

No pricing due to scarcity.
Production 10 Sets
Hot Pack exclusive.

Career Stat Line

Cards Serial #'d from 251-500:	3-5X
Print run 101-250:	4-6X
Print run 61-100:	4-8X
Print run 26-60:	8-15X

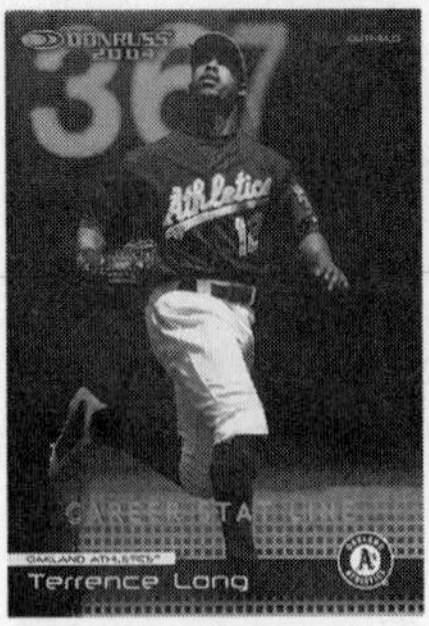

No pricing for P/R 25 or less.
Numbered to career statistic.

Season Stat Line

Print run 101-261:	4-6X
Print run 61-100:	4-8X
Print run 26-60:	8-15X

No pricing for P/R 25 or less.
Numbered to 2003 statistic.

All-Stars

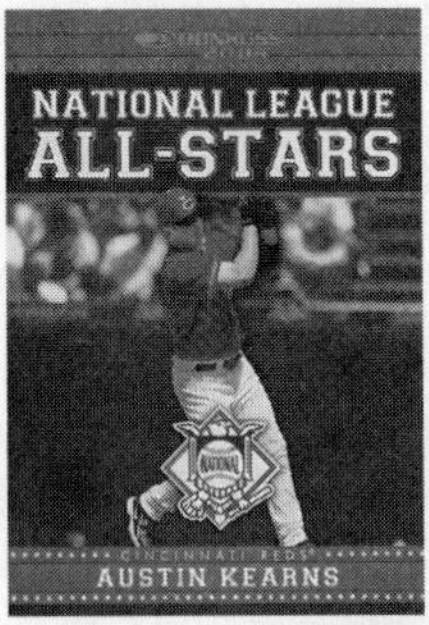

		NM/M
Complete Set (20):		40.00
Common Player:		1.50
Production 1,000 Sets		
Black:		1-2X
Production 250 Sets		
1	Alex Rodriguez	5.00
2	Roger Clemens	5.00
3	Ichiro Suzuki	3.00
4	Barry Zito	1.50
5	Garret Anderson	1.50
6	Derek Jeter	5.00
7	Manny Ramirez	2.00
8	Pedro J. Martinez	2.00
9	Alfonso Soriano	2.50
10	Carlos Delgado	1.50
11	Barry Bonds	5.00
12	Andruw Jones	2.00
13	Scott Rolen	2.00
14	Austin Kearns	1.50
15	Mark Prior	4.00
16	Vladimir Guerrero	2.00
17	Jeff Bagwell	2.00
18	Mike Piazza	3.00
19	Albert Pujols	5.00
20	Randy Johnson	2.50

Bat Kings

		NM/M
Common Player:		5.00
Studio Current Player:		1.5X
Production 50		
Studio Retired:		No Pricing
Production 25		
1	Alex Rodriguez/250	10.00
2	Albert Pujols/250	15.00
3	Chipper Jones/250	12.00
4	Lance Berkman/250	5.00
5	Cal Ripken Jr./100	50.00
6	George Brett/100	30.00
7	Don Mattingly/100	40.00
8	Roberto Clemente/100	75.00

Craftsmen

		NM/M
Complete Set (15):		40.00
Common Player:		2.00
Production 2,000 Sets		
Black:		1-2X
Production 275 Sets		
Master Craftsmen:		1-2X
Production 150 Sets		
1	Alex Rodriguez	5.00
2	Mark Prior	4.00
3	Ichiro Suzuki	3.00
4	Barry Bonds	5.00

5	Ken Griffey Jr.	3.00
6	Alfonso Soriano	3.00
7	Mike Piazza	3.00
8	Chipper Jones	3.00
9	Derek Jeter	5.00
10	Randy Johnson	2.50
11	Sammy Sosa	4.00
12	Roger Clemens	4.00
13	Nomar Garciaparra	4.00
14	Greg Maddux	3.00
15	Albert Pujols	3.00

Diamond Kings Insert

		NM/M
Complete Set (25):		80.00
Common Player:		2.00
Production 2,500 Sets		
Studio Series:		1-2X
Production 250 Sets		
Black:		1.5-2X
Production 100 Sets		
1	Derek Jeter	8.00
2	Greg Maddux	6.00
3	Albert Pujols	8.00
4	Ichiro Suzuki	6.00
5	Alex Rodriguez	6.00
6	Roger Clemens	6.00
7	Andruw Jones	3.00
8	Barry Bonds	8.00
9	Jeff Bagwell	3.00
10	Randy Johnson	3.00
11	Scott Rolen	3.00
12	Lance Berkman	2.00
13	Barry Zito	2.00
14	Manny Ramirez	3.00
15	Carlos Delgado	2.50
16	Alfonso Soriano	4.00
17	Todd Helton	3.00
18	Mike Mussina	2.00
19	Austin Kearns	2.00
20	Nomar Garciaparra	6.00
21	Chipper Jones	4.00
22	Mark Prior	4.00
23	Jim Thome	3.00
24	Vladimir Guerrero	3.00
25	Pedro J. Martinez	3.00

Elite Series

		NM/M
Complete Set (15):		60.00
Common Player:		2.00
Production 1,500 Sets		
Black:		1-2X
Production 150 Sets		
Dominators:		No Pricing
Production 25 Sets		
1	Albert Pujols	8.00
2	Barry Zito	3.00
3	Gary Sheffield	3.00
4	Mike Mussina	3.00
5	Lance Berkman	2.00
6	Alfonso Soriano	4.00
7	Randy Johnson	3.00
8	Nomar Garciaparra	8.00
9	Austin Kearns	3.00
10	Manny Ramirez	3.00

11	Mark Prior	6.00
12	Alex Rodriguez	6.00
13	Derek Jeter	8.00
14	Barry Bonds	8.00
15	Roger Clemens	6.00

Inside View

		NM/M
Complete Set (25):		50.00
Common Player:		1.00
Production 1,250 Sets		
1	Derek Jeter	5.00
2	Greg Maddux	3.00
3	Albert Pujols	5.00
4	Ichiro Suzuki	3.00
5	Alex Rodriguez	4.00
6	Roger Clemens	5.00
7	Andruw Jones	1.50
8	Barry Bonds	5.00
9	Jeff Bagwell	2.00
10	Randy Johnson	2.00
11	Scott Rolen	2.00
12	Lance Berkman	1.00
13	Barry Zito	1.50
14	Manny Ramirez	2.00
15	Carlos Delgado	1.50
16	Alfonso Soriano	2.00
17	Todd Helton	2.00
18	Mike Mussina	1.50
19	Austin Kearns	1.50
20	Nomar Garciaparra	4.00
21	Chipper Jones	3.00
22	Mark Prior	4.00
23	Jim Thome	2.00
24	Vladimir Guerrero	2.00
25	Pedro J. Martinez	2.50

Jersey Kings

		NM/M
Quantity produced listed		
Studio Current Player:		1.5X
Production 50		
Studio Retired:		No Pricing
Production 25		
1	Alfonso Soriano/250	10.00
2	Sammy Sosa/250	15.00
3	Roger Clemens/250	15.00
4	Nomar Garciaparra/250	12.00
5	Mark Prior/250	10.00
6	Vladimir Guerrero/250	8.00
7	Don Mattingly/100	40.00
8	Roberto Clemente/100	80.00
9	George Brett/100	35.00
10	Nolan Ryan/100	40.00
11	Cal Ripken Jr./100	55.00
12	Mike Schmidt/100	40.00

Longball Leaders

		NM/M
Complete Set (10):		20.00
Common Player:		1.50
Production 1,500 Sets		
Black:		1-2X
Production 250 Sets		
Die-Cuts:		1.5-3X
Production 50 Sets		
1	Barry Bonds	5.00

2	Alfonso Soriano	3.00
3	Adam Dunn	1.50
4	Alex Rodriguez	5.00
5	Jim Thome	2.00
6	Garret Anderson	1.50
7	Juan Gonzalez	2.00
8	Jeff Bagwell	2.00
9	Gary Sheffield	1.50
10	Sammy Sosa	4.00

Mound Marvels

		NM/M
Complete Set (15):		20.00
Common Player:		1.00
Production 750 Sets		
Black:		1-2X
Production 175 Sets		
1	Mark Prior	4.00
2	Curt Schilling	1.50
3	Mike Mussina	1.50
4	Kevin Brown	1.50
5	Pedro J. Martinez	2.50
6	Mark Mulder	1.00
7	Kerry Wood	1.50
8	Greg Maddux	3.00
9	Kevin Millwood	1.00
10	Barry Zito	1.50
11	Roger Clemens	5.00
12	Randy Johnson	2.50
13	Hideo Nomo	1.50
14	Tim Hudson	1.50
15	Tom Glavine	1.50

Power Alley Red

		NM/M
Complete Set (20):		50.00
Common Player:		2.00
Production 2,500 Sets		
Red Die-Cut:		1-2X
Production 250 Sets		
Blues:		1X
Production 1,000 Sets		
Blue Die-Cuts:		1.5-2X
Production 100 Sets		
Purples:		1-2X
Production 250 Sets		
Purple Die-Cuts:		No Pricing
Production 25 Sets		
Yellows:		1.5-2X
Production 100 Sets		
Yellow Die-Cuts:		No Pricing
Production 10 Sets		
Greens:		No Pricing
Production 25 Sets		
Green Die-Cuts:		No Pricing
Production 5 Sets		
1	Albert Pujols	8.00
2	Mike Piazza	5.00
3	Carlos Delgado	2.00
4	Barry Bonds	8.00
5	Jim Edmonds	2.00
6	Nomar Garciaparra	6.00
7	Alfonso Soriano	4.00
8	Alex Rodriguez	6.00
9	Lance Berkman	2.00
10	Scott Rolen	3.00
11	Manny Ramirez	3.00

12	Rafael Palmeiro	3.00
13	Sammy Sosa	6.00
14	Adam Dunn	2.00
15	Andruw Jones	2.00
16	Jim Thome	3.00
17	Jason Giambi	3.00
18	Jeff Bagwell	3.00
19	Juan Gonzalez	3.00
20	Austin Kearns	2.00

Production Line OPS

		NM/M
Complete Set (10):		25.00
Varying quanties produced		
Black:		1-2X
Production 125 Sets		
Die-Cuts:		1-2X
Production 100 Sets		
1	Albert Pujols/1,106	5.00
2	Barry Bonds/1,278	5.00
3	Gary Sheffield/1,023	1.50
4	Todd Helton/1,088	2.00
5	Scott Rolen/910	3.00
6	Manny Ramirez/1,014	3.00
7	Alex Rodriguez/995	5.00
8	Jim Thome/958	3.00
9	Jason Giambi/939	3.00
10	Frank Thomas/952	3.00

Production Line Slugging

		NM/M
Complete Set (10):		25.00
Varying quantities produced		
Black:		1-2X
Production 75 Sets		
Die-Cuts:		1-2X
Production 100 Sets		
1	Alex Rodriguez/604	6.00
2	Frank Thomas/562	3.00
3	Garret Anderson/541	2.00
4	Albert Pujols/667	6.00
5	Sammy Sosa/553	5.00
6	Gary Sheffield/604	2.00
7	Manny Ramirez/587	3.00
8	Jim Edmonds/617	2.00
9	Barry Bonds/688	6.00
10	Todd Helton/630	3.00

Production Line OBP

		NM/M
Complete Set (10):		25.00
Common Player:		2.00
Die-Cuts:		1-2X
Production 100 Sets		
Black:		2-3X
Production 40 Sets		
1	Todd Helton/458	3.00
2	Albert Pujols/439	6.00
3	Larry Walker/422	2.00
4	Barry Bonds/529	6.00
5	Chipper Jones/402	4.00
6	Manny Ramirez/427	3.00
7	Gary Sheffield/419	2.00
8	Lance Berkman/412	2.00
9	Alex Rodriguez/396	6.00
10	Jason Giambi/412	3.00

Production Line Average

		NM/M
Complete Set (10):		35.00
Common Player:		
Die-Cuts:		1-2X
Production 100 Sets		
Black:		2-3X
Production 35 Sets		
1	Gary Sheffield/330	2.00
2	Ichiro Suzuki/312	5.00
3	Todd Helton/358	3.00
4	Manny Ramirez/325	3.00
5	Garret Anderson/315	2.00
6	Barry Bonds/341	8.00
7	Albert Pujols/359	8.00
8	Derek Jeter/324	8.00
9	Nomar Garciaparra/301	6.00
10	Hank Blalock/300	3.00

Timber & Threads

		NM/M
Common Player:		4.00
Inserted 1:40		
Studio Series:		1.5X
Production 50 Sets		
1	Adam Dunn	6.00
2	Alex Rodriguez - Blue	10.00
3	Alex Rodriguez - White	10.00
4	Andruw Jones	6.00
5	Austin Kearns	6.00
6	Carlos Beltran	4.00
7	Carlos Lee	4.00
8	Frank Thomas	8.00
9	Greg Maddux	10.00
10	Hideo Nomo	10.00

11 Jeff Bagwell 8.00
12 Lance Berkman 4.00
13 Magglio Ordonez 4.00
14 Mike Sweeney 4.00
15 Randy Johnson 8.00
16 Rocco Baldelli 10.00
17 Roger Clemens 12.00
18 Sammy Sosa 12.00
19 Shawn Green 4.00
20 Tom Glavine 6.00
21 Adam Dunn 6.00
22 Andruw Jones 6.00
23 Bobby Abreu 4.00
24 Hank Blalock 6.00
25 Ivan Rodriguez 6.00
26 Jim Edmonds 6.00
27 Josh Phelps 4.00
28 Juan Gonzalez 6.00
29 Lance Berkman 4.00
30 Larry Walker 4.00
31 Magglio Ordonez 4.00
32 Manny Ramirez 8.00
33 Mike Piazza 10.00
34 Nomar Garciaparra 10.00
35 Paul LoDuca 4.00
36 Roberto Alomar 6.00
37 Rocco Baldelli 10.00
38 Sammy Sosa 12.00
39 Vernon Wells 4.00
40 Vladimir Guerrero 8.00

2004 Donruss Classics

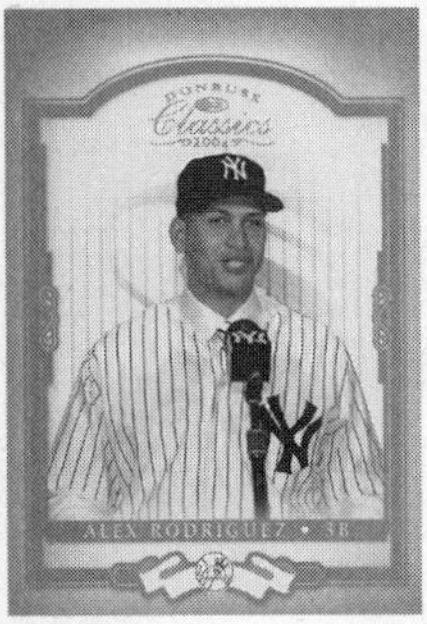

NM/M

Complete Set (213):
Common Player: .40
Common (151-210): 3.00
Production 1,999
Pack (6): 6.00
Box (18): 90.00
1 Albert Pujols 2.50
2 Derek Jeter 3.00
3 Hank Blalock .50
4 Shannon Stewart .40
5 Jason Giambi 1.00
6 Carlos Lee .40
7 Trot Nixon .40
8 Bret Boone .50
9 Mark Mulder .40
10 Mariano Rivera .50
11 Scott Podsednik .75
12 Jim Edmonds .50
13 Mike Lowell .50
14 Robin Ventura .40
15 Brian Giles .50
16 Jose Vidro .40
17 Manny Ramirez .75
18 Alex Rodriquez 2.50
19 Carlos Beltran .50
20 Hideki Matsui 2.50
21 Johan Santana .40
22 Richie Sexson .50
23 Chipper Jones 1.00
24 Steve Finley .40
25 Mark Prior 1.50
26 Alexis Rios .40
27 Rafael Palmeiro .75
28 Jorge Posada .50
29 Barry Zito .50
30 Jamie Moyer .40
31 Preston Wilson .40
32 Miguel Cabrera .75
33 Pedro Martinez 1.00
34 Curt Schilling .75
35 Hee Seop Choi .40
36 Dontrelle Willis .50
37 Rafael Soriano .40
38 Richard Fischer .40
39 Brian Tallet .40
40 Jose Castillo .40
41 Wade Miller .40
42 Jose Contreras .40
43 Runelvys Hernandez .40
44 Joe Borchard .40
45 Kazuhisa Ishii .40
46 Jose Reyes .50
47 Adam Dunn .50
48 Randy Johnson 1.00
49 Brandon Phillips .40
50 Scott Rolen 1.00
51 Ken Griffey Jr. 1.50
52 Tom Glavine .50
53 Cliff Lee .50
54 Chien-Ming Wang .50
55 Roy Oswalt .50
56 Austin Kearns .50
57 Jhonny Peralta .40
58 Greg Maddux 1.50
59 Mark Grace .50
60 Jae Weong Seo .40
61 Nic Jackson .40
62 Roger Clemens 2.50
63 Jimmy Gobble .40
64 Travis Hafner .40
65 Paul Konerko .40
66 Jerome Williams .40
67 Ryan Klesko .50
68 Alexis Gomez .40
69 Omar Vizquel .40
70 Zach Day .40
71 Rickey Henderson .50
72 Morgan Ensberg .40
73 Josh Beckett .75
74 Garrett Atkins .40
75 Sean Casey .40
76 Julio Franco .40
77 Lyle Overbay .40
78 Josh Phelps .40
79 Juan Gonzalez .75
80 Rich Harden .40
81 Bernie Williams .50
82 Torii Hunter .50
83 Angel Berroa .40
84 Jody Gerut .40
85 Roberto Alomar .50
86 Byung-Hyun Kim .40
87 Jay Gibbons .40
88 Chone Figgins .40
89 Fred McGriff .50
90 Rich Aurilia .40
91 Xavier Nady .40
92 Marlon Byrd .40
93 Mike Piazza 1.50
94 Vladimir Guerrero 1.00
95 Shawn Green .50
96 Jeff Kent .50
97 Ivan Rodriguez .75
98 Jay Payton .40
99 Barry Larkin .50
100 Mike Sweeney .40
101 Adrian Beltre .40
102 Robby Hammock .40
103 Orlando Hudson .40
104 Mark Teixeira .50
105 Hong-Chih Kuo .40
106 Eric Chavez .50
107 Nick Johnson .40
108 Jacque Jones .40
109 Ken Harvey .40
110 Aramis Ramirez .40
111 Victor Martinez .40
112 Joe Crede .40
113 Jason Varitek .40
114 Troy Glaus .50
115 Billy Wagner .40
116 Kerry Wood 1.00
117 Hideo Nomo .50
118 Brandon Webb .40
119 Craig Biggio .40
120 Orlando Cabrera .40
121 Sammy Sosa 2.00
122 Bobby Abreu .50
123 Andruw Jones .75
124 Jeff Bagwell .75
125 Jim Thome 1.00
126 Javy Lopez .50
127 Luis Castillo .40
128 Todd Helton .75
129 Roy Halladay .50
130 Mike Mussina .50
131 Eric Byrnes .40
132 Eric Hinske .40
133 Nomar Garciaparra 2.00
134 Edgar Martinez .50
135 Rocco Baldelli .50
136 Miguel Tejada .50
137 Alfonso Soriano 1.00
138 Carlos Delgado .75
139 Rafael Furcal .50
140 Ichiro Suzuki 2.00
141 Aubrey Huff .40
142 Garret Anderson .50
143 Vernon Wells .40
144 Magglio Ordonez .50
145 Brett Myers .40
146 Luis Gonzalez .40
147 Lance Berkman .50
148 Frank Thomas .75
149 Gary Sheffield .50
150 Tim Hudson .50
151 Duke Snider 3.00
152 Carl Yastrzemski 4.00
153 Whitey Ford 3.00
154 Cal Ripken Jr. 8.00
155 Dwight Gooden 2.00
156 Warren Spahn 4.00
157 Bob Gibson 3.00
158 Don Mattingly 6.00
159 Jack Morris 2.00
160 Jim Bunning 2.00
161 Fergie Jenkins 2.00
162 Brooks Robinson 3.00
163 George Kell 2.00
164 Darryl Strawberry 2.00
165 Robin Roberts 2.00
166 Monte Irvin 2.00
167 Ernie Banks 4.00
168 Wade Boggs 3.00
169 Gaylord Perry 2.00
170 Keith Hernandez 2.00
171 Lou Brock 3.00
172 Frank Robinson 3.00
173 Nolan Ryan 8.00
174 Stan Musial 5.00
175 Eddie Murray 3.00
176 Byron Gettis 3.00
177 Merkin Valdez **RC** 5.00
178 Rickie Weeks 3.00
179 Akinori Otsuka **RC** 3.00
180 Brian Bruney 3.00
181 Freddy Guzman **RC** 3.00
182 Brendan Harris 3.00
183 John Gall **RC** 3.00
184 Jason Kubel 3.00
185 Delmon Young 4.00
186 Ryan Howard 3.00
187 Adam Loewen 3.00
188 J.D. Durbin 3.00
189 Dan Haren 3.00
190 Dustin McGowan 3.00
191 Chad Gaudin 3.00
192 Preston Larrison 3.00
193 Ramon Nivar 3.00
194 Ronald Belisario **RC** 3.00
195 Mike Gosling 3.00
196 Kevin Youkilis 3.00
197 Ryan Wagner 3.00
198 Bubba Nelson 3.00
199 Edwin Jackson 3.00
200 Chris Burke 3.00
201 Carlos Hines **RC** 3.00
202 Greg Dobbs **RC** 3.00
203 Jamie Brown **RC** 3.00
204 David Crouthers 3.00
205 Ian Snell **RC** 5.00
206 Gary Carter 3.00
207 Dale Murphy 3.00
208 Ryne Sandberg 5.00
209 Phil Niekro 2.00
210 Don Sutton 2.00
211 Alex Rodriguez/Yankees/SP 5.00
212 Alfonso Soriano/Rangers/SP 1.00
213 Greg Maddux/Cubs/SP 3.00

Timeless Tributes Green

Cards (1-150): 4-6X
Cards (151-210): 1-2X
Production 50 Sets

Timeless Tributes Platinum

No Pricing
Production One Set

Timeless Tributes Red

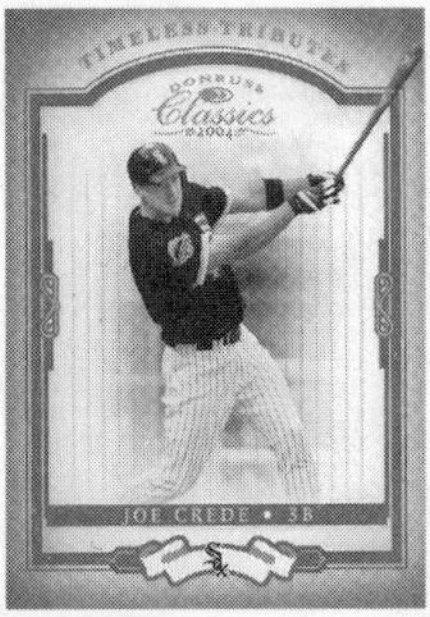

Red (1-150): 2-4X
Red (151-210): 1-1.5X
Production 100 Sets

Classic Singles Jersey

NM/M

Quantity produced listed
Prime: No Pricing
Production One Set
2 Nolan Ryan/50 35.00
3 Stan Musial/15 50.00
6 Eddie Murray/100 10.00
7 Roy Campanella/Pants/50 20.00
8 Robin Yount/100 15.00
9 Roberto Clemente/25 75.00
10 Don Mattingly/100 20.00
11 Bob Gibson/15 25.00
12 Carl Yastrzemski/50 20.00
13 Mark Grace/25 20.00
14 Jack Morris/100 6.00
15 Rickey Henderson/25 20.00
16 Reggie Jackson/50 15.00
17 Pee Wee Reese/25 25.00
18 Marty Marion/100 6.00
19 Tommy John/100 6.00
20 Roger Maris/25 50.00
21 Cal Ripken Jr./25 75.00
22 Red Schoendienst/25 10.00
23 Willie Stargell/100 15.00
24 Paul Molitor/100 10.00
25 Whitey Ford/50 25.00
26 Alan Trammell/100 10.00
27 Sammy Sosa/50 20.00
28 Bobby Doerr/50 8.00
29 Rod Carew/100 10.00
30 Yogi Berra/15 35.00
31 Phil Rizzuto/25 20.00
32 George Brett/25 40.00

Classic Singles Bat

NM/M

Quantity produced listed
1 Babe Ruth/15 250.00
3 Stan Musial/25 30.00
4 Ted Williams/25 100.00
5 Lou Gehrig/50 125.00
6 Eddie Murray/50 15.00
7 Roy Campanella/50 20.00
8 Robin Yount/50 20.00
9 Roberto Clemente/25 70.00
10 Don Mattingly/50 25.00
12 Carl Yastrzemski/50 20.00
13 Mark Grace/50 15.00
15 Rickey Henderson/50 15.00
16 Reggie Jackson/50 15.00
17 Pee Wee Reese/50 15.00
20 Roger Maris/25 40.00
21 Cal Ripken Jr./50 60.00
23 Willie Stargell/50 15.00
24 Paul Molitor/50 20.00
26 Alan Trammell/50 12.00
27 Sammy Sosa/50 20.00
28 Bobby Doerr/50 8.00
29 Rod Carew/50 15.00
30 Yogi Berra/25 20.00
32 George Brett/50 30.00

Classic Singles Jersey-Bat

NM/M

Quantity produced listed
Prime: No Pricing
Production One Set
2 Nolan Ryan/25 50.00
3 Stan Musial/15 45.00
6 Eddie Murray/25 25.00
7 Roy Campanella/Pants/25 35.00
8 Robin Yount/25 40.00
9 Roberto Clemente/25 125.00
10 Don Mattingly/25 40.00
12 Carl Yastrzemski/25 50.00
13 Mark Grace/25 20.00
15 Rickey Henderson/25 25.00
16 Reggie Jackson/25 25.00
17 Pee Wee Reese/25 25.00
20 Roger Maris/15 75.00
21 Cal Ripken Jr./25 75.00
23 Willie Stargell/25 20.00
24 Paul Molitor/25 25.00
26 Alan Trammell/25 20.00
27 Sammy Sosa/25 25.00
28 Bobby Doerr/25 25.00
29 Rod Carew/25 30.00
30 Yogi Berra/15 40.00
32 George Brett/25 50.00

Classic Combos Jersey

NM/M

Quantity produced listed
Prime: No Pricing
Production One Set
1 Babe Ruth Pants, Lou Gehrig Pants/15 500.00
2 Roy Campanella Pants, Pee Wee Reese/25 30.00
3 Ted Williams, Carl Yastrzemski/15 200.00
4 Roberto Clemente, Willie Stargell/25 85.00
5 Eddie Murray, Cal Ripken Jr./25 75.00
6 Roger Maris, Yogi Berra/25 65.00
8 Whitey Ford, Yogi Berra/25 30.00
9 Marty Marion, Stan Musial/25 40.00
10 Nolan Ryan, Rod Carew/25 40.00
11 Don Mattingly, Rickey Henderson/50 40.00
12 Jack Morris, Alan Trammell/50 15.00
13 Whitey Ford, Phil Rizzuto/25 30.00
14 Marty Marion, Red Schoendienst/25 15.00
15 Robin Yount, Paul Molitor/50 40.00
16 Mark Grace, Sammy Sosa/50 30.00
17 Ted Williams, Bobby Doerr/15 150.00
18 Reggie Jackson, Rod Carew/50 25.00

Classic Combos Bat

NM/M

Quantity produced listed
1 Babe Ruth, Lou Gehrig/25 375.00
2 Roy Campanella, Pee Wee Reese/50 25.00
3 Ted Williams, Carl Yastrzemski/25 125.00
4 Roberto Clemente, Willie Stargell/25 100.00
5 Eddie Murray, Cal Ripken Jr./50 50.00
6 Roger Maris, Yogi Berra/25 65.00
10 Nolan Ryan, Rod Carew/50 35.00
11 Don Mattingly, Rickey Henderson/50 40.00

15	Robin Yount, Paul Molitor/50	40.00
16	Mark Grace, Sammy Sosa/50	30.00
17	Ted Williams, Bobby Doerr/25	80.00
18	Reggie Jackson, Rod Carew/50	25.00

Classic Combos Quad

NM/M

Quantity produced listed
Prime: No Pricing
Production One Set

2	Roy Campanella/Pants, Pee Wee Reese/25	50.00
3	Ted Williams, Carl Yastrzemski/15	250.00
4	Roberto Clemente, Willie Stargell/25	200.00
5	Eddie Murray, Cal Ripken Jr./25	125.00
6	Roger Maris, Yogi Berra/15	150.00
10	Nolan Ryan, Rod Carew/25	70.00
11	Don Mattingly, Rickey Henderson/25	80.00
15	Robin Yount, Paul Molitor/25	75.00
16	Mark Grace, Sammy Sosa/25	60.00
17	Ted Williams, Bobby Doerr/15	200.00
18	Reggie Jackson, Rod Carew/25	40.00

Dress Code Jersey

NM/M

Common Player: 4.00
Production 100 Sets
Number: 1X
Production 100 Sets
Prime: 2X
Production 25 Sets

1	Derek Jeter	25.00
2	Kerry Wood	15.00
3	Nomar Garciaparra	10.00
4	Jacque Jones	4.00
5	Mark Teixeira	6.00
6	Troy Glaus	6.00
7	Todd Helton	6.00
8	Miguel Tejada	6.00
9	Mike Piazza	10.00
11	Mike Sweeney	4.00
12	Albert Pujols	15.00
13	Rickey Henderson	8.00
14	Chipper Jones	8.00
15	Don Mattingly	25.00
16	Shawn Green	5.00
17	Mark Grace	10.00
18	Jason Giambi	8.00
19	Barry Zito	6.00
20	Sammy Sosa	12.00
21	Jay Gibbons	4.00
22	Rafael Palmeiro	8.00
23	Frank Thomas	8.00
24	Manny Ramirez	8.00
25	Mike Mussina	8.00
26	Magglio Ordonez	8.00
27	Rocco Baldelli	6.00
28	Andruw Jones	6.00
29	Torii Hunter	6.00
30	Ivan Rodriguez	6.00
31	Jeff Bagwell	6.00
32	Mark Mulder	6.00
33	Trot Nixon	4.00
34	Cal Ripken Jr./25	80.00
35	Dontrelle Willis	6.00
36	Hank Blalock	6.00
37	Brandon Webb	4.00
38	Miguel Cabrera	12.00
39	Hideo Nomo	8.00
40	Shannon Stewart	4.00
41	Tim Hudson	6.00
42	Pedro Martinez	8.00
43	Hee Seop Choi	4.00
44	Randy Johnson	8.00
45	Tony Gwynn	10.00
46	Mark Prior	10.00

47	Eric Chavez	6.00
48	Alex Rodriguez	10.00
49	Johan Santana	4.00
50	Alfonso Soriano	8.00

Dress Code Bat

NM/M

Common Player: 5.00
Production 50 Sets
Combo Material: 1-1.5X
Production 50 Sets

1	Derek Jeter	25.00
2	Kerry Wood	15.00
3	Nomar Garciaparra	15.00
4	Jacque Jones	5.00
5	Mark Teixeira	6.00
6	Troy Glaus	8.00
7	Todd Helton	10.00
8	Miguel Tejada	6.00
9	Mike Piazza	12.00
11	Mike Sweeney	5.00
12	Albert Pujols	20.00
13	Rickey Henderson	10.00
14	Chipper Jones	10.00
15	Don Mattingly	25.00
16	Shawn Green	5.00
17	Mark Grace	10.00
18	Jason Giambi	8.00
19	Barry Zito	8.00
20	Sammy Sosa	15.00
22	Rafael Palmeiro	10.00
23	Frank Thomas	10.00
24	Manny Ramirez	8.00
25	Mike Mussina	10.00
26	Magglio Ordonez	6.00
27	Rocco Baldelli	12.00
28	Andruw Jones	8.00
29	Torii Hunter	6.00
30	Ivan Rodriguez	10.00
31	Jeff Bagwell	10.00
32	Mark Mulder	6.00
33	Trot Nixon	10.00
34	Cal Ripken Jr.	60.00
35	Dontrelle Willis	8.00
36	Hank Blalock	8.00
37	Brandon Webb	8.00
38	Miguel Cabrera	10.00
39	Hideo Nomo	10.00
41	Tim Hudson	8.00
42	Pedro Martinez	12.00
43	Hee Seop Choi	6.00
44	Randy Johnson	10.00
45	Tony Gwynn	15.00
46	Mark Prior	10.00
47	Eric Chavez	8.00
48	Alex Rodriguez	15.00
50	Alfonso Soriano	12.00

Dress Code Combos Signature

NM/M

Quantity produced listed
Prime: No Pricing
Production One Set

4	Jacque Jones/Jsy/25	15.00
21	Jay Gibbons/Jsy/25	25.00
32	Mark Mulder/Jsy/25	35.00
33	Trot Nixon/Jsy/25	50.00
35	Dontrelle Willis/Jsy/25	40.00
38	Miguel Cabrera/Jsy/25	70.00
40	Shannon Stewart/Jsy/25	20.00
49	Johan Santana Jsy/25	40.00

Famous Foursomes

NM/M

Production 99 Sets

1	Roy Campanella, Pee Wee Reese, Jackie Robinson, Duke Snider	15.00
2	Stan Musial, Bob Gibson, Red Schoendienst, Clete Boyer	15.00

Famous Foursomes Jersey

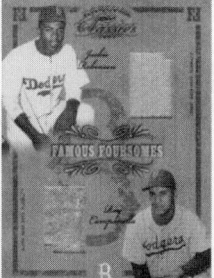

No Pricing
Production 10 Sets
Prime: No Pricing
Production One Set

Legendary Lumberjacks

NM/M

Common Player: 2.00

Production 1,000 Sets
Spikes: 1-2X
Production 100 Sets
Hats: 2-3X
Production 50 Sets
Jackets: 2-3X
Production 50 Sets
Jerseys: 1X
Production 500 Sets
Leather: 1-2X
Production 100 Sets
Pants: 2-3X
Production 50 Sets

1	Tony Gwynn	3.00
2	Mike Schmidt	5.00
3	Johnny Bench	4.00
4	Roger Maris	5.00
5	Ted Williams	8.00
6	George Brett	6.00
7	Carlton Fisk	2.00
8	Reggie Jackson	3.00
9	Joe Morgan	2.00
10	Bo Jackson	3.00
11	Stan Musial	4.00
12	Andre Dawson	2.00
13	Rickey Henderson	2.00
14	Cal Ripken Jr.	8.00
15	Dale Murphy	2.00
16	Kirby Puckett	4.00
17	Don Mattingly	5.00
18	Brooks Robinson	3.00
19	Orlando Cepeda	2.00
20	Reggie Jackson	3.00
21	Roberto Clemente	6.00
22	Ernie Banks	4.00
23	Frank Robinson	3.00
24	Harmon Killebrew	3.00
25	Willie Stargell	3.00
26	Al Kaline	4.00
27	Carl Yastrzemski	4.00
28	Duke Snider	3.00
29	Dave Winfield	2.00
30	Eddie Murray	3.00
31	Eddie Matthews	3.00
32	Gary Carter	2.00
33	Rod Carew	3.00
34	Jimmie Foxx	4.00
35	Mel Ott	3.00
36	Paul Molitor	2.00
37	Thurman Munson	4.00
38	Rogers Hornsby	3.00
39	Robin Yount	4.00
40	Wade Boggs	3.00
41	Jackie Robinson	5.00
42	Rickey Henderson	2.00
43	Ty Cobb	5.00
44	Yogi Berra	3.00
45	Roy Campanella	3.00
46	Luis Aparicio	3.00
47	Phil Rizzuto	3.00
48	Roger Maris	3.00
49	Reggie Jackson	3.00
50	Lou Gehrig	4.00
51	Rafael Palmeiro	3.00
52	Sammy Sosa	3.00
53	Roger Clemens	6.00
54	Nolan Ryan	3.00
55	Steve Carlton	3.00
56	Rod Carew	3.00
57	Whitey Ford	3.00
58	Fergie Jenkins	2.00
59	Babe Ruth	3.00
60	R Henderson	2.00

Legendary Lumberjacks Material

NM/M

Quantity produced listed

1	Tony Gwynn/100	15.00
2	Mike Schmidt/100	15.00
3	Johnny Bench/100	12.00
4	Roger Maris /25	40.00
5	Ted Williams/25	100.00
6	George Brett/100	25.00
7	Carlton Fisk/100	10.00
8	Reggie Jackson /100	12.00
9	Joe Morgan/100	5.00
10	Bo Jackson/100	8.00
11	Stan Musial/25	35.00
12	Andre Dawson/100	5.00
13	R Henderson/100	10.00

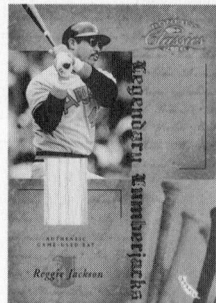

14	Cal Ripken Jr./100	40.00
15	Dale Murphy/100	12.00
16	Kirby Puckett/100	15.00
17	Don Mattingly/100	20.00
18	Brooks Robinson/100	15.00
19	Orlando Cepeda/100	5.00
20	Reggie Jackson/100	12.00
21	Roberto Clemente/25	65.00
22	Ernie Banks/100	15.00
23	Frank Robinson/100	15.00
24	Harmon Killebrew/100	20.00
25	Willie Stargell/100	15.00
26	Al Kaline/100	15.00
27	Carl Yastrzemski/100	15.00
28	Dave Winfield/100	5.00
30	Eddie Murray/100	15.00
31	Eddie Mathews/50	20.00
32	Gary Carter/100	8.00
33	Rod Carew/100	10.00
35	Mel Ott/25	35.00
36	Paul Molitor/100	10.00
37	Thurman Munson/50	20.00
38	Rogers Hornsby/25	50.00
39	Robin Yount/100	15.00
40	Wade Boggs/100	10.00
42	Rickey Henderson/50	10.00
44	Yogi Berra/25	20.00
45	Roy Campanella/25	30.00
46	Luis Aparicio/100	8.00
48	Roger Maris/25	40.00
49	Reggie Jackson/100	15.00
50	Lou Gehrig/25	125.00
51	Rafael Palmeiro/100	8.00
52	Sammy Sosa/100	15.00
56	Rod Carew/100	8.00
60	R Henderson/100	10.00

Legendary Leather Material

NM/M

Quantity produced listed

16	Kirby Puckett/Fld Glv/25	40.00
32	Gary Carter/Fld Glv/25	35.00
51	Rafael Palmeiro/Fld Glv/25	25.00
52	Sammy Sosa/Btg Glv/25	50.00
55	Steve Carlton/Fld Glv/25	15.00
58	Fergie Jenkins/Fld Glv/25	15.00

Legendary Jerseys Material

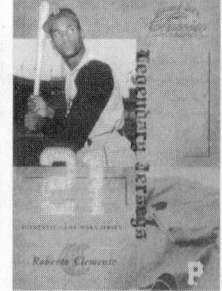

NM/M

Quantity produced listed
Number: 1X
Production 3-50
No pricing for production 15 or less.
Prime: No Pricing
Production One Set

1	Tony Gwynn/50	20.00
2	Mike Schmidt/25	35.00
3	Johnny Bench/50	15.00
6	George Brett/25	50.00
7	Carlton Fisk/50	10.00
8	Reggie Jackson/25	30.00
9	Joe Morgan/25	15.00
10	Bo Jackson/25	50.00
12	Andre Dawson/50	10.00
13	R Henderson/25	20.00
14	Cal Ripken Jr./25	85.00
15	Dale Murphy/25	30.00
16	Kirby Puckett/50	15.00

17 Don Mattingly/50 25.00
18 Brooks Robinson/50 20.00
19 Orlando Cepeda/50 8.00
20 Reggie Jackson/25 25.00
21 Roberto Clemente/25 75.00
23 Frank Robinson/50 10.00
24 Harmon Killebrew/50 15.00
25 Willie Stargell/50 20.00
27 Carl Yastrzemski/50 25.00
29 Dave Winfield/50 10.00
30 Eddie Murray/50 20.00
31 Eddie Mathews/25 25.00
32 Gary Carter/50 8.00
33 Rod Carew/25 20.00
36 Paul Molitor/50 15.00
39 Robin Yount/50 25.00
40 Wade Boggs/50 15.00
42 Rickey Henderson/25 25.00
44 Yogi Berra/15 35.00
46 Luis Aparicio/50 8.00
47 Phil Rizzuto/25 20.00
48 Roger Maris/25 40.00
49 Reggie Jackson/50 15.00
51 Rafael Palmeiro/50 10.00
52 Sammy Sosa/50 20.00
53 Roger Clemens/50 25.00
p4 Nolan Ryan/50 30.00
55 Steve Carlton/50 8.00
56 Rod Carew/50 15.00
57 Whitey Ford/25 35.00
59 Babe Ruth/5

Legendary Spikes Material

NM/M

Quantity produced listed
13 R Henderson/Yanks/25 30.00
17 Don Mattingly/50 40.00
29 Dave Winfield/50 15.00
42 Rickey Henderson/A's/25 30.00
51 Rafael Palmeiro/25 25.00
52 Sammy Sosa/50 30.00
60 R Henderson/Angels/25 30.00

Legendary Pants Material

NM/M

Quantity produced listed
1 Tony Gwynn/25 25.00
12 Andre Dawson/25 10.00
24 Harmon Killebrew/50 20.00
26 Al Kaline/50 20.00
45 Roy Campanella/25 25.00
46 Luis Aparicio/50 10.00
47 Phil Rizzuto/50 15.00
48 Roger Maris/A's/25 30.00
51 Rafael Palmeiro/25 20.00
56 Rod Carew/Angels/50 15.00
57 Whitey Ford/25 25.00
58 Fergie Jenkins/25 20.00
59 Babe Ruth/3

Legendary Jackets Material

NM/M

Production 100 Sets
2 Mike Schmidt 15.00
8 Reggie Jackson/A's 15.00
17 Don Mattingly 20.00
32 Gary Carter 5.00
54 Nolan Ryan 30.00
56 Rod Carew/Angels 10.00

Legendary Hats Material

NM/M

Quantity produced listed
1 Tony Gwynn/10
2 Mike Schmidt/25 50.00
6 George Brett/25 60.00
14 Cal Ripken Jr./25 100.00
16 Kirby Puckett/25 30.00
20 Reggie Jackson/Yanks/25 25.00
22 Ernie Banks/25 35.00
29 Dave Winfield/25 15.00
40 Wade Boggs/25 25.00
42 Rickey Henderson/A'S/25 20.00
49 Reggie Jackson/Angels/25 25.00
51 Rafael Palmeiro/25 20.00
52 Sammy Sosa/25 30.00
55 Steve Carlton/25 15.00
56 Rod Carew/Angels/25 20.00
60 R Henderson/Angels/25 20.00

Membership

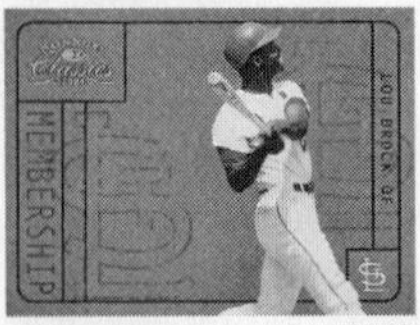

NM/M

Complete Set (25): 70.00
Common Player: 2.00
Production 2,499 Sets
1 Stan Musial 4.00
2 Ted Williams 5.00
3 Early Wynn 2.00
4 Roberto Clemente 5.00
5 Al Kaline 4.00
6 Bob Gibson 3.00
7 Lou Brock 2.00
8 Carl Yastrzemski 4.00
9 Gaylord Perry 2.00
10 Fergie Jenkins 2.00
11 Steve Carlton 2.00
12 Reggie Jackson 3.00
13 Rod Carew 3.00
14 Bert Blyleven 2.00
15 Mike Schmidt 4.00
16 Nolan Ryan 6.00
17 Robin Yount 4.00
18 George Brett 6.00
19 Eddie Murray 3.00
20 Tony Gwynn 3.00
21 Cal Ripken Jr. 8.00
22 Randy Johnson 4.00
23 Sammy Sosa 5.00
24 Rafael Palmeiro 3.00
25 Roger Clemens 5.00

Membership VIP Bat

NM/M

Quantity produced listed
1 Stan Musial/25 40.00
2 Ted Williams/25 100.00
4 Roberto Clemente/25 65.00
5 Al Kaline/25 20.00
7 Lou Brock/25 20.00
8 Carl Yastrzemski/25 25.00
11 Steve Carlton/25 15.00
12 Reggie Jackson/25 25.00
13 Rod Carew/25 20.00
15 Mike Schmidt/25 30.00
17 Robin Yount/25 25.00
19 Eddie Murray/25 25.00
20 Tony Gwynn/25 25.00
22 Randy Johnson/25 20.00
23 Sammy Sosa/25 30.00
24 Rafael Palmeiro/25 20.00
25 Roger Clemens/25 25.00

Membership VIP Combos Material

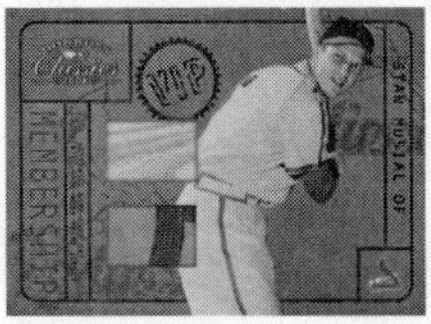

NM/M

Quantity produced listed
Prime: No Pricing
Production One Set
1 Stan Musial/Bat-Jsy/15 40.00
4 Roberto Clemente/ Bat-Jsy/25 100.00
5 Al Kaline/Bat-Pants/25 30.00
8 Carl Yastrzemski/ Bat-Jsy/25 50.00
10 Fergie Jenkins/ Fld Glv-Pants/25 15.00
11 Steve Carlton/Bat-Jsy/25 15.00
12 Reggie Jackson/ Bat-Jsy/25 30.00
13 Rod Carew/Bat-Pants/25 25.00
15 Mike Schmidt/Bat-Jsy/25 40.00
16 Nolan Ryan/Bat-Jsy/25 50.00
17 Robin Yount/Bat-Jsy/25 40.00
18 George Brett/Bat-Jsy/25 50.00
19 Eddie Murray/Bat-Jsy/25 30.00
20 Tony Gwynn/Bat-Jsy/25 40.00
21 Cal Ripken Jr./Bat-Jsy/25 80.00
22 Randy Johnson/Bat-Jsy/25 25.00
23 Sammy Sosa/Bat-Jsy/25 35.00
24 Rafael Palmeiro/Bat-Jsy/25 25.00
25 Roger Clemens/Bat-Jsy/25 30.00

Membership VIP Combos Signature

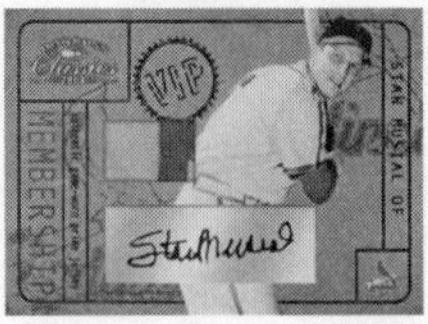

NM/M

Quantity produced listed
Prime: No Pricing
Production One Set
5 Al Kaline/Pants/25 50.00
9 Gaylord Perry/Jsy/50 15.00
10 Fergie Jenkins/Pants/50 20.00
11 Steve Carlton/Jsy/25 40.00
14 Bert Blyleven/Jsy/50 15.00

Membership VIP Signatures

NM/M

Quantity produced listed
5 Al Kaline/20 50.00
9 Gaylord Perry/50 15.00
10 Fergie Jenkins/50 20.00
11 Steve Carlton/20 30.00
14 Bert Blyleven/50 10.00

Membership VIP Jersey

NM/M

Quantity produced listed
Prime: No Pricing
Production One Set
1 Stan Musial/15 40.00
4 Roberto Clemente/25 75.00
5 Al Kaline/Pants/25 20.00
8 Carl Yastrzemski/25 30.00
9 Gaylord Perry/25 10.00
10 Fergie Jenkins/Pants/25 15.00
11 Steve Carlton/25 15.00
12 Reggie Jackson/25 25.00
13 Rod Carew/25 20.00
14 Bert Blyleven/25 10.00
15 Mike Schmidt/25 30.00
16 Nolan Ryan/25 35.00
17 Robin Yount/25 25.00
18 George Brett/25 40.00
19 Eddie Murray/25 25.00
20 Tony Gwynn/25 25.00
21 Cal Ripken Jr./25 85.00
22 Randy Johnson/25 20.00
23 Sammy Sosa/25 30.00
24 Rafael Palmeiro/25 20.00
25 Roger Clemens/25 25.00

October Heroes

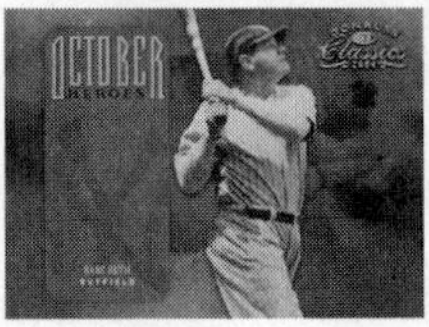

NM/M

Production 2,499 Sets
1 Reggie Jackson 3.00
2 Bob Gibson 3.00
3 Carlton Fisk 2.00
4 Whitey Ford 2.00
5 George Brett 5.00
6 Roberto Clemente 5.00
7 Roy Campanella 3.00
8 Babe Ruth 6.00

October Heroes Bat

NM/M

Quantity produced listed
1 Reggie Jackson/25 25.00
3 Carlton Fisk/25 25.00
6 Roberto Clemente/25 65.00
7 Roy Campanella/25 25.00

October Heroes Combos Mat.

NM/M

Quantity produced listed
1 Reggie Jackson/Bat-Hat/25 40.00
3 Carlton Fisk/Bat-Jsy/25 30.00
5 George Brett/Bat-Jsy/25 50.00
7 Roy Campanella/ Bat-Pants/25 35.00

October Heroes Combos Sig.

NM/M

Quantity produced listed
4 Whitey Ford/Jsy/50 45.00

October Heroes Fabric

NM/M

Quantity produced listed
2 Bob Gibson/Jsy/15 30.00
3 Carlton Fisk/Jsy/25 20.00
4 Whitey Ford/Jsy/25 20.00
5 George Bret/Jsy/25 40.00
7 Roy Campanella/Pants/25 20.00

October Heroes Signature

NM/M

Quantity produced listed
4 Whitey Ford/50 40.00

Significant Signatures Green

NM/M

Quantity produced listed
3 Hank Blalock/25 40.00
4 Shannon Stewart/50 10.00
7 Trot Nixon/25 30.00
13 Mike Lowell/25 25.00
14 Robin Ventura/25 15.00
19 Carlos Beltran/25 50.00
21 Johan Santana/50 35.00
24 Steve Finley/25 25.00
26 Alexis Rios/100 25.00
32 Miguel Cabrera/50 50.00
36 Dontrelle Willis/25 25.00
37 Rafael Soriano/100 6.00
38 Richard Fischer/100 6.00
39 Brian Tallet/100 6.00
40 Jose Castillo/100 6.00
41 Wade Miller/25 20.00
43 Runelvys Hernandez/20 10.00
44 Joe Borchard/50 8.00
47 Adam Dunn/25 30.00
49 Brandon Phillips/50 6.00
53 Cliff Lee/50 20.00
54 Chien-Ming Wang/50 150.00
57 Jhonny Peralta/100 6.00
60 Jae Weong Seo/50 15.00
61 Nic Jackson/100 8.00
63 Jimmy Gobble/45 10.00
64 Travis Hafner/50 12.00
66 Jerome Williams/50 20.00
68 Alexis Gomez/50 6.00
70 Zach Day/50 8.00
72 Morgan Ensberg/50 8.00
74 Garrett Atkins/99 6.00
77 Lyle Overbay/100 15.00
78 Josh Phelps/25 10.00
79 Juan Gonzalez/25 45.00
80 Rich Harden/50 15.00
84 Jody Gerut/50 15.00
87 Jay Gibbons/50 15.00
88 Chone Figgins/50 10.00
98 Jay Payton/50 10.00
99 Barry Larkin/25 40.00
102 Robby Hammock/50 6.00
103 Orlando Hudson/50 8.00
105 Hong-Chih Kuo/50 30.00
106 Eric Chavez/25 35.00
108 Jacque Jones/50 10.00
109 Ken Harvey/100 8.00
110 Aramis Ramirez/50 20.00
111 Victor Martinez/50 20.00
112 Joe Crede/50 10.00
113 Jason Varitek/25 40.00
118 Brandon Webb/25 15.00
121 Sammy Sosa/21 150.00
127 Luis Castillo/25 10.00
134 Edgar Martinez/25 40.00
145 Brett Myers/50 8.00
149 Gary Sheffield/25 25.00
151 Duke Snider/25 35.00
153 Whitey Ford/25 40.00
155 Dwight Gooden/50 20.00
158 Don Mattingly/25 100.00
159 Jack Morris/50 10.00
160 Jim Bunning/25 25.00
161 Fergie Jenkins/50 15.00
163 George Kell/50 15.00
164 Darryl Strawberry/50 20.00
165 Robin Roberts/25 30.00
166 Monte Irvin/25 20.00
167 Ernie Banks/25 60.00
168 Wade Boggs/25 40.00
169 Gaylord Perry/50 10.00
170 Keith Hernandez/50 20.00
172 Frank Robinson/25 30.00
173 Nolan Ryan/25 120.00
174 Stan Musial/25 70.00
175 Eddie Murray/25 50.00
176 Byron Gettis/100 6.00
177 Merkin Valdez/100 20.00
178 Rickie Weeks/25 30.00
180 Brian Bruney/100 6.00
181 Freddy Guzman/100 6.00
182 Brendan Harris/100 6.00
183 John Gall/100 8.00
184 Jason Kubel/100 12.00
185 Delmon Young/50 30.00
186 Ryan Howard/100 80.00
187 Adam Loewen/100 15.00
188 J.D. Durbin/100 8.00
189 Dan Haren/100 10.00
190 Dustin McGowan/100 10.00
191 Chad Gaudin/100 6.00
192 Preston Larrison/100 6.00
193 Ramon Nivar/100 6.00
195 Mike Gosling/100 6.00
196 Kevin Youkilis/100 15.00
197 Ryan Wagner/100 10.00
198 Bubba Nelson/100 8.00
199 Edwin Jackson/100 10.00
200 Chris Burke/100 6.00
201 Carlos Hines/100 10.00
202 Greg Dobbs/50 6.00
203 Jamie Brown/100 8.00
204 David Crouthers/100 6.00
205 Ian Snell/100 30.00
206 Gary Carter/50 25.00
207 Dale Murphy/50 40.00
208 Ryne Sandberg/50 75.00
209 Phil Niekro/50 20.00
210 Don Sutton/50 15.00

Significant Signatures Red

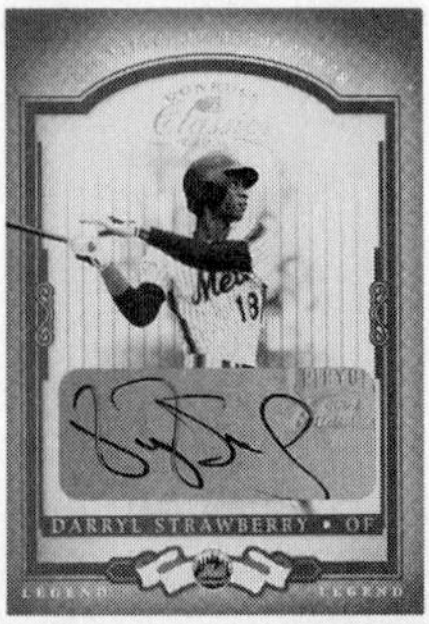

NM/M
Quantity produced listed
3 Hank Blalock/50 30.00
4 Shannon Stewart/100 8.00
6 Carlos Lee/25 20.00
7 Trot Nixon/50 20.00
9 Mark Mulder/25 30.00
12 Jim Edmonds/25 30.00
13 Mike Lowell/50 20.00
14 Robin Ventura/50 10.00
16 Jose Vidro/25 20.00
19 Carlos Beltran/25 50.00
21 Johan Santana/100 30.00
24 Steve Finley/100 20.00
26 Alexis Rios/250 25.00
27 Rafael Palmeiro/25 65.00
28 Jorge Posada/25 45.00
32 Miguel Cabrera/100 40.00
36 Dontrelle Willis/100 25.00
37 Rafael Soriano/250 6.00
38 Richard Fischer/250 6.00
39 Brian Tallet/250 6.00
40 Jose Castillo/250 6.00
41 Wade Miller/92 15.00
42 Jose Contreras/25 25.00
43 Runelvys Hernandez/50 8.00
44 Joe Borchard/250 6.00
47 Adam Dunn/25 30.00
49 Brandon Phillips/70 6.00
50 Scott Rolen/25 35.00
53 Cliff Lee/100 15.00
54 Chien-Ming Wang/250 100.00
55 Roy Oswalt/25 30.00
56 Austin Kearns/25 20.00
57 Jhonny Peralta/250 6.00
60 Jae Weong Seo/100 10.00
61 Nic Jackson/250 8.00
63 Jimmy Gobble/200 10.00
64 Travis Hafner/100 12.00
65 Paul Konerko/25 15.00
66 Jerome Williams/250 20.00
68 Alexis Gomez/100 6.00
70 Zach Day/100 8.00
72 Morgan Ensberg/100 8.00
74 Garrett Atkins/245 6.00
76 Julio Franco/25 20.00
77 Lyle Overbay/250 15.00
78 Josh Phelps/50 8.00
79 Juan Gonzalez/25 45.00
80 Rich Harden/150 10.00
82 Torii Hunter/25 30.00
84 Jody Gerut/100 15.00
87 Jay Gibbons/100 15.00
88 Chone Figgins/100 10.00
90 Rich Aurilia/25 15.00
92 Marlon Byrd/25 15.00
98 Jay Payton/100 8.00
99 Barry Larkin/25 40.00
102 Robby Hammock/150 6.00
103 Orlando Hudson/100 8.00
105 Hong-Chih Kuo/100 30.00
106 Eric Chavez/25 35.00
107 Nick Johnson/25 15.00
108 Jacque Jones/100 10.00
109 Ken Harvey/250 8.00
110 Aramis Ramirez/100 20.00
111 Victor Martinez/99 20.00
112 Joe Crede/250 10.00
113 Jason Varitek/50 35.00
114 Troy Glaus/25 30.00
118 Brandon Webb/50 15.00
119 Craig Biggio/25 30.00
120 Orlando Cabrera/50 10.00
121 Sammy Sosa/25 150.00
122 Bobby Abreu/25 15.00
123 Andruw Jones/25 30.00
124 Jeff Bagwell/25 65.00
127 Luis Castillo/50 10.00
131 Eric Byrnes/25 10.00
132 Eric Hinske/25 15.00
134 Edgar Martinez/50 30.00
135 Rocco Baldelli/25 40.00
143 Vernon Wells/25 15.00
144 Magglio Ordonez/25 30.00
145 Brett Myers/100 8.00
149 Gary Sheffield/50 20.00
150 Tim Hudson/25 40.00
151 Duke Snider/50 30.00
153 Whitey Ford/50 40.00
155 Dwight Gooden/100 20.00
156 Warren Spahn/25 45.00
158 Don Mattingly/25 100.00
159 Jack Morris/100 10.00
160 Jim Bunning/100 20.00
161 Fergie Jenkins/100 15.00
163 George Kell/100 15.00
164 Darryl Strawberry/100 20.00
165 Robin Roberts/100 15.00
166 Monte Irvin/100 15.00
167 Ernie Banks/50 50.00
168 Wade Boggs/50 30.00
169 Gaylord Perry/100 10.00
170 Keith Hernandez/100 20.00
171 Lou Brock/25 30.00
172 Frank Robinson/50 25.00
173 Nolan Ryan/50 85.00
174 Stan Musial/50 60.00
175 Eddie Murray/50 50.00
176 Byron Gettis/250 6.00
177 Merkin Valdez/250 15.00
178 Rickie Weeks/250 25.00
180 Brian Bruney/250 6.00
181 Freddy Guzman/250 6.00
182 Brendan Harris/250 6.00
183 John Gall/250 8.00
184 Jason Kubel/250 10.00
185 Delmon Young/100 30.00
186 Ryan Howard/250 70.00
187 Adam Loewen/250 15.00
188 J.D. Durbin/250 8.00
189 Dan Haren/250 10.00
190 Dustin McGowan/250 10.00
191 Chad Gaudin/250 6.00
192 Preston Larrison/250 6.00
193 Ramon Nivar/250 6.00
195 Mike Gosling/250 6.00
196 Kevin Youkilis/250 15.00
197 Ryan Wagner/250 10.00
198 Bubba Nelson/250 8.00
199 Edwin Jackson/250 10.00
200 Chris Burke/250 6.00
201 Carlos Hines/250 10.00
202 Greg Dobbs/100 6.00
203 Jamie Brown/250 8.00
204 David Crouthers/250 6.00
205 Ian Snell/250 25.00
206 Gary Carter/100 20.00
207 Dale Murphy/50 40.00
208 Ryne Sandberg/25 85.00
209 Phil Niekro/100 15.00
210 Don Sutton/100 15.00

Team Colors Jersey

NM/M
Quantity produced listed
Prime: No Pricing
Production One Set
1 Lenny Dykstra/
Mets Fld Glv/25 15.00
2 Steve Garvey/100 6.00
3 Eric Davis/25 15.00
5 Nolan Ryan/50 30.00
6 Bobby Doerr/25 20.00
7 Paul Molitor/100 10.00
8 Dale Murphy/50 20.00
9 Harold Baines/100 8.00
10 Dwight Gooden/50 10.00
11 Jose Canseco/100 15.00
12 Jim Rice/100 8.00
13 Will Clark/50 25.00
14 Alan Trammell/100 8.00
15 Lee Smith/100 5.00
16 Dwight Evans/50 15.00
17 Tony Oliva/100 8.00
18 Dave Parker/Pirates/25 10.00
19 Jack Morris/100 5.00
20 Luis Tiant/100 6.00
21 Andre Dawson/Expos/100 6.00
22 Darryl Strawberry/Dgr/100 8.00
23 George Foster/100 5.00
24 Marty Marion/50 6.00
25 Dennis Eckersley/100 6.00
26 Bo Jackson/50 30.00
27 Cal Ripken Jr./100 35.00
28 Deion Sanders/50 8.00
29 Don Mattingly/Jkt/100 20.00
30 Mark Grace/50 15.00
31 Fred Lynn/50 8.00
33 Ernie Banks/25 30.00
34 Gary Carter/Jkt/100 8.00
37 Keith Hernandez/25 15.00
38 Tony Gwynn/50 15.00
39 Jim Palmer/25 15.00
40 Red Schoendienst/25 15.00
41 Steve Carlton/25 15.00
42 Wade Boggs/25 25.00
43 Tommy John/100 5.00
44 Luis Aparicio/25 10.00
46 Andre Dawson/Cubs/25 15.00
47 Bert Blyleven/100 5.00
48 Darryl Strawberry/Mets/100 8.00
49 Dave Parker/Reds/100 5.00

Team Colors Bat

NM/M
Quantity produced listed
2 Steve Garvey/50 10.00
3 Eric Davis/25 15.00
4 Al Oliver/50 8.00
6 Bobby Doerr/25 20.00
7 Paul Molitor/50 15.00
8 Dale Murphy/50 20.00
11 Jose Canseco/50 20.00
12 Jim Rice/50 12.00
13 Will Clark/50 25.00
14 Alan Trammell/50 12.00
16 Dwight Evans/50 15.00
18 Dave Parker/Pirates/25 10.00
21 Andre Dawson/Expos/50 10.00
22 Darryl Strawberry/Dgr/50 10.00
23 George Foster/50 8.00
26 Bo Jackson/50 30.00
27 Cal Ripken Jr./50 50.00
28 Deion Sanders/25 15.00
29 Don Mattingly/Jkt/50 25.00
30 Mark Grace/50 15.00
31 Fred Lynn/50 8.00
33 Ernie Banks/25 30.00
34 Gary Carter/50 12.00
35 Roger Maris/25 40.00
36 Ron Santo/50 12.00
38 Tony Gwynn/50 15.00
40 Red Schoendienst/25 15.00
41 Steve Carlton/25 15.00
42 Wade Boggs/25 25.00
44 Luis Aparicio/25 10.00
46 Andre Dawson/Cubs/25 12.00
48 Darryl Strawberry/Mets/50 10.00
49 Dave Parker/Reds/50 8.00

Team Colors Combos Material

NM/M
Production 25 Sets
Prime: No Pricing
Production One Set
2 Steve Garvey/Bat-Jsy 15.00
3 Eric Davis/Bat-Jsy 20.00
5 Nolan Ryan/Bat-Jsy 50.00
6 Bobby Doerr/Bat-Jsy 25.00
7 Paul Molitor/Bat-Jsy 25.00
8 Dale Murphy/Bat-Jsy 25.00
11 Jose Canseco/Bat-Jsy 30.00
12 Jim Rice/Bat-Jsy 25.00
13 Will Clark/Bat-Jst 40.00
14 Alan Trammell/Bat-Jsy 30.00
16 Dwight Evans/Bat-Jsy 25.00
18 Dave Parker/Pirates Bat-Jsy 20.00
21 Andre Dawson/
Expos Bat-Jsy 15.00
22 Darryl Strawberry/
Dgr Bat-Jsy 20.00
23 George Foster/Bat-Jsy 10.00
26 Bo Jackson/Bat-Jsy 40.00
27 Cal Ripken Jr./Bat-Jsy 65.00
28 Deion Sanders/Bat-Jsy 25.00
29 Don Mattingly/Bat-Jsy 45.00
30 Mark Grace/Bat-Jsy 25.00
33 Ernie Banks/Bat-Jsy 45.00
34 Gary Carter/Bat-Jacket 25.00
38 Tony Gwynn/Bat-Jsy 40.00
40 Red Schoendienst/Bat-Jsy 15.00
41 Steve Carlton/Bat-Jsy 20.00
42 Wade Boggs/Bat-Jsy 25.00
44 Luis Aparicio/Bat-Jsy 15.00
46 Andre Dawson/
Cubs Bat-Jsy 15.00
48 Darryl Strawberry/
Mets Bat-Jsy 20.00
49 Dave Parker/Reds Bat-Jsy 20.00

Team Colors Combos Signature

NM/M
Quantity produced listed
Prime: No Pricing
Production One Set
1 Lenny Dykstra/
Mets Fld Glv/100 15.00
2 Steve Garvey/Jsy/100 15.00
3 Eric Davis/Jsy/100 25.00
4 Al Oliver/Bat/100 20.00
6 Bobby Doerr/Jsy/100 20.00
9 Harold Baines/Jsy/100 20.00
10 Dwight Gooden/Jsy/100 25.00
12 Jim Rice/Jsy/100 25.00
14 Alan Trammell/Jsy/100 25.00
15 Lee Smith/Jsy/100 20.00
16 Dwight Evans/Jsy/100 25.00
17 Tony Oliva/Jsy/100 20.00
18 Dave Parker/
Pirates Jsy/100 15.00
19 Jack Morris/Jsy/100 20.00
20 Luis Tiant/Jsy/100 20.00
21 Andre Dawson/
Expos Jsy/50 25.00
22 Darryl Strawberry/
Dgr Jsy/100 25.00
23 George Foster/Jsy/100 20.00
24 Marty Marion/Jsy/100 20.00
25 Dennis Eckersley/Jsy/100 25.00
31 Fred Lynn/Jsy/100 20.00
33 Ernie Banks/Jsy/25 90.00
34 Gary Carter/Jkt/50 40.00
36 Ron Santo/Bat/25 50.00
37 Keith Hernandez/Jsy/25 45.00
39 Jim Palmer/Jsy/50 35.00
40 Red Schoendienst/Jsy/100 15.00
41 Steve Carlton Jsy/50 40.00
43 Tommy John/Jsy/100 20.00
44 Luis Aparicio/Jsy/100 15.00
46 Andre Dawson/Cubs Jsy/50 25.00
47 Bert Blyleven/Jsy/100 25.00
48 Darryl Strawberry/
Mets Jsy/100 25.00
49 Dave Parker/Reds Jsy/100 15.00
50 Lenny Dykstra/
Phils Btg Glv/30 25.00

Team Colors Signatures

NM/M
Quantity produced listed
1 Lenny Dykstra/Mets/50 15.00
2 Steve Garvey/50 25.00
3 Eric Davis/50 20.00
4 Al Oliver/50 15.00
6 Bobby Doerr/50 20.00
9 Harold Baines/50 25.00
10 Dwight Gooden/50 20.00
12 Jim Rice/50 20.00
14 Alan Trammell/50 20.00
15 Lee Smith/50 15.00
16 Dwight Evans/50 15.00
17 Tony Oliva/50 20.00
18 Dave Parker/Pirates/50 15.00
19 Jack Morris/50 10.00
20 Luis Tiant/50 15.00
21 Andre Dawson/Expos/25 25.00
23 George Foster/50 15.00
24 Marty Marion/50 15.00
25 Dennis Eckersley/50 25.00
31 Fred Lynn/50 15.00
34 Gary Carter/20 35.00
37 Keith Hernandez/25 35.00
39 Jim Palmer/20 20.00
40 Red Schoendienst/50 15.00
41 Steve Carlton/20 35.00
43 Tommy John/50 15.00
44 Luis Aparicio/50 20.00
45 Bob Feller/50 20.00
46 Andre Dawson/Cubs/25 25.00
47 Bert Blyleven/50 12.00
48 Darryl Strawberry/Mets/50 20.00
49 Dave Parker/Reds/50 15.00
50 Lenny Dykstra/Phils/50 15.00

Timeless Triples

NM/M
Complete Set (6): 40.00
Common Player:
Production 500 Sets
1 Ted Williams, Carl Yastrzemski,
Carlton Fisk 10.00
2 Lou Gehrig, Roger Maris,
Thurman Munson 8.00
3 Brooks Robinson,
Frank Robinson,
Cal Ripken Jr. 10.00
4 Roger Clemens, Andy Pettitte,
Roy Oswalt 6.00
5 Greg Maddux, Mark Prior,
Kerry Wood 8.00
6 Alex Rodriguez, Derek Jeter,
Gary Sheffield 10.00

Timeless Triples Bat

NM/M
Production 25 Sets
1 Ted Williams, Carl Yastrzemski,
Carlton Fisk 185.00
2 Lou Gehrig, Roger Maris,
Thurman Munson 200.00
3 Brooks Robinson,
Frank Robinson,
Cal Ripken Jr. 140.00

Timeless Triples Jersey

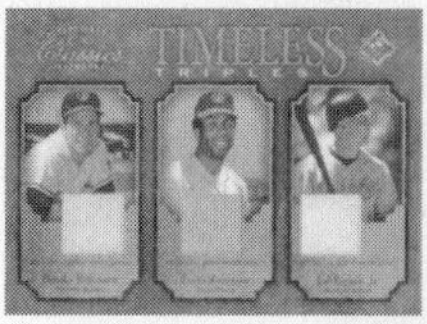

NM/M
Quantity produced listed
Prime: No Pricing
Production One Set
3 Brooks Robinson,
Frank Robinson,
Cal Ripken Jr./25 140.00

2004 Donruss Diamond Kings

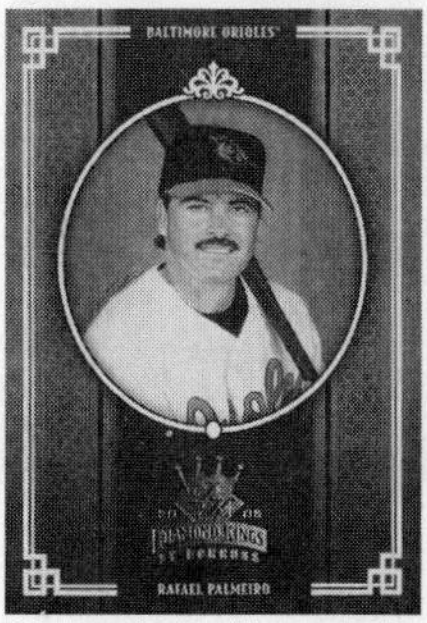

NM/M
Complete Set (175): 75.00
Common Player: .25
Common (151-175): 1.50
Pack (5): 7.50
Box (12): 80.00
1 Alex Rodriguez 2.50
2 Andruw Jones .75
3 Nomar Garciaparra 2.00
4 Kerry Wood .75
5 Magglio Ordonez .50
6 Victor Martinez .25
7 Jeremy Bonderman .25
8 Josh Beckett .75
9 Jeff Kent .40
10 Carlos Beltran .50
11 Hideo Nomo .50
12 Richie Sexson .50
13 Jose Vidro .25
14 Jae Weong Seo .25
15 Alfonso Soriano 1.00
16 Barry Zito .50
17 Brett Myers .25
18 Brian Giles .40
19 Edgar Martinez .40
20 Jim Edmonds .50
21 Rocco Baldelli .75
22 Mark Teixeira .50
23 Carlos Delgado .75
24 Julius Matos .25

25	Jose Reyes	.50
26	Marlon Byrd	.25
27	Albert Pujols	2.50
28	Vernon Wells	.40
29	Garret Anderson	.50
30	Jerome Williams	.25
31	Chipper Jones	1.00
32	Rich Harden	.25
33	Manny Ramirez	.75
34	Derek Jeter	3.00
35	Brandon Webb	.25
36	Mark Prior	1.50
37	Roy Halladay	.50
38	Frank Thomas	.75
39	Rafael Palmeiro	.75
40	Adam Dunn	.50
41	Aubrey Huff	.25
42	Todd Helton	.75
43	Matt Morris	.40
44	Dontrelle Willis	.40
45	Lance Berkman	.50
46	Mike Sweeney	.25
47	Kazuhisa Ishii	.25
48	Torii Hunter	.50
49	Vladimir Guerrero	1.00
50	Mike Piazza	1.50
51	Alexis Rios	.25
52	Shannon Stewart	.25
53	Eric Hinske	.25
54	Jason Jennings	.25
55	Jason Giambi	1.00
56	Brandon Claussen	.25
57	Joe Thurston	.25
58	Ramon Nivar	.25
59	Jay Gibbons	.25
60	Eric Chavez	.50
61	Jimmy Gobble	.25
62	Walter Young	.25
63	Mark Grace	.50
64	Austin Kearns	.50
65	Bobby Abreu	.25
66	Hee Seop Choi	.25
67	Brandon Phillips	.25
68	Rickie Weeks	.50
69	Luis Gonzalez	.50
70	Mariano Rivera	.50
71	Jason Lane	.25
72	Xavier Nady	.25
73	Runelvys Hernandez	.25
74	Aramis Ramirez	.25
75	Ichiro Suzuki	2.00
76	Cliff Lee	.25
77	Chris Snelling	.25
78	Ryan Wagner	.25
79	Miguel Tejada	.50
80	Juan Gonzalez	.75
81	Joe Borchard	.25
82	Gary Sheffield	.50
83	Wade Miller	.25
84	Jeff Bagwell	.75
85	Ryan Church	.25
86	Adrian Beltre	.25
87	Jeff Baker	.25
88	Adam Loewen	.25
89	Bernie Williams	.50
90	Pedro J. Martinez	1.00
91	Carlos Rivera	.25
92	Junior Spivey	.25
93	Tim Hudson	.50
94	Troy Glaus	.50
95	Ken Griffey Jr.	1.50
96	Alexis Gomez	.25
97	Antonio Perez	.25
98	Dan Haren	.25
99	Ivan Rodriguez	.75
100	Randy Johnson	1.00
101	Lyle Overbay	.25
102	Oliver Perez	.25
103	Miguel Cabrera	.75
104	Scott Rolen	1.00
105	Roger Clemens	2.00
106	Brian Tallet	.25
107	Nic Jackson	.25
108	Angel Berroa	.25
109	Hank Blalock	.50
110	Ryan Klesko	.40
111	Jose Castillo	.25
112	Paul Konerko	.25
113	Greg Maddux	1.50
114	Mark Mulder	.50
115	Pat Burrell	.50
116	Garrett Atkins	.25
117	Jeremy Guthrie	.25
118	Orlando Cabrera	.25
119	Nick Johnson	.25
120	Tom Glavine	.50
121	Morgan Ensberg	.25
122	Sean Casey	.25
123	Orlando Hudson	.25
124	Hideki Matsui	2.50
125	Craig Biggio	.25
126	Adam LaRoche	.25
127	Hong-Chih Kuo	.25
128	Paul LoDuca	.25
129	Shawn Green	.50
130	Luis Castillo	.25
131	Joe Crede	.25
132	Ken Harvey	.25
133	Freddy Sanchez	.25
134	Roy Oswalt	.50
135	Curt Schilling	.75
136	Alfredo Amezaga	.25
137	Chien-Ming Wang	.50
138	Barry Larkin	.50
139	Trot Nixon	.25
140	Jim Thome	1.00
141	Bret Boone	.40
142	Jacque Jones	.25
143	Travis Hafner	.25
144	Sammy Sosa	2.00
145	Mike Mussina	.50
146	Vinnie Chulk	.25
147	Chad Gaudin	.25
148	Delmon Young	.50
149	Mike Lowell	.40
150	Rickey Henderson	.50
151	Roger Clemens	4.00
152	Mark Grace	2.00
153	Rickey Henderson	2.00
154	Alex Rodriguez	5.00
155	Rafael Palmeiro	2.00
156	Greg Maddux	3.00
157	Mike Piazza	3.00
158	Mike Mussina	1.50
159	Dale Murphy	1.50
160	Cal Ripken Jr.	6.00
161	Carl Yastrzemski	2.00
162	Marty Marion	1.50
163	Don Mattingly	4.00
164	Robin Yount	2.00
165	Andre Dawson	1.50
166	Jim Palmer	1.50
167	George Brett	5.00
168	Whitey Ford	2.00
169	Roy Campanella	2.00
170	Roger Maris	4.00
171	Duke Snider	2.00
172	Steve Carlton	2.00
173	Stan Musial	3.00
174	Nolan Ryan	6.00
175	Deion Sanders	1.50

Bronze

Bronze (1-150): 4-6X
Bronze (151-175): 2-3X
Production 100 Sets
Bronze Sepia: 2-3X
Production 100

Platinum

Platinum: No Pricing
Production One Set
Platinum Sepia: No Pricing
Production One Set

Silver

Silver (1-150): 5-10X
Silver (151-175): 2-4X
Production 50 Sets
Silver Sepia: 2-4X
Production 50

Framed Bronze

Framed Bronze (1-150): 2-3X
Framed Bronze (151-175): 1-2X
Framed Bronze Sepia: 1-2X
Inserted 1:6

Framed Silver

Framed Silver (1-150): 4-8X
Framed Silver (151-175): 2-3X
Production 100 Sets
Framed Silver Sepia: 2-3X
Production 100

Framed Platinum

Framed Platinum: No Pricing
Production One Set

Diamond Cut Bat

NM/M

Common Player: 6.00
Production 100 unless noted.

1	Alex Rodriguez	15.00
2	Nomar Garciaparra	12.00
3	Hideo Nomo	8.00
4	Alfonso Soriano	10.00
6	Edgar Martinez	8.00
7	Rocco Baldelli	10.00
8	Mark Teixeira	10.00
9	Albert Pujols	20.00
10	Vernon Wells	8.00
11	Garret Anderson	8.00
14	Brandon Webb	6.00
15	Mark Prior	15.00
16	Rafael Palmeiro	10.00
17	Adam Dunn	10.00
18	Dontrelle Willis	8.00
19	Kazuhisa Ishii	6.00
20	Torii Hunter	8.00
21	Vladimir Guerrero	10.00
22	Mike Piazza	15.00
23	Jason Giambi	10.00
26	Bobby Abreu	6.00
27	Hee Seop Choi	6.00
28	Rickie Weeks	12.00
30	Troy Glaus	8.00
31	Ivan Rodriguez	10.00
32	Hank Blalock	10.00
33	Greg Maddux	15.00
34	Nick Johnson	6.00
35	Shawn Green	8.00
36	Sammy Sosa	15.00
37	Dale Murphy/50	15.00
38	Cal Ripken Jr./50	50.00
39	Carl Yastrzemski	15.00
41	Don Mattingly	25.00
43	George Brett/50	40.00
46	Steve Carlton/50	15.00
47	Stan Musial/25	40.00
48	Nolan Ryan/50	35.00
49	Deion Sanders/50	15.00
50	Roberto Clemente/25	120.00

Diamond Cut Jersey

NM/M

Common Player: 6.00
Production 100 unless noted.

1	Alex Rodriguez	15.00
2	Nomar Garciaparra	15.00
3	Hideo Nomo/50	15.00
4	Alfonso Soriano	10.00
5	Brett Myers/50	10.00
6	Edgar Martinez	8.00
7	Rocco Baldelli	12.00
8	Mark Teixeira	10.00
9	Albert Pujols	20.00
10	Vernon Wells	8.00
11	Garret Anderson/50	8.00
12	Jerome Williams	8.00
13	Rich Harden	8.00
14	Brandon Webb	6.00
15	Mark Prior	15.00
16	Rafael Palmeiro	10.00
17	Adam Dunn	10.00
18	Dontrelle Willis	8.00
19	Kazuhisa Ishii	6.00
20	Torii Hunter	8.00
21	Vladimir Guerrero/50	15.00
22	Mike Piazza	15.00
23	Jason Giambi	10.00
25	Ramon Nivar	6.00
26	Bobby Abreu	6.00
27	Hee Seop Choi	6.00
30	Troy Glaus	8.00
31	Ivan Rodriguez	10.00
32	Hank Blalock	10.00
33	Greg Maddux	15.00
34	Nick Johnson	6.00
35	Shawn Green	8.00
36	Sammy Sosa	15.00
37	Dale Murphy/50	20.00
38	Cal Ripken Jr./50	50.00
39	Carl Yastrzemski	20.00
40	Marty Marion/50	15.00
41	Don Mattingly	25.00
42	Jim Palmer/25	20.00
43	George Brett/50	35.00
44	Whitey Ford/25	25.00
46	Steve Carlton/50	15.00
48	Nolan Ryan/50	40.00
49	Deion Sanders/50	15.00

Diamond Cut Signature

NM/M

Many not priced due to scarcity.

7	Rocco Baldelli/25	45.00
8	Mark Teixeira/25	30.00
13	Rich Harden/50	25.00
14	Brandon Webb/50	30.00
20	Torii Hunter/25	30.00
24	Ryan Wagner/50	20.00
25	Ramon Nivar/50	10.00
28	Rickie Weeks/50	30.00
29	Adam Loewen/50	20.00
32	Hank Blalock/25	30.00
40	Marty Marion/25	25.00
41	Don Mattingly/23	110.00
42	Jim Palmer/22	45.00
46	Steve Carlton/32	35.00
48	Nolan Ryan/34	125.00

Diamond Cut Combo

NM/M

Common Player: 10.00
Production 50 unless noted.

1	Alex Rodriguez	30.00
2	Nomar Garciaparra	25.00
3	Hideo Nomo/25	30.00
4	Alfonso Soriano	15.00
6	Edgar Martinez/25	15.00
7	Rocco Baldelli/25	25.00
8	Mark Teixeira/25	20.00
9	Albert Pujols	40.00
10	Vernon Wells/25	15.00
11	Garret Anderson/25	15.00
14	Brandon Webb/25	15.00
15	Mark Prior	20.00
16	Rafael Palmeiro/25	20.00
17	Adam Dunn/25	15.00
18	Dontrelle Willis/25	20.00
19	Kazuhisa Ishii/25	15.00
20	Torii Hunter/25	15.00
21	Vladimir Guerrero/25	25.00
22	Mike Piazza	20.00
23	Jason Giambi/25	25.00
26	Bobby Abreu	10.00
27	Hee Seop Choi	10.00
30	Troy Glaus/25	20.00
31	Ivan Rodriguez/25	20.00
32	Hank Blalock/25	20.00
33	Greg Maddux	25.00
34	Nick Johnson/25	12.00
35	Shawn Green/25	15.00
36	Sammy Sosa	25.00
41	Don Mattingly/23	50.00
42	Jim Palmer/22	20.00
46	Steve Carlton/32	20.00
48	Nolan Ryan/34	50.00
49	Deion Sanders/24	25.00
50	Roberto Clemente/21	150.00

Diamond Cut Signature Combo

NM/M

Varying quantities produced

40	Marty Marion/25	30.00
46	Steve Carlton/32	45.00

DK Combos Bronze

NM/M

Varying quantities produced

26	Marlon Byrd/Bat-Jsy/30	20.00
32	Rich Harden/Jsy-Jsy/15	50.00
53	Eric Hinske/Bat-Jsy/30	20.00
57	Joe Thurston/Bat-Jsy/25	15.00
59	Jay Gibbons/Jsy-Jsy/15	35.00
65	Bob Abreu/Bat-Jsy/15	25.00
74	Aramis Ramirez/Bat-Bat/15	25.00
92	Junior Spivey/Bat-Jsy/15	30.00
101	Lyle Overbay/Bat-Jsy/30	15.00
103	Miguel Cabrera/Bat-Jsy/30	35.00
108	Angel Berroa/Bat-Pants/30	15.00
109	Hank Blalock/Bat-Jsy/30	35.00
111	Jose Castillo/Bat-Bat/15	15.00
121	Morgan Ensberg/Bat-Jsy/30	15.00
123	Orlando Hudson/Bat-Jsy/30	15.00
126	Adam LaRoche/Bat-Bat/30	15.00
130	Luis Castillo/Bat-Jsy/30	15.00
143	Travis Hafner/Bat-Jsy/30	12.00
147	Chad Gaudin/Jsy-Jsy/25	12.00

DK Combos Gold

Gold Combos: No Pricing
Production 1-5
Gold Combos Sepia: No Pricing
Production One Set

DK Combos Silver

NM/M

Varying quantities produced

26	Marlon Byrd/Bat-Jsy/15	15.00
101	Lyle Overbay/Bat-Jsy/15	15.00
102	Miguel Cabrera/Bat-Jsy/15	50.00
108	Angel Berroa/Bat-Pants/15	20.00
109	Hank Blalock/Bat-Jsy/15	50.00
121	Morgan Ensberg/Bat-Jsy/15	20.00
123	Orlando Hudson/Bat-Jsy/15	15.00
126	Adam LaRoche/Bat-Bat/15	20.00

DK Combos Platinum

Platinum Combos: No Pricing
Production One Set
Platinum Combos Sepia: No Pricing
Production One Set

DK Combos Framed Bronze

NM/M

Varying quantities produced

26	Marlon Byrd/Bat-Jsy/25	12.00
35	Brandon Webb/Bat-Jsy/25	25.00
53	Eric Hinske Bat-Jsy/25	15.00
57	Joe Thurston/Bat-Jsy/25	12.00
59	Jay Gibbons/Jsy-Jsy/25	15.00
62	Walter Young/Bat-Bat/25	12.00
65	Bobby Abreu/Bat-Jsy/25	15.00
71	Jason Lane/Bat-Hat/25	15.00
74	Aramis Ramirez/Bat-Bat/25	20.00
77	Chris Snelling/Bat-Bat/25	12.00
81	Joe Borchard/Bat-Jsy/25	10.00
92	Junior Spivey/Bat-Jsy/25	12.00
97	Antonio Perez/Bat-Pants/25	12.00
98	Dan Haren/Bat-Jsy/25	15.00
101	Lyle Overbay/Bat-Jsy/25	10.00
103	Miguel Cabrera/Bat-Jsy/25	40.00
107	Nic Jackson/Bat-Bat/25	10.00
108	Angel Berroa/Bat-Pants/25	12.00
109	Hank Blalock/Bat-Jsy/25	30.00
110	Ryan Klesko/Bat-Jsy/15	20.00
111	Jose Castillo/Bat-Bat/25	10.00
121	Morgan Ensberg/Bat-Jsy/25	15.00
123	Orlando Hudson/Bat-Jsy/25	12.00
126	Adam LaRoche/Bat-Bat/25	15.00
127	Hong-Chih Kuo/Bat-Bat/25	10.00
130	Luis Castillo/Bat-Jsy/25	12.00
136	Alfredo Amezaga/ Bat-Jsy/15	15.00
143	Travis Hafner/Bat-Jsy/15	15.00
147	Chad Gaudin/Jsy-Jsy/25	10.00

DK Combos Framed Gold

Framed Gold Combos: No Pricing
Production 1-5
Framed Gold Sepia: No Pricing
Production 1-5

DK Combos Framed Platinum

Framed Platinum: No Pricing
Production One Set

DK Combos Framed Silver

Framed Silver: No Pricing
Production 1-15
Framed Silver Sepia: No Pricing
Production 1-5

DK Materials Bronze

NM/M

Common Player:
No pricing for production 15 or less.
Framed Bronze: 1-1.5X
Production 5-100
Framed Bronze Sepia: 1.5-2X
Production 5-50
Silver: 1-2X
Production 5-50
Silver Sepia: 1.5-2X
Production 1-30
Framed Silver: 1-2X
Production 5-75
Framed Silver Sepia: 1.5-2X
Production 1-30
Gold: 1.5-2X
Production 1-50
Gold Sepia: No Pricing
Production 1-15
Framed Gold: 1.5-2X
Production 5-50
Framed Gold Sepia: No Pricing
Production 1-15
Platinums: No Pricing
All Platinums limited to one set.
1 Alex Rodriguez/Bat-Jsy/150 20.00
2 Andruw Jones/Bat-Jsy/150 8.00
3 Nomar Garciaparra/ Bat-Jsy/150 15.00
4 Kerry Wood/Bat-Jsy/150 15.00
5 Magglio Ordonez/ Bat-Jsy/150 8.00
6 Victor Martinez/Bat-Bat/100 6.00
7 Jeremy Bonderman/ Jsy-Jsy/30 10.00
8 Josh Beckett/Bat-Jsy/150 10.00
9 Jeff Kent/Bat-Jsy/150 8.00
10 Carlos Beltran/Bat-Jsy/150 8.00
11 Hideo Nomo/Bat-Jsy/150 10.00
12 Richie Sexson/Bat-Jsy/150 10.00
13 Jose Vidro/Bat-Jsy/50 8.00
14 Jae Weong Seo/Jsy-Jsy/100 8.00
15 Alfonso Soriano/ Bat-Jsy/150 10.00
16 Barry Zito/Bat-Jsy/100 10.00
17 Brett Myers/Jsy-Jsy/30 10.00
18 Brian Giles/Bat-Bat/100 8.00
19 Edgar Martinez/Bat-Jsy/150 8.00
20 Jim Edmonds/Bat-Jsy/150 8.00
21 Rocco Baldelli/Bat-Jsy/100 12.00
22 Mark Teixeira/Bat-Jsy/100 8.00
23 Carlos Delgado/Bat-Jsy/150 8.00
25 Jose Reyes/Bat-Jsy/100 8.00
26 Marlon Byrd/Bat-Jsy/100 8.00
27 Albert Pujols/Bat-Jsy/150 25.00
28 Vernon Wells/Bat-Jsy/150 8.00
29 Garret Anderson/Bat-Jsy/15 20.00
30 Jerome Williams/ Jsy-Jsy/100 8.00
31 Chipper Jones/Bat-Jsy/150 12.00
32 Rich Harden Jsy-Jsy/100 8.00
33 Manny Ramirez/ Bat-Jsy/150 10.00
34 Derek Jeter/Base-Base/100 20.00
35 Brandon Webb/Bat-Jsy/100 8.00
36 Mark Prior/Bat-Jsy/100 15.00
37 Roy Halladay/Jsy-Jsy/100 8.00
38 Frank Thomas/Bat-Jsy/150 12.00
39 Rafael Palmeiro/ Bat-Jsy/150 10.00
40 Adam Dunn/Bat-Jsy/150 8.00
41 Aubrey Huff/Bat-Jsy/30 10.00
42 Todd Helton/Bat-Jsy/150 10.00
43 Matt Morris/Jsy-Jsy/100 8.00
44 Dontrelle Willis/Bat-Jsy/100 10.00
45 Lance Berkman/Bat-Jsy/150 6.00
46 Mike Sweeney/Bat-Jsy/100 8.00
47 Kazuhisa Ishii/Bat-Jsy/100 8.00
48 Torii Hunter Bat-Jsy/100 8.00
49 Vladimir Guerrero/ Bat-Jsy/100 15.00
50 Mike Piazza/Bat-Jsy/150 15.00
51 Alexis Rios/Bat-Bat/150 12.00
52 Shannon Stewart/ Bat-Bat/100 6.00
53 Eric Hinske/Bat-Jsy/100 6.00
54 Jason Jennings/Bat-Jsy/150 6.00
55 Jason Giambi/Bat-Jsy/150 10.00
57 Joe Thurston/Bat-Jsy/150 6.00
58 Ramon Nivar/Bat-Jsy/100 6.00
59 Jay Gibbons/Jsy-Jsy/100 8.00
60 Eric Chavez/Bat-Jsy/150 8.00
62 Walter Young/Bat-Bat/100 6.00
63 Mark Grace/Bat-Jsy/150 10.00
64 Austin Kearns/Bat-Jsy/150 8.00
65 Bob Abreu/Bat-Jsy/150 6.00
66 Hee Seop Choi/Bat-Jsy/100 6.00
67 Brandon Phillips/Bat-Bat/100 6.00
68 Rickie Weeks/Bat-Bat/100 15.00
69 Luis Gonzalez/Bat-Jsy/150 6.00
70 Mariano Rivera/Jsy-Jsy/100 10.00
71 Jason Lane 15.00
73 Runelvys Hernandez/ Jsy-Jsy/30 8.00
75 Ichiro Suzuki/Ball-Base/15 50.00
77 Chris Snelling/Bat-Bat/30 8.00
79 Miguel Tejada/Bat-Jsy/150 8.00
80 Juan Gonzalez/Bat-Jsy/150 8.00
82 Gary Sheffield/Bat-Jsy/150 8.00
83 Wade Miller/Bat-Jsy/50 6.00
84 Jeff Bagwell/Bat-Jsy/150 15.00
86 Adrian Beltre/Bat-Jsy/100 6.00
87 Jeff Baker/Bat-Bat/100 6.00
89 Bernie Williams/ Bat-Jsy/150 10.00
90 Pedro J. Martinez/ Bat-Jsy/100 15.00
92 Junior Spivey/Bat-Jsy/100 8.00
93 Tim Hudson/Bat-Jsy/150 8.00
94 Troy Glaus/Bat-Jsy/100 8.00
95 Ken Griffey Jr./ Base-Base/100 15.00
96 Alexis Gomez/Bat-Bat/30 10.00
97 Antonio Perez/Bat-Pants/100 6.00
98 Dan Haren/Bat-Jsy/100 6.00
99 Ivan Rodriguez/Bat-Jsy/150 10.00
100 Randy Johnson/ Bat-Jsy/100 12.00
101 Lyle Overbay/Bat-Jsy/100 6.00
103 Miguel Cabrera/Bat-Jsy/100 15.00
104 Scott Rolen/Bat-Jsy/100 10.00
105 Roger Clemens/ Bat-Jsy/100 20.00
107 Nic Jackson/Bat-Bat/100 6.00
108 Angel Berroa/Bat-Pants/30 10.00
109 Hank Blalock/Bat-Jsy/100 10.00
110 Ryan Klesko/Bat-Jsy/100 8.00
111 Jose Castillo/Bat-Bat/100 6.00
112 Paul Konerko/Bat-Jsy/100 6.00
113 Greg Maddux/Bat-Jsy/100 15.00
114 Mark Mulder/Bat-Jsy/100 8.00
115 Pat Burrell/Bat-Jsy/100 8.00
116 Garrett Atkins/Jsy-Jsy/100 6.00
118 Orlando Cabrera/Bat-Jsy/100 8.00
119 Nick Johnson/Bat-Jsy/100 6.00
120 Tom Glavine/Bat-Jsy/100 10.00
121 Morgan Ensberg/Bat-Jsy/100 6.00
123 Orlando Hudson/Bat-Jsy/100 6.00
124 Hideki Matsui/Ball-Base/15 70.00
125 Craig Biggio/Bat-Jsy/100 8.00
126 Adam LaRoche/Bat-Bat/100 8.00
127 Hong-Chih Kuo/Bat-Bat/100 6.00
128 Paul LoDuca/Bat-Jsy/100 6.00
129 Shawn Green/Bat-Jsy/100 8.00
130 Luis Castillo/Bat-Jsy/100 6.00
132 Ken Harvey/Bat-Bat/100 6.00
133 Freddy Sanchez/Bat-Bat/100 6.00
134 Roy Oswalt/Bat-Jsy/100 8.00
135 Curt Schilling/Bat-Jsy/100 8.00
136 Alfredo Amezaga/ Bat-Jsy/15 15.00
139 Trot Nixon/Bat-Bat/100 10.00
140 Jim Thome/Bat-Jsy/100 15.00
141 Bret Boone/Bat-Jsy/100 8.00
142 Jacque Jones/Bat-Jsy/100 8.00
143 Todd Hafner/Bat-Jsy/100 8.00
144 Sammy Sosa/Bat-Jsy/100 20.00
145 Mike Mussina/Bat-Jsy/100 12.00
147 Chad Gaudin/Jsy-Jsy/100 6.00
149 Mike Lowell/Bat-Jsy/100 8.00
150 Rickey Henderson/ Bat-Jsy/100 15.00
151 Roger Clemens/ FB Bat-Jsy/100 20.00
153 Rickey Henderson/ FB Bat-Jsy/30 30.00
154 Alex Rodriguez/ FB Bat-Jsy/100 20.00
155 Rafael Palmeiro/ FB Bat-Jsy/100 10.00
156 Greg Maddux/ FB Bat-Bat/100 15.00
157 Mike Piazza/FB Bat-Jsy/100 15.00
158 Mike Mussina/ FB Bat-Jsy/100 12.00
159 Dale Murphy/ LGD Bat-Jsy/30 20.00
160 Cal Ripken Jr./ LGD Bat-Jsy/100 50.00
161 Carl Yastrzemski/ LGD Bat-Jsy/100 25.00
162 Marty Marion/ LGD Jsy-Jsy/30 10.00
163 Don Mattingly/ LGD Bat-Jsy/100 25.00
164 Robin Yount LGD Bat-Jsy/100 25.00
165 Andre Dawson/ LGD Bat-Jsy/30 15.00
167 George Brett/ LGD Bat-Jsy/30 50.00
168 Whitey Ford/ LGD Jsy-Pants/30 20.00
172 Steve Carlton/ LGD Bat-Jsy/100 15.00
173 Stan Musial/ LGD Bat-Jsy/30 25.00
174 Nolan Ryan/ LGD Bat-Jsy/30 50.00
175 Deion Sanders/ LGD Bat-Jsy/100 12.00

DK Signatures Bronze

NM/M

No Pricing For Prod. less than 15.
Framed Bronze: 1X
Production 1-50
Bronze Sepia: No Pricing
Production 1-15
6 Victor Martinez/200 10.00
13 Jose Vidro/200 10.00
14 Jae Weong Seo/200 15.00
17 Brett Myers/200 10.00
19 Edgar Martinez/25 40.00
26 Marlon Byrd/200 10.00
32 Rich Harden/200 15.00
35 Brandon Webb/25 30.00
41 Aubrey Huff/100 12.00
48 Torii Hunter/100 20.00
51 Alexis Rios/200 20.00
52 Shannon Stewart/200 10.00
53 Eric Hinske/25 20.00
56 Brandon Claussen/200 10.00
57 Joe Thurston/200 8.00
58 Ramon Nivar/100 10.00
59 Jay Gibbons/25 25.00
61 Jimmy Gobble/100 15.00
62 Walter Young/200 8.00
67 Brandon Phillips/100 6.00
68 Rickie Weeks/30 30.00
71 Jason Lane/200 8.00
73 Runelvys Hernandez/50 10.00
74 Aramis Ramirez/100 15.00
76 Cliff Lee/200 15.00
77 Chris Snelling/200 8.00
78 Ryan Wagner/100 15.00
81 Joe Borchard/200 8.00
85 Ryan Church/200 8.00
87 Jeff Baker/100 10.00
88 Adam Loewen/100 20.00
91 Carlos Rivera/100 8.00
92 Junior Spivey/25 20.00
96 Alexis Gomez/200 8.00
97 Antonio Perez/46 10.00
98 Dan Haren/100 12.00
101 Lyle Overbay/200 8.00
102 Oliver Perez/200 8.00
103 Miguel Cabrera/100 35.00
106 Brian Tallet/200 8.00
107 Nic Jackson/200 8.00
108 Angel Berroa/25 15.00
109 Hank Blalock/25 35.00
111 Jose Castillo/200 8.00
114 Mark Mulder/25 30.00
116 Garrett Atkins/100 8.00
117 Jeremy Guthrie/200 8.00
118 Orlando Cabrera/75 12.00
121 Morgan Ensberg/200 10.00
123 Orlando Hudson/100 10.00
126 Adam LaRoche/100 15.00
127 Hong-Chih Kuo/25 75.00
130 Luis Castillo/25 20.00
131 Joe Crede/100 8.00
132 Ken Harvey/200 8.00
133 Freddy Sanchez/50 10.00
136 Alfredo Amezaga/90 8.00
137 Chien-Ming Wang/25 125.00
142 Jacque Jones/25 20.00
143 Travis Hafner/200 10.00
146 Vinnie Chulk/200 8.00
147 Chad Gaudin/100 8.00
149 Mike Lowell/25 20.00

DK Signatures Gold

NM/M

Many not priced due to scarcity.
Framed Gold: No Pricing
Production 1-5
Gold Sepia: No Pricing
Production 1-5
32 Rich Harden/50 20.00
51 Alexis Rios/50 25.00
56 Brandon Claussen/50 15.00
57 Joe Thurston/50 10.00
62 Walter Young/50 10.00
71 Jason Lane/40 15.00
77 Chris Snelling/50 10.00
81 Joe Borchard/50 15.00
85 Ryan Church/50 10.00
96 Alexis Gomez/50 10.00
101 Lyle Overbay/50 10.00
102 Oliver Perez/50 10.00
106 Brian Tallet/50 10.00
107 Nic Jackson/50 15.00
121 Morgan Ensberg/48 15.00
146 Vinnie Chulk/50 10.00

DK Signatures Silver

NM/M

No pricing for prod. less than 15.
Framed Silver: 1.5-2X
Production 1-25
Silver Sepia: No Pricing
Production 1-10
6 Victor Martinez/49 15.00
13 Jose Vidro/20 20.00
14 Jae Weong Seo/80 20.00
17 Brett Myers/90 15.00
26 Marlon Byrd/100 10.00
32 Rich Harden/100 15.00
35 Brandon Webb/15 35.00
41 Aubrey Huff/40 15.00
51 Alexis Rios/100 20.00
52 Shannon Stewart/30 15.00
56 Brandon Claussen/100 10.00
57 Joe Thurston/100 8.00
58 Ramon Nivar/30 15.00
61 Jimmy Gobble/30 20.00
62 Walter Young/100 8.00
67 Brandon Phillips/30 10.00
68 Rickie Weeks/20 40.00
71 Jason Lane/100 8.00
73 Runelvys Hernandez/30 10.00
74 Aramis Ramirez/30 25.00
76 Cliff Lee/100 15.00
77 Chris Snelling/100 8.00
78 Ryan Wagner/30 20.00
81 Joe Borchard/100 8.00
85 Ryan Church/100 8.00
87 Jeff Baker/30 15.00
88 Adam Loewen/30 25.00
96 Alexis Gomez/100 8.00
98 Dan Haren/30 15.00
101 Lyle Overbay/100 8.00
102 Oliver Perez/100 8.00
103 Miguel Cabrera/30 40.00
106 Brian Tallet/100 8.00
107 Nic Jackson/100 8.00
109 Hank Blalock/30 35.00
111 Jose Castillo/100 8.00
116 Garrett Atkins/30 10.00
117 Jeremy Guthrie/30 15.00
121 Morgan Ensberg/50 15.00
123 Orlando Hudson/30 15.00
126 Adam LaRoche/30 20.00
131 Joe Crede/35 12.00
132 Ken Harvey/30 15.00
136 Alfredo Amezaga/30 10.00
143 Travis Hafner/30 15.00
146 Vinnie Chulk/100 8.00
147 Chad Gaudin/30 10.00

DK Signatures Platinum

No Pricing
Production One Set
Framed Platinum: No Pricing
Platinum Sepia: No Pricing
Production One Set

Gallery of Stars

NM/M

Complete Set (15): 50.00
Common Player: 2.00
Inserted 1:37
1 Nolan Ryan 8.00
2 Cal Ripken Jr. 8.00
3 George Brett 6.00
4 Don Mattingly 6.00
5 Deion Sanders 2.00
6 Mike Piazza 4.00
7 Hideo Nomo 2.00
8 Rickey Henderson 2.00
9 Roger Clemens 6.00
10 Greg Maddux 4.00
11 Albert Pujols 6.00
12 Alex Rodriguez 6.00
13 Dale Murphy 3.00
14 Mark Prior 4.00
15 Dontrelle Willis 2.00

Gallery of Stars Autograph

No Pricing

Heritage Collection

NM/M

Complete Set (25): 75.00
Common Player: 2.00
Inserted 1:22
1 Dale Murphy 3.00
2 Cal Ripken Jr. 8.00
3 Carl Yastrzemski 4.00
4 Don Mattingly 6.00
5 Jim Palmer 2.00
6 Andre Dawson 2.00
7 Roy Campanella 3.00
8 George Brett 6.00
9 Duke Snider 3.00
10 Marty Marion 2.00
11 Deion Sanders 2.00
12 Whitey Ford 3.00
13 Stan Musial 5.00
14 Nolan Ryan 8.00
15 Steve Carlton 2.00
16 Robin Yount 3.00
17 Albert Pujols 6.00
18 Alex Rodriguez 6.00
19 Mike Piazza 4.00
20 Roger Clemens 6.00
21 Hideo Nomo 2.00
22 Mark Prior 4.00
23 Roger Maris 5.00
24 Greg Maddux 4.00
25 Mark Grace 2.00

Heritage Collection Auto.

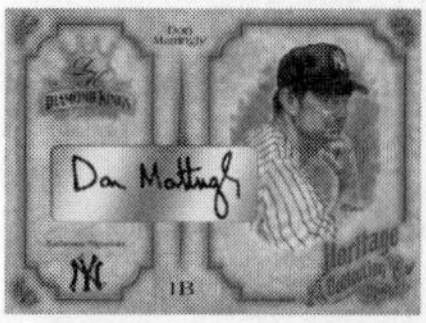

No Pricing

Heritage Collection Bat

NM/M

Production 50 unless noted.
1 Dale Murphy 20.00
2 Cal Ripken Jr. 40.00
3 Carl Yastrzemski 20.00
4 Don Mattingly 30.00
6 Andre Dawson/25 20.00
7 Roy Campanella/25 30.00
8 George Brett/25 40.00
11 Deion Sanders 10.00
13 Stan Musial/25 35.00
14 Nolan Ryan/25 40.00

15	Steve Carlton/25	20.00
16	Robin Yount	20.00
17	Albert Pujols	25.00
18	Alex Rodriguez	25.00
19	Mike Piazza	15.00
20	Roger Clemens	25.00
21	Hideo Nomo	15.00
22	Mark Prior	15.00
23	Roger Maris/25	50.00
24	Greg Maddux	15.00
25	Mark Grace	10.00

Heritage Collection Jersey

		NM/M
Production 50 unless noted.		
1	Dale Murphy	15.00
2	Cal Ripken Jr.	40.00
3	Carl Yastrzemski	20.00
4	Don Mattingly	30.00
6	Andre Dawson/25	20.00
7	Roy Campanella/25	30.00
8	George Brett/25	40.00
10	Marty Marion	10.00
11	Deion Sanders	15.00
12	Whitey Ford/25	40.00
14	Nolan Ryan/25	40.00
15	Steve Carlton/25	20.00
16	Robin Yount	20.00
17	Albert Pujols	25.00
18	Alex Rodriguez	25.00
19	Mike Piazza	15.00
20	Roger Clemens	25.00
21	Hideo Nomo	15.00
22	Mark Prior	15.00
23	Roger Maris/25	50.00
24	Greg Maddux	15.00
25	Mark Grace	10.00

HOF Heroes

		NM/M
Common Player:		2.50
1	George Brett/1,000	6.00
2	George Brett/500	8.00
3	George Brett/250	12.00
4	Mike Schmidt/1,000	5.00
5	Mike Schmidt/250	8.00
6	Nolan Ryan/1,000	8.00
7	Nolan Ryan/500	10.00
8	Nolan Ryan/250	15.00
9	Roberto Clemente/1,000	6.00
10	Roberto Clemente/500	10.00
11	Roberto Clemente/250	15.00
12	Roberto Clemente/100	20.00
13	Carl Yastrzemski/1,000	4.00
14	Robin Yount/1,000	4.00
15	Whitey Ford/1,000	4.00
16	Duke Snider/1,000	4.00
17	Duke Snider/1,000	8.00
18	Carlton Fisk/1,000	3.00
19	Ozzie Smith/1,000	5.00
20	Kirby Puckett/1,000	4.00
21	Bobby Doerr/1,000	2.50
22	Frank Robinson/1,000	3.00
23	Ralph Kiner/1,000	2.50
24	Al Kaline/1,000	4.00
25	Bob Feller/1,000	3.00
26	Yogi Berra/1,000	4.00
27	Stan Musial/1,000	5.00
28	Stan Musial/500	8.00
29	Stan Musial/250	10.00
30	Jim Palmer/1,000	2.50
31	Johnny Bench/1,000	4.00
32	Steve Carlton/1,000	3.00
33	Gary Carter/1,000	3.00
34	Roy Campanella/1,000	3.00
35	Roy Campanella/250	8.00

HOF Heroes Bat

		NM/M
Production 25 unless noted.		
1	George Brett	35.00
2	George Brett	35.00
3	George Brett	35.00
4	Mike Schmidt	35.00
5	Mike Schmidt	35.00
6	Nolan Ryan	40.00
7	Nolan Ryan	40.00
8	Nolan Ryan	40.00
13	Carl Yastrzemski	30.00
14	Robin Yount	35.00
18	Carlton Fisk	25.00

19	Ozzie Smith	30.00
20	Kirby Puckett	30.00
21	Bobby Doerr	20.00
22	Frank Robinson	15.00
23	Ralph Kiner	15.00
24	Al Kaline	25.00
31	Johnny Bench	25.00
32	Steve Carlton	20.00
33	Gary Carter	20.00
34	Roy Campanella	30.00
35	Roy Campanella	30.00

HOF Heroes Combo

Stan Musial

		NM/M
Production 25 unless noted.		
1	George Brett	50.00
2	George Brett	50.00
3	George Brett	50.00
4	Mike Schmidt	40.00
5	Mike Schmidt	40.00
6	Nolan Ryan	50.00
7	Nolan Ryan	50.00
8	Nolan Ryan	50.00
13	Carl Yastrzemski	40.00
14	Robin Yount	40.00
15	Whitey Ford	30.00
18	Carlton Fisk	30.00
19	Ozzie Smith	40.00
20	Kirby Puckett	40.00
21	Bobby Doerr	25.00
23	Ralph Kiner	20.00
24	Al Kaline	35.00
32	Steve Carlton	30.00
33	Gary Carter	25.00
34	Roy Campanella	40.00
35	Roy Campanella	40.00

HOF Heroes Jersey

		NM/M
Production 25 unless noted.		
1	George Brett	35.00
2	George Brett	35.00
3	George Brett	35.00
4	Mike Schmidt	35.00
5	Mike Schmidt	35.00
6	Nolan Ryan	40.00
7	Nolan Ryan	40.00
8	Nolan Ryan	40.00
13	Carl Yastrzemski	30.00
14	Robin Yount	35.00
15	Whitey Ford	30.00
18	Carlton Fisk	25.00
19	Ozzie Smith	30.00
20	Kirby Puckett	30.00
21	Bobby Doerr	20.00
24	Al Kaline	25.00
32	Steve Carlton	20.00
33	Gary Carter	20.00
34	Roy Campanella	30.00
35	Roy Campanella	30.00

HOF Heroes Signature

		NM/M
Many not priced.		
14	Robin Yount/19	70.00
15	Whitey Ford/16	50.00
22	Frank Robinson/20	50.00
25	Bob Feller/19	40.00
30	Jim Palmer/22	40.00
32	Steve Carlton/32	35.00

Recollection Autographs

		NM/M
Varying quantities produced		
6	Clint Barmes	
	03 DK Black/82	10.00
8	Clint Barmes 03 DK Blue/72	10.00
	Carlos Beltran 02 DK/23	20.00
9	Carlos Beltran 03 DK/99	15.00
10	Adrian Beltre 02 DK/40	10.00
19	Chris Burke 03 DK/150	10.00
20	Marlon Byrd 02 DK/23	15.00
21	Marlon Byrd 03 DK/100	10.00
24	Kevin Cash 03 DK/103	10.00
25	Jose Cruz 85 DK/59	10.00
26	J.D. Durbin 03 DK/151	10.00
27	Jim Edmonds 03 DK/24	25.00
32	Julio Franco 87 DK/25	20.00
33	Freddy Garcia 03 DK/50	20.00
38	Jay Gibbons 03 DK/100	12.00
39	Brendan Harris 03 DK/150	8.00

42	Runelvys Hernandez	
	02 DK/100	8.00
43	Eric Hinske 03 DK/20	20.00
44	Tim Hudson 02 DK/25	30.00
45	Tim Hudson 03 DK/25	30.00
46	Aubrey Huff 03 DK/99	15.00
49	Jason Jennings 03 DK/50	10.00
50	Tommy John	
	88 DK Black/62	15.00
52	Howard Johnson 90 DK/52	10.00
54	Austin Kearns 02 DK/25	30.00
55	Austin Kearns 03 DK/25	30.00
59	Preston Larrison	
	03 DK Black/74	10.00
60	Preston Larrison	
	03 DK Blue/77	10.00
67	Dustin McGowan 03 DK/159	8.00
69	Melvin Mora 03 DK/101	8.00
71	Jack Morris 03 DK/60	10.00
72	Jack Morris 03 DK Her/19	20.00
74	Dale Murphy	
	03 DK Blue/47	30.00
82	Magglio Ordonez 03 DK/25	30.00
85	Dave Parker 82 DK/20	30.00
86	Dave Parker 90 DK/18	30.00
88	Jorge Posada 02 DK/25	50.00
89	Mark Prior 03 DK/25	100.00
92	Mike Rivera 02 DK/24	15.00
97	Ivan Rodriguez 03 DK/22	40.00
100	Rodrigo Rosario 02 DK/50	8.00
105	Ron Santo 02 DK/29	35.00
106	Richie Sexson 02 DK/25	25.00
107	Richie Sexson 03 DK/25	25.00
109	Chris Snelling 02 DK/46	12.00
119	Shannon Stewart 02 DK/50	15.00
120	Shannon Stewart	
	03 DK Black/92	12.00
126	Gorman Thomas	
	82 DK Black/22	20.00
127	Gorman Thomas	
	82 DK Blue/20	20.00
128	Alan Trammell 02 DK/29	30.00
129	Alan Trammell	
	02 DK Her/25	30.00
130	Robin Ventura 03 DK/25	20.00
131	Jose Vidro 03 DK/25	20.00
132	Rickie Weeks 03 DK/52	40.00
133	Kevin Youkilis 03 DK/153	15.00

Team Timeline

		NM/M
Complete Set (19):		65.00
Common Duo:		2.00
Inserted 1:29		
1	Deion Sanders, Andruw Jones	2.00
2	Rickie Weeks, Robin Yount	3.00
3	Don Mattingly, Whitey Ford	8.00
4	Chipper Jones, Dale Murphy	4.00
5	Nomar Garciaparra, Bobby Doerr	5.00
6	Mark Prior, Sammy Sosa	5.00
7	Hideo Nomo, Kazuhisa Ishii	2.00
8	Andre Dawson, Mark Grace	3.00
9	Roger Clemens, Carl Yastrzemski	6.00
10	Mike Mussina, Cal Ripken Jr.	8.00
11	Stan Musial, Albert Pujols	6.00
12	Jim Palmer, Mike Mussina	2.00
13	Marty Marion, Stan Musial	4.00
14	George Brett, Mike Sweeney	6.00
15	Roger Clemens, Roger Maris	6.00
16	Duke Snider, Shawn Green	3.00
17	Jim Thome, Mike Schmidt	4.00
18	Nolan Ryan, Alex Rodriguez	8.00
19	Roy Campanella, Mike Piazza	4.00

Team Timeline Bat

		NM/M
Production 25 unless noted.		
1	Deion Sanders, Andruw Jones	15.00
2	Rickie Weeks, Robin Yount	30.00
3	Don Mattingly, Whitey Ford	60.00
4	Chipper Jones, Dale Murphy	35.00
5	Nomar Garciaparra, Bobby Doerr	30.00
6	Mark Prior, Sammy Sosa	40.00
7	Hideo Nomo, Kazuhisa Ishii	40.00
8	Andre Dawson, Mark Grace	20.00
9	Roger Clemens, Carl Yastrzemski	50.00
10	Mike Mussina, Cal Ripken Jr.	75.00
11	Stan Musial, Albert Pujols	65.00
12	Jim Palmer, Mike Mussina	25.00
14	George Brett, Mike Sweeney	60.00
15	Roger Clemens, Roger Maris	60.00
17	Jim Thome, Mike Schmidt	40.00
18	Nolan Ryan, Alex Rodriguez	40.00
19	Roy Campanella, Mike Piazza	40.00

Team Timeline Jersey

		NM/M
Production 25 Sets		
Prime:		No Pricing
Production One Set		
1	Deion Sanders, Andruw Jones	15.00
2	Rickie Weeks, Robin Yount	30.00

3	Don Mattingly, Whitey Ford	60.00
4	Chipper Jones,	35.00
5	Nomar Garciaparra, Bobby Doerr	30.00
6	Mark Prior, Sammy Sosa	40.00
7	Hideo Nomo, Kazuhisa Ishii	40.00
8	Andre Dawson, Mark Grace	20.00
9	Roger Clemens, Carl Yastrzemski	50.00
10	Mike Mussina, Cal Ripken Jr.	75.00
14	George Brett, Mike Sweeney	30.00
15	Roger Clemens, Roger Maris	60.00
17	Jim Thome, Mike Schmidt	40.00
18	Nolan Ryan, Alex Rodriguez	60.00
19	Roy Campanella, Mike Piazza	40.00

Timeline

		NM/M
Common Player:		3.00
Inserted 1:92		
1	Roger Clemens	6.00
2	Mark Grace	3.00
3	Mike Mussina	3.00
4	Mike Piazza	4.00
5	Nolan Ryan	8.00
6	Rickey Henderson	3.00

Timeline Bat

		NM/M
Production 25 Sets		
1	Roger Clemens	35.00
2	Mark Grace	25.00
3	Mike Mussina	20.00
4	Mike Piazza	35.00
5	Nolan Ryan	50.00
6	Rickey Henderson	20.00

Timeline Jersey

		NM/M
Production 25 Sets		
Prime:		No Pricing
Production One Set		
1	Roger Clemens	35.00
2	Mark Grace	25.00
3	Mike Mussina	20.00
4	Mike Piazza	35.00
5	Nolan Ryan	50.00
6	Rickey Henderson	20.00

2004 Donruss Elite

		NM/M
Complete Set (205):		
Common Player:		.25
Common Auto. (151-180):		5.00
Production 250-1,000		
Common (181-200):		2.00
Production 1,000		
Pack (5):		5.00
Box (24):		100.00
1	Troy Glaus	.40
2	Darin Erstad	.25
3	Garret Anderson	.40

JASON BARTLETT

4	Tim Salmon	.40
5	Bartolo Colon	.40
6	Jose Guillen	.25
7	Miguel Tejada	.40
8	Adam Loewen	.25
9	Jay Gibbons	.25
10	Melvin Mora	.25
11	Javy Lopez	.40
12	Pedro J. Martinez	.75
13	Curt Schilling	.50
14	David Ortiz	.50
15	Keith Foulke	.25
16	Nomar Garciaparra	1.00
17	Magglio Ordonez	.40
18	Frank Thomas	.50
19	Carlos Lee	.40
20	Paul Konerko	.25
21	Mark Buehrle	.25
22	Jody Gerut	.25
23	Victor Martinez	.25
24	C.C. Sabathia	.25
25	Ellis Burks	.25
26	Bobby Higginson	.25
27	Jeremy Bonderman	.25
28	Fernando Vina	.25
29	Carlos Pena	.25
30	Dmitri Young	.25
31	Carlos Beltran	.50
32	Benito Santiago	.25
33	Mike Sweeney	.25
34	Angel Berroa	.25
35	Runelvys Hernandez	.25
36	Johan Santana	.25
37	Doug Mientkiewicz	.25
38	Shannon Stewart	.25
39	Torii Hunter	.40
40	Derek Jeter	2.00
41	Jason Giambi	.50
42	Bernie Williams	.50
43	Alfonso Soriano	.50
44	Gary Sheffield	.50
45	Mike Mussina	.50
46	Jorge Posada	.40
47	Hideki Matsui	1.00
48	Kevin Brown	.40
49	Javier Vazquez	.40
50	Mariano Rivera	.50
51	Eric Chavez	.40
52	Tim Hudson	.40
53	Mark Mulder	.40
54	Barry Zito	.40
55	Ichiro Suzuki	1.00
56	Edgar Martinez	.40
57	Bret Boone	.40
58	John Olerud	.25
59	Scott Spiezio	.25
60	Aubrey Huff	.40
61	Rocco Baldelli	.40
62	Jose Cruz Jr.	.40
63	Delmon Young	.40
64	Mark Teixeira	.50
65	Hank Blalock	.50
66	Michael Young	.40
67	Alex Rodriguez	2.00
68	Carlos Delgado	.50
69	Eric Hinske	.25
70	Roy Halladay	.40
71	Vernon Wells	.40
72	Randy Johnson	.75
73	Richie Sexson	.50
74	Brandon Webb	.40
75	Luis Gonzalez	.50
76	Steve Finley	.25
77	Chipper Jones	.75
78	Andruw Jones	.50
79	Marcus Giles	.25
80	Rafael Furcal	.25
81	J.D. Drew	.40
82	Sammy Sosa	1.50
83	Kerry Wood	.75
84	Mark Prior	1.00
85	Derrek Lee	.40
86	Moises Alou	.40
87	Corey Patterson	.40
88	Ken Griffey Jr.	1.00
89	Austin Kearns	.40
90	Adam Dunn	.50
91	Barry Larkin	.50
92	Todd Helton	.50
93	Larry Walker	.40
94	Preston Wilson	.25

95	Charles Johnson	.25
96	Luis Castillo	.25
97	Josh Beckett	.40
98	Mike Lowell	.40
99	Miguel Cabrera	.75
100	Juan Pierre	.25
101	Dontrelle Willis	.40
102	Andy Pettitte	.40
103	Wade Miller	.25
104	Jeff Bagwell	.50
105	Craig Biggio	.40
106	Lance Berkman	.40
107	Jeff Kent	.40
108	Roy Oswalt	.40
109	Hideo Nomo	.40
110	Adrian Beltre	.25
111	Paul LoDuca	.25
112	Shawn Green	.40
113	Fred McGriff	.40
114	Eric Gagne	.40
115	Geoff Jenkins	.40
116	Rickie Weeks	.40
117	Scott Podsednik	.40
118	Nick Johnson	.25
119	Orlando Cabrera	.25
120	Jose Vidro	.25
121	Kazuo Matsui RC	5.00
122	Tom Glavine	.40
123	Al Leiter	.25
124	Mike Piazza	1.00
125	Jose Reyes	.50
126	Mike Cameron	.25
127	Pat Burrell	.40
128	Jim Thome	.75
129	Mike Lieberthal	.25
130	Bobby Abreu	.40
131	Kip Wells	.25
132	Jack Wilson	.40
133	Pokey Reese	.25
134	Brian Giles	.40
135	Sean Burroughs	.25
136	Ryan Klesko	.40
137	Trevor Hoffman	.25
138	Jason Schmidt	.40
139	J.T. Snow	.25
140	A.J. Pierzynski	.25
141	Ray Durham	.25
142	Jim Edmonds	.40
143	Albert Pujols	1.50
144	Edgar Renteria	.40
145	Scott Rolen	.75
146	Matt Morris	.25
147	Ivan Rodriguez	.50
148	Vladimir Guerrero	.75
149	Greg Maddux	1.00
150	Kevin Millwood	.40
151	Hector Gimenez AU/750 RC	5.00
152	Willy Taveras AU/750 RC	15.00
153	Ruddy Yan AU/750	5.00
154	Graham Koonce AU/750	8.00
155	Jose Capellan AU/750 RC	15.00
156	Onil Joseph AU/750 RC	5.00
157	John Gall AU/1000 RC	10.00
158	Carlos Hines AU/750 RC	5.00
159	Jerry Gil AU/750 RC	5.00
160	Mike Gosling AU/750	5.00
161	Jason Frasor AU/750 RC	5.00
162	Justin Knoedler AU/750 RC	5.00
163	Merkin Valdez AU/500 RC	5.00
164	Angel Chavez AU/1000 RC	5.00
165	Ivan Ochoa AU/750	5.00
166	Greg Dobbs AU/750 RC	5.00
167	Ronald Belisario AU/750 RC	5.00
168	Aarom Baldiris AU/750 RC	10.00
169	Kazuo Matsui RC	
170	David Crouthers AU/750	5.00
171	Freddy Guzman AU/750 RC	10.00
172	Akinori Otsuka AU/250 RC	25.00
173	Ian Snell AU/750 RC	30.00
174	Nick Regilio AU/1000 RC	5.00
175	Jamie Brown AU/750 RC	5.00
176	Jerome Gamble AU/750 RC	5.00
177	Roberto Novoa AU/1000 RC	5.00
178	Sean Henn AU/1000	10.00
179	Ramon Ramirez AU/1000 RC	10.00
180	Jason Bartlett AU/1000 RC	10.00
181	Bob Gibson/RET	2.00
182	Cal Ripken Jr./RET	8.00
183	Carl Yastrzemski/RET	4.00
184	Dale Murphy/RET	3.00
185	Don Mattingly/RET	6.00
186	Eddie Murray/RET	2.00
187	George Brett/RET	6.00
188	Jackie Robinson/RET	4.00
189	Jim Palmer/RET	2.00
190	Lou Gehrig/RET	5.00
191	Mike Schmidt/RET	5.00
192	Ozzie Smith/RET	5.00
193	Nolan Ryan/RET	8.00
194	Reggie Jackson/RET	3.00
195	Roberto Clemente/RET	6.00
196	Robin Yount/RET	4.00
197	Stan Musial/RET	5.00
198	Ted Williams/RET	8.00
199	Tony Gwynn/RET	3.00
200	Ty Cobb/RET	5.00
201	James Gandolfini/FG	3.00
202	Freddy Adu/FG	3.00
203	Summer Sanders/FG	1.50
204	Janet Evans/FG	1.50
205	Brandi Chastain/FG	1.50

Aspirations

GRAHAM KOONCE

Cards (1-150) print run 61-99:	4-8X
(1-150) p/r 41-60:	6-10X
(1-150) p/r 21-40:	8-15X
Autos. (151-180):	.75-1.5X
(181-200):	2-3X
Production 19-99	

Status

SHAWN GREEN

Cards (1-150) print run 61-81:	4-8X
(1-150) p/r 41-60:	6-10X
(1-150) p/r 21-40:	8-15X
Autos. (151-180):	.75-1X
(181-200):	3-4X
Production 1-81	

Status Gold

Gold (1-150):	10-20X
Gold (151-180):	No Pricing
Gold (181-200):	3-6X
Production 24 Sets	

Back 2 Back Jacks

NM/M

Singles Production 25-125
Duals Production 25-50

1	Albert Pujols/125	15.00
2	Alex Rodriguez/125	10.00
3	Alfonso Soriano/125	8.00
4	Andruw Jones/125	5.00
5	Chipper Jones/125	8.00
6	Derek Jeter/125	20.00
7	Frank Thomas/125	8.00
8	Miguel Cabrera/125	8.00
9	Jason Giambi/125	8.00
10	Jim Thome/125	8.00
11	Mike Piazza/125	10.00
12	Nomar Garciaparra/125	35.00
13	Sammy Sosa/125	10.00
14	Shawn Green/125	4.00
15	Vladimir Guerrero/125	8.00
16	Andruw Jones,	
	Chipper Jones/50	20.00
17	Alfonso Soriano,	
	Derek Jeter/50	30.00
18	Jeff Bagwell,	
	Lance Berkman/50	15.00
19	Alex Rodriguez,	
	Rafael Palmeiro/50	20.00
20	Adam Dunn,	
	Austin Kearns/25	20.00
21	Al Kaline/50	15.00
22	Babe Ruth/50	140.00
23	Cal Ripken Jr./100	40.00
24	Dale Murphy/100	10.00
25	Don Mattingly/100	15.00
26	George Brett/100	20.00
27	Lou Gehrig/100	85.00
28	Mike Schmidt/100	15.00
29	Roberto Clemente/100	50.00
30	Roy Campanella/100	15.00
31	Babe Ruth,	
	Roger Maris/25	200.00
32	Harmon Killebrew,	
	Kirby Puckett/50	35.00
33	Paul Molitor,	
	Robin Yount/50	40.00

34	Reggie Jackson/50	15.00
35	Lou Gehrig, Ty Cobb/50	200.00
36	Don Mattingly,	
	Jason Giambi/50	25.00
37	Ted Williams,	
	Nomar Garciaparra/50	75.00
38	Andre Dawson,	
	Sammy Sosa/50	25.00
39	Dale Murphy,	
	Chipper Jones/50	15.00
40	Stan Musial,	
	Jim Edmonds/50	25.00

Back 2 Back Jacks Combos

NM/M

Singles Production 25-50
Duals Production 10-25

1	Albert Pujols/Bat-Jsy/50	30.00
2	Alex Rodriguez/Bat-Jsy/50	20.00
3	Alfonso Soriano/Bat-Jsy/50	15.00
4	Andruw Jones/Bat-Jsy/50	8.00
5	Chipper Jones/Bat-Jsy/50	12.00
6	Derek Jeter/Bat-Jsy/50	35.00
7	Frank Thomas/Bat-Jsy/50	15.00
8	Miguel Cabrera/Bat-Jsy/50	15.00
9	Jason Giambi/Bat-Jsy/50	15.00
10	Jim Thome/Bat-Jsy/50	15.00
11	Mike Piazza/Bat-Jsy/50	20.00
12	Nomar Garciaparra/	
	Bat-Jsy/50	20.00
13	Sammy Sosa/Bat-Jsy/50	20.00
14	Shawn Green/Bat-Jsy/50	6.00
15	Vladimir Guerrero/	
	Bat-Jsy/50	15.00
16	Andruw Jones,	
	Chipper Jones/25	30.00
17	Alfonso Soriano,	
	Lance Berkman/25	50.00
18	Jeff Bagwell,	
	Lance Berkman/25	20.00
19	Alex Rodriguez,	
	Rafael Palmeiro/25	30.00
20	Adam Dunn,	
	Austin Kearns/25	20.00
21	Al Kaline/Bat-Jsy/50	25.00
22	Babe Ruth/Bat-Jsy/25	350.00
23	Cal Ripken Jr./Bat-Jsy/50	60.00
24	Dale Murphy/Bat-Jsy/50	15.00
25	Don Mattingly/Bat-Jsy/50	25.00
26	George Brett/Bat-Jsy/50	30.00
27	Lou Gehrig/Bat-Jsy/25	150.00
28	Mike Schmidt/Bat-Jsy/25	30.00
29	Roberto Clemente/	
	Bat-Jsy/50	80.00
30	Roy Campanella/Bat-Jsy/25	25.00
31	Babe Ruth,	
	Roger Maris/10	185.00
32	Harmon Killebrew,	
	Kirby Puckett/25	50.00
33	Paul Molitor,	
	Robin Yount/25	50.00
34	Reggie Jackson/25	25.00
35	Lou Gehrig, Ty Cobb/25	350.00
36	Don Mattingly,	
	Jason Giambi/25	35.00
37	Ted Williams,	
	Nomar Garciaparra	140.00
38	Andre Dawson,	
	Sammy Sosa	40.00
39	Dale Murphy,	
	Chipper Jones	20.00
40	Jim Thome/Bat-Jsy, Jim Edmonds	35.00

Back to the Future

NM/M

#1-6	
Production 500	
#6-9	
Production 250	
Black:	1-2X
Production 25 or 50	
Gold:	.75-1.5X
Production 50 or 100	
Red:	1X
Production 125 or 250	

1	Tim Hudson	2.00
2	Rich Harden	1.50
3	Alex Rodriguez/Rgr	5.00
4	Hank Blalock	3.00
5	Sammy Sosa	5.00
6	Hee Seop Choi	1.50
7	Tim Hudson, Rich Harden	3.00
8	Alex Rodriguez,	
	Hank Blalock	6.00
9	Sammy Sosa,	
	Hee Seop Choi	6.00

Back to the Future Bats

NM/M

#1-6	
Production 200	
#8-9	

Production 100
1	Tim Hudson	4.00
3	Alex Rodriguez	10.00
4	Hank Blalock	6.00
5	Sammy Sosa	10.00
6	Hee Seop Choi	4.00
8	Alex Rodriguez, Hank Blalock	12.00
9	Sammy Sosa, Hee Seop Choi	12.00

Back to the Future Jerseys

NM/M

#1-6
Production 200
#7-9
Production 100
Prime: 1.5-2X
Production 25 or 50

1	Tim Hudson	4.00
2	Rich Harden	4.00
3	Alex Rodriguez/Rgr	10.00
4	Hank Blalock	6.00
5	Sammy Sosa	10.00
6	Hee Seop Choi	4.00
7	Tim Hudson, Rich Harden	8.00
8	Alex Rodriguez, Hank Blalock	12.00
9	Sammy Sosa, Hee Seop Choi	12.00

Career Best

NM/M

Common Player: 1.00
Production 1,000 Sets
Black: 2X
Production 100 Sets
Gold Print Run 200-390: 1.5X
Gold P/R 101-200: 2X
Gold P/R 50-100: 3X
Gold P/R 26-50: 3-5X
Gold P/R 15-25: 5-8X

1	Albert Pujols	3.00
2	Alex Rodriguez	3.00
3	Alfonso Soriano	1.50
4	Andruw Jones	1.00
5	Barry Zito	1.00
6	Cal Ripken Jr.	5.00
7	Chipper Jones	1.50
8	Curt Schilling	1.00
9	Derek Jeter	4.00
10	Don Mattingly	4.00
11	Dontrelle Willis	1.00
12	Doc Gooden	1.00
13	Eddie Murray	1.50
14	Frank Thomas	1.50
15	Gary Sheffield	1.00
16	George Brett	4.00
17	Greg Maddux	2.00
18	Hideo Nomo	1.00
19	Ichiro Suzuki	2.00
20	Ivan Rodriguez	1.50
21	Jason Giambi	1.50
22	Jeff Bagwell	1.50
23	Jim Thome	1.50
24	Kerry Wood	1.50
25	Lance Berkman	1.00
26	Magglio Ordonez	1.00
27	Mark Prior	2.00
28	Mike Piazza	2.00
29	Mike Schmidt	3.00
30	Nomar Garciaparra	2.50
31	Pedro J. Martinez	2.00
32	Randy Johnson	2.00
33	Roger Clemens	3.00
34	Sammy Sosa	2.50
35	Tony Gwynn	1.50

Career Best Bats

NM/M

Production 100 Or 200
Combo Print Run 50: 1-2X
Combo P/R 25: 2X
Production 25 or 50

1	Albert Pujols/200	15.00
2	Alex Rodriguez/200	10.00
3	Alfonso Soriano/200	8.00
4	Andruw Jones/200	5.00
5	Barry Zito/200	4.00
6	Cal Ripken Jr./200	25.00
7	Chipper Jones/200	8.00
8	Curt Schilling/200	5.00
9	Derek Jeter/200	15.00
10	Don Mattingly/200	15.00
11	Dontrelle Willis/100	6.00
12	Doc Gooden/200	6.00
13	Eddie Murray/200	4.00
14	Frank Thomas/200	8.00
15	Gary Sheffield/200	5.00
16	George Brett/200	15.00
17	Greg Maddux/100	10.00
18	Hideo Nomo/100	8.00
20	Ivan Rodriguez/200	8.00
21	Jason Giambi/200	8.00
22	Jeff Bagwell/200	6.00
23	Jim Thome/200	8.00
24	Kerry Wood/100	10.00
25	Lance Berkman/200	4.00
26	Magglio Ordonez/200	4.00
27	Mark Prior/100	8.00
28	Mike Piazza/200	10.00
29	Mike Schmidt/100	10.00
30	Nomar Garciaparra/200	10.00
31	Pedro J. Martinez/200	8.00
32	Randy Johnson/200	8.00
33	Roger Clemens/200	15.00
34	Sammy Sosa/200	10.00
35	Tony Gwynn/50	15.00

Career Best Jerseys

NM/M

Quantity produced listed
Prime: 1.5-2X
Production 25-50

1	Albert Pujols/200	15.00
2	Alex Rodriguez/200	10.00
3	Alfonso Soriano/200	8.00
4	Andruw Jones/200	5.00
5	Barry Zito/200	4.00
6	Cal Ripken Jr./50	40.00
7	Chipper Jones/200	5.00
8	Curt Schilling/200	5.00
9	Derek Jeter/200	15.00
10	Don Mattingly/50	20.00
11	Dontrelle Willis/200	6.00
12	Doc Gooden/200	6.00
13	Eddie Murray/200	6.00
14	Frank Thomas/200	8.00
15	Gary Sheffield/200	5.00
16	George Brett/50	25.00
17	Greg Maddux/200	10.00
18	Hideo Nomo/200	8.00
20	Ivan Rodriguez/200	8.00
21	Jason Giambi/200	8.00
22	Jeff Bagwell/200	6.00
23	Jim Thome/200	8.00
24	Kerry Wood/200	10.00
25	Lance Berkman/200	4.00
26	Magglio Ordonez/200	4.00
27	Mark Prior/200	8.00
28	Mike Piazza/200	10.00
29	Mike Schmidt/100	10.00
30	Nomar Garciaparra/200	10.00
31	Pedro J. Martinez/200	8.00
32	Randy Johnson/200	8.00
33	Roger Clemens/200	15.00
34	Sammy Sosa/200	10.00
35	Tony Gwynn/50	15.00

Fans of the Game Autographs

NM/M

201	James Gandolfini	120.00
202	Freddy Adu	80.00
203	Summer Sanders	25.00
204	Janet Evans	25.00
205	Brandi Chastain	35.00

Passing the Torch

NM/M

#1-30
Production 1,000
#31-45
Production 500
Black: 1-2X
Production 50 or 100
Blue: 1X
Production 125 or 250
Gold: 1.5-3X
Production 25 or 50
Green: .75-1X
Production 250 or 500

1	Whitey Ford	3.00
2	Andy Pettitte	1.50
3	Willie McCovey	2.00
4	Will Clark	3.00
5	Stan Musial	4.00
6	Albert Pujols	5.00
7	Andre Dawson	2.00
8	Vladimir Guerrero	2.00
9	Dale Murphy	2.00
10	Chipper Jones	2.00
11	Joe Morgan	1.50
12	Barry Larkin	1.50
13	Jim "Catfish" Hunter	1.50
14	Tim Hudson	1.50
15	Jim Rice	1.50
16	Manny Ramirez	2.00
17	Greg Maddux	2.50
18	Mark Prior	2.00
19	Don Mattingly	4.00
20	Jason Giambi	2.00
21	Roy Campanella	2.00
22	Mike Piazza	3.00
23	Ozzie Smith	2.00
24	Scott Rolen	4.00
25	Roger Clemens	4.00
26	Mike Mussina	2.00
27	Babe Ruth	6.00
28	Roger Maris	4.00
29	Nolan Ryan	6.00
30	Roy Oswalt	1.50
31	Whitey Ford, Andy Pettitte	3.00
32	Willie McCovey, Will Clark	3.00
33	Stan Musial, Albert Pujols	6.00
34	Andre Dawson, Vladimir Guerrero	3.00
35	Dale Murphy, Chipper Jones	3.00
36	Joe Morgan, Barry Larkin	3.00
37	Jim "Catfish" Hunter, Tim Hudson	2.00
38	Jim Rice, Manny Ramirez	3.00
39	Greg Maddux, Mark Prior	4.00
40	Don Mattingly, Jason Giambi	8.00
41	Roy Campanella, Mike Piazza	5.00
42	Ozzie Smith, Scott Rolen	5.00
43	Roger Clemens, Mike Mussina	5.00
44	Babe Ruth, Roger Maris	10.00
45	Nolan Ryan, Roy Oswalt	6.00

Passing the Torch Autographs

NM/M

Quantity produced listed
Many not priced due to scarcity.

4	Will Clark/15	100.00
7	Andre Dawson/50	15.00
9	Dale Murphy/50	30.00
11	Joe Morgan/15	25.00
14	Tim Hudson/15	45.00
15	Jim Rice/50	15.00
18	Mark Prior/15	80.00
24	Scott Rolen/15	50.00
30	Roy Oswalt/50	15.00

Passing the Torch Bats

NM/M

Quantity produced listed

2	Andy Pettitte/200	4.00
4	Willie McCovey/100	6.00
5	Will Clark/100	10.00
6	Stan Musial/100	25.00
7	Albert Pujols/200	15.00
8	Andre Dawson/100	8.00
9	Vladimir Guerrero/200	10.00
10	Chipper Jones/200	8.00
11	Joe Morgan/200	4.00
12	Barry Larkin/200	5.00
14	Tim Hudson/200	5.00
15	Jim Rice/200	5.00
16	Manny Ramirez/200	8.00
17	Greg Maddux/200	10.00
18	Mark Prior/200	8.00
19	Don Mattingly/100	15.00
20	Jason Giambi/200	8.00
21	Roy Campanella/200	30.00
22	Mike Piazza/200	10.00
23	Ozzie Smith/200	15.00
24	Scott Rolen/200	8.00
25	Roger Clemens/200	15.00
26	Mike Mussina/200	8.00
27	Babe Ruth/25	150.00
28	Roger Maris/50	50.00
29	Nolan Ryan/100	25.00
30	Roy Oswalt/200	4.00
32	Willie McCovey, Will Clark/50	20.00
33	Stan Musial, Albert Pujols/50	50.00
34	Andre Dawson, Vladimir Guerrero/50	20.00
35	Dale Murphy, Chipper Jones/50	20.00
36	Joe Morgan, Barry Larkin/50	15.00
38	Jim Rice, Manny Ramirez/50	20.00
39	Greg Maddux, Mark Prior/50	25.00
40	Don Mattingly, Jason Giambi/50	35.00
41	Roy Campanella, Mike Piazza/25	35.00
42	Ozzie Smith, Scott Rolen/50	30.00
43	Roger Clemens, Mike Mussina/50	30.00
44	Babe Ruth, Roger Maris/25	200.00
45	Nolan Ryan, Roy Oswalt/50	35.00

Passing the Torch Jerseys

NM/M

Quantity produced listed

1	Whitey Ford/100	15.00
2	Andy Pettitte/200	8.00
3	Willie McCovey/100	6.00
4	Will Clark/100	10.00
5	Stan Musial/100	25.00
6	Albert Pujols/200	15.00
7	Andre Dawson/200	8.00
8	Vladimir Guerrero/200	8.00
9	Dale Murphy/100	10.00
10	Chipper Jones/200	8.00
11	Joe Morgan/100	4.00
12	Barry Larkin/200	5.00
13	Jim "Catfish" Hunter/100	5.00
14	Tim Hudson/200	5.00
15	Jim Rice/200	5.00
16	Manny Ramirez/200	8.00
18	Mark Prior/200	8.00
19	Don Mattingly/100	15.00
20	Jason Giambi/200	8.00
21	Roy Campanella/50	30.00
22	Mike Piazza/200	10.00
23	Ozzie Smith/100	12.00
24	Scott Rolen/200	8.00
25	Roger Clemens/200	15.00
26	Mike Mussina/200	8.00
27	Babe Ruth/25	300.00
28	Roger Maris/50	50.00
29	Nolan Ryan/100	25.00
30	Roy Oswalt/200	4.00
31	Whitey Ford, Andy Pettitte/50	20.00
32	Willie McCovey, Will Clark/50	20.00
33	Stan Musial, Albert Pujols/50	50.00
34	Andre Dawson, Vladimir Guerrero/50	20.00
35	Dale Murphy, Chipper Jones/50	20.00
36	Joe Morgan, Barry Larkin/50	15.00
37	Jim "Catfish" Hunter, Tim Hudson/50	15.00
38	Jim Rice, Manny Ramirez/50	20.00
40	Don Mattingly, Jason Giambi/50	35.00
41	Roy Campanella, Mike Piazza	35.00
42	Ozzie Smith, Scott Rolen/50	30.00
43	Roger Clemens, Mike Mussina/50	30.00
45	Nolan Ryan, Roy Oswalt/50	35.00

Recollection Autographs

NM/M

Common Autograph: 8.00

1	Jeremy Affeldt 01/25	15.00
2	Erick Almonte 01/26	10.00
4	Jeff Baker 02/25	30.00
5	Brandon Berger 01/25	8.00
6	Marlon Byrd 01/24	25.00
8	Ryan Drese 02/45	8.00
9	Brandon Duckworth 01/16	15.00
10	Casey Fossum 01/23	15.00

11	Geronimo Gil 01/25	8.00
13	Jeremy Guthrie 02/25	20.00
14	Nic Jackson 02/95	8.00
21	Ricardo Rodriguez 01/25	8.00
23	Bud Smith 01/25	8.00
25	Junior Spivey 01/20	20.00
26	Tim Spooneybarger 01/25	10.00
28	Martin Vargas 01/37	8.00

Team

NM/M

Production 1,500 Sets
Black: 1X-2X
Production 150 Sets
Gold: 1-1.5X
Production 250 Sets

1	Cal Ripken Jr., Eddie Murray, Jim Palmer	8.00
2	Derek Jeter, Roger Clemens, Bernie Williams, Andy Pettitte	4.00
3	Johnny Bench, Tony Perez, George Foster, Dave Concepcion	4.00
4	Josh Beckett, Dontrelle Willis, Ivan Rodriguez	2.00
5	Randy Johnson, Curt Schilling, Luis Gonzalez, Mark Grace	2.00
6	Derek Jeter, Wade Boggs, Darryl Strawberry	5.00
7	Chipper Jones, Tom Glavine, Greg Maddux, Ryan Klesko	4.00
8	Dwight Gooden, Gary Carter, Darryl Strawberry	2.00
9	Jackie Robinson, Roy Campanella, Duke Snider	3.00
10	Phil Rizzuto, Yogi Berra, Whitey Ford	2.00
11	Stan Musial, Curt Schilling, Marty Marion, Enos Slaughter	4.00

Team Bats

NM/M

Production 100 Sets

2	Derek Jeter, Roger Clemens, Bernie Williams, Andy Pettitte	30.00
3	Johnny Bench, Tony Perez, George Foster, Dave Concepcion	50.00
4	Josh Beckett, Dontrelle Willis, Ivan Rodriguez	15.00
5	Randy Johnson, Curt Schilling, Luis Gonzalez, Mark Grace	25.00
6	Derek Jeter, Wade Boggs, Darryl Strawberry	30.00
7	Chipper Jones, Tom Glavine, Greg Maddux, Ryan Klesko	25.00
8	Dwight Gooden, Gary Carter, Darryl Strawberry	20.00

Team Jerseys

NM/M

Production 100 unless noted.

1	Cal Ripken Jr., Eddie Murray, Jim Palmer	50.00
2	Derek Jeter, Roger Clemens, Bernie Williams, Andy Pettitte	40.00
4	Josh Beckett, Dontrelle Willis, Ivan Rodriguez	15.00
5	Randy Johnson, Curt Schilling, Luis Gonzalez, Mark Grace	25.00
6	Derek Jeter, Wade Boggs, Darryl Strawberry	30.00
7	Chipper Jones, Tom Glavine, Greg Maddux, Ryan Klesko	25.00
9	Jackie Robinson, Roy Campanella, Duke Snider	75.00
10	Phil Rizzuto, Yogi Berra, Whitey Ford	35.00
11	Stan Musial, Curt Schilling, Marty Marion, Enos Slaughter	50.00

Throwback Threads

NM/M

Quantity produced listed
Prime: 1.5-3X
Prime Singles Production 10-25
Prime Duals Production 5-15

1	Albert Pujols/150	60.00
2	Alex Rodriguez/Rgr/150	125.00
3	Alfonso Soriano/150	175.00
4	Chipper Jones/150	120.00
5	Derek Jeter/150	15.00
6	Greg Maddux/150	10.00
7	Hideo Nomo/150	8.00
8	Miguel Cabrera/150	8.00
9	Ivan Rodriguez/150	8.00
10	Jason Giambi/150	8.00
11	Jeff Bagwell/150	8.00
12	Lance Berkman/150	4.00
13	Mark Prior/150	8.00
14	Mike Piazza/150	10.00
15	Nomar Garciaparra/150	10.00
16	Pedro J. Martinez/150	8.00
17	Randy Johnson/150	8.00
18	Sammy Sosa/150	10.00
19	Shawn Green/150	4.00
20	Vladimir Guerrero/150	8.00
21	Adam Dunn, Austin Kearns/75	20.00
22	Barry Zito, Mark Mulder/75	10.00
23	Curt Schilling/75	10.00
24	Derek Jeter, Jason Giambi/75	25.00
25	Dontrelle Willis, Josh Beckett/75	15.00
26	Frank Thomas, Magglio Ordonez/75	15.00
27	Jim Thome/75	15.00
28	Kerry Wood, Mark Prior/75	25.00
29	Hank Blalock, Mark Teixeira/75	15.00
30	Albert Pujols, Scott Rolen/75	40.00
31	Babe Ruth/50	280.00
32	Cal Ripken Jr./100	40.00
33	Carl Yastrzemski/100	20.00
34	Deion Sanders/100	10.00
35	Don Mattingly/100	20.00
36	George Brett/100	20.00
37	Jim Palmer/100	8.00
38	Kirby Puckett/100	15.00
39	Lou Gehrig/100	125.00
40	Mark Grace/100	10.00
41	Mike Schmidt/100	20.00
42	Nolan Ryan/100	25.00
43	Ozzie Smith/100	20.00
44	Reggie Jackson/100	10.00
45	Rickey Henderson/100	10.00
46	Roberto Clemente/100	75.00
47	Roger Clemens/100	15.00
48	Roger Maris/100	40.00
49	Roy Campanella/Pants/100	20.00
50	Tony Gwynn/100	15.00
51	Babe Ruth, Lou Gehrig/25	400.00
52	Cal Ripken Jr., Eddie Murray/50	50.00
53	Ted Williams, Carl Yastrzemski/50	85.00
54	Andre Dawson, Gary Carter/50	20.00
55	Reggie Jackson, Rod Carew/50	20.00
56	Derek Jeter, Phil Rizzuto/50	40.00
57	Nolan Ryan, Roy Oswalt/50	40.00
58	Roger Clemens, Mike Mussina/50	25.00
59	Albert Pujols, Stan Musial/50	40.00
60	Nomar Garciaparra, Stan Musial/50	85.00

Throwback Threads Autographs

NM/M

Production 25 Sets
Prime: No Pricing

Production 5-10

9	Ivan Rodriguez/25	60.00
13	Mark Prior/25	80.00
18	Sammy Sosa/25	175.00
35	Don Mattingly/25	120.00
37	Jim Palmer/25	40.00

Throwback Threads Prime

No Pricing

Turn of the Century

Stars (1-150): 2-3X
Production 750
Stars (181-200): 1X
Production 250

2004 Donruss Elite Extra Edition

NM/M

Complete Set (288):
Common (1-150): .25
Common (206-215): 2.00
Production 1,000
Common Auto.(216-355): 6.00
Common No Auto. (234-254): 3.00
No Auto. Production 1,000
Pack (5): 14.00
Box (12): 150.00
Note: Cards 151-205 do not exist.

1	Troy Glaus	.40
2	John Lackey	.25
3	Garret Anderson	.40
4	Francisco Rodriguez	.25
5	Casey Kotchman	.25
6	Jose Guillen	.25
7	Miguel Tejada	.50
8	Rafael Palmeiro	.50
9	Jay Gibbons	.25
10	Melvin Mora	.25
11	Javy Lopez	.25
12	Pedro Martinez	.75
13	Curt Schilling	.75
14	David Ortiz	.75
15	Manny Ramirez	.75
16	Nomar Garciaparra	1.00
17	Magglio Ordonez	.25
18	Frank Thomas	.75
19	Esteban Loaiza	.25
20	Paul Konerko	.50
21	Mark Buehrle	.25
22	Jody Gerut	.25
23	Victor Martinez	.40
24	C.C. Sabathia	.25
25	Travis Hafner	.50
26	Cliff Lee	.25

27	Jeremy Bonderman	.40
28	Dallas McPherson	.25
29	Jermaine Dye	.25
30	Carlos Guillen	.25
31	Carlos Beltran	.50
32	Ken Harvey	.25
33	Mike Sweeney	.25
34	Angel Berroa	.25
35	Joe Nathan	.25
36	Johan Santana	.50
37	Jacque Jones	.25
38	Shannon Stewart	.25
39	Torii Hunter	.40
40	Derek Jeter	2.00
41	Jason Giambi	.50
42	Danny Graves	.25
43	Alfonso Soriano	.75
44	Gary Sheffield	.50
45	Mike Mussina	.50
46	Jorge Posada	.50
47	Hideki Matsui	1.00
48	Francisco Cordero	.25
49	Javier Vazquez	.25
50	Mariano Rivera	.40
51	Eric Chavez	.40
52	Tim Hudson	.40
53	Mark Mulder	.40
54	Barry Zito	.40
55	Ichiro Suzuki	1.50
56	Edgar Martinez	.25
57	Bret Boone	.25
58	Lew Ford	.25
59	B.J. Upton	.40
60	Aubrey Huff	.25
61	Rocco Baldelli	.25
62	Carl Crawford	.40
63	Delmon Young	.40
64	Mark Teixeira	.40
65	Hank Blalock	.50
66	Michael Young	.25
67	Alex Rodriguez	1.50
68	Carlos Delgado	.40
69	Milton Bradley	.25
70	Roy Halladay	.40
71	Vernon Wells	.25
72	Randy Johnson	.75
73	Bobby Crosby	.25
74	Lyle Overbay	.25
75	Luis Gonzalez	.25
76	Steve Finley	.25
77	Chipper Jones	.75
78	Andruw Jones	.40
79	Marcus Giles	.25
80	Rafael Furcal	.25
81	J.D. Drew	.40
82	Sammy Sosa	1.00
83	Kerry Wood	.40
84	Mark Prior	.75
85	Derrek Lee	.50
86	Moises Alou	.40
87	Carlos Zambrano	.40
88	Ken Griffey Jr.	1.00
89	Austin Kearns	.40
90	Adam Dunn	.50
91	Barry Larkin	.40
92	Todd Helton	.50
93	Larry Walker	.40
94	Preston Wilson	.25
95	Sean Casey	.25
96	Luis Castillo	.25
97	Josh Beckett	.25
98	Mike Lowell	.25
99	Miguel Cabrera	.75
100	Brad Penny	.25
101	Dontrelle Willis	.50
102	Andy Pettitte	.40
103	Wade Miller	.25
104	Jeff Bagwell	.50
105	Craig Biggio	.40
106	Lance Berkman	.40
107	Jeff Kent	.25
108	Roy Oswalt	.40
109	Hideo Nomo	.40
110	Adrian Beltre	.25
111	Paul LoDuca	.25
112	Shawn Green	.25
113	Roger Clemens	2.00
114	Eric Gagne	.40
115	Danny Kolb	.25
116	Rickie Weeks	.25
117	Scott Podsednik	.25
118	Livan Hernandez	.25
119	Orlando Cabrera	.25
120	Jose Vidro	.25
121	David Wright	1.50
122	Tom Glavine	.40
123	Al Leiter	.25
124	Mike Piazza	1.00
125	Jose Reyes	.50
126	Richard Hidalgo	.25
127	Eric Milton	.25
128	Jim Thome	.75
129	Mike Lieberthal	.25
130	Bobby Abreu	.40
131	Kip Wells	.25
132	Jack Wilson	.25
133	Jason Bay	.25
134	Brian Giles	.25
135	Sean Burroughs	.25
136	Khalil Greene	.25
137	Jake Peavy	.40
138	Jason Schmidt	.40
139	J.T. Snow	.25
140	Craig Wilson	.25
141	Chase Utley	.50

142 Jim Edmonds .40
143 Albert Pujols 2.00
144 Edgar Renteria .40
145 Scott Rolen .75
146 Matt Morris .25
147 Ivan Rodriguez .50
148 Vladimir Guerrero .75
149 Greg Maddux 1.00
150 Ben Sheets .40
206 Will Clark 2.00
207 Nolan Ryan 8.00
208 Bob Feller 2.00
209 Red Schoendienst 2.00
210 Brooks Robinson 3.00
211 Al Kaline 3.00
212 Ozzie Smith 4.00
213 Maury Wills 2.00
214 Steve Carlton 2.00
215 Duke Snider 3.00
216 Scott Lewis/Auto./603 **RC** 10.00
217 Josh Johnson/Auto./597 **RC** 10.00
218 Jeff Fiorentino/Auto./597 **RC** 10.00
219 Grant Hansen/Auto./599 **RC** 6.00
220 Yovani Gallardo/Auto./803 **RC** 50.00
221 Eddie Prasch/Auto./603 **RC** 10.00
222 Danny Hill/Auto./603 **RC** 6.00
223 Chuck Lofgren/Auto./803 **RC** 15.00
224 Blake Johnson/Auto./811 **RC** 10.00
225 Cory Dunlap/Auto./599 **RC** 15.00
226 Carlos Vasquez/Auto./869 **RC** 8.00
227 Jesse Crain/Auto./1000 **RC** 10.00
228 Yhency Brazoban/Auto./1000 **RC** 6.00
229 Abe Alvarez/Auto./1000 **RC** 8.00
230 Scott Kazmir/Auto./350 60.00
231 J.A. Happ/Auto./1195 **RC** 8.00
232 Mark Jecmen/Auto./1047 **RC** 6.00
234 Kameron Loe/1000 **RC** 3.00
235 Ervin Santana/1000 **RC** 5.00
239 Josh Karp/1000 **RC** 3.00
242 Alberto Callaspo/1000 **RC** 3.00
243 Jesse Hoover/Auto./1191 **RC** 8.00
246 Justin Hoyman/Auto./1124 **RC** 8.00
247 Juan Cedeno/1000 **RC** 3.00
250 Jake Dittler/1000 4.00
252 Benjamin Zobrist/Auto./1178 **RC** 10.00
253 Jeff Salazar/1000 **RC** 3.00
254 Fausto Carmona/1000 **RC** 4.00
256 Jorge Vasquez/Auto./1000 **RC** 6.00
257 Rafael Gonzalez/Auto./603 **RC** 6.00
258 Andrew Dobies/Auto./601 **RC** 10.00
259 Colby Miller/Auto./997 **RC** 6.00
260 K.C. Herren/Auto./735 **RC** 10.00
261 Ryan Meaux/Auto./546 **RC** 6.00
262 Dustin Pedroia/Auto./1114 **RC** 85.00
263 Fernando Nieve/Auto./1000 **RC** 10.00
264 Mariano Gomez/Auto./1000 **RC** 6.00
265 Eric Campbell/Auto./260 **RC** 50.00
266 Billy Killian/Auto./703 **RC** 6.00
267 Mike Rouse/Auto./999 6.00
268 Kyle Bono/Auto./1203 **RC** 8.00
269 Mitch Einertson/Auto./1047 **RC** 10.00
270 Scott Proctor/Auto./1000 **RC** 8.00
271 Tim Bittner/Auto./1000 **RC** 6.00
272 Christian Garcia/Auto./799 **RC** 10.00
273 Yadier Molina/Auto./1000 **RC** 20.00
275 Charles Thomas/Auto./907 **RC** 8.00
276 Travis Blackley/Auto./1000 **RC** 8.00
277 Frankie Francisco/Auto./1000 **RC** 6.00
278 Dioner Navarro/Auto./1000 **RC** 10.00
279 Joey Gathright/Auto./1000 **RC** 8.00
280 Kazuhito Tadano/Auto./1000 **RC** 15.00
281 Matt Bush/Auto./1100 **RC** 20.00
282 David Haehnel/Auto./865 **RC** 8.00
283 Tommy Hottovy/Auto./825 **RC** 8.00
284 Chris Carter/Auto./973 **RC** 25.00
285 Mark Rogers/Auto./578 **RC** 15.00
286 Jeremy Sowers/Auto./537 **RC** 25.00
287 Homer Bailey/Auto./1571 **RC** 25.00
288 Mike Butia/Auto./825 **RC** 8.00
289 Chris Nelson/Auto./465 **RC** 20.00
290 Thomas Diamond/Auto./1055 **RC** 15.00
291 Neil Walker/Auto./1343 **RC** 25.00
292 Sean Gamble/Auto./1229 **RC** 8.00
293 Bill Bray/Auto./1073 **RC** 6.00
294 Reid Brignac/Auto./522 **RC** 50.00
295 Ryan Klosterman/Auto./865 **RC** 6.00
296 David Purcey/Auto./1485 **RC** 8.00
297 Scott Elbert/Auto./1617 **RC** 25.00
298 Josh Fields/Auto./961 **RC** 25.00
299 Chris Lambert/Auto./954 **RC** 8.00
300 Trevor Plouffe/Auto./1329 **RC** 15.00
301 Greg Golson/Auto./1334 **RC** 20.00
302 Josh Baker/Auto./525 **RC** 8.00
303 Phillip Hughes/Auto./1485 **RC** 50.00
304 Matt Macri/Auto./979 **RC** 10.00
305 Kyle Waldrop/Auto./823 **RC** 10.00
306 Richie Robnett/Auto./1575 **RC** 15.00
307 Taylor Tankersley/Auto./1073 **RC** 8.00
308 Blake DeWitt/Auto./1562 **RC** 25.00
309 Daryl Jones/Auto./575 **RC** 15.00
310 Eric Hurley/Auto./1021 **RC** 30.00
311 J.P. Howell/Auto./1453 **RC** 10.00
312 Zach Jackson/Auto./1069 **RC** 8.00
313 Justin Orenduff/Auto./473 **RC** 10.00
314 Tyler Lumsden/Auto./473 **RC** 10.00
315 Matt Fox/Auto./473 **RC** 12.00
316 Danny Putnam/Auto./473 **RC** 10.00
317 Jon Poterson/Auto./464 **RC** 15.00
318 Gio Gonzalez/Auto./473 **RC** 30.00
319 Jay Rainville/Auto./823 **RC** 12.00
320 Huston Street/Auto./709 **RC** 25.00
321 Jeff Marquez/Auto./493 **RC** 15.00
322 Eric Beattie/Auto./930 **RC** 8.00
323 B.J. Szymanski/Auto./1327 **RC** 8.00
324 Seth Smith/Auto./1065 **RC** 15.00
325 Robert Johnson/Auto./790 **RC** 8.00
326 Wes Whisler/Auto./473 **RC** 8.00
327 Billy Buckner/Auto./673 **RC** 8.00
328 Jon Zeringue/Auto./473 **RC** 15.00
329 Curtis Thigpen/Auto./673 **RC** 10.00
330 Donny Lucy/Auto./573 **RC** 6.00
331 Mike Ferris/Auto./558 **RC** 10.00
332 Anthony Swarzak/Auto./370 **RC** 25.00
333 Jason Jaramillo/Auto./573 **RC** 8.00
334 Hunter Pence/Auto./672 **RC** 80.00
335 Mike Rozier/Auto./628 **RC** 8.00
336 Kurt Suzuki/Auto./473 **RC** 15.00
337 Jason Vargas/Auto./621 **RC** 15.00
338 Brian Bixler/Auto./665 **RC** 10.00
340 Dexter Fowler/Auto./623 **RC** 60.00
341 Mark Trumbo/Auto./1321 **RC** 20.00
342 Jeff Frazier/Auto./423 **RC** 15.00
343 Steven Register/Auto./673 **RC** 8.00
344 Michael Schlact/Auto./477 **RC** 8.00
345 Garrett Mock/Auto./471 **RC** 12.00
346 Eric Haberer/Auto./473 **RC** 8.00
347 Matt Tuiasosopo/Auto./473 **RC** 20.00
348 Jason Windsor/Auto./473 **RC** 15.00
349 Grant Johnson/Auto./815 **RC** 10.00
350 J.C. Holt/Auto./673 **RC** 10.00
351 Joseph Bauserman/Auto./472 **RC** 8.00
352 Jamar Walton/Auto./481 **RC** 15.00
353 Eric Patterson/Auto.1571 **RC** 15.00
354 Tyler Johnson/Auto./775 **RC** 15.00
355 Nick Adenhart/Auto./653 **RC** 60.00

Aspirations

1-150 print run 61-99: 4-8X
1-150 p/r 41-60: 6-12X
1-150 p/r 26-40: 8-15X
1-150 p/r 25 or less: No Pricing
206-355 p/r 51-99: 1-2X No auto.
216-355 p/r 61-99: .4-1X Auto.
216-355 p/r 41-60: .5-1X Auto.
216-355 p/r 26-40: .75-1X Auto.
No Pricing print run 25 or less.

Aspirations Gold

Gold (1-150): 10-20X
Gold (206-215): 3-6X
Gold (216-355): No Pricing
Production 25 Sets

Status

1-150 print run 61-99: 4-8X
1-150 p/r 41-60: 6-12X
1-150 p/r 26-40: 8-15X
1-150 p/r 25 or less: No Pricing
206-355 p/r 51-99: 1-2X No Auto.
216-355 p/r 61-99: .4-1X Auto.
216-355 p/r 41-60: .5-1X Auto.
216-355 p/r 26-40: .75-1X Auto.
No pricing print run 25 or less.

Status Gold

No Pricing
Production 10 Sets

Turn of the Century

(1-150): 3-5X
Production 250 Sets
(206-215): 2-3X
(216-355 no auto.): .5-1X
(216-355 auto.): .2-.5X
206-355 production 100

Back to Back Picks Signatures

NM/M

Quantity produced listed
1 Delmon Young, Rickie Weeks/25 40.00
3 Adam Dunn, Austin Kearns/25 50.00
5 Michael Young, Vernon Wells/25 35.00
6 Brian Roberts, Larry Bigbie/50 30.00
7 Ron Cey, Steve Garvey/50 35.00
8 Bill Madlock, Dave Parker/50 40.00
9 Derrek Lee, Torii Hunter, Trot Nixon/50 50.00
11 Chris Nelson, Matt Bush, Reid Brignac/250 65.00
12 B.J. Szymanski, Greg Golson, Jeff Frazier/250 40.00
13 Mark Trumbo, Nick Adenhart, Tyler Johnson/100 50.00
14 Chris Carter, Danny Putnam, Mark Jecmen/100 40.00
15 Billy Killian, Daryl Jones, Matt Bush/100 40.00
16 Blake DeWitt, Justin Orenduff, Scott Elbert/250 40.00
17 Jay Rainville, Kyle Waldrop, Trevor Plouffe/250 40.00
18 Jeff Marquez, Jon Poterson, Phillip Hughes/100 60.00
19 Wes Whisler, Tyler Lumsden, Wes Whisler/100 40.00
20 Curtis Thigpen, David Purcey, Zach Jackson/100 40.00

Career Best All-Stars

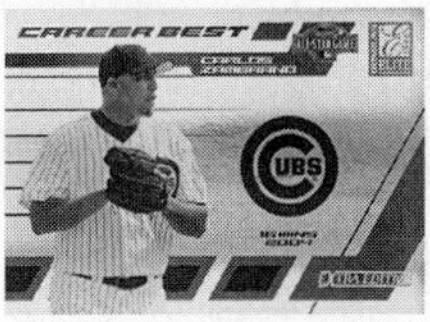

NM/M

Common Player:
Production 500 Sets
1 Randy Johnson 3.00
2 David Ortiz 3.00
3 Edgar Renteria 2.00
4 Victor Martinez 2.00
5 Albert Pujols 6.00
6 Hideki Matsui 5.00
7 Mariano Rivera 2.00
8 Carlos Zambrano 2.00
9 Hank Blalock 2.00
10 Michael Young 2.00
11 Mike Piazza 4.00
12 Alfonso Soriano 3.00
13 Carl Crawford 2.00
14 Scott Rolen 3.00
15 Vladimir Guerrero 3.00
16 Lance Berkman 2.00
17 Todd Helton 3.00
18 Curt Schilling 3.00
19 Francisco Cordero 2.00
20 Mark Mulder 2.00
21 Sammy Sosa 4.00
22 Roger Clemens 6.00
23 Miguel Cabrera 3.00
24 Manny Ramirez 3.00
25 Jim Thome 3.00

Career Best A-S Jersey

NM/M

Production 50 Sets
Prime: 1X-2X
Production 5-25
No pricing 15 or less.
1 Randy Johnson 15.00
2 David Ortiz 15.00
3 Edgar Renteria 8.00
4 Victor Martinez 8.00
5 Albert Pujols 25.00
6 Hideki Matsui 40.00
7 Mariano Rivera 10.00
8 Carlos Zambrano 8.00
9 Hank Blalock 10.00
10 Michael Young 8.00
11 Mike Piazza 20.00
12 Alfonso Soriano 15.00
13 Carl Crawford 8.00
14 Scott Rolen 15.00
15 Vladimir Guerrero 15.00
16 Lance Berkman 8.00
17 Todd Helton 10.00
18 Curt Schilling 15.00
19 Francisco Cordero 8.00
20 Mark Mulder 8.00
21 Sammy Sosa 20.00
22 Roger Clemens 20.00
23 Miguel Cabrera 12.00
24 Manny Ramirez 15.00
25 Jim Thome 15.00

Career Best A-S Jersey Prime

NM/M

2 David Ortiz/25 25.00
4 Victor Martinez/25 15.00
5 Albert Pujols/25 40.00
6 Hideki Matsui/25 75.00
8 Carlos Zambrano/25 15.00
9 Hank Blalock/25 20.00
10 Michael Young/25 15.00
11 Mike Piazza/25 30.00
12 Alfonso Soriano/25 25.00
13 Carl Crawford/25 15.00
14 Scott Rolen/25 25.00
15 Vladimir Guerrero/25 25.00
16 Lance Berkman/25 15.00
17 Todd Helton/25 20.00
18 Curt Schilling/25 25.00
20 Mark Mulder/25 15.00
21 Sammy Sosa/25 30.00
22 Roger Clemens/25 40.00
23 Miguel Cabrera/25 20.00
24 Manny Ramirez/25 25.00
25 Jim Thome/25 25.00

Career Best A-S Sig. Black

No Pricing
Production 1-5

Career Best A-S Sign. Gold

No Pricing
Production 1-10

Career Best A-S Signature Jersey Gold

NM/M

Production 1-25
2 David Ortiz/25 75.00
3 Edgar Renteria/25 40.00
4 Victor Martinez/25 40.00
8 Carlos Zambrano/25 40.00
10 Michael Young/25 35.00
13 Carl Crawford/25 30.00
19 Francisco Cordero/25 20.00

Career Best A-S Signature Jersey Prime

No Pricing
Production 1-10

Draft Class

NM/M

Common Duo: 2.00
Production 500 Sets
1 Johnny Bench, Nolan Ryan 10.00
2 Bert Blyleven, Dwight Evans 2.00
3 Jim Rice, Keith Hernandez 2.00
4 Dennis Eckersley, Gary Carter 3.00
5 Fred Lynn, Robin Yount 5.00
6 Andre Dawson, Lee Smith 2.00
7 Alan Trammell, Jack Morris 2.00
8 Harold Baines, Paul Molitor 3.00
9 Cal Ripken Jr., Kirk Gibson 10.00
10 Don Mattingly, Orel Hershiser 6.00
11 Darryl Strawberry, Eric Davis 2.00
12 Dwight Gooden, Jose Canseco 3.00
13 Rafael Palmeiro, Randy Johnson 4.00
14 Curt Schilling, Gary Sheffield 3.00
15 Mike Piazza, Robin Ventura 4.00
16 Frank Thomas, Jeff Bagwell 3.00
17 Chipper Jones, Mike Mussina 3.00
18 Garret Anderson, Jorge Posada 2.00
19 Scott Rolen, Torii Hunter 3.00
20 Kerry Wood, Todd Helton 3.00
21 Eric Chavez, Roy Oswalt 2.00
22 Johnny Estrada, Vernon Wells 2.00
23 Lance Berkman, Tim Hudson 2.00
24 Mark Buehrle, Mark Mulder 2.00
25 C.C. Sabathia, Sean Burroughs 2.00

26 Albert Pujols, Barry Zito 6.00
27 Rich Harden, Rocco Baldelli 2.00
28 Bobby Crosby, Mark Teixeira 2.00
29 Casey Kotchman, Mark Prior 3.00
30 Dewon Brazelton, Jeremy Bonderman 2.00
31 J.C. Holt, Jon Zeringue 3.00
32 Kyle Bono, Matt Fox 3.00
33 Dexter Fowler, Mike Rozier 3.00
34 Huston Street, J.P. Howell 3.00
35 Grant Johnson, Matt Macri 3.00
36 Eric Beattie, Jeff Frazier 3.00
37 Jason Windsor, Kurt Suzuki 5.00
38 Josh Fields, Matt Tuiasosopo 6.00
39 Joseph Bauserman, K.C. Herren 3.00
40 Chris Lambert, Eric Haberer, Matt Tuiasosopo 3.00

Passing the Torch

NM/M

Common Duo: 3.00
Production 500 Sets
1 Dennis Eckersley, Huston Street 4.00
2 Matt Bush, Tony Gwynn 6.00
3 Homer Bailey, Tom Seaver 4.00
4 Bob Feller,Jeremy Sowers 3.00
5 Josh Fields, Robin Ventura 3.00
6 Nolan Ryan, Thomas Diamond 8.00
7 Eric Patterson, Ryne Sandberg 6.00
8 Richie Robnett, Rickey Henderson 4.00
9 Mike Ferris, Stan Musial 5.00
10 Bobby Doerr, Dustin Pedroia 3.00

Passing the Torch Autograph Black

No Pricing
Production 5-10 Sets

Passing the Torch Autograph Gold

NM/M

Production 5-25
2 Matt Bush, Tony Gwynn/25 90.00
4 Bob Feller, Jeremy Sowers/25 60.00
10 Bobby Doerr, Dustin Pedroia/25 80.00

Round Numbers

NM/M

Common Player: 2.00
Production 500 Sets
1 Ozzie Smith 4.00
2 Derek Jeter 6.00
3 Alex Rodriguez 5.00
4 Paul Molitor 3.00
5 George Brett 6.00
6 Delmon Young 2.00
7 Dontrelle Willis 2.00
8 Gary Carter 2.00
9 Reggie Jackson 3.00
10 Andre Dawson 2.00
11 Neil Walker 2.00
12 Laynce Nix 2.00
13 Matt Bush 6.00
14 Lyle Overbay 2.00
15 Carlos Beltran 3.00
16 Todd Helton 3.00
17 Mark Grace 2.00
18 Fred Lynn 2.00
19 Robin Yount 4.00
20 Mike Schmidt 6.00
21 Roger Clemens 6.00
22 Will Clark 3.00
23 Don Mattingly 5.00
24 Blake DeWitt 2.00
25 Rafael Palmeiro 3.00
26 Wade Boggs 3.00
27 Mark Rogers 5.00
28 Billy Buckner 3.00
29 Jeff Baker 2.00
30 Nolan Ryan 8.00
31 Mike Piazza 4.00
32 Alexis Rios 2.00
33 Eddie Murray 3.00
34 Jose Canseco 3.00
35 Mike Mussina 3.00
36 Eric Beattie 3.00
37 Keith Hernandez 2.00
38 Michael Young 2.00
39 Dwight Evans 2.00
40 Scott Elbert 3.00
41 Adrian Gonzalez 2.00
42 Johnny Bench 3.00
43 Dennis Eckersley 2.00
44 Dale Murphy 3.00
45 Ryne Sandberg 4.00
46 David Wright 3.00
47 Hank Blalock 3.00
48 Orel Hershiser 2.00
49 Sean Casey 2.00
50 Albert Pujols 6.00

Round Numbers Signature

NM/M

Production 5-250
1 Ozzie Smith/25 65.00
4 Paul Molitor/25 35.00
6 Delmon Young/50 25.00
7 Dontrelle Willis/25 20.00
8 Gary Carter/50 20.00
10 Andre Dawson/50 20.00
11 Neil Walker/250 20.00
12 Laynce Nix/50 20.00
13 Matt Bush/100 40.00
14 Lyle Overbay/50 15.00
15 Carlos Beltran/25 50.00
17 Mark Grace/25 35.00
18 Fred Lynn/50 15.00
20 Mike Schmidt/25 85.00
22 Will Clark/20 60.00
23 Don Mattingly/25 80.00
24 Blake DeWitt/250 30.00
27 Mark Rogers/100 40.00
28 Billy Buckner/100 15.00
32 Alexis Rios/50 15.00
34 Jose Canseco/25 50.00
36 Eric Beattie/100 10.00
37 Keith Hernandez/50 20.00
38 Michael Young/50 20.00
39 Dwight Evans/50 25.00
40 Scott Elbert/250 15.00
41 Adrian Gonzalez/50 10.00
43 Dennis Eckersley/50 30.00
44 Dale Murphy/50 30.00
46 David Wright/25 75.00
47 Hank Blalock/25 20.00
49 Sean Casey/25 15.00

Signature

NM/M

Production 1-50
132 Jack Wilson/25 25.00
133 Jason Bay/25 25.00
231 J.A. Happ/50 10.00
233 Mark Jecmen/50 8.00
234 Kameron Loe/50 20.00
235 Ervin Santana/50 50.00
239 Josh Karp/50 15.00
243 Jesse Hoover/50 10.00
246 Justin Hoyman/50 15.00
247 Juan Cedeno/50 15.00
252 Benjamin Zobrist/50 10.00
253 Jeff Salazar/50 30.00
254 Fausto Carmona/50 20.00

Signature Aspirations

NM/M

Production 1-100
Golds: No Pricing
Production 1-25
216 Scott Lewis/50 15.00
217 Josh Johnson/50 15.00
218 Jeff Fiorentino/50 25.00
219 Grant Hansen/50 8.00
220 Yovani Gallardo/50 80.00
221 Eddie Prasch/50 10.00
222 Danny Hill/50 8.00
223 Chuck Lofgren/50 40.00
224 Blake Johnson/50 15.00
225 Cory Dunlap/50 20.00
226 Carlos Vasquez/50 10.00
227 Jesse Crain/50 15.00
228 Yhency Brazoban/50 10.00
229 Abe Alvarez/50 10.00
256 Jorge Vasquez/50 8.00
257 Rafael Gonzalez/50 8.00
258 Andrew Dobies/50 15.00
259 Colby Miller/49 10.00
260 K.C. Herren/50 15.00
261 Ryan Meaux/50 10.00
262 Dustin Pedroia/50 175.00
263 Fernando Nieve/50 8.00
264 Mariano Gomez/50 8.00
266 Billy Killian/50 8.00
267 Mike Rouse/50 10.00
268 Kyle Bono/50 10.00
269 Mitch Einertson/50 25.00
270 Scott Proctor/50 15.00
271 Tim Bittner/50 8.00
272 Christian Garcia/50 10.00
273 Yadier Molina/50 30.00
274 Justin Leone/50 15.00
275 Charles Thomas/50 15.00
276 Travis Blackley/50 10.00
277 Frankie Francisco/50 10.00
278 Dioner Navarro/50 15.00
279 Joey Gathright/50 10.00
280 Kazuhito Tadano/50 20.00
281 Matt Bush/100 30.00
282 David Haehnel/100 10.00
283 Tommy Hottovy/100 10.00
284 Chris Carter/100 30.00
286 Jeremy Sowers/100 40.00
287 Homer Bailey/100 30.00
288 Mike Butia/100 10.00
289 Chris Nelson/100 40.00
290 Thomas Diamond/100 30.00
291 Neil Walker/100 30.00
292 Sean Gamble/100 10.00
293 Bill Bray/100 8.00
294 Reid Brignac/50 75.00
295 Ryan Klosterman/100 8.00
296 David Purcey/100 10.00
297 Scott Elbert/100 50.00
298 Josh Fields/100 40.00
299 Chris Lambert/100 10.00
300 Trevor Plouffe/100 25.00
301 Greg Golson/100 20.00
302 Josh Baker/100 10.00
303 Phillip Hughes/100 75.00
304 Matt Macri/50 12.00
305 Kyle Waldrop/100 25.00
306 Richie Robnett/100 25.00
307 Taylor Tankersley/100 10.00
308 Blake DeWitt/100 40.00
309 Daryl Jones/50 25.00
310 Eric Hurley/100 40.00
311 J.P. Howell/100 10.00
312 Zach Jackson/100 20.00
313 Justin Orenduff/100 20.00
314 Tyler Lumsden/100 15.00
315 Matt Fox/100 15.00
316 Danny Putnam/100 15.00
317 Jon Poterson/100 20.00
318 Gio Gonzalez/100 40.00
319 Jay Rainville/100 25.00
320 Huston Street/100 40.00
321 Jeff Marquez/100 15.00
322 Eric Beattie/100 10.00
323 B.J. Szymanski/100 10.00
324 Seth Smith/100 30.00
325 Robert Johnson/100 10.00
326 Wes Whisler/50 10.00
327 Billy Buckner/50 10.00
328 Jon Zeringue/100 30.00
329 Curtis Thigpen/50 12.00
330 Donny Lucy/50 10.00
331 Mike Ferris/100 12.00
333 Jason Jaramillo/100 10.00
334 Hunter Pence/50 125.00
335 Mike Rozier/50 10.00
336 Kurt Suzuki/100 25.00
337 Jason Vargas/50 40.00
338 Brian Bixler/50 10.00
340 Dexter Fowler/50 100.00
341 Mark Trumbo/50 40.00
342 Jeff Frazier/100 20.00
343 Steven Register/50 10.00
344 Michael Schlact/50 10.00
345 Garrett Mock/50 15.00
346 Eric Haberer/50 10.00
347 Matt Tuiasosopo/100 30.00
348 Jason Windsor/50 20.00
349 Grant Johnson/50 10.00
350 J.C. Holt/50 10.00
351 Joseph Bauserman/50 10.00
352 Jamar Walton/50 10.00
353 Eric Patterson/100 35.00
354 Tyler Johnson/50 25.00
355 Nick Adenhart/100 80.00

Signature Status

NM/M

Production 1-50
Golds: No Pricing
Production 1-10
221 Eddie Prasch/25 15.00
224 Blake Johnson/25 20.00
229 Abe Alvarez/25 15.00
257 Rafael Gonzalez/25 10.00
268 Kyle Bono/25 15.00
272 Christian Garcia/25 15.00
276 Travis Blackley/25 15.00
281 Matt Bush/50 40.00
282 David Haehnel/50 15.00
283 Tommy Hottovy/50 15.00
284 Chris Carter/50 40.00
286 Jeremy Sowers/50 40.00
287 Homer Bailey/50 40.00
288 Mike Butia/50 15.00
289 Chris Nelson/50 40.00
290 Thomas Diamond/50 40.00
291 Neil Walker/50 40.00
292 Sean Gamble/50 15.00
293 Bill Bray/50 10.00
294 Reid Brignac/50 80.00
295 Ryan Klosterman/50 10.00
296 David Purcey/50 15.00
297 Scott Elbert/50 60.00
298 Josh Fields/50 50.00
299 Chris Lambert/50 15.00
300 Trevor Plouffe/50 25.00
301 Greg Golson/50 35.00
302 Josh Baker/50 15.00
303 Phillip Hughes/50 100.00
304 Matt Macri/50 15.00
305 Kyle Waldrop/50 25.00
306 Richie Robnett/50 25.00
307 Taylor Tankersley/50 15.00
308 Blake DeWitt/50 50.00
309 Daryl Jones/50 30.00
310 Eric Hurley/50 50.00
311 J.P. Howell/50 20.00
312 Zach Jackson/50 15.00
313 Justin Orenduff/50 20.00
314 Tyler Lumsden/50 20.00
315 Matt Fox/50 20.00
316 Danny Putnam/50 20.00
317 Jon Poterson/50 20.00
318 Gio Gonzalez/50 50.00
319 Jay Rainville/50 35.00
320 Huston Street/50 50.00
321 Jeff Marquez/50 20.00
322 Eric Beattie/50 15.00
323 B.J. Szymanski/50 15.00
324 Seth Smith/50 40.00
325 Robert Johnson/50 15.00
326 Wes Whisler/50 15.00
327 Billy Buckner/50 15.00
328 Jon Zeringue/50 35.00
329 Curtis Thigpen/50 12.00
330 Donny Lucy/50 15.00
331 Mike Ferris/50 15.00
333 Jason Jaramillo/50 15.00
334 Hunter Pence/50 125.00
335 Mike Rozier/50 15.00
336 Kurt Suzuki/50 25.00
337 Jason Vargas/50 50.00
338 Brian Bixler/50 15.00
340 Dexter Fowler/50 100.00
341 Mark Trumbo/50 40.00
342 Jeff Frazier/50 20.00
343 Steven Register/50 10.00
344 Michael Schlact/50 10.00
345 Garrett Mock/50 15.00
346 Eric Haberer/50 10.00
347 Matt Tuiasosopo/50 40.00
348 Jason Windsor/50 20.00
349 Grant Johnson/50 10.00
350 J.C. Holt/50 10.00
351 Joseph Bauserman/50 10.00
352 Jamar Walton/50 25.00
353 Eric Patterson/50 35.00
354 Tyler Johnson/50 15.00
355 Nick Adenhart/50 120.00

Signature Turn of Century

NM/M

216 Scott Lewis/100 12.00
217 Josh Johnson/100 12.00
218 Jeff Fiorentino/100 10.00
219 Grant Hansen/100 8.00
220 Yovani Gallardo/100 60.00
221 Eddie Prasch/100 10.00
222 Danny Hill/100 8.00
223 Chuck Lofgren/100 25.00
224 Blake Johnson/100 20.00
225 Cory Dunlap/100 20.00
226 Carlos Vasquez/100 10.00
227 Jesse Crain/100 15.00
228 Yhency Brazoban/100 10.00
229 Abe Alvarez/100 10.00
246 Justin Hoyman/250 10.00
252 Benjamin Zobrist/150 10.00
256 Jorge Vasquez/100 8.00
257 Rafael Gonzalez/100 8.00
258 Andrew Dobies/100 15.00
259 Colby Miller/100 10.00
260 K.C. Herren/100 15.00
261 Ryan Meaux/100 10.00
262 Dustin Pedroia/100 120.00
263 Fernando Nieve/100 10.00
264 Mariano Gomez/100 10.00
266 Billy Killian/100 15.00
267 Mike Rouse/100 10.00
268 Kyle Bono/100 10.00
269 Mitch Einertson/100 15.00
270 Scott Proctor/100 10.00
271 Tim Bittner/100 8.00
272 Christian Garcia/100 10.00
273 Yadier Molina/100 30.00
274 Justin Leone/100 15.00
275 Charles Thomas/100 15.00
276 Travis Blackley/100 10.00
277 Frankie Francisco/100 10.00
278 Dioner Navarro/100 15.00
279 Joey Gathright/100 15.00
280 Kazuhito Tadano/100 15.00
281 Matt Bush/250 20.00
282 David Haehnel/250 8.00
283 Tommy Hottovy/250 8.00
284 Chris Carter/250 25.00
285 Mark Rogers/100 25.00
286 Jeremy Sowers/250 25.00
287 Homer Bailey/250 30.00
288 Mike Butia/250 8.00
289 Chris Nelson/100 25.00
290 Thomas Diamond/250 25.00
291 Neil Walker/242 25.00
292 Sean Gamble/250 8.00
293 Bill Bray/250 8.00
294 Reid Brignac/100 60.00
295 Ryan Klosterman/250 8.00
296 David Purcey/250 8.00
297 Scott Elbert/250 40.00
298 Josh Fields/250 40.00
299 Chris Lambert/250 15.00
300 Trevor Plouffe/250 15.00
301 Greg Golson/250 20.00
302 Josh Baker/100 10.00
303 Phillip Hughes/250 60.00
304 Matt Macri/250 15.00
305 Kyle Waldrop/250 15.00
306 Richie Robnett/250 15.00
307 Taylor Tankersley/250 10.00
308 Blake DeWitt/250 25.00
309 Daryl Jones/250 15.00
310 Eric Hurley/250 30.00
311 J.P. Howell/250 10.00
312 Zach Jackson/250 10.00
313 Justin Orenduff/100 15.00
314 Tyler Lumsden/250 10.00
315 Matt Fox/250 12.00
316 Danny Putnam/250 12.00
317 Jon Poterson/238 12.00
318 Gio Gonzalez/250 30.00
319 Jay Rainville/250 20.00
320 Huston Street/250 25.00
321 Jeff Marquez/250 10.00
322 Eric Beattie/250 8.00
323 B.J. Szymanski/250 8.00
324 Seth Smith/250 20.00
325 Robert Johnson/100 10.00
326 Wes Whisler/100 8.00
327 Billy Buckner/100 10.00
328 Jon Zeringue/250 20.00
329 Curtis Thigpen/100 10.00
330 Donny Lucy/100 8.00
331 Mike Ferris/250 10.00
332 Anthony Swarzak/100 25.00

333 Jason Jaramillo/250 8.00
334 Hunter Pence/200 100.00
335 Mike Rozier/250 8.00
336 Kurt Suzuki/250 20.00
337 Jason Vargas/200 20.00
338 Brian Bixler/200 8.00
340 Dexter Fowler/250 60.00
341 Mark Trumbo/250 25.00
342 Jeff Frazier/50 20.00
343 Steven Register/200 8.00
344 Michael Schlact/200 8.00
345 Garrett Mock/200 15.00
346 Eric Haberer/100 8.00
347 Matt Tuiasosopo/250 25.00
348 Jason Windsor/100 15.00
349 Grant Johnson/250 8.00
350 J.C. Holt/100 8.00
351 Joseph Bauserman/100 8.00
352 Jamar Walton/200 12.00
353 Eric Patterson/250 25.00
354 Tyler Johnson/250 15.00
355 Nick Adenhart/100 75.00

Throwback Threads

NM/M

Production 50 Sets
1 Roger Maris 60.00
2 Ted Williams 80.00
3 Cal Ripken Jr. 75.00
4 Duke Snider 20.00
5 George Brett 40.00

Throwback Threads Auto.

No Pricing

2004 Donruss Leather & Lumber

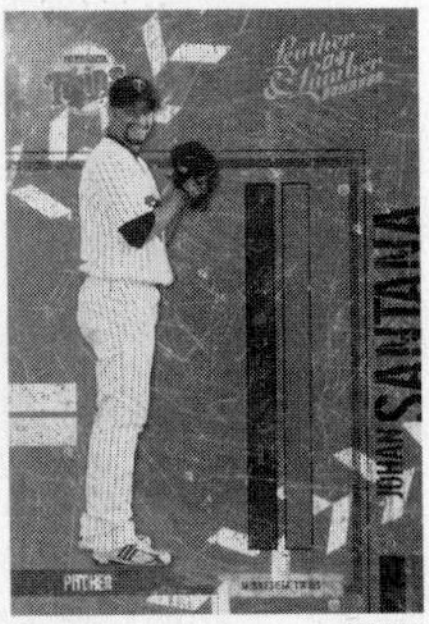

NM/M

Complete Set (175):
Common Player (1-150): .25
Common Auto. (151-173): 6.00
Production 500
Pack (5): 5.00
Box (24): 100.00
1 Bartolo Colon .25
2 Garret Anderson .50
3 Tim Salmon .40
4 Troy Glaus .50
5 Vladimir Guerrero 1.00
6 Brandon Webb .25
7 Luis Gonzalez .40
8 Randy Johnson 1.00
9 Richie Sexson .50
10 Shea Hillenbrand .25
11 Adam LaRoche .25
12 Andruw Jones .50
13 Chipper Jones 1.00
14 Dale Murphy .75
15 J.D. Drew .50
16 Marcus Giles .25
17 Rafael Furcal .25
18 Cal Ripken Jr. 3.00
19 Javy Lopez .50
20 Jay Gibbons .25
21 Luis Matos .25
22 Miguel Tejada .50
23 Rafael Palmeiro .75
24 Curt Schilling .75
25 Jason Varitek .40
26 Manny Ramirez .75
27 Nomar Garciaparra 1.50
28 Pedro J. Martinez 1.00
29 Trot Nixon .25
30 Greg Maddux 1.50
31 Kerry Wood 1.00
32 Mark Prior 1.00
33 Ryne Sandberg 1.50
34 Sammy Sosa 2.00
35 Carlos Lee .25
36 Frank Thomas .75
37 Magglio Ordonez .40
38 Paul Konerko .25
39 Adam Dunn .75
40 Austin Kearns .25
41 Barry Larkin .50
42 Ken Griffey Jr. 1.50
43 Ryan Wagner .25
44 C.C. Sabathia .25
45 Jody Gerut .25
46 Omar Vizquel .25
47 Larry Walker .40
48 Preston Wilson .25
49 Todd Helton .75
50 Alan Trammell .25
51 Ivan Rodriguez .75
52 Jeremy Bonderman .25
53 Dontrelle Willis .25
54 Josh Beckett .50
55 Luis Castillo .25
56 Miguel Cabrera 1.00
57 Mike Lowell .25
58 Andy Pettitte .40
59 Craig Biggio .40
60 Jeff Bagwell .75
61 Jeff Kent .40
62 Lance Berkman .40
63 Roger Clemens 2.50
64 Roy Oswalt .40
65 Angel Berroa .25
66 Carlos Beltran .75
67 George Brett 2.00
68 Juan Gonzalez .50
69 Mike Sweeney .25
70 Eric Gagne .50
71 Hideo Nomo .50
72 Kazuhisa Ishii .25
73 Paul LoDuca .25
74 Shawn Green .50
75 Geoff Jenkins .25
76 Junior Spivey .25
77 Rickie Weeks .25
78 Robin Yount .75
79 Scott Podsednik .25
80 Jacque Jones .25
81 Johan Santana .50
82 Shannon Stewart .25
83 Torii Hunter .40
84 Andre Dawson .50
85 Chad Cordero .25
86 Jose Vidro .25
87 Nick Johnson .25
88 Orlando Cabrera .40
89 Gary Carter .50
90 Jae Weong Seo .25
91 Jose Reyes .50
92 Mike Piazza 1.50
93 Tom Glavine .50
94 Alex Rodriguez 2.50
95 Bernie Williams .50
96 Derek Jeter 2.50
97 Don Mattingly 2.00
98 Gary Sheffield .50
99 Hideki Matsui 1.50
100 Jason Giambi .50
101 Jorge Posada .50
102 Mike Mussina .50
103 Barry Zito .50
104 Bobby Crosby .25
105 Eric Chavez .40
106 Jermaine Dye .25
107 Mark Mulder .40
108 Rich Harden .25
109 Rickey Henderson .25
110 Tim Hudson .40
111 Bobby Abreu .40
112 Brett Myers .25
113 Jim Thome 1.00
114 Kevin Millwood .25
115 Marlon Byrd .25
116 Mike Schmidt 2.00
117 Pat Burrell .25
118 Dave Parker .25
119 Jason Bay .25
120 Jason Kendall .25
121 Brian Giles .25
122 Jay Payton .25
123 Ryan Klesko .25
124 Tony Gwynn 1.00
125 Edgardo Alfonzo .25
126 Jason Schmidt .50
127 Jerome Williams .25
128 Bret Boone .25
129 Edgar Martinez .25
130 Ichiro Suzuki 2.00
131 Jamie Moyer .25
132 John Olerud .25
133 Albert Pujols 2.00
134 Edgar Renteria .40
135 Jim Edmonds .50
136 Matt Morris .25
137 Scott Rolen 1.00
138 Aubrey Huff .25
139 Carl Crawford .25
140 Delmon Young .25
141 Rocco Baldelli .25
142 Alfonso Soriano 1.00
143 Hank Blalock .75
144 Mark Teixeira .50
145 Michael Young .25
146 Nolan Ryan 2.50
147 Carlos Delgado .50
148 Eric Hinske .25
149 Roy Halladay .25
150 Vernon Wells .25
151 Andres Blanco **RC** 8.00
152 Kevin Cave **RC** 6.00
153 Ryan Meaux **RC** 6.00
154 Tim Bausher **RC** 6.00
155 Jesse Harper **RC** 6.00
156 Mike Wuertz **RC** 8.00
157 Colby Miller **RC** 8.00
158 Donald Kelly **RC** 6.00
159 Edwin Moreno **RC** 8.00
160 Mike Johnston **RC** 6.00
161 Orlando Rodriguez **RC** 6.00
162 Phil Stockman **RC** 8.00
163 Yadier Molina **RC** 8.00
164 Jorge Vasquez **RC** 6.00
165 Scott Proctor **RC** 8.00
166 Jake Woods 6.00
167 Aarom Baldiris **RC** 8.00
168 Jason Bartlett **RC** 6.00
169 Casey Daigle **RC** 6.00
170 Dennis Sarfate **RC** 6.00
171 Edwardo Sierra **RC** 8.00
172 Merkin Valdez **RC** 8.00
173 Eddy Rodriguez **RC** 8.00
174 Kazuo Matsui **RC** 8.00
175 David Aardsma **RC** 4.00

Gold

Stars (1-150): 10-15X
SP's (151-175): No Pricing
Production 25 Sets

Platinum

No Pricing
Production One Set

Silver

Stars (1-150): 4-8X
SP's (151-175): .5X
Production 100 Sets

B/W

NM/M

Common Player: 1.50
Production 1,000 Sets
Gold B/W: 4-6X
Production 25 Sets
Silver B/W: 2-3X
Production 100 Sets
Platinum B/W: No Pricing
Production One Set
13 Chipper Jones 2.00
14 Dale Murphy 1.50
18 Cal Ripken Jr. 8.00
27 Nomar Garciaparra 3.00
30 Greg Maddux 2.50
32 Mark Prior 1.50
33 Ryne Sandberg 3.00
34 Sammy Sosa 3.00
63 Roger Clemens 4.00
67 George Brett 4.00
78 Robin Yount 3.00
89 Gary Carter 1.50
92 Mike Piazza 3.00
94 Alex Rodriguez 5.00
96 Derek Jeter 5.00
97 Don Mattingly 4.00
99 Hideki Matsui 3.00
109 Rickey Henderson 1.50
116 Mike Schmidt 3.00
124 Tony Gwynn 2.00
130 Ichiro Suzuki 4.00
133 Albert Pujols 4.00
142 Alfonso Soriano 2.00
146 Nolan Ryan 5.00
174 Kazuo Matsui 6.00

Bat-Spikes

NM/M

Bat/Glove: .75-1.5X
Production 1-50
Bat/Ball: .75-1.5X
Production 5-25
No pricing 15 or less.
Barrel/Jersey: No Pricing
Production 1-5
1 Andruw Jones/25 15.00
3 Angel Berroa/25 10.00
6 Barry Zito/25 15.00
7 Ben Sheets/50 10.00
8 Brad Penny/50 8.00
9 Brian Giles/50 8.00
10 Carlos Lee/50 8.00
11 Corey Patterson/50 15.00
13 Don Mattingly/25 40.00
15 Gary Carter/50 12.00
17 Ivan Rodriguez/50 15.00
18 Jack Cust/50 8.00
19 Jason Jennings/50 8.00
21 Jim Edmonds/50 10.00
22 Joe Borchard/50 8.00
23 Joe Crede/50 8.00
24 Josh Beckett/25 15.00
25 Josh Phelps/50 8.00
26 Juan Pierre/50 8.00
27 Kenny Lofton/50 8.00
29 Lance Berkman/25 15.00
30 Magglio Ordonez/25 10.00
31 Marcus Giles/50 10.00
32 Mark Buehrle/50 8.00
33 Mark Prior/25 20.00
34 Mark Teixeira/25 15.00
35 Marlon Byrd/50 8.00
38 Nick Johnson/25 10.00
39 Orlando Hudson/50 8.00
40 Paul LoDuca/25 10.00
41 Rafael Palmeiro/25 20.00
43 Roy Oswalt/25 15.00
44 Ryan Klesko/50 10.00
46 Sean Casey/50 10.00
48 Travis Hafner/50 15.00
49 Victor Martinez/50 10.00
50 Wade Miller/50 10.00

Cuts

NM/M

Common Player:
1 Adam Dunn/192 20.00

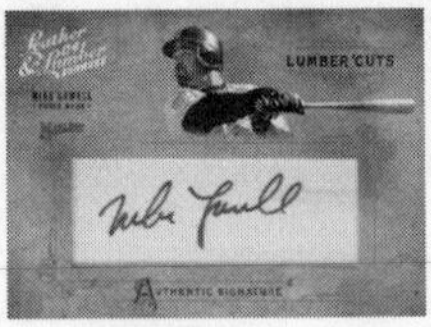

2 Al Kaline/192 35.00
3 Alfonso Soriano/160 40.00
4 Andre Dawson/224 15.00
5 Angel Berroa/224 10.00
6 Harmon Killebrew/192 35.00
7 Bob Gibson/96 30.00
8 Brooks Robinson/192 30.00
9 Cal Ripken Jr./32 200.00
10 Dale Murphy/224 25.00
11 Darryl Strawberry/224 15.00
12 Delmon Young/192 20.00
13 Don Mattingly/96 65.00
14 Duke Snider/96 30.00
15 Dwight Gooden/224 15.00
16 Ozzie Smith/96 60.00
18 Garret Anderson/224 15.00
19 Gary Carter/160 20.00
20 George Kell/224 15.00
21 Hank Blalock/224 20.00
22 Jim Palmer/192 20.00
23 Kirk Gibson/160 15.00
24 Lou Brock/192 25.00
25 Ryne Sandberg/160 50.00
26 Mark Prior/160 40.00
27 Miguel Cabrera/224 25.00
28 Mike Lowell/160 15.00
29 Nolan Ryan/96 100.00
30 Luis Aparicio/224 15.00
31 Paul Molitor/160 30.00
32 Red Schoendienst/224 25.00
33 Rickie Weeks/224 10.00
34 Ron Santo/224 25.00
35 Roy Oswalt/224 20.00
36 Stan Musial/96 60.00
37 Steve Carlton/192 20.00
38 Tony Gwynn/192 35.00
39 Vernon Wells/160 10.00
40 Will Clark/192 35.00
41 Bob Feller/224 25.00
42 Bobby Doerr/224 20.00
44 Ralph Kiner/224 30.00
45 Torii Hunter/224 15.00
46 Rollie Fingers/224 15.00
47 Steve Garvey/224 15.00
48 Alan Trammell/224 15.00
49 Maury Wills/224 15.00
50 Gaylord Perry/224 15.00

Cuts Glove

NM/M

Quantity produced listed
1 Adam Dunn/192 20.00
2 Al Kaline/192 35.00
3 Alfonso Soriano/160 40.00
4 Andre Dawson/224 15.00
5 Angel Berroa/224 10.00
6 Harmon Killebrew/192 35.00
7 Bob Gibson/96 30.00
8 Brooks Robinson/192 30.00
9 Cal Ripken Jr./32 200.00
10 Dale Murphy/224 25.00
11 Darryl Strawberry/224 15.00
12 Delmon Young/192 20.00
13 Don Mattingly/96 65.00
14 Duke Snider/96 30.00
15 Dwight Gooden/224 15.00
16 Ozzie Smith/96 60.00
18 Garret Anderson/224 15.00
19 Gary Carter/160 20.00
20 George Kell/224 15.00
21 Hank Blalock/224 20.00
22 Jim Palmer/192 20.00
23 Kirk Gibson/160 15.00
24 Lou Brock/192 25.00
25 Ryne Sandberg/160 50.00
26 Mark Prior/160 40.00
27 Miguel Cabrera/224 25.00
28 Mike Lowell/160 15.00
29 Nolan Ryan/96 100.00
30 Luis Aparicio/224 15.00
31 Paul Molitor/160 30.00
32 Red Schoendienst/224 25.00
33 Rickie Weeks/224 10.00
34 Ron Santo/224 25.00
35 Roy Oswalt/224 20.00
36 Stan Musial/96 60.00
37 Steve Carlton/192 20.00
38 Tony Gwynn/192 35.00
39 Vernon Wells/160 10.00
40 Will Clark/192 35.00
41 Bob Feller/224 25.00
42 Bobby Doerr/224 20.00
44 Ralph Kiner/224 30.00
45 Torii Hunter/224 15.00
46 Rollie Fingers/224 15.00
47 Steve Garvey/224 15.00
48 Alan Trammell/224 15.00
49 Maury Wills/224 15.00
50 Gaylord Perry/224 15.00

Fans of the Game

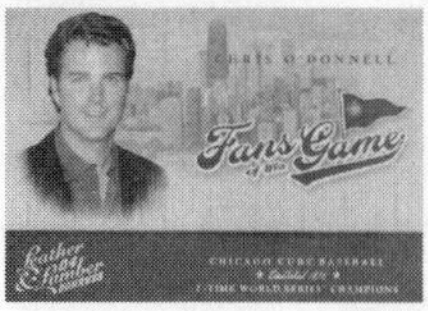

NM/M

Inserted 1:24
1 John Travolta 4.00
2 Dennis Haysbert 2.00
3 Chris O'Donnell 2.00
4 Abby Wambach 3.00
5 Jules Asner 3.00

Fans of the Game Sign.

NM/M

Common Auto.: 20.00
1 John Travolta/SP EXCH 220.00
2 Dennis Haysbert 25.00
3 Chris O'Donnell 20.00
4 Abby Wambach 50.00
5 Jules Asner 50.00

Hall of Fame

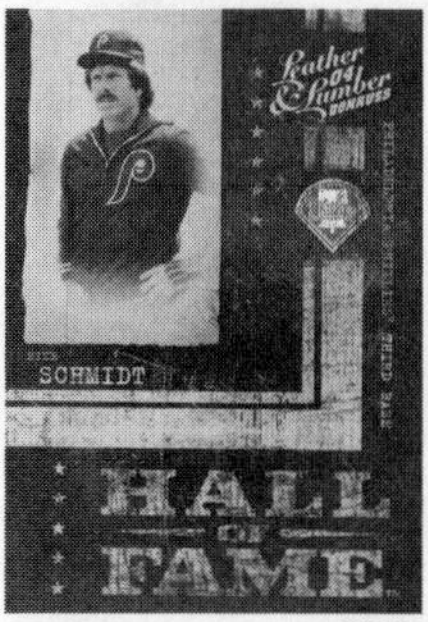

NM/M

Common Player: 2.00
Quantity produced listed
Silver: 1-2X
Production 100 Sets
1 Carl Yastrzemski/1989 4.00
2 Carlton Fisk/2000 2.00
3 George Brett/1999 5.00
4 Johnny Bench/1989 4.00
5 Mike Schmidt/1995 5.00
6 Nolan Ryan/1999 6.00
7 Ozzie Smith/2002 4.00
8 Robin Yount/1999 4.00
9 Rod Carew/1991 3.00
10 Tom Seaver/1992 3.00

Hall of Fame Materials

NM/M

Quantity produced listed
1 Carl Yastrzemski/Jsy/250 15.00
2 Carlton Fisk/Jsy/250 10.00
3 George Brett/Jsy/250 15.00
4 Johnny Bench/Jsy/100 15.00
5 Mike Schmidt/Jkt/250 15.00
6 Nolan Ryan/Pants/100 25.00
7 Ozzie Smith/Jsy/100 20.00
8 Robin Yount/Jsy/250 12.00
9 Rod Carew/Jkt/250 10.00
10 Tom Seaver/Jsy/200 15.00

Leather Materials

NM/M

Quantity produced listed
1 Garret Anderson/Ball/50 8.00
2 Albert Pujols/Ball/50 25.00
3 John Smoltz/Ball/50 20.00
4 Cal Ripken Jr./Ball/50 75.00
5 Ichiro Suzuki/Ball/50 60.00
6 Pedro J. Martinez/Ball/50 15.00
7 Shawn Green/Ball/50 8.00
8 Juan Gonzalez/Ball/50 10.00
9 Mariano Rivera/Ball/50 10.00
10 Jason Giambi/Ball/50 10.00
11 Dave Parker/Btg Glv/25 20.00
12 Dwight Gooden/Btg Glv/25 20.00
13 Eric Munson/Btg Glv/50 8.00
14 Frank Thomas/Btg Glv/50 20.00
15 Joe Carter/Btg Glv/50 10.00
16 Jose Canseco/Btg Glv/50 20.00
17 Paul O'Neill/Btg Glv/50 20.00
18 Tony Gwynn/Btg Glv/50 30.00
19 Wade Boggs/Btg Glv/25 20.00
20 Xavier Nady/Btg Glv/50 8.00
22 Alex Rodriguez/Fld Glv/25 35.00
23 Chipper Jones/Fld Glv/25 30.00
24 Derek Jeter/Fld Glv/25 50.00
25 Jack Wilson/Fld Glv/50 8.00
26 Lenny Dykstra/Fld Glv/50 10.00
27 Mark Grace/Fld Glv/50 15.00
28 Steve Carlton/Fld Glv/50 12.00
29 Tony Perez/Fld Glv/25 15.00
31 Bernie Williams/Spikes/50 10.00
32 Eddie Murray/Spikes/50 30.00
33 Frank Robinson/Spikes/50 10.00
34 Greg Maddux/Spikes/25 30.00
35 Harmon Killebrew/Spikes/25 35.00

Leather Cuts Ball

No Pricing
Production 5-10

Leather in Leather

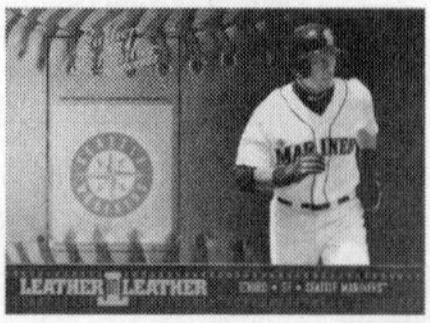

NM/M

Common Player:
Production 2,499 Sets
Silver: 1-2X
Production 100 Sets
1 Garret Anderson/BB 1.50
2 Albert Pujols/BB 5.00
3 John Smoltz/BB 1.50
4 Cal Ripken Jr./BB 8.00
5 Ichiro Suzuki/BB 5.00
6 Pedro J. Martinez/BB 2.00
7 Shawn Green/BB 1.50
8 Juan Gonzalez/BB 1.50
9 Mariano Rivera/BB 1.50
10 Jason Giambi/BB 1.50
11 Dave Parker/BG 1.50
12 Dwight Gooden/BG 1.50
13 Eric Munson/BG 1.50
14 Frank Thomas/BG 2.00
15 Joe Carter/BG 1.50
16 Jose Canseco/BG 2.00
17 Paul O'Neill/BG 1.50
18 Tony Gwynn/BG 3.00
19 Wade Boggs/BG 2.00
20 Xavier Nady/BG 1.50
21 Albert Pujols/FG 5.00
22 Alex Rodriguez/FG 6.00
23 Chipper Jones/FG 3.00
24 Derek Jeter/FG 6.00
25 Jack Wilson/FG 1.50
26 Lenny Dykstra/FG 1.50
27 Mark Grace/FG 2.00
28 Steve Carlton/FG 2.00
29 Tony Perez/FG 2.00
30 Vladimir Guerrero/FG 3.00
31 Bernie Williams/SH 2.00
32 Eddie Murray/SH 3.00
33 Frank Robinson/SH 3.00
34 Greg Maddux/SH 4.00
35 Harmon Killebrew/SH 3.00
36 Manny Ramirez/SH 2.00
37 Mike Piazza/SH 4.00
38 Paul Molitor/SH 3.00
39 Sammy Sosa/SH 4.00
40 Tim Hudson/SH 2.00

Materials Jersey

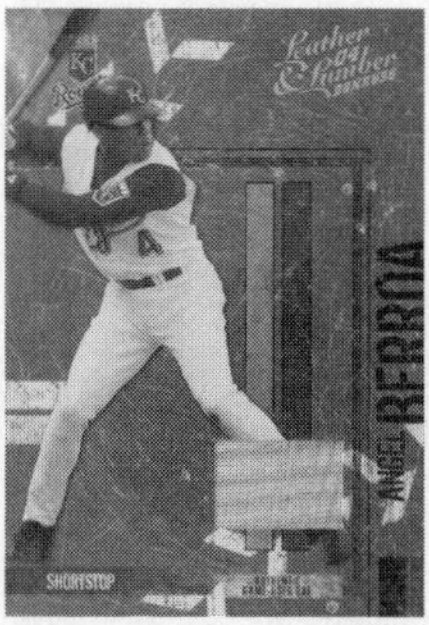

NM/M

Common Jersey: 4.00
Quantity produced listed
MLB Logo: No Pricing
Production One Set
Prime: 1-1.25X
Production 1-25
No pricing 15 or less.
Barrel: No Pricing
Production 1-5
2 Garret Anderson/50 8.00
3 Tim Salmon/250 4.00
4 Troy Glaus/200 4.00
6 Brandon Webb/100 4.00
7 Luis Gonzalez/250 4.00
8 Randy Johnson/100 10.00
12 Andruw Jones/250 4.00
13 Chipper Jones/250 8.00
14 Dale Murphy/250 10.00
16 Marcus Giles/250 4.00
17 Rafael Furcal/250 4.00
18 Cal Ripken Jr./100 30.00
19 Javy Lopez/150 4.00
20 Jay Gibbons/250 4.00
21 Luis Matos/250 4.00
22 Miguel Tejada/250 6.00
23 Rafael Palmeiro/250 8.00
25 Jason Varitek/250 8.00
26 Manny Ramirez/250 8.00
28 Pedro J. Martinez/250 8.00
29 Trot Nixon/25 10.00
30 Greg Maddux/100 10.00
31 Kerry Wood/250 10.00
32 Mark Prior/250 8.00
33 Ryne Sandberg/50 30.00
34 Sammy Sosa/250 10.00
35 Carlos Lee/250 4.00
36 Frank Thomas/250 8.00
37 Maggilo Ordonez/250 4.00
38 Paul Konerko/250 4.00
39 Adam Dunn/250 8.00
40 Austin Kearns/250 4.00
41 Barry Larkin/250 6.00
44 C.C. Sabathia/250 4.00
45 Jody Gerut/250 4.00
46 Omar Vizquel/250 4.00
47 Larry Walker/250 4.00
48 Preston Wilson/250 4.00
49 Todd Helton 8.00
50 Alan Trammell/50 10.00
51 Ivan Rodriguez/100 10.00
52 Jeremy Bonderman/150 4.00
53 Dontrelle Willis/100 4.00
54 Josh Beckett/250 4.00
55 Luis Castillo/250 4.00
56 Miguel Cabrera/50 15.00
57 Mike Lowell/25 10.00
58 Andy Pettitte/25 15.00
59 Craig Biggio/250 4.00
60 Jeff Bagwell/250 8.00
61 Jeff Kent/250 4.00
62 Lance Berkman/250 4.00
64 Roy Oswalt/250 4.00
65 Angel Berroa/50 6.00
66 Carlos Beltran/250 6.00
67 George Brett/250 15.00
69 Mike Sweeney/100 4.00
71 Hideo Nomo/250 6.00
72 Kazuhisa Ishii/250 4.00
73 Paul LoDuca/250 4.00
74 Shawn Green/250 4.00
75 Geoff Jenkins/250 4.00
78 Robin Yount/250 10.00
80 Jacque Jones/250 10.00
81 Johan Santana/250 8.00
82 Shannon Stewart/250 4.00
83 Torii Hunter/250 4.00
84 Andre Dawson/50 10.00
86 Jose Vidro/100 4.00
88 Orlando Cabrera/100 4.00
89 Gary Carter/250 8.00
90 Jae Weong Seo/100 4.00
91 Jose Reyes/250 6.00
92 Mike Piazza/250 10.00
93 Tom Glavine/250 6.00
95 Bernie Williams/250 6.00
96 Derek Jeter/150 20.00
97 Don Mattingly/250 15.00
99 Hideki Matsui/250 20.00
100 Jason Giambi/250 4.00
101 Jorge Posada/50 10.00
102 Mike Mussina/100 8.00
103 Barry Zito/250 4.00
105 Eric Chavez/100 4.00
107 Mark Mulder/250 4.00
108 Rich Harden/50 8.00
109 Rickey Henderson/100 10.00
110 Tim Hudson/250 4.00
111 Bobby Abreu/250 4.00
112 Brett Myers/250 4.00
113 Jim Thome/250 8.00
114 Kevin Millwood/250 4.00
115 Marlon Byrd/250 4.00
116 Mike Schmidt/50 25.00
117 Pat Burrell/250 4.00
118 Dave Parker/250 8.00
120 Jason Kendall/50 6.00
123 Ryan Klesko/250 4.00
124 Tony Gwynn/100 12.00
127 Jerome Williams/200 4.00
129 Edgar Martinez/250 6.00
131 Jamie Moyer/250 4.00
132 John Olerud/150 4.00
133 Albert Pujols/250 15.00
134 Edgar Renteria/100 6.00
135 Jim Edmonds/250 4.00
136 Matt Morris/250 4.00
137 Scott Rolen/250 8.00
138 Aubrey Huff/100 4.00
139 Carl Crawford/250 4.00
141 Rocco Baldelli/250 4.00
143 Hank Blalock/250 6.00
146 Nolan Ryan/100 30.00
147 Carlos Delgado/250 4.00
148 Eric Hinske/100 4.00
149 Roy Halladay/100 4.00
150 Vernon Wells/250 4.00

Materials Jersey B/W

NM/M

Common Player: 5.00
Jersey Prime B/W: No Pricing
Production 1-25
13 Chipper Jones/250 8.00
14 Dale Murphy/250 8.00
18 Cal Ripken Jr./100 35.00
30 Greg Maddux/100 10.00
32 Mark Prior/250 8.00
33 Ryne Sandberg/50 30.00
34 Sammy Sosa/250 12.00
67 George Brett/250 15.00
78 Robin Yount/150 10.00
89 Gary Carter/250 5.00
92 Mike Piazza/250 10.00
96 Derek Jeter/100 20.00
97 Don Mattingly/250 15.00
99 Hideki Matsui/250 20.00
109 Rickey Henderson/250 8.00
116 Mike Schmidt/50 25.00
124 Tony Gwynn/100 10.00
133 Albert Pujols/250 15.00
146 Nolan Ryan/100 25.00
174 Kazuo Matsui/50 25.00

Materials Bat B/W

NM/M

Production 100 unless noted.
13 Chipper Jones 8.00
14 Dale Murphy 10.00
18 Cal Ripken Jr. 30.00
27 Nomar Garciaparra 10.00
30 Greg Maddux 10.00
32 Mark Prior 8.00
33 Ryne Sandberg/50 30.00
34 Sammy Sosa 12.00
63 Roger Clemens/50 20.00
67 George Brett 15.00
78 Robin Yount 12.00
89 Gary Carter 8.00
92 Mike Piazza 10.00
94 Alex Rodriguez 10.00
96 Derek Jeter 20.00
97 Don Mattingly 20.00
109 Rickey Henderson 10.00
116 Mike Schmidt 15.00
124 Tony Gwynn 10.00
133 Albert Pujols 20.00
142 Alfonso Soriano 8.00
146 Nolan Ryan/25 65.00
174 Kazuo Matsui 20.00

Naturals

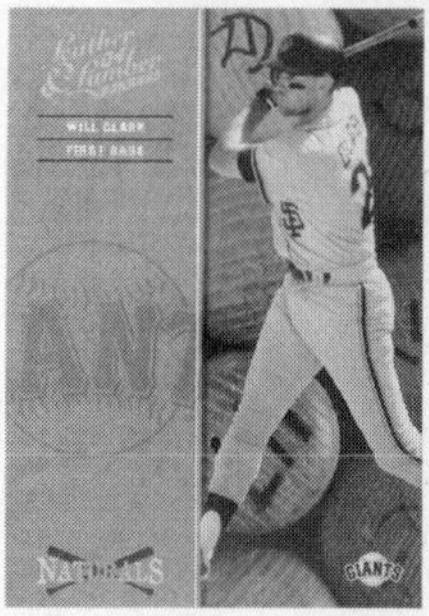

NM/M

Common Player: 1.50
Production 1,499 Sets
Silver: 1-2X
Production 100 Sets
1 Eric Chavez 1.50
2 Garret Anderson 1.50
3 Lance Berkman 1.50
4 Paul Molitor 3.00
5 Rafael Palmeiro 2.00
6 Ralph Kiner 3.00
7 Todd Helton 2.00
8 Tony Gwynn 4.00
9 Wade Boggs 2.00
10 Will Clark 2.00

Naturals Materials Bat

NM/M

Barrel: No Pricing
Production 1-5
1 Eric Chavez/20 12.00
2 Garret Anderson/250 5.00
3 Lance Berkman/250 5.00
4 Paul Molitor/250 8.00
5 Rafael Palmeiro/250 8.00
6 Ralph Kiner/250 10.00
7 Todd Helton/250 8.00
8 Tony Gwynn/250 12.00
9 Wade Boggs/250 8.00
10 Will Clark/250 10.00

Pennants/Pinstripes

NM/M

Common Player: 1.50
Production 1,499 Sets
Gold: 1-2X
Production 100 Sets
1 Reggie Jackson 2.50
2 Mike Schmidt 5.00
3 Steve Carlton 2.00
4 Dwight Gooden 1.50
5 Darryl Strawberry 1.50

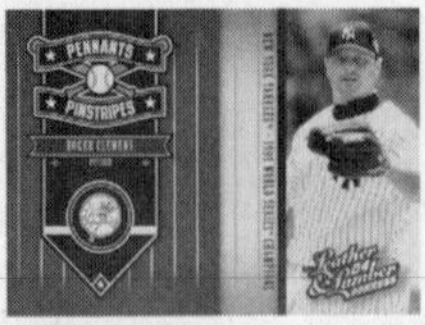

6 Roger Clemens 5.00
7 Curt Schilling 2.00
8 Mark Grace 2.00
9 Ivan Rodriguez 2.00
10 Josh Beckett 1.50

Pennants/Pinstripes Materials

NM/M

Quantity produced listed
1 Reggie Jackson/Pants/100 10.00
2 Mike Schmidt/Jsy/25 35.00
3 Steve Carlton/Jsy/100 8.00
4 Dwight Gooden/Jsy/250 8.00
5 Darryl Strawberry/Pants/250 5.00
6 Roger Clemens/Jsy/250 10.00
7 Curt Schilling/Jsy/250 6.00
8 Mark Grace/Jsy/250 8.00
9 Ivan Rodriguez/Jsy/250 8.00
10 Josh Beckett/Jsy/100 5.00

Rivals

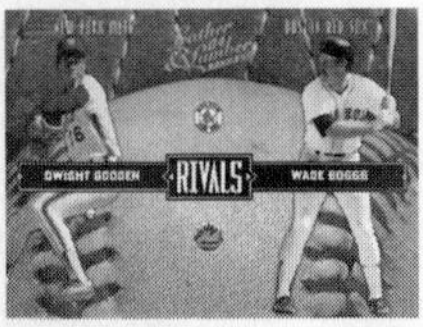

NM/M

Common Duo:
Production 1,499 Sets
Silver: 1-2X
Production 100 Sets
1 Derek Jeter, Nomar Garciaparra 6.00
2 Mark Prior, Albert Pujols 4.00
3 Warren Spahn, Stan Musial 4.00
4 Don Sutton, Reggie Jackson 2.00
5 Roger Clemens, Mike Piazza 4.00
6 Dennis Eckersley, M. Williams 1.50
7 Kerry Wood, Frank Thomas 3.00
8 Jim Palmer, Willie Stargell 2.00
9 Tom Seaver, Mike Schmidt 5.00
10 Jack Morris, George Brett 5.00
11 Randy Johnson, Todd Helton 2.00
12 Tommy John, Rod Carew 2.00
13 Pedro J. Martinez, Jason Giambi 2.00
14 Dwight Gooden, Wade Boggs 1.50
15 Bob Gibson, Ernie Banks 3.00
16 Hideo Nomo, Barry Larkin 1.50
17 Roy Halladay, Vladimir Guerrero 2.00
18 Greg Maddux, Jeff Bagwell 3.00
19 Barry Zito, Alex Rodriguez 5.00
20 Steve Carlton, Andre Dawson 1.50
21 Mariano Rivera, Chipper Jones 2.00
22 Tom Glavine, Manny Ramirez 2.00
23 Whitey Ford, Harmon Killebrew 2.00
24 Carl Yastrzemski, Jim "Catfish" Hunter 2.00
25 Nolan Ryan, Robin Ventura 5.00
26 Carlton Fisk, Joe Morgan 1.50
27 Phil Rizzuto, Duke Snider 2.00
28 Fergie Jenkins, Lou Brock 1.50
29 Jose Canseco, Will Clark 1.50
30 Mike Mussina, Josh Beckett 1.50
31 Rickey Henderson, Ivan Rodriguez 2.00
32 Don Mattingly, Eddie Murray 5.00
33 Troy Glaus, Eric Chavez 1.50
34 Ryne Sandberg, Steve Garvey 3.00
35 Bob Gibson, Roger Maris 4.00
36 Roger Clemens, Cal Ripken Jr. 8.00
37 Orel Hershiser, Darryl Strawberry 1.50
38 Curt Schilling, Paul Molitor 2.00
39 Ichiro Suzuki, Hideki Matsui 5.00
40 Sammy Sosa, Jim Thome 4.00

Rivals Materials

NM/M

Quantity produced listed
1 Derek Jeter/Jsy, Nomar Garciaparra/Bat/250 25.00
2 Mark Prior/Jsy, Albert Pujols/Jsy/250 20.00
3 Warren Spahn/Pants, Stan Musial/Jsy/100 30.00

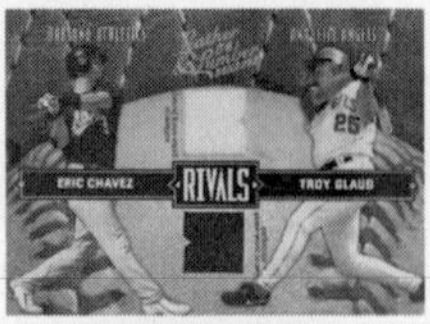

5 Roger Clemens/Jsy, Mike Piazza/Jsy/250 20.00
7 Kerry Wood/Jsy, Frank Thomas/Jsy/250 10.00
8 Jim Palmer/Jsy, Willie Stargell/Jsy/250 12.00
9 Tom Seaver/Jsy, Mike Schmidt/Jsy/250 20.00
10 Jack Morris/Jsy, George Brett/Jsy/250 15.00
11 Randy Johnson/Jsy, Todd Helton/Jsy/250 12.00
12 Tommy John/Pants, Rod Carew/Jkt/250 12.00
13 Pedro J. Martinez/Jsy, Jason Giambi/Jsy/250 12.00
14 Dwight Gooden/Jsy, Wade Boggs/Jsy/250 10.00
15 Bob Gibson/Jsy, Ernie Banks/Pants/100 20.00
16 Hideo Nomo/Jsy, Barry Larkin/Jsy/250 10.00
17 Roy Halladay/Jsy, Vladimir Guerrero/Jsy/250 10.00
18 Greg Maddux/Jsy, Jeff Bagwell/Jsy/250 15.00
19 Barry Zito/Jsy, Alex Rodriguez/Jsy/250 15.00
20 Steve Carlton/Jsy, Andre Dawson/Jsy/250 10.00
22 Tom Glavine/Jsy, Manny Ramirez/Jsy/250 10.00
23 Whitey Ford/Pants, Harmon Killebrew/Jsy/100 35.00
24 Carl Yastrzemski/Jsy, Jim "Catfish" Hunter/Jsy/250 20.00
25 Nolan Ryan/Pants, Robin Ventura/Jsy/250 25.00
26 Carlton Fisk/Jsy, Joe Morgan/Jsy/250 10.00
28 Fergie Jenkins/Pants, Lou Brock/Jsy/100 20.00
29 Jose Canseco/Bat, Will Clark/Bat/250 15.00
30 Mike Mussina/Jsy, Josh Beckett/Jsy/250 10.00
31 Rickey Henderson/Jsy, Ivan Rodriguez/Jsy/250 10.00
32 Don Mattingly/Pants, Eddie Murray/Jsy/250 20.00
33 Troy Glaus/Jsy, Eric Chavez/Jsy/250 8.00
34 Ryne Sandberg/Jsy, Steve Garvey/Jsy/250 20.00
35 Bob Gibson/Jsy, Roger Maris/Jsy/100 40.00
36 Roger Clemens/Jsy, Cal Ripken Jr./Pants/250 30.00
38 Curt Schilling/Jsy, Paul Molitor/Bat/250 12.00
39 Ichiro Suzuki/Base, Hideki Matsui/Base/250 40.00
40 Sammy Sosa/Jsy, Jim Thome/Jsy/250 12.00

Signatures Bronze

NM/M

Quantity produced listed 8.00
2 Garret Anderson/25 25.00
10 Shea Hillenbrand/100 10.00
11 Adam LaRoche/100 10.00
14 Dale Murphy/25 35.00
16 Marcus Giles/50 15.00
17 Rafael Furcal/25 20.00
20 Jay Gibbons/100 10.00
21 Luis Matos/100 10.00
35 Carlos Lee/100 10.00
39 Adam Dunn/25 30.00
44 C.C. Sabathia/100 15.00
48 Preston Wilson/50 15.00
50 Alan Trammell/50 20.00
52 Jeremy Bonderman/100 10.00
56 Miguel Cabrera/50 30.00
65 Angel Berroa/100 10.00
66 Carlos Beltran/100 25.00
79 Scott Podsednik/100 10.00
80 Jacque Jones/100 10.00
81 Johan Santana/100 40.00
82 Shannon Stewart/100 10.00
83 Torii Hunter/50 15.00
84 Andre Dawson/100 15.00
85 Chad Cordero/100 8.00
86 Jose Vidro/100 10.00
88 Orlando Cabrera/100 10.00
104 Bobby Crosby/100 20.00
106 Jermaine Dye/100 15.00
108 Rich Harden/50 20.00
115 Marlon Byrd/25 15.00
119 Jason Bay/100 15.00
122 Jay Payton/50 10.00
138 Aubrey Huff/50 15.00
139 Carl Crawford/50 20.00
145 Michael Young/100 15.00
151 Andres Blanco/50 10.00
152 Kevin Cave/50 10.00
153 Ryan Meaux/50 10.00
154 Tim Bausher/50 10.00
155 Jesse Harper/50 10.00
156 Mike Wuertz/50 10.00
158 Donald Kelly/50 8.00
159 Edwin Moreno/50 8.00
160 Mike Johnston/50 8.00
161 Orlando Rodriguez/50 8.00
164 Jorge Vasquez/50 10.00
166 Jake Woods/50 10.00
167 Aarom Baldiris/50 10.00
170 Dennis Sarfate/50 8.00
173 Eddy Rodriguez/50 10.00

Signatures Bronze B/W

No Pricing
Production 1-25

Signatures Gold

NM/M

Quantity produced listed
2 Garret Anderson/25 25.00
10 Shea Hillenbrand/25 20.00
11 Adam LaRoche/25 15.00
14 Dale Murphy/25 35.00
16 Marcus Giles/25 20.00
17 Rafael Furcal/25 20.00
20 Jay Gibbons/25 15.00
21 Luis Matos/25 15.00
35 Carlos Lee/25 15.00
39 Adam Dunn/25 30.00
44 C.C. Sabathia/25 20.00
45 Jody Gerut/25 20.00
48 Preston Wilson/25 20.00
50 Alan Trammell/25 25.00
52 Jeremy Bonderman/25 15.00
56 Miguel Cabrera/25 35.00
65 Angel Berroa/25 10.00
66 Carlos Beltran/25 40.00
79 Scott Podsednik/25 20.00
80 Jacque Jones/25 20.00
81 Johan Santana/25 50.00
82 Shannon Stewart/25 20.00
83 Torii Hunter/25 20.00
84 Andre Dawson/25 20.00
85 Chad Cordero/25 10.00
86 Jose Vidro/25 15.00
88 Orlando Cabrera/25 15.00
104 Bobby Crosby/25 30.00
106 Jermaine Dye/25 20.00
115 Marlon Byrd/25 15.00
119 Jason Bay/25 25.00
122 Jay Payton/25 15.00
138 Aubrey Huff/25 20.00
139 Carl Crawford/25 25.00
145 Michael Young/25 30.00
151 Andres Blanco/50 10.00
152 Kevin Cave/50 10.00
153 Ryan Meaux/50 10.00
154 Tim Bausher/50 10.00
155 Jesse Harper/50 10.00
156 Mike Wuertz/50 10.00
158 Donald Kelly/50 8.00
159 Edwin Moreno/50 8.00
160 Mike Johnston/50 8.00
161 Orlando Rodriguez/50 8.00
164 Jorge Vasquez/50 10.00
166 Jake Woods/50 10.00
167 Aarom Baldiris/50 10.00
168 Jason Bartlett/50 12.00
170 Dennis Sarfate/50 8.00
173 Eddy Rodriguez/50 10.00

Signatures Gold B/W

No Pricing
Production 1-25

Signatures Silver

NM/M

Quantity produced listed
2 Garret Anderson/50 20.00
10 Shea Hillenbrand/50 15.00
11 Adam LaRoche/50 15.00
14 Dale Murphy/50 25.00
16 Marcus Giles/50 15.00
17 Rafael Furcal/50 15.00
20 Jay Gibbons/50 10.00
21 Luis Matos/50 10.00
29 Trot Nixon/25 35.00
32 Mark Prior/25 40.00
35 Carlos Lee/50 10.00
39 Adam Dunn/25 30.00
40 Austin Kearns/25 20.00
43 Ryan Wagner/50 10.00
44 C.C. Sabathia/50 15.00
45 Jody Gerut/50 15.00
48 Preston Wilson/50 15.00
50 Alan Trammell/50 20.00
52 Jeremy Bonderman/50 10.00
56 Miguel Cabrera/50 30.00
65 Angel Berroa/50 10.00
66 Carlos Beltran/50 30.00
73 Paul LoDuca/25 20.00
79 Scott Podsednik/50 15.00
80 Jacque Jones/50 15.00
81 Johan Santana/50 40.00
82 Shannon Stewart/50 15.00
83 Torii Hunter/50 15.00
84 Andre Dawson/50 15.00
85 Chad Cordero/50 8.00
86 Jose Vidro/50 10.00
88 Orlando Cabrera/50 12.00
104 Bobby Crosby/50 25.00
106 Jermaine Dye/50 15.00
107 Mark Mulder/25 20.00
108 Rich Harden/50 20.00
115 Marlon Byrd/50 10.00
119 Jason Bay/50 20.00
122 Jay Payton/50 10.00
138 Aubrey Huff/50 15.00
139 Carl Crawford/50 20.00
143 Hank Blalock/50 25.00
145 Michael Young/50 20.00
150 Vernon Wells/50 15.00
151 Andres Blanco/100 10.00
152 Kevin Cave/100 10.00
153 Ryan Meaux/100 8.00
154 Tim Bausher/100 8.00
155 Jesse Harper/100 8.00
156 Mike Wuertz/100 10.00
158 Donald Kelly/100 6.00
159 Edwin Moreno/100 6.00
160 Mike Johnston/100 6.00
161 Orlando Rodriguez/100 6.00
164 Jorge Vasquez/100 8.00
166 Jake Woods/100 8.00
167 Aarom Baldiris/100 8.00
170 Dennis Sarfate/100 6.00
173 Eddy Rodriguez/100 8.00

Signatures Silver B/W

No Pricing
Production 1-25

Signatures Platinum

No Pricing
Production One Set

Signatures Platinum B/W

No Pricing
Production One Set

2004 Donruss Studio

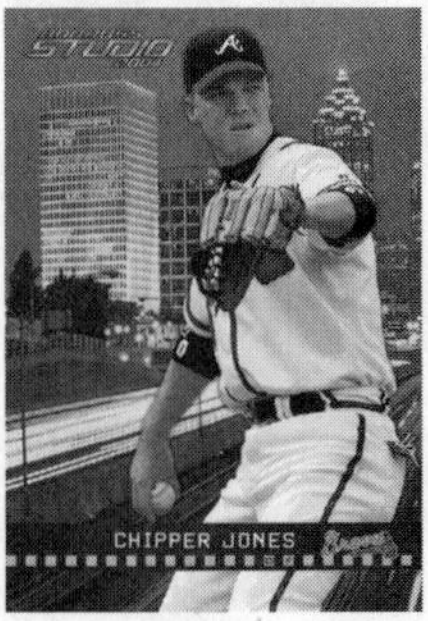

NM/M

Complete Set (220):
Common Player: .15
Common SP (201-221): 6.00
Production 400-800:
Pack (6): 4.00
Box (24): 75.00
1 Bartolo Colon .15
2 Garret Anderson .40
3 Tim Salmon .25
4 Troy Glaus .40
5 Vladimir Guerrero .75
6 Brandon Webb .15
7 Brian Bruney .15
8 Casey Fossum .15
9 Luis Gonzales .25
10 Randy Johnson 1.00
11 Richie Sexson .40
12 Robby Hammock .15
13 Roberto Alomar .40
14 Shea Hillenbrand .15
15 Steve Finley .15
16 Adam LaRoche .15
17 Andruw Jones .50
18 Bubba Nelson .15
19 Chipper Jones .75
20 Dale Murphy .50
21 J.D. Drew .25
22 Marcus Giles .15
23 Michael Hessman .15
24 Rafael Furcal .25
25 Warren Spahn .50
26 Adam Loewen .15
27 Cal Ripken Jr. 3.00
28 Javy Lopez .40
29 Jay Gibbons .15
30 Luis Matos .15
31 Miguel Tejada .40
32 Rafael Palmeiro .50
33 Curt Schilling .50
34 Jason Varitek .25
35 Kevin Youkilis .15
36 Manny Ramirez .50
37 Nomar Garciaparra 1.50
38 Pedro Martinez .75
39 Trot Nixon .25
40 Aramis Ramirez .40
41 Brendan Harris .15
42 Derrek Lee .25
43 Ernie Banks 1.00

44 Greg Maddux 1.00
45 Kerry Wood .75
46 Mark Prior 1.00
47 Ryne Sandberg 1.00
48 Sammy Sosa 1.50
49 Todd Wellemeyer .15
50 Carlos Lee .15
51 Edwin Almonte .15
52 Frank Thomas .50
53 Joe Borchard .15
54 Joe Crede .15
55 Magglio Ordonez .25
56 Adam Dunn .50
57 Austin Kearns .25
58 Barry Larkin .40
59 Brandon Larson .15
60 Ken Griffey Jr. 1.00
61 Ryan Wagner .15
62 Sean Casey .25
63 Brian Tallet .15
64 C.C. Sabathia .15
65 Jeremy Guthrie .15
66 Jody Gerut .15
67 Travis Hafner .25
68 Clint Barmes .15
69 Jeff Baker .15
70 Joe Kennedy .15
71 Larry Walker .25
72 Preston Wilson .15
73 Todd Helton .50
74 Dmitri Young .15
75 Ivan Rodriguez .50
76 Jeremy Bonderman .15
77 Preston Larrison .15
78 Dontrelle Willis .15
79 Josh Beckett .50
80 Juan Pierre .15
81 Luis Castillo .15
82 Miguel Cabrera .75
83 Mike Lowell .25
84 Andy Pettitte .25
85 Chris Burke .15
86 Craig Biggio .25
87 Jeff Bagwell .50
88 Jeff Kent .25
89 Lance Berkman .25
90 Morgan Ensberg .15
91 Richard Hidalgo .15
92 Roger Clemens 1.50
93 Roy Oswalt .25
94 Wade Miller .15
95 Angel Berroa .15
96 Byron Gettis .15
97 Carlos Beltran .25
98 Juan Gonzalez .50
99 Mike Sweeney .15
100 Duke Snider .50
101 Edwin Jackson .15
102 Eric Gagne .50
103 Hideo Nomo .40
104 Hong-Chih Kuo .15
105 Kazuhisa Ishii .15
106 Paul Lo Duca .15
107 Robin Ventura .15
108 Shawn Green .25
109 Junior Spivey .15
110 Lyle Overbay .25
111 Rickie Weeks .25
112 Scott Podsednik .25
113 J.D. Durbin .15
114 Jacque Jones .15
115 Jason Kubel .15
116 Johan Santana .15
117 Shannon Stewart .15
118 Torii Hunter .25
119 Brad Wilkerson .15
120 Jose Vidro .15
121 Nick Johnson .15
122 Orlando Cabrera .15
123 Zach Day .15
124 Gary Carter .40
125 Jae Weong Seo .15
126 Kazuo Matsui **RC** 5.00
127 Mike Piazza 1.00
128 Tom Glavine .40
129 Alex Rodriguez 2.00
130 Bernie Williams .40
131 Chien-Ming Wang .50
132 Derek Jeter 2.00
133 Don Mattingly 2.00
134 Gary Sheffield .40
135 Hideki Matsui 1.00
136 Jason Giambi .50
137 Javier Vazquez .25
138 Jorge Posada .40
139 Jose Contreras .15
140 Kevin Brown .25
141 Mariano Rivera .40
142 Mike Mussina .40
143 Whitey Ford .50
144 Barry Zito .25
145 Eric Chavez .25
146 Mark Mulder .25
147 Rich Harden .15
148 Tim Hudson .25
149 Bobby Abreu .25
150 Jim Thome .75
151 Kevin Millwood .25
152 Marlon Byrd .15
153 Mike Schmidt 1.00
154 Ryan Howard .75
155 Jack Wilson .15
156 Jason Kendall .15
157 Akinori Otsuka **RC** 1.00
158 Brian Giles .25
159 David Wells .15
160 Jay Payton .15
161 Phil Nevin .15
162 Ryan Klesko .15
163 Sean Burroughs .15
164 A.J. Pierzynski .15
165 J.T. Snow .15
166 Jason Schmidt .25
167 Jerome Williams .15
168 Merkin Valdez **RC** 1.00
169 Will Clark .50
170 Bret Boone .25
171 Chris Snelling .15
172 Edgar Martinez .25
173 Ichiro Suzuki 1.00
174 Jamie Moyer .15
175 Randy Winn .15
176 Rich Aurilia .15
177 Shigetoshi Hasegawa .15
178 Albert Pujols 1.50
179 Dan Haren .15
180 Edgar Renteria .25
181 Jim Edmonds .25
182 Matt Morris .25
183 Scott Rolen .75
184 Stan Musial 1.00
185 Aubrey Huff .15
186 Chad Gaudin .15
187 Delmon Young .15
188 Fred McGriff .25
189 Rocco Baldelli .25
190 Alfonso Soriano .75
191 Hank Blalock .50
192 Mark Teixeira .50
193 Nolan Ryan 2.50
194 Alexis Rios .15
195 Carlos Delgado .50
196 Dustin McGowan .15
197 Guillermo Quiroz .15
198 Josh Phelps .15
199 Roy Halladay .25
200 Vernon Wells .25
201 Mike Gosling/AU/400 8.00
202 Ronny Cedeno/AU/76 **RC** 8.00
203 Ronald Belisario/AU/400 **RC** 8.00
204 Justin Hampson/AU/800 **RC** 6.00
205 Carlos Vasquez/AU/800 **RC** 6.00
206 Lincoln Holdzkom/AU/800 **RC** 6.00
207 Casey Daigle/AU/550 **RC** 6.00
208 Jason Bartlett/AU/700 **RC** 6.00
209 Mariano Gomez/AU/800 **RC** 8.00
210 Mike House/AU/800 **RC** 6.00
211 Chris Shelton/AU/800 **RC** 25.00
212 Dennis Sarfate/AU/800 **RC** 8.00
213 Shingo Takatsu/AU/400 **RC** 35.00
214 Justin Leone/AU/800 **RC** 15.00
215 Cory Sullivan/AU/800 **RC** 8.00
216 Mike Wuertz/AU/800 **RC** 8.00
217 Tim Bausher/AU/800 **RC** 8.00
218 Jesse Harper/AU/800 **RC** 8.00
219 Ryan Meaux/AU/800 **RC** 8.00
221 Kevin Cave/AU/800 **RC** 8.00

Proofs Gold

Gold (1-200): 5-10X
Gold (201-225): .5X
#220, 222-225 exist only in parallel set
Production 50 Sets

Proofs Platinum

No Pricing
Production 10 Sets

Proofs Silver

Silver (1-200): 3-6X
Silver (201-225): .25X
#220, 222-225 exist only in parallel set
Production 100 Sets

Big League Challenge

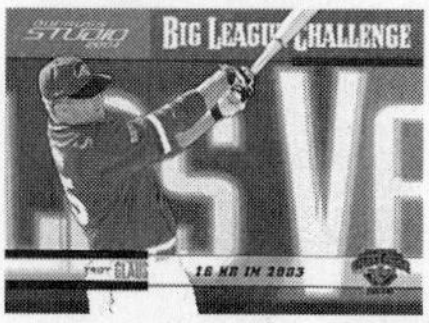

NM/M

Production 999 Sets 6.00
Die-Cut: 1X
Production 500 Sets
1 Albert Pujols Left 6.00
2 Albert Pujols Right 6.00
3 Alex Rodriguez Rgr Left 5.00
4 Alex Rodriguez Rgr Right 5.00
5 Magglio Ordonez 2.00
6 Rafael Palmeiro 3.00
7 Troy Glaus Follow 2.00
8 Troy Glaus Start 2.00
9 Albert Pujols Bat Up 6.00
10 Alex Rodriguez Rgr Bat Up 5.00

Big League Challenge Material

NM/M

Production 100 Sets 15.00
Combo: 1-2X

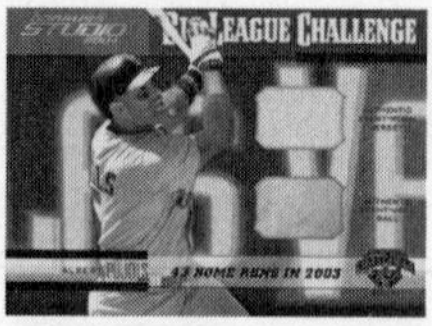

Production 50 Sets
1 Albert Pujols/Jsy 15.00
2 Albert Pujols/Pants 15.00
3 Alex Rodriquez/Rgr/Jsy 10.00
4 Alex Rodriquez/Rgr/Pants 10.00
5 Magglio Ordonez/Jsy 5.00
6 Rafael Palmeiro/Jsy 8.00
7 Troy Glaus/Jsy 6.00
8 Troy Glaus/Pants 6.00
9 Albert Pujols/Hat 20.00
10 Alex Rodriquez/Rgr/Hat 15.00

Diamond Cuts Combo Material

NM/M

Quantity produced listed 15.00
1 Derek Jeter/Bat/Jsy/50 40.00
2 Greg Maddux/Bat/Jsy/50 25.00
4 Miguel Cabrera/Bat/Jsy/50 20.00
5 Mark Mulder/Bat/Jsy/50 15.00
6 Rafael Furcal/Bat/Jsy/50 10.00
7 Mark Prior/Bat/Jsy/50 20.00
8 Roy Oswalt/Bat/Jsy/50 10.00
9 Dontrelle Willis/Bat/Jsy/25 15.00
10 Jay Gibbons/Bat/Jsy/50 10.00
11 Josh Beckett/Bat/Jsy/50 15.00
12 Angel Berroa/Bat/Jsy/50 10.00
13 Adam Dunn/Bat/Jsy/50 15.00
14 Hank Blalock/Bat/Jsy/50 15.00
15 Carlos Beltran/Bat/Jsy/50 15.00
16 Shannon Stewart/Bat/Jsy/50 10.00
17 Aubrey Huff/Bat/Jsy/50 10.00
18 Jeff Bagwell/Bat/Jsy/50 20.00
19 Trot Nixon/Bat/Jsy/50 15.00
20 Nolan Ryan/Jket/Jsy/50 40.00
21 Tony Gwynn/Bat/Jsy/50 30.00
22 Andre Dawson/Bat/Jsy/50 15.00
23 Don Mattingly/Bat/Jkt/50 40.00
24 Dale Murphy/Bat/Jsy/50 20.00
25 Gary Carter/Bat/Jsy/50 15.00

Diamond Cuts Combo Material Signature

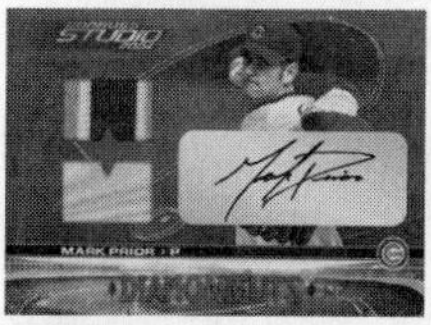

No Pricing
Production 1-5 Sets

Diamond Cuts Material Bat

NM/M

Quantity produced listed 8.00
1 Derek Jeter/100 25.00
2 Greg Maddux/100 10.00
3 Nomar Garciaparra/200 10.00
4 Miguel Cabrera/200 8.00
5 Mark Mulder/200 6.00
6 Rafael Furcal/200 4.00
7 Mark Prior/200 8.00
8 Roy Oswalt/200 4.00
9 Dontrelle Willis/100 6.00
10 Jay Gibbons/200 4.00
11 Josh Beckett/200 6.00
12 Angel Berroa/200 4.00
13 Adam Dunn/200 8.00
14 Hank Blalock/200 8.00
15 Carlos Beltran/200 6.00
16 Shannon Stewart/200 4.00
17 Aubrey Huff/200 4.00
18 Jeff Bagwell/200 8.00
19 Trot Nixon/200 6.00
21 Tony Gwynn/200 10.00
22 Andre Dawson/200 6.00
23 Don Mattingly/200 15.00
24 Dale Murphy/200 10.00
25 Gary Carter/200 6.00

Diamond Cuts Material Jersey

NM/M

Production 250 Sets 8.00
1 Derek Jeter 20.00
2 Greg Maddux 10.00
3 Nomar Garciaparra 10.00
4 Miguel Cabrera 8.00
5 Mark Mulder 6.00
6 Rafael Furcal 4.00
7 Mark Prior 8.00
8 Roy Oswalt 4.00
9 Dontrelle Willis 6.00
10 Jay Gibbons 4.00
11 Josh Beckett 6.00
12 Angel Berroa 4.00
13 Adam Dunn 8.00
14 Hank Blalock 8.00
15 Carlos Beltran 6.00
16 Shannon Stewart 4.00
17 Aubrey Huff 4.00
18 Jeff Bagwell 8.00
19 Trot Nixon 6.00
20 Nolan Ryan/Jkt 25.00
21 Tony Gwynn 10.00
22 Andre Dawson 6.00
23 Don Mattingly/Jkt 15.00
24 Dale Murphy 10.00
25 Gary Carter 6.00

Fans of the Game

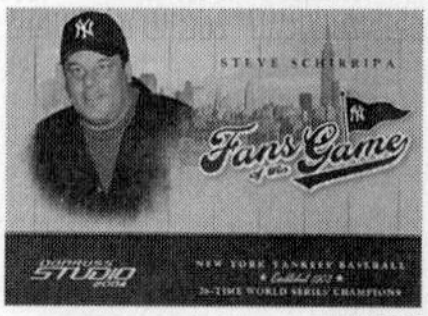

NM/M

216 Regis Philbin 3.00
217 Denis Leary 3.00
218 Bode Miller 3.00
219 Steve Schirripa 2.00
220 Adam Mesh 2.00

Fans of the Game Autographs

NM/M

216 Regis Philbin 40.00
217 Denis Leary 30.00
218 Bode Miller 20.00
219 Steve Schirripa 25.00
220 Adam Mesh 25.00

Game Day Souvenirs Number

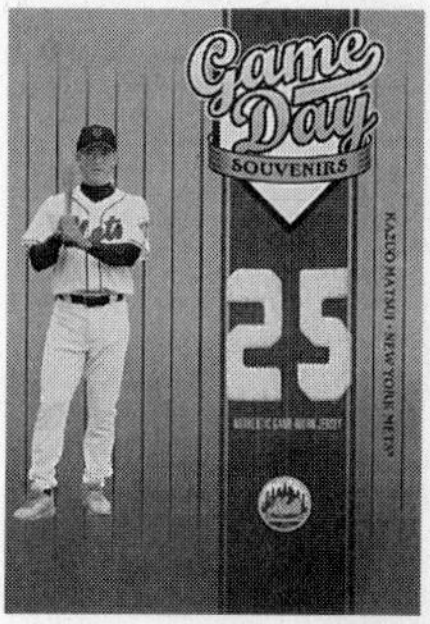

NM/M

Quantity produced listed 4.00
Position: .5-1X
Production 25-300
1 Garret Anderson/Jsy/300 4.00
2 Troy Glaus/Jsy/300 6.00
3 Vladimir Guerrero/Jsy/300 8.00
4 Steve Finley/Jsy/250 4.00
5 Luis Gonzalez/Jsy/25 4.00
6 Richie Sexson/Jsy/250 6.00
7 Andruw Jones/Jsy/300 6.00
8 Chipper Jones/Jsy/250 8.00
9 Rafael Furcal/Jsy/250 4.00
13 Curt Schilling/Jsy/300 6.00
14 Pedro Martinez/Jsy/300 8.00
15 David Ortiz/Jsy/300 8.00
16 Sammy Sosa/Jsy/300 10.00
17 Corey Patterson/Jsy/250 6.00
18 Moises Alou/Jsy/300 6.00
19 Magglio Ordonez/Jsy/250 4.00
20 Paul Konerko/Jsy/300 4.00
21 Frank Thomas/Jsy/300 8.00
22 Austin Kearns/Jsy/50 8.00
23 Sean Casey/Jsy/200 6.00
24 Adam Dunn/Jsy/200 10.00
25 Omar Vizquel/Jsy/250 4.00
26 C.C. Sabathia/Jsy/300 4.00
27 Jody Gerut/Jsy/250 4.00
28 Todd Helton/Jsy/300 8.00
29 Vinny Castilla/Jsy/300 4.00
30 Jeromy Burnitz/Jsy/300 4.00
31 Fernando Vina/Jsy/150 4.00
32 Ivan Rodriguez/Jsy/300 8.00
33 Jeremy Bonderman/Jsy/300 4.00
34 Mike Lowell/Jsy/225 4.00
35 Luis Castillo/Jsy/250 4.00
36 Miguel Cabrera/Jsy/250 8.00
37 Roger Clemens/Jsy/300 10.00
38 Andy Pettitte/Jsy/300 6.00
39 Jeff Bagwell/Jsy/300 6.00
40 Mike Sweeney/Jsy/150 4.00
41 Carlos Beltran/Jsy/200 6.00
42 Angel Berroa/Jsy/100 6.00
43 Paul Lo Duca/Jsy/75 6.00
44 Shawn Green/Jsy/300 4.00
45 Adrian Beltre/Jsy/150 4.00
46 Ben Sheets/Jsy/300 6.00
47 Geoff Jenkins/Jsy/250 4.00
48 Junior Spivey/Jsy/300 4.00
49 Doug Mientkiewicz/Jsy/100 4.00
50 Shannon Stewart/Jsy/100 4.00

51	Torii Hunter/Jsy/300	6.00
52	Livan Hernandez/Jsy/300	4.00
53	Jose Vidro/Jsy/200	4.00
54	Orlando Cabrera/Jsy/300	4.00
55	Mike Piazza/Jsy/250	8.00
56	Mike Cameron/Jsy/250	4.00
57	Kazuo Matsui/Jsy/200	30.00
58	Derek Jeter/Jsy/50	30.00
59	Jason Giambi/Jsy/50	10.00
61	Barry Zito/Jsy/200	6.00
62	Eric Chavez/Jsy/150	4.00
63	Eric Byrnes/Jsy/150	4.00
65	Jim Thome/Jsy/300	8.00
66	Jimmy Rollins/Jsy/250	4.00
67	Jason Kendall/Jsy/250	4.00
68	Craig Wilson/Jsy/300	4.00
69	Jack Wilson/Jsy/250	4.00
70	Ryan Klesko/Jsy/250	4.00
71	Brian Giles/Jsy/300	4.00
72	Sean Burroughs/Jsy/300	4.00
73	A.J. Pierzynski/Jsy/300	4.00
74	J.T. Snow/Jsy/300	4.00
75	Michael Tucker/Jsy/300	4.00
77	Edgar Martinez/Jsy/50	10.00
79	Scott Rolen/Jsy/300	8.00
80	Albert Pujols/Jsy/300	15.00
81	Jim Edmonds/Jsy/300	6.00
82	Aubrey Huff/Jsy/100	4.00
83	Tino Martinez/Jsy/100	4.00
84	Rocco Baldelli/Jsy/100	6.00
85	Alfonso Soriano/Jsy/200	8.00
86	Michael Young/Jsy/250	4.00
87	Hank Blalock/Jsy/200	6.00
88	Eric Hinske/Jsy/200	4.00
89	Carlos Delgado/Jsy/300	4.00
90	Vernon Wells/Jsy/250	4.00

Game Day Souvenirs Signature Number

No Pricing
Production Five Sets

Heritage

		NM/M
Production 999 Sets		4.00
Die-Cut:		2-3X
Production 100 Sets		
1	George Brett	6.00
2	Nolan Ryan	8.00
3	Cal Ripken Jr.	8.00
4	Mike Schmidt	5.00
5	Roberto Clemente	6.00
6	Don Mattingly	5.00
7	Dale Murphy	4.00
8	Ryne Sandberg	5.00
9	Harmon Killebrew	4.00
10	Stan Musial	5.00

Heritage Material Bat

		NM/M
Production 50 Sets		15.00
1	George Brett	30.00
3	Cal Ripken Jr.	40.00
4	Mike Schmidt	20.00
5	Roberto Clemente	60.00
6	Don Mattingly	30.00
7	Dale Murphy	15.00
8	Ryne Sandberg	30.00
9	Harmon Killebrew	15.00
10	Stan Musial	35.00

Heritage Material Jersey

		NM/M
Quantity produced listed		15.00
1	George Brett/200	15.00
2	Nolan Ryan/Jkt/200	20.00
3	Cal Ripken Jr./200	30.00
4	Mike Schmidt/Pants/200	15.00
5	Roberto Clemente/50	60.00
6	Don Mattingly/Jkt/200	15.00
7	Dale Murphy/200	8.00
8	Ryne Sandberg/200	20.00
9	Harmon Killebrew/Pants/200	15.00
10	Stan Musial/100	20.00

Heritage Signature Material Jersey

No Pricing
Production Five Sets

Heroes of the Hall

		NM/M
Production 999 Sets		4.00
Die-Cut:		1X
Production 500 Sets		
1	Fergie Jenkins	3.00
2	Gary Carter	3.00
3	Gaylord Perry	3.00
4	George Brett	6.00
5	Jim Palmer	3.00
6	Nolan Ryan	8.00
7	Paul Molitor	4.00

8	Rod Carew	4.00
9	Steve Carlton	3.00
10	Robin Yount	5.00

Heroes of the Hall Mat. Bat

		NM/M
Production 100 Sets		8.00
2	Gary Carter	8.00
4	George Brett	20.00
7	Paul Molitor	10.00
8	Rod Carew	8.00
9	Steve Carlton	8.00
10	Robin Yount	15.00

Heroes of the Hall Mat. Jsy

		NM/M
Production 200 Unless Noted		
Prime:		No Pricing
Production 10 Sets		
1	Fergie Jenkins/Pants	8.00
2	Gary Carter	8.00
3	Gaylord Perry/100	8.00
4	George Brett	15.00
5	Jim Palmer	8.00
6	Nolan Ryan	25.00
7	Paul Molitor	10.00
8	Rod Carew	10.00
9	Steve Carlton	8.00
10	Robin Yount	15.00

Heroes of the Hall Material Signature

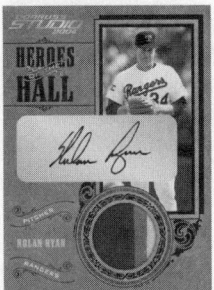

No Pricing
Production 1-10

Masterstrokes Combo Material

		NM/M
Production 50 Sets		10.00
1	Todd Helton/Bat-Jsy/50	15.00
2	Jose Vidro/Bat-Jsy/50	8.00
3	Edgar Renteria/Bat-Jsy/50	10.00
4	Mike Lowell/Bat-Jsy/50	10.00
5	Gary Sheffield/Bat-Jsy/50	10.00
6	Albert Pujols/Bat-Jsy/50	30.00
7	Javy Lopez/Bat-Jsy/50	10.00
8	Carlos Delgado/Bat-Jsy/50	10.00
9	Bret Boone/Bat-Jsy/50	8.00
10	Alex Rodriguez/ Rgr Bat-Jsy/50	20.00
11	Vernon Wells/Bat-Jsy/50	8.00
12	Manny Ramirez/Bat-Jsy/50	10.00
13	Jorge Posada/Bat-Jsy/50	10.00
14	Edgar Martinez/Bat-Jsy/50	10.00
15	Bernie Williams/Bat-Jsy/50	10.00
16	Magglio Ordonez/Bat-Jsy/50	8.00
17	Garret Anderson/Bat-Jsy/50	8.00
18	Eric Chavez/Bat-Jsy/50	8.00
19	Alfonso Soriano/Bat-Jsy/50	15.00
20	Jason Giambi/Bat-Jsy/50	10.00
21	Jeff Kent/Bat-Jsy/50	8.00
22	Scott Rolen/Bat-Jsy/50	20.00
23	Vladimir Guerrero/ Bat-Jsy/50	20.00
24	Sammy Sosa/Bat-Jsy/50	25.00
25	Mike Piazza/Bat-Jsy/50	20.00

Masterstrokes Combo Material Signature

No Pricing
Production 1-10

Masterstrokes Material Bat

		NM/M
Production 200 Sets		6.00
1	Todd Helton	8.00
2	Jose Vidro	4.00
3	Edgar Renteria	6.00
4	Mike Lowell	4.00
5	Gary Sheffield	6.00
6	Albert Pujols	15.00
7	Javy Lopez	6.00
8	Carlos Delgado	6.00
9	Bret Boone	4.00
10	Alex Rodriguez	10.00
11	Vernon Wells	4.00
12	Manny Ramirez	6.00
13	Jorge Posada	6.00
14	Edgar Martinez	4.00
15	Bernie Williams	6.00
16	Magglio Ordonez	4.00
17	Garret Anderson	4.00
18	Eric Chavez	4.00
19	Alfonso Soriano	8.00
20	Jason Giambi	6.00
21	Jeff Kent	4.00
22	Scott Rolen	8.00
23	Vladimir Guerrero	8.00
24	Sammy Sosa	10.00
25	Mike Piazza	8.00

Masterstrokes Material Jersey

		NM/M
Prime:		No Pricing
Production Five Sets		
1	Todd Helton/250	8.00
2	Jose Vidro/250	4.00
3	Edgar Renteria/250	6.00
4	Mike Lowell/250	4.00
5	Gary Sheffield/250	6.00
6	Albert Pujols/250	15.00
7	Javy Lopez/250	6.00
8	Carlos Delgado/250	6.00
9	Bret Boone/250	4.00
10	Alex Rodriguez/250	10.00
11	Vernon Wells/250	4.00
12	Manny Ramirez/250	6.00
13	Jorge Posada/250	6.00
14	Edgar Martinez/250	4.00
15	Bernie Williams/250	6.00
16	Magglio Ordonez/250	4.00
17	Garret Anderson/250	6.00
18	Eric Chavez/250	4.00
19	Alfonso Soriano/150	8.00
20	Jason Giambi/250	6.00
21	Jeff Kent/250	4.00
22	Scott Rolen/250	8.00
23	Vladimir Guerrero/250	8.00
24	Sammy Sosa/250	10.00
25	Mike Piazza/250	8.00

Players Collection Jersey

		NM/M
Common Jersey:		
Production 150 Sets		
Platinum:		1-2X
Production 50 Sets		
1	Adam Dunn/AS	6.00
2	Adam Dunn/Gray	6.00
3	Adam Dunn/White	6.00
4	Alex Rodriguez	10.00
5	Alex Rodriguez/AS	10.00
6	Alex Rodriguez/Blue	10.00
7	Alex Rodriguez/White	10.00
8	Andruw Jones/Home	6.00
9	Andruw Jones/Road	6.00
10	Austin Kearns	6.00
11	Brandon Webb	4.00
12	C.C. Sabathia	4.00
13	Cal Ripken Jr.	25.00
14	Carlos Beltran	6.00
15	Carlos Delgado	6.00
16	Carlos Lee	4.00
17	Chipper Jones/Home	8.00
18	Chipper Jones/Road	8.00
19	Craig Biggio	6.00
20	Curt Schilling	6.00
21	David Wells	4.00
22	Don Mattingly	20.00
23	Dontrelle Willis	6.00
24	Frank Thomas/Black	8.00
25	Frank Thomas/White	8.00
26	Fred McGriff	4.00
27	Garret Anderson/AS	6.00
28	Gary Sheffield	6.00
29	Gary Sheffield	6.00
30	Greg Maddux/Gray	8.00
31	Hank Blalock/Home	6.00
32	Hank Blalock/Road	6.00
33	Hee Seop Choi	4.00
34	Hideo Nomo	6.00
35	Hideo Nomo/Gray	6.00
36	Hideo Nomo/White	6.00
37	Ivan Rodriguez	6.00
38	Ivan Rodriguez	6.00
39	Jason Giambi/Home	6.00
40	Jim Edmonds	6.00
41	Jim Thorne	8.00
42	John Olerud	6.00
43	John Smoltz	6.00
44	Josh Beckett	6.00
45	Josh Phelps	4.00
46	Juan Gonzalez	6.00
47	Juan Gonzalez	6.00
48	Kazuhisa Ishii	4.00
49	Lance Berkman	6.00
50	Larry Walker/Home	4.00
51	Larry Walker/Road	4.00
52	Luis Gonzalez/AS	4.00
53	Magglio Ordonez/Home	4.00
54	Magglio Ordonez/Road	4.00
55	Manny Ramirez	8.00
56	Manny Ramirez/AS	8.00
57	Mark Prior Home	8.00
58	Mark Prior Road	8.00
59	Mark Teixeira	6.00
60	Mike Mussina	6.00
61	Mike Piazza/AS	8.00
62	Mike Piazza/Black	8.00
63	Mike Piazza/White	8.00
64	Nomar Garciaparra/Gray	8.00
65	Nomar Garciaparra/White	8.00
66	Pat Burrell	6.00
67	Paul Konerko	4.00
68	Paul Lo Duca	4.00
69	Pedro Martinez	8.00
70	Rafael Furcal	4.00
71	Rafael Palmeiro/Blue	6.00
72	Rafael Palmeiro/Gray	6.00
73	Ramon Hernandez	4.00
74	Rickey Henderson	6.00
75	Rickey Henderson/Black	6.00
76	Rickey Henderson/White	6.00
77	Roberto Alomar	6.00
78	Roberto Alomar	6.00
79	Robin Ventura/AS	4.00
80	Roger Clemens/Away	10.00
81	Roger Clemens/Home	10.00
82	Roy Halladay	6.00
83	Sammy Sosa/AS	12.00
84	Sammy Sosa/Gray	12.00
85	Sammy Sosa/White	12.00
86	Scott Rolen	8.00
87	Shannon Stewart	4.00
88	Shawn Green/Blue	4.00
89	Shawn Green/Gray	4.00
90	Shawn Green/White	4.00
91	Terrence Long	4.00
92	Tim Hudson	6.00
93	Todd Helton/Away	8.00
94	Todd Helton/Home	8.00
95	Tom Glavine	6.00
96	Tom Glavine	6.00
97	Torii Hunter	6.00
98	Vernon Wells	4.00
99	Vladimir Guerrero	8.00
100	Vladimir Guerrero/AS	8.00

Private Signings Silver

		NM/M
2	Garret Anderson/25	25.00
6	Brandon Webb/25	15.00
7	Brian Bruney/200	5.00
8	Casey Fossum/63	8.00
14	Shea Hillenbrand/25	20.00
16	Adam LaRoche/25	15.00
18	Bubba Nelson/250	8.00
22	Marcus Giles/25	30.00
24	Rafael Furcal/25	25.00
26	Adam Loewen/25	20.00
29	Jay Gibbons/50	15.00
30	Luis Matos/250	10.00
35	Kevin Youkilis/250	20.00
39	Trot Nixon/25	50.00
44	Aramis Ramirez/25	25.00
41	Brendan Harris/100	8.00
43	Ernie Banks/25	75.00
48	Sammy Sosa/21	150.00
50	Carlos Lee/25	20.00

30	Luis Matos/100	10.00
35	Kevin Youkilis/100	25.00
40	Aramis Ramirez/16	35.00
41	Brendan Harris/75	10.00
49	Todd Wellemeyer/50	10.00
50	Carlos Lee/45	15.00
51	Edwin Almonte/56	10.00
53	Joe Borchard/25	10.00
54	Joe Crede/24	15.00
57	Austin Kearns/28	15.00
59	Brandon Larson/16	15.00
61	Ryan Wagner/38	10.00
63	Brian Tallet/50	10.00
65	Jeremy Guthrie/67	8.00
66	Jody Gerut/25	20.00
67	Travis Hafner/34	25.00
68	Clint Barmes/36	10.00
69	Jeff Baker/62	10.00
70	Joe Kennedy/37	15.00
73	Todd Helton/17	50.00
77	Preston Larrison/56	10.00
78	Dontrelle Willis/35	40.00
82	Miguel Cabrera/24	60.00
85	Chris Burke/46	8.00
89	Lance Berkman/17	50.00
90	Morgan Ensberg/25	15.00
96	Byron Gettis/100	8.00
97	Carlos Beltran/25	50.00
98	Juan Gonzalez/22	35.00
100	Duke Snider/25	50.00
101	Edwin Jackson/50	25.00
104	Hong-Chih Kuo/100	40.00
105	Kazuhisa Ishii/17	50.00
106	Paul Lo Duca/16	30.00
107	Robin Ventura/25	30.00
108	Shawn Green/15	30.00
109	Junior Spivey/37	15.00
112	Scott Podsednik/20	25.00
113	J.D. Durbin/31	15.00
114	Jacque Jones/25	25.00
116	Johan Santana/57	25.00
117	Shannon Stewart/23	15.00
121	Nick Johnson/21	15.00
122	Orlando Cabrera/18	25.00
124	Gary Carter/25	30.00
125	Jae Weong Seo/25	15.00
131	Chien-Ming Wang/100	125.00
147	Rich Harden/53	20.00
152	Marlon Byrd/29	15.00
154	Ryan Howard/100	75.00
160	Jay Payton/17	20.00
167	Jerome Williams/50	25.00
168	Merkin Valdez/100	15.00
171	Chris Snelling/32	10.00
177	Shigetoshi Hasegawa/17	75.00
179	Dan Haren/100	10.00
184	Stan Musial/25	80.00
185	Aubrey Huff/19	25.00
186	Chad Gaudin/100	5.00
187	Delmon Young/73	20.00
192	Mark Teixeira/25	25.00
194	Alexis Rios/50	20.00
196	Dustin McGowan/50	10.00
198	Josh Phelps/17	15.00

Private Signings Platinum
No Pricing
Production 1-10

Rally Caps

		NM/M
Production 999 Sets		
Die-Cut:		1X
Production 500 Sets		
1	Adam Dunn	2.00
2	Adrian Beltre	1.50
3	Albert Pujols	5.00
4	Alex Rodriguez	4.00
5	Andruw Jones	2.00
6	Angel Berroa	1.50
7	Aubrey Huff	1.50
8	Austin Kearns	1.50
9	Ben Sheets	2.00
10	Brad Penny	1.50
11	Carlos Beltran	2.00
12	Carlos Lee	1.50
13	Casey Fossum	1.50
14	Eric Hinske	1.50
15	Geoff Jenkins	1.50
16	Jack Wilson	1.50
17	Jason Jennings	1.50
18	Joe Kennedy	1.50
19	Lance Berkman	2.00
20	Magglio Ordonez	1.50
21	Kerry Wood	3.00
22	Mark Buehrle	1.50
23	Mark Prior	3.00
24	Mark Teixeira	2.00
25	Michael Cuddyer	1.50
26	Jeff Conine	1.50
27	Mike Mussina	2.50
28	Mike Piazza	4.00
29	Jose Reyes	2.00

51	Edwin Almonte/227	5.00
53	Joe Borchard/100	5.00
59	Brandon Larson/100	5.00
61	Ryan Wagner/50	10.00
63	Brian Tallet/250	5.00
65	Jeremy Guthrie/89	8.00
66	Jody Gerut/100	10.00
67	Travis Hafner/100	15.00
68	Clint Barmes/100	8.00
70	Joe Kennedy/100	5.00
72	Preston Wilson/25	25.00
77	Preston Larrison/100	8.00
81	Luis Castillo/25	15.00
82	Miguel Cabrera/25	60.00
85	Chris Burke/100	5.00
90	Morgan Ensberg/50	15.00
96	Byron Gettis/250	10.00
97	Carlos Beltran/50	35.00
100	Duke Snider/50	40.00
101	Edwin Jackson/100	15.00
104	Hong-Chih Kuo/250	30.00
105	Kazuhisa Ishii/5	10.00
106	Paul Lo Duca/25	25.00
107	Robin Ventura/25	30.00
109	Junior Spivey/10	15.00
112	Scott Podsednik/100	20.00
113	J.D. Durbin/250	5.00
114	Jacque Jones/50	20.00
115	Jason Kubel/100	15.00
116	Johan Santana/25	25.00
117	Shannon Stewart/25	15.00
120	Jose Vidro/15	30.00
122	Orlando Cabrera/15	25.00
124	Gary Carter/50	25.00
131	Chien-Ming Wang/243	100.00
133	Don Mattingly/25	75.00
134	Gary Sheffield/25	25.00
147	Rich Harden/200	15.00
154	Ryan Howard/250	65.00
160	Jay Payton/50	10.00
167	Jerome Williams/57	25.00
168	Merkin Valdez/250	10.00
169	Will Clark/50	75.00
171	Chris Snelling/200	5.00
177	Shigetoshi Hasegawa/25	75.00
179	Dan Haren/250	8.00
184	Stan Musial/25	80.00
185	Aubrey Huff/250	10.00
186	Chad Gaudin/100	5.00
187	Delmon Young/25	40.00
192	Mark Teixeira/23	25.00
193	Nolan Ryan/34	100.00
194	Alexis Rios/250	15.00
196	Dustin McGowan/115	10.00
197	Guillermo Quiroz/120	8.00

Private Signings Gold

		NM/M
2	Garret Anderson/16	35.00
6	Brandon Webb/55	10.00
7	Brian Bruney/100	5.00
14	Shea Hillenbrand/28	25.00
16	Adam LaRoche/25	15.00
18	Bubba Nelson/100	10.00
22	Marcus Giles/25	30.00
23	Michael Hessman/25	15.00
29	Jay Gibbons/25	20.00

30	Paul Lo Duca	1.50
31	Pedro Martinez	2.00
32	Roy Oswalt	2.00
33	Ryan Klesko	1.50
34	Sammy Sosa	4.00
35	Tim Hudson	1.50
36	Todd Helton	2.00
37	Torii Hunter	2.00
38	Vernon Wells	1.50
39	Craig Wilson	1.50
40	Edgar Renteria	1.50

Spirit of the Game

		NM/M
Production 999 Sets		
Die-Cut:		1X
Production 500 Sets		
1	Sammy Sosa	4.00
2	Alex Rodriguez/Rgr	4.00
3	Nomar Garciaparra	4.00
4	Derek Jeter	6.00
5	Albert Pujols	5.00
6	Roger Clemens	5.00
7	Mark Prior	3.00
8	Randy Johnson	2.00
9	Pedro Martinez	2.00
10	Vladimir Guerrero	2.00
11	Todd Helton	2.00
12	Jeff Bagwell	2.00
13	Mike Mussina	1.50
14	Josh Beckett	1.50
15	Hideo Nomo	1.50
16	Mike Piazza	4.00
17	Don Mattingly	5.00
18	George Brett	5.00
19	Nolan Ryan	8.00
20	Cal Ripken Jr.	8.00

Spirit of the Game Material Bat

		NM/M
1	Sammy Sosa/100	15.00
2	Alex Rodriguez/Rgr/100	10.00
3	Nomar Garciaparra/100	10.00
4	Derek Jeter/100	20.00
5	Albert Pujols/100	15.00
6	Roger Clemens/50	20.00
7	Mark Prior/100	8.00
8	Randy Johnson/100	10.00
9	Pedro Martinez/100	10.00
10	Vladimir Guerrero/100	10.00
11	Todd Helton/100	10.00
12	Jeff Bagwell/100	8.00
13	Mike Mussina/100	10.00
14	Josh Beckett/100	8.00
15	Hideo Nomo/100	10.00
16	Mike Piazza/100	10.00
17	Don Mattingly/100	20.00
18	George Brett/100	20.00
20	Cal Ripken Jr./50	50.00

Spirit of the Game Material Jersey

		NM/M
Prime:		No Pricing
Production 1-5		
1	Sammy Sosa/200	10.00
2	Alex Rodriguez/200	10.00
3	Nomar Garciaparra/200	10.00
4	Derek Jeter/200	20.00
5	Albert Pujols/100	20.00
6	Mark Prior/200	8.00
7	Randy Johnson/100	10.00
9	Pedro Martinez/200	10.00
11	Todd Helton/100	10.00
12	Jeff Bagwell/200	8.00
13	Mike Mussina/200	8.00
14	Josh Beckett/200	8.00
15	Hideo Nomo/200	8.00
16	Mike Piazza/200	12.00
17	Don Mattingly/Jkt/200	15.00
18	George Brett/200	15.00
19	Nolan Ryan/100	40.00
20	Cal Ripken Jr./100	40.00

Spirit of the Game Material Signature Jersey

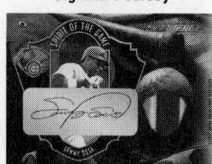

No Pricing
Production 1-5

Stars

		NM/M
Inserted 1:5		
Gold:		1.5-3X
Production 100 Sets		
Platinum:		3-5X
Production 25 Sets		
1	Albert Pujols	3.00
2	Alex Rodriguez	4.00
3	Alfonso Soriano	1.50
4	Andy Pettitte	.50
5	Angel Berroa	.50
6	Aubrey Huff	.50
7	Austin Kearns	.75
8	Barry Zito	.75
9	Brian Giles	.75
10	Carlos Delgado	.75
11	Chipper Jones	1.50
12	Craig Biggio	.75
13	Curt Schilling	1.00
14	Derek Jeter	4.00
15	Edgar Martinez	.50
16	Eric Gagne	1.00
17	Frank Thomas	1.00
18	Hank Blalock	1.00
19	Hideki Matsui	3.00
20	Hideo Nomo	.75
21	Ichiro Suzuki	2.00
22	Ivan Rodriguez	1.00
23	Jason Kendall	.50
24	Jason Schmidt	.75
25	Jeff Bagwell	1.00
26	Jim Edmonds	1.00
27	Jim Thome	1.50
28	Josh Beckett	.75
29	Kazuo Matsui	4.00
30	Ken Griffey Jr.	2.50
31	Larry Walker	.50
32	Magglio Ordonez	.50
33	Manny Ramirez	1.00
34	Mark Mulder	.75
35	Mark Prior	2.00
36	Mark Teixeira	1.00
37	Miguel Tejada	1.00
38	Mike Mussina	1.00
39	Mike Piazza	2.50
40	Pedro Martinez	1.00
41	Randy Johnson	1.50
42	Roger Clemens	3.00
43	Roy Halladay	.50
44	Russ Ortiz	.50
45	Sammy Sosa	3.00
46	Scott Podsednik	.50
47	Tim Hudson	.75
48	Todd Helton	1.50
49	Vernon Wells	.50
50	Vladimir Guerrero	2.00

2004 Donruss Team Heroes

PEDRO MARTINEZ

		NM/M
Complete Set (465):		75.00
Common Player:		.25
Common SP (441-465):		.50
Pack (8):		2.00
Box (24):		40.00
1	Troy Glaus	.40
2	Garret Anderson	.40
3	John Lackey	.25
4	Jarrod Washburn	.25
5	Bengie Molina	.25
6	Adam Kennedy	.25
7	Francisco Rodriguez	.25
8	Darin Erstad	.25
9	Ramon Ortiz	.25
10	Chone Figgins	.25
11	Rich Fischer	.25
12	David Eckstein	.25
13	Troy Percival	.25

14	Tim Salmon	.40
15	Nolan Ryan Angels	2.00
16	Luis Gonzalez	.40
17	Matt Kata	.25
18	Randy Johnson	.75
19	Oscar Villarreal	.25
20	Tim Olson	.25
21	Rob Hammock	.25
22	Alex Cintron	.25
23	Brian Bruney	.25
24	Brandon Webb	.25
25	Greg Aquino	.25
26	Shea Hillenbrand	.25
27	Steve Finley	.25
28	Rod Barajas	.25
29	Mike Hampton	.25
30	Adam LaRoche	.25
31	Russ Ortiz	.25
32	Chipper Jones	.75
33	John Smoltz	.40
34	Andruw Jones	.50
35	Bubba Nelson	.25
36	Johnny Estrada	.25
37	Marcus Giles	.25
38	Rafael Furcal	.25
39	Horacio Ramirez	.25
40	Dale Murphy	.40
41	Gaylord Perry Braves	.25
42	Mark DeRosa	.25
43	Adam Loewen	.25
44	Jerry Hairston Jr.	.25
45	Jose Morban	.25
46	Daniel Cabrera	.25
47	Jay Gibbons	.25
48	Larry Bigbie	.25
49	Luis Matos	.25
50	Rodrigo Lopez	.25
51	Melvin Mora	.25
52	Cal Ripken Jr.	2.50
53	Geronimo Gil	.25
54	Tony Batista	.25
55	Jason Johnson	.25
56	Jason Varitek	.25
57	Bill Mueller	.25
58	Todd Walker	.25
59	Trot Nixon	.40
60	Tim Wakefield	.25
61	Kevin Youkilis	.25
62	David Ortiz	.50
63	Johnny Damon	.40
64	Derek Lowe	.25
65	Pedro J. Martinez	.75
66	Carl Yastrzemski	.75
67	Bobby Doerr	.25
68	Matt Clement	.25
69	Sammy Sosa	1.50
70	Randall Simon	.25
71	Nate Frese	.25
72	Carlos Zambrano	.40
73	Moises Alou	.40
74	Mark Prior	1.00
75	Jason Dubois	.25
76	Nic Jackson	.25
77	Corey Patterson	.40
78	John Webb	.25
79	Kerry Wood	.75
80	Aramis Ramirez	.40
81	Brendan Harris	.25
82	Kenny Lofton	.40
83	Alex Gonzalez	.25
84	Gary Matthews Sr.	.25
85	Mark Grace	.40
86	Mark Grudzielanek	.25
87	Joe Borowski	.25
88	Joe Crede	.25
89	Mark Buehrle	.25
90	Paul Konerko	.40
91	Magglio Ordonez	.40
92	Corwin Malone	.25
93	Frank Thomas	.50
94	Jose Valentin	.25
95	Miguel Olivo	.25
96	Esteban Loaiza	.25
97	Carlos Lee	.40
98	Harold Baines	.25
99	Jason LaRue	.25
100	Sean Casey	.40
101	Adam Dunn	.50
102	Josh Hall	.25
103	Danny Graves	.25
104	Barry Larkin	.40
105	Ken Griffey Jr.	1.00
106	Brandon Claussen	.25
107	Austin Kearns	.40
108	D'Angelo Jimenez	.25
109	Ryan Wagner	.25
110	Tim Hummel	.25
111	Johnny Bench	1.00
112	Eric Davis	.25
113	Jose Rijo	.25
114	Travis Hafner	.40
115	Jody Gerut	.25
116	Fernando Cabrera	.25
117	Jhonny Peralta	.25
118	Ryan Church	.25
119	Francisco Cruceta	.25
120	Omar Vizquel	.40
121	Jason Davis	.25
122	Jeremy Guthrie	.25
123	C.C. Sabathia	.25
124	Milton Bradley	.25
125	Cliff Lee	.25
126	Victor Martinez	.25
127	Bob Feller	.50
128	Casey Blake	.25
129	Josh Bard	.25
130	Billy Traber	.25
131	Coco Crisp	.25
132	Larry Walker	.40
133	Jason Jennings	.25
134	Garrett Atkins	.25
135	Rene Reyes	.25
136	Chin-Hui Tsao	.25
137	Preston Wilson	.25
138	Jeff Baker	.25
139	Charles Johnson	.25
140	Shawn Chacon	.25
141	Todd Helton	.50
142	Jay Payton	.25
143	Omar Infante	.25
144	Bobby Higginson	.25
145	Dmitri Young	.25
146	Jorge Cordova	.25
147	Jeremy Bonderman	.25
148	Brandon Inge	.25
149	Franklyn German	.25
150	Nook Logan	.25
151	Alex Sanchez	.25
152	Craig Monroe	.25
153	Preston Larrison	.25
154	Carlos Pena	.25
155	Alan Trammell	.50
156	Jack Morris	.25
157	Eric Munson	.25
158	Mike Maroth	.25
159	Josh Beckett	.40
160	Josh Willingham	.25
161	Mike Lowell	.40
162	Luis Castillo	.25
163	Wilson Valdez	.25
164	Miguel Cabrera	.75
165	Alex Gonzalez	.25
166	Carl Pavano	.25
167	Dontrelle Willis	.40
168	Juan Pierre	.25
169	Juan Encarnacion	.25
170	Brad Penny	.25
171	Ivan Rodriguez Marlins	.50
172	Josh Wilson	.25
173	Jeff Conine	.25
174	Mark Redman	.25
175	A.J. Burnett	.25
176	Jeff Bagwell	.50
177	Octavio Dotel	.25
178	Craig Biggio	.40
179	John Buck	.25
180	Rodrigo Rosario	.25
181	Tommy Whiteman	.25
182	Kirk Saarloos	.25
183	Jason Lane	.25
184	Wade Miller	.25
185	Lance Berkman	.40
186	Roy Oswalt	.40
187	Tim Redding	.25
188	Jeff Kent	.40
189	Chris Burke	.25
190	Morgan Ensberg	.25
191	Nolan Ryan Astros	2.00
192	Geoff Blum	.25
193	Jeremy Affeldt	.25
194	Mike Sweeney	.25
195	Angel Berroa	.25
196	Jimmy Gobble	.25
197	Ken Harvey	.25
198	Carlos Beltran	.50
199	Alexis Gomez	.25
200	Byron Gettis	.25
201	Mike MacDougal	.25
202	David DeJesus	.25
203	Runelvys Hernandez	.25
204	George Brett	1.50
205	Amos Otis	.25
206	Joe Randa	.25
207	Aaron Guiel	.25
208	Eric Gagne	.40
209	Shawn Green	.40
210	Kevin Brown	.40
211	Cesar Izturis	.25
212	Kazuhisa Ishii	.25
213	Joe Thurston	.25
214	Odalis Perez	.25
215	Rickey Henderson	.50
216	Hideo Nomo	.40
217	Hong-Chih Kuo	.25
218	Edwin Jackson	.25
219	Paul LoDuca	.25
220	Adrian Beltre	.40
221	Duke Snider	.75
222	Steve Garvey	.50
223	Rickie Weeks	.40
224	Bill Hall	.25
225	Doug Davis	.25
226	Geoff Jenkins	.40
227	Matt Childers	.25
228	Dan Kolb	.25
229	Scott Podsednik	.40
230	Pedro Liriano	.25
231	Ben Sheets	.40
232	Robin Yount	.75
233	Gorman Thomas	.25
234	Ben Oglivie	.25
235	Matt LeCroy	.25
236	Cristian Guzman	.25
237	Lew Ford	.25
238	J.C. Romero	.25
239	Rob Bowen	.25
240	Corey Koskie	.25
241	Jacque Jones	.25
242	Brad Radke	.25
243	Shannon Stewart	.25
244	J.D. Durbin	.25
245	Doug Mientkiewicz	.25
246	Jason Kubel	.25
247	Torii Hunter	.40
248	Johan Santana	.25
249	Kirby Puckett	.75
250	Luis Rivas	.25
251	Orlando Cabrera	.25
252	Tony Armas Jr.	.25
253	Brad Wilkerson	.25
254	Endy Chavez	.25
255	Jose Vidro	.25
256	Zach Day	.25
257	Livan Hernandez	.25
258	Terrmel Sledge	.25
259	Michael Barrett	.25
260	Gary Carter	.50
261	Andre Dawson	.50
262	Craig Brazell	.25
263	Mike Piazza	1.00
264	Jeff Duncan	.25
265	Jason Anderson	.25
266	Tom Glavine	.40
267	Danny Garcia	.25
268	Ty Wigginton	.25
269	Al Leiter	.25
270	Jeremy Griffiths	.25
271	Jose Reyes	.40
272	Prentice Redman	.25
273	Cliff Floyd	.25
274	Jae Weong Seo	.25
275	Nolan Ryan/Mets	2.00
276	Keith Hernandez	.25
277	Jason Phillips	.25
278	Kazuo Matsui **RC**	3.00
279	Jose Contreras	.25
280	Aaron Boone	.25
281	Mike Mussina	.40
282	Jason Giambi	.50
283	Hideki Matsui	1.00
284	Derek Jeter	2.00
285	Mariano Rivera	.40
286	Chien-Ming Wang	.40
287	Bernie Williams	.40
288	Alfonso Soriano/Yanks	.50
289	Jorge Posada	.40
290	Michel Hernandez	.25
291	Erick Almonte	.25
292	Don Mattingly	1.50
293	Roger Clemens/Yanks	1.50
294	Gaylord Perry/Rgr	.25
295	Tommy John	.25
296	Tim Hudson	.40
297	Rich Harden	.25
298	Eric Chavez	.40
299	Adam Morrissey	.25
300	Mark Mulder	.40
301	Eric Byrnes	.25
302	Jermaine Dye	.25
303	Barry Zito	.40
304	Erubiel Durazo	.25
305	Mark Ellis	.25
306	Bobby Crosby	.25
307	Shane Bazzell	.25
308	Mario Ramos	.25
309	Jose Canseco	.50
310	Placido Polanco	.25
311	Jimmy Rollins	.25
312	Jim Thome	.75
313	Brett Myers	.25
314	Jason Michaels	.25
315	Vicente Padilla	.25
316	Bobby Abreu	.40
317	Ryan Howard	.50
318	Chase Utley	.50
319	Pat Burrell	.40
320	Randy Wolf	.25
321	Franklin Perez	.25
322	Marlon Byrd	.25
323	Kevin Millwood	.40
324	Mike Lieberthal	.25
325	Anderson Machado	.25
326	Travis Chapman	.25
327	Steve Carlton	.50
328	Greg Luzinski	.25
329	David Bell	.25
330	Craig Wilson	.40
331	Kris Benson	.25
332	Jose Castillo	.25
333	Josh Fogg	.25
334	Jason Kendall	.25
335	Walter Young	.25
336	Oliver Perez	.25
337	Jason Bay	.25
338	Duaner Sanchez	.25
339	Jack Wilson	.40
340	Carlos Rivera	.25
341	Kip Wells	.25
342	Freddy Sanchez	.25
343	Roberto Clemente	2.00
344	Al Oliver	.25
345	Phil Nevin	.25
346	Trevor Hoffman	.25
347	Ryan Klesko	.40
348	Khalil Greene	.25
349	Freddy Guzman **RC**	.25
350	Brian Giles	.40
351	Brian Lawrence	.25
352	Sean Burroughs	.25
353	Ben Howard	.25
354	Xavier Nady	.25
355	Mark Loretta	.25
356	Ramon Vazquez	.25
357	Tony Gwynn	.75
358	Adam Eaton	.25
359	Merkin Valdez **RC**	.75
360	Kevin Correia	.25
361	Edgardo Alfonzo	.25
362	Mike Cameron	.25
363	Ray Durham	.25
364	Jesse Foppert	.25
365	Robb Nen	.25
366	Marquis Grissom	.25
367	Jerome Williams	.25
368	Jason Schmidt	.40
369	Will Clark	.50
370	Bret Boone	.40
371	Freddy Garcia	.25
372	Dan Wilson	.25
373	Rett Johnson	.25
374	Kazuhiro Sasaki	.25
375	Ichiro Suzuki	1.00
376	Edgar Martinez	.40
377	Jamie Moyer	.25
378	Joel Pineiro	.25
379	Carlos Guillen	.25
380	Randy Winn	.25
381	J.J. Putz	.25
382	John Olerud	.40
383	Matt Thornton	.25
384	Rafael Soriano	.25
385	Gil Meche	.25
386	Albert Pujols	1.50
387	Woody Williams	.25
388	Dan Haren	.25
389	Matt Morris	.40
390	Jim Edmonds	.40
391	Edgar Renteria	.40
392	Scott Rolen	.75
393	J.D. Drew	.40
394	Bo Hart	.25
395	Stan Musial	1.00
396	Red Schoendienst	.25
397	Terry Pendleton	.25
398	Mike Matheny	.25
399	Dewon Brazelton	.25
400	Chad Gaudin	.25
401	Aubrey Huff	.25
402	Victor Zambrano	.25
403	Antonio Perez	.25
404	Carl Crawford	.25
405	Joe Kennedy	.25
406	Pete LaForest	.25
407	Delmon Young	.40
408	Rocco Baldelli	.40
409	Doug Waechter	.25
410	Brian Stokes	.25
411	Edwin Almonte	.25
412	Toby Hall	.25
413	Lance Carter	.25
414	Greg Maddux/Braves	1.00
415	Hank Blalock	.50
416	Colby Lewis	.25
417	Mark Teixeira	.40
418	Gerald Laird	.25
419	Ricardo Rodriguez	.25
420	Ben Kozlowski	.25
421	Kevin Mench	.25
422	Michael Young	.25
423	Ramon Nivar	.25
424	Laynce Nix	.25
425	Nolan Ryan/Rgr	2.00
426	Einar Diaz	.25
427	Carlos Delgado	.40
428	Eric Hinske	.25
429	Dustin McGowan	.25
430	Frank Catalanotto	.25
431	Kevin Cash	.25
432	Roy Halladay	.40
433	Orlando Hudson	.25
434	Francisco Rosario	.25
435	Guillermo Quiroz	.25
436	Vernon Wells	.25
437	Josh Phelps	.25
438	Alexis Rios	.25
439	Reed Johnson	.25
440	Chris Woodward	.25
441	Bartolo Colon/SP	.50
442	Richie Sexson/SP	.75
443	Greg Maddux/Cubs/SP	2.00
444	Javy Lopez/SP	.75
445	Gary Sheffield/SP	.75
446	Curt Schilling/SP	1.00
447	Nomar Garciaparra/SP	2.50
448	Manny Ramirez/SP	1.50
449	Derrek Lee/SP	.75
450	Roberto Alomar/SP	.75
451	Ivan Rodriguez/Tigers/SP	1.50
452	Junior Spivey/SP	.50
453	Alfonso Soriano/Rgr/SP	1.00
454	Vladimir Guerrero/SP	1.50
455	Nick Johnson/SP	.50
456	Javier Vazquez/SP	.50
457	Andy Pettitte/SP	.75
458	Miguel Tejada/SP	.75
459	Rich Aurilia/SP	.50
460	A.J. Pierzynski/SP	.50
461	Raul Ibanez/SP	.50
462	Roger Clemens/Astros/SP	3.00
463	Juan Gonzalez/SP	1.00
464	Rafael Palmeiro/SP	1.00
465	Alex Rodriguez/Yanks/SP	4.00

Showdown Bronze

Bronze (1-440): 3-5X
Bronze (441-465): 2-3X
Production 150 Sets

Showdown Gold

No Pricing
Production 10 Sets

Showdown Silver

Silver (1-440): 5-10X
Silver (441-465): 3-5X
Production 50 Sets

Autographs

NM/M
Inserted 1:24

10	Chone Figgins	10.00
11	Rich Fischer	5.00
17	Matt Kata	5.00
19	Oscar Villarreal	5.00
20	Tim Olson	5.00
21	Rob Hammock/57	10.00
23	Brian Bruney	5.00
25	Greg Aquino	5.00
35	Bubba Nelson	5.00
45	Jose Morban	5.00
46	Daniel Cabrera	5.00
61	Kevin Youkilis/50	15.00
71	Nate Frese	5.00
75	Jason Dubois	5.00
76	Nic Jackson	5.00
78	John Webb	5.00
81	Brendan Harris	10.00
84	Gary Matthews Sr.	10.00
92	Corwin Malone	5.00
102	Josh Hall/25	15.00
106	Brandon Claussen	10.00
110	Tim Hummel	5.00
116	Francisco Cabrera	5.00
117	Jhonny Peralta	8.00
118	Ryan Church	5.00
119	Francisco Cruceta/75	8.00
146	Jorge Cordova	5.00
149	Franklyn German	5.00
150	Nook Logan	5.00
153	Preston Larrison	8.00
160	Josh Willingham	8.00
163	Wilson Valdez	8.00
172	Josh Wilson	5.00
180	Rodrigo Rosario	8.00
181	Tommy Whiteman	5.00
187	Tim Redding/22	10.00
189	Chris Burke	5.00
197	Ken Harvey	15.00
200	Byron Gettis	8.00
205	Amos Otis	10.00
211	Cesar Izturis	8.00
225	Doug Davis	8.00
227	Matt Childers	5.00
230	Pedro Liriano	5.00
233	Gorman Thomas	15.00
234	Ben Oglivie/86	15.00
237	Lew Ford	10.00
238	J.C. Romero	5.00
239	Rob Bowen	5.00
246	Jason Kubel/50	15.00
258	Termel Sledge	5.00
262	Craig Brazell	5.00
264	Jeff Duncan	8.00
265	Jason Anderson	5.00
267	Danny Garcia	5.00
270	Jeremy Griffiths	8.00
272	Prentice Redman	8.00
291	Erick Almonte/66	8.00
307	Shane Bazzell	5.00
308	Mario Ramos	5.00
314	Jason Michaels/42	8.00
321	Franklin Perez	5.00
325	Anderson Machado/50	10.00
326	Travis Chapman	5.00
328	Greg Luzinski	15.00
331	Kris Benson	10.00
335	Walter Young/67	10.00
338	Duaner Sanchez	5.00
353	Ben Howard	5.00
359	Merkin Valdez/50	20.00
360	Kevin Correia	5.00
373	Rett Johnson/76	8.00
381	J.J. Putz	5.00
383	Matt Thornton/50	8.00
384	Rafael Soriano	8.00
406	Pete LaForest	5.00
410	Brian Stokes	5.00
411	Edwin Almonte	5.00
419	Ricardo Rodriguez	5.00
420	Ben Kozlowski	5.00
431	Kevin Cash	5.00
434	Francisco Rosario/48	8.00

2004 Donruss Throwback Threads

NM/M

Complete Set (250):		
Common Player:		
Common (201-225):		1.50
Common (226-250):		3.00
Production 1,000		
Hobby Pack (5):		5.00
Hobby Box (24):		90.00
1	Bartolo Colon	.15
2	Darin Erstad	.25
3	David Eckstein	.15
4	Garret Anderson	.25
5	Tim Salmon	.25
6	Troy Glaus	.25
7	Vladimir Guerrero	.75
8	Brandon Webb	.15
9	Luis Gonzalez	.25
10	Randy Johnson	.75
11	Richie Sexson	.40
12	Roberto Alomar	.50
13	Shea Hillenbrand	.15
14	Steve Finley	.15
15	Adam LaRoche	.15
16	Andruw Jones	.50
17	Chipper Jones	.75
18	J.D. Drew	.25
19	John Smoltz	.25
20	Rafael Furcal	.15
21	Russ Ortiz	.15
22	Javy Lopez	.25
23	Jay Gibbons	.15
24	Larry Bigbie	.15
25	Luis Matos	.15
26	Melvin Mora	.15
27	Miguel Tejada	.40
28	Rafael Palmeiro	.50
29	Curt Schilling	.50
30	David Ortiz	.75
31	Derek Lowe	.15
32	Jason Varitek	.15
33	Johnny Damon	.25
34	Manny Ramirez	.50
35	Nomar Garciaparra	1.00
36	Pedro J. Martinez	.75
37	Trot Nixon	.15
38	Aramis Ramirez	.40
39	Corey Patterson	.25
40	Derrek Lee	.25
41	Greg Maddux	1.00
42	Kerry Wood	.75
43	Mark Prior	.75
44	Sammy Sosa	1.50
45	Carlos Lee	.15
46	Esteban Loaiza	.15
47	Frank Thomas	.50
48	Joe Borchard	.15
49	Magglio Ordonez	.25
50	Mark Buehrle	.15
51	Paul Konerko	.15
52	Adam Dunn	.50
53	Austin Kearns	.25
54	Barry Larkin	.40
55	Brandon Larson	.15
56	Ken Griffey Jr.	1.00
57	Ryan Wagner	.15
58	Sean Casey	.15
59	C.C. Sabathia	.15
60	Jody Gerut	.15
61	Omar Vizquel	.15
62	Travis Hafner	.25
63	Victor Martinez	.25
64	Charles Johnson	.15
65	Garrett Atkins	.15
66	Jason Jennings	.15
67	Joe Kennedy	.15
68	Larry Walker	.25
69	Preston Wilson	.15
70	Todd Helton	.50
71	Ivan Rodriguez	.50
72	Jeremy Bonderman	.15
73	A.J. Burnett	.15
74	Brad Penny	.15
75	Dontrelle Willis	.25
76	Josh Beckett	.50
77	Juan Pierre	.15
78	Luis Castillo	.15
79	Miguel Cabrera	.75
80	Mike Lowell	.25
81	Andy Pettitte	.25
82	Craig Biggio	.25
83	Jeff Bagwell	.50
84	Jeff Kent	.25
85	Lance Berkman	.25
86	Morgan Ensberg	.15
87	Richard Hidalgo	.15
88	Roger Clemens	1.50
89	Roy Oswalt	.25
90	Wade Miller	.15
91	Angel Berroa	.15
92	Carlos Beltran	.50
93	Juan Gonzalez	.40
94	Ken Harvey	.15
95	Mike Sweeney	.15
96	Runelvys Hernandez	.15
97	Adrian Beltre	.40
98	Edwin Jackson	.15
99	Eric Gagne	.40
100	Hideo Nomo	.25
101	Hong-Chih Kuo	.15
102	Kazuhisa Ishii	.15
103	Paul LoDuca	.15
104	Shawn Green	.25
105	Ben Sheets	.25
106	Geoff Jenkins	.15
107	Junior Spivey	.15
108	Rickie Weeks	.25
109	Scott Podsednik	.25
110	Corey Koskie	.15
111	Doug Mientkiewicz	.15
112	Jacque Jones	.15
113	Joe Mays	.15
114	Johan Santana	.25
115	Shannon Stewart	.15
116	Torii Hunter	.25
117	Brad Wilkerson	.15
118	Carl Everett	.15
119	Chad Cordero	.15
120	Jose Vidro	.15
121	Nick Johnson	.15
122	Orlando Cabrera	.15
123	Al Leiter	.15
124	Cliff Floyd	.15
125	Jae Weong Seo	.15
126	Jose Reyes	.25
127	Mike Cameron	.15
128	Mike Piazza	1.00
129	Tom Glavine	.25
130	Alex Rodriguez	2.00
131	Bernie Williams	.40
132	Chien-Ming Wang	.40
133	Derek Jeter	2.00
134	Gary Sheffield	.50
135	Hideki Matsui	1.00
136	Jason Giambi	.25
137	Javier Vazquez	.15
138	Jorge Posada	.25
139	Jose Contreras	.15
140	Kevin Brown	.15
141	Mariano Rivera	.25
142	Mike Mussina	.40
143	Barry Zito	.25
144	Bobby Crosby	.15
145	Eric Chavez	.25
146	Erubiel Durazo	.15
147	Jermaine Dye	.15
148	Mark Kotsay	.15
149	Mark Mulder	.25
150	Rich Harden	.15
151	Tim Hudson	.25
152	Billy Wagner	.15
153	Bobby Abreu	.25
154	Brett Myers	.15
155	Jim Thome	.75
156	Jimmy Rollins	.25
157	Kevin Millwood	.15
158	Marlon Byrd	.15
159	Pat Burrell	.25
160	Jason Bay	.25
161	Jason Kendall	.15
162	Brian Giles	.25
163	Jay Payton	.15
164	Ryan Klesko	.15
165	Edgardo Alfonzo	.15
166	Jason Schmidt	.40
167	Jerome Williams	.15
168	Todd Linden	.15
169	Bret Boone	.15
170	Edgar Martinez	.25
171	Freddy Garcia	.15
172	Ichiro Suzuki	1.50
173	Jamie Moyer	.15
174	John Olerud	.15
175	Shigetoshi Hasegawa	.15
176	Albert Pujols	1.50
177	Dan Haren	.15
178	Edgar Renteria	.25
179	Jim Edmonds	.25
180	Matt Morris	.25
181	Scott Rolen	.75
182	Aubrey Huff	.15
183	Carl Crawford	.25
184	Chad Gaudin	.15
185	Delmon Young	.25
186	Dewon Brazelton	.15
187	Fred McGriff	.25
188	Rocco Baldelli	.15
189	Alfonso Soriano	.75
190	Hank Blalock	.25
191	Laynce Nix	.15
192	Mark Teixeira	.25
193	Michael Young	.15
194	Carlos Delgado	.40
195	Eric Hinske	.15
196	Frank Catalanotto	.15
197	Josh Phelps	.15
198	Orlando Hudson	.15
199	Roy Halladay	.15
200	Vernon Wells	.15
201	Dale Murphy	2.00
202	Cal Ripken Jr.	10.00
203	Fred Lynn	1.50
204	Wade Boggs	2.00
205	Nolan Ryan	6.00
206	Rod Carew	2.00
207	Andre Dawson	1.50
208	Ernie Banks	3.00
209	Ryne Sandberg	5.00
210	Bo Jackson	3.00
211	Carlton Fisk	3.00
212	Dave Concepcion	1.50
213	Alan Trammell	1.50
214	George Brett	5.00
215	Robin Yount	4.00
216	Gary Carter	1.50
217	Darryl Strawberry	1.50
218	Dwight Gooden	1.50
219	Babe Ruth	6.00
220	Don Mattingly	5.00
221	Reggie Jackson	3.00
222	Mike Schmidt	5.00
223	Tony Gwynn	4.00
224	Keith Hernandez	2.00
225	Hector Gimenez RC	3.00
226	Graham Koonce	3.00
227	John Gall RC	5.00
228	Jerry Gil RC	3.00
229	Jason Frasor RC	3.00
230	Justin Knoedler RC	3.00
231	Ivan Ochoa RC	3.00
232	Greg Dobbs RC	3.00
233	Ronald Belisario RC	3.00
234	Jerome Gamble RC	3.00
235	Roberto Novoa RC	3.00
236	Sean Henn	4.00
237	Willy Taveras RC	3.00
238	Ramon Ramirez RC	3.00
239	Kazuo Matsui RC	8.00
240	Akinori Otsuka RC	4.00
241	Jason Bartlett RC	3.00
242	Fernando Nieve RC	3.00
243	Freddy Guzman RC	3.00
244	Aarom Baldiris RC	5.00
245	Merkin Valdez RC	5.00
246	Mike Gosling	3.00
247	Shingo Takatsu RC	8.00
248	William Bergolla RC	3.00
249	Shawn Hill RC	3.00
250	Justin Germano RC	3.00

Blast From the Past

NM/M

Common Player:		1.50
Production 1,500 Sets		
Spectrum:		2-3X
Production 100 Sets		
1	Albert Pujols	5.00
2	Alex Rodriguez	4.00
3	Babe Ruth	6.00
4	Cal Ripken Jr.	8.00
5	Carlton Fisk	2.00

6	Eddie Mathews	3.00
7	Eddie Murray	2.00
8	Ernie Banks	3.00
9	Frank Robinson	2.00
10	George Foster	1.50
11	Harmon Killebrew	3.00
12	Jim Rice	1.50
13	Jim Thome	2.00
14	Johnny Bench	3.00
15	Jose Canseco	2.00
16	Juan Gonzalez	2.00
17	Ken Griffey Jr.	3.00
18	Mike Piazza	4.00
19	Mike Schmidt	5.00
20	Reggie Jackson	2.00
21	Roger Maris	3.00
22	Sammy Sosa	4.00
23	Stan Musial	4.00
24	Willie McCovey	2.00
25	Willie Stargell	2.00

Blast From the Past Bat

NM/M
Production 250 unless noted.

1	Albert Pujols	15.00
2	Alex Rodriguez	10.00
3	Babe Ruth/50	150.00
4	Cal Ripken Jr.	25.00
5	Carlton Fisk	8.00
6	Eddie Mathews	10.00
7	Eddie Murray	8.00
8	Ernie Banks	10.00
9	Frank Robinson	8.00
10	George Foster	6.00
11	Harmon Killebrew	10.00
12	Jim Rice	8.00
13	Jim Thome	8.00
14	Johnny Bench	10.00
15	Jose Canseco/100	10.00
16	Juan Gonzalez	8.00
18	Mike Piazza	10.00
19	Mike Schmidt	15.00
20	Reggie Jackson	8.00
21	Roger Maris	30.00
22	Sammy Sosa	10.00
23	Stan Musial	15.00
24	Willie McCovey	8.00
25	Willie Stargell	8.00

Century Coll. Material

NM/M
All Jersey unless noted.
Prime: 1.5-3X
Production 10-25
Combo: .75-2X
Production 5-50
Combo Prime: 2-3X
Production 5-25
No pricing 15 or less.

1	Alan Trammell/250	8.00
2	Alex Rodriguez/250	10.00
3	Alfonso Soriano/250	8.00
4	Andre Dawson/250	6.00
5	Andy Pettitte/250	6.00
6	Bert Blyleven/250	6.00
7	Bo Jackson/250	12.00
8	Bobby Doerr/250	8.00
9	Brooks Robinson/25	30.00
10	Carl Yastrzemski/250	15.00
11	Carlos Delgado/250	4.00
12	Carlton Fisk Jkt/250	8.00
13	Curt Schilling/250	6.00
14	Darryl Strawberry/250	6.00
15	Dave Concepcion/250	6.00
16	Dave Parker/250	8.00
17	Dennis Eckersley/250	8.00
18	Don Sutton/250	6.00
19	Duke Snider/250	10.00
20	Dwight Gooden/250	6.00
21	Eddie Mathews/25	25.00
22	Enos Slaughter/100	8.00
23	Ernie Banks/Pants/250	15.00
24	Frankie Frisch/Jkt/250	12.00
25	Frank Robinson/50	10.00
26	Frank Thomas/250	8.00
27	Garret Anderson/250	6.00
28	Gary Carter/250	6.00
29	Gary Sheffield/250	6.00
30	Harmon Killebrew/50	25.00
31	Harold Baines/250	6.00
32	Hideo Nomo/250	6.00
33	Jack Morris/250	6.00
34	Jason Giambi/250	6.00
35	Jeff Kent/250	4.00
36	Jim "Catfish" Hunter/250	6.00
37	Jim Palmer/50	10.00
38	Jim Rice/250	8.00
39	Jim Thome/250	10.00
40	John Smoltz/250	8.00
41	Johnny Mize/Pants/250	8.00
42	Jose Canseco/250	8.00
43	Juan Gonzalez/250	6.00
44	Juan Marichal/250	8.00
45	Keith Hernandez/250	8.00
46	Kerry Wood/250	10.00
47	Kevin Brown/250	4.00
48	Lance Berkman/250	6.00
49	Larry Walker/250	6.00
50	Lee Smith/250	6.00
51	Lenny Dykstra/Bat/250	8.00
52	Luis Tiant/250	6.00
53	Magglio Ordonez/250	4.00
54	Manny Ramirez/250	8.00
55	Mariano Rivera/100	8.00
56	Mark Grace/250	8.00
57	Mark Mulder/250	8.00
58	Mark Teixeira/150	6.00
59	Marty Marion/25	15.00
60	Mike Mussina/Pants/250	8.00
61	Mike Piazza/250	10.00
62	Nellie Fox/Bat/250	15.00
63	Nolan Ryan/Jkt/250	20.00
65	Ozzie Smith/250	12.00
66	Pedro J. Martinez/250	8.00
67	Pee Wee Reese/Bat/250	8.00
68	Phil Niekro/250	8.00
69	Phil Rizzuto/Pants/250	10.00
70	Rafael Palmeiro/250	8.00
71	Ralph Kiner/Bat/250	8.00
72	Randy Johnson/250	10.00
73	Reggie Jackson/Jkt/250	8.00
74	Rickey Henderson/250	8.00
75	Roberto Alomar/250	6.00
76	Robin Ventura/250	4.00
77	Rod Carew/250	8.00
78	Roger Clemens/250	15.00
79	Ron Santo/Bat/250	10.00
80	Scott Rolen/250	6.00
81	Shawn Green/250	6.00
82	Steve Garvey/250	6.00
83	Tim Hudson/250	4.00
84	Tom Glavine/250	6.00
85	Tom Seaver/25	30.00
86	Adam Dunn/250	8.00
87	Tommy John/250	8.00
88	Tommy Lasorda/250	8.00
89	Tony Oliva/250	8.00
90	Tony Perez/Bat/250	8.00
91	Torii Hunter/250	4.00
92	Troy Glaus/250	4.00
93	Vernon Wells/250	4.00
94	Vladimir Guerrero/250	8.00
95	Wade Boggs/250	8.00
96	Warren Spahn/100	20.00
97	Will Clark/Bat/250	10.00
98	Willie McCovey/250	8.00
99	Willie Stargell/250	8.00
100	George Foster/250	8.00

Century Coll. Sign. Mat.

NM/M
All Jersey unless noted.
Prime: No Pricing
Production 5-10
Combo: .75-1.5X
Production 5-25
No pricing 15 or less.
Combo Prime: No Pricing
Production 5-10

1	Alan Trammell/50	25.00
3	Alfonso Soriano/50	40.00
4	Andre Dawson/50	25.00
6	Bert Blyleven/50	20.00
8	Bobby Doerr/50	25.00
14	Darryl Strawberry/50	25.00
15	Dave Concepcion/50	25.00
16	Dave Parker/50	20.00
17	Dennis Eckersley/50	40.00
18	Don Sutton/50	25.00
19	Dwight Gooden/50	25.00
27	Garret Anderson/50	25.00
28	Gary Carter/50	25.00
29	Gary Sheffield/25	30.00
31	Harold Baines/50	25.00
33	Jack Morris/50	25.00
37	Jim Palmer/25	25.00
38	Jim Rice/50	25.00
42	Jose Canseco/25	50.00
44	Juan Marichal/50	25.00
45	Keith Hernandez/50	25.00
50	Lee Smith/50	15.00
51	Lenny Dykstra/Bat/50	25.00
52	Luis Tiant/50	15.00
53	Magglio Ordonez/50	25.00
56	Mark Grace/50	40.00
57	Mark Mulder/50	25.00
58	Mark Teixeira/25	40.00
59	Marty Marion/50	25.00
68	Phil Niekro/50	25.00
71	Ralph Kiner Bat/50	40.00
75	Roberto Alomar/25	50.00
76	Robin Ventura/50	20.00
82	Steve Garvey/50	25.00
87	Tommy John/50	15.00
90	Tony Perez Bat/25	40.00
91	Torii Hunter/25	30.00
93	Vernon Wells/25	25.00
94	Vladimir Guerrero/50	40.00
100	George Foster/50	20.00

Century Stars

NM/M
Common Player: 1.50
Production 1,500 Sets
Spectrum: 1.5-3X
Production 100 Sets

1	Al Kaline	2.00
2	Albert Pujols	5.00
3	Alex Rodriguez	4.00
4	Barry Larkin	2.00
5	Barry Zito	1.50
6	Billy Williams	1.50
7	Bob Feller	1.50
8	Bob Gibson	3.00
9	Cal Ripken Jr.	8.00
10	Chipper Jones	3.00
11	Curt Schilling	2.00
12	Dale Murphy	2.00
13	Dave Parker	1.50
14	Derek Jeter	6.00
15	Don Drysdale	1.50
16	Don Mattingly	5.00
17	Eddie Murray	2.00
18	Fergie Jenkins	2.00
19	Gary Carter	2.00
20	George Brett	5.00
21	Greg Maddux	3.00
22	Ivan Rodriguez	2.00
23	Jeff Bagwell	2.00
24	Joe Morgan	2.00
25	Johnny Bench	3.00
26	Kirby Puckett	3.00
27	Lou Boudreau	1.50
28	Lou Brock	1.50
29	Luis Aparicio	1.50
30	Manny Ramirez	2.00
31	Mark Prior	2.00
32	Miguel Tejada	2.00
33	Mike Mussina	2.00
34	Mike Piazza	4.00
35	Mike Schmidt	5.00
36	Nolan Ryan	6.00
37	Nomar Garciaparra	4.00
38	Ozzie Smith	3.00
39	Paul Molitor	3.00
40	Pedro J. Martinez	3.00
41	Rafael Palmeiro	2.00
42	Randy Johnson	3.00
43	Red Schoendienst	1.50
44	Reggie Jackson	3.00
45	Rickey Henderson	2.00
46	Roberto Alomar	2.00
47	Roberto Clemente	5.00
48	Robin Yount	3.00
49	Rod Carew	2.00
50	Roger Clemens	5.00
51	Ryne Sandberg	4.00
52	Sammy Sosa	3.00
53	Stan Musial	4.00
54	Steve Carlton	2.00
55	Todd Helton	2.00
56	Tom Glavine	2.00
57	Tom Seaver	3.00
58	Tony Gwynn	3.00
59	Wade Boggs	2.00
60	Whitey Ford	2.00

Century Stars Material

NM/M
All Jersey unless noted.
Prime: No Pricing
Production Five Sets

1	Al Kaline/Pants/25	30.00
2	Albert Pujols/50	25.00
4	Barry Larkin/50	10.00
5	Barry Zito/50	6.00
6	Billy Williams/50	8.00
8	Bob Gibson/25	20.00
9	Cal Ripken Jr./50	60.00
10	Chipper Jones/50	10.00
11	Curt Schilling/50	8.00
12	Dale Murphy/50	12.00
13	Dave Parker/50	8.00
14	Derek Jeter/50	35.00
15	Don Drysdale/50	12.00
16	Don Mattingly/Jkt/50	20.00
17	Eddie Murray/50	15.00
18	Fergie Jenkins/Pants/25	12.00
19	Gary Carter/Pants/50	8.00
20	George Brett/50	25.00
21	Greg Maddux/50	15.00
22	Ivan Rodriguez/50	12.00
23	Jeff Bagwell/50	10.00
24	Joe Morgan/25	10.00
25	Johnny Bench/50	20.00
26	Kirby Puckett/50	15.00
27	Lou Boudreau/50	8.00
28	Lou Brock/25	20.00
29	Luis Aparicio/Pants/50	8.00
30	Manny Ramirez/50	10.00
31	Mark Prior/50	8.00
32	Miguel Tejada/50	8.00
33	Mike Mussina/50	10.00
34	Mike Piazza/50	20.00
35	Mike Schmidt/50	20.00
36	Nolan Ryan/50	35.00
37	Nomar Garciaparra/50	15.00
38	Ozzie Smith/50	15.00
40	Pedro J. Martinez/50	10.00
41	Rafael Palmeiro/25	15.00
42	Randy Johnson/50	12.00
43	Red Schoendienst/50	8.00
44	Reggie Jackson/Pants/50	15.00
45	Rickey Henderson/50	12.00
46	Roberto Alomar/50	12.00
48	Robin Yount/50	15.00
49	Rod Carew/Jkt/50	10.00
50	Roger Clemens/50	15.00
51	Ryne Sandberg/50	20.00
52	Sammy Sosa/50	15.00
54	Steve Carlton/25	15.00
55	Todd Helton/50	12.00
56	Tom Glavine/50	15.00
57	Tom Seaver/50	15.00
58	Tony Gwynn/50	15.00
59	Wade Boggs/50	10.00

Century Stars Signature

NM/M
Signature Material: No Pricing
Production Five Sets
Sig. Material Prime: No Pricing
Production Five Sets

1	Al Kaline/25	50.00
6	Billy Williams/25	35.00
7	Bob Feller/25	30.00
8	Bob Gibson/25	35.00
12	Dale Murphy/50	40.00
13	Dave Parker/25	15.00
18	Fergie Jenkins/25	25.00
19	Gary Carter/25	15.00
24	Joe Morgan/25	30.00
28	Lou Brock/25	35.00
29	Luis Aparicio/25	20.00
35	Mike Schmidt/25	60.00
38	Ozzie Smith/25	75.00
53	Stan Musial/25	75.00

Dynasty

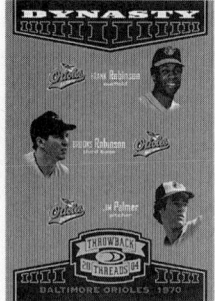

NM/M
Common Player: 3.00
Production 1,500 Sets
Spectrum: 2-3X
Production 100 Sets

1	Phil Rizzuto, Whitey Ford	3.00
2	Pee Wee Reese, Duke Snider, Tom Lasorda	3.00
3	Jim "Catfish" Hunter, Reggie Jackson	3.00
4	Roger Maris, Whitey Ford	5.00
5	Enos Slaughter, Shawn Marion, Stan Musial	5.00

6 Dwight Gooden, Gary Carter, Darryl Strawberry, Keith Hernandez 3.00
7 Johnny Bench, Tony Perez, Joe Morgan, George Foster 3.00
8 Derek Jeter, Jorge Posada, Bernie Williams, Andy Pettitte 6.00
9 Frank Robinson, Brooks Robinson, Jim Palmer 3.00
10 Willie Stargell, Dave Parker, Bill Madlock 3.00
11 Bob Gibson, Lou Brock, Ken Boyer 3.00
12 Rickey Henderson, Paul Molitor, Joe Carter, Roberto Alomar 3.00

Dynasty Material

NM/M

Quantity produced listed
Prime: No Pricing
Production Five Sets
3 Jim "Catfish" Hunter, Reggie Jackson/25 25.00
6 Dwight Gooden, Gary Carter, Darryl Strawberry, Keith Hernandez/50 35.00
7 Johnny Bench, Tony Perez, Joe Morgan, George Foster/25 80.00
8 Derek Jeter, Jorge Posada, Bernie Williams, Andy Pettitte/50 50.00
10 Willie Stargell, Dave Parker, Bill Madlock/25 30.00
11 Bob Gibson, Lou Brock, Ken Boyer/25 35.00
12 Rickey Henderson, Paul Molitor, Joe Carter, Roberto Alomar/25 60.00

Fans of the Game

NM/M

Inserted 1:24
1 Emilio Estevez 3.00
2 Shannon Elizabeth 3.00
3 Joe Montegna UER 2.00
4 Jamie-Lynn DiScala 2.00
5 Jonathan Silverman 2.00

Fans of the Game Sign.

NM/M

1 Emilio Estevez 40.00
2 Shannon Elizabeth 60.00
3 Joe Montegna UER 20.00
4 Jamie-Lynn DiScala 60.00
5 Jonathan Silverman 20.00

Generations

NM/M

Common Duo: 1.50
Production 1,500 Sets
Spectrum: 2-3X
Production 100 Sets
1 George Brett, Albert Pujols 5.00
2 Wade Boggs, Aubrey Huff 2.00
3 Jim "Catfish" Hunter, Tim Hudson 2.00
4 Steve Garvey, Shawn Green 1.50
5 Tony Gwynn, Garret Anderson 4.00
6 Fergie Jenkins, Mark Prior 2.00
7 Robin Yount, Rickie Weeks 4.00
8 Warren Spahn, Greg Maddux 4.00
9 Brooks Robinson, Cal Ripken Jr., Miguel Tejada 8.00
10 Bobby Doerr, Carl Yastrzemski, Manny Ramirez 5.00
11 Al Kaline, Alan Trammell, Ivan Rodriguez 2.50
12 Tom Seaver, Dwight Gooden, Tom Glavine 3.00
13 Stan Musial, Lou Brock, Jim Edmonds 4.00
14 George Foster, Dave Parker, Austin Kearns 1.50
15 Ed Mathews, Dale Murphy, Chipper Jones 3.00
16 Don Sutton, Nolan Ryan, Roger Clemens 8.00
17 Bernie Williams, Andre Dawson, Sammy Sosa 4.00
18 Whitey Ford, Tommy John, Andy Pettitte 2.00
19 Carlton Fisk, Roger Clemens, Nomar Garciaparra 5.00
20 Shawn Marion, Ozzie Smith, Edgar Renteria 4.00
21 Reggie Jackson, Rickey Henderson, Eric Chavez 2.00
22 Babe Ruth, Don Mattingly, Derek Jeter 8.00
23 Roberto Clemente Jr., Reggie Jackson, Sammy Sosa 6.00
24 Bob Feller, Tom Seaver, Roger Clemens 5.00
25 Ernie Banks, Cal Ripken Jr., Alex Rodriguez 8.00
26 Pee Wee Reese, Ozzie Smith, Derek Jeter 6.00
27 Harmon Killebrew, Mike Schmidt, Alex Rodriguez 5.00
28 Bob Gibson, Dwight Gooden, Josh Beckett 2.00

Generations Material

NM/M

Quantity produced listed
Prime: No Pricing
Production Five Sets
1 George Brett, Albert Pujols/50 40.00
2 Wade Boggs, Aubrey Huff/50 10.00
3 Jim "Catfish" Hunter, Tim Hudson/25 20.00
5 Tony Gwynn, Garret Anderson/50 20.00
6 Fergie Jenkins, Mark Prior/25 15.00
7 Robin Yount, Rickie Weeks/Bat/50 20.00
8 Warren Spahn, Greg Maddux/25 40.00
11 Al Kaline, Alan Trammell, Ivan Rodriguez/Bat/25 40.00
14 George Foster, Dave Parker, Austin Kearns/25 20.00
16 Don Sutton, Nolan Ryan, Roger Clemens/Bat/50 50.00
17 Billy Williams, Andre Dawson, Sammy Sosa/50 30.00
18 Whitey Ford, Tommy John, Andy Pettitte/25 40.00
19 Carlton Fisk, Roger Clemens, Nomar Garciaparra 40.00
20 Marty Marion, Ozzie Smith, Edgar Renteria/25 40.00
21 Reggie Jackson, Rickey Henderson, Eric Chavez/50 30.00
24 Bob Feller, Tom Seaver, Roger Clemens/25 40.00
25 Ernie Banks, Cal Ripken Jr., Alex Rodriguez 65.00
26 Pee Wee Reese, Ozzie Smith, Derek Jeter/25 50.00
27 Harmon Killebrew, Mike Schmidt, Alex Rodriguez/25 50.00
28 Bob Gibson, Dwight Gooden, Josh Beckett/25 30.00

Material

NM/M

Common Player: 4.00
2 Darin Erstad/Jsy/100 6.00
4 Garret Anderson/Jsy/100 6.00
5 Tim Salmon/Jsy/100 6.00
6 Troy Glaus/Jsy/100 6.00
7 Vladimir Guerrero/Bat/100 10.00
8 Brandon Webb/Pants/100 4.00
9 Luis Gonzalez/Jsy/100 4.00
10 Randy Johnson/Jsy/100 10.00
11 Richie Sexson/Bat/50 8.00
12 Roberto Alomar/Bat/100 8.00
14 Steve Finley/Jsy/100 4.00
15 Adam LaRoche/Bat/100 4.00
16 Andruw Jones/Jsy/100 6.00
17 Chipper Jones/Jsy/100 8.00
18 J.D. Drew/Bat/100 6.00
19 John Smoltz/Jsy/100 8.00
20 Rafael Furcal/Jsy/100 4.00
22 Javy Lopez/Bat/100 6.00
23 Jay Gibbons/Jsy/100 4.00
24 Larry Bigbie/Jsy/100 4.00
25 Luis Matos/Jsy/100 4.00
26 Melvin Mora/Jsy/100 4.00
27 Miguel Tejada/Bat/100 6.00
28 Rafael Palmeiro/Jsy/100 8.00
29 Curt Schilling/Bat/100 6.00
30 David Ortiz/Bat/100 10.00
32 Jason Varitek/Jsy/100 8.00
33 Johnny Damon/Bat/100 6.00
34 Manny Ramirez/Jsy/100 8.00
35 Nomar Garciaparra/Jsy/100 8.00
36 Pedro J. Martinez/Jsy/100 8.00
37 Trot Nixon/Bat/100 4.00
38 Aramis Ramirez/Jsy/100 6.00
39 Corey Patterson/Pants/100 6.00
41 Greg Maddux/Bat/100 10.00
42 Kerry Wood/Pants/100 10.00
43 Mark Prior/Jsy/100 6.00
44 Sammy Sosa/Jsy/100 12.00
45 Carlos Lee/Jsy/100 4.00
47 Frank Thomas/Pants/100 8.00
48 Joe Borchard/Jsy/100 4.00
49 Magglio Ordonez/Jsy/100 4.00
50 Mark Buehrle/Jsy/100 4.00
51 Paul Konerko/Jsy/100 4.00
52 Adam Dunn/Jsy/100 8.00
53 Austin Kearns/Jsy/100 6.00
54 Barry Larkin/Jsy/100 6.00
55 Brandon Larson/Fld Glv/100 4.00
58 Sean Casey/Jsy/100 4.00
59 C.C. Sabathia/Jsy/100 4.00
60 Jody Gerut/Jsy/100 4.00
61 Omar Vizquel/Jsy/100 4.00
62 Travis Hafner/Jsy/100 4.00
63 Victor Martinez/Bat/100 6.00
64 Charles Johnson/Bat/100 4.00
65 Garrett Atkins/Jsy/100 4.00
66 Jason Jennings/Jsy/100 4.00
67 Joe Kennedy/Bat/100 4.00
68 Larry Walker/Jsy/100 6.00
69 Preston Wilson/Jsy/100 4.00
70 Todd Helton/Jsy/100 8.00
71 Ivan Rodriguez/Bat/100 8.00
72 Jeremy Bonderman/Jsy/100 4.00
73 A.J. Burnett/Jsy/100 4.00
74 Brad Penny/Jsy/100 4.00
75 Dontrelle Willis/Jsy/100 4.00
76 Josh Beckett/Jsy/100 6.00
77 Juan Pierre/Bat/100 4.00
78 Luis Castillo/Jsy/100 4.00
79 Miguel Cabrera/Jsy/100 8.00
80 Mike Lowell/Jsy/50 8.00
81 Andy Pettitte/Bat/100 6.00
82 Craig Biggio/Jsy/100 6.00
83 Jeff Bagwell/Jsy/100 8.00
84 Jeff Kent/Jsy/100 4.00
85 Lance Berkman/Jsy/100 4.00
86 Morgan Ensberg/Jsy/100 4.00
87 Richard Hidalgo/Pants/100 4.00
88 Roger Clemens/Bat/50 15.00
89 Roy Oswalt/Jsy/100 4.00
90 Wade Miller/Jsy/100 4.00
91 Angel Berroa/Pants/100 4.00
92 Carlos Beltran/Jsy/100 8.00
93 Juan Gonzalez/Bat/100 8.00
94 Ken Harvey/Bat/100 4.00
95 Mike Sweeney/Jsy/100 4.00
96 Runelvys Hernandez/Jsy/100 4.00
97 Adrian Beltre/Jsy/100 6.00
98 Edwin Jackson/Jsy/100 4.00
100 Hideo Nomo/Jsy/100 8.00
101 Hong-Chih Kuo/Bat/100 8.00
102 Kazuhisa Ishii/Jsy/100 4.00
103 Paul LoDuca/Jsy/100 4.00
104 Shawn Green/Jsy/100 6.00
105 Ben Sheets/Jsy/100 6.00
106 Geoff Jenkins/Jsy/100 4.00
107 Junior Spivey/Bat/50 4.00
108 Rickie Weeks/Bat/50 8.00
111 Doug Mientkiewicz/Bat/100 4.00
112 Jacque Jones/Jsy/100 4.00
113 Joe Mays/Jsy/100 4.00
114 Johan Santana/Jsy/100 8.00
115 Shannon Stewart/Jsy/100 4.00
116 Torii Hunter/Jsy/100 6.00
117 Brad Wilkerson/Bat/100 4.00
118 Carl Everett/Bat/100 4.00
120 Jose Vidro/Jsy/100 4.00
121 Nick Johnson/Bat/100 4.00
122 Orlando Cabrera/Jsy/100 4.00
123 Al Leiter/Jsy/100 4.00
124 Cliff Floyd/Bat/100 4.00
125 Jae Weong Seo/Jsy/100 4.00
126 Jose Reyes/Jsy/100 8.00
128 Mike Piazza/Jsy/100 10.00
129 Tom Glavine/Jsy/100 6.00
130 Alex Rodriguez/Bat/100 10.00
131 Bernie Williams/Jsy/100 6.00
133 Derek Jeter/Jsy/100 20.00
134 Gary Sheffield/Bat/100 6.00
135 Hideki Matsui/Jsy/100 20.00
136 Jason Giambi/Jsy/100 6.00
138 Jorge Posada/Jsy/100 6.00
141 Mariano Rivera/Jsy/50 15.00
142 Mike Mussina/Jsy/100 6.00
143 Barry Zito/Jsy/100 4.00
145 Eric Chavez/Jsy/100 4.00
146 Erubiel Durazo/Bat/100 4.00
147 Jermaine Dye/Bat/100 4.00
149 Mark Mulder/Jsy/100 6.00
150 Rich Harden/Jsy/100 4.00
151 Tim Hudson/Jsy/100 6.00
153 Bobby Abreu/Jsy/100 6.00
154 Brett Myers/Jsy/100 4.00
155 Jim Thome/Jsy/100 8.00
157 Kevin Millwood/Jsy/100 4.00
158 Marlon Byrd/Jsy/100 4.00
159 Pat Burrell/Jsy/100 6.00
161 Jason Kendall/Jsy/100 4.00
162 Brian Giles/Bat/100 4.00
164 Ryan Klesko/Jsy/100 4.00
165 Edgardo Alfonzo/Bat/100 4.00
167 Jerome Williams/Jsy/100 4.00
169 Bret Boone/Jsy/29 4.00
170 Edgar Martinez/Jsy/100 8.00
171 Freddy Garcia/Jsy/100 4.00
173 Jamie Moyer/Jsy/100 4.00
174 John Olerud/Jsy/100 4.00
176 Albert Pujols/Jsy/100 20.00
177 Dan Haren/Jsy/100 4.00
178 Edgar Renteria/Jsy/100 6.00
179 Jim Edmonds/Jsy/100 6.00
180 Matt Morris/Jsy/100 4.00
181 Scott Rolen/Jsy/100 8.00
182 Aubrey Huff/Jsy/100 4.00
183 Carl Crawford/Jsy/100 4.00
184 Chad Gaudin/Jsy/100 4.00
185 Delmon Young/Bat/100 6.00
186 Dewon Brazelton/Jsy/100 4.00
187 Fred McGriff/Jsy/100 6.00
188 Rocco Baldelli/Jsy/100 4.00
189 Alfonso Soriano/Bat/100 8.00
190 Hank Blalock/Jsy/100 6.00
191 Laynce Nix/Bat/100 4.00
192 Mark Teixeira/Jsy/23 15.00
193 Michael Young/Bat/100 6.00
194 Carlos Delgado/Jsy/100 6.00
195 Eric Hinske/Jsy/100 4.00
196 Frank Catalanotto/Jsy/100 4.00
197 Josh Phelps/Jsy/100 4.00
198 Orlando Hudson/Jsy/100 4.00
199 Roy Halladay/Jsy/100 4.00
200 Vernon Wells/Jsy/100 4.00
201 Dale Murphy/Jsy/100 12.00
202 Cal Ripken Jr./Jsy/100 30.00
203 Fred Lynn/Bat/100 8.00
204 Wade Boggs/Jsy/100 8.00
205 Nolan Ryan/Jkt/100 25.00
206 Rod Carew/Jkt/100 8.00
207 Andre Dawson/Pants/100 6.00
208 Ernie Banks/Pants/50 20.00
209 Ryne Sandberg/Jsy/50 25.00
210 Bo Jackson/Jsy/100 12.00
211 Carlton Fisk/Jkt/100 10.00
212 Dave Concepcion/Jsy/100 8.00
213 Alan Trammell/Bat/100 8.00
214 George Brett/Jsy/100 15.00
215 Robin Yount/Jsy/100 15.00
216 Gary Carter/Jsy/100 8.00
217 Darryl Strawberry/Pants/100 8.00
218 Dwight Gooden/Jsy/50 8.00
219 Babe Ruth/Jsy/25 400.00
220 Don Mattingly/Jkt/100 15.00
221 Reggie Jackson/Jkt/100 10.00
222 Mike Schmidt/Jkt/100 15.00
223 Tony Gwynn/Jsy/100 10.00
224 Keith Hernandez/Jsy/100 8.00

Player Threads

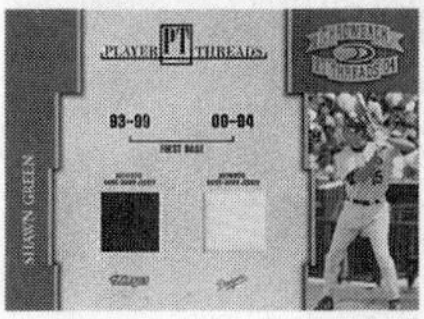

NM/M

Common Player: 4.00
Production 250 Sets
Prime: 2-3X
Production 10-25
No pricing 15 or less.
1 Aaron Boone 4.00
2 Alex Rodriguez/M's-Rgr 15.00
3 Andres Galarraga/Braves-Giants-Rgr 10.00
4 Aramis Ramirez 4.00
5 Bartolo Colon 4.00
6 Ben Grieve/A's-D'Rays 4.00
7 Brad Fullmer 4.00
8 Bret Boone/Braves-M's 4.00
9 Brian Giles 4.00
10 Brian Jordan 4.00
11 Byung-Hyun Kim 4.00
12 Casey Fossum 4.00

13 Cesar Izturis 4.00
14 Chan Ho Park 4.00
15 Charles Johnson 4.00
16 Cliff Floyd 4.00
17 Darryl Strawberry/ Dgr-Met-Ynk 10.00
18 David Ortiz 10.00
19 David Wells/Jays-Yanks 4.00
20 Derrek Lee 6.00
21 Dmitri Young 4.00
22 Edgardo Alfonzo 4.00
23 Ellis Burks 4.00
24 Gary Sheffield/ Braves-Brew-Dgr 8.00
25 Hee Seop Choi 4.00
26 Ivan Rodriguez/Marlins-Rgr 10.00
27 J.D. Drew 6.00
28 Javier Vazquez 4.00
29 Jay Payton 4.00
30 Jeff Kent/Astros-Giants-Jays 4.00
31 Jeromy Burnitz 4.00
32 Jim Thome/Indians-Phils 10.00
33 Joe Kennedy 4.00
34 Joe Torre 8.00
35 Jose Cruz Jr. 4.00
36 Juan Encarnacion 4.00
37 Juan Gonzalez/Indians-Rgr 8.00
38 Juan Pierre 4.00
39 Junior Spivey 4.00
40 Kenny Lofton/Brave-Tribe 8.00
41 Kevin Millwood 6.00
42 Manny Ramirez/ Indians-Sox 12.00
43 Mark Grace/Cubs-D'backs 10.00
44 Mike Hampton 4.00
45 Mike Piazza/ Dgr-Marlins-Mets 20.00
46 Milton Bradley 4.00
47 Moises Alou 6.00
48 Nick Johnson 4.00
49 Nolan Ryan/ Ang/Jkt-Ast/Jkt-Rgr 50.00
50 Preston Wilson/ Marlins-Rockies 6.00
51 Rafael Palmeiro/O's-Rgr 10.00
52 Ray Durham 4.00
53 Reggie Jackson/ A's-Ang-Yank 15.00
54 Reggie Sanders 4.00
55 Rich Aurilia 4.00
56 Richie Sexson 6.00
57 Rickey Henderson/ A's-M's-Yanks/25 50.00
58 Rickey Henderson/ Dgr-Mets-Padres 20.00
59 Robert Fick 4.00
60 Roberto Alomar/Mets-Sox 8.00
61 Roberto Alomar/Indians-O's 8.00
62 Robin Ventura/ Mets-Sox-Yanks 10.00
63 Rondell White/Cubs-Expos 6.00
64 Ryan Klesko/Braves-Padres 6.00
65 Sean Casey 6.00
66 Shannon Stewart/Jays-Twins 6.00
67 Shawn Green/Jays-Dgr 8.00
68 Shea Hillenbrand 4.00
69 Steve Carlton/Giants-Sox 8.00
70 Terrence Long 4.00
71 Tony Batista 4.00
72 Travis Hafner/Indians-Rgr 6.00
73 Travis Lee 4.00
74 Vladimir Guerrero 8.00
75 Wes Helms 4.00

Player Threads Signature

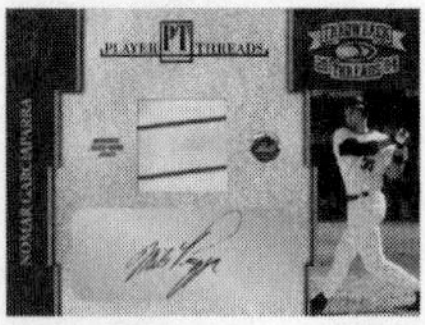

NM/M

Quantity produced listed
4 Aramis Ramirez/25 30.00
17 Darryl Strawberry/ Dgr-Met-Ynk/25 40.00
24 Gary Sheffield/ Brave-Brw-Dgr/25 40.00
28 Javier Vazquez/25 20.00
29 Jay Payton/25 15.00
37 Juan Gonzalez/ Indians-Rgr/25 40.00
39 Junior Spivey/25 15.00
50 Preston Wilson/ Marlins-Rockies/25 25.00
55 Rich Aurilia/25 15.00
62 Robin Ventura/ Mets-Sox-Yanks/25 40.00
68 Shea Hillenbrand/25 20.00
74 Vladimir Guerrero/25 60.00

Signature Marks

NM/M

Common Autograph: 8.00
4 Garret Anderson/25 25.00
8 Brandon Webb/50 10.00
13 Shea Hillenbrand/50 15.00
15 Adam LaRoche/50 10.00

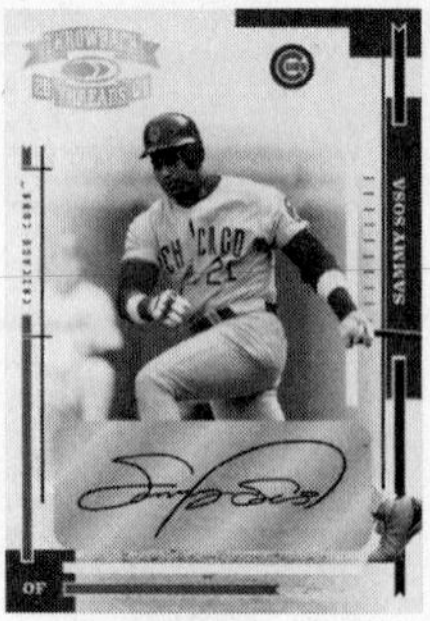

20 Rafael Furcal/25 25.00
23 Jay Gibbons/50 10.00
24 Larry Bigbie/50 20.00
25 Luis Matos/50 10.00
26 Melvin Mora/50 15.00
30 David Ortiz/25 40.00
37 Trot Nixon/25 30.00
40 Derrek Lee/25 30.00
43 Mark Prior/25 40.00
45 Carlos Lee/50 10.00
46 Esteban Loaiza/50 12.00
48 Joe Borchard/25 10.00
50 Mark Buehrle/25 25.00
53 Austin Kearns/25 20.00
55 Brandon Larson/25 15.00
60 Jody Gerut/50 20.00
62 Travis Hafner/50 20.00
63 Victor Martinez/50 25.00
69 Preston Wilson/50 15.00
74 Brad Penny/50 10.00
79 Miguel Cabrera/25 40.00
80 Mike Lowell/25 20.00
86 Morgan Ensberg/50 12.00
89 Roy Oswalt/25 25.00
91 Angel Berroa/25 12.00
92 Carlos Beltran/25 35.00
98 Edwin Jackson/50 15.00
101 Hong-Chih Kuo/50 30.00
109 Scott Podsednik/50 15.00
112 Jacque Jones/50 15.00
114 Johan Santana/25 50.00
115 Shannon Stewart/25 20.00
116 Torii Hunter/25 25.00
119 Chad Cordero/50 8.00
120 Jose Vidro/25 15.00
122 Orlando Cabrera/50 15.00
132 Chien-Ming Wang/25 100.00
147 Jermaine Dye/50 12.00
160 Jason Bay/50 20.00
163 Jay Payton/50 15.00
168 Todd Linden/50 15.00
175 Shigetoshi Hasegawa/25 50.00
177 Dan Haren/50 15.00
181 Scott Rolen/25 50.00
182 Aubrey Huff/50 15.00
184 Chad Gaudin/50 10.00
186 Dewon Brazelton/50 10.00
187 Fred McGriff/25 40.00
189 Alfonso Soriano/25 50.00
193 Michael Young/50 20.00
203 Fred Lynn/50 15.00
207 Andre Dawson/50 20.00
216 Gary Carter/25 25.00
217 Darryl Strawberry/50 20.00
218 Dwight Gooden/50 15.00
224 Keith Hernandez/50 20.00
225 Hector Gimenez/100 8.00
226 Graham Koonce/100 8.00
228 Jerry Gil/100 8.00
229 Jason Frasor/100 8.00
230 Justin Knoedler/50 10.00
233 Ronald Belisario/200 8.00
234 Jerome Gamble/200 8.00
235 Roberto Novoa/200 8.00
236 Sean Henn/200 10.00
237 Willy Taveras/100 8.00
238 Ramon Ramirez/200 10.00
241 Jason Bartlett/25 20.00
242 Fernando Nieve/25 12.00
243 Freddy Guzman/25 20.00
248 William Bergolla/100 10.00
249 Shawn Hill/100 8.00
250 Justin Germano/100 8.00

2004 Donruss Timeless Treasures

NM/M

Complete Set (100): 200.00
Common Player: 1.50
Production 999 Sets
Tin (4): 125.00
1 Albert Pujols 6.00
2 Garret Anderson 2.00
3 Randy Johnson 3.00
4 Alex Rodriguez/Yanks 8.00
5 Manny Ramirez 3.00
6 Mark Prior 4.00
7 Roberto Alomar 2.00
8 Barry Larkin 2.00
9 Todd Helton 2.50
10 Ivan Rodriguez 3.00
11 Jacque Jones 1.50
12 Jeff Kent 2.00
13 Mike Sweeney 1.50
14 Shawn Green 2.00
15 Richie Sexson 2.00
16 Mike Piazza 5.00
17 Vladimir Guerrero 4.00
18 Mike Mussina 2.00
19 Barry Zito 2.00
20 Don Mattingly 6.00
21 Ichiro Suzuki 5.00
22 Rocco Baldelli 2.00
23 Rafael Palmeiro 3.00
24 Carlos Delgado 2.00
25 Roger Clemens 6.00
26 Luis Gonzalez 2.00
27 Gary Sheffield 2.00
28 Jay Gibbons 1.50
29 Nomar Garciaparra 5.00
30 Aramis Ramirez 2.00
31 Frank Thomas 3.00
32 Ryan Wagner 1.50
33 Preston Wilson 1.50
34 Hideki Matsui 4.00
35 Roy Oswalt 2.00
36 Angel Berroa 1.50
37 Kazuhisa Ishii 1.50
38 Scott Podsednik 2.00
39 Torii Hunter 2.00
40 Tom Glavine 2.00
41 Jason Giambi 3.00
42 Eric Chavez 2.00
43 Jim Thome 3.00
44 Tony Gwynn 3.00
45 Edgar Martinez 2.00
46 Jim Edmonds 2.00
47 Delmon Young 2.00
48 Hank Blalock 2.00
49 Vernon Wells 1.50
50 Curt Schilling 2.50
51 Chipper Jones 3.00
52 Cal Ripken Jr. 8.00
53 Jason Varitek 1.50
54 Kerry Wood 3.00
55 Magglio Ordonez 2.00
56 Adam Dunn 2.00
57 Jay Payton 1.50
58 Josh Beckett 2.00
59 Jeff Bagwell 3.00
60 Carlos Beltran 2.00
61 Hideo Nomo 2.00
62 Rickie Weeks 2.00
63 Alfonso Soriano 2.50
64 Miguel Tejada 2.00
65 Bret Boone 2.00
66 Scott Rolen 3.00
67 Aubrey Huff 1.50
68 Juan Gonzalez 2.50
69 Roy Halladay 2.50
70 Brandon Webb 1.50
71 Andruw Jones 2.50
72 Pedro J. Martinez 3.00
73 Carlos Lee 1.50
74 Lance Berkman 2.00
75 Paul LoDuca 1.50
76 Jorge Posada 2.00
77 Tim Hudson 2.00
78 Stan Musial 4.00
79 Mark Teixeira 2.00
80 Trot Nixon 1.50
81 Fred McGriff 1.50
82 Nick Johnson 1.50
83 Nolan Ryan 8.00
84 Ken Griffey Jr. 4.00
85 Mariano Rivera 2.00
86 Mark Mulder 2.00
87 Bob Gibson 2.50
88 Dale Murphy UER 2.50
89 Bernie Williams 2.00
90 Carl Yastrzemski 3.00
91 Sammy Sosa 5.00
92 Miguel Cabrera 4.00
93 Craig Biggio 2.00
94 George Brett 6.00
95 Rickey Henderson 3.00
96 Derek Jeter 8.00
97 Greg Maddux 4.00
98 Bob Abreu 2.00
99 Troy Glaus 2.00
100 Dontrelle Willis 2.00

Bronze

Bronze: 1-2X
Production 100 Sets

Gold

Gold: No Pricing
Production 10 Sets

Platinum

Platinum: No Pricing
Production One Set

Silver

Silver: 2-4X
Production 25 Sets

Award Materials

NM/M

Common Player: 10.00
Quantity produced listed
Prime: 1-2X
Production 1-25
No pricing 10 or less.
Number: .75-1.5X
Production 3-51
No pricing 15 or less.
2 Stan Musial/Jsy/43 25.00
3 Lou Boudreau/Jsy/19 15.00
4 Roger Maris/Pants/61 40.00
5 Roger Maris/Bat/61 40.00
6 Roberto Clemente/Bat/66 60.00
7 Bob Gibson 68 CY/Jsy/68 20.00
8 Bob Gibson 68 MVP/Jsy/68 20.00
9 Tom Seaver/Jsy/19 20.00
10 Fred Lynn/Jsy/75 8.00
11 Jim Rice/Jsy/78 10.00
12 Mike Schmidt 80 MVP/ Jsy/80 15.00
13 Mike Schmidt 80 MVP/ Pants/80 15.00
14 Mike Schmidt 80 MVP/ Stir/80 15.00
15 Mike Schmidt 81 MVP/ Jsy/81 15.00
16 Mike Schmidt 81 MVP/ Bat/81 15.00
17 Dale Murphy/Jsy/82 10.00
18 Mike Schmidt 86 MVP/ Hat/19 35.00
19 Mike Schmidt 86 MVP/ Shoe/19 35.00
20 Mike Schmidt 86 MVP/ Bat/86 15.00
21 Mike Schmidt 86 MVP/ Stir/19 35.00
22 Jose Canseco/Jsy/88 10.00
23 Frank Thomas 93 MVP/ Bat/93 10.00
24 Frank Thomas 93 MVP/ Jsy/93 10.00
25 Jeff Bagwell/Pants/94 10.00
26 Frank Thomas 94 MVP/ Jsy/94 10.00
27 Frank Thomas 94 MVP/ Pants/94 10.00
28 Jeff Bagwell/Bat/94 10.00
29 Pedro J. Martinez 97 CY/ Jsy/97 10.00
30 Ivan Rodriguez/Bat/99 10.00
31 Randy Johnson 00 CY/ Jsy/25 20.00
32 Pedro J. Martinez 00 CY/ Jsy/25 20.00
33 Roger Clemens/Jsy/50 20.00
34 Randy Johnson 02 CY/ Jsy/25 20.00
35 Miguel Tejada/Jsy/25 15.00

Award Mat. Combo Prime

No Pricing
Production 19 Sets

Award Materials Combos

NM/M

Prime: .75-1.5X
Production 19 Sets
4 Roger Maris/ Bat-Pants/25 70.00
12 Mike Schmidt 80M/ Jsy-Pants/25 40.00
13 Mike Schmidt 80M/ Pant-Stir/50 30.00
14 Mike Schmidt 80M/ Jsy-Stir/50 30.00
15 Mike Schmidt 81M/ Bat-Jsy/25 40.00
16 Mike Schmidt 81M/ Bat-Stir/50 30.00
18 Mike Schmidt 86M/ Hat-Shoe/50 30.00
19 Mike Schmidt 86M/ Hat-Bat/50 30.00
20 Mike Schmidt 86M/ Hat-Stir/50 30.00
21 Mike Schmidt 86M/ Bat-Shoe/50 30.00
23 Frank Thomas 93M/ Bat-Jsy/25 25.00
25 Jeff Bagwell/Bat-Jsy/25 25.00
26 Frank Thomas 94M/ Bat-Jsy/25 25.00
35 Miguel Tejada/Bat-Jsy/25 15.00

Award Mater. Combo Sig.

No Pricing
Production Five Sets
Prime: No Pricing
Production One Set

Award Materials Number

No Pricing
Production 3-45

Award Materials Prime

No Pricing
Production 1-25

Award Materials Signature

NM/M

Common Autograph:
Quantity produced listed
Number: 1-2X
Production 1-19
No pricing 10 or less.
Prime: No Pricing
7 Bob Gibson 68 CY/Jsy/19 50.00
8 Bob Gibson 68 MVP/Jsy/19 50.00
10 Fred Lynn Jsy/75 15.00
11 Jim Rice Jsy/78 30.00

Award Mat. Sig. Number
No Pricing

Award Mat. Sig. Prime
No Pricing

Game Day Materials
NM/M
Quantity produced listed
1 Nellie Fox/Bat/58 40.00
2 Frank Robinson/Bat/61 10.00
3 George Brett/Bat/77 20.00
4 George Brett/Hat/82 30.00
5 Nolan Ryan/Hat/19 80.00
6 Cal Ripken Jr./Hat/85 50.00
7 Rod Carew/Hat/19 25.00
8 Ryne Sandberg/Bat/91 20.00
9 Kirby Puckett/Bat/92 15.00
10 Frank Thomas/Bat/93 10.00
12 Tony Gwynn/Pants/99 20.00
13 Vladimir Guerrero/Bat/99 15.00
14 Tony Gwynn/Hat/99 20.00
15 Magglio Ordonez/Hat/15 15.00
16 Rickey Henderson/Bat/50 10.00

Game Day Material Sig.
NM/M
Many not priced due to scarcity.
2 Frank Robinson/Bat/25 40.00
15 Magglio Ordonez/Hat/25 30.00

HOF Materials Barrel
No Pricing
Production One Set

HOF Materials Bat
NM/M
1 Al Kaline/25 25.00
2 Babe Ruth/50 200.00
4 Bobby Doerr/25 10.00
5 Brooks Robinson/25 30.00
6 Carl Yastrzemski/25 30.00
7 Carlton Fisk/25 20.00
8 Dave Winfield/25 15.00
10 Eddie Murray/25 25.00
11 Ernie Banks/25 30.00
13 Frank Robinson/25 15.00
18 Joe Morgan/25 15.00
19 Johnny Bench/25 30.00
21 Kirby Puckett/25 30.00
22 Lou Brock/25 20.00
23 Lou Gehrig/50 125.00
24 Luis Aparicio/25 10.00
25 Mel Ott/25 40.00
26 Orlando Cepeda/25 15.00
27 Pee Wee Reese/25 15.00
28 Phil Rizzuto/25 15.00
29 Red Schoendienst/25 10.00
30 Roberto Clemente/25 65.00
31 Roy Campanella/25 25.00
32 Paul Molitor/25 20.00
33 Ty Cobb/25 100.00
35 Willie McCovey/25 15.00
36 Willie Stargell/25 15.00

HOF Materials Bat Sig.
NM/M
1 Al Kaline/50 40.00
4 Bobby Doerr/50 35.00
5 Brooks Robinson/50 40.00
11 Ernie Banks/25 75.00
13 Frank Robinson/50 35.00
18 Joe Morgan/25 40.00
19 Johnny Bench/25 60.00
22 Lou Brock/50 30.00
24 Luis Aparicio/50 20.00
26 Orlando Cepeda/50 25.00
28 Phil Rizzuto/50 35.00
29 Red Schoendienst/50 25.00
32 Paul Molitor/25 50.00

HOF Mat. Combo Bat-Jsy
NM/M
Quantity produced listed
Prime: No Pricing
Production 1-5
1 Al Kaline/25 40.00
2 Babe Ruth/25 500.00
4 Bobby Doerr/25 15.00
5 Brooks Robinson/50 30.00
6 Carl Yastrzemski/50 40.00
7 Carlton Fisk/50 20.00
8 Dave Winfield/50 15.00
10 Eddie Murray/50 35.00
13 Frank Robinson/50 20.00
18 Joe Morgan/50 15.00
21 Kirby Puckett/50 30.00
22 Lou Brock/50 15.00
23 Lou Gehrig/25 220.00
24 Luis Aparicio/25 20.00
25 Mel Ott/25 60.00
27 Pee Wee Reese/50 20.00
28 Phil Rizzuto/50 20.00
29 Red Schoendienst/25 15.00
30 Roberto Clemente/50 80.00
32 Paul Molitor/50 20.00
35 Willie McCovey/50 15.00
36 Willie Stargell/50 20.00

HOF Material Combo Bat-Jsy Signature
NM/M
Quantity produced listed
Prime: No Pricing
Production 1-5
4 Bobby Doerr/25 30.00
5 Brooks Robinson/25 80.00
11 Ernie Banks/25 80.00
13 Frank Robinson/25 65.00
18 Joe Morgan/25 40.00
22 Lou Brock/25 40.00
24 Luis Aparicio/25 30.00
29 Red Schoendienst/25 40.00
32 Paul Molitor/25 60.00

HOF Material Bat-Jsy Signature Prime
No Pricing

HOF Mat. Combo Bat-Pant
NM/M
Production 25 Sets
1 Al Kaline/25 35.00
2 Babe Ruth/25 350.00
12 Fergie Jenkins/ Fld Glv-Pants/25 15.00
23 Lou Gehrig/25 200.00
24 Luis Aparicio/25 15.00
25 Mel Ott/25 60.00
31 Roy Campanella/25 40.00
33 Ty Cobb/25 200.00

HOF Material Combo Bat-Pant Signature
NM/M
1 Al Kaline/25 75.00
12 Fergie Jenkins/ Fld Glv-Pants/25 35.00
24 Luis Aparicio/25 25.00

HOF Mat. Combo Jsy-Pant
NM/M
2 Babe Ruth/25 500.00
23 Lou Gehrig/25 220.00
24 Luis Aparicio/25 15.00

HOF Material Combo Jsy-Pant Prime
No Pricing

HOF Material Combo Jsy-Pant Signature
NM/M
Prime: No Pricing
Production 1-5
24 Luis Aparicio/25 25.00

HOF Materials Jersey
NM/M
Quantity produced listed
Prime: No Pricing
Production 1-10
Jersey Number: .75-1.5X
Production 1-44
No pricing 15 or less.
2 Babe Ruth/25 500.00
3 Bob Feller/10 10.00
4 Bobby Doerr/25 15.00
5 Brooks Robinson/50 15.00
6 Carl Yastrzemski/50 25.00
7 Carlton Fisk/50 15.00
8 Dave Winfield/50 10.00
10 Eddie Murray/25 25.00
13 Frank Robinson/25 20.00
14 Hal Newhouser/50 10.00
15 Hoyt Wilhelm/50 10.00
17 Jim Palmer/50 10.00
18 Joe Morgan/50 10.00
20 Juan Marichal/50 10.00
21 Kirby Puckett/50 20.00
22 Lou Brock/25 15.00
23 Lou Gehrig/25 140.00
24 Luis Aparicio/25 10.00
25 Mel Ott/25 40.00
27 Pee Wee Reese/50 15.00
28 Phil Rizzuto/50 15.00
29 Red Schoendienst/25 15.00
30 Roberto Clemente/50 60.00
32 Paul Molitor/50 15.00
34 Warren Spahn/50 20.00
35 Willie McCovey/50 10.00
36 Willie Stargell/50 15.00

HOF Material Jsy Number
NM/M
16 Jackie Robinson/42 50.00

HOF Materials Jsy Prime
No Pricing

HOF Materials Jsy Sig.
NM/M
Quantity produced listed
Prime: No Pricing
Production 1-10
Number: 1X
Production 10-25
1 Al Kaline/25 50.00
4 Bobby Doerr/50 30.00
5 Brooks Robinson/25 60.00
13 Frank Robinson/50 35.00
15 Hoyt Wilhelm/25 25.00
17 Jim Palmer/50 30.00
18 Joe Morgan/25 30.00
20 Juan Marichal/50 35.00
22 Lou Brock/50 30.00
24 Luis Aparicio/50 25.00
26 Orlando Cepeda/25 25.00
28 Phil Rizzuto/50 40.00
29 Red Schoendienst/50 20.00
32 Paul Molitor/50 30.00
34 Warren Spahn/25 65.00

HOF Mat. Jsy Sig Number
No Pricing

HOF Mat. Jsy Sig. Prime
NM/M
23 Lou Gehrig/1 (7/04 Auction) 4,950

HOF Materials Pants
NM/M
1 Al Kaline/25 30.00
2 Babe Ruth/50 200.00
12 Fergie Jenkins/25 15.00
23 Lou Gehrig/50 125.00
24 Luis Aparicio/25 15.00
25 Mel Ott/25 40.00
31 Roy Campanella/25 30.00
33 Ty Cobb/25 125.00

HOF Mat. Pants Signature
NM/M
Production 25 Sets
1 Al Kaline 50.00
12 Fergie Jenkins 30.00
24 Luis Aparicio 25.00
28 Phil Rizzuto 40.00

HOF Materials Signature
NM/M
Quantity produced listed
Prime: No Pricing
Production 1-10
1 Al Kaline/25 50.00
3 Bob Feller/25 25.00
5 Brooks Robinson/25 50.00
7 Carlton Fisk/27 50.00
9 Duke Snider/25 40.00
11 Ernie Banks/25 60.00
12 Fergie Jenkins/31 30.00
13 Frank Robinson/20 40.00
15 Hoyt Wilhelm/25 25.00
17 Jim Palmer/22 30.00
20 Juan Marichal/27 30.00
21 Kirby Puckett/34 60.00
22 Lou Brock/20 40.00
26 Orlando Cepeda/30 30.00
28 Phil Rizzuto/25 40.00
29 Red Schoendienst/25 30.00
32 Paul Molitor/25 50.00
34 Warren Spahn/21 50.00
35 Willie McCovey/25 40.00

Home Away Gamers
NM/M
Quantity produced listed
Prime: No Pricing
Production 3-5
1 Babe Ruth/Jsy-Jsy/25 600.00
3 Wade Boggs/Jsy-Jsy/50 15.00
4 Tony Gwynn/Jsy-Jsy/50 30.00
5 Steve Carlton/Jsy-Jsy/50 15.00
7 Ryne Sandberg/Jsy-Jsy/50 35.00
8 Rod Carew/Jsy-Jsy/50 15.00
9 Rickey Henderson/ Jsy-Jsy/50 25.00
11 Ted Williams/Jsy-Jsy/100 85.00
12 Ozzie Smith/Jsy-Jsy/50 25.00
13 Mike Schmidt/Jsy-Jsy/50 30.00
14 Harmon Killebrew/ Jsy-Jsy/50 30.00
15 George Brett/Jsy-Jsy/100 30.00
16 Don Mattingly/Jsy-Jsy/50 35.00
17 Dale Murphy/Jsy-Jsy/50 15.00
18 Cal Ripken Jr./Jsy-Jsy/100 50.00
19 Lou Gehrig/Jsy-Jsy/50 200.00
20 Nolan Ryan/Jsy-Jsy/100 40.00

Home Away Gamers Combos
NM/M
Quantity produced listed
Prime: No Pricing
Production 3-10
1 Babe Ruth/25 800.00
3 Wade Boggs/50 25.00
4 Tony Gwynn/50 40.00
5 Steve Carlton/50 25.00
6 Stan Musial/25 85.00
7 Ryne Sandberg/50 40.00
8 Rod Carew/50 25.00
9 Rickey Henderson/50 35.00
11 Ted Williams/100 150.00
12 Ozzie Smith/50 40.00
13 Mike Schmidt/50 50.00
14 Harmon Killebrew/25 40.00
15 George Brett/100 50.00
16 Don Mattingly/50 60.00
17 Dale Murphy/50 25.00
18 Cal Ripken Jr./100 65.00
19 Lou Gehrig/25 400.00
20 Nolan Ryan/100 65.00

Home Away Gamer Combo Prime
No Pricing

Home Away Gamer Combo Signature
No Pricing
Production 1-5
Prime: No Pricing
Production One Set

Home Away Gamers Prime
No Pricing

Home Away Gamers Sig.

NM/M
5 Steve Carlton/Jsy-Jsy/25 40.00
13 Mike Schmidt/Jsy-Jsy/20 100.00
14 Harmon Killebrew/ Jsy-Jsy/25 90.00
16 Don Mattingly/Jsy-Jsy/25 120.00
17 Dale Murphy/Jsy-Jsy/25 70.00
19 Lou Gehrig/Jsy-Jsy/1 (5/04 Auction) 7,100

Home Run Materials
NM/M
1 Roger Maris/Bat/61 40.00
3 Harmon Killebrew HR 570 Bat/75 20.00
4 Harmon Killebrew HR 565 Bat/75 20.00
5 Jose Canseco/Bat/96 10.00
6 Alex Rodriguez/Bat/100 15.00
7 Sammy Sosa/Jsy/100 15.00
8 Rafael Palmeiro/Jsy/25 20.00
9 Ivan Rodriguez/Jsy/25 20.00

Home Run Material Sig.
No Pricing

Material Ink Bat
NM/M
1 Adam Dunn/25 40.00
2 Alan Trammell/25 35.00
4 Andre Dawson/25 35.00
5 Bo Jackson/25 60.00
7 Dale Murphy/25 40.00
12 Don Mattingly/50 65.00
20 Mark Prior/25 80.00
25 Paul O'Neill/25 40.00
29 Ron Santo/50 35.00
30 Ryne Sandberg/25 85.00
32 Tony Gwynn/25 80.00
34 Will Clark/25 45.00

Material Ink Combos
NM/M
Quantity produced listed
Prime: No Pricing
Production 1-10
1 Adam Dunn/Bat-Jsy/25 40.00
2 Alan Trammell/Bat-Jsy/25 35.00
4 Andre Dawson/Bat-Jsy/25 35.00
5 Bo Jackson/Bat-Jsy/25 60.00
7 Dale Murphy/Bat-Jsy/25 40.00
12 Don Mattingly/Bat-Jsy/25 100.00
17 Jose Canseco/Bat-Jsy/25 50.00
30 Ryne Sandberg/Bat-Jsy/25 85.00
32 Tony Gwynn/Bat-Jsy/25 80.00
34 Will Clark/Bat-Jsy/50 40.00

Material Ink Combo Prime
Quantity produced listed
No Pricing

Material Ink Jersey
NM/M
Quantity produced listed
Number: .75-1X
Production 1-100
No pricing 15 or less.
Prime: .75-1.5X
Production 1-25
No pricing 15 or less.
1 Adam Dunn/25 40.00
2 Alan Trammell/100 20.00
4 Andre Dawson/100 25.00
5 Bo Jackson/25 60.00
7 Dale Murphy/50 35.00
8 Darryl Strawberry/100 25.00
9 Dave Parker/25 20.00
11 Doc Gooden/100 20.00
12 Don Mattingly/50 65.00
13 Dontrelle Willis/25 40.00
15 Ivan Rodriguez/25 50.00
16 Joe Carter/25 30.00
17 Jose Canseco/25 50.00
20 Mark Prior/50 60.00
21 Mark Teixeira/25 30.00
22 Marty Marion/25 25.00
26 Rocco Baldelli/25 40.00
30 Ryne Sandberg/50 75.00
31 Ernie Banks/50 75.00
33 Vladimir Guerrero/25 60.00
34 Will Clark/50 40.00

Material Ink Jsy Number
NM/M
Quantity produced listed

1 Adam Dunn/25 40.00
2 Alan Trammell/100 20.00
4 Andre Dawson/100 20.00
5 Bo Jackson/25 75.00
7 Dale Murphy/50 30.00
8 Darryl Strawberry/100 20.00
9 Dave Parker/25 30.00
11 Doc Gooden/100 15.00
12 Don Mattingly/50 75.00
13 Dontrelle Willis/25 40.00
16 Joe Carter/25 30.00
19 Mark Grace/25 40.00
21 Mark Teixeira/25 40.00
22 Marty Marion/25 20.00
26 Rocco Baldelli/25 25.00
31 Ernie Banks/25 65.00
33 Vladimir Guerrero/25 50.00
34 Will Clark/50 25.00

Milestone Materials
NM/M
Quantity produced listed
Number: .75-1.5X
Production 9-36
Prime: 1-2X
Production 25 Sets

Milestone Material Number
No Pricing

Milestone Material Prime
No Pricing

Milestone Material Signature
NM/M
4 Gaylord Perry/Jsy/82 20.00

Milestone Mat. Sig. Number
NM/M
4 Gaylord Perry/Jsy/82 20.00

Milestone Mat. Sig. Prime
NM/M
Quantity produced listed
4 Gaylord Perry/Jsy/19 30.00

No-Hitters Quad Signature
No Pricing
Production One Set

Rookie Year Materials
NM/M
Quantity produced listed
Prime: No Pricing
Production 5-10
Number: .75-1.5X
Production 3-51
No pricing 15 or less.
1 Stan Musial/Jsy/19 60.00
2 Yogi Berra/Stripe/Jsy/19 40.00
3 Yogi Berra/Gray Jsy/47 25.00
4 Whitey Ford/Jsy/50 20.00
5 Jim "Catfish" Hunter/Jsy/65 10.00
6 Johnny Bench/Bat/68 15.00
7 Mike Schmidt/Bat/72 15.00
8 Gary Carter/Jsy/74 8.00
9 Robin Yount/Jsy/74 20.00
11 Cal Ripken Jr./Bat/81 40.00
12 Kirby Puckett/Bat/84 10.00
13 Roger Clemens/Jsy/84 20.00
15 Gary Sheffield/Jsy/89 8.00
16 Juan Gonzalez/Jsy/89 10.00
17 Randy Johnson/Jsy/89 10.00
18 Ivan Rodriguez/Jsy/91 10.00
20 Pedro J. Martinez/Jsy/92 10.00
21 Mike Piazza/Jsy/93 10.00
22 Hideo Nomo/Jsy/95 10.00
23 Hideo Nomo/Pants/95 10.00
24 Alex Rodriguez/Jsy/95 15.00
26 Scott Rolen/Jsy/96 10.00
27 Andruw Jones/Jsy/96 8.00
28 Nomar Garciaparra/Jsy/97 10.00
29 Vladimir Guerrero/Jsy/97 10.00
31 Alfonso Soriano/Jsy/100 10.00
32 Albert Pujols/White/100 20.00
33 Albert Pujols/Gray/Jsy/100 20.00
34 Albert Pujols/Bat/100 20.00
36 Mark Prior/Blue Jsy/100 10.00
37 Mark Prior/Gray/100 10.00
38 Dontrelle Willis/Jsy/35 15.00

Rookie Year Mat. Combo
NM/M
Quantity produced listed
2 Yogi Berra/Jsy-Jsy/8 60.00
22 Hideo Nomo/Jsy-Pants/16 30.00
36 Mark Prior/Jsy-Jsy/22 30.00
38 Dontrelle Willis/Jsy-Jsy/35 10.00

R.Y. Mat. Combos Prime
NM/M
Quantity produced listed
36 Mark Prior/Jsy-Jsy/22 30.00
38 Dontrelle Willis/
Jsy-Jsy/35 10.00

R.Y. Materials Combos Sig.
NM/M
Quantity produced listed
36 Mark Prior/Jsy-Jsy/22 100.00
38 Dontrelle Willis/Jsy-Jsy/35 40.00

R.Y. Mat. Combo Sig. Prime
NM/M
Quantity produced listed
36 Mark Prior/Jsy/Jsy/22 100.00
38 Dontrelle Willis/Jsy/Jsy/35 40.00

Rookie Year Mat. Dual
NM/M
Production 25 Sets
Prime: No Pricing
Production 10 Sets
40 Roger Clemens/Jsy,
Nomar Garciaparra/Jsy 40.00
41 Pedro J. Martinez/Jsy,
Mike Piazza/Jsy 35.00
42 Mike Piazza/Jsy,
Hideo Nomo/Jsy 35.00
43 Pedro J. Martinez/Jsy,
Hideo Nomo/Jsy 20.00
44 Yogi Berra/Jsy,
Whitey Ford/Jsy 50.00
45 Mike Schmidt/Bat,
Scott Rolen/Jsy 40.00
46 Stan Musial/Jsy,
Albert Pujols/Jsy 75.00
47 Juan Gonzalez/Jsy,
Ivan Rodriguez/Jsy 15.00

R.K. Year Mat. Dual Prime
No Pricing
Production 10 Sets

R.K. Year Mat. Dual Sig.
No Pricing
Production Five Sets

Rookie Year Mat. Number
No Pricing
Quantity produced listed

Rookie Year Mat. Prime
No Pricing
Quantity produced listed

Rookie Year Mat. Sig.

NM/M
Quantity produced listed
Prime: 1X
Production 1-35
Number: 1X
No pricing 15 or less.
1 Stan Musial/Jsy/9 125.00
3 Yogi Berra/Gray Jsy/19 100.00
4 Whitey Ford/Jsy/19 85.00
8 Gary Carter/Jsy/19 35.00
10 Fred Lynn/Jsy/75 15.00
14 Lenny Dykstra/Fld Glv/85 20.00
16 Juan Gonzalez/Jsy/19 40.00
25 Garret Anderson/Jsy/95 20.00
30 Shannon Stewart/Jsy/19 15.00
36 Mark Prior/Blue Jsy/22 80.00
37 Mark Prior/Gray Jsy/22 80.00
38 Dontrelle Willis/Jsy/35 40.00
39 Rocco Baldelli/Jsy/19 40.00

R.K. Year Mat. Sig. Number
No Pricing
Quantity produced listed

R.K. Year Mat. Sig. Prime
No Pricing
Quantity produced listed

Signature Bronze
NM/M
1 Albert Pujols/25 125.00
2 Garret Anderson/16 30.00
4 Alex Rodriguez/25 100.00
6 Manny Ramirez/24 40.00
7 Mark Prior/50 50.00
8 Barry Larkin/25 30.00
9 Todd Helton/17 40.00
14 Shawn Green/15 30.00
17 Vladimir Guerrero 50.00
20 Don Mattingly/50 60.00
23 Rafael Palmeiro/25 45.00
27 Gary Sheffield/50 25.00
37 Kazuhisa Ishii/17 40.00
41 Tom Glavine/25 30.00
42 Eric Chavez/25 25.00
46 Tony Gwynn/50 40.00
47 Jim Edmonds/15 35.00
49 Vernon Wells/25 20.00
50 Curt Schilling/38 40.00
53 Jason Varitek/33 30.00
56 Adam Dunn/25 30.00
58 Josh Beckett/25 30.00
59 Jeff Bagwell/25 50.00
68 Carlos Beltran/15 40.00
71 Andruw Jones/25 30.00
76 Jorge Posada/25 40.00
78 Stan Musial/50 75.00
79 Mark Teixeira/23 35.00
83 Nolan Ryan/50 90.00
87 Bob Gibson/25 40.00
88 Dale Murphy/25 35.00

90 Carl Yastrzemski/25 60.00
91 Sammy Sosa/50 125.00
92 Miguel Cabrera/24 50.00
94 George Brett/25 100.00
95 Rickey Henderson/25 25.00
97 Greg Maddux/31 75.00
100 Dontrelle Willis/35 30.00

Signature Gold
No Pricing
Production 1-11

Signature Silver
NM/M
Quantity produced listed
2 Garret Anderson/10 10.00
6 Mark Prior/22 50.00
17 Vladimir Guerrero/27 50.00
20 Don Mattingly/23 90.00
27 Gary Sheffield/25 35.00
44 Tony Gwynn/19 75.00
47 Delmon Young/25 30.00
68 Juan Gonzalez/22 35.00
76 Jorge Posada/20 40.00
78 Stan Musial/25 75.00
83 Nolan Ryan/34 120.00
88 Dale Murphy/25 40.00
91 Sammy Sosa/21 125.00

Statistical Champions
NM/M
Number: .75-1.5X
Production 1-51
No pricing 15 or less.
Prime: No Pricing
Production 5-10
2 Stan Musial 43 BA/Jsy/19 40.00
3 Ralph Kiner/Bat/49 10.00
4 Stan Musial 57 BA/Jsy/57 30.00
5 Ted Williams/Jsy/25 90.00
6 Warren Spahn/Jsy/25 30.00
7 Eddie Mathews/Jsy/25 40.00
8 Roger Maris 61 HR/Bat/61 40.00
9 Roger Maris 61 HR/
Pants/61 40.00
10 Roger Maris 61 RBI/Bat/61 40.00
11 Roger Maris 61 RBI/
Pants/61 40.00
12 Roberto Clemente/Jsy/19 100.00
13 Frank Robinson/Bat/66 10.00
14 Bob Gibson 68 ERA/Jsy/68 15.00
15 Bob Gibson 68 K/Jsy/68 15.00
17 Tom Seaver/Jsy/19 25.00
18 Harmon Killebrew/Pants/71 15.00
19 Mike Schmidt/Jsy/74 15.00
20 Reggie Jackson/Jsy/19 15.00
22 Rod Carew/Hat/78 15.00
23 Jim Rice 78 HR/Jsy/78 10.00
24 Jim Rice 78 RBI/Jsy/78 10.00
25 Reggie Jackson/Bat/80 15.00
26 Dale Murphy 82 RBI/Jsy/82 15.00
27 Steve Carlton/Jsy/83 10.00
28 Dale Murphy 85 HR/Jsy/85 15.00
29 Wade Boggs 86 BA/Jsy/86 15.00
30 Wade Boggs 87 BA/Jsy/87 15.00
31 Will Clark/Jsy/88 15.00
32 Nolan Ryan 89 K/Jsy/89 20.00
33 Nolan Ryan 90 K/Jsy/90 20.00
34 Nolan Ryan 90 K/Pants/90 20.00
35 Ryne Sandberg/Jsy/90 20.00
36 Roger Clemens 90 K/Jsy/90 20.00
37 George Brett/Jsy/90 20.00
38 Roger Clemens 92 ERA/
Jsy/100 20.00
39 Roger Clemens 96 K/
Jsy/100 20.00
40 Tony Gwynn/Jsy/25 35.00
41 Pedro Martinez/Expos/
Jsy/25 20.00
42 Greg Maddux/Jsy/100 20.00
43 Juan Gonzalez/Pants/25 20.00
44 Manny Ramirez/Bat/25 20.00
45 Nomar Garciaparra 99 BA/
Jsy/100 10.00
47 Nomar Garciaparra 00 BA/
Jsy/100 10.00
48 Todd Helton 00 BA/Jsy/25 15.00
49 Todd Helton 00 RBI/Jsy/25 15.00
50 Troy Glaus/Jsy/25 10.00
51 Randy Johnson 00 K/
Jsy/25 15.00
52 Tom Glavine/Jsy/25 10.00
53 Sammy Sosa 00 HR/
Jsy/100 15.00
54 Alex Rodriguez 01 HR/
Bat/100 15.00
55 Curt Schilling/Jsy/25 10.00
56 Pedro J. Martinez 99 K/
Jsy/25 20.00
57 Alex Rodriguez 01 HR/
Jsy/100 15.00
58 Mark Mulder/Jsy/25 10.00
59 Sammy Sosa 01 RBI/
Jsy/25 15.00
60 Manny Ramirez/Jsy/25 15.00
61 Lance Berkman/Jsy/25 10.00
62 Randy Johnson 02 W/
Jsy/25 15.00
63 Alex Rodriguez 02 HR/
Jsy/100 15.00
64 Alex Rodriguez 02 RBI/
Jsy/100 15.00
65 Alex Rodriguez 02 HR/
Bat/100 15.00

66 Alex Rodriguez 02 RBI/
Bat/100 15.00
67 Pedro J. Martinez 02 K/
Jsy/25 20.00
68 Pedro J. Martinez
02 ERA/Jsy/25 20.00
69 Sammy Sosa 02 HR/
Jsy/100 15.00
70 Jim Thome/Jsy/25 15.00
71 Alex Rodriguez 03 HR/
Bat/100 15.00
72 Albert Pujols/Bat/100 20.00
73 Alex Rodriguez 03 HR/
Jsy/100 15.00
74 Albert Pujols/Jsy/100 20.00

Statistical Champ. Number
No Pricing

Statistical Champ. Prime
No Pricing

Statistical Champ. Sig.
NM/M
Quantity produced listed
Number: .5-1.5X
Production 1-47
Prime: No Pricing
Production 1-10
3 Ralph Kiner/Bat/49 35.00
6 Warren Spahn/Jsy/25 75.00
13 Frank Robinson/Bat/66 40.00
14 Bob Gibson 68 ERA/Jsy/25 50.00
15 Bob Gibson 68 K/Jsy/25 50.00
17 Harmon Killebrew/Jsy/71 50.00
18 Harmon Killebrew/Pants/71 50.00
19 Mike Schmidt/Jsy/25 50.00
20 Reggie Jackson/Jsy/25 65.00
21 Phil Niekro/Jsy/50 30.00
22 Rod Carew/Hat/25 40.00
23 Jim Rice 78 HR/Jsy/78 30.00
24 Jim Rice 78 RBI/Jsy/78 30.00
25 Reggie Jackson/Hat/25 65.00
26 Dale Murphy 82 RBI/Jsy/25 50.00
27 Steve Carlton/Jsy/25 50.00
28 Dale Murphy 85 HR/Jsy/25 50.00
29 Wade Boggs 86 BA/Jsy/25 40.00
30 Wade Boggs 87 BA/Jsy/25 40.00
31 Will Clark/Jsy/88 30.00
32 Nolan Ryan 89 K/Jsy/25 120.00
33 Nolan Ryan 90 K/Jsy/25 120.00
34 Nolan Ryan 90 K/Pants/25 120.00
35 Ryne Sandberg/Jsy/25 80.00
40 Tony Gwynn/Jsy/25 70.00
43 Juan Gonzalez/Pants/19 40.00
50 Troy Glaus/Jsy/25 35.00
52 Tom Glavine/Jsy/20 25.00
53 Sammy Sosa 00 HR/
Jsy/25 150.00
55 Curt Schilling/Jsy/25 50.00
58 Mark Mulder/Jsy/25 30.00
59 Sammy Sosa 01 RBI/
Jsy/25 150.00
61 Lance Berkman/Jsy/20 40.00
62 Sammy Sosa 02 HR/
Jsy/25 150.00

Statistical Champions Signature Number
No Pricing

Statistical Champions Signature Prime
No Pricing

World Series Materials
NM/M
Quantity produced listed
1 Frank Robinson/Bat/61 15.00
2 Ozzie Smith/Jsy/87 15.00
3 Rickey Henderson/Bat/93 15.00
4 Tom Glavine/Jsy/96 10.00
5 Roger Clemens/Jsy/100 15.00

World Series Mat. Prime
NM/M
Quantity produced listed
2 Ozzie Smith/Jsy/19 25.00
4 Tom Glavine/Jsy/19 30.00
5 Roger Clemens/Jsy/20 30.00

World Series Mat. Sig.
NM/M
Quantity produced listed
Prime: No Pricing
Production 9-10
1 Frank Robinson/Bat/19 15.00
4 Tom Glavine/Jsy/19 40.00

2004 Donruss Timelines
NM/M
Complete Set (50): 40.00
Common Player: .75
Pack (5): 40.00
Box (4): 120.00
1 Adam Dunn .75
2 Albert Pujols 3.00
3 Alex Rodriguez 3.00
4 Alfonso Soriano 1.50
6 Andruw Jones 1.00
7 Austin Kearns .75
7 Miguel Cabrera 1.00
8 Barry Zito .75
9 Carlos Beltran .75

#	Player	Price
10	Carlos Delgado	1.00
11	Chipper Jones	2.00
12	Curt Schilling	1.00
13	Derek Jeter	4.00
14	Frank Thomas	1.00
15	Garret Anderson	.75
16	Gary Sheffield	.75
17	Greg Maddux	2.00
18	Hank Blalock	.75
19	Hideki Matsui	3.00
20	Hideo Nomo	.75
21	Ichiro Suzuki	2.00
22	Ivan Rodriguez	1.00
23	Jason Giambi	1.50
24	Jeff Bagwell	1.00
25	Jim Thome	1.50
26	Juan Gonzalez	.75
27	Ken Griffey Jr.	2.00
28	Kevin Brown	.75
29	Kerry Wood	.75
30	Lance Berkman	.75
31	Magglio Ordonez	.75
32	Manny Ramirez	1.00
33	Mark Prior	3.00
34	Mike Mussina	1.00
35	Mike Piazza	2.00
36	Nomar Garciaparra	3.00
37	Pedro J. Martinez	1.50
38	Rafael Palmeiro	1.00
39	Randy Johnson	1.50
40	Richie Sexson	.75
41	Roger Clemens	3.00
42	Roy Halladay	.75
43	Sammy Sosa	2.50
44	Scott Rolen	1.50
45	Shawn Green	.75
46	Tim Hudson	.75
47	Todd Helton	1.00
48	Torii Hunter	.75
49	Vernon Wells	.75
50	Vladimir Guerrero	1.50

Gold
Cards (1-50): 4-6X
Production 25 Sets

Silver
Cards (1-50): 2X
Production 100 Sets

Platinum
No Pricing
Production One Set

Gold Autographs
NM/M
Production 25 Sets

#	Player	Price
		30.00
1	Adam Dunn	40.00
7	Miguel Cabrera	80.00
9	Carlos Beltran	40.00
15	Garret Anderson	30.00
18	Hank Blalock	35.00
22	Ivan Rodriguez	60.00
26	Juan Gonzalez	50.00
31	Magglio Ordonez	40.00
33	Mark Prior	50.00
44	Scott Rolen	45.00
48	Torii Hunter	35.00
49	Vernon Wells	30.00
50	Vladimir Guerrero	70.00

Platinum Autographs
No Pricing
Production One Set

Boys of Summer
NM/M
Complete Set (25): 75.00
Common Player: 3.00
Production 250 Sets
Silver: 1-1.5x
Production 100 Sets
Gold: 3-4X
Production 25 Sets
Platinum: No Pricing
Production One Set

#	Player	Price
1	Alan Trammell	5.00
2	Marty Marion	3.00
3	Andre Dawson	3.00
4	Bo Jackson	5.00
5	Cal Ripken Jr.	10.00
6	Steve Garvey	3.00
7	Dale Murphy	3.00
8	Darren Daulton	3.00
9	Darryl Strawberry	3.00
10	Dave Parker	3.00
11	Doc Gooden	3.00
12	Don Mattingly	6.00
13	Eric Davis	3.00
14	Dwight Evans	3.00
15	Fred Lynn	3.00
16	Graig Nettles	3.00
17	Jay Buhner	3.00
18	Jim Rice	3.00
19	Jose Canseco	3.00
20	Keith Hernandez	3.00
21	Rickey Henderson	3.00
22	Jack Morris	3.00
23	Tony Gwynn	4.00
24	Vida Blue	3.00
25	Will Clark	3.00

Boys of Summer Autographs

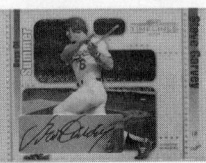

NM/M

#	Player	Price
	Common Autograph:	10.00
2	Marty Marion	10.00
3	Andre Dawson	15.00
6	Steve Garvey	12.00
8	Darren Daulton	10.00
9	Darryl Strawberry	15.00
10	Dave Parker	10.00
11	Doc Gooden	10.00
13	Eric Davis	10.00
15	Fred Lynn	12.00
16	Graig Nettles	15.00
17	Jay Buhner	15.00
20	Keith Hernandez	12.00
22	Jack Morris	12.00
24	Vida Blue	12.00

Boys of Summer Silver Auto.
NM/M
Common Autograph: 12.00
Production 100

#	Player	Price
2	Marty Marion	12.00
3	Andre Dawson	15.00
6	Steve Garvey	20.00
8	Darren Daulton	12.00
9	Darryl Strawberry	18.00
10	Dave Parker	12.00
11	Doc Gooden	20.00
12	Don Mattingly	65.00
13	Eric Davis	12.00
15	Fred Lynn	15.00
16	Graig Nettles	20.00
18	Jim Rice	20.00
20	Keith Hernandez	15.00
22	Jack Morris	15.00
24	Vida Blue	15.00

Boys of Summer Gold Autographs
NM/M
Common Autograph: 20.00
Production 25

#	Player	Price
1	Alan Trammell	35.00
2	Marty Marion	20.00
3	Andre Dawson	20.00
6	Steve Garvey	20.00
8	Darren Daulton	20.00
9	Darryl Strawberry	20.00
10	Dave Parker	20.00
11	Doc Gooden	20.00
12	Don Mattingly	75.00
13	Eric Davis	20.00
14	Dwight Evans	25.00
15	Fred Lynn	25.00
16	Graig Nettles	20.00
17	Jay Buhner	25.00
18	Jim Rice	25.00
20	Keith Hernandez	20.00
22	Jack Morris	20.00
24	Vida Blue	20.00
25	Will Clark	100.00

Boys of Summer Platinum Auto.
No Pricing
Production One Set

Boys of Summer Materials

NM/M
Common Player: 5.00
Combos: 1-2X
Production 100 Sets
Prime: 1-2X
Production 100 Sets

#	Player	Price
3	Andre Dawson	5.00
4	Bo Jackson	10.00
5	Cal Ripken Jr.	20.00
7	Dale Murphy	6.00
9	Darryl Strawberry	5.00
11	Doc Gooden	5.00
12	Don Mattingly	15.00
19	Jose Canseco	6.00
21	Rickey Henderson	8.00
22	Jack Morris	5.00
23	Tony Gwynn	8.00
25	Will Clark	8.00

Boys of Summer Combo Materials
NM/M
Production 100 Sets

#	Player	Price
3	Andre Dawson	10.00
4	Bo Jackson	15.00
5	Cal Ripken Jr.	30.00
7	Dale Murphy	10.00
12	Don Mattingly	25.00
19	Jose Canseco	10.00
21	Rickey Henderson	15.00
23	Tony Gwynn	10.00
25	Will Clark	10.00

Boys of Summer Material Auto.
NM/M
Varying quantities produced

#	Player	Price
3	Andre Dawson/50	25.00
9	Darryl Strawberry/150	25.00
11	Doc Gooden/100	25.00
12	Don Mattingly/25	80.00
22	Jack Morris/150	12.00

Boys of Summer Prime Materials
NM/M
Common Player: 8.00
Production 100 Sets

#	Player	Price
3	Andre Dawson	8.00
4	Bo Jackson	15.00
5	Cal Ripken Jr.	30.00
9	Darryl Strawberry	8.00
11	Doc Gooden	8.00
12	Don Mattingly	25.00
21	Rickey Henderson	15.00
23	Tony Gwynn	12.00
25	Will Clark	12.00

Boys/Summer Prime Materials Autographs
No Pricing
Production One Set

Call to the Hall

NM/M
Complete Set (25): 80.00
Common Player: 3.00
Production 250 Sets
Silver: 1X
Production 100 Sets
Gold: 3-4X
Production 25 Sets
Platinum: No Pricing
Production One Set

#	Player	Price
1	Babe Ruth	10.00
2	Billy Williams	3.00
3	Bob Feller	3.00
4	Bobby Doerr	3.00
5	Carlton Fisk	3.00
6	Gary Carter	3.00
7	George Brett	8.00
8	Carl Yastrzemski	5.00
9	Harmon Killebrew	3.00
10	Jim Palmer	3.00
11	Joe Morgan	3.00
12	Johnny Bench	5.00
13	Kirby Puckett	5.00
14	Gaylord Perry	3.00
15	Mike Schmidt	6.00
16	Nolan Ryan	10.00
17	Ozzie Smith	5.00
18	Phil Rizzuto	3.00
19	Reggie Jackson	4.00
20	Roberto Clemente	6.00
21	Robin Yount	4.00
22	Rod Carew	6.00
23	Rollie Fingers	3.00
24	Steve Carlton	3.00
25	Tom Seaver	4.00

Call to the Hall Autographs

NM/M
Common Autograph: 15.00
Silver Autos.: 1X
Production 100

#	Player	Price
3	Bob Feller	15.00
4	Bobby Doerr	15.00
14	Gaylord Perry	15.00
23	Rollie Fingers	15.00

Call to the Hall Gold Autographs
NM/M
Production 25 Sets

#	Player	Price
2	Billy Williams	25.00
3	Bob Feller	40.00
6	Gary Carter	40.00
10	Jim Palmer	30.00
18	Phil Rizzuto	40.00
24	Steve Carlton	40.00

Call to the Hall Platinum Autographs
No Pricing
Production One Set

Call to the Hall Materials

NM/M
Common Player: 6.00

#	Player	Price
1	Babe Ruth/50	575.00
4	Bobby Doerr	6.00
6	Gary Carter	8.00
7	George Brett	12.00
8	Carl Yastrzemski	12.00
13	Kirby Puckett	10.00
15	Mike Schmidt	12.00
16	Nolan Ryan	20.00
17	Ozzie Smith	8.00
19	Reggie Jackson	8.00
20	Roberto Clemente/100	50.00

Call to the Hall Combo Materials
NM/M
Production 125 Sets

#	Player	Price
6	Gary Carter	12.00
7	George Brett	25.00
13	Kirby Puckett	20.00
15	Mike Schmidt	25.00
16	Nolan Ryan	35.00
19	Reggie Jackson	20.00

Call to the Hall Material Auto.
NM/M
Varying quantities produced

#	Player	Price
4	Bobby Doerr/100	25.00
6	Gary Carter/25	45.00
19	Reggie Jackson/25	50.00

Materials

NM/M
Common Player: 5.00
Combos: 1-2X
Production 125

Primes: 1-2X
Production 125

#	Player	
1	Adam Dunn	5.00
2	Albert Pujols	12.00
3	Alex Rodriguez	10.00
4	Alfonso Soriano	8.00
5	Andruw Jones	5.00
7	Miguel Cabrera/SP	10.00
10	Carlos Delgado	5.00
11	Chipper Jones	8.00
14	Frank Thomas	8.00
17	Greg Maddux	8.00
20	Hideo Nomo	6.00
22	Ivan Rodriguez	6.00
23	Jason Giambi	6.00
24	Jeff Bagwell	6.00
25	Jim Thome	8.00
26	Juan Gonzalez	6.00
30	Lance Berkman	5.00
33	Mark Prior	10.00
35	Mike Piazza	8.00
36	Nomar Garciaparra	10.00
37	Pedro J. Martinez	8.00
39	Randy Johnson	6.00
41	Roger Clemens	10.00
43	Sammy Sosa	10.00
45	Shawn Green	5.00
47	Todd Helton	6.00
49	Vernon Wells	5.00

Materials Combo

NM/M
Common Player: 8.00
Production 125 Sets

#	Player	
1	Adam Dunn	8.00
2	Albert Pujols	20.00
3	Alex Rodriguez	15.00
4	Alfonso Soriano	10.00
5	Andruw Jones	8.00
7	Miguel Cabrera	20.00
11	Chipper Jones	15.00
14	Frank Thomas	12.00
17	Greg Maddux	15.00
20	Hideo Nomo	10.00
25	Jim Thome	12.00
30	Lance Berkman	8.00
33	Mark Prior	20.00
35	Mike Piazza	15.00
36	Nomar Garciaparra	15.00
37	Pedro J. Martinez	12.00
39	Randy Johnson	10.00
41	Roger Clemens	15.00
43	Sammy Sosa	15.00
45	Shawn Green	10.00
47	Todd Helton	10.00

Materials Autographs
NM/M
Varying quantities produced

#	Player	
7	Miguel Cabrera/25	85.00
22	Ivan Rodriguez/25	65.00
33	Mark Prior/50	75.00
49	Vernon Wells/25	25.00

Materials Prime
NM/M
Common Player: 8.00
Production 125 Sets

#	Player	
1	Adam Dunn	8.00
2	Albert Pujols	20.00
3	Alex Rodriguez	20.00
4	Alfonso Soriano	10.00
5	Andruw Jones	8.00
7	Miguel Cabrera	20.00
10	Carlos Delgado	8.00
11	Chipper Jones	15.00
14	Frank Thomas	12.00
17	Greg Maddux	15.00
20	Hideo Nomo	10.00
25	Jim Thome	12.00
30	Lance Berkman	8.00
33	Mark Prior	20.00
35	Mike Piazza	15.00
36	Nomar Garciaparra	15.00
37	Pedro J. Martinez	12.00
39	Randy Johnson	15.00
41	Roger Clemens	15.00
43	Sammy Sosa	15.00
45	Shawn Green	10.00
47	Todd Helton	10.00
49	Vernon Wells	8.00

2004 Donruss World Series

ROGER CLEMENS

NM/M
Complete Set (200):
Common Player: .15
Common SP (176-200): 8.00
Pack (6): 6.00
Box (24): 120.00

#	Player	
1	Bartolo Colon	.15
2	Darin Erstad	.25
3	Garret Anderson	.25
4	Tim Salmon	.25
5	Troy Glaus	.25
6	Vladimir Guerrero	.75
7	Brandon Webb	.15
8	Luis Gonzalez	.15
9	Randy Johnson	.75
10	Roberto Alomar	.40
11	Shea Hillenbrand	.15
12	Steve Finley	.15
13	Andruw Jones	.40
14	Chipper Jones	.75
15	J.D. Drew	.25
16	Marcus Giles	.15
17	Rafael Furcal	.25
18	Javy Lopez	.25
19	Jay Gibbons	.15
20	Luis Matos	.15
21	Melvin Mora	.15
22	Miguel Tejada	.40
23	Rafael Palmeiro	.50
24	Curt Schilling	.75
25	Dwight Evans	.15
26	Fred Lynn	.15
27	Jason Varitek	.25
28	Jim Rice	.25
29	Johnny Damon	.40
30	Luis Tiant	.15
31	Manny Ramirez	.50
32	Nomar Garciaparra	1.00
33	Pedro Martinez	.75
34	Trot Nixon	.15
35	Aramis Ramirez	.25
36	Corey Patterson	.25
37	Derrek Lee	.25
38	Greg Maddux	1.00
39	Kerry Wood	.75
40	Mark Prior	.75
41	Moises Alou	.25
42	Sammy Sosa	1.50
43	Carlos Lee	.15
44	Frank Thomas	.50
45	Luis Aparicio	.15
46	Magglio Ordonez	.25
47	Mark Buehrle	.15
48	Paul Konerko	.15
49	Adam Dunn	.50
50	Austin Kearns	.15
51	Barry Larkin	.25
52	Dave Concepcion	.15
53	George Foster	.15
54	Joe Morgan	.15
55	Sean Casey	.25
56	Tony Perez	.15
57	C.C. Sabathia	.15
58	Jody Gerut	.15
59	Omar Vizquel	.15
60	Victor Martinez	.15
61	Charles Johnson	.15
62	Jeromy Burnitz	.15
63	Larry Walker	.25
64	Preston Wilson	.15
65	Todd Helton	.50
66	Alan Trammell	.15
67	Dmitri Young	.15
68	Ivan Rodriguez	.50
69	Jeremy Bonderman	.15
70	A.J. Burnett	.15
71	Brad Penny	.15
72	Dontrelle Willis	.15
73	Josh Beckett	.40
74	Juan Pierre	.15
75	Luis Castillo	.15
76	Miguel Cabrera	.75
77	Mike Lowell	.25
78	Andy Pettitte	.25
79	Craig Biggio	.25
80	Jeff Bagwell	.50
81	Jeff Kent	.25
82	Lance Berkman	.25
83	Roger Clemens	2.00
84	Roy Oswalt	.25
85	Wade Miller	.15
86	Angel Berroa	.15
87	Carlos Beltran	.50
88	Juan Gonzalez	.40
89	Ken Harvey	.15
90	Mike Sweeney	.15
91	Adrian Beltre	.40
92	Hideo Nomo	.40
93	Kazuhisa Ishii	.15
94	Milton Bradley	.15
95	Orel Hershiser	.15
96	Paul LoDuca	.15
97	Shawn Green	.25
98	Ben Sheets	.25
99	Geoff Jenkins	.15
100	Junior Spivey	.15
101	Rickie Weeks	.15
102	Scott Podsednik	.15
103	Jack Morris	.15
104	Jacque Jones	.15
105	Johan Santana	.50
106	Shannon Stewart	.15
107	Torii Hunter	.25
108	Jose Vidro	.15
109	Orlando Cabrera	.25
110	Al Leiter	.25
111	Darryl Strawberry	.25
112	Dwight Gooden	.15
113	Jose Reyes	.25
114	Kazuo Matsui RC	2.00
115	Keith Hernandez	.15
116	Lenny Dykstra	.15
117	Mike Piazza	1.00
118	Tom Glavine	.40
119	Alex Rodriguez	2.00
120	Bernie Williams	.40
121	Derek Jeter	2.00
122	Gary Sheffield	.50
123	Jason Giambi	.25
124	Javier Vazquez	.25
125	Jorge Posada	.25
126	Kenny Lofton	.15
127	Kevin Brown	.25
128	Mariano Rivera	.25
129	Mike Mussina	.40
130	Barry Zito	.25
131	Eric Chavez	.25
132	Jermaine Dye	.15
133	Mark Mulder	.25
134	Rich Harden	.15
135	Tim Hudson	.25
136	Brett Myers	.15
137	Jim Thome	.75
138	Kevin Millwood	.15
139	Marlon Byrd	.15
140	Mike Lieberthal	.15
141	Pat Burrell	.15
142	Steve Carlton	.25
143	Dave Parker	.15
144	Jason Kendall	.15
145	Brian Giles	.15
146	Jay Payton	.15
147	Ryan Klesko	.15
148	J.T. Snow	.15
149	Jason Schmidt	.25
150	Bret Boone	.15
151	Edgar Martinez	.25
152	Jamie Moyer	.15
153	Rich Aurilia	.15
154	Shigetoshi Hasegawa	.15
155	Albert Pujols	2.00
156	Dan Haren	.15
157	Edgar Renteria	.25
158	Fernando Vina	.15
159	Jim Edmonds	.40
160	Matt Morris	.15
161	Scott Rolen	.75
162	Aubrey Huff	.15
163	Carl Crawford	.15
164	Dewon Brazelton	.15
165	Fred McGriff	.25
166	Rocco Baldelli	.15
167	Alfonso Soriano	.75
168	Hank Blalock	.50
169	Kenny Rogers	.15
170	Mark Teixeira	.25
171	Michael Young	.15
172	Carlos Delgado	.15
173	Eric Hinske	.15
174	Roy Halladay	.25
175	Vernon Wells	.15
176	Ivan Ochoa/Auto./487 RC	8.00
177	Jason Bartlett/ Auto./1,000 RC	8.00
178	Josh Labandeira/ Auto./703 RC	8.00
179	Phil Stockman/ Auto./1,000 RC	8.00
180	Ronny Cedeno/Auto./715 RC	8.00
181	Shawn Camp/ Auto./1,000 RC	8.00
182	Ruddy Yan/Auto./1,000	8.00
183	Roberto Novoa/ Auto./568 RC	10.00
184	Justin Knoedler/ Auto./1,000 RC	8.00
185	Jesse Harper/ Auto./1,000 RC	8.00
186	Jason Szuminski/ Auto./1,000 RC	8.00
187	Jamie Brown/Auto./800 RC	8.00
188	Eddy Rodriguez/ Auto./1,000 RC	8.00
189	Dennis Sarfate/ Auto./1,000 RC	8.00
190	Ryan Meaux/Auto./1,000 RC	8.00
191	Charles Thomas/ Auto./1,000 RC	10.00
192	Frank Francisco/ Auto./1,000 RC	8.00
193	Orlando Rodriguez/ Auto./500 RC	8.00
194	Joey Gathright/ Auto./1,000 RC	10.00
195	Renyel Pinto/ Auto./1,000 RC	10.00
196	Justin Leone/ Auto./1,000 RC	8.00
197	Tim Bausher/Auto./834 RC	8.00
198	Travis Blackley/ Auto./1,000 RC	8.00
199	Yadier Molina/ Auto./500 RC	15.00
200	Brad Halsey/Auto./500 RC	10.00

HoloFoil 100
HoloFoil (1-175): 4-8X
HoloFoil (176-200): .5X
Production 100 Sets

HoloFoil 50
HoloFoil (1-175): 6-12X
HoloFoil (176-200): .75X
Production 50 Sets

HoloFoil 25
HoloFoil (1-175): 10-20X
HoloFoil (176-200): No Pricing
Production 25 Sets

HoloFoil 10
No Pricing
Production 10 Sets

Blue
NM/M
Complete Set (100): 50.00
Common Player: .50
Inserted 1:1
HoloFoil 100: 2-4X
Production 100 Sets
HoloFoil 50: 4-6X
Production 50 Sets
HoloFoil 25: 6-10X
Production 25 Sets
HoloFoil 10: No Pricing
Production 10 Sets

#	Player	
1	Josh Beckett	.50
2	Miguel Cabrera	1.00
3	Derrek Lee	.50
4	Mike Lowell	.50
5	Brad Penny	.50
6	Ivan Rodriguez	1.00
7	Dontrelle Willis	.50
8	Luis Castillo	.50
9	Garret Anderson	.75
10	Troy Glaus	.75
11	John Lackey	.50
12	Chone Figgins	.50
13	Tim Salmon	.50
14	Darin Erstad	.50
15	Troy Percival	.50
16	Steve Finley	.50
17	Mark Grace	.75
18	Randy Johnson	1.00
19	Curt Schilling	1.00
20	Luis Gonzalez	.50
21	Andy Pettitte	.75
22	Bernie Williams	.75
23	Jorge Posada	.75
24	Mariano Rivera	.75
25	Roger Clemens	3.00
26	Jose Canseco	1.00
27	David Justice	.50
28	Paul O'Neill	.75
29	Darryl Strawberry	.50
30	David Wells	.50
31	Wade Boggs	.75
32	Charles Johnson	.50
33	Cliff Floyd	.50
34	Moises Alou	.50
35	Edgar Renteria	.75
36	Chipper Jones	1.50
37	Tom Glavine	.75
38	John Smoltz	.75
39	Greg Maddux	1.50
40	Ryan Klesko	.50
41	Javy Lopez	.50
42	Fred McGriff	.50
43	Roberto Alomar	.75
44	Joe Carter	.50
45	Rickey Henderson	.50
46	Paul Molitor	1.00
47	Jack Morris	.50
48	Jack Morris	.50
49	Kirby Puckett	1.50
50	Eric Davis	.50
51	Barry Larkin	.75
52	Paul O'Neill	.75
53	Dennis Eckersley	.50
54	Jose Canseco	1.00
55	Rickey Henderson	.75
56	Dave Parker	.50
57	Orel Hershiser	.50
58	Kirk Gibson	.50
59	Bert Blyleven	.50
60	Dwight Gooden	.50
61	Gary Carter	.50
62	Lenny Dykstra	.50

63	Keith Hernandez	.50
64	Darryl Strawberry	.50
65	George Brett	3.00
66	Kirk Gibson	.50
67	Alan Trammell	.50
68	Jim Palmer	.75
69	Eddie Murray	.75
70	Cal Ripken Jr.	5.00
71	Keith Hernandez	.50
72	Ozzie Smith	1.50
73	Steve Garvey	.50
74	Steve Carlton	1.00
75	Mike Schmidt	4.00
76	John Candelaria	.50
77	Bert Blyleven	.50
78	Dave Parker	.50
79	Willie Stargell	1.00
80	Reggie Jackson	1.00
81	Johnny Bench	2.00
82	Dave Concepcion	.50
83	George Foster	.50
84	Joe Morgan	.50
85	Tony Perez	.50
86	Rollie Fingers	.50
87	Jim "Catfish" Hunter	.50
88	Reggie Jackson	1.00
89	Al Oliver	.50
90	Roberto Clemente	3.00
91	Willie Stargell	.75
92	Brooks Robinson	1.00
93	Frank Robinson	.75
94	Nolan Ryan	4.00
95	Tom Seaver	1.50
96	Al Kaline	1.00
97	Bob Gibson	1.00
98	Lou Brock	.75
99	Orlando Cepeda	.50
100	Duke Snider	1.00

Blue Signature

NM/M

Quantity produced listed

2	Miguel Cabrera/25	40.00
3	Derrek Lee/25	30.00
5	Brad Penny/25	15.00
9	Garret Anderson/25	20.00
11	John Lackey/50	10.00
12	Chone Figgins/25	15.00
16	Steve Finley/25	20.00
29	Darryl Strawberry/25	20.00
42	Fred McGriff/25	40.00
47	Jack Morris/25	20.00
48	Jack Morris/25	20.00
50	Eric Davis/25	25.00
53	Dennis Eckersley/25	40.00
56	Dave Parker/25	20.00
59	Bert Blyleven/25	25.00
60	Dwight Gooden/25	25.00
62	Lenny Dykstra/25	25.00
63	Keith Hernandez/25	25.00
64	Darryl Strawberry/25	25.00
67	Alan Trammell/25	25.00
68	Jim Palmer/25	25.00
71	Keith Hernandez/25	25.00
76	John Candelaria/25	25.00
77	Bert Blyleven/25	25.00
78	Dave Parker/25	20.00
82	Dave Concepcion/25	20.00
83	George Foster/25	20.00
85	Tony Perez/25	35.00
86	Rollie Fingers/25	25.00
89	Al Oliver/25	25.00

Blue Material Fabric

NM/M

Common Player: 4.00
Quantity produced listed

1	Josh Beckett/Jsy/103	4.00
2	Miguel Cabrera/Jsy/103	8.00
3	Derrek Lee/Jsy/103	6.00
4	Mike Lowell/Jsy/103	4.00
5	Brad Penny/Jsy/103	4.00
6	Ivan Rodriguez/Jsy/103	8.00
7	Dontrelle Willis/Jsy/103	4.00
9	Garret Anderson/Jsy/102	4.00
10	Troy Glaus/Jsy/102	4.00
13	Tim Salmon/Jsy/102	4.00
14	Darin Erstad/Jsy/102	4.00
15	Tony Percival/Jsy/102	4.00
16	Steve Finley/Jsy/101	4.00
18	Randy Johnson/Pants/101	8.00
19	Curt Schilling/Jsy/101	8.00
20	Luis Gonzalez/Jsy/101	4.00
21	Andy Pettitte/Jsy/100	6.00
22	Bernie Williams/Jsy/100	6.00
24	Mariano Rivera/Jsy/100	6.00
25	Roger Clemens/Jsy/100	12.00
29	Darryl Strawberry/Jsy/99	6.00
30	David Wells/Jsy/99	4.00
31	Wade Boggs/Jsy/96	8.00
32	Charles Johnson/Jsy/97	4.00
33	Cliff Floyd/Jsy/97	4.00
36	Chipper Jones/Jsy/95	8.00
37	Tom Glavine/Jsy/95	6.00
39	Greg Maddux/Jsy/95	10.00
40	Ryan Klesko/Jsy/95	4.00
41	Javy Lopez/Jsy/95	4.00
51	Barry Larkin/Jsy/90	8.00
54	Jose Canseco/Jsy/89	10.00
55	Rickey Henderson/Jsy/89	12.00
57	Orel Hershiser/Jsy/88	8.00
59	Bert Blyleven/Jsy/87	6.00
60	Dwight Gooden/Jsy/86	6.00
61	Gary Carter/Jkt/86	6.00
64	Darryl Strawberry/Jsy/86	6.00
65	George Brett/Jsy/85	20.00
68	Jim Palmer/Pants/83	8.00
69	Eddie Murray/Jsy/83	15.00
70	Cal Ripken Jr./Jsy/83	40.00
71	Keith Hernandez/Jsy/82	6.00
74	Steve Carlton/Jsy/80	6.00
75	Mike Schmidt/Jkt/80	15.00
78	Dave Parker/Jsy/79	6.00
79	Willie Stargell/Jsy/79	8.00
80	Reggie Jackson/Jsy/78	8.00
81	Johnny Bench/Jsy/75	12.00
82	Dave Concepcion/Jsy/75	4.00
83	George Foster/Jsy/75	4.00
86	Rollie Fingers/Jsy/74	4.00
87	Jim "Catfish" Hunter/Jsy/74	8.00
88	Reggie Jackson/Jkt/73	8.00
91	Willie Stargell/Jsy/71	8.00
98	Lou Brock/Jkt/67	8.00
100	Duke Snider/Pants/55	10.00

Blue Material Fabric AL/NL

NM/M

Common Player: 4.00
Quantity produced listed

1	Josh Beckett/Jsy/100	4.00
2	Miguel Cabrera/Jsy/100	8.00
3	Derrek Lee/Jsy/100	4.00
4	Mike Lowell/Jsy/100	4.00
5	Brad Penny/Jsy/103	4.00
6	Ivan Rodriguez/Jsy/100	8.00
7	Dontrelle Willis/Jsy/100	4.00
9	Garret Anderson/Jsy/100	4.00
10	Troy Glaus/Jsy/100	4.00
13	Tim Salmon/Jsy/100	4.00
14	Darin Erstad/Jsy/100	4.00
15	Tony Percival/Jsy/100	4.00
16	Steve Finley/Jsy/100	4.00
18	Randy Johnson/Pants/100	8.00
19	Curt Schilling/Jsy/100	8.00
20	Luis Gonzalez/Jsy/100	4.00
21	Andy Pettitte/Jsy/100	6.00
22	Bernie Williams/Jsy/100	6.00
24	Mariano Rivera/Jsy/100	6.00
25	Roger Clemens/Jsy/100	15.00
29	Darryl Strawberry/Jsy/100	4.00
30	David Wells/Jsy/100	4.00
31	Wade Boggs/Jsy/100	8.00
32	Charles Johnson/Jsy/100	4.00
33	Cliff Floyd/Jsy/100	4.00
36	Chipper Jones/Jsy/100	8.00
37	Tom Glavine/Jsy/100	6.00
39	Greg Maddux/Jsy/100	10.00
40	Ryan Klesko/Jsy/100	4.00
41	Javy Lopez/Jsy/10	4.00
51	Barry Larkin/Jsy/100	8.00
54	Jose Canseco/Jsy/100	10.00
55	Rickey Henderson/Jsy/100	10.00
57	Orel Hershiser/Jsy/100	8.00
59	Bert Blyleven/Jsy/50	8.00
60	Dwight Gooden/Jsy/100	6.00
61	Gary Carter/Jkt/100	6.00
64	Darryl Strawberry/Jsy/100	6.00
65	George Brett/Jsy/50	25.00
68	Jim Palmer/Pants/50	8.00
69	Eddie Murray/Jsy/50	15.00
70	Cal Ripken Jr./Jsy/50	65.00
71	Keith Hernandez/Jsy/50	8.00
74	Steve Carlton/Jsy/50	8.00
75	Mike Schmidt/Jkt/50	25.00
78	Dave Parker/Jsy/50	8.00
79	Willie Stargell/Jsy/50	15.00
80	Reggie Jackson/Jsy/50	15.00
82	Dave Concepcion/Jsy/50	8.00
83	George Foster/Jsy/50	8.00
86	Rollie Fingers/Jsy/50	8.00
87	Jim "Catfish" Hunter/Jsy/50	15.00
88	Reggie Jackson/Jkt/50	15.00
91	Willie Stargell/Jsy/50	15.00
98	Lou Brock/Jkt/50	15.00
100	Duke Snider/Pants/50	15.00

Blue Material Bat

NM/M

Common Player: 5.00
Production 50 Sets

1	Josh Beckett	8.00
2	Miguel Cabrera	12.00
3	Derrek Lee	8.00
4	Mike Lowell	5.00
5	Brad Penny	5.00
6	Ivan Rodriguez	12.00
8	Luis Castillo	5.00
9	Garret Anderson	5.00
10	Troy Glaus	8.00
13	Tim Salmon	5.00
14	Darin Erstad	5.00
17	Mark Grace	12.00
19	Curt Schilling	12.00
20	Luis Gonzalez	5.00
21	Andy Pettitte	5.00
22	Bernie Williams	8.00
23	Jorge Posada	10.00
25	Roger Clemens	20.00
27	David Justice	5.00
28	Paul O'Neill	10.00
29	Darryl Strawberry	10.00
31	Wade Boggs	15.00
32	Charles Johnson	5.00
33	Cliff Floyd	5.00
34	Moises Alou	8.00
35	Edgar Renteria	8.00
36	Chipper Jones	15.00
37	Tom Glavine	10.00
39	Greg Maddux	20.00
40	Ryan Klesko	5.00
41	Javy Lopez	5.00
42	Fred McGriff	8.00
43	Roberto Alomar	8.00
44	Joe Carter	5.00
45	Rickey Henderson	15.00
46	Paul Molitor	15.00
49	Kirby Puckett	15.00
50	Eric Davis	5.00
51	Barry Larkin	8.00
52	Paul O'Neill	8.00
55	Rickey Henderson	15.00
56	Dave Parker	8.00
58	Kirk Gibson	10.00
60	Dwight Gooden	8.00
61	Gary Carter	8.00
62	Lenny Dykstra	5.00
63	Keith Hernandez	5.00
64	Darryl Strawberry	5.00
65	George Brett	25.00
66	Kirk Gibson	8.00
67	Alan Trammell	8.00
69	Eddie Murray	20.00
70	Cal Ripken Jr.	70.00
71	Keith Hernandez	8.00
72	Ozzie Smith	20.00
73	Steve Garvey	5.00
74	Steve Carlton	10.00
75	Mike Schmidt	25.00
78	Dave Parker	8.00
79	Willie Stargell	15.00
80	Reggie Jackson	15.00
81	Johnny Bench	20.00
82	Dave Concepcion	5.00
83	George Foster	5.00
84	Joe Morgan	8.00
85	Tony Perez	8.00
88	Reggie Jackson	15.00
89	Al Oliver	5.00
90	Roberto Clemente	60.00
91	Willie Stargell	15.00
92	Brooks Robinson	15.00
93	Frank Robinson	10.00
96	Al Kaline	15.00
98	Lou Brock	15.00
99	Orlando Cepeda	10.00

Face Off

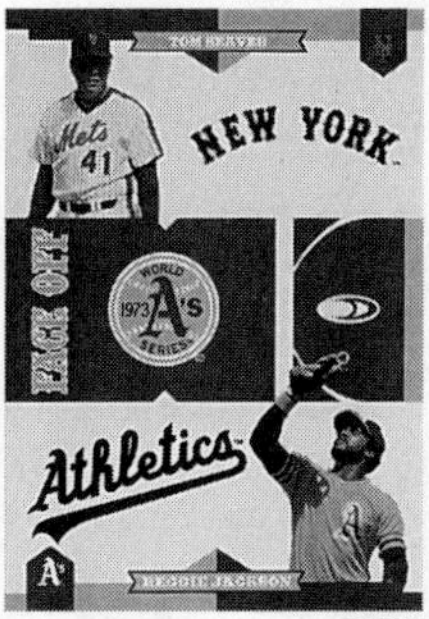

NM/M

Complete Set (20): 75.00
Common Duo: 2.00
Production 500 Sets
HoloFoil: 2-4X
Production 25 Sets

1	Roger Clemens, Mike Piazza	6.00
2	Mike Mussina, Ivan Rodriguez	3.00
3	Mark Grace, Jorge Posada	4.00
4	Greg Maddux, Jim Thome	5.00
5	Rickey Henderson, Curt Schilling	4.00
6	Kirby Puckett, Tom Glavine	4.00
7	Dennis Eckersley, Will Clark	3.00
8	Bernie Williams, Randy Johnson	4.00
9	Cal Ripken Jr., Steve Carlton	12.00
10	Tom Seaver, Reggie Jackson	4.00
11	Mike Schmidt, George Brett	8.00
12	Wade Boggs, Keith Hernandez	3.00
13	Dwight Gooden, Dwight Evans	2.00
14	Johnny Bench, Jim "Catfish" Hunter	4.00
15	Jim Palmer, Dave Parker	4.00
16	Bob Gibson, Al Kaline	4.00
17	Carl Yastrzemski, Lou Brock	6.00
18	Duke Snider, Whitey Ford	4.00
19	Carlton Fisk, Tony Perez	4.00
20	Roberto Clemente, Frank Robinson	8.00

Face Off Material

NM/M

Common Duo: 10.00
Quantity produced listed

1	Roger Clemens/Jsy, Mike Piazza/Jsy/100	25.00
2	Mike Mussina/Jsy, Ivan Rodriguez/Jsy/100	20.00

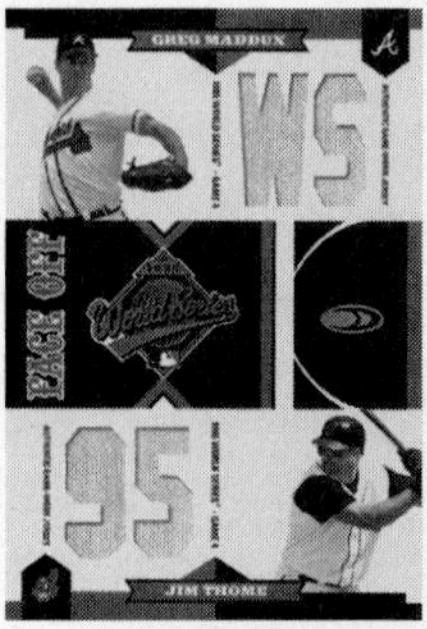

4	Greg Maddux/Jsy, Jim Thome/Jsy/25	35.00
5	Rickey Henderson/Jsy, Curt Schilling/Jsy/100	15.00
6	Kirby Puckett/Jsy, Tom Glavine/Jsy/100	25.00
8	Bernie Williams/Jsy, Randy Johnson/Pants/100	20.00
9	Cal Ripken Jr./Jsy, Steve Carlton/Jsy/50	75.00
11	Mike Schmidt/Jkt, George Brett/Jsy/50	40.00
13	Dwight Gooden/Jsy, Dwight Evans/Jsy/50	25.00
15	Jim Palmer/Jsy, Dave Parker/Jsy/50	10.00
17	Carl Yastrzemski/Jsy, Lou Brock/Jkt/50	40.00
18	Duke Snider/Pants, Whitey Ford/Jsy/50	25.00
19	Carlton Fisk/Jsy, Tony Perez/Fld Glv/50	20.00

Fans of the Game

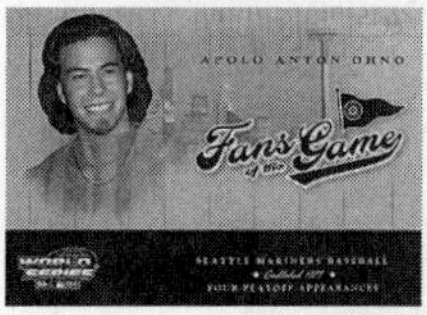

NM/M

Complete Set (5): 8.00
Common Player: 1.50
Inserted 1:24

1	Val Kilmer	2.00
2	Stan Lee	2.00
3	Apolo Anton Ohno	1.50
4	Gene Shalit	1.50
5	Leeann Tweeden	1.50

Fans of the Game Signatures

NM/M

Common Autograph: 20.00

1	Val Kilmer	50.00
2	Stan Lee	50.00
3	Apolo Anton Ohno	30.00
4	Gene Shalit	20.00
5	Leeann Tweeden	35.00

Legends of the Fall

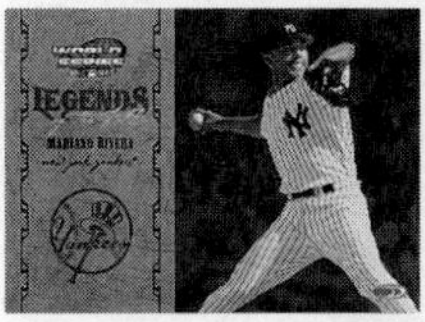

NM/M

Complete Set (20): 75.00
Common Player: 3.00
Production 500 Sets
HoloFoil: 2-4X
Production 25 Sets

1	Bob Gibson	4.00
2	Brooks Robinson	4.00
3	Cal Ripken Jr.	12.00
4	Carl Yastrzemski	6.00
5	Carlton Fisk	4.00
6	Derek Jeter	8.00
7	Duke Snider	4.00
8	Eddie Murray	4.00
9	Frank Robinson	3.00
10	Gary Carter	3.00
11	George Brett	8.00
12	Jim Palmer	3.00
13	Johnny Bench	4.00
14	Marco Rivera	3.00
15	Mike Schmidt	8.00
16	Phil Rizzuto	3.00

17 Red Schoendienst 3.00
18 Reggie Jackson 4.00
19 Rickey Henderson 3.00
20 Whitey Ford 4.00

Legends of the Fall Material

NM/M

Common Player: 5.00
Quantity produced listed
1 Bob Gibson/Jsy/50 12.00
2 Brooks Robinson/Bat/100 10.00
3 Cal Ripken Jr./Jkt/100 40.00
4 Carl Yastrzemski/Bat/50 10.00
5 Carlton Fisk/Bat/50 10.00
7 Duke Snider/Pants/50 15.00
8 Eddie Murray/Jsy/50 15.00
9 Frank Robinson/Bat/100 5.00
10 Gary Carter/Jkt/100 5.00
11 George Brett/Bat/50 25.00
12 Jim Palmer/Pants/25 12.00
13 Johnny Bench/Bat/100 12.00
14 Marco Rivera/Jsy/100 8.00
15 Mike Schmidt/Jkt/50 25.00
16 Phil Rizzuto/Pants/50 10.00
17 Red Schoendienst/Bat/100 5.00
18 Reggie Jackson/Bat/100 10.00
19 Rickey Henderson/Bat/100 10.00

Legends of the Fall Signature

NM/M

Common Player:
2 Brooks Robinson/25 30.00
9 Frank Robinson/25 35.00
10 Gary Carter/25 25.00
12 Jim Palmer/25 25.00
16 Phil Rizzuto/25 30.00
17 Red Schoendienst/50 20.00

Legends of the Fall Signature Material

NM/M

Quantity produced listed
1 Bob Gibson/Jsy/25 40.00
2 Brooks Robinson/Bat/50 35.00
7 Duke Snider/Pants/50 35.00
9 Frank Robinson/Bat/50 30.00
10 Gary Carter/Jkt/50 25.00
12 Jim Palmer/Pants/25 25.00
13 Johnny Bench/Bat/25 70.00
16 Phil Rizzuto/Pants/50 35.00
17 Red Schoendienst/Bat/100 20.00

Material Bat

NM/M

Common Player: 4.00
Production 100 Sets
2 Darin Erstad 4.00
3 Garret Anderson 4.00
4 Tim Salmon 4.00
5 Troy Glaus 4.00
6 Vladimir Guerrero 8.00
8 Luis Gonzalez 4.00
13 Andruw Jones 6.00
14 Chipper Jones 8.00
15 J.D. Drew 4.00
16 Marcus Giles 4.00
17 Rafael Furcal 4.00
18 Javy Lopez 4.00
19 Jay Gibbons 4.00
22 Miguel Tejada 6.00
23 Rafael Palmeiro 8.00
25 Dwight Evans 4.00
26 Fred Lynn 4.00
27 Jason Varitek 8.00
28 Jim Rice 6.00
29 Johnny Damon 10.00
31 Manny Ramirez 8.00
32 Nomar Garciaparra 10.00
33 Pedro Martinez 8.00
34 Trot Nixon 4.00
35 Aramis Ramirez 6.00
37 Derrek Lee 6.00
40 Mark Prior 6.00
41 Moises Alou 4.00
42 Sammy Sosa 12.00
43 Carlos Lee 4.00
44 Frank Thomas 8.00
45 Luis Aparicio 4.00
46 Magglio Ordonez 4.00
47 Mark Buehrle 4.00
48 Paul Konerko 4.00
49 Adam Dunn/Jsy 8.00
50 Austin Kearns 4.00
51 Barry Larkin 8.00
52 Dave Concepcion 4.00
53 George Foster 4.00
54 Joe Morgan 6.00
55 Sean Casey 4.00
56 Tony Perez 4.00
59 Omar Vizquel 4.00
60 Victor Martinez 4.00
61 Charles Johnson 4.00
63 Larry Walker 4.00
64 Preston Wilson 8.00
65 Todd Helton 8.00
66 Alan Trammell 4.00
68 Ivan Rodriguez 8.00
71 Brad Penny 4.00
73 Josh Beckett 6.00
74 Juan Pierre 4.00
75 Luis Castillo 4.00
76 Miguel Cabrera 8.00
77 Mike Lowell 4.00
78 Andy Pettitte 6.00
79 Craig Biggio 6.00
80 Jeff Bagwell 8.00
81 Jeff Kent 4.00
82 Lance Berkman 4.00
83 Roger Clemens 15.00
84 Roy Oswalt 4.00
86 Angel Berroa 4.00
87 Carlos Beltran 8.00
88 Juan Gonzalez 6.00
89 Ken Harvey 4.00
90 Mike Sweeney 4.00
91 Adrian Beltre 6.00
93 Kazuhisa Ishii 4.00
96 Paul LoDuca 4.00
97 Shawn Green 4.00
98 Ben Sheets 4.00
99 Geoff Jenkins 4.00
104 Jacque Jones 4.00
106 Shannon Stewart 4.00
107 Torii Hunter 6.00
108 Jose Vidro 4.00
109 Orlando Cabrera 6.00
111 Darryl Strawberry 6.00
112 Dwight Gooden 6.00
113 Jose Reyes 6.00
114 Kazuo Matsui 10.00
115 Keith Hernandez 6.00
116 Lenny Dykstra 4.00
118 Tom Glavine 8.00
122 Gary Sheffield 8.00
123 Jason Giambi 4.00
125 Jorge Posada 8.00
126 Kenny Lofton 4.00
127 Kevin Brown 4.00
129 Mike Mussina 8.00
131 Eric Chavez 4.00
132 Jermaine Dye 4.00
133 Mark Mulder 4.00
135 Tim Hudson 6.00
137 Jim Thome 8.00
139 Marlon Byrd 4.00
141 Pat Burrell 4.00
142 Steve Carlton 6.00
143 Dave Parker 4.00
145 Brian Giles 4.00
147 Ryan Klesko 4.00
151 Edgar Martinez 4.00
153 Rich Aurilia 4.00
155 Albert Pujols 15.00
156 Dan Haren 4.00
157 Edgar Renteria 6.00
159 Jim Edmonds 6.00
161 Scott Rolen 8.00
162 Aubrey Huff 4.00
165 Fred McGriff 4.00
166 Rocco Baldelli 4.00
167 Alfonso Soriano 8.00
168 Hank Blalock 8.00
170 Mark Teixeira 6.00
171 Michael Young 4.00
172 Carlos Delgado 4.00
175 Vernon Wells 4.00

Material Fabric AL/NL

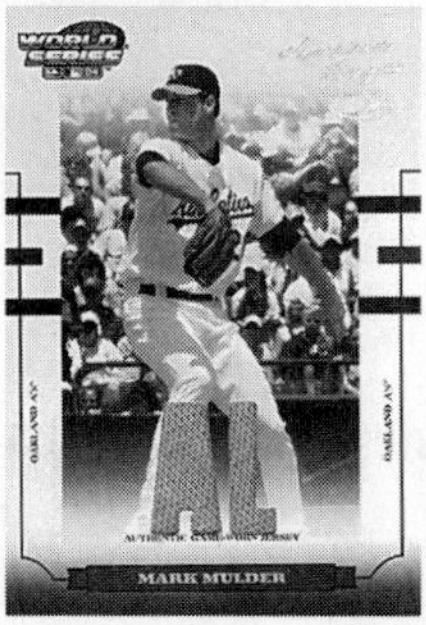

NM/M

Common Player: 4.00
Production 250 unless noted.
2 Darin Erstad/Jsy 4.00
3 Garret Anderson/Jsy 4.00
4 Tim Salmon/Jsy 4.00
5 Troy Glaus/Jsy 4.00
6 Vladimir Guerrero/Jsy 8.00
7 Brandon Webb/Pants 4.00
8 Luis Gonzalez/Jsy 4.00
9 Randy Johnson/Pants/100 10.00
12 Steve Finley/Jsy 4.00
13 Andruw Jones/Jsy 6.00
14 Chipper Jones/Jsy 8.00
16 Marcus Giles/Jsy 4.00
17 Rafael Furcal/Jsy 4.00
19 Jay Gibbons/Jsy 4.00
20 Luis Matos/Jsy 4.00
21 Melvin Mora/Jsy 4.00
22 Miguel Tejada/Jsy 6.00
23 Rafael Palmeiro/Jsy/100 8.00
25 Dwight Evans/Jsy 4.00
26 Fred Lynn/Jsy 4.00
28 Jim Rice/Jsy 6.00
31 Manny Ramirez/Jsy 8.00
33 Pedro Martinez/Jsy 8.00
35 Aramis Ramirez/Jsy 6.00
38 Greg Maddux/Jsy/100 12.00
39 Kerry Wood/Pants 8.00
40 Mark Prior/Jsy 6.00
42 Sammy Sosa/Jsy 10.00
43 Carlos Lee/Jsy 4.00
44 Frank Thomas/Jsy 8.00
47 Mark Buehrle/Jsy 4.00
48 Paul Konerko/Jsy 4.00
49 Adam Dunn/Jsy 8.00
50 Austin Kearns/Jsy 4.00
52 Dave Concepcion/Jsy 4.00
57 C.C. Sabathia/Jsy 4.00
58 Jody Gerut/Jsy 4.00
59 Omar Vizquel/Jsy 4.00
60 Victor Martinez/Jsy 4.00
63 Larry Walker/Jsy 8.00
64 Preston Wilson/Jsy 4.00
65 Todd Helton/Jsy 8.00
70 A.J. Burnett/Jsy 4.00
71 Brad Penny/Jsy 4.00
72 Dontrelle Willis/Jsy 4.00
73 Josh Beckett/Jsy 6.00
76 Miguel Cabrera/Jsy 8.00
77 Mike Lowell/Jsy 4.00
79 Craig Biggio/Jsy 6.00
80 Jeff Bagwell/Pants 8.00
81 Jeff Kent/Jsy 4.00
82 Lance Berkman/Jsy 4.00
86 Angel Berroa/Pants 4.00
90 Mike Sweeney/Jsy 4.00
91 Adrian Beltre/Jsy 6.00
92 Hideo Nomo/Jsy 8.00
93 Kazuhisa Ishii/Jsy 4.00
95 Orel Hershiser/Jsy/100 6.00
96 Paul LoDuca/Jsy 4.00
97 Shawn Green/Jsy 6.00
98 Ben Sheets/Jsy 4.00
99 Geoff Jenkins/Jsy 4.00
104 Jacque Jones/Jsy 4.00
105 Johan Santana/Jsy 8.00
106 Shannon Stewart/Jsy 4.00
110 Al Leiter/Jsy 4.00
111 Darryl Strawberry/Jsy 4.00
117 Mike Piazza/Jsy 10.00
118 Tom Glavine/Jsy 8.00
120 Bernie Williams/Jsy 6.00
123 Jason Giambi/Jsy 4.00
128 Mariano Rivera/Jsy 6.00
129 Mike Mussina/Jsy 8.00
130 Barry Zito/Jsy 4.00
131 Eric Chavez/Jsy 4.00
133 Mark Mulder/Jsy 4.00
135 Tim Hudson/Jsy 4.00
136 Brett Myers/Jsy 4.00
137 Jim Thome/Jsy 8.00
138 Kevin Millwood/Jsy 4.00
139 Marlon Byrd/Jsy 4.00
141 Pat Burrell/Jsy 4.00
142 Steve Carlton/Jsy/100 6.00
143 Dave Parker/Jsy/100 4.00
147 Ryan Klesko/Jsy 4.00
152 Jamie Moyer/Jsy 4.00
155 Albert Pujols/Jsy/100 15.00
156 Dan Haren/Jsy 4.00
159 Jim Edmonds/Jsy 6.00
161 Scott Rolen/Jsy 8.00
162 Aubrey Huff/Jsy 4.00
163 Carl Crawford/Jsy 4.00
164 Dewon Brazelton/Jsy 4.00
165 Fred McGriff/Jsy 4.00
166 Rocco Baldelli/Jsy 4.00
168 Hank Blalock/Jsy 8.00
174 Roy Halladay/Jsy 4.00
175 Vernon Wells/Jsy 4.00

Material Fabric Number

NM/M

Common Player:
5 Troy Glaus/Jsy/25 10.00
6 Vladimir Guerrero/Jsy/27 20.00
7 Brandon Webb/Pants/55 6.00
8 Luis Gonzalez/Jsy/20 8.00
9 Randy Johnson/Pants/51 15.00
13 Andruw Jones/Jsy/25 10.00
16 Marcus Giles/Jsy/22 8.00
19 Jay Gibbons/Jsy/31 8.00
23 Rafael Palmeiro/Jsy/25 15.00
25 Dwight Evans/Jsy/24 15.00
26 Fred Lynn/Jsy/19 10.00
30 Luis Tiant/Jsy/23 8.00
31 Manny Ramirez/Jsy/24 20.00
33 Pedro Martinez/Jsy/45 15.00
38 Greg Maddux/Jsy/31 20.00
39 Kerry Wood/Pants/34 20.00
40 Mark Prior/Jsy/22 15.00
42 Sammy Sosa/Jsy/21 25.00
43 Carlos Lee/Jsy/45 6.00
44 Frank Thomas/Jsy/35 15.00
46 Magglio Ordonez/Jsy/30 8.00
47 Mark Buehrle/Jsy/56 6.00
49 Adam Dunn/Jsy/44 12.00
50 Austin Kearns/Jsy/28 10.00
57 C.C. Sabathia/Jsy/52 6.00
60 Victor Martinez/Jsy/41 8.00
63 Larry Walker/Jsy/33 10.00
64 Preston Wilson/Jsy/44 6.00
65 Todd Helton/Jsy/17 25.00
70 A.J. Burnett/Jsy/34 6.00
71 Brad Penny/Jsy/31 6.00
72 Dontrelle Willis/Jsy/35 6.00
76 Miguel Cabrera/Jsy/24 20.00
90 Mike Sweeney/Jsy/29 10.00
91 Adrian Beltre/Jsy/29 15.00
95 Orel Hershiser/Jsy/55 8.00
105 Johan Santana/Jsy/57 15.00
106 Shannon Stewart/Jsy/23 8.00
107 Torii Hunter/Jsy/48 10.00
110 Al Leiter/Jsy/22 10.00
117 Mike Piazza/Jsy/31 20.00
118 Tom Glavine/Jsy/47 12.00
120 Bernie Williams/Jsy/51 12.00
123 Jason Giambi/Jsy/25 10.00
125 Jorge Posada/Jsy/20 15.00
128 Mariano Rivera/Jsy/42 10.00
129 Mike Mussina/Jsy/35 15.00
130 Barry Zito/Jsy/75 8.00
133 Mark Mulder/Jsy/20 15.00
136 Brett Myers/Jsy/39 6.00
137 Jim Thome/Jsy/25 20.00
138 Kevin Millwood/Jsy/34 8.00
139 Marlon Byrd/Jsy/29 8.00
142 Steve Carlton/Jsy/32 12.00
143 Dave Parker/Jsy/39 8.00
147 Ryan Klesko/Jsy/30 10.00
152 Jamie Moyer/Jsy/50 6.00
156 Dan Haren/Jsy/55 6.00
159 Jim Edmonds/Jsy/15 15.00
161 Scott Rolen/Jsy/27 25.00
164 Dewon Brazelton/Jsy/45 6.00
165 Fred McGriff/Jsy/29 15.00
174 Roy Halladay/Jsy/32 8.00

MVP

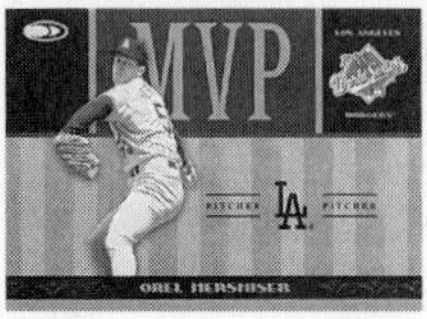

NM/M

Complete Set (15): 35.00
Common Player: 2.00
Production 1,000 Sets
HoloFoil: 2-4X
Production 50 Sets
1 Whitey Ford 3.00
2 Bob Gibson 3.00
3 Frank Robinson 2.00
4 Brooks Robinson 3.00
5 Roberto Clemente 6.00
6 Reggie Jackson 3.00
7 Rollie Fingers 2.00
8 Johnny Bench 4.00
9 Reggie Jackson 3.00
10 Mike Schmidt 6.00
11 Alan Trammell 2.00
12 Orel Hershiser 2.00
13 Jack Morris 2.00
14 Paul Molitor 4.00
15 Tom Glavine 3.00

MVP Material

NM/M

Quantity produced listed
1 Whitey Ford/Jsy/50 10.00
2 Bob Gibson/Jsy/50 10.00
3 Frank Robinson/Jsy/25 12.00
6 Reggie Jackson/Jkt/100 10.00
7 Rollie Fingers/Jsy/100 5.00
9 Reggie Jackson/Jsy/25 20.00
10 Mike Schmidt/Jsy/50 25.00
12 Orel Hershiser/Jsy/100 5.00
15 Tom Glavine/Jsy/100 8.00

MVP Signature

NM/M

Quantity produced listed
11 Alan Trammell/25 20.00
13 Jack Morris/25 20.00

MVP Signature Material

NM/M

Quantity produced listed
2 Bob Gibson/Jsy/50 35.00
3 Frank Robinson/Shoe/50 40.00
7 Rollie Fingers/Jsy/100 15.00
12 Orel Hershiser/Jsy/25 25.00

October Heroes

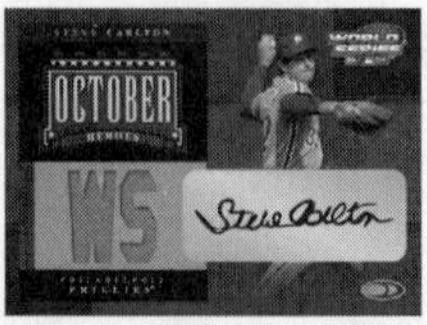

NM/M

Complete Set (20): 40.00
Common Player: 2.00
Production 500 Sets
HoloFoil: 2-4X
Production 25 Sets
1 Alan Trammell 2.00
2 Andy Pettitte 3.00
3 Jim "Catfish" Hunter 2.00
4 Chipper Jones 4.00
5 Dave Concepcion 2.00

6	David Wells	2.00
7	Jack Morris	2.00
8	Joe Morgan	3.00
9	Josh Beckett	2.00
10	Kirby Puckett	4.00
11	Kirk Gibson	2.00
12	Marty Marion	4.00
13	Miguel Cabrera	4.00
14	Paul Molitor	4.00
15	Paul O'Neill	2.00
16	Randy Johnson	4.00
17	Roger Clemens	6.00
18	Steve Carlton	3.00
19	Steve Garvey	2.00
20	Wade Boggs	3.00

October Heroes Material

		NM/M
Common Player:		4.00
1	Alan Trammell/Jsy/25	10.00
2	Andy Pettitte/Jsy/100	4.00
3	Jim "Catfish" Hunter/Jsy/25	15.00
4	Chipper Jones/Jsy/100	8.00
5	Dave Concepcion/Jsy/50	4.00
6	David Wells/Jsy/25	8.00
9	Josh Beckett/Jsy/100	4.00
10	Kirby Puckett/Jsy/25	25.00
12	Marty Marion/Jsy/25	10.00
13	Miguel Cabrera/Jsy/100	8.00
16	Randy Johnson/Pants/50	12.00
17	Roger Clemens/Jsy/100	12.00
18	Steve Carlton/Jsy/100	6.00
19	Steve Garvey/Jsy/100	4.00
20	Wade Boggs/Jsy/100	8.00

October Heroes Signatures

		NM/M
Quantity produced listed		
1	Alan Trammell/25	25.00
5	Dave Concepcion/25	20.00
7	Jack Morris/25	20.00
12	Marty Marion/25	20.00
13	Miguel Cabrera/25	40.00
18	Steve Carlton/25	35.00
19	Steve Garvey/25	20.00

October Heroes Signature Material

		NM/M
Quantity produced listed		
1	Alan Trammell/Jsy/100	20.00
5	Dave Concepcion/Jsy/100	15.00
12	Marty Marion/Jsy/100	15.00
13	Miguel Cabrera/Jsy/100	30.00
18	Steve Carlton/Jsy/100	35.00
19	Steve Garvey/Jsy/100	15.00

October Legends

		NM/M
Complete Set (20):		60.00
Common Player:		2.00
Production 500 Sets		
HoloFoil:		2-4X
Production 25 Sets		
1	Bob Gibson	4.00
2	Cal Ripken Jr.	10.00
3	Carl Yastrzemski	6.00
4	Carlton Fisk	3.00
5	Duke Snider	4.00
6	Eddie Murray	4.00
7	Frank Robinson	3.00
8	George Brett	8.00
9	Joe Morgan	2.00
10	Johnny Bench	4.00
11	Lou Brock	3.00
12	Mike Schmidt	8.00
13	Paul Molitor	4.00
14	Phil Rizzuto	3.00
15	Reggie Jackson	4.00
16	Robin Yount	4.00
17	Stan Musial	6.00
18	Steve Carlton	2.00
19	Whitey Ford	3.00
20	Willie McCovey	2.00

October Legends Materials

		NM/M
Common Player:		5.00
Quantity produced listed		
1	Bob Gibson/Jsy/50	10.00
2	Cal Ripken Jr./Jsy/50	50.00
3	Carl Yastrzemski/Jsy/50	20.00
4	Carlton Fisk/Bat/100	8.00
5	Duke Snider/Jsy/25	20.00
6	Eddie Murray/Jsy/50	10.00
7	Frank Robinson/Jsy/50	8.00
8	George Brett/Jsy/50	25.00
10	Johnny Bench/Jsy/25	15.00
11	Lou Brock/Jkt/100	8.00
12	Mike Schmidt/Jkt/100	15.00
14	Phil Rizzuto/Pants/25	15.00
15	Reggie Jackson/Jsy/100	8.00
16	Robin Yount/Jsy/100	10.00
18	Steve Carlton/Jsy/100	5.00
19	Whitey Ford/Pants/25	15.00
20	Willie McCovey/Jsy/25	15.00

October Legends Signature

		NM/M
Quantity produced listed		
11	Lou Brock/25	35.00
14	Phil Rizzuto/25	35.00
18	Steve Carlton/25	30.00

October Legends Signature Material

		NM/M
Quantity produced listed		
1	Bob Gibson/Jsy/50	40.00
5	Duke Snider/Jsy/50	40.00
7	Frank Robinson/Jsy/50	30.00
11	Lou Brock/Jkt/100	25.00
13	Paul Molitor/Jsy/25	40.00
14	Phil Rizzuto/Pants/25	30.00
16	Robin Yount/Jsy/25	65.00
17	Stan Musial/Jsy/25	90.00
18	Steve Carlton/Jsy/100	25.00
19	Whitey Ford/Pants/25	40.00
20	Willie McCovey/Jsy/25	40.00

Playoff All-Stars

		NM/M
Complete Set (20):		50.00
Common Player:		2.00
Production 500 Sets		
HoloFoil:		2-4X
Production 25 Sets		
1	Mark Prior	3.00
2	Sammy Sosa	6.00
3	Steve Finley	2.00
4	David Ortiz	4.00
5	Mike Piazza	5.00
6	Edgar Martinez	2.00
7	Roy Oswalt	2.00
8	Johan Santana	3.00
9	Jacque Jones	2.00
10	Will Clark	2.00
11	Albert Pujols	8.00
12	Andre Dawson	3.00
13	Nolan Ryan	10.00
14	Fred Lynn	2.00
15	Jim Rice	2.00
16	Dwight Evans	2.00
17	Harmon Killebrew	4.00
18	Maury Wills	2.00
19	Mark Mulder	2.00
20	Frank Thomas	8.00

Playoff All-Stars Material 1

		NM/M
Quantity produced listed		
1	Mark Prior/Jsy/100	6.00
2	Sammy Sosa/Jsy/100	10.00
3	Steve Finley/Jsy/100	4.00
4	David Ortiz/Jsy/100	10.00
5	Mike Piazza/Jsy/100	10.00
6	Edgar Martinez/Jsy/100	6.00
7	Roy Oswalt/Jsy/100	4.00
8	Johan Santana/Jsy/100	8.00
9	Jacque Jones/Jsy/100	4.00
10	Will Clark/Bat/100	10.00
11	Albert Pujols/Jsy/100	20.00
12	Andre Dawson/Jsy/100	6.00
13	Nolan Ryan/Jsy/100	25.00
14	Fred Lynn/Jsy/50	6.00
15	Jim Rice/Jsy/50	6.00
16	Dwight Evans/Jsy/50	6.00
18	Harmon Killebrew/Jsy/50	20.00
19	Mark Mulder/Jsy/100	6.00
20	Frank Thomas/Jsy/100	8.00

Playoff All-Stars Material 2

		NM/M
Common Dual:		6.00
1	Mark Prior/Jsy/100	8.00
2	Sammy Sosa/Jsy/100	15.00
3	Steve Finley/Jsy-Jsy/100	6.00
4	David Ortiz/Bat-Jsy/100	20.00
5	Mike Piazza/Bat/100	15.00
6	Edgar Martinez/Bat-Jsy/100	10.00
7	Roy Oswalt/Bat/100	6.00
8	Johan Santana/Jsy-Jsy/100	10.00
9	Jacque Jones/Bat-Jsy/100	6.00
11	Albert Pujols/Jsy-Jsy/100	25.00
12	Andre Dawson/Bat-Jsy/100	8.00
13	Nolan Ryan/Jkt-Jsy/50	40.00
14	Fred Lynn/Bat-Jsy/50	8.00
15	Jim Rice/Bat-Jsy/50	10.00
16	Dwight Evans/Bat-Jsy/50	6.00
17	Harmon Killebrew/Bat-Jsy/50	25.00
19	Mark Mulder/Bat-Jsy/100	6.00
20	Frank Thomas/Bat-Jsy/100	12.00

Playoff All-Stars Material 3

		NM/M
Common Triple:		10.00
1	Mark Prior/Bat-Hat-Jsy/100	15.00
2	Sammy Sosa/ Bat-Jsy/100	20.00
3	Steve Finley/ Jsy-Jsy/100	10.00
4	David Ortiz/ Bat-Jsy/100	25.00
5	Mike Piazza/ Bat-Jsy/100	20.00
6	Edgar Martinez/ Bat-Jsy/50	10.00
7	Roy Oswalt/ Bat-Fld Glv-Jsy/100	10.00
9	Jacque Jones/ Bat-Jsy/50	10.00
11	Albert Pujols/ Bat-Jsy/50	40.00
12	Andre Dawson/ Bat-Hat-Jsy/100	10.00
13	Nolan Ryan/ Bat-Jsy/50	65.00
15	Jim Rice/ Bat-Jsy/100	10.00
16	Dwight Evans/ Bat-Hat-Jsy/100	10.00
17	Harmon Killebrew/ Bat-Jsy-Shoe/25	50.00
20	Frank Thomas/ Jsy-Jsy-Pants/100	20.00

Playoff All-Stars Signature

		NM/M
Quantity produced listed		
1	Mark Prior/25	40.00
3	Steve Finley/25	20.00
4	David Ortiz/25	60.00
7	Roy Oswalt/25	20.00
8	Johan Santana/25	40.00
9	Jacque Jones/25	20.00
10	Will Clark/25	20.00
12	Andre Dawson/25	20.00
13	Nolan Ryan/25	125.00
14	Fred Lynn/25	20.00
15	Jim Rice/25	25.00
16	Dwight Evans/25	30.00
18	Maury Wills/25	20.00

All-Stars Sig. Material 1

		NM/M
Quantity produced listed		
Material 2:		.75-1.5X
Production 5-100		
Material 3:		.75-1.5X
Production 5-100		
3	Steve Finley/Jsy/100	15.00
4	David Ortiz/Jsy/100	50.00
6	Edgar Martinez/Jsy/50	30.00
7	Roy Oswalt/Jsy/100	15.00
8	Johan Santana/Jsy/100	35.00
9	Jacque Jones/Jsy/100	15.00
10	Will Clark/Bat/100	65.00
12	Andre Dawson/Jsy/100	20.00
14	Fred Lynn/Jsy/25	20.00
15	Jim Rice/Jsy/25	25.00
16	Dwight Evans/Jsy/50	30.00
19	Mark Mulder/Jsy/25	30.00
20	Frank Thomas/Jsy/25	50.00

Records

		NM/M
Complete Set (5):		10.00
Common Player:		3.00
Production 1,000 Sets		
HoloFoil:		2-4X
Production 50 Sets		
1	Lou Brock	3.00
2	Yogi Berra	4.00
3	Reggie Jackson	3.00
4	Bob Gibson	3.00
5	Whitey Ford	3.00

Records Material

		NM/M
Quantity produced listed		
1	Lou Brock/Bat/100	10.00
2	Yogi Berra/Bat/50	20.00
3	Reggie Jackson/Bat/25	20.00
5	Whitey Ford/Pants/25	20.00

Records Signature

		NM/M
Common Player:		
1	Lou Brock/25	30.00

Records Signature Material

		NM/M
Quantity produced listed		
1	Lou Brock/Bat/100	25.00
3	Reggie Jackson/Bat/20	40.00

Signature

		NM/M
Common Autograph:		10.00
201-222 Exclusive to Red Sox Champs Sets		
3	Garret Anderson/25	25.00
7	Brandon Webb/25	10.00
11	Shea Hillenbrand/25	20.00
12	Steve Finley/25	15.00
16	Marcus Giles/25	15.00
17	Rafael Furcal/25	20.00
19	Jay Gibbons/25	10.00
21	Luis Matos/25	20.00
21	Melvin Mora/25	20.00
25	Dwight Evans/25	30.00
26	Fred Lynn/25	20.00
28	Jim Rice/25	25.00
30	Luis Tiant/25	20.00
34	Trot Nixon/25	25.00
35	Aramis Ramirez/25	35.00
37	Derrek Lee/25	30.00
40	Mark Prior/25	40.00
43	Carlos Lee/25	10.00
45	Luis Aparicio/25	20.00
46	Magglio Ordonez/25	20.00
47	Mark Buehrle/25	20.00
49	Adam Dunn/25	40.00
51	Austin Kearns/25	20.00
52	Dave Concepcion/25	15.00
53	George Foster/25	15.00
56	Tony Perez/25	35.00
57	C.C. Sabathia/25	20.00
58	Jody Gerut/25	10.00
60	Victor Martinez/25	25.00
64	Preston Wilson/25	15.00
66	Alan Trammell/25	25.00
69	Jeremy Bonderman/25	10.00
71	Brad Penny/25	10.00
76	Miguel Cabrera/25	40.00
84	Roy Oswalt/25	20.00
85	Wade Miller/25	10.00
86	Angel Berroa/25	10.00
87	Carlos Beltran/25	50.00
89	Ken Harvey/25	10.00
94	Milton Bradley/25	20.00
96	Paul LoDuca/25	25.00
101	Rickie Weeks/25	20.00
102	Scott Podsednik/25	20.00
103	Jack Morris/25	20.00
104	Jacque Jones/25	15.00
105	Jason Giambi/25	50.00
106	Shannon Stewart/25	15.00
107	Torii Hunter/25	25.00
108	Jose Vidro/25	10.00
109	Orlando Cabrera/25	40.00
111	Darryl Strawberry/25	25.00
112	Dwight Gooden/25	25.00
115	Keith Hernandez/25	25.00
116	Lenny Dykstra/25	20.00
132	Jermaine Dye/25	20.00
133	Mark Mulder/25	25.00
134	Rich Harden/25	25.00
139	Marlon Byrd/25	10.00
142	Steve Carlton/25	35.00
143	Dave Parker/25	25.00
146	Jay Payton/25	10.00
148	J.T. Snow/25	15.00
154	Shigetoshi Hasegawa/25	10.00
156	Dan Haren/25	15.00
162	Aubrey Huff/25	25.00
163	Carl Crawford/25	20.00
164	Dewon Brazelton/25	10.00
168	Hank Blalock/25	25.00
170	Mark Teixeira/25	35.00
171	Michael Young/25	20.00

Signature Trio

		NM/M
Quantity produced listed		
2	Derrek Lee, Brad Penny, Mike Lowell/25	40.00
3	Garret Anderson, John Lackey, Chone Figgins/25	75.00
8	Roberto Alomar, Paul Molitor, Jack Morris/25	125.00
9	Eric Davis, Barry Larkin, Paul O'Neill/25	100.00
10	Dennis Eckersley, Jose Canseco, Dave Parker/25	125.00

11	Keith Hernandez, Dwight Gooden, Gary Carter/25	75.00
12	Lenny Dykstra, George Foster, Darryl Strawberry/25	65.00
13	Alan Trammell, Kirk Gibson, Jack Morris/25	100.00
15	Bert Blyleven, John Candelaria, Dave Parker/25	75.00

Souvenirs Playoff

		NM/M
Common Player:		5.00
Production 100 Sets		
1	Chipper Jones/Ball	10.00
2	Randy Johnson/Ball	10.00
3	Albert Pujols/Ball	20.00
4	Jason Schmidt/Ball	8.00
5	Gary Sheffield/Ball	8.00
6	Miguel Tejada/Ball	8.00
7	J.D. Drew/Ball	8.00
8	John Smoltz/Ball	10.00
9	Eric Milton/Ball	5.00
10	Mark Grace/Ball	10.00
11	Tim Hudson/Ball	8.00
12	Jeff Bagwell/Ball	10.00
13	Jim Edmonds/Ball	8.00
14	Sammy Sosa/Ball	15.00
15	Albert Pujols/Ball	20.00

Souvenirs World Series

		NM/M
Common Player:		5.00
Production 100 Sets		
1	Jason Schmidt/Ball	8.00
2	Troy Glaus/Base	5.00
3	Reggie Sanders/Base	5.00
4	Tim Salmon/Base	5.00
5	Garret Anderson/Base	5.00
6	Francisco Rodriguez/Base	5.00
7	Rich Aurilia/Ball	5.00
8	Jeff Kent/Ball	5.00
9	Darin Erstad/Base	5.00
10	Troy Glaus/Base	5.00
11	Jeff Kent/Ball	5.00
12	Scott Spiezio/Base	5.00
13	Tony Percival/Base	5.00
14	Garret Anderson/Base	5.00
15	Darin Erstad/Base	5.00

Triple Threads

		NM/M
Common Player:		10.00
1	Josh Beckett, Miguel Cabrera, Mike Lowell/100	15.00
2	Luis Castillo, Ivan Rodriguez, Dontrelle Willis/100	20.00
3	Garret Anderson, Troy Glaus, Tim Salmon/100	20.00
4	Curt Schilling, Mark Grace, Randy Johnson/50	25.00
5	Jorge Posada, Bernie Williams, Roger Clemens/50	25.00
6	Andy Pettitte, Wade Boggs, Mariano Rivera/50	20.00
7	Charles Johnson, Cliff Floyd, Moises Alou/100	10.00
8	Chipper Jones, Tom Glavine, Greg Maddux/100	30.00
9	Joe Carter, Rickey Henderson, David Wells/100	25.00
10	Eric Davis, Barry Larkin, Paul O'Neill/100	20.00
11	Dwight Gooden, Gary Carter, Darryl Strawberry/100	20.00
12	Frank White, Willie Wilson, George Brett/100	30.00
13	Jim Palmer, Eddie Murray, Cal Ripken Jr./50	125.00
14	Willie Stargell, Dave Parker, Bill Madlock/100	20.00
15	Johnny Bench, Joe Morgan, Tony Perez/100	35.00
16	Dave Concepcion, George Foster, Johnny Bench/50	40.00
17	Al Oliver, Roberto Clemente, Willie Stargell/50	80.00
18	Jim Palmer, Frank Robinson, Brooks Robinson/50	25.00
19	Bob Gibson, Lou Brock, Orlando Cepeda/50	25.00
20	Stan Musial, Red Schoendienst, Marty Marion/50	40.00

2004 Donruss World Series Champions

	NM/M
Complete Boxed Set (25):	25.00
Common Player:	.50
201 Curt Schilling	3.00
202 Pedro Martinez	3.00
203 Derek Lowe	.50
204 Tim Wakefield	.50
205 Bronson Arroyo	.50
206 Mike Timlin	.50
207 Curt Leskanic	.50
208 Mike Myers	.50
209 Alan Embree	.50
210 Keith Foulke	.50
211 Jason Varitek	2.00
212 Doug Mirabelli	.50
213 Doug Mientkiewicz	.50
214 Mark Bellhorn	.50
215 Pokey Reese	.50
216 Orlando Cabrera	1.00
217 Bill Mueller	.50
218 Kevin Youkilis	.50
219 Manny Ramirez	3.00
220 Johnny Damon	3.00
221 Dave Roberts	.50
222 Trot Nixon	.50
223 Gabe Kapler	.50
224 David Ortiz	3.00

Box Topper

	NM/M
Inserted 1:Set	
WS1 World Series Champions	2.00

2005 Donruss

	NM/M
Complete Set (400):	120.00
Common Player:	.15
Common SP (1-70, 371-400):	1.00
Inserted 1:6	
Pack (10):	2.50
Box (24):	50.00
1 Garret Anderson	1.00
2 Vladimir Guerrero	2.00
3 Manny Ramirez	2.00
4 Kerry Wood	2.00
5 Sammy Sosa	3.00
6 Magglio Ordonez	1.00
7 Adam Dunn	1.50
8 Todd Helton	1.50
9 Josh Beckett	1.00
10 Miguel Cabrera	2.00
11 Lance Berkman	1.00
12 Carlos Beltran	1.50
13 Shawn Green	1.00
14 Roger Clemens	4.00
15 Mike Piazza	2.50
16 Alex Rodriguez	3.00
17 Derek Jeter	4.00
18 Mark Mulder	1.00
19 Jim Thome	2.00
20 Albert Pujols	3.00
21 Scott Rolen	2.00
22 Aubrey Huff	1.00
23 Alfonso Soriano	2.00
24 Hank Blalock	1.50
25 Vernon Wells	1.00
26 Kazuo Matsui	1.50
27 B.J. Upton	1.50
28 Charles Thomas	1.00
29 Akinori Otsuka	1.00
30 David Aardsma	1.00
31 Travis Blackley	1.00
32 Brad Halsey	1.00
33 David Wright	5.00
34 Kazuhito Tadano	1.00
35 Casey Kotchman	1.50
36 Khalil Greene	2.00
37 Adrian Gonzalez	1.00
38 Zack Greinke	1.00
39 Chad Cordero	1.00
40 Scott Kazmir	4.00
41 Jeremy Guthrie	1.00
42 Noah Lowry	1.00
43 Chase Utley	1.00
44 Billy Traber	1.00
45 Aarom Baldiris	1.00
46 Abe Alvarez	1.00
47 Angel Chavez	1.00
48 Joe Mauer	1.00
49 Joey Gathright	1.00
50 John Gall	1.00
51 Ronald Belisario	1.00
52 Ryan Wing	1.00
53 Scott Proctor	1.00
54 Yadier Molina	1.00
55 Carlos Hines	1.00
56 Frankie Francisco	1.00
57 Graham Koonce	1.00
58 Jake Woods	1.00
59 Jason Bartlett	1.00
60 Mike Rouse	1.00
61 Phil Stockman	1.00
62 Renyel Pinto	1.00
63 Roberto Novoa	1.00
64 Ryan Meaux	1.00
65 David Crouthers	1.00
66 Justin Knoedler	1.00
67 Justin Leone	1.00
68 Nick Regilio	1.00
69 Mike Gosling	1.00
70 Onil Joseph	1.00
71 Bartolo Colon	.15
72 Brad Fullmer	.15
73 Chone Figgins	.15
74 Darin Erstad	.25
75 Francisco Rodriguez	.15
76 Garret Anderson	.25
77 Jarrod Washburn	.15
78 John Lackey	.15
79 Jose Guillen	.15
80 Robb Quinlan	.15
81 Tim Salmon	.25
82 Troy Glaus	.25
83 Troy Percival	.15
84 Vladimir Guerrero	.50
85 Brandon Webb	.15
86 Casey Fossum	.15
87 Luis Gonzalez	.15
88 Randy Johnson	.50
89 Richie Sexson	.25
90 Robby Hammock	.15
91 Roberto Alomar	.25
92 Adam LaRoche	.15
93 Andruw Jones	.25
94 Bubba Nelson	.15
95 Chipper Jones	.50
96 J.D. Drew	.25
97 John Smoltz	.25
98 Johnny Estrada	.15
99 Marcus Giles	.15
100 Mike Hampton	.15
101 Nick Green	.15
102 Rafael Furcal	.15
103 Russ Ortiz	.15
104 Adam Loewen	.15
105 Brian Roberts	.15
106 Javy Lopez	.25
107 Jay Gibbons	.15
108 Larry Bigbie	.15
109 Luis Matos	.15
110 Melvin Mora	.15
111 Miguel Tejada	.40
112 Rafael Palmeiro	.40
113 Rodrigo Lopez	.15
114 Sidney Ponson	.15
115 Bill Mueller	.15
116 Byung-Hyun Kim	.15
117 Curt Schilling	.40
118 David Ortiz	.40
119 Derek Lowe	.15
120 Doug Mientkiewicz	.15
121 Jason Varitek	.25
122 Johnny Damon	.25
123 Keith Foulke	.15
124 Kevin Youkilis	.15
125 Manny Ramirez	.50
126 Orlando Cabrera	.25
127 Pedro J. Martinez	.25
128 Trot Nixon	.15
129 Aramis Ramirez	.25
130 Carlos Zambrano	.25
131 Corey Patterson	.15
132 Derrek Lee	.25
133 Greg Maddux	.75
134 Kerry Wood	.50
135 Mark Prior	.50
136 Matt Clement	.15
137 Moises Alou	.25
138 Nomar Garciaparra	1.00
139 Sammy Sosa	1.00
140 Todd Walker	.15
141 Angel Guzman	.15
142 Billy Koch	.15
143 Carlos Lee	.15
144 Frank Thomas	.40
145 Magglio Ordonez	.25
146 Mark Buehrle	.15
147 Paul Konerko	.25
148 Wilson Valdez	.15
149 Adam Dunn	.40
150 Austin Kearns	.15
151 Barry Larkin	.25
152 Benito Santiago	.15
153 Jason LaRue	.15
154 Ken Griffey Jr.	.75
155 Ryan Wagner	.15
156 Sean Casey	.15
157 Brandon Phillips	.15
158 Brian Tallet	.15
159 C.C. Sabathia	.15
160 Cliff Lee	.15
161 Jeremy Guthrie	.15
162 Jody Gerut	.15
163 Matt Lawton	.15
164 Omar Vizquel	.15
165 Travis Hafner	.15
166 Victor Martinez	.25
167 Charles Johnson	.15
168 Garrett Atkins	.15
169 Jason Jennings	.15
170 Jay Payton	.15
171 Jeromy Burnitz	.15
172 Joe Kennedy	.15
173 Larry Walker	.25
174 Preston Wilson	.15
175 Todd Helton	.40
176 Vinny Castilla	.15
177 Bobby Higginson	.15
178 Brandon Inge	.15
179 Carlos Guillen	.15
180 Carlos Pena	.15
181 Craig Monroe	.15
182 Dmitri Young	.15
183 Eric Munson	.15
184 Fernando Vina	.15
185 Ivan Rodriguez	.40
186 Jeremy Bonderman	.15
187 Rondell White	.15
188 A.J. Burnett	.15
189 Dontrelle Willis	.25
190 Guillermo Mota	.15
191 Hee Seop Choi	.15
192 Jeff Conine	.15
193 Josh Beckett	.25
194 Juan Encarnacion	.15
195 Juan Pierre	.15
196 Luis Castillo	.15
197 Miguel Cabrera	.50
198 Mike Lowell	.15
199 Paul LoDuca	.15
200 Andy Pettitte	.25
201 Brad Ausmus	.15
202 Carlos Beltran	.40
203 Chris Burke	.15
204 Craig Biggio	.25
205 Jeff Bagwell	.40
206 Jeff Kent	.25
207 Lance Berkman	.25
208 Morgan Ensberg	.15
209 Octavio Dotel	.15
210 Roger Clemens	1.50
211 Roy Oswalt	.25
212 Tim Redding	.15
213 Angel Berroa	.15
214 Juan Gonzalez	.25
215 Ken Harvey	.15
216 Mike Sweeney	.15
217 Adrian Beltre	.25
218 Brad Penny	.15
219 Eric Gagne	.25
220 Hideo Nomo	.15
221 Hong-Chih Kuo	.15
222 Jeff Weaver	.15
223 Kazuhisa Ishii	.15
224 Milton Bradley	.15
225 Shawn Green	.25
226 Steve Finley	.15
227 Danny Kolb	.15
228 Geoff Jenkins	.15
229 Junior Spivey	.15
230 Lyle Overbay	.15
231 Rickie Weeks	.15
232 Scott Podsednik	.15
233 Brad Radke	.15
234 Corey Koskie	.15
235 Cristian Guzman	.15
236 Dustan Mohr	.15
237 Eddie Guardado	.15
238 J.D. Durbin	.15
239 Jacque Jones	.15
240 Joe Nathan	.15
241 Johan Santana	.40
242 Lew Ford	.15
243 Michael Cuddyer	.15
244 Shannon Stewart	.15
245 Torii Hunter	.15
246 Brad Wilkerson	.15
247 Carl Everett	.15
248 Jeff Fassero	.15
249 Jose Vidro	.15
250 Livan Hernandez	.15
251 Michael Barrett	.15
252 Tony Batista	.15
253 Zach Day	.15
254 Al Leiter	.15
255 Cliff Floyd	.15
256 Jae Weong Seo	.15
257 John Olerud	.15
258 Jose Reyes	.40
259 Mike Cameron	.15
260 Mike Piazza	1.00
261 Richard Hidalgo	.15

262	Tom Glavine	.25
263	Vance Wilson	.15
264	Alex Rodriguez	1.50
265	Armando Benitez	.15
266	Bernie Williams	.25
267	Bubba Crosby	.15
268	Chien-Ming Wang	.40
269	Derek Jeter	1.50
270	Esteban Loaiza	.15
271	Gary Sheffield	.25
272	Hideki Matsui	1.00
273	Jason Giambi	.25
274	Javier Vazquez	.15
275	Jorge Posada	.25
276	Jose Contreras	.25
277	Kenny Lofton	.15
278	Kevin Brown	.15
279	Mariano Rivera	.25
280	Mike Mussina	.25
281	Barry Zito	.25
282	Bobby Crosby	.15
283	Eric Byrnes	.15
284	Eric Chavez	.25
285	Erubiel Durazo	.15
286	Jermaine Dye	.15
287	Mark Kotsay	.15
288	Mark Mulder	.25
289	Rich Harden	.15
290	Tim Hudson	.15
291	Billy Wagner	.15
292	Bobby Abreu	.25
293	Brett Myers	.15
294	Eric Milton	.15
295	Jim Thome	.50
296	Jimmy Rollins	.25
297	Kevin Millwood	.15
298	Marlon Byrd	.15
299	Mike Lieberthal	.15
300	Pat Burrell	.15
301	Randy Wolf	.15
302	Craig Wilson	.15
303	Jack Wilson	.15
304	Jacob Cruz	.15
305	Jason Bay	.15
306	Jason Kendall	.15
307	Jose Castillo	.15
308	Kip Wells	.15
309	Brian Giles	.15
310	Brian Lawrence	.15
311	Chris Oxspring	.15
312	David Wells	.15
313	Freddy Guzman	.15
314	Jake Peavy	.15
315	Mark Loretta	.15
316	Ryan Klesko	.15
317	Sean Burroughs	.15
318	Trevor Hoffman	.15
319	Xavier Nady	.15
320	A.J. Pierzynski	.15
321	Edgardo Alfonzo	.15
322	J.T. Snow	.15
323	Jason Schmidt	.25
324	Jerome Williams	.15
325	Kirk Rueter	.15
326	Bret Boone	.15
327	Bucky Jacobsen	.15
328	Edgar Martinez	.15
329	Freddy Garcia	.15
330	Ichiro Suzuki	1.00
331	Jamie Moyer	.15
332	Joel Pineiro	.15
333	Scott Spiezio	.15
334	Shigetoshi Hasegawa	.15
335	Albert Pujols	1.50
336	Edgar Renteria	.25
337	Jason Isringhausen	.15
338	Jim Edmonds	.15
339	Matt Morris	.15
340	Mike Matheny	.15
341	Reggie Sanders	.15
342	Scott Rolen	.50
343	Woody Williams	.15
344	Jeff Suppan	.15
345	Aubrey Huff	.15
346	Carl Crawford	.15
347	Chad Gaudin	.15
348	Delmon Young	.15
349	Dewon Brazelton	.15
350	Jose Cruz Jr.	.15
351	Rocco Baldelli	.25
352	Tino Martinez	.15
353	Toby Hall	.15
354	Alfonso Soriano	.40
355	Brian Jordan	.15
356	Francisco Cordero	.15
357	Hank Blalock	.40
358	Kenny Rogers	.15
359	Kevin Mench	.15
360	Laynce Nix	.15
361	Mark Teixeira	.25
362	Michael Young	.15
363	Alex Gonzalez	.15
364	Alexis Rios	.15
365	Carlos Delgado	.25
366	Eric Hinske	.15
367	Frank Catalanotto	.15
368	Josh Phelps	.15
369	Roy Halladay	.15
370	Vernon Wells	.15
371	Vladimir Guerrero	2.00
372	Randy Johnson	2.00
373	Chipper Jones	2.00
374	Miguel Tejada	1.50
375	Pedro Martinez	2.00
376	Sammy Sosa	3.00
377	Frank Thomas	1.50
378	Ken Griffey Jr.	3.00
379	Victor Martinez	1.00

380	Todd Helton	1.50
381	Ivan Rodriguez	1.50
382	Miguel Cabrera	2.00
383	Roger Clemens	4.00
384	Ken Harvey	1.00
385	Eric Gagne	1.50
386	Lyle Overbay	1.00
387	Shannon Stewart	1.00
388	Brad Wilkerson	1.00
389	Mike Piazza	2.50
390	Alex Rodriguez	3.00
391	Mark Mulder	1.00
392	Jim Thome	2.00
393	Jack Wilson	1.00
394	Khalil Greene	1.50
395	Jason Schmidt	1.00
396	Ichiro Suzuki	3.00
397	Albert Pujols	4.00
398	Rocco Baldelli	1.00
399	Alfonso Soriano	1.50
400	Vernon Wells	1.00

25th Anniversary

Stars:	10-20X
SP's (1-70, 371-400):	3-6X
Production 25 Sets	

Press Proofs Black

No Pricing
Production 10 Sets

Press Proofs Blue

Blue (71-370):	4-8X
Blue SP's:	2-3X
Production 100 Sets	

Press Proofs Gold

Gold (71-370):	10-20X
Gold SP's:	3-6X
Production 25 Sets	

Press Proofs Red

Red (71-370):	2-4X
Red SP's:	.75-1.5X
Production 200 Sets	

Stat Line Career

	NM/M
#71-370 print run 201-400:	2-4X
71-370 p/r 101-200:	3-6X
71-370 p/r 51-100:	4-8X
71-370 p/r 26-50:	6-12X
71-370 p/r 25 or less:	No Pricing
SP's print run 200 or more:	1-2X
SP's p/r 101-200:	1.5-2X
SP's p/r 51-100:	2-4X
SP's p/r 26-50:	3-5X
SP's p/r 25 or less:	No Pricing

Cards are numbered to career statistic.

Stat Line Season

	NM/M
#71-370 print run 101-200:	3-6X
71-370 p/r 51-100:	4-8X
71-370 p/r 26-50:	6-12X
71-370 p/r 25 or less:	No Pricing
SP's p/r 101 or more 1.5-2X	
SP's p/r 51-100:	2-4X

SP's p/r 26-50:	3-5X
SP's p/r 25 or less:	No Pricing

Cards are numbered to season statistic.

'85 Reprints

	NM/M
Complete Set (12):	40.00
Common Player:	2.00
Production 1,985 Sets	
1	Eddie Murray	3.00
2	George Brett	6.00
3	Nolan Ryan	8.00
4	Mike Schmidt	6.00
5	Tony Gwynn	3.00
6	Cal Ripken Jr.	10.00
7		
8	Dwight Gooden	2.00
9	Roger Clemens	8.00
10	Don Mattingly	6.00
11	Kirby Puckett	4.00
12	Orel Hershiser	2.00

'85 Reprints Material

		NM/M
Production 85 Sets		
1	Eddie Murray/Jsy	20.00
2	George Brett/Jsy	35.00
3	Nolan Ryan/Jkt	40.00
4	Mike Schmidt/Jkt	35.00
5	Tony Gwynn/Jsy	20.00
6	Cal Ripken Jr./Jsy	50.00
9	Roger Clemens/Jsy	40.00
10	Don Mattingly/Jsy	35.00
11	Kirby Puckett/Jsy	20.00
12	Orel Hershiser/Jsy	10.00

All-Stars AL

		NM/M
Common Player:		2.00
Production 1,000 Sets		
Gold:		1-2X
Production 100 Sets		
1	Alex Rodriguez	6.00
2	Alfonso Soriano	3.00
3	Curt Schilling	2.00
4	Derek Jeter	8.00
5	Hank Blalock	2.00
6	Hideki Matsui	6.00
7	Ichiro Suzuki	6.00
8	Ivan Rodriguez	3.00
9	Jason Giambi	2.00
10	Manny Ramirez	3.00
11	Mark Mulder	2.00
12	Michael Young	2.00
13	Tim Hudson	2.00
14	Victor Martinez	2.00
15	Vladimir Guerrero	3.00

All-Stars NL

		NM/M
Common Player:		2.00
Production 1,000 Sets		
Gold:		1-2X
Production 100 Sets		
1	Albert Pujols	8.00
2	Ben Sheets	2.00
3	Edgar Renteria	2.00
4	Eric Gagne	2.00
5	Jack Wilson	2.00
6	Jason Schmidt	2.00
7	Jeff Kent	2.00
8	Jim Thome	3.00
9	Ken Griffey Jr.	4.00
10	Mike Piazza	4.00
11	Roger Clemens	8.00
12	Sammy Sosa	5.00
13	Scott Rolen	3.00
14	Sean Casey	2.00
15	Todd Helton	2.00

Autographs

No Pricing

Bat Kings

		NM/M
Common Player:		5.00
Quantity produced listed		
1	Garret Anderson/250	5.00
2	Vladimir Guerrero/250	8.00
3	Cal Ripken Jr./100	50.00
4	Manny Ramirez/250	8.00
5	Kerry Wood/250	8.00
6	Sammy Sosa/250	12.00
7	Magglio Ordonez/250	5.00

8	Adam Dunn/250	8.00
9	Todd Helton/250	8.00
10	Josh Beckett/250	5.00
11	Miguel Cabrera/250	8.00
12	Lance Berkman/250	5.00
13	Carlos Beltran/250	8.00
14	Shawn Green/250	5.00
15	Roger Clemens/100	15.00
16	Mike Piazza/250	12.00
17	Nolan Ryan/100	50.00
18	Mark Mulder/250	5.00
19	Jim Thome/250	10.00
20	Albert Pujols/250	20.00
21	Scott Rolen/250	10.00
22	Aubrey Huff/250	5.00
23	Alfonso Soriano/250	8.00

Bat Kings Signatures

No Pricing
Production 5 or 10

2005 Donruss Cal Ripken 10th Anniversary

	NM/M
Cal Ripken Jr.	4.00

Craftsmen

		NM/M
Complete Set (30):		40.00
Common Player:		1.00
Production 1,000 Sets		
Black:		1.5-2X
Production 100 Sets		
Master:		1-2X
Production 250 Sets		
Master Black:		No Pricing
Production 10 Sets		
1	Albert Pujols	5.00
2	Alex Rodriguez	4.00
3	Alfonso Soriano	2.00
4	Andruw Jones	1.00
5	Carlos Beltran	1.50
6	Derek Jeter	5.00
7	Greg Maddux	2.50
8	Hank Blalock	1.50
9	Ichiro Suzuki	4.00
10	Jeff Bagwell	1.50
11	Jim Thome	2.00
12	Josh Beckett	1.00
13	Ken Griffey Jr.	2.50
14	Manny Ramirez	2.00
15	Mark Mulder	1.00
16	Mark Prior	2.00
17	Mark Teixeira	1.00
18	Miguel Tejada	1.50
19	Mike Mussina	1.50
20	Mike Piazza	2.50
21	Nomar Garciaparra	3.00
22	Pedro Martinez	2.00
23	Rafael Palmeiro	1.50
24	Randy Johnson	2.00
25	Roger Clemens	5.00
26	Sammy Sosa	3.00
27	Scott Rolen	2.00
28	Tim Hudson	1.00
29	Vernon Wells	1.00
30	Vladimir Guerrero	2.00

Diamond Kings Inserts

		NM/M
Complete Set (25):		40.00
Common Player:		1.50
Production 2,005 Sets		
Studio:		1.5-2X
Production 250 Sets		
Studio Black:		1.5-3X
Production 100 Sets		
1	Garret Anderson	1.50

2	Vladimir Guerrero	2.00
3	Manny Ramirez	2.00
4	Kerry Wood	1.50
5	Sammy Sosa	4.00
6	Magglio Ordonez	1.50
7	Adam Dunn	1.50
8	Todd Helton	1.50
9	Josh Beckett	1.50
10	Miguel Cabrera	2.00
11	Lance Berkman	1.50
12	Carlos Beltran	2.00
13	Shawn Green	1.50
14	Roger Clemens	6.00
15	Mike Piazza	3.00
16	Alex Rodriguez	5.00
17	Derek Jeter	6.00
18	Mark Mulder	1.50
19	Jim Thome	2.00
20	Albert Pujols	6.00
21	Scott Rolen	2.00
22	Aubrey Huff	1.50
23	Alfonso Soriano	2.00
24	Hank Blalock	1.50
25	Vernon Wells	1.50

Elite Series

		NM/M
Complete Set (25):		50.00
Common Player:		2.00
Production 1,500 Sets		
Black:		1-2X
Production 100 Sets		
Dominator:		1-1.5X
Production 250 Sets		
Dominator Black:		3-5X
Production 25 Sets		
1	Albert Pujols	6.00
2	Alex Rodriguez	5.00
3	Alfonso Soriano	2.00
4	Derek Jeter	6.00
5	Hank Blalock	1.50
6	Ichiro Suzuki	5.00
7	Ivan Rodriguez	2.00
8	Jim Thome	2.00
9	Ken Griffey Jr.	3.00
10	Manny Ramirez	3.00
11	Mark Mulder	1.50
12	Mark Prior	2.00
13	Michael Young	1.50
14	Miguel Cabrera	2.00
15	Miguel Tejada	2.00
16	Mike Piazza	3.00
17	Nomar Garciaparra	4.00
18	Rafael Palmeiro	2.00
19	Randy Johnson	2.00
20	Roger Clemens	6.00
21	Sammy Sosa	4.00
22	Scott Rolen	2.00
23	Tim Hudson	1.50
24	Todd Helton	1.50
25	Vladimir Guerrero	2.00

Fans of the Game

		NM/M
Complete Set (5):		10.00
1	Jesse Ventura	3.00
2	John C. McGinley	2.00
3	Susie Essman	2.00
4	Dean Cain	2.00
5	Meat Loaf	3.00

Fans of the Game Signatures

		NM/M
1	Jesse Ventura	50.00
2	John C. McGinley/SP/300	50.00
3	Susie Essman	60.00
4	Dean Cain/SP/250	90.00
5	Meat Loaf	60.00

Jersey Kings

		NM/M
Common Player:		5.00
1	Garret Anderson/250	5.00
2	Vladimir Guerrero/250	8.00
3	Cal Ripken Jr./100	50.00
4	Manny Ramirez/250	8.00
5	Kerry Wood/250	10.00
6	Sammy Sosa/250	12.00
7	Magglio Ordonez/250	5.00
8	Adam Dunn/250	8.00
9	Todd Helton/250	8.00
10	Josh Beckett/250	5.00
11	Miguel Cabrera/250	8.00
12	Lance Berkman/250	8.00
13	Carlos Beltran/250	8.00
14	Shawn Green/250	5.00
15	Roger Clemens/250	15.00
16	Mike Piazza/250	8.00
17	Nolan Ryan/100	50.00
18	Mark Mulder/250	5.00
19	Jim Thome/250	8.00
20	Albert Pujols/250	20.00
21	Scott Rolen/250	10.00
22	Aubrey Huff/250	8.00
23	Alfonso Soriano/250	8.00
24	Hank Blalock/250	8.00
25	Vernon Wells/250	5.00

Jersey Kings Signatures

No Pricing
Production 5 or 10

Longball Leaders

		NM/M
Complete Set (15):		30.00
Common Player:		2.00
Black:		1-2X
Production 250 Sets		
Die-Cut:		2-3X
Production 50 Sets		
Black Die-Cut:		No Pricing
Production 10 Sets		
1	Adam Dunn	3.00
2	Adrian Beltre	3.00
3	Albert Pujols	6.00
4	Alex Rodriguez	5.00
5	David Ortiz	3.00
6	Hank Blalock	3.00
7	J.D. Drew	2.00
8	Jeromy Burnitz	2.00
9	Jim Edmonds	2.50
10	Jim Thome	3.00
11	Manny Ramirez	3.00
12	Mark Teixeira	2.00
13	Moises Alou	3.00
14	Paul Konerko	2.00
15	Steve Finley	2.00

Mound Marvels

		NM/M
Complete Set (15):		40.00
Common Player:		2.00
Production 1,000 Sets		
Black:		No Pricing
Production 10 Sets		
1	Curt Schilling	4.00
2	Dontrelle Willis	2.00
3	Eric Gagne	4.00
4	Greg Maddux	6.00
5	John Smoltz	3.00
6	Kenny Rogers	2.00
7	Kerry Wood	4.00
8	Mariano Rivera	3.00
9	Mark Mulder	2.00
10	Mark Prior	4.00
11	Mike Mussina	3.00
12	Pedro Martinez	4.00
13	Randy Johnson	4.00
14	Roger Clemens	8.00
15	Tim Hudson	2.00

Power Alley Red

	NM/M
Common Player:	1.50
Production 2,500 Sets	
Black:	No Pricing
Production 10 Sets	
Black Die-Cut:	No Pricing
Production Five Sets	
Blue:	1X
Production 1,000 Sets	
Blue Die-Cut:	2-3X
Production 100 Sets	
Green:	3-5X
Production 25 Sets	
Green Die-Cut:	No Pricing
Production 10 Sets	
Purple:	1-2X
Production 250 Sets	
Purple Die-Cut:	2-3X
Production 50 Sets	
Red Die-Cut:	1-2X

Production 250 Sets		
Yellow:		2-3X
Production 100 Sets		
Yellow Die-Cut:		3-5X
Production 25 Sets		
1	Adam Dunn	2.00
2	Adrian Beltre	2.00
3	Albert Pujols	6.00
4	Alex Rodriguez	5.00
5	Alfonso Soriano	3.00
6	Gary Sheffield	2.00
7	Hank Blalock	2.00
8	Hideki Matsui	4.00
9	J.D. Drew	1.50
10	Jeromy Burnitz	1.50
11	Jim Edmonds	2.00
12	Jim Thome	3.00
13	Ken Griffey Jr.	3.00
14	Manny Ramirez	2.00
15	Mark Teixeira	1.50
16	Miguel Cabrera	2.00
17	Miguel Tejada	2.00
18	Mike Lowell	1.50
19	Mike Piazza	3.00
20	Moises Alou	1.50
21	Paul Konerko	1.50
22	Sammy Sosa	4.00
23	Scott Rolen	3.00
24	Todd Helton	2.00
25	Vladimir Guerrero	3.00

Production Line BA

		NM/M
Common Player:		3.00
Black:		2-3X
Production 25 Sets		
Die-Cut:		1X
Production 100 Sets		
Black Die-Cut:		No Pricing
Production 10 Sets		
1	Ichiro Suzuki/372	8.00
2	Ivan Rodriguez/334	5.00
3	Juan Pierre/326	3.00
4	Adrian Beltre/334	5.00
5	Albert Pujols/331	10.00
6	Mark Loretta/335	3.00
7	Melvin Mora/340	3.00
8	Sean Casey/324	3.00
9	Todd Helton/347	5.00
10	Vladimir Guerrero/337	5.00

Production Line OBP

		NM/M
Common Player:		3.00
Black:		2-3X
Production 25 Sets		
Die-Cut:		1X
Production 100 Sets		
Black Die-Cut:		No Pricing
Production 10 Sets		
1	Albert Pujols/415	8.00
2	Bobby Abreu/428	3.00
3	Lance Berkman/450	3.00
4	J.D. Drew/436	4.00
5	Jorge Posada/400	4.00
6	Ichiro Suzuki/414	8.00
7	Manny Ramirez/397	4.00
8	Melvin Mora/419	3.00
9	Todd Helton/469	4.00
10	Travis Hafner/410	3.00

Production Line OPS

		NM/M
Common Player:		3.00
Black:		1.5-2X
Production 50 Sets		
Die-Cut:		1X
Production 100 Sets		
Black Die-Cut:		2-3X
Production 25 Sets		
1	Albert Pujols/1,072	8.00
2	Bobby Abreu/983	4.00
3	Lance Berkman/1,017	3.00
4	J.D. Drew/1,006	3.00
5	Jorge Posada/977	4.00
6	Ichiro Suzuki/1,016	3.00
7	Manny Ramirez/1,009	4.00
8	Melvin Mora/1,007	4.00
9	Todd Helton/1,088	4.00
10	Travis Hafner/993	3.00

Production Line Slugging

		NM/M
Common Player:		3.00
Black:		1.5-2X
Production 50 Sets		
Die-Cut:		1X
Production 100 Sets		
Black Die-Cut:		2-3X
Production 25 Sets		
1	Adrian Beltre/629	4.00
2	Albert Pujols/657	8.00
3	Todd Helton/620	4.00
4	J.D. Drew/569	3.00
5	Jim Edmonds/643	3.00
6	Jim Thome/581	4.00
7	Vladimir Guerrero/598	4.00
8	Manny Ramirez/613	4.00
9	Scott Rolen/598	4.00
10	Travis Hafner/583	3.00

Rookies

		NM/M
Common Player:		2.00
Inserted 1:23		
Black:		No Pricing
Production 10 Sets		
Blue:		1X
Production 100 Sets		
Gold:		2-3X
Production 25 Sets		
Red:		.75-1X
Production 200 Sets		
1	Fernando Nieve	2.00
2	Frankie Francisco	2.00
3	Jorge Vasquez	2.00
4	Travis Blackley	2.00
5	Joey Gathright	4.00
6	Kazuhito Tadano	2.00
7	Edwin Moreno	2.00
8	Lance Cormier	2.00
9	Justin Knoedler	2.00
10	Orlando Rodriguez	2.00
11	Renyel Pinto	2.00
12	Justin Leone	2.00
13	Dennis Sarfate	2.00
14	Sam Narron	2.00
15	Yadier Molina	4.00
16	Carlos Vasquez	2.00
17	Ryan Wing	2.00
18	Brad Halsey	2.00
19	Ryan Meaux	2.00
20	Mike Wuertz	2.00
21	Shawn Camp	2.00
22	Ruddy Yan	2.00
23	Donald Kelly	2.00
24	Jake Woods	2.00
25	Colby Miller	2.00
26	Abe Alvarez	2.00
27	Mike Rouse	2.00
28	Phil Stockman	2.00
29	Kevin Cave	2.00
30	Chris Shelton	4.00
31	Tim Bittner	2.00
32	Mariano Gomez	2.00
33	Angel Chavez	2.00
34	Carlos Hines	2.00
35	Aarom Baldiris	2.00
36	Kazuo Matsui	5.00
37	Nick Regilio	2.00
38	Ivan Ochoa	2.00
39	Graham Koonce	2.00
40	Merkin Valdez	3.00
41	Greg Dobbs	2.00
42	Chris Oxspring	2.00
43	David Crouthers	2.00
44	Freddy Guzman	2.00
45	Akinori Otsuka	3.00
46	Jesse Crain	2.00
47	Casey Daigle	2.00
48	Roberto Novoa	2.00
49	Eddy Rodriguez	2.00
50	Jason Bartlett	2.00

Rookies Autographs

		NM/M
Common Autographs:		5.00
1	Fernando Nieve	5.00
2	Frankie Francisco	5.00
3	Jorge Vasquez	5.00
4	Travis Blackley	5.00
5	Joey Gathright	8.00

7	Edwin Moreno	5.00
8	Lance Cormier	5.00
9	Justin Knoedler	5.00
10	Orlando Rodriguez	5.00
11	Renyel Pinto	5.00
13	Dennis Sarfate	5.00
15	Yadier Molina	10.00
16	Carlos Vasquez	8.00
17	Ryan Wing/SP	10.00
18	Brad Halsey	8.00
19	Ryan Meaux	5.00
20	Mike Wuertz	5.00
22	Ruddy Yan	5.00
23	Donald Kelly	5.00
24	Jake Woods	5.00
25	Colby Miller	5.00
26	Abe Alvarez	8.00
27	Mike Rouse/SP	8.00
28	Phil Stockman	5.00
29	Kevin Cave	5.00
30	Chris Shelton/SP	10.00
31	Tim Bittner	5.00
32	Mariano Gomez	5.00
33	Angel Chavez	5.00
34	Carlos Hines	5.00
35	Aarom Baldiris	5.00
37	Nick Regilio	5.00
38	Ivan Ochoa	5.00
39	Graham Koonce	5.00
42	Chris Oxspring	5.00
43	David Crouthers	5.00
48	Roberto Novoa	5.00
49	Eddy Rodriguez	5.00
50	Jason Bartlett	5.00

Rookies Stat Line Career

Print run 201-316:	1X
Print run 101-200:	1X
Print run 51-100:	1-1.5X
Print run 26-50:	1-2X
Print run 25 or less:	No Pricing

Cards are numbered to career statistic.

Rookies Stat Line Season

Print run 101-200:	1X
Print run 51-100:	1-1.5X
Print run 26-50:	1-2X
Print run 25 or less:	No Pricing

Cards are numbered to season statistic.

Timber and Threads Bat

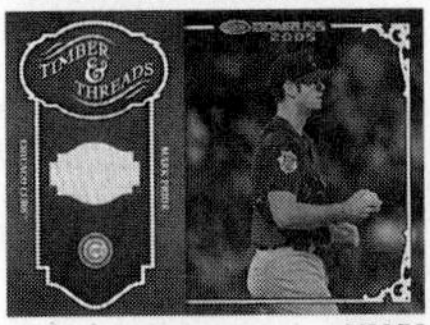

		NM/M
Common Player:		5.00
1	Albert Pujols	15.00
2	Alfonso Soriano	8.00
3	Andre Dawson	8.00
4	Austin Kearns	5.00
5	Brad Penny	5.00
6	Carlos Beltran	8.00
7	Carlos Lee	5.00
8	Chipper Jones	8.00
9	Dale Murphy	8.00
10	Don Mattingly	20.00
11	Frank Thomas	8.00
12	Garret Anderson	5.00
13	Gary Carter	8.00
14	Hank Blalock	8.00
15	Jacque Jones	5.00
17	Jay Gibbons	5.00
18	Jeff Bagwell	8.00
20	Jermaine Dye	5.00
21	Jim Thome	8.00
22	Jose Vidro	5.00
23	Lance Berkman	5.00
24	Laynce Nix	5.00
25	Magglio Ordonez	5.00
26	Marcus Giles	5.00
27	Mark Prior	10.00
28	Mark Teixeira	5.00
29	Melvin Mora	5.00
30	Michael Young	5.00
31	Miguel Cabrera	8.00
32	Mike Lowell	5.00
33	Roy Oswalt	5.00
34	Sammy Sosa	10.00
35	Scott Rolen	10.00
36	Sean Burroughs	5.00
37	Sean Casey	5.00
38	Shannon Stewart	5.00
39	Torii Hunter	5.00
40	Travis Hafner	5.00

Timber and Threads Bat Signature

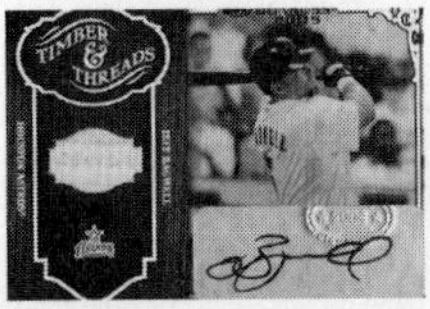

No Pricing
Production 5 or 10

Timber and Threads Combo

		NM/M
1	Albert Pujols/Bat-Jsy	25.00
2	Alfonso Soriano/Bat-Jsy	10.00
3	Andre Dawson/Bat-Jsy	8.00
4	Austin Kearns/Bat-Jsy	8.00
5	Brad Penny/Bat-Jsy	6.00
6	Carlos Beltran/Bat-Jsy	12.00
7	Carlos Lee/Bat-Jsy	6.00
8	Chipper Jones/Bat-Jsy	12.00
9	Dale Murphy/Bat-Jsy	10.00
10	Don Mattingly/Bat-Jsy	25.00
11	Frank Thomas/Bat-Jsy	12.00
12	Garret Anderson/Bat-Jsy	8.00
13	Gary Carter/Bat-Jsy	10.00
14	Hank Blalock/Bat-Jsy	10.00
15	Jacque Jones/Bat-Jsy	6.00
17	Jay Gibbons/Bat-Jsy	6.00
18	Jeff Bagwell/Bat-Jsy	12.00
20	Jermaine Dye/Bat-Jsy	6.00
21	Jim Thome/Bat-Jsy	12.00
22	Jose Vidro/Bat-Jsy	6.00
23	Lance Berkman/Bat-Jsy	6.00
24	Laynce Nix/Bat-Jsy	6.00
25	Magglio Ordonez/Bat-Jsy	8.00
26	Marcus Giles/Bat-Jsy	6.00
27	Mark Prior/Bat-Jsy	15.00
28	Mark Teixeira/Bat-Jsy	8.00
29	Melvin Mora/Bat-Jsy	6.00
30	Michael Young/Bat-Jsy	8.00
31	Miguel Cabrera/Bat-Jsy	12.00
32	Mike Lowell/Bat-Jsy	8.00
33	Roy Oswalt/Bat-Jsy	8.00
34	Sammy Sosa/Bat-Jsy	15.00
35	Scott Rolen/Bat-Jsy	15.00
36	Sean Burroughs/Bat-Jsy	6.00
37	Sean Casey/Bat-Jsy	6.00
38	Shannon Stewart/Bat-Jsy	6.00
39	Torii Hunter/Bat-Jsy	8.00
40	Travis Hafner/Bat-Jsy	8.00

Timber and Threads Combo Signture

No Pricing
Production 5 or 10

Timber and Threads Jersey

		NM/M
Common Player:		5.00
1	Albert Pujols	15.00
2	Alfonso Soriano	8.00
4	Austin Kearns	5.00
5	Brad Penny	5.00
6	Carlos Beltran	8.00
7	Carlos Lee	5.00
9	Dale Murphy	8.00
10	Don Mattingly	25.00
11	Frank Thomas	8.00
12	Garret Anderson	5.00
13	Gary Carter	8.00
14	Hank Blalock	8.00
15	Jacque Jones	5.00
17	Jay Gibbons	5.00
18	Jeff Bagwell	8.00
19	Jeremy Bonderman	5.00
20	Jermaine Dye	5.00
21	Jim Thome	8.00
22	Jose Vidro	5.00
23	Lance Berkman	5.00
24	Laynce Nix	5.00
25	Magglio Ordonez	5.00
26	Marcus Giles	5.00
27	Mark Prior	10.00
28	Mark Teixeira	5.00
29	Melvin Mora	5.00
30	Michael Young	5.00
31	Miguel Cabrera	8.00
32	Mike Lowell	5.00
33	Roy Oswalt	5.00
34	Sammy Sosa	10.00
35	Scott Rolen	10.00
36	Sean Burroughs	5.00
37	Sean Casey	5.00
38	Shannon Stewart	5.00
39	Torii Hunter	5.00
40	Travis Hafner	5.00

Timber and Threads Jersey Signature

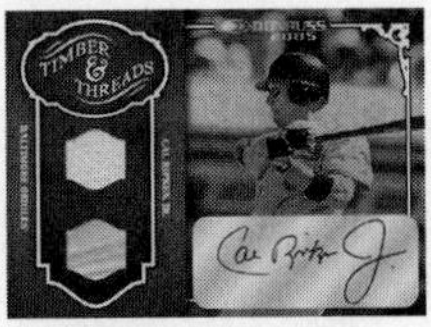

No Pricing
Production 5 or 10

2005 Donruss Champions

		NM/M
Complete Set (450):		
Common Player:		.25
Pack (8):		3.75
Box (24):		75.00
1	Adam Dunn	.50
2	Albert Pujols	2.00
3	Albert Pujols	2.00
4	Ichiro Suzuki	1.50
5	Alex Rodriguez	2.00
6	Andruw Jones	.50
7	Carlos Beltran	.50
8	Derrek Lee	.50
9	Hideki Matsui	1.50
10	Ichiro Suzuki	1.50
11	Ichiro Suzuki	1.50
12	Jeff Kent	.25
13	Ken Griffey Jr.	1.50
14	Ken Griffey Jr.	1.50
15	Sammy Sosa	1.00
16	Sean Casey	.25
17	Troy Glaus	.40
18	Derek Jeter	2.00
19	Cal Ripken Jr.	2.00
20	Roberto Alomar	.40
21	B.J. Surhoff	.25
22	Brian Jordan	.25
23	Corey Koskie	.25
24	Doug Davis	.25
25	Jason Varitek	.50
26	Jim Edmonds	.40
27	Kevin Mench	.25
28	Roberto Alomar	.40
29	Tony Armas Jr.	.25
30	Ramon Ortiz	.25
31	Rodrigo Lopez	.25
32	Andres Galarraga	.25
33	Brian Lawrence	.25
34	Jay Payton	.25
35	Ryan Ludwick	.25
36	Hee Seop Choi	.25
37	J.D. Drew	.25
38	Raul Mondesi	.25
39	Brian Jordan	.25
40	Luis Matos	.25
41	Russell Branyan	.25
42	Tony Gwynn	.75
43	Francisco Rodriguez	.25
44	Frank Robinson	.75
45	Jeff Bagwell	.50
46	Tony Gwynn	.75
47	Tony Gwynn	.75
48	Will Clark	.50
49	Antonio Perez	.25
50	Rickey Henderson	.50
51	Brian Lawrence	.25
52	Carlos Beltran	.50
53	Chris Snelling	.25
54	Darryl Strawberry	.25
55	Doug Mientkiewicz	.25
56	Edgardo Alfonzo	.25
57	Eric Chavez	.25
58	Eric Davis	.25
59	Guillermo Quiroz	.25
60	J.D. Drew	.25
61	J.D. Drew	.25
62	Walter Young	.25
63	John Kruk	.25
64	Jose Reyes	.50
65	Jose Vidro	.25
66	Josh Phelps	.25
67	Larry Walker	.25
68	Lyle Overbay	.25
69	Manny Ramirez	.75
70	Marlon Byrd	.25
71	Matt Williams	.25
72	Melvin Mora	.25
73	Nook Logan	.25
74	Orlando Hudson	.25
75	Orlando Hudson	.25
76	Orlando Hudson	.25
77	Paul Konerko	.50
78	Raul Mondesi	.25
79	Reed Johnson	.25
80	Ryan Ludwick	.25
81	So Taguchi	.25
82	Toby Hall	.25
83	Todd Helton	.50
84	Tommy John	.25
85	Tony Clark	.25
86	Victor Martinez	.40
87	Vladimir Guerrero	.75
88	Wade Boggs	.40
89	Roberto Clemente	1.50
90	Angel Berroa	.25
91	Termel Sledge	.25
92	Andres Galarraga	.25
93	Brooks Robinson	.50
94	Brooks Robinson	.50
95	Dennis Tankersley	.25
96	Don Mattingly	1.00
97	Ricardo Rodriguez	.25
98	Deivi Cruz	.25
99	Deivi Cruz	.25
100	Pete LaForest	.25
101	Roger Clemens	2.00
102	Frankie Francisco	.25
103	Kevin Millwood	.25
104	Tony Womack	.25
105	Jeff Bagwell	.50
106	Billy Martin	.25
107	J.T. Snow	.25
108	Juan Uribe	.25
109	Ryan Dempster	.25
110	Toby Hall	.25
111	Dennis Tankersley	.25
112	Freddy Garcia	.25
113	Garrett Atkins	.25
114	Troy Glaus	.40
115	Gabe Kapler	.25
116	Jeff Kent	.25
117	Rondell White	.25
118	C.C. Sabathia	.25
119	Javier Vazquez	.25
120	Mike Cameron	.25
121	Pat Burrell	.25
122	Lew Ford	.25
123	Brad Radke	.25
124	Preston Wilson	.25
125	Ray Durham	.25
126	Vernon Wells	.25
127	Bo Jackson	.50
128	Dmitri Young	.25
129	Doug Davis	.25
130	Brandon Duckworth	.25
131	Brandon Backe	.25
132	Juan Encarnacion	.25
133	Mike Maroth	.25
134	Sean Casey	.25
135	Travis Hafner	.40
136	Wes Helms	.25
137	Randy Johnson	.75
138	Larry Walker	.25
139	Luis Gonzalez	.25
140	John Olerud	.25
141	Kazuhisa Ishii	.25
142	Mike Lowell	.25
143	Kevin Millwood	.25
144	Chad Gaudin	.25
145	Bret Boone	.25
146	Cliff Floyd	.25
147	Dale Murphy	.25
148	Rickey Henderson	.50
149	Ricardo Rodriguez	.25
150	Richard Hidalgo	.25
151	Joe Kennedy	.25
152	Juan Pierre	.25
153	Juan Pierre **RC**	.25
154	Lance Berkman	.50
155	Joe Borchard	.25
156	Craig Monroe	.25
157	Abraham Nunez	.25
158	Willie Wilson	.25
159	Carlos Lee	.25
160	Carl Everett	.25
161	Frank White	.25
162	Craig Biggio	.40
163	Jason Varitek	.50
164	Magglio Ordonez	.25
165	Carlos Delgado	.50
166	Casey Kotchman	.25
167	Kenny Lofton	.25
168	Gil Hodges	.25
169	Rafael Furcal	.25
170	Ramon Vazquez	.25
171	Jeff Bagwell	.50
172	Jason Lane	.25
173	Nomar Garciaparra	.75
174	Willie Harris	.25
175	Adam Dunn	.50
176	Jose Cruz Jr.	.25
177	Robin Ventura	.25
178	Al Oliver	.25
179	Wily Mo Pena	.25
180	Erubiel Durazo	.25
181	Joey Gathright	.25
182	Luis Castillo	.25
183	Mark Teixeira	.50
184	Delmon Young	.25
185	Esteban Loaiza	.25
186	Bo Jackson	.50
187	Freddy Sanchez	.25
188	Jason Bay	.50
189	Rickey Henderson	.50
190	Shawn Green	.25
191	Roger Cedeno	.25
192	Hideki Matsui	1.50
193	Andruw Jones	.50
194	David Wright	1.00
195	Cesar Izturis	.25
196	Chipper Jones	.75
197	Troy Glaus	.40
198	Cliff Floyd	.25
199	Jason Jennings	.25
200	Mike Lowell	.25
201	Johnny Damon	.75
202	Aramis Ramirez	.40
203	John Smoltz	.40
204	Alan Trammell	.25
205	Moises Alou	.25
206	Randy Johnson	.75
207	Reggie Sanders	.25
208	Rickey Henderson	.50
209	Runelvys Hernandez	.25
210	Ryan Klesko	.25
211	Casey Fossum	.25
212	Robert Fick	.25
213	Al Oliver	.25
214	Kazuo Matsui	.25
215	Pedro Martinez	.75
216	Roberto Alomar	.50
217	Greg Maddux	1.50
218	Mark Ellis	.25
219	Shawn Green	.25
220	Shawn Green	.25
221	Willie McCovey	.50
222	Rafael Furcal	.25
223	Richie Ashburn	.25
224	Edgar Martinez	.25
225	Carlos Delgado	.25
226	David Justice	.25
227	Jose Cruz	.25
228	Larry Walker	.25
229	Miguel Tejada	.50
230	Andres Galarraga	.25

231	Trot Nixon	.25
232	Willie Mays	1.50
233	Dennis Eckersley	.25
234	Michael Barrett	.25
235	Jose Cruz Jr.	.25
236	Nolan Ryan	2.00
237	Hal Newhouser	.25
238	Roger Clemens	2.00
239	Victor Martinez	.40
240	Sean Burroughs	.25
241	Andres Galarraga	.25
242	Cal Ripken Jr.	2.00
243	Doug Mientkiewicz	.25
244	Hank Aaron	2.00
245	Vladimir Guerrero	.75
246	Reggie Jackson	.75
247	Terrence Long	.25
248	Tommy Lasorda	.25
249	Bert Blyleven	.25
250	Ken Boyer	.25
251	Maury Wills	.25
252	Lou Brock	.25
253	Don Sutton	.25
254	Enos Slaughter	.25
255	Ernie Banks	.75
256	Gaylord Perry	.25
257	Joe Carter	.25
258	Keith Hernandez	.25
259	Orlando Cabrera	.25
260	Phil Niekro	.25
261	Robin Ventura	.25
262	Rod Carew	.50
263	Rollie Fingers	.25
264	Sammy Sosa	1.00
265	Byung-Hyun Kim	.25
266	Zach Day	.25
267	Richie Ashburn	.25
268	Mike Piazza	1.00
269	Tommy John	.25
270	Craig Biggio	.50
271	Hideki Matsui	1.50
272	Cesar Izturis	.25
273	Paul Molitor	.50
274	Steve Carlton	.50
275	Justin Morneau	.50
276	Albert Pujols	2.00
277	John Olerud	.25
278	Austin Kearns	.25
279	Travis Hafner	.40
280	Charles Johnson	.25
281	Craig Wilson	.25
282	Joe Carter	.25
283	Josh Beckett	.40
284	Dale Murphy	.25
285	Robert Fick	.25
286	David Justice	.25
287	Kirby Puckett	.75
288	Juan Encarnacion	.25
289	Moises Alou	.25
290	Shannon Stewart	.25
291	Alfonso Soriano	.75
292	Jacque Jones	.25
293	Pee Wee Reese	.25
294	Deion Sanders	.50
295	Richard Hidalgo	.25
296	Rocco Baldelli	.25
297	Bill Hall	.25
298	Mike Sweeney	.25
299	Paul Molitor	.50
300	Will Clark	.50
301	Torii Hunter	.40
302	Jim Thome	.75
303	Kevin Mench	.25
304	John Buck	.25
305	Joe Morgan	.25
306	Wilson Betemit	.25
307	Ivan Rodriguez	.50
308	Michael Young	.25
309	Moises Alou	.25
310	So Taguchi	.25
311	Rickey Henderson	.50
312	Kenny Lofton	.25
313	Rickey Henderson	.50
314	Shannon Stewart	.25
315	Fred Lynn	.25
316	Mark Prior	.50
317	Tony Perez	.25
318	Dontrelle Willis	.25
319	Xavier Nady	.25
320	Juan Uribe	.25
321	Chipper Jones	.75
322	Joe Crede	.25
323	Kerry Wood	.40
324	Eric Hinske	.25
325	Carlos Lee	.25
326	Joe Borchard	.25
327	Sean Casey	.25
328	Joe Kennedy	.25
329	Brandon Duckworth	.25
330	Willie Mays	1.50
331	Andruw Jones	.50
332	Brandon Claussen	.25
333	Brandon Claussen	.25
334	Brian Giles	.25
335	Gary Sheffield	.40
336	Mark Grace	.40
337	Ryne Sandberg	.75
338	Sammy Sosa	1.00
339	Steve Carlton	.25
340	Vernon Wells	.40
341	Wade Miller	.25
342	Andre Dawson	.25
343	Darryl Strawberry	.25
344	Nolan Ryan	2.00
345	Curt Schilling	.75
346	Bo Jackson	.50
347	Darin Erstad	.25
348	Alfonso Soriano	.75
349	A.J. Burnett	.25
350	David Ortiz	.75
351	George Foster	.25
352	Rafael Palmeiro	.50
353	Alan Trammell	.25
354	Willie Mays	1.50
355	Bernie Williams	.50
356	Phil Niekro	.25
357	Hank Blalock	.40
358	Miguel Cabrera	.75
359	Carl Yastrzemski	.75
360	Aramis Ramirez	.40
361	Frank Thomas	.75
362	Tony Oliva	.25
363	Roger Clemens	2.00
364	Adam Loewen	.25
365	Alex Cintron	.25
366	Alfredo Simon	.25
367	Angel Guzman	.25
368	Anthony Lerew	.25
369	Ben Hendrickson	.25
370	Brandon McCarthy **RC**	1.50
371	Bubba Nelson	.25
372	Clint Nageotte	.25
373	Eddy Rodriguez	.25
374	Edwin Moreno	.25
375	J.J. Putz	.25
376	Jake Woods	.25
377	Jeff Suppan	.25
378	Jeremy Affeldt	.25
379	Jose Castillo	.25
380	Justin Leone	.25
381	Justin Verlander **RC**	4.00
382	Marlon Byrd	.25
383	Mike Gosling	.25
384	Prince Fielder	5.00
385	Randy Wolf	.25
386	Raul Ibanez	.25
387	Raul Tablado **RC**	.50
388	Rick Dempsey	.25
389	Roberto Novoa	.25
390	Russ Ortiz	.25
391	Ryan Wing	.25
392	Scot Shields	.25
393	Steve Stone	.25
394	Tadahito Iguchi **RC**	1.50
395	Todd Wellemeyer	.25
396	Travis Blackley	.25
397	Troy Percival	.25
398	Wilson Valdez	.25
399	Kevin Youkilis	.25
400	Jose Guillen	.25
401	Duke Snider	.25
402	Jeff Niemann **RC**	1.00
403	Johan Santana	.50
404	Nellie Fox	.25
405	Nellie Fox	.25
406	Marlon Byrd	.25
407	Mike Piazza	1.00
408	Bobby Higginson	.25
409	Don Mattingly	1.00
410	Jayson Werth	.25
411	Al Kaline	.50
412	Bobby Higginson	.25
413	Roger Cedeno	.25
414	Roger Cedeno	.25
415	Roger Cedeno	.25
416	Roger Cedeno	.25
417	Roger Cedeno	.25
418	Magglio Ordonez	.25
419	Don Mattingly	1.00
420	Morgan Ensberg	.25
421	Charles Johnson	.25
422	Albert Pujols	2.00
423	Dave Righetti	.25
424	Roy Halladay	.50
425	Tom Seaver	.75
426	Early Wynn	.25
427	Bob Gibson	.50
428	Doug Mientkiewicz	.25
429	Jason Varitek	.50
430	Tom Glavine	.25
431	Erik Bedard	.25
432	Pedro Martinez	.75
433	David Ortiz	.75
434	Kazuhisa Ishii	.25
435	Trevor Hoffman	.25
436	Paul Molitor	.50
437	Derrek Lee	.50
438	Fergie Jenkins	.25
439	Tony Gwynn	.75
440	Jeff Bagwell	.50
441	Steve Carlton	.25
442	Adam Dunn	.50
443	Sean Casey	.25
444	Geoff Jenkins	.25
445	Derek Jeter	2.00
446	J.T. Snow	.25
447	Kenny Lofton	.25
448	Benito Santiago	.25
449	Tim Salmon	.25
450	Ichiro Suzuki	1.50

Press Plates

No Pricing
Production one set per color.

Impressions

Stars: 1.5-3X
Inserted 1:3

Impressions Black

No Pricing
Production 5 Sets

Impressions Blue

Stars: 2-4X
Production 100 Sets

Impressions Gold

Stars: 3-5X
Production 50 Sets

Impressions Green

No Pricing
Production 25 Sets

Impressions Orange

Stars: 2-4X
Production 75 Sets

Impressions Red

Stars: 1.5-2X
Production 250 Sets

Impressions Autograph

NM/M

Tier 1 Production 101-250
Tier 2 Production 251-500
Tier 3 Production 501-800
Tier 4 Production 801-1,200
Tier 5 Production 1,201-1,500
Cards are not serial numbered.

19	Cal Ripken Jr./65	140.00
42	Tony Gwynn/65	35.00
44	Frank Robinson/59	25.00
46	Tony Gwynn/65	35.00
47	Tony Gwynn/61	35.00
206	Randy Johnson/62	65.00
242	Cal Ripken Jr./25	160.00
262	Rod Carew/37	25.00
279	Travis Hafner/49	20.00
297	Bill Hall/52	10.0
322	Joe Crede/34	20.00
364	Adam Loewen T1	10.00
365	Alex Cintron T1	10.00
366	Alfredo Simon T2	8.00
367	Angel Guzman T2	8.00
369	Ben Hendrickson T3	8.00
371	Bubba Nelson T2	8.00
372	Clint Nageotte T2	8.00
373	Eddy Rodriguez/89	8.00
374	Edwin Moreno/55	10.00
375	J.J. Putz T3	8.00
376	Jake Woods T1	8.00
377	Jeff Suppan T4	12.00
378	Jeremy Affeldt T1	8.00
379	Jose Castillo T1	8.00
380	Justin Leone T2	8.00
382	Marlon Byrd T1	10.00
383	Mike Gosling/93	8.00
385	Randy Wolf T1	10.00
386	Raul Ibanez T1	10.00
387	Raul Tablado/74	10.00
388	Rick Dempsey T4	10.00
389	Roberto Novoa T2	8.00
390	Russ Ortiz/49	15.00
391	Ryan Wing T1	8.00
392	Scot Shields T5	8.00
393	Steve Stone/65	15.00
395	Todd Wellemeyer/92	10.00
396	Travis Blackley/87	8.00
397	Troy Percival T1	10.00
398	Wilson Valdez T5	8.00
399	Kevin Youkilis T2	20.00
401	Duke Snider/30	35.00
402	Jeff Niemann/77	15.00
403	Johan Santana/29	40.00
423	Dave Righetti T1	15.00
425	Tom Seaver/28	40.00

Impressions Ball

NM/M

Production 1-100

55	Doug Mientkiewicz/25	8.00
57	Eric Chavez/45	5.00
175	Adam Dunn/25	10.00
192	Hideki Matsui/40	40.00
193	Andruw Jones/30	10.00
197	Troy Glaus/78	8.00
276	Albert Pujols/76	20.00
277	John Olerud/53	5.00
286	David Justice/30	8.00
292	Jacque Jones/37	5.00
301	Torii Hunter/55	8.00
316	Mark Prior/31	8.00
348	Alfonso Soriano/75	8.00
350	David Ortiz/100	10.00
352	Rafael Palmeiro/65	8.00
390	Russ Ortiz/50	5.00

Impressions Batting Glove

NM/M

Production 44-145

306	Wilson Betemit/145	5.00
320	Juan Uribe/125	5.00
322	Joe Crede/89	8.00
325	Carlos Lee/71	8.00
334	Brian Giles/44	8.00
419	Don Mattingly/125	15.00

Impressions Button

Production 1-16

Impressions Combos

NM/M

Production 1-210
Prime: .75-2X
Production 1-50

302A	Jim Thome/105	8.00
302B	Jim Thome/45	10.00
303	Kevin Mench/175	5.00
304	John Buck/150	5.00
305	Joe Morgan/80	8.00
306A	Wilson Betemit/210	5.00
306B	Wilson Betemit/65	5.00
307A	Ivan Rodriguez/175	8.00
307B	Ivan Rodriguez/35	10.00
308A	Michael Young/180	8.00
308B	Michael Young/50	8.00
310	So Taguchi/150	8.00
311	Rickey Henderson/40	15.00
313	Rickey Henderson/85	15.00
315A	Fred Lynn/60	5.00
316A	Mark Prior/53	8.00
317	Tony Perez/62	8.00
319A	Xavier Nady/50	5.00
320	Juan Uribe/59	5.00
322A	Joe Crede/190	8.00
322B	Joe Crede/40	10.00
323A	Kerry Wood/33	8.00
324A	Eric Hinske/132	5.00
325A	Carlos Lee/52	8.00
326A	Joe Borchard/57	5.00
332A	Brandon Claussen/165	5.00
334A	Brian Giles/90	8.00
342A	Andre Dawson/165	8.00
342B	Andre Dawson/50	10.00
343	Darryl Strawberry/73	8.00
345	Curt Schilling/89	10.00
350A	David Ortiz/53	15.00
352	Rafael Palmeiro/201	8.00
355	Bernie Williams/43	8.00
357	Hank Blalock/47	5.00
359	Carl Yastrzemski/73	15.00
362	Tony Oliva/93	8.00

Impressions Fielding Glove

NM/M

Production 26-250

317	Tony Perez/49	10.00
319	Xavier Nady/97	5.00
321	Chipper Jones/26	30.00
328	Joe Kennedy/130	5.00
331	Andruw Jones/82	10.00
332	Brandon Claussen/250	5.00
336	Mark Grace/186	10.00
337	Ryne Sandberg/64	20.00
339	Steve Carlton/86	8.00
341	Wade Miller/117	5.00
420	Morgan Ensberg/87	5.00

Impressions Hat

NM/M

Production 1-250

313	Rickey Henderson/219	10.00
314	Shannon Stewart/250	5.00
316	Mark Prior/250	8.00
329	Brandon Duckworth/157	5.00
332	Brandon Claussen/250	5.00
340	Vernon Wells/26	8.00

Impressions Material

NM/M

Tier 1 Production 101-250
Tier 2 Production 251-500
Tier 3 Production 501-800
Tier 4 Production 801-1,200
Tier 5 Production 1,201-1,500
Cards are not serial numbered.
Prime: 1-2.5X
No pricing production 25 or less.

21	B.J. Surhoff T5	4.00
22	Brian Jordan T5	4.00
23	Corey Koskie T5	4.00
24	Doug Davis T5	4.00
25	Jason Varitek T5	8.00
26	Jim Edmonds/65	6.00
27	Kevin Mench T5	4.00
28	Roberto Alomar T5	6.00
29	Tony Armas Jr. T5	4.00
30	Ramon Ortiz T5	4.00
31	Rodrigo Lopez T5	4.00
32	Andres Galarraga T4	4.00
33	Brian Lawrence T5	4.00
34	Jay Payton T5	4.00
36	Hee Seop Choi T5	4.00
37	J.D. Drew T4	4.00
38	Raul Mondesi T4	4.00
39	Brian Jordan T4	4.00
40	Luis Matos T5	4.00
41	Russell Branyan T4	4.00
42	Tony Gwynn T4	8.00
43	Francisco Rodriguez T4	4.00
44	Frank Robinson T5	10.00
45	Jeff Bagwell T5	6.00
46	Tony Gwynn T5	8.00
47	Tony Gwynn T5	8.00
48	Will Clark T5	8.00
50	Rickey Henderson T3	10.00
51	Brian Lawrence T4	4.00
52	Carlos Beltran T5	8.00
53	Chris Snelling T5	4.00
54	Darryl Strawberry/50	6.00
55	Doug Mientkiewicz T5	4.00
56	Edgardo Alfonzo T5	4.00
57	Eric Chavez T5	6.00
58	Eric Davis T5	4.00
59	Guillermo Quiroz T5	4.00
60	J.D. Drew T5	4.00
61	J.D. Drew T5	4.00
62	Walter Young T4	4.00
63	John Kruk T5	6.00

64 Jose Reyes T5 8.00
65 Jose Vidro T5 4.00
66 Josh Phelps T5 4.00
67 Larry Walker T5 6.00
68 Lyle Overbay T5 4.00
69 Manny Ramirez T1 10.00
70 Marlon Byrd T5 4.00
71 Matt Williams T5 6.00
72 Melvin Mora T5 4.00
73 Nook Logan T5 4.00
74 Orlando Hudson T5 4.00
75 Orlando Hudson T5 4.00
76 Orlando Hudson T5 4.00
77 Paul Konerko T5 6.00
78 Raul Mondesi T4 4.00
79 Reed Johnson T5 4.00
81 So Taguchi T4 4.00
82 Toby Hall T5 4.00
83 Todd Helton T2 8.00
84 Tommy John T5 4.00
85 Tony Clark T4 4.00
86 Victor Martinez T5 6.00
87 Vladimir Guerrero/51 10.00
88 Wade Boggs T5 6.00
89 Roberto Clemente T5 35.00
90 Angel Berroa T5 4.00
91 Termel Sledge T5 4.00
92 Andres Galarraga T4 4.00
93 Brooks Robinson T5 10.00
94 Brooks Robinson T4 10.00
95 Dennis Tankersley T4 4.00
96 Don Mattingly T4 15.00
97 Ricardo Rodriguez T4 4.00
98 Deivi Cruz T5 4.00
99 Deivi Cruz T3 4.00
100 Pete LaForest T4 4.00
101 Rickey Henderson T3 15.00
102 Frankie Francisco T4 4.00
103 Kevin Millwood T4 4.00
104 Tony Womack T4 4.00
105 Jeff Bagwell T4 6.00
106 Billy Martin T3 8.00
107 J.T. Snow T3 4.00
108 Juan Uribe T4 4.00
109 Ryan Dempster T3 4.00
110 Toby Hall T4 4.00
111 Dennis Tankersley T3 4.00
112 Freddy Garcia T4 4.00
113 Garrett Atkins T4 4.00
114 Troy Glaus T3 4.00
115 Gabe Kapler T4 4.00
116 Jeff Kent T4 4.00
117 Rondell White T3 4.00
118 C.C. Sabathia T3 4.00
119 Javier Vazquez T4 4.00
120 Mike Cameron T3 4.00
121 Pat Burrell T3 6.00
122 Lew Ford T3 4.00
123 Brad Radke T3 4.00
124 Preston Wilson T3 4.00
125 Ray Durham T3 4.00
126 Vernon Wells T3 6.00
127 Bo Jackson T3 8.00
128 Dmitri Young T3 4.00
129 Doug Davis T3 4.00
130 Brandon Duckworth T3 4.00
131 Brandon Backe T3 4.00
132 Juan Encarnacion T3 4.00
133 Mike Maroth T3 4.00
134 Sean Casey T4 4.00
135 Travis Hafner T3 6.00
136 Wes Helms T3 4.00
137 Randy Johnson T3 8.00
138 Larry Walker T2 4.00
139 Luis Gonzalez T2 4.00
140 John Olerud T1 4.00
141 Kazuhisa Ishii T4 4.00
142 Mike Lowell T2 4.00
143 Kevin Millwood T2 4.00
144 Chad Gaudin T2 4.00
145 Bret Boone T2 4.00
146 Cliff Floyd T2 4.00
147A Dale Murphy T3 6.00
148 Rickey Henderson T4 10.00
149 Ricardo Rodriguez T2 10.00
150 Richard Hidalgo T3 4.00
151 Joe Kennedy T4 4.00
152 Juan Pierre T4 4.00
153 Juan Pierre T4 4.00
154 Lance Berkman T4 6.00
155 Joe Borchard T4 4.00
156 Craig Monroe T4 4.00
157 Abraham Nunez T1 4.00
158 Willie Wilson T4 4.00
159 Carlos Lee T3 6.00
160 Carl Everett T4 4.00
161 Frank White T4 4.00
162 Craig Biggio T4 6.00
163 Jason Varitek T4 8.00
164 Magglio Ordonez T4 4.00
165 Carlos Delgado T4 6.00
166 Casey Kotchman T4 4.00
167 Kenny Lofton T4 4.00
168 Gil Hodges T4 15.00
169 Rafael Furcal T3 4.00
170 Ramon Vazquez T3 4.00
171 Jeff Bagwell T3 6.00
172 Jason Lane T3 4.00
173 Nomar Garciaparra T3 8.00
174 Willie Harris T3 4.00
175 Adam Dunn T3 6.00
176 Jose Cruz Jr. T3 4.00
177 Robin Ventura T3 4.00
178 Al Oliver T3 4.00
179 Wily Mo Pena T3 4.00
180 Erubiel Durazo T3 4.00
181 Joey Gathright T3 4.00
182 Luis Castillo T3 4.00
183 Mark Teixeira T3 8.00
184 Delmon Young T3 8.00
185 Esteban Loaiza T3 4.00
186 Bo Jackson T3 8.00
187 Freddy Sanchez T3 4.00
188 Jason Bay T3 6.00
189 Rickey Henderson T3 10.00
190 Shawn Green T2 4.00
191 Roger Cedeno T4 4.00
192 Hideki Matsui T3 15.00
193 Andruw Jones T3 8.00
194 David Wright T3 10.00
195 Cesar Izturis T2 4.00
196 Chipper Jones T3 8.00
197 Troy Glaus T3 6.00
198 Cliff Floyd T3 6.00
199 Jason Jennings T2 4.00
200 Mike Lowell T2 4.00
201 Johnny Damon T2 10.00
202 Aramis Ramirez T1 6.00
203 John Smoltz T2 6.00
204 Alan Trammell T2 6.00
205 Moises Alou T2 4.00
206 Randy Johnson T2 8.00
207 Reggie Sanders T2 4.00
208 Rickey Henderson T2 10.00
209 Runelvys Hernandez T2 4.00
210 Ryan Klesko T2 4.00
211 Casey Fossum T2 4.00
212 Robert Fick T2 4.00
213 Al Oliver T2 4.00
214 Kazuo Matsui T2 4.00
215 Pedro Martinez T2 8.00
216 Roberto Alomar T1 6.00
217 Greg Maddux T1 10.00
218 Mark Ellis T2 4.00
219 Shawn Green T1 4.00
220 Shawn Green T1 4.00
221 Willie McCovey T2 6.00
222 Rafael Furcal T1 4.00
223 Richie Ashburn T1 6.00
225 Carlos Delgado T2 6.00
226 David Justice T2 4.00
227 Jose Cruz T2 4.00
228 Larry Walker T1 4.00
229 Miguel Tejada T1 6.00
230 Andres Galarraga T1 4.00
231 Trot Nixon T1 6.00
232 Willie Mays T2 30.00
233 Dennis Eckersley T1 4.00
234 Michael Barrett T1 4.00
235 Jose Cruz Jr. T1 4.00
236 Nolan Ryan T1 20.00
237 Hal Newhouser T1 6.00
238 Roger Clemens T1 15.00
239 Victor Martinez/50 6.00
240 Sean Burroughs/90 4.00
241 Andres Galarraga/84 4.00
242 Cal Ripken Jr. T1 40.00
243 Doug Mientkiewicz/68 4.00
244 Hank Aaron/60 40.00
246 Reggie Jackson/35 8.00
247 Terrence Long/73 4.00
265 Byung-Hyun Kim T2 4.00
266 Zach Day T2 4.00
267 Richie Ashburn T2 6.00
268 Mike Piazza T2 10.00
269 Tommy John T1 4.00
270 Craig Biggio T1 6.00
271 Hideki Matsui T1 15.00
272 Cesar Izturis T1 4.00
273 Paul Molitor T1 8.00
274 Steve Carlton/40 6.00
275 Justin Morneau T2 6.00
276 Albert Pujols T2 15.00
277 John Olerud T2 4.00
278 Austin Kearns T2 4.00
279 Travis Hafner T2 6.00
280 Charles Johnson T2 4.00
281 Craig Wilson T2 4.00
282 Joe Carter T2 4.00
283 Josh Beckett T2 6.00
284 Dale Murphy/42 8.00
285 Robert Fick T2 4.00
286 David Justice T2 4.00
287 Kirby Puckett T2 8.00
288 Juan Encarnacion T2 4.00
289 Moises Alou T2 4.00
290 Shannon Stewart T2 4.00
291 Alfonso Soriano T2 8.00
292 Jacque Jones T2 4.00
293 Pee Wee Reese T2 8.00
294 Deion Sanders/81 8.00
295 Richard Hidalgo T2 4.00
296 Rocco Baldelli T2 4.00
297 Bill Hall T2 4.00
298 Mike Sweeney T1 4.00
299 Paul Molitor T2 8.00
300 Will Clark T1 8.00
301 Torii Hunter T1 6.00
305 Joe Morgan/95 8.00
311 Rickey Henderson T1 10.00
315 Fred Lynn/40 4.00
318 Dontrelle Willis/51 8.00
342 Andre Dawson/25 8.00
350 David Ortiz T1 8.00
351 George Foster T1 4.00
353 Alan Trammell T1 6.00
354 Willie Mays T1 30.00
355 Bernie Williams T1 6.00
356 Phil Niekro T1 6.00
357 Hank Blalock T1 6.00
358 Miguel Cabrera T1 8.00
359 Carl Yastrzemski/47 8.00
360 Aramis Ramirez/57 6.00
361 Frank Thomas T1 8.00
404 Nellie Fox T5 6.00
405 Nellie Fox T5 6.00
406 Marlon Byrd T5 4.00
407 Mike Piazza T2 10.00
408 Bobby Higginson T4 4.00
410 Jayson Werth T5 4.00
411 Al Kaline T4 8.00
412 Bobby Higginson T3 4.00
413 Roger Cedeno T4 4.00
414 Roger Cedeno T4 4.00
415 Roger Cedeno T4 4.00
416 Roger Cedeno T4 4.00
417 Roger Cedeno T4 4.00
418 Magglio Ordonez T5 4.00
424 Roy Halladay/89 6.00
426 Early Wynn T1 6.00
427 Bob Gibson/36 8.00
428 Doug Mientkiewicz T5 4.00
429 Jason Varitek T2 8.00
430 Tom Glavine T1 6.00
431 Erik Bedard T2 4.00
432 Pedro Martinez T2 8.00
433 David Ortiz T3 8.00
434 Kazuhisa Ishii T2 4.00
435 Trevor Hoffman T2 4.00
436 Paul Molitor T1 6.00
437 Derrek Lee T1 8.00
439 Tony Gwynn T5 8.00
440 Jeff Bagwell T4 6.0

Impressions Shoe

NM/M

Production 2-226
310 So Taguchi/226 5.00
312 Kenny Lofton/103 5.00
323 Kerry Wood/89 6.00
324 Eric Hinske/133 5.00
326 Joe Borchard/200 5.00
327 Sean Casey/51 5.00
338 Sammy Sosa/75 10.00
421 Charles Johnson/196 5.00

MLB Logo Patch

No Pricing
Production 1-7

Recollection Autographs

NM/M

Production 1-319
BBR1 Brian Bruney/151 8.00
SB1 Sean Burroughs/72 8.00
MB1 Marlon Byrd/319 8.00
MB2 Marlon Byrd/25 12.00
MB3 Marlon Byrd/25 12.00
MB4 Marlon Byrd/23 12.00
MB5 Marlon Byrd/35 12.00
EC2 Eric Chavez/33 15.00
RD1 Rob Dibble/33 10.00
JD4 Jermaine Dye/33 15.00
CF2 Chone Figgins/68 15.00
JG1 Jason Giambi/25 30.00
JG2 Jason Giambi/25 30.00
JG3 Jason Giambi/25 30.00
JGI1 Jay Gibbons/27 10.00
GG1 Geronimo Gil/40 8.00
BG3 Bobby Grich/68 10.00
JGU1 Jose Guillen/35 10.00
RHA1 Rich Harden/33 10.00
DH1 Danny Haren/146 10.00
RHO1 Ryan Howard/150 200.00
THU2 Torii Hunter/72 15.00
RI1 Raul Ibanez/72 10.00
JJ2 Jacque Jones/32 15.00
PK1 Paul Konerko/33 20.00
JK1 Jason Kubel/151 10.00
BL1 Barry Larkin/33 25.00
CLE2 Cliff Lee/73 20.00
ML2 Mike Lieberthal/27 10.00
MLO1 Mike Lowell/33 10.00
BM4 Bill Madlock/35 15.00
EM3 Edgar Martinez/35 20.00
EM9 Edgar Martinez/33 20.00
WM2 Wade Miller/89 10.00
JM6 Jack Morris/74 10.00
BN1 Bubba Nelson/147 8.00
TN1 Trot Nixon/33 15.00
BO1 Ben Oglivie/44 15.00
BO2 Ben Oglivie/81 10.00
BO3 Ben Oglivie/28 15.00
BO6 Ben Oglivie/62 10.00
BO7 Ben Oglivie/132 10.00
MO4 Magglio Ordonez/33 15.00
MO5 Magglio Ordonez/33 15.00
RO1 Roy Oswalt/73 15.00
GQ1 Guillermo Quiroz/149 8.00
AR2 Aramis Ramirez/34 25.00
AR3 Aramis Ramirez/33 25.00
RR1 Ricardo Rodriguez/63 8.00
JS1 Jae Weong Seo/33 15.00
CS1 Chris Snelling/47 8.00
SS1 Shannon Stewart 10.00
JV2 Jose Vidro/71 8.00
BW2 Brandon Webb/51 15.00
TW1 Todd Wellemeyer/146 8.00
VW1 Vernon Wells/33 15.00
VW2 Vernon Wells/49 15.00

2005 Donruss Classics

NM/M

Complete Set (250):
Common Player (1-200): .25

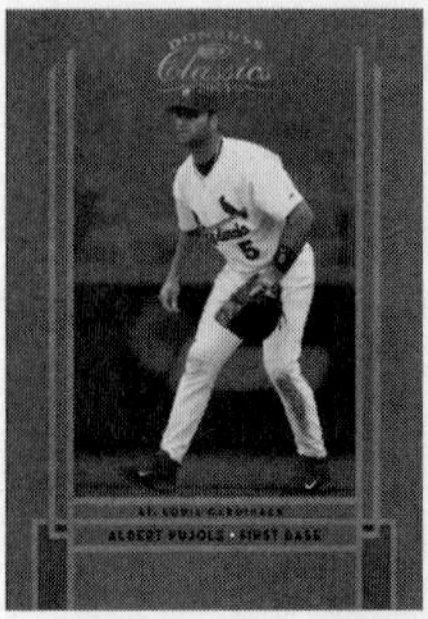

Common Auto. (201-225): 6.00
Common SP (226-250): 3.00
Production 1,000
Pack (5): 8.00
Box (18): 120.00
1 Scott Rolen 1.00
2 Derek Jeter 3.00
3 Jose Vidro .25
4 Johnny Damon 1.00
5 Nomar Garciaparra 2.00
6 Jose Guillen .25
7 Trot Nixon .25
8 Mark Loretta .25
9 Jody Gerut .25
10 Miguel Tejada .75
11 Barry Larkin .50
12 Jeff Kent .40
13 Carl Crawford .25
14 Paul Konerko .40
15 Jim Edmonds .50
16 Garret Anderson .40
17 Jay Gibbons .25
18 Moises Alou .40
19 Mike Lowell .25
20 Mark Mulder .40
21 Josh Beckett .50
22 Tim Salmon .25
23 Shannon Stewart .25
24 Miguel Cabrera 1.00
25 Jim Thome 1.00
26 Kevin Youkilis .25
27 Justin Morneau .75
28 Austin Kearns .25
29 Cliff Lee .25
30 Ken Griffey Jr. 1.50
31 Mike Piazza 1.50
32 Roy Halladay .40
33 Larry Walker .50
34 David Ortiz 1.00
35 Dontrelle Willis .50
36 Craig Wilson .25
37 Jeff Suppan .25
38 Curt Schilling 1.00
39 Larry Bigbie .25
40 Rich Harden .40
41 Victor Martinez .40
42 Jorge Posada .50
43 Joey Gathright .25
44 Adam Dunn .75
45 Pedro Martinez 1.00
46 Dallas McPherson .50
47 Tom Glavine .40
48 Torii Hunter .40
49 Angel Berroa .25
50 Mark Prior 1.00
51 Ichiro Suzuki 2.00
52 C.C. Sabathia .25
53 Bobby Abreu .50
54 Shigetoshi Hasegawa .25
55 Brandon Webb .50
56 Mark Buehrle .50
57 Johan Santana .75
58 Francisco Rodriguez .25
59 Roy Oswalt .50
60 Mike Sweeney .25
61 Jake Peavy .50
62 Akinori Otsuka .25
63 Dioner Navarro .25
64 Kazuhito Tadano .25
65 Ryan Wagner .25
66 Abe Alvarez .25
67 Mark Teixeira .75
68 Jermaine Dye .25
69 Todd Walker .25
70 Octavio Dotel .25
71 Frank Thomas .75
72 Javy Lopez .50
73 Scott Podsednik .25
74 B.J. Upton .25
75 Barry Zito .40
76 Raul Ibanez .25
77 Orlando Cabrera .25
78 Sean Burroughs .25
79 Esteban Loaiza .25
80 Jason Schmidt .50
81 Vinny Castilla .25
82 Shingo Takatsu .25
83 Juan Pierre .25
84 David Dellucci .25
85 Travis Blackley .25
86 Brad Penny .25

87	Nick Johnson	.25
88	Brian Roberts	.50
89	Kazuo Matsui	.25
90	Mike Lieberthal	.25
91	Craig Biggio	.40
92	Sean Casey	.25
93	Andy Pettitte	.50
94	Milton Bradley	.40
95	Rocco Baldelli	.25
96	Adrian Gonzalez	.25
97	Chad Tracy	.25
98	Chad Cordero	.25
99	Albert Pujols	3.00
100	Jason Kubel	.25
101	Rafael Furcal	.25
102	Jack Wilson	.25
103	Eric Chavez	.40
104	Casey Kotchman	.25
105	Jeff Bagwell	.75
106	Melvin Mora	.25
107	Bobby Crosby	.25
108	Preston Wilson	.25
109	Hank Blalock	.75
110	Vernon Wells	.40
111	Francisco Cordero	.25
112	Steve Finley	.25
113	Omar Vizquel	.25
114	Eric Byrnes	.25
115	Tim Hudson	.50
116	Aramis Ramirez	.50
117	Lance Berkman	.40
118	Shea Hillenbrand	.25
119	Aubrey Huff	.25
120	Lew Ford	.25
121	Sammy Sosa	2.00
122	Marcus Giles	.25
123	Rickie Weeks	.25
124	Manny Ramirez	1.00
125	Jason Giambi	.40
126	Adam LaRoche	.25
127	Vladimir Guerrero	1.00
128	Ken Harvey	.25
129	Adrian Beltre	.50
130	Magglio Ordonez	.25
131	Greg Maddux	1.50
132	Russ Ortiz	.25
133	Jason Varitek	.75
134	Kerry Wood	1.00
135	Mike Mussina	.75
136	Joe Nathan	.25
137	Troy Glaus	.50
138	Carlos Zambrano	.50
139	Ben Sheets	.50
140	Jae Weong Seo	.25
141	Derrek Lee	.50
142	Carlos Beltran	.50
143	John Lackey	.25
144	Aaron Rowand	.25
145	Dewon Brazelton	.25
146	Jason Bay	.25
147	Alfonso Soriano	1.00
148	Travis Hafner	.25
149	Ryan Church	.25
150	Bret Boone	.25
151	Bernie Williams	.50
152	Wade Miller	.25
153	Zack Greinke	.25
154	Scott Kazmir	.25
155	Hideki Matsui	2.00
156	Livan Hernandez	.25
157	Jose Capellan	.25
158	David Wright	1.00
159	Chone Figgins	.25
160	Jeremy Reed	.25
161	J.D. Drew	.40
162	Hideo Nomo	.50
163	Merkin Valdez	.25
164	Shawn Green	.40
165	Alexis Rios	.25
166	Johnny Estrada	.25
167	Danny Graves	.25
168	Carlos Lee	.25
169	John Van Benschoten	.25
170	Randy Johnson	1.00
171	Randy Wolf	.25
172	Luis Gonzalez	.40
173	Chipper Jones	1.00
174	Delmon Young	.50
175	Edwin Jackson	.25
176	Carlos Delgado	.50
177	Matt Clement	.25
178	Jacque Jones	.25
179	Gary Sheffield	.50
180	Laynce Nix	.25
181	Tom Gordon	.25
182	Jose Castillo	.25
183	Andruw Jones	.50
184	Brian Giles	.40
185	Paul LoDuca	.25
186	Roger Clemens	3.00
187	Todd Helton	.75
188	Keith Foulke	.25
189	Jeremy Bonderman	.25
190	Troy Percival	.25
191	Michael Young	.25
192	Carlos Guillen	.25
193	Rafael Palmeiro	.75
194	Brett Myers	.25
195	Carl Pavano	.40
196	Alex Rodriguez	2.50
197	Lyle Overbay	.25
198	Ivan Rodriguez	.75
199	Khalil Greene	.40
200	Edgar Renteria	.40

201	Justin Verlander AU/400 RC	40.00
202	Miguel Negron AU/1,300 RC	6.00
204	Paul Reynoso AU/1,200 RC	8.00
205	Colter Bean AU/1,200 RC	8.00
206	Raul Tablado AU/1,200 RC	8.00
207	Mark McLemore AU/1,500 RC	8.00
208	Russel Rohlicek AU/1,200 RC	8.00
210	Chris Seddon AU/785 RC	8.00
213	Mike Morse AU/1,200 RC	6.00
215	Randy Messenger AU/1,200 RC	8.00
217	Carlos Ruiz AU/1,200 RC	8.00
218	Chris Roberson AU/1,200 RC	8.00
219	Ryan Speier AU/1,200 RC	8.00
221	Ambiorix Burgos AU/750 RC	8.00
223	David Gassner AU/1,200 RC	6.00
224	Sean Tracey AU/1,200 RC	8.00
225	Casey Rogowski AU/1,500 RC	8.00
226	Billy Williams	3.00
227	Ralph Kiner	3.00
228	Ozzie Smith	5.00
229	Rod Carew	3.00
230	Nolan Ryan	8.00
231	Fergie Jenkins	3.00
232	Paul Molitor	4.00
233	Carlton Fisk	4.00
234	Rollie Fingers	3.00
235	Lou Brock	3.00
236	Gaylord Perry	3.00
237	Don Mattingly	6.00
238	Maury Wills	4.00
239	Luis Aparicio	3.00
240	George Brett	8.00
241	Mike Schmidt	6.00
242	Joe Morgan	3.00
243	Dennis Eckersley	3.00
244	Reggie Jackson	4.00
245	Bobby Doerr	3.00
246	Bob Feller	3.00
247	Cal Ripken Jr.	10.00
248	Harmon Killebrew	4.00
249	Frank Robinson	4.00
250	Stan Musial	5.00

Timeless Tributes Gold

Gold (1-200):	4-8X
Gold (201-225):	.4-.75X
Gold (226-250):	2-4X
Production 50 Sets	

Timeless Tributes Silver

Gold (1-200):	2-4X
Gold (201-225):	.25X
Gold (226-250):	1-2X
Production 100 Sets	

Timeless Tributes Platinum
No Pricing
Production One Set

Classic Combos

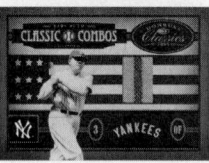

NM/M

Common Combo:	4.00
Production 400 Sets	
Gold:	2-4X
Production 25 Sets	
Platinum:	No Pricing
Production One Set	

33	Babe Ruth, Ted Williams	10.00
34	Roberto Clemente, Vladimir Guerrero	8.00
35	Willie Mays, Willie McCovey	8.00
36	Yogi Berra, Mike Piazza	6.00
37	Sandy Koufax, Nolan Ryan	30.00
38	Harmon Killebrew, Mike Schmidt	8.00
39	Whitey Ford, Randy Johnson	4.00
40	Cal Ripken Jr., George Brett	15.00
41	Hank Aaron, Stan Musial	8.00
42	Carl Yastrzemski, Frank Robinson	6.00
43	Bob Feller, Roger Clemens	6.00
44	Bob Gibson, Tom Seaver	4.00
45	Roger Maris, Jim Thome	4.00
46	Albert Pujols, Don Mattingly	8.00
47	Duke Snider, Sammy Sosa	4.00
48	Rickey Henderson, Bo Jackson	4.00
49	Ernie Banks, Reggie Jackson	4.00
50	Burleigh Grimes, Greg Maddux	6.00

Classic Combos Bat
No Pricing
Production Five Sets

Classic Combos Jersey
NM/M

Production 5-50
Prime: No Pricing
Production 1-5

38	Harmon Killebrew, Mike Schmidt/50	30.00
39	Whitey Ford, Randy Johnson/25	25.00
40	Cal Ripken Jr., George Brett/50	50.00
45	Roger Maris, Jim Thome/25	50.00
46	Albert Pujols, Don Mattingly/50	40.00
47	Duke Snider, Sammy Sosa/25	30.00
48	Rickey Henderson, Bo Jackson/50	25.00

Classic Combos Materials
NM/M

Production 1-25
Prime: No Pricing
Production Five Sets

46	Albert Pujols, Don Mattingly/25	50.00
48	Rickey Henderson, Bo Jackson/25	30.00

Classic Combos Materials HR
NM/M

Production 1-25

46	Albert Pujols, Don Mattingly/25	50.00
48	Rickey Henderson, Bo Jackson/25	30.00

Classic Combos Signature
No Pricing
Production One Set

Classic Combos Signature Bat
No Pricing
Production One Set

Classic Combos Signature Jersey
No Pricing
Production 1-5

Classic Combos Signature Material
No Pricing
Production One Set

Classic Combos Signature Materials HR
No Pricing
Production One Set

Classic Singles
NM/M

Complete Set (32):	120.00
Common Player:	3.00

Production 400 Sets	
Gold:	2-4X
Production 25 Sets	
Platinum:	No Pricing
Production One Set	

1	Hank Aaron	8.00
2	Tom Seaver	4.00
3	Harmon Killebrew	4.00
4	Paul Molitor	4.00
5	Brooks Robinson	4.00
6	Stan Musial	5.00
7	Bobby Doerr	3.00
8	Cal Ripken Jr.	12.00
9	Phil Niekro	3.00
10	Eddie Murray	4.00
11	Randy Johnson	4.00
12	Steve Carlton	3.00
13	Rickey Henderson	3.00
14	Ernie Banks	4.00
15	Curt Schilling	4.00
16	Whitey Ford	4.00
17	Al Kaline	4.00
18	Gary Carter	3.00
19	Robin Yount	4.00
20	Johnny Bench	4.00
21	Bob Feller	3.00
22	Jim Palmer	3.00
23	Don Mattingly	6.00
24	Willie Mays	6.00
25	Dave Righetti	3.00
26	Roger Clemens	6.00
27	Juan Marichal	3.00
28	Tony Gwynn	4.00
29	Nolan Ryan	8.00
30	Carlton Fisk	3.00
31	Greg Maddux	5.00
32	Sandy Koufax	25.00

Classic Singles Bat
NM/M

Production 25-50

1	Hank Aaron/25	50.00
2	Tom Seaver/50	15.00
4	Paul Molitor/50	15.00
5	Brooks Robinson/50	15.00
6	Stan Musial/25	30.00
7	Bobby Doerr/25	10.00
8	Cal Ripken Jr./25	70.00
9	Phil Niekro/50	8.00
10	Eddie Murray/50	15.00
11	Randy Johnson/25	20.00
12	Steve Carlton/25	10.00
13	Rickey Henderson/50	8.00
14	Ernie Banks/50	20.00
17	Al Kaline/25	25.00
18	Gary Carter/50	8.00
19	Robin Yount/50	15.00
20	Johnny Bench/25	20.00
23	Don Mattingly/25	30.00
24	Willie Mays/25	50.00
28	Tony Gwynn/50	15.00
29	Nolan Ryan/25	40.00
30	Carlton Fisk/50	15.00

Classic Singles Jersey
NM/M

Production 10-100
Prime: No Pricing
Production 1-5

2	Tom Seaver/25	20.00
3	Harmon Killebrew/25	15.00
4	Paul Molitor/50	15.00
5	Brooks Robinson/50	15.00
7	Bobby Doerr/Pants/100	15.00
8	Cal Ripken Jr./25	70.00
9	Phil Niekro/50	8.00
10	Eddie Murray/50	15.00
11	Randy Johnson/100	12.00
12	Steve Carlton/25	12.00
13	Rickey Henderson/100	12.00
14	Ernie Banks/25	25.00
15	Curt Schilling/25	15.00
16	Whitey Ford/25	20.00
18	Gary Carter/100	8.00
19	Robin Yount/50	15.00
20	Johnny Bench/25	15.00
21	Bob Feller/Pants/25	20.00
22	Jim Palmer/100	8.00
23	Don Mattingly/100	25.00
24	Willie Mays/50	50.00
25	Dave Righetti/50	8.00
26	Roger Clemens/25	25.00
27	Juan Marichal/50	10.00
28	Tony Gwynn/100	15.00
29	Nolan Ryan/50	30.00
30	Carlton Fisk/25	15.00
31	Greg Maddux/100	15.00
32	Sandy Koufax/25	375.00

Classic Singles Materials
NM/M

Production 10-25
Prime: No Pricing
Production 10-25

2	Tom Seaver/Bat-Jsy/25	20.00
3	Harmon Killebrew/Bat-Jys/25	20.00
4	Paul Molitor/Bat-Jsy/25	20.00
5	Brooks Robinson/Bat-Jsy/25	20.00
7	Bobby Doerr/Bat-Pants/25	10.00
11	Randy Johnson/Bat-Jsy/25	15.00
12	Steve Carlton/Bat-Jsy/25	15.00

13 Rickey Henderson/
Bat-Jsy/25 30.00
18 Gary Carter/Bat-Jsy/25 15.00
19 Robin Yount/Bat-Jsy/25 25.00
20 Johnny Bench/Bat-Jsy/25 25.00
23 Don Mattingly/Bat-Jsy/25 35.00
28 Tony Gwynn/Bat-Jsy/25 25.00
29 Nolan Ryan/Bat-Jsy/25 40.00
30 Carlton Fisk/Bat-Jsy/25 15.00

Classic Singles Materials HR

NM/M

Production 10-25
2 Tom Seaver/Bat-Jsy/25 20.00
3 Harmon Killebrew/
Bat-Jsy/25 25.00
4 Paul Molitor/Bat-Jsy/25 20.00
5 Brooks Robinson/
Bat-Jsy/25 20.00
7 Bobby Doerr/Bat-Pants/25 10.00
11 Randy Johnson/Bat-Jsy/25 20.00
12 Steve Carlton/Bat-Pants/25 15.00
13 Rickey Henderson/
Bat-Jsy/25 30.00
18 Gary Carter/Bat-Jsy/25 15.00
19 Robin Yount/Bat-Jsy/25 25.00
20 Johnny Bench/Bat-Jsy/25 25.00
23 Don Mattingly/Bat-Jsy/25 35.00
24 Willie Mays/Bat-Jsy/10
28 Tony Gwynn/Bat-Jsy/25 25.00

Classic Singles Signature

No Pricing
Production 1-5

Classic Singles Signature Bat

No Pricing
Production 1-10

Classic Singles Signature Jersey

No Pricing
Production 1-5

Classic Singles Signture Materials

No Pricing
Production 1-10

Classic Singles Signature Materials HR

No Pricing
Production 1-10

Dress Code Bat

NM/M

Production 50-100
1 Albert Pujols/100 25.00
2 Bernie Williams/50 10.00
4 Carlos Beltran/100 10.00
5 Chipper Jones/100 10.00
7 David Ortiz/100 12.00
8 Hank Blalock/100 6.00
9 Hideki Matsui/100 30.00
10 Jim Edmonds/100 8.00
11 Jim Thome/100 10.00
14 Mark Prior/50 8.00
15 Mark Teixeira/100 6.00
16 Miguel Cabrera/100 8.00
17 Miguel Tejada/100 6.00
18 Mike Piazza/100 12.00
22 Sammy Sosa/100 12.00
23 Scott Rolen/100 10.00
26 Torii Hunter/100 6.00
30 Vladimir Guerrero/100 10.00

Dress Code Jersey Number

NM/M

Production 5-57
1 Albert Pujols/5
2 Bernie Williams/51 10.00
4 Carlos Beltran/15 20.00
6 Curt Schilling/38 15.00
7 David Ortiz/34 20.00
9 Hideki Matsui/55 30.00
11 Jim Thome/25 15.00
12 Johan Santana/57 12.00
13 Mark Mulder/20 10.00
14 Mark Prior/22 15.00
15 Mark Teixeira/23 10.00
16 Miguel Cabrera/24 15.00
18 Mike Piazza/31 20.00
19 Pedro J. Martinez/45 10.00
20 Randy Johnson/Pants/51 12.00
21 Roger Clemens/23 25.00
22 Sammy Sosa/21 20.00
23 Scott Rolen/27 15.00
26 Torii Hunter/48 6.00
27 Travis Hafner/48 6.00
29 Victor Martinez/51 8.00
30 Vladimir Guerrero/27 20.00

Dress Code Jersey Prime

NM/M

Production 25 Sets
1 Albert Pujols 75.00
2 Bernie Williams 20.00
3 Carl Crawford 12.00
4 Carlos Beltran 25.00
5 Chipper Jones 30.00
6 Curt Schilling 30.00
7 David Ortiz 30.00
8 Hank Blalock 20.00
10 Jim Edmonds 20.00
11 Jim Thome 25.00
12 Johan Santana 30.00
13 Mark Mulder 20.00
14 Mark Prior 20.00
15 Mark Teixeira 15.00
16 Miguel Cabrera 25.00
17 Miguel Tejada 25.00
18 Mike Piazza 30.00
19 Pedro J. Martinez 25.00
20 Randy Johnson 30.00
21 Roger Clemens 50.00
22 Sammy Sosa 30.00
23 Scott Rolen 30.00
24 Tim Hudson 20.00
25 Todd Helton 20.00
26 Torii Hunter 15.00
27 Travis Hafner 10.00
28 Vernon Wells 10.00
29 Victor Martinez 15.00
30 Vladimir Guerrero 30.00

Dress Code Materials

NM/M

Production 5-100
Prime: No Pricing
Production Five Sets
1 Albert Pujols/Bat-Jsy/100 25.00
2 Bernie Williams/Bat-Jsy/50 10.00
4 Carlos Beltran/
Bat-Bat/Jsy/100 10.00
5 Chipper Jones/Bat-Jsy/100 12.00
6 Curt Schilling/Bat-Jsy/50 15.00
7 David Ortiz/Bat-Hat/100 15.00
8 Hank Blalock/Bat-Jsy/100 8.00
9 Hideki Matsui/Bat-Jsy/100 30.00
10 Jim Edmonds 10.00
11 Jim Thome/Jsy-Jsy/100 12.00
15 Mark Teixeira/Bat-Jsy/100 8.00
16 Miguel Cabrera/Jsy-Jsy/100 10.00
17 Miguel Tejada/Bat-Jsy/100 8.00
18 Mike Piazza/Bat-Jsy/100 12.00
19 Pedro J. Martinez/
Bat-Jsy/100 12.00
22 Sammy Sosa/Bat-Jsy/100 12.00
23 Scott Rolen/Bat-Jsy/100 12.00
25 Todd Helton/Jsy-Jsy/50 12.00
26 Torii Hunter/Bat-Jsy/100 8.00
27 Travis Hafner/Jsy-Shoes/50 8.00
28 Vernon Wells/Jsy-Jsy/50 8.00
29 Victor Martinez/Jsy-Jsy/50 8.00
30 Vladimir Guerrero/
Bat-Jsy/100 12.00

Dress Code Signature Bat

NM/M

Production 1-25
7 David Ortiz/25 50.00
8 Hank Blalock/25 30.00
16 Miguel Cabrera/25 50.00
26 Torii Hunter/25 30.00
27 Travis Hafner/25 25.00
28 Vernon Wells/25 25.00

Dress Code Signature Jersey

NM/M

Production 5-25
7 David Ortiz/25 50.00
8 Hank Blalock/25 30.00
12 Johan Santana/25 50.00
16 Miguel Cabrera/25 50.00
26 Torii Hunter/25 30.00
27 Travis Hafner/25 25.00
28 Vernon Wells/25 25.00
29 Victor Martinez/25 25.00

Dress Code Sign. Jersey Number

NM/M

Production 1-25
Prime: No Pricing
Production 1-5
7 David Ortiz/25 50.00
8 Hank Blalock/25 30.00
12 Johan Santana/25 50.00
26 Torii Hunter/25 30.00
27 Travis Hafner/25 25.00
29 Victor Martinez/25 25.00

Dress Code Signature Materials

No Pricing
Production 1-5

Home Run Heroes

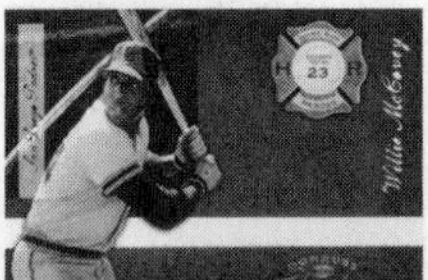

NM/M

Complete Set (50): 90.00
Common Player: 1.50
Production 1,000 Sets
Gold: 2-4X
Production 50 Sets
Platinum: No Pricing
Production One Set
1 Mike Schmidt 4.00
2 Ken Griffey Jr. 4.00
3 Babe Ruth 6.00
4 Duke Snider 2.00
5 Johnny Bench 3.00
6 Stan Musial 3.00
7 Willie McCovey 2.00
8 Willie Stargell 2.00
9 Ted Williams 5.00
10 Frank Thomas 2.00
11 Gary Sheffield 2.00
12 Jim Thome 2.00
13 Harmon Killebrew 2.00
14 Ernie Banks 3.00
15 George Foster 1.50
16 Albert Pujols 5.00
17 Tony Perez 1.50
18 Richie Sexson 1.50
19 Juan Gonzalez 1.50
20 Frank Robinson 2.00
21 Sammy Sosa 3.00
22 Jeff Bagwell 1.50
23 Mark Teixeira 1.50
24 Willie Mays 5.00
25 Rafael Palmeiro 2.00
26 Billy Williams 1.50
27 Vladimir Guerrero 2.00
28 Gary Carter 2.00
29 Fred McGriff 1.50
30 Orlando Cepeda 1.50
31 Dave Winfield 2.00
32 Shawn Green 1.50
33 Jose Canseco 1.50
34 Hideki Matsui 4.00
35 Roger Maris 4.00
36 Andre Dawson 2.00
37 Paul Konerko 1.50
38 Darryl Strawberry 1.50
39 Dave Parker 1.50
40 Adam Dunn 2.00
41 Ralph Kiner 2.00
42 Miguel Tejada 2.00
43 Dale Murphy 2.00
44 Hank Aaron 6.00
45 Mike Piazza 3.00
46 Reggie Jackson 2.00
47 Adrian Beltre 2.00
48 Cal Ripken Jr. 8.00
49 Manny Ramirez 3.00
50 Alex Rodriguez 5.00

Home Run Heroes Jersey HR

NM/M

Production 1-66
Prime: No Pricing
Production One Set
1 Mike Schmidt/48 25.00
3 Babe Ruth/25 165.00
5 Johnny Bench/45 15.00
7 Willie McCovey/23 15.00
8 Willie Stargell/48 15.00
9 Ted Williams/43 60.00
10 Frank Thomas/43 12.00
11 Gary Sheffield/36 8.00
12 Jim Thome/47 15.00
13 Harmon Killebrew/49 20.00
14 Ernie Banks Pants/47 20.00
15 Gene Foster/25 10.00
16 Albert Pujols/46 35.00
18 Richie Sexson/45 8.00
19 Juan Gonzalez/47 8.00
21 Sammy Sosa/66 12.00
22 Jeff Bagwell/47 10.00
23 Mark Teixeira/38 8.00
24 Willie Mays/51 50.00
25 Rafael Palmeiro/47 10.00
26 Billy Williams/26 10.00
27 Vladimir Guerrero/44 12.00
28 Gary Carter/31 10.00
29 Fred McGriff/32 12.00
30 Orlando Cepeda/Pants/46 8.00
31 Dave Winfield/34 10.00
32 Shawn Green/49 8.00
33 Jose Canseco/44 10.00
34 Hideki Matsui/Pants/31 40.00
35 Roger Maris/Pants/19 50.00
36 Andre Dawson/49 8.00
38 Darryl Strawberry/24 10.00
39 Dave Parker/34 8.00
40 Adam Dunn/46 10.00
42 Miguel Tejada/34 10.00
43 Dale Murphy/44 12.00
44 Hank Aaron/47 50.00
45 Mike Piazza/40 15.00
46 Reggie Jackson/39 12.00
47 Adrian Beltre/48 8.00
48 Cal Ripken Jr./34 50.00
49 Manny Ramirez/43 12.00

Home Run Heroes Materials

NM/M

Production 1-66
Prime: No Pricing
Production One Set
1 Mike Schmidt/Bat-Jsy/48 30.00
3 Babe Ruth/Bat-Jsy/25 300.00
5 Johnny Bench/Bat-Jsy/45 20.00
7 Willie McCovey/Bat-Jsy/23 20.00
8 Willie Stargell/Bat-Jsy/48 20.00
9 Ted Williams/Bat-Jsy/43 85.00
10 Frank Thomas/Jsy-Jsy/43 15.00
11 Gary Sheffield/Bat-Jsy/36 10.00
12 Jim Thome/Bat-Jsy/47 15.00
13 Harmon Killebrew/
Bat-Jsy/49 25.00
14 Ernie Banks/Bat-Pants/47 25.00
15 George Foster/Bat-Jsy/52 10.00
16 Albert Pujols/Jsy-Jsy/46 40.00
17 Tony Perez/Bat-Fld Glv/24 15.00
18 Richie Sexson/Bat-Jsy/45 10.00
19 Juan Gonzalez/Bat-Jsy/47 10.00
21 Sammy Sosa/Bat-Jsy/66 15.00
22 Jeff Bagwell/Bat-Jsy/47 12.00
23 Mark Teixeira/Bat-Jsy/38 10.00
24 Willie Mays/Bat-Jsy/51 50.00
25 Rafael Palmeiro/Bat-Jsy/47 12.00
26 Billy Williams/Bat-Jsy/26 10.00
27 Vladimir Guerrero/
Bat-Jsy/44 15.00
28 Gary Carter/Bat-Jsy/31 12.00
29 Fred McGriff/Bat-Jsy/32 15.00
30 Orlando Cepeda/
Bat-Pants/34 12.00
31 Dave Winfield/Bat-Jsy/34 15.00
32 Shawn Green/Bat-Jsy/49 10.00
33 Jose Canseco/Hat-Jsy/44 12.00
34 Hideki Matsui/Bat-Pants/31 60.00
35 Roger Maris/Bat-Pants/19 50.00
36 Andre Dawson/Bat-Jsy/49 10.00
38 Darryl Strawberry/
Jsy-Pants/24 12.00
39 Dave Parker/Bat-Jsy/34 12.00
40 Adam Dunn/Bat-Jsy/46 15.00
42 Miguel Tejada/Bat-Jsy/34 15.00
43 Dale Murphy/Jsy-Jsy/44 15.00
44 Hank Aaron/Bat-Jsy/47 50.00
45 Mike Piazza/Jsy-Jsy/40 15.00
46 Reggie Jackson/Bat-Jsy/39 15.00
47 Adrian Beltre/Bat-Jsy/48 12.00
48 Cal Ripken Jr./Bat-Jsy/34 60.00
49 Manny Ramirez/Jsy-Jsy/43 15.00

Home Rune Heroes Signature

No Pricing
Production 1-10

Home Run Heroes Signature Materials

No Pricing
Production 1-10

Legendary Lumberjacks

NM/M

Common Player: 2.00
Production 400 Sets
Gold: 2-4X
Production 50 Sets
Platinum: No Pricing
Production One Set
1 Al Kaline 4.00
2 Babe Ruth 8.00
3 Billy Williams 2.00
4 Bob Feller 3.00
5 Bob Gibson 3.00
6 Brooks Robinson 4.00
7 Cal Ripken Jr. 10.00
8 Carlton Fisk 3.00
9 Dennis Eckersley 2.00
10 Don Mattingly 6.00
11 Duke Snider 3.00
12 Eddie Murray 3.00
13 Ernie Banks 4.00
14 Fergie Jenkins 2.00
15 Frank Robinson 4.00
16 Gaylord Perry 2.00
17 George Brett 6.00
18 George Kell 2.00
19 Harmon Killebrew 4.00
20 Jim Palmer 2.00
21 Joe Morgan 2.00
22 Johnny Bench 5.00
23 Juan Marichal 2.00
24 Lou Brock 3.00
25 Maury Wills 2.00
26 Mike Schmidt 6.00
27 Nolan Ryan 8.00
28 Ozzie Smith 4.00
29 Paul Molitor 3.00
30 Pee Wee Reese 2.00
31 Phil Niekro 2.00
32 Phil Rizzuto 3.00
33 Ralph Kiner 2.00
34 Reggie Jackson 3.00
35 Rickey Henderson 3.00
36 Roberto Clemente 8.00
37 Robin Yount 4.00
38 Rod Carew 2.00
39 Roger Maris 5.00
40 Stan Musial 5.00
41 Steve Carlton 2.00
42 Ted Williams 8.00
43 Tom Seaver 3.00
44 Tony Gwynn 3.00
45 Tony Perez 2.00
46 Wade Boggs 3.00
47 Warren Spahn 4.00
48 Whitey Ford 4.00
49 Willie McCovey 3.00
50 Yogi Berra 4.00

Legendary Lumberjacks Bat

NM/M

Production 1-50
2 Babe Ruth/25 200.00
6 Brooks Robinson/50 15.00
7 Cal Ripken Jr./50 50.00
8 Carlton Fisk/50 10.00
10 Don Mattingly/50 25.00

12	Eddie Murray/50	15.00
13	Ernie Banks/50	15.00
15	Frank Robinson/50	15.00
17	George Brett/50	15.00
19	Harmon Killebrew/50	15.00
21	Joe Morgan/50	10.00
22	Johnny Bench/50	15.00
24	Lou Brock/50	10.00
26	Mike Schmidt/50	20.00
28	Ozzie Smith/50	15.00
29	Paul Molitor/50	12.00
30	Pee Wee Reese/50	10.00
34	Reggie Jackson/50	12.00
35	Rickey Henderson/50	12.00
36	Roberto Clemente/50	50.00
37	Robin Yount/50	15.00
38	Rod Carew/50	10.00
39	Roger Maris/25	40.00
40	Stan Musial/25	25.00
42	Ted Williams/25	60.00
44	Tony Gwynn/50	15.00
46	Wade Boggs/50	12.00
49	Willie McCovey/50	12.00
50	Yogi Berra/25	25.00

Legendary Lumberjacks Jersey

NM/M

Production 1-50

3	Billy Williams/25	12.00
6	Brooks Robinson/25	20.00
7	Cal Ripken Jr./50	50.00
8	Carlton Fisk/25	15.00
10	Don Mattingly/50	25.00
12	Eddie Murray/50	15.00
13	Ernie Banks/25	20.00
19	Harmon Killebrew/25	20.00
22	Johnny Bench/25	20.00
24	Lou Brock/25	12.00
25	Maury Wills/25	12.00
26	Mike Schmidt/25	25.00
28	Ozzie Smith/25	20.00
29	Paul Molitor/25	12.00
34	Reggie Jackson/25	15.00
35	Rickey Henderson/50	12.00
37	Robin Yount/50	15.00

Legendary Lumberjacks Jersey HR

NM/M

Production 1-25

6	Brooks Robinson/25	20.00
7	Cal Ripken Jr./25	60.00
10	Don Mattingly/25	30.00
12	Eddie Murray/25	20.00
29	Paul Molitor/25	20.00
35	Rickey Henderson/25	20.00
37	Robin Yount/25	20.00
44	Tony Gwynn/25	20.00
45	Tony Perez/25	15.00
46	Wade Boggs/25	15.00
49	Willie McCovey/25	15.00

Legendary Lumberjacks Materials

NM/M

Production 1-50

2	Babe Ruth/Bat-Jsy/25	300.00
6	Brooks Robinson/Bat-Jsy/50	20.00
7	Cal Ripken Jr./Bat-Jsy/50	60.00
8	Carlton Fisk/Bat-Jsy/25	15.00
10	Don Mattingly/Bat-Jsy/50	30.00
12	Eddie Murray/Bat-Jsy/50	15.00
13	Ernie Banks/Bat-Jsy/25	25.00
19	Harmon Killebrew/Bat-Jsy/25	25.00
22	Johnny Bench/Bat-Jsy/50	20.00
24	Lou Brock/Bat-Jsy/50	12.00
26	Mike Schmidt/Bat-Jsy/50	25.00
29	Paul Molitor/Bat-Jsy/50	20.00
34	Reggie Jackson/Bat-Jsy/50	20.00
35	Rickey Henderson/Bat-Jsy/50	15.00
37	Robin Yount/Bat-Jsy/50	20.00
38	Rod Carew/Bat-Jsy/50	20.00
44	Tony Gwynn/Bat-Jsy/50	20.00
46	Wade Boggs/Bat-Jsy/50	15.00
49	Willie McCovey/Bat-Jsy/44	15.00

Legendary Players

NM/M

Common Player:	1.50

Production 800 Sets

Gold:	2-3X

Production 75 Sets

Platinum:	No Pricing

Production One Set

1	Al Kaline	3.00
2	Babe Ruth	6.00
3	Billy Williams	1.50
4	Bob Feller	2.00
5	Bob Gibson	2.00
6	Brooks Robinson	2.00
7	Cal Ripken Jr.	8.00
8	Carlton Fisk	2.00
9	Dennis Eckersley	2.00
10	Don Mattingly	5.00
11	Duke Snider	2.00
12	Eddie Murray	2.00
13	Ernie Banks	3.00
14	Fergie Jenkins	1.50
15	Frank Robinson	3.00
16	Gaylord Perry	1.50
17	George Brett	5.00
18	George Kell	1.50
19	Harmon Killebrew	3.00
20	Jim Palmer	1.50
21	Joe Morgan	1.50
22	Johnny Bench	4.00
23	Juan Marichal	1.50
24	Lou Brock	2.00
25	Maury Wills	1.50
26	Mike Schmidt	5.00
27	Nolan Ryan	6.00
28	Ozzie Smith	3.00
29	Paul Molitor	2.00
30	Pee Wee Reese	1.50
31	Phil Niekro	1.50
32	Phil Rizzuto	2.00
33	Ralph Kiner	1.50
34	Reggie Jackson	2.00
35	Rickey Henderson	2.00
36	Roberto Clemente	6.00
37	Robin Yount	3.00
38	Rod Carew	2.00
39	Roger Maris	4.00
40	Stan Musial	4.00
41	Steve Carlton	1.50
42	Ted Williams	6.00
43	Tom Seaver	2.00
44	Tony Gwynn	2.00
45	Tony Perez	1.50
46	Wade Boggs	2.00
47	Warren Spahn	3.00
48	Whitey Ford	3.00
49	Willie McCovey	2.00
50	Yogi Berra	4.00

Legendary Players Hat

NM/M

Production 1-25

10	Don Mattingly/25	30.00
13	Ernie Banks/25	20.00
17	George Brett/25	30.00
20	Jim Palmer/25	10.00
26	Mike Schmidt/25	30.00
28	Ozzie Smith/25	25.00
37	Robin Yount/25	25.00
44	Tony Gwynn/25	25.00

Legendary Players Jacket

NM/M

Production 25 Sets

7	Cal Ripken Jr.	60.00
8	Carlton Fisk	12.00
10	Don Mattingly	40.00
24	Lou Brock	15.00
26	Mike Schmidt	35.00
27	Nolan Ryan	50.00
34	Reggie Jackson	15.00
35	Rickey Henderson	20.00
38	Rod Carew	20.00
42	Ted Williams	85.00

Legendary Players Jersey Number

NM/M

Production 1-44

Prime:	No Pricing

Production One Set

3	Billy Williams/26	10.00
8	Carlton Fisk/72	10.00
9	Dennis Eckersley/43	10.00
10	Don Mattingly/23	30.00
12	Eddie Murray/33	15.00
16	Gaylord Perry/36	8.00
20	Jim Palmer/22	10.00
23	Juan Marichal/27	10.00
24	Lou Brock/20	15.00
25	Maury Wills/30	8.00
26	Mike Schmidt/20	30.00
27	Nolan Ryan/34	40.00
31	Phil Niekro/35	8.00
35	Rickey Henderson/24	15.00
37	Robin Yount/19	25.00
38	Rod Carew/29	15.00
41	Steve Carlton/32	10.00
43	Tom Seaver/41	15.00
44	Tony Gwynn/19	20.00
45	Tony Perez/24	10.00
46	Wade Boggs/26	15.00
47	Warren Spahn/24	20.00
49	Willie McCovey/44	12.00

Legendary Players Leather

NM/M

Production 10-25

10	Don Mattingly/Btg Glv/25	40.00
14	Fergie Jenkins/Fld Glv/25	15.00
26	Mike Schmidt/Fld Glv/25	40.00
35	Rickey Henderson/Btg Glv/25	25.00
41	Steve Carlton/Fld Glv/25	15.00
44	Tony Gwynn/Btg Glv/25	30.00
45	Tony Perez/Fld Glv/25	15.00

Legendary Players Pants

NM/M

Production 1-25

4	Bob Feller/19	20.00
7	Cal Ripken Jr./25	60.00
11	Duke Snider/25	20.00
12	Eddie Murray/25	20.00
14	Fergie Jenkins/25	10.00
20	Jim Palmer/25	10.00
23	Juan Marichal/25	10.00
28	Ozzie Smith/25	25.00
29	Paul Molitor/25	15.00
35	Rickey Henderson/25	20.00
38	Rod Carew/25	15.00
39	Roger Maris/25	50.00
43	Tom Seaver/25	15.00
44	Tony Gwynn/25	20.00
47	Warren Spahn/24	20.00
49	Willie McCovey/25	15.00

Legendary Players Signature

No Pricing

Production 1-10

Legendary Players Spikes

NM/M

Production 1-25

15	Frank Robinson/25	20.00
44	Tony Gwynn/25	30.00

Membership

NM/M

Common Player:	1.50

Production 1,000 Sets

Gold:	2-4X

Production 50 Sets

Platinum:	No Pricing

Production One Set

1	Bobby Doerr	1.50
2	Tom Seaver	2.00
3	Cal Ripken Jr.	8.00
4	Paul Molitor	2.00
5	Brooks Robinson	2.00
6	Al Kaline	4.00
7	Steve Carlton	2.00
8	Carl Yastrzemski	4.00
9	Bob Feller	2.00
10	Fred Lynn	1.50
11	Luis Aparicio	1.50
12	Hank Aaron	6.00
13	Willie Mays	6.00
14	Bob Gibson	3.00
15	Joe Morgan	2.00
16	Whitey Ford	3.00
17	Don Sutton	1.50
18	Harmon Killebrew	3.00
19	Tony Gwynn	3.00
20	Lou Brock	1.50
21	Dennis Eckersley	1.50
22	Jim Palmer	1.50
23	Don Mattingly	5.00
24	Carlton Fisk	2.00
25	Gaylord Perry	1.50
26	Mike Schmidt	5.00
27	Nolan Ryan	6.00
28	Sandy Koufax	10.00
29	Rod Carew	2.00
30	Maury Wills	1.50

Membership VIP Bat

NM/M

Production 25 Sets

1	Bobby Doerr	10.00
2	Tom Seaver	20.00
3	Cal Ripken Jr.	60.00
4	Paul Molitor	15.00
5	Brooks Robinson	15.00
6	Al Kaline	15.00
7	Steve Carlton	10.00
8	Carl Yastrzemski	20.00
10	Fred Lynn	8.00
11	Luis Aparicio	8.00
12	Hank Aaron	40.00
13	Willie Mays	50.00
15	Joe Morgan	20.00
18	Harmon Killebrew	20.00
19	Tony Gwynn	20.00
20	Lou Brock	15.00
23	Don Mattingly	30.00
24	Carlton Fisk	15.00
29	Rod Carew	12.00

Membership VIP Jersey

NM/M

Production 5-50

Prime:	No Pricing

Production One Set

7	Steve Carlton/25	10.00
10	Fred Lynn/25	10.00
11	Luis Aparicio/25	10.00
15	Joe Morgan/25	10.00
17	Don Sutton/50	8.00
19	Tony Gwynn/50	15.00
20	Lou Brock/25	15.00
21	Dennis Eckersley/50	8.00
22	Jim Palmer/25	10.00
23	Don Mattingly/25	30.00
24	Carlton Fisk/25	15.00
25	Gaylord Perry/50	8.00
26	Mike Schmidt/50	20.00
27	Nolan Ryan/50	40.00
29	Rod Carew/50	10.00

Membership VIP Materials

NM/M

Production 5-25

Prime:	No Pricing

Production One Set

1	Bobby Doerr/Bat-Pants/25	10.00
2	Tom Seaver/Bat-Jsy/25	20.00
3	Cal Ripken Jr./Bat-Jsy/25	75.00
4	Paul Molitor/Bat-Jsy/25	20.00
5	Brooks Robinson/Bat-Jsy/25	25.00
7	Steve Carlton/Bat-Jsy/25	15.00
10	Fred Lynn/Bat-Jsy/25	10.00
11	Luis Aparicio/Bat-Jsy/25	10.00
15	Joe Morgan/Bat-Jsy/25	12.00
18	Harmon Killebrew/Bat-Jsy/25	25.00
19	Tony Gwynn/Bat-Jsy/25	25.00
20	Lou Brock/Bat-Jsy/25	25.00
23	Don Mattingly/Bat-Jsy/25	35.00
27	Nolan Ryan/Bat-Jsy/25	50.00
29	Rod Carew/Bat-Jsy/25	20.00

Membership VIP Materials Awards

No Pricing

Production 5-10

Membership VIP Materials HOF

No Pricing

Production 10 Sets

Membership VIP Materials HR

NM/M

Production 6-49

1	Bobby Doerr/Jsy-Pants/27	15.00
3	Cal Ripken Jr./Jsy-Pants/34	60.00
4	Paul Molitor/Bat-Jsy/22	15.00
8	Carl Yastrzemski/Bat-Jsy/44	25.00
10	Fred Lynn/Bat-Jsy/39	8.00
12	Hank Aaron/Bat-Jsy/47	50.00
15	Joe Morgan/Bat-Jsy/27	12.00
18	Harmon Killebrew/Bat-Jsy/49	20.00
20	Lou Brock/Bat-Jsy/21	15.00
23	Don Mattingly/Bat-Jsy/35	40.00
24	Carlton Fisk/Bat-Jsy/37	15.00
26	Mike Schmidt/Bat-Jsy/48	25.00

Membership VIP Materials Stats

No Pricing

Production 10 Sets

Membership VIP Signature

No Pricing

Production 1-5

Membership VIP Signature Bat

No Pricing

Production 1-10

Membership VIP Signature Jersey

No Pricing

Production 1-10

Membership VIP Signature Material

NM/M

Production 1-25

Prime:	No Pricing

Production One Set

1	Bobby Doerr/Bat-Pants/25	35.00
10	Fred Lynn/Bat-Jsy/25	30.00
11	Luis Aparicio/Bat-Jsy/25	30.00
20	Lou Brock/Bat-Jsy/25	50.00

Membership VIP Signature Material Awards

No Pricing

Production 1-10

Membership VIP Signature Materials HOF

No Pricing

Production 1-10

Membership VIP Signature Materials HR

No Pricing

Production 1-10

Membership VIP Signature Material Stats

No Pricing

Production 5-10

Significant Signatures Silver

NM/M

Production 1-200

Gold:	.75-1.5X

Production 1-100

No pricing 20 or less.

Platinum:	No Pricing

Production One Set

17	Jay Gibbons/25	15.00
22	Tim Salmon/100	15.00
23	Kevin Youkilis/25	12.00
29	Cliff Lee/200	15.00

37	Jeff Suppan/200	10.00
39	Larry Bigbie/100	15.00
40	Rich Harden/100	15.00
41	Victor Martinez/25	20.00
43	Joey Gathright/100	8.00
61	Jake Peavy/25	40.00
63	Dioner Navarro/100	15.00
64	Kazuhito Tadano/100	15.00
65	Ryan Wagner/50	10.00
66	Abe Alvarez/100	15.00
68	Jermaine Dye/25	15.00
69	Todd Walker/25	15.00
70	Octavio Dotel/25	15.00
73	Scott Podsednik/25	20.00
76	Raul Ibanez/50	10.00
77	Orlando Cabrera/25	20.00
79	Esteban Loaiza/50	15.00
84	David Dellucci/50	20.00
85	Travis Blackley/200	8.00
86	Brad Penny/25	15.00
88	Brian Roberts/100	35.00
90	Mike Lieberthal/25	15.00
94	Milton Bradley/100	15.00
96	Adrian Gonzalez/200	12.00
97	Chad Tracy/100	10.00
98	Chad Cordero/100	8.00
100	Jason Kubel/200	12.00
102	Jack Wilson/100	10.00
104	Casey Kotchman/100	12.00
106	Melvin Mora/100	15.00
107	Bobby Crosby/100	15.00
111	Francisco Cordero/50	15.00
114	Eric Byrnes/50	10.00
118	Shea Hillenbrand/25	15.00
119	Aubrey Huff/25	20.00
120	Lew Ford/25	20.00
126	Adam LaRoche/25	15.00
128	Ken Harvey/50	10.00
132	Russ Ortiz/25	15.00
133	Jason Varitek	10.00
136	Joe Nathan/100	20.00
138	Carlos Zambrano/25	35.00
143	John Lackey/200	10.00
145	Dewon Brazelton/200	10.00
146	Jason Bay/25	25.00
148	Travis Hafner/100	12.00
152	Wade Miller/50	12.00
154	Scott Kazmir/25	35.00
156	Livan Hernandez/25	15.00
158	David Wright/25	85.00
159	Chone Figgins/50	12.00
163	Merkin Valdez/200	10.00
165	Alexis Rios/50	15.00
166	Johnny Estrada/200	10.00
167	Danny Graves/50	15.00
168	Carlos Lee/25	25.00
171	Randy Wolf/25	15.00
175	Edwin Jackson/25	12.00
178	Jacque Jones/25	15.00
180	Laynce Nix/200	10.00
181	Tom Gordon/25	15.00
182	Jose Castillo/100	12.00
188	Keith Foulke/25	60.00
189	Jeremy Bonderman/50	20.00
190	Troy Percival/25	15.00
194	Brett Myers/50	15.00
197	Lyle Overbay/25	20.00
202	Miguel Negron/100	8.00
204	Paulino Reynoso/100	8.00
205	Colter Bean/100	10.00
206	Raul Tablado/100	8.00
207	Mark McLemore/100	8.00
208	Russel Rohlicek/100	8.00
210	Chris Seddon/100	8.00
213	Mike Morse/100	20.00
217	Carlos Ruiz/100	15.00
218	Chris Roberson/100	8.00
219	Ryan Speier/100	8.00
221	Ambiorix Burgos/100	8.00
223	David Gassner/100	10.00
224	Sean Tracey/100	8.00
225	Casey Rogowski/100	8.00
236	Gaylord Perry/LGD/25	25.00
245	Bobby Doerr/LGD/25	25.00
246	Bob Feller/LGD/25	30.00

Stars of Summer

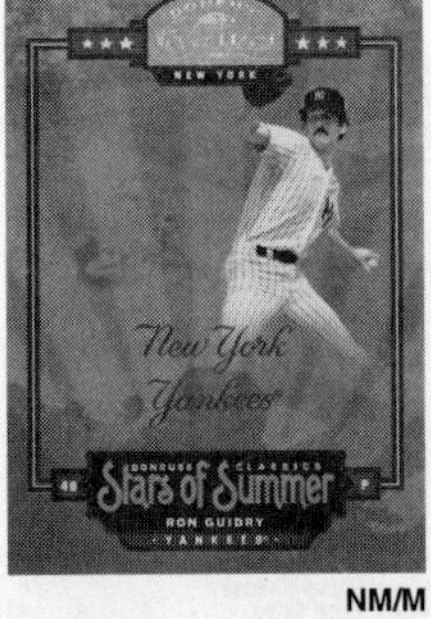

NM/M

Common Player: 1.50
Production 1,000 Sets
Gold: 2-4X
Production 50 Sets
Platinum: No Pricing
Production One Set

1	Andre Dawson	2.00
2	Bert Blyleven	2.00
3	Bill Madlock	1.50
4	Dale Murphy	3.00
5	Darryl Strawberry	2.00
6	Dave Parker	2.00
7	Dave Righetti	2.00
8	Dwight Evans	2.00
9	Dwight Gooden	2.00
10	Fred Lynn	1.50
11	George Foster	2.00
12	Harold Baines	2.00
13	Jack Morris	1.50
14	Jim Rice	3.00
15	Keith Hernandez	2.00
16	Kirk Gibson	2.00
17	Luis Aparicio	2.00
18	Mark Grace	2.00
19	Marty Marion	1.50
20	Orel Hershiser	2.00
21	Ron Guidry	3.00
22	Ron Santo	2.00
23	Steve Garvey	2.00
24	Tony Oliva	2.00
25	Will Clark	3.00

Stars of Summer Material

NM/M

Production 100-250

1	Andre Dawson/Jsy/250	8.00
2	Bert Blyleven/Jsy/150	8.00
3	Bill Madlock/Bat/250	5.00
4	Dale Murphy/Jsy/100	12.00
5	Darryl Strawberry/Jsy/250	8.00
6	Dave Parker/Jsy/100	10.00
7	Dave Righetti/Jsy/150	8.00
8	Dwight Evans/Bat/250	8.00
9	Dwight Gooden/Bat/150	8.00
10	Fred Lynn/Jsy/100	5.00
11	George Foster/Bat/250	5.00
12	Harold Baines/Jsy/250	5.00
13	Jack Morris/Jsy/100	5.00
14	Jim Rice/Pants/250	8.00
15	Keith Hernandez/Bat/100	5.00
16	Kirk Gibson/Jsy/250	8.00
17	Luis Aparicio/Bat/250	8.00
18	Mark Grace/Bat/250	10.00
22	Ron Santo/Bat/150	10.00
23	Steve Garvey/Jsy/250	8.00
24	Tony Oliva/Jsy/250	8.00
25	Will Clark/Bat/250	10.00

Stars of Summer Signature Material

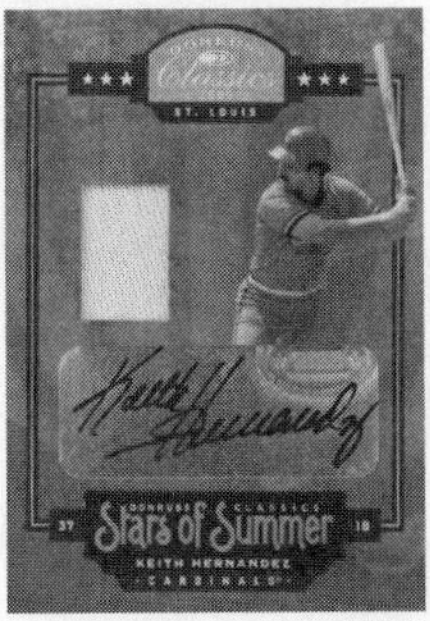

NM/M

Production 25-100

1	Andre Dawson/Jsy/100	20.00
2	Bert Blyleven/Jsy/50	20.00
3	Bill Madlock/Bat/100	20.00
4	Dale Murphy/Jsy/25	40.00
6	Dave Parker/Jsy/50	20.00
7	Dave Righetti/Jsy/50	20.00
8	Dwight Evans/Jsy/50	30.00
9	Dwight Gooden/Bat/25	25.00
10	Fred Lynn/Jsy/100	15.00
11	George Foster/Bat/50	20.00
12	Harold Baines/Jsy/100	25.00
13	Jack Morris/Jsy/100	15.00
14	Jim Rice/Pants/50	25.00
15	Keith Hernandez/Jsy/50	20.00
16	Kirk Gibson/Jsy/25	40.00
17	Luis Aparicio/Bat/50	20.00
18	Mark Grace/Bat/25	40.00
22	Ron Santo/Bat/50	35.00
23	Steve Garvey/Jsy/50	20.00
24	Tony Oliva/Jsy/50	20.00
25	Will Clark/Bat/25	40.00

Team Colors

NM/M

Common Player: 1.50
Production 800 Sets
Gold: 2-4X
Production 50 Sets
Platinum: No Pricing
Production One Set

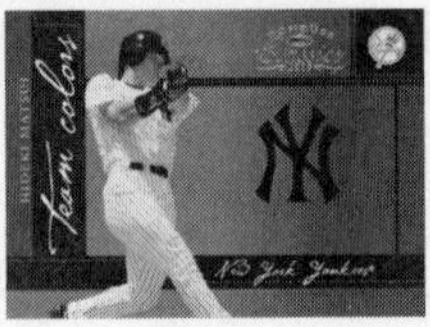

1	Adam Dunn	2.00
2	Albert Pujols	6.00
3	Andruw Jones	2.00
4	Aramis Ramirez	2.00
5	Aubrey Huff	1.50
6	Bobby Abreu	2.00
7	Cal Ripken Jr.	8.00
8	Carlos Lee	1.50
9	Craig Biggio	2.00
10	Derrek Lee	2.00
11	Garret Anderson	2.00
12	Gary Carter	2.00
13	Geoff Jenkins	1.50
14	Greg Maddux	4.00
15	Hank Blalock	2.00
16	Hideki Matsui	5.00
17	Jake Peavy	2.00
18	Jim Edmonds	2.00
19	Jim Palmer	2.00
20	Jose Guillen	1.50
21	Jose Vidro	1.50
22	Juan Pierre	1.50
23	Lew Ford	1.50
24	Lyle Overbay	1.50
25	Manny Ramirez	3.00
26	Mark Loretta	1.50
27	Mark Teixeira	3.00
28	Melvin Mora	1.50
29	Michael Young	2.00
30	Miguel Cabrera	4.00
31	Mike Lowell	1.50
32	Mike Mussina	2.00
33	Milton Bradley	2.00
34	Randy Johnson	4.00
35	Roger Clemens	6.00
36	Sean Casey	2.00
37	Shawn Green	2.00
38	Steve Carlton	2.00
39	Todd Helton	2.00
40	Travis Hafner	1.50

Team Colors Bat

NM/M

Production 100 Sets

1	Adam Dunn	8.00
2	Albert Pujols	20.00
3	Andruw Jones	5.00
4	Aramis Ramirez	8.00
7	Cal Ripken Jr.	30.00
9	Craig Biggio	8.00
10	Derrek Lee	8.00
11	Garret Anderson	5.00
12	Gary Carter	5.00
15	Hank Blalock	8.00
16	Hideki Matsui	30.00
18	Jim Edmonds	10.00
21	Jose Vidro	5.00
22	Juan Pierre	5.00
23	Lew Ford	5.00
27	Mark Teixeira	8.00
28	Melvin Mora	5.00
29	Michael Young	5.00
30	Miguel Cabrera	10.00
31	Mike Lowell	5.00
36	Sean Casey	5.00
37	Shawn Green	5.00

Team Colors Materials

NM/M

Production 25-100
Prime: No Pricing
Production Five Sets

1	Adam Dunn/Bat-Jsy/100	10.00
2	Albert Pujols/Bat-Jsy/100	25.00
3	Andruw Jones/Bat-Jsy/100	8.00
4	Aramis Ramirez/ Bat-Jsy/100	10.00
6	Bobby Abreu/Jsy-Jsy/100	10.00
7	Cal Ripken Jr./Bat-Jsy/100	40.00
8	Carlos Lee/Jsy-Jsy/100	8.00
9	Craig Biggio/Bat-Jsy/100	10.00
11	Garret Anderson/Bat-Jsy/50	8.00
12	Gary Carter/Bat-Jsy/50	8.00
13	Geoff Jenkins/Jsy-Pants/100	8.00
15	Hank Blalock/Bat-Jsy/100	10.00
16	Hideki Matsui/Bat-Jsy/50	45.00
18	Jim Edmonds/Bat-Jkt/100	12.00
19	Jim Palmer/Jsy-Pants/25	12.00
21	Jose Vidro/Bat-Jsy/50	8.00
23	Lew Ford/Bat-Jsy/100	8.00
25	Manny Ramirez/ Jsy-Jsy/100	15.00
27	Mark Teixeira/Bat-Jsy/100	10.00
28	Melvin Mora/Bat-Jsy/50	8.00
29	Michael Young/ Bat-Jsy/100	8.00
30	Miguel Cabrera/ Bat-Jsy/100	15.00
31	Mike Lowell/Bat-Jsy/100	8.00
36	Sean Casey/Bat-Jsy/100	8.00
37	Shawn Green/Bat-Jsy/100	8.00
39	Todd Helton/Jsy-Jsy/50	10.00

Team Colors Signature

NM/M

Production 1-25

4	Aramis Ramirez/25	40.00
5	Aubrey Huff/25	20.00
8	Carlos Lee/25	25.00
17	Jake Peavy/25	40.00
20	Jose Guillen/25	25.00
21	Jose Vidro/25	20.00
23	Lew Ford/25	20.00
24	Lyle Overbay/25	25.00
26	Mark Loretta/25	25.00
28	Melvin Mora/25	25.00
33	Milton Bradley/25	25.00
40	Travis Hafner/25	20.00

Team Colors Signature Bat

NM/M

Production 5-25

1	Adam Dunn/25	40.00
4	Aramis Ramirez/25	40.00
5	Aubrey Huff/25	20.00
10	Derrek Lee/25	35.00
11	Garret Anderson/25	25.00
15	Hank Blalock/25	30.00
21	Jose Vidro/25	20.00
23	Lew Ford/25	20.00
29	Michael Young/25	20.00

Team Colors Signature Jersey

NM/M

Production 1-25
Prime: No Pricing
Production One Set

1	Adam Dunn/25	40.00
4	Aramis Ramirez/25	40.00
5	Aubrey Huff/25	20.00
8	Carlos Lee/25	25.00
11	Garret Anderson/25	25.00
12	Gary Carter/25	25.00
15	Hank Blalock/25	30.00
21	Jose Vidro/25	20.00
23	Lew Ford/25	20.00
24	Lyle Overbay/25	25.00
28	Melvin Mora/25	25.00
29	Michael Young/25	20.00
40	Travis Hafner/25	20.00

Team Colors Signature Materials

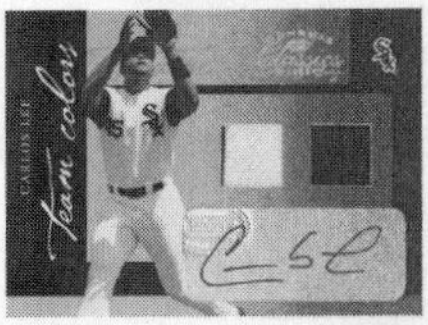

NM/M

Production 5-25
Prime: No Pricing
Production One Set

4	Aramis Ramirez/Bat-Jsy/25	50.00
5	Aubrey Huff/Jsy-Jsy/25	25.00
8	Carlos Lee/Jsy-Jsy/25	30.00
11	Garret Anderson/Bat-Jsy/25	30.00
15	Hank Blalock/Bat-Jsy/25	40.00
21	Jose Vidro/Bat-Jsy/25	25.00
23	Lew Ford/Bat-Jsy/25	25.00
28	Melvin Mora/Bat-Jsy/25	30.00
29	Michael Young/Bat-Jsy/25	30.00
40	Travis Hafner/Jsy-Jsy/25	25.00

2005 Donruss Classics Texas Rangers Hall of Fame

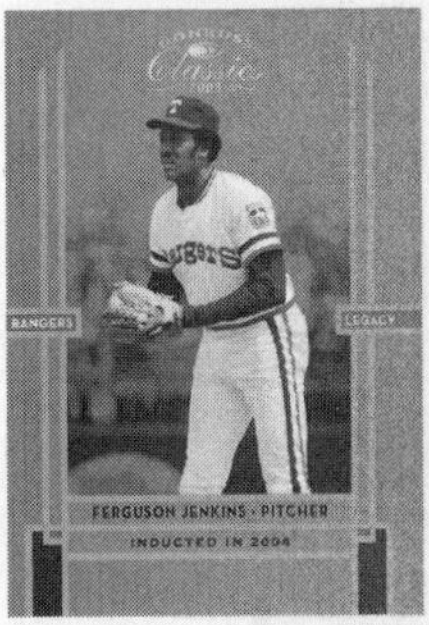

NM/M

Complete Set (9): 7.00
Common Player: .25

(1)	Buddy Bell	.50
(2)	Mark Holtz (Broadcaster)	.25
(3)	Charlie Hough	.50
(4)	Ferguson Jenkins	.50
(5)	Johnny Oates	.50
(6)	Nolan Ryan	5.00

(7) Jim Sundberg .50
(8) Tom Vandergriff (Broadcaster) .25
(9) John Wetteland .50

2005 Donruss Diamond Kings

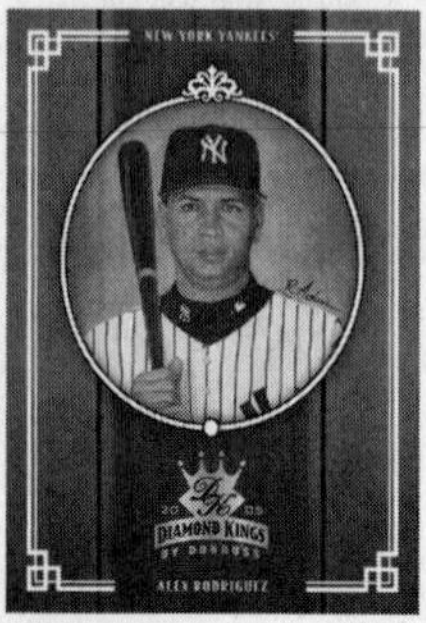

	NM/M
Complete Set (300):	85.00
Complete Update Set (150):	40.00
Common Player:	.25
Pack (5):	8.00
Box (12):	75.00
Update Pack (5):	5.00
Update Box (16):	75.00

1 Garret Anderson .40
2 Vladimir Guerrero .75
3 Jose Guillen .40
4 Troy Glaus .40
5 Tim Salmon .25
6 Casey Kotchman .25
7 Chone Figgins .25
8 Robb Quinlan .25
9 Francisco Rodriguez .25
10 Troy Percival .25
11 Randy Johnson .75
12 Brandon Webb .25
13 Richie Sexson .40
14 Shea Hillenbrand .25
15 Chad Tracy .25
16 Alex Cintron .25
17 Luis Gonzalez .25
18 Rafael Furcal .25
19 Andruw Jones .50
20 Marcus Giles .25
21 John Smoltz .50
22 Adam LaRoche .25
23 Russ Ortiz .25
24 J.D. Drew .25
25 Chipper Jones .75
26 Nick Green .25
27 Rafael Palmeiro .50
28 Miguel Tejada .50
29 Javy Lopez .25
30 Luis Matos .25
31 Larry Bigbie .25
32 Rodrigo Lopez .25
33 Brian Roberts .25
34 Melvin Mora .25
35 Adam Loewen .25
36 Manny Ramirez .75
37 Jason Varitek .50
38 Trot Nixon .25
39 Curt Schilling .75
40 Keith Foulke .25
41 Pedro Martinez .75
42 Johnny Damon .75
43 Kevin Youkilis .25
44 Orlando Cabrera .25
45 Abe Alvarez .25
46 David Ortiz .75
47 Kerry Wood .75
48 Mark Prior .75
49 Aramis Ramirez .50
50 Greg Maddux 1.00
51 Carlos Zambrano .40
52 Derrek Lee .50
53 Corey Patterson .40
54 Moises Alou .40
55 Matt Clement .25
56 Sammy Sosa 1.50
57 Nomar Garciaparra 1.00
58 Todd Walker .25
59 Angel Guzman .25
60 Magglio Ordonez .25
61 Carlos Lee .25
62 Joe Crede .25
63 Paul Konerko .25
64 Shingo Takatsu .25
65 Frank Thomas .50
66 Freddy Garcia .25
67 Aaron Rowand .25
68 Jose Contreras .25
69 Adam Dunn .50
70 Austin Kearns .25
71 Barry Larkin .40
72 Ken Griffey Jr. 1.00
73 Ryan Wagner .25
74 Sean Casey .25
75 Danny Graves .25
76 C.C. Sabathia .25
77 Jody Gerut .25
78 Omar Vizquel .25
79 Victor Martinez .40
80 Matt Lawton .25
81 Jake Westbrook .25
82 Kazuhito Tadano .25
83 Travis Hafner .25
84 Todd Helton .50
85 Preston Wilson .25
86 Matt Holiday .25
87 Jeromy Burnitz .25
88 Vinny Castilla .25
89 Jeremy Bonderman .25
90 Ivan Rodriguez .50
91 Carlos Guillen .25
92 Brandon Inge .25
93 Rondell White .25
94 Dontrelle Willis .25
95 Miguel Cabrera .75
96 Josh Beckett .40
97 Mike Lowell .25
98 Luis Castillo .25
99 Juan Pierre .25
100 Paul LoDuca .25
101 Guillermo Mota .25
102 Craig Biggio .25
103 Lance Berkman .25
104 Roy Oswalt .25
105 Roger Clemens 2.00
106 Jeff Kent .25
107 Morgan Ensberg .25
108 Jeff Bagwell .50
109 Carlos Beltran .50
110 Angel Berroa .25
111 Mike Sweeney .25
112 Jeremy Affeldt .25
113 Zack Greinke .25
114 Juan Gonzalez .25
115 Andres Blanco .25
116 Shawn Green .25
117 Milton Bradley .25
118 Adrian Beltre .50
119 Hideo Nomo .50
120 Steve Finley .25
121 Eric Gagne .25
122 Brad Penny .25
123 Scott Podsednik .25
124 Ben Sheets .40
125 Lyle Overbay .25
126 Junior Spivey .25
127 Bill Hall .25
128 Rickie Weeks .25
129 Jacque Jones .25
130 Torii Hunter .40
131 Johan Santana .50
132 Lew Ford .25
133 Joe Mauer .75
134 Justin Morneau .50
135 Jason Kubel .25
136 Jose Vidro .25
137 Chad Cordero .25
138 Brad Wilkerson .25
139 Nick Johnson .25
140 Livan Hernandez .25
141 Tom Glavine .40
142 Jae Weong Seo .25
143 Jose Reyes .50
144 Al Leiter .25
145 Mike Piazza 1.00
146 Kazuo Matsui .25
147 Richard Hidalgo .25
148 David Wright .75
149 Mariano Rivera .50
150 Mike Mussina .50
151 Alex Rodriguez 1.50
152 Derek Jeter 2.00
153 Jorge Posada .50
154 Jason Giambi .25
155 Gary Sheffield .50
156 Bubba Crosby .25
157 Javier Vazquez .25
158 Kevin Brown .25
159 Tom Gordon .25
160 Esteban Loaiza .25
161 Hideki Matsui 1.50
162 Eric Chavez .40
163 Mark Mulder .40
164 Barry Zito .40
165 Tim Hudson .40
166 Jermaine Dye .25
167 Octavio Dotel .25
168 Bobby Crosby .25
169 Mark Kotsay .25
170 Scott Hatteberg .25
171 Jim Thome .75
172 Bobby Abreu .40
173 Kevin Millwood .25
174 Mike Lieberthal .25
175 Jimmy Rollins .50
176 Chase Utley .50
177 Randy Wolf .25
178 Craig Wilson .25
179 Jason Kendall .25
180 Jack Wilson .25
181 Jose Castillo .25
182 Robert Mackowiak .25
183 Oliver Perez .25
184 Oliver Perez .25
185 Sean Burroughs .25
186 Jay Payton .25
187 Brian Giles .25
188 Akinori Otsuka .25
189 Jake Peavy .25
190 Phil Nevin .25
191 Mark Loretta .25
192 Khalil Greene .40
193 Trevor Hoffman .25
194 Freddy Guzman .25
195 Jerome Williams .25
196 Jason Schmidt .40
197 Todd Linden .25
198 Merkin Valdez .25
199 J.T. Snow .25
200 A.J. Pierzynski .25
201 Edgar Martinez .40
202 Ichiro Suzuki 1.50
203 Raul Ibanez .25
204 Bret Boone .25
205 Shigetoshi Hasegawa .25
206 Miguel Olivo .25
207 Bucky Jacobsen .25
208 Jamie Moyer .25
209 Jim Edmonds .50
210 Scott Rolen .75
211 Edgar Renteria .50
212 Dan Haren .25
213 Matt Morris .25
214 Albert Pujols 2.00
215 Larry Walker .40
216 Jason Isringhausen .25
217 Chris Carpenter .25
218 Jason Marquis .25
219 Jeff Suppan .25
220 Aubrey Huff .25
221 Carl Crawford .25
222 Rocco Baldelli .25
223 Fred McGriff .25
224 Dewon Brazelton .25
225 B.J. Upton .40
226 Joey Gathright .25
227 Scott Kazmir .40
228 Hank Blalock .50
229 Mark Teixeira .50
230 Michael Young .25
231 Adrian Gonzalez .25
232 Laynce Nix .25
233 Alfonso Soriano .75
234 Rafael Palmeiro .50
235 Kevin Mench .25
236 David Dellucci .25
237 Francisco Cordero .25
238 Kenny Rogers .25
239 Roy Halladay .25
240 Carlos Delgado .40
241 Alexis Rios .25
242 Vernon Wells .25
243 Yadier Molina .25
244 Rene Rivera .25
245 Logan Kensing .25
246 Gavin Floyd .25
247 Russ Adams .25
248 Dioner Navarro .25
249 Ryan Howard 1.00
250 Ryan Church .25
251 Jeff Francis .25
252 John Van Benschoten .25
253 Yhency Brazoban .25
254 David Krynzel .25
255 Victor Diaz .25
256 Jairo Garcia .25
257 Scott Proctor .25
258 Shawn Hill .25
259 Jeff Baker .25
260 Matt Peterson .25
261 Josh Kroeger .25
262 Grady Sizemore .40
263 Clint Nageotte .25
264 Andy Green .25
265 Justin Verlander **RC** 2.00
266 Jim Thome .75
267 Larry Walker .40
268 Ivan Rodriguez .50
269 Brad Penny .25
270 Carlos Beltran .50
271 Paul LoDuca .25
272 Orlando Cabrera .25
273 Nomar Garciaparra 1.00
274 Esteban Loaiza .25
275 Richard Hidalgo .25
276 John Olerud .25
277 Greg Maddux 1.00
278 Roger Clemens 2.00
279 Alfonso Soriano .75
280 Dale Murphy .50
281 Cal Ripken Jr. 4.00
282 Dwight Evans .25
283 Ron Santo .25
284 Andre Dawson .50
285 Harold Baines .25
286 Jack Morris .25
287 Kirk Gibson .25
288 Bo Jackson .75
289 Orel Hershiser .25
290 Maury Wills .25
291 Tony Oliva .25
292 Darryl Strawberry .25
293 Roger Maris 1.00
294 Don Mattingly 2.00
295 Rickey Henderson .50
296 Dave Stewart .25
297 Dave Parker .25
298 Steve Garvey .25
299 Matt Williams .25
300 Keith Hernandez .25
301 John Lackey .25
302 Vladimir Guerrero .75
303 Garret Anderson .25
304 Dallas McPherson .25
305 Orlando Cabrera .25
306 Steve Finley .25
307 Luis Gonzalez .25
308 Randy Johnson .75
309 Scott Hairston .25
310 Shawn Green .25
311 Troy Glaus .40
312 Javier Vazquez .25
313 Russ Ortiz .25
314 Chipper Jones .75
315 Johnny Estrada .25
316 Andruw Jones .50
317 Tim Hudson .50
318 Danny Kolb .25
319 Jay Gibbons .25
320 Melvin Mora .25
321 Rafael Palmeiro .50
322 Val Majewski .25
323 David Ortiz .75
324 Manny Ramirez .75
325 Edgar Renteria .25
326 Matt Clement .25
327 Curt Schilling .75
328 Sammy Sosa 1.00
329 Mark Prior .75
330 Greg Maddux 1.00
331 Nomar Garciaparra 1.00
332 Frank Thomas .50
333 Mark Buehrle .25
334 Jermaine Dye .25
335 Scott Podsednik .25
336 Sean Casey .25
337 Adam Dunn .50
338 Ken Griffey Jr. 1.00
339 Travis Hafner .25
340 Victor Martinez .25
341 Cliff Lee .25
342 Todd Helton .50
343 Preston Wilson .25
344 Ivan Rodriguez .50
345 Dmitri Young .25
346 Nate Robertson .25
347 Miguel Cabrera .75
348 Jeff Bagwell .40
349 Andy Pettitte .40
350 Roger Clemens 2.00
351 Ken Harvey .25
352 Danny Bautista .25
353 Hideo Nomo .50
354 Kazuhisa Ishii .25
355 Edwin Jackson .25
356 J.D. Drew .25
357 Jeff Kent .25
358 Geoff Jenkins .25
359 Carlos Lee .25
360 Shannon Stewart .25
361 Joe Nathan .25
362 Johan Santana .50
363 Mike Piazza 1.00
364 Hideki Matsui .25
365 Carlos Beltran .50
366 Pedro Martinez .75
367 Ambiorix Concepcion **RC** .40
368 Hideki Matsui 1.50
369 Bernie Williams .40
370 Gary Sheffield .50
371 Randy Johnson .75
372 Jaret Wright .25
373 Carl Pavano .25
374 Derek Jeter 2.00
375 Alex Rodriguez 1.50
376 Eric Byrnes .25
377 Rich Harden .25
378 Mark Mulder .40
379 Nick Swisher .25
380 Eric Chavez .25
381 Jason Kendall .25
382 Marlon Byrd .25
383 Pat Burrell .25
384 Brett Myers .25
385 Jim Thome .50
386 Jason Bay .25
387 Jake Peavy .25
388 Moises Alou .25
389 Omar Vizquel .25
390 Travis Blackley .25
391 Jose Lopez .25
392 Jeremy Reed .25
393 Adrian Beltre .25
394 Richie Sexson .25
395 Wladimir Balentien **RC** 1.50
396 Ichiro Suzuki 1.50
397 Albert Pujols 2.00
398 Scott Rolen .75
399 Mark Mulder .40
400 David Eckstein .25
401 Delmon Young .25
402 Aubrey Huff .25
403 Alfonso Soriano .50
404 Hank Blalock .25
405 Richard Hidalgo .25
406 Vernon Wells .25
407 Orlando Hudson .25
408 Alexis Rios .25
409 Shea Hillenbrand .25
410 Jose Guillen .25
411 Vinny Castilla .25
412 Jose Vidro .25
413 Nick Johnson .25
414 Livan Hernandez .25
415 Miguel Tejada .50
416 Gary Sheffield .50
417 Curt Schilling .75
418 Rafael Palmeiro .50
419 Scott Rolen .75
420 Aramis Ramirez .40
421 Vladimir Guerrero .75
422 Steve Finley .25

423 Roger Clemens 2.00
424 Mike Piazza 1.00
425 Ivan Rodriguez .50
426 David Justice .25
427 Mark Grace .40
428 Alan Trammell .25
429 Bert Blyleven .25
430 Dwight Gooden .25
431 Deion Sanders .25
432 Joe Torre .25
433 Jose Canseco .40
434 Tony Gwynn .75
435 Will Clark .40
436 Marty Marion .25
437 Nolan Ryan 3.00
438 Billy Martin .25
439 Carlos Delgado .25
440 Magglio Ordonez .25
441 Sammy Sosa 1.00
442 Keiichi Yabu **RC** .50
443 Yuniesky Betancourt **RC** 1.00
444 Jeff Niemann **RC** 1.50
445 Brandon McCarthy **RC** 1.50
446 Philip Humber **RC** 1.50
447 Tadahito Iguchi **RC** 2.00
448 Cal Ripken Jr. 4.00
449 Ryne Sandberg 2.00
450 Willie Mays 2.00

Non-Canvas

No Pricing
Production 20 Sets

Bronze

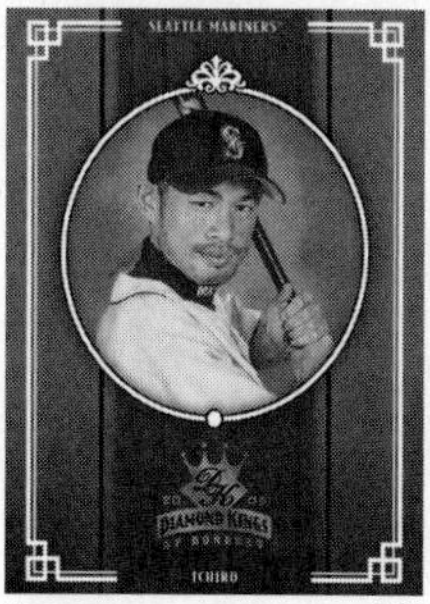

Stars: 3-5X
Production 100 Sets
Update Bronze (301-450): 3-5X
Production 50

Gold

Golds: 5-10X
Production 25 Sets
Gold Update (301-450): No Pricing
Production 10 Sets

Platinum

No Pricing
Production One Set
Framed Platinums: No Pricing
Production One Set

Silver

Silvers: 4-8X
Production 50 Sets
Update (301-450): No Pricing
Production 25 Sets

Framed Black

Stars: 5-10X
Production 25 Sets

Framed Blue

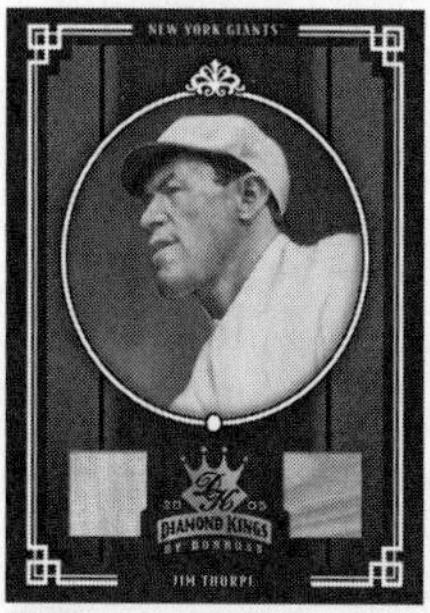

Stars: 5-10X
Production 25 Sets

Framed Green

Stars: 4-8X
Production 50 Sets

Framed Red

Stars: 1-3X
Inserted 1:3

Diamond Cuts Bat

NM/M

Common Player: 4.00
1 Adam Dunn/200 8.00
2 Adrian Beltre/200 6.00
3 Alfonso Soriano/50 8.00
4 Andruw Jones/200 4.00
5 Andy Pettitte/50 6.00
6 Aramis Ramirez/100 6.00
7 Brian Giles/200 4.00
10 Carlos Beltran/200 8.00
12 Craig Wilson/200 4.00
13 Curt Schilling/50 10.00
14 Darin Erstad/200 4.00
16 Derrek Lee/200 6.00
17 Fred McGriff/100 4.00
19 Ivan Rodriguez/200 8.00
20 Jason Bay/200 4.00
21 Jason Giambi/100 4.00
22 Jay Gibbons/200 4.00
23 Jeff Kent/200 4.00
24 John Olerud/200 4.00
25 Juan Gonzalez/200 4.00
27 Kazuhisa Ishii/50 6.00
28 Kevin Brown/100 4.00
29 Larry Walker/200 6.00
31 Mark Teixeira/200 6.00
32 Melvin Mora/50 6.00
33 Michael Young/200 4.00
34 Miguel Tejada/100 8.00
35 Mike Mussina/50 8.00
36 Paul LoDuca/200 4.00
37 Preston Wilson/200 4.00
38 Randy Johnson/50 10.00
39 Richie Sexson/200 6.00
40 Roger Clemens/50 15.00
41 Scott Rolen/100 8.00
42 Sean Burroughs/200 4.00
43 Sean Casey/200 4.00
44 Shannon Stewart/200 4.00
45 Shawn Green/200 4.00
47 Tim Salmon/200 4.00
48 Tom Glavine/200 6.00
49 Torii Hunter/200 6.00

Diamond Cuts Combos

NM/M

Common Player: 6.00
Prime: No Pricing
Production One Set
1 Adam Dunn/Bat-Jsy/100 10.00
2 Adrian Beltre/Bat-Jsy/100 8.00
3 Alfonso Soriano/
Bat-Jsy/100 10.00
4 Andruw Jones/Bat-Jsy/100 8.00
5 Andy Pettitte/Jsy-Jsy/100 10.00
6 Aramis Ramirez/Bat-Jsy/100 8.00
7 Brian Giles/Bat-Jsy/100 6.00
10 Carlos Beltran/Bat-Jsy/50 15.00
11 Carlos Lee/Jsy-Jsy/100 6.00
12 Craig Wilson/Bat-Jsy/100 6.00
13 Curt Schilling/Bat-Jsy/100 12.00
14 Darin Erstad/Bat-Jsy/100 6.00
17 Fred McGriff/Bat-Jsy/100 6.00
19 Ivan Rodriguez/Bat-Jsy/100 10.00
21 Jason Giambi/Bat-Jsy/50 8.00
22 Jay Gibbons/Bat-Jsy/50 8.00
23 Jeff Kent/Bat-Jsy/100 6.00
24 John Olerud/Bat-Jsy/200 6.00
25 Juan Gonzalez/Bat-Pants/100 8.00
27 Kazuhisa Ishii/Bat-Jsy/100 8.00
28 Kevin Brown/Bat-Jsy/100 6.00
29 Larry Walker/Bat-Jsy/100 8.00
31 Mark Teixeira/Bat-Jsy/100 10.00
34 Miguel Tejada/Jsy-Jsy/100 10.00
35 Mike Mussina/Bat-Pants/50 12.00
36 Paul LoDuca/Bat-Jsy/50 8.00
37 Preston Wilson/Bat-Jsy/100 6.00
38 Randy Johnson/Bat-Jsy/50 15.00
40 Roger Clemens/Bat-Jsy/50 20.00
44 Shannon Stewart/
Bat-Jsy/100 6.00
45 Shawn Green/Bat-Jsy/100 6.00
48 Tom Glavine/Bat-Jsy/100 8.00
49 Torii Hunter/Bat-Jsy/25 8.00

Diamond Cuts Jersey

NM/M

Common Player: 4.00
Prime: No Pricing
Production One Set
1 Adam Dunn/50 10.00
2 Adrian Beltre/200 6.00
3 Alfonso Soriano/50 8.00
4 Andruw Jones/200 4.00
5 Andy Pettitte/100 6.00
6 Aramis Ramirez/200 6.00
7 Brian Giles/200 4.00
8 C.C. Sabathia/200 4.00
9 Carl Crawford/200 4.00
10 Carlos Beltran/200 8.00
11 Carlos Lee/200 4.00
12 Craig Wilson/200 4.00
13 Curt Schilling/50 10.00
14 Darin Erstad/200 4.00
17 Fred McGriff/200 4.00
18 Greg Maddux/50 12.00
19 Ivan Rodriguez/200 8.00
20 Jason Bay/200 4.00
21 Jason Giambi/200 4.00
22 Jay Gibbons/100 4.00
23 Jeff Kent/200 4.00
24 John Olerud/200 4.00
25 Juan Gonzalez/Pants/200 4.00
26 Junior Spivey/200 4.00
27 Kazuhisa Ishii/200 6.00
28 Kevin Brown/200 4.00
29 Larry Walker Rockies/200 6.00
30 Lyle Overbay/200 4.00
31 Mark Teixeira/100 6.00
32 Melvin Mora/200 4.00
33 Michael Young/200 4.00
34 Miguel Tejada/200 8.00
35 Mike Mussina/100 8.00
36 Paul LoDuca/50 6.00
37 Preston Wilson/200 4.00
38 Randy Johnson/200 8.00
39 Richie Sexson/200 6.00
40 Roger Clemens/50 15.00
41 Scott Rolen/50 10.00
42 Sean Burroughs/200 4.00
43 Sean Casey/200 4.00
44 Shannon Stewart/100 4.00
45 Shawn Green/200 4.00
46 Steve Finley/200 4.00
48 Tom Glavine/200 6.00
50 Travis Hafner/100 4.00

Diamond Cuts Signature

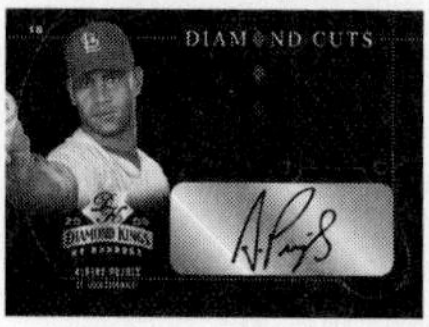

NM/M

Production 1-100
8 C.C. Sabathia/25 20.00
9 Carl Crawford/50 20.00
11 Carlos Lee/100 15.00
12 Craig Wilson/100 15.00
20 Jason Bay/100 15.00
22 Jay Gibbons/100 10.00
30 Lyle Overbay/100 15.00
32 Melvin Mora/50 15.00
44 Shannon Stewart/25 20.00
47 Tim Salmon/100 20.00
50 Travis Hafner/100 15.00

Diamond Cuts Signature Bat

NM/M

Production 5-100
1 Adam Dunn/25 40.00
2 Adrian Beltre/50 35.00
6 Aramis Ramirez/100 30.00
10 Carlos Beltran/50 40.00
12 Craig Wilson/100 15.00
16 Derrek Lee/100 20.00
17 Fred McGriff/25 50.00
22 Jay Gibbons/100 10.00
31 Mark Teixeira/25 40.00
33 Michael Young/100 20.00
36 Paul LoDuca/25 25.00
43 Sean Casey/25 25.00
44 Shannon Stewart/25 20.00
49 Torii Hunter/25 25.00

Diamond Cuts Sign. Combos

NM/M

Production 1-100
Prime: No Pricing
Production One Set
1 Adam Dunn/Bat-Jsy/25 40.00
2 Adrian Beltre/Bat-Bat/25 40.00
6 Aramis Ramirez/
Bat-Jsy/100 30.00
8 C.C. Sabathia/Jsy-Jsy/50 25.00
11 Carlos Lee/Jsy-Jsy/50 20.00
12 Craig Wilson/Bat-Bat/100 15.00
17 Fred McGriff/Bat-Jsy/25 50.00
22 Jay Gibbons/Bat-Bat/50 10.00
25 Juan Gonzalez/Bat-Jsy/100 25.00
27 Kazuhisa Ishii/Bat-Jsy/25 50.00
31 Mark Teixeira/Bat-Bat/25 40.00
33 Michael Young/Bat-Jsy/50 25.00
36 Paul LoDuca/Bat-Bat/25 25.00
43 Sean Casey/Bat-Jsy/25 25.00
44 Shannon Stewart/
Bat-Jsy/25 20.00
49 Torii Hunter/Bat-Jsy/25 25.00
50 Travis Hafner/Bat-Jsy/25 25.00
51 Aramis Ramirez/Jsy/24 25.00
60 Victor Martinez/25 20.00

Diamond Cuts Sign. Jersey

NM/M

Production 5-100
Prime: No Pricing
Production One Set
2 Adrian Beltre/100 25.00
6 Aramis Ramirez/100 30.00
8 C.C. Sabathia/100 15.00
9 Carl Crawford/50 20.00
11 Carlos Lee/100 15.00
12 Craig Wilson/100 15.00
30 Lyle Overbay/100 15.00
31 Mark Teixeira/25 40.00
32 Melvin Mora/50 15.00
33 Michael Young/100 20.00
36 Paul LoDuca/25 25.00
42 Sean Burroughs/50 10.00
43 Sean Casey/25 25.00
44 Shannon Stewart/25 20.00
46 Steve Finley/25 25.00
50 Travis Hafner/50 20.00
57 Mark Mulder/25 25.00
60 Victor Martinez/25 20.00

Heritage Collection

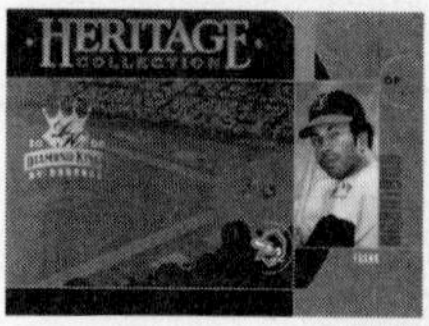

NM/M

Common Player: 1.50
Inserted 1:21
#26-35 inserted 1:76
#26-35 are DK Update exclusive
1 Andre Dawson 1.50
2 Bob Gibson 2.50
3 Cal Ripken Jr. 8.00
4 Dale Murphy 2.00
5 Darryl Strawberry 1.50
6 Dennis Eckersley 1.50
7 Don Mattingly 6.00
8 Duke Snider 3.00
9 Dwight Gooden 1.50
10 Eddie Murray 3.00
11 Frank Robinson 3.00
12 Gary Carter 2.00
13 George Brett 6.00
14 Harmon Killebrew 3.00
15 Jack Morris 1.50
16 Jim Palmer 1.50
17 Lou Brock 2.00
18 Mike Schmidt 6.00
19 Nolan Ryan 8.00
20 Ozzie Smith 4.00
21 Phil Niekro 1.50
22 Rod Carew 2.00
23 Rollie Fingers 1.50
24 Steve Carlton 1.50
25 Tony Gwynn 3.00
26 Curt Schilling 3.00
27 Bobby Doerr 1.50
28 Edgar Martinez 1.50
29 Jim Thorpe 4.00
30 Mark Grace 1.50
31 Matt Williams 1.50
32 Paul Molitor 2.50
33 Robin Yount 4.00
34 Ryne Sandberg 5.00
35 Will Clark 2.00

Heritage Collection Bat

NM/M

Production 50-100
1 Andre Dawson/50 8.00
3 Cal Ripken Jr./100 40.00
4 Dale Murphy/100 10.00
5 Darryl Strawberry/50 8.00
7 Don Mattingly/100 20.00
9 Dwight Gooden/100 5.00
10 Eddie Murray/100 15.00
11 Frank Robinson/50 8.00
12 Gary Carter/100 5.00
13 George Brett/100 15.00
14 Harmon Killebrew/100 10.00
17 Lou Brock/100 8.00
18 Mike Schmidt/100 20.00
19 Nolan Ryan/50 30.00
20 Ozzie Smith/100 15.00
21 Phil Niekro/50 8.00
22 Rod Carew/100 8.00
24 Steve Carlton/100 5.00
25 Tony Gwynn/100 10.00

Heritage Collection Combos

NM/M

Production 25-100
Prime: No Pricing
Production One Set
1 Andre Dawson/Bat-Jsy/50 8.00
3 Cal Ripken Jr./Bat-Jsy/50 60.00
4 Dale Murphy/Bat-Jsy/25 20.00
7 Don Mattingly/Bat-Jkt/100 25.00
8 Duke Snider/Jsy-Pants/25 20.00
9 Dwight Gooden/Bat-Jsy/50 10.00
10 Eddie Murray/Bat-Jsy/100 20.00
14 Harmon Killebrew/
Bat-Jsy/100 15.00
16 Jim Palmer/Jsy-Pants/100 10.00
17 Lou Brock/Bat-Jkt/50 10.00
18 Mike Schmidt/Bat-Jsy/100 25.00
19 Nolan Ryan/Jsy-Pants/50 40.00
20 Ozzie Smith/Bat-Pants/100 20.00
21 Phil Niekro/Bat-Jsy/50 10.00
22 Rod Carew/Bat-Jsy/100 10.00
24 Steve Carlton/Bat-Jsy/100 8.00
25 Tony Gwynn/Bat-Jsy/50 15.00

Heritage Collection Jersey

NM/M

Production 25-100
Prime: No Pricing
Production One Set
1 Andre Dawson/100 8.00
2 Bob Gibson/50 10.00

3 Cal Ripken Jr./100 40.00
4 Dale Murphy/100 10.00
5 Darryl Strawberry/25 10.00
6 Dennis Eckersley/100 5.00
7 Don Mattingly/100 20.00
8 Duke Snider/50 15.00
9 Dwight Gooden/100 5.00
10 Eddie Murray/100 15.00
12 Gary Carter/100 5.00
13 George Brett/50 20.00
14 Harmon Killebrew/100 10.00
15 Jack Morris/100 5.00
16 Jim Palmer/100 5.00
17 Lou Brock/100 8.00
18 Mike Schmidt/Jkt/100 20.00
19 Nolan Ryan/100 25.00
20 Ozzie Smith/Pants/100 15.00
21 Phil Niekro/50 8.00
22 Rod Carew/100 8.00
23 Rollie Fingers/50 8.00
24 Steve Carlton/50 8.00
25 Tony Gwynn/100 10.00

Heritage Coll. Signature

NM/M

Production 1-50
1 Andre Dawson/50 25.00
5 Darryl Strawberry/50 25.00
9 Dwight Gooden/25 25.00
15 Jack Morris/50 20.00
23 Rollie Fingers/25 40.00

Heritage Coll. Sign. Bat

NM/M

Production 5-100
#26-35 are DK Update exclusive
1 Andre Dawson/50 25.00
4 Dale Murphy/25 40.00
7 Don Mattingly/25 75.00
9 Dwight Gooden/100 25.00
11 Frank Robinson/25 40.00
14 Harmon Killebrew/50 50.00
17 Lou Brock/50 35.00
20 Ozzie Smith/25 65.00
21 Phil Niekro/20 30.00
22 Rod Carew/25 40.00
24 Steve Carlton/25 40.00
25 Tony Gwynn/25 50.00
28 Edgar Martinez/25 40.00
31 Matt Williams/25 35.00
35 Will Clark/25 40.00

Heritage Coll. Sign. Combos

NM/M

Production 5-100
#26-35 are DK Update exclusive
Prime: No Pricing
Production One Set
1 Andre Dawson/Bat-Jsy/50 25.00
4 Dale Murphy/Bat-Jsy/25 40.00
6 Dennis Eckersley/ Jsy-Jsy/50 25.00
7 Don Mattingly/Bat-Jkt/25 80.00
9 Dwight Gooden/ Bat-Jsy/100 25.00
12 Gary Carter/Jkt-Jsy/50 25.00
14 Harmon Killebrew/ Bat-Bat/25 50.00
15 Jack Morris/Jsy-Jsy/25 30.00
16 Jim Palmer/ Jsy-Pants/25 30.00
17 Lou Brock/Bat-Jsy/50 40.00
21 Phil Niekro/Bat-Jsy/50 25.00
22 Rod Carew/Bat-Jkt/25 40.00
24 Steve Carlton/Bat-Jsy/25 40.00
25 Tony Gwynn/Bat-Jsy/25 50.00
27 Bobby Doerr/Jsy/Pants/25 25.00
28 Edgar Martinez/Bat/Jsy/25 40.00
31 Matt Williams/Bat/Jsy/25 35.00
35 Will Clark/Bat/Jsy/25 40.00

Heritage Coll. Sign. Jersey

NM/M

Production 5-100
#26-35 are DK Update exclusive
Prime: No Pricing
Production One Set
1 Andre Dawson/100 25.00
2 Bob Gibson/25 40.00
4 Dale Murphy/50 40.00
5 Darryl Strawberry/ Pants/100 20.00
6 Dennis Eckersley/50 25.00
7 Don Mattingly/25 85.00
8 Duke Snider/50 35.00
9 Dwight Gooden/100 20.00
11 Frank Robinson/25 40.00
12 Gary Carter/50 25.00
14 Harmon Killebrew/50 50.00
15 Jack Morris/100 15.00
16 Jim Palmer/25 35.00
17 Lou Brock/50 35.00
20 Ozzie Smith/25 60.00
21 Phil Niekro/25 30.00
22 Rod Carew/25 40.00
23 Rollie Fingers/25 30.00
24 Steve Carlton/25 40.00
27 Bobby Doerr/25 25.00
28 Edgar Martinez/25 35.00
31 Matt Williams/25 35.00
35 Will Clark/25 40.00

HOF Heroes

NM/M

#51-100 are DK Update exclusive

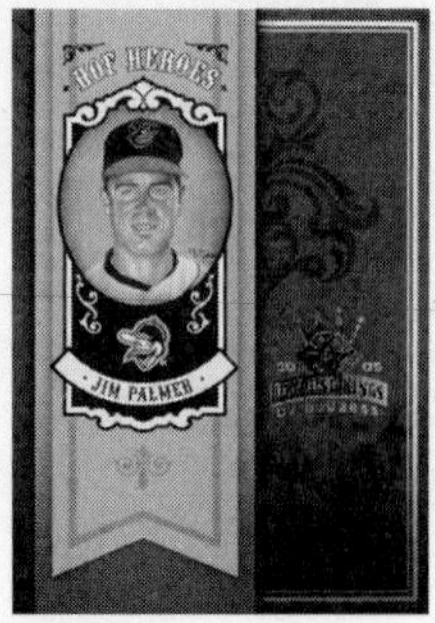

Common Player: 1.50
Inserted 1:5
Non Canvas: No Pricing
Production 20 Sets
Bronze: 1-2X
Production 100 Sets
Gold: 3-5X
Production 25 Sets
Platinum: No Pricing
Production One Set
Silver: 2-4X
Production 50 Sets
Frame Black: 3-5X
Production 25 Sets
Frame Blue: 1-2X
Production 100 Sets
Frame Green: 2-4X
Production 50 Sets
Frame Red: 1X
Inserted 1:18
1 Phil Niekro 1.50
2 Brooks Robinson 2.00
3 Jim Palmer 2.00
4 Carl Yastrzemski 3.00
5 Ted Williams 5.00
6 Duke Snider 3.00
7 Burleigh Grimes 1.50
8 Don Sutton 1.50
9 Nolan Ryan 6.00
10 Fergie Jenkins 1.50
11 Carlton Fisk 2.00
12 Tom Seaver 2.00
13 Bob Feller 2.00
14 Nolan Ryan 6.00
15 George Brett 5.00
16 Warren Spahn 3.00
17 Paul Molitor 3.00
18 Rod Carew 3.00
19 Harmon Killebrew 3.00
20 Monte Irvin 2.00
21 Gary Carter 1.50
22 Phil Rizzuto 2.00
23 Babe Ruth 6.00
24 Reggie Jackson 2.00
25 Mike Schmidt 5.00
26 Roberto Clemente 5.00
27 Juan Marichal 1.50
28 Willie McCovey 2.00
29 Stan Musial 4.00
30 Ozzie Smith 3.00
31 Dennis Eckersley 1.50
32 Phil Niekro 1.50
33 Jim Palmer 2.00
34 Carl Yastrzemski 3.00
35 Duke Snider 3.00
36 Don Sutton 1.50
37 Nolan Ryan 6.00
38 Carlton Fisk 2.00
39 Tom Seaver 2.00
40 Bob Feller 2.00
41 Nolan Ryan 6.00
42 George Brett 5.00
43 Harmon Killebrew 3.00
44 Gary Carter 1.50
45 Mike Schmidt 5.00
46 Stan Musial 4.00
47 Ozzie Smith 3.00
48 Dennis Eckersley 1.50
49 Fergie Jenkins 1.50
50 Brooks Robinson 2.00
51 Eddie Murray 2.00
52 Frank Robinson 2.00
53 Carlton Fisk 1.50
54 Ted Williams 5.00
55 Rod Carew 2.00
56 Ernie Banks 3.00
57 Luis Aparicio 1.50
58 Johnny Bench 3.00
59 Al Kaline 2.00
60 George Kell 1.50
61 Robin Yount 3.00
62 Nolan Ryan 6.00
63 Whitey Ford 1.50
64 Reggie Jackson 2.00
65 Babe Ruth 6.00
66 Rollie Fingers 1.50
67 Steve Carlton 1.50
68 Robin Roberts 1.50
69 Ralph Kiner 1.50
70 Willie Stargell 2.00
71 Roberto Clemente 5.00
72 Gaylord Perry 1.50
73 Bob Gibson 2.00
74 Lou Brock 1.50
75 Frankie Frisch 1.50
76 Eddie Murray 2.00
77 Frank Robinson 2.00
78 Carlton Fisk 1.50
79 Ted Williams 5.00
80 Rod Carew 2.00
81 Ernie Banks 3.00
82 Luis Aparicio 1.50
83 Johnny Bench 3.00
84 Al Kaline 2.00
85 Willie Mays 5.00
86 Robin Yount 3.00
87 Nolan Ryan 5.00
88 Whitey Ford 2.00
89 Reggie Jackson 2.00
90 Babe Ruth 6.00
91 Rollie Fingers 1.50
92 Steve Carlton 1.50
93 Wade Boggs 2.00
94 Wade Boggs 2.00
95 Willie Stargell 2.00
96 Roberto Clemente 5.00
97 Gaylord Perry 1.50
98 Bob Gibson 2.00
99 Lou Brock 1.50
100 Frankie Frisch 1.50

HOF Heroes Materials Bronze

NM/M

Production 1-100
No pricing 20 or less.
Gold: .75-1.5X
Production 1-25
Silver: .75-1.5X
Production 10-50
Framed Black: No Pricing
Production 1-10
Framed Blue: .75-1.5X
Production 1-25
Framed Red: .75-1.5X
Production 10-50
1 Phil Niekro/Bat-Jsy/100 8.00
2 Brooks Robinson/ Bat-Jsy/100 12.00
3 Jim Palmer/Jsy-Pants/100 8.00
4 Carl Yastrzemski/ Bat-Pants/50 20.00
6 Duke Snider/Jsy-Pants/50 15.00
7 Burleigh Grimes/ Pants-Pants/25 75.00
8 Don Sutton/Jsy-Jsy/100 8.00
9 Nolan Ryan/Bat-Jkt/50 40.00
10 Fergie Jenkins/ Pants-Pants/100 8.00
11 Carlton Fisk/Bat-Jkt/100 12.00
12 Tom Seaver/Jsy-Pants/50 15.00
13 Bob Feller/Pants-Pants/25 20.00
14 Nolan Ryan/Bat-Jkt/25 40.00
15 George Brett/Bat-Bat/25 40.00
16 Warren Spahn/ Jsy-Pants/25 30.00
17 Paul Molitor/Bat-Jsy/100 15.00
18 Rod Carew/Bat-Jsy/50 15.00
19 Harmon Killebrew/ Bat-Jsy/50 20.00
21 Gary Carter/Bat-Jsy/100 8.00
23 Babe Ruth/Bat-Pants/25 300.00
24 Reggie Jackson/Bat-Jkt/100 15.00
25 Mike Schmidt/Bat-Jkt/50 30.00
26 Roberto Clemente/ Bat-Bat/50 60.00
27 Juan Marichal/ Pants-Pants/25 12.00
28 Willie McCovey/ Jsy-Pants/100 10.00
29 Stan Musial/Bat-Bat/25 30.00
30 Ozzie Smith/Bat-Pants/100 20.00
31 Dennis Eckersley/ Jsy-Jsy/100 8.00
32 Phil Niekro/Bat-Jsy/100 8.00
33 Jim Palmer/Jsy-Pants/25 12.00
34 Carl Yastrzemski/ Bat-Pants/25 30.00
35 Duke Snider/Jsy-Pants 20.00
36 Don Sutton/Jsy-Jsy/100 8.00
37 Nolan Ryan/Bat-Jkt/25 50.00
38 Carlton Fisk/Bat-Jkt/100 12.00
39 Tom Seaver/Bat-Jsy/25 20.00
40 Bob Feller/Pants-Pants/25 20.00
41 Nolan Ryan/Bat-Jkt/25 50.00
42 George Brett/Bat-Bat/25 40.00
43 Harmon Killebrew/ Bat-Jsy/25 25.00
44 Gary Carter/Bat-Jsy/100 8.00
45 Mike Schmidt/Bat-Jsy/25 40.00
46 Stan Musial/Bat-Bat/25 30.00
47 Ozzie Smith/Bat-Pants/100 20.00
48 Dennis Eckersley/ Jsy-Jsy/100 8.00
49 Fergie Jenkins/ Pants-Pants/25 12.00
50 Brooks Robinson/ Bat-Jsy/25 20.00
51 Eddie Murray/Bat/Pants/50 12.00
52 Frank Robinson/Bat/Bat/50 12.00
53 Carlton Fisk/Bat/Bat/50 10.00
55 Rod Carew/Bat/Jsy/50 12.00
56 Ernie Banks/Bat/Pants/50 15.00
57 Luis Aparicio/Bat/Bat/50 8.00
58 Johnny Bench/Bat/Jsy/50 15.00
59 Al Kaline/Bat/Bat/25 20.00
61 Robin Yount/Bat/Jsy/50 15.00
62 Nolan Ryan/Bat/Jsy/25 50.00
63 Whitey Ford/Jsy/Jsy/25 25.00
64 Reggie Jackson/Jsy/Jsy/50 15.00
66 Rollie Fingers/Jsy/Jsy/50 8.00
67 Steve Carlton/Bat/Jsy/50 10.00
70 Willie Stargell/Bat/Bat/50 15.00
72 Gaylord Perry/Jsy/Jsy/50 8.00
73 Bob Gibson/Jsy/Jsy/25 15.00
74 Lou Brock/Bat/Jsy/50 12.00
76 Eddie Murray/Bat/Bat/50 12.00
77 Frank Robinson/Bat/Bat/50 12.00
78 Carlton Fisk/Bat/Bat/50 12.00
80 Rod Carew/Bat/Jkt/50 12.00
81 Ernie Banks/Bat/Jsy/25 15.00
82 Luis Aparicio/Bat/Bat/50 8.00
83 Johnny Bench/Bat/Jsy/50 15.00
86 Robin Yount/Bat/Jsy/50 15.00
87 Nolan Ryan/Bat/Jsy/25 40.00
88 Whitey Ford/Jsy/Jsy/25 25.00
89 Reggie Jackson/Jsy/Jsy/50 15.00
91 Rollie Fingers/Jsy/Jsy/50 8.00
92 Steve Carlton/Bat/Jsy/50 10.00
95 Willie Stargell/Jsy/Jsy/50 15.00
97 Gaylord Perry/Jsy/Jsy/50 8.00
99 Lou Brock/Bat/Jsy/50 10.00

HOF Heroes Signatures Bronze

NM/M

Production 1-25
No pricing 20 or less.
Gold: No Pricing
Production 1-10
Platinum: No Pricing
Production One Set
Silver: 1X
Production 1-25
Framed Blue: No Pricing
Production One Set
Framed Black: No Pricing
Production One Set
Framed Green: No Pricing
Production 1-10
Framed Red: No Pricing
Production 1-25
Cards #52-99 are seeded in DK Update
13 Bob Feller/25 35.00
40 Bob Feller/25 35.00
52 Frank Robinson/25 35.00
57 Luis Aparicio/25 15.00
59 Al Kaline/25 40.00
66 Rollie Fingers/25 15.00
67 Steve Carlton/25 20.00
68 Robin Roberts/25 20.00
69 Ralph Kiner/25 35.00
72 Gaylord Perry/15 15.00
74 Lou Brock/25 35.00
82 Luis Aparicio/25 15.00
84 Al Kaline/25 40.00
91 Rollie Fingers/25 15.00
92 Steve Carlton/25 20.00
93 Wade Boggs/Yanks/25 30.00
94 Wade Boggs/Sox/25 30.00
97 Gaylord Perry/25 15.00
99 Lou Brock/25 35.00

Signature Materials Bronze

NM/M

Production 5-50
No pricing 20 or less.
Gold: .75-1.5X
Production 5-25
Platinum: No Pricing
Production One Set
Silver: .75-1X
Production 5-50
Framed Black: No Pricing
Production 5-10
Framed Blue: .75-1.5X
Production 5-25
Framed Green: No Pricing
Production 1-10
Framed Red: .75-1.5X
Production 1-25
#53-99 are found in DK Update
2 Brooks Robinson/ Bat-Jsy/25 50.00
3 Jim Palmer/Jsy-Pants/25 40.00
6 Duke Snider/Jsy-Pants/25 40.00
8 Don Sutton/Jsy-Jsy/25 30.00
10 Fergie Jenkins/ Pants-Pants/25 30.00
13 Bob Feller/Pants-Pants/50 35.00
18 Rod Carew/Bat-Jsy/50 40.00
19 Harmon Killebrew/ Bat-Jsy/25 50.00
21 Gary Carter/Bat-Jsy/50 25.00
27 Juan Marichal/ Pants-Pants/25 40.00
28 Willie McCovey/ Jsy-Pants/25 50.00
29 Stan Musial/Bat-Bat/25 85.00
30 Ozzie Smith/Bat-Pants/25 75.00
31 Dennis Eckersley/ Jsy-Jsy/25 35.00
32 Phil Niekro/Bat-Jsy/25 30.00
33 Jim Palmer/Jsy-Pants/25 40.00
35 Duke Snider/Jsy-Pants/25 40.00
36 Don Sutton/Jsy-Jsy/25 30.00
40 Bob Feller/Pants-Pants/50 35.00
43 Harmon Killebrew/ Bat-Jsy/50 40.00
44 Gary Carter/Bat-Jsy/50 25.00
47 Ozzie Smith/Bat-Pants/25 75.00
48 Dennis Eckersley/ Jsy-Jsy/50 25.00

49 Fergie Jenkins/
Pants-Pants/50 30.00
50 Brooks Robinson/
Bat-Jsy/25 50.00
61 Robin Yount/Bat-Jsy/25 50.00
66 Rollie Fingers/Jsy-Jsy/50 15.00
72 Gaylord Perry/Jsy-Jsy/50 15.00
74 Lou Brock/Jsy-Jsy/50 30.00
80 Rod Carew/Bat-Jsy/50 25.00
99 Lou Brock/Bat-Jsy/25 40.00

Materials Bronze

NM/M

Production 10-200
No pricing 20 or less.
Gold: .75-1.5X
Production 25-50
Silver: .75-1.5X
Production 25-100
Platinum: No Pricing
Production One Set
Framed Black: No Pricing
Production 10 Sets
Framed Blue: .75-1.5X
Production 50 Sets
Framed Green:
Production 25 Sets
Framed Red: .75-1.5X
Production 25-100
#302-450 are found in DK Update
1 Garret Anderson/
Bat-Jsy/200 5.00
2 Vladimir Guerrero/
Bat-Jsy/200 10.00
4 Troy Glaus/Bat-Jsy/200 5.00
5 Tim Salmon/Bat-Jsy/200 5.00
7 Chone Figgins/Bat-Jsy/200 5.00
10 Tony Percival/Jsy-Jsy/200 5.00
12 Brandon Webb/
Bat-Pants/200 5.00
13 Richie Sexson/Bat-Bat/200 8.00
17 Luis Gonzalez/Jsy-Jsy/200 5.00
18 Rafael Furcal/Bat-Jsy/200 5.00
19 Andruw Jones/Bat-Jsy/200 8.00
21 John Smoltz/Jsy-Jsy/200 8.00
24 J.D. Drew/Bat-Bat/200 5.00
25 Chipper Jones/Bat-Jsy/200 10.00
27 Rafael Palmeiro/Bat-Jsy/200 8.00
28 Miguel Tejada/Bat-Jsy/200 10.00
29 Javy Lopez/Bat-Jsy/25 10.00
30 Luis Matos/Jsy-Jsy/100 5.00
31 Larry Bigbie/Jsy-Jsy/200 5.00
32 Rodrigo Lopez/Jsy-Jsy/200 5.00
34 Melvin Mora/Bat-Jsy/200 5.00
36 Manny Ramirez/
Bat-Jsy/200 10.00
38 Trot Nixon/Bat-Bat/200 10.00
39 Curt Schilling/Bat-Jsy/200 10.00
41 Pedro Martinez/Bat-Jsy/200 10.00
42 Johnny Damon/Bat-Bat/200 15.00
43 Kevin Youkilis/Bat-Bat/200 5.00
46 David Ortiz/Bat-Jsy/200 10.00
47 Kerry Wood/Jsy-Pants/200 10.00
48 Mark Prior/Bat-Jsy/200 8.00
49 Aramis Ramirez/Bat-Jsy/200 8.00
50 Greg Maddux/Bat-Jsy/100 15.00
51 Carlos Zambrano/
Jsy-Jsy/200 8.00
52 Derrek Lee/Bat-Bat/200 8.00
54 Moises Alou/Bat-Bat/200 8.00
56 Sammy Sosa/Bat-Jsy/200 10.00
57 Nomar Garciaparra/
Bat-Bat/200 10.00
60 Magglio Ordonez/
Bat-Jsy/200 5.00
61 Carlos Lee/Bat-Jsy/200 5.00
62 Joe Crede/Bat-Bat/200 5.00
65 Frank Thomas/Bat-Jsy/200 8.00
69 Adam Dunn/Bat-Jsy/200 8.00
70 Austin Kearns/Bat-Bat/200 5.00
74 Sean Casey/Jsy-Pants/200 5.00
76 C.C. Sabathia/Jsy-Jsy/200 5.00
77 Jody Gerut/Bat-Jsy/200 5.00
78 Omar Vizquel/Bat-Jsy/200 5.00
79 Victor Martinez/Bat-Jsy/200 5.00
80 Matt Lawton/Bat-Bat/200 5.00
84 Todd Helton/Bat-Jsy/200 8.00
85 Preston Wilson/Bat-Jsy/200 5.00
90 Ivan Rodriguez/Bat-Jsy/200 8.00
92 Brandon Inge/Bat-Jsy/200 5.00
94 Dontrelle Willis/Jsy-Jsy/200 5.00
95 Miguel Cabrera/Bat-Jsy/200 10.00
96 Josh Beckett/Bat-Bat/100 5.00
97 Mike Lowell/Bat-Jsy/100 5.00
98 Luis Castillo/Bat-Bat/200 5.00
99 Juan Pierre/Bat-Bat/200 5.00
100 Paul LoDuca/Bat-Bat/200 5.00
102 Craig Biggio/Bat-Pants/200 5.00
103 Lance Berkman/Bat-Jsy/200 5.00
104 Roy Oswalt/Jsy-Jsy/200 5.00
105 Roger Clemens/Bat-Jsy/200 15.00
106 Jeff Kent/Bat-Jsy/100 5.00
108 Jeff Bagwell/Bat-Jsy/200 8.00
109 Carlos Beltran/Bat-Jsy/200 8.00
110 Angel Berroa/Bat-Bat/200 5.00
111 Mike Sweeney/Bat-Jsy/200 5.00
112 Jeremy Affeldt/
Pants-Pants/200 5.00
114 Juan Gonzalez/Bat-Jsy/200 8.00
116 Shawn Green/Bat-Jsy/200 5.00
118 Adrian Beltre/Bat-Jsy/200 8.00
119 Hideo Nomo/Bat-Jsy/200 8.00
123 Scott Podsednik/Jsy-Jsy/200 5.00
124 Ben Sheets/Bat-Pants/200 8.00
125 Lyle Overbay/Jsy-Jsy/200 5.00
126 Junior Spivey/Jsy-Jsy/200 5.00
127 Bill Hall/Bat-Jsy/200 5.00
129 Jacque Jones/Bat-Jsy/200 5.00
130 Torii Hunter/Bat-Jsy/200 5.00
131 Johan Santana/Jsy-Jsy/200 10.00
132 Lew Ford/Bat-Jsy/200 5.00
136 Jose Vidro/Bat-Jsy/200 5.00
138 Brad Wilkerson/Bat-Bat/100 5.00
139 Nick Johnson/Bat-Bat/100 5.00
140 Livan Hernandez/Jsy-Jsy/25 5.00
141 Tom Glavine/Bat-Bat/200 8.00
143 Jose Reyes/Bat-Jsy/200 6.00
144 Al Leiter/Jsy-Jsy/200 5.00
145 Mike Piazza/Jsy-Jsy/100 15.00
146 Kazuo Matsui/Bat-Jsy/200 8.00
147 Richard Hidalgo/Bat-Bat/200 5.00
149 Mariano Rivera/Jsy-Jsy/100 8.00
150 Mike Mussina/Bat-Jsy/200 8.00
153 Jorge Posada/Bat-Jsy/200 8.00
154 Jason Giambi/Bat-Jsy/200 5.00
155 Gary Sheffield/Bat-Jsy/200 8.00
158 Kevin Brown/Bat-Bat/100 5.00
160 Esteban Loaiza/Bat-Bat/100 5.00
161 Hideki Matsui/
Jsy-Pants/200 20.00
162 Eric Chavez/Bat-Jsy/200 5.00
163 Mark Mulder/Bat-Bat/25 10.00
164 Barry Zito/Bat-Jsy/200 5.00
165 Tim Hudson/Bat-Jsy/200 8.00
166 Jermaine Dye/Bat-Jsy/200 5.00
168 Bobby Crosby/Jsy-Jsy/200 8.00
171 Jim Thome/Bat-Jsy/200 8.00
172 Bobby Abreu/Jsy-Jsy/200 8.00
173 Kevin Millwood/Jsy-Jsy/200 5.00
178 Craig Wilson/Bat-Jsy/200 5.00
180 Jack Wilson/Bat-Bat/200 5.00
181 Jose Castillo/Bat-Bat/200 5.00
184 Jason Bay/Bat-Jsy/200 5.00
185 Sean Burroughs/Bat-Jsy/200 8.00
187 Brian Giles/Bat-Bat/100 5.00
193 Trevor Hoffman/Jsy-Jsy/200 5.00
199 J.T. Snow/Jsy-Jsy/25 5.00
200 A.J. Pierzynski/Jsy-Jsy/100 5.00
201 Edgar Martinez/Bat-Bat/200 5.00
204 Bret Boone/Jsy-Jsy/200 5.00
208 Jamie Moyer/Jsy-Jsy/50 5.00
209 Jim Edmonds/Bat-Jsy/200 8.00
210 Scott Rolen/Bat-Jsy/200 10.00
211 Edgar Renteria/Bat-Jsy/200 8.00
212 Dan Haren/Bat-Jsy/100 5.00
213 Matt Morris/Jsy-Jsy/100 5.00
214 Albert Pujols/Jsy-Jsy/200 20.00
215 Larry Walker/Bat-Bat/200 8.00
220 Aubrey Huff/Bat-Bat/100 5.00
221 Carl Crawford/Jsy-Jsy/200 5.00
222 Rocco Baldelli/Bat-Jsy/200 5.00
223 Fred McGriff/Bat-Jsy/200 5.00
224 Dewon Brazelton/
Jsy-Jsy/200 5.00
225 B.J. Upton/Bat-Bat/200 8.00
226 Joey Gathright/Bat-Jsy/200 5.00
228 Hank Blalock/Bat-Jsy/100 8.00
229 Mark Teixeira/Bat-Jsy/200 8.00
230 Michael Young/Bat-Jsy/200 5.00
232 Laynce Nix/Bat-Jsy/200 5.00
233 Alfonso Soriano/Bat-Jsy/200 8.00
234 Rafael Palmeiro/Bat-Jsy/200 8.00
235 Kevin Mench/Bat-Jsy/200 5.00
236 David Dellucci/Jsy-Jsy/200 8.00
237 Francisco Cordero/
Jsy-Jsy/200 5.00
239 Roy Halladay/Jsy-Jsy/200 5.00
240 Carlos Delgado/Bat-Jsy/200 5.00
242 Vernon Wells/Bat-Jsy/200 5.00
267 Larry Walker/Jsy-Jsy/200 8.00
268 Ivan Rodriguez/Jsy-Jsy/200 8.00
269 Brad Penny/Bat-Jsy/200 5.00
270 Carlos Beltran/Bat-Jsy/200 8.00
271 Paul LoDuca/Bat-Jsy/200 5.00
273 Nomar Garciaparra/
Bat-Bat/100 10.00
274 Esteban Loiaza/Bat-Bat/100 5.00
275 Richard Hidalgo/
Jkt-Pants/200 5.00
276 John Olerud/Bat-Jsy/200 5.00
277 Greg Maddux/Jsy-Jsy/200 12.00
278 Roger Clemens/Bat-Jsy/200 15.00
279 Alfonso Soriano/Bat-Jsy/200 8.00
280 Dale Murphy/Jsy-Jsy/200 8.00
281 Cal Ripken Jr./Bat-Jsy/200 30.00
282 Dwight Evans/Bat-Jsy/200 8.00
283 Ron Santo/Bat-Bat/200 10.00
284 Andre Dawson/Bat-Jsy/100 8.00
285 Harold Baines/Bat-Jsy/200 8.00
286 Jack Morris/Jsy-Jsy/100 8.00
287 Kirk Gibson/Bat-Jsy/200 5.00
288 Bo Jackson/Bat-Jsy/200 10.00
289 Orel Hershiser/Jsy-Jsy/50 8.00
291 Tony Oliva/Bat-Jsy/200 10.00
292 Darryl Strawberry/
Bat-Jsy/100 8.00
293 Roger Maris/Bat-Jsy/100 50.00
294 Don Mattingly/Bat-Jsy/100 25.00
295 Rickey Henderson/
Bat-Jsy/100 10.00
297 Dave Parker/Bat-Jsy/200 8.00
298 Steve Garvey/Bat-Jsy/200 8.00
299 Matt Williams/Jsy-Jsy/200 8.00
300 Keith Hernandez/Bat-Jsy/200 8.00
302 Vladimir Guerrero/
Jsy-Jsy/200 10.00
303 Garret Anderson/Bat-Jsy/200 5.00
307 Luis Gonzalez/Jsy-Jsy/200 5.00
310 Shawn Green/Bat-Bat/200 5.00
311 Troy Glaus/Bat-Bat/200 5.00
314 Chipper Jones/Jsy-Jsy/100 10.00
315 Johnny Estrada/Jsy-Jsy/200 5.00
316 Andruw Jones/Bat-Jsy/200 8.00
319 Jay Gibbons/Bat-Bat/200 5.00
320 Melvin Mora/Jsy-Jsy/200 5.00
321 Rafael Palmeiro/Bat-Jsy/200 8.00
323 David Ortiz/Bat-Jsy/200 10.00
324 Manny Ramirez/
Bat-Jsy/200 10.00
327 Curt Schilling/Jsy-Jsy/200 10.00
328 Sammy Sosa/Bat-Jsy/100 10.00
329 Mark Prior/Bat-Jsy/200 8.00
330 Greg Maddux/Jsy-Jsy/25 15.00
332 Frank Thomas/
Bat-Pants/200 10.00
333 Mark Buehrle/Bat-Jsy/200 5.00
336 Sean Casey/Bat-Jsy/200 5.00
337 Adam Dunn/Bat-Jsy/200 8.00
339 Travis Hafner/Jsy-Jsy/100 5.00
340 Victor Martinez/Bat-Jsy/100 5.00
341 Cliff Lee/Jsy-Jsy/200 5.00
342 Todd Helton/Bat-Jsy/25 8.00
343 Preston Wilson/Jsy-Jsy/200 5.00
344 Ivan Rodriguez/Bat-Jsy/200 8.00
347 Miguel Cabrera/Bat-Jsy/200 10.00
348 Jeff Bagwell/Bat-Jsy/200 8.00
349 Andy Pettitte/Bat-Jsy/200 8.00
350 Roger Clemens/Bat-Jsy/100 15.00
351 Ken Harvey/Jsy-Jsy/200 5.00
353 Hideo Nomo/Bat-Jsy/200 8.00
354 Kazuhisa Ishii/Jsy-Jsy/200 5.00
355 Edwin Jackson/Jsy-Jsy/200 5.00
356 J.D. Drew/Bat-Bat/200 5.00
357 Jeff Kent/Bat-Bat/25 5.00
358 Geoff Jenkins/Jsy-Pants/200 5.00
359 Carlos Lee/Bat-Bat/200 5.00
360 Shannon Stewart/
Jsy-Jsy/200 5.00
362 Johan Santana/Jsy-Jsy/100 10.00
363 Mike Piazza/Jsy-Jsy/100 12.00
364 Kazuo Matsui/Jsy-Jsy/100 5.00
366 Pedro Martinez/Bat-Bat/100 10.00
368 Hideki Matsui/Bat-Jsy/100 20.00
369 Bernie Williams/Bat-Jsy/200 8.00
370 Gary Sheffield/Bat-Jsy/100 8.00
373 Randy Johnson/Bat-Bat/25 10.00
378 Mark Mulder/Bat-Bat/50 8.00
380 Eric Chavez/Jsy-Jsy/100 5.00
382 Marlon Byrd/Bat-Jsy/200 5.00
383 Pat Burrell/Jsy-Jsy/200 5.00
385 Jim Thome/Bat-Bat/200 8.00
388 Moises Alou/Bat-Bat/200 5.00
393 Adrian Beltre/Bat-Bat/50 5.00
394 Richie Sexson/Bat-Bat/200 5.00
397 Albert Pujols/Bat-Jsy/200 20.00
398 Scott Rolen/Bat-Jsy/200 10.00
401 Delmon Young/Bat-Bat/200 5.00
402 Aubrey Huff/Bat-Bat/50 5.00
403 Alfonso Soriano/Bat-Jsy/200 8.00
404 Hank Blalock/Bat-Jsy/200 5.00
405 Richard Hidalgo/Bat-Bat/200 5.00
406 Vernon Wells/Jsy-Jsy/200 5.00
407 Orlando Hudson/Bat-Bat/200 5.00
412 Jose Vidro/Bat-Jsy/5 5.00
415 Miguel Tejada/Jsy-Jsy/200 8.00
416 Gary Sheffield/Bat-Bat/200 8.00
417 Curt Schilling/Jsy-Jsy/200 10.00
418 Rafael Palmeiro/Bat-Pants/50 8.00
419 Scott Rolen/Bat-Jsy/200 10.00
420 Aramis Ramirez/Jsy-Jsy/200 8.00
421 Vladimir Guerrero/
Bat-Bat/200 10.00
422 Steve Finley/Jsy-Jsy/200 5.00
423 Roger Clemens/Bat-Jsy/200 15.00
424 Mike Piazza/Jsy-Jsy/200 12.00
425 Ivan Rodriguez/Bat-Jsy/200 8.00
426 David Justice/Jsy-Jsy/200 5.00
427 Mark Grace/Bat-Jsy/25 8.00
428 Alan Trammell/Bat-Jsy/100 5.00
430 Dwight Gooden/Bat-Jsy/200 5.00
431 Deion Sanders/Bat-Jsy/200 8.00
432 Joe Torre/Bat-Bat/100 5.00
433 Jose Canseco/Jsy-Jsy/100 8.00
434 Tony Gwynn/Bat-Pants/200 10.00
435 Will Clark/Bat-Jsy/100 8.00
436 Marty Marion/Jsy-Jsy/1
437 Nolan Ryan/Bat-Jsy/50 15.00
438 Billy Martin/Jsy-Pants/200 10.00
439 Carlos Delgado/Bat-Bat/100 5.00
440 Magglio Ordonez/
Bat-Bat/200 5.00
441 Sammy Sosa/Bat-Bat/25 10.00
449 Ryne Sandberg/Bat-Jsy/100 10.00

Recollection Autographs Gold

No Pricing
Production One Set
Silver: No Pric
Production One Set
Platinum: No P
Production One Set

Signature Bronze

Production 1-100
No pricing 20 or less.
Black: X
Production One Set
Gold: .5X
Production 1-50
Silver: icing
Production 1-100
Platinum: 5-1.5X
Production One Se
Framed Blue:
Production 1-50
Framed Green: .75-1.5X
Production 1-25
Framed Red: .75-1.5X
Production 1-100
#303-450 found in DK Update
1 Garret Anderson/10
3 Jose Guillen/100 15.00
5 Tim Salmon/100 20.00
6 Casey Kotchman/100 15.00
7 Chone Figgins/100 15.00
8 Robb Quinlan/100 8.00
9 Francisco Rodriguez/50 40.00
10 Troy Percival/50 15.00
14 Shea Hillenbrand/100 10.00
15 Chad Tracy/100 10.00
16 Alex Cintron/100 8.00
22 Adam LaRoche/50 10.00
23 Russ Ortiz/50 12.00
26 Nick Green/100 8.00
30 Luis Matos/100 10.00
31 Larry Bigbie/100 10.00
32 Rodrigo Lopez/100 15.00
33 Brian Roberts/100 25.00
34 Melvin Mora/100 15.00
40 Keith Foulke/50 40.00
43 Kevin Youkilis/100 10.00
44 Orlando Cabrera/50 20.00
45 Abe Alvarez/100 8.00
51 Carlos Zambrano/50 30.00
58 Todd Walker/50 15.00
59 Angel Guzman/100 15.00
61 Carlos Lee/100 15.00
73 Ryan Wagner/100 10.00
75 Danny Graves/100 12.00
76 C.C. Sabathia/50 20.00
77 Jody Gerut/100 8.00
79 Victor Martinez/50 20.00
82 Kazuhito Tadano/100 20.00
83 Travis Hafner/100 15.00
89 Jeremy Bonderman/100 15.00
92 Brandon Inge/100 10.00
101 Guillermo Mota/50 10.00
107 Morgan Ensberg/100 10.00
112 Jeremy Affeldt/100 10.00
117 Milton Bradley/100 15.00
122 Brad Penny/100 10.00
123 Scott Podsednik/50 15.00
125 Lyle Overbay/100 12.00
127 Bill Hall/100 8.00
132 Lew Ford/100 15.00
135 Jason Kubel/100 15.00
137 Chad Cordero/100 10.00
140 Livan Hernandez/25 15.00
156 Bubba Crosby/100 10.00
159 Tom Gordon/25 20.00
160 Esteban Loaiza/100 10.0
166 Jermaine Dye/50 15
167 Octavio Dotel/50 15
168 Bobby Crosby/100 00
174 Mike Lieberthal/100 .00
177 Randy Wolf/100 .00
178 Craig Wilson/100 2.00
180 Jack Wilson/100 10.00
181 Jose Castillo/100 15.00
184 Jason Bay/100 10.00
186 Jay Payton/50 30.00
189 Jake Peavy/50 8.00
194 Freddy Guzman/1 10.00
197 Todd Linden/50 10.00
198 Merkin Valdez/1 10.00
203 Raul Ibanez/10 8.00
206 Miguel Olivo/0 12.00
207 Bucky Jacob 15.00
208 Jamie Moy 12.00
212 Dan Haren 10.00
219 Jeff Sup 15.00
220 Aubrey 25 20.00
221 Carl C ton/100 8.00
224 Dew ht/100 10.00
226 Joe r/25 25.00
227 Sc ung/50 20.00
230 nzalez/100 10.00
231 ix/100 15.00
232 ellucci/100 20.00
236 sco Cordero/100 15.00
237 Rios/100 15.00
24 er Navarro/100 15.00
ncy Brazoban/100 10.00
tt Proctor/100 8.00
att Peterson/100 8.00
rad Penny/50 10.00
Orlando Cabrera/50 15.00
Esteban Loaiza/100 10.00
Andre Dawson/50 20.00
Harold Baines/100 15.00
6 Jack Morris/100 10.00
90 Maury Wills/100 15.00
92 Darryl Strawberry/100 15.00
297 Dave Parker/100 20.00
299 Matt Williams/25 25.00
303 Garret Anderson/50 15.00
304 Dallas McPherson/100 10.00
305 Orlando Cabrera/25 10.00
306 Steve Finley/50 10.00
313 Russ Ortiz/50 10.00
315 Johnny Estrada/100 8.00
318 Danny Kolb/100 8.00
319 Jay Gibbons/50 8.00
320 Melvin Mora/50 10.00
325 Edgar Renteria/50 15.00
333 Mark Buehrle/50 20.00
336 Sean Casey/25 15.00
339 Travis Hafner/50 15.00
340 Victor Martinez/50 10.00

341 Cliff Lee/100 15.00
343 Preston Wilson/50 15.00
351 Ken Harvey/100 8.00
355 Edwin Jackson/100 8.00
359 Carlos Lee/100 10.00
360 Shannon Stewart/25 15.00
361 Joe Nathan/100 15.00
376 Eric Byrnes/100 8.00
377 Rich Harden/100 15.00
378 Mark Mulder/25 20.00
380 Eric Chavez/25 15.00
382 Marlon Byrd/100 8.00
384 Brett Myers/100 10.00
386 Jason Bay/50 15.00
387 Jake Peavy/50 25.00
402 Aubrey Huff/50 15.00
407 Orlando Hudson/25 10.00
410 Jose Guillen/25 15.00
429 Bert Blyleven/50 10.00
430 Dwight Gooden/50 15.00
436 Marty Marion/50 15.00

Signature Materials Bronze

NM/M

Production 1-200
No pricing 20 or less.
Platinum: No Pricing
Production One Set
Framed Black: No Pricing
Production 1-10
Framed Blue: No Pricing
Production 1-50
Framed Green: 1-2X
Production 1-25
Framed Red: .75-1.5X
Production 1-100
1 Garret Anderson/ Bat-Jsy/50 25.00
7 Chone Figgins/Bat-Jsy/200 15.00
18 Rafael Furcal/Bat-Jsy/50 20.00
19 Andruw Jones/Bat-Jsy/25 35.00
31 Larry Bigbie/Jsy-Jsy/200 15.00
32 Rodrigo Lopez/Jsy-Jsy/200 15.00
38 Trot Nixon/Jsy-Jsy/100 30.00
46 David Ortiz/Bat-Jsy/100 50.00
48 Mark Prior/Bat-Jsy/25 40.00
49 Aramis Ramirez/ Bat-Jsy/100 25.00
51 Carlos Zambrano/ Jsy-Jsy/200 25.00
52 Derrek Lee/Bat-Bat/100 20.00
61 Carlos Lee/Bat-Jsy/100 10.00
76 C.C. Sabathia/Jsy-Jsy/100 20.00
Omar Vizquel/Jsy-Jsy/25 40.00
Miguel Cabrera/Bat-Jsy/25 50.00
1 Carlos Beltran/Bat-Jsy/50 40.00
11 Jeremy Affeldt/ Pants-Pants/100 10.00
127 ll Hall/Bat-Bat/100 10.00
129 que Jones/Bat-Jsy/50 20.00
131 n Santana/Jsy-Jsy/50 40.00
132 Nord/Bat-Jsy/200 15.00
139 Johnson/Bat-Bat/50 12.00
153 Eric sada/Bat-Jsy/25 40.00
162 Craig z/Bat-Jsy/25 25.00
178 Sean n/Bat-Jsy/200 15.00
185 Bat-Jsy ghs/
201 Edgar M 10.00
211 Edgar Re /Bat-Bat/25 40.00
221 Carl Craw at-Jsy/50 30.00
229 Mark Teixei -Jsy/200 15.00
230 Michael Youn sy/25 40.00
232 Laynce Nix/Ba y/100 20.00
233 Alfonso Sorian 00 12.00
239 Roy Halladay/Jsy /25 50.00
269 Brad Penny/Bat-Js 25.00
280 Dale Murphy/Jsy-J 10.00
282 Dwight Evans/Bat-J 35.00
283 Ron Santo/Bat-Bat/1 25.00
284 Andre Dawson/Bat-Jsy 5.00
286 Jack Morris/Jsy-Jsy/10 .00
287 Kirk Gibson/Bat-Jsy/25 00
289 Orel Hershiser/Jsy-Jsy/2 0
291 Tony Oliva/Bat-Jsy/100
294 Don Mattingly/Bat-Jsy/25
297 Dave Parker/Bat-Jsy/100
298 Steve Garvey/Bat-Jsy/50
300 Keith Hernandez/ Bat-Jsy/100 20
303 Garret Anderson/Bat-Jsy/50 20.
315 Johnny Estrada/ Jsy-Jsy/50 12.00
319 Jay Gibbons/Bat-Bat/50 12.00
320 Melvin Mora/Jsy-Jsy/50 15.00
323 David Ortiz/Jsy-Jsy/25 50.00
333 Mark Buehrle/Jsy-Jsy/25 25.00
339 Travis Hafner/Jsy-Jsy/25 25.00
340 Victor Martinez/Jsy-Jsy/25 20.00
341 Cliff Lee/Jsy-Jsy/25 20.00
343 Preston Wilson/Bat-Jsy/25 20.00
351 Ken Harvey/Jsy-Jsy/25 12.00
382 Marlon Byrd/Bat-Jsy/50 12.00
401 Delmon Young/Bat-Bat/25 25.00
407 Orlando Hudson/Bat-Bat/25 12.00
419 Scott Rolen/Bat-Jsy/25 30.00
428 Alan Trammell/Bat-Jsy/25 25.00
430 Dwight Gooden/Bat-Jsy/25 25.00
434 Tony Gwynn/Bat-Jsy/25 40.00

Signature Materials Gold

NM/M

Production 1-50
7 Chone Figgins/Bat-Jsy/50 20.00
18 Rafael Furcal/Bat-Jsy/25 30.00
31 Larry Bigbie/Jsy-Jsy/50 20.00
32 Rodrigo Lopez/Jsy-Jsy/50 20.00
46 David Ortiz/Bat-Jsy/50 60.00
49 Aramis Ramirez/Bat-Jsy/50 35.00
51 Carlos Zambrano/ Jsy-Jsy/50 35.00
76 C.C. Sabathia/Jsy-Jsy/50 25.00
104 Roy Oswalt/Jsy-Jsy/50 30.00
112 Jeremy Affeldt/ Pants-Pants/50 15.00
127 Bill Hall/Bat-Bat/50 15.00
129 Jacque Jones/Bat-Jsy/50 20.00
132 Lew Ford/Bat-Jsy/50 20.00
178 Craig Wilson/Bat-Jsy/50 20.00
221 Carl Crawford/Jsy-Jsy/50 20.00
230 Michael Young/Bat-Jsy/50 25.00
269 Brad Penny/Bat-Jsy/50 15.00
280 Dale Murphy/Jsy-Jsy/25 50.00
282 Dwight Evans/Bat-Jsy/25 30.00
283 Ron Santo/Bat-Bat/50 45.00
284 Andre Dawson/Bat-Jsy/50 30.00
285 Harold Baines/Bat-Jsy/50 25.00
286 Jack Morris/Jsy-Jsy/50 25.00
291 Tony Oliva/Bat-Jsy/50 30.00
297 Dave Parker/Bat-Jsy/50 30.00
299 Matt Williams/Jsy-Jsy/25 35.00

Signature Materials Silver

NM/M

Production 1-100
7 Chone Figgins/Bat-Jsy/100 15.00
18 Rafael Furcal/Bat-Jsy/25 30.00
31 Larry Bigbie/Jsy-Jsy/100 15.00
32 Rodrigo Lopez/Jsy-Jsy/100 15.00
46 David Ortiz/Bat-Jsy/50 60.00
49 Aramis Ramirez/Bat-Jsy/50 35.00
51 Carlos Zambrano/ Jsy-Jsy/100 30.00
61 Carlos Lee/Bat-Jsy/100 10.00
76 C.C. Sabathia/ Jsy-Jsy/100 20.00
104 Roy Oswalt/Jsy-Jsy/50 30.00
112 Jeremy Affeldt/ Pants-Pants/100 10.00
127 Bill Hall/Bat-Bat/100 10.00
129 Jacque Jones/ Bat-Jsy/50 20.00
132 Lew Ford/Bat-Jsy/100 15.00
178 Craig Wilson/ Bat-Jsy/100 15.00
221 Carl Crawford/ Jsy-Jsy/100 15.00
230 Michael Young/ Bat-Jsy/50 25.00
232 Laynce Nix/Bat-Jsy/100 15.00
269 Brad Penny/Bat-Jsy/50 15.00
280 Dale Murphy/Jsy-Jsy/25 50.00
282 Dwight Evans/ Bat-Jsy/25 30.00
283 Ron Santo/Bat-Bat/50 45.00
284 Andre Dawson/ Bat-Jsy/50 30.00
285 Harold Baines/ Bat-Jsy/50 25.00
286 Jack Morris/Jsy-Jsy/50 25.00
291 Tony Oliva/Bat-Jsy/50 30.00
297 Dave Parker/Bat-Jsy/50 30.00
298 Steve Garvey/Bat-Jsy/25 30.00
299 Matt Williams/Jsy-Jsy/25 35.00
300 Keith Hernandez/Bat-Jsy/50 25.00

Team Timeline

NM/M

Complete Set (25): 65.00
Common Duo: 1.50
Inserted 1:21
#26-30 found in DK Update
1 Albert Pujols, Scott Rolen 6.00
2 Roger Clemens, Andy Pettitte 6.00
3 Tim Hudson, Mark Mulder 1.50
4 Hank Blalock, Mark Teixeira 2.00
5 Miguel Cabrera, Mike Lowell 2.00
6 Greg Maddux, Sammy Sosa 4.00
7 Miguel Tejada, Cal Ripken Jr. 8.00
8 Vladimir Guerrero, Reggie Jackson 3.00
9 Mike Schmidt, Jim Thome 4.00
10 Chipper Jones, Greg Maddux 4.00
George Brett, Ken Harvey 5.00
Don Mattingly, Hideki Matsui 5.00
Torii Hunter, han Santana 2.00
los Delgado,Vernon Wells 1.50
Helton, Larry Walker 2.00
1 Snider,
18 Beltre 2.00
, Ivan Rodriguez 3.00
19 meiro,
ay 2.00
20 rez,
21 ski 3.00
22 R son Bay 1.50
23 No dam Dunn 3.00
24 Gar Overbay 4.00
25 Carlt Johnson 8.00
26 Nolan azza 4.00
27 Roger C omas 3.00
28 Cal Ripke a 8.00
29 Willie Ma ell 8.00
30 Albert Pujo a 8.00
8.00
8.00

Team Timeline Materials Bat

NM/M

Production 25-100
2 Roger Clemens, Andy Pettitte/50 25.00
5 Miguel Cabrera, Mike Lowell/100 15.00
8 Vladimir Guerrero, Reggie Jackson/75 20.00
9 Mike Schmidt, Jim Thome/50 30.00
12 Don Mattingly, Hideki Matsui/50 50.00
15 Todd Helton, Larry Walker/100 10.00
17 Al Kaline, Ivan Rodriguez/25 30.00
18 Rafael Palmeiro, Eddie Murray/100 15.00
21 Johnny Bench, Adam Dunn/100 15.00
22 Robin Yount, Lyle Overbay/100 20.00
23 Nolan Ryan, Randy Johnson/25 40.00

Team Timeline Materials Jersey

NM/M

Common Duo: 8.00
Production 100 Sets
Prime: No Pricing
Production One Set
#26-30 found in DK Update
1 Albert Pujols, Scott Rolen 40.00
2 Roger Clemens, Andy Pettitte 25.00
3 Tim Hudson, Mark Mulder 8.00
4 Hank Blalock, Mark Teixeira 10.00
7 Miguel Tejada, Cal Ripken Jr. 40.00
8 Vladimir Guerrero, Reggie Jackson 15.00
9 Mike Schmidt/Jkt, Jim Thome 30.00
10 Chipper Jones, Greg Maddux 20.00
12 Don Mattingly/Jkt, Hideki Matsui 50.00
14 Carlos Delgado, Vernon Wells 8.00
15 Todd Helton, Larry Walker 10.00
16 Duke Snider, Adrian Beltre 10.00
18 Rafael Palmeiro, Eddie Murray 15.00
19 Manny Ramirez, Carl Yastrzemski 25.00
21 Johnny Bench, Adam Dunn 15.00
22 Robin Yount, Lyle Overbay 15.00
23 Nolan Ryan, Randy Johnson
24 Gary Carter, Mike Piazza 15.00
25 Carlton Fisk, Frank Thomas 15.00
26 Nolan Ryan, Mike Piazza 30.00
27 Roger Clemens, Jeff Bagwell 20.00
30 Albert Pujols, Stan Musial 40.00

Timeline

NM/M

Complete Set (25): 50.00
Common Player: 1.50
Inserted 1:21
#26-30 found in DK Update
1 Roger Clemens 6.00
2 Nolan Ryan 8.00
3 Carlos Beltran 3.00
4 Ivan Rodriguez 3.00
5 Jim Thome 3.00
6 Mike Piazza 4.00
7 Miguel Tejada 3.00
8 Rafael Palmeiro 2.00
9 Greg Maddux 4.00
10 Tom Glavine 1.50
11 Vladimir Guerrero 3.00
12 Curt Schilling 3.00
13 Mike Mussina 2.00
14 Rickey Henderson 2.00
15 Scott Rolen 3.00
16 Alfonso Soriano 3.00
17 Gary Sheffield 2.00
18 Carlton Fisk 2.00
19 Aramis Ramirez 2.00
20 Mark Grace 1.50
21 Jason Giambi 1.50
22 Juan Gonzalez 1.50
23 Brad Penny 1.50
24 Nomar Garciaparra 4.00
25 Larry Walker 2.00
26 Curt Schilling 2.00
27 Reggie Jackson 2.00
28 Gary Carter 1.50
29 Roger Clemens 6.00
30 Nolan Ryan 8.00

Timeline Materials Bat

NM/M

Production 25-100
1 Roger Clemens 30.00
2 Nolan Ryan 50.00
3 Carlos Beltran 10.00
4 Ivan Rodriguez 10.00
5 Jim Thome 20.00
8 Rafael Palmeiro 10.00
9 Greg Maddux 30.00
10 Tom Glavine 10.00
11 Vladimir Guerrero 15.00
12 Curt Schilling 20.00
13 Mike Mussina 10.00
14 Rickey Henderson 10.00
15 Scott Rolen 20.00
17 Gary Sheffield 10.00
18 Carlton Fisk 10.00
19 Aramis Ramirez 10.00
20 Mark Grace 10.00
22 Juan Gonzalez 10.00
25 Larry Walker 10.00

Timeline Materials Jersey

NM/M

Production 50-200
Prime: No Pricing
Production One Set
#26-30 found in DK Update
1 Roger Clemens 15.00
2 Nolan Ryan 25.00
3 Carlos Beltran 10.00
4 Ivan Rodriguez 8.00
6 Mike Piazza 15.00
7 Miguel Tejada 10.00
8 Rafael Palmeiro 10.00
9 Greg Maddux 15.00
11 Vladimir Guerrero 15.00
12 Curt Schilling 10.00
13 Mike Mussina 10.00
14 Rickey Henderson 10.00
15 Scott Rolen 15.00
16 Alfonso Soriano 10.00
18 Carlton Fisk 10.00
19 Aramis Ramirez 10.00
21 Jason Giambi 8.00
22 Juan Gonzalez 8.00
26 Curt Schilling 10.00
27 Reggie Jackson 10.00
28 Gary Carter 8.00
29 Roger Clemens 15.00
30 Nolan Ryan 25.00

Update B/W

B/W: 1X
Inserted 1:2

Silver B/W

Silvers: 4-8X
Production 50 Sets

Update Gallery of Stars

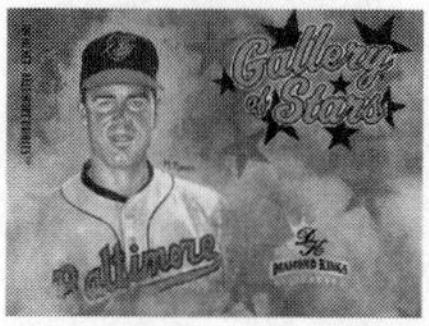

NM/M

Complete Set (25): 30.00
Common Player: 1.50
Inserted 1:8
1 Andre Dawson 1.50
2 Bob Feller 2.00
3 Bobby Doerr 1.50
4 C.C. Sabathia 1.50
5 Carl Crawford 1.50
6 Dale Murphy 2.00
7 Danny Kolb 1.50
8 Darryl Strawberry 1.50
9 Dave Parker 1.50
10 David Ortiz 3.00
11 Dwight Gooden 1.50
12 Garret Anderson 1.50
13 Jack Morris 1.50
14 Jacque Jones 1.50
15 Jim Palmer 2.00
16 Johan Santana 3.00
17 Ken Harvey 1.50
18 Lyle Overbay 1.50
19 Marty Marion 1.50
20 Melvin Mora 1.50
21 Michael Young 1.50
22 Miguel Cabrera 3.00
23 Preston Wilson 1.50
24 Sean Casey 1.50
25 Victor Martinez 1.50

Update Gallery of Stars Bat

NM/M

Production 50-200
1 Andre Dawson/50 8.00
3 Bobby Doerr/100 4.00
6 Dale Murphy/100 8.00
8 Darryl Strawberry/100 4.00
9 Dave Parker/200 4.00
10 David Ortiz/200 10.00
11 Dwight Gooden/100 4.00
12 Garret Anderson/100 4.00
18 Lyle Overbay/50 4.00
21 Michael Young/200 4.00

22 Miguel Cabrera/100 8.00
23 Preston Wilson/200 4.00
24 Sean Casey/200 4.00

Update Gallery of Star Combo

NM/M

Production 50-200 5.00
Prime: No Pricing
Production One Set
1 Andre Dawson/100 10.00
3 Bobby Doerr/100 8.00
4 C.C. Sabathia/100 5.00
6 Dale Murphy/100 10.00
9 Dave Parker/200 5.00
10 David Ortiz/200 12.00
11 Dwight Gooden/100 5.00
12 Garret Anderson/100 6.00
14 Jacque Jones/50 5.00
15 Jim Palmer/50 8.00
18 Lyle Overbay/50 5.00
21 Michael Young/200 5.00
22 Miguel Cabrera/200 10.00
23 Preston Wilson/200 5.00
24 Sean Casey/200 5.00

Update Gallery of Stars Jsy

NM/M

Production 25-100
Prime: No Pricing
Production One Set
1 Andre Dawson/100 6.00
2 Bob Feller/50 8.00
3 Bobby Doerr/100 6.00
4 C.C. Sabathia/100 4.00
5 Carl Crawford/100 4.00
6 Dale Murphy/100 8.00
8 Darryl Strawberry/25 6.00
9 Dave Parker/100 4.00
10 David Ortiz/100 8.00
11 Dwight Gooden/25 4.00
12 Garret Anderson/50 4.00
13 Jack Morris/100 4.00
14 Jacque Jones/100 4.00
15 Jim Palmer/50 6.00
17 Ken Harvey/100 4.00
18 Lyle Overbay/100 4.00
20 Melvin Mora/100 4.00
21 Michael Young/100 4.00
22 Miguel Cabrera/100 8.00
23 Preston Wilson/100 4.00
24 Sean Casey/100 4.00
25 Victor Martinez/25 6.00

Update Gallery of Stars Auto.

NM/M

Production 5-100
1 Andre Dawson/100 15.00
2 Bob Feller/100 25.00
3 Bobby Doerr/100 15.00
4 C.C. Sabathia/25 20.00
5 Carl Crawford/100 12.00
6 Dale Murphy/100 20.00
7 Danny Kolb/100 10.00
8 Darryl Strawberry/100 15.00
9 Dave Parker/100 12.00
11 Dwight Gooden/100 15.00
13 Jack Morris/100 12.00
14 Jacque Jones/50 10.00
17 Ken Harvey/100 8.00
18 Lyle Overbay/50 10.00
19 Marty Marion/25 20.00
20 Melvin Mora/100 12.00
25 Victor Martinez/100 12.00

Update Gallery of Stars Bat Autograph

NM/M

Production 5-200
1 Andre Dawson/25 25.00
3 Bobby Doerr/200 15.00
9 Dave Parker/200 15.00
11 Dwight Gooden/100 20.00
12 Garret Anderson/100 15.00
14 Jacque Jones/100 15.00
17 Ken Harvey/25 12.00
21 Michael Young/100 15.00
22 Miguel Cabrera/50 35.00
24 Sean Casey/50 20.00

Update Gallery of Stars Combo Autograph

NM/M

Production 25-200
Prime: No Pricing
Production One Set
1 Andre Dawson/50 25.00
3 Bobby Doerr/200 20.00
6 Dale Murphy/50 30.00
9 Dave Parker/100 15.00
10 David Ortiz/50 40.00
11 Dwight Gooden/100 20.00
12 Garret Anderson/50 20.00
14 Jacque Jones/50 20.00
15 Jim Palmer/25 25.00
17 Ken Harvey/25 15.00
21 Michael Young/50 20.00
22 Miguel Cabrera/50 35.00
24 Sean Casey/25 20.00
25 Victor Martinez/100 20.00

Update Gallery of Stars Jersey Autograph

NM/M

Production 25-100
Prime: No Pricing
Production One Set
1 Andre Dawson/25 25.00
2 Bob Feller/50 30.00
3 Bobby Doerr/100 15.00
4 C.C. Sabathia/100 15.00
5 Carl Crawford/50 15.00
6 Dale Murphy/50 25.00
9 Dave Parker/100 15.00
10 David Ortiz/50 40.00
11 Dwight Gooden/50 20.00
12 Garret Anderson/50 20.00
13 Jack Morris/50 15.00
14 Jacque Jones/25 20.00
15 Jim Palmer/25 25.00
17 Ken Harvey/100 8.00
18 Lyle Overbay/100 10.00
19 Marty Marion/25 20.00
20 Melvin Mora/100 15.00
24 Sean Casey/25 20.00
25 Victor Martinez/100 20.00

Update HOF Sluggers

NM/M

Common Player: 2.00
1 Duke Snider 2.00
2 Eddie Murray 2.00
3 Frank Robinson 2.00
4 George Brett 5.00
5 Harmon Killebrew 3.00
6 Mike Schmidt 5.00
7 Reggie Jackson 3.00
8 Roberto Clemente 6.00
9 Stan Musial 4.00
10 Willie Mays 5.00

Update HOF Sluggers Jersey

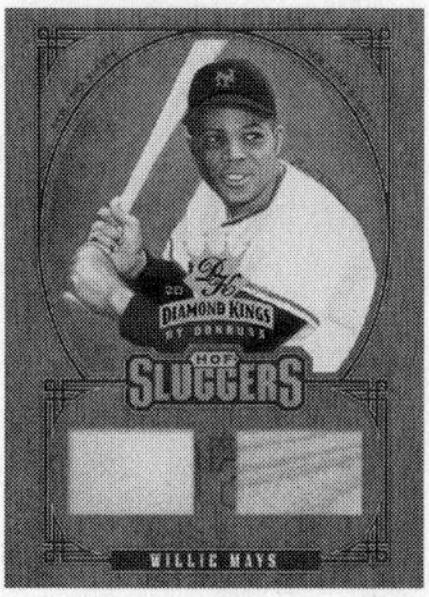

NM/M

Production 5-50
1 Duke Snider/Pants/25 10.00
2 Eddie Murray/50 10.00
5 Harmon Killebrew/25 15.00
6 Mike Schmidt/50 15.00
7 Reggie Jackson/Pants/50 8.00
9 Stan Musial/Pants/25 20.00
10 Willie Mays/Pants/50 25.00

Update Masters of the Game

NM/M

Common Player: 2.00
1 Albert Pujols 4.00
2 Cal Ripken Jr. 6.00
3 Don Mattingly 4.00
4 Greg Maddux 3.00
5 Jim Thorpe 4.00
6 Nolan Ryan 5.00
7 Randy Johnson 2.00
8 Roberto Clemente 6.00
9 Roger Clemens 4.00
10 Willie Mays 4.00

Update Masters of the Game Jersey

NM/M

Production 25-50
1 Albert Pujols/50 20.00
2 Cal Ripken Jr./50 30.00
3 Don Mattingly/25 20.00
4 Greg Maddux/50 10.00
5 Jim Thorpe/25 250.00
6 Nolan Ryan/50 20.00
7 Randy Johnson/25 10.00
9 Roger Clemens/50 10.00
10 Willie Mays/Pants/25 30.00

2005 Donruss Elite

NM/M

Complete Set (200):
Common Player (1-150): .25
Common SP (151-170): 3.00
Production 1,250
Common Auto. (171-200): 8.00
Production 500 to 1,500
Pack (5): 5.00
Box (20): 90.00
1 Bartolo Colon .25
2 Casey Kotchman .25
3 Chone Figgins .25
4 Darin Erstad .25
5 Garret Anderson .40
6 Jose Guillen .25
7 Vladimir Guerrero .75

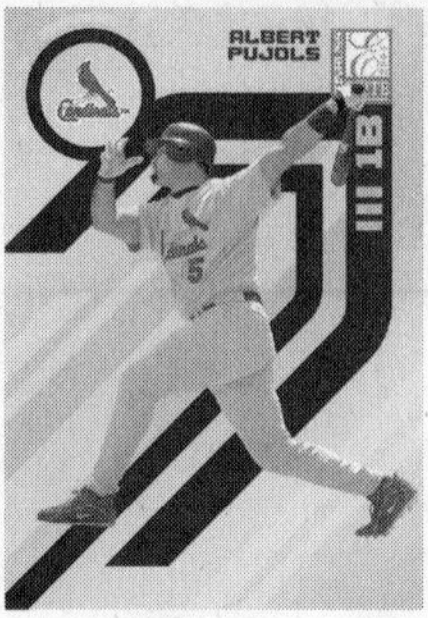

8 Luis Gonzalez .25
9 Randy Johnson .75
10 Troy Glaus .40
11 Andruw Jones .40
12 Chipper Jones .75
13 J.D. Drew .25
14 John Smoltz .40
15 Johnny Estrada .25
16 Marcus Giles .25
17 Rafael Furcal .25
18 Javy Lopez .40
19 Jay Gibbons .25
20 Melvin Mora .25
21 Miguel Tejada .50
22 Rafael Palmeiro .50
23 Sidney Ponson .25
24 Curt Schilling .75
25 David Ortiz .75
26 Derek Lowe .25
27 Jason Varitek .40
28 Johnny Damon .75
29 Manny Ramirez .75
30 Pedro Martinez .75
31 Aramis Ramirez .40
32 Carlos Zambrano .40
33 Corey Patterson .25
34 Derrek Lee .50
35 Greg Maddux 1.00
36 Kerry Wood .50
37 Mark Prior .75
38 Moises Alou .40
39 Nomar Garciaparra 1.00
40 Sammy Sosa 1.00
41 Carlos Lee .25
42 Frank Thomas .50
43 Jermaine Dye .25
44 Magglio Ordonez .25
45 Mark Buehrle .25
46 Paul Konerko .25
47 Adam Dunn .50
48 Austin Kearns .25
49 Barry Larkin .40
50 Ken Griffey Jr. 1.00
51 Sean Casey .25
52 C.C. Sabathia .25
53 Cliff Lee .25
54 Travis Hafner .25
55 Victor Martinez .25
56 Jeromy Burnitz .25
57 Preston Wilson .25
58 Todd Helton .50
59 Brandon Inge .25
60 Ivan Rodriguez .50
61 Jeremy Bonderman .25
62 Troy Percival .25
63 Dontrelle Willis .40
64 Josh Beckett .40
65 Juan Pierre .25
66 Miguel Cabrera .75
67 Mike Lowell .25
68 Paul LoDuca .25
69 Andy Pettitte .40
70 Brad Ausmus .25
71 Carlos Beltran .50
72 Craig Biggio .40
73 Jeff Bagwell .50
74 Lance Berkman .40
75 Roger Clemens 2.00
76 Roy Oswalt .25
77 Juan Gonzalez .25
78 Mike Sweeney .25
79 Zack Greinke .25
80 Adrian Beltre .25
81 Hideo Nomo .25
82 Jeff Kent .25
83 Milton Bradley .25
84 Shawn Green .25
85 Steve Finley .25
86 Ben Sheets .25
87 Lyle Overbay .25
88 Scott Podsednik .25
89 Lew Ford .25
90 Shannon Stewart .25
91 Torii Hunter .25
92 David Wright .75
93 Jose Reyes .50
94 Kazuo Matsui .25
95 Mike Piazza 1.00
96 Tom Glavine .40
97 Alex Rodriguez 1.50
98 Bernie Williams .40
99 Derek Jeter 2.00
100 Gary Sheffield .50
101 Hideki Matsui 1.50
102 Jason Giambi .25
103 Kevin Brown .25
104 Mike Mussina .40
105 Barry Zito .25
106 Bobby Crosby .40
107 Eric Chavez .40
108 Jason Kendall .25
109 Mark Mulder .40
110 Bobby Abreu .40
111 Jim Thome .75
112 Kevin Millwood .25
113 Pat Burrell .25
114 Craig Wilson .25
115 Jack Wilson .25
116 Jason Bay .40
117 Brian Giles .25
118 Khalil Greene .40
119 Mark Loretta .25
120 Ryan Klesko .25
121 Sean Burroughs .25
122 Edgardo Alfonzo .25
123 J.T. Snow .25
124 Jason Schmidt .25
125 Omar Vizquel .25
126 Ichiro Suzuki 1.50
127 Jamie Moyer .25
128 Bret Boone .25
129 Richie Sexson .40
130 Albert Pujols 2.00
131 Edgar Renteria .40
132 Jeff Suppan .25
133 Jim Edmonds .40
134 Larry Walker .40
135 Scott Rolen .75
136 Aubrey Huff .25
137 B.J. Upton .25
138 Carl Crawford .25
139 Rocco Baldelli .25
140 Alfonso Soriano .75
141 Hank Blalock .40
142 Kenny Rogers .25
143 Laynce Nix .25
144 Mark Teixeira .50
145 Michael Young .25
146 Carlos Delgado .40
147 Eric Hinske .25
148 Roy Halladay .25
149 Vernon Wells .25
150 Jose Vidro .25
151 Bob Gibson 3.00
152 Brooks Robinson 3.00
153 Cal Ripken Jr. 10.00
154 Carl Yastrzemski 4.00
155 Don Mattingly 5.00
156 Eddie Murray 3.00
157 Ernie Banks 4.00
158 Frank Robinson 3.00
159 George Brett 5.00
160 Harmon Killebrew 4.00
161 Johnny Bench 4.00
162 Mike Schmidt 5.00
163 Nolan Ryan 6.00
164 Paul Molitor 4.00
165 Stan Musial 5.00
166 Steve Carlton 3.00
167 Tony Gwynn 4.00
168 Warren Spahn 4.00
169 Willie Mays 6.00
170 Willie McCovey 3.00
171 Miguel Negron AU/1,500 **RC** 8.00
172 Mike Morse AU/1,000 **RC** 15.00
173 Wladimir Balentien AU/1,500 **RC** 10.00
174 Alberto Concepcion AU/651 **RC** 10.00
175 Ubaldo Jimenez AU/500 **RC** 10.00
176 Justin Verlander AU/500 **RC** 50.00
177 Ryan Speier AU/1,000 **RC** 8.00
178 Geovany Soto AU/500 **RC** 50.00
179 Mark McLemore AU/1,200 **RC** 8.00
180 Ambiorix Burgos AU/599 **RC** 8.00
181 Chris Roberson AU/1,000 **RC** 10.00
182 Colter Bean AU/625 **RC** 10.00
183 Erick Threets AU/500 **RC** 8.00
184 Carlos Ruiz AU/1,000 **RC** 15.00
186 Jared Gothreaux AU/1,500 **RC** 10.00
187 Luis Hernandez AU/1,000 **RC** 8.00
188 Agustin Montero/1,000 **RC** 2.00
189 Paulino Reynoso/1,000 **RC** 2.00
190 Garrett Jones AU/500 **RC** 8.00
191 Sean Thompson AU/500 **RC** 8.00
192 Matt Lindstrom AU/1,500 **RC** 8.00
193 Nate McLouth AU/500 **RC** 15.00
194 Luke Scott AU/671 **RC** 25.00
195 Keith Hattig AU/500 10.00
196 Jason Hammel AU/1,500 **RC** 10.00
197 Danny Rueckel AU/671 **RC** 8.00
198 Justin Wechsler AU/500 **RC** 8.00
199 Chris Resop AU/500 **RC** 15.00
200 Jeff Miller AU/500 **RC** 10.00

Aspirations

Cards (1-150) print run 61-99: 4-8X
(1-150) p/r 41-60: 6-10X
(1-150) p/r 21-40: 8-15X
(151-170) p/r 36-80: 1.5-3X
Autos. (171-200) p/r 40-99: .5-1.5X
No pricing production 20 or less.
Production 15-99

Status

Cards (1-150) print run 61-81: 4-8X
(1-150) p/r 41-60: 6-10X
(1-150) p/r 21-40: 8-15X
(151-170) p/r 36-81: 1.5-3X
Autos. (171-200) p/r 40-81: .5-1.5X
No pricing production 20 or less.
Production 1-81

Status Gold

Gold (1-150): 10-20X
Gold (151-170): 3-5X
Gold (171-200): No Pricing
Production 24 Sets

Turn of the Century

Stars (1-150): 2-3X
Production 750
(151-170): 1X
Production 250
Rookies (171-200): .25-1X
Production 500

Back 2 Back Jacks

NM/M

Production 25-200
1 Adam Dunn/200 8.00
3 Albert Pujols/100 15.00
4 Babe Ruth/50 160.00
5 Cal Ripken Jr./100 30.00
6 David Ortiz/200 10.00
7 Eddie Murray/150 8.00
8 Ernie Banks/50 15.00
9 Frank Robinson/50 8.00
10 Gary Sheffield/200 5.00
11 George Foster/125 5.00
12 Don Mattingly/10 15.00
13 Hideki Matsui/25 30.00
14 Jason Giambi/50 5.00
16 Jim Rice/125 8.00
17 Jim Thome/200 8.00
18 Johnny Bench/125 10.00
19 Lance Berkman/200 5.00
20 Manny Ramirez/200 8.00
21 Mike Piazza/200 10.00
22 Mike Schmidt/125 15.00
23 Rafael Palmeiro/200 8.00
24 Reggie Jackson/125 10.00
25 Sammy Sosa/100 10.00
26 Scott Rolen/200 8.00
27 Stan Musial/125 15.00
28 Willie Mays/50 40.00
29 Kirk Gibson/125 5.00
30 Will Clark/125 5.00
31 Willie Mays, Sammy Sosa/50 50.00
32 Eddie Murray, Mike Piazza/50 20.00
33 Mike Schmidt, Jim Thome/50 30.00
34 Rafael Palmeiro, Kirk Gibson/50 10.00
35 Jim Rice, Manny Ramirez/50 15.00
36 Adrian Beltre, Will Clark/50 15.00
37 Reggie Jackson, David Ortiz/50 15.00
38 Johnny Bench, Adam Dunn/50 20.00

Back 2 Back Jacks Combos

NM/M

1 Adam Dunn/Bat-Jsy/100 10.00
2 Adrian Beltre/Bat-Jsy/100 8.00
5 Cal Ripken Jr./Bat-Jsy/50 40.00
6 David Ortiz/Bat-Jsy/50 12.00
7 Eddie Murray/Bat-Jsy/50 10.00
8 Ernie Banks/Bat-Jsy/10 20.00
10 Gary Sheffield/Bat-Jsy/100 8.00
11 George Foster/Bat-Jsy/50 8.00
12 Don Mattingly/Bat-Jsy/50 20.00
13 Hideki Matsui/Bat-Jsy/25 40.00
14 Jason Giambi/Bat-Jsy/50 8.00
15 Jim Edmonds/Bat-Jsy/100 10.00
17 Jim Thome/Bat-Jsy/100 8.00
18 Johnny Bench/Bat-Jsy/50 15.00
19 Lance Berkman/Bat-Jsy/100 8.00
20 Manny Ramirez/Bat-Jsy/100 12.00
21 Mike Piazza/Bat-Jsy/50 15.00
22 Mike Schmidt/Bat-Jsy/50 20.00
23 Rafael Palmeiro/Bat-Jsy/50 10.00
24 Reggie Jackson/Bat-Jsy/50 15.00
25 Sammy Sosa/Bat-Jsy/100 15.00
26 Scott Rolen/Bat-Jsy/100 12.00
27 Stan Musial/Bat-Pants/50 25.00
28 Willie Mays/Bat-Jsy/50 60.00
29 Kirk Gibson/Bat-Jsy/50 10.00
30 Will Clark/Bat-Jsy/50 12.00
32 Eddie Murray, Mike Piazza/25 30.00
33 Mike Schmidt, Jim Thome/25 50.00
34 Rafael Palmeiro, Kirk Gibson/25 20.00

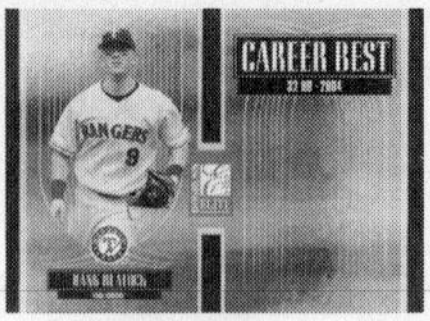

35 Jim Rice, Manny Ramirez/50 25.00
36 Adrian Beltre, Will Clark/50 15.00
37 Reggie Jackson, David Ortiz/25 30.00
38 Johnny Bench, Adam Dunn/25 30.00
40 Cal Ripken Jr., Albert Pujols/25 100.00

Career Best

NM/M

Common Player: 1.00
Production 1,500 Sets
Black: 1-2X
Production 150 Sets
Blue: 1-2X
Production 250 Sets
Gold: 1-1.5X
Production 500 Sets
1 Adam Dunn 1.50
2 Adrian Beltre 1.00
3 Albert Pujols 4.00
4 Andruw Jones 1.50
5 Ben Sheets 1.00
6 Bo Jackson 2.00
7 Brooks Robinson 2.00
8 Cal Ripken Jr. 6.00
9 Dale Murphy 1.50
10 Don Mattingly 3.00
11 Eddie Murray 1.50
12 George Brett 3.00
13 Hank Blalock 1.50
14 Ichiro Suzuki 3.00
15 Jim Thome 1.50
16 Kerry Wood 1.50
17 Lance Berkman 1.00
18 Mark Prior 2.00
19 Mark Teixeira 1.50
20 Mike Schmidt 3.00
21 Pedro Martinez 2.00
22 Randy Johnson 2.00
23 Rickey Henderson 1.50
24 Sammy Sosa 3.00
25 Tony Gwynn 2.00

Career Best Bats

NM/M

Production 50-250
1 Adam Dunn/250 8.00
2 Adrian Beltre/250 5.00
3 Albert Pujols/250 15.00
4 Andruw Jones/250 5.00
5 Ben Sheets/250 5.00
6 Bo Jackson/250 10.00
7 Brooks Robinson/250 8.00
8 Cal Ripken Jr./150 25.00
9 Dale Murphy/150 10.00
10 Don Mattingly/250 12.00
11 Eddie Murray/250 8.00
12 George Brett/250 15.00
13 Hank Blalock/250 8.00
15 Jim Thome/100 8.00
16 Kerry Wood/100 8.00
17 Lance Berkman/250 5.00
18 Mark Prior/150 6.00
19 Mark Teixeira/250 8.00
20 Mike Schmidt/250 12.00
21 Pedro Martinez/100 10.00
22 Randy Johnson/100 10.00
23 Rickey Henderson/250 8.00
24 Sammy Sosa/100 10.00
25 Tony Gwynn/100 10.00

Career Best Combos

NM/M

Production 25-150 10.00
1 Adam Dunn/Bat-Jsy/150 10.00
2 Adrian Beltre/Bat-Jsy/150 8.00
3 Albert Pujols/Bat-Jsy/150 20.00
4 Andruw Jones/Bat-Jsy/150 8.00
5 Ben Sheets/Bat-Jsy/150 8.00
6 Bo Jackson/Bat-Jsy/25 20.00
7 Brooks Robinson/Bat-Jsy/25 20.00
8 Cal Ripken Jr./Bat-Jsy/25 40.00
9 Dale Murphy/Bat-Jsy/25 10.00
10 Don Mattingly/Bat-Jsy/25 20.00
11 Eddie Murray/Bat-Jsy/25 12.00
12 George Brett/Bat-Jsy/25 25.00
13 Hank Blalock/Bat-Jsy/150 10.00
15 Jim Thome/Bat-Jsy/150 10.00
16 Kerry Wood/Bat-Pants/150 10.00
17 Lance Berkman/Bat-Jsy/150 8.00
18 Mark Prior/Bat-Jsy/150 8.00
19 Mark Teixeira/Bat-Jsy/150 12.00
21 Pedro Martinez/Bat-Jsy/125 10.00
23 Rickey Henderson/Bat-Jsy/25 15.00
24 Sammy Sosa/Bat-Jsy/150 12.00
25 Tony Gwynn/Bat-Jsy/25 15.00

Career Best Jerseys

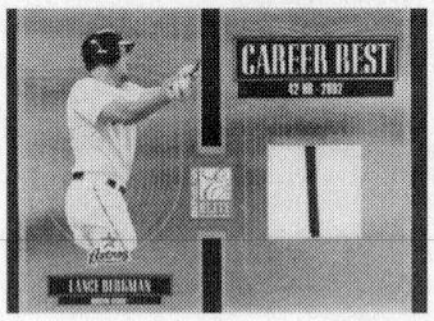

NM/M

Production 100-250
1 Adam Dunn/250 8.00
2 Adrian Beltre/250 5.00
3 Albert Pujols/250 15.00
4 Andruw Jones/250 5.00
5 Ben Sheets/250 5.00
6 Bo Jackson/250 10.00
7 Brooks Robinson/50 10.00
8 Cal Ripken Jr./150 25.00
9 Dale Murphy/100 10.00
10 Don Mattingly/150 12.00
11 Eddie Murray/100 8.00
12 George Brett/100 15.00
13 Hank Blalock/250 8.00
15 Jim Thome/250 8.00
16 Kerry Wood/250 8.00
17 Lance Berkman/250 5.00
18 Mark Prior/250 6.00
19 Mark Teixeira/250 8.00
20 Mike Schmidt/100 12.00
21 Pedro Martinez/250 8.00
22 Randy Johnson/100 10.00
23 Rickey Henderson/50 10.00
24 Sammy Sosa/250 10.00
25 Tony Gwynn/250 10.00

Face 2 Face

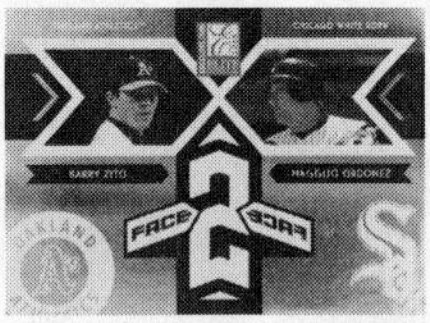

NM/M

Complete Set (20): 35.00
Common Duo:
Production 1,500 Sets
Black: 1-1.5X
Production 500 Sets
Gold: 1-2X
Production 250 Sets
Red: 1X
Production 750 Sets
1 Roger Clemens, Scott Rolen 3.00
2 Greg Maddux, Jeff Bagwell 3.00
3 Mark Prior, Mike Piazza 3.00
4 Mike Mussina, Ivan Rodriguez 2.00
5 Josh Beckett, Sammy Sosa 2.00
6 Roy Oswalt, Miguel Cabrera 2.00
7 Roger Clemens, Albert Pujols 4.00
8 Pedro Martinez, Vladimir Guerrero 2.00
9 Randy Johnson, Jim Edmonds 2.00
10 Curt Schilling, Derek Jeter 4.00
11 Kerry Wood, Lance Berkman 1.50
12 Tim Hudson, Garret Anderson 1.00
13 Pedro Martinez, Gary Sheffield 2.00
14 Barry Zito, Magglio Ordonez 1.00
15 Kerry Wood, Shawn Green 1.50
16 Mike Mussina, Miguel Tejada 2.00
17 Randy Johnson, Albert Pujols 4.00
18 Nolan Ryan, George Brett 4.00
19 Tom Seaver, Mike Schmidt 3.00
20 Jim Palmer, Harmon Killebrew 2.00

Face 2 Face Bats

NM/M

Production 25-150
3 Mark Prior, Mike Piazza/10 8.00
4 Mike Mussina, Ivan Rodriguez/100 8.00
5 Josh Beckett, Sammy Sosa/50 10.00
6 Roy Oswalt, Miguel Cabrera/100 10.00
8 Pedro Martinez, Vladimir Guerrero/50 10.00
9 Randy Johnson, Jim Edmonds/50 10.00
11 Kerry Wood, Lance Berkman/150 8.00
12 Tim Hudson, Garret Anderson/150 8.00
13 Pedro Martinez, Gary Sheffield/150 10.00
14 Barry Zito, Maggio Ordonez/50 8.00
15 Kerry Wood, Shawn Green/150 8.00
18 Nolan Ryan, George Brett/100 25.00
19 Tom Seaver, Mike Schmidt/150 15.00

Face 2 Face Combos

NM/M

Production 25-250
1 Roger Clemens/Jsy, Scott Rolen/Bat/100 15.00
2 Greg Maddux/Jsy, Jeff Bagwell/Bat/100 10.00
3 Mark Prior/Jsy, Mike Piazza/Bat/250 8.00
4 Mike Mussina/Jsy, Ivan Rodriguez/Bat/250 8.00
5 Josh Beckett/Jsy, Sammy Sosa/Bat/250 10.00
6 Roy Oswalt/Jsy, Miguel Cabrera/Bat/250 8.00
8 Pedro Martinez/Jsy, Vladimir Guerrero/Bat/75 10.00
11 Kerry Wood/Bat, Lance Berkman/Jsy/250 8.00
12 Tim Hudson/Jsy, Garret Anderson/Bat/100 8.00
13 Pedro Martinez/Bat, Gary Sheffield/Jsy/75 12.00
14 Barry Zito/Jsy, Maggio Ordonez/Bat/250 8.00
15 Kerry Wood/Jsy, Shawn Green/Bat/250 8.00
16 Mike Mussina/Jsy, Miguel Tejada/Bat/250 10.00
19 Tom Seaver/Jsy, Mike Schmidt/Bat/50 20.00

Face 2 Face Jerseys

NM/M

Production 25-200
1 Roger Clemens, Scott Rolen/200 15.00
2 Greg Maddux, Jeff Bagwell/75 10.00
3 Mark Prior, Mike Piazza/200 8.00
4 Mike Mussina, Ivan Rodriguez/200 8.00
5 Josh Beckett, Sammy Sosa/200 12.00
6 Roy Oswalt, Miguel Cabrera/200 8.00
7 Roger Clemens, Albert Pujols/200 20.00
8 Pedro Martinez, Vladimir Guerrero/75 10.00
11 Kerry Wood, Lance Berkman/200 8.00
12 Tim Hudson, Garret Anderson/75 8.00
13 Pedro Martinez, Gary Sheffield/75 10.00
14 Barry Zito, Maggio Ordonez/200 8.00
15 Kerry Wood, Shawn Green/200 8.00
16 Mike Mussina, Miguel Tejada/200 10.00
17 Randy Johnson, Albert Pujols/75 20.00
19 Tom Seaver, Mike Schmidt/50 20.00

Passing the Torch

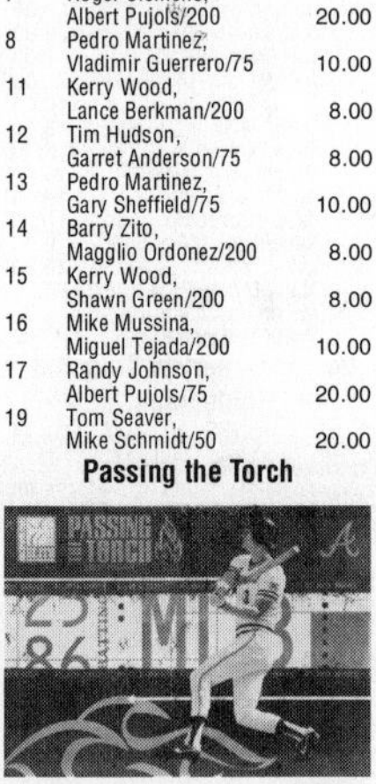

NM/M

Common Player: 1.50
1-30 Production 1,000
31-45 Production 500
Black: 2-3X
1-30 Production 50
31-45 Production 25
Gold: 1-2X
1-30 Production 100
31-45 Production 50
Green: 1-1.5X
1-30 Production 250
31-45 Production 125
Red: 1X
1-30 Production 500
31-45 Production 250
1 Adrian Beltre 1.50
2 Albert Pujols 5.00
3 Alex Rodriguez 4.00
4 Andruw Jones 1.50
5 Babe Ruth 6.00
6 Ben Sheets 1.50
7 Brooks Robinson 2.00

8	Cal Ripken Jr.	8.00
9	Carl Yastrzemski	3.00
10	Dale Murphy	2.00
11	David Ortiz	2.00
12	Derek Jeter	5.00
13	Don Mattingly	4.00
14	George Brett	4.00
15	Greg Maddux	3.00
16	Hank Blalock	1.50
17	Jeff Bagwell	1.50
18	Johnny Bench	3.00
19	Magglio Ordonez	1.50
20	Mark Prior	2.00
21	Mark Teixeira	2.00
22	Miguel Cabrera	2.00
23	Mike Schmidt	3.00
24	Nolan Ryan	6.00
25	Pedro Martinez	2.00
26	Sammy Sosa	3.00
27	Scott Rolen	2.00
28	Tom Seaver	2.00
29	Vladimir Guerrero	2.00
30	Willie Mays	4.00
31	Carlton Fisk, Magglio Ordonez	3.00
32	Nolan Ryan, Ben Sheets	8.00
33	Babe Ruth, Alex Rodriguez	8.00
34	Cal Ripken Jr., B.J. Upton	10.00
35	Willie Mays, Andruw Jones	5.00
36	George Brett, Hank Blalock	5.00
37	Greg Maddux, Whitey Ford	4.00
38	Harmon Killebrew, Mark Prior	3.00
39	Tom Seaver, Mark Prior	3.00
40	Don Mattingly, Mark Teixeira	5.00
41	Stan Musial, Carlos Beltran	5.00
42	Dale Murphy, Lance Berkman	3.00
43	Willie McCovey, Jeff Bagwell	3.00
44	Andre Dawson, Miguel Cabrera	3.00
45	Brooks Robinson, Scott Rolen	4.00

Passing the Torch Autographs

		NM/M
Production 5-100		
1	Adrian Beltre/75	15.00
6	Ben Sheets/75	15.00
7	Brooks Robinson/100	25.00
10	Dale Murphy/100	20.00
13	Don Mattingly/50	50.00
18	Johnny Bench/25	50.00
19	Magglio Ordonez/75	10.00
20	Mark Prior/25	40.00
21	Mark Teixeira/25	25.00
22	Miguel Cabrera/75	25.00
23	Mike Schmidt/25	50.00
27	Scott Rolen/25	40.00
28	Tom Seaver/25	50.00
31	Carlton Fisk, Magglio Ordonez/25	50.00
44	Andre Dawson, Miguel Cabrera/25	50.00
45	Brooks Robinson, Scott Rolen/25	75.00

Passing the Torch Bats

		NM/M
Production 25-250		
1	Adrian Beltre/250	4.00
2	Albert Pujols/250	15.00
4	Andruw Jones/250	4.00
6	Ben Sheets/250	4.00
7	Brooks Robinson/250	10.00
8	Cal Ripken Jr./150	25.00
9	Carl Yastrzemski/150	10.00
10	Dale Murphy/150	6.00
12	David Ortiz/250	8.00
13	Don Mattingly/150	10.00
14	George Brett/150	10.00
16	Hank Blalock/250	4.00
17	Jeff Bagwell/250	6.00
18	Johnny Bench/150	10.00
19	Magglio Ordonez/250	4.00
20	Mark Prior/50	10.00
21	Mark Teixeira/250	4.00
22	Miguel Cabrera/250	8.00
23	Mike Schmidt/150	10.00
24	Nolan Ryan/50	20.00
25	Pedro Martinez/150	8.00
26	Sammy Sosa/250	8.00
27	Scott Rolen/250	8.00
28	Tom Seaver/150	8.00
29	Vladimir Guerrero/250	8.00
30	Willie Mays/50	30.00
31	Carlton Fisk, Magglio Ordonez/250	6.00
32	Nolan Ryan,Ben Sheets/50	35.00
34	Cal Ripken Jr., B.J. Upton/50	50.00
35	Willie Mays, Andruw Jones/50	35.00
36	George Brett, Hank Blalock/150	15.00
39	Tom Seaver, Mark Prior/25	20.00
40	Don Mattingly, Mark Teixeira/150	15.00
42	Dale Murphy, Lance Berkman/50	12.00

43	Willie McCovey, Jeff Bagwell/25	20.00
44	Andre Dawson, Miguel Cabrera/150	10.00
45	Brooks Robinson, Scott Rolen/150	15.00

Passing the Torch Jerseys

		NM/M
Production 25-250		
1	Adrian Beltre/250	4.00
2	Albert Pujols/250	15.00
4	Andruw Jones/250	4.00
6	Ben Sheets/250	4.00
8	Cal Ripken Jr./250	20.00
9	Carl Yastrzemski/Pants/50	10.00
10	Dale Murphy/250	6.00
11	David Ortiz/250	8.00
13	Don Mattingly/150	10.00
14	George Brett/50	12.00
15	Greg Maddux/250	10.00
16	Hank Blalock/250	4.00
17	Jeff Bagwell/250	6.00
18	Johnny Bench/Pants/150	10.00
19	Magglio Ordonez/250	4.00
20	Mark Prior/250	6.00
21	Mark Teixeira/250	6.00
22	Miguel Cabrera/250	8.00
23	Mike Schmidt/150	10.00
24	Nolan Ryan/50	20.00
25	Pedro Martinez/250	8.00
26	Sammy Sosa/250	8.00
27	Scott Rolen/250	8.00
28	Tom Seaver/250	8.00
29	Vladimir Guerrero/250	8.00
31	Carlton Fisk, Magglio Ordonez/50	8.00
32	Nolan Ryan, Ben Sheets/50	35.00
34	Cal Ripken Jr., B.J. Upton/50	50.00
35	Willie Mays, Andruw Jones/50	35.00
36	George Brett, Hank Blalock/50	15.00
39	Tom Seaver, Mark Prior/25	20.00
40	Don Mattingly, Mark Teixeira/100	15.00
42	Dale Murphy, Lance Berkman/50	10.00
43	Willie McCovey, Jeff Bagwell/50	15.00
44	Andre Dawson, Miguel Cabrera/100	10.00

Recollection Autographs

No Pricing
Production 10-25

Teams

		NM/M
Common Card:		2.00
Production 1,500 Sets		
Black:		1-2X
Production 250 Sets		
Blue:		1X
Production 1,000 Sets		
Gold:		2-3X
Production 100 Sets		
Green:		1-1.5X
Production 750 Sets		
Red:		1-1.5X
Production 500 Sets		
1	Manny Ramirez, Pedro Martinez, David Ortiz	4.00
2	Albert Pujols, Scott Rolen, Jim Edmonds	4.00
3	Roger Clemens, Jeff Bagwell, Lance Berkman, Craig Biggio	4.00
4	Miguel Cabrera, Josh Beckett, Mike Lowell	2.00
5	Kerry Wood, Mark Prior, Sammy Sosa, Greg Maddux	4.00
6	Adrian Beltre, Shawn Green, Hideo Nomo, Kazuhisa Ishii	2.00
7	Cal Ripken Jr., Eddie Murray, Jim Palmer	8.00

8	George Brett, Bo Jackson, Frank White	4.00
9	Roger Clemens, Mike Mussina, Alfonso Soriano, Bernie Williams	4.00
10	Tom Glavine, Greg Maddux, Ryan Klesko, David Justice	4.00

Teams Bats

		NM/M
Production 50-100		
1	Manny Ramirez, Pedro Martinez, David Ortiz/100	20.00
2	Albert Pujols, Scott Rolen, Jim Edmonds/100	40.00
3	Roger Clemens, Jeff Bagwell, Lance Berkman, Craig Biggio/50	35.00
4	Miguel Cabrera, Josh Beckett, Mike Lowell/100	10.00
6	Adrian Beltre, Shawn Green, Hideo Nomo, Kazuhisa Ishii/50	20.00
8	George Brett, Bo Jackson, Frank White/100	25.00

Teams Jerseys

		NM/M
Production 50-150		
1	Manny Ramirez, Pedro Martinez, David Ortiz/150	20.00
2	Albert Pujols, Scott Rolen, Jim Edmonds/150	30.00
3	Roger Clemens, Jeff Bagwell, Lance Berkman, Craig Biggio/150	25.00
4	Miguel Cabrera, Josh Beckett, Mike Lowell/50	15.00
5	Kerry Wood, Mark Prior, Sammy Sosa, Greg Maddux/150	25.00
6	Adrian Beltre, Shawn Green, Hideo Nomo, Kazuhisa Ishii/50	20.00
7	Cal Ripken Jr., Eddie Murray, Jim Palmer/100	35.00
9	Roger Clemens, Mike Mussina, Alfonso Soriano, Bernie Williams/100	25.00
10	Tom Glavine, Greg Maddux, Ryan Klesko, David Justice/100	30.00

Throwback Threads

		NM/M
Production 10-200		
1	Albert Pujols/200	15.00
3	Bert Blyleven/200	4.00
4	Bobby Doerr/Pants/200	6.00
6	Cal Ripken Jr./150	25.00
7	Carl Yastrzemski/Pants/150	12.00
8	Dale Murphy/150	9.00
9	Dennis Eckersley/50	8.00
10	Don Mattingly/200	10.00
11	Don Sutton/100	4.00
13	Early Wynn/50	6.00
14	Eddie Murray/100	8.00
16	Greg Maddux/150	8.00
17	Harmon Killebrew/100	8.00
18	Hoyt Wilhelm/150	6.00
19	Jim Edmonds/200	8.00
21	Lou Boudreau/100	8.00
22	Lou Brock/100	8.00
23	Miguel Cabrera/200	8.00
24	Mike Mussina/150	8.00
25	Mike Piazza/150	8.00
26	Mike Schmidt/150	15.00
27	Nolan Ryan/50	20.00
28	Phil Niekro/100	6.00
29	Randy Johnson/150	8.00
30	Rickey Henderson/150	8.00
31	Sammy Sosa/150	8.00
32	Scott Rolen/200	8.00
34	Steve Carlton/100	8.00
36	Tommy John/150	6.00
37	Vladimir Guerrero/200	8.00
38	Whitey Ford/25	15.00
39	Willie Mays/50	40.00
40	Willie McCovey/150	8.00
46	Lou Brock, Bo Jackson, Rickey Henderson/100	15.00
49	Deion Sanders/150	15.00
50	Nolan Ryan, Curt Schilling/100	25.00
51	Don Sutton, Greg Maddux/100	15.00
52	Harmon Killebrew, Rafael Palmeiro/100	15.00
53	Dale Murphy, Dwight Evans/150	12.00
55	Carl Yastrzemski, Vladimir Guerrero/50	15.00
56	Eddie Murray, Mike Piazza/50	12.00
57	Johnny Bench, Ivan Rodriguez/50	12.00
58	Jim Palmer, Tim Hudson/50	10.00
59	Cal Ripken Jr., Hank Blalock/50	15.00
60	Jim Rice, Manny Ramirez/100	12.00

Throwback Threads Autographs

		NM/M
Production 5-100		
Prime:		No Pricing
Production 1-10		
3	Bert Blyleven/100	15.00
4	Bobby Doerr/Pants/100	20.00
5	Brooks Robinson/50	30.00
8	Dale Murphy/100	25.00
9	Dennis Eckersley/75	20.00
10	Don Sutton/50	20.00
17	Harmon Killebrew/75	30.00
20	Jim Palmer/75	15.00
22	Lou Brock/Jkt/75	30.00
23	Miguel Cabrera/75	30.00

Throwback Threads Prime

No Pricing
Production 1-25

2005 Donruss Greats

		NM/M
Complete Set (150):		50.00
Common Player:		.50
Pack (5):		9.00
Box (15):		120.00
1	Al Kaline	.75
2	Alan Trammell	.50
3	Andre Dawson	.50
4	Barry Larkin	.50
5	Bert Blyleven	.50
6	Billy Williams	.50
7	Bo Jackson	1.00
8	Bob Feller	.75
9	Bobby Doerr	.50
10	Brooks Robinson	1.00
11	Cal Ripken Jr.	4.00
12	Dale Murphy	.50
13	Darryl Strawberry	.50
14	Dave Parker	.50
15	Dave Stewart	.50
16	David Cone	.50
17	Dennis Eckersley	.50
18	Don Larsen	.50
19	Don Mattingly	2.00
20	Don Sutton	.50
21	Duke Snider	1.00
22	Dwight Evans	.50
23	Dwight Gooden	.50
24	Earl Weaver	.50
25	Fergie Jenkins	.50
26	Frank Robinson	1.00
27	Fred Lynn	.50
28	Gary Carter	.50
29	Gaylord Perry	.50
30	George Brett	2.50
31	George Foster	.50
32	George Kell	.50
33	Harmon Killebrew	1.50
34	Harold Baines	.50
35	Harold Reynolds	.50
36	Jack Morris	.50
37	Jim Abbott	.50
38	Jim Bunning	.50
39	Jim Palmer	.50
40	Jim Rice	.50
41	Jim Leyritz	.50
42	Joe Morgan	.50
43	John Kruk	.50
44	Johnny Bench	2.00
45	Johnny Podres	.50
46	Jose Canseco	1.00
47	Juan Marichal	.50
48	Keith Hernandez	.50
49	Kent Hrbek	.50
50	Kirby Puckett	2.00
51	Lee Smith	.50
52	Lenny Dykstra	.50
53	Luis Aparicio	.50
54	Luis Tiant	.50
55	Mark Grace	.50
56	Marty Marion	.50
57	Matt Williams	.50
58	Maury Wills	.50
59	Mike Schmidt	2.00
60	Minnie Minoso	.50
61	Nolan Ryan	3.00
62	Ozzie Smith	1.00
63	Paul Molitor	.75
64	Phil Rizzuto	.75
65	Ralph Kiner	.50
66	Randy Jones	.50
67	Red Schoendienst	.50
68	Rich "Goose" Gossage	.50
69	Rob Dibble	.50
70	Robin Roberts	.50
71	Rod Carew	.50
72	Rollie Fingers	.50
73	Ron Guidry	.50
74	Ron Santo	.50
75	Ryne Sandberg	2.00
76	Stan Musial	2.00
77	Steve Carlton	.50
78	Steve Garvey	.50
79	Steve Stone	.50
80	Terry Pendleton	.50
81	Terry Steinbach	.50
82	Tom Seaver	1.00
83	Tommy John	.50
84	Tony Gwynn	1.00
85	Tony Oliva	.50
86	Whitey Ford	1.00
87	Will Clark	.75

88 Willie Mays 3.00
89 Willie McCovey 1.00
90 Roberto Clemente 2.50
91 Roger Maris 2.00
92 Bob Gibson .75
93 Carl Yastrzemski 1.50
94 Jim "Catfish" Hunter .50
95 Warren Spahn 1.00
96 Reggie Jackson 1.00
97 Lou Brock .75
98 Joe Morgan .50
99 Carlton Fisk .50
100 Eddie Murray .50
101 Roger Clemens 3.00
102 Greg Maddux 2.00
103 Derek Jeter 3.00
104 Albert Pujols 3.00
105 Ken Griffey Jr. 2.00
106 Alex Rodriguez 3.00
107 Mike Piazza 1.50
108 Manny Ramirez 1.00
109 Sammy Sosa 1.00
110 Rafael Palmeiro .75
111 Randy Johnson 1.00
112 Vladimir Guerrero 1.00
113 Ichiro Suzuki 2.00
114 David Ortiz 1.00
115 Miguel Cabrera 1.00
116 Frank Thomas 1.00
117 Pedro Martinez 1.00
118 Chipper Jones 1.00
119 Todd Helton .75
120 Alfonso Soriano 1.00
121 Ivan Rodriguez .75
122 Carlos Delgado .75
123 Carlos Beltran .75
124 Jeff Kent .50
125 Curt Schilling .75
126 Derrek Lee .75
127 Jason Bay .50
128 Mark Teixeira .75
129 Craig Biggio .50
130 Miguel Tejada .50
131 Johan Santana .75
132 Jim Thome .75
133 Tim Hudson .50
134 Barry Zito .50
135 Mark Mulder .50
136 Hideki Matsui 2.00
137 John Smoltz .50
138 Mark Prior .75
139 Andruw Jones .75
140 Adam Dunn .75
141 Prince Fielder 4.00
142 Tadahito Iguchi **RC** 2.00
143 Randy Johnson 1.00
144 Pedro Martinez 1.00
145 Alex Rodriguez 3.00
146 Roger Clemens 3.00
147 Vladimir Guerrero 1.00
148 Greg Maddux 2.00
149 Ken Griffey Jr. 2.00
150 Roger Clemens 3.00

Gold Holofoil

Gold Holofoil: 3-4X
Production 100 Sets

Platinum Holofoil

Platinum Holofoil: 3-5X
Production 50 Sets

Silver Holofoil

Silver Holofoil: 1-2X
Inserted 1:3

Dodger Blues Brooklyn Material

NM/M
Common Player: 10.00
Prime: No Pricing
Production 10
1 Sandy Koufax/43 140.00
2 Duke Snider/27 40.00
3 Burleigh Grimes 40.00
4 Tommy Lasorda 10.00

Dodger Blues Brooklyn Signature Material

NM/M
1 Sandy Koufax/37 300.00

Dodger Blues LA Material

NM/M
Common Player: 10.00
Prime: No Pricing
Production 1-10
1 Sandy Koufax/43 140.00
2 Duke Snider/55 35.00
4 Tommy Lasorda 10.00
5 Orel Hershiser 10.00
6 Don Sutton 10.00

Dodger Blues LA Signature Material

NM/M
Production 10-37
Prime: No Pricing
Production 1-5
1 Sandy Koufax/37 300.00

Hall of Fame Souvenirs

NM/M
Common Player: 2.00
1 Willie Mays/Giants 4.00
2 Hank Aaron/Mil 4.00
3 Hank Aaron/Atl 4.00
4 Willie Mays/Mets 4.00
5 Nolan Ryan 6.00
6 Roberto Clemente/Kneeling 4.00
7 Nellie Fox 2.00
8 Pee Wee Reese 3.00
9 Babe Ruth 6.00
10 Bobby Doerr 2.00
11 Brooks Robinson 3.00
12 Carlton Fisk 3.00
13 Eddie Murray 3.00
14 Ernie Banks 4.00
15 Frank Robinson 3.00
16 Gary Carter 2.00
17 Hack Wilson 2.00
18 Harmon Killebrew 4.00
19 Joe Morgan 2.00
20 Kirby Puckett 4.00
21 Lou Brock 3.00
22 Orlando Cepeda 2.00
23 Red Schoendienst 2.00
24 Richie Ashburn 2.00
25 Stan Musial 5.00
26 Roberto Clemente/Standing 6.00
27 Wade Boggs/Sox 3.00
28 Wade Boggs/Yanks 3.00

Hall of Fame Souvenirs Material Bat

NM/M
Common Player: 10.00
1 Willie Mays 25.00
2 Hank Aaron 25.00
3 Hank Aaron 25.00
4 Willie Mays 25.00
5 Nolan Ryan/30 25.00
6 Roberto Clemente 40.00
7 Nellie Fox 10.00
8 Pee Wee Reese 10.00
9 Babe Ruth 140.00
11 Brooks Robinson 10.00
12 Carlton Fisk 10.00
13 Eddie Murray 10.00
14 Ernie Banks 15.00
15 Frank Robinson 8.00
16 Gary Carter 8.00
17 Hack Wilson 30.00
18 Harmon Killebrew 10.00
19 Joe Morgan 8.00
20 Kirby Puckett 10.00
21 Lou Brock 8.00
22 Orlando Cepeda 8.00
23 Red Schoendienst 8.00
24 Richie Ashburn 8.00
25 Stan Musial 20.00
26 Roberto Clemente 40.00
27 Wade Boggs 10.00
28 Wade Boggs 10.00

HOF Souvenirs Material Combo

NM/M
Common Combo: 10.00
1 Willie Mays/Giants 50.00
2 Hank Aaron/Mil 50.00
3 Hank Aaron/Atl 50.00
4 Willie Mays/25 50.00
5 Nolan Ryan/25 40.00
8 Pee Wee Reese/38 25.00
9 Babe Ruth/50 300.00
10 Bobby Doerr 10.00
11 Brooks Robinson/29 20.00
12 Carlton Fisk 10.00
13 Eddie Murray 10.00
14 Ernie Banks 20.00
16 Gary Carter 10.00
18 Harmon Killebrew 15.00
23 Red Schoendienst 10.00
26 Roberto Clemente 75.00
27 Wade Boggs 15.00
28 Wade Boggs 25.00

HOF Souvenirs Material Jersey

NM/M
Common Player: 10.00
1 Willie Mays/25 40.00
2 Hank Aaron/25 40.00
3 Hank Aaron/25 40.00
4 Willie Mays/25 40.00
5 Nolan Ryan/25 25.00
9 Babe Ruth/25 225.00
10 Bobby Doerr 10.00
12 Carlton Fisk 10.00
24 Richie Ashburn 10.00
25 Stan Musial 25.00
27 Wade Boggs 12.00

Hall of Fame Souvenirs Signature

No Pricing

HOF Souvenirs Signature Material Bat

NM/M
No pricing production 22 or less.
10 Bobby Doerr 20.00
11 Brooks Robinson 30.00
12 Carlton Fisk 30.00
15 Frank Robinson 20.00
16 Gary Carter 20.00
18 Harmon Killebrew 30.00
19 Joe Morgan 20.00
20 Kirby Puckett/52 90.00
21 Lou Brock 25.00
22 Orlando Cepeda 20.00
23 Red Schoendienst 25.00
25 Stan Musial/50 60.00

HOF Souvenirs Signature Material Combo

NM/M
Common Signature: 20.00
10 Bobby Doerr 20.00
11 Brooks Robinson 40.00
12 Carlton Fisk/50 40.00
15 Frank Robinson/39 30.00
16 Gary Carter 20.00
18 Harmon Killebrew 30.00
19 Joe Morgan/23 25.00
20 Kirby Puckett/45 125.00
22 Orlando Cepeda 25.00
25 Stan Musial 80.00
27 Wade Boggs/50 40.00
28 Wade Boggs/31 40.00

HOF Souvenirs Signature Material Jersey

NM/M
Common Signature: 20.00
10 Bobby Doerr 20.00
11 Brooks Robinson 40.00
12 Carlton Fisk 30.00
15 Frank Robinson 30.00
16 Gary Carter/63 20.00
18 Harmon Killebrew 30.00
22 Orlando Cepeda/68 20.00
23 Red Schoendienst 25.00
25 Stan Musial 65.00
27 Wade Boggs/50 40.00
28 Wade Boggs/3 40.00

Redbirds Material

NM/M
Common Player: 8.00
Prime: No Pricing
Production 1-25
1 Stan Musial/w/Glove Jsy T2 35.00
2 Ozzie Smith/Jkt T4 20.00
3 Enos Slaughter/Jsy T4 15.00
4 Frankie Frisch/Jkt T3 20.00
5 Lou Brock/Jsy T2 15.00
6 Bob Gibson/Jsy T2 20.00
7 Ken Boyer/Jsy T3 25.00
8 Lee Smith/Jsy T4 8.00
9 Albert Pujols/Jsy T2 30.00
10 Stan Musial/ w/Bant Pants T2 35.00

Redbirds Signature Material

NM/M
Production 5-50
Prime: No Pricing
Production 1-5
8 Lee Smith/50 20.00

Signature Gold HoloFoil

NM/M
Tier 1 Production 1-50
Tier 2 Production 51-100
Tier 3 Production 101-250
Tier 4 Production 251-800
Tier 5 Production 801-1200
Tier 6 Production 1201-2000
Cards are not serial numbered.
1 Al Kaline T2 30.00
2 Alan Trammell T3 15.00
3 Andre Dawson T5 10.00
4 Barry Larkin T2/55 30.00
5 Bert Blyleven T4 10.00
6 Billy Williams T2/55 15.00
7 Bo Jackson T1/35 50.00
8 Bob Feller T6 15.00
9 Bobby Doerr T5 20.00
10 Brooks Robinson T2 30.00
11 Cal Ripken Jr. T3 120.00
12 Dale Murphy T3 20.00
13 Darryl Strawberry T6 15.00
14 Dave Parker T3 10.00
15 Dave Stewart T4 10.00
16 David Cone T2 15.00
17 Dennis Eckersley T2 20.00
18 Don Larsen T4 20.00
19 Don Mattingly T1/45 75.00
20 Don Sutton T3 15.00
21 Duke Snider T2/55 25.00
22 Dwight Evans T3 15.00
23 Dwight Gooden T4 15.00
24 Earl Weaver T4 15.00
25 Fergie Jenkins T3 15.00
26 Frank Robinson T2 25.00
27 Fred Lynn T4 10.00
28 Gary Carter T2/55 15.00
29 Gaylord Perry T3 15.00
30 George Brett T1/35 75.00
31 George Foster T5 10.00
32 George Kell T6 15.00
33 Harmon Killebrew T2/55 30.00
34 Harold Baines T4 10.00
35 Harold Reynolds T4 10.00
36 Jack Morris T5 10.00
37 Jim Abbott T4 10.00
38 Jim Bunning T2 25.00
39 Jim Palmer T3 15.00
40 Jim Rice T2 20.00
41 Jim Leyritz T3 10.00
42 Joe Morgan T1/35 20.00
43 John Kruk T2 20.00
44 Johnny Bench T1/35 50.00
45 Johnny Podres T6 10.00
46 Jose Canseco T1/45 35.00
47 Juan Marichal T2 20.00
48 Keith Hernandez T5 15.00
49 Kent Hrbek T5 10.00
50 Kirby Puckett T1/35 85.00
51 Lee Smith T5 10.00
52 Lenny Dykstra T4 10.00
53 Luis Aparicio T3 15.00
54 Luis Tiant T3 15.00
55 Mark Grace T1/45 25.00
56 Marty Marion T4 15.00
57 Matt Williams T5 15.00
58 Maury Wills T4 15.00
59 Mike Schmidt T1/35 50.00
60 Minnie Minoso T5 15.00
61 Nolan Ryan T2/75 80.00
62 Ozzie Smith T2/55 40.00
63 Paul Molitor T2/55 30.00
64 Phil Rizzuto T2/55 30.00
65 Ralph Kiner T5 25.00
66 Randy Jones T4 10.00
67 Red Schoendienst T3 10.00
68 Rich "Goose" Gossage T3 10.00
69 Rob Dibble T4 30.00
70 Robin Roberts T2 30.00
71 Rod Carew T2/55 25.00
72 Rollie Fingers T3 15.00
73 Ron Guidry T3 25.00
74 Ron Santo T3 20.00
75 Ryne Sandberg T1/35 60.00
76 Stan Musial 20.00
77 Steve Carlton T2 15.00
78 Steve Garvey T3 15.00
79 Steve Stone T5 15.00
81 Terry Steinbach T3 10.00
82 Tom Seaver T1/35 40.00
83 Tommy John T6 10.00
84 Tony Gwynn T1/45 40.00
85 Tony Oliva T5 15.00
86 Whitey Ford T1/35 40.00
87 Will Clark T2/55 25.00
88 Willie Mays T2 150.00
89 Willie McCovey T1/45 35.00

Signature Platinum HoloFoil

NM/M
Production 1-50
Cards are not serial #'d.
3 Andre Dawson 15.00
5 Bert Blyleven 15.00
8 Bob Feller 25.00
9 Bobby Doerr 20.00
13 Darryl Strawberry 15.00
14 Dave Parker 15.00
18 Don Larsen 30.00
23 Dwight Gooden 20.00
25 Fergie Jenkins 25.00
27 Fred Lynn 15.00
31 George Foster 15.00
32 George Kell 25.00
34 Harold Baines 20.00
35 Harold Reynolds 15.00
36 Jack Morris 15.00
39 Jim Palmer 25.00
45 Johnny Podres 20.00
48 Keith Hernandez 15.00
49 Kent Hrbek 20.00
51 Lee Smith 20.00
52 Lenny Dykstra 20.00
54 Luis Tiant 20.00
56 Marty Marion 25.00
57 Matt Williams 20.00
58 Maury Wills 20.00
60 Minnie Minoso 25.00
65 Ralph Kiner 40.00
66 Randy Jones 15.00
67 Red Schoendienst 25.00
69 Rob Dibble 15.00
74 Ron Santo 30.00
79 Steve Stone 20.00
81 Terry Steinbach 15.00
83 Tommy John 15.00
85 Tony Oliva 20.00

Souvenirs

NM/M
Common Player: 2.00
1 Jim Thorpe 4.00
2 Joe Carter 2.00
3 Will Clark 3.00
4 Cal Ripken Jr. 6.00
5 Dwight Evans 2.00
6 George Foster 2.00
7 Steve Garvey 2.00
8 Don Mattingly 4.00
9 Deion Sanders 3.00
10 Ron Santo 3.00
11 Alan Trammell 2.00
12 Robin Ventura 2.00
13 Matt Williams 3.00

Souvenirs Material Bat

NM/M
Common Player: 5.00
2 Joe Carter 5.00
3 Will Clark 8.00
5 Dwight Evans 5.00

6 George Foster 5.00
7 Steve Garvey 5.00
8 Don Mattingly 15.00
9 Deion Sanders 8.00
10 Ron Santo 8.00
11 Alan Trammell 8.00
12 Robin Ventura 5.00
13 Matt Williams 5.00

Souvenirs Material Combo

NM/M

Common Combo:
2 Joe Carter/50 10.00
3 Will Clark 12.00
9 Deion Sanders 12.00
11 Alan Trammell 10.00
13 Matt Williams 10.00

Souvenirs Material Jersey

NM/M

Common Player: 5.00
1 Jim Thorpe 120.00
3 Will Clark 10.00
4 Cal Ripken Jr. 25.00
9 Deion Sanders 10.00
11 Alan Trammell/68 10.00
12 Robin Ventura/48 5.00
13 Matt Williams 8.00

Souvenirs Signature

NM/M

Common Auto.: 15.00
3 Will Clark 25.00
5 Dwight Evans/25 20.00
7 Steve Garvey 15.00
10 Ron Santo 25.00
11 Alan Trammell 20.00

Souvenirs Signature Material Bat

NM/M

Common Player: 15.00
3 Will Clark 25.00
5 Dwight Evans 20.00
7 Steve Garvey 15.00
10 Ron Santo 25.00
11 Alan Trammell 20.00
12 Robin Ventura 15.00

Souvenirs Signature Material Combo

NM/M

Common Player: 20.00
3 Will Clark 30.00
7 Steve Garvey 20.00
11 Alan Trammell 20.00

Souvenirs Signature Material Jersey

NM/M

Common Player: 15.00
3 Will Clark 25.00
5 Dwight Evans 25.00
7 Steve Garvey 15.00
11 Alan Trammell 20.00

Sox Nation Material

NM/M

Common Player: 10.00
Prime: No Pricing
Production 1-10
1 Ted Williams 75.00
2 Bobby Doerr 20.00
3 Roger Clemens/55 40.00
4 Carl Yastrzemski 25.00
5 Carl Yastrzemski 25.00
6 Jim Rice 15.00
7 Jim Rice 15.00
8 Joe Cronin 15.00
9 Joe Cronin 15.00
10 Carlton Fisk 20.00
11 Fred Lynn 10.00
12 Wade Boggs 25.00
13 Wade Boggs/55 25.00

Sox Nation Signature Material

NM/M

Prime: No Pricing
Production 1-5
2 Bobby Doerr/50 25.00
6 Jim Rice/50 25.00
7 Jim Rice/50 25.00
11 Fred Lynn/50 15.00

Yankee Clippings Material

NM/M

Common Player: 8.00
Prime: No Pricing
Production 1-33
2 Babe Ruth 300.00
3 Billy Martin 40.00
4 Billy Martin 40.00
5 Bobby Murcer 15.00
6 Bucky Dent 10.00
7 Jim "Catfish" Hunter 15.00
8 Jim "Catfish" Hunter 15.00
9 Darryl Strawberry 8.00
10 Dave Righetti 8.00
11 Dave Winfield 10.00
12 Deion Sanders 15.00
13 Deion Sanders 15.00
14 Don Mattingly 35.00
15 Elston Howard 15.00
16 Graig Nettles 10.00
17 Roger Clemens/43 50.00
18 Luis Tiant 8.00
19 Mickey Rivers 15.00
20 Phil Rizzuto 15.00
21 Reggie Jackson 20.00
22 Rickey Henderson 15.00
23 Roger Maris 50.00
24 Roger Maris 50.00
25 Ron Guidry 15.00
26 Sparky Lyle 8.00
27 Phil Niekro 20.00
28 Tommy John 20.00
29 Whitey Ford 40.00
30 Yogi Berra 60.00

Yankee Clippings Signature Material

NM/M

Prime: No Pricing
Production 1-5
9 Darryl Strawberry/25 30.00
18 Luis Tiant/50 30.00
20 Phil Rizzuto/25 60.00
25 Ron Guidry/25 50.00
28 Tommy John/25 30.00

2005 Donruss Leather & Lumber

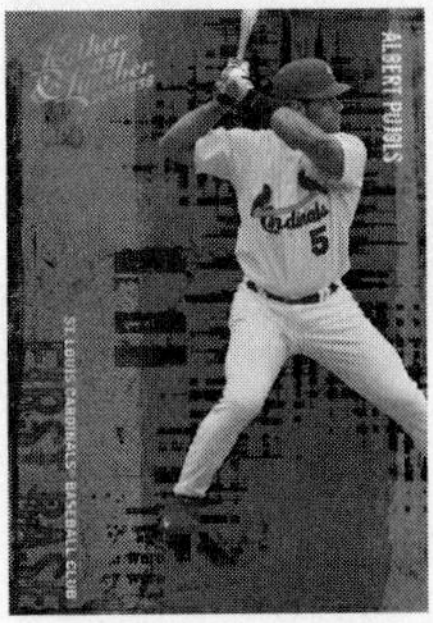

NM/M

Complete Set (177):
Common Player (1-150): .25
Common Auto. (151-175): 8.00
Production 256
Card #176 doesn't exist.
Pack (5): 7.00
Box (18): 100.00
1 Adam Dunn .50
2 Adrian Beltre .40
3 Akinori Otsuka .25
4 Al Leiter .25
5 Albert Pujols 2.00
6 Alex Rodriguez 1.50
7 Alfonso Soriano .75
8 Andy Pettitte .40
9 Aramis Ramirez .40
10 Aubrey Huff .25
11 Austin Kearns .25
12 Barry Larkin .40
13 Barry Zito .40
14 Bartolo Colon .25
15 Bernie Williams .40
16 Bobby Abreu .40
17 Bobby Crosby .40
18 Brad Penny .25
19 Brian Giles .25
20 C.C. Sabathia .25
21 Carl Crawford .25
22 Carl Pavano .25
23 Carlos Beltran .50
24 Carlos Delgado .40
25 Carlos Lee .40
26 Carlos Zambrano .40
27 Casey Kotchman .25
28 Chipper Jones .75
29 Chone Figgins .25
30 Craig Biggio .40
31 Craig Monroe .25
32 Cristian Guzman .25
33 Curt Schilling .75
34 Danny Haren .25
35 Darin Erstad .25
36 David Dellucci .25
37 David Ortiz .75
38 David Wells .25
39 Derek Jeter 2.00
40 Dontrelle Willis .40
41 Edgar Renteria .40
42 Eric Gagne .40
43 Frank Thomas .50
44 Garret Anderson .40
45 Gary Sheffield .50
46 Geoff Jenkins .25
47 Greg Maddux 1.50
48 Hideo Nomo .40
49 Ichiro Suzuki 1.50
50 Ivan Rodriguez .50
51 J.D. Drew .25
52 Jake Peavy .40
53 Jamie Moyer .25
54 Jason Giambi .40
55 Jason Kendall .25
56 Jason Schmidt .40
57 Jason Varitek .40
58 Javy Lopez .40
59 Jay Gibbons .25
60 Jeff Bagwell .50
61 Jeff Bagwell .25
62 Jeremy Bonderman .25
63 Jermaine Dye .25
64 Jim Edmonds .40
65 Jim Thome .50
66 Joe Nathan .25
67 Johan Santana .50
68 John Olerud .25
69 John Smoltz .40
70 Johnny Damon .75
71 Johnny Estrada .25
72 Jose Reyes .50
73 Jose Vidro .25
74 Josh Beckett .40
75 Juan Pierre .25
76 Junior Spivey .25
77 Justin Morneau .40
78 Kazuhisa Ishii .25
79 Kazuo Matsui .25
80 Ken Griffey Jr. 1.50
81 Kerry Wood .40
82 Kevin Brown .25
83 Kevin Millwood .25
84 Khalil Greene .40
85 Lance Berkman .25
86 Larry Walker .40
87 Laynce Nix .25
88 Lyle Overbay .25
89 Magglio Ordonez .25
90 Manny Ramirez .50
91 Marcus Giles .25
92 Mark Loretta .25
93 Mark Mulder .40
94 Mark Prior .50
95 Mark Teixeira .40
96 Melvin Mora .25
97 Michael Young .25
98 Miguel Tejada .50
99 Mike Lieberthal .25
100 Mike Lowell .25
101 Mike Mussina .40
102 Mike Piazza 1.00
103 Milton Bradley .25
104 Moises Alou .40
105 Morgan Ensberg .25
106 Nomar Garciaparra 1.00
107 Omar Vizquel .25
108 Paul Konerko .40
109 Paul LoDuca .25
110 Pedro Martinez .75
111 Rafael Furcal .25
112 Rafael Palmeiro .40
113 Randy Johnson .75
114 Richie Sexson .40
115 Rocco Baldelli .25
116 Roger Clemens 2.00
117 Roy Halladay .40
118 Sammy Sosa .75
119 Scott Podsednik .25
120 Scott Rolen .75
121 Sean Burroughs .25
122 Sean Casey .25
123 Shannon Stewart .25
124 Shawn Green .40
125 Steve Finley .25
126 Tim Hudson .40
127 Tim Salmon .25
128 Todd Helton .50
129 Tom Glavine .40
130 Torii Hunter .40
131 Travis Hafner .25
132 Troy Glaus .40
133 Troy Percival .25
134 Vernon Wells .25
135 Victor Martinez .25
136 Vladimir Guerrero .75
137 Andre Dawson .40
138 Brooks Robinson .75
139 Cal Ripken Jr. 3.00
140 Dale Murphy .50
141 Darryl Strawberry .40
142 George Brett 2.00
143 Harmon Killebrew 1.00
144 Jim Palmer .50
145 Lou Brock .75
146 Mike Schmidt 2.00
147 Nolan Ryan 2.00
148 Steve Carlton .50
149 Tony Gwynn 1.00
150 Willie Mays 2.00
151 Agustin Montero **RC** 10.00
152 Carlos Ruiz **RC** 15.00
153 Casey Rogowski **RC** 8.00
154 Chris Resop **RC** 15.00
155 Chris Roberson **RC** 15.00
156 Colter Bean **RC** 15.00
157 Danny Rueckel **RC** 8.00
158 David Gassner **RC** 10.00
159 Geovany Soto **RC** 15.00
160 John Hattig Jr. **RC** 8.00
161 Justin Wechsler **RC** 10.00
162 Luke Scott **RC** 25.00
163 Mark McLemore **RC** 10.00
164 Miguel Negron **RC** 8.00
165 Mike Morse **RC** 20.00
166 Nate McLouth **RC** 8.00
167 Philip Humber **RC** 20.00
168 Randy Messenger **RC** 8.00
169 Raul Tablado **RC** 8.00
170 Russel Rohlicek **RC** 8.00
171 Ryan Speier **RC** 8.00
172 Scott Munter **RC** 10.00
173 Sean Thompson **RC** 10.00
174 Sean Tracey **RC** 10.00
175 Wladimir Balentien **RC** 15.00
177 Norihiro Nakamura/128 **RC** 75.00

Gold

Gold (1-150): 4-8X
Production 50 Sets

Silver

Silver (1-150): 3-5X
Production 100 Sets

Platinum

Platinum: No Pricing
Production One Set

Big Bang

NM/M

Common Player: 1.50
Production 2,000 Sets
Gold: 1-2X
Production 100 Sets
Silver: 1-2X
Production 200 Sets
Platinum: No Pricing
Production One Set
1 Adam Dunn 2.00
2 Adrian Beltre 1.50
3 Albert Pujols 6.00
4 Alex Rodriguez 5.00
5 Chipper Jones 2.00
6 Dale Murphy 2.00
7 Darryl Strawberry 1.50
8 Dave Parker 1.50
9 David Ortiz 2.00
10 Duke Snider 2.00
11 Frank Robinson 2.00
12 Gary Sheffield 1.50
13 George Foster 1.50
14 Harmon Killebrew 3.00
15 Jim Edmonds 2.00
16 Jim Rice 1.50
17 Jim Thome 2.00
18 Ken Griffey Jr. 4.00
19 Manny Ramirez 2.00
20 Matt Williams 1.50
21 Mike Piazza 3.00
22 Mike Schmidt 5.00
23 Rafael Palmeiro 2.00
24 Sammy Sosa 3.00
25 Ted Williams 5.00

Big Bang Bat

NM/M

Production 50-250
3 Albert Pujols/250 15.00
8 Dave Parker/250 4.00
9 David Ortiz/250 8.00
11 Frank Robinson/100 8.00
13 George Foster/250 4.00
16 Jim Rice/50 6.00
19 Manny Ramirez/250 8.00
22 Mike Schmidt/100 15.00
23 Rafael Palmeiro/250 6.00
24 Sammy Sosa/250 8.00
25 Ted Williams/100 60.00

Big Bang Combos

NM/M

Production 25-100
Prime: No Pricing
Production Five Sets
1 Adam Dunn/Bat-Jsy/25 12.00
2 Adrian Beltre/Bat-Jsy/25 8.00
3 Albert Pujols/Bat-Jsy/100 25.00
7 Darryl Strawberry/Jsy-Pants/100 8.00
8 Dave Parker/Bat-Jsy/100 8.00
9 David Ortiz/Bat-Jsy/100 15.00
15 Jim Edmonds/Jsy-Jsy/100 10.00
16 Jim Rice/Jsy-Jsy/100 10.00
19 Manny Ramirez/Bat-Jsy/100 12.00
20 Matt Williams/Jsy-Jsy/100 8.00
21 Mike Piazza/Bat-Jsy/50 15.00
22 Mike Schmidt/Bat-Jsy/100 20.00
23 Rafael Palmeiro/Bat-Jsy/100 10.00
24 Sammy Sosa/Bat-Jsy/100 12.00

Big Bang Jersey

NM/M

Production 25-250
Prime: No Pricing
Production Five Sets
1 Adam Dunn/250 6.00
3 Albert Pujols/250 15.00
5 Chipper Jones/250 8.00
6 Dale Murphy/250 8.00
7 Darryl Strawberry/Pants/250 6.00
8 Dave Parker/250 4.00
9 David Ortiz/250 8.00
10 Duke Snider/25 12.00
12 Gary Sheffield/250 6.00
14 Harmon Killebrew/100 10.00
15 Jim Edmonds/250 6.00
16 Jim Rice/Pants/250 6.00
17 Jim Thome/250 8.00
19 Manny Ramirez/100 8.00

20	Matt Williams/250	6.00
21	Mike Piazza/250	10.00
22	Mike Schmidt/100	15.00
23	Rafael Palmeiro/Pants/250	6.00
24	Sammy Sosa/250	8.00
25	Ted Williams/Jkt/250	40.00

Big Bang Signatures

No Pricing
Production 1-10

Game Ball Signatures

NM/M

Production 1-50

1	Ben Grieve/50	10.00
3	Eli Marrero/24	12.00
4	Jeff Fassero/24	25.00
5	Jose Guillen/47	25.00
7	Mark Grudzielanek/23	30.00
9	Paul Konerko/45	25.00

Great Gloves

NM/M

Common Player: 1.50
Production 2,000 Sets
Gold: 2-3X
Production 50 Sets
Silver: 1-2X
Production 100 Sets
Platinum: No Pricing
Production One Set

1	Austin Kearns	1.50
2	Gary Carter	2.00
3	Ivan Rodriguez	2.00
4	Mark Grace	2.00
5	Mark Teixeira	2.00
6	Mike Schmidt	5.00
7	Omar Vizquel	1.50
8	Scott Rolen	3.00
9	Tony Gwynn	3.00
10	Willie Mays	5.00

Great Gloves Fielding Glv

NM/M

Production 25 Sets

1	Austin Kearns/25	10.00
2	Gary Carter/25	20.00
3	Ivan Rodriguez/25	15.00
4	Mark Grace/25	20.00
5	Mark Teixeira/25	15.00
6	Mike Schmidt/25	40.00
9	Tony Gwynn/25	20.00

Great Gloves Jersey

NM/M

Production 25-50
Prime: No Pricing
Production Five Sets

1	Austin Kearns/50	8.00
2	Gary Carter/50	8.00
3	Ivan Rodriguez/50	8.00
4	Mark Grace/50	10.00
5	Mark Teixeira/50	8.00
6	Mike Schmidt/50	20.00
7	Omar Vizquel/50	8.00
8	Scott Rolen/50	10.00
9	Tony Gwynn/50	12.00
10	Willie Mays/25	40.00

Hitters Inc.

NM/M

Common Player: 1.50
Production 2,000 Sets
Gold: 2-3X
Production 50 Sets
Silver: 1-2X
Production 100 Sets
Platinum: No Pricing
Production One Set

1	Albert Pujols	6.00
2	Alfonso Soriano	2.00
3	Cal Ripken Jr.	8.00
4	Don Mattingly	5.00
5	Dwight Evans	1.50
6	George Brett	5.00
7	Hank Blalock	1.50
8	Ichiro Suzuki	5.00
9	Ivan Rodriguez	2.00
10	Jack Wilson	1.50
11	Keith Hernandez	1.50
12	Larry Walker	2.00
13	Lou Brock	2.00
14	Lyle Overbay	1.50
15	Michael Young	1.50
16	Paul Molitor	2.00
17	Rod Carew	2.00
18	Sean Casey	1.50
19	Steve Garvey	1.50
20	Todd Helton	2.00
21	Tony Gwynn	3.00
22	Travis Hafner	1.50
23	Ted Williams	6.00
24	Wade Boggs	2.00
25	Willie Mays	5.00

Hitters Inc. Bat

NM/M

Production 25-100

1	Albert Pujols/100	15.00
2	Alfonso Soriano/50	6.00
3	Cal Ripken Jr./100	25.00
4	Don Mattingly/100	15.00
5	Dwight Evans/100	6.00
6	George Brett/50	15.00
7	Hank Blalock/50	6.00
9	Ivan Rodriguez/100	6.00
10	Jack Wilson/100	4.00
12	Larry Walker/100	6.00
13	Lou Brock/100	8.00
15	Michael Young/100	4.00
16	Paul Molitor/100	8.00
17	Rod Carew/100	8.00
18	Sean Casey/100	4.00
19	Steve Garvey/100	6.00
21	Tony Gwynn/100	10.00
23	Ted Williams/50	60.00
24	Wade Boggs/100	8.00
25	Willie Mays/25	40.00

Hitters Inc. Jersey

NM/M

Production 25-100

1	Albert Pujols/100	15.00
2	Alfonso Soriano/100	6.00
3	Cal Ripken Jr./100	25.00
4	Don Mattingly/100	15.00
5	Dwight Evans/100	6.00
7	Hank Blalock/100	4.00
9	Ivan Rodriguez/100	6.00
10	Jack Wilson/100	4.00
12	Larry Walker/100	6.00
13	Lou Brock/50	8.00
14	Lyle Overbay/100	4.00
16	Paul Molitor/100	8.00
17	Rod Carew/100	8.00
18	Sean Casey/100	4.00
19	Steve Garvey/100	6.00
20	Todd Helton/100	8.00
21	Tony Gwynn/100	10.00
22	Travis Hafner/100	4.00
23	Ted Williams/Jkt/100	40.00
24	Wade Boggs/100	8.00
25	Willie Mays/25	40.00

Hitters Inc. Signatures

No Pricing
Production 5-10

Hitters Inc. Signature Bat

NM/M

Production 5-25

5	Dwight Evans/25	20.00
7	Hank Blalock/25	25.00
10	Jack Wilson/25	15.00
13	Lou Brock/25	30.00
15	Michael Young/25	20.00
18	Sean Casey/25	15.00
19	Steve Garvey/25	30.00

Hitters Inc. Sign. Jersey

NM/M

Production 5-25

5	Dwight Evans/25	20.00
7	Hank Blalock/25	25.00
10	Jack Wilson/25	15.00
13	Lou Brock/25	30.00
14	Lyle Overbay/25	15.00
18	Sean Casey/25	15.00
19	Steve Garvey/25	30.00
22	Travis Hafner/25	20.00

Leather Cuts

NM/M

Production 1-128

2	Andre Dawson/128	15.00
3	Bert Blyleven/128	15.00
4	Lee Smith/32	15.00
5	Billy Williams/64	15.00
6	Bob Feller/128	25.00
7	Joe Pepitone/128	20.00
8	Bobby Doerr/128	15.00
9	Juan Marichal/112	20.00
12	Dale Murphy/96	25.00
13	Darryl Strawberry/128	15.00
14	Johnny Podres/128	20.00
18	Duke Snider/128	25.00
20	Dwight Gooden/128	15.00
23	Fred Lynn/128	15.00
24	Justin Morneau/128	20.00
25	Gaylord Perry/128	15.00
27	George Foster/128	15.00
28	Harmon Killebrew/64	30.00
29	Jack Morris/128	15.00
30	Jim Palmer/128	15.00
31	Jim Rice/128	15.00
33	John Kruk/128	20.00
34	Randy Jones/128	15.00
35	Keith Hernandez/128	15.00
36	Lenny Dykstra/128	15.00
37	Lou Brock/64	35.00
38	Luis Aparicio/128	15.00
39	Lyle Overbay/128	10.00
40	Maury Wills/128	15.00
41	Earl Weaver/128	15.00
42	Miguel Cabrera/64	40.00
44	Monte Irvin/96	20.00
47	Red Schoendienst/128	15.00
48	Rich "Goose" Gossage/128	20.00
50	Minnie Minoso/128	20.00
51	Sean Casey/64	15.00
54	Steve Stone/128	15.00
55	Tommy John/128	15.00
57	Victor Martinez/128	15.00
61	Lee Smith/128	15.00

Leather Cuts Bat

NM/M

Production 6-128

1	Al Kaline/58	40.00
10	Cal Ripken Jr./60	125.00
13	Darryl Strawberry/96	20.00
19	Dwight Evans/128	25.00
20	Dwight Gooden/128	15.00
22	Frank Robinson/40	25.00
23	Fred Lynn/96	15.00
27	George Foster/128	15.00
31	Jim Rice/32	25.00
36	Lenny Dykstra/128	15.00
37	Lou Brock/128	30.00
38	Luis Aparicio/128	15.00
39	Lyle Overbay/128	10.00
51	Sean Casey/32	15.00
55	Tommy John/128	15.00
57	Victor Martinez/128	15.00

Leather Cuts Jersey

NM/M

Production 1-128

2	Andre Dawson/128	20.00
3	Bert Blyleven/128	15.00
4	Lee Smith/96	15.00
8	Bobby Doerr/Pants/128	20.00
9	Juan Marichal/112	20.00
10	Cal Ripken Jr./60	125.00
12	Dale Murphy/96	25.00
13	Darryl Strawberry/96	20.00
15	Dave Righetti/48	20.00
16	David Cone/120	15.00
19	Dwight Evans/44	30.00
20	Dwight Gooden/128	15.00
21	Fergie Jenkins/Pants/96	15.00
23	Fred Lynn/96	15.00
25	Gaylord Perry/128	15.00
28	Harmon Killebrew/32	40.00
29	Jack Morris/64	15.00
31	Jim Rice/Pants/128	20.00
33	John Kruk/128	20.00
35	Keith Hernandez/32	20.00
36	Lenny Dykstra/128	15.00
38	Luis Aparicio/128	15.00
39	Lyle Overbay/128	10.00
42	Miguel Cabrera/64	40.00
51	Sean Casey/32	15.00
55	Tommy John/128	15.00
57	Victor Martinez/128	15.00

Lumber Cuts

NM/M

Production 1-128

1	Al Kaline/6	
2	Andre Dawson/128	15.00
3	Bert Blyleven/128	15.00
4	Lee Smith/32	20.00
5	Billy Williams/64	20.00
6	Bob Feller/128	25.00
7	Joe Pepitone/128	20.00
8	Bobby Doerr/128	20.00
9	Juan Marichal/112	20.00
12	Dale Murphy/96	25.00
13	Darryl Strawberry/128	15.00
14	Johnny Podres/128	15.00
18	Duke Snider/128	25.00
20	Dwight Gooden/128	15.00
21	Fergie Jenkins/96	15.00
23	Fred Lynn/128	15.00
24	Justin Morneau/128	20.00
25	Gaylord Perry/128	15.00
27	George Foster/128	10.00
28	Harmon Killebrew/64	30.00
29	Jack Morris/128	15.00
30	Jim Palmer/128	15.00
31	Jim Rice/128	15.00
33	John Kruk/128	20.00
34	Randy Jones/128	15.00
35	Keith Hernandez/128	15.00
36	Lenny Dykstra/128	15.00
37	Lou Brock/64	35.00
38	Luis Aparicio/128	15.00
39	Lyle Overbay/128	10.00
40	Maury Wills/128	15.00
41	Earl Weaver/128	15.00
42	Miguel Cabrera/64	40.00
44	Monte Irvin/96	20.00
46	Kent Hrbek/128	15.00
47	Red Schoendienst/128	20.00
48	Rich "Goose" Gossage/128	15.00
50	Minnie Minoso/128	20.00
51	Sean Casey/64	15.00
54	Steve Stone/128	15.00
55	Tommy John/128	15.00
57	Victor Martinez/128	15.00
61	Lee Smith/128	15.00

Lumber Cuts Bat

NM/M

Production 6-128

1	Al Kaline	40.00
10	Cal Ripken Jr./60	125.00
13	Darryl Strawberry/96	20.00
19	Dwight Evans/128	25.00
20	Dwight Gooden/128	15.00
22	Frank Robinson/40	25.00
23	Fred Lynn/96	15.00
27	George Foster/128	15.00
31	Jim Rice/32	25.00
36	Lenny Dykstra/128	15.00
37	Lou Brock/128	30.00
38	Luis Aparicio/128	15.00
39	Lyle Overbay/128	10.00
51	Sean Casey/32	15.00
55	Tommy John/128	15.00
57	Victor Martinez/128	15.00

Lumber Cuts Jersey

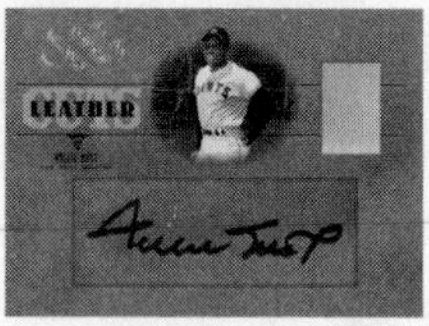

NM/M

Production 7-128

2	Andre Dawson/128	20.00
3	Bert Blyleven/128	15.00
4	Lee Smith/96	15.00
8	Bobby Doerr/Pants/128	20.00
9	Juan Marichal/112	20.00
10	Cal Ripken Jr./60	125.00
12	Dale Murphy/96	25.00
13	Darryl Strawberry/96	20.00
15	Dave Righetti/48	20.00
16	David Cone/120	15.00
19	Dwight Evans/44	30.00
20	Dwight Gooden/128	15.00
21	Fergie Jenkins/Pants/96	15.00
23	Fred Lynn/96	15.00
25	Gaylord Perry/128	15.00
28	Harmon Killebrew/32	40.00
29	Jack Morris/64	15.00
31	Jim Rice/Pants/128	20.00
33	John Kruk/128	20.00
35	Keith Hernandez/32	20.00
36	Lenny Dykstra/128	15.00
38	Luis Aparicio/128	15.00
39	Lyle Overbay/128	10.00
42	Miguel Cabrera/64	40.00
51	Sean Casey/32	15.00
55	Tommy John/128	15.00
57	Victor Martinez/128	15.00

Lumber/Leather

NM/M

Common Player: 1.50
Production 2,000 Sets
Gold: 2-3X
Production 50 Sets
Silver: 1-2X
Production 100 Sets
Platinum: No Pricing
Production One Set

1	Albert Pujols	6.00
2	Alex Rodriguez	5.00
3	Alfonso Soriano	2.00
4	Cal Ripken Jr.	8.00
5	Carlos Lee	2.00
6	Derek Jeter	6.00
7	Don Mattingly	5.00
8	Ichiro Suzuki	4.00
9	Ivan Rodriguez	2.00
10	Jack Wilson	1.50
11	Josh Beckett	1.50
12	Ken Griffey Jr.	4.00
13	Lance Berkman	1.50
14	Magglio Ordonez	1.50
15	Mark Grace	2.00
16	Mark Prior	2.00
17	Mark Teixeira	2.00
18	Mike Schmidt	4.00
19	Nolan Ryan	6.00
20	Nomar Garciaparra	3.00
21	Paul LoDuca	1.50
22	Rafael Palmeiro	2.00
23	Randy Johnson	2.00
24	Richie Sexson	2.00
25	Rickey Henderson	2.00
26	Roger Clemens	6.00
27	Ryan Klesko	1.50
28	Stan Musial	3.00
29	Steve Carlton	2.00
30	Tim Hudson	2.00
31	Tony Gwynn	2.00
32	Travis Hafner	1.50
33	Victor Martinez	1.50
34	Wade Boggs	2.00
35	Willie Mays	5.00

Lumber/Leather Barrel

No Pricing
Production One Set

L/L Barrel-Jersey

No Pricing
Production One Set

L/L Bat-Btg Glove

NM/M

Production 1-25

3	Alfonso Soriano/25	15.00
5	Carlos Lee/25	12.00
7	Don Mattingly/25	40.00
9	Ivan Rodriguez/25	15.00
13	Lance Berkman/25	15.00
14	Magglio Ordonez/25	10.00
18	Mike Schmidt/25	40.00
21	Paul LoDuca/25	10.00
22	Rafael Palmeiro/25	15.00
24	Richie Sexson/25	15.00
25	Rickey Henderson/25	20.00
27	Ryan Klesko/25	10.00
31	Tony Gwynn/25	20.00

L/L Bat-Fld Glove

NM/M

Production 5-25
5 Carlos Lee/25 12.00
9 Ivan Rodriguez/25 15.00
10 Jack Wilson/25 10.00
13 Lance Berkman/25 15.00
15 Mark Grace/25 20.00
16 Mark Prior/25 20.00
18 Mike Schmidt/25 40.00
21 Paul LoDuca/25 10.00
22 Rafael Palmeiro/25 15.00
24 Richie Sexson/25 15.00
27 Ryan Klesko/25 10.00
29 Steve Carlton/25 15.00
30 Tim Hudson/25 15.00
31 Tony Gwynn/25 20.00

Lumber/Leather Bat-Spikes

NM/M

Production 1-25
1 Albert Pujols/25 40.00
5 Carlos Lee/25 12.00
9 Ivan Rodriguez/25 15.00
11 Josh Beckett/25 12.00
13 Lance Berkman/25 15.00
14 Magglio Ordonez/25 10.00
16 Mark Prior/25 20.00
21 Paul LoDuca/25 10.00
22 Rafael Palmeiro/25 15.00
24 Richie Sexson/25 15.00
25 Rickey Henderson/25 20.00
27 Ryan Klesko/25 10.00
30 Tim Hudson/25 15.00
31 Tony Gwynn/25 20.00

Materials Barrel

No Pricing
Production 1-4

Materials Bat

NM/M

Production 25-250
1 Adam Dunn/250 6.00
2 Adrian Beltre/100 4.00
5 Albert Pujols/250 15.00
7 Alfonso Soriano/100 6.00
8 Andy Pettitte/100 6.00
9 Aramis Ramirez/100 6.00
10 Aubrey Huff/250 4.00
11 Austin Kearns/100 4.00
12 Barry Larkin/200 6.00
13 Barry Zito/25 8.00
15 Bernie Williams/250 6.00
18 Brad Penny/75 4.00
19 Brian Giles/50 6.00
23 Carlos Beltran/100 8.00
24 Carlos Delgado/250 4.00
25 Carlos Lee/150 4.00
27 Casey Kotchman/250 4.00
29 Chone Figgins/250 4.00
30 Craig Biggio/250 6.00
31 Craig Monroe/250 4.00
33 Curt Schilling/100 8.00
35 Darin Erstad/250 4.00
37 David Ortiz/250 8.00
40 Dontrelle Willis/250 6.00
43 Frank Thomas/50 8.00
44 Garret Anderson/250 4.00
46 Geoff Jenkins/50 4.00
47 Greg Maddux/250 10.00
51 J.D. Drew/250 4.00
57 Jason Varitek/100 6.00
58 Javy Lopez/250 4.00
59 Jay Gibbons/250 4.00
60 Jeff Bagwell/250 6.00
61 Jeff Kent/250 4.00
68 John Olerud/250 4.00
72 Jose Reyes/250 6.00
73 Jose Vidro/250 4.00
75 Juan Pierre/250 4.00
81 Kerry Wood/100 6.00
82 Kevin Brown/100 4.00
85 Lance Berkman/250 4.00
87 Laynce Nix/250 4.00
89 Magglio Ordonez/250 4.00
90 Manny Ramirez/100 8.00
94 Mark Prior/100 6.00
97 Michael Young/250 4.00
104 Moises Alou/250 4.00
106 Nomar Garciaparra/100 8.00
109 Paul LoDuca/250 4.00
111 Rafael Furcal/250 4.00
112 Rafael Palmeiro/250 6.00
114 Richie Sexson/250 4.00
115 Rocco Baldelli/250 8.00
118 Sammy Sosa/100 4.00
122 Sean Casey/100 4.00
123 Shannon Stewart/50 4.00
124 Shawn Green/250 4.00
126 Tim Hudson/50 6.00
127 Tim Salmon/250 4.00
129 Tom Glavine/250 4.00
130 Torii Hunter/250 4.00
132 Troy Glaus/250 4.00
138 Brooks Robinson/100 8.00
139 Cal Ripken Jr./50 30.00
145 Lou Brock/100 8.00
146 Mike Schmidt/50 15.00
147 Nolan Ryan/50 25.00
149 Tony Gwynn/100 10.00
150 Willie Mays/25 40.00

Materials Jersey

NM/M

Production 20-250
1 Adam Dunn/150 6.00
5 Albert Pujols/250 15.00
7 Alfonso Soriano/150 6.00
8 Andy Pettitte/150 6.00
9 Aramis Ramirez/250 4.00
10 Aubrey Huff/250 4.00
12 Barry Larkin/250 6.00
13 Barry Zito/150 4.00
15 Bernie Williams/150 6.00
16 Bobby Abreu/250 4.00
17 Bobby Crosby/150 4.00
20 C.C. Sabathia/250 4.00
21 Carl Crawford/200 4.00
26 Carlos Zambrano/250 6.00
27 Casey Kotchman/140 4.00
28 Chipper Jones/250 8.00
29 Chone Figgins/200 4.00
30 Craig Biggio/200 6.00
33 Curt Schilling/250 8.00
35 Darin Erstad/150 4.00
36 David Dellucci/250 4.00
37 David Ortiz/250 8.00
40 Dontrelle Willis/250 4.00
43 Frank Thomas/Pants/150 8.00
44 Garret Anderson/250 4.00
45 Gary Sheffield/250 6.00
46 Geoff Jenkins/250 4.00
47 Greg Maddux/25 15.00
48 Hideo Nomo/250 6.00
50 Ivan Rodriguez/150 6.00
53 Jamie Moyer/50 6.00
54 Jason Giambi/250 4.00
57 Jason Varitek/100 10.00
58 Javy Lopez/150 4.00
59 Jay Gibbons/75 4.00
60 Jeff Bagwell/250 6.00
62 Jeremy Bonderman/150 4.00
64 Jim Edmonds/250 6.00
65 Jim Thome/150 6.00
67 Johan Santana/250 8.00
69 John Smoltz/250 6.00
70 Johnny Damon/250 8.00
71 Johnny Estrada/250 4.00
72 Jose Reyes/150 6.00
73 Jose Vidro/150 4.00
74 Josh Beckett/50 4.00
76 Junior Spivey/250 4.00
77 Justin Morneau/250 6.00
78 Kazuhisa Ishii/250 4.00
79 Kazuo Matsui/250 4.00
81 Kerry Wood/Pants/150 6.00
85 Lance Berkman/250 4.00
86 Larry Walker/250 4.00
87 Laynce Nix/250 4.00
88 Lyle Overbay/200 4.00
90 Manny Ramirez/250 8.00
91 Marcus Giles/150 4.00
94 Mark Prior/250 6.00
95 Mark Teixeira/250 6.00
96 Melvin Mora/100 4.00
97 Michael Young/25 8.00
98 Miguel Tejada/250 6.00
100 Mike Lowell/250 4.00
101 Mike Mussina/250 6.00
102 Mike Piazza/250 8.00
105 Morgan Ensberg/150 4.00
108 Paul Konerko/150 4.00
111 Rafael Furcal/150 4.00
112 Rafael Palmeiro/150 6.00
115 Rocco Baldelli/250 4.00
116 Roger Clemens/150 10.00
117 Roy Halladay/150 4.00
119 Scott Podsednik/250 4.00
120 Scott Rolen/250 6.00
121 Sean Burroughs/150 4.00
122 Sean Casey/250 4.00
123 Shannon Stewart/150 4.00
128 Todd Helton/250 6.00
130 Torii Hunter/250 4.00
131 Travis Hafner 6.00
134 Vernon Wells/250 4.00
135 Victor Martinez/150 4.00
136 Vladimir Guerrero/250 8.00
137 Andre Dawson/50 8.00
139 Cal Ripken Jr./250 20.00
140 Dale Murphy/250 6.00
141 Darryl Strawberry/Pants/150 4.00
143 Harmon Killebrew/100 8.00
145 Lou Brock/Jkt/250 8.00
146 Mike Schmidt/50 15.00
147 Nolan Ryan/250 15.00
148 Steve Carlton/25 10.00
149 Tony Gwynn/250 8.00
150 Willie Mays/Pants/25 40.00

Naturals Barrel

No Pricing
Production 1-3

Naturals Bat

NM/M

Production 25-100
1 Andruw Jones/100 6.00
2 Bernie Williams/100 6.00
3 Brooks Robinson/100 8.00
4 Cal Ripken Jr./100 25.00
5 Casey Kotchman/100 4.00
6 Craig Biggio/100 6.00
7 Craig Wilson/100 4.00
8 David Ortiz/100 10.00
9 Eddie Murray/100 8.00
10 Javy Lopez/100 4.00
11 Jeff Bagwell/100 6.00
12 Lance Berkman/100 4.00
13 Magglio Ordonez/100 4.00
14 Michael Young/100 4.00
15 Rafael Palmeiro/100 6.00
16 Reggie Jackson/100 8.00
17 Rickey Henderson/100 8.00
18 Rocco Baldelli/100 4.00
19 Sammy Sosa/100 8.00
20 Shawn Green/100 4.00
21 Ted Williams/50 50.00
22 Tony Gwynn/100 10.00
23 Wade Boggs/100 8.00
24 Will Clark/100 8.00
25 Willie Mays/25 40.00

Naturals Combos

NM/M

Production 25-100
Prime: No Pricing
Production Five Sets
1 Andruw Jones/Bat-Jsy/100 8.00
2 Bernie Williams/Bat-Jsy/100 8.00
3 Brooks Robinson/Bat-Jsy/25 15.00
4 Cal Ripken Jr./Bat-Jsy/100 30.00
5 Casey Kotchman/Bat-Jsy/100 6.00
6 Craig Biggio/Bat-Jsy/100 8.00
7 Craig Wilson/Bat-Jsy/100 6.00
8 David Ortiz/Bat-Jsy/100 12.00
9 Eddie Murray/Bat-Jsy/100 10.00
10 Javy Lopez/Bat-Jsy/100 6.00
11 Jeff Bagwell/Bat-Jsy/100 8.00
12 Lance Berkman/Bat-Jsy/100 6.00
13 Magglio Ordonez/Bat-Jsy/25 8.00
14 Michael Young/Bat-Jsy/100 6.00
15 Rafael Palmeiro/Bat-Jsy/100 8.00
16 Reggie Jackson/Bat-Jsy/50 12.00
17 Rickey Henderson/Bat-Jkt/100 10.00
18 Rocco Baldelli/Bat-Jsy/100 6.00
19 Sammy Sosa/Bat-Jsy/100 10.00
20 Shawn Green/Bat-Jsy/100 6.00
21 Ted Williams/Bat-Jkt/50 60.00
22 Tony Gwynn/Bat-Jsy/100 12.00
23 Wade Boggs/Bat-Jsy/100 10.00
24 Will Clark/Bat-Jsy/50 10.00
25 Willie Mays/Bat-Jsy/25 50.00

Naturals

NM/M

Common Player: 1.50
Production 2,000 Sets
Gold: 2-3X
Production 50 Sets
Silver: 1-2X
Production 100 Sets
Platinum: No Pricing
Production One Set
1 Andruw Jones 2.00
2 Bernie Williams 1.50
3 Brooks Robinson 2.00
4 Cal Ripken Jr. 8.00
5 Casey Kotchman 1.50
6 Craig Biggio 2.00
7 Craig Wilson 1.50
8 David Ortiz 3.00
9 Eddie Murray 2.00
10 Javy Lopez 1.50
11 Jeff Bagwell 2.00
12 Lance Berkman 1.50
13 Magglio Ordonez 1.50
14 Michael Young 1.50
15 Rafael Palmeiro 2.00
16 Reggie Jackson 2.00
17 Rickey Henderson 2.00
18 Rocco Baldelli 1.50
19 Sammy Sosa 4.00
20 Shawn Green 1.50
21 Ted Williams 6.00
22 Tony Gwynn 3.00
23 Wade Boggs 2.00
24 Will Clark 2.00
25 Willie Mays 5.00

Naturals Jersey

NM/M

Production 25-100
Prime: No Pricing
Production Five Sets
1 Andruw Jones/100 6.00
2 Bernie Williams/100 6.00
4 Cal Ripken Jr./100 25.00
5 Casey Kotchman/100 4.00
6 Craig Biggio/100 6.00
7 Craig Wilson/100 4.00
8 David Ortiz/100 10.00
9 Eddie Murray/100 8.00
10 Javy Lopez/100 4.00
11 Jeff Bagwell/100 6.00
12 Lance Berkman/100 4.00
13 Magglio Ordonez/50 4.00
14 Michael Young/50 4.00
15 Rafael Palmeiro/100 6.00
16 Reggie Jackson/100 8.00
17 Rickey Henderson/Jkt/100 8.00
18 Rocco Baldelli/100 4.00
19 Sammy Sosa/100 8.00
20 Shawn Green/100 4.00
21 Ted Williams/Jkt/100 40.00
22 Tony Gwynn/100 10.00
23 Wade Boggs/100 8.00
24 Will Clark/50 8.00
25 Willie Mays/25 40.00

Rivals

NM/M

Common Duo: 1.50
Production 2,000 Sets
Gold: 2-3X
Production 50 Sets
Silver: 1-2X
Production 100 Sets
Platinum: No Pricing
Production One Set
1 Ichiro Suzuki, Hideki Matsui 5.00
2 Mark Mulder, Vladimir Guerrero 2.00
3 Tim Hudson, Mark Teixeira 2.00
4 Roger Clemens, Albert Pujols 6.00
5 Greg Maddux, Jeff Bagwell 4.00
6 Randy Johnson, Adrian Beltre 3.00
7 Kerry Wood, Larry Walker 2.00
8 Mike Mussina, Manny Ramirez 2.00
9 C.C. Sabathia, Torii Hunter 1.50
10 Josh Beckett, Chipper Jones 2.00
11 Derek Jeter, Miguel Tejada 6.00
12 Alex Rodriguez, Hank Blalock 5.00
13 Carlos Beltran,Sammy Sosa 3.00
14 Mark Prior, Jim Thome 2.00
15 Miguel Cabrera, Andruw Jones 2.00
16 Johan Santana, Magglio Ordonez 2.00
17 Josh Beckett, Craig Biggio 2.00
18 Adam Dunn, Shawn Green 2.00
19 J. Morris, Rod Carew 2.00
20 Jim Palmer, Paul Molitor 2.00
21 Mike Schmidt, George Brett 5.00
22 Cal Ripken Jr., Don Mattingly 8.00
23 Bob Gibson, Ernie Banks 4.00
24 Eddie Murray, Bert Blyleven 3.00
25 Warren Spahn, Willie Mays 6.00

Rivals Bat

NM/M

Production 50-100
3 Tim Hudson, Mark Teixeira/50 10.00
4 Roger Clemens, Albert Pujols/100 25.00
5 Greg Maddux, Jeff Bagwell/100 15.00
7 Kerry Wood, Larry Walker/100 15.00
10 Josh Beckett, Chipper Jones/50 15.00
13 Carlos Beltran, Sammy Sosa/100 15.00
14 Mark Prior, Jim Thome/50 15.00
18 Adam Dunn, Shawn Green/100 10.00
21 Mike Schmidt, George Brett/100 20.00
22 Cal Ripken Jr., Don Mattingly/100 30.00

Rivals Jersey

NM/M

Production 50-250
Prime: No Pricing
Production Five Sets
2 Mark Mulder, Vladimir Guerrero/100 10.00
3 Tim Hudson, Mark Teixeira/250 10.00
4 Roger Clemens, Albert Pujols/100 20.00
5 Greg Maddux, Jeff Bagwell/250 10.00
7 Kerry Wood, Larry Walker/250 8.00
9 C.C. Sabathia, Torii Hunter/150 6.00
10 Josh Beckett/Pants, Chipper Jones/150 10.00
13 Carlos Beltran, Sammy Sosa/250 10.00
14 Mark Prior, Jim Thome/250 10.00
15 Miguel Cabrera, Andruw Jones/250 10.00
16 Johan Santana, Magglio Ordonez/100 10.00
18 Adam Dunn, Shawn Green/100 10.00
19 J. Morris, Rod Carew/250 10.00
21 Mike Schmidt, George Brett/100 15.00
22 Cal Ripken Jr., Don Mattingly/100 40.00
23 Bob Gibson, Ernie Banks/50 15.00
24 Eddie Murray, Bert Blyleven 10.00
25 Warren Spahn/Pants, Willie Mays/Pants/50 60.00

Signatures Gold

NM/M

Production 5-100
Platinum: No Pricing
Production One Set

1 Adam Dunn/25 35.00
2 Adrian Beltre/25 25.00
3 Akinori Otsuka/50 30.00
10 Aubrey Huff/50 15.00
11 Austin Kearns/25 15.00
17 Bobby Crosby/100 15.00
18 Brad Penny/100 10.00
25 Carlos Lee/100 15.00
26 Carlos Zambrano/100 25.00
27 Casey Kotchman/100 10.00
29 Chone Figgins/100 15.00
31 Craig Monroe/100 15.00
34 Danny Haren/100 10.00
36 David Dellucci/100 15.00
52 Jake Peavy/100 25.00
53 Jamie Moyer/100 15.00
59 Jay Gibbons/100 10.00
62 Jeremy Bonderman/100 10.00
63 Jermaine Dye/100 12.00
66 Joe Nathan/100 15.00
71 Johnny Estrada/50 10.00
87 Laynce Nix/100 10.00
88 Lyle Overbay/100 10.00
92 Mark Loretta/100 15.00
99 Mike Lieberthal/100 10.00
103 Milton Bradley/100 12.00
105 Morgan Ensberg/100 12.00
108 Paul Konerko/25 20.00
111 Rafael Furcal/50 15.00
117 Roy Halladay/25 25.00
119 Scott Podsednik/50 15.00
121 Sean Burroughs/100 8.00
122 Sean Casey/25 15.00
123 Shannon Stewart/100 8.00
125 Steve Finley/50 15.00
126 Tim Hudson/25 30.00
127 Tim Salmon/100 15.00
130 Torii Hunter/25 20.00
131 Travis Hafner/100 12.00
133 Troy Percival/50 15.00
134 Vernon Wells/25 15.00
135 Victor Martinez/100 15.00
137 Andre Dawson/100 15.00
138 Brooks Robinson/25 30.00
140 Dale Murphy/50 25.00
141 Darryl Strawberry/100 15.00
143 Harmon Killebrew/50 30.00
144 Jim Palmer/25 20.00
145 Lou Brock/25 30.00
146 Mike Schmidt/25 60.00
148 Steve Carlton/50 25.00
149 Tony Gwynn/25 50.00

Signatures Lumber Cuts

NM/M

Production 256 Sets
151 Agustin Montero 8.00
152 Carlos Ruiz 8.00
153 Casey Rogowski 10.00
154 Chris Resop 15.00
155 Chris Roberson 10.00
156 Colter Bean 10.00
157 Danny Rueckel 8.00
158 David Gassner 8.00
159 Geovany Soto 15.00
160 John Hattig Jr. 8.00
161 Justin Wechsler 8.00
162 Luke Scott 15.00
163 Mark McLemore 8.00
164 Miguel Negron 8.00
165 Mike Morse 40.00
166 Nate McLouth/254 15.00
167 Philip Humber 20.00
168 Randy Messenger 8.00
169 Raul Tablado 8.00
170 Russel Rohlicek 8.00
171 Ryan Speier 8.00
172 Scott Munter 12.00
173 Sean Thompson 10.00
174 Sean Tracey 10.00
175 Wladimir Balentien 15.00
177 Norihiro Nakamura/128 75.00

2005 Donruss Signature

NM/M

Complete Set (159):
Common Player (1-150): 1.00
Common Dual Auto. (151-156):
Triple Auto. (157-158):
Inserted 1:51
Quad Auto. (#159): No Pricing
Inserted 1:626
Pack (5): 60.00
Box (4): 200.00
1 Scot Shields 1.00
2 Tim Salmon 1.50
3 Chone Figgins 1.00
4 Dallas McPherson 1.00
5 John Lackey 1.00
6 Ervin Santana 1.00
7 Casey Kotchman 1.00
8 Steve Finley 1.00
9 Brandon Webb 1.00
10 Chad Tracy 1.00
11 Russ Ortiz 1.00
12 Alex Cintron 1.00
13 Marcus Giles 1.00
14 Ichiro Suzuki 5.00
15 Tadahito Iguchi **RC** 4.00
16 Chipper Jones 2.50
17 Cal Ripken Jr. 6.00
18 Rick Dempsey 1.00
19 Adam Loewen 1.00
20 Eric Byrnes 1.00
21 Luis Matos 1.00
22 Miguel Tejada 1.50
23 Brooks Robinson 3.00
24 Kevin Youkilis 1.50
25 Keith Foulke 1.00
26 Trot Nixon 1.00
27 Edgar Renteria 1.00
28 Luis Tiant 1.00
29 Todd Walker 1.00
30 Mark Grace 2.00
31 Steve Stone 1.00
32 Ron Santo 2.00
33 Mike Wuertz 1.00
34 Russel Rohlicek **RC** 2.00
35 Ryne Sandberg 4.00
36 Andre Dawson 1.50
37 Aramis Ramirez 1.50
38 Derrek Lee 2.00
39 Paulino Reynoso **RC** 1.50
40 Jose Contreras 1.00
41 Freddy Garcia 1.00
42 Mark Buehrle 1.50
43 Bubba Nelson 1.00
44 Eric Davis 1.00
45 Adam Dunn 2.00
46 Travis Hafner 1.50
47 Larry Bigbie 1.00
48 Todd Helton 2.00
49 Chris Shelton 1.00
50 Willie Mays 5.00
51 Craig Monroe 1.00
52 Ivan Rodriguez 2.00
53 Miguel Cabrera 2.50
54 Chris Resop **RC** 1.50
55 Paul LoDuca 1.00
56 Luke Scott **RC** 3.00
57 Brandon Backe 1.00
58 Mark McLemore **RC** 1.50
59 Devon Lowery **RC** 1.50
60 Jeremy Affeldt 1.00
61 Duke Snider 2.00
62 Johnny Podres 1.00
63 Rickie Weeks 1.50
64 Ben Sheets 1.50
65 Carlos Lee 1.50
66 Lew Ford 1.00
67 Travis Bowyer **RC** 1.50
68 Garrett Jones **RC** 1.50
69 Joe Nathan 1.00
70 Kent Hrbek 1.00
71 J.D. Durbin 1.00
72 Shannon Stewart 1.00
73 Torii Hunter 1.50
74 Kirby Puckett 4.00
75 Danny Graves 1.00
76 Jae Weong Seo 1.00
77 Matt Lindstrom **RC** 1.50
78 Dwight Gooden 1.00
79 Carlos Beltran 2.00
80 Mike Piazza 3.00
81 Tom Gordon 1.00
82 Adam LaRoche 1.00
83 Dave Righetti 1.00
84 Joe Pepitone 1.00
85 Gary Sheffield 2.00
86 Jim Leyritz 1.00
87 Rich "Goose" Gossage 1.00
88 Don Larsen 1.00
89 Bernie Williams 1.50
90 Jorge Posada 2.00
91 Octavio Dotel 1.00
92 Rollie Fingers 1.00
93 Dennis Eckersley 1.50
94 Rich Harden 1.00
95 Art Howe 1.00
96 Jose Canseco 2.00
97 Barry Zito 1.50
98 Eric Chavez 1.50
99 Rickey Henderson 2.00
100 Chris Roberson **RC** 1.50
101 Eude Brito **RC** 1.50
102 Randy Wolf 1.00
103 Mike Lieberthal 1.00
104 John Kruk 1.00
105 Lenny Dykstra 1.00
106 Carlos Ruiz **RC** 1.50
107 Bobby Abreu 1.50
108 Bill Madlock 1.00
109 Mike Johnston 1.00
110 Ian Snell 1.00
111 Freddy Sanchez 1.00
112 Jose Castillo 1.00
113 Jeff Miller **RC** 1.50
114 John Candelaria 1.00
115 Jason Bay 1.50
116 Mark Loretta 1.00
117 Sean Thompson **RC** 1.50
118 Akinori Otsuka 1.00
119 Omar Vizquel 1.00
120 Will Clark 1.50
121 Clint Nageotte 1.00
122 J.J. Putz 1.00
123 Raul Ibanez 1.00
124 Wladimir Balentien **RC** 3.00
125 Jamie Moyer 1.00
126 Adrian Beltre 1.00
127 Richie Sexson 1.50
128 Edgar Martinez 1.00
129 Jeff Suppan 1.00
130 Marty Marion 1.00
131 Keith Hernandez 1.00
132 Ozzie Smith 4.00
133 Mark Mulder 1.00
134 Lee Smith 1.00
135 Jim Edmonds 1.50
136 Nomar Garciaparra 2.50
137 Delmon Young 1.50
138 Jason Hammel **RC** 1.50
139 Agustin Montero **RC** 1.50
140 Francisco Cordero 1.00
141 Michael Young 1.50
142 Al Oliver 1.00
143 David Dellucci 1.00
144 Nolan Ryan 6.00
145 Rafael Palmeiro 1.50
146 Alexis Rios 1.00
147 Jose Guillen 1.00
148 Danny Rueckel **RC** 1.50
149 Jose Vidro 1.00
150 Preston Wilson 1.00
151 Rickie Weeks, Prince Fielder 60.00
152 Hayden Penn, Adam Loewen 20.00
153 Akinori Otsuka, Keiichi Yabu **RC** 25.00
154 Brandon McCarthy, Anibal Sanchez **RC** 30.00
157 Jeff Niemann, Justin Verlander, Philip Humber **RC** 50.00
158 Wladimir Balentien, Ambiorix Concepcion, Miguel Negron **RC** 15.00
159 Justin Verlander, Jeff Niemann, Tony Pena, Ubaldo Jimenez 80.00

Autograph Gold MS

NM/M

Production 5-50
1 Scot Shields/50 10.00
2 Tim Salmon/50 15.00
3 Chone Figgins/50 15.00
4 Dallas McPherson/50 10.00
5 John Lackey/25 20.00
6 Ervin Santana/50 20.00
9 Brandon Webb/50 20.00
10 Chad Tracy/50 10.00
11 Russ Ortiz/50 10.00
12 Alex Cintron/50 10.00
17 Cal Ripken Jr./50 100.00
18 Rick Dempsey/50 10.00
19 Adam Loewen/50 10.00
20 Eric Byrnes/50 10.00
21 Luis Matos/50 10.00
24 Kevin Youkilis/50 15.00
25 Keith Foulke/50 20.00
26 Trot Nixon/50 20.00
27 Edgar Renteria/50 20.00
28 Luis Tiant/25 20.00
29 Todd Walker/50 10.00
30 Mark Grace/25 25.00
31 Steve Stone/50 20.00
32 Ron Santo/50 35.00
34 Russel Rohlicek/50 10.00
35 Ryne Sandberg/50 75.00
43 Bubba Nelson/50 10.00
47 Larry Bigbie/50 15.00
49 Chris Shelton/43 15.00
53 Miguel Cabrera/50 30.00
54 Chris Resop/50 10.00
56 Luke Scott/25 40.00
59 Devon Lowery/50 10.00
61 Duke Snider/50 35.00
62 Johnny Podres/25 25.00
63 Rickie Weeks/50 20.00
64 Ben Sheets/50 20.00
66 Lew Ford/50 10.00
67 Travis Bowyer/50 10.00
68 Garrett Jones/50 10.00
69 Joe Nathan/50 15.00
70 Kent Hrbek/25 20.00
71 J.D. Durbin/50 10.00
75 Danny Graves/50 10.00
76 Jae Weong Seo/50 20.00
77 Matt Lindstrom/50 10.00
81 Tom Gordon/50 15.00
82 Adam LaRoche/25 20.00
83 Dave Righetti/50 20.00
84 Joe Pepitone/25 25.00
85 Gary Sheffield/50 25.00
86 Jim Leyritz/25 25.00
87 Rich "Goose" Gossage/25 20.00
88 Don Larsen/25 25.00
91 Octavio Dotel/50 10.00
92 Rollie Fingers/50 20.00
93 Dennis Eckersley/50 25.00
94 Rich Harden/50 20.00
97 Barry Zito/50 20.00
100 Chris Roberson/50 10.00
101 Eude Brito/50 10.00
102 Randy Wolf/50 10.00
103 Mike Lieberthal/50 15.00
104 John Kruk/25 25.00
106 Carlos Ruiz/50 10.00
110 Ian Snell/34 10.00
116 Mark Loretta/50 15.00
117 Sean Thompson/50 10.00
119 Omar Vizquel/50 25.00
121 Clint Nageotte/50 10.00
122 J.J. Putz/50 10.00
123 Raul Ibanez/50 10.00
124 Wladimir Balentien/50 10.00
125 Jamie Moyer/25 15.00
129 Jeff Suppan/50 15.00
130 Marty Marion/50 20.00
131 Keith Hernandez/50 20.00
132 Ozzie Smith/50 50.00
133 Mark Mulder/25 20.00
137 Delmon Young/25 30.00
139 Agustin Montero/50 10.00
140 Francisco Cordero/50 10.00
142 Al Oliver/25 20.00
143 David Dellucci/25 15.00
146 Alexis Rios/50 15.00
147 Jose Guillen/50 15.00
148 Danny Rueckel/50 10.00

Autograph Material Bat Gold

NM/M

Production 1-50
Platinum: No Pricing
Production 1-25
3 Chone Figgins/50 20.00
7 Casey Kotchman/25 20.00
24 Kevin Youkilis/25 20.00
65 Carlos Lee/25 20.00
108 Bill Madlock/50 15.00
111 Freddy Sanchez/42 20.00
119 Omar Vizquel/50 25.00
146 Alexis Rios/50 20.00

Autograph Material Bat Silver

NM/M

Cards are not serial numbered.
3 Chone Figgins/50 20.00
108 Bill Madlock 15.00
119 Omar Vizquel 15.00

Autograph Material Button Platinum

No Pricing
Production 1-6

Autograph Material Combo Gold

NM/M

Production 1-46
Platinum: No Pricing
Production 1-25
17 Cal Ripken Jr./46 125.00
30 Mark Grace/25 40.00

Autograph Material Combo Silver

NM/M

Cards are not serial numbered.
17 Cal Ripken Jr./100 100.00
30 Mark Grace/50 35.00

Autograph Material Jersey Number Platinum

NM/M

Production 1-25
9 Brandon Webb/25 20.00
21 Luis Matos/25 15.00
26 Trot Nixon/25 20.00
57 Brandon Backe/25 15.00
76 Jae Weong Seo/25 20.00
93 Dennis Eckersley/25 25.00

Autograph Material Jersey Position Gold

NM/M

Production 1-50
9 Brandon Webb/50 15.00
21 Luis Matos/50 15.00
26 Trot Nixon/50 20.00
30 Mark Grace/25 30.00
57 Brandon Backe/50 10.00
76 Jae Weong Seo/50 20.00
93 Dennis Eckersley/50 25.00

Autograph Material Jersey Silver

NM/M

Cards are not serial numbered.
21 Luis Matos 10.00
26 Trot Nixon/71 20.00
30 Mark Grace 20.00
60 Jeremy Affeldt/36 10.00
76 Jae Weong Seo/86 20.00
93 Dennis Eckersley/50 25.00
104 John Kruk/75 20.00
130 Marty Marion/38 20.00

Autograph Platinum MS

NM/M

Production 1-25
1 Scot Shields/25 15.00
2 Tim Salmon/25 20.00
3 Chone Figgins/25 20.00
4 Dallas McPherson/25 15.00
6 Ervin Santana/25 25.00
9 Brandon Webb/25 20.00
10 Chad Tracy/25 15.00
11 Russ Ortiz/25 15.00
12 Alex Cintron/25 15.00
17 Cal Ripken Jr./25 125.00
18 Rick Dempsey/25 15.00
19 Adam Loewen/25 15.00
20 Eric Byrnes/25 15.00
21 Luis Matos/25 15.00
24 Kevin Youkilis/25 20.00
25 Keith Foulke/25 25.00
26 Trot Nixon/25 25.00
27 Edgar Renteria/25 25.00
29 Todd Walker/25 15.00
31 Steve Stone/25 25.00
32 Ron Santo/25 40.00
34 Russel Rohlicek/25 10.00
35 Ryne Sandberg/25 90.00

43	Bubba Nelson/25	15.00
47	Larry Bigbie/25	15.00
54	Chris Resop/25	10.00
59	Devon Lowery/25	10.00
61	Duke Snider/25	40.00
63	Rickie Weeks/25	20.00
66	Lew Ford/25	10.00
67	Travis Bowyer/25	10.00
68	Garrett Jones/25	10.00
69	Joe Nathan/25	20.00
71	J.D. Durbin/25	15.00
75	Danny Graves/25	10.00
76	Jae Weong Seo/25	25.00
77	Matt Lindstrom/25	15.00
81	Tom Gordon/25	15.00
83	Dave Righetti/25	25.00
85	Gary Sheffield/25	25.00
91	Octavio Dotel/25	10.00
92	Rollie Fingers/25	25.00
94	Rich Harden/25	25.00
97	Barry Zito/25	25.00
100	Chris Roberson/25	10.00
101	Eude Brito/25	10.00
102	Randy Wolf/25	15.00
103	Mike Lieberthal/25	20.00
106	Carlos Ruiz/25	15.00
110	Ian Snell/25	15.00
116	Mark Loretta/25	20.00
117	Sean Thompson/25	15.00
119	Omar Vizquel/25	30.00
121	Clint Nageotte/25	10.00
122	J.J. Putz/25	10.00
123	Raul Ibanez/25	15.00
124	Wladimir Balentien/25	10.00
129	Jeff Suppan/25	20.00
130	Marty Marion/25	25.00
131	Keith Hernandez/25	25.00
132	Ozzie Smith/25	60.00
139	Agustin Montero/25	10.00
140	Francisco Cordero/25	15.00
146	Alexis Rios/25	20.00
147	Jose Guillen/25	15.00
148	Danny Rueckel/25	15.00

Autograph Silver

NM/M

Cards are not serial numbered.

1	Scot Shields	8.00
2	Tim Salmon	10.00
3	Chone Figgins	10.00
4	Dallas McPherson	8.00
5	John Lackey	15.00
6	Ervin Santana/25	25.00
9	Brandon Webb	15.00
10	Chad Tracy	8.00
11	Russ Ortiz	8.00
12	Alex Cintron	5.00
17	Cal Ripken Jr.	85.00
18	Rick Dempsey	8.00
19	Adam Loewen	8.00
20	Eric Byrnes	8.00
24	Kevin Youkilis	15.00
25	Keith Foulke	15.00
26	Trot Nixon	15.00
27	Edgar Renteria	15.00
28	Luis Tiant	15.00
29	Todd Walker	8.00
30	Mark Grace	20.00
31	Steve Stone	15.00
32	Ron Santo	25.00
33	Mike Wuertz	10.00
34	Russel Rohlicek/60	10.00
35	Ryne Sandberg	50.00
39	Paulino Reynoso/86	10.00
43	Bubba Nelson	8.00
47	Larry Bigbie/92	10.00
53	Miguel Cabrera	20.00
54	Chris Resop	8.00
56	Luke Scott	20.00
58	Mark McLemore/43	15.00
59	Devon Lowery	8.00
61	Duke Snider	25.00
62	Johnny Podres/99	20.00
63	Rickie Weeks	15.00
64	Ben Sheets	15.00
66	Lew Ford	8.00
67	Travis Bowyer	8.00
68	Garrett Jones	8.00
69	Joe Nathan	10.00
70	Kent Hrbek	15.00
71	J.D. Durbin/39	10.00
75	Danny Graves	5.00
76	Jae Weong Seo	15.00
77	Matt Lindstrom	8.00
79	Carlos Beltran/37	25.00
81	Tom Gordon	10.00
82	Adam LaRoche/53	15.00
83	Dave Righetti	15.00
84	Joe Pepitone	20.00
85	Gary Sheffield	20.00
86	Jim Leyritz/93	15.00
87	Rich "Goose" Gossage/65	15.00
91	Octavio Dotel	8.00
92	Rollie Fingers	15.00
94	Rich Harden	15.00
97	Barry Zito/26	25.00
100	Chris Roberson	8.00
101	Eude Brito	8.00
102	Randy Wolf	8.00
103	Mike Lieberthal	10.00
104	John Kruk	15.00
109	Mike Johnston	10.00
113	Jeff Miller/49	10.00
114	John Candelaria/43	20.00
116	Mark Loretta	10.00
117	Sean Thompson	8.00
118	Akinori Otsuka/52	20.00
119	Omar Vizquel/100	20.00
121	Clint Nageotte	5.00
122	J.J. Putz	5.00
123	Raul Ibanez	8.00
124	Wladimir Balentien	8.00
125	Jamie Moyer	10.00
129	Jeff Suppan	10.00
130	Marty Marion	15.00
131	Keith Hernandez	15.00
132	Ozzie Smith/94	40.00
133	Mark Mulder	10.00
137	Delmon Young/99	20.00
138	Jason Hammel/57	10.00
139	Agustin Montero	8.00
140	Francisco Cordero	8.00
144	Nolan Ryan/62	80.00
146	Alexis Rios	10.00
147	Jose Guillen	10.00
148	Danny Rueckel	8.00

Autograph Silver Notation

NM/M

Cards are not serial numbered.

11	Russ Ortiz/84	12.00
17	Cal Ripken Jr./25	125.00
81	Tom Gordon	10.00
105	Lenny Dykstra/41	15.00
131	Keith Hernandez/34	15.00
147	Jose Guillen	8.00

Club Autograph Barrel

No Pricing
Production 1-4

Club Autograph Bat

NM/M

Cards are not serial numbered.

1	Paul O'Neill/32	35.00
2	Alan Trammell/70	20.00
3	Barry Larkin	20.00
4	Carlton Fisk/34	35.00
5	Dale Murphy/100	20.00
6	Frank Thomas	35.00
7	Magglio Ordonez	15.00
8	Mark Teixeira/100	25.00
10	Omar Vizquel	20.00
11	Steve Garvey	15.00

Hall of Fame

NM/M

Common Player:		2.00
Inserted 1:3		
1	Al Kaline	4.00
2	Billy Williams	2.00
3	Bobby Doerr	2.00
4	Gaylord Perry	2.00
5	George Brett	6.00
6	Hank Aaron	6.00
7	Mike Schmidt	5.00
8	Nolan Ryan	8.00
9	Robin Roberts	2.00
10	Phil Niekro	2.00
11	Phil Rizzuto	4.00
12	Ralph Kiner	3.00
13	Rod Carew	3.00
14	Ryne Sandberg	6.00
15	Stan Musial	5.00
16	Steve Carlton	3.00
17	Tom Seaver	4.00
18	Willie McCovey	3.00
19	Willie Mays	6.00
20	Duke Snider	4.00
21	Rollie Fingers	2.00
22	Monte Irvin	3.00
23	Ozzie Smith	5.00
24	Johnny Bench	4.00
25	Luis Aparicio	2.00
26	Whitey Ford	4.00
27	Orlando Cepeda	3.00
28	Jim Bunning	2.00
29	Earl Weaver	2.00
30	Frank Robinson	3.00
31	Babe Ruth	8.00
32	Yogi Berra	4.00
33	Wade Boggs	4.00
34	Ted Williams	6.00
35	Roberto Clemente	6.00
36	Nellie Fox	3.00
37	Joe Morgan	3.00
38	Harmon Killebrew	4.00
39	Carlton Fisk	3.00
40	Babe Ruth	8.00

Hall of Fame Autograph

NM/M

Cards are not serial numbered.

1	Al Kaline/82	40.00
2	Billy Williams/42	20.00
3	Bobby Doerr/25	25.00
4	Gaylord Perry	15.00
8	Nolan Ryan/25	100.00
9	Robin Roberts	15.00
11	Phil Rizzuto	35.00
14	Ryne Sandberg/55	60.00
15	Stan Musial/56	60.00
18	Willie McCovey	25.00
20	Duke Snider	35.00
21	Rollie Fingers	15.00
22	Monte Irvin	20.00
24	Johnny Bench	40.00
27	Orlando Cepeda	25.00
28	Jim Bunning/25	25.00

Hall of Fame Autograph Bat

NM/M

Cards are not serial numbered.

12	Ralph Kiner/97	40.00
25	Luis Aparicio/100	20.00
33	Wade Boggs/56	30.00

Hall of Fame Autograph Combo

NM/M

Cards are not serial numbered.

14	Ryne Sandberg/100	75.00
15	Stan Musial/100	75.00
16	Steve Carlton/50	25.00
17	Tom Seaver/50	50.00
18	Willie McCovey/50	40.00

Hall of Fame Autograph Jersey

NM/M

Cards are not serial numbered.

2	Billy Williams/35	25.00
4	Gaylord Perry/100	20.00
6	Hank Aaron/25	250.00
8	Nolan Ryan/50	100.00
11	Phil Rizzuto/100	40.00
14	Ryne Sandberg/35	75.00
15	Stan Musial/50	75.00
16	Steve Carlton/25	30.00
17	Tom Seaver/25	50.00
18	Willie McCovey/25	40.00
21	Rollie Fingers/84	20.00
24	Johnny Bench/100	50.00
26	Whitey Ford/33	40.00

Hall of Fame Autograph MS

NM/M

Production 1-25

2	Billy Williams/25	25.00
4	Gaylord Perry/25	20.00
8	Nolan Ryan/25	100.00
9	Robin Roberts/25	20.00
20	Duke Snider/25	40.00
21	Rollie Fingers/25	20.00
22	Monte Irvin/25	25.00
23	Ozzie Smith/25	60.00
24	Johnny Bench/25	60.00
26	Whitey Ford/25	40.00
27	Orlando Cepeda/25	30.00
28	Jim Bunning/25	25.00
29	Earl Weaver/25	20.00

Hall of Fame Bat

No Pricing
Cards are not serial numbered.

Hall of Fame Combo

NM/M

Cards are not serial numbered.

6	Hank Aaron	40.00
31	Babe Ruth/79	300.00
34	Ted Williams	60.00

Hall of Fame Jersey

NM/M

Cards are not serial numbered.

2	Billy Williams/25	8.00
3	Bobby Doerr/100	10.00
4	Gaylord Perry	8.00
6	Hank Aaron	25.00
8	Nolan Ryan/30	40.00
10	Phil Niekro	10.00
11	Phil Rizzuto	15.00
13	Rod Carew	12.00
15	Stan Musial/66	20.00
16	Steve Carlton	10.00
19	Willie Mays	25.00
21	Rollie Fingers/33	8.00
23	Ozzie Smith/47	20.00
24	Johnny Bench/51	15.00
34	Ted Williams	40.00

HOF Combos Autograph

NM/M

Cards are not serial numbered.

41	Harmon Killebrew, Rod Carew/25	80.00
42	Ryne Sandberg, Wade Boggs/100	70.00
43	Nolan Ryan, George Brett/36	120.00
44	Phil Rizzuto, Steve Carlton/100	50.00
45	Tom Seaver, Rollie Fingers/100	40.00
46	Jim Palmer, Joe Morgan/25	40.00
47	Bobby Doerr, Willie McCovey/51	40.00
48	Harmon Killebrew, Luis Aparicio/25	65.00
49	Duke Snider, Al Kaline/25	75.00
50	Frank Robinson, Jim Palmer/25	40.00
51	Bobby Doerr, Carlton Fisk/25	50.00
52	Joe Morgan, Johnny Bench/25	75.00
53	Duke Snider, Don Sutton/100	50.00
54	Phil Rizzuto, Whitey Ford/57	60.00
55	Johnny Bench, Carlton Fisk/25	75.00
57	Steve Carlton, Whitey Ford/25	50.00
58	Jim Palmer, Tom Seaver/32	50.00
59	Reggie Jackson, Rollie Fingers/49	60.00
60	Duke Snider, Stan Musial	85.00

HOF Quads Autograph

NM/M

Cards are not serial numbered.

72	Jim Bunning, Mike Schmidt, Robin Roberts, Steve Carlton/38	100.00
74	Billy Williams, Lou Brock, Monte Irvin, Ralph Kiner/41	100.00
75	Fergie Jenkins, Gaylord Perry, Tom Seaver, Bob Gibson/50	100.00
76	Nolan Ryan, Don Sutton, Tom Seaver, Steve Carlton/50	80.00

HOF Six Autograph

No Pricing

HOF Trios Autograph

NM/M

Cards are not serial numbered.

64	Joe Morgan, Ryne Sandberg, Bobby Doerr/63	85.00
65	Ozzie Smith, Phil Rizzuto, Luis Aparicio/50	100.00
67	Ralph Kiner, Frank Robinson, Reggie Jackson/25	85.00
68	Gaylord Perry, Bob Gibson, Fergie Jenkins/50	75.00
69	Bob Gibson, Stan Musial, Ozzie Smith/100	140.00

INKcredible Combos

NM/M

Cards are not serial numbered.

1	Francisco Rodriguez, Troy Percival	25.00
2	Francisco Rodriguez, Scot Shields	15.00
3	Scot Shields, Troy Percival	15.00
6	Paul Molitor, Rickie Weeks/28	20.00
9	Ron Cey, Ron Santo/25	50.00
11	Don Sutton, Steve Garvey/100	30.00
12	Billy Ripken, Cal Ripken Jr.	90.00
13	Jim Palmer, Rick Dempsey/100	25.00
15	Mark Loretta, Sean Burroughs	10.00
17	Brett Myers, Randy Wolf	10.00
19	Justin Morneau, Kent Hrbek/36	25.00
20	Frank Thomas, Paul Konerko/50	50.00
21	Luis Aparicio, Minnie Minoso	20.00
22	Cal Ripken Jr., Tony Gwynn/100	125.00
24	Jose Guillen, Tim Salmon	10.00
25	Dallas McPherson, Kevin Youkilis	15.00
26	Esteban Loaiza, Jose Guillen	10.00
31	Jason Kubel, Lew Ford	10.00
32	Danny Graves, Matt Lindstrom	10.00
33	Garret Anderson, Tim Salmon	25.00
34	Clint Nageotte, J.J. Putz	10.00

INKredible Quads

NM/M

Cards are not serial numbered.

60	Jose Guillen, Marlon Byrd, Junior Spivey, Esteban Loiaza	50.00
61	Marlon Byrd, Jose Guillen, Livan Hernandez, Esteban Loiaza	50.00
63	Dwight Evans, Jim Rice, Luis Tiant, Carlton Fisk/73	100.00
65	Hideo Nomo, Shigetoshi Hasegawa, Akinori Otsuka, So Taguchi/45	300.00

INKcredible Six

NM/M

Cards are not serial numbered.

67	St. Louis Cardinals	240.00

INKcredible Trios

NM/M

Cards are not serial numbered.

35	Scot Shields, Troy Percival, Francisco Rodriguez	30.00
36	Barry Zito, Mark Mulder, Tim Hudson/37	80.00
38	Roy Halladay, Vernon Wells, Alex Rios/25	40.00
40	Duke Snider, Johnny Podres, Maury Wills/100	60.00

42 Keith Hernandez, Lenny Dykstra, Jesse Orosco/80 40.00
43 Esteban Loaiza, Jose Guillen, Paul Byrd 30.00
44 Cal Ripken Jr., Jim Palmer, Rick Dempsey/80 150.00
45 Brett Myers, Randy Wolf, Mike Lieberthal 30.00
46 Jacque Jones, Lew Ford, Jason Kubel/91 30.00
47 Randy Jones, Ozzie Smith, Rollie Fingers/36 80.00
48 Ron Guidry, "Goose" Gossage, Luis Tiant 40.00
49 Ron Guidry, 'Goose" Gossage, Dave Righetti 40.00
50 Ozzie Smith, Cal Ripken Jr., Alan Trammell/99 180.00
51 Wade Boggs, Ryne Sandberg, Tony Gwynn/95 140.00
52 Earl Weaver, Cal Ripken Jr., Frank Robinson/38 150.00
53 Harmon Killebrew, Rod Carew, Kent Hrbek/28 100.00
54 Minnie Minoso, Luis Aparicio, Carlton Fisk/25 60.00

K-Force

NM/M

Inserted 1:7
1 Nolan Ryan 8.00
2 Steve Carlton 3.00
3 Roger Clemens 8.00
4 Randy Johnson 4.00
5 Tom Seaver 4.00
6 Don Sutton 2.00
7 Gaylord Perry 2.00
8 Fergie Jenkins 2.00
9 Bob Gibson 4.00
10 Greg Maddux 4.00
11 David Cone 2.00
12 Bob Feller 3.00
13 Johan Santana 4.00
14 Roy Halladay 3.00
15 Juan Marichal 3.00

K-Force Autograph

NM/M

Cards are not serial numbered.
1 Nolan Ryan 75.00
2 Steve Carlton/33 20.00
6 Don Sutton 10.00
7 Gaylord Perry/75 15.00
8 Fergie Jenkins/55 20.00
10 Greg Maddux/25 80.00
11 David Cone 10.00
12 Bob Feller/39 25.00
13 Johan Santana/55 30.00
15 Juan Marichal 15.00

K-Force Autograph Material

NM/M

Cards are not serial numbered.
1 Nolan Ryan/100 90.00
2 Steve Carlton 15.00
6 Don Sutton/80 15.00
7 Gaylord Perry/50 20.00
8 Fergie Jenkins/41 25.00
9 Bob Gibson/41 40.00
10 Greg Maddux/25 90.00
11 David Cone 15.00
12 Bob Feller/30 25.00
15 Juan Marichal/58 20.00

K-Force Autograph MS

NM/M

Production 1-25
1 Nolan Ryan/25 100.00
2 Steve Carlton/25 20.00
6 Don Sutton/25 20.00
7 Gaylord Perry/25 25.00
8 Fergie Jenkins/25 25.00
10 Greg Maddux/25 90.00
11 David Cone/25 20.00
12 Bob Feller/25 25.00
13 Johan Santana/25 40.00
15 Juan Marichal/25 25.00

Milestone Marks

NM/M

Common Player: 2.00
Inserted 1:10
1 Duke Snider 4.00
2 Nolan Ryan 8.00
3 Gaylord Perry 2.00
4 Johnny Bench 4.00
5 Willie McCovey 3.00
6 Stan Musial 5.00
7 Randi Johnson 4.00
9 Gary Carter 3.00
10 Tony Gwynn 4.00
2.00

Milestone Marks Autograph

NM/M

Cards are not serial numbered.
1 Duke Snider 25.00
2 Nolan Ryan 75.00
3 Gaylord Perry 15.00
4 Johnny Bench 30.00
5 Willie McCovey/44 30.00
6 Stan Musial 50.00

Milestone Marks Autograph Material Bat

No Pricing
Cards are not serial numbered.

Milestone Marks Autograph Material Combo

NM/M

Inserted 1:210
Cards are not serial numbered.
7 Randy Johnson/25 75.00
10 Tony Gwynn 30.00

Milestone Marks Autograph Material Jersey

NM/M

Cards are not serial numbered
3 Gaylord Perry/100 10.00
5 Willie McCovey 30.00
10 Tony Gwynn/75 30.00

Milestone Marks Autograph MS

NM/M

Production 20-25
1 Duke Snider/25 40.00
2 Nolan Ryan/25 100.00
3 Gaylord Perry/25 20.00
4 Johnny Bench/25 40.00
5 Willie McCovey/25 35.00
6 Stan Musial/25 80.00
10 Tony Gwynn/25 50.00

Notable Nicknames

NM/M

Production 100 Sets
Master Series: No Pricing
GM Greg Maddux Bulldog 300.00
IR Ivan Rodriguez Pudge 50.00
OS Ozzie Smith Wizard 60.00

Stamps Autograph Centennial

NM/M

Production 3-81
Pro Ball: .75-1X
Production 3-81
2 Cal Ripken Jr./50 125.00
4 Duke Snider/81 30.00
6 Orlando Cepeda/48 25.00
7 Don Larsen/50 25.00
10 Cal Ripken Jr./50 125.00

Stamps Autograph Material Centennial

NM/M

Production 2-50
Pro Ball: .75-1X
Production 1-50
2 Cal Ripken Jr./50 140.00
10 Cal Ripken Jr./50 140.00

Stamps Centennial Autograph

No Pricing
Production 1-2

Stamps Material Centennial

NM/M

Production 40-100
Pro Ball: .75-1X
Production 40-100
2 Cal Ripken Jr./50 40.00
5 Harmon Killebrew/70 15.00
8 Adrian Beltre/100 8.00
10 Cal Ripken Jr./50 40.00
11 Jim Thorpe/68 140.00
12 Willie Mays/100 40.00
13 Roger Maris/100 40.00

Stars Autograph

NM/M

Cards are not serial numbered.
1 Mark Teixeira/42 30.00
2 Scott Rolen 25.00
3 Roy Oswalt/85 20.00
5 Morgan Ensberg 15.00
6 Mark Grace/86 25.00
7 Gary Sheffield/82 25.00
8 Sean Casey 15.00
10 Ryne Sandberg 50.00

Stars Autograph Material Bat

NM/M

Cards are not serial numbered.
1 Mark Teixeira/100 25.00
3 Roy Oswalt 15.00
4 Hideo Nomo/36 200.00
6 Mark Grace 25.00
7 Gary Sheffield 25.00
11 Stan Musial/38 75.00
12 Joe Torre/44 40.00
13 Wade Boggs/40 30.00
14 Barry Larkin 25.00
15 Dale Murphy/100 25.00

Stars Autograph Material Jersey

NM/M

Cards are not serial numbered.
2 Scott Rolen 25.00
4 Hideo Nomo/50 200.00
6 Mark Grace/43 35.00
7 Gary Sheffield/43 30.00
8 Sean Casey/52 20.00
11 Stan Musial/44 80.00
12 Joe Torre/50 40.00
15 Dale Murphy 25.00

Stars Autograph MS

NM/M

Production 1-25
1 Mark Teixeira/25 35.00
2 Scott Rolen/25 35.00
3 Roy Oswalt/25 25.00
5 Morgan Ensberg/25 20.00
6 Mark Grace/25 40.00
7 Gary Sheffield/25 40.00
8 Sean Casey/25 20.00
10 Ryne Sandberg/25 75.00
14 Barry Larkin/25 35.00

Stats Autograph

NM/M

Cards are not serial numbered.
4 Alfonso Soriano 25.00
9 Miguel Cabrera 30.00
10 Mark Teixeira/41 30.00

Stats Autograph Material Bat

NM/M

Cards are not serial numbered.
4 Alfonso Soriano 25.00
5 Don Mattingly/25 75.00
10 Mark Teixeira 25.00

Stats Autograph Material Combo

NM/M

Cards are not serial numbered.
1 Tony Gwynn 30.00
4 Alfonso Soriano/25 30.00

Stats Autograph Material Jersey

NM/M

Cards are not serial numbered.
1 Tony Gwynn/25 50.00
2 Johan Santana/100 30.00
3 Orel Hershiser/25 25.00
8 Victor Martinez/25 25.00

Stats Autograph MS

NM/M

Production 1-25
1 Tony Gwynn/25 50.00
2 Johan Santana/25 40.00
3 Orel Hershiser/25 25.00
4 Alfonso Soriano/25 30.00
5 Don Mattingly/25 75.00
8 Victor Martinez/25 25.00
9 Miguel Cabrera/25 40.00
10 Mark Teixeira/25 35.00

2005 Donruss Studio

NM/M

Complete Set (300):
Common Player: .25
Pack (6): 4.00
Box (24): 90.00
1 Casey Kotchman .25
2 Chone Figgins .25
3 Dallas McPherson .25
4 Darin Erstad .25
5 Ervin Santana .25
6 Garret Anderson .40
7 Norihiro Nakamura **RC** 2.00
8 John Lackey .25
9 Orlando Cabrera .25
10 Robb Quinlan .25
11 Steve Finley .25
12 Tim Salmon .25
13 Vladimir Guerrero .75
14 Brandon Webb .25
15 Craig Counsell .25
16 Javier Vazquez .25
17 Luis Gonzalez .25
18 Tony Pena **RC** .40
19 Russ Ortiz .25
20 Scott Hairston .25
21 Shawn Green .25
22 Jose Cruz Jr. .25
23 Troy Glaus .40
24 Adam LaRoche .25
25 Andruw Jones .50
26 Chipper Jones .75
27 Danny Kolb .25
28 John Smoltz .40
29 Johnny Estrada .25
30 Marcus Giles .25
31 Nick Green .25
32 Rafael Furcal .25
33 Tim Hudson .40
34 Brian Roberts .25
35 Javy Lopez .25
36 Jay Gibbons .25
37 Melvin Mora .25
38 Miguel Tejada .50
39 Rafael Palmeiro .50
40 Rodrigo Lopez .25
41 Sidney Ponson .25
42 Abe Alvarez .25
43 Bill Mueller .25
44 Curt Schilling .75
45 David Ortiz .75
46 David Wells .25
47 Edgar Renteria .25
48 Jason Varitek .50
49 Jay Payton .25
50 Johnny Damon .75
51 Juan Cedeno .25
52 Manny Ramirez .75
53 Matt Clement .25
54 Trot Nixon .25
55 Wade Miller .25
56 Aramis Ramirez .40
57 Carlos Zambrano .40
58 Corey Patterson .25
59 Derrek Lee .50
60 Greg Maddux 1.50
61 Kerry Wood .40
62 Mark Prior .75
63 Nomar Garciaparra .75
64 Sammy Sosa 1.00
65 Todd Walker .25
66 A.J. Pierzynski .25
67 Aaron Rowand .25
68 Frank Thomas .50
69 Freddy Garcia .25
70 Jermaine Dye .25
71 Mark Buehrle .40
72 Paul Konerko .40
73 Tadahito Iguchi **RC** 3.00
74 Pedro Lopez **RC** .40
75 Scott Podsednik .25
76 Shingo Takatsu .25
77 Adam Dunn .50
78 Austin Kearns .25
79 Barry Larkin .50
80 Bubba Nelson .25
81 Danny Graves .25
82 Eric Milton .25
83 Ken Griffey Jr. 1.50
84 Ryan Wagner .25
85 Sean Casey .25
86 C.C. Sabathia .25
87 Cliff Lee .25
88 Fausto Carmona .25
89 Grady Sizemore .40
90 Jake Westbrook .25
91 Jody Gerut .25
92 Juan Gonzalez .40
93 Kazuhito Tadano .25
94 Travis Hafner .25
95 Victor Martinez .25
96 Charles Johnson .25
97 Clint Barmes .25
98 Cory Sullivan .25
99 Jeff Baker .25
100 Jeff Francis .25
101 Jeff Salazar .25
102 Jeromy Burnitz .25
103 Joe Kennedy .25
104 Matt Holliday .50
105 Preston Wilson .25
106 Todd Helton .50
107 Ubaldo Jimenez **RC** .40
108 Brandon Inge .25
109 Carlos Guillen .25
110 Carlos Pena .25
111 Craig Monroe .25
112 Ivan Rodriguez .50
113 Jeremy Bonderman .25
114 Justin Verlander **RC** 2.00
115 Magglio Ordonez .25
116 Troy Percival .25
117 Vance Wilson .25
118 A.J. Burnett .25
119 Al Leiter .25
120 Dontrelle Willis .40
121 Josh Beckett .40
122 Juan Pierre .25
123 Miguel Cabrera .75
124 Mike Lowell .25
125 Paul LoDuca .25
126 Randy Messenger **RC** .40
127 Yorman Bazardo **RC** .40
128 Andy Pettitte .40
129 Brad Lidge .25
130 Chris Burke .25
131 Craig Biggio .40
132 Fernando Nieve .25
133 Jason Lane .25
134 Jeff Bagwell .50
135 Lance Berkman .40
136 Morgan Ensberg .25
137 Roger Clemens 2.00
138 Roy Oswalt .25
139 Ambiorix Burgos **RC** .40
140 David DeJesus .25
141 Jeremy Affeldt .25
142 Jose Lima .25
143 Ken Harvey .25
144 Mike MacDougal .25
145 Mike Sweeney .25
146 Terrence Long .25
147 Zack Greinke .25
148 Brad Penny .25
149 Derek Lowe .25
150 Dioner Navarro .25
151 Edwin Jackson .25
152 Eric Gagne .25
153 Hee Seop Choi .25
154 Hideo Nomo .50
155 J.D. Drew .40
156 Jeff Kent .25
157 Jeff Weaver .25
158 Milton Bradley .25
159 Yhency Brazoban .25
160 Ben Sheets .40
161 Bill Hall .25

162 Carlos Lee .25
163 Gustavo Chacin .25
164 Geoff Jenkins .25
165 Jose Capellan .25
166 Lyle Overbay .25
167 Rickie Weeks .40
168 Jacque Jones .25
169 Joe Mauer .50
170 Joe Nathan .25
171 Johan Santana .50
172 Justin Morneau .40
173 Lew Ford .25
174 Michael Cuddyer .25
175 Shannon Stewart .25
176 Torii Hunter .25
177 Brad Radke .25
178 Ambiorix Concepcion **RC** .40
179 Carlos Beltran .50
180 David Wright .75
181 Jose Reyes .50
182 Kazuo Matsui .25
183 Kris Benson .25
184 Mike Piazza 1.00
185 Pedro Martinez .75
186 Philip Humber **RC** 1.00
187 Tom Glavine .40
188 Alex Rodriguez 1.50
189 Carl Pavano .25
190 Derek Jeter 2.00
191 Yuniesky Betancourt **RC** 1.00
192 Hideki Matsui 1.50
193 Jorge Posada .40
194 Kevin Brown .25
195 Mariano Rivera .40
196 Mike Mussina .40
197 Randy Johnson .75
198 Scott Proctor .25
199 Tom Gordon .25
200 Barry Zito .40
201 Bobby Crosby .40
202 Danny Haren .25
203 Eric Chavez .40
204 Keiichi Yabu **RC** .40
205 Jason Kendall .25
206 Joe Blanton .25
207 Mark Kotsay .25
208 Nick Swisher .25
209 Octavio Dotel .25
210 Rich Harden .40
211 Billy Wagner .25
212 Bobby Abreu .40
213 Chase Utley .50
214 Gavin Floyd .25
215 Jim Thome .50
216 Jimmy Rollins .50
217 Jon Lieber .25
218 Kenny Lofton .25
219 Mike Lieberthal .25
220 Pat Burrell .25
221 Randy Wolf .25
222 Craig Wilson .25
223 Jack Wilson .25
224 Jason Bay .25
225 John Van Benschoten .25
226 Jose Castillo .25
227 Kip Wells .25
228 Matt Lawton .25
229 Akinori Otsuka .25
230 Brian Giles .25
231 Freddy Guzman .25
232 Jake Peavy .40
233 Khalil Greene .40
234 Mark Loretta .25
235 Sean Burroughs .25
236 Trevor Hoffman .25
237 Woody Williams .25
238 Armando Benitez .25
239 Edgardo Alfonzo .25
240 Erick Threets **RC** .40
241 Jason Schmidt .40
242 Marquis Grissom .25
243 Merkin Valdez .25
244 Michael Tucker .25
245 Moises Alou .40
246 Omar Vizquel .25
247 Adrian Beltre .40
248 Bret Boone .25
249 Bucky Jacobsen .25
250 Clint Nageotte .25
251 Ichiro Suzuki 1.50
252 J.J. Putz .25
253 Jeremy Reed .25
254 Miguel Olivo .25
255 Mike Morse **RC** 2.00
256 Richie Sexson .40
257 Wladimir Balentien **RC** 1.00
258 Albert Pujols 2.00
259 Jason Isringhausen .25
260 Jeff Suppan .25
261 Jim Edmonds .40
262 Larry Walker .40
263 Mark Mulder .40
264 Rick Ankiel .25
265 Scott Rolen .75
266 Yadier Molina .25
267 Aubrey Huff .25
268 B.J. Upton .25
269 Carl Crawford .25
270 Chris Seddon **RC** .40
271 Delmon Young .25
272 Dewon Brazelton .25
273 Jeff Niemann **RC** 1.00
274 Rocco Baldelli .25
275 Scott Kazmir .25
276 Adrian Gonzalez .25
277 Alfonso Soriano .75
278 Francisco Cordero .25
279 Hank Blalock .40
280 Kameron Loe .25
281 Kenny Rogers .25
282 Laynce Nix .25
283 Mark Teixeira .40
284 Michael Young .25
285 Corey Koskie .25
286 David Bush .25
287 Frank Catalanotto .25
288 Gabe Gross .25
289 Raul Tablado **RC** .40
290 Roy Halladay .40
291 Shea Hillenbrand .25
292 Vernon Wells .25
293 Chad Cordero .25
294 Cristian Guzman .25
295 Jose Guillen .25
296 Jose Vidro .25
297 Josh Karp .25
298 Livan Hernandez .25
299 Nick Johnson .25
300 Vinny Castilla .25

Proofs Gold

Stars: 8-12X
Production 25 Sets

Proofs Platinum

No Pricing
Production 10 Sets

Proofs Silver

Stars: 3-5X
Production 100 Sets

Autographs

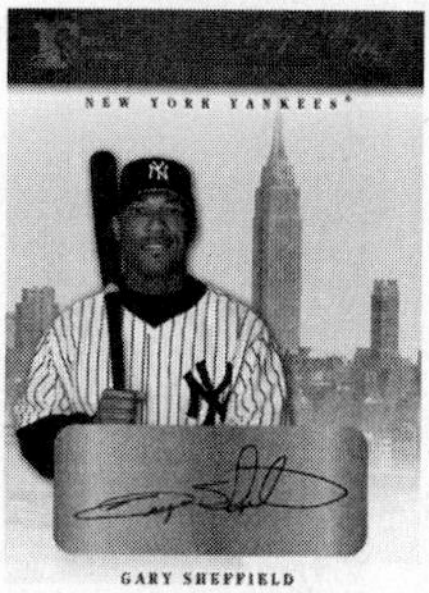

No Pricing

Diamond Cuts

NM/M
Common Player: 1.00
Production 1,250 Sets
Die-Cut: 1-1.5X
Production 250 Sets
Die-Cut Gold: 1.5-3X
Production 75 Sets
1 Roger Clemens 4.00
2 Manny Ramirez 1.50
3 Francisco Rodriguez 1.00
4 Brian Roberts 1.00
5 Javy Lopez 1.00
6 Vernon Wells 1.00
7 Johan Santana 1.50
8 Torii Hunter 1.00
9 Mike Mussina 1.50
10 Sammy Sosa 2.50
11 Ryan Wagner 1.00
12 Jack Wilson 1.00
13 Ichiro Suzuki 3.00
14 Greg Maddux 3.00
15 Albert Pujols 4.00
16 Jeremy Bonderman 1.00
17 Johnny Estrada 1.00
18 Mark Buehrle 1.00
19 Jorge Posada 1.00
20 Carl Crawford 1.00
21 Paul Konerko 1.00
22 Victor Martinez 1.00
23 Jose Vidro 1.00
24 Jim Thome 1.50
25 Andruw Jones 1.50

Diamond Cuts Bat

NM/M
Production 5-300
1 Roger Clemens/50 15.00
2 Manny Ramirez/200 8.00
5 Javy Lopez/300 4.00
8 Torii Hunter/300 4.00
10 Sammy Sosa/25 15.00
12 Jack Wilson/300 4.00
14 Greg Maddux/225 10.00
15 Albert Pujols/300 15.00
21 Paul Konerko/50 6.00
22 Victor Martinez/300 4.00
23 Jose Vidro/300 4.00
25 Andruw Jones/300 6.00

Diamond Cuts Combo

NM/M
Production 5-50
Prime: No Pricing
Production 10 Sets
1 Roger Clemens/Bat-Jsy/50 20.00
2 Manny Ramirez/Bat-Jsy/50 12.00
3 Freddy Rodriguez/Jsy-Jsy/50 10.00
5 Javy Lopez/Bat-Jsy/50 8.00
6 Vernon Wells/Jsy-Jsy/50 8.00
8 Torii Hunter/Bat-Jsy/50 8.00
10 Sammy Sosa/Jsy-Jsy/50 12.00
11 Ryan Wagner/Jsy-Jsy/50 8.00
12 Jack Wilson/Bat-Jsy/50 8.00
14 Greg Maddux/Bat-Jsy/50 15.00
15 Albert Pujols/Bat-Jsy/50 30.00
17 Johnny Estrada/Fld Glve-Jsy/50 10.00
21 Paul Konerko/Jsy-Jsy/50 10.00
22 Victor Martinez/Bat-Jsy/50 10.00
23 Jose Vidro/Bat-Jsy/50 8.00
24 Jim Thome/Jsy-Jsy/45 12.00
25 Andruw Jones/Bat-Jsy/50 10.00

Diamond Cuts Jersey

NM/M
Production 15-250
Prime: No Pricing
Production 5-10
1 Roger Clemens/125 10.00
2 Manny Ramirez/250 8.00
3 Francisco Rodriguez/250 4.00
4 Brian Roberts/250 6.00
5 Javy Lopez/250 4.00
6 Vernon Wells/250 4.00
7 Johan Santana/175 8.00
8 Torii Hunter/250 4.00
9 Mike Mussina/250 6.00
10 Sammy Sosa/250 8.00
11 Ryan Wagner/250 4.00
14 Greg Maddux/250 8.00
15 Albert Pujols/250 20.00
16 Jeremy Bonderman/250 4.00
17 Johnny Estrada/250 4.00
18 Mark Buehrle/250 4.00
19 Jorge Posada/250 4.00
20 Carl Crawford/250 4.00
21 Paul Konerko/250 4.00
22 Victor Martinez/250 4.00
23 Jose Vidro/175 4.00
24 Jim Thome/250 6.00
25 Andruw Jones/250 6.00

Diamond Cuts Signature Combo

NM/M
Production 25-50
Prime: No Pricing
Production 10 Sets
3 Freddy Rodriguez/Jsy-Jsy/25 40.00
6 Vernon Wells/Jsy-Jsy/25 25.00
8 Torii Hunter/Bat-Jsy/50 20.00
11 Ryan Wagner/Jsy-Jsy/50 15.00
12 Jack Wilson/Bat-Jsy/50 20.00
16 Jeremy Bonderman/Jsy-Jsy/50 20.00
17 Johnny Estrada/Fld Glv-Jsy/50 15.00
21 Paul Konerko/Jsy-Jsy/25 25.00

Heritage

NM/M
Common Player: 1.00
Production 1,000 Sets
Die-Cut: 1-1.5X
Production 200 Sets
Die-Cut Gold: 2-3X
Production 50 Sets
1 Rickey Henderson 1.50
2 Jeff Bagwell 1.50
3 Steve Garvey 1.00
4 Albert Pujols 5.00
5 Don Mattingly 4.00
6 Frank Thomas 1.50
7 Tony Gwynn 2.00
8 Gary Sheffield 1.50
9 Dale Murphy 1.50
10 Kerry Wood 1.50
11 Cal Ripken Jr. 6.00
12 Miguel Cabrera 2.00
13 Dwight Gooden 1.00
14 Barry Zito 1.00
15 Darryl Strawberry 1.00

Heritage Bat

NM/M
Production 150 Sets
1 Rickey Henderson 8.00
2 Jeff Bagwell 6.00
3 Steve Garvey 4.00
4 Albert Pujols 15.00
5 Don Mattingly 10.00
6 Frank Thomas 6.00
7 Tony Gwynn 8.00
8 Gary Sheffield 6.00
9 Dale Murphy 6.00
11 Cal Ripken Jr. 20.00
12 Miguel Cabrera 6.00
13 Dwight Gooden 4.00
15 Darryl Strawberry 4.00

Heritage Combo

NM/M
Production 10-50
Prime: No Pricing
Production 10 Sets
1 Rickey Henderson/Bat-Jsy/50 15.00
2 Jeff Bagwell/Bat-Jsy/50 10.00
3 Steve Garvey/Bat-Jsy/50 10.00
4 Albert Pujols/Bat-Jsy/50 25.00
5 Don Mattingly/Bat-Jsy/50 20.00
6 Frank Thomas/Bat-Jsy/50 10.00
7 Tony Gwynn/Bat-Jsy/50 15.00
8 Gary Sheffield/Bat-Jsy/50 10.00
9 Dale Murphy/Bat-Jsy/50 12.00
10 Kerry Wood/Jsy-Pants/25 10.00
11 Cal Ripken Jr./Bat-Jsy/50 4.00
12 Miguel Cabrera/Bat-Jsy/50 12.00
13 Dwight Gooden/Bat-Jsy/50 10.00
15 Darryl Strawberry/Bat-Jsy/50 10.00

Heritage Jersey

NM/M
Production 50-250
Prime: No Pricing
Production 10 Sets
1 Rickey Henderson/250 8.00
2 Jeff Bagwell/250 6.00
3 Steve Garvey/250 4.00
4 Albert Pujols/250 15.00
5 Don Mattingly/250 12.00
6 Frank Thomas/250 6.00
7 Tony Gwynn/250 8.00
9 Dale Murphy/250 6.00
10 Kerry Wood/250 6.00
11 Cal Ripken Jr./250 20.00
12 Miguel Cabrera/50 8.00
13 Dwight Gooden/250 4.00
14 Barry Zito/250 4.00
15 Darryl Strawberry/250 4.00

Heritage Signature Combo

NM/M
Production 10-50
Prime: No Pricing
Production 5-10
3 Steve Garvey/Bat-Jsy/50 25.00
5 Don Mattingly/Bat-Jsy/25 75.00
9 Dale Murphy/Bat-Jsy/25 40.00
11 Cal Ripken Jr./Bat-Jsy/50 160.00
12 Miguel Cabrera/Bat-Jsy/25 50.00
13 Dwight Gooden/Bat-Jsy/25 25.00
15 Darryl Strawberry/Bat-Jsy/25 25.00

Heroes of the Hall

NM/M
Common Player: 2.00
Production 350 Sets
Die-Cut: 1-1.5X
Production 75 Sets
Die-Cut Gold: 2-3X
Production 25 Sets
1 Luis Aparicio 2.00
2 Dennis Eckersley 2.00
3 Brooks Robinson 4.00
4 Carlton Fisk 4.00
5 Tom Seaver 4.00
6 Paul Molitor 4.00
7 Rod Carew 3.00
8 George Brett 6.00
9 Nolan Ryan 8.00
10 Mike Schmidt 6.00
11 Willie Mays 6.00
12 Gary Carter 2.00
13 Lou Brock 2.00
14 Steve Carlton 2.00
15 Harmon Killebrew 4.00

Heroes of the Hall Bat

NM/M
Production 100-150
1 Luis Aparicio/150 4.00
3 Brooks Robinson/150 8.00
4 Carlton Fisk/150 6.00
6 Paul Molitor/150 8.00
8 George Brett/150 12.00
10 Mike Schmidt/125 15.00
11 Willie Mays/100 35.00
12 Gary Carter/125 6.00
13 Lou Brock/150 6.00
15 Harmon Killebrew/150 8.00

Heroes of the Hall Combo

NM/M
Production 25-50
Prime: No Pricing
Production 5-10
1 Luis Aparicio/Bat-Jsy/50 10.00
2 Dennis Eckersley/Jsy-Pants/50 10.00
3 Brooks Robinson/Bat-Jsy/25 15.00
4 Carlton Fisk/Bat-Jsy/50 12.00
5 Tom Seaver/Jsy-Pants/50 15.00
6 Paul Molitor/Bat-Jsy/50 15.00
7 Rod Carew/Bat-Jsy/50 12.00
8 George Brett/Bat-Jsy/50 20.00
9 Nolan Ryan/Bat-Jsy/50 25.00
10 Mike Schmidt/Bat-Jsy/50 20.00
11 Willie Mays/Bat-Jsy/25 60.00
12 Gary Carter/Jsy-Pants/50 10.00
13 Lou Brock/Bat-Jkt/50 15.00
15 Harmon Killebrew/Bat-Jsy/50 15.00

Heroes of the Hall Jersey

NM/M

Production 50-150
Prime: No Pricing
Production 5-10
1 Luis Aparicio/150 4.00
2 Dennis Eckersley/150 6.00
3 Brooks Robinson/50 10.00
4 Carlton Fisk/150 6.00
5 Tom Seaver/150 8.00
6 Paul Molitor/150 8.00
7 Rod Carew/150 6.00
8 George Brett/150 12.00
9 Nolan Ryan/100 20.00
10 Mike Schmidt/100 15.00
11 Willie Mays/50 40.00
12 Gary Carter/150 6.00
14 Steve Carlton/150 4.00
15 Harmon Killebrew/150 8.00

Heroes of the Hall Signature Combo

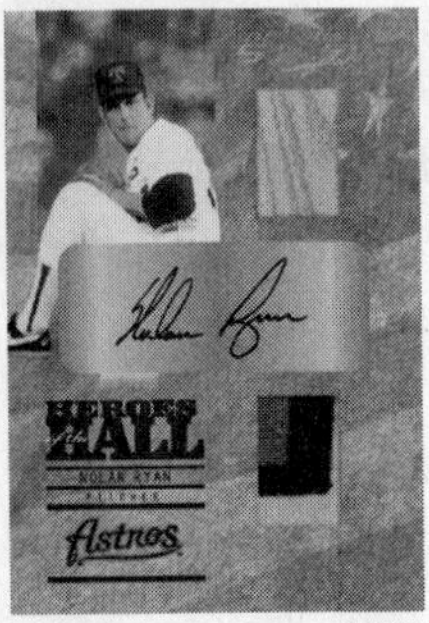

NM/M

Production 5-50
Prime: No Pricing
Production 5-10
1 Luis Aparicio/Bat-Jsy/50 20.00
2 Dennis Eckersley/Jsy-Pants/25 30.00
4 Carlton Fisk/Bat-Jsy/25 40.00
6 Paul Molitor/Bat-Jsy/25 35.00
14 Steve Carlton/Bat-Jsy/25 35.00
15 Harmon Killebrew/Bat-Jsy/25 40.00

Masterstrokes

NM/M

Common Player: 1.50
Production 750 Sets
Die-Cut: 1-1.5X
Production 150 Sets
Die-Cut Gold: 1.5-2X
Production 50 Sets
1 Hideki Matsui 6.00
2 David Ortiz 3.00
3 Aramis Ramirez 2.00
4 Lance Berkman 1.50
5 Ichiro Suzuki 6.00
6 Mike Piazza 4.00
7 Ivan Rodriguez 2.00
8 Hideo Nomo 2.00
9 Jeff Bagwell 2.00
10 Travis Hafner 1.50
11 Casey Kotchman 1.50
12 Jim Edmonds 2.00
13 Michael Young 1.50
14 Lyle Overbay 1.50
15 Eric Chavez 2.00
16 Jason Bay 1.50
17 Hank Blalock 2.00
18 Frank Thomas 2.00
19 Craig Biggio 2.00
20 Miguel Cabrera 3.00
21 Vladimir Guerrero 3.00
22 Sammy Sosa 4.00
23 Chipper Jones 3.00
24 Rafael Palmeiro 2.00
25 Adam Dunn 2.00

Masterstrokes Bat

NM/M

Production 25-250
1 Hideki Matsui/25 30.00
2 David Ortiz/250 8.00
3 Aramis Ramirez/35 8.00
4 Lance Berkman/250 4.00
6 Mike Piazza/100 10.00
7 Ivan Rodriguez/250 6.00
9 Jeff Bagwell/250 6.00
10 Travis Hafner/250 4.00
11 Casey Kotchman/250 4.00
13 Michael Young/250 4.00
14 Lyle Overbay/250 4.00
16 Jason Bay/250 4.00
17 Hank Blalock/50 6.00
18 Frank Thomas/250 6.00
19 Craig Biggio/250 6.00
20 Miguel Cabrera/250 6.00
21 Vladimir Guerrero/250 8.00
22 Sammy Sosa/200 8.00
23 Chipper Jones/250 6.00
25 Adam Dunn/250 6.00

Masterstrokes Combo

NM/M

Production 15-50
Prime: No Pricing
Production 10 Sets
2 David Ortiz/Bat-Jsy/50 15.00
3 Aramis Ramirez/Jsy-Jsy/50 10.00
4 Lance Berkman/Bat-Jsy/50 8.00
6 Mike Piazza/Jsy-Jsy/50 15.00
7 Ivan Rodriguez/Bat-Jsy/50 10.00
8 Hideo Nomo/Jsy-Jsy/50 12.00
9 Jeff Bagwell/Bat-Jsy/50 10.00
10 Travis Hafner/Bat-Jsy/50 8.00
11 Casey Kotchman/Bat-Jsy/50 8.00
12 Jim Edmonds/Jsy-Jsy/50 10.00
13 Michael Young/Bat-Jsy/50 10.00
14 Lyle Overbay/Bat-Jsy/50 8.00
15 Eric Chavez/Bat-Jsy/50 10.00
16 Jason Bay/Bat-Jsy/50 8.00
17 Hank Blalock/Jsy-Jsy/50 10.00
18 Frank Thomas/Bat-Jsy/50 12.00
19 Craig Biggio/Bat-Jsy/50 10.00
20 Miguel Cabrera/Bat-Jsy/50 15.00
21 Vladimir Guerrero/Bat-Jsy/50 15.00
22 Sammy Sosa/Bat-Jsy/50 15.00
23 Chipper Jones/Bat-Jsy/50 12.00
24 Rafael Palmeiro/Bat-Pants/50 12.00
25 Adam Dunn/Bat-Jsy/50 10.00

Masterstrokes Jersey

NM/M

Production 40-250
Prime: No Pricing
Production 10 Sets
1 Hideki Matsui/250 20.00
2 David Ortiz/250 8.00
3 Aramis Ramirez/250 6.00
4 Lance Berkman/250 4.00
6 Mike Piazza/250 8.00
7 Ivan Rodriguez/250 6.00
8 Hideo Nomo/250 6.00
9 Jeff Bagwell/250 6.00
10 Travis Hafner/200 4.00
11 Casey Kotchman/250 4.00
12 Jim Edmonds/250 6.00
13 Michael Young/150 4.00
14 Lyle Overbay/250 4.00
15 Eric Chavez/250 4.00
16 Jason Bay/150 4.00
17 Hank Blalock/250 4.00
18 Frank Thomas/250 6.00
19 Craig Biggio/250 6.00
20 Miguel Cabrera/250 6.00
21 Vladimir Guerrero/50 10.00
22 Sammy Sosa/250 8.00
23 Chipper Jones/225 6.00
24 Rafael Palmeiro/40 8.00
25 Adam Dunn/250 6.00

Masterstrokes Signature Combo

NM/M

Production 5-50
Prime: No Pricing
Production 5-10
10 Travis Hafner/Bat-Jsy/50 25.00
11 Casey Kotchman/Bat-Jsy/50 20.00
14 Lyle Overbay/Bat-Jsy/50 12.00
15 Eric Chavez/Bat-Jsy/25 25.00
16 Jason Bay/Bat-Jsy/25 25.00
17 Hank Blalock/Jsy-Jsy/25 30.00
20 Miguel Cabrera/Bat-Jsy/25 50.00

Portraits Zenith White

NM/M

Common Player: 2.00
Production 70 Sets
Parallel #'d 40-60: .75-1X
Parallel #'d 20-35: .75-1.5X
No pricing 15 or less.
1 Ozzie Smith 6.00
2 Derek Jeter 8.00
3 Eric Chavez 2.00
4 Duke Snider 4.00
5 Albert Pujols 8.00
6 Stan Musial 6.00
7 Ivan Rodriguez 3.00
8 Cal Ripken Jr. 15.00
9 Hank Blalock 2.00
10 Chipper Jones 3.00
11 Gary Sheffield 2.00
12 Alfonso Soriano 3.00
13 Carl Crawford 2.00
14 Lou Brock 4.00
15 Jim Edmonds 3.00
16 Bo Jackson 4.00
17 Todd Helton 3.00
18 Javy Lopez 2.00
19 Tony Gwynn 5.00
20 Mark Mulder 2.00
21 Sammy Sosa 4.00
22 Roger Clemens 6.00
23 Don Mattingly 8.00
24 Willie Mays 8.00
25 Andruw Jones 3.00
26 Steve Garvey 2.00
27 Scott Rolen 3.00
28 George Brett 8.00
29 Rod Carew 4.00
30 Ken Griffey Jr. 6.00
31 Mike Piazza 5.00
32 Steve Carlton 3.00
33 Larry Walker 3.00
34 Kerry Wood 2.00
35 Frank Thomas 3.00
36 Lance Berkman 2.00
37 Nomar Garciaparra 4.00
38 Curt Schilling 3.00
39 Carl Yastrzemski 6.00
40 Mark Grace 3.00
41 Tom Seaver 4.00
42 Mariano Rivera 3.00
43 Carlos Beltran 3.00
44 Reggie Jackson 4.00
45 Pedro Martinez 4.00
46 Richie Sexson 2.00
47 Tom Glavine 2.00
48 Torii Hunter 2.00
49 Ron Guidry 2.00
50 Michael Young 2.00
51 Ichiro Suzuki 6.00
52 C.C. Sabathia 2.00
53 Johnny Bench 4.00
54 Mark Teixeira 3.00
55 Hideki Matsui 6.00
56 Mike Mussina 3.00
57 Johan Santana 3.00
58 Fergie Jenkins 2.00
59 Hideo Nomo 3.00
60 Nolan Ryan 10.00
61 Whitey Ford 4.00
62 Jim Thome 3.00
63 Gary Carter 3.00
64 Randy Johnson 3.00
65 Vladimir Guerrero 3.00
66 Harmon Killebrew 4.00
67 Tim Hudson 3.00
68 Josh Beckett 2.00
69 Eddie Murray 4.00
70 Greg Maddux 5.00
71 J.D. Drew 2.00
72 Bob Feller 4.00
73 Adrian Beltre 2.00
74 Wade Boggs 4.00
75 Barry Zito 2.00
76 David Ortiz 3.00
77 Mike Schmidt 8.00
78 Miguel Cabrera 4.00
79 Carlos Delgado 2.00
80 Andre Dawson 2.00
81 Garret Anderson 2.00
82 Rickey Henderson 3.00
83 Shawn Green 2.00
84 Dale Murphy 3.00
85 Alex Rodriguez 6.00
86 Mark Prior 3.00
87 Paul Molitor 4.00
88 Jeff Bagwell 3.00
89 Eric Gagne 2.00
90 Troy Glaus 2.00
91 Robin Yount 4.00
92 Miguel Tejada 3.00
93 Kirk Gibson 2.00
94 Manny Ramirez 3.00
95 Rafael Palmeiro 3.00
96 Maury Wills 2.00
97 Craig Biggio 2.00
98 Jim Palmer 3.00
99 Adam Dunn 3.00
100 Carlton Fisk 3.00

Private Signings Gold

NM/M

Common Autograph: 8.00
Production 50 Sets
1 Casey Kotchman 20.00
2 Chone Figgins 10.00
5 Ervin Santana 10.00
6 Garret Anderson 15.00
9 Orlando Cabrera 15.00
10 Robb Quinlan 8.00
11 Steve Finley 15.00
12 Tim Salmon 15.00
14 Brandon Webb 10.00
18 Tony Pena 10.00
19 Russ Ortiz 10.00
24 Adam LaRoche 12.00
27 Danny Kolb 10.00
29 Johnny Estrada 10.00
31 Nick Green 8.00
32 Rafael Furcal 15.00
34 Brian Roberts 20.00
36 Jay Gibbons 10.00
40 Rodrigo Lopez 10.00
47 Edgar Renteria 25.00
49 Jay Payton 10.00
51 Juan Cedeno 8.00
53 Matt Clement 30.00
54 Trot Nixon 20.00
55 Wade Miller 10.00
57 Carlos Zambrano 25.00
59 Derrek Lee 40.00
65 Todd Walker 12.00
70 Jermaine Dye 15.00
71 Mark Buehrle 25.00
72 Paul Konerko 15.00
76 Shingo Takatsu 20.00
78 Austin Kearns 10.00
80 Bubba Nelson 8.00
81 Danny Graves 8.00
84 Ryan Wagner 8.00
87 Cliff Lee 15.00
88 Fausto Carmona 8.00
91 Jody Gerut 10.00
93 Kazuhito Tadano 15.00
94 Travis Hafner 15.00
98 Cory Sullivan 8.00
101 Jeff Salazar 8.00
103 Joe Kennedy 8.00
108 Brandon Inge 10.00
111 Craig Monroe 10.00
113 Jeremy Bonderman 15.00
114 Justin Verlander
116 Troy Percival 15.00
117 Vance Wilson 8.00
123 Miguel Cabrera 35.00
127 Yorman Bazardo 10.00
133 Jason Lane 8.00
136 Morgan Ensberg 15.00
141 Jeremy Affeldt 8.00
143 Ken Harvey 8.00
148 Brad Penny 10.00
150 Dioner Navarro 15.00
151 Edwin Jackson 10.00
158 Milton Bradley 12.00
159 Yhency Brazoban 8.00
161 Bill Hall 10.00
162 Carlos Lee 15.00
166 Lyle Overbay 8.00
168 Jacque Jones 8.00
170 Joe Nathan 12.00
173 Lew Ford 10.00
175 Shannon Stewart 10.00
191 Yuniesky Betancourt 30.00
198 Scott Proctor 10.00
199 Tom Gordon 12.00
201 Bobby Crosby 20.00
202 Danny Haren 10.00
209 Octavio Dotel 10.00
210 Rich Harden 15.00
219 Mike Lieberthal 15.00
221 Randy Wolf 8.00
222 Craig Wilson 8.00
223 Jack Wilson 10.00
224 Jason Bay 15.00
226 Jose Castillo 10.00
229 Akinori Otsuka 20.00
231 Freddy Guzman 8.00
232 Jake Peavy 30.00
234 Mark Loretta 12.00
235 Sean Burroughs 8.00
243 Merkin Valdez 10.00
246 Omar Vizquel 8.00
249 Bucky Jacobsen 10.00
250 Clint Nageotte 15.00
252 J.J. Putz 15.00
254 Miguel Olivo 8.00
260 Jeff Suppan 12.00
266 Yadier Molina 12.00
267 Aubrey Huff 12.00
268 B.J. Upton 20.00
269 Carl Crawford 20.00
271 Delmon Young 25.00
272 Dewon Brazelton 10.00
276 Adrian Gonzalez 10.00
278 Francisco Cordero 10.00
280 Kameron Loe 10.00
282 Laynce Nix 10.00
284 Michael Young 15.00
291 Shea Hillenbrand 12.00
293 Chad Cordero 12.00
295 Jose Guillen 12.00
297 Josh Karp 8.00
298 Livan Hernandez 15.00
299 Nick Johnson 15.00

Private Signings Silver

NM/M

Common Autograph: 8.00
Production 100 Sets
1 Casey Kotchman 15.00
2 Chone Figgins 8.00
5 Ervin Santana 8.00
9 Orlando Cabrera 12.00
12 Tim Salmon 12.00
18 Tony Pena 8.00
19 Russ Ortiz 8.00
24 Adam LaRoche 10.00
27 Danny Kolb 8.00
31 Nick Green 8.00
34 Brian Roberts 15.00
36 Jay Gibbons 8.00
49 Jay Payton 8.00
51 Juan Cedeno 8.00
55 Wade Miller 8.00
57 Carlos Zambrano 20.00
65 Todd Walker 10.00
70 Jermaine Dye 12.00
80 Bubba Nelson 8.00
81 Danny Graves 8.00
84 Ryan Wagner 8.00
87 Cliff Lee 15.00
88 Fausto Carmona 8.00
91 Jody Gerut 8.00
94 Travis Hafner 12.00
98 Cory Sullivan 8.00
101 Jeff Salazar 8.00
103 Joe Kennedy 8.00
108 Brandon Inge 8.00
111 Craig Monroe 8.00
113 Jeremy Bonderman 12.00
117 Vance Wilson 8.00
127 Yorman Bazardo 8.00
127 Yorman Bazardo 8.00
133 Jason Lane 8.00
136 Morgan Ensberg 12.00
141 Jeremy Affeldt 8.00

143	Ken Harvey	8.00
150	Dioner Navarro	12.00
151	Edwin Jackson	8.00
158	Milton Bradley	10.00
159	Yhency Brazoban	8.00
161	Bill Hall	8.00
162	Carlos Lee	12.00
166	Lyle Overbay	8.00
170	Joe Nathan	10.00
173	Lew Ford	8.00
191	Yuniesky Betancourt	25.00
198	Scott Proctor	8.00
201	Bobby Crosby	10.00
202	Danny Haren	8.00
209	Octavio Dotel	8.00
210	Rich Harden	12.00
219	Mike Lieberthal	12.00
221	Randy Wolf	8.00
222	Craig Wilson	8.00
223	Jack Wilson	8.00
224	Jason Bay	10.00
226	Jose Castillo	8.00
231	Freddy Guzman	8.00
232	Jake Peavy	25.00
234	Mark Loretta	10.00
250	Clint Nageotte	8.00
252	J.J. Putz	8.00
260	Jeff Suppan	10.00
276	Adrian Gonzalez	8.00
278	Francisco Cordero	8.00
280	Kameron Loe	8.00
282	Laynce Nix	8.00
291	Shea Hillenbrand	10.00
293	Chad Cordero	10.00
295	Jose Guillen	10.00
297	Josh Karp	8.00
298	Livan Hernandez	12.00

Spirit of the Game

NM/M

Common Player: 1.50
Production 600 Sets
Die-Cut: 1-1.5X
Production 125 Sets
Die-Cut Gold: 2-4X
Production 25 Sets

1	Mark Prior	3.00
2	Sean Casey	1.50
3	Ichiro Suzuki	6.00
4	Andruw Jones	2.00
5	Francisco Cordero	1.50
6	Ben Sheets	2.00
7	Rocco Baldelli	1.50
8	Rafael Furcal	1.50
9	Angel Berroa	1.50
10	Roy Oswalt	1.50
11	Jose Reyes	1.50
12	Shannon Stewart	1.50
13	Greg Maddux	5.00
14	Alfonso Soriano	3.00
15	Curt Schilling	3.00
16	Jody Gerut	1.50
17	Brandon Webb	1.50
18	Josh Beckett	2.00
19	Laynce Nix	1.50
20	Scott Rolen	3.00

Spirit of the Game Bat

NM/M

Production 75-300

1	Mark Prior/300	6.00
4	Andruw Jones/300	6.00
6	Ben Sheets/300	4.00
7	Rocco Baldelli/300	4.00
8	Rafael Furcal/300	4.00
9	Angel Berroa/300	4.00
11	Jose Reyes/300	4.00
12	Shannon Stewart/75	4.00
13	Greg Maddux/300	8.00
14	Alfonso Soriano/225	6.00
16	Jody Gerut/300	4.00
17	Brandon Webb/300	4.00
19	Laynce Nix/300	4.00

Spirit of the Game Combo

NM/M

Production 50 Sets
Prime: No Pricing
Production 10 Sets

1	Mark Prior/Bat-Jsy	12.00
2	Sean Casey/Jsy-Jsy	6.00
4	Andruw Jones/Bat-Jsy	8.00
6	Ben Sheets/Bat-Jsy	8.00
7	Rocco Baldelli/Bat-Jsy	6.00
8	Rafael Furcal/Bat-Jsy	6.00
10	Roy Oswalt/Bat-Jsy	8.00
11	Jose Reyes/Bat-Jsy	8.00
12	Shannon Stewart/Jsy-Jsy	6.00
13	Greg Maddux/Bat-Jsy	15.00
14	Alfonso Soriano/Jsy-Jsy	12.00
15	Curt Schilling/Bat-Jsy	12.00
16	Jody Gerut/Bat-Jsy	6.00
19	Laynce Nix/Bat-Jsy	6.00
20	Scott Rolen/Jsy-Jsy	12.00

Spirit of the Game Jersey

NM/M

Production 125-250
Prime: No Pricing
Production 10 Sets

1	Mark Prior/250	6.00
2	Sean Casey/250	4.00
4	Andruw Jones/250	6.00
5	Francisco Cordero/250	4.00
6	Ben Sheets/250	4.00
7	Rocco Baldelli/250	4.00
8	Rafael Furcal/250	4.00
10	Roy Oswalt/250	4.00
11	Jose Reyes/250	4.00
12	Shannon Stewart/250	4.00
13	Greg Maddux/250	8.00
14	Alfonso Soriano/250	6.00
15	Curt Schilling/250	6.00
16	Jody Gerut/125	4.00
18	Josh Beckett/250	4.00
19	Laynce Nix/250	4.00
20	Scott Rolen/250	6.00

Spirit of the Game Signature Combo

NM/M

Production 10-25
Prime: No Pricing
Production 5-10

2	Sean Casey/Jsy-Jsy/25	20.00
8	Rafael Furcal/Bat-Jsy/25	25.00
12	Shannon Stewart/ Jsy-Jsy/25	20.00
16	Jody Gerut/Bat-Jsy/25	15.00
19	Laynce Nix/Bat-Jsy/25	15.00

Stars

NM/M

Common Player: 1.00
Inserted 1:6
Gold: 1-2X
Production 500 Sets
Platinum: 2-4X
Production 50 Sets

1	Carlos Beltran	1.50
2	Sean Casey	1.00
3	Ichiro Suzuki	3.00
4	Vladimir Guerrero	1.50
5	Tim Hudson	1.50
6	Alex Rodriguez	4.00
7	Miguel Tejada	1.50
8	Curt Schilling	1.50
9	Roger Clemens	4.00
10	Ben Sheets	1.00
11	Todd Helton	1.50
12	Mark Mulder	1.00
13	Scott Podsednik	1.00
14	Victor Martinez	1.00
15	Mark Prior	1.50
16	Ivan Rodriguez	1.50
17	Dontrelle Willis	1.00
18	Andy Pettitte	1.00
19	Khalil Greene	1.50
20	Jeff Kent	1.00
21	Paul Konerko	1.00
22	Joe Mauer	1.50
23	Bobby Crosby	1.00
24	Pedro Martinez	2.00
25	John Smoltz	1.00
26	Derek Jeter	4.00
27	Moises Alou	1.00
28	Rich Harden	1.00
29	Jim Thome	1.50
30	Jason Bay	2.00
31	Aramis Ramirez	3.00
32	Carlos Lee	1.00
33	B.J. Upton	1.00
34	Nomar Garciaparra	1.00
35	Ken Griffey Jr.	1.00
36	Darin Erstad	1.00
37	Larry Walker	1.00
38	Jose Vidro	1.00
39	Zack Greinke	1.00
40	Michael Young	1.00
41	David Wright	2.00
42	Albert Pujols	4.00
43	Vernon Wells	1.00
44	Mark Teixeira	1.50
45	Jacque Jones	1.00
46	Brian Giles	1.00
47	Austin Kearns	1.00
48	Omar Vizquel	1.00
49	Randy Johnson	1.50
50	Jason Varitek	1.50

2005 Donruss Throwback Threads

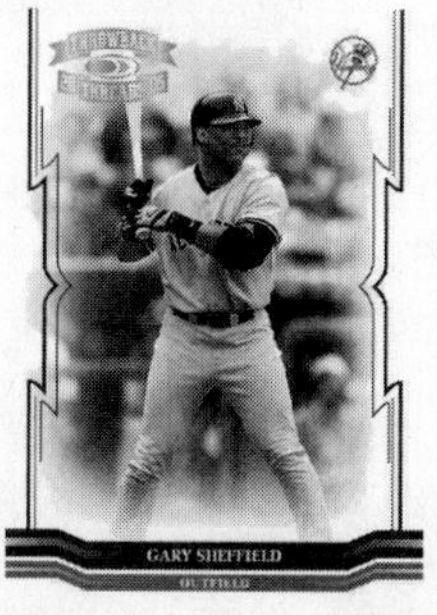

NM/M

Complete Set (300):
Common Player: .20
Pack (5): 3.00
Box (24): 65.00

1	Luis Castillo	.20
2	Derek Jeter	1.50
3	Eric Chavez	.20
4	Angel Berroa	.20
5	Jeff Bagwell	.40
6	J.T. Snow	.20
7	Craig Biggio	.30
8	Michael Barrett	.20
9	Hank Blalock	.40
10	Chipper Jones	.50
11	Jacque Jones	.20
12	Mark Teixeira	.50
13	Omar Vizquel	.20
14	Paul LoDuca	.20
15	Jim Edmonds	.30
16	Aramis Ramirez	.30
17	Lance Berkman	.30
18	Javy Lopez	.30
19	Adam LaRoche	.20
20	Jorge Posada	.40
21	Sean Casey	.20
22	Mark Prior	.40
23	Phil Nevin	.20
24	Manny Ramirez	.50
25	Andruw Jones	.40
26	Matt Lawton	.20
27	Vladimir Guerrero	.50
28	Austin Kearns	.20
29	John Smoltz	.40
30	Ken Griffey Jr.	1.00
31	Mike Piazza	.75
32	Jason Jennings	.20
33	Jason Varitek	.40
34	David Ortiz	.50
35	Mike Mussina	.40
36	Joe Nathan	.20
37	Kenny Rogers	.20
38	Carlos Zambrano	.30
39	Eric Byrnes	.20
40	Clint Barmes	.20
41	Danny Kolb	.20
42	Mariano Rivera	.40
43	Joey Gathright	.20
44	Adam Dunn	.40
45	Carlos Lee	.20
46	Yhency Brazoban	.20
47	Roy Oswalt	.30
48	Torii Hunter	.20
49	Scott Podsednik	.20
50	Jason Hammel **RC**	.40
51	Ichiro Suzuki	1.00
52	C.C. Sabathia	.20
53	Bobby Abreu	.40
54	Jon Garland	.20
55	Brandon Webb	.20
56	Mark Buehrle	.30
57	Johan Santana	.50
58	Mike Sweeney	.20
59	Tadahito Iguchi **RC**	1.50
60	Edgar Renteria	.20
61	Aaron Rowand	.20
62	Craig Wilson	.20
63	J.D. Drew	.30
64	Bobby Crosby	.40
65	Justin Morneau	.50
66	Scott Rolen	.50
67	Jose Vidro	.20
68	Carlos Beltran	.40
69	Jeff Weaver	.20
70	Jason Schmidt	.30
71	Brad Wilkerson	.20
72	Yuniesky Betancourt **RC**	1.50
73	Octavio Dotel	.20
74	Mike Cameron	.20
75	Barry Zito	.40
76	Woody Williams	.20
77	Russel Rohlicek **RC**	.40
78	Mark Kotsay	.20
79	Jeff Suppan	.20
80	Eric Gagne	.40
81	Tim Salmon	.40
82	Troy Glaus	.40
83	Kevin Mench	.20
84	Ivan Rodriguez	.40
85	Sean Burroughs	.20
86	Dallas McPherson	.20
87	Jamie Moyer	.20
88	Orlando Cabrera	.20
89	Wladimir Balentien **RC**	1.00
90	Philip Humber **RC**	1.00
91	Francisco Cordero	.20
92	Danny Graves	.20
93	Bucky Jacobsen	.20
94	Cliff Lee	.40
95	Oliver Perez	.20
96	Jake Peavy	.30
97	Doug Mientkiewicz	.20
98	Brad Radke	.20
99	Jeremy Reed	.20
100	Garret Anderson	.30
101	Rafael Furcal	.20
102	Jack Wilson	.20
103	Bernie Williams	.20
104	Josh Beckett	.20
105	Albert Pujols	1.50
106	Ubaldo Jimenez **RC**	.40
107	Richard Hidalgo	.20
108	Luke Scott **RC**	1.00
109	Hideo Nomo	.40
110	Vernon Wells	.30
111	Richie Sexson	.40
112	Chad Cordero	.20
113	Alex Rodriguez	1.50
114	Paul Konerko	.30
115	Carlos Guillen	.20
116	Francisco Rodriguez	.20
117	Johnny Damon	.50
118	David Wright	1.00
119	Lyle Overbay	.20
120	Brian Roberts	.20
121	Sammy Sosa	1.00
122	Roger Clemens	1.50
123	Rickie Weeks	.50
124	Larry Bigbie	.20
125	Rafael Palmeiro	.40
126	Jason Giambi	.30
127	Hideki Matsui	1.00
128	Brad Lidge	.20
129	Jeremy Affeldt	.20
130	Mike MacDougal	.20
131	Troy Percival	.20
132	Matt Morris	.20
133	David Gassner **RC**	.40
134	Kerry Wood	.40
135	Dontrelle Willis	.40
136	Michael Young	.30
137	Andy Pettitte	.40
138	Kris Benson	.20
139	Miguel Negron **RC**	.40
140	Rich Harden	.40
141	Bret Boone	.20
142	Danny Rueckel **RC**	.40
143	Jeff Niemann **RC**	1.00
144	Randy Messenger **RC**	.40
145	Pedro Martinez	.50
146	Kazuhisa Ishii	.20
147	Carlos Delgado	.30
148	Tom Glavine	.30
149	Russ Ortiz	.20
150	Gavin Floyd	.20
151	Randy Johnson	.50
152	Prince Fielder	10.00
153	Nomar Garciaparra	.75
154	Pat Burrell	.30
155	Melvin Mora	.20
156	Jose Reyes	.50
157	Trot Nixon	.20
158	B.J. Upton	.20
159	Jody Gerut	.20
160	Juan Pierre	.20
161	Miguel Tejada	.40
162	Barry Larkin	.40
163	Carl Crawford	.20
164	Ben Sheets	.30
165	Tim Hudson	.40
166	Darin Erstad	.20
167	Todd Helton	.40
168	Luis Gonzalez	.30
169	Mark Mulder	.30
170	David Dellucci	.20
171	Marcus Giles	.20
172	Shannon Stewart	.20
173	Zack Greinke	.20
174	Miguel Cabrera	.50
175	Nick Johnson	.20
176	Derrek Lee	.50
177	Jim Thome	.40
178	Ken Harvey	.20
179	Ambiorix Concepcion **RC**	.40
180	Roy Halladay	.30
181	Larry Walker	.40
182	Greg Maddux	1.00
183	Frank Thomas	.50
184	Travis Hafner	.30
185	Matt Holliday	.50
186	Victor Martinez	.20
187	Jason Isringhausen	.20
188	Bill Mueller	.20
189	Dewon Brazelton	.20
190	Adrian Beltre	.40
191	Tim Wakefield	.20
192	Alexis Rios	.20
193	Alfonso Soriano	.50
194	Fernando Vina	.20
195	Armando Benitez	.20
196	Bartolo Colon	.30
197	A.J. Burnett	.20
198	Milton Bradley	.20
199	Brad Penny	.20
200	Rocco Baldelli	.20
201	Curt Schilling	.50
202	Ryan Wagner	.20
203	Preston Wilson	.20
204	Akinori Otsuka	.20
205	Bill McCarthy **RC**	.40
206	Edgardo Alfonzo	.20
207	Mike Lieberthal	.20
208	Shea Hillenbrand	.20
209	Tom Gordon	.20
210	Kip Wells	.20
211	Frank Catalanotto	.20
212	Casey Kotchman	.20
213	Justin Verlander **RC**	1.50
214	Brandon Inge	.20
215	Terrmel Sledge	.20
216	Gary Sheffield	.40
217	Steve Finley	.20
218	Kenny Lofton	.20
219	Chris Carpenter	.30
220	Danny Haren	.20
221	Brett Myers	.20
222	Joe Mauer	.50
223	David Wells	.20
224	Brian Giles	.20
225	Moises Alou	.30
226	Casey Rogowski **RC**	.40
227	Chase Utley	.50

228 Corey Koskie .20
229 Derek Lowe .20
230 Erick Threets **RC** .40
231 Grady Sizemore .40
232 Jason Lane .20
233 Jeremy Bonderman .20
234 Livan Hernandez .20
235 Ryan Klesko .20
236 Sidney Ponson .20
237 Jimmy Rollins .40
238 Eric Milton .20
239 Shingo Takatsu .20
240 Scott Kazmir .20
241 Shawn Green .30
242 Nick Swisher .20
243 Shawn Chacon .20
244 Javier Vazquez .20
245 Mark Loretta .20
246 Dmitri Young .20
247 Charles Johnson .20
248 Magglio Ordonez .30
249 Sean Thompson **RC** .40
250 Jared Gothreaux **RC** .40
251 Kevin Millwood .20
252 Mike Lowell .20
253 Cristian Guzman .20
254 Nate McLouth **RC** 2.00
255 Delmon Young .40
256 Jeromy Burnitz .20
257 Garrett Atkins .20
258 Junior Spivey .20
259 Morgan Ensberg .20
260 Chone Figgins .20
261 Hayden Penn **RC** .50
262 Jason Bay .40
263 Jose Cruz Jr. .20
264 Khalil Greene .40
265 Ray Durham .20
266 Juan Gonzalez .40
267 Jeff Kent .20
268 Dioner Navarro .20
269 Rodrigo Lopez .20
270 Geoff Jenkins .20
271 Jermaine Dye .20
272 Orlando Hudson .20
273 Jose Lima .20
274 Jeff Francis .20
275 Luis Matos .20
276 Jason Kendall .20
277 Mike Hampton .20
278 Al Kaline .75
279 Bert Blyleven .20
280 Bill Madlock .20
281 Cal Ripken Jr. 3.00
282 Dale Murphy .50
283 Gary Carter .50
284 George Brett 2.00
285 Harmon Killebrew 1.00
286 Harold Baines .40
287 John Kruk .50
288 Keith Hernandez .40
289 Willie Mays 3.00
290 Matt Williams .20
291 Nolan Ryan 2.50
292 Paul Molitor .50
293 Reggie Jackson .75
294 Rickey Henderson .50
295 Ron Cey .20
296 Ryne Sandberg 1.00
297 Ted Williams 2.50
298 Tom Seaver .50
299 Tony Gwynn .75
300 Babe Ruth/SP 20.00

Century Stars

NM/M

Common Player: 1.00
Spectrum: 1.5-3X
Production 100 Sets
1 Bobby Doerr 1.00
2 Derek Jeter 4.00
3 Harmon Killebrew 1.50
4 Paul Molitor 1.50
5 Brooks Robinson 1.50
6 Steve Garvey 1.00
7 Ivan Rodriguez 1.00
8 Carl Yastrzemski 2.50
9 Nomar Garciaparra 2.00
10 Miguel Tejada 1.00
11 Edgar Martinez 1.00
12 Kevin Brown 1.00
13 Alex Rodriguez 3.00
14 Carlton Fisk 1.00
15 Craig Biggio 1.00
16 Dwight Gooden 1.00
17 Jim Palmer 1.00
18 Ken Griffey Jr. 2.00
19 Bob Feller 1.50
20 Don Sutton 1.00
21 Al Kaline 1.50
22 Roger Clemens 4.00
23 Kirk Gibson 1.00
24 Willie Mays 3.00
25 Frank Robinson 1.00
26 Randy Johnson 1.50
27 Jim "Catfish" Hunter 1.00
28 Austin Kearns 1.00
29 John Smoltz 1.00
30 Nolan Ryan 4.00
31 Duke Snider 1.50
32 Bernie Williams 1.00
33 David Wells 1.00
34 Bo Jackson 1.50
35 Mike Mussina 1.00
36 Gaylord Perry 1.00
37 Andre Dawson 1.00
38 Curt Schilling 1.50
39 Darryl Strawberry 1.00
40 Willie McCovey 1.00
41 Tom Seaver 1.50
42 Mariano Rivera 1.00
43 Dennis Eckersley 1.00
44 David Cone 1.00
45 Bret Boone 1.00
46 Will Clark 1.00
47 Jack Morris 1.00
48 Ichiro Suzuki 3.00
49 Alan Trammell 1.00
50 Cal Ripken Jr. 4.00

Century Stars Material

NM/M

Common Player: 4.00
Production 20-50
Prime: No Pricing
Production Five Sets
1 Bobby Doerr/Pants/50 8.00
3 Harmon Killebrew/Jsy/50 15.00
4 Paul Molitor/Jsy/50 10.00
5 Brooks Robinson/Bat/50 10.00
6 Steve Garvey/Jsy/50 4.00
7 Ivan Rodriguez/Jsy/50 8.00
8 Carl Yastrzemski/Jsy/50 15.00
10 Miguel Tejada/Jsy/50 6.00
11 Edgar Martinez/Jsy/50 6.00
12 Kevin Brown/Jsy/50 4.00
14 Carlton Fisk/Jsy/50 8.00
15 Craig Biggio/Jsy/50 8.00
16 Dwight Gooden/Jsy/50 4.00
17 Jim Palmer/Jsy/50 6.00
20 Don Sutton/Jsy/50 4.00
21 Al Kaline/Bat/50 15.00
22 Roger Clemens/Jsy/50 15.00
23 Kirk Gibson/Jsy/50 4.00
25 Frank Robinson/Bat/50 6.00
26 Randy Johnson/Jsy/50 8.00
28 Austin Kearns/Jsy/50 4.00
29 John Smoltz/Jsy/50 8.00
30 Nolan Ryan/Jkt/50 25.00
32 Bernie Williams/Jsy/50 6.00
33 David Wells/Jsy/50 4.00
34 Bo Jackson/Jsy/50 10.00
35 Mike Mussina/Jsy/50 8.00
36 Gaylord Perry/Jsy/50 6.00
37 Andre Dawson/Jsy/50 6.00
38 Curt Schilling/Jsy/50 8.00
39 Darryl Strawberry/Jsy/50 6.00
40 Willie McCovey/Jsy/50 8.00
42 Mariano Rivera/Jsy/50 10.00
43 Dennis Eckersley/Jsy/50 6.00
44 David Cone/Jsy/50 4.00
45 Bret Boone/Jsy/50 4.00
47 Jack Morris/Jsy/50 4.00
49 Alan Trammell/Jsy/50 6.00
50 Cal Ripken Jr./Jsy/50 30.00

Century Stars Sign. Mat.

No Pricing
Production 10 Sets
Prime: No Pricing
Production Five Sets

Dynasty

NM/M

Common Trio: 2.00
Spectrum: 1.25X
Production 100 Sets
1 Reggie Jackson, Jim "Catfish" Hunter, Sparky Lyle 2.00
2 Cal Ripken Jr., Jim Palmer, Eddie Murray 8.00
3 Dwight Gooden, Gary Carter, Darryl Strawberry 2.00
4 Rickey Henderson, Dennis Eckersley, Jose Canseco 2.00
5 Chipper Jones, Greg Maddux, David Justice 3.00
6 Roger Clemens, Alfonso Soriano, Bernie Williams 6.00
7 Randy Johnson, Curt Schilling, Matt Williams 3.00
8 Troy Glaus, Garret Anderson, Francisco Rodriguez 2.00
9 Josh Beckett, Miguel Cabrera, Mike Lowell 2.00
10 Curt Schilling, Manny Ramirez, Jason Varitek 8.00

Dynasty Material

NM/M

Production 20-50
Prime: No Pricing
Production Five Sets
1 Reggie Jackson/Pants, Jim "Catfish" Hunter/Pants, Sparky Lyle/Pants/50 20.00
2 Cal Ripken Jr./Jsy, Jim Palmer/Jsy, Eddie Murray/Jsy/50 40.00
3 Dwight Gooden/Jsy, Gary Carter/Jsy, Darryl Strawberry/Pants/20 15.00
4 Rickey Henderson/Jsy, Dennis Eckersley/Pants, Jose Canseco/Jsy/50 35.00
5 Chipper Jones/Jsy, Greg Maddux/Jsy, David Justice/Jsy/50 25.00
6 Roger Clemens/Jsy, Alfonso Soriano/Jsy, Bernie Williams/Jsy/50 30.00
7 Randy Johnson/Jsy, Curt Schilling/Jsy, Matt Williams/Jsy/50 20.00
8 Troy Glaus/Jsy, Garret Anderson/Jsy, Francisco Rodriguez/Jsy/50 15.00
10 Curt Schilling/Jsy, Manny Ramirez/Jsy, Jason Varitek/Jsy/50 40.00

Generations

NM/M

Common Player: 2.00
Spectrum: 1-2.5X
Production 100 Sets
1 Duke Snider, Reggie Jackson, Sammy Sosa 2.00
2 Rod Carew, John Kruk, Eric Chavez 2.00
3 Bo Jackson, Deion Sanders, Brian Jordan 3.00
4 Brett George, Tony Gwynn, Todd Helton 4.00
5 Babe Ruth, Ted Williams, Willie Mays 5.00
6 Rickey Henderson, Lenny Dykstra, Ichiro Suzuki 3.00
7 Keith Hernandez, Don Mattingly, Casey Kotchman 3.00
8 Wade Boggs, Mark Grace, Hank Blalock 2.00
9 Gary Carter, Ivan Rodriguez, Victor Martinez 2.00
10 Gaylord Perry, Morris, Greg Maddux 2.00
11 Joe Morgan, Ryne Sandberg, Alfonso Soriano 3.00
12 Juan Marichal, Luis Tiant, Pedro Martinez 2.00
13 Stan Musial, Carl Yastrzemski, Lance Berkman 3.00
14 Johnny Bench, Carlton Fisk, Mike Piazza 3.00
15 Harmon Killebrew, Cal Ripken Jr., Albert Pujols 5.00
16 Frank Robinson, Andre Dawson, Gary Sheffield 2.00
17 Bob Feller, Roger Clemens, Kerry Wood 4.00
18 Steve Carlton, Tom Glavine, Barry Zito 2.00
19 Murray, Rafael Palmeiro, Mark Teixeira 2.00
20 Brooks Robinson, Mike Schmidt, Scott Rolen 3.00
21 Luis Aparicio, Omar Vizquel, Rafael Furcal 2.00
22 Don Sutton, David Cone, Roy Oswalt 2.00
23 Fred Lynn, Dale Murphy, Jim Edmonds 2.00
24 Ozzie, Barry Larkin, B.J. Upton 3.00
25 Gibson, Nolan Ryan, Mark Prior 4.00

Generations Material

NM/M

Production 20-50
Prime: No Pricing
Production 10 Sets
2 Rod Carew/Jsy, John Kruk/Jsy, Eric Chavez/Jsy/50 15.00
3 Bo Jackson/Jsy, Deion Sanders/Jsy, Brian Jordan/Jsy/50 25.00
4 Brett George/Jsy, Tony Gwynn/Jsy, Todd Helton/Jsy/50 25.00
7 Keith Hernandez/Jsy, Don Mattingly/Pants, Casey Kotchman/Jsy/20 30.00
8 Wade Boggs/Jsy, Mark Grace/Jsy, Hank Blalock/Jsy/50 15.00
9 Gary Carter/Jsy, Ivan Rodriguez/Jsy, Victor Martinez/Jsy/50 15.00
10 Gaylord Perry/Jsy, Morris/Jsy, Greg Maddux/Jsy/50 25.00
11 Joe Morgan/Jsy, Ryne Sandberg/Jsy, Alfonso Soriano/Jsy/50 35.00
12 Juan Marichal/Pants, Luis Tiant/Pants, Pedro Martinez/Jsy/50 20.00
14 Johnny Bench/Pants, Carlton Fisk/Jsy, Mike Piazza/Jsy/50 20.00
15 Harmon Killebrew/Jsy, Cal Ripken Jr./Jsy, Albert Pujols/Jsy/50 50.00
16 Frank Robinson/Bat, Andre Dawson/Jsy, Gary Sheffield/Jsy/20 15.00
17 Bob Feller/Pants, Roger Clemens/Jsy, Kerry Wood/Jsy/20 50.00
18 Steve Carlton/Jsy, Tom Glavine/Jsy, Barry Zito/Jsy/50 20.00
19 Murray/Jsy, Rafael Palmeiro/Jsy, Mark Teixeira/Jsy/50 20.00

Material Bat

NM/M

Common Player: 4.00
Production 5-250
1 Luis Castillo/250 4.00
4 Angel Berroa/250 4.00
5 Jeff Bagwell/250 6.00
7 Craig Biggio/250 6.00
14 Paul LoDuca/250 4.00
17 Lance Berkman/250 4.00
18 Javy Lopez/250 4.00
21 Sean Casey/50 6.00
25 Andruw Jones/250 6.00
26 Matt Lawton/250 4.00
28 Austin Kearns/250 4.00
32 Jason Jennings/250 4.00
33 Jason Varitek/50 12.00
34 David Ortiz/250 8.00
43 Joey Gathright/250 4.00
48 Torii Hunter/250 4.00
55 Brandon Webb/250 4.00
58 Mike Sweeney/250 4.00
62 Craig Wilson/250 4.00
63 J.D. Drew/250 4.00
67 Jose Vidro/250 4.00
68 Carlos Beltran/250 6.00
81 Tim Salmon/250 4.00
82 Troy Glaus/250 4.00
83 Kevin Mench/250 4.00
101 Rafael Furcal/150 4.00
102 Jack Wilson/25 4.00
103 Bernie Williams/250 4.00
107 Richard Hidalgo/250 4.00
111 Richie Sexson/100 6.00
121 Sammy Sosa/50 8.00
123 Rickie Weeks/25 6.00
125 Rafael Palmeiro/250 6.00
135 Dontrelle Willis/50 6.00
136 Michael Young/250 4.00
141 Bret Boone/50 4.00
147 Carlos Delgado/250 4.00
148 Tom Glavine/250 4.00
153 Nomar Garciaparra/150 8.00
154 Pat Burrell/150 4.00
156 Jose Reyes/50 6.00
158 B.J. Upton/250 6.00
159 Jody Gerut/250 4.00
160 Juan Pierre/250 4.00
162 Barry Larkin/100 6.00
164 Ben Sheets/250 4.00
165 Tim Hudson/50 6.00
166 Darin Erstad/250 4.00
168 Luis Gonzalez/25 6.00
169 Mark Mulder/35 6.00
174 Miguel Cabrera/50 10.00
175 Nick Johnson/250 4.00
176 Derrek Lee/50 8.00
192 Alex Rios/50 4.00
197 A.J. Burnett/250 4.00
200 Rocco Baldelli/250 4.00
203 Preston Wilson/150 4.00
206 Edgardo Alfonzo/250 4.00
212 Casey Kotchman/250 4.00
215 Terrmel Sledge/250 4.00
218 Kenny Lofton/150 4.00
224 Brian Giles/35 6.00
225 Moises Alou/250 6.00
232 Jason Lane/250 4.00
235 Ryan Klesko/25 4.00
241 Shawn Green/250 4.00
247 Charles Johnson/250 4.00
248 Magglio Ordonez/250 4.00
252 Mike Lowell/50 4.00
255 Delmon Young/250 4.00
259 Morgan Ensberg/25 6.00
260 Chone Figgins/250 4.00
262 Jason Bay/175 6.00
265 Ray Durham/200 4.00
266 Juan Gonzalez/250 6.00
267 Jeff Kent/250 4.00
272 Orlando Hudson/250 4.00
280 Bill Madlock/100 4.00
281 Cal Ripken Jr./150 25.00
283 Gary Carter/25 8.00
284 George Brett/25 25.00
286 Harold Baines/50 6.00
288 Keith Hernandez/25 8.00
289 Willie Mays/25 35.00
291 Nolan Ryan/50 25.00
292 Paul Molitor/150 6.00
293 Reggie Jackson/25 10.00
294 Rickey Henderson/250 8.00
296 Ryne Sandberg/50 15.00
297 Ted Williams/25 50.00
299 Tony Gwynn/50 10.00
300 Babe Ruth/25 180.00

Material Combo

NM/M

Common Player: 6.00
Production 10-100
Prime: 1-2X
Production 5-40
No pricing 20 or less.
1 Luis Castillo/Bat-Jsy/90 6.00
3 Eric Chavez/Bat-Jsy/25 8.00
5 Jeff Bagwell/Bat-Jsy/100 8.00
7 Craig Biggio/Bat-Jsy/25 10.00
12 Mark Teixeira/Bat-Jsy/25 10.00
17 Lance Berkman/Bat-Jsy/100 6.00
21 Sean Casey/Bat-Jsy/100 6.00
22 Mark Prior/Bat-Jsy/25 10.00
25 Andruw Jones/Bat-Jsy/100 8.00
32 Jason Jennings/Bat-Jsy/100 6.00

34 David Ortiz/Bat-Jsy/25 20.00
43 Joey Gathright/Bat-Jsy/50 6.00
55 Brandon Webb/ Bat-Pants/100 6.00
58 Mike Sweeney/Bat-Jsy/65 6.00
62 Craig Wilson/Bat-Jsy/100 6.00
67 Jose Vidro/Bat-Jsy/100 6.00
83 Kevin Mench/Bat-Jsy/100 6.00
101 Rafael Furcal/Bat-Jsy/50 6.00
103 Bernie Williams/Bat-Jsy/50 8.00
104 Josh Beckett/Bat-Jsy/25 8.00
110 Vernon Wells/Hat-Jsy/100 6.00
124 Larry Bigbie/Jsy-Jsy/100 6.00
126 Jason Giambi/Jsy-Jsy/100 8.00
136 Michael Young/Bat-Jsy/50 8.00
146 Kazuhisa Ishii/Hat-Jsy/25 10.00
154 Pat Burrell/Bat-Jsy/50 8.00
156 Jose Reyes/Bat-Jsy/25 8.00
157 Trot Nixon/Bat-Jsy/25 10.00
160 Juan Pierre/Bat-Fld Glv/95 6.00
164 Ben Sheets/Bat-Jsy/100 8.00
168 Luis Gonzalez/Jsy-Jsy/100 6.00
171 Marcus Giles/Hat-Jsy/50 6.00
172 Shannon Stewart/Jsy-Jsy/30 6.00
174 Miguel Cabrera/Bat-Jsy/25 12.00
180 Roy Halladay/Jsy-Jsy/85 8.00
183 Frank Thomas/Hat-Jsy/25 15.00
186 Victor Martinez/ Fld Glv-Jsy/40 8.00
197 A.J. Burnett/Bat-Jsy/100 6.00
200 Rocco Baldelli/Bat-Jsy/100 6.00
201 Curt Schilling/Bat-Jsy/25 12.00
202 Ryan Wagner/Jsy-Jsy/100 6.00
203 Preston Wilson/Bat-Jsy/85 6.00
212 Casey Kotchman/Bat-Jsy/50 6.00
218 Kenny Lofton/ Bat-Fld Glv/100 6.00
232 Jason Lane/Bat-Hat/50 6.00
235 Ryan Klesko/Hat-Jsy/100 6.00
252 Mike Lowell/Bat-Jsy/100 6.00
257 Garrett Atkins/Jsy-Jsy/100 6.00
259 Morgan Ensberg/Hat-Jsy/100 8.00
260 Chone Figgins/Bat-Jsy/50 6.00
262 Jason Bay/Bat-Jsy/40 8.00
272 Orlando Hudson/Bat-Jsy/40 6.00
275 Luis Matos/Jsy-Jsy/50 6.00
281 Cal Ripken Jr./Bat-Jsy/50 40.00
283 Gary Carter/Jsy-Pants/25 15.00
284 George Brett/Bat-Jsy/25 30.00
286 Harold Baines/Bat-Jsy/50 10.00
288 Keith Hernandez/Bat-Jsy/25 10.00
289 Willie Mays/Bat-Pants/25 50.00
291 Nolan Ryan/Bat-Jsy/50 25.00
292 Paul Molitor/Bat-Jsy/50 15.00
293 Reggie Jackson/Bat-Jsy/25 15.00
294 Rickey Henderson/ Bat-Jsy/50 15.00
296 Ryne Sandberg/Bat-Jsy/50 25.00
297 Ted Williams/Bat-Jsy/25 75.00
298 Tom Seaver/Jsy-Pants/25 15.00
299 Tony Gwynn/Jsy-Pants/50 15.00
300 Babe Ruth/Bat-Jsy/25 375.00

Material Jersey

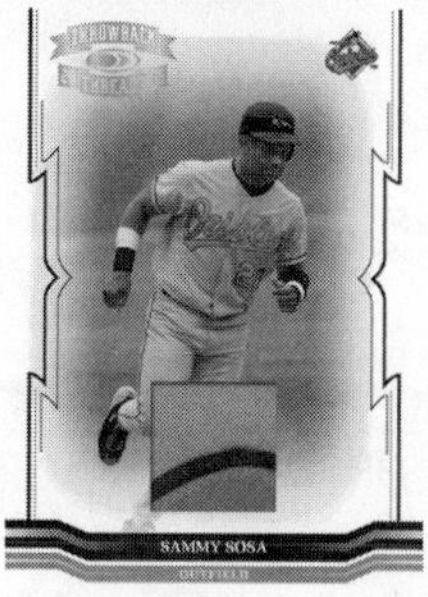

NM/M
Common Player: 4.00
Production 5-250
Prime: 1-2X
Production 10-100
No pricing 20 or less.
1 Luis Castillo/45 4.00
3 Eric Chavez/250 4.00
5 Jeff Bagwell/250 6.00
6 J.T. Snow/250 4.00
7 Craig Biggio/50 6.00
9 Hank Blalock/25 6.00
10 Chipper Jones/250 8.00
11 Jacque Jones/250 4.00
12 Mark Teixeira/150 6.00
15 Jim Edmonds/250 6.00
16 Aramis Ramirez/250 6.00
17 Lance Berkman/250 4.00
18 Javy Lopez/250 4.00
20 Jorge Posada/250 6.00
21 Sean Casey/250 4.00
22 Mark Prior/50 8.00
23 Phil Nevin/50 4.00
24 Manny Ramirez/250 8.00
25 Andruw Jones/250 6.00
27 Vladimir Guerrero/250 8.00
28 Austin Kearns/250 4.00
29 John Smoltz/250 8.00
31 Mike Piazza/250 8.00
32 Jason Jennings/250 4.00
34 David Ortiz/250 10.00
35 Mike Mussina/250 6.00
38 Carlos Zambrano/250 6.00
42 Mariano Rivera/50 8.00
43 Joey Gathright/100 4.00
44 Adam Dunn/250 6.00
47 Roy Oswalt/250 4.00
48 Torii Hunter/100 4.00
52 C.C. Sabathia/250 4.00
53 Bobby Abreu/250 4.00
56 Mark Buehrle/250 4.00
57 Johan Santana/250 6.00
58 Mike Sweeney/75 4.00
62 Craig Wilson/250 4.00
64 Bobby Crosby/100 6.00
66 Scott Rolen/250 6.00
67 Jose Vidro/75 4.00
74 Mike Cameron/250 4.00
75 Barry Zito/250 4.00
83 Kevin Mench/250 4.00
84 Ivan Rodriguez/250 6.00
87 Jamie Moyer/50 4.00
91 Francisco Cordero/250 4.00
94 Cliff Lee/250 4.00
98 Brad Radke/250 4.00
100 Garret Anderson/50 6.00
101 Rafael Furcal/100 4.00
103 Bernie Williams/250 6.00
104 Josh Beckett/25 6.00
105 Albert Pujols/250 15.00
109 Hideo Nomo/250 8.00
110 Vernon Wells/250 4.00
114 Paul Konerko/250 4.00
116 Francisco Rodriguez/250 4.00
117 Johnny Damon/250 8.00
118 David Wright/250 10.00
119 Lyle Overbay/250 4.00
120 Brian Roberts/100 4.00
122 Roger Clemens/100 12.00
124 Larry Bigbie/200 4.00
125 Rafael Palmeiro/250 6.00
126 Jason Giambi/250 6.00
127 Hideki Matsui/250 15.00
134 Kerry Wood/250 6.00
135 Dontrelle Willis/250 6.00
136 Michael Young/250 4.00
137 Andy Pettitte/250 6.00
141 Bret Boone/250 4.00
146 Kazuhisa Ishii/250 4.00
147 Carlos Delgado/250 4.00
148 Tom Glavine/250 4.00
154 Pat Burrell/250 4.00
155 Melvin Mora/250 4.00
156 Jose Reyes/200 6.00
157 Trot Nixon/250 4.00
158 B.J. Upton/250 4.00
159 Jody Gerut/100 4.00
161 Miguel Tejada/35 8.00
162 Barry Larkin/40 8.00
163 Carl Crawford/40 4.00
164 Ben Sheets/250 6.00
166 Darin Erstad/25 6.00
167 Todd Helton/150 6.00
168 Luis Gonzalez/250 4.00
170 David Dellucci/150 4.00
172 Shannon Stewart/250 4.00
174 Miguel Cabrera/100 8.00
176 Derrek Lee/250 8.00
177 Jim Thome/250 6.00
178 Ken Harvey/150 4.00
180 Roy Halladay/250 4.00
182 Greg Maddux/250 8.00
186 Victor Martinez/250 4.00
189 Dewon Brazelton/250 4.00
190 Adrian Beltre/250 4.00
193 Alfonso Soriano/250 8.00
197 A.J. Burnett/250 4.00
200 Rocco Baldelli/250 4.00
201 Curt Schilling/250 8.00
202 Ryan Wagner/250 4.00
203 Preston Wilson/250 4.00
211 Frank Catalanotto/250 4.00
212 Casey Kotchman/250 4.00
214 Brandon Inge/250 4.00
221 Brett Myers/50 4.00
232 Jason Lane/95 4.00
233 Jeremy Bonderman/250 4.00
234 Livan Hernandez/250 4.00
235 Ryan Klesko/250 4.00
237 Jimmy Rollins/35 6.00
252 Mike Lowell/250 4.00
257 Garrett Atkins/250 4.00
258 Junior Spivey/250 4.00
259 Morgan Ensberg/150 4.00
260 Chone Figgins/250 4.00
262 Jason Bay/250 6.00
269 Rodrigo Lopez/250 4.00
270 Geoff Jenkins/250 4.00
275 Luis Matos/250 4.00
279 Bert Blyleven/50 6.00
281 Cal Ripken Jr./50 30.00
282 Dale Murphy/25 10.00
283 Gary Carter/50 8.00
284 George Brett/50 15.00
285 Harmon Killebrew/25 15.00
286 Harold Baines/50 6.00
287 John Kruk/50 8.00
289 Willie Mays/Pants/25 40.00
290 Matt Williams/50 8.00
291 Nolan Ryan/50 25.00
292 Paul Molitor/50 10.00
293 Reggie Jackson/25 8.00
294 Rickey Henderson/50 10.00
295 Ron Cey/50 6.00
296 Ryne Sandberg/50 15.00
297 Ted Williams/25 60.00
298 Tom Seaver/25 15.00
299 Tony Gwynn/50 12.00
300 Babe Ruth/25 200.00

Player Timelines

NM/M
Common Player: 1.00
Spectrum: 1-2.5X
Production 100 Sets
1 Dale Murphy 2.00
2 Greg Maddux 3.00
3 Tom Glavine 2.00
4 David Ortiz 3.00
5 Bo Jackson 2.00
6 Lyle Overbay 1.00
7 Tommy John 1.00
8 Shawn Green 1.00
9 Aramis Ramirez 1.50
10 Javy Lopez 1.00
11 Vladimir Guerrero 3.00
12 Travis Hafner 1.00
13 Junior Spivey 1.00
14 Alfonso Soriano 2.00
15 Andre Dawson 1.00
16 Sammy Sosa 3.00
17 Andy Pettitte 1.50
18 Jim Edmonds 1.50
19 Willie McCovey 2.00
20 Scott Rolen 2.00
21 Jermaine Dye 1.00
22 Pedro Martinez 2.50
23 Don Sutton 1.00
24 Randy Johnson 2.00
25 Nolan Ryan 3.00
26 Dennis Eckersley 1.00
27 Reggie Jackson 2.00
28 Deion Sanders 1.00
29 Curt Schilling 2.00
30 Rickey Henderson 1.00
31 Mike Piazza 2.00
32 Gary Carter 1.00
33 Roberto Alomar 1.00
34 Hideo Nomo 1.00
35 Andres Galarraga 1.00
36 Juan Gonzalez 1.00
37 Roger Clemens 4.00
38 Jeff Kent 1.00
39 Steve Carlton 1.00
40 Wade Boggs 1.50

Player Timeline Material

NM/M
Production 25-250
1 Dale Murphy/50 10.00
2 Greg Maddux/100 10.00
3 Tom Glavine/50 8.00
4 David Ortiz/250 10.00
5 Bo Jackson/100 12.00
6 Lyle Overbay/250 4.00
7 Tommy John/Pants/250 4.00
8 Shawn Green/100 4.00
9 Aramis Ramirez/250 6.00
10 Javy Lopez/100 4.00
11 Vladimir Guerrero/25 15.00
12 Travis Hafner/25 8.00
13 Junior Spivey/250 4.00
14 Alfonso Soriano/100 6.00
16 Sammy Sosa/250 8.00
17 Andy Pettitte/100 8.00
18 Jim Edmonds/100 8.00
19 Willie McCovey/Pants/50 12.00
20 Scott Rolen/50 10.00
21 Jermaine Dye/100 4.00
22 Pedro Martinez/50 12.00
23 Don Sutton/25 10.00
24 Randy Johnson/50 15.00
25 Nolan Ryan/Jkt/50 40.00
27 Reggie Jackson/Pants/50 15.00
28 Deion Sanders/25 15.00
29 Curt Schilling/50 10.00
30 Rickey Henderson/ Pants/100 15.00
31 Mike Piazza/50 15.00
32 Gary Carter/Pants/50 10.00
33 Roberto Alomar/250 8.00
34 Hideo Nomo/50 15.00
35 Andres Galarraga/250 6.00
36 Juan Gonzalez/25 8.00
37 Roger Clemens/25 30.00
38 Jeff Kent/50 6.00

Player Timelines Sign. Mat.

NM/M
Production 5-50
Prime: No Pricing
Production 5-10
1 Dale Murphy/50 30.00
6 Lyle Overbay/50 12.00
7 Tommy John/Pants/50 15.00
12 Travis Hafner/25 20.00
13 Junior Spivey/50 12.00
15 Andre Dawson/25 25.00
21 Jermaine Dye/50 15.00
23 Don Sutton/25 20.00
32 Gary Carter/Pants/50 20.00
36 Juan Gonzalez/25 40.00

Polo Grounds 85 HIT Long Fly

NM/M
Common Player: 1.50
Production 85 Sets

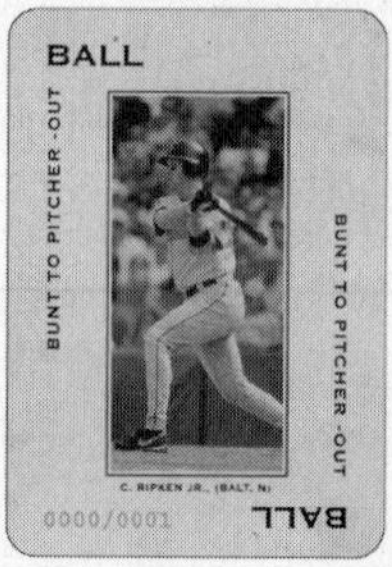

Parallel #'d 40-75: .75-1.5X
Parallel #'d 20-35: 1-2X
No pricing 15 or less.
1 Ken Griffey Jr. 4.00
2 Roger Clemens 6.00
3 Barry Zito 2.00
4 Alex Rodriguez 5.00
5 Melvin Mora 1.50
6 Kevin Brown 1.50
7 Chipper Jones 3.00
8 Scott Kazmir 2.00
9 Kip Wells 1.50
10 Khalil Greene 2.00
11 Kevin Millwood 1.50
12 Kerry Wood 2.00
13 Mark Kotsay 1.50
14 Jeff Bagwell 2.00
15 Hank Blalock 2.00
16 Scott Rolen 2.00
17 Lance Berkman 2.00
18 Mike Mussina 2.00
19 Jim Edmonds 2.00
20 Jorge Posada 2.00
21 Curt Schilling 3.00
22 Vernon Wells 1.50
23 Pedro Martinez 3.00
24 Jeremy Reed 1.50
25 Hideki Matsui 4.00
26 Steve Finley 1.50
27 Gavin Floyd 1.50
28 Darin Erstad 1.50
29 Bernie Williams 2.00
30 Mark Mulder 2.00
31 Rafael Palmeiro 2.00
32 Andruw Jones 2.00
33 Roy Halladay 2.00
34 Dontrelle Willis 2.00
35 Bret Boone 1.50
36 Andy Pettitte 2.00
37 Vladimir Guerrero 3.00
38 Randy Johnson 3.00
39 Michael Young 2.00
40 Frank Thomas 2.00
41 Todd Helton 2.00
42 Johan Santana 3.00
43 Mark Teixeira 2.00
44 Justin Morneau 1.50
45 Brad Radke 1.50
46 Dallas McPherson 1.50
47 Tim Hudson 2.00
48 Carl Crawford 1.50
49 Eric Gagne 2.00
50 Mark Prior 3.00
51 Tom Glavine 2.00
52 Craig Biggio 2.00
53 John Smoltz 2.00
54 Manny Ramirez 3.00
55 Ivan Rodriguez 2.00
56 Gary Sheffield 2.00
57 Josh Beckett 2.00
58 Miguel Tejada 2.00
59 Bobby Abreu 2.00
60 Ichiro Suzuki 4.00
61 Sammy Sosa 2.50
62 Garret Anderson 2.00
63 Sean Casey 1.50
64 Troy Glaus 2.00
65 Larry Walker 2.00
66 Alfonso Soriano 2.00
67 Luis Gonzalez 2.00
68 Eric Chavez 2.00
69 Adrian Beltre 2.00
70 Miguel Cabrera 3.00
71 Carlos Beltran 2.00
72 Jim Thome 2.00
73 David Ortiz 3.00
74 Adam Dunn 2.00
75 Jacque Jones 1.50
76 Shawn Green 1.50
77 Victor Martinez 1.50
78 Torii Hunter 1.50
79 Carlos Lee 1.50
80 C.C. Sabathia 1.50
81 Joe Mauer 2.00
82 Kris Benson 1.50
83 Zack Greinke 1.50
84 Greg Maddux 4.00
85 David Wright 4.00
86 Mike Piazza 4.00
87 Johnny Damon 3.00
88 Derek Jeter 6.00
89 B.J. Upton 1.50

90 Albert Pujols 6.00
91 Cal Ripken Jr. 6.00
92 Nolan Ryan 5.00
93 George Brett 5.00
94 Don Mattingly 4.00
95 Ryne Sandberg 4.00
96 Rickey Henderson 3.00
97 Robin Yount 3.00
98 Mike Schmidt 4.00
99 Tony Gwynn 3.00
100 Willie Mays 5.00

Signature Marks

NM/M

Production 5-1,000
4 Angel Berroa/25 12.00
19 Adam LaRoche/50 20.00
36 Joe Nathan/25 20.00
38 Carlos Zambrano/25 30.00
39 Eric Byrnes/50 10.00
41 Danny Kolb/25 10.00
45 Carlos Lee/25 20.00
49 Scott Podsednik/20 20.00
52 C.C. Sabathia/25 15.00
56 Mark Buehrle/25 30.00
62 Craig Wilson/50 10.00
64 Bobby Crosby/100 15.00
67 Jose Vidro/25 12.00
73 Octavio Dotel/25 12.00
77 Russel Rohlicek/250 5.00
81 Tim Salmon/50 20.00
85 Sean Burroughs/25 10.00
87 Jamie Moyer/25 15.00
88 Orlando Cabrera/25 20.00
90 Philip Humber/50 20.00
91 Francisco Cordero/50 10.00
92 Danny Graves/25 10.00
93 Bucky Jacobsen/64 8.00
94 Cliff Lee/50 15.00
96 Jake Peavy/25 35.00
101 Rafael Furcal/25 20.00
102 Jack Wilson/100 10.00
108 Luke Scott/250 15.00
110 Vernon Wells/25 15.00
112 Chad Cordero/25 15.00
114 Paul Konerko/25 20.00
116 Francisco Rodriguez/25 20.00
118 David Wright/25 85.00
119 Lyle Overbay/25 10.00
120 Brian Roberts/100 15.00
124 Larry Bigbie/75 8.00
129 Jeremy Affeldt/50 8.00
131 Troy Percival/25 15.00
133 David Gassner/1,000 5.00
136 Michael Young/25 20.00
139 Miguel Negron/250 5.00
140 Rich Harden/50 25.00
142 Danny Rueckel/250 5.00
144 Randy Messenger/500 5.00
149 Russ Ortiz/25 15.00
157 Trot Nixon/25 25.00
158 B.J. Upton/25 20.00
159 Jody Gerut/25 10.00
170 David Dellucci/50 15.00
172 Shannon Stewart/25 15.00
175 Nick Johnson/25 15.00
176 Derrek Lee/25 40.00
178 Ken Harvey/50 8.00
179 Ambiorix Concepcion/500 8.00
184 Travis Hafner/50 15.00
189 Dewon Brazelton/66 8.00
192 Alexis Rios/25 15.00
198 Milton Bradley/100 12.00
199 Brad Penny/25 10.00
202 Ryan Wagner/25 10.00
204 Akinori Otsuka/25 20.00
207 Mike Lieberthal/25 10.00
208 Shea Hillenbrand/25 20.00
209 Tom Gordon/25 20.00
212 Casey Kotchman/100 10.00
213 Justin Verlander/50 40.00
220 Danny Haren/25 20.00
226 Casey Rogowski/250 5.00
230 Erick Threets/500 5.00
232 Jason Lane/25 10.00
233 Jeremy Bonderman/50 15.00
234 Livan Hernandez/25 15.00
239 Shingo Takatsu/25 20.00
245 Mark Loretta/25 20.00
250 Jared Gothreaux/1,000 5.00
254 Nate McLouth/1,000 15.00
258 Junior Spivey/25 10.00
259 Morgan Ensberg/25 20.00
260 Chone Figgins/50 10.00
262 Jason Bay/186 15.00
268 Dioner Navarro/75 8.00
271 Jermaine Dye/25 15.00
272 Orlando Hudson/100 8.00
275 Luis Matos/50 10.00
279 Bert Blyleven/25 15.00
280 Bill Madlock/50 15.00
281 Cal Ripken Jr./25 150.00
282 Dale Murphy/25 30.00
286 Harold Baines/25 15.00
288 Keith Hernandez/25 15.00
290 Matt Williams/25 30.00

Throwback Collection

NM/M

Common Player: 1.00
Spectrum: 1-2.5X
Production 100 Sets
1 Billy Martin 2.00
2 Tony Gwynn 2.00
3 Babe Ruth 4.00
4 Angel Berroa 1.00
5 Jeff Bagwell 1.50
6 Tony Oliva 1.00
7 Ivan Rodriguez 1.50
8 Gary Carter 1.50
9 Ted Williams 4.00
10 Chipper Jones 2.00
11 Al Oliver 1.00
12 Roberto Alomar 1.00
13 Omar Vizquel 1.00
14 Ernie Banks 2.00
15 Carlos Beltran 1.50
16 Garret Anderson 1.00
17 Mark Grace 1.00
18 Jason Giambi 1.00
19 Dave Righetti 1.00
20 Mike Schmidt 3.00
21 Roger Clemens 4.00
22 Juan Gonzalez 1.50
23 Carlos Delgado 1.00
24 Manny Ramirez 2.00
25 Jim Thome 1.50
26 Wade Boggs 2.00
27 Luis Tiant 1.00
28 Kerry Wood 1.50
29 Rod Carew 1.50
30 Dwight Evans 1.00
31 Mike Piazza 2.00
32 Billy Williams 1.00
33 Larry Walker 1.00
34 Nolan Ryan 4.00
35 Edgar Renteria 1.00
36 Greg Maddux 2.50
37 Gaylord Perry 1.00
38 Curt Schilling 2.00
39 Dave Parker 1.00
40 Andruw Jones 1.50
41 Orlando Cepeda 1.50
42 Fergie Jenkins 1.00
43 Kirby Puckett 2.00
44 Reggie Jackson 2.00
45 Bob Gibson 2.00
46 Rickey Henderson 2.00
47 Lee Smith 1.00
48 Lou Brock 1.50
49 Fred Lynn 1.00
50 Lance Berkman 1.00
51 Shawn Green 1.00
52 Hoyt Wilhelm 1.00
53 Sammy Sosa 2.50
54 Tim Hudson 1.50
55 Matt Williams 1.00
56 Marty Marion 1.00
57 Eric Chavez 1.00
58 Rafael Palmeiro 1.50
59 Randy Johnson 2.00
60 David Ortiz 2.00
61 Hank Blalock 1.00
62 Jim Rice 1.00
63 Mark Mulder 1.50
64 Kazuo Matsui 1.00
65 Pedro Martinez 2.00
66 Sean Casey 1.00
67 Carlos Lee 1.00
68 Stan Musial 3.00
69 Fred McGriff 1.00
70 Darryl Strawberry 1.00
71 Tommy John 1.00
72 Hideo Nomo 1.00
73 Johnny Bench 2.00
74 Cal Ripken Jr. 5.00
75 Harold Baines 1.00

Throwback Coll. Material

NM/M

Production 5-500
Prime: 1-2X
Production 5-25
No pricing 20 or less.
1 Billy Martin/Pants/250 8.00
2 Tony Gwynn/Jsy/250 8.00
4 Angel Berroa/Pants/100 4.00
5 Jeff Bagwell/Jsy/250 6.00
6 Tony Oliva/Jsy/250 4.00
7 Ivan Rodriguez/Jsy/500 6.00
8 Gary Carter/Pants/250 4.00
10 Chipper Jones/Jsy/250 6.00
11 Al Oliver/Jsy/250 4.00
12 Roberto Alomar/Jsy/500 6.00
13 Omar Vizquel/Jsy/500 4.00
15 Carlos Beltran/Jsy/500 6.00
16 Garret Anderson/Jsy/50 4.00
17 Mark Grace/Jsy/250 6.00
18 Jason Giambi/Jsy/500 4.00
19 Dave Righetti/Jsy/250 4.00
21 Roger Clemens/Jsy/250 10.00
22 Juan Gonzalez/Jsy/150 4.00
23 Carlos Delgado/Jsy/150 4.00
24 Manny Ramirez/Jsy/50 10.00
25 Jim Thome/Jsy/500 4.00
26 Wade Boggs/Jsy/250 6.00
27 Luis Tiant/Pants/500 4.00
28 Kerry Wood/Jsy/50 4.00
29 Rod Carew/Jkt/250 6.00
30 Dwight Evans/Jsy/50 6.00
31 Mike Piazza/Jsy/250 8.00
32 Billy Williams/Jsy/100 4.00
33 Larry Walker/Jsy/500 4.00
34 Nolan Ryan/Pants/100 15.00
35 Edgar Renteria/Jsy/500 4.00
36 Greg Maddux/Jsy/375 8.00
37 Gaylord Perry/Jsyu/250 4.00
38 Curt Schilling/Jsy/500 4.00
39 Dave Parker/Jsy/50 4.00
40 Andruw Jones/Jsy/500 4.00
41 Orlando Cepeda/Pants/250 4.00
42 Fergie Jenkins/Jsy/250 4.00
43 Kirby Puckett/Jsy/400 6.00
44 Reggie Jackson/Jsy/250 6.00
45 Bob Gibson/Jsy/100 8.00
46 Rickey Henderson/Jsy/500 6.00
47 Lee Smith/Jsy/250 4.00
49 Fred Lynn/Jsy/250 4.00
50 Lance Berkman/Jsy/500 4.00
51 Shawn Green/Jsy/500 4.00
52 Hoyt Wilhelm/Jsy/250 4.00
53 Sammy Sosa/Jsy/500 8.00
54 Tim Hudson/Jsy/500 4.00
55 Matt Williams/Jsy/250 4.00
57 Eric Chavez/Jsy/500 4.00
58 Rafael Palmeiro/Jsy/500 6.00
59 Randy Johnson/Jsy/250 6.00
60 David Ortiz/Jsy/500 8.00
61 Hank Blalock/Jsy/50 4.00
62 Jim Rice/Pants/250 4.00
63 Mark Mulder/Jsy/100 4.00
64 Kazuo Matsui/Jsy/500 4.00
65 Pedro Martinez/Jsy/250 6.00
66 Sean Casey/Jsy/500 4.00
67 Carlos Lee/Jsy/500 4.00
68 Stan Musial/Pants/100 20.00
69 Fred McGriff/Jsy/500 4.00
70 Darryl Strawberry/Jsy/250 4.00
71 Tommy John/Jsy/250 4.00
72 Hideo Nomo/Jsy/500 6.00
73 Johnny Bench/Pants/100 8.00
74 Cal Ripken Jr./Jsy/250 20.00
75 Harold Baines/Jsy/250 4.00

Throwback Col. Mat. Combo

NM/M

Production 5-100
1 Billy Martin/Jsy-Pants/100 10.00
2 Tony Gwynn/Jsy-Pants/100 12.00
4 Angel Berroa/Bat-Pants/100 4.00
5 Jeff Bagwell/Jsy-Pants/100 8.00
6 Tony Oliva/Bat-Jsy/100 6.00
7 Ivan Rodriguez/ Chest Prot-Jsy/100 8.00
8 Gary Carter/Jsy-Pants/100 4.00
10 Chipper Jones/Bat-Jsy/100 8.00
11 Al Oliver/Bat-Jsy/100 6.00
12 Roberto Alomar/Bat-Jsy/100 8.00
13 Omar Vizquel/Bat-Jsy/100 6.00
15 Carlos Beltran/Bat-Jsy/100 8.00
17 Mark Grace/Bat-Jsy/50 10.00
18 Jason Giambi/Jsy-Jsy/100 6.00
19 Dave Righetti/Jsy-Jsy/100 6.00
21 Roger Clemens/ Jsy-Jsy/100 15.00
22 Juan Gonzalez/Bat-Jsy/100 6.00
23 Carlos Delgado/Bat-Jsy/100 4.00
26 Wade Boggs/Bat-Jsy/100 10.00
29 Rod Carew/Jkt-Jsy/100 10.00
33 Larry Walker/Jsy-Jsy/100 6.00
34 Nolan Ryan/Bat-Pants/100 20.00
36 Greg Maddux/Jsy-Jsy/100 12.00
38 Curt Schilling/Jsy-Jsy/100 6.00
40 Andruw Jones/Bat-Jsy/100 8.00
41 Orlando Cepeda/ Bat-Pants/100 8.00
43 Kirby Puckett/Bat-Jsy/100 12.00
44 Reggie Jackson/ Bat-Jsy/100 10.00
46 Rickey Henderson/ Bat-Jsy/100 10.00
47 Lee Smith/Jsy-Jsy/100 6.00
49 Fred Lynn/Bat-Jsy/100 4.00
50 Lance Berkman/Bat-Jsy/100 4.00
51 Shawn Green/Bat-Jsy/100 4.00
52 Hoyt Wilhelm/Jsy-Jsy/100 4.00
53 Sammy Sosa/Hat-Jsy/100 8.00
54 Tim Hudson/Jsy-Jsy/100 4.00
57 Eric Chavez/Jsy-Jsy/50 6.00
58 Rafael Palmeiro/Bat-Jsy/100 8.00
59 Randy Johnson/ Jsy-Pants/100 10.00
60 David Ortiz/Bat-Jsy/100 10.00
61 Hank Blalock/Jsy-Jsy/50 6.00
62 Jim Rice/Jsy-Pants/100 6.00
64 Kazuo Matsui/Bat-Jsy/100 4.00
65 Pedro Martinez/Jsy-Jsy/100 8.00
66 Sean Casey/Jsy-Pants/100 4.00
67 Carlos Lee/Hat-Jsy/100 4.00
69 Fred McGriff/Bat-Jsy/100 8.00
70 Darryl Strawberry/ Jsy-Jsy/100 6.00
71 Tommy John/Bat-Jsy/100 4.00
73 Johnny Bench/ Bat-Pants/100 12.00
74 Cal Ripken Jr./Bat-Jsy/100 30.00
75 Harold Baines/Bat-Jsy/100 4.00

Throwback Col. Sign. Mat.

NM/M

Production 5-50
2 Tony Gwynn/Jsy/50 40.00
4 Angel Berroa/Pants/50 10.00
6 Tony Oliva/Jsy/50 20.00
8 Gary Carter/Pants/50 20.00
12 Roberto Alomar/Jsy/50 30.00
13 Omar Vizquel/Jsy/50 30.00
15 Carlos Beltran/Jsy/50 30.00
17 Mark Grace/Jsy/50 30.00
19 Dave Righetti/Jsy/50 20.00
26 Wade Boggs/Jsy/50 35.00
27 Luis Tiant/Pants/50 20.00
29 Rod Carew/Jkt/50 30.00
30 Dwight Evans/Jsy/25 25.00
32 Billy Williams/Jsy/50 20.00

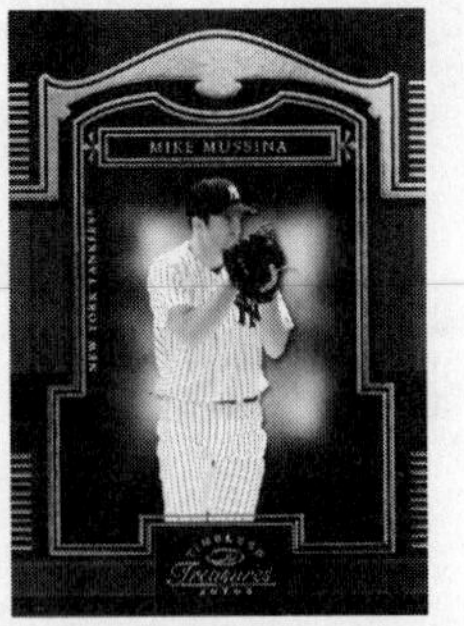

35 Edgar Renteria/Jsy/50 20.00
37 Gaylord Perry/Jsy/50 15.00
39 Dave Parker/Jsy/50 20.00
41 Orlando Cepeda/Pants/25 25.00
42 Fergie Jenkins/Jsy/50 20.00
44 Reggie Jackson/Jsy/25 50.00
45 Bob Gibson/Jsy/25 40.00
49 Fred Lynn/Jsy/50 20.00
54 Tim Hudson/Jsy/25 25.00
55 Matt Williams/Jsy/50 30.00
57 Eric Chavez/Jsy/50 20.00
62 Jim Rice/Pants/50 25.00
63 Mark Mulder/Jsy/50 20.00
66 Sean Casey/Jsy/50 20.00
67 Carlos Lee/Jsy/50 20.00
68 Stan Musial/Pants/25 75.00
70 Darryl Strawberry/Jsy/50 20.00
71 Tommy John/Jsy/50 15.00
75 Harold Baines/Jsy/50 15.00

Throwback Collectible Signature Material Combo

NM/M

Production 5-25
2 Tony Gwynn/Jsy-Pants/25 50.00
4 Angel Berroa/Bat-Pants/25 15.00
6 Tony Oliva/Bat-Jsy/25 25.00
8 Gary Carter/Jsy-Pants/25 25.00
12 Roberto Alomar/Bat-Jsy/25 40.00
15 Carlos Beltran/Bat-Jsy/25 35.00
17 Mark Grace/Bat-Jsy/25 35.00
19 Dave Righetti/Jsy-Jsy/25 25.00
26 Wade Boggs/Bat-Jsy/25 40.00
29 Rod Carew/Jkt-Jsy/25 40.00
44 Reggie Jackson/Bat-Jsy/25 50.00
49 Fred Lynn/Bat-Jsy/25 25.00
62 Jim Rice/Jsy-Pants/25 30.00
67 Carlos Lee/Hat-Jsy/25 25.00
68 Stan Musial/Bat-Pants/25 75.00
70 Darryl Strawberry/ Jsy-Jsy/25 20.00
75 Harold Baines/Bat-Jsy/25 20.00

Century Proof Blue

Blue (1-299): 3-6X
Production 150 Sets

Century Proof Gold

Gold (1-299): 3-6X
Production 100 Sets

Century Proof Green

Green (1-299): 3-6X

Cent. Proof Platinum Blue

No Pricing
Production 10 Sets

2005 Donruss Timeless Treasures

NM/M

Complete Set (100):
Common Player: 1.50
Production 799 Sets
Tin (4): 100.00
1 David Ortiz 3.00
2 Derek Jeter 8.00
3 Edgar Renteria 2.00
4 Paul Molitor 3.00
5 Jeff Bagwell 2.00
6 Melvin Mora 1.50
7 Bobby Crosby 1.50
8 Cal Ripken Jr. 10.00
9 Hank Blalock 2.00
10 Hideo Nomo 2.00
11 Gary Sheffield 2.00
12 Alfonso Soriano 3.00
13 Carl Crawford 1.50
14 Paul Konerko 1.50
15 Jim Edmonds 2.00
16 Garret Anderson 2.00
17 Lance Berkman 1.50
18 Javy Lopez 1.50
19 Tony Gwynn 3.00
20 Mark Mulder 1.50
21 Sammy Sosa 5.00
22 Roger Clemens 8.00
23 Mark Teixeira 2.00
24 Miguel Cabrera 3.00
25 Jim Thome 3.00
26 Mike Piazza 4.00

27	Vladimir Guerrero	3.00
28	Austin Kearns	1.50
29	Rod Carew	3.00
30	Ken Griffey Jr.	5.00
31	Mike Piazza	4.00
32	David Wright	3.00
33	Jason Varitek	2.00
34	Kerry Wood	3.00
35	Frank Thomas	2.00
36	Mark Prior	3.00
37	Mike Mussina	2.00
38	Curt Schilling	3.00
39	Greg Maddux	4.00
40	Miguel Tejada	3.00
41	Tom Seaver	3.00
42	Mariano Rivera	2.00
43	Jason Giambi	1.50
44	Roy Oswalt	1.50
45	Pedro Martinez	3.00
46	Jeff Niemann **RC**	5.00
47	Tom Glavine	1.50
48	Torii Hunter	1.50
49	Scott Rolen	3.00
50	Curt Schilling	3.00
51	Randy Johnson	3.00
52	C.C. Sabathia	1.50
53	Rafael Palmeiro	2.00
54	Jake Peavy	2.00
55	Hideki Matsui	6.00
56	Ichiro Suzuki	6.00
57	Johan Santana	3.00
58	Todd Helton	2.00
59	Justin Verlander **RC**	8.00
60	Kazuo Matsui	1.50
61	Rafael Palmeiro	2.00
62	Sean Casey	1.50
63	Nolan Ryan	8.00
64	Magglio Ordonez	1.50
65	Craig Biggio	2.00
66	Vernon Wells	1.50
67	Manny Ramirez	3.00
68	Aramis Ramirez	2.00
69	Omar Vizquel	1.50
70	Eric Gagne	1.50
71	Troy Glaus	2.00
72	Carlton Fisk	2.00
73	Victor Martinez	1.50
74	Adrian Beltre	2.00
75	Barry Zito	1.50
76	Josh Beckett	2.00
77	Michael Young	1.50
78	Eric Chavez	1.50
79	Hideo Nomo	2.00
80	Andruw Jones	2.00
81	Ivan Rodriguez	2.00
82	Don Mattingly	6.00
83	Larry Walker	2.00
84	Philip Humber **RC**	5.00
85	Juan Gonzalez	1.50
86	Tim Hudson	2.00
87	Alex Rodriguez	6.00
88	Greg Maddux	4.00
89	J.D. Drew	2.00
90	Shawn Green	1.50
91	Roger Clemens	8.00
92	Nomar Garciaparra	4.00
93	Andy Pettitte	2.00
94	Khalil Greene	1.50
95	Mike Schmidt	5.00
96	Carlos Beltran	2.00
97	Mike Mussina	2.00
98	Ben Sheets	1.50
99	Chipper Jones	3.00
100	Albert Pujols	8.00

Bronze

Bronze: 1-2X
Production 100 Sets

Gold

Gold: 3-5X
Production 25 Sets

Platinum

No Pricing
Production One Set

Silver

Gold: 2-3X
Production 50 Sets

Award Materials Number

NM/M

Production 1-29
Prime: No Pricing
Production 1-5.

9	Jim Palmer/Pants/22	12.00
10	Rod Carew/Jsy/29	15.00
12	Mike Schmidt/Jsy/20	25.00
13	Robin Yount/Jsy/19	25.00
15	Roger Clemens/Jsy/21	25.00

Award Mat. Sign. Number

No Pricing
Production 1-5

Award Material Sign. Year

NM/M

Production 1-25
Prime: No Pricing
Production 1-5

6	Johnny Bench/Jsy/25	60.00
9	Jim Palmer/Pants/25	35.00
10	Rod Carew/Jsy/25	50.00
12	Mike Schmidt/Jsy/25	75.00
14	Dale Murphy/Jsy/25	50.00

Award Materials Year

NM/M

Production 1-99

1	Lou Boudreau/Jsy/48	20.00
2	Roger Maris/Pants/61	40.00
6	Johnny Bench/Jsy/72	15.00
9	Jim Palmer/Pants/76	10.00
12	Mike Schmidt/Jsy/81	20.00
13	Robin Yount/Jsy/89	15.00
14	Dale Murphy/Jsy/83	10.00
15	Roger Clemens/Jsy/86	20.00
16	Cal Ripken Jr./Jsy/91	40.00
17	Tom Glavine/Jsy/91	8.00
18	Frank Thomas/Jsy/94	10.00
19	Jeff Bagwell/Pants/94	8.00
20	Randy Johnson/Jsy/95	10.00
21	Pedro Martinez/Jsy/97	10.00
22	Ivan Rodriguez/Jsy/99	10.00

Game Day Materials

NM/M

Production 5-100

1	Rod Carew/Hat/25	20.00
2	Kirby Puckett/Bat/100	15.00
5	Nellie Fox/Bat/25	60.00
6	Vladimir Guerrero/ Fld Glv/25	15.00
7	Tony Gwynn/Jsy/100	15.00
8	Rickey Henderson/Bat/100	10.00
9	David Ortiz/Hat/100	15.00
10	Carlos Beltran/Jsy/50	10.00

Game Day Material Sign.

NM/M

Production 3-25

7	Tony Gwynn/Jsy/25	50.00

Gamers NY

NM/M

Production 25 Sets

1	Jim Thorpe/Jsy-Jsy/25	450.00
2	Willie Mays/Jsy-Pants/25	75.00
3	Nolan Ryan/Bat-Jsy/25	65.00

Gamers NY Signatures

NM/M

Production 25 Sets

2	Willie Mays/Jsy-Pants/25	250.00
3	Nolan Ryan/Bat-Jsy/25	125.00

HOF Cuts

No Pricing
Production 1-10

HOF Cuts Materials

No Pricing
Production 1-10

HOF Materials Barrel

No Pricing
Production One Set

HOF Materials Bat

NM/M

Production 5-50

1	Pee Wee Reese/25	20.00
3	Harmon Killebrew/25	20.00
4	Hack Wilson/50	65.00
5	Brooks Robinson/50	20.00
6	Stan Musial/50	30.00
8	Carl Yastrzemski/50	20.00
9	Ted Williams/50	50.00
11	Luis Aparicio/25	15.00
12	Bobby Doerr/25	15.00
14	Ernie Banks/50	20.00
15	Ralph Kiner/25	20.00
20	Mike Schmidt/50	20.00
21	Roberto Clemente/50	75.00
24	Willie Mays/50	40.00
25	Willie Stargell/25	25.00
26	Frank Robinson/50	10.00
28	Reggie Jackson/50	15.00
30	Orlando Cepeda/50	10.00
34	Nolan Ryan/50	30.00
35	George Brett/50	25.00
39	Nellie Fox/50	40.00
43	Johnny Bench/50	20.00
44	Hank Aaron/50	40.00
50	Al Kaline/50	20.00

HOF Materials Combos

NM/M

Production 1-25
Prime: No Pricing
Production 1-5

3	Harmon Killebrew/ Bat-Jsy/25	25.00
5	Brooks Robinson/ Bat-Jsy/25	30.00
6	Stan Musial/Bat-Jsy/25	40.00
8	Carl Yastrzemski/ Bat-Jsy/25	30.00
9	Ted Williams/Bat-Jsy/25	85.00
12	Bobby Doerr/Bat-Pants/25	15.00
14	Ernie Banks/Bat-Jsy/25	25.00
18	Willie McCovey/ Jsy-Pants/25	25.00
20	Mike Schmidt/Bat-Jsy/25	30.00
24	Willie Mays/Bat-Jsy/25	75.00
25	Willie Stargell/Bat-Jsy/25	30.00
28	Reggie Jackson/Bat-Jsy/25	30.00
29	Warren Spahn/ Jsy-Pants/25	30.00
34	Nolan Ryan/Jsy-Pants/25	50.00
35	George Brett/Bat-Jsy/25	30.00
43	Johnny Bench/Bat-Jsy/25	25.00
44	Hank Aaron/Bat-Jsy/25	60.00

HOF Materials Hat

No Pricing

HOF Materials Jersey

NM/M

Production 1-100
Prime: No Pricing
Production 1-5

3	Harmon Killebrew/100	15.00
5	Brooks Robinson/50	15.00
6	Stan Musial/100	25.00
8	Carl Yastrzemski/100	15.00
9	Ted Williams/100	60.00
14	Ernie Banks/100	15.00
16	Whitey Ford/100	15.00
17	Duke Snider/25	20.00
18	Willie McCovey/25	20.00
20	Mike Schmidt/50	25.00
22	Jim Palmer/25	12.00
23	Enos Slaughter/50	15.00
24	Willie Mays/100	40.00
25	Willie Stargell/50	20.00
28	Reggie Jackson/25	25.00
29	Warren Spahn/25	25.00
31	Hoyt Wilhelm/50	10.00
32	Sandy Koufax/25	250.00
33	Hal Newhouser/50	10.00
34	Nolan Ryan/50	30.00
35	George Brett/50	25.00
37	Jim "Catfish" Hunter/25	15.00
38	Frankie Frisch Jkt/50	15.00
40	Lou Boudreau/25	15.00
43	Johnny Bench/50	15.00
44	Hank Aaron/100	40.00
45	Joe Cronin/50	20.00
49	Early Wynn/50	15.00

HOF Mat. Jersey Number

NM/M

Production 1-44

18	Willie McCovey/44	15.00
20	Mike Schmidt/20	30.00
22	Jim Palmer/22	12.00
24	Willie Mays/24	65.00
28	Reggie Jackson/44	15.00
29	Warren Spahn/21	25.00
31	Hoyt Wilhelm/31	10.00
32	Sandy Koufax/32	250.00
34	Nolan Ryan/34	30.00
37	Jim "Catfish" Hunter/29	15.00
44	Hank Aaron/44	50.00
49	Early Wynn/24	15.00

HOF Materials Pants

NM/M

Production 1-50

6	Stan Musial/50	30.00
8	Carl Yastrzemski/50	20.00
12	Bobby Doerr/50	10.00
17	Duke Snider/25	20.00
18	Willie McCovey/50	15.00
19	Bob Feller/25	20.00
22	Jim Palmer/25	10.00
24	Willie Mays/50	40.00
29	Warren Spahn/25	25.00
30	Orlando Cepeda/50	10.00
34	Nolan Ryan/50	25.00
42	Burleigh Grimes/50	75.00
43	Johnny Bench/50	15.00
45	Joe Cronin/50	20.00
46	Fergie Jenkins/50	10.00
50	Al Kaline/1	

HOF Material Sign. Bat

NM/M

Production 1-25

3	Harmon Killebrew/25	50.00
5	Brooks Robinson/25	50.00
6	Stan Musial/25	85.00
11	Luis Aparicio/25	25.00
12	Bobby Doerr/25	25.00
15	Ralph Kiner/25	50.00
20	Mike Schmidt/25	75.00
24	Willie Mays/25	240.00
26	Frank Robinson/25	40.00
30	Orlando Cepeda/25	25.00
34	Nolan Ryan/25	120.00
43	Johnny Bench/25	60.00
50	Al Kaline/25	50.00

HOF Mat. Sign. Combos

NM/M

Production 1-25
Prime: No Pricing
Production 1-5

3	Harmon Killebrew/ Bat-Jsy/25	65.00
5	Brooks Robinson/ Bat-Jsy/25	65.00
6	Stan Musial/Bat-Jsy/25	100.00
12	Bobby Doerr/Bat-Pants/25	30.00
18	Willie McCovey/ Jsy-Pants/25	60.00
20	Mike Schmidt/Bat-Jsy/25	85.00
24	Willie Mays/Bat-Jsy/25	250.00
30	Orlando Cepeda/ Bat-Pants/25	30.00
34	Nolan Ryan/Jsy-Pants/25	120.00
43	Johnny Bench/Bat-Jsy/25	60.00

HOF Materials Sign. Hat

No Pricing
Production 5-10

HOF Mat. Sign. Jersey

NM/M

Production 1-25
Prime: No Pricing
Production 1-5

3	Harmon Killebrew/25	50.00
5	Brooks Robinson/25	50.00
6	Stan Musial/25	85.00
17	Duke Snider/25	40.00
18	Willie McCovey/25	50.00
20	Mike Schmidt/25	75.00
22	Jim Palmer/25	40.00
24	Willie Mays/25	240.00
34	Nolan Ryan/25	120.00
43	Johnny Bench/25	60.00

HOF Material Sign. Pants

NM/M

Production 1-50

6	Stan Musial/25	85.00
12	Bobby Doerr/50	25.00
17	Duke Snider/25	40.00
18	Willie McCovey/25	50.00
22	Jim Palmer/25	40.00
24	Willie Mays/25	240.00
30	Orlando Cepeda/25	25.00
34	Nolan Ryan/25	120.00
43	Johnny Bench/25	60.00
46	Fergie Jenkins/25	30.00

HOF Silver

NM/M

Common Player: 4.00
Production 500 Sets
Gold: 2-4X
Production 25 Sets
Platinum: No Pricing
Production One Set

1	Pee Wee Reese	4.00
2	Red Schoendienst	4.00
3	Harmon Killebrew	5.00
4	Hack Wilson	5.00
5	Brooks Robinson	5.00
6	Stan Musial	6.00
7	Al Simmons	4.00
8	Carl Yastrzemski	5.00
9	Ted Williams	8.00
10	Phil Rizzuto	4.00
11	Luis Aparicio	4.00
12	Bobby Doerr	4.00
13	Bob Lemon	4.00
14	Ernie Banks	5.00
15	Ralph Kiner	4.00
16	Whitey Ford	4.00
17	Duke Snider	4.00
18	Willie McCovey	4.00
19	Bob Feller	4.00
20	Mike Schmidt	6.00
21	Roberto Clemente	8.00
22	Jim Palmer	4.00
23	Enos Slaughter	4.00
24	Willie Mays	8.00
25	Willie Stargell	4.00
26	Frank Robinson	4.00
27	Carl Hubbell	4.00
28	Reggie Jackson	4.00
29	Warren Spahn	5.00
30	Orlando Cepeda	4.00
31	Hoyt Wilhelm	4.00
32	Sandy Koufax	15.00
33	Hal Newhouser	4.00
34	Nolan Ryan	8.00
35	George Brett	6.00
36	Bill Dickey	4.00
37	Jim "Catfish" Hunter	4.00
38	Frankie Frisch	4.00
39	Nellie Fox	4.00
40	Lou Boudreau	4.00
41	Hank Greenberg	5.00
42	Burleigh Grimes	4.00
43	Johnny Bench	5.00
44	Hank Aaron	8.00
45	Joe Cronin	4.00
46	Fergie Jenkins	4.00
47	Luke Appling	4.00
48	Yogi Berra	5.00
49	Early Wynn	4.00
50	Al Kaline	5.00

Home Road Gamers Duos

NM/M

Production 1-100
Prime: No Pricing
Production 1-10

3	Babe Ruth/Jsy-Jsy/25	450.00
4	Paul Molitor/ Jsy-Pants/100	15.00
7	Ivan Rodriguez/ Jsy-Jsy/100	10.00
9	Ted Williams/Jsy-Jsy/25	85.00
10	Andre Dawson/Jsy-Jsy/25	15.00
11	Darryl Strawberry/ Jsy-Jsy/25	12.00
14	Ernie Banks/Jsy-Jsy/25	30.00
15	Jim Edmonds/Jsy-Jsy/25	15.00
16	Bo Jackson/Jsy-Jsy/25	20.00
17	Mark Grace/Jsy-Jsy/100	15.00
18	Albert Pujols/Jsy-Jsy/100	25.00
19	Tony Gwynn/Jsy-Jsy/100	15.00
20	Cal Ripken Jr./Jsy-Jsy/100	40.00
21	Chipper Jones/Jsy-Jsy/50	15.00

23 Don Mattingly/Jsy-Jsy/100 25.00
24 Willie Mays/Jsy-Jsy/25 80.00
25 Tony Oliva/Jsy-Jsy/50 10.00
28 Reggie Jackson/ Jsy-Jsy/100 15.00
29 Rod Carew/Jsy-Jsy/100 15.00
30 Harmon Killebrew/ Jsy-Jsy/25 25.00
32 Nolan Ryan/Jsy-Jsy/100 30.00
33 Eddie Murray/ Jsy-Pants/100 15.00
35 Rickey Henderson/ Jsy-Jsy/50 15.00
36 Jim Rice/Jsy-Jsy/50 12.00
37 Hoyt Wilhelm/Jsy-Jsy/50 10.00
38 Curt Schilling/Jsy-Jsy/100 10.00
42 Greg Maddux/Jsy-Jsy/100 15.00
43 Dennis Eckersley/ Jsy-Jsy/50 10.00
44 Willie McCovey/ Jsy-Pants/100 15.00
45 Willie Stargell/Jsy-Jsy/50 20.00
46 Mike Mussina/Jsy-Pants/50 15.00
47 Gary Carter/Jsy-Jsy/50 15.00
48 Dale Murphy/Jsy-Jsy/50 15.00
49 Mike Piazza/Jsy-Jsy/50 20.00
50 Jim Palmer/Jsy-Pants/100 10.00

Home Road Gamers Signature Duos

NM/M

Production 1-25
4 Paul Molitor/Jsy-Pants/25 60.00
11 Darryl Strawberry/ Jsy-Jsy/25 30.00
17 Mark Grace/Jsy-Jsy/25 50.00
19 Tony Gwynn/Jsy-Jsy/25 50.00
23 Don Mattingly/Jsy-Jsy/25 80.00
25 Tony Oliva/Jsy-Jsy/25 30.00
29 Rod Carew/Jsy-Jsy/25 50.00
30 Harmon Killebrew/ Jsy-Jsy/25 50.00
36 Jim Rice/Jsy-Jsy/25 35.00
43 Dennis Eckersley/ Jsy-Jsy/25 30.00
44 Willie McCovey/ Jsy-Pants/25 50.00
47 Gary Carter/Jsy-Jsy/25 30.00
48 Dale Murphy/Jsy-Jsy/25 50.00
50 Jim Palmer/Jsy-Pants/25 40.00

Home Road Gamer Signature Trios

NM/M

Production 1-25
Prime: No Pricing
Production 1-5
4 Paul Molitor/ Bat-Jsy-Pants/25 75.00
11 Darryl Strawberry/ Fld Glv-Jsy-Jsy/25 40.00
17 Mark Grace/Bat-Jsy-Jsy/25 60.00
19 Tony Gwynn/ Jsy-Jsy-Jsy/25 70.00
25 Tony Oliva/Bat-Jsy-Jsy/25 35.00
29 Rod Carew/Bat-Jsy-Jsy/25 60.00
30 Harmon Killebrew/ Bat-Jsy-Jsy/25 70.00
36 Jim Rice/Bat-Jsy-Jsy/25 40.00

Home Road Gamers Trios

NM/M

Production 1-100
Prime: No Pricing
Production 1-10
4 Paul Molitor/ Bat-Jsy-Pants/100 25.00
7 Ivan Rodriguez/ Jsy-Jsy-Jsy/100 15.00
9 Ted Williams/ Bat-Jsy-Jsy/25 120.00
11 Darryl Strawberry/ Fld Glv-Jsy-Jsy/25 20.00
14 Ernie Banks/ Bat-Jsy-Jsy/25 40.00
15 Jim Edmonds/ Bat-Jsy-Jsy/25 25.00
17 Mark Grace/ Bat-Jsy-Jsy/100 20.00
18 Albert Pujols/ Bat-Jsy-Jsy/100 40.00
19 Tony Gwynn/ Jsy-Jsy-Jsy/100 25.00
20 Cal Ripken Jr./ Jsy-Jsy-Jsy/100 60.00
21 Chipper Jones/ Bat-Jsy-Jsy/25 20.00
23 Don Mattingly/ Bat-Jsy-Jsy/100 30.00
24 Willie Mays/Bat-Jsy-Jsy/25 75.00
25 Tony Oliva/Bat-Jsy-Jsy/25 20.00
28 Reggie Jackson/ Bat-Jsy-Jsy/100 20.00
29 Rod Carew/ Bat-Jsy-Jsy/100 20.00
30 Harmon Killebrew/ Bat-Jsy-Jsy/25 35.00
32 Nolan Ryan/ Jkt-Jsy-Jsy/100 35.00
33 Eddie Murray/ Jsy-Jsy-Pants/100 20.00
35 Rickey Henderson/ Bat-Jsy-Jsy/100 20.00
36 Jim Rice/Bat-Jsy-Jsy/25 20.00
38 Curt Schilling/ Bat-Jsy-Jsy/50 15.00
44 Willie McCovey/ Bat-Jsy-Pants/100 20.00
45 Willie Stargell/ Bat-Jsy-Jsy/50 25.00
46 Mike Mussina/ Bat-Jsy-Pants/25 35.00
47 Gary Carter/Bat-Jsy-Jsy/50 25.00
48 Dale Murphy/ Bat-Jsy-Jsy/25 30.00
49 Mike Piazza/Jsy-Jsy-Jsy/25 35.00

Home Run Materials

NM/M

Production 1-100
1 Ernie Banks/Bat/60 15.00
2 Roger Maris/Bat/61 50.00
4 Johnny Bench/Pants/71 10.00
5 Harmon Killebrew/Bat/75 10.00
6 Jose Canseco/Bat/25 15.00
8 Sammy Sosa/Jsy/100 10.00
9 Jim Thome/Jsy/50 10.00
10 Rafael Palmeiro/Jsy/50 8.00

Home Run Materials Sig.

NM/M

Production 3-25
1 Ernie Banks/Bat/25 60.00
4 Johnny Bench/Pants/25 60.00
5 Harmon Killebrew/Bat/25 50.00

Material Ink Bat

No Pricing
Production 1-10

Material Ink Combos

NM/M

Production 1-25
Prime: No Pricing
Production 1-5
2 Fred Lynn/Bat-Jsy/25 35.00
8 Gary Carter/Bat-Jsy/25 30.00
10 Andre Dawson/Bat-Jsy/25 30.00
11 Luis Aparicio/Bat-Jsy/25 30.00
14 Darryl Strawberry/ Bat-Jsy/25 30.00
27 Carlton Fisk/Bat-Jsy/25 40.00
37 Miguel Cabrera/Bat-Jsy/25 50.00
39 Dave Parker/Bat-Jsy/25 25.00
48 Mark Grace/Bat-Jsy/25 40.00

Material Ink Jersey

NM/M

Production 1-50
2 Fred Lynn/50 15.00
3 Dale Murphy/50 30.00
4 Paul Molitor/50 30.00
5 Alan Trammell/50 15.00
8 Gary Carter/50 20.00
10 Andre Dawson/50 20.00
11 Luis Aparicio/50 15.00
14 Darryl Strawberry/50 15.00
18 Kirk Gibson/50 20.00
20 Don Sutton/25 20.00
23 Don Mattingly/Jkt/25 75.00
24 Tony Perez/50 25.00
27 Carlton Fisk/25 40.00
29 Fred McGriff/25 40.00
30 John Kruk/25 50.00
32 Dwight Evans/50 25.00
33 Gary Sheffield/25 50.00
34 Bo Jackson/25 65.00
36 Gaylord Perry/50 20.00
39 Dave Parker/25 20.00
42 Harmon Killebrew/50 50.00
43 Dennis Eckersley/25 25.00
44 Willie McCovey/25 50.00
46 Luis Tiant/50 20.00
48 Mark Grace/25 40.00

Mat. Ink Jersey Number

NM/M

Production 1-44
2 Fred Lynn/19 30.00
14 Darryl Strawberry/44 20.00
20 Don Sutton/20 25.00
22 Mark Prior/22 50.00
23 Don Mattingly/Jkt/23 80.00
24 Tony Perez/34 30.00
27 Carlton Fisk/27 40.00
29 Fred McGriff/29 40.00
30 John Kruk/29 50.00
32 Dwight Evans/24 35.00
36 Gaylord Perry/36 20.00
40 Mark Teixeira/23 40.00
43 Dennis Eckersley/43 20.00
44 Willie McCovey/44 40.00
46 Luis Tiant/27 25.00

Milestone Material Number

NM/M

Production 1-31
2 Nolan Ryan/Jsy/30 35.00
10 Greg Maddux/Jsy/31 20.00

Milestone Material Year

NM/M

Production 10-25
Prime: No Pricing
Production 1-10
1 Roger Maris/Pants/25 40.00
2 Nolan Ryan/Jsy/25 30.00
5 Steve Garvey/Jsy/25 10.00
6 Wade Boggs/Jsy/25 20.00
7 Tony Gwynn/Jsy/25 20.00
8 Sammy Sosa/Jsy/25 20.00
9 Randy Johnson/Jsy/25 15.00
10 Greg Maddux/Jsy/25 20.00

No-Hitters

NM/M

Production 3-25
7 Dennis Eckersley, Bert Blyleven/25 35.00
8 Juan Marichal, Gaylord Perry/25 35.00
9 Jim Palmer, Bob Gibson/25 40.00

Salutations Signature

NM/M

Production 1-24
1 Al Kaline/24 70.00
5 Dale Murphy/24 50.00
7 Duke Snider/24 50.00
11 Johnny Bench/24 60.00
19 Steve Carlton/24 40.00

Signature Bronze

NM/M

Production 10-100
Platinum: No Pricing
Production One Set
3 Edgar Renteria/50 30.00
4 Paul Molitor/100 25.00
7 Bobby Crosby/25 25.00
8 Cal Ripken Jr./25 200.00
9 Hank Blalock/50 20.00
11 Gary Sheffield/50 35.00
12 Alfonso Soriano/50 25.00
14 Paul Konerko/50 20.00
15 Jim Edmonds/50 30.00
16 Garret Anderson/50 20.00
19 Tony Gwynn/100 40.00
20 Mark Mulder/100 20.00
23 Mark Teixeira/50 30.00
24 Miguel Cabrera/50 30.00
28 Austin Kearns/50 15.00
29 Rod Carew/100 25.00
32 David Wright/25 75.00
34 Kerry Wood/50 35.00
36 Mark Prior/100 40.00
41 Tom Seaver/100 40.00
44 Roy Oswalt/25 20.00
46 Jeff Niemann/100 35.00
48 Torii Hunter/50 20.00
49 Scott Rolen/50 40.00
52 C.C. Sabathia/25 25.00
53 Rafael Palmeiro/25 50.00
57 Johan Santana/50 40.00
59 Justin Verlander/100 30.00
61 Rafael Palmeiro/25 50.00
62 Sean Casey/25 20.00
63 Nolan Ryan/100 85.00
64 Magglio Ordonez/50 15.00
65 Craig Biggio/50 30.00
66 Vernon Wells/25 20.00
67 Manny Ramirez/25 50.00
69 Omar Vizquel/50 40.00
72 Carlton Fisk/100 25.00
73 Victor Martinez/50 15.00
74 Adrian Beltre/50 25.00
75 Barry Zito/50 20.00
76 Josh Beckett/25 35.00
77 Michael Young/50 20.00
78 Eric Chavez/50 15.00
82 Don Mattingly/100 60.00
84 Philip Humber/100 25.00
85 Juan Gonzalez/50 25.00
86 Tim Hudson/50 30.00
90 Shawn Green/25 30.00
95 Mike Schmidt/100 50.00
98 Ben Sheets/25 25.00
99 Chipper Jones/25 60.00

Signature Gold

NM/M

Production 3-25
4 Paul Molitor/25 35.00
19 Tony Gwynn/25 50.00
20 Mark Mulder/25 30.00
29 Rod Carew/25 35.00
36 Mark Prior/25 50.00
41 Tom Seaver/25 60.00
63 Nolan Ryan/25 120.00
72 Carlton Fisk/25 35.00
82 Don Mattingly/25 80.00
95 Mike Schmidt/25 85.00

Signature Silver

NM/M

Production 5-50
3 Edgar Renteria/25 40.00
4 Paul Molitor/50 30.00
9 Hank Blalock/25 25.00
11 Gary Sheffield/25 40.00
12 Alfonso Soriano/25 35.00
14 Paul Konerko/25 25.00
15 Jim Edmonds/25 35.00
16 Garret Anderson/25 25.00
19 Tony Gwynn/50 60.00
20 Mark Mulder/50 25.00
23 Mark Teixeira/25 40.00
24 Miguel Cabrera/25 40.00
28 Austin Kearns/25 20.00
29 Rod Carew/50 30.00
34 Kerry Wood/25 40.00
36 Mark Prior/50 40.00
41 Tom Seaver/50 50.00
46 Jeff Niemann/50 40.00
48 Torii Hunter/25 25.00
49 Scott Rolen/25 50.00
57 Johan Santana/25 50.00
59 Justin Verlander/50 35.00
63 Nolan Ryan/50 100.00
64 Magglio Ordonez/25 20.00
65 Craig Biggio/25 35.00
69 Omar Vizquel/25 40.00
72 Carlton Fisk/50 25.00
73 Victor Martinez/25 20.00
74 Adrian Beltre/25 25.00
75 Barry Zito/25 20.00
77 Michael Young/25 20.00
78 Eric Chavez/25 20.00
82 Don Mattingly/50 60.00
84 Philip Humber/50 30.00
85 Juan Gonzalez/25 30.00
86 Tim Hudson/25 40.00
95 Mike Schmidt/50 65.00

World Series Materials

NM/M

Production 1-100
1 Frank Robinson/Bat/100 10.00
3 Carl Yastrzemski/Bat/100 25.00
4 Jack Morris/Jsy/50 8.00
5 Wade Boggs/Bat/100 12.00
8 Andruw Jones/Jsy/100 8.00
10 Darryl Strawberry/Jsy/25 10.00

2005 Donruss Zenith

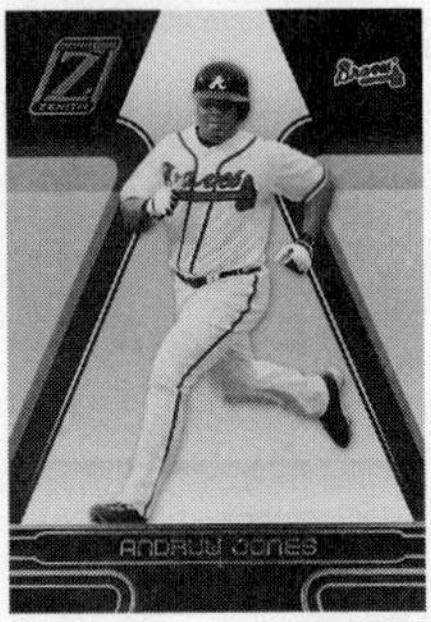

NM/M

Complete Set (250): 50.00
Common Player: .25
Hobby Pack (5): 5.00
Hobby Box (18): 80.00
1 Curt Schilling .50
2 Jim Edmonds .40
3 Ichiro Suzuki 1.50
4 Jody Gerut .25
5 Carlos Beltran .50
6 Miguel Tejada .50
7 Ted Lilly .25
8 Bobby Abreu .40
9 Mark Teixeira .50
10 Manny Ramirez .75
11 Eric Gagne .40
12 Adrian Beltre .40
13 Dmitri Young .25
14 Alfonso Soriano .50
15 Vladimir Guerrero .75
16 Carl Crawford .25
17 David Ortiz .75
18 Jose Guillen .25
19 Miguel Cabrera .75
20 Alex Rodriguez 2.00
21 Brad Lidge .25
22 Francisco Rodriguez .25
23 Carlos Lee .25
24 Ben Sheets .40
25 Jason Schmidt .25
26 Cesar Izturis .25
27 Corey Patterson .25
28 Marcus Giles .25
29 Melvin Mora .25
30 Yadier Molina .25
31 Juan Pierre .25
32 Aubrey Huff .25
33 Rafael Furcal .25
34 David Dellucci .25
35 Jake Peavy .40
36 Aramis Ramirez .40
37 Javy Lopez .25
38 Aaron Rowand .25
39 Raul Ibanez .25
40 Jason Bay .40
41 Michael Young .25
42 Ivan Rodriguez .50
43 Derrek Lee .50
44 Adam Dunn .50
45 Eric Chavez .40
46 Pedro Martinez .75
47 Roy Oswalt .40
48 Kevin Millwood .25
49 Carlos Delgado .40
50 Derek Jeter 2.00
51 Johnny Damon .50
52 Richie Sexson .40
53 Nomar Garciaparra .75
54 Edgar Renteria .25

#	Player	Price
55	Carl Pavano	.25
56	Tim Wakefield	.25
57	Michael Barrett	.25
58	Johnny Estrada	.25
59	Jeff Kent	.25
60	Mark Loretta	.25
61	Greg Maddux	1.00
62	Hank Blalock	.40
63	Moises Alou	.25
64	Brad Radke	.25
65	Brad Wilkerson	.25
66	Sean Casey	.25
67	Oliver Perez	.40
68	Scott Hatteberg	.25
69	Mike Lowell	.25
70	Kazuo Matsui	.25
71	Mark Prior	.50
72	Hideki Matsui	1.50
73	Geoff Jenkins	.25
74	Gary Sheffield	.50
75	A.J. Burnett	.25
76	Vernon Wells	.25
77	Kenny Rogers	.25
78	Jose Reyes	.50
79	Victor Martinez	.25
80	Jorge Posada	.40
81	Rich Harden	.25
82	Travis Hafner	.25
83	Bret Boone	.25
84	Chipper Jones	.75
85	Bartolo Colon	.25
86	Scott Podsednik	.25
87	Coco Crisp	.25
88	Luis Castillo	.25
89	John Smoltz	.40
90	Andruw Jones	.50
91	Milton Bradley	.25
92	Torii Hunter	.40
93	Shawn Green	.40
94	Paul Konerko	.25
95	David Wells	.25
96	Scott Rolen	.25
97	Rodrigo Lopez	.25
98	Garret Anderson	.40
99	Tim Hudson	.40
100	Sammy Sosa	.75
101	Jason Varitek	.50
102	Lance Berkman	.40
103	Troy Glaus	.40
104	Carlos Guillen	.25
105	Jeff Bagwell	.50
106	Phil Nevin	.25
107	Freddy Garcia	.25
108	Jake Westbrook	.25
109	Marquis Grissom	.25
110	Johan Santana	.75
111	Kerry Wood	.25
112	Jose Vidro	.25
113	Mike Mussina	.40
114	Josh Beckett	.40
115	Matt Lawton	.25
116	Craig Biggio	.40
117	Reggie Sanders	.25
118	Jason Kendall	.25
119	Larry Walker	.25
120	Roger Clemens	2.00
121	C.C. Sabathia	.25
122	Javier Vazquez	.25
123	Barry Zito	.25
124	Jon Lieber	.25
125	Kris Benson	.25
126	Jacque Jones	.25
127	Ray Durham	.25
128	Mark Kotsay	.25
129	Jack Wilson	.25
130	Bobby Crosby	.50
131	Todd Helton	.50
132	Lyle Overbay	.25
133	Jon Garland	.25
134	Roy Halladay	.40
135	Orlando Cabrera	.25
136	Danny Kolb	.25
137	Austin Kearns	.25
138	Paul LoDuca	.25
139	Magglio Ordonez	.40
140	Rafael Palmeiro	.50
141	Omar Vizquel	.25
142	Mike Piazza	1.00
143	Mark Mulder	.40
144	Dontrelle Willis	.40
145	Tom Glavine	.40
146	Khalil Greene	.25
147	Ken Griffey Jr.	1.50
148	Mike Sweeney	.25
149	Trot Nixon	.25
150	Randy Johnson	.75
151	Doug Mientkiewicz	.25
152	Jeromy Burnitz	.25
153	Brandon Webb	.25
154	Kevin Brown	.25
155	Carlos Zambrano	.40
156	Shingo Takatsu	.25
157	Erubiel Durazo	.25
158	Jason Isringhausen	.25
159	Corey Koskie	.25
160	Aaron Boone	.25
161	Joe Nathan	.25
162	Nick Johnson	.25
163	Michael Tucker	.25
164	Chris Carpenter	.25
165	Preston Wilson	.25
166	J.T. Snow	.25
167	Hideo Nomo	.40
168	Miguel Olivo	.25
169	Jarrod Washburn	.25
170	Derek Lowe	.25
171	Eric Milton	.25
172	Andy Pettitte	.40
173	Jason Giambi	.40
174	Richard Hidalgo	.25
175	Jayson Werth	.25
176	Juan Gonzalez	.40
177	Rocco Baldelli	.25
178	Steve Finley	.25
179	Frank Thomas	.40
180	Kenny Lofton	.25
181	Randy Winn	.25
182	Brandon McCarthy RC	1.50
183	Lew Ford	.25
184	Mike Cameron	.25
185	Carlos Pena	.25
186	Brian Roberts	.25
187	Jeremy Bonderman	.25
188	Luis Gonzalez	.25
189	J.D. Drew	.25
190	Frank Catalanotto	.25
191	John Buck	.25
192	Pat Burrell	.25
193	Ryan Klesko	.25
194	Jermaine Dye	.25
195	Mariano Rivera	.40
196	Angel Berroa	.25
197	Carlos Zambrano	.25
198	Joel Pineiro	.25
199	Jay Gibbons	.25
200	Albert Pujols	2.00
201	Billy Wagner	.25
202	Darin Erstad	.25
203	Jim Thome	.50
204	Adam LaRoche	.25
205	Cliff Floyd	.25
206	Grady Sizemore	.50
207	Garrett Atkins	.25
208	Philip Humber RC	1.00
209	Zack Greinke	.50
210	Wladimir Balentien RC	1.00
211	Ubaldo Jimenez RC	.50
212	Dallas McPherson	.25
213	Justin Verlander RC	3.00
214	Justin Morneau	.50
215	Chase Utley	.50
216	Casey Kotchman	.25
217	Tadahito Iguchi RC	3.00
218	Hanley Ramirez	.50
219	Scott Kazmir	.25
220	J.J. Hardy	.25
221	Ambiorix Concepcion RC	.25
222	Jeff Niemann RC	1.00
223	David Wright	1.00
224	Joe Mauer	.50
225	Rickie Weeks	.25
226	Yuniesky Betancourt RC	1.00
227	Brady Clark	.25
228	Keiichi Yabu RC	.25
229	Delmon Young	.50
230	Nick Swisher	.25
231	George Brett	1.00
232	Ryne Sandberg	1.00
233	Mike Schmidt	1.00
234	Tony Gwynn	.75
235	Rickey Henderson	.50
236	Ozzie Smith	1.00
237	Reggie Jackson	.75
238	Steve Carlton	.40
239	Robin Yount	1.00
240	Tom Seaver	.50
241	Ted Williams	1.50
242	Don Mattingly	1.00
243	Mark Grace	.40
244	Rod Carew	.40
245	Willie Mays	1.50
246	Gary Carter	.40
247	Wade Boggs	.50
248	Dale Murphy	.40
249	Nolan Ryan	2.00
250	Cal Ripken Jr.	3.00

Artist's Proofs Gold

Gold AP (1-250): 5-10X
Production 50 Sets

Artist's Proofs Silver

Silver AP (1-250): 3-5X
Inserted 1:16

Museum Collection

Museum (1-250): 2-3X
Inserted 1:3

Epix Orange Play

	NM/M
Common Player:	1.50
Black Game:	
Production 75 Sets	
Black Moment:	2-3X
Production 25 Sets	
Black Play:	1X
Production 100 Sets	
Black Season:	1-2X
Production 50 Sets	
Blue Game:	1X
Production 350	
Blue Moment:	1X
Production 150 Sets	
Blue Play:	1X
Production 500 Sets	
Blue Season:	1X
Production 250 Sets	
Emerald Game:	1X
Production 100 Sets	
Emerald Moment:	1-2X
Production 50 Sets	
Emerald Play:	1X
Production 150 Sets	
Emerald Season:	1X
Production 75 Sets	
Orange Game:	1X
Production 500 Sets	
Orange Moment:	1X
Production 250 Sets	
Orange Season:	1X
Production 350 Sets	
Purple Game:	1X
Production 250 Sets	
Purple Moment:	1X
Production 100 Sets	
Purple Play:	1X
Production 350 Sets	
Purple Season:	1X
Production 150 Sets	
Red Game:	1X
Production 150 Sets	
Red Moment:	1-2X
Production 50 Sets	
Red Play:	1X
Production 250 Sets	
Red Season:	1X
Production 100 Sets	
1 Vladimir Guerrero	3.00
2 Alex Rodriguez	6.00
3 Johan Santana	3.00
4 Todd Helton	2.00
5 Mark Teixeira	2.00
6 Manny Ramirez	3.00
7 Scott Rolen	2.00
8 Gary Sheffield	3.00
9 Miguel Cabrera	3.00
10 Jim Thome	2.00
11 Eric Chavez	1.50
12 Roger Clemens	6.00
13 Pedro Martinez	3.00
14 Roy Oswalt	1.50
15 Carlos Delgado	1.50
16 Nomar Garciaparra	2.00
17 Hideki Matsui	5.00
18 Shawn Green	1.50
19 Greg Maddux	4.00
20 Ted Williams	6.00
21 Don Mattingly	5.00
22 Cal Ripken Jr.	10.00
23 George Brett	6.00
24 Nolan Ryan	8.00
25 Willie Mays	6.00

Mozaics

	NM/M
Common Trio:	1.00
Inserted 1:8	
1 Pedro Martinez, Carlos Beltran, Tom Glavine	2.00
2 Albert Pujols, Jim Edmonds, Mark Mulder	5.00
3 Sammy Sosa, Miguel Tejada, Rafael Palmeiro	2.00
4 Mark Teixeira, Hank Blalock, Michael Young	2.00
5 Andruw Jones, Rafael Furcal, Johnny Estrada	1.50
6 Bobby Crosby, Eric Chavez, Barry Zito	1.00
7 Shawn Green, Troy Glaus, Luis Gonzalez	1.00
8 Austin Kearns, Adam Dunn, Sean Casey	1.00
9 Jim Thome, Bobby Abreu, Pat Burrell	1.50
10 Lance Berkman, Jeff Bagwell, Craig Biggio	1.50
11 Orlando Cabrera, Steve Finley, Darin Erstad	1.00
12 J.D. Drew, Jeff Kent, Milton Bradley	1.00
13 Dontrelle Willis, Mike Lowell, A.J. Burnett	1.00
14 Adrian Beltre, Jeremy Reed, Richie Sexson	1.00
15 Joe Mauer, Justin Morneau, Jacque Jones	1.00
16 Gary Sheffield, Hideki Matsui, Mike Mussina	4.00

Mozaics Materials Single

	NM/M
Common Player:	4.00
1 Pedro Martinez/Jsy	6.00
2 Albert Pujols/Bat	15.00
3 Miguel Tejada/Jsy	6.00
4 Mark Teixeira/Bat	6.00
5 Andruw Jones/Bat	6.00
7 Luis Gonzalez/Bat	4.00
8 Adam Dunn/Bat	4.00
9 Bobby Abreu/Jsy	4.00
10 Craig Biggio/Bat	4.00
11 Darin Erstad/Bat	4.00
12 J.D. Drew/Bat	4.00
13 A.J. Burnett/Bat	4.00
14 Richie Sexson/Bat	4.00
15 Jacque Jones/Bat	4.00
16 Gary Sheffield/Fld Glv	6.00

Mozaics Materials Triple Jerseys

	NM/M
Production 5-100	
Prime:	No Pricing
Production 5-10	
4 Mark Teixeira, Hank Blalock, Michael Young/100	10.00
6 Bobby Crosby, Eric Chavez, Barry Zito/25	10.00
8 Austin Kearns, Adam Dunn, Sean Casey/100	10.00
9 Jim Thome, Bobby Abreu, Pat Burrell/100	10.00
10 Lance Berkman, Jeff Bagwell, Craig Biggio/100	10.00
16 Gary Sheffield, Hideki Matsui, Mike Mussina/50	25.00

Positions

	NM/M
Common Card:	
Inserted 1:21	
Gold:	1-2X
Production 100 Sets	
1 Randy Johnson, Mark Prior, Roger Clemens	4.00
2 Ivan Rodriguez, Mike Piazza, Victor Martinez	2.00
3 Albert Pujols, Todd Helton, David Ortiz	5.00
4 Marcus Giles, Mark Loretta, Bret Boone	1.00
5 Scott Rolen, Aramis Ramirez, Chipper Jones	2.00
6 Kazuo Matsui, Miguel Tejada, Michael Young	1.50
7 Brian Giles, Manny Ramirez, Shannon Stewart	2.00
8 Rocco Baldelli, Andruw Jones, Vernon Wells	1.50
9 Miguel Cabrera, Lance Berkman, Vladimir Guerrero	2.00

Positions Materials Single

	NM/M
Common Player:	4.00
1 Mark Prior/Bat	6.00
2 Ivan Rodriguez/Bat	6.00
3 Albert Pujols/Bat	15.00
4 Bret Boone/Jsy	4.00
5 Chipper Jones/Bat	6.00
6 Kazuo Matsui/Jsy	4.00
7 Manny Ramirez/Bat	6.00
8 Andruw Jones/Bat	6.00
9 Lance Berkman/Bat	4.00

Positions Materials Triple Jersey

	NM/M
Production 5-100	
2 Ivan Rodriguez, Mike Piazza, Victor Martinez/50	15.00
3 Albert Pujols, Todd Helton, David Ortiz/50	25.00
5 Scott Rolen, Aramis Ramirez, Chipper Jones/100	15.00
6 Kazuo Matsui, Miguel Tejada, Michael Young/75	10.00
8 Rocco Baldelli, Andruw Jones, Vernon Wells/100	10.00
9 Miguel Cabrera, Lance Berkman, Vladimir Guerrero/100	15.00

Positions Materials Triple Jersey Prime

	NM/M
Production 5-25	
2 Ivan Rodriguez, Mike Piazza, Victor Martinez/25	35.00

5 Scott Rolen, Aramis Ramirez, Chipper Jones/25 35.00
6 Kazuo Matsui, Miguel Tejada, Michael Young/25 25.00
7 Brian Giles, Manny Ramirez, Shannon Stewart/25 20.00
8 Rocco Baldelli, Andruw Jones, Vernon Wells/25 25.00
9 Miguel Cabrera, Lance Berkman, Vladimir Guerrero/25 35.00

Red Hot

NM/M

Common Player:
Inserted 1:16
1 Scott Rolen 1.50
2 Johan Santana 1.50
3 Josh Beckett 1.00
4 Aubrey Huff 1.00
5 Alfonso Soriano 1.50
6 Jeff Bagwell 1.50
7 Ted Williams 5.00
8 Mark Prior 1.50
9 Todd Helton 1.50
10 Vladimir Guerrero 2.00

Red Hot Bats

NM/M

Production 50-150
1 Scott Rolen/150 6.00
4 Aubrey Huff/150 4.00
5 Alfonso Soriano/150 6.00
6 Jeff Bagwell/150 6.00
7 Ted Williams/50 40.00
8 Mark Prior/150 6.00
9 Todd Helton/150 6.00
10 Vladimir Guerrero/150 8.00

Red Hot Jerseys

NM/M

Production 25-300
1 Scott Rolen/150 6.00
2 Johan Santana/150 6.00
3 Josh Beckett/300 4.00
4 Aubrey Huff/25 6.00
5 Alfonso Soriano/150 6.00
6 Jeff Bagwell/300 6.00
7 Ted Williams/25 60.00
8 Mark Prior/250 6.00
9 Todd Helton/165 6.00
10 Vladimir Guerrero/150 8.00

Red Hot Jerseys Prime

NM/M

Production 1-25
1 Scott Rolen/25 20.00
2 Johan Santana/25 20.00
3 Josh Beckett/25 15.00
4 Aubrey Huff/25 10.00
5 Alfonso Soriano/25 15.00
6 Jeff Bagwell/25 20.00
8 Mark Prior/25 20.00
9 Todd Helton/25 20.00
10 Vladimir Guerrero/25 25.00

Roll Call Autographs

NM/M

Inserted 1:24
1 Hanley Ramirez 20.00
2 Sean Tracey 8.00
3 Justin Wechsler 8.00
4 Matt Lindstrom 6.00
5 Garrett Jones 8.00
6 Ambiorix Concepcion 8.00
7 Casey Rogowski 8.00
8 Kelly Shoppach 6.00
9 Sean Thompson 8.00
10 Jeff Miller 6.00
11 Chris Resop 10.00
12 Justin Verlander 25.00
13 Geovany Soto 40.00
14 Paulino Reynoso 6.00
15 Chris Roberson 8.00
16 Justin Leone 6.00
17 Jeff Niemann 15.00
18 Mark Woodyard 6.00
19 Raul Tablado 8.00
20 Norihiro Nakamura 40.00
21 Tony Pena 8.00
22 Wladimir Balentien 15.00
23 Miguel Negron 6.00
24 Eude Brito 8.00
25 Ubaldo Jimenez 10.00
26 Mike Morse 10.00
27 Devon Lowery 6.00
28 Philip Humber 12.00
29 Nate McLouth 15.00
30 Jason Hammel 8.00

Spellbound

NM/M

Common Maddux (1-4): 3.00
Common Clemens (5-9): 4.00
Common A-Rod (10-13): 4.00
Common Pujols (14-19): 4.00
Inserted 1:11
1 Greg Maddux/G 3.00
2 Greg Maddux/R 3.00
3 Greg Maddux/E 3.00
4 Greg Maddux/G 3.00
5 Roger Clemens/R 4.00
6 Roger Clemens/O 4.00
7 Roger Clemens/G 4.00
8 Roger Clemens/E 4.00
9 Roger Clemens/R 4.00
10 Alex Rodriguez/A 4.00
11 Alex Rodriguez/L 4.00
12 Alex Rodriguez/E 4.00
13 Alex Rodriguez/X 4.00
14 Albert Pujols/A 4.00
15 Albert Pujols/L 4.00
16 Albert Pujols/B 4.00
17 Albert Pujols/E 4.00
18 Albert Pujols/R 4.00
19 Albert Pujols/T 4.00

Spellbound Jerseys

NM/M

Production 150-250
1 Greg Maddux G/150 12.00
2 Greg Maddux R/150 12.00
3 Greg Maddux E/150 12.00
4 Greg Maddux G/150 12.00
5 Roger Clemens R/150 15.00
6 Roger Clemens O/150 15.00
7 Roger Clemens G/150 15.00
8 Roger Clemens E/150 15.00
9 Roger Clemens R/150 15.00
14 Albert Pujols A/250 15.00
15 Albert Pujols L/250 15.00
16 Albert Pujols B/250 15.00
17 Albert Pujols E/250 15.00
18 Albert Pujols R/250 15.00
19 Albert Pujols T/250 15.00

Spellbound Jerseys Prime

NM/M

Production 10-25
5 Roger Clemens R/25 40.00
6 Roger Clemens O/25 40.00
7 Roger Clemens G/25 40.00
8 Roger Clemens E/25 40.00
9 Roger Clemens R/25 40.00

Team Zenith

NM/M

Common Player:
Inserted 1:31
Gold: 1-2X
Production 100 Sets
1 Ichiro Suzuki 5.00
2 Jim Edmonds 2.00
3 Hideki Matsui 5.00
4 Alex Rodriguez 5.00
5 Derek Jeter 6.00
6 Alfonso Soriano 2.00
7 Jim Thome 2.00
8 Jorge Posada 1.50
9 Barry Zito 1.50
10 Curt Schilling 2.00
11 Willie Mays 4.00

Team Zenith Bats

NM/M

Production 15-25
3 Hideki Matsui/50 25.00
7 Jim Thome/150 6.00
8 Jorge Posada/25 8.00
11 Willie Mays/25 70.00

Team Zenith Jerseys

NM/M

Production 15-300
3 Hideki Matsui/165 20.00
7 Jim Thome/175 6.00
8 Jorge Posada/300 6.00
9 Barry Zito/150 4.00
10 Curt Schilling/150 6.00
11 Willie Mays/175 30.00

Team Zenith Jerseys Prime

NM/M

Production 25 Sets
2 Jim Edmonds/25 15.00
6 Alfonso Soriano/25 15.00
7 Jim Thome/25 20.00
8 Jorge Posada/25 15.00
9 Barry Zito/25 15.00
10 Curt Schilling/25 20.00

White Hot

NM/M

Common Player:
Inserted 1:65
1 Scott Rolen 2.00
2 Johan Santana 2.00
3 Josh Beckett 1.50
4 Aubrey Huff 1.50
5 Alfonso Soriano 2.00
6 Jeff Bagwell 2.00
7 Ted Williams 6.00
8 Mark Prior 2.00
9 Todd Helton 2.00
10 Vladimir Guerrero 2.00

White Hot Bats

NM/M

Production 50 Sets
1 Scott Rolen/50 8.00
4 Aubrey Huff/50 4.00
5 Alfonso Soriano/50 6.00
6 Jeff Bagwell/50 6.00
7 Ted Williams/50 40.00
8 Mark Prior/50 8.00
9 Todd Helton/50 6.00
10 Vladimir Guerrero/50 8.00

White Hot Jerseys

NM/M

Production 1-200
Prime: No Pricing
Production 1-10
1 Scott Rolen/50 8.00
2 Johan Santana/50 8.00
3 Josh Beckett/185 4.00
5 Alfonso Soriano/50 6.00
6 Jeff Bagwell/200 6.00
8 Mark Prior/200 6.00
9 Todd Helton/151 6.00
10 Vladimir Guerrero/50 8.00

Z-Batgraphs

NM/M

Production 1-100
7 Craig Wilson/100 12.00
9 Nick Johnson/100 15.00
11 Dontrelle Willis/25 40.00
24 Angel Berroa/100 8.00
29 Magglio Ordonez/100 10.00
39 Jack Wilson/25 15.00
44 Tony Gwynn/25 50.00
52 Paul Molitor/25 40.00
55 Ryne Sandberg/25 65.00
57 Casey Kotchman/50 20.00
59 Chone Figgins/50 20.00
69 Victor Martinez/25 25.00
90 Michael Young/100 15.00
91 Dale Murphy/100 20.00
97 Carlos Lee/50 20.00
99 Mark Teixeira/25 40.00

Z-Bats

NM/M

Common Player: 4.00
3 Rickey Henderson 8.00
4 Andy Pettitte 4.00
7 Craig Wilson 4.00
9 Nick Johnson 4.00
10 Bernie Williams 6.00
11 Dontrelle Willis 6.00
12 Kenny Lofton 4.00
13 Tom Glavine 4.00
14 Kazuo Matsui/SP 6.00
15 Morgan Ensberg/SP 6.00
16 Mike Piazza 8.00
17 Trot Nixon/SP 8.00
18 Ryan Klesko/SP 6.00
19 B.J. Upton 4.00
21 Omar Vizquel 4.00
22 Shannon Stewart 4.00
23 Preston Wilson 4.00
24 Angel Berroa 4.00
26 Brandon Webb 4.00
27 Rafael Palmeiro 6.00
28 Mike Sweeney 4.00
29 Magglio Ordonez 4.00
30 Cal Ripken Jr. 25.00
31 Johnny Estrada 4.00
32 Austin Kearns 4.00
33 Nolan Ryan 20.00
34 Orlando Cabrera 4.00
35 Roy Oswalt 4.00
37 Lyle Overbay 4.00
39 Jack Wilson 4.00
40 Jacque Jones 4.00
44 Tony Gwynn 8.00
46 Geoff Jenkins 4.00
47 Bo Jackson 8.00
48 Luis Gonzalez 4.00
50 Craig Biggio 4.00
51 Josh Beckett 4.00
52 Paul Molitor 6.00
55 Ryne Sandberg 10.00
56 Jeff Bagwell 6.00
57 Casey Kotchman 4.00
58 Chipper Jones 6.00
60 Paul Konerko 6.00
61 Kevin Mench 4.00
62 David Wright 10.00
64 Andruw Jones 6.00
65 Garret Anderson 4.00
66 Jorge Posada 6.00
68 Travis Hafner 4.00
69 Victor Martinez 4.00
70 Vernon Wells 4.00
71 A.J. Burnett 4.00
73 Mark Prior 6.00
74 Mike Lowell 4.00
76 Brad Wilkerson 4.00
79 Moises Alou 4.00
81 Hank Blalock 4.00
82 J.D. Drew 4.00
83 Reggie Jackson/SP 8.00
84 Mark Buehrle/SP 6.00
87 Adam Dunn 6.00
88 Derrek Lee 6.00
90 Michael Young 4.00
91 Dale Murphy 6.00
92 Aramis Ramirez 4.00
95 Aubrey Huff 4.00
96 Ben Sheets 4.00
97 Carlos Lee 4.00
98 Miguel Cabrera 6.00
99 Mark Teixeira 6.00
100 Albert Pujols 15.00

Z-Combos

NM/M

Production 1-150
Cards are bat/jsy unless noted.
3 Rickey Henderson/100 12.00
7 Craig Wilson/150 6.00
10 Bernie Williams/150 8.00
11 Dontrelle Willis/25 10.00
14 Kazuo Matsui/50 8.00
19 B.J. Upton/25 10.00
26 Brandon Webb/ Bat-Pants/100 6.00
30 Cal Ripken Jr./100 30.00
33 Nolan Ryan/25 40.00
44 Tony Gwynn/100 12.00
47 Bo Jackson/100 12.00
50 Craig Biggio/50 10.00
52 Paul Molitor/50 12.00
53 Kerry Wood/25 10.00
54 Lew Ford/25 8.00
55 Ryne Sandberg/100 20.00
56 Jeff Bagwell/50 10.00
57 Casey Kotchman/50 8.00
58 Chipper Jones/100 10.00
59 Chone Figgins/100 6.00
61 Kevin Mench/100 6.00
64 Andruw Jones/100 10.00
69 Victor Martinez/100 8.00
71 A.J. Burnett/100 6.00
73 Mark Prior/100 10.00
81 Hank Blalock/100 8.00
87 Adam Dunn/25 10.00
88 Derrek Lee/25 12.00
90 Michael Young/100 6.00
91 Dale Murphy/100 10.00
99 Mark Teixeira/Bat-Hat/100 12.00

Z-Combos Prime

NM/M

Production 1-25
All are bat/patch.
3 Rickey Henderson/25 25.00
7 Craig Wilson/25 10.00
10 Bernie Williams/25 15.00
11 Dontrelle Willis/25 15.00
14 Kazuo Matsui/25 10.00
19 B.J. Upton/25 15.00
27 Rafael Palmeiro/25 15.00
30 Cal Ripken Jr./25 65.00
33 Nolan Ryan/25 50.00
44 Tony Gwynn/25 25.00
47 Bo Jackson/25 25.00
55 Ryne Sandberg/25 35.00
56 Jeff Bagwell/25 15.00
57 Casey Kotchman/25 15.00
58 Chipper Jones/25 20.00
61 Kevin Mench/25 10.00
64 Andruw Jones/25 20.00
65 Garret Anderson/25 15.00
69 Victor Martinez/25 15.00
71 A.J. Burnett/25 10.00
73 Mark Prior/25 20.00
74 Mike Lowell/25 15.00
81 Hank Blalock/25 15.00
87 Adam Dunn/25 15.00
88 Derrek Lee/25 20.00
90 Michael Young/25 15.00
91 Dale Murphy/25 20.00
96 Ben Sheets/25 15.00
99 Mark Teixeira/25 25.00

Z-Graphs

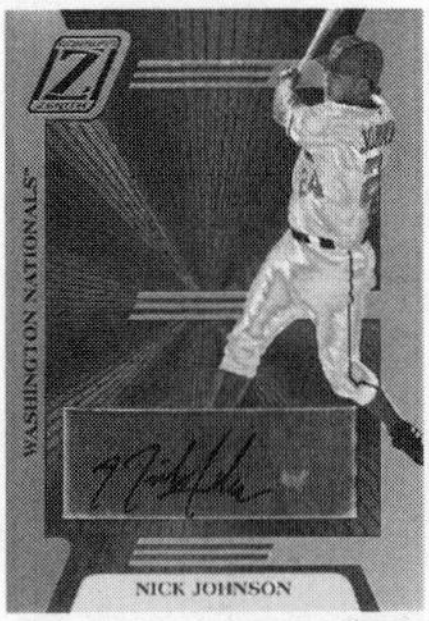

NM/M

Production 1-250
1 Danny Haren/250 10.00
2 Dallas McPherson/250 12.00
5 Jeremy Bonderman/200 15.00
7 Craig Wilson/250 8.00
8 Adam LaRoche/250 12.00
9 Nick Johnson/250 10.00
11 Dontrelle Willis/25 25.00
15 Morgan Ensberg/250 10.00
17 Trot Nixon/100 20.00
19 B.J. Upton/50 20.00
20 Brian Roberts/250 15.00
21 Omar Vizquel/100 20.00
22 Shannon Stewart/100 10.00
24 Angel Berroa/100 8.00
26 Brandon Webb/100 10.00
29 Magglio Ordonez/100 12.00
30 Cal Ripken Jr./100 90.00
31 Johnny Estrada/50 10.00
32 Austin Kearns/100 10.00
33 Nolan Ryan/34 80.00
34 Orlando Cabrera/25 10.00
35 Roy Oswalt/100 15.00
36 Roy Halladay/50 20.00
38 Bobby Crosby/50 20.00
39 Jack Wilson/25 10.00

40 Jacque Jones/100 12.00
41 Eric Byrnes/250 8.00
44 Tony Gwynn/25 40.00
52 Paul Molitor/25 30.00
55 Ryne Sandberg/25 50.00
57 Casey Kotchman/100 12.00
60 Paul Konerko/100 20.00
62 David Wright/100 60.00
63 Milton Bradley/100 12.00
67 Rich Harden/250 15.00
68 Travis Hafner/250 10.00
69 Victor Martinez/25 20.00
70 Vernon Wells/25 15.00
72 Francisco Rodriguez/100 20.00
73 Mark Prior/25 40.00
75 Sean Casey/50 15.00
77 Carlos Zambrano/50 20.00
80 Livan Hernandez/100 12.00
84 Mark Buehrle/100 15.00
85 Keith Foulke/100 20.00
86 Edgar Renteria/50 15.00
88 Derrek Lee/100 25.00
89 Joe Nathan/100 10.00
90 Michael Young/50 15.00
91 Dale Murphy/100 20.00
93 Francisco Cordero/100 8.00
94 Jake Peavy/100 20.00
95 Aubrey Huff/100 10.00
96 Ben Sheets/50 20.00
97 Carlos Lee/25 15.00
98 Miguel Cabrera/25 40.00
99 Mark Teixeira/25 40.00

Z-Jerseygraphs

NM/M

Production 1-100
5 Jeremy Bonderman/100 20.00
7 Craig Wilson/100 10.00
11 Dontrelle Willis/25 35.00
15 Morgan Ensberg/25 20.00
17 Trot Nixon/50 25.00
19 B.J. Upton/50 25.00
20 Brian Roberts/100 20.00
22 Shannon Stewart/100 15.00
31 Johnny Estrada/100 10.00
35 Roy Oswalt/20 25.00
36 Roy Halladay/25 25.00
37 Lyle Overbay/25 15.00
38 Bobby Crosby/25 25.00
40 Jacque Jones/100 15.00
44 Tony Gwynn/25 50.00
52 Paul Molitor/25 35.00
55 Ryne Sandberg/25 65.00
57 Casey Kotchman/50 20.00
59 Chone Figgins/50 20.00
60 Paul Konerko/25 35.00
68 Travis Hafner/50 20.00
69 Victor Martinez/25 25.00
70 Vernon Wells/25 20.00
72 Francisco Rodriguez/100 25.00
73 Mark Prior/25 50.00
75 Sean Casey/25 20.00
80 Livan Hernandez/100 15.00
84 Mark Buehrle/100 20.00
88 Derrek Lee/100 30.00
90 Michael Young/100 20.00
91 Dale Murphy/100 25.00
93 Francisco Cordero/100 12.00
96 Ben Sheets/25 25.00
99 Mark Teixeira/25 50.00

Z-Jerseygraphs Prime

NM/M

Production 1-25
5 Jeremy Bonderman/25 35.00
7 Craig Wilson/25 20.00
11 Dontrelle Willis/25 50.00
17 Trot Nixon/25 40.00
19 B.J. Upton/25 35.00
20 Brian Roberts/25 40.00
22 Shannon Stewart/25 25.00
24 Angel Berroa/25 20.00
31 Johnny Estrada/25 20.00
32 Austin Kearns/25 20.00
35 Roy Oswalt/25 35.00
36 Roy Halladay/25 45.00
40 Jacque Jones/25 25.00
41 Eric Byrnes/25 20.00
44 Tony Gwynn/25 65.00
52 Paul Molitor/25 50.00
55 Ryne Sandberg/25 80.00
57 Casey Kotchman/25 30.00
60 Paul Konerko/25 50.00
68 Travis Hafner/25 35.00
69 Victor Martinez/25 35.00
70 Vernon Wells/25 30.00
72 Francisco Rodriguez/25 40.00
73 Mark Prior/25 60.00
75 Sean Casey/25 30.00
77 Carlos Zambrano/25 30.00
80 Livan Hernandez/25 25.00
84 Mark Buehrle/25 30.00
88 Derrek Lee/25 50.00
90 Michael Young/25 30.00
91 Dale Murphy/25 40.00
93 Francisco Cordero/25 20.00
95 Aubrey Huff/25 25.00
96 Ben Sheets/25 35.00
98 Miguel Cabrera/25 50.00
99 Mark Teixeira/25 60.00

Z-Jerseys

NM/M

Common Player: 4.00
1 Danny Haren 6.00
3 Rickey Henderson 8.00
4 Andy Pettitte 4.00
5 Jeremy Bonderman 4.00
6 Pat Burrell 4.00
7 Craig Wilson 4.00
10 Bernie Williams 4.00
11 Dontrelle Willis 6.00
13 Tom Glavine 4.00
14 Kazuo Matsui 4.00
16 Mike Piazza 8.00
17 Trot Nixon 4.00
18 Ryan Klesko 4.00
19 B.J. Upton 4.00
20 Brian Roberts 4.00
21 Omar Vizquel 4.00
22 Shannon Stewart 4.00
23 Preston Wilson 4.00
25 Garrett Atkins 4.00
27 Rafael Palmeiro 6.00
28 Mike Sweeney 4.00
29 Magglio Ordonez 4.00
30 Cal Ripken Jr. 25.00
32 Austin Kearns 4.00
33 Nolan Ryan 20.00
34 Orlando Cabrera 4.00
35 Roy Oswalt 4.00
36 Roy Halladay 6.00
37 Lyle Overbay 4.00
39 Jack Wilson 4.00
40 Jacque Jones 4.00
41 Eric Byrnes 4.00
42 Barry Zito 4.00
43 C.C. Sabathia 4.00
44 Tony Gwynn 8.00
45 Mike Cameron 4.00
46 Geoff Jenkins 4.00
47 Bo Jackson 8.00
48 Luis Gonzalez 4.00
49 Johnny Damon 6.00
50 Craig Biggio 6.00
51 Josh Beckett 6.00
52 Paul Molitor 8.00
53 Kerry Wood 4.00
54 Lew Ford 4.00
55 Ryne Sandberg 10.00
56 Jeff Bagwell 6.00
57 Casey Kotchman 4.00
58 Chipper Jones 8.00
59 Chone Figgins 4.00
60 Paul Konerko 6.00
61 Kevin Mench 4.00
62 David Wright 10.00
64 Andruw Jones 6.00
65 Garret Anderson 4.00
66 Jorge Posada 6.00
68 Travis Hafner 4.00
69 Victor Martinez 4.00
70 Vernon Wells 4.00
71 A.J. Burnett 4.00
72 Francisco Rodriguez 4.00
73 Mark Prior 6.00
74 Mike Lowell 4.00
75 Sean Casey 4.00
77 Carlos Zambrano 4.00
78 Brad Radke 4.00
79 Moises Alou 4.00
80 Livan Hernandez 4.00
81 Hank Blalock 4.00
82 J.D. Drew 4.00
83 Reggie Jackson 8.00
84 Mark Buehrle 6.00
86 Edgar Renteria 4.00
87 Adam Dunn 6.00
88 Derrek Lee 6.00
90 Michael Young 6.00
91 Dale Murphy 6.00
92 Aramis Ramirez 4.00
93 Francisco Cordero 4.00
95 Aubrey Huff 4.00
96 Ben Sheets 4.00
97 Carlos Lee 4.00
98 Miguel Cabrera 8.00
99 Mark Teixeira 8.00
100 Albert Pujols 15.00

Z-Jerseys Prime

NM/M

Production 1-150
3 Rickey Henderson/150 15.00
4 Andy Pettitte/100 10.00
5 Jeremy Bonderman/150 8.00
6 Pat Burrell/150 8.00
7 Craig Wilson/150 8.00
10 Bernie Williams/50 10.00
11 Dontrelle Willis/100 10.00
14 Kazuo Matsui/150 8.00
17 Trot Nixon/25 12.00
18 Ryan Klesko/150 8.00
19 B.J. Upton/50 10.00
20 Brian Roberts/50 10.00
22 Shannon Stewart/150 8.00
23 Preston Wilson/150 8.00
25 Garrett Atkins/150 8.00
27 Rafael Palmeiro/150 10.00
28 Mike Sweeney/150 8.00
30 Cal Ripken Jr./25 50.00
31 Johnny Estrada/100 8.00
32 Austin Kearns/150 8.00
33 Nolan Ryan/100 30.00
35 Roy Oswalt/100 10.00
36 Roy Halladay/150 10.00
37 Lyle Overbay/100 8.00
40 Jacque Jones/100 8.00
41 Eric Byrnes/50 8.00
42 Barry Zito/150 10.00
43 C.C. Sabathia/150 8.00
44 Tony Gwynn/150 15.00
45 Mike Cameron/150 8.00
46 Geoff Jenkins/50 10.00
47 Bo Jackson/100 20.00
48 Luis Gonzalez/150 8.00
49 Johnny Damon/25 20.00
51 Josh Beckett/150 10.00
52 Paul Molitor/70 15.00
54 Lew Ford/150 8.00
55 Ryne Sandberg/50 25.00
56 Jeff Bagwell/150 12.00
57 Casey Kotchman/50 10.00
58 Chipper Jones/150 15.00
60 Paul Konerko/150 10.00
61 Kevin Mench/150 8.00
64 Andruw Jones/150 12.00
65 Garret Anderson/25 12.00
66 Jorge Posada/50 12.00
68 Travis Hafner/100 10.00
69 Victor Martinez/25 12.00
70 Vernon Wells/150 10.00
71 A.J. Burnett/150 10.00
72 Francisco Rodriguez/100 8.00
73 Mark Prior/50 15.00
74 Mike Lowell/150 8.00
75 Sean Casey/150 8.00
77 Carlos Zambrano/100 10.00
78 Brad Radke/150 8.00
80 Livan Hernandez/50 10.00
81 Hank Blalock/100 10.00
83 Reggie Jackson/150 15.00
84 Mark Buehrle/50 12.00
87 Adam Dunn/150 10.00
88 Derrek Lee/50 15.00
90 Michael Young/50 10.00
91 Dale Murphy/50 20.00
92 Aramis Ramirez/100 10.00
93 Francisco Cordero/50 10.00
95 Aubrey Huff/150 8.00
96 Ben Sheets/150 10.00
98 Miguel Cabrera/150 15.00
99 Mark Teixeira/100 15.00

Z-Team

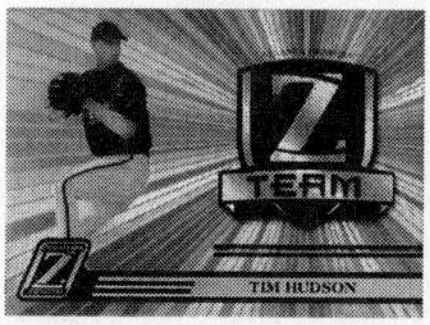

NM/M

Common Player:
Inserted 1:11
Gold: 1-2X
Production 100 Sets
1 Albert Pujols 5.00
2 Carlos Beltran 1.50
3 Randy Johnson 2.00
4 Miguel Tejada 1.50
5 Ichiro Suzuki 4.00
6 Eric Gagne 1.00
7 Adrian Beltre 1.00
8 Alfonso Soriano 1.50
9 Jim Edmonds 1.50
10 David Ortiz 2.00
11 Curt Schilling 2.00
12 Mariano Rivera 1.50
13 Derek Jeter 5.00
14 Ivan Rodriguez 1.50
15 Johnny Damon 2.00
16 Mark Prior 1.50
17 Vernon Wells 1.00
18 Chipper Jones 2.00
19 Torii Hunter 1.00
20 Tim Hudson 1.50
21 Lance Berkman 1.00
22 Troy Glaus 1.00
23 Mike Piazza 2.50
24 Mark Mulder 1.00
25 Ken Griffey Jr. 3.00

2007 Donruss Americana

NM/M

Complete Set (100): 40.00
Common Player: .25
1 John Travolta 1.00
2 Stacy Keibler 2.00
3 Burt Reynolds 1.00
4 Steve Guttenberg .25
5 William Shatner 1.00
6 Lee Majors .50
7 Gretchen Wilson .25
8 Ultimate Warrior .50
9 Barbara Eden .50
10 Carrie Fisher .50
11 Lori Petty .25
12 Morgan Fairchild .50
13 Vince Neil .50
14 Gail Kim .25
15 Cedric the Entertainer .50
16 Corin Nemec .25
17 Billy Dee Williams .50
18 Jim Furyk .50
19 Dick Van Patten .25
20 Debbie Reynolds .25
21 William Fichtner .25
22 Bob Eubanks .25
23 Mike Huckabee 1.00
24 Jack Hanna .25
25 Elliott Gould .25
26 Lou Gossett Jr. .50
27 Catherine Bach .50
28 Tippi Hedren .25
29 Walter Koenig .25
30 Ernest Borgnine .25
31 Cindy Williams .25
32 Cindy Morgan .25
33 Giovanni Ribisi .25
34 Story Musgrave .25
35 Esther Williams .25
36 Connie Mack III .25
37 Gilbert Gottfried .25
38 Burt Ward .50
39 Josh Duhamel .25
40 Larry Hagman .50
41 Catherine Hicks .25
42 Karen Lynn Gorney .25
43 Larry King .50
44 Autumn Reeser .25
45 Mickey Rooney .50
46 Aidan Quinn .25
47 Martin Klebba .25
48 Michael Pare' .25
49 Hugh O'Brian .25
50 Molly Shannon .25
51 Dee Snider .75
52 Melissa Jo Hunter .25
53 Jennie Finch 1.00
54 Henry Winkler .50
55 Neil Patrick Harris .25
56 Val Kilmer .25
57 Peter Marshall .25
58 Clint Howard .25
59 Buzz Aldrin .50
60 Heather Cox .25
61 Angela Simmons .25
62 Richard Kiel .25
63 Leonard Nimoy .50
64 Jan Rooney .25
65 Shirley Jones .25
66 Bruce Jenner .50
67 Tom Green .25
68 Dom DeLuise .25
69 Bobby Allison .50
70 Tony Curtis .25
71 Shawnee Smith .25
72 Wink Martindale .25
73 Tara Conner .25
74 Sheryl Swoopes .25
75 Wayne Newton .50
76 Justine Simmons .25
77 Keiko Agena .25
78 Tom Savini .25
79 David Faustino .25
80 Adam West .50
81 Gina Phillips .25
82 Dawn Wells .25
83 George Allen .25
84 Chris Sarandon .25
85 Amanda Beard .50
86 Katey Sagal .50
87 Ed O'Neill .50
88 Dina Meyer .50
89 Ron Howard .25
90 Randy Owen .25
91 Yunjin Kim .25
92 Chuck Woolery .25
93 Ed McMahon .25
94 Stephanie Powers .25
95 Warwick Davis .25
96 Scott Baio .25
97 Russell Johnson .25
98 Michael Berryman .25
99 Bernie Mac .50
100 Ashley Judd 1.00

Cinema Stars

NM/M

Common Card: 4.00
Production 500 Sets
1 John Travolta 5.00
2 Burt Reynolds 5.00
3 William Shatner 5.00
4 Carrie Fisher 5.00
5 Ron Howard 5.00
6 Elliott Gould 4.00
7 Lou Gossett Jr. 4.00
8 Ernest Borgnine 4.00
9 Giovanni Ribisi 4.00
10 Quentin Tarantino 4.00
11 Shirley Jones 4.00
12 Dom DeLuise 4.00
13 Adam West 4.00
14 Bernie Mac 4.00
15 Ashley Judd 5.00
16 Josh Duhamel 4.00
17 Catherine Bach 4.00
18 Cindy Morgan 4.00
19 Karen Lynn Gorney 4.00
20 Larry Hagman 4.00
21 Lee Majors 4.00
22 Morgan Fairchild 4.00
23 Richard Kiel 4.00
24 Tippi Hedren 4.00
25 Walter Koenig 4.00
26 Burt Ward 4.00
27 Barbara Eden 4.00
28 Cedric the Entertainer 5.00
29 Billy Dee Williams 4.00
30 Leonard Nimoy 5.00

Cinema Stars Directors Cut Signatures

NM/M

Production 10-100
2 Burt Reynolds/25 250.00
3 William Shatner/25 150.00
5 Ron Howard/25 125.00
11 Shirley Jones/25 80.00
12 Dom DeLuise/25 60.00
16 Josh Duhamel/25 80.00
17 Catherine Bach/50 100.00
18 Cindy Morgan/100 40.00
19 Karen Lynn Gorney/50 40.00
20 Larry Hagman/25 100.00
22 Morgan Fairchild/50 60.00
23 Richard Kiel/25 75.00
24 Tippi Hedren/25 100.00
25 Walter Koenig/25 100.00
27 Barbara Eden/25 125.00
29 Billy Dee Williams/25 150.00
30 Leonard Nimoy/25 200.00

Cinema Stars Materials

NM/M

Common Card: 8.00
Production 100-500
Golden Era: 1-1.5X
Production 5-50
Silver Screen: 1-1.5X
Production 25-100
Super Stars: 2-3X
Production 5-25
No pricing production 20 or less.
1 John Travolta/Jkt/500 20.00
2 Burt Reynolds/Shirt/500 15.00
3 William Shatner/Shirt/500 15.00
4 Carrie Fisher/Shirt/250 20.00
6 Elliott Gould/Sweater/500 8.00
7 Lou Gossett Jr./Shirt/500 8.00
8 Ernest Borgnine/Shirt/500 10.00
9 Giovanni Ribisi/Shirt/380 8.00
11 Shirley Jones/Skirt/500 10.00
13 Adam West/Shirt/500 15.00
15 Ashley Judd/Shirt/400 20.00
16 Josh Duhamel/Shirt/350 8.00
17 Catherine Bach/Shirt/500 15.00
18 Cindy Morgan/Shirt/500 8.00
20 Larry Hagman/Shirt/350 10.00
21 Lee Majors/Pajamas/500 10.00
22 Morgan Fairchild/Shirt/100 20.00
24 Tippi Hedren/Dress/500 10.00
26 Burt Ward/Shirt/400 10.00
27 Barbara Eden/Shirt/195 20.00
30 Leonard Nimoy/Shirt/400 15.00

Cinema Stars Signatures

NM/M

Production 10-100
Signature Materials: 1-1.5X
Production 4-25
2 Burt Reynolds/25 80.00
3 William Shatner/25 140.00
4 Carrie Fisher/50 150.00
5 Ron Howard/75 75.00
6 Elliott Gould/100 25.00
7 Lou Gossett/50 30.00
8 Ernest Borgnine/50 60.00
9 Giovanni Ribisi/50 25.00
11 Shirley Jones/50 50.00
12 Dom DeLuise/50 40.00
13 Adam West/50 60.00
14 Bernie Mac/50 50.00
15 Ashley Judd/50 160.00
16 Josh Duhamel/50 50.00
17 Catherine Bach/25 75.00
18 Cindy Morgan/25 25.00
19 Karen Lynn Gorney/25 25.00
20 Larry Hagman/50 75.00
21 Lee Majors/25 60.00
22 Morgan Fairchild/25 60.00
23 Richard Kiel/50 25.00
24 Tippi Hedren/25 75.00
25 Walter Koenig/75 50.00
26 Burt Ward/50 50.00
27 Barbara Eden/50 75.00
28 Cedric the Entertainer/50 30.00
29 Billy Dee Williams/50 50.00
30 Leonard Nimoy/25 120.00

Co-Stars Materials

NM/M

Production 50 unless noted.
Golden Era: No Pricing
Production 10 Sets
Silver Screen: 1-1.5X
Production 25 Sets
1 Marilyn Monroe/Skirt, Bette Davis/Dress 150.00
2 Humphrey Bogart/Shirt, Ingrid Bergman/Dress 100.00
3 James Dean/Robe, Natalie Wood/Dress 100.00
4 Burt Reynolds/Shirt, Jackie Gleason/Coat/100 50.00
5 William Shatner/Shirt, Leonard Nimoy/Shirt/100 50.00
6 Adam West/Shirt, Burt Ward/Shirt/100 40.00
7 Rock Hudson/Jkt, James Dean/Robe 100.00
8 Ed O'Neill/Shirt, Katey Sagal/Blouse/100 30.00
9 Dawn Wells/Shirt, Russell Johnson/Shirt/100 40.00
10 Ernest Borgnine/Shirt, Debbie Reynolds/H'chief 40.00

Co-Stars Signatures

NM/M

Production 50 unless noted
1 S. Smith, D. Meyer 100.00
2 Barbara Eden, Larry Hagman 200.00
3 William Shatner, Leonard Nimoy/25 300.00
4 Adam West, Burt Ward 150.00
5 Ed O'Neill, Katey Sagal 150.00
6 Burt Reynolds, Dom DeLuise/25 150.00
7 Ron Howard, Henry Winkler/25 200.00
8 Billy Dee Williams, Carrie Fisher/25 200.00
9 Mickey Rooney, Jan Rooney/25 150.00
10 Dawn Wells, Russell Johnson 150.00

Hollywood Legends

NM/M

Common Card:
Production 500 Sets
1 James Dean 8.00
2 Ingrid Bergman 4.00
3 Gloria Swanson 4.00
4 Rock Hudson 4.00
5 Bette Davis 6.00
6 Jayne Mansfield 8.00
7 Greta Garbo 4.00
8 Ava Gardner 4.00
9 Mae West 4.00
10 Steve McQueen 4.00
11 Audrey Hepburn 6.00
12 Jean Harlow 4.00
13 Lillian Gish 4.00
14 Carole Lombard 4.00
15 James Cagney 4.00
16 Marilyn Monroe 10.00
17 Mary Pickford 4.00
18 Debbie Reynolds 4.00
19 Ginger Rogers 4.00
20 Glenn Ford 4.00
21 Eleanor Powell 4.00
22 Gene Tierney 4.00
23 Lana Turner 4.00
24 Esther Williams 4.00
25 Natalie Wood 4.00
26 Loretta Young 4.00
27 Humphrey Bogart 4.00
28 Marlon Brando 6.00
29 Dorothy Lamour 4.00
30 Tony Curtis 4.00
31 Bob Denver 4.00
32 Errol Flynn 4.00
33 Peter Sellers 4.00
34 Patricia Neal 4.00
35 Mickey Rooney 4.00
36 Marlene Dietrich 4.00
37 Jimmy Stewart 6.00
38 Yvonne De Carlo 4.00
39 Rudolph Valentino 4.00
40 Bing Crosby 4.00

Hollywood Legends Directors Cut Signatures

NM/M

Production 1-25
24 Esther Williams/25 200.00
34 Patricia Neal/25 150.00

Hollywood Legends Materials

NM/M

Common Card:
Production 25-350
Golden Era: 1-1.5X
Production 5-50
Silver Screen: 1-1.5X
Production 10-100
Super Stars: 2-3X
Production 1-25
1 James Dean/Robe/155 100.00
2 Ingrid Bergman/Dress/250 35.00
3 Gloria Swanson/Dress/350 25.00
4 Rock Hudson/Jkt/250 25.00
5 Bette Davis/Dress/250 35.00
6 Jayne Mansfield/Shirt/325 40.00
7 Greta Garbo/Dress/350 35.00
8 Ava Gardner/Dress/325 35.00
9 Mae West/Coat/350 30.00
10 Steve McQueen/Jkt/350 30.00
11 Audrey Hepburn/Dress/325 50.00
12 Jean Harlow/Coat/325 35.00
13 Lillian Gish/Coat/325 30.00
14 Carole Lombard/Dress/350 30.00
15 James Cagney/Coat/350 35.00
16 Marilyn Monroe/Skirt/250 125.00
17 Mary Pickford/Dress/350 25.00
18 Debbie Reynolds/Handkerchief/25 40.00
19 Ginger Rogers/Coat/325 30.00
20 Glenn Ford/Shirt/350 20.00
21 Eleanor Powell/Tights/350 25.00
22 Gene Tierney/Dress/325 25.00
23 Lana Turner/Dress/325 30.00
24 Esther Williams/Bathing Suit/100 25.00
25 Natalie Wood/Dress/250 40.00
26 Loretta Young/Coat/350 25.00
27 Humphrey Bogart/Shirt/350 50.00
28 Marlon Brando/Pants/325 30.00
29 Dorothy Lamour/Dress/325 30.00
30 Tony Curtis/Shirt/325 20.00
31 Bob Denver/Shirt/350 20.00
32 Errol Flynn/Jkt/325 40.00
33 Peter Sellers/Jkt/325 25.00
34 Patricia Neal/Shawl/350 30.00
35 Mickey Rooney/Shirt/325 25.00
36 Marlene Dietrich/Coat/350 30.00
37 Jimmy Stewart/Coat/325 50.00
38 Yvonne De Carlo/Coat/350 25.00
40 Bing Crosby/Shoes/25 200.00

Hollywood Legends Signatures

NM/M

Production 25 Sets
Signature Materials: 1-1.5X
Production 25 Sets
18 Debbie Reynolds 100.00
24 Esther Williams 100.00
30 Tony Curtis 100.00
35 Mickey Rooney 100.00

Private Signings

NM/M

Production 5-1,250 40.00
1 John Travolta/25 180.00
2 Stacy Keibler/250 50.00
4 Steve Guttenberg/300 20.00
5 William Shatner/25 120.00
7 Gretchen Wilson/200 60.00
8 Ultimate Warrior/250 50.00
9 Barbara Eden/25 75.00
10 Carrie Fisher/25 150.00
11 Lori Petty/200 15.00
12 Morgan Fairchild/150 50.00
13 Vince Neil/250 30.00
14 Gail Kim/250 30.00
15 Cedric the Entertainer/135 30.00
16 Corin Nemec/200 15.00
17 Billy Dee Williams/85 50.00
18 Jim Furyk/100 50.00
19 Dick Van Patten 25.00
21 William Fichtner/100 15.00
22 Bob Eubanks/50 25.00
23 Mike Huckabee/275 50.00
24 Jack Hanna/400 20.00
25 Elliott Gould/200 25.00
26 Lou Gossett Jr./50 30.00
28 Tippi Hedren 40.00
29 Walter Koenig/60 50.00
30 Ernest Borgnine/50 50.00
31 Cindy Williams/25 40.00
32 Cindy Morgan/330 15.00
33 Giovanni Ribisi/100 20.00
34 Story Musgrave/250 25.00
35 Esther Williams/50 75.00
36 Connie Mack III/150 10.00
37 Gilbert Gottfried/450 15.00
38 Burt Ward/25 75.00
39 Josh Duhamel/50 50.00
40 Larry Hagman/50 65.00
41 Catherine Hicks/350 20.00
42 Karen Lynn Gorney/418 10.00
43 Larry King/200 30.00
44 Autumn Reeser/364 25.00
45 Mickey Rooney/25 80.00
46 Aidan Quinn/168 15.00
47 Martin Klebba/1,250 10.00
48 Michael Pare'/1,250 10.00
49 Hugh O'Brian/70 25.00
50 Molly Shannon/250 25.00
51 Dee Snider 25.00
52 Melissa Jo Hunter/1,250 10.00
53 Jennie Finch/500 40.00
54 Henry Winkler/50 80.00
55 Neil Patrick Harris/100 30.00
56 Val Kilmer/100 40.00
57 Peter Marshall/200 15.00
58 Clint Howard/100 25.00
59 Buzz Aldrin/50 150.00
60 Heather Cox/500 25.00
61 Angela Simmons/159 15.00
62 Richard Kiel/100 50.00
63 Leonard Nimoy/25 125.00
64 Jan Rooney/175 20.00
66 Bruce Jenner/250 25.00
67 Tom Green/200 20.00
68 Dom DeLuise/105 40.00
69 Bobby Allison/100 25.00
70 Tony Curtis/25 80.00
71 Shawnee Smith 40.00
72 Wink Martindale/95 15.00
73 Tara Conner/150 40.00
74 Sheryl Swoopes/375 20.00
75 Wayne Newton/110 50.00
76 Justine Simmons/250 10.00
77 Keiko Agena/130 15.00
78 Tom Savini/364 15.00
79 David Faustino/150 20.00
80 Adam West/50 60.00
81 Gina Phillips/350 20.00
82 Dawn Wells/100 50.00
83 George Allen/224 15.00
84 Chris Sarandon/312 10.00
86 Katey Sagal/100 40.00
87 Ed O'Neill/100 50.00
88 Dina Meyer/100 40.00
89 Ron Howard/60 80.00
90 Randy Owen/200 25.00
91 Yunjin Kim/400 30.00
92 Chuck Woolery/100 15.00
93 Ed McMahon/470 25.00
94 Stephanie Powers/100 50.00
95 Warwick Davis/250 10.00
96 Scott Baio/200 25.00
97 Russell Johnson/100 40.00
98 Michael Berryman/314 15.00
99 Bernie Mac/85 40.00
100 Ashley Judd/50 180.00

Sports Legends

NM/M

Common Card: 4.00
Production 500 Sets
1 Willie Mays 8.00
2 Jackie Robinson 8.00
3 Walt Frazier 4.00
4 Lou Gehrig 10.00
5 Jim Courier 4.00
6 Tony Esposito 4.00
7 Martina Navratilova 4.00
8 Stan Musial 8.00
9 Patrick Roy 8.00
10 Larry Bird 8.00

Sports Legends Materials

NM/M

Production 25-500
1 Willie Mays/Jsy/100 40.00
2 Jackie Robinson/Jkt/100 50.00
3 Walt Frazier/Jsy/500 10.00
4 Lou Gehrig/Jsy/100 150.00
5 Jim Courier/Shirt/500 10.00
6 Tony Esposito/Jsy/500 10.00
8 Stan Musial/Jsy/25 40.00

Sports Legends Signatures

NM/M

Production 25-50
Signature Materials: 1X
Production 25-50
1 Willie Mays/25 200.00
3 Walt Frazier/25 50.00
5 Jim Courier/50 40.00
6 Tony Esposito/25 50.00
7 Martina Navratilova/50 75.00
8 Stan Musial/25 75.00
9 Patrick Roy/25 125.00
10 Larry Bird/25 125.00

Stars Materials

NM/M

Common Card: 5.00
Production 10-250 .25
1 John Travolta/Jkt/250 15.00
2 Stacy Keibler/Shirt/195 20.00
3 Burt Reynolds/Shirt/250 15.00
4 Steve Guttenberg/Shirt/250 5.00
5 William Shatner/Shirt/250 15.00
6 Lee Majors/Pajamas/250 10.00
8 Ultimate Warrior/Trunks/95 20.00
9 Barbara Eden/Shirt/50 25.00
10 Carrie Fisher/Shirt/50 25.00
11 Lori Petty/Shirt/250 8.00
12 Morgan Fairchild/Shirt/50 25.00
13 Vince Neil/Shirt/250 10.00
16 Corin Nemec/Shirt/250 8.00
18 Jim Furyk/Shirt/250 15.00
19 Dick Van Patten/Shirt/250 8.00
20 Debbie Reynolds/Handkerchief/25 40.00
21 William Fichtner/Shirt/250 5.00
22 Bob Eubanks/Shirt/250 8.00
23 Mike Huckabee/Shirt/250 10.00
25 Elliott Gould/Sweater/250 8.00
26 Lou Gossett Jr./Shirt/250 8.00
27 Catherine Bach/Shirt/250 15.00
28 Tippi Hedren/Dress/250 15.00
30 Ernest Borgnine/Shirt/100 10.00
31 Cindy Williams/Shirt/100 5.00
32 Cindy Morgan/Shirt/190 8.00
33 Giovanni Ribisi/Shirt/250 8.00
35 Esther Williams/Bathing Suit/100 25.00
36 Connie Mack III/Shirt/250 5.00
37 Gilbert Gottfried/Shirt/100 10.00
38 Burt Ward/Shirt/100 15.00
39 Josh Duhamel/Shirt/100 10.00
40 Larry Hagman/Shirt/100 15.00
45 Mickey Rooney/Shirt/80 25.00
46 Aidan Quinn/Pants/250 5.00
47 Martin Klebba/Shirt/250 5.00
49 Hugh O'Brian/Shirt/250 8.00
52 Melissa Jo Hunter/Shirt/25 25.00
55 Neil Patrick Harris/Shirt/250 8.00
63 Leonard Nimoy/Shirt/100 15.00
65 Shirley Jones/Shirt/100 5.00
66 Bruce Jenner/Shirt/250 8.00
67 Tom Green/Pants/250 5.00
69 Bobby Allison/Shirt/250 8.00
70 Tony Curtis/Shirt/85 20.00
72 Wink Martindale/Shirt/250 5.00
73 Tara Conner/Shirt/100 20.00
77 Keiko Agena/Shirt/250 5.00
79 David Faustino/Shirt/250 8.00
80 Adam West/Shirt/100 20.00
82 Dawn Wells/Shirt/100 15.00
83 George Allen/Pants/250 5.00
85 Amanda Beard/Bathing Suit/25 30.00
86 Katey Sagal/Blouse/250 10.00
87 Ed O'Neill/Shirt/250 10.00
88 Dina Meyer/Shirt/55 15.00

92	Chuck Woolery/Pants/250	5.00
96	Scott Baio/Shirt/250	8.00
97	Russell Johnson/Shirt/100	15.00
100	Ashley Judd/Shirt/100	25.00

Stars Signature Materials

NM/M

Production 10-250

1	John Travolta/Jkt/25	180.00
2	Stacy Keibler/Shirt/250	60.00
3	Burt Reynolds/Shirt/25	80.00
5	William Shatner/Shirt/25	120.00
6	Lee Majors/Pajamas/25	60.00
8	Ultimate Warrior/Trunks/50	75.00
9	Barbara Eden/Shirt/100	60.00
10	Carrie Fisher/Shirt/25	160.00
11	Lori Petty/Shirt/200	15.00
12	Morgan Fairchild/Shirt/150	50.00
13	Vince Neil/Shirt/250	30.00
14	Gail Kim/Trunks/150	30.00
16	Corin Nemec/Shirt/200	15.00
18	Jim Furyk/Shirt/100	50.00
19	Dick Van Patten/Shirt/200	20.00
20	Debbie Reynolds/ Handerkerchief/25	100.00
21	William Fichtner/Shirt/250	15.00
22	Bob Eubanks/Shirt/150	20.00
23	Mike Huckabee/Shirt/225	50.00
26	Lou Gossett Jr./Shirt/50	30.00
27	Catherine Bach/Shirt/22	100.00
28	Tippi Hedren/Dress/25	80.00
30	Ernest Borgnine/Shirt/100	50.00
31	Cindy Williams/Shirt/200	25.00
33	Giovanni Ribisi/Shirt/200	20.00
35	Esther Williams/ Bathing Suit/50	80.00
36	Connie Mack III/Shirt/250	10.00
38	Burt Ward/Shirt/100	50.00
45	Mickey Rooney/Shirt/50	80.00
46	Aidan Quinn/Pants/200	15.00
47	Martin Klebba/Shirt/250	15.00
49	Hugh O'Brian/Shirt/200	30.00
52	Melissa Jo Hunter/ Shirt/250	15.00
55	Neil Patrick Harris/ Shirt/100	25.00
56	Val Kilmer/Coat/100	35.00
63	Leonard Nimoy/Shirt/25	125.00
65	Shirley Jones/Skirt/50	50.00
66	Bruce Jenner/Shirt/250	25.00
67	Tom Green/Pants/200	20.00
69	Bobby Allison/Shirt/100	25.00
70	Tony Curtis/Shirt/50	75.00
72	Wink Martindale/Shirt/150	20.00
73	Tara Conner/Shirt/100	50.00
77	Keiko Agena/Shirt/250	15.00
79	David Faustino/Shirt/200	20.00
80	Adam West/Shirt/50	60.00
82	Dawn Wells/Shirt/100	50.00
83	George Allen/Pants/250	15.00
86	Katey Sagal/Blouse/100	40.00
87	Ed O'Neill/Shirt/100	50.00
88	Dina Meyer/Shirt/100	50.00
94	Stephanie Powers/ Handkerchief/25	60.00
96	Scott Baio/Shirt/100	20.00
97	Russell Johnson/Shirt/100	40.00
100	Ashley Judd/Shirt/50	160.00

2007 Donruss Elite Extra Edition

NM/M

Common (1-92):	.25
Common Auto. (93-142):	8.00
Pack (5):	8.00
Box (20):	140.00

1	Andrew Brackman	1.00
2	Austin Gallagher	1.00
3	Brett Cecil	1.00
4	Darwin Barney	1.00
5	David Price	3.00
6	J.P. Arencibia	1.00
7	Josh Donaldson	.50
8	Brandon Hicks	.25
9	Brian Rike	.25
10	Bryan Morris	.25
11	Cale Iorg	.50
12	Casey Weathers	.25
13	Corey Kluber	.25
14	Daniel Moskos	1.00
15	Danny Payne	.25
16	David Kopp	.50
17	Dellin Betances	.50
18	Derrick Robinson	.25
19	Drew Stubbs	.50
20	Eric Eiland	.50
21	Francisco Pena	.25
22	Greg Reynolds	.25
23	Jeff Samardzija	1.00
24	Jess Todd	.50
25	John Tolisano	.50
26	Jordan Zimmerman	.50
27	Julian Sampson	.25
28	Luke Hochevar	1.00
29	Mat Latos	.50
30	Matt Mangini	.25
31	Matt Spencer	.50
32	Matthew Sweeney	.25
33	Max Scherzer	3.00
34	Mitch Canham	.50
35	Nick Schmidt	.25
36	Paul Kelly	.25
37	Ryan Pope	.75
38	Sam Runion	.50
39	Steven Souza	.50
40	Travis Mattair	.75
41	Trystan Magnuson	1.00
42	Willie Middlebrooks	1.00
43	Zack Cozart	.50
44	James Adkins	.50
45	Cory Luebke	.25
46	Aaron Poreda	.50
47	Clayton Mortensen	.50
48	Bradley Suttle	1.00
49	Tony Butler	.50
50	Zach Britton	.50
51	Scott Cousins	.25
52	Wendell Fairley	1.00
53	Eric Sogard	.50
54	Jonathan Lucroy	.50
55	Lars Davis	.25
56	Demetris Nichols	.25
57	Aaron Gray	.25
58	Daequan Cook	.25
59	Derrick Byars	.25
60	Reyshawn Terry	.25
61	Taurean Green	.25
62	Don Haskins	.25
63	Jerry Tarkanian	.50
64	Rick Majerus	.25
65	Rollie Massimino	.25
66	Ara Parseghian	.25
67	Dale Brown	.25
68	Dean Smith	.50
69	Eddie Sutton	.25
70	Frank Broyles	.25
71	Gene Keady	.25
72	Jim Boeheim	.50
73	Norm Stewart	.25
74	Steve Spurrier	.50
75	Tom Osborne	.25
76	Vince Dooley	.25
77	Jennie Finch	.50
78	Amanda Beard	.50
79	Mike Powell	.25
80	Rebecca Lobo	.25
81	Brandi Chastain	.25
82	Clint Dolezel	.25
83	Elvin Hayes	.50
84	Cobi Jones	.25
85	Bill Walton	.50
86	Sidney Moncrief	.25
87	Dominique Wilkins	.50
88	Summer Sanders	.25
89	Michelle Akers	.25
90	Muggsy Bogues	.25
91	Charlie Culberson	.50
92	Jacob Smolinski	1.00
93	Blake Beaven/Auto./719	15.00
94	Brad Chalk/Auto./613	8.00
95	Brett Anderson/Auto./549	40.00
96	Chris Withrow/Auto./700	20.00
97	Clay Fuller/Auto./674	8.00
98	Damon Sublett/Auto./674	25.00
99	Devin Mesoraco/Auto./674	15.00
100	Drew Cumberland/ Auto./744	15.00
101	Jack McGeary/Auto./674	20.00
102	Jake Arrieta/Auto./949	25.00
103	James Simmons/Auto./624	15.00
104	Jarrod Parker/Auto./499	40.00
105	Jason Dominguez/Auto./744	8.00
106	Jason Heyward/Auto./750	50.00
107	Joe Savery/Auto./750	15.00
108	Jon Gilmore/Auto./819	15.00
109	Jordan Walden/Auto./794	30.00
110	Josh Smoker/Auto./719	25.00
111	Josh Vitters/Auto./769	50.00
112	Julio Borbon/Auto./594	15.00
113	Justin Jackson/Auto./850	10.00
114	Kellen Kulbacki/Auto./549	15.00
115	Kevin Ahrens/Auto./794	25.00
116	Kyle Lotzkar/Auto./611	15.00
117	Madison Bumgarner/ Auto./794	35.00
118	Matt Dominguez/Auto./769	25.00
119	Matt LaPorta/Auto./594	60.00
120	Matt Wieters/Auto./799	100.00
121	Michael Burgess/ Auto./672	25.00
122	Michael Main/Auto./794	15.00
123	Michael Moustakas/ Auto./999	60.00
124	Nathan Vineyard/Auto./700	10.00
125	Neil Ramirez/Auto./774	15.00
126	Nick Hagadone/Auto./544	20.00
127	Peter Kozma/Auto./719	15.00
128	Phillippe Aumont/ Auto./674	40.00
129	Preston Mattingly/ Auto./519	25.00
130	Mystery Redemption	100.00
131	Ross Detwiler/Auto./650	15.00
132	Tim Alderson/Auto./719	25.00
133	Todd Frazier/Auto./774	20.00
134	Wes Roemer/Auto./694	15.00
135	Ben Revere/Auto./700	20.00
136	D.J. Strawberry/Auto./374	10.00
137	Alando Tucker/Auto./494	10.00
138	Jared Jordan/Auto./474	8.00
139	Marc Gasol/Auto./474	8.00
140	Stephane Lasme/Auto./674	8.00
141	Austin Jackson/Auto./794	80.00
142	Beau Mills/Auto./624	25.00

Aspirations

Aspirations (1-92):	4-8X
Non Auto. Aspir. (93-142):	.2-.25X

Production 100 Sets

Status

Status (1-92):	6-10X
Non Auto. Status (93-142):	.2-.3X
Production 50 Sets	
Gold Status (1-92):	8-15X
Non Auto. Gold Status:	No Pricing
Production 25 Sets	

Black Status Autographs

Production One Set

College Ties

NM/M

Common Duo:	2.00
Production 1,500 Sets	
Gold:	1X
Production 500 Sets	
Red:	1.5-3X
Production 100 Sets	

1	Daniel Moskos, David Kopp	2.00
2	Jess Todd, Nick Schmidt	2.00
3	J.P. Arencibia, Julio Borbon	2.00
4	Casey Weathers, David Price	3.00
5	Matt LaPorta, Taurean Green	3.00
6	Amanda Beard, Jennie Finch	3.00
7	Demetris Nichols, Jim Boeheim	2.00
8	Danny Payne, Matt Wieters	2.00
9	Darwin Barney, Mitch Canham	2.00
10	James Adkins, Luke Hochevar	2.00
11	Cory Luebke, Daequan Cook	2.00
12	Brett Cecil, D.J. Strawberry	2.00

College Ties Autograph

NM/M

Production 50 or 100

1	Daniel Moskos, David Kopp/100	15.00
2	Jess Todd, Nick Schmidt/100	15.00
3	J.P. Arencibia, Julio Borbon/100	15.00
4	Casey Weathers, David Price/100	50.00
5	Matt LaPorta, Taurean Green/100	30.00
6	Amanda Beard, Jennie Finch/50	60.00
7	Demetris Nichols, Jim Boeheim/50	15.00
8	Danny Payne, Matt Wieters/100	40.00
9	Darwin Barney, Mitch Canham/100	30.00
10	James Adkins, Luke Hochevar/50	30.00
11	Cory Luebke, Daequan Cook/100	20.00
12	Brett Cecil, D.J. Strawberry/50	10.00

College Ties Jerseys

NM/M

Production 50-500	
Prime:	No Pricing
Production 5-50	

1	Daniel Moskos, David Kopp/75	8.00
6	Amanda Beard, Jennie Finch/50	20.00
9	Darwin Barney, Mitch Canham/500	10.00

Collegiate Patches Autographs

NM/M

Production 25-250

1	Amanda Beard/100	40.00
2	Ara Parseghian/250	30.00
4	Burt Reynolds/25	100.00
5	Dale Brown/250	200.00
6	Dean Smith/250	60.00
7	Eddie Sutton/250	30.00
8	Frank Broyles/250	20.00
9	Gene Keady/250	20.00
10	Jennie Finch/249	50.00
11	Jim Boeheim/250	25.00
12	Sheryl Swoopes/250	20.00
14	Rebecca Lobo/250	20.00
15	Ron Howard/25	75.00
16	Steve Spurrier S.Carolina/100	40.00
17	Tom Osborne/249	40.00
18	Vince Dooley/250	25.00
19	Josh Donaldson/250	20.00
20	Cobi Jones/97	25.00
21	Bill Walton/50	40.00
22	Sidney Moncrief/250	20.00
23	Dominique Wilkins/100	40.00
24	Steve Spurrier Florida/100	40.00
25	Drew Stubbs/250	20.00
26	Andrew Brackman/250	30.00
27	Casey Weathers/250	20.00
28	Daniel Moskos/250	20.00
29	David Price/250	75.00
30	Greg Reynolds/250	15.00
31	J.P. Arencibia/249	20.00
32	Jeff Samardzija/150	50.00
33	Julio Borbon/250	15.00
34	Luke Hochevar/100	25.00
35	Matt LaPorta/250	50.00
36	Matt Mangini/250	20.00
37	Matt Wieters/250	80.00
38	Max Scherzer/182	75.00
39	Mitch Canham/250	25.00
40	Nick Schmidt/250	20.00
41	James Adkins/250	15.00
42	Demetris Nichols/250	10.00
43	Aaron Gray/250	15.00
44	Daequan Cook/250	20.00
45	Derrick Byars/250	10.00
46	Reyshawn Terry/250	15.00
47	Taurean Green/250	15.00
48	Summer Sanders/250	25.00
49	Bobby Hurley/250	20.00
50	Muggsy Bogues/250	25.00
51	Jerry Tarkanian/250	20.00
52	Cale Iorg/250	20.00
53	Lynette Woodard/249	15.00
54	Nick Hagadone/250	20.00
55	Trystan Magnuson/248	15.00
64	Matt Spencer/249	15.00
65	Darwin Barney/250	20.00
67	Connie Mack III/100	15.00
68	Mike Powell/99	25.00

School Colors

NM/M

Common Card:	2.00

Production 1,500 Sets

1	David Price	3.00
2	Daniel Moskos	2.00
3	Greg Reynolds	2.00
4	Matt LaPorta	3.00
5	Matt Wieters	3.00
6	Luke Hochevar	2.00
7	Max Scherzer	4.00
8	Alando Tucker	2.00
9	Daequan Cook	2.00
10	Eddie Sutton	2.00
11	Dean Smith	3.00
12	Steve Spurrier	2.00
13	Tom Osborne	2.00
14	Don Haskins	2.00
15	Jerry Tarkanian	2.00
16	Rick Majerus	2.00
17	Rollie Massimino	2.00
18	Ara Parseghian	2.00
19	Dale Brown	2.00
20	Frank Broyles	2.00
21	Gene Keady	2.00
22	Jim Boeheim	2.00
23	Norm Stewart	2.00
24	Vince Dooley	2.00
25	Bill Walton	3.00
26	Nick Schmidt	2.00
27	Burt Reynolds	3.00
28	Ron Howard	2.00
29	Beau Mills	3.00
30	James Simmons	2.00
31	Joe Savery	2.00
32	Ross Detwiler	2.00
33	J.P. Arencibia	2.00
34	Drew Stubbs	2.00

School Colors Autographs

NM/M

Production 10-50

1	David Price/50	80.00
2	Daniel Moskos/50	15.00
3	Greg Reynolds/50	20.00
4	Matt LaPorta/50	80.00
5	Matt Wieters/50	75.00
6	Luke Hochevar/50	20.00
7	Max Scherzer/50	100.00
8	Alando Tucker/50	15.00
9	Daequan Cook/50	20.00
10	Eddie Sutton/25	30.00
12	Steve Spurrier/25	40.00
13	Tom Osborne/25	40.00
14	Don Haskins/25	20.00
15	Jerry Tarkanian/25	25.00
16	Rick Majerus/25	20.00
18	Ara Parseghian/25	30.00
19	Dale Brown/25	20.00
20	Frank Broyles/25	20.00
21	Gene Keady/25	20.00
22	Jim Boeheim/25	30.00
23	Norm Stewart/25	20.00
24	Vince Dooley/25	25.00
25	Bill Walton/25	30.00
26	Nick Schmidt/50	15.00
29	Beau Mills/50	25.00
30	James Simmons/50	15.00
31	Joe Savery/50	30.00
32	Ross Detwiler/50	15.00
33	J.P. Arencibia/50	20.00
34	Drew Stubbs/50	25.00

Signature Aspirations

NM/M

Production 5-100

1	Andrew Brackman/100	50.00
2	Austin Gallagher/100	35.00
3	Brett Cecil/100	20.00
4	Darwin Barney/100	15.00
5	David Price/100	150.00
6	J.P. Arencibia/100	30.00
7	Josh Donaldson/100	25.00
8	Brandon Hicks/100	20.00
9	Brian Rike/100	20.00
10	Bryan Morris/100	15.00
11	Cale Iorg/100	20.00
12	Casey Weathers/100	20.00
13	Corey Kluber/100	10.00
14	Daniel Moskos/100	15.00
15	Danny Payne/50	15.00

16	David Kopp/36	15.00
17	Dellin Betances/50	40.00
18	Derrick Robinson/100	15.00
19	Drew Stubbs/100	20.00
20	Eric Eiland/100	15.00
21	Francisco Pena/100	20.00
22	Greg Reynolds/100	20.00
24	Jess Todd/50	30.00
25	John Tolisano/100	25.00
26	Jordan Zimmerman/75	25.00
27	Julian Sampson/50	15.00
29	Mat Latos/34	40.00
30	Matt Mangini/80	15.00
31	Matt Spencer/30	20.00
32	Matthew Sweeney/100	20.00
34	Mitch Canham/25	40.00
35	Nick Schmidt/25	20.00
36	Paul Kelly/100	15.00
37	Ryan Pope/100	25.00
38	Sam Runion/50	20.00
39	Steven Souza/100	20.00
40	Travis Mattair/50	25.00
41	Trystan Magnuson/50	20.00
42	Willie Middlebrooks/25	50.00
43	Zack Cozart/25	20.00
44	James Adkins/100	20.00
45	Cory Luebke/100	15.00
46	Aaron Poreda/100	20.00
47	Clayton Mortensen/100	10.00
48	Bradley Suttle/100	25.00
49	Tony Butler/100	20.00
50	Zach Britton/100	20.00
51	Scott Cousins/50	15.00
52	Wendell Fairley/100	35.00
53	Eric Sogard/100	10.00
54	Jonathan Lucroy/100	25.00
55	Lars Davis/100	15.00
56	Demetris Nichols/100	10.00
57	Aaron Gray/100	10.00
58	Daequan Cook/50	20.00
59	Derrick Byars/100	10.00
60	Reyshawn Terry/100	10.00
61	Taurean Green/75	15.00
62	Don Haskins/100	15.00
63	Jerry Tarkanian/50	15.00
64	Rick Majerus/100	15.00
66	Ara Parseghian/100	15.00
67	Dale Brown/25	15.00
69	Eddie Sutton/50	20.00
70	Frank Broyles/100	15.00
71	Gene Keady/50	15.00
72	Jim Boeheim/100	20.00
74	Steve Spurrier/25	40.00
75	Tom Osborne/100	30.00
76	Vince Dooley/50	25.00
77	Jennie Finch/50	50.00
79	Mike Powell/100	20.00
80	Rebecca Lobo/100	30.00
81	Brandi Chastain/50	50.00
82	Clint Dolezel/100	10.00
83	Elvin Hayes/100	20.00
84	Cobi Jones/100	20.00
85	Bill Walton/100	25.00
86	Sidney Moncrief/50	15.00
87	Dominique Wilkins/50	20.00
88	Summer Sanders/50	20.00
89	Michelle Akers/100	15.00
90	Muggsy Bogues/100	15.00
91	Charlie Culberson/100	30.00
92	Jacob Smolinski/100	25.00
93	Blake Beaven/100	25.00
94	Brad Chalk/100	15.00
95	Brett Anderson/100	60.00
96	Chris Withrow/100	30.00
97	Clay Fuller/100	15.00
98	Damon Sublett/50	35.00
99	Devin Mesoraco/100	20.00
100	Drew Cumberland/100	20.00
101	Jack McGeary/100	25.00
102	Jake Arrieta/100	35.00
103	James Simmons/50	15.00
104	Jarrod Parker/50	60.00
105	Jason Dominguez/100	10.00
106	Jason Heyward/100	90.00
107	Joe Savery/100	20.00
108	Jon Gilmore/100	25.00
109	Jordan Walden/50	50.00
110	Josh Smoker/100	40.00
111	Josh Vitters/100	80.00
112	Julio Borbon/100	20.00
113	Justin Jackson/50	25.00
114	Kellen Kulbacki/100	20.00
115	Kevin Ahrens/50	40.00
116	Kyle Lotzkar/100	15.00
117	Madison Bumgarner/50	50.00
118	Matt Dominguez/50	40.00
119	Matt LaPorta/100	60.00
120	Matt Wieters/50	175.00
121	Michael Burgess/50	40.00
122	Michael Main/50	30.00
123	Michael Moustakas/100	120.00
124	Nathan Vineyard/100	15.00
125	Neil Ramirez/100	15.00
126	Nick Hagadone/50	40.00
127	Peter Kozma/100	20.00
128	Phillippe Aumont/100	60.00
129	Preston Mattingly/50	40.00
131	Ross Detwiler/100	25.00
132	Tim Alderson/100	50.00
133	Todd Frazier/100	20.00
134	Wes Roemer/100	15.00
135	Ben Revere/100	30.00
136	D.J. Strawberry/50	15.00
137	Alando Tucker/50	15.00
138	Jared Jordan/50	10.00
139	Marc Gasol/50	15.00
140	Stephane Lasme/100	10.00
141	Austin Jackson/50	100.00
142	Beau Mills/50	40.00

Signature Status

NM/M

Production 1-50
Gold Status: No Pricing
Production 1-10

1	Andrew Brackman/50	60.00
2	Austin Gallagher/50	40.00
3	Brett Cecil/50	25.00
4	Darwin Barney/50	20.00
5	David Price/50	180.00
6	J.P. Arencibia/50	40.00
7	Josh Donaldson/50	40.00
8	Brandon Hicks/50	25.00
9	Brian Rike/50	25.00
10	Bryan Morris/50	20.00
11	Cale Iorg/50	25.00
12	Casey Weathers/50	25.00
13	Corey Kluber/50	10.00
14	Daniel Moskos/50	20.00
15	Danny Payne/25	20.00
16	David Kopp/25	15.00
17	Dellin Betances/25	50.00
18	Derrick Robinson/50	20.00
19	Drew Stubbs/50	25.00
20	Eric Eiland/50	20.00
21	Francisco Pena/50	25.00
22	Greg Reynolds/50	25.00
24	Jess Todd/25	40.00
25	John Tolisano/50	30.00
26	Jordan Zimmerman/25	35.00
27	Julian Sampson/25	20.00
29	Mat Latos/25	40.00
30	Matt Mangini/50	20.00
32	Matthew Sweeney/50	25.00
36	Paul Kelly/50	20.00
37	Ryan Pope/50	30.00
38	Sam Runion/25	25.00
39	Steven Souza/50	25.00
40	Travis Mattair/25	30.00
41	Trystan Magnuson/25	25.00
44	James Adkins/50	25.00
45	Cory Luebke/50	20.00
46	Aaron Poreda/50	25.00
47	Clayton Mortensen/50	15.00
48	Bradley Suttle/50	30.00
49	Tony Butler/50	25.00
50	Zach Britton/50	25.00
52	Wendell Fairley/50	40.00
53	Eric Sogard/50	15.00
54	Jonathan Lucroy/50	30.00
55	Lars Davis/50	20.00
56	Demetris Nichols/50	15.00
57	Aaron Gray/50	15.00
58	Daequan Cook/25	20.00
59	Derrick Byars/50	10.00
60	Reyshawn Terry/50	10.00
61	Taurean Green/29	20.00
62	Don Haskins/50	20.00
63	Jerry Tarkanian/25	20.00
64	Rick Majerus/50	20.00
66	Ara Parseghian/50	20.00
69	Eddie Sutton/25	25.00
70	Frank Broyles/50	20.00
71	Gene Keady/25	20.00
72	Jim Boeheim/50	25.00
75	Tom Osborne/50	40.00
76	Vince Dooley/25	30.00
77	Jennie Finch/25	60.00
79	Mike Powell/50	25.00
80	Rebecca Lobo/50	40.00
81	Brandi Chastain/25	50.00
82	Clint Dolezel/50	10.00
83	Elvin Hayes/50	25.00
84	Cobi Jones/50	25.00
85	Bill Walton/50	30.00
86	Sidney Moncrief/25	20.00
87	Dominique Wilkins/25	25.00
88	Summer Sanders/25	25.00
89	Michelle Akers/50	15.00
90	Muggsy Bogues/50	15.00
91	Charlie Culberson/50	35.00
92	Jacob Smolinski/50	30.00
93	Blake Beaven/50	30.00
94	Brad Chalk/50	20.00
95	Brett Anderson/50	75.00
96	Chris Withrow/50	35.00
97	Clay Fuller/50	20.00
98	Damon Sublett/25	40.00
99	Devin Mesoraco/50	25.00
100	Drew Cumberland/50	25.00
101	Jack McGeary/50	30.00
102	Jake Arrieta/50	40.00
103	James Simmons/25	20.00
104	Jarrod Parker/25	80.00
105	Jason Dominguez/50	15.00
106	Jason Heyward/50	100.00
107	Joe Savery/50	25.00
108	Jon Gilmore/50	30.00
109	Jordan Walden/25	75.00
110	Josh Smoker/50	50.00
111	Josh Vitters/50	100.00
112	Julio Borbon/50	25.00
113	Justin Jackson/25	30.00
114	Kellen Kulbacki/50	25.00
115	Kevin Ahrens/25	50.00
116	Kyle Lotzkar/50	20.00
117	Madison Bumgarner/25	60.00
118	Matt Dominguez/25	50.00
119	Matt LaPorta/50	75.00
120	Matt Wieters/25	200.00
121	Michael Burgess/25	60.00
122	Michael Main/25	40.00
123	Michael Moustakas/50	180.00
124	Nathan Vineyard/50	20.00
125	Neil Ramirez/50	20.00
126	Nick Hagadone/25	60.00
127	Peter Kozma/50	25.00
128	Phillippe Aumont/50	75.00
129	Preston Mattingly/25	50.00
131	Ross Detwiler/50	30.00
132	Tim Alderson/50	60.00
133	Todd Frazier/50	30.00
134	Wes Roemer/50	20.00
135	Ben Revere/50	40.00
136	D.J. Strawberry/25	20.00
137	Alando Tucker/25	20.00
138	Jared Jordan/25	15.00
139	Marc Gasol/25	15.00
340	Stephane Lasme/50	10.00
141	Austin Jackson/25	150.00
142	Beau Mills/25	50.00

Signature Turn of the Century

NM/M

Production 10-500

1	Andrew Brackman/500	35.00
2	Austin Gallagher/500	20.00
3	Brett Cecil/500	20.00
4	Darwin Barney/500	15.00
5	David Price/500	75.00
6	J.P. Arencibia/500	20.00
7	Josh Donaldson/500	20.00
8	Brandon Hicks/419	20.00
9	Brian Rike/500	20.00
10	Bryan Morris/500	15.00
11	Cale Iorg/397	20.00
12	Casey Weathers/500	20.00
13	Corey Kluber/419	8.00
14	Daniel Moskos/500	15.00
15	Danny Payne/394	10.00
16	David Kopp/449	10.00
17	Dellin Betances/494	30.00
18	Derrick Robinson/500	15.00
19	Drew Stubbs/494	20.00
20	Eric Eiland/419	15.00
21	Francisco Pena/396	20.00
22	Greg Reynolds/500	20.00
23	Jeff Samardzija/219	30.00
24	Jess Todd/394	20.00
25	John Tolisano/419	20.00
26	Jordan Zimmerman/469	20.00
27	Julian Sampson/494	10.00
28	Luke Hochevar/158	25.00
29	Mat Latos/499	25.00
30	Matt Mangini/500	15.00
31	Matt Spencer/500	10.00
32	Matthew Sweeney/500	20.00
33	Max Scherzer/250	150.00
34	Mitch Canham/250	25.00
35	Nick Schmidt/209	10.00
36	Paul Kelly/500	15.00
37	Ryan Pope/500	20.00
38	Sam Runion/494	15.00
39	Steven Souza/500	15.00
40	Travis Mattair/494	20.00
41	Trystan Magnuson/246	15.00
42	Willie Middlebrooks/409	30.00
43	Zack Cozart/409	10.00
44	James Adkins/500	15.00
45	Cory Luebke/469	10.00
46	Aaron Poreda/500	15.00
47	Clayton Mortensen/500	8.00
48	Bradley Suttle/500	20.00
49	Tony Butler/419	15.00
50	Zach Britton/437	15.00
51	Scott Cousins/500	8.00
52	Wendell Fairley/500	30.00
53	Eric Sogard/500	8.00
54	Jonathan Lucroy/500	20.00
55	Lars Davis/500	10.00
56	Demetris Nichols/500	8.00
57	Aaron Gray/500	8.00
58	Daequan Cook/494	10.00
59	Derrick Byars/300	8.00
60	Reyshawn Terry/300	8.00
61	Taurean Green/500	10.00
62	Don Haskins/194	15.00
63	Jerry Tarkanian/144	15.00
64	Rick Majerus/194	15.00
66	Ara Parseghian/69	15.00
67	Dale Brown/89	15.00
69	Eddie Sutton/144	15.00
70	Frank Broyles/69	15.00
71	Gene Keady/144	15.00
74	Steve Spurrier/59	25.00
75	Tom Osborne/320	25.00
76	Vince Dooley/91	20.00
77	Jennie Finch/119	50.00
79	Mike Powell/119	20.00
80	Rebecca Lobo/234	25.00
81	Brandi Chastain/94	40.00
82	Clint Dolezel/243	8.00
83	Elvin Hayes/344	15.00
84	Cobi Jones/247	15.00
86	Sidney Moncrief/169	15.00
88	Summer Sanders/169	15.00
89	Michelle Akers/344	10.00
90	Muggsy Bogues/94	15.00
91	Charlie Culberson/500	25.00
92	Jacob Smolinski/500	20.00
93	Blake Beaven/100	25.00
94	Brad Chalk/100	15.00
95	Brett Anderson/145	50.00
96	Chris Withrow/168	30.00
97	Clay Fuller/145	15.00
98	Damon Sublett/220	30.00
99	Devin Mesoraco/145	20.00
100	Drew Cumberland/125	20.00
101	Jack McGeary/145	25.00
102	Jake Arrieta/145	30.00
103	James Simmons/100	15.00
104	Jarrod Parker/55	60.00
105	Jason Dominguez/100	10.00
106	Jason Heyward/169	65.00
107	Joe Savery/119	20.00
108	Jon Gilmore/100	25.00
109	Jordan Walden/100	40.00
110	Josh Smoker/200	30.00
111	Josh Vitters/150	80.00
112	Julio Borbon/100	20.00
113	Justin Jackson/100	20.00
114	Kellen Kulbacki/145	20.00
115	Kevin Ahrens/100	30.00
116	Kyle Lotzkar/100	15.00
117	Madison Bumgarner/100	40.00
118	Matt Dominguez/100	30.00
119	Matt LaPorta/100	60.00
120	Matt Wieters/100	150.00
121	Michael Burgess/100	30.00
122	Michael Main/100	25.00
123	Michael Moustakas/345	70.00
124	Nathan Vineyard/119	15.00
125	Neil Ramirez/145	15.00
126	Nick Hagadone/100	30.00
127	Peter Kozma/100	20.00
128	Phillippe Aumont/120	60.00
129	Preston Mattingly/100	35.00
131	Ross Detwiler/119	25.00
132	Tim Alderson/100	50.00
133	Todd Frazier/145	20.00
134	Wes Roemer/100	15.00
135	Ben Revere/119	30.00
136	D.J. Strawberry/100	10.00
137	Alando Tucker/100	10.00
138	Jared Jordan/100	10.00
139	Marc Gasol/100	10.00
140	Stephane Lasme/145	10.00
141	Austin Jackson/100	80.00
142	Beau Mills/100	30.00

Throwback Threads

NM/M

Common Player: 5.00
Production 500 unless noted.
Prime: No Pricing
Production 3-50

1	Brandi Chastain	20.00
2	Amanda Beard/44	15.00
3	Drew Stubbs	5.00
4	Drew Cumberland	5.00
5	Clint Dolezel	5.00
6	Mat Latos	5.00
7	Brett Cecil	5.00
8	Vince Dooley	8.00
9	Brett Anderson	5.00
10	Casey Weathers/75	5.00
11	Daniel Moskos	5.00
12	Darwin Barney	5.00
13	Kellen Kulbacki	5.00
14	Matt Dominguez	8.00
15	Matt Mangini	5.00
16	Mitch Canham	5.00
18	Willie Middlebrooks	8.00
19	Mike Powell	5.00
20	Steve Spurrier	5.00
21	Dale Brown	5.00
22	Don Haskins	5.00
23	Nick Schmidt	5.00
24	Zack Cozart	5.00

Throwback Threads Auto.

NM/M

Production 50 or 100
Prime Auto.: No Pricing
Production 1-25

1	Brandi Chastain/100	50.00
2	Amanda Beard/50	40.00
3	Drew Stubbs/100	15.00
4	Drew Cumberland/100	15.00
5	Clint Dolezel/100	15.00
6	Mat Latos/100	25.00
9	Brett Anderson/100	50.00
10	Casey Weathers/100	15.00
11	Daniel Moskos/100	15.00
12	Darwin Barney/100	25.00
13	Kellen Kulbacki/100	20.00
14	Matt Dominguez/100	30.00
15	Matt Mangini/100	15.00
16	Mitch Canham/100	20.00
18	Willie Middlebrooks/100	25.00
19	Mike Powell/100	25.00
20	Steve Spurrier/50	40.00
21	Dale Brown/50	25.00
22	Don Haskins/100	15.00
23	Nick Schmidt/100	20.00
24	Zack Cozart/100	15.00

2008 Donruss Celebrity Cuts

NM/M

Complete Set (100):
Common Celebrity: 3.00
Production 499 Sets
Hobby Box (One Pack): 120.00

1	Adam West	3.00
2	Ashley Judd	3.00
3	Angie Dickinson	3.00
4	Barbara Eden	3.00
5	Bernie Mac	3.00
6	Betty Garrett	3.00

7 Billy Dee Williams 3.00
8 Bobby Allison 3.00
9 Burt Reynolds 5.00
10 Burt Ward 3.00
11 Buzz Aldrin 3.00
12 Carrie Fisher 3.00
13 Cedric the Entertainer 3.00
14 Cindy Williams 3.00
15 Dawn Wells 3.00
16 Debbie Reynolds 3.00
17 Dick Van Patten 3.00
18 Dolores Hart 3.00
19 Dom DeLuise 3.00
20 Christina Applegate 3.00
21 Doug Jones 3.00
22 Ed O'Neill 3.00
23 Elliott Gould 3.00
24 Ernest Borgnine 3.00
25 Erik Estrada 3.00
26 Esther Williams 3.00
27 Ed Asner 3.00
28 Joyce DeWitt 3.00
29 Helen Slater 3.00
30 Giovanni Ribisi 3.00
31 Gloria Stuart 3.00
32 Barbara Bush 3.00
33 Henry Winkler 3.00
34 Hugh O'Brian 3.00
35 Jonathan Winters 3.00
36 Julie Newmar 3.00
37 Jackie Robinson 8.00
38 James Dean 5.00
39 Jane Russell 3.00
40 Jerry Lewis 3.00
41 Jim Courier 3.00
42 Kathryn Grayson 3.00
43 John Travolta 5.00
44 Josh Duhamel 3.00
45 Katey Sagal 3.00
46 Knute Rockne 3.00
47 John Wooden 6.00
48 Larry Bird 6.00
49 Larry Hagman 3.00
50 Lee Majors 3.00
51 Leonard Nimoy 5.00
52 Kathie Lee Gifford 3.00
53 Lou Gehrig 8.00
54 Lou Gossett Jr. 3.00
55 Margaret O'Brien 3.00
56 Marilyn Monroe 8.00
57 Lee Meriwether 3.00
58 Marlon Brando 3.00
59 Martina Navratilova 3.00
60 Maud Adams 3.00
61 Mickey Rooney 3.00
62 Molly Shannon 3.00
63 Lindsay Wagner 3.00
64 Mark Hamill 3.00
65 Neil Patrick Harris 3.00
66 George Bush 5.00
67 Patrick Roy 8.00
68 Kurt Russell 3.00
69 Peggy Fleming 3.00
70 Randy Couture 3.00
71 Quentin Tarantino 3.00
72 Richard Kiel 3.00
73 Richard Petty 5.00
74 Robert Wagner 3.00
75 Ricardo Montalban 3.00
76 Ron Howard 3.00
77 Russell Johnson 3.00
78 Scott Baio 3.00
79 Shawnee Smith 3.00
80 Shirley Jones 3.00
81 Stan Musial 6.00
82 Stella Stevens 3.00
83 Stephanie Powers 3.00
84 Steve Guttenberg 3.00
85 Rob Schneider 3.00
86 Ted Williams 8.00
87 Tippi Hedren 3.00
88 Tony Curtis 3.00
89 Tony Esposito 4.00
90 Ultimate Warrior 3.00
91 Val Kilmer 3.00
92 Walt Frazier 3.00
93 Walter Koenig 3.00
94 Wayne Newton 3.00
95 William Shatner 5.00
96 Willie Mays 6.00
97 Willie Nelson 3.00
98 Margot Kidder 3.00
99 Yunjin Kim 3.00
100 Priscilla Barnes 3.00

Century Silver

Silver (1-100): 2X
Production 50 Sets

Century Gold

Gold (1-100): 3-4X
Production 25 Sets

Century Platinum

Production One Set

Century Gold Signatures

NM/M

Production 1-200
Platium Autos.: No Pricing
Production One Set
3 Angie Dickinson/200 40.00
6 Betty Garrett/200 25.00
8 Bobby Allison/200 25.00
10 Burt Ward/5
11 Buzz Aldrin/50 150.00
13 Cedric the Entertainer/200 20.00
15 Dawn Wells/50 40.00
18 Dolores Hart/200 25.00
19 Dom DeLuise/50 30.00
20 Christina Applegate/25 100.00
21 Doug Jones/50 15.00
25 Erik Estrada/25 25.00
27 Ed Asner/200 25.00
28 Joyce DeWitt/100 30.00
29 Helen Slater/200 25.00
30 Giovanni Ribisi/50 25.00
31 Gloria Stuart/100 40.00
33 Henry Winkler/34 60.00
35 Jonathan Winters/100 35.00
36 Julie Newmar/200 50.00
39 Jane Russell/200 50.00
41 Jim Courier/200 20.00
44 Josh Duhamel/50 40.00
48 Larry Bird/50 75.00
52 Kathie Lee Gifford/200 30.00
55 Margaret O'Brien/200 25.00
57 Lee Meriwether/200 30.00
59 Martina Navratilova/100 30.00
62 Molly Shannon/50 20.00
63 Lindsay Wagner/50 40.00
65 Neil Patrick Harris/30 40.00
67 Patrick Roy/75 60.00
69 Peggy Fleming/200 40.00
70 Randy Couture/100 75.00
71 Quentin Tarantino/50 70.00
72 Richard Kiel/50 25.00
73 Richard Petty/200 50.00
74 Robert Wagner/100 25.00
78 Scott Baio/50 20.00
79 Shawnee Smith/50 40.00
81 Stan Musial/100 60.00
83 Stephanie Powers/25 60.00
84 Steve Guttenberg/99 20.00
85 Rob Schneider/36 40.00
87 Tippi Hedren/50 50.00
89 Tony Esposito/50 35.00
90 Ultimate Warrior/50 50.00
92 Walt Frazier/50 35.00
93 Walter Koenig/50 40.00
94 Wayne Newton/50 50.00
96 Willie Mays/50 125.00
97 Willie Nelson/50 150.00
98 Margot Kidder/200 25.00
100 Priscilla Barnes/200 30.00

Award Winners Autos.

NM/M

Production 25-55
1 Ernest Borgnine/55 60.00
2 Lou Gossett Jr./25 60.00
3 Quentin Tarantino/50 85.00

Celebrity Cuts

NM/M

Production 1-25
26 Ernest Borgnine/25 60.00
29 Patricia Neal/25 50.00

Century Materials

NM/M

Production 5-100
Combo Materials: 1-1.5X
Production 5-50
Prime Materials: 1.5-2X
Production 1-50
Combo Prime Materials: No Pricing
Production 1-10
No pricing production 20 or less.
1 Adam West/75 15.00
2 Ashley Judd/50 20.00
4 Barbara Eden/100 20.00
5 Bernie Mac/100 15.00
8 Bobby Allison/100 10.00
9 Burt Reynolds/100 20.00
14 Cindy Williams/100 8.00
15 Dawn Wells/100 15.00
17 Dick Van Patten/100 8.00
20 Christina Applegate/100 20.00
21 Doug Jones/100 10.00
22 Ed O'Neill/100 15.00
23 Elliott Gould/75 10.00
24 Ernest Borgnine/50 10.00
25 Erik Estrada/100 8.00
27 Ed Asner/100 10.00
31 Gloria Stuart/100 25.00
32 Barbara Bush/50 15.00
33 Henry Winkler/50 15.00
34 Hugh O'Brian/50 8.00
35 Jonathan Winters/100 15.00
36 Julie Newmar/100 20.00
37 Jackie Robinson/100 30.00
38 James Dean/100 40.00
39 Jane Russell/100 25.00
40 Jerry Lewis/100 25.00
41 Jim Courier/100 8.00
42 Kathryn Grayson/100 20.00
43 John Travolta/100 20.00
45 Katey Sagal/100 10.00
46 Knute Rockne/100 75.00
48 Larry Bird/100 35.00
49 Larry Hagman/50 8.00
50 Lee Majors/100 10.00
52 Kathie Lee Gifford/100 15.00
53 Lou Gehrig/50 60.00
54 Lou Gossett Jr./50 15.00
55 Margaret O'Brien/100 15.00
56 Marilyn Monroe/100 100.00
57 Lee Meriwether/100 15.00
58 Marlon Brando/100 25.00
59 Martina Navratilova/50 15.00
62 Molly Shannon/100 10.00
65 Neil Patrick Harris/100 10.00
67 Patrick Roy/100 20.00
68 Kurt Russell/100 20.00
70 Randy Couture/100 30.00
73 Richard Petty/100 20.00
77 Russell Johnson/100 15.00
78 Scott Baio/100 8.00
81 Stan Musial/100 25.00
82 Stella Stevens/100 10.00
83 Stephanie Powers/36 20.00
84 Steve Guttenberg/100 10.00
85 Rob Schneider/100 10.00
87 Tippi Hedren/100 20.00
89 Tony Esposito/100 10.00
91 Val Kilmer/100 10.00
92 Walt Frazier/100 15.00
96 Willie Mays/100 25.00
99 Yunjin Kim/100 15.00
100 Priscilla Barnes/100 10.00

Century Signature Materials

NM/M

Production 1-50
Prime Autos.: 1-1.5X
Production 1-50
Combo Autos.: No Pricing
Production 1-10
Combo Prime Autos.: No Pricing
Production 1-25
No pricing production 20 or less.
1 Adam West/25 60.00
8 Bobby Allison/50 30.00
17 Dick Van Patten/50 25.00
21 Doug Jones/50 25.00
27 Ed Asner/50 30.00
33 Henry Winkler/50 60.00
41 Jim Courier/50 25.00
48 Larry Bird/50 90.00
49 Larry Hagman/50 35.00
55 Margaret O'Brien/50 40.00
62 Molly Shannon/50 30.00
85 Rob Schneider/25 50.00
96 Willie Mays/50 125.00

Combo Cuts

No Pricing
Production One Set

Hollywood Letter Autos.

NM/M

Production 45-99
1 Burt Reynolds/45 75.00
2 Debbie Reynolds/99 75.00
3 Ernest Borgnine/99 60.00
4 Lou Gossett Jr./45 50.00
5 Mickey Rooney/45 85.00
6 Ron Howard/72 85.00
7 Tony Curtis/45 75.00
9 Elliott Gould/45 50.00
10 Leonard Nimoy/44 100.00
11 Christina Applegate/45 100.00
12 Ricardo Montalban/45 80.00

Hollywood Icons

NM/M

Common Icon: 4.00
Production 200 Sets
Gold: 2-3X
Production 25 Sets
1 Audrey Hepburn 4.00
2 Ava Gardner 4.00
3 Bette Davis 4.00
4 Bing Crosby 4.00
5 Carole Lombard 4.00
6 Dorothy Lamour 4.00
7 Errol Flynn 4.00
8 Gene Tierney 4.00
9 Ginger Rogers 4.00
10 Gloria Swanson 4.00
11 Greta Garbo 4.00
12 Humphrey Bogart 4.00
13 Ingrid Bergman 4.00
14 Jackie Gleason 4.00
15 James Cagney 4.00
16 James Dean 6.00
17 Jimmy Stewart 6.00
18 Jayne Mansfield 4.00
19 Jean Harlow 4.00
20 Lana Turner 4.00
21 Lillian Gish 4.00
22 Loretta Young 4.00
23 Mae West 4.00
24 Marilyn Monroe 8.00
25 Marlene Dietrich 4.00
26 Marlon Brando 4.00
27 Mary Pickford 4.00
28 Natalie Wood 4.00
29 Rock Hudson 4.00
30 Steve McQueen 4.00
31 Yvonne De Carlo 4.00
32 Patricia Neal 4.00
33 Glenn Ford 4.00
34 Eleanor Powell 4.00
35 Bob Denver 4.00
36 Peter Sellers 4.00
37 Rudolph Valentino 4.00
38 Johnny Weissmuller 4.00
39 Montgomery Clift 4.00
40 Olivia de Havilland 4.00
41 Henry Fonda 4.00
42 John Wayne 6.00
43 Gene Kelly 4.00
44 Ed O'Neill 4.00
45 Katey Sagal 4.00
46 Ron Howard 4.00
47 Wayne Newton 4.00
48 Esther Williams 4.00
49 Ernest Borgnine 4.00
50 Shirley Jones 4.00
51 Lou Gossett Jr. 4.00
52 Debbie Reynolds 4.00
53 Tony Curtis 4.00
54 Mickey Rooney 4.00
55 John Travolta 4.00
56 Burt Reynolds 6.00
57 William Shatner 6.00
58 Lee Majors 4.00
59 Barbara Eden 4.00
60 Carrie Fisher 4.00
61 Elliott Gould 4.00
62 Val Kilmer 4.00
63 Larry Hagman 4.00
64 Quentin Tarantino 4.00
65 Leonard Nimoy 6.00
66 Adam West 4.00
67 Ashley Judd 4.00
68 Frank Sinatra 4.00
69 Fred Astaire 4.00
70 George Burns 4.00
71 Leslie Howard 4.00
72 John Gilbert 4.00
73 Orson Welles 4.00
74 William Holden 4.00
75 Rita Hayworth 4.00

Hollywood Icons Materials

NM/M

Production 100 unless noted.
Combo Materials: 1-1.5X
Production 5-50
Prime Materials: 1.5X
Production 1-50
Combo Prime Materials: No Pricing
Production 1-10
Prime Studio Die-Cuts: No Pricing
Production 1-10
1 Audrey Hepburn 50.00
2 Ava Gardner 20.00
3 Bette Davis 35.00
4 Bing Crosby/50 30.00
5 Carole Lombard 20.00
6 Dorothy Lamour 20.00
7 Errol Flynn 25.00
8 Gene Tierney 20.00
9 Ginger Rogers 25.00
10 Gloria Swanson 20.00
11 Greta Garbo 20.00
12 Humphrey Bogart 35.00
13 Ingrid Bergman 25.00
14 Jackie Gleason 35.00
15 James Cagney 35.00
16 James Dean 50.00
17 Jimmy Stewart 35.00
18 Jayne Mansfield 25.00
19 Jean Harlow 25.00
20 Lana Turner 20.00
21 Lillian Gish 20.00
22 Loretta Young 25.00
23 Mae West 25.00
24 Marilyn Monroe 80.00
25 Marlene Dietrich 20.00
26 Marlon Brando 25.00
27 Mary Pickford 20.00
28 Natalie Wood 35.00
29 Rock Hudson 20.00
30 Steve McQueen 25.00
31 Yvonne De Carlo 25.00
33 Glenn Ford 15.00
34 Eleanor Powell/50 20.00
35 Bob Denver 25.00
36 Peter Sellers 20.00
38 Johnny Weissmuller 30.00
39 Montgomery Clift 25.00
42 John Wayne 60.00
43 Gene Kelly 25.00
44 Ed O'Neill 15.00
45 Katey Sagal 15.00
49 Ernest Borgnine/50 15.00
51 Lou Gossett Jr. 20.00
52 Debbie Reynolds/50 25.00
55 John Travolta 20.00
56 Burt Reynolds 20.00
58 Lee Majors 15.00
59 Barbara Eden/25 35.00
61 Elliott Gould 15.00
62 Val Kilmer 15.00
63 Larry Hagman 15.00
66 Adam West/50 15.00
67 Ashley Judd/25 25.00
71 Leslie Howard 15.00
74 William Holden 20.00

Hollywood Icons Cut Sigs.

NM/M

Production 1-100
31 Yvonne De Carlo/100 80.00
32 Patricia Neal/100 50.00
59 Barbara Eden/40 80.00
64 Quentin Tarantino/100 80.00
66 Adam West/25 125.00
67 Ashley Judd/25 150.00

Hollywood Icons Gold Autos.

NM/M

No Pricing 4.00
Production 1-14
Platinum Autos.: No Pricing
Production One Set

Hollywd Icons Signature Materials

NM/M
Production 1-25 4.00
Prime Autos: No Pricing
Production 1-5
Combo Material Auto.: No Pricing
Production 1-25
Combo Prime Auto.: No Pricing
Production 1-10
56 Burt Reynolds/25 75.00
63 Larry Hagman/25 35.00

Hollywood Icons Quad Die-Cut

NM/M
Production 25 unless noted. 4.00
Prime Quads: No Pricing
Production 1-25
1 Audrey Hepburn 180.00
2 Ava Gardner 50.00
3 Bette Davis 60.00
5 Carole Lombard 50.00
6 Dorothy Lamour 50.00
7 Errol Flynn 60.00
8 Gene Tierney 50.00
9 Ginger Rogers 60.00
10 Gloria Swanson 30.00
13 Ingrid Bergman 60.00
14 Jackie Gleason 60.00
15 James Cagney 75.00
16 James Dean 180.00
17 Jimmy Stewart 120.00
19 Jean Harlow 50.00
20 Lana Turner 50.00
21 Lillian Gish 40.00
22 Loretta Young 50.00
23 Mae West 40.00
24 Marilyn Monroe 200.00
25 Marlene Dietrich 50.00
26 Marlon Brando 60.00
27 Mary Pickford 40.00
30 Steve McQueen 60.00
31 Yvonne De Carlo 40.00
32 Patricia Neal 40.00
33 Glenn Ford 35.00
35 Bob Denver 50.00
36 Peter Sellers 40.00
38 Johnny Weissmuller 50.00
39 Montgomery Clift 60.00
42 John Wayne 120.00
45 Katey Sagal 30.00
55 John Travolta 50.00
56 Burt Reynolds 80.00
58 Lee Majors 30.00
59 Barbara Eden 50.00
62 Val Kilmer 40.00
74 William Holden 60.00

Movie Stars

NM/M
Common Movie Star: 4.00
Production 200 Sets
Gold: 2-3X
Production 25 Sets
Platinum: No Pricing
Production One Set
1 Adam West 4.00
2 Barbara Eden 4.00
3 Billy Dee Williams 4.00
4 Burt Reynolds 6.00
5 Burt Ward 4.00
6 Carrie Fisher 4.00
7 Debbie Reynolds 4.00
8 Ernest Borgnine 4.00
9 Esther Williams 4.00
10 Hugh O'Brian 4.00
11 Josh Duhamel 4.00
12 Larry Hagman 4.00
13 Lee Majors 4.00
14 Leonard Nimoy 6.00
15 Lou Gossett Jr. 4.00
16 Richard Kiel 4.00
17 Ashley Judd 6.00
18 Shirley Jones 4.00
19 Tippi Hedren 4.00
20 Tony Curtis 4.00
21 Walter Koenig 4.00
22 William Shatner 6.00
23 Mickey Rooney 4.00
24 John Travolta 4.00
25 Elliott Gould 4.00
26 Val Kilmer 4.00
27 Patricia Neal 4.00
28 Ricardo Montalban 4.00
29 Rob Schneider 4.00
30 Jerry Lewis 4.00

Movie Stars Gold Signatures

NM/M
Production 2-50
Platinum Autos.: No Pricing
Production 1-10
12 Larry Hagman/50 40.00
16 Richard Kiel/50 30.00
20 Tony Curtis/38 60.00
29 Rob Schneider/25 40.00
30 Jerry Lewis/25 75.00

Movie Stars Materials

NM/M
Production 1-100
Prime Materials: No Pricing
Production 1-20
Combo Materials: 1-1.5X
Production 5-100
Combo Prime Materials: No Pricing
Production 1-25
1 Adam West/50 20.00
2 Barbara Eden/100 25.00
4 Burt Reynolds/100 20.00
7 Debbie Reynolds/50 25.00
10 Hugh O'Brian/100 8.00
11 Josh Duhamel/100 8.00
12 Larry Hagman/100 10.00
13 Lee Majors/100 15.00
15 Lou Gossett Jr./50 15.00
17 Ashley Judd/25 25.00
19 Tippi Hedren/100 15.00
24 John Travolta/100 15.00
25 Elliott Gould/100 10.00
26 Val Kilmer/100 15.00
27 Patricia Neal/100 15.00
28 Ricardo Montalban/50 15.00
29 Rob Schneider/50 15.00
30 Jerry Lewis/50 10.00

Movie Stars Material Auto.

NM/M
Production 1-50 4.00
Prime Auto.: No Pricing
Production 1-5
Combo Material Auto.: 1-1.5X
Production 1-50
Combo Material Prime Auto.: No Pricing
Production 1-10
11 Josh Duhamel/50 40.00
12 Larry Hagman/50 40.00
19 Tippi Hedren/18 50.00
29 Rob Schneider/25 40.00
30 Jerry Lewis/25 75.00

Movie Stars Cut Auto. Var. 1

NM/M
Production 2-40
3 Billy Dee Williams/35 75.00
16 Richard Kiel/25 40.00
23 Mickey Rooney/25 100.00
27 Patricia Neal/25 50.00

Movie Stars Cut Auto. Var. 2

NM/M
Production 2-40
11 Josh Duhamel/22 50.00
19 Tippi Hedren/27 60.00
26 Val Kilmer/20 60.00

Movie Stars Cut Auto. Var. 3

NM/M
Production 2-23
11 Josh Duhamel/23 50.00
26 Val Kilmer/20 60.00

Movie Stars Cut Auto. Var. 4

NM/M
Production 4-20
26 Val Kilmer/20 60.00

Movie Stars Cut Auto. Var. 5

No Pricing
Production 4-15

Movie Stars Cut Auto. Var. 6

NM/M
Production 3-20
26 Val Kilmer/20 60.00

Recollection Collection

NM/M
represents total autos produced
1 Catherine Bach/78 60.00
3 Lee Majors/52 70.00

Stardom Combo Autos.

No Pricing
Production 10 Sets

Stardom Triple Autos.

No Pricing
Production Five Sets

Stardom Quad Autos.

No Pricing
Production Five Sets

2008 Donruss Threads

NM/M
Common Player (1-100): .25
Common Auto (101-150): 8.00
Production 99-1,999
Common Letter Auto. (151-187): 15.00
Production (240-280):
Pack (5): 4.00
Box (24): 85.00
1 Hank Aaron 2.00
2 Dale Murphy .50
3 Brooks Robinson .75
4 Cal Ripken Jr. 2.00
5 Eddie Murray .50
6 Carl Yastrzemski 1.00
7 Carlton Fisk .50
8 Wade Boggs .50
9 Joe Jackson 1.50
10 Johnny Pesky .25
11 Jim Rice .50
12 Fred Lynn .25
13 Duke Snider .75
14 Carl Erskine .25
15 Ernie Banks 1.00
16 Ryne Sandberg 1.00
17 Don Sutton .50
18 Luis Aparicio .50
19 Tom Seaver .75
20 Tony Perez .50
21 Pete Rose 2.00
22 Bob Feller .50
23 Al Kaline .75
24 Mark Fidrych .25
25 Kirk Gibson .25
26 Alan Trammell .25
27 George Brett 1.50
28 Steve Garvey .50
29 Robin Yount .75
30 Harmon Killebrew .75
31 Paul Molitor .50
32 Gary Carter .50
33 George Bush .50
34 Don Larsen .50
35 Don Mattingly 1.00
36 Reggie Jackson .75
37 Tim Raines .25
38 Mike Schmidt 1.00
39 Steve Carlton .50
40 Tony Gwynn .50
41 Juan Marichal .50
42 Willie Mays 1.50
43 Willie McCovey .50
44 Will Clark .25
45 Bob Gibson .50
46 Dennis Eckersley .25
47 Red Schoendienst .25
48 Stan Musial 1.00
49 Nolan Ryan 1.50
50 Frank Howard .25
51 Austin Romine .50
52 Chris Carter .50
53 Jordan Schafer .50
54 Michael Burgess .50
55 John Raynor .25
56 Lars Anderson 2.00
57 Josh Reddick .25
58 Luis Exposito .50
59 Aneury Rodriguez .50
60 Nick Weglarz 1.00
61 Hector Gomez .50
62 Jon Still .25
63 Brandon Hamilton .25
64 Bud Norris .50
65 Danny Duffy .50
66 Jovan Rosa .50
67 Sean O'Sullivan .25
68 Edilio Colina .25
69 Ryan Patterson .25
70 Brent Brewer .25
71 David Bromberg .25
72 Bryan Petersen .25
73 Lucas Duda .25
74 Ruben Tejada .25
75 Andrew Lambo 1.00
76 Jeff Corsaletti .50
77 Alexis Oliveras 1.00
78 Fernando Garcia .25
79 Jairo Heredia .50
80 Jesus Montero 2.00
81 Jose Tabata .50
82 Carlos Gonzalez .50
83 Patrick Ryan .25
84 Sean Doolittle .25
85 Carlos Carrasco .50
86 Luis Cruz .50
87 Yefri Carvajal .25
88 Stolmy Pimentel .50
89 Wilber Bucardo .50
90 Angel Villalona .50
91 Madison Bumgarner 1.00
92 Danny Carroll .25
93 Juan Ramirez .25
94 Louis Marson .75
95 Josh Vitters 1.00
96 Desmond Jennings .25
97 Abraham Almonte .25
98 Mat Gamel 1.00
99 Andrew LeFave .25
100 Elvis Andrus .50
101 Emilio Bonifacio/1,874 8.00
102 Wilin Rosario/999 20.00
103 Carlos Peguero/465 20.00
104 Tyler Flowers/999 40.00
105 Tyler Henson/999 10.00
106 Nevin Griffith/999 8.00
107 Caleb Gindl/465 10.00
108 Jose Ceda/999 8.00
109 Brandon Waring/465 20.00
110 Neftali Soto/500 30.00
111 Ryan Miller/999 8.00
112 Jack Egers/999 8.00
113 Juan Silverio/999 8.00
114 Jhoulys Chacin/1,999 20.00
115 Charlie Furbush/465 8.00
116 Hector Correa/999 8.00
117 Brad James/1,999 8.00
119 Keaton Hayenga/999 10.00
120 Brent Fisher/1,058 8.00
121 Juan Francisco/999 15.00
122 Andrew Romine/875 8.00
123 Mason Tobin/999 10.00
124 Anel De Los Santos/999 8.00
125 Andrew Walker/2,599 15.00
126 Alfredo Silverio/25,999 8.00
127 Mario Martinez/1,375 15.00
128 Taylor Green/999 10.00
129 D.J. Jones/399 15.00
130 Wilson Ramos/999 15.00
131 Trevor Reckling/875 15.00
132 Engel Beltre/465 20.00
133 Scott Moviel/1,000 8.00
134 Josh Tomlin/875 10.00
135 Dominic Brown/999 20.00
136 Neftali Feliz/465 40.00
137 Brian Friday/1,249 8.00
138 Drew Miller/1,999 8.00
139 Steve Garrison/1,999 8.00
140 Mike McBryde/950 8.00
141 Brian Duensing/575 8.00
142 Greg Halman/465 30.00
143 Jharmidy DeJesus/465 25.00
144 Mike Stanton/465 50.00
145 Wilmer Flores/99 80.00
146 Heath Rollins/999 8.00
147 Alex Cobb/999 8.00
148 Omar Poveda/999 8.00
149 Yohermyn Chavez/999 15.00
150 Gerardo Parra/999 10.00
151 Clayton Conner/240 15.00
152 Tyler Kolodny/280 20.00
153 Ryan Kalish/240 30.00
154 Rick Porcello/240 75.00
155 Shane Peterson/240 20.00
156 Tyler Ladendorf/269 15.00
157 Josh Lindblom/240 20.00
158 Tyler Chatwood/240 20.00
159 Logan Morrison/240 50.00
160 Collin DeLome/240 25.00
161 Daniel Cortes/240 20.00
162 Chris Johnson/280 40.00
163 Matt Mitchell/240 15.00
164 Denny Almonte/280 15.00
165 Greg Veloz/250 20.00
166 R.J. Seidel/240 15.00
167 Xavier Avery/250 25.00
168 Quincy Latimore/240 15.00
169 Aaron Shafer/280 15.00
170 Raynor Contreras/270 15.00
171 Waldis Joaquin/280 15.00
172 Jorge Bucardo/280 15.00
173 James Darnell/280 20.00
174 Logan Forsythe/280 15.00
175 Kyle Ginley/240 15.00
176 Ike Davis/250 30.00
177 Max Ramirez/244 20.00
178 Chris Davis/250 50.00
180 Jay Austin/240 25.00
181 Brad Holt/240 25.00
182 Carlos Gutierrez/270 15.00
183 Christian Friedrich/270 15.00
184 Zach Collier/280 20.00
186 Robert Hernandez/269 15.00
187 Christian Marrero/280 20.00

Gold Century Proof

Gold (1-100): 3-6X
Gold (101-150): .2-.25X
Production 50 Sets

Green Century Proof

Green (1-100): 2-4X
Green (101-150): .15-.2X
Production 250 Sets

Platinum Century Proof

Platinum (1-100): 10-15X
Platinum (101-150): .4-.5X
Production 25 Sets

Silver Century Proof

Silver (1-100): 3-5X
Silver (101-150): .2-.25X
Production 100 Sets

Baseball Americana

NM/M
Common Card: 2.00
1 Bud Abbott 2.00
2 Lou Costello 2.00
3 Don Mattingly 4.00
4 Eddie Murray 3.00
5 Ryne Sandberg 4.00
6 Pete Rose 5.00
7 Cal Ripken Jr. 5.00
8 Ernie Banks 3.00
9 George Brett 4.00
10 Mike Schmidt 3.00
11 Johnny Bench 3.00
12 Carlton Fisk 2.00
13 Tony Gwynn 3.00
14 Hank Aaron 5.00
15 Willie Mays 4.00
16 Joe Jackson 4.00
17 Ted Williams 4.00
18 Stan Musial 4.00
19 Nolan Ryan 5.00
20 Bob Feller 2.00
21 Kurt Russell 2.00
22 Burt Lancaster 2.00
23 Tab Hunter 2.00
24 Gary Cooper 2.00
25 Tony Curtis 2.00
26 John Cusack 2.00
27 Bernie Mac 2.00
28 Regis Philbin 2.00
29 Marcia Gay Harden 2.00
30 Albert Brooks 2.00
31 Billy Dee Williams 2.00
32 Esther Williams 2.00
33 Betty Garrett 2.00
34 Karen Allen 2.00
35 Ed Asner 2.00
36 Robert Wagner 2.00
37 Gary Coleman 2.00
38 Ed McMahon 2.00
39 Rob Schneider 2.00

40 Lori Petty 2.00
41 Bob Gibson 3.00
42 Dennis Eckersley 2.00
43 Carl Yastrzemski 4.00
44 Don Drysdale 3.00
45 Satchel Paige 4.00
46 Casey Stengel 3.00
47 Eddie Mathews 4.00
48 Early Wynn 2.00
49 Marilyn Monroe 5.00
50 George Bush 3.00

Baseball Americana Materials

NM/M

Production 1-500
Position: 1-2X
Production 1-250
No pricing prod. under 25
1 Bud Abbott/500 15.00
2 Lou Costello/250 25.00
3 Don Mattingly/100 20.00
4 Eddie Murray/150 10.00
6 Pete Rose/250 35.00
7 Cal Ripken Jr./100 25.00
9 George Brett/75 15.00
10 Mike Schmidt/100 15.00
12 Carlton Fisk/75 5.00
13 Tony Gwynn/250 8.00
17 Ted Williams/100 25.00
19 Nolan Ryan/100 20.00
21 Kurt Russell/500 8.00
22 Burt Lancaster/500 8.00
24 Gary Cooper/500 15.00
25 Tony Curtis/500 8.00
26 John Cusack/500 10.00
27 Bernie Mac/250 8.00
33 Betty Garrett/250 8.00
35 Ed Asner/500 5.00
36 Robert Wagner/500 5.00
38 Ed McMahon/500 5.00
39 Rob Schneider/350 5.00
40 Lori Petty/100 5.00
41 Bob Gibson/100 8.00
42 Dennis Eckersley/100 8.00
43 Carl Yastrzemski/100 15.00
44 Don Drysdale/100 15.00
45 Satchel Paige/100 30.00
46 Casey Stengel/500 15.00
47 Eddie Mathews/100 8.00
48 Early Wynn/100 8.00
49 TBD/500 40.00
50 TBD/500 20.00

Baseball Americana Signatures

NM/M

Production 3-100
3 Don Mattingly/25 50.00
6 Pete Rose/50 125.00
10 Mike Schmidt/25 40.00
11 Johnny Bench/50 40.00
12 Carlton Fisk/50 25.00
13 Tony Gwynn/25 40.00
20 Bob Feller/100 25.00
23 Tab Hunter/100 20.00
27 Bernie Mac/38 70.00
28 Regis Philbin/100 25.00
29 Marcia Gay Harden/100 15.00
30 Albert Brooks/100 25.00
41 Bob Gibson/100 25.00
42 Dennis Eckersley/100 15.00
43 Carl Yastrzemski/25 50.00

Baseball Americana Signature Materials

NM/M

Production 3-100
3 Don Mattingly/25 50.00
6 Pete Rose/50 150.00
7 Cal Ripken Jr./25 100.00
10 Mike Schmidt/25 40.00
11 Johnny Bench/50 40.00
12 Carlton Fisk/50 25.00
13 Tony Gwynn/50 40.00
27 Bernie Mac/100 75.00
41 Bob Gibson/50 25.00

Bats

NM/M

Production 1-500
1 Hank Aaron/500 25.00
9 Joe Jackson/100 300.00
35 Don Mattingly/250 15.00
36 Reggie Jackson/500 8.00
38 Mike Schmidt/500 10.00
42 Willie Mays/50 30.00
52 Chris Carter/500 8.00
53 Jordan Schafer/500 8.00
54 Michael Burgess/500 5.00
70 Brent Brewer/500 5.00
81 Jose Tabata/500 5.00
84 Sean Doolittle/500 8.00
92 Danny Carroll/500 5.00
96 Desmond Jennings/50 5.00
128 Taylor Green/500 5.00
142 Greg Halman/500 8.00
143 Jharmidy DeJesus/500 5.00

Century Collection Materials

NM/M

Production 10-100
Prime: No Pricing
Production 3-10
1 Cal Ripken Jr./100 25.00
2 Ryne Sandberg/75 15.00
3 Pete Rose/100 40.00
4 Fred Lynn/100 8.00
5 Tom Seaver/100 10.00
6 George Brett/50 25.00
7 Don Mattingly/75 20.00
8 Mike Schmidt/100 15.00
9 Tony Gwynn/100 8.00
11 Nolan Ryan/100 15.00
12 Dale Murphy/100 8.00
13 Pete Rose/100 40.00
15 Dave Winfield/100 8.00
16 Paul Molitor/100 6.00
17 Barry Larkin/100 5.00
18 Kirk Gibson/100 5.00
19 Pete Rose/100 40.00
20 Steve Garvey/100 8.00
21 Wade Boggs/100 6.00
22 Ted Williams/100 30.00
23 Steve Carlton/100 5.00
24 Robin Yount/100 10.00
25 Luis Aparicio/100 6.00
26 Jim Rice/100 5.00
27 Jim Palmer/100 6.00
28 Harmon Killebrew/100 10.00
29 Gaylord Perry/100 5.00
30 Gary Carter/100 8.00
31 Eddie Murray/50 10.00
32 Don Drysdale/100 10.00
33 Satchel Paige/100 40.00
34 Casey Stengel/100 15.00
35 Eddie Mathews/100 8.00
36 Dennis Eckersley/100 5.00
37 Carlton Fisk/100 8.00
38 Carl Yastrzemski/100 15.00
39 Early Wynn/100 8.00
40 Lefty Grove/50 100.00

Century Stars

NM/M

Common Player: 1.00
Century Proof: 2-3X
Production 100 Sets
1 Carlton Fisk 1.00
2 Harmon Killebrew 2.00
3 Ryne Sandberg 2.00
4 Cal Ripken Jr. 3.00
5 Mike Schmidt 2.00
6 Tony Gwynn 1.50
7 Pete Rose 2.00
8 Tim Raines 1.00
9 Dale Murphy 1.00
10 Steve Carlton 1.00
11 Bob Gibson 1.50
12 Nolan Ryan 3.00
13 Robin Yount 1.50
14 Paul Molitor 1.00
15 Kirk Gibson 1.00

Century Stars Materials

NM/M

Production 50 or 100
Prime: No Pricing
Production 1-10
1 Carlton Fisk/100 8.00
2 Harmon Killebrew/100 10.00
3 Ryne Sandberg/50 15.00
4 Cal Ripken Jr./100 25.00
5 Mike Schmidt/100 15.00
6 Tony Gwynn/100 8.00
7 Pete Rose/100 40.00
9 Dale Murphy/100 8.00
10 Steve Carlton/100 5.00
11 Bob Gibson/100 10.00
12 Nolan Ryan/100 15.00
13 Robin Yount/100 10.00
14 Paul Molitor/100 6.00
15 Kirk Gibson/50 5.00

Century Legends

NM/M

Common Player: 1.50
Century Proof: 2-3X
Production 100 Sets
1 Stan Musial 2.00
2 Willie Mays 2.00
3 Hank Aaron 3.00
4 Ted Williams 2.00
5 Whitey Ford 1.50
6 Bob Gibson 1.50
7 Joe Jackson 2.00
8 Duke Snider 1.50
9 Ernie Banks 2.00
10 Bob Feller 1.50
11 Nolan Ryan 3.00
12 Mike Schmidt 2.00
13 Carl Yastrzemski 2.00
14 Pete Rose 2.00
15 Harmon Killebrew 2.00

Century Legends Materials

NM/M

Production 1-100
Prime: No Pricing
Production 1-25
1 Stan Musial/25 30.00
4 Ted Williams/50 30.00
6 Bob Gibson/50 10.00
11 Nolan Ryan/100 15.00
12 Mike Schmidt/100 15.00
13 Carl Yastrzemski/100 15.00
14 Pete Rose/100 40.00
15 Harmon Killebrew/100 10.00

College Greats

NM/M

Common Player: 1.00
1 Tom Seaver 2.00
2 Reggie Jackson 2.00
3 Frank Howard 1.00
4 Dave Winfield 2.00
5 Paul Molitor 1.50
6 Barry Larkin 1.00
7 Kirk Gibson 1.00
8 Robin Roberts 1.00
9 Will Clark 1.50
10 Bob Gibson 1.50
11 Steve Garvey 1.00
12 Fred Lynn 1.00

College Greats Signatures

NM/M

Production 5-50
1 Tom Seaver/25 40.00
2 Reggie Jackson/25 50.00
3 Frank Howard/50 25.00
4 Dave Winfield/25 50.00
5 Paul Molitor/25 40.00
6 Barry Larkin/50 50.00
8 Robin Roberts/40 30.00
10 Bob Gibson/50 30.00
12 Fred Lynn/50 30.00

College Greats Signature Combos

No Pricing
Production 5 Sets

Dynasty

NM/M

Common Trio: 3.00
Century Proof: 2-3X
Production 100 Sets
1 Cal Ripken Jr., Eddie Murray, Jim Palmer 3.00
2 Joe Morgan, Johnny Bench, Pete Rose 3.00
3 Juan Marichal, Willie Mays, Willie McCovey 3.00

Dynasty Materials

NM/M

Production 50 or 100
Prime: No Pricing
Production 10 Sets
1 Cal Ripken Jr., Eddie Murray, Jim Palmer/50 30.00
2 Joe Morgan, Johnny Bench, Pete Rose/100 65.00

Diamond Kings

NM/M

Common Player:
Framed Red: 1.5-2X
Production 100 Sets
Gold: 1.5-2X
Production 100 Sets
Silver: 1-2X
Production 250 Sets
Framed Blue: 2-3X
Production 50 Sets
Framed Green: 3-5X
Production 25 Sets
Framed Black: No Pricing
Production 10 Sets
Platinum: 3-5X
Production 25 Sets
1 Jordan Schafer 2.00
2 Nolan Reimold 2.00
3 Matt McBride 2.00
4 Lars Anderson 3.00
5 Blake Wood 2.00
6 Josh Vitters 2.00
7 Chris Valaika 2.00
8 Mark Melancon 2.00
9 Drew Stubbs 2.00
10 Rick Porcello 3.00
11 Anthony Rizzo 2.00
12 Jon Jay 1.00
13 Clay Fuller 1.00
14 Damon Sublett 3.00
15 Brett Anderson 1.00
16 Matt Spencer 1.00
17 Drew Cumberland 1.00
18 Tim Alderson 2.00
19 Madison Bumgarner 2.00
20 Jess Todd 1.00
21 Michael Hollimon 1.00
22 Taylor Teagarden 1.00
23 Daniel McCutchen 1.00
24 Trystan Magnuson 1.00
25 Michael Burgess 1.00
26 Hank Aaron 4.00
27 Cal Ripken Jr. 4.00
28 Jim Palmer 1.50
29 Bobby Doerr 1.50
30 Duke Snider 2.00
31 Rod Carew 1.50
32 Ernie Banks 2.00
33 Ryne Sandberg 3.00
34 Billy Williams 1.50
35 Fergie Jenkins 1.50
36 Pete Rose 3.00
37 George Kell 1.50
38 George Brett 3.00
39 Reggie Jackson 2.00
40 Don Mattingly 3.00
41 Phil Niekro 1.00
42 Whitey Ford 2.00
43 Yogi Berra 2.00
44 Mike Schmidt 2.00
45 Tony Gwynn 2.00
46 Willie Mays 3.00
47 Gaylord Perry 1.00
48 Stan Musial 2.00
49 Lou Brock 1.50
50 Nolan Ryan 3.00
51 Joe Jackson 3.00
52 Gordon Beckham 5.00
53 Derrick Rose 3.00
54 Michael Beasley 3.00
55 O.J. Mayo 3.00
56 Pete Rose 3.00
57 Rick Porcello 3.00
58 Nolan Ryan 3.00

Diamond Kings Materials

NM/M

Production 1-250
Prime: No Pricing
Production 1-25
1 Jordan Schafer/250 5.00
6 Josh Vitters/250 8.00
8 Mark Melancon/125 5.00
9 Drew Stubbs/250 5.00
10 Rick Porcello/250 20.00
13 Clay Fuller/250 5.00
14 Damon Sublett/250 10.00
15 Brett Anderson/250 5.00
16 Matt Spencer/250 8.00
17 Drew Cumberland/250 5.00
18 Tim Alderson/250 8.00
19 Madison Bumgarner/125 15.00
20 Jess Todd/250 8.00
24 Trystan Magnuson/250 10.00
25 Michael Burgess/250 10.00
27 Cal Ripken Jr./200 20.00
33 Ryne Sanberg/50 25.00
36 Pete Rose/250 50.00
38 George Brett/75 20.00
40 Don Mattingly/150 20.00
43 Yogi Berra/25 25.00
44 Mike Schmidt/75 20.00
45 Tony Gwynn/250 8.00
49 Lou Brock/100 20.00
50 Nolan Ryan/50 25.00
56 Pete Rose/100 40.00
57 Rick Porcello 15.00
58 Nolan Ryan 25.00

Diamond Kings Signatures

NM/M

Production 5-500
1 Jordan Schafer/199 15.00
2 Nolan Reimold/500 10.00
3 Matt McBride/500 10.00
4 Lars Anderson/474 35.00
5 Blake Wood/500 10.00
7 Chris Valaika/500 10.00
8 Mark Melancon/238 15.00
9 Drew Stubbs/465 15.00
10 Rick Porcello/300 60.00
15 Brett Anderson/315 15.00
18 Tim Alderson/215 15.00
19 Madison Bumgarner/223 25.00
21 Michael Hollimon/500 10.00
22 Taylor Teagarden/475 15.00
23 Daniel McCutchen/500 10.00
24 Trystan Magnuson/215 10.00
25 Michael Burgess/182 15.00
28 Jim Palmer/100 25.00
29 Bobby Doerr/250 20.00
30 Duke Snider/50 40.00
35 Fergie Jenkins/100 20.00
36 Pete Rose/50 125.00
39 Reggie Jackson/25 40.00
40 Don Mattingly/25 50.00
42 Whitey Ford/100 40.00
44 Mike Schmidt/25 40.00
47 Gaylord Perry/150 20.00
49 Lou Brock/50 25.00
50 Nolan Ryan/25 70.00
56 Pete Rose/25 125.00
57 Rick Porcello/25 80.00
58 Nolan Ryan/25 75.00

Diamond Kings Signatures Materials

NM/M

Production 5-100
Prime: No Pricing
Production 1-10
1 Jordan Schafer/25 25.00
10 Rick Porcello/25 100.00
14 Damon Sublett/25 50.00
18 Tim Alderson/25 25.00
19 Madison Bumgarner/25 40.00
27 Cal Ripken Jr./25 150.00
28 Jim Palmer/25 30.00
36 Pete Rose/25 160.00
40 Don Mattingly/25 60.00
49 Lou Brock/100 35.00
50 Nolan Ryan/25 85.00
56 Pete Rose/25 160.00
57 Rick Porcello/25 100.00

Generations

NM/M

Common Duo: 2.00
Century Proof: 2-3X
Production 100 Sets

1 Dale Murphy, Hank Aaron 3.00
2 Cal Ripken Jr., Eddie Murray 3.00
3 Ernie Banks, Ryne Sandberg 2.00
4 Willie Mays, Willie McCovey 2.00
5 Paul Molitor, Rod Carew 2.00

Generations Materials

NM/M

Production 10-100
Prime: No Pricing
Production 5-10
2 Cal Ripken Jr., Eddie Murray/100 30.00

Jerseys

NM/M

Production 5-500
Prime: No Pricing
Production 1-25
1 Hank Aaron/10
2 Dale Murphy/350 8.00
3 Brooks Robinson/250 8.00
4 Cal Ripken Jr./350 20.00
5 Eddie Murray/250 5.00
6 Carl Yastrzemski/400 10.00
7 Carlton Fisk/150 5.00
8 Wade Boggs/500 8.00
11 Jim Rice/350 5.00
12 Fred Lynn/350 5.00
16 Ryne Sandberg/150 10.00
18 Luis Aparicio/200 5.00
19 Tom Seaver/350 8.00
21 Pete Rose/100 40.00
25 Kirk Gibson/250 5.00
26 Alan Trammell/250 5.00
27 George Brett/250 10.00
28 Steve Garvey/150 5.00
29 Robin Yount/500 10.00
30 Harmon Killebrew/150 10.00
31 Paul Molitor/300 8.00
32 Gary Carter/450 5.00
33 George Bush/500 20.00
35 Don Mattingly/150 20.00
36 Reggie Jackson/350 8.00
38 Mike Schmidt/350 10.00
39 Steve Carlton/250 8.00
40 Tony Gwynn/500 8.00
43 Willie McCovey/500 8.00
44 Will Clark/500 5.00
45 Bob Gibson/100 10.00
46 Dennis Eckersley/250 5.00
47 Red Schoendienst/300 8.00
49 Nolan Ryan/250 15.00
54 Michael Burgess/500 5.00
91 Madison Bumgarner/100 20.00
95 Josh Vitters/500 10.00
146 Heath Rollins/90 5.00
147 Alex Cobb/95 8.00

Signatures Gold

NM/M

Production 10-999
Platinum: No Pricing
Production 5-25
3 Brooks Robinson/50 25.00
4 Cal Ripken Jr./50 80.00
5 Eddie Murray/25 35.00
6 Carl Yastrzemski/50 40.00
7 Carlton Fisk/50 25.00
10 Johnny Pesky/100 15.00
11 Jim Rice/100 20.00
12 Fred Lynn/50 20.00
13 Duke Snider/50 40.00
14 Carl Erskine/75 15.00
16 Ryne Sandberg/50 40.00
17 Don Sutton/100 20.00
18 Luis Aparicio/50 20.00
19 Tom Seaver/50 40.00
20 Tony Perez/25 20.00
21 Pete Rose/75 120.00
22 Bob Feller/100 25.00
23 Al Kaline/50 35.00
24 Mark Fidrych/100 15.00
26 Alan Trammell/75 15.00
28 Steve Garvey/45 20.00
29 Robin Yount/50 25.00
31 Paul Molitor/50 20.00
32 Gary Carter/50 20.00
34 Don Larsen/50 25.00
35 Don Mattingly/50 60.00
36 Reggie Jackson/50 35.00
37 Tim Raines/25 30.00
38 Mike Schmidt/50 50.00
39 Steve Carlton/50 20.00
40 Tony Gwynn/50 35.00
42 Willie Mays/50 80.00
43 Willie McCovey/50 35.00
45 Bob Gibson/50 25.00
46 Dennis Eckersley/50 25.00
47 Red Schoendienst/100 20.00
48 Stan Musial/50 50.00
49 Nolan Ryan/50 75.00
50 Frank Howard/75 15.00
51 Austin Romine/725 20.00
52 Chris Carter/499 15.00
53 Jordan Schafer/275 15.00
54 Michael Burgess/25
55 John Raynor/575 15.00
56 Lars Anderson/499 35.00
57 Josh Reddick/499 30.00
58 Luis Exposito/971 10.00
59 Aneury Rodriguez/975 8.00
60 Nick Weglarz/999 15.00
61 Hector Gomez/499 15.00
62 Jon Still/725 8.00
63 Brandon Hamilton/972 8.00
64 Bud Norris/499 8.00
65 Danny Duffy/499 20.00
66 Jovan Rosa/973 10.00
67 Sean O'Sullivan/499 10.00
68 Edilio Colina/975 8.00
69 Ryan Patterson/775 8.00
70 Brent Brewer/470 8.00
71 David Bromberg/999 8.00
72 Bryan Petersen/475 8.00
73 Lucas Duda/250 10.00
74 Ruben Tejada/999 10.00
76 Jeff Corsaletti/975 10.00
77 Alexis Oliveras/975 10.00
78 Fernando Garcia/975 8.00
79 Jairo Heredia/999 10.00
80 Jesus Montero/975 35.00
81 Jose Tabata/975 15.00
82 Carlos Gonzalez/975 15.00
83 Patrick Ryan/499 8.00
84 Sean Doolittle/249 15.00
85 Carlos Carrasco/999 15.00
86 Luis Cruz/975 10.00
87 Yefri Carvajal/999 8.00
88 Stolmy Pimentel/975 15.00
89 Wilber Bucardo/420 8.00
91 Madison Bumgarner/250 25.00
92 Danny Carroll/999 8.00
93 Juan Ramirez/999 8.00
94 Louis Marson/725 20.00
96 Desmond Jennings/749 10.00
97 Abraham Almonte/975 8.00
99 Andrew LeFave/975 8.00
100 Elvis Andrus/749 10.00
102 Wilin Rosario/100 10.00
104 Tyler Flowers/100 50.00
105 Tyler Henson/100 10.00
106 Nevin Griffith/100 8.00
108 Jose Ceda/100 10.00
111 Ryan Miller/100 10.00
112 Jack Egbert/100 10.00
113 Juan Silverio/100 15.00
114 Jhoulys Chacin/ 30.00
116 Hector Correa/100 10.00
117 Brad James/100 10.00
119 Keaton Hayenga/100 20.00
120 Brent Fisher/100 10.00
121 Juan Francisco/100 25.00
122 Andrew Romine/100 15.00
123 Mason Tobin/100 10.00
124 Anel De Los Santos/100 10.00
126 Alfredo Silverio/100 15.00
127 Mario Martinez/100 10.00
128 Taylor Green/100 20.00
129 D.J. Jones/100 15.00
130 Wilson Ramos/100 15.00
131 Trevor Reckling/100 15.00
133 Scott Moviel/100 10.00
134 Josh Tomlin/100 10.00
135 Dominic Brown/100 25.00
137 Brian Friday/100 10.00
138 Drew Miller/100 10.00
139 Steve Garrison/100 10.00
140 Mike McBryde/100 10.00
141 Brian Duensing/100 10.00
146 Heath Rollins/100 10.00
148 Omar Poveda/100 15.00
149 Yohermyn Chavez/100 15.00
150 Gerardo Parra/100 15.00

E

2000 E-X

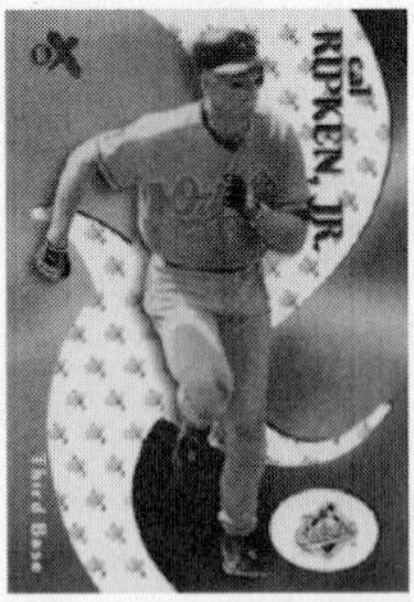

NM/M

Complete Set (90): 80.00
Common Player: .25
Common Prospect (61-90): 3.00
Production 3,499 Sets
Pack: 2.75
Box: 50.00
1 Alex Rodriguez 2.50
2 Jeff Bagwell 1.00
3 Mike Piazza 2.00
4 Tony Gwynn 1.50
5 Ken Griffey Jr. 2.00
6 Juan Gonzalez .40
7 Vladimir Guerrero 1.00
8 Cal Ripken Jr. 3.00
9 Mo Vaughn .25
10 Chipper Jones 1.50
11 Derek Jeter 3.00
12 Nomar Garciaparra 1.50
13 Mark McGwire 2.50
14 Sammy Sosa 1.50
15 Pedro Martinez 1.00
16 Greg Maddux 1.50
17 Frank Thomas .75
18 Shawn Green .50
19 Carlos Beltran .50
20 Roger Clemens 1.75
21 Randy Johnson 1.00
22 Bernie Williams .25
23 Carlos Delgado .50
24 Manny Ramirez .75
25 Freddy Garcia .25
26 Barry Bonds 3.00
27 Tim Hudson .40
28 Larry Walker .25
29 Raul Mondesi .25
30 Ivan Rodriguez .65
31 Magglio Ordonez .25
32 Scott Rolen .65
33 Mike Mussina .40
34 J.D. Drew .40
35 Tom Glavine .50
36 Barry Larkin .25
37 Jim Thome .65
38 Erubiel Durazo .25
39 Curt Schilling .50
40 Orlando Hernandez .25
41 Rafael Palmeiro .65
42 Gabe Kapler .25
43 Mark Grace .25
44 Jeff Cirillo .25
45 Jeromy Burnitz .25
46 Sean Casey .35
47 Kevin Millwood .25
48 Vinny Castilla .25
49 Jose Canseco .50
50 Roberto Alomar .30
51 Craig Biggio .25
52 Preston Wilson .25
53 Jeff Weaver .25
54 Robin Ventura .25
55 Ben Grieve .25
56 Troy Glaus .65
57 Jacque Jones .25
58 Brian Giles .25
59 Kevin Brown .25
60 Todd Helton .65
61 Ben Petrick 3.00
62 Chad Hermansen 3.00
63 Kevin Barker 3.00
64 Matt LeCroy 3.00
65 Brad Penny 4.00
66 D.T. Cromer 3.00
67 Steve Lomasney 3.00
68 Cole Liniak 3.00
69 B.J. Ryan 3.00
70 Wilton Veras 3.00
71 Aaron McNeal **RC** 4.00
72 Nick Johnson 4.00
73 Adam Piatt 3.00
74 Adam Kennedy 3.00
75 Cesar King 3.00
76 Peter Bergeron 3.00
77 Rob Bell 3.00
78 Wily Pena 4.00
79 Ruben Mateo 3.00
80 Kip Wells 3.00
81 Alex Escobar 3.00
82 Danys Baez **RC** 5.00
83 Travis Dawkins 3.00
84 Mark Quinn 3.00
85 Jimmy Anderson 3.00
86 Rick Ankiel 4.00
87 Alfonso Soriano 5.00
88 Pat Burrell 4.00
89 Eric Munson 3.00
90 Josh Beckett 4.00

Essential Credentials Future

NM/M

Common Player: 10.00
1 Alex Rodriguez/60 75.00
2 Jeff Bagwell/59 30.00
3 Mike Piazza/58 50.00
4 Tony Gwynn/57 50.00
5 Ken Griffey Jr./56 50.00
6 Juan Gonzalez/55 15.00
7 Vladimir Guerrero/54 20.00
8 Cal Ripken Jr./53 85.00
9 Mo Vaughn/52 10.00
10 Chipper Jones/51 30.00
11 Derek Jeter/50 85.00
12 Nomar Garciaparra/49 45.00
13 Mark McGwire/48 75.00
14 Sammy Sosa/47 50.00
15 Pedro Martinez/46 30.00
16 Greg Maddux/45 50.00
17 Frank Thomas/44 20.00
18 Shawn Green/43 10.00
19 Carlos Beltran/42 10.00
20 Roger Clemens/41 60.00
21 Randy Johnson/40 30.00
22 Bernie Williams/39 10.00
23 Carlos Delgado/38 15.00
24 Manny Ramirez/37 20.00
25 Freddy Garcia/36 10.00
26 Barry Bonds/35 90.00
27 Tim Hudson/34 20.00
28 Larry Walker/33 10.00
29 Raul Mondesi/32 10.00
30 Ivan Rodriguez/31 15.00
31 Magglio Ordonez/30 10.00
32 Scott Rolen/29 20.00
33 Mike Mussina/28 25.00
34 J.D. Drew/27 20.00
35 Tom Glavine/26 25.00
36 Barry Larkin/25 15.00
37 Jim Thome/24 30.00
38 Erubiel Durazo/23 15.00
39 Curt Schilling/22 25.00
40 Orlando Hernandez/21 15.00
41 Rafael Palmeiro/20 40.00
42 Gabe Kapler/19 15.00
43 Mark Grace/18 15.00
44 Jeff Cirillo/17 15.00
45 Jeromy Burnitz/16 15.00
46 Sean Casey/15 15.00
47 Kevin Millwood/14 20.00
48 Vinny Castilla/13 20.00
49 Jose Canseco/12 40.00
50 Roberto Alomar/11 50.00
51 Craig Biggio/10 50.00
61 Ben Petrick/30 10.00
62 Chad Hermansen/29 10.00
63 Kevin Barker/28 10.00
64 Matt LeCroy/27 10.00
65 Brad Penny/26 10.00
66 D.T. Cromer/25 10.00
67 Steve Lomasney/24 10.00
68 Cole Liniak/23 10.00
69 B.J. Ryan/22 10.00
70 Wilton Veras/21 10.00
71 Aaron McNeal/20 15.00
72 Nick Johnson/19 25.00
73 Adam Piatt/18 15.00
74 Adam Kennedy/17 15.00
75 Cesar King/16 15.00
76 Peter Bergeron/15 15.00
77 Rob Bell/14 15.00
78 Wily Pena/13 15.00
79 Ruben Mateo/12 15.00
80 Kip Wells/11 15.00
81 Alex Escobar/10 20.00

Essential Credentials Now

NM/M

Common Player: 8.00
20 Roger Clemens/20 50.00
21 Randy Johnson/21 30.00
22 Bernie Williams/22 10.00
23 Carlos Delgado/23 25.00
24 Manny Ramirez/24 30.00
25 Freddy Garcia/25 10.00
26 Barry Bonds/26 75.00
27 Tim Hudson/27 15.00
28 Larry Walker/28 10.00
29 Raul Mondesi/29 10.00
30 Ivan Rodriguez/30 15.00
31 Magglio Ordonez/31 10.00
32 Scott Rolen/32 20.00
33 Mike Mussina/33 15.00
34 J.D. Drew/34 20.00
35 Tom Glavine/35 20.00
36 Barry Larkin/36 15.00
37 Jim Thome/37 25.00
38 Erubiel Durazo/38 8.00
39 Curt Schilling/39 20.00
40 Orlando Hernandez/40 8.00
41 Rafael Palmeiro/41 15.00
42 Gabe Kapler/42 8.00
43 Mark Grace/43 8.00
44 Jeff Cirillo/44 8.00
45 Jeromy Burnitz/45 8.00
46 Sean Casey/46 8.00
47 Kevin Millwood/47 8.00
48 Vinny Castilla/48 8.00
49 Jose Canseco/49 15.00
50 Roberto Alomar/50 12.00
51 Craig Biggio/51 15.00
52 Preston Wilson/52 8.00
53 Jeff Weaver/53 8.00
54 Robin Ventura/54 8.00
55 Ben Grieve/55 8.00
56 Troy Glaus/56 15.00
57 Jacque Jones/57 12.00
58 Brian Giles/58 8.00
59 Kevin Brown/59 8.00
60 Todd Helton/60 20.00
74 Adam Kennedy/14 15.00
75 Cesar King/15 15.00
76 Peter Bergeron/16 15.00
77 Rob Bell/17 15.00
78 Wily Pena/18 15.00
79 Ruben Mateo/19 15.00
80 Kip Wells/20 15.00
81 Alex Escobar/21 15.00
82 Danys Baez/22 15.00
83 Travis Dawkins/23 15.00
84 Mark Quinn/24 15.00
85 Jimmy Anderson/25 15.00
86 Rick Ankiel/26 15.00
87 Alfonso Soriano/27 60.00
88 Pat Burrell/28 30.00
89 Eric Munson/29 15.00
90 Josh Beckett/30 20.00

Autographics

NM/M

Common Player: 5.00
Inserted 1:24
Bob Abreu 15.00
Moises Alou 15.00
Rick Ankiel 20.00
Michael Barrett 5.00
Josh Beckett 25.00

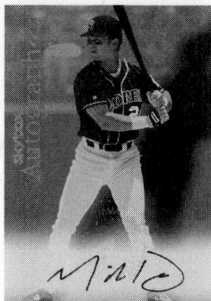

Rob Bell	5.00
Adrian Beltre	15.00
Carlos Beltran	15.00
Wade Boggs	25.00
Barry Bonds	150.00
Kent Bottenfield	5.00
Milton Bradley	10.00
Pat Burrell	15.00
Chris Carpenter	20.00
Sean Casey	8.00
Eric Chavez	8.00
Will Clark	25.00
Johnny Damon	20.00
Mike Darr	5.00
Ben Davis	5.00
Russ Davis	5.00
Carlos Delgado	20.00
Jason Dewey	5.00
Octavio Dotel	5.00
J.D. Drew	10.00
Ray Durham	8.00
Damion Easley	6.00
Kelvim Escobar	6.00
Carlos Febles	6.00
Freddy Garcia	5.00
Jeremy Giambi	5.00
Todd Greene	5.00
Jason Grilli	5.00
Vladimir Guerrero	30.00
Tony Gwynn	40.00
Jerry Hairston Jr.	5.00
Mike Hampton	8.00
Todd Helton	20.00
Trevor Hoffman	10.00
Tim Hudson	15.00
John Jaha	5.00
Derek Jeter	100.00
D'Angelo Jimenez	5.00
Randy Johnson	60.00
Jason Kendall	8.00
Adam Kennedy	8.00
Cesar King	5.00
Paul Konerko	10.00
Mark Kotsay	6.00
Ray Lankford	6.00
Jason LaRue	6.00
Matt Lawton	6.00
Carlos Lee	8.00
Mike Lieberthal	8.00
Cole Liniak	5.00
Steve Lomasney	5.00
Jose Macias	5.00
Greg Maddux	60.00
Edgar Martinez	15.00
Pedro Martinez	60.00
Ruben Mateo	5.00
Gary Matthews Jr.	8.00
Aaron McNeal	5.00
Raul Mondesi	8.00
Orber Moreno	5.00
Warren Morris	5.00
Eric Munson	5.00
Heath Murray	5.00
Mike Mussina	30.00
Joe Nathan	5.00
Rafael Palmeiro	25.00
Jim Parque	6.00
Angel Pena	5.00
Wily Pena	8.00
Pokey Reese	6.00
Matt Riley	5.00
Cal Ripken Jr.	85.00
Alex Rodriguez	75.00
Scott Rolen	20.00
Jimmy Rollins	20.00
B.J. Ryan	5.00
Randall Simon	5.00
Chris Singleton	5.00
Alfonso Soriano	30.00
Shannon Stewart	8.00
Mike Sweeney	8.00
Miguel Tejada	20.00
Frank Thomas	25.00
Wilton Veras	5.00
Billy Wagner	5.00
Jeff Weaver	5.00
Rondell White	8.00
Scott Williamson	5.00
Randy Wolf	5.00
Jaret Wright	5.00
Ed Yarnall	5.00
Kevin Young	5.00

E-Xceptional Red

		NM/M
Complete Set (15):		100.00
Common Player:		4.00
Inserted 1:14		
Blue:		2-3X
Inserted 1:288		
Green:		1-1.5X
Production 999 Sets		
1	Ken Griffey Jr.	8.00
2	Derek Jeter	15.00
3	Nomar Garciaparra	6.00
4	Mark McGwire	10.00
5	Sammy Sosa	6.00
6	Mike Piazza	8.00
7	Alex Rodriguez	10.00
8	Cal Ripken Jr.	15.00
9	Chipper Jones	6.00
10	Pedro Martinez	4.00
11	Jeff Bagwell	4.00
12	Greg Maddux	6.00
13	Roger Clemens	7.00
14	Tony Gwynn	5.00
15	Frank Thomas	4.00

E-Xciting

		NM/M
Complete Set (10):		25.00
Common Player:		1.00
Inserted 1:24		
1	Mark McGwire	6.00
2	Ken Griffey Jr.	4.00
3	Randy Johnson	2.00
4	Sammy Sosa	3.00
5	Manny Ramirez	2.00
6	Jose Canseco	1.00
7	Derek Jeter	6.00
8	Scott Rolen	1.50
9	Juan Gonzalez	1.25
10	Barry Bonds	6.00

E-Xplosive

	NM/M
Complete Set (20):	90.00

Common Player:		2.00
Production 2,499 Sets		
1	Tony Gwynn	6.00
2	Alex Rodriguez	10.00
3	Pedro Martinez	5.00
4	Sammy Sosa	6.00
5	Cal Ripken Jr.	15.00
6	Adam Piatt	2.00
7	Pat Burrell	2.50
8	J.D. Drew	2.50
9	Mike Piazza	8.00
10	Shawn Green	2.50
11	Troy Glaus	4.00
12	Randy Johnson	5.00
13	Juan Gonzalez	2.50
14	Chipper Jones	6.00
15	Ivan Rodriguez	4.00
16	Nomar Garciaparra	6.00
17	Ken Griffey Jr.	8.00
18	Nick Johnson	2.50
19	Mark McGwire	10.00
20	Frank Thomas	5.00

Generation E-X

		NM/M
Complete Set (15):		20.00
Common Player:		1.00
Inserted 1:8		
1	Rick Ankiel	1.00
2	Josh Beckett	1.50
3	Carlos Beltran	2.00
4	Pat Burrell	2.00
5	Freddy Garcia	1.00
6	Alex Rodriguez	5.00
7	Derek Jeter	6.00
8	Tim Hudson	1.50
9	Shawn Green	1.50
10	Eric Munson	1.00
11	Adam Piatt	1.00
12	Adam Kennedy	1.00
13	Nick Johnson	1.00
14	Alfonso Soriano	2.00
15	Nomar Garciaparra	4.00

Genuine Coverage

		NM/M
Common Player:		5.00
Inserted 1:144		
1	Alex Rodriguez	40.00
2	Tom Glavine	10.00
3	Cal Ripken Jr.	50.00
4	Edgar Martinez	5.00
5	Raul Mondesi	5.00
6	Carlos Beltran	5.00
7	Chipper Jones	25.00
8	Barry Bonds	50.00
9	Heath Murray	5.00
10	Tim Hudson	10.00
11	Mike Mussina	10.00
12	Derek Jeter	50.00

2001 E-X

		NM/M
Complete Set (130):		100.00
Common Player:		.25
Common SP (101-130):		4.00
Production Listed		
Pack (5):		4.00
Box (24):		80.00
1	Jason Kendall	.25
2	Derek Jeter	3.00
3	Greg Vaughn	.25
4	Eric Chavez	.40
5	Nomar Garciaparra	1.00
6	Roberto Alomar	.50
7	Barry Larkin	.40
8	Matt Lawton	.25
9	Larry Walker	.25
10	Chipper Jones	1.50
11	Scott Rolen	.75
12	Carlos Lee	.40
13	Adrian Beltre	.40
14	Ben Grieve	.25
15	Mike Sweeney	.25
16	John Olerud	.25
17	Gabe Kapler	.25
18	Brian Giles	.25
19	Luis Gonzalez	.40
20	Sammy Sosa	1.00
21	Roger Clemens	1.50
22	Vladimir Guerrero	1.00
23	Ken Griffey Jr.	2.00
24	Mark McGwire	2.50
25	Orlando Hernandez	.25
26	Shannon Stewart	.25
27	Fred McGriff	.25
28	Lance Berkman	.50
29	Carlos Delgado	.75
30	Mike Piazza	2.00
31	Juan Encarnacion	.25
32	David Justice	.25
33	Greg Maddux	1.50
34	Frank Thomas	1.00
35	Jason Giambi	.75
36	Ruben Mateo	.25
37	Todd Helton	1.00
38	Jim Edmonds	.25
39	Steve Finley	.25
40	Tom Glavine	.40
41	Mo Vaughn	.25
42	Phil Nevin	.25
43	Richie Sexson	.25
44	Craig Biggio	.25
45	Kerry Wood	.50
46	Pat Burrell	.60
47	Edgar Martinez	.25
48	Jim Thome	.40
49	Jeff Bagwell	1.00
50	Bernie Williams	.45
51	Andruw Jones	.50
52	Gary Sheffield	.40
53	Johnny Damon	.50
54	Rondell White	.25
55	J.D. Drew	.50
56	Tony Batista	.25
57	Paul Konerko	.25
58	Rafael Palmeiro	.75
59	Cal Ripken Jr.	3.00
60	Darin Erstad	.50
61	Ivan Rodriguez	.75
62	Barry Bonds	3.00
63	Edgardo Alfonzo	.25
64	Ellis Burks	.25
65	Mike Lieberthal	.25
66	Robin Ventura	.25
67	Richard Hidalgo	.25
68	Magglio Ordonez	.40
69	Kazuhiro Sasaki	.25
70	Miguel Tejada	.50
71	David Wells	.25
72	Troy Glaus	.50
73	Jose Vidro	.25
74	Shawn Green	.50
75	Barry Zito	.50
76	Jermaine Dye	.25
77	Geoff Jenkins	.25
78	Jeff Kent	.25
79	Al Leiter	.25
80	Deivi Cruz	.25
81	Eric Karros	.25
82	Albert Belle	.25
83	Pedro Martinez	1.00
84	Raul Mondesi	.25
85	Preston Wilson	.25
86	Rafael Furcal	.40
87	Rick Ankiel	.50
88	Randy Johnson	1.00
89	Kevin Brown	.25
90	Sean Casey	.35
91	Mike Mussina	.50
92	Alex Rodriguez	2.50
93	Andres Galarraga	.25
94	Juan Gonzalez	.50
95	Manny Ramirez	1.00
96	Mark Grace	.35
97	Carl Everett	.25
98	Tony Gwynn	1.50
99	Mike Hampton	.25
100	Ken Caminiti	.25
101	Jason Hart/1749	4.00
102	Corey Patterson/1199	5.00

103	Timo Perez/1999	4.00
104	Marcus Giles/1999	4.00
105	Ichiro Suzuki/1999 RC	50.00
106	Aubrey Huff/1499	8.00
107	Joe Crede/1999	5.00
108	Larry Barnes/1499	4.00
109	Esix Snead/1499 RC	4.00
110	Kenny Kelly/2249	4.00
111	Justin Miller/2249	4.00
112	Jack Cust/1999	4.00
113	Xavier Nady/999	4.00
114	Eric Munson/1499	4.00
115	Elpidio Guzman/1749 RC	4.00
116	Juan Pierre/2189	4.00
117	Winston Abreu/1749 RC	4.00
118	Keith Ginter/1999	4.00
119	Jace Brewer/2699	4.00
120	Paxton Crawford/2249	4.00
121	Jason Tyner/2249	4.00
122	Tike Redman/1999	4.00
123	John Riedling/2499	4.00
124	Jose Ortiz/1499	4.00
125	Oswaldo Mairena/2499	4.00
126	Eric Byrnes/2249	6.00
127	Brian Cole/999	4.00
128	Adam Piatt/2249	4.00
129	Nate Rolison/2499	4.00
130	Keith McDonald/2249	4.00

Essential Credentials

	NM/M
Stars (1-100):	3-6X
Production 299	
Common (101-130):	10.00
Minor Stars (101-130):	15.00
Production 29	

(See 2001 E-X for checklist and base card values.)

Base Inks

	NM/M
Random Inserts	
Derek Jeter AU/500	100.00

Behind the Numbers

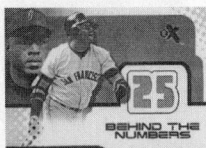

	NM/M
Common Player:	5.00
Inserted 1:33	
1BN	Johnny Bench	10.00
2BN	Wade Boggs	15.00
3BN	George Brett	20.00
4BN	Lou Brock	5.00
5BN	Rollie Fingers	5.00
6BN	Carlton Fisk	10.00
7BN	Reggie Jackson	10.00
8BN	Al Kaline	10.00
9BN	Willie McCovey	5.00
10BN	Willie McCovey	5.00
11BN	Paul Molitor	10.00
12BN	Eddie Murray	10.00
13BN	Jim Palmer	5.00
14BN	Ozzie Smith	15.00
15BN	Nolan Ryan	30.00
16BN	Mike Schmidt	20.00
17BN	Tom Seaver	5.00
18BN	Dave Winfield	5.00
19BN	Ted Williams	75.00

20BN	Robin Yount	10.00
21BN	Brady Anderson	5.00
22BN	Rick Ankiel	5.00
23BN	Albert Belle	5.00
24BN	Adrian Beltre	7.50
25BN	Barry Bonds	30.00
26BN	Eric Chavez	5.00
27BN	J.D. Drew	6.00
28BN	Darin Erstad	5.00
29BN	Troy Glaus	5.00
30BN	Mark Grace	6.00
31BN	Ben Grieve	5.00
32BN	Tony Gwynn	15.00
33BN	Todd Helton	10.00
34BN	Derek Jeter	30.00
35BN	Jeff Kent	5.00
36BN	Jason Kendall	5.00
37BN	Greg Maddux	15.00
38BN	John Olerud	5.00
39BN	Cal Ripken Jr.	30.00
40BN	Chipper Jones	15.00
41BN	John Smoltz	5.00
42BN	Frank Thomas	10.00
43BN	Robin Ventura	5.00
44BN	Bernie Williams	6.00

Behind the Numbers Autograph

	NM/M
Quantity produced listed	
2BN	Wade Boggs/26	75.00
4BN	Lou Brock/20	50.00
5BN	Rollie Fingers/34	40.00
6BN	Carlton Fisk/27	40.00
7BN	Reggie Jackson/44	80.00
10BN	Willie McCovey/44	60.00
12BN	Eddie Murray/33	75.00
13BN	Jim Palmer/22	50.00
15BN	Nolan Ryan/34	250.00
16BN	Mike Schmidt/20	200.00
17BN	Tom Seaver/41	60.00
18BN	Dave Winfield/31	60.00
20BN	Robin Yount/19	150.00
22BN	Rick Ankiel/66	40.00
23BN	Albert Belle/88	20.00
24BN	Adrian Beltre/29	25.00
25BN	Barry Bonds/25	250.00
28BN	Darin Erstad/17	40.00
29BN	Troy Glaus/25	50.00
30BN	Mark Grace/17	50.00
32BN	Tony Gwynn/19	150.00
33BN	Todd Helton/17	75.00
35BN	Jeff Kent/21	50.00
36BN	Jason Kendall/18	40.00
37BN	Greg Maddux/31	250.00
41BN	John Smoltz/29	40.00
42BN	Frank Thomas/35	75.00
44BN	Bernie Williams/51	75.00

Derek Jeter Monumental Moments

	NM/M
2DJMM	Derek Jeter (Edition of 1,996.)	5.00
2DJMM	Derek Jeter (Autographed edition of 96.)	80.00

E-Xtra Innings

	NM/M
Complete Set (10):	30.00
Common Player:	2.00
Inserted 1:20 R	
1XI	Mark McGwire	5.00
2XI	Sammy Sosa	4.00
3XI	Chipper Jones	3.00
4XI	Mike Piazza	4.00
5XI	Cal Ripken Jr.	6.00
6XI	Ken Griffey Jr.	4.00
7XI	Alex Rodriguez	5.00
8XI	Vladimir Guerrero	2.00
9XI	Nomar Garciaparra	4.00
10XI	Derek Jeter	6.00

Prospects Autograph

	NM/M
Common Autograph:	5.00
Prod. #'s Listed	
101	Jason Hart/250	5.00
102	Corey Patterson/800	10.00

103	Timoniel Perez/1000	5.00
104	Marcus Giles/500	5.00
106	Aubrey Huff/500	10.00
107	Joe Crede/500	10.00
108	Larry Barnes/500	5.00
109	Esix Snead/500	5.00
110	Kenny Kelly/250	5.00
111	Justin Miller/250	5.00
112	Jack Cust/1000	10.00
113	Xavier Nady/1000	10.00
114	Eric Munson/500	5.00
115	Elpidio Guzman/250	5.00
116	Juan Pierre/810	5.00
117	Winston Abreu/250	5.00
118	Keith Ginter/500	5.00
119	Jace Brewer/300	5.00
120	Paxton Crawford/250	5.00
121	Jason Tyner/250	5.00
122	Tike Redman/250	5.00
123	John Riedling/500	5.00
124	Jose Ortiz/500	5.00
125	Oswaldo Mairena/500	5.00
126	Eric Byrnes/250	10.00
127	Brian Cole/2000	5.00
128	Adam Piatt/250	5.00
129	Nate Rolison/500	5.00
130	Keith McDonald/250	5.00

Wall of Fame

	NM/M
Common Player:	4.00
Inserted 1:24	
1WF	Robin Yount	8.00
2WF	Paul Molitor	8.00
3WF	Geoff Jenkins	4.00
4WF	Mark McGwire	15.00
5WF	Sammy Sosa	12.00
6WF	Greg Maddux	10.00
7WF	Mike Piazza	12.00
8WF	Cal Ripken Jr.	20.00
9WF	Todd Helton	8.00
10WF	Ken Griffey Jr.	12.00
11WF	Alex Rodriguez	15.00
12WF	Vladimir Guerrero	8.00
13WF	Jeff Bagwell	8.00
14WF	Ivan Rodriguez	6.00
15WF	Juan Gonzalez	8.00
16WF	Barry Bonds	20.00
17WF	Derek Jeter	20.00
18WF	Chipper Jones	10.00
19WF	Frank Thomas	8.00
20WF	Tony Gwynn	10.00
21WF	Nomar Garciaparra	12.00
22WF	Manny Ramirez	8.00
23WF	Andruw Jones	8.00
24WF	Scott Rolen	6.00
25WF	Jason Kendall	4.00
26WF	Roger Clemens	15.00
27WF	Troy Glaus	6.00
28WF	Pedro Martinez	8.00
29WF	Jason Giambi	5.00
30WF	Pat Burrell	5.00

F

1993 Finest

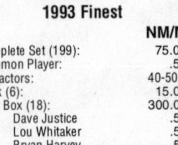

	NM/M
Complete Set (199):	75.00
Common Player:	.50
Refractors:	40-50X
Pack (6):	15.00
Wax Box (18):	300.00
1	Dave Justice	.50
2	Lou Whitaker	.50
3	Bryan Harvey	.50

4	Carlos Garcia	.50
5	Sid Fernandez	.50
6	Brett Butler	.50
7	Scott Cooper	.50
8	B.J. Surhoff	.50
9	Steve Finley	.50
10	Curt Schilling	2.00
11	Jeff Bagwell	4.00
12	Alex Cole	.50
13	John Olerud	.50
14	John Smiley	.50
15	Bip Roberts	.50
16	Albert Belle	.50
17	Duane Ward	.50
18	Alan Trammell	.50
19	Andy Benes	.50
20	Reggie Sanders	.50
21	Todd Zeile	.50
22	Rick Aguilera	.50
23	Dave Hollins	.50
24	Jose Rijo	.50
25	Matt Williams	.50
26	Sandy Alomar	.50
27	Alex Fernandez	.50
28	Ozzie Smith	6.00
29	Ramon Martinez	.50
30	Bernie Williams	1.00
31	Gary Sheffield	1.00
32	Eric Karros	.50
33	Frank Viola	.50
34	Kevin Young	.50
35	Ken Hill	.50
36	Tony Fernandez	.50
37	Tim Wakefield	.50
38	John Kruk	.50
39	Chris Sabo	.50
40	Marquis Grissom	.50
41	Glenn Davis	.50
42	Jeff Montgomery	.50
43	Kenny Lofton	.50
44	John Burkett	.50
45	Darryl Hamilton	.50
46	Jim Abbott	.50
47	Ivan Rodriguez	3.00
48	Eric Young	.50
49	Mitch Williams	.50
50	Harold Reynolds	.50
51	Brian Harper	.50
52	Rafael Palmeiro	3.00
53	Bret Saberhagen	.50
54	Jeff Conine	.50
55	Ivan Calderon	.50
56	Juan Guzman	.50
57	Carlos Baerga	.50
58	Charles Nagy	.50
59	Wally Joyner	.50
60	Charlie Hayes	.50
61	Shane Mack	.50
62	Pete Harnisch	.50
63	George Brett	8.00
64	Lance Johnson	.50
65	Ben McDonald	.50
66	Bobby Bonilla	.50
67	Terry Steinbach	.50
68	Ron Gant	.50
69	Doug Jones	.50
70	Paul Molitor	4.00
71	Brady Anderson	.50
72	Chuck Finley	.50
73	Mark Grace	.75
74	Mike Devereaux	.50
75	Tony Phillips	.50
76	Chuck Knoblauch	.50
77	Tony Gwynn	6.00
78	Kevin Appier	.50
79	Sammy Sosa	6.00
80	Mickey Tettleton	.50
81	Felix Jose	.50
82	Mark Langston	.50
83	Gregg Jefferies	.50
84	Andre Dawson/AS	1.00
85	Greg Maddux/AS	6.00
86	Rickey Henderson/AS	4.00
87	Tom Glavine/AS	2.50
88	Roberto Alomar/AS	1.00
89	Darryl Strawberry/AS	.50
90	Wade Boggs/AS	6.00
91	Bo Jackson/AS	1.00
92	Mark McGwire/AS	6.00
93	Robin Ventura/AS	.50
94	Joe Carter/AS	.50

95	Lee Smith/AS	.50
96	Cal Ripken, Jr./AS	10.00
97	Larry Walker/AS	.50
98	Don Mattingly/AS	8.00
99	Jose Canseco/AS	2.50
100	Dennis Eckersley/AS	3.00
101	Terry Pendleton/AS	.50
102	Frank Thomas/AS	4.00
103	Barry Bonds/AS	10.00
104	Roger Clemens/AS	8.00
105	Ryne Sandberg/AS	6.00
106	Fred McGriff/AS	.50
107	Nolan Ryan/AS	10.00
108	Will Clark/AS	.50
109	Pat Listach/AS	.50
110	Ken Griffey Jr./AS	6.00
111	Cecil Fielder/AS	.50
112	Kirby Puckett/AS	6.00
113	Dwight Gooden/AS	.50
114	Barry Larkin/AS	.50
115	David Cone/AS	.50
116	Juan Gonzalez/AS	2.50
117	Kent Hrbek	.50
118	Tim Wallach	.50
119	Craig Biggio	.50
120	Bobby Kelly	.50
121	Greg Olson	.50
122	Eddie Murray	4.00
123	Wil Cordero	.50
124	Jay Buhner	.50
125	Carlton Fisk	4.00
126	Eric Davis	.50
127	Doug Drabek	.50
128	Ozzie Guillen	.50
129	John Wetteland	.50
130	Andres Galarraga	.50
131	Ken Caminiti	.50
132	Tom Candiotti	.50
133	Pat Borders	.50
134	Kevin Brown	.50
135	Travis Fryman	.50
136	Kevin Mitchell	.50
137	Greg Swindell	.50
138	Benny Santiago	.50
139	Reggie Jefferson	.50
140	Chris Bosio	.50
141	Deion Sanders	.60
142	Scott Erickson	.50
143	Howard Johnson	.50
144	Orestes Destrade	.50
145	Jose Guzman	.50
146	Chad Curtis	.50
147	Cal Eldred	.50
148	Willie Greene	.50
149	Tommy Greene	.50
150	Erik Hanson	.50
151	Bob Welch	.50
152	John Jaha	.50
153	Harold Baines	.50
154	Randy Johnson	4.00
155	Al Martin	.50
156	J.T. Snow **RC**	1.50
157	Mike Mussina	2.50
158	Ruben Sierra	.50
159	Dean Palmer	.50
160	Steve Avery	.50
161	Julio Franco	.50
162	Dave Winfield	4.00
163	Tim Salmon	.50
164	Tom Henke	.50
165	Mo Vaughn	.50
166	John Smoltz	.50
167	Danny Tartabull	.50
168	Delino DeShields	.50
169	Charlie Hough	.50
170	Paul O'Neill	.50
171	Darren Daulton	.50
172	Jack McDowell	.50
173	Junior Felix	.50
174	Jimmy Key	.50
175	George Bell	.50
176	Mike Stanton	.50
177	Len Dykstra	.50
178	Norm Charlton	.50
179	Eric Anthony	.50
180	Bob Dibble	.50
181	Otis Nixon	.50
182	Randy Myers	.50
183	Tim Raines	.50
184	Orel Hershiser	.50
185	Andy Van Slyke	.50
186	Mike Lansing **RC**	1.00
187	Ray Lankford	.50
188	Mike Morgan	.50
189	Moises Alou	.50
190	Edgar Martinez	.50
191	John Franco	.50
192	Robin Yount	5.00
193	Bob Tewksbury	.50
194	Jay Bell	.50
195	Luis Gonzalez	.50
196	Dave Fleming	.50
197	Mike Greenwell	.50
198	David Nied	.50
199	Mike Piazza	10.00

Refractors

		NM/M
Common Player:		15.00
1	Dave Justice	15.00
2	Lou Whitaker	15.00
3	Bryan Harvey/SP	45.00
4	Carlos Garcia	15.00
5	Sid Fernandez	15.00
6	Brett Butler	15.00
7	Scott Cooper	15.00
8	B.J. Surhoff	15.00
9	Steve Finley	15.00
10	Curt Schilling	50.00
11	Jeff Bagwell	100.00
12	Alex Cole	15.00
13	John Olerud	15.00
14	John Smiley	15.00
15	Bip Roberts	15.00
16	Albert Belle	15.00
17	Duane Ward	15.00
18	Alan Trammell	15.00
19	Andy Benes	15.00
20	Reggie Sanders	15.00
21	Todd Zeile	15.00
22	Rick Aguilera	15.00
23	Dave Hollins	15.00
24	Jose Rijo	15.00
25	Matt Williams	15.00
26	Sandy Alomar	15.00
27	Alex Fernandez	15.00
28	Ozzie Smith	100.00
29	Ramon Martinez	15.00
30	Bernie Williams	15.00
31	Gary Sheffield	40.00
32	Eric Karros	15.00
33	Frank Viola	15.00
34	Kevin Young	15.00
35	Ken Hill	15.00
36	Tony Fernandez	15.00
37	Tim Wakefield	15.00
38	John Kruk	15.00
39	Chris Sabo/SP	75.00
40	Marquis Grissom	15.00
41	Glenn Davis/SP	50.00
42	Jeff Montgomery	15.00
43	Kenny Lofton	15.00
44	John Burkett	15.00
45	Darryl Hamilton	15.00
46	Jim Abbott	15.00
47	Ivan Rodriguez	150.00
48	Eric Young	15.00
49	Mitch Williams	15.00
50	Harold Reynolds	15.00
51	Brian Harper	15.00
52	Rafael Palmeiro	75.00
53	Bret Saberhagen	15.00
54	Jeff Conine	15.00
55	Ivan Calderon	15.00
56	Juan Guzman	15.00
57	Carlos Baerga	15.00
58	Charles Nagy	15.00
59	Wally Joyner	15.00
60	Charlie Hayes	15.00
61	Shane Mack	15.00
62	Pete Harnisch	15.00
63	George Brett	125.00
64	Lance Johnson	15.00
65	Ben McDonald	15.00
66	Bobby Bonilla	15.00
67	Terry Steinbach	15.00
68	Ron Gant	15.00
69	Doug Jones	15.00
70	Paul Molitor	100.00
71	Brady Anderson	15.00
72	Chuck Finley	15.00
73	Mark Grace	15.00
74	Mike Devereaux	15.00
75	Tony Phillips	15.00
76	Chuck Knoblauch	15.00
77	Tony Gwynn	100.00
78	Kevin Appier	15.00
79	Sammy Sosa	150.00
80	Mickey Tettleton	15.00
81	Felix Jose	15.00
82	Mark Langston	15.00
83	Gregg Jefferies	15.00
84	Andre Dawson/AS	35.00
85	Greg Maddux/AS	150.00
86	Rickey Henderson/AS	125.00
87	Tom Glavine/AS	50.00
88	Roberto Alomar/AS	45.00
89	Darryl Strawberry/AS	15.00
90	Wade Boggs/AS	100.00
91	Bo Jackson/AS	60.00
92	Mark McGwire/AS	200.00
93	Robin Ventura/AS	15.00
94	Joe Carter/AS/SP	50.00
95	Lee Smith/AS	15.00
96	Cal Ripken, Jr./AS	500.00
97	Larry Walker/AS/SP	100.00
98	Don Mattingly/AS	100.00
99	Jose Canseco/AS	50.00
100	Dennis Eckersley/AS	75.00
101	Terry Pendleton/AS	15.00
102	Frank Thomas/AS/SP	200.00
103	Barry Bonds/AS	300.00
104	Roger Clemens/AS	200.00
105	Ryne Sandberg/AS	125.00
106	Fred McGriff/AS	15.00
107	Nolan Ryan/AS	500.00
108	Will Clark/AS/SP	75.00
109	Pat Listach/AS	15.00
110	Ken Griffey Jr./AS	450.00
111	Cecil Fielder/AS	15.00
112	Kirby Puckett/AS	100.00
113	Dwight Gooden/AS	15.00
114	Barry Larkin/AS	15.00
115	David Cone/AS	15.00
116	Juan Gonzalez/AS/SP	150.00
117	Kent Hrbek	15.00
118	Tim Wallach	15.00
119	Craig Biggio	15.00
120	Bobby Kelly	15.00
121	Greg Olson	15.00
122	Eddie Murray	100.00
123	Wil Cordero	15.00
124	Jay Buhner	15.00
125	Carlton Fisk	75.00
126	Eric Davis	15.00
127	Doug Drabek	15.00
128	Ozzie Guillen	15.00
129	John Wetteland	15.00
130	Andres Galarraga	15.00
131	Ken Caminiti	15.00
132	Tom Candiotti	15.00
133	Pat Borders	15.00
134	Kevin Brown	15.00
135	Travis Fryman	15.00
136	Kevin Mitchell	15.00
137	Greg Swindell	15.00
138	Benny Santiago	15.00
139	Reggie Jefferson	15.00
140	Chris Bosio	15.00
141	Deion Sanders	15.00
142	Scott Erickson	15.00
143	Howard Johnson	15.00
144	Orestes Destrade	15.00
145	Jose Guzman	15.00
146	Chad Curtis	15.00
147	Cal Eldred	15.00
148	Willie Greene/SP	75.00
149	Tommy Greene	15.00
150	Erik Hanson	15.00
151	Bob Welch	15.00
152	John Jaha	15.00
153	Harold Baines	15.00
154	Randy Johnson	100.00
155	Al Martin	15.00
156	J.T. Snow	15.00
157	Mike Mussina	45.00
158	Ruben Sierra	15.00
159	Dean Palmer	15.00
160	Steve Avery	15.00
161	Julio Franco	15.00
162	Dave Winfield	100.00
163	Tim Salmon/SP	50.00
164	Tom Henke	15.00
165	Mo Vaughn	15.00
166	John Smoltz	15.00
167	Danny Tartabull	15.00
168	Delino DeShields	15.00
169	Charlie Hough	15.00
170	Paul O'Neill	15.00
171	Darren Daulton	15.00
172	Jack McDowell	15.00
173	Junior Felix	15.00
174	Jimmy Key	15.00
175	George Bell	15.00
176	Mike Stanton	15.00
177	Len Dykstra	15.00
178	Norm Charlton	15.00
179	Eric Anthony	15.00
180	Bob Dibble	15.00
181	Otis Nixon	15.00
182	Randy Myers	15.00
183	Tim Raines	15.00
184	Orel Hershiser	15.00
185	Andy Van Slyke	15.00
186	Mike Lansing	15.00
187	Ray Lankford	15.00
188	Mike Morgan	15.00
189	Moises Alou	15.00
190	Edgar Martinez	15.00
191	John Franco	15.00
192	Robin Yount	90.00
193	Bob Tewksbury	15.00
194	Jay Bell	15.00
195	Luis Gonzalez	15.00
196	Dave Fleming	15.00
197	Mike Greenwell	15.00
198	David Nied	15.00
199	Mike Piazza	250.00

1993 Finest Promos

		NM/M
Complete Set (3):		25.00
Complete Set, Refractors (3):		1,500
88	Roberto Alomar	3.50
88r	Roberto Alomar (Refractor)	300.00
98	Don Mattingly	10.00
98r	Don Mattingly (Refractor)	500.00
107	Nolan Ryan	15.00
107r	Nolan Ryan (Refractor)	750.00

Jumbo All-Stars

		NM/M
Complete Set (33):		185.00
Common Player:		2.00
84	Andre Dawson	2.50
85	Greg Maddux	10.00
86	Rickey Henderson	7.50
87	Tom Glavine	3.00
88	Roberto Alomar	3.00
89	Darryl Strawberry	2.00
90	Wade Boggs	10.00
91	Bo Jackson	2.00
92	Mark McGwire	20.00
93	Robin Ventura	2.00
94	Joe Carter	2.00
95	Lee Smith	2.00
96	Cal Ripken, Jr.	30.00
97	Larry Walker	2.00
98	Don Mattingly	12.00
99	Jose Canseco	3.50
100	Dennis Eckersley	6.00
101	Terry Pendleton	2.00
102	Frank Thomas	7.50
103	Barry Bonds	30.00
104	Roger Clemens	12.00
105	Ryne Sandberg	10.00
106	Fred McGriff	2.00
107	Nolan Ryan	30.00
108	Will Clark	2.50
109	Pat Listach	2.00
110	Ken Griffey Jr.	15.00
111	Cecil Fielder	2.00
112	Kirby Puckett	10.00
113	Dwight Gooden	2.00
114	Barry Larkin	2.00
115	David Cone	2.00
116	Juan Gonzalez	7.50

1994 Finest

		NM/M
Complete Set (440):		40.00
Common Player:		.15
Refractors:		3X
Series 1 or 2 Pack (7):		1.50
Series 1 or 2 Box (24):		25.00
1	Mike Piazza	3.00
2	Kevin Stocker	.15
3	Greg McMichael	.15
4	Jeff Conine	.15
5	Rene Arocha	.15
6	Aaron Sele	.15
7	Brent Gates	.15
8	Chuck Carr	.15
9	Kirk Rueter	.15
10	Mike Lansing	.15
11	Al Martin	.15
12	Jason Bere	.15
13	Troy Neel	.15
14	Armando Reynoso	.15
15	Jeromy Burnitz	.15
16	Rich Amaral	.15
17	David McCarty	.15
18	Tim Salmon	.15
19	Steve Cooke	.15
20	Wil Cordero	.15
21	Kevin Tapani	.15

22	Deion Sanders	.15
23	Jose Offerman	.15
24	Mark Langston	.15
25	Ken Hill	.15
26	Alex Fernandez	.15
27	Jeff Blauser	.15
28	Royce Clayton	.15
29	Brad Ausmus	.15
30	Ryan Bowen	.15
31	Steve Finley	.15
32	Charlie Hayes	.15
33	Jeff Kent	.15
34	Mike Henneman	.15
35	Andres Galarraga	.15
36	Wayne Kirby	.15
37	Joe Oliver	.15
38	Terry Steinbach	.15
39	Ryan Thompson	.15
40	Luis Alicea	.15
41	Randy Velarde	.15
42	Bob Tewksbury	.15
43	Reggie Sanders	.15
44	Brian Williams	.15
45	Joe Orsulak	.15
46	Jose Lind	.15
47	Dave Hollins	.15
48	Graeme Lloyd	.15
49	Jim Gott	.15
50	Andre Dawson	.40
51	Steve Buechele	.15
52	David Cone	.15
53	Ricky Gutierrez	.15
54	Lance Johnson	.15
55	Tino Martinez	.15
56	Phil Hiatt	.15
57	Carlos Garcia	.15
58	Danny Darwin	.15
59	Dante Bichette	.15
60	Scott Kamieniecki	.15
61	Orlando Merced	.15
62	Brian McRae	.15
63	Pat Kelly	.15
64	Tom Henke	.15
65	Jeff King	.15
66	Mike Mussina	.75
67	Tim Pugh	.15
68	Robby Thompson	.15
69	Paul O'Neill	.15
70	Hal Morris	.15
71	Ron Karkovice	.15
72	Joe Girardi	.15
73	Eduardo Perez	.15
74	Raul Mondesi	.15
75	Mike Gallego	.15
76	Mike Stanley	.15
77	Kevin Roberson	.15
78	Mark McGwire	4.00
79	Pat Listach	.15
80	Eric Davis	.15
81	Mike Bordick	.15
82	Dwight Gooden	.15
83	Mike Moore	.15
84	Phil Plantier	.15
85	Darren Lewis	.15
86	Rick Wilkins	.15
87	Darryl Strawberry	.15
88	Rob Dibble	.15
89	Greg Vaughn	.15
90	Jeff Russell	.15
91	Mark Lewis	.15
92	Gregg Jefferies	.15
93	Jose Guzman	.15
94	Kenny Rogers	.15
95	Mark Lemke	.15
96	Mike Morgan	.15
97	Andujar Cedeno	.15
98	Orel Hershiser	.15
99	Greg Swindell	.15
100	John Smoltz	.15
101	Pedro Martinez	.15
102	Jim Thome	1.00
103	David Segui	.15
104	Charles Nagy	.15
105	Shane Mack	.15
106	John Jaha	.15
107	Tom Candiotti	.15
108	David Wells	.15
109	Bobby Jones	.15
110	Bob Hamelin	.15
111	Bernard Gilkey	.15
112	Chili Davis	.15
113	Todd Stottlemyre	.15
114	Derek Bell	.15
115	Mark McLemore	.15
116	Mark Whiten	.15
117	Mike Devereaux	.15
118	Terry Pendleton	.15
119	Pat Meares	.15
120	Pete Harnisch	.15
121	Moises Alou	.15
122	Jay Buhner	.15
123	Wes Chamberlain	.15
124	Mike Perez	.15
125	Devon White	.15
126	Ivan Rodriguez	1.25
127	Don Slaught	.15
128	John Valentin	.15
129	Jaime Navarro	.15
130	Dave Magadan	.15
131	Brady Anderson	.15
132	Juan Guzman	.15
133	John Wetteland	.15
134	Dave Stewart	.15
135	Scott Servais	.15
136	Ozzie Smith	2.50
137	Darrin Fletcher	.15
138	Jose Mesa	.15
139	Wilson Alvarez	.15
140	Pete Incaviglia	.15
141	Chris Hoiles	.15
142	Darryl Hamilton	.15
143	Chuck Finley	.15
144	Archi Cianfrocco	.15
145	Bill Wegman	.15
146	Joey Cora	.15
147	Darrell Whitmore	.15
148	David Hulse	.15
149	Jim Abbott	.15
150	Curt Schilling	.40
151	Bill Swift	.15
152	Tommy Greene	.15
153	Roberto Mejia	.15
154	Edgar Martinez	.15
155	Roger Pavlik	.15
156	Randy Tomlin	.15
157	J.T. Snow	.15
158	Bob Welch	.15
159	Alan Trammell	.15
160	Ed Sprague	.15
161	Ben McDonald	.15
162	Derrick May	.15
163	Roberto Kelly	.15
164	Bryan Harvey	.15
165	Ron Gant	.15
166	Scott Erickson	.15
167	Anthony Young	.15
168	Scott Cooper	.15
169	Rod Beck	.15
170	John Franco	.15
171	Gary DiSarcina	.15
172	Dave Fleming	.15
173	Wade Boggs	2.50
174	Kevin Appier	.15
175	Jose Bautista	.15
176	Wally Joyner	.15
177	Dean Palmer	.15
178	Tony Phillips	.15
179	John Smiley	.15
180	Charlie Hough	.15
181	Scott Fletcher	.15
182	Todd Van Poppel	.15
183	Mike Blowers	.15
184	Willie McGee	.15
185	Paul Sorrento	.15
186	Eric Young	.15
187	Bret Barberie	.15
188	Manuel Lee	.15
189	Jeff Branson	.15
190	Jim Deshaies	.15
191	Ken Caminiti	.15
192	Tim Raines	.15
193	Joe Grahe	.15
194	Hipolito Pichardo	.15
195	Denny Neagle	.15
196	Jeff Gardner	.15
197	Mike Benjamin	.15
198	Milt Thompson	.15
199	Bruce Ruffin	.15
200	Chris Hammond	.15
201	Tony Gwynn	2.50
202	Robin Ventura	.15
203	Frank Thomas	1.50
204	Kirby Puckett	2.50
205	Roberto Alomar	.30
206	Dennis Eckersley	1.25
207	Joe Carter	.15
208	Albert Belle	.15
209	Greg Maddux	2.50
210	Ryne Sandberg	2.50
211	Juan Gonzalez	.75
212	Jeff Bagwell	1.50
213	Randy Johnson	1.50
214	Matt Williams	.15
215	Dave Winfield	1.50
216	Larry Walker	.15
217	Roger Clemens	2.75
218	Kenny Lofton	.15
219	Cecil Fielder	.15
220	Darren Daulton	.15
221	John Olerud	.15
222	Jose Canseco	.75
223	Rickey Henderson	1.50
224	Fred McGriff	.15
225	Gary Sheffield	.50
226	Jack McDowell	.15
227	Rafael Palmeiro	1.25
228	Travis Fryman	.15
229	Marquis Grissom	.15
230	Barry Bonds	5.00
231	Carlos Baerga	.15
232	Ken Griffey Jr.	3.00
233	Dave Justice	.15
234	Bobby Bonilla	.15
235	Cal Ripken	5.00
236	Sammy Sosa	2.50
237	Len Dykstra	.15
238	Will Clark	.15
239	Paul Molitor	1.50
240	Barry Larkin	.15
241	Bo Jackson	.35
242	Mitch Williams	.15
243	Ron Darling	.15
244	Darryl Kile	.15
245	Geronimo Berroa	.15
246	Gregg Olson	.15
247	Brian Harper	.15
248	Rheal Cormier	.15
249	Rey Sanchez	.15
250	Jeff Fassero	.15
251	Sandy Alomar	.15
252	Chris Bosio	.15
253	Andy Stankiewicz	.15
254	Harold Baines	.15
255	Andy Ashby	.15
256	Tyler Green	.15
257	Kevin Brown	.15
258	Mo Vaughn	.15
259	Mike Harkey	.15
260	Dave Henderson	.15
261	Kent Hrbek	.15
262	Darrin Jackson	.15
263	Bob Wickman	.15
264	Spike Owen	.15
265	Todd Jones	.15
266	Pat Borders	.15
267	Tom Glavine	.45
268	Dave Nilsson	.15
269	Rich Batchelor	.15
270	Delino DeShields	.15
271	Felix Fermin	.15
272	Orestes Destrade	.15
273	Mickey Morandini	.15
274	Otis Nixon	.15
275	Ellis Burks	.15
276	Greg Gagne	.15
277	John Doherty	.15
278	Julio Franco	.15
279	Bernie Williams	.15
280	Rick Aguilera	.15
281	Mickey Tettleton	.15
282	David Nied	.15
283	Johnny Ruffin	.15
284	Dan Wilson	.15
285	Omar Vizquel	.15
286	Willie Banks	.15
287	Erik Pappas	.15
288	Cal Eldred	.15
289	Bobby Witt	.15
290	Luis Gonzalez	.15
291	Greg Pirkl	.15
292	Alex Cole	.15
293	Ricky Bones	.15
294	Denis Boucher	.15
295	John Burkett	.15
296	Steve Trachsel	.15
297	Ricky Jordan	.15
298	Mark Dewey	.15
299	Jimmy Key	.15
300	Mike MacFarlane	.15
301	Tim Belcher	.15
302	Carlos Reyes	.15
303	Greg Harris	.15
304	Brian Anderson **RC**	.15
305	Terry Mulholland	.15
306	Felix Jose	.15
307	Darren Holmes	.15
308	Jose Rijo	.15
309	Paul Wagner	.15
310	Bob Scanlan	.15
311	Mike Jackson	.15
312	Jose Vizcaino	.15
313	Rob Butler	.15
314	Kevin Seitzer	.15
315	Geronimo Pena	.15
316	Hector Carrasco	.15
317	Eddie Murray	1.50
318	Roger Salkeld	.15
319	Todd Hundley	.15
320	Danny Jackson	.15
321	Kevin Young	.15
322	Mike Greenwell	.15
323	Kevin Mitchell	.15
324	Chuck Knoblauch	.15
325	Danny Tartabull	.15
326	Vince Coleman	.15
327	Marvin Freeman	.15
328	Andy Benes	.15
329	Mike Kelly	.15
330	Karl Rhodes	.15
331	Allen Watson	.15
332	Damion Easley	.15
333	Reggie Jefferson	.15
334	Kevin McReynolds	.15
335	Arthur Rhodes	.15
336	Brian Hunter	.15
337	Tom Browning	.15
338	Pedro Munoz	.15
339	Billy Ripken	.15
340	Gene Harris	.15
341	Fernando Vina	.15
342	Sean Berry	.15
343	Pedro Astacio	.15
344	B.J. Surhoff	.15
345	Doug Drabek	.15
346	Jody Reed	.15
347	Ray Lankford	.15
348	Steve Farr	.15
349	Eric Anthony	.15
350	Pete Smith	.15
351	Lee Smith	.15
352	Mariano Duncan	.15
353	Doug Strange	.15
354	Tim Bogar	.15
355	Dave Weathers	.15
356	Eric Karros	.15
357	Randy Myers	.15
358	Chad Curtis	.15
359	Steve Avery	.15
360	Brian Jordan	.15
361	Tim Wallach	.15
362	Pedro Martinez	1.50
363	Bip Roberts	.15
364	Lou Whitaker	.15
365	Luis Polonia	.15
366	Benny Santiago	.15
367	Brett Butler	.15
368	Shawon Dunston	.15
369	Kelly Stinnett	.15
370	Chris Turner	.15
371	Ruben Sierra	.15
372	Greg Harris	.15
373	Xavier Hernandez	.15
374	Howard Johnson	.15
375	Duane Ward	.15
376	Roberto Hernandez	.15
377	Scott Leius	.15
378	Dave Valle	.15
379	Sid Fernandez	.15
380	Doug Jones	.15
381	Zane Smith	.15
382	Craig Biggio	.15
383	Rick White	.15
384	Tom Pagnozzi	.15
385	Chris James	.15
386	Bret Boone	.15
387	Jeff Montgomery	.15
388	Chad Kreuter	.15
389	Greg Hibbard	.15
390	Mark Grace	.15
391	Phil Leftwich	.15
392	Don Mattingly	2.75
393	Ozzie Guillen	.15
394	Gary Gaetti	.15
395	Erik Hanson	.15
396	Scott Brosius	.15
397	Tom Gordon	.15
398	Bill Gullickson	.15
399	Matt Mieske	.15
400	Pat Hentgen	.15
401	Walt Weiss	.15
402	Greg Blosser	.15
403	Stan Javier	.15
404	Doug Henry	.15
405	Ramon Martinez	.15
406	Frank Viola	.15
407	Mike Hampton	.15
408	Andy Van Slyke	.15
409	Bobby Ayala	.15
410	Todd Zeile	.15
411	Jay Bell	.15
412	Denny Martinez	.15
413	Mark Portugal	.15
414	Bobby Munoz	.15
415	Kirt Manwaring	.15
416	John Kruk	.15
417	Trevor Hoffman	.15
418	Chris Sabo	.15
419	Bret Saberhagen	.15
420	Chris Nabholz	.15
421	James Mouton	.15
422	Tony Tarasco	.15
423	Carlos Delgado	.75
424	Rondell White	.15
425	Javier Lopez	.15
426	Chan Ho Park **RC**	1.00
427	Cliff Floyd	.15
428	Dave Staton	.15
429	J.R. Phillips	.15
430	Manny Ramirez	1.50
431	Kurt Abbott	.15
432	Melvin Nieves	.15
433	Alex Gonzalez	.15
434	Rick Helling	.15
435	Danny Bautista	.15
436	Matt Walbeck	.15
437	Ryan Klesko	.15
438	Steve Karsay	.15
439	Salomon Torres	.15
440	Scott Ruffcorn	.15

1994 Finest Bronze

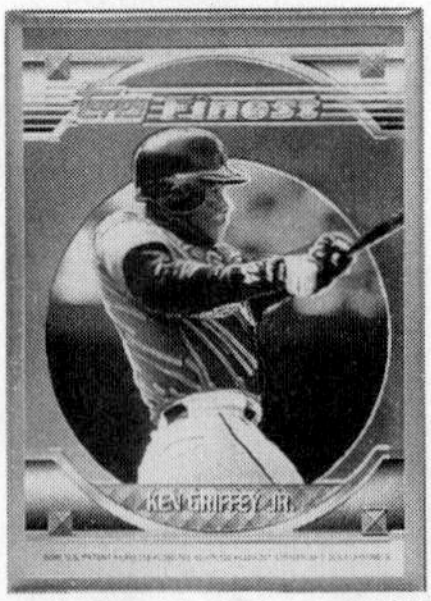

		NM/M
Complete Set (3):		40.00
Common Player:		10.00
1	Barry Bonds	20.00
2	Ken Griffey Jr.	15.00
3	Frank Thomas	10.00

1994 Finest Pre-Production

		NM/M
Complete Set (40):		35.00
Common Player:		1.00
22	Deion Sanders	1.00
23	Jose Offerman	1.00
26	Alex Fernandez	1.00
31	Steve Finley	1.00
35	Andres Galarraga	1.00

Mark McGwire 1B

#	Player	NM/M
43	Reggie Sanders	1.00
47	Dave Hollins	1.00
52	David Cone	1.00
59	Dante Bichette	1.00
61	Orlando Merced	1.00
62	Brian McRae	1.00
66	Mike Mussina	2.50
76	Mike Stanley	1.00
78	Mark McGwire	6.00
79	Pat Listach	1.00
82	Dwight Gooden	1.00
84	Phil Plantier	1.00
90	Jeff Russell	1.00
92	Gregg Jefferies	1.00
93	Jose Guzman	1.00
100	John Smoltz	1.00
102	Jim Thome	3.00
121	Moises Alou	1.00
125	Devon White	1.00
126	Ivan Rodriguez	3.00
130	Dave Magadan	1.00
136	Ozzie Smith	4.00
141	Chris Hoiles	1.00
149	Jim Abbott	1.00
151	Bill Swift	1.00
154	Edgar Martinez	1.00
157	J.T. Snow	1.00
159	Alan Trammell	1.00
163	Roberto Kelly	1.00
166	Scott Erickson	1.00
168	Scott Cooper	1.00
169	Rod Beck	1.00
177	Dean Palmer	1.00
182	Todd Van Poppel	1.00
185	Paul Sorrento	1.00

Refractors

		NM/M
Complete Set (440):		300.00
Common Player:		1.00
Stars/Rookies:		3X

(See 1994 Finest for checklist and base card prices.)

1994 Finest Superstar Jumbos

		NM/M
Complete Set (45):		400.00
Common Player:		4.00
1	Mike Piazza	35.00
18	Tim Salmon	4.00
35	Andres Galarraga	4.00
74	Raul Mondesi	4.00
92	Gregg Jefferies	4.00
201	Tony Gwynn	20.00
203	Frank Thomas	15.00
204	Kirby Puckett	20.00
205	Roberto Alomar	6.00

		NM/M
Complete Set (80):		140.00
Common Player:		1.00
1	Mike Piazza	12.50
2	Kevin Stocker	1.00
3	Greg McMichael	1.00
4	Jeff Conine	1.00
5	Rene Arocha	1.00
6	Aaron Sele	1.00
7	Brent Gates	1.00
8	Chuck Carr	1.00
9	Kirk Rueter	1.00
10	Mike Lansing	1.00
11	Al Martin	1.00
12	Jason Bere	1.00
13	Troy Neel	1.00
14	Armando Reynoso	1.00
15	Jeromy Burnitz	1.00
16	Rich Amaral	1.00
17	David McCarty	1.00
18	Tim Salmon	1.00
19	Steve Cooke	1.00
20	Wil Cordero	1.00
201	Tony Gwynn	7.50
202	Robin Ventura	1.00
203	Frank Thomas	6.00
204	Kirby Puckett	7.50
205	Roberto Alomar	2.00
206	Dennis Eckersley	5.00
207	Joe Carter	1.00
208	Albert Belle	1.00
209	Greg Maddux	7.50
210	Ryne Sandberg	7.50
211	Juan Gonzalez	3.00
212	Jeff Bagwell	2.00
213	Randy Johnson	6.00
214	Matt Williams	1.00
215	Dave Winfield	6.00
216	Larry Walker	1.00
217	Roger Clemens	10.00
218	Kenny Lofton	1.00
219	Cecil Fielder	1.00
220	Darren Daulton	1.00
221	John Olerud	1.00
222	Jose Canseco	4.00
223	Rickey Henderson	6.00
224	Fred McGriff	1.00
225	Gary Sheffield	2.00
226	Jack McDowell	1.00
227	Rafael Palmeiro	5.00
228	Travis Fryman	1.00
229	Marquis Grissom	1.00
230	Barry Bonds	20.00
231	Carlos Baerga	1.00
232	Ken Griffey Jr.	12.50
233	Dave Justice	1.00
234	Bobby Bonilla	1.00
235	Cal Ripken	20.00
236	Sammy Sosa	7.50
237	Len Dykstra	1.00
238	Will Clark	1.00
239	Paul Molitor	6.00
240	Barry Larkin	1.00
421	James Mouton	1.00
422	Tony Tarasco	1.00
423	Carlos Delgado	3.00
424	Rondell White	1.00
425	Javier Lopez	1.00
426	Chan Ho Park	1.00
427	Cliff Floyd	1.00
428	Dave Staton	1.00
429	J.R. Phillips	1.00
430	Manny Ramirez	6.00
431	Kurt Abbott	1.00
432	Melvin Nieves	1.00
433	Alex Gonzalez	1.00
434	Rick Helling	1.00
435	Danny Bautista	1.00
436	Matt Walbeck	1.00
437	Ryan Klesko	1.00
438	Steve Karsay	1.00
439	Salomon Torres	1.00
440	Scott Ruffcorn	1.00

1994 Finest Superstar Sampler

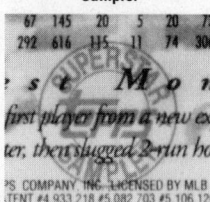

#	Player	Price
207	Joe Carter	4.00
208	Albert Belle	4.00
209	Greg Maddux	20.00
210	Ryne Sandberg	20.00
211	Juan Gonzalez	7.50
212	Jeff Bagwell	15.00
213	Randy Johnson	15.00
214	Matt Williams	4.00
216	Larry Walker	4.00
217	Roger Clemens	30.00
219	Cecil Fielder	4.00
220	Darren Daulton	4.00
221	John Olerud	4.00
222	Jose Canseco	7.50
224	Fred McGriff	4.00
225	Gary Sheffield	6.00
226	Jack McDowell	4.00
227	Rafael Palmeiro	12.00
229	Marquis Grissom	4.00
230	Barry Bonds	65.00
231	Carlos Baerga	4.00
232	Ken Griffey Jr.	35.00
233	Dave Justice	4.00
234	Bobby Bonilla	4.00
235	Cal Ripken Jr.	65.00
237	Len Dykstra	4.00
238	Will Clark	4.00
239	Paul Molitor	15.00
240	Barry Larkin	4.00
258	Mo Vaughn	4.00
267	Tom Glavine	7.50
390	Mark Grace	4.00
392	Don Mattingly	30.00
408	Andy Van Slyke	4.00
427	Cliff Floyd	4.00
430	Manny Ramirez	15.00

1995 Finest

ALBERT BELLE

		NM/M
Complete Set (220):		75.00
Common Player:		.25
Refractors:		5X
Series 1 or 2 Pack (7):		2.00
Series 1 or 2 Wax Box (24):		30.00
1	Raul Mondesi	.25
2	Kurt Abbott	.25
3	Chris Gomez	.25
4	Manny Ramirez	1.50
5	Rondell White	.25
6	William Van Landingham	.25
7	Jon Lieber	.25
8	Ryan Klesko	.25
9	John Hudek	.25
10	Joey Hamilton	.25
11	Bob Hamelin	.25
12	Brian Anderson	.25
13	Mike Lieberthal	.25
14	Rico Brogna	.25
15	Rusty Greer	.25
16	Carlos Delgado	1.00
17	Jim Edmonds	.65
18	Steve Trachsel	.25
19	Matt Walbeck	.25
20	Armando Benitez	.25
21	Steve Karsay	.25
22	Jose Oliva	.25
23	Cliff Floyd	.25
24	Kevin Foster	.25
25	Javier Lopez	.25
26	Jose Valentin	.25
27	James Mouton	.25
28	Hector Carrasco	.25
29	Orlando Miller	.25
30	Garret Anderson	.25
31	Marvin Freeman	.25
32	Brett Butler	.25
33	Roberto Kelly	.25
34	Rod Beck	.25
35	Jose Rijo	.25
36	Edgar Martinez	.25
37	Jim Thome	.65
38	Rick Wilkins	.25
39	Wally Joyner	.25
40	Wil Cordero	.25
41	Tommy Greene	.25
42	Travis Fryman	.25
43	Don Slaught	.25
44	Brady Anderson	.25
45	Matt Williams	.25
46	Rene Arocha	.25
47	Rickey Henderson	1.50
48	Mike Mussina	.75

#	Player	Price
49	Greg McMichael	.25
50	Jody Reed	.25
51	Tino Martinez	.25
52	Dave Clark	.25
53	John Valentin	.25
54	Bret Boone	.25
55	Walt Weiss	.25
56	Kenny Lofton	.25
57	Scott Leius	.25
58	Eric Karros	.25
59	John Olerud	.25
60	Chris Hoiles	.25
61	Sandy Alomar	.25
62	Tim Wallach	.25
63	Cal Eldred	.25
64	Tom Glavine	.50
65	Mark Grace	.25
66	Rey Sanchez	.25
67	Bobby Ayala	.25
68	Dante Bichette	.25
69	Andres Galarraga	.25
70	Chuck Carr	.25
71	Bobby Witt	.25
72	Steve Avery	.25
73	Bobby Jones	.25
74	Delino DeShields	.25
75	Kevin Tapani	.25
76	Randy Johnson	1.50
77	David Nied	.25
78	Pat Hentgen	.25
79	Tim Salmon	.25
80	Todd Zeile	.25
81	John Wetteland	.25
82	Albert Belle	.25
83	Ben McDonald	.25
84	Bobby Munoz	.25
85	Bip Roberts	.25
86	Mo Vaughn	.25
87	Chuck Finley	.25
88	Chuck Knoblauch	.25
89	Frank Thomas	1.50
90	Danny Tartabull	.25
91	Dean Palmer	.25
92	Len Dykstra	.25
93	J.R. Phillips	.25
94	Tom Candiotti	.25
95	Marquis Grissom	.25
96	Barry Larkin	.25
97	Bryan Harvey	.25
98	Dave Justice	.25
99	David Cone	.25
100	Wade Boggs	2.50
101	Jason Bere	.25
102	Hal Morris	.25
103	Fred McGriff	.25
104	Bobby Bonilla	.25
105	Jay Buhner	.25
106	Allen Watson	.25
107	Mickey Tettleton	.25
108	Kevin Appier	.25
109	Ivan Rodriguez	1.00
110	Carlos Garcia	.25
111	Andy Benes	.25
112	Eddie Murray	1.50
113	Mike Piazza	3.50
114	Greg Vaughn	.25
115	Paul Molitor	1.50
116	Terry Steinbach	.25
117	Jeff Bagwell	1.50
118	Ken Griffey Jr.	3.50
119	Gary Sheffield	.75
120	Cal Ripken Jr.	5.00
121	Jeff Kent	.25
122	Jay Bell	.25
123	Will Clark	.25
124	Cecil Fielder	.25
125	Alex Fernandez	.25
126	Don Mattingly	3.00
127	Reggie Sanders	.25
128	Moises Alou	.25
129	Craig Biggio	.25
130	Eddie Williams	.25
131	John Franco	.25
132	John Kruk	.25
133	Jeff King	.25
134	Royce Clayton	.25
135	Doug Drabek	.25
136	Ray Lankford	.25
137	Roberto Alomar	.50
138	Todd Hundley	.25
139	Alex Cole	.25
140	Shawon Dunston	.25
141	John Roper	.25
142	Mark Langston	.25
143	Tom Pagnozzi	.25
144	Wilson Alvarez	.25
145	Scott Cooper	.25
146	Kevin Mitchell	.25
147	Mark Whiten	.25
148	Jeff Conine	.25
149	Chili Davis	.25
150	Luis Gonzalez	.25
151	Juan Guzman	.25
152	Mike Greenwell	.25
153	Mike Henneman	.25
154	Rick Aguilera	.25
155	Dennis Eckersley	1.00
156	Darrin Fletcher	.25
157	Darren Lewis	.25
158	Juan Gonzalez	.75
159	Dave Hollins	.25
160	Jimmy Key	.25
161	Roberto Hernandez	.25
162	Randy Myers	.25
163	Joe Carter	.25
164	Darren Daulton	.25
165	Mike MacFarlane	.25
166	Bret Saberhagen	.25

167	Kirby Puckett	2.50
168	Lance Johnson	.25
169	Mark McGwire	4.00
170	Jose Canseco	.75
171	Mike Stanley	.25
172	Lee Smith	.25
173	Robin Ventura	.25
174	Greg Gagne	.25
175	Brian McRae	.25
176	Mike Bordick	.25
177	Rafael Palmeiro	1.00
178	Kenny Rogers	.25
179	Chad Curtis	.25
180	Devon White	.25
181	Paul O'Neill	.25
182	Ken Caminiti	.25
183	Dave Nilsson	.25
184	Tim Naehring	.25
185	Roger Clemens	3.00
186	Otis Nixon	.25
187	Tim Raines	.25
188	Dennis Martinez	.25
189	Pedro Martinez	1.50
190	Jim Abbott	.25
191	Ryan Thompson	.25
192	Barry Bonds	5.00
193	Joe Girardi	.25
194	Steve Finley	.25
195	John Jaha	.25
196	Tony Gwynn	2.50
197	Sammy Sosa	2.50
198	John Burkett	.25
199	Carlos Baerga	.25
200	Ramon Martinez	.25
201	Aaron Sele	.25
202	Eduardo Perez	.25
203	Alan Trammell	.25
204	Orlando Merced	.25
205	Deion Sanders	.35
206	Robb Nen	.25
207	Jack McDowell	.25
208	Ruben Sierra	.25
209	Bernie Williams	.25
210	Kevin Seitzer	.25
211	Charles Nagy	.25
212	Tony Phillips	.25
213	Greg Maddux	2.50
214	Jeff Montgomery	.25
215	Larry Walker	.25
216	Andy Van Slyke	.25
217	Ozzie Smith	2.50
218	Geronimo Pena	.25
219	Gregg Jefferies	.25
220	Lou Whitaker	.25

Refractors

	NM/M
Complete Set (220):	400.00
Common Player:	1.00
Stars:	5X

(See 1995 Finest for checklist and base card values.)

Bronze League Leaders

		NM/M
Complete Set (6):		20.00
Common Player:		2.50
1	Matt Williams	2.50
2	Tony Gwynn	6.50
3	Jeff Bagwell	5.00
4	Ken Griffey Jr.	9.00

5	Paul O'Neill	2.50
6	Frank Thomas	5.00

Flame Throwers

		NM/M
Complete Set (9):		20.00
Common Player:		1.50
1	Jason Bere	1.50
2	Roger Clemens	8.00
3	Juan Guzman	1.50
4	John Hudek	1.50
5	Randy Johnson	5.00
6	Pedro Martinez	4.00
7	Jose Rijo	1.50
8	Bret Saberhagen	1.50
9	John Wetteland	1.50

Power Kings

		NM/M
Complete Set (18):		35.00
Common Player:		.75
1	Bob Hamelin	.75
2	Raul Mondesi	.75
3	Ryan Klesko	.75
4	Carlos Delgado	1.50
5	Manny Ramirez	3.00
6	Mike Piazza	5.00
7	Jeff Bagwell	3.00
8	Mo Vaughn	.75
9	Frank Thomas	3.00
10	Ken Griffey Jr.	5.00
11	Albert Belle	.75
12	Sammy Sosa	4.00
13	Dante Bichette	.75
14	Gary Sheffield	.75
15	Matt Williams	.75
16	Fred McGriff	.75
17	Barry Bonds	7.50
18	Cecil Fielder	.75

Update

	NM/M
Complete Set (110):	20.00

Common Player:		.25
Refractors:		5X
Wax Pack (7):		1.25
Wax Box (24):		20.00
221	Chipper Jones	2.50
222	Benji Gil	.25
223	Tony Phillips	.25
224	Trevor Wilson	.25
225	Tony Tarasco	.25
226	Roberto Petagine	.25
227	Mike MacFarlane	.25
228	Hideo Nomo **RC**	3.00
229	Mark McLemore	.25
230	Ron Gant	.25
231	Andujar Cedeno	.25
232	Mike Mimbs **RC**	.25
233	Jim Abbott	.25
234	Ricky Bones	.25
235	Marty Cordova	.25
236	Mark Johnson	.25
237	Marquis Grissom	.25
238	Tom Henke	.25
239	Terry Pendleton	.25
240	John Wetteland	.25
241	Lee Smith	.25
242	Jaime Navarro	.25
243	Luis Alicea	.25
244	Scott Cooper	.25
245	Gary Gaetti	.25
246	Edgardo Alfonzo	.25
247	Brad Clontz	.25
248	Dave Mlicki	.25
249	Dave Winfield	1.50
250	Mark Grudzielanek **RC**	.50
251	Alex Gonzalez	.25
252	Kevin Brown	.25
253	Esteban Loaiza	.25
254	Vaughn Eshelman	.25
255	Bill Swift	.25
256	Brian McRae	.25
257	Bobby Higginson **RC**	.50
258	Jack McDowell	.25
259	Scott Stahoviak	.25
260	Jon Nunnally	.25
261	Charlie Hayes	.25
262	Jacob Brumfield	.25
263	Chad Curtis	.25
264	Heathcliff Slocumb	.25
265	Mark Whiten	.25
266	Mickey Tettleton	.25
267	Jose Mesa	.25
268	Doug Jones	.25
269	Trevor Hoffman	.25
270	Paul Sorrento	.25
271	Shane Andrews	.25
272	Brett Butler	.25
273	Curtis Goodwin	.25
274	Larry Walker	.25
275	Phil Plantier	.25
276	Ken Hill	.25
277	Vinny Castilla	.25
278	Billy Ashley	.25
279	Derek Jeter	6.00
280	Bob Tewksbury	.25
281	Jose Offerman	.25
282	Glenallen Hill	.25
283	Tony Fernandez	.25
284	Mike Devereaux	.25
285	John Burkett	.25
286	Geronimo Berroa	.25
287	Quilvio Veras	.25
288	Jason Bates	.25
289	Lee Tinsley	.25
290	Derek Bell	.25
291	Jeff Fassero	.25
292	Ray Durham	.25
293	Chad Ogea	.25
294	Bill Pulsipher	.25
295	Phil Nevin	.25
296	Carlos Perez **RC**	.25
297	Roberto Kelly	.25
298	Tim Wakefield	.25
299	Jeff Manto	.25
300	Brian Hunter	.25
301	C.J. Nitkowski	.25
302	Dustin Hermanson	.25
303	John Mabry	.25
304	Orel Hershiser	.25
305	Ron Villone	.25
306	Sean Bergman	.25
307	Tom Goodwin	.25
308	Al Reyes	.25
309	Todd Stottlemyre	.25
310	Rich Becker	.25
311	Joey Cora	.25
312	Ed Sprague	.25
313	John Smoltz	.25
314	Frank Castillo	.25
315	Chris Hammond	.25
316	Ismael Valdes	.25
317	Pete Harnisch	.25
318	Bernard Gilkey	.25
319	John Kruk	.25
320	Marc Newfield	.25
321	Brian Johnson	.25
322	Mark Portugal	.25
323	David Hulse	.25
324	Luis Ortiz	.25
325	Mike Benjamin	.25
326	Brian Jordan	.25
327	Shawn Green	.75
328	Joe Oliver	.25
329	Felipe Lira	.25
330	Andre Dawson	.75

Update Refractors

	NM/M
Complete Set (110):	100.00
Common Player:	1.00
Stars:	5X

(See 1995 Finest Update for checklist andbase card values.)

1996 Finest

		NM/M
Complete Set (359):		300.00
Bronze Set (220):		60.00
Common Bronze:		.15
Silver Set (91):		90.00
Typical Silver:		.50
Gold Set (47):		200.00
Typical Gold:		2.00
Series 1 Pack (6):		1.50
Series 1 Wax Box (24):		30.00
Series 2 Pack (6):		1.50
Series 2 Wax Box (24):		30.00
1	Greg Maddux/S	3.00
2	Bernie Williams/S	.50
3	Ivan Rodriguez/S	1.50
4	Marty Cordova/S	2.00
5	Roberto Hernandez	.15
6	Tony Gwynn/G	7.50
7	Barry Larkin/S	.50
8	Terry Pendleton	.15
9	Albert Belle/G	2.00
10	Ray Lankford/S	.50
11	Mike Piazza/S	4.00
12	Ken Caminiti	.15
13	Larry Walker/S	.50
14	Matt Williams/S	.50
15	Dan Miceli	.15
16	Chipper Jones	2.00
17	John Wetteland	.15
18	Kirby Puckett/G	7.50
19	Tim Naehring	.15
20	Karim Garcia/G	2.00
21	Eddie Murray	1.25
22	Tim Salmon/S	.50
23	Kevin Appier	.15
24	Ken Griffey Jr.	3.00
25	Cal Ripken Jr./G	15.00
26	Brian McRae	.15
27	Pedro Martinez	1.25
28	Brian Jordan	.15
29	Mike Fetters	.15
30	Carlos Delgado	.65
31	Shane Reynolds	.15
32	Terry Steinbach	.15
33	Hideo Nomo/G	2.50
34	Mark Leiter	.15
35	Edgar Martinez/S	.50
36	David Segui	.15
37	Gregg Jefferies/S	.50
38	Bill Pulsipher/S	.50
39	Ryne Sandberg/G	7.50
40	Fred McGriff	.15
41	Shawn Green/S	.75
42	Jeff Bagwell/S	5.00
43	Jim Abbott/S	.50
44	Glenallen Hill	.15
45	Brady Anderson	.15
46	Roger Clemens/S	3.50
47	Jim Thome	.60
48	Frank Thomas	1.25
49	Chuck Knoblauch	.15
50	Lenny Dykstra	.15
51	Jason Isringhausen/G	2.00
52	Rondell White/S	.50
53	Tom Pagnozzi	.15
54	Dennis Eckersley/S	1.50
55	Ricky Bones	.15
56	David Justice	.15
57	Steve Avery	.15
58	Robby Thompson	.15
59	Hideo Nomo/S	1.00
60	Gary Sheffield/S	.75
61	Tony Gwynn	2.00
62	Will Clark/S	.50
63	Denny Neagle	.15
64	Mo Vaughn/S	2.00
65	Bret Boone/S	.50
66	Dante Bichette/G	2.00
67	Robin Ventura	.15
68	Rafael Palmeiro/S	1.50
69	Carlos Baerga/S	.50

70	Kevin Seitzer	.15
71	Ramon Martinez	.15
72	Tom Glavine/S	1.00
73	Garret Anderson/S	.50
74	Mark McGwire/G	12.00
75	Brian Hunter	.15
76	Alan Benes	.15
77	Randy Johnson/S	2.00
78	Jeff King/S	.50
79	Kirby Puckett/S	3.00
80	Ozzie Guillen	.15
81	Kenny Lofton/G	2.00
82	Benji Gil	.15
83	Jim Edmonds/G	2.00
84	Cecil Fielder/S	.50
85	Todd Hundley	.15
86	Reggie Sanders/S	.50
87	Pat Hentgen	.15
88	Ryan Klesko/S	.50
89	Chuck Finley	.15
90	Mike Mussina/G	2.50
91	John Valentin/S	.50
92	Derek Jeter	4.00
93	Paul O'Neill	.15
94	Darrin Fletcher	.15
95	Manny Ramirez/S	2.00
96	Delino DeShields	.15
97	Tim Salmon	.15
98	John Olerud	.15
99	Vinny Castilla/S	.50
100	Jeff Conine/G	2.00
101	Tim Wakefield	.15
102	Johnny Damon/G	3.50
103	Dave Stevens	.15
104	Orlando Merced	.15
105	Barry Bonds/G	15.00
106	Jay Bell	.15
107	John Burkett	.15
108	Chris Hoiles	.15
109	Carlos Perez/S	.50
110	Dave Nilsson	.15
111	Rod Beck	.15
112	Craig Biggio/S	.50
113	Mike Piazza	3.00
114	Mark Langston	.15
115	Juan Gonzalez/S	1.00
116	Rico Brogna	.15
117	Jose Canseco/G	3.00
118	Tom Goodwin	.15
119	Bryan Rekar	.15
120	David Cone	.15
121	Ray Durham/S	.50
122	Andy Pettitte	.40
123	Chili Davis	.15
124	John Smoltz	.15
125	Heathcliff Slocumb	.15
126	Dante Bichette	.15
127	C.J. Nitkowski/S	.50
128	Alex Gonzalez	.15
129	Jeff Montgomery	.15
130	Raul Mondesi/S	.50
131	Denny Martinez	.15
132	Mel Rojas	.15
133	Derek Bell	.15
134	Trevor Hoffman	.15
135	Ken Griffey Jr./G	9.00
136	Darren Daulton	.15
137	Pete Schourek	.15
138	Phil Nevin	.15
139	Andres Galarraga	.15
140	Chad Fonville	.15
141	Chipper Jones/G	8.00
142	Lee Smith/S	.50
143	Joe Carter/S	.50
144	J.T. Snow	.15
145	Greg Maddux/G	7.50
146	Barry Bonds	4.00
147	Orel Hershiser	.15
148	Quilvio Veras	.15
149	Will Clark	.15
150	Jose Rijo	.15
151	Mo Vaughn/S	.50
152	Travis Fryman	.15
153	Frank Rodriguez/S	.50
154	Alex Fernandez	.15
155	Wade Boggs	2.00
156	Troy Percival	.15
157	Moises Alou	.15
158	Javy Lopez	.15
159	Jason Giambi	.50
160	Steve Finley/S	.50
161	Jeff Bagwell/S	2.00
162	Mark McGwire	3.50
163	Eric Karros	.15
164	Jay Buhner/G	2.00
165	Cal Ripken Jr./S	6.00
166	Mickey Tettleton	.15
167	Barry Larkin	.15
168	Lyle Mouton/S	.50
169	Ruben Sierra	.15
170	Bill Swift	.15
171	Sammy Sosa/S	3.00
172	Chad Curtis	.15
173	Dean Palmer	.15
174	John Franco/S	.50
175	Bobby Bonilla	.15
176	Greg Colbrunn	.15
177	Jose Mesa	.15
178	Mike Greenwell	.15
179	Greg Vaughn/S	.50
180	Mark Wohlers/S	.50
181	Doug Drabek	.15
182	Paul O'Neill/S	.50
183	Wilson Alvarez	.15
184	Marty Cordova	.15
185	Hal Morris	.15
186	Frank Thomas/G	6.00
187	Carlos Garcia	.15
188	Albert Belle/S	.50
189	Mark Grace/S	.50
190	Marquis Grissom	.15
191	Checklist	.15
192	Chipper Jones/G	8.00
193	Will Clark	.15
194	Paul Molitor	1.25
195	Kenny Rogers	.15
196	Reggie Sanders	.15
197	Roberto Alomar/G	2.50
198	Dennis Eckersley/G	4.00
199	Raul Mondesi	.15
200	Lance Johnson	.15
201	Alvin Mormon	.15
202	George Arias/G	2.00
203	Jack McDowell	.15
204	Randy Myers	.15
205	Harold Baines	.15
206	Marty Cordova	.15
207	Rich Hunter **RC**	.15
208	Al Leiter	.15
209	Greg Gagne	.15
210	Ben McDonald	.15
211	Ernie Young/S	.50
212	Terry Adams	.15
213	Paul Sorrento	.15
214	Albert Belle	.15
215	Mike Blowers	.15
216	Jim Edmonds	.15
217	Felipe Crespo	.15
218	Fred McGriff/S	.50
219	Shawon Dunston	.15
220	Jimmy Haynes	.15
221	Jose Canseco	.50
222	Eric Davis	.15
223	Kimera Bartee/S	.50
224	Tim Raines	.15
225	Tony Phillips	.15
226	Charlie Hayes	.15
227	Eric Owens	.15
228	Roberto Alomar	.30
229	Rickey Henderson/S	2.00
230	Sterling Hitchcock/S	.50
231	Bernard Gilkey/S	.50
232	Hideo Nomo/G	2.50
233	Kenny Lofton	.15
234	Ryne Sandberg/S	3.00
235	Greg Maddux/S	3.00
236	Mark McGwire	3.50
237	Jay Buhner	.15
238	Craig Biggio	.15
239	Todd Stottlemyre/S	.50
240	Barry Bonds	4.00
241	Jason Kendall/S	.50
242	Paul O'Neill/S	.50
243	Chris Snopek/G	2.00
244	Ron Gant	.15
245	Paul Wilson	.15
246	Todd Hollandsworth	.15
247	Todd Zeile	.15
248	David Justice	.15
249	Tim Salmon/G	2.00
250	Moises Alou	.15
251	Bob Wolcott	.15
252	David Wells	.15
253	Juan Gonzalez	.65
254	Andres Galarraga	.15
255	Dave Hollins	.15
256	Devon White/S	.50
257	Sammy Sosa	2.00
258	Ivan Rodriguez	.75
259	Bip Roberts	.15
260	Tino Martinez	.15
261	Chuck Knoblauch/S	.50
262	Mike Stanley	.15
263	Wally Joyner/S	.50
264	Butch Huskey	.15
265	Jeff Conine	.15
266	Matt Williams/G	2.00
267	Mark Grace	.15
268	Jason Schmidt	.15
269	Otis Nixon	.15
270	Randy Johnson/G	5.00
271	Kirby Puckett	2.00
272	Andy Fox/S **RC**	.50
273	Andy Benes	.15
274	Sean Berry/S	.50
275	Mike Piazza	3.00
276	Rey Ordonez	.15
277	Benito Santiago/S	.50
278	Gary Gaetti	.15
279	Paul Molitor/G	5.00
280	Robin Ventura	.15
281	Cal Ripken Jr.	4.00
282	Carlos Baerga	.15
283	Roger Cedeno	.15
284	Chad Mottola/S	.50
285	Terrell Wade	.15
286	Kevin Brown	.15
287	Rafael Palmeiro	1.00
288	Mo Vaughn	.15
289	Dante Bichette/S	.50
290	Cecil Fielder/G	2.00
291	Doc Gooden/S	.50
292	Bob Tewksbury	.15
293	Kevin Mitchell/S	.50
294	Livan Hernandez/G **RC**	2.00
295	Russ Davis/S	.50
296	Chan Ho Park/S	.50
297	T.J. Mathews	.15
298	Manny Ramirez	1.25
299	Jeff Bagwell	1.25
300	Marty Janzen/G **RC**	2.00
301	Wade Boggs	2.00
302	Larry Walker/S	.50
303	Steve Gibralter	.15
304	B.J. Surhoff	.15
305	Ken Griffey Jr./S	4.00
306	Royce Clayton	.15
307	Sal Fasano	.15
308	Ron Gant/G	2.00
309	Gary Sheffield	.40
310	Ken Hill	.15
311	Joe Girardi	.15
312	Matt Lawton **RC**	.15
313	Billy Wagner/S	.50
314	Julio Franco	.15
315	Joe Carter	.15
316	Brooks Kieschnick	.15
317	Mike Grace/S **RC**	.50
318	Heathcliff Slocumb	.15
319	Barry Larkin	.15
320	Tony Gwynn	2.00
321	Ryan Klesko/G	2.00
322	Frank Thomas	1.25
323	Edgar Martinez	.15
324	Jermaine Dye/G	2.00
325	Henry Rodriguez	.15
326	Marvin Benard **RC**	.50
327	Kenny Lofton/S	.50
328	Derek Bell/S	.50
329	Ugueth Urbina	.15
330	Jason Giambi/G	3.00
331	Roger Salkeld	.15
332	Edgar Renteria	.15
333	Ryan Klesko	.15
334	Ray Lankford	.15
335	Edgar Martinez/G	2.00
336	Justin Thompson	.15
337	Gary Sheffield/S	.75
338	Rey Ordonez/G	2.00
339	Mark Clark	.15
340	Ruben Rivera	.15
341	Mark Grace/S	.50
342	Matt Williams	.15
343	Francisco Cordova **RC**	.25
344	Cecil Fielder	.15
345	Andres Galarraga/S	.50
346	Brady Anderson/S	.50
347	Sammy Sosa/G	7.50
348	Mark Grudzielanek	.15
349	Ron Coomer	.15
350	Derek Jeter/S	6.00
351	Rich Aurilia	.15
352	Jose Herrera	.15
353	Jay Buhner/S	.50
354	Juan Gonzalez/G	2.50
355	Craig Biggio/G	2.00
356	Tony Clark	.15
357	Tino Martinez/S	.50
358	Dan Naulty **RC**	.15
359	Checklist	.15

Refractors

	NM/M
Complete Set (359):	900.00
Bronze Set (220):	300.00
Common Bronze:	1.00
Bronze Stars:	4X
Silver Set (91):	250.00
Typical Silver:	2.00
Silver Stars:	2.5X
Gold Set (48):	600.00
Typical Gold:	6.00
Gold Stars:	2X

(See 1996 Finest for checklist and base card values.)

1997 Finest

	NM/M
Complete Set (350):	200.00
Bronze Set (200):	15.00
Common Bronze:	.15
Silver Set (100):	75.00
Typical Silver:	.50
Embossed Silvers:	2X
Gold Set (50):	150.00
Typical Gold:	2.00
Embossed Die-Cut Golds:	1.5X
Series 1 or 2 Pack (6):	1.50
Series 1 or 2 Wax Box (24):	25.00

1	Barry Bonds/B	2.00
2	Ryne Sandberg/B	.75
3	Brian Jordan/B	.15

4	Rocky Coppinger/B	.15
5	Dante Bichette/B	.15
6	Al Martin/B	.15
7	Charles Nagy/B	.15
8	Otis Nixon/B	.15
9	Mark Johnson/B	.15
10	Jeff Bagwell/B	.60
11	Ken Hill/B	.15
12	Willie Adams/B	.15
13	Raul Mondesi/B	.15
14	Reggie Sanders/B	.15
15	Derek Jeter/B	2.00
16	Jermaine Dye/B	.15
17	Edgar Renteria/B	.15
18	Travis Fryman/B	.15
19	Roberto Hernandez/B	.15
20	Sammy Sosa/B	.75
21	Garret Anderson/B	.15
22	Rey Ordonez/B	.15
23	Glenallen Hill/B	.15
24	Dave Nilsson/B	.15
25	Kevin Brown/B	.15
26	Brian McRae/B	.15
27	Joey Hamilton/B	.15
28	Jamey Wright/B	.15
29	Frank Thomas/B	.60
30	Mark McGwire/B	1.50
31	Ramon Martinez/B	.15
32	Jaime Bluma/B	.15
33	Frank Rodriguez/B	.15
34	Andy Benes/B	.15
35	Jay Buhner/B	.15
36	Justin Thompson/B	.15
37	Darin Erstad/B	.30
38	Gregg Jefferies/B	.15
39	Jeff D'Amico/B	.15
40	Pedro Martinez/B	.60
41	Nomar Garciaparra/B	.75
42	Jose Valentin/B	.15
43	Pat Hentgen/B	.15
44	Will Clark/B	.15
45	Bernie Williams/B	.15
46	Luis Castillo/B	.15
47	B.J. Surhoff/B	.15
48	Greg Gagne/B	.15
49	Pete Schourek/B	.15
50	Mike Piazza/B	1.00
51	Dwight Gooden/B	.15
52	Javy Lopez/B	.15
53	Chuck Finley/B	.15
54	James Baldwin/B	.15
55	Jack McDowell/B	.15
56	Royce Clayton/B	.15
57	Carlos Delgado/B	.35
58	Neifi Perez/B	.15
59	Eddie Taubensee/B	.15
60	Rafael Palmeiro/B	.50
61	Marty Cordova/B	.15
62	Wade Boggs/B	.75
63	Rickey Henderson/B	.60
64	Mike Hampton/B	.15
65	Troy Percival/B	.15
66	Barry Larkin/B	.15
67	Jermaine Allensworth/B	.15
68	Mark Clark/B	.15
69	Mike Lansing/B	.15
70	Mark Grudzielanek/B	.15
71	Todd Stottlemyre/B	.15
72	Juan Guzman/B	.15
73	John Burkett/B	.15
74	Wilson Alvarez/B	.15
75	Ellis Burks/B	.15
76	Bobby Higginson/B	.15
77	Ricky Bottalico/B	.15
78	Omar Vizquel/B	.15
79	Paul Sorrento/B	.15
80	Denny Neagle/B	.15
81	Roger Pavlik/B	.15
82	Mike Lieberthal/B	.15
83	Devon White/B	.15
84	John Olerud/B	.15
85	Kevin Appier/B	.15
86	Joe Girardi/B	.15
87	Paul O'Neill/B	.15
88	Mike Sweeney/B	.15
89	John Smiley/B	.15
90	Ivan Rodriguez/B	.50
91	Randy Myers/B	.15
92	Bip Roberts/B	.15
93	Jose Mesa/B	.15
94	Paul Wilson/B	.15

95 Mike Mussina/B	.30
96 Ben McDonald/B	.15
97 John Mabry/B	.15
98 Tom Goodwin/B	.15
99 Edgar Martinez/B	.15
100 Andruw Jones/B	.60
101 Jose Canseco/S	.75
102 Billy Wagner/S	.50
103 Dante Bichette/S	.50
104 Curt Schilling/S	1.00
105 Dean Palmer/S	.50
106 Larry Walker/S	.50
107 Bernie Williams/S	.50
108 Chipper Jones/S	2.00
109 Gary Sheffield/S	1.00
110 Randy Johnson/S	1.50
111 Roberto Alomar/S	.75
112 Todd Walker/S	.50
113 Sandy Alomar/S	.50
114 John Jaha/S	.50
115 Ken Caminiti/S	.50
116 Ryan Klesko/S	.50
117 Mariano Rivera/S	.75
118 Jason Giambi/S	1.00
119 Lance Johnson/S	.50
120 Robin Ventura/S	.50
121 Todd Hollandsworth/S	.50
122 Johnny Damon/S	.75
123 William Van Landingham/S	.50
124 Jason Kendall/S	.50
125 Vinny Castilla/S	.50
126 Harold Baines/S	.50
127 Joe Carter/S	.50
128 Craig Biggio/S	.50
129 Tony Clark/S	.50
130 Ron Gant/S	.50
131 David Segui/S	.50
132 Steve Trachsel/S	1.00
133 Scott Rolen/S	.50
134 Mike Stanley/S	5.00
135 Cal Ripken Jr./S	.50
136 John Smoltz/S	.50
137 Bobby Jones/S	1.50
138 Manny Ramirez/S	3.00
139 Ken Griffey Jr./S	.50
140 Chuck Knoblauch/S	.50
141 Mark Grace/S	.50
142 Chris Snopek/S	.75
143 Hideo Nomo/S	.50
144 Tim Salmon/S	.50
145 David Cone/S	.50
146 Eric Young/S	.50
147 Jeff Brantley/S	1.00
148 Jim Thome/S	.50
149 Trevor Hoffman/S	.75
150 Juan Gonzalez/S	8.00
151 Mike Piazza/G	4.00
152 Ivan Rodriguez/G	2.00
153 Mo Vaughn/G	8.00
154 Brady Anderson/G	4.00
155 Mark McGwire/G	2.00
156 Rafael Palmeiro/G	7.50
157 Barry Larkin/G	5.00
158 Greg Maddux/G	6.00
159 Jeff Bagwell/G	2.00
160 Frank Thomas/G	5.00
161 Ken Caminiti/G	2.00
162 Andruw Jones/G	5.00
163 Dennis Eckersley/G	4.00
164 Jeff Conine/G	2.00
165 Jim Edmonds/G	2.00
166 Derek Jeter/G	12.00
167 Vladimir Guerrero/G	6.00
168 Sammy Sosa/G	5.00
169 Tony Gwynn/G	6.00
170 Andres Galarraga/G	2.00
171 Todd Hundley/G	2.00
172 Jay Buhner/G	2.00
173 Paul Molitor/G	6.00
174 Kenny Lofton/G	2.00
175 Barry Bonds/G	12.00
176 Gary Sheffield/B	.35
177 Dmitri Young/B	.15
178 Jay Bell/B	.15
179 David Wells/B	.15
180 Walt Weiss/B	.15
181 Paul Molitor/B	.60
182 Jose Guillen/B	.15
183 Al Leiter/B	.15
184 Mike Fetters/B	.15
185 Mark Langston/B	.15
186 Fred McGriff/B	.15
187 Darrin Fletcher/B	.15
188 Brant Brown/B	.15
189 Geronimo Berroa/B	.15
190 Jim Thome/B	.50
191 Jose Vizcaino/B	.15
192 Andy Ashby/B	.15
193 Rusty Greer/B	.15
194 Brian Hunter/B	.15
195 Chris Hoiles/B	.15
196 Orlando Merced/B	.15
197 Brett Butler/B	.15
198 Derek Bell/B	.15
199 Bobby Bonilla/B	.15
200 Alex Ochoa/B	.15
201 Wally Joyner/B	.15
202 Mo Vaughn/B	.15
203 Doug Drabek/B	.15
204 Tino Martinez/B	.30
205 Roberto Alomar/B	.75
206 Brian Giles/B **RC**	.15
207 Todd Worrell/B	.15
208 Alan Benes/B	.15
209 Jim Leyritz/B	.15
210 Darryl Hamilton/B	.15
211 Jimmy Key/B	.15
212 Juan Gonzalez/B	.35
213 Vinny Castilla/B	.15
214 Chuck Knoblauch/B	.15
215 Tony Phillips/B	.15
216 Jeff Cirillo/B	.15
217 Carlos Garcia/B	.15
218 Brooks Kieschnick/B	.15
219 Marquis Grissom/B	.15
220 Dan Wilson/B	.15
221 Greg Vaughn/B	.15
222 John Wetteland/B	.15
223 Andres Galarraga/B	.15
224 Ozzie Guillen/B	.15
225 Kevin Elster/B	.15
226 Bernard Gilkey/B	.15
227 Mike MacFarlane/B	.15
228 Heathcliff Slocumb/B	.15
229 Wendell Magee Jr./B	.15
230 Carlos Baerga/B	.15
231 Kevin Seitzer/B	.15
232 Henry Rodriguez/B	.15
233 Roger Clemens/B	1.00
234 Mark Wohlers/B	.15
235 Eddie Murray/B	.60
236 Todd Zeile/B	.15
237 J.T. Snow/B	.15
238 Ken Griffey Jr./B	1.00
239 Sterling Hitchcock/B	.15
240 Albert Belle/B	.15
241 Terry Steinbach/B	.15
242 Robb Nen/B	.15
243 Mark McLemore/B	.15
244 Jeff King/B	.15
245 Tony Clark/B	.15
246 Tim Salmon/B	.15
247 Benito Santiago/B	.15
248 Robin Ventura/B	.15
249 Bubba Trammell/B **RC**	.15
250 Chili Davis/B	.15
251 John Valentin/B	.15
252 Cal Ripken Jr./B	2.00
253 Matt Williams/B	.15
254 Jeff Kent/B	.15
255 Eric Karros/B	.15
256 Ray Lankford/B	.15
257 Ed Sprague/B	.15
258 Shane Reynolds/B	.15
259 Jaime Navarro/B	.15
260 Eric Davis/B	.15
261 Orel Hershiser/B	.15
262 Mark Grace/B	.15
263 Rod Beck/B	.15
264 Ismael Valdes/B	.15
265 Manny Ramirez/B	.60
266 Ken Caminiti/B	.15
267 Tim Naehring/B	.15
268 Jose Rosado/B	.15
269 Greg Colbrunn/B	.15
270 Dean Palmer/B	.15
271 David Justice/B	.15
272 Scott Spiezio/B	.15
273 Chipper Jones/B	.75
274 Mel Rojas/B	.15
275 Bartolo Colon/B	.15
276 Darin Erstad/S	1.00
277 Sammy Sosa/S	2.00
278 Rafael Palmeiro/S	1.00
279 Frank Thomas/S	1.50
280 Ruben Rivera/S	.50
281 Hal Morris/S	.50
282 Jay Buhner/S	.50
283 Kenny Lofton/S	.50
284 Jose Canseco/S	.75
285 Alex Fernandez/S	.50
286 Todd Helton/S	1.25
287 Andy Pettitte/S	1.00
288 John Franco/S	.15
289 Ivan Rodriguez/S	1.25
290 Ellis Burks/S	.50
291 Julio Franco/S	.50
292 Mike Piazza/S	3.00
293 Brian Jordan/S	.50
294 Greg Maddux/S	2.00
295 Bob Abreu/S	.50
296 Rondell White/S	.50
297 Moises Alou/S	.50
298 Tony Gwynn/S	2.00
299 Deion Sanders/S	.50
300 Jeff Montgomery/S	.50
301 Ray Durham/S	.50
302 John Wasdin/S	.50
303 Ryne Sandberg/S	2.00
304 Delino DeShields/S	.50
305 Mark McGwire/S	4.00
306 Andruw Jones/S	1.50
307 Kevin Orie/S	.50
308 Matt Williams/S	.50
309 Karim Garcia/S	.50
310 Derek Jeter/S	5.00
311 Mo Vaughn/S	.50
312 Brady Anderson/S	.50
313 Barry Bonds/S	5.00
314 Steve Finley/S	.50
315 Vladimir Guerrero/S	1.50
316 Matt Morris/S	.50
317 Tom Glavine/S	1.00
318 Jeff Bagwell/S	1.50
319 Albert Belle/S	.50
320 Hideki Irabu/S **RC**	1.00
321 Andres Galarraga/S	.50
322 Cecil Fielder/S	.50
323 Barry Larkin/S	.50
324 Todd Hundley/S	.50
325 Fred McGriff/S	.50
326 Gary Sheffield/S	3.00
327 Craig Biggio/G	2.00
328 Raul Mondesi/G	2.00
329 Edgar Martinez/G	2.00
330 Chipper Jones/G	8.00
331 Bernie Williams/G	2.00
332 Juan Gonzalez/G	3.00
333 Ron Gant/G	2.00
334 Cal Ripken Jr./G	12.00
335 Larry Walker/G	2.00
336 Matt Williams/G	2.00
337 Jose Cruz Jr./G	2.00
338 Joe Carter/G	2.00
339 Wilton Guerrero/G	2.00
340 Cecil Fielder/G	2.00
341 Todd Walker/G	2.00
342 Ken Griffey Jr./G	10.00
343 Ryan Klesko/G	2.00
344 Roger Clemens/G	10.00
345 Hideo Nomo/G	3.00
346 Dante Bichette/G	2.00
347 Albert Belle/G	2.00
348 Randy Johnson/G	6.00
349 Manny Ramirez/G	6.00
350 John Smoltz/G	2.00

Embossed/Die-Cut Gold Stars: 1.5X
(See 1997 Finest for checklist and base card values.)

1998 Finest

1997 Finest Samples

	NM/M
Complete Set (5):	15.00
Common Player:	2.50
1 Barry Bonds	3.50
15 Derek Jeter	3.50
30 Mark McGwire	3.00
143 Hideo Nomo	2.50
159 Jeff Bagwell	2.50

Refractors

	NM/M
Common Bronze:	2.00
Bronze Stars:	6X
Typical Silver:	3.00
Silver Stars:	3X
Typical Gold:	8.00
Gold Stars:	2X
Typical Embossed Silver:	7.50
Embossed Silver Stars:	7X
Typical Embossed Gold:	20.00
Embossed Gold Stars:	5X

(See 1997 Finest for cheklist and base card values.)

Embossed

	NM/M
Common Embossed Silver:	1.00
Embossed Silver Stars:	2X
Common Embossed Gold:	3.00

	NM/M
Complete Set (275):	30.00
Common Player:	.15
No-Protector:	2.5X
Refractors:	4X
No-Protector Refractor:	8X
Pack (6):	1.50
Wax Box (24):	25.00
Jumbo Pack (13):	2.50
Jumbo Box (12):	25.00
1 Larry Walker	.15
2 Andruw Jones	.75
3 Ramon Martinez	.15
4 Geronimo Berroa	.15
5 David Justice	.15
6 Rusty Greer	.15
7 Chad Ogea	.15
8 Tom Goodwin	.15
9 Tino Martinez	.15
10 Jose Guillen	.15
11 Jeffrey Hammonds	.15
12 Brian McRae	.15
13 Jeremi Gonzalez	.15
14 Craig Counsell	.15
15 Mike Piazza	1.50
16 Greg Maddux	1.00
17 Todd Greene	.15
18 Rondell White	.15
19 Kirk Rueter	.15
20 Tony Clark	.15
21 Brad Radke	.15
22 Jaret Wright	.15
23 Carlos Delgado	.50
24 Dustin Hermanson	.15
25 Gary Sheffield	.40
26 Jose Canseco	.35
27 Kevin Young	.15
28 David Wells	.15
29 Mariano Rivera	.25
30 Reggie Sanders	.15
31 Mike Cameron	.15
32 Bobby Witt	.15
33 Kevin Orie	.15
34 Royce Clayton	.15
35 Edgar Martinez	.15
36 Neifi Perez	.15
37 Kevin Appier	.15
38 Darryl Hamilton	.15
39 Michael Tucker	.15
40 Roger Clemens	1.25
41 Carl Everett	.15
42 Mike Sweeney	.15
43 Pat Meares	.15
44 Brian Giles	.15
45 Matt Morris	.15
46 Jason Dickson	.15
47 Rich Loiselle	.15
48 Joe Girardi	.15
49 Steve Trachsel	.15
50 Ben Grieve	.15
51 Jose Vizcaino	.15
52 Hideki Irabu	.15
53 J.T. Snow	.15
54 Mike Hampton	.15
55 Dave Nilsson	.15

#	Player	Price
56	Alex Fernandez	.15
57	Brett Tomko	.15
58	Wally Joyner	.15
59	Kelvim Escobar	.15
60	Roberto Alomar	.30
61	Todd Jones	.15
62	Paul O'Neill	.15
63	Jamie Moyer	.15
64	Mark Wohlers	.15
65	Jose Cruz Jr.	.15
66	Troy Percival	.15
67	Rick Reed	.15
68	Will Clark	.15
69	Jamey Wright	.15
70	Mike Mussina	.35
71	David Cone	.15
72	Ryan Klesko	.15
73	Scott Hatteberg	.15
74	James Baldwin	.15
75	Tony Womack	.15
76	Carlos Perez	.15
77	Charles Nagy	.15
78	Jeromy Burnitz	.15
79	Shane Reynolds	.15
80	Cliff Floyd	.15
81	Jason Kendall	.15
82	Chad Curtis	.15
83	Matt Karchner	.15
84	Ricky Bottalico	.15
85	Sammy Sosa	1.00
86	Javy Lopez	.15
87	Jeff Kent	.15
88	Shawn Green	.25
89	Devon White	.15
90	Tony Gwynn	1.00
91	Bob Tewksbury	.15
92	Derek Jeter	2.50
93	Eric Davis	.15
94	Jeff Fassero	.15
95	Denny Neagle	.15
96	Ismael Valdes	.15
97	Tim Salmon	.15
98	Mark Grudzielanek	.15
99	Curt Schilling	.35
100	Ken Griffey Jr.	1.50
101	Edgardo Alfonzo	.15
102	Vinny Castilla	.15
103	Jose Rosado	.15
104	Scott Erickson	.15
105	Alan Benes	.15
106	Shannon Stewart	.15
107	Delino DeShields	.15
108	Mark Loretta	.15
109	Todd Hundley	.15
110	Chuck Knoblauch	.15
111	Quinton McCracken	.15
112	F.P. Santangelo	.15
113	Gerald Williams	.15
114	Omar Vizquel	.15
115	John Valentin	.15
116	Damion Easley	.15
117	Matt Lawton	.15
118	Jim Thome	.60
119	Sandy Alomar	.15
120	Albert Belle	.15
121	Chris Stynes	.15
122	Butch Huskey	.15
123	Shawn Estes	.15
124	Terry Adams	.15
125	Ivan Rodriguez	.60
126	Ron Gant	.15
127	John Mabry	.15
128	Jeff Shaw	.15
129	Jeff Montgomery	.15
130	Justin Thompson	.15
131	Livan Hernandez	.15
132	Ugueth Urbina	.15
133	Doug Glanville	.15
134	Troy O'Leary	.15
135	Cal Ripken Jr.	2.50
136	Quilvio Veras	.15
137	Pedro Astacio	.15
138	Willie Greene	.15
139	Lance Johnson	.15
140	Nomar Garciaparra	1.00
141	Jose Offerman	.15
142	Scott Rolen	.60
143	Derek Bell	.15
144	Johnny Damon	.35
145	Mark McGwire	2.00
146	Chan Ho Park	.15
147	Edgar Renteria	.15
148	Eric Young	.15
149	Craig Biggio	.15
150	Checklist 1-150	.15
151	Frank Thomas	.75
152	John Wetteland	.15
153	Mike Lansing	.15
154	Pedro Martinez	.75
155	Rico Brogna	.15
156	Kevin Brown	.15
157	Alex Rodriguez	2.00
158	Wade Boggs	1.00
159	Richard Hidalgo	.15
160	Mark Grace	.15
161	Jose Mesa	.15
162	John Olerud	.15
163	Tim Belcher	.15
164	Chuck Finley	.15
165	Brian Hunter	.15
166	Joe Carter	.15
167	Stan Javier	.15
168	Jay Bell	.15
169	Ray Lankford	.15
170	John Smoltz	.15
171	Ed Sprague	.15
172	Jason Giambi	.50
173	Todd Walker	.15

#	Player	Price
174	Paul Konerko	.15
175	Rey Ordonez	.15
176	Dante Bichette	.15
177	Bernie Williams	.15
178	Jon Nunnally	.15
179	Rafael Palmeiro	.60
180	Jay Buhner	.15
181	Devon White	.15
182	Jeff D'Amico	.15
183	Walt Weiss	.15
184	Scott Spiezio	.15
185	Moises Alou	.15
186	Carlos Baerga	.15
187	Todd Zeile	.15
188	Gregg Jefferies	.15
189	Mo Vaughn	.15
190	Terry Steinbach	.15
191	Ray Durham	.15
192	Robin Ventura	.15
193	Jeff Reed	.15
194	Ken Caminiti	.15
195	Eric Karros	.15
196	Wilson Alvarez	.15
197	Gary Gaetti	.15
198	Andres Galarraga	.15
199	Alex Gonzalez	.15
200	Garret Anderson	.15
201	Andy Benes	.15
202	Harold Baines	.15
203	Ron Coomer	.15
204	Dean Palmer	.15
205	Reggie Jefferson	.15
206	John Burkett	.15
207	Jermaine Allensworth	.15
208	Bernard Gilkey	.15
209	Jeff Bagwell	.75
210	Kenny Lofton	.15
211	Bobby Jones	.15
212	Bartolo Colon	.15
213	Jim Edmonds	.15
214	Pat Hentgen	.15
215	Matt Williams	.15
216	Bob Abreu	.15
217	Jorge Posada	.15
218	Marty Cordova	.15
219	Ken Hill	.15
220	Steve Finley	.15
221	Jeff King	.15
222	Quinton McCracken	.15
223	Matt Stairs	.15
224	Darin Erstad	.35
225	Fred McGriff	.15
226	Marquis Grissom	.15
227	Doug Glanville	.15
228	Tom Glavine	.35
229	John Franco	.15
230	Darren Bragg	.15
231	Barry Larkin	.15
232	Trevor Hoffman	.15
233	Brady Anderson	.15
234	Al Martin	.15
235	B.J. Surhoff	.15
236	Ellis Burks	.15
237	Randy Johnson	.75
238	Mark Clark	.15
239	Tony Saunders	.15
240	Hideo Nomo	.40
241	Brad Fullmer	.15
242	Chipper Jones	1.00
243	Jose Valentin	.15
244	Manny Ramirez	.75
245	Derrek Lee	.50
246	Jimmy Key	.15
247	Tim Naehring	.15
248	Bobby Higginson	.15
249	Charles Johnson	.15
250	Chili Davis	.15
251	Tom Gordon	.15
252	Mike Lieberthal	.15
253	Billy Wagner	.15
254	Juan Guzman	.15
255	Todd Stottlemyre	.15
256	Brian Jordan	.15
257	Barry Bonds	2.50
258	Dan Wilson	.15
259	Paul Molitor	.75
260	Juan Gonzalez	.40
261	Francisco Cordova	.15
262	Cecil Fielder	.15
263	Travis Lee	.15
264	Kevin Tapani	.15
265	Raul Mondesi	.15
266	Travis Fryman	.15
267	Armando Benitez	.15
268	Pokey Reese	.15
269	Rick Aguilera	.15
270	Andy Pettitte	.35
271	Jose Vizcaino	.15
272	Kerry Wood	.40
273	Vladimir Guerrero	.75
274	John Smiley	.15
275	Checklist 151-275	.15

Refractors

PEDRO ASTACIO — Pitcher · Rockies

	NM/M
Complete Set (275):	200.00
Common Player:	1.00
Stars/Rookies:	4X

(See 1998 Finest for checklist and base card values.)

No-Protector

BEN GRIEVE — Outfielder · Athletics

	NM/M
Complete Set (275):	150.00
Common Player:	.50
Stars/Rookies:	2.5X

(See 1998 Finest for checklist and base card values.)

No-Protector Refractor

JAY BELL — Shortstop · Diamondbacks

	NM/M
Complete Set (275):	400.00
Common Player:	2.00
Stars/Rookies:	8X

(See 1998 Finest for checklist and base card values.)

Pre-Production

		NM/M
Complete Set (5):		8.00
Common Player:		2.00
1	Nomar Garciaparra	2.25
2	Mark McGwire	3.00
3	Ivan Rodriguez	2.00
4	Ken Griffey Jr.	2.50
5	Roger Clemens	2.25

Centurions

		NM/M
Complete Set (20):		75.00
Common Player:		1.50
Production 500 Sets		
Refractors (75 Sets):		4X
C1	Andruw Jones	4.50
C2	Vladimir Guerrero	4.50
C3	Nomar Garciaparra	6.00
C4	Scott Rolen	3.50
C5	Ken Griffey Jr.	8.00
C6	Jose Cruz Jr.	1.50
C7	Barry Bonds	12.00
C8	Mark McGwire	10.00
C9	Juan Gonzalez	2.50
C10	Jeff Bagwell	4.50
C11	Frank Thomas	4.50
C12	Paul Konerko	2.00
C13	Alex Rodriguez	10.00
C14	Mike Piazza	8.00
C15	Travis Lee	1.50
C16	Chipper Jones	6.00
C17	Larry Walker	1.50
C18	Mo Vaughn	1.50
C19	Livan Hernandez	1.50
C20	Jaret Wright	1.50

Jumbo

CHIPPER JONES — Third Base · Braves

CHIPPER JONES — Third Base · Braves

		NM/M
Complete Set (16):		30.00
Common Player:		1.00
Refractors:		1.5X
	FIRST SERIES	
1	Mark McGwire	4.00
2	Cal Ripken Jr.	5.00
3	Nomar Garciaparra	2.00
4	Mike Piazza	3.00
5	Greg Maddux	2.00
6	Jose Cruz Jr.	1.00
7	Roger Clemens	2.50
8	Ken Griffey Jr.	3.00
	SECOND SERIES	
1	Frank Thomas	1.50
2	Bernie Williams	1.00
3	Randy Johnson	1.50
4	Chipper Jones	2.00
5	Manny Ramirez	1.50
6	Barry Bonds	5.00
7	Juan Gonzalez	1.25
8	Jeff Bagwell	1.50

Mystery Finest

MARK McGWIRE — First Base

		NM/M
Complete Set (50):		125.00
Common Player:		1.50
Refractors:		4X
M1	Frank Thomas, Ken Griffey Jr.	3.00

M2	Frank Thomas, Mike Piazza	3.00
M3	Frank Thomas, Mark McGwire	4.00
M4	Frank Thomas, Frank Thomas	2.00
M5	Ken Griffey Jr., Mike Piazza	3.00
M6	Ken Griffey Jr., Mark McGwire	4.00
M7	Ken Griffey Jr., Ken Griffey Jr.	4.00
M8	Mike Piazza, Mark McGwire	4.00
M9	Mike Piazza, Mike Piazza	4.00
M10	Mark McGwire, Mark McGwire	6.00
M11	Nomar Garciaparra, Jose Cruz Jr.	2.50
M12	Nomar Garciaparra, Derek Jeter	5.00
M13	Nomar Garciaparra, Andruw Jones	2.50
M14	Nomar Garciaparra, Nomar Garciaparra	3.00
M15	Jose Cruz Jr., Derek Jeter	5.00
M16	Jose Cruz Jr., Andruw Jones	1.50
M17	Jose Cruz Jr., Jose Cruz Jr.	1.50
M18	Derek Jeter, Andruw Jones	5.00
M19	Derek Jeter, Derek Jeter	7.50
M20	Andruw Jones, Andruw Jones	2.00
M21	Cal Ripken Jr., Tony Gwynn	5.00
M22	Cal Ripken Jr., Barry Bonds	5.00
M23	Cal Ripken Jr., Greg Maddux	5.00
M24	Cal Ripken Jr., Cal Ripken Jr.	7.50
M25	Tony Gwynn, Barry Bonds	5.00
M26	Tony Gwynn, Greg Maddux	2.50
M27	Tony Gwynn, Tony Gwynn	3.00
M28	Barry Bonds, Greg Maddux	5.00
M29	Barry Bonds, Barry Bonds	7.50
M30	Greg Maddux, Greg Maddux	3.00
M31	Juan Gonzalez, Larry Walker	5.00
M32	Juan Gonzalez, Andruw Galarraga	1.50
M33	Juan Gonzalez, Chipper Jones	2.50
M34	Juan Gonzalez, Juan Gonzalez	1.50
M35	Larry Walker, Andres Galarraga	1.50
M36	Larry Walker, Chipper Jones	2.50
M37	Larry Walker, Larry Walker	1.50
M38	Andres Galarraga, Chipper Jones	2.50
M39	Andres Galarraga, Andres Galarraga	1.50
M40	Chipper Jones, Chipper Jones	3.00
M41	Gary Sheffield, Sammy Sosa	3.00
M42	Gary Sheffield, Jeff Bagwell	3.00
M43	Gary Sheffield, Tino Martinez	1.50
M44	Gary Sheffield, Gary Sheffield	2.00
M45	Sammy Sosa, Jeff Bagwell	3.00
M46	Sammy Sosa, Tino Martinez	3.00
M47	Sammy Sosa, Sammy Sosa	3.00
M48	Jeff Bagwell, Tino Martinez	1.50
M49	Jeff Bagwell, Jeff Bagwell	2.00
M50	Tino Martinez, Tino Martinez	1.50

Mystery Finest 2

		NM/M
Complete Set (40):		100.00
Common Player:		1.50
Refractors:		4X
M1	Nomar Garciaparra, Frank Thomas	3.50
M2	Nomar Garciaparra, Albert Belle	3.50
M3	Nomar Garciaparra, Scott Rolen	3.50
M4	Frank Thomas, Albert Belle	2.50
M5	Frank Thomas, Scott Rolen	2.50
M6	Albert Belle, Scott Rolen	1.50
M7	Ken Griffey Jr., Jose Cruz	4.00
M8	Ken Griffey Jr., Alex Rodriguez	6.00

M9	Ken Griffey Jr., Roger Clemens	4.50
M10	Jose Cruz, Alex Rodriguez	6.00
M11	Jose Cruz, Roger Clemens	3.00
M12	Alex Rodriguez, Roger Clemens	6.00
M13	Mike Piazza, Barry Bonds	6.00
M14	Mike Piazza, Derek Jeter	6.00
M15	Mike Piazza, Bernie Williams	5.00
M16	Barry Bonds, Derek Jeter	6.50
M17	Barry Bonds, Bernie Williams	4.00
M18	Derek Jeter, Bernie Williams	6.00
M19	Mark McGwire, Jeff Bagwell	4.50
M20	Mark McGwire, Mo Vaughn	5.00
M21	Mark McGwire, Jim Thome	5.00
M22	Jeff Bagwell, Mo Vaughn	2.00
M23	Jeff Bagwell, Jim Thome	1.50
M24	Mo Vaughn, Jim Thome	1.50
M25	Juan Gonzalez, Travis Lee	1.50
M26	Juan Gonzalez, Ben Grieve	1.50
M27	Juan Gonzalez, Fred McGriff	1.50
M28	Travis Lee, Ben Grieve	1.50
M29	Travis Lee, Fred McGriff	1.50
M30	Ben Grieve, Fred McGriff	1.50
M31	Albert Belle, Albert Belle	1.50
M32	Scott Rolen, Scott Rolen	2.00
M33	Alex Rodriguez, Alex Rodriguez	6.00
M34	Roger Clemens, Roger Clemens	4.00
M35	Bernie Williams, Bernie Williams	1.50
M36	Mo Vaughn, Mo Vaughn	1.50
M37	Jim Thome, Jim Thome	2.00
M38	Travis Lee, Travis Lee	1.50
M39	Fred McGriff, Fred McGriff	1.50
M40	Ben Grieve, Ben Grieve	1.50

Mystery Finest Jumbo

		NM/M
Complete Set (3):		12.50
Common Card:		4.00
Refractor:		1.5X
1	Ken Griffey Jr., Alex Rodriguez	4.00
2	Derek Jeter, Bernie Williams	5.00
3	Mark McGwire, Jeff Bagwell	4.00

Power Zone

NM/M

Complete Set (20):		25.00
Common Player:		.50
1	Ken Griffey Jr.	3.00
2	Jeff Bagwell	2.00
3	Jose Cruz Jr.	.50
4	Barry Bonds	5.00
5	Mark McGwire	4.00
6	Jim Thome	1.50
7	Mo Vaughn	.50
8	Gary Sheffield	1.00
9	Andres Galarraga	.50
10	Nomar Garciaparra	2.50
11	Rafael Palmeiro	1.50
12	Sammy Sosa	2.50
13	Jay Buhner	.50
14	Tony Clark	.50
15	Mike Piazza	3.00
16	Larry Walker	.50
17	Albert Belle	.50
18	Tino Martinez	.50
19	Juan Gonzalez	1.25
20	Frank Thomas	2.00

Stadium Stars

		NM/M
Complete Set (24):		95.00
Common Player:		1.00
SS1	Ken Griffey Jr.	8.00
SS2	Alex Rodriguez	10.00
SS3	Mo Vaughn	1.00
SS4	Nomar Garciaparra	6.00
SS5	Frank Thomas	4.50
SS6	Albert Belle	1.00
SS7	Derek Jeter	12.00
SS8	Chipper Jones	6.00
SS9	Cal Ripken Jr.	12.00
SS10	Jim Thome	3.00
SS11	Mike Piazza	8.00

SS12	Juan Gonzalez	2.50
SS13	Jeff Bagwell	4.50
SS14	Sammy Sosa	6.00
SS15	Jose Cruz Jr.	1.00
SS16	Gary Sheffield	2.00
SS17	Larry Walker	1.00
SS18	Tony Gwynn	6.00
SS19	Mark McGwire	10.00
SS20	Barry Bonds	12.00
SS21	Tino Martinez	1.00
SS22	Manny Ramirez	4.50
SS23	Ken Caminiti	1.00
SS24	Andres Galarraga	1.00

The Man

		NM/M
Complete Set (20):		125.00
Common Player:		1.50
Refractors:		3X
TM1	Ken Griffey Jr.	10.00
TM2	Barry Bonds	15.00
TM3	Frank Thomas	6.00
TM4	Chipper Jones	7.50
TM5	Cal Ripken Jr.	15.00
TM6	Nomar Garciaparra	7.50
TM7	Mark McGwire	12.50
TM8	Mike Piazza	10.00
TM9	Derek Jeter	15.00
TM10	Alex Rodriguez	12.50
TM11	Jose Cruz Jr.	1.50
TM12	Larry Walker	1.50
TM13	Jeff Bagwell	6.00
TM14	Tony Gwynn	7.50
TM15	Travis Lee	2.00
TM16	Juan Gonzalez	6.00
TM17	Scott Rolen	4.50
TM18	Randy Johnson	6.00
TM19	Roger Clemens	9.00
TM20	Greg Maddux	7.50

1999 Finest

	NM/M
Complete Set (300):	80.00

Complete Series 1 (150):		30.00
Complete Series 2 (150):		50.00
Common Player:		.15
Common SP (101-150, 251-300):		.50
Star Refractors:		6X
SP Refractors:		3X
Star Gold Refractors:		15X
SP Gold Refractors:		10X
Pack (6):		1.50
Wax Box (24):		30.00
1	Darin Erstad	.35
2	Javy Lopez	.15
3	Vinny Castilla	.15
4	Jim Thome	.60
5	Tino Martinez	.15
6	Mark Grace	.15
7	Shawn Green	.40
8	Dustin Hermanson	.15
9	Kevin Young	.15
10	Tony Clark	.15
11	Scott Brosius	.15
12	Craig Biggio	.15
13	Brian McRae	.15
14	Chan Ho Park	.15
15	Manny Ramirez	1.00
16	Chipper Jones	1.50
17	Rico Brogna	.15
18	Quinton McCracken	.15
19	J.T. Snow Jr.	.15
20	Tony Gwynn	1.50
21	Juan Guzman	.15
22	John Valentin	.15
23	Rick Helling	.15
24	Sandy Alomar	.15
25	Frank Thomas	1.00
26	Jorge Posada	.15
27	Dmitri Young	.15
28	Rick Reed	.15
29	Kevin Tapani	.15
30	Troy Glaus	.75
31	Kenny Rogers	.15
32	Jeremy Burnitz	.15
33	Mark Grudzielanek	.15
34	Mike Mussina	.50
35	Scott Rolen	.75
36	Neifi Perez	.15
37	Brad Radke	.15
38	Darryl Strawberry	.15
39	Robb Nen	.15
40	Moises Alou	.15
41	Eric Young	.15
42	Livan Hernandez	.15
43	John Wetteland	.15
44	Matt Lawton	.15
45	Ben Grieve	.15
46	Fernando Tatis	.15
47	Travis Fryman	.15
48	David Segui	.15
49	Bob Abreu	.15
50	Nomar Garciaparra	1.50
51	Paul O'Neill	.15
52	Jeff King	.15
53	Francisco Cordova	.15
54	John Olerud	.15
55	Vladimir Guerrero	1.00
56	Fernando Vina	.15
57	Shane Reynolds	.15
58	Chuck Finley	.15
59	Rondell White	.15
60	Greg Vaughn	.15
61	Ryan Minor	.15
62	Tom Gordon	.15
63	Damion Easley	.15
64	Ray Durham	.15
65	Orlando Hernandez	.15
66	Bartolo Colon	.15
67	Jaret Wright	.15
68	Royce Clayton	.15
69	Tim Salmon	.15
70	Mark McGwire	2.50
71	Alex Gonzalez	.15
72	Tom Glavine	.40
73	David Justice	.15
74	Omar Vizquel	.15
75	Juan Gonzalez	.50
76	Bobby Higginson	.15
77	Todd Walker	.15
78	Dante Bichette	.15
79	Kevin Millwood	.15
80	Roger Clemens	1.75
81	Kerry Wood	.50
82	Cal Ripken Jr.	3.00
83	Jay Bell	.15
84	Barry Bonds	3.00
85	Alex Rodriguez	2.50
86	Doug Glanville	.15
87	Jason Kendall	.15
88	Sean Casey	.25
89	Aaron Sele	.15
90	Derek Jeter	3.00
91	Andy Ashby	.15
92	Rusty Greer	.15
93	Rod Beck	.15
94	Matt Williams	.15
95	Mike Piazza	2.00
96	Wally Joyner	.15
97	Barry Larkin	.15
98	Eric Milton	.15
99	Gary Sheffield	.50
100	Greg Maddux	1.50
101	Ken Griffey Jr./Gem	4.00
102	Frank Thomas/Gem	2.00
103	Nomar Garciaparra/Gem	3.00
104	Mark McGwire/Gem	5.00
105	Alex Rodriguez/Gem	5.00
106	Tony Gwynn/Gem	3.00
107	Juan Gonzalez/Gem	.75

108	Jeff Bagwell/Gem	2.00
109	Sammy Sosa/Gem	3.00
110	Vladimir Guerrero/Gem	2.00
111	Roger Clemens/Gem	3.50
112	Barry Bonds/Gem	6.00
113	Darin Erstad/Gem	.50
114	Mike Piazza/Gem	4.00
115	Derek Jeter/Gem	6.00
116	Chipper Jones/Gem	3.00
117	Larry Walker/Gem	.50
118	Scott Rolen/Gem	1.50
119	Cal Ripken Jr./Gem	6.00
120	Greg Maddux/Gem	3.00
121	Troy Glaus	1.50
122	Ben Grieve	.50
123	Ryan Minor	.50
124	Kerry Wood	.50
125	Travis Lee	.50
126	Adrian Beltre	.50
127	Brad Fullmer	.50
128	Aramis Ramirez	.50
129	Eric Chavez	.50
130	Todd Helton	1.50
131	Pat Burrell RC	4.00
132	Ryan Mills RC	.50
133	Austin Kearns RC	3.00
134	Josh McKinley RC	.50
135	Adam Everett RC	.75
136	Marlon Anderson	.50
137	Bruce Chen	.50
138	Matt Clement	.50
139	Alex Gonzalez	.50
140	Roy Halladay	.50
141	Calvin Pickering	.50
142	Randy Wolf	.50
143	Ryan Anderson	.50
144	Ruben Mateo	.50
145	Alex Escobar RC	.50
146	Jeremy Giambi	.50
147	Lance Berkman	.50
148	Michael Barrett	.50
149	Preston Wilson	.50
150	Gabe Kapler	.50
151	Roger Clemens	1.75
152	Jay Buhner	.15
153	Brad Fullmer	.15
154	Ray Lankford	.15
155	Jim Edmonds	.15
156	Jason Giambi	.60
157	Bret Boone	.15
158	Jeff Cirillo	.15
159	Rickey Henderson	1.00
160	Edgar Martinez	.15
161	Ron Gant	.15
162	Mark Kotsay	.15
163	Trevor Hoffman	.15
164	Jason Schmidt	.15
165	Brett Tomko	.15
166	David Ortiz	.50
167	Dean Palmer	.15
168	Hideki Irabu	.15
169	Mike Cameron	.15
170	Pedro Martinez	1.00
171	Tom Goodwin	.15
172	Brian Hunter	.15
173	Al Leiter	.15
174	Charles Johnson	.15
175	Curt Schilling	.50
176	Robin Ventura	.15
177	Travis Lee	.15
178	Jeff Shaw	.15
179	Ugueth Urbina	.15
180	Roberto Alomar	.30
181	Cliff Floyd	.15
182	Adrian Beltre	.25
183	Tony Womack	.15
184	Brian Jordan	.15
185	Randy Johnson	1.00
186	Mickey Morandini	.15
187	Todd Hundley	.15
188	Jose Valentin	.15
189	Eric Davis	.15
190	Ken Caminiti	.15
191	David Wells	.15
192	Ryan Klesko	.15
193	Garret Anderson	.15
194	Eric Karros	.15
195	Ivan Rodriguez	.75
196	Aramis Ramirez	.15
197	Mike Lieberthal	.15
198	Will Clark	.15
199	Rey Ordonez	.15
200	Ken Griffey Jr.	2.00
201	Jose Guillen	.15
202	Scott Erickson	.15
203	Paul Konerko	.15
204	Johnny Damon	.40
205	Larry Walker	.15
206	Denny Neagle	.15
207	Jose Offerman	.15
208	Andy Pettitte	.30
209	Bobby Jones	.15
210	Kevin Brown	.15
211	John Smoltz	.15
212	Henry Rodriguez	.15
213	Tim Belcher	.15
214	Carlos Delgado	.50
215	Andruw Jones	1.00
216	Andy Benes	.15
217	Fred McGriff	.15
218	Edgar Renteria	.15
219	Miguel Tejada	.25
220	Bernie Williams	.15
221	Justin Thompson	.15
222	Marty Cordova	.15
223	Delino DeShields	.15
224	Ellis Burks	.15

225	Kenny Lofton	.15
226	Steve Finley	.15
227	Eric Chavez	.25
228	Jose Cruz Jr.	.15
229	Marquis Grissom	.15
230	Jeff Bagwell	1.00
231	Jose Canseco	.50
232	Edgardo Alfonzo	.15
233	Richie Sexson	.15
234	Jeff Kent	.15
235	Rafael Palmeiro	.75
236	David Cone	.15
237	Gregg Jefferies	.15
238	Mike Lansing	.15
239	Mariano Rivera	.25
240	Albert Belle	.15
241	Chuck Knoblauch	.15
242	Derek Bell	.15
243	Pat Hentgen	.15
244	Andres Galarraga	.15
245	Mo Vaughn	.15
246	Wade Boggs	1.50
247	Devon White	.15
248	Todd Helton	.75
249	Raul Mondesi	.15
250	Sammy Sosa	1.50
251	Nomar Garciaparra	3.00
252	Mark McGwire	5.00
253	Alex Rodriguez	5.00
254	Juan Gonzalez	.75
255	Vladimir Guerrero	2.00
256	Ken Griffey Jr.	4.00
257	Mike Piazza	4.00
258	Derek Jeter	6.00
259	Albert Belle	.50
260	Greg Vaughn	.50
261	Sammy Sosa	3.00
262	Greg Maddux	3.00
263	Frank Thomas	2.00
264	Mark Grace	.50
265	Ivan Rodriguez	1.25
266	Roger Clemens	3.50
267	Mo Vaughn	.50
268	Jim Thome	.75
269	Darin Erstad	.65
270	Chipper Jones	2.50
271	Larry Walker	.50
272	Cal Ripken Jr.	6.00
273	Scott Rolen	1.25
274	Randy Johnson	2.00
275	Tony Gwynn	2.50
276	Barry Bonds	6.00
277	Sean Burroughs RC	1.50
278	J.M. Gold RC	.50
279	Carlos Lee	.50
280	George Lombard	.50
281	Carlos Beltran	1.50
282	Fernando Seguignol	.50
283	Eric Chavez	.65
284	Carlos Pena RC	3.00
285	Corey Patterson RC	2.00
286	Alfonso Soriano RC	12.00
287	Nick Johnson RC	2.00
288	Jorge Toca RC	.50
289	A.J. Burnett RC	1.00
290	Andy Brown RC	.50
291	Doug Mientkiewicz RC	1.00
292	Bobby Seay RC	.50
293	Chip Ambres RC	.50
294	C.C. Sabathia RC	3.00
295	Choo Freeman RC	1.00
296	Eric Valent RC	.50
297	Matt Belisle RC	.50
298	Jason Tyner RC	.50
299	Masao Kida RC	.50
300	Hank Aaron, Mark McGwire (Homerun Kings)	3.00

Refractors

ABREU
PHILADELPHIA PHILLIES

	NM/M
Complete Set (300):	750.00
Common Player:	1.00
Stars:	6X
SP's:	3X

(See 1999 Finest for checklist and base card values.)

Gold Refractors

	NM/M
Common Player:	3.00
Stars:	15X

DETROIT TIGERS

SP's:	10X

(See 1999 Finest for checklist and base card values.)

Complements

	NM/M
Complete Set (7):	25.00
Common Player:	2.50
Inserted 1:56	
Dual-Refractors:	2X
Inserted 1:168	
1	Mike Piazza, Ivan Rodriguez	4.00
2	Tony Gwynn, Wade Boggs	3.00
3	Kerry Wood, Roger Clemens	3.50
4	Juan Gonzalez, Sammy Sosa	3.00
5	Derek Jeter, Nomar Garciaparra	6.00
6	Mark McGwire, Frank Thomas	5.00
7	Vladimir Guerrero, Andruw Jones	2.50

Double Feature

	NM/M
Complete Set (7):	30.00
Common Player:	2.00
Dual-Refractors:	2X
1	Ken Griffey Jr., Alex Rodriguez	10.00
2	Chipper Jones, Andruw Jones	6.00
3	Darin Erstad, Mo Vaughn	2.00
4	Craig Biggio, Jeff Bagwell	4.00
5	Ben Grieve, Eric Chavez	2.00
6	Albert Belle, Cal Ripken Jr.	10.00
7	Scott Rolen, Pat Burrell	3.00

Franchise Records

BARRY BONDS
FRANCHISE RECORDS

	NM/M
Complete Set (10):	35.00
Common Player:	2.00
Refractors:	3X
1	Frank Thomas	2.50

2	Ken Griffey Jr.	5.00
3	Mark McGwire	6.00
4	Juan Gonzalez	2.00
5	Nomar Garciaparra	3.00
6	Mike Piazza	5.00
7	Cal Ripken Jr.	7.50
8	Sammy Sosa	3.00
9	Barry Bonds	7.50
10	Tony Gwynn	3.00

Future's Finest

FUTURE'S FINEST
ALEX GONZALEZ

	NM/M
Complete Set (10):	35.00
Common Player:	2.00
1	Pat Burrell	10.00
2	Troy Glaus	12.50
3	Eric Chavez	3.00
4	Ryan Anderson	2.00
5	Ruben Mateo	2.00
6	Gabe Kapler	2.00
7	Alex Gonzalez	2.00
8	Michael Barrett	2.00
9	Lance Berkman	2.00
10	Fernando Seguignol	2.00

Hank Aaron Award Contenders

HANK AARON AWARD CONTENDERS
VLADIMIR GUERRERO

	NM/M
Complete Set (9):	20.00
Common Player:	2.00
Refractors:	3X
1	Juan Gonzalez	2.00
2	Vladimir Guerrero	2.50
3	Nomar Garciaparra	3.00
4	Albert Belle	2.00
5	Frank Thomas	2.50
6	Sammy Sosa	3.00
7	Alex Rodriguez	5.00
8	Ken Griffey Jr.	4.00
9	Mark McGwire	5.00

Leading Indicators

LEADING INDICATORS
SAMMY SOSA (9)

	NM/M
Complete Set (10):	20.00

Common Player:		.50
Inserted 1:24		
L1	Mark McGwire	5.00
L2	Sammy Sosa	3.00
L3	Ken Griffey Jr.	4.00
L4	Greg Vaughn	.50
L5	Albert Belle	.50
L6	Juan Gonzalez	.75
L7	Andres Galarraga	.50
L8	Alex Rodriguez	5.00
L9	Barry Bonds	6.00
L10	Jeff Bagwell	1.50

Milestones

		NM/M
Complete Set (40):		125.00
Common Hits (1-10):		.50
Common Homeruns (11-20):		2.00
Common RBI (21-30):		1.00
Common Doubles (31-40):		2.00
1	Tony Gwynn	1.50
2	Cal Ripken Jr.	3.00
3	Wade Boggs	1.50
4	Ken Griffey Jr.	2.00
5	Frank Thomas	1.00
6	Barry Bonds	3.00
7	Travis Lee	.50
8	Alex Rodriguez	2.50
9	Derek Jeter	3.00
10	Vladimir Guerrero	1.00
11	Mark McGwire	8.00
12	Ken Griffey Jr.	7.00
13	Vladimir Guerrero	4.00
14	Alex Rodriguez	8.00
15	Barry Bonds	10.00
16	Sammy Sosa	5.00
17	Albert Belle	2.00
18	Frank Thomas	4.00
19	Jose Canseco	3.00
20	Mike Piazza	7.00
21	Jeff Bagwell	2.00
22	Barry Bonds	6.00
23	Ken Griffey Jr.	4.00
24	Albert Belle	1.00
25	Juan Gonzalez	1.50
26	Vinny Castilla	1.00
27	Mark McGwire	5.00
28	Alex Rodriguez	5.00
29	Nomar Garciaparra	3.00
30	Frank Thomas	2.50
31	Barry Bonds	10.00
32	Albert Belle	2.00
33	Ben Grieve	2.00
34	Craig Biggio	2.00
35	Vladimir Guerrero	4.00
36	Nomar Garciaparra	5.00
37	Alex Rodriguez	7.00
38	Derek Jeter	10.00
39	Ken Griffey Jr.	7.00
40	Brad Fulmer	2.00

Peel & Reveal

	NM/M
Complete Set (20):	40.00
Common Player:	1.00
Hyperplaid:	1.5X
Stadium Stars:	2.5X

1	Kerry Wood	1.50
2	Mark McGwire	5.00
3	Sammy Sosa	3.00
4	Ken Griffey Jr.	4.00
5	Nomar Garciaparra	3.00
6	Greg Maddux	3.00
7	Derek Jeter	6.00
8	Andres Galarraga	1.00
9	Alex Rodriguez	5.00
10	Frank Thomas	2.00
11	Roger Clemens	3.50
12	Juan Gonzalez	1.50
13	Ben Grieve	1.00
14	Jeff Bagwell	2.00
15	Todd Helton	2.00
16	Chipper Jones	3.00
17	Barry Bonds	6.00
18	Travis Lee	1.00
19	Vladimir Guerrero	2.00
20	Pat Burrell	1.50

Prominent Figures

		NM/M
Complete Set (50):		250.00
Common Home Runs (1-10); #d to 70:		3.00
Common Slugging % (11-20); #d to 847:		1.00
Common Batting Ave. (21-30); #d to 424:		1.75
Common RBIs (31-40); #d to 190:		2.00
Common Total Bases (41-50); #d to 457:		1.75
1	Mark McGwire (HR)	25.00
2	Sammy Sosa (HR)	10.00
3	Ken Griffey Jr. (HR)	15.00
4	Mike Piazza (HR)	15.00
5	Juan Gonzalez (HR)	5.00
6	Greg Vaughn (HR)	3.00
7	Alex Rodriguez (HR)	25.00
8	Manny Ramirez (HR)	7.50
9	Jeff Bagwell (HR)	7.50
10	Andres Galarraga (HR)	3.00
11	Mark McGwire (S%)	6.00
12	Sammy Sosa (S%)	5.00
13	Juan Gonzalez (S%)	2.50
14	Ken Griffey Jr. (S%)	5.00
15	Barry Bonds (S%)	7.50
16	Greg Vaughn (S%)	1.00
17	Larry Walker (S%)	1.00
18	Andres Galarraga (S%)	1.00
19	Jeff Bagwell (S%)	2.50
20	Albert Belle (S%)	1.00
21	Tony Gwynn (BA)	5.00
22	Mike Piazza (BA)	6.00
23	Larry Walker (BA)	1.75
24	Alex Rodriguez (BA)	7.50
25	John Olerud (BA)	1.75
26	Frank Thomas (BA)	3.50
27	Bernie Williams (BA)	1.75
28	Chipper Jones (BA)	5.00
29	Jim Thome (BA)	2.50
30	Barry Bonds (BA)	9.00
31	Juan Gonzalez (RBI)	3.00
32	Sammy Sosa (RBI)	9.00
33	Mark McGwire (RBI)	20.00
34	Albert Belle (RBI)	2.00
35	Ken Griffey Jr. (RBI)	15.00
36	Jeff Bagwell (RBI)	6.00
37	Chipper Jones (RBI)	10.00
38	Vinny Castilla (RBI)	2.00
39	Alex Rodriguez (RBI)	20.00
40	Andres Galarraga (RBI)	2.00
41	Sammy Sosa (TB)	6.00
42	Mark McGwire (TB)	7.50
43	Albert Belle (TB)	1.75
44	Ken Griffey Jr. (TB)	6.00
45	Jeff Bagwell (TB)	3.50
46	Juan Gonzalez (TB)	3.50
47	Barry Bonds (TB)	9.00
48	Vladimir Guerrero (TB)	3.50
49	Larry Walker (TB)	1.75
50	Alex Rodriguez (TB)	7.50

Split Screen

	NM/M
Complete Set (14):	30.00
Common Card:	1.00
Dual-Refractor:	2X

1	Mark McGwire, Sammy Sosa	4.00

2	Ken Griffey Jr., Alex Rodriguez	4.00
3	Nomar Garciaparra, Derek Jeter	5.00
4	Barry Bonds, Albert Belle	4.00
5	Cal Ripken Jr., Tony Gwynn	4.00
6	Manny Ramirez, Juan Gonzalez	1.50
7	Frank Thomas, Andres Galarraga	1.50
8	Scott Rolen, Chipper Jones	2.00
9	Ivan Rodriguez, Mike Piazza	3.00
10	Kerry Wood, Roger Clemens	2.50
11	Greg Maddux, Tom Glavine	2.00
12	Troy Glaus, Eric Chavez	1.50
13	Ben Grieve, Todd Helton	1.00
14	Travis Lee, Pat Burrell	2.50

Team Finest

		NM/M
Complete Set (20):		25.00
Common Blue:		1.00
Production 1,500 Sets		
Blue Refractors:		3X
Production 150 Sets		
Reds:		1.5X
Production 500 Sets		
Red Refractors:		7X
Production 50 Sets		
Golds:		2X
Production 250 Sets		
Gold Refractors:		10X
Production 25 Sets		
1	Greg Maddux	2.50
2	Mark McGwire	4.50
3	Sammy Sosa	2.50
4	Juan Gonzalez	1.25
5	Alex Rodriguez	4.50
6	Travis Lee	1.00
7	Roger Clemens	2.75
8	Darin Erstad	1.25
9	Todd Helton	1.75
10	Mike Piazza	3.50
11	Kerry Wood	1.25
12	Ken Griffey Jr.	3.50
13	Frank Thomas	2.00
14	Jeff Bagwell	2.00
15	Nomar Garciaparra	2.50
16	Derek Jeter	6.00
17	Chipper Jones	2.50
18	Barry Bonds	6.00
19	Tony Gwynn	2.50
20	Ben Grieve	1.00

2000 Finest

	NM/M
Complete Set (286):	250.00
Complete Series 1 (147):	175.00
Complete Series 2 (140):	125.00
Common Player:	.25
Common Rookie (101-120):	4.00
Production 2,000	
Common Rookie (247-266):	4.00
Production 3,000	
Common Counterpart (267-276):	.75
Inserted 1:8	
Common Gem (136-145):	1.50
Inserted 1:24	
Pack (6):	2.00
Series 1 & 2 Box (24):	40.00

1	Nomar Garciaparra	2.00
2	Chipper Jones	1.50
3	Erubiel Durazo	.25
4	Robin Ventura	.25
5	Garret Anderson	.25
6	Dean Palmer	.25
7	Mariano Rivera	.35
8	Rusty Greer	.25

MARK GRACE

9	Jim Thome	.25
10	Jeff Bagwell	1.00
11	Jason Giambi	.75
12	Jeromy Burnitz	.25
13	Mark Grace	.35
14	Russ Ortiz	.25
15	Kevin Brown	.25
16	Kevin Millwood	.25
17	Scott Williamson	.25
18	Orlando Hernandez	.25
19	Todd Walker	.25
20	Carlos Beltran	.50
21	Ruben Rivera	.25
22	Curt Schilling	.40
23	Brian Giles	.25
24	Eric Karros	.25
25	Preston Wilson	.25
26	Al Leiter	.25
27	Juan Encarnacion	.25
28	Tim Salmon	.40
29	B.J. Surhoff	.25
30	Bernie Williams	.45
31	Lee Stevens	.25
32	Pokey Reese	.25
33	Mike Sweeney	.25
34	Corey Koskie	.25
35	Roberto Alomar	.40
36	Tim Hudson	.40
37	Tom Glavine	.40
38	Jeff Kent	.25
39	Mike Lieberthal	.25
40	Barry Larkin	.25
41	Paul O'Neill	.25
42	Rico Brogna	.25
43	Brian Daubach	.25
44	Rich Aurilia	.25
45	Vladimir Guerrero	1.00
46	Luis Castillo	.25
47	Bartolo Colon	.25
48	Kevin Appier	.25
49	Mo Vaughn	.25
50	Alex Rodriguez	2.50
51	Randy Johnson	1.00
52	Kris Benson	.25
53	Tony Clark	.25
54	Chad Allen	.25
55	Larry Walker	.25
56	Freddy Garcia	.25
57	Paul Konerko	.35
58	Edgardo Alfonzo	.25
59	Brady Anderson	.25
60	Derek Jeter	3.00
61	Mike Hampton	.25
62	Jeff Cirillo	.25
63	Shannon Stewart	.25
64	Greg Maddux	1.50
65	Mark McGwire	2.50
66	Gary Sheffield	.50
67	Kevin Young	.25
68	Tony Gwynn	1.50
69	Rey Ordonez	.25
70	Cal Ripken Jr.	3.00
71	Todd Helton	1.00
72	Brian Jordan	.25
73	Jose Canseco	.50
74	Luis Gonzalez	.40
75	Barry Bonds	3.00
76	Jermaine Dye	.25
77	Jose Offerman	.25
78	Magglio Ordonez	.40
79	Fred McGriff	.25
80	Ivan Rodriguez	.60
81	Josh Hamilton	.50
82	Vernon Wells	.50
83	Mark Mulder	.35
84	John Patterson	.25
85	Nick Johnson	.50
86	Pablo Ozuna	.25
87	A.J. Burnett	.25
88	Jack Cust	.25
89	Adam Piatt	.25
90	Rob Ryan	.25
91	Sean Burroughs (Prospects)	.35
92	D'Angelo Jimenez	.25
93	Chad Hermansen	.25
94	Rob Fick	.25
95	Ruben Mateo	.25
96	Alex Escobar	.25
97	Willi Mo Pena	.25
98	Corey Patterson	.50

#	Player	Price
99	Eric Munson	.25
100	Pat Burrell	.75
101	Michael Tejera RC	4.00
102	Bobby Bradley RC	4.00
103	Larry Bigbie RC	6.00
104	B.J. Garbe RC	4.00
105	Josh Kalinowski RC	4.00
106	Brett Myers RC	15.00
107	Chris Mears RC	4.00
108	Aaron Rowand RC	10.00
109	Corey Myers RC	4.00
110	John Sneed RC	4.00
111	Ryan Christensen RC	4.00
112	Kyle Snyder RC	4.00
113	Mike Paradis RC	4.00
114	Chance Caple RC	4.00
115	Ben Christiansen RC	4.00
116	Brad Baker RC	4.00
117	Rob Purvis RC	4.00
118	Rick Asadoorian RC	4.00
119	Ruben Salazar RC	4.00
120	Julio Zuleta RC	4.00
121	Ken Griffey Jr., Alex Rodriguez	4.00
122	Nomar Garciaparra, Derek Jeter	5.00
123	Mark McGwire, Sammy Sosa	4.00
124	Randy Johnson, Pedro Martinez	2.00
125	Mike Piazza, Ivan Rodriguez	3.00
126	Manny Ramirez, Roberto Alomar	2.00
127	Chipper Jones, Andruw Jones	3.00
128	Ken Griffey Jr., Tony Gwynn	5.00
129	Jeff Bagwell, Craig Biggio	1.50
130	Vladimir Guerrero, Barry Bonds	5.00
131	Alfonso Soriano, Nick Johnson	2.00
132	Josh Hamilton, Pat Burrell	1.50
133	Corey Patterson, Ruben Mateo	.75
134	Larry Walker, Todd Helton	1.50
135	Edgardo Alfonzo, Rey Ordonez	.75
136	Derek Jeter	10.00
137	Alex Rodriguez	8.00
138	Chipper Jones	5.00
139	Mike Piazza	6.00
140	Mark McGwire	8.00
141	Ivan Rodriguez	2.00
142	Cal Ripken Jr.	10.00
143	Vladimir Guerrero	3.00
144	Randy Johnson	3.00
145	Jeff Bagwell	3.00
146	Ken Griffey Jr. field	1.50
146a	Ken Griffey Jr. press	1.50
147	Andruw Jones	1.00
148	Kerry Wood	.50
149	Jim Edmonds	.25
150	Pedro Martinez	1.00
151	Warren Morris	.25
152	Trevor Hoffman	.25
153	Eric Young	.25
154	Andy Pettitte	.40
155	Frank Thomas	1.00
156	Damion Easley	.25
157	Cliff Floyd	.25
158	Ben Davis	.25
159	John Valentin	.25
160	Rafael Palmeiro	.65
161	Andy Ashby	.25
162	J.D. Drew	.40
163	Jay Bell	.25
164	Adam Kennedy	.25
165	Manny Ramirez	1.00
166	John Halama	.25
167	Octavio Dotel	.25
168	Darin Erstad	.40
169	Jose Lima	.25
170	Andres Galarraga	.25
171	Scott Rolen	.75
172	Delino DeShields	.25
173	J.T. Snow Jr.	.25
174	Tony Womack	.25
175	John Olerud	.25
176	Jason Kendall	.25
177	Carlos Lee	.25
178	Eric Milton	.25
179	Jeff Cirillo	.25
180	Gabe Kapler	.25
181	Greg Vaughn	.25
182	Denny Neagle	.25
183	Tino Martinez	.25
184	Doug Mientkiewicz	.25
185	Juan Gonzalez	1.00
186	Ellis Burks	.25
187	Mike Hampton	.25
188	Royce Clayton	.25
189	Mike Mussina	.50
190	Carlos Delgado	.50
191	Ben Grieve	.25
192	Fernando Tatis	.25
193	Matt Williams	.25
194	Rondell White	.25
195	Shawn Green	.50
196	Justin Thompson	.25
197	Troy Glaus	1.00
198	Roger Cedeno	.25
199	Ray Lankford	.25
200	Sammy Sosa	2.00
201	Kenny Lofton	.25
202	Edgar Martinez	.25
203	Mark Kotsay	.25
204	David Wells	.25
205	Craig Biggio	.25
206	Ray Durham	.25
207	Troy O'Leary	.25
208	Rickey Henderson	.75
209	Bob Abreu	.25
210	Neifi Perez	.25
211	Carlos Febles	.25
212	Chuck Knoblauch	.25
213	Moises Alou	.25
214	Omar Vizquel	.25
215	Vinny Castilla	.25
216	Javy Lopez	.25
217	Johnny Damon	.40
218	Roger Clemens	1.75
219	Miguel Tejada	.40
220	Deion Sanders	.35
221	Matt Lawton	.25
222	Albert Belle	.25
223	Adrian Beltre	.50
224	Dante Bichette	.25
225	Raul Mondesi	.25
226	Mike Piazza	2.00
227	Brad Penn	.25
228	Kip Wells	.25
229	Adam Everett	.25
230	Eddie Yarnall	.25
231	Matt LeCroy	.25
232	Ryan Anderson	.25
233	Rick Ankiel	.25
234	Daryle Ward	.25
235	Rafael Furcal	.25
236	Dee Brown	.25
237	Travis Dawkins	.25
238	Eric Valent	.25
239	Peter Bergeron	.25
240	Alfonso Soriano	1.50
241	John Patterson	.25
242	Jorge Toca	.25
243	Ryan Anderson	.25
244	Jason Dallaero	.25
245	Jason Grilli	.25
246	Chad Hermansen	.25
247	Scott Downs RC	4.00
248	Keith Reed RC	4.00
249	Edgar Cruz RC	4.00
250	Wes Anderson RC	4.00
251	Lyle Overbay RC	10.00
252	Mike Lamb RC	4.00
253	Vince Faison RC	4.00
254	Chad Alexander RC	4.00
255	Chris Wakeland	4.00
256	Aaron McNeal RC	4.00
257	Tomokazu Ohka RC	4.00
258	Ty Howington RC	6.00
259	Javier Colina RC	4.00
260	Jason Jennings	4.00
261	Ramon Santiago RC	4.00
262	Johan Santana RC	150.00
263	Quincey Foster RC	4.00
264	Junior Brignac RC	4.00
265	Rico Washington RC	4.00
266	Scott Sobkowiak RC	4.00
267	Pedro Martinez, Rick Ankiel	2.00
268	Manny Ramirez, Vladimir Guerrero	2.00
269	A.J. Burnett, Mark Mulder	.75
270	Mike Piazza, Eric Munson	2.50
271	Josh Hamilton, Corey Patterson	1.00
272	Ken Griffey Jr., Sammy Sosa	3.00
273	Derek Jeter, Alfonso Soriano	5.00
274	Mark McGwire, Pat Burrell	4.00
275	Chipper Jones, Cal Ripken Jr.	5.00
276	Nomar Garciaparra, Alex Rodriguez	8.00
277	Pedro Martinez	3.00
278	Tony Gwynn	5.00
279	Barry Bonds	10.00
280	Juan Gonzalez	3.00
281	Larry Walker	1.50
282	Nomar Garciaparra	8.00
283	Ken Griffey Jr.	6.00
284	Manny Ramirez	3.00
285	Shawn Green	2.00
286	Sammy Sosa	6.00

Refractor

AL LEITER

Stars (1-100):	5-10X
Inserted 1:24	
Rookies (101-120,247-266):	.5-1X
Production 500 Sets	
Features (121-135):	2-3X
Inserted 1:96	
Counterparts (267-276):	2-3X
Inserted 1:96	
Gems (136-145,277-286):	2-3X
Inserted 1:288	

Gold Refractor

Stars (1-100):	20-40X
Inserted 1:240	
Rookies (101-120, 247-266):	1-2X
Production 100 Sets	
Features:	4-8X
Inserted 1:960	
Counterparts:	4-8X
Inserted 1:960	
Gems:	5-10X
Inserted 1:2,880	

Ballpark Bounties

Scott Rolen

		NM/M
Complete Set (30):		85.00
Complete Series 1 (15):		45.00
Complete Series 2 (15):		45.00
Common Player:		1.50
Inserted 1:24		
1	Chipper Jones	5.00
2	Mike Piazza	6.00
3	Vladimir Guerrero	3.00
4	Sammy Sosa	6.00
5	Nomar Garciaparra	6.00
6	Manny Ramirez	3.00
7	Jeff Bagwell	3.00
8	Scott Rolen	2.00
9	Carlos Beltran	2.50
10	Pedro Martinez	3.00
11	Greg Maddux	5.00
12	Josh Hamilton	2.00
13	Adam Piatt	1.50
14	Pat Burrell	2.00
15	Alfonso Soriano	3.00
16	Alex Rodriguez	8.00
17	Derek Jeter	10.00
18	Cal Ripken Jr.	10.00
19	Larry Walker	1.50
20	Barry Bonds	10.00
21	Ken Griffey Jr.	6.00
22	Mark McGwire	8.00
23	Ivan Rodriguez	2.00
24	Andruw Jones	2.50
25	Todd Helton	2.50
26	Randy Johnson	3.00
27	Ruben Mateo	1.50
28	Corey Patterson	1.50
29	Sean Burroughs	1.50
30	Eric Munson	1.50

Dream Cast

		NM/M
Complete Set (10):		40.00
Common Player:		2.00
Inserted 1:36		
1	Mark McGwire	8.00
2	Roberto Alomar	2.00

3	Chipper Jones	5.00
4	Derek Jeter	10.00
5	Barry Bonds	10.00
6	Ken Griffey Jr.	6.00
7	Sammy Sosa	6.00
8	Mike Piazza	6.00
9	Pedro Martinez	3.00
10	Randy Johnson	3.00

Finest Moments

3,000 Hits

		NM/M
Complete Set (4):		6.00
Common Player:		1.00
Inserted 1:9		
Refractor:		1-2X
Inserted 1:20		
1	Chipper Jones	3.00
2	Ivan Rodriguez	1.50
3	Tony Gwynn	3.00
4	Wade Boggs	3.00

For The Record

CHIPPER JONES Atlanta Braves

		NM/M
Complete Set (30):		300.00
Common Player:		8.00
1A	Derek Jeter/318	20.00
1B	Derek Jeter/408	20.00
1C	Derek Jeter/314	20.00
2A	Mark McGwire/330	15.00
2B	Mark McGwire/402	15.00
2C	Mark McGwire/330	15.00
3A	Ken Griffey Jr./331	10.00
3B	Ken Griffey Jr./405	10.00
3C	Ken Griffey Jr./327	10.00
4A	Alex Rodriguez/331	15.00
4B	Alex Rodriguez/405	15.00
4C	Alex Rodriguez/327	15.00
5A	Nomar Garciaparra/310	10.00
5B	Nomar Garciaparra/390	10.00
5C	Nomar Garciaparra/302	10.00
6A	Cal Ripken Jr./333	20.00
6B	Cal Ripken Jr./410	20.00
6C	Cal Ripken Jr./318	20.00
7A	Sammy Sosa/355	10.00
7B	Sammy Sosa/400	10.00
7C	Sammy Sosa/353	10.00
8A	Manny Ramirez/325	8.00
8B	Manny Ramirez/410	8.00
8C	Manny Ramirez/325	8.00
9A	Mike Piazza/338	10.00
9B	Mike Piazza/410	10.00
9C	Mike Piazza/338	10.00
10A	Chipper Jones/335	9.00
10B	Chipper Jones/401	10.00
10C	Chipper Jones/330	10.00

Gems Oversized

		NM/M
Complete Set (20):		50.00
Common Player:		1.00
Inserted 1:Box		
1	Derek Jeter	6.00
2	Alex Rodriguez	5.00
3	Chipper Jones	3.00
4	Mike Piazza	4.00
5	Mark McGwire	5.00
6	Ivan Rodriguez	1.25

#	Player	NM/M
7	Cal Ripken Jr.	6.00
8	Vladimir Guerrero	2.00
9	Randy Johnson	2.00
10	Jeff Bagwell	2.00
11	Nomar Garciaparra	4.00
12	Ken Griffey Jr.	4.00
13	Manny Ramirez	2.00
14	Shawn Green	1.50
15	Sammy Sosa	4.00
16	Pedro Martinez	2.00
17	Tony Gwynn	2.00
18	Barry Bonds	6.00
19	Juan Gonzalez	1.50
20	Larry Walker	1.00

Going the Distance

MIKE PIAZZA

		NM/M
Complete Set (12):		45.00
Common Player:		3.00
Inserted 1:24		
1	Tony Gwynn	3.50
2	Alex Rodriguez	6.00
3	Derek Jeter	8.00
4	Chipper Jones	4.00
5	Nomar Garciaparra	4.00
6	Sammy Sosa	4.00
7	Ken Griffey Jr.	4.00
8	Vladimir Guerrero	3.00
9	Mark McGwire	6.00
10	Mike Piazza	4.00
11	Manny Ramirez	3.00
12	Cal Ripken Jr.	3.00

Moments Autographs

1999 NL MVP

		NM/M
Common Autograph:		25.00
Inserted 1:425		
1	Chipper Jones	50.00
2	Ivan Rodriguez	25.00
3	Tony Gwynn	50.00
4	Wade Boggs	25.00

2001 Finest

	NM/M
Complete Set (140):	250.00

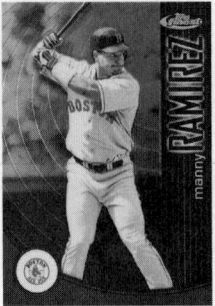

Common Player:		.25
Common Standout Veteran (10):		5.00
Production 1999		
Common Rookie (111-140):		4.00
Production 999		
Pack (6):		8.00
Box (20):		140.00
1	Mike Piazza/SV	10.00
2	Andruw Jones	.50
3	Jason Giambi	.75
4	Fred McGriff	.25
5	Vladimir Guerrero/SV	6.00
6	Adrian Gonzalez	.40
7	Pedro Martinez	1.00
8	Mike Lieberthal	.25
9	Warren Morris	.25
10	Juan Gonzalez	.50
11	Jose Canseco	.50
12	Jose Valentin	.25
13	Jeff Cirillo	.25
14	Pokey Reese	.25
15	Scott Rolen	.75
16	Greg Maddux	1.50
17	Carlos Delgado	.50
18	Rick Ankiel	.50
19	Steve Finley	.25
20	Shawn Green	.40
21	Orlando Cabrerra	.25
22	Roberto Alomar	.40
23	John Olerud	.25
24	Albert Belle	.25
25	Edgardo Alfonzo	.25
26	Rafael Palmeiro	.75
27	Mike Sweeney	.25
28	Bernie Williams	.40
29	Larry Walker	.25
30	Barry Bonds/SV	15.00
31	Orlando Hernandez	.25
32	Randy Johnson	1.00
33	Shannon Stewart	.25
34	Mark Grace	.40
35	Alex Rodriguez/SV	12.00
36	Tino Martinez	.40
37	Carlos Febles	.25
38	Al Leiter	.25
39	Omar Vizquel	.25
40	Chuck Knoblauch	.25
41	Tim Salmon	.40
42	Brian Jordan	.25
43	Edgar Renteria	.25
44	Preston Wilson	.25
45	Mariano Rivera	.50
46	Gabe Kapler	.25
47	Jason Kendall	.25
48	Rickey Henderson	.75
49	Luis Gonzalez	.40
50	Tom Glavine	.50
51	Jeromy Burnitz	.25
52	Garret Anderson	.25
53	Craig Biggio	.25
54	Vinny Castilla	.25
55	Jeff Kent	.25
56	Gary Sheffield	.50
57	Jorge Posada	.25
58	Sean Casey	.40
59	Johnny Damon	.50
60	Dean Palmer	.25
61	Todd Helton	.75
62	Barry Larkin	.50
63	Robin Ventura	.25
64	Kenny Lofton	.25
65	Sammy Sosa/SV	8.00
66	Rafael Furcal	.40
67	Jay Bell	.25
68	J.T. Snow Jr.	.25
69	Jose Vidro	.25
70	Ivan Rodriguez	.75
71	Jermaine Dye	.25
72	Chipper Jones/SV	10.00
73	Fernando Vina	.25
74	Ben Grieve	.25
75	Mark McGwire/SV	10.00
76	Matt Williams	.25
77	Mark Grudzielanek	.25
78	Mike Hampton	.25
79	Brian Giles	.25
80	Tony Gwynn	1.50
81	Carlos Beltran	.50
82	Ray Durham	.25
83	Brad Radke	.25
84	David Justice	.25
85	Frank Thomas	1.00
86	Todd Zeile	.25
87	Pat Burrell	.75
88	Jim Thome	.25
89	Greg Vaughn	.25
90	Ken Griffey Jr./SV	10.00
91	Mike Mussina	.50
92	Magglio Ordonez	.50
93	Bobby Abreu	.50
94	Alex Gonzalez	.25
95	Kevin Brown	.25
96	Jay Buhner	.25
97	Roger Clemens	2.00
98	Nomar Garciaparra/SV	5.00
99	Derek Lee	.50
100	Derek Jeter/SV	15.00
101	Adrian Beltre	.40
102	Geoff Jenkins	.25
103	Javy Lopez	.25
104	Raul Mondesi	.25
105	Troy Glaus	.50
106	Jeff Bagwell	.75
107	Eric Karros	.25
108	Mo Vaughn	.25
109	Cal Ripken Jr.	3.00
110	Manny Ramirez	1.00
111	Scott Heard	4.00
112	Luis Montanez RC	5.00
113	Ben Diggins	4.00
114	Shaun Boyd RC	4.00
115	Sean Burnett	4.00
116	Carmen Cali RC	4.00
117	Derek Thompson	4.00
118	David Parrish RC	4.00
119	Dominic Rich RC	4.00
120	Chad Petty RC	4.00
121	Steve Smyth RC	4.00
122	John Lackey	6.00
123	Matt Galante RC	4.00
124	Danny Borrell RC	4.00
125	Bob Keppel RC	4.00
126	Justin Wayne RC	4.00
127	J.R. House	4.00
128	Brian Sellier RC	4.00
129	Dan Moylan RC	4.00
130	Scott Pratt RC	4.00
131	Victor Hall RC	4.00
132	Joel Pineiro	4.00
133	Josh Axelson RC	4.00
134	Jose Reyes RC	120.00
135	Greg Runser RC	4.00
136	Bryan Hebson RC	4.00
137	Sammy Serrano RC	4.00
138	Kevin Joseph RC	4.00
139	Juan Richardson RC	4.00
140	Mark Fischer RC	4.00

Refractors

Stars (1-110):	4-8X
Production 499	
SP's:	.5-1.5X
Production 399	
Cards (111-140):	1-2X
Production 241	

Autographed

		NM/M
Common Player:		5.00
Inserted 1:22		
MB	Milton Bradley	15.00
SB	Sean Burnett	5.00
BKC	Brian Cole	5.00
JC	Joe Crede	10.00
BC	Brad Creese	5.00
BD	Ben Diggins	5.00
CD	Chad Durham	5.00
TF	Troy Farnsworth	5.00
RF	Rafael Furcal	15.00
KG	Keith Ginter	5.00
AG	Adrian Gonzalez	20.00
JHH	Josh Hamilton	40.00
JH	Jason Hart	5.00
JRH	J.R. House	5.00
AH	Adam Hyzdu	5.00
DKC	David Kelton	5.00
AK	Adam Kennedy	5.00
DK	David Krynzal	5.00
ML	Mike Lamb	5.00
TL	Terrence Long	5.00
KM	Kevin Mench	5.00
BM	Ben Molina	8.00
JM	Justin Morneau	75.00
CM	Chad Mottola	5.00
JO	Jose Ortiz	5.00
DP	David Parrish	5.00
DCP	Corey Patterson	8.00
JP	Jay Payton	5.00
CP	Carlos Pena	10.00
AP	Albert Pujols	300.00
MQ	Mark Quinn	5.00
MR	Mark Redman	5.00
BS	Ben Sheets	15.00
JS	Juan Silvestre	5.00
JNS	Jamal Strong	5.00
BZ	Barry Zito	15.00

All-Stars

Mike Piazza

		NM/M
Complete Set (10):		30.00
Common Player:		2.00
Inserted 1:10		
Refractors:		1.5-2X
Inserted 1:40		
1	Mark McGwire	4.00
2	Derek Jeter	6.00
3	Alex Rodriguez	5.00
4	Chipper Jones	4.00
5	Nomar Garciaparra	2.00
6	Sammy Sosa	2.00
7	Mike Piazza	4.00
8	Barry Bonds	6.00
9	Vladimir Guerrero	2.00
10	Ken Griffey Jr.	4.00

Moments

Finest Moments — CAL RIPKEN 3000th Hit

		NM/M
Complete Set (25):		45.00
Common Player:		1.00
Inserted 1:12		
Refractors:		1.5-2X
Inserted 1:40		
1	Pat Burrell	2.00
2	Adam Kennedy	1.00
3	Mike Lamb	1.00
4	Rafael Furcal	1.50
5	Terrence Long	1.00
6	Jay Payton	1.00
7	Mark Quinn	1.00
8	Ben Molina	1.00
9	Kazuhiro Sasaki	1.00
10	Mark Redman	1.00
11	Barry Bonds	8.00
12	Alex Rodriguez	6.00
13	Roger Clemens	5.00
14	Jim Edmonds	1.00
15	Jason Giambi	2.00
16	Todd Helton	2.50
17	Troy Glaus	2.00
18	Carlos Delgado	2.00
19	Darin Erstad	2.00
20	Cal Ripken Jr.	8.00
21	Paul Molitor	3.00
22	Robin Yount	2.50
23	George Brett	5.00
24	Dave Winfield	2.50
25	Wade Boggs	3.00

Moments Autographs

		NM/M
Inserted 1:250		
BB	Barry Bonds	150.00
GB	George Brett	75.00
JG	Jason Giambi	25.00
TG	Troy Glaus	20.00
TH	Todd Helton	30.00
PM	Paul Molitor	30.00
EM	Eddie Murray	20.00

Finest Moments

CR	Cal Ripken Jr.	125.00
DW	Dave Winfield	20.00
RY	Robin Yount	50.00

Origins

Complete Set (15):	18.00
Common Player:	1.00
Inserted 1:7	
Refractors:	1.5-2X
Inserted 1:40	
1	Derek Jeter	5.00
2	Jason Kendall	1.00
3	Jose Vidro	1.00
4	Preston Wilson	1.00
5	Jim Edmonds	1.00
6	Vladimir Guerrero	2.00
7	Andruw Jones	1.50
8	Scott Rolen	1.50
9	Edgardo Alfonzo	1.00
10	Mike Sweeney	1.00
11	Alex Rodriguez	4.00
12	Jermaine Dye	1.00
13	Charles Johnson	1.00
14	Darren Dreifort	1.00
15	Neifi Perez	1.00

2002 Finest

Complete Set (110):	125.00
Common Player:	.25
Common SP Auto. (101-110):	8.00
Pack (5):	4.00
Box (18):	60.00
1	Mike Mussina	.50
2	Steve Sparks	.25
3	Randy Johnson	1.00
4	Orlando Cabrera	.25
5	Jeff Kent	.25
6	Carlos Delgado	.75
7	Ivan Rodriguez	.75
8	Jose Cruz	.25
9	Jason Giambi	.75

10	Brad Penny	.25
11	Moises Alou	.25
12	Mike Piazza	2.00
13	Ben Grieve	.25
14	Derek Jeter	3.00
15	Roy Oswalt	.40
16	Pat Burrell	.65
17	Preston Wilson	.25
18	Kevin Brown	.25
19	Barry Bonds	3.00
20	Phil Nevin	.25
21	Juan Gonzalez	1.00
22	Carlos Beltran	.60
23	Chipper Jones	1.50
24	Curt Schilling	.50
25	Jorge Posada	.40
26	Alfonso Soriano	1.00
27	Cliff Floyd	.25
28	Rafael Palmeiro	.75
29	Terrence Long	.25
30	Ken Griffey Jr.	2.00
31	Jason Kendall	.25
32	Jose Vidro	.25
33	Jermaine Dye	.25
34	Bobby Higginson	.25
35	Albert Pujols	2.50
36	Miguel Tejada	.40
37	Jim Edmonds	.25
38	Barry Zito	.40
39	Jimmy Rollins	.50
40	Rafael Furcal	.25
41	Omar Vizquel	.25
42	Kazuhiro Sasaki	.25
43	Brian Giles	.25
44	Darin Erstad	.50
45	Mariano Rivera	.40
46	Troy Percival	.25
47	Mike Sweeney	.25
48	Vladimir Guerrero	1.00
49	Troy Glaus	1.00
50	Hideo Nomo	.65
51	Edgardo Alfonzo	.25
52	Roger Clemens	1.75
53	Eric Chavez	.40
54	Alex Rodriguez	2.50
55	Cristian Guzman	.25
56	Jeff Bagwell	1.00
57	Bernie Williams	.40
58	Kerry Wood	.60
59	Ryan Klesko	.25
60	Ichiro Suzuki	2.00
61	Larry Walker	.25
62	Nomar Garciaparra	2.00
63	Craig Biggio	.25
64	J.D. Drew	.40
65	Juan Pierre	.25
66	Roberto Alomar	.50
67	Luis Gonzalez	.40
68	Bud Smith	.25
69	Magglio Ordonez	.25
70	Scott Rolen	1.00
71	Tsuyoshi Shinjo	.25
72	Reggie Sanders	.25
73	Garret Anderson	.25
74	Tim Hudson	.40
75	Adam Dunn	.75
76	Gary Sheffield	.50
77	Johnny Damon	.40
78	Todd Helton	1.00
79	Geoff Jenkins	.25
80	Shawn Green	.40
81	C.C. Sabathia	.50
82	Kazuhisa Ishii **RC**	2.00
83	Rich Aurilia	.25
84	Mike Hampton	.25
85	Ben Sheets	.25
86	Andruw Jones	1.00
87	Richie Sexson	.25
88	Jim Thome	.25
89	Sammy Sosa	2.00
90	Greg Maddux	1.50
91	Pedro Martinez	1.00
92	Jeromy Burnitz	.25
93	Raul Mondesi	.25
94	Bret Boone	.25
95	Jerry Hairston Jr.	.25
96	Carlos Pena	.25
97	Juan Cruz	.25
98	Morgan Ensberg	.25
99	Nathan Haynes	.25
100	Xavier Nady	.25
101	Nic Jackson/Auto. **RC**	10.00
102	Mauricio Lara/Auto. **RC**	8.00
103	Freddy Sanchez/Auto. **RC**	20.00
104	Clint Nageotte/Auto. **RC**	15.00
105	Beltran Perez/Auto. **RC**	8.00
106	Garrett Gentry/Auto. **RC**	8.00
107	Chad Qualls/Auto. **RC**	8.00
108	Jason Bay/Auto. **RC**	30.00
109	Michael Hill/Auto. **RC**	8.00
110	Brian Tallet/Auto.	10.00

Refractors

Star Refractors:	2-5X
Numbered to 499	
X-Fractors:	3-6X
Numbered to 299	
X-Fractor Protector:	5-10X
X-Fract. Protector (101-110):	1-2X
Numbered to 99	

Bat Relics

NM/M

Common Player:	5.00
Inserted 1:72	

BB	Barry Bonds	25.00
BBO	Bret Boone	5.00
NG	Nomar Garciaparra	15.00
LG	Luis Gonzalez	5.00
TG	Tony Gwynn	10.00
TH	Todd Helton	8.00
AJ	Andruw Jones	5.00
CJ	Chipper Jones	10.00
MP	Mike Piazza	10.00
AP	Albert Pujols	20.00
AR	Alex Rodriguez	10.00
IR	Ivan Rodriguez	8.00
TS	Tsuyoshi Shinjo	5.00
AS	Alfonso Soriano	8.00
BW	Bernie Williams	8.00

Moments Autographs

NM/M

Common Autograph:	10.00
Inserted 1:18	
LA	Luis Aparicio	15.00
YB	Yogi Berra	30.00
JB	Jim Bunning	15.00
BG	Bob Gibson	25.00
GG	Rich "Goose" Gossage	10.00
FJ	Fergie Jenkins	15.00
DL	Don Larsen	15.00
DM	Don Mattingly	75.00
GP	Gaylord Perry	10.00
BR	Bobby Richardson	10.00
BRO	Brooks Robinson	35.00
JS	Johnny Sain	10.00
MS	Mike Schmidt	50.00
RS	Red Schoendienst	10.00
BT	Bobby Thomson	15.00

Team Topps Legends

No Pricing
Common Autograph

Uniform Relics

NM/M

Common Player:	5.00
Inserted 1:24	
RA	Roberto Alomar	8.00
JB	Jeff Bagwell	8.00
BB	Barry Bonds	20.00
BBO	Bret Boone	5.00
CD	Carlos Delgado	8.00
LG	Luis Gonzalez	8.00
MG	Mark Grace	8.00
SG	Shawn Green	5.00
TG	Tony Gwynn	10.00
TH	Todd Helton	8.00
RH	Rickey Henderson	15.00
AJ	Andruw Jones	8.00

CJ	Chipper Jones	10.00
GM	Greg Maddux	10.00
PM	Pedro Martinez	10.00
HN	Hideo Nomo	20.00
RP	Rafael Palmeiro	10.00
MP	Mike Piazza	10.00
AR	Alex Rodriguez	10.00
IR	Ivan Rodriguez	8.00
CS	Curt Schilling	10.00
TS	Tsuyoshi Shinjo	5.00
FT	Frank Thomas	8.00
LW	Larry Walker	5.00

2003 Finest

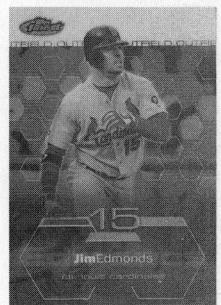

NM/M

Complete Set (110):	
Common Player:	.25
Common Auto. (101-110):	10.00
Pack (5):	4.00
Box (18):	50.00
1	Sammy Sosa	1.00
2	Paul Konerko	.25
3	Todd Helton	.75
4	Mike Lowell	.25
5	Lance Berkman	.25
6	Kazuhisa Ishii	.25
7	A.J. Pierzynski	.25
8	Jose Vidro	.25
9	Roberto Alomar	.40
10	Derek Jeter	3.00
11	Barry Zito	.25
12	Jimmy Rollins	.75
13	Brian Giles	.25
14	Ryan Klesko	.25
15	Rich Aurilia	.25
16	Jim Edmonds	.25
17	Aubrey Huff	.25
18	Ivan Rodriguez	.50
19	Eric Hinske	.25
20	Barry Bonds	3.00
21	Darin Erstad	.40
22	Curt Schilling	.50
23	Andruw Jones	.50
24	Jay Gibbons	.25
25	Nomar Garciaparra	.50
26	Kerry Wood	.50
27	Magglio Ordonez	.50
28	Austin Kearns	.50
29	Jason Jennings	.25
30	Jason Giambi	.50
31	Tim Hudson	.40
32	Edgar Martinez	.25
33	Carl Crawford	.25
34	Hee Seop Choi	.50
35	Vladimir Guerrero	.75
36	Jeff Kent	.25
37	John Smoltz	.25
38	Frank Thomas	.75
39	Cliff Floyd	.25
40	Mike Piazza	1.50
41	Mark Prior	.50
42	Tim Salmon	.40
43	Shawn Green	.50
44	Bernie Williams	.40
45	Jim Thome	.25
46	John Olerud	.25
47	Orlando Hudson	.25
48	Mark Teixeira	.75
49	Gary Sheffield	.50
50	Ichiro Suzuki	2.00
51	Tom Glavine	.40
52	Torii Hunter	.25
53	Craig Biggio	.25
54	Carlos Beltran	.75
55	Bartolo Colon	.25
56	Jorge Posada	.35
57	Pat Burrell	.50
58	Edgar Renteria	.25
59	Rafael Palmeiro	.50
60	Alfonso Soriano	.75
61	Brandon Phillips	.25
62	Luis Gonzalez	.40
63	Manny Ramirez	.75
64	Garret Anderson	.25
65	Ken Griffey Jr.	1.50
66	A.J. Burnett	.25
67	Mike Sweeney	.25
68	Doug Mientkiewicz	.25
69	Eric Chavez	.50
70	Adam Dunn	.75
71	Shea Hillenbrand	.25

72	Troy Glaus	.50
73	Rodrigo Lopez	.25
74	Moises Alou	.25
75	Chipper Jones	1.50
76	Bobby Abreu	.25
77	Mark Mulder	.40
78	Kevin Brown	.25
79	Josh Beckett	.75
80	Larry Walker	.25
81	Randy Johnson	.75
82	Greg Maddux	1.50
83	Johnny Damon	.40
84	Omar Vizquel	.25
85	Jeff Bagwell	.50
86	Carlos Pena	.25
87	Roy Oswalt	.40
88	Richie Sexson	.25
89	Roger Clemens	1.25
90	Miguel Tejada	.40
91	Vicente Padilla	.25
92	Phil Nevin	.25
93	Edgardo Alfonzo	.25
94	Bret Boone	.25
95	Albert Pujols	2.00
96	Carlos Delgado	.50
97	Marlon Byrd	.25
98	Scott Rolen	.50
99	Pedro J. Martinez	.75
100	Alex Rodriguez	2.00
101	Adam LaRoche	15.00
102	Andy Marte RC	15.00
103	Daryl Clark RC	10.00
104	J.D. Durbin RC	10.00
105	Craig Brazell RC	10.00
106	Brian Burgamy RC	10.00
107	Tyler Johnson RC	10.00
108	Joey Gomes	10.00
109	Bryan Bullington RC	10.00
110	Byron Gettis RC	10.00

Refractors

Stars (1-100):	2-4X
Rookie Autos.(101-110):	.75-1.5X
Inserted 1:6	

X-Fractors

Stars (1-100):	5-10X
Rookie Autos. (101-110):	1-2.5X
Production 99 Sets	
X-Fractor Golds (1-100):	3-6X
Golds Rk Autos. (101-110):	1-2X
Production 199 Sets	

Bat Relics

		NM/M
Common Player:		8.00
Inserted 1:6		
JB	Jeff Bagwell	8.00
LB	Lance Berkman	8.00
WB	Wade Boggs	8.00
BB	Barry Bonds	20.00
RC	Rod Carew	10.00
RCL	Roger Clemens	15.00
AD	Adam Dunn	8.00
NG	Nomar Garciaparra	20.00
TH	Todd Helton	8.00
RH	Rickey Henderson	10.00
CJ	Chipper Jones	15.00
AK	Austin Kearns	8.00
GM	Greg Maddux	15.00
PM	Paul Molitor	8.00
DM	Dale Murphy	15.00
RP	Rafael Palmeiro	8.00
MP	Mike Piazza	15.00
KP	Kirby Puckett	15.00
AP	Albert Pujols	25.00
MR	Manny Ramirez	15.00
CR	Cal Ripken Jr.	35.00
AR	Alex Rodriguez	12.00
IR	Ivan Rodriguez	8.00
MS	Mike Schmidt	20.00
AS	Alfonso Soriano	10.00
MT	Miguel Tejada	8.00
JT	Jim Thome	10.00

Moments Autographs

		NM/M
Common Player:		10.00
EB	Ernie Banks	60.00
PB	Paul Blair	10.00

LB	Lou Brock	25.00
GC	Gary Carter	15.00
OC	Orlando Cepeda	15.00
GF	George Foster	15.00
GG	Rich "Goose" Gossage	15.00
KH	Keith Hernandez	15.00
DL	Don Larsen	15.00
WMA	Willie Mays	150.00
JP	Jim Palmer	15.00
GP	Gaylord Perry	15.00
JS	Johnny Sain	10.00

Team Topps Legends Autograph

	NM/M
Common Autograph:	10.00
Luis Aparicio	15.00
Paul Blair	10.00
Lou Brock	25.00
Rich "Goose" Gossage	15.00
Al Kaline	35.00
Don Larsen	20.00
Vern Law	12.00
Stan Musial	75.00
Brooks Robinson	

Uniform Relics

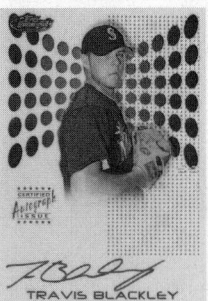

		NM/M
Common Player:		5.00
BB	Barry Bonds	20.00
EC	Eric Chavez	5.00
AD	Adam Dunn	10.00
LG	Luis Gonzalez	5.00
TH	Todd Helton	8.00
RJ	Randy Johnson	8.00
AJ	Andruw Jones	8.00
CJ	Chipper Jones	10.00
GM	Greg Maddux	12.00
WM	Willie Mays	30.00
MM	Mark Mulder	6.00
RO	Roy Oswalt	5.00
RP	Rafael Palmeiro	8.00
MP	Mike Piazza	12.00
AP	Albert Pujols	15.00
AR	Alex Rodriguez	15.00
MR	Manny Ramirez	8.00
CS	Curt Schilling	5.00
AS	Alfonso Soriano	10.00
SS	Sammy Sosa	15.00
MSW	Mike Sweeney	5.00
LW	Larry Walker	5.00

2004 Finest

		NM/M
Complete Set (122):		
Common Player:		.40
Common Star Relic (101-110):		8.00
Inserted 1:42		
Common FYP Autograph (111-122):		10.00
Inserted 1:18		
Pack (5):		6.00
Box (18):		85.00
Mini-Box (6):		30.00
1	Juan Pierre	.40
2	Derek Jeter	3.00
3	Garret Anderson	.50
4	Javy Lopez	.50
5	Corey Patterson	.50
6	Todd Helton	.75
7	Roy Oswalt	.50
8	Shawn Green	.50
9	Vladimir Guerrero	1.00
10	Jorge Posada	.50
11	Jason Kendall	.40
12	Scott Rolen	1.00
13	Randy Johnson	1.00
14	Bill Mueller	.40
15	Magglio Ordonez	.50
16	Larry Walker	.50
17	Lance Berkman	.50
18	Richie Sexson	.75
19	Orlando Cabrera	.40
20	Alfonso Soriano	1.00
21	Kevin Millwood	.50
22	Edgar Martinez	.50
23	Aubrey Huff	.40
24	Carlos Delgado	.75
25	Vernon Wells	.40
26	Mark Teixeira	.40
27	Troy Glaus	.50
28	Jeff Kent	.50
29	Hideo Nomo	.50
30	Torii Hunter	.50
31	Hank Blalock	.50
32	Brandon Webb	.40
33	Tony Batista	.40
34	Bret Boone	.40
35	Ryan Klesko	.50
36	Barry Zito	.50
37	Aaron Boone	.40
38	Geoff Jenkins	.50
39	Jeff Bagwell	.75
40	Dontrelle Willis	.75
41	Adam Dunn	.75
42	Mark Buehrle	.40
43	Esteban Loaiza	.40
44	Angel Berroa	.40
45	Ivan Rodriguez	.75
46	Jose Vidro	.40
47	Mark Mulder	.50
48	Marlon Byrd	.40
49	Jim Edmonds	.50
50	Eric Gagne	.50
51	Marcus Giles	.40
52	Curt Schilling	.75
53	Ken Griffey Jr.	1.50
54	Jason Schmidt	.50
55	Miguel Tejada	.50
56	Dmitri Young	.40
57	Mike Lowell	.40
58	Mike Sweeney	.40
59	Scott Podsednik	.75
60	Miguel Cabrera	1.00
61	Johan Santana	.40
62	Bernie Williams	.50
63	Eric Chavez	.50
64	Bobby Abreu	.50
65	Brian Giles	.50
66	Michael Young	.40
67	Paul LoDuca	.40
68	Austin Kearns	.40
69	Jody Gerut	.40
70	Kerry Wood	1.00
71	Luis Matos	.40
72	Greg Maddux	1.50
73	Alex Rodriguez	4.00
74	Mike Lieberthal	.40
75	Jim Thome	1.00
76	Javier Vazquez	.40
77	Bartolo Colon	.50
78	Manny Ramirez	.75
79	Jacque Jones	.40
80	Johnny Damon	.50
81	Carlos Beltran	.75
82	C.C. Sabathia	.50
83	Preston Wilson	.40
84	Luis Castillo	.40
85	Kevin Brown	.50
86	Shannon Stewart	.40
87	Cliff Floyd	.40
88	Mike Mussina	.50
89	Rafael Furcal	.40
90	Roy Halladay	.50
91	Frank Thomas	.75
92	Melvin Mora	.40
93	Andruw Jones	.75
94	Luis Gonzalez	.50
95	David Ortiz	.75
96	Gary Sheffield	.50
97	Tim Hudson	.50
98	Phil Nevin	.40
99	Ichiro Suzuki	2.00
100	Albert Pujols	2.50
101	Nomar Garciaparra	15.00
102	Sammy Sosa	15.00
103	Josh Beckett	8.00
104	Jason Giambi	8.00
105	Rocco Baldelli	8.00
106	Jose Reyes	8.00
107	Chipper Jones	10.00
108	Pedro J. Martinez	10.00
109	Mike Piazza	8.00
110	Mark Prior	8.00
111	Craig Ansman RC	10.00
112	Jeff Allison	15.00
113	David Murphy	20.00
114	Jason Hirsh	20.00
115	Matt Moses	20.00
116	Estee Harris RC	10.00
117	Logan Kensing RC	10.00
118	Lastings Milledge	40.00
119	Merkin Valdez RC	15.00
120	Travis Blackley RC	15.00
121	Vito Chiaravalloti RC	15.00
122	Dioner Navarro RC	25.00

Refractor

Refractor (1-100):	2-4X
Inserted 1:6	
Refractor (101-110):	1-2X
Inserted 1:156	
Refractor (111-122):	1-2X
Inserted 1:132	

Gold Refractor

Gold Refractor (1-100):	6-12X
Gold Refr. (101-110):	1.5-2X
Gold Refr. (111-122):	2-4X
Production 50 Sets	

Uncirculated X-Fractor

Stars (1-100):	4-8X
Relics (101-110):	1-2X
Autographs (111-122):	1-2X
Inserted as a box topper.	
Production 139 Sets	

Moments Autographs

		NM/M
Common Autograph:		10.00
JA	Jim Abbott	15.00
VB	Vida Blue	12.00
OC	Orlando Cepeda	12.00
LD	Lenny Dykstra	10.00
GS	George Foster	10.00
EK	Ed Kranepool	10.00
WM	Willie Mays	100.00
JP	Johnny Podres	10.00
DS	Duke Snider	40.00
RY	Robin Yount	75.00

Relics

		NM/M
Common Player:		4.00
JB	Jeff Bagwell	8.00
RB1	Rocco Baldelli/Jsy	6.00
RB3	Rocco Baldelli/Jsy	6.00
JPB1	Josh Beckett	8.00
LB1	Lance Berkman/Bat	5.00
LB2	Lance Berkman/Jsy	5.00
AB	Angel Berroa	4.00
HB1	Hank Blalock/Bat	8.00
HB2	Hank Blalock/Jsy	8.00
PB	Pat Burrell	10.00

SB	Sean Burroughs	5.00
MB	Marlon Byrd	4.00
MC	Miguel Cabrera	10.00
EC	Eric Chavez	6.00
AD	Adam Dunn	8.00
DE	Darin Erstad	8.00
NG	Nomar Garciaparra	12.00
TG	Troy Glaus	6.00
AG	Adrian Gonzalez	4.00
LG	Luis Gonzalez	4.00
SG	Shawn Green	6.00
VG	Vladimir Guerrero	8.00
CG	Cristian Guzman	4.00
RH	Rich Harden	5.00
TH1	Todd Helton/Bat	8.00
TH2	Todd Helton/Jsy	8.00
TH	Tim Hudson	5.00
TKH1	Torii Hunter/Bat	6.00
TKH2	Torii Hunter/Jsy	6.00
KI	Kazuhisa Ishii	4.00
RJ	Randy Johnson	8.00
AJ	Andruw Jones	6.00
JL	Javy Lopez	6.00
DL	Derek Lowe	6.00
ML1	Mike Lowell/Jsy	5.00
ML2	Mike Lowell/Jsy	5.00
GM	Greg Maddux	10.00
KM	Kevin Millwood	6.00
MM	Mark Mulder	4.00
BM1	Brett Myers/Jsy	4.00
BM2	Brett Myers/Jsy	4.00
MO1	Magglio Ordonez/Jsy	6.00
MO2	Magglio Ordonez/Bat	6.00
RP1	Rafael Palmeiro/Bat	8.00
RP2	Rafael Palmeiro/Jsy	8.00
RP3	Rafael Palmeiro/Jsy	8.00
AP	Andy Pettitte	6.00
JP	Juan Pierre	4.00
MP	Mark Prior	10.00
AP1	Albert Pujols/Jsy	15.00
AP2	Albert Pujols/Bat	15.00
JR1	Jose Reyes/Jsy	8.00
JR2	Jose Reyes/Bat	8.00
JR3	Jose Reyes/Jsy	8.00
MR	Mariano Rivera	10.00
AR1	Alex Rodriguez/Rngrs	10.00
AR2	Alex Rodriguez/Yanks	20.00
IR1	Ivan Rodriguez/Jsy	4.00
IR2	Ivan Rodriguez/Jsy	8.00
IR3	Ivan Rodriguez/Bat	8.00
SR	Scott Rolen	8.00
CCS	C.C. Sabathia	6.00
KS	Kazuhiro Sasaki	4.00
CS	Curt Schilling	6.00
GS	Gary Sheffield	8.00
JS	John Smoltz	8.00
AS	Alfonso Soriano	8.00
SS	Sammy Sosa	12.00
MT1	Miguel Tejada/Bat	6.00
MT2	Miguel Tejada/Jsy	6.00
FT	Frank Thomas	8.00
JT	Jim Thome	10.00
LW	Larry Walker	4.00
VW	Vernon Wells	5.00
BW	Bernie Williams	6.00
DW	Dontrelle Willis	6.00
PW	Preston Wilson	4.00
KW1	Kerry Wood/Jsy	10.00
KW2	Kerry Wood/Bat	10.00
DY	Delmon Young	8.00
BZ	Barry Zito	8.00

2005 Finest

		NM/M
Complete Set (166):		
Common Player:		.40
Common Auto. (141-156):		10.00
Production 970, unless noted.		
Pack (5):		10.00
Box (18):		150.00
1	Alexis Rios	.40
2	Hank Blalock	.50
3	Bobby Abreu	.50
4	Curt Schilling	1.00
5	Albert Pujols	3.00
6	Aaron Rowand	.40
7	B.J. Upton	.50
8	Andruw Jones	.50
9	Jeff Francis	.40
10	Sammy Sosa	1.00
11	Aramis Ramirez	.75
12	Carl Pavano	.40
13	Bartolo Colon	.40
14	Greg Maddux	2.00
15	Scott Kazmir	.50
16	Melvin Mora	.40
17	Brandon Backe	.40
18	Bobby Crosby	.40
19	Carlos Lee	.50
20	Carl Crawford	.50
21	Brian Giles	.40
22	Jeff Bagwell	.75
23	J.D. Drew	.50
24	C.C. Sabathia	.50
25	Alfonso Soriano	1.00
26	Chipper Jones	1.00
27	Austin Kearns	.40
28	Carlos Delgado	.50
29	Jack Wilson	.40
30	Dmitri Young	.40
31	Carlos Guillen	.40
32	Jim Thome	1.00
33	Eric Chavez	.50
34	Jason Schmidt	.40
35	Brad Radke	.40
36	Frank Thomas	.75
37	Darin Erstad	.40
38	Javier Vazquez	.40
39	Garret Anderson	.50
40	David Ortiz	1.00
41	Javy Lopez	.40
42	Geoff Jenkins	.40
43	Jose Vidro	.40
44	Aubrey Huff	.40
45	Bernie Williams	.50
46	Dontrelle Willis	.50
47	Jim Edmonds	.50
48	Ivan Rodriguez	.50
49	Gary Sheffield	.50
50	Alex Rodriguez	2.50
51	John Buck	.40
52	Andy Pettitte	.50
53	Ichiro Suzuki	2.50
54	Johnny Estrada	.40
55	Jake Peavy	.50
56	Carlos Zambrano	.50
57	Jose Reyes	1.00
58	Bret Boone	.40
59	Jason Bay	.50
60	David Wright	1.50
61	Jeromy Burnitz	.40
62	Corey Patterson	.50
63	Juan Pierre	.40
64	Zack Greinke	.40
65	Mike Lowell	.40
66	Ken Griffey Jr.	2.00
67	Marcus Giles	.40
68	Edgar Renteria	.50
69	Ken Harvey	.40
70	Pedro Martinez	1.00
71	Johnny Damon	.50
72	Lyle Overbay	.40
73	Mike Maroth	.40
74	Jorge Posada	.50
75	Carlos Beltran	.75
76	Mark Buehrle	.50
77	Khalil Greene	.40
78	Josh Beckett	.75
79	Mark Loretta	.40
80	Rafael Palmeiro	.75
81	Justin Morneau	.75
82	Rocco Baldelli	.50
83	Ben Sheets	.50
84	Kerry Wood	.50
85	Miguel Tejada	.75
86	Magglio Ordonez	.50
87	Livan Hernandez	.40
88	Kazuo Matsui	.40
89	Manny Ramirez	1.00
90	Hideki Matsui	2.00
91	Jeff Kent	.50
92	Matt Lawton	.40
93	Richie Sexson	.50
94	Mike Mussina	.75
95	Adam Dunn	.75
96	Johan Santana	.75
97	Nomar Garciaparra	.50
98	Michael Young	.50
99	Victor Martinez	.50
100	Barry Bonds	3.00
101	Oliver Perez	.40
102	Randy Johnson	1.00
103	Mark Mulder	.50
104	Pat Burrell	.40
105	Mike Sweeney	.40
106	Mark Teixeira	.75
107	Paul LoDuca	.40
108	Jon Lieber	.40
109	Mike Piazza	1.50
110	Roger Clemens	2.00
111	Rafael Furcal	.50
112	Troy Glaus	.50
113	Miguel Cabrera	1.00
114	Randy Wolf	.40
115	Lance Berkman	.75
116	Mark Prior	.50
117	Rich Harden	.50
118	Preston Wilson	.40
119	Roy Oswalt	.50
120	Luis Gonzalez	.40
121	Ronnie Belliard	.40
122	Sean Casey	.50
123	Barry Zito	.50
124	Larry Walker	.50
125	Derek Jeter	3.00
126	Tim Hudson	.50
127	Tom Glavine	.50
128	Scott Rolen	1.00
129	Torii Hunter	.50
130	Paul Konerko	.75
131	Shawn Green	.40
132	Travis Hafner	.50
133	Vernon Wells	.50
134	Sidney Ponson	.40
135	Vladimir Guerrero	1.00
136	Mark Kotsay	.40
137	Todd Helton	.75
138	Adrian Beltre	.50
139	Wily Mo Pena	.40
140	Joe Mauer	.75
141	Brian Stavisky RC	10.00
142	Nate McLouth RC	20.00
143	Glen Perkins/375 RC	20.00
144	Chip Cannon RC	15.00
145	Shane Costa RC	10.00
146	Wes Swackhamer RC	15.00
147	Kevin Melillo RC	15.00
148	Billy Butler RC	40.00
149	Landon Powell RC	15.00
150	Scott Mathieson RC	10.00
151	Chris Roberson RC	10.00
152	Chad Orvella/375 RC	15.00
153	Eric Nielsen RC	10.00
154	Matt Campbell RC	10.00
155	Mike Rogers RC	10.00
156	Melky Cabrera RC	25.00
157	Nolan Ryan	3.00
158	Bo Jackson	1.00
159	Wade Boggs	1.00
160	Andre Dawson	.75
161	Dave Winfield	1.00
162	Reggie Jackson	1.00
163	David Justice	.50
164	Dale Murphy	1.00
165	Paul O'Neill	.75
166	Tom Seaver	1.50

Refractors
Refrac. (1-140, 157-166): 2-4X
Autograph (141-156): .5-1X
Production 399 Sets

Refractors Black
Refrac. (1-140, 157-166): 4-8X
Autograph (141-156): 1-2X
Production 99 Sets

Refractors Blue

Refrac. (1-140, 157-166): 2-4X
Autograph (141-156): .5-1X
Production 299 Sets

Refractors Gold
Refrac. (1-140, 157-166): 5-10X
Autograph (141-156): 2-4X
Production 49 Sets

Refractors Green
Refrac. (1-140, 157-166): 2-4X
Autograph (141-156): .5-1.5X
Production 199 Sets

Refractors White Framed
No Pricing
Production One Set

X-Fractor
Refrac. (1-140, 157-166): 2-4X
Autograph (141-156): .5-1X
Production 250 Sets

X-Fractor Black
Refrac. (1-140, 157-166): 8-15X
Autograph (141-156): No Pricing
Production 25 Sets

X-Fractor Blue
Refrac. (1-140, 157-166): 3-5X
Autograph (141-156): .5-1.5X
Production 150 Sets

X-Fractor Gold
No Pricing
Production 10 Sets

X-Fractor Green
Refrac. (1-140, 157-166): 5-10X
Autograph (141-156): 1.5-3X
Production 50 Sets

X-Fractor White Framed
No Pricing
Production One Set

Super Fractor
No Pricing
Production One Set

Printing Plates

No Pricing
Production one set for each color.

Autographs

		NM/M
X-Fractor:		1.5-2X
Production 25 Sets		
JB	Jason Bay	25.00
CB	Carlos Beltran	30.00
BB	Barry Bonds	150.00
MB	Milton Bradley	15.00
EC	Eric Chavez	20.00
JE	Johnny Estrada	15.00
EG	Eric Gagne	30.00
KM	Kevin Millar	25.00
DO	David Ortiz	50.00
MR	Mariano Rivera	60.00
JS	Johan Santana	40.00
GS	Gary Sheffield	30.00
AS	Alfonso Soriano	30.00
JST	Jacob Stevens	10.00
DW	David Wright	80.00

Alex Rodriguez Finest Moments Autograph

		NM/M
Production 13 Sets		
A-Rod Auto. 1-49:		150.00
FAM1-49	Alex Rodriguez	150.00

Alex Rodriguez Finest Moments

	NM/M
A-Rod 1-49:	10.00
Production 190 Sets	
FAM1-49 Alex Rodriguez	10.00

Finest Moment Autographs

	NM/M
Production 50	
PM Pedro Martinez	75.00
CS Curt Schilling	120.00

2 of a Kind Autographs
No Pricing
Production 13

2006 Finest

	NM/M
Complete Set (155):	
Common Player:	.40
Common Auto. (141-155):	10.00
Pack (5):	9.00
Box (18):	150.00
1 Vladimir Guerrero	1.00
2 Troy Glaus	.50
3 Andruw Jones	.75
4 Miguel Tejada	.75
5 Manny Ramirez	1.00
6 Curt Schilling	1.00
7 Mark Prior	.50
8 Kerry Wood	.50
9 Tadahito Iguchi	.50
10 Freddy Garcia	.40
11 Ryan Howard	1.50
12 Mark Buehrle	.50
13 Wily Mo Pena	.40
14 C.C. Sabathia	.75
15 Garret Anderson	.40
16 Shawn Green	.40
17 Rafael Furcal	.75
18 Jeff Francoeur	.75
19 Ken Griffey Jr.	2.00
20 Derrek Lee	.75
21 Paul Konerko	.75
22 Rickie Weeks	.50
23 Magglio Ordonez	.75
24 Juan Pierre	.40
25 Felix Hernandez	1.00
26 Roger Clemens	3.00
27 Zack Greinke	.40
28 Johan Santana	1.00
29 Jose Reyes	1.00
30 Bobby Crosby	.40
31 Jason Schmidt	.40
32 Khalil Greene	.40
33 Richie Sexson	.50
34 Mark Mulder	.40
35 Mark Teixeira	.75
36 Nick Johnson	.40
37 Vernon Wells	.50
38 Scott Kazmir	.75
39 Jim Edmonds	.50
40 Adrian Beltre	.50
41 Dan Johnson	.40
42 Carlos Lee	.75
43 Lance Berkman	.75
44 Josh Beckett	.75
45 Morgan Ensberg	.40
46 Garrett Atkins	.75
47 Chase Utley	1.00
48 Joe Mauer	.75
49 Travis Hafner	.75
50 Alex Rodriguez	3.00
51 Austin Kearns	.40
52 Scott Podsednik	.40
53 Jose Contreras	.40
54 Greg Maddux	2.00
55 Hideki Matsui	2.00
56 Matt Clement	.40
57 Javy Lopez	.40
58 Tim Hudson	.75
59 Luis Gonzalez	.50
60 Bartolo Colon	.50
61 Marcus Giles	.40
62 Justin Morneau	.75
63 Nomar Garciaparra	.75
64 Robinson Cano	1.00
65 Ervin Santana	.50
66 Brady Clark	.40
67 Edgar Renteria	.40
68 Jon Garland	.40
69 Felipe Lopez	.40
70 Ivan Rodriguez	.75
71 Dontrelle Willis	.50
72 Carlos Guillen	.75
73 J.D. Drew	.40
74 Rich Harden	.50
75 Albert Pujols	3.00
76 Livan Hernandez	.40
77 Roy Halladay	.50
78 Hank Blalock	.50
79 David Wright	1.50
80 Jimmy Rollins	1.00
81 John Smoltz	.75
82 Miguel Cabrera	1.00
83 David DeJesus	.40
84 Torii Hunter	.50
85 Adam Dunn	.75
86 Randy Johnson	1.00
87 Roy Oswalt	.75
88 Bobby Abreu	.75
89 Rocco Baldelli	.40
90 Ichiro Suzuki	2.00
91 Jorge Cantu	.40
92 Jack Wilson	.40
93 Jose Vidro	.40
94 Kevin Millwood	.50
95 David Ortiz	1.00
96 Victor Martinez	.75
97 Jeremy Bonderman	.40
98 Todd Helton	.75
99 Carlos Beltran	.75
100 Barry Bonds	3.00
101 Jeff Kent	.50
102 Mike Sweeney	.40
103 Ben Sheets	.50
104 Melvin Mora	.40
105 Gary Sheffield	.75
106 Craig Wilson	.40
107 Chris Carpenter	.75
108 Michael Young	.50
109 Gustavo Chacin	.40
110 Chipper Jones	1.00
111 Mark Loretta	.50
112 Andy Pettitte	.75
113 Carlos Delgado	.75
114 Pat Burrell	.50
115 Jason Bay	.50
116 Brian Roberts	.50
117 Joe Crede	.40
118 Jake Peavy	.75
119 Aubrey Huff	.40
120 Pedro Martinez	1.00
121 Jorge Posada	.75
122 Barry Zito	.50
123 Scott Rolen	.75
124 Brett Myers	.40
125 Derek Jeter	3.00
126 Eric Chavez	.50
127 Carl Crawford	.50
128 Jim Thome	.75
129 Johnny Damon	1.00
130 Alfonso Soriano	.75
131 Clint Barmes	.40
132 Dustin Nippert (RC)	1.00
133 Hanley Ramirez (RC)	2.00
134 Matt Capps (RC)	1.00
135 Miguel Perez (RC)	1.00
136 Tom Gorzelanny (RC)	1.00
137 Charlton Jimerson (RC)	1.00
138 Bryan Bullington (RC)	1.00
139 Kenji Johjima RC	4.00
140 Craig Hansen RC	2.00
141 Craig Breslow RC	10.00
142 Adam Wainwright (RC)	20.00
143 Joey Devine RC	10.00
144 Hong-Chih Kuo (RC)	30.00
145 Jason Botts (RC)	10.00
146 Josh Johnson (RC)	10.00
147 Jason Bergmann RC	10.00
148 Scott Olsen (RC)	15.00
149 Darrell Rasner (RC)	10.00
150 Daniel Ortmeier (RC)	10.00
151 Chuck James (RC)	15.00
152 Ryan Garko (RC)	15.00
153 Nelson Cruz (RC)	10.00
154 Anthony Lerew (RC)	10.00
155 Francisco Liriano (RC)	20.00

Refractor
Stars (1-140):	2-4X
Autos. (141-155):	.5-1X
Production 399 Sets	

Black Refractor
Stars (1-140):	4-8X
Autos. (141-155):	1-2X
Production 99 Sets	

Blue Refractor
Stars (1-140):	2-5X
Autos. (141-155):	.75-1X
Production 299 Sets	

Gold Refractor
Stars (1-140):	6-12X
Autos. (141-155):	2-3X
Production 49 Sets	

Green Refractor
Stars (1-140):	2-5X
Autos. (141-155):	.75-1.5X
Production 199 Sets	

SuperFractor
No Pricing
Production One Set

White Framed Refractor
No Pricing
Production One Set

Black X-Fractor
Stars (1-140):	8-15X
Autos. (141-155):	No Pricing
Production 25 Sets	

Blue X-Fractor
Stars (1-140):	3-5X
Autos. (141-155):	1-1.5X
Production 150 Sets	

Gold X-Fractor
No Pricing
Production 10 Sets

Green X-Fractor
Stars (1-140):	6-12X
Autos. (141-155):	2-3X
Production 50 Sets	

X-Fractor
Stars (1-140):	2-5X
Autos. (141-155):	.75-1X
Production 250 Sets	

Autographs
	NM/M
Common Auto.:	8.00
X-Fractor:	1-2X
Production 25 Sets	
SuperFractor:	No Pricing
Production One Set	
Printing plates one set per color.	
JB Jason Bay	15.00
MC Miguel Cabrera	30.00
RC Robinson Cano	30.00
EC Eric Chavez	8.00
MG Marcus Giles	8.00
VG Vladimir Guerrero	30.00
JG Jose Guillen	8.00
RH Rich Harden	10.00
KJ Kenji Johjima	80.00
AJ Andruw Jones	15.00
CJ Chipper Jones	60.00
DL Derrek Lee	30.00
RO Roy Oswalt	25.00
AR Alex Rodriguez	160.00
GS Gary Sheffield	8.00
DWI Dontrelle Willis	10.00
CW Craig Wilson	8.00
DW David Wright	60.00

Barry Bonds Finest Moments Autographs
No Pricing

Barry Bonds Finest Moments

	NM/M
Common Bonds:	10.00
Production 425 Sets	
Gold Refractor:	1-2X
Production 199 Sets	
1-25 Barry Bonds	10.00

Mickey Mantle Finest Moments
	NM/M
Common Mantle:	10.00
Production 850 Sets	
Refractor:	1X
Production 399 Sets	
Blue Refractor:	1-1.5X
Production 299 Sets	
Green Refractor:	1-2X
Production 199 Sets	
Black Refractor:	1.5-3X
Production 99 Sets	
Gold Refractor:	3-4X
Production 49 Sets	
X-Fractor:	1-1.5X
Production 150 Sets	
Blue X-Fractor:	1-2X
Production 150 Sets	
Green X-Fractor:	3-4X
Production 50 Sets	
Black X-Fractor:	4-6X
Production 25 Sets	

Gold X-Fractor:	No Pricing
Production 10 Sets	
1-20 Mickey Mantle	10.00

Mickey Mantle Finest Moments Cut Signature
No Pricing
Production One Set

2007 Finest

	NM/M
Complete Set (165):	
Common Player (1-135):	.25
Common RC (136-150):	1.00
Common RC Auto. (151-165):	10.00
Pack (5):	8.00
Box (18):	125.00
1 David Wright	2.00
2 Jered Weaver	.50
3 Chipper Jones	1.00
4 Magglio Ordonez	.50
5 Ben Sheets	.50
6 Nick Johnson	.25
7 Melvin Mora	.25
8 Chien-Ming Wang	1.00
9 Andre Ethier	.50
10 Carlos Beltran	1.00
11 Ryan Zimmerman	1.00
12 Troy Glaus	.50
13 Hanley Ramirez	.75
14 Mark Buehrle	.50
15 Dan Uggla	.50
16 Richie Sexson	.75
17 Scott Kazmir	.50
18 Garrett Atkins	.25
19 Matt Cain	.50
20 Jorge Posada	.50
21 Brett Myers	.50
22 Jeff Francoeur	.50
23 Scott Rolen	1.00
24 Derrek Lee	.75
25 Manny Ramirez	1.00
26 Johnny Damon	1.00
27 Mark Teixeira	1.00
28 Mark Prior	.75
29 Victor Martinez	.50
30 Greg Maddux	2.00
31 Prince Fielder	1.50
32 Jeremy Bonderman	.50
33 Paul LoDuca	.25
34 Brandon Webb	.50
35 Robinson Cano	1.00
36 Josh Beckett	.75
37 David DeJesus	.25
38 Kenny Rogers	.25
39 Jim Thome	1.00
40 Brian McCann	.50
41 Lance Berkman	.50
42 Adam Dunn	.75
43 Rocco Baldelli	.50
44 Brian Roberts	.50
45 Vladimir Guerrero	1.00
46 Dontrelle Willis	.50
47 Eric Chavez	.25
48 Carlos Zambrano	.50
49 Ivan Rodriguez	1.00
50 Alex Rodriguez	3.00
51 Curt Schilling	1.00
52 Carlos Delgado	.75
53 Matt Holliday	1.00
54 Mark Teahen	.25
55 Frank Thomas	1.00
56 Grady Sizemore	.75
57 Aramis Ramirez	.50
58 Rafael Furcal	.50
59 David Ortiz	1.00
60 Paul Konerko	.50
61 Barry Zito	.25
62 Travis Hafner	.50
63 Nick Swisher	.50
64 Johan Santana	1.00
65 Miguel Tejada	.75
66 Carl Crawford	.50
67 Kenji Johjima	.50
68 Derek Jeter	3.00
69 Francisco Liriano	.50
70 Ken Griffey Jr.	2.00
71 Pat Burrell	.50
72 Adrian Gonzalez	.50
73 Miguel Cabrera	1.00
74 Albert Pujols	3.00

75 Justin Verlander .75
76 Carlos Lee .50
77 John Smoltz .50
78 Orlando Hudson .25
79 Joe Mauer .50
80 Freddy Sanchez .25
81 Bobby Abreu .50
82 Pedro Martinez 1.00
83 Vernon Wells .50
84 Justin Morneau .75
85 Bill Hall .50
86 Jason Schmidt .50
87 Michael Young .50
88 Tadahito Iguchi .25
89 Kevin Millwood .50
90 Randy Johnson 1.00
91 Roy Halladay .50
92 Mike Lowell .50
93 Jake Peavy .50
94 Jason Varitek .75
95 Todd Helton .75
96 Mark Loretta .25
97 Gary Matthews .25
98 Ryan Howard 2.00
99 Jose Reyes 1.00
100 Chris Carpenter .50
101 Hideki Matsui 2.00
102 Brian Giles .25
103 Torii Hunter .50
104 Rich Harden .25
105 Ichiro Suzuki 2.00
106 Chase Utley 1.00
107 Nicholas Markakis .50
108 Marcus Giles .25
109 Gary Sheffield .75
110 Jim Edmonds .50
111 Brandon Phillips .50
112 Roy Oswalt .50
113 Jeff Kent .50
114 Jason Bay .50
115 Raul Ibanez .25
116 Stephen Drew .50
117 Hank Blalock .50
118 Tom Glavine .50
119 Andruw Jones .75
120 Alfonso Soriano 1.00
121 Mariano Rivera .50
122 Garret Anderson .25
123 Erik Bedard .50
124 Huston Street .25
125 Austin Kearns .50
126 Jermaine Dye .25
127 C.C. Sabathia .50
128 Joe Nathan .25
129 Craig Monroe .25
130 Aubrey Huff .25
131 Billy Wagner .25
132 Jorge Cantu .25
133 Trevor Hoffman .25
134 Ronnie Belliard .25
135 B.J. Ryan .25
136 Adam Lind **(RC)** 1.00
137 Hector Gimenez **(RC)** 1.00
138 Shawn Riggans **(RC)** 1.00
139 Joaquin Arias **(RC)** 1.00
140 Drew Anderson **(RC)** 1.00
141 Mike Rabelo **RC** 1.00
142 Chris Narveson **(RC)** 1.00
143 Ryan Feierabend **(RC)** 1.00
144 Vinny Rottino **(RC)** 2.00
145 Jon Knott **(RC)** 1.00
146 Oswaldo Navarro **RC** 1.00
147 Brian Stokes **(RC)** 1.00
148 Glen Perkins **(RC)** 1.00
149 Mitch Maier **(RC)** 1.00
150 Delmon Young **(RC)** 2.00
151 Andrew Miller/Auto. **RC** 20.00
152 Troy Tulowitzki/Auto. **(RC)** 20.00
153 Philip Humber/Auto. **(RC)** 15.00
154 Kevin Kouzmanoff/ Auto. **(RC)** 15.00
155 Michael Bourn/Auto. **(RC)** 15.00
156 Miguel Montero/Auto. **(RC)** 15.00
157 David Murphy/Auto. **(RC)** 15.00
158 Ryan Sweeney/Auto. **(RC)** 15.00
159 Jeff Baker/Auto. **(RC)** 10.00
160 Jeff Salazar/Auto. **(RC)** 10.00
161 Jose Garcia/Auto. **(RC)** 10.00
162 Josh Fields/Auto. **(RC)** 15.00
163 Delwyn Young/Auto. **(RC)** 15.00
164 Fred Lewis/Auto. **(RC)** 10.00
165 Scott Moore/Auto. **(RC)** 15.00

Printing Plates

Production one set per color.

SuperFractor

Production One Set

X-Fractor

X-Fractor (1-135): 10-20X
RC Autos.: No Pricing
Production 25 Sets

Gold Refractor

Gold Refractor (1-150): 5-10X
Production 50
RC Autos.: 2X
Production 49

Black Refractor

Black Refractor (1-150): 4-8X
RC Autos.: 1.5X
Production 99 Sets

Green Refractor

Green Refractor (1-150): 2-5X
RC Autos.: 1-1.5X
Production 199 Sets

Blue Refractor

Blue Refractor (1-150): 2-5X
Production 399 Sets
RC Autos.: .75-1X
Production 299

Refractor

Refractor (1-150): 2-4X
RC Autographs: .5-1X
Production 399 only autos serial #'d.

Rookies Finest Moments Autograph

NM/M
Common Autograph: 10.00
Refractors: No Pricing
Production 25 Sets
DO David Ortiz 50.00
DW David Wright 75.00
JN Joe Nathan 10.00
AR Alex Rodriguez 125.00
TH Travis Hafner 20.00
RH Ryan Howard 100.00
AS Anibal Sanchez 15.00
BP Brandon Phillips 10.00
CH Cole Hamels 40.00
DWW Dontrelle Willis 15.00
LM Lastings Milledge 25.00
RC Robinson Cano 50.00
MN Michael Napoli 20.00
DU Dan Uggla 15.00
BW Brad Wilkerson 10.00
MC Melky Cabrera 25.00
AW Adam Wainwright 30.00
CQ Carlos Quentin 15.00
RJH Rich Hill 20.00
YP Yusmeiro Petit 15.00
FC Fausto Carmona 15.00
CJ Chuck James 15.00
JM Justin Morneau 25.00
RZ Ryan Zimmerman 25.00
RM Russell Martin 20.00
JP Jonathan Papelbon 50.00
HR Hanley Ramirez 25.00
MTC Matt Cain 25.00
DY Delmon Young 20.00

Dual Rookies Finest Moments Autograph

NM/M
Refractors: No Pricing
Production 25 Sets
VR Justin Verlander, Hanley Ramirez 60.00
US Dan Uggla, Anibal Sanchez 25.00
RP Mariano Rivera, Jorge Posada 80.00
OP Roy Oswalt, Mark Prior 40.00
UW Chase Utley, David Wright 100.00
CY Robinson Cano, Michael Young 50.00
HR Travis Hafner, Manny Ramirez 40.00
WW Chien-Ming Wang, Brandon Webb 175.00
JH Chuck James, Cole Hamels 40.00
MNA Russell Martin, Michael Napoli 20.00
PO Yusmeiro Petit, Scott Olsen 20.00
PP Jonathan Papelbon, Dustin Pedroia 75.00
CC Eric Chavez, Miguel Cabrera 40.00
UG Dan Uggla, Marcus Giles 15.00
CK Nelson Cruz, Matthew Kemp 25.00
HJ Rich Hill, Josh Johnson 30.00
HM Cole Hamels, Brett Myers 60.00
MC Lastings Milledge, Melky Cabrera 35.00
CR Matt Cain, Anthony Reyes 25.00
ZC Joel Zumaya, Fausto Carmona 20.00
BM Jason Bay, Justin Morneau 35.00
MG Russell Martin, Ryan Garko 25.00
MN Kendry Morales, Michael Napoli 25.00
MK Lastings Milledge, Matthew Kemp 30.00
RU Hanley Ramirez, Dan Uggla 40.00

A-Rod Road to 500

Common A-Rod (26-50): 2.00
Inserted 2:Box

Ryan Howard HR History

NM/M
Common Howard (1-58): 4.00
Inserted 2:Box
Production 459 Sets
Refractor: 1.5-2X
Production 149 Sets
X-Fractor: 2-4X
Production 50 Sets
Gold Refractor: No Pricing
Production One Set

Mantle Cut Signature

Production One

Rookies Finest Moments

NM/M
Common Player: .50
Refractor: 2-3X
Blue Refractor: 2-4X
Production 299 Sets
Green Refractor: 2-4X
Production 199 Sets
Black Refractor: 4-6X
Production 99 Sets
Gold Refractor: 4-8X
Production 50 Sets
X-Fractor: 10-15X
Production 25 Sets
AD Adam Dunn 1.00
AJ Andruw Jones 1.50
AP Albert Pujols 4.00
AR Alex Rodriguez 4.00
CB Carlos Beltran 1.50
CC Carl Crawford .50
CJ Chipper Jones 1.50
DJ Derek Jeter 4.00
DL Derrek Lee 1.50
DO David Ortiz 1.50
DW David Wright 2.50
DWW Dontrelle Willis .50
HM Hideki Matsui 2.50
IS Ichiro Suzuki 2.50
JB Jason Bay 1.00
JM Joe Mauer 1.00
JR Jose Reyes 2.00
KG Ken Griffey Jr. 3.00
MC Miguel Cabrera 1.50
MP Mike Piazza 2.00
MR Manny Ramirez 1.50
MT Miguel Tejada 1.00
NG Nomar Garciaparra 1.50
RH Ryan Howard 3.00
VG Vladimir Guerrero 1.50
AS Anibal Sanchez .50
JP Jonathan Papelbon 1.50
DU Dan Uggla .50
HR Hanley Ramirez 1.00
JV Justin Verlander 1.00
FL Francisco Liriano 1.00
SD Stephen Drew 1.00
JW Jered Weaver 1.00
JS Jeremy Sowers .50
KJ Kenji Johjima 1.00
MCA Melky Cabrera 1.00
NM Nicholas Markakis 1.00
PF Prince Fielder 2.00
RM Russell Martin .50
AE Andre Ethier 1.00
MK Matthew Kemp 1.00
JH Jason Hirsh .50
CH Cole Hamels 2.00
JBA Josh Barfield .50
IK Ian Kinsler .50
AW Adam Wainwright 1.00
JST Brian Stokes .50
MN Michael Napoli .50
CQ Carlos Quentin 1.00
NC Nelson Cruz .50

Rookie Redemption

NM/M
Complete Set (10):
Common Card: 10.00
Inserted 1:3 Mini Box
1 Hideki Okajima **RC** 10.00
2 Elijah Dukes **RC** 10.00
3 Akinori Iwamura **RC** 10.00
4 Tim Lincecum **RC** 30.00
5 Daisuke Matsuzaka **RC** 20.00
6 Ryan Braun **(RC)** 20.00
7 Daisuke Matsuzaka, Hideki Okajima 10.00
8 Justin Upton **RC** 25.00
9 Phil Hughes **(RC)** 15.00
10 Joba Chamberlain/ Auto. **RC** 100.00

2008 Finest

NM/M
Common Player (1-125): .25
Common RC (126-150): 1.00
Common RC Auto. (151-166): 10.00
Pack (5): 10.00
Box (15): 140.00
1 Daisuke Matsuzaka 2.00
2 Justin Upton 1.00
3 Andruw Jones .50
4 John Lackey .50
5 Brandon Phillips .50
6 Ryan Zimmerman .50
7 Tim Lincecum .75
8 Johnny Damon .75
9 Garrett Atkins .50
10 Magglio Ordonez .50
11 Tom Gorzelanny .25
12 Eric Chavez .25
13 Troy Tulowitzki 1.00
14 Mike Lowell .50
15 Brandon Webb .50
16 Chipper Jones 1.00
17 Alex Gordon .75
18 Ken Griffey Jr. 2.00
19 Roy Oswalt .50
20 Miguel Cabrera 1.00
21 Chase Utley 1.00
22 Scott Kazmir .50
23 Kenji Johjima .25
24 Frank Thomas 1.00
25 Ryan Braun 1.50
26 Carlos Pena .50
27 Robinson Cano .75
28 Ben Sheets .50
29 Russell Martin .50
30 Joe Mauer .50
31 Gary Sheffield .50
32 Carlos Zambrano .50
33 Jermaine Dye .25
34 Dan Uggla .25
35 Erik Bedard .50
36 Tim Hudson .50
37 David Ortiz 1.00
38 Tom Glavine .50
39 Adrian Gonzalez .50
40 Jorge Posada .50
41 Noah Lowry .25
42 Vernon Wells .50
43 Johan Santana 1.00
44 Dmitri Young .25
45 Manny Ramirez 1.00
46 Jim Edmonds .25
47 Roy Halladay .50
48 Delmon Young .50
49 Nick Swisher .25
50 David Wright 1.50
51 Paul Konerko .50
52 Curt Schilling .75
53 Torii Hunter .50
54 Gary Matthews Jr. .25
55 Derrek Lee .75
56 John Smoltz .50
57 Adam Dunn .75
58 C.C. Sabathia .50
59 Chris Young .50
60 Jake Peavy .50
61 Joba Chamberlain 1.50
62 Jason Bay .50
63 Chris Carpenter .50
64 Jimmy Rollins .75
65 Grady Sizemore .75
66 Joe Blanton .25
67 Justin Morneau .50
68 Lance Berkman .50
69 Jeff Francis .25
70 Nicholas Markakis .50
71 Orlando Cabrera .50
72 Barry Zito .25
73 Eric Byrnes .50
74 Brian McCann .50
75 Albert Pujols 3.00
76 Josh Beckett .75
77 Jim Thome .75
78 Fausto Carmona .50
79 Brad Hawpe .25
80 Prince Fielder 1.00
81 Justin Verlander .75
82 Billy Butler .25
83 J.J. Hardy .25
84 Hideki Matsui 1.50
85 Matt Holliday .75
86 Bobby Crosby .25
87 Orlando Hudson .25
88 Ichiro Suzuki 2.00
89 Troy Glaus .50
90 Hanley Ramirez 1.00
91 Carlos Beltran .75
92 Mark Buehrle .25
93 Andy Pettitte .50
94 Mark Teixeira .75
95 Curtis Granderson .75
96 Cole Hamels .50
97 Jarrod Saltalamacchia .25
98 Carl Crawford .50
99 Dontrelle Willis .25
100 Alex Rodriguez 3.00
101 Brad Penny .25
102 Michael Young .25
103 Greg Maddux 1.50
104 Brian Roberts .50
105 Hunter Pence .75
106 Aaron Harang .25
107 Ivan Rodriguez .50
108 Danny Haren .50
109 Freddy Sanchez .25
110 Alfonso Soriano 1.00
111 Hank Blalock .25
112 Chien-Ming Wang 1.00
113 Carlos Delgado .50
114 Aramis Ramirez .50
115 Jose Reyes 1.00
116 Victor Martinez .50
117 Carlos Lee .50
118 Jeff Kent .25
119 Miguel Tejada .50
120 Vladimir Guerrero 1.00
121 Travis Hafner .50
122 Todd Helton .50
123 Chris Young .50
124 Derek Jeter 3.00
125 Ryan Howard 1.50
126 Alberto Gonzalez **(RC)** 1.00
127 Felipe Paulino **RC** 1.00
128 Donny Lucy **(RC)** 1.00
129 Nick Blackburn **RC** 4.00
130 Luke Hochevar **RC** 3.00
131 Bronson Sardinha **(RC)** 1.00
132 Heath Phillips **RC** 1.00
133 Bryan Bullington **(RC)** 1.00
134 Jeff Clement **(RC)** 4.00
135 Josh Banks **(RC)** 1.00
136 Emilio Bonifacio **RC** 1.00
137 Ryan Hanigan **RC** 1.00
138 Erick Threets **(RC)** 1.00
139 Seth Smith **(RC)** 1.00

140	Billy Buckner **(RC)**	1.00
141	Bill Murphy **(RC)**	1.00
142	Radhames Liz **RC**	1.00
143	Joey Votto **(RC)**	2.00
144	Mel Stocker **RC**	2.00
145	Dan Meyer **(RC)**	1.00
146	Rob Johnson **(RC)**	1.00
147	Josh Newman **RC**	1.00
148	Daniel Giese **(RC)**	1.00
149	Luis Mendoza **(RC)**	1.00
150	Wladimir Balentien **(RC)**	2.00
151	Brandon Jones/Auto. **RC**	15.00
152	Rich Thompson/Auto. **(RC)**	10.00
153	Chin-Lung Hu/Auto. **(RC)**	50.00
154	Chris Seddon/Auto. **(RC)**	10.00
155	Steve Pearce/Auto. **RC**	20.00
156	Lance Broadway/Auto. **RC**	10.00
157	Nyjer Morgan/Auto. **(RC)**	15.00
158	Jonathan Meloan/Auto. **RC**	10.00
159	Josh Anderson/Auto. **(RC)**	10.00
160	Clay Buchholz/Auto. **(RC)**	40.00
161	Joe Koshansky/Auto. **(RC)**	10.00
162	Clint Sammons/Auto. **(RC)**	15.00
163	Daric Barton/Auto. **(RC)**	15.00
164	Ross Detwiler/Auto. **RC**	20.00
165	Sam Fuld/Auto. **RC**	15.00
166	Justin Ruggiano/Auto. **RC**	10.00

Refractor

Refractor (1-150): 2-4X
RC Autographs: 1X
Production 499 only autos serial #'d.

Blue Refractor

Blue Refractor (1-150): 2-5X
Production 299 Sets
RC Autos.: .75-1X
Production 399

Green Refractor

Green Refractor (1-150): 2-5X
RC Autos.: 1-1.5X
Production 199 Sets

Black Refractor

Black Refractor (1-150): 4-8X
RC Autos.: 1.5X
Production 99 Sets

Gold Refractor

Gold Refractor (1-150): 5-10X
RC Autos.: 2X
Production 50 Sets

Red Refractor

Red Refractor (1-150): 8-15X
RC Autos.: 3-4X
Production 25 Sets

White X-Fractor

Production One Set

Printing Plates

Production one set per color.

Moments

NM/M

Common Player: .50
Refractor: 2-3X
Blue Refractor: 2-4X
Production 299 Sets
Green Refractor: 2-4X
Production 199 Sets
Black Refractor: 4-6X
Production 99 Sets
Gold Refractor: 4-8X
Production 50 Sets
Red Refractor: 8-15X
Production 25 Sets

AR	Alex Rodriguez	3.00
JT	Jim Thome	1.00
SS	Sammy Sosa	1.00
TG	Tom Glavine	1.00
TH	Trevor Hoffman	.50
RA	Rick Ankiel	1.00
MB	Mark Buehrle	.50
JV	Justin Verlander	1.00
CB	Clay Buchholz	1.00
FT	Frank Thomas	1.00
CG	Curtis Granderson	1.00
DW	David Wright	2.00
RH	Ryan Howard	2.00
PM	Pedro Martinez	1.00
ROH	Roy Halladay	1.00
TT	Troy Tulowitzki	1.00
JS	John Smoltz	1.00
PF	Prince Fielder	2.00
IS	Ichiro Suzuki	2.00
CP	Carlos Pena	1.00
DJ	Derek Jeter	3.00
JR	Jose Reyes	2.00
AP	Andy Pettitte	.50
TOH	Todd Helton	1.00
ISS	Ichiro Suzuki	2.00
DO	David Ortiz	2.00
BP	Brandon Phillips	1.00
JSA	Jarrod Saltalamacchia	.50
BW	Brandon Webb	1.00
APU	Albert Pujols	3.00
CF	Chone Figgins	.50
MH	Matt Holliday	1.50
DH	Danny Haren	.50
FH	Felix Hernandez	1.00
EB	Eric Byrnes	.50
AG	Adrian Gonzalez	.75
VG	Vladimir Guerrero	1.00
RB	Ryan Braun	1.50
HP	Hunter Pence	1.00
FC	Fausto Carmona	.50
HR	Hanley Ramirez	1.50
AS	Andrew Sonnanstine	.50
CH	Cole Hamels	1.00
JAS	Johan Santana	1.50
MR	Mark Reynolds	.50
JMC	Miguel Cabrera	1.50
BPB	Brian Bannister	.50
DL	Derrek Lee	1.00
ME	Mark Ellis	.50
CS	C.C. Sabathia	1.00

Moments Autographs

NM/M

Common Auto.: 10.00
Red Refractor: No Pricing
Production 25 Sets

RH	Ryan Howard	60.00
BP	Brandon Phillips	20.00
JC	Jack Cust	15.00
JR	Jose Reyes	50.00
HR	Hanley Ramirez	25.00
RB	Ryan Braun	40.00
ME	Mark Ellis	10.00
JD	Justin Duchscherer	10.00
MR	Mark Reynolds	15.00
AS	Andrew Sonnanstine	10.00
DW	David Wright	60.00
NM	Nicholas Markakis	30.00
MC	Miguel Cabrera	30.00
BPB	Brian Bannister	15.00
CH	Cole Hamels	30.00
JA	Jeremy Accardo	10.00
PH	Phil Hughes	20.00
JS	Jarrod Saltalamacchia	15.00
CMW	Chien-Ming Wang	125.00
CG	Curtis Granderson	30.00
RZ	Ryan Zimmerman	20.00
JH	Josh Hamilton	15.00
FC	Fausto Carmona	15.00
VG	Vladimir Guerrero	35.00

Rookie Redemption

NM/M

Common Redemption:
Inserted 1:15

1	Johnny Cueto	15.00
2	Jay Bruce/Auto.	60.00
3	Kosuke Fukudome	25.00
4	Jeff Samardzija	20.00
5	Chris Davis	20.00
6	Justin Masterson	15.00
7	Clayton Kershaw	15.00
8	Daniel Murphy	20.00
9	Denard Span	15.00
10	Jed Lowrie/Auto.	25.00

Topps Team Favorites

NM/M

Complete Set (8): 10.00
Common Player: 1.00
Refractors: 2-4X

JR	Jose Reyes	3.00
DW	David Wright	4.00
MC	Melky Cabrera	1.50
RC	Robinson Cano	2.00
AS	Alfonso Soriano	2.00
FP	Felix Pie	1.50
EC	Eric Chavez	1.00
BC	Bobby Crosby	1.00

Topps Team Favorites Autographs

NM/M

Production 100 Sets
Red Refractor: No Pricing
Production 25 Sets

JR	Jose Reyes	50.00
DW	David Wright	60.00
MC	Melky Cabrera	30.00
RC	Robinson Cano	40.00
AS	Alfonso Soriano	30.00
FP	Felix Pie	15.00
EC	Eric Chavez	10.00
BC	Bobby Crosby	10.00

Topps Team Favorites Cut Signatures

No Pricing
Production One Set

Topps Team Favorites Dual

NM/M

Common Duo: 2.00
Red Refractor: No Pricing
Production 25 Sets

RW	Jose Reyes, David Wright	4.00
CC	Melky Cabrera, Robinson Cano	3.00
SP	Alfonso Soriano, Felix Pie	2.00
EB	Eric Chavez, Bobby Crosby	2.00

Topps Team Favorites Dual Autographs

NM/M

Production 74 Sets
Red Refractor: No Pricing
Production 25 Sets

RW	Jose Reyes, David Wright	180.00
CC	Melky Cabrera, Robinson Cano	80.00
SP	Alfonso Soriano, Felix Pie	50.00
EB	Eric Chavez, Bobby Crosby	25.00

1993 Flair

NM/M

Complete Set (300): 15.00
Common Player: .10
Pack (10): 1.50
Wax Box (24): 20.00

1	Steve Avery	.10
2	Jeff Blauser	.10
3	Ron Gant	.10
4	Tom Glavine	.25
5	Dave Justice	.10
6	Mark Lemke	.10
7	Greg Maddux	1.00
8	Fred McGriff	.10
9	Terry Pendleton	.10
10	Deion Sanders	.15
11	John Smoltz	.10
12	Mike Stanton	.10
13	Steve Buechele	.10
14	Mark Grace	.10
15	Greg Hibbard	.10
16	Derrick May	.10
17	Chuck McElroy	.10
18	Mike Morgan	.10
19	Randy Myers	.10
20	Ryne Sandberg	1.00
21	Dwight Smith	.10
22	Sammy Sosa	1.00
23	Jose Vizcaino	.10
24	Tim Belcher	.10
25	Rob Dibble	.10
26	Roberto Kelly	.10
27	Barry Larkin	.10
28	Kevin Mitchell	.10
29	Hal Morris	.10
30	Joe Oliver	.10
31	Jose Rijo	.10
32	Bip Roberts	.10
33	Chris Sabo	.10
34	Reggie Sanders	.10
35	Dante Bichette	.10
36	Willie Blair	.10
37	Jerald Clark	.10
38	Alex Cole	.10
39	Andres Galarraga	.10
40	Joe Girardi	.10
41	Charlie Hayes	.10
42	Chris Jones	.10
43	David Nied	.10
44	Eric Young	.10
45	Alex Arias	.10
46	Jack Armstrong	.10
47	Bret Barberie	.10
48	Chuck Carr	.10
49	Jeff Conine	.10
50	Orestes Destrade	.10
51	Chris Hammond	.10
52	Bryan Harvey	.10
53	Benito Santiago	.10
54	Gary Sheffield	.35
55	Walt Weiss	.10
56	Eric Anthony	.10
57	Jeff Bagwell	.75
58	Craig Biggio	.10
59	Ken Caminiti	.10
60	Andujar Cedeno	.10
61	Doug Drabek	.10
62	Steve Finley	.10
63	Luis Gonzalez	.10
64	Pete Harnisch	.10
65	Doug Jones	.10
66	Darryl Kile	.10
67	Greg Swindell	.10
68	Brett Butler	.10
69	Jim Gott	.10
70	Orel Hershiser	.10
71	Eric Karros	.10
72	Pedro Martinez	.75
73	Ramon Martinez	.10
74	Roger McDowell	.10
75	Mike Piazza	1.50
76	Jody Reed	.10
77	Tim Wallach	.10
78	Moises Alou	.10
79	Greg Colbrunn	.10
80	Wil Cordero	.10
81	Delino DeShields	.10
82	Jeff Fassero	.10
83	Marquis Grissom	.10
84	Ken Hill	.10
85	Mike Lansing **RC**	.25
86	Dennis Martinez	.10
87	Larry Walker	.10
88	John Wetteland	.10
89	Bobby Bonilla	.10
90	Vince Coleman	.10
91	Dwight Gooden	.10
92	Todd Hundley	.10
93	Howard Johnson	.10
94	Eddie Murray	.75
95	Joe Orsulak	.10
96	Bret Saberhagen	.10
97	Darren Daulton	.10
98	Mariano Duncan	.10
99	Len Dykstra	.10
100	Jim Eisenreich	.10
101	Tommy Greene	.10
102	Dave Hollins	.10
103	Pete Incaviglia	.10
104	Danny Jackson	.10
105	John Kruk	.10
106	Terry Mulholland	.10
107	Curt Schilling	.25
108	Mitch Williams	.10
109	Stan Belinda	.10
110	Jay Bell	.10
111	Steve Cooke	.10
112	Carlos Garcia	.10
113	Jeff King	.10
114	Al Martin	.10
115	Orlando Merced	.10
116	Don Slaught	.10
117	Andy Van Slyke	.10
118	Tim Wakefield	.10
119	Rene Arocha **RC**	.10
120	Bernard Gilkey	.10
121	Gregg Jefferies	.10
122	Ray Lankford	.10
123	Donovan Osborne	.10
124	Tom Pagnozzi	.10
125	Erik Pappas	.10
126	Geronimo Pena	.10
127	Lee Smith	.10
128	Ozzie Smith	1.00
129	Bob Tewksbury	.10
130	Mark Whiten	.10
131	Derek Bell	.10
132	Andy Benes	.10
133	Tony Gwynn	1.00
134	Gene Harris	.10
135	Trevor Hoffman	.10
136	Phil Plantier	.10
137	Rod Beck	.10
138	Barry Bonds	2.50
139	John Burkett	.10
140	Will Clark	.10
141	Royce Clayton	.10
142	Mike Jackson	.10
143	Darren Lewis	.10
144	Kirt Manwaring	.10
145	Willie McGee	.10
146	Bill Swift	.10
147	Robby Thompson	.10
148	Matt Williams	.10
149	Brady Anderson	.10
150	Mike Devereaux	.10
151	Chris Hoiles	.10
152	Ben McDonald	.10
153	Mark McLemore	.10
154	Mike Mussina	.40
155	Gregg Olson	.10
156	Harold Reynolds	.10
157	Cal Ripken, Jr.	2.50
158	Rick Sutcliffe	.10
159	Fernando Valenzuela	.10
160	Roger Clemens	1.25
161	Scott Cooper	.10
162	Andre Dawson	.30
163	Scott Fletcher	.10
164	Mike Greenwell	.10
165	Greg Harris	.10
166	Billy Hatcher	.10
167	Jeff Russell	.10
168	Mo Vaughn	.10
169	Frank Viola	.10
170	Chad Curtis	.10

171	Chili Davis	.10
172	Gary DiSarcina	.10
173	Damion Easley	.10
174	Chuck Finley	.10
175	Mark Langston	.10
176	Luis Polonia	.10
177	Tim Salmon	.10
178	Scott Sanderson	.10
179	J.T. Snow RC	.50
180	Wilson Alvarez	.10
181	Ellis Burks	.10
182	Joey Cora	.10
183	Alex Fernandez	.10
184	Ozzie Guillen	.10
185	Roberto Hernandez	.10
186	Bo Jackson	.20
187	Lance Johnson	.10
188	Jack McDowell	.10
189	Frank Thomas	.75
190	Robin Ventura	.10
191	Carlos Baerga	.10
192	Albert Belle	.10
193	Wayne Kirby	.10
194	Derek Lilliquist	.10
195	Kenny Lofton	.10
196	Carlos Martinez	.10
197	Jose Mesa	.10
198	Eric Plunk	.10
199	Paul Sorrento	.10
200	John Doherty	.10
201	Cecil Fielder	.10
202	Travis Fryman	.10
203	Kirk Gibson	.10
204	Mike Henneman	.10
205	Chad Kreuter	.10
206	Scott Livingstone	.10
207	Tony Phillips	.10
208	Mickey Tettleton	.10
209	Alan Trammell	.10
210	David Wells	.10
211	Lou Whitaker	.10
212	Kevin Appier	.10
213	George Brett	1.25
214	David Cone	.10
215	Tom Gordon	.10
216	Phil Hiatt	.10
217	Felix Jose	.10
218	Wally Joyner	.10
219	Jose Lind	.10
220	Mike Macfarlane	.10
221	Brian McRae	.10
222	Jeff Montgomery	.10
223	Cal Eldred	.10
224	Darryl Hamilton	.10
225	John Jaha	.10
226	Pat Listach	.10
227	Graeme Lloyd RC	.10
228	Kevin Reimer	.10
229	Bill Spiers	.10
230	B.J. Surhoff	.10
231	Greg Vaughn	.10
232	Robin Yount	.75
233	Rick Aguilera	.10
234	Jim Deshaies	.10
235	Brian Harper	.10
236	Kent Hrbek	.10
237	Chuck Knoblauch	.10
238	Shane Mack	.10
239	David McCarty	.10
240	Pedro Munoz	.10
241	Mike Pagliarulo	.10
242	Kirby Puckett	1.00
243	Dave Winfield	.75
244	Jim Abbott	.10
245	Wade Boggs	1.00
246	Pat Kelly	.10
247	Jimmy Key	.10
248	Jim Leyritz	.10
249	Don Mattingly	1.25
250	Matt Nokes	.10
251	Paul O'Neill	.10
252	Mike Stanley	.10
253	Danny Tartabull	.10
254	Bob Wickman	.10
255	Bernie Williams	.10
256	Mike Bordick	.10
257	Dennis Eckersley	.60
258	Brent Gates	.10
259	Goose Gossage	.10
260	Rickey Henderson	.75
261	Mark McGwire	2.00
262	Ruben Sierra	.10
263	Terry Steinbach	.10
264	Bob Welch	.10
265	Bobby Witt	.10
266	Rich Amaral	.10
267	Chris Bosio	.10
268	Jay Buhner	.10
269	Norm Charlton	.10
270	Ken Griffey Jr.	1.50
271	Erik Hanson	.10
272	Randy Johnson	.75
273	Edgar Martinez	.10
274	Tino Martinez	.10
275	Dave Valle	.10
276	Omar Vizquel	.10
277	Kevin Brown	.10
278	Jose Canseco	.45
279	Julio Franco	.10
280	Juan Gonzalez	.40
281	Tom Henke	.10
282	David Hulse	.10
283	Rafael Palmeiro	.65
284	Dean Palmer	.10
285	Ivan Rodriguez	.65
286	Nolan Ryan	2.50
287	Roberto Alomar	.25
288	Pat Borders	.10
289	Joe Carter	.10
290	Juan Guzman	.10
291	Pat Hentgen	.10
292	Paul Molitor	.75
293	John Olerud	.10
294	Ed Sprague	.10
295	Dave Stewart	.10
296	Duane Ward	.10
297	Devon White	.10
298	Checklist	.05
299	Checklist	.05
300	Checklist	.05

1993 Flair Promos

BRYAN HARVEY

		NM/M
Complete Set (8):		200.00
Common Player:		10.00
(1)	Will Clark	10.00
(2)	Darren Daulton	10.00
(3)	Andres Galarraga	10.00
(4)	Bryan Harvey	10.00
(5)	David Justice	10.00
(6)	Jody Reed	10.00
(7)	Nolan Ryan	100.00
(8)	Sammy Sosa	60.00

Wave of the Future

		NM/M
Complete Set (20):		6.00
Common Player:		.15
1	Jason Bere	.15
2	Jeremy Burnitz	.15
3	Russ Davis	.15
4	Jim Edmonds	.25
5	Cliff Floyd	.15
6	Jeffrey Hammonds	.15
7	Trevor Hoffman	.15
8	Domingo Jean	.15
9	David McCarty	.15
10	Bobby Munoz	.15
11	Brad Pennington	.15
12	Mike Piazza	3.00
13	Manny Ramirez	2.00
14	John Roper	.15
15	Tim Salmon	.25
16	Aaron Sele	.15
17	Allen Watson	.15
18	Rondell White	.15
19	Darell Whitmore	.15
20	Nigel Wilson	.15

1994 Flair

		NM/M
Complete Set (450):		60.00
Common Player:		.10
Series 1 Pack (10):		1.50
Series 1 Box (24):		20.00
Series 2 Pack (10):		3.00
Series 2 Box (24):		50.00
1	Harold Baines	.10
2	Jeffrey Hammonds	.10
3	Chris Hoiles	.10
4	Ben McDonald	.10
5	Mark McLemore	.10

6	Jamie Moyer	.10
7	Jim Poole	.10
8	Cal Ripken, Jr.	3.00
9	Chris Sabo	.10
10	Scott Bankhead	.10
11	Scott Cooper	.10
12	Danny Darwin	.10
13	Andre Dawson	.30
14	Billy Hatcher	.10
15	Aaron Sele	.10
15a	Aaron Sele/OPS	2.00
16	John Valentin	.10
17	Dave Valle	.10
18	Mo Vaughn	.10
19	Brian Anderson RC	.50
20	Gary DiSarcina	.10
21	Jim Edmonds	.10
22	Chuck Finley	.10
23	Bo Jackson	.20
24	Mark Leiter	.10
25	Greg Myers	.10
26	Eduardo Perez	.10
27	Tim Salmon	.10
28	Wilson Alvarez	.10
29	Jason Bere	.10
30	Alex Fernandez	.10
31	Ozzie Guillen	.10
32	Joe Hall	.10
33	Darrin Jackson	.10
34	Kirk McCaskill	.10
35	Tim Raines	.10
36	Frank Thomas	1.00
37	Carlos Baerga	.10
38	Albert Belle	.10
39	Mark Clark	.10
40	Wayne Kirby	.10
41	Dennis Martinez	.10
42	Charles Nagy	.10
43	Manny Ramirez	1.00
44	Paul Sorrento	.10
45	Jim Thome	.65
46	Eric Davis	.10
47	John Doherty	.10
48	Junior Felix	.10
49	Cecil Fielder	.10
50	Kirk Gibson	.10
51	Mike Moore	.10
52	Tony Phillips	.10
53	Alan Trammell	.10
54	Kevin Appier	.10
55	Stan Belinda	.10
56	Vince Coleman	.10
57	Greg Gagne	.10
58	Bob Hamelin	.10
59	Dave Henderson	.10
60	Wally Joyner	.10
61	Mike Macfarlane	.10
62	Jeff Montgomery	.10
63	Ricky Bones	.10
64	Jeff Bronkey	.10
65	Alex Diaz	.10
66	Cal Eldred	.10
67	Darryl Hamilton	.10
68	John Jaha	.10
69	Mark Kiefer	.10
70	Kevin Seitzer	.10
71	Turner Ward	.10
72	Rich Becker	.10
73	Scott Erickson	.10
74	Keith Garagozzo	.10
75	Kent Hrbek	.10
76	Scott Leius	.10
77	Kirby Puckett	1.50
78	Matt Walbeck	.10
79	Dave Winfield	1.00
80	Mike Gallego	.10
81	Xavier Hernandez	.10
82	Jimmy Key	.10
83	Jim Leyritz	.10
84	Don Mattingly	1.75
85	Matt Nokes	.10
86	Paul O'Neill	.10
87	Melido Perez	.10
88	Danny Tartabull	.10
89	Mike Bordick	.10
90	Ron Darling	.10
91	Dennis Eckersley	.75
92	Stan Javier	.10
93	Steve Karsay	.10
94	Mark McGwire	2.50
95	Troy Neel	.10

96	Terry Steinbach	.10
97	Bill Taylor	.10
98	Eric Anthony	.10
99	Chris Bosio	.10
100	Tim Davis	.10
101	Felix Fermin	.10
102	Dave Fleming	.10
103	Ken Griffey Jr.	2.00
104	Ken Hibbard	.10
105	Reggie Jefferson	.10
106	Tino Martinez	.10
107	Jack Armstrong	.10
108	Will Clark	.10
109	Juan Gonzalez	.50
110	Rick Helling	.10
111	Tom Henke	.10
112	David Hulse	.10
113	Manuel Lee	.10
114	Doug Strange	.10
115	Roberto Alomar	.25
116	Joe Carter	.10
117	Carlos Delgado	.50
118	Pat Hentgen	.10
119	Paul Molitor	1.00
120	John Olerud	.10
121	Dave Stewart	.10
122	Todd Stottlemyre	.10
123	Mike Timlin	.10
124	Jeff Blauser	.10
125	Tom Glavine	.30
126	Dave Justice	.10
127	Mike Kelly	.10
128	Ryan Klesko	.10
129	Javier Lopez	.10
130	Greg Maddux	1.50
131	Fred McGriff	.10
132	Kent Mercker	.10
133	Mark Wohlers	.10
134	Willie Banks	.10
135	Steve Buechele	.10
136	Shawon Dunston	.10
137	Jose Guzman	.10
138	Glenallen Hill	.10
139	Randy Myers	.10
140	Karl Rhodes	.10
141	Ryne Sandberg	1.50
142	Steve Trachsel	.10
143	Bret Boone	.10
144	Tom Browning	.10
145	Hector Carrasco	.10
146	Barry Larkin	.10
147	Hal Morris	.10
148	Jose Rijo	.10
149	Reggie Sanders	.10
150	John Smiley	.10
151	Dante Bichette	.10
152	Ellis Burks	.10
153	Joe Girardi	.10
154	Mike Harkey	.10
155	Roberto Mejia	.10
156	Marcus Moore	.10
157	Armando Reynoso	.10
158	Bruce Ruffin	.10
159	Eric Young	.10
160	Kurt Abbott RC	.10
161	Jeff Conine	.10
162	Orestes Destrade	.10
163	Chris Hammond	.10
164	Bryan Harvey	.10
165	Dave Magadan	.10
166	Gary Sheffield	.40
167	David Weathers	.10
168	Andujar Cedeno	.10
169	Tom Edens	.10
170	Luis Gonzalez	.10
171	Pete Harnisch	.10
172	Todd Jones	.10
173	Darryl Kile	.10
174	James Mouton	.10
175	Scott Servais	.10
176	Mitch Williams	.10
177	Pedro Astacio	.10
178	Orel Hershiser	.10
179	Raul Mondesi	.10
180	Jose Offerman	.10
181	Chan Ho Park RC	1.00
182	Mike Piazza	2.00
183	Cory Snyder	.10
184	Tim Wallach	.10
185	Todd Worrell	.10
186	Sean Berry	.10
187	Wil Cordero	.10
188	Darrin Fletcher	.10
189	Cliff Floyd	.10
190	Marquis Grissom	.10
191	Rod Henderson	.10
192	Ken Hill	.10
193	Pedro Martinez	1.00
194	Kirk Rueter	.10
195	Jeromy Burnitz	.10
196	John Franco	.10
197	Dwight Gooden	.10
198	Todd Hundley	.10
199	Bobby Jones	.10
200	Jeff Kent	.10
201	Mike Maddux	.10
202	Ryan Thompson	.10
203	Jose Vizcaino	.10
204	Darren Daulton	.10
205	Len Dykstra	.10
206	Jim Eisenreich	.10
207	Dave Hollins	.10
208	Danny Jackson	.10
209	Doug Jones	.10
210	Jeff Juden	.10

211	Ben Rivera	.10
212	Kevin Stocker	.10
213	Milt Thompson	.10
214	Jay Bell	.10
215	Steve Cooke	.10
216	Mark Dewey	.10
217	Al Martin	.10
218	Orlando Merced	.10
219	Don Slaught	.10
220	Zane Smith	.10
221	Rick White	.10
222	Kevin Young	.10
223	Rene Arocha	.10
224	Rheal Cormier	.10
225	Brian Jordan	.10
226	Ray Lankford	.10
227	Mike Perez	.10
228	Ozzie Smith	1.50
229	Mark Whiten	.10
230	Todd Zeile	.10
231	Derek Bell	.10
232	Archi Cianfrocco	.10
233	Ricky Gutierrez	.10
234	Trevor Hoffman	.10
235	Phil Plantier	.10
236	Dave Staton	.10
237	Wally Whitehurst	.10
238	Todd Benzinger	.10
239	Barry Bonds	3.00
240	John Burkett	.10
241	Royce Clayton	.10
242	Bryan Hickerson	.10
243	Mike Jackson	.10
244	Darren Lewis	.10
245	Kirt Manwaring	.10
246	Mark Portugal	.10
247	Salomon Torres	.10
248	Checklist	.10
249	Checklist	.10
250	Checklist	.10
251	Brady Anderson	.10
252	Mike Devereaux	.10
253	Sid Fernandez	.10
254	Leo Gomez	.10
255	Mike Mussina	.40
256	Mike Oquist	.10
257	Rafael Palmeiro	.75
258	Lee Smith	.10
259	Damon Berryhill	.10
260	Wes Chamberlain	.10
261	Roger Clemens	1.75
262	Gar Finnvold	.10
263	Mike Greenwell	.10
264	Tim Naehring	.10
265	Otis Nixon	.10
266	Ken Ryan	.10
267	Chad Curtis	.10
268	Chili Davis	.10
269	Damion Easley	.10
270	Jorge Fabregas	.10
271	Mark Langston	.10
272	Phil Leftwich	.10
273	Harold Reynolds	.10
274	J.T. Snow	.10
275	Joey Cora	.10
276	Julio Franco	.10
277	Roberto Hernandez	.10
278	Lance Johnson	.10
279	Ron Karkovice	.10
280	Jack McDowell	.10
281	Robin Ventura	.10
282	Sandy Alomar Jr.	.10
283	Kenny Lofton	.10
284	Jose Mesa	.10
285	Jack Morris	.10
286	Eddie Murray	1.00
287	Chad Ogea	.10
288	Eric Plunk	.10
289	Paul Shuey	.10
290	Omar Vizquel	.10
291	Danny Bautista	.10
292	Travis Fryman	.10
293	Greg Gohr	.10
294	Chris Gomez	.10
295	Mickey Tettleton	.10
296	Lou Whitaker	.10
297	David Cone	.10
298	Gary Gaetti	.10
299	Tom Gordon	.10
300	Felix Jose	.10
301	Jose Lind	.10
302	Brian McRae	.10
303	Mike Fetters	.10
304	Brian Harper	.10
305	Pat Listach	.10
306	Matt Mieske	.10
307	Dave Nilsson	.10
308	Jody Reed	.10
309	Greg Vaughn	.10
310	Bill Wegman	.10
311	Rick Aguilera	.10
312	Alex Cole	.10
313	Denny Hocking	.10
314	Chuck Knoblauch	.10
315	Shane Mack	.10
316	Pat Meares	.10
317	Kevin Tapani	.10
318	Jim Abbott	.10
319	Wade Boggs	1.00
320	Sterling Hitchcock	.10
321	Pat Kelly	.10
322	Terry Mulholland	.10
323	Luis Polonia	.10
324	Mike Stanley	.10
325	Bob Wickman	.10

326	Bernie Williams	.10
327	Mark Acre	.10
328	Geronimo Berroa	.10
329	Scott Brosius	.10
330	Brent Gates	.10
331	Rickey Henderson	1.00
332	Carlos Reyes	.10
333	Ruben Sierra	.10
334	Bobby Witt	.10
335	Bobby Ayala	.10
336	Jay Buhner	.10
337	Randy Johnson	1.00
338	Edgar Martinez	.10
339	Bill Risley	.10
340	Alex Rodriguez RC	40.00
341	Roger Salkeld	.10
342	Dan Wilson	.10
343	Kevin Brown	.10
344	Jose Canseco	.45
345	Dean Palmer	.10
346	Ivan Rodriguez	.75
347	Kenny Rogers	.10
348	Pat Borders	.10
349	Juan Guzman	.10
350	Ed Sprague	.10
351	Devon White	.10
352	Steve Avery	.10
353	Roberto Kelly	.10
354	Mark Lemke	.10
355	Greg McMichael	.10
356	Terry Pendleton	.10
357	John Smoltz	.10
358	Mike Stanton	.10
359	Tony Tarasco	.10
360	Mark Grace	.10
361	Derrick May	.10
362	Rey Sanchez	.10
363	Sammy Sosa	1.50
364	Rick Wilkins	.10
365	Jeff Brantley	.10
366	Tony Fernandez	.10
367	Chuck McElroy	.10
368	Kevin Mitchell	.10
369	John Roper	.10
370	Johnny Ruffin	.10
371	Deion Sanders	.15
372	Marvin Freeman	.10
373	Andres Galarraga	.10
374	Charlie Hayes	.10
375	Nelson Liriano	.10
376	David Nied	.10
377	Walt Weiss	.10
378	Bret Barberie	.10
379	Jerry Browne	.10
380	Chuck Carr	.10
381	Greg Colbrunn	.10
382	Charlie Hough	.10
383	Kurt Miller	.10
384	Benito Santiago	.10
385	Jeff Bagwell	1.00
386	Craig Biggio	.10
387	Ken Caminiti	.10
388	Doug Drabek	.10
389	Steve Finley	.10
390	John Hudek	.10
391	Orlando Miller	.10
392	Shane Reynolds	.10
393	Brett Butler	.10
394	Tom Candiotti	.10
395	Delino DeShields	.10
396	Kevin Gross	.10
397	Eric Karros	.10
398	Ramon Martinez	.10
399	Henry Rodriguez	.10
400	Moises Alou	.10
401	Jeff Fassero	.10
402	Mike Lansing	.10
403	Mel Rojas	.10
404	Larry Walker	.10
405	John Wetteland	.10
406	Gabe White	.10
407	Bobby Bonilla	.10
408	Josias Manzanillo	.10
409	Bret Saberhagen	.10
410	David Segui	.10
411	Mariano Duncan	.10
412	Tommy Greene	.10
413	Billy Hatcher	.10
414	Ricky Jordan	.10
415	John Kruk	.10
416	Bobby Munoz	.10
417	Curt Schilling	.30
418	Fernando Valenzuela	.10
419	David West	.10
420	Carlos Garcia	.10
421	Brian Hunter	.10
422	Jeff King	.10
423	Jon Lieber	.10
424	Ravelo Manzanillo	.10
425	Denny Neagle	.10
426	Andy Van Slyke	.10
427	Bryan Eversgerd	.10
428	Bernard Gilkey	.10
429	Gregg Jefferies	.10
430	Tom Pagnozzi	.10
431	Bob Tewksbury	.10
432	Allen Watson	.10
433	Andy Ashby	.10
434	Andy Benes	.10
435	Donnie Elliott	.10
436	Tony Gwynn	1.50
437	Joey Hamilton	.10
438	Tim Hyers	.10
439	Luis Lopez	.10
440	Bip Roberts	.10

441	Scott Sanders	.10
442	Rod Beck	.10
443	Dave Burba	.10
444	Darryl Strawberry	.10
445	Bill Swift	.10
446	Robby Thompson	.10
447	William Van Landingham RC	.10
448	Matt Williams	.10
449	Checklist	.10
450	Checklist	.10

Hot Gloves

		NM/M
Complete Set (10):		40.00
Common Player:		2.00
1	Barry Bonds	10.00
2	Will Clark	2.00
3	Ken Griffey Jr.	7.50
4	Kenny Lofton	2.00
5	Greg Maddux	5.00
6	Don Mattingly	6.50
7	Kirby Puckett	5.00
8	Cal Ripken, Jr.	10.00
9	Tim Salmon	2.00
10	Matt Williams	2.00

Hot Numbers

		NM/M
Complete Set (10):		15.00
Common Player:		.50
1	Roberto Alomar	1.00
2	Carlos Baerga	.50
3	Will Clark	.50
4	Fred McGriff	.50
5	Paul Molitor	3.00
6	John Olerud	.50
7	Mike Piazza	4.50
8	Cal Ripken, Jr.	6.00
9	Ryne Sandberg	4.00
10	Frank Thomas	3.00

Infield Power

		NM/M
Complete Set (10):		5.00
Common Player:		.25
1	Jeff Bagwell	.75
2	Will Clark	.25
3	Darren Daulton	.25
4	Don Mattingly	1.25
5	Fred McGriff	.25
6	Rafael Palmeiro	.65
7	Mike Piazza	1.50
8	Cal Ripken, Jr.	2.50
9	Frank Thomas	.75
10	Matt Williams	.25

Outfield Power

		NM/M
Complete Set (10):		5.00
Common Player:		.30
1	Albert Belle	.30
2	Barry Bonds	2.00
3	Joe Carter	.30
4	Len Dykstra	.30
5	Juan Gonzalez	.45
6	Ken Griffey Jr.	1.50
7	Dave Justice	.30
8	Kirby Puckett	1.00
9	Tim Salmon	.30
10	Dave Winfield	.75

Wave of the Future 1

		NM/M
Complete Set (10):		6.00
Common Player:		.25
1	Kurt Abbott	.25
2	Carlos Delgado	5.00
3	Steve Karsay	.25
4	Ryan Klesko	.25
5	Javier Lopez	.25
6	Raul Mondesi	.25
7	James Mouton	.25
8	Chan Ho Park	.25
9	Dave Staton	.25
10	Rick White	.25

Wave of the Future 2

		NM/M
Complete Set (10):		22.50
Common Player:		.50
1	Mark Acre	.50
2	Chris Gomez	.50
3	Joey Hamilton	.50
4	John Hudek	.50
5	Jon Lieber	.50
6	Matt Mieske	.50
7	Orlando Miller	.50
8	Alex Rodriguez	20.00
9	Tony Tarasco	.50
10	Bill VanLandingham	.50

1995 Flair

		NM/M
Complete Set (432):		30.00
Common Player:		.10
Series 1 or 2 Pack (9):		1.00
Series 1 or 2 Wax Box (24):		15.00
1	Brady Anderson	.10
2	Harold Baines	.10
3	Leo Gomez	.10

4	Alan Mills	.10
5	Jamie Moyer	.10
6	Mike Mussina	.40
7	Mike Oquist	.10
8	Arthur Rhodes	.10
9	Cal Ripken Jr.	3.00
10	Roger Clemens	1.75
11	Scott Cooper	.10
12	Mike Greenwell	.10
13	Aaron Sele	.10
14	John Valentin	.10
15	Mo Vaughn	.10
16	Chad Curtis	.10
17	Gary DiSarcina	.10
18	Chuck Finley	.10
19	Andrew Lorraine	.10
20	Spike Owen	.10
21	Tim Salmon	.10
22	J.T. Snow	.10
23	Wilson Alvarez	.10
24	Jason Bere	.10
25	Ozzie Guillen	.10
26	Mike LaValliere	.10
27	Frank Thomas	1.00
28	Robin Ventura	.10
29	Carlos Baerga	.10
30	Albert Belle	.10
31	Jason Grimsley	.10
32	Dennis Martinez	.10
33	Eddie Murray	1.00
34	Charles Nagy	.10
35	Manny Ramirez	1.00
36	Paul Sorrento	.10
37	John Doherty	.10
38	Cecil Fielder	.10
39	Travis Fryman	.10
40	Chris Gomez	.10
41	Tony Phillips	.10
42	Lou Whitaker	.10
43	David Cone	.10
44	Gary Gaetti	.10
45	Mark Gubicza	.10
46	Bob Hamelin	.10
47	Wally Joyner	.10
48	Rusty Meacham	.10
49	Jeff Montgomery	.10
50	Ricky Bones	.10
51	Cal Eldred	.10
52	Pat Listach	.10
53	Matt Mieske	.10
54	Dave Nilsson	.10
55	Greg Vaughn	.10
56	Bill Wegman	.10
57	Chuck Knoblauch	.10
58	Scott Leius	.10
59	Pat Mahomes	.10
60	Pat Meares	.10
61	Pedro Munoz	.10
62	Kirby Puckett	1.50
63	Wade Boggs	1.00
64	Jimmy Key	.10
65	Jim Leyritz	.10
66	Don Mattingly	1.75
67	Paul O'Neill	.10
68	Melido Perez	.10
69	Danny Tartabull	.10
70	John Briscoe	.10
71	Scott Brosius	.10
72	Ron Darling	.10
73	Brent Gates	.10
74	Rickey Henderson	1.00
75	Stan Javier	.10
76	Mark McGwire	2.50
77	Todd Van Poppel	.10
78	Bobby Ayala	.10
79	Mike Blowers	.10
80	Jay Buhner	.10
81	Ken Griffey Jr.	2.00
82	Randy Johnson	1.00
83	Tino Martinez	.10
84	Jeff Nelson	.10
85	Alex Rodriguez	2.50
86	Will Clark	.10
87	Jeff Frye	.10
88	Juan Gonzalez	.50
89	Rusty Greer	.10
90	Darren Oliver	.10
91	Dean Palmer	.10
92	Ivan Rodriguez	.75
93	Matt Whiteside	.10
94	Roberto Alomar	.25
95	Joe Carter	.10
96	Tony Castillo	.10
97	Juan Guzman	.10
98	Pat Hentgen	.10
99	Mike Huff	.10
100	John Olerud	.10
101	Woody Williams	.10
102	Roberto Kelly	.10
103	Ryan Klesko	.10
104	Javier Lopez	.10
105	Greg Maddux	1.50
106	Fred McGriff	.10
107	Jose Oliva	.10
108	John Smoltz	.10
109	Tony Tarasco	.10
110	Mark Wohlers	.10
111	Jim Bullinger	.10
112	Shawon Dunston	.10
113	Derrick May	.10
114	Randy Myers	.10
115	Karl Rhodes	.10
116	Rey Sanchez	.10
117	Steve Trachsel	.10
118	Eddie Zambrano	.10
119	Bret Boone	.10
120	Brian Dorsett	.10
121	Hal Morris	.10
122	Jose Rijo	.10
123	John Roper	.10
124	Reggie Sanders	.10
125	Pete Schourek	.10
126	John Smiley	.10
127	Ellis Burks	.10
128	Vinny Castilla	.10
129	Marvin Freeman	.10
130	Andres Galarraga	.10
131	Mike Munoz	.10
132	David Nied	.10
133	Bruce Ruffin	.10
134	Walt Weiss	.10
135	Eric Young	.10
136	Greg Colbrunn	.10
137	Jeff Conine	.10
138	Jeremy Hernandez	.10
139	Charles Johnson	.10
140	Robb Nen	.10
141	Gary Sheffield	.40
142	Dave Weathers	.10
143	Jeff Bagwell	1.00
144	Craig Biggio	.10
145	Tony Eusebio	.10
146	Luis Gonzalez	.10
147	John Hudek	.10
148	Darryl Kile	.10
149	Dave Veres	.10
150	Billy Ashley	.10
151	Pedro Astacio	.10
152	Rafael Bournigal	.10
153	Delino DeShields	.10
154	Raul Mondesi	.10
155	Mike Piazza	2.00
156	Rudy Seanez	.10
157	Ismael Valdes	.10
158	Tim Wallach	.10
159	Todd Worrell	.10
160	Moises Alou	.10
161	Cliff Floyd	.10
162	Gil Heredia	.10
163	Mike Lansing	.10
164	Pedro Martinez	1.00
165	Kirk Rueter	.10
166	Tim Scott	.10
167	Jeff Shaw	.10
168	Rondell White	.10
169	Bobby Bonilla	.10
170	Rico Brogna	.10
171	Todd Hundley	.10
172	Jeff Kent	.10
173	Jim Lindeman	.10
174	Joe Orsulak	.10
175	Bret Saberhagen	.10
176	Toby Borland	.10
177	Darren Daulton	.10
178	Lenny Dykstra	.10
179	Jim Eisenreich	.10
180	Tommy Greene	.10
181	Tony Longmire	.10
182	Bobby Munoz	.10
183	Kevin Stocker	.10
184	Jay Bell	.10
185	Steve Cooke	.10
186	Ravelo Manzanillo	.10
187	Al Martin	.10
188	Denny Neagle	.10
189	Don Slaught	.10
190	Paul Wagner	.10
191	Rene Arocha	.10
192	Bernard Gilkey	.10
193	Jose Oquendo	.10
194	Tom Pagnozzi	.10
195	Ozzie Smith	1.50
196	Allen Watson	.10
197	Mark Whiten	.10
198	Andy Ashby	.10
199	Donnie Elliott	.10
200	Bryce Florie	.10
201	Tony Gwynn	1.50
202	Trevor Hoffman	.10
203	Brian Johnson	.10
204	Tim Mauser	.10
205	Bip Roberts	.10
206	Rod Beck	.10
207	Barry Bonds	3.00
208	Royce Clayton	.10
209	Darren Lewis	.10
210	Mark Portugal	.10
211	Kevin Rogers	.10
212	William Van Landingham	.10
213	Matt Williams	.10
214	Checklist	.10
215	Checklist	.10
216	Checklist	.10
217	Bret Barberie	.10
218	Armando Benitez	.10
219	Kevin Brown	.10
220	Sid Fernandez	.10
221	Chris Hoiles	.10
222	Doug Jones	.10
223	Ben McDonald	.10
224	Rafael Palmeiro	.75
225	Andy Van Slyke	.10
226	Jose Canseco	.40
227	Vaughn Eshelman	.10
228	Mike Macfarlane	.10
229	Tim Naehring	.10
230	Frank Rodriguez	.10
231	Lee Tinsley	.10
232	Mark Whiten	.10
233	Garret Anderson	.10
234	Chili Davis	.10
235	Jim Edmonds	.10
236	Mark Langston	.10
237	Troy Percival	.10
238	Tony Phillips	.10
239	Lee Smith	.10
240	Jim Abbott	.10
241	James Baldwin	.10
242	Mike Devereaux	.10
243	Ray Durham	.10
244	Alex Fernandez	.10
245	Roberto Hernandez	.10
246	Lance Johnson	.10
247	Ron Karkovice	.10
248	Tim Raines	.10
249	Sandy Alomar Jr.	.10
250	Orel Hershiser	.10
251	Julian Tavarez	.10
252	Jim Thome	.65
253	Omar Vizquel	.10
254	Dave Winfield	1.00
255	Chad Curtis	.10
256	Kirk Gibson	.10
257	Mike Henneman	.10
258	Bob Higginson **RC**	.25
259	Felipe Lira	.10
260	Rudy Pemberton	.10
261	Alan Trammell	.10
262	Kevin Appier	.10
263	Pat Borders	.10
264	Tom Gordon	.10
265	Jose Lind	.10
266	Jon Nunnally	.10
267	Dilson Torres	.10
268	Michael Tucker	.10
269	Jeff Cirillo	.10
270	Darryl Hamilton	.10
271	David Hulse	.10
272	Mark Kiefer	.10
273	Graeme Lloyd	.10
274	Joe Oliver	.10
275	Al Reyes	.10
276	Kevin Seitzer	.10
277	Rick Aguilera	.10
278	Marty Cordova	.10
279	Scott Erickson	.10
280	LaTroy Hawkins	.10
281	Brad Radke	.10
282	Kevin Tapani	.10
283	Tony Fernandez	.10
284	Sterling Hitchcock	.10
285	Pat Kelly	.10
286	Jack McDowell	.10
287	Andy Pettitte	.30
288	Mike Stanley	.10
289	John Wetteland	.10
290	Bernie Williams	.10
291	Mark Acre	.10
292	Geronimo Berroa	.10
293	Dennis Eckersley	.75
294	Steve Ontiveros	.10
295	Ruben Sierra	.10
296	Terry Steinbach	.10
297	Dave Stewart	.10
298	Todd Stottlemyre	.10
299	Darren Bragg	.10
300	Joey Cora	.10
301	Edgar Martinez	.10
302	Bill Risley	.10
303	Ron Villone	.10
304	Dan Wilson	.10
305	Benji Gil	.10
306	Wilson Heredia	.10
307	Mark McLemore	.10
308	Otis Nixon	.10
309	Kenny Rogers	.10
310	Jeff Russell	.10
311	Mickey Tettleton	.10
312	Bob Tewksbury	.10
313	David Cone	.10
314	Carlos Delgado	.50
315	Alex Gonzalez	.10
316	Shawn Green	.40
317	Paul Molitor	1.00
318	Ed Sprague	.10
319	Devon White	.10
320	Steve Avery	.10
321	Jeff Blauser	.10
322	Brad Clontz	.10
323	Tom Glavine	.30
324	Marquis Grissom	.10
325	Chipper Jones	1.50
326	Dave Justice	.10
327	Mark Lemke	.10
328	Kent Mercker	.10
329	Jason Schmidt	.10
330	Steve Buechele	.10
331	Kevin Foster	.10
332	Mark Grace	.10
333	Brian McRae	.10
334	Sammy Sosa	1.50
335	Ozzie Timmons	.10
336	Rick Wilkins	.10
337	Hector Carrasco	.10
338	Ron Gant	.10
339	Barry Larkin	.10
340	Deion Sanders	.15
341	Benito Santiago	.10
342	Roger Bailey	.10
343	Jason Bates	.10
344	Dante Bichette	.10
345	Joe Girardi	.10
346	Bill Swift	.10
347	Mark Thompson	.10
348	Larry Walker	.10
349	Kurt Abbott	.10
350	John Burkett	.10
351	Chuck Carr	.10
352	Andre Dawson	.30
353	Chris Hammond	.10
354	Charles Johnson	.10
355	Terry Pendleton	.10
356	Quilvio Veras	.10
357	Derek Bell	.10
358	Jim Dougherty	.10
359	Doug Drabek	.10
360	Todd Jones	.10
361	Orlando Miller	.10
362	James Mouton	.10
363	Phil Plantier	.10
364	Shane Reynolds	.10
365	Todd Hollandsworth	.10
366	Eric Karros	.10
367	Ramon Martinez	.10
368	Hideo Nomo **RC**	3.00
369	Jose Offerman	.10
370	Antonio Osuna	.10
371	Todd Williams	.10
372	Shane Andrews	.10
373	Wil Cordero	.10
374	Jeff Fassero	.10
375	Darrin Fletcher	.10
376	Mark Grudzielanek **RC**	.50
377	Carlos Perez **RC**	.25
378	Mel Rojas	.10
379	Tony Tarasco	.10
380	Edgardo Alfonzo	.10
381	Brett Butler	.10
382	Carl Everett	.10
383	John Franco	.10
384	Pete Harnisch	.10
385	Bobby Jones	.10
386	Dave Mlicki	.10
387	Jose Vizcaino	.10
388	Ricky Bottalico	.10
389	Tyler Green	.10
390	Charlie Hayes	.10
391	Dave Hollins	.10
392	Gregg Jefferies	.10
393	Michael Mimbs **RC**	.10
394	Mickey Morandini	.10
395	Curt Schilling	.30
396	Heathcliff Slocumb	.10
397	Jason Christiansen	.10
398	Midre Cummings	.10
399	Carlos Garcia	.10
400	Mark Johnson	.10
401	Jeff King	.10
402	Jon Lieber	.10
403	Esteban Loaiza	.10
404	Orlando Merced	.10
405	Gary Wilson **RC**	.10
406	Scott Cooper	.10
407	Tom Henke	.10
408	Ken Hill	.10
409	Danny Jackson	.10
410	Brian Jordan	.10
411	Ray Lankford	.10
412	John Mabry	.10
413	Todd Zeile	.10
414	Andy Benes	.10
415	Andres Berumen	.10
416	Ken Caminiti	.10
417	Andujar Cedeno	.10
418	Steve Finley	.10
419	Joey Hamilton	.10
420	Dustin Hermanson	.10
421	Melvin Nieves	.10
422	Roberto Petagine	.10
423	Eddie Williams	.10
424	Glenallen Hill	.10
425	Kirt Manwaring	.10
426	Terry Mulholland	.10
427	J.R. Phillips	.10
428	Joe Rosselli	.10
429	Robby Thompson	.10
430	Checklist	.10
431	Checklist	.10
432	Checklist	.10

Cal Ripken, Jr. Enduring Flair

		NM/M
Complete Set (15):		40.00
Common Card:		4.00
1	Rookie Of The Year	4.00
2	1st MVP Season	4.00
3	World Series Highlight	4.00
4	Family Tradition	4.00
5	8,243 Consecutive Innings	4.00
6	95 Consecutive Errorless Games	4.00
7	All-Star MVP	4.00
8	1,000th RBI	4.00
9	287th Home Run	4.00
10	2,000th Consecutive Game	4.00
11	Record-tying Game	6.00

12	Record-breaking Game	6.00
13	Defensive Prowess	6.00
14	Literacy Work	6.00
15	2,153 and Counting	6.00

Hot Gloves

		NM/M
Complete Set (12):		35.00
Common Player:		1.25
1	Roberto Alomar	2.00
2	Barry Bonds	10.00
3	Ken Griffey Jr.	7.50
4	Marquis Grissom	1.25
5	Barry Larkin	1.25
6	Darren Lewis	1.25
7	Kenny Lofton	1.25
8	Don Mattingly	6.00
9	Cal Ripken Jr.	10.00
10	Ivan Rodriguez	2.50
11	Devon White	1.25
12	Matt Williams	1.25

Hot Numbers

		NM/M
Complete Set (10):		10.00
Common Player:		.50
1	Jeff Bagwell	1.00
2	Albert Belle	.50
3	Barry Bonds	2.25
4	Ken Griffey Jr.	2.00
5	Kenny Lofton	.50
6	Greg Maddux	1.25
7	Mike Piazza	2.00
8	Cal Ripken Jr.	2.25
9	Frank Thomas	1.00
10	Matt Williams	.50

Infield Power

		NM/M
Complete Set (10):		4.00
Common Player:		.25
1	Jeff Bagwell	.75
2	Darren Daulton	.25
3	Cecil Fielder	.25

4	Andres Galarraga	.25
5	Fred McGriff	.25
6	Rafael Palmeiro	.65
7	Mike Piazza	1.50
8	Frank Thomas	1.00
9	Mo Vaughn	.25
10	Matt Williams	.25

Outfield Power

		NM/M
Complete Set (10):		4.00
Common Player:		.25
1	Albert Belle	.25
2	Dante Bichette	.25
3	Barry Bonds	2.00
4	Jose Canseco	.50
5	Joe Carter	.25
6	Juan Gonzalez	.50
7	Ken Griffey Jr.	1.00
8	Kirby Puckett	.75
9	Gary Sheffield	.50
10	Ruben Sierra	.25

Today's Spotlight

		NM/M
Complete Set (12):		15.00
Common Player:		1.00
1	Jeff Bagwell	3.00
2	Jason Bere	1.00
3	Cliff Floyd	1.00
4	Chuck Knoblauch	1.00
5	Kenny Lofton	1.00
6	Javier Lopez	1.00
7	Raul Mondesi	1.00
8	Mike Mussina	1.50
9	Mike Piazza	5.00
10	Manny Ramirez	3.00
11	Tim Salmon	1.00
12	Frank Thomas	3.00

Wave Of The Future

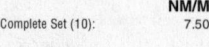

	NM/M
Complete Set (10):	7.50

Common Player:		.35
1	Jason Bates	.25
2	Armando Benitez	.25
3	Marty Cordova	.25
4	Ray Durham	.25
5	Vaughn Eshelman	.25
6	Carl Everett	.25
7	Shawn Green	1.50
8	Dustin Hermanson	.25
9	Chipper Jones	4.00
10	Hideo Nomo	1.50

1996 Flair

		NM/M
Complete Set (400):		50.00
Common Player:		.15
Pack (9):		3.00
Wax Box (18):		40.00
1	Roberto Alomar	.30
2	Brady Anderson	.15
3	Bobby Bonilla	.15
4	Scott Erickson	.15
5	Jeffrey Hammonds	.15
6	Jimmy Haynes	.15
7	Chris Hoiles	.15
8	Kent Mercker	.15
9	Mike Mussina	.50
10	Randy Myers	.15
11	Rafael Palmeiro	.75
12	Cal Ripken Jr.	3.00
(12p)	Cal Ripken Jr./OPS (No card #.)	3.00
13	B.J. Surhoff	.15
14	David Wells	.15
15	Jose Canseco	.50
16	Roger Clemens	1.75
17	Wil Cordero	.15
18	Tom Gordon	.15
19	Mike Greenwell	.15
20	Dwayne Hosey	.15
21	Jose Malave	.15
22	Tim Naehring	.15
23	Troy O'Leary	.15
24	Aaron Sele	.15
25	Heathcliff Slocumb	.15
26	Mike Stanley	.15
27	Jeff Suppan	.15
28	John Valentin	.15
29	Mo Vaughn	.15
30	Tim Wakefield	.15
31	Jim Abbott	.15
32	Garret Anderson	.15
33	George Arias	.15
34	Chili Davis	.15
35	Gary DiSarcina	.15
36	Jim Edmonds	.15
37	Chuck Finley	.15
38	Todd Greene	.15
39	Mark Langston	.15
40	Troy Percival	.15
41	Tim Salmon	.15
42	Lee Smith	.15
43	J.T. Snow	.15
44	Randy Velarde	.15
45	Tim Wallach	.15
46	Wilson Alvarez	.15
47	Harold Baines	.15
48	Jason Bere	.15
49	Ray Durham	.15
50	Alex Fernandez	.15
51	Ozzie Guillen	.15
52	Roberto Hernandez	.15
53	Ron Karkovice	.15
54	Darren Lewis	.15
55	Lyle Mouton	.15
56	Tony Phillips	.15
57	Chris Snopek	.15
58	Kevin Tapani	.15
59	Danny Tartabull	.15
30	Frank Thomas	1.00
61	Robin Ventura	.15
62	Sandy Alomar	.15
63	Carlos Baerga	.15
64	Albert Belle	.15
65	Julio Franco	.15
66	Orel Hershiser	.15
67	Kenny Lofton	.15
68	Dennis Martinez	.15
69	Jack McDowell	.15
70	Jose Mesa	.15
71	Eddie Murray	1.00
72	Charles Nagy	.15
73	Tony Pena	.15
74	Manny Ramirez	1.00
75	Julian Tavarez	.15
76	Jim Thome	.65
77	Omar Vizquel	.15
78	Chad Curtis	.15
79	Cecil Fielder	.15
80	Travis Fryman	.15
81	Chris Gomez	.15
82	Bob Higginson	.15
83	Mark Lewis	.15
84	Felipe Lira	.15
85	Alan Trammell	.15
86	Kevin Appier	.15
87	Johnny Damon	.50
88	Tom Goodwin	.15
89	Mark Gubicza	.15
90	Bob Hamelin	.15
91	Keith Lockhart	.15
92	Jeff Montgomery	.15
93	Jon Nunnally	.15
94	Bip Roberts	.15
95	Michael Tucker	.15
96	Joe Vitiello	.15
97	Ricky Bones	.15
98	Chuck Carr	.15
99	Jeff Cirillo	.15
100	Mike Fetters	.15
101	John Jaha	.15
102	Mike Matheny	.15
103	Ben McDonald	.15
104	Matt Mieske	.15
105	Dave Nilsson	.15
106	Kevin Seitzer	.15
107	Steve Sparks	.15
108	Jose Valentin	.15
109	Greg Vaughn	.15
110	Rick Aguilera	.15
111	Rich Becker	.15
112	Marty Cordova	.15
113	LaTroy Hawkins	.15
114	Dave Hollins	.15
115	Roberto Kelly	.15
116	Chuck Knoblauch	.15
117	Matt Lawton RC	.50
118	Pat Meares	.15
119	Paul Molitor	1.00
120	Kirby Puckett	1.50
121	Brad Radke	.15
122	Frank Rodriguez	.15
123	Scott Stahoviak	.15
124	Matt Walbeck	.15
125	Wade Boggs	1.00
126	David Cone	.15
127	Joe Girardi	.15
128	Dwight Gooden	.15
129	Derek Jeter	3.00
130	Jimmy Key	.15
131	Jim Leyritz	.15
132	Tino Martinez	.15
133	Paul O'Neill	.15
134	Andy Pettitte	.40
135	Tim Raines	.15
136	Ruben Rivera	.15
137	Kenny Rogers	.15
138	Ruben Sierra	.15
139	John Wetteland	.15
140	Bernie Williams	.15
141	Tony Batista RC	.50
142	Allen Battle	.15
143	Geronimo Berroa	.15
144	Mike Bordick	.15
145	Scott Brosius	.15
146	Steve Cox	.15
147	Brent Gates	.15
148	Jason Giambi	.65
149	Doug Johns	.15
150	Mark McGwire	2.50
151	Pedro Munoz	.15
152	Ariel Prieto	.15
153	Terry Steinbach	.15
154	Todd Van Poppel	.15
155	Bobby Ayala	.15
156	Chris Bosio	.15
157	Jay Buhner	.15
158	Joey Cora	.15
159	Russ Davis	.15
160	Ken Griffey Jr.	2.00
161	Sterling Hitchcock	.15
162	Randy Johnson	1.00

163	Edgar Martinez	.15
164	Alex Rodriguez	2.50
165	Paul Sorrento	.15
166	Dan Wilson	.15
167	Will Clark	.15
168	Benji Gil	.15
169	Juan Gonzalez	.50
170	Rusty Greer	.15
171	Kevin Gross	.15
172	Darryl Hamilton	.15
173	Mike Henneman	.15
174	Ken Hill	.15
175	Mark McLemore	.15
176	Dean Palmer	.15
177	Roger Pavlik	.15
178	Ivan Rodriguez	.75
179	Mickey Tettleton	.15
180	Bobby Witt	.15
181	Joe Carter	.15
182	Felipe Crespo	.15
183	Alex Gonzalez	.15
184	Shawn Green	.40
185	Juan Guzman	.15
186	Erik Hanson	.15
187	Pat Hentgen	.15
188	Sandy Martinez RC	.15
189	Otis Nixon	.15
190	John Olerud	.15
191	Paul Quantrill	.15
192	Bill Risley	.15
193	Ed Sprague	.15
194	Steve Avery	.15
195	Jeff Blauser	.15
196	Brad Clontz	.15
197	Jermaine Dye	.15
198	Tom Glavine	.40
199	Marquis Grissom	.15
200	Chipper Jones	1.50
201	David Justice	.15
202	Ryan Klesko	.15
203	Mark Lemke	.15
204	Javier Lopez	.15
205	Greg Maddux	1.50
206	Fred McGriff	.15
207	Greg McMichael	.15
208	Wonderful Monds	.15
209	Jason Schmidt	.15
210	John Smoltz	.15
211	Mark Wohlers	.15
212	Jim Bullinger	.15
213	Frank Castillo	.15
214	Kevin Foster	.15
215	Luis Gonzalez	.15
216	Mark Grace	.15
217	Robin Jennings RC	.15
218	Doug Jones	.15
219	Dave Magadan	.15
220	Brian McRae	.15
221	Jaime Navarro	.15
222	Rey Sanchez	.15
223	Ryne Sandberg	1.50
224	Scott Servais	.15
225	Sammy Sosa	1.50
226	Ozzie Timmons	.15
227	Bret Boone	.15
228	Jeff Branson	.15
229	Jeff Brantley	.15
230	Dave Burba	.15
231	Vince Coleman	.15
232	Steve Gibralter	.15
233	Mike Kelly	.15
234	Barry Larkin	.15
235	Hal Morris	.15
236	Mark Portugal	.15
237	Jose Rijo	.15
238	Reggie Sanders	.15
239	Pete Schourek	.15
240	John Smiley	.15
241	Eddie Taubensee	.15
242	Jason Bates	.15
243	Dante Bichette	.15
244	Ellis Burks	.15
245	Vinny Castilla	.15
246	Andres Galarraga	.15
247	Darren Holmes	.15
248	Curt Leskanic	.15
249	Steve Reed	.15
250	Kevin Ritz	.15
251	Bret Saberhagen	.15
252	Bill Swift	.15
253	Larry Walker	.15
254	Walt Weiss	.15
255	Eric Young	.15
256	Kurt Abbott	.15
257	Kevin Brown	.15
258	John Burkett	.15
259	Greg Colbrunn	.15
260	Jeff Conine	.15
261	Andre Dawson	.40
262	Chris Hammond	.15
263	Charles Johnson	.15
264	Al Leiter	.15
265	Robb Nen	.15
266	Terry Pendleton	.15
267	Pat Rapp	.15
268	Gary Sheffield	.50
269	Quivilo Veras	.15
270	Devon White	.15
271	Bob Abreu	.15
272	Jeff Bagwell	1.00
273	Derek Bell	.15
274	Sean Berry	.15
275	Craig Biggio	.15
276	Doug Drabek	.15
277	Tony Eusebio	.15
278	Richard Hidalgo	.15
279	Brian Hunter	.15
280	Todd Jones	.15
281	Derrick May	.15
282	Orlando Miller	.15
283	James Mouton	.15
284	Shane Reynolds	.15
285	Greg Swindell	.15
286	Mike Blowers	.15
287	Brett Butler	.15
288	Tom Candiotti	.15
289	Roger Cedeno	.15
290	Delino DeShields	.15
291	Greg Gagne	.15
292	Karim Garcia	.15
293	Todd Hollandsworth	.15
294	Eric Karros	.15
295	Ramon Martinez	.15
296	Raul Mondesi	.15
297	Hideo Nomo	.50
298	Mike Piazza	2.00
299	Ismael Valdes	.15
300	Todd Worrell	.15
301	Moises Alou	.15
302	Shane Andrews	.15
303	Yamil Benitez	.15
304	Jeff Fassero	.15
305	Darrin Fletcher	.15
306	Cliff Floyd	.15
307	Mark Grudzielanek	.15
308	Mike Lansing	.15
309	Pedro Martinez	1.00
310	Ryan McGuire	.15
311	Carlos Perez	.15
312	Mel Rojas	.15
313	David Segui	.15
314	Rondell White	.15
315	Edgardo Alfonzo	.15
316	Rico Brogna	.15
317	Carl Everett	.15
318	John Franco	.15
319	Bernard Gilkey	.15
320	Todd Hundley	.15
321	Jason Isringhausen	.15
322	Lance Johnson	.15
323	Bobby Jones	.15
324	Jeff Kent	.15
325	Rey Ordonez	.15
326	Bill Pulsipher	.15
327	Jose Vizcaino	.15
328	Paul Wilson	.15
329	Ricky Bottalico	.15
330	Darren Daulton	.15
331	David Doster RC	.15
332	Lenny Dykstra	.15
333	Jim Eisenreich	.15
334	Sid Fernandez	.15
335	Gregg Jefferies	.15
336	Mickey Morandini	.15
337	Benito Santiago	.15
338	Curt Schilling	.40
339	Kevin Stocker	.15
340	David West	.15
341	Mark Whiten	.15
342	Todd Zeile	.15
343	Jay Bell	.15
344	John Ericks	.15
345	Carlos Garcia	.15
346	Charlie Hayes	.15
347	Jason Kendall	.15
348	Jeff King	.15
349	Mike Kingery	.15
350	Al Martin	.15
351	Orlando Merced	.15
352	Dan Miceli	.15
353	Denny Neagle	.15
354	Alan Benes	.15
355	Andy Benes	.15
356	Royce Clayton	.15
357	Dennis Eckersley	.75
358	Gary Gaetti	.15
359	Ron Gant	.15
360	Brian Jordan	.15
361	Ray Lankford	.15
362	John Mabry	.15
363	T.J. Mathews	.15
364	Mike Morgan	.15
365	Donovan Osborne	.15
366	Tom Pagnozzi	.15
367	Ozzie Smith	1.50
368	Todd Stottlemyre	.15
369	Andy Ashby	.15
370	Brad Ausmus	.15
371	Ken Caminiti	.15
372	Andujar Cedeno	.15
373	Steve Finley	.15
374	Tony Gwynn	1.50
375	Joey Hamilton	.15
376	Rickey Henderson	1.00
377	Trevor Hoffman	.15
378	Wally Joyner	.15
379	Marc Newfield	.15
380	Jody Reed	.15
381	Bob Tewksbury	.15
382	Fernando Valenzuela	.15
383	Rod Beck	.15
384	Barry Bonds	3.00
385	Mark Carreon	.15
386	Shawon Dunston	.15
387	Osvaldo Fernandez RC	.40
388	Glenallen Hill	.15
389	Stan Javier	.15
390	Mark Leiter	.15
391	Kirt Manwaring	.15
392	Robby Thompson	.15
393	William Van Landingham	.15
394	Allen Watson	.15
395	Matt Williams	.15
396	Checklist	.15
397	Checklist	.15
398	Checklist	.15
399	Checklist	.15
400	Checklist	.15

Diamond Cuts

		NM/M
Complete Set (12):		25.00
Common Player:		1.00
1	Jeff Bagwell	2.50
2	Albert Belle	1.00
3	Barry Bonds	6.00
4	Juan Gonzalez	1.25
5	Ken Griffey Jr.	4.00
6	Greg Maddux	3.00
7	Eddie Murray	2.50
8	Mike Piazza	4.00
9	Cal Ripken Jr.	6.00
10	Frank Thomas	2.50
11	Mo Vaughn	1.00
12	Matt Williams	1.00

Hot Gloves

		NM/M
Complete Set (10):		60.00
Common Player:		3.00
1	Roberto Alomar	4.00
2	Barry Bonds	15.00
3	Will Clark	3.00
4	Ken Griffey Jr.	10.00
5	Kenny Lofton	3.00
6	Greg Maddux	7.50
7	Mike Piazza	10.00
8	Cal Ripken Jr.	15.00
9	Ivan Rodriguez	6.00
10	Matt Williams	3.00

Powerline

		NM/M
Complete Set (10):		6.00
Common Player:		.25
1	Albert Belle	.25
2	Barry Bonds	2.00
3	Juan Gonzalez	.35
4	Ken Griffey Jr.	.75
5	Mark McGwire	1.00
6	Mike Piazza	.75
7	Manny Ramirez	.50
8	Sammy Sosa	.65
9	Frank Thomas	.50
10	Matt Williams	.25

1996 Flair Promotional Sheet

	NM/M
Complete Sheet:	5.00

Manny Ramirez, Cal Ripken Jr., Matt Williams, Information Card

Wave of the Future

		NM/M
Complete Set (20):		30.00
Common Player:		2.00
1	Bob Abreu	3.00
2	George Arias	2.00
3	Tony Batista	2.00
4	Alan Benes	2.00
5	Yamil Benitez	2.00
6	Steve Cox	2.00
7	David Doster	2.00
8	Jermaine Dye	2.00
9	Osvaldo Fernandez	2.00
10	Karim Garcia	3.00
11	Steve Gibralter	2.00
12	Todd Greene	2.00
13	Richard Hidalgo	2.00
14	Robin Jennings	2.00
15	Jason Kendall	2.00
16	Jose Malave	2.00
17	Wonderful Monds	2.00
18	Rey Ordonez	2.00
19	Ruben Rivera	2.00
20	Paul Wilson	2.00

1997 Flair Showcase Row 2 (Style)

		NM/M
Complete Set (180):		15.00
Common Showtime (1-60):		.15
Common Showpiece (61-120):		.25
Common Showstopper (121-180):		.20
A-Rod Glove Exchange:		125.00
Pack (5):		2.00
Wax Box (24):		35.00
1	Andruw Jones	1.25
2	Derek Jeter	3.00
3	Alex Rodriguez	2.25
4	Paul Molitor	1.25
5	Jeff Bagwell	1.25
6	Scott Rolen	1.00
7	Kenny Lofton	.15
8	Cal Ripken Jr.	3.00
9	Brady Anderson	.15
10	Chipper Jones	1.50
11	Todd Greene	.15

12	Todd Walker	.15
13	Billy Wagner	.15
14	Craig Biggio	.15
15	Kevin Orie	.15
16	Hideo Nomo	.65
17	Kevin Appier	.15
18	Bubba Trammell RC	.25
19	Juan Gonzalez	.65
20	Randy Johnson	1.25
21	Roger Clemens	1.75
22	Johnny Damon	.35
23	Ryne Sandberg	1.50
24	Ken Griffey Jr.	2.00
25	Barry Bonds	3.00
26	Nomar Garciaparra	1.50
27	Vladimir Guerrero	1.25
28	Ron Gant	.15
29	Joe Carter	.15
30	Tim Salmon	.15
31	Mike Piazza	2.00
32	Barry Larkin	.15
33	Manny Ramirez	1.25
34	Sammy Sosa	1.50
35	Frank Thomas	1.25
36	Melvin Nieves	.15
37	Tony Gwynn	1.50
38	Gary Sheffield	.35
39	Darin Erstad	.50
40	Ken Caminiti	.15
41	Jermaine Dye	.15
42	Mo Vaughn	.15
43	Raul Mondesi	.15
44	Greg Maddux	1.00
45	Chuck Knoblauch	.15
46	Andy Pettitte	.50
47	Deion Sanders	.25
48	Albert Belle	.15
49	Jamey Wright	.15
50	Rey Ordonez	.15
51	Bernie Williams	.15
52	Mark McGwire	2.25
53	Mike Mussina	.50
54	Bob Abreu	.20
55	Reggie Sanders	.15
56	Brian Jordan	.15
57	Ivan Rodriguez	1.00
58	Roberto Alomar	.30
59	Tim Naehring	.15
60	Edgar Renteria	.15
61	Dean Palmer	.25
62	Benito Santiago	.25
63	David Cone	.25
64	Carlos Delgado	.75
65	Brian Giles RC	.75
66	Alex Ochoa	.25
67	Rondell White	.25
68	Robin Ventura	.25
69	Eric Karros	.25
70	Jose Valentin	.25
71	Rafael Palmeiro	1.00
72	Chris Snopek	.25
73	David Justice	.25
74	Tom Glavine	.45
75	Rudy Pemberton	.25
76	Larry Walker	.75
77	Jim Thome	.75
78	Charles Johnson	.25
79	Dante Powell	.25
80	Derrek Lee	.75
81	Jason Kendall	.25
82	Todd Hollandsworth	.25
83	Bernard Gilkey	.25
84	Mel Rojas	.25
85	Dmitri Young	.25
86	Bret Boone	.25
87	Pat Hentgen	.25
88	Bobby Bonilla	.25
89	John Wetteland	.25
90	Todd Hundley	.25
91	Wilton Guerrero	.25
92	Geronimo Berroa	.25
93	Al Martin	.25
94	Danny Tartabull	.25
95	Brian McRae	.25
96	Steve Finley	.25
97	Todd Stottlemyre	.25
98	John Smoltz	.25
99	Matt Williams	.25
100	Eddie Murray	1.25
101	Henry Rodriguez	.25
102	Marty Cordova	.25
103	Juan Guzman	.25
104	Chili Davis	.25
105	Eric Young	.25
106	Jeff Abbott	.25
107	Shannon Stewart	.25
108	Rocky Coppinger	.25
109	Jose Canseco	.65
110	Dante Bichette	.25
111	Dwight Gooden	.25
112	Scott Brosius	.25
113	Steve Avery	.25
114	Andres Galarraga	.25
115	Sandy Alomar Jr.	.25
116	Ray Lankford	.25
117	Jorge Posada	.25
118	Ryan Klesko	.25
119	Jay Buhner	.25
120	Jose Guillen	.25
121	Paul O'Neill	.20
122	Jimmy Key	.20
123	Hal Morris	.20
124	Travis Fryman	.20
125	Jim Edmonds	.20
126	Jeff Cirillo	.20
127	Fred McGriff	.20
128	Alan Benes	.20
129	Derek Bell	.20
130	Tony Graffanino	.20
131	Shawn Green	.40
132	Denny Neagle	.20
133	Alex Fernandez	.20
134	Mickey Morandini	.20
135	Royce Clayton	.20
136	Jose Mesa	.20
137	Edgar Martinez	.20
138	Curt Schilling	.40
139	Lance Johnson	.20
140	Andy Benes	.20
141	Charles Nagy	.20
142	Mariano Rivera	.40
143	Mark Wohlers	.20
144	Ken Hill	.20
145	Jay Bell	.20
146	Bob Higginson	.20
147	Mark Grudzielanek	.20
148	Ray Durham	.20
149	John Olerud	.20
150	Joey Hamilton	.20
151	Trevor Hoffman	.20
152	Dan Wilson	.20
153	J.T. Snow	.20
154	Marquis Grissom	.20
155	Yamil Benitez	.20
156	Rusty Greer	.20
157	Darryl Kile	.20
158	Ismael Valdes	.20
159	Jeff Conine	.20
160	Darren Daulton	.20
161	Chan Ho Park	.20
162	Troy Percival	.20
163	Wade Boggs	1.50
164	Dave Nilsson	.20
165	Vinny Castilla	.20
166	Kevin Brown	.20
167	Dennis Eckersley	1.00
168	Wendell Magee Jr.	.20
169	John Jaha	.20
170	Garret Anderson	.20
171	Jason Giambi	.75
172	Mark Grace	.15
173	Tony Clark	.20
174	Moises Alou	.20
175	Brett Butler	.20
176	Cecil Fielder	.20
177	Chris Widger	.20
178	Doug Drabek	.20
179	Ellis Burks	.20
180	Shigetosi Hasegawa	.20

Row 1 (Grace)

NM/M

Complete Set (180): 50.00
Common Showstopper (1-60): .35
Stars: 1.5X
Common Showtime (#61-120): .25
Stars: 1X
Common Showpiece (#121-180): .60
Stars: 1.5X
(See 1997 Flair Showcase Row 2 for checklist and base card values.)

Row 0 (Showcase)

NM/M

Complete Set (180): 200.00
Common Showpiece (1-60): 1.50
Stars: 2X
Common Showstopper (61-120): .75
Stars: 4X
Common Showtime (121-180): .35
Stars: 3X
(See 1997 Flair Showcase Row 2 for checklist and base card values.)

Legacy Collection

NM/M

Common Player: 10.00
Stars: 25X
(See 1997 Flair Showcase Row 2 for checklist and base card values.)

Legacy Masterpiece

NM/M

Common Player: 100.00
(Star values undetermined.)

Diamond Cuts

NM/M

Complete Set (20):		55.00
Common Player:		1.50
1	Jeff Bagwell	3.00
2	Albert Belle	1.50
3	Ken Caminiti	1.50
4	Juan Gonzalez	2.00
5	Ken Griffey Jr.	4.50
6	Tony Gwynn	4.00
7	Todd Hundley	1.50
8	Andruw Jones	3.00
9	Chipper Jones	4.00
10	Greg Maddux	4.00
11	Mark McGwire	5.00
12	Mike Piazza	4.00
13	Derek Jeter	6.00
14	Manny Ramirez	3.00
15	Cal Ripken Jr.	6.00
16	Alex Rodriguez	5.00

17	Frank Thomas	3.00
18	Mo Vaughn	1.50
19	Bernie Williams	1.50
20	Matt Williams	1.50
Complete Set (15):		125.00
Common Player:		2.50
1	Roberto Alomar	3.00
2	Barry Bonds	20.00
3	Juan Gonzalez	6.00
4	Ken Griffey Jr.	15.00
5	Marquis Grissom	2.50
6	Derek Jeter	20.00
7	Chipper Jones	12.00
8	Barry Larkin	2.50
9	Kenny Lofton	2.50
10	Greg Maddux	12.00
11	Mike Piazza	15.00
12	Cal Ripken Jr.	20.00
13	Alex Rodriguez	17.50
14	Ivan Rodriguez	7.50
15	Frank Thomas	4.00

1997 Flair Showcase Promo Strip

NM/M

Complete Strip (3): 5.00

Wave of the Future

NM/M

Complete Set (27):		10.00
Common Player:		.25
1	Todd Greene	.25
2	Andruw Jones	1.50
3	Randall Simon	.25
4	Wady Almonte	.25
5	Pat Cline	.25
6	Jeff Abbott	.25
7	Justin Towle	.25
8	Richie Sexson	.25
9	Bubba Trammell	.25
10	Bob Abreu	.35
11	David Arias (Last name actually Ortiz.)	9.00
12	Todd Walker	.25
13	Orlando Cabrera	.25
14	Vladimir Guerrero	1.50
15	Ricky Ledee	.25
16	Jorge Posada	.25
17	Ruben Rivera	.25
18	Scott Spiezio	.25
19	Scott Rolen	1.00
20	Emil Brown	.25
21	Jose Guillen	.25
22	T.J. Staton	.25
23	Elieser Marrero	.25
24	Fernando Tatis	.25
25	Ryan Jones	.25
WF1	Hideki Irabu	.25
WF2	Jose Cruz Jr.	.25

1998 Flair Showcase Row 3

NM/M

Complete Set (120):		20.00
Common Player (1-30):		.25
Common Player (31-60):		.25
Common Player (61-90):		.35
Common Player (91-120):		.45
Pack (5):		2.50
Wax Box (24):		45.00
1	Ken Griffey Jr.	2.00
2	Travis Lee	.25
3	Frank Thomas	1.25
4	Ben Grieve	.25
5	Nomar Garciaparra	1.50
6	Jose Cruz Jr.	.25
7	Alex Rodriguez	2.50
8	Cal Ripken Jr.	3.00
9	Mark McGwire	2.50
10	Chipper Jones	1.50
11	Paul Konerko	.40
12	Todd Helton	1.00

13	Greg Maddux	1.50
14	Derek Jeter	3.00
15	Jaret Wright	.25
16	Livan Hernandez	.25
17	Mike Piazza	2.00
18	Juan Encarnacion	.25
19	Tony Gwynn	1.50
20	Scott Rolen	1.00
21	Roger Clemens	1.75
22	Tony Clark	.25
23	Albert Belle	.25
24	Mo Vaughn	.25
25	Andruw Jones	1.25
26	Jason Dickson	.25
27	Fernando Tatis	.25
28	Ivan Rodriguez	.75
29	Ricky Ledee	.25
30	Darin Erstad	.50
31	Brian Rose	.25
32	Magglio Ordonez RC	3.00
33	Larry Walker	.25
34	Bobby Higginson	.25
35	Chili Davis	.25
36	Barry Bonds	3.00
37	Vladimir Guerrero	1.25
38	Jeff Bagwell	1.25
39	Kenny Lofton	.25
40	Ryan Klesko	.25
41	Mike Cameron	.25
42	Charles Johnson	.25
43	Andy Pettitte	.40
44	Juan Gonzalez	1.25
45	Tim Salmon	.25
46	Hideki Irabu	.25
47	Paul Molitor	1.25
48	Edgar Renteria	.25
49	Manny Ramirez	1.25
50	Jim Edmonds	.25
51	Bernie Williams	.25
52	Roberto Alomar	.40
53	David Justice	.25
54	Rey Ordonez	.25
55	Ken Caminiti	.25
56	Jose Guillen	.25
57	Randy Johnson	1.25
58	Brady Anderson	.25
59	Hideo Nomo	.50
60	Tino Martinez	.25
61	John Smoltz	.35
62	Joe Carter	.35
63	Matt Williams	.35
64	Robin Ventura	.35
65	Barry Larkin	.35
66	Dante Bichette	.35
67	Travis Fryman	.35
68	Gary Sheffield	.60
69	Eric Karros	.35
70	Matt Stairs	.35
71	Al Martin	.35
72	Jay Buhner	.35
73	Ray Lankford	.35
74	Carlos Delgado	.65
75	Edgardo Alfonzo	.35
76	Rondell White	.35
77	Chuck Knoblauch	.35
78	Raul Mondesi	.35
79	Johnny Damon	.60
80	Matt Morris	.35
81	Tom Glavine	.60
82	Kevin Brown	.35
83	Garret Anderson	.35
84	Mike Mussina	.40
85	Pedro Martinez	1.25
86	Craig Biggio	.35
87	Darryl Kile	.35
88	Rafael Palmeiro	.75
89	Jim Thome	.60
90	Andres Galarraga	.35
91	Sammy Sosa	1.50
92	Willie Greene	.45
93	Vinny Castilla	.45
94	Justin Thompson	.45
95	Jeff King	.45
96	Jeff Cirillo	.45
97	Mark Grudzielanek	.45
98	Brad Radke	.45
99	John Olerud	.65
100	Curt Schilling	.65
101	Steve Finley	.45
102	J.T. Snow	.45
103	Edgar Martinez	.45

104	Wilson Alvarez	.45
105	Rusty Greer	.45
106	Pat Hentgen	.45
107	David Cone	.45
108	Fred McGriff	.45
109	Jason Giambi	.75
110	Tony Womack	.45
111	Bernard Gilkey	.45
112	Alan Benes	.45
113	Mark Grace	.45
114	Reggie Sanders	.45
115	Moises Alou	.45
116	John Jaha	.45
117	Henry Rodriguez	.45
118	Dean Palmer	.45
119	Mike Lieberthal	.45
120	Shawn Estes	.45

Row 2

	NM/M
Complete Set (120):	40.00
Common Player:	.50
Stars:	1.5-2X

Row 1

(See 1998 Flair Showcase Row 3 for checklist and base card values.)

Complete Set (1-120):	100.00
Commons (1-30):	1.00
Stars:	2X
Commons (31-60):	1.25
Stars:	3X
Commons (61-90):	.35
Stars:	1X
Commons (91-120):	.75
Stars:	1.5X

Row 0

(See 1998 Flair Showcase Row 3 for checklist and base cards values.)

Complete Set (120):	350.00
Common Player (1-30):	5.00
Stars:	10X
Common Player (31-60):	3.00
Stars:	8X
Common Player (61-90):	2.00
Stars:	6X
Common Player (91-120):	.75
Stars:	4X

(See 1998 Flair Showcase Row 3 for checklist and base card values.)

Legacy Masterpiece

	NM/M
Common Player:	50.00

(Values Undetermined)

Legacy Collection

	NM/M
Common Player:	7.50
Stars:	25X

(See 1998 Flair Showcase Row 3 for checklist and base card values.)

Perfect 10

	NM/M
Complete Set (10):	1,600
Common Player:	100.00
1	Ken Griffey Jr.	200.00
2	Cal Ripken Jr.	300.00
3	Frank Thomas	125.00
4	Mike Piazza	200.00
5	Greg Maddux	150.00
6	Nomar Garciaparra	150.00
7	Mark McGwire	250.00
8	Scott Rolen	100.00
9	Alex Rodriguez	250.00
10	Roger Clemens	175.00

1998 Flair Showcase Promo Strip

	NM/M
Complete Promo Strip:	5.00

Wave of the Future

	NM/M
Complete Set (12):	10.00
Common Player:	.50
WF1	Travis Lee	.50
WF2	Todd Helton	5.00
WF3	Ben Grieve	.50
WF4	Juan Encarnacion	.50
WF5	Brad Fullmer	.50
WF6	Ruben Rivera	.50
WF7	Paul Konerko	.75
WF8	Derek Lee	1.50
WF9	Mike Lowell	.50
WF10	Magglio Ordonez	2.00
WF11	Rich Butler	.50
WF12	Eli Marrero	.50

1999 Flair Showcase Row 3 (Power)

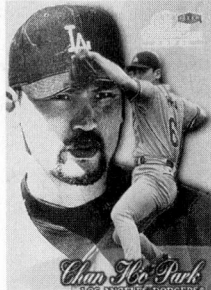

	NM/M
Complete Set (144):	25.00
Common Player:	.25
Pack (5):	3.00
Wax Box (24):	45.00
1	Mark McGwire	2.50
2	Sammy Sosa	1.50
3	Ken Griffey Jr.	2.00
4	Chipper Jones	1.50
5	Ben Grieve	.25
6	J.D. Drew	.75
7	Jeff Bagwell	1.00
8	Cal Ripken Jr.	3.00
9	Tony Gwynn	1.50
10	Nomar Garciaparra	1.50
11	Travis Lee	.35
12	Troy Glaus	.75
13	Mike Piazza	2.00
14	Alex Rodriguez	2.50
15	Kevin Brown	.25
16	Darin Erstad	.50
17	Scott Rolen	.50
18	Micah Bowie RC	.25
19	Juan Gonzalez	.50
20	Kerry Wood	.50
21	Roger Clemens	1.75
22	Derek Jeter	3.00
23	Pat Burrell RC	3.00
24	Tim Salmon	.25
25	Barry Bonds	3.00
26	Roosevelt Brown RC	.25
27	Vladimir Guerrero	1.00
28	Randy Johnson	1.00
29	Mo Vaughn	.50
30	Fernando Seguignol	.25
31	Greg Maddux	1.50
32	Tony Clark	.25
33	Eric Chavez	.40
34	Kris Benson	.25
35	Frank Thomas	1.00
36	Mario Encarnacion	.25
37	Gabe Kapler	.25
38	Jeremy Giambi	.25
39	Peter Tucci RC	.25
40	Manny Ramirez	1.00
41	Albert Belle	.25
42	Warren Morris	.25
43	Michael Barrett	.25
44	Andruw Jones	1.00
45	Carlos Delgado	.60
46	Jaret Wright	.25
47	Juan Encarnacion	.25
48	Scott Hunter	.25
49	Tino Martinez	.25
50	Craig Biggio	.25
51	Jim Thome	.60
52	Vinny Castilla	.25
53	Tom Glavine	.40
54	Bob Higginson	.25
55	Moises Alou	.25
56	Robin Ventura	.25
57	Bernie Williams	.25
58	Pedro J. Martinez	1.00
59	Greg Vaughn	.25
60	Ray Lankford	.25
61	Jose Canseco	.40
62	Ivan Rodriguez	.75
63	Shawn Green	.40
64	Rafael Palmeiro	.75
65	Ellis Burks	.25
66	Jason Kendall	.25
67	David Wells	.25
68	Rondell White	.25
69	Gary Sheffield	.40
70	Ken Caminiti	.25
71	Cliff Floyd	.25
72	Larry Walker	.25
73	Bartolo Colon	.25
74	Barry Larkin	.25
75	Calvin Pickering	.25
76	Jim Edmonds	.25
77	Henry Rodriguez	.25
78	Roberto Alomar	.40
79	Andres Galarraga	.25
80	Richie Sexson	.25

81	Todd Helton	.75
82	Damion Easley	.25
83	Livan Hernandez	.25
84	Carlos Beltran	.60
85	Todd Hundley	.25
86	Todd Walker	.25
87	Scott Brosius	.25
88	Bob Abreu	.25
89	Corey Koskie	.25
90	Ruben Rivera	.25
91	Edgar Renteria	.25
92	Quinton McCracken	.25
93	Bernard Gilkey	.25
94	Shannon Stewart	.25
95	Dustin Hermanson	.25
96	Mike Caruso	.25
97	Alex Gonzalez	.25
98	Raul Mondesi	.25
99	David Cone	.25
100	Curt Schilling	.40
101	Brian Giles	.25
102	Edgar Martinez	.25
103	Rolando Arrojo	.25
104	Derek Bell	.25
105	Denny Neagle	.25
106	Marquis Grissom	.25
107	Bret Boone	.25
108	Mike Mussina	.50
109	John Smoltz	.25
110	Brett Tomko	.25
111	David Justice	.25
112	Andy Pettitte	.40
113	Eric Karros	.25
114	Dante Bichette	.25
115	Jeromy Burnitz	.25
116	Paul Konerko	.40
117	Steve Finley	.25
118	Ricky Ledee	.25
119	Edgardo Alfonzo	.25
120	Dean Palmer	.25
121	Rusty Greer	.25
122	Luis Gonzalez	.25
123	Randy Winn	.25
124	Jeff Kent	.25
125	Doug Glanville	.25
126	Justin Thompson	.25
127	Bret Saberhagen	.25
128	Wade Boggs	1.50
129	Al Leiter	.25
130	Paul O'Neill	.25
131	Chan Ho Park	.25
132	Johnny Damon	.60
133	Darryl Kile	.25
134	Reggie Sanders	.25
135	Kevin Millwood	.25
136	Charles Johnson	.25
137	Ray Durham	.25
138	Rico Brogna	.25
139	Matt Williams	.25
140	Sandy Alomar	.25
141	Jeff Cirillo	.25
142	Devon White	.25
143	Andy Benes	.25
144	Mike Stanley	.25
	Checklist Card	.05

Row 2 (Passion)

	NM/M
Complete Set (144):	65.00
Common Player:	.25
Showdown (1-48):	2X
Showpiece (49-96):	1X
Showtime (97-144):	1X

(See 1999 Flair Showcase Row 3 for checklist and base card values.)

Row 1 (Showcase)

	NM/M
Complete Set (144):	300.00

Common Showpiece (1-48):	2.00
Showpiece Stars:	5X
Common Showtime (49-96):	1.00
Showtime Stars:	3X
Common Showdown (97-144):	.50
Showdown Stars:	2X

(See 1999 Flair Showcase Row 1 for checklist and base card values.)

Legacy Masterpiece

	NM/M
Common Legacy:	6.00
Legacy Stars:	20X
Common Masterpiece:	50.00

(See 1999 Flair Showcase for checklist.)

Measure of Greatness

	NM/M
Complete Set (15):	100.00
Common Player:	3.00

Production 500 Sets

1	Roger Clemens	7.50
2	Nomar Garciaparra	6.50
3	Juan Gonzalez	3.00
4	Ken Griffey Jr.	9.00
5	Vladimir Guerrero	5.00
6	Tony Gwynn	6.50
7	Derek Jeter	15.00
8	Chipper Jones	8.00
9	Mark McGwire	12.50
10	Mike Piazza	9.00
11	Manny Ramirez	5.00
12	Cal Ripken Jr.	15.00
13	Alex Rodriguez	12.50
14	Sammy Sosa	6.50
15	Frank Thomas	5.00

Wave of the Future

	NM/M
Complete Set (15):	40.00
Common Player:	1.50

Production 1,000 Sets

1	Kerry Wood	4.00
2	Ben Grieve	1.50
3	J.D. Drew	4.00
4	Juan Encarnacion	1.50
5	Travis Lee	2.00
6	Todd Helton	7.50
7	Troy Glaus	7.50
8	Ricky Ledee	1.50
9	Eric Chavez	2.00
10	Ben Davis	1.50
11	George Lombard	1.50
12	Jeremy Giambi	1.50
13	Roosevelt Brown	1.50
14	Pat Burrell	6.00
15	Preston Wilson	1.50

2003 Flair Greats of the Game

	NM/M
Complete Set (95):	35.00
Common Player:	.40
Pack (5):	6.00
Box (20):	100.00

1	Ozzie Smith	1.00
2	Red Schoendienst	.40
3	Harmon Killebrew	1.50
4	Ralph Kiner	.40
5	Johnny Bench	2.00
6	Al Kaline	1.00
7	Bobby Doerr	.40
8	Cal Ripken Jr.	4.00
9	Enos Slaughter	.40
10	Phil Rizzuto	1.00
11	Luis Aparicio	.40
12	Pee Wee Reese	.40
13	Richie Ashburn	.40
14	Ernie Banks	2.00
15	Earl Weaver	.40
16	Whitey Ford	1.50
17	Brooks Robinson	1.00
18	Lou Boudreau	.40
19	Robin Yount	1.00
20	Mike Schmidt	2.50
21	Bob Lemon	.40
22	Stan Musial	2.50
23	Joe Morgan	.60
24	Early Wynn	.40
25	Willie Stargell	.75
26	Yogi Berra	2.00
27	Juan Marichal	.40
28	Rick Ferrell	.40
29	Rod Carew	.75
30	Jim Bunning	.40
31	Ferguson Jenkins	.40
32	Steve Carlton	.75
33	Larry Doby	.40
34	Nolan Ryan	4.00
35	Phil Niekro	.40
36	Billy Williams	.40
37	Hal Newhouser	.40
38	Bob Feller	.75
39	Lou Brock	.75
40	Monte Irvin	.75
41	Eddie Mathews	1.00
42	Rollie Fingers	.40
43	Gaylord Perry	.40
44	Reggie Jackson	1.50
45	Bob Gibson	1.00
46	Robin Roberts	.40
47	Tom Seaver	1.00
48	Willie McCovey	.40
49	Hoyt Wilhelm	.40
50	George Kell	.40
51	Warren Spahn	1.00
52	Jim "Catfish" Hunter	.40
53	Dom DiMaggio	.40
54	Joe Medwick	.40
55	Johnny Pesky	.40
56	Steve Garvey	.40
57	Harry Heilmann	.40
58	Dave Winfield	.75
59	Andre Dawson	.40
60	Jimmie Foxx	1.00
61	Buddy Bell	.40
62	Gabby Hartnett	.40
63	Babe Ruth	4.00
64	Dizzy Dean	1.50
65	Hank Greenberg	.40
66	Don Drysdale	.75
67	Gary Carter	.40
68	Wade Boggs	.75
69	Tony Perez	.40
70	Mickey Cochrane	.75
71	Bill Dickey	.40
72	George Brett	3.00
73	Honus Wagner	3.00
74	George Sisler	1.00
75	Walter Johnson	2.00
76	Ron Santo	.40
77	Roy Campanella	1.00
78	Roger Maris	2.50
79	Kirby Puckett	2.50
80	Alan Trammell	.40
81	Don Mattingly	4.00
82	Ty Cobb	3.00
83	Lou Gehrig	3.00
84	Jackie Robinson	3.00
85	Billy Martin	.75
86	Paul Molitor	.75
87	Duke Snider	1.00
88	Thurman Munson	1.50
89	Luke Appling	.40
90	Ernie Lombardi	.40
91	Rube Waddell	.40
92	Travis Jackson	.40
93	Joe Sewell	.40
94	King Kelly	.40
95	Heinie Manush	.40
	Common Home Team (96-133):	2.00
96HT	Bobby Doerr	2.00
97HT	Johnny Pesky	2.00
98HT	Wade Boggs	3.00
99HT	Tony Conigliaro	2.00
100HT	Carlton Fisk	3.00
101HT	Rico Petrocelli	2.00
102HT	Jim Rice	2.00
103HT	Al Lopez	2.00
104HT	Pee Wee Reese	2.00
105HT	Tommy Lasorda	2.00
106HT	Gil Hodges	3.00
107HT	Jackie Robinson	6.00
108HT	Duke Snider	4.00
109HT	Don Drysdale	4.00
110HT	Steve Garvey	2.00
111HT	Hoyt Wilhelm	2.00
112HT	Juan Marichal	3.00
113HT	Monte Irvin	3.00
114HT	Willie McCovey	3.00
115HT	Travis Jackson	2.00
116HT	Bobby Bonds	2.00
117HT	Orlando Cepeda	2.00
118HT	Whitey Ford	4.00
119HT	Phil Rizzuto	4.00
120HT	Reggie Jackson	4.00
121HT	Yogi Berra	5.00
122HT	Roger Maris	6.00
123HT	Don Mattingly	10.00
124HT	Babe Ruth	10.00
125HT	Dave Winfield	3.00
126HT	Bob Gibson	4.00
127HT	Enos Slaughter	2.00
128HT	Joe Medwick	2.00
129HT	Lou Brock	3.00
130HT	Ozzie Smith	5.00
131HT	Stan Musial	6.00
132HT	Steve Carlton	3.00
133HT	Dizzy Dean	4.00

Ballpark Heroes

	NM/M
Complete Set (9):	25.00
Common Player:	.40
Inserted 1:10	

1BH	Nolan Ryan	5.00
2BH	Babe Ruth	5.00
3BH	Honus Wagner	3.00
4BH	Ty Cobb	4.00
5BH	Ernie Banks	3.00
6BH	Mike Schmidt	3.00
7BH	Duke Snider	2.00
8BH	Cal Ripken Jr.	5.00
9BH	Stan Musial	3.00

Classic Numbers

	NM/M
Complete Set (13):	50.00
Common Player:	3.00
Inserted 1:20	

1CN	Jackie Robinson	6.00
2CN	Willie McCovey	3.00
3CN	Brooks Robinson	3.00
4CN	Reggie Jackson	6.00
5CN	Ozzie Smith	6.00
6CN	Johnny Bench	6.00
7CN	Yogi Berra	6.00
8CN	Cal Ripken Jr.	10.00
9CN	George Brett	8.00
10CN	Thurman Munson	5.00
11CN	Joe Morgan	3.00
12CN	Nolan Ryan	10.00
13CN	Steve Carlton	3.00

Classic Numbers Game-Used

	NM/M
Common Player:	10.00
Inserted 1:24	
Willie McCovey	12.00
George Brett	20.00
Joe Morgan	10.00
Yogi Berra	20.00
Cal Ripken Jr.	25.00
Nolan Ryan	35.00
Ozzie Smith	15.00
Johnny Bench	15.00
Ryne Sandberg	25.00
Thurman Munson	20.00
Steve Carlton	10.00

Classic Numbers Dual-Side

	NM/M
Common Card:	25.00
Production 250 Sets	
Yogi Berra,	
Thurman Munson	45.00
Nolan Ryan, Steve Carlton	65.00
Johnny Bench,	
Thurman Munson	35.00
Cal Ripken Jr., Ozzie Smith	60.00
Joe Morgan,	
Ryne Sandberg	35.00
Willie McCovey,	
Johnny Bench	25.00
Yogi Berra, Cal Ripken Jr.	50.00
George Brett, Nolan Ryan	75.00

HOF Postmark

	NM/M
Production 2,002	
Ozzie Smith	20.00
Ozzie Smith/Auto./202	100.00

Bat Rack Triple

	NM/M
Common Card:	15.00
Production 300	
Eddie Murray, Cal Ripken Jr.,	
Brooks Robinson	75.00
Ryne Sandberg, Ron Santo,	
Billy Williams	45.00
Johnny Bench, Joe Morgan,	
Tony Perez	35.00
Eddie Mathews, Paul Molitor,	
Robin Yount	40.00
Tommie Agee, Jerry Grote,	
Bud Harrelson	15.00
Reggie Jackson, Don Mattingly,	
Dave Winfield	45.00
Dave Parker, Willie Stargell	20.00

Bat Rack Quad

	NM/M
Common Card:	50.00
Numbered to 150.	
Don Mattingly, Joe Morgan,	
Cal Ripken Jr.,	
Brooks Robinson	90.00
Ryne Sandberg, Ron Santo,	
Billy Williams,	
Andre Dawson	60.00
Dave Winfield, Cal Ripken Jr.,	
Paul Molitor,	
Robin Yount	80.00
Eddie Murray, Eddie Mathews,	
Reggie Jackson,	
Willie McCovey	50.00

Cut of History

	NM/M
Common Player:	5.00

Inserted 1:10

Paul O'Neill	5.00
Dennis Eckersley	8.00
Jim Palmer	6.00
Graig Nettles	8.00
Frank Baker	30.00
Wade Boggs	8.00
Roger Maris	60.00
Jim "Catfish" Hunter	8.00
Alan Trammell	12.00
Eddie Murray	20.00
Steve Carlton	10.00
Tom Seaver	8.00
Gary Carter	8.00
Phil Niekro	6.00
Luis Aparicio	8.00
Reggie Jackson	12.00
Fergie Jenkins	8.00
Kirby Puckett	15.00
Billy Martin	15.00
Joe Medwick	25.00
Buddy Bell	5.00
Early Wynn	10.00
Cal Ripken Jr.	25.00
Hoyt Wilhelm	8.00
Willie McCovey	10.00

Cut of History Autograph

	NM/M
Common Player:	
Alan Trammell/211	25.00
Steve Carlton/506	30.00
Cal Ripken Jr/155	150.00
Johnny Bench/161	50.00

Greats of the Grain

	NM/M
Production 50 Sets	
1GOG Ty Cobb	100.00
2GOG Mike Schmidt	50.00
3GOG Babe Ruth	140.00
4GOG Lou Gehrig	80.00
5GOG George Brett	160.00
6GOG Stan Musial	75.00
7GOG Don Mattingly	110.00
8GOG Cal Ripken Jr.	100.00
9GOG Eddie Mathews	75.00

Home Team Cut

	NM/M
Common Player:	8.00
Patch:	2-5X
Production 25 Sets	
Wade Boggs	15.00
Carlton Fisk	20.00
Jim Rice	15.00
Pee Wee Reese	15.00
Duke Snider	20.00
Steve Garvey	10.00
Tommy Lasorda	15.00
Juan Marichal	10.00
Bobby Bonds	8.00
Willie McCovey	10.00
Billy Martin	15.00
Roger Maris	65.00
Reggie Jackson	15.00
Dave Winfield	12.00
Red Schoendienst	8.00
Ozzie Smith	35.00
Joe Medwick	25.00

Sweet Swatch Jersey

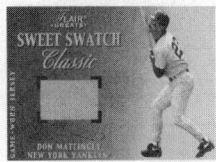

	NM/M
Common Player:	15.00
Jerry Coleman/528	15.00
Ryne Sandberg/374	25.00
Johnny Bench/410	20.00
Paul Molitor/592	15.00
Cal Ripken Jr/557	45.00
Gil Hodges/545	20.00
Carlton Fisk/1,200	15.00
Nolan Ryan/590	40.00
Tom Seaver/385	20.00
Don Mattingly/880	35.00
Jose Canseco/1,329	15.00
George Brett/384	30.00
Jim Palmer/335	15.00
Kirby Puckett/445	20.00
Juan Marichal/385	15.00
Robin Yount/340	25.00
Andre Dawson/335	15.00

Sweet Swatch Bat

	NM/M
Common Player:	15.00
Cal Ripken Jr./305	40.00
George Brett/320	30.00
Johnny Bench/175	20.00
Reggie Jackson/155	20.00
Don Mattingly/340	40.00
Willie McCovey/155	15.00
Jose Canseco/175	25.00

Kirby Puckett/251	30.00
Orlando Cepeda/165	15.00
Eddie Mathews/185	40.00
Pee Wee Reese/165	30.00
Andre Dawson/310	15.00

Sweet Swatch Jersey Auto.

	NM/M
Common Autograph:	
Cal Ripken Jr/40	240.00
Johnny Bench/40	130.00
Alan Trammell/40	75.00

2003 Flair

	NM/M
Complete Set (125):	
Common Player:	.25
Common SP (91-125):	4.00
Production 500	
Pack (5):	3.50
Box (20):	50.00
1 Hideo Nomo	.60
2 Derek Jeter	3.00
3 Junior Spivey	.25
4 Rich Aurilia	.25
5 Luis Gonzalez	.35
6 Sean Burroughs	.25
7 Pedro J. Martinez	1.00
8 Randy Winn	.25
9 Carlos Delgado	.50
10 Pat Burrell	.50
11 Barry Larkin	.25
12 Roberto Alomar	.40
13 Tony Batista	.25
14 Barry Bonds	3.00
15 Craig Biggio	.25
16 Ivan Rodriguez	.65
17 Javier Vazquez	.25
18 Joe Borchard	.25
19 Josh Phelps	.25
20 Omar Vizquel	.25
21 Tom Glavine	.40
22 Darin Erstad	.50
23 Hee Seop Choi	.25
24 Roger Clemens	1.75
25 Michael Cuddyer	.25
26 Mike Sweeney	.25
27 Phil Nevin	.25
28 Torii Hunter	.25
29 Vladimir Guerrero	1.00
30 Ellis Burks	.25
31 Jimmy Rollins	.50
32 Ken Griffey Jr.	2.00
33 Magglio Ordonez	.40
34 Mark Prior	1.00
35 Mike Lieberthal	.25
36 Jorge Posada	.30
37 Rodrigo Lopez	.25
38 Todd Helton	1.00
39 Adam Kennedy	.25
40 Curt Schilling	.25
41 Jim Thome	.25
42 Josh Beckett	.25
43 Carlos Pena	.25
44 Jason Kendall	.25
45 Sammy Sosa	2.00
46 Scott Rolen	.75
47 Alex Rodriguez	2.50
48 Aubrey Huff	.25
49 Bobby Abreu	.25
50 Jeff Kent	.25
51 Joe Randa	.25
52 Lance Berkman	.25
53 Orlando Cabrera	.25
54 Richie Sexson	.25
55 Albert Pujols	2.00
56 Alfonso Soriano	.50
57 Greg Maddux	1.50
58 Jason Giambi	.75
59 Jeff Bagwell	1.00
60 Kerry Wood	.50
61 Manny Ramirez	1.00
62 Eric Chavez	.40
63 Preston Wilson	.25
64 Shawn Green	.50
65 Shea Hillenbrand	.25
66 Austin Kearns	.75
67 Cliff Floyd	.25
68 Edgardo Alfonzo	.25
69 J.D. Drew	.40
70 Larry Walker	.25

---

71 Mike Piazza	2.00
72 Andruw Jones	.75
73 Ben Grieve	.25
74 Eric Hinske	.25
75 Geoff Jenkins	.25
76 Kazuhiro Sasaki	.25
77 Matt Morris	.25
78 Miguel Tejada	.40
79 Aramis Ramirez	.25
80 Troy Glaus	1.00
81 Ichiro Suzuki	2.00
82 Mark Teixeira	.50
83 Nomar Garciaparra	2.00
84 Chipper Jones	1.50
85 Frank Thomas	1.00
86 Paul LoDuca	.25
87 Bernie Williams	.35
88 Adam Dunn	.75
89 Randy Johnson	1.00
90 Barry Zito	.40
91 Lew Ford RC	8.00
92 Joe Valentine RC	3.00
93 Jhonny Peralta	4.00
94 Hideki Matsui RC	20.00
95 Francisco Rosario RC	3.00
96 Adam LaRoche	4.00
97 Josh Hall RC	6.00
98 Chien-Ming Wang RC	25.00
99 Josh Willingham RC	6.00
100 Guillermo Quiroz RC	6.00
101 Termel Sledge RC	3.00
102 Prentice Redman RC	6.00
103 Matt Bruback RC	6.00
104 Alejandro Machado RC	3.00
105 Shane Victorino RC	3.00
106 Chris Waters RC	3.00
107 Jose Contreras RC	8.00
108 Pete LaForest RC	3.00
109 Nook Logan RC	3.00
110 Hector Luna RC	8.00
111 Daniel Cabrera RC	6.00
112 Matt Kata RC	6.00
113 Rontrez Johnson RC	6.00
114 Josh Stewart RC	8.00
115 Michael Hessman RC	3.00
116 Felix Sanchez RC	3.00
117 Michel Hernandez RC	3.00
118 Arnaldo Munoz RC	3.00
119 Ian Ferguson RC	3.00
120 Clint Barmes RC	6.00
121 Brian Stokes RC	3.00
122 Craig Brazell RC	6.00
123 John Webb	3.00
124 Tim Olson RC	6.00
125 Jeremy Bonderman	10.00

Row 1

Stars (1-90):	5-10X
Rookies (91-125):	.75-1.5X
Production 150 Sets	
Row 2:	No Pricing
Production 25 Sets	

Diamond Cuts

	NM/M
Common Player:	4.00
Inserted 1:10	
Golds:	1-2X
Production 100 Sets	
1DC Alex Rodriguez	12.00
2DC Roberto Alomar	4.00
3DC Scott Rolen	5.00
4DC Alfonso Soriano	6.00
5DC Chipper Jones	7.50
6DC Pat Burrell	5.00
7DC Derek Jeter	15.00
8DC Mike Piazza	10.00
9DC J.D. Drew	4.00
10DC Vladimir Guerrero	6.00
11DC Greg Maddux	7.50
12DC Barry Zito	4.00
13DC Troy Glaus	5.00
14DC Roy Oswalt	4.00
15DC Roger Clemens	9.00

Hot Numbers

	NM/M
Common Player:	15.00
Production 100 Sets	
1HN Alex Rodriguez	35.00
2HN Roberto Alomar	20.00
3HN Scott Rolen	30.00
4HN Alfonso Soriano	30.00
5HN Chipper Jones	25.00
6HN Pat Burrell	25.00
7HN Derek Jeter	40.00
8HN Mike Piazza	30.00
9HN J.D. Drew	15.00
10HN Vladimir Guerrero	20.00
11HN Greg Maddux	30.00
12HN Barry Zito	15.00
13HN Troy Glaus	15.00

14HN	Roy Oswalt	15.00
15HN	Roger Clemens	

Hot Numbers Dual

No Pricing
Production 25 Sets

Power Tools

		NM/M
Common Player:		5.00
Production 500 Sets		
Golds:		1-1.5X
Production 100 Sets		
1PT	Nomar Garciaparra	15.00
2PT	Derek Jeter	25.00
3PT	Sammy Sosa	12.00
4PT	Miguel Tejada	5.00
5PT	Austin Kearns	10.00
6PT	Jason Giambi	8.00
7PT	Adam Dunn	8.00
8PT	Jim Thome	8.00
9PT	Lance Berkman	6.00
10PT	Alfonso Soriano	15.00
12PT	Alex Rodriguez	15.00
13PT	Mike Piazza	10.00
14PT	Bernie Williams	8.00
15PT	Jeff Bagwell	8.00
16PT	Andruw Jones	8.00
17PT	Scott Rolen	12.00
19PT	Juan Gonzalez	6.00

Power Tools - Dual

		NM/M
Common Duo:		
Production 200 Sets		
1PTD	Nomar Garciaparra, Derek Jeter	40.00
2PTD	Pat Burrell, Jim Thome	
3PTD	Adam Dunn, Austin Kearns	25.00
4PTD	Jim Thome, Sammy Sosa	15.00
5PTD	Alex Rodriguez, Nomar Garciaparra	20.00
6PTD	Jason Giambi, Bernie Williams	15.00
7PTD	Derek Jeter, Alfonso Soriano	25.00
8PTD	Lance Berkman, Jeff Bagwell	10.00
9PTD	Miguel Tejada, Alex Rodriguez	20.00
10PTD	Jason Giambi, Mike Piazza	20.00

Sweet Swatch

	NM/M
Common Player:	5.00
Production 250 Sets	
Derek Jeter	20.00
Sammy Sosa	15.00
Hideo Nomo	20.00
Vladimir Guerrero	6.00
Jason Giambi	8.00
Nomar Garciaparra	15.00
Randy Johnson	12.00
Miguel Tejada	5.00
Pedro J. Martinez	10.00
Adam Dunn	8.00
Roger Clemens	15.00
Mark Prior	10.00
Chipper Jones	10.00
Alex Rodriguez	15.00
Bernie Williams	6.00
Lance Berkman	6.00
Kazuhiro Sasaki	6.00
Alfonso Soriano	12.00

Sweet Swatch Patch

	NM/M
Common Player:	15.00
Production 50 Sets	
Sammy Sosa	50.00
Hideo Nomo	50.00
Jason Giambi	20.00
Nomar Garciaparra	45.00
Randy Johnson	40.00
Miguel Tejada	15.00
Pedro J. Martinez	40.00
Adam Dunn	35.00
Roger Clemens	50.00

	Mark Prior	25.00
	Alex Rodriguez	45.00
	Bernie Williams	20.00
	Kazuhiro Sasaki	30.00
	Alfonso Soriano	35.00

Sweet Swatch Oversized

	NM/M
Common Player:	6.00
1:Hobby Box	
Masterpiece One-of-One's exist.	
Derek Jeter/150	20.00
Sammy Sosa/279	15.00
Hideo Nomo/970	12.00
Jason Giambi/350	15.00
Nomar Garciaparra/727	15.00
Randy Johnson/274	15.00
Miguel Tejada/518	6.00
Pedro Martinez/1,480	10.00
Adam Dunn/1,090	8.00
Roger Clemens/97	25.00
Mark Prior/1,195	10.00
Chipper Jones/80	15.00
Alex Rodriguez/150	15.00
Bernie Williams/1,420	8.00
Lance Berkman/1,465	6.00
Kazuhiro Sasaki/505	10.00

Sweet Swatch Patch Oversized

	NM/M
Common Player:	15.00
Derek Jeter/35	75.00
Sammy Sosa/190	40.00
Hideo Nomo/114	50.00
Vladimir Guerrero/290	35.00
Nomar Garciaparra/124	40.00
Miguel Tejada/183	15.00
Pedro Martinez/185	40.00
Adam Dunn/130	30.00
Mark Prior/290	25.00
Chipper Jones/284	25.00
Alex Rodriguez/298	40.00
Bernie Williams/123	25.00
Lance Berkman/287	25.00
Kazuhiro Sasaki/90	40.00

Sweet Swatch Dual Oversized

No Pricing
Production 25 Sets

Sweet Swatch Autograph Oversized

	NM/M
Common Player:	
Golds:	1.5-2X
Production 25, Jeter 50	
Masterpiece One-of-Ones exist.	
Derek Jeter/312	90.00
Randy Johnson/218	60.00
Adam Dunn/218	30.00
Jeff Bagwell/218	40.00

Wave of the Future

		NM/M
Common Player:		3.00
Production 500 Sets		
Golds:		1-2X
Production 100 Sets		
1WOF	Francisco Rodriguez	3.00
2WOF	Carl Crawford	4.00
3WOF	Austin Kearns	10.00
4WOF	Hank Blalock	8.00
5WOF	Marlon Byrd	3.00
6WOF	Michael Restovich	3.00
7WOF	Joe Borchard	3.00
8WOF	Sean Burroughs	4.00
9WOF	Aubrey Huff	3.00
10WOF	Josh Phelps	5.00

2006 Flair Showcase

	NM/M
Complete Set (200):	
Common Player (1-100):	.50
Common Player (101-150):	1.50
Inserted 1:4 Hobby	
Common Player (151-200):	2.00
Inserted 1:8 Hobby	
Pack (5):	3.00
Box (18):	50.00
1 Jeremy Hermida	.50
2 Albert Pujols	3.00

3	Ryan Shealy	.50
4	Mark Prior	.50
5	Chuck James	1.00
6	Shawn Green	.50
7	Rickie Weeks	.75
8	Roy Halladay	.75
9	Luis Gonzalez	.50
10	David Ortiz	1.50
11	Josh Beckett	1.00
12	Gary Sheffield	.75
13	Jose Reyes	1.00
14	Brandon Watson	.50
15	Tadahito Iguchi	.50
16	Rich Harden	.50
17	Skip Schumaker	.50
18	Vladimir Guerrero	1.00
19	Chris Carpenter	.75
20	Brian Roberts	.50
21	Roy Oswalt	.75
22	Ben Johnson	.50
23	Todd Helton	.75
24	Wilbert Nieves	.50
25	Michael Young	.50
26	A.J. Burnett	.50
27	J.D. Drew	.50
28	Adrian Beltre	.50
29	Tim Hudson	.50
30	Jake Peavy	.75
31	Magglio Ordonez	.75
32	Brad Wilkerson	.50
33	Ryan Freel	.50
34	Javier Vazquez	.50
35	Tom Glavine	.75
36	Jason Bergmann **RC**	1.00
37	Marcus Giles	.50
38	Jim Thome	.75
39	Ichiro Suzuki	2.00
40	Jeff Harris **RC**	.75
41	Miguel Cabrera	1.00
42	Nomar Garciaparra	.75
43	Brian Giles	.50
44	Jeremy Accardo **RC**	1.00
45	Taylor Buchholz	.50
46	Mike Jacobs	.50
47	Chris Denorfia	.50
48	Ivan Rodriguez	.50
49	Mike Piazza	1.00
50	Curt Schilling	1.00
51	Kelly Stoppach	.50
52	Jason Kubel	.50
53	Craig Biggio	.75
54	Livan Hernandez	.50
55	Joe Mauer	.75
56	Scott Feldman **RC**	1.00
57	Garret Anderson	.50
58	Steve Stemle **RC**	1.00
59	Boof Bonser	.75
60	Jose Guillen	.50
61	Rafael Furcal	.75
62	John Van Benschoten	.50
63	Dontrelle Willis	.75
64	Jose Vidro	.50
65	David Wright	2.00
66	Alfonso Soriano	1.00
67	Scott Podsednik	.50
68	Felix Hernandez	.75
69	Richie Sexson	.75
70	Jeff Francoeur	.75
71	Conor Jackson	.50
72	Javy Lopez	.50
73	Jonathan Papelbon **(RC)**	5.00
74	Frank Thomas	.75
75	Greg Maddux	2.00
76	Josh Rupe **(RC)**	.50
77	Eric Chavez	.50
78	Ben Sheets	.50
79	Chase Utley	1.00
80	Derrek Lee	.75
81	Manny Ramirez	1.00
82	Pedro Martinez	1.00
83	Hideki Matsui	2.00
84	Jeremy Bonderman	.50
85	Ronny Cedeno	.50
86	Trevor Hoffman	.50
87	Mark Buehrle	.50
88	Jason Bay	.75
89	Reggie Sanders	.50
90	Brian Anderson **(RC)**	.50
91	Travis Hafner	.75
92	Carlos Beltran	.50
93	Cody Ross **(RC)**	.50

94	Melvin Mora	.50
95	Chris Duffy	.50
96	Vernon Wells	.50
97	Bartolo Colon	.50
98	Aubrey Huff	.50
99	Paul Konerko	.75
100	Cesar Izturis	.50
101	Josh Willingham **(RC)**	1.50
102	Matt Cain **(RC)**	2.00
103	Macay McBride **(RC)**	1.50
104	Jeff Mathis	1.50
105	Alex Rodriguez	8.00
106	Justin Morneau	2.00
107	Felipe Lopez	1.50
108	Justin Verlander **(RC)**	8.00
109	Ryan Howard	5.00
110	Mike Sweeney	1.50
111	Scott Rolen	2.00
112	Hank Blalock	1.50
113	Kerry Wood	1.50
114	B.J. Ryan	1.50
115	Garrett Atkins	2.00
116	Carlos Delgado	2.00
117	Zack Greinke	2.00
118	Chad Cordero	1.50
119	Julio Lugo	1.50
120	Bobby Crosby	1.50
121	Barry Zito	1.50
122	Jhonny Peralta	1.50
123	Miguel Tejada	2.50
124	Grady Sizemore	3.00
125	Derek Jeter	8.00
126	Cliff Lee	1.50
127	Khalil Greene	1.50
128	Lance Berkman	2.00
129	Huston Street	1.50
130	Jermaine Dye	2.00
131	Chone Figgins	2.00
132	Torii Hunter	2.00
133	Jorge Cantu	1.50
134	Jason Giambi	2.00
135	Johan Santana	3.00
136	Chad Tracy	1.50
137	Troy Glaus	2.00
138	Moises Alou	2.00
139	Jason Schmidt	1.50
140	Ken Griffey Jr.	6.00
141	Jason Varitek	3.00
142	John Smoltz	2.50
143	Andy Pettitte	2.00
144	Jeff Kent	2.00
145	Coco Crisp	1.50
146	Jonny Gomes	1.50
147	Aaron Rowand	1.50
148	Mike Mussina	2.50
149	Johnny Damon	4.00
150	Edgar Renteria	1.50
151	Scott Kazmir	2.00
152	Lyle Overbay	2.00
153	Placido Polanco	2.00
154	Mariano Rivera	3.00
155	Hanley Ramirez **(RC)**	3.00
156	Morgan Ensberg	2.00
157	Kenny Rogers	2.00
158	Brad Lidge	2.00
159	A.J. Pierzynski	2.00
160	Aramis Ramirez	3.00
161	Mark Teixeira	3.00
162	Carl Crawford	3.00
163	Ryan Zimmerman **(RC)**	8.00
164	Adam Dunn	3.00
165	Joe Nathan	2.00
166	Juan Pierre	2.00
167	Pat Burrell	3.00
168	Carlos Lee	3.00
169	Billy Wagner	2.00
170	Prince Fielder **(RC)**	10.00
171	Randy Johnson	4.00
172	Andruw Jones	3.00
173	Francisco Rodriguez	2.00
174	Robinson Cano	3.00
175	Matt Holliday	3.00
176	Jim Edmonds	2.00
177	Josh Barfield **(RC)**	2.00
178	Chipper Jones	4.00
179	Bobby Jenks	2.00
180	Carlos Zambrano	3.00
181	Bobby Abreu	2.00
182	Brandon Webb	2.00
183	Kevin Millwood	2.00
184	Zachary Duke	2.00
185	Randy Winn	2.00
186	Eric Gagne	2.00
187	Kenji Johjima **RC**	5.00
188	John Patterson	2.00
189	Mark Loretta	2.00
190	Anderson Hernandez **(RC)**	2.00
191	Chris Resop **(RC)**	2.00
192	Ian Kinsler **(RC)**	5.00
193	Francisco Liriano **(RC)**	5.00
194	Noah Lowry	2.00
195	Brett Myers	2.00
196	Rocco Baldelli	2.00
197	Cliff Floyd	2.00
198	Sean Casey	2.00
199	Geoff Jenkins	2.00
200	Clint Barmes	2.00

Legacy Blue

Blue (1-100):	2-4X
Blue (101-150):	1-1.5X

Blue (151-200): 1X
Production 150 Sets

Legacy Emerald

Emerald (1-100): 2-4X
Emerald (101-150): 1-1.5X
Emerald (151-200): 1X
Production 150 Sets

Printing Plates

No Pricing
Production one set per color.

Autographs

		NM/M
Common Autograph:		8.00
BA	Bronson Arroyo	20.00
JB	Jason Bay	15.00
HB	Hank Blalock	10.00
BO	Jeremy Bonderman	15.00
SC	Sean Casey/SP	15.00
GC	Gustavo Chacin	10.00
BC	Brandon Claussen	10.00
CH	Chad Cordero	8.00
CO	Craig Counsell	10.00
CA	Carl Crawford	15.00
CC	Coco Crisp	15.00
KG	Ken Griffey Jr./SP	75.00
JG	Jose Guillen	8.00
TH	Travis Hafner/SP	15.00
AH	Aaron Harang	15.00
LH	Livan Hernandez	8.00
CI	Cesar Izturis	8.00
MK	Mark Kotsay	8.00
CL	Cliff Lee	15.00
JM	Justin Morneau	15.00
XN	Xavier Nady	10.00
RO	Roy Oswalt/SP	15.00
WP	Wily Mo Pena	10.00
JH	Jhonny Peralta	10.00
JP	Joel Pineiro	10.00
RA	Aramis Ramirez	15.00
AR	Aaron Rowand	15.00
CU	Chase Utley/SP/100	40.00
JV	Javier Vazquez/SP	8.00
OV	Omar Vizquel	20.00
RZ	Ryan Zimmerman	30.00

Fresh Ink

		NM/M
Common Auto.:		8.00
GA	Garrett Atkins	10.00
CB	Clint Barmes/SP	10.00
JB	Joe Blanton	10.00
MC	Miguel Cabrera/SP	25.00

MA	Matt Cain/SP	25.00
BC	Bobby Crosby	8.00
DD	David DeJesus	10.00
GF	Gavin Floyd	15.00
JG	Jonny Gomes	8.00
KG	Khalil Greene/SP	25.00
ZG	Zack Greinke	10.00
HA	Rich Harden	15.00
DH	Danny Haren	10.00
RH	Rich Hill	15.00
TI	Tadahito Iguchi	40.00
SK	Scott Kazmir	15.00
CK	Casey Kotchman	10.00
NL	Noah Lowry	8.00
VM	Victor Martinez	15.00
BM	Brandon McCarthy	8.00
OP	Odalis Perez	8.00
RE	Jeremy Reed	8.00
BR	Brian Roberts	15.00
ES	Ervin Santana	15.00
JS	Johan Santana/SP	50.00
CS	Chris Shelton	8.00
HS	Huston Street	15.00
MT	Mark Teahen	8.00
DW	Dontrelle Willis	10.00
WR	David Wright/SP/100	60.00
KY	Kevin Youkilis	15.00
MY	Michael Young/SP/100	20.00

Lettermen

No Pricing
Production 3-9

Showcase Signatures

		NM/M
Production 35 Sets		
JE	Jeremy Bonderman	30.00
SC	Sean Casey	20.00
CD	Chad Cordero	10.00
JG	Jose Guillen	10.00
AH	Aaron Harang	20.00
HA	Rich Harden	30.00
CI	Cesar Izturis	10.00
XN	Xavier Nady	20.00
RO	Roy Oswalt	20.00
WM	Wily Mo Pena	20.00
PE	Jhonny Peralta	15.00
BR	Brian Roberts	30.00
CS	Chris Shelton	20.00
KY	Kevin Youkilis	20.00
RZ	Ryan Zimmerman	50.00

Stitches

		NM/M
Common Player:		4.00
Inserted 1:9		
BA	Bobby Abreu	6.00
MA	Moises Alou	6.00
RB	Rocco Baldelli	6.00
JO	Josh Beckett	8.00
CB	Carlos Beltran	8.00
AB	Adrian Beltre	4.00
LB	Lance Berkman	6.00
HB	Hank Blalock	6.00
BO	Jeremy Bonderman	6.00
MB	Mark Buehrle	4.00
MC	Miguel Cabrera	10.00
RC	Robinson Cano	12.00
JC	Jorge Cantu	6.00
EC	Eric Chavez	6.00
CO	Michael Collins	4.00
CA	Carl Crawford	4.00
BC	Bobby Crosby	4.00
JD	Johnny Damon	10.00
CD	Carlos Delgado	6.00
DR	J.D. Drew	6.00
AD	Adam Dunn	6.00
JE	Jim Edmonds	6.00
RF	Rafael Furcal	6.00
EG	Eric Gagne	6.00
FG	Freddy Garcia	4.00
JG	Jason Giambi	6.00
BG	Brian Giles	4.00
TG	Tom Glavine	8.00
LG	Luis Gonzalez	4.00
GR	Khalil Greene	4.00
KG	Ken Griffey Jr.	10.00
VG	Vladimir Guerrero	8.00
TR	Travis Hafner	6.00
RH	Roy Halladay	6.00
RI	Rich Harden	6.00
HA	J.J. Hardy	4.00
TH	Todd Helton	8.00
HO	Trevor Hoffman	4.00
MH	Matt Holliday	8.00
HU	Tim Hudson	6.00
TO	Torii Hunter	6.00
DJ	Derek Jeter	20.00
RJ	Randy Johnson	8.00
AJ	Andruw Jones	6.00
CJ	Chipper Jones	8.00
JJ	Jacque Jones	4.00
SK	Scott Kazmir	6.00
JK	Jeff Kent	6.00
CL	Carlos Lee	4.00
DL	Derrek Lee	8.00
PL	Paul LoDuca	4.00
JL	Javy Lopez	4.00
GM	Greg Maddux	10.00
PM	Pedro Martinez	10.00
KM	Kazuo Matsui	6.00
DM	Daisuke Matsuzaka	50.00
JM	Joe Mauer	8.00
KE	Kevin Millwood	4.00
MM	Mike Mussina	8.00
TN	Trot Nixon	8.00
DO	David Ortiz	10.00
JP	Jake Peavy	6.00
AN	Andy Pettitte	6.00
MI	Mike Piazza	10.00
MP	Mark Prior	6.00
AP	Albert Pujols	20.00
AR	Aramis Ramirez	6.00
MR	Manny Ramirez	8.00
RE	Jeremy Reed	4.00
JR	Jose Reyes	10.00
BR	Brian Roberts	4.00
FR	Francisco Rodriguez	4.00
IR	Ivan Rodriguez	8.00
SR	Scott Rolen	8.00
CC	C.C. Sabathia	4.00
JS	Johan Santana	8.00
CS	Curt Schilling	8.00
JA	Jason Schmidt	6.00
RS	Richie Sexson	6.00
BS	Ben Sheets	4.00
GS	Gary Sheffield	8.00
SM	John Smoltz	8.00
AS	Alfonso Soriano	8.00
SW	Mike Sweeney	4.00
MT	Mark Teixeira	8.00
TE	Miguel Tejada	8.00
FT	Frank Thomas	10.00
JT	Jim Thome	8.00
JU	Juan Uribe	4.00
JV	Jason Varitek	10.00
OV	Omar Vizquel	8.00
RW	Rickie Weeks	5.00
VW	Vernon Wells	8.00
DW	Dontrelle Willis	6.00
PW	Preston Wilson	4.00
KW	Kerry Wood	4.00
WR	David Wright	15.00
MY	Michael Young	6.00
BZ	Barry Zito	4.00

Hot Gloves

		NM/M
Common Player:		10.00
Inserted 1:108 Hobby		
1	Derrek Lee	15.00
2	Andruw Jones	10.00
3	Bobby Abreu	10.00
4	Luis Castillo	10.00
5	Mike Matheny	10.00
6	Cesar Izturis	10.00
7	Craig Biggio	10.00
8	Darin Erstad	10.00
9	Derek Jeter	40.00
10	Eric Chavez	10.00
11	Greg Maddux	40.00
12	Ichiro Suzuki	35.00
13	Ivan Rodriguez	10.00
14	J.T. Snow	10.00
15	Jim Edmonds	10.00
16	Steve Finley	10.00
17	Kenny Rogers	10.00
18	Jason Varitek	20.00
19	Ken Griffey Jr.	40.00
20	Mark Teixeira	15.00
21	Orlando Hudson	10.00
22	Mike Hampton	10.00
23	Mike Mussina	15.00
24	Vernon Wells	15.00
25	Omar Vizquel	10.00
26	Alex Rodriguez	40.00
27	Mike Cameron	10.00
28	Scott Rolen	15.00
29	Todd Helton	15.00
30	Torii Hunter	15.00

Hot Numbers

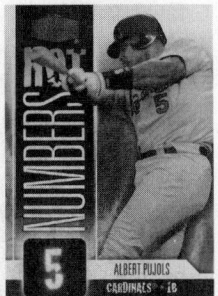

		NM/M
Common Player:		1.50
Inserted 1:6 Hobby		
1	Albert Pujols	8.00
2	Alex Rodriguez	8.00
3	Andruw Jones	2.00
4	Bobby Abreu	1.50
5	Chipper Jones	3.00
6	Curt Schilling	2.00
7	David Ortiz	3.00
8	David Wright	5.00
9	Derek Jeter	8.00
10	Derrek Lee	3.00
11	Eric Gagne	1.50
12	Greg Maddux	5.00
13	Hideki Matsui	5.00
14	Ichiro Suzuki	5.00
15	Ivan Rodriguez	2.00
16	Johan Santana	3.00
17	Johnny Damon	3.00
18	Ken Griffey Jr.	5.00
19	Manny Ramirez	3.00
20	Mark Prior	1.50
21	Mark Teixeira	2.00
22	Miguel Cabrera	3.00
23	Miguel Tejada	2.00

24	Pedro Martinez	3.00
25	Randy Johnson	3.00
26	Rickie Weeks	1.50
27	Roger Clemens	5.00
28	Todd Helton	2.00
29	Torii Hunter	1.50
30	Vladimir Guerrero	3.00

Wave of the Future

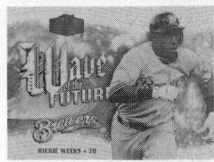

		NM/M
Common Player:		1.00
Inserted 1:2		
WF-1	Jeremy Hermida	1.00
WF-2	Kelly Stoppach	1.00
WF-3	Adam Wainwright	1.00
WF-4	Ryan Zimmerman	4.00
WF-5	Josh Willingham	1.00
WF-6	Brandon McCarthy	1.00
WF-7	Conor Jackson	1.00
WF-8	Grady Sizemore	2.00
WF-9	Curtis Granderson	1.50
WF-10	Jose Capellan	1.00
WF-11	Mike Jacobs	1.00
WF-12	Gavin Floyd	1.00
WF-13	Hanley Ramirez	2.00
WF-14	Jason Kubel	1.00
WF-15	Nate McLouth	1.00
WF-16	Felix Hernandez	1.50
WF-17	Jeff Francoeur	1.00
WF-18	Wilbert Nieves	1.00
WF-19	Cody Ross	1.00
WF-20	Justin Verlander	5.00
WF-21	Ben Johnson	1.00
WF-22	Guillermo Quiroz	1.00
WF-23	Jonathan Papelbon	4.00
WF-24	Prince Fielder	4.00
WF-25	Rickie Weeks	1.50
WF-26	Robinson Cano	2.00
WF-27	Kenji Johjima	3.00
WF-28	Anderson Hernandez	1.00
WF-29	Yuniesky Betancourt	1.00
WF-30	Zachary Duke	1.00

WBC Classic Moments

		NM/M
Common Player:		1.50
Inserted 1:8		
CM-1	Adam Stern	1.50
CM-2	Jason Bay	2.00
CM-3	Wei Wang	1.50
CM-4	Yung-Chi Chen	3.00
CM-5	Pedro Luis Lazo	2.00
CM-6	Yoandy Garlobo	1.50

CM-7 Ormari Romero 1.50
CM-8 Frederich Cepeda 1.50
CM-9 Yulieski Gourriel 1.50
CM-10 Yadel Marti 1.50
CM-11 David Ortiz 2.50
CM-12 Albert Pujols 5.00
CM-13 Adrian Beltre 1.50
CM-14 Alberto Castillo 1.50
CM-15 Odalis Perez 1.50
CM-16 Jason Grilli 1.50
CM-17 Daisuke Matsuzaka 5.00
CM-18 Sadaharu Oh 10.00
CM-19 Nobuhiko Matsunaka 3.00
CM-20 Ichiro Suzuki 5.00
CM-21 Akinori Otsuka 3.00
CM-22 Koji Uehara 3.00
CM-23 Kosuke Fukudome 5.00
CM-24 Daisuke Matsuzaka 5.00
CM-25 Ichiro Suzuki 5.00
CM-26 Seung-Yeop Lee 2.00
CM-27 Seung-Yeop Lee 2.00
CM-28 Jong Beom Lee 1.50
CM-29 Jae Weong Seo 1.50
CM-30 Chan Ho Park 1.50
CM-31 Hee Seop Choi 1.50
CM-32 Jorge Cantu 1.50
CM-33 Oliver Perez 1.50
CM-34 Vinny Castilla 1.50
CM-35 Esteban Loaiza 1.50
CM-36 Shairon Martis 1.50
CM-37 Bernie Williams 2.00
CM-38 Javier Vazquez 1.50
CM-39 Carlos Beltran 2.00
CM-40 Bernie Williams 2.00
CM-41 Roger Clemens 5.00
CM-42 Ken Griffey Jr. 5.00
CM-43 Alex Rodriguez 5.00
CM-44 Derrek Lee 2.00
CM-45 Derek Jeter 5.00
CM-46 Chipper Jones 2.00
CM-47 Miguel Cabrera 2.00
CM-48 Francisco Rodriguez 1.50
CM-49 Victor Martinez 1.50
CM-50 Freddy Garcia 1.50

1981 Fleer

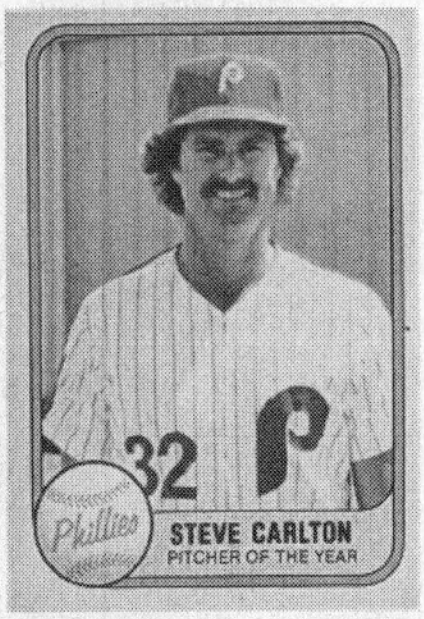

NM/M

Complete Set (660):
Common Player:
Wax Pack (17):
Wax Box (38):
Vending Box (500):
1 Pete Rose 2.25
2 Larry Bowa .04
3 Manny Trillo .05
4 Bob Boone .04
5a Mike Schmidt/Portrait 2.00
5b Mike Schmidt/Btg 1.50
6a Steve Carlton ("Lefty" on front.) .70
6b Steve Carlton (Pitcher of the Year on front, date 1066 on back.) 1.50
6c Steve Carlton (Pitcher of the Year on front, date 1966 on back.) 2.00
7a Tug McGraw (Game Saver on front.) .40
7b Tug McGraw (Pitcher on front.) .06
8 Larry Christenson .05
9 Bake McBride .05
10 Greg Luzinski .06
11 Ron Reed .05
12 Dickie Noles .05
13 Keith Moreland **RC** .11
14 Bob Walk **RC** .06
15 Lonnie Smith .05
16 Dick Ruthven .05
17 Sparky Lyle .06
18 Greg Gross .05
19 Garry Maddox .06
20 Nino Espinosa .05
21 George Vukovich .05
22 John Vukovich .05
23 Ramon Aviles .05
24a Kevin Saucier (Ken Saucier on back.) .08
24b Kevin Saucier (Kevin Saucier on back.) .40
25 Randy Lerch .05
26 Del Unser .05
27 Tim McCarver .11
28a George Brett/Btg 1.50
28b George Brett/Portrait 1.50
29a Willie Wilson/Portrait .40
29b Willie Wilson/Btg .11
30 Paul Splittorff .05
31 Dan Quisenberry .06
32a Amos Otis/Btg .40
32b Amos Otis/Portrait .08
33 Steve Busby .05
34 U.L. Washington .05
35 Dave Chalk .05
36 Darrell Porter .05
37 Marty Pattin .05
38 Larry Gura .05
39 Renie Martin .05
40 Rich Gale .05
41a Hal McRae (Dark blue "Royals" on front.) .30
41b Hal McRae (Light blue "Royals" on front.) .08
42 Dennis Leonard .05
43 Willie Aikens .05
44 Frank White .05
45 Clint Hurdle .05
46 John Wathan .05
47 Pete LaCock .05
48 Rance Mulliniks .05
49 Jeff Twitty .05
50 Jamie Quirk .05
51 Art Howe .05
52 Ken Forsch .05
53 Vern Ruhle .05
54 Joe Niekro .04
55 Frank LaCorte .05
56 J.R. Richard .04
57 Nolan Ryan 3.00
58 Enos Cabell .05
59 Cesar Cedeno .04
60 Jose Cruz .04
61 Bill Virdon .05
62 Terry Puhl .05
63 Joaquin Andujar .05
64 Alan Ashby .05
65 Joe Sambito .05
66 Denny Walling .05
67 Jeff Leonard .05
68 Luis Pujols .05
69 Bruce Bochy .05
70 Rafael Landestoy .05
71 Dave Smith **RC** .05
72 Danny Heep **RC** .05
73 Julio Gonzalez .05
74 Craig Reynolds .05
75 Gary Woods .05
76 Dave Bergman .05
77 Randy Niemann .05
78 Joe Morgan .70
79a Reggie Jackson/Portrait 2.00
79b Reggie Jackson/Btg 1.50
80 Bucky Dent .08
81 Tommy John .08
82 Luis Tiant .04
83 Rick Cerone .05
84 Dick Howser .05
85 Lou Piniella .08
86 Ron Davis .05
87a Graig Nettles (Craig on back.) 3.50
87b Graig Nettles (Graig on back.) .11
88 Ron Guidry .08
89 Rich Gossage .08
90 Rudy May .05
91 Gaylord Perry .60
92 Eric Soderholm .05
93 Bob Watson .05
94 Bobby Murcer .08
95 Bobby Brown .05
96 Jim Spencer .05
97 Tom Underwood .05
98 Oscar Gamble .05
99 Johnny Oates .05
100 Fred Stanley .05
101 Ruppert Jones .05
102 Dennis Werth .05
103 Joe Lefebvre .05
104 Brian Doyle .05
105 Aurelio Rodriguez .05
106 Doug Bird .05
107 Mike Griffin .05
108 Tim Lollar .05
109 Willie Randolph .05
110 Steve Garvey .25
111 Reggie Smith .06
112 Don Sutton .60
113 Burt Hooton .05
114a Davy Lopes (Davey) (No finger on back.) .05
114b Davy Lopes (Davey) (Small finger on back.) .40
115 Dusty Baker .04
116 Tom Lasorda .08
117 Bill Russell .06
118 Jerry Reuss .05
119 Terry Forster .05
120a Bob Welch (Bob on back.) .08
120b Bob Welch (Robert) .40
121 Don Stanhouse .05
122 Rick Monday .05
123 Derrel Thomas .05
124 Joe Ferguson .05
125 Rick Sutcliffe .08
126a Ron Cey (No finger on back.) .06
126b Ron Cey (Small finger on back.) .40
127 Dave Goltz .05
128 Jay Johnstone .05
129 Steve Yeager .05
130 Gary Weiss .05
131 Mike Scioscia **RC** .40
132 Vic Davalillo .05
133 Doug Rau .05
134 Pepe Frias .05
135 Mickey Hatcher .05
136 Steve Howe **RC** .08
137 Robert Castillo .05
138 Gary Thomasson .05
139 Rudy Law .05
140 Fernando Valenzuela **RC** 1.25
141 Manny Mota .05
142 Gary Carter .70
143 Steve Rogers .05
144 Warren Cromartie .05
145 Andre Dawson .30
146 Larry Parrish .05
147 Rowland Office .05
148 Ellis Valentine .05
149 Dick Williams .05
150 Bill Gullickson **RC** .11
151 Elias Sosa .05
152 John Tamargo .05
153 Chris Speier .05
154 Ron LeFlore .05
155 Rodney Scott .05
156 Stan Bahnsen .05
157 Bill Lee .06
158 Fred Norman .05
159 Woodie Fryman .05
160 Dave Palmer .05
161 Jerry White .05
162 Roberto Ramos .05
163 John D'Acquisto .05
164 Tommy Hutton .05
165 Charlie Lea **RC** .11
166 Scott Sanderson .05
167 Ken Macha .05
168 Tony Bernazard .05
169 Jim Palmer .70
170 Steve Stone .08
171 Mike Flanagan .05
172 Al Bumbry .05
173 Doug DeCinces .05
174 Scott McGregor .05
175 Mark Belanger .05
176 Tim Stoddard .05
177a Rick Dempsey (No finger on front.) .05
177b Rick Dempsey (Small finger on front.) .40
178 Earl Weaver .20
179 Tippy Martinez .05
180 Dennis Martinez .06
181 Sammy Stewart .05
182 Rich Dauer .05
183 Lee May .05
184 Eddie Murray .70
185 Benny Ayala .05
186 John Lowenstein .05
187 Gary Roenicke .05
188 Ken Singleton .06
189 Dan Graham .05
190 Terry Crowley .05
191 Kiko Garcia .05
192 Dave Ford .05
193 Mark Corey .05
194 Lenn Sakata .05
195 Doug DeCinces .05
196 Johnny Bench .70
197 Dave Concepcion .04
198 Ray Knight .04
199 Ken Griffey .08
200 Tom Seaver .70
201 Dave Collins .05
202 George Foster .04
203 Junior Kennedy .05
204 Frank Pastore .05
205 Dan Driessen .06
206 Hector Cruz .05
207 Paul Moskau .05
208 Charlie Leibrandt **RC** .20
209 Harry Spilman .05
210 Joe Price **RC** .05
211 Tom Hume .05
212 Joe Nolan .05
213 Doug Bair .05
214 Mario Soto .05
215a Bill Bonham (No finger on back.) .05
215b Bill Bonham (Small finger on back.) .40
216a George Foster (Slugger on front.) .20
216b George Foster (Outfield on front.) .11
217 Paul Householder .05
218 Ron Oester .05
219 Sam Mejias .05
220 Sheldon Burnside .05
221 Carl Yastrzemski .70
222 Jim Rice .30
223 Fred Lynn .04
224 Carlton Fisk .70
225 Rick Burleson .05
226 Dennis Eckersley .60
227 Butch Hobson .05
228 Tom Burgmeier .05
229 Garry Hancock .05
230 Don Zimmer .05
231 Steve Renko .05
232 Dwight Evans .04
233 Mike Torrez .05
234 Bob Stanley .05
235 Jim Dwyer .05
236 Dave Stapleton .05
237 Glenn Hoffman .05
238 Jerry Remy .05
239 Dick Drago .05
240 Bill Campbell .05
241 Tony Perez .60
242 Phil Niekro .60
243 Dale Murphy .25
244 Bob Horner .04
245 Jeff Burroughs .05
246 Rick Camp .05
247 Bob Cox .20
248 Bruce Benedict .05
249 Gene Garber .05
250 Jerry Royster .05
251a Gary Matthews (No finger on back.) .05
251b Gary Matthews (Small finger on back.) .40
252 Chris Chambliss .05
253 Luis Gomez .05
254 Bill Nahorodny .05
255 Doyle Alexander .05
256 Brian Asselstine .05
257 Biff Pocoroba .05
258 Mike Lum .05
259 Charlie Spikes .05
260 Glenn Hubbard .06
261 Tommy Boggs .05
262 Al Hrabosky .05
263 Rick Matula .05
264 Preston Hanna .05
265 Larry Bradford .05
266 Rafael Ramirez **RC** .05
267 Larry McWilliams .05
268 Rod Carew .70
269 Bobby Grich .04
270 Carney Lansford .05
271 Don Baylor .04
272 Joe Rudi .05
273 Dan Ford .05
274 Jim Fregosi .06
275 Dave Frost .05
276 Frank Tanana .05
277 Dickie Thon .05
278 Jason Thompson .05
279 Rick Miller .05
280 Bert Campaneris .05
281 Tom Donohue .05
282 Brian Downing .05
283 Fred Patek .05
284 Bruce Kison .05
285 Dave LaRoche .05
286 Don Aase .05
287 Jim Barr .05
288 Alfredo Martinez .05
289 Larry Harlow .05
290 Andy Hassler .05
291 Dave Kingman .04
292 Bill Buckner .04
293 Rick Reuschel .05
294 Bruce Sutter .60
295 Jerry Martin .05
296 Scot Thompson .05
297 Ivan DeJesus .05
298 Steve Dillard .05
299 Dick Tidrow .05
300 Randy Martz .05
301 Lenny Randle .05
302 Lynn McGlothen .05
303 Cliff Johnson .05
304 Tim Blackwell .05
305 Dennis Lamp .05
306 Bill Caudill .05
307 Carlos Lezcano .05
308 Jim Tracy .06
309 Doug Capilla .05
310 Willie Hernandez .05
311 Mike Vail .05
312 Mike Krukow .05
313 Barry Foote .05
314 Larry Biittner .05
315 Mike Tyson .05
316 Lee Mazzilli .05
317 John Stearns .05
318 Alex Trevino .05
319 Craig Swan .05
320 Frank Taveras .05
321 Steve Henderson .05
322 Neil Allen .05
323 Mark Bomback .05
324 Mike Jorgensen .05
325 Joe Torre .20
326 Elliott Maddox .05
327 Pete Falcone .05
328 Ray Burris .05
329 Claudell Washington .05
330 Doug Flynn .05
331 Joel Youngblood .05
332 Bill Almon .05
333 Tom Hausman .05
334 Pat Zachry .05
335 Jeff Reardon **RC** 1.50
336 Wally Backman **RC** .11
337 Dan Norman .05
338 Jerry Morales .05
339 Ed Farmer .05
340 Bob Molinaro .05
341 Todd Cruz .05

342a	Britt Burns **RC** (No finger on front.)	.08
342b	Britt Burns **RC** (Small finger on front.)	.40
343	Kevin Bell	.05
344	Tony LaRussa	.20
345	Steve Trout	.05
346	Harold Baines **RC**	2.25
347	Richard Wortham	.05
348	Wayne Nordhagen	.05
349	Mike Squires	.05
350	Lamar Johnson	.05
351	Rickey Henderson	2.00
352	Francisco Barrios	.05
353	Thad Bosley	.05
354	Chet Lemon	.05
355	Bruce Kimm	.05
356	Richard Dotson **RC**	.05
357	Jim Morrison	.05
358	Mike Proly	.05
359	Greg Pryor	.05
360	Dave Parker	.04
361	Omar Moreno	.05
362a	Kent Tekulve (1071 Waterbury on back)	.11
362b	Kent Tekulve (1971 Waterbury on back)	.40
363	Willie Stargell	.70
364	Phil Garner	.05
365	Ed Ott	.05
366	Don Robinson	.05
367	Chuck Tanner	.05
368	Jim Rooker	.05
369	Dale Berra	.05
370	Jim Bibby	.05
371	Steve Nicosia	.05
372	Mike Easler	.05
373	Bill Robinson	.05
374	Lee Lacy	.05
375	John Candelaria	.05
376	Manny Sanguillen	.05
377	Rick Rhoden	.05
378	Grant Jackson	.05
379	Tim Foli	.05
380	Rod Scurry **RC**	.05
381	Bill Madlock	.04
382a	Kurt Bevacqua (Photo reversed, backwards "P" on cap.)	.11
382b	Kurt Bevacqua (Correct photo.)	.40
383	Bert Blyleven	.08
384	Eddie Solomon	.05
385	Enrique Romo	.05
386	John Milner	.05
387	Mike Hargrove	.05
388	Jorge Orta	.05
389	Toby Harrah	.06
390	Tom Veryzer	.05
391	Miguel Dilone	.05
392	Dan Spillner	.05
393	Jack Brohamer	.05
394	Wayne Garland	.05
395	Sid Monge	.05
396	Rick Waits	.05
397	Joe Charboneau **RC**	.40
398	Gary Alexander	.05
399	Jerry Dybzinski	.05
400	Mike Stanton	.05
401	Mike Paxton	.05
402	Gary Gray	.05
403	Rick Manning	.05
404	Bo Diaz	.05
405	Ron Hassey	.05
406	Ross Grimsley	.05
407	Victor Cruz	.05
408	Len Barker	.05
409	Bob Bailor	.05
410	Otto Velez	.05
411	Ernie Whitt	.05
412	Jim Clancy	.05
413	Barry Bonnell	.05
414	Dave Stieb	.04
415	Damaso Garcia **RC**	.08
416	John Mayberry	.05
417	Roy Howell	.05
418	Dan Ainge **RC**	2.25
419a	Jesse Jefferson (Pirates on back.)	.08
419b	Jesse Jefferson (Blue Jays on back.)	.40
420	Joey McLaughlin	.05
421	Lloyd Moseby **RC**	.08
422	Al Woods	.05
423	Garth Iorg	.05
424	Doug Ault	.05
425	Ken Schrom **RC**	.05
426	Mike Willis	.05
427	Steve Braun	.05
428	Bob Davis	.05
429	Jerry Garvin	.05
430	Alfredo Griffin	.05
431	Bob Mattick	.05
432	Vida Blue	.04
433	Jack Clark	.04
434	Willie McCovey	.70
435	Mike Ivie	.05
436a	Darrel Evans (Darrel on front.)	.11
436b	Darrell Evans (Darrell on front.)	.40
437	Terry Whitfield	.05
438	Rennie Stennett	.05
439	John Montefusco	.05
440	Jim Wohlford	.05
441	Bill North	.05
442	Milt May	.05
443	Max Venable	.05
444	Ed Whitson	.05
445	Al Holland **RC**	.05
446	Randy Moffitt	.05
447	Bob Knepper	.06
448	Gary Lavelle	.05
449	Greg Minton	.05
450	Johnnie LeMaster	.05
451	Larry Herndon	.05
452	Rich Murray	.05
453	Joe Pettini	.05
454	Allen Ripley	.05
455	Dennis Littlejohn	.05
456	Tom Griffin	.05
457	Alan Hargesheimer	.05
458	Joe Strain	.05
459	Steve Kemp	.05
460	Sparky Anderson	.20
461	Alan Trammell	.04
462	Mark Fidrych	.20
463	Lou Whitaker	.04
464	Dave Rozema	.05
465	Milt Wilcox	.05
466	Champ Summers	.05
467	Lance Parrish	.04
468	Dan Petry	.05
469	Pat Underwood	.05
470	Rick Peters	.05
471	Al Cowens	.05
472	John Wockenfuss	.05
473	Tom Brookens	.05
474	Richie Hebner	.05
475	Jack Morris	.04
476	Jim Lentine	.05
477	Bruce Robbins	.05
478	Mark Wagner	.05
479	Tim Corcoran	.05
480a	Stan Papi (Pitcher on front.)	.11
480b	Stan Papi (Shortstop on front.)	.40
481	Kirk Gibson **RC**	3.75
482	Dan Schatzeder	.05
483	Amos Otis	.04
484	Dave Winfield	.70
485	Rollie Fingers	.60
486	Gene Richards	.05
487	Randy Jones	.05
488	Ozzie Smith	1.50
489	Gene Tenace	.05
490	Bill Fahey	.05
491	John Curtis	.05
492	Dave Cash	.05
493a	Tim Flannery (Photo reversed, batting righty.)	.11
493b	Tim Flannery (Photo correct, batting lefty.)	.40
494	Jerry Mumphrey	.05
495	Bob Shirley	.05
496	Steve Mura	.05
497	Eric Rasmussen	.05
498	Broderick Perkins	.05
499	Barry Evans	.05
500	Chuck Baker	.05
501	Luis Salazar **RC**	.06
502	Gary Lucas	.05
503	Mike Armstrong	.05
504	Jerry Turner	.05
505	Dennis Kinney	.05
506	Willy Montanez (Willie)	.05
507	Gorman Thomas	.05
508	Ben Oglivie	.05
509	Larry Hisle	.05
510	Sal Bando	.05
511	Robin Yount	.70
512	Mike Caldwell	.05
513	Sixto Lezcano	.05
514a	Jerry Augustine (Billy Travers photo.)	.11
514b	Billy Travers (Correct name with photo.)	.40
515	Paul Molitor	.70
516	Moose Haas	.05
517	Bill Castro	.05
518	Jim Slaton	.05
519	Lary Sorensen	.05
520	Bob McClure	.05
521	Charlie Moore	.05
522	Jim Gantner	.05
523	Reggie Cleveland	.05
524	Don Money	.05
525	Billy Travers	.05
526	Buck Martinez	.05
527	Dick Davis	.05
528	Ted Simmons	.05
529	Garry Templeton	.05
530	Ken Reitz	.05
531	Tony Scott	.05
532	Ken Oberkfell	.05
533	Bob Sykes	.05
534	Keith Smith	.05
535	John Littlefield	.05
536	Jim Kaat	.04
537	Bob Forsch	.05
538	Mike Phillips	.05
539	Terry Landrum **RC**	.05
540	Leon Durham **RC**	.08
541	Terry Kennedy	.05
542	George Hendrick	.05
543	Dane Iorg	.05
544	Mark Littell (Photo actually Jeff Little.)	.05
545	Keith Hernandez	.04
546	Silvio Martinez	.05
547a	Pete Vuckovich (Photo actually Don Hood.)	.11
547b	Don Hood (Correct name with photo.)	.40
548	Bobby Bonds	.08
549	Mike Ramsey	.05
550	Tom Herr	.05
551	Roy Smalley	.05
552	Jerry Koosman	.05
553	Ken Landreaux	.05
554	John Castino	.05
555	Doug Corbett	.05
556	Bombo Rivera	.05
557	Ron Jackson	.05
558	Butch Wynegar	.05
559	Hosken Powell	.05
560	Pete Redfern	.05
561	Roger Erickson	.05
562	Glenn Adams	.05
563	Rick Sofield	.05
564	Geoff Zahn	.05
565	Pete Mackanin	.05
566	Mike Cubbage	.05
567	Darrell Jackson	.05
568	Dave Edwards	.05
569	Rob Wilfong	.05
570	Sal Butera	.05
571	Jose Morales	.05
572	Rick Langford	.05
573	Mike Norris	.05
574	Rickey Henderson	2.00
575	Tony Armas	.05
576	Dave Revering	.05
577	Jeff Newman	.05
578	Bob Lacey	.05
579	Brian Kingman (Photo actually Alan Wirth.)	.05
580	Mitchell Page	.05
581	Billy Martin	.20
582	Rob Picciolo	.05
583	Mike Heath	.05
584	Mickey Klutts	.05
585	Orlando Gonzalez	.05
586	Mike Davis **RC**	.05
587	Wayne Gross	.05
588	Matt Keough	.05
589	Steve McCatty	.05
590	Dwayne Murphy	.05
591	Mario Guerrero	.05
592	Dave McKay	.05
593	Jim Essian	.05
594	Dave Heaverlo	.05
595	Maury Wills	.08
596	Juan Beniquez	.05
597	Rodney Craig	.05
598	Jim Anderson	.05
599	Floyd Bannister	.05
600	Bruce Bochte	.05
601	Julio Cruz	.05
602	Ted Cox	.05
603	Dan Meyer	.05
604	Larry Cox	.05
605	Bill Stein	.05
606	Steve Garvey	.25
607	Dave Roberts	.05
608	Leon Roberts	.05
609	Reggie Walton	.05
610	Dave Edler	.05
611	Larry Milbourne	.05
612	Kim Allen	.05
613	Mario Mendoza	.05
614	Tom Paciorek	.05
615	Glenn Abbott	.05
616	Joe Simpson	.05
617	Mickey Rivers	.05
618	Jim Kern	.05
619	Jim Sundberg	.05
620	Richie Zisk	.06
621	Jon Matlack	.06
622	Fergie Jenkins	.60
623	Pat Corrales	.05
624	Ed Figueroa	.05
625	Buddy Bell	.04
626	Al Oliver	.04
627	Doc Medich	.05
628	Bump Wills	.05
629	Rusty Staub	.04
630	Pat Putnam	.05
631	John Grubb	.05
632	Danny Darwin	.05
633	Ken Clay	.05
634	Jim Norris	.05
635	John Butcher	.05
636	Dave Roberts	.05
637	Billy Sample	.05
638	Carl Yastrzemski	.70
639	Cecil Cooper	.05
640	Mike Schmidt	1.50
641a	Checklist 1-50 (41 Hal McRae)	.08
641b	Checklist 1-50 (41 Hal McRae Double Threat)	.08
642	Checklist 51-109	.05
643	Checklist 110-168	.05
644a	Checklist 169-220 (202 George Foster)	.08
644b	Checklist 169-220 (202 George Foster "Slugger")	.08
(645a)	Larry Bowa, Pete Rose, Mike Schmidt Triple Threat (No number on back.)	1.50
645b	Pete Rose, Larry Bowa, Mike Schmidt Triple Threat (Number on back.)	1.50
646	Checklist 221-267	.05
647	Checklist 268-315	.05
648	Checklist 316-359	.05
649	Checklist 360-408	.05
650	Reggie Jackson	1.50
651	Checklist 409-458	.05
652a	Checklist 459-509 (483 Aurelio Lopez)	.08
652b	Checklist 459-506 (No 483.)	.08
653	Willie Wilson	.04
654a	Checklist 507-550 (514 Jerry Augustine)	.08
654b	Checklist 507-550 (514 Billy Travers)	.08
655	George Brett	2.25
656	Checklist 551-593	.05
657	Tug McGraw	.04
658	Checklist 594-637	.05
659a	Checklist 640-660 (Last number on front is 551.)	.08
659b	Checklist 640-660 (Last number on front is 483.)	.11
660a	Steve Carlton (Date 1066 on back.)	.70
660b	Steve Carlton (Date 1966 on back.)	1.50

1982 Fleer

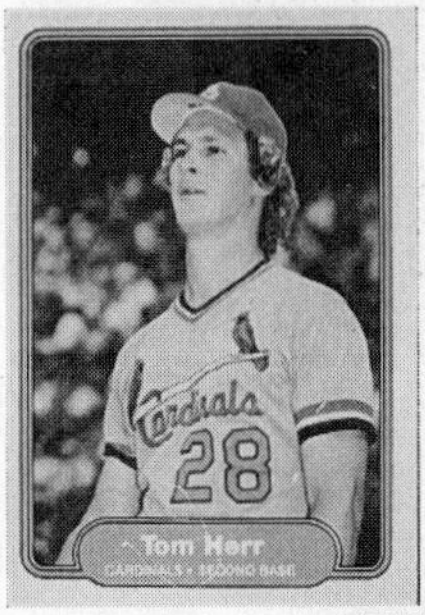

		NM/M
Complete Set (660):		45.00
Common Player:		.05
Wax Pack (15):		3.00
Wax Box (36):		85.00
Cello Pack (28):		4.00
Cello Box (24):		85.00
Vending Box (500):		40.00
1	Dusty Baker	.05
2	Robert Castillo	.05
3	Ron Cey	.05
4	Terry Forster	.05
5	Steve Garvey	.30
6	Dave Goltz	.05
7	Pedro Guerrero	.05
8	Burt Hooton	.05
9	Steve Howe	.05
10	Jay Johnstone	.05
11	Ken Landreaux	.05
12	Davey Lopes	.05
13	Mike Marshall **RC**	.15
14	Bobby Mitchell	.05
15	Rick Monday	.05
16	Tom Niedenfuer **RC**	.05
17	Ted Power **RC**	.05
18	Jerry Reuss	.05
19	Ron Roenicke	.05
20	Bill Russell	.05
21	Steve Sax **RC**	.45
22	Mike Scioscia	.05
23	Reggie Smith	.05
24	Dave Stewart **RC**	1.50
25	Rick Sutcliffe	.05
26	Derrel Thomas	.05
27	Fernando Valenzuela	.10
28	Bob Welch	.05
29	Steve Yeager	.05
30	Bobby Brown	.05
31	Rick Cerone	.05
32	Ron Davis	.05
33	Bucky Dent	.10
34	Barry Foote	.05
35	George Frazier	.05
36	Oscar Gamble	.05
37	Rich Gossage	.10
38	Ron Guidry	.10
39	Reggie Jackson	1.50
40	Tommy John	.10
41	Rudy May	.05
42	Larry Milbourne	.05
43	Jerry Mumphrey	.05
44	Bobby Murcer	.10
45	Gene Nelson **RC**	.05
46	Graig Nettles	.10
47	Johnny Oates	.05
48	Lou Piniella	.10
49	Willie Randolph	.05
50	Rick Reuschel	.05
51	Dave Revering	.05
52	Dave Righetti **RC**	.45
53	Aurelio Rodriguez	.05
54	Bob Watson	.05
55	Dennis Werth	.05
56	Dave Winfield	1.00

57	Johnny Bench	1.00
58	Bruce Berenyi	.05
59	Larry Biittner	.05
60	Scott Brown	.05
61	Dave Collins	.05
62	Geoff Combe	.05
63	Dave Concepcion	.05
64	Dan Driessen	.05
65	Joe Edelen	.05
66	George Foster	.05
67	Ken Griffey	.05
68	Paul Householder	.05
69	Tom Hume	.05
70	Junior Kennedy	.05
71	Ray Knight	.05
72	Mike LaCoss	.05
73	Rafael Landestoy	.05
74	Charlie Leibrandt	.05
75	Sam Mejias	.05
76	Paul Moskau	.05
77	Joe Nolan	.05
78	Mike O'Berry	.05
79	Ron Oester	.05
80	Frank Pastore	.05
81	Joe Price	.05
82	Tom Seaver	1.00
83	Mario Soto	.05
84	Mike Vail	.05
85	Tony Armas	.05
86	Shooty Babitt	.05
87	Dave Beard	.05
88	Rick Bosetti	.05
89	Keith Drumright	.05
90	Wayne Gross	.05
91	Mike Heath	.05
92	Rickey Henderson	1.00
93	Cliff Johnson	.05
94	Jeff Jones	.05
95	Matt Keough	.05
96	Brian Kingman	.05
97	Mickey Klutts	.05
98	Rick Langford	.05
99	Steve McCatty	.05
100	Dave McKay	.05
101	Dwayne Murphy	.05
102	Jeff Newman	.05
103	Mike Norris	.05
104	Bob Owchinko	.05
105	Mitchell Page	.05
106	Rob Picciolo	.05
107	Jim Spencer	.05
108	Fred Stanley	.05
109	Tom Underwood	.05
110	Joaquin Andujar	.05
111	Steve Braun	.05
112	Bob Forsch	.05
113	George Hendrick	.05
114	Keith Hernandez	.05
115	Tom Herr	.05
116	Dane Iorg	.05
117	Jim Kaat	.10
118	Tito Landrum	.05
119	Sixto Lezcano	.05
120	Mark Littell	.05
121	John Martin	.05
122	Silvio Martinez	.05
123	Ken Oberkfell	.05
124	Darrell Porter	.05
125	Mike Ramsey	.05
126	Orlando Sanchez	.05
127	Bob Shirley	.05
128	Lary Sorensen	.05
129	Bruce Sutter	.75
130	Bob Sykes	.05
131	Garry Templeton	.05
132	Gene Tenace	.05
133	Jerry Augustine	.05
134	Sal Bando	.05
135	Mark Brouhard	.05
136	Mike Caldwell	.05
137	Reggie Cleveland	.05
138	Cecil Cooper	.05
139	Jamie Easterly	.05
140	Marshall Edwards	.05
141	Rollie Fingers	.75
142	Jim Gantner	.05
143	Moose Haas	.05
144	Larry Hisle	.05
145	Roy Howell	.05
146	Rickey Keeton	.05
147	Randy Lerch	.05
148	Paul Molitor	1.00
149	Don Money	.05
150	Charlie Moore	.05
151	Ben Oglivie	.05
152	Ted Simmons	.05
153	Jim Slaton	.05
154	Gorman Thomas	.05
155	Robin Yount	1.00
156	Pete Vukovich	.05
157	Benny Ayala	.05
158	Mark Belanger	.05
159	Al Bumbry	.05
160	Terry Crowley	.05
161	Rich Dauer	.05
162	Doug DeCinces	.05
163	Rick Dempsey	.05
164	Jim Dwyer	.05
165	Mike Flanagan	.05
166	Dave Ford	.05
167	Dan Graham	.05
168	Wayne Krenchicki	.05
169	John Lowenstein	.05
170	Dennis Martinez	.05
171	Tippy Martinez	.05
172	Scott McGregor	.05
173	Jose Morales	.05
174	Eddie Murray	1.00
175	Jim Palmer	1.00
176	Cal Ripken, Jr. **RC**	40.00
177	Gary Roenicke	.05
178	Lenn Sakata	.05
179	Ken Singleton	.05
180	Sammy Stewart	.05
181	Tim Stoddard	.05
182	Steve Stone	.05
183	Stan Bahnsen	.05
184	Ray Burris	.05
185	Gary Carter	1.00
186	Warren Cromartie	.05
187	Andre Dawson	.50
188	Terry Francona **RC**	.05
189	Woodie Fryman	.05
190	Bill Gullickson	.05
191	Grant Jackson	.05
192	Wallace Johnson	.05
193	Charlie Lea	.05
194	Bill Lee	.05
195	Jerry Manuel	.05
196	Brad Mills	.05
197	John Milner	.05
198	Rowland Office	.05
199	David Palmer	.05
200	Larry Parrish	.05
201	Mike Phillips	.05
202	Tim Raines	.25
203	Bobby Ramos	.05
204	Jeff Reardon	.05
205	Steve Rogers	.05
206	Scott Sanderson	.05
207	Rodney Scott	
	(Photo actually Tim Raines.)	.10
208	Elias Sosa	.05
209	Chris Speier	.05
210	Tim Wallach **RC**	1.00
211	Jerry White	.05
212	Alan Ashby	.05
213	Cesar Cedeno	.05
214	Jose Cruz	.05
215	Kiko Garcia	.05
216	Phil Garner	.05
217	Danny Heep	.05
218	Art Howe	.05
219	Bob Knepper	.05
220	Frank LaCorte	.05
221	Joe Niekro	.05
222	Joe Pittman	.05
223	Terry Puhl	.05
224	Luis Pujols	.05
225	Craig Reynolds	.05
226	J.R. Richard	.05
227	Dave Roberts	.05
228	Vern Ruhle	.05
229	Nolan Ryan	3.00
230	Joe Sambito	.05
231	Tony Scott	.05
232	Dave Smith	.05
233	Harry Spilman	.05
234	Don Sutton	.75
235	Dickie Thon	.05
236	Denny Walling	.05
237	Gary Woods	.05
238	Luis Aguayo **RC**	.05
239	Ramon Aviles	.05
240	Bob Boone	.05
241	Larry Bowa	.05
242	Warren Brusstar	.05
243	Steve Carlton	1.00
244	Larry Christenson	.05
245	Dick Davis	.05
246	Greg Gross	.05
247	Sparky Lyle	.05
248	Garry Maddox	.05
249	Gary Matthews	.05
250	Bake McBride	.05
251	Tug McGraw	.05
252	Keith Moreland	.05
253	Dickie Noles	.05
254	Mike Proly	.05
255	Ron Reed	.05
256	Pete Rose	2.50
257	Dick Ruthven	.05
258	Mike Schmidt	2.00
259	Lonnie Smith	.05
260	Manny Trillo	.05
261	Del Unser	.05
262	George Vukovich	.05
263	Tom Brookens	.05
264	George Cappuzzello	.05
265	Marty Castillo	.05
266	Al Cowens	.05
267	Kirk Gibson	.05
268	Richie Hebner	.05
269	Ron Jackson	.05
270	Lynn Jones	.05
271	Steve Kemp	.05
272	Rick Leach **RC**	.25
273	Aurelio Lopez	.05
274	Jack Morris	.05
275	Kevin Saucier	.05
276	Lance Parrish	.05
277	Rick Peters	.05
278	Dan Petry	.05
279	David Rozema	.05
280	Stan Papi	.05
281	Dan Schatzeder	.05
282	Champ Summers	.05
283	Alan Trammell	.05
284	Lou Whitaker	.05
285	Milt Wilcox	.05
286	John Wockenfuss	.05
287	Gary Allenson	.05
288	Tom Burgmeier	.05
289	Bill Campbell	.05
290	Mark Clear	.05
291	Steve Crawford	.05
292	Dennis Eckersley	.75
293	Dwight Evans	.05
294	Rich Gedman **RC**	.10
295	Garry Hancock	.05
296	Glenn Hoffman	.05
297	Bruce Hurst	.05
298	Carney Lansford	.05
299	Rick Miller	.05
300	Reid Nichols	.05
301	Bob Ojeda **RC**	.25
302	Tony Perez	.75
303	Chuck Rainey	.05
304	Jerry Remy	.05
305	Jim Rice	.50
306	Joe Rudi	.05
307	Bob Stanley	.05
308	Dave Stapleton	.05
309	Frank Tanana	.05
310	Mike Torrez	.05
311	John Tudor	.05
312	Carl Yastrzemski	1.00
313	Buddy Bell	.05
314	Steve Comer	.05
315	Danny Darwin	.05
316	John Ellis	.05
317	John Grubb	.05
318	Rick Honeycutt	.05
319	Charlie Hough	.05
320	Ferguson Jenkins	.75
321	John Henry Johnson	.05
322	Jim Kern	.05
323	Jon Matlack	.05
324	Doc Medich	.05
325	Mario Mendoza	.05
326	Al Oliver	.05
327	Pat Putnam	.05
328	Mickey Rivers	.05
329	Leon Roberts	.05
330	Billy Sample	.05
331	Bill Stein	.05
332	Jim Sundberg	.05
333	Mark Wagner	.05
334	Bump Wills	.05
335	Bill Almon	.05
336	Harold Baines	.05
337	Ross Baumgarten	.05
338	Tony Bernazard	.05
339	Britt Burns	.05
340	Richard Dotson	.05
341	Jim Essian	.05
342	Ed Farmer	.05
343	Carlton Fisk	1.00
344	Kevin Hickey	.05
345	Lamarr Hoyt (LaMarr)	.05
346	Lamar Johnson	.05
347	Jerry Koosman	.05
348	Rusty Kuntz	.05
349	Dennis Lamp	.05
350	Ron LeFlore	.05
351	Chet Lemon	.05
352	Greg Luzinski	.05
353	Bob Molinaro	.05
354	Jim Morrison	.05
355	Wayne Nordhagen	.05
356	Greg Pryor	.05
357	Mike Squires	.05
358	Steve Trout	.05
359	Alan Bannister	.05
360	Len Barker	.05
361	Bert Blyleven	.10
362	Joe Charboneau	.10
363	John Denny	.05
364	Bo Diaz	.05
365	Miguel Dilone	.05
366	Jerry Dybzinski	.05
367	Wayne Garland	.05
368	Mike Hargrove	.05
369	Toby Harrah	.05
370	Ron Hassey	.05
371	Von Hayes **RC**	.25
372	Pat Kelly	.05
373	Duane Kuiper	.05
374	Rick Manning	.05
375	Sid Monge	.05
376	Jorge Orta	.05
377	Dave Rosello	.05
378	Dan Spillner	.05
379	Mike Stanton	.05
380	Andre Thornton	.05
381	Tom Veryzer	.05
382	Rick Waits	.05
383	Doyle Alexander	.05
384	Vida Blue	.05
385	Fred Breining	.05
386	Enos Cabell	.05
387	Jack Clark	.05
388	Darrell Evans	.05
389	Tom Griffin	.05
390	Larry Herndon	.05
391	Al Holland	.05
392	Gary Lavelle	.05
393	Johnnie LeMaster	.05
394	Jerry Martin	.05
395	Milt May	.05
396	Greg Minton	.05
397	Joe Morgan	1.00
398	Joe Pettini	.05
399	Alan Ripley	.05
400	Billy Smith	.05
401	Rennie Stennett	.05
402	Ed Whitson	.05
403	Jim Wohlford	.05
404	Willie Aikens	.05
405	George Brett	2.00
406	Ken Brett	.05
407	Dave Chalk	.05
408	Rich Gale	.05
409	Cesar Geronimo	.05
410	Larry Gura	.05
411	Clint Hurdle	.05
412	Mike Jones	.05
413	Dennis Leonard	.05
414	Renie Martin	.05
415	Lee May	.05
416	Hal McRae	.05
417	Darryl Motley	.05
418	Rance Mulliniks	.05
419	Amos Otis	.05
420	Ken Phelps **RC**	.05
421	Jamie Quirk	.05
422	Dan Quisenberry	.05
423	Paul Splittorff	.05
424	U.L. Washington	.05
425	John Wathan	.05
426	Frank White	.05
427	Willie Wilson	.05
428	Brian Asselstine	.05
429	Bruce Benedict	.05
430	Tom Boggs	.05
431	Larry Bradford	.05
432	Rick Camp	.05
433	Chris Chambliss	.05
434	Gene Garber	.05
435	Preston Hanna	.05
436	Bob Horner	.05
437	Glenn Hubbard	.05
438a	Al Hrabosky	
	(All Hrabosky, 5'1" on back.)	4.50
438b	Al Hrabosky	
	(Al Hrabosky, 5'1" on back.)	1.00
438c	Al Hrabosky	
	(Al Hrabosky, 5'10" on back.)	.25
439	Rufino Linares	.05
440	Rick Mahler **RC**	.05
441	Ed Miller	.05
442	John Montefusco	.05
443	Dale Murphy	.50
444	Phil Niekro	.75
445	Gaylord Perry	.75
446	Biff Pocoroba	.05
447	Rafael Ramirez	.05
448	Jerry Royster	.05
449	Claudell Washington	.05
450	Don Aase	.05
451	Don Baylor	.05
452	Juan Beniquez	.05
453	Rick Burleson	.05
454	Bert Campaneris	.05
455	Rod Carew	1.00
456	Bob Clark	.05
457	Brian Downing	.05
458	Dan Ford	.05
459	Ken Forsch	.05
460	Dave Frost	.05
461	Bobby Grich	.05
462	Larry Harlow	.05
463	John Harris	.05
464	Andy Hassler	.05
465	Butch Hobson	.05
466	Jesse Jefferson	.05
467	Bruce Kison	.05
468	Fred Lynn	.05
469	Angel Moreno	.05
470	Ed Ott	.05
471	Fred Patek	.05
472	Steve Renko	.05
473	Mike Witt **RC**	.10
474	Geoff Zahn	.05
475	Gary Alexander	.05
476	Dale Berra	.05
477	Kurt Bevacqua	.05
478	Jim Bibby	.05
479	John Candelaria	.05
480	Victor Cruz	.05
481	Mike Easler	.05
482	Tim Foli	.05
483	Lee Lacy	.05
484	Vance Law	.05
485	Bill Madlock	.05
486	Willie Montanez	.05
487	Omar Moreno	.05
488	Steve Nicosia	.05
489	Dave Parker	.05
490	Tony Pena	.05
491	Pascual Perez	.05
492	Johnny Ray **RC**	.05
493	Rick Rhoden	.05
494	Bill Robinson	.05
495	Don Robinson	.05
496	Enrique Romo	.05
497	Rod Scurry	.05
498	Eddie Solomon	.05
499	Willie Stargell	1.00
500	Kent Tekulve	.05
501	Jason Thompson	.05
502	Glenn Abbott	.05
503	Jim Anderson	.05
504	Floyd Bannister	.05
505	Bruce Bochte	.05
506	Jeff Burroughs	.05
507	Bryan Clark	.05
508	Ken Clay	.05
509	Julio Cruz	.05
510	Dick Drago	.05

511 Gary Gray .05
512 Dan Meyer .05
513 Jerry Narron .05
514 Tom Paciorek .05
515 Casey Parsons .05
516 Lenny Randle .05
517 Shane Rawley .05
518 Joe Simpson .05
519 Richie Zisk .05
520 Neil Allen .05
521 Bob Bailor .05
522 Hubie Brooks .05
523 Mike Cubbage .05
524 Pete Falcone .05
525 Doug Flynn .05
526 Tom Hausman .05
527 Ron Hodges .05
528 Randy Jones .05
529 Mike Jorgensen .05
530 Dave Kingman .05
531 Ed Lynch .05
532 Mike Marshall .05
533 Lee Mazzilli .05
534 Dyar Miller .05
535 Mike Scott .05
536 Rusty Staub .05
537 John Stearns .05
538 Craig Swan .05
539 Frank Taveras .05
540 Alex Trevino .05
541 Ellis Valentine .05
542 Mookie Wilson .05
543 Joel Youngblood .05
544 Pat Zachry .05
545 Glenn Adams .05
546 Fernando Arroyo .05
547 John Verhoeven .05
548 Sal Butera .05
549 John Castino .05
550 Don Cooper .05
551 Doug Corbett .05
552 Dave Engle .05
553 Roger Erickson .05
554 Danny Goodwin .05
555a Darrell Jackson (Black cap.) .65
555b Darrell Jackson (Red cap w/speck of white.) 3.00
555c Darrell Jackson (Red cap w/white T.) .10
556 Pete Mackanin .05
557 Jack O'Connor .05
558 Hosken Powell .05
559 Pete Redfern .05
560 Roy Smalley .05
561 Chuck Baker .05
562 Gary Ward .05
563 Rob Wilfong .05
564 Al Williams .05
565 Butch Wynegar .05
566 Randy Bass .05
567 Juan Bonilla .05
568 Danny Boone .05
569 John Curtis .05
570 Juan Eichelberger .05
571 Barry Evans .05
572 Tim Flannery .05
573 Ruppert Jones .05
574 Terry Kennedy .05
575 Joe Lefebvre .05
576a John Littlefield (Pitching lefty.) 80.00
576b John Littlefield (Pitching righty.) .05
577 Gary Lucas .05
578 Steve Mura .05
579 Broderick Perkins .05
580 Gene Richards .05
581 Luis Salazar .05
582 Ozzie Smith 1.50
583 John Urrea .05
584 Chris Welsh .05
585 Rick Wise .05
586 Doug Bird .05
587 Tim Blackwell .05
588 Bobby Bonds .10
589 Bill Buckner .05
590 Bill Caudill .05
591 Hector Cruz .05
592 Jody Davis **RC** .10
593 Ivan DeJesus .05
594 Steve Dillard .05
595 Leon Durham .05
596 Rawly Eastwick .05
597 Steve Henderson .05
598 Mike Krukow .05
599 Mike Lum .05
600 Randy Martz .05
601 Jerry Morales .05
602 Ken Reitz .05
603a Lee Smith **RC** (Cubs logo reversed on back.) 2.50
603b Lee Smith **RC** (corrected) 2.50
604 Dick Tidrow .05
605 Jim Tracy .05
606 Mike Tyson .05
607 Ty Waller .05
608 Danny Ainge .50
609 Jorge Bell **RC** 1.00
610 Mark Bomback .05
611 Barry Bonnell .05
612 Jim Clancy .05
613 Damaso Garcia .05
614 Jerry Garvin .05
615 Alfredo Griffin .05
616 Garth Iorg .05
617 Luis Leal .05
618 Ken Macha .05
619 John Mayberry .05
620 Joey McLaughlin .05
621 Lloyd Moseby .05
622 Dave Stieb .05
623 Jackson Todd .05
624 Willie Upshaw .05
625 Otto Velez .05
626 Ernie Whitt .05
627 Al Woods .05
628 1981 All-Star Game .05
629 Bucky Dent, Frank White All-Star Infielders .05
630 Dave Concepcion, Dan Driessen, George Foster Big Red Machine .10
631 Bruce Sutter Top N.L. Relief Pitcher .30
632 Steve Carlton, Carlton Fisk Steve & Carlton .25
633 Carl Yastrzemski 3000th Game, May 25, 1981 .35
634 Johnny Bench, Tom Seaver Dynamic Duo .30
635 Gary Carter, Fernando Valenzuela West Meets East .20
636a Fernando Valenzuela N.L. Strikeout King ("...led the National League...") .50
636b Fernando Valenzuela N.L. Strikeout King ("... led the National League...") .25
637 Mike Schmidt Home Run King .50
638 Gary Carter, Dave Parker N.L. All-Stars .25
639 Len Barker, Bo Diaz Perfect Game! .05
640 Pete Rose, Pete Rose, Jr. (Re-Pete) 2.00
641 Steve Carlton, Mike Schmidt, Lonnie Smith Phillies' Finest .50
642 Dwight Evans, Fred Lynn Red Sox Reunion .10
643 Rickey Henderson Most Hits and Runs 1.00
644 Rollie Fingers Most Saves 1981 A.L. .15
645 Tom Seaver Most 1981 Wins .25
646a Reggie Jackson, Dave Winfield Yankee Powerhouse (Comma after "outfielder" on back.) 1.50
646b Reggie Jackson, Dave Winfield Yankee Powerhouse (No comma.) 2.00
647 Checklist 1-56 .05
648 Checklist 57-109 .05
649 Checklist 110-156 .05
650 Checklist 157-211 .05
651 Checklist 212-262 .05
652 Checklist 263-312 .05
653 Checklist 313-358 .05
654 Checklist 359-403 .05
655 Checklist 404-449 .05
656 Checklist 450-501 .05
657 Checklist 502-544 .05
658 Checklist 545-585 .05
659 Checklist 586-627 .05
660 Checklist 628-646 .05

1983 Fleer

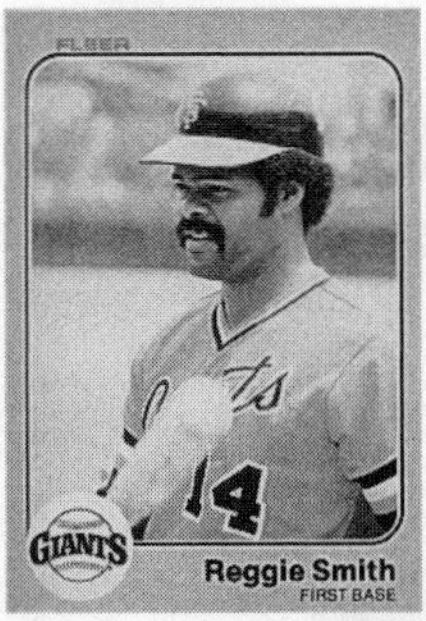

	NM/M
Complete Set (660):	40.00
Common Player:	.05
Wax Pack (15):	3.00
Wax Box (38):	100.00
Cello Pack (28):	4.00
Cello Box (24):	80.00
Vending Box (500):	35.00

1 Joaquin Andujar .05
2 Doug Bair .05
3 Steve Braun .05
4 Glenn Brummer .05
5 Bob Forsch .05
6 David Green .05
7 George Hendrick .05
8 Keith Hernandez .05
9 Tom Herr .05
10 Dane Iorg .05
11 Jim Kaat .10
12 Jeff Lahti .05
13 Tito Landrum .05
14 Dave LaPoint **RC** .05
15 Willie McGee **RC** 1.50
16 Steve Mura .05
17 Ken Oberkfell .05
18 Darrell Porter .05
19 Mike Ramsey .05
20 Gene Roof .05
21 Lonnie Smith .05
22 Ozzie Smith 1.50
23 John Stuper .05
24 Bruce Sutter .65
25 Gene Tenace .05
26 Jerry Augustine .05
27 Dwight Bernard .05
28 Mark Brouhard .05
29 Mike Caldwell .05
30 Cecil Cooper .05
31 Jamie Easterly .05
32 Marshall Edwards .05
33 Rollie Fingers .65
34 Jim Gantner .05
35 Moose Haas .05
36 Roy Howell .05
37 Peter Ladd .05
38 Bob McClure .05
39 Doc Medich .05
40 Paul Molitor .75
41 Don Money .05
42 Charlie Moore .05
43 Ben Oglivie .05
44 Ed Romero .05
45 Ted Simmons .05
46 Jim Slaton .05
47 Don Sutton .65
48 Gorman Thomas .05
49 Pete Vuckovich .05
50 Ned Yost .05
51 Robin Yount .75
52 Benny Ayala .05
53 Bob Bonner .05
54 Al Bumbry .05
55 Terry Crowley .05
56 Storm Davis **RC** .10
57 Rich Dauer .05
58 Rick Dempsey .05
59 Jim Dwyer .05
60 Mike Flanagan .05
61 Dan Ford .05
62 Glenn Gulliver .05
63 John Lowenstein .05
64 Dennis Martinez .05
65 Tippy Martinez .05
66 Scott McGregor .05
67 Eddie Murray .75
68 Joe Nolan .05
69 Jim Palmer .75
70 Cal Ripken, Jr. 6.00
71 Gary Roenicke .05
72 Lenn Sakata .05
73 Ken Singleton .05
74 Sammy Stewart .05
75 Tim Stoddard .05
76 Don Aase .05
77 Don Baylor .05
78 Juan Beniquez .05
79 Bob Boone .05
80 Rick Burleson .05
81 Rod Carew .75
82 Bobby Clark .05
83 Doug Corbett .05
84 John Curtis .05
85 Doug DeCinces .05
86 Brian Downing .05
87 Joe Ferguson .05
88 Tim Foli .05
89 Ken Forsch .05
90 Dave Goltz .05
91 Bobby Grich .05
92 Andy Hassler .05
93 Reggie Jackson 1.50
94 Ron Jackson .05
95 Tommy John .10
96 Bruce Kison .05
97 Fred Lynn .05
98 Ed Ott .05
99 Steve Renko .05
100 Luis Sanchez .05
101 Rob Wilfong .05
102 Mike Witt .05
103 Geoff Zahn .05
104 Willie Aikens .05
105 Mike Armstrong .05
106 Vida Blue .05
107 Bud Black **RC** .50
108 George Brett 2.00
109 Bill Castro .05
110 Onix Concepcion .05
111 Dave Frost .05
112 Cesar Geronimo .05
113 Larry Gura .05
114 Steve Hammond .05
115 Don Hood .05
116 Dennis Leonard .05
117 Jerry Martin .05
118 Lee May .05
119 Hal McRae .05
120 Amos Otis .05
121 Greg Pryor .05
122 Dan Quisenberry .05
123 Don Slaught **RC** .20
124 Paul Splittorff .05
125 U.L. Washington .05
126 John Wathan .05
127 Frank White .05
128 Willie Wilson .05
129 Steve Bedrosian .05
130 Bruce Benedict .05
131 Tommy Boggs .05
132 Brett Butler .05
133 Rick Camp .05
134 Chris Chambliss .05
135 Ken Dayley .05
136 Gene Garber .05
137 Terry Harper .05
138 Bob Horner .05
139 Glenn Hubbard .05
140 Rufino Linares .05
141 Rick Mahler .05
142 Dale Murphy .50
143 Phil Niekro .65
144 Pascual Perez .05
145 Biff Pocoroba .05
146 Rafael Ramirez .05
147 Jerry Royster .05
148 Ken Smith .05
149 Bob Walk .05
150 Claudell Washington .05
151 Bob Watson .05
152 Larry Whisenton .05
153 Porfirio Altamirano .05
154 Marty Bystrom .05
155 Steve Carlton .75
156 Larry Christenson .05
157 Ivan DeJesus .05
158 John Denny .05
159 Bob Dernier .05
160 Bo Diaz .05
161 Ed Farmer .05
162 Greg Gross .05
163 Mike Krukow .05
164 Garry Maddox .05
165 Gary Matthews .05
166 Tug McGraw .05
167 Bob Molinaro .05
168 Sid Monge .05
169 Ron Reed .05
170 Bill Robinson .05
171 Pete Rose 3.00
172 Dick Ruthven .05
173 Mike Schmidt 2.00
174 Manny Trillo .05
175 Ozzie Virgil .05
176 George Vukovich .05
177 Gary Allenson .05
178 Luis Aponte .05
179 Wade Boggs **RC** 10.00
180 Tom Burgmeier .05
181 Mark Clear .05
182 Dennis Eckersley .65
183 Dwight Evans .05
184 Rich Gedman .05
185 Glenn Hoffman .05
186 Bruce Hurst .05
187 Carney Lansford .05
188 Rick Miller .05
189 Reid Nichols .05
190 Bob Ojeda .05
191 Tony Perez .65
192 Chuck Rainey .05
193 Jerry Remy .05
194 Jim Rice .35
195 Bob Stanley .05
196 Dave Stapleton .05
197 Mike Torrez .05
198 John Tudor .05
199 Julio Valdez .05
200 Carl Yastrzemski .75
201 Dusty Baker .05
202 Joe Beckwith .05
203 Greg Brock **RC** .05
204 Ron Cey .05
205 Terry Forster .05
206 Steve Garvey .30
207 Pedro Guerrero .05
208 Burt Hooton .05
209 Steve Howe .05
210 Ken Landreaux .05
211 Mike Marshall .05
212 Candy Maldonado **RC** .05
213 Rick Monday .05
214 Tom Niedenfuer .05
215 Jorge Orta .05
216 Jerry Reuss .05
217 Ron Roenicke .05
218 Vicente Romo .05
219 Bill Russell .05
220 Steve Sax .05
221 Mike Scioscia .05
222 Dave Stewart .05
223 Derrel Thomas .05
224 Fernando Valenzuela .05
225 Bob Welch .05
226 Ricky Wright .05
227 Steve Yeager .05
228 Bill Almon .05
229 Harold Baines .05
230 Salome Barojas .05
231 Tony Bernazard .05
232 Britt Burns .05
233 Richard Dotson .05
234 Ernesto Escarrega .05
235 Carlton Fisk .75
236 Jerry Hairston Sr. .05
237 Kevin Hickey .05
238 LaMarr Hoyt .05
239 Steve Kemp .05
240 Jim Kern .05

241	Ron Kittle **RC**	.25
242	Jerry Koosman	.05
243	Dennis Lamp	.05
244	Rudy Law	.05
245	Vance Law	.05
246	Ron LeFlore	.05
247	Greg Luzinski	.05
248	Tom Paciorek	.05
249	Aurelio Rodriguez	.05
250	Mike Squires	.05
251	Steve Trout	.05
252	Jim Barr	.05
253	Dave Bergman	.05
254	Fred Breining	.05
255	Bob Brenly	.05
256	Jack Clark	.05
257	Chili Davis	.05
258	Darrell Evans	.05
259	Alan Fowlkes	.05
260	Rich Gale	.05
261	Atlee Hammaker	.05
262	Al Holland	.05
263	Duane Kuiper	.05
264	Bill Laskey	.05
265	Gary Lavelle	.05
266	Johnnie LeMaster	.05
267	Renie Martin	.05
268	Milt May	.05
269	Greg Minton	.05
270	Joe Morgan	.75
271	Tom O'Malley	.05
272	Reggie Smith	.05
273	Guy Sularz	.05
274	Champ Summers	.05
275	Max Venable	.05
276	Jim Wohlford	.05
277	Ray Burris	.05
278	Gary Carter	.75
279	Warren Cromartie	.05
280	Andre Dawson	.40
281	Terry Francona	.05
282	Doug Flynn	.05
283	Woody Fryman	.05
284	Bill Gullickson	.05
285	Wallace Johnson	.05
286	Charlie Lea	.05
287	Randy Lerch	.05
288	Brad Mills	.05
289	Dan Norman	.05
290	Al Oliver	.05
291	David Palmer	.05
292	Tim Raines	.05
293	Jeff Reardon	.05
294	Steve Rogers	.05
295	Scott Sanderson	.05
296	Dan Schatzeder	.05
297	Bryn Smith	.05
298	Chris Speier	.05
299	Tim Wallach	.05
300	Jerry White	.05
301	Joel Youngblood	.05
302	Ross Baumgarten	.05
303	Dale Berra	.05
304	John Candelaria	.05
305	Dick Davis	.05
306	Mike Easler	.05
307	Richie Hebner	.05
308	Lee Lacy	.05
309	Bill Madlock	.05
310	Larry McWilliams	.05
311	John Milner	.05
312	Omar Moreno	.05
313	Jim Morrison	.05
314	Steve Nicosia	.05
315	Dave Parker	.05
316	Tony Pena	.05
317	Johnny Ray	.05
318	Rick Rhoden	.05
319	Don Robinson	.05
320	Enrique Romo	.05
321	Manny Sarmiento	.05
322	Rod Scurry	.05
323	Jim Smith	.05
324	Willie Stargell	.75
325	Jason Thompson	.05
326	Kent Tekulve	.05
327a	Tom Brookens (Narrow (1/4") brown box at bottom on back.)	.45
327b	Tom Brookens (Wide (1-1/4") brown box at bottom on back.)	.05
328	Enos Cabell	.05
329	Kirk Gibson	.05
330	Larry Herndon	.05
331	Mike Ivie	.05
332	Howard Johnson **RC**	1.00
333	Lynn Jones	.05
334	Rick Leach	.05
335	Chet Lemon	.05
336	Jack Morris	.05
337	Lance Parrish	.05
338	Larry Pashnick	.05
339	Dan Petry	.05
340	Dave Rozema	.05
341	Dave Rucker	.05
342	Elias Sosa	.05
343	Dave Tobik	.05
344	Alan Trammell	.05
345	Jerry Turner	.05
346	Jerry Ujdur	.05
347	Pat Underwood	.05
348	Lou Whitaker	.05
349	Milt Wilcox	.05
350	Glenn Wilson **RC**	.05
351	John Wockenfuss	.05
352	Kurt Bevacqua	.05
353	Juan Bonilla	.05
354	Floyd Chiffer	.05
355	Luis DeLeon	.05
356	Dave Dravecky **RC**	.30
357	Dave Edwards	.05
358	Juan Eichelberger	.05
359	Tim Flannery	.05
360	Tony Gwynn **RC**	15.00
361	Ruppert Jones	.05
362	Terry Kennedy	.05
363	Joe Lefebvre	.05
364	Sixto Lezcano	.05
365	Tim Lollar	.05
366	Gary Lucas	.05
367	John Montefusco	.05
368	Broderick Perkins	.05
369	Joe Pittman	.05
370	Gene Richards	.05
371	Luis Salazar	.05
372	Eric Show **RC**	.05
373	Garry Templeton	.05
374	Chris Welsh	.05
375	Alan Wiggins	.05
376	Rick Cerone	.05
377	Dave Collins	.05
378	Roger Erickson	.05
379	George Frazier	.05
380	Oscar Gamble	.05
381	Goose Gossage	.10
382	Ken Griffey	.05
383	Ron Guidry	.10
384	Dave LaRoche	.05
385	Rudy May	.05
386	John Mayberry	.05
387	Lee Mazzilli	.05
388	Mike Morgan	.05
389	Jerry Mumphrey	.05
390	Bobby Murcer	.10
391	Graig Nettles	.10
392	Lou Piniella	.10
393	Willie Randolph	.05
394	Shane Rawley	.05
395	Dave Righetti	.05
396	Andre Robertson	.05
397	Roy Smalley	.05
398	Dave Winfield	.75
399	Butch Wynegar	.05
400	Chris Bando	.05
401	Alan Bannister	.05
402	Len Barker	.05
403	Tom Brennan	.05
404	Carmelo Castillo **RC**	.05
405	Miguel Dilone	.05
406	Jerry Dybzinski	.05
407	Mike Fischlin	.05
408	Ed Glynn (Photo actually Bud Anderson.)	.05
409	Mike Hargrove	.05
410	Toby Harrah	.05
411	Ron Hassey	.05
412	Von Hayes	.05
413	Rick Manning	.05
414	Bake McBride	.05
415	Larry Milbourne	.05
416	Bill Nahorodny	.05
417	Jack Perconte	.05
418	Larry Sorensen	.05
419	Dan Spillner	.05
420	Rick Sutcliffe	.05
421	Andre Thornton	.05
422	Rick Waits	.05
423	Eddie Whitson	.05
424	Jesse Barfield	.05
425	Barry Bonnell	.05
426	Jim Clancy	.05
427	Damaso Garcia	.05
428	Jerry Garvin	.05
429	Alfredo Griffin	.05
430	Garth Iorg	.05
431	Roy Lee Jackson	.05
432	Luis Leal	.05
433	Buck Martinez	.05
434	Joey McLaughlin	.05
435	Lloyd Moseby	.05
436	Rance Mulliniks	.05
437	Dale Murray	.05
438	Wayne Nordhagen	.05
439	Gene Petralli **RC**	.05
440	Hosken Powell	.05
441	Dave Stieb	.05
442	Willie Upshaw	.05
443	Ernie Whitt	.05
444	Al Woods	.05
445	Alan Ashby	.05
446	Jose Cruz	.05
447	Kiko Garcia	.05
448	Phil Garner	.05
449	Danny Heep	.05
450	Art Howe	.05
451	Bob Knepper	.05
452	Alan Knicely	.05
453	Ray Knight	.05
454	Frank LaCorte	.05
455	Mike LaCoss	.05
456	Randy Moffitt	.05
457	Joe Niekro	.05
458	Terry Puhl	.05
459	Luis Pujols	.05
460	Craig Reynolds	.05
461	Bert Roberge	.05
462	Vern Ruhle	.05
463	Nolan Ryan	4.00
464	Joe Sambito	.05
465	Tony Scott	.05
466	Dave Smith	.05
467	Harry Spilman	.05
468	Dickie Thon	.05
469	Denny Walling	.05
470	Larry Andersen	.05
471	Floyd Bannister	.05
472	Jim Beattie	.05
473	Bruce Bochte	.05
474	Manny Castillo	.05
475	Bill Caudill	.05
476	Bryan Clark	.05
477	Al Cowens	.05
478	Julio Cruz	.05
479	Todd Cruz	.05
480	Gary Gray	.05
481	Dave Henderson	.05
482	Mike Moore **RC**	.05
483	Gaylord Perry	.65
484	Dave Revering	.05
485	Joe Simpson	.05
486	Mike Stanton	.05
487	Rick Sweet	.05
488	Ed Vande Berg **RC**	.05
489	Richie Zisk	.05
490	Doug Bird	.05
491	Larry Bowa	.05
492	Bill Buckner	.05
493	Bill Campbell	.05
494	Jody Davis	.05
495	Leon Durham	.05
496	Steve Henderson	.05
497	Willie Hernandez	.05
498	Fergie Jenkins	.65
499	Jay Johnstone	.05
500	Junior Kennedy	.05
501	Randy Martz	.05
502	Jerry Morales	.05
503	Keith Moreland	.05
504	Dickie Noles	.05
505	Mike Proly	.05
506	Allen Ripley	.05
507	Ryne Sandberg **RC**	10.00
508	Lee Smith	1.00
509	Pat Tabler	.05
510	Dick Tidrow	.05
511	Bump Wills	.05
512	Gary Woods	.05
513	Tony Armas	.05
514	Dave Beard	.05
515	Jeff Burroughs	.05
516	John D'Acquisto	.05
517	Wayne Gross	.05
518	Mike Heath	.05
519	Rickey Henderson	.75
520	Cliff Johnson	.05
521	Matt Keough	.05
522	Brian Kingman	.05
523	Rick Langford	.05
524	Davey Lopes	.05
525	Steve McCatty	.05
526	Dave McKay	.05
527	Dan Meyer	.05
528	Dwayne Murphy	.05
529	Jeff Newman	.05
530	Mike Norris	.05
531	Bob Owchinko	.05
532	Joe Rudi	.05
533	Jimmy Sexton	.05
534	Fred Stanley	.05
535	Tom Underwood	.05
536	Neil Allen	.05
537	Wally Backman	.05
538	Bob Bailor	.05
539	Hubie Brooks	.05
540	Carlos Diaz	.05
541	Pete Falcone	.05
542	George Foster	.05
543	Ron Gardenhire	.05
544	Brian Giles	.05
545	Ron Hodges	.05
546	Randy Jones	.05
547	Mike Jorgensen	.05
548	Dave Kingman	.05
549	Ed Lynch	.05
550	Jesse Orosco	.05
551	Rick Ownbey	.05
552	Charlie Puleo **RC**	.05
553	Gary Rajsich	.05
554	Mike Scott	.05
555	Rusty Staub	.05
556	John Stearns	.05
557	Craig Swan	.05
558	Ellis Valentine	.05
559	Tom Veryzer	.05
560	Mookie Wilson	.05
561	Pat Zachry	.05
562	Buddy Bell	.05
563	John Butcher	.05
564	Steve Comer	.05
565	Danny Darwin	.05
566	Bucky Dent	.05
567	John Grubb	.05
568	Rick Honeycutt	.05
569	Dave Hostetler	.05
570	Charlie Hough	.05
571	Lamar Johnson	.05
572	Jon Matlack	.05
573	Paul Mirabella	.05
574	Larry Parrish	.05
575	Mike Richardt	.05
576	Mickey Rivers	.05
577	Billy Sample	.05
578	Dave Schmidt **RC**	.05
579	Bill Stein	.05
580	Jim Sundberg	.05
581	Frank Tanana	.05
582	Mark Wagner	.05
583	George Wright	.05
584	Johnny Bench	.75
585	Bruce Berenyi	.05
586	Larry Biittner	.05
587	Cesar Cedeno	.05
588	Dave Concepcion	.05
589	Dan Driessen	.05
590	Greg Harris	.05
591	Ben Hayes	.05
592	Paul Householder	.05
593	Tom Hume	.05
594	Wayne Krenchicki	.05
595	Rafael Landestoy	.05
596	Charlie Leibrandt	.05
597	Eddie Milner **RC**	.05
598	Ron Oester	.05
599	Frank Pastore	.05
600	Joe Price	.05
601	Tom Seaver	.75
602	Bob Shirley	.05
603	Mario Soto	.05
604	Alex Trevino	.05
605	Mike Vail	.05
606	Duane Walker	.05
607	Tom Brunansky	.05
608	Bobby Castillo	.05
609	John Castino	.05
610	Ron Davis	.05
611	Lenny Faedo	.05
612	Terry Felton	.05
613	Gary Gaetti **RC**	.35
614	Mickey Hatcher	.05
615	Brad Havens	.05
616	Kent Hrbek	.05
617	Randy S. Johnson	.05
618	Tim Laudner	.05
619	Jeff Little	.05
620	Bob Mitchell	.05
621	Jack O'Connor	.05
622	John Pacella	.05
623	Pete Redfern	.05
624	Jesus Vega	.05
625	Frank Viola **RC**	1.00
626	Ron Washington	.05
627	Gary Ward	.05
628	Al Williams	.05
629	Mark Clear, Dennis Eckersley, Carl Yastrzemski Red Sox All-Stars	.25
630	Terry Bulling, Gaylord Perry 300 Career Wins	.10
631	Dave Concepcion, Manny Trillo Pride of Venezuela	.10
632	Buddy Bell, Robin Yount All-Star Infielders	.20
633	Kent Hrbek, Dave Winfield Mr. Vet & Mr. Rookie	.25
634	Pete Rose, Willie Stargell Fountain of Youth	.40
635	Toby Harrah, Andre Thornton Big Chiefs	.05
636	Lonnie Smith, Ozzie Smith "Smith Bros."	.15
637	Gary Carter, Bo Diaz Base Stealers' Threat	.10
638	Gary Carter, Carlton Fisk All-Star Catchers	.15
639	Rickey Henderson/IA	.50
640	Reggie Jackson, Ben Oglivie Home Run Threats	.25
641	Joel Youngblood Two Teams - Same Day	.05
642	Len Barker, Ron Hassey Last Perfect Game	.05
643	Vida Blue Blue	.05
644	Bud Black Black &	.05
645	Reggie Jackson Power	.30
646	Rickey Henderson Speed &	.30
647	Checklist 1-51	.05
648	Checklist 52-103	.05
649	Checklist 104-152	.05
650	Checklist 153-200	.05
651	Checklist 201-251	.05
652	Checklist 252-301	.05
653	Checklist 302-351	.05
654	Checklist 352-399	.05
655	Checklist 400-444	.05
656	Checklist 445-489	.05
657	Checklist 490-535	.05
658	Checklist 536-583	.05
659	Checklist 584-628	.05
660	Checklist 629-646	.05

1984 Fleer

		NM/M
Complete Set (660):		40.00
Common Player:		.05
Wax Pack (15):		2.50
Wax Box (36):		75.00
Cello Pack (28):		4.50
Cello Box (24):		85.00
Vending Box (500):		40.00
1	Mike Boddicker	.05
2	Al Bumbry	.05
3	Todd Cruz	.05
4	Rich Dauer	.05
5	Storm Davis	.05
6	Rick Dempsey	.05
7	Jim Dwyer	.05
8	Mike Flanagan	.05
9	Dan Ford	.05
10	John Lowenstein	.05

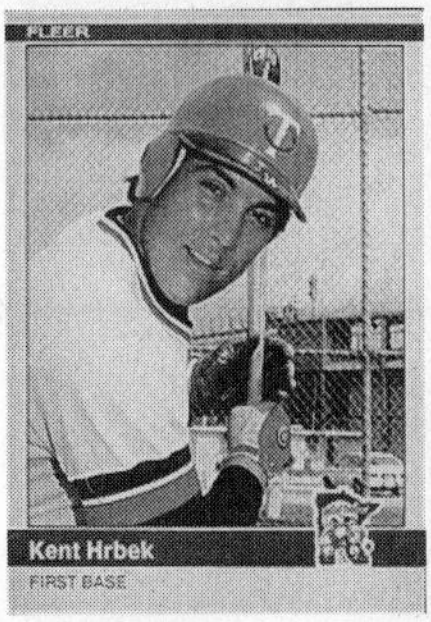
FLEER
Kent Hrbek
FIRST BASE

11 Dennis Martinez .05
12 Tippy Martinez .05
13 Scott McGregor .05
14 Eddie Murray 1.00
15 Joe Nolan .05
16 Jim Palmer 1.00
17 Cal Ripken, Jr. 4.00
18 Gary Roenicke .05
19 Lenn Sakata .05
20 John Shelby **RC** .05
21 Ken Singleton .05
22 Sammy Stewart .05
23 Tim Stoddard .05
24 Marty Bystrom .05
25 Steve Carlton 1.00
26 Ivan DeJesus .05
27 John Denny .05
28 Bob Dernier .05
29 Bo Diaz .05
30 Kiko Garcia .05
31 Greg Gross .05
32 Kevin Gross **RC** .05
33 Von Hayes .05
34 Willie Hernandez .05
35 Al Holland .05
36 Charles Hudson **RC** .05
37 Joe Lefebvre .05
38 Sixto Lezcano .05
39 Garry Maddox .05
40 Gary Matthews .05
41 Len Matuszek .05
42 Tug McGraw .05
43 Joe Morgan 1.00
44 Tony Perez .75
45 Ron Reed .05
46 Pete Rose 3.00
47 Juan Samuel **RC** .25
48 Mike Schmidt 2.50
49 Ozzie Virgil .05
50 Juan Agosto **RC** .05
51 Harold Baines .05
52 Floyd Bannister .05
53 Salome Barojas .05
54 Britt Burns .05
55 Julio Cruz .05
56 Richard Dotson .05
57 Jerry Dybzinski .05
58 Carlton Fisk 1.00
59 Scott Fletcher .05
60 Jerry Hairston Sr. .05
61 Kevin Hickey .05
62 Marc Hill .05
63 LaMarr Hoyt .05
64 Ron Kittle .05
65 Jerry Koosman .05
66 Dennis Lamp .05
67 Rudy Law .05
68 Vance Law .05
69 Greg Luzinski .05
70 Tom Paciorek .05
71 Mike Squires .05
72 Dick Tidrow .05
73 Greg Walker **RC** .05
74 Glenn Abbott .05
75 Howard Bailey .05
76 Doug Bair .05
77 Juan Berenguer .05
78 Tom Brookens .05
79 Enos Cabell .05
80 Kirk Gibson .05
81 John Grubb .05
82 Larry Herndon .05
83 Wayne Krenchicki .05
84 Rick Leach .05
85 Chet Lemon .05
86 Aurelio Lopez .05
87 Jack Morris .05
88 Lance Parrish .05
89 Dan Petry .05
90 Dave Rozema .05
91 Alan Trammell .05
92 Lou Whitaker .05
93 Milt Wilcox .05
94 Glenn Wilson .05
95 John Wockenfuss .05
96 Dusty Baker .05
97 Joe Beckwith .05
98 Greg Brock .05
99 Jack Fimple .05
100 Pedro Guerrero .05
101 Rick Honeycutt .05
102 Burt Hooton .05
103 Steve Howe .05
104 Ken Landreaux .05
105 Mike Marshall .05
106 Rick Monday .05
107 Jose Morales .05
108 Tom Niedenfuer .05
109 Alejandro Pena **RC** .05
110 Jerry Reuss .05
111 Bill Russell .05
112 Steve Sax .05
113 Mike Scioscia .05
114 Derrel Thomas .05
115 Fernando Valenzuela .05
116 Bob Welch .05
117 Steve Yeager .05
118 Pat Zachry .05
119 Don Baylor .05
120 Bert Campaneris .05
121 Rick Cerone .05
122 Ray Fontenot **RC** .05
123 George Frazier .05
124 Oscar Gamble .05
125 Goose Gossage .10
126 Ken Griffey .05
127 Ron Guidry .10
128 Jay Howell .05
129 Steve Kemp .05
130 Matt Keough .05
131 Don Mattingly **RC** 20.00
132 John Montefusco .05
133 Omar Moreno .05
134 Dale Murray .05
135 Graig Nettles .05
136 Lou Piniella .10
137 Willie Randolph .05
138 Shane Rawley .05
139 Dave Righetti .05
140 Andre Robertson .05
141 Bob Shirley .05
142 Roy Smalley .05
143 Dave Winfield 1.00
144 Butch Wynegar .05
145 Jim Acker **RC** .05
146 Doyle Alexander .05
147 Jesse Barfield .05
148 George Bell .05
149 Barry Bonnell .05
150 Jim Clancy .05
151 Dave Collins .05
152 Tony Fernandez **RC** .50
153 Damaso Garcia .05
154 Dave Geisel .05
155 Jim Gott .05
156 Alfredo Griffin .05
157 Garth Iorg .05
158 Roy Lee Jackson .05
159 Cliff Johnson .05
160 Luis Leal .05
161 Buck Martinez .05
162 Joey McLaughlin .05
163 Randy Moffitt .05
164 Lloyd Moseby .05
165 Rance Mulliniks .05
166 Jorge Orta .05
167 Dave Stieb .05
168 Willie Upshaw .05
169 Ernie Whitt .05
170 Len Barker .05
171 Steve Bedrosian .05
172 Bruce Benedict .05
173 Brett Butler .05
174 Rick Camp .05
175 Chris Chambliss .05
176 Ken Dayley .05
177 Pete Falcone .05
178 Terry Forster .05
179 Gene Garber .05
180 Terry Harper .05
181 Bob Horner .05
182 Glenn Hubbard .05
183 Randy Johnson .05
184 Craig McMurtry **RC** .05
185 Donnie Moore .05
186 Dale Murphy .60
187 Phil Niekro .75
188 Pascual Perez .05
189 Biff Pocoroba .05
190 Rafael Ramirez .05
191 Jerry Royster .05
192 Claudell Washington .05
193 Bob Watson .05
194 Jerry Augustine .05
195 Mark Brouhard .05
196 Mike Caldwell .05
197 Tom Candiotti **RC** .25
198 Cecil Cooper .05
199 Rollie Fingers .75
200 Jim Gantner .05
201 Bob L. Gibson .05
202 Moose Haas .05
203 Roy Howell .05
204 Pete Ladd .05
205 Rick Manning .05
206 Bob McClure .05
207 Paul Molitor 1.00
208 Don Money .05
209 Charlie Moore .05
210 Ben Oglivie .05
211 Chuck Porter .05
212 Ed Romero .05
213 Ted Simmons .05
214 Jim Slaton .05
215 Don Sutton .75
216 Tom Tellmann .05
217 Pete Vuckovich .05
218 Ned Yost .05
219 Robin Yount 1.00
220 Alan Ashby .05
221 Kevin Bass .05
222 Jose Cruz .05
223 Bill Dawley **RC** .05
224 Frank DiPino .05
225 Bill Doran **RC** .05
226 Phil Garner .05
227 Art Howe .05
228 Bob Knepper .05
229 Ray Knight .05
230 Frank LaCorte .05
231 Mike LaCoss .05
232 Mike Madden .05
233 Jerry Mumphrey .05
234 Joe Niekro .05
235 Terry Puhl .05
236 Luis Pujols .05
237 Craig Reynolds .05
238 Vern Ruhle .05
239 Nolan Ryan 4.00
240 Mike Scott .05
241 Tony Scott .05
242 Dave Smith .05
243 Dickie Thon .05
244 Denny Walling .05
245 Dale Berra .05
246 Jim Bibby .05
247 John Candelaria .05
248 Jose DeLeon **RC** .05
249 Mike Easler .05
250 Cecilio Guante .05
251 Richie Hebner .05
252 Lee Lacy .05
253 Bill Madlock .05
254 Milt May .05
255 Lee Mazzilli .05
256 Larry McWilliams .05
257 Jim Morrison .05
258 Dave Parker .05
259 Tony Pena .05
260 Johnny Ray .05
261 Rick Rhoden .05
262 Don Robinson .05
263 Manny Sarmiento .05
264 Rod Scurry .05
265 Kent Tekulve .05
266 Gene Tenace .05
267 Jason Thompson .05
268 Lee Tunnell **RC** .05
269 Marvell Wynne **RC** .05
270 Ray Burris .05
271 Gary Carter 1.00
272 Warren Cromartie .05
273 Andre Dawson .30
274 Doug Flynn .05
275 Terry Francona .05
276 Bill Gullickson .05
277 Bob James .05
278 Charlie Lea .05
279 Bryan Little .05
280 Al Oliver .05
281 Tim Raines .05
282 Bobby Ramos .05
283 Jeff Reardon .05
284 Steve Rogers .05
285 Scott Sanderson .05
286 Dan Schatzeder .05
287 Bryn Smith .05
288 Chris Speier .05
289 Manny Trillo .05
290 Mike Vail .05
291 Tim Wallach .05
292 Chris Welsh .05
293 Jim Wohlford .05
294 Kurt Bevacqua .05
295 Juan Bonilla .05
296 Bobby Brown .05
297 Luis DeLeon .05
298 Dave Dravecky .05
299 Tim Flannery .05
300 Steve Garvey .25
301 Tony Gwynn 2.00
302 Andy Hawkins **RC** .10
303 Ruppert Jones .05
304 Terry Kennedy .05
305 Tim Lollar .05
306 Gary Lucas .05
307 Kevin McReynolds **RC** .25
308 Sid Monge .05
309 Mario Ramirez .05
310 Gene Richards .05
311 Luis Salazar .05
312 Eric Show .05
313 Elias Sosa .05
314 Garry Templeton .05
315 Mark Thurmond **RC** .05
316 Ed Whitson .05
317 Alan Wiggins .05
318 Neil Allen .05
319 Joaquin Andujar .05
320 Steve Braun .05
321 Glenn Brummer .05
322 Bob Forsch .05
323 David Green .05
324 George Hendrick .05
325 Tom Herr .05
326 Dane Iorg .05
327 Jeff Lahti .05
328 Dave LaPoint .05
329 Willie McGee .05
330 Ken Oberkfell .05
331 Darrell Porter .05
332 Jamie Quirk .05
333 Mike Ramsey .05
334 Floyd Rayford .05
335 Lonnie Smith .05
336 Ozzie Smith 2.00
337 John Stuper .05
338 Bruce Sutter .75
339 Andy Van Slyke **RC** 1.00
340 Dave Von Ohlen .05
341 Willie Aikens .05
342 Mike Armstrong .05
343 Bud Black .05
344 George Brett 2.50
345 Onix Concepcion .05
346 Keith Creel .05
347 Larry Gura .05
348 Don Hood .05
349 Dennis Leonard .05
350 Hal McRae .05
351 Amos Otis .05
352 Gaylord Perry .75
353 Greg Pryor .05
354 Dan Quisenberry .05
355 Steve Renko .05
356 Leon Roberts .05
357 Pat Sheridan **RC** .05
358 Joe Simpson .05
359 Don Slaught .05
360 Paul Splittorff .05
361 U.L. Washington .05
362 John Wathan .05
363 Frank White .05
364 Willie Wilson .05
365 Jim Barr .05
366 Dave Bergman .05
367 Fred Breining .05
368 Bob Brenly .05
369 Jack Clark .05
370 Chili Davis .05
371 Mark Davis .05
372 Darrell Evans .05
373 Atlee Hammaker .05
374 Mike Krukow .05
375 Duane Kuiper .05
376 Bill Laskey .05
377 Gary Lavelle .05
378 Johnnie LeMaster .05
379 Jeff Leonard .05
380 Randy Lerch .05
381 Renie Martin .05
382 Andy McGaffigan .05
383 Greg Minton .05
384 Tom O'Malley .05
385 Max Venable .05
386 Brad Wellman .05
387 Joel Youngblood .05
388 Gary Allenson .05
389 Luis Aponte .05
390 Tony Armas .05
391 Doug Bird .05
392 Wade Boggs 2.00
393 Dennis Boyd **RC** .05
394 Mike Brown .05
395 Mark Clear .05
396 Dennis Eckersley .75
397 Dwight Evans .05
398 Rich Gedman .05
399 Glenn Hoffman .05
400 Bruce Hurst .05
401 John Henry Johnson .05
402 Ed Jurak .05
403 Rick Miller .05
404 Jeff Newman .05
405 Reid Nichols .05
406 Bob Ojeda .05
407 Jerry Remy .05
408 Jim Rice .05
409 Bob Stanley .05
410 Dave Stapleton .05
411 John Tudor .05
412 Carl Yastrzemski 1.50
413 Buddy Bell .05
414 Larry Biittner .05
415 John Butcher .05
416 Danny Darwin .05
417 Bucky Dent .05
418 Dave Hostetler .05
419 Charlie Hough .05
420 Bobby Johnson .05
421 Odell Jones .05
422 Jon Matlack .05
423 Pete O'Brien **RC** .05
424 Larry Parrish .05
425 Mickey Rivers .05
426 Billy Sample .05
427 Dave Schmidt .05
428 Mike Smithson **RC** .05
429 Bill Stein .05
430 Dave Stewart .05
431 Jim Sundberg .05
432 Frank Tanana .05
433 Dave Tobik .05
434 Wayne Tolleson .05
435 George Wright .05
436 Bill Almon .05
437 Keith Atherton **RC** .05
438 Dave Beard .05
439 Tom Burgmeier .05
440 Jeff Burroughs .05
441 Chris Codiroli **RC** .05
442 Tim Conroy **RC** .05
443 Mike Davis .05
444 Wayne Gross .05
445 Garry Hancock .05
446 Mike Heath .05

447 Rickey Henderson 1.00
448 Don Hill **RC** .05
449 Bob Kearney .05
450 Bill Krueger .05
451 Rick Langford .05
452 Carney Lansford .05
453 Davey Lopes .05
454 Steve McCatty .05
455 Dan Meyer .05
456 Dwayne Murphy .05
457 Mike Norris .05
458 Ricky Peters .05
459 Tony Phillips .05
460 Tom Underwood .05
461 Mike Warren .05
462 Johnny Bench 1.50
463 Bruce Berenyi .05
464 Dann Bilardello .05
465 Cesar Cedeno .05
466 Dave Concepcion .05
467 Dan Driessen .05
468 Nick Esasky **RC** .05
469 Rich Gale .05
470 Ben Hayes .05
471 Paul Householder .05
472 Tom Hume .05
473 Alan Knicely .05
474 Eddie Milner .05
475 Ron Oester .05
476 Kelly Paris .05
477 Frank Pastore .05
478 Ted Power .05
479 Joe Price .05
480 Charlie Puleo .05
481 Gary Redus **RC** .05
482 Bill Scherrer .05
483 Mario Soto .05
484 Alex Trevino .05
485 Duane Walker .05
486 Larry Bowa .05
487 Warren Brusstar .05
488 Bill Buckner .05
489 Bill Campbell .05
490 Ron Cey .05
491 Jody Davis .05
492 Leon Durham .05
493 Mel Hall .05
494 Fergie Jenkins .75
495 Jay Johnstone .05
496 Craig Lefferts **RC** .10
497 Carmelo Martinez **RC** .05
498 Jerry Morales .05
499 Keith Moreland .05
500 Dickie Noles .05
501 Mike Proly .05
502 Chuck Rainey .05
503 Dick Ruthven .05
504 Ryne Sandberg 2.00
505 Lee Smith .05
506 Steve Trout .05
507 Gary Woods .05
508 Juan Beniquez .05
509 Bob Boone .05
510 Rick Burleson .05
511 Rod Carew 1.00
512 Bobby Clark .05
513 John Curtis .05
514 Doug DeCinces .05
515 Brian Downing .05
516 Tim Foli .05
517 Ken Forsch .05
518 Bobby Grich .05
519 Andy Hassler .05
520 Reggie Jackson 1.50
521 Ron Jackson .05
522 Tommy John .10
523 Bruce Kison .05
524 Steve Lubratich .05
525 Fred Lynn .05
526 Gary Pettis **RC** .05
527 Luis Sanchez .05
528 Daryl Sconiers .05
529 Ellis Valentine .05
530 Rob Wilfong .05
531 Mike Witt .05
532 Geoff Zahn .05
533 Bud Anderson .05
534 Chris Bando .05
535 Alan Bannister .05
536 Bert Blyleven .10
537 Tom Brennan .05
538 Jamie Easterly .05
539 Juan Eichelberger .05
540 Jim Essian .05
541 Mike Fischlin .05
542 Julio Franco .05
543 Mike Hargrove .05
544 Toby Harrah .05
545 Ron Hassey .05
546 Neal Heaton **RC** .05
547 Bake McBride .05
548 Broderick Perkins .05
549 Lary Sorensen .05
550 Dan Spillner .05
551 Rick Sutcliffe .05
552 Pat Tabler .05
553 Gorman Thomas .05
554 Andre Thornton .05
555 George Vukovich .05
556 Darrell Brown .05
557 Tom Brunansky .05
558 Randy Bush **RC** .05
559 Bobby Castillo .05
560 John Castino .05
561 Ron Davis .05
562 Dave Engle .05
563 Lenny Faedo .05
564 Pete Filson .05
565 Gary Gaetti .05
566 Mickey Hatcher .05
567 Kent Hrbek .05
568 Rusty Kuntz .05
569 Tim Laudner .05
570 Rick Lysander .05
571 Bobby Mitchell .05
572 Ken Schrom .05
573 Ray Smith .05
574 Tim Teufel **RC** .05
575 Frank Viola .05
576 Gary Ward .05
577 Ron Washington .05
578 Len Whitehouse .05
579 Al Williams .05
580 Bob Bailor .05
581 Mark Bradley .05
582 Hubie Brooks .05
583 Carlos Diaz .05
584 George Foster .05
585 Brian Giles .05
586 Danny Heep .05
587 Keith Hernandez .05
588 Ron Hodges .05
589 Scott Holman .05
590 Dave Kingman .05
591 Ed Lynch .05
592 Jose Oquendo **RC** .05
593 Jesse Orosco .05
594 Junior Ortiz **RC** .05
595 Tom Seaver 1.00
596 Doug Sisk **RC** .05
597 Rusty Staub .05
598 John Stearns .05
599 Darryl Strawberry .25
600 Craig Swan .05
601 Walt Terrell **RC** .05
602 Mike Torrez .05
603 Mookie Wilson .05
604 Jamie Allen .05
605 Jim Beattie .05
606 Tony Bernazard .05
607 Manny Castillo .05
608 Bill Caudill .05
609 Bryan Clark .05
610 Al Cowens .05
611 Dave Henderson .05
612 Steve Henderson .05
613 Orlando Mercado .05
614 Mike Moore .05
615 Ricky Nelson .05
616 Spike Owen **RC** .10
617 Pat Putnam .05
618 Ron Roenicke .05
619 Mike Stanton .05
620 Bob Stoddard .05
621 Rick Sweet .05
622 Roy Thomas .05
623 Ed Vande Berg .05
624 Matt Young **RC** .05
625 Richie Zisk .05
626 Fred Lynn '83 All-Star Game Record Breaker .05
627 Manny Trillo '83 All-Star Game Record Breaker .05
628 Steve Garvey N.L. Iron Man .10
629 Rod Carew A.L. Batting Runner-Up .15
630 Wade Boggs A.L. Batting Champion .50
631 Tim Raines Letting Go Of The Raines .10
632 Al Oliver Double Trouble .05
633 Steve Sax All-Star Second Base .05
634 Dickie Thon All-Star Shortstop .05
635 Tippy Martinez, Dan Quisenberry Ace Firemen .05
636 Joe Morgan, Tony Perez, Pete Rose Reds Reunited .75
637 Bob Boone, Lance Parrish Backstop Stars .05
638 George Brett, Gaylord Perry The Pine Tar Incident, 7/24/83 .25
639 Bob Forsch, Dave Righetti, Mike Warren 1983 No-Hitters .05
640 Johnny Bench, Carl Yastrzemski Retiring Superstars .50
641 Gaylord Perry Going Out In Style .05
642 Steve Carlton 300 Club & Strikeout Record .10
643 Joe Altobelli, Paul Owens The Managers .05
644 Rick Dempsey The MVP .05
645 Mike Boddicker The Rookie Winner .05
646 Scott McGregor The Clincher .05
647 Joe Altobelli Checklist: Orioles/Royals .05
648 Paul Owens Checklist: Phillies/Giants .05
649 Tony LaRussa Checklist: White Sox/Red Sox .05
650 Sparky Anderson Checklist: Tigers/Rangers .10
651 Tommy Lasorda Checklist: Dodgers/A's .10
652 Billy Martin Checklist: Yankees/Reds .05
653 Bobby Cox Checklist: Blue Jays/Cubs .10
654 Joe Torre Checklist: Braves/Angels .10
655 Rene Lacheman Checklist: Brewers/Indians .05
656 Bob Lillis Checklist: Astros/Twins .05
657 Chuck Tanner Checklist: Pirates/Mets .05
658 Bill Virdon Checklist: Expos/Mariners .05
659 Dick Williams Checklist: Padres/Specials .05
660 Whitey Herzog Checklist: Cardinals/Specials .05

Update

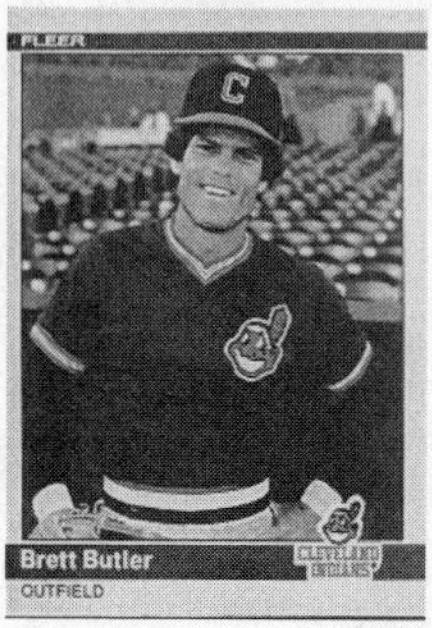

	NM/M
Complete Set (132):	250.00
Common Player:	.25

1 Willie Aikens .25
2 Luis Aponte .25
3 Mark Bailey .25
4 Bob Bailor .25
5 Dusty Baker .25
6 Steve Balboni .25
7 Alan Bannister .25
8 Marty Barrett .25
9 Dave Beard .25
10 Joe Beckwith .25
11 Dave Bergman .25
12 Tony Bernazard .25
13 Bruce Bochte .25
14 Barry Bonnell .25
15 Phil Bradley .25
16 Fred Breining .25
17 Mike Brown .25
18 Bill Buckner .25
19 Ray Burris .25
20 John Butcher .25
21 Brett Butler .25
22 Enos Cabell .25
23 Bill Campbell .25
24 Bill Caudill .25
25 Bobby Clark .25
26 Bryan Clark .25
27 Roger Clemens **RC** 175.00
28 Jaime Cocanower .25
29 Ron Darling **RC** 1.00
30 Alvin Davis **RC** .25
31 Bob Dernier .25
32 Carlos Diaz .25
33 Mike Easler .25
34 Dennis Eckersley 4.00
35 Jim Essian .25
36 Darrell Evans .25
37 Mike Fitzgerald .25
38 Tim Foli .25
39 John Franco **RC** 3.00
40 George Frazier .25
41 Rich Gale .25
42 Barbaro Garbey .25
43 Dwight Gooden **RC** 7.50
44 Goose Gossage .40
45 Wayne Gross .25
46 Mark Gubicza 1.00
47 Jackie Gutierrez .25
48 Toby Harrah .25
49 Ron Hassey .25
50 Richie Hebner .25
51 Willie Hernandez .25
52 Ed Hodge .25
53 Ricky Horton .25
54 Art Howe .25
55 Dane Iorg .25
56 Brook Jacoby .25
57 Dion James **RC** .25
58 Mike Jeffcoat **RC** .25
59 Ruppert Jones .25
60 Bob Kearney .25
61 Jimmy Key **RC** 1.00
62 Dave Kingman .25
63 Brad Komminsk **RC** .25
64 Jerry Koosman .25
65 Wayne Krenchicki .25
66 Rusty Kuntz .25
67 Frank LaCorte .25
68 Dennis Lamp .25
69 Tito Landrum .25
70 Mark Langston **RC** 4.00
71 Rick Leach .25
72 Craig Lefferts .25
73 Gary Lucas .25
74 Jerry Martin .25
75 Carmelo Martinez .25
76 Mike Mason **RC** .25
77 Gary Matthews .25
78 Andy McGaffigan .25
79 Joey McLaughlin .25
80 Joe Morgan 5.00
81 Darryl Motley .25
82 Graig Nettles .40
83 Phil Niekro 3.00
84 Ken Oberkfell .25
85 Al Oliver .25
86 Jorge Orta .25
87 Amos Otis .25
88 Bob Owchinko .25
89 Dave Parker .25
90 Jack Perconte .25
91 Tony Perez 3.00
92 Gerald Perry .25
93 Kirby Puckett **RC** 75.00
94 Shane Rawley .25
95 Floyd Rayford .25
96 Ron Reed .25
97 R.J. Reynolds .25
98 Gene Richards .25
99 Jose Rijo **RC** 1.00
100 Jeff Robinson .25
101 Ron Romanick .25
102 Pete Rose 10.00
103 Bret Saberhagen **RC** 5.00
104 Scott Sanderson .25
105 Dick Schofield **RC** .25
106 Tom Seaver 7.50
107 Jim Slaton .25
108 Mike Smithson .25
109 Lary Sorensen .25
110 Tim Stoddard .25
111 Jeff Stone .25
112 Champ Summers .25
113 Jim Sundberg .25
114 Rick Sutcliffe .35
115 Craig Swan .25
116 Derrel Thomas .25
117 Gorman Thomas .25
118 Alex Trevino .25
119 Manny Trillo .25
120 John Tudor .25
121 Tom Underwood .25
122 Mike Vail .25
123 Tom Waddell .25
124 Gary Ward .25
125 Terry Whitfield .25
126 Curtis Wilkerson .25
127 Frank Williams .25
128 Glenn Wilson .25
129 John Wockenfuss .25
130 Ned Yost .25
131 Mike Young **RC** .25
132 Checklist 1-132 .10

1985 Fleer

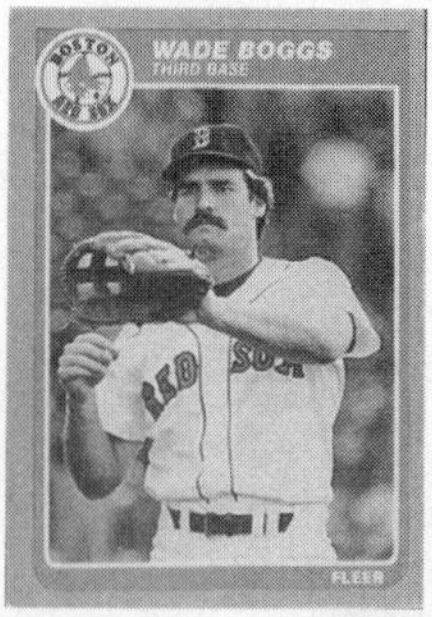

	NM/M
Unopened Factory Set (660):	50.00
Complete Set (660):	40.00
Common Player:	.05
Wax Pack (15):	4.50
Wax Box (36):	150.00
Cello Pack (28):	6.00
Cello Box (24):	150.00
Rack Pack (45):	8.00
Vending Box (500):	35.00

1 Doug Bair .05
2 Juan Berenguer .05
3 Dave Bergman .05
4 Tom Brookens .05
5 Marty Castillo .05
6 Darrell Evans .05
7 Barbaro Garbey .05
8 Kirk Gibson .05
9 John Grubb .05
10 Willie Hernandez .05
11 Larry Herndon .05
12 Howard Johnson .05
13 Ruppert Jones .05
14 Rusty Kuntz .05
15 Chet Lemon .05

16	Aurelio Lopez	.05
17	Sid Monge	.05
18	Jack Morris	.05
19	Lance Parrish	.05
20	Dan Petry	.05
21	Dave Rozema	.05
22	Bill Scherrer	.05
23	Alan Trammell	.05
24	Lou Whitaker	.05
25	Milt Wilcox	.05
26	Kurt Bevacqua	.05
27	Greg Booker **RC**	.05
28	Bobby Brown	.05
29	Luis DeLeon	.05
30	Dave Dravecky	.05
31	Tim Flannery	.05
32	Steve Garvey	.40
33	Goose Gossage	.10
34	Tony Gwynn	2.00
35	Greg Harris	.05
36	Andy Hawkins	.05
37	Terry Kennedy	.05
38	Craig Lefferts	.05
39	Tim Lollar	.05
40	Carmelo Martinez	.05
41	Kevin McReynolds	.05
42	Graig Nettles	.05
43	Luis Salazar	.05
44	Eric Show	.05
45	Garry Templeton	.05
46	Mark Thurmond	.05
47	Ed Whitson	.05
48	Alan Wiggins	.05
49	Rich Bordi	.05
50	Larry Bowa	.05
51	Warren Brusstar	.05
52	Ron Cey	.05
53	Henry Cotto **RC**	.05
54	Jody Davis	.05
55	Bob Dernier	.05
56	Leon Durham	.05
57	Dennis Eckersley	.75
58	George Frazier	.05
59	Richie Hebner	.05
60	Dave Lopes	.05
61	Gary Matthews	.05
62	Keith Moreland	.05
63	Rick Reuschel	.05
64	Dick Ruthven	.05
65	Ryne Sandberg	2.00
66	Scott Sanderson	.05
67	Lee Smith	.05
68	Tim Stoddard	.05
69	Rick Sutcliffe	.05
70	Steve Trout	.05
71	Gary Woods	.05
72	Wally Backman	.05
73	Bruce Berenyi	.05
74	Hubie Brooks	.05
75	Kelvin Chapman	.05
76	Ron Darling	.05
77	Sid Fernandez	.05
78	Mike Fitzgerald	.05
79	George Foster	.05
80	Brent Gaff	.05
81	Ron Gardenhire	.05
82	Dwight Gooden	.25
83	Tom Gorman	.05
84	Danny Heep	.05
85	Keith Hernandez	.05
86	Ray Knight	.05
87	Ed Lynch	.05
88	Jose Oquendo	.05
89	Jesse Orosco	.05
90	Rafael Santana **RC**	.05
91	Doug Sisk	.05
92	Rusty Staub	.05
93	Darryl Strawberry	.10
94	Walt Terrell	.05
95	Mookie Wilson	.05
96	Jim Acker	.05
97	Willie Aikens	.05
98	Doyle Alexander	.05
99	Jesse Barfield	.05
100	George Bell	.05
101	Jim Clancy	.05
102	Dave Collins	.05
103	Tony Fernandez	.05
104	Damaso Garcia	.05
105	Jim Gott	.05
106	Alfredo Griffin	.05
107	Garth Iorg	.05
108	Roy Lee Jackson	.05
109	Cliff Johnson	.05
110	Jimmy Key	.05
111	Dennis Lamp	.05
112	Rick Leach	.05
113	Luis Leal	.05
114	Buck Martinez	.05
115	Lloyd Moseby	.05
116	Rance Mulliniks	.05
117	Dave Stieb	.05
118	Willie Upshaw	.05
119	Ernie Whitt	.05
120	Mike Armstrong	.05
121	Don Baylor	.05
122	Marty Bystrom	.05
123	Rick Cerone	.05
124	Joe Cowley	.05
125	Brian Dayett	.05
126	Tim Foli	.05
127	Ray Fontenot	.05
128	Ken Griffey	.05
129	Ron Guidry	.10
130	Toby Harrah	.05
131	Jay Howell	.05
132	Steve Kemp	.05
133	Don Mattingly	2.50
134	Bobby Meacham	.05
135	John Montefusco	.05
136	Omar Moreno	.05
137	Dale Murray	.05
138	Phil Niekro	.75
139	Mike Pagliarulo **RC**	.20
140	Willie Randolph	.05
141	Dennis Rasmussen	.05
142	Dave Righetti	.05
143	Jose Rijo	.05
144	Andre Robertson	.05
145	Bob Shirley	.05
146	Dave Winfield	1.00
147	Butch Wynegar	.05
148	Gary Allenson	.05
149	Tony Armas	.05
150	Marty Barrett	.05
151	Wade Boggs	2.00
152	Dennis Boyd	.05
153	Bill Buckner	.05
154	Mark Clear	.05
155	Roger Clemens	25.00
156	Steve Crawford	.05
157	Mike Easler	.05
158	Dwight Evans	.05
159	Rich Gedman	.05
160	Jackie Gutierrez	.05
161	Bruce Hurst	.05
162	John Henry Johnson	.05
163	Rick Miller	.05
164	Reid Nichols	.05
165	Al Nipper **RC**	.05
166	Bob Ojeda	.05
167	Jerry Remy	.05
168	Jim Rice	.25
169	Bob Stanley	.05
170	Mike Boddicker	.05
171	Al Bumbry	.05
172	Todd Cruz	.05
173	Rich Dauer	.05
174	Storm Davis	.05
175	Rick Dempsey	.05
176	Jim Dwyer	.05
177	Mike Flanagan	.05
178	Dan Ford	.05
179	Wayne Gross	.05
180	John Lowenstein	.05
181	Dennis Martinez	.05
182	Tippy Martinez	.05
183	Scott McGregor	.05
184	Eddie Murray	1.00
185	Joe Nolan	.05
186	Floyd Rayford	.05
187	Cal Ripken, Jr.	4.00
188	Gary Roenicke	.05
189	Lenn Sakata	.05
190	John Shelby	.05
191	Ken Singleton	.05
192	Sammy Stewart	.05
193	Bill Swaggerty	.05
194	Tom Underwood	.05
195	Mike Young	.05
196	Steve Balboni	.05
197	Joe Beckwith	.05
198	Bud Black	.05
199	George Brett	2.50
200	Onix Concepcion	.05
201	Mark Gubicza **RC**	.50
202	Larry Gura	.05
203	Mark Huismann	.05
204	Dane Iorg	.05
205	Danny Jackson	.05
206	Charlie Leibrandt	.05
207	Hal McRae	.05
208	Darryl Motley	.05
209	Jorge Orta	.05
210	Greg Pryor	.05
211	Dan Quisenberry	.05
212	Bret Saberhagen	.25
213	Pat Sheridan	.05
214	Don Slaught	.05
215	U.L. Washington	.05
216	John Wathan	.05
217	Frank White	.05
218	Willie Wilson	.05
219	Neil Allen	.05
220	Joaquin Andujar	.05
221	Steve Braun	.05
222	Danny Cox	.05
223	Bob Forsch	.05
224	David Green	.05
225	George Hendrick	.05
226	Tom Herr	.05
227	Ricky Horton **RC**	.05
228	Art Howe	.05
229	Mike Jorgensen	.05
230	Kurt Kepshire	.05
231	Jeff Lahti	.05
232	Tito Landrum	.05
233	Dave LaPoint	.05
234	Willie McGee	.05
235	Tom Nieto **RC**	.05
236	Terry Pendleton **RC**	1.00
237	Darrell Porter	.05
238	Dave Rucker	.05
239	Lonnie Smith	.05
240	Ozzie Smith	2.00
241	Bruce Sutter	.75
242	Andy Van Slyke	.05
243	Dave Von Ohlen	.05
244	Larry Andersen	.05
245	Bill Campbell	.05
246	Steve Carlton	1.00
247	Tim Corcoran	.05
248	Ivan DeJesus	.05
249	John Denny	.05
250	Bo Diaz	.05
251	Greg Gross	.05
252	Kevin Gross	.05
253	Von Hayes	.05
254	Al Holland	.05
255	Charles Hudson	.05
256	Jerry Koosman	.05
257	Joe Lefebvre	.05
258	Sixto Lezcano	.05
259	Garry Maddox	.05
260	Len Matuszek	.05
261	Tug McGraw	.05
262	Al Oliver	.05
263	Shane Rawley	.05
264	Juan Samuel	.05
265	Mike Schmidt	2.50
266	Jeff Stone **RC**	.05
267	Ozzie Virgil	.05
268	Glenn Wilson	.05
269	John Wockenfuss	.05
270	Darrell Brown	.05
271	Tom Brunansky	.05
272	Randy Bush	.05
273	John Butcher	.05
274	Bobby Castillo	.05
275	Ron Davis	.05
276	Dave Engle	.05
277	Pete Filson	.05
278	Gary Gaetti	.05
279	Mickey Hatcher	.05
280	Ed Hodge	.05
281	Kent Hrbek	.05
282	Houston Jimenez	.05
283	Tim Laudner	.05
284	Rick Lysander	.05
285	Dave Meier	.05
286	Kirby Puckett	8.00
287	Pat Putnam	.05
288	Ken Schrom	.05
289	Mike Smithson	.05
290	Tim Teufel	.05
291	Frank Viola	.05
292	Ron Washington	.05
293	Don Aase	.05
294	Juan Beniquez	.05
295	Bob Boone	.05
296	Mike Brown	.05
297	Rod Carew	1.00
298	Doug Corbett	.05
299	Doug DeCinces	.05
300	Brian Downing	.05
301	Ken Forsch	.05
302	Bobby Grich	.05
303	Reggie Jackson	2.00
304	Tommy John	.10
305	Curt Kaufman	.05
306	Bruce Kison	.05
307	Fred Lynn	.05
308	Gary Pettis	.05
309	Ron Romanick **RC**	.05
310	Luis Sanchez	.05
311	Dick Schofield	.05
312	Daryl Sconiers	.05
313	Jim Slaton	.05
314	Derrel Thomas	.05
315	Rob Wilfong	.05
316	Mike Witt	.05
317	Geoff Zahn	.05
318	Len Barker	.05
319	Steve Bedrosian	.05
320	Bruce Benedict	.05
321	Rick Camp	.05
322	Chris Chambliss	.05
323	Jeff Dedmon **RC**	.05
324	Terry Forster	.05
325	Gene Garber	.05
326	Albert Hall **RC**	.05
327	Terry Harper	.05
328	Bob Horner	.05
329	Glenn Hubbard	.05
330	Randy Johnson	.05
331	Brad Komminsk	.05
332	Rick Mahler	.05
333	Craig McMurtry	.05
334	Donnie Moore	.05
335	Dale Murphy	.40
336	Ken Oberkfell	.05
337	Pascual Perez	.05
338	Gerald Perry	.05
339	Rafael Ramirez	.05
340	Jerry Royster	.05
341	Alex Trevino	.05
342	Claudell Washington	.05
343	Alan Ashby	.05
344	Mark Bailey **RC**	.05
345	Kevin Bass	.05
346	Enos Cabell	.05
347	Jose Cruz	.05
348	Bill Dawley	.05
349	Frank DiPino	.05
350	Bill Doran	.05
351	Phil Garner	.05
352	Bob Knepper	.05
353	Mike LaCoss	.05
354	Jerry Mumphrey	.05
355	Joe Niekro	.05
356	Terry Puhl	.05
357	Craig Reynolds	.05
358	Vern Ruhle	.05
359	Nolan Ryan	4.00
360	Joe Sambito	.05
361	Mike Scott	.05
362	Dave Smith	.05
363	Julio Solano **RC**	.05
364	Dickie Thon	.05
365	Denny Walling	.05
366	Dave Anderson	.05
367	Bob Bailor	.05
368	Greg Brock	.05
369	Carlos Diaz	.05
370	Pedro Guerrero	.05
371	Orel Hershiser **RC**	3.00
372	Rick Honeycutt	.05
373	Burt Hooton	.05
374	Ken Howell **RC**	.05
375	Ken Landreaux	.05
376	Candy Maldonado	.05
377	Mike Marshall	.05
378	Tom Niedenfuer	.05
379	Alejandro Pena	.05
380	Jerry Reuss	.05
381	R.J. Reynolds **RC**	.05
382	German Rivera	.05
383	Bill Russell	.05
384	Steve Sax	.05
385	Mike Scioscia	.05
386	Franklin Stubbs **RC**	.05
387	Fernando Valenzuela	.05
388	Bob Welch	.05
389	Terry Whitfield	.05
390	Steve Yeager	.05
391	Pat Zachry	.05
392	Fred Breining	.05
393	Gary Carter	1.00
394	Andre Dawson	.25
395	Miguel Dilone	.05
396	Dan Driessen	.05
397	Doug Flynn	.05
398	Terry Francona	.05
399	Bill Gullickson	.05
400	Bob James	.05
401	Charlie Lea	.05
402	Bryan Little	.05
403	Gary Lucas	.05
404	David Palmer	.05
405	Tim Raines	.05
406	Mike Ramsey	.05
407	Jeff Reardon	.05
408	Steve Rogers	.05
409	Dan Schatzeder	.05
410	Bryn Smith	.05
411	Mike Stenhouse	.05
412	Tim Wallach	.05
413	Jim Wohlford	.05
414	Bill Almon	.05
415	Keith Atherton	.05
416	Bruce Bochte	.05
417	Tom Burgmeier	.05
418	Ray Burris	.05
419	Bill Caudill	.05
420	Chris Codiroli	.05
421	Tim Conroy	.05
422	Mike Davis	.05
423	Jim Essian	.05
424	Mike Heath	.05
425	Rickey Henderson	1.00
426	Donnie Hill	.05
427	Dave Kingman	.05
428	Bill Krueger	.05
429	Carney Lansford	.05
430	Steve McCatty	.05
431	Joe Morgan	1.00
432	Dwayne Murphy	.05
433	Tony Phillips	.05
434	Lary Sorensen	.05
435	Mike Warren	.05
436	Curt Young **RC**	.05
437	Luis Aponte	.05
438	Chris Bando	.05
439	Tony Bernazard	.05
440	Bert Blyleven	.10
441	Brett Butler	.05
442	Ernie Camacho	.05
443	Joe Carter	.25
444	Carmelo Castillo	.05
445	Jamie Easterly	.05
446	Steve Farr **RC**	.05
447	Mike Fischlin	.05
448	Julio Franco	.05
449	Mel Hall	.05
450	Mike Hargrove	.05
451	Neal Heaton	.05
452	Brook Jacoby	.05
453	Mike Jeffcoat **RC**	.05
454	Don Schulze **RC**	.05
455	Roy Smith	.05
456	Pat Tabler	.05
457	Andre Thornton	.05
458	George Vukovich	.05
459	Tom Waddell	.05
460	Jerry Willard	.05
461	Dale Berra	.05
462	John Candelaria	.05
463	Jose DeLeon	.05
464	Doug Frobel	.05
465	Cecilio Guante	.05
466	Brian Harper	.05
467	Lee Lacy	.05
468	Bill Madlock	.05
469	Lee Mazzilli	.05
470	Larry McWilliams	.05
471	Jim Morrison	.05
472	Tony Pena	.05
473	Johnny Ray	.05
474	Rick Rhoden	.05
475	Don Robinson	.05

476	Rod Scurry	.05
477	Kent Tekulve	.05
478	Jason Thompson	.05
479	John Tudor	.05
480	Lee Tunnell	.05
481	Marvell Wynne	.05
482	Salome Barojas	.05
483	Dave Beard	.05
484	Jim Beattie	.05
485	Barry Bonnell	.05
486	Phil Bradley **RC**	.05
487	Al Cowens	.05
488	Alvin Davis	.05
489	Dave Henderson	.05
490	Steve Henderson	.05
491	Bob Kearney	.05
492	Mark Langston	.15
493	Larry Milbourne	.05
494	Paul Mirabella	.05
495	Mike Moore	.05
496	Edwin Nunez	.05
497	Spike Owen	.05
498	Jack Perconte	.05
499	Ken Phelps	.05
500	Jim Presley **RC**	.05
501	Mike Stanton	.05
502	Bob Stoddard	.05
503	Gorman Thomas	.05
504	Ed Vande Berg	.05
505	Matt Young	.05
506	Juan Agosto	.05
507	Harold Baines	.05
508	Floyd Bannister	.05
509	Britt Burns	.05
510	Julio Cruz	.05
511	Richard Dotson	.05
512	Jerry Dybzinski	.05
513	Carlton Fisk	1.00
514	Scott Fletcher	.05
515	Jerry Hairston Sr.	.05
516	Marc Hill	.05
517	LaMarr Hoyt	.05
518	Ron Kittle	.05
519	Rudy Law	.05
520	Vance Law	.05
521	Greg Luzinski	.05
522	Gene Nelson	.05
523	Tom Paciorek	.05
524	Ron Reed	.05
525	Bert Roberge	.05
526	Tom Seaver	1.00
527	Roy Smalley	.05
528	Dan Spillner	.05
529	Mike Squires	.05
530	Greg Walker	.05
531	Cesar Cedeno	.05
532	Dave Concepcion	.05
533	Eric Davis **RC**	2.00
534	Nick Esasky	.05
535	Tom Foley	.05
536	John Franco	.05
537	Brad Gulden	.05
538	Tom Hume	.05
539	Wayne Krenchicki	.05
540	Andy McGaffigan	.05
541	Eddie Milner	.05
542	Ron Oester	.05
543	Bob Owchinko	.05
544	Dave Parker	.05
545	Frank Pastore	.05
546	Tony Perez	.75
547	Ted Power	.05
548	Joe Price	.05
549	Gary Redus	.05
550	Pete Rose	3.00
551	Jeff Russell	.05
552	Mario Soto	.05
553	Jay Tibbs **RC**	.05
554	Duane Walker	.05
555	Alan Bannister	.05
556	Buddy Bell	.05
557	Danny Darwin	.05
558	Charlie Hough	.05
559	Bobby Jones	.05
560	Odell Jones	.05
561	Jeff Kunkel **RC**	.05
562	Mike Mason **RC**	.05
563	Pete O'Brien	.05
564	Larry Parrish	.05
565	Mickey Rivers	.05
566	Billy Sample	.05
567	Dave Schmidt	.05
568	Donnie Scott	.05
569	Dave Stewart	.05
570	Frank Tanana	.05
571	Wayne Tolleson	.05
572	Gary Ward	.05
573	Curtis Wilkerson	.05
574	George Wright	.05
575	Ned Yost	.05
576	Mark Brouhard	.05
577	Mike Caldwell	.05
578	Bobby Clark	.05
579	Jaime Cocanower	.05
580	Cecil Cooper	.05
581	Rollie Fingers	.75
582	Jim Gantner	.05
583	Moose Haas	.05
584	Dion James	.05
585	Pete Ladd	.05
586	Rick Manning	.05
587	Bob McClure	.05
588	Paul Molitor	1.00
589	Charlie Moore	.05
590	Ben Oglivie	.05
591	Chuck Porter	.05
592	Randy Ready **RC**	.05
593	Ed Romero	.05
594	Bill Schroeder	.05
595	Ray Searage	.05
596	Ted Simmons	.05
597	Jim Sundberg	.05
598	Don Sutton	.75
599	Tom Tellmann	.05
600	Rick Waits	.05
601	Robin Yount	1.00
602	Dusty Baker	.05
603	Bob Brenly	.05
604	Jack Clark	.05
605	Chili Davis	.05
606	Mark Davis	.05
607	Dan Gladden **RC**	.25
608	Atlee Hammaker	.05
609	Mike Krukow	.05
610	Duane Kuiper	.05
611	Bob Lacey	.05
612	Bill Laskey	.05
613	Gary Lavelle	.05
614	Johnnie LeMaster	.05
615	Jeff Leonard	.05
616	Randy Lerch	.05
617	Greg Minton	.05
618	Steve Nicosia	.05
619	Gene Richards	.05
620	Jeff Robinson **RC**	.05
621	Scot Thompson	.05
622	Manny Trillo	.05
623	Brad Wellman	.05
624	Frank Williams **RC**	.05
625	Joel Youngblood	.05
626	Cal Ripken, Jr./IA	1.00
627	Mike Schmidt/IA	.50
628	Sparky Anderson Giving the Signs	.05
629	Rickey Henderson, Dave Winfield A.L. Pitcher's Nightmare	.50
630	Ryne Sandberg, Mike Schmidt N.L. Pitcher's Nightmare	1.00
631	Gary Carter, Steve Garvey, Ozzie Smith, Darryl Strawberry N.L. All-Stars	.25
632	Gary Carter, Charlie Lea All-Star Game Winning Battery	.10
633	Steve Garvey, Goose Gossage N.L. Pennant Clinchers	.10
634	Dwight Gooden, Juan Samuel N.L. Rookie Phenoms	.05
635	Willie Upshaw Toronto's Big Guns	.05
636	Lloyd Moseby Toronto's Big Guns	.05
637	Al Holland Holland	.05
638	Lee Tunnell Tunnell	.05
639	Reggie Jackson/IA	.50
640	Pete Rose/IA	.75
641	Cal Ripken, Jr., Cal Ripken, Sr. Father & Son	1.00
642	Cubs team	.10
643	Jack Morris, David Palmer, Mike Witt 1984's Two Perfect Games & One No-Hitter	.05
644	Willie Lozado, Vic Mata Major League Prospect	.05
645	Kelly Gruber, Randy O'Neal **RC** Major League Prospect	.15
646	Jose Roman, Joel Skinner **RC** Major League Prospect	.05
647	Steve Kiefer, Danny Tartabull **RC** Major League Prospect	.50
648	Rob Deer, Alejandro Sanchez **RC** Major League Prospect	.25
649	Shawon Dunston, Bill Hatcher **RC** Major League Prospect	1.00
650	Mike Bielecki, Ron Robinson **RC** Major League Prospect	.10
651	Zane Smith, Paul Zuvella **RC** Major League Prospect	.10
652	Glenn Davis, Joe Hesketh **RC** Major League Prospect	.20
653	Steve Jeltz, John Russell **RC** Major League Prospect	.10
654	Checklist 1-95	.05
655	Checklist 96-195	.05
656	Checklist 196-292	.05
657	Checklist 293-391	.05
658	Checklist 392-481	.05
659	Checklist 482-575	.05
660	Checklist 576-660	.05

Update

		NM/M
Complete Set (132):		5.00
Common Player:		.10
1	Don Aase	.10
2	Bill Almon	.10
3	Dusty Baker	.10
4	Dale Berra	.10
5	Karl Best	.10
6	Tim Birtsas	.10
7	Vida Blue	.10
8	Rich Bordi	.10
9	Daryl Boston	.10
10	Hubie Brooks	.10
11	Chris Brown	.10
12	Tom Browning	.10
13	Al Bumbry	.10
14	Tim Burke	.10
15	Ray Burris	.10
16	Jeff Burroughs	.10
17	Ivan Calderon	.10

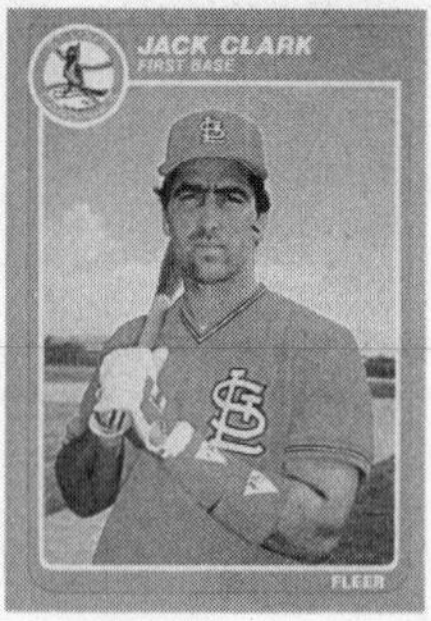

18	Jeff Calhoun	.10
19	Bill Campbell	.10
20	Don Carman	.10
21	Gary Carter	.50
22	Bobby Castillo	.10
23	Bill Caudill	.10
24	Rick Cerone	.10
25	Jack Clark	.10
26	Pat Clements	.10
27	Stewart Cliburn	.10
28	Vince Coleman	.10
29	Dave Collins	.10
30	Fritz Connally	.10
31	Henry Cotto	.10
32	Danny Darwin	.10
33	Darren Daulton **RC**	1.00
34	Jerry Davis	.10
35	Brian Dayett	.10
36	Ken Dixon	.10
37	Tommy Dunbar	.10
38	Mariano Duncan	.10
39	Bob Fallon	.10
40	Brian Fisher	.10
41	Mike Fitzgerald	.10
42	Ray Fontenot	.10
43	Greg Gagne	.10
44	Oscar Gamble	.10
45	Jim Gott	.10
46	David Green	.10
47	Alfredo Griffin	.10
48	Ozzie Guillen **RC**	2.00
49	Toby Harrah	.10
50	Ron Hassey	.10
51	Rickey Henderson	3.00
52	Steve Henderson	.10
53	George Hendrick	.10
54	Teddy Higuera	.10
55	Al Holland	.10
56	Burt Hooton	.10
57	Jay Howell	.10
58	LaMarr Hoyt	.10
59	Tim Hulett	.10
60	Bob James	.10
61	Cliff Johnson	.10
62	Howard Johnson	.10
63	Ruppert Jones	.10
64	Steve Kemp	.10
65	Bruce Kison	.10
66	Mike LaCoss	.10
67	Lee Lacy	.10
68	Dave LaPoint	.10
69	Gary Lavelle	.10
70	Vance Law	.10
71	Manny Lee	.10
72	Sixto Lezcano	.10
73	Tim Lollar	.10
74	Urbano Lugo	.10
75	Fred Lynn	.10
76	Steve Lyons	.10
77	Mickey Mahler	.10
78	Ron Mathis	.10
79	Len Matuszek	.10
80	Oddibe McDowell	.10
81	Roger McDowell	.10
82	Donnie Moore	.10
83	Ron Musselman	.10
84	Al Oliver	.10
85	Joe Orsulak	.10
86	Dan Pasqua	.10
87	Chris Pittaro	.10
88	Rick Reuschel	.10
89	Earnie Riles	.10
90	Jerry Royster	.10
91	Dave Rozema	.10
92	Dave Rucker	.10
93	Vern Ruhle	.10
94	Mark Salas	.10
95	Luis Salazar	.10
96	Joe Sambito	.10
97	Billy Sample	.10
98	Alex Sanchez	.10
99	Calvin Schiraldi	.10
100	Rick Schu	.10
101	Larry Sheets	.10
102	Ron Shepherd	.10
103	Nelson Simmons	.10
104	Don Slaught	.10
105	Roy Smalley	.10
106	Lonnie Smith	.10
107	Nate Snell	.10
108	Lary Sorensen	.10
109	Chris Speier	.10
110	Mike Stenhouse	.10
111	Tim Stoddard	.10
112	John Stuper	.10
113	Jim Sundberg	.10
114	Bruce Sutter	.40
115	Don Sutton	.50
116	Bruce Tanner	.10
117	Kent Tekulve	.10
118	Walt Terrell	.10
119	Mickey Tettleton **RC**	1.00
120	Rich Thompson	.10
121	Louis Thornton	.10
122	Alex Trevino	.10
123	John Tudor	.10
124	Jose Uribe	.10
125	Dave Valle	.10
126	Dave Von Ohlen	.10
127	Curt Wardle	.10
128	U.L. Washington	.10
129	Ed Whitson	.10
130	Herm Winningham	.10
131	Rich Yett	.10
132	Checklist	.10

1986 Fleer

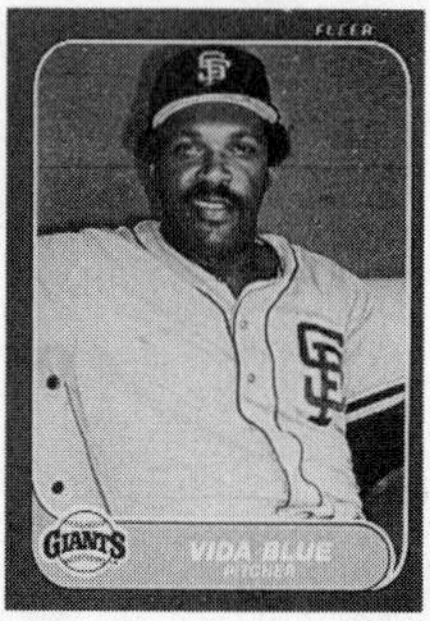

		NM/M
Unopened Fact. Set (660):		30.00
Complete Set (660):		25.00
Common Player:		.05
Wax Pack (15):		1.50
Wax Box (36):		45.00
Cello Pack (28):		2.00
Cello Box (24):		40.00
Rack Pack (45):		4.00
Rack Box (24):		65.00
1	Steve Balboni	.05
2	Joe Beckwith	.05
3	Buddy Biancalana	.05
4	Bud Black	.05
5	George Brett	2.00
6	Onix Concepcion	.05
7	Steve Farr	.05
8	Mark Gubicza	.05
9	Dane Iorg	.05
10	Danny Jackson	.05
11	Lynn Jones	.05
12	Mike Jones	.05
13	Charlie Leibrandt	.05
14	Hal McRae	.05
15	Omar Moreno	.05
16	Darryl Motley	.05
17	Jorge Orta	.05
18	Dan Quisenberry	.05
19	Bret Saberhagen	.05
20	Pat Sheridan	.05
21	Lonnie Smith	.05
22	Jim Sundberg	.05
23	John Wathan	.05
24	Frank White	.05
25	Willie Wilson	.05
26	Joaquin Andujar	.05
27	Steve Braun	.05
28	Bill Campbell	.05
29	Cesar Cedeno	.05
30	Jack Clark	.05
31	Vince Coleman	.05
32	Danny Cox	.05
33	Ken Dayley	.05
34	Ivan DeJesus	.05
35	Bob Forsch	.05
36	Brian Harper	.05
37	Tom Herr	.05
38	Ricky Horton	.05
39	Kurt Kepshire	.05
40	Jeff Lahti	.05
41	Tito Landrum	.05
42	Willie McGee	.05
43	Tom Nieto	.05
44	Terry Pendleton	.05
45	Darrell Porter	.05
46	Ozzie Smith	1.50
47	John Tudor	.05
48	Andy Van Slyke	.05
49	Todd Worrell **RC**	.25
50	Jim Acker	.05
51	Doyle Alexander	.05
52	Jesse Barfield	.05
53	George Bell	.05
54	Jeff Burroughs	.05
55	Bill Caudill	.05

56	Jim Clancy	.05
57	Tony Fernandez	.05
58	Tom Filer	.05
59	Damaso Garcia	.05
60	Tom Henke	.05
61	Garth Iorg	.05
62	Cliff Johnson	.05
63	Jimmy Key	.05
64	Dennis Lamp	.05
65	Gary Lavelle	.05
66	Buck Martinez	.05
67	Lloyd Moseby	.05
68	Rance Mulliniks	.05
69	Al Oliver	.05
70	Dave Stieb	.05
71	Louis Thornton	.05
72	Willie Upshaw	.05
73	Ernie Whitt	.05
74	Rick Aguilera **RC**	.75
75	Wally Backman	.05
76	Gary Carter	1.00
77	Ron Darling	.05
78	Len Dykstra **RC**	2.00
79	Sid Fernandez	.05
80	George Foster	.05
81	Dwight Gooden	.05
82	Tom Gorman	.05
83	Danny Heep	.05
84	Keith Hernandez	.05
85	Howard Johnson	.05
86	Ray Knight	.05
87	Terry Leach	.05
88	Ed Lynch	.05
89	Roger McDowell	.05
90	Jesse Orosco	.05
91	Tom Paciorek	.05
92	Ronn Reynolds	.05
93	Rafael Santana	.05
94	Doug Sisk	.05
95	Rusty Staub	.05
96	Darryl Strawberry	.05
97	Mookie Wilson	.05
98	Neil Allen	.05
99	Don Baylor	.05
100	Dale Berra	.05
101	Rich Bordi	.05
102	Marty Bystrom	.05
103	Joe Cowley	.05
104	Brian Fisher **RC**	.05
105	Ken Griffey	.05
106	Ron Guidry	.10
107	Ron Hassey	.05
108	Rickey Henderson	1.00
109	Don Mattingly	2.00
110	Bobby Meacham	.05
111	John Montefusco	.05
112	Phil Niekro	.75
113	Mike Pagliarulo	.05
114	Dan Pasqua	.05
115	Willie Randolph	.05
116	Dave Righetti	.05
117	Andre Robertson	.05
118	Billy Sample	.05
119	Bob Shirley	.05
120	Ed Whitson	.05
121	Dave Winfield	1.00
122	Butch Wynegar	.05
123	Dave Anderson	.05
124	Bob Bailor	.05
125	Greg Brock	.05
126	Enos Cabell	.05
127	Bobby Castillo	.05
128	Carlos Diaz	.05
129	Mariano Duncan	.05
130	Pedro Guerrero	.05
131	Orel Hershiser	.05
132	Rick Honeycutt	.05
133	Ken Howell	.05
134	Ken Landreaux	.05
135	Bill Madlock	.05
136	Candy Maldonado	.05
137	Mike Marshall	.05
138	Len Matuszek	.05
139	Tom Niedenfuer	.05
140	Alejandro Pena	.05
141	Jerry Reuss	.05
142	Bill Russell	.05
143	Steve Sax	.05
144	Mike Scioscia	.05
145	Fernando Valenzuela	.05
146	Bob Welch	.05
147	Terry Whitfield	.05
148	Juan Beniquez	.05
149	Bob Boone	.05
150	John Candelaria	.05
151	Rod Carew	1.00
152	Stewart Cliburn **RC**	.05
153	Doug DeCinces	.05
154	Brian Downing	.05
155	Ken Forsch	.05
156	Craig Gerber	.05
157	Bobby Grich	.05
158	George Hendrick	.05
159	Al Holland	.05
160	Reggie Jackson	1.50
161	Ruppert Jones	.05
162	Urbano Lugo **RC**	.05
163	Kirk McCaskill **RC**	.25
164	Donnie Moore	.05
165	Gary Pettis	.05
166	Ron Romanick	.05
167	Dick Schofield	.05
168	Daryl Sconiers	.05
169	Jim Slaton	.05
170	Don Sutton	.75
171	Mike Witt	.05
172	Buddy Bell	.05
173	Tom Browning	.05
174	Dave Concepcion	.05
175	Eric Davis	.05
176	Bo Diaz	.05
177	Nick Esasky	.05
178	John Franco	.05
179	Tom Hume	.05
180	Wayne Krenchicki	.05
181	Andy McGaffigan	.05
182	Eddie Milner	.05
183	Ron Oester	.05
184	Dave Parker	.05
185	Frank Pastore	.05
186	Tony Perez	.75
187	Ted Power	.05
188	Joe Price	.05
189	Gary Redus	.05
190	Ron Robinson	.05
191	Pete Rose	2.50
192	Mario Soto	.05
193	John Stuper	.05
194	Jay Tibbs	.05
195	Dave Van Gorder	.05
196	Max Venable	.05
197	Juan Agosto	.05
198	Harold Baines	.05
199	Floyd Bannister	.05
200	Britt Burns	.05
201	Julio Cruz	.05
202	Joel Davis **RC**	.05
203	Richard Dotson	.05
204	Carlton Fisk	1.00
205	Scott Fletcher	.05
206	Ozzie Guillen	.05
207	Jerry Hairston Sr.	.05
208	Tim Hulett	.05
209	Bob James	.05
210	Ron Kittle	.05
211	Rudy Law	.05
212	Bryan Little	.05
213	Gene Nelson	.05
214	Reid Nichols	.05
215	Luis Salazar	.05
216	Tom Seaver	1.00
217	Dan Spillner	.05
218	Bruce Tanner	.05
219	Greg Walker	.05
220	Dave Wehrmeister	.05
221	Juan Berenguer	.05
222	Dave Bergman	.05
223	Tom Brookens	.05
224	Darrell Evans	.05
225	Barbaro Garbey	.05
226	Kirk Gibson	.05
227	John Grubb	.05
228	Willie Hernandez	.05
229	Larry Herndon	.05
230	Chet Lemon	.05
231	Aurelio Lopez	.05
232	Jack Morris	.05
233	Randy O'Neal	.05
234	Lance Parrish	.05
235	Dan Petry	.05
236	Alex Sanchez	.05
237	Bill Scherrer	.05
238	Nelson Simmons	.05
239	Frank Tanana	.05
240	Walt Terrell	.05
241	Alan Trammell	.05
242	Lou Whitaker	.05
243	Milt Wilcox	.05
244	Hubie Brooks	.05
245	Tim Burke **RC**	.05
246	Andre Dawson	.35
247	Mike Fitzgerald	.05
248	Terry Francona	.05
249	Bill Gullickson	.05
250	Joe Hesketh	.05
251	Bill Laskey	.05
252	Vance Law	.05
253	Charlie Lea	.05
254	Gary Lucas	.05
255	David Palmer	.05
256	Tim Raines	.05
257	Jeff Reardon	.05
258	Bert Roberge	.05
259	Dan Schatzeder	.05
260	Bryn Smith	.05
261	Randy St. Claire	.05
262	Scot Thompson	.05
263	Tim Wallach	.05
264	U.L. Washington	.05
265	Mitch Webster **RC**	.05
266	Herm Winningham **RC**	.05
267	Floyd Youmans **RC**	.05
268	Don Aase	.05
269	Mike Boddicker	.05
270	Rich Dauer	.05
271	Storm Davis	.05
272	Rick Dempsey	.05
273	Ken Dixon	.05
274	Jim Dwyer	.05
275	Mike Flanagan	.05
276	Wayne Gross	.05
277	Lee Lacy	.05
278	Fred Lynn	.05
279	Tippy Martinez	.05
280	Dennis Martinez	.05
281	Scott McGregor	.05
282	Eddie Murray	1.00
283	Floyd Rayford	.05
284	Cal Ripken, Jr.	3.00
285	Gary Roenicke	.05
286	Larry Sheets	.05
287	John Shelby	.05
288	Nate Snell	.05
289	Sammy Stewart	.05
290	Alan Wiggins	.05
291	Mike Young	.05
292	Alan Ashby	.05
293	Mark Bailey	.05
294	Kevin Bass	.05
295	Jeff Calhoun	.05
296	Jose Cruz	.05
297	Glenn Davis	.05
298	Bill Dawley	.05
299	Frank DiPino	.05
300	Bill Doran	.05
301	Phil Garner	.05
302	Jeff Heathcock **RC**	.05
303	Charlie Kerfeld **RC**	.05
304	Bob Knepper	.05
305	Ron Mathis	.05
306	Jerry Mumphrey	.05
307	Jim Pankovits	.05
308	Terry Puhl	.05
309	Craig Reynolds	.05
310	Nolan Ryan	3.00
311	Mike Scott	.05
312	Dave Smith	.05
313	Dickie Thon	.05
314	Denny Walling	.05
315	Kurt Bevacqua	.05
316	Al Bumbry	.05
317	Jerry Davis	.05
318	Luis DeLeon	.05
319	Dave Dravecky	.05
320	Tim Flannery	.05
321	Steve Garvey	.30
322	Goose Gossage	.05
323	Tony Gwynn	1.50
324	Andy Hawkins	.05
325	LaMarr Hoyt	.05
326	Roy Lee Jackson	.05
327	Terry Kennedy	.05
328	Craig Lefferts	.05
329	Carmelo Martinez	.05
330	Lance McCullers **RC**	.05
331	Kevin McReynolds	.05
332	Graig Nettles	.05
333	Jerry Royster	.05
334	Eric Show	.05
335	Tim Stoddard	.05
336	Garry Templeton	.05
337	Mark Thurmond	.05
338	Ed Wojna	.05
339	Tony Armas	.05
340	Marty Barrett	.05
341	Wade Boggs	1.50
342	Dennis Boyd	.05
343	Bill Buckner	.05
344	Mark Clear	.05
345	Roger Clemens	2.00
346	Steve Crawford	.05
347	Mike Easler	.05
348	Dwight Evans	.05
349	Rich Gedman	.05
350	Jackie Gutierrez	.05
351	Glenn Hoffman	.05
352	Bruce Hurst	.05
353	Bruce Kison	.05
354	Tim Lollar	.05
355	Steve Lyons	.05
356	Al Nipper	.05
357	Bob Ojeda	.05
358	Jim Rice	.30
359	Bob Stanley	.05
360	Mike Trujillo	.05
361	Thad Bosley	.05
362	Warren Brusstar	.05
363	Ron Cey	.05
364	Jody Davis	.05
365	Bob Dernier	.05
366	Shawon Dunston	.05
367	Leon Durham	.05
368	Dennis Eckersley	.75
369	Ray Fontenot	.05
370	George Frazier	.05
371	Bill Hatcher	.05
372	Dave Lopes	.05
373	Gary Matthews	.05
374	Ron Meredith	.05
375	Keith Moreland	.05
376	Reggie Patterson	.05
377	Dick Ruthven	.05
378	Ryne Sandberg	1.50
379	Scott Sanderson	.05
380	Lee Smith	.05
381	Lary Sorensen	.05
382	Chris Speier	.05
383	Rick Sutcliffe	.05
384	Steve Trout	.05
385	Gary Woods	.05
386	Bert Blyleven	.10
387	Tom Brunansky	.05
388	Randy Bush	.05
389	John Butcher	.05
390	Ron Davis	.05
391	Dave Engle	.05
392	Frank Eufemia	.05
393	Pete Filson	.05
394	Gary Gaetti	.05
395	Greg Gagne	.05
396	Mickey Hatcher	.05
397	Kent Hrbek	.05
398	Tim Laudner	.05
399	Rick Lysander	.05
400	Dave Meier	.05
401	Kirby Puckett	1.50
402	Mark Salas	.05
403	Ken Schrom	.05
404	Roy Smalley	.05
405	Mike Smithson	.05
406	Mike Stenhouse	.05
407	Tim Teufel	.05
408	Frank Viola	.05
409	Ron Washington	.05
410	Keith Atherton	.05
411	Dusty Baker	.05
412	Tim Birtsas **RC**	.05
413	Bruce Bochte	.05
414	Chris Codiroli	.05
415	Dave Collins	.05
416	Mike Davis	.05
417	Alfredo Griffin	.05
418	Mike Heath	.05
419	Steve Henderson	.05
420	Donnie Hill	.05
421	Jay Howell	.05
422	Tommy John	.10
423	Dave Kingman	.05
424	Bill Krueger	.05
425	Rick Langford	.05
426	Carney Lansford	.05
427	Steve McCatty	.05
428	Dwayne Murphy	.05
429	Steve Ontiveros **RC**	.05
430	Tony Phillips	.05
431	Jose Rijo	.05
432	Mickey Tettleton	.05
433	Luis Aguayo	.05
434	Larry Andersen	.05
435	Steve Carlton	1.00
436	Don Carman **RC**	.05
437	Tim Corcoran	.05
438	Darren Daulton	.05
439	John Denny	.05
440	Tom Foley	.05
441	Greg Gross	.05
442	Kevin Gross	.05
443	Von Hayes	.05
444	Charles Hudson	.05
445	Garry Maddox	.05
446	Shane Rawley	.05
447	Dave Rucker	.05
448	John Russell	.05
449	Juan Samuel	.05
450	Mike Schmidt	2.00
451	Rick Schu	.05
452	Dave Shipanoff	.05
453	Dave Stewart	.05
454	Jeff Stone	.05
455	Kent Tekulve	.05
456	Ozzie Virgil	.05
457	Glenn Wilson	.05
458	Jim Beattie	.05
459	Karl Best	.05
460	Barry Bonnell	.05
461	Phil Bradley	.05
462	Ivan Calderon **RC**	.05
463	Al Cowens	.05
464	Alvin Davis	.05
465	Dave Henderson	.05
466	Bob Kearney	.05
467	Mark Langston	.05
468	Bob Long	.05
469	Mike Moore	.05
470	Edwin Nunez	.05
471	Spike Owen	.05
472	Jack Perconte	.05
473	Jim Presley	.05
474	Donnie Scott	.05
475	Bill Swift	.05
476	Danny Tartabull	.05
477	Gorman Thomas	.05
478	Roy Thomas	.05
479	Ed Vande Berg	.05
480	Frank Wills	.05
481	Matt Young	.05
482	Ray Burris	.05
483	Jaime Cocanower	.05
484	Cecil Cooper	.05
485	Danny Darwin	.05
486	Rollie Fingers	.75
487	Jim Gantner	.05
488	Bob Gibson	.05
489	Moose Haas	.05
490	Teddy Higuera **RC**	.05
491	Paul Householder	.05
492	Pete Ladd	.05
493	Rick Manning	.05
494	Bob McClure	.05
495	Paul Molitor	1.00
496	Charlie Moore	.05
497	Ben Oglivie	.05
498	Randy Ready	.05
499	Earnie Riles **RC**	.05
500	Ed Romero	.05
501	Bill Schroeder	.05
502	Ray Searage	.05
503	Ted Simmons	.05
504	Pete Vuckovich	.05
505	Rick Waits	.05
506	Robin Yount	1.00
507	Len Barker	.05
508	Steve Bedrosian	.05
509	Bruce Benedict	.05
510	Rick Camp	.05
511	Rick Cerone	.05
512	Chris Chambliss	.05
513	Jeff Dedmon	.05
514	Terry Forster	.05
515	Gene Garber	.05

516	Terry Harper	.05
517	Bob Horner	.05
518	Glenn Hubbard	.05
519	Joe Johnson **RC**	.05
520	Brad Komminsk	.05
521	Rick Mahler	.05
522	Dale Murphy	.30
523	Ken Oberkfell	.05
524	Pascual Perez	.05
525	Gerald Perry	.05
526	Rafael Ramirez	.05
527	Steve Shields **RC**	.05
528	Zane Smith	.05
529	Bruce Sutter	.75
530	Milt Thompson **RC**	.05
531	Claudell Washington	.05
532	Paul Zuvella	.05
533	Vida Blue	.05
534	Bob Brenly	.05
535	Chris Brown **RC**	.05
536	Chili Davis	.05
537	Mark Davis	.05
538	Rob Deer	.05
539	Dan Driessen	.05
540	Scott Garrelts	.05
541	Dan Gladden	.05
542	Jim Gott	.05
543	David Green	.05
544	Atlee Hammaker	.05
545	Mike Jeffcoat	.05
546	Mike Krukow	.05
547	Dave LaPoint	.05
548	Jeff Leonard	.05
549	Greg Minton	.05
550	Alex Trevino	.05
551	Manny Trillo	.05
552	Jose Uribe **RC**	.05
553	Brad Wellman	.05
554	Frank Williams	.05
555	Joel Youngblood	.05
556	Alan Bannister	.05
557	Glenn Brummer	.05
558	Steve Buechele **RC**	.05
559	Jose Guzman **RC**	.05
560	Toby Harrah	.05
561	Greg Harris	.05
562	Dwayne Henry **RC**	.05
563	Burt Hooton	.05
564	Charlie Hough	.05
565	Mike Mason	.05
566	Oddibe McDowell **RC**	.05
567	Dickie Noles	.05
568	Pete O'Brien	.05
569	Larry Parrish	.05
570	Dave Rozema	.05
571	Dave Schmidt	.05
572	Don Slaught	.05
573	Wayne Tolleson	.05
574	Duane Walker	.05
575	Gary Ward	.05
576	Chris Welsh	.05
577	Curtis Wilkerson	.05
578	George Wright	.05
579	Chris Bando	.05
580	Tony Bernazard	.05
581	Brett Butler	.05
582	Ernie Camacho	.05
583	Joe Carter	.05
584	Carmello Castillo (Carmelo)	.05
585	Jamie Easterly	.05
586	Julio Franco	.05
587	Mel Hall	.05
588	Mike Hargrove	.05
589	Neal Heaton	.05
590	Brook Jacoby	.05
591	Otis Nixon **RC**	.25
592	Jerry Reed	.05
593	Vern Ruhle	.05
594	Pat Tabler	.05
595	Rich Thompson	.05
596	Andre Thornton	.05
597	Dave Von Ohlen	.05
598	George Vukovich	.05
599	Tom Waddell	.05
600	Curt Wardle	.05
601	Jerry Willard	.05
602	Bill Almon	.05
603	Mike Bielecki	.05
604	Sid Bream	.05
605	Mike Brown	.05
606	Pat Clements **RC**	.05
607	Jose DeLeon	.05
608	Denny Gonzalez	.05
609	Cecilio Guante	.05
610	Steve Kemp	.05
611	Sam Khalifa	.05
612	Lee Mazzilli	.05
613	Larry McWilliams	.05
614	Jim Morrison	.05
615	Joe Orsulak **RC**	.25
616	Tony Pena	.05
617	Johnny Ray	.05
618	Rick Reuschel	.05
619	R.J. Reynolds	.05
620	Rick Rhoden	.05
621	Don Robinson	.05
622	Jason Thompson	.05
623	Lee Tunnell	.05
624	Jim Winn	.05
625	Marvell Wynne	.05
626	Dwight Gooden/IA	.05
627	Don Mattingly/IA	.50
628	Pete Rose (4,192 Hits)	1.00
629	Rod Carew (3,000 Hits)	.25
630	Phil Niekro, Tom Seaver (300 Wins)	.25
631	Don Baylor Ouch!	.05
632	Tim Raines, Darryl Strawberry Instant Offense	.05
633	Cal Ripken, Jr., Alan Trammell Shortstops Supreme	1.00
634	Wade Boggs, George Brett Boggs & "Hero"	1.00
635	Bob Horner, Dale Murphy Braves Dynamic Duo	.25
636	Vince Coleman, Willie McGee Cardinal Ignitors	.25
637	Vince Coleman Terror on the Basepaths	.05
638	Dwight Gooden, Pete Rose Charlie Hustle & Dr. K	.50
639	Wade Boggs, Don Mattingly 1984 and 1985 A.L. Batting Champs	1.00
640	Steve Garvey, Dale Murphy, Dave Parker N.L. West Sluggers	.25
641	Dwight Gooden, Fernando Valenzuela Staff Aces	.10
642	Jimmy Key, Dave Stieb Blue Jay Stoppers	.05
643	Carlton Fisk, Rich Gedman A.L. All-Star Backstops	.10
644	Benito Santiago, Gene Walter **RC** Major League Prospect	1.00
645	Colin Ward, Mike Woodard **RC** Major League Prospect	.10
646	Kal Daniels, Paul O'Neill **RC** Major League Prospect	2.00
647	Andres Galarraga, Fred Toliver **RC** Major League Prospect	3.00
648	Curt Ford, Bob Kipper **RC** Major League Prospect	.10
649	Jose Canseco, Eric Plunk **RC** Major League Prospect	5.00
650	Mark McLemore, Gus Polidor **RC** Major League Prospect	.75
651	Mickey Brantley, Rob Woodward **RC** Major League Prospect	.10
652	Mark Funderburk, Billy Joe Robidoux **RC** Major League Prospect	.10
653	Cecil Fielder, Cory Snyder **RC** Major League Prospect	1.50
654	Checklist 1-97	.05
655	Checklist 98-196	.05
656	Checklist 197-291	.05
657	Checklist 292-385	.05
658	Checklist 386-482	.05
659	Checklist 483-578	.05
660	Checklist 579-660	.05

Update

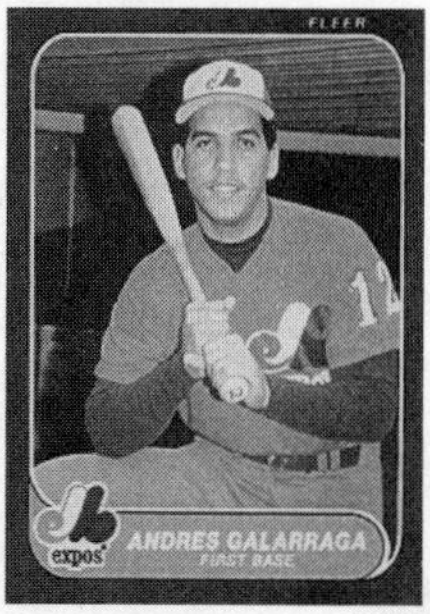

		NM/M
Unopened Fact. Set (132):		40.00
Complete Set (132):		30.00
Common Player:		.05
1	Mike Aldrete	.05
2	Andy Allanson	.05
3	Neil Allen	.05
4	Joaquin Andujar	.05
5	Paul Assenmacher	.05
6	Scott Bailes	.05
7	Jay Baller	.05
8	Scott Bankhead	.05
9	Bill Bathe	.05
10	Don Baylor	.05
11	Billy Beane	.05
12	Steve Bedrosian	.05
13	Juan Beniquez	.05
14	Barry Bonds **RC**	25.00
15	Bobby Bonilla **RC**	1.00
16	Rich Bordi	.05
17	Bill Campbell	.05
18	Tom Candiotti	.05
19	John Cangelosi	.05
20	Jose Canseco	4.00
21	Chuck Cary	.05
22	Juan Castillo	.05
23	Rick Cerone	.05
24	John Cerutti	.05
25	Will Clark **RC**	1.00
26	Mark Clear	.05
27	Darnell Coles	.05
28	Dave Collins	.05
29	Tim Conroy	.05
30	Ed Correa	.05
31	Joe Cowley	.05
32	Bill Dawley	.05
33	Rob Deer	.05
34	John Denny	.05
35	Jim DeShaies	.05
36	Doug Drabek **RC**	1.00
37	Mike Easler	.05
38	Mark Eichhorn	.05
39	Dave Engle	.05
40	Mike Fischlin	.05
41	Scott Fletcher	.05
42	Terry Forster	.05
43	Terry Francona	.05
44	Andres Galarraga	.50
45	Lee Guetterman	.05
46	Bill Gullickson	.05
47	Jackie Gutierrez	.05
48	Moose Haas	.05
49	Billy Hatcher	.05
50	Mike Heath	.05
51	Guy Hoffman	.05
52	Tom Hume	.05
53	Pete Incaviglia **RC**	.50
54	Dane Iorg	.05
55	Chris James	.05
56	Stan Javier	.05
57	Tommy John	.15
58	Tracy Jones	.05
59	Wally Joyner **RC**	1.00
60	Wayne Krenchicki	.05
61	John Kruk **RC**	1.00
62	Mike LaCoss	.05
63	Pete Ladd	.05
64	Dave LaPoint	.05
65	Mike LaValliere	.05
66	Rudy Law	.05
67	Dennis Leonard	.05
68	Steve Lombardozzi	.05
69	Aurelio Lopez	.05
70	Mickey Mahler	.05
71	Candy Maldonado	.05
72	Roger Mason	.05
73	Greg Mathews	.05
74	Andy McGaffigan	.05
75	Joel McKeon	.05
76	Kevin Mitchell **RC**	.50
77	Bill Mooneyham	.05
78	Omar Moreno	.05
79	Jerry Mumphrey	.05
80	Al Newman	.05
81	Phil Niekro	.50
82	Randy Niemann	.05
83	Juan Nieves	.05
84	Bob Ojeda	.05
85	Rick Ownbey	.05
86	Tom Paciorek	.05
87	David Palmer	.05
88	Jeff Parrett	.05
89	Pat Perry	.05
90	Dan Plesac	.05
91	Darrell Porter	.05
92	Luis Quinones	.05
93	Rey Quinonez	.05
94	Gary Redus	.05
95	Jeff Reed	.05
96	Bip Roberts	.05
97	Billy Joe Robidoux	.05
98	Gary Roenicke	.05
99	Ron Roenicke	.05
100	Angel Salazar	.05
101	Joe Sambito	.05
102	Billy Sample	.05
103	Dave Schmidt	.05
104	Ken Schrom	.05
105	Ruben Sierra **RC**	.75
106	Ted Simmons	.05
107	Sammy Stewart	.05
108	Kurt Stillwell	.05
109	Dale Sveum	.05
110	Tim Teufel	.05
111	Bob Tewksbury	.05
112	Andres Thomas	.05
113	Jason Thompson	.05
114	Milt Thompson	.05
115	Rob Thompson	.05
116	Jay Tibbs	.05
117	Fred Toliver	.05
118	Wayne Tolleson	.05
119	Alex Trevino	.05
120	Manny Trillo	.05
121	Ed Vande Berg	.05
122	Ozzie Virgil	.05
123	Tony Walker	.05
124	Gene Walter	.05
125	Duane Ward	.05
126	Jerry Willard	.05
127	Mitch Williams	.05
128	Reggie Williams	.05
129	Bobby Witt	.05
130	Marvell Wynne	.05
131	Steve Yeager	.05
132	Checklist	.05

1987 Fleer

		NM/M
Unopened Fact. Set (672):		65.00
Complete Set (660):		50.00
Common Player:		.05
Wax Pack (15/17):		3.00
Wax Box (36):		100.00
Cello Pack (28):		5.00

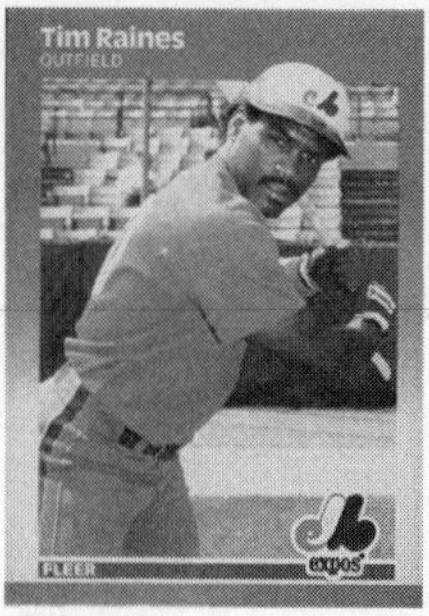

Cello Box (24):		100.00
Rack Pack (51):		8.00
Rack Box (24):		160.00
1	Rick Aguilera	.05
2	Richard Anderson	.05
3	Wally Backman	.05
4	Gary Carter	.75
5	Ron Darling	.05
6	Len Dykstra	.05
7	Kevin Elster **RC**	.15
8	Sid Fernandez	.05
9	Dwight Gooden	.05
10	Ed Hearn **RC**	.05
11	Danny Heep	.05
12	Keith Hernandez	.05
13	Howard Johnson	.05
14	Ray Knight	.05
15	Lee Mazzilli	.05
16	Roger McDowell	.05
17	Kevin Mitchell	.05
18	Randy Niemann	.05
19	Bob Ojeda	.05
20	Jesse Orosco	.05
21	Rafael Santana	.05
22	Doug Sisk	.05
23	Darryl Strawberry	.05
24	Tim Teufel	.05
25	Mookie Wilson	.05
26	Tony Armas	.05
27	Marty Barrett	.05
28	Don Baylor	.05
29	Wade Boggs	1.00
30	Oil Can Boyd	.05
31	Bill Buckner	.05
32	Roger Clemens	2.00
33	Steve Crawford	.05
34	Dwight Evans	.05
35	Rich Gedman	.05
36	Dave Henderson	.05
37	Bruce Hurst	.05
38	Tim Lollar	.05
39	Al Nipper	.05
40	Spike Owen	.05
41	Jim Rice	.30
42	Ed Romero	.05
43	Joe Sambito	.05
44	Calvin Schiraldi	.05
45	Tom Seaver	.75
46	Jeff Sellers **RC**	.05
47	Bob Stanley	.05
48	Sammy Stewart	.05
49	Larry Andersen	.05
50	Alan Ashby	.05
51	Kevin Bass	.05
52	Jeff Calhoun	.05
53	Jose Cruz	.05
54	Danny Darwin	.05
55	Glenn Davis	.05
56	Jim Deshaies **RC**	.10
57	Bill Doran	.05
58	Phil Garner	.05
59	Billy Hatcher	.05
60	Charlie Kerfeld	.05
61	Bob Knepper	.05
62	Dave Lopes	.05
63	Aurelio Lopez	.05
64	Jim Pankovits	.05
65	Terry Puhl	.05
66	Craig Reynolds	.05
67	Nolan Ryan	3.00
68	Mike Scott	.05
69	Dave Smith	.05
70	Dickie Thon	.05
71	Tony Walker	.05
72	Denny Walling	.05
73	Bob Boone	.05
74	Rick Burleson	.05
75	John Candelaria	.05
76	Doug Corbett	.05
77	Doug DeCinces	.05
78	Brian Downing	.05
79	Chuck Finley **RC**	1.00
80	Terry Forster	.05
81	Bobby Grich	.05
82	George Hendrick	.05
83	Jack Howell	.05
84	Reggie Jackson	1.00
85	Ruppert Jones	.05
86	Wally Joyner	.05
87	Gary Lucas	.05
88	Kirk McCaskill	.05

89	Donnie Moore	.05
90	Gary Pettis	.05
91	Vern Ruhle	.05
92	Dick Schofield	.05
93	Don Sutton	.65
94	Rob Wilfong	.05
95	Mike Witt	.05
96	Doug Drabek	.05
97	Mike Easler	.05
98	Mike Fischlin	.05
99	Brian Fisher	.05
100	Ron Guidry	.10
101	Rickey Henderson	.75
102	Tommy John	.10
103	Ron Kittle	.05
104	Don Mattingly	2.00
105	Bobby Meacham	.05
106	Joe Niekro	.05
107	Mike Pagliarulo	.05
108	Dan Pasqua	.05
109	Willie Randolph	.05
110	Dennis Rasmussen	.05
111	Dave Righetti	.05
112	Gary Roenicke	.05
113	Rod Scurry	.05
114	Bob Shirley	.05
115	Joel Skinner	.05
116	Tim Stoddard	.05
117	Bob Tewksbury **RC**	.35
118	Wayne Tolleson	.05
119	Claudell Washington	.05
120	Dave Winfield	.75
121	Steve Buechele	.05
122	Ed Correa **RC**	.05
123	Scott Fletcher	.05
124	Jose Guzman	.05
125	Toby Harrah	.05
126	Greg Harris	.05
127	Charlie Hough	.05
128	Pete Incaviglia	.05
129	Mike Mason	.05
130	Oddibe McDowell	.05
131	Dale Mohorcic **RC**	.05
132	Pete O'Brien	.05
133	Tom Paciorek	.05
134	Larry Parrish	.05
135	Geno Petralli	.05
136	Darrell Porter	.05
137	Jeff Russell	.05
138	Ruben Sierra	.05
139	Don Slaught	.05
140	Gary Ward	.05
141	Curtis Wilkerson	.05
142	Mitch Williams **RC**	.10
143	Bobby Witt **RC**	.10
144	Dave Bergman	.05
145	Tom Brookens	.05
146	Bill Campbell	.05
147	Chuck Cary **RC**	.05
148	Darnell Coles	.05
149	Dave Collins	.05
150	Darrell Evans	.05
151	Kirk Gibson	.05
152	John Grubb	.05
153	Willie Hernandez	.05
154	Larry Herndon	.05
155	Eric King **RC**	.05
156	Chet Lemon	.05
157	Dwight Lowry	.05
158	Jack Morris	.05
159	Randy O'Neal	.05
160	Lance Parrish	.05
161	Dan Petry	.05
162	Pat Sheridan	.05
163	Jim Slaton	.05
164	Frank Tanana	.05
165	Walt Terrell	.05
166	Mark Thurmond	.05
167	Alan Trammell	.05
168	Lou Whitaker	.05
169	Luis Aguayo	.05
170	Steve Bedrosian	.05
171	Don Carman	.05
172	Darren Daulton	.05
173	Greg Gross	.05
174	Kevin Gross	.05
175	Von Hayes	.05
176	Charles Hudson	.05
177	Tom Hume	.05
178	Steve Jeltz	.05
179	Mike Maddux **RC**	.05
180	Shane Rawley	.05
181	Gary Redus	.05
182	Ron Roenicke	.05
183	Bruce Ruffin **RC**	.10
184	John Russell	.05
185	Juan Samuel	.05
186	Dan Schatzeder	.05
187	Mike Schmidt	2.00
188	Rick Schu	.05
189	Jeff Stone	.05
190	Kent Tekulve	.05
191	Milt Thompson	.05
192	Glenn Wilson	.05
193	Buddy Bell	.05
194	Tom Browning	.05
195	Sal Butera	.05
196	Dave Concepcion	.05
197	Kal Daniels	.05
198	Eric Davis	.05
199	John Denny	.05
200	Bo Diaz	.05
201	Nick Esasky	.05
202	John Franco	.05
203	Bill Gullickson	.05
204	Barry Larkin **RC**	2.00
205	Eddie Milner	.05
206	Rob Murphy **RC**	.05
207	Ron Oester	.05
208	Dave Parker	.05
209	Tony Perez	.65
210	Ted Power	.05
211	Joe Price	.05
212	Ron Robinson	.05
213	Pete Rose	2.50
214	Mario Soto	.05
215	Kurt Stillwell **RC**	.05
216	Max Venable	.05
217	Chris Welsh	.05
218	Carl Willis **RC**	.05
219	Jesse Barfield	.05
220	George Bell	.05
221	Bill Caudill	.05
222	John Cerutti **RC**	.05
223	Jim Clancy	.05
224	Mark Eichhorn **RC**	.10
225	Tony Fernandez	.05
226	Damaso Garcia	.05
227	Kelly Gruber	.05
228	Tom Henke	.05
229	Garth Iorg	.05
230	Cliff Johnson	.05
231	Joe Johnson	.05
232	Jimmy Key	.05
233	Dennis Lamp	.05
234	Rick Leach	.05
235	Buck Martinez	.05
236	Lloyd Moseby	.05
237	Rance Mulliniks	.05
238	Dave Stieb	.05
239	Willie Upshaw	.05
240	Ernie Whitt	.05
241	Andy Allanson **RC**	.05
242	Scott Bailes **RC**	.05
243	Chris Bando	.05
244	Tony Bernazard	.05
245	John Butcher	.05
246	Brett Butler	.05
247	Ernie Camacho	.05
248	Tom Candiotti	.05
249	Joe Carter	.05
250	Carmen Castillo	.05
251	Julio Franco	.05
252	Mel Hall	.05
253	Brook Jacoby	.05
254	Phil Niekro	.65
255	Otis Nixon	.05
256	Dickie Noles	.05
257	Bryan Oelkers	.05
258	Ken Schrom	.05
259	Don Schulze	.05
260	Cory Snyder	.05
261	Pat Tabler	.05
262	Andre Thornton	.05
263	Rich Yett **RC**	.05
264	Mike Aldrete **RC**	.05
265	Juan Berenguer	.05
266	Vida Blue	.05
267	Bob Brenly	.05
268	Chris Brown	.05
269	Will Clark	.05
270	Chili Davis	.05
271	Mark Davis	.05
272	Kelly Downs **RC**	.05
273	Scott Garrelts	.05
274	Dan Gladden	.05
275	Mike Krukow	.05
276	Randy Kutcher **RC**	.05
277	Mike LaCoss	.05
278	Jeff Leonard	.05
279	Candy Maldonado	.05
280	Roger Mason	.05
281	Bob Melvin	.05
282	Greg Minton	.05
283	Jeff Robinson	.05
284	Harry Spilman	.05
285	Rob Thompson **RC**	.05
286	Jose Uribe	.05
287	Frank Williams	.05
288	Joel Youngblood	.05
289	Jack Clark	.05
290	Vince Coleman	.05
291	Tim Conroy	.05
292	Danny Cox	.05
293	Ken Dayley	.05
294	Curt Ford	.05
295	Bob Forsch	.05
296	Tom Herr	.05
297	Ricky Horton	.05
298	Clint Hurdle	.05
299	Jeff Lahti	.05
300	Steve Lake	.05
301	Tito Landrum	.05
302	Mike LaValliere **RC**	.05
303	Greg Mathews **RC**	.05
304	Willie McGee	.05
305	Jose Oquendo	.05
306	Terry Pendleton	.05
307	Pat Perry	.05
308	Ozzie Smith	1.50
309	Ray Soff	.05
310	John Tudor	.05
311	Andy Van Slyke	.05
312	Todd Worrell	.05
313	Dann Bilardello	.05
314	Hubie Brooks	.05
315	Tim Burke	.05
316	Andre Dawson	.35
317	Mike Fitzgerald	.05
318	Tom Foley	.05
319	Andres Galarraga	.05
320	Joe Hesketh	.05
321	Wallace Johnson	.05
322	Wayne Krenchicki	.05
323	Vance Law	.05
324	Dennis Martinez	.05
325	Bob McClure	.05
326	Andy McGaffigan	.05
327	Al Newman **RC**	.05
328	Tim Raines	.05
329	Jeff Reardon	.05
330	Luis Rivera **RC**	.05
331	Bob Sebra **RC**	.05
332	Bryn Smith	.05
333	Jay Tibbs	.05
334	Tim Wallach	.05
335	Mitch Webster	.05
336	Jim Wohlford	.05
337	Floyd Youmans	.05
338	Chris Bosio **RC**	.25
339	Glenn Braggs **RC**	.05
340	Rick Cerone	.05
341	Mark Clear	.05
342	Bryan Clutterbuck **RC**	.05
343	Cecil Cooper	.05
344	Rob Deer	.05
345	Jim Gantner	.05
346	Ted Higuera	.05
347	John Henry Johnson	.05
348	Tim Leary	.05
349	Rick Manning	.05
350	Paul Molitor	.75
351	Charlie Moore	.05
352	Juan Nieves	.05
353	Ben Oglivie	.05
354	Dan Plesac **RC**	.10
355	Ernest Riles	.05
356	Billy Joe Robidoux	.05
357	Bill Schroeder	.05
358	Dale Sveum **RC**	.05
359	Gorman Thomas	.05
360	Bill Wegman	.05
361	Robin Yount	.75
362	Steve Balboni	.05
363	Scott Bankhead **RC**	.05
364	Buddy Biancalana	.05
365	Bud Black	.05
366	George Brett	2.00
367	Steve Farr	.05
368	Mark Gubicza	.05
369	Bo Jackson	.75
370	Danny Jackson	.05
371	Mike Kingery **RC**	.05
372	Rudy Law	.05
373	Charlie Leibrandt	.05
374	Dennis Leonard	.05
375	Hal McRae	.05
376	Jorge Orta	.05
377	Jamie Quirk	.05
378	Dan Quisenberry	.05
379	Bret Saberhagen	.05
380	Angel Salazar	.05
381	Lonnie Smith	.05
382	Jim Sundberg	.05
383	Frank White	.05
384	Willie Wilson	.05
385	Joaquin Andujar	.05
386	Doug Bair	.05
387	Dusty Baker	.05
388	Bruce Bochte	.05
389	Jose Canseco	.65
390	Chris Codiroli	.05
391	Mike Davis	.05
392	Alfredo Griffin	.05
393	Moose Haas	.05
394	Donnie Hill	.05
395	Jay Howell	.05
396	Dave Kingman	.05
397	Carney Lansford	.05
398	David Leiper **RC**	.05
399	Bill Mooneyham **RC**	.05
400	Dwayne Murphy	.05
401	Steve Ontiveros	.05
402	Tony Phillips	.05
403	Eric Plunk	.05
404	Jose Rijo	.05
405	Terry Steinbach **RC**	.50
406	Dave Stewart	.05
407	Mickey Tettleton	.05
408	Dave Von Ohlen	.05
409	Jerry Willard	.05
410	Curt Young	.05
411	Bruce Bochy	.05
412	Dave Dravecky	.05
413	Tim Flannery	.05
414	Steve Garvey	.25
415	Goose Gossage	.10
416	Tony Gwynn	1.50
417	Andy Hawkins	.05
418	LaMarr Hoyt	.05
419	Terry Kennedy	.05
420	John Kruk	.05
421	Dave LaPoint	.05
422	Craig Lefferts	.05
423	Carmelo Martinez	.05
424	Lance McCullers	.05
425	Kevin McReynolds	.05
426	Graig Nettles	.05
427	Bip Roberts	.05
428	Jerry Royster	.05
429	Benito Santiago	.05
430	Eric Show	.05
431	Bob Stoddard	.05
432	Garry Templeton	.05
433	Gene Walter	.05
434	Ed Whitson	.05
435	Marvell Wynne	.05
436	Dave Anderson	.05
437	Greg Brock	.05
438	Enos Cabell	.05
439	Mariano Duncan	.05
440	Pedro Guerrero	.05
441	Orel Hershiser	.05
442	Rick Honeycutt	.05
443	Ken Howell	.05
444	Ken Landreaux	.05
445	Bill Madlock	.05
446	Mike Marshall	.05
447	Len Matuszek	.05
448	Tom Niedenfuer	.05
449	Alejandro Pena	.05
450	Dennis Powell	.05
451	Jerry Reuss	.05
452	Bill Russell	.05
453	Steve Sax	.05
454	Mike Scioscia	.05
455	Franklin Stubbs	.05
456	Alex Trevino	.05
457	Fernando Valenzuela	.05
458	Ed Vande Berg	.05
459	Bob Welch	.05
460	Reggie Williams **RC**	.05
461	Don Aase	.05
462	Juan Beniquez	.05
463	Mike Boddicker	.05
464	Juan Bonilla	.05
465	Rich Bordi	.05
466	Storm Davis	.05
467	Rick Dempsey	.05
468	Ken Dixon	.05
469	Jim Dwyer	.05
470	Mike Flanagan	.05
471	Jackie Gutierrez	.05
472	Brad Havens	.05
473	Lee Lacy	.05
474	Fred Lynn	.05
475	Scott McGregor	.05
476	Eddie Murray	.75
477	Tom O'Malley	.05
478	Cal Ripken, Jr.	3.00
479	Larry Sheets	.05
480	John Shelby	.05
481	Nate Snell	.05
482	Jim Traber	.05
483	Mike Young	.05
484	Neil Allen	.05
485	Harold Baines	.05
486	Floyd Bannister	.05
487	Daryl Boston	.05
488	Ivan Calderon	.05
489	John Cangelosi **RC**	.05
490	Steve Carlton	.75
491	Joe Cowley	.05
492	Julio Cruz	.05
493	Bill Dawley	.05
494	Jose DeLeon	.05
495	Richard Dotson	.05
496	Carlton Fisk	.75
497	Ozzie Guillen	.05
498	Jerry Hairston Sr.	.05
499	Ron Hassey	.05
500	Tim Hulett	.05
501	Bob James	.05
502	Steve Lyons	.05
503	Joel McKeon **RC**	.05
504	Gene Nelson	.05
505	Dave Schmidt	.05
506	Ray Searage	.05
507	Bobby Thigpen **RC**	.15
508	Greg Walker	.05
509	Jim Acker	.05
510	Doyle Alexander	.05
511	Paul Assenmacher **RC**	.05
512	Bruce Benedict	.05
513	Chris Chambliss	.05
514	Jeff Dedmon	.05
515	Gene Garber	.05
516	Ken Griffey	.05
517	Terry Harper	.05
518	Bob Horner	.05
519	Glenn Hubbard	.05
520	Rick Mahler	.05
521	Omar Moreno	.05
522	Dale Murphy	.35
523	Ken Oberkfell	.05
524	Ed Olwine	.05
525	David Palmer	.05
526	Rafael Ramirez	.05
527	Billy Sample	.05
528	Ted Simmons	.05
529	Zane Smith	.05
530	Bruce Sutter	.65
531	Andres Thomas **RC**	.05
532	Ozzie Virgil	.05
533	Allan Anderson **RC**	.05
534	Keith Atherton	.05
535	Billy Beane	.05
536	Bert Blyleven	.10
537	Tom Brunansky	.05
538	Randy Bush	.05
539	George Frazier	.05
540	Gary Gaetti	.05
541	Greg Gagne	.05
542	Mickey Hatcher	.05
543	Neal Heaton	.05
544	Kent Hrbek	.05
545	Roy Lee Jackson	.05
546	Tim Laudner	.05
547	Steve Lombardozzi	.05
548	Mark Portugal **RC**	.10

549	Kirby Puckett	1.50
550	Jeff Reed	.05
551	Mark Salas	.05
552	Roy Smalley	.05
553	Mike Smithson	.05
554	Frank Viola	.05
555	Thad Bosley	.05
556	Ron Cey	.05
557	Jody Davis	.05
558	Ron Davis	.05
559	Bob Dernier	.05
560	Frank DiPino	.05
561	Shawon Dunston	.05
562	Leon Durham	.05
563	Dennis Eckersley	.65
564	Terry Francona	.05
565	Dave Gumpert	.05
566	Guy Hoffman	.05
567	Ed Lynch	.05
568	Gary Matthews	.05
569	Keith Moreland	.05
570	Jamie Moyer RC	.05
571	Jerry Mumphrey	.05
572	Ryne Sandberg	1.00
573	Scott Sanderson	.05
574	Lee Smith	.05
575	Chris Speier	.05
576	Rick Sutcliffe	.05
577	Manny Trillo	.05
578	Steve Trout	.05
579	Karl Best	.05
580	Scott Bradley	.05
581	Phil Bradley	.05
582	Mickey Brantley	.05
583	Mike Brown	.05
584	Alvin Davis	.05
585	Lee Guetterman RC	.05
586	Mark Huismann	.05
587	Bob Kearney	.05
588	Pete Ladd	.05
589	Mark Langston	.05
590	Mike Moore	.05
591	Mike Morgan	.05
592	John Moses	.05
593	Ken Phelps	.05
594	Jim Presley	.05
595	Rey Quinonez (Quinones) RC	.05
596	Harold Reynolds	.05
597	Billy Swift	.05
598	Danny Tartabull	.05
599	Steve Yeager	.05
600	Matt Young	.05
601	Bill Almon	.05
602	Rafael Belliard RC	.05
603	Mike Bielecki	.05
604	Barry Bonds	40.00
605	Bobby Bonilla	.05
606	Sid Bream	.05
607	Mike Brown	.05
608	Pat Clements	.05
609	Mike Diaz RC	.05
610	Cecilio Guante	.05
611	Barry Jones RC	.05
612	Bob Kipper	.05
613	Larry McWilliams	.05
614	Jim Morrison	.05
615	Joe Orsulak	.05
616	Junior Ortiz	.05
617	Tony Pena	.05
618	Johnny Ray	.05
619	Rick Reuschel	.05
620	R.J. Reynolds	.05
621	Rick Rhoden	.05
622	Don Robinson	.05
623	Bob Walk	.05
624	Jim Winn	.05
625	Jose Canseco, Pete Incaviglia Youthful Power	.15
626	Phil Niekro, Don Sutton 300 Game Winners	.25
627	Don Aase, Dave Righetti A.L. Firemen	.05
628	Jose Canseco, Wally Joyner Rookie All-Stars	.15
629	Gary Carter, Dwight Gooden, Keith Hernandez, Darryl Strawberry Magic Mets	.15
630	Mike Krukow, Mike Scott N.L. Best Righties	.05
631	John Franco, Fernando Valenzuela Sensational Southpaws	.05
632	Bob Horner Count 'Em	.10
633	Jose Canseco, Kirby Puckett, Jim Rice A.L. Pitcher's Nightmare	.25
634	Gary Carter, Roger Clemens All Star Battery	.50
635	Steve Carlton 4,000 Strikeouts	.15
636	Glenn Davis, Eddie Murray Big Bats At First Sack	.15
637	Wade Boggs, Keith Hernandez On Base	.25
638	Don Mattingly, Darryl Strawberry Sluggers From Left Side	.50
639	Dave Parker, Ryne Sandberg Former MVP's	.25
640	Roger Clemens, Dwight Gooden Dr. K. & Super K	.50
641	Charlie Hough, Mike Witt A.L. West Stoppers	.05
642	Tim Raines, Juan Samuel Doubles & Triples	.05

643	Harold Baines, Jesse Barfield Outfielders With Punch	.05
644	Dave Clark, Greg Swindell RC Major League Prospects	.35
645	Ron Karkovice, Russ Morman RC Major League Prospects	.25
646	Willie Fraser, Devon White RC Major League Prospects	1.00
647	Jerry Browne, Mike Stanley RC Major League Prospects	.25
648	Phil Lombardi, Dave Magadan RC Major League Prospects	.20
649	Ralph Bryant, Jose Gonzalez RC Major League Prospects	.10
650	Randy Asadoor, Jimmy Jones RC Major League Prospects	.10
651	Marvin Freeman, Tracy Jones RC Major League Prospects	.10
652	Kevin Seitzer, John Stefero Major League Prospects	.25
653	Steve Fireovid, Rob Nelson RC Major League Prospects	.10
654	Checklist 1-95	.05
655	Checklist 96-192	.05
656	Checklist 193-288	.05
657	Checklist 289-384	.05
658	Checklist 385-483	.05
659	Checklist 484-578	.05
660	Checklist 579-660	.05

Update

		NM/M
Complete Set (132):		9.00
Common Player:		.05
1	Scott Bankhead	.05
2	Eric Bell	.05
3	Juan Beniquez	.05
4	Juan Berenguer	.05
5	Mike Birkbeck	.05
6	Randy Bockus	.05
7	Rod Booker	.05
8	Thad Bosley	.05
9	Greg Brock	.05
10	Bob Brower	.05
11	Chris Brown	.05
12	Jerry Browne	.05
13	Ralph Bryant	.05
14	DeWayne Buice	.05
15	Ellis Burks	.05
16	Casey Candaele	.05
17	Steve Carlton	.50
18	Juan Castillo	.05
19	Chuck Crim	.05
20	Mark Davidson	.05
21	Mark Davis	.05
22	Storm Davis	.05
23	Bill Dawley	.05
24	Andre Dawson	.30
25	Brian Dayett	.05
26	Rick Dempsey	.05
27	Ken Dowell	.05
28	Dave Dravecky	.05
29	Mike Dunne	.05
30	Dennis Eckersley	.40
31	Cecil Fielder	.05
32	Brian Fisher	.05
33	Willie Fraser	.05
34	Ken Gerhart	.05
35	Jim Gott	.05
36	Dan Gladden	.05
37	Mike Greenwell	.05
38	Cecilio Guante	.05
39	Albert Hall	.05
40	Atlee Hammaker	.05
41	Mickey Hatcher	.05
42	Mike Heath	.05
43	Neal Heaton	.05
44	Mike Henneman	.05
45	Guy Hoffman	.05
46	Charles Hudson	.05
47	Chuck Jackson	.05
48	Mike Jackson	.05
49	Reggie Jackson	.75
50	Chris James	.05
51	Dion James	.05
52	Stan Javier	.05
53	Stan Jefferson	.05
54	Jimmy Jones	.05
55	Tracy Jones	.05
56	Terry Kennedy	.05
57	Mike Kingery	.05

58	Ray Knight	.05
59	Gene Larkin	.05
60	Mike LaValliere	.05
61	Jack Lazorko	.05
62	Terry Leach	.05
63	Rick Leach	.05
64	Craig Lefferts	.05
65	Jim Lindeman	.05
66	Bill Long	.05
67	Mike Loynd	.05
68	Greg Maddux RC	8.00
69	Bill Madlock	.05
70	Dave Magadan	.05
71	Joe Magrane	.05
72	Fred Manrique	.05
73	Mike Mason	.05
74	Lloyd McClendon	.05
75	Fred McGriff	.05
76	Mark McGwire	3.00
77	Mark McLemore	.05
78	Kevin McReynolds	.05
79	Dave Meads	.05
80	Greg Minton	.05
81	John Mitchell	.05
82	Kevin Mitchell	.05
83	John Morris	.05
84	Jeff Musselman	.05
85	Randy Myers	.05
86	Gene Nelson	.05
87	Joe Niekro	.05
88	Tom Nieto	.05
89	Reid Nichols	.05
90	Matt Nokes	.05
91	Dickie Noles	.05
92	Edwin Nunez	.05
93	Jose Nunez	.05
94	Paul O'Neill	.05
95	Jim Paciorek	.05
96	Lance Parrish	.05
97	Bill Pecota	.05
98	Tony Pena	.05
99	Luis Polonia	.05
100	Randy Ready	.05
101	Jeff Reardon	.05
102	Gary Redus	.05
103	Rick Rhoden	.05
104	Wally Ritchie	.05
105	Jeff Robinson	.05
106	Mark Salas	.05
107	Dave Schmidt	.05
108	Kevin Seitzer	.05
109	John Shelby	.05
110	John Smiley	.05
111	Lary Sorensen	.05
112	Chris Speier	.05
113	Randy St. Claire	.05
114	Jim Sundberg	.05
115	B.J. Surhoff	.05
116	Greg Swindell	.05
117	Danny Tartabull	.05
118	Dorn Taylor	.05
119	Lee Tunnell	.05
120	Ed Vande Berg	.05
121	Andy Van Slyke	.05
122	Gary Ward	.05
123	Devon White	.05
124	Alan Wiggins	.05
125	Bill Wilkinson	.05
126	Jim Winn	.05
127	Frank Williams	.05
128	Ken Williams	.05
129	Matt Williams RC	1.00
130	Herm Winningham	.05
131	Matt Young	.05
132	Checklist 1-132	.05

1987 Fleer Glossy Tin

	NM/M
Unopened Set (672):	75.00
Complete Set (672):	50.00
Common Player:	.05
(Single star cards valued at .75-1X regular-issue 1987 Fleer.)	

1987 Fleer Update Glossy Tin

	NM/M
Unopened Set (132):	12.00
Complete Set (132):	7.50
Common Player:	.10
(Star cards valued at .75-1X regular version 1987 Fleer updates.)	

1988 Fleer

	NM/M
Retail Factory Set (672):	12.00
Hobby Factory Set (672):	10.00
Complete Set (660):	8.00
Common Player:	.05
Wax Pack (15):	.75
Wax Box (36):	12.00
Cello Pack (28):	1.25
Cello Box (24):	16.00
1	Keith Atherton	.05

Alan Trammell
SHORTSTOP

2	Don Baylor	.05
3	Juan Berenguer	.05
4	Bert Blyleven	.10
5	Tom Brunansky	.05
6	Randy Bush	.05
7	Steve Carlton	.50
8	Mark Davidson RC	.05
9	George Frazier	.05
10	Gary Gaetti	.05
11	Greg Gagne	.05
12	Dan Gladden	.05
13	Kent Hrbek	.05
14	Gene Larkin RC	.05
15	Tim Laudner	.05
16	Steve Lombardozzi	.05
17	Al Newman	.05
18	Joe Niekro	.05
19	Kirby Puckett	.65
20	Jeff Reardon	.05
21a	Dan Schatzader (Incorrect spelling.)	.10
21b	Dan Schatzader (Correct spelling.)	.05
22	Roy Smalley	.05
23	Mike Smithson	.05
24	Les Straker RC	.05
25	Frank Viola	.05
26	Jack Clark	.05
27	Vince Coleman	.05
28	Danny Cox	.05
29	Bill Dawley	.05
30	Ken Dayley	.05
31	Doug DeCinces	.05
32	Curt Ford	.05
33	Bob Forsch	.05
34	David Green	.05
35	Tom Herr	.05
36	Ricky Horton	.05
37	Lance Johnson RC	.25
38	Steve Lake	.05
39	Jim Lindeman	.05
40	Joe Magrane RC	.10
41	Greg Mathews	.05
42	Willie McGee	.05
43	John Morris	.05
44	Jose Oquendo	.05
45	Tony Pena	.05
46	Terry Pendleton	.05
47	Ozzie Smith	.65
48	John Tudor	.05
49	Lee Tunnell	.05
50	Todd Worrell	.05
51	Doyle Alexander	.05
52	Dave Bergman	.05
53	Tom Brookens	.05
54	Darrell Evans	.05
55	Kirk Gibson	.05
56	Mike Heath	.05
57	Mike Henneman	.05
58	Willie Hernandez	.05
59	Larry Herndon	.05
60	Eric King	.05
61	Chet Lemon	.05
62	Scott Lusader RC	.05
63	Bill Madlock	.05
64	Jack Morris	.05
65	Jim Morrison	.05
66	Matt Nokes	.05
67	Dan Petry	.05
68a	Jeff Robinson RC (Born 12-13-60 on back.)	.25
68b	Jeff Robinson RC (Born 12/14/61 on back.)	.10
69	Pat Sheridan	.05
70	Nate Snell	.05
71	Frank Tanana	.05
72	Walt Terrell	.05
73	Mark Thurmond	.05
74	Alan Trammell	.05
75	Lou Whitaker	.05
76	Mike Aldrete	.05
77	Bob Brenly	.05
78	Will Clark	.05
79	Chili Davis	.05
80	Kelly Downs	.05
81	Dave Dravecky	.05
82	Scott Garrelts	.05
83	Atlee Hammaker	.05
84	Dave Henderson	.05
85	Mike Krukow	.05
86	Mike LaCoss	.05

87	Craig Lefferts	.05
88	Jeff Leonard	.05
89	Candy Maldonado	.05
90	Ed Milner	.05
91	Bob Melvin	.05
92	Kevin Mitchell	.05
93	Jon Perlman **RC**	.05
94	Rick Reuschel	.05
95	Don Robinson	.05
96	Chris Speier	.05
97	Harry Spilman	.05
98	Robbie Thompson	.05
99	Jose Uribe	.05
100	Mark Wasinger **RC**	.05
101	Matt Williams	.05
102	Jesse Barfield	.05
103	George Bell	.05
104	Juan Beniquez	.05
105	John Cerutti	.05
106	Jim Clancy	.05
107	Rob Ducey **RC**	.05
108	Mark Eichhorn	.05
109	Tony Fernandez	.05
110	Cecil Fielder	.05
111	Kelly Gruber	.05
112	Tom Henke	.05
113	Garth Iorq (Iorg)	.05
114	Jimmy Key	.05
115	Rick Leach	.05
116	Manny Lee	.05
117	Nelson Liriano **RC**	.05
118	Fred McGriff	.05
119	Lloyd Moseby	.05
120	Rance Mulliniks	.05
121	Jeff Musselman	.05
122	Jose Nunez **RC**	.05
123	Dave Stieb	.05
124	Willie Upshaw	.05
125	Duane Ward	.05
126	Ernie Whitt	.05
127	Rick Aguilera	.05
128	Wally Backman	.05
129	Mark Carreon **RC**	.10
130	Gary Carter	.50
131	David Cone	.05
132	Ron Darling	.05
133	Len Dykstra	.05
134	Sid Fernandez	.05
135	Dwight Gooden	.05
136	Keith Hernandez	.05
137	Gregg Jefferies **RC**	.50
138	Howard Johnson	.05
139	Terry Leach	.05
140	Barry Lyons **RC**	.05
141	Dave Magadan	.05
142	Roger McDowell	.05
143	Kevin McReynolds	.05
144	Keith Miller **RC**	.05
145	John Mitchell **RC**	.05
146	Randy Myers	.05
147	Bob Ojeda	.05
148	Jesse Orosco	.05
149	Rafael Santana	.05
150	Doug Sisk	.05
151	Darryl Strawberry	.05
152	Tim Teufel	.05
153	Gene Walter	.05
154	Mookie Wilson	.05
155	Jay Aldrich **RC**	.05
156	Chris Bosio	.05
157	Glenn Braggs	.05
158	Greg Brock	.05
159	Juan Castillo	.05
160	Mark Clear	.05
161	Cecil Cooper	.05
162	Chuck Crim **RC**	.05
163	Rob Deer	.05
164	Mike Felder	.05
165	Jim Gantner	.05
166	Ted Higuera	.05
167	Steve Kiefer	.05
168	Rick Manning	.05
169	Paul Molitor	.50
170	Juan Nieves	.05
171	Dan Plesac	.05
172	Earnest Riles	.05
173	Bill Schroeder	.05
174	Steve Stanicek **RC**	.05
175	B.J. Surhoff	.05
176	Dale Sveum	.05
177	Bill Wegman	.05
178	Robin Yount	.50
179	Hubie Brooks	.05
180	Tim Burke	.05
181	Casey Candaele	.05
182	Mike Fitzgerald	.05
183	Tom Foley	.05
184	Andres Galarraga	.05
185	Neal Heaton	.05
186	Wallace Johnson	.05
187	Vance Law	.05
188	Dennis Martinez	.05
189	Bob McClure	.05
190	Andy McGaffigan	.05
191	Reid Nichols	.05
192	Pascual Perez	.05
193	Tim Raines	.05
194	Jeff Reed	.05
195	Bob Sebra	.05
196	Bryn Smith	.05
197	Randy St. Claire	.05
198	Tim Wallach	.05
199	Mitch Webster	.05
200	Herm Winningham	.05
201	Floyd Youmans	.05
202	Brad Arnsberg **RC**	.05
203	Rick Cerone	.05
204	Pat Clements	.05
205	Henry Cotto	.05
206	Mike Easler	.05
207	Ron Guidry	.10
208	Bill Gullickson	.05
209	Rickey Henderson	.50
210	Charles Hudson	.05
211	Tommy John	.10
212	Roberto Kelly **RC**	.25
213	Ron Kittle	.05
214	Don Mattingly	.75
215	Bobby Meacham	.05
216	Mike Pagliarulo	.05
217	Dan Pasqua	.05
218	Willie Randolph	.05
219	Rick Rhoden	.05
220	Dave Righetti	.05
221	Jerry Royster	.05
222	Tim Stoddard	.05
223	Wayne Tolleson	.05
224	Gary Ward	.05
225	Claudell Washington	.05
226	Dave Winfield	.50
227	Buddy Bell	.05
228	Tom Browning	.05
229	Dave Concepcion	.05
230	Kal Daniels	.05
231	Eric Davis	.05
232	Bo Diaz	.05
233	Nick Esasky	.05
234	John Franco	.05
235	Guy Hoffman	.05
236	Tom Hume	.05
237	Tracy Jones	.05
238	Bill Landrum **RC**	.05
239	Barry Larkin	.05
240	Terry McGriff	.05
241	Rob Murphy	.05
242	Ron Oester	.05
243	Dave Parker	.05
244	Pat Perry	.05
245	Ted Power	.05
246	Dennis Rasmussen	.05
247	Ron Robinson	.05
248	Kurt Stillwell	.05
249	Jeff Treadway **RC**	.05
250	Frank Williams	.05
251	Steve Balboni	.05
252	Bud Black	.05
253	Thad Bosley	.05
254	George Brett	.75
255	John Davis **RC**	.05
256	Steve Farr	.05
257	Gene Garber	.05
258	Jerry Gleaton	.05
259	Mark Gubicza	.05
260	Bo Jackson	.10
261	Danny Jackson	.05
262	Ross Jones **RC**	.05
263	Charlie Leibrandt	.05
264	Bill Pecota **RC**	.05
265	Melido Perez **RC**	.05
266	Jamie Quirk	.05
267	Dan Quisenberry	.05
268	Bret Saberhagen	.05
269	Angel Salazar	.05
270	Kevin Seitzer	.05
271	Danny Tartabull	.05
272	Gary Thurman **RC**	.05
273	Frank White	.05
274	Willie Wilson	.05
275	Tony Bernazard	.05
276	Jose Canseco	.30
277	Mike Davis	.05
278	Storm Davis	.05
279	Dennis Eckersley	.40
280	Alfredo Griffin	.05
281	Rick Honeycutt	.05
282	Jay Howell	.05
283	Reggie Jackson	.65
284	Dennis Lamp	.05
285	Carney Lansford	.05
286	Mark McGwire	.85
287	Dwayne Murphy	.05
288	Gene Nelson	.05
289	Steve Ontiveros	.05
290	Tony Phillips	.05
291	Eric Plunk	.05
292	Luis Polonia **RC**	.15
293	Rick Rodriguez **RC**	.05
294	Terry Steinbach	.05
295	Dave Stewart	.05
296	Curt Young	.05
297	Luis Aguayo	.05
298	Steve Bedrosian	.05
299	Jeff Calhoun	.05
300	Don Carman	.05
301	Todd Frohwirth **RC**	.05
302	Greg Gross	.05
303	Kevin Gross	.05
304	Von Hayes	.05
305	Keith Hughes **RC**	.05
306	Mike Jackson **RC**	.05
307	Chris James	.05
308	Steve Jeltz	.05
309	Mike Maddux	.05
310	Lance Parrish	.05
311	Shane Rawley	.05
312	Wally Ritchie **RC**	.05
313	Bruce Ruffin	.05
314	Juan Samuel	.05
315	Mike Schmidt	.75
316	Rick Schu	.05
317	Jeff Stone	.05
318	Kent Tekulve	.05
319	Milt Thompson	.05
320	Glenn Wilson	.05
321	Rafael Belliard	.05
322	Barry Bonds	1.00
323	Bobby Bonilla	.05
324	Sid Bream	.05
325	John Cangelosi	.05
326	Mike Diaz	.05
327	Doug Drabek	.05
328	Mike Dunne **RC**	.05
329	Brian Fisher	.05
330	Brett Gideon **RC**	.05
331	Terry Harper	.05
332	Bob Kipper	.05
333	Mike LaValliere	.05
334	Jose Lind **RC**	.15
335	Junior Ortiz	.05
336	Vicente Palacios **RC**	.05
337	Bob Patterson **RC**	.05
338	Al Pedrique **RC**	.05
339	R.J. Reynolds	.05
340	John Smiley	.05
341	Andy Van Slyke	.05
342	Bob Walk	.05
343	Marty Barrett	.05
344	Todd Benzinger **RC**	.05
345	Wade Boggs	.65
346	Tom Bolton **RC**	.05
347	Oil Can Boyd	.05
348	Ellis Burks	.05
349	Roger Clemens	.75
350	Steve Crawford	.05
351	Dwight Evans	.05
352	Wes Gardner **RC**	.05
353	Rich Gedman	.05
354	Mike Greenwell	.05
355	Sam Horn **RC**	.05
356	Bruce Hurst	.05
357	John Marzano **RC**	.05
358	Al Nipper	.05
359	Spike Owen	.05
360	Jody Reed **RC**	.15
361	Jim Rice	.20
362	Ed Romero	.05
363	Kevin Romine	.05
364	Joe Sambito	.05
365	Calvin Schiraldi	.05
366	Jeff Sellers	.05
367	Bob Stanley	.05
368	Scott Bankhead	.05
369	Phil Bradley	.05
370	Scott Bradley	.05
371	Mickey Brantley	.05
372	Mike Campbell **RC**	.05
373	Alvin Davis	.05
374	Lee Guetterman	.05
375	Dave Hengel **RC**	.05
376	Mike Kingery	.05
377	Mark Langston	.05
378	Edgar Martinez **RC**	1.00
379	Mike Moore	.05
380	Mike Morgan	.05
381	John Moses	.05
382	Donnell Nixon **RC**	.05
383	Edwin Nunez	.05
384	Ken Phelps	.05
385	Jim Presley	.05
386	Rey Quinones	.05
387	Jerry Reed	.05
388	Harold Reynolds	.05
389	Dave Valle	.05
390	Bill Wilkinson **RC**	.05
391	Harold Baines	.05
392	Floyd Bannister	.05
393	Daryl Boston	.05
394	Ivan Calderon	.05
395	Jose DeLeon	.05
396	Richard Dotson	.05
397	Carlton Fisk	.50
398	Ozzie Guillen	.05
399	Ron Hassey	.05
400	Donnie Hill	.05
401	Bob James	.05
402	Dave LaPoint	.05
403	Bill Lindsey **RC**	.05
404	Bill Long **RC**	.05
405	Steve Lyons	.05
406	Fred Manrique **RC**	.05
407	Jack McDowell **RC**	.25
408	Gary Redus	.05
409	Ray Searage	.05
410	Bobby Thigpen	.05
411	Greg Walker	.05
412	Kenny Williams **RC**	.05
413	Jim Winn	.05
414	Jody Davis	.05
415	Andre Dawson	.25
416	Brian Dayett	.05
417	Bob Dernier	.05
418	Frank DiPino	.05
419	Shawon Dunston	.05
420	Leon Durham	.05
421	Les Lancaster **RC**	.10
422	Ed Lynch	.05
423	Greg Maddux	.75
424	Dave Martinez	.05
425a	Keith Moreland (Bunting, photo actually Jody Davis.)	2.00
425b	Keith Moreland (Standing upright, correct photo.)	.05
426	Jamie Moyer	.05
427	Jerry Mumphrey	.05
428	Paul Noce **RC**	.05
429	Rafael Palmeiro	.40
430	Wade Rowdon	.05
431	Ryne Sandberg	.65
432	Scott Sanderson	.05
433	Lee Smith	.05
434	Jim Sundberg	.05
435	Rick Sutcliffe	.05
436	Manny Trillo	.05
437	Juan Agosto	.05
438	Larry Andersen	.05
439	Alan Ashby	.05
440	Kevin Bass	.05
441	Ken Caminiti **RC**	.25
442	Rocky Childress **RC**	.05
443	Jose Cruz	.05
444	Danny Darwin	.05
445	Glenn Davis	.05
446	Jim Deshaies	.05
447	Bill Doran	.05
448	Ty Gainey	.05
449	Billy Hatcher	.05
450	Jeff Heathcock	.05
451	Bob Knepper	.05
452	Rob Mallicoat **RC**	.05
453	Dave Meads **RC**	.05
454	Craig Reynolds	.05
455	Nolan Ryan	1.00
456	Mike Scott	.05
457	Dave Smith	.05
458	Denny Walling	.05
459	Robbie Wine **RC**	.05
460	Gerald Young **RC**	.05
461	Bob Brower	.05
462a	Jerry Browne (White player, photo actually Bob Brower.)	2.00
462b	Jerry Browne (Black player, correct photo.)	.05
463	Steve Buechele	.05
464	Edwin Correa	.05
465	Cecil Espy **RC**	.05
466	Scott Fletcher	.05
467	Jose Guzman	.05
468	Greg Harris	.05
469	Charlie Hough	.05
470	Pete Incaviglia	.05
471	Paul Kilgus **RC**	.05
472	Mike Loynd	.05
473	Oddibe McDowell	.05
474	Dale Mohorcic	.05
475	Pete O'Brien	.05
476	Larry Parrish	.05
477	Geno Petralli	.05
478	Jeff Russell	.05
479	Ruben Sierra	.05
480	Mike Stanley	.05
481	Curtis Wilkerson	.05
482	Mitch Williams	.05
483	Bobby Witt	.05
484	Tony Armas	.05
485	Bob Boone	.05
486	Bill Buckner	.05
487	DeWayne Buice **RC**	.05
488	Brian Downing	.05
489	Chuck Finley	.05
490	Willie Fraser	.05
491	Jack Howell	.05
492	Ruppert Jones	.05
493	Wally Joyner	.05
494	Jack Lazorko	.05
495	Gary Lucas	.05
496	Kirk McCaskill	.05
497	Mark McLemore	.05
498	Darrell Miller	.05
499	Greg Minton	.05
500	Donnie Moore	.05
501	Gus Polidor	.05
502	Johnny Ray	.05
503	Mark Ryal	.05
504	Dick Schofield	.05
505	Don Sutton	.40
506	Devon White	.05
507	Mike Witt	.05
508	Dave Anderson	.05
509	Tim Belcher	.05
510	Ralph Bryant	.05
511	Tim Crews **RC**	.15
512	Mike Devereaux **RC**	.10
513	Mariano Duncan	.05
514	Pedro Guerrero	.05
515	Jeff Hamilton	.05
516	Mickey Hatcher	.05
517	Brad Havens	.05
518	Orel Hershiser	.05
519	Shawn Hillegas **RC**	.05
520	Ken Howell	.05
521	Tim Leary	.05
522	Mike Marshall	.05
523	Steve Sax	.05
524	Mike Scioscia	.05
525	Mike Sharperson	.05
526	John Shelby	.05
527	Franklin Stubbs	.05
528	Fernando Valenzuela	.05
529	Bob Welch	.05
530	Matt Young	.05
531	Jim Acker	.05
532	Paul Assenmacher	.05
533	Jeff Blauser **RC**	.10
534	Joe Boever **RC**	.05
535	Martin Clary	.05
536	Kevin Coffman **RC**	.05
537	Jeff Dedmon	.05
538	Ron Gant **RC**	.50
539	Tom Glavine **RC**	2.00
540	Ken Griffey	.05

541	Al Hall	.05
542	Glenn Hubbard	.05
543	Dion James	.05
544	Dale Murphy	.20
545	Ken Oberkfell	.05
546	David Palmer	.05
547	Gerald Perry	.05
548	Charlie Puleo	.05
549	Ted Simmons	.05
550	Zane Smith	.05
551	Andres Thomas	.05
552	Ozzie Virgil	.05
553	Don Aase	.05
554	Jeff Ballard **RC**	.05
555	Eric Bell	.05
556	Mike Boddicker	.05
557	Ken Dixon	.05
558	Jim Dwyer	.05
559	Ken Gerhart	.05
560	Rene Gonzales **RC**	.05
561	Mike Griffin	.05
562	John Hayban (Habyan)	.05
563	Terry Kennedy	.05
564	Ray Knight	.05
565	Lee Lacy	.05
566	Fred Lynn	.05
567	Eddie Murray	.50
568	Tom Niedenfuer	.05
569	Bill Ripken **RC**	.05
570	Cal Ripken, Jr.	1.00
571	Dave Schmidt	.05
572	Larry Sheets	.05
573	Pete Stanicek **RC**	.05
574	Mark Williamson **RC**	.05
575	Mike Young	.05
576	Shawn Abner	.05
577	Greg Booker	.05
578	Chris Brown	.05
579	Keith Comstock **RC**	.05
580	Joey Cora **RC**	.05
581	Mark Davis	.05
582	Tim Flannery	.05
583	Goose Gossage	.05
584	Mark Grant	.05
585	Tony Gwynn	.65
586	Andy Hawkins	.05
587	Stan Jefferson	.05
588	Jimmy Jones	.05
589	John Kruk	.05
590	Shane Mack **RC**	.10
591	Carmelo Martinez	.05
592	Lance McCullers	.05
593	Eric Nolte **RC**	.05
594	Randy Ready	.05
595	Luis Salazar	.05
596	Benito Santiago	.05
597	Eric Show	.05
598	Garry Templeton	.05
599	Ed Whitson	.05
600	Scott Bailes	.05
601	Chris Bando	.05
602	Jay Bell **RC**	.50
603	Brett Butler	.05
604	Tom Candiotti	.05
605	Joe Carter	.05
606	Carmen Castillo	.05
607	Brian Dorsett **RC**	.05
608	John Farrell **RC**	.05
609	Julio Franco	.05
610	Mel Hall	.05
611	Tommy Hinzo **RC**	.05
612	Brook Jacoby	.05
613	Doug Jones **RC**	.10
614	Ken Schrom	.05
615	Cory Snyder	.05
616	Sammy Stewart	.05
617	Greg Swindell	.05
618	Pat Tabler	.05
619	Ed Vande Berg	.05
620	Eddie Williams **RC**	.05
621	Rich Yett	.05
622	Wally Joyner, Cory Snyder Slugging Sophomores	.10
623	George Bell, Pedro Guerrero Dominican Dynamite	.05
624	Jose Canseco, Mark McGwire Oakland's Power Team	.50
625	Dan Plesac, Dave Righetti Classic Relief	.05
626	Jack Morris, Bret Saberhagen, Mike Witt All Star Righties	.05
627	Steve Bedrosian, John Franco Game Closers	.05
628	Ryne Sandberg, Ozzie Smith Masters of the Double Play	.50
629	Mark McGwire Rookie Record Setter	.50
630	Todd Benzinger, Ellis Burks, Mike Greenwell Changing the Guard in Boston	.10
631	Tony Gwynn, Tim Raines N.L. Batting Champs	.20
632	Orel Hershiser, Mike Scott Pitching Magic	.05
633	Mark McGwire, Pat Tabler Big Bats At First	.50
634	Tony Gwynn, Vince Coleman Hitting King and the Thief	.15
635	Tony Fernandez, Cal Ripken, Jr., Alan Trammell A.L. Slugging Shortstops	.40
636	Gary Carter, Mike Schmidt Tried and True Sluggers	.40
637	Eric Davis Crunch Time	.05
638	Matt Nokes, Kirby Puckett A.L. All Stars	.25
639	Keith Hernandez, Dale Murphy N.L. All Stars	.10
640	Bill Ripken, Cal Ripken, Jr. The "O's" Brothers	.50
641	Mark Grace, Darrin Jackson **RC** Major League Prospects	1.00
642	Damon Berryhill, Jeff Montgomery **RC** Major League Prospects	.20
643	Felix Fermin, Jessie Reid **RC** Major League Prospects	.05
644	Greg Myers, Greg Tabor **RC** Major League Prospects	.05
645	Jim Eppard, Joey Meyer Major League Prospects	.05
646	Adam Peterson, Randy Velarde **RC** Major League Prospects	.10
647	Chris Gwynn, Peter Smith **RC** Major League Prospects	.15
648	Greg Jelks, Tom Newell **RC** Major League Prospects	.05
649	Mario Diaz, Clay Parker **RC** Major League Prospects	.05
650	Jack Savage, Todd Simmons **RC** Major League Prospects	.05
651	John Burkett, Kirt Manwaring **RC** Major League Prospects	.30
652	Dave Otto, Walt Weiss **RC** Major League Prospects	.25
653	Randell Byers (Randall), Jeff King **RC** Major League Prospects	.25
654a	Checklist 1-101 (21 is Schatzader)	.10
654b	Checklist 1-101 (21 is Schatzeder)	.05
655	Checklist 102-201	.05
656	Checklist 202-296	.05
657	Checklist 297-390	.05
658	Checklist 391-483	.05
659	Checklist 484-575	.05
660	Checklist 576-660	.05

Update

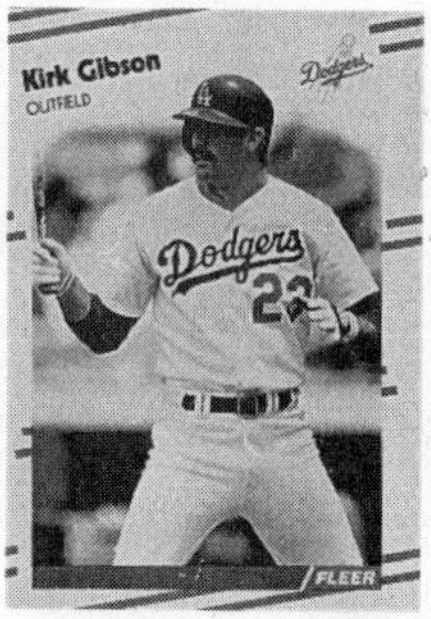

Kirk Gibson
OUTFIELD
Dodgers
FLEER

		NM/M
Complete Set (132):		5.00
Common Player:		.05
1	Jose Bautista	.05
2	Joe Orsulak	.05
3	Doug Sisk	.05
4	Craig Worthington	.05
5	Mike Boddicker	.05
6	Rick Cerone	.05
7	Larry Parrish	.05
8	Lee Smith	.10
9	Mike Smithson	.05
10	John Trautwein	.05
11	Sherman Corbett	.05
12	Chili Davis	.05
13	Jim Eppard	.05
14	Bryan Harvey	.05
15	John Davis	.05
16	Dave Gallagher	.05
17	Ricky Horton	.05
18	Dan Pasqua	.05
19	Melido Perez	.05
20	Jose Segura	.05
21	Andy Allanson	.05
22	Jon Perlman	.05
23	Domingo Ramos	.05
24	Rick Rodriguez	.05
25	Willie Upshaw	.05
26	Paul Gibson	.05
27	Don Heinkel	.05
28	Ray Knight	.05
29	Gary Pettis	.05
30	Luis Salazar	.05
31	Mike MacFarlane	.05
32	Jeff Montgomery	.05
33	Ted Power	.05
34	Israel Sanchez	.05
35	Kurt Stillwell	.05
36	Pat Tabler	.05
37	Don August	.05
38	Darryl Hamilton	.05
39	Jeff Leonard	.05
40	Joey Meyer	.05
41	Allan Anderson	.05
42	Brian Harper	.05
43	Tom Herr	.05
44	Charlie Lea	.05
45	John Moses	.05
46	John Candelaria	.05
47	Jack Clark	.05
48	Richard Dotson	.05
49	Al Leiter	.05
50	Rafael Santana	.05
51	Don Slaught	.05
52	Todd Burns	.05
53	Dave Henderson	.05
54	Doug Jennings	.05
55	Dave Parker	.05
56	Walt Weiss	.05
57	Bob Welch	.05
58	Henry Cotto	.05
59	Marion Diaz (Mario)	.05
60	Mike Jackson	.05
61	Bill Swift	.05
62	Jose Cecena	.05
63	Ray Hayward	.05
64	Jim Steels	.05
65	Pat Borders	.05
66	Sil Campusano	.05
67	Mike Flanagan	.05
68	Todd Stottlemyre	.05
69	David Wells	.05
70	Jose Alvarez	.05
71	Paul Runge	.05
72	Cesar Jimenez (German)	.05
73	Pete Smith	.05
74	John Smoltz **RC**	1.50
75	Damon Berryhill	.05
76	Goose Gossage	.05
77	Mark Grace	.10
78	Darrin Jackson	.05
79	Vance Law	.05
80	Jeff Pico	.05
81	Gary Varsho	.05
82	Tim Birtsas	.05
83	Rob Dibble	.05
84	Danny Jackson	.05
85	Paul O'Neill	.05
86	Jose Rijo	.05
87	Chris Sabo **RC**	.25
88	John Fishel	.05
89	Craig Biggio **RC**	4.00
90	Terry Puhl	.05
91	Rafael Ramirez	.05
92	Louie Meadows	.05
93	Kirk Gibson	.05
94	Alfredo Griffin	.05
95	Jay Howell	.05
96	Jesse Orosco	.05
97	Alejandro Pena	.05
98	Tracy Woodson	.05
99	John Dopson	.05
100	Brian Holman	.05
101	Rex Hudler	.05
102	Jeff Parrett	.05
103	Nelson Santovenia	.05
104	Kevin Elster	.05
105	Jeff Innis	.05
106	Mackey Sasser	.05
107	Phil Bradley	.05
108	Danny Clay	.05
109	Greg Harris	.05
110	Ricky Jordan	.05
111	David Palmer	.05
112	Jim Gott	.05
113	Tommy Gregg (Photo actually Randy Milligan.)	.05
114	Barry Jones	.05
115	Randy Milligan	.05
116	Luis Alicea	.05
117	Tom Brunansky	.05
118	John Costello	.05
119	Jose DeLeon	.05
120	Bob Horner	.05
121	Scott Terry	.05
122	Roberto Alomar **RC**	1.50
123	Dave Leiper	.05
124	Keith Moreland	.05
125	Mark Parent	.05
126	Dennis Rasmussen	.05
127	Randy Bockus	.05
128	Brett Butler	.05
129	Donell Nixon	.05
130	Earnest Riles	.05
131	Roger Samuels	.05
132	Checklist	.05

1988 Fleer Glossy Tin

	NM/M
Complete Set (672):	20.00
Common Player:	.15

(Star cards valued 1-1.5X regular-issue 1988 Fleer.)

1988 Fleer Update Glossy Tin

	NM/M
Complete Set (132):	9.00
Common Player:	.15

(Star cards valued about 2X regular-issue1988 Fleer Updates.)

1989 Fleer

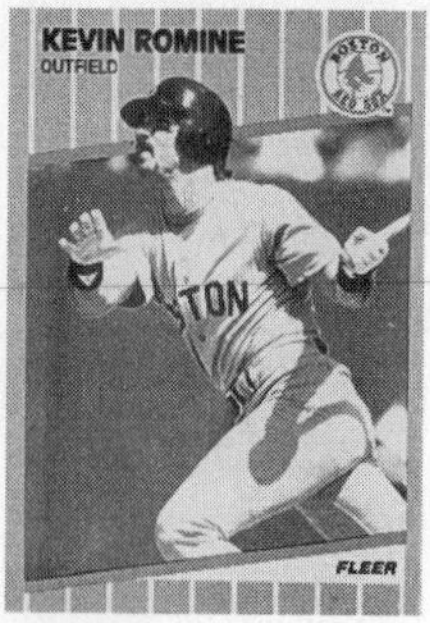

KEVIN ROMINE
OUTFIELD
FLEER

		NM/M
Retail Factory Set (660):		17.50
Hobby Factory Set (672):		20.00
Complete Set (660):		15.00
Common Player:		.05
Wax Pack (15):		1.00
Wax Box (36):		25.00
Cello Pack (36):		1.50
Cello Box (24):		20.00
Rack Pack (42+1):		1.50
Rack Box (24):		25.00
1	Don Baylor	.05
2	Lance Blankenship **RC**	.05
3	Todd Burns **RC**	.05
4	Greg Cadaret	.05
5	Jose Canseco	.35
6	Storm Davis	.05
7	Dennis Eckersley	.35
8	Mike Gallego	.05
9	Ron Hassey	.05
10	Dave Henderson	.05
11	Rick Honeycutt	.05
12	Glenn Hubbard	.05
13	Stan Javier	.05
14	Doug Jennings **RC**	.05
15	Felix Jose **RC**	.05
16	Carney Lansford	.05
17	Mark McGwire	.65
18	Gene Nelson	.05
19	Dave Parker	.05
20	Eric Plunk	.05
21	Luis Polonia	.05
22	Terry Steinbach	.05
23	Dave Stewart	.05
24	Walt Weiss	.05
25	Bob Welch	.05
26	Curt Young	.05
27	Rick Aguilera	.05
28	Wally Backman	.05
29	Mark Carreon	.05
30	Gary Carter	.40
31	David Cone	.05
32	Ron Darling	.05
33	Len Dykstra	.05
34	Kevin Elster	.05
35	Sid Fernandez	.05
36	Dwight Gooden	.05
37	Keith Hernandez	.05
38	Gregg Jefferies	.05
39	Howard Johnson	.05
40	Terry Leach	.05
41	Dave Magadan	.05
42	Bob McClure	.05
43	Roger McDowell	.05
44	Kevin McReynolds	.05
45	Keith Miller	.05
46	Randy Myers	.05
47	Bob Ojeda	.05
48	Mackey Sasser	.05
49	Darryl Strawberry	.05
50	Tim Teufel	.05
51	Dave West **RC**	.05
52	Mookie Wilson	.05
53	Dave Anderson	.05
54	Tim Belcher	.05
55	Mike Davis	.05
56	Mike Devereaux	.05
57	Kirk Gibson	.05
58	Alfredo Griffin	.05
59	Chris Gwynn	.05
60	Jeff Hamilton	.05
61a	Danny Heep (Home: San Antonio, TX)	.25
61b	Danny Heep (Home: Lake Hills, TX)	.05
62	Orel Hershiser	.05
63	Brian Holton	.05
64	Jay Howell	.05
65	Tim Leary	.05
66	Mike Marshall	.05
67	Ramon Martinez **RC**	.25
68	Jesse Orosco	.05
69	Alejandro Pena	.05
70	Steve Sax	.05
71	Mike Scioscia	.05
72	Mike Sharperson	.05
73	John Shelby	.05
74	Franklin Stubbs	.05
75	John Tudor	.05
76	Fernando Valenzuela	.05
77	Tracy Woodson	.05
78	Marty Barrett	.05
79	Todd Benzinger	.05
80	Mike Boddicker	.05
81	Wade Boggs	.50
82	"Oil Can" Boyd	.05
83	Ellis Burks	.05
84	Rick Cerone	.05

85	Roger Clemens	.75
86	Steve Curry **RC**	.05
87	Dwight Evans	.05
88	Wes Gardner	.05
89	Rich Gedman	.05
90	Mike Greenwell	.05
91	Bruce Hurst	.05
92	Dennis Lamp	.05
93	Spike Owen	.05
94	Larry Parrish	.05
95	Carlos Quintana **RC**	.05
96	Jody Reed	.05
97	Jim Rice	.25
98a	Kevin Romine (Batting follow-thru, photo actually Randy Kutcher.)	.25
98b	Kevin Romine (Arms crossed on chest, correct photo.)	.25
99	Lee Smith	.05
100	Mike Smithson	.05
101	Bob Stanley	.05
102	Allan Anderson	.05
103	Keith Atherton	.05
104	Juan Berenguer	.05
105	Bert Blyleven	.10
106	Eric Bullock **RC**	.05
107	Randy Bush	.05
108	John Christensen	.05
109	Mark Davidson	.05
110	Gary Gaetti	.05
111	Greg Gagne	.05
112	Dan Gladden	.05
113	German Gonzalez **RC**	.05
114	Brian Harper	.05
115	Tom Herr	.05
116	Kent Hrbek	.05
117	Gene Larkin	.05
118	Tim Laudner	.05
119	Charlie Lea	.05
120	Steve Lombardozzi	.05
121a	John Moses (Home: Phoenix, AZ)	.25
121b	John Moses (Home: Tempe, AZ)	.05
122	Al Newman	.05
123	Mark Portugal	.05
124	Kirby Puckett	.50
125	Jeff Reardon	.05
126	Fred Toliver	.05
127	Frank Viola	.05
128	Doyle Alexander	.05
129	Dave Bergman	.05
130a	Tom Brookens (Mike Heath stats on back.)	.50
130b	Tom Brookens (Correct stats on back.)	.05
131	Paul Gibson **RC**	.05
132a	Mike Heath(Tom Brookens stats on back.)	.50
132b	Mike Heath (Correct stats on back.)	.05
133	Don Heinkel **RC**	.05
134	Mike Henneman	.05
135	Guillermo Hernandez	.05
136	Eric King	.05
137	Chet Lemon	.05
138	Fred Lynn	.05
139	Jack Morris	.05
140	Matt Nokes	.05
141	Gary Pettis	.05
142	Ted Power	.05
143	Jeff Robinson	.05
144	Luis Salazar	.05
145	Steve Searcy **RC**	.05
146	Pat Sheridan	.05
147	Frank Tanana	.05
148	Alan Trammell	.05
149	Walt Terrell	.05
150	Jim Walewander	.05
151	Lou Whitaker	.05
152	Tim Birtsas	.05
153	Tom Browning	.05
154	Keith Brown **RC**	.05
155	Norm Charlton **RC**	.15
156	Dave Concepcion	.05
157	Kal Daniels	.05
158	Eric Davis	.05
159	Bo Diaz	.05
160	Rob Dibble	.05
161	Nick Esasky	.05
162	John Franco	.05
163	Danny Jackson	.05
164	Barry Larkin	.05
165	Rob Murphy	.05
166	Paul O'Neill	.05
167	Jeff Reed	.05
168	Jose Rijo	.05
169	Ron Robinson	.05
170	Chris Sabo	.05
171	Candy Sierra **RC**	.05
172	Van Snider **RC**	.05
173a	Jeff Treadway (Blue "target" above head.)	75.00
173b	Jeff Treadway (No "target.")	.05
174	Frank Williams	.05
175	Herm Winningham	.05
176	Jim Adduci	.05
177	Don August	.05
178	Mike Birkbeck	.05
179	Chris Bosio	.05
180	Glenn Braggs	.05
181	Greg Brock	.05
182	Mark Clear	.05
183	Chuck Crim	.05
184	Rob Deer	.05
185	Tom Filer	.05
186	Jim Gantner	.05
187	Darryl Hamilton	.05
188	Ted Higuera	.05
189	Odell Jones	.05
190	Jeffrey Leonard	.05
191	Joey Meyer	.05
192	Paul Mirabella	.05
193	Paul Molitor	.40
194	Charlie O'Brien	.05
195	Dan Plesac	.05
196	Gary Sheffield **RC**	1.00
197	B.J. Surhoff	.05
198	Dale Sveum	.05
199	Bill Wegman	.05
200	Robin Yount	.40
201	Rafael Belliard	.05
202	Barry Bonds	.75
203	Bobby Bonilla	.05
204	Sid Bream	.05
205	Benny Distefano	.05
206	Doug Drabek	.05
207	Mike Dunne	.05
208	Felix Fermin	.05
209	Brian Fisher	.05
210	Jim Gott	.05
211	Bob Kipper	.05
212	Dave LaPoint	.05
213	Mike LaValliere	.05
214	Jose Lind	.05
215	Junior Ortiz	.05
216	Vicente Palacios	.05
217	Tom Prince	.05
218	Gary Redus	.05
219	R.J. Reynolds	.05
220	Jeff Robinson	.05
221	John Smiley	.05
222	Andy Van Slyke	.05
223	Bob Walk	.05
224	Glenn Wilson	.05
225	Jesse Barfield	.05
226	George Bell	.05
227	Pat Borders	.05
228	John Cerutti	.05
229	Jim Clancy	.05
230	Mark Eichhorn	.05
231	Tony Fernandez	.05
232	Cecil Fielder	.05
233	Mike Flanagan	.05
234	Kelly Gruber	.05
235	Tom Henke	.05
236	Jimmy Key	.05
237	Rick Leach	.05
238	Manny Lee	.05
239	Nelson Liriano	.05
240	Fred McGriff	.05
241	Lloyd Moseby	.05
242	Rance Mulliniks	.05
243	Jeff Musselman	.05
244	Dave Stieb	.05
245	Todd Stottlemyre	.05
246	Duane Ward	.05
247	David Wells	.05
248	Ernie Whitt	.05
249	Luis Aguayo	.05
250a	Neil Allen (Home: Sarasota, FL)	.25
250b	Neil Allen (Home: Syosset, NY)	.05
251	John Candelaria	.05
252	Jack Clark	.05
253	Richard Dotson	.05
254	Rickey Henderson	.40
255	Tommy John	.10
256	Roberto Kelly	.05
257	Al Leiter	.05
258	Don Mattingly	.60
259	Dale Mohorcic	.05
260	Hal Morris **RC**	.25
261	Scott Nielsen	.05
262	Mike Pagliarulo	.05
263	Hipolito Pena **RC**	.05
264	Ken Phelps	.05
265	Willie Randolph	.05
266	Rick Rhoden	.05
267	Dave Righetti	.05
268	Rafael Santana	.05
269	Steve Shields	.05
270	Joel Skinner	.05
271	Don Slaught	.05
272	Claudell Washington	.05
273	Gary Ward	.05
274	Dave Winfield	.40
275	Luis Aquino	.05
276	Floyd Bannister	.05
277	George Brett	.60
278	Bill Buckner	.05
279	Nick Capra **RC**	.05
280	Jose DeJesus **RC**	.05
281	Steve Farr	.05
282	Jerry Gleaton	.05
283	Mark Gubicza	.05
284	Tom Gordon **RC**	.25
285	Bo Jackson	.10
286	Charlie Leibrandt	.05
287	Mike Macfarlane **RC**	.10
288	Jeff Montgomery	.05
289	Bill Pecota	.05
290	Jamie Quirk	.05
291	Bret Saberhagen	.05
292	Kevin Seitzer	.05
293	Kurt Stillwell	.05
294	Pat Tabler	.05
295	Danny Tartabull	.05
296	Gary Thurman	.05
297	Frank White	.05
298	Willie Wilson	.05
299	Roberto Alomar	.20
300	Sandy Alomar, Jr. **RC**	.25
301	Chris Brown	.05
302	Mike Brumley	.05
303	Mark Davis	.05
304	Mark Grant	.05
305	Tony Gwynn	.50
306	Greg Harris **RC**	.05
307	Andy Hawkins	.05
308	Jimmy Jones	.05
309	John Kruk	.05
310	Dave Leiper	.05
311	Carmelo Martinez	.05
312	Lance McCullers	.05
313	Keith Moreland	.05
314	Dennis Rasmussen	.05
315	Randy Ready	.05
316	Benito Santiago	.05
317	Eric Show	.05
318	Todd Simmons	.05
319	Garry Templeton	.05
320	Dickie Thon	.05
321	Ed Whitson	.05
322	Marvell Wynne	.05
323	Mike Aldrete	.05
324	Brett Butler	.05
325	Will Clark	.05
326	Kelly Downs	.05
327	Dave Dravecky	.05
328	Scott Garrelts	.05
329	Atlee Hammaker	.05
330	Charlie Hayes **RC**	.10
331	Mike Krukow	.05
332	Craig Lefferts	.05
333	Candy Maldonado	.05
334	Kirt Manwaring	.05
335	Bob Melvin	.05
336	Kevin Mitchell	.05
337	Donell Nixon	.05
338	Tony Perezchica **RC**	.05
339	Joe Price	.05
340	Rick Reuschel	.05
341	Earnest Riles	.05
342	Don Robinson	.05
343	Chris Speier	.05
344	Robby Thompson	.05
345	Jose Uribe	.05
346	Matt Williams	.05
347	Trevor Wilson **RC**	.15
348	Juan Agosto	.05
349	Larry Andersen	.05
350a	Alan Ashby ("Throws Right")	.25
350b	Alan Ashby ("Throws Right")	.05
351	Kevin Bass	.05
352	Buddy Bell	.05
353	Craig Biggio	.05
354	Danny Darwin	.05
355	Glenn Davis	.05
356	Jim Deshaies	.05
357	Bill Doran	.05
358	John Fishel **RC**	.05
359	Billy Hatcher	.05
360	Bob Knepper	.05
361	Louie Meadows **RC**	.05
362	Dave Meads	.05
363	Jim Pankovits	.05
364	Terry Puhl	.05
365	Rafael Ramirez	.05
366	Craig Reynolds	.05
367	Mike Scott	.05
368	Nolan Ryan	.75
369	Dave Smith	.05
370	Gerald Young	.05
371	Hubie Brooks	.05
372	Tim Burke	.05
373	John Dopson **RC**	.05
374	Mike Fitzgerald	.05
375	Tom Foley	.05
376	Andres Galarraga	.05
377	Neal Heaton	.05
378	Joe Hesketh	.05
379	Brian Holman **RC**	.05
380	Rex Hudler	.05
381a	Randy Johnson **RC** (Marlboro ad on scoreboard.)	40.00
381b	Randy Johnson (Ad partially obscured.)	10.00
381c	Randy Johnson **RC** (Ad completely blacked out.)	3.00
382	Wallace Johnson	.05
383	Tracy Jones	.05
384	Dave Martinez	.05
385	Dennis Martinez	.05
386	Andy McGaffigan	.05
387	Otis Nixon	.05
388	Johnny Paredes **RC**	.05
389	Jeff Parrett	.05
390	Pascual Perez	.05
391	Tim Raines	.05
392	Luis Rivera	.05
393	Nelson Santovenia **RC**	.05
394	Bryn Smith	.05
395	Tim Wallach	.05
396	Andy Allanson	.05
397	Rod Allen **RC**	.05
398	Scott Bailes	.05
399	Tom Candiotti	.05
400	Joe Carter	.05
401	Carmen Castillo	.05
402	Dave Clark	.05
403	John Farrell	.05
404	Julio Franco	.05
405	Don Gordon	.05
406	Mel Hall	.05
407	Brad Havens	.05
408	Brook Jacoby	.05
409	Doug Jones	.05
410	Jeff Kaiser **RC**	.05
411	Luis Medina **RC**	.05
412	Cory Snyder	.05
413	Greg Swindell	.05
414	Ron Tingley **RC**	.05
415	Willie Upshaw	.05
416	Ron Washington	.05
417	Rich Yett	.05
418	Damon Berryhill	.05
419	Mike Bielecki	.05
420	Doug Dascenzo **RC**	.05
421	Jody Davis	.05
422	Andre Dawson	.25
423	Frank DiPino	.05
424	Shawon Dunston	.05
425	"Goose" Gossage	.10
426	Mark Grace	.05
427	Mike Harkey **RC**	.05
428	Darrin Jackson	.05
429	Les Lancaster	.05
430	Vance Law	.05
431	Greg Maddux	.50
432	Jamie Moyer	.05
433	Al Nipper	.05
434	Rafael Palmeiro	.35
435	Pat Perry	.05
436	Jeff Pico **RC**	.05
437	Ryne Sandberg	.50
438	Calvin Schiraldi	.05
439	Rick Sutcliffe	.05
440a	Manny Trillo ("Throws Rig")	.35
440b	Manny Trillo ("Throws Right")	.05
441	Gary Varsho **RC**	.05
442	Mitch Webster	.05
443	Luis Alicea	.05
444	Tom Brunansky	.05
445	Vince Coleman	.05
446	John Costello **RC**	.05
447	Danny Cox	.05
448	Ken Dayley	.05
449	Jose DeLeon	.05
450	Curt Ford	.05
451	Pedro Guerrero	.05
452	Bob Horner	.05
453	Tim Jones **RC**	.05
454	Steve Lake	.05
455	Joe Magrane	.05
456	Greg Mathews	.05
457	Willie McGee	.05
458	Larry McWilliams	.05
459	Jose Oquendo	.05
460	Tony Pena	.05
461	Terry Pendleton	.05
462	Steve Peters **RC**	.05
463	Ozzie Smith	.50
464	Scott Terry	.05
465	Denny Walling	.05
466	Todd Worrell	.05
467	Tony Armas	.05
468	Dante Bichette **RC**	.25
469	Bob Boone	.05
470	Terry Clark **RC**	.05
471	Stew Cliburn	.05
472	Mike Cook **RC**	.05
473	Sherman Corbett **RC**	.05
474	Chili Davis	.05
475	Brian Downing	.05
476	Jim Eppard	.05
477	Chuck Finley	.05
478	Willie Fraser	.05
479	Bryan Harvey	.05
480	Jack Howell	.05
481	Wally Joyner	.05
482	Jack Lazorko	.05
483	Kirk McCaskill	.05
484	Mark McLemore	.05
485	Greg Minton	.05
486	Dan Petry	.05
487	Johnny Ray	.05
488	Dick Schofield	.05
489	Devon White	.05
490	Mike Witt	.05
491	Harold Baines	.05
492	Daryl Boston	.05
493	Ivan Calderon	.05
494	Mike Diaz	.05
495	Carlton Fisk	.40
496	Dave Gallagher **RC**	.05
497	Ozzie Guillen	.05
498	Shawn Hillegas	.05
499	Lance Johnson	.05
500	Barry Jones	.05
501	Bill Long	.05
502	Steve Lyons	.05
503	Fred Manrique	.05
504	Jack McDowell	.05
505	Donn Pall **RC**	.05
506	Kelly Paris	.05
507	Dan Pasqua	.05
508	Ken Patterson **RC**	.05
509	Melido Perez	.05
510	Jerry Reuss	.05
511	Mark Salas	.05
512	Bobby Thigpen	.05
513	Mike Woodard	.05
514	Bob Brower	.05
515	Steve Buechele	.05
516	Jose Cecena **RC**	.05
517	Cecil Espy	.05
518	Scott Fletcher	.05
519	Cecilio Guante	.05
520	Jose Guzman	.05
521	Ray Hayward	.05

522	Charlie Hough	.05
523	Pete Incaviglia	.05
524	Mike Jeffcoat	.05
525	Paul Kilgus	.05
526	Chad Kreuter RC	.15
527	Jeff Kunkel	.05
528	Oddibe McDowell	.05
529	Pete O'Brien	.05
530	Geno Petralli	.05
531	Jeff Russell	.05
532	Ruben Sierra	.05
533	Mike Stanley	.05
534	Ed Vande Berg	.05
535	Curtis Wilkerson	.05
536	Mitch Williams	.05
537	Bobby Witt	.05
538	Steve Balboni	.05
539	Scott Bankhead	.05
540	Scott Bradley	.05
541	Mickey Brantley	.05
542	Jay Buhner	.05
543	Mike Campbell	.05
544	Darnell Coles	.05
545	Henry Cotto	.05
546	Alvin Davis	.05
547	Mario Diaz	.05
548	Ken Griffey Jr. RC	6.00
549	Erik Hanson RC	.05
550	Mike Jackson	.05
551	Mark Langston	.05
552	Edgar Martinez	.05
553	Bill McGuire RC	.05
554	Mike Moore	.05
555	Jim Presley	.05
556	Rey Quinones	.05
557	Jerry Reed	.05
558	Harold Reynolds	.05
559	Mike Schooler RC	.05
560	Bill Swift	.05
561	Dave Valle	.05
562	Steve Bedrosian	.05
563	Phil Bradley	.05
564	Don Carman	.05
565	Bob Dernier	.05
566	Marvin Freeman	.05
567	Todd Frohwirth	.05
568	Greg Gross	.05
569	Kevin Gross	.05
570	Greg Harris	.05
571	Von Hayes	.05
572	Chris James	.05
573	Steve Jeltz	.05
574	Ron Jones RC	.05
575	Ricky Jordan RC	.05
576	Mike Maddux	.05
577	David Palmer	.05
578	Lance Parrish	.05
579	Shane Rawley	.05
580	Bruce Ruffin	.05
581	Juan Samuel	.05
582	Mike Schmidt	.60
583	Kent Tekulve	.05
584	Milt Thompson	.05
585	Jose Alvarez RC	.05
586	Paul Assenmacher	.05
587	Bruce Benedict	.05
588	Jeff Blauser	.05
589	Terry Blocker RC	.05
590	Ron Gant	.05
591	Tom Glavine	.30
592	Tommy Gregg	.05
593	Albert Hall	.05
594	Dion James	.05
595	Rick Mahler	.05
596	Dale Murphy	.25
597	Gerald Perry	.05
598	Charlie Puleo	.05
599	Ted Simmons	.05
600	Pete Smith	.05
601	Zane Smith	.05
602	John Smoltz	.50
603	Bruce Sutter	.35
604	Andres Thomas	.05
605	Ozzie Virgil	.05
606	Brady Anderson	.05
607	Jeff Ballard	.05
608	Jose Bautista RC	.05
609	Ken Gerhart	.05
610	Terry Kennedy	.40
611	Eddie Murray	.40
612	Carl Nichols	.05
613	Tom Niedenfuer	.05
614	Joe Orsulak	.05
615	Oswaldo Peraza RC (Oswald)	.05
616a	Bill Ripken (Vulgarity on bat knob.)	8.00
616b	Bill Ripken (Scribble over vulgarity.)	6.00
616c	Bill Ripken (Black box over vulgarity.)	.10
616d	Bill Ripken (Vulgarity whited out.(Many fake "white out" cards exist, created by erasures.)	250.00
616e	Billy Ripken (Strip cut out of bottom of card.)	.10
617	Cal Ripken, Jr.	.75
618	Dave Schmidt	.05
619	Rick Schu	.05
620	Larry Sheets	.05
621	Doug Sisk	.05
622	Pete Stanicek	.05
623	Mickey Tettleton	.05
624	Jay Tibbs	.05
625	Jim Traber	.05
626	Mark Williamson	.05
627	Craig Worthington RC	.05

628	Jose Canseco Speed and Power	.20
629	Tom Browning Pitcher Perfect	.05
630	Roberto Alomar, Sandy Alomar, Jr. Like Father Like Sons	.20
631	Will Clark, Rafael Palmeiro N.L. All-Stars	.10
632	Will Clark, Darryl Strawberry Homeruns Coast to Coast	.05
633	Wade Boggs, Carney Lansford Hot Corner's Hot Hitters	.25
634	Jose Canseco, Mark McGwire, Terry Steinbach Triple A's	.40
635	Mark Davis, Dwight Gooden Dual Heat	.05
636	David Cone, Danny Jackson N.L. Pitching Power	.05
637	Bobby Bonilla, Chris Sabo Cannon Arms	.05
638	Andres Galarraga, Gerald Perry Double Trouble	.05
639	Eric Davis Power Center	.05
640	Cameron Drew, Steve Wilson RC Major League Prospects	.05
641	Kevin Brown, Kevin Reimer RC Major League Prospects	.30
642	Jerald Clark, Brad Pounders RC Major League Prospects	.05
643	Mike Capel, Drew Hall RC Major League Prospects	.05
644	Joe Girardi, Rolando Roomes RC Major League Prospects	.20
645	Marty Brown, Lenny Harris RC Major League Prospects	.15
646	Luis de los Santos, Jim Campbell RC Major League Prospects	.05
647	Miguel Garcia, Randy Kramer RC Major League Prospects	.05
648	Torey Lovullo, Robert Palacios RC Major League Prospects	.05
649	Jim Corsi, Bob Milacki RC Major League Prospects	.05
650	Grady Hall, Mike Rochford RC Major League Prospects	.05
651	Vance Lovelace, Terry Taylor RC Major League Prospects	.05
652	Dennis Cook, Ken Hill RC Major League Prospects	.20
653	Scott Service, Shane Turner RC Major LeagueProspects	.05
654	Checklist 1-101	.05
655	Checklist 102-200	.05
656	Checklist 201-298	.05
657	Checklist 299-395	.05
658	Checklist 396-490	.05
659	Checklist 491-584	.05
660	Checklist 585-660	.05

Update

ROBIN VENTURA
THIRD BASE

NM/M

Complete Set (132):		6.00
Common Player:		.05
1	Phil Bradley	.05
2	Mike Devereaux	.05
3	Steve Finley	.05
4	Kevin Hickey	.05
5	Brian Holton	.05
6	Bob Milacki	.05
7	Randy Milligan	.05
8	John Dopson	.05
9	Nick Esasky	.05
10	Rob Murphy	.05
11	Jim Abbott	.25
12	Bert Blyleven	.10
13	Jeff Manto	.05
14	Bob McClure	.05
15	Lance Parrish	.05
16	Lee Stevens	.05
17	Claudell Washington	.05
18	Mark Davis	.05
19	Eric King	.05
20	Ron Kittle	.05
21	Matt Merullo	.05
22	Steve Rosenberg	.05
23	Robin Ventura	.25
24	Keith Atherton	.05
25	Joey (Albert) Belle RC	1.00
26	Jerry Browne	.05
27	Felix Fermin	.05

28	Brad Komminsk	.05
29	Pete O'Brien	.05
30	Mike Brumley	.05
31	Tracy Jones	.05
32	Mike Schwabe	.05
33	Gary Ward	.05
34	Frank Williams	.05
35	Kevin Appier RC	.25
36	Bob Boone	.05
37	Luis de los Santos	.05
38	Jim Eisenreich	.05
39	Jaime Navarro RC	.05
40	Bill Spiers	.05
41	Greg Vaughn RC	.25
42	Randy Veres	.05
43	Wally Backman	.05
44	Shane Rawley	.05
45	Steve Balboni	.05
46	Jesse Barfield	.05
47	Alvaro Espinoza	.05
48	Bob Geren	.05
49	Mel Hall	.05
50	Andy Hawkins	.05
51	Hensley Meulens	.05
52	Steve Sax	.05
53	Deion Sanders RC	.75
54	Rickey Henderson	.40
55	Mike Moore	.05
56	Tony Phillips	.05
57	Greg Briley	.05
58	Gene Harris	.05
59	Randy Johnson	2.00
60	Jeffrey Leonard	.05
61	Dennis Powell	.05
62	Omar Vizquel	.05
63	Kevin Brown	.05
64	Julio Franco	.05
65	Jamie Moyer	.05
66	Rafael Palmeiro	.35
67	Nolan Ryan	1.00
68	Francisco Cabrera	.05
69	Junior Felix	.05
70	Al Leiter	.05
71	Alex Sanchez	.05
72	Geronimo Berroa	.05
73	Derek Lilliquist	.05
74	Lonnie Smith	.05
75	Jeff Treadway	.05
76	Paul Kilgus	.05
77	Lloyd McClendon	.05
78	Scott Sanderson	.05
79	Dwight Smith	.05
80	Jerome Walton	.05
81	Mitch Williams	.05
82	Steve Wilson	.05
83	Todd Benzinger	.05
84	Ken Griffey	.05
85	Rick Mahler	.05
86	Rolando Roomes	.05
87	Scott Scudder	.05
88	Jim Clancy	.05
89	Rick Rhoden	.05
90	Dan Schatzeder	.05
91	Mike Morgan	.05
92	Eddie Murray	.40
93	Willie Randolph	.05
94	Ray Searage	.05
95	Mike Aldrete	.05
96	Kevin Gross	.05
97	Mark Langston	.05
98	Spike Owen	.05
99	Zane Smith	.05
100	Don Aase	.05
101	Barry Lyons	.05
102	Juan Samuel	.05
103	Wally Whitehurst	.05
104	Dennis Cook	.05
105	Len Dykstra	.05
106	Charlie Hayes	.05
107	Tommy Herr	.05
108	Ken Howell	.05
109	Ken Kruk	.05
110	Roger McDowell	.05
111	Terry Mulholland	.05
112	Jeff Parrett	.05
113	Neal Heaton	.05
114	Jeff King	.05
115	Randy Kramer	.05
116	Bill Landrum	.05
117	Cris Carpenter	.05
118	Frank DiPino	.05
119	Ken Hill	.05
120	Dan Quisenberry	.05
121	Milt Thompson	.05
122	Todd Zeile RC	.25
123	Jack Clark	.05
124	Bruce Hurst	.05
125	Mark Parent	.05
126	Bip Roberts	.05
127	Jeff Brantley	.05
128	Terry Kennedy	.05
129	Mike LaCoss	.05
130	Greg Litton	.05
131	Mike Schmidt	.65
132	Checklist	.05

1989 Fleer Glossy Tin

NM/M

Unopened Set (672):	75.00
Complete Set (672):	50.00

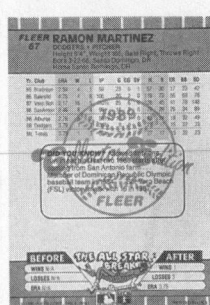

Common Player: .25
(Star cards valued at 3-4X regular 1989 Fleer cards.)

1990 Fleer

GEORGE BRETT   FIRST BASE

NM/M

Factory Hobby Set (672):		12.50
Retail Hobby Set (660):		12.00
Complete Set (660):		10.00
Common Player:		.05
Wax Pack (15):		.50
Wax Box (36):		10.00
Cello Pack (33):		1.00
Cello Box (24):		12.00
1	Lance Blankenship	.05
2	Todd Burns	.05
3	Jose Canseco	.30
4	Jim Corsi	.05
5	Storm Davis	.05
6	Dennis Eckersley	.35
7	Mike Gallego	.05
8	Ron Hassey	.05
9	Dave Henderson	.05
10	Rickey Henderson	.40
11	Rick Honeycutt	.05
12	Stan Javier	.05
13	Felix Jose	.05
14	Carney Lansford	.05
15	Mark McGwire	.65
16	Mike Moore	.05
17	Gene Nelson	.05
18	Dave Parker	.05
19	Tony Phillips	.05
20	Terry Steinbach	.05
21	Dave Stewart	.05
22	Walt Weiss	.05
23	Bob Welch	.05
24	Curt Young	.05
25	Paul Assenmacher	.05
26	Damon Berryhill	.05
27	Mike Bielecki	.05
28	Kevin Blankenship	.05
29	Andre Dawson	.25
30	Shawon Dunston	.05
31	Joe Girardi	.05
32	Mark Grace	.05
33	Mike Harkey	.05
34	Paul Kilgus	.05
35	Les Lancaster	.05
36	Vance Law	.05
37	Greg Maddux	.50
38	Lloyd McClendon	.05
39	Jeff Pico	.05
40	Ryne Sandberg	.50
41	Scott Sanderson	.05
42	Dwight Smith	.05
43	Rick Sutcliffe	.05
44	Jerome Walton RC	.05
45	Mitch Webster	.05
46	Curt Wilkerson	.05
47	Dean Wilkins RC	.05
48	Mitch Williams	.05
49	Steve Wilson	.05
50	Steve Bedrosian	.05
51	Mike Benjamin RC	.05
52	Jeff Brantley RC	.10
53	Brett Butler	.05
54	Will Clark	.05

55	Kelly Downs	.05
56	Scott Garrelts	.05
57	Atlee Hammaker	.05
58	Terry Kennedy	.05
59	Mike LaCoss	.05
60	Craig Lefferts	.05
61	Greg Litton **RC**	.05
62	Candy Maldonado	.05
63	Kirt Manwaring	.05
64	Randy McCament **RC**	.05
65	Kevin Mitchell	.05
66	Donell Nixon	.05
67	Ken Oberkfell	.05
68	Rick Reuschel	.05
69	Ernest Riles	.05
70	Don Robinson	.05
71	Pat Sheridan	.05
72	Chris Speier	.05
73	Robby Thompson	.05
74	Jose Uribe	.05
75	Matt Williams	.05
76	George Bell	.05
77	Pat Borders	.05
78	John Cerutti	.05
79	Junior Felix **RC**	.05
80	Tony Fernandez	.05
81	Mike Flanagan	.05
82	Mauro Gozzo **RC**	.05
83	Kelly Gruber	.05
84	Tom Henke	.05
85	Jimmy Key	.05
86	Manny Lee	.05
87	Nelson Liriano	.05
88	Lee Mazzilli	.05
89	Fred McGriff	.05
90	Lloyd Moseby	.05
91	Rance Mulliniks	.05
92	Alex Sanchez	.05
93	Dave Steib	.05
94	Todd Stottlemyre	.05
95	Duane Ward	.05
96	David Wells	.05
97	Ernie Whitt	.05
98	Frank Wills	.05
99	Mookie Wilson	.05
100	Kevin Appier	.05
101	Luis Aquino	.05
102	Bob Boone	.05
103	George Brett	.60
104	Jose DeJesus	.05
105	Luis de los Santos	.05
106	Jim Eisenreich	.05
107	Steve Farr	.05
108	Tom Gordon	.05
109	Mark Gubicza	.05
110	Bo Jackson	.10
111	Terry Leach	.05
112	Charlie Leibrandt	.05
113	Rick Luecken **RC**	.05
114	Mike Macfarlane	.05
115	Jeff Montgomery	.05
116	Bret Saberhagen	.05
117	Kevin Seitzer	.05
118	Kurt Stillwell	.05
119	Pat Tabler	.05
120	Danny Tartabull	.05
121	Gary Thurman	.05
122	Frank White	.05
123	Willie Wilson	.05
124	Matt Winters **RC**	.05
125	Jim Abbott	.05
126	Tony Armas	.05
127	Dante Bichette	.05
128	Bert Blyleven	.10
129	Chili Davis	.05
130	Brian Downing	.05
131	Mike Fetters **RC**	.05
132	Chuck Finley	.05
133	Willie Fraser	.05
134	Bryan Harvey	.05
135	Jack Howell	.05
136	Wally Joyner	.05
137	Jeff Manto **RC**	.05
138	Kirk McCaskill	.05
139	Bob McClure	.05
140	Greg Minton	.05
141	Lance Parrish	.05
142	Dan Petry	.05
143	Johnny Ray	.05
144	Dick Schofield	.05
145	Lee Stevens **RC**	.05
146	Claudell Washington	.05
147	Devon White	.05
148	Mike Witt	.05
149	Roberto Alomar	.20
150	Sandy Alomar, Jr.	.05
151	Andy Benes	.05
152	Jack Clark	.05
153	Pat Clements	.05
154	Joey Cora	.05
155	Mark Davis	.05
156	Mark Grant	.05
157	Tony Gwynn	.50
158	Greg Harris	.05
159	Bruce Hurst	.05
160	Darrin Jackson	.05
161	Chris James	.05
162	Carmelo Martinez	.05
163	Mike Pagliarulo	.05
164	Mark Parent	.05
165	Dennis Rasmussen	.05
166	Bip Roberts	.05
167	Benito Santiago	.05
168	Calvin Schiraldi	.05
169	Eric Show	.05
170	Garry Templeton	.05
171	Ed Whitson	.05
172	Brady Anderson	.05
173	Jeff Ballard	.05
174	Phil Bradley	.05
175	Mike Devereaux	.05
176	Steve Finley	.05
177	Pete Harnisch	.05
178	Kevin Hickey	.05
179	Brian Holton	.05
180	Ben McDonald **RC**	.15
181	Bob Melvin	.05
182	Bob Milacki	.05
183	Randy Milligan	.05
184	Gregg Olson	.05
185	Joe Orsulak	.05
186	Bill Ripken	.05
187	Cal Ripken, Jr.	.75
188	Dave Schmidt	.05
189	Larry Sheets	.05
190	Mickey Tettleton	.05
191	Mark Thurmond	.05
192	Jay Tibbs	.05
193	Jim Traber	.05
194	Mark Williamson	.05
195	Craig Worthington	.05
196	Don Aase	.05
197	Blaine Beatty **RC**	.05
198	Mark Carreon	.05
199	Gary Carter	.40
200	David Cone	.05
201	Ron Darling	.05
202	Kevin Elster	.05
203	Sid Fernandez	.05
204	Dwight Gooden	.05
205	Keith Hernandez	.05
206	Jeff Innis **RC**	.05
207	Gregg Jefferies	.05
208	Howard Johnson	.05
209	Barry Lyons	.05
210	Dave Magadan	.05
211	Kevin McReynolds	.05
212	Jeff Musselman	.05
213	Randy Myers	.05
214	Bob Ojeda	.05
215	Juan Samuel	.05
216	Mackey Sasser	.05
217	Darryl Strawberry	.05
218	Tim Teufel	.05
219	Frank Viola	.05
220	Juan Agosto	.05
221	Larry Anderson	.05
222	Eric Anthony **RC**	.10
223	Kevin Bass	.05
224	Craig Biggio	.05
225	Ken Caminiti	.05
226	Jim Clancy	.05
227	Danny Darwin	.05
228	Glenn Davis	.05
229	Jim Deshaies	.05
230	Bill Doran	.05
231	Bob Forsch	.05
232	Brian Meyer	.05
233	Terry Puhl	.05
234	Rafael Ramirez	.05
235	Rick Rhoden	.05
236	Dan Schatzeder	.05
237	Mike Scott	.05
238	Dave Smith	.05
239	Alex Trevino	.05
240	Glenn Wilson	.05
241	Gerald Young	.05
242	Tom Brunansky	.05
243	Cris Carpenter	.05
244	Alex Cole **RC**	.05
245	Vince Coleman	.05
246	John Costello	.05
247	Ken Dayley	.05
248	Jose DeLeon	.05
249	Frank DiPino	.05
250	Pedro Guerrero	.05
251	Ken Hill	.05
252	Joe Magrane	.05
253	Willie McGee	.05
254	John Morris	.05
255	Jose Oquendo	.05
256	Tony Pena	.05
257	Terry Pendleton	.05
258	Ted Power	.05
259	Dan Quisenberry	.05
260	Ozzie Smith	.50
261	Scott Terry	.05
262	Milt Thompson	.05
263	Denny Walling	.05
264	Todd Worrell	.05
265	Todd Zeile	.05
266	Marty Barrett	.05
267	Mike Boddicker	.05
268	Wade Boggs	.50
269	Ellis Burks	.05
270	Rick Cerone	.05
271	Roger Clemens	.60
272	John Dopson	.05
273	Nick Esasky	.05
274	Dwight Evans	.05
275	Wes Gardner	.05
276	Rich Gedman	.05
277	Mike Greenwell	.05
278	Danny Heep	.05
279	Eric Hetzel	.05
280	Dennis Lamp	.05
281	Rob Murphy	.05
282	Joe Price	.05
283	Carlos Quintana	.05
284	Jody Reed	.05
285	Luis Rivera	.05
286	Kevin Romine	.05
287	Lee Smith	.05
288	Mike Smithson	.05
289	Bob Stanley	.05
290	Harold Baines	.05
291	Kevin Brown	.05
292	Steve Buechele	.05
293	Scott Coolbaugh **RC**	.05
294	Jack Daugherty **RC**	.05
295	Cecil Espy	.05
296	Julio Franco	.05
297	Juan Gonzalez **RC**	2.00
298	Cecilio Guante	.05
299	Drew Hall	.05
300	Charlie Hough	.05
301	Pete Incaviglia	.05
302	Mike Jeffcoat	.05
303	Chad Kreuter	.05
304	Jeff Kunkel	.05
305	Rick Leach	.05
306	Fred Manrique	.05
307	Jamie Moyer	.05
308	Rafael Palmeiro	.35
309	Geno Petralli	.05
310	Kevin Reimer	.05
311	Kenny Rogers **RC**	.10
312	Jeff Russell	.05
313	Nolan Ryan	.75
314	Ruben Sierra	.05
315	Bobby Witt	.05
316	Chris Bosio	.05
317	Glenn Braggs	.05
318	Greg Brock	.05
319	Chuck Crim	.05
320	Rob Deer	.05
321	Mike Felder	.05
322	Tom Filer	.05
323	Tony Fossas **RC**	.05
324	Jim Gantner	.05
325	Darryl Hamilton	.05
326	Ted Higuera	.05
327	Mark Knudson	.05
328	Bill Krueger	.05
329	Tim McIntosh **RC**	.05
330	Paul Molitor	.40
331	Jaime Navarro	.05
332	Charlie O'Brien	.05
333	Jeff Peterek **RC**	.05
334	Dan Plesac	.05
335	Jerry Reuss	.05
336	Gary Sheffield	.35
337	Bill Spiers **RC**	.05
338	B.J. Surhoff	.05
339	Greg Vaughn	.05
340	Robin Yount	.40
341	Hubie Brooks	.05
342	Tim Burke	.05
343	Mike Fitzgerald	.05
344	Tom Foley	.05
345	Andres Galarraga	.05
346	Damaso Garcia	.05
347	Marquis Grissom **RC**	.50
348	Kevin Gross	.05
349	Joe Hesketh	.05
350	Jeff Huson **RC**	.05
351	Wallace Johnson	.05
352	Mark Langston	.05
353a	Dave Martinez (Yellow 90.)	6.00
353b	Dave Martinez (Red 90.)	.05
354	Dennis Martinez	.05
355	Andy McGaffigan	.05
356	Otis Nixon	.05
357	Spike Owen	.05
358	Pascual Perez	.05
359	Tim Raines	.05
360	Nelson Santovenia	.05
361	Bryn Smith	.05
362	Zane Smith	.05
363	Larry Walker **RC**	.75
364	Tim Wallach	.05
365	Rick Aguilera	.05
366	Allan Anderson	.05
367	Wally Backman	.05
368	Doug Baker	.05
369	Juan Berenguer	.05
370	Randy Bush	.05
371	Carmen Castillo	.05
372	Mike Dyer **RC**	.05
373	Gary Gaetti	.05
374	Greg Gagne	.05
375	Dan Gladden	.05
376	German Gonzalez	.05
377	Brian Harper	.05
378	Kent Hrbek	.05
379	Gene Larkin	.05
380	Tim Laudner	.05
381	John Moses	.05
382	Al Newman	.05
383	Kirby Puckett	.50
384	Shane Rawley	.05
385	Jeff Reardon	.05
386	Roy Smith	.05
387	Gary Wayne **RC**	.05
388	Dave West	.05
389	Tim Belcher	.05
390	Tim Crews	.05
391	Mike Davis	.05
392	Rick Dempsey	.05
393	Kirk Gibson	.05
394	Jose Gonzalez	.05
395	Alfredo Griffin	.05
396	Jeff Hamilton	.05
397	Lenny Harris	.05
398	Mickey Hatcher	.05
399	Orel Hershiser	.05
400	Jay Howell	.05
401	Mike Marshall	.05
402	Ramon Martinez	.05
403	Mike Morgan	.05
404	Eddie Murray	.40
405	Alejandro Pena	.05
406	Willie Randolph	.05
407	Mike Scioscia	.05
408	Ray Searage	.05
409	Fernando Valenzuela	.05
410	Jose Vizcaino **RC**	.10
411	John Wetteland **RC**	.20
412	Jack Armstrong	.05
413	Todd Benzinger	.05
414	Tim Birtsas	.05
415	Tom Browning	.05
416	Norm Charlton	.05
417	Eric Davis	.05
418	Rob Dibble	.05
419	John Franco	.05
420	Ken Griffey Sr.	.05
421	Chris Hammond **RC**	.15
422	Danny Jackson	.05
423	Barry Larkin	.05
424	Tim Leary	.05
425	Rick Mahler	.05
426	Joe Oliver **RC**	.05
427	Paul O'Neill	.05
428	Luis Quinones	.05
429	Jeff Reed	.05
430	Jose Rijo	.05
431	Ron Robinson	.05
432	Rolando Roomes	.05
433	Chris Sabo	.05
434	Scott Scudder **RC**	.05
435	Herm Winningham	.05
436	Steve Balboni	.05
437	Jesse Barfield	.05
438	Mike Blowers **RC**	.05
439	Tom Brookens	.05
440	Greg Cadaret	.05
441	Alvaro Espinoza	.05
442	Bob Geren **RC**	.05
443	Lee Guetterman	.05
444	Mel Hall	.05
445	Andy Hawkins	.05
446	Roberto Kelly	.05
447	Don Mattingly	.60
448	Lance McCullers	.05
449	Hensley Meulens	.05
450	Dale Mohorcic	.05
451	Clay Parker	.05
452	Eric Plunk	.05
453	Dave Righetti	.05
454	Deion Sanders	.10
455	Steve Sax	.05
456	Don Slaught	.05
457	Walt Terrell	.05
458	Dave Winfield	.40
459	Jay Bell	.05
460	Rafael Belliard	.05
461	Barry Bonds	.75
462	Bobby Bonilla	.05
463	Sid Bream	.05
464	Benny Distefano	.05
465	Doug Drabek	.05
466	Jim Gott	.05
467	Billy Hatcher	.05
468	Neal Heaton	.05
469	Jeff King	.05
470	Bob Kipper	.05
471	Randy Kramer	.05
472	Bill Landrum	.05
473	Mike LaValliere	.05
474	Jose Lind	.05
475	Junior Ortiz	.05
476	Gary Redus	.05
477	Rick Reed **RC**	.05
478	R.J. Reynolds	.05
479	Jeff Robinson	.05
480	John Smiley	.05
481	Andy Van Slyke	.05
482	Bob Walk	.05
483	Andy Allanson	.05
484	Scott Bailes	.05
485	Albert Belle	.05
486	Bud Black	.05
487	Jerry Browne	.05
488	Tom Candiotti	.05
489	Joe Carter	.05
490	David Clark	.05
491	John Farrell	.05
492	Felix Fermin	.05
493	Brook Jacoby	.05
494	Dion James	.05
495	Doug Jones	.05
496	Brad Komminsk	.05
497	Rod Nichols	.05
498	Pete O'Brien	.05
499	Steve Olin **RC**	.05
500	Jesse Orosco	.05
501	Joel Skinner	.05
502	Cory Snyder	.05
503	Greg Swindell	.05
504	Rich Yett	.05
505	Scott Bankhead	.05
506	Scott Bradley	.05
507	Greg Briley	.05
508	Jay Buhner	.05
509	Darnell Coles	.05
510	Keith Comstock	.05
511	Henry Cotto	.05
512	Alvin Davis	.05
513	Ken Griffey Jr.	.65

514 Erik Hanson .05
515 Gene Harris .05
516 Brian Holman .05
517 Mike Jackson .05
518 Randy Johnson .40
519 Jeffrey Leonard .05
520 Edgar Martinez .05
521 Dennis Powell .05
522 Jim Presley .05
523 Jerry Reed .05
524 Harold Reynolds .05
525 Mike Schooler .05
526 Bill Swift .05
527 David Valle .05
528 Omar Vizquel .05
529 Ivan Calderon .05
530 Carlton Fisk .40
531 Scott Fletcher .05
532 Dave Gallagher .05
533 Ozzie Guillen .05
534 Greg Hibbard **RC** .05
535 Shawn Hillegas .05
536 Lance Johnson .05
537 Eric King .05
538 Ron Kittle .05
539 Steve Lyons .05
540 Carlos Martinez .05
541 Tom McCarthy **RC** .05
542 Matt Merullo **RC** .05
543 Donn Pall .05
544 Dan Pasqua .05
545 Ken Patterson .05
546 Melido Perez .05
547 Steve Rosenberg .05
548 Sammy Sosa **RC** 5.00
549 Bobby Thigpen .05
550 Robin Ventura .05
551 Greg Walker .05
552 Don Carman .05
553 Pat Combs **RC** .05
554 Dennis Cook .05
555 Darren Daulton .05
556 Len Dykstra .05
557 Curt Ford .05
558 Charlie Hayes .05
559 Von Hayes .05
560 Tom Herr .05
561 Ken Howell .05
562 Steve Jeltz .05
563 Ron Jones .05
564 Ricky Jordan .05
565 John Kruk .05
566 Steve Lake .05
567 Roger McDowell .05
568 Terry Mulholland .05
569 Dwayne Murphy .05
570 Jeff Parrett .05
571 Randy Ready .05
572 Bruce Ruffin .05
573 Dickie Thon .05
574 Jose Alvarez .05
575 Geronimo Berroa .05
576 Jeff Blauser .05
577 Joe Boever .05
578 Marty Clary .05
579 Jody Davis .05
580 Mark Eichhorn .05
581 Darrell Evans .05
582 Ron Gant .05
583 Tom Glavine .25
584 Tommy Greene **RC** .05
585 Tommy Gregg .05
586 Dave Justice **RC** .40
587 Mark Lemke .05
588 Derek Lilliquist .05
589 Oddibe McDowell .05
590 Kent Mercker **RC** .05
591 Dale Murphy .20
592 Gerald Perry .05
593 Lonnie Smith .05
594 Pete Smith .05
595 John Smoltz .05
596 Mike Stanton **RC** .05
597 Andres Thomas .05
598 Jeff Treadway .05
599 Doyle Alexander .05
600 Dave Bergman .05
601 Brian Dubois **RC** .05
602 Paul Gibson .05
603 Mike Heath .05
604 Mike Henneman .05
605 Guillermo Hernandez .05
606 Shawn Holman **RC** .05
607 Tracy Jones .05
608 Chet Lemon .05
609 Fred Lynn .05
610 Jack Morris .05
611 Matt Nokes .05
612 Gary Pettis .05
613 Kevin Ritz **RC** .05
614 Jeff Robinson .05
615 Steve Searcy .05
616 Frank Tanana .05
617 Alan Trammell .05
618 Gary Ward .05
619 Lou Whitaker .05
620 Frank Williams .05
621a George Brett Players of the Decade - 1980 (... 10 .390 hitting ...) 1.00
621b George Brett Players of the Decade - 1980 .25
622 Fernando Valenzuela Players of the Decade - 1981 .05
623 Dale Murphy Players of the Decade - 1982 .05
624a Cal Ripkin, Jr. Players of the Decade - 1983 (Ripken) 1.50
624b Cal Ripken, Jr. Players of the Decade - 1983 .30
625 Ryne Sandberg Players of the Decade - 1984 .25
626 Don Mattingly Players of the Decade - 1985 .30
627 Roger Clemens Players of the Decade - 1986 .30
628 George Bell Players of the Decade - 1987 .05
629 Jose Canseco Players of the Decade - 1988 .10
630a Will Clark Players of the Decade - 1989 (Total bases 32.) .35
630b Will Clark Players of the Decade - 1989 (Total bases 321.) .05
631 Mark Davis, Mitch Williams Game Savers .05
632 Wade Boggs, Mike Greenwell Boston Igniters .15
633 Mark Gubicza, Jeff Russell Starter & Stopper .05
634 Tony Fernandez, Cal Ripken Jr. League's Best Shortstops .30
635 Kirby Puckett, Bo Jackson Human Dynamos .20
636 Mike Scott, Nolan Ryan 300 Strikeout Club .30
637 Will Clark, Kevin Mitchell The Dymanic Duo .05
638 Don Mattingly, Mark McGwire A.L. All-Stars .65
639 Howard Johnson, Ryne Sandberg N.L. East Rivals .20
640 Rudy Seanez, Colin Charland **RC** Major League Prospects .05
641 George Canale, Kevin Maas **RC** Major League Prospects .10
642 Kelly Mann, Dave Hansen **RC** Major League Prospects .05
643 Greg Smith, Stu Tate **RC** Major League Prospects .05
644 Tom Drees, Dan Howitt **RC** Major LeagueProspects .05
645 Mike Roesler, Derrick May **RC** Major League Prospects .05
646 Scott Hemond, Mark Gardner **RC** Major League Prospects .10
647 John Orton, Scott Leius **RC** Major League Prospects .10
648 Rich Monteleone, Dana Williams **RC** Major League Prospects .05
649 Mike Huff, Steve Frey **RC** Major League Prospects .05
650 Chuck McElroy, Moises Alou **RC** Major League Prospects .50
651 Bobby Rose, Mike Hartley **RC** Major League Prospects .10
652 Matt Kinzer, Wayne Edwards **RC** Major League Prospects .05
653 Delino DeShields, Jason Grimsley **RC** Major League Prospects .15
654 Athletics, Cubs, Giants & Blue Jays (Checklist) .05
655 Royals, Angels, Padres & Orioles (Checklist) .05
656 Mets, Astros, Cardinals & Red Sox (Checklist) .05
657 Rangers, Brewers, Expos & Twins (Checklist) .05
658 Dodgers, Reds, Yankees & Pirates (Checklist) .05
659 Indians, Mariners, White Sox & Phillies (Checklist) .05
660 Braves, Tigers & Special Cards (Checklist) .05

Update

NM/M

Complete Set (132): 5.00
Common Player: .05
1 Steve Avery .05
2 Francisco Cabrera .05
3 Nick Esasky .05
4 Jim Kremers .05
5 Greg Olson .05
6 Jim Presley .05
7 Shawn Boskie .05
8 Joe Kraemer .05
9 Luis Salazar .05
10 Hector Villanueva .05
11 Glenn Braggs .05
12 Mariano Duncan .05
13 Billy Hatcher .05
14 Tim Layana .05
15 Hal Morris .05
16 Javier Ortiz .05
17 Dave Rohde .05
18 Eric Yelding .05
19 Hubie Brooks .05
20 Kal Daniels .05
21 Dave Hansen .05
22 Mike Hartley .05
23 Stan Javier .05
24 Jose Offerman .05
25 Juan Samuel .05
26 Dennis Boyd .05
27 Delino DeShields .05
28 Steve Frey .05
29 Mark Gardner .05
30 Chris Nabholz .05
31 Bill Sampen .05
32 Dave Schmidt .05
33 Daryl Boston .05
34 Chuck Carr .05
35 John Franco .05
36 Todd Hundley **RC** .25
37 Julio Machado .05
38 Alejandro Pena .05
39 Darren Reed .05
40 Kelvin Torve .05
41 Darrel Akerfelds .05
42 Jose DeJesus .05
43 Dave Hollins .05
44 Carmelo Martinez .05
45 Brad Moore .05
46 Dale Murphy .15
47 Wally Backman .05
48 Stan Belinda .05
49 Bob Patterson .05
50 Ted Power .05
51 Don Slaught .05
52 Geronimo Pena .05
53 Lee Smith .05
54 John Tudor .05
55 Joe Carter .05
56 Tom Howard .05
57 Craig Lefferts .05
58 Rafael Valdez .05
59 Dave Anderson .05
60 Kevin Bass .05
61 John Burkett .05
62 Gary Carter .40
63 Rick Parker .05
64 Trevor Wilson .05
65 Chris Hoiles .05
66 Tim Hulett .05
67 Dave Johnson .05
68 Curt Schilling .35
69 David Segui .05
70 Tom Brunansky .05
71 Greg Harris .05
72 Dana Kiecker .05
73 Tim Naehring .05
74 Tony Pena .05
75 Jeff Reardon .05
76 Jerry Reed .05
77 Mark Eichhorn .05
78 Mark Langston .05
79 John Orton .05
80 Luis Polonia .05
81 Dave Winfield .40
82 Cliff Young .05
83 Wayne Edwards .05
84 Alex Fernandez .05
85 Craig Grebeck .05
86 Scott Radinsky .05
87 Frank Thomas 3.00
88 Beau Allred .05
89 Sandy Alomar, Jr. .05
90 Carlos Baerga **RC** .10
91 Kevin Bearse .05
92 Chris James .05
93 Candy Maldonado .05
94 Jeff Manto .05
95 Cecil Fielder .05
96 Travis Fryman **RC** .25
97 Lloyd Moseby .05
98 Edwin Nunez .05
99 Tony Phillips .05
100 Larry Sheets .05
101 Mark Davis .05
102 Storm Davis .05
103 Gerald Perry .05
104 Terry Shumpert .05
105 Edgar Diaz .05
106 Dave Parker .05
107 Tim Drummond .05
108 Junior Ortiz .05
109 Park Pittman .05
110 Kevin Tapani .05
111 Oscar Azocar .05
112 Jim Leyritz .05
113 Kevin Maas .05
114 Alan Mills .05
115 Matt Nokes .05
116 Pascual Perez .05
117 Ozzie Canseco .05
118 Scott Sanderson .05
119 Tino Martinez .05
120 Jeff Schaefer .05
121 Matt Young .05
122 Brian Bohanon .05
123 Jeff Huson .05
124 Ramon Manon .05
125 Gary Mielke .05
126 Willie Blair .05
127 Glenallen Hill .05
128 John Olerud **RC** .35
129 Luis Sojo .05
130 Mark Whiten .05
131 Nolan Ryan Three Decades of No Hitters 1.00
132 Checklist .05

1991 Fleer

NM/M

Unopened Factory Set (732): 12.00
Complete Set (720): 10.00
Common Player: .05
Wax Pack (15): .50
Wax Box (36): 12.50
Jumbo Wax Pack (53): 1.25
Jumbo Wax Box (24): 20.00
Cello Pack (30): 1.00
Cello Box (24): 16.00
1 Troy Afenir **RC** .05
2 Harold Baines .05
3 Lance Blankenship .05
4 Todd Burns .05
5 Jose Canseco .30
6 Dennis Eckersley .35
7 Mike Gallego .05
8 Ron Hassey .05
9 Dave Henderson .05
10 Rickey Henderson .40
11 Rick Honeycutt .05
12 Doug Jennings .05
13 Joe Klink **RC** .05
14 Carney Lansford .05
15 Darren Lewis **RC** .05
16 Willie McGee .05
17a Mark McGwire (Six-line career summary.) .65
17b Mark McGwire (Seven-line career summary.) .65
18 Mike Moore .05
19 Gene Nelson .05
20 Dave Otto .05
21 Jamie Quirk .05
22 Willie Randolph .05
23 Scott Sanderson .05
24 Terry Steinbach .05
25 Dave Stewart .05
26 Walt Weiss .05
27 Bob Welch .05
28 Curt Young .05
29 Wally Backman .05
30 Stan Belinda **RC** .05
31 Jay Bell .05
32 Rafael Belliard .05
33 Barry Bonds .75
34 Bobby Bonilla .05
35 Sid Bream .05
36 Doug Drabek .05
37 Carlos Garcia **RC** .10
38 Neal Heaton .05
39 Jeff King .05
40 Bob Kipper .05
41 Bill Landrum .05
42 Mike LaValliere .05
43 Jose Lind .05
44 Carmelo Martinez .05
45 Bob Patterson .05
46 Ted Power .05
47 Gary Redus .05
48 R.J. Reynolds .05
49 Don Slaught .05
50 John Smiley .05
51 Zane Smith .05
52 Randy Tomlin **RC** .10
53 Andy Van Slyke .05
54 Bob Walk .05
55 Jack Armstrong .05
56 Todd Benzinger .05
57 Glenn Braggs .05
58 Keith Brown .05
59 Tom Browning .05
60 Norm Charlton .05
61 Eric Davis .05
62 Rob Dibble .05
63 Bill Doran .05
64 Mariano Duncan .05
65 Chris Hammond .05
66 Billy Hatcher .05

67	Danny Jackson	.05
68	Barry Larkin	.05
69	Tim Layana **RC**	.05
70	Terry Lee **RC**	.05
71	Rick Mahler	.05
72	Hal Morris	.05
73	Randy Myers	.05
74	Ron Oester	.05
75	Joe Oliver	.05
76	Paul O'Neill	.05
77	Luis Quinones	.05
78	Jeff Reed	.05
79	Jose Rijo	.05
80	Chris Sabo	.05
81	Scott Scudder	.05
82	Herm Winningham	.05
83	Larry Andersen	.05
84	Marty Barrett	.05
85	Mike Boddicker	.05
86	Wade Boggs	.50
87	Tom Bolton	.05
88	Tom Brunansky	.05
89	Ellis Burks	.05
90	Roger Clemens	.55
91	Scott Cooper	.05
92	John Dopson	.05
93	Dwight Evans	.05
94	Wes Gardner	.05
95	Jeff Gray **RC**	.05
96	Mike Greenwell	.05
97	Greg Harris	.05
98	Daryl Irvine **RC**	.05
99	Dana Kiecker **RC**	.05
100	Randy Kutcher	.05
101	Dennis Lamp	.05
102	Mike Marshall	.05
103	John Marzano	.05
104	Rob Murphy	.05
105a	Tim Naehring **RC** (Seven-line career summary.)	.05
105b	Tim Naehring **RC** (Nine-line career summary.)	.05
106	Tony Pena	.05
107	Phil Plantier **RC**	.05
108	Carlos Quintana	.05
109	Jeff Reardon	.05
110	Jerry Reed	.05
111	Jody Reed	.05
112	Luis Rivera	.05
113a	Kevin Romine (One-line career summary.)	.05
113b	Kevin Romine (Two-line career summary.)	.05
114	Phil Bradley	.05
115	Ivan Calderon	.05
116	Wayne Edwards	.05
117	Alex Fernandez	.05
118	Carlton Fisk	.40
119	Scott Fletcher	.05
120	Craig Grebeck **RC**	.05
121	Ozzie Guillen	.05
122	Greg Hibbard	.05
123	Lance Johnson	.05
124	Barry Jones	.05
125a	Ron Karkovice (Two-line career summary.)	.05
125b	Ron Karkovice (One-line career summary.)	.05
126	Eric King	.05
127	Steve Lyons	.05
128	Carlos Martinez	.05
129	Jack McDowell	.05
130	Donn Pall	.05
131	Dan Pasqua	.05
132	Ken Patterson	.05
133	Melido Perez	.05
134	Adam Peterson	.05
135	Scott Radinsky **RC**	.05
136	Sammy Sosa	.50
137	Bobby Thigpen	.05
138	Frank Thomas	.40
139	Robin Ventura	.05
140	Daryl Boston	.05
141	Chuck Carr **RC**	.05
142	Mark Carreon	.05
143	David Cone	.05
144	Ron Darling	.05
145	Kevin Elster	.05
146	Sid Fernandez	.05
147	John Franco	.05
148	Dwight Gooden	.05
149	Tom Herr	.05
150	Todd Hundley	.05
151	Gregg Jefferies	.05
152	Howard Johnson	.05
153	Dave Magadan	.05
154	Kevin McReynolds	.05
155	Keith Miller	.05
156	Bob Ojeda	.05
157	Tom O'Malley	.05
158	Alejandro Pena	.05
159	Darren Reed **RC**	.05
160	Mackey Sasser	.05
161	Darryl Strawberry	.05
162	Tim Teufel	.05
163	Kelvin Torve	.05
164	Julio Valera	.05
165	Frank Viola	.05
166	Wally Whitehurst	.05
167	Jim Acker	.05
168	Derek Bell **RC**	.10
169	George Bell	.05
170	Willie Blair **RC**	.05
171	Pat Borders	.05
172	John Cerutti	.05
173	Junior Felix	.05
174	Tony Fernandez	.05
175	Kelly Gruber	.05
176	Tom Henke	.05
177	Glenallen Hill	.05
178	Jimmy Key	.05
179	Manny Lee	.05
180	Fred McGriff	.05
181	Rance Mulliniks	.05
182	Greg Myers	.05
183	John Olerud	.05
184	Luis Sojo	.05
185	Dave Steib	.05
186	Todd Stottlemyre	.05
187	Duane Ward	.05
188	David Wells	.05
189	Mark Whiten **RC**	.05
190	Ken Williams	.05
191	Frank Wills	.05
192	Mookie Wilson	.05
193	Don Aase	.05
194	Tim Belcher	.05
195	Hubie Brooks	.05
196	Dennis Cook	.05
197	Tim Crews	.05
198	Kal Daniels	.05
199	Kirk Gibson	.05
200	Jim Gott	.05
201	Alfredo Griffin	.05
202	Chris Gwynn	.05
203	Dave Hansen	.05
204	Lenny Harris	.05
205	Mike Hartley	.05
206	Mickey Hatcher	.05
207	Carlos Hernandez **RC**	.05
208	Orel Hershiser	.05
209	Jay Howell	.05
210	Mike Huff	.05
211	Stan Javier	.05
212	Ramon Martinez	.05
213	Mike Morgan	.05
214	Eddie Murray	.40
215	Jim Neidlinger **RC**	.05
216	Jose Offerman	.05
217	Jim Poole **RC**	.05
218	Juan Samuel	.05
219	Mike Scioscia	.05
220	Ray Searage	.05
221	Mike Sharperson	.05
222	Fernando Valenzuela	.05
223	Jose Vizcaino	.05
224	Mike Aldrete	.05
225	Scott Anderson **RC**	.05
226	Dennis Boyd	.05
227	Tim Burke	.05
228	Delino DeShields	.05
229	Mike Fitzgerald	.05
230	Tom Foley	.05
231	Steve Frey	.05
232	Andres Galarraga	.05
233	Mark Gardner	.05
234	Marquis Grissom	.05
235	Kevin Gross	.05
236	Drew Hall	.05
237	Dave Martinez	.05
238	Dennis Martinez	.05
239	Dale Mohorcic	.05
240	Chris Nabholz **RC**	.05
241	Otis Nixon	.05
242	Junior Noboa	.05
243	Spike Owen	.05
244	Tim Raines	.05
245	Mel Rojas **RC**	.10
246	Scott Ruskin **RC**	.05
247	Bill Sampen **RC**	.05
248	Nelson Santovenia	.05
249	Dave Schmidt	.05
250	Larry Walker	.05
251	Tim Wallach	.05
252	Dave Anderson	.05
253	Kevin Bass	.05
254	Steve Bedrosian	.05
255	Jeff Brantley	.05
256	John Burkett	.05
257	Brett Butler	.05
258	Gary Carter	.40
259	Will Clark	.05
260	Steve Decker **RC**	.05
261	Kelly Downs	.05
262	Scott Garrelts	.05
263	Terry Kennedy	.05
264	Mike LaCoss (Photo on back actually Ken Oberkfell.)	.05
265	Mark Leonard **RC**	.05
266	Greg Litton	.05
267	Kevin Mitchell	.05
268	Randy O'Neal	.05
269	Rick Parker **RC**	.05
270	Rick Reuschel	.05
271	Ernest Riles	.05
272	Don Robinson	.05
273	Robby Thompson	.05
274	Mark Thurmond	.05
275	Jose Uribe	.05
276	Matt Williams	.05
277	Trevor Wilson	.05
278	Gerald Alexander **RC**	.05
279	Brad Arnsberg	.05
280	Kevin Belcher **RC**	.05
281	Joe Bitker **RC**	.05
282	Kevin Brown	.05
283	Steve Buechele	.05
284	Jack Daugherty	.05
285	Julio Franco	.05
286	Juan Gonzalez	.20
287	Bill Haselman **RC**	.05
288	Charlie Hough	.05
289	Jeff Huson	.05
290	Pete Incaviglia	.05
291	Mike Jeffcoat	.05
292	Jeff Kunkel	.05
293	Gary Mielke	.05
294	Jamie Moyer	.05
295	Rafael Palmeiro	.35
296	Geno Petralli	.05
297	Gary Pettis	.05
298	Kevin Reimer	.05
299	Kenny Rogers	.05
300	Jeff Russell	.05
301	John Russell	.05
302a	Nolan Ryan (First horizontal line between 1979/1980.)	.75
302b	Nolan Ryan (First horizontal line between 1980/1981.)	.75
303	Ruben Sierra	.05
304	Bobby Witt	.05
305	Jim Abbott	.05
306	Kent Anderson	.05
307	Dante Bichette	.05
308	Bert Blyleven	.05
309	Chili Davis	.05
310	Brian Downing	.05
311	Mark Eichhorn	.05
312	Mike Fetters	.05
313	Chuck Finley	.05
314	Willie Fraser	.05
315	Bryan Harvey	.05
316	Donnie Hill	.05
317	Wally Joyner	.05
318	Mark Langston	.05
319	Kirk McCaskill	.05
320	John Orton	.05
321	Lance Parrish	.05
322	Luis Polonia	.05
323	Johnny Ray	.05
324	Bobby Rose	.05
325	Dick Schofield	.05
326	Rick Schu	.05
327a	Lee Stevens (Six-line career summary.)	.05
327b	Lee Stevens (Seven-line career summary.)	.05
328	Devon White	.05
329	Dave Winfield	.40
330	Cliff Young **RC**	.05
331	Dave Bergman	.05
332	Phil Clark **RC**	.05
333	Darnell Coles	.05
334	Milt Cuyler	.05
335	Cecil Fielder	.05
336	Travis Fryman	.05
337	Paul Gibson	.05
338	Jerry Don Gleaton	.05
339	Mike Heath	.05
340	Mike Henneman	.05
341	Chet Lemon	.05
342	Lance McCullers	.05
343	Jack Morris	.05
344	Lloyd Moseby	.05
345	Edwin Nunez	.05
346	Clay Parker	.05
347	Dan Petry	.05
348	Tony Phillips	.05
349	Jeff Robinson	.05
350	Mark Salas	.05
351	Mike Schwabe **RC**	.05
352	Larry Sheets	.05
353	John Shelby	.05
354	Frank Tanana	.05
355	Alan Trammell	.05
356	Gary Ward	.05
357	Lou Whitaker	.05
358	Beau Allred	.05
359	Sandy Alomar,Jr.	.05
360	Carlos Baerga	.05
361	Kevin Bearse **RC**	.05
362	Tom Brookens	.05
363	Jerry Browne	.05
364	Tom Candiotti	.05
365	Alex Cole	.05
366	John Farrell	.05
367	Felix Fermin	.05
368	Keith Hernandez	.05
369	Brook Jacoby	.05
370	Chris James	.05
371	Dion James	.05
372	Doug Jones	.05
373	Candy Maldonado	.05
374	Steve Olin	.05
375	Jesse Orosco	.05
376	Rudy Seanez	.05
377	Joel Skinner	.05
378	Cory Snyder	.05
379	Greg Swindell	.05
380	Sergio Valdez	.05
381	Mike Walker **RC**	.05
382	Colby Ward **RC**	.05
383	Turner Ward **RC**	.05
384	Mitch Webster	.05
385	Kevin Wickander	.05
386	Darrel Akerfelds	.05
387	Joe Boever	.05
388a	Rod Booker (No 1981 stats.)	.05
388b	Rod Booker (1981 stats included)	.05
389	Sil Campusano	.05
390	Don Carman	.05
391	Wes Chamberlain **RC**	.05
392	Pat Combs	.05
393	Darren Daulton	.05
394	Jose DeJesus	.05
395	Len Dykstra	.05
396	Jason Grimsley	.05
397	Charlie Hayes	.05
398	Von Hayes	.05
399	Dave Hollins **RC**	.05
400	Ken Howell	.05
401	Ricky Jordan	.05
402	John Kruk	.05
403	Steve Lake	.05
404	Chuck Malone **RC**	.05
405	Roger McDowell	.05
406	Chuck McElroy	.05
407	Mickey Morandini **RC**	.05
408	Terry Mulholland	.05
409	Dale Murphy	.15
410	Randy Ready	.05
411	Bruce Ruffin	.05
412	Dickie Thon	.05
413	Paul Assenmacher	.05
414	Damon Berryhill	.05
415	Mike Bielecki	.05
416	Shawn Boskie **RC**	.05
417	Dave Clark	.05
418	Doug Dascenzo	.05
419a	Andre Dawson (No 1976 stats.)	.25
419b	Andre Dawson (1976 stats included)	.25
420	Shawon Dunston	.05
421	Joe Girardi	.05
422	Mark Grace	.05
423	Mike Harkey	.05
424	Les Lancaster	.05
425	Bill Long	.05
426	Greg Maddux	.50
427	Derrick May	.05
428	Jeff Pico	.05
429	Domingo Ramos	.05
430	Luis Salazar	.05
431	Ryne Sandberg	.50
432	Dwight Smith	.05
433	Greg Smith	.05
434	Rick Sutcliffe	.05
435	Gary Varsho	.05
436	Hector Villanueva **RC**	.05
437	Jerome Walton	.05
438	Curtis Wilkerson	.05
439	Mitch Williams	.05
440	Steve Wilson	.05
441	Marvell Wynne	.05
442	Scott Bankhead	.05
443	Scott Bradley	.05
444	Greg Briley	.05
445	Mike Brumley	.05
446	Jay Buhner	.05
447	Dave Burba **RC**	.05
448	Henry Cotto	.05
449	Alvin Davis	.05
450	Ken Griffey Jr.	.60
451	Erik Hanson	.05
452	Gene Harris	.05
453	Brian Holman	.05
454	Mike Jackson	.05
455	Randy Johnson	.40
456	Jeffrey Leonard	.05
457	Edgar Martinez	.05
458	Tino Martinez	.05
459	Pete O'Brien	.05
460	Harold Reynolds	.05
461	Mike Schooler	.05
462	Bill Swift	.05
463	David Valle	.05
464	Omar Vizquel	.05
465	Matt Young	.05
466	Brady Anderson	.05
467	Jeff Ballard	.05
468	Juan Bell	.05
469a	Mike Devereaux ("Six" last word in career summary top line.)	.05
469b	Mike Devereaux ("Runs" last word in career summary top line.)	.05
470	Steve Finley	.05
471	Dave Gallagher	.05
472	Leo Gomez **RC**	.05
473	Rene Gonzales	.05
474	Pete Harnisch	.05
475	Kevin Hickey	.05
476	Chris Hoiles **RC**	.10
477	Sam Horn	.05
478	Tim Hulett	.05
479	Dave Johnson	.05
480	Ron Kittle	.05
481	Ben McDonald	.05
482	Bob Melvin	.05
483	Bob Milacki	.05
484	Randy Milligan	.05
485	John Mitchell **RC**	.05
486	Gregg Olson	.05
487	Joe Orsulak	.05
488	Joe Price	.05
489	Bill Ripken	.05
490	Cal Ripken, Jr.	.75
491	Curt Schilling	.25
492	David Segui **RC**	.10
493	Anthony Telford **RC**	.05
494	Mickey Tettleton	.05
495	Mark Williamson	.05
496	Craig Worthington	.05
497	Juan Agosto	.05
498	Eric Anthony	.05
499	Craig Biggio	.05
500	Ken Caminiti	.05
501	Casey Candaele	.05

502	Andujar Cedeno **RC**	.05
503	Danny Darwin	.05
504	Mark Davidson	.05
505	Glenn Davis	.05
506	Jim Deshaies	.05
507	Luis Gonzalez **RC**	1.00
508	Bill Gullickson	.05
509	Xavier Hernandez	.05
510	Brian Meyer	.05
511	Ken Oberkfell	.05
512	Mark Portugal	.05
513	Rafael Ramirez	.05
514	Karl Rhodes **RC**	.10
515	Mike Scott	.05
516	Mike Simms **RC**	.05
517	Dave Smith	.05
518	Franklin Stubbs	.05
519	Glenn Wilson	.05
520	Eric Yelding	.05
521	Gerald Young	.05
522	Shawn Abner	.05
523	Roberto Alomar	.20
524	Andy Benes	.05
525	Joe Carter	.05
526	Jack Clark	.05
527	Joey Cora	.05
528	Paul Faries **RC**	.05
529	Tony Gwynn	.50
530	Atlee Hammaker	.05
531	Greg Harris	.05
532	Thomas Howard **RC**	.05
533	Bruce Hurst	.05
534	Craig Lefferts	.05
535	Derek Lilliquist	.05
536	Fred Lynn	.05
537	Mike Pagliarulo	.05
538	Mark Parent	.05
539	Dennis Rasmussen	.05
540	Bip Roberts	.05
541	Richard Rodriguez **RC**	.05
542	Benito Santiago	.05
543	Calvin Schiraldi	.05
544	Eric Show	.05
545	Phil Stephenson	.05
546	Garry Templeton	.05
547	Ed Whitson	.05
548	Eddie Williams	.05
549	Kevin Appier	.05
550	Luis Aquino	.05
551	Bob Boone	.05
552	George Brett	.55
553	Jeff Conine **RC**	.30
554	Steve Crawford	.05
555	Mark Davis	.05
556	Storm Davis	.05
557	Jim Eisenreich	.05
558	Steve Farr	.05
559	Tom Gordon	.05
560	Mark Gubicza	.05
561	Bo Jackson	.10
562	Mike Macfarlane	.05
563	Brian McRae **RC**	.10
564	Jeff Montgomery	.05
565	Bill Pecota	.05
566	Gerald Perry	.05
567	Bret Saberhagen	.05
568	Jeff Schulz **RC**	.05
569	Kevin Seitzer	.05
570	Terry Shumpert **RC**	.05
571	Kurt Stillwell	.05
572	Danny Tartabull	.05
573	Gary Thurman	.05
574	Frank White	.05
575	Willie Wilson	.05
576	Chris Bosio	.05
577	Greg Brock	.05
578	George Canale	.05
579	Chuck Crim	.05
580	Rob Deer	.05
581	Edgar Diaz **RC**	.05
582	Tom Edens **RC**	.05
583	Mike Felder	.05
584	Jim Gantner	.05
585	Darryl Hamilton	.05
586	Ted Higuera	.05
587	Mark Knudson	.05
588	Bill Krueger	.05
589	Tim McIntosh	.05
590	Paul Mirabella	.05
591	Paul Molitor	.40
592	Jaime Navarro	.05
593	Dave Parker	.05
594	Dan Plesac	.05
595	Ron Robinson	.05
596	Gary Sheffield	.30
597	Bill Spiers	.05
598	B.J. Surhoff	.05
599	Greg Vaughn	.05
600	Randy Veres	.05
601	Robin Yount	.40
602a	Rick Aguilera (Five-line career summary.)	.05
602b	Rick Aguilera (Four-line career summary.)	.05
603	Allan Anderson	.05
604	Juan Berenguer	.05
605	Randy Bush	.05
606	Carmen Castillo	.05
607	Tim Drummond	.05
608	Scott Erickson **RC**	.10
609	Gary Gaetti	.05
610a	Greg Gagne (Horizontal lines under 82 Ft. Lauderdale, 84 Toledo and 87 Twins.)	.05
610b	Greg Gagne (Horizontal lines under 82 Orlando, 84 Twins and 88 Twins.)	.05
611	Dan Gladden	.05
612	Mark Guthrie	.05
613	Brian Harper	.05
614	Kent Hrbek	.05
615	Gene Larkin	.05
616	Terry Leach	.05
617	Nelson Liriano	.05
618	Shane Mack	.05
619	John Moses	.05
620	Pedro Munoz **RC**	.05
621	Al Newman	.05
622	Junior Ortiz	.05
623	Kirby Puckett	.50
624	Roy Smith	.05
625	Kevin Tapani	.05
626	Gary Wayne	.05
627	David West	.05
628	Cris Carpenter	.05
629	Vince Coleman	.05
630	Ken Dayley	.05
631	Jose DeLeon	.05
632	Frank DiPino	.05
633	Bernard Gilkey **RC**	.25
634	Pedro Guerrero	.05
635	Ken Hill	.05
636	Felix Jose	.05
637	Ray Lankford **RC**	.25
638	Joe Magrane	.05
639	Tom Niedenfuer	.05
640	Jose Oquendo	.05
641	Tom Pagnozzi	.05
642	Terry Pendleton	.05
643	Mike Perez **RC**	.05
644	Bryn Smith	.05
645	Lee Smith	.05
646	Ozzie Smith	.50
647	Scott Terry	.05
648	Bob Tewksbury	.05
649	Milt Thompson	.05
650	John Tudor	.05
651	Denny Walling	.05
652	Craig Wilson **RC**	.05
653	Todd Worrell	.05
654	Todd Zeile	.05
655	Oscar Azocar **RC**	.05
656	Steve Balboni	.05
657	Jesse Barfield	.05
658	Greg Cadaret	.05
659	Chuck Cary	.05
660	Rick Cerone	.05
661	Dave Eiland	.05
662a	Alvaro Espinoza (No 1979-80 stats.)	.05
662b	Alvaro Espinoza (1979-80 stats included)	.05
663	Bob Geren	.05
664	Lee Guetterman	.05
665	Mel Hall	.05
666a	Andy Hawkins (No 1978 stats.)	.05
666b	Andy Hawkins (1978 stats included)	.05
667	Jimmy Jones	.05
668	Roberto Kelly	.05
669	Dave LaPoint	.05
670	Tim Leary	.05
671	Jim Leyritz **RC**	.10
672	Kevin Maas	.05
673	Don Mattingly	.60
674	Matt Nokes	.05
675	Pascual Perez	.05
676	Eric Plunk	.05
677	Dave Righetti	.05
678	Jeff Robinson	.05
679	Steve Sax	.05
680	Mike Witt	.05
681	Steve Avery	.05
682	Mike Bell	.05
683	Jeff Blauser	.05
684	Francisco Cabrera	.05
685	Tony Castillo	.05
686	Marty Clary	.05
687	Nick Esasky	.05
688	Ron Gant	.05
689	Tom Glavine	.25
690	Mark Grant	.05
691	Tommy Gregg	.05
692	Dwayne Henry	.05
693	Dave Justice	.05
694	Jimmy Kremers **RC**	.05
695	Charlie Leibrandt	.05
696	Mark Lemke	.05
697	Oddibe McDowell	.05
698	Greg Olson **RC**	.05
699	Jeff Parrett	.05
700	Jim Presley	.05
701	Victor Rosario **RC**	.05
702	Lonnie Smith	.05
703	Pete Smith	.05
704	John Smoltz	.05
705	Mike Stanton	.05
706	Andres Thomas	.05
707	Jeff Treadway	.05
708	Jim Vatcher **RC**	.05
709	Ryne Sandberg, Cecil Fielder Home Run Kings	.10
710	Barry Bonds, Ken Griffey Jr. Second Generation Superstars	.65
711	Bobby Bonilla, Barry Larkin NLCS Team Leaders	.05
712	Bobby Thigpen, John Franco Top Game Savers	.05
713	Andre Dawson, Ryne Sandberg Chicago's 100 Club	.10
714	Athletics, Pirates, Reds, Red Sox Checklists	.05
715	Dodgers	.05
716	Expos, Giants, Rangers, Angels Checklists	.05
717	Tigers, Indians, Phillies, Cubs Checklists	.05
718	Checklists (Mariners, Orioles, Astros, Padres)	.05
719	Royals, Brewers, Twins, Cardinals Checklists	.05
720	Checklists (Yankees, Braves, Super Stars)	.05

Update

		NM/M
Complete Set (132):		3.00
Common Player:		.05
1	Glenn Davis	.05
2	Dwight Evans	.05
3	Jose Mesa	.05
4	Jack Clark	.05
5	Danny Darwin	.05
6	Steve Lyons	.05
7	Mo Vaughn	.05
8	Floyd Bannister	.05
9	Gary Gaetti	.05
10	Dave Parker	.05
11	Joey Cora	.05
12	Charlie Hough	.05
13	Matt Merullo	.05
14	Warren Newson	.05
15	Tim Raines	.05
16	Albert Belle	.05
17	Glenallen Hill	.05
18	Shawn Hillegas	.05
19	Mark Lewis	.05
20	Charles Nagy	.05
21	Mark Whiten	.05
22	John Cerutti	.05
23	Rob Deer	.05
24	Mickey Tettleton	.05
25	Warren Cromartie	.05
26	Kirk Gibson	.05
27	David Howard	.05
28	Brent Mayne	.05
29	Dante Bichette	.05
30	Mark Lee	.05
31	Julio Machado	.05
32	Edwin Nunez	.05
33	Willie Randolph	.05
34	Franklin Stubbs	.05
35	Bill Wegman	.05
36	Chili Davis	.05
37	Chuck Knoblauch	.05
38	Scott Leius	.05
39	Jack Morris	.05
40	Mike Pagliarulo	.05
41	Lenny Webster	.05
42	John Habyan	.05
43	Steve Howe	.05
44	Jeff Johnson	.05
45	Scott Kamieniecki	.05
46	Pat Kelly	.05
47	Hensley Meulens	.05
48	Wade Taylor	.05
49	Bernie Williams	.20
50	Kirk Dressendorfer	.05
51	Ernest Riles	.05
52	Rich DeLucia	.05
53	Tracy Jones	.05
54	Bill Krueger	.05
55	Alonzo Powell	.05
56	Jeff Schaefer	.05
57	Russ Swan	.05
58	John Barfield	.05
59	Rich Gossage	.10
60	Jose Guzman	.05
61	Dean Palmer	.05
62	Ivan Rodriguez **RC**	1.50
63	Roberto Alomar	.20
64	Tom Candiotti	.05
65	Joe Carter	.05
66	Ed Sprague	.05
67	Pat Tabler	.05
68	Mike Timlin	.05
69	Devon White	.05
70	Rafael Belliard	.05
71	Juan Berenguer	.05
72	Sid Bream	.05
73	Marvin Freeman	.05
74	Kent Mercker	.05
75	Otis Nixon	.05
76	Terry Pendleton	.05
77	George Bell	.05
78	Danny Jackson	.05
79	Chuck McElroy	.05
80	Gary Scott	.05
81	Heathcliff Slocumb	.05
82	Dave Smith	.05
83	Rick Wilkins	.05
84	Freddie Benavides	.05
85	Ted Power	.05
86	Mo Sanford	.05
87	Jeff Bagwell **RC**	2.00
88	Steve Finley	.05
89	Pete Harnisch	.05
90	Darryl Kile	.05
91	Brett Butler	.05
92	John Candelaria	.05
93	Gary Carter	.40
94	Kevin Gross	.05
95	Bob Ojeda	.05
96	Darryl Strawberry	.05
97	Ivan Calderon	.05
98	Ron Hassey	.05
99	Gilberto Reyes	.05
100	Hubie Brooks	.05
101	Rick Cerone	.05
102	Vince Coleman	.05
103	Jeff Innis	.05
104	Pete Schourek	.05
105	Andy Ashby	.05
106	Wally Backman	.05
107	Darrin Fletcher	.05
108	Tommy Greene	.05
109	John Morris	.05
110	Mitch Williams	.05
111	Lloyd McClendon	.05
112	Orlando Merced	.05
113	Vicente Palacios	.05
114	Gary Varsho	.05
115	John Wehner	.05
116	Rex Hudler	.05
117	Tim Jones	.05
118	Geronimo Pena	.05
119	Gerald Perry	.05
120	Larry Andersen	.05
121	Jerald Clark	.05
122	Scott Coolbaugh	.05
123	Tony Fernandez	.05
124	Darrin Jackson	.05
125	Fred McGriff	.05
126	Jose Mota	.05
127	Tim Teufel	.05
128	Bud Black	.05
129	Mike Felder	.05
130	Willie McGee	.05
131	Dave Righetti	.05
132	Checklist	.05

1992 Fleer

		NM/M
Unopened Factory Set (732):		17.50
Complete Set (720):		8.00
Common Player:		.05
Wax Pack (15):		.45
Wax Box (36):		10.00
Cello Pack (35):		1.00
Cello Box (24):		16.00
1	Brady Anderson	.05
2	Jose Bautista	.05
3	Juan Bell	.05
4	Glenn Davis	.05
5	Mike Devereaux	.05
6	Dwight Evans	.05
7	Mike Flanagan	.05
8	Leo Gomez	.05
9	Chris Hoiles	.05
10	Sam Horn	.05
11	Tim Hulett	.05
12	Dave Johnson	.05
13	Chito Martinez **RC**	.05
14	Ben McDonald	.05
15	Bob Melvin	.05
16	Luis Mercedes **RC**	.10
17	Jose Mesa	.05
18	Bob Milacki	.05
19	Randy Milligan	.05
20	Mike Mussina	.30
21	Gregg Olson	.05

22	Joe Orsulak	.05
23	Jim Poole	.05
24	Arthur Rhodes **RC**	.10
25	Billy Ripken	.05
26	Cal Ripken, Jr.	1.00
27	David Segui	.05
28	Roy Smith	.05
29	Anthony Telford	.05
30	Mark Williamson	.05
31	Craig Worthington	.05
32	Wade Boggs	.55
33	Tom Bolton	.05
34	Tom Brunansky	.05
35	Ellis Burks	.05
36	Jack Clark	.05
37	Roger Clemens	.60
38	Danny Darwin	.05
39	Mike Greenwell	.05
40	Joe Hesketh	.05
41	Daryl Irvine	.05
42	Dennis Lamp	.05
43	Tony Pena	.05
44	Phil Plantier	.05
45	Carlos Quintana	.05
46	Jeff Reardon	.05
47	Jody Reed	.05
48	Luis Rivera	.05
49	Mo Vaughn	.05
50	Jim Abbott	.05
51	Kyle Abbott	.05
52	Ruben Amaro Jr. **RC**	.05
53	Scott Bailes	.05
54	Chris Beasley **RC**	.05
55	Mark Eichhorn	.05
56	Mike Fetters	.05
57	Chuck Finley	.05
58	Gary Gaetti	.05
59	Dave Gallagher	.05
60	Donnie Hill	.05
61	Bryan Harvey	.05
62	Wally Joyner	.05
63	Mark Langston	.05
64	Kirk McCaskill	.05
65	John Orton	.05
66	Lance Parrish	.05
67	Luis Polonia	.05
68	Bobby Rose	.05
69	Dick Schofield	.05
70	Luis Sojo	.05
71	Lee Stevens	.05
72	Dave Winfield	.50
73	Cliff Young	.05
74	Wilson Alvarez	.05
75	Esteban Beltre **RC**	.05
76	Joey Cora	.05
77	Brian Drahman **RC**	.05
78	Alex Fernandez	.05
79	Carlton Fisk	.50
80	Scott Fletcher	.05
81	Craig Grebeck	.05
82	Ozzie Guillen	.05
83	Greg Hibbard	.05
84	Charlie Hough	.05
85	Mike Huff	.05
86	Bo Jackson	.10
87	Lance Johnson	.05
88	Ron Karkovice	.05
89	Jack McDowell	.05
90	Matt Merullo	.05
91	Warren Newson **RC**	.05
92	Donn Pall	.05
93	Dan Pasqua	.05
94	Ken Patterson	.05
95	Melido Perez	.05
96	Scott Radinsky	.05
97	Tim Raines	.05
98	Sammy Sosa	.55
99	Bobby Thigpen	.05
100	Frank Thomas	.50
101	Robin Ventura	.05
102	Mike Aldrete	.05
103	Sandy Alomar, Jr.	.05
104	Carlos Baerga	.05
105	Albert Belle	.05
106	Willie Blair	.05
107	Jerry Browne	.05
108	Alex Cole	.05
109	Felix Fermin	.05
110	Glenallen Hill	.05
111	Shawn Hillegas	.05
112	Chris James	.05
113	Reggie Jefferson	.05
114	Doug Jones	.05
115	Eric King	.05
116	Mark Lewis	.05
117	Carlos Martinez	.05
118	Charles Nagy	.05
119	Rod Nichols	.05
120	Steve Olin	.05
121	Jesse Orosco	.05
122	Rudy Seanez	.05
123	Joel Skinner	.05
124	Greg Swindell	.05
125	Jim Thome	.50
126	Mark Whiten	.05
127	Scott Aldred	.05
128	Andy Allanson	.05
129	John Cerutti	.05
130	Milt Cuyler	.05
131	Mike Dalton **RC**	.05
132	Rob Deer	.05
133	Cecil Fielder	.05
134	Travis Fryman	.05
135	Dan Gakeler **RC**	.05
136	Paul Gibson	.05
137	Bill Gullickson	.05
138	Mike Henneman	.05
139	Pete Incaviglia	.05
140	Mark Leiter **RC**	.05
141	Scott Livingstone **RC**	.10
142	Lloyd Moseby	.05
143	Tony Phillips	.05
144	Mark Salas	.05
145	Frank Tanana	.05
146	Walt Terrell	.05
147	Mickey Tettleton	.05
148	Alan Trammell	.05
149	Lou Whitaker	.05
150	Kevin Appier	.05
151	Luis Aquino	.05
152	Todd Benzinger	.05
153	Mike Boddicker	.05
154	George Brett	.60
155	Storm Davis	.05
156	Jim Eisenreich	.05
157	Kirk Gibson	.05
158	Tom Gordon	.05
159	Mark Gubicza	.05
160	David Howard **RC**	.05
161	Mike Macfarlane	.05
162	Brent Mayne	.05
163	Brian McRae	.05
164	Jeff Montgomery	.05
165	Bill Pecota	.05
166	Harvey Pulliam **RC**	.05
167	Bret Saberhagen	.05
168	Kevin Seitzer	.05
169	Terry Shumpert	.05
170	Kurt Stillwell	.05
171	Danny Tartabull	.05
172	Gary Thurman	.05
173	Dante Bichette	.05
174	Kevin Brown	.05
175	Chuck Crim	.05
176	Jim Gantner	.05
177	Darryl Hamilton	.05
178	Ted Higuera	.05
179	Darren Holmes	.05
180	Mark Lee	.05
181	Julio Machado	.05
182	Paul Molitor	.50
183	Jaime Navarro	.05
184	Edwin Nunez	.05
185	Dan Plesac	.05
186	Willie Randolph	.05
187	Ron Robinson	.05
188	Gary Sheffield	.30
189	Bill Spiers	.05
190	B.J. Surhoff	.05
191	Dale Sveum	.05
192	Greg Vaughn	.05
193	Bill Wegman	.05
194	Robin Yount	.50
195	Rick Aguilera	.05
196	Allan Anderson	.05
197	Steve Bedrosian	.05
198	Randy Bush	.05
199	Larry Casian	.05
200	Chili Davis	.05
201	Scott Erickson	.05
202	Greg Gagne	.05
203	Dan Gladden	.05
204	Brian Harper	.05
205	Kent Hrbek	.05
206	Chuck Knoblauch	.05
207	Gene Larkin	.05
208	Terry Leach	.05
209	Scott Leius	.05
210	Shane Mack	.05
211	Jack Morris	.05
212	Pedro Munoz	.05
213	Denny Neagle **RC**	.10
214	Al Newman	.05
215	Junior Ortiz	.05
216	Mike Pagliarulo	.05
217	Kirby Puckett	.55
218	Paul Sorrento	.05
219	Kevin Tapani	.05
220	Lenny Webster	.05
221	Jesse Barfield	.05
222	Greg Cadaret	.05
223	Dave Eiland	.05
224	Alvaro Espinoza	.05
225	Steve Farr	.05
226	Bob Geren	.05
227	Lee Guetterman	.05
228	John Habyan	.05
229	Mel Hall	.05
230	Steve Howe	.05
231	Mike Humphreys **RC**	.05
232	Scott Kamieniecki **RC**	.10
233	Pat Kelly	.05
234	Roberto Kelly	.05
235	Tim Leary	.05
236	Kevin Maas	.05
237	Don Mattingly	.60
238	Hensley Meulens	.05
239	Matt Nokes	.05
240	Pascual Perez	.05
241	Eric Plunk	.05
242	John Ramos **RC**	.05
243	Scott Sanderson	.05
244	Steve Sax	.05
245	Wade Taylor **RC**	.05
246	Randy Velarde	.05
247	Bernie Williams	.05
248	Troy Afenir	.05
249	Harold Baines	.05
250	Lance Blankenship	.05
251	Mike Bordick **RC**	.10
252	Jose Canseco	.30
253	Steve Chitren	.05
254	Ron Darling	.05
255	Dennis Eckersley	.45
256	Mike Gallego	.05
257	Dave Henderson	.05
258	Rickey Henderson	.50
259	Rick Honeycutt	.05
260	Brook Jacoby	.05
261	Carney Lansford	.05
262	Mark McGwire	.75
263	Mike Moore	.05
264	Gene Nelson	.05
265	Jamie Quirk	.05
266	Joe Slusarski **RC**	.10
267	Terry Steinbach	.05
268	Dave Stewart	.05
269	Todd Van Poppel	.05
270	Walt Weiss	.05
271	Bob Welch	.05
272	Curt Young	.05
273	Scott Bradley	.05
274	Greg Briley	.05
275	Jay Buhner	.05
276	Henry Cotto	.05
277	Alvin Davis	.05
278	Rich DeLucia	.05
279	Ken Griffey Jr.	.65
280	Erik Hanson	.05
281	Brian Holman	.05
282	Mike Jackson	.05
283	Randy Johnson	.50
284	Tracy Jones	.05
285	Bill Krueger	.05
286	Edgar Martinez	.05
287	Tino Martinez	.05
288	Rob Murphy	.05
289	Pete O'Brien	.05
290	Alonzo Powell	.05
291	Harold Reynolds	.05
292	Mike Schooler	.05
293	Russ Swan	.05
294	Bill Swift	.05
295	Dave Valle	.05
296	Omar Vizquel	.05
297	Gerald Alexander	.05
298	Brad Arnsberg	.05
299	Kevin Brown	.05
300	Jack Daugherty	.05
301	Mario Diaz	.05
302	Brian Downing	.05
303	Julio Franco	.05
304	Juan Gonzalez	.25
305	Rich Gossage	.10
306	Jose Guzman	.05
307	Jose Hernandez **RC**	.05
308	Jeff Huson	.05
309	Mike Jeffcoat	.05
310	Terry Mathews **RC**	.05
311	Rafael Palmeiro	.45
312	Dean Palmer	.05
313	Geno Petralli	.05
314	Gary Pettis	.05
315	Kevin Reimer	.05
316	Ivan Rodriguez	.45
317	Kenny Rogers	.05
318	Wayne Rosenthal **RC**	.05
319	Jeff Russell	.05
320	Nolan Ryan	1.00
321	Ruben Sierra	.05
322	Jim Acker	.05
323	Roberto Alomar	.20
324	Derek Bell	.05
325	Pat Borders	.05
326	Tom Candiotti	.05
327	Joe Carter	.05
328	Rob Ducey	.05
329	Kelly Gruber	.05
330	Juan Guzman **RC**	.25
331	Tom Henke	.05
332	Jimmy Key	.05
333	Manny Lee	.05
334	Al Leiter	.05
335	Bob MacDonald **RC**	.05
336	Candy Maldonado	.05
337	Rance Mulliniks	.05
338	Greg Myers	.05
339	John Olerud	.05
340	Ed Sprague **RC**	.10
341	Dave Stieb	.05
342	Todd Stottlemyre	.05
343	Mike Timlin **RC**	.10
344	Duane Ward	.05
345	David Wells	.05
346	Devon White	.05
347	Mookie Wilson	.05
348	Eddie Zosky	.05
349	Steve Avery	.05
350	Mike Bell	.05
351	Rafael Belliard	.05
352	Juan Berenguer	.05
353	Jeff Blauser	.05
354	Sid Bream	.05
355	Francisco Cabrera	.05
356	Marvin Freeman	.05
357	Ron Gant	.05
358	Tom Glavine	.30
359	Brian Hunter **RC**	.05
360	Dave Justice	.05
361	Charlie Leibrandt	.05
362	Mark Lemke	.05
363	Kent Mercker	.05
364	Keith Mitchell **RC**	.05
365	Greg Olson	.05
366	Terry Pendleton	.05
367	Armando Reynoso **RC**	.05
368	Deion Sanders	.10
369	Lonnie Smith	.05
370	Pete Smith	.05
371	John Smoltz	.05
372	Mike Stanton	.05
373	Jeff Treadway	.05
374	Mark Wohlers **RC**	.05
375	Paul Assenmacher	.05
376	George Bell	.05
377	Shawn Boskie	.05
378	Frank Castillo **RC**	.05
379	Andre Dawson	.25
380	Shawon Dunston	.05
381	Mark Grace	.05
382	Mike Harkey	.05
383	Danny Jackson	.05
384	Les Lancaster	.05
385	Cedric Landrum **RC**	.05
386	Greg Maddux	.55
387	Derrick May	.05
388	Chuck McElroy	.05
389	Ryne Sandberg	.55
390	Heathcliff Slocumb **RC**	.10
391	Dave Smith	.05
392	Dwight Smith	.05
393	Rick Sutcliffe	.05
394	Hector Villanueva	.05
395	Chico Walker **RC**	.05
396	Jerome Walton	.05
397	Rick Wilkins **RC**	.15
398	Jack Armstrong	.05
399	Freddie Benavides **RC**	.05
400	Glenn Braggs	.05
401	Tom Browning	.05
402	Norm Charlton	.05
403	Eric Davis	.05
404	Rob Dibble	.05
405	Bill Doran	.05
406	Mariano Duncan	.05
407	Kip Gross **RC**	.05
408	Chris Hammond	.05
409	Billy Hatcher	.05
410	Chris Jones **RC**	.05
411	Barry Larkin	.05
412	Hal Morris	.05
413	Randy Myers	.05
414	Joe Oliver	.05
415	Paul O'Neill	.05
416	Ted Power	.05
417	Luis Quinones	.05
418	Jeff Reed	.05
419	Jose Rijo	.05
420	Chris Sabo	.05
421	Reggie Sanders	.05
422	Scott Scudder	.05
423	Glenn Sutko	.05
424	Eric Anthony	.05
425	Jeff Bagwell	.50
426	Craig Biggio	.05
427	Ken Caminiti	.05
428	Casey Candaele	.05
429	Mike Capel	.05
430	Andujar Cedeno	.05
431	Jim Corsi	.05
432	Mark Davidson	.05
433	Steve Finley	.05
434	Luis Gonzalez	.05
435	Pete Harnisch	.05
436	Dwayne Henry	.05
437	Xavier Hernandez	.05
438	Jimmy Jones	.05
439	Darryl Kile **RC**	.05
440	Rob Mallicoat **RC**	.05
441	Andy Mota **RC**	.05
442	Al Osuna	.05
443	Mark Portugal	.05
444	Scott Servais **RC**	.10
445	Mike Simms	.05
446	Gerald Young	.05
447	Tim Belcher	.05
448	Brett Butler	.05
449	John Candelaria	.05
450	Gary Carter	.50
451	Dennis Cook	.05
452	Tim Crews	.05
453	Kal Daniels	.05
454	Jim Gott	.05
455	Alfredo Griffin	.05
456	Kevin Gross	.05
457	Chris Gwynn	.05
458	Lenny Harris	.05
459	Orel Hershiser	.05
460	Jay Howell	.05
461	Stan Javier	.05
462	Eric Karros	.05
463	Ramon Martinez	.05
464	Roger McDowell	.05
465	Mike Morgan	.05
466	Eddie Murray	.50
467	Jose Offerman	.05
468	Bob Ojeda	.05
469	Juan Samuel	.05
470	Mike Scioscia	.05
471	Darryl Strawberry	.05
472	Bret Barberie **RC**	.10
473	Brian Barnes	.05
474	Eric Bullock	.05
475	Ivan Calderon	.05
476	Delino DeShields	.05
477	Jeff Fassero **RC**	.10
478	Mike Fitzgerald	.05
479	Steve Frey	.05
480	Andres Galarraga	.05
481	Mark Gardner	.05

482	Marquis Grissom	.05
483	Chris Haney **RC**	.05
484	Barry Jones	.05
485	Dave Martinez	.05
486	Dennis Martinez	.05
487	Chris Nabholz	.05
488	Spike Owen	.05
489	Gilberto Reyes	.05
490	Mel Rojas	.05
491	Scott Ruskin	.05
492	Bill Sampen	.05
493	Larry Walker	.05
494	Tim Wallach	.05
495	Daryl Boston	.05
496	Hubie Brooks	.05
497	Tim Burke	.05
498	Mark Carreon	.05
499	Tony Castillo	.05
500	Vince Coleman	.05
501	David Cone	.05
502	Kevin Elster	.05
503	Sid Fernandez	.05
504	John Franco	.05
505	Dwight Gooden	.05
506	Todd Hundley	.05
507	Jeff Innis	.05
508	Gregg Jefferies	.05
509	Howard Johnson	.05
510	Dave Magadan	.05
511	Terry McDaniel **RC**	.05
512	Kevin McReynolds	.05
513	Keith Miller	.00
514	Charlie O'Brien	.05
515	Mackey Sasser	.05
516	Pete Schourek **RC**	.05
517	Julio Valera	.05
518	Frank Viola	.05
519	Wally Whitehurst	.05
520	Anthony Young **RC**	.05
521	Andy Ashby **RC**	.10
522	Kim Batiste **RC**	.05
523	Joe Boever	.05
524	Wes Chamberlain	.05
525	Pat Combs	.05
526	Danny Cox	.05
527	Darren Daulton	.05
528	Jose DeJesus	.05
529	Len Dykstra	.05
530	Darrin Fletcher	.05
531	Tommy Greene	.05
532	Jason Grimsley	.05
533	Charlie Hayes	.05
534	Von Hayes	.05
535	Dave Hollins	.05
536	Ricky Jordan	.05
537	John Kruk	.05
538	Jim Lindeman	.05
539	Mickey Morandini	.05
540	Terry Mulholland	.05
541	Dale Murphy	.20
542	Randy Ready	.05
543	Wally Ritchie	.05
544	Bruce Ruffin	.05
545	Steve Searcy	.05
546	Dickie Thon	.05
547	Mitch Williams	.05
548	Stan Belinda	.05
549	Jay Bell	.05
550	Barry Bonds	1.00
551	Bobby Bonilla	.05
552	Steve Buechele	.05
553	Doug Drabek	.05
554	Neal Heaton	.05
555	Jeff King	.05
556	Bob Kipper	.05
557	Bill Landrum	.05
558	Mike LaValliere	.05
559	Jose Lind	.05
560	Lloyd McClendon	.05
561	Orlando Merced	.05
562	Bob Patterson	.05
563	Joe Redfield **RC**	.05
564	Gary Redus	.05
565	Rosario Rodriguez	.05
566	Don Slaught	.05
567	John Smiley	.05
568	Zane Smith	.05
569	Randy Tomlin	.05
570	Andy Van Slyke	.05
571	Gary Varsho	.05
572	Bob Walk	.05
573	John Wehner **RC**	.05
574	Juan Agosto	.05
575	Cris Carpenter	.05
576	Jose DeLeon	.05
577	Rich Gedman	.05
578	Bernard Gilkey	.05
579	Pedro Guerrero	.05
580	Ken Hill	.05
581	Rex Hudler	.05
582	Felix Jose	.05
583	Ray Lankford	.05
584	Omar Olivares	.05
585	Jose Oquendo	.05
586	Tom Pagnozzi	.05
587	Geronimo Pena	.05
588	Mike Perez	.05
589	Gerald Perry	.05
590	Bryn Smith	.05
591	Lee Smith	.05
592	Ozzie Smith	.55
593	Scott Terry	.05
594	Bob Tewksbury	.05
595	Milt Thompson	.05
596	Todd Zeile	.05

597	Larry Andersen	.05
598	Oscar Azocar	.05
599	Andy Benes	.05
600	Ricky Bones **RC**	.05
601	Jerald Clark	.05
602	Pat Clements	.05
603	Paul Faries	.05
604	Tony Fernandez	.05
605	Tony Gwynn	.55
606	Greg Harris	.05
607	Thomas Howard	.05
608	Bruce Hurst	.05
609	Darrin Jackson	.05
610	Tom Lampkin	.05
611	Craig Lefferts	.05
612	Jim Lewis **RC**	.05
613	Mike Maddux	.05
614	Fred McGriff	.05
615	Jose Melendez **RC**	.05
616	Jose Mota **RC**	.05
617	Dennis Rasmussen	.05
618	Bip Roberts	.05
619	Rich Rodriguez	.05
620	Benito Santiago	.05
621	Craig Shipley **RC**	.05
622	Tim Teufel	.05
623	Kevin Ward **RC**	.05
624	Ed Whitson	.05
625	Dave Anderson	.05
626	Kevin Bass	.05
627	Rod Beck **RC**	.10
628	Bud Black	.05
629	Jeff Brantley	.05
630	John Burkett	.05
631	Will Clark	.05
632	Royce Clayton	.05
633	Steve Decker	.05
634	Kelly Downs	.05
635	Mike Felder	.05
636	Scott Garrelts	.05
637	Eric Gunderson	.05
638	Bryan Hickerson **RC**	.05
639	Darren Lewis	.05
640	Greg Litton	.05
641	Kirt Manwaring	.05
642	Paul McClellan **RC**	.05
643	Willie McGee	.05
644	Kevin Mitchell	.05
645	Francisco Olivares	.05
646	Mike Remlinger **RC**	.10
647	Dave Righetti	.05
648	Robby Thompson	.05
649	Jose Uribe	.05
650	Matt Williams	.05
651	Trevor Wilson	.05
652	Tom Goodwin	.05
653	Terry Bross	.05
654	Mike Christopher **RC**	.05
655	Kenny Lofton	.05
656	Chris Cron **RC**	.05
657	Willie Banks	.05
658	Pat Rice **RC**	.05
659a	Rob Mauer **RC**	
	(Last name misspelled.)	.75
659b	Rob Maurer **RC** (Corrected)	.05
660	Don Harris	.05
661	Henry Rodriguez	.05
662	Cliff Brantley **RC**	.05
663	Mike Linskey **RC**	.05
664	Gary Disarcina	.05
665	Gil Heredia **RC**	.10
666	Vinny Castilla **RC**	.50
667	Paul Abbott	.05
668	Monty Fariss	.05
669	Jarvis Brown **RC**	.05
670	Wayne Kirby **RC**	.05
671	Scott Brosius **RC**	.05
672	Bob Hamelin	.05
673	Joel Johnston **RC**	.05
674	Tim Spehr **RC**	.05
675	Jeff Gardner **RC**	.05
676	Rico Rossy **RC**	.05
677	Roberto Hernandez **RC**	.20
678	Ted Wood **RC**	.05
679	Cal Eldred	.05
680	Sean Berry	.05
681	Rickey Henderson	.20
682	Nolan Ryan	.25
683	Dennis Martinez	.05
684	Wilson Alvarez	.05
685	Joe Carter	.05
686	Dave Winfield	.20
687	David Cone	.05
688	Jose Canseco	.15
689	Howard Johnson	.05
690	Julio Franco	.05
691	Terry Pendleton	.05
692	Cecil Fielder	.05
693	Scott Erickson	.05
694	Tom Glavine	.05
695	Dennis Martinez	.05
696	Bryan Harvey	.05
697	Lee Smith	.05
698	Roberto & Sandy Alomar,	
	Roberto & Sandy Alomar	
	Super Siblings	.10
699	Bobby Bonilla, Will Clark	
	The Indispensables	.05
700	Mark Wohlers, Kent Mercker,	
	Alejandro Pena Teamwork	.05
701	Chris Jones, Bo Jackson,	
	Gregg Olson, Frank Thomas	
	Tiger Tandems	.05
702	Brett Butler, Paul Molitor	
	The Ignitors	.10

703	Cal Ripken Jr., Joe Carter	
	The Indispensables II	.20
704	Barry Larkin, Kirby Puckett	
	Power Packs	.15
705	Mo Vaughn, Cecil Fielder	
	Today and Tomorrow	.05
706	Ramon Martinez, Ozzie Guillen	
	Teenage Sensations	.05
707	Harold Baines, Wade Boggs	
	Designated Hitters	.20
708	Robin Yount	.35
709	Ken Griffey Jr.	.60
710	Nolan Ryan	.75
711	Cal Ripken, Jr.	.75
712	Frank Thomas	.50
713	Dave Justice	.05
714	Checklist 1-101	.05
715	Checklist 102-194	.05
716	Checklist 195-296	.05
717	Checklist 297-397	.05
718	Checklist 398-494	.05
719	Checklist 495-596	.05
720a	Checklist 597-720	
	(659 Rob Mauer)	.05
720b	Checklist 597-720	
	(659 Rob Maurer)	.05

All-Stars

KIRBY PUCKETT

FLEER ALL-STARS

		NM/M
Complete Set (24):		8.00
Common Player:		.10
1	Felix Jose	.10
2	Tony Gwynn	1.25
3	Barry Bonds	3.00
4	Bobby Bonilla	.10
5	Mike LaValliere	.10
6	Tom Glavine	.40
7	Ramon Martinez	.10
8	Lee Smith	.10
9	Mickey Tettleton	.10
10	Scott Erickson	.10
11	Frank Thomas	.75
12	Danny Tartabull	.10
13	Will Clark	.10
14	Ryne Sandberg	1.25
15	Terry Pendleton	.10
16	Barry Larkin	.10
17	Rafael Palmeiro	.65
18	Julio Franco	.10
19	Robin Ventura	.10
20	Cal Ripken, Jr.	3.00
21	Joe Carter	.10
22	Kirby Puckett	1.25
23	Ken Griffey Jr.	2.25
24	Jose Canseco	.50

Lumber Co.

THE LUMBER CO.

		NM/M
Complete Set (9):		5.00
Common Player:		.25
1	Cecil Fielder	.25
2	Mickey Tettleton	.25
3	Darryl Strawberry	.25
4	Ryne Sandberg	1.00
5	Jose Canseco	.40
6	Matt Williams	.25
7	Cal Ripken, Jr.	2.00

8	Barry Bonds	2.00
9	Ron Gant	.25

Roger Clemens

ROGER CLEMENS
CAREER HIGHLIGHTS

		NM/M
Complete Set (15):		6.00
Common Card:		.50
Autographed Card:		40.00
1	Quiet Storm	.50
2	Courted by the Mets and	
	Twins	.50
3	The Show	.50
4	A Rocket Launched	.50
5	Time of Trial	.50
6	Break Through	.50
7	Play it Again Roger	.50
8	Business as Usual	.50
9	Heee's Back	.50
10	Blood, Sweat and Tears	.50
11	Prime of Life	.50
12	Man for Every Season	.50
13	Cooperstown Bound	1.50
14	The Heat of the Moment	1.50
15	Final Words	1.50

Rookie Sensations

ROOKIE SENSATIONS

TODD VAN POPPEL
ATHLETICS

		NM/M
Complete Set (20):		13.50
Common Player:		.35
1	Frank Thomas	6.00
2	Todd Van Poppel	.35
3	Orlando Merced	.35
4	Jeff Bagwell	6.00
5	Jeff Fassero	.35
6	Darren Lewis	.35
7	Milt Cuyler	.35
8	Mike Timlin	.35
9	Brian McRae	.35
10	Chuck Knoblauch	.35
11	Rich DeLucia	.35
12	Ivan Rodriguez	4.50
13	Juan Guzman	.35
14	Steve Chitren	.35
15	Mark Wohlers	.35
16	Wes Chamberlain	.35
17	Ray Lankford	.35
18	Chito Martinez	.35
19	Phil Plantier	.35
20	Scott Leius	.35

Smoke 'N Heat

		NM/M
Complete Set (12):		7.50
Common Player:		.25
1	Lee Smith	.25
2	Jack McDowell	.25
3	David Cone	.25
4	Roger Clemens	2.00
5	Nolan Ryan	3.00
6	Scott Erickson	.25
7	Tom Glavine	.50
8	Dwight Gooden	.25
9	Andy Benes	.25

STEVE AVERY

10	Steve Avery	.25
11	Randy Johnson	1.00
12	Jim Abbott	.25

Team Leaders

RAFAEL PALMEIRO

		NM/M
Complete Set (20):		10.00
Common Player:		.50
1	Don Mattingly	2.00
2	Howard Johnson	.50
3	Chris Sabo	.50
4	Carlton Fisk	1.25
5	Kirby Puckett	1.50
6	Cecil Fielder	.50
7	Tony Gwynn	1.50
8	Will Clark	.50
9	Bobby Bonilla	.50
10	Len Dykstra	.50
11	Tom Glavine	.75
12	Rafael Palmeiro	1.00
13	Wade Boggs	1.50
14	Joe Carter	.50
15	Ken Griffey Jr.	2.50
16	Darryl Strawberry	.50
17	Cal Ripken, Jr.	3.00
18	Danny Tartabull	.50
19	Jose Canseco	.75
20	Andre Dawson	.50

Update

RYAN THOMPSON — OUTFIELD

		NM/M
Complete Set (136):		60.00
Common Player:		.05
H1	Ken Griffey Jr. 1992 All-Star Game MVP	1.50
H2	Robin Yount 3000 Career Hits	.50
H3	Jeff Reardon Major League Career Saves Record	.10
H4	Cecil Fielder Record RBI Performance	.05
1	Todd Frohwirth	.05
2	Alan Mills	.05
3	Rick Sutcliffe	.05
4	John Valentin RC	.25
5	Frank Viola	.05
6	Bob Zupcic	.05
7	Mike Butcher	.05
8	Chad Curtis RC	.50
9	Damion Easley RC	.25
10	Tim Salmon	.50
11	Julio Valera	.05
12	George Bell	.05
13	Roberto Hernandez	.05
14	Shawn Jeter	.05
15	Thomas Howard	.05
16	Jesse Levis	.05
17	Kenny Lofton	.05
18	Paul Sorrento	.05
19	Rico Brogna	.05
20	John Doherty	.05
21	Dan Gladden	.05
22	Buddy Groom	.05
23	Shawn Hare	.05
24	John Kiely	.05
25	Kurt Knudsen	.05
26	Gregg Jefferies	.05
27	Wally Joyner	.05
28	Kevin Koslofski	.05
29	Kevin McReynolds	.05
30	Rusty Meacham	.05
31	Keith Miller	.05
32	Hipolito Pichardo	.05
33	James Austin	.05
34	Scott Fletcher	.05
35	John Jaha RC	.05
36	Pat Listach	.05
37	Dave Nilsson	.05
38	Kevin Seitzer	.05
39	Tom Edens	.05
40	Pat Mahomes	.05
41	John Smiley	.05
42	Charlie Hayes	.05
43	Sam Militello	.05
44	Andy Stankiewicz	.05
45	Danny Tartabull	.05
46	Bob Wickman	.05
47	Jerry Browne	.05
48	Kevin Campbell	.05
49	Vince Horsman	.05
50	Troy Neel	.05
51	Ruben Sierra	.05
52	Bruce Walton	.05
53	Willie Wilson	.05
54	Bret Boone	.50
55	Dave Fleming	.05
56	Kevin Mitchell	.05
57	Jeff Nelson RC	.05
58	Shane Turner	.05
59	Jose Canseco	.65
60	Jeff Frye RC	.05
61	Damilo Leon	.05
62	Roger Pavlik	.05
63	David Cone	.05
64	Pat Hentgen	.05
65	Randy Knorr	.05
66	Jack Morris	.05
67	Dave Winfield	1.00
68	David Nied RC	.05
69	Otis Nixon	.05
70	Alejandro Pena	.05
71	Jeff Reardon	.05
72	Alex Arias	.05
73	Jim Bullinger	.05
74	Mike Morgan	.05
75	Rey Sanchez	.05
76	Bob Scanlan	.05
77	Sammy Sosa	3.00
78	Scott Bankhead	.05
79	Tim Belcher	.05
80	Steve Foster	.05
81	Willie Greene	.05
82	Bip Roberts	.05
83	Scott Ruskin	.05
84	Greg Swindell	.05
85	Juan Guerrero	.05
86	Butch Henry	.05
87	Doug Jones	.05
88	Brian Williams	.05
89	Tom Candiotti	.05
90	Eric Davis	.05
91	Carlos Hernandez	.05
92	Mike Piazza RC	45.00
93	Mike Sharperson	.05
94	Eric Young	.05
95	Moises Alou	.05
96	Greg Colbrunn	.05
97	Wil Cordero	.05
98	Ken Hill	.05
99	John Vander Wal	.05
100	John Wetteland	.05
101	Bobby Bonilla	.05
102	Eric Hilman	.05
103	Pat Howell	.05
104	Jeff Kent RC	15.00
105	Dick Schofield	.05
106	Ryan Thompson RC	.05
107	Chico Walker	.05
108	Juan Bell	.05
109	Jeff Grotewold	.05
110	Mariano Duncan	.05
111	Ben Rivera	.65
112	Curt Schilling	.65
113	Victor Cole	.05
114	Al Martin	.05
115	Roger Mason	.05
116	Blas Minor	.05
117	Tim Wakefield	4.00
118	Mark Clark RC	.05
119	Rheal Cormier	.05
120	Donovan Osborne	.05
121	Todd Worrell	.05
122	Jeremy Hernandez	.05
123	Randy Myers	.05
124	Frank Seminara	.05
125	Gary Sheffield	.75
126	Dan Walters	.05
127	Steve Hosey	.05
128	Mike Jackson	.05
129	Jim Pena	.05
130	Cory Snyder	.05
131	Bill Swift	.05
132	Checklist	.05

1993 Fleer

BRETT BUTLER · LOS ANGELES DODGERS · OF

		NM/M
Complete Set (720):		10.00
Common Player:		.05
Series 1 or 2 Pack (15):		.50
Series 1 or 2 Box (36):		12.50
1	Steve Avery	.05
2	Sid Bream	.05
3	Ron Gant	.05
4	Tom Glavine	.25
5	Brian Hunter	.05
6	Ryan Klesko	.05
7	Charlie Leibrandt	.05
8	Kent Mercker	.05
9	David Nied	.05
10	Otis Nixon	.05
11	Greg Olson	.05
12	Terry Pendleton	.05
13	Deion Sanders	.10
14	John Smoltz	.05
15	Mike Stanton	.05
16	Mark Wohlers	.05
17	Paul Assenmacher	.05
18	Steve Buechele	.05
19	Shawon Dunston	.05
20	Mark Grace	.05
21	Derrick May	.05
22	Chuck McElroy	.05
23	Mike Morgan	.05
24	Rey Sanchez	.05
25	Ryne Sandberg	.60
26	Bob Scanlan	.05
27	Sammy Sosa	.60
28	Rick Wilkins	.05
29	Bobby Ayala RC	.05
30	Tim Belcher	.05
31	Jeff Branson RC	.05
32	Norm Charlton	.05
33	Steve Foster RC	.05
34	Willie Greene	.05
35	Chris Hammond	.05
36	Milt Hill	.05
37	Hal Morris	.05
38	Joe Oliver	.05
39	Paul O'Neill	.05
40	Tim Pugh RC	.05
41	Jose Rijo	.05
42	Bip Roberts	.05
43	Chris Sabo	.05
44	Reggie Sanders	.05
45	Eric Anthony	.05
46	Jeff Bagwell	.50
47	Craig Biggio	.05
48	Joe Boever	.05
49	Casey Candaele	.05
50	Steve Finley	.05
51	Luis Gonzalez	.05
52	Pete Harnisch	.05
53	Xavier Hernandez	.05
54	Doug Jones	.05
55	Eddie Taubensee	.05
56	Brian Williams	.05
57	Pedro Astacio RC	.10
58	Todd Benzinger	.05
59	Brett Butler	.05
60	Tom Candiotti	.05
61	Lenny Harris	.05
62	Carlos Hernandez	.05
63	Orel Hershiser	.05
64	Eric Karros	.05
65	Ramon Martinez	.05
66	Jose Offerman	.05
67	Mike Scioscia	.05
68	Mike Sharperson	.05
69	Eric Young RC	.10
70	Moises Alou	.05
71	Ivan Calderon	.05
72	Archi Cianfrocco RC	.05
73	Wil Cordero	.05
74	Delino DeShields	.05
75	Mark Gardner	.05
76	Ken Hill	.05
77	Tim Laker RC	.05
78	Chris Nabholz	.05
79	Mel Rojas	.05
80	John Vander Wal RC	.10
81	Larry Walker	.05
82	Tim Wallach	.05
83	John Wetteland	.05
84	Bobby Bonilla	.05
85	Daryl Boston	.05
86	Sid Fernandez	.05
87	Eric Hillman RC	.05
88	Todd Hundley	.05
89	Howard Johnson	.05
90	Jeff Kent	.05
91	Eddie Murray	.50
92	Bill Pecota	.05
93	Bret Saberhagen	.05
94	Dick Schofield	.05
95	Pete Schourek	.05
96	Anthony Young	.05
97	Ruben Amaro Jr.	.05
98	Juan Bell	.05
99	Wes Chamberlain	.05
100	Darren Daulton	.05
101	Mariano Duncan	.05
102	Mike Hartley	.05
103	Ricky Jordan	.05
104	John Kruk	.05
105	Mickey Morandini	.05
106	Terry Mulholland	.05
107	Ben Rivera RC	.05
108	Curt Schilling	.25
109	Keith Shepherd RC	.05
110	Stan Belinda	.05
111	Jay Bell	.05
112	Barry Bonds	1.00
113	Jeff King	.05
114	Mike LaValliere	.05
115	Jose Lind	.05
116	Roger Mason	.05
117	Orlando Merced	.05
118	Bob Patterson	.05
119	Don Slaught	.05
120	Zane Smith	.05
121	Randy Tomlin	.05
122	Andy Van Slyke	.05
123	Tim Wakefield RC	.10
124	Rheal Cormier	.05
125	Bernard Gilkey	.05
126	Felix Jose	.05
127	Ray Lankford	.05
128	Bob McClure	.05
129	Donovan Osborne	.05
130	Tom Pagnozzi	.05
131	Geronimo Pena	.05
132	Mike Perez	.05
133	Lee Smith	.05
134	Bob Tewksbury	.05
135	Todd Worrell	.05
136	Todd Zeile	.05
137	Jerald Clark	.05
138	Tony Gwynn	.60
139	Greg Harris	.05
140	Jeremy Hernandez	.05
141	Darrin Jackson	.05
142	Mike Maddux	.05
143	Fred McGriff	.05
144	Jose Melendez	.05
145	Rich Rodriguez	.05
146	Frank Seminara	.05
147	Gary Sheffield	.35
148	Kurt Stillwell	.05
149	Dan Walters RC	.05
150	Rod Beck	.05
151	Bud Black	.05
152	Jeff Brantley	.05
153	John Burkett	.05
154	Will Clark	.05
155	Royce Clayton	.05
156	Mike Jackson	.05
157	Darren Lewis	.05
158	Kirt Manwaring	.05
159	Willie McGee	.05
160	Cory Snyder	.05
161	Bill Swift	.05
162	Trevor Wilson	.05
163	Brady Anderson	.05
164	Glenn Davis	.05
165	Mike Devereaux	.05
166	Todd Frohwirth	.05
167	Leo Gomez	.05
168	Chris Hoiles	.05
169	Ben McDonald	.05
170	Randy Milligan	.05
171	Alan Mills	.05
172	Mike Mussina	.30
173	Gregg Olson	.05
174	Arthur Rhodes	.05
175	David Segui	.05
176	Ellis Burks	.05
177	Roger Clemens	.65
178	Scott Cooper	.05
179	Danny Darwin	.05
180	Tony Fossas	.05
181	Paul Quantrill RC	.10
182	Jody Reed	.05
183	John Valentin RC	.10
184	Mo Vaughn	.05
185	Frank Viola	.05

186	Bob Zupcic	.05
187	Jim Abbott	.05
188	Gary DiSarcina	.05
189	Damion Easley **RC**	.10
190	Junior Felix	.05
191	Chuck Finley	.05
192	Joe Grahe	.05
193	Bryan Harvey	.05
194	Mark Langston	.05
195	John Orton	.05
196	Luis Polonia	.05
197	Tim Salmon	.05
198	Luis Sojo	.05
199	Wilson Alvarez	.05
200	George Bell	.05
201	Alex Fernandez	.05
202	Craig Grebeck	.05
203	Ozzie Guillen	.05
204	Lance Johnson	.05
205	Ron Karkovice	.05
206	Kirk McCaskill	.05
207	Jack McDowell	.05
208	Scott Radinsky	.05
209	Tim Raines	.05
210	Frank Thomas	.50
211	Robin Ventura	.05
212	Sandy Alomar Jr.	.05
213	Carlos Baerga	.05
214	Dennis Cook	.05
215	Thomas Howard	.05
216	Mark Lewis	.05
217	Derek Lilliquist	.05
218	Kenny Lofton	.05
219	Charles Nagy	.05
220	Steve Olin	.05
221	Paul Sorrento	.05
222	Jim Thome	.40
223	Mark Whiten	.05
224	Milt Cuyler	.05
225	Rob Deer	.05
226	John Doherty **RC**	.05
227	Cecil Fielder	.05
228	Travis Fryman	.05
229	Mike Henneman	.05
230	John Kiely **RC**	.05
231	Kurt Knudsen **RC**	.05
232	Scott Livingstone	.05
233	Tony Phillips	.05
234	Mickey Tettleton	.05
235	Kevin Appier	.05
236	George Brett	.65
237	Tom Gordon	.05
238	Gregg Jefferies	.05
239	Wally Joyner	.05
240	Kevin Koslofski **RC**	.05
241	Mike Macfarlane	.05
242	Brian McRae	.05
243	Rusty Meacham	.05
244	Keith Miller	.05
245	Jeff Montgomery	.05
246	Hipolito Pichardo **RC**	.05
247	Ricky Bones	.05
248	Cal Eldred	.05
249	Mike Fetters	.05
250	Darryl Hamilton	.05
251	Doug Henry	.05
252	John Jaha	.05
253	Pat Listach	.05
254	Paul Molitor	.50
255	Jaime Navarro	.05
256	Kevin Seitzer	.05
257	B.J. Surhoff	.05
258	Greg Vaughn	.05
259	Bill Wegman	.05
260	Robin Yount	.50
261	Rick Aguilera	.05
262	Chili Davis	.05
263	Scott Erickson	.05
264	Greg Gagne	.05
265	Mark Guthrie	.05
266	Brian Harper	.05
267	Kent Hrbek	.05
268	Terry Jorgensen	.05
269	Gene Larkin	.05
270	Scott Leius	.05
271	Pat Mahomes	.05
272	Pedro Munoz	.05
273	Kirby Puckett	.60
274	Kevin Tapani	.05
275	Carl Willis	.05
276	Steve Farr	.05
277	John Habyan	.05
278	Mel Hall	.05
279	Charlie Hayes	.05
280	Pat Kelly	.05
281	Don Mattingly	.65
282	Sam Militello	.05
283	Matt Nokes	.05
284	Melido Perez	.05
285	Andy Stankiewicz	.05
286	Danny Tartabull	.05
287	Randy Velarde	.05
288	Bob Wickman	.05
289	Bernie Williams	.05
290	Lance Blankenship	.05
291	Mike Bordick	.05
292	Jerry Browne	.05
293	Dennis Eckersley	.40
294	Rickey Henderson	.50
295	Vince Horsman **RC**	.05
296	Mark McGwire	.85
297	Jeff Parrett	.05
298	Ruben Sierra	.05
299	Terry Steinbach	.05
300	Walt Weiss	.05
301	Bob Welch	.05
302	Willie Wilson	.05
303	Bobby Witt	.05
304	Bret Boone	.05
305	Jay Buhner	.05
306	Dave Fleming	.05
307	Ken Griffey Jr.	.75
308	Erik Hanson	.05
309	Edgar Martinez	.05
310	Tino Martinez	.05
311	Jeff Nelson	.05
312	Dennis Powell	.05
313	Mike Schooler	.05
314	Russ Swan	.05
315	Dave Valle	.05
316	Omar Vizquel	.05
317	Kevin Brown	.05
318	Todd Burns	.05
319	Jose Canseco	.35
320	Julio Franco	.05
321	Jeff Frye	.05
322	Juan Gonzalez	.30
323	Jose Guzman	.05
324	Jeff Huson	.05
325	Dean Palmer	.05
326	Kevin Reimer	.05
327	Ivan Rodriguez	.40
328	Kenny Rogers	.05
329	Dan Smith	.05
330	Roberto Alomar	.20
331	Derek Bell	.05
332	Pat Borders	.05
333	Joe Carter	.05
334	Kelly Gruber	.05
335	Tom Henke	.05
336	Jimmy Key	.05
337	Manuel Lee	.05
338	Candy Maldonado	.05
339	John Olerud	.05
340	Todd Stottlemyre	.05
341	Duane Ward	.05
342	Devon White	.05
343	Dave Winfield	.50
344	Edgar Martinez	.05
345	Cecil Fielder	.05
346	Kenny Lofton	.05
347	Jack Morris	.05
348	Roger Clemens	.35
349	Fred McGriff	.05
350	Barry Bonds	.60
351	Gary Sheffield	.05
352	Darren Daulton	.05
353	Dave Hollins	.05
354	Pedro Martinez, Ramon Martinez Brothers In Blue	.25
355	Ivan Rodriguez, Kirby Puckett Power Packs	.25
356	Ryne Sandberg, Gary Sheffield Triple Threats	.20
357	Roberto Alomar, Chuck Knoblauch, Carlos Baerga Infield Trifecta	.05
358	Checklist	.05
359	Checklist	.05
360	Checklist	.05
361	Rafael Belliard	.05
362	Damon Berryhill	.05
363	Mike Bielecki	.05
364	Jeff Blauser	.05
365	Francisco Cabrera	.05
366	Marvin Freeman	.05
367	Dave Justice	.05
368	Mark Lemke	.05
369	Alejandro Pena	.05
370	Jeff Reardon	.05
371	Lonnie Smith	.05
372	Pete Smith	.05
373	Shawn Boskie	.05
374	Jim Bullinger	.05
375	Frank Castillo	.05
376	Doug Dascenzo	.05
377	Andre Dawson	.25
378	Mike Harkey	.05
379	Greg Hibbard	.05
380	Greg Maddux	.60
381	Ken Patterson	.05
382	Jeff Robinson	.05
383	Luis Salazar	.05
384	Dwight Smith	.05
385	Jose Vizcaino	.05
386	Scott Bankhead	.05
387	Tom Browning	.05
388	Darnell Coles	.05
389	Rob Dibble	.05
390	Bill Doran	.05
391	Dwayne Henry	.05
392	Cesar Hernandez	.05
393	Roberto Kelly	.05
394	Barry Larkin	.05
395	Dave Martinez	.05
396	Kevin Mitchell	.05
397	Jeff Reed	.05
398	Scott Ruskin	.05
399	Greg Swindell	.05
400	Dan Wilson	.05
401	Andy Ashby	.05
402	Freddie Benavides	.05
403	Dante Bichette	.05
404	Willie Blair	.05
405	Denis Boucher	.05
406	Vinny Castilla	.05
407	Braulio Castillo	.05
408	Alex Cole	.05
409	Andres Galarraga	.05
410	Joe Girardi	.05
411	Butch Henry	.05
412	Darren Holmes	.05
413	Calvin Jones	.05
414	Steve Reed **RC**	.05
415	Kevin Ritz	.05
416	Jim Tatum **RC**	.05
417	Jack Armstrong	.05
418	Bret Barberie	.05
419	Ryan Bowen	.05
420	Cris Carpenter	.05
421	Chuck Carr	.05
422	Scott Chiamparino	.05
423	Jeff Conine	.05
424	Jim Corsi	.05
425	Steve Decker	.05
426	Chris Donnels	.05
427	Monty Fariss	.05
428	Bob Natal	.05
429	Pat Rapp **RC**	.05
430	Dave Weathers	.05
431	Nigel Wilson **RC**	.05
432	Ken Caminiti	.05
433	Andujar Cedeno	.05
434	Tom Edens	.05
435	Juan Guerrero	.05
436	Pete Incaviglia	.05
437	Jimmy Jones	.05
438	Darryl Kile	.05
439	Rob Murphy	.05
440	Al Osuna	.05
441	Mark Portugal	.05
442	Scott Servais	.05
443	John Candelaria	.05
444	Tim Crews	.05
445	Eric Davis	.05
446	Tom Goodwin	.05
447	Jim Gott	.05
448	Kevin Gross	.05
449	Dave Hansen	.05
450	Jay Howell	.05
451	Roger McDowell	.05
452	Bob Ojeda	.05
453	Henry Rodriguez	.05
454	Darryl Strawberry	.05
455	Mitch Webster	.05
456	Steve Wilson	.05
457	Brian Barnes	.05
458	Sean Berry	.05
459	Jeff Fassero	.05
460	Darrin Fletcher	.05
461	Marquis Grissom	.05
462	Dennis Martinez	.05
463	Spike Owen	.05
464	Matt Stairs	.05
465	Sergio Valdez	.05
466	Kevin Bass	.05
467	Vince Coleman	.05
468	Mark Dewey	.05
469	Kevin Elster	.05
470	Tony Fernandez	.05
471	John Franco	.05
472	Dave Gallagher	.05
473	Paul Gibson	.05
474	Dwight Gooden	.05
475	Lee Guetterman	.05
476	Jeff Innis	.05
477	Dave Magadan	.05
478	Charlie O'Brien	.05
479	Willie Randolph	.05
480	Mackey Sasser	.05
481	Ryan Thompson	.05
482	Chico Walker	.05
483	Kyle Abbott	.05
484	Bob Ayrault	.05
485	Kim Batiste	.05
486	Cliff Brantley	.05
487	Jose DeLeon	.05
488	Len Dykstra	.05
489	Tommy Greene	.05
490	Jeff Grotewold	.05
491	Dave Hollins	.05
492	Danny Jackson	.05
493	Stan Javier	.05
494	Tom Marsh	.05
495	Greg Matthews	.05
496	Dale Murphy	.15
497	Todd Pratt **RC**	.05
498	Mitch Williams	.05
499	Danny Cox	.05
500	Doug Drabek	.05
501	Carlos Garcia	.05
502	Lloyd McClendon	.05
503	Denny Neagle	.05
504	Gary Redus	.05
505	Bob Walk	.05
506	John Wehner	.05
507	Luis Alicea	.05
508	Mark Clark	.05
509	Pedro Guerrero	.05
510	Rex Hudler	.05
511	Brian Jordan	.05
512	Omar Olivares	.05
513	Jose Oquendo	.05
514	Gerald Perry	.05
515	Bryn Smith	.05
516	Craig Wilson	.05
517	Tracy Woodson	.05
518	Larry Anderson	.05
519	Andy Benes	.05
520	Jim Deshaies	.05
521	Bruce Hurst	.05
522	Randy Myers	.05
523	Benito Santiago	.05
524	Tim Scott	.05
525	Tim Teufel	.05
526	Mike Benjamin	.05
527	Dave Burba	.05
528	Craig Colbert	.05
529	Mike Felder	.05
530	Bryan Hickerson	.05
531	Chris James	.05
532	Mark Leonard	.05
533	Greg Litton	.05
534	Francisco Oliveras	.05
535	John Patterson	.05
536	Jim Pena	.05
537	Dave Righetti	.05
538	Robby Thompson	.05
539	Jose Uribe	.05
540	Matt Williams	.05
541	Storm Davis	.05
542	Sam Horn	.05
543	Tim Hulett	.05
544	Craig Lefferts	.05
545	Chito Martinez	.05
546	Mark McLemore	.05
547	Luis Mercedes	.05
548	Bob Milacki	.05
549	Joe Orsulak	.05
550	Billy Ripken	.05
551	Cal Ripken, Jr.	1.00
552	Rick Sutcliffe	.05
553	Jeff Tackett	.05
554	Wade Boggs	.60
555	Tom Brunansky	.05
556	Jack Clark	.05
557	John Dopson	.05
558	Mike Gardiner	.05
559	Mike Greenwell	.05
560	Greg Harris	.05
561	Billy Hatcher	.05
562	Joe Hesketh	.05
563	Tony Pena	.05
564	Phil Plantier	.05
565	Luis Rivera	.05
566	Herm Winningham	.05
567	Matt Young	.05
568	Bert Blyleven	.05
569	Mike Butcher	.05
570	Chuck Crim	.05
571	Chad Curtis **RC**	.15
572	Tim Fortugno	.05
573	Steve Frey	.05
574	Gary Gaetti	.05
575	Scott Lewis	.05
576	Lee Stevens	.05
577	Ron Tingley	.05
578	Julio Valera	.05
579	Shawn Abner	.05
580	Joey Cora	.05
581	Chris Cron	.05
582	Carlton Fisk	.50
583	Roberto Hernandez	.05
584	Charlie Hough	.05
585	Terry Leach	.05
586	Donn Pall	.05
587	Dan Pasqua	.05
588	Steve Sax	.05
589	Bobby Thigpen	.05
590	Albert Belle	.05
591	Felix Fermin	.05
592	Glenallen Hill	.05
593	Brook Jacoby	.05
594	Reggie Jefferson	.05
595	Carlos Martinez	.05
596	Jose Mesa	.05
597	Rod Nichols	.05
598	Junior Ortiz	.05
599	Eric Plunk	.05
600	Ted Power	.05
601	Scott Scudder	.05
602	Kevin Wickander	.05
603	Skeeter Barnes	.05
604	Mark Carreon	.05
605	Dan Gladden	.05
606	Bill Gullickson	.05
607	Chad Kreuter	.05
608	Mark Leiter	.05
609	Mike Munoz	.05
610	Rich Rowland	.05
611	Frank Tanana	.05
612	Walt Terrell	.05
613	Alan Trammell	.05
614	Lou Whitaker	.05
615	Luis Aquino	.05
616	Mike Boddicker	.05
617	Jim Eisenreich	.05
618	Mark Gubicza	.05
619	David Howard	.05
620	Mike Magnante	.05
621	Brent Mayne	.05
622	Kevin McReynolds	.05
623	Eddie Pierce **RC**	.05
624	Bill Sampen	.05
625	Steve Shifflett	.05
626	Gary Thurman	.05
627	Curtis Wilkerson	.05
628	Chris Bosio	.05
629	Scott Fletcher	.05
630	Jim Gantner	.05
631	Dave Nilsson	.05
632	Jesse Orosco	.05
633	Dan Plesac	.05
634	Ron Robinson	.05
635	Bill Spiers	.05
636	Franklin Stubbs	.05
637	Willie Banks	.05
638	Randy Bush	.05
639	Chuck Knoblauch	.05
640	Shane Mack	.05

641	Mike Pagliarulo	.05
642	Jeff Reboulet	.05
643	John Smiley	.05
644	Mike Trombley RC	.05
645	Gary Wayne	.05
646	Lenny Webster	.05
647	Tim Burke	.05
648	Mike Gallego	.05
649	Dion James	.05
650	Jeff Johnson	.05
651	Scott Kamieniecki	.05
652	Kevin Maas	.05
653	Rich Monteleone	.05
654	Jerry Nielsen	.05
655	Scott Sanderson	.05
656	Mike Stanley	.05
657	Gerald Williams	.05
658	Curt Young	.05
659	Harold Baines	.05
660	Kevin Campbell	.05
661	Ron Darling	.05
662	Kelly Downs	.05
663	Eric Fox	.05
664	Dave Henderson	.05
665	Rick Honeycutt	.05
666	Mike Moore	.05
667	Jamie Quirk	.05
668	Jeff Russell	.05
669	Dave Stewart	.05
670	Greg Briley	.05
671	Dave Cochrane	.05
672	Henry Cotto	.05
673	Rich DeLucia	.05
674	Brian Fisher	.05
675	Mark Grant	.05
676	Randy Johnson	.50
677	Tim Leary	.05
678	Pete O'Brien	.05
679	Lance Parrish	.05
680	Harold Reynolds	.05
681	Shane Turner	.05
682	Jack Daugherty	.05
683	David Hulse RC	.05
684	Terry Mathews	.05
685	Al Newman	.05
686	Edwin Nunez	.05
687	Rafael Palmeiro	.40
688	Roger Pavlik	.05
689	Geno Petralli	.05
690	Nolan Ryan	1.00
691	David Cone	.05
692	Alfredo Griffin	.05
693	Juan Guzman	.05
694	Pat Hentgen	.05
695	Randy Knorr	.05
696	Bob MacDonald	.05
697	Jack Morris	.05
698	Ed Sprague	.05
699	Dave Stieb	.05
700	Pat Tabler	.05
701	Mike Timlin	.05
702	David Wells	.05
703	Eddie Zosky	.05
704	Gary Sheffield	.05
705	Darren Daulton	.05
706	Marquis Grissom	.05
707	Greg Maddux	.10
708	Bill Swift	.05
709	Juan Gonzalez	.15
710	Mark McGwire	.50
711	Cecil Fielder	.05
712	Albert Belle (Round Trippers)	.05
713	Joe Carter	.05
714	Frank Thomas, Cecil Fielder Power Brokers	.10
715	Larry Walker, Darren Daulton Unsung Heroes	.05
716	Edgar Martinez, Robin Ventura Hot Corner Hammers	.05
717	Roger Clemens, Dennis Eckersley Start to Finish	.25
718	Checklist	.05
719	Checklist	.05
720	Checklist	.05

All-Stars

		NM/M
Complete Set A.L. (12):		6.00
Complete Set N.L. (12):		3.75
Common Player:		.15
AMERICAN LEAGUE		
1	Frank Thomas	.85
2	Roberto Alomar	.40
3	Edgar Martinez	.15
4	Pat Listach	.15
5	Cecil Fielder	.15
6	Juan Gonzalez	.40
7	Ken Griffey Jr.	2.00
8	Joe Carter	.15
9	Kirby Puckett	1.00
10	Brian Harper	.15
11	Dave Fleming	.15
12	Jack McDowell	.15
NATIONAL LEAGUE		
1	Fred McGriff	.15
2	Delino DeShields	.15
3	Gary Sheffield	.40
4	Barry Larkin	.15
5	Felix Jose	.15
6	Larry Walker	.15
7	Barry Bonds	2.50
8	Andy Van Slyke	.15
9	Darren Daulton	.15
10	Greg Maddux	.75
11	Tom Glavine	.25
12	Lee Smith	.15

Golden Moments

		NM/M
Complete Set (6):		4.00
Common Player:		.25
SERIES 1		2.00
(1)	George Brett	1.50
(2)	Mickey Morandini	.25
(3)	Dave Winfield	.50
SERIES 2		2.00
(1)	Dennis Eckersley	.40
(2)	Bip Roberts	.25
(3)	Frank Thomas, Juan Gonzalez	1.50

Major League Prospects

		NM/M
Complete Set (36):		7.50
Common Player:		.15
SERIES 1		5.00
1	Melvin Nieves	.15
2	Sterling Hitchcock	.15
3	Tim Costo	.15
4	Manny Alexander	.15
5	Alan Embree	.15
6	Kevin Young	.15
7	J.T. Snow	.15
8	Russ Springer	.15
9	Billy Ashley	.15
10	Kevin Rogers	.15
11	Steve Hosey	.15
12	Eric Wedge	.15
13	Mike Piazza	3.50
14	Jesse Levis	.15
15	Rico Brogna	.15
16	Alex Arias	.15
17	Rod Brewer	.15
18	Troy Neel	.15
SERIES 2		2.50
1	Scooter Tucker	.15
2	Kerry Woodson	.15
3	Greg Colbrunn	.15
4	Pedro Martinez	1.50
5	Dave Silvestri	.15
6	Kent Bottenfield	.15
7	Rafael Bournigal	.15
8	J.T. Bruett	.15
9	Dave Mlicki	.15
10	Paul Wagner	.15
11	Mike Williams	.15
12	Henry Mercedes	.15
13	Scott Taylor	.15
14	Dennis Moeller	.15
15	Javier Lopez	.15
16	Steve Cooke	.15
17	Pete Young	.15
18	Ken Ryan	.15

ProVisions

GARY SHEFFIELD

		NM/M
Complete Set (6):		3.00
Common Player:		.40
SERIES 1		2.00
1	Roberto Alomar	.65
2	Dennis Eckersley	1.00
3	Gary Sheffield	.75
SERIES 2		1.00
1	Andy Van Slyke	.40
2	Tom Glavine	.75
3	Cecil Fielder	.40

Rookie Sensations

		NM/M
Complete Set (20):		6.25
Common Player:		.25
SERIES 1		3.00
1	Kenny Lofton	.50
2	Cal Eldred	.25
3	Pat Listach	.25
4	Roberto Hernandez	.25
5	Dave Fleming	.25
6	Eric Karros	.25
7	Reggie Sanders	.25
8	Derrick May	.25
9	Mike Perez	.25
10	Donovan Osborne	.25
SERIES 2		2.00
1	Moises Alou	.50
2	Pedro Astacio	.25
3	Jim Austin	.25
4	Chad Curtis	.25
5	Gary DiSarcina	.25
6	Scott Livingstone	.25
7	Sam Militello	.25
8	Arthur Rhodes	.25
9	Tim Wakefield	.35
10	Bob Zupcic	.25

Team Leaders

		NM/M
Complete Set (20):		12.50
Common Player:		.40
SERIES 1		10.00
1	Kirby Puckett	1.25
2	Mark McGwire	3.00
3	Pat Listach	.40
4	Roger Clemens	1.50
5	Frank Thomas	1.00
6	Carlos Baerga	.40
7	Brady Anderson	.40
8	Juan Gonzalez	.50
9	Roberto Alomar	.60
10	Ken Griffey Jr.	2.00
SERIES 2		4.00
1	Will Clark	.40
2	Terry Pendleton	.40
3	Ray Lankford	.40

4	Eric Karros	.40
5	Gary Sheffield	.75
6	Ryne Sandberg	1.25
7	Marquis Grissom	.40
8	John Kruk	.40
9	Jeff Bagwell	1.00
10	Andy Van Slyke	.40

Tom Glavine Career Highlights

		NM/M
Complete Set (15):		5.00
Common Card:		.50
Autographed Card:		30.00
1-15	Tom Glavine	.50

Final Edition

		NM/M
Complete Set (310):		7.50
Common Player:		.05
1	Steve Bedrosian	.05
2	Jay Howell	.05
3	Greg Maddux	.65
4	Greg McMichael RC	.05
5	Tony Tarasco RC	.05
6	Jose Bautista	.05
7	Jose Guzman	.05
8	Greg Hibbard	.05
9	Candy Maldonado	.05
10	Randy Myers	.05
11	Matt Walbeck RC	.05
12	Turk Wendell	.05
13	Willie Nelson	.05
14	Greg Cadaret	.05
15	Roberto Kelly	.05
16	Randy Milligan	.05
17	Kevin Mitchell	.05
18	Jeff Reardon	.05
19	John Roper	.05
20	John Smiley	.05
21	Andy Ashby	.05
22	Dante Bichette	.05
23	Willie Blair	.05
24	Pedro Castellano	.05

25 Vinny Castilla .05
26 Jerald Clark .05
27 Alex Cole .05
28 Scott Fredrickson **RC** .05
29 Jay Gainer **RC** .05
30 Andres Galarraga .05
31 Joe Girardi .05
32 Ryan Hawblitzel .05
33 Charlie Hayes .05
34 Darren Holmes .05
35 Chris Jones .05
36 David Nied .05
37 J. Owens **RC** .05
38 Lance Painter **RC** .05
39 Jeff Parrett .05
40 Steve Reed **RC** .05
41 Armando Reynoso .05
42 Bruce Ruffin .05
43 Danny Sheaffer **RC** .05
44 Keith Shepherd .05
45 Jim Tatum .05
46 Gary Wayne .05
47 Eric Young .05
48 Luis Aquino .05
49 Alex Arias .05
50 Jack Armstrong .05
51 Bret Barberie .05
52 Geronimo Berroa .05
53 Ryan Bowen .05
54 Greg Briley .05
55 Chris Carpenter .05
56 Chuck Carr .05
57 Jeff Conine .05
58 Jim Corsi .05
59 Orestes Destrade .05
60 Junior Felix .05
61 Chris Hammond .05
62 Bryan Harvey .05
63 Charlie Hough .05
64 Joe Klink .05
65 Richie Lewis **RC** .05
66 Mitch Lyden **RC** .05
67 Bob Natal .05
68 Scott Pose **RC** .05
69 Rich Renteria .05
70 Benito Santiago .05
71 Gary Sheffield .15
72 Matt Turner **RC** .05
73 Walt Weiss .05
74 Darrell Whitmore **RC** .05
75 Nigel Wilson .05
76 Kevin Bass .05
77 Doug Drabek .05
78 Tom Edens .05
79 Chris James .05
80 Greg Swindell .05
81 Omar Daal **RC** .05
82 Raul Mondesi .05
83 Jody Reed .05
84 Cory Snyder .05
85 Rick Trlicek .05
86 Tim Wallach .05
87 Todd Worrell .05
88 Tavo Alvarez .05
89 Frank Bolick .05
90 Kent Bottenfield .05
91 Greg Colbrunn .05
92 Cliff Floyd .05
93 Lou Frazier **RC** .05
94 Mike Gardiner .05
95 Mike Lansing **RC** .25
96 Bill Risley .05
97 Jeff Shaw .05
98 Kevin Baez .05
99 Tim Bogar **RC** .05
100 Jeromy Burnitz .05
101 Mike Draper .05
102 Darrin Jackson .05
103 Mike Maddux .05
104 Joe Orsulak .05
105 Doug Saunders .05
106 Frank Tanana .05
107 Dave Telgheder .05
108 Larry Anderson .05
109 Jim Eisenreich .05
110 Pete Incaviglia .05
111 Danny Jackson .05
112 David West .05
113 Al Martin .05
114 Blas Minor .05
115 Dennis Moeller .05
116 Will Pennyfeather .05
117 Rich Robertson .05
118 Ben Shelton .05
119 Lonnie Smith .05
120 Freddie Toliver .05
121 Paul Wagner .05
122 Kevin Young .05
123 Rene Arocha **RC** .05
124 Gregg Jefferies .05
125 Paul Kilgus .05
126 Les Lancaster .05
127 Joe Magrane .05
128 Rob Murphy .05
129 Erik Pappas .05
130 Stan Royer .05
131 Ozzie Smith .65
132 Tom Urbani .05
133 Mark Whiten .05
134 Derek Bell .05
135 Doug Brocall .05
136 Phil Clark .05
137 Mark Ettles **RC** .05
138 Jeff Gardner .05
139 Pat Gomez **RC** .05
140 Ricky Gutierrez .05
141 Gene Harris .05
142 Kevin Higgins **RC** .05
143 Trevor Hoffman .05
144 Phil Plantier .05
145 Kerry Taylor **RC** .05
146 Guillermo Velasquez .05
147 Wally Whitehurst .05
148 Tim Worrell **RC** .05
149 Todd Benzinger .05
150 Barry Bonds 2.00
151 Greg Brummett .05
152 Mark Carreon .05
153 Dave Martinez .05
154 Jeff Reed .05
155 Kevin Rogers .05
156 Harold Baines .05
157 Damon Buford .05
158 Paul Carey **RC** .05
159 Jeffrey Hammonds .05
160 Jamie Moyer .05
161 Sherman Obando **RC** .05
162 John O'Donoghue **RC** .05
163 Brad Pennington .05
164 Jim Poole .05
165 Harold Reynolds .05
166 Fernando Valenzuela .05
167 Jack Voight **RC** .05
168 Mark Williamson .05
169 Scott Bankhead .05
170 Greg Blosser .05
171 Jim Byrd **RC** .05
172 Ivan Calderon .05
173 Andre Dawson .25
174 Scott Fletcher .05
175 Jose Melendez .05
176 Carlos Quintana .05
177 Jeff Russell .05
178 Aaron Sele .05
179 Rod Correia **RC** .05
180 Chili Davis .05
181 Jim Edmonds **RC** 3.00
182 Rene Gonzales .05
183 Hilly Hathaway **RC** .05
184 Torey Lovullo .05
185 Greg Myers .05
186 Gene Nelson .05
187 Troy Percival .05
188 Scott Sanderson .05
189 Darryl Scott **RC** .05
190 J.T. Snow **RC** .50
191 Russ Springer .05
192 Jason Bere .05
193 Rodney Bolton .05
194 Ellis Burks .05
195 Bo Jackson .15
196 Mike LaValliere .05
197 Scott Ruffcorn .05
198 Jeff Schwartz **RC** .05
199 Jerry DiPoto .05
200 Alvaro Espinoza .05
201 Wayne Kirby .05
202 Tom Kramer **RC** .05
203 Jesse Levis .05
204 Manny Ramirez .50
205 Jeff Treadway .05
206 Bill Wertz **RC** .05
207 Cliff Young .05
208 Matt Young .05
209 Kirk Gibson .05
210 Greg Gohr .05
211 Bill Krueger .05
212 Bob MacDonald .05
213 Mike Moore .05
214 David Wells .05
215 Billy Brewer **RC** .05
216 David Cone .05
217 Greg Gagne .05
218 Mark Gardner .05
219 Chis Haney .05
220 Phil Hiatt .05
221 Jose Lind .05
222 Juan Bell .05
223 Tom Brunansky .05
224 Mike Ignasiak .05
225 Joe Kmak .05
226 Tom Lampkin .05
227 Graeme Lloyd **RC** .05
228 Carlos Maldonado .05
229 Matt Mieske .05
230 Angel Miranda .05
231 Troy O'Leary **RC** .10
232 Kevin Reimer .05
233 Larry Casian .05
234 Jim Deshaies .05
235 Eddie Guardado **RC** .10
236 Chip Hale .05
237 Mike Maksudian **RC** .05
238 David McCarty .05
239 Pat Meares **RC** .05
240 George Tsamis **RC** .05
241 Dave Winfield .50
242 Jim Abbott .05
243 Wade Boggs .65
244 Andy Cook **RC** .05
245 Russ Davis **RC** .10
246 Mike Humphreys .05
247 Jimmy Key .05
248 Jim Leyritz .05
249 Bobby Munoz .05
250 Paul O'Neill .05
251 Spike Owen .05
252 Dave Silvestri .05
253 Marcos Armas **RC** .05
254 Brent Gates .05
255 Goose Gossage .25
256 Scott Lydy **RC** .05
257 Henry Mercedes .05
258 Mike Mohler **RC** .05
259 Troy Neel .05
260 Edwin Nunez .05
261 Craig Paquette .05
262 Kevin Seitzer .05
263 Rich Amaral .05
264 Mike Blowers .05
265 Chris Bosio .05
266 Norm Charlton .05
267 Jim Converse **RC** .05
268 John Cummings **RC** .05
269 Mike Felder .05
270 Mike Hampton .05
271 Bill Haselman .05
272 Dwayne Henry .05
273 Greg Litton .05
274 Mackey Sasser .05
275 Lee Tinsley .05
276 David Wainhouse .05
277 Jeff Bronkey **RC** .05
278 Benji Gil .05
279 Tom Henke .05
280 Charlie Leibrandt .05
281 Robb Nen .05
282 Bill Ripken .05
283 Jon Shave **RC** .05
284 Doug Strange .05
285 Matt Whiteside **RC** .05
286 Scott Brow **RC** .05
287 Willie Canate **RC** .05
288 Tony Castillo .05
289 Domingo Cedeno **RC** .05
290 Darnell Coles .05
291 Danny Cox .05
292 Mark Eichhorn .05
293 Tony Fernandez .05
294 Al Leiter .05
295 Paul Molitor .50
296 Dave Stewart .05
297 Woody Williams **RC** .05
298 Checklist .05
299 Checklist .05
300 Checklist .05

DIAMOND TRIBUTE

1DT Wade Boggs .65
2DT George Brett .75
3DT Andre Dawson .25
4DT Carlton Fisk .50
5DT Paul Molitor .50
6DT Nolan Ryan 2.00
7DT Lee Smith .05
8DT Ozzie Smith .65
9DT Dave Winfield .50
10DT Robin Yount .50

1994 Fleer

NM/M

Complete Set (720): 12.50
Common Player: .05
Pack (15): .50
Wax Box (36): 12.50
1 Brady Anderson .05
2 Harold Baines .05
3 Mike Devereaux .05
4 Todd Frohwirth .05
5 Jeffrey Hammonds .05
6 Chris Hoiles .05
7 Tim Hulett .05
8 Ben McDonald .05
9 Mark McLemore .05
10 Alan Mills .05
11 Jamie Moyer .05
12 Mike Mussina .40
13 Gregg Olson .05
14 Mike Pagliarulo .05
15 Brad Pennington .05
16 Jim Poole .05
17 Harold Reynolds .05
18 Arthur Rhodes .05
19 Cal Ripken, Jr. 2.00
20 David Segui .05
21 Rick Sutcliffe .05
22 Fernando Valenzuela .05
23 Jack Voigt .05
24 Mark Williamson .05
25 Scott Bankhead .05
26 Roger Clemens 1.00
27 Scott Cooper .05
28 Danny Darwin .05
29 Andre Dawson .25
30 Rob Deer .05
31 John Dopson .05
32 Scott Fletcher .05
33 Mike Greenwell .05
34 Greg Harris .05
35 Billy Hatcher .05
36 Bob Melvin .05
37 Tony Pena .05
38 Paul Quantrill .05
39 Carlos Quintana .05
40 Ernest Riles .05
41 Jeff Russell .05
42 Ken Ryan .05
43 Aaron Sele .05
44 John Valentin .05
45 Mo Vaughn .05
46 Frank Viola .05
47 Bob Zupcic .05
48 Mike Butcher .05
49 Rod Correia .05
50 Chad Curtis .05
51 Chili Davis .05
52 Gary DiSarcina .05
53 Damion Easley .05
54 Jim Edmonds .05
55 Chuck Finley .05
56 Steve Frey .05
57 Rene Gonzales .05
58 Joe Grahe .05
59 Hilly Hathaway .05
60 Stan Javier .05
61 Mark Langston .05
62 Phil Leftwich .05
63 Torey Lovullo .05
64 Joe Magrane .05
65 Greg Myers .05
66 Ken Patterson .05
67 Eduardo Perez .05
68 Luis Polonia .05
69 Tim Salmon .20
69a Tim Salmon/OPS 2.00
70 J.T. Snow .05
71 Ron Tingley .05
72 Julio Valera .05
73 Wilson Alvarez .05
74 Tim Belcher .05
75 George Bell .05
76 Jason Bere .05
77 Rod Bolton .05
78 Ellis Burks .05
79 Joey Cora .05
80 Alex Fernandez .05
81 Craig Grebeck .05
82 Ozzie Guillen .05
83 Roberto Hernandez .05
84 Bo Jackson .10
85 Lance Johnson .05
86 Ron Karkovice .05
87 Mike LaValliere .05
88 Kirk McCaskill .05
89 Jack McDowell .05
90 Warren Newson .05
91 Dan Pasqua .05
92 Scott Radinsky .05
93 Tim Raines .05
94 Steve Sax .05
95 Jeff Schwarz .05
96 Frank Thomas .75
97 Robin Ventura .05
98 Sandy Alomar, Jr. .05
99 Carlos Baerga .05
100 Albert Belle .05
101 Mark Clark .05
102 Jerry DiPoto .05
103 Alvaro Espinoza .05
104 Felix Fermin .05
105 Jeremy Hernandez .05
106 Reggie Jefferson .05
107 Wayne Kirby .05
108 Tom Kramer .05
109 Mark Lewis .05
110 Derek Lilliquist .05
111 Kenny Lofton .05
112 Candy Maldonado .05
113 Jose Mesa .05
114 Jeff Mutis .05
115 Charles Nagy .05
116 Bob Ojeda .05
117 Junior Ortiz .05
118 Eric Plunk .05
119 Manny Ramirez .75
120 Paul Sorrento .05
121 Jim Thome .60
122 Jeff Treadway .05
123 Bill Wertz .05
124 Skeeter Barnes .05
125 Milt Cuyler .05
126 Eric Davis .05
127 John Doherty .05
128 Cecil Fielder .05
129 Travis Fryman .05
130 Kirk Gibson .05
131 Dan Gladden .05
132 Greg Gohr .05
133 Chris Gomez .05
134 Bill Gullickson .05
135 Mike Henneman .05
136 Kurt Knudsen .05
137 Chad Kreuter .05
138 Bill Krueger .05
139 Scott Livingstone .05
140 Bob MacDonald .05
141 Mike Moore .05

142	Tony Phillips	.05
143	Mickey Tettleton	.05
144	Alan Trammell	.05
145	David Wells	.05
146	Lou Whitaker	.05
147	Kevin Appier	.05
148	Stan Belinda	.05
149	George Brett	1.00
150	Billy Brewer	.05
151	Hubie Brooks	.05
152	David Cone	.05
153	Gary Gaetti	.05
154	Greg Gagne	.05
155	Tom Gordon	.05
156	Mark Gubicza	.05
157	Chris Gwynn	.05
158	John Habyan	.05
159	Chris Haney	.05
160	Phil Hiatt	.05
161	Felix Jose	.05
162	Wally Joyner	.05
163	Jose Lind	.05
164	Mike Macfarlane	.05
165	Mike Magnante	.05
166	Brent Mayne	.05
167	Brian McRae	.05
168	Kevin McReynolds	.05
169	Keith Miller	.05
170	Jeff Montgomery	.05
171	Hipolito Pichardo	.05
172	Rico Rossy	.05
173	Juan Bell	.05
174	Ricky Bones	.05
175	Cal Eldred	.05
176	Mike Fetters	.05
177	Darryl Hamilton	.05
178	Doug Henry	.05
179	Mike Ignasiak	.05
180	John Jaha	.05
181	Pat Listach	.05
182	Graeme Lloyd	.05
183	Matt Mieske	.05
184	Angel Miranda	.05
185	Jaime Navarro	.05
186	Dave Nilsson	.05
187	Troy O'Leary	.05
188	Jesse Orosco	.05
189	Kevin Reimer	.05
190	Kevin Seitzer	.05
191	Bill Spiers	.05
192	B.J. Surhoff	.05
193	Dickie Thon	.05
194	Jose Valentin	.05
195	Greg Vaughn	.05
196	Bill Wegman	.05
197	Robin Yount	.75
198	Rick Aguilera	.05
199	Willie Banks	.05
200	Bernardo Brito	.05
201	Larry Casian	.05
202	Scott Erickson	.05
203	Eddie Guardado	.05
204	Mark Guthrie	.05
205	Chip Hale	.05
206	Brian Harper	.05
207	Mike Hartley	.05
208	Kent Hrbek	.05
209	Terry Jorgensen	.05
210	Chuck Knoblauch	.05
211	Gene Larkin	.05
212	Shane Mack	.05
213	David McCarty	.05
214	Pat Meares	.05
215	Pedro Munoz	.05
216	Derek Parks	.05
217	Kirby Puckett	.85
218	Jeff Reboulet	.05
219	Kevin Tapani	.05
220	Mike Trombley	.05
221	George Tsamis	.05
222	Carl Willis	.05
223	Dave Winfield	.75
224	Jim Abbott	.05
225	Paul Assenmacher	.05
226	Wade Boggs	.85
227	Russ Davis	.05
228	Steve Farr	.05
229	Mike Gallego	.05
230	Paul Gibson	.05
231	Steve Howe	.05
232	Dion James	.05
233	Domingo Jean	.05
234	Scott Kamieniecki	.05
235	Pat Kelly	.05
236	Jimmy Key	.05
237	Jim Leyritz	.05
238	Kevin Maas	.05
239	Don Mattingly	1.00
240	Rich Monteleone	.05
241	Bobby Munoz	.05
242	Matt Nokes	.05
243	Paul O'Neill	.05
244	Spike Owen	.05
245	Melido Perez	.05
246	Lee Smith	.05
247	Mike Stanley	.05
248	Danny Tartabull	.05
249	Randy Velarde	.05
250	Bob Wickman	.05
251	Bernie Williams	.20
252	Mike Aldrete	.05
253	Marcos Armas	.05
254	Lance Blankenship	.05
255	Mike Bordick	.05
256	Scott Brosius	.05
257	Jerry Browne	.05
258	Ron Darling	.05
259	Kelly Downs	.05
260	Dennis Eckersley	.60
261	Brent Gates	.05
262	Goose Gossage	.05
263	Scott Hemond	.05
264	Dave Henderson	.05
265	Rick Honeycutt	.05
266	Vince Horsman	.05
267	Scott Lydy	.05
268	Mark McGwire	1.50
269	Mike Mohler	.05
270	Troy Neel	.05
271	Edwin Nunez	.05
272	Craig Paquette	.05
273	Ruben Sierra	.05
274	Terry Steinbach	.05
275	Todd Van Poppel	.05
276	Bob Welch	.05
277	Bobby Witt	.05
278	Rich Amaral	.05
279	Mike Blowers	.05
280	Bret Boone	.05
281	Chris Bosio	.05
282	Jay Buhner	.05
283	Norm Charlton	.05
284	Mike Felder	.05
285	Dave Fleming	.05
286	Ken Griffey Jr.	1.25
287	Erik Hanson	.05
288	Bill Haselman	.05
289	Brad Holman **RC**	.05
290	Randy Johnson	.75
291	Tim Leary	.05
292	Greg Litton	.05
293	Dave Magadan	.05
294	Edgar Martinez	.05
295	Tino Martinez	.05
296	Jeff Nelson	.05
297	Erik Plantenberg **RC**	.05
298	Mackey Sasser	.05
299	Brian Turang **RC**	.05
300	Dave Valle	.05
301	Omar Vizquel	.05
302	Brian Bohanon	.05
303	Kevin Brown	.05
304	Jose Canseco	.40
305	Mario Diaz	.05
306	Julio Franco	.05
307	Juan Gonzalez	.75
308	Tom Henke	.05
309	David Hulse	.05
310	Manuel Lee	.05
311	Craig Lefferts	.05
312	Charlie Leibrandt	.05
313	Rafael Palmeiro	.75
314	Dean Palmer	.05
315	Roger Pavlik	.05
316	Dan Peltier	.05
317	Geno Petralli	.05
318	Gary Redus	.05
319	Ivan Rodriguez	.65
320	Kenny Rogers	.05
321	Nolan Ryan	2.00
322	Doug Strange	.05
323	Matt Whiteside	.05
324	Roberto Alomar	.30
325	Pat Borders	.05
326	Joe Carter	.05
327	Tony Castillo	.05
328	Darnell Coles	.05
329	Danny Cox	.05
330	Mark Eichhorn	.05
331	Tony Fernandez	.05
332	Alfredo Griffin	.05
333	Juan Guzman	.05
334	Rickey Henderson	.75
335	Pat Hentgen	.05
336	Randy Knorr	.05
337	Al Leiter	.05
338	Paul Molitor	.75
339	Jack Morris	.05
340	John Olerud	.05
341	Dick Schofield	.05
342	Ed Sprague	.05
343	Dave Stewart	.05
344	Todd Stottlemyre	.05
345	Mike Timlin	.05
346	Duane Ward	.05
347	Turner Ward	.05
348	Devon White	.05
349	Woody Williams	.05
350	Steve Avery	.05
351	Steve Bedrosian	.05
352	Rafael Belliard	.05
353	Damon Berryhill	.05
354	Jeff Blauser	.05
355	Sid Bream	.05
356	Francisco Cabrera	.05
357	Marvin Freeman	.05
358	Ron Gant	.05
359	Tom Glavine	.25
360	Jay Howell	.05
361	Dave Justice	.05
362	Ryan Klesko	.05
363	Mark Lemke	.05
364	Javier Lopez	.05
365	Greg Maddux	.85
366	Fred McGriff	.05
367	Greg McMichael	.05
368	Kent Mercker	.05
369	Otis Nixon	.05
370	Greg Olson	.05
371	Bill Pecota	.05
372	Terry Pendleton	.05
373	Deion Sanders	.05
374	Pete Smith	.05
375	John Smoltz	.05
376	Mike Stanton	.05
377	Tony Tarasco	.05
378	Mark Wohlers	.05
379	Jose Bautista	.05
380	Shawn Boskie	.05
381	Steve Buechele	.05
382	Frank Castillo	.05
383	Mark Grace	.10
384	Jose Guzman	.05
385	Mike Harkey	.05
386	Greg Hibbard	.05
387	Glenallen Hill	.05
388	Steve Lake	.05
389	Derrick May	.05
390	Chuck McElroy	.05
391	Mike Morgan	.05
392	Randy Myers	.05
393	Dan Plesac	.05
394	Kevin Roberson	.05
395	Rey Sanchez	.05
396	Ryne Sandberg	.85
397	Bob Scanlan	.05
398	Dwight Smith	.05
399	Sammy Sosa	1.25
400	Jose Vizcaino	.05
401	Rick Wilkins	.05
402	Willie Wilson	.05
403	Eric Yelding	.05
404	Bobby Ayala	.05
405	Jeff Branson	.05
406	Tom Browning	.05
407	Jacob Brumfield	.05
408	Tim Costo	.05
409	Rob Dibble	.05
410	Willie Greene	.05
411	Thomas Howard	.05
412	Roberto Kelly	.05
413	Bill Landrum	.05
414	Barry Larkin	.05
415	Larry Luebbers **RC**	.05
416	Kevin Mitchell	.05
417	Hal Morris	.05
418	Joe Oliver	.05
419	Tim Pugh	.05
420	Jeff Reardon	.05
421	Jose Rijo	.05
422	Bip Roberts	.05
423	John Roper	.05
424	Johnny Ruffin	.05
425	Chris Sabo	.05
426	Juan Samuel	.05
427	Reggie Sanders	.05
428	Scott Service	.05
429	John Smiley	.05
430	Jerry Spradlin **RC**	.05
431	Kevin Wickander	.05
432	Freddie Benavides	.05
433	Dante Bichette	.05
434	Willie Blair	.05
435	Daryl Boston	.05
436	Kent Bottenfield	.05
437	Vinny Castilla	.05
438	Jerald Clark	.05
439	Alex Cole	.05
440	Andres Galarraga	.05
441	Joe Girardi	.05
442	Greg Harris	.05
443	Charlie Hayes	.05
444	Darren Holmes	.05
445	Chris Jones	.05
446	Roberto Mejia	.05
447	David Nied	.05
448	J. Owens	.05
449	Jeff Parrett	.05
450	Steve Reed	.05
451	Armando Reynoso	.05
452	Bruce Ruffin	.05
453	Mo Sanford	.05
454	Danny Sheaffer	.05
455	Jim Tatum	.05
456	Gary Wayne	.05
457	Eric Young	.05
458	Luis Aquino	.05
459	Alex Arias	.05
460	Jack Armstrong	.05
461	Bret Barberie	.05
462	Ryan Bowen	.05
463	Chuck Carr	.05
464	Jeff Conine	.05
465	Henry Cotto	.05
466	Orestes Destrade	.05
467	Chris Hammond	.05
468	Bryan Harvey	.05
469	Charlie Hough	.05
470	Joe Klink	.05
471	Richie Lewis	.05
472	Bob Natal **RC**	.05
473	Pat Rapp **RC**	.05
474	Rich Renteria **RC**	.10
475	Rich Rodriguez	.05
476	Benito Santiago	.05
477	Gary Sheffield	.35
478	Matt Turner	.05
479	David Weathers	.05
480	Walt Weiss	.05
481	Darrell Whitmore	.05
482	Eric Anthony	.05
483	Jeff Bagwell	.75
484	Kevin Bass	.05
485	Craig Biggio	.05
486	Ken Caminiti	.05
487	Andujar Cedeno	.05
488	Chris Donnels	.05
489	Doug Drabek	.05
490	Steve Finley	.05
491	Luis Gonzalez	.25
492	Pete Harnisch	.05
493	Xavier Hernandez	.05
494	Doug Jones	.05
495	Todd Jones	.05
496	Darryl Kile	.05
497	Al Osuna	.05
498	Mark Portugal	.05
499	Scott Servais	.05
500	Greg Swindell	.05
501	Eddie Taubensee	.05
502	Jose Uribe	.05
503	Brian Williams	.05
504	Billy Ashley	.05
505	Pedro Astacio	.05
506	Brett Butler	.05
507	Tom Candiotti	.05
508	Omar Daal	.05
509	Jim Gott	.05
510	Kevin Gross	.05
511	Dave Hansen	.05
512	Carlos Hernandez	.05
513	Orel Hershiser	.05
514	Eric Karros	.05
515	Pedro Martinez	.75
516	Ramon Martinez	.05
517	Roger McDowell	.05
518	Raul Mondesi	.05
519	Jose Offerman	.05
520	Mike Piazza	1.25
521	Jody Reed	.05
522	Henry Rodriguez	.05
523	Mike Sharperson	.05
524	Cory Snyder	.05
525	Darryl Strawberry	.05
526	Rick Trlicek	.05
527	Tim Wallach	.05
528	Mitch Webster	.05
529	Steve Wilson	.05
530	Todd Worrell	.05
531	Moises Alou	.05
532	Brian Barnes	.05
533	Sean Berry	.05
534	Greg Colbrunn	.05
535	Delino DeShields	.05
536	Jeff Fassero	.05
537	Darrin Fletcher	.05
538	Cliff Floyd	.05
539	Lou Frazier	.05
540	Marquis Grissom	.05
541	Butch Henry	.05
542	Ken Hill	.05
543	Mike Lansing	.05
544	Brian Looney **RC**	.05
545	Dennis Martinez	.05
546	Chris Nabholz	.05
547	Randy Ready	.05
548	Mel Rojas	.05
549	Kirk Rueter	.05
550	Tim Scott	.05
551	Jeff Shaw	.05
552	Tim Spehr	.05
553	John VanderWal	.05
554	Larry Walker	.05
555	John Wetteland	.05
556	Rondell White	.05
557	Tim Bogar	.05
558	Bobby Bonilla	.05
559	Jeromy Burnitz	.05
560	Sid Fernandez	.05
561	John Franco	.05
562	Dave Gallagher	.05
563	Dwight Gooden	.05
564	Eric Hillman	.05
565	Todd Hundley	.05
566	Jeff Innis	.05
567	Darrin Jackson	.05
568	Howard Johnson	.05
569	Bobby Jones	.05
570	Jeff Kent	.05
571	Mike Maddux	.05
572	Jeff McKnight	.05
573	Eddie Murray	.75
574	Charlie O'Brien	.05
575	Joe Orsulak	.05
576	Bret Saberhagen	.05
577	Pete Schourek	.05
578	Dave Telgheder	.05
579	Ryan Thompson	.05
580	Anthony Young	.05
581	Ruben Amaro	.05
582	Larry Andersen	.05
583	Kim Batiste	.05
584	Wes Chamberlain	.05
585	Darren Daulton	.05
586	Mariano Duncan	.05
587	Len Dykstra	.05
588	Jim Eisenreich	.05
589	Tommy Greene	.05
590	Dave Hollins	.05
591	Pete Incaviglia	.05
592	Danny Jackson	.05
593	Ricky Jordan	.05
594	John Kruk	.05
595	Roger Mason	.05
596	Mickey Morandini	.05
597	Terry Mulholland	.05
598	Todd Pratt	.05
599	Ben Rivera	.05
600	Curt Schilling	.25
601	Kevin Stocker	.05

602	Milt Thompson	.05
603	David West	.05
604	Mitch Williams	.05
605	Jay Bell	.05
606	Dave Clark	.05
607	Steve Cooke	.05
608	Tom Foley	.05
609	Carlos Garcia	.05
610	Joel Johnston	.05
611	Jeff King	.05
612	Al Martin	.05
613	Lloyd McClendon	.05
614	Orlando Merced	.05
615	Blas Minor	.05
616	Denny Neagle	.05
617	Mark Petkovsek RC	.05
618	Tom Prince	.05
619	Don Slaught	.05
620	Zane Smith	.05
621	Randy Tomlin	.05
622	Andy Van Slyke	.05
623	Paul Wagner	.05
624	Tim Wakefield	.05
625	Bob Walk	.05
626	Kevin Young	.05
627	Luis Alicea	.05
628	Rene Arocha	.05
629	Rod Brewer	.05
630	Rheal Cormier	.05
631	Bernard Gilkey	.05
632	Lee Guetterman	.05
633	Gregg Jefferies	.05
634	Brian Jordan	.05
635	Les Lancaster	.05
636	Ray Lankford	.05
637	Rob Murphy	.05
638	Omar Olivares	.05
639	Jose Oquendo	.05
640	Donovan Osborne	.05
641	Tom Pagnozzi	.05
642	Erik Pappas	.05
643	Geronimo Pena	.05
644	Mike Perez	.05
645	Gerald Perry	.05
646	Ozzie Smith	.85
647	Bob Tewksbury	.05
648	Allen Watson	.05
649	Mark Whiten	.05
650	Tracy Woodson	.05
651	Todd Zeile	.05
652	Andy Ashby	.05
653	Brad Ausmus	.05
654	Billy Bean	.05
655	Derek Bell	.05
656	Andy Benes	.05
657	Doug Brocail	.05
658	Jarvis Brown	.05
659	Archi Cianfrocco	.05
660	Phil Clark	.05
661	Mark Davis	.05
662	Jeff Gardner	.05
663	Pat Gomez	.05
664	Ricky Gutierrez	.05
665	Tony Gwynn	.85
666	Gene Harris	.05
667	Kevin Higgins	.05
668	Trevor Hoffman	.05
669	Pedro A. Martinez RC	.05
670	Tim Mauser	.05
671	Melvin Nieves	.05
672	Phil Plantier	.05
673	Frank Seminara	.05
674	Craig Shipley	.05
675	Kerry Taylor	.05
676	Tim Teufel	.05
677	Guillermo Velasquez	.05
678	Wally Whitehurst	.05
679	Tim Worrell	.05
680	Rod Beck	.05
681	Mike Benjamin	.05
682	Todd Benzinger	.05
683	Bud Black	.05
684	Barry Bonds	2.00
685	Jeff Brantley	.05
686	Dave Burba	.05
687	John Burkett	.05
688	Mark Carreon	.05
689	Will Clark	.10
690	Royce Clayton	.05
691	Bryan Hickerson	.05
692	Mike Jackson	.05
693	Darren Lewis	.05
694	Kirt Manwaring	.05
695	Dave Martinez	.05
696	Willie McGee	.05
697	John Patterson	.05
698	Jeff Reed	.05
699	Kevin Rogers	.05
700	Scott Sanderson	.05
701	Steve Scarsone	.05
702	Billy Swift	.05
703	Robby Thompson	.05
704	Matt Williams	.05
705	Trevor Wilson	.05
706	Fred McGriff, Ron Gant, Dave Justice "Brave New World"	.10
707	Paul Molitor, John Olerud "1-2 Punch"	.10
708	Mike Mussina, Jack McDowell "American Heat"	.10
709	Lou Whitaker, Alan Trammell "Together Again"	.05
710	Rafael Palmeiro, Juan Gonzalez "Lone Star Lumber"	.20

711	Brett Butler, Tony Gwynn "Batmen"	.10
712	Kirby Puckett, Chuck Knoblauch "Twin Peaks"	.20
713	Mike Piazza, Eric Karros "Back to Back"	.25
714	Checklist	.05
715	Checklist	.05
716	Checklist	.05
717	Checklist	.05
718	Checklist	.05
719	Checklist	.05
720	Checklist	.05

All-Stars

		NM/M
Complete Set (50):		10.00
Common Player:		.10
1	Roberto Alomar	.20
2	Carlos Baerga	.10
3	Albert Belle	.10
4	Wade Boggs	.75
5	Joe Carter	.10
6	Scott Cooper	.10
7	Cecil Fielder	.10
8	Travis Fryman	.10
9	Juan Gonzalez	.60
10	Ken Griffey Jr.	1.50
11	Pat Hentgen	.10
12	Randy Johnson	.60
13	Jimmy Key	.10
14	Mark Langston	.10
15	Jack McDowell	.10
16	Paul Molitor	.60
17	Jeff Montgomery	.10
18	Mike Mussina	.40
19	John Olerud	.10
20	Kirby Puckett	.75
21	Cal Ripken, Jr.	2.00
22	Ivan Rodriguez	.50
23	Frank Thomas	.65
24	Greg Vaughn	.10
25	Duane Ward	.10
26	Steve Avery	.10
27	Rod Beck	.10
28	Jay Bell	.10
29	Andy Benes	.10
30	Jeff Blauser	.10
31	Barry Bonds	2.00
32	Bobby Bonilla	.10
33	John Burkett	.10
34	Darren Daulton	.10
35	Andres Galarraga	.10
36	Tom Glavine	.30
37	Mark Grace	.25
38	Marquis Grissom	.10
39	Tony Gwynn	.75
40	Bryan Harvey	.10
41	Dave Hollins	.10
42	Dave Justice	.10
43	Darryl Kile	.10
44	John Kruk	.10
45	Barry Larkin	.10
46	Terry Mulholland	.10
47	Mike Piazza	1.50
48	Ryne Sandberg	.75
49	Gary Sheffield	.30
50	John Smoltz	.10

All-Rookie Team

		NM/M
Complete Set (9):		3.00
Common Player:		.25
Exchange Card:		.25
1	Kurt Abbott	.25
2	Rich Becker	.25
3	Carlos Delgado	2.00
4	Jorge Fabregas	.25
5	Bob Hamelin	.25
6	John Hudek	.25
7	Tim Hyers	.25

8	Luis Lopez	.25
9	James Mouton	.25

Award Winners

		NM/M
Complete Set (6):		4.50
Common Player:		.25
1	Frank Thomas	.75
2	Barry Bonds	2.00
3	Jack McDowell	.25
4	Greg Maddux	1.00
5	Tim Salmon	.50
6	Mike Piazza	1.50

Golden Moments

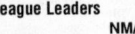
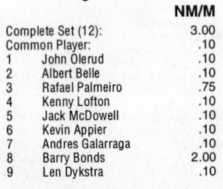

		NM/M
Complete Set (10):		5.00
Common Player:		.10
1	Mark Whiten "Four in One"	.10
2	Carlos Baerga "Left and Right"	.10
3	Dave Winfield "3,000 Hit Club"	.50
4	Ken Griffey Jr. "Eight Straight"	1.50
5	Bo Jackson "Triumphant Return"	.25
6	George Brett "Farewell to Baseball"	1.00
7	Nolan Ryan "Farewell to Baseball"	2.00
8	Fred McGriff "Thirty Times Six"	.10
9	Frank Thomas "Enters 5th Dimension"	.75
10	Chris Bosio, Jim Abbott, Darryl Kile "The No-Hit Parade"	.10

League Leaders

		NM/M
Complete Set (12):		3.00
Common Player:		.10
1	John Olerud	.10
2	Albert Belle	.10
3	Rafael Palmeiro	.75
4	Kenny Lofton	.10
5	Jack McDowell	.10
6	Kevin Appier	.10
7	Andres Galarraga	.10
8	Barry Bonds	2.00
9	Len Dykstra	.10

10	Chuck Carr	.10
11	Tom Glavine	.30
12	Greg Maddux	1.00

Lumber Co.

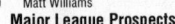

		NM/M
Complete Set (10):		7.50
Common Player:		.40
1	Albert Belle	.40
2	Barry Bonds	2.50
3	Ron Gant	.40
4	Juan Gonzalez	1.00
5	Ken Griffey Jr.	2.00
6	Dave Justice	.40
7	Fred McGriff	.40
8	Rafael Palmeiro	.75
9	Frank Thomas	1.25
10	Matt Williams	.40

Major League Prospects

		NM/M
Complete Set (35):		4.00
Common Player:		.10
1	Kurt Abbott	.10
2	Brian Anderson	.10
3	Rich Aude	.10
4	Cory Bailey	.10
5	Danny Bautista	.10
6	Marty Cordova	.10
7	Tripp Cromer	.10
8	Midre Cummings	.10
9	Carlos Delgado	1.50
10	Steve Dreyer	.10
11	Steve Dunn	.10
12	Jeff Granger	.10
13	Tyrone Hill	.10
14	Denny Hocking	.10
15	John Hope	.10
16	Butch Huskey	.10
17	Miguel Jimenez	.10
18	Chipper Jones	2.50
19	Steve Karsay	.10
20	Mike Kelly	.10

21	Mike Lieberthal	.20
22	Albie Lopez	.10
23	Jeff McNeely	.10
24	Dan Miceli	.10
25	Nate Minchey	.10
26	Marc Newfield	.10
27	Darren Oliver	.10
28	Luis Ortiz	.10
29	Curtis Pride	.10
30	Roger Salkeld	.10
31	Scott Sanders	.10
32	Dave Staton	.10
33	Salomon Torres	.10
34	Steve Trachsel	.10
35	Chris Turner	.10

ProVisions

NM/M

Complete Set (9):		4.00
Common Player:		.25
1	Darren Daulton	.25
2	John Olerud	.25
3	Matt Williams	.25
4	Carlos Baerga	.25
5	Ozzie Smith	1.00
6	Juan Gonzalez	.75
7	Jack McDowell	.25
8	Mike Piazza	2.00
9	Tony Gwynn	1.00

Rookie Sensations

NM/M

Complete Set (20):		6.00
Common Player:		.25
1	Rene Arocha	.25
2	Jason Bere	.25
3	Jeromy Burnitz	.25
4	Chuck Carr	.25
5	Jeff Conine	.25
6	Steve Cooke	.25
7	Cliff Floyd	.25
8	Jeffrey Hammonds	.25
9	Wayne Kirby	.25
10	Mike Lansing	.25
11	Al Martin	.25
12	Greg McMichael	.25
13	Troy Neel	.25
14	Mike Piazza	4.00
15	Armando Reynoso	.25
16	Kirk Rueter	.25
17	Tim Salmon	1.00
18	Aaron Sele	.25
19	J.T. Snow	1.00
20	Kevin Stocker	.25

Tim Salmon
A.L. Rookie of the Year

NM/M

Complete Set (15):	12.50
Common Card:	1.00
Autograph/2,000:	15.00

1-12	Tim Salmon	1.00
13-15	Tim Salmon	1.50

Smoke N' Heat

NM/M

Complete Set (12):		10.00
Common Player:		.20
1	Roger Clemens	4.00
2	David Cone	.25
3	Juan Guzman	.25
4	Pete Harnisch	.25
5	Randy Johnson	2.00
6	Mark Langston	.25
7	Greg Maddux	3.00
8	Mike Mussina	1.00
9	Jose Rijo	.25
10	Nolan Ryan	5.00
11	Curt Schilling	1.00
12	John Smoltz	.75

Team Leaders

NM/M

Complete Set (28):		7.50
Common Player:		.10
1	Cal Ripken, Jr.	2.00
2	Mo Vaughn	.50
3	Tim Salmon	.15
4	Frank Thomas	.50
5	Carlos Baerga	.10
6	Cecil Fielder	.10
7	Brian McRae	.10
8	Greg Vaughn	.10
9	Kirby Puckett	.65
10	Don Mattingly	.75
11	Mark McGwire	1.50
12	Ken Griffey Jr.	1.00
13	Juan Gonzalez	.50
14	Paul Molitor	.50
15	Dave Justice	.10
16	Ryne Sandberg	.65
17	Barry Larkin	.10
18	Andres Galarraga	.10
19	Gary Sheffield	.25
20	Jeff Bagwell	.50

21	Mike Piazza	1.00
22	Marquis Grissom	.10
23	Bobby Bonilla	.10
24	Len Dykstra	.10
25	Jay Bell	.10
26	Gregg Jefferies	.10
27	Tony Gwynn	.65
28	Will Clark	.15

Update

NM/M

Complete Set (210):		50.00
Common Player:		.05
1	Mark Eichhorn	.05
2	Sid Fernandez	.05
3	Leo Gomez	.05
4	Mike Oquist	.05
5	Rafael Palmeiro	.60
6	Chris Sabo	.05
7	Dwight Smith	.05
8	Lee Smith	.05
9	Damon Berryhill	.05
10	Wes Chamberlain	.05
11	Gar Finnvold	.05
12	Chris Howard	.05
13	Tim Naehring	.05
14	Otis Nixon	.05
15	Brian Anderson	.05
16	Jorge Fabregas	.05
17	Rex Hudler	.05
18	Bo Jackson	.15
19	Mark Leiter	.05
20	Spike Owen	.05
21	Harold Reynolds	.05
22	Chris Turner	.05
23	Dennis Cook	.05
24	Jose DeLeon	.05
25	Julio Franco	.05
26	Joe Hall	.05
27	Darrin Jackson	.05
28	Dane Johnson	.05
29	Norberto Martin	.05
30	Scott Sanderson	.05
31	Jason Grimsley	.05
32	Dennis Martinez	.05
33	Jack Morris	.05
34	Eddie Murray	.75
35	Chad Ogea	.05
36	Tony Pena	.05
37	Paul Shuey	.05
38	Omar Vizquel	.05
39	Danny Bautista	.05
40	Tim Belcher	.05
41	Joe Boever	.05
42	Storm Davis	.05
43	Junior Felix	.05
44	Mike Gardiner	.05
45	Buddy Groom	.05
46	Juan Samuel	.05
47	Vince Coleman	.05
48	Bob Hamelin	.05
49	Dave Henderson	.05
50	Rusty Meacham	.05
51	Terry Shumpert	.05
52	Jeff Bronkey	.05
53	Alex Diaz	.05
54	Brian Harper	.05
55	Jose Mercedes	.05
56	Jody Reed	.05
57	Bob Scanlan	.05
58	Turner Ward	.05
59	Rich Becker	.05
60	Alex Cole	.05
61	Denny Hocking	.05
62	Scott Leius	.05
63	Pat Mahomes	.05
64	Carlos Pulido	.05
65	Dave Stevens	.05
66	Matt Walbeck	.05
67	Xavier Hernandez	.05
68	Sterling Hitchcock	.05
69	Terry Mulholland	.05
70	Luis Polonia	.05
71	Gerald Williams	.05
72	Mark Acre	.05
73	Geronimo Berroa	.05
74	Rickey Henderson	.75
75	Stan Javier	.05
76	Steve Karsay	.05
77	Carlos Reyes	.05
78	Bill Taylor	.05

79	Eric Anthony	.05
80	Bobby Ayala	.05
81	Tim Davis	.05
82	Felix Fermin	.05
83	Reggie Jefferson	.05
84	Keith Mitchell	.05
85	Bill Risley	.05
86	Alex Rodriguez RC	40.00
87	Roger Salkeld	.05
88	Dan Wilson	.05
89	Cris Carpenter	.05
90	Will Clark	.10
91	Jeff Frye	.05
92	Rick Helling	.05
93	Chris James	.05
94	Oddibe McDowell	.05
95	Billy Ripken	.05
96	Carlos Delgado	.60
97	Alex Gonzalez	.05
98	Shawn Green	.50
99	Darren Hall	.05
100	Mike Huff	.05
101	Mike Kelly	.05
102	Roberto Kelly	.05
103	Charlie O'Brien	.05
104	Jose Oliva	.05
105	Gregg Olson	.05
106	Willie Banks	.05
107	Jim Bullinger	.05
108	Chuck Crim	.05
109	Shawon Dunston	.05
110	Karl Rhodes	.05
111	Steve Trachsel	.05
112	Anthony Young	.05
113	Eddie Zambrano	.05
114	Bret Boone	.05
115	Jeff Brantley	.05
116	Hector Carrasco	.05
117	Tony Fernandez	.05
118	Tim Fortugno	.05
119	Erik Hanson	.05
120	Chuck McElroy	.05
121	Deion Sanders	.05
122	Ellis Burks	.05
123	Marvin Freeman	.05
124	Mike Harkey	.05
125	Howard Johnson	.05
126	Mike Kingery	.05
127	Nelson Liriano	.05
128	Marcus Moore	.05
129	Mike Munoz	.05
130	Kevin Ritz	.05
131	Walt Weiss	.05
132	Kurt Abbott	.05
133	Jerry Browne	.05
134	Greg Colbrunn	.05
135	Jeremy Hernandez	.05
136	Dave Magadan	.05
137	Kurt Miller	.05
138	Robb Nen	.05
139	Jesus Taverez	.05
140	Sid Bream	.05
141	Tom Edens	.05
142	Tony Eusebio	.05
143	John Hudek	.05
144	Brian Hunter	.05
145	Orlando Miller	.05
146	James Mouton	.05
147	Shane Reynolds	.05
148	Rafael Bournigal	.05
149	Delino DeShields	.05
150	Garey Ingram	.05
151	Chan Ho Park	.05
152	Wil Cordero	.05
153	Pedro Martinez	.75
154	Randy Milligan	.05
155	Lenny Webster	.05
156	Rico Brogna	.05
157	Josias Manzanillo	.05
158	Kevin McReynolds	.05
159	Mike Remlinger	.05
160	David Segui	.05
161	Pete Smith	.05
162	Kelly Stinnett	.05
163	Jose Vizcaino	.05
164	Billy Hatcher	.05
165	Doug Jones	.05
166	Mike Lieberthal	.05
167	Tony Longmire	.05
168	Bobby Munoz	.05
169	Paul Quantrill	.05
170	Heathcliff Slocumb	.05
171	Fernando Valenzuela	.05
172	Mark Dewey	.05
173	Brian Hunter	.05
174	Jon Lieber	.05
175	Ravelo Manzanillo	.05
176	Dan Miceli	.05
177	Rick White	.05
178	Bryan Eversgerd	.05
179	John Habyan	.05
180	Terry McGriff	.05
181	Vicente Palacios	.05
182	Rich Rodriguez	.05
183	Rick Sutcliffe	.05
184	Donnie Elliott	.05
185	Joey Hamilton	.05
186	Tim Hyers	.05
187	Luis Lopez	.05
188	Ray McDavid	.05
189	Bip Roberts	.05
190	Scott Sanders	.05
191	Eddie Williams	.05
192	Steve Frey	.05
193	Pat Gomez	.05

194 Rich Monteleone .05
195 Mark Portugal .05
196 Darryl Strawberry .05
197 Salomon Torres .05
198 W. Van Landingham .05
199 Checklist .05
200 Checklist .05

DIAMOND TRIBUTE .05

DT1 Barry Bonds 2.00
DT2 Joe Carter .05
DT3 Will Clark .10
DT4 Roger Clemens 1.50
DT5 Tony Gwynn 1.00
DT6 Don Mattingly 1.50
DT7 Fred McGriff .05
DT8 Eddie Murray .75
DT9 Kirby Puckett 1.00
DT10 Cal Ripken Jr. 2.00

1995 Fleer

NM/M

Complete Set (600): 15.00
Common Player: .05
Pack (12): .75
Wax Box (36): 17.50

1 Brady Anderson .05
2 Harold Baines .05
3 Damon Buford .05
4 Mike Devereaux .05
5 Mark Eichhorn .05
6 Sid Fernandez .05
7 Leo Gomez .05
8 Jeffrey Hammonds .05
9 Chris Hoiles .05
10 Rick Krivda .05
11 Ben McDonald .05
12 Mark McLemore .05
13 Alan Mills .05
14 Jamie Moyer .05
15 Mike Mussina .40
16 Mike Oquist .05
17 Rafael Palmeiro .65
18 Arthur Rhodes .05
19 Cal Ripken, Jr. 2.50
20 Chris Sabo .05
21 Lee Smith .05
22 Jack Voight .05
23 Damon Berryhill .05
24 Tom Brunansky .05
25 Wes Chamberlain .05
26 Roger Clemens 1.25
27 Scott Cooper .05
28 Andre Dawson .25
29 Gar Finnvold .05
30 Tony Fossas .05
31 Mike Greenwell .05
32 Joe Hesketh .05
33 Chris Howard .05
34 Chris Nabholz .05
35 Tim Naehring .05
36 Otis Nixon .05
37 Carlos Rodriguez .05
38 Rich Rowland .05
39 Ken Ryan .05
40 Aaron Sele .05
41 John Valentin .05
42 Mo Vaughn .05
43 Frank Viola .05
44 Danny Bautista .05
45 Joe Boever .05
46 Milt Cuyler .05
47 Storm Davis .05
48 John Doherty .05
49 Junior Felix .05
50 Cecil Fielder .05
51 Travis Fryman .05
52 Mike Gardiner .05
53 Kirk Gibson .05
54 Chris Gomez .05
55 Buddy Groom .05
56 Mike Henneman .05
57 Chad Kreuter .05
58 Mike Moore .05
59 Tony Phillips .05
60 Juan Samuel .05
61 Mickey Tettleton .05
62 Alan Trammell .05
63 David Wells .05
64 Lou Whitaker .05
65 Jim Abbott .05
66 Joe Ausanio .05
67 Wade Boggs 1.00
68 Mike Gallego .05
69 Xavier Hernandez .05
70 Sterling Hitchcock .05
71 Steve Howe .05
72 Scott Kamieniecki .05
73 Pat Kelly .05
74 Jimmy Key .05
75 Jim Leyritz .05
76 Don Mattingly 1.25
77 Terry Mulholland .05
78 Paul O'Neill .05
79 Melido Perez .05
80 Luis Polonia .05
81 Mike Stanley .05
82 Danny Tartabull .05
83 Randy Velarde .05
84 Bob Wickman .05
85 Bernie Williams .10
86 Gerald Williams .05
87 Roberto Alomar .10
88 Pat Borders .05
89 Joe Carter .05
90 Tony Castillo .05
91 Brad Cornett .05
92 Carlos Delgado .50
93 Alex Gonzalez .05
94 Shawn Green .40
95 Juan Guzman .05
96 Darren Hall .05
97 Pat Hentgen .05
98 Mike Huff .05
99 Randy Knorr .05
100 Al Leiter .05
101 Paul Molitor .75
102 John Olerud .05
103 Dick Schofield .05
104 Ed Sprague .05
105 Dave Stewart .05
106 Todd Stottlemyre .05
107 Devon White .05
108 Woody Williams .05
109 Wilson Alvarez .05
110 Paul Assenmacher .05
111 Jason Bere .05
112 Dennis Cook .05
113 Joey Cora .05
114 Jose DeLeon .05
115 Alex Fernandez .05
116 Julio Franco .05
117 Craig Grabоeck .05
118 Ozzie Guillen .05
119 Roberto Hernandez .05
120 Darrin Jackson .05
121 Lance Johnson .05
122 Ron Karkovice .05
123 Mike LaValliere .05
124 Norberto Martin .05
125 Kirk McCaskill .05
126 Jack McDowell .05
127 Tim Raines .05
128 Frank Thomas .75
129 Robin Ventura .05
130 Sandy Alomar Jr. .05
131 Carlos Baerga .05
132 Albert Belle .05
133 Mark Clark .05
134 Alvaro Espinoza .05
135 Jason Grimsley .05
136 Wayne Kirby .05
137 Kenny Lofton .05
138 Albie Lopez .05
139 Dennis Martinez .05
140 Jose Mesa .05
141 Eddie Murray .75
142 Charles Nagy .05
143 Tony Pena .05
144 Eric Plunk .05
145 Manny Ramirez .75
146 Jeff Russell .05
147 Paul Shuey .05
148 Paul Sorrento .05
149 Jim Thome .65
150 Omar Vizquel .05
151 Dave Winfield .75
152 Kevin Appier .05
153 Billy Brewer .05
154 Vince Coleman .05
155 David Cone .05
156 Gary Gaetti .05
157 Greg Gagne .05
158 Tom Gordon .05
159 Mark Gubicza .05
160 Bob Hamelin .05
161 Dave Henderson .05
162 Felix Jose .05
163 Wally Joyner .05
164 Jose Lind .05
165 Mike Macfarlane .05
166 Mike Magnante .05
167 Brent Mayne .05
168 Brian McRae .05
169 Rusty Meacham .05
170 Jeff Montgomery .05
171 Hipolito Pichardo .05
172 Terry Shumpert .05
173 Michael Tucker .05
174 Ricky Bones .05
175 Jeff Cirillo **RC** .30
176 Alex Diaz .05
177 Cal Eldred .05
178 Mike Fetters .05
179 Darryl Hamilton .05
180 Brian Harper .05
181 John Jaha .05
182 Pat Listach .05
183 Graeme Lloyd .05
184 Jose Mercedes .05
185 Matt Mieske .05
186 Dave Nilsson .05
187 Jody Reed .05
188 Bob Scanlan .05
189 Kevin Seitzer .05
190 Bill Spiers .05
191 B.J. Surhoff .05
192 Jose Valentin .05
193 Greg Vaughn .05
194 Turner Ward .05
195 Bill Wegman .05
196 Rick Aguilera .05
197 Rich Becker .05
198 Alex Cole .05
199 Marty Cordova .05
200 Steve Dunn .05
201 Scott Erickson .05
202 Mark Guthrie .05
203 Chip Hale .05
204 LaTroy Hawkins .05
205 Denny Hocking .05
206 Chuck Knoblauch .05
207 Scott Leius .05
208 Shane Mack .05
209 Pat Mahomes .05
210 Pat Meares .05
211 Pedro Munoz .05
212 Kirby Puckett 1.00
213 Jeff Reboulet .05
214 Dave Stevens .05
215 Kevin Tapani .05
216 Matt Walbeck .05
217 Carl Willis .05
218 Brian Anderson .05
219 Chad Curtis .05
220 Chili Davis .05
221 Gary DiSarcina .05
222 Damion Easley .05
223 Jim Edmonds .05
224 Chuck Finley .05
225 Joe Grahe .05
226 Rex Hudler .05
227 Bo Jackson .10
228 Mark Langston .05
229 Phil Leftwich .05
230 Mark Leiter .05
231 Spike Owen .05
232 Bob Patterson .05
233 Troy Percival .05
234 Eduardo Perez .05
235 Tim Salmon .10
236 J.T. Snow .05
237 Chris Turner .05
238 Mark Acre .05
239 Geronimo Berroa .05
240 Mike Bordick .05
241 John Briscoe .05
242 Scott Brosius .05
243 Ron Darling .05
244 Dennis Eckersley .65
245 Brent Gates .05
246 Rickey Henderson .75
247 Stan Javier .05
248 Steve Karsay .05
249 Mark McGwire 2.00
250 Troy Neel .05
251 Steve Ontiveros .05
252 Carlos Reyes .05
253 Ruben Sierra .05
254 Terry Steinbach .05
255 Bill Taylor .05
256 Todd Van Poppel .05
257 Bobby Witt .05
258 Rich Amaral .05
259 Eric Anthony .05
260 Bobby Ayala .05
261 Mike Blowers .05
262 Chris Bosio .05
263 Jay Buhner .05
264 John Cummings .05
265 Tim Davis .05
266 Felix Fermin .05
267 Dave Fleming .05
268 Goose Gossage .05
269 Ken Griffey Jr. 1.50
270 Reggie Jefferson .05
271 Randy Johnson .75
272 Edgar Martinez .05
273 Tino Martinez .05
274 Greg Pirkl .05
275 Bill Risley .05
276 Roger Salkeld .05
277 Luis Sojo .05
278 Mac Suzuki .05
279 Dan Wilson .05
280 Kevin Brown .05
281 Jose Canseco .40
282 Cris Carpenter .05
283 Will Clark .10
284 Jeff Frye .05
285 Juan Gonzalez .65
286 Rick Helling .05
287 Tom Henke .05
288 David Hulse .05
289 Chris James .05
290 Manuel Lee .05
291 Oddibe McDowell .05
292 Dean Palmer .05
293 Roger Pavlik .05
294 Bill Ripken .05
295 Ivan Rodriguez .65
296 Kenny Rogers .05
297 Doug Strange .05
298 Matt Whiteside .05
299 Steve Avery .05
300 Steve Bedrosian .05
301 Rafael Belliard .05
302 Jeff Blauser .05
303 Dave Gallagher .05
304 Tom Glavine .30
305 Dave Justice .05
306 Mike Kelly .05
307 Roberto Kelly .05
308 Ryan Klesko .05
309 Mark Lemke .05
310 Javier Lopez .05
311 Greg Maddux 1.00
312 Fred McGriff .05
313 Greg McMichael .05
314 Kent Mercker .05
315 Charlie O'Brien .05
316 Jose Oliva .05
317 Terry Pendleton .05
318 John Smoltz .05
319 Mike Stanton .05
320 Tony Tarasco .05
321 Terrell Wade .05
322 Mark Wohlers .05
323 Kurt Abbott .05
324 Luis Aquino .05
325 Bret Barberie .05
326 Ryan Bowen .05
327 Jerry Browne .05
328 Chuck Carr .05
329 Matias Carrillo .05
330 Greg Colbrunn .05
331 Jeff Conine .05
332 Mark Gardner .05
333 Chris Hammond .05
334 Bryan Harvey .05
335 Richie Lewis .05
336 Dave Magadan .05
337 Terry Mathews .05
338 Robb Nen .05
339 Yorkis Perez .05
340 Pat Rapp .05
341 Benito Santiago .05
342 Gary Sheffield .40
343 Dave Weathers .05
344 Moises Alou .05
345 Sean Berry .05
346 Wil Cordero .05
347 Joe Eischen .05
348 Jeff Fassero .05
349 Darrin Fletcher .05
350 Cliff Floyd .05
351 Marquis Grissom .05
352 Butch Henry .05
353 Gil Heredia .05
354 Ken Hill .05
355 Mike Lansing .05
356 Pedro Martinez .75
357 Mel Rojas .05
358 Kirk Rueter .05
359 Tim Scott .05
360 Jeff Shaw .05
361 Larry Walker .05
362 Lenny Webster .05
363 John Wetteland .05
364 Rondell White .05
365 Bobby Bonilla .05
366 Rico Brogna .05
367 Jeromy Burnitz .05
368 John Franco .05
369 Dwight Gooden .05
370 Todd Hundley .05
371 Jason Jacome .05
372 Bobby Jones .05
373 Jeff Kent .05
374 Jim Lindeman .05
375 Josias Manzanillo .05
376 Roger Mason .05
377 Kevin McReynolds .05
378 Joe Orsulak .05
379 Bill Pulsipher .05
380 Bret Saberhagen .05
381 David Segui .05
382 Pete Smith .05
383 Kelly Stinnett .05
384 Ryan Thompson .05
385 Jose Vizcaino .05
386 Toby Borland .05
387 Ricky Bettalico .05
388 Darren Daulton .05
389 Mariano Duncan .05
390 Len Dykstra .05
391 Jim Eisenreich .05
392 Tommy Greene .05
393 Dave Hollins .05
394 Pete Incaviglia .05
395 Danny Jackson .05
396 Doug Jones .05
397 Ricky Jordan .05
398 John Kruk .05
399 Mike Lieberthal .05
400 Tony Longmire .05
401 Mickey Morandini .05
402 Bobby Munoz .05
403 Curt Schilling .25
404 Heathcliff Slocumb .05
405 Kevin Stocker .05
406 Fernando Valenzuela .05
407 David West .05
408 Willie Banks .05
409 Jose Bautista .05
410 Steve Buechele .05
411 Jim Bullinger .05

412	Chuck Crim	.05
413	Shawon Dunston	.05
414	Kevin Foster	.05
415	Mark Grace	.10
416	Jose Hernandez	.05
417	Glenallen Hill	.05
418	Brooks Kieschnick	.05
419	Derrick May	.05
420	Randy Myers	.05
421	Dan Plesac	.05
422	Karl Rhodes	.05
423	Rey Sanchez	.05
424	Sammy Sosa	1.50
425	Steve Trachsel	.05
426	Rick Wilkins	.05
427	Anthony Young	.05
428	Eddie Zambrano	.05
429	Bret Boone	.05
430	Jeff Branson	.05
431	Jeff Brantley	.05
432	Hector Carrasco	.05
433	Brian Dorsett	.05
434	Tony Fernandez	.05
435	Tim Fortugno	.05
436	Erik Hanson	.05
437	Thomas Howard	.05
438	Kevin Jarvis	.05
439	Barry Larkin	.05
440	Chuck McElroy	.05
441	Kevin Mitchell	.05
442	Hal Morris	.05
443	Jose Rijo	.05
444	John Roper	.05
445	Johnny Ruffin	.05
446	Deion Sanders	.05
447	Reggie Sanders	.05
448	Pete Schourek	.05
449	John Smiley	.05
450	Eddie Taubensee	.05
451	Jeff Bagwell	.75
452	Kevin Bass	.05
453	Craig Biggio	.05
454	Ken Caminiti	.05
455	Andujar Cedeno	.05
456	Doug Drabek	.05
457	Tony Eusebio	.05
458	Mike Felder	.05
459	Steve Finley	.05
460	Luis Gonzalez	.10
461	Mike Hampton	.05
462	Pete Harnisch	.05
463	John Hudek	.05
464	Todd Jones	.05
465	Darryl Kile	.05
466	James Mouton	.05
467	Shane Reynolds	.05
468	Scott Servais	.05
469	Greg Swindell	.05
470	Dave Veres	.05
471	Brian Williams	.05
472	Jay Bell	.05
473	Jacob Brumfield	.05
474	Dave Clark	.05
475	Steve Cooke	.05
476	Midre Cummings	.05
477	Mark Dewey	.05
478	Tom Foley	.05
479	Carlos Garcia	.05
480	Jeff King	.05
481	Jon Lieber	.05
482	Ravelo Manzanillo	.05
483	Al Martin	.05
484	Orlando Merced	.05
485	Danny Miceli	.05
486	Denny Neagle	.05
487	Lance Parrish	.05
488	Don Slaught	.05
489	Zane Smith	.05
490	Andy Van Slyke	.05
491	Paul Wagner	.05
492	Rick White	.05
493	Luis Alicea	.05
494	Rene Arocha	.05
495	Rheal Cormier	.05
496	Bryan Eversgerd	.05
497	Bernard Gilkey	.05
498	John Habyan	.05
499	Gregg Jefferies	.05
500	Brian Jordan	.05
501	Ray Lankford	.05
502	John Mabry	.05
503	Terry McGriff	.05
504	Tom Pagnozzi	.05
505	Vicente Palacios	.05
506	Geronimo Pena	.05
507	Gerald Perry	.05
508	Rich Rodriguez	.05
509	Ozzie Smith	1.00
510	Bob Tewksbury	.05
511	Allen Watson	.05
512	Mark Whiten	.05
513	Todd Zeile	.05
514	Dante Bichette	.05
515	Willie Blair	.05
516	Ellis Burks	.05
517	Marvin Freeman	.05
518	Andres Galarraga	.05
519	Joe Girardi	.05
520	Greg Harris	.05
521	Charlie Hayes	.05
522	Mike Kingery	.05
523	Nelson Liriano	.05
524	Mike Munoz	.05
525	David Nied	.05
526	Steve Reed	.05

527	Kevin Ritz	.05
528	Bruce Ruffin	.05
529	John Vander Wal	.05
530	Walt Weiss	.05
531	Eric Young	.05
532	Billy Ashley	.05
533	Pedro Astacio	.05
534	Rafael Bournigal	.05
535	Brett Butler	.05
536	Tom Candiotti	.05
537	Omar Daal	.05
538	Delino DeShields	.05
539	Darren Dreifort	.05
540	Kevin Gross	.05
541	Orel Hershiser	.05
542	Garey Ingram	.05
543	Eric Karros	.05
544	Ramon Martinez	.05
545	Raul Mondesi	.05
546	Chan Ho Park	.05
547	Mike Piazza	1.50
548	Henry Rodriguez	.05
549	Rudy Seanez	.05
550	Ismael Valdes	.05
551	Tim Wallach	.05
552	Todd Worrell	.05
553	Andy Ashby	.05
554	Brad Ausmus	.05
555	Derek Bell	.05
556	Andy Benes	.05
557	Phil Clark	.05
558	Donnie Elliott	.05
559	Ricky Gutierrez	.05
560	Tony Gwynn	1.00
561	Joey Hamilton	.05
562	Trevor Hoffman	.05
563	Luis Lopez	.05
564	Pedro Martinez	.05
565	Tim Mauser	.05
566	Phil Plantier	.05
567	Bip Roberts	.05
568	Scott Sanders	.05
569	Craig Shipley	.05
570	Jeff Tabaka	.05
571	Eddie Williams	.05
572	Rod Beck	.05
573	Mike Benjamin	.05
574	Barry Bonds	2.50
575	Dave Burba	.05
576	John Burkett	.05
577	Mark Carreon	.05
578	Royce Clayton	.05
579	Steve Frey	.05
580	Bryan Hickerson	.05
581	Mike Jackson	.05
582	Darren Lewis	.05
583	Kirt Manwaring	.05
584	Rich Monteleone	.05
585	John Patterson	.05
586	J.R. Phillips	.05
587	Mark Portugal	.05
588	Joe Rosselli	.05
589	Darryl Strawberry	.05
590	Bill Swift	.05
591	Robby Thompson	.05
592	William Van Landingham	.05
593	Matt Williams	.05
594	Checklist	.05
595	Checklist	.05
596	Checklist	.05
597	Checklist	.05
598	Checklist	.05
599	Checklist	.05
600	Checklist	.05

All-Stars

		NM/M
Complete Set (25):		8.00
Common Card:		.20
1	Ivan Rodriguez, Mike Piazza	.75
2	Frank Thomas, Gregg Jefferies	.50
3	Roberto Alomar, Mariano Duncan	.40
4	Wade Boggs, Matt Williams	.65
5	Cal Ripken, Jr., Ozzie Smith	1.50
6	Joe Carter, Barry Bonds	1.50
7	Ken Griffey Jr., Tony Gwynn	.75
8	Kirby Puckett, Dave Justice	.65
9	Jimmy Key, Greg Maddux	.65
10	Chuck Knoblauch, Wil Cordero	.20
11	Scott Cooper, Ken Caminiti	.20
12	Will Clark, Carlos Garcia	.50
13	Paul Molitor, Jeff Bagwell	.50
14	Travis Fryman, Craig Biggio	.20
15	Mickey Tettleton, Fred McGriff	.20
16	Kenny Lofton, Moises Alou	.20
17	Albert Belle, Marquis Grissom	.20
18	Paul O'Neill, Dante Bichette	.20
19	David Cone, Ken Hill	.20
20	Mike Mussina, Doug Drabek	.50
21	Randy Johnson, John Hudek	.50
22	Pat Hentgen, Danny Jackson	.20
23	Wilson Alvarez, Rod Beck	.20
24	Lee Smith, Randy Myers	.20
25	Jason Bere, Doug Jones	.20

All-Fleer 9

		NM/M
Complete Set (9):		4.00
Common Player:		.25
1	Mike Piazza	1.00
2	Frank Thomas	.50
3	Roberto Alomar	.40
4	Cal Ripken Jr.	2.50
5	Matt Williams	.25
6	Barry Bonds	2.50
7	Ken Griffey Jr.	1.00
8	Tony Gwynn	.65
9	Greg Maddux	.65

All-Rookies

		NM/M
Complete Set (9):		1.50
Common Player:		.25
Trade card: 2X		.12
1	Edgardo Alfonzo	.25
2	Jason Bates	.25
3	Brian Boehringer	.25
4	Darren Bragg	.25
5	Brad Clontz	.25
6	Jim Dougherty	.25
7	Todd Hollandsworth	.25
8	Rudy Pemberton	.25
9	Frank Rodriguez	.25

Award Winners

		NM/M
Complete Set (6):		4.00
Common Player:		.25
1	Frank Thomas	1.50
2	Jeff Bagwell	1.50
3	David Cone	.25
4	Greg Maddux	2.00
5	Bob Hamelin	.25
6	Raul Mondesi	.25

League Leaders

		NM/M
Complete Set (10):		4.00
Common Player:		.25
1	Paul O'Neill	.25
2	Ken Griffey Jr.	1.50
3	Kirby Puckett	.75
4	Jimmy Key	.25
5	Randy Johnson	.65
6	Tony Gwynn	.75
7	Matt Williams	.25
8	Jeff Bagwell	.50
9	Greg Maddux, Ken Hill	.75
10	Andy Benes	.25

Lumber Company

		NM/M
Complete Set (10):		12.00
Common Player:		.40
1	Jeff Bagwell	1.50
2	Albert Belle	.40
3	Barry Bonds	3.50
4	Jose Canseco	.75
5	Joe Carter	.40
6	Ken Griffey Jr.	2.50
7	Fred McGriff	.40
8	Kevin Mitchell	.40
9	Frank Thomas	1.75
10	Matt Williams	.40

Major League Prospects

		NM/M
Complete Set (10):		6.00
Common Player:		.25
1	Garret Anderson	.50
2	James Baldwin	.25
3	Alan Benes	.25
4	Armando Benitez	.25
5	Ray Durham	.25
6	Brian Hunter	.25
7a	Derek Jeter (No licensor logos on back.)	4.00
7b	Derek Jeter (Licensor logos on back.)	4.00
8	Charles Johnson	.25
9	Orlando Miller	.25
10	Alex Rodriguez	3.00

Pro-Visions

		NM/M
Complete Set (6):		2.00
Common Player:		.25
1	Mike Mussina	.40
2	Raul Mondesi	.25

3	Jeff Bagwell	.75
4	Greg Maddux	1.00
5	Tim Salmon	.25
6	Manny Ramirez	.75

Rookie Sensations

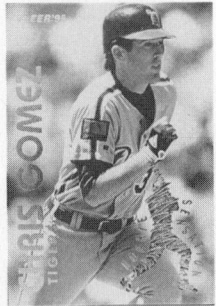

		NM/M
Complete Set (20):		5.00
Common Player:		.25
1	Kurt Abbott	.25
2	Rico Brogna	.25
3	Hector Carrasco	.25
4	Kevin Foster	.25
5	Chris Gomez	.25
6	Darren Hall	.25
7	Bob Hamelin	.25
8	Joey Hamilton	.25
9	John Hudek	.25
10	Ryan Klesko	.25
11	Javier Lopez	.25
12	Matt Mieske	.25
13	Raul Mondesi	.25
14	Manny Ramirez	4.00
15	Shane Reynolds	.25
16	Bill Risley	.25
17	Johnny Ruffin	.25
18	Steve Trachsel	.25
19	William Van Landingham	.25
20	Rondell White	.25

Team Leaders

		NM/M
Complete Set (28):		50.00
Common Card:		.50
1	Cal Ripken, Jr.,	
	Mike Mussina	7.50
2	Mo Vaughn, Roger Clemens	4.50
3	Tim Salmon, Chuck Finley	.75
4	Frank Thomas,	
	Jack McDowell	2.50
5	Albert Belle, Dennis Martinez	.50
6	Cecil Fielder, Mike Moore	.50
7	Bob Hamelin, David Cone	.50

8	Greg Vaughn, Ricky Bones	.50
9	Kirby Puckett, Rick Aguilera	3.00
10	Don Mattingly, Jimmy Key	4.50
11	Ruben Sierra,	
	Dennis Eckersley	1.50
12	Ken Griffey Jr.,	
	Randy Johnson	6.00
13	Jose Canseco, Kenny Rogers	1.00
14	Joe Carter, Pat Hentgen	.50
15	Dave Justice,	
	Greg Maddux	3.00
16	Sammy Sosa,	
	Steve Trachsel	5.00
17	Kevin Mitchell, Jose Rijo	.50
18	Dante Bichette,	
	Bruce Ruffin	.50
19	Jeff Conine, Robb Nen	.50
20	Jeff Bagwell,	
	Doug Drabek	2.50
21	Mike Piazza,	
	Ramon Martinez	5.00
22	Moises Alou, Ken Hill	.50
23	Bobby Bonilla,	
	Bret Saberhagen	.50
24	Darren Daulton,	
	Danny Jackson	.50
25	Jay Bell, Zane Smith	.50
26	Gregg Jefferies,	
	Bob Tewksbury	.50
27	Tony Gwynn, Andy Benes	3.00
28	Matt Williams, Rod Beck	.50

Update

		NM/M
Complete Set (200):		7.00
Common Player:		.05
Pack (12):		.50
Wax Box (36):		7.50
1	Manny Alexander	.05
2	Bret Barberie	.05
3	Armando Benitez	.05
4	Kevin Brown	.05
5	Doug Jones	.05
6	Sherman Obando	.05
7	Andy Van Slyke	.05
8	Stan Belinda	.05
9	Jose Canseco	.30
10	Vaughn Eshelman	.05
11	Mike Macfarlane	.05
12	Troy O'Leary	.05
13	Steve Rodriguez	.05
14	Lee Tinsley	.05
15	Tim Vanegmond	.05
16	Mark Whiten	.05
17	Sean Bergman	.05
18	Chad Curtis	.05
19	John Flaherty	.05
20	Bob Higginson RC	.15
21	Felipe Lira	.05
22	Shannon Penn	.05
23	Todd Steverson	.05
24	Sean Whiteside	.05
25	Tony Fernandez	.05
26	Jack McDowell	.05
27	Andy Pettitte	.15
28	John Wetteland	.05
29	David Cone	.05
30	Mike Timlin	.05
31	Duane Ward	.05
32	Jim Abbott	.05
33	James Baldwin	.05
34	Mike Devereaux	.05
35	Ray Durham	.05
36	Tim Fortugno	.05
37	Scott Ruffcorn	.05
38	Chris Sabo	.05
39	Paul Assenmacher	.05
40	Bob Black	.05
41	Orel Hershiser	.05
42	Julian Tavarez	.05
43	Dave Winfield	.60
44	Pat Borders	.05
45	Melvin Bunch RC	.05
46	Tom Goodwin	.05
47	Jon Nunnally	.05
48	Joe Randa	.05
49	Dilson Torres RC	.05
50	Joe Vitiello	.05
51	David Hulse	.05
52	Scott Karl	.05
53	Mark Kiefer	.05

54	Derrick May	.05
55	Joe Oliver	.05
56	Al Reyes	.05
57	Steve Sparks RC	.05
58	Jerald Clark	.05
59	Eddie Guardado	.05
60	Kevin Maas	.05
61	David McCarty	.05
62	Brad Radke RC	.50
63	Scott Stahoviak	.05
64	Garret Anderson	.05
65	Shawn Boskie	.05
66	Mike James	.05
67	Tony Phillips	.05
68	Lee Smith	.05
69	Mitch Williams	.05
70	Jim Corsi	.05
71	Mark Harkey	.05
72	Dave Stewart	.05
73	Todd Stottlemyre	.05
74	Joey Cora	.05
75	Chad Kreuter	.05
76	Jeff Nelson	.05
77	Alex Rodriguez	2.00
78	Ron Villone	.05
79	Bob Wells RC	.05
80	Jose Alberro RC	.05
81	Terry Burrows	.05
82	Kevin Gross	.05
83	Wilson Heredia	.05
84	Mark McLemore	.05
85	Otis Nixon	.05
86	Jeff Russell	.05
87	Mickey Tettleton	.05
88	Bob Tewksbury	.05
89	Pedro Borbon	.05
90	Marquis Grissom	.05
91	Chipper Jones	.75
92	Mike Mordecai	.05
93	Jason Schmidt	.15
94	John Burkett	.05
95	Andre Dawson	.25
96	Matt Dunbar RC	.05
97	Charles Johnson	.05
98	Terry Pendleton	.05
99	Rich Scheid	.05
100	Quilvio Veras	.05
101	Bobby Witt	.05
102	Eddie Zosky	.05
103	Shane Andrews	.05
104	Reid Cornelius	.05
105	Chad Fonville RC	.05
106	Mark Grudzielanek RC	.25
107	Roberto Kelly	.05
108	Carlos Perez RC	.05
109	Tony Tarasco	.05
110	Brett Butler	.05
111	Carl Everett	.05
112	Pete Harnisch	.05
113	Doug Henry	.05
114	Kevin Lomon	.05
115	Blas Minor	.05
116	Dave Mlicki	.05
117	Ricky Otero RC	.05
118	Norm Charlton	.05
119	Tyler Green	.05
120	Gene Harris	.05
121	Charlie Hayes	.05
122	Gregg Jefferies	.05
123	Michael Mimbs RC	.05
124	Paul Quantrill	.05
125	Frank Castillo	.05
126	Brian McRae	.05
127	Jaime Navarro	.05
128	Mike Perez	.05
129	Tanyon Sturtze	.05
130	Ozzie Timmons	.05
131	John Courtright	.05
132	Ron Gant	.05
133	Xavier Hernandez	.05
134	Brian Hunter	.05
135	Benito Santiago	.05
136	Pete Smith	.05
137	Scott Sullivan	.05
138	Derek Bell	.05
139	Doug Brocail	.05
140	Ricky Gutierrez	.05
141	Pedro Martinez	.05
142	Orlando Miller	.05
143	Phil Plantier	.05
144	Craig Shipley	.05
145	Rich Aude	.05
146	Jason Christiansen RC	.05
147	Freddy Garcia RC	.25
148	Jim Gott	.05
149	Mark Johnson RC	.05
150	Esteban Loaiza	.05
151	Dan Plesac	.05
152	Gary Wilson RC	.05
153	Allen Battle	.05
154	Terry Bradshaw	.05
155	Scott Cooper	.05
156	Tripp Cromer	.05
157	John Frascatore	.05
158	John Habyan	.05
159	Tom Henke	.05
160	Ken Hill	.05
161	Danny Jackson	.05
162	Donovan Osborne	.05
163	Tom Urbani	.05
164	Roger Bailey	.05
165	Jorge Brito RC	.05
166	Vinny Castilla	.05
167	Darren Holmes	.05
168	Roberto Mejia	.05

169	Bill Swift	.05
170	Mark Thompson	.05
171	Larry Walker	.05
172	Greg Hansell	.05
173	Dave Hansen	.05
174	Carlos Hernandez	.05
175	Hideo Nomo RC	2.00
176	Jose Offerman	.05
177	Antonio Osuna	.05
178	Reggie Williams	.05
179	Todd Williams	.05
180	Andres Berumen	.05
181	Ken Caminiti	.05
182	Andujar Cedeno	.05
183	Steve Finley	.05
184	Bryce Florie	.05
185	Dustin Hermanson	.05
186	Ray Holbert	.05
187	Melvin Nieves	.05
188	Roberto Petagine	.05
189	Jody Reed	.05
190	Fernando Valenzuela	.05
191	Brian Williams	.05
192	Mark Dewey	.05
193	Glenallen Hill	.05
194	Chris Hook RC	.05
195	Terry Mulholland	.05
196	Steve Scarsone	.05
197	Trevor Wilson	.05
198	Checklist	.05
199	Checklist	.05
200	Checklist	.05

Update Diamond Tribute

		NM/M
Complete Set (10):		6.00
Common Player:		.25
1	Jeff Bagwell	.75
2	Albert Belle	.25
3	Barry Bonds	3.00
4	David Cone	.25
5	Dennis Eckersley	.50
6	Ken Griffey Jr.	1.50
7	Rickey Henderson	.60
8	Greg Maddux	1.00
9	Frank Thomas	.75
10	Matt Williams	.25

Update Smooth Leather

		NM/M
Complete Set (10):		7.50
Common Player:		.25
1	Roberto Alomar	.50
2	Barry Bonds	2.50
3	Ken Griffey Jr.	1.50
4	Marquis Grissom	.25
5	Darren Lewis	.25
6	Kenny Lofton	.50
7	Don Mattingly	1.00
8	Cal Ripken Jr.	2.50
9	Ivan Rodriguez	.75
10	Matt Williams	.25

Update Rookie Update

		NM/M
Complete Set (10):		4.00
Common Player:		.10

1	Shane Andrews	.10
2	Ray Durham	.10
3	Shawn Green	.40
4	Charles Johnson	.10
5	Chipper Jones	1.50
6	Esteban Loaiza	.10
7	Hideo Nomo	1.00
8	Jon Nunnally	.10
9	Alex Rodriguez	2.00
10	Julian Tavarez	.10

Update Soaring Stars

		NM/M
Complete Set (9):		3.50
Common Player:		.15
1	Moises Alou	.35
2	Jason Bere	.25
3	Jeff Conine	.25
4	Cliff Floyd	.25
5	Pat Hentgen	.25
6	Kenny Lofton	.25
7	Raul Mondesi	.25
8	Mike Piazza	3.00
9	Tim Salmon	.35

Update Headliners

		NM/M
Complete Set (20):		8.00
Common Player:		.10
1	Jeff Bagwell	.50
2	Albert Belle	.15
3	Barry Bonds	3.00
4	Jose Canseco	.40
5	Joe Carter	.15
6	Will Clark	.25
7	Roger Clemens	2.00
8	Lenny Dykstra	.15
9	Cecil Fielder	.15
10	Juan Gonzalez	.40
11	Ken Griffey Jr.	2.00
12	Kenny Lofton	.15
13	Greg Maddux	.75
14	Fred McGriff	.15
15	Mike Piazza	1.50
16	Kirby Puckett	.75
17	Tim Salmon	.15
18	Frank Thomas	.50
19	Mo Vaughn	.15
20	Matt Williams	.15

1996 Fleer

		NM/M
Complete Set (600):		20.00
Common Player:		.05
Complete Tiffany Set (600):		100.00

Tiffanies:		2X
Pack (11):		.75
Wax Box (36):		16.00
1	Manny Alexander	.05
2	Brady Anderson	.05
3	Harold Baines	.05
4	Armando Benitez	.05
5	Bobby Bonilla	.05
6	Kevin Brown	.05
7	Scott Erickson	.05
8	Curtis Goodwin	.05
9	Jeffrey Hammonds	.05
10	Jimmy Haynes	.05
11	Chris Hoiles	.05
12	Doug Jones	.05
13	Rick Krivda	.05
14	Jeff Manto	.05
15	Ben McDonald	.05
16	Jamie Moyer	.05
17	Mike Mussina	.50
18	Jesse Orosco	.05
19	Rafael Palmeiro	.65
20	Cal Ripken Jr.	2.50
20(p)	Cal Ripken Jr./OPS	2.50
21	Rick Aguilera	.05
22	Luis Alicea	.05
23	Stan Belinda	.05
24	Jose Canseco	.50
25	Roger Clemens	1.25
26	Vaughn Eshelman	.05
27	Mike Greenwell	.05
28	Erik Hanson	.05
29	Dwayne Hosey	.05
30	Mike Macfarlane	.05
31	Tim Naehring	.05
32	Troy O'Leary	.05
33	Aaron Sele	.05
34	Zane Smith	.05
35	Jeff Suppan	.05
36	Lee Tinsley	.05
37	John Valentin	.05
38	Mo Vaughn	.05
39	Tim Wakefield	.05
40	Jim Abbott	.05
41	Brian Anderson	.05
42	Garret Anderson	.05
43	Chili Davis	.05
44	Gary DiSarcina	.05
45	Damion Easley	.05
46	Jim Edmonds	.05
47	Chuck Finley	.05
48	Todd Greene	.05
49	Mike Harkey	.05
50	Mike James	.05
51	Mark Langston	.05
52	Greg Myers	.05
53	Orlando Palmeiro	.05
54	Bob Patterson	.05
55	Troy Percival	.05
56	Tony Phillips	.05
57	Tim Salmon	.10
58	Lee Smith	.05
59	J.T. Snow	.05
60	Randy Velarde	.05
61	Wilson Alvarez	.05
62	Luis Andujar RC	.05
63	Jason Bere	.05
64	Ray Durham	.05
65	Alex Fernandez	.05
66	Ozzie Guillen	.05
67	Roberto Hernandez	.05
68	Lance Johnson	.05
69	Matt Karchner	.05
70	Ron Karkovice	.05
71	Norberto Martin	.05
72	Dave Martinez	.05
73	Kirk McCaskill	.05
74	Lyle Mouton	.05
75	Tim Raines	.05
76	Mike Sirotka RC	.05
77	Frank Thomas	.75
78	Larry Thomas	.05
79	Robin Ventura	.05
80	Sandy Alomar Jr.	.05
81	Paul Assenmacher	.05
82	Carlos Baerga	.05
83	Albert Belle	.05
84	Mark Clark	.05
85	Alan Embree	.05
86	Alvaro Espinoza	.05
87	Orel Hershiser	.05

88	Ken Hill	.05
89	Kenny Lofton	.05
90	Dennis Martinez	.05
91	Jose Mesa	.05
92	Eddie Murray	.75
93	Charles Nagy	.05
94	Chad Ogea	.05
95	Tony Pena	.05
96	Herb Perry	.05
97	Eric Plunk	.05
98	Jim Poole	.05
99	Manny Ramirez	.75
100	Paul Sorrento	.05
101	Julian Travarez	.05
102	Jim Thome	.60
103	Omar Vizquel	.05
104	Dave Winfield	.75
105	Danny Bautista	.05
106	Joe Boever	.05
107	Chad Curtis	.05
108	John Doherty	.05
109	Cecil Fielder	.05
110	John Flaherty	.05
111	Travis Fryman	.05
112	Chris Gomez	.05
113	Bob Higginson	.05
114	Mark Lewis	.05
115	Jose Lima	.05
116	Felipe Lira	.05
117	Brian Maxcy	.05
118	C.J. Nitkowski	.05
119	Phil Plantier	.05
120	Clint Sodowsky	.05
121	Alan Trammell	.05
122	Lou Whitaker	.05
123	Kevin Appier	.05
124	Johnny Damon	.35
125	Gary Gaetti	.05
126	Tom Goodwin	.05
127	Tom Gordon	.05
128	Mark Gubicza	.05
129	Bob Hamelin	.05
130	David Howard	.05
131	Jason Jacome	.05
132	Wally Joyner	.05
133	Keith Lockhart	.05
134	Brent Mayne	.05
135	Jeff Montgomery	.05
136	Jon Nunnally	.05
137	Juan Samuel	.05
138	Mike Sweeney RC	.50
139	Michael Tucker	.05
140	Joe Vitiello	.05
141	Ricky Bones	.05
142	Chuck Carr	.05
143	Jeff Cirillo	.05
144	Mike Fetters	.05
145	Darryl Hamilton	.05
146	David Hulse	.05
147	John Jaha	.05
148	Scott Karl	.05
149	Mark Kiefer	.05
150	Pat Listach	.05
151	Mark Loretta	.05
152	Mike Matheny	.05
153	Matt Mieske	.05
154	Dave Nilsson	.05
155	Joe Oliver	.05
156	Al Reyes	.05
157	Kevin Seitzer	.05
158	Steve Sparks	.05
159	B.J. Surhoff	.05
160	Jose Valentin	.05
161	Greg Vaughn	.05
162	Fernando Vina	.05
163	Rich Becker	.05
164	Ron Coomer	.05
165	Marty Cordova	.05
166	Chuck Knoblauch	.05
167	Matt Lawton RC	.30
168	Pat Meares	.05
169	Paul Molitor	.75
170	Pedro Munoz	.05
171	Jose Parra	.05
172	Kirby Puckett	1.00
173	Brad Radke	.05
174	Jeff Reboulet	.05
175	Rich Robertson	.05
176	Frank Rodriguez	.05
177	Scott Stahoviak	.05
178	Dave Stevens	.05
179	Matt Walbeck	.05
180	Wade Boggs	1.00
181	David Cone	.05
182	Tony Fernandez	.05
183	Joe Girardi	.05
184	Derek Jeter	2.50
185	Scott Kamieniecki	.05
186	Pat Kelly	.05
187	Jim Leyritz	.05
188	Tino Martinez	.05
189	Don Mattingly	1.25
190	Jack McDowell	.05
191	Jeff Nelson	.05
192	Paul O'Neill	.05
193	Melido Perez	.05
194	Andy Pettitte	.30
195	Mariano Rivera	.15
196	Ruben Sierra	.05
197	Mike Stanley	.05
198	Darryl Strawberry	.05
199	John Wetteland	.05
200	Bob Wickman	.05
201	Bernie Williams	.10
202	Mark Acre	.05

203	Geronimo Berroa	.05
204	Mike Bordick	.05
205	Scott Brosius	.05
206	Dennis Eckersley	.65
207	Brent Gates	.05
208	Jason Giambi	.60
209	Rickey Henderson	.75
210	Jose Herrera	.05
211	Stan Javier	.05
212	Doug Johns	.05
213	Mark McGwire	2.00
214	Steve Ontiveros	.05
215	Craig Paquette	.05
216	Ariel Prieto	.05
217	Carlos Reyes	.05
218	Terry Steinbach	.05
219	Todd Stottlemyre	.05
220	Danny Tartabull	.05
221	Todd Van Poppel	.05
222	John Wasdin	.05
223	George Williams	.05
224	Steve Wojciechowski	.05
225	Rich Amaral	.05
226	Bobby Ayala	.05
227	Tim Belcher	.05
228	Andy Benes	.05
229	Chris Bosio	.05
230	Darren Bragg	.05
231	Jay Buhner	.05
232	Norm Charlton	.05
233	Vince Coleman	.05
234	Joey Cora	.05
235	Russ Davis	.05
236	Alex Diaz	.05
237	Felix Fermin	.05
238	Ken Griffey Jr.	1.75
239	Sterling Hitchcock	.05
240	Randy Johnson	.75
241	Edgar Martinez	.05
242	Bill Risley	.05
243	Alex Rodriquez	2.00
244	Luis Sojo	.05
245	Dan Wilson	.05
246	Bob Wolcott	.05
247	Will Clark	.10
248	Jeff Frye	.05
249	Benji Gil	.05
250	Juan Gonzalez	.65
251	Rusty Greer	.05
252	Kevin Gross	.05
253	Roger McDowell	.05
254	Mark McLemore	.05
255	Otis Nixon	.05
256	Luis Ortiz	.05
257	Mike Pagliarulo	.05
258	Dean Palmer	.05
259	Roger Pavlik	.05
260	Ivan Rodriguez	.65
261	Kenny Rogers	.05
262	Jeff Russell	.05
263	Mickey Tettleton	.05
264	Bob Tewksbury	.05
265	Dave Valle	.05
266	Matt Whiteside	.05
267	Roberto Alomar	.10
268	Joe Carter	.05
269	Tony Castillo	.05
270	Domingo Cedeno	.05
271	Timothy Crabtree	.05
272	Carlos Delgado	.60
273	Alex Gonzalez	.05
274	Shawn Green	.20
275	Juan Guzman	.05
276	Pat Hentgen	.05
277	Al Leiter	.05
278	Sandy Martinez RC	.05
279	Paul Menhart	.05
280	John Olerud	.05
281	Paul Quantrill	.05
282	Ken Robinson	.05
283	Ed Sprague	.05
284	Mike Timlin	.05
285	Steve Avery	.05
286	Rafael Belliard	.05
287	Jeff Blauser	.05
288	Pedro Borbon	.05
289	Brad Clontz	.05
290	Mike Devereaux	.05
291	Tom Glavine	.25
292	Marquis Grissom	.05
293	Chipper Jones	1.00
294	David Justice	.05
295	Mike Kelly	.05
296	Ryan Klesko	.05
297	Mark Lemke	.05
298	Javier Lopez	.05
299	Greg Maddux	1.00
300	Fred McGriff	.05
301	Greg McMichael	.05
302	Kent Mercker	.05
303	Mike Mordecai	.05
304	Charlie O'Brien	.05
305	Eduardo Perez	.05
306	Luis Polonia	.05
307	Jason Schmidt	.05
308	John Smoltz	.05
309	Terrell Wade	.05
310	Mark Wohlers	.05
311	Scott Bullett	.05
312	Jim Bullinger	.05
313	Larry Casian	.05
314	Frank Castillo	.05
315	Shawon Dunston	.05
316	Kevin Foster	.05
317	Matt Franco	.05

318	Luis Gonzalez	.10
319	Mark Grace	.10
320	Jose Hernandez	.05
321	Mike Hubbard	.05
322	Brian McRae	.05
323	Randy Myers	.05
324	Jaime Navarro	.05
325	Mark Parent	.05
326	Mike Perez	.05
327	Rey Sanchez	.05
328	Ryne Sandberg	1.00
329	Scott Servais	.05
330	Sammy Sosa	1.50
331	Ozzie Timmons	.05
332	Steve Trachsel	.05
333	Todd Zeile	.05
334	Bret Boone	.10
335	Jeff Branson	.05
336	Jeff Brantley	.05
337	Dave Burba	.05
338	Hector Carrasco	.05
339	Mariano Duncan	.05
340	Ron Gant	.05
341	Lenny Harris	.05
342	Xavier Hernandez	.05
343	Thomas Howard	.05
344	Mike Jackson	.05
345	Barry Larkin	.05
346	Darren Lewis	.05
347	Hal Morris	.05
348	Eric Owens	.05
349	Mark Portugal	.05
350	Jose Rijo	.05
351	Reggie Sanders	.05
352	Benito Santiago	.05
353	Pete Schourek	.05
354	John Smiley	.05
355	Eddie Taubensee	.05
356	Jerome Walton	.05
357	David Wells	.05
358	Roger Bailey	.05
359	Jason Bates	.05
360	Dante Bichette	.05
361	Ellis Burks	.05
362	Vinny Castilla	.05
363	Andres Galarraga	.05
364	Darren Holmes	.05
365	Mike Kingery	.05
366	Curt Leskanic	.05
367	Quinton McCracken	.05
368	Mike Munoz	.05
369	David Nied	.05
370	Steve Reed	.05
371	Bryan Rekar	.05
372	Kevin Ritz	.05
373	Bruce Ruffin	.05
374	Bret Saberhagen	.05
375	Bill Swift	.05
376	John Vander Wal	.05
377	Larry Walker	.05
378	Walt Weiss	.05
379	Eric Young	.05
380	Kurt Abbott	.05
381	Alex Arias	.05
382	Jerry Browne	.05
383	John Burkett	.05
384	Greg Colbrunn	.05
385	Jeff Conine	.05
386	Andre Dawson	.35
387	Chris Hammond	.05
388	Charles Johnson	.05
389	Terry Mathews	.05
390	Robb Nen	.05
391	Joe Orsulak	.05
392	Terry Pendleton	.05
393	Pat Rapp	.05
394	Gary Sheffield	.45
395	Jesus Tavarez	.05
396	Marc Valdes	.05
397	Quilvio Veras	.05
398	Randy Veres	.05
399	Devon White	.05
400	Jeff Bagwell	.75
401	Derek Bell	.05
402	Craig Biggio	.05
403	John Cangelosi	.05
404	Jim Dougherty	.05
405	Doug Drabek	.05
406	Tony Eusebio	.05
407	Ricky Gutierrez	.05
408	Mike Hampton	.05
409	Dean Hartgraves	.05
410	John Hudek	.05
411	Brian Hunter	.05
412	Todd Jones	.05
413	Darryl Kile	.05
414	Dave Magadan	.05
415	Derrick May	.05
416	Orlando Miller	.05
417	James Mouton	.05
418	Shane Reynolds	.05
419	Greg Swindell	.05
420	Jeff Tabaka	.05
421	Dave Veres	.05
422	Billy Wagner	.05
423	Donne Wall **RC**	.05
424	Rick Wilkins	.05
425	Billy Ashley	.05
426	Mike Blowers	.05
427	Brett Butler	.05
428	Tom Candiotti	.05
429	Juan Castro	.05
430	John Cummings	.05
431	Delino DeShields	.05
432	Joey Eischen	.05
433	Chad Fonville	.05
434	Greg Gagne	.05
435	Dave Hansen	.05
436	Carlos Hernandez	.05
437	Todd Hollandsworth	.05
438	Eric Karros	.05
439	Roberto Kelly	.05
440	Ramon Martinez	.05
441	Raul Mondesi	.05
442	Hideo Nomo	.65
443	Antonio Osuna	.05
444	Chan Ho Park	.05
445	Mike Piazza	1.75
446	Felix Rodriguez	.05
447	Kevin Tapani	.05
448	Ismael Valdes	.05
449	Todd Worrell	.05
450	Moises Alou	.05
451	Shane Andrews	.05
452	Yamil Benitez	.05
453	Sean Berry	.05
454	Wil Cordero	.05
455	Jeff Fassero	.05
456	Darrin Fletcher	.05
457	Cliff Floyd	.05
458	Mark Grudzielanek	.05
459	Gil Heredia	.05
460	Tim Laker	.05
461	Mike Lansing	.05
462	Pedro Martinez	.75
463	Carlos Perez	.05
464	Curtis Pride	.05
465	Mel Rojas	.05
466	Kirk Rueter	.05
467	F.P. Santangelo **RC**	.05
468	Tim Scott	.05
469	David Segui	.05
470	Tony Tarasco	.05
471	Rondell White	.05
472	Edgardo Alfonzo	.05
473	Tim Bogar	.05
474	Rico Brogna	.05
475	Damon Buford	.05
476	Paul Byrd	.05
477	Carl Everett	.10
478	John Franco	.05
479	Todd Hundley	.05
480	Butch Huskey	.05
481	Jason Isringhausen	.05
482	Bobby Jones	.05
483	Chris Jones	.05
484	Jeff Kent	.10
485	Dave Mlicki	.05
486	Robert Person	.05
487	Bill Pulsipher	.05
488	Kelly Stinnett	.05
489	Ryan Thompson	.05
490	Jose Vizcaino	.05
491	Howard Battle	.05
492	Toby Borland	.05
493	Ricky Bottalico	.05
494	Darren Daulton	.05
495	Lenny Dykstra	.05
496	Jim Eisenreich	.05
497	Sid Fernandez	.05
498	Tyler Green	.05
499	Charlie Hayes	.05
500	Gregg Jefferies	.05
501	Kevin Jordan	.05
502	Tony Longmire	.05
503	Tom Marsh	.05
504	Michael Mimbs	.05
505	Mickey Morandini	.05
506	Gene Schall	.05
507	Curt Schilling	.25
508	Heathcliff Slocumb	.05
509	Kevin Stocker	.05
510	Andy Van Slyke	.05
511	Lenny Webster	.05
512	Mark Whiten	.05
513	Mike Williams	.05
514	Jay Bell	.05
515	Jacob Brumfield	.05
516	Jason Christiansen	.05
517	Dave Clark	.05
518	Midre Cummings	.05
519	Angelo Encarnacion	.05
520	John Ericks	.05
521	Carlos Garcia	.05
522	Mark Johnson	.05
523	Jeff King	.05
524	Nelson Liriano	.05
525	Esteban Loaiza	.05
526	Al Martin	.05
527	Orlando Merced	.05
528	Dan Miceli	.05
529	Ramon Morel	.05
530	Denny Neagle	.05
531	Steve Parris	.05
532	Dan Plesac	.05
533	Don Slaught	.05
534	Paul Wagner	.05
535	John Wehner	.05
536	Kevin Young	.05
537	Allen Battle	.05
538	David Bell	.05
539	Alan Benes	.05
540	Scott Cooper	.05
541	Tripp Cromer	.05
542	Tony Fossas	.05
543	Bernard Gilkey	.05
544	Tom Henke	.05
545	Brian Jordan	.05
546	Ray Lankford	.05
547	John Mabry	.05
548	T.J. Mathews	.05
549	Mike Morgan	.05
550	Jose Oliva	.05
551	Jose Oquendo	.05
552	Donovan Osborne	.05
553	Tom Pagnozzi	.05
554	Mark Petkovsek	.05
555	Danny Sheaffer	.05
556	Ozzie Smith	1.00
557	Mark Sweeney	.05
558	Allen Watson	.05
559	Andy Ashby	.05
560	Brad Ausmus	.05
561	Willie Blair	.05
562	Ken Caminiti	.05
563	Andujar Cedeno	.05
564	Glenn Dishman	.05
565	Steve Finley	.05
566	Bryce Florie	.05
567	Tony Gwynn	1.00
568	Joey Hamilton	.05
569	Dustin Hermanson	.05
570	Trevor Hoffman	.05
571	Brian Johnson	.05
572	Marc Kroon	.05
573	Scott Livingstone	.05
574	Marc Newfield	.05
575	Melvin Nieves	.05
576	Jody Reed	.05
577	Bip Roberts	.05
578	Scott Sanders	.05
579	Fernando Valenzuela	.05
580	Eddie Williams	.05
581	Rod Beck	.05
582	Marvin Benard **RC**	.10
583	Barry Bonds	2.50
584	Jamie Brewington	.05
585	Mark Carreon	.05
586	Royce Clayton	.05
587	Shawn Estes	.05
588	Glenallen Hill	.05
589	Mark Leiter	.05
590	Kirt Manwaring	.05
591	David McCarty	.05
592	Terry Mulholland	.05
593	John Patterson	.05
594	J.R. Phillips	.05
595	Deion Sanders	.05
596	Steve Scarsone	.05
597	Robby Thompson	.05
598	Sergio Valdez	.05
599	William Van Landingham	.05
600	Matt Williams	.05

1996 Fleer Tiffany

	NM/M
Complete Set (600):	100.00
Common Player:	.15
Stars:	2X

(See 1996 Fleer for checklist and base card values.)

1996 Fleer Baseball '96 Team Sets

	NM/M
Complete Set (180):	27.00
Common Player:	.09

Atlanta Braves Team Set:		4.00
1	Steve Avery	.10
2	Jeff Blauser	.10
3	Brad Clontz	.10
4	Tom Glavine	.35
5	Marquis Grissom	.10
6	Chipper Jones	1.25
7	David Justice	.10
8	Ryan Klesko	.10
9	Mark Lemke	.10
10	Javier Lopez	.10
11	Greg Maddux	1.25
12	Fred McGriff	.10
13	Greg McMichael	.10
14	Eddie Perez	.10
15	Jason Schmidt	.10
16	John Smoltz	.10
17	Terrell Wade	.10
18	Mark Wohlers	.10
19	Logo Card	.10
20	Checklist	.10
Baltimore Orioles Team Set:		5.00
1	Roberto Alomar	.20
2	Brady Anderson	.10
3	Armando Benitez	.10
4	Bobby Bonilla	.10
5	Scott Erickson	.10
6	Jeffrey Hammonds	.10
7	Jimmy Haynes	.10
8	Chris Hoiles	.10
9	Rick Krivda	.10
10	Kent Mercker	.10
11	Mike Mussina	.45
12	Randy Myers	.10
13	Jesse Orosco	.10
14	Rafael Palmeiro	.75
15	Cal Ripken Jr.	2.50
16	B.J. Surhoff	.10
17	Tony Tarasco	.10
18	David Wells	.10
19	Logo Card	.10
20	Checklist	.10
Boston Red Sox Team Set:		3.00
1	Stan Belinda	.10
2	Jose Canseco	.50
3	Roger Clemens	2.00
4	Wil Cordero	.10
5	Vaughn Eshelman	.10
6	Tom Gordon	.10
7	Mike Greenwell	.10
8	Dwayne Hosey	.10
9	Kevin Mitchell	.10
10	Tim Naehring	.10
11	Troy O'Leary	.10
12	Aaron Sele	.10
13	Heathcliff Slocumb	.10
14	Mike Stanley	.10
15	Jeff Suppan	.10
16	John Valentin	.10
17	Mo Vaughn	.10
18	Tim Wakefield	.10
19	Logo Card	.10
20	Checklist	.10
Chicago Cubs Team Set:		4.00
1	Terry Adams	.10
2	Jim Bullinger	.10
3	Frank Castillo	.10
4	Kevin Foster	.10
5	Leo Gomez	.10
6	Luis Gonzalez	.20
7	Mark Grace	.15
8	Jose Hernandez	.10
9	Robin Jennings **RC**	.10
10	Doug Jones	.10
11	Brooks Kieschnick	.10
12	Brian McRae	.10
13	Jaime Navarro	.10
14	Rey Sanchez	.10
15	Ryne Sandberg	1.25
16	Scott Servais	.10
17	Sammy Sosa	1.50
18	Steve Trachsel	.10
19	Logo Card	.10
20	Checklist	.10
Chicago White Sox Team Set:		4.00
1	Wilson Alvarez	.10
2	Harold Baines	.10
3	Jason Bere	.10
4	Ray Durham	.10
5	Alex Fernandez	.10
6	Ozzie Guillen	.10
7	Roberto Hernandez	.10
8	Matt Karchner	.10
9	Ron Karkovice	.10
10	Darren Lewis	.10
11	Dave Martinez	.10
12	Lyle Mouton	.10
13	Tony Phillips	.10
14	Chris Snopek	.10
15	Kevin Tapani	.10
16	Danny Tartabull	.10
17	Frank Thomas	1.00
18	Robin Ventura	.10
19	Logo Card	.10
20	Checklist	.10
Cleveland Indians Team Set:		4.00
1	Sandy Alomar Jr.	.10
2	Paul Assenmacher	.10
3	Carlos Baerga	.10
4	Albert Belle	.09
5	Orel Hershiser	.10
6	Kenny Lofton	.10
7	Dennis Martinez	.10
8	Jose Mesa	.10
9	Eddie Murray	1.00
10	Charles Nagy	.10

11	Tony Pena	.10
12	Herb Perry	.10
13	Eric Plunk	.10
14	Jim Poole	.10
15	Manny Ramirez	1.00
16	Julian Tavarez	.10
17	Jim Thome	.75
18	Omar Vizquel	.10
19	Logo Card	.10
20	Checklist	.10
Colorado Rockies Team Set:		**2.75**
1	Jason Bates	.10
2	Dante Bichette	.10
3	Ellis Burks	.10
4	Vinny Castilla	.10
5	Andres Galarraga	.10
6	Darren Holmes	.10
7	Curt Leskanic	.10
8	Quinton McCracken	.10
9	Mike Munoz	.10
10	Jayhawk Owens	.10
11	Steve Reed	.10
12	Kevin Ritz	.10
13	Bret Saberhagen	.10
14	Bill Swift	.10
15	John Vander Wal	.10
16	Larry Walker	.10
17	Walt Weiss	.10
18	Eric Young	.10
19	Logo Card	.10
20	Checklist	.10
L.A. Dodgers Team Set:		**4.00**
1	Mike Blowers	.10
2	Brett Butler	.10
3	Tom Candiotti	.10
4	Roger Cedeno	.10
5	Delino DeShields	.10
6	Chad Fonville	.10
7	Greg Gagne	.10
8	Karim Garcia	.15
9	Todd Hollandsworth	.10
10	Eric Karros	.10
11	Ramon Martinez	.10
12	Raul Mondesi	.10
13	Hideo Nomo	.75
14	Antonio Osuna	.10
15	Chan Ho Park	.10
16	Mike Piazza	2.00
17	Ismael Valdes	.10
18	Todd Worrell	.10
19	Logo Card	.10
20	Checklist	.10
Texas Rangers Team Set:		**2.75**
1	Mark Brandenburg	.10
2	Damon Buford	.10
3	Will Clark	.15
4	Kevin Elster	.10
5	Benji Gil	.10
6	Juan Gonzalez	.75
7	Rusty Greer	.10
8	Kevin Gross	.10
9	Darryl Hamilton	.10
10	Ken Hill	.10
11	Mark McLemore	.10
12	Dean Palmer	.10
13	Roger Pavlik	.10
14	Ivan Rodriguez	.75
15	Mickey Tettleton	.10
16	Dave Valle	.10
17	Ed Vosberg	.10
18	Matt Whiteside	.10
19	Logo Card	.10
20	Checklist	.10

Checklists

		NM/M
Complete Set (10):		**5.00**
Common Player:		**.25**
1	Barry Bonds	2.00
2	Ken Griffey Jr.	1.00
3	Chipper Jones	.75
4	Greg Maddux	.75
5	Mike Piazza	1.00
6	Manny Ramirez	.60
7	Cal Ripken Jr.	2.00
8	Frank Thomas	.60
9	Mo Vaughn	.25
10	Matt Williams	.25

Golden Memories

	NM/M
Complete Set (10):	**6.00**
Common Player:	**.10**

1	Albert Belle	.10
2	Barry Bonds, Sammy Sosa	1.50
3	Greg Maddux	1.00
4	Edgar Martinez	.10
5	Ramon Martinez	.10
6	Mark McGwire	1.50
7	Eddie Murray	.75
8	Cal Ripken Jr.	2.00
9	Frank Thomas	.75
10	Alan Trammell, Lou Whitaker	.10

Lumber Company

		NM/M
Complete Set (12):		**12.50**
Common Player:		**.50**
1	Albert Belle	.50
2	Dante Bichette	.50
3	Barry Bonds	3.00
4	Ken Griffey Jr.	1.50
5	Mark McGwire	2.00
6	Mike Piazza	1.50
7	Manny Ramirez	1.00
8	Tim Salmon	.60
9	Sammy Sosa	1.25
10	Frank Thomas	1.00
11	Mo Vaughn	.50
12	Matt Williams	.50

Post-Season Glory

		NM/M
Complete Set (5):		**1.50**
Common Player:		**.15**
1	Tom Glavine	.25
2	Ken Griffey Jr.	1.00
3	Orel Hershiser	.15
4	Randy Johnson	.50
5	Jim Thome	.50

Prospects

	NM/M
Complete Set (10):	**1.00**
Common Player:	**.15**

1	Yamil Benitez	.15
2	Roger Cedeno	.15
3	Tony Clark	.15
4	Micah Franklin	.15
5	Karim Garcia	.30
6	Todd Greene	.15
7	Alex Ochoa	.15
8	Ruben Rivera	.15
9	Chris Snopek	.15
10	Shannon Stewart	.15

Road Warriors

		NM/M
Complete Set (10):		**9.00**
Common Player:		**.40**
1	Derek Bell	.40
2	Tony Gwynn	1.25
3	Greg Maddux	1.25
4	Mark McGwire	2.50
5	Mike Piazza	2.00
6	Manny Ramirez	1.00
7	Tim Salmon	.50
8	Frank Thomas	1.00
9	Mo Vaughn	.40
10	Matt Williams	.40

Rookie Sensations

		NM/M
Complete Set (15):		**5.00**
Common Player:		**.25**
1	Garret Anderson	.40
2	Marty Cordova	.25
3	Johnny Damon	1.00
4	Ray Durham	.25
5	Carl Everett	.25
6	Shawn Green	.50
7	Brian Hunter	.25
8	Jason Isringhausen	.25
9	Charles Johnson	.25
10	Chipper Jones	2.00
11	John Mabry	.25
12	Hideo Nomo	.50
13	Troy Percival	.25
14	Andy Pettitte	.50
15	Quilvio Veras	.25

Smoke 'N Heat

	NM/M
Complete Set (10):	**4.00**
Common Player:	**.15**
1 Kevin Appier	.15
2 Roger Clemens	1.50
3 David Cone	.15
4 Chuck Finley	.15

5	Randy Johnson	.75
6	Greg Maddux	1.00
7	Pedro Martinez	.75
8	Hideo Nomo	.50
9	John Smoltz	.30
10	Todd Stottlemyre	.15

Team Leaders

		NM/M
Complete Set (28):		**30.00**
Common Player:		**.50**
1	Cal Ripken Jr.	6.00
2	Mo Vaughn	.50
3	Jim Edmonds	1.00
4	Frank Thomas	2.00
5	Kenny Lofton	.50
6	Travis Fryman	.50
7	Gary Gaetti	.50
8	B.J. Surhoff	.50
9	Kirby Puckett	2.50
10	Don Mattingly	3.00
11	Mark McGwire	4.00
12	Ken Griffey Jr.	3.00
13	Juan Gonzalez	1.00
14	Joe Carter	.50
15	Greg Maddux	2.50
16	Sammy Sosa	3.00
17	Barry Larkin	.50
18	Dante Bichette	.50
19	Jeff Conine	.50
20	Jeff Bagwell	2.00
21	Mike Piazza	3.00
22	Rondell White	.50
23	Rico Brogna	.50
24	Darren Daulton	.50
25	Jeff King	.50
26	Ray Lankford	.50
27	Tony Gwynn	2.50
28	Barry Bonds	6.00

Tomorrow's Legends

		NM/M
Complete Set (10):		**3.50**
Common Player:		**.25**
1	Garret Anderson	.25
2	Jim Edmonds	.50
3	Brian Hunter	.25
4	Jason Isringhausen	.25
5	Charles Johnson	.25
6	Chipper Jones	2.00
7	Ryan Klesko	.25
8	Hideo Nomo	1.00
9	Manny Ramirez	1.50
10	Rondell White	.25

Zone

		NM/M
Complete Set (12):		**20.00**
Common Player:		**.75**
1	Albert Belle	.75
2	Barry Bonds	6.00
3	Ken Griffey Jr.	4.00
4	Tony Gwynn	3.00
5	Randy Johnson	2.00
6	Kenny Lofton	.75
7	Greg Maddux	3.00
8	Edgar Martinez	.75

9	Mike Piazza	4.00
10	Frank Thomas	2.00
11	Mo Vaughn	.75
12	Matt Williams	.75

Update

		NM/M
Complete Set (250):		12.00
Common Player:		.05
Complete Tiffany Set (250):		40.00
Tiffany Stars:		2X
Pack (11):		1.00
Wax Box (24):		15.00
1	Roberto Alomar	.10
2	Mike Devereaux	.05
3	Scott McClain RC	.05
4	Roger McDowell	.05
5	Kent Mercker	.05
6	Jimmy Myers	.05
7	Randy Myers	.05
8	B.J. Surhoff	.05
9	Tony Tarasco	.05
10	David Wells	.05
11	Wil Cordero	.05
12	Tom Gordon	.05
13	Reggie Jefferson	.05
14	Jose Malave	.05
15	Kevin Mitchell	.05
16	Jamie Moyer	.05
17	Heathcliff Slocumb	.05
18	Mike Stanley	.05
19	George Arias	.05
20	Jorge Fabregas	.05
21	Don Slaught	.05
22	Randy Velarde	.05
23	Harold Baines	.05
24	Mike Cameron RC	.75
25	Darren Lewis	.05
26	Tony Phillips	.05
27	Bill Simas	.05
28	Chris Snopek	.05
29	Kevin Tapani	.05
30	Danny Tartabull	.05
31	Julio Franco	.05
32	Jack McDowell	.05
33	Kimera Bartee	.05
34	Mark Lewis	.05
35	Melvin Nieves	.05
36	Mark Parent	.05
37	Eddie Williams	.05
38	Tim Belcher	.05
39	Sal Fasano	.05
40	Chris Haney	.05
41	Mike Macfarlane	.05
42	Jose Offerman	.05
43	Joe Randa	.05
44	Bip Roberts	.05
45	Chuck Carr	.05
46	Bobby Hughes	.05
47	Graeme Lloyd	.05
48	Ben McDonald	.05
49	Kevin Wickander	.05
50	Rick Aguilera	.05
51	Mike Durant	.05
52	Chip Hale	.05
53	LaTroy Hawkins	.05
54	Dave Hollins	.05
55	Roberto Kelly	.05
56	Paul Molitor	.75
57	Dan Naulty RC	.05
58	Mariano Duncan	.05
59	Andy Fox RC	.05
60	Joe Girardi	.05
61	Dwight Gooden	.05
62	Jimmy Key	.05
63	Matt Luke RC	.05
64	Tino Martinez	.05
65	Jeff Nelson	.05
66	Tim Raines	.05
67	Ruben Rivera	.05
68	Kenny Rogers	.05
69	Gerald Williams	.05
70	Tony Batista RC	.50
71	Allen Battle	.05
72	Jim Corsi	.05
73	Steve Cox	.05
74	Pedro Munoz	.05
75	Phil Plantier	.05
76	Scott Spiezio	.05
77	Ernie Young	.05
78	Russ Davis	.05
79	Sterling Hitchcock	.05
80	Edwin Hurtado	.05
81	Raul Ibanez RC	.05
82	Mike Jackson	.05
83	Ricky Jordan	.05
84	Paul Sorrento	.05
85	Doug Strange	.05
86	Mark Brandenburg	.05
87	Damon Buford	.05
88	Kevin Elster	.05
89	Darryl Hamilton	.05
90	Ken Hill	.05
91	Ed Vosberg	.05
92	Craig Worthington	.05
93	Tilson Brito	.05
94	Giovanni Carrara	.05
95	Felipe Crespo	.05
96	Erik Hanson	.05
97	Marty Janzen RC	.05
98	Otis Nixon	.05
99	Charlie O'Brien	.05
100	Robert Perez	.05
101	Paul Quantrill	.05
102	Bill Risley	.05
103	Juan Samuel	.05
104	Jermaine Dye	.05
105	Wonderful Monds	.05
106	Dwight Smith	.05
107	Jerome Walton	.05
108	Terry Adams	.05
109	Leo Gomez	.05
110	Robin Jennings RC	.05
111	Doug Jones	.05
112	Brooks Kieschnick	.05
113	Dave Magadan	.05
114	Jason Maxwell RC	.05
115	Rodney Myers	.05
116	Eric Anthony	.05
117	Vince Coleman	.05
118	Eric Davis	.05
119	Steve Gibralter	.05
120	Curtis Goodwin	.05
121	Willie Greene	.05
122	Mike Kelly	.05
123	Marcus Moore	.05
124	Chad Mottola	.05
125	Chris Sabo	.05
126	Roger Salkeld	.05
127	Pedro Castellano	.05
128	Trenidad Hubbard	.05
129	Jayhawk Owens	.05
130	Jeff Reed	.05
131	Kevin Brown	.05
132	Al Leiter	.05
133	Matt Mantei RC	.05
134	Dave Weathers	.05
135	Devon White	.05
136	Sean Berry	.05
137	Doug Brocail	.05
138	Richard Hidalgo	.05
139	Alvin Morman	.05
140	Mike Blowers	.05
141	Roger Cedeno	.05
142	Greg Gagne	.05
143	Karim Garcia	.10
144	Wilton Guerrero RC	.05
145	Israel Alcantara RC	.05
146	Omar Daal	.05
147	Ryan McGuire	.05
148	Sherman Obando	.05
149	Jose Paniagua	.05
150	Henry Rodriguez	.05
151	Andy Stankiewicz	.05
152	Dave Veres	.05
153	Juan Acevedo	.05
154	Mark Clark	.05
155	Bernard Gilkey	.05
156	Pete Harnisch	.05
157	Lance Johnson	.05
158	Brent Mayne	.05
159	Rey Ordonez	.05
160	Kevin Roberson	.05
161	Paul Wilson	.05
162	David Doster RC	.05
163	Mike Grace RC	.05
164	Rich Hunter RC	.05
165	Pete Incaviglia	.05
166	Mike Lieberthal	.05
167	Terry Mulholland	.05
168	Ken Ryan	.05
170	Benito Santiago	.05
171	Kevin Sefcik RC	.05
172	Lee Tinsley	.05
173	Todd Zeile	.05
174	Francisco Cordova RC	.05
175	Danny Darwin	.05
176	Charlie Hayes	.05
177	Jason Kendall	.05
178	Mike Kingery	.05
179	Jon Lieber	.05
180	Zane Smith	.05
181	Luis Alicea	.05
182	Cory Bailey	.05
183	Andy Benes	.05
184	Pat Borders	.05
185	Mike Busby RC	.05
186	Royce Clayton	.05
187	Dennis Eckersley	.65
188	Gary Gaetti	.05
189	Ron Gant	.05
190	Aaron Holbert	.05
191	Willie McGee	.05
192	Miguel Mejia RC	.05
193	Jeff Parrett	.05
194	Todd Stottlemyre	.05
195	Sean Bergman	.05
196	Archi Cianfrocco	.05
197	Rickey Henderson	.75
198	Wally Joyner	.05
199	Craig Shipley	.05
200	Bob Tewksbury	.05
201	Tim Worrell	.05
202	Rich Aurilia RC	.05
203	Doug Creek	.05
204	Shawon Dunston	.05
205	Osvaldo Fernandez RC	.05
206	Mark Gardner	.05
207	Stan Javier	.05
208	Marcus Jensen	.05
209	Chris Singleton RC	.05
210	Allen Watson	.05
211	Jeff Bagwell	.75
212	Derek Bell	.05
213	Albert Belle	.05
214	Wade Boggs	1.00
215	Barry Bonds	2.00
216	Jose Canseco	.50
217	Marty Cordova	.05
218	Jim Edmonds	.05
219	Cecil Fielder	.05
220	Andres Galarraga	.05
221	Juan Gonzalez	.65
222	Mark Grace	.10
223	Ken Griffey Jr.	1.50
224	Tony Gwynn	1.00
225	Jason Isringhausen	.05
226	Derek Jeter	2.00
227	Randy Johnson	.75
228	Chipper Jones	1.00
229	Ryan Klesko	.05
230	Barry Larkin	.05
231	Kenny Lofton	.05
232	Greg Maddux	1.00
233	Raul Mondesi	.05
234	Hideo Nomo	.65
235	Mike Piazza	1.50
236	Manny Ramirez	.75
237	Cal Ripken Jr.	2.00
238	Tim Salmon	.10
239	Ryne Sandberg	1.00
240	Reggie Sanders	.05
241	Gary Sheffield	.30
242	Sammy Sosa	1.25
243	Frank Thomas	.75
244	Mo Vaughn	.05
245	Matt Williams	.05
246	Checklist	.05
247	Checklist	.05
248	Checklist	.05
249	Checklist	.05
250	Checklist	.05

Update Tiffany

		NM/M
Complete Set (250):		45.00
Common Player:		.15
Glossy Stars:		2X

(See 1996 Fleer Update for checklist and base card values.)

Update Diamond Tribute

		NM/M
Complete Set (10):		50.00
Common Player:		4.00
1	Wade Boggs	6.00
2	Barry Bonds	10.00
3	Ken Griffey Jr.	7.50
4	Tony Gwynn	6.00
5	Rickey Henderson	4.00
6	Greg Maddux	6.00
7	Eddie Murray	4.00
8	Cal Ripken Jr.	10.00
9	Ozzie Smith	6.00
10	Frank Thomas	5.00

Update Headliners

		NM/M
Complete Set (20):		20.00
Common Player:		.25
1	Roberto Alomar	.50
2	Jeff Bagwell	1.00
3	Albert Belle	.25
4	Barry Bonds	3.50
5	Cecil Fielder	.25
6	Juan Gonzalez	.75
7	Ken Griffey Jr.	2.25
8	Tony Gwynn	1.50
9	Randy Johnson	1.00
10	Chipper Jones	1.50
11	Ryan Klesko	.25
12	Kenny Lofton	.25
13	Greg Maddux	1.50
14	Hideo Nomo	.75
15	Mike Piazza	2.25
16	Manny Ramirez	1.00
17	Cal Ripken Jr.	3.50
18	Tim Salmon	.40
19	Frank Thomas	1.00
20	Matt Williams	.25

Update New Horizons

		NM/M
Complete Set (20):		2.00
Common Player:		.25
1	Bob Abreu	.45
2	George Arias	.25
3	Tony Batista	.25
4	Steve Cox	.25
5	David Doster	.25
6	Jermaine Dye	.25
7	Andy Fox	.25
8	Mike Grace	.25
9	Todd Greene	.25
10	Wilton Guerrero	.25
11	Richard Hidalgo	.25
12	Raul Ibanez	.25
13	Robin Jennings	.25
14	Marcus Jensen	.25
15	Jason Kendall	.35
16	Brooks Kieschnick	.25
17	Ryan McGuire	.25
18	Miguel Mejia	.25
19	Rey Ordonez	.25
20	Paul Wilson	.25

Update Smooth Leather

		NM/M
Complete Set (10):		7.00
Common Player:		.40
1	Roberto Alomar	.50
1p	Roberto Alomar (Promo)	2.00
2	Barry Bonds	2.50
3	Will Clark	.45
4	Ken Griffey Jr.	1.75
5	Kenny Lofton	.40
6	Greg Maddux	1.00
7	Raul Mondesi	.40
8	Rey Ordonez	.40
9	Cal Ripken Jr.	2.50
9p	Cal Ripken Jr. (Promo)	6.00
10	Matt Williams	.40

Update Soaring Stars

		NM/M
Complete Set (10):		6.00
Common Player:		.25
1	Jeff Bagwell	.75
2	Barry Bonds	2.00
3	Juan Gonzalez	.75
4	Ken Griffey Jr.	1.50
5	Chipper Jones	1.00
6	Greg Maddux	1.00
7	Mike Piazza	1.50
8	Manny Ramirez	.75
9	Frank Thomas	.75
10	Matt Williams	.25

1997 Fleer

		NM/M
Complete Set (761):		100.00
Complete Series 1 Set (500):		30.00
Complete Series 2 Set (261):		70.00
Common Player:		.05
Complete Tiffany Set (1-761):		500.00
Tiffany Stars/RC's:		8X
A. Jones Circa AU/200:		35.00
Series 2 Pack (10):		3.00
Series 2 Wax Box (36):		90.00
1	Roberto Alomar	.10
2	Brady Anderson	.05
3	Bobby Bonilla	.05
4	Rocky Coppinger	.05
5	Cesar Devarez	.05
6	Scott Erickson	.05
7	Jeffrey Hammonds	.05
8	Chris Hoiles	.05
9	Eddie Murray	1.00
10	Mike Mussina	.40
11	Randy Myers	.05
12	Rafael Palmeiro	.75
13	Cal Ripken Jr.	2.50
14	B.J. Surhoff	.05
15	David Wells	.05
16	Todd Zeile	.05
17	Darren Bragg	.05
18	Jose Canseco	.40
19	Roger Clemens	1.75
20	Wil Cordero	.05
21	Jeff Frye	.05
22	Nomar Garciaparra	1.75
23	Tom Gordon	.05
24	Mike Greenwell	.05
25	Reggie Jefferson	.05
26	Jose Malave	.05
27	Tim Naehring	.05
28	Troy O'Leary	.05
29	Heathcliff Slocumb	.05
30	Mike Stanley	.05
31	John Valentin	.05
32	Mo Vaughn	.05
33	Tim Wakefield	.05
34	Garret Anderson	.05
35	George Arias	.05
36	Shawn Boskie	.05
37	Chili Davis	.05
38	Jason Dickson	.05
39	Gary DiSarcina	.05
40	Jim Edmonds	.05
41	Darin Erstad	.10
42	Jorge Fabregas	.05
43	Chuck Finley	.05
44	Todd Greene	.05
45	Mike Holtz **RC**	.05
46	Rex Hudler	.05
47	Mike James	.05
48	Mark Langston	.05
49	Troy Percival	.05
50	Tim Salmon	.15
51	Jeff Schmidt	.05
52	J.T. Snow	.05
53	Randy Velarde	.05
54	Wilson Alvarez	.05
55	Harold Baines	.05
56	James Baldwin	.05
57	Jason Bere	.05
58	Mike Cameron	.05
59	Ray Durham	.05
60	Alex Fernandez	.05
61	Ozzie Guillen	.05
62	Roberto Hernandez	.05
63	Ron Karkovice	.05
64	Darren Lewis	.05
65	Dave Martinez	.05
66	Lyle Mouton	.05
67	Greg Norton	.05
68	Tony Phillips	.05
69	Chris Snopek	.05
70	Kevin Tapani	.05
71	Danny Tartabull	.05
72	Frank Thomas	1.00
73	Robin Ventura	.05
74	Sandy Alomar Jr.	.05
75	Albert Belle	.05
76	Mark Carreon	.05
77	Julio Franco	.05
78	Brian Giles **RC**	1.00
79	Orel Hershiser	.05
80	Kenny Lofton	.05
81	Dennis Martinez	.05
82	Jack McDowell	.05
83	Jose Mesa	.05
84	Charles Nagy	.05
85	Chad Ogea	.05
86	Eric Plunk	.05
87	Manny Ramirez	1.00
88	Kevin Seitzer	.05
89	Julian Tavarez	.05
90	Jim Thome	.65
91	Jose Vizcaino	.05
92	Omar Vizquel	.05
93	Brad Ausmus	.05
94	Kimera Bartee	.05
95	Raul Casanova	.05
96	Tony Clark	.05
97	John Cummings	.05
98	Travis Fryman	.05
99	Bob Higginson	.05
100	Mark Lewis	.05
101	Felipe Lira	.05
102	Phil Nevin	.05
103	Melvin Nieves	.05
104	Curtis Pride	.05
105	A.J. Sager	.05
106	Ruben Sierra	.05
107	Justin Thompson	.05
108	Alan Trammell	.05
109	Kevin Appier	.05
110	Tim Belcher	.05
111	Jaime Bluma	.05
112	Johnny Damon	.35
113	Tom Goodwin	.05
114	Chris Haney	.05
115	Keith Lockhart	.05
116	Mike Macfarlane	.05
117	Jeff Montgomery	.05
118	Jose Offerman	.05
119	Craig Paquette	.05
120	Joe Randa	.05
121	Bip Roberts	.05
122	Jose Rosado	.05
123	Mike Sweeney	.05
124	Michael Tucker	.05
125	Jeromy Burnitz	.05
126	Jeff Cirillo	.05
127	Jeff D'Amico	.05
128	Mike Fetters	.05
129	John Jaha	.05
130	Scott Karl	.05
131	Jesse Levis	.05
132	Mark Loretta	.05
133	Mike Matheny	.05
134	Ben McDonald	.05
135	Matt Mieske	.05
136	Marc Newfield	.05
137	Dave Nilsson	.05
138	Jose Valentin	.05
139	Fernando Vina	.05
140	Bob Wickman	.05
141	Gerald Williams	.05
142	Rick Aguilera	.05
143	Rich Becker	.05
144	Ron Coomer	.05
145	Marty Cordova	.05
146	Roberto Kelly	.05
147	Chuck Knoblauch	.05
148	Matt Lawton	.05
149	Pat Meares	.05
150	Travis Miller	.05
151	Paul Molitor	1.00
152	Greg Myers	.05
153	Dan Naulty	.05
154	Kirby Puckett	1.50
155	Brad Radke	.05
156	Frank Rodriguez	.05
157	Scott Stahoviak	.05
158	Dave Stevens	.05
159	Matt Walbeck	.05
160	Todd Walker	.05
161	Wade Boggs	1.50
162	David Cone	.05
163	Mariano Duncan	.05
164	Cecil Fielder	.05
165	Joe Girardi	.05
166	Dwight Gooden	.05
167	Charlie Hayes	.05
168	Derek Jeter	2.50
169	Jimmy Key	.05
170	Jim Leyritz	.05
171	Tino Martinez	.05
172	Ramiro Mendoza **RC**	.10
173	Jeff Nelson	.05
174	Paul O'Neill	.05
175	Andy Pettitte	.35
176	Mariano Rivera	.15
177	Ruben Rivera	.05
178	Kenny Rogers	.05
179	Darryl Strawberry	.05
180	John Wetteland	.05
181	Bernie Williams	.10
182	Willie Adams	.05
183	Tony Batista	.05
184	Geronimo Berroa	.05
185	Mike Bordick	.05
186	Scott Brosius	.05
187	Bobby Chouinard	.05
188	Jim Corsi	.05
189	Brent Gates	.05
190	Jason Giambi	.50
191	Jose Herrera	.05
192	Damon Mashore **RC**	.05
193	Mark McGwire	2.25
194	Mike Mohler	.05
195	Scott Spiezio	.05
196	Terry Steinbach	.05
197	Bill Taylor	.05
198	John Wasdin	.05
199	Steve Wojciechowski	.05
200	Ernie Young	.05
201	Rich Amaral	.05
202	Jay Buhner	.05
203	Norm Charlton	.05
204	Joey Cora	.05
205	Russ Davis	.05
206	Ken Griffey Jr.	2.00
207	Sterling Hitchcock	.05
208	Brian Hunter	.05
209	Raul Ibanez	.05
210	Randy Johnson	1.00
211	Edgar Martinez	.05
212	Jamie Moyer	.05
213	Alex Rodriguez	2.25
214	Paul Sorrento	.05
215	Matt Wagner	.05
216	Bob Wells	.05
217	Dan Wilson	.05
218	Damon Buford	.05
219	Will Clark	.10
220	Kevin Elster	.05
221	Juan Gonzalez	.75
222	Rusty Greer	.05
223	Kevin Gross	.05
224	Darryl Hamilton	.05
225	Mike Henneman	.05
226	Ken Hill	.05
227	Mark McLemore	.05
228	Darren Oliver	.05
229	Dean Palmer	.05
230	Roger Pavlik	.05
231	Ivan Rodriguez	.75
232	Mickey Tettleton	.05
233	Bobby Witt	.05
234	Jacob Brumfield	.05
235	Joe Carter	.05
236	Tim Crabtree	.05
237	Carlos Delgado	.50
238	Huck Flener	.05
239	Alex Gonzalez	.05
240	Shawn Green	.20
241	Juan Guzman	.05
242	Pat Hentgen	.05
243	Marty Janzen	.05
244	Sandy Martinez	.05
245	Otis Nixon	.05
246	Charlie O'Brien	.05
247	John Olerud	.05
248	Robert Perez	.05
249	Ed Sprague	.05
250	Mike Timlin	.05
251	Steve Avery	.05
252	Jeff Blauser	.05
253	Brad Clontz	.05
254	Jermaine Dye	.05
255	Tom Glavine	.30
256	Marquis Grissom	.05
257	Andruw Jones	1.00
258	Chipper Jones	1.50
259	David Justice	.05
260	Ryan Klesko	.05
261	Mark Lemke	.05
262	Javier Lopez	.05
263	Greg Maddux	1.50
264	Fred McGriff	.05
265	Greg McMichael	.05
266	Denny Neagle	.05
267	Terry Pendleton	.05
268	Eddie Perez	.05
269	John Smoltz	.05
270	Terrell Wade	.05
271	Mark Wohlers	.05
272	Terry Adams	.05
273	Brant Brown	.05
274	Leo Gomez	.05
275	Luis Gonzalez	.10
276	Mark Grace	.10
277	Tyler Houston	.05
278	Robin Jennings	.05
279	Brooks Kieschnick	.05
280	Brian McRae	.05
281	Jaime Navarro	.05
282	Ryne Sandberg	1.50
283	Scott Servais	.05
284	Sammy Sosa	1.75
285	Dave Swartzbaugh **RC**	.05
286	Amaury Telemaco	.05
287	Steve Trachsel	.05
288	Pedro Valdes **RC**	.05
289	Turk Wendell	.05
290	Bret Boone	.05
291	Jeff Branson	.05
292	Jeff Brantley	.05
293	Eric Davis	.05
294	Willie Greene	.05
295	Thomas Howard	.05
296	Barry Larkin	.05
297	Kevin Mitchell	.05
298	Hal Morris	.05
299	Chad Mottola	.05
300	Joe Oliver	.05
301	Mark Portugal	.05
302	Roger Salkeld	.05
303	Reggie Sanders	.05
304	Pete Schourek	.05
305	John Smiley	.05
306	Eddie Taubensee	.05
307	Dante Bichette	.05
308	Ellis Burks	.05
309	Vinny Castilla	.05
310	Andres Galarraga	.05
311	Curt Leskanic	.05
312	Quinton McCracken	.05
313	Neifi Perez	.05
314	Jeff Reed	.05
315	Steve Reed	.05
316	Armando Reynoso	.05
317	Kevin Ritz	.05
318	Bruce Ruffin	.05
319	Larry Walker	.05
320	Walt Weiss	.05
321	Jamey Wright	.05
322	Eric Young	.05
323	Kurt Abbott	.05
324	Alex Arias	.05
325	Kevin Brown	.05
326	Luis Castillo	.05
327	Greg Colbrunn	.05
328	Jeff Conine	.05
329	Andre Dawson	.25
330	Charles Johnson	.05
331	Al Leiter	.05
332	Ralph Milliard	.05
333	Robb Nen	.05
334	Pat Rapp	.05
335	Edgar Renteria	.05
336	Gary Sheffield	.35
337	Devon White	.05
338	Bob Abreu	.05
339	Jeff Bagwell	1.00
340	Derek Bell	.05
341	Sean Berry	.05
342	Craig Biggio	.05
343	Doug Drabek	.05
344	Tony Eusebio	.05
345	Ricky Gutierrez	.05
346	Mike Hampton	.05
347	Brian Hunter	.05
348	Todd Jones	.05
349	Darryl Kile	.05
350	Derrick May	.05
351	Orlando Miller	.05
352	James Mouton	.05
353	Shane Reynolds	.05
354	Billy Wagner	.05
355	Donne Wall	.05
356	Mike Blowers	.05
357	Brett Butler	.05
358	Roger Cedeno	.05
259	Chad Curtis	.05
360	Delino DeShields	.05
361	Greg Gagne	.05
362	Karim Garcia	.10
363	Wilton Guerrero	.05
364	Todd Hollandsworth	.05
365	Eric Karros	.05
366	Ramon Martinez	.05
367	Raul Mondesi	.05
368	Hideo Nomo	.75
369	Antonio Osuna	.05
370	Chan Ho Park	.05

371 Mike Piazza 2.00
372 Ismael Valdes .05
373 Todd Worrell .05
374 Moises Alou .05
375 Shane Andrews .05
376 Yamil Benitez .05
377 Jeff Fassero .05
378 Darrin Fletcher .05
379 Cliff Floyd .05
380 Mark Grudzielanek .05
381 Mike Lansing .05
382 Barry Manuel .05
383 Pedro Martinez 1.00
384 Henry Rodriguez .05
385 Mel Rojas .05
386 F.P. Santangelo .05
387 David Segui .05
388 Ugueth Urbina .05
389 Rondell White .05
390 Edgardo Alfonzo .05
391 Carlos Baerga .05
392 Mark Clark .05
393 Alvaro Espinoza .05
394 John Franco .05
395 Bernard Gilkey .05
396 Pete Harnisch .05
397 Todd Hundley .05
398 Butch Huskey .05
399 Jason Isringhausen .05
400 Lance Johnson .05
401 Bobby Jones .05
402 Alex Ochoa .05
403 Rey Ordonez .05
404 Robert Person .05
405 Paul Wilson .05
406 Matt Beech .05
407 Ron Blazier .05
408 Ricky Bottalico .05
409 Lenny Dykstra .05
410 Jim Eisenreich .05
411 Bobby Estalella .05
412 Mike Grace .05
413 Gregg Jefferies .05
414 Mike Lieberthal .05
415 Wendell Magee Jr. .05
416 Mickey Morandini .05
417 Ricky Otero .05
418 Scott Rolen .75
419 Ken Ryan .05
420 Benito Santiago .05
421 Curt Schilling .25
422 Kevin Sefcik .05
423 Jermaine Allensworth .05
424 Trey Beamon .05
425 Jay Bell .05
426 Francisco Cordova .05
427 Carlos Garcia .05
428 Mark Johnson .05
429 Jason Kendall .05
430 Jeff King .05
431 Jon Lieber .05
432 Al Martin .05
433 Orlando Merced .05
434 Ramon Morel .05
435 Matt Ruebel .05
436 Jason Schmidt .05
437 Marc Wilkins **RC** .05
438 Alan Benes .05
439 Andy Benes .05
440 Royce Clayton .05
441 Dennis Eckersley .65
442 Gary Gaetti .05
443 Ron Gant .05
444 Aaron Holbert .05
445 Brian Jordan .05
446 Ray Lankford .05
447 John Mabry .05
448 T.J. Mathews .05
449 Willie McGee .05
450 Donovan Osborne .05
451 Tom Pagnozzi .05
452 Ozzie Smith 1.50
453 Todd Stottlemyre .05
454 Mark Sweeney .05
455 Dmitri Young .05
456 Andy Ashby .05
457 Ken Caminiti .05
458 Archi Cianfrocco .05
459 Steve Finley .05
460 John Flaherty .05
461 Chris Gomez .05
462 Tony Gwynn 1.50
463 Joey Hamilton .05
464 Rickey Henderson 1.00
465 Trevor Hoffman .05
466 Brian Johnson .05
467 Wally Joyner .05
468 Jody Reed .05
469 Scott Sanders .05
470 Bob Tewksbury .05
471 Fernando Valenzuela .05
472 Greg Vaughn .05
473 Tim Worrell .05
474 Rich Aurilia .05
475 Rod Beck .05
476 Marvin Benard .05
477 Barry Bonds 2.50
478 Jay Canizaro .05
479 Shawon Dunston .05
480 Shawn Estes .05
481 Mark Gardner .05
482 Glenallen Hill .05
483 Stan Javier .05
484 Marcus Jensen .05
485 Bill Mueller **RC** 1.50
486 William Van Landingham .05
487 Allen Watson .05
488 Rick Wilkins .05
489 Matt Williams .05
489p Matt Williams ("PROMOTIONAL SAMPLE") 1.50
490 Desi Wilson .05
491 Albert Belle Checklist .05
492 Ken Griffey Jr. Checklist .85
493 Andruw Jones Checklist .40
494 Chipper Jones Checklist .60
495 Mark McGwire Checklist 1.00
496 Paul Molitor Checklist .45
497 Mike Piazza Checklist .85
498 Cal Ripken Jr. Checklist 1.25
499 Alex Rodriguez Checklist 1.00
500 Frank Thomas Checklist .45
501 Kenny Lofton .05
502 Carlos Perez .05
503 Tim Raines .05
504 Danny Patterson **RC** .05
505 Derrick May .05
506 Dave Hollins .05
507 Felipe Crespo .05
508 Brian Banks .05
509 Jeff Kent .05
510 Bubba Trammell **RC** .25
511 Robert Person .05
512 David Arias **RC** (Ortiz) 40.00
513 Ryan Jones .05
514 David Justice .05
515 Will Cunnane .05
516 Russ Johnson .05
517 John Burkett .05
518 Robinson Checo **RC** .05
519 Ricardo Rincon **RC** .05
520 Woody Williams .05
521 Rick Helling .05
522 Jorge Posada .05
523 Kevin Orie .05
524 Fernando Tatis **RC** .15
525 Jermaine Dye .05
526 Brian Hunter .05
527 Greg McMichael .05
528 Matt Wagner .05
529 Richie Sexson .05
530 Scott Ruffcorn .05
531 Luis Gonzalez .10
532 Mike Johnson .05
533 Mark Petkovsek .05
534 Doug Drabek .05
535 Jose Canseco .40
536 Bobby Bonilla .05
537 J.T. Snow .05
538 Shawon Dunston .05
539 John Ericks .05
540 Terry Steinbach .05
541 Jay Bell .05
542 Joe Borowski .05
543 David Wells .05
544 Justin Towle **RC** .10
545 Mike Blowers .05
546 Shannon Stewart .05
547 Rudy Pemberton .05
548 Bill Swift .05
549 Osvaldo Fernandez .05
550 Eddie Murray 1.00
551 Don Wengert .05
552 Brad Ausmus .05
553 Carlos Garcia .05
554 Jose Guillen .05
555 Rheal Cormier .05
556 Doug Brocail .05
557 Rex Hudler .05
558 Armando Benitez .05
559 Elieser Marrero .05
560 Ricky Ledee **RC** .25
561 Bartolo Colon .05
562 Quilvio Veras .05
563 Alex Fernandez .05
564 Darren Dreifort .05
565 Benji Gil .05
566 Kent Mercker .05
567 Glendon Rusch .05
568 Ramon Tatis **RC** .05
569 Roger Clemens 1.75
570 Mark Lewis .05
571 Emil Brown **RC** .05
572 Jaime Navarro .05
573 Sherman Obando .05
574 John Wasdin .05
575 Calvin Maduro .05
576 Todd Jones .05
577 Orlando Merced .05
578 Cal Eldred .05
579 Mark Gubicza .05
580 Michael Tucker .05
581 Tony Saunders **RC** .05
582 Garvin Alston .05
583 Joe Roa .05
584 Brady Raggio **RC** .05
585 Jimmy Key .05
586 Marc Sagmoen **RC** .05
587 Jim Bullinger .05
588 Yorkis Perez .05
589 Jose Cruz Jr. **RC** .75
590 Mike Stanton .05
591 Deivi Cruz **RC** .25
592 Steve Karsay .05
593 Mike Trombley .05
594 Doug Glanville .05
595 Scott Sanders .05
596 Thomas Howard .05
597 T.J. Staton .05
598 Garrett Stephenson .05
599 Rico Brogna .05
600 Albert Belle .05
601 Jose Vizcaino .05
602 Chili Davis .05
603 Shane Mack .05
604 Jim Eisenreich .05
605 Todd Zeile .05
606 Brian Boehringer .05
607 Paul Shuey .05
608 Kevin Tapani .05
609 John Wetteland .05
610 Jim Leyritz .05
611 Ray Montgomery .05
612 Doug Bochtler .05
613 Wady Almonte .05
614 Danny Tartabull .05
615 Orlando Miller .05
616 Bobby Ayala .05
617 Tony Graffanino .05
618 Marc Valdes .05
619 Ron Villone .05
620 Derrek Lee .05
621 Greg Colbrunn .05
622 Felix Heredia **RC** .10
623 Carl Everett .05
624 Mark Thompson .05
625 Jeff Granger .05
626 Damian Jackson .05
627 Mark Leiter .05
628 Chris Holt .05
629 Dario Veras **RC** .05
630 Dave Burba .05
631 Darryl Hamilton .05
632 Mark Acre .05
633 Fernando Hernandez .05
634 Terry Mulholland .05
635 Dustin Hermanson .05
636 Delino DeShields .05
637 Steve Avery .05
638 Tony Womack **RC** .10
639 Mark Whiten .05
640 Marquis Grissom .05
641 Xavier Hernandez .05
642 Eric Davis .05
643 Bob Tewksbury .05
644 Dante Powell .05
645 Carlos Castillo .05
646 Chris Widger .05
647 Moises Alou .05
648 Pat Listach .05
649 Edgar Ramos .05
650 Deion Sanders .05
651 John Olerud .05
652 Todd Dunwoody .05
653 Randall Simon **RC** .10
654 Dan Carlson .05
655 Matt Williams .05
656 Jeff King .05
657 Luis Alicea .05
658 Brian Moehler .05
659 Ariel Prieto .05
660 Kevin Elster .05
661 Mark Hutton .05
662 Aaron Sele .05
663 Graeme Lloyd .05
664 John Burke .05
665 Mel Rojas .05
666 Sid Fernandez .05
667 Pedro Astacio .05
668 Jeff Abbott .05
669 Darren Daulton .05
670 Mike Bordick .05
671 Sterling Hitchcock .05
672 Damion Easley .05
673 Armando Reynoso .05
674 Pat Cline .05
675 Orlando Cabrera **RC** .50
676 Alan Embree .05
677 Brian Bevil .05
678 David Weathers .05
679 Cliff Floyd .05
680 Joe Randa .05
681 Bill Haselman .05
682 Jeff Fassero .05
683 Matt Morris .05
684 Mark Portugal .05
685 Lee Smith .05
686 Pokey Reese .05
687 Benito Santiago .05
688 Brian Johnson .05
689 Brent Brede **RC** .05
690 Shigetosi Hasegawa .05
691 Julio Santana .05
692 Steve Kline .05
693 Julian Tavarez .05
694 John Hudek .05
695 Manny Alexander .05
696 Roberto Alomar (Encore) .10
697 Jeff Bagwell (Encore) .45
698 Barry Bonds (Encore) 1.25
699 Ken Caminiti (Encore) .05
700 Juan Gonzalez (Encore) .35
701 Ken Griffey Jr. (Encore) .85
702 Tony Gwynn (Encore) .60
703 Derek Jeter (Encore) 1.25
704 Andruw Jones (Encore) .45
705 Chipper Jones (Encore) .60
706 Barry Larkin (Encore) .05
707 Greg Maddux (Encore) .60
708 Mark McGwire (Encore) 1.00
709 Paul Molitor (Encore) .45
710 Hideo Nomo (Encore) .35
711 Andy Pettitte (Encore) .30
712 Mike Piazza (Encore) .85
713 Manny Ramirez (Encore) .45
714 Cal Ripken Jr. (Encore) 1.25
715 Alex Rodriguez (Encore) 1.00
716 Ryne Sandberg (Encore) .60
717 John Smoltz (Encore) .05
718 Frank Thomas (Encore) .50
719 Mo Vaughn (Encore) .05
720 Bernie Williams (Encore) .10
721 Tim Salmon Checklist .05
722 Greg Maddux Checklist .60
723 Cal Ripken Jr. Checklist 1.25
724 Mo Vaughn Checklist .05
725 Ryne Sandberg Checklist .45
726 Frank Thomas Checklist .50
727 Barry Larkin Checklist .05
728 Manny Ramirez Checklist .45
729 Andres Galarraga Checklist .05
730 Tony Clark Checklist .05
731 Gary Sheffield Checklist .20
732 Jeff Bagwell Checklist .40
733 Kevin Appier Checklist .05
734 Mike Piazza Checklist .85
735 Jeff Cirillo Checklist .05
736 Paul Molitor Checklist .40
737 Henry Rodriguez Checklist .05
738 Todd Hundley Checklist .05
739 Derek Jeter Checklist 1.25
740 Mark McGwire Checklist 1.00
741 Curt Schilling Checklist .15
742 Jason Kendall Checklist .05
743 Tony Gwynn Checklist .60
744 Barry Bonds Checklist 1.25
745 Ken Griffey Jr. Checklist .85
746 Brian Jordan Checklist .05
747 Juan Gonzalez Checklist .40
748 Joe Carter Checklist .05
749 Arizona Diamondbacks .05
750 Tampa Bay Devil Rays .05
751 Hideki Irabu **RC** .15
752 Jeremi Gonzalez **RC** .15
753 Mario Valdez **RC** .05
754 Aaron Boone .05
755 Brett Tomko .05
756 Jaret Wright **RC** 1.00
757 Ryan McGuire .05
758 Jason McDonald .05
759 Adrian Brown **RC** .05
760 Keith Foulke **RC** .25
761 Checklist .05

Tiffany

NM/M

Complete Set (761): 500.00
Common Player: 1.00
Stars/Rcs: 8X
(See 1997 Fleer for checklist and base card values.)
512 David Arias (Ortiz) 140.00

Bleacher Blasters

NM/M

Complete Set (10): 40.00
Common Player: 1.50
1 Albert Belle 1.50
2 Barry Bonds 10.00
3 Juan Gonzalez 2.00
4 Ken Griffey Jr. 6.00
5 Mark McGwire 8.00
6 Mike Piazza 6.00
7 Alex Rodriguez 8.00
8 Frank Thomas 4.00
9 Mo Vaughn 1.50
10 Matt Williams 1.50

Decade of Excellence

NM/M

Complete Set (12): 35.00
Common Player: 1.50
Rare Tradition: 12X
1 Wade Boggs 4.50
2 Barry Bonds 9.00
3 Roger Clemens 6.00
4 Tony Gwynn 4.50
5 Rickey Henderson 3.00
6 Greg Maddux 4.50
7 Mark McGwire 6.00
8 Paul Molitor 3.00
9 Eddie Murray 3.00
10 Cal Ripken Jr. 9.00

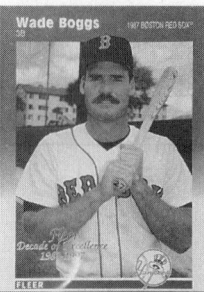

Wade Boggs

		4.50
11	Ryne Sandberg	4.50
12	Matt Williams	1.50

Diamond Tribute

		NM/M
Complete Set (12):		120.00
Common Player:		3.00
1	Albert Belle	3.00
2	Barry Bonds	20.00
3	Juan Gonzalez	5.00
4	Ken Griffey Jr.	12.50
5	Tony Gwynn	10.00
6	Greg Maddux	10.00
7	Mark McGwire	15.00
8	Eddie Murray	8.00
9	Mike Piazza	12.50
10	Cal Ripken Jr.	20.00
11	Alex Rodriguez	15.00
12	Frank Thomas	8.00

Golden Memories

		NM/M
Complete Set (10):		6.00
Common Player:		.25
1	Barry Bonds	2.00
2	Dwight Gooden	.25
3	Todd Hundley	.25
4	Mark McGwire	1.50
5	Paul Molitor	.75
6	Eddie Murray	.75
7	Hideo Nomo	.50
8	Mike Piazza	1.25
9	Cal Ripken Jr.	2.00
10	Ozzie Smith	1.00

Goudey Greats

		NM/M
Complete Set (15):		20.00
Common Player:		.50
Foils:		15X
1	Barry Bonds	4.00
2	Ken Griffey Jr.	3.00
3	Tony Gwynn	2.00
4	Derek Jeter	4.00
5	Chipper Jones	2.00
6	Kenny Lofton	.50
7	Greg Maddux	2.00
8	Mark McGwire	3.50
9	Eddie Murray	1.50
10	Mike Piazza	3.00
11	Cal Ripken Jr.	4.00
12	Alex Rodriguez	3.50
13	Ryne Sandberg	2.00
14	Frank Thomas	1.50
15	Mo Vaughn	.50

Headliners

		NM/M
Complete Set (20):		5.00
Common Player:		.10
1	Jeff Bagwell	.25
2	Albert Belle	.10
3	Barry Bonds	1.00
4	Ken Caminiti	.10
5	Juan Gonzalez	.20
6	Ken Griffey Jr.	.60
7	Tony Gwynn	.40
8	Derek Jeter	1.00
9	Andruw Jones	.25
10	Chipper Jones	.40
11	Greg Maddux	.40
12	Mark McGwire	.75
13	Paul Molitor	.25
14	Eddie Murray	.25
15	Mike Piazza	.60
16	Cal Ripken Jr.	1.00
17	Alex Rodriguez	.75
18	Ryne Sandberg	.40
19	John Smoltz	.20
20	Frank Thomas	.25

Lumber Company

		NM/M
Complete Set (18):		45.00
Common Player:		1.00
1	Brady Anderson	1.00
2	Jeff Bagwell	3.00
3	Albert Belle	1.00
4	Barry Bonds	8.00
5	Jay Buhner	1.00
6	Ellis Burks	1.00
7	Andres Galarraga	1.00
8	Juan Gonzalez	2.00
9	Ken Griffey Jr.	5.00
10	Todd Hundley	1.00
11	Ryan Klesko	1.00
12	Mark McGwire	6.00
13	Mike Piazza	5.00
14	Alex Rodriguez	6.00
15	Gary Sheffield	2.00
16	Sammy Sosa	4.00
17	Frank Thomas	3.00
18	Mo Vaughn	1.00

New Horizons

		NM/M
Complete Set (15):		2.00
Common Player:		.05
1	Bob Abreu	.10
2	Jose Cruz Jr.	.05
3	Darin Erstad	.10
4	Nomar Garciaparra	.75
5	Vladimir Guerrero	.60
6	Wilton Guerrero	.05
7	Jose Guillen	.05
8	Hideki Irabu	.05
9	Andruw Jones	.60
10	Kevin Orie	.05
11	Scott Rolen	.50
12	Scott Spiezio	.05
13	Bubba Trammell	.05
14	Todd Walker	.05
15	Dmitri Young	.05

Night & Day

		NM/M
Complete Set (10):		45.00
Common Player:		1.00
1	Barry Bonds	12.00
2	Ellis Burks	1.00
3	Juan Gonzalez	2.00
4	Ken Griffey Jr.	6.00
5	Mark McGwire	7.50
6	Mike Piazza	6.00
7	Manny Ramirez	4.00
8	Alex Rodriguez	8.00
9	John Smoltz	2.00
10	Frank Thomas	4.00

Rookie Sensations

		NM/M
Complete Set (20):		6.00
Common Player:		.25
1	Jermaine Allensworth	.25
2	James Baldwin	.25
3	Alan Benes	.25
4	Jermaine Dye	.25
5	Darin Erstad	.50
6	Todd Hollandsworth	.25
7	Derek Jeter	2.50
8	Jason Kendall	.25
9	Alex Ochoa	.25
10	Rey Ordonez	.25
11	Edgar Renteria	.25
12	Bob Abreu	.50
13	Nomar Garciaparra	1.50
14	Wilton Guerrero	.25
15	Andruw Jones	1.00

16	Wendell Magee	.25
17	Neifi Perez	.25
18	Scott Rolen	.75
19	Scott Spiezio	.25
20	Todd Walker	.25

Soaring Stars

		NM/M
Complete Set (12):		10.00
Common Player:		.25
Glowing:		6X
1	Albert Belle	.25
2	Barry Bonds	2.00
3	Juan Gonzalez	.50
4	Ken Griffey Jr.	1.25
5	Derek Jeter	2.00
6	Andruw Jones	.60
7	Chipper Jones	1.00
8	Greg Maddux	1.00
9	Mark McGwire	1.50
10	Mike Piazza	1.25
11	Alex Rodriguez	1.50
12	Frank Thomas	.75

Team Leaders

		NM/M
Complete Set (28):		25.00
Common Player:		.25
1	Cal Ripken Jr.	5.00
2	Mo Vaughn	.25
3	Jim Edmonds	.40
4	Frank Thomas	1.50
5	Albert Belle	.25
6	Bob Higginson	.25
7	Kevin Appier	.25
8	John Jaha	.25
9	Paul Molitor	1.50
10	Andy Pettitte	.65
11	Mark McGwire	4.00
12	Ken Griffey Jr.	3.00
13	Juan Gonzalez	.75
14	Pat Hentgen	.25
15	Chipper Jones	2.00
16	Mark Grace	.35
17	Barry Larkin	.25
18	Ellis Burks	.25
19	Gary Sheffield	.60
20	Jeff Bagwell	1.50
21	Mike Piazza	3.00
22	Henry Rodriguez	.25
23	Todd Hundley	.25
24	Curt Schilling	.60
25	Jeff King	.25
26	Brian Jordan	.25
27	Tony Gwynn	1.50
28	Barry Bonds	5.00

Zone

		NM/M
Complete Set (20):		80.00
Common Player:		1.50
1	Jeff Bagwell	5.00
2	Albert Belle	1.50
3	Barry Bonds	15.00
4	Ken Caminiti	1.50
5	Andres Galarraga	1.50
6	Juan Gonzalez	2.50
7	Ken Griffey Jr.	8.00
8	Tony Gwynn	6.00
9	Chipper Jones	6.00
10	Greg Maddux	6.00
11	Mark McGwire	10.00
12	Dean Palmer	1.50
13	Andy Petitte	3.00
14	Mike Piazza	8.00
15	Alex Rodriguez	12.00
16	Gary Sheffield	2.50
17	John Smoltz	2.50

18	Frank Thomas	5.00
19	Jim Thome	4.00
20	Matt Williams	1.50

1998 Fleer

	NM/M
Complete Set (600):	65.00
Complete Series 1 (350):	40.00
Complete Series 2 (250):	25.00
Common Player:	.05
Series 1 or 2 Pack (10):	1.00
Series 1 or 2 Wax Box (36):	20.00

1	Ken Griffey Jr.	1.50
2	Derek Jeter	2.50
3	Gerald Williams	.05
4	Carlos Delgado	.50
5	Nomar Garciaparra	1.50
6	Gary Sheffield	.30
7	Jeff King	.05
8	Cal Ripken Jr.	2.50
9	Matt Williams	.05
10	Chipper Jones	1.00
11	Chuck Knoblauch	.05
12	Mark Grudzielanek	.05
13	Edgardo Alfonzo	.05
14	Andres Galarraga	.05
15	Tim Salmon	.15
16	Reggie Sanders	.05
17	Tony Clark	.05
18	Jason Kendall	.05
19	Juan Gonzalez	.65
20	Ben Grieve	.10
21	Roger Clemens	1.25
22	Raul Mondesi	.05
23	Robin Ventura	.05
24	Derrek Lee	.05
25	Mark McGwire	2.00
26	Luis Gonzalez	.10
27	Kevin Brown	.05
28	Kirk Rueter	.05
29	Bobby Estalella	.05
30	Shawn Green	.35
31	Greg Maddux	1.00
32	Jorge Velandia	.05
33	Larry Walker	.05
34	Joey Cora	.05
35	Frank Thomas	.85
36	Curtis King **RC**	.05
37	Aaron Boone	.05
38	Curt Schilling	.25
39	Bruce Aven	.05
40	Ben McDonald	.05
41	Andy Ashby	.05
42	Jason McDonald	.05
43	Eric Davis	.05
44	Mark Grace	.10
45	Pedro Martinez	.75
46	Lou Collier	.05
47	Chan Ho Park	.05
48	Shane Halter	.05
49	Brian Hunter	.05
50	Jeff Bagwell	.75
51	Bernie Williams	.10
52	J.T. Snow	.05
53	Todd Greene	.05
54	Shannon Stewart	.05
55	Darren Bragg	.05
56	Fernando Tatis	.05
57	Darryl Kile	.05
58	Chris Stynes	.05
59	Javier Valentin	.05
60	Brian McRae	.05
61	Tom Evans	.05
62	Randall Simon	.05
63	Darrin Fletcher	.05
64	Jaret Wright	.05
65	Luis Ordaz	.05
66	Jose Canseco	.40
67	Edgar Renteria	.05
68	Jay Buhner	.05
69	Paul Konerko	.10
70	Adrian Brown	.05
71	Chris Carpenter	.05
72	Mike Lieberthal	.05
73	Dean Palmer	.05
74	Jorge Fabregas	.05
75	Stan Javier	.05
76	Damion Easley	.05
77	David Cone	.05
78	Aaron Sele	.05
79	Antonio Alfonseca	.05
80	Bobby Jones	.05
81	David Justice	.05
82	Jeffrey Hammonds	.05
83	Doug Glanville	.05
84	Jason Dickson	.05
85	Brad Radke	.05
86	David Segui	.05
87	Greg Vaughn	.05
88	Mike Cather **RC**	.05
89	Alex Fernandez	.05
90	Billy Taylor	.05
91	Jason Schmidt	.05
92	Mike DeJean **RC**	.05
93	Domingo Cedeno	.05
94	Jeff Cirillo	.05
95	Manny Aybar **RC**	.10
96	Jaime Navarro	.05
97	Dennis Reyes	.05
98	Barry Larkin	.05
99	Troy O'Leary	.05
100	Alex Rodriguez	2.00
100p	Alex Rodriguez/OPS	2.00
101	Pat Hentgen	.05
102	Bubba Trammell	.05
103	Glendon Rusch	.05
104	Kenny Lofton	.05
105	Craig Biggio	.05
106	Kelvim Escobar	.05
107	Mark Kotsay	.05
108	Rondell White	.05
109	Darren Oliver	.05
110	Jim Thome	.65
111	Rich Becker	.05
112	Chad Curtis	.05
113	Dave Hollins	.05
114	Bill Mueller	.05
115	Antone Williamson	.05
116	Tony Womack	.05
117	Randy Myers	.05
118	Rico Brogna	.05
119	Pat Watkins	.05
120	Eli Marrero	.05
121	Jay Bell	.05
122	Kevin Tapani	.05
123	Todd Erdos **RC**	.10
124	Neifi Perez	.05
125	Todd Hundley	.05
126	Jeff Abbott	.05
127	Todd Zeile	.05
128	Travis Fryman	.05
129	Sandy Alomar	.05
130	Fred McGriff	.05
131	Richard Hidalgo	.05
132	Scott Spiezio	.05
133	John Valentin	.05
134	Quilvio Veras	.05
135	Mike Lansing	.05
136	Paul Molitor	.75
137	Randy Johnson	.75
138	Harold Baines	.05
139	Doug Jones	.05
140	Abraham Nunez	.05
141	Alan Benes	.05
142	Matt Perisho	.05
143	Chris Clemons	.05
144	Andy Pettitte	.30
145	Jason Giambi	.40
146	Moises Alou	.05
147	Chad Fox **RC**	.05
148	Felix Martinez	.05
149	Carlos Mendoza **RC**	.05
150	Scott Rolen	.65
151	Jose Cabrera **RC**	.05
152	Justin Thompson	.05
153	Ellis Burks	.05
154	Pokey Reese	.05
155	Bartolo Colon	.05
156	Ray Durham	.05
157	Ugueth Urbina	.05
158	Tom Goodwin	.05
159	David Dellucci **RC**	.25
160	Rod Beck	.05
161	Ramon Martinez	.05
162	Joe Carter	.05
163	Kevin Orie	.05
164	Trevor Hoffman	.05
165	Emil Brown	.05
166	Robb Nen	.05
167	Paul O'Neill	.05
168	Ryan Long	.05
169	Ray Lankford	.05
170	Ivan Rodriguez	.65
171	Rick Aguilera	.05
172	Deivi Cruz	.05
173	Ricky Bottalico	.05
174	Garret Anderson	.05
175	Jose Vizcaino	.05
176	Omar Vizquel	.05
177	Jeff Blauser	.05
178	Orlando Cabrera	.05
179	Russ Johnson	.05
180	Matt Stairs	.05
181	Will Cunnane	.05
182	Adam Riggs	.05
183	Matt Morris	.05
184	Mario Valdez	.05
185	Larry Sutton	.05
186	Marc Pisciotta **RC**	.05
187	Dan Wilson	.05
188	John Franco	.05
189	Darren Daulton	.05
190	Todd Helton	.75
191	Brady Anderson	.05
192	Ricardo Rincon	.05
193	Kevin Stocker	.05
194	Jose Valentin	.05
195	Ed Sprague	.05
196	Ryan McGuire	.05
197	Scott Eyre **RC**	.05
198	Steve Finley	.05
199	T.J. Mathews	.05
200	Mike Piazza	1.50
201	Mark Wohlers	.05
202	Brian Giles	.05
203	Eduardo Perez	.05
204	Shigetosi Hasegawa	.05
205	Mariano Rivera	.15
206	Jose Rosado	.05
207	Michael Coleman	.05
208	James Baldwin	.05
209	Russ Davis	.05
210	Billy Wagner	.05
211	Sammy Sosa	1.50
212	Frank Catalanotto **RC**	.15
213	Delino DeShields	.05
214	John Olerud	.05
215	Heath Murray	.05
216	Jose Vidro	.05
217	Jim Edmonds	.05
218	Shawon Dunston	.05
219	Homer Bush	.05
220	Midre Cummings	.05
221	Tony Saunders	.05
222	Jeromy Burnitz	.05
223	Enrique Wilson	.05
224	Chili Davis	.05
225	Jerry DiPoto	.05
226	Dante Powell	.05
227	Javier Lopez	.05
228	Kevin Polcovich **RC**	.10
229	Deion Sanders	.05
230	Jimmy Key	.05
231	Rusty Greer	.05
232	Reggie Jefferson	.05
233	Ron Coomer	.05
234	Bobby Higginson	.05
235	Magglio Ordonez **RC**	2.00
236	Miguel Tejada	.25
237	Rick Gorecki	.05
238	Charles Johnson	.05
239	Lance Johnson	.05
240	Derek Bell	.05
241	Will Clark	.10
242	Brady Raggio	.05
243	Orel Hershiser	.05
244	Vladimir Guerrero	.75
245	John LeRoy	.05
246	Shawn Estes	.05
247	Brett Tomko	.05
248	Dave Nilsson	.05
249	Edgar Martinez	.05
250	Tony Gwynn	1.00
251	Mark Bellhorn	.05
252	Jed Hansen	.05
253	Butch Huskey	.05
254	Eric Young	.05
255	Vinny Castilla	.05
256	Hideki Irabu	.05
257	Mike Cameron	.05
258	Juan Encarnacion	.05
259	Brian Rose	.05
260	Brad Ausmus	.05
261	Dan Serafini	.05
262	Willie Greene	.05
263	Troy Percival	.05
264	Jeff Wallace **RC**	.05
265	Richie Sexson	.05
266	Rafael Palmeiro	.65
267	Brad Fullmer	.05
268	Jeremi Gonzalez	.05
269	Rob Stanifer **RC**	.05
270	Mickey Morandini	.05
271	Andruw Jones	.75
272	Royce Clayton	.05
273	Takashi Kashiwada	.05
274	Steve Woodard **RC**	.10
275	Jose Cruz Jr.	.05
276	Keith Foulke	.05
277	Brad Rigby	.05
278	Tino Martinez	.05
279	Todd Jones	.05
280	John Wetteland	.05
281	Alex Gonzalez	.05
282	Ken Cloude	.05
283	Jose Guillen	.05
284	Danny Clyburn	.05
285	David Ortiz	.05
286	John Thomson	.05
287	Kevin Appier	.05
288	Ismael Valdes	.05
289	Gary DiSarcina	.05
290	Todd Dunwoody	.05
291	Wally Joyner	.05
292	Charles Nagy	.05
293	Jeff Shaw	.05
294	Kevin Millwood **RC**	1.00
295	Rigo Beltran **RC**	.05
296	Jeff Frye	.05
297	Oscar Henriquez	.05
298	Mike Thurman	.05
299	Garrett Stephenson	.05
300	Barry Bonds	2.50
301	Roger Clemens	.75
302	David Cone	.05
303	Hideki Irabu	.05
304	Randy Johnson	.40
305	Greg Maddux	.50
306	Pedro Martinez	.35
307	Mike Mussina	.25
308	Andy Pettitte	.15
309	Curt Schilling	.10
310	John Smoltz	.05
311	Roger Clemens	1.00
312	Jose Cruz Jr.	.25
313	Nomar Garciaparra	1.00
314	Ken Griffey Jr.	1.00
315	Tony Gwynn	.75
316	Hideki Irabu	.25
317	Randy Johnson	.60
318	Mark McGwire	1.50
319	Curt Schilling	.35
320	Larry Walker	.15
321	Jeff Bagwell	.60
322	Albert Belle	.15
323	Barry Bonds	1.50
324	Jay Buhner	.15
325	Tony Clark	.15
326	Jose Cruz Jr.	.15
327	Andres Galarraga	.15
328	Juan Gonzalez	.30
329	Ken Griffey Jr.	.85
330	Andruw Jones	.60
331	Tino Martinez	.15
332	Mark McGwire	1.00
333	Rafael Palmeiro	.50
334	Mike Piazza	.85
335	Manny Ramirez	.65
336	Alex Rodriguez	1.00
337	Frank Thomas	.65
338	Jim Thome	.65
339	Mo Vaughn	.15
340	Larry Walker	.15
341	Jose Cruz Jr. Checklist	.15
342	Ken Griffey Jr. Checklist	.65
343	Derek Jeter Checklist	1.00
344	Andruw Jones Checklist	.40
345	Chipper Jones Checklist	.50
346	Greg Maddux Checklist	.50
347	Mike Piazza Checklist	.65
348	Cal Ripken Jr. Checklist	1.00
349	Alex Rodriguez Checklist	.75
350	Frank Thomas Checklist	.45
351	Mo Vaughn	.05
352	Andres Galarraga	.05
353	Roberto Alomar	.10
354	Darin Erstad	.10
355	Albert Belle	.05
356	Matt Williams	.05
357	Darryl Kile	.05
358	Kenny Lofton	.05
359	Orel Hershiser	.05
360	Bob Abreu	.05
361	Chris Widger	.05
362	Glenallen Hill	.05
363	Chili Davis	.05
364	Kevin Brown	.05
365	Marquis Grissom	.05
366	Livan Hernandez	.05
367	Moises Alou	.05
368	Matt Lawton	.05
369	Rey Ordonez	.05
370	Kenny Rogers	.05
371	Lee Stevens	.05
372	Wade Boggs	1.00
373	Luis Gonzalez	.05
374	Jeff Conine	.05
375	Esteban Loaiza	.05
376	Jose Canseco	.40
377	Henry Rodriguez	.05
378	Dave Burba	.05
379	Todd Hollandsworth	.05
380	Ron Gant	.05
381	Pedro Martinez	.75
382	Ryan Klesko	.05
383	Derrek Lee	.05
384	Doug Glanville	.05
385	David Wells	.05
386	Ken Caminiti	.05
387	Damon Hollins	.05
388	Manny Ramirez	.75
389	Mike Mussina	.45
390	Jay Bell	.05
391	Mike Piazza	1.50
392	Mike Lansing	.05
393	Mike Hampton	.05
394	Geoff Jenkins	.05
395	Jimmy Haynes	.05
396	Scott Servais	.05
397	Kent Mercker	.05
398	Jeff Kent	.05
399	Kevin Elster	.05

400	Masato Yoshii RC	.50
401	Jose Vizcaino	.05
402	Javier Martinez	.05
403	David Segui	.05
404	Tony Saunders	.05
405	Karim Garcia	.05
406	Armando Benitez	.05
407	Joe Randa	.05
408	Vic Darensbourg	.05
409	Sean Casey	.20
410	Eric Milton	.05
411	Trey Moore	.05
412	Mike Stanley	.05
413	Tom Gordon	.05
414	Hal Morris	.05
415	Braden Looper	.05
416	Mike Kelly	.05
417	John Smoltz	.05
418	Roger Cedeno	.05
419	Al Leiter	.05
420	Chuck Knoblauch	.05
421	Felix Rodriguez	.05
422	Bip Roberts	.05
423	Ken Hill	.05
424	Jermaine Allensworth	.05
425	Esteban Yan	.05
426	Scott Karl	.05
427	Sean Berry	.05
428	Rafael Medina	.05
429	Javier Vazquez	.05
430	Rickey Henderson	.75
431	Adam Butler RC	.05
432	Todd Stottlemyre	.05
433	Yamil Benitez	.05
434	Sterling Hitchcock	.05
435	Paul Sorrento	.05
436	Bobby Ayala	.05
437	Tim Raines	.05
438	Chris Hoiles	.05
439	Rod Beck	.05
440	Donnie Sadler	.05
441	Charles Johnson	.05
442	Russ Ortiz	.05
443	Pedro Astacio	.05
444	Wilson Alvarez	.05
445	Mike Blowers	.05
446	Todd Zeile	.05
447	Mel Rojas	.05
448	F.P. Santangelo	.05
449	Dmitri Young	.05
450	Brian Anderson	.05
451	Cecil Fielder	.05
452	Roberto Hernandez	.05
453	Todd Walker	.05
454	Tyler Green	.05
455	Jorge Posada	.05
456	Geronimo Berroa	.05
457	Jose Silva	.05
458	Bobby Bonilla	.05
459	Walt Weiss	.05
460	Darren Dreifort	.05
461	B.J. Surhoff	.05
462	Quinton McCracken	.05
463	Derek Lowe	.05
464	Jorge Fabregas	.05
465	Joey Hamilton	.05
466	Brian Jordan	.05
467	Allen Watson	.05
468	John Jaha	.05
469	Heathcliff Slocumb	.05
470	Gregg Jefferies	.05
471	Scott Brosius	.05
472	Chad Ogea	.05
473	A.J. Hinch	.05
474	Bobby Smith	.05
475	Brian Moehler	.05
476	DaRond Stovall	.05
477	Kevin Young	.05
478	Jeff Suppan	.05
479	Marty Cordova	.05
480	John Halama RC	.25
481	Bubba Trammell	.05
482	Mike Caruso	.05
483	Eric Karros	.05
484	Jamey Wright	.05
485	Mike Sweeney	.05
486	Aaron Sele	.05
487	Cliff Floyd	.05
488	Jeff Brantley	.05
489	Jim Leyritz	.05
490	Denny Neagle	.05
491	Travis Fryman	.05
492	Carlos Baerga	.05
493	Eddie Taubensee	.05
494	Darryl Strawberry	.05
495	Brian Johnson	.05
496	Randy Myers	.05
497	Jeff Blauser	.05
498	Jason Wood	.05
499	Rolando Arrojo RC	.25
500	Johnny Damon	.05
501	Jose Mercedes	.05
502	Tony Batista	.05
503	Mike Piazza	1.50
504	Hideo Nomo	.65
505	Chris Gomez	.05
506	Jesus Sanchez RC	.05
507	Al Martin	.05
508	Brian Edmondson	.05
509	Joe Girardi	.05
510	Shayne Bennett	.05
511	Joe Carter	.05
512	Dave Mlicki	.05
513	Rich Butler RC	.10
514	Dennis Eckersley	.65
515	Travis Lee	.10
516	John Mabry	.05
517	Jose Mesa	.05
518	Phil Nevin	.05
519	Raul Casanova	.05
520	Mike Fetters	.05
521	Gary Sheffield	.30
522	Terry Steinbach	.05
523	Steve Trachsel	.05
524	Josh Booty	.05
525	Darryl Hamilton	.05
526	Mark McLemore	.05
527	Kevin Stocker	.05
528	Bret Boone	.05
529	Shane Andrews	.05
530	Robb Nen	.05
531	Carl Everett	.05
532	LaTroy Hawkins	.05
533	Fernando Vina	.05
534	Michael Tucker	.05
535	Mark Langston	.05
536	Mickey Mantle	2.00
537	Bernard Gilkey	.05
538	Francisco Cordova	.05
539	Mike Bordick	.05
540	Fred McGriff	.05
541	Cliff Politte	.05
542	Jason Varitek	.05
543	Shawon Dunston	.05
544	Brian Meadows	.05
545	Pat Meares	.05
546	Carlos Perez	.05
547	Desi Relaford	.05
548	Antonio Osuna	.05
549	Devon White	.05
550	Sean Runyan	.05
551	Mickey Morandini	.05
552	Dave Martinez	.05
553	Jeff Fassero	.05
554	Ryan Jackson RC	.05
555	Stan Javier	.05
556	Jaime Navarro	.05
557	Jose Offerman	.05
558	Mike Lowell RC	1.00
559	Darrin Fletcher	.05
560	Mark Lewis	.05
561	Dante Bichette	.05
562	Chuck Finley	.05
563	Kerry Wood	.35
564	Andy Benes	.05
565	Freddy Garcia	.05
566	Tom Glavine	.25
567	Jon Nunnally	.05
568	Miguel Cairo	.05
569	Shane Reynolds	.05
570	Roberto Kelly	.05
571	Jose Cruz Jr. Checklist	.25
572	Ken Griffey Jr. Checklist	.65
573	Mark McGwire Checklist	.75
574	Cal Ripken Jr. Checklist	1.00
575	Frank Thomas Checklist	.45
576	Jeff Bagwell	1.00
577	Barry Bonds	3.00
578	Tony Clark	.25
579	Roger Clemens	2.00
580	Jose Cruz Jr.	.25
581	Nomar Garciaparra	1.50
582	Juan Gonzalez	1.00
583	Ben Grieve	.25
584	Ken Griffey Jr.	2.00
585	Tony Gwynn	1.50
586	Derek Jeter	3.00
587	Randy Johnson	1.00
588	Chipper Jones	1.50
589	Greg Maddux	1.50
590	Mark McGwire	2.50
591	Andy Pettitte	.45
592	Paul Molitor	1.00
593	Cal Ripken Jr.	3.00
594	Alex Rodriguez	2.50
595	Scott Rolen	.50
596	Curt Schilling	.50
597	Frank Thomas	1.25
598	Jim Thome	.75
599	Larry Walker	.25
600	Bernie Williams	.30

Decade of Excellence

		NM/M
Complete Set (12):		35.00
Common Player:		1.00
Inserted 1:72		
Rare Traditions:		3X
Inserted 1:720		
1	Roberto Alomar	1.50
2	Barry Bonds	8.00
3	Roger Clemens	5.00
4	David Cone	1.00
5	Andres Galarraga	1.00
6	Mark Grace	1.00
7	Tony Gwynn	4.00
8	Randy Johnson	3.00
9	Greg Maddux	4.00
10	Mark McGwire	6.00
11	Paul O'Neill	1.00
12	Cal Ripken Jr.	8.00

Diamond Standouts

		NM/M
Complete Set (20):		25.00
Common Player:		.50
1	Jeff Bagwell	1.00
2	Barry Bonds	4.00
3	Roger Clemens	2.00
4	Jose Cruz Jr.	.50
5	Andres Galarraga	.50
6	Nomar Garciaparra	2.00
7	Juan Gonzalez	.75
8	Ken Griffey Jr.	2.00
9	Derek Jeter	4.00
10	Randy Johnson	1.00
11	Chipper Jones	1.50
12	Kenny Lofton	.50
13	Greg Maddux	1.50
14	Pedro Martinez	1.00
15	Mark McGwire	3.00
16	Mike Piazza	2.00
17	Alex Rodriguez	3.00
18	Curt Schilling	.75
19	Frank Thomas	1.00
20	Larry Walker	.50

Diamond Tribute

		NM/M
Complete Set (10):		90.00
Common Player:		5.00
DT1	Jeff Bagwell	7.50
DT2	Roger Clemens	10.00
DT3	Nomar Garciaparra	10.00
DT4	Juan Gonzalez	5.00
DT5	Ken Griffey Jr.	12.00
DT6	Mark McGwire	15.00
DT7	Mike Piazza	12.00
DT8	Cal Ripken Jr.	20.00
DT9	Alex Rodriguez	15.00
DT10	Frank Thomas	7.50

In the Clutch

		NM/M
Complete Set (15):		25.00
Common Player:		.40
IC1	Jeff Bagwell	1.00
IC2	Barry Bonds	5.00
IC3	Roger Clemens	2.00
IC4	Jose Cruz Jr.	.40
IC5	Nomar Garciaparra	2.00
IC6	Juan Gonzalez	.75
IC7	Ken Griffey Jr.	2.50
IC8	Tony Gwynn	1.50
IC9	Derek Jeter	5.00
IC10	Chipper Jones	1.50
IC11	Greg Maddux	1.50
IC12	Mark McGwire	4.00
IC13	Mike Piazza	2.50
IC14	Frank Thomas	1.00
IC15	Larry Walker	.40

Lumber Company

		NM/M
Complete Set (15):		50.00
Common Player:		.75
Inserted 1:36 R		
1	Jeff Bagwell	2.50
2	Barry Bonds	8.00
3	Jose Cruz Jr.	.75
4	Nomar Garciaparra	4.00
5	Juan Gonzalez	1.50
6	Ken Griffey Jr.	5.00
7	Tony Gwynn	3.00
8	Chipper Jones	3.00
9	Tino Martinez	.75
10	Mark McGwire	6.00
11	Mike Piazza	5.00
12	Cal Ripken Jr.	8.00
13	Alex Rodriguez	6.00
14	Frank Thomas	2.50
15	Larry Walker	.75

1998 Fleer Mantle & Sons

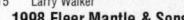

	NM/M
Mickey Mantle, Danny Mantle, David Mantle	3.00

Mickey Mantle Monumental Moments

		NM/M
Complete Set (10):		40.00
Common Card:		5.00
Inserted 1:68		
Gold (51 Sets):		3X
1	Armed and Dangerous	5.00
2	Getting Ready in Spring Training	5.00
3	Mantle and Rizzuto Celebrate	5.00
4	Posed for Action	5.00
5	Signed, Sealed and Ready to Deliver	5.00
6	Triple Crown 1956 Season	5.00
7	Number 7 . . .	5.00
8	Mantle's Powerful Swing . . .	5.00

9	Old-Timers Day Introduction	5.00
10	Portrait of Determination	5.00

Promising Forecast

NM/M

Complete Set (20):		7.00
Common Player:		.25
Inserted 1:12		
PF1	Rolando Arrojo	.25
PF2	Sean Casey	.40
PF3	Brad Fullmer	.25
PF4	Karim Garcia	.35
PF5	Ben Grieve	.25
PF6	Todd Helton	3.00
PF7	Richard Hidalgo	.25
PF8	A.J. Hinch	.25
PF9	Paul Konerko	.35
PF10	Mark Kotsay	.25
PF11	Derrek Lee	1.00
PF12	Travis Lee	.35
PF13	Eric Milton	.25
PF14	Magglio Ordonez	.50
PF15	David Ortiz	.50
PF16	Brian Rose	.25
PF17	Miguel Tejada	.40
PF18	Jason Varitek	.35
PF19	Enrique Wilson	.25
PF20	Kerry Wood	1.00

Rookie Sensations

NM/M

Complete Set (20):		12.00
Common Player:		.50
Inserted 1:18		
1	Mike Cameron	.50
2	Jose Cruz Jr.	.50
3	Jason Dickson	.50
4	Kelvim Escobar	.50
5	Nomar Garciaparra	3.00
6	Ben Grieve	.50
7	Vladimir Guerrero	3.00
8	Wilton Guerrero	.50
9	Jose Guillen	.50

10	Todd Helton	2.00
11	Livan Hernandez	.50
12	Hideki Irabu	.50
13	Andruw Jones	3.00
14	Matt Morris	.50
15	Magglio Ordonez	1.00
16	Neifi Perez	.50
17	Scott Rolen	2.00
18	Fernando Tatis	.50
19	Brett Tomko	.50
20	Jaret Wright	.50

The Power Game

NM/M

Complete Set (20):		30.00
Common Player:		.50
Inserted 1:36		
1	Jeff Bagwell	2.00
2	Albert Belle	.50
3	Barry Bonds	6.00
4	Tony Clark	.50
5	Roger Clemens	3.50
6	Jose Cruz Jr.	.50
7	Andres Galarraga	.50
8	Nomar Garciaparra	3.50
9	Juan Gonzalez	1.00
10	Ken Griffey Jr.	4.00
11	Randy Johnson	2.00
12	Greg Maddux	3.00
13	Pedro Martinez	2.00
14	Tino Martinez	.50
15	Mark McGwire	5.00
16	Mike Piazza	4.00
17	Curt Schilling	.75
18	Frank Thomas	2.00
19	Jim Thome	2.00
20	Larry Walker	.50

Zone

NM/M

Complete Set (15):		130.00
Common Player:		4.00
Inserted 1:288		
1	Jeff Bagwell	7.50
2	Barry Bonds	25.00
3	Roger Clemens	10.00
4	Jose Cruz Jr.	4.00
5	Nomar Garciaparra	10.00
6	Juan Gonzalez	6.00
7	Ken Griffey Jr.	12.00
8	Tony Gwynn	9.00
9	Chipper Jones	9.00
10	Greg Maddux	9.00
11	Mark McGwire	15.00
12	Mike Piazza	12.00
13	Alex Rodriguez	20.00
14	Frank Thomas	7.50
15	Larry Walker	4.00

Vintage '63

NM/M

Complete Set (126):		20.00
Complete Series 1 (63):		10.00
Complete Series 2 (63):		10.00
Common Player:		.10
Classics (63 Sets):		20X
1	Jason Dickson	.10

MARK McGWIRE
St. Louis Cardinals,—18

2	Tim Salmon	.25
3	Andruw Jones	.75
4	Chipper Jones	1.00
5	Kenny Lofton	.10
6	Greg Maddux	1.00
7	Rafael Palmeiro	.65
8	Cal Ripken Jr.	2.50
9	Nomar Garciaparra	1.25
10	Mark Grace	.10
11	Sammy Sosa	1.25
12	Frank Thomas	.75
13	Deion Sanders	.10
14	Sandy Alomar	.10
15	David Justice	.10
16	Jim Thome	.75
17	Matt Williams	.10
18	Jaret Wright	.10
19	Vinny Castilla	.10
20	Andres Galarraga	.10
21	Todd Helton	.75
22	Larry Walker	.10
23	Tony Clark	.10
24	Moises Alou	.10
25	Kevin Brown	.10
26	Charles Johnson	.10
27	Edgar Renteria	.10
28	Gary Sheffield	.50
29	Jeff Bagwell	.75
30	Craig Biggio	.10
31	Raul Mondesi	.10
32	Mike Piazza	1.50
33	Chuck Knoblauch	.10
34	Paul Molitor	.75
35	Vladimir Guerrero	.75
36	Pedro Martinez	.75
37	Todd Hundley	.10
38	Derek Jeter	2.50
39	Tino Martinez	.10
40	Paul O'Neill	.10
41	Andy Pettitte	.35
42	Mariano Rivera	.20
43	Bernie Williams	.20
44	Ben Grieve	.35
45	Scott Rolen	.65
46	Curt Schilling	.45
47	Jason Kendall	.10
48	Tony Womack	.10
49	Ray Lankford	.10
50	Mark McGwire	2.00
51	Matt Morris	.10
52	Tony Gwynn	1.00
53	Barry Bonds	2.50
54	Jay Buhner	.10
55	Ken Griffey Jr.	1.50
56	Randy Johnson	.75
57	Edgar Martinez	.10
58	Alex Rodriguez	2.00
59	Juan Gonzalez	.65
60	Rusty Greer	.10
61	Ivan Rodriguez	.65
62	Roger Clemens	1.25
63	Jose Cruz Jr.	.10
	Checklist #1-63	.10
64	Darin Erstad	.20
65	Jay Bell	.10
66	Andy Benes	.10
67	Mickey Mantle	2.00
68	Karim Garcia	.10
69	Travis Lee	.10
70	Matt Williams	.10
71	Andres Galarraga	.10
72	Tom Glavine	.35
73	Ryan Klesko	.10
74	Denny Neagle	.10
75	John Smoltz	.10
76	Roberto Alomar	.20
77	Joe Carter	.10
78	Mike Mussina	.50
79	B.J. Surhoff	.10
80	Dennis Eckersley	.65
81	Pedro Martinez	.75
82	Mo Vaughn	.10
83	Jeff Blauser	.10
84	Henry Rodriguez	.10
85	Albert Belle	.10
86	Sean Casey	.25
87	Travis Fryman	.10
88	Kenny Lofton	.10
89	Darryl Kile	.10
90	Mike Lansing	.10
91	Bobby Bonilla	.10

92	Cliff Floyd	.10
93	Livan Hernandez	.10
94	Derrek Lee	.10
95	Moises Alou	.10
96	Shane Reynolds	.10
97	Jeff Conine	.10
98	Johnny Damon	.35
99	Eric Karros	.10
100	Hideo Nomo	.65
101	Marquis Grissom	.10
102	Matt Lawton	.10
103	Todd Walker	.10
104	Gary Sheffield	.50
105	Bernard Gilkey	.10
106	Rey Ordonez	.10
107	Chili Davis	.10
108	Chuck Knoblauch	.10
109	Charles Johnson	.10
110	Rickey Henderson	.75
111	Bob Abreu	.10
112	Doug Glanville	.10
113	Gregg Jefferies	.10
114	Al Martin	.10
115	Kevin Young	.10
116	Ron Gant	.10
117	Kevin Brown	.10
118	Ken Caminiti	.10
119	Joey Hamilton	.10
120	Jeff Kent	.10
121	Wade Boggs	1.00
122	Quinton McCracken	.10
123	Fred McGriff	.10
124	Paul Sorrento	.10
125	Jose Canseco	.50
126	Randy Myers	.10
	Checklist #64-126	.10

Vintage '63 Classic

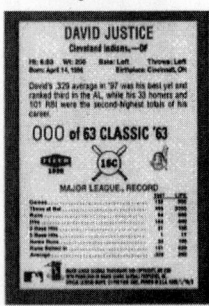

NM/M

Complete Set (128):		650.00
Common Player:		4.00
Stars/RC's:		20X

(See 1998 Fleer Vintage '63 for checklist and base card values.)

1998 Fleer Update

NM/M

Complete Set (100):		12.50
Common Player:		.05
U1	Mark McGwire	.75
U2	Sammy Sosa	.45
U3	Roger Clemens	.45
U4	Barry Bonds	1.00
U5	Kerry Wood	.20
U6	Paul Molitor	.25
U7	Ken Griffey Jr.	.50
U8	Cal Ripken Jr.	1.00
U9	David Wells	.05
U10	Alex Rodriguez	.75
U11	Angel Pena RC	.25
U12	Bruce Chen	.05
U13	Craig Wilson	.05
U14	Orlando Hernandez RC	1.50
U15	Aramis Ramirez	.10
U16	Aaron Boone	.05
U17	Bob Henley	.05
U18	Juan Guzman	.05
U19	Darryl Hamilton	.05

U20	Jay Payton	.05
U21	Jeremy Powell **RC**	.05
U22	Ben Davis	.05
U23	Preston Wilson	.10
U24	Jim Parque **RC**	.15
U25	Odalis Perez **RC**	.25
U26	Ron Belliard	.05
U27	Royce Clayton	.05
U28	George Lombard	.05
U29	Tony Phillips	.05
U30	Fernando Seguignol **RC**	.15
U31	Armando Rios **RC**	.10
U32	Jerry Hairston Jr. **RC**	.25
U33	Justin Baughman **RC**	.05
U34	Seth Greisinger	.05
U35	Alex Gonzalez	.05
U36	Michael Barrett	.05
U37	Carlos Beltran	.35
U38	Ellis Burks	.05
U39	Jose Jimenez	.05
U40	Carlos Guillen	.05
U41	Marlon Anderson	.05
U42	Scott Elarton	.05
U43	Glenallen Hill	.05
U44	Shane Monahan	.05
U45	Dennis Martinez	.05
U46	Carlos Febles **RC**	.20
U47	Carlos Perez	.05
U48	Wilton Guerrero	.05
U49	Randy Johnson	.45
U50	Brian Simmons **RC**	.05
U51	Carlton Loewer	.05
U52	Mark DeRosa **RC**	.50
U53	Tim Young **RC**	.05
U54	Gary Gaetti	.05
U55	Eric Chavez	.25
U56	Carl Pavano	.15
U57	Mike Stanley	.05
U58	Todd Stottlemyre	.05
U59	Gabe Kapler **RC**	.50
U60	Mike Jerzembeck **RC**	.05
U61	Mitch Meluskey **RC**	.15
U62	Bill Pulsipher	.05
U63	Derrick Gibson	.05
U64	John Rocker **RC**	.75
U65	Calvin Pickering	.05
U66	Blake Stein	.05
U67	Fernando Tatis	.05
U68	Gabe Alvarez	.05
U69	Jeffrey Hammonds	.05
U70	Adrian Beltre	.25
U71	Ryan Bradley **RC**	.10
U72	Edgar Clemente **RC**	.05
U73	Rick Croushore **RC**	.05
U74	Matt Clement	.15
U75	Dermal Brown	.05
U76	Paul Bako	.05
U77	Placido Polanco **RC**	1.00
U78	Jay Tessmer	.05
U79	Jarrod Washburn	.05
U80	Kevin Witt	.05
U81	Mike Metcalfe	.05
U82	Daryle Ward	.05
U83	Benj Sampson **RC**	.05
U84	Mike Kinkade **RC**	.20
U85	Randy Winn	.05
U86	Jeff Shaw	.05
U87	Troy Glaus **RC**	4.00
U88	Hideo Nomo	.35
U89	Mark Grudzielanek	.05
U90	Mike Frank **RC**	.05
U91	Bobby Howry **RC**	.10
U92	Ryan Minor **RC**	.15
U93	Corey Koskie **RC**	1.00
U94	Matt Anderson **RC**	.20
U95	Joe Carter	.05
U96	Paul Konerko	.15
U97	Sidney Ponson	.05
U98	Jeremy Giambi **RC**	.25
U99	Jeff Kubenka **RC**	.05
U100	J.D. Drew **RC**	5.00

1999 Fleer

	NM/M
Complete Set (600):	25.00
Common Player:	.05
Warning Track:	2X
Inserted 1:1 R	
Pack (10):	1.00
Wax Box (36):	25.00

1	Mark McGwire	2.00
2	Sammy Sosa	1.25
3	Ken Griffey Jr.	1.50
4	Kerry Wood	.30
5	Derek Jeter	2.50
6	Stan Musial	2.00
7	J.D. Drew	.65
7p	J.D. Drew/OPS	1.50
8	Cal Ripken Jr.	2.50
9	Alex Rodriguez	2.00
10	Travis Lee	.15
11	Andres Galarraga	.05
12	Nomar Garciaparra	1.25
13	Albert Belle	.05
14	Barry Larkin	.05
15	Dante Bichette	.05
16	Tony Clark	.05
17	Moises Alou	.05
18	Rafael Palmeiro	.65
19	Raul Mondesi	.05
20	Vladimir Guerrero	.75
21	John Olerud	.05
22	Bernie Williams	.10
23	Ben Grieve	.05
24	Scott Rolen	.65
25	Jeromy Burnitz	.05
26	Ken Caminiti	.05
27	Barry Bonds	2.50
28	Todd Helton	.75
29	Juan Gonzalez	.65
30	Roger Clemens	1.25
31	Andruw Jones	.75
32	Mo Vaughn	.05
33	Larry Walker	.05
34	Frank Thomas	.75
35	Manny Ramirez	.75
36	Randy Johnson	.75
37	Vinny Castilla	.05
38	Juan Encarnacion	.05
39	Jeff Bagwell	.75
40	Gary Sheffield	.50
41	Mike Piazza	1.50
42	Richie Sexson	.05
43	Tony Gwynn	1.00
44	Chipper Jones	1.00
45	Jim Thome	.65
46	Craig Biggio	.05
47	Carlos Delgado	.40
48	Greg Vaughn	.05
49	Greg Maddux	1.00
50	Troy Glaus	.65
51	Roberto Alomar	.10
52	Dennis Eckersley	.60
53	Mike Caruso	.05
54	Bruce Chen	.05
55	Aaron Boone	.05
56	Bartolo Colon	.05
57	Derrick Gibson	.05
58	Brian Anderson	.05
59	Gabe Alvarez	.05
60	Todd Dunwoody	.05
61	Rod Beck	.05
62	Derek Bell	.05
63	Francisco Cordova	.05
64	Johnny Damon	.25
65	Adrian Beltre	.15
66	Garret Anderson	.05
67	Armando Benitez	.05
68	Edgardo Alfonzo	.05
69	Ryan Bradley	.05
70	Eric Chavez	.30
71	Bobby Abreu	.05
72	Andy Ashby	.05
73	Ellis Burks	.05
74	Jeff Cirillo	.05
75	Jay Buhner	.05
76	Ron Gant	.05
77	Rolando Arrojo	.05
78	Will Clark	.10
79	Chris Carpenter	.05
80	Jim Edmonds	.05
81	Tony Batista	.05
82	Shane Andrews	.05
83	Mark DeRosa	.05
84	Brady Anderson	.05
85	Tony Gordon	.05
86	Brant Brown	.05
87	Ray Durham	.05
88	Ron Coomer	.05
89	Bret Boone	.05
90	Travis Fryman	.05
91	Darryl Kile	.05
92	Paul Bako	.05
93	Cliff Floyd	.05
94	Scott Elarton	.05
95	Jeremy Giambi	.05
96	Darren Dreifort	.05
97	Marquis Grissom	.05
98	Marty Cordova	.05
99	Fernando Seguignol	.05
100	Orlando Hernandez	.05
101	Jose Cruz Jr.	.05
102	Jason Giambi	.60
103	Damion Easley	.05
104	Freddy Garcia	.05
105	Marlon Anderson	.05
106	Kevin Brown	.05
107	Joe Carter	.05
108	Russ Davis	.05
109	Brian Jordan	.05
110	Wade Boggs	1.00
111	Tom Goodwin	.05
112	Scott Brosius	.05
113	Darin Erstad	.10
114	Jay Bell	.05
115	Tom Glavine	.25
116	Pedro Martinez	.75
117	Mark Grace	.10
118	Russ Ortiz	.05
119	Magglio Ordonez	.10
120	Sean Casey	.15
121	Rafael Roque **RC**	.05
122	Brian Giles	.05
123	Mike Lansing	.05
124	David Cone	.05
125	Alex Gonzalez	.05
126	Carl Everett	.05
127	Jeff King	.05
128	Charles Johnson	.05
129	Geoff Jenkins	.05
130	Corey Koskie	.05
131	Brad Fullmer	.05
132	Al Leiter	.05
133	Rickey Henderson	.75
134	Rico Brogna	.05
135	Jose Guillen	.05
136	Matt Clement	.05
137	Carlos Guillen	.05
138	Orel Hershiser	.05
139	Ray Lankford	.05
140	Miguel Cairo	.05
141	Chuck Finley	.05
142	Rusty Greer	.05
143	Kelvim Escobar	.05
144	Ryan Klesko	.05
145	Andy Benes	.05
146	Eric Davis	.05
147	David Wells	.05
148	Trot Nixon	.05
149	Jose Hernandez	.05
150	Mark Johnson	.05
151	Mike Frank	.05
152	Joey Hamilton	.05
153	David Justice	.05
154	Mike Mussina	.40
155	Neifi Perez	.05
156	Luis Gonzalez	.10
157	Livan Hernandez	.05
158	Dermal Brown	.05
159	Jose Lima	.05
160	Eric Karros	.05
161	Ronnie Belliard	.05
162	Matt Lawton	.05
163	Dustin Hermanson	.05
164	Brian McRae	.05
165	Mike Kinkade	.05
166	A.J. Hinch	.05
167	Doug Glanville	.05
168	Hideo Nomo	.65
169	Jason Kendall	.05
170	Steve Finley	.05
171	Jeff Kent	.05
172	Ben Davis	.05
173	Edgar Martinez	.05
174	Eli Marrero	.05
175	Quinton McCracken	.05
176	Rick Helling	.05
177	Tom Evans	.05
178	Carl Pavano	.10
179	Todd Greene	.05
180	Omar Daal	.05
181	George Lombard	.05
182	Ryan Minor	.05
183	Troy O'Leary	.05
184	Robb Nen	.05
185	Mickey Morandini	.05
186	Robin Ventura	.05
187	Pete Harnisch	.05
188	Kenny Lofton	.05
189	Eric Milton	.05
190	Bobby Higginson	.05
191	Jamie Moyer	.05
192	Mark Kotsay	.05
193	Shane Reynolds	.05
194	Carlos Febles	.05
195	Jeff Kubenka	.05
196	Chuck Knoblauch	.05
197	Kenny Rogers	.05
198	Bill Mueller	.05
199	Shane Monahan	.05
200	Matt Morris	.05
201	Fred McGriff	.05
202	Ivan Rodriguez	.65
203	Kevin Witt	.05
204	Troy Percival	.05
205	David Dellucci	.05
206	Kevin Millwood	.05
207	Jerry Hairston Jr.	.05
208	Mike Stanley	.05
209	Henry Rodriguez	.05
210	Trevor Hoffman	.05
211	Craig Wilson	.05
212	Reggie Sanders	.05
213	Carlton Loewer	.05
214	Omar Vizquel	.05
215	Gabe Kapler	.05
216	Derrek Lee	.05
217	Billy Wagner	.05
218	Dean Palmer	.05
219	Chan Ho Park	.05
220	Fernando Vina	.05
221	Roy Halladay	.05
222	Paul Molitor	.75
223	Ugueth Urbina	.05
224	Rey Ordonez	.05
225	Ricky Ledee	.05
226	Scott Spiezio	.05
227	Wendell Magee Jr.	.05
228	Aramis Ramirez	.05
229	Brian Simmons	.05
230	Fernando Tatis	.05
231	Bobby Smith	.05
232	Aaron Sele	.05
233	Shawn Green	.20
234	Mariano Rivera	.15
235	Tim Salmon	.10
236	Andy Fox	.05
237	Denny Neagle	.05
238	John Valentin	.05
239	Kevin Tapani	.05
240	Paul Konerko	.10
241	Robert Fick	.05
242	Edgar Renteria	.05
243	Brett Tomko	.05
244	Daryle Ward	.05
245	Carlos Beltran	.30
246	Angel Pena	.05
247	Steve Woodard	.05
248	David Ortiz	.05
249	Justin Thompson	.05
250	Rondell White	.05
251	Jaret Wright	.05
252	Ed Sprague	.05
253	Jay Payton	.05
254	Mike Lowell	.05
255	Orlando Cabrera	.05
256	Jason Schmidt	.05
257	David Segui	.05
258	Paul Sorrento	.05
259	John Wetteland	.05
260	Devon White	.05
261	Odalis Perez	.05
262	Calvin Pickering	.05
263	Alex Ramirez	.05
264	Preston Wilson	.05
265	Brad Radke	.05
266	Walt Weiss	.05
267	Tim Young	.05
268	Tino Martinez	.05
269	Matt Stairs	.05
270	Curt Schilling	.25
271	Tony Womack	.05
272	Ismael Valdes	.05
273	Wally Joyner	.05
274	Armando Rios	.05
275	Andy Pettitte	.25
276	Bubba Trammell	.05
277	Todd Zeile	.05
278	Shannon Stewart	.05
279	Matt Williams	.05
280	John Rocker	.05
281	B.J. Surhoff	.05
282	Eric Young	.05
283	Dmitri Young	.05
284	John Smoltz	.05
285	Todd Walker	.05
286	Paul O'Neill	.05
287	Blake Stein	.05
288	Kevin Young	.05
289	Quilvio Veras	.05
290	Kirk Rueter	.05
291	Randy Winn	.05
292	Miguel Tejada	.05
293	J.T. Snow	.05
294	Michael Tucker	.05
295	Jay Tessmer	.05
296	Scott Erickson	.05
297	Tim Wakefield	.05
298	Jeff Abbott	.05
299	Eddie Taubensee	.05
300	Darryl Hamilton	.05
301	Kevin Orie	.05
302	Jose Offerman	.05
303	Scott Karl	.05
304	Chris Widger	.05
305	Todd Hundley	.05
306	Desi Relaford	.05
307	Sterling Hitchcock	.05
308	Delino DeShields	.05
309	Alex Gonzalez	.05
310	Justin Baughman	.05
311	Jamey Wright	.05
312	Wes Helms	.05
313	Dante Powell	.05
314	Jim Abbott	.05
315	Manny Alexander	.05
316	Harold Baines	.05
317	Danny Graves	.05
318	Sandy Alomar	.05
319	Pedro Astacio	.05
320	Jermaine Allensworth	.05
321	Matt Anderson	.05
322	Chad Curtis	.05
323	Antonio Osuna	.05
324	Brad Ausmus	.05
325	Steve Trachsel	.05
326	Mike Blowers	.05
327	Brian Bohanon	.05
328	Chris Gomez	.05
329	Valerio de los Santos	.05
330	Rich Aurilia	.05
331	Michael Barrett	.05
332	Rick Aguilera	.05
333	Adrian Brown	.05
334	Bill Spiers	.05
335	Matt Beech	.05
336	David Bell	.05
337	Juan Acevedo	.05
338	Jose Canseco	.50
339	Wilson Alvarez	.05
340	Luis Alicea	.05
341	Jason Dickson	.05
342	Mike Bordick	.05
343	Ben Ford	.05
344	Keith Lockhart	.05
345	Jason Christiansen	.05

#	Player	Value
346	Darren Bragg	.05
347	Doug Brocail	.05
348	Jeff Blauser	.05
349	James Baldwin	.05
350	Jeffrey Hammonds	.05
351	Ricky Bottalico	.05
352	Russ Branyon	.05
353	Mark Brownson	.05
354	Dave Berg	.05
355	Sean Bergman	.05
356	Jeff Conine	.05
357	Shayne Bennett	.05
358	Bobby Bonilla	.05
359	Bob Wickman	.05
360	Carlos Baerga	.05
361	Chris Fussell	.05
362	Chili Davis	.05
363	Jerry Spradlin	.05
364	Carlos Hernandez	.05
365	Roberto Hernandez	.05
366	Marvin Benard	.05
367	Ken Cloude	.05
368	Tony Fernandez	.05
369	John Burkett	.05
370	Gary DiSarcina	.05
371	Alan Benes	.05
372	Karim Garcia	.05
373	Carlos Perez	.05
374	Damon Buford	.05
375	Mark Clark	.05
376	Edgard Clemente **RC**	.05
377	Chad Bradford	.05
378	Frank Catalanotto	.05
379	Vic Darensbourg	.05
380	Sean Berry	.05
381	Dave Burba	.05
382	Sal Fasano	.05
383	Steve Parris	.05
384	Roger Cedeno	.05
385	Chad Fox	.05
386	Wilton Guerrero	.05
387	Dennis Cook	.05
388	Joe Girardi	.05
389	LaTroy Hawkins	.05
390	Ryan Christenson	.05
391	Paul Byrd	.05
392	Lou Collier	.05
393	Jeff Fassero	.05
394	Jim Leyritz.	.05
395	Shawn Estes	.05
396	Mike Kelly	.05
397	Rich Croushore	.05
398	Royce Clayton	.05
399	Rudy Seanez	.05
400	Darrin Fletcher	.05
401	Shigetosi Hasegawa	.05
402	Bernard Gilkey	.05
403	Juan Guzman	.05
404	Jeff Frye	.05
405	Marino Santana	.05
406	Alex Fernandez	.05
407	Gary Gaetti	.05
408	Dan Miceli	.05
409	Mike Cameron	.05
410	Mike Remlinger	.05
411	Joey Cora	.05
412	Mark Gardner	.05
413	Aaron Ledesma	.05
414	Jerry Dipoto	.05
415	Ricky Gutierrez	.05
416	John Franco	.05
417	Mendy Lopez	.05
418	Hideki Irabu	.05
419	Mark Grudzielanek	.05
420	Bobby Hughes	.05
421	Pat Meares	.05
422	Jimmy Haynes	.05
423	Bob Henley	.05
424	Bobby Estalella	.05
425	Jon Lieber	.05
426	Giomar Guevara **RC**	.05
427	Jose Jimenez	.05
428	Deivi Cruz	.05
429	Jonathan Johnson	.05
430	Ken Hill	.05
431	Craig Grebeck	.05
432	Jose Rosado	.05
433	Danny Klassen	.05
434	Bobby Howry	.05
435	Gerald Williams	.05
436	Omar Olivares	.05
437	Chris Hoiles	.05
438	Seth Greisinger	.05
439	Scott Hatteberg	.05
440	Jeremi Gonzalez	.05
441	Wil Cordero	.05
442	Jeff Montgomery	.05
443	Chris Stynes	.05
444	Tony Saunders	.05
445	Einar Diaz	.05
446	Laril Gonzalez	.05
447	Ryan Jackson	.05
448	Mike Hampton	.05
449	Todd Hollandsworth	.05
450	Gabe White	.05
451	John Jaha	.05
452	Bret Saberhagen	.05
453	Otis Nixon	.05
454	Steve Kline	.05
455	Butch Huskey	.05
456	Mike Jerzembeck	.05
457	Wayne Gomes	.05
458	Mike Macfarlane	.05
459	Jesus Sanchez	.05
460	Al Martin	.05

#	Player	Value
461	Dwight Gooden	.05
462	Ruben Rivera	.05
463	Pat Hentgen	.05
464	Jose Valentin	.05
465	Vladimir Nunez	.05
466	Charlie Hayes	.05
467	Jay Powell	.05
468	Raul Ibanez	.05
469	Kent Mercker	.05
470	John Mabry	.05
471	Woody Williams	.05
472	Roberto Kelly	.05
473	Jim Mecir	.05
474	Dave Hollins	.05
475	Rafael Medina	.05
476	Darren Lewis	.05
477	Felix Heredia	.05
478	Brian Hunter	.05
479	Matt Mantei	.05
480	Richard Hidalgo	.05
481	Bobby Jones	.05
482	Hal Morris	.05
483	Ramiro Mendoza	.05
484	Matt Luke	.05
485	Esteban Loaiza	.05
486	Mark Loretta	.05
487	A.J. Pierzynski	.05
488	Charles Nagy	.05
489	Kevin Sefcik	.05
490	Jason McDonald	.05
491	Jeremy Powell	.05
492	Scott Servais	.05
493	Abraham Nunez	.05
494	Stan Spencer	.05
495	Stan Javier	.05
496	Jose Paniagua	.05
497	Gregg Jefferies	.05
498	Gregg Olson	.05
499	Derek Lowe	.05
500	Willis Otanez	.05
501	Brian Moehler	.05
502	Glenallen Hill	.05
503	Bobby Jones	.05
504	Greg Norton	.05
505	Mike Jackson	.05
506	Kirt Manwaring	.05
507	Eric Weaver	.05
508	Mitch Meluskey	.05
509	Todd Jones	.05
510	Mike Matheny	.05
511	Benj Sampson	.05
512	Tony Phillips	.05
513	Mike Thurman	.05
514	Jorge Posada	.05
515	Bill Taylor	.05
516	Mike Sweeney	.05
517	Jose Silva	.05
518	Mark Lewis	.05
519	Chris Peters	.05
520	Brian Johnson	.05
521	Mike Timlin	.05
522	Mark McLemore	.05
523	Dan Plesac	.05
524	Kelly Stinnett.	.05
525	Sidney Ponson.	.05
526	Jim Parque	.05
527	Tyler Houston	.05
528	John Thomson	.05
529	Mike Metcalfe	.05
530	Robert Person	.05
531	Marc Newfield	.05
532	Javier Vazquez	.05
533	Terry Steinbach	.05
534	Turk Wendell	.05
535	Tim Raines	.05
536	Brian Meadows	.05
537	Mike Lieberthal	.05
538	Ricardo Rincon	.05
539	Dan Wilson	.05
540	John Johnstone	.05
541	Todd Stottlemyre	.05
542	Ramon Stocker	.05
543	Ramon Martinez	.05
544	Mike Simms	.05
545	Paul Quantrill	.05
546	Matt Walbeck	.05
547	Turner Ward	.05
548	Bill Pulsipher	.05
549	Donnie Sadler	.05
550	Lance Johnson	.05
551	Bill Simas	.05
552	Jeff Reed	.05
553	Jeff Shaw	.05
554	Joe Randa	.05
555	Paul Shuey	.05
556	Mike Redmond	.05
557	Sean Runyan	.05
558	Enrique Wilson	.05
559	Scott Radinsky	.05
560	Larry Sutton	.05
561	Masato Yoshii	.05
562	David Nilsson	.05
563	Mike Trombley	.05
564	Darryl Strawberry	.05
565	Dave Mlicki	.05
566	Placido Polanco	.05
567	Yorkis Perez	.05
568	Esteban Yan	.05
569	Lee Stevens	.05
570	Steve Sinclair	.05
571	Jarrod Washburn	.05
572	Lenny Webster	.05
573	Mike Sirotka	.05
574	Jason Varitek	.05
575	Terry Mulholland	.05

#	Player	Value
576	Adrian Beltre	.10
577	Eric Chavez	.20
578	J.D. Drew	.35
579	Juan Encarnacion	.05
580	Nomar Garciaparra	.65
581	Troy Glaus	.35
582	Ben Grieve	.05
583	Vladimir Guerrero	.40
584	Todd Helton	.35
585	Derek Jeter	1.25
586	Travis Lee	.10
587	Alex Rodriguez	1.00
588	Scott Rolen	.30
589	Richie Sexson	.05
590	Kerry Wood	.20
591	Ken Griffey Jr. (Checklist)	.75
592	Chipper Jones (Checklist)	.50
593	Alex Rodriguez (Checklist)	1.00
594	Sammy Sosa (Checklist)	.65
595	Mark McGwire (Checklist)	1.00
596	Cal Ripken Jr. (Checklist)	1.25
597	Nomar Garciaparra (Checklist)	.65
598	Derek Jeter (Checklist)	1.25
599	Kerry Wood (Checklist)	.20
600	J.D. Drew (Checklist)	.40

Warning Track Collection

NM/M

Complete Set (600):	160.00
Common Player:	.50
Stars:	2X

(See 1999 Fleer for checklist and base card values.)

Date With Destiny

NM/M

Complete Set (10):	300.00
Common Player:	20.00
Production 100 Sets	
1	Barry Bonds	60.00
2	Roger Clemens	35.00
3	Ken Griffey Jr.	40.00
4	Tony Gwynn	30.00
5	Greg Maddux	30.00
6	Mark McGwire	50.00
7	Mike Piazza	40.00
8	Cal Ripken Jr.	60.00
9	Alex Rodriguez	50.00
10	Frank Thomas	20.00

Diamond Magic

NM/M

Complete Set (15):	50.00
Common Player:	1.00
Inserted 1:96	
1	Barry Bonds	9.00
2	Roger Clemens	4.50
3	Nomar Garciaparra	4.50
4	Ken Griffey Jr.	5.00
5	Tony Gwynn	3.75
6	Orlando Hernandez	1.00
7	Derek Jeter	9.00
8	Randy Johnson	3.00
9	Chipper Jones	3.75
10	Greg Maddux	3.75
11	Mark McGwire	6.00
12	Alex Rodriguez	7.50

Chipper Jones

13	Sammy Sosa	4.50
14	Bernie Williams	1.50
15	Kerry Wood	2.00

Going Yard

NM/M

Complete Set (15):	4.00
Common Player:	.10
Inserted 1:18	
1	Moises Alou	.10
2	Albert Belle	.10
3	Jose Canseco	.30
4	Vinny Castilla	.10
5	Andres Galarraga	.10
6	Juan Gonzalez	.20
7	Ken Griffey Jr.	.75
8	Chipper Jones	.50
9	Mark McGwire	1.00
10	Rafael Palmeiro	.35
11	Mike Piazza	.75
12	Alex Rodriguez	1.00
13	Sammy Sosa	.65
14	Greg Vaughn	.10
15	Mo Vaughn	.10

Golden Memories

NM/M

Complete Set (15):	45.00
Common Player:	.75
Inserted 1:54	
1	Albert Belle	.75
2	Barry Bonds	7.50
3	Roger Clemens	4.50
4	Nomar Garciaparra	4.50
5	Juan Gonzalez	1.50
6	Ken Griffey Jr.	3.75
7	Randy Johnson	2.75
8	Greg Maddux	3.25
9	Mark McGwire	5.00
10	Mike Piazza	3.75
11	Cal Ripken Jr.	7.50
12	Alex Rodriguez	6.00
13	Sammy Sosa	4.50
14	David Wells	.75
15	Kerry Wood	2.00

1999 Fleer Home Run Heroes

		NM/M
Complete Set (4):		7.50
Common Player:		1.50
1	Mark McGwire (Tradition)	3.00
2	Sammy Sosa	
	(Sports Illustrated)	2.00
3	Mike Piazza	
	(SkyBox Thunder)	2.00
4	Nomar Garciaparra	
	(SkyBox Thunder)	2.00

Rookie Flashback

		NM/M
Complete Set (15):		5.00
Common Player:		.25
Inserted 1:6		
1	Matt Anderson	.25
2	Rolando Arrojo	.25
3	Adrian Beltre	.50
4	Mike Caruso	.25
5	Eric Chavez	.40
6	J.D. Drew	.75
7	Juan Encarnacion	.25
8	Brad Fullmer	.25
9	Troy Glaus	1.50
10	Ben Grieve	.25
11	Todd Helton	1.50
12	Orlando Hernandez	.25
13	Travis Lee	.40
14	Richie Sexson	.25
15	Kerry Wood	.65

Stan Musial Monumental Moments

		NM/M
Complete Set (10):		15.00
Common Musial:		2.00
Autographed Card:		60.00
1	Life in Donora	2.00
2	Values	2.00
3	In the Beginning	2.00

4	In the Navy	2.00
5	The 1948 Season	
	(W/Red Schoendienst.)	2.00
6	Success Stories	
	(W/Pres. Kennedy.)	2.00
7	Mr. Cardinal	2.00
8	Most Valuable Player	2.00
9	... baseball's perfect knight	2.00
10	Hall of Fame	2.00

Starting Nine

	NM/M
Common Player:	20.00
(Star and rookie cards valued at 200-250X base versions.)	

Vintage '61

		NM/M
Complete Set (50):		7.50
Common Player:		.05
Inserted 1:1		
1	Mark McGwire	.75
2	Sammy Sosa	.50
3	Ken Griffey Jr.	.60
4	Kerry Wood	.25
5	Derek Jeter	1.00
6	Stan Musial	.75
7	J.D. Drew	.30
8	Cal Ripken Jr.	1.00
9	Alex Rodriguez	.75
10	Travis Lee	.10
11	Andres Galarraga	.05
12	Nomar Garciaparra	.50
13	Albert Belle	.05
14	Barry Larkin	.05
15	Dante Bichette	.05
16	Tony Clark	.05
17	Moises Alou	.05
18	Rafael Palmeiro	.30
19	Raul Mondesi	.05
20	Vladimir Guerrero	.35
21	John Olerud	.05
22	Bernie Williams	.10
23	Ben Grieve	.05
24	Scott Rolen	.30
25	Jeromy Burnitz	.05
26	Ken Caminiti	.05
27	Barry Bonds	1.00
28	Todd Helton	.35
29	Juan Gonzalez	.35
30	Roger Clemens	.50
31	Andruw Jones	.35
32	Mo Vaughn	.05
33	Larry Walker	.05
34	Frank Thomas	.35
35	Manny Ramirez	.35
36	Randy Johnson	.35
37	Vinny Castilla	.05
38	Juan Encarnacion	.05
39	Jeff Bagwell	.35
40	Gary Sheffield	.25
41	Mike Piazza	.60
42	Richie Sexson	.05
43	Tony Gwynn	.45
44	Chipper Jones	.45
45	Jim Thome	.30
46	Craig Biggio	.05

47	Carlos Delgado	.25
48	Greg Vaughn	.05
49	Greg Maddux	.45
50	Troy Glaus	.35

1999 Fleer Update

		NM/M
Complete Set (150):		25.00
Common Player:		.10
1	Rick Ankiel RC	5.00
2	Peter Bergeron RC	.25
3	Pat Burrell RC	1.50
4	Eric Munson RC	.35
5	Alfonso Soriano RC	3.00
6	Tim Hudson RC	2.00
7	Erubiel Durazo RC	.25
8	Chad Hermansen	.10
9	Jeff Zimmerman	.10
10	Jesus Pena RC	.10
11	Ramon Hernandez	.10
12	Trent Durrington RC	.25
13	Tony Armas Jr.	.10
14	Mike Fyhrie RC	.10
15	Danny Kolb RC	.25
16	Mike Porzio RC	.10
17	Will Brunson RC	.10
18	Mike Duvall RC	.10
19	Doug Mientkiewicz RC	.75
20	Gabe Molina RC	.15
21	Luis Vizcaino RC	.20
22	Robinson Cancel RC	.10
23	Brett Laxton RC	.25
24	Joe McEwing RC	.25
25	Justin Speier RC	.20
26	Kip Wells RC	.25
27	Armando Almanza RC	.10
28	Joe Davenport RC	.10
29	Yamid Haad RC	.10
30	John Halama	.10
31	Adam Kennedy	.10
32	Vicente Padilla RC	.25
33	Travis Dawkins RC	.25
34	Ryan Rupe RC	.25
35	B.J. Ryan RC	.25
36	Chance Sanford RC	.10
37	Anthony Shumaker RC	.10
38	Ryan Glynn RC	.10
39	Matt Herges RC	.20
40	Ben Molina	.10
41	Scott Williamson	.10
42	Eric Gagne RC	1.50
43	John McDonald RC	.10
44	Scott Sauerbeck RC	.10
45	Mike Venafro RC	.10
46	Edwards Guzman RC	.10
47	Richard Barker RC	.10
48	Braden Looper	.10
49	Chad Meyers RC	.10
50	Scott Strickland RC	.10
51	Billy Koch	.10
52	Dave Newhan RC	.10
53	David Riske RC	.10
54	Jose Santiago	.10
55	Miguel Del Toro RC	.10
56	Orber Moreno RC	.10
57	Dave Roberts	.10
58	Tim Byrdak RC	.10
59	David Lee RC	.10
60	Guillermo Mota RC	.15
61	Wilton Veras RC	.15
62	Joe Mays RC	.35
63	Jose Fernandez RC	.10
64	Ray King RC	.10
65	Chris Petersen RC	.10
66	Vernon Wells	.15
67	Ruben Mateo	.10
68	Ben Petrick	.10
69	Chris Tremie RC	.10
70	Lance Berkman	.10
71	Dan Smith	.10
72	Carlos Hernandez RC	.10
73	Chad Harville RC	.25
74	Damaso Marte	.15
75	Aaron Myette RC	.15
76	Willis Roberts RC	.10
77	Erik Sabel RC	.10
78	Hector Almonte RC	.10
79	Kris Benson	.10
80	Pat Daneker RC	.10
81	Freddy Garcia RC	.50
82	Byung-Hyun Kim RC	.25

83	Wily Pena RC	1.00
84	Dan Wheeler RC	.15
85	Tim Harikkala RC	.10
86	Derrin Ebert RC	.10
87	Horacio Estrada RC	.10
88	Liu Rodriguez RC	.10
89	Jordan Zimmerman RC	.10
90	A.J. Burnett RC	.40
91	Doug Davis RC	.10
92	Robert Ramsey RC	.10
93	Ryan Franklin RC	.10
94	Charlie Greene RC	.10
95	Bo Porter RC	.10
96	Jorge Toca RC	.10
97	Casey Blake RC	.20
98	Amaury Garcia RC	.10
99	Jose Molina RC	.10
100	Melvin Mora RC	1.00
101	Joe Nathan RC	.10
102	Juan Pena RC	.25
103	Dave Borkowski RC	.10
104	Eddie Gaillard RC	.10
105	Rob Radlosky RC	.10
106	Brett Hinchliffe RC	.10
107	Carlos Lee	.10
108	Rob Ryan RC	.10
109	Jeff Weaver RC	.50
110	Ed Yarnall	.10
111	Nelson Cruz RC	.10
112	Cleatus Davidson RC	.10
113	Tim Kubinski RC	.10
114	Sean Spencer RC	.10
115	Joe Winkelsas RC	.10
116	Chris Clapinski RC	.10
117	Tom Davey RC	.10
118	Warren Morris	.10
119	Dan Murray RC	.10
120	Jose Nieves RC	.10
121	Mark Quinn RC	.10
122	Josh Beckett RC	10.00
123	Chad Allen RC	.10
124	Mike Figga	.10
125	Beiker Graterol RC	.10
126	Aaron Scheffer RC	.10
127	Wiki Gonzalez RC	.10
128	Ramon E. Martinez	.10
129	Matt Riley RC	.25
130	Chris Woodward RC	.10
131	Albert Belle	.10
132	Roger Cedeno	.10
133	Roger Clemens	.75
134	Brian Giles	.10
135	Rickey Henderson	.60
136	Randy Johnson	.60
137	Brian Jordan	.10
138	Paul Konerko	.15
139	Hideo Nomo	.50
140	Kenny Rogers	.10
141	Wade Boggs	.65
142	Jose Canseco	.45
143	Roger Clemens	.75
144	David Cone	.10
145	Tony Gwynn	.65
146	Mark McGwire	1.00
147	Cal Ripken Jr.	1.50
148	Alex Rodriguez	1.00
149	Fernando Tatis	.10
150	Robin Ventura	.10

1999 Fleer Brilliants

		NM/M
Complete Set (175):		60.00
Common Player:		.25
Common SP (126-175):		.50
Blues (1:3):		1.5X
SP Blues (1:6):		1X
Golds:		8X
SP Golds:		3X
Production 99 Sets		
24 Karat Golds:		40X
SP's:		15X
Production 24 Sets		
Pack (5):		2.00
Wax Box (24):		32.50
1	Mark McGwire	2.50
2	Derek Jeter	3.00
3	Nomar Garciaparra	1.75
4	Travis Lee	.25
5	Jeff Bagwell	.75
6	Andres Galarraga	.25
7	Pedro Martinez	.75

8	Cal Ripken Jr.	3.00
9	Vladimir Guerrero	.75
10	Chipper Jones	1.50
11	Rusty Greer	.25
12	Omar Vizquel	.25
13	Quinton McCracken	.25
14	Jaret Wright	.25
15	Mike Mussina	.50
16	Jason Giambi	.60
17	Tony Clark	.25
18	Troy O'Leary	.25
19	Troy Percival	.25
20	Kerry Wood	.25
21	Vinny Castilla	.25
22	Chris Carpenter	.25
23	Richie Sexson	.25
24	Ken Griffey Jr.	2.00
25	Barry Bonds	3.00
26	Carlos Delgado	.60
27	Frank Thomas	.75
28	Manny Ramirez	.75
29	Shawn Green	.50
30	Mike Piazza	2.00
31	Tino Martinez	.25
32	Dante Bichette	.25
33	Scott Rolen	.65
34	Gabe Alvarez	.25
35	Raul Mondesi	.25
36	Damion Easley	.25
37	Jeff Kent	.25
38	Al Leiter	.25
39	Alex Rodriguez	2.50
40	Jeff King	.25
41	Mark Grace	.25
42	Larry Walker	.25
43	Moises Alou	.25
44	Juan Gonzalez	.65
45	Rolando Arrojo	.25
46	Tom Glavine	.45
47	Johnny Damon	.45
48	Livan Hernandez	.25
49	Craig Biggio	.25
50	Dmitri Young	.25
51	Chan Ho Park	.25
52	Todd Walker	.25
53	Derrek Lee	.25
54	Todd Helton	.75
55	Ray Lankford	.25
56	Jim Thome	.65
57	Matt Lawton	.25
58	Matt Anderson	.25
59	Jose Offerman	.25
60	Eric Karros	.25
61	Orlando Hernandez	.25
62	Ben Grieve	.25
63	Bobby Abreu	.25
64	Kevin Young	.25
65	John Olerud	.25
66	Sammy Sosa	1.75
67	Andy Ashby	.25
68	Juan Encarnacion	.25
69	Shane Reynolds	.25
70	Bernie Williams	.35
71	Mike Cameron	.25
72	Troy Glaus	.75
73	Gary Sheffield	.60
74	Jeromy Burnitz	.25
75	Mike Caruso	.25
76	Chuck Knoblauch	.25
77	Kenny Rogers	.25
78	David Cone	.25
79	Tony Gwynn	1.50
80	Aramis Ramirez	.25
81	Paul O'Neill	.25
82	Charles Nagy	.25
83	Javy Lopez	.25
84	Scott Erickson	.25
85	Trevor Hoffman	.25
86	Andruw Jones	.75
87	Ray Durham	.25
88	Jorge Posada	.25
89	Edgar Martinez	.25
90	Tim Salmon	.35
91	Bobby Higginson	.25
92	Adrian Beltre	.45
93	Jason Kendall	.25
94	Henry Rodriguez	.25
95	Greg Maddux	1.50
96	David Justice	.25
97	Ivan Rodriguez	.65
98	Curt Schilling	.45
99	Matt Williams	.25
100	Darin Erstad	.50
101	Rafael Palmeiro	.65
102	David Wells	.25
103	Barry Larkin	.25
104	Robin Ventura	.25
105	Edgar Renteria	.25
106	Andy Pettitte	.50
107	Albert Belle	.25
108	Steve Finley	.25
109	Fernando Vina	.25
110	Rondell White	.25
111	Kevin Brown	.25
112	Jose Canseco	.50
113	Roger Clemens	1.75
114	Todd Hundley	.25
115	Will Clark	.35
116	Jim Edmonds	.25
117	Randy Johnson	.75
118	Denny Neagle	.25
119	Brian Jordan	.25
120	Dean Palmer	.25
121	Roberto Alomar	.45
122	Ken Caminiti	.25

123	Brian Giles	.25
124	Todd Stottlemyre	.25
125	Mo Vaughn	.25
126	J.D. Drew	1.00
127	Ryan Minor	.50
128	Gabe Kapler	.50
129	Jeremy Giambi	.50
130	Eric Chavez	1.00
131	Ben Davis	.50
132	Rob Fick	.50
133	George Lombard	.50
134	Calvin Pickering	.50
135	Preston Wilson	.50
136	Corey Koskie	.75
137	Russell Branyan	.50
138	Bruce Chen	.50
139	Matt Clement	.75
140	Pat Burrell **RC**	2.50
141	Freddy Garcia **RC**	1.00
142	Brian Simmons	.50
143	Carlos Febles	.50
144	Carlos Guillen	.50
145	Fernando Seguignol	.50
146	Carlos Beltran	1.00
147	Edgard Clemente	.50
148	Mitch Meluskey	.50
149	Ryan Bradley	.50
150	Marlon Anderson	.50
151	A.J. Burnett **RC**	1.00
152	Scott Hunter **RC**	.50
153	Mark Johnson	.50
154	Angel Pena	.50
155	Roy Halladay	.75
156	Chad Allen **RC**	.50
157	Trot Nixon	.75
158	Ricky Ledee	.50
159	Gary Bennett **RC**	.50
160	Micah Bowie **RC**	.60
161	Doug Mientkiewicz	.50
162	Danny Klassen	.50
163	Willis Otanez	.50
164	Jin Ho Cho	.50
165	Mike Lowell	.60
166	Armando Rios	.50
167	Tom Evans	.50
168	Michael Barrett	.50
169	Alex Gonzalez	.50
170	Masao Kida **RC**	.60
171	Peter Tucci **RC**	.50
172	Luis Saturria	.50
173	Kris Benson	.50
174	Mario Encarnacion **RC**	.50
175	Roosevelt Brown **RC**	.50

Blue/Golds

NM/M

Brilliants Blue Common:	.50
Brilliants Blue Stars:	1.5X
Brilliants Blue Rookies:	1X
Brilliants Gold Common:	3.00
Brilliants Gold Stars:	8X
Brilliants Gold Rookies:	3X
Brilliants 24K Gold Common:	10.00
Brilliants 24K Gold Stars:	40X
Brilliants 24K Gold Rookies:	15X

(See 1999 Fleer Brilliants for checklist and base card values.)

1999 Fleer Brilliants Sample

NM/M
J.D. Drew 3.00

Illuminators

NM/M

Complete Set (15):		10.00
Common Player:		.75
Inserted 1:10		
1	Kerry Wood	2.00
2	Ben Grieve	.75
3	J.D. Drew	1.50
4	Juan Encarnacion	.75
5	Travis Lee	.75
6	Todd Helton	3.00
7	Troy Glaus	2.00
8	Ricky Ledee	.75
9	Eric Chavez	1.50
10	Ben Davis	.75
11	George Lombard	.75
12	Jeremy Giambi	.75
13	Richie Sexson	.75
14	Corey Koskie	.75
15	Russell Branyan	.75

Shining Stars

NM/M

Complete Set (15):		30.00
Common Player:		1.50
Inserted 1:20		
Pulsars:		4X
Inserted 1:400		
1	Ken Griffey Jr.	2.50
2	Mark McGwire	3.00
3	Sammy Sosa	2.25
4	Derek Jeter	4.00
5	Nomar Garciaparra	2.25
6	Alex Rodriguez	3.00
7	Mike Piazza	2.50
8	Juan Gonzalez	1.50
9	Chipper Jones	2.00
10	Cal Ripken Jr.	4.00
11	Frank Thomas	1.50
12	Greg Maddux	2.00
13	Roger Clemens	2.25
14	Vladimir Guerrero	1.50
15	Manny Ramirez	1.50

1999 Fleer Mystique

NM/M

Complete Set (160):		125.00
Common Player:		.20
Common SP (1-100):		.75
Common (101-150):		1.00
Production 2,999 Sets		
Common (151-160):		2.00
Production 2,500 Sets		
Pack (4):		3.00
Wax Box (24):		60.00
1	Ken Griffey Jr./SP	2.50
2	Livan Hernandez	.20
3	Jeff Kent	.20
4	Brian Jordan	.20
5	Kevin Young	.20
6	Vinny Castilla	.20
7	Orlando Hernandez/SP	.75
8	Bobby Abreu	.20
9	Vladimir Guerrero/SP	1.50

10	Chuck Knoblauch	.20
11	Nomar Garciaparra/SP	2.25
12	Jeff Bagwell	1.00
13	Todd Walker	.20
14	Johnny Damon	.45
15	Mike Caruso	.20
16	Cliff Floyd	.20
17	Andy Pettitte	.35
18	Cal Ripken Jr./SP	4.00
19	Brian Giles	.20
20	Robin Ventura	.20
21	Alex Gonzalez	.20
22	Randy Johnson	.75
23	Raul Mondesi	.20
24	Ken Caminiti	.20
25	Tom Glavine	.40
26	Derek Jeter/SP	4.00
27	Carlos Delgado	.50
28	Adrian Beltre	.35
29	Tino Martinez	.20
30	Todd Helton	1.00
31	Juan Gonzalez/SP	1.25
32	Henry Rodriguez	.20
33	Jim Thome	.65
34	Paul O'Neill	.20
35	Scott Rolen/SP	1.25
36	Rafael Palmeiro	.65
37	Will Clark	.25
38	Todd Hundley	.20
39	Andruw Jonesv	1.50
40	Luis Rolando Arrojo	.20
41	Barry Larkin	.20
42	Tim Salmon	.25
43	Rondell White	.20
44	Curt Schilling	.40
45	Chipper Jones/SP	2.00
46	Jeromy Burnitz	.20
47	Mo Vaughn	.20
48	Tony Clark	.20
49	Fernando Tatis	.20
50	Dmitri Young	.20
51	Wade Boggs	1.50
52	Rickey Henderson	.75
53	Manny Ramirez/SP	1.50
54	Edgar Martinez	.20
55	Jason Giambi	.65
56	Jason Kendall	.20
57	Eric Karros	.20
58	Jose Canseco/SP	1.00
59	Shawn Green	.40
60	Ellis Burks	.20
61	Derek Bell	.20
62	Shannon Stewart	.20
63	Roger Clemens/SP	2.25
64	Sean Casey/SP	.75
65	Jose Offerman	.20
66	Sammy Sosa/SP	2.25
67	Frank Thomas/SP	1.50
68	Tony Gwynn/SP	2.00
69	Roberto Alomar	.35
70	Mark McGwire/SP	3.00
71	Troy Glaus	1.00
72	Ray Durham	.20
73	Jeff Cirillo	.20
74	Alex Rodriguez/SP	3.00
75	Jose Cruz Jr.	.20
76	Juan Encarnacion	.20
77	Mark Grace	.20
78	Barry Bonds/SP	4.00
79	Ivan Rodriguez/SP	1.25
80	Greg Vaughn	.20
81	Greg Maddux/SP	2.00
82	Albert Belle	.20
83	John Olerud	.20
84	Kenny Lofton	.20
85	Bernie Williams	.30
86	Matt Williams	.20
87	Ray Lankford	.20
88	Darin Erstad	.40
89	Ben Grieve	.20
90	Craig Biggio	.20
91	Dean Palmer	.20
92	Reggie Sanders	.20
93	Dante Bichette	.20
94	Pedro Martinez/SP	1.50
95	Larry Walker	.20
96	David Wells	.20
97	Travis Lee/SP	.75
98	Mike Piazza/SP	2.50
99	Mike Mussina	.45
100	Kevin Brown	.20
101	Ruben Mateo	1.00

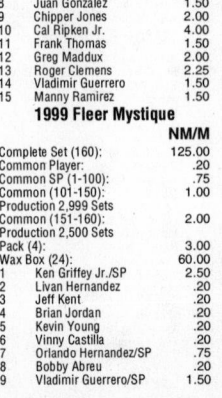

102	Roberto Ramirez	1.00
103	Glen Barker RC	1.00
104	Clay Bellinger RC	1.00
105	Carlos Guillen	1.00
106	Scott Schoeneweis	1.00
107	Creighton Gubanich	1.00
108	Scott Williamson	1.00
109	Edwards Guzman RC	1.00
110	A.J. Burnett RC	4.00
111	Jeremy Giambi	1.00
112	Trot Nixon	1.50
113	J.D. Drew	3.00
114	Roy Halladay	1.50
115	Jose Macias RC	2.00
116	Corey Koskie	2.00
117	Ryan Rupe RC	1.50
118	Scott Hunter	1.00
119	Rob Fick	1.00
120	McKay Christensen	1.50
121	Carlos Febles	2.00
122	Gabe Kapler	1.50
123	Jeff Liefer	1.00
124	Warren Morris	1.00
125	Chris Pritchett	1.00
126	Torii Hunter	3.00
127	Armando Rios	1.00
128	Ricky Ledee	1.00
129	Kelly Dransfeldt RC	1.00
130	Jeff Zimmerman	1.50
131	Eric Chavez	2.00
132	Freddy Garcia	3.00
133	Jose Jimenez	1.00
134	Pat Burrell RC	20.00
135	Joe McEwing RC	1.50
136	Kris Benson	1.00
137	Joe Mays RC	2.00
138	Rafael Roque	1.00
139	Cristian Guzman	1.50
140	Michael Barrett	1.50
141	Doug Mientkiewicz	1.50
142	Jeff Weaver RC	4.00
143	Mike Lowell	1.50
144	Jason Phillips RC	2.00
145	Marlon Anderson	1.50
146	Brett Hinchliffe RC	1.00
147	Matt Clement	1.50
148	Terrence Long	1.00
149	Carlos Beltran	2.50
150	Preston Wilson	1.50
151	Ken Griffey Jr.	2.00
152	Mark McGwire	3.00
153	Sammy Sosa	1.50
154	Mike Piazza	2.00
155	Alex Rodriguez	3.00
156	Nomar Garciaparra	1.50
157	Cal Ripken Jr.	4.00
158	Greg Maddux	1.50
159	Derek Jeter	4.00
160	Juan Gonzalez	1.00
	Checklist Card	.10

Gold

	NM/M
Common Player:	1.00
Stars (1-100):	1.5X
Inserted 1:8	

(See 1999 Fleer Mystique for checklist and base card values.)

Masterpiece

	NM/M
Common Player:	50.00

(Because of their unique nature star Masterpiece values cannot be determined.)

Destiny

	NM/M
Complete Set (10):	35.00
Common Player:	2.00
Production 999 Sets	
1 Tony Gwynn	5.00
2 Juan Gonzalez	3.00
3 Scott Rolen	4.00
4 Nomar Garciaparra	6.00
5 Orlando Hernandez	2.00
6 Andruw Jones	4.00
7 Vladimir Guerrero	4.00
8 Darin Erstad	2.00

JUAN GONZALEZ 287/999

9	Manny Ramirez	4.00
10	Roger Clemens	6.00

Established

Mark McGwire 83/100

	NM/M
Complete Set (10):	300.00
Common Player:	15.00
Production 100 Sets	
1 Ken Griffey Jr.	30.00
2 Derek Jeter	60.00
3 Chipper Jones	20.00
4 Greg Maddux	20.00
5 Mark McGwire	45.00
6 Mike Piazza	30.00
7 Cal Ripken Jr.	60.00
8 Alex Rodriguez	45.00
9 Sammy Sosa	25.00
10 Frank Thomas	15.00

Feel the Game

	NM/M
Common Player:	10.00
Adrian Beltre/Shoe/430	15.00
J.D. Drew/Jsy/450	15.00
Juan Gonzalez/Bat Glove/415	10.00
Tony Gwynn/Jsy/435	15.00
Kevin Millwood/Jsy/435	10.00
Alex Rodriguez/Bat Glove/345	30.00
Frank Thomas/Jsy/450	15.00

Fresh Ink

	NM/M
Complete Set (26):	300.00
Common Player:	4.00
Inserted 1:48	
Roberto Alomar/500	10.00
Michael Barrett/1,000	6.00
Kris Benson/500	8.00
Micah Bowie/1,000	4.00
A.J. Burnett/500	10.00
Pat Burrell/500	15.00
Ken Caminiti/250	10.00
Jose Canseco/250	25.00
Sean Casey/1,000	8.00
Edgard Clemente/1,000	4.00
Bartolo Colon/500	8.00
J.D. Drew/400	15.00
Juan Encarnacion/1,000	4.00
Troy Glaus/400	15.00
Juan Gonzalez/250	15.00
Shawn Green/250	15.00
Tony Gwynn/250	30.00
Chipper Jones/500	35.00

056/200

Gabe Kapler/750	6.00
Barry Larkin/250	25.00
Doug Mientkiewiczc	6.00
Alex Rodriguez/200	80.00
Scott Rolen/140	30.00
Fernando Tatis/750	4.00
Robin Ventura/500	6.00
Todd Walker/1,000	6.00

Prophetic

J.D. DREW 1267/1999

	NM/M
Complete Set (10):	15.00
Common Player:	1.00
Production 1,999 Sets	
1 Eric Chavez	1.50
2 J.D. Drew	2.00
3 A.J. Burnett	1.00
4 Ben Grieve	1.00
5 Gabe Kapler	1.00
6 Todd Helton	2.50
7 Troy Glaus	4.00
8 Travis Lee	1.00
9 Pat Burrell	5.00
10 Kerry Wood	1.50

2000 Fleer Focus

MIKE PIAZZA (Bat) Catches

	NM/M
Complete Set (250):	100.00
Common Player:	.15
Common Prospect (226-250):	4.00
Production 2,999 Sets	
Common Portrait (226-250):	8.00
Portraits:	2X
Production 999 Sets	
Pack:	2.00
Wax Box (24):	35.00
1 Nomar Garciaparra	1.25
2 Adrian Beltre	.35
3 Miguel Tejada	.35
4 Joe Randa	.15
5 Larry Walker	.15
6 Jeff Weaver	.15
7 Jay Bell	.15

8	Ivan Rodriguez	.50
9	Edgar Martinez	.15
10	Desi Relaford	.15
11	Derek Jeter	2.50
12	Delino DeShields	.15
13	Craig Biggio	.15
14	Chuck Knoblauch	.15
15	Chuck Finley	.15
16	Brett Tomko	.15
17	Bobby Higginson	.15
18	Pedro Martinez	.75
19	Troy O'Leary	.15
20	Rickey Henderson	.75
21	Robb Nen	.15
22	Rolando Arrojo	.15
23	Rondell White	.15
24	Royce Clayton	.15
25	Rusty Greer	.15
26	Stan Spencer	.15
27	Steve Finley	.15
28	Tom Goodwin	.15
29	Troy Percival	.15
30	Wilton Guerrero	.15
31	Roberto Alomar	.30
32	Mike Hampton	.15
33	Michael Barrett	.15
34	Curt Schilling	.40
35	Bill Mueller	.15
36	Bernie Williams	.30
37	John Smoltz	.15
38	B.J. Surhoff	.15
39	Pete Harnisch	.15
40	Juan Encarnacion	.15
41	Derrek Lee	.15
42	Jeff Shaw	.15
43	David Cone	.15
44	Jason Christiansen	.15
45	Jeff Kent	.15
46	Randy Johnson	.75
47	Todd Walker	.15
48	Jose Lima	.15
49	Jason Giambi	.50
50	Ken Griffey Jr.	1.50
51	Bartolo Colon	.15
52	Mike Lieberthal	.15
53	Shane Reynolds	.15
54	Travis Lee	.15
55	Travis Fryman	.15
56	John Valentin	.15
57	Joey Hamilton	.15
58	Jay Buhner	.15
59	Brad Radke	.15
60	A.J. Burnett	.15
61	Roy Halladay	.25
62	Raul Mondesi	.15
63	Matt Mantei	.15
64	Mark Grace	.15
65	David Justice	.15
66	Billy Wagner	.15
67	Eric Milton	.15
68	Eric Chavez	.25
69	Doug Glanville	.15
70	Ray Durham	.15
71	Mike Sirotka	.15
72	Greg Vaughn	.15
73	Brian Jordan	.15
74	Alex Gonzalez	.15
75	Alex Rodriguez	2.00
76	David Nilsson	.15
77	Robin Ventura	.15
78	Kevin Young	.15
79	Wilson Alvarez	.15
80	Matt Williams	.15
81	Ismael Valdes	.15
82	Kenny Lofton	.15
83	Carlos Beltran	.45
84	Doug Mientkiewicz	.15
85	Wally Joyner	.15
86	J.D. Drew	.35
87	Carlos Delgado	.50
88	Tony Womack	.15
89	Eric Young	.15
90	Manny Ramirez	.75
91	Johnny Damon	.15
92	Torii Hunter	.25
93	Kenny Rogers	.15
94	Trevor Hoffman	.15
95	John Wetteland	.15
96	Ray Lankford	.15
97	Tom Glavine	.30
98	Carlos Lee	.15
99	Richie Sexson	.15
100	Carlos Febles	.15
101	Chad Allen	.15
102	Sterling Hitchcock	.15
103	Joe McEwing	.15
104	Justin Thompson	.15
105	Jim Edmonds	.15
106	Kerry Wood	.40
107	Jim Thome	.65
108	Jeremy Giambi	.15
109	Mike Piazza	1.50
110	Darryl Kile	.15
111	Darin Erstad	.30
112	Kyle Farnsworth	.15
113	Omar Vizquel	.15
114	Orber Moreno	.15
115	Al Leiter	.15
116	John Olerud	.15
117	Aaron Sele	.15
118	Chipper Jones	1.00
119	Paul Konerko	.25
120	Chris Singleton	.15
121	Fernando Vina	.15
122	Andy Ashby	.15

123	Eli Marrero	.15
124	Edgar Renteria	.15
125	Roberto Hernandez	.15
126	Andruw Jones	.75
127	Magglio Ordonez	.25
128	Bob Wickman	.15
129	Tony Gwynn	1.00
130	Mark McGwire	2.00
131	Albert Belle	.15
132	Pokey Reese	.15
133	Tony Clark	.15
134	Jeff Bagwell	.75
135	Mark Grudzielanek	.15
136	Dustin Hermanson	.15
137	Reggie Sanders	.15
138	Ryan Rupe	.15
139	Kevin Millwood	.15
140	Bret Saberhagen	.15
141	Juan Guzman	.15
142	Alex Gonzalez	.15
143	Gary Sheffield	.30
144	Roger Clemens	1.25
145	Ben Grieve	.15
146	Bobby Abreu	.15
147	Brian Giles	.15
148	Quinton McCracken	.15
149	Freddy Garcia	.15
150	Erubiel Durazo	.15
151	Sidney Ponson	.15
152	Scott Williamson	.15
153	Ken Caminiti	.15
154	Vladimir Guerrero	.75
155	Andy Pettitte	.25
156	Edwards Guzman	.15
157	Shannon Stewart	.15
158	Greg Maddux	1.00
159	Mike Stanley	.15
160	Sean Casey	.25
161	Cliff Floyd	.15
162	Devon White	.15
163	Scott Brosius	.15
164	Marlon Anderson	.15
165	Jason Kendall	.15
166	Ryan Klesko	.15
167	Sammy Sosa	1.25
168	Frank Thomas	.75
169	Geoff Jenkins	.15
170	Jason Schmidt	.15
171	Dan Wilson	.15
172	Jose Canseco	.40
173	Troy Glaus	.75
174	Mariano Rivera	.20
175	Scott Rolen	.65
176	J.T. Snow	.15
177	Rafael Palmeiro	.65
178	A.J. Hinch	.15
179	Jose Offerman	.15
180	Jeff Cirillo	.15
181	Dean Palmer	.15
182	Jose Rosado	.15
183	Armando Benitez	.15
184	Brady Anderson	.15
185	Cal Ripken Jr.	2.50
186	Barry Larkin	.15
187	Damion Easley	.15
188	Moises Alou	.15
189	Todd Hundley	.15
190	Tim Hudson	.25
191	Livan Hernandez	.15
192	Fred McGriff	.15
193	Orlando Hernandez	.25
194	Tim Salmon	.20
195	Mike Mussina	.40
196	Todd Helton	.75
197	Juan Gonzalez	.50
198	Kevin Brown	.15
199	Ugueth Urbina	.15
200	Matt Stairs	.15
201	Shawn Estes	.15
202	Gabe Kapler	.15
203	Javy Lopez	.15
204	Henry Rodriguez	.15
205	Dante Bichette	.15
206	Jeromy Burnitz	.15
207	Todd Zeile	.15
208	Rico Brogna	.15
209	Warren Morris	.15
210	David Segui	.15
211	Vinny Castilla	.15
212	Mo Vaughn	.15
213	Charles Johnson	.15
214	Neifi Perez	.15
215	Shawn Green	.40
216	Carl Pavano	.15
217	Tino Martinez	.15
218	Barry Bonds	2.50
219	David Wells	.15
220	Paul O'Neill	.15
221	Masato Yoshii	.15
222	Kris Benson	.15
223	Fernando Tatis	.15
224	Lee Stevens	.15
225	Jose Cruz Jr.	.15
226	Rick Ankiel	4.00
227	Matt Riley	4.00
228	Norm Hutchins	4.00
229	Ruben Mateo	4.00
230	Ben Petrick	4.00
231	Mario Encarnacion	4.00
232	Nick Johnson	6.00
233	Adam Piatt	6.00
234	Mike Darr	4.00
235	Chad Hermansen	4.00
236	Wily Pena	6.00
237	Octavio Dotel	4.00

238	Vernon Wells	6.00
239	Daryle Ward	4.00
240	Adam Kennedy	4.00
241	Angel Pena	4.00
242	Lance Berkman	6.00
243	Gabe Molina	4.00
244	Steve Lomasney	4.00
245	Jacob Cruz	4.00
246	Mark Quinn	4.00
247	Eric Munson	4.00
248	Alfonso Soriano	6.00
249	Kip Wells	4.00
250	Josh Beckett	6.00
	Checklist #171	.05
	Checklist #172-25, Inserts	.05
	Checklist Inserts	.05

Green

JAVY LOPEZ

	NM/M
Common Player:	3.00
Stars:	5-10X
Yng Stars & RC's (226-250):	1-2X

Production 300 Sets
(See 2000 Fleer Focus for checklist and base card values.)

Masterpiece

	NM/M
Common Player:	100.00

(Values undetermined due to rarity and fluctuating demand. See 2000 Fleer Focusfor checklist.)

Masterpiece Errors

DAVID SEGUI
Blue Jays • First Base

		NM/M
Complete Set (25):		250.00
Common Player:		4.00
50M	Ken Griffey Jr.	100.00
202M	Gabe Kapler	8.00
203M	Javy Lopez	6.00
204M	Henry Rodriguez	4.00
205M	Dante Bichette	5.00
206M	Jeromy Burnitz	5.00
207M	Todd Zeile	4.00
208M	Rico Brogna	4.00
209M	Warren Morris	4.00
210M	David Segui	4.00
211M	Vinny Castilla	5.00
212M	Mo Vaughn	6.00
213M	Charles Johnson	5.00
214M	Neifi Perez	5.00
215M	Shawn Green	20.00
216M	Carl Pavano	4.00
217M	Tino Martinez	5.00
218M	Barry Bonds	30.00
219M	David Wells	8.00
220M	Paul O'Neill	6.00
221M	Masato Yoshii	5.00
222M	Kris Benson	8.00
223M	Fernando Tatis	6.00
224M	Lee Stevens	4.00
225M	Jose Cruz Jr.	6.00

Club 3000

	NM/M
Complete Set (3):	4.00
Common Player:	1.50

(1)	Steve Carlton	1.50
(2)	Paul Molitor	1.50
(3)	Stan Musial	1.50

Club 3000 Memorabilia

	NM/M
Steve Carlton/Bat/325	25.00
Steve Carlton/Hat/65	75.00
Steve Carlton/Jsy/750	20.00
Steve Carlton/ Bat/Hat/Jsy/25	200.00
Paul Molitor/Bat/355	30.00
Paul Molitor/Hat/65	85.00
Paul Molitor/Jsy/975	20.00
Paul Molitor/Bat/Jsy/100	60.00
Stan Musial/Bat/325	50.00
Stan Musial/Hat/65	125.00
Stan Musial/Jsy/975	35.00
Stan Musial/Bat/Jsy/100	80.00

Feel the Game

ALEX RODRIGUEZ

	NM/M
Common Player:	5.00
Inserted 1:288	
Adrian Beltre	7.50
Tom Glavine	10.00
Vladimir Guerrero	15.00
Randy Johnson	15.00
Javy Lopez	5.00
Alex Rodriguez	30.00
Scott Rolen	10.00
Cal Ripken Jr.	40.00
Tim Salmon	6.00
Miguel Tejada	10.00

Focal Points

		NM/M
Complete Set (15):		15.00
Common Player:		.75
Inserted 1:6		
1	Mark McGwire	2.50
2	Tony Gwynn	1.00

3	Nomar Garciaparra	2.00
4	Juan Gonzalez	.75
5	Jeff Bagwell	.75
6	Chipper Jones	1.00
7	Cal Ripken Jr.	3.00
8	Alex Rodriguez	2.50
9	Scott Rolen	.75
10	Vladimir Guerrero	.75
11	Mike Piazza	1.50
12	Frank Thomas	.75
13	Ken Griffey Jr.	1.50
14	Sammy Sosa	1.50
15	Derek Jeter	3.00

Focus Pocus

ALEX RODRIGUEZ

		NM/M
Complete Set (10):		12.00
Common Player:		1.00
Inserted 1:14		
1	Cal Ripken Jr.	3.00
2	Tony Gwynn	1.50
3	Nomar Garciaparra	2.00
4	Juan Gonzalez	1.00
5	Mike Piazza	2.00
6	Mark McGwire	2.50
7	Chipper Jones	1.50
8	Ken Griffey Jr.	2.00
9	Derek Jeter	3.00
10	Alex Rodriguez	2.50

Future Vision

Chad Hermansen
Pittsburgh Pirates

		NM/M
Complete Set (15):		8.00
Common Player:		.40
Inserted 1:9		
1	Rick Ankiel	.50
2	Matt Riley	.40
3	Ruben Mateo	.40
4	Ben Petrick	.40
5	Mario Encarnacion	.40
6	Octavio Dotel	.40
7	Vernon Wells	.65
8	Adam Kennedy	.40
9	Lance Berkman	.40
10	Chad Hermansen	.40
11	Mark Quinn	.40
12	Eric Munson	.40
13	Alfonso Soriano	2.00
14	Kip Wells	.40
15	Josh Beckett	.75

Fresh Ink

	NM/M
Common Player:	5.00
Inserted 1:96	
Chad Allen	5.00
Michael Barrett	5.00
Josh Beckett	30.00
Rob Bell	5.00
Adrian Beltre	15.00
Milton Bradley	8.00
Rico Brogna	5.00
Mike Cameron	8.00
Eric Chavez	15.00
Bruce Chen	5.00
Johnny Damon	20.00
Ben Davis	5.00

J.D. Drew		15.00
Erubiel Durazo		10.00
Jeremy Giambi		6.00
Jason Giambi		25.00
Doug Glanville		6.00
Troy Glaus		25.00
Shawn Green		20.00
Mike Hampton		10.00
Tim Hudson		15.00
John Jaha		5.00
Derek Jeter		150.00
D'Angelo Jimenez		5.00
Nick Johnson		8.00
Andruw Jones		20.00
Jason Kendall		10.00
Adam Kennedy		6.00
Mike Lieberthal		8.00
Edgar Martinez		15.00
Aaron McNeal		5.00
Kevin Millwood		10.00
Mike Mussina		30.00
Magglio Ordonez		15.00
Eric Owens		5.00
Rafael Palmeiro		20.00
Wily Pena		15.00
Adam Piatt		8.00
Cal Ripken Jr.		100.00
Alex Rodriguez		65.00
Scott Rolen		20.00
Tim Salmon		15.00
Chris Singleton		5.00
Mike Sweeney		10.00
Jose Vidro		8.00
Rondell White		8.00
Jaret Wright		5.00

2000 Fleer Gamers

		NM/M
Complete Set (120):		50.00
Common Player (1-90):		.15
Common (91-110):		1.00
Inserted 1:3		
Common (111-120):		1.50
Inserted 1:8		
Pack:		2.00
Wax Box:		35.00
1	Cal Ripken Jr.	2.00
2	Derek Jeter	2.00
3	Alex Rodriguez	1.50
4	Alex Gonzalez	.15
5	Nomar Garciaparra	1.25
6	Brian Giles	.15
7	Chris Singleton	.15
8	Kevin Brown	.15
9	J.D. Drew	.25
10	Raul Mondesi	.15
11	Sammy Sosa	1.25
12	Carlos Beltran	.50
13	Eric Chavez	.15
14	Gabe Kapler	.15
15	Tim Salmon	.25
16	Manny Ramirez	.75
17	Orlando Hernandez	.15
18	Jeff Kent	.15
19	Juan Gonzalez	.75
20	Moises Alou	.15
21	Jason Giambi	.50
22	Ivan Rodriguez	.60

23	Geoff Jenkins	.15
24	Ken Griffey Jr.	1.25
25	Mark McGwire	1.50
26	Jose Canseco	.40
27	Roberto Alomar	.40
28	Craig Biggio	.15
29	Scott Rolen	.65
30	Vinny Castilla	.15
31	Greg Maddux	1.00
32	Pedro J. Martinez	.75
33	Mike Piazza	1.25
34	Albert Belle	.25
35	Frank Thomas	.75
36	Bobby Abreu	.15
37	Edgar Martinez	.15
38	Pokey Reese	.15
39	Preston Wilson	.15
40	Mike Lieberthal	.15
41	Andruw Jones	.75
42	Damion Easley	.15
43	Mike Cameron	.15
44	Todd Walker	.15
45	Jason Kendall	.15
46	Sean Casey	.25
47	Corey Koskie	.15
48	Warren Morris	.15
49	Andres Galarraga	.15
50	Dean Palmer	.15
51	Jose Vidro	.15
52	Brian Jordan	.15
53	Tony Clark	.15
54	Vladimir Guerrero	.75
55	Mo Vaughn	.15
56	Richie Sexson	.15
57	Tino Martinez	.15
58	Eric Owens	.15
59	Matt Williams	.15
60	Omar Vizquel	.15
61	Rickey Henderson	.75
62	J.T. Snow	.15
63	Mark Grace	.25
64	Carlos Febles	.15
65	Paul O'Neill	.15
66	Randy Johnson	.75
67	Kenny Lofton	.15
68	Roger Cedeno	.15
69	Shawn Green	.35
70	Chipper Jones	1.00
71	Jeff Cirillo	.15
72	Robin Ventura	.15
73	Paul Konerko	.15
74	Jeromy Burnitz	.15
75	Ben Grieve	.15
76	Troy Glaus	.75
77	Jim Thome	.15
78	Bernie Williams	.25
79	Barry Bonds	2.00
80	Ray Durham	.15
81	Adrian Beltre	.15
82	Ray Lankford	.15
83	Carlos Delgado	.50
84	Erubiel Durazo	.15
85	Larry Walker	.15
86	Edgardo Alfonzo	.15
87	Rafael Palmeiro	.65
88	Magglio Ordonez	.25
89	Jeff Bagwell	.75
90	Tony Gwynn	1.00
91	Norm Hutchins	1.00
92	Derrick Turnbow **RC**	1.50
93	Matt Riley	1.00
94	David Eckstein	1.00
95	Dernell Stenson	1.00
96	Joe Crede	1.00
97	Ben Petrick	1.00
98	Eric Munson	1.00
99	Pablo Ozuna	1.00
100	Josh Beckett	3.00
101	Aaron McNeal **RC**	1.50
102	Milton Bradley	1.50
103	Alex Escobar	1.50
104	Alfonso Soriano (Next Gamers)	4.00
105	Wily Pena	1.50
106	Nick Johnson	1.50
107	Adam Piatt	1.00
108	Pat Burrell	2.00
109	Rick Ankiel	1.00
110	Vernon Wells	2.00
111	Alex Rodriguez	3.00
112	Cal Ripken Jr.	4.00
113	Mark McGwire	3.00
114	Ken Griffey Jr.	2.00
115	Mike Piazza	2.00
116	Nomar Garciaparra	3.00
117	Derek Jeter	4.00
118	Chipper Jones	1.50
119	Sammy Sosa	2.00
120	Tony Gwynn	1.50

Extra

Stars (1-90):		5-10X
Inserted 1:24		
Next Gamers (91-110):		1-2X
Inserted 1:36		
Fame Game (110-120):		1-2X

Inserted 1:36
(See Fleer Gamers for checklist and base card values.)

Cal to Greatness

		NM/M
Complete Set (15):		100.00
Common Ripken (1-5):		3.00
Inserted 1:9		
Common Ripken (6-10):		6.00
Inserted 1:25		
Common Ripken (11-15):		20.00
Inserted 1:144		
1-5	Cal Ripken Jr.	3.00
6-10	Cal Ripken Jr.	6.00
11-15	Cal Ripken Jr.	20.00

Change the Game

		NM/M
Complete Set (15):		50.00
Common Player:		1.50
Inserted 1:24		
1	Alex Rodriguez	6.00
2	Cal Ripken Jr.	7.50
3	Chipper Jones	3.00
4	Derek Jeter	7.50
5	Ken Griffey Jr.	4.00
6	Mark McGwire	6.00
7	Mike Piazza	4.00
8	Nomar Garciaparra	4.00
9	Sammy Sosa	4.00
10	Tony Gwynn	3.00
11	Ivan Rodriguez	1.50
12	Pedro Martinez	2.00
13	Juan Gonzalez	2.00
14	Vladimir Guerrero	2.00
15	Manny Ramirez	2.00

Determined

		NM/M
Complete Set (15):		25.00
Common Player:		.50
Inserted 1:12		
1	Nomar Garciaparra	2.50
2	Chipper Jones	2.00
3	Derek Jeter	4.00

4	Mike Piazza	2.50
5	Jeff Bagwell	1.00
6	Mark McGwire	3.00
7	Greg Maddux	2.00
8	Sammy Sosa	2.50
9	Ken Griffey Jr.	2.50
10	Alex Rodriguez	3.00
11	Tony Gwynn	2.00
12	Cal Ripken Jr.	4.00
13	Barry Bonds	4.00
14	Juan Gonzalez	1.00
15	Sean Casey	.50

Lumber

		NM/M
Common Player:		5.00
Inserted 1:36		
1	Alex Rodriguez	30.00
2	Carlos Delgado	10.00
3	Jose Vidro	5.00
4	Carlos Febles	5.00
5	J.D. Drew	7.50
6	Mike Cameron	5.00
7	Derek Jeter	40.00
8	Eric Chavez	6.00
9	Cal Ripken Jr.	40.00
10	Gabe Kapler	5.00
11	Damion Easley	5.00
12	Frank Thomas	15.00
13	Chris Singleton	5.00
14	Norm Hutchins	5.00
15	Pokey Reese	5.00
16	Rafael Palmeiro	12.00
17	Ray Durham	5.00
18	Ray Lankford	5.00
19	Roger Cedeno	5.00
20	Shawn Green	5.00
21	Wade Boggs	20.00
22	Roberto Alomar	7.50
23	Moises Alou	5.00
24	Adrian Beltre	6.00
25	Barry Bonds	40.00
26	Jason Giambi	10.00
27	Jason Kendall	5.00
28	Paul Konerko	5.00
29	Mike Lieberthal	5.00
30	Edgar Martinez	5.00
31	Raul Mondesi	5.00
32	Scott Rolen	12.00
33	Alfonso Soriano	10.00
34	Ivan Rodriguez	10.00
35	Magglio Ordonez	7.50
36	Chipper Jones	20.00
37	Sean Casey	6.00
38	Edgardo Alfonzo	5.00
39	Robin Ventura	5.00
40	Bernie Williams	6.00
41	Vladimir Guerrero	15.00
42	Tony Clark	5.00
43	Carlos Beltran	10.00
44	Warren Morris	5.00
45	Jim Thome	5.00
46	Jeromy Burnitz	5.00
47	Matt Williams	5.00
48	Erubiel Durazo	5.00

Lumber Autograph

		NM/M
Common Player:		15.00
Inserted 1:287		
1	Derek Jeter	150.00
2	Eric Chavez	20.00
3	Rafael Palmeiro	40.00
4	Shawn Green	35.00
5	Roberto Alomar	45.00
6	Paul Konerko	15.00
7	Sean Casey	15.00
8	Alex Rodriguez	80.00
9	Robin Ventura	20.00
10	Erubiel Durazo	15.00
11	Tony Clark	15.00
12	Alfonso Soriano	60.00

2000 Fleer Greats of the Game

Satchel Paige
of the
St. Louis Browns

		NM/M
Complete Set (108):		50.00
Common Player:		.50
Pack (6):		10.00
Wax Box (24):		200.00
1	Mickey Mantle	8.00
2	Gil Hodges	1.00
3	Monte Irvin	1.00
4	Satchel Paige	2.50
5	Roy Campanella	2.00
6	Richie Ashburn	1.00
7	Roger Maris	3.00
8	Ozzie Smith	2.00
9	Reggie Jackson	2.50
10	Eddie Mathews	2.50
11	Dave Righetti	.50
12	Dave Winfield	1.00
13	Lou Whitaker	.50
14	Phil Garner	.50
15	Ron Cey	.50
16	Brooks Robinson	2.50
17	Bruce Sutter	.50
18	Dave Parker	.50
19	Johnny Bench	2.50
20	Fernando Valenzuela	.50
21	George Brett	4.00
22	Paul Molitor	2.00
23	Hoyt Wilhelm	.50
24	Luis Aparicio	.50
25	Frank White	.50
26	Herb Score	.50
27	Kirk Gibson	.50
28	Mike Schmidt	3.00
29	Don Baylor	.50
30	Joe Pepitone	.50
31	Hal McRae	.50
32	Lee Smith	.50
33	Nolan Ryan	7.00
33	Nolan Ryan/OPS	5.00
34	Bill Mazeroski	.75
35	Bobby Doerr	.50
36	Duke Snider	1.00
37	Dick Groat	.50
38	Larry Doby	.50
39	Kirby Puckett	2.00
40	Steve Carlton	1.00
41	Dennis Eckersley	.50
42	Jim Bunning	.50
43	Ron Guidry	.50
44	Alan Trammell	1.00
45	Bob Feller	1.50
46	Dave Concepcion	.50
47	Dwight Evans	.50
48	Enos Slaughter	.50
49	Tom Seaver	2.50
50	Tony Oliva	1.00
51	Mel Stottlemyre	.50
52	Tommy John	.50
53	Willie McCovey	1.00
54	Red Schoendienst	.50
55	Gorman Thomas	.50
56	Ralph Kiner	.50
57	Robin Yount	2.00
58	Andre Dawson	1.00
59	Al Kaline	2.50
60	Dom DiMaggio	.50
61	Juan Marichal	1.00
62	Jack Morris	.50
63	Warren Spahn	1.50
64	Preacher Roe	.50
65	Darrell Evans	.50
66	Jim Bouton	.50
67	Rocky Colavito	.75
68	Bob Gibson	1.50

69	Whitey Ford	1.50
70	Moose Skowron	.50
71	Boog Powell	1.00
72	Al Lopez	.50
73	Lou Brock	1.00
74	Mickey Lolich	.50
75	Rod Carew	2.00
76	Bob Lemon	.50
77	Frank Howard	.50
78	Phil Rizzuto	1.50
79	Carl Yastrzemski	2.00
80	Rico Carty	.50
81	Jim Kaat	.50
82	Bert Blyleven	.50
83	George Kell	.50
84	Jim Palmer	1.00
85	Maury Wills	1.00
86	Jim Rice	.50
87	Joe Carter	.50
88	Clete Boyer	.50
89	Yogi Berra	2.00
90	Cecil Cooper	.50
91	Davey Johnson	.50
92	Lou Boudreau	.50
93	Orlando Cepeda	1.00
94	Tommy Henrich	.50
95	Hank Bauer	.50
96	Don Larsen	1.50
97	Vida Blue	1.00
98	Ben Oglivie	.50
99	Don Mattingly	5.00
100	Dale Murphy	1.00
101	Ferguson Jenkins	1.00
102	Bobby Bonds	.75
103	Dick Allen	.50
104	Stan Musial	3.00
105	Gaylord Perry	.50
106	Willie Randolph	.50
107	Willie Stargell	1.50
108	Checklist	.50

Autographs

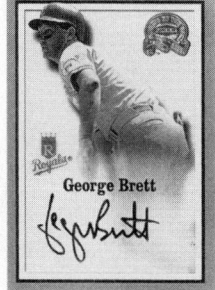

George Brett

		NM/M
Common Player:		10.00
Inserted 1:6		
	Luis Aparicio	25.00
	Hank Bauer	10.00
	Don Baylor	20.00
	Johnny Bench	200.00
	Yogi Berra	180.00
	Vida Blue	20.00
	Bert Blyleven	10.00
	Bobby Bonds	40.00
	Lou Boudreau	120.00
	Jim Bouton	20.00
	Clete Boyer	15.00
	George Brett (275 or less)	300.00
	Lou Brock	40.00
	Jim Bunning	20.00
	Rod Carew	50.00
	Steve Carlton	20.00
	Joe Carter/SP	75.00
	Orlando Cepeda	25.00
	Ron Cey	15.00
	Rocky Colavito	30.00
	Dave Concepcion	
	(Black autograph.)	15.00
	Dave Concepcion	
	(Red autograph.)	15.00
	Cecil Cooper	10.00
	Andre Dawson	25.00
	Dom DiMaggio	75.00
	Bobby Doerr	15.00
	Darrell Evans	15.00
	Bob Feller	30.00
	Whitey Ford	
	(300 or less)	150.00
	Phil Garner	10.00
	Bob Gibson	40.00
	Kirk Gibson	20.00
	Dick Groat	25.00
	Ron Guidry	20.00
	Tommy Henrich	
	(300 or less)	180.00
	Frank Howard	20.00
	Reggie Jackson	
	(250 or less)	180.00
	Ferguson Jenkins	20.00
	Tommy John	10.00
	Davey Johnson	10.00
	Jim Kaat	20.00

	Al Kaline	50.00
	George Kell	20.00
	Ralph Kiner	30.00
	Don Larsen	25.00
	Mickey Lolich	10.00
	Juan Marichal	40.00
	Eddie Mathews	150.00
	Don Mattingly	
	(300 or less)	350.00
	Bill Mazeroski	50.00
	Willie McCovey	150.00
	Hal McRae	10.00
	Paul Molitor	50.00
	Jack Morris	10.00
	Dale Murphy	40.00
	Stan Musial	150.00
	Ben Oglivie	10.00
	Tony Oliva	15.00
	Jim Palmer/SP	150.00
	Dave Parker	20.00
	Joe Pepitone	10.00
	Gaylord Perry	15.00
	Boog Powell	15.00
	Kirby Puckett	
	(200 or less)	350.00
	Willie Randolph	20.00
	Jim Rice	30.00
	Dave Righetti	15.00
	Phil Rizzuto	
	(200 or less)	200.00
	Brooks Robinson	40.00
	Preacher Roe	15.00
	Nolan Ryan	180.00
	Mike Schmidt	
	(175 or less)	500.00
	Red Schoendienst	20.00
	Herb Score	25.00
	Tom Seaver	100.00
	Moose Skowron	20.00
	Enos Slaughter	30.00
	Lee Smith	10.00
	Ozzie Smith/SP	200.00
	Duke Snider/SP	200.00
	Warren Spahn/SP	275.00
	Bruce Sutter	15.00
	Gorman Thomas	10.00
	Alan Trammell	20.00
	Frank White	10.00
	Hoyt Wilhelm	15.00
	Maury Wills	15.00
	Dave Winfield	300.00
	Carl Yastrzemski	75.00
	Robin Yount/SP	250.00

Memorable Moments Auto.

		NM/M
Common Player:		60.00
1	Ron Guidry/78	75.00
2	Nolan Ryan/99	300.00
3	Herb Score/55	40.00
4	Tom Seaver/69	180.00

Retrospection

REGGIE JACKSON

		NM/M
Complete Set (15):		75.00
Common Player:		4.00
Inserted 1:6		
1	Rod Carew	4.00
2	Stan Musial	8.00
3	Nolan Ryan	15.00
4	Tom Seaver	6.00
5	Brooks Robinson	5.00
6	Al Kaline	6.00
7	Mike Schmidt	10.00
8	Thurman Munson	8.00
9	Steve Carlton	4.00
10	Roger Maris	8.00
11	Duke Snider	5.00
12	Yogi Berra	6.00
13	Carl Yastrzemski	5.00
14	Reggie Jackson	6.00
15	Johnny Bench	8.00

Yankees Clippings

		NM/M
Common Player:		20.00
Inserted 1:48		
1	Mickey Mantle	200.00
2	Ron Guidry	40.00
3	Don Larsen	40.00

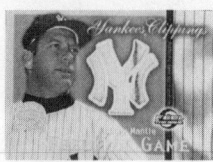

Yankees Clippings

4	Elston Howard	40.00
5	Mel Stottlemyre	25.00
6	Don Mattingly	100.00
7	Reggie Jackson	50.00
8	Tommy John	20.00
9	Dave Winfield	25.00
10	Willie Randolph	20.00
11	Tommy Henrich	20.00
12	Billy Martin	50.00
13	Dave Righetti	20.00
14	Joe Pepitone	20.00
15	Thurman Munson	80.00

2000 Fleer Impact

Roger Clemens P

		NM/M
Complete Set (200):		15.00
Common Player:		.10
Pack (10):		1.00
Box (36):		20.00
1	Cal Ripken Jr.	1.50
2	Jose Canseco	.25
3	Manny Ramirez	.60
4	Bernie Williams	.30
5	Troy Glaus	.60
6	Jeff Bagwell	.60
7	Corey Koskie	.10
8	Barry Larkin	.10
9	Mark Quinn	.10
10	Russ Ortiz	.10
11	Tim Salmon	.15
12	Preston Wilson	.10
13	Mo Vaughn	.10
14	Ray Lankford	.10
15	Sterling Hitchcock	.10
16	Al Leiter	.10
17	Jim Morris	.10
18	Freddy Garcia	.10
19	Adrian Beltre	.20
20	Eric Chavez	.20
21	Robinson Cancel	.10
22	Edgar Renteria	.10
23	John Jaha	.10
24	Chuck Finley	.10
25	Andres Galarraga	.10
26	Paul Byrd	.10
27	John Halama	.10
28	Eric Karros	.10
29	Mike Piazza	1.00
30	Ryan Rupe	.10
31	Frank Thomas	.60
32	Randy Velarde	.10
33	Bobby Abreu	.10
34	Randy Johnson	.60
35	Matt Williams	.10
36	Tony Gwynn	.75
37	Dean Palmer	.10
38	Aaron Sele	.10
39	Rondell White	.10
40	Erubiel Durazo	.10
41	Curt Schilling	.25
42	Kip Wells	.10
43	Craig Biggio	.10
44	Tom Glavine	.25
45	Trevor Hoffman	.10
46	Greg Vaughn	.10
47	Edgar Martinez	.10
48	Magglio Ordonez	.20
49	Mark Mulder	.10
50	John Rocker	.10
51	Kenny Rogers	.10
52	Gary Sheffield	.25
53	Brian Simmons	.10
54	Tony Womack	.10
55	Ken Caminiti	.10
56	Jeff Cirillo	.10
57	Ray Durham	.10
58	Mike Lieberthal	.10
59	Ruben Mateo	.10
60	Mike Cameron	.10

61	Rusty Greer	.10
62	Alex Rodriguez	1.25
63	Robin Ventura	.10
64	Pokey Reese	.10
65	Jose Lima	.10
66	Neifi Perez	.10
67	Rafael Palmeiro	.50
68	Scott Rolen	.50
69	Mike Hampton	.10
70	Sammy Sosa	1.00
71	Mike Stanley	.10
72	Dan Wilson	.10
73	Kerry Wood	.50
74	Mike Mussina	.30
75	Masato Yoshii	.10
76	Peter Bergeron	.10
77	Carlos Delgado	.50
78	Juan Encarnacion	.10
79	Nomar Garciaparra	1.00
80	Jason Kendall	.10
81	Pedro Martinez	.60
82	Darin Erstad	.40
83	Larry Walker	.10
84	Rick Ankiel	.10
85	Scott Erickson	.10
86	Roger Clemens	.85
87	Matt Lawton	.10
88	Jon Lieber	.10
89	Shane Reynolds	.10
90	Ivan Rodriguez	.50
91	Pat Burrell	.50
92	Kent Bottenfield	.10
93	David Cone	.10
94	Mark Grace	.15
95	Paul Konerko	.10
96	Eric Milton	.10
97	Lee Stevens	.10
98	B.J. Surhoff	.10
99	Billy Wagner	.10
100	Ken Griffey Jr.	1.00
101	Randy Wolf	.10
102	Henry Rodriguez	.10
103	Carlos Beltran	.40
104	Rich Aurilia	.10
105	Chipper Jones	.75
106	Homer Bush	.10
107	Johnny Damon	.10
108	J.D. Drew	.40
109	Orlando Hernandez	.10
110	Brad Radke	.10
111	Wilton Veras	.10
112	Dmitri Young	.10
113	Jermaine Dye	.10
114	Kris Benson	.10
115	Derek Jeter	1.50
116	Cole Liniak	.10
117	Jim Thome	.10
118	Pedro Astacio	.10
119	Carlos Febles	.10
120	Darryl Kile	.10
121	Alfonso Soriano	.50
122	Michael Barrett	.10
123	Ellis Burks	.10
124	Chad Hermansen	.10
125	Trot Nixon	.10
126	Bobby Higginson	.10
127	Rick Helling	.10
128	Chris Carpenter	.10
129	Vinny Castilla	.10
130	Brian Giles	.10
131	Todd Helton	.60
132	Jason Varitek	.10
133	Rob Ducey	.10
134	Octavio Dotel	.10
135	Adam Kennedy	.10
136	Jeff Kent	.10
137	Aaron Boone	.10
138	Todd Walker	.10
139	Jeromy Burnitz	.10
140	Roberto Hernandez	.10
141	Matt LeCroy	.10
142	Ugueth Urbina	.10
143	David Wells	.10
144	Luis Gonzalez	.25
145	Andruw Jones	.50
146	Juan Gonzalez	.60
147	Moises Alou	.10
148	Michael Tejera	.10
149	Brian Jordan	.10
150	Mark McGwire	1.25
151	Shawn Green	.25
152	Jay Bell	.10
153	Fred McGriff	.10
154	Rey Ordonez	.10
155	Matt Stairs	.10
156	A.J. Burnett	.10
157	Omar Vizquel	.10
158	Damion Easley	.10
159	Dante Bichette	.10
160	Javy Lopez	.10
161	Fernando Seguignol	.10
162	Richie Sexson	.10
163	Vladimir Guerrero	.60
164	Kevin Young	.10
165	Josh Beckett	.10
166	Albert Belle	.10
167	Cliff Floyd	.10
168	Gabe Kapler	.10
169	Nick Johnson	.15
170	Raul Mondesi	.10
171	Warren Morris	.10
172	Kenny Lofton	.10
173	Reggie Sanders	.10
174	Mike Sweeney	.10
175	Robert Fick	.10
176	Barry Bonds	1.50

177	Luis Castillo	.10
178	Roger Cedeno	.10
179	Jim Edmonds	.10
180	Geoff Jenkins	.10
181	Adam Piatt	.10
182	Phil Nevin	.10
183	Roberto Alomar	.30
184	Kevin Brown	.10
185	D.T. Cromer	.10
186	Jason Giambi	.50
187	Fernando Tatis	.10
188	Brady Anderson	.10
189	Tony Clark	.10
190	Alex Fernandez	.10
191	Matt Blank	.10
192	Greg Maddux	.75
193	Kevin Millwood	.10
194	Jason Schmidt	.10
195	Shannon Stewart	.10
196	Rolando Arrojo	.10
197	Darren Dreifort	.10
198	Ben Grieve	.10
199	Bartolo Colon	.10
200	Sean Casey	.10

Autographics

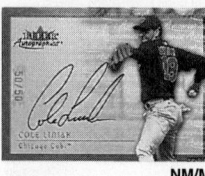

		NM/M
Common Player:		5.00
Inserted 1:216		
Silvers:		1-2X
Production 250 Sets		
Golds:		1-2X
Production 50 Sets		
1	Bobby Abreu	15.00
2	Marlon Anderson	5.00
3	Rick Ankiel	15.00
4	Rob Bell	5.00
5	Carlos Beltran	15.00
6	Wade Boggs	30.00
7	Barry Bonds	200.00
8	Milton Bradley	8.00
9	Pat Burrell	25.00
10	Orlando Cabrera	10.00
11	Chris Carpenter	5.00
12	Sean Casey	8.00
13	Carlos Delgado	20.00
14	J.D. Drew	15.00
15	Ray Durham	8.00
16	Kelvim Escobar	6.00
17	Vladimir Guerrero	30.00
18	Tony Gwynn	35.00
19	Jerry Hairston Jr.	5.00
20	Todd Helton	25.00
21	Nick Johnson	8.00
22	Jason Kendall	8.00
23	Mark Kotsay	8.00
24	Cole Liniak	5.00
25	Jose Macias	5.00
26	Greg Maddux	60.00
27	Ruben Mateo	8.00
28	Ober Moreno	5.00
29	Eric Munson	8.00
30	Joe Nathan	5.00
31	Angel Pena	5.00
32	Adam Piatt	6.00
33	Matt Riley	5.00
34	Cal Ripken Jr.	100.00
35	Alex Rodriguez	75.00
36	Scott Rolen	25.00
37	Jimmy Rollins	15.00
38	B.J. Ryan	5.00
39	Alfonso Soriano	40.00
40	Frank Thomas	25.00
41	Wilton Veras	5.00
42	Billy Wagner	10.00
43	Jeff Weaver	8.00
44	Scott Williamson	6.00

Genuine Coverage

		NM/M
Common Player:		5.00
Inserted 1:720		
1	Alex Rodriguez	65.00
2	Cole Liniak	5.00
3	Barry Bonds	75.00
4	Ben Davis	5.00
5	Bobby Abreu	7.50
6	Mike Sweeney	7.50
7	Rafael Palmeiro	35.00
8	Carlos Lee	5.00
9	Glen Barker	5.00

10	Jason Giambi	30.00
11	Jacque Jones	7.50
12	Joe Nathan	5.00
13	Jason LaRue	5.00
14	Magglio Ordonez	7.50
15	Shannon Stewart	5.00
16	Matt Lawton	5.00
17	Trevor Hoffman	5.00

Mighty Fine in '99

		NM/M
Complete Set (40):		8.00
Common Player:		.15
Inserted 1:1		
1	Clay Bellinger	.15
2	Scott Brosius	.15
3	Roger Clemens	.75
4	David Cone	.15
5	Chad Curtis	.15
6	Chili Davis	.15
7	Joe Girardi	.15
8	Jason Grimsley	.15
9	Orlando Hernandez	.15
10	Hideki Irabu	.15
11	Derek Jeter	2.00
12	Chuck Knoblauch	.15
13	Ricky Ledee	.15
14	Jim Leyritz	.15
15	Tino Martinez	.15
16	Ramiro Mendoza	.15
17	Jeff Nelson	.15
18	Paul O'Neill	.15
19	Andy Pettitte	.25
20	Jorge Posada	.25
21	Mariano Rivera	.25
22	Luis Sojo	.15
23	Mike Stanton	.15
24	Allen Watson	.15
25	Bernie Williams	.30
26	Chipper Jones	.60
27	Ivan Rodriguez	.45
28	Randy Johnson	.50
29	Pedro Martinez	.50
30	Scott Williamson	.15
31	Carlos Beltran	.40
32	Mark McGwire	1.50
33	Ken Griffey Jr.	1.00
34	Robin Ventura	.15
35	Tony Gwynn	.60
36	Wade Boggs	.50
37	Cal Ripken Jr.	2.00
38	Jose Canseco	.40
39	Alex Rodriguez	1.50
40	Fernando Tatis	.15

Point of Impact

		NM/M
Complete Set (10):		20.00
Common Player:		1.00
Inserted 1:30		
1	Ken Griffey Jr.	2.00
2	Mark McGwire	3.00
3	Sammy Sosa	2.00
4	Jeff Bagwell	1.00
5	Derek Jeter	4.00
6	Chipper Jones	1.50
7	Nomar Garciaparra	2.00
8	Cal Ripken Jr.	4.00
9	Barry Bonds	4.00
10	Alex Rodriguez	3.00

2000 Fleer Mystique

		NM/M
Complete Set (175):		350.00
Common Player:		.20
Common 126-175:		6.00
Production 2,000 Sets		
Pack (5):		3.00
Box (20):		50.00
1	Derek Jeter	3.00
2	David Justice	.20
3	Kevin Brown	.20
4	Jason Giambi	.75
5	Jose Canseco	.50
6	Mark Grace	.30
7	Hideo Nomo	.65
8	Edgardo Alfonzo	.20
9	Barry Bonds	3.00
10	Pedro Martinez	1.00
11	Juan Gonzalez	1.00
12	Vladimir Guerrero	1.00
13	Chuck Finley	.20
14	Brian Jordan	.20
15	Richie Sexson	.20
16	Chan Ho Park	.20
17	Tim Hudson	.40
18	Fred McGriff	.20
19	Darin Erstad	.60
20	Chris Singleton	.20
21	Jeff Bagwell	1.00
22	David Cone	.20
23	Edgar Martinez	.20
24	Greg Maddux	1.50
25	Jim Thome	.20
26	Eric Karros	.20
27	Bobby Abreu	.20
28	Greg Vaughn	.20
29	Kevin Millwood	.20
30	Omar Vizquel	.20
31	Marquis Grissom	.20
32	Mike Lieberthal	.20
33	Gabe Kapler	.20
34	Brady Anderson	.20
35	Jeff Cirillo	.20
36	Geoff Jenkins	.20
37	Scott Rolen	.75
38	Rafael Palmeiro	.65
39	Randy Johnson	1.00
40	Barry Larkin	.20
41	Johnny Damon	.40
42	Andy Pettitte	.40
43	Mark McGwire	2.50
44	Albert Belle	.20
45	Derrick Gibson	.20
46	Corey Koskie	.20
47	Curt Schilling	.50
48	Ivan Rodriguez	.65
49	Mike Mussina	.50
50	Todd Helton	1.00
51	Matt Lawton	.20
52	Jason Kendall	.20
53	Kenny Rogers	.20
54	Cal Ripken Jr.	3.00
55	Larry Walker	.20
56	Eric Milton	.20
57	Warren Morris	.20
58	Carlos Delgado	.50
59	Kerry Wood	.65
60	Cliff Floyd	.20
61	Mike Piazza	2.00
62	Jeff Kent	.20
63	Sammy Sosa	2.00
64	Alex Fernandez	.20
65	Mike Hampton	.20
66	Livan Hernandez	.20
67	Matt Williams	.20
68	Roberto Alomar	.45
69	Jermaine Dye	.20
70	Bernie Williams	.35
71	Edgar Renteria	.20
72	Tom Glavine	.40
73	Bartolo Colon	.20
74	Jason Varitek	.20
75	Eric Chavez	.40
76	Fernando Tatis	.40
77	Adrian Beltre	.40
78	Paul Konerko	.20
79	Mike Lowell	.20
80	Robin Ventura	.20
81	Russ Ortiz	.20
82	Troy Glaus	1.00

83	Frank Thomas	1.00
84	Craig Biggio	.20
85	Orlando Hernandez	.20
86	John Olerud	.20
87	Chipper Jones	1.50
88	Manny Ramirez	1.00
89	Shawn Green	.40
90	Ben Grieve	.20
91	Vinny Castilla	.20
92	Tim Salmon	.35
93	Dante Bichette	.20
94	Ken Caminiti	.20
95	Andruw Jones	.75
96	Alex Rodriguez	2.50
97	Erubiel Durazo	.20
98	Sean Casey	.30
99	Carlos Beltran	.50
100	Paul O'Neill	.20
101	Ray Lankford	.20
102	Troy O'Leary	.20
103	Bobby Higginson	.20
104	Rondell White	.20
105	Tony Gwynn	1.50
106	Jim Edmonds	.20
107	Magglio Ordonez	.40
108	Preston Wilson	.20
109	Roger Clemens	1.75
110	Ken Griffey Jr.	2.00
111	Nomar Garciaparra	2.00
112	Juan Encarnacion	.20
113	Michael Barrett	.20
114	Matt Clement	.20
115	David Wells	.20
116	Mo Vaughn	.20
117	Mike Cameron	.20
118	Jose Lima	.20
119	Tino Martinez	.20
120	J.D. Drew	.40
121	Carl Everett	.20
122	Tony Clark	.20
123	Brad Radke	.20
124	Kevin Young	.20
125	Raul Mondesi	.20
126	Cole Liniak	6.00
127	Alfonso Soriano	8.00
128	Lance Berkman	8.00
129	Danny Young	6.00
130	Francisco Cordero	6.00
131	Rob Fick	6.00
132	Matt LeCroy	6.00
133	Adam Piatt	6.00
134	Derrick Turnbow **RC**	6.00
135	Mark Quinn	6.00
136	Kip Wells	6.00
137	Rob Bell	6.00
138	Brad Penny	6.00
139	Pat Burrell	10.00
140	Danys Baez **RC**	6.00
141	Chad Hermansen	6.00
142	Steve Lomasney	6.00
143	Peter Bergeron	6.00
144	Jimmy Anderson	6.00
145	Mike Darr	6.00
146	Jacob Cruz	6.00
147	Kazuhiro Sasaki **RC**	10.00
148	Ben Petrick	6.00
149	Rick Ankiel	8.00
150	Aaron McNeal **RC**	6.00
152	Octavio Dotel	6.00
153	Juan Pena	6.00
153	Nick Johnson	8.00
154	Wilton Veras	6.00
155	Wily Pena	6.00
156	Mark Mulder	6.00
157	Daryle Ward	6.00
158	Chad Durbin **RC**	6.00
159	Angel Pena	6.00
160	Dewayne Wise	6.00
161	Tarrik Brock	6.00
162	Marcus Jensen	6.00
163	Kevin Barker	6.00
164	B.J. Ryan	6.00
165	Cesar King	6.00
166	Geoff Blum	6.00
167	Ruben Mateo	6.00
168	Ramon Ortiz	6.00
169	Eric Munson	6.00
170	Josh Beckett	8.00
171	Rafael Furcal	6.00
172	Matt Riley	6.00
173	Johan Santana **RC**	60.00
174	Mark Johnson	6.00
175	Adam Kennedy	6.00

Gold

Stars (1-125):		4-8X
SP's (126-175):		1X
Inserted 1:20		

(See 2000 Fleer Mystique for checklist
and base card values.)

Club 3000

		NM/M
Complete Set (3):		6.00

Common Player:		1.50
Inserted 1:20		
1	Cal Ripken Jr.	5.00
2	Bob Gibson	1.50
3	Dave Winfield	1.50

Club 3000 Memorabilia

		NM/M
	Cal Ripken Jr./Jsy/825	40.00
	Cal Ripken Jr./Bat/265	75.00
	Cal Ripken Jr./Hat/55	120.00
	Cal Ripken Jr./	
	Bat, Jsy/100	100.00
	Bob Gibson/Jsy/825	20.00
	Bob Gibson/Bat/265	30.00
	Bob Gibson/Bat, Jsy/100	50.00
	Bob Gibson/Hat, Jsy/100	50.00
	Bob Gibson/Hat/55	75.00
	Dave Winfield/Jsy/825	15.00
	Dave Winfield/Bat/270	25.00
	Dave Winfield/Bat, Jsy/100	50.00
	Dave Winfield/Hat/55	60.00

Dave Winfield Autograph Memorabilia

		NM/M
Complete Set (2):		
1	Dave Winfield/Bat/20	140.00
2	Dave Winfield/Helmet/40	125.00

Diamond Dominators

		NM/M
Complete Set (10):		15.00
Common Player:		.75
Inserted 1:5		
1	Manny Ramirez	1.00
2	Pedro Martinez	1.00
3	Sean Casey	.75
4	Vladimir Guerrero	1.00
5	Sammy Sosa	1.50
6	Nomar Garciaparra	1.50
7	Mark McGwire	2.50
8	Ken Griffey Jr.	1.50
9	Derek Jeter	3.00
10	Alex Rodriguez	2.50

Feel the Game

		NM/M
Common Player:		5.00
Inserted 1:120		
1	Tony Gwynn/Jsy	20.00
2	Alex Rodriguez/Jsy	25.00
3	Chipper Jones/Jsy	20.00
4	Cal Ripken Jr./Jsy	40.00
5	Derek Jeter/Pants	40.00
6	Alex Rodriguez/Bat	30.00
7	Frank Thomas/Bat	15.00
8	Barry Bonds/Bat	40.00
9	Carlos Beltran/Bat	5.00
10	Shawn Green/Bat	8.00
11	Michael Barrett/Bat	5.00
12	Rafael Palmeiro/Bat	10.00
13	Vladimir Guerrero/Bat	15.00
14	Pat Burrell/Bat	12.00

Fresh Ink

		NM/M
Common Player:		5.00
Inserted 1:40		
1	Chad Allen	5.00
2	Glen Barker	5.00
3	Michael Barrett	5.00
4	Josh Beckett	30.00
5	Rob Bell	5.00
6	Lance Berkman	25.00
7	Kent Bottenfield	5.00
8	Milton Bradley	8.00
9	Orlando Cabrera	10.00
10	Sean Casey	10.00
11	Roger Cedeno	6.00
12	Will Clark	25.00
13	Russ Davis	5.00
14	Carlos Delgado	15.00
15	Einar Diaz	5.00
16	J.D. Drew	10.00
17	Erubiel Durazo	10.00
18	Damion Easley	5.00
19	Carlos Febles	5.00
20	Doug Glanville	6.00
21	Alex Gonzalez	5.00
22	Tony Gwynn	40.00
23	Mike Hampton	8.00
24	Bobby Howry	5.00
25	John Jaha	5.00
26	Nick Johnson	10.00
27	Andruw Jones	20.00
28	Adam Kennedy	8.00
29	Mike Lieberthal	5.00
30	Jose Macias	5.00
31	Ruben Mateo	8.00
32	Raul Mondesi	8.00
33	Heath Murray	5.00
34	Mike Mussina	30.00
35	Hideo Nomo	250.00
36	Magglio Ordonez	15.00
37	Eric Owens	5.00
38	Adam Piatt	5.00
39	Cal Ripken Jr.	100.00
40	Tim Salmon	15.00
41	Chris Singleton	5.00
42	J.T. Snow	8.00
43	Mike Sweeney	10.00
44	Wilton Veras	5.00
45	Jose Vidro	8.00
46	Rondell White	10.00
47	Jaret Wright	5.00

High Praise

		NM/M
Complete Set (10):		18.00
Common Player:		.75
Inserted 1:20		
1	Mark McGwire	3.00
2	Ken Griffey Jr.	2.00
3	Alex Rodriguez	3.00
4	Derek Jeter	4.00
5	Sammy Sosa	2.00
6	Mike Piazza	2.00
7	Nomar Garciaparra	2.00
8	Cal Ripken Jr.	4.00
9	Tony Gwynn	1.50
10	Shawn Green	.75

Rookie I.P.O.

		NM/M
Complete Set (10):		8.00
Common Player:		.50
Inserted 1:10		
1	Josh Beckett	1.00
2	Eric Munson	.50
3	Pat Burrell	2.00
4	Alfonso Soriano	1.50
5	Rick Ankiel	.50
6	Ruben Mateo	.50
7	Mark Quinn	.50
8	Kip Wells	.50
9	Ben Petrick	.50
10	Nick Johnson	.75

Seismic Activity

		NM/M
Complete Set (10):		45.00
Common Player:		3.00
Inserted 1:40		
Richter parallel:		3-5X
Production 100 Sets		
1	Ken Griffey Jr.	5.00
2	Sammy Sosa	5.00
3	Derek Jeter	10.00
4	Mark McGwire	8.00
5	Manny Ramirez	3.00
6	Mike Piazza	5.00
7	Vladimir Guerrero	3.00
8	Chipper Jones	4.00
9	Alex Rodriguez	8.00
10	Jeff Bagwell	3.00

Supernaturals

		NM/M
Complete Set (10):		15.00
Common Player:		1.00
Inserted 1:10		
1	Alex Rodriguez	3.00
2	Chipper Jones	1.75
3	Derek Jeter	4.00
4	Ivan Rodriguez	1.00
5	Ken Griffey Jr.	2.00

6	Mark McGwire	3.00
7	Mike Piazza	2.00
8	Nomar Garciaparra	2.00
9	Sammy Sosa	2.00
10	Vladimir Guerrero	1.50

2000 Fleer Showcase

		NM/M
Complete Set (140):		200.00
Common Player (1-100):		.25
Common (101-115):		6.00
Production 1,000 Sets		
Common (116-140):		4.00
Production 2,000 Sets		
Pack (5):		2.50
Box (24):		50.00
1	Alex Rodriguez	2.50
2	Derek Jeter	3.00
3	Jeromy Burnitz	.25
4	John Olerud	.25
5	Paul Konerko	.25
6	Johnny Damon	.40
7	Curt Schilling	.50
8	Barry Larkin	.25
9	Adrian Beltre	.40
10	Scott Rolen	.75
11	Carlos Delgado	.50
12	Pedro J. Martinez	1.00
13	Todd Helton	1.00
14	Jacque Jones	.25
15	Jeff Kent	.25
16	Darin Erstad	.65
17	Juan Encarnacion	.25
18	Roger Clemens	1.75
19	Tony Gwynn	1.50
20	Nomar Garciaparra	2.00
21	Roberto Alomar	.40
22	Matt Lawton	.25
23	Rich Aurilia	.25
24	Charles Johnson	.25
25	Jim Thome	.25
26	Eric Milton	.25
27	Barry Bonds	3.00
28	Albert Belle	.25
29	Travis Fryman	.25
30	Ken Griffey Jr.	2.00
31	Phil Nevin	.25
32	Chipper Jones	1.50
33	Craig Biggio	.25
34	Mike Hampton	.25
35	Fred McGriff	.25
36	Cal Ripken Jr.	3.00
37	Manny Ramirez	1.00
38	Jose Vidro	.25
39	Trevor Hoffman	.25
40	Tom Glavine	.50
41	Frank Thomas	1.00
42	Chris Widger	.25
43	J.D. Drew	.50
44	Andres Galarraga	.25
45	Pokey Reese	.25
46	Mike Piazza	2.00
47	Kevin Young	.25
48	Sean Casey	.25
49	Carlos Beltran	.60
50	Jason Kendall	.25
51	Vladimir Guerrero	1.00
52	Jermaine Dye	.25
53	Brian Giles	.25
54	Andruw Jones	1.00
55	Richard Hidalgo	.25
56	Robin Ventura	.25
57	Ivan Rodriguez	.65
58	Greg Maddux	1.50
59	Billy Wagner	.25
60	Ruben Mateo	.25
61	Troy Glaus	1.00
62	Dean Palmer	.25
63	Eric Chavez	.40
64	Edgar Martinez	.25
65	Randy Johnson	1.00
66	Preston Wilson	.25
67	Orlando Hernandez	.25
68	Jim Edmonds	.25
69	Carl Everett	.25
70	Larry Walker	.25
71	Ron Belliard	.25
72	Sammy Sosa	2.00
73	Matt Williams	.25
74	Cliff Floyd	.25
75	Bernie Williams	.40
76	Fernando Tatis	.25
77	Steve Finley	.25
78	Jeff Bagwell	1.00
79	Edgardo Alfonzo	.25
80	Jose Canseco	.40
81	Magglio Ordonez	.40
82	Shawn Green	.40
83	Bobby Abreu	.25
84	Tony Batista	.25
85	Mo Vaughn	.25
86	Juan Gonzalez	1.00
87	Paul O'Neill	.25
88	Mark McGwire	2.50
89	Mark Grace	.35
90	Kevin Brown	.25
91	Ben Grieve	.25
92	Shannon Stewart	.25
93	Erubiel Durazo	.25
94	Antonio Alfonseca	.25
95	Jeff Cirillo	.25
96	Greg Vaughn	.25
97	Kerry Wood	.60
98	Geoff Jenkins	.25
99	Jason Giambi	.75
100	Rafael Palmeiro	.65
101	Rafael Furcal	6.00
102	Pablo Ozuna	6.00
103	Brad Penny	6.00
104	Mark Mulder	8.00
105	Adam Piatt	6.00
106	Mike Lamb **RC**	6.00
107	Kazuhiro Sasaki **RC**	15.00
108	Aaron McNeal **RC**	6.00
109	Pat Burrell	8.00
110	Rick Ankiel	6.00
111	Eric Munson	6.00
112	Josh Beckett	8.00
113	Adam Kennedy	6.00
114	Alex Escobar	8.00
115	Chad Hermansen	6.00
116	Kip Wells	4.00
117	Matt LeCroy	4.00
118	Julio Ramirez	4.00
119	Ben Petrick	4.00
120	Nick Johnson	6.00
121	Gookie Dawkins	4.00
122	Julio Zuleta **RC**	4.00
123	Alfonso Soriano	4.00
124	Keith McDonald **RC**	4.00
125	Kory DeHaan	4.00
126	Vernon Wells	6.00
127	Dernell Stenson	4.00
128	David Eckstein	4.00
129	Robert Fick	4.00
130	Cole Liniak	4.00
131	Mark Quinn	4.00
132	Eric Gagne	5.00
133	Wily Pena	4.00
134	Andy Thompson **RC**	4.00
135	Steve Sisco **RC**	4.00
136	Paul Rigdon **RC**	6.00
137	Rob Bell	4.00
138	Carlos Guillen	5.00
139	Jimmy Rollins	5.00
140	Jason Conti	4.00

Legacy

Stars (1-100):	30-50X
Prospects (101-140):	3-6X
Production 20 Sets	
(See 2000 Fleer Showcase for checklist and base card values.)	

2000 Fleer Showcase Masterpiece
(Because of each card's unique nature, catalog values cannot be presented.)

Club 3000

	NM/M
Common Player:	3.00
Inserted 1:24	

1	Lou Brock	2.00
2	Nolan Ryan	8.00

Club 3000 Memorabilia

	NM/M
Lou Brock/Jsy/680	15.00
Lou Brock/Bat/270	25.00
Lou Brock/	
Hat, Bat, Jsy/25	100.00
Nolan Ryan/Jsy/780	40.00
Nolan Ryan/Hat/65	120.00
Nolan Ryan/Bat/265	60.00
Nolan Ryan/Bat, Jsy/100	120.00

Consummate Prose

Consummate Prose
Sammy Sosa

		NM/M
Complete Set (15):		20.00
Common Player:		.50
Inserted 1:6		
1	Jeff Bagwell	1.50
2	Alex Rodriguez	3.00
3	Chipper Jones	2.00
4	Derek Jeter	4.00
5	Manny Ramirez	1.50
6	Tony Gwynn	2.00
7	Sammy Sosa	2.50
8	Ivan Rodriguez	1.00
9	Greg Maddux	2.00
10	Ken Griffey Jr.	2.50
11	Rick Ankiel	.50
12	Cal Ripken Jr.	4.00
13	Pedro Martinez	1.50
14	Mike Piazza	2.50
15	Mark McGwire	3.00

Feel the Game

Troy Glaus

		NM/M
Common Player:		5.00
Inserted 1:72		
1	Barry Bonds	30.00
2	Gookie Dawkins	5.00
3	Darin Erstad	8.00
4	Troy Glaus	10.00
5	Scott Rolen	10.00
6	Alex Rodriguez	25.00
7	Andruw Jones	10.00
8	Robin Ventura	5.00
9	Sean Casey	5.00
10	Cal Ripken Jr.	40.00

Final Answer

		NM/M
Complete Set (10):		20.00
Common Player:		1.00
Inserted 1:10		
1	Alex Rodriguez	3.00
2	Vladimir Guerrero	1.00
3	Cal Ripken Jr.	4.00
4	Sammy Sosa	2.00
5	Barry Bonds	4.00
6	Derek Jeter	4.00
7	Ken Griffey Jr.	2.00
8	Mike Piazza	2.00

9	Nomar Garciaparra	2.00
10	Mark McGwire	3.00

Fresh Ink

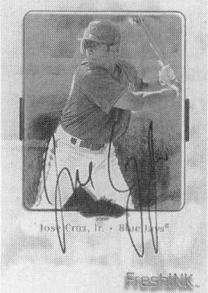

		NM/M
Common Player:		5.00
Inserted 1:24		
1	Rick Ankiel	20.00
2	Josh Beckett	30.00
3	Barry Bonds	200.00
4	A.J. Burnett	10.00
5	Pat Burrell	15.00
6	Ken Caminiti	8.00
7	Sean Casey	10.00
8	Jose Cruz Jr.	10.00
9	Gookie Dawkins	5.00
10	Erubiel Durazo	10.00
11	Juan Encarnacion	8.00
12	Darin Erstad	15.00
13	Rafael Furcal	15.00
14	Nomar Garciaparra	100.00
15	Jason Giambi	20.00
16	Jeremy Giambi	6.00
17	Brian Giles	15.00
18	Troy Glaus	20.00
20	Vladimir Guerrero	30.00
21	Chad Hermansen	5.00
23	Trevor Hoffman	8.00
24	Randy Johnson	60.00
25	Andruw Jones	15.00
26	Jason Kendall	8.00
27	Paul Konerko	10.00
28	Mike Lowell	10.00
29	Aaron McNeal	5.00
30	Warren Morris	5.00
31	Paul O'Neill	20.00
32	Magglio Ordonez	10.00
33	Pablo Ozuna	5.00
34	Brad Penny	8.00
35	Ben Petrick	5.00
36	Pokey Reese	5.00
37	Cal Ripken Jr.	125.00
38	Alex Rodriguez	75.00
39	Scott Rolen	30.00
40	Jose Vidro	8.00
41	Kip Wells	5.00

License to Skill

		NM/M
Complete Set (10):		25.00
Common Player:		1.50
Inserted 1:20		
1	Vladimir Guerrero	2.00
2	Pedro J. Martinez	2.00
3	Nomar Garciaparra	4.00
4	Ivan Rodriguez	1.50
5	Mark McGwire	4.00
6	Derek Jeter	6.00
7	Ken Griffey Jr.	4.00
8	Randy Johnson	2.00

9	Sammy Sosa	4.00
10	Alex Rodriguez	5.00

Long Gone

		NM/M
Complete Set (10):		25.00
Common Player:		2.00
Inserted 1:20		
1	Sammy Sosa	4.00
2	Derek Jeter	6.00
3	Nomar Garciaparra	4.00
4	Juan Gonzalez	2.00
5	Vladimir Guerrero	2.00
6	Barry Bonds	6.00
7	Jeff Bagwell	2.00
8	Alex Rodriguez	5.00
9	Ken Griffey Jr.	4.00
10	Mark McGwire	5.00

Noise of Summer

		NM/M
Complete Set (10):		15.00
Common Player:		1.00
Inserted 1:10		
1	Chipper Jones	1.50
2	Jeff Bagwell	1.00
3	Manny Ramirez	1.00
4	Mark McGwire	3.00
5	Ken Griffey Jr.	2.00
6	Mike Piazza	2.00
7	Pedro J. Martinez	1.00
8	Alex Rodriguez	3.00
9	Derek Jeter	4.00
10	Randy Johnson	1.00

Prospect Showcase First

Prospects (101-140):		1-2X

Production 500 Sets
(See Prospects subset in 2000 Fleer
Showcase for checklist and base values.)

Sweet Sigs

		NM/M
Common Player:		10.00
Inserted 1:250		
1	Nomar Garciaparra/53	150.00
2	Alex Rodriguez/67	200.00
3	Tony Gwynn	40.00
4	Roger Clemens/79	140.00
5	Scott Rolen	50.00
6	Greg Maddux	80.00
7	Jose Cruz Jr.	15.00
8	Tony Womack	10.00
9	Jay Buhner	10.00
10	Nolan Ryan	125.00

2000 Fleer Tradition

		NM/M
Complete Set (450):		50.00
Common Player:		.10
Complete Glossy Factory Set (500):		450.00
Complete Glossy Factory Set (455):		75.00
Glossy (1-450):		1-2X
Common Glossy (451-500):		8.00
Five Glossy (451-500) per factory set.		
1,000 produced (451-500)		
Pack (10):		1.50
Wax Box:		35.00
1	AL HRs	.50
2	NL HRs	.50
3	AL RBIs	.50
4	NL RBIs	.50
5	AL Avg.	.50
6	NL Avg.	.15
7	AL Wins	.20
8	NL Wins	.40
9	AL ERA	.20
10	NL ERA	.25
11	Matt Mantei	.10
12	John Rocker	.10
13	Kyle Farnsworth	.10
14	Juan Guzman	.10
15	Manny Ramirez	.75
16	Matt Riley-P,	
	Calvin Pickering-1B	.10
17	Tony Clark	.10
18	Brian Meadows	.10
19	Orber Moreno	.10
20	Eric Karros	.10
21	Steve Woodard	.10
22	Scott Brosius	.10
23	Gary Bennett	.10
24	Jason Wood-3B,	
	Dave Borkowski-P	.10
25	Joe McEwing	.10
26	Juan Gonzalez	.75
27	Roy Halladay	.25
28	Trevor Hoffman	.10
29	Arizona Diamondbacks	.10
30	Domingo Guzman-P,	
	Wiki Gonzalez-C	.25
31	Bret Boone	.10

32	Nomar Garciaparra	2.00
33	Bo Porter	.10
34	Eddie Taubensee	.10
35	Pedro Astacio	.10
36	Derek Bell	.10
37	Jacque Jones	.10
38	Ricky Ledee	.10
39	Jeff Kent	.10
40	Matt Williams	.10
41	Alfonso Soriano-SS,	
	D'Angelo Jimenez-3B	.75
42	B.J. Surhoff	.10
43	Denny Neagle	.10
44	Omar Vizquel	.10
45	Jeff Bagwell	.75
46	Mark Grudzielanek	.10
47	LaTroy Hawkins	.10
48	Orlando Hernandez	.10
49	Ken Griffey Jr.	2.00
50	Fernando Tatis	.10
51	Quilvio Veras	.10
52	Wayne Gomes	.10
53	Rick Helling	.10
54	Shannon Stewart	.10
55	Dermal Brown-OF,	
	Mark Quinn-OF	.20
56	Randy Johnson	1.00
57	Greg Maddux	1.50
58	Mike Cameron	.10
59	Matt Anderson	.10
60	Milwaukee Brewers	.10
61	Derrek Lee	.10
62	Mike Sweeney	.10
63	Fernando Vina	.10
64	Orlando Cabrera	.20
65	Doug Glanville	.10
66	Stan Spencer	.10
67	Ray Lankford	.10
68	Kelly Dransfeldt	.10
69	Alex Gonzalez	.10
70	Russell Branyan-3B,	
	Danny Peoples-OF	.10
71	Jim Edmonds	.10
72	Brady Anderson	.10
73	Mike Stanley	.10
74	Travis Fryman	.10
75	Carlos Febles	.10
76	Bobby Higginson	.10
77	Carlos Perez	.10
78	Steve Cox-1B,	
	Alex Sanchez-OF	.10
79	Dustin Hermanson	.10
80	Kenny Rogers	.10
81	Miguel Tejada	.25
82	Ben Davis	.10
83	Reggie Sanders	.10
84	Eric Davis	.10
85	J.D. Drew	.45
86	Ryan Rupe	.10
87	Bobby Smith	.10
88	Jose Cruz Jr.	.10
89	Carlos Delgado	.50
90	Toronto Blue Jays	.10
91	Denny Stark-P,	
	Gil Meche-P	.25
92	Randy Velarde	.10
93	Aaron Boone	.10
94	Javy Lopez	.10
95	Johnny Damon	.25
96	Jon Lieber	.10
97	Montreal Expos	.10
98	Mark Kotsay	.10
99	Luis Gonzalez	.25
100	Larry Walker	.25
101	Adrian Beltre	.25
102	Alex Ochoa	.10
103	Michael Barrett	.10
104	Tampa Bay Devil Rays	.10
105	Rey Ordonez	.10
106	Derek Jeter	3.00
107	Mike Lieberthal	.10
108	Ellis Burks	.10
109	Steve Finley	.10
110	Ryan Klesko	.10
111	Steve Avery	.10
112	Dave Veres	.10
113	Cliff Floyd	.10
114	Shane Reynolds	.10
115	Kevin Brown	.10
116	David Nilsson	.10
117	Mike Trombley	.10
118	Todd Walker	.10
119	John Olerud	.10
120	Chuck Knoblauch	.10
121	Nomar Garciaparra	2.00
122	Trot Nixon	.10
123	Erubiel Durazo	.10
124	Edwards Guzman	.10
125	Curt Schilling	.50
126	Brian Jordan	.10
127	Cleveland Indians	.10
128	Benito Santiago	.10
129	Frank Thomas	.75
130	Neifi Perez	.10
131	Alex Fernandez	.10
132	Jose Lima	.10
133	Jorge Toca-1B,	
	Melvin Mora-OF	.10
134	Scott Karl	.10
135	Brad Radke	.10
136	Paul O'Neill	.10
137	Kris Benson	.10
138	Colorado Rockies	.10
139	Jason Phillips	.10
140	Robb Nen	.10
141	Ken Hill	.10
142	Charles Johnson	.10

143	Paul Konerko	.10
144	Dmitri Young	.10
145	Justin Thompson	.10
146	Mark Loretta	.10
147	Edgardo Alfonzo	.10
148	Armando Benitez	.10
149	Octavio Dotel	.10
150	Wade Boggs	1.50
151	Ramon Hernandez	.10
152	Freddy Garcia	.10
153	Edgar Martinez	.10
154	Ivan Rodriguez	.65
155	Kansas City Royals	.10
156	Cleatus Davidson-2B,	
	Cristian Guzman-SS	.10
157	Andy Benes	.10
158	Todd Dunwoody	.10
159	Pedro Martinez	1.00
160	Mike Caruso	.10
161	Mike Sirotka	.10
162	Houston Astros	.10
163	Darryl Kile	.10
164	Chipper Jones	1.50
165	Carl Everett	.10
166	Geoff Jenkins	.10
167	Dan Perkins	.10
168	Andy Pettitte	.25
169	Francisco Cordova	.10
170	Jay Buhner	.10
171	Jay Bell	.10
172	Andruw Jones	.75
173	Bobby Howry	.10
174	Chris Singleton	.10
175	Todd Helton	.75
176	A.J. Burnett	.10
177	Marquis Grissom	.10
178	Eric Milton	.10
179	Los Angeles Dodgers	.10
180	Kevin Appier	.10
181	Brian Giles	.10
182	Tom Davey	.10
183	Mo Vaughn	.10
184	Jose Hernandez	.10
185	Jim Parque	.10
186	Derrick Gibson	.10
187	Bruce Aven	.10
188	Jeff Cirillo	.10
189	Doug Mientkiewicz	.10
190	Eric Chavez	.25
191	Al Martin	.10
192	Tom Glavine	.25
193	Butch Huskey	.10
194	Ray Durham	.10
195	Greg Vaughn	.10
196	Vinny Castilla	.10
197	Ken Caminiti	.10
198	Joe Mays	.10
199	Chicago White Sox	.10
200	Mariano Rivera	.20
201	Mark McGwire	2.50
202	Pat Meares	.10
203	Andres Galarraga	.10
204	Tom Gordon	.10
205	Henry Rodriguez	.10
206	Brett Tomko	.10
207	Dante Bichette	.10
208	Craig Biggio	.10
209	Matt Lawton	.10
210	Tino Martinez	.10
211	Aaron Myette-P, Josh Paul-C	.10
212	Warren Morris	.10
213	San Diego Padres	.10
214	Ramon E. Martinez	.10
215	Troy Percival	.10
216	Jason Johnson	.10
217	Carlos Lee	.10
218	Scott Williamson	.10
219	Jeff Weaver	.10
220	Ronnie Belliard	.10
221	Jason Giambi	.65
222	Ken Griffey Jr.	2.00
223	John Halama	.10
224	Brett Hinchliffe	.10
225	Wilson Alvarez	.10
226	Rolando Arrojo	.10
227	Ruben Mateo	.10
228	Rafael Palmeiro	.65
229	David Wells	.10
230	Eric Gagne-P, Jeff Williams-P	.10
231	Tim Salmon	.30
232	Mike Mussina	.50
233	Magglio Ordonez	.25
234	Ron Villone	.10
235	Antonio Alfonseca	.10
236	Jeromy Burnitz	.10
237	Ben Grieve	.10
238	Giomar Guevara	.10
239	Garret Anderson	.10
240	John Smoltz	.10
241	Mark Grace	.15
242	Cole Liniak-3B, Jose Molina-C	.10
243	Damion Easley	.10
244	Jeff Montgomery	.10
245	Kenny Lofton	.10
246	Masato Yoshii	.10
247	Philadelphia Phillies	.10
248	Raul Mondesi	.10
249	Marlon Anderson	.10
250	Shawn Green	.40
251	Sterling Hitchcock	.10
252	Randy Wolf-P,	
	Anthony Shumaker-P	.10
253	Jeff Fassero	.10
254	Eli Marrero	.10
255	Cincinnati Reds	.10
256	Rick Ankiel-P,	
	Adam Kennedy-2B	.50

257	Darin Erstad	.60
258	Albert Belle	.20
259	Bartolo Colon	.10
260	Bret Saberhagen	.10
261	Carlos Beltran	.50
262	Glenallen Hill	.10
263	Gregg Jefferies	.10
264	Matt Clement	.10
265	Miguel Del Toro	.10
266	Robinson Cancel-C, Kevin Barker-1B	.10
267	San Francisco Giants	.10
268	Kent Bottenfield	.10
269	Fred McGriff	.10
270	Chris Carpenter	.10
271	Atlanta Braves	.10
272	Wilton Veras-3B, Tomokazu Ohka-P **RC**	.50
273	Will Clark	.20
274	Troy O'Leary	.10
275	Sammy Sosa	2.00
276	Travis Lee	.15
277	Sean Casey	.25
278	Ron Gant	.10
279	Roger Clemens	1.75
280	Phil Nevin	.10
281	Mike Piazza	2.00
282	Mike Lowell	.10
283	Kevin Millwood	.10
284	Joe Randa	.10
285	Jeff Shaw	.10
286	Jason Varitek	.10
287	Harold Baines	.10
288	Gabe Kapler	.10
289	Chuck Finley	.10
290	Carl Pavano	.10
291	Brad Ausmus	.10
292	Brad Fullmer	.10
293	Boston Red Sox	.10
294	Bob Wickman	.10
295	Billy Wagner	.10
296	Shawn Estes	.10
297	Gary Sheffield	.40
298	Fernando Seguignol	.10
299	Omar Olivares	.10
300	Baltimore Orioles	.10
301	Matt Stairs	.10
302	Andy Ashby	.10
303	Todd Greene	.10
304	Jesse Garcia	.10
305	Kerry Wood	.50
306	Roberto Alomar	.40
307	New York Mets	.10
308	Dean Palmer	.10
309	Mike Hampton	.10
310	Devon White	.10
311	Chad Hermansen-OF, Mike Garcia-P	.10
312	Tim Hudson	.40
313	John Franco	.10
314	Jason Schmidt	.10
315	J.T. Snow	.10
316	Ed Sprague	.10
317	Chris Widger	.10
318	Ben Petrick-C, Luther Hackman-P **RC**	.25
319	Jose Mesa	.10
320	Jose Canseco	.50
321	John Wetteland	.10
322	Minnesota Twins	.10
323	Jeff DaVanon-OF, Brian Cooper-P	.25
324	Tony Womack	.10
325	Rod Beck	.10
326	Mickey Morandini	.10
327	Pokey Reese	.10
328	Jaret Wright	.10
329	Glen Barker	.10
330	Darren Dreifort	.10
331	Torii Hunter	.15
332	Tony Armas Jr.-P, Peter Bergeron-OF	.10
333	Hideki Irabu	.10
334	Desi Relaford	.10
335	Barry Bonds	3.00
336	Gary DiSarcina	.10
337	Gerald Williams	.10
338	John Valentin	.10
339	David Justice	.10
340	Juan Encarnacion	.10
341	Jeremy Giambi	.10
342	Chan Ho Park	.10
343	Vladimir Guerrero	1.00
344	Robin Ventura	.10
345	Bobby Abreu	.10
346	Tony Gwynn	1.50
347	Jose Jimenez	.10
348	Royce Clayton	.10
349	Kelvim Escobar	.10
350	Chicago Cubs	.10
351	Travis Dawkins-SS, Jason LaRue-C	.10
352	Barry Larkin	.10
353	Cal Ripken Jr.	3.00
353s	Cal Ripken Jr./OPS	4.00
354	Alex Rodriguez	2.50
355	Todd Stottlemyre	.10
356	Terry Adams	.10
357	Pittsburgh Pirates	.10
358	Jim Thome	.10
359	Corey Lee-P, Doug Davis-P	.10
360	Moises Alou	.10
361	Todd Hollandsworth	.10
362	Marty Cordova	.10
363	David Cone	.10
364	Joe Nathan-P, Wilson Delgado-SS	.10
365	Paul Byrd	.10
366	Edgar Renteria	.10
367	Rusty Greer	.10
368	David Segui	.10
369	New York Yankees	.50
370	Daryle Ward-OF/1B, Carlos Hernandez-2B	.10
371	Troy Glaus	.75
372	Delino DeShields	.10
373	Jose Offerman	.10
374	Sammy Sosa	2.00
375	Sandy Alomar Jr.	.10
376	Masao Kida	.10
377	Richard Hidalgo	.10
378	Ismael Valdes	.10
379	Ugueth Urbina	.10
380	Darryl Hamilton	.10
381	John Jaha	.10
382	St. Louis Cardinals	.10
383	Scott Sauerbeck	.10
384	Russ Ortiz	.10
385	Jamie Moyer	.10
386	Dave Martinez	.10
387	Todd Zeile	.10
388	Anaheim Angels	.10
389	Rob Ryan-OF, Nick Bierbrodt-P	.10
390	Rickey Henderson	.75
391	Alex Rodriguez	2.50
392	Texas Rangers	.10
393	Roberto Hernandez	.10
394	Tony Batista	.10
395	Oakland Athletics	.10
396	Randall Simon-1B, David Cortes-P **RC**	.20
397	Gregg Olson	.10
398	Sidney Ponson	.10
399	Micah Bowie	.10
400	Mark McGwire	2.50
401	Florida Marlins	.10
402	Chad Allen	.10
403	Casey Blake-3B, Vernon Wells-OF	.10
404	Pete Harnisch	.10
405	Preston Wilson	.10
406	Richie Sexson	.10
407	Rico Brogna	.10
408	Todd Hundley	.10
409	Wally Joyner	.10
410	Tom Goodwin	.10
411	Joey Hamilton	.10
412	Detroit Tigers	.10
413	Michael Tejera-P, Ramon Castro-C	.25
414	Alex Gonzalez	.10
415	Jermaine Dye	.10
416	Jose Rosado	.10
417	Wilton Guerrero	.10
418	Rondell White	.10
419	Al Leiter	.10
420	Bernie Williams	.25
421	A.J. Hinch	.10
422	Pat Burrell	.50
423	Scott Rolen	.65
424	Jason Kendall	.10
425	Kevin Young	.10
426	Eric Owens	.10
427	Derek Jeter	1.00
428	Livan Hernandez	.10
429	Russ Davis	.10
430	Dan Wilson	.10
431	Quinton McCracken	.10
432	Homer Bush	.10
433	Seattle Mariners	.10
434	Chad Harville-P, Luis Vizcaino-P	.10
435	Carlos Beltran	.45
436	Scott Williamson	.10
437	Pedro Martinez	.75
438	Randy Johnson	.75
439	Ivan Rodriguez	.60
440	Chipper Jones	.75
441	Bernie Williams AL Division	.15
442	Pedro Martinez AL Division	.50
443	Derek Jeter AL Champ	1.00
444	Brian Jordan NL Division	.10
445	Todd Pratt NL Division	.10
446	Kevin Millwood NL Champ	.10
447	Orlando Hernandez World Series	.10
448	Derek Jeter World Series	1.00
449	Chad Curtis World Series	.10
450	Roger Clemens World Series	.75
451	Carlos Casimiro **RC**	8.00
452	Adam Melhuse **RC**	8.00
453	Adam Bernero **RC**	8.00
454	Dusty Allen **RC**	8.00
455	Chan Perry **RC**	8.00
456	Damian Rolls **RC**	8.00
457	Josh Phelps **RC**	10.00
458	Barry Zito **RC**	25.00
459	Hector Ortiz **RC**	8.00
460	Juan Pierre **RC**	15.00
461	Jose Ortiz **RC**	15.00
462	Chad Zerbe **RC**	8.00
463	Julio Zuleta **RC**	8.00
464	Eric Byrnes **RC**	25.00
465	Wilfredo Rodriguez **RC**	10.00
466	Wascar Serrano **RC**	8.00
467	Aaron McNeal **RC**	8.00
468	Paul Rigdon **RC**	8.00
469	John Snyder **RC**	8.00
470	J.C. Romero **RC**	8.00
471	Talmadge Nunnari **RC**	8.00
472	Mike Lamb **RC**	8.00
473	Ryan Kohlmeier **RC**	8.00
474	Rodney Lindsey **RC**	8.00
475	Elvis Pena **RC**	8.00
476	Alex Cabrera **RC**	10.00
477	Chris Richard **RC**	8.00
478	Pedro Feliz **RC**	10.00
479	Ross Gload **RC**	8.00
480	Timoniel Perez **RC**	8.00
481	Jason Woolf **RC**	8.00
482	Kenny Kelly **RC**	8.00
483	Sang-Hoon Lee **RC**	8.00
484	John Riedling **RC**	8.00
485	Chris Wakeland	8.00
486	Britt Reames **RC**	8.00
487	Greg LaRocca **RC**	8.00
488	Randy Keisler **RC**	8.00
489	Xavier Nady **RC**	20.00
490	Keith Ginter **RC**	10.00
491	Joey Nation **RC**	8.00
492	Kazuhiro Sasaki **RC**	8.00
493	Lesli Brea **RC**	8.00
494	Jace Brewer **RC**	8.00
495	Yohanny Valera **RC**	8.00
496	Adam Piatt	10.00
497	Nate Rolison	8.00
498	Aubrey Huff	10.00
499	Jason Tyner	8.00
500	Corey Patterson	10.00

Club 3000

		NM/M
Complete Set (3):		5.00
Common Player:		3.00
Inserted 1:36		
(1)	George Brett	4.00
(2)	Rod Carew	2.00
(3)	Robin Yount	2.00

Club 3000 Memorabilia

	NM/M
George Brett/Bat/250	60.00
George Brett/Hat/100	75.00
George Brett/Jsy/445	30.00
George Brett/Bat, Jsy/100	90.00
Rod Carew/Bat/225	30.00
Rod Carew/Hat/100	50.00
Rod Carew/Jsy/440	20.00
Rod Carew/Bat, Jsy/100	65.00
Robin Yount/Bat/250	40.00
Robin Yount/Hat/100	60.00
Robin Yount/Jsy/440	30.00
Robin Yount/Bat, Jsy/100	75.00

Dividends

		NM/M
Complete Set (15):		15.00
Common Player:		.50
Inserted 1:6		
1	Alex Rodriguez	2.50
2	Ben Grieve	.50
3	Cal Ripken Jr.	3.00
4	Chipper Jones	1.50
5	Derek Jeter	3.00
6	Frank Thomas	1.00
7	Jeff Bagwell	1.00
8	Sammy Sosa	2.00
9	Tony Gwynn	1.50
10	Scott Rolen	.75
11	Nomar Garciaparra	2.00
12	Mike Piazza	2.00
13	Mark McGwire	2.50
14	Ken Griffey Jr.	2.00
15	Juan Gonzalez	1.00

Fresh Ink

	NM/M
Common Player:	5.00
Inserted 1:144	
Rick Ankiel	15.00
Carlos Beltran	25.00
Pat Burrell	15.00
Miguel Cairo	5.00
Sean Casey	8.00
Will Clark	30.00
Mike Darr	5.00
J.D. Drew	10.00
Erubiel Durazo	10.00
Carlos Febles	6.00
Freddy Garcia	8.00
Greg Maddux	80.00
Jason Grilli	5.00
Vladimir Guerrero	35.00
Tony Gwynn	40.00
Jerry Hairston Jr.	8.00
Tim Hudson	15.00
John Jaha	5.00
D'Angelo Jimenez	5.00
Andruw Jones	20.00
Gabe Kapler	6.00
Cesar King	5.00
Jason LaRue	6.00
Mike Lieberthal	8.00
Pedro Martinez	50.00
Gary Matthews Jr.	5.00
Orber Moreno	5.00
Eric Munson	5.00
Rafael Palmeiro	35.00
Jim Parque	6.00
Willi Mo Pena	15.00
Cal Ripken Jr.	100.00
Alex Rodriguez	80.00
Tim Salmon	15.00
Chris Singleton	5.00
Alfonso Soriano	50.00
Ed Yarnall	5.00

Glossy Lumberjacks

		NM/M
Common Player:		8.00
One per factory set.		
Production listed		
1	Edgardo Alfonzo/145	10.00
2	Roberto Alomar/627	10.00
3	Moises Alou/529	8.00
4	Carlos Beltran/489	8.00
5	Adrian Beltre/127	10.00
7	Barry Bonds/305	40.00
9	Pat Burrell/45	25.00
10	Sean Casey/50	15.00
11	Eric Chavez/259	10.00
12	Tony Clark/70	10.00
13	Carlos Delgado/70	20.00
14	J.D. Drew/135	10.00
15	Erubiel Durazo/70	10.00
17	Carlos Febles/120	10.00
18	Jason Giambi/220	15.00
19	Shawn Green/429	10.00
20	Vladimir Guerrero/809	15.00
21	Derek Jeter/180	50.00
22	Chipper Jones/725	15.00
23	Gabe Kapler/160	8.00
25	Paul Konerko/70	10.00
27	Mike Lieberthal/45	10.00
28	Edgar Martinez/211	10.00
29	Raul Mondesi/458	8.00
30	Warren Morris/35	10.00
31	Magglio Ordonez/190	10.00
32	Rafael Palmeiro/49	15.00
33	Pokey Reese/110	8.00
34	Cal Ripken/235	50.00
35	Alex Rodriguez/292	25.00
36	Ivan Rodriguez/602	10.00
37	Scott Rolen/502	10.00
38	Chris Singleton/68	8.00
39	Alfonso Soriano/285	15.00
40	Frank Thomas/489	10.00
41	Jim Thome/479	10.00
42	Robin Ventura/114	10.00

43	Jose Vidro/60	10.00
44	Bernie Williams/215	10.00
45	Matt Williams/152	8.00

Grasskickers

		NM/M
Complete Set (15):		50.00
Common Player:		2.00
Inserted 1:30		
1	Tony Gwynn	3.00
2	Scott Rolen	2.00
3	Nomar Garciaparra	4.00
4	Mike Piazza	4.00
5	Mark McGwire	6.00
6	Frank Thomas	2.00
7	Cal Ripken Jr.	8.00
8	Chipper Jones	3.00
9	Greg Maddux	3.00
10	Ken Griffey Jr.	4.00
11	Juan Gonzalez	2.00
12	Derek Jeter	8.00
13	Sammy Sosa	4.00
14	Roger Clemens	3.50
15	Alex Rodriguez	6.00

Hall's Well

		NM/M
Complete Set (15):		50.00
Common Player:		1.50
Inserted 1:30		
1	Mark McGwire	6.00
2	Alex Rodriguez	6.00
3	Cal Ripken Jr.	8.00
4	Chipper Jones	3.00
5	Derek Jeter	8.00
6	Frank Thomas	2.00
7	Greg Maddux	3.00
8	Juan Gonzalez	2.00
9	Ken Griffey Jr.	4.00
10	Mike Piazza	4.00
11	Nomar Garciaparra	4.00
12	Sammy Sosa	4.00
13	Roger Clemens	3.50
14	Ivan Rodriguez	1.50
15	Tony Gwynn	3.00

2000 Fleer Tradition Japan Commemorative Sheet

NM/M

Derek Jeter, Chipper Jones, Pedro Martinez, Mike Piazza, Cal Ripken Jr., Ivan Rodriguez, Sammy Sosa, Mo Vaughn 20.00

2000 Fleer Tradition Opening Day 2K

		NM/M
Complete Set (8):		6.00
Common Player:		.50
9	Cal Ripken Jr.	2.00
10	Alex Rodriguez	2.00
11	Mike Piazza	1.00
12	Jeff Bagwell	.75

Mike Piazza
New York Mets

Inserted 1:3		
1	Rick Ankiel	.40
2	Matt Riley	.25
3	Wilton Veras	.25
4	Ben Petrick	.25
5	Chad Hermansen	.25
6	Peter Bergeron	.25
7	Mark Quinn	.25
8	Russell Branyan	.25
9	Alfonso Soriano	1.50
10	Randy Wolf	.50
11	Ben Davis	.25
12	Jeff DaVanon	.25
13	D'Angelo Jimenez	.25
14	Vernon Wells	1.00
15	Adam Kennedy	.40
13	Randy Johnson	.75
14	Jason Kendall	.50
15	Magglio Ordonez	.50
16	Carlos Delgado	.50

Ripken Collection

CAL RIPKEN, JR.
THIRD BASE
BALTIMORE ORIOLES

		NM/M
Complete Set (10):		50.00
Common Card:		6.00
Inserted 1:30		
(Inserted at the rate of 1:30 packs.)		

Ten-4

		NM/M
Complete Set (10):		20.00
Common Player:		2.00
Inserted 1:18		
1	Sammy Sosa	2.00
2	Nomar Garciaparra	2.00
3	Mike Piazza	2.00
4	Mark McGwire	3.00
5	Ken Griffey Jr.	2.00
6	Juan Gonzalez	1.00
7	Derek Jeter	4.00
8	Chipper Jones	1.50
9	Cal Ripken Jr.	4.00
10	Alex Rodriguez	3.00

Who To Watch

		NM/M
Complete Set (15):		5.00
Common Player:		.25

2000 Fleer Tradition Update

CHAD DURBIN
KANSAS CITY ROYALS • PITCHER

		NM/M
Complete Set (150):		20.00
Common Player:		.15
1	Ken Griffey Jr.	.50
2	Cal Ripken Jr.	1.00
3	Randy Velarde	.15
4	Fred McGriff	.15
5	Derek Jeter	1.00
6	Tom Glavine	.25
7	Brent Mayne	.15
8	Alex Ochoa	.15
9	Scott Sheldon	.15
10	Randy Johnson	.35
11	Daniel Garibay RC	.15
12	Brad Fullmer	.15
13	Kazuhiro Sasaki RC	.50
14	Andy Tracy	.15
15	Bret Boone	.15
16	Chad Durbin RC	.25
17	Mark Buehrle RC	1.50
18	Julio Zuleta RC	.15
19	Jeremy Giambi	.15
20	Gene Stechschulte RC	.15
21	Lou Pote, Bengie Molina	.15
22	Darrell Einertson	.15
23	Ken Griffey Jr.	.75
24	Jeff Sparks, Dan Wheeler	.15
25	Aaron Fultz RC	.15
26	Derek Bell	.15
27	Rob Bell, D.T. Cromer	.15
28	Rob Fick	.15
29	Darryl Kile	.15
30	Clayton Andrews, John Bate	.15
31	Dave Veres	.15
32	Hector Mercado RC	.15
33	Willie Morales	.15
34	Kelly Wunsch, Kip Wells	.15
35	Hideki Irabu	.15
36	Sean DePaula	.15
37	Dewayne Wise, Chris Woodward	.15
38	Curt Schilling	.25
39	Mark Johnson	.15
40	Mike Cameron	.15
41	Scott Sheldon, Tom Evans	.15
42	Brett Tomko	.15
43	Johan Santana RC	15.00
44	Andy Benes	.15
45	Matt LeCroy, Mark Redman	.15
46	Ryan Klesko	.15
47	Andy Ashby	.15
48	Octavio Dotel	.15
49	Eric Byrnes RC	1.00
50	Not Issued	
51	Kenny Rogers	.15
52	Ben Weber	.15
53	Matt Blank, Scott Strickland	.15
54	Tom Goodwin	.15
55	Jim Edmonds	.15
56	Derrick Turnbow RC	.25
57	Mark Mulder	.15
58	Tarrik Brock, Ruben Quevedo	.15
59	Danny Young	.15
60	Fernando Vina	.15
61	Justin Brunette RC	.15
62	Jimmy Anderson	.15
63	Reggie Sanders	.15
64	Adam Kennedy	.15
65	Jesse Garcia, B.J. Ryan	.15
66	Al Martin	.15
67	Kevin Walker	.15
68	Brad Penny	.15
69	B.J. Surhoff	.15
70	Geoff Blum, Trace Coquillette	.15
71	Jose Jimenez	.15
72	Chuck Finley	.15
73	Valerio De Los Santos, Everett Stull	.15
74	Terry Adams	.15
75	Rafael Furcal	.15
76	Mike Darr, John Roskos	.15
77	Quivio Veras	.15
78	Armando Almanza	.15
79	Greg Vaughn	.15
80	Keith McDonald RC	.15
81	Eric Cammack	.15
82	Horacio Estrada, Ray King	.15
83	Kory DeHaan	.15
84	Kevin Hodges	.15
85	Mike Lamb RC	.25
86	Shawn Green	.40
87	Dan Reichert, Jason Rakers	.15
88	Adam Piatt	.15
89	Mike Garcia	.15
90	Rodrigo Lopez RC	1.00
91	John Olerud	.15
92	Barry Zito, Terrence Long	1.00
93	Jimmy Rollins	.25
94	Denny Neagle	.15
95	Rickey Henderson	.50
96	Adam Eaton, Buddy Carlyle	.15
97	Brian O'Connor	.15
98	Andy Thompson	.15
99	Jason Boyd	.15
100	Carlos Guillen, Joel Piniero	.15
101	Raul Gonzalez	.15
102	Brandon Kolb RC	.15
103	Jason Maxwell, Mike Lincoln	.15
104	Luis Matos RC	.25
105	Morgan Burkhart RC	.50
106	Ismael Villegas, Steve Sisco	.15
107	David Justice	.15
108	Pablo Ozuna	.15
109	Jose Canseco	.40
110	Alex Cora, Shawn Gilbert	.15
111	Will Clark	.25
112	Keith Luuloa, Eric Weaver	.15
113	Bruce Chen	.15
114	Adam Hyzdu	.15
115	Scott Forster, Yovanny Lara	.15
116	Allen McDill, Jose Macias	.15
117	Kevin Nicholson	.15
118	Israel Alcantara, Tim Young	.15
119	Juan Alvarez	.15
120	Julio Lugo, Mitch Meluskey	.15
121	B.J. Waszgis	.15
122	Jeff D'Amico, Brett Laxton	.15
123	Ricky Ledee	.15
124	Mark DeRosa, Jason Marquis	.15
125	Alex Cabrera RC	.50
126	Gary Matthews, Augie Ojeda	.15
127	Richie Sexson	.15
128	Santiago Perez, Hector Ramirez	.15
129	Rondell White	.15
130	Craig House RC	.15
131	Kevin Beirne, Jon Garland	.15
132	Wayne Franklin	.15
133	Henry Rodriguez	.15
134	Jay Payton, Jim Mann	.15
135	Ron Gant	.15
136	Paxton Crawford, Sang-Hoon Lee	.25
137	Kent Bottenfield	.15
138	Rocky Biddle RC	.15
139	Travis Lee	.15
140	Ryan Vogelsong	.15
141	Jason Conti, Geraldo Guzman	.15
142	Tim Drew, Mark Watson	.15
143	John Parrish, Chris Richard	.15
144	Javier Cardona, Brandon Villafuetre	.15
145	Tike Redman, Steve Sparks	.15
146	Brian Schneider, Matt Skrmetta	.15
147	Pasqual Coco, Leo Estrella	.15
148	Lorenzo Barcelo, Joe Crede	.15
149	Jace Brewer RC	.25
150	Milton Bradley, Tomas de la Rosa	.15

Mantle Pieces

		NM/M
Inserted 1:80 Sets		
1	Mickey Mantle	150.00

2001 Fleer Authority

		NM/M
Complete Set (150):		265.00
Common Player:		.25
Common (101-150):		3.00
Production 2,001		
Pack (5):		6.00
Box (22 + 2 Graded Packs):		120.00
1	Mark Grace	.40
2	Paul Konerko	.40
3	Sean Casey	.25
4	Jim Thome	.40
5	Todd Helton	.75

#	Player	Price
6	Tony Clark	.25
7	Jeff Bagwell	.50
8	Mike Sweeney	.25
9	Eric Karros	.25
10	Richie Sexson	.25
11	Doug Mientkiewicz	.25
12	Ryan Klesko	.25
13	John Olerud	.25
14	Mark McGwire	2.00
15	Fred McGriff	.25
16	Rafael Palmeiro	.50
17	Carlos Delgado	.50
18	Roberto Alomar	.40
19	Craig Biggio	.25
20	Jose Vidro	.25
21	Edgardo Alfonzo	.25
22	Jeff Kent	.25
23	Bret Boone	.25
24	Rafael Furcal	.40
25	Nomar Garciaparra	.50
26	Barry Larkin	.40
27	Cristian Guzman	.25
28	Derek Jeter	2.50
29	Miguel Tejada	.50
30	Jimmy Rollins	.75
31	Rich Aurilia	.25
32	Alex Rodriguez	2.00
33	Cal Ripken Jr.	2.50
34	Troy Glaus	.50
35	Matt Williams	.25
36	Chipper Jones	1.00
37	Jeff Cirillo	.25
38	Robin Ventura	.25
39	Eric Chavez	.25
40	Scott Rolen	.50
41	Phil Nevin	.25
42	Mike Piazza	1.00
43	Jorge Posada	.40
44	Jason Kendall	.25
45	Ivan Rodriguez	.50
46	Frank Thomas	.75
47	Edgar Martinez	.25
48	Darin Erstad	.25
49	Tim Salmon	.25
50	Luis Gonzalez	.25
51	Andruw Jones	.50
52	Carl Everett	.25
53	Manny Ramirez	.75
54	Sammy Sosa	.75
55	Rondell White	.25
56	Magglio Ordonez	.40
57	Ken Griffey Jr.	1.50
58	Juan Gonzalez	.50
59	Larry Walker	.25
60	Bobby Higginson	.25
61	Cliff Floyd	.25
62	Preston Wilson	.25
63	Moises Alou	.25
64	Lance Berkman	.50
65	Richard Hidalgo	.25
66	Jermaine Dye	.25
67	Mark Quinn	.25
68	Shawn Green	.50
69	Gary Sheffield	.40
70	Jeromy Burnitz	.25
71	Geoff Jenkins	.25
72	Vladimir Guerrero	.75
73	Bernie Williams	.40
74	Johnny Damon	.50
75	Jason Giambi	.50
76	Bobby Abreu	.40
77	Pat Burrell	.50
78	Brian Giles	.25
79	Tony Gwynn	1.00
80	Barry Bonds	2.50
81	J.D. Drew	.40
82	Jim Edmonds	.25
83	Greg Vaughn	.25
84	Raul Mondesi	.25
85	Shannon Stewart	.25
86	Randy Johnson	.75
87	Curt Schilling	.50
88	Tom Glavine	.50
89	Greg Maddux	1.50
90	Pedro Martinez	.75
91	Kerry Wood	.50
92	David Wells	.25
93	Bartolo Colon	.25
94	Mike Hampton	.25
95	Kevin Brown	.25
96	Al Leiter	.25
97	Roger Clemens	2.00
98	Mike Mussina	.50

#	Player	Price
99	Tim Hudson	.40
100	Kazuhiro Sasaki	.25
101	Ichiro Suzuki RC	35.00
102	Albert Pujols RC	75.00
103	Drew Henson RC	5.00
104	Adam Pettyjohn RC	3.00
105	Adrian Hernandez RC	3.00
106	Andy Morales RC	3.00
107	Tsuyoshi Shinjo RC	4.00
108	Juan Uribe RC	3.00
109	Jack Wilson RC	5.00
110	Jason Smith RC	3.00
111	Junior Spivey RC	4.00
112	Wilson Betemit RC	3.00
113	Elpidio Guzman RC	3.00
114	Esix Snead RC	3.00
115	Winston Abreu RC	3.00
116	Jeremy Owens RC	3.00
117	Jay Gibbons RC	5.00
118	Luis Lopez RC	3.00
119	Ryan Freel RC	4.00
120	Rafael Soriano RC	4.00
121	Johnny Estrada RC	5.00
122	Bud Smith RC	3.00
123	Jackson Melian RC	3.00
124	Matt White RC	3.00
125	Travis Hafner RC	10.00
126	Morgan Ensberg RC	5.00
127	Endy Chavez RC	3.00
128	Bret Prinz RC	3.00
129	Juan Diaz RC	3.00
130	Erick Almonte RC	4.00
131	Rob Mackowiak RC	3.00
132	Carlos Valderrama RC	3.00
133	Wilkin Ruan RC	3.00
134	Angel Berroa RC	5.00
135	Henry Mateo RC	3.00
136	Bill Ortega RC	3.00
137	Billy Sylvester RC	3.00
138	Andres Torres RC	3.00
139	Nate Frese RC	3.00
140	Casey Fossum RC	4.00
141	Ricardo Rodriguez RC	3.00
142	Brian Roberts RC	8.00
143	Carlos Garcia RC	3.00
144	Brian Lawrence RC	4.00
145	Cory Aldridge RC	3.00
146	Mark Teixeira RC	25.00
147	Juan Cruz RC	3.00
148	Brandon Duckworth RC	3.00
149	Dewon Brazelton RC	3.00
150	Mark Prior RC	8.00

Prominence

Stars (1-100):	5-10X
Production 125	
SP's (101-150):	3-5X
Production 75	

(See 2001 Fleer Authority for checklist and base card values.)

Graded

Mint:	1-1.5X
NrMt+:	.8-1X
NrMt:	.4-.6X

No Multipliers for Gem Mint.
(See 2001 Fleer Authority for checklist and base card values.)

Authority Figures

NM/M

Complete Set (20):		75.00
Common Card:		2.00
1AF	Mark McGwire, Albert Pujols	8.00
2AF	Kazuhiro Sasaki, Ichiro Suzuki	8.00
3AF	Derek Jeter, Drew Henson	10.00
4AF	Ken Griffey Jr., Jackson Melian	6.00
5AF	Wilson Betemit, Chipper Jones	4.50
6AF	Jeff Bagwell, Morgan Ensberg	4.00
7AF	Cal Ripken Jr., Jay Gibbons	10.00
8AF	Mike Piazza, Tsuyoshi Shinjo	6.00
9AF	Luis Gonzalez, Junior Spivey	2.00
10AF	Barry Bonds, Carlos Valderrama	10.00
11AF	Todd Helton, Juan Uribe	4.00
12AF	Roger Clemens, Adrian Hernandez	5.00
13AF	Alex Rodriguez, Travis Hafner	8.00
14AF	Scott Rolen, Johnny Estrada	3.00
15AF	Brian Giles, Rob Mackowiak	2.00
16AF	Randy Johnson, Bret Prinz	4.00
17AF	Carlos Delgado, Luis Lopez	3.00
18AF	Manny Ramirez, Juan Diaz	4.00
19AF	Mike Sweeney, Endy Chavez	2.00
20AF	Sammy Sosa, Jaisen Randolph	6.00

Derek Jeter Monumental Moments

NM/M

MM4	Derek Jeter/2000	5.00
MM4AU	Derek Jeter/Auto./100	100.00

Derek Jeter Reprint Autographs

NM/M

Production 500		
1DJRA	Derek Jeter/500	80.00

Diamond Cuts

NM/M

Common Player:	4.00

Seal of Approval

NM/M

Complete Set (15):		45.00
Common Player:		1.50
1SA	Derek Jeter	6.00
2SA	Alex Rodriguez	5.00
3SA	Nomar Garciaparra	4.00
4SA	Cal Ripken Jr.	6.00
5SA	Mike Piazza	4.00
6SA	Mark McGwire	5.00
7SA	Tony Gwynn	3.00
8SA	Barry Bonds	6.00
9SA	Greg Maddux	3.00
10SA	Chipper Jones	3.00
11SA	Roger Clemens	3.50

Inserted 1:10

Rick Ankiel/Shoe	4.00
Jeff Bagwell/Jsy	8.00
Adrian Beltre/Hat	4.00
Craig Biggio/Bat	4.00
Barry Bonds/Hat	35.00
Barry Bonds/Jsy	20.00
Barry Bonds/Pants	20.00
Barry Bonds/Shoe	30.00
Barry Bonds/Wristband/100	50.00
Kevin Brown/Hat	6.00
Kevin Brown/Pants	4.00
Eric Byrnes/Bat	4.00
Sean Casey/Jsy	4.00
Eric Chavez/Hat	6.00
Chipper Jones/Jsy	10.00
Chipper Jones/Bat	10.00
Bartolo Colon/Hat	6.00
Erubiel Durazo/Bat	4.00
Ray Durham/Bat	4.00
Jim Edmonds/Hat	6.00
Jim Edmonds/Shoe	10.00
Darin Erstad/Hat	6.00
Carlos Febles/Bat	4.00
Carlos Febles/Shoe	4.00
Rafael Furcal/Hat	6.00
Juan Gonzalez/Bat Glv	10.00
Juan Gonzalez/Hat	8.00
Luis Gonzalez	6.00
Shawn Green/Bat Glv	10.00
Shawn Green/Bat	6.00
Vladimir Guerrero/Bat	8.00
Tony Gwynn/Bat	8.00
Mike Hampton/Hat	5.00
Mike Hampton/Shoe	5.00
Jerry Hairston Jr./Hat	4.00
Jason Hart/Bat	4.00
Todd Helton/Jsy	8.00
Todd Helton/Pants	8.00
Orlando Hernandez/Bat	4.00
Richard Hidalgo/Bat	4.00
Richard Hidalgo/Bat Glv	15.00
Derek Jeter/Bat	30.00
Derek Jeter/Bat Glv	60.00
Derek Jeter/Jsy	30.00
Derek Jeter/Pants	30.00
Derek Jeter/Shoe	40.00
Randy Johnson/Hat	30.00
Andruw Jones/Bat	6.00
Andruw Jones/Hat	8.00
Jason Kendall/Hat	4.00
Barry Larkin/Jsy	5.00
Matt Lawton/Hat	6.00
Mike Lieberthal/Bat Glv	6.00
Kenny Lofton/Bat	4.00
Edgar Martinez/Bat	8.00
Pedro Martinez/Shoe	10.00
Raul Mondesi/Bat	4.00
Raul Mondesi/Bat Glv	6.00
Hideo Nomo/Bat	15.00
Hideo Nomo/Hat	40.00
Magglio Ordonez/Bat Glv	8.00
Magglio Ordonez/Hat	6.00
David Ortiz/Bat	4.00
Rafael Palmeiro/Bat	8.00
Rafael Palmeiro/Hat	10.00
Chan Ho Park/Hat	5.00
Mike Piazza/Bat	15.00
Mike Piazza/Jsy	15.00
Mike Piazza/Shoe	25.00
Albert Pujols/Pants	30.00
Manny Ramirez/Bat	8.00
Manny Ramirez/Bat Glv	15.00
Manny Ramirez/Hat	15.00
Cal Ripken Jr./Bat Glv	65.00
Cal Ripken Jr./Pants	25.00
Ivan Rodriguez/Bat Glv	10.00
Ivan Rodriguez/Hat	10.00
Ivan Rodriguez/Pants	8.00
Ivan Rodriguez/Shoe	10.00
Scott Rolen/Hat	10.00
Jared Sandberg/Bat	4.00
Deion Sanders/Jsy	4.00
Tsuyoshi Shinjo/Wristband	10.00
Tsuyoshi Shinjo/Bat	6.00
J.T. Snow	4.00
Alfonso Soriano/Hat	20.00
Ichiro Suzuki/Bat	50.00
Ichiro Suzuki/Hat	65.00
Mike Sweeney/Hat	6.00
Miguel Tejada/Hat	6.00
Frank Thomas/Bat	8.00
Frank Thomas/Hat	10.00
Jim Thome/Bat	8.00
Larry Walker/Bat	4.00
Larry Walker/Jsy	4.00
Bernie Williams/Bat	6.00
Brian Giles/Pants	5.00

12SA	Ken Griffey Jr.	4.00
13SA	Vladimir Guerrero	2.00
14SA	Sammy Sosa	4.00
15SA	Todd Helton	1.50

2001 Fleer Boston Red Sox 100th Anniversary

		NM/M
Complete Set (100):		40.00
Common Player:		.25
Pack (5):		6.00
Box (24):		125.00
1	Carl Yastrzemski	2.50
2	Mel Parnell	.25
3	Birdie Tebbetts	.25
4	Tex Hughson	.25
5	Nomar Garciaparra	4.00
6	Fred Lynn	.50
7	John Valentin	.25
8	Rico Petrocelli	.25
9	Ted Williams	5.00
10	Roger Clemens	3.00
11	Luis Aparicio	.40
12	Cy Young	1.50
13	Carlton Fisk	1.00
14	Pedro Martinez	2.00
15	Joe Dobson	.25
16	Babe Ruth	5.00
17	Doc Cramer	.25
18	Pete Runnels	.25
19	Tony Conigliaro	.25
20	Bill Monbouquette	.25
21	Boo Ferriss	.25
22	Harry Hooper	.25
23	Tony Armas	.25
24	Joe Cronin	1.00
25	Rick Ferrell	.25
26	Wade Boggs	2.25
27	Don Baylor	.25
28	Jeff Reardon	.25
29	Smokey Joe Wood	.25
30	Mo Vaughn	.40
31	Walt Dropo	.25
32	Vern Stephens	.25
33	Bernie Carbo	.25
34	George Scott	.25
35	Lefty Grove	1.00
36	Dom DiMaggio	1.00
37	Dennis Eckersley	.75
38	Johnny Pesky	.25
39	Jim Lonborg	.25
40	Jimmy Piersall	.25
41	Tris Speaker	1.50
42	Frank Malzone	.25
43	Bobby Doerr	.75
44	Jimmie Foxx	2.00
45	Tony Pena	.25
46	Billy Goodman	.25
47	Jim Rice	.25
48	Reggie Smith	.25
49	Bill Buckner	.25
50	Earl Wilson	.25
51	Rick Burleson	.25
52	George Kell	.25
53	Dick Radatz	.25
54	Dwight Evans	.25
55	Luis Tiant	.25

56	Elijah "Pumpsie" Green	.25
57	Gene Conley	.25
58	Jackie Jensen	.25
59	Mike Fornieles	.25
60	Dutch Leonard	.25
61	Jake Stahl	.25
62	Don Schwall	.25
63	Jimmy Collins	.25
64	Herb Pennock	.25
65	Red Ruffing	.50
66	Carney Lansford	.25
67	Dick Stuart	.25
68	Dave Morehead	.25
69	Harry Agganis	.25
70	Lou Boudreau	.25
71	Joe Morgan	.75
72	Don Zimmer	.75
73	Tom Yawkey	.25
74	Jean Yawkey	.25
75	Origin of the Red Sox	.25
76	First Season	.25
77	World Series History	.25
78	Carl Yastrzemski	1.00
79	Carlton Fisk	.50
80	Dom DiMaggio	.50
81	Wade Boggs	.75
82	Nomar Garciaparra	2.00
83	Pedro Martinez	1.00
84	Ted Williams	2.50
85	Jim Rice	.25
86	Fred Lynn	.25
87	Mo Vaughn	.25
88	Bobby Doerr	.40
89	Bernie Carbo	.25
90	Dennis Eckersley	.35
91	Jimmy Piersall	.25
92	Luis Tiant	.25
93	Jimmy Fund signage	.25
94	Green Monster w/Ads	.25
95	Green Monster w/All-Star logo	.25
96	Ladder shot on Green Monster	.25
97	Manual Scoreboard	.25
98	Panoramic of Fenway	.25
99	Lansdowne St.	.25
100	1999 All-Star Game	.25

Autograph Caps

		NM/M
One cap per Deluxe box		
(1)	Wade Boggs	75.00
(2)	Bill Buckner	30.00
(3)	Bernie Carbo	30.00
(4)	Roger Clemens	150.00
(6)	Bobby Doerr	40.00
(7)	Dennis Eckersley	50.00
(8)	Dwight Evans	40.00
(10)	Nomar Garciaparra	80.00
(11)	Jim Lonborg	30.00
(12)	Johnny Pesky	40.00
(13)	Rico Petrocelli	30.00
(14)	Jimmy Piersall	30.00
(15)	Jim Rice	40.00
(16)	Luis Tiant	40.00

BoSox Sigs

		NM/M
Common Autograph:		15.00
Inserted 1:96		
	Wade Boggs	80.00
	Bill Buckner	30.00
	Bernie Carbo	20.00
	Roger Clemens/100	200.00
	Dom DiMaggio	75.00
	Bobby Doerr	40.00
	Dwight Evans	50.00
	Carlton Fisk	80.00
	Nomar Garciaparra	70.00
	Jim Lonborg	20.00
	Fred Lynn	40.00
	Rico Petrocelli	25.00
	Jim Rice	40.00
	Luis Tiant	30.00
	Carl Yastrzemski/200	180.00

Field the Game

		NM/M
Complete Set (4):		75.00
(1)	Piece of Green Monster outfield wall	20.00
(2)	Piece of base from 100th anniver. game	20.00

(3)	Piece of baseball from 100th anniv. game	20.00
(4)	anniv. game	20.00

Splendid Splinters

		NM/M
Complete Set (15):		20.00
Common Player:		1.00
Inserted 1:10		
SS1	Babe Ruth	6.00
SS2	Dom DiMaggio	1.50
SS3	Carlton Fisk	2.00
SS4	Carl Yastrzemski	3.00
SS5	Nomar Garciaparra	5.00
SS6	Wade Boggs	2.50
SS7	Ted Williams	5.00
SS8	Jim Rice	1.00
SS9	Mo Vaughn	1.00
SS10	Tris Speaker	2.00
SS11	Dwight Evans	1.00
SS12	Jimmie Foxx	2.50
SS13	Bobby Doerr	1.50
SS14	Fred Lynn	1.00
SS15	Johnny Pesky	1.00

Splendid Splinters Game Bat

		NM/M
Common Player:		15.00
Inserted 1:96		
	Babe Ruth/SP/100	400.00
	Carl Yastrzemski	75.00
	Nomar Garciaparra	30.00
	Wade Boggs	25.00
	Ted Williams/SP/100	200.00
	Jim Rice	15.00
	Dwight Evans	15.00
	Jimmie Foxx/SP/100	200.00

Threads

		NM/M
Common Player:		15.00
Inserted 1:96		
	Wade Boggs	25.00
	Roger Clemens	50.00
	Dwight Evans	15.00
	Carlton Fisk/100	40.00
	Pedro Martinez/100	40.00
	Jim Rice	20.00
	Ted Williams/100	180.00
	Carl Yastrzemski	50.00
	Don Zimmer	15.00

Yawkey's Heroes

	NM/M
Complete Set (20):	15.00

Common Player:		.50
Inserted 1:4		
1YH	Bobby Doerr	.75
2YH	Dom DiMaggio	1.00
3YH	Jim Rice	.50
4YH	Wade Boggs	1.50
5YH	Carlton Fisk	1.00
6YH	Nomar Garciaparra	3.00
7YH	Dennis Eckersley	1.00
8YH	Carl Yastrzemski	2.00
9YH	Ted Williams	4.00
10YH	Tony Conigliaro	.75
11YH	Tony Armas	.50
12YH	Joe Cronin	1.00
13YH	Mo Vaughn	.50
14YH	Johnny Pesky	.50
15YH	Jim Lonborg	.50
16YH	Luis Tiant	.50
17YH	Tony Pena	.50
18YH	Dwight Evans	.50
19YH	Fred Lynn	.75
20YH	Jimmy Piersall	.50

2001 Fleer Cal Ripken Jr. Commemoratives

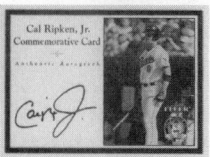

	NM/M
Cal Ripken Jr. (1982 Reprint)	10.00
Cal Ripken Jr. (Autograph card.)	125.00

2001 Fleer Focus

		NM/M
Complete Set (240):		100.00
Common Player:		.15
Common Prospect (201-224):		3.00
Common Prospect (225-250):		3.00
Pack (10):		2.50
Box (24):		50.00
1	Derek Jeter	2.00
2	Manny Ramirez	.75
3	Ken Griffey Jr.	1.50
4	Ken Caminiti	.15
5	Joe Randa	.15
6	Jason Kendall	.15
7	Ron Coomer	.15
8	Rondell White	.15
9	Tino Martinez	.15
10	Nomar Garciaparra	.50
11	Tony Batista	.15
12	Todd Stottlemyre	.15
13	Ryan Klesko	.15
14	Darin Erstad	.50
15	Todd Walker	.15
16	Al Leiter	.15
17	Carl Everett	.15
18	Bobby Abreu	.25
19	Raul Mondesi	.15
20	Vladimir Guerrero	.75
21	Mike Bordick	.15
22	Aaron Sele	.15
23	Ray Lankford	.15
24	Roger Clemens	1.00
25	Kevin Young	.15
26	Brad Radke	.15
27	Todd Hundley	.15
28	Ellis Burks	.15
29	Lee Stevens	.15
30	Eric Karros	.15
31	Darren Dreifort	.15
32	Ivan Rodriguez	.50
33	Pedro Martinez	.75
34	Travis Fryman	.15
35	Garret Anderson	.15
36	Rafael Palmeiro	.50
37	Jason Giambi	.50
38	Jeromy Burnitz	.15
39	Robin Ventura	.15

40	Derek Bell	.15
41	Carlos Guillen	.25
42	Albert Belle	.15
43	Henry Rodriguez	.15
44	Brian Jordan	.15
45	Mike Sweeney	.15
46	Ruben Rivera	.15
47	Greg Maddux	1.00
48	Corey Koskie	.15
49	Sandy Alomar Jr.	.15
50	Mike Mussina	.40
51	Tom Glavine	.40
52	Aaron Boone	.15
53	Frank Thomas	.75
54	Kenny Lofton	.15
55	Danny Graves	.15
56	Jose Valentin	.15
57	Travis Lee	.15
58	Jim Edmonds	.15
59	Jim Thome	.25
60	Steve Finley	.15
61	Shawn Green	.45
62	Lance Berkman	.40
63	Mark Quinn	.15
64	Randy Johnson	.75
65	Dmitri Young	.15
66	Andy Pettitte	.40
67	Paul O'Neill	.15
68	Gil Heredia	.15
69	Russell Branyan	.15
70	Alex Rodriguez	1.50
71	Geoff Jenkins	.15
72	Eric Chavez	.25
73	Cal Ripken Jr.	2.00
74	Mark Kotsay	.15
75	Jeff D'Amico	.15
76	Tony Womack	.15
77	Eric Milton	.15
78	Joe Girardi	.15
79	Peter Bergeron	.15
80	Miguel Tejada	.50
81	Luis Gonzalez	.25
82	Doug Glanville	.15
83	Gerald Williams	.15
84	Troy O'Leary	.15
85	Brian Giles	.15
86	Miguel Cairo	.15
87	Magglio Ordonez	.40
88	Rick Helling	.15
89	Bruce Chen	.15
90	Jason Varitek	.15
91	Mike Lieberthal	.15
92	Shawn Estes	.15
93	Rick Ankiel	.25
94	Tim Salmon	.25
95	Jacque Jones	.15
96	Johnny Damon	.50
97	Larry Walker	.15
98	Ruben Mateo	.15
99	Brad Fullmer	.15
100	Edgardo Alfonzo	.15
101	Mark Mulder	.15
102	Tony Gwynn	1.00
103	Mike Cameron	.15
104	Richie Sexson	.15
105	Barry Larkin	.25
106	Mike Piazza	1.00
107	Eric Young	.15
108	Edgar Renteria	.15
109	Todd Zeile	.15
110	Luis Castillo	.15
111	Sammy Sosa	1.00
112	David Justice	.15
113	Delino DeShields	.15
114	Mariano Rivera	.40
115	Edgar Martinez	.15
116	Ray Durham	.15
117	Brady Anderson	.15
118	Eric Owens	.15
119	Alex Gonzalez	.15
120	Jay Buhner	.15
121	Greg Vaughn	.15
122	Mike Lowell	.25
123	Marquis Grissom	.15
124	Matt Williams	.15
125	Dean Palmer	.15
126	Troy Glaus	.40
127	Bret Boone	.15
128	David Ortiz	.75
129	Glenallen Hill	.15
130	Chipper Jones	1.00
131	Tony Clark	.15
132	Terrence Long	.15
133	Chuck Finley	.15
134	Jeff Bagwell	.75
135	J.T. Snow	.15
136	Andruw Jones	.50
137	Carlos Delgado	.50
138	Mo Vaughn	.15
139	Derrek Lee	.40
140	Bobby Estalella	.15
141	Kerry Wood	.50
142	Jose Vidro	.15
143	Ben Grieve	.15
144	Barry Bonds	2.00
145	Javy Lopez	.15
146	Adam Kennedy	.15
147	Jeff Cirillo	.15
148	Cliff Floyd	.15
149	Carl Pavano	.25
150	Bobby Higginson	.15
151	Kevin Brown	.15
152	Fernando Tatis	.15
153	Matt Lawton	.15
154	Damion Easley	.15
155	Curt Schilling	.40
156	Mark McGwire	1.00
157	Mark Grace	.40
158	Adrian Beltre	.40
159	Jorge Posada	.40
160	Richard Hidalgo	.15
161	Vinny Castilla	.15
162	Bernie Williams	.40
163	John Olerud	.15
164	Todd Helton	.75
165	Craig Biggio	.25
166	David Wells	.15
167	Phil Nevin	.15
168	Andres Galarraga	.15
169	Moises Alou	.25
170	Denny Neagle	.15
171	Jeffrey Hammonds	.15
172	Sean Casey	.30
173	Gary Sheffield	.40
174	Carlos Lee	.25
175	Juan Encarnacion	.15
176	Roberto Alomar	.40
177	Kenny Rogers	.15
178	Charles Johnson	.15
179	Shannon Stewart	.15
180	B.J. Surhoff	.15
181	Paul Konerko	.25
182	Jermaine Dye	.15
183	Scott Rolen	.50
184	Fred McGriff	.15
185	Juan Gonzalez	.40
186	Carlos Beltran	.40
187	Jay Payton	.15
188	Chad Hermansen	.15
189	Pat Burrell	.50
190	Omar Vizquel	.15
191	Trot Nixon	.15
192	Mike Hampton	.15
193	Kris Benson	.15
194	Gabe Kapler	.15
195	Rickey Henderson	.75
196	J.D. Drew	.45
197	Pokey Reese	.15
198	Jeff Kent	.15
199	Jose Cruz Jr.	.15
200	Preston Wilson	.15
201	Eric Munson 2,499	3.00
202	Alex Cabrera 2,499	3.00
203	Nate Rolison 2,499	3.00
204	Julio Zuleta 2,499	3.00
205	Chris Richard 2,499	3.00
206	Dernell Stenson 2,499	3.00
207	Aaron McNeal 2,499	3.00
208	Aubrey Huff 2,999	5.00
209	Mike Lamb 2,999	3.00
210	Xavier Nady 2,999	4.00
211	Joe Crede 2,999	4.00
212	Ben Petrick 3,499	3.00
213	Morgan Burkhart 3,499	3.00
214	Jason Tyner 1,999	3.00
215	Juan Pierre 1,999	5.00
216	Adam Dunn 1,999	5.00
117	Adam Piatt 1,999	3.00
218	Eric Byrnes 1,999	4.00
219	Corey Patterson 1,999	4.00
220	Kenny Kelly 1,999	3.00
221	Tike Redman 1,999	3.00
222	Luis Matos 1,999	3.00
223	Timoniel Perez 1,999	3.00
224	Vernon Wells 1,999	3.00
225	Barry Zito 4,999	4.00
226	Adam Bernero 4,999	3.00
227	Kazuhiro Sasaki 4,999	3.00
228	Oswaldo Mairena 4,999	3.00
229	Mark Buehrle 4,999	4.00
230	Ryan Dempster 4,999	3.00
231	Tim Hudson 4,999	5.00
232	Scott Downs 4,999	3.00
233	A.J. Burnett 4,999	4.00
234	Adam Eaton 4,999	3.00
235	Paxton Crawford 4,999	3.00
236	Jace Brewer 3,999	3.00
237	Jose Ortiz 3,999	3.00
238	Rafael Furcal 3,999	4.00
239	Julio Lugo 3,999	3.00
240	Tomas de la Rosa 3,999	3.00

Green

Focus
RAY DURHAM
CHICAGO WHITE SOX
SECOND BASE

	NM/M
Common Player:	1.00

Random inserts in packs.
Stated print runs listed below.

1	Derek Jeter/339	10.00
2	Manny Ramirez/351	4.00
3	Ken Griffey Jr./271	8.00
4	Ken Caminiti/303	1.00
5	Joe Randa/304	1.00
6	Jason Kendall/270	1.50
7	Ron Coomer/270	1.00
8	Rondell White/258	1.50
9	Tino Martinez/258	2.00
10	Nomar Garciaparra/372	10.00
11	Tony Batista/263	1.00
12	Todd Stottlemyre/491	1.00
13	Ryan Klesko/283	1.50
14	Darin Erstad/355	1.50
15	Todd Walker/290	1.00
16	Al Leiter/320	1.00
17	Carl Everett/300	1.00
18	Bobby Abreu/316	1.50
19	Raul Mondesi/271	1.00
20	Vladimir Guerrero/345	5.00
21	Mike Bordick/285	1.00
22	Aaron Sele/451	1.00
23	Ray Lankford/253	1.00
24	Roger Clemens/370	10.00
25	Kevin Young/258	1.00
26	Brad Radke/445	1.00
27	Todd Hundley/284	1.00
28	Ellis Burks/344	1.00
29	Lee Stevens/265	1.00
30	Eric Karros/250	1.00
31	Darren Dreifort/416	1.00
32	Ivan Rodriguez/347	4.00
33	Pedro Martinez/174	5.00
34	Travis Fryman/321	1.50
35	Garret Anderson/286	2.00
36	Rafael Palmeiro/288	3.00
37	Jason Giambi/333	5.00
38	Jeromy Burnitz/232	1.00
39	Robin Ventura/232	1.50
40	Derek Bell/266	1.00
41	Carlos Guillen/257	1.00
42	Albert Belle/281	1.00
43	Henry Rodriguez/256	1.00
44	Brian Jordan/264	1.00
45	Mike Sweeney/333	1.00
46	Ruben Rivera/208	1.00
47	Greg Maddux/300	8.00
48	Corey Koskie/300	1.00
49	Sandy Alomar Jr./289	1.00
50	Mike Mussina/379	3.00
51	Tom Glavine/340	2.00
52	Aaron Boone/285	1.00
53	Frank Thomas/328	4.00
54	Kenny Lofton/278	2.00
55	Danny Graves/256	1.00
56	Jose Valentin/273	1.00
57	Travis Lee/235	1.00
58	Jim Edmonds/295	2.00
59	Jim Thome/269	4.00
60	Steve Finley/280	1.00
61	Shawn Green/269	2.00
62	Lance Berkman/297	2.00
63	Mark Quinn/294	1.00
64	Randy Johnson/264	5.00
65	Dmitri Young/303	1.00
66	Andy Pettitte/435	2.00
67	Paul O'Neill/283	2.00
68	Gil Heredia/412	1.00
69	Russell Branyan/238	1.00
70	Alex Rodriguez/316	10.00
71	Geoff Jenkins/303	1.50
72	Eric Chavez/277	2.00
73	Cal Ripken Jr./256	15.00
74	Mark Kotsay/298	1.00
75	Jeff D'Amico/266	1.00
76	Tony Womack/271	1.00
77	Eric Milton/486	1.00
78	Joe Girardi/278	1.00
79	Peter Bergeron/245	1.00
80	Miguel Tejada/275	2.00
81	Luis Gonzalez/311	2.00
82	Doug Glanville/275	1.00
83	Gerald Williams/274	1.00
84	Troy O'Leary/261	1.00
85	Brian Giles/315	2.00
86	Miguel Cairo/261	1.00
87	Magglio Ordonez/315	2.00
88	Rick Helling/448	1.00
89	Bruce Chen/329	1.00
90	Jason Varitek/248	1.00
91	Mike Lieberthal/278	1.00
92	Shawn Estes/426	1.00
93	Rick Ankiel/350	1.00
94	Tim Salmon/290	2.00
95	Jacque Jones/285	1.00
96	Johnny Damon/327	1.50
97	Larry Walker/309	2.00
98	Ruben Mateo/291	1.00
99	Brad Fullmer/295	1.00
100	Edgardo Alfonzo/324	1.00
101	Mark Mulder/544	2.00
102	Tony Gwynn/323	5.00
103	Mike Cameron/267	1.00
104	Richie Sexson/272	2.00
105	Barry Larkin/313	2.00
106	Mike Piazza/324	8.00
107	Eric Young/297	1.00
108	Edgar Renteria/278	1.00
109	Todd Zeile/268	1.00
110	Luis Castillo/334	1.00
111	Sammy Sosa/320	10.00
112	David Justice/286	1.50
113	Delino DeShields/296	1.00
114	Mariano Rivera/285	1.50
115	Edgar Martinez/324	2.00
116	Ray Durham/280	1.00
117	Brady Anderson/257	1.00
118	Eric Owens/293	1.00
119	Alex Gonzalez/252	1.00
120	Jay Buhner/253	1.00
121	Greg Vaughn/254	1.00
122	Mike Lowell/270	1.00
123	Marquis Grissom/244	1.00
124	Matt Williams/275	1.50
125	Dean Palmer/256	1.00
126	Troy Glaus/284	3.00
127	Bret Boone/251	1.50
128	David Ortiz/282	1.00
129	Glenallen Hill/293	1.00
130	Chipper Jones/311	8.00
131	Tony Clark/274	1.00
132	Terrence Long/288	1.00
133	Chuck Finley/417	1.00
134	Jeff Bagwell/310	4.00
135	J.T. Snow/284	1.00
136	Andruw Jones/303	3.00
137	Carlos Delgado/344	3.00
138	Mo Vaughn/272	1.50
139	Derek Lee/281	1.50
140	Bobby Estalella/234	1.00
141	Kerry Wood/480	3.00
142	Jose Vidro/330	1.00
143	Ben Grieve/279	1.00
144	Barry Bonds/306	12.00
145	Javy Lopez/287	2.00
146	Adam Kennedy/266	1.00
147	Jeff Cirillo/326	1.00
148	Cliff Floyd/300	1.00
149	Carl Pavano/306	1.00
150	Bobby Higginson/300	1.00
151	Kevin Brown/258	2.00
152	Fernando Tatis/253	1.00
153	Matt Lawton/305	1.00
154	Damion Easley/259	1.00
155	Curt Schilling/381	3.00
156	Mark McGwire/305	10.00
157	Mark Grace/280	2.50
158	Adrian Beltre/290	1.50
159	Jorge Posada/287	2.00
160	Richard Hidalgo/314	1.00
161	Vinny Castilla/221	1.00
162	Bernie Williams/307	3.00
163	John Olerud/285	1.50
164	Todd Helton/372	4.00
165	Craig Biggio/268	1.50
166	David Wells/411	1.00
167	Phil Nevin/303	1.00
168	Andres Galarraga/302	1.00
169	Moises Alou/355	2.00
170	Denny Neagle/452	1.00
171	Jeffrey Hammonds/335	1.00
172	Sean Casey/315	1.00
173	Gary Sheffield/325	2.00
174	Carlos Lee/301	1.00
175	Juan Encarnacion/289	1.00
176	Roberto Alomar/310	3.00
177	Kenny Rogers/455	1.00
178	Charles Johnson/304	1.00
179	Shannon Stewart/319	1.00
180	B.J. Surhoff/291	1.00
181	Paul Konerko/298	1.00
182	Jermaine Dye/321	1.00
183	Scott Rolen/298	4.00
184	Fred McGriff/277	2.00
185	Juan Gonzalez/289	4.00
186	Carlos Beltran/247	1.50
187	Jay Payton/291	1.50
188	Chad Hermansen/185	1.00
189	Pat Burrell/260	3.00
190	Omar Vizquel/287	2.00
191	Trot Nixon/276	1.00
192	Mike Hampton/314	1.00
193	Kris Benson/385	1.00
194	Gabe Kapler/302	1.00
195	Rickey Henderson/233	3.00
196	J.D. Drew/295	2.00
197	Pokey Reese/255	1.00
198	Jeff Kent/334	1.50
199	Jose Cruz Jr./242	1.00
200	Preston Wilson/264	1.00
201	Eric Munson/252	1.00
202	Alex Cabrera/263	1.00
203	Nate Rolison/77	1.00
204	Julio Zuleta/294	1.00
205	Chris Richard/265	1.00
206	Dernell Stenson/268	1.00
207	Aaron McNeal/310	1.00
208	Aubrey Huff/287	1.00
209	Mike Lamb/278	1.00
211	Joe Crede/357	2.00
212	Ben Petrick/322	1.00
213	Morgan Burkhart/288	1.00
214	Jason Tyner/226	1.00
215	Juan Pierre/310	3.00
216	Adam Dunn/281	4.00
217	Adam Piatt/299	1.00
218	Eric Byrnes/300	1.00
219	Corey Patterson/167	2.00
220	Kenny Kelly/252	1.00
221	Tike Redman/333	1.00
222	Luis Matos/225	1.00
223	Timo Perez/286	1.00
224	Vernon Wells/243	2.00
225	Barry Zito/272	3.00
226	Adam Bernero/419	1.00
227	Kazuhiro Sasaki/316	2.00
228	Oswaldo Mairena/18	5.00
229	Mark Buehrle/421	1.50
230	Ryan Dempster/366	1.00

231	Tim Hudson/414	2.00
232	Scott Downs/529	1.00
233	A.J. Burnett/479	1.00
234	Adam Eaton/413	1.00
235	Paxton Crawford/341	1.00
237	Jose Ortiz/182	1.00
238	Rafael Furcal/295	2.00
239	Julio Lugo/283	1.00
240	Tomas De La Rosa/288	1.00

Autographics

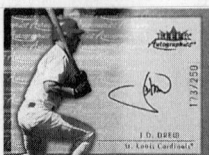

	NM/M
Common Player:	5.00
Inserted 1:72	
Silvers:	1-1.5X
Production 250 Sets	
Golds:	1-1.5X
Production 50 Sets	
Roberto Alomar	30.00
Rick Ankiel	20.00
Albert Belle	5.00
Adrian Beltre	15.00
Lance Berkman	25.00
Barry Bonds	150.00
Jeromy Burnitz	5.00
Pat Burrell	10.00
Sean Casey	8.00
Eric Chavez	10.00
Carlos Delgado	10.00
J.D. Drew	10.00
Jermaine Dye	5.00
Jim Edmonds	10.00
Troy Glaus	15.00
Ben Grieve	5.00
Tony Gwynn	30.00
Randy Johnson	40.00
Chipper Jones	50.00
Mike Lamb	5.00
Mike Lieberthal	5.00
Terrence Long	5.00
Greg Maddux	75.00
Edgar Martinez	15.00
Kevin Millwood	10.00
Mike Mussina	25.00
Corey Patterson	10.00
Jay Payton	8.00
Juan Pierre	8.00
Brad Radke	5.00
Scott Rolen	20.00
Gary Sheffield	15.00
Fernando Tatis	5.00
Robin Ventura	5.00
Kerry Wood	20.00

Bat Company

		NM/M
Complete Set (10):		25.00
Common Player:		1.00
Inserted 1:24		
1	Barry Bonds	5.00
2	Mark McGwire	4.00
3	Sammy Sosa	3.00
4	Ken Griffey Jr.	3.00
5	Mike Piazza	3.00
6	Derek Jeter	5.00
7	Gary Sheffield	1.00
8	Frank Thomas	1.50
9	Chipper Jones	2.00
10	Alex Rodriguez	4.00

Big Innings

	NM/M
Complete Set (25):	15.00
Common Player:	.50
Inserted 1:6	
VIP:	5-10X
Production 50 Sets	

1	Rick Ankiel	.50
2	Andruw Jones	1.00
3	Brian Giles	.50
4	Derek Jeter	4.00
5	Rafael Furcal	.50
6	Richie Sexson	.50
7	Jay Payton	.50
8	Carlos Delgado	.75
9	Jermaine Dye	.50
10	Darin Erstad	.75
11	Pat Burrell	.75
12	Richard Hidalgo	.50
13	Adrian Beltre	.60
14	Todd Helton	1.00
15	Vladimir Guerrero	1.00
16	Nomar Garciaparra	2.00
17	Gabe Kapler	.50
18	Carlos Lee	.50
19	J.D. Drew	.60
20	Troy Glaus	1.00
21	Scott Rolen	1.00
22	Alex Rodriguez	3.00
23	Magglio Ordonez	.60
24	Miguel Tejada	.60
25	Ruben Mateo	.50

Diamond Vision

		NM/M
Complete Set (15):		25.00
Common Player:		1.00
Inserted 1:12		
1	Derek Jeter	4.00
2	Nomar Garciaparra	2.50
3	Cal Ripken Jr.	4.00
4	Jeff Bagwell	1.50
5	Mark McGwire	3.00
6	Ken Griffey Jr.	2.50
7	Pedro Martinez	1.50
8	Carlos Delgado	1.00
9	Chipper Jones	2.00
10	Barry Bonds	4.00
11	Mike Piazza	2.50
12	Sammy Sosa	2.50
13	Alex Rodriguez	3.00
14	Frank Thomas	1.50
15	Randy Johnson	1.50

Feel the Game

	NM/M
Common Player:	5.00
Inserted 1:72	
Moises Alou	6.00
Brady Anderson	5.00
Dante Bichette	5.00
Jermaine Dye	5.00
Brian Giles	5.00
Juan Gonzalez	8.00
Rickey Henderson	15.00
Javy Lopez	5.00
Tino Martinez	6.00
Phil Nevin	5.00
Matt Stairs	5.00
Shannon Stewart	5.00
Jose Vidro	5.00

ROY Collection

		NM/M
Complete Set (25):		75.00
Common Player:		2.00
Inserted 1:24		
1	Luis Aparicio	2.00
2	Johnny Bench	3.00
3	Joe Black	2.00
4	Rod Carew	2.00
5	Orlando Cepeda	2.00
6	Carlton Fisk	2.00
7	Ben Grieve	2.00
8	Frank Howard	2.00
9	Derek Jeter	10.00
10	Fred Lynn	3.00
11	Willie Mays	8.00
12	Willie McCovey	2.00
13	Mark McGwire	8.00
14	Raul Mondesi	2.00
15	Thurman Munson	4.00
16	Eddie Murray	2.00
17	Mike Piazza	6.00
18	Cal Ripken Jr.	10.00
19	Frank Robinson	2.00
20	Jackie Robinson	8.00
21	Scott Rolen	3.00
22	Tom Seaver	2.00
23	Fernando Valenzuela	2.00
24	David Justice	2.00
25	Billy Williams	2.00

ROY Collection Memorabilia

		NM/M
Common Player:		8.00
Inserted 1:288		
1	Luis Aparicio/Bat	8.00
2	Johnny Bench/Jsy	15.00
3	Orlando Cepeda/Bat	8.00
4	Carlton Fisk/Bat	10.00
5	Ben Grieve/Jsy	8.00
6	Frank Howard/Bat	8.00
7	Derek Jeter/Jsy	50.00
8	Fred Lynn/Bat	8.00
9	Willie Mays/Jsy	60.00
10	Willie McCovey/Bat	10.00
11	Mark McGwire/Ball	50.00
12	Raul Mondesi/Bat	8.00
13	Thurman Munson/Bat	30.00
14	Eddie Murray/Jsy	10.00
15	Mike Piazza/Base	15.00
16	Cal Ripken/Jsy	50.00
17	Frank Robinson/Jsy	10.00
18	Jackie Robinson/Jsy	60.00
19	Scott Rolen/Jsy	15.00
20	Tom Seaver/Jsy	15.00
22	David Justice/Jsy	8.00

ROY Collection Signed Mem.

		NM/M
Common Player:		25.00
1	Luis Aparicio/Jsy/56	40.00
2	Johnny Bench/68	85.00
3	Orlando Cepeda/58	30.00
4	Carlton Fisk/72	50.00
5	Ben Grieve/98	25.00
6	Frank Howard/60	25.00
7	Derek Jeter/96	200.00
8	Fred Lynn/75	25.00
9	Willie Mays/Jsy/51	200.00
10	Willie McCovey/Bat/59	40.00
11	Raul Mondesi/94	25.00
12	Eddie Murray/77	50.00
13	Cal Ripken/82	250.00
14	Frank Robinson/Bat/225	50.00
15	Scott Rolen/97	50.00
16	Tom Seaver/67	90.00
18	David Justice/90	25.00

2001 Fleer Futures

Pedro Martinez • Boston Red Sox • 45

		NM/M
Complete Set (220):		20.00
Common Player:		.15
Pack (8):		1.50
Box (28):		30.00
1	Darin Erstad	.40
2	Manny Ramirez	.75
3	Troy O'Leary	.15
4	Darryl Kile	.15
5	Mark Quinn	.15
6	Brian Giles	.15
7	Randy Johnson	.75
8	Todd Walker	.15
9	Mike Piazza	1.50
10	Fred McGriff	.15
11	Sammy Sosa	1.00
12	Chan Ho Park	.15
13	John Rocker	.15
14	Luis Castillo	.15
15	Eric Chavez	.25
16	Carlos Delgado	.50
17	Sean Casey	.25
18	Corey Koskie	.15
19	John Olerud	.15
20	Nomar Garciaparra	.50
21	Craig Biggio	.25
22	Pat Burrell	.40
23	Bengie Molina	.15
24	Jim Thome	.50
25	Rey Ordonez	.15
26	Fernando Tatis	.15
27	Eric Young	.15
28	Eric Karros	.15
29	Adam Eaton	.15
30	Brian Jordan	.15
31	Jorge Posada	.25
32	Gabe Kapler	.15
33	Keith Foulke	.15
34	Ron Coomer	.15
35	Chipper Jones	1.00
36	Miguel Tejada	.25
37	David Wells	.15
38	Carlos Lee	.15
39	Barry Bonds	2.00
40	Derrek Lee	.15
41	Tim Hudson	.25
42	Billy Koch	.15
43	Dmitri Young	.15
44	Vladimir Guerrero	.75
45	Rickey Henderson	.75
46	Jeff Bagwell	.75
47	Robert Person	.15
48	Brady Anderson	.15
49	Lance Berkman	.15
50	Mike Lieberthal	.15
51	Adam Kennedy	.15
52	Russ Branyan	.15
53	Robin Ventura	.15
54	Mark McGwire	2.00
55	Tony Gwynn	1.00
56	Matt Williams	.15
57	Jeff Cirillo	.15
58	Roger Clemens	1.25
59	Ivan Rodriguez	.50
60	Brad Radke	.15
61	Kazuhiro Sasaki	.15
62	Cal Ripken Jr.	2.50
63	Ken Caminiti	.15
64	Bobby Abreu	.15
65	Troy Glaus	.50
66	Sandy Alomar Jr.	.15
67	Jose Vidro	.15
68	Pedro Martinez	.75
69	Kevin Young	.15
70	Jay Bell	.15
71	Larry Walker	.15
72	Derek Jeter	2.50
73	Miguel Cairo	.15
74	Magglio Ordonez	.15
75	Jeromy Burnitz	.15
76	J.T. Snow	.15
77	Andres Galarraga	.15
78	Ryan Dempster	.15
79	Ken Griffey Jr.	1.50
80	Aaron Sele	.15
81	Tom Glavine	.25
82	Hideo Nomo	.50
83	Orlando Hernandez	.15
84	Tony Batista	.15
85	Aaron Boone	.15
86	Jacque Jones	.15
87	Delino DeShields	.15
88	Garret Anderson	.15
89	Fernando Seguignol	.15
90	Jim Edmonds	.15
91	Frank Thomas	.75
92	Adrian Beltre	.30
93	Ellis Burks	.15
94	Andruw Jones	.50
95	Tony Clark	.15
96	Danny Graves	.15
97	Alex Rodriguez	2.00
98	Mike Mussina	.40
99	Scott Elarton	.15
100	Jason Giambi	.50
101	Jay Payton	.15
102	Gerald Williams	.15
103	Kerry Wood	.50
104	Shawn Green	.35
105	Greg Maddux	1.00
106	Juan Encarnacion	.15
107	Bernie Williams	.30
108	Mike Lamb	.15
109	Charles Johnson	.15
110	Richie Sexson	.15
111	Jeff Kent	.15
112	Albert Belle	.15

113	Cliff Floyd	.15
114	Ben Grieve	.15
115	Tim Salmon	.25
116	Carl Pavano	.15
117	Rick Ankiel	.25
118	Dante Bichette	.15
119	Johnny Damon	.30
120	Brian Anderson	.15
121	Roberto Alomar	.40
122	Mike Hampton	.15
123	Greg Vaughn	.15
124	Carl Everett	.15
125	Moises Alou	.15
126	Jason Kendall	.15
127	Omar Vizquel	.15
128	Mark Grace	.25
129	Kevin Brown	.15
130	Phil Nevin	.15
131	Kevin Millwood	.15
132	Bobby Higginson	.15
133	Ruben Mateo	.15
134	Luis Gonzalez	.25
135	Dean Palmer	.15
136	Mariano Rivera	.25
137	Rick Helling	.15
138	Paul Konerko	.15
139	Marquis Grissom	.15
140	Robb Nen	.15
141	Javy Lopez	.15
142	Preston Wilson	.15
143	Terrence Long	.15
144	Shannon Stewart	.15
145	Barry Larkin	.15
146	Cristian Guzman	.15
147	Jay Buhner	.15
148	Jermaine Dye	.15
149	Kris Benson	.15
150	Curt Schilling	.15
151	Todd Helton	.50
152	Paul O'Neill	.50
153	Rafael Palmeiro	.15
154	Ray Durham	.15
155	Geoff Jenkins	.15
156	Livan Hernandez	.15
157	Rafael Furcal	.15
158	Juan Gonzalez	.50
159	Tino Martinez	.15
160	Raul Mondesi	.15
161	Matt Lawton	.15
162	Edgar Martinez	.15
163	Richard Hidalgo	.15
164	Scott Rolen	.50
165	Chuck Finley	.15
166	Edgardo Alfonzo	.15
167	J.D. Drew	.35
168	Trot Nixon	.15
169	Carlos Beltran	.50
170	Ryan Klesko	.15
171	Mo Vaughn	.15
172	Kenny Lofton	.15
173	Al Leiter	.15
174	Rondell White	.15
175	Mike Sweeney	.15
176	Trevor Hoffman	.15
177	Steve Finley	.15
178	Jeffrey Hammonds	.15
179	David Justice	.15
180	Gary Sheffield	.40
181	Eric Munson	.15
182	Luis Matos	.15
183	Alex Cabrera	.15
184	Randy Keisler	.15
185	Nate Rolison	.15
186	Jason Hart	.15
187	Timo Perez	.15
188	Adam Bernero	.15
189	Barry Zito	.50
190	Ryan Kohlmeier	.15
191	Joey Nation	.15
192	Oswaldo Mairena	.15
193	Aubrey Huff	.15
194	Mark Buehrle	.15
195	Jace Brewer	.15
196	Julio Zuleta	.15
197	Xavier Nady	.15
198	Vernon Wells	.25
199	Joe Crede	.15
200	Scott Downs	.15
201	Ben Petrick	.15
202	A.J. Burnett	.15
203	Esix Snead RC	.15
204	Dernell Stenson	.15
205	Jose Ortiz	.15
206	Paxton Crawford	.15
207	Jason Tyner	.15
208	Jimmy Rollins	.25
209	Juan Pierre	.25
210	Keith Ginter	.15
211	Adam Dunn	.40
212	Larry Barnes	.15
213	Adam Piatt	.15
214	Rodney Lindsey	.15
215	Eric Byrnes	.15
216	Julio Lugo	.15
217	Corey Patterson	.25
218	Reggie Taylor	.15
219	Kenny Kelly	.15
220	Tike Redman	.15

Black Gold

Production 499 Sets: 3-6X
(See 2001 Fleer Futures for checklist
and base card values.)

Bases Loaded

		NM/M
Common Player:		4.00
Inserted 1:134		
BL1	Ken Griffey Jr.	10.00
BL2	Mark McGwire	12.00
BL3	Carlos Delgado	4.00
BL4	Chipper Jones	7.50
BL5	Nomar Garciaparra	10.00
BL6	Cal Ripken Jr.	15.00
BL7	Sammy Sosa	10.00
BL8	Jeff Bagwell	6.00
BL9	Vladimir Guerrero	6.00
BL10	Tony Gwynn	7.50
BL11	Frank Thomas	6.00
BL12	Mike Piazza	10.00
BL13	Jason Giambi	5.00
BL14	Troy Glaus	6.00
BL15	Pat Burrell	4.00

Bats to the Future

		NM/M
Complete Set (25):		60.00
Common Player:		1.00
Inserted 1:28		
1BF	Mike Schmidt	6.00
2BF	Carlton Fisk	3.00
3BF	Paul Molitor	3.00
4BF	Vladimir Guerrero	3.00
5BF	Dave Parker	1.00
6BF	Chipper Jones	5.00
7BF	Carlos Delgado	2.00
8BF	Tony Gwynn	5.00
9BF	Reggie Jackson	5.00
10BF	Eddie Murray	1.50
11BF	Robin Yount	3.00
12BF	Alan Trammell	1.00
13BF	Frank Thomas	3.00
14BF	Cal Ripken Jr.	6.00
15BF	Don Mattingly	6.00
16BF	Jim Rice	1.00
17BF	Juan Gonzalez	3.00
18BF	Todd Helton	3.00
19BF	George Brett	6.00
20BF	Barry Bonds	8.00
21BF	Kirk Gibson	1.00
22BF	Matt Williams	1.00
23BF	Dave Winfield	1.50
24BF	Ryne Sandberg	3.00
25BF	Ivan Rodriguez	2.00

Bats to the Future Game Bat

		NM/M
Common Player:		5.00
Inserted 1:114		
1BF	Mike Schmidt	25.00
2BF	Carlton Fisk	10.00
3BF	Paul Molitor	15.00
4BF	Vladimir Guerrero	8.00
5BF	Dave Parker	5.00
6BF	Chipper Jones	10.00
7BF	Chris Delgado	8.00
8BF	Tony Gwynn	10.00
9BF	Reggie Jackson	10.00
10BF	Eddie Murray	8.00
11BF	Robin Yount	15.00
12BF	Alan Trammell	5.00
13BF	Frank Thomas	8.00
14BF	Cal Ripken Jr.	30.00
15BF	Don Mattingly	30.00
16BF	Jim Rice	5.00
17BF	Juan Gonzalez	8.00
18BF	Todd Helton	8.00
19BF	George Brett	25.00
20BF	Barry Bonds	25.00
21BF	Kirk Gibson	5.00
22BF	Matt Williams	5.00
23BF	Dave Winfield	8.00
24BF	Ryne Sandberg	15.00
25BF	Ivan Rodriguez	8.00

Bats to the Future Game Bat Autograph

		NM/M
Common Autograph:		40.00
Production 50 Sets		
1BF	Mike Schmidt	150.00
2BF	Carlton Fisk	60.00
3BF	Paul Molitor	50.00
4BF	Vladimir Guerrero	80.00
5BF	Dave Parker	40.00
6BF	Chipper Jones	75.00
7BF	Carlos Delgado	50.00
8BF	Tony Gwynn	75.00
9BF	Reggie Jackson	70.00
10BF	Eddie Murray	70.00
11BF	Robin Yount	80.00
12BF	Alan Trammell	40.00
13BF	Frank Thomas	60.00
14BF	Cal Ripken Jr.	200.00
15BF	Don Mattingly	150.00
16BF	Jim Rice	40.00
17BF	Juan Gonzalez	60.00
18BF	Todd Helton	60.00
19BF	George Brett	150.00
20BF	Barry Bonds	150.00
21BF	Kirk Gibson	40.00
22BF	Matt Williams	40.00
23BF	Dave Winfield	60.00
24BF	Ryne Sandberg	125.00
25BF	Ivan Rodriguez	60.00

Characteristics

		NM/M
Complete Set (15):		20.00
Common Player:		.75
Inserted 1:9		
1C	Derek Jeter	4.00
2C	Mark McGwire	3.00
3C	Nomar Garciaparra	2.50
4C	Sammy Sosa	2.50
5C	Pedro Martinez	1.50
6C	Chipper Jones	2.00
7C	Cal Ripken Jr.	4.00
8C	Todd Helton	1.50
9C	Jim Edmonds	.75
10C	Ken Griffey Jr.	2.50
11C	Alex Rodriguez	3.00
12C	Mike Piazza	2.50
13C	Vladimir Guerrero	1.50
14C	Frank Thomas	1.50
15C	Carlos Delgado	1.00

Hot Commodities

		NM/M
Complete Set (10):		20.00
Common Player:		1.00
Inserted 1:14		
1HC	Mark McGwire	3.00
2HC	Ken Griffey Jr.	2.50
3HC	Derek Jeter	4.00
4HC	Cal Ripken Jr.	4.00
5HC	Chipper Jones	2.00
6HC	Barry Bonds	4.00
7HC	Mike Piazza	2.50
8HC	Sammy Sosa	2.50
9HC	Alex Rodriguez	3.00
10HC	Frank Thomas	1.00

September Call-Ups Memorabilia

		NM/M
Common Card:		4.00
Production 200 Sets		
184	Randy Keisler/Cap/Cleat	4.00
185	Nate Rolison/Bat	4.00
187	Timoniel Perez/Bat	4.00
191	Joey Nation/Glv	4.00
192	Oswaldo Mairena/Glv	4.00
195	Jace Brewer/Bat	4.00
197	Xavier Nady/Glv	6.00
199	Joe Crede/Bat	6.00
205	Jose Ortiz/Bat	6.00
208	Jimmy Rollins/Glv	6.00
210	Keith Ginter/Bat	6.00
214	Rodney Lindsey/Bat	4.00
217	Corey Patterson/Bat	8.00
218	Reggie Taylor/Bat	4.00
219	Kenny Kelly/Bat	4.00

2001 Fleer Game Time

		NM/M
Complete Set (121):		
Common Player:		.15
Common (91-121):		3.00
Production 2,000		
Pack (5):		4.00
Box (24):		80.00
1	Derek Jeter	2.00
2	Nomar Garciaparra	.50

3	Alex Rodriguez	1.50
4	Jason Kendall	.15
5	Barry Bonds	2.00
6	David Wells	.15
7	Craig Biggio	.25
8	Adrian Beltre	.40
9	Pat Burrell	.40
10	Rafael Palmeiro	.50
11	Jim Thome	.25
12	Mike Lowell	.20
13	Trevor Hoffman	.15
14	Pokey Reese	.15
15	Juan Encarnacion	.15
16	Shawn Green	.15
17	Kerry Wood	.50
18	Richard Hidalgo	.15
19	Scott Rolen	.50
20	Jeff Kent	.25
21	Alex Gonzalez	.15
22	Matt Williams	.15
23	Mike Sweeney	.15
24	Edgar Martinez	.15
25	Sammy Sosa	.75
26	Bobby Higginson	.15
27	Kevin Brown	.15
28	Mike Lieberthal	.15
29	Pedro J. Martinez	.75
30	Jeff Weaver	.15
31	Greg Maddux	1.00
32	Mike Hampton	.15
33	Vladimir Guerrero	.75
34	Greg Vaughn	.15
35	Manny Ramirez	.75
36	Carlos Beltran	.40
37	Eric Chavez	.25
38	Troy Glaus	.50
39	Todd Helton	.50
40	Gary Sheffield	.40
41	Brady Anderson	.15
42	Juan Gonzalez	.50
43	Tim Hudson	.40
44	Kenny Lofton	.15
45	Al Leiter	.15
46	Eric Owens	.15
47	Roberto Alomar	.40
48	Preston Wilson	.15
49	Tony Gwynn	1.00
50	Cal Ripken Jr.	2.00
51	Ben Petrick	.15
52	Jason Giambi	.50
53	Ben Grieve	.15
54	Albert Belle	.15
55	Jose Vidro	.15
56	Barry Zito	.25
57	Ivan Rodriguez	.50
58	Jeff Bagwell	.50
59	Geoff Jenkins	.15
60	Roger Clemens	1.00
61	John Olerud	.15
62	Randy Johnson	.75
63	Matt Lawton	.15
64	Mark McGwire	1.50
65	Brad Radke	.15
66	Frank Thomas	.75
67	Edgardo Alfonzo	.15
68	Brian Giles	.15
69	J.T. Snow	.15
70	Carlos Delgado	.50
71	Chipper Jones	1.00
72	Mark Quinn	.15
73	Mike Mussina	.40
74	Rick Ankiel	.50
75	Rafael Furcal	.25
76	Jim Edmonds	.15
77	Vinny Castilla	.15
78	Sean Casey	.25
79	Derek Lee	.15
80	Mike Piazza	1.00
81	Warren Morris	.15
82	Tim Salmon	.25
83	Jeromy Burnitz	.15
84	Freddy Garcia	.15
85	Ken Griffey Jr.	1.00
86	Andruw Jones	.40
87	Darryl Kile	.15
88	Magglio Ordonez	.25
89	Bernie Williams	.15
90	Timo Perez	.15
91	Ichiro Suzuki RC	30.00
92	Larry Barnes, Darin Erstad	3.00
93	Jaisen Randolph RC	3.00
94	Paul Phillips RC	3.00
95	Esix Snead RC	3.00
96	Matt White RC	3.00
97	Ryan Freel RC	3.00
98	Winston Abreu RC	3.00
99	Junior Spivey RC	3.00
100	Randy Keisler, Roger Clemens	5.00
101	Brian Cole, Mike Piazza	4.00
102	Aubrey Huff, Chipper Jones	4.00
103	Corey Patterson, Sammy Sosa	5.00
104	Sun-Woo Kim, Pedro Martinez	4.00
105	Drew Henson RC	4.00
106	Claudio Vargas RC	3.00
107	Cesar Izturis, Rafael Furcal	3.00
108	Paxton Crawford, Pedro Martinez	4.00
109	Adrian Hernandez RC	3.00
110	Jace Brewer, Derek Jeter	3.00
111	Andy Morales RC	3.00
112	Wilson Betemit RC	3.00

113	Juan Diaz RC	3.00
114	Erick Almonte RC	3.00
115	Nick Punto RC	3.00
116	Tsuyoshi Shinjo RC	3.00
117	Jay Gibbons RC	3.00
118	Andres Torres RC	3.00
119	Alexis Gomez RC	3.00
120	Wilken Ruan RC	3.00
121	Albert Pujols RC	60.00

Next Game Extra

Cards (91-121):	2-3X
Production 200 Sets	

(See 2001 Fleer Game Time #91-121 for checklist and base card values.)

Derek Jeter's Monumental Moments

NM/M

Complete Set (2):		
1JM	Derek Jeter/1996	8.00
1JMS	Derek Jeter/Auto./96	80.00

Famers Lumber

NM/M

Common Player:		8.00
Production 100 Sets		
1FL	Luis Aparicio	8.00
2FL	Hank Bauer	8.00
3FL	Paul Blair	8.00
4FL	Bobby Bonds	8.00
5FL	Orlando Cepeda	8.00
6FL	Roberto Clemente	100.00
7FL	Rocky Colavito	10.00
8FL	Bucky Dent	8.00
9FL	Bill Dickey	10.00
10FL	Larry Doby	10.00
11FL	Carlton Fisk	10.00
12FL	Hank Greenberg	25.00
13FL	Elston Howard	8.00
14FL	Frank Howard	8.00
15FL	Reggie Jackson	15.00
16FL	Harmon Killebrew	20.00
17FL	Tony Lazzeri	8.00
18FL	Roger Maris	60.00
19FL	Johnny Mize	10.00
20FL	Thurman Munson	40.00
21FL	Tony Perez	10.00
22FL	Jim Rice	8.00
23FL	Phil Rizzuto	10.00
24FL	Bill Skowron	8.00
25FL	Enos Slaughter	10.00
26FL	Duke Snider	15.00
27FL	Willie Stargell	8.00
28FL	Bill Terry	8.00
29FL	Ted Williams	100.00

Famers Lumber Autograph

NM/M

Common Player:		40.00
Production 25 Sets		
1FLS	Hank Bauer	40.00
2FLS	Bobby Bonds	50.00
3FLS	Orlando Cepeda	50.00
4FLS	Rocky Colavito	50.00
5FLS	Bucky Dent	40.00
6FLS	Larry Doby	50.00
7FLS	Carlton Fisk	65.00
8FLS	Frank Howard	40.00
9FLS	Reggie Jackson	100.00
10FLS	Harmon Killebrew	120.00
11FLS	Tony Perez	40.00
12FLS	Jim Rice	40.00
13FLS	Phil Rizzuto	60.00
14FLS	Bill Skowron	40.00
15FLS	Enos Slaughter	40.00
16FLS	Duke Snider	75.00

Let's Play Two!

NM/M

Complete Set (15):		30.00
Common Player:		1.50
Inserted 1:24		
1LT	Derek Jeter, Nomar Garciaparra	4.00
2LT	Mark McGwire, Sammy Sosa	3.00
3LT	Pedro J. Martinez, Randy Johnson	1.50

4LT	Vladimir Guerrero, Carlos Delgado	1.50
5LT	Mike Piazza, Roger Clemens	2.50
6LT	Alex Rodriguez, Miguel Tejada	3.00
7LT	Troy Glaus, Chipper Jones	2.00
8LT	Derek Jeter, Alex Rodriguez	4.00
9LT	Cal Ripken Jr., Derek Jeter	4.00
10LT	Jason Giambi, Mark McGwire	3.00
11LT	Jeff Bagwell, Craig Biggio	1.50
12LT	Tom Glavine, Greg Maddux	2.00
13LT	Ken Griffey Jr., Barry Bonds	4.00
14LT	Manny Ramirez, Pedro J. Martinez	1.50
15LT	Alex Rodriguez, Ivan Rodriguez	3.00

Lumber

JUAN GONZALEZ (Cleveland Indians)

NM/M

Common Player:		4.00
Inserted 1:40		
1GL	Roberto Alomar	6.00
2GL	Rick Ankiel	6.00
3GL	Adrian Beltre	6.00
4GL	Barry Bonds	25.00
5GL	Kevin Brown	4.00
7GL	Ken Caminiti	4.00
8GL	Eric Chavez	5.00
9GL	Carlos Delgado	5.00
10GL	J.D. Drew	5.00
11GL	Erubiel Durazo	4.00
12GL	Carl Everett	4.00
13GL	Rafael Furcal	4.00
14GL	Brian Giles	5.00
15GL	Juan Gonzalez	6.00
16GL	Todd Helton	8.00
18GL	Randy Johnson	10.00
19GL	Chipper Jones	10.00
20GL	Pedro J. Martinez	10.00
21GL	Tino Martinez	5.00
23GL	Cal Ripken/SP/275	40.00
24GL	Ivan Rodriguez	8.00
25GL	Frank Thomas	8.00
26GL	Jim Thome	8.00
27GL	Bernie Williams	8.00
28GL	Nomar Garciaparra	15.00

New Order

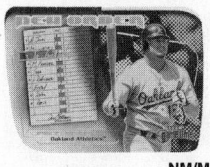

Oakland Athletics

NM/M

Complete Set (15):		30.00
Common Player:		1.50
Inserted 1:12		
1NO	Derek Jeter	6.00
2NO	Nomar Garciaparra	4.00
3NO	Alex Rodriguez	5.00
4NO	Mark McGwire	5.00
5NO	Sammy Sosa	4.00
6NO	Carlos Delgado	1.50
7NO	Troy Glaus	1.50
8NO	Jason Giambi	1.50
9NO	Mike Piazza	4.00
10NO	Todd Helton	1.50
11NO	Vladimir Guerrero	2.00
12NO	Manny Ramirez	1.50
13NO	Frank Thomas	1.50
14NO	Ken Griffey Jr.	4.00
15NO	Chipper Jones	3.00

Sticktoitness

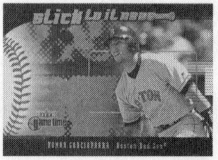

NM/M

Complete Set (20):		15.00
Common Player:		.50
Inserted 1:8		
1S	Derek Jeter	4.00
2S	Nomar Garciaparra	3.00
3S	Alex Rodriguez	3.00

4S	Jeff Bagwell	1.00
5S	Bernie Williams	.50
6S	Eric Chavez	.60
7S	Richard Hidalgo	.50
8S	Ichiro Suzuki	2.00
9S	Troy Glaus	.75
10S	Magglio Ordonez	.50
11S	Corey Patterson	.50
12S	Todd Helton	1.00
13S	Jim Edmonds	.50
14S	Rafael Furcal	.50
15S	Mo Vaughn	.50
16S	Pat Burrell	.65
17S	Adrian Beltre	.60
18S	Andruw Jones	1.00
19S	Manny Ramirez	1.00
20S	Sean Casey	.65

Uniformity

ANDRES GALARRAGA (Texas Rangers)

NM/M

Common Player:		4.00
Inserted 1:25		
1GU	Andres Galarraga	4.00
2GU	Barry Bonds	20.00
3GU	Ben Petrick	4.00
4GU	Brad Radke	4.00
5GU	Brian Jordan	4.00
6GU	Carlos Guillen	4.00
7GU	Fernando Seguignol	4.00
8GU	Fred McGriff	4.00
9GU	Gary Sheffield	5.00
10GU	Greg Maddux	15.00
11GU	Ivan Rodriguez	8.00
12GU	Jay Buhner	4.00
13GU	Jeromy Burnitz	4.00
14GU	John Olerud	4.00
15GU	Kevin Brown	4.00
16GU	Larry Walker	4.00
17GU	Magglio Ordonez	4.00
18GU	Matt Williams	4.00
19GU	Robin Ventura	4.00
20GU	Rondell White	4.00
21GU	Tony Gwynn	15.00
22GU	Troy Glaus	6.00
23GU	Vladimir Guerrero	8.00

2001 Fleer Genuine

Troy Glaus

NM/M

Complete Set (130):		150.00
Common Player:		.25
Common (101-130):		3.00
Production 1,500		
Pack (5):		3.00
Box (24):		60.00
1	Derek Jeter	3.00
2	Nomar Garciaparra	.75
3	Alex Rodriguez	2.50
4	Frank Thomas	1.00
5	Travis Fryman	.25
6	Gary Sheffield	.40
7	Jason Giambi	.75
8	Trevor Hoffman	.25
9	Todd Helton	.75
10	Ivan Rodriguez	.75
11	Roberto Alomar	.40
12	Barry Zito	.40
13	Kevin Brown	.25
14	Shawn Green	.40
15	Kenny Lofton	.25
16	Jeff Weaver	.25
17	Geoff Jenkins	.25
18	Carlos Delgado	.50
19	Mark Grace	.40
20	Ken Griffey Jr.	2.00
21	David Justice	.25
22	Brian Giles	.25
23	Scott Williamson	.25
24	Richie Sexson	.25

25	John Olerud	.25
26	Sammy Sosa	1.00
27	Bobby Higginson	.25
28	Matt Lawton	.25
29	Vinny Castilla	.25
30	Alex S. Gonzalez	.25
31	Manny Ramirez	1.00
32	Brad Radke	.25
33	Cal Ripken Jr.	3.00
34	Richard Hidalgo	.25
35	Al Leiter	.25
36	Freddy Garcia	.25
37	Juan Encarnacion	.25
38	Corey Koskie	.25
39	Greg Vaughn	.25
40	Rafael Palmeiro	.50
41	Vladimir Guerrero	1.00
42	Troy Glaus	.50
43	Mike Hampton	.25
44	Jose Vidro	.25
45	Ryan Rupe	.25
46	Troy O'Leary	.25
47	Ben Petrick	.25
48	Mike Lieberthal	.25
49	Mike Sweeney	.25
50	Scott Rolen	.50
51	Albert Belle	.25
52	Mark Quinn	.25
53	Mike Piazza	1.50
54	Mark McGwire	1.50
55	Brady Anderson	.25
56	Carlos Beltran	.45
57	Michael Barrett	.25
58	Jason Kendall	.25
59	Jim Edmonds	.25
60	Matt Williams	.25
61	Pokey Reese	.25
62	Bernie Williams	.40
63	Barry Bonds	3.00
64	David Wells	.25
65	Chipper Jones	1.50
66	Jim Parque	.25
67	Derek Lee	.50
68	Darin Erstad	.40
69	Edgar Martinez	.25
70	Kerry Wood	.50
71	Omar Vizquel	.25
72	Jeromy Burnitz	.25
73	Warren Morris	.25
74	Rick Ankiel	.50
75	Andruw Jones	.50
76	Paul Konerko	.40
77	Mike Lowell	.40
78	Roger Clemens	1.50
79	Tim Hudson	.40
80	Rafael Furcal	.40
81	Craig Biggio	.40
82	Edgardo Alfonzo	.25
83	Pat Burrell	.50
84	Adrian Beltre	.40
85	Tony Gwynn	1.50
86	J.T. Snow	.25
87	Randy Johnson	1.00
88	Sean Casey	.25
89	Preston Wilson	.25
90	Mike Mussina	.50
91	Eric Chavez	.25
92	Tim Salmon	.25
93	Pedro Martinez	1.00
94	Darryl Kile	.25
95	Greg Maddux	1.50
96	Magglio Ordonez	.40
97	Jeff Bagwell	.50
98	Timo Perez	.25
99	Jeff Kent	.40
100	Eric Owens	.25
101	Ichiro Suzuki RC	30.00
102	Elpidio Guzman RC	3.00
103	Tsuyoshi Shinjo RC	3.00
104	Travis Hafner RC	8.00
105	Larry Barnes RC	3.00
106	Jaisen Randolph RC	3.00
107	Paul Phillips RC	3.00
108	Erick Almonte RC	3.00
109	Nick Punto RC	3.00
110	Jack Wilson RC	3.00
111	Jeremy Owens RC	3.00
112	Esix Snead RC	3.00
113	Jay Gibbons RC	3.00
114	Adrian Hernandez RC	3.00
115	Matt White RC	3.00
116	Ryan Freel RC	5.00
117	Martin Vargas RC	3.00
118	Winston Abreu RC	3.00
119	Junior Spivey RC	3.00
120	Paxton Crawford	3.00
121	Randy Keisler	3.00
122	Juan Diaz RC	3.00
123	Aaron Rowand	4.00
124	Toby Hall	3.00
125	Brian Cole	3.00
126	Aubrey Huff	4.00
127	Corey Patterson	4.00
128	Sun-Woo Kim	3.00
129	Jace Brewer	3.00
130	Cesar Izturis	3.00

Final Cut

	NM/M
Common Player:	4.00
Inserted 1:30	
Miguel Tejada/SP/170	6.00
Barry Bonds/SP/330	30.00
Robin Ventura	4.00
Greg Maddux	15.00

Andruw Jones/SP/135	10.00
J.D. Drew/SP/75	10.00
Chipper Jones	10.00
Tim Salmon	4.00
Edgar Martinez/SP/130	8.00
Troy Glaus	8.00
Frank Thomas	8.00
Pokey Reese	4.00
Larry Walker	4.00
Ivan Rodriguez/120	10.00
Scott Rolen	8.00
Cal Ripken Jr.	30.00
Tony Gwynn	10.00
Wade Boggs	8.00
George Brett	30.00
Sean Casey	4.00
Bob Gibson	6.00
Matt Williams	6.00
Robin Yount	6.00
Ron Guidry	4.00
(Not officially released.)	150.00
Reggie Jackson	
(Not officially released.)	250.00
Don Larsen	
(Not officially released.)	140.00

Genuine Coverage PLUS

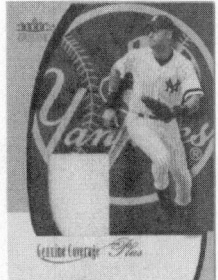

	NM/M
Common Player:	5.00
Production 150 Sets	
Troy Glaus	5.00
Randy Johnson	10.00
Andruw Jones	5.00
Frank Thomas	8.00
Darin Erstad	5.00
Chipper Jones	15.00
Derek Jeter	25.00
Tony Gwynn	15.00
Barry Bonds	25.00
Cal Ripken Jr.	25.00

High Interest

	NM/M
Complete Set (15):	25.00
Common Player:	1.50
Inserted 1:23	
1HI Derek Jeter	6.00
2HI Nomar Garciaparra	1.50
3HI Greg Maddux	3.00
4HI Todd Helton	2.00
5HI Sammy Sosa	2.50
6HI Jeff Bagwell	1.50
7HI Jason Giambi	1.50
8HI Frank Thomas	2.00
9HI Andruw Jones	1.50
10HI Jim Edmonds	1.50
11HI Bernie Williams	1.50
12HI Randy Johnson	2.00
13HI Ken Griffey Jr.	4.00
14HI Pedro Martinez	2.00
15HI Mark McGwire	4.00

Material Issue

	NM/M
Common Player:	5.00
Inserted 1:30	
Randy Johnson	10.00
Scott Rolen	8.00
Robin Ventura	5.00
Tony Gwynn	15.00
Troy Glaus	5.00
Kevin Millwood	5.00
Chipper Jones	15.00
Tom Glavine	8.00
Pedro Martinez/SP/60	25.00
Greg Maddux	15.00
Frank Thomas	10.00
Curt Schilling/SP/120	10.00
Edgar Martinez	5.00
Darin Erstad	5.00
J.D. Drew	5.00
Cal Ripken Jr.	30.00
Nolan Ryan	40.00
Steve Carlton	15.00

Names of the Game - Autographs

	NM/M
Common Player:	25.00
Yogi Berra	60.00
Orlando Cepeda	20.00
Rocky Colavito	60.00
Andre Dawson	20.00
Bucky Dent	20.00
Rollie Fingers	20.00
Carlton Fisk	40.00
Whitey Ford	40.00
Reggie Jackson	50.00
Randy Johnson	60.00
Chipper Jones	50.00
Harmon Killebrew	60.00
Don Mattingly	90.00
Willie McCovey	25.00
Cal Ripken Jr.	150.00
Ivan Rodriguez	40.00
Preacher Roe	35.00
Nolan Ryan	100.00
Tom Seaver	50.00
Bill Skowron	25.00
Enos Slaughter	30.00
Duke Snider	40.00

Names of the Game - Game Used

	NM/M
Common Player:	10.00
Production 50 Sets	
Yogi Berra/Bat	25.00
Orlando Cepeda/Bat	10.00
Rocky Colavito/Bat	20.00
Andre Dawson/Jsy	10.00
Bucky Dent/Bat	10.00
Rollie Fingers/Jsy	10.00
Carlton Fisk/Bat	15.00
Whitey Ford/Jsy	25.00
Jimmie Foxx/Bat	80.00
Hank Greenberg/Bat	50.00
"Catfish" Hunter/Jsy	10.00
Reggie Jackson/Jsy	20.00
Randy Johnson/Jsy	30.00
Chipper Jones/Bat	30.00
Harmon Killebrew/Bat	25.00
Tony Lazzeri/Bat	10.00
Don Mattingly/Bat	40.00
Willie McCovey/Bat	20.00
Johnny Mize/Bat	15.00
Pee Wee Reese/Jsy	15.00
Cal Ripken Jr./Bat	60.00
Phil Rizzuto/Bat	20.00
Ivan Rodriguez/Bat	25.00
Preacher Roe/Jsy	15.00
Babe Ruth/Bat	300.00
Nolan Ryan/Jsy	50.00
Tom Seaver/Jsy	25.00
Bill Skowron/Bat	10.00
Enos Slaughter/Bat	10.00
Duke Snider/Bat	25.00
Willie Stargell/Bat	25.00
Bill Terry/Bat	10.00
Ted Williams/Bat	150.00
Hack Wilson/Bat	75.00

Pennant Aggression

	NM/M
Complete Set (10):	20.00
Inserted 1:23	
1PA Derek Jeter	5.00
2PA Alex Rodriguez	5.00
3PA Nomar Garciaparra	1.50
4PA Mark McGwire	3.00
5PA Ken Griffey Jr.	4.00
6PA Mike Piazza	3.00
7PA Sammy Sosa	2.00
8PA Barry Bonds	4.00
9PA Chipper Jones	3.00
10PA Pedro Martinez	2.00

Tip of the Cap

	NM/M
Common Player:	5.00
Production 150 Sets	
Barry Bonds	30.00
Eric Chavez	5.00
Shawn Green	5.00
Vladimir Guerrero	15.00
Randy Johnson	20.00
Andruw Jones	5.00
Javy Lopez	5.00
Rafael Palmeiro	10.00
Ivan Rodriguez	10.00
Miguel Tejada	8.00
Roberto Alomar	8.00
Pedro Martinez	15.00

@ LG (At Large)

	NM/M
Complete Set (15):	40.00
Common Player:	1.50
Inserted 1:23	
1AL Derek Jeter	8.00
2AL Nomar Garciaparra	3.00
3AL Mark McGwire	5.00
4AL Pedro Martinez	3.00
5AL Tony Gwynn	3.00
6AL Roger Clemens	4.00
7AL Ivan Rodriguez	2.00

8AL	Sammy Sosa	4.00
9AL	Magglio Ordonez	1.50
10AL	Jason Giambi	2.00
11AL	Carlos Delgado	2.00
12AL	Chipper Jones	4.00
13AL	Mike Piazza	4.00
14AL	Cal Ripken Jr.	8.00
15AL	Ken Griffey Jr.	4.00

2001 Fleer Greats of the Game

Robin Yount Milwaukee Brewers

		NM/M
Complete Set (137):		50.00
Common Player:		.25
Hobby Pack (5):		10.00
Hobby Box (24):		200.00
1	Roberto Clemente	2.50
2	George "Sparky" Anderson	.25
3	Babe Ruth	4.00
4	Paul Molitor	1.00
5	Don Larsen	.25
6	Cy Young	1.00
7	Billy Martin	.50
8	Lou Brock	1.00
9	Fred Lynn	.25
10	Johnny Vander Meer	.25
11	Harmon Killebrew	1.00
12	Dave Winfield	1.00
13	Orlando Cepeda	.25
14	Johnny Mize	.75
15	Walter Johnson	1.00
16	Roy Campanella	1.00
17	Monte Irvin	.50
18	Mookie Wilson	.25
19	Elston Howard	.25
20	Walter Alston	.25
21	Rollie Fingers	.25
22	Brooks Robinson	1.00
23	Hank Greenberg	1.00
24	Maury Wills	.25
25	Rich Gossage	.25
26	Leon Day	.25
27	Jimmie Foxx	2.00
28	Alan Trammell	.50
29	Dennis Martinez	.25
30	Don Drysdale	.75
31	Bob Feller	.75
32	Jackie Robinson	3.00
33	Whitey Ford	1.00
34	Enos Slaughter	.25
35	Rod Carew	.75
36	Eddie Mathews	1.00
37	Ron Cey	.25
38	Thurman Munson	1.00
39	Henry Kimbro	.25
40	Ty Cobb	3.00
41	Rocky Colavito	.50
42	Satchel Paige	.50
43	Andre Dawson	.50
44	Phil Rizzuto	1.00
45	Roger Maris	2.50
46	Bobby Bonds	.25
47	Joe Carter	.25
48	Christy Mathewson	.75
49	Tony Lazzeri	.25
50	Gil Hodges	.25
51	Ray Dandridge	.25
52	Gaylord Perry	.25
53	Ernie Banks	2.00
54	Lou Gehrig	3.00
55	George Kell	.25
56	Wes Parker	.25
57	Sam Jethroe	.25
58	Joe Morgan	.50
59	Steve Garvey	.50
60	Joe Torre	.75
61	Roger Craig	.25
62	Warren Spahn	1.00
63	Willie McCovey	.25
64	Cool Papa Bell	1.00
65	Frank Robinson	1.00
66	Richie Allen	.25
67	Bucky Dent	.25
68	George Foster	.25
69	Hoyt Wilhelm	.25
70	Phil Niekro	.25
71	Buck Leonard	.25
72	Preacher Roe	.25
73	Yogi Berra	1.50
74	Joe Black	.25
75	Nolan Ryan	4.00
76	Pop Lloyd	.25
77	Lester Lockett	.25

78	Paul Blair	.25
79	Ryne Sandberg	2.00
80	Bill Perkins	.25
81	Frank Howard	.25
82	Hack Wilson	1.00
83	Robin Yount	1.00
84	Harry Heilmann	.25
85	Mike Schmidt	3.00
86	Vida Blue	.25
87	George Brett	3.00
88	Juan Marichal	.50
89	Tom Seaver	1.50
90	Bill Skowron	.25
91	Don Mattingly	2.00
92	Jim Bunning	.25
93	Eddie Murray	1.00
94	Tommy Lasorda	.50
95	Pee Wee Reese	.50
96	Bill Dickey	.25
97	Ozzie Smith	1.50
98	Dale Murphy	.25
99	Artie Wilson	.25
100	Bill Terry	.25
101	Jim "Catfish" Hunter	.25
102	Don Sutton	.25
103	Luis Aparicio	.25
104	Reggie Jackson	1.50
105	Ted Radcliffe	.25
106	Carl Erskine	.25
107	Johnny Bench	2.00
108	Carl Furillo	.25
109	Stan Musial	2.00
110	Carlton Fisk	.75
111	Rube Foster	.25
112	Tony Oliva	.25
113	Hank Bauer	.25
114	Jim Rice	.25
115	Willie Mays	3.00
116	Ralph Kiner	.50
117	Al Kaline	1.00
118	Billy Williams	.25
119	Buck O'Neil	.25
120	Tony Perez	.25
121	Dave Parker	.25
122	Kirk Gibson	.25
123	Lou Piniella	.25
124	Ted Williams	4.00
125	Steve Carlton	.75
126	Dizzy Dean	.25
127	Willie Stargell	.25
128	Joe Niekro	.25
129	Lloyd Waner	.25
130	Wade Boggs	2.00
131	Wilmer Fields	.25
132	Bill Mazeroski	.50
133	Duke Snider	1.00
134	Smoky Joe Williams	.25
135	Bob Gibson	1.50
136	Jim Palmer	.75
137	Oscar Charleston	.25

Autographs

Andre Dawson Chicago Cubs

		NM/M
Common Player:		10.00
Inserted 1:8		
1	Richie Allen	10.00
2	George "Sparky" Anderson	10.00
3	Luis Aparicio	10.00
4	Ernie Banks/SP/250	100.00
5	Hank Bauer	10.00
6	Johnny Bench/SP/400	80.00
7	Yogi Berra/SP/500	60.00
8	Joe Black	10.00
9	Paul Blair	10.00
9a	Paul Blair/Double Signed	10.00
10	Vida Blue	10.00
11	Wade Boggs	40.00
12	Bobby Bonds	25.00
13	George Brett/SP/247	150.00
14	Lou Brock/SP/500	40.00
15	Jim Bunning	25.00
16	Rod Carew	20.00
17	Steve Carlton	25.00
18	Joe Carter	10.00
19	Orlando Cepeda	15.00
20	Ron Cey	10.00
21	Rocky Colavito	40.00
22	Roger Craig	10.00
23	Andre Dawson	15.00
24	Bucky Dent	10.00
25	Larry Doby	35.00
26	Carl Erskine	10.00
27	Bob Feller	15.00

28	Wilmer Fields	10.00
29	Rollie Fingers	10.00
30	Carlton Fisk	40.00
31	Whitey Ford	30.00
32	George Foster	10.00
33	Steve Garvey/SP/400	40.00
34	Bob Gibson	20.00
35	Kirk Gibson	20.00
36	Rich Gossage	10.00
37	Frank Howard	10.00
38	Monte Irvin	10.00
39	Reggie Jackson/SP/400	85.00
40	Sam Jethroe	10.00
41	Al Kaline	30.00
42	George Kell	15.00
43	Harmon Killebrew	30.00
44	Ralph Kiner	20.00
45	Don Larsen	15.00
46	Tommy Lasorda/SP/400	50.00
47	Lester Lockett	10.00
48	Fred Lynn	10.00
49	Juan Marichal	20.00
50	Dennis Martinez	10.00
51	Don Mattingly	75.00
52	Willie Mays/SP/100	450.00
53	Bill Mazeroski	20.00
54	Willie McCovey	20.00
55	Paul Molitor	25.00
56	Joe Morgan	10.00
57	Dale Murphy	30.00
58	Eddie Murray/SP/140	200.00
59	Stan Musial/SP/525	100.00
60	Joe Niekro	10.00
61	Phil Niekro	10.00
62	Tony Oliva	40.00
63	Buck O'Neil	40.00
64	Jim Palmer/SP/600	25.00
65	Dave Parker	10.00
66	Tony Perez	20.00
67	Gaylord Perry	10.00
68	Lou Piniella	10.00
69	Ted Radcliffe	25.00
70	Jim Rice	10.00
71	Phil Rizzuto/SP/425	50.00
72	Brooks Robinson	25.00
73	Frank Robinson	20.00
74	Preacher Roe	20.00
75	Nolan Ryan/SP/650	100.00
76	Ryne Sandberg	50.00
77	Mike Schmidt/SP/213	200.00
78	Tom Seaver	50.00
79	Bill Skowron	10.00
80	Enos Slaughter	15.00
81	Ozzie Smith	50.00
82	Duke Snider/SP/600	60.00
83	Warren Spahn	50.00
84	Willie Stargell (Redemption card only, none signed.)	20.00
85	Don Sutton	10.00
86	Joe Torre/SP/500	40.00
87	Alan Trammell	15.00
88	Hoyt Wilhelm	10.00
89	Billy Williams	10.00
90	Maury Wills	10.00
91	Artie Wilson	10.00
92	Mookie Wilson	10.00
93	Dave Winfield/SP/370	50.00
94	Robin Yount/SP/400	100.00

Dodger Blues

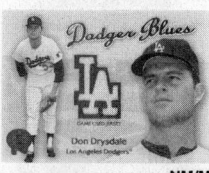

Don Drysdale
Los Angeles Dodgers

		NM/M
Common Player:		10.00
Inserted 1:36		
(1)	Walter Alston/Jsy	10.00
(2)	Walt Alston/Uniform	10.00
(3)	Roy Campanella/ Uniform/SP	100.00
(4)	Roger Craig/Jsy	10.00
(5)	Don Drysdale/Jsy	25.00
(6)	Carl Furillo/Jsy	10.00
(7)	Steve Garvey/Jsy	10.00
(8)	Gil Hodges/Uniform	20.00
(9)	Wes Parker/Bat	10.00
(10)	Wes Parker/Jsy	10.00
(11)	Pee Wee Reese/Jsy	20.00
(12)	Jackie Robinson/ Uniform/SP	150.00
(13)	Preacher Roe/Jsy	20.00
(14)	Duke Snider/Bat/SP	100.00
(15)	Don Sutton/Jsy	10.00

Feel the Game Classics

		NM/M
		5.00
Common Player:		
Inserted 1:72		
1	Luis Aparicio/Bat	5.00
2	George Brett/Jsy	30.00
3	Lou Brock/Jsy	15.00
4	Orlando Cepeda/Bat	10.00
5	Whitey Ford/Jsy	15.00
6	Hank Greenberg/Bat	50.00
7	Elston Howard/Bat	5.00
8	"Catfish" Hunter/Jsy	8.00
9	Harmon Killebrew/Bat	15.00
10	Roger Maris/Bat	50.00
11	Eddie Mathews/Bat	15.00
12	W. McCovey/Bat/SP/200	15.00
13	Johnny Mize/Bat	5.00
14	Paul Molitor/Jsy	10.00
15	Jim Palmer/Jsy	10.00
16	Tony Perez/Bat	5.00
17	Brooks Robinson/Bat/144	25.00
18	Babe Ruth/Bat/250	200.00
19	Mike Schmidt/Jsy	25.00
20	Tom Seaver/Jsy	20.00
21	Enos Slaughter	10.00
22	Willie Stargell	10.00
23	Hack Wilson	40.00
24	Harry Heilmann	5.00

Retrospection Collection

MIKE SCHMIDT
Philadelphia Phillies

		NM/M
Complete Set (10):		20.00
Common Player:		1.00
Inserted 1:6		
1	Babe Ruth	5.00
2	Stan Musial	3.00
3	Jimmie Foxx	3.00
4	Roberto Clemente	4.00
5	Ted Williams	4.00
6	Mike Schmidt	4.00
7	Cy Young	1.50
8	Satchel Paige	2.00
9	Hank Greenberg	2.00
10	Jim Bunning	1.00

2001 Fleer Legacy

		NM/M
Complete Set (105):		
Common Player:		.50
Common (91-105):		8.00
Production 799 Sets		
Pack (5):		8.00
Box (15 + Cap):		140.00
1	Pedro J. Martinez	1.50
2	Andruw Jones	1.50
3	Mike Hampton	.50
4	Gary Sheffield	.65
5	Barry Zito	.65
6	J.D. Drew	.75
7	Charles Johnson	.50
8	David Wells	.50
9	Kazuhiro Sasaki	.50
10	Vladimir Guerrero	1.50
11	Pat Burrell	.75
12	Ruben Mateo	.50
13	Greg Maddux	2.00
14	Sean Casey	.65
15	Craig Biggio	.50
16	Bernie Williams	.65
17	Jeff Kent	.50
18	Nomar Garciaparra	1.00
19	Cal Ripken Jr.	4.00
20	Larry Walker	.50
21	Adrian Beltre	.65
22	Johnny Damon	.75
23	Rick Ankiel	.50
24	Matt Williams	.50
25	Magglio Ordonez	.50

#	Player	Price
26	Richard Hidalgo	.50
27	Robin Ventura	.50
28	Jason Kendall	.50
29	Tony Batista	.50
30	Chipper Jones	2.00
31	Jim Thome	.50
32	Kevin Brown	.50
33	Mike Mussina	.65
34	Mark McGwire	3.00
35	Darin Erstad	.75
36	Manny Ramirez	1.50
37	Bobby Higginson	.50
38	Richie Sexson	.50
39	Jason Giambi	1.00
40	Alex Rodriguez	3.00
41	Mark Grace	.65
42	Ken Griffey Jr.	2.50
43	Moises Alou	.50
44	Edgardo Alfonzo	.50
45	Phil Nevin	.50
46	Rafael Palmeiro	1.25
47	Javy Lopez	.50
48	Juan Gonzalez	1.50
49	Jermaine Dye	.50
50	Roger Clemens	2.25
51	Barry Bonds	4.00
52	Carl Everett	.50
53	Ben Sheets	.50
54	Juan Encarnacion	.50
55	Jeromy Burnitz	.50
56	Miguel Tejada	.65
57	Ben Grieve	.50
58	Randy Johnson	1.50
59	Frank Thomas	1.50
60	Preston Wilson	.50
61	Mike Piazza	2.00
62	Brian Giles	.50
63	Carlos Delgado	1.00
64	Tom Glavine	.75
65	Roberto Alomar	.65
66	Mike Sweeney	.50
67	Orlando Hernandez	.50
68	Edgar Martinez	.50
69	Tim Salmon	.75
70	Kerry Wood	1.00
71	Jack Wilson RC	3.00
72	Matt Lawton	.50
73	Scott Rolen	1.25
74	Ivan Rodriguez	1.25
75	Steve Finley	.50
76	Barry Larkin	.50
77	Jeff Bagwell	1.50
78	Derek Jeter	4.00
79	Tony Gwynn	2.00
80	Raul Mondesi	.50
81	Rafael Furcal	.50
82	Todd Helton	1.50
83	Shawn Green	.75
84	Tim Hudson	.65
85	Jim Edmonds	.50
86	Troy Glaus	1.50
87	Sammy Sosa	2.50
88	Cliff Floyd	.50
89	Jose Vidro	.50
90	Bobby Abreu	.50
91	Drew Henson/Auto. RC	15.00
92	Andy Morales/Auto. RC	8.00
93	Wilson Betemit/Auto. RC	20.00
94	Elpidio Guzman RC	8.00
95	Esix Snead RC	8.00
96	Winston Abreu RC	8.00
97	Jeremy Owens RC	8.00
99	Junior Spivey RC	10.00
100	Jaisen Randolph RC	8.00
101	Ichiro Suzuki RC	50.00
102	Albert Pujols/499 RC	150.00
102	Albert Pujols/Auto./300 RC	350.00
103	Tsuyoshi Shinjo RC	10.00
104	Jay Gibbons RC	10.00
105	Juan Uribe RC	10.00

Ultimate Legacy

Stars (1-90):	3-5X
Rookies (91-100):	.3-.75X
Rookies (101-105):	.75-1X
Production 250 Sets	

(See 2001 Fleer Legacy for checklist and base card values.)

Autographed MLB Fitted Cap

	NM/M
Common Player:	25.00

Inserted one per box.

Player	Price
Edgardo Alfonzo	25.00
Roberto Alomar	50.00
Ernie Banks/100	125.00
Adrian Beltre	40.00
Johnny Bench/100	125.00
Lance Berkman	60.00
Yogi Berra/200	120.00
Craig Biggio	40.00
Barry Bonds	250.00
Jeromy Burnitz	25.00
Pat Burrell	40.00
Steve Carlton	40.00
Sean Casey	25.00
Orlando Cepeda	30.00
Eric Chavez	25.00
Tony Clark	25.00
Roger Clemens/100	200.00
Johnny Damon	60.00
Dom DiMaggio/200	75.00
J.D. Drew	40.00
Jermaine Dye	40.00
Darin Erstad	25.00
Carlton Fisk/150	80.00
Rafael Furcal	40.00
Nomar Garciaparra/150	120.00
Jason Giambi	50.00
Troy Glaus	40.00
Tom Glavine	60.00
Juan Gonzalez	40.00
Luis Gonzalez	30.00
Tony Gwynn	85.00
Drew Henson	25.00
Derek Jeter	250.00
Andruw Jones	40.00
David Justice	30.00
Paul Konerko	40.00
Don Mattingly	150.00
Willie McCovey	30.00
Paul Molitor	50.00
Stan Musial/200	125.00
Mike Mussina	50.00
Jim Palmer	40.00
Corey Patterson	25.00
Kirby Puckett/200	125.00
Cal Ripken/200	200.00
Brooks Robinson	60.00
Ivan Rodriguez	50.00
Scott Rolen	50.00
Nolan Ryan/150	200.00
Mike Schmidt/150	125.00
Tom Seaver/100	125.00
Ben Sheets	40.00
Ozzie Smith	100.00
Duke Snider	50.00
Miguel Tejada	50.00
Jim Thome	60.00
Matt Williams	25.00
Dave Winfield/150	75.00
Carl Yastrzemski/150	100.00
Robin Yount	100.00
Barry Zito	40.00

Hit Kings

	NM/M
Common Player:	5.00
Inserted 1:13	
Stan Musial	15.00
Barry Bonds	25.00
Corey Patterson	5.00
Shawn Green	5.00
Ralph Kiner	5.00
Troy O'Leary	5.00
Ivan Rodriguez	5.00
Jose Vidro	5.00
Carlos Beltran	5.00
Jose Canseco	5.00
Juan Encarnacion	5.00
Reggie Jackson	10.00
Ruben Mateo	5.00
Juan Pierre	5.00
Tim Salmon	5.00
Adrian Beltre	5.00
Roger Cedeno	5.00
Troy Glaus	5.00
Jason Kendall	5.00
Rick Ankiel	8.00
Andruw Jones	5.00
Jim Thome	5.00
Tony Batista	5.00
George Brett	20.00
Vladimir Guerrero	10.00
Billy Martin	5.00
Magglio Ordonez	5.00
Johnny Damon	8.00

Hit Kings Short Prints

	NM/M
Common Player:	15.00
Production 100 Sets	
Robin Yount	20.00
Scott Rolen	15.00

Johnny Bench	25.00
Steve Garvey	15.00
Joe Morgan	15.00
Frank Thomas	20.00
Eddie Mathews	20.00
Tony Gwynn	25.00
Roger Clemens	40.00
Wade Boggs	25.00

Hot Gloves

	NM/M
Inserted 1:180	
1HG	Andruw Jones	15.00
2HG	Mike Mussina	15.00
3HG	Roberto Alomar	15.00
4HG	Tony Gwynn	30.00
5HG	Bernie Williams	15.00
6HG	Ivan Rodriguez	15.00
7HG	Ken Griffey Jr.	40.00
8HG	Robin Ventura	15.00
9HG	Cal Ripken Jr.	75.00
10HG	Jeff Bagwell	20.00
11HG	Mark McGwire	50.00
12HG	Rafael Palmeiro	15.00
13HG	Scott Rolen	15.00
14HG	Barry Bonds	60.00
15HG	Greg Maddux	40.00

MLB Game Issue - Base/Ball/Jersey

	NM/M
Common Card:	25.00
Production 50 Sets	
Derek Jeter	100.00
Cal Ripken Jr.	100.00
Todd Helton	30.00
Tony Gwynn	50.00
Chipper Jones	50.00
Frank Thomas	30.00
Barry Bonds	100.00
Troy Glaus	25.00
Pat Burrell	25.00
Scott Rolen	30.00

MLB Game Issue - Base

	NM/M
Common Player:	4.00
Inserted 1:52	
1GI	Mark McGwire	15.00
2GI	Ken Griffey Jr.	10.00
3GI	Sammy Sosa	8.00
4GI	Mike Piazza	10.00
5GI	Alex Rodriguez	15.00
6GI	Derek Jeter	15.00
7GI	Cal Ripken Jr.	20.00
8GI	Todd Helton	6.00
9GI	Tony Gwynn	8.00
10GI	Chipper Jones	10.00
11GI	Frank Thomas	6.00
12GI	Barry Bonds	20.00
13GI	Troy Glaus	4.00
14GI	Pat Burrell	4.00
15GI	Scott Rolen	5.00

MLB Game Issue - Base/Ball

	NM/M
Common Player:	10.00
Production 100 Sets	
Mark McGwire	50.00
Ken Griffey Jr.	40.00
Sammy Sosa	25.00
Mike Piazza	40.00
Alex Rodriguez	50.00
Derek Jeter	60.00
Cal Ripken Jr.	60.00
Todd Helton	15.00
Tony Gwynn	25.00
Chipper Jones	25.00
Frank Thomas	15.00
Barry Bonds	60.00
Troy Glaus	10.00
Pat Burrell	10.00
Scott Rolen	12.50

Tailor Made

	NM/M
Common Player:	4.00
Inserted 1:15	
2TM	Cal Ripken Jr.	40.00
3TM	Orlando Cepeda	6.00
4TM	Willie McCovey	6.00
5TM	Dave Winfield	6.00
6TM	Don Mattingly	25.00
7TM	Nolan Ryan	40.00
8TM	Manny Ramirez	8.00
9TM	Edgardo Alfonzo	4.00
10TM	Rondell White	4.00
11TM	Lou Piniella	4.00
12TM	Ivan Rodriguez	8.00
13TM	J.D. Drew	4.00
14TM	Barry Bonds	40.00
15TM	Greg Maddux	15.00
16TM	Rick Ankiel	6.00
17TM	Carlos Delgado	8.00
18TM	Kevin Brown	4.00
20TM	Reggie Jackson	10.00
21TM	Shawn Green	4.00
22TM	Jason Kendall	8.00
23TM	Rafael Palmeiro	8.00
24TM	Todd Helton	8.00
25TM	Curt Schilling	6.00

2001 Fleer Platinum

	NM/M
Complete Set (301):	140.00
Common Player:	.15
Common SP (251-300):	1.00
Inserted 1:6	
Card #301 Production 1,500	
Pack (10):	5.00
Box (24):	100.00
1	Bobby Abreu	.15
2	Brad Radke	.15
3	Bill Mueller	.15
4	Adam Eaton	.15
5	Antonio Alfonseca	.15
6	Manny Ramirez	.75
7	Adam Kennedy	.15
8	Jose Valentin	.15
9	Jaret Wright	.15

10 Aramis Ramirez .15
11 Jeff Kent .15
12 Juan Encarnacion .15
13 Sandy Alomar Jr. .15
14 Joe Randa .15
15 Darryl Kile .15
16 Darren Dreifort .15
17 Matt Kinney .15
18 Pokey Reese .15
19 Ryan Klesko .15
20 Shawn Estes .15
21 Moises Alou .15
22 Edgar Renteria .15
23 Chuck Knoblauch .15
24 Carl Everett .15
25 Garret Anderson .15
26 Shane Reynolds .15
27 Billy Koch .15
28 Carlos Febles .15
29 Brian Anderson .15
30 Armando Rios .15
31 Ryan Kohlmeier .15
32 Steve Finley .15
33 Brady Anderson .15
34 Cal Ripken Jr. 2.50
35 Paul Konerko .15
36 Chuck Finley .15
37 Rick Ankiel .25
38 Mariano Rivera .25
39 Corey Koskie .15
40 Cliff Floyd .15
41 Kevin Appier .15
42 Henry Rodriguez .15
43 Mark Kotsay .15
44 Brook Fordyce .15
45 Brad Ausmus .15
46 Alfonso Soriano .50
47 Ray Lankford .15
48 Keith Foulke .15
49 Rich Aurilia .15
50 Alex Rodriguez 2.00
51 Eric Byrnes .15
52 Travis Fryman .15
53 Jeff Bagwell .75
54 Scott Rolen .65
55 Matt Lawton .15
56 Brad Fullmer .15
57 Tony Batista .15
58 Nate Rolison .15
59 Carlos Lee .15
60 Rafael Furcal .15
61 Jay Bell .15
62 Jimmy Rollins .25
63 Derrek Lee .15
64 Andres Galarraga .15
65 Derek Bell .15
66 Tim Salmon .25
67 Travis Lee .15
68 Kevin Millwood .15
69 Albert Belle .15
70 Kazuhiro Sasaki .15
71 Al Leiter .15
72 Britt Reames .15
73 Carlos Beltran .45
74 Curt Schilling .50
75 Curtis Leskanic .15
76 Jeremy Giambi .15
77 Adrian Beltre .35
78 David Segui .15
79 Mike Lieberthal .15
80 Brian Giles .15
81 Marvin Benard .15
82 Aaron Sele .15
83 Kenny Lofton .15
84 Doug Glanville .15
85 Kris Benson .15
86 Richie Sexson .15
87 Javy Lopez .15
88 Doug Mientkiewicz .15
89 Peter Bergeron .15
90 Gary Sheffield .40
91 Derek Lowe .15
92 Tom Glavine .40
93 Lance Berkman .15
94 Chris Singleton .15
95 Mike Lowell .25
96 Luis Gonzalez .30
97 Dante Bichette .15
98 Mike Sirotka .15
99 Julio Lugo .15
100 Juan Gonzalez .75
101 Craig Biggio .15
102 Armando Benitez .15
103 Greg Maddux 1.00
104 Mark Grace .25
105 John Smoltz .15
106 J.T. Snow .15
107 Al Martin .15
108 Danny Graves .15
109 Barry Bonds 2.50
110 Lee Stevens .15
111 Pedro Martinez .75
112 Shawn Green .40
113 Bret Boone .15
114 Matt Stairs .15
115 Tino Martinez .15
116 Rusty Greer .15
117 Mike Bordick .15
118 Garrett Stephenson .15
119 Edgar Martinez .15
120 Ben Grieve .15
121 Milton Bradley .15
122 Aaron Boone .15
123 Ruben Mateo .15
124 Ken Griffey Jr. 1.50
125 Russell Branyan .15
126 Shannon Stewart .15
127 Fred McGriff .15
128 Ben Petrick .15
129 Kevin Brown .15
130 B.J. Surhoff .15
131 Mark McGwire 2.00
132 Carlos Guillen .15
133 Adrian Brown .15
134 Mike Sweeney .15
135 Eric Milton .15
136 Cristian Guzman .15
137 Ellis Burks .15
138 Fernando Tatis .15
139 Ben Molina .15
140 Tony Gwynn 1.00
141 Jeromy Burnitz .15
142 Miguel Tejada .25
143 Raul Mondesi .15
144 Jeffrey Hammonds .15
145 Pat Burrell .40
146 Frank Thomas .75
147 Eric Munson .15
148 Mike Hampton .15
149 Mike Cameron .15
150 Jim Thome .15
151 Mike Mussina .50
152 Rick Helling .15
153 Ken Caminiti .15
154 John Vander Wal .15
155 Denny Neagle .15
156 Robb Nen .15
157 Jose Canseco .50
158 Mo Vaughn .15
159 Phil Nevin .15
160 Pat Hentgen .15
161 Sean Casey .25
162 Greg Vaughn .15
163 Trot Nixon .15
164 Roberto Hernandez .15
165 Vinny Castilla .15
166 Robin Ventura .15
167 Alex Ochoa .15
168 Orlando Hernandez .15
169 Luis Castillo .15
170 Quilvio Veras .15
171 Troy O'Leary .15
172 Livan Hernandez .15
173 Roger Cedeno .15
174 Jose Vidro .15
175 John Olerud .15
176 Richard Hidalgo .15
177 Eric Chavez .25
178 Fernando Vina .15
179 Chris Stynes .15
180 Bobby Higginson .15
181 Bruce Chen .15
182 Omar Vizquel .15
183 Rey Ordonez .15
184 Trevor Hoffman .15
185 Jeff Cirillo .15
186 Billy Wagner .15
187 David Ortiz .15
188 Tim Hudson .40
189 Tony Clark .15
190 Larry Walker .15
191 Eric Owens .15
192 Aubrey Huff .15
193 Royce Clayton .15
194 Todd Walker .15
195 Rafael Palmeiro .65
196 Todd Hundley .15
197 Roger Clemens 1.50
198 Jeff Weaver .15
199 Dean Palmer .15
200 Geoff Jenkins .15
201 Matt Clement .15
202 David Wells .15
203 Chan Ho Park .15
204 Hideo Nomo .65
205 Bartolo Colon .15
206 John Wetteland .15
207 Corey Patterson .15
208 Freddy Garcia .15
209 David Cone .15
210 Rondell White .15
211 Carl Pavano .15
212 Charles Johnson .15
213 Ron Coomer .15
214 Matt Williams .15
215 Jay Payton .15
216 Nick Johnson .15
217 Deivi Cruz .15
218 Scott Elarton .15
219 Neifi Perez .15
220 Jason Isringhausen .15
221 Jose Cruz .15
222 Gerald Williams .15
223 Timo Perez .15
224 Damion Easley .15
225 Jeff D'Amico (Photo actually Jamey Wright.) .15
226 Preston Wilson .15
227 Robert Person .15
228 Jacque Jones .15
229 Johnny Damon .25
230 Tony Womack .15
231 Adam Piatt .15
232 Brian Jordan .15
233 Ben Davis .15
234 Kerry Wood .50
235 Mike Piazza 1.50
236 David Justice .15
237 Dave Veres .15
238 Eric Young .15
239 Juan Pierre .15
240 Gabe Kapler .15
241 Ryan Dempster .15
242 Dmitri Young .15
243 Jorge Posada .35
244 Eric Karros .15
245 J.D. Drew .25
246 Todd Zeile .15
247 Mark Quinn .15
248 Kenny Kelly .15
249 Jermaine Dye .15
250 Barry Zito .30
251 Jason Hart, Larry Barnes 1.00
252 Ichiro Suzuki, Elpidio Guzman **RC** 20.00
253 Tsuyoshi Shinjo, Brian Cole 1.00
254 John Barnes, Adrian Hernandez **RC** 1.00
255 Jason Tyner, Jace Brewer 1.00
256 Brian Buchanan, Luis Rivas 1.00
257 Brent Abernathy, Jose Ortiz 1.00
258 Marcus Giles, Keith Ginter 1.00
259 Tike Redman, Jaisen Randolph **RC** 1.00
260 Dane Sardinha, David Espinosa 1.00
261 Josh Beckett, Craig House 1.00
262 Jack Cust, Hiram Bocachica 1.00
263 Alex Escobar, Esix Snead **RC** 1.00
264 Chris Richard, Vernon Wells 1.00
265 Pedro Feliz, Xavier Nady 1.00
266 Brandon Inge, Joe Crede 1.00
267 Ben Sheets, Roy Oswalt 1.00
268 Drew Henson, Andy Morales **RC** 2.00
269 C.C. Sabathia, Justin Miller 1.00
270 David Eckstein, Jason Gabrowski 1.00
271 Dee Brown, Chris Wakeland 1.00
272 Junior Spivey, Alex Cintron 1.00
273 Elvis Pena, Juan Uribe **RC** 1.00
274 Carlos Pena, Jason Romano 1.00
275 Winston Abreu, Wilson Betemit **RC** 1.50
276 Jose Mieses, Nick Neugebauer 1.00
277 Shea Hillenbrand, Dernell Stenson 1.00
278 Jared Sandberg, Toby Hall 1.00
279 Jay Gibbons, Ivanon Coffie 1.00
280 Pablo Ozuna, Santiago Perez 1.00
281 Nomar Garciaparra/AS 2.00
282 Derek Jeter/AS 6.00
283 Jason Giambi/AS 2.50
284 Magglio Ordonez/AS 1.00
285 Ivan Rodriguez/AS 2.00
286 Troy Glaus/AS 1.50
287 Carlos Delgado/AS 1.50
288 Darin Erstad/AS 1.00
289 Bernie Williams/AS 2.00
290 Roberto Alomar/AS 1.50
291 Barry Larkin/AS 1.50
292 Chipper Jones/AS 4.00
293 Vladimir Guerrero/AS 2.00
294 Sammy Sosa/AS 2.50
295 Todd Helton/AS 2.00
296 Randy Johnson/AS 3.00
297 Jason Kendall/AS 1.00
298 Jim Edmonds/AS 1.50
299 Andruw Jones/AS 2.00
300 Edgardo Alfonzo/AS 1.00
301 Albert Pujols, Donaldo Mendez **RC** 80.00

Platinum Edition

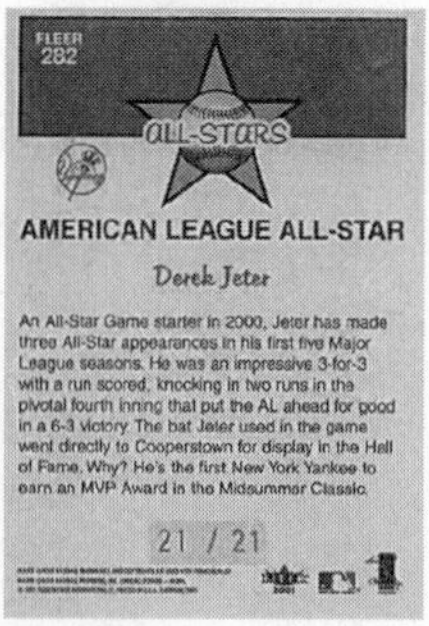
FLEER
282
ALL-STARS
AMERICAN LEAGUE ALL-STAR
Derek Jeter
An All-Star Game starter in 2000, Jeter has made three All-Star appearances in his first five Major League seasons. He was an impressive 3-for-3 with a run scored, knocking in two runs in the pivotal fourth inning that put the AL ahead for good in a 6-3 victory. The bat Jeter used in the game went directly to Cooperstown for display in the Hall of Fame. Why? He's the first New York Yankee to earn an MVP Award in the Midsummer Classic.
21 / 21

Cards (1-250): 4-8X
Production 201 Sets
SP's (251-280): 8-20X
SP's (281-300): 5-10X
SP Production 21 Sets
(See 2001 Fleer Platinum for checklist and base card values.)

Classic Combinations

Classic Combinations
Tony Gwynn
Ted Williams
San Diego Sluggers

NM/M

Common Card: 4.00
#1-10 Numbered to 250
11-20 Numbered to 500
21-30 Numbered to 1,000
31-40 Numbered to 2,000

1CC Derek Jeter, Alex Rodriguez 20.00
2CC Willie Mays, Willie McCovey 15.00
3CC Lou Gehrig, Babe Ruth 20.00
4CC Mark McGwire, Ken Griffey Jr. 15.00
5CC Johnny Bench, Roy Campanella 10.00
6CC Ted Williams, Nomar Garciaparra 20.00
7CC Yogi Berra, Mike Piazza 15.00
8CC Ernie Banks, Sammy Sosa 12.00
9CC Nolan Ryan, Randy Johnson 25.00
10CC Roberto Clemente, Vladimir Guerrero 15.00
11CC Lou Gehrig, Stan Musial 15.00
12CC Bill Mazeroski, Roberto Clemente 10.00
13CC Ernie Banks, Alex Rodriguez 10.00
14CC Phil Rizzuto, Derek Jeter 10.00
15CC Mike Piazza, Johnny Bench 8.00
16CC Mark McGwire, Sammy Sosa 10.00
17CC Ted Williams, Tony Gwynn 12.00
18CC Eddie Mathews, Mike Schmidt 10.00
19CC Barry Bonds, Willie Mays 10.00
20CC Nolan Ryan, Pedro Martinez 15.00
21CC Barry Bonds, Ken Griffey Jr. 10.00
22CC Willie McCovey, Reggie Jackson 5.00
23CC Roberto Clemente, Sammy Sosa 8.00
24CC Willie Mays, Ernie Banks 8.00
25CC Eddie Mathews, Chipper Jones 5.00
26CC Mike Schmidt, Brooks Robinson 6.00
27CC Stan Musial, Mark McGwire 8.00
28CC Ted Williams, Roger Maris 8.00
29CC Yogi Berra, Roy Campanella 5.00
30CC Johnny Bench, Tony Perez 5.00
31CC Bill Mazeroski, Joe Carter 3.00
32CC Mike Piazza, Roy Campanella 5.00
33CC Ernie Banks, Craig Biggio 4.00
34CC Frank Robinson, Brooks Robinson 4.00
35CC Mike Schmidt, Scott Rolen 5.00
36CC Roger Maris, Mark McGwire 10.00
37CC Stan Musial, Tony Gwynn 4.00
38CC Ted Williams, Bill Terry 6.00
39CC Derek Jeter, Reggie Jackson 6.00
40CC Yogi Berra, Bill Dickey 4.00

Classic Combinations Memorabilia

Classic Combinations
Ted Williams
Bill Terry
14/25

NM/M

Production 25 Sets
1 Yogi Berra, Bill Dickey 75.00
2 Yogi Berra, Roy Campanella 100.00
3 Roberto Clemente, Vladimir Guerrero 150.00
4 Eddie Mathews, Chipper Jones 80.00
5 Willie McCovey, Reggie Jackson 75.00
6 Phil Rizzuto, Derek Jeter 180.00
7 Brooks Robinson, Frank Robinson 75.00
8 Brooks Robinson, Mike Schmidt 120.00
9 Mike Schmidt, Scott Rolen 100.00
10 Ted Williams, Bill Terry 200.00
11 Ted Williams, Tony Gwynn 250.00

Grandstand Greats

NM/M

Complete Set (20): 25.00
Common Player: 1.00
Inserted 1:12

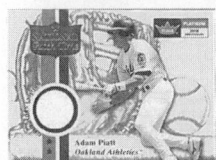

1GG	Chipper Jones	2.00
2GG	Alex Rodriguez	3.00
3GG	Jeff Bagwell	1.00
4GG	Troy Glaus	1.00
5GG	Manny Ramirez	1.50
6GG	Derek Jeter	4.00
7GG	Tony Gwynn	2.00
8GG	Greg Maddux	2.00
9GG	Nomar Garciaparra	1.50
10GG	Sammy Sosa	1.50
11GG	Mike Piazza	2.00
12GG	Barry Bonds	4.00
13GG	Mark McGwire	2.50
14GG	Vladimir Guerrero	1.50
15GG	Ivan Rodriguez	1.00
16GG	Ken Griffey Jr.	2.50
17GG	Todd Helton	1.50
18GG	Cal Ripken Jr.	4.00
19GG	Pedro Martinez	1.50
20GG	Frank Thomas	1.50

Nameplates

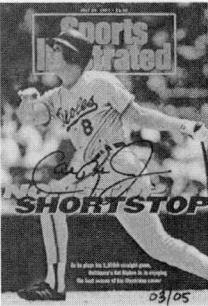

NM/M

Common Player: 15.00
Inserted 1:12

	Cal Ripken/19	200.00
	Cal Ripken/21	200.00
	Cal Ripken/23	200.00
	Cal Ripken/110	100.00
	Randy Johnson/99	40.00
	Nolan Ryan/40	200.00
	Javy Lopez/49	20.00
	Frank Thomas/35	40.00
	Frank Thomas/75	30.00
	Frank Thomas/80	30.00
	Jeffrey Hammonds/135	15.00
	Larry Walker/79	15.00
	Larry Walker/85	15.00
	Dave Winfield/80	20.00
	Vladimir Guerrero/80	25.00
	Vladimir Guerrero/90	25.00
	Kevin Millwood/130	15.00
	Mike Mussina/91	25.00
	Edgar Martinez/87	25.00
	Edgar Martinez/120	20.00
	Scott Rolen/65	30.00
	Ivan Rodriguez/177	25.00
	Manny Ramirez/75	25.00
	Manny Ramirez/105	25.00
	J.D. Drew/170	15.00
	Greg Maddux/180	50.00
	Chipper Jones/95	40.00
	Carlos Beltran/90	15.00
	Adrian Beltre	15.00
	Matt Williams/175	15.00
	Curt Schilling	20.00
	Pedro Martinez/120	30.00
	Robin Ventura/99	15.00
	Tom Glavine/125	15.00
	Tony Gwynn/35	75.00
	Tony Gwynn/65	40.00
	Tony Gwynn/90	40.00
	Troy Glaus/85	20.00
	Sean Casey/21	25.00
	Darin Erstad/39	25.00
	Stan Musial/30	150.00

National Patch Time

NM/M

Common Player: 4.00
Inserted 1:24 H

	Tony Gwynn	8.00
	Manny Ramirez	6.00
	Freddy Garcia	4.00
	Rondell White	4.00
	Ivan Rodriguez	5.00
	Brady Anderson	4.00

	Adam Piatt	4.00
	Carl Everett	4.00
	Magglio Ordonez	5.00
	Edgardo Alfonzo	4.00
	Jason Kendall	4.00
	Greg Maddux	8.00
	Cal Ripken Jr.	30.00
	Fred McGriff	4.00
	Pedro Martinez	6.00
	Roger Clemens	10.00
	Wade Boggs	8.00
	George Brett	15.00
	Ozzie Smith	8.00
	Dave Winfield	6.00
	Tom Seaver	6.00
	Rollie Fingers	4.00
	Mike Schmidt	15.00
	Eddie Murray	6.00
	Nolan Ryan	30.00
	Jeff Cirillo	4.00
	Mike Mussina	5.00
	Carl Yastrzemski	
	(Not officially issued.)	

Rack Pack Autographs

NM/M

Common Player: 5.00

	Hank Aaron/1997/90	200.00
	Roger Clemens/ 1998/125	100.00
	Jose Cruz Jr./1997	5.00
	Bob Gibson/1998/300	25.00
	Ben Grieve/100	6.00
	Tony Gwynn/1998/125	50.00
	Wes Helms/1997	5.00
	Harmon Killebrew/ 1998/300	30.00
	Paul Konerko/135	20.00
	Willie Mays/1997/115	125.00
	Willie Mays/1998/120	125.00
	Kirby Puckett/1997/105	75.00
	Brooks Robinson/1998/40	75.00
	Frank Robinson/1998/115	20.00
	Scott Rolen/1998/150	25.00
	Alex Rodriguez/1997/94	100.00
	Alex Rodriguez/1998/150	75.00

Tickets

No Pricing

Tickets Autographs

No Pricing

20th Anniversary Reprints

NM/M

Complete Set (18): 25.00
Common Player: .50
Inserted 1:8

1AR	Cal Ripken Jr.	4.00
2AR	Wade Boggs	1.50
3AR	Ryne Sandberg	1.50
4AR	Tony Gwynn	1.50
5AR	Don Mattingly	3.00
6AR	Roger Clemens	2.00
7AR	Kirby Puckett	1.50
8AR	Jose Canseco	.75
9AR	Barry Bonds	4.00
10AR	Ken Griffey Jr.	2.50
11AR	Sammy Sosa	2.50
12AR	Ivan Rodriguez	.75
13AR	Jeff Bagwell	1.00
14AR	J.D. Drew	.75
15AR	Troy Glaus	1.00
16AR	Rick Ankiel	.50
17AR	Xavier Nady	.50
18AR	Jose Ortiz	.50

2001 Fleer Platinum RC

ALEX RODRIGUEZ RANGERS

NM/M

Complete Set (300):		150.00
Common Player:		.15
Common (502-601):		1.00
Inserted 1:3 Hobby		
Pack (10):		7.00
Box (24):		140.00
302	Shawn Wooten	.15
303	Todd Walker	.15
304	Brian Buchanan	.15
305	Jim Edmonds	.25
306	Jarrod Washburn	.15
307	Jose Rijo	.15
308	Tim Raines	.15
309	Matt Morris	.15
310	Troy Glaus	.40
311	Barry Larkin	.40
312	Javier Vazquez	.15
313	Placido Polanco	.15
314	Darin Erstad	.25
315	Marty Cordova	.15
316	Vladimir Guerrero	.75
317	Kerry Robinson	.15
318	Byung-Hyun Kim	.15
319	C.C. Sabathia	.15
320	Edgardo Alfonzo	.15
321	Jason Tyner	.15
322	Reggie Sanders	.15
323	Roberto Alomar	.50
324	Matt Lawton	.15
325	Brent Abernathy	.15
326	Randy Johnson	.75
327	Todd Helton	.75
328	Andy Pettitte	.40
329	Josh Beckett	.50
330	Mark DeRosa	.15
331	Jose Ortiz	.15
332	Derek Jeter	2.00
333	Toby Hall	.15
334	Wes Helms	.15
335	Jose Macias	.15
336	Bernie Williams	.50
337	Ivan Rodriguez	.75
338	Chipper Jones	1.50
339	Brandon Inge	.15
340	Jason Giambi	.75
341	Frank Catalanotto	.15
342	Andruw Jones	.50
343	Carlos Hernandez RC	.40
344	Jermaine Dye	.15
345	Mike Lamb	.15
346	Ken Caminiti	.15
347	A.J. Burnett	.15
348	Terrence Long	.15
349	Ruben Sierra	.15
350	Marcus Giles	.15
351	Wade Miller	.15
352	Mark Mulder	.25
353	Carlos Delgado	.50
354	Chris Richard	.15
355	Daryle Ward	.15
356	Brad Penny	.15
357	Vernon Wells	.25
358	Jason Johnson	.15
359	Tim Redding	.15
360	Marlon Anderson	.15
361	Carlos Pena	.15
362	Nomar Garciaparra	.75
363	Roy Oswalt	.40
364	Todd Ritchie	.15
365	Jose Mesa	.15
366	Shea Hillenbrand	.15
367	Dee Brown	.15
368	Jason Kendall	.15
369	Vinny Castilla	.15
370	Fred McGriff	.25
371	Neifi Perez	.15
372	Xavier Nady	.15
373	Abraham Nunez	.15
374	Jon Lieber	.15
375	Paul LoDuca	.15
376	Bubba Trammell	.15

377	Brady Clark	.15
378	Joel Pineiro	.15
379	Mark Grudzielanek	.15
380	D'Angelo Jimenez	.15
381	Junior Herndon	.15
382	Magglio Ordonez	.40
383	Ben Sheets	.25
384	John Vander Wal	.15
385	Pedro Astacio	.15
386	Jose Canseco	.40
387	Jose Hernandez	.15
388	Eric Davis	.15
389	Sammy Sosa	1.00
390	Mark Buehrle	.15
391	Mark Loretta	.15
392	Andres Galarraga	.25
393	Scott Spiezio	.15
394	Joe Crede	.15
395	Luis Rivas	.15
396	David Bell	.15
397	Einar Diaz	.15
398	Adam Dunn	.75
399	A.J. Pierzynski	.15
400	Jamie Moyer	.15
401	Nick Johnson	.15
402	Freddy Garcia	4.00
403	Hideo Nomo	.40
404	Mark Mulder	.25
405	Steve Sparks	.15
406	Mariano Rivera	.25
407	Mark Buehrle, Mike Mussina	.25
408	Randy Johnson	.50
409	Randy Johnson	.50
410	Curt Schilling, Matt Morris	.25
411	Greg Maddux	.75
412	Robb Nen	.15
413	Randy Johnson	.50
414	Barry Bonds	1.00
415	Jason Giambi	.40
416	Ichiro Suzuki	2.50
417	Ichiro Suzuki	2.50
418	Alex Rodriguez	1.00
419	Bret Boone	.25
420	Ichiro Suzuki	2.50
421	Alex Rodriguez	1.00
422	Jason Giambi	.40
423	Alex Rodriguez	1.00
424	Larry Walker	.25
425	Rich Aurilia	.15
426	Barry Bonds	1.00
427	Sammy Sosa	.75
428	Jimmy Rollins, Juan Pierre	.25
429	Sammy Sosa	.75
430	Lance Berkman	.25
431	Sammy Sosa	.75
432	Carlos Delgado	.25
433	Alex Rodriguez	1.00
434	Greg Vaughn	.15
435	Albert Pujols	10.00
436	Ichiro Suzuki	2.50
437	Barry Bonds	1.00
438	Phil Nevin	.15
439	Brian Giles	.25
440	Bobby Abreu	.25
441	Jason Giambi	.40
442	Derek Jeter	1.00
443	Mike Piazza	.75
444	Vladimir Guerrero	.50
445	Corey Koskie	.15
446	Richie Sexson	.25
447	Shawn Green	.25
448	Mike Sweeney	.15
449	Jeff Bagwell	.40
450	Cliff Floyd	.15
451	Roger Cedeno	.15
452	Todd Helton	.40
453	Juan Gonzalez	.30
454	Sean Casey	.15
455	Magglio Ordonez	.25
456	Sammy Sosa	.75
457	Manny Ramirez	.40
458	Jeff Conine	.15
459	Chipper Jones	.50
460	Luis Gonzalez	.25
461	Troy Glaus	.25
462	Ivan Rodriguez	.40
463	Luis Gonzalez, Jack Cust	.25
464	Jim Thome, C.C. Sabathia	.25
465	Jason Hart, Jason Giambi	.25
466	Jeff Bagwell, Roy Oswalt	.30
467	Sammy Sosa, Corey Patterson	.50
468	Mike Piazza, Alex Escobar	.25
469	Ken Griffey Jr., Adam Dunn	.75
470	Roger Clemens, Nick Johnson	.75
471	Cliff Floyd, Josh Beckett	.15
472	Cal Ripken Jr., Jerry Hairston Jr.	.75
473	Phil Nevin, Xavier Nady	.15
474	Scott Rolen, Jimmy Rollins	.40
475	Barry Larkin, David Espinosa	.25
476	Larry Walker, Jose Ortiz	.25
477	Chipper Jones, Marcus Giles	.40
478	Craig Biggio, Keith Ginter	.15
479	Magglio Ordonez, Aaron Rowand	.25
480	Alex Rodriguez, Carlos Pena	.75
481	Derek Jeter, Alfonso Soriano	.75
482	Curt Schilling	
	(Post Season Glory)	.20
483	(Post Season Glory)	.25
484	(Post Season Glory)	.25
485	(Post Season Glory)	.25
486	(Post Season Glory)	.25

#	Player	Price
487	(Post Season Glory)	.25
488	(Post Season Glory)	.25
489	Rudolph Giuliani (Post Season Glory)	.50
490	George Bush (Post Season Glory)	.50
491	(Post Season Glory)	.25
492	(Post Season Glory)	.25
493	(Post Season Glory)	.25
494	Derek Jeter (Post Season Glory)	.75
495	(Post Season Glory)	.25
496	(Post Season Glory)	.25
497	(Post Season Glory)	.25
498	(Post Season Glory)	.25
499	(Post Season Glory)	.25
500	(Post Season Glory)	.25
501	(Post Season Glory)	.25
502	Josh Fogg RC	1.00
503	Elpidio Guzman	1.00
504	Corky Miller RC	1.00
505	Cesar Crespo RC	1.00
506	Carlos Garcia RC	1.00
507	Carlos Valderrama RC	1.00
508	Joe Kennedy RC	1.00
509	Henry Mateo RC	1.00
510	Brandon Duckworth RC	1.00
511	Ichiro Suzuki RC	15.00
512	Zach Day RC	1.00
513	Ryan Freel RC	1.50
514	Brian Lawrence RC	1.00
515	Alexis Gomez RC	1.00
516	Will Ohman RC	1.00
517	Juan Diaz RC	1.00
518	Juan Moreno RC	1.00
519	Rob Mackowiak RC	1.00
520	Horacio Ramirez RC	1.50
521	Albert Pujols	75.00
522	Tsuyoshi Shinjo	1.00
523	Ryan Drese RC	1.00
524	Angel Berroa RC	1.00
525	Josh Towers RC	2.50
526	Junior Spivey	1.00
527	Greg Miller RC	1.00
528	Esix Snead RC	1.00
529	Mark Prior RC	5.00
530	Drew Henson	1.00
531	Brian Reith RC	1.00
532	Andres Torres RC	1.00
533	Casey Fossum RC	1.00
534	Wilmy Caceres RC	1.00
535	Matt White RC	1.00
536	Wilkin Ruan RC	1.00
537	Rick Bauer RC	1.00
538	Morgan Ensberg RC	1.00
539	Geronimo Gil RC	1.00
540	Dewon Brazelton RC	1.00
541	Johnny Estrada RC	1.50
542	Claudio Vargas RC	1.00
543	Donaldo Mendez RC	1.00
544	Kyle Lohse RC	2.00
545	Nate Frese RC	1.00
546	Christian Parker RC	1.00
547	Blaine Neal RC	1.00
548	Travis Hafner RC	4.00
549	Billy Sylvester RC	1.00
550	Adam Pettyjohn	1.00
551	Bill Ortega	1.00
552	Jose Acevedo RC	1.00
553	Steve Green RC	1.00
554	Jay Gibbons RC	1.00
555	Bert Snow RC	1.00
556	Erick Almonte RC	1.00
557	Jeremy Owens RC	1.00
558	Sean Douglass RC	1.00
559	Jason Smith RC	1.00
560	Ricardo Rodriguez RC	1.00
561	Mark Teixeira RC	15.00
562	Tyler Walker RC	1.00
563	Juan Uribe RC	1.50
564	Bud Smith RC	1.00
565	Angel Santos RC	1.00
566	Brandon Lyon RC	1.00
567	Eric Hinske RC	2.50
568	Nick Punto RC	1.00
569	Winston Abreu RC	1.00
570	Jason Phillips RC	1.00
571	Rafael Soriano RC	1.50
572	Wilson Betemit	1.00
573	Endy Chavez RC	1.00
574	Juan Cruz RC	1.00
575	Cory Aldridge RC	1.00
576	Adrian Hernandez	1.00
577	Brandon Larson RC	1.50
578	Bret Prinz RC	1.00
579	Jackson Melian RC	1.00
580	Dave Maurer RC	1.00
581	Jason Michaels RC	1.00
582	Travis Phelps RC	1.00
583	Cody Ransom RC	1.00
584	Benito Baez RC	1.00
585	Brian Roberts RC	1.00
586	Nate Teut RC	1.00
587	Jack Wilson RC	1.00
588	Willie Harris RC	1.00
589	Martin Vargas RC	1.00
590	Steve Torrealba RC	1.00
591	Stubby Clapp RC	1.00
592	Danny Wright RC	1.00
593	Mike Rivera RC	1.00
594	Luis Pineda RC	1.00
595	Lance Davis RC	1.00
596	Ramon Vazquez RC	1.50
597	Dustan Mohr RC	1.00
598	Troy Mattes RC	1.00
599	Grant Balfour RC	1.00
600	Jared Fernandez RC	1.00
601	Jorge Julio RC	1.00

E-X

#	Player	Price
131	Albert Pujols/499 RC	250.00
132	Bud Smith/499 RC	8.00
133	Tsuyoshi Shinjo/499 RC	8.00
134	Wilson Betemit/499 RC	10.00
135	Adrian Hernandez/499 RC	8.00
136	Jackson Melian/499	8.00
137	Jay Gibbons/499 RC	8.00
138	Johnny Estrada/499 RC	10.00
139	Morgan Ensberg/499 RC	10.00
140	Drew Henson/499 RC	10.00

Focus

#	Player	Price
241	Tsuyoshi Shinjo/999 RC	5.00
242	Wilson Betemit/999 RC	5.00
243	Jeremy Owens/999 RC	5.00
244	Drew Henson/999 RC	5.00
245	Albert Pujols/999 RC	100.00
246	Travis Hafner/999 RC	10.00
247	Ichiro Suzuki/999 RC	40.00
248	Elpidio Guzman/999 RC	5.00
249	Matt White/999 RC	5.00
250	Junior Spivey/999 RC	5.00

Futures

#	Player	Price
221	Drew Henson/2,499 RC	5.00
222	Johnny Estrada/2,499 RC	3.00
223	Elpidio Guzman/2,499 RC	3.00
224	Albert Pujols/2,499 RC	60.00
225	Wilson Betemit/2,499 RC	4.00
226	Mark Teixeira/2,499 RC	15.00
227	Tsuyoshi Shinjo/2,499 RC	3.00
228	Matt White/2,499 RC	3.00
229	Adrian Hernandez/2,499 RC	3.00
230	Ichiro Suzuki/2,499 RC	30.00

Triple Crown

#	Player	Price
301	Elpidio Guzman/2,999 RC	2.00
302	Drew Henson/2,999 RC	2.00
303	Bud Smith/2,999 RC	2.00
304	Carlos Valderrama/2,999 RC	2.00
305	Tsuyoshi Shinjo/2,999 RC	2.00
306	Ichiro Suzuki/2,999 RC	25.00
307	Jackson Melian/2,999	2.00
308	Morgan Ensberg/2,999 RC	2.00
309	Albert Pujols/2,999 RC	75.00
310	Johnny Estrada/2,999 RC	5.00

Ultra

#	Player	Price
276	Junior Spivey, Juan Uribe RC	4.00
277	Albert Pujols, Bud Smith RC	50.00
278	Ichiro Suzuki, Tsuyoshi Shinjo RC	20.00
279	Drew Henson, Jackson Melian	3.00
280	Matt White, Adrian Hernandez RC	2.00

Platinum

Cards (302-501): 4-8X
Production 201
SP's (502-601):
Production 21 not priced.
(See 2001 Fleer Platinum RC for checklist and base card values.)

Lumberjacks

NM/M

Common Player: 4.00
Inserted 1:1 Rack Pack

Player	Price
Barry Bonds	20.00
Derek Jeter	20.00
Luis Gonzalez	4.00
Mike Sweeney	4.00
Albert Pujols	15.00
Tony Gwynn	10.00
Adam Dunn	5.00
J.D. Drew	4.00
Brian Giles	4.00
Adrian Beltre	5.00
Bret Boone	4.00
Chipper Jones	10.00
Cliff Floyd	4.00
Darin Erstad	4.00
Gary Sheffield	6.00
Manny Ramirez	8.00
Mike Piazza	12.00
Todd Helton	8.00
Ivan Rodriguez	8.00
Lance Berkman	6.00
Vladimir Guerrero	8.00
Drew Henson	4.00
Cristian Guzman	4.00
Roberto Alomar	5.00
Moises Alou	4.00
Larry Walker	4.00

Lumberjacks Autographs

NM/M

Production 100 Sets

Player	Price
Barry Bonds	200.00
J.D. Drew	40.00
Adam Dunn	60.00
Luis Gonzalez	20.00
Derek Jeter	150.00
Albert Pujols	500.00
Cal Ripken Jr.	150.00
Mike Sweeney	20.00

National Patch Time

NM/M

Common Player: 4.00
Inserted 1:24 H

Player	Price
Edgardo Alfonzo	4.00
Brady Anderson	4.00
Adrian Beltre	6.00
Barry Bonds	20.00
Jeromy Burnitz	4.00
Eric Chavez	4.00
Roger Clemens	15.00
J.D. Drew	4.00
Darin Erstad	4.00
Carl Everett	4.00
Freddy Garcia	4.00
Jason Giambi	8.00
Juan Gonzalez	4.00
Mark Grace	4.00
Shawn Green	4.00
Ben Grieve	4.00
Vladimir Guerrero	8.00
Tony Gwynn	10.00
Randy Johnson	8.00
Chipper Jones	10.00
David Justice	4.00
Jeff Kent	4.00
Greg Maddux	10.00
Fred McGriff	4.00
John Olerud	4.00
Magglio Ordonez	4.00
Jorge Posada	6.00
Cal Ripken Jr.	20.00
Mariano Rivera	6.00
Ivan Rodriguez	6.00
Scott Rolen	4.00
Kazuhiro Sasaki	4.00
Aaron Sele	4.00
Gary Sheffield	6.00
John Smoltz	6.00
Frank Thomas	8.00
Mo Vaughn	4.00
Robin Ventura	4.00
Bernie Williams	6.00
Carlos Delgado	6.00
Chan Ho Park	4.00
Todd Helton	8.00
Craig Biggio	4.00
Jeff Bagwell	8.00
Paul LoDuca	4.00

Prime Numbers

NM/M

Common Player: 8.00
Inserted 1:12 Jumbo Pack

#	Player	Price
1PN	Jeff Bagwell	15.00
2PN	Cal Ripken Jr.	50.00
3PN	Barry Bonds	50.00
4PN	Todd Helton	15.00
5PN	Derek Jeter	50.00
6PN	Tony Gwynn	20.00
7PN	Kazuhiro Sasaki	8.00
8PN	Chan Ho Park	8.00
9PN	Sean Casey	10.00
10PN	Chipper Jones	20.00
11PN	Pedro Martinez	15.00
12PN	Mike Piazza	30.00
13PN	Carlos Delgado	10.00
14PN	Craig Biggio	8.00
15PN	Roger Clemens	25.00

Winning Combinations

NM/M

Common Card: 3.00
Varying quantities produced

1WC	Derek Jeter, Ozzie Smith/2,000	8.00
2WC	Barry Bonds, Mark McGwire/500	10.00
3WC	Ichiro Suzuki, Albert Pujols/250	30.00
4WC	Ted Williams, Manny Ramirez/1,000	10.00
5WC	Tony Gwynn, Cal Ripken/250	15.00
6WC	Mike Piazza, Derek Jeter/500	10.00
7WC	Dave Winfield, Tony Gwynn/2,000	5.00
8WC	Hideo Nomo, Ichiro Suzuki/2,000	10.00
9WC	Cal Ripken, Ozzie Smith/1,000	10.00
10WC	Mark McGwire, Albert Pujols/2,000	10.00
11WC	Jeff Bagwell, Craig Biggio/1,000	3.00
12WC	Bobby Bonds, Barry Bonds/250	10.00
13WC	Ted Williams, Stan Musial/250	10.00
14WC	Babe Ruth, Reggie Jackson/500	15.00
15WC	Kazuhiro Sasaki, Ichiro Suzuki/500	10.00
16WC	Nolan Ryan, Roger Clemens/500	15.00
17WC	Roger Clemens, Derek Jeter/250	15.00
18WC	Ivan Rodriguez, Mike Piazza/500	6.00
19WC	Vladimir Guerrero, Sammy Sosa/2,000	6.00
20WC	Barry Bonds, Sammy Sosa/250	10.00
21WC	Roger Clemens, Greg Maddux/1,000	8.00
22WC	Juan Gonzalez, Manny Ramirez/2,000	3.00
23WC	Todd Helton, Jason Giambi/2,000	3.00
24WC	Jeff Bagwell, Lance Berkman/2,000	3.00
25WC	Mike Sweeney, George Brett/1,000	6.00
26WC	Luis Gonzalez, Babe Ruth/2,000	10.00
27WC	Bill Skowron, Don Mattingly/250	10.00
28WC	Yogi Berra, Cal Ripken/2,000	10.00
29WC	Pedro Martinez, Nomar Garciaparra/500	8.00
30WC	Ted Kluszewski, Frank Robinson/1,000	3.00
31WC	Curt Schilling, Randy Johnson/1,000	5.00
32WC	Ken Griffey Jr., Cal Ripken/500	10.00
33WC	Mike Piazza, Johnny Bench/1,000	6.00
34WC	Stan Musial, Albert Pujols/500	10.00
35WC	Jackie Robinson, Nellie Fox/500	8.00
36WC	Lefty Grove, Steve Carlton/250	5.00
37WC	Ty Cobb, Tony Gwynn/250	10.00
38WC	Albert Pujols, Frank Robinson/1,000	10.00
39WC	Ryne Sandberg, Sammy Sosa/500	10.00
40WC	Cal Ripken Jr., Lou Gehrig/250	20.00

2001 Fleer Premium

NM/M

Complete Set (235):
Common Player: .15
Common SP (201-230): 3.00
Production 1,999
Cards 231-235 are redemptions.
Hobby Pack (8): 4.00
Hobby Box (24): 75.00

#	Player	Price
1	Cal Ripken Jr.	2.00
2	Derek Jeter	2.00
3	Edgardo Alfonzo	.15
4	Luis Castillo	.15
5	Mike Lieberthal	.15
6	Kazuhiro Sasaki	.15
7	Jeff Kent	.15
8	Eric Karros	.15

#	Player	Price
9	Tom Glavine	.40
10	Jeromy Burnitz	.15
11	Travis Fryman	.15
12	Ron Coomer	.15
13	Jeff D'Amico	.15
14	Carlos Febles	.15
15	Kevin Brown	.15
16	Deivi Cruz	.15
17	Tino Martinez	.15
18	Bobby Abreu	.15
19	Roger Clemens	1.00
20	Jeffrey Hammonds	.15
21	Peter Bergeron	.15
22	Ray Lankford	.15
23	Scott Rolen	.60
24	Jermaine Dye	.15
25	Rusty Greer	.15
26	Frank Thomas	.75
27	Jeff Bagwell	.75
28	Cliff Floyd	.15
29	Chris Singleton	.15
30	Steve Finley	.15
31	Orlando Hernandez	.15
32	Tom Goodwin	.15
33	Larry Walker	.15
34	Mike Sweeney	.15
35	Tim Hudson	.30
36	Kerry Wood	.40
37	Mike Lowell	.15
38	Andruw Jones	.75
39	Alex S. Gonzalez	.15
40	Juan Gonzalez	.75
41	J.D. Drew	.25
42	Mark McLemore	.15
43	Royce Clayton	.15
44	Paul O'Neill	.15
45	Carlos Beltran	.45
46	Phil Nevin	.15
47	Rondell White	.15
48	Gerald Williams	.15
49	Geoff Jenkins	.15
50	Marvin Benard	.15
51	Alex Rodriguez	1.50
52	Moises Alou	.15
53	Mike Lansing	.15
54	Omar Vizquel	.15
55	Eric Chavez	.30
56	Mark Quinn	.15
57	Mike Lamb	.15
58	Rick Ankiel	.25
59	Lance Berkman	.60
60	Jeff Conine	.15
61	B.J. Surhoff	.15
62	Todd Helton	.75
63	J.T. Snow	.15
64	John Vander Wal	.15
65	Johnny Damon	.25
66	Bobby Higginson	.15
67	Carlos Delgado	.40
68	Shawn Green	.35
69	Mike Redmond	.15
70	Mike Piazza	1.25
71	Adrian Beltre	.35
72	Juan Encarnacion	.15
73	Chipper Jones	1.00
74	Garret Anderson	.15
75	Paul Konerko	.15
76	Barry Larkin	.15
77	Tony Gwynn	1.00
78	Rafael Palmeiro	.60
79	Randy Johnson	.75
80	Mark Grace	.25
81	Javy Lopez	.15
82	Gabe Kapler	.15
83	Henry Rodriguez	.15
84	Raul Mondesi	.15
85	Adam Piatt	.15
86	Marquis Grissom	.15
87	Charles Johnson	.15
88	Sean Casey	.25
89	Manny Ramirez	.75
90	Curt Schilling	.40
91	Fernando Tatis	.15
92	Derek Bell	.15
93	Tony Clark	.15
94	Homer Bush	.15
95	Nomar Garciaparra	1.25
96	Vinny Castilla	.15
97	Ben Davis	.15
98	Carl Everett	.15
99	Damion Easley	.15
100	Craig Biggio	.40
101	Todd Hollandsworth	.15
102	Jay Payton	.15
103	Gary Sheffield	.35
104	Sandy Alomar Jr.	.15
105	Doug Glanville	.15
106	Barry Bonds	2.00
107	Tim Salmon	.25
108	Terrence Long	.15
109	Jorge Posada	.30
110	Jose Offerman	.15
111	Edgar Martinez	.15
112	Jeremy Giambi	.15
113	Dean Palmer	.15
114	Roberto Alomar	.35
115	Aaron Boone	.15
116	Adam Kennedy	.15
117	Joe Randa	.15
118	Jose Vidro	.15
119	Tony Batista	.15
120	Kevin Young	.15
121	Preston Wilson	.15
122	Jason Kendall	.15
123	Mark Kotsay	.15

#	Player	Price
124	Timoniel Perez	.15
125	Eric Young	.15
126	Greg Maddux	1.00
127	Richard Hidalgo	.15
128	Brian Giles	.15
129	Fred McGriff	.15
130	Troy Glaus	.75
131	Todd Walker	.15
132	Brady Anderson	.15
133	Jim Edmonds	.15
134	Ben Grieve	.15
135	Greg Vaughn	.15
136	Robin Ventura	.15
137	Sammy Sosa	1.25
138	Rich Aurilia	.15
139	Jose Valentin	.15
140	Trot Nixon	.15
141	Troy Percival	.15
142	Bernie Williams	.35
143	Warren Morris	.15
144	Jacque Jones	.15
145	Danny Bautista	.15
146	A.J. Pierzynski	.15
147	Mark McGwire	1.50
148	Rafael Furcal	.15
149	Ray Durham	.15
150	Mike Mussina	.40
151	Jay Bell	.15
152	David Wells	.15
153	Ken Caminiti	.15
154	Jim Thome	.15
155	Ivan Rodriguez	.60
156	Milton Bradley	.15
157	Ken Griffey Jr.	1.25
158	Al Leiter	.15
159	Corey Koskie	.15
160	Shannon Stewart	.15
161	Mo Vaughn	.15
162	Pedro Martinez	.75
163	Todd Hundley	.15
164	Darin Erstad	.60
165	Ruben Rivera	.15
166	Richie Sexson	.15
167	Andres Galarraga	.15
168	Darryl Kile	.15
169	Jose Cruz Jr.	.15
170	David Justice	.15
171	Vladimir Guerrero	.75
172	Jeff Cirillo	.15
173	John Olerud	.15
174	Devon White	.15
175	Ron Belliard	.15
176	Pokey Reese	.15
177	Mike Hampton	.15
178	David Ortiz	.15
179	Magglio Ordonez	.15
180	Ruben Mateo	.15
181	Carlos Lee	.15
182	Matt Williams	.15
183	Miguel Tejada	.25
184	Scott Elarton	.15
185	Bret Boone	.15
186	Pat Burrell	.40
187	Brad Radke	.15
188	Brian Jordan	.15
189	Matt Lawton	.15
190	Al Martin	.15
191	Albert Belle	.15
192	Tony Womack	.15
193	Roger Cedeno	.15
194	Travis Lee	.15
195	Dmitri Young	.15
196	Jay Buhner	.15
197	Jason Giambi	.50
198	Jason Tyner	.15
199	Ben Petrick	.15
200	Jose Canseco	.40
201	Nick Johnson	3.00
202	Jace Brewer	3.00
203	Ryan Freel RC	4.00
204	Jaisen Randolph RC	3.00
205	Marcus Giles	3.00
206	Claudio Vargas RC	3.00
207	Brian Cole	3.00
208	Scott Hodges	3.00
209	Winston Abreu RC	3.00
210	Shea Hillenbrand	3.00
211	Larry Barnes	3.00
212	Paul Phillips RC	3.00
213	Pedro Santana RC	3.00
214	Ivanon Coffie	3.00
215	Junior Spivey RC	3.00
216	Donzell McDonald	3.00
217	Vernon Wells	3.00
218	Corey Patterson	3.00
219	Sang-Hoon Lee	3.00
220	Jack Cust	4.00
221	Jason Romano	3.00
222	Jack Wilson RC	5.00
223	Adam Everett	3.00
224	Esix Snead RC	3.00
225	Jason Hart	3.00
226	Joe Lawrence	3.00
227	Brandon Inge	3.00
228	Alex Escobar	3.00
229	Abraham Nunez	3.00
230	Jared Sandberg	3.00
231	Ichiro Suzuki RC	40.00
232	Tsuyoshi Shinjo RC	3.00
233	Albert Pujols RC	75.00
234	Wilson Betemit RC	5.00
235	Drew Henson RC	5.00

Star Ruby

Stars (1-200):	5-10X
SPs (201-230):	.4-.8X
Production 125 Sets	

(See 2001 Fleer Premium for checklist and base card values.)

A Time for Heroes

	NM/M
Complete Set (20):	25.00
Common Player:	1.00
Inserted 1:20	
Darin Erstad	1.00
Alex Rodriguez	4.00
Shawn Green	1.00
Jeff Bagwell	1.50
Sammy Sosa	3.00
Derek Jeter	5.00
Nomar Garciaparra	1.50
Carlos Delgado	1.00
Pat Burrell	1.00
Tony Gwynn	2.50
Chipper Jones	2.50
Jason Giambi	1.00
Magglio Ordonez	1.00
Troy Glaus	1.00
Ivan Rodriguez	1.00
Andruw Jones	1.00
Vladimir Guerrero	2.00
Ken Griffey Jr.	3.00
J.D. Drew	1.00
Todd Helton	1.50

A Time for Heroes Mem.

	NM/M
Common Player:	4.00
Inserted 1:82	
Shawn Green	5.00
Derek Jeter	25.00
Pat Burrell	5.00
Chipper Jones	10.00
Jason Giambi	8.00
Troy Glaus	5.00
Ivan Rodriguez	6.00
Andruw Jones	8.00
J.D. Drew	4.00
Todd Helton	8.00

Brother Wood

	NM/M
Common Player:	4.00
Inserted 1:108	
1BW	Vladimir Guerrero	8.00
2BW	Andruw Jones	4.00
3BW	Corey Patterson	4.00
4BW	Magglio Ordonez	5.00
5BW	Jason Giambi	5.00
6BW	Rafael Palmeiro	5.00
7BW	Eric Chavez	4.00
8BW	Pat Burrell	5.00
9BW	Adrian Beltre	5.00

Decades of Excellence

	NM/M
Complete Set (50):	140.00

2000s

Common Player:	1.00
Inserted 1:12	
Card #17 does not exist.	
Babe Ruth, Lou Gehrig	10.00
Lloyd Waner	1.00
Jimmie Foxx	3.00
Hank Greenberg	2.00
Ted Williams	8.00
Johnny Mize	2.00
Enos Slaughter	1.00
Jackie Robinson	6.00
Stan Musial	5.00
Duke Snider	3.00
Eddie Mathews	3.00
Roy Campanella	2.50
Yogi Berra	4.00
Pee Wee Reese	2.00
Phil Rizzuto	2.00
Al Kaline	4.00
Frank Howard	1.00
Roberto Clemente	8.00
Bob Gibson	3.00
Roger Maris	4.00
Don Drysdale	2.50
Maury Wills	1.00
Tom Seaver	2.50
Reggie Jackson	3.00
Johnny Bench	4.00
Carlton Fisk	2.50
Rod Carew	2.00
Steve Carlton	1.00
Mike Schmidt	6.00
Nolan Ryan	10.00
Rickey Henderson	3.00
Roger Clemens	5.00
Don Mattingly	6.00
George Brett	6.00
Greg Maddux	5.00
Cal Ripken Jr.	10.00
Chipper Jones	5.00
Barry Bonds	10.00
Ivan Rodriguez	2.50
Sammy Sosa,	
Mark McGwire	8.00
Ken Griffey Jr.	6.00
Tony Gwynn	4.00
Vladimir Guerrero	3.00
Shawn Green	1.00
Alex Rodriguez, Derek Jeter,	
Nomar Garciaparra	4.00
Pat Burrell	2.00
Rick Ankiel	1.00
Eric Chavez	1.00
Troy Glaus	2.00

Decades of Excellence Auto.

	NM/M
Common Autograph:	20.00
Production #'s listed.	
1	Rick Ankiel/99	40.00
2	Johnny Bench/67	65.00
3	Barry Bonds/86	150.00
4	George Brett/73	100.00
5	Rod Carew/67	40.00
6	Steve Carlton/65	30.00
7	Eric Chavez/98	20.00
8	Carlton Fisk/69	50.00
9	Bob Gibson/59	40.00
10	Tony Gwynn/82	60.00
11	Reggie Jackson/67	50.00
12	Chipper Jones/93	65.00
13	Al Kaline/53	80.00
14	Don Mattingly/82	100.00
15	Cal Ripken Jr./82	150.00
16	Nolan Ryan/66	125.00
17	Mike Schmidt/72	80.00
18	Tom Seaver/67	50.00
19	Enos Slaughter/38	40.00
20	Maury Wills/59	20.00

Decades of Excellence Mem.

	NM/M
Common Player:	8.00
Inserted 1:217 H	
1	Rick Ankiel/Jsy	8.00
2	Barry Bonds/Jsy	25.00
3	Pat Burrell/Jsy	10.00
4	Roy Campanella/Bat/50	50.00
5	Eric Chavez/Bat	8.00

6	Roberto Clemente/Bat/50	100.00
7	Carlton Fisk/Uni.	15.00
8	Jimmie Foxx/Bat/50	80.00
9	Shawn Green/Bat	8.00
10	Tony Gwynn/Jsy	15.00
11	Reggie Jackson/Jsy	15.00
12	Greg Maddux/Jsy	20.00
13	Roger Maris/Uni.	40.00
14	Pee Wee Reese/Jsy	8.00
15	Cal Ripken/Jsy/50	35.00
16	Ivan Rodriguez/Bat	8.00
17	Nolan Ryan/Jsy	40.00
18	Mike Schmidt/Jsy	20.00
19	Tom Seaver/Jsy	15.00
20	Duke Snider/Bat	15.00
21	Ted Williams/Jsy/50	100.00

Derek Jeter Monumental Moments

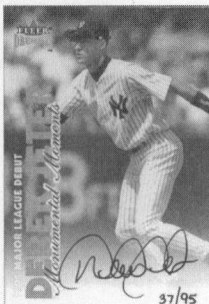

NM/M

Numbered to 1,995.
Autograph numbered to 95.

DJMM	Derek Jeter	8.00
DJMM	Derek Jeter/Auto./95	80.00

Diamond Dominators

NM/M

Common Player: 4.00
Inserted 1:51

1DD	Troy Glaus	5.00
2DD	Darin Erstad	4.00
3DD	J.D. Drew	4.00
4DD	Barry Bonds	20.00
5DD	Roger Clemens	15.00
6DD	Vladimir Guerrero	8.00
7DD	Tony Gwynn	10.00
8DD	Greg Maddux	15.00
9DD	Cal Ripken Jr.	25.00
10DD	Ivan Rodriguez	5.00
11DD	Frank Thomas	8.00
12DD	Bernie Williams	4.00
13DD	Jeromy Burnitz	4.00
14DD	Juan Gonzalez	4.00

Diamond Dominators Patches

NM/M

Common Player: 15.00
Production 100 Sets

1DD	Troy Glaus	25.00
2DD	Darin Erstad	20.00
3DD	J.D. Drew	15.00
4DD	Barry Bonds	75.00
5DD	Roger Clemens	60.00
6DD	Vladimir Guerrero	25.00
7DD	Tony Gwynn	50.00
8DD	Greg Maddux	50.00
9DD	Cal Ripken Jr.	75.00
10DD	Ivan Rodriguez	20.00
11DD	Frank Thomas	25.00
12DD	Bernie Williams	20.00
13DD	Jeromy Burnitz	15.00
14DD	Juan Gonzalez	25.00

Grip It and Rip It

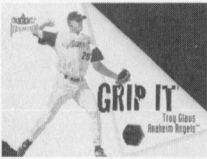

NM/M

Complete Set (15): 10.00

	Common Player:	.50
	Inserted 1:6	
1GRP	Roger Clemens, Derek Jeter	2.00
2GRP	Scott Rolen, Pat Burrell	.50
3GRP	Greg Maddux, Andruw Jones	1.00
4GRP	Shannon Stewart, Carlos Delgado	.50
5GRP	Shawn Estes, Barry Bonds	2.00
6GRP	Cal Eldred, Frank Thomas	.50
7GRP	Mark McGwire, Jim Edmonds	2.00
8GRP	Jose Vidro, Vladimir Guerrero	.75
9GRP	Pedro Martinez, Nomar Garciaparra	1.50
10GRP	Tom Glavine, Chipper Jones	1.00
11GRP	Ken Griffey Jr., Sean Casey	1.00
12GRP	Jeff Bagwell, Moises Alou	.50
13GRP	Troy Glaus, Darin Erstad	.50
14GRP	Mike Piazza, Robin Ventura	1.00
15GRP	Eric Chavez, Jason Giambi	.50

Grip It and Rip It Plus

NM/M

Common Card: 8.00

200 Base/Bat Produced		
100 Ball/Bat Produced		
	Roger Clemens, Derek Jeter/100	50.00
	Scott Rolen, Pat Burrell/200	8.00
	Greg Maddux, Andruw Jones/100	40.00
	Shannon Stewart, Carlos Delgado/200	8.00
	Shawn Estes, Barry Bonds/100	50.00
	Cal Eldred, Frank Thomas/200	15.00
	Mark McGwire, Jim Edmonds/100	60.00
	Jose Vidro, Vladimir Guerrero/200	15.00
	Pedro Martinez, Nomar Garciaparra/100	50.00
	Tom Glavine, Chipper Jones/200	15.00
	Ken Griffey Jr., Sean Casey/200	20.00
	Jeff Bagwell, Moises Alou/200	10.00
	Troy Glaus, Darin Erstad/200	10.00
	Mike Piazza, Robin Ventura/100	40.00
	Eric Chavez, Jason Giambi/200	10.00

Home Field Advantage

NM/M

Complete Set (15): 60.00
Common Player: 2.00
Inserted 1:72

	Mike Piazza	6.00
	Derek Jeter	10.00
	Ken Griffey Jr.	6.00
	Carlos Delgado	2.00
	Chipper Jones	5.00
	Alex Rodriguez	8.00
	Sammy Sosa	4.00
	Scott Rolen	3.00
	Nomar Garciaparra	3.00
	Todd Helton	3.00
	Vladimir Guerrero	3.00
	Jeff Bagwell	3.00
	Barry Bonds	10.00
	Cal Ripken Jr.	10.00
	Mark McGwire	8.00

Home Field Advantage Game Wall

NM/M

Common Player: 6.00
Production 100 Sets

	Mike Piazza	15.00
	Derek Jeter	25.00
	Ken Griffey Jr.	15.00
	Carlos Delgado	6.00
	Chipper Jones	10.00
	Alex Rodriguez	20.00
	Sammy Sosa	8.00
	Scott Rolen	8.00
	Nomar Garciaparra	10.00
	Todd Helton	8.00

	Vladimir Guerrero	8.00
	Jeff Bagwell	8.00
	Barry Bonds	25.00
	Cal Ripken Jr.	25.00
	Mark McGwire	20.00

Solid Performers

NM/M

Complete Set (15): 30.00
Common Player: 1.50
Inserted 1:20

1SP	Mark McGwire	4.00
2SP	Alex Rodriguez	4.00
3SP	Nomar Garciaparra	2.50
4SP	Derek Jeter	5.00
5SP	Vladimir Guerrero	1.50
6SP	Todd Helton	1.50
7SP	Chipper Jones	2.00
8SP	Mike Piazza	2.50
9SP	Ivan Rodriguez	1.50
10SP	Tony Gwynn	2.00
11SP	Cal Ripken Jr.	5.00
12SP	Barry Bonds	5.00
13SP	Jeff Bagwell	1.50
14SP	Ken Griffey Jr.	2.50
15SP	Sammy Sosa	2.50

Solid Performers Game Base

NM/M

Common Player: 5.00
Production 150 Sets

1SP	Mark McGwire	15.00
2SP	Alex Rodriguez	15.00
3SP	Nomar Garciaparra	12.00
4SP	Derek Jeter	20.00
5SP	Vladimir Guerrero	8.00
6SP	Todd Helton	8.00
7SP	Chipper Jones	10.00
8SP	Mike Piazza	12.00
9SP	Ivan Rodriguez	8.00
10SP	Tony Gwynn	10.00
11SP	Cal Ripken Jr.	20.00
12SP	Barry Bonds	20.00
13SP	Jeff Bagwell	8.00
14SP	Ken Griffey Jr.	12.00
15SP	Sammy Sosa	12.00

2001 Fleer Showcase

NM/M

Complete Set (160): .25
Common Player: .25
Common SP (116-125): 8.00
Production 500
Common SP (126-145): 3.00
Production 1,500
Common SP (146-160): 3.00
Production 2,000
Pack (5): 8.00
Box (24): 160.00

1	Tony Gwynn	1.50
2	Barry Larkin	.25
3	Chan Ho Park	.25
4	Darin Erstad	.65
5	Rafael Furcal	.25
6	Roger Cedeno	.25
7	Timo Perez	.25
8	Rick Ankiel	.25

9	Pokey Reese	.25
10	Jeromy Burnitz	.25
11	Phil Nevin	.25
12	Matt Williams	.25
13	Mike Hampton	.25
14	Fernando Tatis	.25
15	Kazuhiro Sasaki	.25
16	Jim Thome	.25
17	Geoff Jenkins	.25
18	Jeff Kent	.25
19	Tom Glavine	.40
20	Dean Palmer	.25
21	Todd Zeile	.25
22	Edgar Renteria	.25
23	Andruw Jones	1.00
24	Juan Encarnacion	.25
25	Robin Ventura	.25
26	J.D. Drew	.25
27	Ray Durham	.25
28	Richard Hidalgo	.25
29	Eric Chavez	.35
30	Rafael Palmeiro	.75
31	Steve Finley	.25
32	Jeff Weaver	.25
33	Al Leiter	.25
34	Jim Edmonds	.25
35	Garret Anderson	.25
36	Larry Walker	.25
37	Jose Vidro	.25
38	Mike Cameron	.25
39	Brady Anderson	.25
40	Mike Lowell	.25
41	Bernie Williams	.35
42	Gary Sheffield	.40
43	John Smoltz	.25
44	Mike Mussina	.40
45	Greg Vaughn	.25
46	Juan Gonzalez	.75
47	Matt Lawton	.25
48	Robb Nen	.25
49	Brad Radke	.25
50	Edgar Martinez	.25
51	Mike Bordick	.25
52	Shawn Green	.40
53	Carl Everett	.25
54	Adrian Beltre	.40
55	Kerry Wood	.50
56	Kevin Brown	.25
57	Brian Giles	.25
58	Greg Maddux	1.50
59	Preston Wilson	.25
60	Orlando Hernandez	.25
61	Ben Grieve	.25
62	Jermaine Dye	.25
63	Travis Lee	.25
64	Jose Cruz Jr.	.25
65	Rondell White	.25
66	Carlos Beltran	.45
67	Scott Rolen	.75
68	Brad Fullmer	.25
69	David Wells	.25
70	Mike Sweeney	.25
71	Barry Zito	.40
72	Tony Batista	.25
73	Curt Schilling	.40
74	Jeff Cirillo	.25
75	Edgardo Alfonzo	.25
76	John Olerud	.25
77	Carlos Lee	.25
78	Moises Alou	.25
79	Tim Hudson	.35
80	Andres Galarraga	.25
81	Roberto Alomar	.45
82	Richie Sexson	.25
83	Trevor Hoffman	.25
84	Omar Vizquel	.25
85	Jacque Jones	.25
86	J.T. Snow	.25
87	Sean Casey	.25
88	Craig Biggio	.40
89	Mariano Rivera	.35
90	Rusty Greer	.25
91	Barry Bonds	3.00
92	Pedro Martinez	3.00
93	Cal Ripken Jr.	3.00
94	Pat Burrell	.50
95	Chipper Jones	1.50
96	Magglio Ordonez	.25
97	Jeff Bagwell	1.00
98	Randy Johnson	1.00
99	Frank Thomas	1.00
100	Jason Kendall	.25
101	Nomar Garciaparra	6.00
102	Mark McGwire	8.00
103	Troy Glaus	3.00
104	Ivan Rodriguez	2.50
105	Manny Ramirez	3.00
106	Derek Jeter	10.00
107	Alex Rodriguez	8.00
108	Ken Griffey Jr.	6.00
109	Todd Helton	3.00
110	Sammy Sosa	6.00
111	Vladimir Guerrero	3.00
112	Mike Piazza	6.00
113	Roger Clemens	5.00
114	Jason Giambi	2.50
115	Carlos Delgado	2.00
116	Ichiro Suzuki **RC**	75.00
117	Morgan Ensberg **RC**	8.00
118	Carlos Valderrama **RC**	8.00
119	Erick Almonte **RC**	8.00
120	Tsuyoshi Shinjo **RC**	8.00
121	Albert Pujols **RC**	150.00
122	Wilson Betemit **RC**	10.00
123	Adrian Hernandez **RC**	8.00
124	Jackson Melian **RC**	8.00
125	Drew Henson **RC**	10.00

126	Paul Phillips RC	3.00
127	Esix Snead RC	3.00
128	Ryan Freel RC	4.00
129	Junior Spivey RC	3.00
130	Elpidio Guzman RC	3.00
131	Juan Diaz RC	3.00
132	Andres Torres RC	3.00
133	Jay Gibbons RC	3.00
134	Bill Ortega	3.00
135	Alexis Gomez RC	3.00
136	Wilken Ruan RC	3.00
137	Henry Mateo RC	3.00
138	Juan Uribe RC	3.00
139	Johnny Estrada RC	3.00
140	Jaisen Randolph RC	3.00
141	Eric Hinske RC	4.00
142	Jack Wilson RC	5.00
143	Cody Ransom RC	3.00
144	Nate Frese RC	3.00
145	John Grabow RC	3.00
146	Christian Parker RC	3.00
147	Brian Lawrence RC	3.00
148	Brandon Duckworth RC	3.00
149	Winston Abreu RC	4.00
150	Horacio Ramirez RC	4.00
151	Nick Maness RC	3.00
152	Blaine Neal RC	3.00
153	Billy Sylvester RC	3.00
154	David Elder RC	3.00
155	Bert Snow RC	3.00
156	Claudio Vargas RC	3.00
157	Martin Vargas RC	3.00
158	Grant Balfour RC	3.00
159	Randy Keisler RC	3.00
160	Zach Day RC	3.00

Legacy

Stars (1-100):	10-15X
Avant (101-115):	2-4X
RC's (116-125):	.75-1.5X
RC's (126-160):	1-2X
Production 50 Sets	

Autographics

	NM/M
Common Player:	5.00
Silvers:	1X
Production 250 Sets	
Golds:	1-2X
Production 50 Sets	
Roberto Alomar	25.00
Rick Ankiel	15.00
Albert Belle	8.00
Carlos Beltran	25.00
Adrian Beltre	10.00
Milton Bradley	8.00
Dee Brown	5.00
Jeromy Burnitz	5.00
Pat Burrell	15.00
Sean Casey	8.00
Joseph Crede	5.00
Jose Cruz Jr.	5.00
Ryan Dempster	5.00
J.D. Drew	15.00
Adam Dunn	15.00
Erubiel Durazo	5.00
Jermaine Dye	10.00
David Eckstein	8.00
Alex Escobar	5.00
Seth Etherton	5.00
Adam Everett	5.00
Carlos Febles	5.00
Troy Glaus	10.00
Ben Grieve	5.00
Toby Hall	5.00
Todd Helton	20.00
Shea Hillenbrand	5.00
Aubrey Huff	8.00
D'Angelo Jimenez	5.00
Paul Konerko	10.00
Mike Lamb	5.00
Matt Lawton	5.00
Derrek Lee	15.00
Mike Lieberthal	5.00
Mike Lowell	15.00
Julio Lugo	5.00
Jason Marquis	5.00
Edgar Martinez	15.00
Kevin Millwood	10.00
Eric Milton	5.00
Bengie Molina	8.00
Mike Mussina	25.00
Russ Ortiz	5.00
Corey Patterson	8.00
Jay Payton	5.00
Adam Piatt	5.00
Juan Pierre	8.00
Brad Radke	5.00
John Rocker	5.00
Alex Rodriguez	75.00
Scott Rolen	20.00
Richie Sexson	8.00
Gary Sheffield	15.00
Shannon Stewart	5.00

Miguel Tejada	25.00
Robin Ventura	5.00
Jose Vidro	5.00
Billy Wagner	8.00
Kip Wells	5.00
Rondell White	5.00
Preston Wilson	5.00
Kerry Wood	20.00
Julio Zuleta	5.00

Awards Showcase

	NM/M
Complete Set (20):	25.00
Common Player:	1.00
Inserted 1:20 Retail	
Derek Jeter	5.00
Derek Jeter	5.00
Jason Giambi	1.50
Jeff Kent	1.00
Pedro Martinez	2.00
Randy Johnson	2.00
Kazuhiro Sasaki	1.00
Rafael Furcal	1.50
Carlos Delgado	1.50
Todd Helton	2.00
Ivan Rodriguez	1.50
Darin Erstad	1.00
Bernie Williams	1.50
Greg Maddux	3.00
Jim Edmonds	1.00
Andruw Jones	1.00
Nomar Garciaparra	1.50
Todd Helton	2.00
Troy Glaus	1.50
Sammy Sosa	3.00

Awards Showcase Autos.

	NM/M
Production 25 Sets	
Johnny Bench	100.00
Yogi Berra	90.00
George Brett	200.00
Steve Carlton	60.00
Roger Clemens	150.00
Andre Dawson	40.00
Whitey Ford	80.00
Tom Glavine	50.00
Juan Gonzalez	40.00
Reggie Jackson	80.00
Randy Johnson	90.00
Chipper Jones	80.00
Harmon Killebrew	75.00
Fred Lynn	25.00
Greg Maddux	150.00
Don Mattingly	150.00
Willie McCovey	40.00
Jim Palmer	40.00
Jim Rice	25.00
Brooks Robinson	60.00
Frank Robinson	50.00
Ivan Rodriguez	50.00
Mike Schmidt	100.00
Tom Seaver	100.00

Awards Showcase Mem.

	NM/M
Common Player:	10.00
Production 100 Sets	
Johnny Bench	20.00
Yogi Berra	15.00
George Brett	40.00
Lou Brock	10.00
Roy Campanella	25.00
Steve Carlton	10.00
Roger Clemens	40.00
Andre Dawson	10.00
Whitey Ford	15.00
Jimmie Foxx	50.00
Kirk Gibson	10.00
Tom Glavine	10.00
Juan Gonzalez	10.00
Elston Howard	10.00
Jim "Catfish" Hunter	10.00
Reggie Jackson	15.00
Randy Johnson	20.00
Chipper Jones	15.00
Harmon Killebrew	20.00
Greg Maddux	25.00
Don Mattingly	40.00

Willie McCovey	10.00
Jim Palmer	10.00
Jim Rice	10.00
Brooks Robinson	20.00
Frank Robinson	15.00
Jackie Robinson	75.00
Ivan Rodriguez	15.00
Mike Schmidt	40.00
Tom Seaver	15.00
Willie Stargell	15.00
Ted Williams	100.00
Robin Yount	25.00

Derek Jeter's Monumental Moments

	NM/M
Production 2,000:	
MM5 Derek Jeter	8.00
Derek Jeter/Auto./100	80.00

Showcase Sticks

	NM/M
Common Player:	4.00
Inserted 1:24	
Roberto Alomar	6.00
Adrian Beltre	6.00
Pat Burrell	6.00
J.D. Drew	4.00
Juan Gonzalez	6.00
Andruw Jones	4.00
Chipper Jones	10.00
Magglio Ordonez	4.00
Ivan Rodriguez	6.00
Scott Rolen	8.00
Frank Thomas	8.00
Roger Cedeno	4.00
Shawn Green	4.00
Richard Hidalgo	4.00
Tony Clark	4.00
Preston Wilson	4.00
Barry Bonds	25.00
Rafael Furcal	6.00
Randy Johnson	8.00
Vladimir Guerrero	8.00
Al Kaline	10.00
George Kell	4.00
Jason Kendall	4.00
Carlos Delgado	5.00
Adam Piatt	4.00
Alex Gonzalez	4.00
Jorge Posada	6.00
Jose Vidro	4.00
Roger Clemens	20.00
Steve Finley	4.00
Reggie Jackson	8.00
Shannon Stewart	4.00
Rick Ankiel	8.00
Jim Thome	8.00
Tsuyoshi Shinjo	4.00
Ichiro Suzuki	25.00

Sweet Sigs

	NM/M
Common Player:	10.00
Inserted 1:24	
Prices for Lumber	
Wall:	1X
Leather:	1-1.5X
Bobby Abreu	15.00
Wilson Betemit	10.00
Russell Branyan	10.00
Pat Burrell	20.00
Eric Chavez	15.00
Rafael Furcal	15.00
Nomar Garciaparra	75.00
Juan Gonzalez	20.00
Elpidio Guzman	10.00

Drew Henson	10.00
Brandon Inge	10.00
Derek Jeter	125.00
Andruw Jones	25.00
Willie Mays	180.00
Jackson Melian	10.00
Xavier Nady	10.00
Jose Ortiz	10.00
Ben Sheets	15.00
Mike Sweeney	10.00
Miguel Tejada	25.00
Albert Pujols	400.00

2001 Fleer Tradition

		NM/M
Complete Set (450):		35.00
Common Player:		.15
Comp. Factory Set (485):		100.00
Pack (10):		2.00
Box (36):		55.00
1	Andres Galarraga	.15
2	Armando Rios	.15
3	Julio Lugo	.15
4	Darryl Hamilton	.15
5	Dave Veres	.15
6	Edgardo Alfonzo	.15
7	Brook Fordyce	.15
8	Eric Karros	.15
9	Neifi Perez	.15
10	Jim Edmonds	.15
11	Barry Larkin	.25
12	Trot Nixon	.15
13	Andy Pettitte	.40
14	Jose Guillen	.15
15	David Wells	.15
16	Magglio Ordonez	.25
17	David Segui	.15
18	Juan Encarnacion	.15
19	Robert Person	.15
20	Quilvio Veras	.15
21	Mo Vaughn	.15
22	B.J. Surhoff	.15
23	Ken Caminiti	.15
24	Frank Catalanotto	.15
25	Luis Gonzalez	.25
26	Pete Harnisch	.15
27	Alex Gonzalez	.15
28	Mark Quinn	.15
29	Luis Castillo	.15
30	Rick Helling	.15
31	Barry Bonds	2.00
32	Warren Morris	.15
33	Aaron Boone	.15
34	Ricky Gutierrez	.15
35	Preston Wilson	.15
36	Erubiel Durazo	.15
37	Jermaine Dye	.25
38	John Rocker	.15
39	Mark Grudzielanek	.15
40	Pedro Martinez	.75
41	Phil Nevin	.15
42	Luis Matos	.15
43	Orlando Hernandez	.15
44	Steve Cox	.15
45	James Baldwin	.15
46	Rafael Furcal	.25
47	Todd Zeile	.15
48	Elmer Dessens	.15
49	Russell Branyan	.15
50	Juan Gonzalez	.40
51	Mac Suzuki	.15
52	Adam Kennedy	.15
53	Randy Velarde	.15
54	David Bell	.15
55	Royce Clayton	.15
56	Greg Colbrunn	.15
57	Rey Ordonez	.15
58	Kevin Millwood	.15
59	Fernando Vina	.15
60	Eddie Taubensee	.15
61	Enrique Wilson	.15
62	Jay Bell	.15
63	Brian Moehler	.15
64	Brad Fullmer	.15
65	Ben Petrick	.15
66	Orlando Cabrera	.25
67	Shane Reynolds	.15
68	Mitch Meluskey	.15
69	Jeff Shaw	.15
70	Chipper Jones	1.00
71	Tomo Ohka	.15
72	Ruben Rivera	.15
73	Mike Sirotka	.15
74	Scott Rolen	.50
75	Glendon Rusch	.15
76	Miguel Tejada	.40
77	Brady Anderson	.15
78	Bartolo Colon	.15
79	Ron Coomer	.15
80	Gary DiSarcina	.15
81	Geoff Jenkins	.15
82	Billy Koch	.15

83	Mike Lamb	.15
84	Alex Rodriguez	1.50
85	Denny Neagle	.15
86	Michael Tucker	.15
87	Edgar Renteria	.15
88	Brian Anderson	.15
89	Glenallen Hill	.15
90	Aramis Ramirez	.25
91	Rondell White	.15
92	Tony Womack	.15
93	Jeffrey Hammonds	.15
94	Freddy Garcia	.15
95	Bill Mueller	.15
96	Mike Lieberthal	.15
97	Michael Barrett	.15
98	Derrek Lee	.40
99	Bill Spiers	.15
100	Derek Lowe	.15
101	Javy Lopez	.15
102	Adrian Beltre	.40
103	Jim Parque	.15
104	Marquis Grissom	.15
105	Eric Chavez	.25
106	Todd Jones	.15
107	Eric Owens	.15
108	Roger Clemens	1.00
109	Denny Hocking	.15
110	Roberto Hernandez	.15
111	Albert Belle	.15
112	Troy Glaus	.40
113	Ivan Rodriguez	.50
114	Carlos Guillen	.15
115	Chuck Finley	.15
116	Dmitri Young	.15
117	Paul Konerko	.25
118	Damon Buford	.15
119	Fernando Tatis	.15
120	Larry Walker	.15
121	Jason Kendall	.15
122	Matt Williams	.15
123	Henry Rodriguez	.15
124	Placido Polanco	.15
125	Bobby Estalella	.15
126	Pat Burrell	.50
127	Mark Loretta	.15
128	Moises Alou	.25
129	Tino Martinez	.25
130	Milton Bradley	.25
131	Todd Hundley	.15
132	Keith Foulke	.15
133	Robert Fick	.15
134	Cristian Guzman	.15
135	Rusty Greer	.15
136	John Olerud	.15
137	Mariano Rivera	.25
138	Jeromy Burnitz	.15
139	Dave Burba	.15
140	Ken Griffey Jr.	1.50
141	Tony Gwynn	1.00
142	Carlos Delgado	.50
143	Edgar Martinez	.15
144	Ramon Hernandez	.15
145	Pedro Astacio	.15
146	Ray Lankford	.15
147	Mike Mussina	.40
148	Ray Durham	.15
149	Lee Stevens	.15
150	Jay Canizaro	.15
151	Adrian Brown	.15
152	Mike Piazza	1.00
153	Cliff Floyd	.15
154	Jose Vidro	.15
155	Jason Giambi	.50
156	Andruw Jones	.40
157	Robin Ventura	.15
158	Gary Sheffield	.40
159	Jeff D'Amico	.15
160	Chuck Knoblauch	.15
161	Roger Cedeno	.15
162	Jim Thome	.25
163	Peter Bergeron	.15
164	Kerry Wood	.50
165	Gabe Kapler	.15
166	Corey Koskie	.15
167	Doug Glanville	.15
168	Brent Mayne	.15
169	Scott Spiezio	.15
170	Steve Karsay	.15
171	Al Martin	.15
172	Fred McGriff	.15
173	Gabe White	.15
174	Alex Gonzalez	.15
175	Mike Darr	.15
176	Bengie Molina	.15
177	Ben Grieve	.15
178	Marlon Anderson	.15
179	Brian Giles	.15
180	Jose Valentin	.15
181	Brian Jordan	.15
182	Randy Johnson	.75
183	Ricky Ledee	.15
184	Russ Ortiz	.15
185	Mike Lowell	.15
186	Curtis Leskanic	.15
187	Bobby Abreu	.25
188	Derek Jeter	2.00
189	Lance Berkman	.40
190	Roberto Alomar	.40
191	Darin Erstad	.40
192	Richie Sexson	.15
193	Alex Ochoa	.15
194	Carlos Febles	.15
195	David Ortiz	.75
196	Shawn Green	.25
197	Mike Sweeney	.15
198	Vladimir Guerrero	.75
199	Jose Jimenez	.15
200	Travis Lee	.15
201	Rickey Henderson	.75
202	Bob Wickman	.15
203	Miguel Cairo	.15
204	Steve Finley	.15
205	Tony Batista	.15
206	Jamey Wright	.15
207	Terrence Long	.15
208	Trevor Hoffman	.15
209	John Vander Wal	.15
210	Greg Maddux	1.00
211	Tim Salmon	.25
212	Herbert Perry	.15
213	Marvin Benard	.15
214	Jose Offerman	.15
215	Jay Payton	.15
216	Jon Lieber	.15
217	Mark Kotsay	.15
218	Scott Brosius	.15
219	Scott Williamson	.15
220	Omar Vizquel	.15
221	Mike Hampton	.15
222	Richard Hidalgo	.15
223	Rey Sanchez	.15
224	Matt Lawton	.15
225	Bruce Chen	.15
226	Ryan Klesko	.15
227	Garret Anderson	.15
228	Kevin Brown	.15
229	Mike Cameron	.15
230	Tony Clark	.15
231	Curt Schilling	.40
232	Vinny Castilla	.15
233	Carl Pavano	.15
234	Eric Davis	.15
235	Darrin Fletcher	.15
236	Matt Stairs	.15
237	Octavio Dotel	.15
238	Mark Grace	.25
239	John Smoltz	.25
240	Matt Clement	.15
241	Ellis Burks	.15
242	Charles Johnson	.15
243	Jeff Bagwell	.50
244	Derek Bell	.15
245	Nomar Garciaparra	.50
246	Jorge Posada	.40
247	Ryan Dempster	.15
248	J.T. Snow	.15
249	Eric Young	.15
250	Daryle Ward	.15
251	Joe Randa	.15
252	Travis Fryman	.15
253	Mike Williams	.15
254	Jacque Jones	.15
255	Scott Elarton	.15
256	Mark McGwire	1.00
257	Jay Buhner	.15
258	Randy Wolf	.15
259	Sammy Sosa	.75
260	Chan Ho Park	.15
261	Damion Easley	.15
262	Rick Ankiel	.50
263	Frank Thomas	.75
264	Kris Benson	.15
265	Luis Alicea	.15
266	Jeremy Giambi	.15
267	Geoff Blum	.15
268	Joe Girardi	.15
269	Livan Hernandez	.15
270	Jeff Conine	.15
271	Danny Graves	.15
272	Craig Biggio	.25
273	Jose Canseco	.40
274	Tom Glavine	.50
275	Ruben Mateo	.15
276	Jeff Kent	.25
277	Kevin Young	.15
278	A.J. Burnett	.15
279	Dante Bichette	.15
280	Sandy Alomar Jr.	.15
281	John Wetteland	.15
282	Torii Hunter	.25
283	Jarrod Washburn	.15
284	Rich Aurilia	.15
285	Jeff Cirillo	.15
286	Fernando Seguignol	.15
287	Darren Dreifort	.15
288	Deivi Cruz	.15
289	Pokey Reese	.15
290	Garrett Stephenson	.15
291	Pat Boone	.15
292	Tim Hudson	.40
293	John Flaherty	.15
294	Shannon Stewart	.15
295	Shawn Estes	.15
296	Wilton Guerrero	.15
297	Delino DeShields	.15
298	David Justice	.15
299	Harold Baines	.15
300	Al Leiter	.15
301	Wil Cordero	.15
302	Antonio Alfonseca	.15
303	Sean Casey	.25
304	Carlos Beltran	.40
305	Brad Radke	.15
306	Jason Varitek	.25
307	Shigetosi Hasegawa	.15
308	Todd Stottlemyre	.15
309	Raul Mondesi	.15
310	Mike Bordick	.15
311	Darryl Kile	.15
312	Dean Palmer	.15
313	Johnny Damon	.50
314	Todd Helton	.75
315	Chad Hermansen	.15
316	Kevin Appier	.15
317	Greg Vaughn	.15
318	Robb Nen	.15
319	Jose Cruz Jr.	.15
320	Ron Belliard	.15
321	Bernie Williams	.40
322	Melvin Mora	.15
323	Kenny Lofton	.15
324	Armando Benitez	.15
325	Carlos Lee	.25
326	Damian Jackson	.15
327	Eric Milton	.15
328	J.D. Drew	.40
329	Byung-Hyun Kim	.15
330	Chris Stynes	.15
331	Kazuhiro Sasaki	.15
332	Troy O'Leary	.15
333	Pat Hentgen	.15
334	Brad Ausmus	.15
335	Todd Walker	.15
336	Jason Isringhausen	.15
337	Gerald Williams	.15
338	Aaron Sele	.15
339	Paul O'Neill	.25
340	Cal Ripken Jr.	2.00
341	Manny Ramirez	.75
342	Will Clark	.40
343	Mark Redman	.15
344	Bubba Trammell	.15
345	Troy Percival	.15
346	Chris Singleton	.15
347	Rafael Palmeiro	.50
348	Carl Everett	.15
349	Andy Benes	.15
350	Bobby Higginson	.15
351	Alex Cabrera	.15
352	Barry Zito	.40
353	Jace Brewer	.15
354	Paxton Crawford	.15
355	Oswaldo Mairena	.15
356	Joe Crede	.15
357	A.J. Pierzynski	.15
358	Daniel Garibay	.15
359	Jason Tyner	.15
360	Nate Rolison	.15
361	Scott Downs	.15
362	Keith Ginter	.15
363	Juan Pierre	.15
364	Adam Bernero	.15
365	Chris Richard	.15
366	Joey Nation	.15
367	Aubrey Huff	.15
368	Adam Eaton	.15
369	Jose Ortiz	.15
370	Eric Munson	.15
371	Matt Kinney	.15
372	Eric Byrnes	.40
373	Keith McDonald	.15
374	Matt Wise	.15
375	Timo Perez	.15
376	Julio Zuleta	.15
377	Jimmy Rollins	.50
378	Xavier Nady	.25
379	Ryan Kohlmeier	.15
380	Corey Patterson	.15
381	Todd Helton	.40
382	Moises Alou	.15
383	Vladimir Guerrero	.40
384	Luis Castillo	.15
385	Jeffrey Hammonds	.15
386	Nomar Garciaparra	.40
387	Carlos Delgado	.25
388	Darin Erstad	.15
389	Manny Ramirez	.40
390	Mike Sweeney	.15
391	Sammy Sosa	.50
392	Barry Bonds	1.00
393	Jeff Bagwell	.40
394	Richard Hidalgo	.15
395	Vladimir Guerrero	.40
396	Troy Glaus	.25
397	Frank Thomas	.40
398	Carlos Delgado	.25
399	David Justice	.15
400	Jason Giambi	.25
401	Randy Johnson	.40
402	Kevin Brown	.15
403	Greg Maddux	.50
404	Al Leiter	.15
405	Mike Hampton	.15
406	Pedro Martinez	.40
407	Roger Clemens	.50
408	Mike Sirotka	.15
409	Mike Mussina	.25
410	Bartolo Colon	.15
411	World Series Update	.15
412	World Series Update	.15
413	World Series Update	.15
414	World Series Update	.15
415	World Series Update	.15
416	World Series Update	.15
417	World Series Update	.15
418	World Series Update	.15
419	World Series Update	.15
420	World Series Update	.15
421	Atlanta Braves	.15
422	New York Mets	.15
423	Florida Marlins	.15
424	Philadelphia Phillies	.15
425	Montreal Expos	.15
426	St. Louis Cardinals	.15
427	Cincinnati Reds	.15
428	Chicago Cubs	.15
429	Milwaukee Brewers	.15
430	Houston Astros	.15
431	Pittsburgh Pirates	.15
432	San Francisco Giants	.15
433	Arizona Diamondbacks	.15
434	Los Angeles Dodgers	.15
435	Colorado Rockies	.15
436	San Diego Padres	.15
437	New York Yankees	.15
438	Boston Red Sox	.15
439	Baltimore Orioles	.15
440	Toronto Blue Jays	.15
441	Tampa Bay Devil Rays	.15
442	Chicago White Sox	.15
443	Cleveland Indians	.15
444	Detroit Tigers	.15
445	Kansas City Royals	.15
446	Minnesota Twins	.15
447	Seattle Mariners	.15
448	Oakland Athletics	.15
449	Anaheim Angels	.15
450	Texas Rangers	.15
451	Albert Pujols **RC**	50.00
452	Ichiro Suzuki **RC**	15.00
453	Tsuyoshi Shinjo **RC**	.50
454	Johnny Estrada **RC**	.75
455	Elpidio Guzman **RC**	.40
456	Adrian Hernandez **RC**	.25
457	Rafael Soriano **RC**	.75
458	Drew Henson **RC**	1.00
459	Juan Uribe **RC**	.75
460	Matt White **RC**	.40
461	Endy Chavez **RC**	.25
462	Bud Smith **RC**	.25
463	Morgan Ensberg **RC**	.50
464	Jay Gibbons **RC**	1.00
465	Jackson Melian **RC**	.25
466	Junior Spivey **RC**	.50
467	Juan Cruz **RC**	.50
468	Wilson Betemit **RC**	.40
469	Alexis Gomez **RC**	.25
470	Mark Teixeira **RC**	10.00
471	Erick Almonte **RC**	.25
472	Travis Hafner **RC**	4.00
473	Carlos Valderrama **RC**	.25
474	Brandon Duckworth **RC**	.50
475	Ryan Freel **RC**	.50
476	Wilkin Ruan **RC**	.25
477	Andres Torres **RC**	.25
478	Josh Towers **RC**	.50
479	Kyle Lohse **RC**	.50
480	Jason Michaels **RC**	.25
481	Alfonso Soriano	.50
482	C.C. Sabathia	.40
483	Roy Oswalt	.25
484	Ben Sheets	.25
485	Adam Dunn	.50

Diamond Tributes

		NM/M
Complete Set (30):		35.00
Common Player:		.50
Inserted 1:7		
1	Jackie Robinson	2.00
2	Mike Piazza	2.00
3	Alex Rodriguez	3.00
4	Barry Bonds	4.00
5	Nomar Garciaparra	1.00
6	Roger Clemens	2.00
7	Ivan Rodriguez	.75
8	Cal Ripken Jr.	4.00
9	Manny Ramirez	1.00
10	Chipper Jones	1.50
11	Barry Larkin	.50
12	Carlos Delgado	.75
13	J.D. Drew	.60
14	Carl Everett	.50
15	Todd Helton	1.00
16	Greg Maddux	2.00
17	Scott Rolen	.75
18	Troy Glaus	1.00
19	Brian Giles	.50
20	Jeff Bagwell	1.00
21	Sammy Sosa	1.50
22	Randy Johnson	1.00
23	Andruw Jones	.75
24	Ken Griffey Jr.	2.00
25	Mark McGwire	2.50
26	Derek Jeter	4.00
27	Vladimir Guerrero	1.00
28	Frank Thomas	1.00
29	Pedro Martinez	1.00
30	Bernie Williams	.50

Grass Roots

		NM/M
Complete Set (15):		25.00
Common Player:		1.00
Inserted 1:18		
1	Derek Jeter	4.00
2	Greg Maddux	2.00

#	Player	Price
3	Sammy Sosa	1.50
4	Alex Rodriguez	3.00
5	Vladimir Guerrero	1.00
6	Scott Rolen	1.00
7	Frank Thomas	1.50
8	Nomar Garciaparra	1.00
9	Cal Ripken Jr.	4.00
10	Mike Piazza	2.50
11	Ivan Rodriguez	1.00
12	Chipper Jones	2.00
13	Tony Gwynn	2.00
14	Ken Griffey Jr.	2.50
15	Mark McGwire	3.00

Lumber Company

		NM/M
Complete Set (20):		25.00
Common Player:		.50
Inserted 1:12		
1	Vladimir Guerrero	1.50
2	Mo Vaughn	.50
3	Ken Griffey Jr.	2.50
4	Juan Gonzalez	1.00
5	Tony Gwynn	2.00
6	Jim Edmonds	.50
7	Jason Giambi	1.00
8	Alex Rodriguez	3.00
9	Derek Jeter	4.00
10	Darin Erstad	1.00
11	Andruw Jones	1.00
12	Cal Ripken Jr.	4.00
13	Magglio Ordonez	.75
14	Nomar Garciaparra	1.00
15	Chipper Jones	1.50
16	Sean Casey	.50
17	Shawn Green	.50
18	Mike Piazza	2.50
19	Sammy Sosa	2.50
20	Barry Bonds	4.00

Season Pass
No Pricing

Stitches in Time

		NM/M
Complete Set (25):		40.00
Common Player:		1.50
Inserted 1:18		
1	Henry Kimbro	1.50
2	Ernie Banks	3.00
3	James "Cool Papa" Bell	2.00
4	Joe Black	1.50
5	Roy Campanella	2.00
6	Ray Dandridge	1.50
7	Leon Day	1.50
8	Larry Doby	2.00
9	Josh Gibson	2.00
10	Elston Howard	2.00
11	Monte Irvin	2.00
12	Buck Leonard	2.00
13	Max Manning	1.50
14	Willie Mays	6.00
15	Buck O'Neil	2.00
16	Satchel Paige	3.00
17	Ted Radcliffe	2.00
18	Jackie Robinson	4.00
19	Bill Perkins	1.50
20	Andrew "Rube" Foster	2.00
21	William "Judy" Johnson	1.50
22	Oscar Charleston	1.50
23	John Henry "Pop" Lloyd	1.50
24	Artie Wilson	1.50
25	Sam Jethroe	1.50

Stitches in Time Autos.

		NM/M
Common Autograph:		20.00
2	Ernie Banks	60.00
4	Joe Black	25.00

#	Player	Price
11	Monte Irvin	40.00
14	Willie Mays	150.00
15	Buck O'Neil	50.00
17	Ted Radcliffe	40.00
24	Artie Wilson	20.00

Stitches in Time Game-Used

		NM/M
Common Card:		25.00
5	Roy Campanella	60.00
8	Larry Doby/Bat	30.00
10	Elston Howard/Bat	30.00
14	Willie Mays/Jsy	125.00
18	Jackie Robinson/Jsy	100.00

Turn Back the Clock

		NM/M
Common Card:		8.00
Inserted 1:352		
1	Tom Glavine	10.00
2	Greg Maddux	30.00
3	Sean Casey	8.00
4	Pokey Reese	8.00
5	Jason Giambi	15.00
6	Tim Hudson	8.00
7	Larry Walker	8.00
8	Jeffrey Hammonds	8.00
9	Scott Rolen	15.00
10	Pat Burrell	10.00
11	Chipper Jones	20.00
13	Troy Glaus	15.00
14	Tony Gwynn	20.00
15	Cal Ripken Jr.	50.00
16	Tom Glavine, Greg Maddux	75.00
17	Sean Casey, Pokey Reese	30.00
18	Chipper Jones, Greg Maddux	100.00
19	Larry Walker, Jeffrey Hammonds	40.00
20	Scott Rolen, Pat Burrell	40.00
21	Jason Giambi, Tim Hudson	40.00

Warning Track

		NM/M
Complete Set (25):		120.00
Common Player:		2.00
Inserted 1:72		
1	Josh Gibson	5.00
2	Willie Mays	10.00
3	Mark McGwire	10.00
4	Barry Bonds	15.00
5	Jose Canseco	4.00
6	Ken Griffey Jr.	10.00
7	Cal Ripken Jr.	15.00
8	Rafael Palmeiro	5.00
9	Sammy Sosa	5.00
10	Juan Gonzalez	4.00
11	Frank Thomas	6.00
12	Jeff Bagwell	5.00
13	Gary Sheffield	2.50
14	Larry Walker	2.00
15	Mike Piazza	10.00
16	Larry Doby	4.00
17	Roy Campanella	5.00
18	Manny Ramirez	6.00
19	Chipper Jones	8.00
20	Alex Rodriguez	12.00
21	Ivan Rodriguez	5.00
22	Vladimir Guerrero	6.00
23	Nomar Garciaparra	4.00
24	Andres Galarraga	2.00
25	Jim Thome	2.00

2001 Fleer Triple Crown

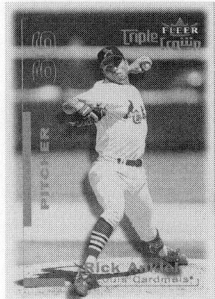

		NM/M
Complete Set (300):		25.00
Common Player:		.15
Pack (10):		2.00
Box (24):		40.00
1	Derek Jeter	2.00
2	Vladimir Guerrero	.75
3	Henry Rodriguez	.15
4	Jason Giambi	.50
5	Nomar Garciaparra	.75
6	Jeff Kent	.15
7	Garret Anderson	.15
8	Todd Helton	.75
9	Barry Bonds	2.00
10	Preston Wilson	.15
11	Troy Glaus	.40
12	Geoff Jenkins	.15
13	Jim Edmonds	.15
14	Bobby Higginson	.15
15	Mark Quinn	.15
16	Barry Larkin	.25
17	Richie Sexson	.15
18	Fernando Tatis	.15
19	John Vander Wal	.15
20	Darin Erstad	.40
21	Shawn Green	.40
22	Scott Rolen	.50
23	Tony Batista	.15
24	Phil Nevin	.15
25	Tim Salmon	.25
26	Gary Sheffield	.35
27	Ben Grieve	.15
28	Jermaine Dye	.15
29	Andres Galarraga	.15
30	Adrian Beltre	.40
31	Rafael Palmeiro	.50
32	J.T. Snow	.15
33	Edgardo Alfonzo	.15
34	Paul Konerko	.25
35	Jim Thome	.25
36	Andruw Jones	.40
37	Mike Sweeney	.15
38	Jose Cruz Jr.	.15
39	David Ortiz	.75
40	Pat Burrell	.40
41	Chipper Jones	1.00
42	Jeff Bagwell	.50
43	Raul Mondesi	.15
44	Rondell White	.15
45	Edgar Martinez	.15
46	Cal Ripken Jr.	2.00
47	Moises Alou	.25
48	Shannon Stewart	.15
49	Tino Martinez	.25
50	Jason Kendall	.15
51	Richard Hidalgo	.15
52	Albert Belle	.15
53	Jay Payton	.15
54	Cliff Floyd	.15
55	Rusty Greer	.15
56	Matt Williams	.15
57	Sammy Sosa	1.00
58	Carl Everett	.15
59	Carlos Delgado	.50
60	Jeremy Giambi	.15
61	Jose Canseco	.40
62	David Segui	.15
63	Jose Vidro	.15
64	Matt Stairs	.15
65	Travis Fryman	.15
66	Ken Griffey Jr.	1.50
67	Mike Piazza	1.25
68	Mark McGwire	1.50
69	Craig Biggio	.25
70	Eric Chavez	.25
71	Mo Vaughn	.15
72	Matt Lawton	.15
73	Miguel Tejada	.25
74	Brian Giles	.15
75	Sean Casey	.25
76	Robin Ventura	.15
77	Ivan Rodriguez	.50
78	Dean Palmer	.15
79	Frank Thomas	.75
80	Bernie Williams	.40
81	Juan Encarnacion	.15
82	John Olerud	.15
83	Rich Aurilia	.15
84	Juan Gonzalez	.40
85	Ray Durham	.15
86	Steve Finley	.15
87	Ken Caminiti	.15
88	Roberto Alomar	.40
89	Jeromy Burnitz	.15
90	J.D. Drew	.15
91	Lance Berkman	.40
92	Gabe Kapler	.15
93	Larry Walker	.15
94	Alex Rodriguez	1.50
95	Jeffrey Hammonds	.15
96	Magglio Ordonez	.25
97	David Justice	.15
98	Eric Karros	.15
99	Manny Ramirez	.75
100	Paul O'Neill	.15
101	Ron Gant	.15
102	Erubiel Durazo	.15
103	Jason Varitek	.15
104	Chan Ho Park	.15
105	Corey Koskie	.15
106	Jeff Conine	.15
107	Kevin Tapani	.15
108	Mike Lowell	.25
109	Tim Hudson	.25
110	Bobby Abreu	.25
111	Bret Boone	.15
112	David Wells	.15
113	Brian Jordan	.15
114	Mitch Meluskey	.15
115	Terrence Long	.15
116	Matt Clement	.15
117	Fernando Vina	.15
118	Luis Alicea	.15
119	Jay Bell	.15
120	Mark Grace	.25
121	Carlos Febles	.15
122	Mark Redman	.15
123	Kevin Jordan	.15
124	Pat Meares	.15
125	Mark McLemore	.15
126	Chris Singleton	.15
127	Trot Nixon	.15
128	Carlos Beltran	.40
129	Lee Stevens	.15
130	Kris Benson	.15
131	Jay Buhner	.15
132	Greg Vaughn	.15
133	Eric Young	.15
134	Tony Womack	.15
135	Roger Cedeno	.15
136	Travis Lee	.15
137	Marvin Benard	.15
138	Aaron Sele	.15
139	Rick Ankiel	.50
140	Ruben Mateo	.15
141	Randy Johnson	.75
142	Jason Tyner	.15
143	Mike Redmond	.15
144	Ron Coomer	.15
145	Scott Elarton	.15
146	Javy Lopez	.15
147	Carlos Lee	.25
148	Tony Clark	.15
149	Roger Clemens	1.00
150	Mike Lieberthal	.15
151	Shawn Estes	.15
152	Vinny Castilla	.15
153	Alex Gonzalez	.15
154	Troy Percival	.15
155	Pokey Reese	.15
156	Todd Hollandsworth	.15
157	Marquis Grissom	.15
158	Greg Maddux	1.00
159	Dante Bichette	.15
160	Hideo Nomo	.40
161	Jacque Jones	.15
162	Kevin Young	.15
163	B.J. Surhoff	.15
164	Eddie Taubensee	.15
165	Neifi Perez	.15
166	Orlando Hernandez	.15
167	Francisco Cordova	.15
168	Miguel Cairo	.15
169	Rafael Furcal	.25

170 Sandy Alomar Jr. .15
171 Jeff Cirillo .15
172 A.J. Pierzynski .15
173 Fred McGriff .15
174 Mike Mussina .40
175 Aaron Boone .15
176 Nick Johnson .15
177 Kent Bottenfield .15
178 Felipe Crespo .15
179 Ryan Minor .15
180 Charles Johnson .15
181 Damion Easley .15
182 Michael Barrett .15
183 Doug Glanville .15
184 Ben Davis .15
185 Rickey Henderson .75
186 Edgard Clemente .15
187 Dmitri Young .15
188 Tom Goodwin .15
189 Mike Hampton .15
190 Gerald Williams .15
191 Omar Vizquel .15
192 Ben Petrick .15
193 Brad Radke .15
194 Russ Davis .15
195 Milton Bradley .15
196 John Parrish .15
197 Todd Hundley .15
198 Carl Pavano .15
199 Bruce Chen .15
200 Royce Clayton .15
201 Homer Bush .15
202 Mark Grudzielanek .15
203 Mike Lansing .15
204 Daryle Ward .15
205 Jeff D'Amico .15
206 Ray Lankford .15
207 Curt Schilling .40
208 Pedro Martinez .75
209 Johnny Damon .50
210 Al Leiter .15
211 Ruben Rivera .15
212 Kazuhiro Sasaki .15
213 Will Clark .25
214 Rick Helling .15
215 Adam Piatt .15
216 Joe Girardi .15
217 A.J. Burnett .15
218 Mike Bordick .15
219 Mike Cameron .15
220 Tony Gwynn 1.00
221 Deivi Cruz .15
222 Bubba Trammell .15
223 Scott Erickson .15
224 Kerry Wood .50
225 Derrek Lee .50
226 Peter Bergeron .15
227 Chris Gomez .15
228 Al Martin .15
229 Brady Anderson .15
230 Ramon Martinez .15
231 Darryl Kile .15
232 Devon White .15
233 Charlie Hayes .15
234 Aramis Ramirez .40
235 Mike Lamb .15
236 Tom Glavine .50
237 Troy O'Leary .15
238 Joe Randa .15
239 Dustin Hermanson .15
240 Adam Kennedy .15
241 Jose Valentin .15
242 Derek Bell .15
243 Mark Kotsay .15
244 Ron Belliard .15
245 Warren Morris .15
246 Ozzie Guillen .15
247 Andy Ashby .15
248 Jose Offerman .15
249 Kevin Brown .15
250 Jorge Posada .40
251 Alex Cabrera .15
252 Chan Perry .15
253 Augie Ojeda .15
254 Santiago Perez .15
255 Grant Roberts .15
256 Dusty Allen .15
257 Elvis Pena .15
258 Matt Kinney .15
259 Timoniel Perez .15
260 Adam Eaton .15
261 Geraldo Guzman .15
262 Damian Rolls .15
263 Alfonso Soriano .50
264 Corey Patterson .15
265 Juan Alvarez .15
266 Shawn Gilbert .15
267 Adam Bernero .15
268 Ben Weber .15
269 Tike Redman .15
270 Willie Morales .15
271 Tomas De La Rosa .15
272 Rodney Lindsey .15
273 Carlos Casimiro .15
274 Jim Mann .15
275 Pasqual Coco .15
276 Julio Zuleta .15
277 Damon Minor .15
278 Jose Ortiz .15
279 Eric Munson .15
280 Andy Thompson .15
281 Aubrey Huff .15
282 Chris Richard .15
283 Ross Gload .15
284 Travis Dawkins .15
285 Tim Drew .15
286 Barry Zito .40
287 Andy Tracy .15
288 Julio Lugo .15
289 Matt DeWitt .15
290 Keith McDonald .15
291 J.C. Romero .15
292 Adam Melhuse .15
293 Ryan Kohlmeier .15
294 John Bale .15
295 Eric Cammack .15
296 Morgan Burkhart .15
297 Kory DeHaan .15
298 Raul Gonzalez .15
299 Hector Ortiz .15
300 Talmadge Nunnari .15

Blue

NM/M
Common Player: 3.00
Produced to # of 2000 HR's
1 Derek Jeter/15 150.00
2 Vladimir Guerrero/44 25.00
3 Henry Rodriguez/20 3.00
4 Jason Giambi/43 15.00
5 Nomar Garciaparra/21 25.00
6 Jeff Kent/33 8.00
7 Garret Anderson/35 8.00
8 Todd Helton/42 15.00
9 Barry Bonds/49 40.00
10 Preston Wilson/31 3.00
11 Troy Glaus/47 10.00
12 Geoff Jenkins/34 8.00
13 Jim Edmonds/42 10.00
14 Bobby Higginson/30 3.00
15 Mark Quinn/20 5.00
16 Barry Larkin/11 15.00
17 Richie Sexson/30 10.00
18 Fernando Tatis/18 3.00
19 John Vander Wal/24 3.00
20 Darin Erstad/25 10.00
21 Shawn Green/24 10.00
22 Scott Rolen/26 15.00
23 Tony Batista/41 3.00
24 Phil Nevin/31 3.00
25 Tim Salmon/34 5.00
26 Gary Sheffield/43 8.00
27 Ben Grieve/27 5.00
28 Jermaine Dye/33 3.00
29 Andres Galarraga/28 5.00
30 Adrian Beltre/20 8.00
31 Rafael Palmeiro/39 10.00
32 J.T. Snow/19 5.00
33 Edgardo Alfonzo/25 5.00
34 Paul Konerko/21 5.00
35 Jim Thome/37 15.00
36 Andruw Jones/36 10.00
37 Mike Sweeney/29 3.00
38 Jose Cruz Jr./31 3.00
39 David Ortiz/10 8.00
40 Pat Burrell/18 15.00
41 Chipper Jones/36 15.00
42 Jeff Bagwell/47 10.00
43 Raul Mondesi/24 5.00
44 Rondell White/13 10.00
45 Edgar Martinez/37 5.00
46 Cal Ripken Jr./15 150.00
47 Moises Alou/30 5.00
48 Shannon Stewart/21 3.00
49 Tino Martinez/16 5.00
50 Jason Kendall/14 5.00
51 Richard Hidalgo/44 3.00
52 Albert Belle/23 3.00
53 Jay Payton/17 3.00
54 Cliff Floyd/22 3.00
55 Rusty Greer/8 8.00
56 Matt Williams/12 10.00
57 Sammy Sosa/50 25.00
58 Carl Everett/34 3.00
59 Carlos Delgado/41 5.00
60 Jeremy Giambi/10 5.00
61 Jose Canseco/15 10.00
62 David Segui/19 3.00
63 Jose Vidro/24 3.00
64 Matt Stairs/21 3.00
65 Travis Fryman/22 5.00
66 Ken Griffey Jr./40 15.00
67 Mike Piazza/38 15.00
68 Mark McGwire/32 20.00
69 Craig Biggio/8 10.00
70 Eric Chavez/26 10.00
71 Mo Vaughn/36 5.00
72 Matt Lawton/13 5.00
73 Miguel Tejada/30 10.00
74 Brian Giles/35 5.00
75 Sean Casey/20 5.00
76 Robin Ventura/24 5.00
77 Ivan Rodriguez/27 8.00
78 Dean Palmer/29 3.00
79 Frank Thomas/43 10.00
80 Bernie Williams/30 8.00
81 Juan Encarnacion/14 5.00
82 John Olerud/14 5.00
83 Rich Aurilia/20 3.00
84 Juan Gonzalez/22 8.00
85 Ray Durham/17 5.00
86 Steve Finley/35 3.00
87 Ken Caminiti/15 5.00
88 Roberto Alomar/19 15.00
89 Jeromy Burnitz/31 3.00
90 J.D. Drew/18 8.00
91 Lance Berkman/21 8.00
92 Gabe Kapler/14 8.00
93 Larry Walker/9 10.00
94 Alex Rodriguez/41 20.00
95 Jeffrey Hammonds/20 3.00
96 Magglio Ordonez/32 5.00
97 David Justice/41 5.00
98 Eric Karros/31 3.00
99 Manny Ramirez/38 10.00
100 Paul O'Neill/18 8.00

Green

NM/M
Common Player: 1.00
Produced to # of 2000 RBI's
1 Derek Jeter/73 20.00
2 Vladimir Guerrero/123 5.00
3 Henry Rodriguez/61 1.00
4 Jason Giambi/137 5.00
5 Nomar Garciaparra/96 10.00
6 Jeff Kent/125 3.00
7 Garret Anderson/117 3.00
8 Todd Helton/147 5.00
9 Barry Bonds/106 20.00
10 Preston Wilson/121 1.00
11 Troy Glaus/102 4.00
12 Geoff Jenkins/94 3.00
13 Jim Edmonds/108 4.00
14 Bobby Higginson/102 1.00
15 Mark Quinn/78 1.00
16 Barry Larkin/41 4.00
17 Richie Sexson/91 4.00
18 Fernando Tatis/64 1.00
19 John Vander Wal/94 1.00
20 Darin Erstad/100 3.00
21 Shawn Green/99 3.00
22 Scott Rolen/89 4.00
23 Tony Batista/114 1.00
24 Phil Nevin/107 1.00
25 Tim Salmon/97 3.00
26 Gary Sheffield/109 3.00
27 Ben Grieve/104 1.00
28 Jermaine Dye/118 1.00
29 Andres Galarraga/100 1.50
30 Adrian Beltre/85 1.00
31 Rafael Palmeiro/120 3.00
32 J.T. Snow/96 1.00
33 Edgardo Alfonzo/94 1.00
34 Paul Konerko/97 1.50
35 Jim Thome/106 4.00
36 Andruw Jones/104 4.00
37 Mike Sweeney/144 1.00
38 Jose Cruz Jr./76 1.00
39 David Ortiz/63 1.00
40 Pat Burrell/79 4.00
41 Chipper Jones/111 8.00
42 Jeff Bagwell/132 5.00
43 Raul Mondesi/67 2.00
44 Rondell White/61 1.50
45 Edgar Martinez/145 2.00
46 Cal Ripken Jr./56 25.00
47 Moises Alou/114 1.00
48 Shannon Stewart/69 1.00
49 Tino Martinez/91 2.00
50 Jason Kendall/58 1.00
51 Richard Hidalgo/122 1.00
52 Albert Belle/103 1.00
53 Jay Payton/62 1.00
54 Cliff Floyd/91 1.00
55 Rusty Greer/65 1.00
56 Matt Williams/47 2.00
57 Sammy Sosa/138 10.00
58 Carl Everett/108 1.00
59 Carlos Delgado/137 3.00
60 Jeremy Giambi/50 1.00
61 Jose Canseco/49 5.00
62 David Segui/103 1.00
63 Jose Vidro/97 1.00
64 Matt Stairs/81 1.00
65 Travis Fryman/106 2.00
66 Ken Griffey Jr./118 10.00
67 Mike Piazza/113 10.00
68 Mark McGwire/73 15.00
69 Craig Biggio/35 4.00
70 Eric Chavez/86 4.00
71 Mo Vaughn/117 3.00
72 Matt Lawton/88 1.00
73 Miguel Tejada/115 4.00
74 Brian Giles/123 3.00
75 Sean Casey/85 2.00
76 Robin Ventura/84 2.00
77 Ivan Rodriguez/83 5.00
78 Dean Palmer/102 1.00
79 Frank Thomas/143 5.00
80 Bernie Williams/121 4.00
81 Juan Encarnacion/72 1.00
82 John Olerud/103 3.00
83 Rich Aurilia/79 1.00
84 Juan Gonzalez/67 5.00
85 Ray Durham75 1.00
86 Steve Finley/96 1.00
87 Ken Caminiti/45 1.00
88 Roberto Alomar/89 5.00
89 Jeromy Burnitz/98 1.00
90 J.D. Drew/57 3.00
91 Lance Berkman/67 2.00
92 Gabe Kapler/66 2.00
93 Larry Walker/51 3.00
94 Alex Rodriguez/132 15.00
95 Jeffrey Hammonds/106 1.00
96 Magglio Ordonez/126 3.00
97 David Justice/118 3.00
98 Eric Karros/106 1.00
99 Manny Ramirez/122 5.00
100 Paul O'Neill/100 2.00

Red

Common Player (1-100):
Stars: 4-8X
Produced to 2000 Bat Avg.
(See 2001 Fleer Triple Crown #1-100 for checklist and base card values.)

Autographics

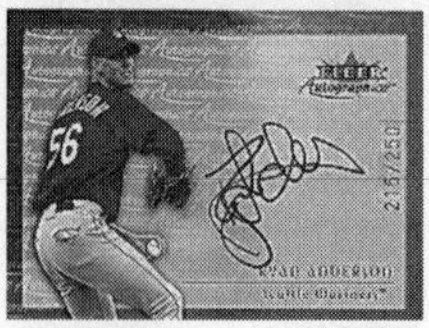

NM/M
Common Autograph: 5.00
Inserted 1:72
Silvers: 1X
Production 250 Sets
Golds: 1-2X
Production 50 Sets
1 Roberto Alomar 30.00
2 Jimmy Anderson 5.00
3 Ryan Anderson 5.00
4 Rick Ankiel 15.00
5 Adrian Beltre 15.00
6 Peter Bergeron 5.00
7 Lance Berkman 15.00
8 Barry Bonds 150.00
9 Milton Bradley 8.00
10 Dee Brown 5.00
11 Roosevelt Brown 5.00
12 Pat Burrell 15.00
13 Sean Casey 8.00
14 Eric Chavez 10.00
15 Giuseppe Chiaramonte 5.00
16 Joe Crede 5.00
17 Jose Cruz Jr. 5.00
18 Carlos Delgado 10.00
19 Ryan Dempster 5.00
20 Adam Dunn 15.00
21 David Eckstein 5.00
22 Jim Edmonds 10.00
23 Troy Glaus 15.00
24 Chad Green 5.00
25 Tony Gwynn 30.00
26 Todd Helton 20.00
27 Chad Hermansen 5.00
28 Shea Hillenbrand 6.00
29 Aubrey Huff 6.00
30 Randy Johnson 40.00
31 Chipper Jones 40.00
32 Mike Lamb 5.00
33 Corey Lee 5.00
34 Steve Lomasney 5.00
35 Terrence Long 5.00
36 Julio Lugo 5.00
37 Jason Marquis 5.00
38 Bengie Molina 8.00
39 Mike Mussina 25.00
40 Pablo Ozuna 5.00
41 Corey Patterson 10.00
42 Jay Payton 6.00
43 Wily Pena 10.00
44 Josh Phelps 8.00
45 Adam Piatt 5.00
46 Matt Riley 5.00
47 Alex Rodriguez 80.00
48 Alex Sanchez 5.00
49 Gary Sheffield 15.00
50 Alfonso Soriano 40.00
51 Shannon Stewart 6.00
52 Fernando Tatis 5.00
53 Jose Vidro 5.00
54 Preston Wilson 8.00
55 Kerry Wood 25.00
56 Julio Zuleta 5.00

Crowning Achievements

NM/M
Complete Set (15): 15.00
Common Player: .50
Inserted 1:9
1 Troy Glaus 1.00
2 Mark McGwire 2.50
3 Barry Larkin, Craig Biggio .50
4 Ken Griffey Jr. 2.00
5 Rafael Palmeiro .75
6 Alex Rodriguez 2.50
7 Roger Clemens 1.75
8 Mike Piazza 2.00
9 Cal Ripken Jr. 3.00
10 Randy Johnson 1.00
11 Jeff Bagwell 1.00
12 Sammy Sosa 2.00
13 Greg Maddux 1.50
14 Barry Bonds 3.00
15 Fred McGriff .50

Crowns of Gold

NM/M
Common Player: 4.00
Random inserts in Hobby packs.
Rick Ankiel/Jsy 4.00
Steve Carlton/Jsy 10.00
Roger Clemens/Jsy 40.00
Carlos Delgado/Bat 8.00
Darin Erstad/Bat 6.00
Jimmie Foxx/Bat 100.00
Todd Helton/Bat 10.00
Randy Johnson/Jsy 15.00

Frank Robinson/Bat	10.00
Gary Sheffield/Jsy	8.00
Frank Thomas/Bat	10.00
Ted Williams/Bat	200.00

Crowns of Gold Autograph

NM/M

Random inserts in Hobby packs.

Steve Carlton/Jsy/72	80.00
Roger Clemens/Jsy/98	150.00
Frank Robinson/Bat/66	80.00

Feel the Game

NM/M

Common Player:	4.00
Inserted 1:72	
Golds:	1.5-2X
Production 50 Sets	
Adrian Beltre	6.00
Dante Bichette	4.00
Roger Cedeno	4.00
Ben Davis	4.00
Carlos Delgado	6.00
J.D. Drew	6.00
Jason Giambi	6.00
Brian Giles	4.00
Juan Gonzalez	4.00
Richard Hidalgo	4.00
Chipper Jones	10.00
Eric Karros	4.00
Javy Lopez	4.00
Tino Martinez	4.00
Raul Mondesi	4.00
Phil Nevin	4.00
Chan Ho Park	4.00
Ivan Rodriguez	6.00
Shannon Stewart	4.00
Frank Thomas	8.00
Jose Vidro	4.00
Matt Williams	4.00
Preston Wilson	4.00

Future Threats

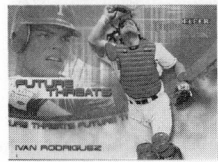

NM/M

Complete Set (15):	15.00
Common Player:	.50
Inserted 1:7	
1 Derek Jeter	3.00
2 Alex Rodriguez	2.50
3 Magglio Ordonez,	
Shawn Green	.50
4 Larry Walker	.50
5 Vladimir Guerrero	1.00
6 Nomar Garciaparra	2.00
7 Ken Griffey Jr.	2.00
8 Barry Bonds	3.00
9 Chipper Jones	1.50
10 Todd Helton	1.00
11 Ivan Rodriguez	.75
12 Jeff Bagwell	1.00
13 Frank Thomas	1.00
14 Carlos Delgado	.65
15 Mike Piazza	2.00

Glamour Boys

NM/M

Complete Set (15):	40.00
Common Player:	1.50
Inserted 1:24	
1 Derek Jeter	6.00
2 Vladimir Guerrero	2.00
3 Scott Rolen, Jeff Bagwell	1.50
4 Sammy Sosa	4.00
5 Ken Griffey Jr.	4.00
6 Mark McGwire	5.00
7 Ivan Rodriguez	1.50

8	Mike Piazza	4.00
9	Nomar Garciaparra	4.00
10	Cal Ripken Jr.	6.00
11	Tony Gwynn	3.00
12	Barry Bonds	6.00
13	Randy Johnson	2.00
14	Alex Rodriguez	5.00
15	Pedro Martinez	2.00

2002 Fleer

NM/M

Complete Set (540):		75.00
Common Player:		.15
Pack (10):		2.00
Box (24):		40.00
1	Darin Erstad	.15
2	Randy Johnson	.25
3	Chipper Jones	.50
4	Jay Gibbons	.15
5	Nomar Garciaparra	.50
6	Sammy Sosa	.50
7	Frank Thomas	.50
8	Ken Griffey Jr.	.75
9	Jim Thome	.25
10	Todd Helton	.25
11	Jeff Weaver	.15
12	Cliff Floyd	.15
13	Jeff Bagwell	.25
14	Mike Sweeney	.15
15	Adrian Beltre	.25
16	Richie Sexson	.15
17	Brad Radke	.15
18	Vladimir Guerrero	.50
19	Mike Piazza	.50
20	Derek Jeter	1.00
21	Eric Chavez	.15
22	Pat Burrell	.15
23	Brian Giles	.15
24	Trevor Hoffman	.15
25	Barry Bonds	1.00
26	Ichiro Suzuki	.75
27	Albert Pujols	1.00
28	Ben Grieve	.15
29	Alex Rodriguez	1.00
30	Carlos Delgado	.25
31	Miguel Tejada	.25
32	Todd Hollandsworth	.15
33	Marlon Anderson	.15
34	Kerry Robinson	.15
35	Chris Richard	.15
36	Jamey Wright	.15
37	Ray Lankford	.15
38	Mike Bordick	.15
39	Danny Graves	.15
40	A.J. Pierzynski	.15
41	Shannon Stewart	.15
42	Tony Armas Jr.	.15
43	Brad Ausmus	.15
44	Alfonso Soriano	.50
45	Junior Spivey	.15
46	Brent Mayne	.15
47	Jim Thome	.25
48	Dan Wilson	.15
49	Geoff Jenkins	.15
50	Kris Benson	.15
51	Rafael Furcal	.15
52	Wiki Gonzalez	.15

53	Jeff Kent	.15
54	Curt Schilling	.40
55	Ken Harvey	.15
56	Roosevelt Brown	.15
57	David Segui	.15
58	Mario Valdez	.15
59	Adam Dunn	.50
60	Bob Howry	.15
61	Michael Barrett	.15
62	Garret Anderson	.15
63	Kelvim Escobar	.15
64	Ben Grieve	.15
65	Randy Johnson	.75
66	Jose Offerman	.15
67	Jason Kendall	.15
68	Joel Pineiro	.15
69	Alex Escobar	.15
70	Chris George	.15
71	Bobby Higginson	.15
72	Nomar Garciaparra	1.50
73	Pat Burrell	.40
74	Lee Stevens	.15
75	Felipe Lopez	.15
76	Al Leiter	.15
77	Jim Edmonds	.15
78	Al Levine	.15
79	Raul Mondesi	.15
80	Jose Valentin	.15
81	Matt Clement	.15
82	Richard Hidalgo	.15
83	Jamie Moyer	.15
84	Brian Schneider	.15
85	John Franco	.15
86	Brian Buchanan	.15
87	Roy Oswalt	.25
88	Johnny Estrada	.15
89	Marcus Giles	.15
90	Carlos Valderrama	.15
91	Mark Mulder	.15
92	Mark Grace	.25
93	Andy Ashby	.15
94	Woody Williams	.15
95	Ben Petrick	.15
96	Roy Halladay	.30
97	Fred McGriff	.25
98	Shawn Green	.40
99	Todd Hundley	.15
100	Carlos Febles	.15
101	Jason Marquis	.15
102	Mike Redmond	.15
103	Shane Halter	.15
104	Trot Nixon	.15
105	Jeremy Giambi	.15
106	Carlos Delgado	.50
107	Richie Sexson	.15
108	Russ Ortiz	.15
109	David Ortiz	.25
110	Curtis Leskanic	.15
111	Jay Payton	.15
112	Travis Phelps	.15
113	J.T. Snow	.15
114	Edgar Renteria	.15
115	Freddy Garcia	.15
116	Cliff Floyd	.15
117	Charles Nagy	.15
118	Tony Batista	.15
119	Rafael Palmeiro	.65
120	Darren Dreifort	.15
121	Warren Morris	.15
122	Augie Ojeda	.15
123	Rusty Greer	.15
124	Esteban Yan	.15
125	Corey Patterson	.15
126	Matt Ginter	.15
127	Matt Lawton	.15
128	Miguel Batista	.15
129	Randy Winn	.15
130	Eric Milton	.15
131	Jack Wilson	.15
132	Sean Casey	.25
133	Mike Sweeney	.15
134	Jason Tyner	.15
135	Carlos Hernandez	.15
136	Shea Hillenbrand	.15
137	Shawn Wooten	.15
138	Peter Bergeron	.15
139	Travis Lee	.15
140	Craig Wilson	.15
141	Carlos Guillen	.15
142	Chipper Jones	1.00
143	Gabe Kapler	.15
144	Raul Ibanez	.15
145	Eric Chavez	.25
146	D'Angelo Jimenez	.15
147	Chad Hermansen	.15
148	Joe Kennedy	.15
149	Mariano Rivera	.25
150	Jeff Bagwell	.75
151	Joe McEwing	.15
152	Ronnie Belliard	.15
153	Desi Relaford	.15
154	Vinny Castilla	.15
155	Tim Hudson	.25
156	Wilton Guerrero	.15
157	Raul Casanova	.15
158	Edgardo Alfonzo	.15
159	Derrek Lee	.15
160	Phil Nevin	.15
161	Roger Clemens	1.25
162	Jason LaRue	.15
163	Brian Lawrence	.15
164	Adrian Beltre	.30
165	Troy Glaus	.75
166	Jeff Weaver	.15
167	B.J. Surhoff	.15

168	Eric Byrnes	.15
169	Mike Sirotka	.15
170	Bill Haselman	.15
171	Javier Vazquez	.15
172	Sidney Ponson	.15
173	Adam Everett	.15
174	Bubba Trammell	.15
175	Robb Nen	.15
176	Barry Larkin	.25
177	Tony Graffanino	.15
178	Rich Garces	.15
179	Juan Uribe	.15
180	Tom Glavine	.25
181	Eric Karros	.15
182	Michael Cuddyer	.15
183	Wade Miller	.15
184	Matt Williams	.15
185	Matt Morris	.15
186	Rickey Henderson	.75
187	Trevor Hoffman	.15
188	Wilson Betemit	.15
189	Steve Karsay	.15
190	Frank Catalanotto	.15
191	Jason Schmidt	.15
192	Roger Cedeno	.15
193	Magglio Ordonez	.15
194	Pat Hentgen	.15
195	Mike Lieberthal	.15
196	Andy Pettitte	.30
197	Jay Gibbons	.15
198	Rolando Arrojo	.15
199	Joe Mays	.15
200	Aubrey Huff	.15
201	Nelson Figueroa	.15
202	Paul Konerko	.25
203	Ken Griffey Jr.	1.50
204	Brandon Duckworth	.15
205	Sammy Sosa	1.50
206	Carl Everett	.15
207	Scott Rolen	.65
208	Orlando Hernandez	.15
209	Todd Helton	.75
210	Preston Wilson	.15
211	Gil Meche	.15
212	Bill Mueller	.15
213	Craig Biggio	.15
214	Dean Palmer	.15
215	Randy Wolf	.15
216	Jeff Suppan	.15
217	Jimmy Rollins	.25
218	Alexis Gomez	.15
219	Ellis Burks	.15
220	Ramon E. Martinez	.15
221	Ramiro Mendoza	.15
222	Einar Diaz	.15
223	Brent Abernathy	.15
224	Darin Erstad	.25
225	Reggie Taylor	.15
226	Jason Jennings	.15
227	Ray Durham	.15
228	John Parrish	.15
229	Kevin Young	.15
230	Xavier Nady	.15
231	Juan Cruz	.15
232	Greg Norton	.15
233	Barry Bonds	2.00
234	Kip Wells	.15
235	Paul LoDuca	.15
236	Javy Lopez	.25
237	Luis Castillo	.15
238	Tom Gordon	.15
239	Mike Mordecai	.15
240	Damian Rolls	.15
241	Julio Lugo	.15
242	Ichiro Suzuki	1.00
243	Tony Womack	.15
244	Matt Anderson	.15
245	Carlos Lee	.15
246	Alex Rodriguez	1.75
247	Bernie Williams	.30
248	Scott Sullivan	.15
249	Mike Hampton	.15
250	Orlando Cabrera	.15
251	Benito Santiago	.15
252	Steve Finley	.15
253	Dave Williams	.15
254	Adam Kennedy	.15
255	Omar Vizquel	.15
256	Garrett Stephenson	.15
257	Fernando Tatis	.15
258	Mike Piazza	1.50
259	Scott Spiezio	.15
260	Jacque Jones	.15
261	Russell Branyan	.15
262	Mark McLemore	.15
263	Mitch Meluskey	.15
264	Marlon Byrd	.15
265	Kyle Farnsworth	.15
266	Billy Sylvester	.15
267	C.C. Sabathia	.15
268	Mark Buehrle	.15
269	Geoff Blum	.15
270	Bret Prinz	.15
271	Placido Polanco	.15
272	John Olerud	.15
273	Pedro J. Martinez	.75
274	Doug Mientkiewicz	.15
275	Jason Bere	.15
276	Bud Smith	.15
277	Terrence Long	.15
278	Troy Percival	.15
279	Derek Jeter	2.00
280	Eric Owens	.15
281	Jay Bell	.15
282	Mike Cameron	.15

#	Player	Price
283	Joe Randa	.15
284	Brian Roberts	.15
285	Ryan Klesko	.15
286	Ryan Dempster	.15
287	Cristian Guzman	.15
288	Tim Salmon	.25
289	Mark Johnson	.15
290	Brian Giles	.15
291	Jon Lieber	.15
292	Fernando Vina	.15
293	Mike Mussina	.40
294	Juan Pierre	.15
295	Carlos Beltran	.40
296	Vladimir Guerrero	.75
297	Orlando Merced	.15
298	Jose Hernandez	.15
299	Mike Lamb	.15
300	David Eckstein	.15
301	Mark Loretta	.15
302	Greg Vaughn	.15
303	Jose Vidro	.15
304	Jose Ortiz	.15
305	Mark Grudzielanek	.15
306	Rob Bell	.15
307	Elmer Dessens	.15
308	Tomas Perez	.15
309	Jerry Hairston Jr.	.15
310	Mike Stanton	.15
311	Todd Walker	.15
312	Jason Varitek	.15
313	Masato Yoshii	.15
314	Ben Sheets	.15
315	Roberto Hernandez	.15
316	Eli Marrero	.15
317	Josh Beckett	.50
318	Robert Fick	.15
319	Aramis Ramirez	.15
320	Bartolo Colon	.15
321	Kenny Kelly	.15
322	Luis Gonzalez	.25
323	John Smoltz	.15
324	Homer Bush	.15
325	Kevin Millwood	.15
326	Manny Ramirez	.75
327	Armando Benitez	.15
328	Luis Alicea	.15
329	Mark Kotsay	.15
330	Felix Rodriguez	.15
331	Eddie Taubensee	.15
332	John Burkett	.15
333	Ramon Ortiz	.15
334	Daryle Ward	.15
335	Jarrod Washburn	.15
336	Benji Gil	.15
337	Mike Lowell	.15
338	Larry Walker	.15
339	Andruw Jones	.75
340	Scott Elarton	.15
341	Tony McKnight	.15
342	Frank Thomas	.50
343	Kevin Brown	.15
344	Jermaine Dye	.15
345	Luis Rivas	.15
346	Jeff Conine	.15
347	Bobby Kielty	.15
348	Jeffrey Hammonds	.15
349	Keith Foulke	.15
350	Dave Martinez	.15
351	Adam Eaton	.15
352	Brandon Inge	.15
353	Tyler Houston	.15
354	Bobby Abreu	.15
355	Ivan Rodriguez	.65
356	Doug Glanville	.15
357	Jorge Julio	.15
358	Kerry Wood	.15
359	Eric Munson	.15
360	Joe Crede	.15
361	Denny Neagle	.15
362	Vance Wilson	.15
363	Neifi Perez	.15
364	Darryl Kile	.15
365	Jose Macias	.15
366	Michael Coleman	.15
367	Erubiel Durazo	.15
368	Darrin Fletcher	.15
369	Matt White	.15
370	Marvin Benard	.15
371	Brad Penny	.15
372	Chuck Finley	.15
373	Delino DeShields	.15
374	Adrian Brown	.15
375	Corey Koskie	.15
376	Kazuhiro Sasaki	.15
377	Brent Butler	.15
378	Paul Wilson	.15
379	Scott Williamson	.15
380	Mike Young	.15
381	Toby Hall	.15
382	Shane Reynolds	.15
383	Tom Goodwin	.15
384	Seth Etherton	.15
385	Billy Wagner	.15
386	Josh Phelps	.15
387	Kyle Lohse	.15
388	Jeremy Fikac	.15
389	Jorge Posada	.30
390	Bret Boone	.15
391	Matt Mantei	.15
392	Alex Gonzalez	.15
393	Scott Strickland	.15
394	Charles Johnson	.15
395	Charles Johnson	.15
396	Ramon Hernandez	.15
397	Damian Jackson	.15
398	Albert Pujols	1.50
399	Gary Bennett	.15
400	Edgar Martinez	.15
401	Carl Pavano	.15
402	Chris Gomez	.15
403	Jaret Wright	.15
404	Lance Berkman	.15
405	Robert Person	.15
406	Brook Fordyce	.15
407	Adam Pettyjohn	.15
408	Chris Carpenter	.15
409	Rey Ordonez	.15
410	Eric Gagne	.25
411	Damion Easley	.15
412	A.J. Burnett	.15
413	Aaron Boone	.15
414	J.D. Drew	.25
415	Kelly Stinnett	.15
416	Mark Quinn	.15
417	Brad Radke	.15
418	Jose Cruz Jr.	.15
419	Greg Maddux	1.00
420	Steve Cox	.15
421	Torii Hunter	.15
422	Sandy Alomar	.15
423	Barry Zito	.40
424	Bill Hall	.15
425	Marquis Grissom	.15
426	Rich Aurilia	.15
427	Royce Clayton	.15
428	Travis Fryman	.15
429	Pablo Ozuna	.15
430	David Dellucci	.15
431	Vernon Wells	.15
432	Gregg Zaun	.15
433	Alex Gonzalez	.15
434	Hideo Nomo	.40
435	Jeromy Burnitz	.15
436	Gary Sheffield	.25
437	Tino Martinez	.15
438	Tsuyoshi Shinjo	.15
439	Chan Ho Park	.15
440	Tony Clark	.15
441	Brad Fullmer	.15
442	Jason Giambi	.50
443	Billy Koch	.15
444	Mo Vaughn	.15
445	Alex Ochoa	.15
446	Darren Lewis	.15
447	John Rocker	.15
448	Scott Hatteberg	.15
449	Brady Anderson	.15
450	Chuck Knoblauch	.15
451	Pokey Reese	.15
452	Brian Jordan	.15
453	Albie Lopez	.15
454	David Bell	.15
455	Juan Gonzalez	.75
456	Terry Adams	.15
457	Kenny Lofton	.25
458	Shawn Estes	.15
459	Josh Fogg	.15
460	Dmitri Young	.15
461	Johnny Damon	.25
462	Chris Singleton	.15
463	Ricky Ledee	.15
464	Dustin Hermanson	.15
465	Aaron Sele	.15
466	Chris Stynes	.15
467	Matt Stairs	.15
468	Kevin Appier	.15
469	Omar Daal	.15
470	Moises Alou	.15
471	Juan Encarnacion	.15
472	Robin Ventura	.15
473	Eric Hinske	.15
474	Rondell White	.15
475	Carlos Pena	.15
476	Craig Paquette	.15
477	Marty Cordova	.15
478	Brett Tomko	.15
479	Reggie Sanders	.15
480	Roberto Alomar	.15
481	Jeff Cirillo	.15
482	Todd Zeile	.15
483	John Vander Wal	.15
484	Rick Helling	.15
485	Jeff D'Amico	.15
486	David Justice	.15
487	Jason Isringhausen	.15
488	Shigetoshi Hasegawa	.15
489	Eric Young	.15
490	David Wells	.15
491	Ruben Sierra	.15
492	Aaron Cook RC	.50
493	Takahito Nomura RC	.50
494	Austin Kearns RC	.50
495	Kazuhisa Ishii RC	2.00
496	Mark Teixeira	.50
497	Rene Reyes RC	.50
498	Tim Spooneybarger	.15
499	Ben Broussard	.15
500	Eric Cyr RC	.25
501	Anastacio Martinez RC	.50
502	Morgan Ensberg	.15
503	Steve Kent RC	.25
504	Franklin Nunez RC	.25
505	Adam Walker RC	.25
506	Anderson Machado RC	.50
507	Ryan Drese	.15
508	Luis Ugueto RC	.25
509	Jorge Nunez RC	.25
510	Colby Lewis	.15
511	Ron Calloway RC	.25
512	Hansel Izquierdo RC	.50
513	Jason Lane	.15
514	Rafael Soriano	.15
515	Jackson Melian	.15
516	Edwin Almonte RC	.50
517	Satoru Komiyama RC	.50
518	Corey Thurman RC	.25
519	Jorge De La Rosa RC	.50
520	Victor Martinez	.15
521	Dewan Brazleton	.15
522	Marlon Byrd	.50
523	Jae Weong Seo	.15
524	Orlando Hudson	.15
525	Sean Burroughs	.15
526	Ryan Langerhans	.15
527	David Kelton	.15
528	So Taguchi RC	.50
529	Tyler Walker	.15
530	Hank Blalock	.50
531	Mark Prior	.75
532	Yankee Stadium	.50
533	Fenway Park	.50
534	Wrigley Field	.50
535	Dodger Stadium	.15
536	Camden Yards	.15
537	PacBell Park	.15
538	Jacobs Field	.15
539	SAFECO Field	.15
540	Miller Field	.15

Mini

Mini (1-540):		8-15X
Production 50 Sets		
Retail Exclusive		

Tiffany

Stars (1-540):		4-8X
Production 200 Sets		

Barry Bonds Career Highlights

	NM/M
Complete Set (10):	40.00
Common Bonds 1-3:	3.00
Common 4-6 inserted 1:125 H.	4.00
7-9 1:250 H	6.00
#10 1:383	6.00
1CH-3CHBarry Bonds	3.00
4CH-6CHBarry Bonds	4.00
5CH-6CHBarry Bonds	4.00
7CH-10CHBarry Bonds	6.00

Barry Bonds Career Highlights Autographs

No Pricing
25 Sets Produced

2002 Fleer Barry Bonds 600 HR Supers

	NM/M
Barry Bonds (Facsimile signature.)	55.00
Barry Bonds (Autograph w/bat chip.)	250.00

2002 Fleer Barry Bonds Chasing History

	NM/M
Barry Bonds	125.00

2002 Fleer Barry Bonds 4X MVP Super

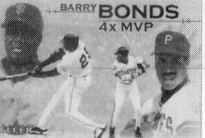

	NM/M
Barry Bonds	15.00

Classic Cuts Autographs

	NM/M
Inserted 1:432	
LA-A Luis Aparicio	15.00
RC-A Ron Cey	8.00
HK-A Harmon Killebrew	35.00
JM-A Juan Marichal	15.00
GP-A Gaylord Perry/SP/225	15.00
PR-A Phil Rizzuto/SP/125	50.00
BR-A Brooks Robinson/SP/200	40.00

Classic Cuts Game Used

	NM/M
Common Player:	5.00
Inserted 1:24	
SA-P Sparky Anderson/Pants	5.00
HB-B Hank Bauer/Bat	5.00
JB-J Johnny Bench/Jsy	15.00
PB-B Paul Blair/Bat	5.00
WB-B Wade Boggs/Bat/99	20.00
WB-J Wade Boggs/Jsy	10.00
BB-B Bobby Bonds/Bat	5.00
BB-J Bobby Bonds/Jsy	5.00
GB-B George Brett/Bat/250	30.00
GB-J George Brett/Jsy/250	30.00
SC-P Steve Carlton/Pants	6.00
OC-P Orlando Cepeda/Pants	5.00
AD-J Andre Dawson/Jsy	8.00
BD-B Bill Dickey/Bat/200	20.00
LD-B Larry Doby/Bat/250	10.00
DE-B Dwight Evans/Bat/250	5.00
DE-J Dwight Evans/Jsy	5.00
RF-J Rollie Fingers/Jsy	5.00
CF-B Carlton Fisk/Bat	10.00
CF-J Carlton Fisk/Jsy/150	20.00
NF-B Nellie Fox/Bat/200	20.00
SG-B Steve Garvey/Bat	5.00
KG-B Kirk Gibson/Bat	5.00
GH-B Gil Hodges/Bat/200	15.00
CH-J Jim Hunter/Jsy	10.00
BJ-J Bo Jackson/Jsy	10.00
RJ-P Reggie Jackson/Pants	10.00
GK-B George Kell/Bat/150	25.00
TK-B Ted Kluszewski/Bat/200	15.00
TK-P Ted Kluszewski/Pants	10.00
RM-P Roger Maris/Pants/200	60.00
EM-B Eddie Mathews/Bat/200	20.00
DM-B Don Mattingly/Bat/200	50.00
DM-J Don Mattingly/Jsy	40.00
WM-J Willie McCovey/Jsy/300	10.00
PM-B Paul Molitor/Bat/250	25.00
JM-B Joe Morgan/Bat/250	8.00
EM-B Eddie Murray/Bat	10.00
EM-J Eddie Murray/Jsy	10.00
JP-J Jim Palmer/Jsy/273	6.00
DP-B Dave Parker/Bat	5.00
TP-B Tony Perez/Bat/250	10.00
TP-J Tony Perez/Jsy	8.00
LP-P Lou Piniella/Pants	5.00
KP-J Kirby Puckett/Jsy	15.00
JR-B Jim Rice/Bat/225	4.00
CR-BG Cal Ripken Jr./Btg Glv/100	75.00
CR-FG Cal Ripken Jr./Fld Glv/50	125.00
CR-J Cal Ripken Jr./Jsy	35.00
CR-P Cal Ripken Jr./Pants/200	40.00
BR-B Brooks Robinson/Bat/250	15.00
NR-J Nolan Ryan/Jsy	50.00
NR-P Nolan Ryan/Pants/200	60.00
RS-B Ryne Sandberg/Bat	25.00
OS-J Ozzie Smith/Jsy/250	15.00
WS-B Willie Stargell/Bat/250	15.00
JT-J Joe Torre/Jsy/125	15.00
AT-B Alan Trammell/Bat	10.00
EW-J Earl Weaver/Jsy	5.00
HW-P Hoyt Wilhelm/Pants/150	15.00
TW-B Ted Williams/Bat	85.00
TW-P Ted Williams/Pants	120.00
DW-B Dave Winfield/Bat	8.00
DW-J Dave Winfield/Jsy/231	10.00
DW-P Dave Winfield/Pants/45	8.00
RY-B Robin Yount/Bat	15.00

Classic Cuts Game Used Autographs

	NM/M
Varying quantities produced	
LA-B Luis Aparicio/Bat/45	25.00
RF-J Rollie Fingers/Jsy/35	
BR-B Brooks Robinson/Bat/45	80.00

Diamond Standouts

	NM/M
Complete Set (10):	40.00

Common Player: 2.00
Production 1,200 Sets
1DS	Mike Piazza	4.00
2DS	Derek Jeter	8.00
3DS	Ken Griffey Jr.	4.00
4DS	Barry Bonds	8.00
5DS	Sammy Sosa	4.00
6DS	Alex Rodriguez	6.00
7DS	Ichiro Suzuki	4.00
8DS	Greg Maddux	3.00
9DS	Jason Giambi	2.00
10DS	Nomar Garciaparra	4.00

Golden Memories

NM/M
Complete Set (15): 20.00
Common Player: 1.00
Inserted 1:24
1GM	Frank Thomas	1.50
2GM	Derek Jeter	4.00
3GM	Albert Pujols	3.00
4GM	Barry Bonds	4.00
5GM	Alex Rodriguez	3.00
6GM	Randy Johnson	1.50
7GM	Jeff Bagwell	1.50
8GM	Greg Maddux	2.00
9GM	Ivan Rodriguez	1.00
10GM	Ichiro Suzuki	2.50
11GM	Mike Piazza	2.50
12GM	Pat Burrell	1.00
13GM	Rickey Henderson	1.50
14GM	Vladimir Guerrero	1.50
15GM	Sammy Sosa	2.50

Headliners

NM/M
Complete Set (20): 10.00
Common Player: .25
Inserted 1:8
1HL	Randy Johnson	.75
2HL	Alex Rodriguez	1.50
3HL	Todd Helton	.75
4HL	Pedro J. Martinez	.75
5HL	Ichiro Suzuki	1.50
6HL	Vladimir Guerrero	.75
7HL	Derek Jeter	2.00
8HL	Adam Dunn	.40
9HL	Luis Gonzalez	.25
10HL	Kazuhiro Sasaki	.25
11HL	Sammy Sosa	1.25
12HL	Jason Giambi	.60
13HL	Ken Griffey Jr.	1.25
14HL	Roger Clemens	1.00
15HL	Brandon Duckworth	.25
16HL	Nomar Garciaparra	1.25
17HL	Bud Smith	.25
18HL	Juan Gonzalez	.75
19HL	Chipper Jones	1.00
20HL	Barry Bonds	2.00

Rookie Flashback

NM/M
Complete Set (20): 6.00
Common Player: .25
Inserted 1:3 Retail
1RF	Bret Prinz	.25
2RF	Albert Pujols	2.00
3RF	C.C. Sabathia	.25
4RF	Ichiro Suzuki	1.50
5RF	Juan Cruz	.25
6RF	Jay Gibbons	.50
7RF	Bud Smith	.25
8RF	Johnny Estrada	.25
9RF	Roy Oswalt	.50
10RF	Tsuyoshi Shinjo	.25
11RF	Brandon Duckworth	.25
12RF	Jackson Melian	.25
13RF	Josh Beckett	1.00
14RF	Morgan Ensberg	.25
15RF	Brian Lawrence	.25
16RF	Eric Hinske	.25
17RF	Juan Uribe	.25
18RF	Matt White	.25
19RF	Junior Spivey	.25
20RF	Wilson Betemit	.25

Rookie Sensations

NM/M
Complete Set (20): 40.00
Common Player: 2.00
Production 1,500 Sets
1RS	Bret Prinz	2.00
2RS	Albert Pujols	10.00
3RS	C.C. Sabathia	2.00
4RS	Ichiro Suzuki	8.00
5RS	Juan Cruz	2.00
6RS	Jay Gibbons	3.00
7RS	Bud Smith	2.00
8RS	Johnny Estrada	2.00
9RS	Roy Oswalt	4.00
10RS	Tsuyoshi Shinjo	2.00
11RS	Brandon Duckworth	2.00
12RS	Jackson Melian	2.00
13RS	Josh Beckett	4.00
14RS	Morgan Ensberg	2.00
15RS	Brian Lawrence	2.00
16RS	Eric Hinske	2.00
17RS	Juan Uribe	2.00
18RS	Matt White	2.00
19RS	Junior Spivey	2.00
20RS	Wilson Betemit	2.00

Then and Now

NM/M
Common Card: 5.00
Production 275 Sets
1TN	Eddie Mathews, Chipper Jones	5.00
2TN	Willie McCovey, Barry Bonds	15.00
3TN	Johnny Bench, Mike Piazza	5.00
4TN	Ernie Banks, Alex Rodriguez	8.00
5TN	Rickey Henderson, Ichiro Suzuki	10.00
6TN	Tom Seaver, Roger Clemens	10.00
7TN	Juan Marichal, Pedro J. Martinez	5.00
8TN	Reggie Jackson, Derek Jeter	15.00
9TN	Nolan Ryan, Kerry Wood	20.00
10TN	Joe Morgan, Ken Griffey Jr.	10.00

2002 Fleer Box Score

NM/M
Complete Set (310):
Common Player: .25
Common (126-150): 3.00
Production 2,499
Complete Rising Star Set (40): 30.00
Common (151-190): 1.00
Complete Intl. Set (40): 18.00
Common (191-230): 1.00
Complete All-Star Set (40): 20.00
Common (231-270): 1.00
Comp. Cooperstown Set (40): 30.00
Common Cooperstown (271-310): 1.00
Print run for all subsets is 2,950.
Pack (7):
Box (18 Packs + Supp. Box): 80.00
1	Derek Jeter	2.00
2	Kevin Brown	.25
3	Nomar Garciaparra	1.25
4	Mark Buehrle	.25
5	Mike Piazza	1.25
6	David Justice	.25
7	Tino Martinez	.25
8	Paul Konerko	.25
9	Larry Walker	.25
10	Ben Sheets	.25
11	Mike Cameron	.25
12	David Wells	.25
13	Barry Zito	.35
14	Pat Burrell	.45
15	Mike Mussina	.50
16	Bud Smith	.25
17	Brian Jordan	.25
18	Chris Singleton	.25
19	Daryle Ward	.25
20	Russ Ortiz	.25
21	Jason Kendall	.25
22	Kerry Wood	.65
23	Jeff Weaver	.25
24	Tony Armas	.25
25	Toby Hall	.25
26	Brian Giles	.25
27	Juan Pierre	.25
28	Ken Griffey Jr.	1.25
29	Mike Sweeney	.25
30	John Smoltz	.25
31	Sean Casey	.35
32	Jeremy Giambi	.25
33	Mike Lieberthal	.25
34	Rich Aurilia	.25
35	Matt Lawton	.25
36	Dmitri Young	.25
37	Wade Miller	.25
38	Jason Giambi	.65
39	Jeff Cirillo	.25
40	Mark Grace	.35
41	Frank Thomas	.75
42	Preston Wilson	.25
43	Brad Radke	.25
44	Greg Maddux	1.00
45	Adam Dunn	.25
46	Roy Oswalt	.35
47	Troy Glaus	.75
48	Edgar Martinez	.25
49	Billy Koch	.25
50	Chipper Jones	1.00
51	Lance Berkman	.25
52	Shannon Stewart	.25
53	Eddie Guardado	.25
54	C.C. Sabathia	.25
55	Craig Biggio	.25
56	Roger Clemens	1.00
57	Jimmy Rollins	.25
58	Carlos Delgado	.50
59	Tony Clark	.25
60	Mike Hampton	.25
61	Jeromy Burnitz	.25
62	Jorge Posada	.35
63	Todd Helton	.75
64	Richie Sexson	.25
65	Ryan Klesko	.25
66	Cliff Floyd	.25
67	Eric Milton	.25
68	Scott Rolen	.65
69	Steve Finley	.25
70	Ray Durham	.25
71	Jeff Bagwell	.75
72	Geoff Jenkins	.25
73	Jamie Moyer	.25
74	David Eckstein	.25
75	Johnny Damon	.40
76	Pokey Reese	.25
77	Mo Vaughn	.25
78	Trevor Hoffman	.25
79	Albert Pujols	1.50
80	Ben Grieve	.25
81	Matt Morris	.25
82	Aubrey Huff	.25
83	Darin Erstad	.60
84	Garret Anderson	.25
85	Jacque Jones	.25
86	Matt Anderson	.25
87	Jose Vidro	.25
88	Carlos Lee	.25
89	Jeff Suppan	.25
90	Al Leiter	.25
91	Jeff Kent	.25
92	Randy Johnson	.75
93	Moises Alou	.25
94	Bobby Higginson	.25
95	Phil Nevin	.25
96	Alex Rodriguez	1.50
97	Luis Gonzalez	.40
98	A.J. Burnett	.25
99	Torii Hunter	.25
100	Ivan Rodriguez	.60
101	Pedro J. Martinez	.75
102	Brady Anderson	.25
103	Paul LoDuca	.25
104	Eric Chavez	.35
105	Tim Salmon	.35
106	Javier Vazquez	.25
107	Bret Boone	.25
108	Greg Vaughn	.25
109	J.D. Drew	.40
110	Jay Gibbons	.25
111	Jim Thome	.25
112	Shawn Green	.40
113	Tim Hudson	.35
114	John Olerud	.25
115	Raul Mondesi	.25
116	Curt Schilling	.50
117	Corey Patterson	.25
118	Robert Fick	.25
119	Corey Koskie	.25
120	Juan Gonzalez	.75
121	Jerry Hairston Jr.	.25
122	Gary Sheffield	.40
123	Mark Mulder	.25
124	Barry Bonds	2.00
125	Jim Edmonds	.25
126	Franklyn German RC	3.00
127	Rodrigo Rosario RC	3.00
128	Ryan Ludwick RC	3.00
129	Jorge de la Rosa RC	4.00
130	Jason Lane	3.00
131	Brian Mallette RC	3.00
132	Chris Baker RC	3.00
133	Kyle Kane RC	3.00
134	Doug DeVore RC	3.00
135	Raul Chavez RC	3.00
136	Miguel Asencio RC	3.00
137	Luis Garcia	3.00
138	Nick Johnson	3.00
139	Michael Crudale RC	3.00
140	P.J. Bevis RC	3.00
141	Josh Hancock RC	3.00
142	Jeremy Lambert RC	3.00
143	Ben Broussard	3.00
144	John Ennis RC	3.00
145	Wilson Valdez RC	3.00
146	Eric Good RC	3.00
147	Elio Serrano RC	3.00
148	Jaime Cerda RC	3.00
149	Hank Blalock	5.00
150	Brandon Duckworth	3.00
151	Drew Henson	1.50
152	Kazuhisa Ishii RC	3.00
153	Earl Snyder RC	1.00
154	J.M. Gold	1.00
155	Satoru Komiyama RC	1.00
156	Marlon Byrd	1.00
157	So Taguchi RC	2.00
158	Eric Hinske	1.00
159	Mark Prior	3.00
160	Jorge Padilla RC	1.50
161	Rene Reyes RC	1.00
162	Jorge Nunez RC	1.00
163	Nelson Castro RC	1.00
164	Anderson Machado RC	2.00
165	Mark Teixeira	2.00
166	Orlando Hudson	1.00
167	Edwin Almonte RC	1.00
168	Luis Ugueto RC	1.00
169	Felix Escalona RC	1.00
170	Ron Calloway RC	1.00
171	Kevin Mench	1.00
172	Takahito Nomura RC	1.00
173	Sean Burroughs	1.00
174	Steve Kent RC	1.00
175	Jorge Sosa RC	1.00
176	Mike Moriarty RC	1.00
177	Carlos Pena	1.00
178	Anastacio Martinez RC	1.00
179	Reed Johnson RC	1.00
180	Juan Brito RC	1.00
181	Wilson Betemit	1.00
182	Mike Rivera	1.00
183	David Espinosa	1.00
184	Todd Donovan RC	1.00
185	Morgan Ensberg	1.00
186	Dewon Brazelton	1.00
187	Ben Howard RC	1.00
188	Austin Kearns	2.00
189	Josh Beckett	2.00
190	Brandon Backe RC	1.50
191	Ichiro Suzuki	4.00
192	Tsuyoshi Shinjo	1.00
193	Hideo Nomo	2.00
194	Kazuhiro Sasaki	1.00
195	Edgardo Alfonzo	1.00
196	Chan Ho Park	1.00
197	Carlos Hernandez	1.00
198	Byung Kim	1.00
199	Omar Vizquel	1.00
200	Freddy Garcia	1.00
201	Richard Hidalgo	1.00
202	Magglio Ordonez	1.00
203	Bobby Abreu	1.00
204	Roger Cedeno	1.00
205	Andruw Jones	2.00
206	Mariano Rivera	1.50
207	Jose Macias	1.00
208	Orlando Hernandez	1.00
209	Rafael Palmeiro	1.00
210	Danys Baez	1.00
211	Bernie Williams	1.25
212	Carlos Beltran	3.00
213	Roberto Alomar	1.50

214	Jose Cruz Jr.	1.00
215	Ryan Dempster	1.00
216	Erubiel Durazo	1.00
217	Carlos Pena	1.00
218	Sammy Sosa	4.00
219	Adrian Beltre	1.50
220	Aramis Ramirez	1.00
221	Alfonso Soriano	2.00
222	Vladimir Guerrero	2.00
223	Juan Uribe	1.00
224	Cristian Guzman	1.00
225	Manny Ramirez	2.00
226	Juan Cruz	1.00
227	Ramon Ortiz	1.00
228	Juan Encarnacion	1.00
229	Bartolo Colon	1.00
230	Miguel Tejada	1.25
231	Cal Ripken Jr.	6.00
232	Derek Jeter	6.00
233	Pedro J. Martinez	2.00
234	Roberto Alomar	1.50
235	Sandy Alomar	1.00
236	Mike Piazza	4.00
237	Jeff Conine	1.00
238	Fred McGriff	1.00
239	Kirby Puckett	3.00
240	Ken Griffey Jr.	4.00
241	Roger Clemens	3.50
242	Joe Morgan	1.00
243	Willie McCovey	1.00
244	Brooks Robinson	1.00
245	Juan Marichal	1.00
246	Todd Helton	2.00
247	Alex Rodriguez	5.00
248	Barry Bonds	6.00
249	Nomar Garciaparra	4.00
250	Jeff Bagwell	2.00
251	Kenny Lofton	1.00
252	Barry Larkin	1.00
253	Tom Glavine	1.50
254	Magglio Ordonez	1.00
255	Randy Johnson	2.00
256	Chipper Jones	3.00
257	Kevin Brown	1.00
258	Rickey Henderson	1.50
259	Greg Maddux	3.00
260	Jim Thome	1.00
261	Rafael Palmeiro	1.50
262	Frank Thomas	2.00
263	Manny Ramirez	2.00
264	Travis Fryman	1.00
265	Gary Sheffield	1.25
266	Bernie Williams	1.25
267	Matt Williams	1.00
268	Ivan Rodriguez	1.50
269	Mike Mussina	1.25
270	Larry Walker	1.00
271	Jim Palmer	1.00
272	Cal Ripken Jr.	6.00
273	Brooks Robinson	1.00
274	Bobby Doerr	1.00
275	Ernie Banks	2.00
276	Fergie Jenkins	1.00
277	Luis Aparicio	1.00
278	Hoyt Wilhelm	1.00
279	Tom Seaver	1.50
280	Joe Morgan	1.00
281	Lou Boudreau	1.00
282	Larry Doby	1.00
283	Jim Bunning	1.00
284	George Kell	1.00
285	Pee Wee Reese	1.50
286	Eddie Mathews	1.00
287	Robin Yount	2.00
288	Rod Carew	1.00
289	Monte Irvin	1.00
290	Yogi Berra	2.00
291	Whitey Ford	1.00
292	Reggie Jackson	2.00
293	Rollie Fingers	1.00
294	Jim "Catfish" Hunter	1.00
295	Richie Ashburn	1.00
296	Willie Stargell	1.00
297	Ralph Kiner	1.00
298	Orlando Cepeda	1.00
299	Juan Marichal	1.00
300	Gaylord Perry	1.00
301	Willie McCovey	1.00
302	Red Schoendienst	1.00
303	Nolan Ryan	8.00
304	Bob Gibson	1.00
305	Al Kaline	1.00
306	Harmon Killebrew	1.00
307	Stan Musial	3.00
308	Phil Rizzuto	1.00
309	Mike Schmidt	4.00
310	Enos Slaughter	1.00

First Edition

Cards (1-125):	4-8X
Cards (126-150):	.5-1X
Cards (151-310):	1-2X
Production 100 Sets	

All-Star Lineup

	NM/M
Common Card:	15.00
1:All-Stars Box	
Derek Jeter, Nomar Garciaparra,	
Alex Rodriguez	50.00
Joe Morgan, Willie McCovey,	
Brooks Robinson	15.00
Alex Rodriguez, Ivan Rodriguez,	
Rafael Palmeiro	20.00

Derek Jeter, Mike Mussina,	
Bernie Williams	35.00
Barry Bonds, Cal Ripken Jr.,	
Frank Thomas	60.00
Cal Ripken Jr., Derek Jeter,	
Roberto Alomar,	
Pedro J. Martinez	60.00
Mike Piazza, Barry Bonds,	
Ken Griffey Jr.,	
Jeff Bagwell	40.00
Roger Clemens, Greg Maddux,	
Randy Johnson,	
Pedro J. Martinez	35.00
Todd Helton, Roberto Alomar,	
Alex Rodriguez,	
Chipper Jones	25.00
Ken Griffey Jr., Barry Bonds,	
Larry Walker,	
Manny Ramirez	35.00

Amazing Greats

	NM/M
Complete Set (20):	20.00
Common Player:	.50
Inserted 1:5	
1AG	Derek Jeter	4.00
2AG	Barry Bonds	4.00
3AG	Mike Piazza	2.50
4AG	Ivan Rodriguez	.75
5AG	Todd Helton	1.00
6AG	Nomar Garciaparra	2.50
7AG	Jim Thome	.50
8AG	Bernie Williams	.50
9AG	Kazuhiro Sasaki	.50
10AG	Torii Hunter	.50
11AG	Bret Boone	.50
12AG	Tim Hudson	.50
13AG	Randy Johnson	1.00
14AG	Rafael Palmeiro	.75
15AG	Scott Rolen	.75
16AG	Carlos Delgado	.75
17AG	Chipper Jones	2.00
18AG	Lance Berkman	.50
19AG	Frank Thomas	1.00
20AG	Greg Maddux	2.00

Amazing Greats Single Swatch

	NM/M
Common Player:	5.00
Inserted 1:13	
Dual Swatches:	1-2X
Inserted 1:90	
Derek Jeter	20.00
Barry Bonds	20.00
Mike Piazza	10.00
Ivan Rodriguez	8.00
Nomar Garciaparra	15.00
Jim Thome/Bat	10.00
Bernie Williams	8.00
Kazuhiro Sasaki	5.00
Torii Hunter	6.00
Bret Boone	5.00
Rafael Palmeiro	8.00
Scott Rolen	8.00
Carlos Delgado	8.00
Lance Berkman	5.00
Frank Thomas	8.00
Greg Maddux	10.00

Amazing Greats Patch

	NM/M
Common Player:	15.00
Production 150 Sets	
Derek Jeter	50.00
Barry Bonds	50.00
Mike Piazza	25.00
Ivan Rodriguez	25.00
Nomar Garciaparra	40.00
Bernie Williams	25.00
Kazuhiro Sasaki	15.00
Torii Hunter	25.00
Bret Boone	15.00
Rafael Palmeiro	25.00
Scott Rolen	25.00
Carlos Delgado	20.00
Lance Berkman	15.00
Frank Thomas	25.00
Greg Maddux	30.00

Bat Rack

	NM/M
Common Card:	20.00
Production 300 Sets	
1BR	Derek Jeter, Alfonso Soriano,	
	Bernie Williams	60.00
2BR	Mike Piazza, Roberto Alomar,	
	Mo Vaughn	30.00
3BR	Jeff Bagwell, Lance Berkman,	
	Craig Biggio	30.00
4BR	Eric Chavez, Miguel Tejada,	
	Carlos Pena	15.00

5BR	Alex Rodriguez, Ivan Rodriguez,	
	Rafael Palmeiro	30.00
6BR	Chipper Jones, Gary Sheffield,	
	Andruw Jones	20.00
7BR	Carlos Delgado, Jim Thome,	
	Frank Thomas	20.00
8BR	Derek Jeter, Nomar Garciaparra,	
	Alex Rodriguez	60.00
9BR	Barry Bonds, Adam Dunn,	
	Chipper Jones	35.00
10BR	Magglio Ordonez, Juan Gonzalez,	
	Manny Ramirez	20.00

Bat Rack Quad

	NM/M
Common Card	25.00
Production 150 Sets	
Torii Hunter, Cristian Guzman,	
Frank Thomas,	
Magglio Ordonez	25.00
Alex Rodriguez, Ivan Rodriguez,	
Eric Chavez, Miguel Tejada	40.00
Mike Piazza, Roberto Alomar,	
Alfonso Soriano,	
Derek Jeter	80.00
Barry Bonds, Lance Berkman,	
Alex Rodriguez,	
Nomar Garciaparra	75.00
Barry Bonds, Chipper Jones,	
Mike Piazza,	
Ivan Rodriguez	75.00
Derek Jeter, Miguel Tejada,	
Nomar Garciaparra,	
Alex Rodriguez	75.00
Roberto Alomar, Mo Vaughn,	
Jeff Bagwell,	
Craig Biggio	25.00
Jim Palmer, Carlos Delgado,	
Jim Thome,	
Frank Thomas	25.00
Magglio Ordonez, Bernie Williams,	
Juan Gonzalez,	
Manny Ramirez	25.00
Chipper Jones, Adam Dunn,	
Jeff Bagwell, Mo Vaughn	25.00
Alex Rodriguez, Jim Palmer,	
Bernie Williams,	
Alfonso Soriano	40.00
Carlos Pena, Eric Chavez,	
Carlos Delgado,	
Juan Gonzalez	20.00
Adam Dunn, Lance Berkman,	
Jim Thome,	
Manny Ramirez	25.00

Box Score Debuts

	NM/M
Complete Set (15):	40.00
Common Player:	2.50
Production 2,002 Sets	
1	Hank Blalock	6.00
2	Eric Hinske	3.00
3	Kazuhisa Ishii	5.00
4	Sean Burroughs	3.00
5	Andres Torres	2.50
6	Satoru Komiyama	2.50
7	Mark Prior	10.00
8	Kevin Mench	2.50
9	Austin Kearns	3.00
10	Earl Snyder	2.50
11	Jon Rauch	2.50
12	Jason Lane	2.50
13	Ben Howard	2.50
14	Bobby Hill	2.50
15	Dennis Tankersley	2.50

Classic Miniatures

	NM/M
Complete Set (40):	25.00
Stars:	1.5-3X Base Card
Production 2,950 Sets	
One set per classic mini box.	
First Editions:	4-8X
Production 100 Sets	

Classic Miniatures Game-Used

	NM/M
Common Player:	6.00
One per Classic Mini box.	
Derek Jeter/Bat	20.00
Mike Piazza/Jsy	10.00
Adam Dunn/Jsy	8.00
Chipper Jones/Bat	10.00
Roger Clemens/Jsy	15.00
Alex Rodriguez/Jsy	10.00
Pedro Martinez/Jsy	10.00
Jim Thome/Bat	10.00
Curt Schilling/Jsy	8.00
Barry Bonds/Bat	20.00

Hall of Fame Material

	NM/M
Common Player:	8.00
1:Cooperstown Box	
Jim Palmer/Jsy	8.00
Cal Ripken Jr/Jsy	25.00
Brooks Robinson/Bat	10.00
Joe Morgan/Bat	8.00
Eddie Mathews/Bat	10.00
Robin Yount/Jsy	15.00
Reggie Jackson/Jsy	10.00
"Catfish" Hunter/Jsy	8.00
Willie McCovey/Jsy	8.00
Nolan Ryan/Jsy	30.00

Press Clippings

	NM/M
Complete Set (20):	90.00
Common Player:	4.00
Inserted 1:90	
1PC	Mark Mulder	4.00
2PC	Curt Schilling	6.00
3PC	Alfonso Soriano	7.50
4PC	Jeff Bagwell	7.50
5PC	J.D. Drew	5.00
6PC	Pedro J. Martinez	7.50
7PC	Bobby Abreu	4.00
8PC	Alex Rodriguez	12.00
9PC	Mike Sweeney	4.00
10PC	Carlos Pena	4.00
11PC	Josh Beckett	6.00
12PC	Roger Clemens	9.00
13PC	Manny Ramirez	7.50
14PC	Adam Dunn	6.00
15PC	Kazuhisa Ishii	4.00
16PC	Ken Griffey Jr.	10.00
17PC	Sammy Sosa	10.00
18PC	Ichiro Suzuki	9.00
19PC	Albert Pujols	15.00
20PC	Troy Glaus	7.50

Press Clippings Game-Used

	NM/M
Common Player:	5.00
Inserted 1:13	
Mark Mulder/Jsy	5.00
Curt Schilling/Jsy	8.00
Alfonso Soriano/Bat	10.00
Jeff Bagwell/Jsy	8.00
J.D. Drew/Jsy	5.00
Pedro Martinez/Jsy	10.00
Bobby Abreu/Jsy	5.00
Alex Rodriguez/Jsy	10.00
Mike Sweeney/Jsy	5.00
Carlos Pena/Jsy	5.00
Josh Beckett/Jsy	8.00
Manny Ramirez/Jsy	10.00
Adam Dunn/Jsy	6.00
Kazuhisa Ishii/Jsy	10.00
Ken Griffey Jr./Base	15.00
Sammy Sosa/Base	15.00
Ichiro Suzuki/Base	15.00
Albert Pujols/Base	10.00
Troy Glaus/Base	5.00

Wave of the Future

	NM/M
Common Player:	4.00
1: Rising Stars Box	
1WF	Drew Henson/Bat	5.00
2WF	Kazuhisa Ishii/Bat	5.00
3WF	Marlon Byrd/Jsy	4.00
4WF	So Taguchi/Bat	4.00
5WF	Jorge Padilla/Pants/75	10.00
6WF	Rene Reyes/Jsy	4.00
7WF	Mark Teixeira/100	10.00
8WF	Carlos Pena/Bat	4.00
9WF	Austin Kearns/Pants	6.00
10WF	Josh Beckett/Jsy/50	15.00

World Piece

	NM/M
Common Player:	4.00
1:International Box	
1WP	Ichiro Suzuki/Base	20.00
2WP	Tsuyoshi Shinjo/Bat	4.00
3WP	Hideo Nomo/Jsy	20.00
4WP	Kazuhiro Sasaki/Jsy	4.00
5WP	Chan Ho Park/Jsy	4.00
6WP	Magglio Ordonez/Jsy	6.00
7WP	Andruw Jones/Jsy	8.00
8WP	Rafael Palmeiro/Jsy	10.00
9WP	Bernie Williams/Jsy	10.00
10WP	Roberto Alomar/Bat	6.00

2002 Fleer E-X

	NM/M
Complete Set (140):	
Common Player:	.25
Common SP (101-125):	3.00
Common (126-140):	5.00
Inserted 1:24	
Pack (4):	2.50
Box (24):	40.00
1	Alex Rodriguez	1.50

2	Albert Pujols	1.50
3	Ken Griffey Jr.	1.25
4	Vladimir Guerrero	.75
5	Sammy Sosa	1.25
6	Ichiro Suzuki	1.25
7	Jorge Posada	.35
8	Matt Williams	.25
9	Adrian Beltre	.40
10	Pat Burrell	.40
11	Roger Cedeno	.25
12	Tony Clark	.25
13	Steve Finley	.25
14	Rafael Furcal	.25
15	Rickey Henderson	.75
16	Richard Hidalgo	.25
17	Jason Kendall	.25
18	Tino Martinez	.25
19	Scott Rolen	.65
20	Shannon Stewart	.25
21	Jose Vidro	.25
22	Preston Wilson	.25
23	Raul Mondesi	.25
24	Lance Berkman	.25
25	Rick Ankiel	.25
26	Kevin Brown	.25
27	Jeromy Burnitz	.25
28	Jeff Cirillo	.25
29	Carl Everett	.25
30	Eric Chavez	.35
31	Freddy Garcia	.25
32	Mark Grace	.35
33	David Justice	.25
34	Fred McGriff	.25
35	Mike Mussina	.50
36	John Olerud	.25
37	Magglio Ordonez	.25
38	Curt Schilling	.50
39	Aaron Sele	.25
40	Robin Ventura	.25
41	Adam Dunn	.50
42	Jeff Bagwell	.75
43	Barry Bonds	2.00
44	Roger Clemens	1.00
45	Cliff Floyd	.25
46	Jason Giambi	.50
47	Juan Gonzalez	.75
48	Luis Gonzalez	.35
49	Cristian Guzman	.25
50	Todd Helton	.75
51	Derek Jeter	2.00
52	Rafael Palmeiro	.65
53	Mike Sweeney	.25
54	Ben Grieve	.25
55	Phil Nevin	.25
56	Mike Piazza	1.25
57	Moises Alou	.25
58	Ivan Rodriguez	.65
59	Manny Ramirez	.75
60	Brian Giles	.25
61	Jim Thome	.25
62	Larry Walker	.25
63	Bobby Abreu	.25
64	Troy Glaus	.75
65	Garret Anderson	.25
66	Roberto Alomar	.40
67	Bret Boone	.25
68	Marty Cardova	.25
69	Craig Biggio	.25
70	Omar Vizquel	.25
71	Jermaine Dye	.25
72	Darin Erstad	.60
73	Carlos Delgado	.50
74	Nomar Garciaparra	1.25
75	Greg Maddux	1.00
76	Tom Glavine	.40
77	Frank Thomas	.75
78	Shawn Green	.40
79	Bobby Higginson	.25
80	Jeff Kent	.25
81	Chuck Knoblauch	.25
82	Paul Konerko	.25
83	Carlos Lee	.25
84	Jon Lieber	.25
85	Paul LoDuca	.25
86	Mike Lowell	.25
87	Edgar Martinez	.25
88	Doug Mientkiewicz	.25
89	Pedro J. Martinez	.75
90	Randy Johnson	.75
91	Aramis Ramirez	.25
92	J.D. Drew	.40
93	Chris Richard	.25
94	Jimmy Rollins	.50
95	Ryan Klesko	.25
96	Gary Sheffield	.40
97	Chipper Jones	1.00
98	Greg Vaughn	.25
99	Mo Vaughn	.25
100	Bernie Williams	.35
101	John Foster/2,999 **RC**	3.00
102	Jorge De La Rosa/2,999 **RC**	4.00
103	Edwin Almonte/2,999 **RC**	3.00
104	Chris Booker/2,999 **RC**	3.00
105	Victor Alvarez/2,999 **RC**	3.00
106	Clifford Bartosh2,999 **RC**	3.00
107	Felix Escalona/2,999 **RC**	3.00
108	Corey Thurman/2,999 **RC**	3.00
109	Kazuhisa Ishii/2,999 **RC**	6.00
110	Miguel Ascencio/2,999 **RC**	3.00
111	P.J. Bevis/2,499 **RC**	3.00
112	Gustavo Chacin/2,499 **RC**	3.00
113	Steve Kent/2,499 **RC**	3.00
114	Takahito Nomura/2,499 **RC**	3.00
115	Adam Walker/2,499 **RC**	3.00
116	So Taguchi/2,499 **RC**	5.00
117	Reed Johnson/2,499 **RC**	5.00
118	Rodrigo Rosario/2,499 **RC**	3.00
119	Luis Martinez/2,499 **RC**	4.00
120	Satoru Komiyama/2,499 **RC**	3.00
121	Sean Burroughs/1,999	3.00
122	Hank Blalock/1,999	5.00
123	Marlon Byrd/1,999	3.00
124	Nick Johnson/1,999	3.00
125	Mark Teixeira/1,999	5.00
126	David Espinosa	3.00
127	Adrian Burnside **RC**	3.00
128	Mark Corey **RC**	3.00
129	Matt Thornton	3.00
130	Dane Sardinha	3.00
131	Juan Rivera	3.00
132	Austin Kearns	5.00
134	Ben Broussard	3.00
135	Orlando Hudson	3.00
136	Carlos Pena	3.00
137	Kenny Kelly	3.00
138	Bill Hall	3.00
139	Ron Chiavacci	3.00
140	Mark Prior	6.00

Essential Credentials Now

Quantity produced listed

19	Scott Rolen/Bat/19	45.00
22	Preston Wilson/Bat/22	15.00
24	Lance Berkman/Bat/24	20.00
25	Rick Ankiel/Jsy/25	15.00
26	Kevin Brown/Jsy/26	20.00
27	Jeromy Burnitz/Bat/27	20.00
28	Jeff Cirillo/Jsy/28	15.00
29	Carl Everett/Jsy/29	15.00
30	Eric Chavez/Bat/30	20.00
31	Freddy Garcia/Jsy/31	15.00
32	Mark Grace/Jsy/32	20.00
33	David Justice/Jsy/33	15.00
34	Fred McGriff/Jsy/34	15.00
35	Mike Mussina/Jsy/35	25.00
36	John Olerud/Jsy/36	10.00
37	Maggio Ordonez/Jsy/37	15.00
38	Curt Schilling/Jsy/38	20.00
39	Aaron Sele/Jsy/39	10.00
40	Robin Ventura/Jsy/40	10.00
41	Adam Dunn/Bat/41	15.00
42	Jeff Bagwell/Jsy/42	20.00
43	Barry Bonds/Pants/43	75.00
44	Roger Clemens/Bat/44	50.00
45	Cliff Floyd/Bat/45	10.00
46	Jason Giambi/Base/46	15.00
47	Juan Gonzalez/Jsy/47	15.00
48	Luis Gonzalez/Base/48	10.00
49	Cristian Guzman/Bat/49	10.00
50	Todd Helton/Base/50	15.00
51	Derek Jeter/Bat/51	60.00
52	Rafael Palmeiro/Bat/52	20.00
53	Mike Sweeney/Bat/53	10.00
54	Ben Grieve/Jsy/54	5.00
55	Phil Nevin/Bat/55	8.00
56	Mike Piazza/Base/56	20.00
57	Moises Alou/Bat/57	10.00
58	Ivan Rodriguez/Jsy/58	15.00
59	Manny Ramirez/Base/59	10.00
60	Brian Giles/Bat/60	10.00
61	Jim Thome/61	15.00
62	Larry Walker/62	5.00
63	Bobby Abreu/63	5.00
64	Troy Glaus/64	8.00
65	Garret Anderson/65	8.00
66	Roberto Alomar/66	8.00
67	Bret Boone/67	5.00
68	Marty Cordova/68	4.00
69	Craig Biggio/69	5.00
70	Omar Vizquel/70	4.00
71	Jermaine Dye/71	4.00
72	Darin Erstad/72	5.00
73	Carlos Delgado/73	6.00
74	Nomar Garciaparra/74	15.00
75	Greg Maddux/75	15.00
76	Tom Glavine/76	5.00
77	Frank Thomas/77	8.00
78	Shawn Green/78	6.00
79	Bobby Higginson/79	4.00
80	Jeff Kent/80	5.00
81	Chuck Knoblauch/81	4.00
82	Paul Konerko/82	5.00
83	Carlos Lee/83	5.00
84	Jon Lieber/84	5.00
85	Paul LoDuca/85	5.00
86	Mike Lowell/86	6.00
87	Edgar Martinez/87	6.00
88	Doug Mientkiewicz/88	5.00
89	Pedro J. Martinez/89	10.00
90	Randy Johnson/90	10.00
91	Aramis Ramirez/91	6.00
92	J.D. Drew/92	6.00
93	Chris Richard/93	4.00
94	Jimmy Rollins/94	10.00
95	Ryan Klesko/95	6.00
96	Gary Sheffield/96	6.00
97	Chipper Jones/97	10.00
98	Greg Vaughn/98	4.00
99	Mo Vaughn/99	5.00
100	Bernie Williams/100	6.00
101	John Foster NT/101	4.00
102	Jorge De La Rosa NT/102	4.00
103	Edwin Almonte NT/103	4.00
104	Chris Booker NT/104	4.00
105	Victor Alvarez NT/105	4.00
106	Clifford Bartosh NT/106	4.00
107	Felix Escalona NT/107	4.00
108	Corey Thurman NT/108	4.00
109	Kazuhisa Ishii NT/109	10.00
110	Miguel Asencio NT/110	4.00
111	P.J. Bevis NT/111	4.00
112	Gustavo Chacin NT/112	4.00
113	Steve Kent NT/113	4.00
114	Takahito Nomura NT/114	4.00
115	Adam Walker NT/115	4.00
116	So Taguchi NT/116	6.00
117	Reed Johnson NT/117	6.00
118	Rodrigo Rosario NT/118	4.00
119	Luis Martinez NT/119	4.00
120	Satoru Komiyama NT/120	4.00
121	Sean Burroughs NT/121	5.00
122	Hank Blalock NT/122	6.00
123	Marlon Byrd NT/123	4.00
124	Nick Johnson NT/124	4.00
125	Mark Teixeira NT/125	6.00

Essential Credentials Future

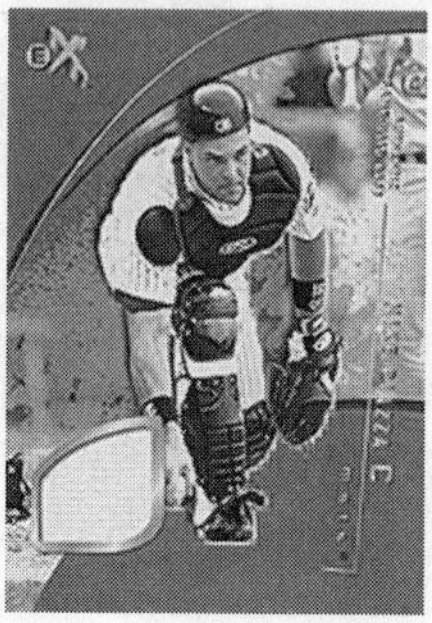

NM/M

Quantity produced listed

1	Alex Rodriguez/Jsy/60	30.00
2	Albert Pujols/Base/59	25.00
3	Ken Griffey Jr./Base/58	20.00
4	Vladimir Guerrero/Base/57	15.00
5	Sammy Sosa/Base/56	25.00
6	Ichiro Suzuki/Base/55	40.00
7	Jorge Posada/Bat/54	12.00
8	Matt Williams/Bat/53	8.00
9	Adrian Beltre/Bat/52	8.00
10	Pat Burrell/Bat/51	10.00
11	Roger Cedeno/Bat/50	8.00
12	Tony Clark/Bat/49	8.00
13	Steve Finley/Bat/48	8.00
14	Rafael Furcal/Bat/47	12.00
15	Rickey Henderson/Bat/46	20.00
16	Richard Hidalgo/Bat/45	10.00
17	Jason Kendall/Bat/44	10.00
18	Tino Martinez/Bat/43	15.00
19	Scott Rolen/Bat/42	20.00
20	Shannon Stewart/Bat/41	10.00
21	Jose Vidro/Bat/40	10.00
22	Preston Wilson/Bat/39	10.00
23	Raul Mondesi/Bat/38	10.00
24	Lance Berkman/Bat/37	10.00
25	Rick Ankiel/Jsy/36	8.00
26	Kevin Brown/Jsy/35	10.00
27	Jeromy Burnitz/Bat/34	8.00
28	Jeff Cirillo/Jsy/33	8.00
29	Carl Everett/Jsy/32	8.00
30	Eric Chavez/Bat/31	10.00
31	Freddy Garcia/Jsy/30	10.00
32	Mark Grace/Jsy/29	20.00
33	David Justice/Jsy/28	15.00
34	Fred McGriff/Jsy/27	15.00
37	Magglio Ordonez/Jsy/24	15.00
38	Curt Schilling/Jsy/23	30.00
61	Jim Thome/125	8.00
62	Larry Walker/124	4.00
63	Bobby Abreu/123	4.00
64	Troy Glaus/122	6.00
65	Garret Anderson/121	6.00
66	Roberto Alomar/120	6.00
67	Bret Boone/119	6.00
68	Marty Cordova/118	4.00
69	Craig Biggio/117	4.00
70	Omar Vizquel/116	4.00
71	Jermaine Dye/115	4.00
72	Darin Erstad/114	4.00
73	Carlos Delgado/113	6.00
74	Nomar Garciaparra/112	10.00
75	Greg Maddux/111	10.00
76	Tom Glavine/110	6.00
77	Frank Thomas/109	6.00
78	Shawn Green/108	5.00
79	Bobby Higginson/107	3.00
80	Jeff Kent/106	4.00
81	Chuck Knoblauch/105	3.00
82	Paul Konerko/104	3.00
83	Carlos Lee/103	3.00
84	Jon Lieber/102	3.00
85	Paul LoDuca/101	3.00
86	Mike Lowell/100	4.00
87	Edgar Martinez/99	4.00
88	Doug Mientkiewicz/98	3.00
89	Pedro J. Martinez/97	8.00
90	Randy Johnson/96	8.00
91	Aramis Ramirez/95	4.00
92	J.D. Drew/94	4.00
93	Chris Richard/93	3.00
94	Jimmy Rollins/92	4.00
95	Ryan Klesko/91	4.00
96	Gary Sheffield/90	4.00
97	Chipper Jones/89	8.00
98	Greg Vaughn/88	3.00
99	Mo Vaughn/87	3.00
100	Bernie Williams/86	5.00
101	John Foster NT/85	3.00
102	Jorge De La Rosa NT/84	3.00
103	Edwin Almonte NT/83	3.00
104	Chris Booker NT/82	3.00
105	Victor Alvarez NT/81	3.00
106	Clifford Bartosh NT/80	3.00
107	Felix Escalona NT/79	3.00
108	Corey Thurman NT/78	3.00
109	Kazuhisa Ishii NT/77	12.00
110	Miguel Asencio NT/76	3.00
111	P.J. Bevis NT/75	3.00
112	Gustavo Chacin NT/74	3.00
113	Steve Kent NT/73	3.00
114	Takahito Nomura NT/72	3.00
115	Adam Walker NT/71	3.00
116	So Taguchi NT/70	6.00
117	Reed Johnson NT/69	6.00
118	Rodrigo Rosario NT/68	4.00
119	Luis Martinez NT/67	5.00
120	Satoru Komiyama NT/66	4.00
121	Sean Burroughs NT/65	5.00
122	Hank Blalock NT/64	6.00
123	Marlon Byrd NT/63	4.00
124	Nick Johnson NT/62	4.00
125	Mark Teixeira NT/61	6.00

Barry Bonds 4X MVP

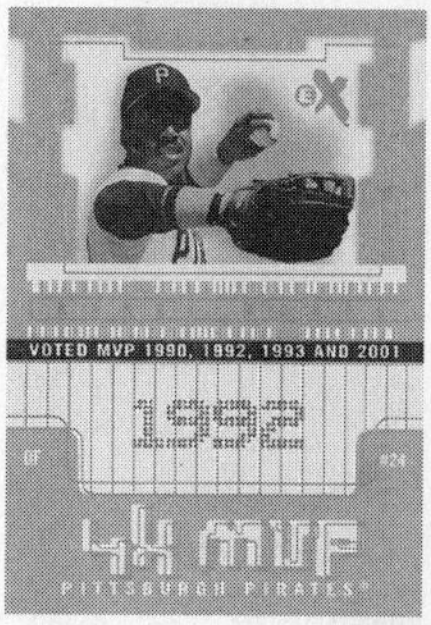

NM/M

Complete Set (4):		20.00
Common Bonds:		6.00
1BB4X	Barry Bonds/1990	6.00
2BB4X	Barry Bonds/1,992	6.00
3BB4X	Barry Bonds/1,993	6.00
4BB4X	Barry Bonds/2,001	6.00

Behind the Numbers

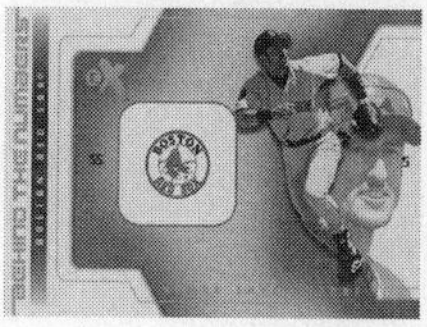

NM/M

Complete Set (35):		75.00
Common Player:		1.00
Inserted 1:8		
1BTN	Ichiro Suzuki	5.00
2BTN	Jason Giambi	2.50
3BTN	Mike Piazza	5.00
4BTN	Brian Giles	1.00
5BTN	Barry Bonds	8.00
6BTN	Pedro J. Martinez	3.00
7BTN	Nomar Garciaparra	5.00
8BTN	Randy Johnson	3.00
9BTN	Craig Biggio	1.00
10BTN	Manny Ramirez	3.00
11BTN	Mike Mussina	1.50
12BTN	Kerry Wood	2.50
13BTN	Jim Edmonds	1.00
14BTN	Ivan Rodriguez	2.50
15BTN	Jeff Bagwell	3.00
16BTN	Roger Clemens	4.50
17BTN	Chipper Jones	4.00
18BTN	Shawn Green	1.25
19BTN	Albert Pujols	6.00
20BTN	Andruw Jones	3.00
21BTN	Luis Gonzalez	1.00
22BTN	Todd Helton	3.00
23BTN	Jorge Posada	1.25
24BTN	Scott Rolen	2.50
25BTN	Ben Sheets	1.00
26BTN	Alfonso Soriano	2.50
27BTN	Greg Maddux	4.00
28BTN	Gary Sheffield	1.25
29BTN	Barry Zito	1.25
30BTN	Alex Rodriguez	6.00
31BTN	Larry Walker	1.00
32BTN	Derek Jeter	8.00
33BTN	Ken Griffey Jr.	5.00
34BTN	Vladimir Guerrero	3.00
35BTN	Sammy Sosa	5.00

Behind the Numbers Game Jersey

		NM/M
Common Player:		5.00
Inserted 1:24		
1	Jeff Bagwell	10.00
2	Craig Biggio/Pants	5.00
4	Roger Clemens	20.00
5	Jim Edmonds	5.00
6	Brian Giles	5.00
7	Luis Gonzalez	5.00
8	Shawn Green	5.00
9	Todd Helton	8.00
10	Derek Jeter/SP	30.00
11	Randy Johnson/SP	10.00
12	Andruw Jones	8.00
13	Chipper Jones	10.00
14	Greg Maddux	10.00
15	Pedro J. Martinez	10.00
16	Mike Mussina	10.00
17	Mike Piazza/Pants	10.00
18	Jorge Posada	8.00
19	Manny Ramirez	8.00
20	Alex Rodriguez	10.00
21	Ivan Rodriguez	8.00
22	Scott Rolen	8.00
23	Alfonso Soriano/SP	10.00
24	Barry Zito	6.00

Behind the Numbers Game Jersey Dual

No Pricing
Production 25 Sets

Derek Jeter 4X Champ

		NM/M
Complete Set (4):		20.00
Common Jeter:		6.00
1DJFX	Derek Jeter/1996	6.00
2DJFX	Derek Jeter/1998	6.00
3DJFX	Derek Jeter/1999	6.00
4DJFX	Derek Jeter/2000	6.00

Game Essentials

		NM/M
Common Player:		5.00
	Carlos Beltran	5.00
	Kevin Brown	5.00
	Jeromy Burnitz	5.00
	Carlos Delgado	8.00
	Jason Hart/SP	8.00
	Rickey Henderson	20.00
	Drew Henson/Shoe	5.00
	Drew Henson/Glv	8.00
	Derek Jeter/Shoe	40.00
	Jason Kendall	5.00
	Jeff Kent	10.00
	Barry Larkin/Glv	20.00
	Javy Lopez	5.00
	Raul Mondesi/Btg Glv	5.00
	Rafael Palmeiro	10.00
	Adam Piatt	5.00
	Brad Radke	5.00
	Cal Ripken Jr.	30.00
	Mariano Rivera	10.00
	Alex Rodriguez/Btg Glv	15.00
	Ivan Rodriguez/Shoe	10.00
	Kazuhiro Sasaki	5.00
	J.T. Snow	5.00
	Mo Vaughn	5.00
	Robin Ventura	8.00
	Jose Vidro	5.00
	Matt Williams	5.00

HardWear

		NM/M
Complete Set (10):		60.00
Common Player:		4.00
Inserted 1:72 Hobby		
1HW	Ivan Rodriguez	4.00
2HW	Mike Piazza	8.00
3HW	Derek Jeter	15.00
4HW	Barry Bonds	15.00
5HW	Todd Helton	4.00
6HW	Roberto Alomar	4.00
7HW	Albert Pujols	10.00
8HW	Ichiro Suzuki	10.00
9HW	Ken Griffey Jr.	8.00
10HW	Jason Giambi	5.00

Hit and Run

		NM/M
Complete Set (30):		50.00
Common Player:		1.00
Inserted 1:12		
1	Adam Dunn	1.00
2	Derek Jeter	6.00
3	Frank Thomas	2.00
4	Albert Pujols	5.00
5	J.D. Drew	1.00
6	Richard Hidalgo	1.00
7	John Olerud	1.00
8	Roberto Alomar	1.00
9	Pat Burrell	1.50
10	Darin Erstad	1.50
11	Mark Grace	1.00
12	Chipper Jones	3.00
13	Jose Vidro	1.00
14	Cliff Floyd	1.00
15	Mo Vaughn	1.00
16	Nomar Garciaparra	4.00
17	Ivan Rodriguez	1.50
18	Luis Gonzalez	1.00
19	Jason Giambi	1.50
20	Bernie Williams	1.00
21	Mike Piazza	4.00
22	Barry Bonds	6.00
23	Jose Ortiz	1.00
24	Magglio Ordonez	1.00
25	Troy Glaus	2.00
26	Alex Rodriguez	5.00
27	Ichiro Suzuki	8.00
28	Sammy Sosa	4.00
29	Ken Griffey Jr.	4.00
30	Vladimir Guerrero	2.00

Hit and Run Game Base

		NM/M
Inserted 1:120		
1	J.D. Drew	4.00
2	Adam Dunn	6.00
3	Jason Giambi	6.00
4	Troy Glaus	6.00
5	Ken Griffey Jr.	10.00
6	Vladimir Guerrero	8.00
7	Albert Pujols	15.00
8	Sammy Sosa	10.00
9	Ichiro Suzuki	15.00
10	Bernie Williams	6.00

Hit and Run Game Bat

		NM/M
Common Player:		4.00
Inserted 1:24		
1	Roberto Alomar	6.00
2	J.D. Drew	4.00
3	Darin Erstad	4.00
4	Cliff Floyd	4.00
5	Nomar Garciaparra	15.00
6	Luis Gonzalez	6.00
7	Richard Hidalgo	4.00
8	Derek Jeter	25.00
9	Chipper Jones	8.00
10	John Olerud	4.00
11	Magglio Ordonez	6.00
12	Jose Ortiz	4.00
13	Mike Piazza	10.00
14	Alex Rodriguez	15.00
15	Ivan Rodriguez	8.00
16	Frank Thomas	8.00
17	Mo Vaughn	4.00
18	Jose Vidro	4.00
19	Bernie Williams	4.00

Hit and Run Game Bat and Base

		NM/M
Common Player:		10.00
Inserted 1:240		
1	Roberto Alomar	15.00
2	Barry Bonds/SP	50.00
3	Nomar Garciaparra	30.00
4	Derek Jeter	40.00
5	Chipper Jones	15.00
6	Mike Piazza	20.00
7	Alex Rodriguez	25.00
8	Mo Vaughn	10.00

2002 Fleer Fall Classic

		NM/M
Complete Set (100):		30.00
Common Player:		.25
Common SP:		3.00
Inserted 1:18 Hobby		
Pack (5):		5.00
Box (24):		100.00
1	Rabbit Maranville	.25
2	Tris Speaker	.75
3	Harmon Killebrew	1.00
4	Lou Gehrig	2.00
5	Lou Boudreau	.25
6	Al Kaline	1.00
7	Paul Molitor	1.00
7	Paul Molitor/Brewers	4.00
8	Cal Ripken Jr.	3.00
9	Yogi Berra	1.00
10	Phil Rizzuto	.75
11	Luis Aparicio	.25
11	Luis Aparicio/Orioles	4.00
12	Stan Musial	2.00
13	Mel Ott	.75
14	Larry Doby	.25
15	Ozzie Smith	1.00
16	Babe Ruth	4.00
16	Babe Ruth/Red Sox	10.00
17	Red Schoendienst	.25
17	Red Schoendienst/Cards	3.00
18	Rollie Fingers	.25
19	Thurman Munson	1.50
20	Lou Brock	.50
21	Paul O'Neill	.25
21	Paul O'Neill/Reds	3.00
22	Jim Palmer	.50
23	Kirby Puckett	1.00
24	Tony Perez	.25
24	Tony Perez/Phila.	3.00
25	Don Larsen	.75
26	Steve Garvey	.25
26	Steve Garvey/Padres	3.00
27	Jim "Catfish" Hunter	.25
27	"Catfish" Hunter/Yanks	4.00
28	Juan Marichal	.50
29	Pee Wee Reese	.50
30	Orlando Cepeda	.25
31	Rich "Goose" Gossage	.25
32	Ray Knight	.25
33	Eddie Murray	.75
34	Nolan Ryan	3.00
35	Alan Trammell	.50
36	Grover Alexander	.75
37	Joe Carter	.25
38	Rogers Hornsby	1.00
39	Jimmie Foxx	1.00
40	Mike Schmidt	1.50
41	Eddie Mathews	1.00
42	Jackie Robinson	1.50
43	Eddie Collins	.25
43	Eddie Collins/White Sox	3.00
44	Willie McCovey	.25
45	Bob Gibson	1.00
46	Keith Hernandez	.50
46	Keith Hernandez/Cards	4.00
47	Brooks Robinson	1.00
48	Mordecai Brown	.25
49	Gary Carter	.50
50	Kirk Gibson	.25
50	Kirk Gibson/Tigers	3.00

		NM/M
51	Johnny Mize	.25
52	Johnny Podres	.25
53	Darrell Porter	.25
54	Willie Stargell	.75
55	Lenny Dykstra	.25
55	Lenny Dykstra/Phila.	3.00
56	Christy Mathewson	.75
57	Walter Johnson	1.00
58	Whitey Ford	.75
59	Lefty Grove	.50
60	Duke Snider	.75
61	Cy Young	1.00
62	Dave Winfield	.75
62	Dave Winfield/Yanks	5.00
63	Robin Yount	1.00
64	Fred Lynn	.25
65	Ty Cobb	2.00
66	Joe Morgan	.25
67	Bill Mazeroski	.25
68	Frank Baker	.25
69	Chief Bender	.25
70	Carlton Fisk	.50
71	Jerry Coleman	.25
72	Frankie Frisch	.25
73	Wade Boggs	1.00
73	Wade Boggs/Yanks	4.00
74	Johnny Bench	.75
75	Roger Maris	2.00
75	Roger Maris/Cards	8.00
76	Dom DiMaggio	.25
77	George Brett	3.00
78	Dave Parker	.25
78	Dave Parker/A's	3.00
79	Hank Greenberg	.25
80	Pepper Martin	.25
81	Graig Nettles	.25
81	Graig Nettles/Padres	3.00
82	Dennis Eckersley	.50
83	Donn Clendenon	.25
84	Tom Seaver	1.00
85	Honus Wagner	1.50
86	Reggie Jackson	.75
86	Reggie Jackson/A's	5.00
87	Goose Goslin	.25
87	Goose Goslin/Tigers	3.00
88	Tony Kubek	.25
89	Roy Campanella	1.00
90	Steve Carlton/Cards	4.00
91	Lou Gehrig, Mel Ott	2.00
92	Eddie Collins, Joe Morgan	.25
93	George Brett,	
	Mike Schmidt	2.00
94	Cal Ripken Jr., Ozzie Smith	3.00
95	Thurman Munson,	
	Johnny Bench	1.50
96	Willie Stargell, Stan Musial,	
	Pepper Martin	1.00
97	Babe Ruth, Kirby Puckett,	
	Reggie Jackson	3.00
98	Cy Young, Bob Gibson	1.00
99	Whitey Ford, Steve Carlton	1.00
100	Paul Molitor, Lou Brock	.50

Championship Gold

Golds:	5-10X
Gold SP's:	1-2X
Production 50 Sets	

HOF Plaque

		NM/M
Complete Set (30):		90.00
Common Player:		3.00
#'d to HOF induction year		
1HOF	Babe Ruth	8.00
2HOF	Christy Mathewson	3.00
3HOF	Honus Wagner	4.00
4HOF	Ty Cobb	5.00
5HOF	Walter Johnson	4.00
6HOF	Cy Young	4.00
7HOF	Tris Speaker	3.00
8HOF	Eddie Collins	3.00
9HOF	Lou Gehrig	6.00
10HOF	Jimmie Foxx	4.00
11HOF	Jackie Robinson	6.00
12HOF	Stan Musial	5.00
13HOF	Yogi Berra	4.00
14HOF	Duke Snider	4.00
15HOF	Juan Marichal	3.00
16HOF	Luis Aparicio	3.00
17HOF	Pee Wee Reese	3.00
18HOF	Willie McCovey	3.00

19HOF	Willie Stargell	3.00
20HOF	Johnny Bench	5.00
21HOF	Joe Morgan	3.00
22HOF	Jim Palmer	3.00
23HOF	Tom Seaver	5.00
24HOF	Reggie Jackson	4.00
25HOF	Steve Carlton	3.00
26HOF	George Brett	6.00
27HOF	Nolan Ryan	8.00
28HOF	Robin Yount	4.00
29HOF	Kirby Puckett	5.00
30HOF	Ozzie Smith	4.00

MVP Collection Game-Used

NM/M

Common Player: 5.00
Inserted 1:100
Golds: .75-2X
Production 100 Sets

JB	Johnny Bench/200	20.00
DC	Donn Clendenon	5.00
RF	Rollie Fingers/200	5.00
RJOK	Reggie Jackson/50	5.00
RJNY	Reggie Jackson	10.00
RK	Ray Knight	5.00
PM	Paul Molitor/250	15.00
DP	Darrell Porter/250	5.00
BR	Brooks Robinson/250	20.00
WS	Willie Stargell/200	10.00
AT	Alan Trammell	10.00

MVP Collection Patch

NM/M

Numbered to MVP year.

JB	Johnny Bench/76	45.00
RF	Rollie Fingers/74	20.00
RJNY	Reggie Jackson/77	40.00
BR	Brooks Robinson/70	40.00
AT	Alan Trammell/84	30.00

October Legends

NM/M

Common Player: 5.00
Inserted 1:48
Golds: .75-1.5X
Production 100 Sets

Joe Morgan	5.00
Wade Boggs/60	20.00
Keith Hernandez/100	15.00
Robin Yount	10.00
Eddie Murray	10.00
Lenny Dykstra/200	8.00
Paul O'Neill	8.00
Red Schoendienst/210	8.00
Pepper Martin/50	15.00
Keith Hernandez/150	20.00
Willie Stargell/225	12.00
George Brett	20.00
Dave Parker/50	10.00
Tony Perez	5.00
Rollie Fingers	5.00
Gary Carter/200	10.00
Dennis Eckersley	5.00
Juan Marichal	8.00
Pee Wee Reese/200	15.00
Roger Maris	60.00
Duke Snider/200	15.00
Darrell Porter/150	5.00
Willie McCovey/150	10.00
Paul Molitor/150	15.00

October Legends Dual

NM/M

Common Card: 10.00
SP's Noted

Rollie Fingers, Dennis Eckersley, Keith Hernandez, Red Schoendienst	12.00
Joe Morgan, Tony Perez	10.00
Wade Boggs, Keith Hernandez	20.00
Lenny Dykstra, Gary Carter	12.00
Robin Yount, Paul Molitor/150	35.00
Roger Maris, Paul O'Neill/200	50.00
Duke Snider, Pee Wee Reese/200	25.00
Juan Marichal, Willie McCovey	15.00
George Brett, Darrell Porter/150	35.00
Willie Stargell, Dave Parker	15.00
Gary Carter, Keith Hernandez	10.00
Cal Ripken Jr., Eddie Murray/200	40.00
Cal Ripken Jr., Eddie Murray/100	50.00
Pepper Martin, Frankie Frisch	15.00

Pennant Chase

NM/M

Common Player: 10.00
Inserted 1:48 Hobby

Yogi Berra/Pants/150	20.00
Carlton Fisk/Bat	10.00
Reggie Jackson/Jsy	10.00
Fred Lynn/Bat	10.00
Thurman Munson/Bat	30.00
Wade Boggs/Jsy	10.00
Dave Winfield/Bat	10.00

Pennant Chase Dual

NM/M

Production 50 Sets

CFRJ	Carlton Fisk/Bat, Reggie Jackson/Jsy	30.00
FLTM	Fred Lynn/Bat, Thurman Munson/Bat	50.00
WBDW	Wade Boggs/Jsy, Dave Winfield/Bat	30.00

Rival Factions

NM/M

Common Card: 2.00
1-24 #'d to 1,000
25-36 #'d to 500
37-43 #'d to 50

1RF	Carlton Fisk, Thurman Munson	3.00
2RF	Frank Baker, Babe Ruth	8.00
3RF	Jimmie Foxx, Lou Gehrig	6.00
4RF	Steve Carlton, Nolan Ryan	8.00
5RF	Mordecai Brown, Honus Wagner	3.00
6RF	Frankie Frisch, Duke Snider	3.00
7RF	Ozzie Smith, Alan Trammell	3.00
8RF	Larry Doby, Jackie Robinson	5.00
9RF	Steve Garvey, Tony Perez	2.00
10RF	Johnny Bench, Willie Stargell	4.00
11RF	Ty Cobb, Eddie Collins	5.00
12RF	Reggie Jackson, Brooks Robinson	4.00
13RF	Yogi Berra, Roy Campanella	4.00
14RF	Orlando Cepeda, Willie McCovey	2.00
15RF	Al Kaline, Jim Palmer	4.00
16RF	George Brett, Kirby Puckett	6.00
17RF	Bob Gibson, Tom Seaver	4.00
18RF	Cal Ripken Jr., Robin Yount	8.00
19RF	Johnny Mize, Mel Ott	3.00
20RF	Stan Musial, Pee Wee Reese	4.00
21RF	Hank Greenburg, Lefty Grove	2.00
22RF	Dave Parker, Mike Schmidt	3.00
23RF	Bill Mazeroski, Joe Morgan	3.00
24RF	Johnny Bench, Carlton Fisk	5.00
25RF	George Brett, Mike Schmidt	8.00
26RF	Pee Wee Reese, Phil Rizzuto	4.00
27RF	Cal Ripken Jr., Alan Trammell	15.00
28RF	Tom Seaver, Jim "Catfish" Hunter	4.00
29RF	Ty Cobb, Honus Wagner	5.00
30RF	Steve Carlton, Lefty Grove	3.00
31RF	Ozzie Smith, Robin Yount	8.00
32RF	Frankie Frisch, Joe Morgan	3.00
33RF	Hank Greenberg, Jackie Robinson	5.00
34RF	Jimmie Foxx, Pepper Martin	5.00
35RF	Lou Gehrig, Cal Ripken Jr.	40.00
36RF	Ozzie Smith, Honus Wagner	40.00
37RF	Reggie Jackson, Dave Winfield	20.00
38RF	Ty Cobb, Rogers Hornsby	35.00
39RF	Babe Ruth, Roger Maris	50.00
40RF	Yogi Berra, Thurman Munson	20.00
41RF	Nolan Ryan, Tom Seaver	50.00
42RF	Joe Morgan, Jackie Robinson	20.00
43RF	Jimmie Foxx, Mel Ott	25.00

Rival Factions Game-Used Single

NM/M

Common Card: 8.00
Inserted 1:32

Carlton Fisk, Thurman Munson	25.00
Frank Baker, Babe Ruth	25.00
Jimmie Foxx, Lou Gehrig	35.00
Steve Carlton, Nolan Ryan	25.00
Frankie Frisch, Duke Snider	20.00
Ozzie Smith, Alan Trammell	15.00
Larry Doby, Jackie Robinson	10.00
Steve Garvey, Tony Perez	10.00
Johnny Bench, Willie Stargell	10.00
Reggie Jackson, Brooks Robinson	12.00
Orlando Cepeda, Willie McCovey	10.00
Al Kaline, Jim Palmer	10.00
George Brett, Kirby Puckett	25.00
Bob Gibson, Tom Seaver	20.00
Cal Ripken Jr., Robin Yount	30.00
Stan Musial, Pee Wee Reese	25.00
Hank Greenberg, Lefty Grove	20.00
Bill Mazeroski, Joe Morgan	8.00
Johnny Bench, Carlton Fisk	10.00
George Brett, Mike Schmidt	25.00
Pee Wee Reese, Phil Rizzuto	15.00
Cal Ripken Jr., Alan Trammell	35.00
Steve Carlton, Lefty Grove	15.00
Ozzie Smith, Robin Yount	15.00
Frankie Frisch, Joe Morgan	25.00
Hank Greenberg, Jackie Robinson	20.00
Jimmie Foxx, Pepper Martin	30.00
Lou Gehrig, Cal Ripken Jr.	40.00
Reggie Jackson, Dave Winfield	10.00
Babe Ruth, Roger Maris	60.00
Nolan Ryan, Tom Seaver	35.00

Rival Factions Game-Used Dual

NM/M

Common Card: 12.00

Carlton Fisk, Thurman Munson	30.00
Steve Carlton, Nolan Ryan	40.00
Frankie Frisch, Duke Snider	15.00
Ozzie Smith, Alan Trammell	25.00
Larry Doby, Jackie Robinson/75	60.00
Steve Garvey, Tony Perez	10.00
Johnny Bench, Willie Stargell	20.00
Reggie Jackson, Brooks Robinson	20.00
Orlando Cepeda, Willie McCovey/200	15.00
George Brett, Kirby Puckett	40.00
Cal Ripken Jr., Robin Yount	30.00
Johnny Bench, Carlton Fisk	20.00
Cal Ripken Jr., Alan Trammell	30.00
Jim "Catfish" Hunter, Tom Seaver	15.00
Ozzie Smith, Robin Yount	25.00
Frankie Frisch, Joe Morgan	15.00
Hank Greenberg, Jackie Robinson/50	100.00
Jimmie Foxx, Pepper Martin/200	40.00
Reggie Jackson, Dave Winfield/150	20.00
Yogi Berra, Thurman Munson	40.00
Nolan Ryan, Tom Seaver	45.00
Joe Morgan, Jackie Robinson/50	50.00

Rival Factions Dual Patch

NM/M

Production 50 Sets	12.00
Carlton Fisk, Thurman Munson	60.00
Steve Carlton, Nolan Ryan	100.00
Ozzie Smith, Alan Trammell	50.00
Steve Garvey, Tony Perez	30.00
Johnny Bench, Willie Stargell	50.00
Cal Ripken Jr., Robin Yount	125.00
Johnny Bench, Carlton Fisk	50.00
Cal Ripken Jr., Alan Trammell	100.00
Ozzie Smith, Robin Yount	60.00
Reggie Jackson, Dave Winfield	40.00

Series of Champions

NM/M

Complete Set (19): 25.00
Common Player: 1.00
Inserted 1:6

1	Yogi Berra	2.00
2	Wade Boggs	2.00
3	Dave Parker	1.00
4	Joe Carter	1.00
5	Kirk Gibson	1.00
6	Reggie Jackson	2.00
7	Tony Kubek	1.00
8	Don Larsen	1.00
9	Bill Mazeroski	1.00
10	Eddie Murray	1.50
11	Graig Nettles	1.00
12	Tony Perez	1.00
13	Phil Rizzuto	1.50
14	Mike Schmidt	2.50
15	Red Schoendienst	1.00
16	Duke Snider	2.00
17	Ty Cobb	2.50
18	Lou Gehrig	3.00
19	Babe Ruth	4.00

Series of Champions Game-Used

NM/M

Common Player: 5.00
Inserted 1:36
Golds: .75-1.5X
Production 100 Sets
Bat Knob numbered to 10 not priced.

Yogi Berra/Bat	15.00
Wade Boggs/Jsy	10.00
Dave Parker/Bat	5.00
Joe Carter/Bat	5.00
Kirk Gibson/Bat	5.00
Reggie Jackson/Bat	10.00
Tony Kubek/Bat	10.00
Eddie Murray/Bat	10.00
Graig Nettles/Bat	5.00
Tony Perez/Bat	5.00
Red Schoendienst/Jsy	5.00
Duke Snider/Bat	10.00
Babe Ruth/Bat/25	180.00

2002 Fleer Flair

NM/M

Complete Set (138):
Common Player: .25
Common (101-138): 3.00
Production 1,750
Pack (5): 4.00
Hobby Box (20): 70.00

1	Scott Rolen	.75
2	Derek Jeter	3.00
3	Sean Casey	.40
4	Hideo Nomo	.75
5	Craig Biggio	.25
6	Randy Johnson	1.00
7	J.D. Drew	.50
8	Greg Maddux	1.50
9	Paul LoDuca	.25
10	John Olerud	.25
11	Barry Larkin	.25
12	Mark Grace	.35
13	Jimmy Rollins	.50
14	Todd Helton	.25
15	Jim Edmonds	.25
16	Roy Oswalt	.35
17	Phil Nevin	.25
18	Tim Salmon	.35
19	Magglio Ordonez	.25
20	Roger Clemens	1.75
21	Raul Mondesi	.25
22	Edgar Martinez	.25
23	Pedro J. Martinez	1.00
24	Edgardo Alfonzo	.25
25	Bernie Williams	.35
26	Gary Sheffield	.40
27	D'Angelo Jimenez	.25

28	Toby Hall	.25
29	Joe Mays	.25
30	Alfonso Soriano	.75
31	Mike Piazza	2.00
32	Lance Berkman	.25
33	Jim Thome	.25
34	Ben Sheets	.25
35	Brandon Inge	.25
36	Luis Gonzalez	.35
37	Jeff Kent	.25
38	Ben Grieve	.25
39	Carlos Delgado	.50
40	Pat Burrell	.50
41	Mark Buehrle	.25
42	Cristian Guzman	.25
43	Shawn Green	.40
44	Nomar Garciaparra	2.00
45	Carlos Beltran	.60
46	Troy Glaus	.75
47	Paul Konerko	.25
48	Moises Alou	.25
49	Kerry Wood	.75
50	Jose Vidro	.25
51	Juan Encarnacion	.25
52	Bobby Abreu	.25
53	C.C. Sabathia	.25
54	Alex Rodriguez	2.50
55	Albert Pujols	2.50
56	Bret Boone	.25
57	Orlando Hernandez	.25
58	Jason Kendall	.25
59	Tim Hudson	.40
60	Darin Erstad	.60
61	Mike Mussina	.40
62	Ken Griffey Jr.	2.00
63	Adrian Beltre	.35
64	Jeff Bagwell	1.00
65	Vladimir Guerrero	1.00
66	Mike Sweeney	.25
67	Sammy Sosa	2.00
68	Andruw Jones	.75
69	Richie Sexson	.25
70	Matt Morris	.25
71	Ivan Rodriguez	.75
72	Shannon Stewart	.25
73	Barry Bonds	3.00
74	Matt Williams	.25
75	Jason Giambi	.60
76	Brian Giles	.25
77	Cliff Floyd	.25
78	Tino Martinez	.25
79	Juan Gonzalez	1.00
80	Frank Thomas	1.00
81	Ichiro Suzuki	2.00
82	Barry Zito	.35
83	Chipper Jones	1.50
84	Adam Dunn	.75
85	Kazuhiro Sasaki	.25
86	Mark Quinn	.25
87	Rafael Palmeiro	.60
88	Jeromy Burnitz	.25
89	Curt Schilling	.50
90	Chris Richards	.25
91	Jon Leiber	.25
92	Doug Mientkiewicz	.25
93	Roberto Alomar	.40
94	Rich Aurilia	.25
95	Eric Chavez	.35
96	Larry Walker	.25
97	Manny Ramirez	1.00
98	Tony Clark	.25
99	Tsuyoshi Shinjo	.25
100	Josh Beckett	.50
101	Dewon Brazelton	3.00
102	Jeremy Lambert RC	3.00
103	Andres Torres	3.00
104	Matt Childers RC	4.00
105	Wilson Betemit	3.00
106	Willie Harris	3.00
107	Drew Henson	4.00
108	Rafael Soriano	3.00
109	Carlos Valderrama	3.00
110	Victor Martinez	6.00
111	Juan Rivera	3.00
112	Felipe Lopez	3.00
113	Brandon Duckworth	3.00
114	Jeremy Owens	3.00
115	Aaron Cook RC	3.00
116	Derrick Lewis	3.00
117	Mark Teixeira	6.00
118	Ken Harvey	5.00
119	Tim Spooneybarger	3.00
120	Bill Hall	3.00
121	Adam Pettyjohn	3.00
122	Ramon Castro	3.00
123	Marlon Byrd	4.00
124	Matt White	3.00
125	Eric Cyr RC	3.00
126	Morgan Ensberg	3.00
127	Horacio Ramirez	4.00
128	Ron Calloway RC	3.00
129	Nick Punto	3.00
130	Joe Kennedy	3.00
131	So Taguchi RC	5.00
132	Austin Kearns	4.00
133	Mark Prior	6.00
134	Kazuhisa Ishii RC	8.00
135	Steve Torrealba	3.00
136	Adam Walker RC	3.00
137	Travis Hafner	4.00
138	Zach Day	3.00

Collection

Collection (1-100):		4-6X
Production 175		

Collection (101-138):		1-2X
Production 50		

Hot Numbers

	NM/M
Common Player:	15.00
Production 100 Sets	
Manny Ramirez	30.00
Randy Johnson	30.00
Curt Schilling	25.00
Pedro J. Martinez	30.00
Nomar Garciaparra	50.00
Barry Larkin	15.00
Todd Helton	30.00
Larry Walker	15.00
Sean Casey	20.00
Jeff Bagwell	30.00
Craig Biggio	15.00
Shawn Green	20.00
Edgardo Alfonzo	15.00
Mike Piazza	50.00
Derek Jeter	75.00
Chipper Jones	40.00
Jim Edmonds	15.00
J.D. Drew	20.00
Ivan Rodriguez	25.00
Rafael Palmeiro	25.00
Alex Rodriguez	60.00
Greg Maddux	40.00
Carlos Delgado	20.00

Jersey Heights

	NM/M
Common Player:	4.00
Inserted 1:18 Hobby	
1JH	Edgardo Alfonzo	4.00
2JH	Jeff Bagwell	8.00
3JH	Craig Biggio	4.00
4JH	Barry Bonds	20.00
5JH	Sean Casey	4.00
6JH	Roger Clemens	15.00
7JH	Carlos Delgado	6.00
8JH	J.D. Drew	6.00
9JH	Jim Edmonds	6.00
10JH	Nomar Garciaparra	15.00
11JH	Shawn Green	5.00
12JH	Todd Helton	8.00
13JH	Derek Jeter	20.00
14JH	Randy Johnson	8.00
15JH	Chipper Jones	8.00
16JH	Barry Larkin	6.00
17JH	Greg Maddux	10.00
18JH	Pedro J. Martinez	8.00
19JH	Rafael Palmeiro	8.00
20JH	Mike Piazza	10.00
21JH	Manny Ramirez	8.00
22JH	Alex Rodriguez	15.00
23JH	Ivan Rodriguez	6.00
24JH	Curt Schilling	6.00
25JH	Alex Rodriguez	15.00

Jersey Heights (Dual)

	NM/M
Common Card:	15.00
Production 100 Sets	
Randy Johnson,	
Curt Schilling	30.00
Pedro J. Martinez,	
Nomar Garciaparra	50.00
Edgardo Alfonzo,	
Mike Piazza	30.00
Derek Jeter,	
Roger Clemens	75.00
Greg Maddux,	
Chipper Jones	40.00
Jim Edmonds, Jeff Bagwell	30.00
Jeff Bagwell, Craig Biggio	25.00
Rafael Palmeiro,	
Ivan Rodriguez	25.00
Carlos Delgado,	
Shawn Green	20.00
Todd Helton, Larry Walker	20.00
Sean Casey, Barry Larkin	25.00
Alex Rodriguez,	
Manny Ramirez	40.00

Power Tools

	NM/M
Common Player:	4.00
Inserted 1:19	
Golds:	1-2.5X

ALEX RODRIGUEZ Texas Rangers®

AUTHENTIC GAME-USED BAT

Power Tools

Production 100		
1PT	Roberto Alomar	6.00
2PT	Jeff Bagwell/150	8.00
3PT	Craig Biggio	4.00
4PT	Barry Bonds	15.00
5PT	Bret Boone	4.00
6PT	Pat Burrell/225	6.00
7PT	Eric Chavez	5.00
8PT	Carlos Delgado	6.00
9PT	J.D. Drew/150	8.00
10PT	Jim Edmonds	6.00
11PT	Juan Gonzalez	6.00
12PT	Luis Gonzalez	4.00
13PT	Shawn Green	5.00
15PT	Derek Jeter	25.00
16PT	Doug Mientkiewicz	4.00
17PT	Magglio Ordonez	4.00
18PT	Rafael Palmeiro/100	6.00
19PT	Mike Piazza	10.00
20PT	Alex Rodriguez	15.00
21PT	Ivan Rodriguez	8.00
22PT	Scott Rolen/42	15.00
23PT	Reggie Sanders/120	5.00
24PT	Gary Sheffield	5.00
25PT	Tsuyoshi Shinjo	5.00
26PT	Miguel Tejada	5.00
27PT	Frank Thomas	15.00
28PT	Jim Thome/225	15.00
29PT	Larry Walker	4.00
30PT	Bernie Williams	6.00

Power Tools Dual

	NM/M
Common Card:	10.00
Inserted 1:40	
Golds:	1-2.5X
Production 50 Sets	
1	Eric Chavez,	
	Miguel Tejada	10.00
2	Barry Bonds,	
	Tsuyoshi Shinjo	25.00
3	Jim Edmonds, J.D. Drew	15.00
4	Jeff Bagwell,	
	Craig Biggio	15.00
5	Bernie Williams,	
	Derek Jeter	35.00
6	Roberto Alomar,	
	Mike Piazza	20.00
7	Sean Casey,	
	Jim Thome/40	30.00
8	Pat Burrell, Scott Rolen	15.00
9	Gary Sheffield,	
	Shawn Green	10.00
10	Ivan Rodriguez,	
	Alex Rodriguez	15.00
11	Juan Gonzalez,	
	Rafael Palmeiro	15.00
12	Magglio Ordonez,	
	Frank Thomas	15.00
13	Larry Walker,	
	Todd Helton/225	10.00
14	Luis Gonzalez,	
	Reggie Sanders	10.00
15	Doug Mientkiewicz,	
	Bret Boone	10.00

Sweet Swatch Autographs

	NM/M
Common Player:	15.00
Quantity produced listed	
Golds:	No Pricing
Production 15 Sets	
Derek Jeter/375	100.00
Barry Bonds/35	200.00
Drew Henson/785	40.00
Mark Teixeira/185	40.00
Dewon Brazelton/185	15.00
Mark Prior/285	40.00
Marlon Byrd/185	15.00
Ozzie Smith/185	65.00
Ron Cey/285	20.00
Paul Molitor/85	50.00
Maury Wills/285	20.00
Dale Murphy/285	60.00
David Espinosa/485	15.00
Dane Sardinha/485	15.00
Ben Sheets/85	20.00
Tony Perez/115	20.00
Brooks Robinson/185	50.00
So Taguchi/335	30.00
Al Kaline/285	50.00
Kazuhisa Ishii/335	30.00

	Albert Pujols/50	125.00
	Don Mattingly/85	150.00

Sweet Swatch Game-Used

	NM/M
Common Player:	8.00
1:Hobby Box	
Jeff Bagwell/490	10.00
Josh Beckett/500	10.00
Darin Erstad/525	8.00
Freddy Garcia/620	8.00
Brian Giles/445	10.00
Juan Gonzalez/505	10.00
Mark Grace/795	15.00
Derek Jeter/525	40.00
Jason Kendall/990	10.00
Paul LoDuca/440	10.00
Greg Maddux/475	15.00
Magglio Ordonez/495	10.00
Rafael Palmeiro/535	10.00
Mike Piazza/1,000	15.00
Alex Rodriguez/550	25.00
Ivan Rodriguez/475	10.00
Tim Salmon/465	8.00
Kazuhiro Sasaki/770	8.00
Alfonso Soriano/775	10.00
Larry Walker/430	8.00
Ted Williams/250	125.00

Sweet Swatch Patch

	NM/M
Common Player:	25.00
Random Box Topper	
Jeff Bagwell/45	75.00
Josh Beckett/60	55.00
Darin Erstad/50	40.00
Freddy Garcia/50	40.00
Juan Gonzalez/55	75.00
Mark Grace/75	60.00
Jason Kendall/120	25.00
Paul LoDuca/50	35.00
Greg Maddux/50	90.00
Magglio Ordonez/55	40.00
Rafael Palmeiro/60	40.00
Mike Piazza/95	100.00
Alex Rodriguez/50	90.00
Ivan Rodriguez/50	60.00
Tim Salmon/40	40.00
Kazuhiro Sasaki/80	50.00
Alfonso Soriano/35	65.00
Larry Walker/40	40.00

2002 Fleer Focus Jersey Edition

CHIPPER JONES

	NM/M
Complete Set (260):	60.00
Common Player:	.15
Common (226-260):	1.00
Inserted 1:4	
Pack (10):	2.00
Box (24):	40.00
1	Mike Piazza	1.50
2	Jason Giambi	.50
3	Jim Thome	.35
4	John Olerud	.15
5	J.D. Drew	.30
6	Richard Hidalgo	.15
7	Rusty Greer	.15
8	Tony Batista	.15
9	Omar Vizquel	.15
10	Randy Johnson	.75
11	Cristian Guzman	.15
12	Mark Grace	.25
13	Jeff Cirillo	.15
14	Mike Cameron	.15
15	Jeromy Burnitz	.15
16	Pokey Reese	.15
17	Richie Sexson	.15
18	Joe Randa	.15
19	Aramis Ramirez	.15
20	Pedro J. Martinez	.75
21	Todd Hollandsworth	.15
22	Rondell White	.15
23	Tsuyoshi Shinjo	.15
24	Melvin Mora	.15
25	Tim Hudson	.30
26	Darrin Fletcher	.15
27	Bill Mueller	.15
28	Jeff Weaver	.15
29	Tony Clark	.15

30	Tom Glavine	.40
31	Jarrod Washburn	.15
32	Greg Vaughn	.15
33	Lee Stevens	.15
34	Charles Johnson	.15
35	Lance Berkman	.15
36	Bud Smith	.15
37	Keith Foulke	.15
38	Ben Davis	.15
39	Daryle Ward	.15
40	Bernie Williams	.30
41	Dean Palmer	.15
42	Mark Mulder	.15
43	Jason LaRue	.15
44	Jay Gibbons	.15
45	Brandon Duckworth	.15
46	Carlos Delgado	.40
47	Barry Zito	.25
48	Matt Morris	.15
49	J.T. Snow	.15
50	Albert Pujols	1.50
51	Brad Fullmer	.15
52	Damion Easley	.15
53	Pat Burrell	.40
54	Kevin Brown	.15
55	Todd Walker	.15
56	Rich Garces	.15
57	Carlos Pena	.15
58	Paul LoDuca	.15
59	Mike Lieberthal	.15
60	Barry Larkin	.15
61	Jon Lieber	.15
62	Jose Cruz	.15
63	Mo Vaughn	.15
64	Ivan Rodriguez	.60
65	Jorge Posada	.25
66	Magglio Ordonez	.15
67	Juan Encarnacion	.15
68	Shawn Estes	.15
69	Kevin Appier	.15
70	Jeff Bagwell	.75
71	Tim Wakefield	.15
72	Shannon Stewart	.15
73	Scott Rolen	.65
74	Bobby Higginson	.15
75	Jim Edmonds	.15
76	Adam Dunn	.50
77	Eric Chavez	.30
78	Adrian Beltre	.30
79	Jason Varitek	.15
80	Barry Bonds	2.50
81	Edgar Renteria	.15
82	Raul Mondesi	.15
83	Eric Karros	.15
84	Ken Griffey Jr.	1.50
85	Jermaine Dye	.15
86	Carlos Beltran	.40
87	Mark Quinn	.15
88	Terrence Long	.15
89	Shawn Green	.40
90	Nomar Garciaparra	1.50
91	Sean Casey	.25
92	Homer Bush	.15
93	Bobby Abreu	.15
94	Jamey Wright	.15
95	Tony Womack	.15
96	Larry Walker	.15
97	Doug Mientkiewicz	.15
98	Jimmy Rollins	.40
99	Brady Anderson	.15
100	Derek Jeter	2.50
101	Kevin Young	.15
102	Juan Pierre	.15
103	Edgar Martinez	.15
104	Corey Koskie	.15
105	Jeffrey Hammonds	.15
106	Luis Gonzalez	.25
107	Travis Fryman	.15
108	Kerry Wood	.50
109	Rafael Palmeiro	.60
110	Ichiro Suzuki	1.00
111	Russ Ortiz	.15
112	Jeff Kent	.15
113	Scott Erickson	.15
114	Bruce Chen	.15
115	Craig Biggio	.15
116	Robin Ventura	.15
117	Alex Rodriguez	2.00
118	Roy Oswalt	.25
119	Fred McGriff	.15
120	Juan Gonzalez	.75
121	David Justice	.15
122	Pat Hentgen	.15
123	Hideo Nomo	.65
124	Ramon Ortiz	.15
125	David Ortiz	.25
126	Phil Nevin	.15
127	Ryan Dempster	.15
128	Toby Hall	.15
129	Vladimir Guerrero	.75
130	Chipper Jones	1.00
131	Russell Branyan	.15
132	Jose Vidro	.15
133	Bubba Trammell	.15
134	Tino Martinez	.15
135	Greg Maddux	1.00
136	Derrek Lee	.15
137	Troy Glaus	.75
138	Joe Crede	.15
139	Steve Cox	.15
140	Sammy Sosa	1.50
141	Corey Patterson	.15
142	Vernon Wells	.15
143	Matt Lawton	.15
144	Gabe Kapler	.15
145	Johnny Damon	.25
146	Marty Cordova	.15
147	Moises Alou	.15
148	Fernando Tatis	.15
149	Tanyon Sturtze	.15
150	Roger Clemens	1.25
151	Paul Konerko	.15
152	Chan Ho Park	.15
153	Marcus Giles	.15
154	David Eckstein	.15
155	Mike Lowell	.15
156	Preston Wilson	.15
157	John Vander Wal	.15
158	Tim Salmon	.25
159	Andy Pettitte	.35
160	Mike Mussina	.40
161	Doug Davis	.15
162	Peter Bergeron	.15
163	Rich Aurilia	.15
164	Eric Milton	.15
165	Geoff Jenkins	.15
166	Todd Helton	.75
167	Bret Boone	.15
168	Kris Benson	.15
169	Brian Anderson	.15
170	Roberto Alomar	.40
171	Javier Vazquez	.15
172	Scott Schoeneweis	.15
173	Ryan Klesko	.15
174	Jacque Jones	.15
175	Andruw Jones	.75
176	Aubrey Huff	.15
177	Mark Buehrle	.15
178	Josh Beckett	.40
179	Ben Sheets	.15
180	Curt Schilling	.40
181	C.C. Sabathia	.15
182	Denny Neagle	.15
183	Jamie Moyer	.15
184	Jason Kendall	.15
185	Dee Brown	.15
186	Frank Thomas	.75
187	Damian Rolls	.15
188	Carlos Lee	.15
189	Kevin Jarvis	.15
190	Manny Ramirez	.75
191	Cliff Floyd	.15
192	Freddy Garcia	.15
193	Orlando Cabrera	.15
194	Mike Sweeney	.15
195	Gary Sheffield	.35
196	Rafael Furcal	.15
197	Esteban Loaiza	.15
198	Mike Hampton	.15
199	Brian Giles	.15
200	Darin Erstad	.60
201	David Wells	.15
202	Kenny Lofton	.15
203	Aaron Sele	.15
204	Jason Schmidt	.15
205	Javy Lopez	.15
206	Dmitri Young	.15
207	Darryl Kile	.15
208	Matt Williams	.15
209	Joe Kennedy	.15
210	Chuck Knoblauch	.15
211	Brian Jordan	.15
212	Roberto Person	.15
213	Alex Ochoa	.15
214	Steve Finley	.15
215	Ben Petrick	.15
216	Al Leiter	.15
217	Mark Kotsay	.15
218	Miguel Tejada	.35
219	David Segui	.15
220	A.J. Burnett	.15
221	Marlon Anderson	.15
222	Wiki Gonzalez	.15
223	Jeff Suppan	.15
224	Dave Roberts	.15
225	Jose Hernandez	.15
226	Angel Berroa	1.00
227	Sean Burroughs	1.00
228	Luis Martinez RC	1.00
229	Adrian Burnside RC	1.00
230	John Ennis RC	1.00
231	Anastacio Martinez RC	1.00
232	Hank Blalock	2.00
233	Eric Hinske	1.00
234	Chris Booker RC	1.00
235	Colin Young RC	1.00
236	Mark Corey RC	1.00
237	Satoru Komiyama RC	1.00
238	So Taguchi RC	2.50
239	Elio Serrano RC	1.00
240	Reed Johnson RC	2.00
241	Jeremy Lambert RC	1.00
242	Chris Baker RC	1.00
243	Orlando Hudson	1.00
244	Travis Hughes RC	1.00
245	Kevin Frederick RC	1.00
246	Rodrigo Rosario RC	1.00
247	Jeremy Ward RC	1.00
248	Kazuhisa Ishii RC	4.00
249	Austin Kearns	1.00
250	Kyle Kane RC	1.00
251	Cam Esslinger RC	1.00
252	Jeff Austin RC	1.00
253	Brian Mallette RC	1.00
254	Mark Prior	4.00
255	Mark Teixeira	2.00
256	Carlos Valderrama	1.00
257	Jason Hart	1.00
258	Takahito Nomura RC	1.00
259	Matt Thornton	1.00
260	Marlon Byrd	1.00

Century

Cards (1-225):	6-10X
Cards (226-260):	.75-1.5X
Production 101-199	

Blue Chips

	NM/M
Complete Set (15):	10.00
Common Player:	.50
Inserted 1:6	
1BC Albert Pujols	3.00
2BC Sean Burroughs	.50
3BC Vernon Wells	.50
4BC Adam Dunn	1.50
5BC Pat Burrell	1.00
6BC Juan Pierre	.50
7BC Russell Branyan	.50
8BC Carlos Pena	.50
9BC Toby Hall	.50
10BC Hank Blalock	1.00
11BC Alfonso Soriano	1.50
12BC Jimmy Rollins	.75
13BC Jose Ortiz	.50
14BC Eric Hinske	.50
15BC Nick Johnson	.50

Blue Chips Game-Used

	NM/M
Inserted 1:96 Hobby	
Russell Branyan/Jsy	8.00
Nick Johnson/Jsy	10.00
Nick Johnson/Patch/100	20.00

International Diamond Co.

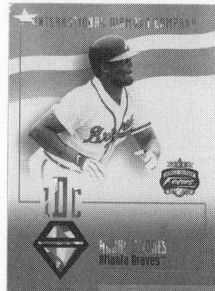

		NM/M
Complete Set (25):		25.00
Common Player:		1.00
Inserted 1:8		
1	Bobby Abreu	1.00
2	Adrian Beltre	1.00
3	Jorge Posada	1.00
4	Vladimir Guerrero	3.00
5	Rafael Palmeiro	2.00
6	Sammy Sosa	4.00
7	Larry Walker	1.00
8	Manny Ramirez	3.00
9	Ichiro Suzuki	4.00
10	Jose Cruz	1.00
11	Juan Gonzalez	3.00
12	Bernie Williams	1.00
13	Ivan Rodriguez	2.00
14	Moises Alou	1.00
15	Cristian Guzman	1.00
16	Andruw Jones	3.00
17	Aramis Ramirez	1.00
18	Raul Mondesi	1.00
19	Edgar Martinez	1.00
20	Magglio Ordonez	1.00
21	Roberto Alomar	1.50
22	Chan Ho Park	1.00
23	Kazuhiro Sasaki	1.00
24	Tsuyoshi Shinjo	1.00
25	Hideo Nomo	3.00

International Diamond Company Game-Used

	NM/M
Common Player:	5.00
Inserted 1:144	
Jorge Posada/Jsy	15.00
Rafael Palmeiro/Jsy	8.00
Manny Ramirez/Jsy	10.00
Ivan Rodriguez/Jsy	6.00
Andruw Jones/Jsy	6.00
Aramis Ramirez/Jsy	5.00
Raul Mondesi/Jsy	5.00

Edgar Martinez/Jsy	6.00
Chan Ho Park/Jsy	5.00
Kazuhiro Sasaki/Jsy	6.00
Hideo Nomo/Jsy	20.00

International Diamond Company Patch

	NM/M
Common Player:	15.00
Production 100	
Manny Ramirez	25.00
Ivan Rodriguez	25.00
Raul Mondesi	15.00
Edgar Martinez	20.00
Chan Ho Park	20.00
Hideo Nomo	75.00

Jersey Number Parallel

(1-225) print run 26-50:	10-25X
(1-225) p/r 51-75:	8-15X
(1-225) p/r 76-99:	5-10X
Produced to player's jsy #.	

K Corps

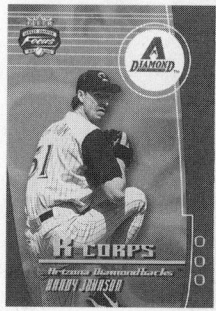

		NM/M
Complete Set (15):		20.00
Common Player:		1.00
Inserted 1:12		
1KC	Roger Clemens	5.00
2KC	Randy Johnson	3.00
3KC	Tom Glavine	1.50
4KC	Josh Beckett	1.50
5KC	Matt Morris	1.00
6KC	Curt Schilling	1.50
7KC	Greg Maddux	4.00
8KC	Tim Hudson	1.00
9KC	Roy Oswalt	1.00
10KC	Kerry Wood	2.00
11KC	Barry Zito	1.00
12KC	Kevin Brown	1.00
13KC	Ryan Dempster	1.00
14KC	Ben Sheets	1.00
15KC	Pedro J. Martinez	3.00

K Corps Game-Used

	NM/M
Common Player:	5.00
Inserted 1:96	
2KC Randy Johnson/Jsy	15.00
6KC Curt Schilling/Jsy	10.00
7KC Greg Maddux/Jsy	15.00
11KC Barry Zito/Jsy	8.00
12KC Kevin Brown/Jsy	5.00
15KC Pedro Martinez/Jsy	10.00

K Corps Patch

	NM/M
Production 100	
Curt Schilling	20.00
Kevin Brown	20.00
Pedro Martinez	30.00

Kings of Swing

	NM/M
Complete Set (20):	80.00
Common Player:	2.00
Inserted 1:48	

1KS	Barry Bonds	10.00
2KS	Mike Piazza	6.00
3KS	Albert Pujols	8.00
4KS	Todd Helton	3.00
5KS	Ken Griffey Jr.	6.00
6KS	Alex Rodriguez	8.00
7KS	Sammy Sosa	6.00
8KS	Troy Glaus	3.00
9KS	Derek Jeter	10.00
10KS	Ichiro Suzuki	6.00
11KS	Manny Ramirez	3.00
12KS	Roberto Alomar	2.00
13KS	Juan Gonzalez	3.00
14KS	Shawn Green	2.00
15KS	Vladimir Guerrero	3.00
16KS	Nomar Garciaparra	6.00
17KS	Adam Dunn	2.00
18KS	Jason Giambi	2.50
19KS	Edgar Martinez	2.00
20KS	Chipper Jones	4.00

Kings of Swing Game-Used

	NM/M
Common Player:	5.00
Inserted 1:108	
Mike Piazza	15.00
Todd Helton	8.00
Alex Rodriguez	15.00
Derek Jeter	30.00
Manny Ramirez	8.00
Shawn Green	5.00
Edgar Martinez	5.00
Chipper Jones	10.00

Kings of Swing Patch

	NM/M
Production 100	
Todd Helton	25.00
Manny Ramirez	25.00
Shawn Green	20.00
Edgar Martinez	25.00
Mike Piazza	40.00

Larger Than Life

		NM/M
Common Player:		4.00
Inserted 1:240		
1LL	Jason Giambi	6.00
2LL	Carlos Delgado	5.00
3LL	Alex Rodriguez	20.00
4LL	Preston Wilson	4.00
5LL	Frank Thomas	9.00
6LL	Nomar Garciaparra	15.00
7LL	Jim Edmonds	4.00
8LL	Jim Thome	4.00
9LL	Barry Bonds	25.00
10LL	Mo Vaughn	4.00
11LL	Ichiro Suzuki	20.00
12LL	Ivan Rodriguez	5.00
13LL	Gary Sheffield	4.00
14LL	Derek Jeter	25.00
15LL	Jeff Bagwell	9.00
16LL	Mike Piazza	15.00
17LL	J.D. Drew	4.00
18LL	Sammy Sosa	15.00
19LL	Albert Pujols	20.00
20LL	Luis Gonzalez	4.00

Larger Than Life Game-Used

	NM/M
Common Player:	5.00
Inserted 1:144	
Alex Rodriguez/Jsy	15.00
Preston Wilson/Jsy	5.00
Frank Thomas/Jsy	10.00
Jim Edmonds/Jsy	6.00
Mo Vaughn/Jsy	5.00
Ivan Rodriguez/Jsy	8.00
Derek Jeter/Jsy	25.00
Jeff Bagwell/Jsy/SP/20	25.00
Mike Piazza/Jsy	15.00
Luis Gonzalez/Jsy	5.00

Larger Than Life Patch

	NM/M
Common Player:	15.00
Production 100	
Preston Wilson	15.00
Frank Thomas	25.00
Jim Edmonds	15.00
Ivan Rodriguez	25.00

Mike Piazza	40.00
Luis Gonzalez	15.00

Lettermen

No Pricing
Production One Set

Materialistic Away

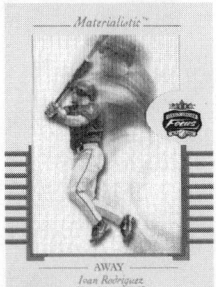

	NM/M
Complete Set (15):	75.00
Common Player:	4.00
Inserted 1:24	
Home:	1.5-3X
Production 50 Sets	
Away Oversized:	.5-1X
One per hobby box.	
Home Oversized:	2-4X
Production 50 Sets	

1MA	Derek Jeter	12.00
2MA	Alex Rodriguez	10.00
3MA	Mike Piazza	8.00
4MA	Ivan Rodriguez	4.00
5MA	Chipper Jones	6.00
6MA	Todd Helton	5.00
7MA	Nomar Garciaparra	8.00
8MA	Barry Bonds	12.00
9MA	Ichiro Suzuki	8.00
10MA	Ken Griffey Jr.	8.00
11MA	Jason Giambi	4.00
12MA	Sammy Sosa	8.00
13MA	Albert Pujols	10.00
14MA	Pedro J. Martinez	5.00
15MA	Vladimir Guerrero	5.00

2002 Fleer Genuine

	NM/M
Complete Set (140):	
Common Player:	.15
Common (101-140):	3.00
Production 2,002	
Pack (5):	3.00
Box (20):	50.00

1	Alex Rodriguez	2.50
2	Manny Ramirez	.75
3	Jim Thome	.15
4	Eric Milton	.15
5	Todd Helton	.75
6	Mike Mussina	.50
7	Ichiro Suzuki	1.50
8	Randy Johnson	1.00
9	Mark Mulder	.15
10	Johnny Damon	.25
11	Sean Casey	.25
12	Albert Pujols	2.50
13	Mark Grace	.25
14	Moises Alou, Mark Mulder	.15
15	Raul Mondesi, Roberto Alomar	.15
16	Cliff Floyd, Scott Rolen	.30
17	Vladimir Guerrero, Tom Glavine	.40
18	Pat Burrell, Bobby Abreu	.25
19	Ryan Klesko, Nomar Garciaparra	.50
20	Mike Hampton, Darin Erstad	.15
21	Shawn Green, Cliff Floyd	.15
22	Rich Aurilia, Tim Hudson	.15
23	Matt Morris, Jim Thome	.15
24	Curt Schilling, Nolan Ryan	1.00
25	Kevin Brown, Reggie Jackson	.25
26	Adrian Beltre, Rafael Palmeiro	.30
27	Joe Mays, Ken Griffey Jr.	.75
28	Luis Gonzalez, Sammy Sosa	.75
29	Barry Larkin, Vladimir Guerrero	.40
30	A.J. Burnett, Ichiro Suzuki	.75
31	Eric Munson	.15
32	Juan Gonzalez	.75
33	Lance Berkman	.15
34	Fred McGriff	.15
35	Paul Konerko	.15
36	Pedro J. Martinez	.75
37	Adam Dunn	.50
38	Jeromy Burnitz	.15
39	Mike Sweeney	.15
40	Bret Boone	.15
41	Ken Griffey Jr.	2.00
42	Eric Chavez	.25
43	Mark Quinn	.15
44	Roberto Alomar	.35
45	Bobby Abreu	.15
46	Bartolo Colon	.15
47	Jimmy Rollins	.25
48	Chipper Jones	1.00
49	Ben Sheets	.15
50	Freddy Garcia	.15
51	Sammy Sosa	2.00
52	Rafael Palmeiro	.65
53	Preston Wilson	.15
54	Troy Glaus	.75
55	Josh Beckett	.50
56	C.C. Sabathia	.15
57	Magglio Ordonez	.15
58	Brian Giles	.15
59	Darin Erstad	.60
60	Gary Sheffield	.35
61	Paul LoDuca	.15
62	Derek Jeter	3.00
63	Greg Maddux	1.50
64	Kerry Wood	.65
65	Toby Hall	.15
66	Barry Bonds	3.00
67	Jeff Bagwell	.75
68	Jason Kendall	.15
69	Richard Hidalgo	.15
70	J.D. Drew	.30
71	Tom Glavine	.25
72	Javier Vazquez	.15
73	Doug Mientkiewicz	.15
74	Jason Giambi	.50
75	Carlos Delgado	.40
76	Aramis Ramirez	.15
77	Torii Hunter	.15
78	Ivan Rodriguez	.65
79	Charles Johnson	.15
80	Jeff Kent	.15
81	Jacque Jones	.15
82	Larry Walker	.15
83	Cristian Guzman	.15
84	Jermaine Dye	.15
85	Roger Clemens	1.75
86	Mike Piazza	2.00
87	Craig Biggio	.15
88	Phil Nevin	.15
89	Jeff Cirillo	.15
90	Barry Zito	.25
91	Ryan Dempster	.15
92	Mark Buehrle	.15
93	Nomar Garciaparra	2.00
94	Frank Thomas	.75
95	Jim Edmonds	.15
96	Geoff Jenkins	.15
97	Scott Rolen	.65
98	Tim Hudson	.25
99	Shannon Stewart	.15
100	Richie Sexson	.15
101	Orlando Hudson	3.00
102	Doug DeVore RC	3.00
103	Rene Reyes RC	3.00
104	Steve Bechler RC	4.00
105	Jorge Nunez RC	3.00
106	Mitch Wylie RC	3.00
107	Jaime Cerda RC	3.00
108	Brandon Puffer RC	3.00
109	Tyler Yates RC	6.00
110	Bill Hall	3.00
111	Peter Zamora RC	3.00
112	Jeff Deardorff RC	3.00
113	J.J. Putz RC	3.00
114	Scotty Layfield RC	3.00
115	Brandon Backe RC	3.00
116	Andy Pratt RC	3.00
117	Mark Prior	8.00
118	Franklyn German RC	3.00
119	Todd Donovan RC	3.00
120	Franklin Nunez RC	3.00
121	Adam Walker RC	3.00
122	Ron Calloway RC	3.00
123	Tim Kalita RC	3.00
124	Kazuhisa Ishii RC	8.00
125	Mark Teixeira	5.00
126	Nate Field RC	3.00
127	Nelson Castro RC	3.00
128	So Taguchi RC	8.00
129	Marlon Byrd	3.00
130	Drew Henson	3.00
131	Kenny Kelly	3.00
132	John Ennis RC	3.00
133	Anastacio Martinez RC	3.00
134	Matt Guerrier	3.00
135	Tom Wilson RC	3.00
136	Ben Howard RC	4.00
137	Chris Baker RC	3.00
138	Kevin Frederick RC	3.00
159	Wilson Valdez RC	3.00
140	Austin Kearns	4.00

Bat's Incredible

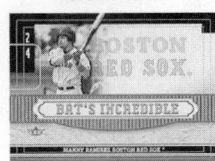

		NM/M
Complete Set (25):		60.00
Common Player:		1.50
Inserted 1:10		
1BI	Todd Helton	2.00
2BI	Chipper Jones	3.00
3BI	Luis Gonzalez	1.50
4BI	Barry Bonds	8.00
5BI	Jason Giambi	2.00
6BI	Alex Rodriguez	6.00
7BI	Manny Ramirez	2.00
8BI	Jeff Bagwell	2.00
9BI	Shawn Green	1.50
10BI	Albert Pujols	6.00
11BI	Paul LoDuca	1.50
12BI	Mike Piazza	5.00
13BI	Derek Jeter	8.00
14BI	Edgar Martinez	1.50
15BI	Juan Gonzalez	2.00
16BI	Magglio Ordonez	1.50
17BI	Jermaine Dye	1.50
18BI	Larry Walker	1.50
19BI	Phil Nevin	1.50
20BI	Ivan Rodriguez	1.50
21BI	Ichiro Suzuki	5.00
22BI	J.D. Drew	1.50
23BI	Vladimir Guerrero	2.00
24BI	Sammy Sosa	5.00
25BI	Ken Griffey Jr.	5.00

Bat's Incredible Game-used

	NM/M
Common Player:	5.00
Inserted 1:20	
Todd Helton	10.00
Chipper Jones	10.00
J.D. Drew	8.00
Alex Rodriguez	15.00
Manny Ramirez	10.00
Shawn Green	6.00
Derek Jeter	20.00
Edgar Martinez	8.00
Juan Gonzalez	8.00
Jermaine Dye	5.00
Phil Nevin	5.00
Ivan Rodriguez	10.00

Genuine Ink

	NM/M
Common Autograph	15.00
Production varies	
Barry Bonds/150	150.00
Ron Cey/175	15.00
Derek Jeter/150	125.00
Al Kaline/300	60.00
Don Mattingly/50	100.00
Paul Molitor	50.00
Dale Murphy/700	40.00
Phil Rizzuto/700	30.00
Brooks Robinson/140	60.00
Maury Willis/975	15.00

Leaders

	NM/M
Complete Set (15):	25.00
Common Player:	1.00
Inserted 1:6	
1GL Sammy Sosa	4.00
2GL Todd Helton	2.00
3GL Alex Rodriguez	4.00
4GL Roger Clemens	3.00
5GL Barry Bonds	5.00
6GL Randy Johnson	2.00
7GL Albert Pujols	4.00
8GL Curt Schilling	1.00
9GL Bernie Williams	1.00
10GL Ken Griffey Jr.	4.00
11GL Pedro J. Martinez	2.00
12GL Juan Gonzalez	2.00
13GL Hideo Nomo	2.00
14GL Bret Boone	1.00
15GL Ichiro Suzuki	4.00

Leaders Game-Used

	NM/M
Common Player:	8.00
Inserted 1:16	
Todd Helton	10.00
Alex Rodriguez	15.00
Roger Clemens	15.00
Barry Bonds	20.00
Randy Johnson	10.00
Curt Schilling	8.00
Bernie Williams	8.00
Pedro J. Martinez	10.00
Hideo Nomo	15.00

Tip of the Cap

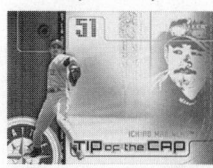

	NM/M
Complete Set (25):	40.00
Common Player:	.50
Inserted 1:6	
1TC Alex Rodriguez	6.00
2TC Derek Jeter	8.00
3TC Kazuhiro Sasaki	.50
4TC Barry Bonds	8.00
5TC J.D. Drew	.75
6TC Tsuyoshi Shinjo	.50
7TC Alfonso Soriano	1.50
8TC Albert Pujols	6.00
9TC Tom Seaver	1.50
10TC Drew Henson	.75
11TC Dave Winfield	1.50
12TC Carlos Delgado	.50
13TC Lou Boudreau	.50
14TC Shawn Green	.75
15TC Roger Clemens	3.00
16TC Randy Johnson	1.50
17TC Sammy Sosa	4.00
18TC Rafael Palmeiro	1.25
19TC Ken Griffey Jr.	5.00
20TC Ichiro Suzuki	5.00
21TC Eric Chavez	.65
22TC Andruw Jones	1.50

23TC Miguel Tejada	.65
24TC Pedro J. Martinez	1.50
25TC Tim Salmon	.50

Tip of the Cap Game-Used

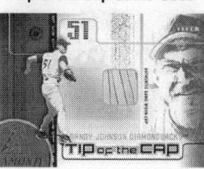

	NM/M
Common Player:	
Alex Rodriguez/670	20.00
Barry Bonds/32	75.00
Tom Seaver/224	25.00
Drew Henson/361	15.00
Dave Winfield/363	15.00
Carlos Delgado/219	15.00
Lou Boudreau/303	20.00
Randy Johnson/74	30.00
Rafael Palmeiro/300	20.00
Andruw Jones/19	40.00
Miguel Tejada/225	15.00

Touch 'Em All

	NM/M
Complete Set (25):	60.00
Common Player:	1.50
Inserted 1:10	
1 Derek Jeter	8.00
2 Sammy Sosa	5.00
3 Albert Pujols	6.00
4 Vladimir Guerrero	3.00
5 Ken Griffey Jr.	5.00
6 Nomar Garciaparra	5.00
7 Luis Gonzalez	1.50
8 Barry Bonds	8.00
9 Manny Ramirez	2.50
10 Jason Giambi	2.00
11 Chipper Jones	4.00
12 Ichiro Suzuki	5.00
13 Alex Rodriguez	6.00
14 Juan Gonzalez	2.50
15 Todd Helton	2.50
16 Roberto Alomar	1.50
17 Jeff Bagwell	2.50
18 Mike Piazza	3.00
19 Gary Sheffield	1.50
20 Ivan Rodriguez	2.00
21 Frank Thomas	2.50
22 Bobby Abreu	1.50
23 J.D. Drew	1.50
24 Scott Rolen	2.00
25 Darin Erstad	1.50

Touch 'Em All Base

	NM/M
Common Player:	4.00
Production 350 Sets	
Derek Jeter	15.00
Sammy Sosa	10.00
Albert Pujols	15.00
Vladimir Guerrero	10.00
Ken Griffey Jr.	10.00
Nomar Garciaparra	10.00
Luis Gonzalez	5.00
Barry Bonds	15.00
Manny Ramirez	8.00
Jason Giambi	8.00
Chipper Jones	8.00
Ichiro Suzuki	15.00
Alex Rodriguez	10.00
Juan Gonzalez	8.00
Todd Helton	8.00
Roberto Alomar	6.00
Jeff Bagwell	8.00
Mike Piazza	10.00
Gary Sheffield	6.00
Ivan Rodriguez	8.00
Frank Thomas	8.00
Bobby Abreu	4.00

J.D. Drew	4.00
Scott Rolen	8.00
Darin Erstad	4.00

Names of the Game

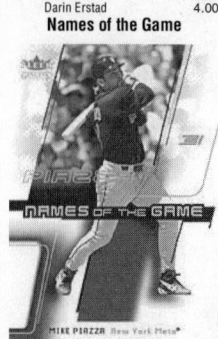

MIKE PIAZZA New York Mets®

	NM/M
Complete Set (30):	60.00
Common Player:	1.00
Inserted 1:10 H, 1:20 R	
1 Mike Piazza	5.00
2 Chipper Jones	4.00
3 Jim Edmonds	1.00
4 Barry Larkin	1.00
5 Frank Thomas	3.00
6 Manny Ramirez	3.00
7 Carlos Delgado	1.50
8 Brian Giles	1.00
9 Kerry Wood	2.00
10 Derek Jeter	8.00
11 Adam Dunn	2.00
12 Gary Sheffield	1.50
13 Luis Gonzalez	1.00
14 Mark Mulder	1.00
15 Roberto Alomar	1.50
16 Scott Rolen	2.50
17 Tom Glavine	1.50
18 Bobby Abreu	1.00
19 Nomar Garciaparra	5.00
20 Darin Erstad	2.00
21 Cliff Floyd	1.00
22 Tim Hudson	1.00
23 Jim Thome	1.00
24 Nolan Ryan	8.00
25 Reggie Jackson	3.00
26 Rafael Palmeiro	2.00
27 Ken Griffey Jr.	5.00
28 Sammy Sosa	5.00
29 Vladimir Guerrero	3.00
30 Ichiro Suzuki	5.00

Names of the Game Memorabilia

NOLAN RYAN Texas Rangers®

	NM/M
Common Player:	5.00
1:24 H, 1:100 R	
1 Roberto Alomar	10.00
2 Carlos Delgado	8.00
3 Jim Edmonds	8.00
4 Darin Erstad	5.00
5 Cliff Floyd	5.00
6 Nomar Garciaparra/SP/90	60.00
7 Brian Giles	5.00
8 Luis Gonzalez	5.00
9 Tim Hudson	8.00
10 Derek Jeter	30.00
11 Chipper Jones	10.00
12 Barry Larkin	8.00
13 Mark Mulder	8.00
14 Rafael Palmeiro	10.00
15 Mike Piazza	15.00
16 Manny Ramirez	8.00
17 Scott Rolen	10.00
18 Nolan Ryan	40.00
19 Jim Thome	10.00

2002 Fleer Greats of the Game

	NM/M
Complete Set (100):	45.00

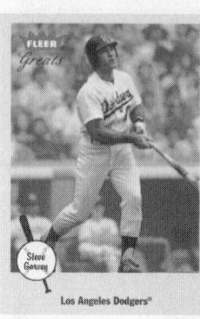

Los Angeles Dodgers®

	NM/M
Common Player:	.40
Pack (5):	5.00
Box (24):	100.00
1 Cal Ripken Jr.	6.00
2 Paul Molitor	1.50
3 Roberto Clemente	4.00
4 Cy Young	1.50
5 Tris Speaker	.75
6 Lou Brock	.50
7 Fred Lynn	.40
8 Harmon Killebrew	1.50
9 Ted Williams	6.00
10 Dave Winfield	1.00
11 Orlando Cepeda	.40
12 Johnny Mize	.40
13 Walter Johnson	1.50
14 Roy Campanella	1.50
15 George Sisler	.40
16 Bo Jackson	1.00
17 Rollie Fingers	.40
18 Brooks Robinson	1.50
19 Billy Williams	.40
20 Maury Wills	.40
21 Jimmie Foxx	1.50
22 Alan Trammell	.40
23 Rogers Hornsby	1.50
24 Don Drysdale	1.00
25 Bob Feller	.75
26 Jackie Robinson	5.00
27 Whitey Ford	1.50
28 Enos Slaughter	.40
29 Rod Carew	1.00
30 Eddie Mathews	1.50
31 Ron Cey	.40
32 Thurman Munson	2.00
33 Ty Cobb	3.00
34 Rocky Colavito	.75
35 Satchel Paige	1.50
36 Andre Dawson	.75
37 Phil Rizzuto	.75
38 Roger Maris	3.00
39 Earl Weaver	.40
40 Joe Carter	.40
41 Christy Mathewson	1.50
42 Tony Lazzeri	.40
43 Gil Hodges	.75
44 Gaylord Perry	.40
45 Steve Carlton	1.00
46 George Kell	.40
47 Mickey Cochrane	1.00
48 Joe Morgan	.60
49 Steve Garvey	.40
50 Bob Gibson	1.50
51 Lefty Grove	.40
52 Warren Spahn	1.50
53 Willie McCovey	.75
54 Frank Robinson	1.50
55 Rich "Goose" Gossage	.40
56 Hank Bauer	.40
57 Hoyt Wilhelm	.40
58 Mel Ott	1.00
59 Preacher Roe	.75
60 Yogi Berra	1.50
61 Nolan Ryan	6.00
62 Dizzy Dean	.75
63 Ryne Sandberg	2.00
64 Frank Howard	.40
65 Hack Wilson	.40
66 Robin Yount	1.50
67 Al Kaline	1.50
68 Mike Schmidt	2.00
69 Vida Blue	.40
70 George Brett	3.00
71 Sparky Anderson	.40
72 Tom Seaver	1.50
73 Bill "Moose" Skowron	.40
74 Don Mattingly	2.50
75 Carl Yastrzemski	1.50
76 Eddie Murray	1.00
77 Jim Palmer	1.00
78 Bill Dickey	.75
79 Ozzie Smith	1.50
80 Dale Murphy	.75
81 Nap Lajoie	1.00
82 Jim "Catfish" Hunter	1.00
83 Duke Snider	1.00
84 Luis Aparicio	.40
85 Reggie Jackson	1.50
86 Honus Wagner	1.50
87 Johnny Bench	2.00
88 Stan Musial	3.00

89	Carlton Fisk	.75
90	Tony Oliva	.75
91	Wade Boggs	2.00
92	Jim Rice	.40
93	Bill Mazeroski	.40
94	Ralph Kiner	.40
95	Tony Perez	.40
96	Kirby Puckett	2.00
97	Bobby Bonds	.75
98	Bill Terry	.40
99	Juan Marichal	.75
100	Hank Greenberg	1.00

Autographs

		NM/M
	Common Autograph:	10.00
	Inserted 1:24	
SA	Sparky Anderson	15.00
LA	Luis Aparicio	15.00
HB	Hank Bauer	10.00
JB	Johnny Bench	50.00
YB	Yogi Berra	40.00
PB	Paul Blair	10.00
VB	Vida Blue	15.00
WB	Wade Boggs	20.00
BB	Bobby Bonds	15.00
GB	George Brett/150	125.00
LB	Lou Brock/250	25.00
RC	Rod Carew/250	40.00
SC	Steve Carlton	15.00
JC	Joe Carter	15.00
OC	Orlando Cepeda	15.00
CE	Ron Cey	10.00
CO	Rocky Colavito	35.00
AD	Andre Dawson	15.00
BF	Bob Feller	15.00
RF	Rollie Fingers	15.00
CF	Carlton Fisk/100	65.00
WF	Whitey Ford	40.00
SG	Steve Garvey	15.00
BG	Bob Gibson/200	30.00
RG	Rich "Goose" Gossage	10.00
FH	Frank Howard	15.00
RJ	Reggie Jackson/150	70.00
AK	Al Kaline	40.00
GK	George Kell	15.00
HK	Harmon Killebrew	30.00
RK	Ralph Kiner/250	25.00
FL	Fred Lynn	15.00
JM	Juan Marichal	15.00
DM	Don Mattingly/300	75.00
BM	Bill Mazeroski/200	20.00
WM	Willie McCovey	25.00
PM	Paul Molitor	25.00
JM	Joe Morgan	15.00
MU	Dale Murphy	40.00
EM	Eddie Murray/250	70.00
SM	Stan Musial/200	75.00
TO	Tony Oliva	15.00
JP	Jim Palmer	20.00
DP	Dave Parker	10.00
TP	Tony Perez	15.00
GP	Gaylord Perry/4	60.00
KP	Kirby Puckett/250	60.00
JR	Jim Rice	15.00
CR	Cal Ripken Jr./100	180.00
PR	Phil Rizzuto/300	50.00
BR	Brooks Robinson	30.00
FR	Frank Robinson/250	30.00
PR	Preacher Roe	15.00
NR	Nolan Ryan/150	100.00
RS	Ryne Sandberg/200	75.00
MS	Mike Schmidt/150	100.00
TS	Tom Seaver/150	50.00
BS	Bill "Moose" Skowron	15.00
ES	Enos Slaughter	15.00
OS	Ozzie Smith/300	65.00
DS	Duke Snider	25.00
WS	Warren Spahn	50.00
AT	Alan Trammell	20.00
HW	Hoyt Wilhelm	15.00
BW	Billy Williams	15.00
MW	Maury Wills	15.00
DW	Dave Winfield/250	75.00
CY	Carl Yastrzemski/200	75.00
RY	Robin Yount	70.00

Dueling Duos

	NM/M
Complete Set (29):	90.00

		2.00
Common Player:		2.00
Inserted 1:6		
1DD	Johnny Bench, Carlton Fisk	4.00
2DD	Roy Campanella, Yogi Berra	5.00
3DD	Stan Musial, Ted Williams	8.00
4DD	Carl Yastrzemski, Reggie Jackson	3.00
5DD	Babe Ruth, Jimmie Foxx	8.00
6DD	Steve Carlton, Nolan Ryan	8.00
7DD	Wade Boggs, Don Mattingly	6.00
8DD	Brooks Robinson, Roger Maris	5.00
9DD	Paul Molitor, Don Mattingly	6.00
10DD	Sparky Anderson, Earl Weaver	2.00
11DD	Bob Gibson, Duke Snider	3.00
12DD	Yogi Berra, Gil Hodges	4.00
13DD	Joe Morgan, Ryne Sandberg	3.00
14DD	Tony Perez, Carl Yastrzemski	3.00
15DD	Jimmie Foxx, Bill Dickey	3.00
16DD	Ralph Kiner, Duke Snider	2.00
17DD	Nellie Fox, Rocky Colavito	2.00
18DD	Willie McCovey, Johnny Bench	3.00
19DD	Duke Snider, Eddie Mathews	4.00
20DD	Reggie Jackson, Jim Rice	3.00
21DD	Eddie Murray, Jim Rice	2.00
22DD	Paul Molitor, Dave Winfield	3.00
23DD	Robin Yount, Dave Winfield	3.00
24DD	Enos Slaughter, Ted Kluszewski	3.00
25DD	Wade Boggs, George Brett	4.00
26DD	George Brett, Eddie Murray	4.00
27DD	George Brett, Cal Ripken Jr.	8.00
28DD	Kirby Puckett, Don Mattingly	6.00
29DD	George Brett, Mike Schmidt	5.00

Dueling Duos Autograph
No Pricing
Production 25 Sets

ling Duos Game-Used Dual
No Pricing
Production 25 Sets

Dueling Duos G-U Single

	NM/M
Common Card:	15.00
Inserted 1:24	
Johnny Bench, Carlton Fisk	20.00
Roy Campanella, Yogi Berra	25.00
Carl Yastrzemski, Reggie Jackson	25.00
Babe Ruth, Jimmie Foxx/75	50.00
Kirby Puckett, Don Mattingly	
Steve Carlton, Nolan Ryan	80.00
Wade Boggs, Don Mattingly	25.00
Brooks Robinson, Roger Maris	25.00
Paul Molitor, Don Mattingly	25.00
Sparky Anderson, Earl Weaver	10.00
Bob Gibson, Duke Snider/200	20.00
Yogi Berra, Gil Hodges	25.00
Joe Morgan, Ryne Sandberg	25.00
Tony Perez, Carl Yastrzemski	25.00
Jimmie Foxx, Bill Dickey	20.00
Ralph Kiner, Duke Snider	20.00
Nellie Fox, Rocky Colavito	20.00
Willie McCovey, Johnny Bench	25.00
Duke Snider, Eddie Mathews	20.00
Reggie Jackson, Jim Rice	20.00
Eddie Murray, Jim Rice	15.00
Paul Molitor, Dave Winfield	15.00
Robin Yount, Dave Winfield	15.00
Enos Slaughter, Ted Kluszewski	10.00

Wade Boggs, George Brett	25.00
George Brett, Eddie Murray	20.00
George Brett, Cal Ripken Jr.	40.00

Through the Years Level 1

	NM/M
Common Player:	10.00
Inserted 1:24	
George Brett	25.00
Reggie Jackson/A's	15.00
Reggie Jackson/Angels	15.00
Ted Williams/350	100.00
Robin Yount	20.00
Willie McCovey	10.00
Paul Molitor/Brewers	15.00
Paul Molitor/Blue Jays	15.00
Jim Palmer	15.00
Brooks Robinson	15.00
Carl Yastrzemski	25.00
Don Mattingly	25.00
Carlton Fisk/Hitting	15.00
Carlton Fisk/Fielding	15.00
Nolan Ryan	40.00
Eddie Murray	10.00
Wade Boggs	15.00
Tony Perez	10.00
Ted Kluszewski	10.00
Bo Jackson/Royals	15.00
Bo Jackson/White Sox	15.00
Johnny Bench	20.00
Jackie Robinson	65.00
Hoyt Wilhelm	10.00
Vida Blue	10.00
Dave Winfield	15.00
Frank Robinson	15.00
Jim Rice	10.00
Jim Rice	10.00
Cal Ripken/Hitting	40.00
Cal Ripken/Fielding	40.00

Through the Years Level 2

	NM/M
Common Player:	25.00
Production 100 Sets	
George Brett	80.00
Reggie Jackson	30.00
Ted Williams	120.00
Robin Yount	40.00
Willie McCovey	30.00
Paul Molitor	40.00
Jim Palmer	25.00
Carl Yastrzemski	65.00
Don Mattingly	60.00
Carlton Fisk	30.00
Nolan Ryan	75.00
Eddie Murray	25.00
Wade Boggs	30.00
Ted Kluszewski	25.00
Bo Jackson/Royals	30.00
Bo Jackson/White Sox	30.00
Johnny Bench	40.00
Dave Winfield	25.00
Jim Rice	25.00
Jim Rice	25.00
Cal Ripken Jr.	60.00
Cal Ripken Jr.	60.00

Through the Years Level 3
No Pricing
Production 25 Sets

Through the Years Patch Edition

	NM/M
Common Player:	25.00
Production 100 Sets	
George Brett	80.00
Reggie Jackson/A's	30.00
Reggie Jackson/Angels	30.00
Ted Williams	120.00
Robin Yount	50.00
Willie McCovey	40.00
Paul Molitor/Brewers	40.00
Paul Molitor/Blue Jays	40.00
Jim Palmer	25.00
Carl Yastrzemski	75.00
Don Mattingly	60.00
Carlton Fisk	30.00
Carlton Fisk	30.00
Nolan Ryan	75.00
Eddie Murray	30.00
Wade Boggs	30.00
Tony Perez	25.00
Ted Kluszewski	30.00
Bo Jackson/Royals	40.00
Bo Jackson/White Sox	40.00
Johnny Bench	30.00
Dave Winfield	30.00
Frank Robinson	30.00
Jim Rice	25.00
Jim Rice	25.00
Cal Ripken Jr.	80.00
Cal Ripken Jr.	80.00

2002 Fleer Hot Prospects

		NM/M
Complete Set (125):		
Common Player:		.25
Common (81-105):		8.00
Production 1,000		
Common (106-125):		3.00
Production 1,500		
Pack (5):		4.00
Box (18):		50.00
1	Derek Jeter	3.00
2	Garret Anderson	.25
3	Scott Rolen	.75
4	Bret Boone	.25
5	Lance Berkman	.25
6	Andruw Jones	1.00
7	Ivan Rodriguez	.75
8	Bernie Williams	.35
9	Cristian Guzman	.25
10	Mo Vaughn	.25
11	Troy Glaus	1.00
12	Tim Salmon	.35
13	Jason Giambi	.65
14	Cliff Floyd	.25
15	Tim Hudson	.35
16	Curt Schilling	.40
17	Sammy Sosa	2.00
18	Alex Rodriguez	2.50
19	Chuck Knoblauch	.25
20	Jason Kendall	.25
21	Ben Sheets	.25
22	Nomar Garciaparra	2.00
23	Ryan Klesko	.25
24	Greg Vaughn	.25
25	Rafael Palmeiro	.75
26	Miguel Tejada	.35
27	Shea Hillenbrand	.25
28	Jim Thome	.25
29	Randy Johnson	1.00
30	Barry Larkin	.25
31	Paul LoDuca	.25
32	Pedro J. Martinez	1.00
33	Luis Gonzalez	.35
34	Carlos Delgado	.50
35	Richie Sexson	.25
36	Albert Pujols	2.25
37	Bobby Abreu	.25
38	Gary Sheffield	.40
39	Magglio Ordonez	.25
40	Eric Chavez	.35
41	Jeff Bagwell	1.00
42	Doug Mientkiewicz	.25
43	Moises Alou	.25
44	Todd Helton	1.00
45	Ichiro Suzuki	2.00
46	Jose Cruz Jr.	.25
47	Freddy Garcia	.25
48	Tino Martinez	.25
49	Roger Clemens	1.75
50	Greg Maddux	1.50
51	Mike Piazza	2.00
52	Roberto Alomar	.50
53	Adam Dunn	.50
54	Kerry Wood	.75
55	Edgar Martinez	.25
56	Ken Griffey Jr.	2.00
57	Juan Gonzalez	1.00
58	Pat Burrell	.50
59	Corey Koskie	.25
60	Jose Vidro	.25
61	Ben Grieve	.25
62	Barry Bonds	3.00
63	Raul Mondesi	.25
64	Jimmy Rollins	.50
65	Mike Sweeney	.50
66	Josh Beckett	.50
67	Chipper Jones	1.50
68	Jeff Kent	.25
69	Tony Batista	.25
70	Phil Nevin	.25
71	Brian Jordan	.25
72	Rich Aurilia	.25
73	Brian Giles	.25
74	Frank Thomas	1.00
75	Larry Walker	.25
76	Shawn Green	.40
77	Manny Ramirez	1.00
78	Craig Biggio	.25
79	Vladimir Guerrero	1.00
80	Jeromy Burnitz	.25

81	Mark Teixeira	10.00
82	Corey Thurman RC	8.00
83	Mark Prior	15.00
84	Marlon Byrd	8.00
85	Austin Kearns RC	10.00
86	Satoru Komiyama RC	8.00
87	So Taguchi RC	12.00
88	Jorge Padilla RC	8.00
89	Rene Reyes RC	8.00
90	Jorge Nunez RC	8.00
91	Ron Calloway RC	8.00
92	Kazuhisa Ishii RC	10.00
93	Dewon Brazelton	8.00
94	Angel Berroa RC	8.00
95	Felix Escalona RC	8.00
96	Sean Burroughs	8.00
97	Brandon Duckworth	8.00
98	Hank Blalock	10.00
99	Eric Hinske	8.00
100	Carlos Pena	8.00
101	Morgan Ensberg	8.00
102	Ryan Ludwick	8.00
103	Chris Snelling RC	8.00
104	Jason Lane	8.00
105	Drew Henson	10.00
106	Bobby Kielty	3.00
107	Earl Snyder RC	3.00
108	Nate Field RC	3.00
109	Juan Diaz	3.00
110	Ryan Anderson	3.00
111	Esteban German	3.00
112	Takahito Nomura RC	3.00
113	David Kelton	3.00
114	Steve Kent RC	3.00
115	Colby Lewis	3.00
116	Jason Simontacchi RC	3.00
117	Rodrigo Rosario RC	3.00
118	Ben Howard RC	3.00
119	Hansel Izquierdo RC	3.00
120	John Ennis RC	3.00
121	Anderson Machado RC	3.00
122	Luis Ugueto RC	3.00
123	Anastacio Martinez RC	3.00
124	Reed Johnson RC	6.00
125	Juan Cruz	3.00

Co-Stars

Complete Set (15):		25.00
Common Card:		1.00
Inserted 1:6		
1CS	Barry Bonds, Alex Rodriguez	6.00
2CS	Derek Jeter, Nomar Garciaparra	5.00
3CS	Andruw Jones, Chipper Jones	3.00
4CS	Juan Gonzalez, Jim Thome	2.00
5CS	Pedro J. Martinez, Randy Johnson	2.00
6CS	Adam Dunn, Pat Burrell	1.50
7CS	Frank Thomas, Manny Ramirez	2.00
8CS	Jeff Bagwell, Lance Berkman	2.00
9CS	So Taguchi, Kazuhisa Ishii	4.00
10CS	Jimmy Rollins, Miguel Tejada	2.00
11CS	Morgan Ensberg, Carlos Pena	1.00
12CS	Adam Dunn, Austin Kearns	2.00
13CS	Vladimir Guerrero, Scott Rolen	3.00
14CS	Drew Henson, Xavier Nady	1.00
15CS	Mike Piazza, Ivan Rodriguez	4.00

Future Swatch Autograph

		NM/M
Common Auto.		
Production 100		
83	Mark Prior	40.00
87	So Taguchi	20.00
89	Rene Reyes	10.00
105	Drew Henson	20.00

Inside Barry Bonds

	NM/M
Common Bonds:	15.00
1BB Barry Bonds/Pants/1,000	15.00
2BB Barry Bonds/Pants/900	20.00
3BB Barry Bonds/Jsy/800	20.00
4BB Barry Bonds/Bat/700	20.00
5BB Barry Bonds/Base/600	15.00
6BB Barry Bonds/Cleat/500	25.00
7BB Barry Bonds/Glv/400	25.00
8BB Barry Bonds/Cap/300	30.00

Jerseygraphs

		NM/M
Common Player:		10.00
Inserted 1:186		
DJ	Derek Jeter/108	150.00
BB	Barry Bonds/65	250.00
CJ	Chipper Jones/100	80.00
DH	Drew Henson	30.00
ST	So Taguchi/100	25.00
DE	David Espinosa	10.00
DS	Dane Sardinha	10.00
AB	Adrian Beltre/169	35.00

MLB Hot Materials

		NM/M
Common Player:		5.00
Inserted 1:9		
Red Hots:		1-2X
Production 500 Sets		
AD	Adam Dunn	8.00
AR	Alex Rodriguez	10.00
BB	Bret Boone	5.00
BB2	Barry Bonds	20.00
BD	Brandon Duckworth	5.00
BG	Brian Giles	5.00
BW	Bernie Williams	8.00
CD	Carlos Delgado	6.00
CG	Cristian Guzman	5.00
CP	Carlos Pena	6.00
CP	Corey Patterson	6.00
CS	Curt Schilling	8.00
FT	Frank Thomas	10.00
GK	Gabe Kapler	5.00
GM	Greg Maddux	15.00
GS	Gary Sheffield	8.00
IR	Ivan Rodriguez	10.00
JB	Josh Beckett	8.00
JB2	Jeff Bagwell/108	20.00
JG	Juan Gonzalez	8.00
JT	Jim Thome	10.00
JU	Juan Uribe	5.00
LB	Lance Berkman	8.00
MM	Mark Mulder	8.00
MA	Moises Alou	6.00
MP	Mike Piazza	15.00
MS	Mike Sweeney	5.00
NJ	Nick Johnson	5.00
PL	Paul LoDuca	5.00
PM	Pedro J. Martinez	10.00
RF	Rafael Furcal	5.00
RO	Roy Oswalt	5.00
RP	Rafael Palmeiro	10.00
SB	Sean Burroughs/350	10.00
SG	Shawn Green	8.00
TA	Tony Armas Jr.	5.00
TH	Torii Hunter	5.00
TM	Tino Martinez	5.00
VW	Vernon Wells	5.00
KI	Kazuhisa Ishii/70	
TH	Todd Helton	8.00
MO	Magglio Ordonez	8.00
FG	Freddy Garcia	5.00
ST	So Taguchi	8.00

MLB Hot Tandems

	NM/M
Common Card:	10.00
Production 100 Sets	
Red Hots 10 Sets:	No Pricing
Adam Dunn, Lance Berkman	15.00
Alex Rodriguez, Ivan Rodriguez	30.00
Bret Boone, Freddy Garcia	10.00
Barry Bonds, Kazuhisa Ishii	40.00
Brandon Duckworth, Roy Oswalt	10.00
Bernie Williams, Jorge Posada	15.00
Carlos Delgado, Vernon Wells	10.00
Cristian Guzman, Torii Hunter	10.00
Carlos Pena, Corey Patterson	10.00
Curt Schilling, Greg Maddux	25.00
Frank Thomas, Magglio Ordonez	15.00
Gabe Kapler, Rafael Palmeiro	12.00
Gary Sheffield, Rafael Furcal	10.00
Josh Beckett, Roy Oswalt	10.00
Brandon Duckworth, Josh Beckett	15.00
Jeff Bagwell, Lance Berkman	15.00
Juan Gonzalez, Rafael Palmeiro	15.00
Jim Thome, Shawn Green	15.00
Paul LoDuca, Shawn Green	10.00
Juan Uribe, Miguel Tejada	15.00
Mark Mulder, Miguel Tejada	15.00
Moises Alou, Magglio Ordonez	10.00
Jorge Posada, Mike Piazza	25.00
Mike Sweeney, Todd Helton	15.00
Carlos Pena, Nick Johnson	10.00
Curt Schilling, Pedro J. Martinez	25.00
Tony Armas Jr., Freddy Garcia	10.00
Tino Martinez, Todd Helton	15.00
Barry Bonds, Derek Jeter	60.00
Kazuhisa Ishii, Derek Jeter	40.00
Juan Uribe, Cristian Guzman	10.00
Kazuhisa Ishii, So Taguchi	20.00
Adam Dunn, Corey Patterson	15.00
Bernie Williams, Nick Johnson	10.00
Bret Boone, Torii Hunter	10.00
Greg Maddux, Pedro J. Martinez	20.00
Sean Burroughs, Drew Henson	10.00
Kazuhisa Ishii, Satoru Komiyama	20.00
Kazuhisa Ishii, Mark Prior	20.00
Hank Blalock, Austin Kearns	15.00
Hank Blalock, Mark Teixeira	15.00
Marlon Byrd, Jorge Padilla	10.00
Marlon Byrd, Austin Kearns	10.00
Gabe Kapler, Juan Gonzalez	15.00
Jeff Bagwell, Mike Piazza	25.00

We're Number One

		NM/M
Complete Set (10):		35.00
Common Player:		1.50
Inserted 1:15		
1WN	Derek Jeter	8.00
2WN	Barry Bonds	8.00
3WN	Ken Griffey Jr.	5.00
4WN	Roger Clemens	4.50
5WN	Alex Rodriguez	6.00
6WN	J.D. Drew	1.50
7WN	Chipper Jones	4.00
8WN	Manny Ramirez	3.00
9WN	Nomar Garciaparra	3.00
10WN	Todd Helton	3.00

We're Number One Memorabilia

	NM/M
Common Player:	5.00
Inserted 1:25	
Derek Jeter/Jsy	25.00
Barry Bonds/Jsy	20.00
Ken Griffey Jr./Base	15.00
Alex Rodriguez/Jsy	15.00
J.D. Drew/Jsy	5.00
Chipper Jones/Jsy	10.00
Manny Ramirez/Jsy	10.00
Nomar Garciaparra/Jsy	10.00
Todd Helton/Jsy	10.00

We're Number One Autograph

	NM/M
Common Player:	
Derek Jeter/92	
Barry Bonds/85	200.00

2002 Fleer Maximum

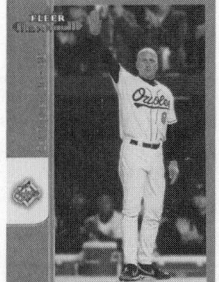

		NM/M
Complete Set (270):		
Common Player:		.15
Common (201-250):		5.00
Production 500		
Common (251-270):		.50
Inserted 1:Hobby Pack		
Pack (15):		2.50
Box (16):		35.00
1	Barry Bonds	2.00
2	Alex Rodriguez	1.50
3	Jim Edmonds	.15
4	Manny Ramirez	.75
5	Jeff Bagwell	.75
6	Kazuhiro Sasaki	.15
7	Jason Giambi	.50
8	J.D. Drew	.25
9	Barry Larkin	.15
10	Chipper Jones	1.00
11	Rafael Palmeiro	.65
12	Roberto Alomar	.35
13	Randy Johnson	.75
14	Juan Gonzalez	.75
15	Gary Sheffield	.25
16	Larry Walker	.15
17	Todd Helton	.75
18	Ivan Rodriguez	.65
19	Greg Maddux	1.00
20	Mike Piazza	1.25
21	Tsuyoshi Shinjo	.15
22	Luis Gonzalez	.25
23	Pedro Martinez	.75
24	Albert Pujols	1.50
25	Jose Canseco	.35
26	Edgar Martinez	.15
27	Moises Alou	.15
28	Vladimir Guerrero	.75
29	Shawn Green	.35
30	Miguel Tejada	.25
31	Bernie Williams	.30
32	Frank Thomas	.75
33	Jim Thome	.15
34	Derek Jeter	2.00
35	Julio Lugo	.15
36	Mo Vaughn	.15
37	Steve Cox	.15
38	Brad Radke	.15
39	Brian Jordan	.15
40	Garret Anderson	.15
41	Ichiro Suzuki	1.25
42	Mike Lieberthal	.15
43	Preston Wilson	.15
44	Bud Smith	.15
45	Curt Schilling	.40
46	Eric Chavez	.25
47	Javier Vazquez	.15
48	Jose Ortiz	.15
49	Mike Sweeney	.15
50	Travis Fryman	.15
51	Brady Anderson	.15
52	Chan Ho Park	.15
53	C.C. Sabathia	.15
54	Jack Wilson	.25
55	Joe Crede	.15
56	Mike Mussina	.40
57	Sean Casey	.30
58	Bobby Abreu	.15
59	Joe Randa	.15
60	Jose Vidro	.15
61	Juan Uribe	.15
62	Mark Grace	.25
63	Matt Morris	.15
64	Omar Vizquel	.15
65	Darryl Kile	.15
66	Dee Brown	.15
67	Fernando Tatis	.15
68	Jeff Cirillo	.15
69	Johnny Damon	.25
70	Milton Bradley	.15
71	Reggie Sanders	.15
72	Al Leiter	.15
73	Andres Galarraga	.15
74	Ellis Burks	.15
75	Jermaine Dye	.15
76	Juan Pierre	.15
77	Junior Spivey	.15
78	Mark Quinn	.15
79	Ben Sheets	.15
80	Brad Fullmer	.15
81	Bubba Trammell	.15
82	Dante Bichette	.15
83	Ken Griffey Jr.	1.25
84	Paul O'Neill	.15
85	Robert Fick	.15
86	Bret Boone	.15
87	Raul Mondesi	.15
88	Josh Beckett	.40
89	Geoff Jenkins	.15
90	Ramon Ortiz	.15
91	Robin Ventura	.15
92	Tom Glavine	.30
93	Jimmy Rollins	.15
94	Jamie Moyer	.15
95	Magglio Ordonez	.15
96	Mike Lowell	.15
97	Ryan Dempster	.15
98	Scott Schoeneweis	.15
99	Todd Zeile	.15
100	A.J. Burnett	.15
101	Aaron Sele	.15
102	Cal Ripken Jr.	2.00
103	Carlos Beltran	.45
104	David Eckstein	.15
105	Jason Marquis	.15
106	Matt Lawton	.15
107	Ben Grieve	.15
108	Brian Giles	.15
109	Josh Towers	.15
110	Lance Berkman	.15
111	Sammy Sosa	1.25
112	Torii Hunter	.15
113	Aubrey Huff	.15
114	Craig Biggio	.15
115	Doug Mientkiewicz	.15
116	Fred McGriff	.15
117	Jason Johnson	.15
118	Pat Burrell	.25
119	Aaron Boone	.15
120	Carlos Delgado	.50
121	Nomar Garciaparra	1.25
122	Richie Sexson	.15
123	Russ Ortiz	.15
124	Tim Hudson	.25
125	Tony Clark	.15

#	Player	Price
126	Jeromy Burnitz	.15
127	Jose Cruz	.15
128	Juan Encarnacion	.15
129	Mark Mulder	.15
130	Mike Hampton	.15
131	Rich Aurilia	.15
132	Trot Nixon	.15
133	Greg Vaughn	.15
134	Jacque Jones	.15
135	Jason Kendall	.15
136	Jay Gibbons	.15
137	Mark Buehrle	.15
138	Richard Hidalgo	.15
139	Rondell White	.15
140	Cristian Guzman	.15
141	Andy Pettitte	.30
142	Chris Richard	.15
143	Paul LoDuca	.15
144	Phil Nevin	.15
145	Ray Durham	.15
146	Todd Walker	.15
147	Bartolo Colon	.15
148	Ben Petrick	.15
149	Freddy Garcia	.15
150	Jon Lieber	.15
151	Jose Hernandez	.15
152	Matt Williams	.15
153	Shannon Stewart	.15
154	Adrian Beltre	.30
155	Carlos Lee	.15
156	Frank Catalanotto	.15
157	Jorge Posada	.30
158	Pokey Reese	.15
159	Ryan Klesko	.15
160	Ugueth Urbina	.15
161	Adam Dunn	.50
162	Alfonso Soriano	.50
163	Ben Davis	.15
164	Paul Konerko	.25
165	Eric Karros	.25
166	Jeff Weaver	.15
167	Ruben Sierra	.15
168	Bobby Higginson	.15
169	Eric Milton	.15
170	Kerry Wood	.65
171	Roy Oswalt	.30
172	Scott Rolen	.65
173	Tim Salmon	.25
174	Aramis Ramirez	.25
175	Jason Tyner	.15
176	Juan Cruz	.15
177	Keith Foulke	.15
178	Kevin Brown	.25
179	Roger Clemens	1.00
180	Tony Batista	.15
181	Andruw Jones	.75
182	Cliff Floyd	.15
183	Darin Erstad	.25
184	Joe Mays	.15
185	Mike Cameron	.15
186	Robert Person	.15
187	Jeff Kent	.25
188	Gabe Kapler	.25
189	Jason Jennings	.15
190	Jason Varitek	.15
191	Barry Zito	.25
192	Rickey Henderson	.75
193	Tino Martinez	.25
194	Brandon Duckworth	.15
195	Corey Koskie	.15
196	Derrek Lee	.25
197	Javy Lopez	.25
198	John Olerud	.25
199	Terrance Long	.15
200	Troy Glaus	.75
201	Scott MacRae	5.00
202	Scott Chiasson	5.00
203	Bart Miadich	5.00
204	Brian Bowles	5.00
205	David Williams	5.00
206	Victor Zambrano	5.00
207	Joe Beimel	5.00
208	Scott Stewart	5.00
209	Bob File	5.00
210	Ryan Jensen	5.00
211	Jason Karnuth	5.00
212	Brandon Knight	5.00
213	Andy Shibilo RC	5.00
214	Chad Ricketts RC	5.00
215	Mark Prior	8.00
216	Chad Paronto	5.00
217	Corky Miller	5.00
218	Luis Pineda	5.00
219	Ramon Vazquez	5.00
220	Tony Cogan	5.00
221	Roy Smith	5.00
222	Mark Lukasiewicz	5.00
223	Mike Rivera	5.00
224	Brad Voyles	5.00
225	Jamie Burke RC	5.00
226	Justin Duchscherer	5.00
227	Eric Cyr RC	5.00
228	Mark Lukasiewicz	5.00
229	Marlon Byrd	5.00
230	Chris Piersoll RC	5.00
231	Ramon Vazquez	5.00
232	Tony Cogan	5.00
233	Roy Smith	5.00
234	Franklin Nunez RC	5.00
235	Corky Miller	5.00
236	Jorge Nunez RC	5.00
237	Joe Beimel	5.00
238	Eric Knott	5.00
239	Victor Zambrano	5.00
240	Jason Karnuth	5.00
241	Jason Middlebrook	5.00
242	Scott Stewart	5.00
243	Tim Spooneybarger	5.00
244	David Williams	5.00
245	Bart Miadich	5.00
246	Mike Koplove	5.00
247	Ryan Jensen	5.00
248	Jeremy Fikac	5.00
249	Bob File	5.00
250	Craig Monroe	5.00
251	Albert Pujols	2.00
252	Ichiro Suzuki	2.00
253	Nomar Garciaparra	2.00
254	Barry Bonds	3.00
255	Jason Giambi	.75
256	Derek Jeter	3.00
257	Roberto Alomar	.75
258	Roger Clemens	2.00
259	Mike Piazza	1.50
260	Vladimir Guerrero	1.00
261	Todd Helton	.75
262	Shawn Green	1.00
263	Chipper Jones	1.00
264	Pedro Martinez	1.00
265	Pat Burrell	.50
266	Sammy Sosa	2.00
267	Ken Griffey Jr.	1.50
268	Cal Ripken Jr.	3.00
269	Kerry Wood	1.00
270	Alex Rodriguez	2.50

Power

		NM/M
Complete Set (25):		40.00
Inserted 1:20 Retail		
1	Luis Gonzalez	1.00
2	Jimmy Rollins	1.00
3	Larry Walker	1.00
4	Frank Thomas	2.00
5	Manny Ramirez	2.00
6	Barry Bonds	8.00
7	Jim Thome	1.00
8	Tsuyoshi Shinjo	1.00
9	Bernie Williams	1.00
10	Chipper Jones	3.00
11	Shawn Green	1.50
12	Drew Henson	1.00
13	Juan Gonzalez	2.00
14	Jim Edmonds	1.00
15	Moises Alou	1.00
16	Roberto Alomar	1.50
17	Jose Canseco	1.50
18	Ivan Rodriguez	1.50
19	Barry Larkin	1.00
20	Mike Piazza	5.00
21	Gary Sheffield	1.00
22	J.D. Drew	1.00
23	Alex Rodriguez	6.00
24	Jason Giambi	1.50
25	Todd Helton	2.00

America's Game

		NM/M
Complete Set (25):		25.00
Common Player:		.50
Inserted 1:10 Retail		
1	Pedro Martinez	1.50
2	Miguel Tejada	.75
3	Randy Johnson	1.50
4	Barry Bonds	5.00
5	Rafael Palmeiro	1.00
6	Mike Piazza	3.00
7	Greg Maddux	2.50
8	Jeff Bagwell	1.50
9	Edgar Martinez	.50
10	Albert Pujols	4.00
11	Todd Helton	1.50
12	Chipper Jones	2.50
13	Luis Gonzalez	1.00
14	Jason Giambi	1.00
15	Kazuhiro Sasaki	.50
16	Dave Winfield	1.00
17	Reggie Jackson	1.50
18	Tom Glavine	.75
19	Carlos Delgado	.75
20	Bobby Abreu	.50
21	Larry Walker	.50
22	J.D. Drew	.75
23	Alex Rodriguez	4.00
24	Frank Thomas	1.50
25	C.C. Sabathia	.50

Americas Game Jersey

		NM/M
Common Player:		8.00
Inserted 1:24 H, 1:72 R		
1	Jeff Bagwell	10.00
2	Craig Biggio	8.00
3	Barry Bonds	25.00
4	Carlos Delgado	8.00
5	J.D. Drew	5.00
6	Jason Giambi	10.00
7	Tom Glavine	10.00
8	Luis Gonzalez	5.00
9	Todd Helton	10.00
10	Reggie Jackson	10.00
11	Randy Johnson	10.00
12	Chipper Jones	10.00
13	Greg Maddux	10.00
14	Edgar Martinez	8.00
15	Pedro Martinez	10.00
16	Rafael Palmeiro	10.00
17	Chan Ho Park	5.00
18	Mike Piazza	10.00
19	Albert Pujols	20.00
20	Kazuhiro Sasaki	5.00
21	Miguel Tejada	5.00
22	Frank Thomas	10.00
23	Larry Walker	5.00
24	Dave Winfield	5.00

Americas Game Stars and Stripes

No Pricing
Production 25 Sets

Coverage

		NM/M
Common Player:		15.00
Production 100 Sets		
1	Roberto Alomar/Bat	25.00
2	Jeff Bagwell/Jsy	20.00
3	Barry Bonds/Bat	50.00
4	Jose Canseco/Bat	25.00
5	J.D. Drew/Bat	25.00
6	Jim Edmonds/Bat	20.00
7	Jason Giambi/Bat	25.00
8	Juan Gonzalez/Bat	25.00
9	Barry Larkin/Jsy	15.00
10	Todd Helton/Jsy	20.00
11	Randy Johnson/Jsy	40.00
12	Chipper Jones/Bat	40.00
13	Greg Maddux/Jsy	40.00
14	Pedro Martinez/Jsy	30.00
15	Rafael Palmeiro/Pants	25.00
16	Albert Pujols/Jsy	50.00
17	Manny Ramirez/Bat	20.00
18	Alex Rodriguez/Bat	30.00
19	Ivan Rodriguez/Bat	20.00
20	Kazuhiro Sasaki/Jsy	20.00
21	Gary Sheffield/Bat	20.00
22	Tsuyoshi Shinjo/Bat	15.00

Coverage Autographs

		NM/M
Quantity produced listed		
1	Barry Bonds/Pants/50	200.00
2	J.D. Drew/Bat/100	25.00
3	Jim Edmonds/Bat/100	25.00
4	Drew Henson/Bat/100	25.00
5	Chipper Jones/Bat/50	60.00
6	Albert Pujols/Jsy	150.00
7	Gary Sheffield/Bat/100	30.00

Derek Jeter Legacy Collection

		NM/M
Inserted 1:236		
DJ	Derek Jeter/Bat	20.00
DJ	Derek Jeter/Bat/Auto./222	150.00
DJ	Derek Jeter/Jsy	20.00
DJ	Derek Jeter/Jsy/Auto.	200.00

Fencebusters Autographed

	NM/M
Numbered to 2001 HR Total.	
Barry Bonds/73	275.00

Maximum Power Bat

		NM/M
Common Player:		5.00
Inserted 1:24 H		
Golds:		3-4X
Production 25 Sets		
	Luis Gonzalez	5.00
	Larry Walker	5.00
	Frank Thomas	10.00
	Manny Ramirez	10.00
	Barry Bonds	25.00
	Jim Thome	10.00
	Tsuyoshi Shinjo	5.00
	Bernie Williams/175	25.00
	Chipper Jones	10.00
	Shawn Green	5.00
	Juan Gonzalez	8.00
	Jim Edmonds	10.00
	Moises Alou	10.00
	Roberto Alomar	10.00
	Jose Canseco	10.00
	Ivan Rodriguez	10.00
	Barry Larkin/50	40.00
	Mike Piazza	15.00
	Gary Sheffield	8.00
	J.D. Drew/200	8.00
	Alex Rodriguez	15.00
	Jason Giambi	10.00
	Todd Helton	8.00

To The Max

Stars (1-200):	4-6X
Print Run 200-500	
Stars (1-200):	4-8X
Print Run 121-199	
Stars (1-200):	6-12X
Print Run 75-120	
Stars (1-200):	10-25X
Print Run 40-75	
Stars (1-200):	15-40X
Print Run 20-39	
Rookies (201-250):	.5-1X
Production 100	
Impact (251-270):	2-4X
Production 200-400	

2002 Fleer Platinum

Roger Clemens PITCHER

		NM/M
Complete Set (302):		125.00
Common Player:		.15
Common (251-260):		2.00
Common (261-302):		1.50
Inserted 1:3 H, 1:6 Retail		
Hobby Pack (10):		2.00
Hobby Box (24):		35.00
Rack Box:		70.00
1	Garrett Anderson	.15
2	Randy Johnson	.65
3	Chipper Jones	.75
4	David Cone	.15
5	Corey Patterson	.15
6	Carlos Lee	.15
7	Barry Larkin	.15
8	Jim Thome	.15
9	Larry Walker	.15
10	Randall Simon	.15
11	Charles Johnson	.15
12	Richard Hidalgo	.15
13	Mark Quinn	.15
14	Paul LoDuca	.15
15	Cristian Guzman	.15
16	Orlando Cabrera	.15
17	Al Leiter	.15
18	Nick Johnson	.15
19	Eric Chavez	.25
20	Miguel Tejada	.25
21	Mike Lieberthal	.15
22	Robert Mackowiak	.15
23	Ryan Klesko	.15
24	Jeff Kent	.15
25	Edgar Martinez	.15
26	Steve Kline	.15
27	Toby Hall	.15

28 Rusty Greer .15
29 Jose Cruz Jr. .15
30 Darin Erstad .50
31 Reggie Sanders .15
32 Javy Lopez .15
33 Carl Everett .15
34 Sammy Sosa 1.00
35 Magglio Ordonez .15
36 Todd Walker .15
37 Omar Vizquel .15
38 Matt Anderson .15
39 Jeff Weaver .15
40 Derrek Lee .15
41 Julio Lugo .15
42 Joe Randa .15
43 Chan Ho Park .15
44 Torii Hunter .15
45 Vladimir Guerrero .65
46 Rey Ordonez .15
47 Tino Martinez .15
48 Johnny Damon .25
49 Barry Zito .25
50 Robert Person .15
51 Aramis Ramirez .15
52 Mark Kotsay .15
53 Jason Schmidt .15
54 Jamie Moyer .15
55 David Justice .15
56 Aubrey Huff .15
57 Rick Helling .15
58 Carlos Delgado .40
59 Troy Glaus .65
60 Curt Schilling .40
61 Greg Maddux .75
62 Nomar Garciaparra 1.00
63 Kerry Wood .50
64 Frank Thomas .65
65 Dmitri Young .15
66 Alex Ochoa .15
67 Jose Macias .15
68 Antonio Alfonseca .15
69 Mike Lowell .15
70 Wade Miller .15
71 Mike Sweeney .15
72 Gary Sheffield .25
73 Corey Koskie .15
74 Lee Stevens .15
75 Jay Payton .15
76 Mike Mussina .40
77 Jermaine Dye .15
78 Bobby Abreu .15
79 Scott Rolen .50
80 Todd Ritchie .15
81 D'Angelo Jimenez .15
82 Rob Nenn .15
83 John Olerud .15
84 Matt Morris .15
85 Joe Kennedy .15
86 Gabe Kapler .15
87 Chris Carpenter .15
88 David Eckstein .15
89 Matt Williams .15
90 John Smoltz .15
91 Pedro J. Martinez .65
92 Eric Young .15
93 Jose Valentin .15
94 Erubiel Durazo .15
95 Jeff Cirillo .15
96 Brandon Inge .15
97 Josh Beckett .40
98 Preston Wilson .15
99 Damian Jackson .15
100 Adrian Beltre .25
101 Jeromy Burnitz .15
102 Joe Mays .15
103 Michael Barrett .15
104 Mike Piazza 1.00
105 Brady Anderson .15
106 Jason Giambi .40
107 Marlon Anderson .15
108 Jimmy Rollins .25
109 Jack Wilson .15
110 Brian Lawrence .15
111 Russ Ortiz .15
112 Kazuhiro Sasaki .15
113 Placido Polanco .15
114 Damian Rolls .15
115 Rafael Palmeiro .50
116 Brad Fullmer .15
117 Tim Salmon .25
118 Tony Womack .15
119 Tony Batista .15
120 Trot Nixon .15
121 Mark Buehrle .15
122 Derek Jeter 1.50
123 Ellis Burks .15
124 Mike Hampton .15
125 Roger Cedeno .15
126 A.J. Burnett .15
127 Moises Alou .15
128 Billy Wagner .15
129 Kevin Brown .15
130 Jose Hernandez .15
131 Doug Mientkiewicz .15
132 Javier Vazquez .15
133 Tsuyoshi Shinjo .15
134 Andy Pettitte .30
135 Tim Hudson .25
136 Pat Burrell .40
137 Brian Giles .15
138 Kevin Young .15
139 Xavier Nady .15
140 J.T. Snow .15
141 Aaron Sele .15
142 Albert Pujols 1.25
143 Jason Tyner .15
144 Ivan Rodriguez .50
145 Raul Mondesi .15
146 Matt Lawton .15
147 Rafael Furcal .15
148 Jeff Conine .15
149 Hideo Nomo .60
150 Jose Canseco .30
151 Aaron Boone .15
152 Bartolo Colon .15
153 Todd Helton .65
154 Tony Clark .15
155 Pablo Ozuna .15
156 Jeff Bagwell .65
157 Carlos Beltran .50
158 Shawn Green .25
159 Geoff Jenkins .15
160 Eric Milton .15
161 Jose Vidro .15
162 Robin Ventura .15
163 Jorge Posada .25
164 Terrence Long .15
165 Brandon Duckworth .15
166 Chad Hermansen .15
167 Ben Davis .15
168 Phil Nevin .15
169 Bret Boone .15
170 J.D. Drew .25
171 Edgar Renteria .15
172 Randy Winn .15
173 Alex Rodriguez 1.50
174 Shannon Stewart .15
175 Steve Finley .15
176 Marcus Giles .15
177 Jay Gibbons .15
178 Manny Ramirez .65
179 Ray Durham .15
180 Sean Casey .25
181 Travis Fryman .15
182 Denny Neagle .15
183 Deivi Cruz .15
184 Luis Castillo .15
185 Lance Berkman .15
186 Dee Brown .15
187 Jeff Shaw .15
188 Mark Loretta .15
189 David Ortiz .25
190 Edgardo Alfonzo .15
191 Roger Clemens .75
192 Mariano Rivera .25
193 Jeremy Giambi .15
194 Johnny Estrada .15
195 Craig Wilson .15
196 Adam Eaton .15
197 Rich Aurilia .15
198 Mike Cameron .15
199 Jim Edmonds .15
200 Fernando Vina .15
201 Greg Vaughn .15
202 Mike Young .15
203 Vernon Wells .15
204 Luis Gonzalez .25
205 Tom Glavine .30
206 Chris Richard .15
207 Jon Lieber .15
208 Keith Foulke .15
209 Rondell White .15
210 Bernie Williams .30
211 Juan Pierre .15
212 Juan Encarnacion .15
213 Ryan Dempster .15
214 Tim Redding .15
215 Jeff Suppan .15
216 Mark Grudzielanek .15
217 Richie Sexson .15
218 Brad Radke .15
219 Armando Benitez .15
220 Orlando Hernandez .15
221 Alfonso Soriano .40
222 Mark Mulder .15
223 Travis Lee .15
224 Jason Kendall .15
225 Trevor Hoffman .15
226 Barry Bonds 1.50
227 Freddy Garcia .15
228 Darryl Kile .15
229 Ben Grieve .15
230 Frank Catalanotto .15
231 Ruben Sierra .15
232 Homer Bush .15
233 Mark Grace .25
234 Andruw Jones .60
235 Brian Roberts .15
236 Fred McGriff .15
237 Paul Konerko .15
238 Ken Griffey Jr. 1.00
239 John Burkett .15
240 Juan Uribe .15
241 Bobby Higginson .15
242 Cliff Floyd .15
243 Craig Biggio .15
244 Neifi Perez .15
245 Eric Karros .15
246 Ben Sheets .15
247 Tony Armas Jr. .15
248 Mo Vaughn .15
249 David Wells .15
250 Juan Gonzalez .60
251 Barry Bonds 5.00
252 Sammy Sosa 3.00
253 Ken Griffey Jr. 3.00
254 Roger Clemens 4.00
255 Greg Maddux 2.50
256 Chipper Jones 1.50
257 Alex Rodriguez, Derek Jeter, Nomar Garciaparra 5.00
258 Roberto Alomar 1.50
259 Jeff Bagwell 1.50
260 Mike Piazza 3.00
261 Mark Teixeira 2.00
262 Mark Prior 2.00
263 Alex Escobar 1.50
264 C.C. Sabathia 1.50
265 Drew Henson 1.50
266 Wilson Betemit 1.50
267 Roy Oswalt 1.50
268 Adam Dunn 2.00
269 Bud Smith 1.50
270 Dewon Brazelton 1.50
271 Brandon Backe, Jason Standridge 1.50
272 Wilfredo Rodriguez, Carlos Hernandez 1.50
273 Geronimo Gil, Luis Rivera 1.50
274 Carlos Pena, Jovanny Cedeno 1.50
275 Austin Kearns, Ben Broussard 1.50
276 Jorge De La Rosa, Kenny Kelly 1.50
277 Ryan Drese, Victor Martinez 1.50
278 Joel Pinero, Nate Cornejo 1.50
279 David Kelton, Carlos Zambrano 1.50
281 Donnie Bridges, Wilkin Ruan 1.50
282 Wily Mo Pena, Brandon Claussen 2.00
283 Jason Jennings, Rene Reyes **RC** 1.50
284 Steve Green, Alfredo Amezaga 1.50
285 Eric Hinske, Felipe Lopez 1.50
286 Anderson Machado, Brad Baisley 1.50
287 Carlos Garcia, Sean Douglass 1.50
288 Pat Strange, Jae Weong Seo 1.50
289 Marcus Thames, Alex Graman 1.50
290 Matt Childers, Hansel Izquierdo **RC** 1.50
291 Ron Calloway, Adam Walker **RC** 1.50
292 J.R. House, J.J. Davis 1.50
293 Ryan Anderson, Rafael Soriano 1.50
294 Mike Bynum, Dennis Tankersley 1.50
295 Kurt Ainsworth, Carlos Valderrama 1.50
296 Billy Hall, Cristian Guerrero 1.50
297 Miguel Olivo, Danny Wright 1.50
298 Marlon Byrd, Jorge Padilla **RC** 1.50
299 Juan Cruz, Ben Christensen 1.50
300 Adam Johnson, Michael Restovich 1.50
301 So Taguchi **RC** 2.00
302 Kazuhisa Ishii **RC** 3.00

Edition

Stars (1-250): 4-8X
Production 202
Cards 251-302: No Pricing
Production 22

Barry Bonds RC Autograph

NM/M

73 Cards Autographed
Barry Bonds 400.00

Buy Back Autographs

No Pricing

Clubhouse Collection Memorabilia

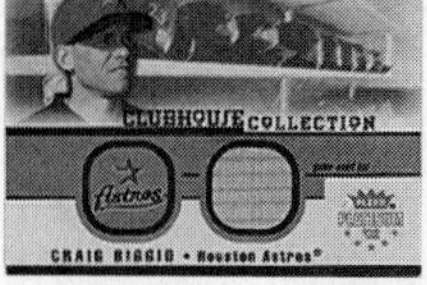
CLUBHOUSE COLLECTION
CRAIG BIGGIO • Houston Astros

NM/M

Common Player: 5.00
Inserted 1:32
Edgardo Alfonzo/Jsy 5.00
Rick Ankiel/Jsy 5.00
Craig Biggio/Bat 8.00
Adrian Beltre/Jsy 5.00
Sean Casey/Jsy 8.00
Barry Bonds/Jsy 25.00
Scott Rolen/Jsy 10.00
Eric Chavez/Jsy 8.00
Roger Clemens/Jsy 25.00
Carlos Delgado/Jsy 8.00
J.D. Drew/Jsy 5.00
Darin Erstad/Jsy 5.00
Jim Thome/Bat 10.00
Juan Gonzalez/Bat 8.00
Nomar Garciaparra/Jsy 15.00
Todd Helton/Jsy 8.00
Derek Jeter/Pants 25.00
Randy Johnson/Jsy 10.00
Andruw Jones/Jsy 8.00
Tim Hudson/Jsy 5.00
Jason Kendall/Jsy 5.00
Johnny Damon/Bat 5.00
Paul LoDuca/Jsy 5.00
Greg Maddux/Jsy 10.00
Pedro Martinez/Jsy 10.00
Raul Mondesi/Bat 5.00
Magglio Ordonez/Jsy 5.00
Mike Piazza/Jsy 10.00
Manny Ramirez/Jsy 8.00
Mariano Rivera/Jsy 8.00
Ivan Rodriguez/Jsy 10.00
Alex Rodriguez/Jsy 15.00
Kazuhiro Sasaki/Jsy 5.00
Frank Thomas/Jsy 10.00
Curt Schilling/Jsy 8.00
Gary Sheffield/Bat 6.00
Omar Vizquel/Jsy 5.00

Clubhouse Collection - Dual

CLUBHOUSE COLLECTION
DARIN ERSTAD • Anaheim Angels

NM/M

Common Card: 10.00
Inserted 1:96
Edgardo Alfonzo 10.00
Rick Ankiel 8.00
Craig Biggio
Adrian Beltre 10.00
Barry Bonds 40.00
Sean Casey 10.00
Eric Chavez 10.00
Roger Clemens 30.00
Carlos Delgado 10.00
J.D. Drew 10.00
Darin Erstad 10.00
Jim Thome 20.00
Juan Gonzalez 15.00
Nomar Garciaparra 30.00
Derek Jeter 40.00
Randy Johnson 20.00
Andruw Jones 10.00
Johnny Damon 10.00
Paul LoDuca 10.00
Greg Maddux 20.00
Pedro J. Martinez 20.00
Magglio Ordonez 10.00
Mike Piazza 30.00
Manny Ramirez 15.00
Mariano Rivera 15.00
Ivan Rodriguez 20.00
Alex Rodriguez 25.00
Scott Rolen 20.00
Kazuhiro Sasaki 10.00
Curt Schilling 20.00
Gary Sheffield 10.00
Frank Thomas 20.00
Jim Thome 20.00
Omar Vizquel 10.00

Cornerstones

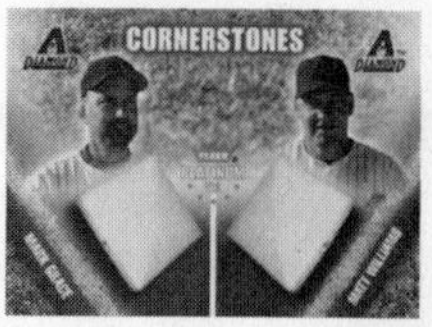
CORNERSTONES

NM/M

Complete Set (40): 120.00
Inserted 1:12 Jumbo
1 Bill Terry, Johnny Mize 1.50
2 Cal Ripken Jr., Eddie Murray 10.00
3 Eddie Mathews, Chipper Jones 3.00
4 Albert Pujols, George Sisler 6.00
5 Sean Casey, Tony Perez 1.50
6 Jimmie Foxx, Scott Rolen 4.00
7 Wade Boggs, George Brett 8.00
8 Rod Carew, Troy Glaus 1.50
9 Jeff Bagwell, Rafael Palmeiro 2.00
10 Willie Stargell, Pie Traynor 2.00
11 Cal Ripken Jr., Brooks Robinson 10.00
12 Tony Perez, Ted Kluszewski 1.50
13 Jason Giambi, Don Mattingly 8.00
14 Hank Greenberg, Jimmie Foxx 4.00
15 Ernie Banks, Willie McCovey 3.00
16 Jim Thome, Travis Fryman 3.00
17 Ted Kluszewski, Sean Casey 1.50
18 Gil Hodges, Johnny Mize 3.00
19 Brooks Robinson, Boog Powell 3.00

20 Bill Terry, George Sisler 2.00
21 Wade Boggs, Don Mattingly 8.00
22 Jason Giambi, Carlos Delgado 2.50
23 Willie Stargell, Bill Madlock 2.00
24 Mark Grace, Matt Williams 2.00
25 Paul Molitor, George Brett 8.00
26 Carlos Delgado, Mo Vaughn 1.50
27 Bill Terry, Willie McCovey 1.50
28 Mike Sweeney, George Brett 8.00
29 Eddie Mathews, Ernie Banks 4.00
30 Eric Karros, Gil Hodges 1.50
31 Paul Molitor, Don Mattingly 8.00
32 Brooks Robinson,Rod Carew 3.00
33 Chipper Jones, Albert Pujols 8.00
34 Harry Heilmann, Hank Greenberg 1.50
35 Frank Thomas, Carlos Delgado 2.50
36 Jeff Bagwell, Todd Helton 2.00
37 Rafael Palmeiro, Fred McGriff 2.00
38 Cal Ripken Jr., Wade Boggs 10.00
39 Orlando Cepeda, Willie McCovey 2.00
40 John Olerud, Mark Grace 2.00

Cornerstones Numbered

NM/M

Complete Set (40):
#1-10: Production 250
#11-20: Production 250
#21-30: Production 1,000
#31-40: Production 2,000
1 Bill Terry, Johnny Mize 10.00
2 Cal Ripken Jr., Eddie Murray 30.00
3 Eddie Mathews, Chipper Jones 10.00
4 Albert Pujols, George Sisler 20.00
5 Sean Casey, Tony Perez 8.00
6 Jimmie Foxx, Scott Rolen 10.00
7 Wade Boggs, George Brett 20.00
8 Rod Carew, Troy Glaus 10.00
9 Jeff Bagwell, Rafael Palmeiro 10.00
10 Willie Stargell, Pie Traynor 8.00
11 Cal Ripken Jr., Brooks Robinson 20.00
12 Tony Perez, Ted Kluszewski 5.00
13 Jason Giambi, Don Mattingly 15.00
14 Hank Greenberg, Jimmie Foxx 8.00
15 Ernie Banks, Willie McCovey 8.00
16 Jim Thome, Travis Fryman 6.00
17 Ted Kluszewski,Sean Casey 5.00
18 Gil Hodges, Johnny Mize 5.00
19 Brooks Robinson, Boog Powell 8.00
20 Bill Terry, George Sisler 5.00
21 Wade Boggs, Don Mattingly 10.00
22 Jason Giambi/Yanks, Carlos Delgado 3.00
23 Willie Stargell, Bill Madlock 4.00
24 Mark Grace, Matt Williams 4.00
25 Paul Molitor, George Brett 10.00
26 Carlos Delgado, Mo Vaughn 3.00
27 Bill Terry, Willie McCovey 4.00
28 Mike Sweeney, George Brett 10.00
29 Eddie Mathews, Ernie Banks 4.00
30 Eric Karros, Gil Hodges 3.00
31 Paul Molitor, Don Mattingly 8.00
32 Brooks Robinson,Rod Carew 3.00
33 Chipper Jones,Albert Pujols 6.00
34 Harry Heilmann, Hank Greenburg 3.00
35 Frank Thomas, Carlos Delgado 3.00
36 Jeff Bagwell, Todd Helton 3.00
37 Rafael Palmeiro, Fred McGriff 3.00
38 Cal Ripken Jr., Wade Boggs 8.00
39 Orlando Cepeda, Willie McCovey 3.00
40 John Olerud, Mark Grace 3.00

Cornerstones Memorabilia

No Pricing
Production 25 Sets

Fencebusters

NM/M

Common Player: 5.00
Rack Pack Exclusive
Derek Jeter 20.00
J.D. Drew 6.00
Brian Giles 5.00
Moises Alou 5.00
Rafael Palmeiro 6.00
Jeff Bagwell 8.00
Mike Piazza 15.00
Manny Ramirez 8.00
Tino Martinez 5.00
Jim Thome 5.00
Andruw Jones 8.00
Shawn Green 6.00
Frank Thomas 8.00
Miguel Tejada 6.00
Luis Gonzalez 5.00
Alex Rodriguez 12.50
Larry Walker 5.00
Barry Bonds 20.00
Todd Helton 8.00
Chipper Jones 10.00
Roberto Alomar 6.00
Jim Edmonds 5.00

National Patch Time

NM/M

Common Player: 20.00
Inserted 1:12 Jumbo
Barry Bonds/75 100.00
Todd Helton/110 40.00
Ivan Rodriguez/225 40.00
Kazuhiro Sasaki/310 20.00
Derek Jeter/65 100.00
Cal Ripken Jr/350 80.00
Darin Erstad/315 20.00
Jose Canseco/150 40.00
Miguel Tejada/55 35.00
Greg Maddux/775 30.00
Juan Gonzalez/50 50.00
J.D. Drew/210 25.00
Manny Ramirez/100 40.00
Pedro Martinez/45 50.00
Carlos Delgado/70 30.00
Magglio Ordonez/85 30.00
Pat Burrell/285 25.00
Adam Dunn/75 40.00
Alex Rodriguez/325 50.00

Wheelhouse

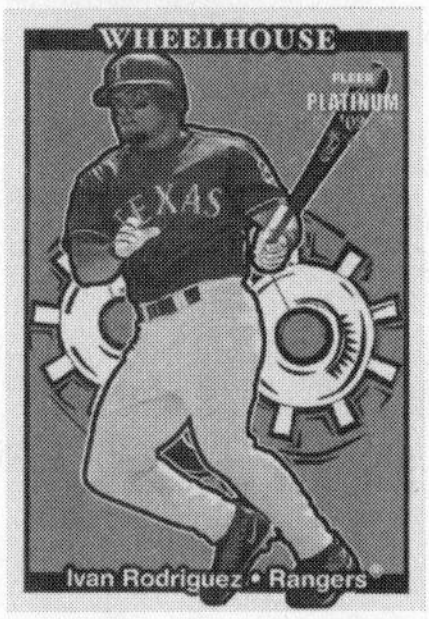

NM/M

Complete Set (20): 40.00
Common Player: 1.00
Inserted 1:12
1WH Derek Jeter 6.00
2WH Barry Bonds 6.00
3WH Luis Gonzalez 1.00
4WH Jason Giambi 1.00
5WH Ivan Rodriguez 1.50
6WH Mike Piazza 4.00
7WH Troy Glaus 1.50
8WH Nomar Garciaparra 4.00
9WH Juan Gonzalez 1.50
10WH Sammy Sosa 4.00
11WH Albert Pujols 5.00
12WH Ken Griffey Jr. 4.00
13WH Scott Rolen 1.00
14WH Jeff Bagwell 1.50
15WH Ichiro Suzuki 4.00
16WH Todd Helton 1.50
17WH Chipper Jones 3.00
18WH Alex Rodriguez 4.00
19WH Vladimir Guerrero 2.00
20WH Manny Ramirez 1.50

2002 Fleer Premium

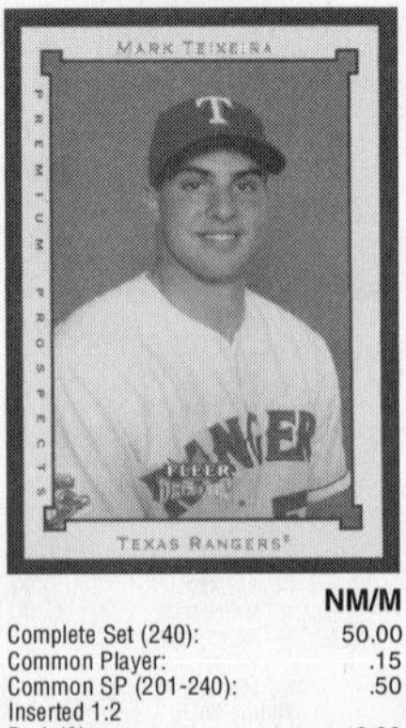

NM/M

Complete Set (240): 50.00
Common Player: .15
Common SP (201-240): .50
Inserted 1:2
Pack (8): 2.00
Box (24): 35.00
1 Garret Anderson .20
2 Derek Jeter 2.50
3 Ken Griffey Jr. 1.50
4 Luis Castillo .15
5 Richie Sexson .20
6 Mike Mussina .40
7 Ricky Henderson .75
8 Bud Smith .15
9 David Eckstein .15
10 Nomar Garciaparra 1.50
11 Barry Larkin .20
12 Cliff Floyd .15
13 Ben Sheets .20
14 Jorge Posada .30
15 Phil Nevin .15
16 Fernando Vina .15
17 Darin Erstad .65
18 Shea Hillenbrand .15
19 Todd Walker .15
20 Charles Johnson .15
21 Cristian Guzman .15
22 Mariano Rivera .30
23 Bubba Trammell .15
24 Brent Abernathy .15
25 Troy Glaus .75
26 Pedro J. Martinez .75
27 Dmitri Young .15
28 Derrek Lee .20
29 Torii Hunter .20
30 Alfonso Soriano .65
31 Rich Aurilia .15
32 Ben Grieve .15
33 Tim Salmon .30
34 Trot Nixon .15
35 Roberto Alomar .40
36 Mike Lowell .20
37 Jacque Jones .15
38 Bernie Williams .30
39 Barry Bonds 2.50
40 Toby Hall .15
41 Mo Vaughn .20
42 Hideo Nomo .65
43 Travis Fryman .15
44 Preston Wilson .15
45 Corey Koskie .15
46 Eric Chavez .30
47 Andres Galarraga .15
48 Greg Vaughn .15
49 Shawn Wooten .15
50 Manny Ramirez .75
51 Juan Gonzalez .75
52 Moises Alou .20
53 Joe Mays .15
54 Johnny Damon .35
55 Jeff Kent .20
56 Frank Catalanotto .15
57 Steve Finley .15
58 Jason Varitek .15
59 Kenny Lofton .20
60 Jeff Bagwell .75
61 Doug Mientkiewicz .15
62 Jermaine Dye .15
63 John Vander Wal .15
64 Gabe Kapler .15
65 Luis Gonzalez .30
66 Jon Lieber .15
67 C.C. Sabathia .15
68 Lance Berkman .20
69 Eric Milton .15
70 Jason Giambi .50
71 Ichiro Suzuki 1.50
72 Rafael Palmeiro .65
73 Mark Grace .30
74 Fred McGriff .20
75 Jim Thome .20
76 Craig Biggio .20
77 A.J. Pierzynski .15
78 Ramon Hernandez .15
79 Paul Abbott .15
80 Alex Rodriguez 2.00
81 Randy Johnson .75
82 Corey Patterson .20
83 Omar Vizquel .20
84 Richard Hidalgo .15
85 Luis Rivas .15
86 Tim Hudson .30
87 Bret Boone .20
88 Ivan Rodriguez .60
89 Junior Spivey .15
90 Sammy Sosa 1.50
91 Jeff Cirillo .15
92 Roy Oswalt .30
93 Orlando Cabrera .15
94 Terrence Long .15
95 Mike Cameron .15
96 Homer Bush .15
97 Reggie Sanders .15
98 Rondell White .20
99 Mike Hampton .15
100 Carlos Beltran .50
101 Vladimir Guerrero .75
102 Miguel Tejada .30
103 Freddy Garcia .15
104 Jose Cruz Jr. .15
105 Curt Schilling .45
106 Kerry Wood .65
107 Todd Helton .75
108 Neifi Perez .15
109 Javier Vazquez .15
110 Barry Zito .30
111 Edgar Martinez .20
112 Carlos Delgado .50
113 Matt Williams .20
114 Eric Young .15
115 Alex Ochoa .15
116 Mark Quinn .15
117 Jose Vidro .15
118 Bobby Abreu .20
119 David Bell .15
120 Brad Fullmer .15
121 Rafael Furcal .15
122 Ray Durham .15
123 Jose Ortiz .15
124 Joe Randa .15
125 Edgardo Alfonzo .15
126 Marlon Anderson .15
127 Jamie Moyer .15
128 Alex Gonzalez .15
129 Marcus Giles .15
130 Keith Foulke .15
131 Juan Pierre .15
132 Mike Sweeney .15
133 Matt Lawton .15
134 Pat Burrell .40
135 John Olerud .20
136 Raul Mondesi .20
137 Tom Glavine .40
138 Paul Konerko .20
139 Larry Walker .20
140 Adrian Beltre .35
141 Al Leiter .20
142 Mike Lieberthal .15
143 Kazuhiro Sasaki .15
144 Shannon Stewart .15
145 Andruw Jones .75
146 Carlos Lee .15
147 Roger Cedeno .15
148 Kevin Brown .20
149 Jay Payton .15
150 Scott Rolen .65
151 J.D. Drew .35
152 Chipper Jones 1.00
153 Magglio Ordonez .20
154 Tony Clark .15
155 Shawn Green .35
156 Mike Piazza 1.50
157 Jimmy Rollins .25
158 Jim Edmonds .20
159 Javy Lopez .20
160 Chris Singleton .15
161 Juan Encarnacion .15
162 Eric Karros .15
163 Tsuyoshi Shinjo .15
164 Brian Giles .20
165 Darryl Kile .15
166 Greg Maddux 1.00
167 Frank Thomas .75
168 Shane Halter .15
169 Paul LoDuca .15
170 Robin Ventura .15
171 Jason Kendall .15
172 Jason Hart .15
173 Brady Anderson .15
174 Jose Valentin .15
175 Bobby Higginson .15
176 Gary Sheffield .40
177 Roger Clemens 1.25
178 Aramis Ramirez .20
179 Matt Morris .20
180 Jeff Conine .15
181 Aaron Boone .15
182 Jose Macias .15
183 Jeromy Burnitz .15
184 Carl Everett .15
185 Trevor Hoffman .15
186 Placido Polanco .15
187 Jay Gibbons .15
188 Sean Casey .35
189 Josh Beckett .40
190 Jeffrey Hammonds .15
191 Chuck Knoblauch .15
192 Ryan Klesko .15
193 Albert Pujols 1.75
194 Chris Richard .15
195 Adam Dunn .50
196 A.J. Burnett .15
197 Geoff Jenkins .25
198 Tino Martinez .15
199 Ray Lankford .15
200 Edgar Renteria .20
201 Eric Cyr **RC** 1.00
202 Travis Phelps .50
203 Rick Bauer .50
204 Mark Prior 2.00
205 Wilson Betemit .50
206 Dewon Brazelton .50
207 Cody Ransom .50
208 Donnie Bridges .50
209 Justin Duchscherer .50
210 Nate Cornejo .50
211 Jason Romano .50
212 Juan Cruz .50
213 Pedro Santana .50
214 Ryan Drese .50
215 Bert Snow .50
216 Nate Frese .50
217 Rafael Soriano .50
218 Franklin Nunez **RC** .50
219 Tim Spooneybarger .50
220 Willie Harris .50
221 Billy Sylvester .50
222 Carlos Hernandez .50
223 Mark Teixeira 3.00
224 Adrian Hernandez .50
225 Andres Torres .50
226 Marlon Byrd .50
227 Juan Rivera .50
228 Adam Johnson .50
229 Justin Kaye .50
230 Kyle Kessel .50
231 Horacio Ramirez .50
232 Brandon Larson .50

233	Luis Lopez	.50
234	Robert Mackowiak	.50
235	Henry Mateo	.50
236	Corky Miller	.50
237	Greg Miller	.50
238	Dustan Mohr	.50
239	Bill Ortega	.50
240	Billy Hall	.50

Star Ruby

Stars (1-200):	4-8X
SP's (201-240):	1-2X
Production 125 Sets	

Diamond Stars

	NM/M
Complete Set (20):	100.00
Common Player:	2.00
Inserted 1:72	
1DS Pedro J. Martinez	4.00
2DS Derek Jeter	15.00
3DS Sammy Sosa	8.00
4DS Ken Griffey Jr.	8.00
5DS Chipper Jones	5.00
6DS Roger Clemens	10.00
7DS Ichiro Suzuki	8.00
8DS Jeff Bagwell	4.00
9DS Luis Gonzalez	2.00
10DS Manny Ramirez	4.00
11DS Alex Rodriguez	12.50
12DS Kazuhiro Sasaki	2.00
13DS Mike Piazza	8.00
14DS Vladimir Guerrero	4.00
15DS Randy Johnson	4.00
16DS Ivan Rodriguez	3.00
17DS Nomar Garciaparra	8.00
18DS Barry Bonds	15.00
19DS Todd Helton	4.00
20DS Greg Maddux	5.00

Diamond Stars Autograph

	NM/M
Numbered to 100	
Derek Jeter	125.00

Diamond Stars Game-Used

	NM/M
Common Player:	5.00
Inserted 1:105	
Barry Bonds/Jsy	20.00
Manny Ramirez/Jsy	8.00
Ivan Rodriguez/Jsy	8.00
Kazuhiro Sasaki/Jsy	5.00
Roger Clemens	20.00
Alex Rodriguez	15.00
Derek Jeter	25.00
Chipper Jones	10.00
Todd Helton	8.00
Luis Gonzalez	5.00
Mike Piazza	10.00
Nomar Garciaparra	25.00

Diamond Stars Game-Used Premium

	NM/M
Production 75 Sets	
Barry Bonds	60.00
Roger Clemens	60.00
Todd Helton	30.00
Chipper Jones	30.00
Manny Ramirez	25.00
Alex Rodriguez	50.00
Ivan Rodriguez	25.00
Luis Gonzalez	25.00
Mike Piazza	40.00
Kazuhiro Sasaki	20.00

Diamond Stars Dual Game-Used

	NM/M
Numbered to 100.	
Barry Bonds	60.00
Todd Helton	20.00
Derek Jeter	60.00
Chipper Jones	30.00
Mike Piazza	35.00
Manny Ramirez	25.00
Alex Rodriguez	40.00

Diamond Stars Dual Game-Used Premium

No Pricing
Production 25 Sets

International Pride

	NM/M
Complete Set (15):	10.00
Common Player:	.50
Inserted 1:6	
1IP Larry Walker	.50
2IP Albert Pujols	3.00
3IP Juan Gonzalez	.75
4IP Ichiro Suzuki	2.00
5IP Rafael Palmeiro	.65
6IP Carlos Delgado	.50
7IP Kazuhiro Sasaki	.50
8IP Vladimir Guerrero	.75
9IP Bobby Abreu	.50
10IP Ivan Rodriguez	.60
11IP Tsuyoshi Shinjo	.50
12IP Pedro J. Martinez	.75
13IP Andruw Jones	.75
14IP Sammy Sosa	2.00
15IP Chan Ho Park	.50

International Pride Game-Used

	NM/M
Common Player:	5.00
Inserted 1:90	
Carlos Delgado/Jsy	8.00
Juan Gonzalez/Jsy	8.00
Andruw Jones/Jsy	8.00
Pedro Martinez/Jsy	10.00
Rafael Palmeiro/Jsy	8.00
Chan Ho Park/Jsy	5.00
Albert Pujols/Jsy	20.00
Ivan Rodriguez/Bat	10.00
Kazuhiro Sasaki/Jsy	5.00
Tsuyoshi Shinjo/Jsy	5.00

International Pride Premium

	NM/M
Production 75 Sets	15.00
Carlos Delgado	25.00
Juan Gonzalez	40.00
Andruw Jones	40.00
Pedro J. Martinez	40.00
Chan Ho Park	15.00
Ivan Rodriguez	25.00
Tsuyoshi Shinjo	15.00
Rafael Palmeiro	25.00
Albert Pujols	75.00
Kazuhiro Sasaki	15.00

Legendary Dynasties

	NM/M
Complete Set (36):	125.00
Common Player:	1.50
Inserted 1:18	
Gold:	1X
Production 300 Sets	
1LD Honus Wagner	4.00
2LD Christy Mathewson	4.00
3LD Lou Gehrig	8.00
4LD Babe Ruth	12.00
5LD Jimmie Foxx	4.00
6LD Lefty Grove	2.00
7LD Al Simmons	1.50
8LD Bill Dickey	1.50
9LD Stan Musial	5.00
10LD Enos Slaughter	1.50
11LD Johnny Mize	2.00
12LD Yogi Berra	3.00
13LD Whitey Ford	3.00
14LD Jackie Robinson	8.00
15LD Duke Snider	3.00
16LD Roger Maris	3.00
17LD Jim Palmer	2.00
18LD Don Drysdale	2.00
19LD Brooks Robinson	3.00
20LD Rollie Fingers	1.50
21LD Reggie Jackson	3.00
22LD Joe Morgan	2.00
23LD Johnny Bench	5.00
24LD Thurman Munson	4.00
25LD Jose Canseco	2.50
26LD Tom Glavine	2.00
27LD Chipper Jones	4.00
28LD Greg Maddux	5.00
29LD Roberto Alomar	3.00
30LD David Cone	1.50
31LD Jim Thome	3.00
32LD Manny Ramirez	3.00
33LD Roger Clemens	6.00
34LD Derek Jeter	8.00
35LD Bernie Williams	2.50
36LD Alfonso Soriano	3.00

Legendary Dynasties Autographs

	NM/M
#'d to World Series Year	
Johnny Bench/76	80.00
Yogi Berra/51	60.00
Reggie Jackson/73	60.00
Derek Jeter/96	125.00

Legendary Dynasties Game-Used

	NM/M
Common Player:	8.00
Inserted 1:120	
Roberto Alomar/Jsy	8.00
Johnny Bench/Jsy	15.00
Yogi Berra/Bat/SP/75	50.00
Roger Clemens/Jsy	25.00
Bill Dickey/Jsy	25.00
Rollie Fingers/Jsy	8.00
Reggie Jackson/Bat	25.00
Derek Jeter/Bat	30.00
Chipper Jones/Jsy	10.00
Roger Maris/Pants/SP	50.00
Johnny Mize/Bat	15.00
Joe Morgan/Bat	8.00
Thurman.Munson/Bat	35.00
Jim Palmer/Jsy	10.00
Manny Ramirez/Jsy	10.00
Brooks Robinson/Bat	30.00
Jackie Robinson/SP/150	60.00
Babe Ruth/Bat	200.00
Duke Snider/Bat	30.00
Alfonso Soriano/Bat	10.00
Bernie Williams/Jsy	8.00

Legendary Dynasties Premium

	NM/M
Numbered to Highest win total.	
Rollie Fingers/93	15.00
Roger Clemens/114	50.00
Roger Maris/109	70.00
Roberto Alomar/96	25.00
Reggie Jackson/93	30.00
Manny Ramirez/99	25.00
Johnny Bench/108	35.00
Jim Palmer/109	20.00
Derek Jeter/114	80.00
Alfonso Soriano/99	30.00
Chipper Jones/106	30.00
Bernie Williams/114	20.00

On Base!

	NM/M
Complete Set (30):	125.00
Common Player:	2.00
#'d to 2001 OBP	
10B Frank Thomas/316	5.00
20B Ivan Rodriguez/347	5.00
30B Nomar Garciaparra/352	10.00
40B Ken Griffey Jr./365	8.00
50B Juan Gonzalez/370	4.00
60B Shawn Green/372	3.00
70B Vladimir Guerrero/377	5.00
80B Derek Jeter/377	15.00
90B Scott Rolen/378	5.00
100B Ichiro Suzuki/381	10.00
110B Mike Piazza/384	10.00
120B Bernie Williams/395	3.00
130B Moises Alou/396	3.00
140B Jeff Bagwell/397	4.00
150B Alex Rodriguez/399	10.00
160B Albert Pujols/403	10.00
170B Manny Ramirez/405	4.00
180B Carlos Delgado/408	4.00
190B Jim Edmonds/410	3.00
200B Roberto Alomar/415	3.00
210B Jim Thome/416	4.00
220B Gary Sheffield/417	3.00
230B Chipper Jones/427	5.00
240B Luis Gonzalez/429	2.00
250B Lance Berkman/430	3.00
260B Todd Helton/432	4.00
270B Sammy Sosa/437	10.00
280B Larry Walker/449	2.00
290B Jason Giambi/477	4.00
300B Barry Bonds/515	12.00

On Base! Game-Used

	NM/M
Common Player:	5.00

Production 100 Sets

Roberto Alomar	8.00
Moises Alou	5.00
Jeff Bagwell	8.00
Lance Berkman	5.00
Barry Bonds	20.00
Carlos Delgado	8.00
Jim Edmonds	6.00
Nomar Garciaparra	15.00
Jason Giambi	8.00
Juan Gonzalez	8.00
Luis Gonzalez	5.00
Shawn Green	5.00
Ken Griffey Jr.	20.00
Vladimir Guerrero	8.00
Todd Helton	8.00
Derek Jeter	25.00
Chipper Jones	10.00
Mike Piazza	15.00
Albert Pujols	20.00
Manny Ramirez	10.00
Alex Rodriguez	15.00
Ivan Rodriguez	10.00
Scott Rolen	10.00
Gary Sheffield	6.00
Sammy Sosa	20.00
Ichiro Suzuki	25.00
Frank Thomas	10.00
Jim Thome	8.00
Larry Walker	5.00
Bernie Williams	6.00

2002 Fleer Showcase

	NM/M
Complete Set (166):	225.00
Common Player:	.25
Common (126-141):	5.00
Production 500	
Common (141-166):	4.00
Production 1,500	
Pack (5):	3.00
Box (24):	60.00
1 Albert Pujols	2.00
2 Pedro J. Martinez	.75
3 Frank Thomas	.75
4 Gary Sheffield	.40
5 Roberto Alomar	.40
6 Luis Gonzalez	.35
7 Bobby Abreu	.25
8 Carlos Lee	.25
9 Preston Wilson	.25
10 Todd Helton	.75
11 Juan Gonzalez	.75
12 Chuck Knoblauch	.25
13 Jason Kendall	.25
14 Aaron Sele	.25
15 Greg Vaughn	.25
16 Fred McGriff	.25
17 Doug Mientkiewicz	.25
18 Richard Hidalgo	.25
19 Alfonso Soriano	.50
20 Matt Williams	.25
21 Bobby Higginson	.25
22 Mo Vaughn	.25
23 Andruw Jones	.75
24 Omar Vizquel	.25
25 Bret Boone	.25
26 Bernie Williams	.35
27 Rafael Furcal	.25
28 Jeff Bagwell	.75
29 Marty Cardova	.25
30 Lance Berkman	.25
31 Vernon Wells	.25
32 Garret Anderson	.25
33 Larry Bigbie	.25
34 Steve Finley	.25
35 Barry Bonds	3.00
36 Eric Chavez	.35
37 Tony Clark	.25
38 Roger Clemens	1.50
39 Adam Dunn	.50
40 Roger Cedeno	.25
41 Carlos Delgado	.50
42 Jermaine Dye	.25
43 Brian Jordan	.25
44 Darin Erstad	.65
45 Paul LoDuca	.25
46 Jim Edmonds	.50
47 Tom Glavine	.50
48 Cliff Floyd	.25
49 Jon Lieber	.25
50 Adrian Beltre	.40
51 Joel Pineiro	.25

#	Player	Price
52	Jim Thome	.25
53	Jimmy Rollins	.40
54	Pat Burrell	.40
55	Jeromy Burnitz	.25
56	Larry Walker	.25
57	Damon Minor	.25
58	John Olerud	.25
59	Carlos Beltran	.50
60	Vladimir Guerrero	.75
61	David Justice	.25
62	Phil Nevin	.25
63	Tino Martinez	.25
64	Curt Schilling	.75
65	Corey Patterson	.25
66	Aubrey Huff	.25
67	Mark Grace	.35
68	Rafael Palmeiro	.65
69	Jorge Posada	.35
70	Craig Biggio	.25
71	Manny Ramirez	.75
72	Mark Quinn	.25
73	Raul Mondesi	.25
74	Shawn Green	.40
75	Brian Giles	.25
76	Paul Konerko	.25
77	Troy Glaus	.75
78	Mike Mussina	.40
79	Greg Maddux	1.00
80	Edgar Martinez	.25
81	Jose Vidro	.25
82	Scott Rolen	.65
83	Ben Grieve	.25
84	Jeff Kent	.25
85	Magglio Ordonez	.25
86	Freddy Garcia	.25
87	Ivan Rodriguez	.65
88	Pokey Reese	.25
89	Shannon Stewart	.25
90	Randy Johnson	.75
91	Cristian Guzman	.25
92	Tsuyoshi Shinjo	.25
93	Steve Cox	.25
94	Mike Sweeney	.25
95	Robert Fick	.25
96	Sean Casey	.40
97	Tim Hudson	.35
98	Bud Smith	.25
99	Corey Koskie	.25
100	Richie Sexson	.25
101	Aramis Ramirez	.25
102	Barry Larkin	.25
103	Rich Aurilia	.25
104	Charles Johnson	.25
105	Ryan Klesko	.25
106	Ben Sheets	.25
107	J.D. Drew	.40
108	Jay Gibbons	.25
109	Kerry Wood	.65
110	C.C. Sabathia	.25
111	Eric Munson	.25
112	Josh Beckett	.40
113	Javier Vasquez	.25
114	Barry Zito	.35
115	Kazuhiro Sasaki	.25
116	Bubba Trammell	.25
117	Russell Branyan	.25
118	Todd Walker	.25
119	Mike Hampton	.25
120	Jeff Weaver	.25
121	Geoff Jenkins	.25
122	Edgardo Alfonzo	.25
123	Mike Lieberthal	.25
124	Mike Lowell	.25
125	Kevin Brown	.25
126	Derek Jeter	8.00
127	Ichiro Suzuki	5.00
128	Nomar Garciaparra	5.00
129	Ken Griffey Jr.	5.00
130	Jason Giambi	5.00
131	Alex Rodriguez	6.00
132	Chipper Jones	5.00
133	Mike Piazza	5.00
134	Sammy Sosa	5.00
135	Hideo Nomo	5.00
136	Kazuhisa Ishii RC	8.00
137	Satoru Komiyama RC	5.00
138	So Taguchi RC	6.00
139	Jorge Padilla RC	5.00
140	Rene Reyes RC	5.00
141	Jorge Nunez RC	5.00
142	Nelson Castro RC	4.00
143	Anderson Machado RC	4.00
144	Edwin Almonte RC	4.00
145	Luis Ugueto RC	4.00
146	Felix Escalona RC	4.00
147	Ron Calloway RC	4.00
148	Hansel Izquierdo RC	4.00
149	Mark Teixeira RC	6.00
150	Orlando Hudson RC	4.00
151	Aaron Cook RC	4.00
152	Aaron Taylor RC	4.00
153	Takahito Nomura RC	4.00
154	Matt Thornton RC	4.00
155	Mark Prior RC	6.00
156	Reed Johnson RC	6.00
157	Doug DeVore RC	4.00
158	Ben Howard RC	4.00
159	Francis Beltran RC	4.00
160	Brian Mallette RC	4.00
161	Sean Burroughs RC	6.00
162	Michael Restovich RC	4.00
163	Austin Kearns RC	6.00
164	Marlon Byrd RC	4.00
165	Hank Blalock RC	6.00
166	Mike Rivera	4.00

Legacy

Stars (1-125): 3-5X
Legacy (126-166): 1X
Production 175 Sets

Baseball's Best

		NM/M
Complete Set (20):		40.00
Common Player:		1.00
Inserted 1:8		
1	Derek Jeter	5.00
2	Barry Bonds	5.00
3	Mike Piazza	3.00
4	Alex Rodriguez	4.00
5	Pat Burrell	1.00
6	Rafael Palmeiro	1.00
7	Nomar Garciaparra	3.00
8	Todd Helton	1.50
9	Roger Clemens	2.50
10	Shawn Green	1.00
11	Chipper Jones	2.00
12	Pedro J. Martinez	1.50
13	Luis Gonzalez	1.00
14	Randy Johnson	1.50
15	Ichiro Suzuki	3.00
16	Ken Griffey Jr.	3.00
17	Vladimir Guerrero	1.50
18	Sammy Sosa	3.00
19	Jason Giambi	1.00
20	Albert Pujols	4.00

Baseball's Best Memorabilia

	NM/M
Common Player:	5.00
Inserted 1:24	
Golds:	1-2X
Production 100 Sets	
Derek Jeter/Jsy	20.00
Barry Bonds/Jsy	20.00
Mike Piazza/Jsy	10.00
Alex Rodriguez/Bat	15.00
Rafael Palmeiro/Jsy	8.00
Nomar Garciaparra/Jsy	10.00
Todd Helton/Bat	8.00
Roger Clemens/Jsy	15.00
Shawn Green/Jsy	5.00
Chipper Jones/Jsy	10.00
Pedro Martinez/Jsy	8.00
Luis Gonzalez/Jsy	5.00
Randy Johnson/Jsy	10.00
Ichiro Suzuki/Base	15.00
Ken Griffey Jr./Base	10.00
Vladimir Guerrero/Base	8.00
Sammy Sosa/Base	10.00
Jason Giambi/Base	8.00
Albert Pujols/Base	10.00

Baseball's Best Silver Auto.

	NM/M
Serial numbered to 400.	
Derek Jeter	125.00
Barry Bonds	200.00

Baseball's Best Gold Auto.

	NM/M
Serial numbered to 100.	
Derek Jeter	150.00
Barry Bonds	225.00

Derek Jeter's Legacy Collec.

	NM/M
Complete Set (22):	80.00
Common Jeter:	5.00
Production 1,000 Sets	
1-22 Derek Jeter	5.00

Derek Jeter's Legacy Collection Memorabilia

	NM/M
Quantity produced listed	
Derek Jeter/Jsy/300	75.00
Derek Jeter/Combo Jsy/175	90.00
Derek Jeter/World Series Ball/50	100.00
Derek Jeter/Glv/425	60.00

Sweet Sigs Wall

		NM/M
Common Player:		8.00
1	Bobby Abreu/70	20.00
2	Russell Branyan/200	8.00
5	Eric Chavez/108	15.00
6	Rafael Furcal/207	10.00
8	Brandon Inge/187	8.00
9	Jackson Melian/146	8.00
10	Xavier Nady/286	8.00
11	Jose Ortiz/116	8.00
12	Ben Sheets/150	20.00
13	Mike Sweeney/371	10.00

Sweet Sigs Lumber

		NM/M
Common Player:		5.00
1	Bobby Abreu/231	10.00
2	Russell Branyan/425	8.00
3	Pat Burrell/115	10.00
4	Sean Casey/64	20.00
5	Eric Chavez/256	10.00
6	Rafael Furcal/530	10.00
8	Brandon Inge/528	5.00
9	Jackson Melian/636	5.00
10	Xavier Nady/589	5.00
11	Jose Ortiz/515	8.00
12	Ben Sheets/458	15.00
13	Mike Sweeney/495	10.00

Sweet Sigs Leather

		NM/M
Common Player:		8.00
2	Russell Branyan/90	10.00
6	Rafael Furcal/92	15.00
8	Brandon Inge/122	8.00
10	Xavier Nady/301	8.00
11	Jose Ortiz/50	10.00
12	Ben Sheets/60	25.00
13	Mike Sweeney/103	15.00

2002 Fleer Tradition

		NM/M
Complete Set (500):		175.00
Common Player:		.15
Common SP (1-100):		1.50
Inserted 1:2		
Pack (10):		2.00
Box (36):		50.00
1	Barry Bonds	10.00
2	Cal Ripken Jr.	10.00
3	Tony Gwynn	5.00
4	Brad Radke	1.50
5	Jose Ortiz	1.50
6	Mark Mulder	1.50
7	Jon Lieber	1.50
8	John Olerud	1.50
9	Phil Nevin	1.50
10	Craig Biggio	1.50
11	Pedro Martinez	4.00
12	Fred McGriff	1.50
13	Vladimir Guerrero	4.00
14	Jason Giambi	3.00
15	Mark Kotsay	1.50
16	Bud Smith	1.50
17	Kevin Brown	1.50
18	Darin Erstad	3.00
19	Julio Franco	1.50
20	C.C. Sabathia	1.50
21	Larry Walker	1.50
22	Doug Mientkiewicz	1.50
23	Luis Gonzalez	2.00
24	Albert Pujols	8.00
25	Brian Lawrence	1.50
26	Al Leiter	1.50
27	Mike Sweeney	1.50
28	Jeff Weaver	1.50
29	Matt Morris	1.50
30	Hideo Nomo	4.00
31	Tom Glavine	2.50
32	Magglio Ordonez	1.50
33	Roberto Alomar	2.50
34	Roger Cedeno	1.50
35	Greg Vaughn	1.50
36	Chan Ho Park	1.50
37	Rich Aurilia	1.50
38	Tsuyoshi Shinjo	1.50
39	Eric Young	1.50
40	Bobby Higginson	1.50
41	Marlon Anderson	1.50
42	Mark Grace	2.00
43	Steve Cox	1.50
44	Cliff Floyd	1.50
45	Brian Roberts	1.50
46	Paul Konerko	1.50
47	Brandon Duckworth	1.50
48	Josh Beckett	2.50
49	David Ortiz	2.50
50	Geoff Jenkins	1.50
51	Ruben Sierra	1.50
52	John Franco	1.50
53	Einar Diaz	1.50
54	Luis Castillo	1.50
55	Mark Quinn	1.50
56	Shea Hillenbrand	1.50
57	Rafael Palmeiro	3.00
58	Paul O'Neill	1.50
59	Andruw Jones	4.00
60	Lance Berkman	1.50
61	Jimmy Rollins	2.00
62	Jose Hernandez	1.50
63	Rusty Greer	1.50
64	Wade Miller	1.50
65	David Eckstein	1.50
66	Jose Valentin	1.50
67	Javier Vazquez	1.50
68	Roger Clemens	6.00
69	Omar Vizquel	1.50
70	Roy Oswalt	1.50
71	Shannon Stewart	1.50
72	Byung-Hyun Kim	1.50
73	Jay Gibbons	1.50
74	Barry Larkin	1.50
75	Brian Giles	1.50
76	Andres Galarraga	1.50
77	Sammy Sosa	6.00
78	Manny Ramirez	4.00
79	Carlos Delgado	2.50
80	Jorge Posada	1.50
81	Todd Ritchie	1.50
82	Russ Ortiz	1.50
83	Brent Mayne	1.50
84	Mike Mussina	3.00
85	Raul Mondesi	1.50
86	Mark Loretta	1.50
87	Tim Raines	1.50
88	Ichiro Suzuki	6.00
89	Juan Pierre	1.50
90	Adam Dunn	2.50
91	Jason Tyner	1.50
92	Miguel Tejada	1.50
93	Elpidio Guzman	1.50
94	Freddy Garcia	1.50
95	Marcus Giles	1.50
96	Junior Spivey	1.50
97	Aramis Ramirez	1.50
98	Jose Rijo	1.50
99	Paul LoDuca	1.50
100	Mike Cameron	1.50
101	Alex Hernandez	.15
102	Benji Gil	.15
103	Benito Santiago	.15
104	Bobby Abreu	.15
105	Brad Penny	.15
106	Calvin Murray	.15
107	Chad Durbin	.15
108	Chris Singleton	.15
109	Chris Carpenter	.15
110	David Justice	.15
111	Eric Chavez	.25
112	Fernando Tatis	.15
113	Frank Castillo	.15
114	Jason LaRue	.15
115	Jim Edmonds	.15
116	Joe Kennedy	.15
117	Jose Jimenez	.15
118	Josh Towers	.15
119	Junior Herndon	.15
120	Luke Prokopec	.15
121	Mac Suzuki	.15
122	Mark DeRosa	.15
123	Marty Cordova	.15
124	Michael Tucker	.15
125	Michael Young	.15
126	Robin Ventura	.15
127	Shane Halter	.15
128	Shane Reynolds	.15
129	Tony Womack	.15
130	A.J. Pierzynski	.15
131	Aaron Rowand	.15
132	Antonio Alfonseca	.15
133	Arthur Rhodes	.15
134	Bob Wickman	.15
135	Brady Clark	.15
136	Chad Hermansen	.15
137	Marlon Byrd	.15
138	Dan Wilson	.15
139	David Cone	.15
140	Dean Palmer	.15
141	Denny Neagle	.15
142	Derek Jeter	2.50
143	Erubiel Durazo	.15
144	Felix Rodriguez	.15

145	Jason Hart	.15
146	Jay Bell	.15
147	Jeff Suppan	.15
148	Jeff Zimmerman	.15
149	Kerry Wood	.65
150	Kerry Robinson	.15
151	Kevin Appier	.15
152	Michael Barrett	.15
153	Mo Vaughn	.15
154	Rafael Furcal	.15
155	Sidney Ponson	.15
156	Terry Adams	.15
157	Tim Redding	.15
158	Toby Hall	.15
159	Aaron Sele	.15
160	Bartolo Colon	.15
161	Brad Ausmus	.15
162	Carlos Pena	.15
163	Jace Brewer	.15
164	David Wells	.15
165	David Segui	.15
166	Derek Lowe	.15
167	Derek Bell	.15
168	Jason Grabowski	.15
169	Johnny Damon	.25
170	Jose Mesa	.15
171	Juan Encarnacion	.15
172	Ken Caminiti	.15
173	Ken Griffey Jr.	1.50
174	Luis Rivas	.15
175	Mariano Rivera	.25
176	Mark Grudzielanek	.15
177	Mark McGwire	2.00
178	Mike Bordick	.15
179	Mike Hampton	.15
180	Nick Bierbrodt	.15
181	Paul Byrd	.15
182	Robb Nen	.15
183	Ryan Dempster	.15
184	Ryan Klesko	.15
185	Scott Spiezio	.15
186	Scott Strickland	.15
187	Todd Zeile	.15
188	Tom Gordon	.15
189	Troy Glaus	.75
190	Matt Williams	.15
191	Wes Helms	.15
192	Jerry Hairston Jr.	.15
193	Brook Fordyce	.15
194	Nomar Garciaparra	1.50
195	Kevin Tapani	.15
196	Mark Buehrle	.15
197	Dmitri Young	.15
198	John Rocker	.15
199	Juan Uribe	.15
200	Matt Anderson	.15
201	Alex Gonzalez	.15
202	Julio Lugo	.15
203	Roberto Hernandez	.15
204	Richie Sexson	.15
205	Corey Koskie	.15
206	Tony Armas Jr.	.15
207	Rey Ordonez	.15
208	Orlando Hernandez	.15
209	Pokey Reese	.15
210	Mike Lieberthal	.15
211	Kris Benson	.15
212	Jermaine Dye	.15
213	Livan Hernandez	.15
214	Bret Boone	.15
215	Dustin Hermanson	.15
216	Placido Polanco	.15
217	Jesus Colome	.15
218	Alex Gonzalez	.15
219	Adam Everett	.15
220	Adam Piatt	.15
221	Brad Fullmer	.15
222	Brian Buchanan	.15
223	Chipper Jones	1.00
224	Chuck Finley	.15
225	David Bell	.15
226	Jack Wilson	.25
227	Jason Bere	.15
228	Jeff Conine	.15
229	Jeff Bagwell	.75
230	Joe McEwing	.15
231	Kip Wells	.15
232	Mike Lansing	.15
233	Neifi Perez	.15
234	Omar Daal	.15
235	Reggie Sanders	.15
236	Shawn Wooten	.15
237	Shawn Chacon	.15
238	Shawn Estes	.15
239	Steve Sparks	.15
240	Steve Kline	.15
241	Tino Martinez	.15
242	Tyler Houston	.15
243	Xavier Nady	.15
244	Bengie Molina	.15
245	Ben Davis	.15
246	Casey Fossum	.15
247	Chris Stynes	.15
248	Danny Graves	.15
249	Pedro Feliz	.15
250	Darren Oliver	.15
251	Dave Veres	.15
252	Deivi Cruz	.15
253	Desi Relaford	.15
254	Devon White	.15
255	Edgar Martinez	.15
256	Eric Munson	.15
257	Eric Karros	.15
258	Homer Bush	.15
259	Jason Kendall	.15
260	Javy Lopez	.15
261	Keith Foulke	.15
262	Keith Ginter	.15
263	Nick Johnson	.15
264	Pat Burrell	.35
265	Ricky Gutierrez	.15
266	Russ Johnson	.15
267	Steve Finley	.15
268	Terrence Long	.15
269	Tony Batista	.15
270	Torii Hunter	.15
271	Vinny Castilla	.15
272	A.J. Burnett	.15
273	Adrian Beltre	.35
274	Alex Rodriguez	2.00
275	Armando Benitez	.15
276	Billy Koch	.15
277	Brady Anderson	.15
278	Brian Jordan	.15
279	Carlos Febles	.15
280	Daryle Ward	.15
281	Eli Marrero	.15
282	Garret Anderson	.15
283	Jack Cust	.15
284	Jacque Jones	.15
285	Jamie Moyer	.15
286	Jeffrey Hammonds	.15
287	Jim Thome	.15
288	Jon Garland	.15
289	Jose Offerman	.15
290	Matt Stairs	.15
291	Orlando Cabrera	.15
292	Ramiro Mendoza	.15
293	Ray Durham	.15
294	Rickey Henderson	.75
295	Rob Mackowiak	.15
296	Scott Rolen	.65
297	Tim Hudson	.25
298	Todd Helton	.75
299	Tony Clark	.15
300	B.J. Surhoff	.15
301	Bernie Williams	.30
302	Bill Mueller	.15
303	Chris Richard	.15
304	Craig Paquette	.15
305	Curt Schilling	.40
306	Damian Jackson	.15
307	Derrek Lee	.15
308	Eric Milton	.15
309	Frank Catalanotto	.15
310	J.T. Snow	.15
311	Jared Sandberg	.15
312	Jason Varitek	.15
313	Jeff Cirillo	.15
314	Jeromy Burnitz	.15
315	Joe Crede	.15
316	Joel Pineiro	.15
317	Jose Cruz Jr.	.15
318	Kevin Young	.15
319	Marquis Grissom	.15
320	Moises Alou	.15
321	Randall Simon	.15
322	Royce Clayton	.15
323	Tim Salmon	.25
324	Travis Fryman	.15
325	Travis Lee	.15
326	Vance Wilson	.15
327	Jarrod Washburn	.15
328	Ben Petrick	.15
329	Ben Grieve	.15
330	Carl Everett	.15
331	Eric Byrnes	.15
332	Doug Glanville	.15
333	Edgardo Alfonzo	.15
334	Ellis Burks	.15
335	Gabe Kapler	.15
336	Gary Sheffield	.25
337	Greg Maddux	1.00
338	J.D. Drew	.25
339	Jamey Wright	.15
340	Jeff Kent	.15
341	Jeremy Giambi	.15
342	Joe Randa	.15
343	Joe Mays	.15
344	Jose Macias	.15
345	Kazuhiro Sasaki	.15
346	Mike Kinkade	.15
347	Mike Lowell	.15
348	Randy Johnson	.75
349	Randy Wolf	.15
350	Richard Hidalgo	.15
351	Ron Coomer	.15
352	Sandy Alomar	.15
353	Sean Casey	.25
354	Trevor Hoffman	.15
355	Adam Eaton	.15
356	Alfonso Soriano	.50
357	Barry Zito	.25
358	Billy Wagner	.15
359	Brent Abernathy	.15
360	Bret Prinz	.15
361	Carlos Beltran	.40
362	Carlos Guillen	.15
363	Charles Johnson	.15
364	Cristian Guzman	.15
365	Damion Easley	.15
366	Darryl Kile	.15
367	Delino DeShields	.15
368	Eric Davis	.15
369	Frank Thomas	.75
370	Ivan Rodriguez	.65
371	Jay Payton	.15
372	Jeff D'Amico	.15
373	John Burkett	.15
374	Melvin Mora	.15
375	Ramon Ortiz	.15
376	Robert Person	.15
377	Russell Branyan	.15
378	Shawn Green	.25
379	Todd Hollandsworth	.15
380	Tony McKnight	.15
381	Trot Nixon	.15
382	Vernon Wells	.15
383	Troy Percival	.15
384	Albie Lopez	.15
385	Alex Ochoa	.15
386	Andy Pettitte	.25
387	Brandon Inge	.15
388	Bubba Trammell	.15
389	Corey Patterson	.15
390	Damian Rolls	.15
391	Dee Brown	.15
392	Edgar Renteria	.15
393	Eric Gagne	.35
394	Jason Johnson	.15
395	Jeff Nelson	.15
396	John Vander Wal	.15
397	Johnny Estrada	.15
398	Jose Canseco	.40
399	Juan Gonzalez	.75
400	Kevin Millwood	.15
401	Lee Stevens	.15
402	Matt Lawton	.15
403	Mike Lamb	.15
404	Octavio Dotel	.15
405	Ramon Hernandez	.15
406	Ruben Quevedo	.15
407	Todd Walker	.15
408	Troy O'Leary	.15
409	Wascar Serrano	.15
410	Aaron Boone	.15
411	Aubrey Huff	.15
412	Ben Sheets	.15
413	Carlos Lee	.15
414	Chuck Knoblauch	.15
415	Steve Karsay	.15
416	Dante Bichette	.15
417	David Dellucci	.15
418	Esteban Loaiza	.15
419	Fernando Vina	.15
420	Ismael Valdes	.15
421	Jason Isringhausen	.15
422	Jeff Shaw	.15
423	John Smoltz	.15
424	Jose Vidro	.15
425	Kenny Lofton	.15
426	Mark Little	.15
427	Mark McLemore	.15
428	Marvin Benard	.15
429	Mike Piazza	1.50
430	Pat Hentgen	.15
431	Preston Wilson	.15
432	Rick Helling	.15
433	Robert Fick	.15
434	Rondell White	.15
435	Adam Kennedy	.15
436	David Espinosa	.15
437	Dewon Brazelton	.15
438	Drew Henson	.25
439	Juan Cruz	.15
440	Jason Jennings	.15
441	Carlos Garcia	.15
442	Carlos Hernandez	.15
443	Wilkin Ruan	.15
444	Wilson Betemit	.15
445	Horacio Ramirez	.15
446	Danys Baez	.15
447	Abraham Nunez	.15
448	Josh Hamilton	.50
449	Chris George	.15
450	Rick Bauer	.15
451	Donnie Bridges	.15
452	Erick Almonte	.15
453	Cory Aldridge	.15
454	Ryan Drese	.15
455	Jason Romano	.15
456	Corky Miller	.15
457	Rafael Soriano	.15
458	Mark Prior	.75
459	Mark Teixeira	.50
460	Adrian Hernandez	.15
461	Tim Spooneybarger	.15
462	Bill Ortega	.15
463	D'Angelo Jimenez	.15
464	Andres Torres	.15
465	Alexis Gomez	.15
466	Angel Berroa	.15
467	Henry Mateo	.15
468	Endy Chavez	.15
469	Billy Sylvester	.15
470	Nate Frese	.15
471	Luis Gonzalez	.25
472	Barry Bonds	2.50
473	Rich Aurilia	.15
474	Albert Pujols	2.00
475	Todd Helton	.75
476	Moises Alou	.15
477	Lance Berkman	.15
478	Brian Giles	.15
479	Cliff Floyd	.15
480	Sammy Sosa	1.50
481	Shawn Green	.30
482	Jon Lieber	.15
483	Matt Morris	.15
484	Curt Schilling	.40
485	Randy Johnson	.75
486	Manny Ramirez	.75
487	Ichiro Suzuki	1.50
488	Juan Gonzalez	.75
489	Derek Jeter	2.50
490	Alex Rodriguez	2.00
491	Bret Boone	.15
492	Roberto Alomar	.30
493	Jason Giambi	.50
494	Rafael Palmeiro	.65
495	Doug Mientkiewicz	.15
496	Jim Thome	.15
497	Freddy Garcia	.15
498	Mark Buehrle	.15
499	Mark Mulder	.15
500	Roger Clemens	1.25

Diamond Tributes

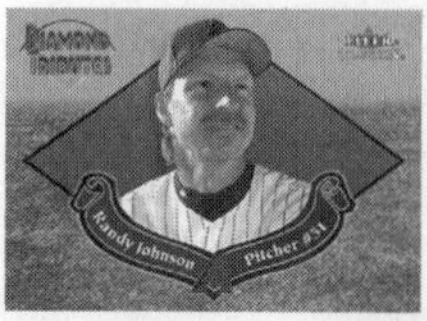

		NM/M
Complete Set (15):		15.00
Common Player:		.50
Inserted 1:6		
1DT	Cal Ripken Jr.	3.00
2DT	Tony Gwynn	1.00
3DT	Derek Jeter	3.00
4DT	Pedro Martinez	.75
5DT	Mark McGwire	2.50
6DT	Sammy Sosa	2.00
7DT	Barry Bonds	3.00
8DT	Roger Clemens	1.50
9DT	Mike Piazza	2.00
10DT	Alex Rodriguez	2.50
11DT	Randy Johnson	.75
12DT	Chipper Jones	1.00
13DT	Nomar Garciaparra	2.00
14DT	Ichiro Suzuki	2.00
15DT	Jason Giambi	.50

Grass Roots

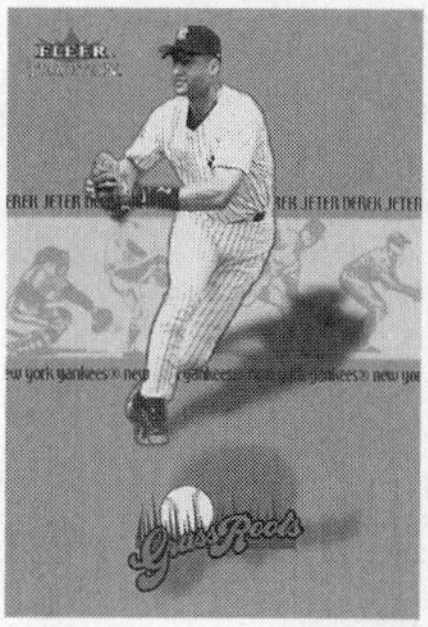

		NM/M
Complete Set (10):		15.00
Common Player:		.75
Inserted 1:18		
1GR	Barry Bonds	5.00
2GR	Alex Rodriguez	4.00
3GR	Derek Jeter	5.00
4GR	Greg Maddux	2.50
5GR	Ivan Rodriguez	1.00
6GR	Cal Ripken Jr.	5.00
7GR	Bernie Williams	.75
8GR	Jeff Bagwell	1.50
9GR	Scott Rolen	1.00
10GR	Larry Walker	.75

Grass Roots Patch

		NM/M
Production 50 Sets		
	Barry Bonds	100.00
	Alex Rodriguez	75.00
	Greg Maddux	50.00
	Ivan Rodriguez	25.00
	Cal Ripken Jr.	100.00
	Bernie Williams	25.00
	Jeff Bagwell	40.00
	Scott Rolen	30.00
	Larry Walker	20.00

Heads Up

		NM/M
Complete Set (10):		45.00
Common Player:		1.00
Inserted 1:36		
1HU	Derek Jeter	8.00
2HU	Ichiro Suzuki	5.00
3HU	Sammy Sosa	5.00
4HU	Mike Piazza	5.00
5HU	Ken Griffey Jr.	5.00
6HU	Alex Rodriguez	6.00
7HU	Barry Bonds	8.00
8HU	Nomar Garciaparra	5.00

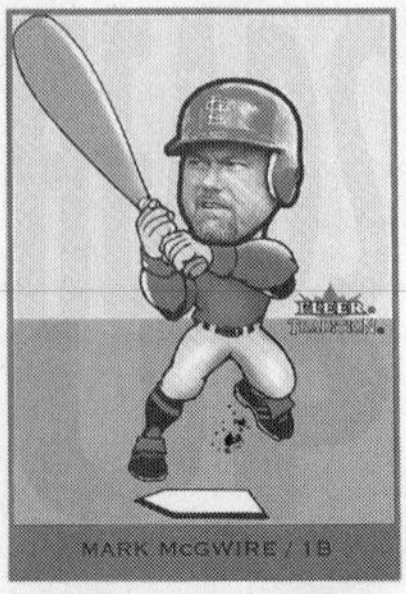
MARK McGWIRE / 1B

9HU	Mark McGwire	6.00
10HU	Cal Ripken Jr.	8.00

Lumber Company

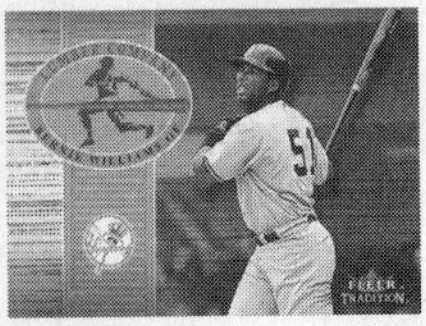

		NM/M
Complete Set (30):		40.00
Common Player:		1.00
Inserted 1:12		
1LC	Moises Alou	1.00
2LC	Luis Gonzalez	1.00
3LC	Todd Helton	2.50
4LC	Mike Piazza	4.00
5LC	J.D. Drew	1.50
6LC	Albert Pujols	5.00
7LC	Chipper Jones	3.00
8LC	Manny Ramirez	2.50
9LC	Miguel Tejada	1.00
10LC	Curt Schilling	1.50
11LC	Alex Rodriguez	5.00
12LC	Barry Larkin	1.00
13LC	Nomar Garciaparra	4.00
14LC	Cliff Floyd	1.00
15LC	Alfonso Soriano	1.50
16LC	Sean Casey	1.00
17LC	Scott Rolen	2.00
18LC	Jose Ortiz	1.00
19LC	Corey Patterson	1.00
20LC	Joe Crede	1.00
21LC	Jace Brewer	1.00
22LC	Derek Jeter	6.00
23LC	Jim Thome	1.00
24LC	Frank Thomas	2.50
25LC	Shawn Green	1.00
26LC	Drew Henson	1.00
27LC	Jimmy Rollins	1.50
28LC	Dave Justice	1.00
29LC	Roberto Alomar	1.50
30LC	Bernie Williams	1.00

Lumber Company Game- Used

	NM/M
Common Player:	5.00
Inserted 1:72	
Moises Alou	5.00
Luis Gonzalez	5.00
Todd Helton	8.00
Mike Piazza	12.00
J.D. Drew	6.00
Albert Pujols	15.00
Chipper Jones	10.00
Manny Ramirez	8.00
Miguel Tejada	6.00
Curt Schilling	6.00
Alex Rodriguez	15.00
Barry Larkin	5.00
Nomar Garciaparra	12.00
Cliff Floyd	5.00
Alfonso Soriano	8.00
Sean Casey	6.00
Scott Rolen	8.00
Jose Ortiz	5.00
Corey Patterson	5.00
Joe Crede	5.00
Jace Brewer	5.00
Derek Jeter	25.00
Jim Thome	5.00
Frank Thomas	8.00
Shawn Green	5.00
Drew Henson	5.00
Jimmy Rollins	5.00
Dave Justice	5.00
Roberto Alomar	6.00
Bernie Williams	5.00

This Day in History

		NM/M
Complete Set (29):		120.00
Common Player:		1.50
Inserted 1:18		

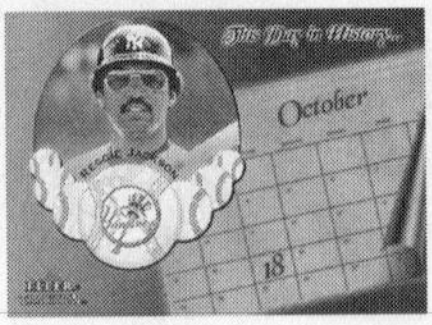
This Day in History
October
18

1	Cal Ripken Jr.	10.00
2	Barry Bonds	10.00
3	George Brett	4.00
4	Tony Gwynn	3.00
5	Nolan Ryan	10.00
6	Reggie Jackson	3.00
7	Paul Molitor	2.00
8	Ichiro Suzuki	5.00
9	Alex Rodriguez	8.00
10	Don Mattingly	6.00
11	Sammy Sosa	5.00
12	Mark McGwire	8.00
13	Derek Jeter	10.00
14	Roger Clemens	4.00
15	Jim "Catfish" Hunter	1.50
16	Greg Maddux	3.00
17	Ken Griffey Jr.	5.00
18	Gil Hodges	1.50
19	Edgar Martinez	1.50
20	Mike Piazza	5.00
21	Jimmie Foxx	1.50
22	Albert Pujols	6.00
23	Chipper Jones	3.00
24	Not Issued	
25	Jeff Bagwell	2.00
26	Nomar Garciaparra	5.00
27	Randy Johnson	2.00
28	Todd Helton	2.00
29	Ted Kluszewski	1.50
30	Ivan Rodriguez	1.75

This Day in History Autographs

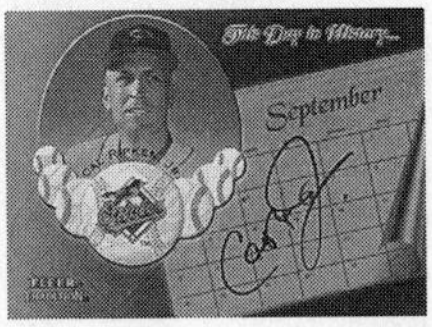
This Day in History
September

		NM/M
Common Player:		
3	Derek Jeter/100	100.00
4	Randy Johnson/75	50.00
5	Don Mattingly/50	90.00
7	Albert Pujols/50	200.00
8	Cal Ripken Jr./50	125.00

This Day in History Game Used

	NM/M
Common Player:	
Jeff Bagwell/Bat/100	15.00
Barry Bonds/Jsy/250	40.00
Roger Clemens/Jsy/150	30.00
Jimmie Foxx/Bat/250	40.00
Todd Helton/Bat/150	15.00
Jim "Catfish" Hunter/ Jsy/250	15.00
Derek Jeter/Jsy/250	40.00
Greg Maddux/Jsy/100	20.00
Mike Piazza/Bat/150	20.00
Alex Rodriguez/Hat/250	30.00

2002 Fleer Tradition Update

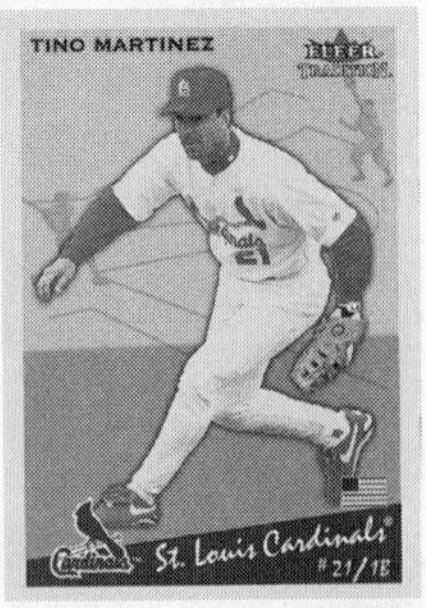
TINO MARTINEZ
St. Louis Cardinals
#21/1B

		NM/M
Complete Set (400):		75.00
Common Player:		.15
Common SP (1-100):		.50
Inserted 1:1		
Pack (10):		1.50
Box (36):		35.00
1	P.J. Bevis **RC**	.50
2	Michael Crudale **RC**	.50
3	Ben Howard **RC**	.75
4	Travis Driskill **RC**	.50
5	Reed Johnson **RC**	.50
6	Kyle Kane **RC**	.50
7	Deivis Santos	.50
8	Tim Kalita **RC**	.50
9	Brandon Puffer **RC**	.50
10	Chris Snelling **RC**	1.00
11	Juan Brito **RC**	.50
12	Tyler Yates **RC**	.50
13	Victor Alvarez **RC**	.50
14	Takahito Nomura **RC**	.50
15	Ron Calloway **RC**	.50
16	Satoru Komiyama **RC**	.50
17	Julius Matos **RC**	.50
18	Jorge Nunez **RC**	.50
19	Anderson Machado **RC**	.50
20	Scotty Layfield **RC**	.50
21	Aaron Cook **RC**	.50
22	Alex Pelaez **RC**	.50
23	Corey Thurman **RC**	.50
24	Nelson Castro **RC**	.50
25	Jeff Austin **RC**	.50
26	Felix Escalona **RC**	.50
27	Luis Ugueto **RC**	.50
28	Jaime Cerda **RC**	.50
29	J.J. Trujillo **RC**	.50
30	Rodrigo Rosario **RC**	.50
31	Jorge Padilla **RC**	.50
32	Shawn Sedlacek **RC**	.50
33	Nate Field **RC**	.50
34	Earl Snyder **RC**	.75
35	Miguel Asencio **RC**	.50
36	Ken Huckaby **RC**	.50
37	Valentino Pascucci	.50
38	So Taguchi **RC**	1.00
39	Brian Mallette **RC**	.50
40	Kazuhisa Ishii **RC**	2.00
41	Matt Thornton	.50
42	Mark Corey	.50
43	Kirk Saarloos	.50
44	Brandon Bracke	.50
45	Hansel Izquierdo **RC**	.50
46	Rene Reyes **RC**	.50
47	Luis Garcia	.50
48	Jason Simontacchi **RC**	.50
49	John Ennis **RC**	.75
50	Franklyn German **RC**	.50
51	Aaron Guiel **RC**	.50
52	Howie Clark **RC**	.50
53	David Ross **RC**	.50
54	Walt McKeel	.50
55	Francis Beltran **RC**	.50
56	Barry Wesson **RC**	.50
57	Runelvys Hernandez **RC**	.50
58	Oliver Perez **RC**	2.00
59	Ryan Bukvich **RC**	.50
60	Steve Kent **RC**	.50
61	Julio Mateo **RC**	.50
62	Jason Jimenez	.50
63	Jayson Durocher **RC**	.75
64	Kevin Frederick **RC**	.50
65	Kevin Gryboski **RC**	.50
66	Edwin Almonte **RC**	.50
67	John Foster **RC**	.50
68	Doug DeVore **RC**	1.00
69	Tom Shearn **RC**	.50
70	Colin Young **RC**	.50
71	Jon Adkins **RC**	.50
72	Wilbert Nieves **RC**	.50
73	Matt Duff	.50
74	Carl Sadler **RC**	.50
75	Jason Kershner	.50
76	Brandon Backe **RC**	.50
77	Wilson Valdez **RC**	.50
78	Chris Baker **RC**	.50
79	Ryan Jamison	.50
80	Steve Bechler **RC**	.75
81	Allan Simpson **RC**	.50
82	Aaron Taylor **RC**	.50
83	Kevin Cash **RC**	.50
84	Chone Figgins **RC**	1.00
85	Clay Condrey **RC**	.50
86	Shane Nance **RC**	.50
87	Freddy Sanchez **RC**	.50
88	Jim Rushford **RC**	.50
89	Jeriome Robertson **RC**	.50
90	Trey Lunsford **RC**	.50
91	Cody McKay **RC**	.50
92	Trey Hodges **RC**	.50
93	Hee Seop Choi	1.00
94	Joe Borchard	.50
95	Orlando Hudson	.50
96	Carl Crawford	.50
97	Mark Prior	2.00
98	Brett Myers	.50
99	Kenny Lofton	.50
100	Cliff Floyd	.50
101	Randy Winn	.15
102	Ryan Dempster	.15
103	Josh Phelps	.15
104	Marcus Giles	.15
105	Rickey Henderson	.75
106	Jose Leon	.15
107	Tino Martinez	.15
108	Greg Norton	.15
109	Odalis Perez	.15
110	J.C. Romero	.15
111	Gary Sheffield	.35
112	Ismael Valdes	.15
113	Juan Acevedo	.15
114	Ben Broussard	.15
115	Deivi Cruz	.15
116	Geronimo Gil	.15
117	Eric Hinske	.15
118	Ted Lilly	.15
119	Quinton McCracken	.15
120	Antonio Alfonseca	.15
121	Brent Abernathy	.15
122	Johnny Damon	.25
123	Francisco Cordova	.15
124	Sterling Hitchcock	.15
125	Vladimir Nunez	.15
126	Andres Galarraga	.15
127	Timoniel Perez	.15
128	Tsuyoshi Shinjo	.15
129	Joe Girardi	.15
130	Roberto Alomar	.35
131	Ellis Burks	.15
132	Mike DeJean	.15
133	Alex Gonzalez	.15
134	Johan Santana	.35
135	Kenny Lofton	.15
136	Juan Encarnacion	.15
137	Dewon Brazelton	.15
138	Jeromy Burnitz	.15
139	Elmer Dessens	.15
140	Juan Gonzalez	.75
141	Todd Hundley	.15
142	Tomokazu Ohka	.15
143	Robin Ventura	.15
144	Rodrigo Lopez	.15
145	Ruben Sierra	.15
146	Jason Phillips	.15
147	Ryan Rupe	.15
148	Kevin Appier	.15
149	Sean Burroughs	.15
150	Masato Yoshii	.15
151	Juan Diaz	.15
152	Tony Graffanino	.15
153	Raul Ibanez	.15
154	Kevin Mench	.15
155	Pedro Astacio	.15
156	Brent Butler	.15
157	Kirk Rueter	.15
158	Eddie Guardado	.15
159	Hideki Irabu	.15
160	Wendell Magee	.15
161	Antonio Osuna	.15
162	Jose Vizcaino	.15
163	Danny Bautista	.15
164	Vinny Castilla	.15
165	Chris Singleton	.15
166	Mark Redman	.15
167	Olmedo Saenz	.15
168	Scott Erickson	.15
169	Ty Wigginton	.15
170	Jason Isringhausen	.15
171	Lou Merloni	.15
172	Chris Magruder	.15
173	Brandon Berger	.15
174	Roger Cedeno	.15
175	Kelvim Escobar	.15
176	Jose Guillen	.15
177	Damian Jackson	.15
178	Eric Owens	.15
179	Angel Berroa	.15
180	Alex Cintron	.15
181	Jeff Weaver	.15
182	Damon Minor	.15
183	Bobby Estalella	.15
184	David Justice	.15
185	Roy Halladay	.25
186	Brian Jordan	.15
187	Mike Maroth	.15
188	Pokey Reese	.15
189	Rey Sanchez	.15
190	Hank Blalock	.50
191	Jeff Cirillo	.15
192	Dmitri Young	.15
193	Carl Everett	.15
194	Joey Hamilton	.15
195	Jorge Julio	.15
196	Pablo Ozuna	.15
197	Jason Marquis	.15
198	Dustan Mohr	.15
199	Joe Borowski	.15
200	Tony Clark	.15
201	David Wells	.15
202	Josh Fogg	.15
203	Aaron Harang	.15
204	John McDonald	.15
205	John Stephens	.15
206	Chris Reitsma	.15
207	Alex Sanchez	.15
208	Milton Bradley	.15
209	Matt Clement	.15
210	Brad Fullmer	.15
211	Shigetoshi Hasegawa	.15
212	Austin Kearns	.50
213	Damaso Marte	.15
214	Vicente Padilla	.15
215	Raul Mondesi	.15
216	Russell Branyan	.15
217	Bartolo Colon	.15
218	Moises Alou	.15
219	Scott Hatteberg	.15
220	Bobby Kielty	.15
221	Kip Wells	.15
222	Scott Stewart	.15
223	Victor Martinez	.40
224	Marty Cordova	.15
225	Desi Relaford	.15
226	Reggie Sanders	.15
227	Jason Giambi	.50
228	Jimmy Haynes	.15
229	Billy Koch	.15
230	Damian Moss	.15
231	Chan Ho Park	.15
232	Cliff Floyd	.15

233	Todd Zeile	.15
234	Jeremy Giambi	.15
235	Rick Helling	.15
236	Matt Lawton	.15
237	Ramon Martinez	.15
238	Rondell White	.15
239	Scott Sullivan	.15
240	Hideo Nomo	.60
241	Todd Ritchie	.15
242	Ramon Santiago	.15
243	Jake Peavy	.15
244	Brad Wilkerson	.15
245	Reggie Taylor	.15
246	Carlos Pena	.15
247	Willis Roberts	.15
248	Jason Schmidt	.15
249	Mike Williams	.15
250	Alan Zinter	.15
251	Michael Tejera	.15
252	Dave Roberts	.15
253	Scott Schoeneweis	.15
254	Woody Williams	.15
255	John Thomson	.15
256	Ricardo Rodriguez	.15
257	Aaron Sele	.15
258	Paul Wilson	.15
259	Brett Tomko	.15
260	Kenny Rogers	.15
261	Mo Vaughn	.15
262	John Burkett	.15
263	Dennis Stark	.15
264	Ray Durham	.15
265	Scott Rolen	.65
266	Gabe Kapler	.15
267	Todd Hollandsworth	.15
268	Bud Smith	.15
269	Jay Payton	.15
270	Tyler Houston	.15
271	Brian Moehler	.15
272	David Espinosa	.15
273	Placido Polanco	.15
274	John Patterson	.15
275	Adam Hyzdu	.15
276	Albert Pujols	2.00
277	Larry Walker	.15
278	Magglio Ordonez	.15
279	Ryan Klesko	.15
280	Darin Erstad	.60
281	Jeff Kent	.15
282	Paul LoDuca	.15
283	Jim Edmonds	.15
284	Chipper Jones	1.00
285	Bernie Williams	.30
286	Pat Burrell	.40
287	Cliff Floyd	.15
288	Troy Glaus	.75
289	Brian Giles	.15
290	Jim Thome	.15
291	Greg Maddux	1.00
292	Roberto Alomar	.30
293	Jeff Bagwell	.75
294	Rafael Furcal	.15
295	Josh Beckett	.25
296	Carlos Delgado	.35
297	Ken Griffey Jr.	1.50
298	Jason Giambi	.50
299	Paul Konerko	.15
300	Mike Sweeney	.15
301	Alfonso Soriano	.50
302	Shea Hillenbrand	.15
303	Tony Batista	.15
304	Robin Ventura	.15
305	Alex Rodriguez	2.00
306	Nomar Garciaparra	1.50
307	Derek Jeter	2.50
308	Miguel Tejada	.30
309	Omar Vizquel	.15
310	Jorge Posada	.25
311	A.J. Pierzynski	.15
312	Ichiro Suzuki	1.50
313	Manny Ramirez	.75
314	Torii Hunter	.15
315	Garret Anderson	.15
316	Robert Fick	.15
317	Randy Winn	.15
318	Mark Buehrle	.15
319	Freddy Garcia	.15
320	Eddie Guardado	.15
321	Roy Halladay	.25
322	Derek Lowe	.15
323	Pedro J. Martinez	.75
324	Mariano Rivera	.15
325	Kazuhiro Sasaki	.15
326	Barry Zito	.25
327	Johnny Damon	.25
328	Ugueth Urbina	.15
329	Todd Helton	.75
330	Richie Sexson	.15
331	Jose Vidro	.15
332	Luis Castillo	.15
333	Junior Spivey	.15
334	Scott Rolen	.65
335	Mike Lowell	.15
336	Jimmy Rollins	.25
337	Jose Hernandez	.15
338	Mike Piazza	1.50
339	Benito Santiago	.15
340	Sammy Sosa	1.50
341	Barry Bonds	2.50
342	Vladimir Guerrero	.75
343	Lance Berkman	.15
344	Adam Dunn	.40
345	Shawn Green	.25
346	Luis Gonzalez	.25
347	Eric Gagne	.25
348	Tom Glavine	.30
349	Trevor Hoffman	.15
350	Randy Johnson	.75
351	Byung-Hyun Kim	.15
352	Matt Morris	.15
353	Odalis Perez	.15
354	Curt Schilling	.40
355	John Smoltz	.15
356	Mike Williams	.15
357	Andruw Jones	.75
358	Vicente Padilla	.15
359	Mike Remlinger	.15
360	Robb Nen	.15
361	Shawn Green	.25
362	Derek Jeter	2.50
363	Troy Glaus	.75
364	Ken Griffey Jr.	1.50
365	Mike Piazza	1.50
366	Jason Giambi	.50
367	Greg Maddux	1.00
368	Albert Pujols	2.00
369	Pedro J. Martinez	.75
370	Barry Zito	.25
371	Ichiro Suzuki	1.50
372	Nomar Garciaparra	1.50
373	Vladimir Guerrero	.75
374	Randy Johnson	.75
375	Barry Bonds	2.50
376	Sammy Sosa	1.50
377	Hideo Nomo	.75
378	Jeff Bagwell	.75
379	Curt Schilling	.35
380	Jim Thome	.15
381	Todd Helton	.75
382	Roger Clemens	1.25
383	Chipper Jones	1.00
384	Alex Rodriguez	2.00
385	Manny Ramirez	.40
386	Barry Bonds	2.50
387	Jim Thome	.15
388	Adam Dunn	.40
389	Alex Rodriguez	2.00
390	Shawn Green	.25
391	Jason Giambi	.50
392	Lance Berkman	.15
393	Pat Burrell	.40
394	Eric Chavez	.25
395	Mike Piazza	1.50
396	Vladimir Guerrero	.75
397	Paul Konerko	.15
398	Sammy Sosa	1.50
399	Richie Sexson	.15
400	Torii Hunter	.15

Glossy

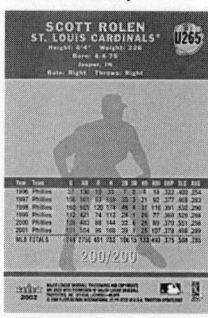

Stars (1-100):	1-2X
Cards (101-400):	4-8X
Production 200 Sets	

Diamond Debuts

		NM/M
Complete Set (15):		10.00
Common Player:		.50
Inserted 1:6		
1DD	Mark Prior	1.50
2DD	Eric Hinske	.50
3DD	Kazuhisa Ishii	.50
4DD	Ben Broussard	.50
5DD	Sean Burroughs	.50
6DD	Austin Kearns	1.00
7DD	Hee Seop Choi	1.00
8DD	Kirk Saarloos	.50
9DD	Orlando Hudson	.50
10DD	So Taguchi	.50
11DD	Kevin Mench	.50
12DD	Carl Crawford	.50
13DD	John Patterson	.50
14DD	Hank Blalock	1.50
15DD	Brett Myers	.50

Grass Roots

		NM/M
Complete Set (10):		15.00
Common Player:		1.00
Inserted 1:24		
1GR	Alfonso Soriano	1.50
2GR	Torii Hunter	1.00
3GR	Andruw Jones	1.50
4GR	Jim Edmonds	1.00
5GR	Shawn Green	1.00
6GR	Todd Helton	1.50
7GR	Nomar Garciaparra	4.00
8GR	Roberto Alomar	1.00
9GR	Vladimir Guerrero	1.50
10GR	Ichiro Suzuki	4.00

Grass Patch

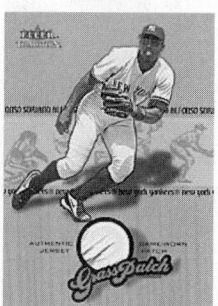

	NM/M
Common Player:	20.00
Production 50 Sets	
Alfonso Soriano	30.00
Torii Hunter	20.00
Andruw Jones	30.00
Jim Edmonds	20.00
Shawn Green	20.00
Nomar Garciaparra	50.00
Roberto Alomar	25.00

Heads Up

		NM/M
Complete Set (10):		25.00
Common Player:		2.00
Inserted 1:48		
1HU	Roger Clemens	6.00
2HU	Adam Dunn	2.00
3HU	Kazuhisa Ishii	1.50
4HU	Barry Zito	1.50
5HU	Pedro J. Martinez	4.00
6HU	Alfonso Soriano	3.00
7HU	Mark Prior	2.00
8HU	Chipper Jones	5.00
9HU	Randy Johnson	4.00
10HU	Lance Berkman	1.50

Heads Up Game-Used

	NM/M
Common Player:	5.00
Production 150 Sets	
Roger Clemens	25.00
Adam Dunn	10.00
Kazuhisa Ishii	5.00
Barry Zito	5.00
Alfonso Soriano	10.00
Mark Prior	10.00
Chipper Jones	15.00
Randy Johnson	15.00
Lance Berkman	5.00
Mike Piazza	20.00
Barry Bonds	50.00

Plays of the Week

		NM/M
Complete Set (30):		35.00
Common Player:		1.00
Inserted 1:12		
1PW	Troy Glaus	1.50
2PW	Andruw Jones	1.50
3PW	Curt Schilling	1.25
4PW	Manny Ramirez	1.50
5PW	Sammy Sosa	2.50
6PW	Magglio Ordonez	1.00
7PW	Ken Griffey Jr.	2.50
8PW	Jim Thome	1.00
9PW	Larry Walker	1.00
10PW	Robert Fick	1.00
11PW	Josh Beckett	1.00
12PW	Roy Oswalt	1.00
13PW	Mike Sweeney	1.00
14PW	Shawn Green	1.00
15PW	Torii Hunter	1.00
16PW	Vladimir Guerrero	1.50
17PW	Mike Piazza	2.50
18PW	Jason Giambi	1.25
19PW	Eric Chavez	1.00
20PW	Pat Burrell	1.25
21PW	Brian Giles	1.00
22PW	Ryan Klesko	1.00
23PW	Barry Bonds	5.00
24PW	Mike Cameron	1.00
25PW	Albert Pujols	4.00
26PW	Alex Rodriguez	4.00
27PW	Carlos Delgado	1.00
28PW	Richie Sexson	1.00
29PW	Jay Gibbons	1.00
30PW	Randy Winn	1.00

New York's Finest

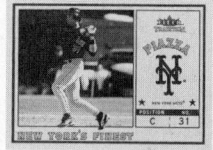

		NM/M
Complete Set (15):		60.00
Common Player:		3.00
Inserted 1:83		
1	Edgardo Alfonzo	3.00
2	Roberto Alomar	4.00
3	Jeromy Burnitz	3.00
4	Satoru Komiyama	3.00
5	Rey Ordonez	3.00
6	Mike Piazza	10.00
7	Mo Vaughn	3.00
8	Roger Clemens	10.00

9	Jason Giambi	5.00
10	Derek Jeter	15.00
11	Mike Mussina	5.00
12	Jorge Posada	3.00
13	Alfonso Soriano	5.00
14	Robin Ventura	3.00
15	Bernie Williams	4.00

N.Y.'s Finest Single Swatch

NM/M

Common Card:	5.00
Inserted 1:112	
Derek Jeter/Jsy, Rey Ordonez	25.00
Alfonso Soriano/Jsy, Roberto Alomar	10.00
Roger Clemens/Jsy, Mike Piazza	15.00
Mike Mussina/Jsy, Mo Vaughn	8.00
Bernie Williams/Jsy, Jeromy Burnitz	8.00
Derek Jeter/Jsy, Satoru Komiyama	25.00
Robin Ventura/Jsy, Edgardo Alfonzo	8.00
Jorge Posada/Jsy, Mike Piazza	8.00
Jason Giambi/Base, Mo Vaughn	8.00
Alfonso Soriano/Jsy, Edgardo Alfonzo	10.00
Derek Jeter, Rey Ordonez/Jsy	5.00
Alfonso Soriano, Roberto Alomar/Jsy	8.00
Roger Clemens, Mike Piazza	15.00
Mike Mussina, Mo Vaughn/Jsy	6.00
Bernie Williams, Jeromy Burnitz/Jsy	5.00
Derek Jeter, Satoru Komiyama/Bat	8.00
Robin Ventura, Edgardo Alfonzo/Jsy	5.00
Jorge Posada, Mike Piazza/Jsy	15.00
Jason Giambi, Mo Vaughn/Jsy	6.00
Alfonso Soriano, Edgardo Alfonzo/Jsy	5.00

N.Y.'s Finest Dual Swatch

NM/M

Common Card:	10.00
Production 100 Sets	
Derek Jeter, Rey Ordonez	75.00
Alfonso Soriano, Roberto Alomar	40.00
Roger Clemens, Mike Piazza	65.00
Mike Mussina, Mo Vaughn	30.00
Bernie Williams, Jeromy Burnitz	20.00
Robin Ventura, Edgardo Alfonzo	10.00

This Day in History

NM/M

Complete Set (25):		40.00
Common Player:		1.00
1	Shawn Green	1.00
2	Ozzie Smith	2.50
3	Derek Lowe	1.00
4	Ken Griffey Jr.	3.00

5	Barry Bonds	5.00
6	Juan Gonzalez	1.50
7	Wade Boggs	2.00
8	Mark Prior	1.50
9	Thurman Munson	2.00
10	Curt Schilling	1.25
11	Jason Giambi	1.25
12	Cal Ripken Jr.	5.00
13	Craig Biggio	1.00
14	Drew Henson	1.00
15	Steve Carlton	1.00
16	Greg Maddux	2.50
17	Adam Dunn	1.00
18	Vladimir Guerrero	2.00
19	Alex Rodriguez	4.00
20	Carlton Fisk	1.50
21	Ichiro Suzuki	3.00
22	Johnny Bench	2.00
23	Kazuhisa Ishii	1.00
24	Derek Jeter	5.00
25	Jim Thome	1.00

This Day in History Memor.

NM/M

Common Player:	5.00
Inserted 1:24	
Shawn Green/Jsy	5.00
Ozzie Smith/Jsy	10.00
Barry Bonds/Bat	15.00
Barry Bonds/Jsy	15.00
Juan Gonzalez/Bat	6.00
Wade Boggs/Jsy	6.00
Wade Boggs/Pants	6.00
Curt Schilling/Jsy	6.00
Craig Biggio/Jsy	5.00
Adam Dunn/Jsy	8.00
Alex Rodriguez/Bat	10.00
Alex Rodriguez/Jsy	10.00
Carlton Fisk/Bat	8.00
Kazuhisa Ishii/Bat	5.00
Derek Jeter/Pants	20.00
Jim Thome/Jsy	8.00
Greg Maddux/Jsy	10.00

This Day in History Auto.

NM/M

Inserted 1:582	
Barry Bonds/150	200.00
Mark Prior/64	40.00
Drew Henson	20.00
Greg Maddux/99	150.00
Derek Jeter	100.00

2002 Fleer Triple Crown

NM/M

Complete Set (270):		30.00
Common Player:		.15
Pack (10):		1.50
Box (24):		30.00
1	Mo Vaughn	.15
2	Derek Jeter	2.00
3	Ken Griffey Jr.	1.25
4	Charles Johnson	.15
5	Geoff Jenkins	.15
6	Chuck Knoblauch	.15
7	Jason Kendall	.15
8	Jim Edmonds	.15
9	David Eckstein	.15
10	Carl Everett	.15
11	Barry Larkin	.15
12	Cliff Floyd	.15
13	Ben Sheets	.15
14	Jeff Conine	.15
15	Brian Giles	.15
16	Darryl Kile	.15
17	Troy Glaus	.65
18	Trot Nixon	.15
19	Jim Thome	.15

20	Preston Wilson	.15
21	Roger Clemens	1.00
22	Chad Hermansen	.15
23	Matt Morris	.15
24	Shawn Wooten	.15
25	Manny Ramirez	.65
26	Roberto Alomar	.30
27	Josh Beckett	.25
28	Jose Hernandez	.25
29	Mike Mussina	.35
30	Jack Wilson	.25
31	Bud Smith	.15
32	Garret Anderson	.15
33	Pedro J. Martinez	.65
34	Travis Fryman	.15
35	Jeff Bagwell	.65
36	Doug Mientkiewicz	.15
37	Andy Pettitte	.25
38	Ryan Klesko	.15
39	Edgar Renteria	.15
40	Mariano Rivera	.25
41	Darin Erstad	.50
42	Hideo Nomo	.50
43	Ellis Burks	.15
44	Craig Biggio	.15
45	Corey Koskie	.15
46	Jason Varitek	.15
47	Xavier Nady	.15
48	Aubrey Huff	.15
49	Tim Salmon	.25
50	Nomar Garciaparra	1.25
51	Juan Gonzalez	.65
52	Moises Alou	.15
53	A.J. Pierzynski	.15
54	Bernie Williams	.30
55	Phil Nevin	.15
56	Ben Grieve	.15
57	Mark Grace	.25
58	Mike Lansing	.15
59	Kenny Lofton	.15
60	Lance Berkman	.15
61	David Ortiz	.25
62	Jason Giambi	.40
63	Mark Kotsay	.15
64	Greg Vaughn	.15
65	Junior Spivey	.15
66	Fred McGriff	.15
67	C.C. Sabathia	.15
68	Richard Hidalgo	.15
69	Torii Hunter	.15
70	Jason Hart	.15
71	Bubba Trammell	.15
72	Jace Brewer	.15
73	Matt Williams	.15
74	Matt Stairs	.15
75	Omar Vizquel	.15
76	Daryle Ward	.15
77	Joe Mays	.15
78	Eric Chavez	.15
79	Andres Galarraga	.15
80	Rafael Palmeiro	.50
81	Steve Finley	.15
82	Eric Young	.15
83	Todd Helton	.65
84	Roy Oswalt	.25
85	Eric Milton	.15
86	Ramon Hernandez	.15
87	Jeff Kent	.15
88	Ivan Rodriguez	.50
89	Luis Gonzalez	.25
90	Corey Patterson	.15
91	Jose Ortiz	.15
92	Mike Sweeney	.15
93	Cristian Guzman	.15
94	Johnny Damon	.25
95	Barry Bonds	2.00
96	Rusty Greer	.15
97	Reggie Sanders	.15
98	Sammy Sosa	1.25
99	Jeff Cirillo	.15
100	Carlos Febles	.15
101	Jose Vidro	.15
102	Jermaine Dye	.15
103	Rich Aurilia	.15
104	Gabe Kapler	.15
105	Randy Johnson	.65
106	Rondell White	.15
107	Ben Petrick	.15
108	Joe Randa	.15
109	Fernando Tatis	.15
110	Tim Hudson	.25
111	John Olerud	.15
112	Alex Rodriguez	1.50
113	Curt Schilling	.40
114	Kerry Wood	.40
115	Alex Ochoa	.15
116	Carlos Beltran	.40
117	Vladimir Guerrero	.65
118	Mark Mulder	.15
119	Bret Boone	.15
120	Carlos Delgado	.35
121	Marcus Giles	.15
122	Paul Konerko	.15
123	Juan Pierre	.15
124	Mark Quinn	.15
125	Edgardo Alfonzo	.15
126	Barry Zito	.25
127	Dan Wilson	.15
128	Jose Cruz Jr.	.15
129	Chipper Jones	.75
130	Ray Durham	.15
131	Larry Walker	.25
132	Neifi Perez	.15
133	Robin Ventura	.15
134	Miguel Tejada	.25

135	Edgar Martinez	.15
136	Raul Mondesi	.15
137	Javy Lopez	.15
138	Jose Canseco	.25
139	Mike Hampton	.15
140	Eric Karros	.15
141	Mike Piazza	1.25
142	Travis Lee	.15
143	Ichiro Suzuki	1.25
144	Shannon Stewart	.15
145	Andruw Jones	.65
146	Frank Thomas	.65
147	Tony Clark	.15
148	Adrian Beltre	.25
149	Matt Lawton	.15
150	Marlon Anderson	.15
151	Freddy Garcia	.15
152	Brian Jordan	.15
153	Carlos Lee	.15
154	Eric Munson	.15
155	Paul LoDuca	.15
156	Jay Payton	.15
157	Scott Rolen	.50
158	Jamie Moyer	.15
159	Tom Glavine	.30
160	Magglio Ordonez	.15
161	Brandon Inge	.15
162	Shawn Green	.25
163	Tsuyoshi Shinjo	.15
164	Mike Lieberthal	.15
165	Kazuhiro Sasaki	.15
166	Greg Maddux	.75
167	Chris Singleton	.15
168	Juan Encarnacion	.15
169	Gary Sheffield	.25
170	Nick Johnson	.15
171	Bobby Abreu	.15
172	Aaron Boone	.15
173	Rafael Furcal	.15
174	Mark Buehrle	.15
175	Bobby Higginson	.15
176	Kevin Brown	.15
177	Tino Martinez	.15
178	Pat Burrell	.30
179	Fernando Vina	.15
180	Jay Gibbons	.15
181	Jose Valentin	.15
182	Derrek Lee	.15
183	Richie Sexson	.15
184	Alfonso Soriano	.50
185	Jimmy Rollins	.15
186	Albert Pujols	1.50
187	Brady Anderson	.15
188	Sean Casey	.25
189	Luis Castillo	.15
190	Jeromy Burnitz	.15
191	Jorge Posada	.25
192	Kevin Young	.15
193	Eli Marrero	.15
194	Shea Hillenbrand	.15
195	Adam Dunn	.40
196	Mike Lowell	.15
197	Jeffrey Hammonds	.15
198	David Justice	.15
199	Aramis Ramirez	.15
200	J.D. Drew	.25
201	Pedro Santana	.15
202	Endy Chavez	.15
203	Donnie Bridges	.15
204	Travis Phelps	.15
205	Drew Henson	.25
206	Angel Berroa	.15
207	George Perez	.15
208	Billy Sylvester	.15
209	Juan Cruz	.15
210	Horacio Ramirez	.15
211	J.J. Davis	.15
212	Cody Ransom	.15
213	Mark Teixeira	.50
214	Nate Frese	.15
215	Brian Rogers	.15
216	Dewon Brazelton	.15
217	Carlos Hernandez	.15
218	Juan Rivera	.15
219	Luis Lopez	.15
220	Benito Baez	.15
221	Bill Ortega	.15
222	Dustan Mohr	.15
223	Corky Miller	.15
224	Tyler Walker	.15
225	Rick Bauer	.15
226	Mark Prior	.50
227	Rafael Soriano	.15
228	Greg Miller	.15
229	Dave Williams	.15
230	Bert Snow	.15
231	Barry Bonds	1.50
232	Rickey Henderson	.50
233	Alex Rodriguez	1.25
234	Luis Gonzalez	.25
235	Derek Jeter	1.50
236	Bud Smith	.15
237	Sammy Sosa	.75
238	Jeff Bagwell	.50
239	Jim Thome	.50
240	Hideo Nomo	.50
241	Greg Maddux	.75
242	Ken Griffey Jr.	1.00
243	Curt Schilling	.25
244	Arizona Diamondbacks	.15
245	Ichiro Suzuki	.75
246	Albert Pujols	1.00
247	Ichiro Suzuki	.75
248	Barry Bonds	1.50
249	Roger Clemens	.65

250	Randy Johnson	.50
251	Todd Helton	.50
252	Rafael Palmeiro	.40
253	Mike Piazza	1.00
254	Alex Rodriguez	1.25
255	Manny Ramirez	.50
256	Ken Griffey Jr.	1.00
257	Jason Giambi	.40
258	Chipper Jones	.65
259	Larry Walker	.15
260	Sammy Sosa	.75
261	Vladimir Guerrero	.50
262	Nomar Garciaparra	.75
263	Randy Johnson	.50
264	Roger Clemens	.65
265	Ichiro Suzuki	1.00
266	Barry Bonds	1.50
267	Paul LoDuca	.15
268	Albert Pujols	1.00
269	Derek Jeter	1.50
270	Adam Dunn	.40

Batting Average Parallel

Gary Sheffield
OUTFIELD

Stars: 4-8X
Numbered to 2001 batting avg.
(See 2002 Fleer Triple Crown for checklist and base card values.)

Home Run Parallel

Stars Print Run 50-75:	10-20X
Stars P/R 31-50:	15-25X
Stars P/R 21-30:	20-40X
Numbered to 2001 HR total.	

RBI parallel

Stars Print Run 101-200:	4-8X
Stars P/R 76-100:	5-10X
Stars P/R 51-75:	6-12X
Stars P/R 25-50:	10-20X
Numbered to 2001 RBI total.	
(See 2002 Fleer Triple Crown for checklist and base card values.)	

Diamond Immortality

Derek Jeter   Yankees

		NM/M
Complete Set (10):		25.00
Common Player:		1.00
Inserted 1:12		
1DI	Derek Jeter	5.00
2DI	Barry Bonds	5.00
3DI	Ricky Henderson	1.00
4DI	Roger Clemens	2.50
5DI	Alex Rodriguez	4.00
6DI	Albert Pujols	4.00
7DI	Nomar Garciaparra	3.00
8DI	Ichiro Suzuki	3.00
9DI	Chipper Jones	2.00
10DI	Ken Griffey Jr.	3.00

Diamond Immortality Game-Used

	NM/M
Inserted 1:129	
Barry Bonds/Jsy	25.00
Roger Clemens/Jsy	20.00
Nomar Garciaparra/Jsy/SP	40.00
Ricky Henderson/Bat	10.00
Derek Jeter/Bat	25.00

	Chipper Jones/Bat	10.00
	Albert Pujols/Jsy	25.00
	Alex Rodriguez/Jsy	20.00

Home Run Kings

		NM/M
Complete Set (25):		100.00
Common Player:		2.00
Inserted 1:24		
1	Ted Williams	10.00
2	Todd Helton	4.00
3	Eddie Murray	2.00
4	Jeff Bagwell	4.00
5	Babe Ruth	15.00
6	Eddie Mathews	5.00
7	Alex Rodriguez	10.00
8	Juan Gonzalez	4.00
9	Chipper Jones	5.00
10	Luis Gonzalez	2.00
11	Johnny Bench	5.00
12	Frank Thomas	4.00
13	Ernie Banks	3.00
14	Jimmie Foxx	4.00
15	Ken Griffey Jr.	8.00
16	Rafael Palmeiro	3.00
17	Sammy Sosa	8.00
18	Reggie Jackson	4.00
19	Barry Bonds	10.00
20	Willie McCovey	2.00
21	Manny Ramirez	4.00
22	Larry Walker	2.00
23	Jason Giambi	4.00
24	Mike Piazza	8.00
25	Jose Canseco	2.00

Home Run Kings Autograph

	NM/M
Common Player:	
Barry Bonds/73	300.00
Alex Rodriguez/52	100.00

Home Run Kings Game-Used

	NM/M
Common Player:	5.00
Inserted 1:155	
Jeff Bagwell/Jsy	10.00
Johnny Bench/Bat/SP	50.00
Barry Bonds/Jsy	25.00
Jimmie Foxx/Bat	40.00
Jason Giambi/Jsy	10.00
Reggie Jackson/Bat	10.00
Eddie Mathews/Bat	15.00
Eddie Murray/Bat	10.00
Rafael Palmeiro/Bat	10.00
Mike Piazza/Jsy	15.00
Manny Ramirez/Bat/SP	50.00
Todd Helton/Bat	10.00
Alex Rodriguez/Bat	15.00
Larry Walker/Bat	5.00
Ted Williams/Bat	100.00

RBI Kings

		NM/M
Complete Set (15):		140.00
Common Player:		4.00
Inserted 1:144		
1	Sammy Sosa	15.00
2	Todd Helton	8.00
3	Albert Pujols	20.00
4	Manny Ramirez	8.00
5	Luis Gonzalez	4.00
6	Shawn Green	4.00
7	Barry Bonds	20.00
8	Ken Griffey Jr.	15.00
9	Alex Rodriguez	20.00
10	Jason Giambi	8.00
11	Jeff Bagwell	8.00
12	Vladimir Guerrero	8.00
13	Juan Gonzalez	8.00
14	Chipper Jones	8.00
15	Mike Piazza	15.00

RBI Kings Game-Used

	NM/M
Common Player:	5.00
Inserted 1:70	
Jeff Bagwell/Jsy	10.00
Barry Bonds/Jsy	25.00
Jason Giambi/Jsy	8.00

Luis Gonzalez/Bat	5.00
Juan Gonzalez/Bat	8.00
Shawn Green/Jsy	6.00
Todd Helton/Jsy	10.00
Mike Piazza/Jsy	15.00
Albert Pujols/Bat/SP	70.00
Manny Ramirez/Bat	10.00
Alex Rodriguez/Shoe	25.00

Season Crowns

		NM/M
Complete Set (10):		25.00
Common Card:		2.00
Inserted 1:12		
1SC	Barry Bonds, Sammy Sosa, Luis Gonzalez	4.00
2SC	Larry Walker, Nomar Garciaparra, Todd Helton	4.00
3SC	Sammy Sosa, Todd Helton, Manny Ramirez	4.00
4SC	Pedro J. Martinez, Derek Jeter, Cal Ripken Jr.	6.00
5SC	Jose Canseco, Barry Bonds, Alex Rodriguez	5.00
6SC	Barry Bonds, Jeff Kent, Chipper Jones	4.00
7SC	Ichiro Suzuki, Jason Giambi, Ivan Rodriguez	3.00
8SC	Curt Schilling, Tom Glavine, Pedro J. Martinez	2.00
9SC	Randy Johnson, Pedro J. Martinez, Greg Maddux	3.00
10SC	Randy Johnson, Curt Schilling, John Smoltz	2.00

Season Crowns Autograph

	NM/M
Jeter #'d to 160.	
Derek Jeter/160	150.00
Barry Bonds/77	250.00

Season Crowns Game-Used

	NM/M
Common Player:	5.00
Inserted 1:90	
Barry Bonds/Jsy	25.00
Sammy Sosa/Base	15.00
Larry Walker/Bat	5.00
Nomar Garciaparra/Jsy	20.00
Todd Helton/Jsy	10.00
Sammy Sosa/Base	15.00
Todd Helton/Jsy	10.00
Manny Ramirez/Jsy	10.00
Pedro Martinez/Jsy	10.00
Derek Jeter/Pants	25.00
Cal Ripken Jr/Bat	60.00
Jose Canseco/Jsy	8.00
Barry Bonds/Jsy	25.00
Alex Rodriguez/Jsy	20.00
Barry Bonds/Jsy	25.00
Jeff Kent/Jsy	5.00
Ichiro Suzuki/Base	25.00
Jason Giambi/Jsy	10.00
Ivan Rodriguez/Jsy	10.00
Curt Schilling/Jsy	10.00
Tom Glavine/Jsy	10.00
Pedro Martinez/Jsy	10.00
Randy Johnson/Jsy	10.00
Greg Maddux/Jsy	15.00
Randy Johnson/Jsy	10.00
Curt Schilling/Jsy	10.00
John Smoltz/Jsy	5.00

Season Crowns Triple Swatch

	NM/M
Production 100 Sets	
Barry Bonds, Sammy Sosa, Luis Gonzalez	100.00
Larry Walker, Nomar Garciaparra, Todd Helton	40.00
Sammy Sosa, Todd Helton, Manny Ramirez	50.00
Barry Bonds, Jeff Kent, Chipper Jones	80.00
Ichiro Suzuki, Jason Giambi, Ivan Rodriguez	80.00
Curt Schilling, Tom Glavine, Pedro J. Martinez	50.00

Randy Johnson, Pedro J. Martinez, Greg Maddux	50.00
Randy Johnson, Curt Schilling, John Smoltz	50.00

2003 Fleer Authentix

		NM/M
Complete Set (160):		
Common Player:		.25
Common (111-125):		3.00
Production 1,850		
Common (126-160):		1.50
Exclusive to Home Team boxes.		
Pack (5):		3.00
Box (24):		50.00
1	Derek Jeter	3.00
2	Tom Glavine	.40
3	Jason Jennings	.25
4	Craig Biggio	.25
5	Miguel Tejada	.40
6	Barry Bonds	3.00
7	Juan Gonzalez	1.00
8	Luis Gonzalez	.40
9	Johnny Damon	.40
10	Ellis Burks	.25
11	Frank Thomas	1.00
12	Richie Sexson	.25
13	Roger Clemens	1.50
14	Matt Morris	.25
15	Troy Glaus	1.00
16	Tony Batista	.25
17	Magglio Ordonez	.25
18	Jose Vidro	.25
19	Barry Zito	.40
20	Chipper Jones	1.50
21	Moises Alou	.25
22	Lance Berkman	.25
23	Jacque Jones	.25
24	Alfonso Soriano	.75
25	Sean Burroughs	.25
26	Scott Rolen	1.00
27	Mark Grace	.35
28	Manny Ramirez	1.00
29	Ken Griffey Jr.	2.00
30	Josh Beckett	.25
31	Kazuhisa Ishii	.25
32	Pat Burrell	1.00
33	Edgar Martinez	.25
34	Tim Salmon	.35
35	Raul Ibanez	.25
36	Vladimir Guerrero	1.00
37	Jermaine Dye	.25
38	Rich Aurilia	.25
39	Rafael Palmeiro	.75
40	Kerry Wood	.75
41	Omar Vizquel	.25
42	Fred McGriff	.25
43	Ben Sheets	.25
44	Bernie Williams	.40
45	Brian Giles	.25
46	Jim Edmonds	.25
47	Garret Anderson	.25
48	Pedro J. Martinez	1.00
49	Adam Dunn	.75
50	A.J. Burnett	.25
51	Eric Gagne	.25
52	Mo Vaughn	.25
53	Bobby Abreu	.25
54	Bret Boone	.25
55	Carlos Delgado	.40
56	Gary Sheffield	.40
57	Sammy Sosa	2.00
58	Jim Thome	.75
59	Jeff Bagwell	1.00
60	David Eckstein	.25
61	Jason Kendall	.25
62	Albert Pujols	2.50
63	Curt Schilling	.40
64	Nomar Garciaparra	2.00
65	Sean Casey	.35
66	Shawn Green	.40
67	Mike Piazza	2.00
68	Ichiro Suzuki	2.00
69	Eric Hinske	.25
70	Greg Maddux	1.50
71	Larry Walker	.25
72	Roy Oswalt	.40
73	Alex Rodriguez	2.50
74	Austin Kearns	.75
75	Cliff Floyd	.25

76	Kevin Brown	.25
77	Jason Giambi	.75
78	Jorge Julio	.25
79	Carlos Lee	.25
80	Mike Sweeney	.25
81	Edgardo Alfonzo	.25
82	Eric Chavez	.40
83	Andruw Jones	1.00
84	Mark Prior	.75
85	Todd Helton	1.00
86	Torii Hunter	.25
87	Ryan Klesko	.25
88	Aubrey Huff	.25
89	Randy Johnson	1.00
90	Barry Larkin	.25
91	Mike Lowell	.25
92	Jimmy Rollins	.40
93	Darin Erstad	.65
94	Jay Gibbons	.25
95	Paul Konerko	.40
96	Bobby Higginson	.25
97	Carlos Beltran	.60
98	Bartolo Colon	.25
99	Jeff Kent	.25
100	Ivan Rodriguez	.65
101	Joe Borchard	.25
102	Mark Teixeira	.50
103	Francisco Rodriguez	.25
104	Chris Snelling	.25
105	Hee Seop Choi	.25
106	Hank Blalock	.50
107	Marlon Byrd	.25
108	Michael Restovich	.25
109	Victor Martinez	.25
110	Lyle Overbay	.25
111	Brian Stokes RC	3.00
112	Josh Hall RC	3.00
113	Chris Waters RC	3.00
114	Lew Ford RC	3.00
115	Ian Ferguson RC	3.00
116	Josh Willingham RC	4.00
117	Josh Stewart RC	3.00
118	Pete LaForest RC	3.00
119	Jose Contreras RC	5.00
120	Termel Sledge RC	3.00
121	Guillermo Quiroz RC	3.00
122	Alejandro Machado RC	3.00
123	Nook Logan RC	3.00
124	Rontrez Johnson RC	3.00
125	Hideki Matsui RC	10.00
126	Phil Rizzuto	3.00
127	Robin Ventura	1.50
128	Andy Pettitte	4.00
129	Mike Mussina	3.00
130	Mariano Rivera	3.00
131	Jeff Weaver	1.50
132	David Wells	1.50
133	Tommy Lasorda	2.00
134	Pee Wee Reese	2.00
135	Hideo Nomo	4.00
136	Adrian Beltre	2.00
137	Chin-Feng Chen	4.00
138	Odalis Perez	1.50
139	Dave Roberts	1.50
140	Bobby Doerr	3.00
141	Jason Varitek	1.50
142	Trot Nixon	1.50
143	Tim Wakefield	1.50
144	John Burkett	1.50
145	Jeremy Giambi	1.50
146	Casey Fossum	1.50
147	Phil Niekro	1.50
148	Warren Spahn	4.00
149	Rafael Furcal	2.00
150	Vinny Castilla	1.50
151	Javy Lopez	1.50
152	Jason Marquis	1.50
153	Mike Hampton	1.50
154	Gaylord Perry	1.50
155	Ruben Sierra	1.50
156	Mike Cameron	1.50
157	Freddy Garcia	1.50
158	Joel Pineiro	1.50
159	Jamie Moyer	1.50
160	Carlos Guillen	1.50

Balcony

Stars (1-110):	3-6X
SP's (111-125):	.5-1.5X
Production 250 Sets	
Club Box (1-110):	5-10X
SP's (111-125):	.75-2X
Production 100 Sets	
Standing Room Only:	No Pricing
Production 25 Sets	

Autographed Authentix

		NM/M
Quantity produced listed		
DJ	Derek Jeter/50	150.00
DJ	Derek Jeter/150	125.00
DJ	Derek Jeter/250	125.00
BB	Barry Bonds/50	200.00
BB	Barry Bonds/150	200.00
BB	Barry Bonds/250	200.00

Autographed Jersey Authentix

		NM/M
Quantity produced listed		
DJ	Derek Jeter/100	150.00
DJ	Derek Jeter/200	150.00
DJ	Derek Jeter/300	125.00
NR	Nolan Ryan/100	185.00
NR	Nolan Ryan/200	150.00
NR	Nolan Ryan/300	125.00

Ballpark Classics

		NM/M
Complete Set (10):		25.00
Common Player:		1.50
Inserted 1:12		
1	Derek Jeter	6.00
2	Randy Johnson	2.00
3	Nomar Garciaparra	4.00
4	Barry Bonds	6.00
5	Alfonso Soriano	2.00
6	Alex Rodriguez	5.00
7	Jim Thome	1.50
8	Chipper Jones	3.00
9	Mike Piazza	4.00
10	Ichiro Suzuki	4.00

Bat Authentix

		NM/M
Common Player:		8.00
Inserted 1:78		
Unripped:		1.5-3X
Production 50 Sets		
AD	Adam Dunn	8.00
NG	Nomar Garciaparra	15.00
JG	Jason Giambi	15.00
VG	Vladimir Guerrero	10.00
DJ	Derek Jeter	30.00
CJ	Chipper Jones	10.00
MR	Manny Ramirez	10.00
SR	Scott Rolen	
SS	Sammy Sosa	15.00
JT	Jim Thome	15.00

Hometown Heroes Memorabilia

		NM/M
Common Player:		8.00
Home Team Box Exclusive		
BB	Bret Boone/Jsy/200	8.00
KB	Kevin Brown/Jsy/150	8.00
CC	Chin-Feng Chen/Jsy/150	35.00
RC	Roger Clemens	25.00
JD	Johnny Damon/Jsy/200	8.00
FG	Freddy Garcia/Jsy/200	8.00
NG	Nomar Garciaparra	25.00
JG	Jason Giambi/Bat/300	20.00
SG	Shawn Green/Jsy/100	8.00
KI	Kazuhisa Ishii/Jsy/100	8.00
DJ	Derek Jeter	40.00
AJ	Andruw Jones/Jsy/150	10.00
CJ	Chipper Jones	15.00
GM	Greg Maddux/Jsy	15.00
EM	Edgar Martinez/Jsy/200	10.00
PM	Pedro Martinez/Jsy/150	15.00
MR	Manny Ramirez	10.00
GS	Gary Sheffield/Jsy/100	8.00
AS	Alfonso Soriano	15.00
I	Ichiro Suzuki/Base/100	30.00

Jersey Authentix

		NM/M
Common Player:		5.00
Inserted 1:10		
Unripped:		1.5-3X
Production 50 Sets		
JB	Jeff Bagwell	8.00
JB2	Josh Beckett	5.00
LB	Lance Berkman	5.00
MB	Mark Buehrle	5.00
PB	Pat Burrell	10.00
SB	Sean Burroughs	5.00
RC	Roger Clemens	15.00
CD	Carlos Delgado	5.00
AD	Adam Dunn	8.00
NG	Nomar Garciaparra	15.00
VG	Vladimir Guerrero	8.00
EH	Eric Hinske	5.00
TH	Torii Hunter	6.00
DJ	Derek Jeter	25.00
RJ	Randy Johnson	8.00

CJ	Chipper Jones		8.00
GM	Greg Maddux		15.00
MP	Mike Piazza		12.00
MR	Manny Ramirez		8.00
AR	Alex Rodriguez		12.00
AS	Alfonso Soriano		10.00
SS	Sammy Sosa		12.00
MT	Miguel Tejada		5.00
KW	Kerry Wood		8.00

Jersey Authentix Game of the Week

		NM/M
Common Card:		10.00
Inserted 1:240		
Unripped:		1.5-3X
Production 50 Sets		
	Derek Jeter, Nomar Garciaparra	45.00
	Mike Piazza, Sammy Sosa	25.00
	Chipper Jones, Pat Burrell	20.00
	Greg Maddux, Randy Johnson	20.00
	Alex Rodriguez, Miguel Tejada	20.00
	Adam Dunn, Lance Berkman	10.00
	Torii Hunter, Alfonso Soriano	15.00
	Derek Jeter, Miguel Tejada	15.00
	Eric Hinske, Torii Hunter	10.00
	Alfonso Soriano, Sammy Sosa	15.00

Ticket Studs

		NM/M
Complete Set (15):		25.00
Common Player:		1.00
Inserted 1:6		
1TS	Curt Schilling	1.00
2TS	Greg Maddux	2.50
3TS	Torii Hunter	1.00
4TS	Mike Piazza	3.00
5TS	Pedro J. Martinez	2.00
6TS	Nomar Garciaparra	3.00
7TS	Derek Jeter	5.00
8TS	Alex Rodriguez	4.00
9TS	Alfonso Soriano	2.00
10TS	Pat Burrell	1.50
11TS	Barry Bonds	5.00
12TS	Jason Giambi	2.50
13TS	Sammy Sosa	2.50
14TS	Vladimir Guerrero	1.50
15TS	Ichiro Suzuki	5.00

2003 Fleer Avant

		NM/M
Complete Set (90):		240.00
Common Player:		.50
Common Retired SP (66-75):		5.00

Production 799		
Common Rk (76-90):		3.00
Production 699		
Pack (4):		4.00
Box (18):		60.00
1	Adam Dunn	.50
2	Barry Zito	.50
3	Preston Wilson	.50
4	Barry Bonds	4.00
5	Hank Blalock	1.00
6	Omar Vizquel	.50
7	Brian Giles	.50
8	Kerry Wood	.75
9	Miguel Tejada	.75
10	Magglio Ordonez	.50
11	Randy Johnson	1.00
12	Jeff Bagwell	1.00
13	Pat Burrell	.75
14	Jason Giambi	.75
15	Mark Prior	.75
16	Roger Clemens	2.00
17	Sammy Sosa	2.50
18	Jay Gibbons	.50
19	Torii Hunter	.75
20	Ichiro Suzuki	2.00
21	Derek Jeter	4.00
22	Tom Glavine	.50
23	Alfonso Soriano	1.00
24	Manny Ramirez	1.00
25	Frank Thomas	1.00
26	Carlos Pena	.50
27	Alex Rodriguez	3.00
28	Edgar Martinez	.50
29	Larry Walker	.50
30	Rafael Palmeiro	.75
31	Mike Piazza	2.00
32	Nomar Garciaparra	2.50
33	Lance Berkman	.50
34	Vladimir Guerrero	1.00
35	Troy Glaus	.75
36	Ivan Rodriguez	.75
37	Mark Mulder	.50
38	Curt Schilling	.75
39	Mike Sweeney	.50
40	Albert Pujols	3.00
41	Tim Hudson	.50
42	Greg Maddux	1.50
43	Shawn Green	.50
44	Scott Rolen	1.00
45	Gary Sheffield	.75
46	Richie Sexson	.75
47	Aubrey Huff	.50
48	Luis Gonzalez	.50
49	Todd Helton	1.00
50	Xavier Nady	.50
51	Juan Gonzalez	1.00
52	Pedro J. Martinez	1.00
53	Garret Anderson	.50
54	Craig Biggio	.50
55	Bret Boone	.50
56	Ken Griffey Jr.	2.00
57	Kevin Millwood	.50
58	Carlos Delgado	.75
59	Chipper Jones	1.50
60	Hideo Nomo	.50
61	Jim Edmonds	.50
62	Austin Kearns	.75
63	Jim Thome	.50
64	Vernon Wells	.50
65	Mike Lowell	.50
66	Whitey Ford	5.00
67	Bob Gibson	5.00
68	Reggie Jackson	5.00
69	Willie McCovey	5.00
70	Phil Rizzuto	5.00
71	Al Kaline	6.00
72	Brooks Robinson	5.00
73	Nolan Ryan	15.00
74	Mike Schmidt	10.00
75	Tom Seaver	6.00
76	Hideki Matsui RC	15.00
77	Rocco Baldelli	4.00
78	Jose Contreras RC	6.00
79	Hee Seop Choi	3.00
80	Jeremy Bonderman	6.00
81	Bo Hart RC	3.00
82	Brandon Webb RC	10.00
83	Ron Calloway	3.00
84	Jesse Foppert	3.00
85	Kyle Snyder	3.00
86	Mark Teixeira	5.00
87	Jose Reyes	5.00
88	Dontrelle Willis	4.00
89	Reed Johnson	3.00
90	Rickie Weeks RC	8.00

Black/White

Stars (1-65):	4-6X
SP's (66-90):	1-2X
Production 199 Sets	

2003 Fleer Avant Sample

Derek Jeter / Yankees

No Pricing

Autographs

		NM/M
Common Autograph:		10.00
Varying quantities produced		
Parallel SP's:		1-1.5X
Production 75 or 150		
DJ	Derek Jeter/75	140.00
MR	Manny Ramirez/100	35.00
VW	Vernon Wells/250	10.00
HB	Hank Blalock/150	25.00
DW	Dontrelle Willis/300	30.00
AK	Al Kaline/200	35.00
BR	Brooks Robinson/300	20.00
BG	Bob Gibson/250	25.00
JR	Jose Reyes/300	30.00
BZ	Barry Zito/150	20.00
EM	Edgar Martinez/246	25.00
BH	Bo Hart/300	15.00
AH	Aubrey Huff/300	15.00
CP	Carlos Pena/150	15.00
MT	Miguel Tejada/150	20.00
ML	Mike Lowell/150	10.00
CB	Craig Biggio/250	15.00
BW	Brandon Webb/300	40.00
RB	Rocco Baldelli/250	30.00

Candid Collection

		NM/M
Complete Set (15):		50.00
Common Player:		2.00
Production 500 Sets		
1CC	Derek Jeter	6.00
2CC	Mike Piazza	4.00
3CC	Albert Pujols	6.00
4CC	Randy Johnson	3.00
5CC	Alex Rodriguez	6.00
6CC	Vladimir Guerrero	3.00
7CC	Troy Glaus	2.00
8CC	Ichiro Suzuki	4.00
9CC	Barry Zito	2.00
10CC	Jim Thome	2.00
11CC	Sammy Sosa	5.00
12CC	Greg Maddux	4.00
13CC	Barry Bonds	8.00
14CC	Jason Giambi	3.00
15CC	Nomar Garciaparra	6.00

Candid Collection Memorabilia

	NM/M
Common Player:	
Production 150 Sets	
Derek Jeter	30.00
Mike Piazza	12.00
Randy Johnson	8.00
Alex Rodriguez	15.00
Barry Zito	8.00
Jim Thome	15.00
Sammy Sosa	15.00
Greg Maddux	15.00
Jason Giambi	10.00
Nomar Garciaparra	15.00

Hall of Frame

	NM/M
Complete Set (14):	80.00
Common Player:	6.00
Production 299 Sets	
1	Richie Ashburn	6.00
2	Rod Carew	8.00
3	Whitey Ford	8.00
4	Bob Gibson	8.00
5	Reggie Jackson	8.00
6	Harmon Killebrew	8.00

7	Willie McCovey	6.00
8	Phil Rizzuto	8.00
9	Al Kaline	10.00
10	Brooks Robinson	8.00
11	Nolan Ryan	15.00
12	Mike Schmidt	10.00
13	Tom Seaver	8.00
14	Warren Spahn	8.00

Hall of Frame Memorabilia

	NM/M
Production 99 Sets	
Reggie Jackson	25.00
Willie McCovey	20.00
Al Kaline	35.00
Nolan Ryan	65.00
Mike Schmidt	40.00

Material

		NM/M
Common Player:		
Production 50 Sets		
RB	Rocco Baldelli	25.00
AR	Alex Rodriguez	25.00
AS	Alfonso Soriano	20.00
SS	Sammy Sosa	20.00
NG	Nomar Garciaparra	20.00
MT	Miguel Tejada	10.00
CJ	Chipper Jones	20.00
RJ	Randy Johnson	15.00
JT	Jim Thome	15.00
GM	Greg Maddux	25.00
JG	Jason Giambi	15.00
VG	Vladimir Guerrero	15.00

On Display

	NM/M
Complete Set (10):	50.00
Common Player:	3.00
Production 399 Sets	
10D	Derek Jeter	6.00
20D	Barry Bonds	8.00
30D	Rocco Baldelli	5.00
40D	Alex Rodriguez	6.00
50D	Alfonso Soriano	6.00
60D	Sammy Sosa	6.00
70D	Nomar Garciaparra	6.00
80D	Hideki Matsui	20.00
90D	Miguel Tejada	3.00
100D	Chipper Jones	5.00

On Display Memorabilia

	NM/M
Common Player:	5.00
Production 250 Sets	
Derek Jeter	20.00
Barry Bonds	15.00
Rocco Baldelli	25.00
Alex Rodriguez	10.00
Alfonso Soriano	10.00
Sammy Sosa	12.00
Nomar Garciaparra	15.00
Hideki Matsui	40.00
Miguel Tejada	5.00
Chipper Jones	10.00

2003 Fleer Box Score

Jim THOME

	NM/M
Complete Set (245):	
Common Player:	.15
Common Box ScoreDebut	
(101-110):	4.00
Production 599	
Common Rookie (111-125):	1.00
Inserted 1:6	
Complete Rising Stars (30):	25.00
Common (126-155):	1.00
Complete All-Stars (30):	20.00
Common (156-185):	.50
Comp. Intl. Road Trip (30):	20.00
Common (186-215):	.50
Comp. Bronx Bombers (30):	30.00
Common (216-245):	.50
Pack (7):	3.00
Box (18 + 1 Supplemental Box):	40.00
1	Troy Glaus	.75
2	Derek Jeter	3.00
3	Alex Rodriguez	2.50
4	Barry Zito	.40
5	Darin Erstad	.60
6	Tim Hudson	.40
7	Josh Beckett	.15
8	Adam Dunn	.60
9	Tim Salmon	.50
10	Ivan Rodriguez	.25
11	Mark Buehrle	.15
12	Sammy Sosa	2.00
13	Vicente Padilla	.15
14	Randy Johnson	1.00
15	Lance Berkman	.15
16	Jim Thome	.75
17	Luis Gonzalez	.25
18	Craig Biggio	.15
19	Cliff Floyd	.15
20	Pat Burrell	.50
21	Matt Morris	.15
22	Torii Hunter	.15
23	Curt Schilling	.40
24	Paul Konerko	.15
25	Jeff Bagwell	.75
26	Mike Piazza	2.00
27	A.J. Burnett	.15
28	Jimmy Rollins	.25
29	Greg Maddux	1.50
30	Jeff Kent	.15
31	Bobby Abreu	.15
32	Chipper Jones	1.50
33	Mike Sweeney	.15
34	Jason Kendall	.15
35	Gary Sheffield	.30
36	Carlos Beltran	.50
37	Brian Giles	.15
38	Jim Edmonds	.15
39	Roger Clemens	1.75
40	Andruw Jones	.75
41	Paul LoDuca	.15
42	Ryan Klesko	.15
43	Jay Gibbons	.15
44	Shawn Green	.40
45	Sean Burroughs	.15
46	Magglio Ordonez	.15
47	Tony Batista	.15
48	J.D. Drew	.45
49	Hideo Nomo	.50
50	Edgardo Alfonzo	.15
51	Nomar Garciaparra	2.00
52	Frank Thomas	.75
53	Kazuhisa Ishii	.15
54	Rich Aurilia	.15
55	Shea Hillenbrand	.15
56	Tom Glavine	.40
57	Richie Sexson	.15
58	Mo Vaughn	.15
59	Barry Bonds	3.00
60	Carlos Delgado	.50
61	Pedro J. Martinez	1.00
62	Jacque Jones	.15
63	Edgar Martinez	.15
64	Manny Ramirez	.75
65	Bret Boone	.15
66	Kerry Wood	.50
67	Roy Oswalt	.40
68	Cristian Guzman	.15
69	Moises Alou	.15
70	Bartolo Colon	.15
71	Ichiro Suzuki	1.50

72	Jose Vidro	.15
73	Scott Rolen	.75
74	Mark Prior	1.00
75	Vladimir Guerrero	.75
76	Albert Pujols	1.50
77	Aubrey Huff	.15
78	Ken Griffey Jr.	2.00
79	Roberto Alomar	.30
80	Ben Grieve	.15
81	Miguel Tejada	.40
82	Austin Kearns	.50
83	Jason Giambi	.75
84	John Olerud	.15
85	Omar Vizquel	.15
86	Juan Gonzalez	.75
87	Larry Walker	.15
88	Jorge Posada	.25
89	Rafael Palmeiro	.65
90	Todd Helton	.75
91	Bernie Williams	.30
92	Garret Anderson	.15
93	Eric Hinske	.15
94	Mike Lowell	.15
95	Jason Jennings	.15
96	Eric Chavez	.30
97	Alfonso Soriano	1.00
98	David Eckstein	.15
99	Bobby Higginson	.15
100	Roy Halladay	.15
101	Robby Hammock RC	4.00
102	Hideki Matsui RC	12.00
103	Chase Utley RC	4.00
104	Oscar Villarreal RC	4.00
105	Jose Contreras RC	8.00
106	Rocco Baldelli	4.00
107	Rontrez Johnson RC	4.00
108	Jeremy Bonderman	6.00
109	Shane Victorino RC	4.00
110	Ron Calloway	4.00
111	Brandon Webb RC	8.00
112	Guillermo Quiroz RC	2.00
113	Clint Barmes RC	2.00
114	Pete LaForest RC	1.00
115	Craig Brazell RC	2.00
116	Todd Wellemeyer RC	1.00
117	Bernie Castro RC	1.00
118	Alejandro Machado RC	1.50
119	Terrmel Sledge RC	1.00
120	Ian Ferguson RC	1.00
121	Lew Ford RC	3.00
122	Nook Logan RC	1.50
123	Mike Nicolas RC	1.00
124	Jeff Duncan RC	1.50
125	Tim Olson RC	1.00
126	Michael Hessman RC	1.00
127	Francisco Rosario RC	1.00
128	Felix Sanchez RC	1.00
129	Andrew Brown RC	1.50
130	Matt Bruback RC	2.00
131	Diegomar Markwell RC	2.00
132	Josh Willingham RC	1.00
133	Wes Obermueller	1.50
134	Phil Seibel RC	2.00
135	Arnie Munoz RC	1.00
136	Matt Kata RC	3.00
137	Joe Valentine RC	1.00
138	Ricardo Rodriguez	1.00
139	Lyle Overbay	2.00
140	Brian Stokes RC	1.00
141	Josh Hall RC	1.50
142	Kevin Hooper	1.00
143	Chien-Ming Wang RC	10.00
144	Prentice Redman RC	1.50
145	Chris Waters RC	1.50
146	Jon Leicester RC	1.00
147	Daniel Cabrera RC	1.50
148	Alfredo Gonzalez RC	1.50
149	Doug Waechter RC	1.50
150	Brandon Larson	1.50
151	Beau Kemp RC	1.50
152	Cory Stewart RC	1.00
153	Francisco Rodriguez	1.00
154	Hee Seop Choi	1.50
155	Mike Neu RC	1.00
156	Derek Jeter	3.00
157	Alex Rodriguez	2.50
158	Nomar Garciaparra	2.00
159	Barry Bonds	2.50
160	Sammy Sosa	1.50
161	Vladimir Guerrero	.75
162	Roger Clemens	2.00
163	Randy Johnson	1.00
164	Greg Maddux	1.50
165	Ken Griffey Jr.	1.50
166	Mike Piazza	2.00
167	Ichiro Suzuki	1.50
168	Barry Larkin	.50
169	Lance Berkman	.50
170	Jim Thome	.75
171	Jason Giambi	1.00
172	Gary Sheffield	.50
173	Ivan Rodriguez	.50
174	Miguel Tejada	.50
175	Manny Ramirez	.75
176	Mike Sweeney	.50
177	Larry Walker	.50
178	Jeff Bagwell	.75
179	Chipper Jones	1.50
180	Craig Biggio	.50
181	Curt Schilling	.50
182	Pedro J. Martinez	1.00
183	Roberto Alomar	.50
184	Bernie Williams	.50
185	Magglio Ordonez	.50
186	Jose Contreras	1.00

187	Rafael Palmeiro	1.00
188	Andruw Jones	.75
189	Bartolo Colon	.50
190	Vladimir Guerrero	.75
191	Pedro Martinez	1.00
192	Albert Pujols	1.50
193	Manny Ramirez	.75
194	Felix Rodriguez	.50
195	Alfonso Soriano	1.00
196	Sammy Sosa	1.50
197	Miguel Tejada	.50
198	Kazuhisa Ishii	.50
199	Hideki Matsui	5.00
200	Hideo Nomo	1.00
201	Tomokazu Ohka	.50
202	Kazuhiro Sasaki	.50
203	Tsuyoshi Shinjo	.50
204	Ichiro Suzuki	1.50
205	Vicente Padilla	.50
206	Carlos Beltran	.50
207	Jose Cruz Jr.	.50
208	Carlos Delgado	.50
209	Juan Gonzalez	.75
210	Jorge Posada	.50
211	Ivan Rodriguez	.50
212	Hee Seop Choi	.50
213	Bobby Abreu	.50
214	Magglio Ordonez	.50
215	Francisco Rodriguez	.50
216	Juan Acevedo	.50
217	Erick Almonte	.50
218	Yogi Berra	1.50
219	Brandon Claussen	1.00
220	Roger Clemens	2.00
221	Jose Contreras	1.00
222	Whitey Ford	1.00
223	Jason Giambi	1.00
225	Michel Hernandez RC	.50
226	Sterling Hitchcock	.50
227	Jim "Catfish" Hunter	.75
228	Reggie Jackson	1.00
229	Derek Jeter	3.00
230	Nick Johnson	.50
231	Hideki Matsui	5.00
232	Raul Mondesi	.50
233	Mike Mussina	.75
234	Andy Pettitte	.50
235	Jorge Posada	.50
236	Mariano Rivera	.50
237	Phil Rizzuto	1.00
238	Enos Slaughter	.50
239	Alfonso Soriano	1.00
240	Robin Ventura	.50
241	Chien-Ming Wang	2.00
242	Jeff Weaver	.50
243	David Wells	.50
244	Bernie Williams	.75
245	Todd Zeile	.50

First Edition

Bobby ABREU

Stars (1-100):	4-8X
Rookies (101-125):	1.5-3X
Production 150 Sets	

All-Star Lineup

	NM/M
Common Card:	15.00
Inserted 1:All-Stars Set	
Derek Jeter, Alex Rodriguez,	
Nomar Garciaparra,	35.00
Barry Bonds, Sammy Sosa,	
Vladimir Guerrero	15.00
Roger Clemens, Randy Johnson,	
Greg Maddux	30.00
Jason Giambi, Alfonso Soriano,	
Derek Jeter	30.00
Craig Biggio, Jeff Bagwell,	
Lance Berkman	30.00
Chipper Jones, Gary Sheffield,	
Greg Maddux	30.00
Ivan Rodriguez, Mike Piazza,	
Randy Johnson,	
Roger Clemens	40.00
Roberto Alomar, Mike Piazza,	
Alfonso Soriano,	
Jason Giambi	45.00
Jim Thome, Roberto Alomar,	
Alex Rodriguez,	
Nomar Garciaparra	40.00

Bat Rack

	NM/M
Common Card:	20.00
Production 250 Sets	
Derek Jeter, Alfonso Soriano,	
Jason Giambi	35.00
Scott Rolen, Miguel Tejada,	
Troy Glaus	20.00
Jim Thome, Torii Hunter,	
Mike Piazza	25.00
Troy Glaus, Nomar Garciaparra,	
Alfonso Soriano	30.00
Lance Berkman,	
Vladimir Guerrero,	
Sammy Sosa	20.00
Chipper Jones, Lance Berkman,	
Vladimir Guerrero	20.00
Torii Hunter, Jason Giambi,	
Nomar Garciaparra	25.00
Derek Jeter, Miguel Tejada,	
Alex Rodriguez	25.00
Scott Rolen, Sammy Sosa,	
Alex Rodriguez	25.00

Bat Rack Quad

	NM/M
Production 50 Sets	
Derek Jeter, Torii Hunter,	
Troy Glaus,	
Miguel Tejada	40.00
Derek Jeter, Mike Piazza,	
Nomar Garciaparra,	
Chipper Jones	60.00
Alex Rodriguez, Jim Thome,	
Sammy Sosa,	
Barry Bonds	50.00

Bronx Bombers Jersey

	NM/M
Common Player:	4.00
Inserted 1:Bronx Bombers Set	
Roger Clemens	15.00
Jason Giambi	12.00
Derek Jeter	20.00
Nick Johnson	4.00
Mike Mussina	10.00
Jorge Posada	8.00
Alfonso Soriano	10.00
Robin Ventura	5.00
Bernie Williams	8.00

Classic Minatures

Kerry WOOD

	NM/M
Complete Set (30):	10.00
Common Player:	.25
1CM Jim Thome	.40
2CM Jason Giambi	.50
3CM Miguel Tejada	.25
4CM Alfonso Soriano	1.00
5CM Ivan Rodriguez	.40
6CM Troy Glaus	.40
7CM Mike Piazza	1.00
8CM Barry Bonds	1.50
9CM Sammy Sosa	1.00
10CM Lance Berkman	.25
11CM Pat Burrell	.25
12CM Chipper Jones	.75
13CM Shawn Green	.25
14CM Manny Ramirez	.50
15CM Ichiro Suzuki	.75
16CM Vladimir Guerrero	.50
17CM Albert Pujols	.75
18CM Ken Griffey Jr.	1.00
19CM Bernie Williams	.40
20CM Austin Kearns	.40
21CM Randy Johnson	.50
22CM Greg Maddux	.75
23CM Roger Clemens	1.00
24CM Hideo Nomo	.25
25CM Pedro J. Martinez	.50
26CM Kerry Wood	.40
27CM Mark Prior	.50
28CM Derek Jeter	1.50
29CM Alex Rodriguez	1.00
30CM Nomar Garciaparra	1.00

Classic Miniatures Mini Jersey

	NM/M
Common Jersey:	4.00

1:Classic Miniatures Box

NG	Nomar Garciaparra	10.00
JG	Jason Giambi	8.00
VG	Vladimir Guerrero	5.00
DJ	Derek Jeter	15.00
AK	Austin Kearns	8.00
GM	Greg Maddux	10.00
HN	Hideo Nomo	10.00
MP	Mark Prior	10.00
MT	Miguel Tejada	4.00
JT	Jim Thome	8.00

Jersey Rack

	NM/M
Common Card:	15.00
Production 350 Sets	
Derek Jeter, Alfonso Soriano,	
Jason Giambi	40.00
Curt Schilling, Randy Johnson,	
Greg Maddux	25.00
Roger Clemens,	
Pedro J. Martinez,	
Barry Zito	30.00
Alex Rodriguez,	
Vladimir Guerrero,	
Sammy Sosa	25.00
Derek Jeter, Nomar Garciaparra,	
Alex Rodriguez	30.00
Lance Berkman, Sammy Sosa,	
Torii Hunter	20.00
Vladimir Guerrero, Jim Thome,	
Alex Rodriguez	20.00
Derek Jeter, Miguel Tejada,	
Nomar Garciaparra	30.00
Alfonso Soriano, Eric Chavez,	
Jim Thome	20.00
Miguel Tejada, Eric Chavez,	
Barry Zito	15.00

Jersey Rack Quad

	NM/M
Common Card:	
Production 150 Sets	
Derek Jeter, Alex Rodriguez,	
Nomar Garciaparra,	
Miguel Tejada	60.00
Jim Thome, Jason Giambi,	
Sammy Sosa,	
Vladimir Guerrero	50.00
Randy Johnson, Greg Maddux,	
Roger Clemens,	
Pedro J. Martinez	60.00
Curt Schilling, Vladimir Guerrero,	
Randy Johnson,	
Alex Rodriguez	40.00
Alfonso Soriano, Jim Thome,	
Sammy Sosa, Eric Chavez	40.00
Eric Chavez, Miguel Tejada,	
Barry Zito,	
Nomar Garciaparra	20.00

Press Clippings

Triple Threat

ALEX RODRIGUEZ SS
TEXAS RANGERS

	NM/M
Complete Set (20):	40.00
Common Player:	1.00
Inserted 1:18	
1PC Derek Jeter	6.00
2PC Nomar Garciaparra	5.00
3PC Miguel Tejada	1.00
4PC Barry Bonds	5.00
5PC Alex Rodriguez	5.00
6PC Sammy Sosa	3.00
7PC Lance Berkman	1.00
8PC Torii Hunter	1.00
9PC Troy Glaus	1.50
10PC Eric Chavez	1.00
11PC Tim Hudson	1.00
12PC Randy Johnson	2.00
13PC Mike Piazza	4.00
14PC Roberto Alomar	1.50
15PC Jim Thome	1.50
16PC Alfonso Soriano	3.00
17PC Roger Clemens	4.00
18PC Pedro J. Martinez	2.00
19PC Mark Prior	1.50
20PC Curt Schilling	1.00

Press Clippings Dual

	NM/M
Complete Set (10):	35.00
Common Player:	2.00

Production 250 Sets

1	Derek Jeter,	
	Nomar Garciaparra	8.00
2	Miguel Tejada, Barry Bonds	6.00
3	Alex Rodriguez,	
	Sammy Sosa	
4	Lance Berkman,Torii Hunter	2.00
5	Troy Glaus, Eric Chavez	2.00
6	Tim Hudson,	
	Randy Johnson	3.00
7	Mike Piazza, Roberto Alomar	5.00
8	Jim Thome,	
	Alfonso Soriano	4.00
9	Roger Clemens,	
	Pedro J. Martinez	5.00
10	Mark Prior, Curt Schilling	2.00

Press Clippings Dual Patch

	NM/M
Common Card:	25.00
Derek Jeter,	
Nomar Garciaparra/100	60.00
Miguel Tejada,	
Troy Glaus/150	25.00
Alex Rodriguez,	
Sammy Sosa/150	80.00
Lance Berkman,	
Torii Hunter/150	30.00
Troy Glaus,	
Eric Chavez/150	30.00
Tim Hudson,	
Randy Johnson/150	30.00
Mike Piazza,	
Roberto Alomar/150	40.00
Jim Thome,	
Alfonso Soriano/100	40.00
Roger Clemens,	
Pedro Martinez/100	50.00
Mark Prior,	
Curt Schilling/150	25.00

Press Clippings Game-Used

Striking Silver & Gold

TODD HELTON 1B
AUTHENTIC GAME-WORN JERSEY

	NM/M
Common Player:	4.00
Inserted 1:12	
Derek Jeter	15.00
Nomar Garciaparra	15.00
Miguel Tejada	4.00
Alex Rodriguez	10.00
Sammy Sosa	12.00
Lance Berkman	4.00
Torii Hunter	6.00
Troy Glaus	5.00
Eric Chavez	4.00
Tim Hudson	4.00
Randy Johnson	8.00
Mike Piazza	12.00
Roberto Alomar	8.00
Jim Thome	10.00
Alfonso Soriano	10.00
Roger Clemens	12.00
Pedro J. Martinez	8.00
Mark Prior	6.00
Curt Schilling	4.00

Wave of the Future

	NM/M
Common Player:	4.00
Inserted 1:Rising Stars Set	
Jeremy Bonderman/Bat	12.00
Ron Calloway/Jsy	4.00
Hee Seop Choi/Jsy	10.00
Brandon Larson/Bat	8.00
Lyle Overbay/Bat	6.00
Francisco Rodriguez/Jsy	6.00
Chase Utley/Jsy	6.00

World Piece

	NM/M
Common Player:	4.00
Inserted 1:Intl. Road Trip Set	
Vladimir Guerrero	6.00
Pedro Martinez	10.00
Sammy Sosa	12.00
Miguel Tejada	4.00
Hideo Nomo	10.00
Jose Cruz Jr.	4.00
Ivan Rodriguez	6.00
Hee Seop Choi	10.00
Francisco Rodriguez	4.00
Kazuhiro Sasaki	4.00

2003 Fleer Double Header

ROBERTO ALOMAR
New York Mets®, 2b

	NM/M
Complete Set (300):	60.00
Common Player:	.20
Common (181-300):	.40
Pack (8):	2.00
Box (20):	35.00

#	Player	Price
1	Ramon Vazquez	.20
2	Derek Jeter	2.00
3	Orlando Hudson	.20
4	Miguel Tejada	.20
5	Steve Finley	.20
6	Brad Wilkerson	.20
7	Craig Biggio	.20
8	Marlon Anderson	.20
9	Phil Nevin	.20
10	Hideo Nomo	.50
11	Barry Larkin	.20
12	Alfonso Soriano	.75
13	Rodrigo Lopez	.20
14	Paul Konerko	.25
15	Carlos Beltran	.50
16	Garret Anderson	.20
17	Kazuhisa Ishii	.20
18	Eddie Guardado	.20
19	Juan Gonzalez	.50
20	Mark Mulder	.20
21	Sammy Sosa	1.25
22	Kazuhiro Sasaki	.20
23	Jose Cruz Jr.	.20
24	Tomokazu Ohka	.20
25	Barry Bonds	2.00
26	Carlos Delgado	.50
27	Scott Rolen	.50
28	Steve Cox	.20
29	Mike Sweeney	.20
30	Ryan Klesko	.20
31	Greg Maddux	1.00
32	Derek Lowe	.20
33	David Wells	.20
34	Kerry Wood	.40
35	Randall Simon	.20
36	Ben Howard	.20
37	Jeff Suppan	.20
38	Curt Schilling	.40
39	Eric Gagne	.20
40	Raul Mondesi	.20
41	Jeffrey Hammonds	.20
42	Mo Vaughn	.20
43	Sidney Ponson	.20
44	Adam Dunn	.50
45	Pedro J. Martinez	.75
46	Jason Simontacchi	.20
47	Tom Glavine	.40
48	Torii Hunter	.20
49	Gabe Kapler	.20
50	Andy Van Hekken	.20
51	Ichiro Suzuki	1.25
52	Andruw Jones	.50
53	Bobby Abreu	.20
54	Junior Spivey	.20
55	Ray Durham	.20
56	Mark Buehrle	.20
57	Drew Henson	.20
58	Brandon Duckworth	.20
59	Robert Mackowiak	.20
60	Josh Beckett	.20
61	Chan Ho Park	.20
62	John Smoltz	.20
63	Jimmy Rollins	.40
64	Orlando Cabrera	.20
65	Johnny Damon	.20
66	Austin Kearns	.40
67	Tsuyoshi Shinjo	.20
68	Tim Hudson	.30
69	Coco Crisp	.20
70	Darin Erstad	.60
71	Jacque Jones	.20
72	Vicente Padilla	.20
73	Hee Seop Choi	.20
74	Shea Hillenbrand	.20
75	Edgardo Alfonzo	.20
76	Pat Burrell	.50
77	Ben Sheets	.20
78	Ivan Rodriguez	.40
79	Josh Phelps	.20
80	Adam Kennedy	.20
81	Eric Chavez	.30
82	Bobby Higginson	.20
83	Nomar Garciaparra	1.50
84	J.D. Drew	.30
85	Carl Crawford	.20
86	Matt Morris	.20
87	Chipper Jones	1.00
88	Luis Gonzalez	.30
89	Richie Sexson	.20
90	Eric Milton	.20
91	Andres Galarraga	.20
92	Paul LoDuca	.20
93	Mark Grace	.30
94	Ben Grieve	.20
95	Mike Lowell	.20
96	Roberto Alomar	.35
97	Wade Miller	.20
98	Sean Casey	.20
99	Roger Clemens	1.25
100	Matt Williams	.20
101	Brian Giles	.20
102	Jim Thome	.20
103	Troy Glaus	.75
104	Joe Borchard	.20
105	Vladimir Guerrero	.75
106	Kevin Mench	.20
107	Omar Vizquel	.20
108	Magglio Ordonez	.20
109	Ken Griffey Jr.	1.50
110	Mike Piazza	1.50
111	Mark Teixeira	.40
112	Jason Jennings	.20
113	Ellis Burks	.20
114	Jason Varitek	.20
115	Larry Walker	.20
116	Frank Thomas	.75
117	Ramon Ortiz	.20
118	Mark Quinn	.20
119	Preston Wilson	.20
120	Carlos Lee	.20
121	Brian Lawrence	.20
122	Tim Salmon	.20
123	Shawn Green	.30
124	Randy Johnson	.75
125	Jeff Bagwell	.75
126	C.C. Sabathia	.20
127	Bernie Williams	.35
128	Roy Oswalt	.30
129	Albert Pujols	.75
130	Reggie Sanders	.20
131	Jeff Conine	.20
132	John Olerud	.20
133	Lance Berkman	.20
134	Geoff Jenkins	.20
135	Jim Edmonds	.20
136	Todd Helton	.65
137	Jason Kendall	.20
138	Robin Ventura	.20
139	Randy Winn	.20
140	Carl Everett	.20
141	Jose Vidro	.20
142	Pokey Reese	.20
143	Edgar Renteria	.20
144	Alex Rodriguez	1.75
145	Doug Mientkiewicz	.20
146	Aramis Ramirez	.20
147	Bobby Hill	.20
148	Jorge Posada	.35
149	Sean Burroughs	.20
150	Jeff Kent	.20
151	Tino Martinez	.20
152	Mark Prior	.50
153	Brad Radke	.20
154	Al Leiter	.20
155	Eric Karros	.20
156	Manny Ramirez	.50
157	Jason Lane	.20
158	Mike Lieberthal	.20
159	Shannon Stewart	.20
160	Robert Fick	.20
161	Derrek Lee	.20
162	Jason Giambi	.50
163	Rafael Palmeiro	.65
164	Jay Payton	.20
165	Adrian Beltre	.20
166	Marlon Byrd	.20
167	Bret Boone	.20
168	Roy Halladay	.20
169	Freddy Garcia	.20
170	Rich Aurilia	.20
171	Jared Sandberg	.20
172	Paul Byrd	.20
173	Gary Sheffield	.30
174	Edgar Martinez	.20
175	Eric Hinske	.20
176	Milton Bradley	.20
177	David Eckstein	.20
178	Jay Gibbons	.20
179	Corey Patterson	.20
180	Barry Zito	.20
181-182	Darin Erstad, Troy Glaus	.50
183-184	Curt Schilling, Randy Johnson	.75
185-186	Andruw Jones, Chipper Jones	1.00
187-188	Tony Batista, Jay Gibbons	.40
189-190	Pedro Martinez, Nomar Garciaparra	1.25
191-192	Sammy Sosa, Kerry Wood	1.00
193-194	Paul Konerko, Joe Borchard	.40
195-196	Austin Kearns, Adam Dunn	.50
197-198	Omar Vizquel, Jim Thome	.50
199-200	Larry Walker, Todd Helton	.40
201-202	Josh Beckett, Luis Castillo	.40
203-204	Craig Biggio, Jeff Bagwell	.50
205-206	Paul Byrd, Mike Sweeney	.40
207-208	Adrian Beltre, Shawn Green	.40
209-210	Jose Hernandez, Richie Sexson	.40
211-212	Jacque Jones, Torii Hunter	.40
213-214	Vladimir Guerrero, Jose Vidro	.75
215-216	Edgardo Alfonzo, Mike Piazza	1.50
217-218	Roger Clemens, Derek Jeter	2.00
219-220	Eric Chavez, Miguel Tejada	.40
221-222	Marlon Byrd, Pat Burrell	.50
223-224	Jason Kendall, Brian Giles	.40
225-226	Phil Nevin, Sean Burroughs	.40
227-228	Jeff Kent, Barry Bonds	2.00
229-230	Kazuhiro Sasaki, Ichiro Suzuki	1.25
231-232	Albert Pujols, J.D. Drew	.75
233-234	Juan Gonzalez, Ivan Rodriguez	.50
235-236	Eric Hinske, Orlando Hudson	.40
237-238	Lance Berkman, Chipper Jones	1.00
239-240	Alex Rodriguez, Derek Jeter	2.00
241-242	Ichiro Suzuki, Hideo Nomo	1.25
243-244	Manny Ramirez, Bernie Williams	.50
245-246	Tom Glavine, Roger Clemens	1.00
247-248	Ken Griffey Jr., Barry Larkin	1.25
249-250	Mark Teixeira, Mark Prior	.40
251-252	Albert Pujols, Drew Henson	.75
253-254	Jason Giambi, Todd Helton	1.00
255-256	Jose Vidro, Alfonso Soriano	.75
257-258	Shea Hillenbrand, Scott Rolen	.50
259-260	Jimmy Rollins, Alex Rodriguez	2.00
261-262	Torii Hunter, Vladimir Guerrero	.75
263-264	Ichiro Suzuki, Sammy Sosa	1.25
265-266	Barry Bonds, Manny Ramirez	2.00
267-268	Mike Piazza, Jorge Posada	1.25
269-270	Robin Yount, Ozzie Smith	1.00
271-272	Josh Hancock, Freddy Sanchez	.40
273-274	Ryan Bukvich, Shawn Sedlacek	.40
275-276	Doug DeVore, Rene Reyes	.40
277-278	Hank Blalock, Travis Hafner	.50
279-280	Eric Junge, Brett Myers	.40
281-282	Brad Lidge, Jeriome Robertson	.40
283-284	Miguel Asencio, Runelvys Hernandez	.40
285-286	Fernando Rodney, Barry Wesson	.40
287-288	Victor Alvarez, David Ross	.40
289-290	Tony Torcato, Chris Snelling	.50
291-292	Kirk Saarloos, Morgan Ensberg	.40
293-294	Josh Bard, Wilbert Nieves	.40
295-296	Jung Bong, Trey Hodges	.40
297-298	Kevin Cash, Reed Johnson	.40
299-300	Chone Figgins, John Lackey	.40

Flip Card Memorabilia

	NM/M
Common Player:	4.00
Inserted 1:20	
Golds:	.75-2X
Production 100 Sets	
1 Roberto Alomar/Bat/200	10.00
2 Jeff Bagwell/Jsy	8.00
3 Adrian Beltre/Jsy	4.00
4 Barry Bonds/Bat/200	15.00
5 Roger Clemens/Jsy/200	12.00
6 J.D. Drew/Jsy	6.00

KERRY WOOD
Chicago Cubs™, p
Game-Worn Jersey

7	Adam Dunn/Jsy/200	10.00
8	Nomar Garciaparra/Jsy/200	15.00
9	Mark Grace/Jsy	8.00
10	Todd Helton/Jsy/200	8.00
11	Derek Jeter/Jsy/200	20.00
12	Randy Johnson/Jsy/200	10.00
13	Chipper Jones/Jsy	8.00
14	Eric Karros/Jsy	4.00
15	Barry Larkin/Jsy/200	8.00
16	Greg Maddux/Jsy/200	10.00
17	Hideo Nomo/Jsy/200	10.00
18	Kazuhisa Ishii/Jsy	6.00
19	Mike Piazza/Jsy/200	10.00
20	Jorge Posada/Jsy/200	8.00
21	Mark Prior/Jsy/200	5.00
22	Alex Rodriguez/Jsy	10.00
23	Kazuhiro Sasaki/Jsy/200	6.00
24	Curt Schilling/Jsy/200	8.00
25	Alfonso Soriano/Jsy	8.00
26	Miguel Tejada/Jsy	8.00
27	Jim Thome/Jsy/200	10.00
28	Robin Ventura/Jsy	4.00
29	Bernie Williams/Jsy/200	8.00
30	Kerry Wood/Jsy/200	10.00

Keystone Combination

	NM/M
Complete Set (10):	25.00
Common Card:	1.00
Inserted 1:10	
1KC Derek Jeter, Bret Boone	6.00
2KC Miguel Tejada, Jeff Kent	1.00
3KC Nomar Garciaparra, Ray Durham	4.00
4KC Omar Vizquel, Roberto Alomar	1.00
5KC Pee Wee Reese, Joe Morgan	1.00
6KC Alex Rodriguez, Craig Biggio	1.00
7KC Orlando Hudson, Jose Vidro	1.00
8KC Phil Rizzuto, Alfonso Soriano	3.00
9KC Alex Rodriguez, Miguel Tejada	5.00
10KC Nomar Garciaparra, Derek Jeter	6.00

Keystone Combination Memorabilia

	NM/M
Common Card:	
Inserted 1:40	
Derek Jeter, Bret Boone/Jsy	8.00
Miguel Tejada, Jeff Kent/Jsy	4.00
N.Garciaparra/Jsy/175, Ray Durham	12.00
Omar Vizquel, Roberto Alomar/Jsy	6.00
Craig Biggio/Jsy, Orlando Hudson	6.00
Jose Vidro/Jsy	4.00
Phil Rizzuto, Alfonso Soriano/Jsy/75	15.00
Alex Rodriguez/Bat, Miguel Tejada	10.00
N.Garciaparra/Jsy/175, Derek Jeter	12.00
Derek Jeter/Jsy/175, Bret Boone	20.00
Derek Jeter/Jsy/175, Nomar Garciaparra	20.00
Alex Rodriguez/Jsy/200, Craig Biggio	10.00
Miguel Tejada/Jsy, Jeff Kent	8.00
Miguel Tejada/Jsy, Alex Rodriguez	8.00

Let's Play, Too!

		NM/M
Complete Set (15):		8.00
Common Player:		.50
Inserted 1:5		
1LPT	Chris Snelling	1.00
2LPT	Kevin Mench	.50
3LPT	Brett Meyers	.50
4LPT	Julius Matos	.50
5LPT	Drew Henson	1.00
6LPT	Joe Borchard	.50
7LPT	Felix Escalona	.50
8LPT	Kirk Saarloos	.50
9LPT	Ben Howard	.50
10LPT	Hee Seop Choi	1.00
11LPT	Rene Reyes	.50
12LPT	Josh Bard	.50
13LPT	Marlon Byrd	.50
14LPT	Coco Crisp	.50
15LPT	Reed Johnson	.50

Matinee Idols

		NM/M
Complete Set (15):		50.00
Common Player:		2.00
Inserted 1:20		
1MI	Yogi Berra	3.00
2MI	Richie Ashburn	3.00
3MI	Whitey Ford	3.00
4MI	Eddie Mathews	3.00
5MI	Jim Palmer	2.00
6MI	Al Kaline	6.00
7MI	Brooks Robinson	3.00
8MI	Willie McCovey	3.00
9MI	Billy Williams	2.00
10MI	Willie Stargell	3.00
11MI	Nolan Ryan	15.00
12MI	Rod Carew	3.00
13MI	Reggie Jackson	4.00
14MI	Tom Seaver	4.00
15MI	Mike Schmidt	6.00

Twin Bill

		NM/M
Complete Set (20):		45.00
Common Player:		1.00
Inserted 1:10		
1a	Barry Bonds	5.00
1b	Lance Berkman	1.00
2a	Derek Jeter	6.00
2b	Alex Rodriguez	5.00
3a	Roger Clemens	3.00
3b	Pedro Martinez	2.00
4a	Roberto Alomar	1.25

4b	Chipper Jones	3.00
5a	Barry Zito	1.00
5b	Ichiro Suzuki	4.00
6a	Sammy Sosa	3.00
6b	Ken Griffey Jr.	4.00
7a	Bernie Williams	1.00
7b	Manny Ramirez	1.50
8a	Nomar Garciaparra	4.00
8b	Derek Jeter	6.00
9a	Randy Johnson	2.00
9b	Greg Maddux	3.00
10a	Albert Pujols	2.00
10b	Adam Dunn	1.50

Twin Bill Single Swatch

		NM/M
Common Player:		1.00
Barry Bonds/Cap/100		25.00
Alex Rodriguez/Cap/100		15.00
Roger Clemens/Cap/100		15.00
Pedro Martinez/Cap/100		12.00
Roberto Alomar/Cap		10.00
Barry Zito/Cap/100		15.00
Bernie Williams/Cap/100		10.00
Manny Ramirez/Cap/75		12.00
Nomar Garciaparra/Cap/100		25.00
Derek Jeter/Cap/100		30.00
Randy Johnson/Cap/100		15.00
Adam Dunn/Cap/100		12.00

Twin Bill Dual Swatch

		NM/M
Common Card:		
Production 50 Sets		
Barry Bonds, Adam Dunn		40.00
Randy Johnson, Barry Zito		35.00

2003 Fleer E-X

		NM/M
Complete Set (102):		125.00
Common Player:		.50
Common SP (83-102):		3.00
Pack (3):		4.00
Box (20):		60.00
1	Troy Glaus	.75
2	Darin Erstad	.75
3	Garret Anderson	.50
4	Curt Schilling	.75
5	Randy Johnson	1.00
6	Luis Gonzalez	.50
7	Greg Maddux	1.50
8	Chipper Jones	1.50
9	Andruw Jones	1.00
10	Melvin Mora	.50
11	Jay Gibbons	.50
12	Nomar Garciaparra	2.00
13	Pedro J. Martinez	1.00
14	Manny Ramirez	1.00
15	Sammy Sosa	2.00
16	Kerry Wood	.75
17	Magglio Ordonez	.50
18	Frank Thomas	1.00
19	Roberto Alomar	.60
20	Barry Larkin	.50
21	Adam Dunn	1.00
22	Austin Kearns	.75
23	Omar Vizquel	.50
24	Larry Walker	.50
25	Todd Helton	1.00
26	Preston Wilson	.50
27	Dmitri Young	.50
28	Ivan Rodriguez	.75
29	Mike Lowell	.50
30	Jeff Kent	.50
31	Jeff Bagwell	1.00
32	Roy Oswalt	.75
33	Craig Biggio	.50
34	Mike Sweeney	.50
35	Carlos Beltran	.75
36	Shawn Green	.60
37	Kazuhisa Ishii	.50
38	Richie Sexson	.50
39	Torii Hunter	.50
40	Jacque Jones	.50
41	Jose Vidro	.50
42	Vladimir Guerrero	1.00
43	Mike Piazza	2.00
44	Tom Glavine	.60
45	Roger Clemens	1.75
46	Jason Giambi	.75

47	Bernie Williams	.60
48	Alfonso Soriano	1.00
49	Mike Mussina	.60
50	Barry Zito	.60
51	Miguel Tejada	.60
52	Eric Chavez	.60
53	Eric Byrnes	.50
54	Jim Thome	.50
55	Kevin Millwood	.50
56	Brian Giles	.50
57	Xavier Nady	.50
58	Barry Bonds	3.00
59	Bret Boone	.50
60	Edgar Martinez	.50
61	Kazuhiro Sasaki	.50
62	Edgar Renteria	.50
63	J.D. Drew	.50
64	Scott Rolen	.50
65	Jim Edmonds	.50
66	Aubrey Huff	.50
67	Alex Rodriguez	2.50
68	Juan Gonzalez	1.00
69	Hank Blalock	.75
70	Mark Teixeira	.75
71	Carlos Delgado	.75
72	Vernon Wells	.50
73	Shea Hillenbrand	.50
74	Gary Sheffield	.60
75	Mark Prior	.50
76	Ken Griffey Jr.	2.00
77	Lance Berkman	.50
78	Hideo Nomo	.75
79	Derek Jeter	3.00
80	Ichiro Suzuki	2.00
81	Albert Pujols	2.50
82	Rafael Palmeiro	.75
83	Jose Reyes	4.00
84	Rocco Baldelli	3.00
85	Hee Seop Choi	3.00
86	Dontrelle Willis	3.00
87	Robby Hammock RC	3.00
88	Brandon Webb RC	10.00
89	Matt Kata RC	3.00
90	Todd Wellemeyer RC	4.00
91	Francisco Cruceta RC	3.00
92	Clint Barmes RC	4.00
93	Jeremy Bonderman	6.00
94	Dave Matranga RC	3.00
95	Ryan Wagner RC	3.00
96	Jeremy Griffiths RC	3.00
97	Hideki Matsui RC	15.00
98	Jose Contreras RC	6.00
99	Chien-Ming Wang RC	25.00
100	Bo Hart RC	3.00
101	Dan Haren RC	5.00
102	Rickie Weeks RC	5.00

Essential Credentials Now/Future

	NM/M
Cards serial numbered 26-50:	6-12X
Cards s/n 51-75:	4-8X
Cards s/n 76-102:	3-5X
SP's (83-102) s/n 83-102:	1-2X
Now is consecutively #'d from 1 to 102.	
Future is consect. #'d from 102 to 1.	

Behind the Numbers

		NM/M
Complete Set (15):		50.00
Common Player:		1.50
Inserted 1:80		
1	Derek Jeter	8.00
2	Alex Rodriguez	8.00
3	Randy Johnson	3.00
4	Chipper Jones	5.00
5	Jim Thome	3.00
6	Alfonso Soriano	4.00
7	Adam Dunn	2.00
8	Nomar Garciaparra	6.00
9	Roger Clemens	6.00
10	Gary Sheffield	1.50
11	Vladimir Guerrero	3.00
12	Greg Maddux	5.00
13	Sammy Sosa	6.00
14	Mike Piazza	5.00
15	Troy Glaus	2.00

Behind the Numbers Game-Used

		NM/M
Common Player:		5.00
Inserted 1:10		
Patch Version:		1.5-2.5X
DJ	Derek Jeter	15.00
AR	Alex Rodriguez	10.00
RJ	Randy Johnson	8.00
CJ	Chipper Jones	8.00
JT	Jim Thome	8.00
AS	Alfonso Soriano	8.00
AD	Adam Dunn	6.00
NG	Nomar Garciaparra	10.00
RC	Roger Clemens	10.00
GS	Gary Sheffield	5.00
VG	Vladimir Guerrero	8.00
GM	Greg Maddux	8.00
SS	Sammy Sosa	10.00
MP	Mike Piazza	8.00
TG	Troy Glaus	5.00
HB	Hank Blalock	5.00
TG	Tom Glavine	5.00
BM	Brett Myers	5.00
LB	Lance Berkman	5.00

RB	Rocco Baldelli	10.00
BZ	Barry Zito	6.00
DW	Dontrelle Willis	10.00
RP	Rafael Palmeiro	6.00
RA	Roberto Alomar	6.00
MB	Marlon Byrd	5.00

Behind the Numbers Autograph

No pricing due to scarcity.
Numbered to jersey number.

Emerald Essentials

		NM/M
Complete Set (10):		60.00
Common Player:		4.00
Inserted 1:240		
1	Austin Kearns	4.00
2	Alfonso Soriano	8.00
3	Miguel Tejada	4.00
4	Troy Glaus	4.00
5	Adam Dunn	4.00
6	Hideo Nomo	4.00
7	Kerry Wood	6.00
8	Nomar Garciaparra	15.00
9	Roger Clemens	15.00
10	Derek Jeter	15.00

Emerald Essentials Game-Used

		NM/M
Common Player:		4.00
Same price for levels #'d 175, 250 & 375		
Patch Versions:		1.5-2.5X
Production 60		
AK	Austin Kearns	6.00
AS	Alfonso Soriano	8.00
MT	Miguel Tejada	4.00
TG	Troy Glaus	6.00
AD	Adam Dunn	6.00
HN	Hideo Nomo	15.00
KW	Kerry Wood	6.00
NG	Nomar Garciaparra	12.00
RC	Roger Clemens	12.00
AR	Alex Rodriguez	10.00

Emerald Essentials Autograph

		NM/M
Common Player:		
Brandon Webb		40.00
Hank Blalock		20.00

Diamond Essentials

		NM/M
Common Player:		5.00
Inserted 1:480		
1DE	Randy Johnson	15.00
2DE	Ichiro Suzuki	25.00
3DE	Albert Pujols	30.00
4DE	Barry Bonds	40.00
5DE	Hideki Matsui	30.00
6DE	Derek Jeter	40.00
7DE	Chipper Jones	20.00
8DE	Sammy Sosa	25.00
9DE	Jeff Bagwell	10.00
10DE	Mike Piazza	20.00
11DE	Pedro J. Martinez	15.00
12DE	Mark Prior	20.00
13DE	Jason Giambi	10.00
14DE	Jose Reyes	5.00
15DE	Alfonso Soriano	15.00

Diamond Essentials Game-Used

		NM/M
Common Player:		8.00
Same price for cards #'d 145, 245 & 345.		
Patch Versions:		1.5-2.5X
Production 55		
RJ	Randy Johnson	8.00
DJ	Derek Jeter	15.00
CJ	Chipper Jones	8.00
SS	Sammy Sosa	12.00
JB	Jeff Bagwell	8.00
MP	Mike Piazza	10.00
PM	Pedro J. Martinez	8.00
MP	Mark Prior	10.00
JG	Jason Giambi	8.00
JR	Jose Reyes	8.00

Diamond Essentials Autograph

	NM/M
Common Player:	
Dontrelle Willis	30.00
Ryan Wagner	20.00
Rocco Baldelli	25.00
Albert Pujols	150.00

X-tra Innings

		NM/M
Complete Set (10):		25.00
Common Player:		1.00
Inserted 1:32		
1XI	Ichiro Suzuki	3.00
2XI	Albert Pujols	4.00
3XI	Barry Bonds	5.00
4XI	Jason Giambi	1.50
5XI	Pedro J. Martinez	2.00
6XI	Mark Prior	3.00
7XI	Derek Jeter	5.00
8XI	Curt Schilling	1.00
9XI	Jeff Bagwell	1.50
10XI	Alex Rodriguez	5.00

2003 Fleer Fall Classic

		NM/M
Complete Set (87):		30.00
Common Player:		.25
Common SP:		
Hobby Pack (5):		4.00
Hobby Box (24):		75.00
1	Rod Carew	.50
2	Bobby Doerr	.25
3	Eddie Mathews	1.00
3	Eddie Mathews/SP/Tigers	
4	Tom Seaver	1.50
5	Lou Brock	.75
6	Nolan Ryan	3.00
6	Nolan Ryan/SP/Astros	10.00
7	Pee Wee Reese	.25
8	Robin Yount	1.00
9	Bob Feller	.50
10	Harmon Killebrew	1.00
11	Hal Newhouser	.25
12	Al Kaline	1.00
13	Hoyt Wilhelm	.25
14	Early Wynn	.25
15	Yogi Berra	1.00
15	Yogi Berra/SP/Mets	4.00
16	Billy Williams	.25
17	Rollie Fingers	.25
18	Sparky Anderson	.25
18	Sparky Anderson/SP/Reds	3.00
19	Lou Boudreau	.25
20	Warren Spahn	1.00
21	Enos Slaughter	.50
22	Luis Aparicio	.50
23	Phil Rizzuto	.75
24	Willie McCovey	.50
25	Joe Morgan	.75
26	Alan Trammell	.75
27	Eddie Murray	.25
28	Lefty Grove	.25
29	Walter Johnson	1.00
30	Roy Campanella	1.00
31	Carlton Fisk	.75
32	Bill Dickey	.25
33	Rogers Hornsby	1.00
33	Rogers Hornsby/SP/Cubs	5.00
34	Wade Boggs	.75
35	Chick Stahl	.25
36	Don Drysdale	.75
36	Don Drysdale/SP/Dodgers	4.00
37	Jose Canseco	.75
38	Roger Maris	2.00
38	Roger Maris/SP/Yanks.	
39	Cal Ripken Jr.	3.00
40	Kiki Cuyler	.25

40	Kiki Cuyler/SP/Cubs	3.00
41	Hank Greenberg	.25
42	Don Larsen	.50
43	Eddie Murray	.75
43	Eddie Murray/SP/Indians	4.00
44	Jimmy Sebring	.25
45	Ozzie Smith	1.50
46	Darryl Strawberry	.25
46	Darryl Strawberry/SP/Yanks.	3.00
47	Dave Parker	.25
48	Gil Hodges	.25
48	Gil Hodges/SP/Mets	3.00
49	Joe Carter	.50
50	Leo Durocher	.25
50	Leo Durocher/SP/Giants	3.00
51	Christy Mathewson	.75
52	Elston Howard	.25
53	Hughie Jennings	.25
54	Nellie Fox	.50
55	Carl Yastrzemski	1.00
56	Frank Robinson	1.00
56	Frank Robinson/SP/Reds	4.00
57	Dennis Eckersley	.50
58	Grover Alexander	.50
58	Grover Alexander/SP/Cards	4.00
59	Carl Hubbell	.25
60	Dave Winfield	.75
61	Honus Wagner	1.50
62	Duke Snider	1.00
62	Duke Snider/SP/Dodgers	5.00
63	Frankie Frisch	.25
63	Frankie Frisch/SP/Cards	3.00
64	Dizzy Dean	.75
65	Bob Gibson	1.00
66	Johnny Bench	1.50
67	Ty Cobb	2.00
68	Lou Gehrig	2.50
69	Jim "Catfish" Hunter	.50
70	Willie Stargell	.75
71	Reggie Jackson	1.00
71	Reggie Jackson/SP/Yanks.	5.00
72	George Brett	2.50
73	Babe Ruth	3.00
73	Babe Ruth/SP/Yanks.	10.00
74	Cy Young	1.00
75	Jim Palmer	.50
76	Mickey Lolich	.25
77	Stan Musial	1.50
78	Steve Carlton	.75
79	Roberto Clemente	2.50
80	John McGraw	.25
81	Paul Molitor	.75
82	Red Ruffing	.25
83	Connie Mack	.25
84	Mike Schmidt	2.00
85	Mickey Cochrane	.50
85	Mickey Cochrane/SP/Tigers	4.00
86	Brooks Robinson	1.00
87	Whitey Ford	.50

Championship Gold

		NM/M
Cards 1-87:		3-6X
Production 50 Sets		

All-American Collection

		NM/M
Common Player:		8.00
OS	Ozzie Smith/100	20.00
TS	Tom Seaver/100	15.00
SM	Stan Musial/100	30.00
CR	Cal Ripken Jr/100	60.00
EM	Eddie Mathews/100	10.00
NR	Nolan Ryan/100	30.00
YB	Yogi Berra/100	15.00
EM	Eddie Murray/100	15.00
FR	Frank Robinson	8.00
DS	Duke Snider	8.00
RJ	Reggie Jackson	8.00
LA	Luis Aparicio/100	10.00
LH	Gil Hodges	8.00
AK	Al Kaline	10.00
BM	Bill Mazeroski/100	10.00
BR	Brooks Robinson/100	15.00
WB	Wade Boggs/100	12.00
AT	Alan Trammell/100	12.00

All American Collection Autograph

		NM/M
Common Autograph:		
Varying quantities produced		
SP version #'d to 100:		1-1.5X
SP version #'d to 50:		1-2X
LA	Luis Aparicio/150	10.00
VB	Vida Blue/450	8.00
RB	Rick Burleson/250	8.00
SC	Steve Carlton/100	20.00
BF	Bob Feller/300	15.00
CF	Carlton Fisk/75	30.00
AK	Al Kaline/325	20.00
HK	Harmon Killebrew/150	30.00
FL	Fred Lynn/275	8.00
BM	Bill Mazeroski/75	20.00
JP	Jim Palmer/100	15.00
BR	Brooks Robinson/325	20.00
PR	Preacher Roe/450	12.00
MS	Mike Schmidt/50	60.00
BS	"Moose" Skowron/150	10.00
OS	Ozzie Smith/50	65.00
DS	Duke Snider/100	25.00
WS	Warren Spahn/75	40.00
AT	Alan Trammell/150	15.00

All American Collection Jersey Autograph

		NM/M
Production 25 Sets		
GB	George Brett	160.00
SC	Steve Carlton	50.00

Legendary Collection

		NM/M
Common Player:		
Inserted 1:Legendary Star Pack		
EM	Eddie Mathews/SP	15.00
NR	Nolan Ryan	30.00
YB	Yogi Berra	15.00
EMY	Eddie Murray	8.00
FR	Frank Robinson	6.00
DS	Duke Snider/SP	10.00
DSy	Darryl Strawberry	5.00
RJ	Reggie Jackson	8.00
RM	Roger Maris/SP	30.00
GH	Gil Hodges/SP	10.00

Pennant Aggression

		NM/M
Complete Set (20):		50.00
Common Player:		3.00
Numbered to pennant year.		
1PA	Ty Cobb/1908	4.00
2PA	Honus Wagner/1909	3.00
3PA	Walter Johnson/1924	3.00
4PA	Jimmie Foxx/1930	3.00
5PA	Frankie Frisch/1931	3.00
6PA	Pee Wee Reese/1947	3.00
7PA	Yogi Berra/1951	4.00
8PA	Roy Campanella/1953	4.00
9PA	Whitey Ford/1961	4.00
10PA	Frank Robinson/1966	3.00
11PA	Carl Yastrzemski/1967	3.00
12PA	Brooks Robinson/1970	3.00
13PA	Johnny Bench/1972	4.00
14PA	Reggie Jackson/1973	3.00
15PA	Jim "Catfish" Hunter/1974	3.00
16PA	Joe Morgan/1975	3.00
17PA	Thurman Munson/1976	4.00
18PA	Willie Stargell/1979	3.00
19PA	Mike Schmidt/1980	4.00
20PA	George Brett/1985	4.00

Pennant Aggression Game-Used

	NM/M
Common Player:	8.00
Production 100	
Patches:	1.5-2X
Production 50	

		NM/M
YB	Yogi Berra	15.00
FR	Frank Robinson	10.00
CY	Carl Yastrzemski	20.00
BR	Brooks Robinson	15.00
JB	Johnny Bench	15.00
RJ	Reggie Jackson	12.00
CH	Jim "Catfish" Hunter	8.00
JM	Joe Morgan	8.00
TM	Thurman Munson	15.00
WS	Willie Stargell	10.00
MS	Mike Schmidt	25.00
GB	George Brett	35.00

Postseason Glory

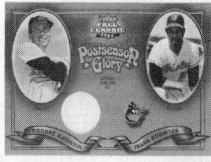

		NM/M
Complete Set (30):		125.00
Common Player:		2.00
#1-15 Numbered to 1,500		
16-25 Numbered to 750		
26-30 Numbered to 100		
1	Carlton Fisk,	
	Carl Yastrzemski	2.00
2	Enos Slaughter, Stan Musial	4.00
3	Reggie Jackson,	
	Thurman Munson	4.00
4	Eddie Plank,	
	Christy Mathewson	3.00
5	Cy Young, Jimmy Sebring	3.00
6	Yogi Berra, Whitey Ford	4.00
7	Mickey Lolich,	
	Alan Trammell	2.00
8	Eddie Mathews,	
	Al Schoendienst	3.00
9	Roy Campanella,	
	Pee Wee Reese	3.00
10	Joe Carter, Bill Mazeroski	2.00
11	Brooks Robinson,	
	Frank Robinson	3.00
12	Tom Seaver, Gil Hodges	3.00
13	Robin Yount, Paul Molitor	2.50
14	Dave Parker, Willie Stargell	2.00
15	Cal Ripken Jr., Jim Palmer	6.00
16	Babe Ruth, Whitey Ford	8.00
18	Lou Brock, Bob Gibson	4.00
19	Mike Schmidt,	
	Brooks Robinson	5.00
20	Johnny Bench,	
	Thurman Munson	5.00
21	Nolan Ryan,	
	Walter Johnson	10.00
22	Don Drysdale,	
	Duke Snider	4.00
23	Joe Carter, Paul Molitor	2.00
24	Hughie Jennings, Ty Cobb	4.00
25	Cal Ripken Jr.,	
	Eddie Murray	3.00
26	Mike Schmidt, Steve Carlton	5.00
27	Roberto Clemente,	
	Willie Stargell	15.00
28	Jim Palmer, Nolan Ryan	25.00
29	Joe Morgan,	
	Johnny Bench	10.00
30	Lou Gehrig, Babe Ruth	25.00

Postseason Glory Dual Game-Used

	NM/M
Production 100	
Single Jerseys:	.5X
Production 150	
Carlton Fisk,	
Carl Yastrzemski	25.00
Reggie Jackson,	
Thurman Munson	25.00
Yogi Berra, Whitey Ford	30.00
Brooks Robinson,	
Frank Robinson	20.00
Robin Yount, Paul Molitor	25.00
Dave Parker, Willie Stargell/	
Single/150	25.00
Lou Brock,	
Bob Gibson/Single/150	10.00
Joe Carter,	
Paul Molitor/Single/150	8.00
Don Drysdale, Duke Snider	25.00
Cal Ripken Jr.,	
Eddie Murray	50.00
Mike Schmidt,	
Steve Carlton	25.00

Jim Palmer, Nolan Ryan	40.00
Joe Morgan, Johnny Bench	25.00
Babe Ruth/Single/150,	
Lou Gehrig	125.00

Postseason Glory Dual Patch

	NM/M
Production 50	
Single Patch:	.5-.75X
Production 75	
Carlton Fisk,	
Carl Yastrzemski	70.00
Robin Yount, Paul Molitor	50.00
Lou Brock, Bob Gibson	50.00
Cal Ripken Jr.,	
Eddie Murray	120.00
Mike Schmidt,	
Steve Carlton	50.00
Jim Palmer, Nolan Ryan	80.00
Joe Morgan, Johnny Bench	50.00
Brooks Robinson,	
Frank Robinson	40.00

Series Contender

	NM/M
Common Player:	
Inserted 1:50 Retail	
Bat Knobs:	Not Priced
Production 9 or 10	
SK	Al Kaline	15.00
BD	Bill Dickey	10.00
DS	Darryl Strawberry	5.00
DM	Don Mattingly	30.00
PR	Phil Rizzuto/SP	10.00
WM	Willie McCovey/SP	10.00
HK	Harmon Killebrew	25.00
CF	Carlton Fisk	6.00
JC	Jose Canseco	10.00

Yankee Penstripes

	NM/M
Production 100	
World Series Edition:	No Pricing
Production 26	
RJ	Reggie Jackson	40.00
BSP	Bill "Moose" Skowron	15.00
WB	Wade Boggs	50.00
DM	Don Mattingly	75.00
DW	Dave Winfield	35.00

2003 Fleer Focus Jersey Edition

	NM/M
Complete Set (180):	45.00
Common Player:	.15
Common Prospect (161-180):	.75
Inserted 1:4	
Pack (7):	1.50
Box (24):	30.00
1	Derek Jeter	2.50
2	Preston Wilson	.15
3	Trevor Hoffman	.15
4	Moises Alou	.15
5	Roberto Alomar	.35
6	Tim Salmon	.25
7	Mike Lowell	.15
8	Barry Bonds	2.50
9	Fred McGriff	.15
10	Mo Vaughn	.15
11	Junior Spivey	.15
12	Roy Oswalt	.25
13	Ichiro Suzuki	1.50
14	Magglio Ordonez	.25
15	Adam Kennedy	.15
16	Randy Johnson	.75
17	Carlos Beltran	.50
18	John Olerud	.15
19	Joe Borchard	.15
20	Alfonso Soriano	.75
21	Curt Schilling	.50
22	Mike Sweeney	.15
23	Tino Martinez	.15
24	Barry Larkin	.15
25	Miguel Tejada	.40
26	Chipper Jones	1.00
27	Kevin Brown	.15
28	J.D. Drew	.15
29	Sean Casey	.15
30	Bernie Williams	.35
31	Troy Percival	.15

32	Jeff Bagwell	.75
33	Kenny Lofton	.15
34	Kerry Wood	.50
35	Armando Benitez	.15
36	David Eckstein	.15
37	Wade Miller	.15
38	Edgar Martinez	.15
39	Mark Prior	.75
40	Mike Piazza	1.50
41	Shea Hillenbrand	.15
42	Bartolo Colon	.15
43	Darin Erstad	.50
44	A.J. Burnett	.15
45	Jeff Kent	.15
46	Corey Patterson	.15
47	Derek Wigginton	.15
48	Troy Glaus	.15
49	Josh Beckett	.15
50	Brian Lawrence	.15
51	Frank Thomas	.75
52	Jason Giambi	.60
53	Luis Gonzalez	.25
54	Raul Ibanez	.15
55	Kazuhiro Sasaki	.15
56	Mark Buehrle	.15
57	Roger Clemens	1.25
58	Matt Williams	.15
59	Joe Randa	.15
60	Jamie Moyer	.15
61	Paul Konerko	.15
62	Mike Mussina	.50
63	Javy Lopez	.15
64	Brian Jordan	.15
65	Scott Rolen	.75
66	Aaron Boone	.15
67	Eric Chavez	.25
68	Mark Grace	.25
69	Shawn Green	.25
70	Albert Pujols	1.25
71	Sammy Sosa	1.50
72	Edgardo Alfonzo	.15
73	Garret Anderson	.15
74	Lance Berkman	.15
75	Bret Boone	.15
76	Joe Crede	.15
77	Al Leiter	.15
78	Jarrod Washburn	.15
79	Craig Biggio	.15
80	Rich Aurilia	.15
81	Adam Dunn	.60
82	Jermaine Dye	.15
83	Tom Glavine	.40
84	Eric Gagne	.15
85	Jared Sandberg	.15
86	Jim Thome	.35
87	Barry Zito	.25
88	Gary Sheffield	.25
89	Paul LoDuca	.15
90	Matt Morris	.15
91	Juan Pierre	.15
92	Randy Wolf	.15
93	Jay Gibbons	.15
94	Brad Radke	.15
95	Carlos Delgado	.35
96	Carlos Pena	.15
97	Brian Giles	.15
98	Rodrigo Lopez	.15
99	Jacque Jones	.15
100	Juan Gonzalez	.75
101	Randall Simon	.15
102	Mike Williams	.15
103	Derek Lowe	.15
104	Brad Wilkerson	.15
105	Eric Hinske	.15
106	Luis Castillo	.15
107	Phil Nevin	.15
108	Manny Ramirez	.75
109	Vladimir Guerrero	.75
110	Roy Halladay	.15
111	Ellis Burks	.15
112	Bobby Abreu	.15
113	Tony Batista	.15
114	Richie Sexson	.15
115	Rafael Palmeiro	.65
116	Todd Helton	.65
117	Pat Burrell	.60
118	John Smoltz	.15
119	Ben Sheets	.15
120	Aubrey Huff	.15
121	Andruw Jones	.75
122	Kazuhisa Ishii	.15
123	Jim Edmonds	.15
124	Austin Kearns	.60
125	Mark Mulder	.25
126	Greg Maddux	1.00
127	Jose Hernandez	.15
128	Ben Grieve	.15
129	Ken Griffey Jr.	1.50
130	Tim Hudson	.35
131	Jorge Julio	.15
132	Torii Hunter	.15
133	Ivan Rodriguez	.65
134	Jason Jennings	.15
135	Jason Kendall	.15
136	Nomar Garciaparra	1.50
137	Michael Cuddyer	.15
138	Shannon Stewart	.15
139	Larry Walker	.15
140	Aramis Ramirez	.15
141	Johnny Damon	.15
142	Orlando Cabrera	.15
143	Vernon Wells	.15
144	Bobby Higginson	.15
145	Sean Burroughs	.15
146	Pedro J. Martinez	.75

147	Jose Vidro	.15
148	Orlando Hudson	.15
149	Robert Fick	.15
150	Ryan Klesko	.15
151	Kevin Millwood	.15
152	Alex Sanchez	.15
153	Randy Winn	.15
154	Omar Vizquel	.15
155	Mike Lieberthal	.15
156	Marty Cordova	.15
157	Cristian Guzman	.15
158	Alex Rodriguez	2.00
159	C.C. Sabathia	.15
160	Jimmy Rollins	.25
161	Josh Willingham **RC**	2.00
162	Lance Niekro	.75
163	Nook Logan **RC**	.75
164	Chase Utley	.75
165	Pete LaForest **RC**	.75
166	Victor Martinez	.75
167	Adam LaRoche	.75
168	Ian Ferguson **RC**	.75
169	Mark Teixeira	.75
170	Chris Waters **RC**	.75
171	Hideki Matsui **RC**	5.00
172	Alejandro Machado **RC**	.75
173	Francisco Rosario **RC**	.75
174	Terrmel Sledge **RC**	1.00
175	Guillermo Quiroz **RC**	.75
176	Lew Ford **RC**	1.00
177	Hank Blalock	.75
178	Lyle Overbay	.75
179	Matt Bruback **RC**	.75
180	Jose Contreras **RC**	3.00

Century Jersey Number

Stars (1-160):	5-10X
Prospects (161-180):	2-4X
Numbered to jsy number + 100.	

Franchise Focus

	NM/M
Complete Set (20):	15.00
Common Player:	.50
Inserted 1:4	
1	Troy Glaus	.75
2	Randy Johnson	1.00
3	Chipper Jones	1.50
4	Nomar Garciaparra	2.00
5	Sammy Sosa	1.50
6	Ken Griffey Jr.	1.50
7	Jeff Bagwell	.75
8	Mike Sweeney	.50
9	Shawn Green	.50
10	Torii Hunter	.50
11	Vladimir Guerrero	1.00
12	Mike Piazza	2.00
13	Jason Giambi	1.00
14	Barry Zito	.50
15	Pat Burrell	.75
16	Barry Bonds	3.00
17	Ichiro Suzuki	1.50
18	Albert Pujols	1.00
19	Alex Rodriguez	2.50
20	Carlos Delgado	.50

Home and Aways

	NM/M
Common Player:	10.00
Inserted 1:288	
Lance Berkman	10.00
J.D. Drew	10.00
Nomar Garciaparra	20.00
Derek Jeter	40.00
Chipper Jones	20.00
Greg Maddux	20.00
Roy Oswalt	10.00
Alex Rodriguez	30.00
Alfonso Soriano	10.00

Materialistic

	NM/M
Common Player:	3.00
Inserted 1:192	
Action Home:	1.5-2.5X
Production 50 Sets	
Portrait Away:	.75-1.5X
Inserted 1:576	
Plus (Memorabilia):	1.5-2.5X
Production 250 Sets	
Portrait Home:	No Pricing

Production One Set	
1M	Greg Maddux	5.00
2M	Roger Clemens	5.00
3M	Nomar Garciaparra	6.00
4M	Derek Jeter	10.00
5M	Mike Piazza	6.00
6M	Pat Burrell	3.00
7M	Alfonso Soriano	5.00
8M	Chipper Jones	5.00
9M	Adam Dunn	3.00
10M	Alex Rodriguez	8.00
11M	Jason Giambi	4.00
12M	Sammy Sosa	4.00
13M	Albert Pujols	4.00
14M	Ken Griffey Jr.	5.00
15M	Ichiro Suzuki	5.00

Materialistic Oversize

	NM/M
Complete Set (16):	60.00
Common Player:	2.00
5-1/4" x 3-3/4" Box Topper	
(1)	Pat Burrell	2.00
(2)	Roger Clemens	6.00
(3)	Adam Dunn	2.00
(4)	Nomar Garciaparra	4.00
(5)	Jason Giambi	2.00
(6)	Ken Griffey Jr.	6.00
(7)	Reggie Jackson	5.00
(8)	Derek Jeter	12.50
(9)	Chipper Jones	5.00
(10)	Greg Maddux	5.00
(11)	Mike Piazza	6.00
(12)	Albert Pujols	10.00
(13)	Alex Rodriguez	10.00
(14)	Alfonso Soriano	2.00
(15)	Sammy Sosa	6.00
(16)	Ichiro Suzuki	7.50

Materialistic Oversize Autographs

	NM/M
Complete Set (3):	200.00
(1)	Reggie Jackson/360	50.00
(2)	Derek Jeter/360	100.00
(3)	Chipper Jones/80	75.00

Materialistic Flannels

Complete Set (15):	
No Pricing	

Shirtified

	NM/M
Complete Set (15):	35.00
Common Player:	1.00
Inserted 1:24	
1 Manny Ramirez	2.00
2 Jarrod Washburn	1.00
3 Greg Maddux	4.00
4 Austin Kearns	2.00
5 Jim Thome	2.00
6 Kazuhisa Ishii	1.00
7 Mike Piazza	5.00
8 Alfonso Soriano	3.00
9 Pat Burrell	2.00
10 Derek Jeter	8.00
11 Miguel Tejada	1.50
12 Roger Clemens	4.00
13 Alex Rodriguez	6.00
14 Barry Bonds	8.00
15 Scott Rolen	2.00

Shirtified Game-Used

	NM/M
Common Player:	
Inserted 1:35	
Patches:	2-3X
Production 200	
Manny Ramirez	8.00
Greg Maddux	12.00
Mike Piazza	10.00
Alfonso Soriano	15.00
Derek Jeter	25.00
Miguel Tejada	6.00
Roger Clemens	12.00
Alex Rodriguez	12.00

Team Colors

	NM/M
Complete Set (20):	20.00
Common Player:	.50
Inserted 1:12	
1TC Alex Rodriguez	3.50
2TC Mark Prior	1.00
3TC Derek Jeter	4.00
4TC Curt Schilling	1.00
5TC Pat Burrell	1.00
6TC Josh Beckett	.50
7TC Sean Burroughs	.50
8TC Troy Glaus	1.00
9TC Torii Hunter	.75
10TC Jeff Bagwell	1.00
11TC Pedro J. Martinez	1.50
12TC Mike Piazza	3.00
13TC Lance Berkman	.75
14TC Nomar Garciaparra	2.50
15TC Chipper Jones	2.00
16TC Eric Chavez	.75
17TC Barry Zito	.75
18TC Barry Bonds	4.00
19TC Adam Dunn	1.00
20TC Randy Johnson	1.50

Team Colors Game-Used

	NM/M
Common Player:	4.00
Inserted 1:28	
Multi-Color:	1.5X
Production 250	
Derek Jeter	25.00
Curt Schilling	5.00
Josh Beckett	4.00
Troy Glaus	8.00
Jeff Bagwell	8.00
Pedro J. Martinez	8.00
Lance Berkman	8.00
Nomar Garciaparra	15.00
Chipper Jones	10.00
Eric Chavez	6.00

Barry Bonds	
Adam Dunn	8.00
Randy Johnson	8.00

2003 Fleer Genuine

	NM/M
Complete Set (130):	150.00
Common Player:	.25
Common Gen. Upside (101-130):	3.00
Production 799	
Pack (5):	2.00
Box (24):	40.00
1 Derek Jeter	3.00
2 Mo Vaughn	.25
3 Adam Dunn	.75
4 Aubrey Huff	.25
5 Jacque Jones	.25
6 Kerry Wood	.60
7 Barry Bonds	3.00
8 Kevin Brown	.25
9 Sammy Sosa	2.00
10 Ray Durham	.25
11 Carlos Beltran	.50
12 Tony Batista	.25
13 Bobby Abreu	.25
14 Craig Biggio	.45
15 Gary Sheffield	.45
16 Jermaine Dye	.25
17 Carlos Pena	.25
18 Tim Salmon	.35
19 Mike Piazza	2.00
20 Moises Alou	.25
21 Edgardo Alfonzo	.25
22 Mike Sweeney	.25
23 Jay Gibbons	.25
24 Kevin Millwood	.25
25 A.J. Burnett	.25
26 Austin Kearns	.75
27 Rafael Palmeiro	.75
28 Vladimir Guerrero	1.00
29 Paul Konerko	.25
30 Scott Rolen	.75
31 Fred McGriff	.25
32 Frank Thomas	1.00
33 John Olerud	.25
34 Eric Gagne	.25
35 Nomar Garciaparra	2.00
36 Ryan Klesko	.25
37 Lance Berkman	.25
38 Andruw Jones	.75
39 Pat Burrell	.60
40 Juan Encarnacion	.25
41 Curt Schilling	.50
42 Jason Giambi	.65
43 Barry Larkin	.25
44 Alex Rodriguez	2.50
45 Kazuhisa Ishii	.25
46 Pedro J. Martinez	1.00
47 Sean Burroughs	.25
48 Roy Oswalt	.40
49 Chipper Jones	1.50
50 Barry Zito	.40
51 Jeff Kent	.25
52 Rodrigo Lopez	.25
53 Jim Thome	.25
54 Ivan Rodriguez	.60
55 Luis Gonzalez	.40
56 Alfonso Soriano	1.00
57 Josh Beckett	.25
58 Junior Spivey	.25
59 Bernie Williams	.40
60 Omar Vizquel	.25
61 Eric Hinske	.25
62 Jose Vidro	.25
63 Bartolo Colon	.25
64 Jim Edmonds	.25
65 Ben Sheets	.25
66 Mark Prior	1.00
67 Edgar Martinez	.25
68 Raul Ibanez	.25
69 Darin Erstad	.40
70 Roger Clemens	1.75
71 C.C. Sabathia	.25
72 Carlos Delgado	.50
73 Tom Glavine	.40
74 Magglio Ordonez	.40
75 Ichiro Suzuki	1.50
76 Johnny Damon	.40
77 Brian Giles	.25
78 Jeff Bagwell	1.00
79 Greg Maddux	1.50
80 Eric Chavez	.40
81 Larry Walker	.25
82 Randy Johnson	1.00
83 Miguel Tejada	.40
84 Todd Helton	.75
85 Jarrod Washburn	.25
86 Troy Glaus	.75
87 Ken Griffey Jr.	2.00
88 Albert Pujols	2.00
89 Torii Hunter	.25
90 Joe Crede	.25
91 Matt Morris	.25
92 Shawn Green	.40
93 Manny Ramirez	1.00
94 Jason Kendall	.25
95 Preston Wilson	.25
96 Garret Anderson	.25
97 Cliff Floyd	.25
98 Sean Casey	.25
99 Juan Gonzalez	.75
100 Richie Sexson	.25
101 Joe Borchard	3.00
102 Josh Stewart RC	3.00
103 Francisco Rodriguez	4.00
104 Jeremy Bonderman	6.00
105 Walter Young	3.00
106 Brandon Webb RC	10.00
107 Lyle Overbay	3.00
108 Jose Contreras RC	6.00
109 Victor Martinez	4.00
110 Hideki Matsui RC	10.00
111 Brian Stokes RC	3.00
112 Daniel Cabrera RC	6.00
113 Josh Willingham RC	3.00
114 Mark Teixeira	4.00
115 Pete LaForest RC	3.00
116 Chris Waters RC	3.00
117 Chien-Ming Wang RC	30.00
118 Ian Ferguson RC	3.00
119 Rocco Baldelli	4.00
120 Terrmel Sledge RC	3.00
121 Hank Blalock	3.00
122 Alejandro Machado RC	3.00
123 Hee Seop Choi	3.00
124 Guillermo Quiroz RC	4.00
125 Chase Utley	4.00
126 Nook Logan RC	3.00
127 Josh Hall RC	3.00
128 Ryan Church	3.00
129 Lew Ford RC	3.00
130 Francisco Rosario RC	3.00

Reflection

Cards 1-100 print run 25-50:	8-15X
Cards 101-130 p/r 101-130:	.5-1.5X
Cards 1-100 p/r 51-80:	4-8X
Cards 1-100 p/r 81-130:	3-5X

Ascending consecutively #'d from 1-130.
Descending consecutively #'d from 130-1.

Article Insider

	NM/M
Common Player:	4.00
Inserted 1:24	
Adam Dunn	5.00
Andruw Jones	6.00
Alex Rodriguez	10.00
Alfonso Soriano	8.00
Chipper Jones	8.00
Curt Schilling	5.00
Derek Jeter	15.00
Don Mattingly	25.00
Greg Maddux	10.00
Jeff Bagwell	6.00
Jason Giambi	10.00
Lance Berkman	4.00
Magglio Ordonez	4.00
Mike Piazza	10.00
Miguel Tejada	4.00
Nomar Garciaparra	15.00
Pat Burrell	4.00
Pedro J. Martinez	8.00
Randy Johnson	6.00
Shawn Green	4.00
Sammy Sosa	10.00
Troy Glaus	5.00
Torii Hunter	5.00
Todd Helton	6.00
Vladimir Guerrero	6.00

Article Insider Autograph

	NM/M
Quantity produced listed	
Lance Berkman/165	25.00
Lance Berkman/100	25.00
Lance Berkman/50	40.00
Derek Jeter/100	125.00
Don Mattingly/170	85.00
Don Mattingly/100	100.00

Long Ball Threats

	NM/M
Complete Set (15):	15.00
Common Card:	.50
Inserted 1:8	
1 Derek Jeter, Nomar Garciaparra	3.00
2 Jim Thome, Pat Burrell	1.00
3 Alex Rodriguez, Rafael Palmeiro	3.00
4 Alfonso Soriano, Hideki Matsui	3.00
5 Torii Hunter, Vladimir Guerrero	1.00
6 Mike Sweeney, Phil Nevin	.50
7 Mike Piazza, Sammy Sosa	2.00
8 Shawn Green, Jason Giambi	1.00
9 Magglio Ordonez, Andruw Jones	1.00
10 Eric Chavez, Carlos Delgado	.75
11 Manny Ramirez, Jeff Bagwell	1.00
12 Scott Rolen, Troy Glaus	1.00
13 Barry Bonds, Miguel Tejada	3.00
14 Albert Pujols, Lance Berkman	2.00
15 Chipper Jones, Todd Helton	1.50

Long Ball Threats Dual Jersey

	NM/M
Common Card:	5.00
Inserted 1:72	
Derek Jeter, Nomar Garciaparra	30.00
Jim Thome, Pat Burrell	15.00
Alex Rodriguez, Rafael Palmeiro	15.00
Torii Hunter, Vladimir Guerrero	10.00
Mike Sweeney, Phil Nevin	5.00
Mike Piazza, Sammy Sosa	20.00
Magglio Ordonez, Andruw Jones	10.00
Scott Rolen, Troy Glaus	10.00
Chipper Jones, Todd Helton	12.00

Long Ball Threats Single Jersey

	NM/M
Common Player:	3.00
Inserted 1:13	
Derek Jeter/Jsy, Nomar Garciaparra	15.00
Derek Jeter, Nomar Garciaparra/Jsy	10.00
Jim Thome/Jsy, Pat Burrell	6.00
Jim Thome, Pat Burrell/Jsy	6.00
Alfonso Soriano/Jsy, Hideki Matsui	8.00
Torii Hunter/Jsy, Vladimir Guerrero	6.00
Torii Hunter, Vladimir Guerrero/Jsy	6.00
Mike Sweeney/Jsy, Phil Nevin	3.00
Mike Sweeney, Phil Nevin/Jsy	3.00

Mike Piazza/Jsy, Sammy Sosa	8.00
Mike Piazza, Sammy Sosa/Jsy	10.00
Shawn Green/Jsy, Jason Giambi	4.00
Magglio Ordonez/Jsy, Andruw Jones	4.00
Eric Chavez, Carlos Delgado/Jsy	5.00
Manny Ramirez/Jsy, Jeff Bagwell	8.00
Manny Ramirez, Jeff Bagwell/Jsy	8.00
Scott Rolen/Jsy, Troy Glaus	6.00
Scott Rolen, Troy Glaus/Jsy	6.00
Barry Bonds, Miguel Tejada/Jsy	5.00
Albert Pujols, Lance Berkman/Jsy	4.00
Chipper Jones/Jsy, Todd Helton	8.00
Chipper Jones, Todd Helton/Jsy	6.00

Long Ball Threats Dual Patch

NM/M

#'d to combined 2002 HR total

Derek Jeter, Nomar Garciaparra/42	80.00
Jim Thome, Pat Burrell/89	30.00
Alex Rodriguez, Rafael Palmeiro/100	50.00
Mike Piazza, Sammy Sosa/82	75.00
Shawn Green, Jason Giambi/83	40.00
Magglio Ordonez, Andruw Jones/73	40.00
Manny Ramirez, Jeff Bagwell/64	40.00
Scott Rolen, Troy Glaus/61	50.00

Tools of the Game 1-Piece

NM/M

Common Player:	
Inserted 1:42	
2-Piece:	1.5-3X
Production 250	
3-Piece:	3-6X
Production 100	
Adam Dunn	6.00
Mike Piazza	8.00
Derek Jeter	15.00
Alex Rodriguez	10.00
Alfonso Soriano	10.00
Jason Giambi	8.00
Sammy Sosa	10.00
Vladimir Guerrero	6.00

Tools of the Game

NM/M

Complete Set (15):		20.00
Common Player:		.75
Inserted 1:20		
1	Adam Dunn	1.00
2	Chipper Jones	2.00
3	Torii Hunter	.75
4	Mike Piazza	1.50
5	Hideki Matsui	8.00
6	Nomar Garciaparra	3.00
7	Derek Jeter	4.00
8	Alex Rodriguez	4.00
9	Alfonso Soriano	2.00
10	Pat Burrell	.75
11	Barry Bonds	4.00
12	Jason Giambi	1.50
13	Sammy Sosa	2.00
14	Vladimir Guerrero	1.00
15	Ichiro Suzuki	2.00

2003 Fleer Hardball

		NM/M
Complete Set (280):		85.00
Common Player:		.15
Common (241-280):		.75
Inserted 1:2 Hobby		
Pack (7):		1.75
Box (24):		30.00
1	Barry Bonds	2.00
2	Derek Jeter	2.00
3	Jason Varitek	.15
4	Magglio Ordonez	.25
5	Ryan Dempster	.15
6	Adam Everett	.15
7	Paul LoDuca	.15
8	Brad Wilkerson	.15
9	Al Leiter	.15
10	Jermaine Dye	.15
11	Robert Mackowiak	.15
12	J.T. Snow	.15
13	Juan Gonzalez	.60
14	Eric Hinske	.15
15	Greg Maddux	1.00
16	Moises Alou	.15
17	Carlos Lee	.15
18	Richard Hidalgo	.15
19	Jorge Posada	.25
20	Mike Lieberthal	.15
21	Jeff Cirillo	.15
22	Corey Patterson	.15
23	C.C. Sabathia	.15
24	Brian Giles	.15
25	Edgar Martinez	.15
26	Trot Nixon	.15
27	Kerry Wood	.50
28	Austin Kearns	.40
29	Lance Berkman	.15
30	Hideo Nomo	.50
31	Brad Radke	.15
32	John Valentin	.15
33	Tim Hudson	.35
34	Aramis Ramirez	.15
35	Kevin Mench	.15
36	Kevin Appier	.15
37	Chris Richard	.15
38	Ruben Mateo	.15
39	Juan Pierre	.15
40	Nick Neugebauer	.15
41	Mike Mussina	.40
42	Rich Aurilia	.15
43	Albert Pujols	1.00
44	Carlos Delgado	.50
45	Junior Spivey	.15
46	Marcus Giles	.15
47	Johnny Damon	.25
48	Mark Prior	.50
49	Omar Vizquel	.15
50	Craig Biggio	.15
51	Chuck Knoblauch	.15
52	Eric Milton	.15
53	Jeromy Burnitz	.15
54	Jim Thome	.15
55	Steve Finley	.15
56	Kevin Millwood	.15
57	Alex Gonzalez	.15
58	Ben Broussard	.15
59	Derrek Lee	.15
60	Joe Randa	.15
61	Doug Mientkiewicz	.15
62	Jason L. Phillips	.15
63	Brett Myers	.15
64	Josh Fogg	.15
65	Reggie Sanders	.15
66	Chipper Jones	1.00
67	Roosevelt Brown	.15
68	Matt Lawton	.15
69	Charles Johnson	.15
70	Mark Quinn	.15
71	Jacque Jones	.15
72	Armando Benitez	.15
73	Bobby Abreu	.15
74	Jason Kendall	.15
75	Jeff Kent	.15
76	Mark Teixeira	.50
77	Garret Anderson	.15
78	Jerry Hairston Jr.	.15
79	Tony Graffanino	.15
80	Josh Beckett	.15
81	Eric Gagne	.15
82	Fernando Tatis	.15
83	Brett Tomko	.15
84	Fernando Vina	.15
85	Rafael Palmeiro	.65
86	Luis Gonzalez	.35
87	Javy Lopez	.15
88	Shea Hillenbrand	.15
89	Hee Seop Choi	.15
90	Preston Wilson	.15
91	Neifi Perez	.15
92	Ray Lankford	.15
93	Tsuyoshi Shinjo	.15
94	Ben Grieve	.15
95	Jarrod Washburn	.15
96	Gary Sheffield	.35
97	Derek Lowe	.15
98	Tony Womack	.15
99	Milton Bradley	.15
100	Brad Penny	.15
101	Mike Sweeney	.15
102	A.J. Pierzynski	.15
103	Edgardo Alfonzo	.15
104	Marlon Byrd	.15
105	Sean Burroughs	.15
106	Kazuhiro Sasaki	.15
107	Damian Rolls	.15
108	Troy Glaus	.60
109	Rafael Furcal	.15
110	Nomar Garciaparra	1.25
111	Josh Bard	.15
112	Alex Gonzalez	.15
113	Cristian Guzman	.15
114	Roger Cedeno	.15
115	Freddy Garcia	.15
116	Travis Phelps	.15
117	Juan Cruz	.15
118	Frank Thomas	.60
119	Jaret Wright	.15
120	Carlos Beltran	.45
121	Ronnie Belliard	.15
122	Roger Clemens	1.00
123	Vicente Padilla	.15
124	Joel Pineiro	.15
125	Jared Sandberg	.15
126	Tom Glavine	.35
127	Matt Clement	.15
128	Aaron Rowand	.15
129	Alex Escobar	.15
130	Randy Wolf	.15
131	Ichiro Suzuki	1.00
132	Toby Hall	.15
133	Scott Spiezio	.15
134	Bobby Higginson	.15
135	A.J. Burnett	.15
136	Cesar Izturis	.15
137	Roberto Alomar	.40
138	Trevor Hoffman	.15
139	Edgar Renteria	.15
140	Rusty Greer	.15
141	David Eckstein	.15
142	Pedro J. Martinez	.75
143	Joe Crede	.15
144	Robert Fick	.15
145	Mike Lowell	.15
146	Brian Jordan	.15
147	Mark Mulder	.25
148	Scott Rolen	.60
149	Ivan Rodriguez	.60
150	Adam Kennedy	.15
151	Ken Griffey Jr.	1.25
152	Larry Walker	.15
153	Carlos Pena	.15
154	Geoff Jenkins	.15
155	Bartolo Colon	.15
156	Mariano Rivera	.25
157	Robb Nen	.15
158	Bret Boone	.15
159	Shannon Stewart	.15
160	Chris Singleton	.15
161	Todd Walker	.15
162	Jay Payton	.15
163	Zach Day	.15
164	Bernie Williams	.40
165	Bubba Trammell	.15
166	Matt Morris	.15
167	Jose Cruz Jr.	.15
168	Mark Grace	.40
169	Andruw Jones	.75
170	Cliff Floyd	.15
171	Antonio Alfonseca	.15
172	Jeff Bagwell	.75
173	Shawn Green	.40
174	Joe Mays	.15
175	Mike Piazza	1.25
176	Adam Piatt	.15
177	Pokey Reese	.15
178	Carl Everett	.15
179	Tim Salmon	.35
180	Rodrigo Lopez	.15
181	Brandon Inge	.15
182	Kazuhisa Ishii	.15
183	Jose Vidro	.15
184	Barry Zito	.40
185	Phil Nevin	.15
186	J.D. Drew	.35
187	Vernon Wells	.15
188	Darin Erstad	.50
189	Barry Larkin	.15
190	Jason Jennings	.15
191	Luis Castillo	.15
192	Alex Beltre	.35
193	Tony Armas	.15
194	Terrence Long	.15
195	Mark Kotsay	.15
196	Tino Martinez	.15
197	Jayson Werth	.15
198	Eric Chavez	.25
199	Matt Williams	.15
200	Jon Lieber	.15
201	Eddie Taubensee	.15
202	Shane Reynolds	.15
203	Alex Sanchez	.15
204	Jason Giambi	.60
205	Jimmy Rollins	.25
206	Jamie Moyer	.15
207	Francisco Rodriguez	.15
208	Marty Cordova	.15
209	Aaron Boone	.15
210	Mike Hampton	.15
211	Mark Redman	.15
212	Richie Sexson	.15
213	Andy Pettitte	.40
214	Livan Hernandez	.15
215	Jason Isringhausen	.15
216	Curt Schilling	.40
217	Manny Ramirez	.75
218	Jose Valentin	.15
219	Brent Butler	.15
220	Billy Wagner	.15
221	Ben Sheets	.15
222	Jeff Weaver	.15
223	Brent Abernathy	.15
224	Jay Gibbons	.15
225	Sean Casey	.15
226	Greg Norton	.15
227	Andy Van Hekken	.15
228	Kevin Brown	.15
229	Orlando Cabrera	.15
230	Scott Hatteberg	.15
231	Ryan Klesko	.15
232	Roy Halladay	.15
233	Randy Johnson	.75
234	Mark Buehrle	.15
235	Todd Helton	.60
236	Jeffrey Hammonds	.15
237	Sidney Ponson	.15
238	Kip Wells	.15
239	John Olerud	.15
240	Aubrey Huff	.15
241	Derek Jeter	4.00
242	Barry Bonds	4.00
243	Ichiro Suzuki	2.00
244	Troy Glaus	1.00
245	Alex Rodriguez	3.00
246	Sammy Sosa	2.00
247	Lance Berkman	.75
248	Jason Giambi	2.00
249	Nomar Garciaparra	2.50
250	Miguel Tejada	.75
251	Albert Pujols	1.50
252	Mike Piazza	2.50
253	Vladimir Guerrero	1.50
254	Shawn Green	.75
255	Todd Helton	.75
256	Ken Griffey Jr.	2.00
257	Torii Hunter	.75
258	Chipper Jones	2.00
259	Alfonso Soriano	1.50
260	Luis Gonzalez	.75
261	Pedro J. Martinez	1.50
262	Tim Hudson	.75
263	Roger Clemens	2.00
264	Greg Maddux	2.00
265	Randy Johnson	1.50
266	Vinnie Chulk	.50
267	Jose Castillo	1.50
268	Craig Brazell RC	1.50
269	Felix Sanchez RC	.50
270	John Webb	.50
271	Josh Hall RC	.50
272	Alexis Rios	.50
273	Phil Seibel RC	.50
274	Prentice Redman RC	1.50
275	Walter Young	1.00
276	Nic Jackson	.50
277	Adam Morrissey	.50
278	Bobby Jenks	.50
279	Rodrigo Rosario	.50
280	Chin-Feng Chen	1.00

Gold

Gold (1-240):	2-3X
Gold (241-280):	1-2X
Inserted 1:4 Hobby	

Platinum

Cards (1-240):	8-15X
Cards (241-280):	3-5X
Production 50 Sets	

Discs

		NM/M
Complete Set (20):		50.00
Common Player:		1.00
Inserted 1:24		
1D	Derek Jeter	8.00
2D	Barry Bonds	8.00
3D	Ichiro Suzuki	4.00
4D	Sammy Sosa	4.00
5D	Nomar Garciaparra	5.00
6D	Lance Berkman	1.50
7D	Jason Giambi	4.00
8D	Mike Piazza	5.00
9D	Shawn Green	1.50
10D	Barry Zito	1.50
11D	Albert Pujols	3.00
12D	Alex Rodriguez	6.00
13D	Tim Salmon	1.00
14D	Eric Chavez	1.00
15D	Ken Griffey Jr.	4.00
16D	Alfonso Soriano	3.00
17D	Vladimir Guerrero	2.50
18D	Francisco Rodriguez	1.00
19D	Miguel Tejada	1.50
20D	Randy Johnson	2.50

On the Ball

		NM/M
Complete Set (15):		20.00
Common Player:		1.00
Inserted 1:12		
1	Derek Jeter	4.00
2	Barry Bonds	4.00
3	Nomar Garciaparra	2.50
4	Alfonso Soriano	1.50
5	Mike Piazza	2.50
6	Alex Rodriguez	3.00
7	Chipper Jones	2.00
8	Randy Johnson	1.50
9	Pedro J. Martinez	1.50
10	Albert Pujols	1.50
11	Vladimir Guerrero	1.50
12	Sammy Sosa	2.00
13	Ichiro Suzuki	2.00
14	Troy Glaus	1.00
15	Jason Giambi	2.00

On the Ball Memorabilia

		NM/M
Common Player:		5.00
Inserted 1:18		
	Derek Jeter/Bat	15.00
	Barry Bonds/Jsy	15.00
	Nomar Garciaparra/Jsy	10.00
	Alfonso Soriano/Jsy	10.00
	Mike Piazza/Jsy	10.00
	Alex Rodriguez/Jsy	10.00
	Chipper Jones/Bat	8.00
	Randy Johnson/Jsy	8.00
	Pedro J. Martinez/Jsy	8.00
	Troy Glaus/Jsy	5.00

Round Trippers

		NM/M
Complete Set (20):		15.00
Common Player:		.50
Inserted 1:8		
1	Alfonso Soriano	1.50
2	Alex Rodriguez	3.00
3	Lance Berkman	.75
4	Shawn Green	.75
5	Pat Burrell	1.00
6	Andruw Jones	.75
7	Garret Anderson	.50
8	Miguel Tejada	.75
9	Mike Piazza	2.50
10	Eric Chavez	.50
11	Rafael Palmeiro	.75
12	Chipper Jones	2.00
13	Manny Ramirez	1.00
14	Jeff Bagwell	1.00
15	Torii Hunter	.75
16	Nomar Garciaparra	2.50
17	Sammy Sosa	2.00
18	Vladimir Guerrero	1.50
19	Troy Glaus	1.00
20	Jason Giambi	2.00

Round Trippers Rounding First

		NM/M
Common Player:		5.00
Quantity produced listed		
Rounding Second:		No Pricing
Production 10 Sets		
Rounding Third:		No Pricing
Production Three Sets		
	Alfonso Soriano/Jsy/228	10.00
	Alex Rodriguez/Jsy/536	12.00
	Lance Berkman/Jsy/557	5.00
	Shawn Green/Bat/249	5.00
	Pat Burrell/Bat/502	10.00
	Andruw Jones/Jsy/569	5.00
	Garret Anderson/Bat/40	20.00
	Miguel Tejada/Jsy/524	5.00
	Mike Piazza/Bat/289	12.00
	Eric Chavez/Jsy/572	5.00
	Rafael Palmeiro/Jsy/515	6.00
	Chipper Jones/Jsy/570	10.00
	Manny Ramirez/Jsy/530	8.00
	Jeff Bagwell/Bat/344	6.00
	Nomar Garciaparra/Bat/529	12.00

Round Numbers

		NM/M
Complete Set (14):		50.00
Common Player:		3.00
Production 1,000 Sets		
1	Nolan Ryan	10.00
2	Al Kaline	6.00
3	Mike Schmidt	6.00
4	Yogi Berra	4.00
5	Brooks Robinson	4.00
6	Tom Seaver	4.00
7	Willie McCovey	3.00
8	Harmon Killebrew	4.00
9	Richie Ashburn	3.00
10	Lou Brock	3.00
11	Jim Palmer	3.00
12	Willie Stargell	4.00
13	Whitey Ford	4.00
14	Robin Yount	5.00

Round Numbers Memorabilia

		NM/M
Inserted 1:288		
	Al Kaline/Jsy	20.00
	Mike Schmidt/Jsy	15.00
	Harmon Killebrew/Bat	30.00
	Lou Brock/Jsy	30.00

Signatures

		NM/M
Bonds 600 HR Inscription:		1-1.5X
	Barry Bonds/255	200.00
	Derek Jeter	110.00

2003 Fleer Hot Prospects

		NM/M
Complete Set (120):		
Common Player:		.25

Common SP (81-120):		4.00
Production 1,250 unless noted.		
Pack (5):		4.00
Box (15):		50.00
1	Derek Jeter	3.00
2	Ryan Klesko	.25
3	Troy Glaus	.75
4	Jeff Kent	.40
5	Frank Thomas	.75
6	Gary Sheffield	.50
7	Jim Edmonds	.40
8	Pat Burrell	.50
9	Jacque Jones	.25
10	Jason Jennings	.25
11	Pedro J. Martinez	1.00
12	Rafael Palmeiro	.50
13	Jason Kendall	.25
14	Tom Glavine	.50
15	Josh Beckett	.25
16	Luis Gonzalez	.40
17	Edgar Martinez	.25
18	Miguel Tejada	.50
19	Fred McGriff	.40
20	Adam Dunn	.50
21	Lance Berkman	.50
22	Magglio Ordonez	.40
23	Darin Erstad	.40
24	Rich Aurilia	.25
25	Mike Piazza	1.50
26	Shawn Green	.50
27	Larry Walker	.40
28	Manny Ramirez	.75
29	Juan Gonzalez	.75
30	Eric Chavez	.50
31	Torii Hunter	.50
32	A.J. Burnett	.25
33	Sammy Sosa	1.50
34	Eric Hinske	.25
35	Brian Giles	.50
36	Mike Sweeney	.25
37	Sean Casey	.25
38	Chipper Jones	1.50
39	Scott Rolen	.75
40	Jason Giambi	1.00
41	Mo Vaughn	.25
42	Roy Oswalt	.25
43	Paul Konerko	.25
44	Tim Salmon	.40
45	Edgardo Alfonzo	.25
46	Jermaine Dye	.25
47	Ben Sheets	.25
48	Todd Helton	.75
49	Greg Maddux	1.50
50	Albert Pujols	2.00
51	Jim Thome	.75
52	Vladimir Guerrero	.75
53	Ivan Rodriguez	.50
54	Nomar Garciaparra	2.00
55	Alex Rodriguez	2.50
56	Alfonso Soriano	1.50
57	Kazuhisa Ishii	.25
58	Austin Kearns	.50
59	Curt Schilling	.50
60	Bret Boone	.40
61	Mark Prior	1.50
62	Garret Anderson	.40
63	Barry Bonds	2.50
64	Roger Clemens	2.00
65	Jeff Bagwell	.75
66	Omar Vizquel	.40
67	Jay Gibbons	.25
68	Aubrey Huff	.25
69	Bobby Abreu	.25
70	Richie Sexson	.50
71	Bobby Higginson	.25
72	Kerry Wood	.50
73	Carlos Delgado	.50
74	Sean Burroughs	.25
75	Jose Vidro	.25
76	Ken Griffey Jr.	1.50
77	Randy Johnson	1.00
78	Ichiro Suzuki	1.50
79	Barry Zito	.50
80	Carlos Beltran	.25
81	Joe Borchard	4.00
82	Mark Teixeira	5.00
83	Brandon Webb RC	15.00
84	Shane Victorino/Auto./400 RC	25.00
85	Hee Seop Choi	4.00
86	Hank Blalock	5.00
87	Brett Myers	4.00
88	Mike Ryan RC	4.00
89	Jesse Foppert	4.00
90	Lyle Overbay	4.00
91	Brian Stokes/Auto./400 RC	10.00
92	Josh Hall/Auto./400 RC	10.00
93	Chris Waters/Auto./400 RC	10.00
94	Lew Ford/Auto./400 RC	20.00
95	Ian Ferguson/Auto./500 RC	8.00
96	Josh Willingham RC	5.00
97	Josh Stewart/Auto./500 RC	8.00
98	Pete LaForest/Auto./500 RC	8.00
99	J.Contreras/Auto./Jsy/300 RC	40.00
100	Terrmel Sledge/Auto./500 RC	8.00
101	Guillermo Quiroz/Auto./500 RC	10.00
102	Alejandro Machado/Auto./500 RC	8.00
103	Nook Logan/Auto./Jsy/400 RC	10.00
104	Robby Hammock/Auto./Jsy/400 RC	10.00
105	Hideki Matsui/Base RC	15.00
106	Wilfredo Ledezma RC	4.00
107	Rocco Baldelli/Jsy	8.00
108	Oscar Villarreal RC	4.00
109	Todd Wellemeyer/Auto./400 RC	15.00
110	Michael Hessman/Auto./400 RC	8.00
111	Jeremy Bonderman/Auto./Jsy/400	25.00
112	Craig Brazell/Auto./400 RC	10.00
113	Francisco Rosario/Auto./Jsy/400 RC	10.00
114	Jeff Duncan/Auto./400 RC	10.00
115	Daniel Cabrera/Auto./Jsy/400 RC	25.00
116	Dontrelle Willis/Auto./Jsy/400	15.00
117	Cory Stewart/Auto./500 RC	10.00
118	Tim Olson/Auto./Jsy/400 RC	10.00
119	Chien-Ming Wang/Auto./Jsy/500 RC	200.00

Class Of...

		NM/M
Common Duo:		10.00
Inserted 1:15		
	Barry Zito, Josh Beckett	10.00
	Pat Burrell, J.D. Drew	12.00
	Mark Prior, Mark Teixeira	15.00
	Austin Kearns, Sean Burroughs	10.00
	Troy Glaus, Lance Berkman	10.00
	Darin Erstad, Todd Helton	10.00
	Manny Ramirez, Shawn Green	10.00
	Matt Morris, Kerry Wood	10.00
	Nomar Garciaparra, Paul Konerko	15.00
	Alex Rodriguez, Torii Hunter	20.00

Cream of the Crop

		NM/M
Complete Set (15):		35.00
Common Player:		1.50
Inserted 1:5		
1	Barry Bonds	5.00
2	Derek Jeter	5.00
3	Ichiro Suzuki	3.00
4	Nomar Garciaparra	3.00
5	Roger Clemens	3.00
6	Alex Rodriguez	4.00
7	Greg Maddux	2.50
8	Mike Piazza	2.50
9	Sammy Sosa	2.50
10	Jason Giambi	2.00
11	Hideki Matsui	6.00
12	Albert Pujols	4.00
13	Vladimir Guerrero	1.50
14	Jim Thome	1.50
15	Pedro J. Martinez	1.50

Hot Materials

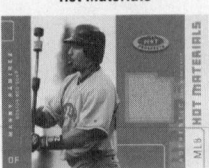

		NM/M
Common Player:		5.00
Production 499 Sets		
Red-Hots:		1-2X
Production 50		
1HM	Derek Jeter	20.00
2HM	Torii Hunter	8.00
3HM	Mark Prior	8.00
4HM	Nomar Garciaparra	15.00
5HM	Sammy Sosa	15.00
6HM	Rafael Palmeiro	6.00
7HM	Hee Seop Choi	10.00
8HM	Mark Teixeira	5.00
9HM	Mike Piazza	10.00
10HM	Pat Burrell	8.00
11HM	Jim Thome	8.00
12HM	Lance Berkman	8.00
13HM	Vladimir Guerrero	6.00
14HM	Troy Glaus	5.00
15HM	Chipper Jones	8.00
16HM	Lyle Overbay	5.00
17HM	Jason Giambi	8.00
18HM	Alex Rodriguez	10.00
19HM	Miguel Tejada	5.00
20HM	Adam Dunn	6.00
21HM	Randy Johnson	8.00
22HM	Josh Beckett	5.00
23HM	Alfonso Soriano	10.00
24HM	Greg Maddux	10.00
25HM	Shawn Green	5.00
26HM	Carlos Delgado	5.00
27HM	Todd Helton	6.00
28HM	Mike Sweeney	5.00
29HM	Manny Ramirez	6.00
30HM	Tom Glavine	5.00

Hot Tandems

	NM/M
Common Duo:	8.00
Production 100 Sets	
Red-Hots numbered to 10.	
Derek Jeter, Chipper Jones	25.00
Derek Jeter, Mike Piazza	25.00
Derek Jeter, Miguel Tejada	25.00
Torii Hunter,	
Lance Berkman	10.00
Mark Prior, Sammy Sosa	25.00
Sammy Sosa, Pat Burrell	20.00
Rafael Palmeiro,	
Mark Teixeira	10.00
Hee Seop Choi,	
Lyle Overbay	15.00
Alex Rodriguez,	
Mark Teixeira	20.00
Mike Piazza, Chipper Jones	15.00
Pat Burrell, Jim Thome	10.00
Lance Berkman, Adam Dunn	8.00
Nomar Garciaparra,	
Miguel Tejada	15.00
Randy Johnson,	
Greg Maddux	12.00
Mark Prior, Josh Beckett	10.00
Miguel Tejada,	
Alex Rodriguez	15.00
Jason Giambi, Jim Thome	10.00

Hot Triple Patch

	NM/M
Production 50 Sets	
Some not priced yet.	
Derek Jeter, Nomar Garciaparra,	
Alex Rodriguez	125.00
Mark Prior, Josh Beckett,	
Greg Maddux	80.00
Mike Piazza, Pat Burrell,	
Jim Thome	50.00
Lance Berkman, Troy Glaus,	
Chipper Jones	50.00
Randy Johnson, Alfonso Soriano,	
Shawn Green	40.00
Derek Jeter, Torii Hunter,	
Mark Prior	75.00
Nomar Garciaparra, Sammy Sosa,	
Mike Piazza	90.00
Pat Burrell, Jim Thome,	
Lance Berkman	40.00

(continued)

Vladimir Guerrero, Troy Glaus,		
Chipper Jones		60.00
Alfonso Soriano, Greg Maddux,		
Shawn Green		60.00

Playergraphs

	NM/M
Common Player:	10.00
Production 400 Sets	
Red-Hots:	1-1.5X
Production 100	
Hank Blalock	20.00
Brett Myers	10.00
Mark Prior	35.00
Carlos Zambrano	20.00
Mark Teixeira	20.00
Francisco Rodriguez	10.00
Roy Oswalt	15.00
Xavier Nady	10.00
Jose Reyes	25.00
Aubrey Huff	10.00

2003 Fleer Mystique

	NM/M
Complete Set (130):	
Common Player:	.25
Common SP (81-130):	3.00
Production 699	
Pack (4):	3.00
Box (20):	40.00
1	Alex Rodriguez	2.50
2	Derek Jeter	3.00
3	Jose Vidro	.25
4	Miguel Tejada	.40
5	Albert Pujols	2.50
6	Rocco Baldelli	.25
7	Jose Reyes	.50
8	Hideo Nomo	.75
9	Hank Blalock	.75
10	Chipper Jones	1.50
11	Barry Larkin	.25
12	Alfonso Soriano	1.00
13	Aramis Ramirez	.25
14	Darin Erstad	.65
15	Jim Edmonds	.25
16	Garret Anderson	.25
17	Todd Helton	1.00
18	Jason Kendall	.25
19	Aubrey Huff	.25
20	Troy Glaus	.75
21	Sammy Sosa	2.00
22	Roger Clemens	1.75
23	Mark Teixeira	.50
24	Barry Bonds	3.00
25	Jim Thome	.25
26	Carlos Delgado	.50
27	Vladimir Guerrero	1.00
28	Austin Kearns	.50
29	Pat Burrell	.75
30	Ken Griffey Jr.	2.00
31	Greg Maddux	1.50
32	Corey Patterson	.25
33	Larry Walker	.25
34	Kerry Wood	.65
35	Frank Thomas	1.00
36	Dontrelle Willis	.25
37	Randy Johnson	1.00
38	Curt Schilling	.40
39	Jay Gibbons	.25
40	Dmitri Young	.25
41	Edgar Martinez	.25
42	Kevin Brown	.25
43	Scott Rolen	1.00
44	Adam Dunn	.75
45	Pedro J. Martinez	1.00
46	Corey Koskie	.25
47	Tom Glavine	.40
48	Torii Hunter	.25
49	Shawn Green	.40
50	Nomar Garciaparra	2.00
51	Bernie Williams	.40
52	Milton Bradley	.25
53	Jason Giambi	.75
54	Mike Lieberthal	.25
55	Jeff Bagwell	1.00
56	Carlos Pena	.25
57	Lance Berkman	.25
58	Jose Cruz Jr.	.25
59	Josh Beckett	.25
60	Mark Mulder	.40
61	Mike Piazza	2.00

62	Mark Prior	1.00
63	Sean Burroughs	.25
64	Angel Berroa	.25
65	Geoff Jenkins	.25
66	Magglio Ordonez	.25
67	Craig Biggio	.25
68	Roberto Alomar	.40
69	Hee Seop Choi	.25
70	J.D. Drew	.25
71	Richie Sexson	.25
72	Brian Giles	.25
73	Gary Sheffield	.50
74	Manny Ramirez	1.00
75	Barry Zito	.45
76	Andruw Jones	1.00
77	Ivan Rodriguez	.65
78	Ichiro Suzuki	2.00
79	Mike Sweeney	.25
80	Vernon Wells	.25
81	Craig Brazell **RC**	5.00
82	Wilfredo Ledezma **RC**	3.00
83	Josh Willingham **RC**	6.00
84	Chien-Ming Wang **RC**	35.00
85	Mike Ryan **RC**	3.00
86	Mike Gallo **RC**	3.00
87	Rickie Weeks **RC**	8.00
88	Brian Stokes **RC**	3.00
89	Humberto Quintero **RC**	3.00
90	Ramon Nivar **RC**	3.00
91	Jeremy Griffiths **RC**	3.00
92	Terrmel Sledge **RC**	4.00
93	Brandon Webb **RC**	20.00
94	David DeJesus **RC**	5.00
95	Doug Waechter **RC**	3.00
96	Jeremy Bonderman **RC**	8.00
97	Felix Sanchez **RC**	3.00
98	Colin Porter **RC**	3.00
99	Francisco Cruceta **RC**	3.00
100	Hideki Matsui **RC**	15.00
101	Chris Waters **RC**	5.00
102	Dan Haren **RC**	5.00
103	Lew Ford **RC**	5.00
104	Oscar Villarreal **RC**	3.00
105	Ryan Wagner **RC**	5.00
106	Prentice Redman **RC**	3.00
107	Josh Stewart **RC**	5.00
108	Carlos Mendez **RC**	3.00
109	Michael Hessman **RC**	5.00
110	Josh Hall **RC**	5.00
111	Daniel Garcia **RC**	5.00
112	Matt Kata **RC**	5.00
113	Michel Hernandez **RC**	5.00
114	Sergio Mitre **RC**	5.00
115	Pete LaForest **RC**	5.00
116	Edwin Jackson **RC**	6.00
117	Matt Diaz **RC**	5.00
118	Greg Aquino **RC**	3.00
119	Jose Contreras **RC**	8.00
120	Jeff Duncan **RC**	6.00
121	Richard Fischer **RC**	5.00
122	Todd Wellemeyer **RC**	6.00
123	Robby Hammock **RC**	5.00
124	Delmon Young **RC**	10.00
125	Clint Barmes **RC**	5.00
126	Phil Seibel **RC**	3.00
127	Bo Hart **RC**	5.00
128	Jon Leicester **RC**	5.00
129	Chad Gaudin **RC**	5.00
130	Guillermo Quiroz **RC**	5.00

Gold

	NM/M
Stars (1-80):	4-8X
Production 150	
SP's (81-130):	1-2X
Production 50	

Awe Pairs

		NM/M
Complete Set (20):		60.00
Common Duo:		2.00
Production 250 Sets		
Golds:		1.5X
#'d to team win total for 2003		
1	Nomar Garciaparra,	
	Pedro J. Martinez	8.00
2	Derek Jeter,	
	Alfonso Soriano	8.00
3	Rocco Baldelli, Aubrey Huff	2.00
4	Carlos Delgado,	
	Vernon Wells	2.00
5	Troy Glaus,	
	Garret Anderson	2.00
6	Ichiro Suzuki, Bret Boone	5.00
7	Alex Rodriguez,	
	Hank Blalock	8.00
8	Chipper Jones,	
	Andruw Jones	5.00
9	Dontrelle Willis, Mike Lowell	3.00
10	Vladimir Guerrero,	
	Orlando Cabrera	4.00
11	Tom Glavine, Mike Piazza	5.00
12	Jim Thome, Mike Lieberthal	3.00
13	Sammy Sosa,	
	Corey Patterson	6.00
14	Jeff Bagwell,	
	Lance Berkman	3.00
15	Geoff Jenkins,	
	Richie Sexson	2.00
16	Albert Pujols, Jim Edmonds	6.00
17	Todd Helton, Larry Walker	3.00
18	Paul LoDuca, Shawn Green	2.00
19	Alex Klesko,	
	Sean Burroughs	2.00
20	Barry Bonds, Rich Aurilia	8.00

Awe Pairs Game-Used

	NM/M
Common Duo:	10.00
Production 100 Sets	
Golds:	No Pricing
Production 10 Sets	
Nomar Garciaparra,	
Pedro J. Martinez	25.00
Derek Jeter,	
Alfonso Soriano	30.00
Rocco Baldelli,	
Aubrey Huff	15.00
Carlos Delgado,	
Vernon Wells	10.00
Troy Glaus,	
Garret Anderson	15.00
Chipper Jones,	
Andruw Jones	15.00
Dontrelle Willis,	
Mike Lowell	25.00
Vladimir Guerrero,	
Orlando Cabrera	10.00
Tom Glavine, Mike Piazza	20.00
Jim Thome,	
Mike Lieberthal	15.00
Sammy Sosa,	
Corey Patterson	20.00
Jeff Bagwell,	
Lance Berkman	15.00
Geoff Jenkins,	
Richie Sexson	10.00
Albert Pujols,	
Jim Edmonds	20.00
Todd Helton, Larry Walker	10.00
Paul LoDuca, Shawn Green	10.00
Ryan Klesko,	
Sean Burroughs	

Diamond Dominators

		NM/M
Complete Set (10):		50.00
Common Player:		3.00
Production 100 Sets		
1	Mike Piazza	8.00
2	Greg Maddux	8.00
3	Alfonso Soriano	5.00
4	Barry Zito	3.00
5	Alex Rodriguez	10.00
6	Roger Clemens	10.00
7	Sammy Sosa	10.00
8	Adam Dunn	3.00
9	Randy Johnson	5.00
10	Pedro J. Martinez	5.00

Diamond Dominators Gold

		NM/M
Some not priced due to scarcity.		
Numbered to jersey number.		
1DD	Mike Piazza/31	25.00
2DD	Greg Maddux/31	25.00
4DD	Barry Zito/75	5.00
8DD	Adam Dunn/44	6.00
9DD	Randy Johnson/51	8.00
10DD	Pedro Martinez/45	10.00

Diamond Dominators Game-Used

		NM/M
Common Player:		6.00
Production 75 Sets		
Golds:		No Pricing
Production 10 Sets		
RC	Roger Clemens	20.00
AD	Adam Dunn	6.00
RJ	Randy Johnson	10.00
GM	Greg Maddux	25.00
PM	Pedro Martinez	12.00
MP	Mike Piazza	15.00
AR	Alex Rodriguez	15.00
AS	Alfonso Soriano	12.00
SS	Sammy Sosa	20.00
BZ	Barry Zito	8.00

Ink Appeal Autographs

		NM/M
Common Player:		15.00
Production 50 Sets		
RB	Rocco Baldelli	40.00
HB	Hank Blalock	35.00
BH	Bo Hart	25.00
AH	Aubrey Huff	15.00
TH	Torii Hunter	20.00
CP	Corey Patterson	15.00
JR	Jose Reyes	30.00
MR	Mike Ryan	15.00
JW	Josh Willingham	15.00

Ink Appeal Gold Autographs

		NM/M
Numbered to jersey number.		
Some not priced due to scarcity.		
BH	Bo Hart/31	50.00
TH	Torii Hunter/48	20.00
MR	Mike Ryan/54	15.00
JW	Josh Willingham/70	12.00

Ink Appeal Dual Autographs

No pricing due to scarcity.
Production 20 Sets
Golds: No Pricing
Production Five Sets

Rare Finds

		NM/M
Complete Set (10):		40.00
Common Trio:		3.00
Production 250 Sets		
1	Jason Giambi, Roger Clemens, Derek Jeter	8.00
2	Randy Johnson, Curt Schilling, Brandon Webb	4.00
3	Nomar Garciaparra, Pedro J. Martinez, Manny Ramirez	8.00
4	Mark Prior, Kerry Wood, Sammy Sosa	5.00
5	Jeff Bagwell, Craig Biggio, Lance Berkman	
6	Austin Kearns, Adam Dunn, Barry Larkin	3.00
7	Jim Edmonds, Scott Rolen, J.D. Drew	3.00
8	Chipper Jones, Andruw Jones, Greg Maddux	5.00
9	Barry Zito, Miguel Tejada, Mark Mulder	3.00
10	Alex Rodriguez, Mark Teixeira, Rafael Palmeiro	8.00

Rare Finds Single Swatch

		NM/M
Common Player:		6.00
Production 150 Sets		
Golds:		No Pricing
Production 15 Sets		
JG	Jason Giambi, Roger Clemens, Derek Jeter	10.00
RC	Jason Giambi, Roger Clemens, Derek Jeter	15.00
DJ	Jason Giambi, Roger Clemens, Derek Jeter	20.00
RJ	Randy Johnson, Curt Schilling, Brandon Webb	8.00
BW	Randy Johnson, Curt Schilling, Brandon Webb	10.00
NG	Nomar Garciaparra, Pedro J. Martinez, Manny Ramirez	15.00
PM	Nomar Garciaparra, Pedro J. Martinez, Manny Ramirez	8.00
MP	Mark Prior, Kerry Wood, Sammy Sosa	10.00
SS	Mark Prior, Kerry Wood, Sammy Sosa	8.00

JB	Jeff Bagwell, Craig Biggio, Lance Berkman	6.00
AK	Austin Kearns, Adam Dunn, Barry Larkin	6.00
BL	Austin Kearns, Adam Dunn, Barry Larkin	6.00
SR	Jim Edmonds, Scott Rolen, J.D. Drew	10.00
JD	Jim Edmonds, Scott Rolen, J.D. Drew	6.00
CJ	Chipper Jones, Andruw Jones, Greg Maddux	10.00
GM	Chipper Jones, Andruw Jones, Greg Maddux	15.00
MT	Barry Zito, Miguel Tejada, Mark Mulder	6.00
MM	Barry Zito, Miguel Tejada, Mark Mulder	6.00
AR	Alex Rodriguez, Mark Teixeira, Rafael Palmeiro	15.00
MT	Alex Rodriguez, Mark Teixeira, Rafael Palmeiro	8.00

Rare Finds Autographs

No Pricing:	
Production 15 Sets	
Auto./Game-Used:	No Pricing
Production Five Sets	

Rare Finds Dual Swatch

		NM/M
Common Dual:		10.00
Production 75 Sets		
Golds:		No Pricing
Production 10 Sets		
	Jason Giambi, Roger Clemens, Derek Jeter	35.00
	Jason Giambi, Roger Clemens, Derek Jeter	40.00
	Randy Johnson, Curt Schilling, Brandon Webb	15.00
	Randy Johnson, Curt Schilling, Brandon Webb	10.00
	Nomar Garciaparra, Pedro J. Martinez, Manny Ramirez	20.00
	Nomar Garciaparra, Pedro J. Martinez, Manny Ramirez	15.00
	Mark Prior, Kerry Wood, Sammy Sosa	15.00
	Mark Prior, Kerry Wood, Sammy Sosa	20.00
	Jeff Bagwell, Craig Biggio, Lance Berkman	10.00
	Austin Kearns, Adam Dunn, Barry Larkin	10.00
	Jim Edmonds, Scott Rolen, J.D. Drew	15.00
	Chipper Jones, Andruw Jones, Greg Maddux	20.00
	Chipper Jones, Andruw Jones, Greg Maddux	20.00
	Barry Zito, Miguel Tejada, Mark Mulder	10.00
	Alex Rodriguez, Mark Teixeira, Rafael Palmeiro	20.00

Rare Finds Triple Swatch

		NM/M
Production 50 Sets		
Golds:		No Pricing
Production Five Sets		
	Jason Giambi, Roger Clemens, Derek Jeter	50.00
	Randy Johnson, Curt Schilling, Brandon Webb	25.00
	Nomar Garciaparra, Pedro J. Martinez, Manny Ramirez	60.00
	Mark Prior, Kerry Wood, Sammy Sosa	40.00
	Jeff Bagwell, Craig Biggio, Lance Berkman	20.00
	Austin Kearns, Adam Dunn, Barry Larkin	20.00
	Jim Edmonds, Scott Rolen, J.D. Drew	25.00
	Chipper Jones, Andruw Jones, Greg Maddux	40.00
	Barry Zito, Miguel Tejada, Mark Mulder	15.00
	Alex Rodriguez, Mark Teixeira, Rafael Palmeiro	40.00

Secret Weapons

		NM/M
Complete Set (10):		25.00
Common Player:		2.00
Production 250 Sets		
Golds:		1X
#'d to career batting average		

1	Hank Blalock	3.00
2	Dontrelle Willis	3.00
3	Jose Reyes	3.00
4	Bo Hart	4.00
5	Corey Patterson	2.00
6	Hideki Matsui	8.00
7	Mark Teixeira	3.00
8	Brandon Webb	3.00
9	Rocco Baldelli	3.00
10	Mark Prior	5.00

Shining Stars

		NM/M
Complete Set (15):		50.00
Common Player:		2.00
Production 300 Sets		
1SS	Derek Jeter	8.00
2SS	Barry Bonds	8.00
3SS	Nomar Garciaparra	6.00
4SS	Austin Kearns	2.00
5SS	Vladimir Guerrero	3.00
6SS	Jim Thome	3.00
7SS	Ichiro Suzuki	5.00
8SS	Jason Giambi	3.00
9SS	Albert Pujols	6.00
10SS	Ken Griffey Jr.	5.00
11SS	Chipper Jones	5.00
12SS	Scott Rolen	3.00
13SS	Manny Ramirez	3.00
14SS	Jeff Bagwell	3.00
15SS	Torii Hunter	2.00

Shining Stars Game-Used

		NM/M
Common Player:		6.00
Production 100 Sets		
Patch:		1.5X
Production 50 Sets		
JB	Jeff Bagwell	8.00
CD	Carlos Delgado	6.00
NG	Nomar Garciaparra	15.00
JG	Jason Giambi	8.00
VG	Vladimir Guerrero	
TH	Todd Helton	8.00
TH	Torii Hunter	8.00
DJ	Derek Jeter	20.00
AJ	Andruw Jones	6.00
CJ	Chipper Jones	10.00
AK	Austin Kearns	6.00
AP	Albert Pujols	15.00
MR	Manny Ramirez	8.00
SR	Scott Rolen	10.00
JT	Jim Thome	8.00

Shining Stars Gold

		NM/M
Numbered to career HR total.		
1SS	Derek Jeter/127	10.00
2SS	Barry Bonds/658	5.00
3SS	Nomar Garciaparra/173	10.00
4SS	Austin Kearns/28	10.00
5SS	Vladimir Guerrero/234	4.00
6SS	Jim Thome/381	3.00
7SS	Ichiro Suzuki/29	30.00
8SS	Jason Giambi/269	3.00
9SS	Albert Pujols/114	8.00
10SS	Ken Griffey Jr./481	4.00
11SS	Chipper Jones/280	4.00
12SS	Scott Rolen/192	4.00
13SS	Manny Ramirez/347	4.00
14SS	Jeff Bagwell/419	4.00
15SS	Torii Hunter/96	4.00

2003 Fleer Patchworks

		NM/M
Complete Set (115):		
Common Player:		.15
Common Prospect (91-115):		3.00
Production 1,500		
Pack (5):		3.00
Box (24):		50.00
1	Luis Castillo	.15
2	Derek Jeter	2.00
3	Vladimir Guerrero	.75
4	Bobby Higginson	.15
5	Pat Burrell	.40
6	Ivan Rodriguez	.60
7	Craig Biggio	.15
8	Troy Glaus	.60
9	Barry Bonds	2.00
10	Hideo Nomo	.60

11	Barry Larkin	.15
12	Roberto Alomar	.35
13	Rodrigo Lopez	.15
14	Eric Chavez	.25
15	Shawn Green	.25
16	Joe Randa	.15
17	Mark Grace	.25
18	Jason Kendall	.15
19	Hee Seop Choi	.15
20	Luis Gonzalez	.25
21	Sammy Sosa	1.25
22	Larry Walker	.15
23	Phil Nevin	.15
24	Manny Ramirez	.75
25	Jim Thome	.75
26	Randy Johnson	.75
27	Jose Vidro	.15
28	Austin Kearns	.35
29	Mike Sweeney	.15
30	Magglio Ordonez	.15
31	Mike Piazza	1.25
32	Eric Hinske	.15
33	Alex Rodriguez	1.50
34	Kerry Wood	.60
35	Matt Morris	.15
36	Lance Berkman	.15
37	Michael Cuddyer	.15
38	Curt Schilling	.40
39	Sean Burroughs	.15
40	Ken Griffey Jr.	1.25
41	Edgardo Alfonzo	.15
42	Carlos Pena	.15
43	Adam Dunn	.50
44	Pedro J. Martinez	.75
45	Miguel Tejada	.35
46	Tom Glavine	.35
47	Torii Hunter	.15
48	Jason Giambi	.50
49	Tony Batista	.15
50	Ben Grieve	.15
51	Ichiro Suzuki	1.25
52	Bobby Abreu	.15
53	Todd Helton	.75
54	Kazuhiro Sasaki	.15
55	Nomar Garciaparra	1.25
56	Francisco Rodriguez	.15
57	Ellis Burks	.15
58	Frank Thomas	.75
59	Greg Maddux	1.00
60	Josh Beckett	.25
61	Brad Wilkerson	.15
62	Joe Borchard	.15
63	Carlos Delgado	.40
64	Alfonso Soriano	.75
65	Chipper Jones	1.00
66	J.D. Drew	.25
67	Mark Prior	.75
68	Rafael Palmeiro	.60
69	Jeff Kent	.15
70	Adrian Beltre	.25
71	Marlon Byrd	.15
72	Orlando Hudson	.15
73	Junior Spivey	.15
74	Jeff Bagwell	.75
75	Barry Zito	.35
76	Roger Clemens	1.00
77	Aubrey Huff	.15
78	Geoff Jenkins	.15
79	Andruw Jones	.75
80	Scott Rolen	.75
81	Omar Vizquel	.15
82	Darin Erstad	.50
83	Bernie Williams	.35
84	Freddy Garcia	.15
85	Richie Sexson	.15
86	Josh Phelps	.15
87	Albert Pujols	1.50
88	Aramis Ramirez	.15
89	Shea Hillenbrand	.15
90	Cristian Guzman	.15
91	Adam LaRoche	3.00
92	David Pember RC	3.00
93	Terrmel Sledge RC	3.00
94	Hideki Matsui RC	10.00
95	Nook Logan RC	3.00
96	Jose Contreras RC	4.00
97	Pete LaForest RC	3.00
98	Richard Fischer RC	3.00
99	Francisco Rosario RC	3.00
100	Josh Willingham RC	4.00
101	Alejandro Machado RC	3.00

102	Lew Ford RC	3.00
103	Joe Valentine RC	3.00
104	Guillermo Quiroz RC	3.00
105	Chien-Ming Wang RC	20.00
106	Jhonny Peralta RC	4.00
107	Shane Victorino RC	8.00
108	Prentice Redman RC	3.00
109	Matt Bruback RC	3.00
110	Lance Niekro	3.00
111	Travis Hughes	3.00
112	Nic Jackson	3.00
113	Hector Luna RC	4.00
114	Cliff Lee	3.00
115	Tim Olson RC	3.00

Star Ruby

Stars (1-90):	4-8X
Prospects (91-115):	1-3X
Production 100 Sets	

Diamond Ink

	NM/M
Quantity signed listed	
Derek Jeter/210	90.00
Derek Jeter/101	125.00
Derek Jeter/50	175.00
Mark Prior/88	40.00
Troy Glaus/351	25.00
Mike Schmidt/194	75.00

Licensed Apparel - Jersey

	NM/M
Common Player:	4.00
Production 500 Sets	
J.D. Drew	8.00
Magglio Ordonez	6.00
Todd Helton	8.00
Paul Konerko	4.00
Shawn Green	6.00
Carlos Beltran	4.00
Kevin Brown	4.00
Shannon Stewart	4.00
Mike Mussina	8.00
Adam Dunn	10.00
Jimmy Rollins	4.00
Darin Erstad	6.00
Chipper Jones	10.00
Mike Piazza	10.00
Derek Jeter	20.00

Licensed Apparel - Patch

	NM/M
Common Player:	10.00
Production 300 Sets	
J.D. Drew	12.00
Magglio Ordonez	15.00
Todd Helton	20.00
Paul Konerko	10.00
Shawn Green	15.00
Carlos Beltran	10.00
Kevin Brown	10.00
Shannon Stewart	10.00
Mike Mussina	15.00
Adam Dunn	20.00
Jimmy Rollins	15.00
Darin Erstad	25.00
Chipper Jones	20.00
Mike Piazza	25.00
Derek Jeter	40.00

National Pastime

	NM/M
Complete Set (25):	40.00
Common Player:	1.00
Inserted 1:12	
1NP	Barry Bonds	6.00
2NP	Kazuhiro Sasaki	1.00
3NP	Mike Piazza	4.00
4NP	Barry Zito	1.50
5NP	Sammy Sosa	3.00
6NP	Pedro J. Martinez	2.00
7NP	Craig Biggio	1.00
8NP	Rafael Palmeiro	1.50
9NP	Greg Maddux	3.00
10NP	Manny Ramirez	2.00
11NP	Adam Dunn	1.50
12NP	Omar Vizquel	1.00
13NP	Hideo Nomo	1.00
14NP	Alex Rodriguez	5.00
15NP	Pat Burrell	1.00
16NP	Nomar Garciaparra	4.00

17NP	Randy Johnson	2.00
18NP	Juan Gonzalez	1.50
19NP	Chipper Jones	3.00
20NP	Frank Thomas	1.50
21NP	Vladimir Guerrero	2.00
22NP	Troy Glaus	2.00
23NP	Albert Pujols	3.00
24NP	Ichiro Suzuki	3.00
25NP	Ken Griffey Jr.	3.00

National Patchtime - Trim

	NM/M
Common Player:	12.00
Production 200 Sets	
Vladimir Guerrero	12.00
Manny Ramirez	15.00
Rafael Palmeiro	12.00
Nomar Garciaparra	25.00
Greg Maddux	20.00
Mike Piazza	20.00
Pedro J. Martinez	20.00
Hideo Nomo	20.00
Alex Rodriguez	25.00
Chipper Jones	20.00
Frank Thomas	20.00

National Patchtime - Number

	NM/M
Common Player:	15.00
Production 75 Sets	
Vladimir Guerrero	20.00
Manny Ramirez	25.00
Craig Biggio	15.00
Rafael Palmeiro	20.00
Nomar Garciaparra	40.00
Greg Maddux	25.00
Sammy Sosa	45.00
Mike Piazza	30.00
Pedro J. Martinez	25.00
Hideo Nomo	25.00
Alex Rodriguez	30.00
Pat Burrell	20.00
Randy Johnson	45.00
Chipper Jones	35.00
Frank Thomas	30.00

National Patchtime - Team Name

	NM/M
Common Player:	15.00
Production 100 Sets	
Vladimir Guerrero	15.00
Rafael Palmeiro	20.00
Nomar Garciaparra	35.00
Sammy Sosa	40.00
Mike Piazza	30.00
Barry Zito	20.00
Hideo Nomo	30.00
Alex Rodriguez	30.00
Pat Burrell	20.00
Randy Johnson	45.00
Chipper Jones	35.00
Troy Glaus	30.00
Omar Vizquel	20.00

National Patchtime - Nameplate

	NM/M
Production 50 Sets	
Vladimir Guerrero	40.00
Rafael Palmeiro	25.00
Nomar Garciaparra	40.00
Greg Maddux	30.00
Sammy Sosa	60.00
Mike Piazza	35.00
Barry Zito	40.00
Hideo Nomo	50.00
Alex Rodriguez	50.00
Pat Burrell	25.00
Randy Johnson	50.00
Chipper Jones	40.00
Frank Thomas	40.00
Troy Glaus	30.00

National Patchtime- Commemorative

| Production 25 Sets: | No Pricing |

National Pastime - MLB Logo

Production One Set
No Pricing

Numbers Game

	NM/M
Complete Set (15):	30.00
Common Player:	1.00
Inserted 1:24	
1	Ichiro Suzuki	3.00
2	Derek Jeter	6.00

3	Alex Rodriguez	5.00
4	Miguel Tejada	1.00
5	Nomar Garciaparra	4.00
6	Jason Giambi	3.00
7	J.D. Drew	1.00
8	Barry Bonds	6.00
9	Alfonso Soriano	2.00
10	Jeff Bagwell	1.50
11	Barry Larkin	1.00
12	Roberto Alomar	1.00
13	Larry Walker	1.00
14	Roger Clemens	3.00
15	Ken Griffey Jr.	3.00

Numbers Game - Jersey

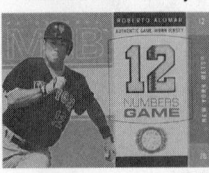

	NM/M
Common Player:	4.00
Inserted 1:25	
Barry Larkin	6.00
Roberto Alomar	4.00
Jeff Bagwell	8.00
Jason Giambi	8.00
Larry Walker	4.00
Derek Jeter	15.00
Alex Rodriguez	10.00
Alfonso Soriano	10.00
Roger Clemens	12.00
Miguel Tejada	5.00

Numbers Game - Patch

	NM/M
Common Player:	10.00
Production 300 Sets	
Barry Larkin	15.00
Roberto Alomar	15.00
Jeff Bagwell	25.00
Jason Giambi	15.00
Larry Walker	10.00
Derek Jeter	40.00
Alex Rodriguez	25.00
Alfonso Soriano	25.00
Roger Clemens	30.00
Miguel Tejada	10.00

Patchworks

	NM/M
Common Player:	8.00
Production 250 Sets	
2	Frank Thomas	12.00
8	Lance Berkman	15.00
9	Kazuhiro Sasaki	15.00
10	Roy Oswalt	15.00
11	Bernie Williams	15.00
12PW	Bob Abreu	15.00
14PW	Greg Maddux	20.00
15PW	Josh Beckett	8.00
16PW	Mark Grace	20.00
17PW	Eric Chavez	10.00
18PW	Andruw Jones	15.00
19PW	Adrian Beltre	8.00

Patchworks - Dual Color

	NM/M
Common Player:	10.00
Production 100 Sets	
Alex Rodriguez	35.00
Frank Thomas	20.00
Vladimir Guerrero	20.00
Roberto Alomar	20.00
Kerry Wood	35.00
Curt Schilling	15.00
Lance Berkman	20.00
Kazuhiro Sasaki	35.00
Roy Oswalt	20.00
Bernie Williams	25.00
Bob Abreu	10.00
Carlos Delgado	12.00
Greg Maddux	25.00
Josh Beckett	10.00
Mark Grace	15.00
Eric Chavez	15.00
Andruw Jones	15.00
Adrian Beltre	10.00

Patchworks - Multi-Color

	NM/M
Common Player:	20.00
Production 50 Sets	
Alex Rodriguez	60.00
Frank Thomas	30.00
Vladimir Guerrero	35.00
Roberto Alomar	35.00
Kerry Wood	40.00
Curt Schilling	20.00
Lance Berkman	25.00
Kazuhiro Sasaki	50.00
Roy Oswalt	40.00
Bernie Williams	35.00
Bob Abreu	25.00
Carlos Delgado	20.00
Greg Maddux	35.00
Josh Beckett	20.00

	Mark Grace	30.00
	Eric Chavez	30.00
	Andruw Jones	30.00
	Adrian Beltre	20.00

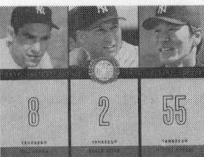

Past, Present, Future

	NM/M
Complete Set (10):	40.00
Common Card:	5.00
Inserted 1:72	
1	Eddie Mathews, Rafael Palmeiro, Alex Rodriguez	5.00
2	Phil Rizzuto, Derek Jeter, Alfonso Soriano	5.00
3	Reggie Jackson, Barry Bonds, Sammy Sosa	6.00
4	Billy Williams, Sammy Sosa, Hee Seop Choi	4.00
5	Joe Morgan, Roberto Alomar, Alfonso Soriano	3.00
6	Yogi Berra, Mike Piazza, Josh Phelps	4.00
7	Nolan Ryan, Roger Clemens, Kerry Wood	6.00
8	Mike Schmidt, Scott Rolen, Eric Hinske	4.00
9	Barry Bonds, Alex Rodriguez, Alfonso Soriano	5.00
10	Yogi Berra, Derek Jeter, Hideki Matsui	6.00

Patch, Present, Future Single

	NM/M
Common Player:	10.00
Production 200 Sets	
Rafael Palmeiro	15.00
Alex Rodriguez	20.00
Derek Jeter	50.00
Alfonso Soriano	50.00
Barry Bonds	50.00
Sammy Sosa	25.00
Sammy Sosa	25.00
Roberto Alomar	25.00
Alfonso Soriano	50.00
Mike Piazza	25.00
Roger Clemens	40.00
Kerry Wood	40.00
Scott Rolen	
Eric Hinske	10.00
Alex Rodriguez	20.00
Alfonso Soriano	50.00
Derek Jeter	50.00

Patch, Present, Future Dual

Production 100 Sets
No Pricing

2003 Fleer Platinum

	NM/M
Complete Set (250):	40.00
Common Player:	.15
Common SP (221-250):	.50
Hobby Pack (10):	1.50
Hobby Box (14 + 4 jumbo + 1 Rack):	35.00
Jumbo Pack:	3.00
Rack Pack:	5.00
1	Barry Bonds	2.50
2	Sean Casey	.25
3	Todd Walker	.15
4	Tony Batista	.15
5	Todd Zeile	.15
6	Ruben Sierra	.15
7	Jose Cruz Jr.	.15
8	Ben Grieve	.15
9	Robert Mackowiak	.15
10	Gary Sheffield	.25
11	Armando Benitez	.15
12	Tim Hudson	.25

13	Eric Milton	.15
14	Andy Pettitte	.40
15	Jeff Bagwell	.75
16	Jeff Kent	.15
17	Joe Randa	.15
18	Benito Santiago	.15
19	Russell Branyan	.15
20	Cliff Floyd	.15
21	Chris Richard	.15
22	Randy Winn	.15
23	Freddy Garcia	.15
24	Derek Lowe	.15
25	Ben Sheets	.15
26	Fred McGriff	.15
27	Bret Boone	.15
28	Jose Hernandez	.15
29	Phil Nevin	.15
30	Mike Piazza	1.50
31	Bobby Abreu	.15
32	Darin Erstad	.50
33	Andruw Jones	.75
34	Brad Wilkerson	.15
35	Brian Lawrence	.15
36	Vladimir Nunez	.15
37	Kazuhiro Sasaki	.15
38	Carlos Delgado	.45
39	Steve Cox	.15
40	Adrian Beltre	.25
41	Josh Bard	.15
42	Randall Simon	.15
43	Johnny Damon	.25
44	Ken Griffey Jr.	1.50
45	Sammy Sosa	1.00
46	Kevin Brown	.15
47	Kazuhisa Ishii	.15
48	Matt Morris	.15
49	Mark Prior	.75
50	Kip Wells	.15
51	Hee Seop Choi	.15
52	Craig Biggio	.15
53	Derek Jeter	2.50
54	Albert Pujols	1.50
55	Joe Borchard	.15
56	Robert Fick	.15
57	Jacque Jones	.15
58	Juan Pierre	.15
59	Bernie Williams	.35
60	Elmer Dessens	.15
61	Al Leiter	.15
62	Curt Schilling	.40
63	Carlos Pena	.15
64	Tino Martinez	.15
65	Fernando Vina	.15
66	Aaron Boone	.15
67	Michael Barrett	.15
68	Frank Thomas	.75
69	J.D. Drew	.25
70	Vladimir Guerrero	.75
71	Shannon Stewart	.15
72	Mark Buehrle	.15
73	Jamie Moyer	.15
74	Brad Radke	.15
75	Mike Williams	.15
76	Ryan Klesko	.15
77	Roberto Alomar	.35
78	Edgardo Alfonzo	.15
79	Matt Williams	.15
80	Edgar Martinez	.15
81	Shawn Green	.25
82	Kenny Lofton	.15
83	Josh Beckett	.15
84	Trevor Hoffman	.15
85	Kevin Millwood	.15
86	Odalis Perez	.15
87	Jarrod Washburn	.15
88	Jason Giambi	.60
89	Eric Young	.15
90	Barry Larkin	.15
91	Aramis Ramirez	.15
92	Ivan Rodriguez	.50
93	Steve Finley	.15
94	Brian Jordan	.15
95	Manny Ramirez	.75
96	Preston Wilson	.15
97	Rodrigo Lopez	.15
98	Ramon Ortiz	.15
99	Jim Thome	.15
100	Luis Castillo	.15
101	Alex Rodriguez	2.00
102	Jared Sandberg	.15
103	Ellis Burks	.15
104	Pat Burrell	.60
105	Brian Giles	.15
106	Mark Kotsay	.15
107	Dave Roberts	.15
108	Roy Halladay	.15
109	Chan Ho Park	.15
110	Erubiel Durazo	.15
111	Bobby Hill	.15
112	Cristian Guzman	.15
113	Troy Glaus	.60
114	Lance Berkman	.15
115	Juan Encarnacion	.15
116	Chipper Jones	1.00
117	Corey Patterson	.15
118	Vernon Wells	.15
119	Matt Clement	.15
120	Billy Koch	.15
121	Hideo Nomo	.50
122	Derrek Lee	.15
123	Todd Helton	.75
124	Sean Burroughs	.15
125	Jason Kendall	.15
126	Dmitri Young	.15
127	Adam Dunn	.60
128	Bobby Higginson	.15
129	Raul Mondesi	.15
130	Bubba Trammell	.15
131	A.J. Burnett	.15
132	Randy Johnson	.75
133	Mark Mulder	.15
134	Mariano Rivera	.25
135	Kerry Wood	.50
136	Mo Vaughn	.15
137	Jimmy Rollins	.25
138	Jose Valentin	.15
139	Brad Fullmer	.15
140	Mike Cameron	.15
141	Luis Gonzalez	.25
142	Kevin Appier	.15
143	Mike Hampton	.15
144	Pedro J. Martinez	.75
145	Javier Vazquez	.15
146	Doug Mientkiewicz	.15
147	Adam Kennedy	.15
148	Rafael Furcal	.15
149	Eric Chavez	.25
150	Mike Lieberthal	.15
151	Moises Alou	.15
152	Jermaine Dye	.15
153	Torii Hunter	.15
154	Trot Nixon	.15
155	Larry Walker	.15
156	Jorge Julio	.15
157	Mike Mussina	.40
158	Kirk Rueter	.15
159	Rafael Palmeiro	.65
160	Pokey Reese	.15
161	Miguel Tejada	.35
162	Robin Ventura	.15
163	Raul Ibanez	.15
164	Roger Cedeno	.15
165	Juan Gonzalez	.65
166	Carlos Lee	.15
167	Tim Salmon	.25
168	Orlando Hernandez	.15
169	Wade Miller	.15
170	Troy Percival	.15
171	Billy Wagner	.15
172	Jeff Conine	.15
173	Junior Spivey	.15
174	Edgar Renteria	.15
175	Scott Rolen	.65
176	Jason Varitek	.15
177	Ben Broussard	.15
178	Jeremy Giambi	.15
179	Gabe Kapler	.15
180	Armando Rios	.15
181	Ichiro Suzuki	2.00
182	Tom Glavine	.35
183	Greg Maddux	1.00
184	Roy Oswalt	.25
185	John Smoltz	.15
186	Eric Karros	.15
187	Alfonso Soriano	.75
188	Nomar Garciaparra	.75
189	Joe Crede	.15
190	Javy Lopez	.15
191	Carlos Beltran	.50
192	Jim Edmonds	.15
193	Geoff Jenkins	.15
194	Magglio Ordonez	.25
195	Daryle Ward	.15
196	Roger Clemens	1.25
197	Byung-Hyun Kim	.15
198	Robb Nen	.15
199	C.C. Sabathia	.15
200	Barry Zito	.35
201	Mark Grace	.25
202	Paul Konerko	.15
203	Mike Sweeney	.15
204	John Olerud	.15
205	Jose Vidro	.15
206	Ray Durham	.15
207	Omar Vizquel	.15
208	Shea Hillenbrand	.15
209	Mike Lowell	.15
210	Aubrey Huff	.15
211	Eric Hinske	.15
212	Paul LoDuca	.15
213	Jay Gibbons	.15
214	Austin Kearns	.50
215	Richie Sexson	.15
216	Garret Anderson	.15
217	Eric Gagne	.15
218	Jason Jennings	.15
219	Damian Moss	.15
220	David Eckstein	.15
221	Mark Teixeira	1.00
222	Bill Hall	.75
223	Bobby Jenks	.50
224	Adam Morrisey	.50
225	Rodrigo Rosario	.50
226	Brett Myers	.75
227	Tony Alvarez	.50
228	Willie Bloomquist	1.00
229	Ben Howard	.50
230	Nic Jackson	.50
231	Carl Crawford	.50
232	Omar Infante	.50
233	Francisco Rodriguez	.50
234	Andy Van Hekken	.50
235	Kirk Saarloos	.50
236	Dusty Wathan RC	.75
237	Jamey Carroll	1.00
238	Jason L. Phillips	1.00
239	Jose Castillo	1.00
240	Arnaldo Munoz RC	1.00
241	Orlando Hudson	.50
242	Drew Henson	.75
243	Jason Lane	.75
244	Vinnie Chulk	1.00
245	Prentice Redman RC	1.00
246	Marlon Byrd	1.00
247	Chin-Feng Chen	1.00
248	Craig Brazell RC	1.00
249	John Webb	1.00
250	Adam LaRoche	1.00

Platinum Finish

Stars (1-220):	5-10X
SP (221-250):	2-4X
Production 100 Sets	

Barry Bonds Chasing History

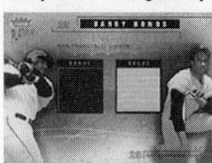

NM/M

Production 250 Sets
Five Player card #'d to 25.

Barry Bonds, Bobby Bonds	35.00
Barry Bonds, Roger Maris	40.00
Barry Bonds, Willie McCovey	35.00
Barry Bonds, Babe Ruth	200.00
Barry Bonds	35.00
Barry Bonds, Babe Ruth, Roger Maris, Willie McCovey, Bobby Bonds	200.00

Guts and Glory

NM/M

Complete Set (20):	12.00
Common Player:	.40
Inserted 1:4	
1GG Jason Giambi	1.00
2GG Alfonso Soriano	.75
3GG Scott Rolen	.50
4GG Ivan Rodriguez	.50
5GG Barry Bonds	1.50
6GG Jim Edmonds	.40
7GG Darin Erstad	.40
8GG Brian Giles	.40
9GG Luis Gonzalez	.40
10GG Adam Dunn	.50
11GG Torii Hunter	.40
12GG Andruw Jones	.40
13GG Sammy Sosa	1.00
14GG Ichiro Suzuki	1.50
15GG Miguel Tejada	.40
16GG Roger Clemens	1.00
17GG Curt Schilling	.40
18GG Nomar Garciaparra	1.50
19GG Derek Jeter	2.00
20GG Alex Rodriguez	1.50

Heart of the Order

NM/M

Complete Set (20):	20.00
Common Card:	.75
Inserted 1:12	
1 Jason Giambi, Derek Jeter, Alfonso Soriano	3.00
2 Todd Helton, Preston Wilson, Larry Walker	.75
3 Rafael Palmeiro, Alex Rodriguez, Ivan Rodriguez	3.00
4 Adam Dunn, Ken Griffey Jr., Austin Kearns	3.00
5 Jeff Bagwell, Craig Biggio, Lance Berkman	1.00
6 Eric Chavez, Miguel Tejada, Jermaine Dye	.75
7 Troy Glaus, Garrett Anderson, Darin Erstad	1.00
8 Mike Piazza, Mo Vaughn, Roberto Alomar	2.50
9 Torii Hunter, Jacque Jones, Corey Koskie	.75
10 Barry Bonds, Jeff Kent, Rich Aurilia	3.00
11 Pat Burrell, Bobby Abreu, Jimmy Rollins	1.50
12 Shawn Green, Adrian Beltre, Paul LoDuca	.75
13 Vladimir Guerrero, Brad Wilkerson, Jose Vidro	1.50
14 Chipper Jones, Andruw Jones, Gary Sheffield	2.00
15 Ichiro Suzuki, Bret Boone, Edgar Martinez	2.50
16 Albert Pujols, Scott Rolen, J.D. Drew	1.50
17 Sammy Sosa, Fred McGriff, Moises Alou	2.00
18 Nomar Garciaparra, Shea Hillenbrand, Manny Ramirez	2.50
19 Frank Thomas, Magglio Ordonez, Paul Konerko	1.00
20 Jason Kendall, Brian Giles, Aramis Ramirez	.75

Heart of the Order Memorabilia

NM/M

Common Card:	5.00
Production 400 Sets	
Jason Giambi, Derek Jeter, Alfonso Soriano/Bat	15.00
Todd Helton/Jsy, Preston Wilson, Larry Walker	8.00
Rafael Palmeiro/Jsy, Alex Rodriguez, Ivan Rodriguez	6.00
Adam Dunn, Ken Griffey Jr., Austin Kearns/Pants	12.00
Troy Glaus, Garrett Anderson, Darin Erstad/Jsy	8.00
Mike Piazza/Jsy, Mo Vaughn, Roberto Alomar	10.00
Barry Bonds, Jeff Kent/Jsy, Rich Aurilia	6.00
Pat Burrell, Bobby Abreu, Jimmy Rollins/Jsy	6.00
Shawn Green, Adrian Beltre/Jsy, Paul LoDuca	5.00
Vladimir Guerrero, Brad Wilkerson, Jose Vidro/Jsy	5.00
Chipper Jones/Jsy, Andruw Jones, Gary Sheffield	10.00
Ichiro Suzuki, Bret Boone/Jsy, Edgar Martinez	5.00
Albert Pujols, Scott Rolen, J.D. Drew/Jsy	8.00
Sammy Sosa/Jsy, Fred McGriff, Moises Alou	12.00
Nomar Garciaparra, Shea Hillenbrand, Manny Ramirez/Jsy	8.00
Frank Thomas, Magglio Ordonez/Jsy, Paul Konerko	5.00
Jason Kendall, Brian Giles/Bat, Aramis Ramirez	5.00

MLB Scouting Report

NM/M

Complete Set (32):	55.00
Common Player:	1.00
Production 400 Sets	
1 Jason Giambi	3.00
2 Paul Konerko	1.00
3 Jim Thome	1.50

4	Alfonso Soriano	2.00
5	Troy Glaus	1.50
6	Eric Hinske	1.00
7	Paul LoDuca	1.00
8	Mike Piazza	4.00
9	Marlon Byrd	1.00
10	Garrett Anderson	1.00
11	Barry Bonds	5.00
12	Pat Burrell	1.50
13	Joe Crede	1.00
14	J.D. Drew	1.00
15	Ken Griffey Jr.	4.00
16	Vladimir Guerrero	2.00
17	Torii Hunter	1.00
18	Chipper Jones	3.00
19	Austin Kearns	1.00
20	Albert Pujols	2.00
21	Manny Ramirez	1.50
22	Gary Sheffield	1.00
23	Sammy Sosa	3.00
24	Ichiro Suzuki	4.00
25	Bernie Williams	1.25
26	Randy Johnson	2.00
27	Greg Maddux	3.00
28	Hideo Nomo	1.00
29	Nomar Garciaparra	4.00
30	Derek Jeter	6.00
31	Alex Rodriguez	5.00
32	Miguel Tejada	1.00

MLB Scouting Report Game- Used

		NM/M
Common Player:		6.00
Production 250 Sets		
3	Jim Thome/Jsy	10.00
4	Alfonso Soriano/Bat	10.00
8	Mike Piazza/Jsy	15.00
11	Barry Bonds/Jsy	20.00
14	J.D. Drew/Jsy	6.00
18	Chipper Jones/Jsy	10.00
19	Austin Kearns/Pants	10.00
21	Manny Ramirez/Jsy	8.00
23	Sammy Sosa/Jsy	15.00
26	Randy Johnson/Jsy	10.00
27	Greg Maddux/Jsy	10.00
28	Hideo Nomo/Jsy	20.00
30	Derek Jeter/Jsy	20.00

Nameplates

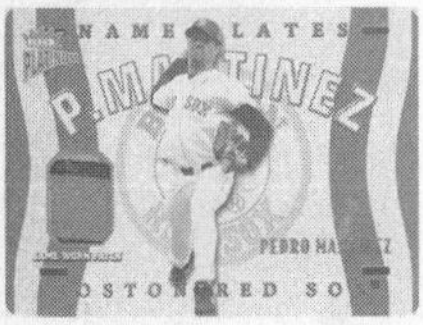

	NM/M
Common Player:	
Jumbo Pack Exclusive	
Barry Larkin/97	30.00
Kazuhiro Sasaki/82	20.00
Greg Maddux/248	25.00
Craig Biggio/152	25.00
Pedro J. Martinez/244	35.00
Barry Zito/248	25.00
Nomar Garciaparra/258	40.00
John Olerud/180	25.00
Ivan Rodriguez/189	20.00
Jeff Bagwell/121	45.00
Chipper Jones/251	40.00
Frank Thomas/58	45.00
Roger Clemens/141	40.00
Mike Piazza/200	35.00
Mark Prior/123	25.00
Manny Ramirez/94	30.00
Kerry Wood/49	45.00
Rafael Palmeiro/245	20.00
Jimmy Rollins/74	20.00
Barry Bonds/251	50.00
Adam Dunn/117	25.00
Alex Rodriguez/248	40.00
Miguel Tejada/225	20.00
Chin-Feng Chen/110	100.00

Portraits

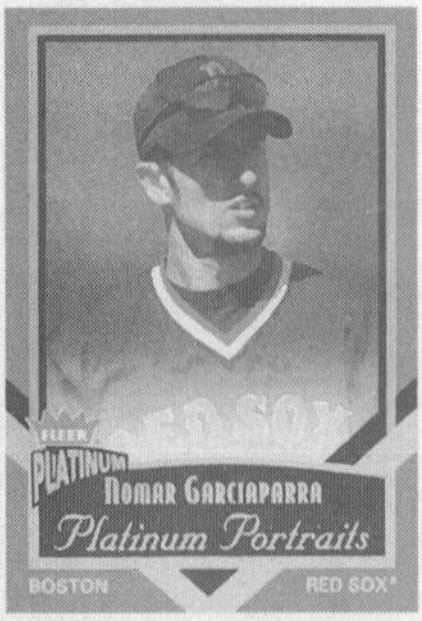

		NM/M
Complete Set (20):		25.00
Common Player:		.75
Inserted 1:20		
1	Josh Beckett	.75
2	Roberto Alomar	1.00
3	Alfonso Soriano	2.00
4	Mike Piazza	3.00
5	Ivan Rodriguez	1.00
6	Edgar Martinez	.75
7	Barry Bonds	4.00
8	Adam Dunn	1.25
9	Juan Gonzalez	1.00
10	Chipper Jones	2.50
11	Albert Pujols	1.50
12	Magglio Ordonez	.75
13	Shea Hillenbrand	.75
14	Larry Walker	.75
15	Pedro J. Martinez	1.50
16	Kerry Wood	1.00
17	Barry Zito	1.00
18	Nomar Garciaparra	3.00
19	Derek Jeter	5.00
20	Alex Rodriguez	4.00

Portraits Game Jersey

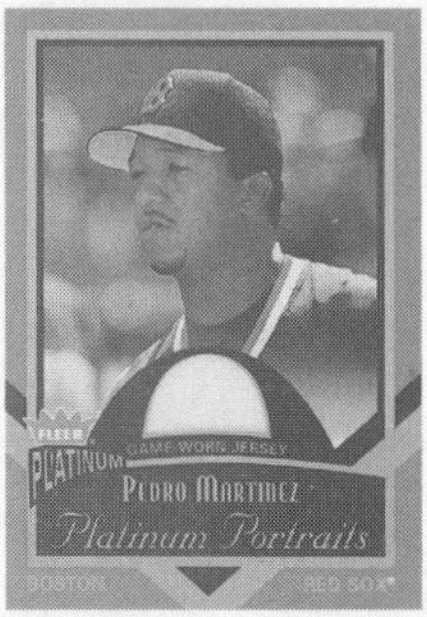

		NM/M
Common Player:		5.00
Inserted 1:86		
4	Mike Piazza	10.00
5	Ivan Rodriguez	6.00
7	Barry Bonds	15.00
8	Adam Dunn	8.00
10	Chipper Jones	8.00
15	Pedro J. Martinez	8.00
16	Kerry Wood	8.00
17	Barry Zito	5.00
18	Nomar Garciaparra	10.00
19	Derek Jeter/SP/150	25.00

Portraits Game Patch

		NM/M
Common Player:		25.00
Production 100 Sets		
4	Mike Piazza	35.00
5	Ivan Rodriguez	25.00
7	Barry Bonds	40.00
8	Adam Dunn	25.00
10	Chipper Jones	25.00
15	Pedro J. Martinez	25.00
16	Kerry Wood	25.00
17	Barry Zito	25.00
18	Nomar Garciaparra	40.00
19	Derek Jeter	45.00

2003 Fleer Rookies & Greats

		NM/M
Complete Set (75):		30.00
Common Player:		.25
Pack (5):		6.00
Box (20):		100.00
1	Troy Glaus	.65
2	Gary Sheffield	.40
3	Sammy Sosa	1.00
4	Mark Prior	.50
5	Dontrelle Willis	.25
6	Shawn Green	.50
7	Vladimir Guerrero	.75
8	Jose Reyes	.50
9	Miguel Tejada	.40
10	Bret Boone	.25
11	Rocco Baldelli	.40
12	Rafael Palmeiro	.65
13	Ichiro Suzuki	1.50
14	Carlos Delgado	.50
15	Garret Anderson	.25
16	Richie Sexson	.25
17	Roger Clemens	1.75
18	Barry Zito	.40
19	Jim Thome	.25
20	Alex Rodriguez	2.50
21	Randy Johnson	.75
22	Chipper Jones	1.00
23	Kerry Wood	.60
24	Ken Griffey Jr.	1.50
25	Ivan Rodriguez	.60
26	Jeff Kent	.25
27	Todd Helton	.75
28	Jeff Bagwell	.75
29	Hideo Nomo	.60
30	Torii Hunter	.25
31	Brian Giles	.25
32	Albert Pujols	2.00
33	Vernon Wells	.25
34	Nomar Garciaparra	.75
35	Magglio Ordonez	.25
36	C.C. Sabathia	.25
37	Preston Wilson	.25
38	Mike Sweeney	.25
39	Jose Vidro	.25
40	Jason Giambi	.60
41	Derek Jeter	3.00
42	Mike Piazza	1.50
43	Rich Harden	.25
44	Jason Kendall	.25
45	Barry Bonds	3.00
46	Barry Larkin	.25
47	Dmitri Young	.25
48	Craig Biggio	.25
49	Angel Berroa	.25
50	Alfonso Soriano	.75
51	Kevin Millwood	.25
52	Edgar Martinez	.25
53	Jim Edmonds	.25
54	Curt Schilling	.40
55	Jay Gibbons	.25
56	Pedro J. Martinez	.75
57	Greg Maddux	1.00
58	Manny Ramirez	.75
59	Frank Thomas	.75
60	Adam Dunn	.60
61	Babe Ruth	3.00
62	Bob Gibson	1.00
63	Willie Stargell	.75
64	Mike Schmidt	2.00
65	Nolan Ryan	3.00
66	Tom Seaver	1.00
67	Brooks Robinson	1.00
68	Willie McCovey	.50
69	Harmon Killebrew	1.00
70	Al Kaline	1.00
71	Reggie Jackson	1.00
72	Eddie Mathews	.75
73	Ralph Kiner	.25
74	Cal Ripken Jr.	3.00
75	Phil Rizzuto	.25
Ultra		
Production 1,500		
U-251	Chien-Ming Wang **RC**	8.00
U-252	Rickie Weeks **RC**	5.00
U-253	Brandon Webb **RC**	6.00
U-254	Hideki Matsui **RC**	8.00
U-255	Michael Hessman **RC**	2.00
U-256	Ryan Wagner **RC**	3.00
U-257	Matt Kata **RC**	3.00
U-258	Edwin Jackson **RC**	6.00
U-259	Jose Contreras **RC**	3.00
U-260	Delmon Young **RC**	8.00
U-261	Bo Hart **RC**	3.00
U-262	Jeff Duncan **RC**	3.00
U-263	Robby Hammock **RC**	2.00
U-264	Jeremy Bonderman	5.00
U-265	Clint Barmes **RC**	2.00
Authentix		
Production 1,250		
A-161	Chien-Ming Wang **RC**	10.00
A-162	Rickie Weeks **RC**	6.00
A-163	Brandon Webb **RC**	6.00
A-164	Craig Brazell **RC**	3.00
A-165	Michael Hessman **RC**	3.00
A-166	Ryan Wagner **RC**	5.00
A-167	Matt Kata **RC**	4.00
A-168	Edwin Jackson **RC**	8.00
A-169	Mike Ryan **RC**	3.00
A-170	Delmon Young **RC**	10.00
A-171	Bo Hart **RC**	4.00
A-172	Jeff Duncan **RC**	4.00
A-173	Robby Hammock **RC**	3.00
A-174	Jeremy Bonderman	5.00
A-175	Clint Barmes **RC**	3.00
Genuine		
Production 1,000		
G-131	Dan Haren	5.00
G-132	Rickie Weeks **RC**	6.00
G-133	Prentice Redman **RC**	4.00
G-134	Craig Brazell **RC**	4.00
G-135	Jon Leicester **RC**	4.00
G-136	Ryan Wagner **RC**	6.00
G-137	Matt Kata **RC**	5.00
G-138	Edwin Jackson **RC**	8.00
G-139	Mike Ryan **RC**	5.00
G-140	Delmon Young **RC**	10.00
G-141	Bo Hart **RC**	5.00
G-142	Jeff Duncan **RC**	5.00
G-143	Robby Hammock **RC**	4.00
G-144	Michael Hessman **RC**	4.00
G-145	Clint Barmes **RC**	4.00
Showcase		
Production 750		
S-136	Chien-Ming Wang **RC**	12.00
S-137	Rickie Weeks **RC**	8.00
S-138	Brandon Webb **RC**	8.00
S-139	Hideki Matsui **RC**	10.00
S-140	Michael Hessman **RC**	4.00
S-141	Ryan Wagner **RC**	6.00
S-142	Bo Hart **RC**	5.00
S-143	Edwin Jackson **RC**	8.00
S-144	Jose Contreras **RC**	6.00
S-145	Delmon Young **RC**	10.00
Flair		
Production 500		
F-126	Jeff Duncan **RC**	6.00
F-127	Rickie Weeks **RC**	10.00
F-128	Brandon Webb **RC**	12.00
F-129	Robby Hammock **RC**	5.00
F-130	Jon Leicester **RC**	5.00
F-131	Ryan Wagner **RC**	8.00
F-132	Bo Hart **RC**	6.00
F-133	Edwin Jackson **RC**	10.00
F-134	Sergio Mitre **RC**	5.00
F-135	Delmon Young **RC**	15.00
Hot Prospects		
Production 250		
H-120	Josh Willingham **RC**	10.00
H-121	Rickie Weeks **RC**	10.00
H-122	Prentice Redman **RC**	8.00
H-123	Mike Ryan **RC**	8.00
H-124	Oscar Villarreal **RC**	8.00
H-125	Ryan Wagner **RC**	10.00
H-126	Bo Hart **RC**	10.00
H-127	Edwin Jackson **RC**	12.00

Boyhood Idols

	NM/M
Common Player:	5.00
Production 615 Sets	
Carlton Fisk	8.00
Joe Carter	5.00
Cal Ripken Jr.	20.00
Mike Schmidt	15.00
Robin Yount	8.00
Joe Morgan	5.00
Jim Palmer	5.00
Harmon Killebrew	8.00
Brooks Robinson	8.00
Frank Howard	5.00
Bill "Moose" Skowron	5.00
Bucky Dent	5.00
Nolan Ryan	20.00
Don Mattingly	20.00

Boyhood Idols Autograph

	NM/M
Production 50 unless noted.	
Carlton Fisk	30.00
Brooks Robinson	35.00
Bucky Dent	20.00

Dynamic Debuts

		NM/M
Complete Set (10):		10.00
Common Player:		.50
Inserted 1:10		
1DD	Rickie Weeks	4.00
2DD	Brandon Webb	1.00
3DD	Jose Reyes	1.00
4DD	Bo Hart	1.00
5DD	Dontrelle Willis	1.00
6DD	Rich Harden	.50
7DD	Ryan Wagner	.50
8DD	Rocco Baldelli	1.00
9DD	Mark Teixeira	1.00
10DD	Hideki Matsui	5.00

Dynamic Debuts Autograph

	NM/M
Common Player:	10.00
Production 100	
Rickie Weeks	20.00
Jose Reyes	35.00
Bo Hart	10.00
Dontrelle Willis	25.00
Ryan Wagner	10.00

Looming Large

		NM/M
Complete Set (15):		30.00
Common Player:		1.50
Production 500 Sets		
Uncommon:		1-2X
Production 150		
Rare:		No Pricing
Production 15		
1LL	Chien-Ming Wang	4.00
2LL	Rickie Weeks	5.00
3LL	Brandon Webb	3.00
4LL	Hideki Matsui	6.00
5LL	Michael Hessman	1.50
6LL	Ryan Wagner	1.50
7LL	Matt Kata	1.50
8LL	Edwin Jackson	1.50
9LL	Jose Contreras	1.50
10LL	Delmon Young	6.00
11LL	Bo Hart	3.00
12LL	Jeff Duncan	1.50
13LL	Robby Hammock	1.50
14LL	Jeremy Bonderman	1.50
15LL	Clint Barmes	1.50

The Naturals

		NM/M
Complete Set (25):		45.00
Common Player:		.50
Inserted 1:5		
Uncommons:		2-4X
Production 75 Sets		
1	Cal Ripken Jr.	5.00
2	Mike Schmidt	3.00
3	Derek Jeter	5.00
4	Joe Carter	.50
5	Nomar Garciaparra	3.00
6	Frank Howard	.50
7	Al Kaline	2.00
8	Albert Pujols	4.00
9	Nolan Ryan	5.00
10	Duke Snider	1.50
11	Alex Rodriguez	4.00
12	Brooks Robinson	1.50
13	Roger Clemens	4.00
14	Sammy Sosa	3.00

15	Jim Palmer	1.00
16	Alfonso Soriano	2.00
17	Don Mattingly	3.00
18	Harmon Killebrew	1.50
19	Bob Feller	.50
20	Reggie Jackson	1.50
21	Ichiro Suzuki	2.50
22	Barry Bonds	5.00
23	Hideki Matsui	4.00
24	Willie Stargell	.50
25	Pee Wee Reese	.50

The Naturals Memorabilia

		NM/M
Common Player:		5.00
Production 250 unless noted.		
CR	Cal Ripken Jr.	30.00
MS	Mike Schmidt	15.00
DJ	Derek Jeter	20.00
JC	Joe Carter	5.00
NG	Nomar Garciaparra	15.00
FH	Frank Howard/400	15.00
AK	Al Kaline	15.00
AP	Albert Pujols	12.00
NR	Nolan Ryan/400	25.00
DS	Duke Snider	10.00
AR	Alex Rodriguez	10.00
BR	Brooks Robinson	10.00
RC	Roger Clemens/400	15.00
JP	Jim Palmer	8.00
AS	Alfonso Soriano	8.00
DM	Don Mattingly	20.00
HK	Harmon Killebrew/400	10.00
RJ	Reggie Jackson/400	10.00

The Naturals Autograph

		NM/M
Common Player:		
Production 50		
	Joe Carter	15.00
	Bob Feller	25.00
	Frank Howard	25.00
	Al Kaline	40.00
	Harmon Killebrew	35.00
	Jim Palmer	15.00
	Cal Ripken Jr.	140.00
	Brooks Robinson	35.00
	Nolan Ryan	100.00
	Duke Snider	25.00

The Naturals Jersey Autograph

		NM/M
Common Player:		
Production 30		
	Joe Carter	25.00
	Frank Howard	25.00
	Al Kaline	60.00
	Harmon Killebrew	50.00
	Jim Palmer	25.00
	Cal Ripken Jr.	150.00
	Brooks Robinson	50.00
	Nolan Ryan	120.00
	Duke Snider	40.00

The Naturals Patch

No Pricing	
Production 25	
Patch Auto.s:	No Pricing
Production 5	

Through the Years

		NM/M
Common Duo:		10.00
Production 360		
Patches:		No Pricing
Production 25		
	Sammy Sosa, Mark Prior	20.00
	Mark Prior, Jose Reyes	10.00
	Nolan Ryan, Hank Blalock	25.00
	Roger Clemens,	
	Chien-Ming Wang	35.00
	Jim Thome, Mike Schmidt	25.00
	Alex Rodriguez,	
	Mark Teixeira,	
	Randy Johnson,	
	Brandon Webb	15.00
	Phil Rizzuto, Jose Reyes	15.00
	Nomar Garciaparra,	
	Bobby Doerr	20.00
	Jason Giambi,	
	Reggie Jackson	15.00
	Derek Jeter, Phil Rizzuto	45.00
	Barry Larkin, Joe Morgan	15.00
	Harmon Killebrew,	
	Torii Hunter	20.00
	Willie McCovey,	
	Barry Bonds	15.00
	Bo Hart, Lou Brock	15.00
	Jose Contreras,	
	Mike Mussina	10.00
	Michael Hessman,	
	Chipper Jones	12.00
	Steve Carlton,	
	Kevin Millwood	12.00
	Robin Yount,	
	Scott Podsednik	20.00
	Eddie Mathews,	
	Chipper Jones	15.00

2003 Fleer Showcase

		NM/M
Complete Set (135):		50.00
Common Player:		.25
Common SP (106-135):		1.00
Inserted 1:4		

Pack (5):	3.00
Box (24):	60.00
1	David Eckstein	.25
2	Curt Schilling	.75
3	Jay Gibbons	.25
4	Kerry Wood	.75
5	Jeff Bagwell	1.00
6	Hideo Nomo	.75
7	Tim Hudson	.40
8	J.D. Drew	.50
9	Josh Phelps	.25
10	Bartolo Colon	.25
11	Bobby Abreu	.25
12	Matt Morris	.25
13	Kazuhiro Sasaki	.25
14	Sean Burroughs	.25
15	Vicente Padilla	.25
16	Jorge Posada	.35
17	Torii Hunter	.25
18	Richie Sexson	.25
19	Lance Berkman	.50
20	Todd Helton	1.00
21	Paul Konerko	.25
22	Pedro J. Martinez	1.00
23	Rodrigo Lopez	.25
24	Gary Sheffield	.35
25	Darin Erstad	.50
26	Nomar Garciaparra	1.00
27	Adam Dunn	.75
28	Jason Giambi	.75
29	Miguel Tejada	.40
30	Chipper Jones	1.50
31	Alex Rodriguez	3.00
32	Barry Bonds	4.00
33	Roger Clemens	2.00
34	Sammy Sosa	1.50
35	Randy Johnson	1.00
36	Tim Salmon	.35
37	Shea Hillenbrand	.25
38	Larry Walker	.25
39	A.J. Burnett	.25
40	Shawn Green	.50
41	Cristian Guzman	.25
42	Bernie Williams	.35
43	Mark Mulder	.25
44	Brian Giles	.25
45	Bret Boone	.25
46	Juan Gonzalez	.75
47	Roy Halladay	.25
48	Wade Miller	.25
49	Jeff Kent	.25
50	Carlos Delgado	.50
51	Mike Lowell	.25
52	Jim Edmonds	.25
53	Ivan Rodriguez	.75
54	Aubrey Huff	.25
55	Ryan Klesko	.25
56	Paul LoDuca	.25
57	Roy Oswalt	.50
58	Omar Vizquel	.25
59	Manny Ramirez	1.00
60	Andruw Jones	1.00
61	Troy Glaus	1.00
62	Ichiro Suzuki	2.50
63	Albert Pujols	2.50
64	Derek Jeter	4.00
65	Mark Prior	1.00
66	Ken Griffey Jr.	2.50
67	Vladimir Guerrero	1.00
68	Mike Piazza	2.50
69	Alfonso Soriano	1.00
70	Greg Maddux	1.50
71	Adam Kennedy	.25
72	Junior Spivey	.25
73	Tom Glavine	.40
74	Derek Lowe	.25
75	Magglio Ordonez	.25
76	Jim Thome	.75
77	Robert Fick	.25
78	Josh Beckett	.25
79	Mike Sweeney	.25
80	Kazuhisa Ishii	.25
81	Roberto Alomar	.40
82	Barry Zito	.25
83	Pat Burrell	.65
84	Scott Rolen	1.00
85	John Olerud	.25
86	Eric Hinske	.25
87	Rafael Palmeiro	.75
88	Edgar Martinez	.25
89	Eric Chavez	.40
90	Jose Vidro	.25

91	Craig Biggio	.25
92	Rich Aurilia	.25
93	Austin Kearns	.75
94	Luis Gonzalez	.40
95	Garrett Anderson	.25
96	Yogi Berra	1.50
97	Al Kaline	1.50
98	Robin Yount	1.00
99	Reggie Jackson	1.00
100	Harmon Killebrew	1.50
101	Eddie Mathews	1.50
102	Willie McCovey	.50
103	Nolan Ryan	4.00
104	Mike Schmidt	2.50
105	Tom Seaver	1.00
106	Francisco Rodriguez	1.00
107	Carl Crawford	1.00
108	Ben Howard	1.00
109	Hank Blalock	1.00
110	Hee Seop Choi	1.00
111	Kirk Saarloos	1.00
112	Lew Ford **RC**	1.00
113	Andy Van Hekken	1.00
114	Drew Henson	1.50
115	Marlon Byrd	1.00
116	Jayson Werth	1.00
117	Willie Bloomquist	1.00
118	Joe Borchard	1.00
119	Mark Teixeira	2.00
120	Bobby Hill	1.00
121	Jason Lane	1.00
122	Omar Infante	1.00
123	Victor Martinez	1.50
124	Jorge Padilla	1.00
125	John Lackey	1.00
126	Anderson Machado	1.00
127	Rodrigo Rosario	1.00
128	Freddy Sanchez	1.00
129	Tony Alvarez	1.00
130	Matt Thornton	1.00
131	Joe Thurston	1.00
132	Brett Myers	1.00
133	Antonio Perez	1.00
134	Chris Snelling	1.00
135	Terrmel Sledge **RC**	1.00

Legacy

Legacy Stars (1-105):	3-6X
SP's (106-135):	1-3X
Production 150 Sets	
Masterpiece 1 of 1 also exists.	

Baseball's Best

		NM/M
Complete Set (15):		40.00
Common Player:		1.50
Inserted 1:24		
1	Curt Schilling	2.00
2	Barry Zito	2.00
3	Torii Hunter	2.00
4	Pedro J. Martinez	4.00
5	Bernie Williams	2.00
6	Magglio Ordonez	1.50
7	Alfonso Soriano	4.00
8	Hideo Nomo	2.00
9	Jason Giambi	5.00
10	Sammy Sosa	4.00
11	Vladimir Guerrero	4.00
12	Ken Griffey Jr.	5.00
13	Troy Glaus	3.00
14	Ichiro Suzuki	6.00
15	Albert Pujols	6.00

Baseball's Best Memorabilia

		NM/M
Common Player:		5.00
Inserted 1:24		
CS	Curt Schilling	6.00

BZ	Barry Zito	6.00
TH	Torii Hunter	8.00
PM	Pedro J. Martinez	10.00
BW	Bernie Williams	8.00
MO	Magglio Ordonez	5.00
AS	Alfonso Soriano	15.00
HN	Hideo Nomo	8.00
JG	Jason Giambi	8.00
SS	Sammy Sosa	15.00

Hot Gloves

		NM/M
Complete Set (10):		15.00
Common Player:		1.00
Inserted 1:8		
1	Greg Maddux	2.00
2	Ivan Rodriguez	1.00
3	Derek Jeter	4.00
4	Mike Piazza	2.50
5	Nomar Garciaparra	2.50
6	Andruw Jones	1.00
7	Scott Rolen	1.00
8	Barry Bonds	3.00
9	Roger Clemens	2.00
10	Alex Rodriguez	3.00

Hot Gloves Memorabilia

		NM/M
Common Player:		5.00
Production 350 Sets		
GM	Greg Maddux	12.00
IR	Ivan Rodriguez	5.00
DJ	Derek Jeter	25.00
MP	Mike Piazza	15.00
NG	Nomar Garciaparra	15.00
AJ	Andruw Jones	6.00
SR	Scott Rolen	15.00
BB	Barry Bonds	25.00
RC	Roger Clemens	15.00
AR	Alex Rodriguez	15.00

Sweet Sigs

		NM/M
Quantity produced listed		
DJ	Derek Jeter/250	130.00
DJ	Derek Jeter/50/Red	185.00
BB	Barry Bonds/90 MVP/150	200.00
BB	Barry Bonds/92 MVP/100	200.00
BB	Barry Bonds/93 MVP/75	200.00

Sweet Stitch

		NM/M
Complete Set (10):		12.00
Common Player:		.75
Inserted 1:8		
1SS	Derek Jeter	4.00
2SS	Randy Johnson	1.50
3SS	Jeff Bagwell	1.00
4SS	Nomar Garciaparra	2.50
5SS	Roger Clemens	2.00
6SS	Todd Helton	.75
7SS	Barry Bonds	3.00
8SS	Alfonso Soriano	1.50
9SS	Miguel Tejada	.75
10SS	Mark Prior	.75

Sweet Stitch Memorabilia

		NM/M
Varying quantities produced		
DJ	Derek Jeter	25.00
RJ	Randy Johnson	8.00
JB	Jeff Bagwell	8.00
NG	Nomar Garciaparra	12.00
RC	Roger Clemens	12.00
TH	Todd Helton	5.00
BB	Barry Bonds	20.00
AS	Alfonso Soriano	12.00

MT	Miguel Tejada	5.00
MP	Mark Prior	10.00

Sweet Stitch Patch

		NM/M
Common Player:		20.00
DJ	Derek Jeter/50	60.00
RJ	Randy Johnson/150	40.00
JB	Jeff Bagwell/150	35.00
NG	Nomar Garciaparra/150	45.00
RC	Roger Clemens/50	45.00
TH	Todd Helton/50	30.00
BB	Barry Bonds/150	75.00
AS	Alfonso Soriano/50	40.00
MT	Miguel Tejada/150	20.00
MP	Mark Prior/150	25.00

Thundersticks

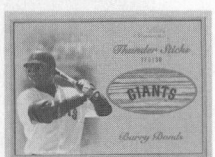

		NM/M
Complete Set (10):		12.00
Common Player:		.75
Inserted 1:8		
1TS	Adam Dunn	1.00
2TS	Alex Rodriguez	3.00
3TS	Barry Bonds	4.00
4TS	Jim Thome	1.00
5TS	Chipper Jones	2.00
6TS	Manny Ramirez	1.00
7TS	Carlos Delgado	.75
8TS	Mike Piazza	2.50
9TS	Shawn Green	.75
10TS	Pat Burrell	1.00

Thundersticks Bat

		NM/M
Common Player:		5.00
Golds:		1-2.5X
Production 99 Sets		
AD	Adam Dunn	10.00
AR	Alex Rodriguez	15.00
BB	Barry Bonds	20.00
JT	Jim Thome	8.00
CJS	Chipper Jones	8.00
MR	Manny Ramirez	8.00
SG	Shawn Green	5.00
PB	Pat Burrell	8.00

2003 Fleer Splendid Splinters

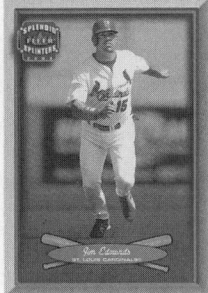

		NM/M
Complete Set (150):		
Common Player:		.20
Common Wood (91-110):		5.00
Production 499		
Common SP (111-140):		1.50
Inserted 1:6		
Common (141-150):		3.00
Production 999		
Pack (5):		3.00
Box (24):		50.00
1	David Eckstein	.20
2	Barry Larkin	.40
3	Edgardo Alfonzo	.20
4	Darin Erstad	.50
5	Ellis Burks	.20
6	Omar Vizquel	.40
7	Bartolo Colon	.20
8	Roberto Alomar	.50
9	Garret Anderson	.40
10	Al Leiter	.20
11	Tim Salmon	.40
12	Larry Walker	.40
13	Jorge Posada	.50
14	Curt Schilling	.50
15	Jason Jennings	.20
16	Jason Giambi	1.00
17	Robert Fick	.20
18	Kazuhiro Sasaki	.20
19	Bernie Williams	.50
20	Junior Spivey	.20
21	Mike Lowell	.20
22	Luis Gonzalez	.40
23	Josh Beckett	.40
24	John Smoltz	.50
25	Mike Mussina	.50
26	Gary Sheffield	.40
27	Tom Glavine	.40
28	Tim Hudson	.40
29	Austin Kearns	.75
30	Andruw Jones	.50
31	Roger Clemens	1.50
32	Mark Mulder	.40
33	Jay Gibbons	.40
34	Jeff Kent	.40
35	Barry Zito	.40
36	Rodrigo Lopez	.20
37	Jeff Bagwell	.75
38	Eric Chavez	.40
39	Pedro J. Martinez	1.00
40	Lance Berkman	.50
41	Bobby Abreu	.40
42	Wade Miller	.20
43	Bret Boone	.20
44	Vicente Padilla	.20
45	Shea Hillenbrand	.20
46	Roy Oswalt	.40
47	Pat Burrell	.75
48	Manny Ramirez	.75
49	Craig Biggio	.40
50	Randy Wolf	.20
51	Kerry Wood	.50
52	Mike Sweeney	.20
53	Brian Giles	.40
54	Kazuhisa Ishii	.20
55	Jason Kendall	.20
56	Hideo Nomo	.40
57	Josh Phelps	.20
58	Sean Burroughs	.20
59	Paul Konerko	.40
60	Shawn Green	.40
61	Ryan Klesko	.40
62	Magglio Ordonez	.40
63	Paul LoDuca	.20
64	Edgar Martinez	.20
65	J.D. Drew	.30
66	Phil Nevin	.20
67	Jim Edmonds	.40
68	Matt Morris	.40
69	Aubrey Huff	.20
70	Adam Dunn	.75
71	John Olerud	.40
72	Juan Gonzalez	.50
73	Scott Rolen	.50
74	Rafael Palmeiro	.50
75	Roy Halladay	.40
76	Kevin Brown	.20
77	Ivan Rodriguez	.50
78	Eric Hinske	.20
79	Frank Thomas	.75
80	Carlos Delgado	.40
81	Bobby Higginson	.20
82	Trevor Hoffman	.20
83	Cliff Floyd	.20
84	Derek Lowe	.20
85	Richie Sexson	.50
86	Rich Aurilia	.20
87	Sean Casey	.20
88	Cristian Guzman	.20
89	Randy Winn	.20
90	Jose Vidro	.20
91	Mark Prior	5.00
92	Derek Jeter	15.00
93	Alex Rodriguez	12.00
94	Greg Maddux	10.00
95	Troy Glaus	5.00
96	Vladimir Guerrero	8.00
97	Todd Helton	8.00
98	Albert Pujols	10.00
99	Torii Hunter	6.00
100	Mike Piazza	10.00
101	Ichiro Suzuki	10.00
102	Sammy Sosa	8.00
103	Ken Griffey Jr.	10.00
104	Nomar Garciaparra	5.00
105	Barry Bonds	15.00
106	Chipper Jones	10.00
107	Jim Thome	5.00
108	Miguel Tejada	5.00
109	Randy Johnson	8.00
110	Alfonso Soriano	8.00
111	Guillermo Quiroz RC	1.50
112	Josh Willingham RC	3.00
113	Alejandro Machado RC	1.50
114	Chris Waters RC	1.50
115	Adam LaRoche	1.50
116	Prentice Redman RC	1.50
117	Jhonny Peralta RC	2.50
118	Francisco Rosario RC	1.50
119	Shane Victorino RC	4.00
120	Chien-Ming Wang RC	15.00
121	Matt Bruback RC	1.50
122	Rontrez Johnson RC	1.50
123	Josh Hall RC	1.50
124	Matt Kata RC	1.50
125	Hector Luna RC	1.50
126	Josh Stewart RC	1.50
127	Craig Brazell RC	1.50
128	Tim Olson RC	1.50
129	Michel Hernandez RC	1.50
130	Michael Hessman RC	1.50
131	Clint Barmes RC	2.00
132	Justin Morneau	2.50
133	Chris Snelling	1.50
134	Bobby Jenks	1.50
135	Tim Hummel RC	1.50
136	Adam Morrissey	1.50
137	Carl Crawford	2.00
138	Garrett Atkins	2.00
139	Jung Bong	1.50
140	Ken Harvey	1.50
141	Chin-Feng Chen	1.50
142	Hee Seop Choi	1.50
143	Lance Niekro	1.50
144	Mark Teixeira	2.00
145	Nook Logan RC	1.50
146	Terrmel Sledge RC	1.50
147	Lew Ford RC	1.50
148	Ian Ferguson RC	1.50
149	Hideki Matsui/499 RC	15.00
150	Jose Contreras RC	6.00

Bat Chips

		NM/M
Common Player:		4.00
Production 425 Sets		
1	Jason Giambi	8.00
2	Jeff Bagwell	8.00
3	Manny Ramirez	8.00
4	Adam Dunn	8.00
5	Derek Jeter	25.00
6	Alex Rodriguez	15.00
7	Troy Glaus	5.00
8	Mike Piazza	15.00
9	Sammy Sosa	12.00
10	Nomar Garciaparra	18.00
11	Barry Bonds	18.00
12	Jim Thome	10.00
13	Miguel Tejada	5.00
14	Alfonso Soriano	10.00
15	Ryan Klesko	4.00
16	Sean Casey	4.00
17	Bernie Williams	8.00
18	Vladimir Guerrero	8.00
19	Gary Sheffield	5.00

Family Tree

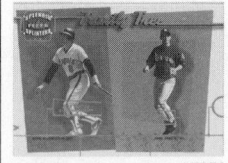

		NM/M
Complete Set (10):		10.00
Common Player:		.50
Inserted 1:8		
1	Lance Niekro, Phil Niekro	.50
2	Bob Boone, Bret Boone	.50
3	Sandy Alomar Jr., Roberto Alomar	.50
4	Ken Griffey Sr., Ken Griffey Jr.	2.00
5	Jason Giambi, Jeremy Giambi	
6	Bobby Bonds, Barry Bonds	3.00
7	Tony Perez, Eduardo Perez	.50
8	Brian Giles, Marcus Giles	.75
9	Felipe Alou, Moises Alou	.75
10	Pedro J. Martinez, Ramon Martinez	1.50

Home Run Club

	NM/M
Complete Set (12):	50.00
Common Player:	2.00
Inserted 1:72	

1	Barry Bonds	10.00
2	Jason Giambi	5.00
3	Sammy Sosa	6.00
4	Jim Thome	4.00
5	Lance Berkman	2.00
6	Alfonso Soriano	5.00
7	Vladimir Guerrero	4.00
8	Shawn Green	2.00
9	Troy Glaus	3.00
10	Pat Burrell	3.00
11	Alex Rodriguez	10.00
12	Mike Piazza	8.00

Home Run Club Autographs

		NM/M
Quantity produced listed		
BB1	Barry Bonds/ Black Ink/150	150.00
CR1	Cal Ripken Jr./ Black Ink/300	100.00
CR2	Cal Ripken Jr./ Blue Ink/150	125.00
CR3	Cal Ripken Jr./Red Ink/50	200.00
DJ1	Derek Jeter/Black Ink/400	80.00
DJ2	Derek Jeter/Blue Ink/250	100.00
DJ3	Derek Jeter/Red Ink/50	125.00

Home Run Club Memorabilia

	NM/M
Common Player:	5.00
Production 599 Sets	
Barry Bonds/Jsy	20.00
Jason Giambi/Bat	8.00
Sammy Sosa/Jsy	12.00
Jim Thome/Bat	8.00
Lance Berkman/Bat	5.00
Alfonso Soriano/Jsy	15.00
Vladimir Guerrero/Jsy	8.00
Shawn Green/Jsy	5.00
Troy Glaus/Bat	6.00
Pat Burrell/Bat	10.00
Alex Rodriguez/Jsy	15.00
Mike Piazza/Jsy	12.00
Todd Helton/Jsy	8.00
Rafael Palmeiro/Jsy	6.00

Knot Hole Gang

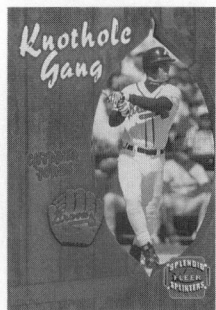

		NM/M
Complete Set (15):		40.00
Common Player:		1.00
Inserted 1:24		
1	Derek Jeter	6.00
2	Barry Bonds	6.00
3	Sammy Sosa	3.00
4	Jason Giambi	3.00
5	Alfonso Soriano	2.00
6	Roger Clemens	3.00
7	Miguel Tejada	1.00
8	Greg Maddux	3.00
9	Randy Johnson	2.00
10	Chipper Jones	3.00
11	Nomar Garciaparra	4.00
12	Alex Rodriguez	5.00
13	Ichiro Suzuki	4.00
14	Vladimir Guerrero	2.00
15	Albert Pujols	2.00

Knot Hole Gang Game-Used

	NM/M
Common Player:	4.00
Inserted 1:40	
Derek Jeter	20.00
Barry Bonds	15.00
Sammy Sosa	10.00
Vladimir Guerrero	8.00
Alfonso Soriano	8.00
Roger Clemens	10.00
Miguel Tejada	5.00
Greg Maddux	10.00
Randy Johnson	8.00
Chipper Jones	8.00
Nomar Garciaparra	12.00
Alex Rodriguez	12.00
Magglio Ordonez	4.00
Lance Berkman	6.00

Knot Hole Gang Patch

	NM/M
Common Player:	15.00
Production 99 Sets	
Derek Jeter	45.00
Barry Bonds	45.00
Sammy Sosa	35.00
Vladimir Guerrero	25.00
Alfonso Soriano	25.00
Roger Clemens	25.00
Miguel Tejada	15.00
Greg Maddux	30.00
Randy Johnson	20.00
Chipper Jones	30.00
Nomar Garciaparra	35.00
Alex Rodriguez	35.00

Knot Hole Gang Triple

No Pricing
Production 29 Sets: No Pricing

Splendid Splinters

		NM/M
Complete Set (10):		15.00
Common Player:		1.00
Inserted 1:12		
1	Derek Jeter	4.00
2	Barry Bonds	4.00
3	Scott Rolen	1.00
4	Nomar Garciaparra	2.50
5	Sammy Sosa	2.00
6	Alfonso Soriano	1.50
7	Alex Rodriguez	3.00
8	Mike Piazza	2.50
9	Manny Ramirez	1.00
10	Jeff Bagwell	1.00

Splendid Splinters G-U

	NM/M
Common Player:	8.00
Production 349 Sets	
Derek Jeter	20.00
Barry Bonds	20.00
Nomar Garciaparra	15.00
Sammy Sosa	10.00
Alfonso Soriano	10.00
Alex Rodriguez	12.00
Mike Piazza	12.00
Manny Ramirez	8.00
Jeff Bagwell	8.00

Splendid Splinters Dual

	NM/M
Production 99 Sets	
Derek Jeter, Alfonso Soriano	40.00
Barry Bonds, Sammy Sosa	50.00
Alex Rodriguez, Nomar Garciaparra	40.00
Mike Piazza, Jeff Bagwell	25.00

2003 Fleer Tradition

FLEER TRADITION
JASON GIAMBI
New York Yankees - First Base

	NM/M
Complete Set (485):	150.00
Common Player:	.15
Common SP (1-100):	1.00
Inserted 1:1	
Hobby Pack (10):	1.50
Hobby Box (40):	40.00

1	Jarrod Washburn, Troy Glaus, Garret Anderson, Ramon Ortiz	1.50
2	Luis Gonzalez, Randy Johnson, Andruw Jones	1.50
3	Andruw Jones, Chipper Jones, Tom Glavine, Kevin Millwood	2.00
4	Tony Batista, Rodrigo Lopez	1.00
5	Manny Ramirez, Nomar Garciaparra, Derek Lowe, Pedro J. Martinez	3.00
6	Sammy Sosa, Matt Clement, Kerry Wood	3.00
7	Mark Buehrle, Magglio Ordonez, Danny Wright	1.00
8	Adam Dunn, Aaron Boone, Jimmy Haynes	1.00
9	C.C. Sabathia, Jim Thome	1.50
10	Todd Helton, Jason Jennings	1.50
11	Randall Simon, Steve Sparks, Mark Redman	1.00
12	Derrek Lee, Mike Lowell, A.J. Burnett	1.00
13	Lance Berkman, Roy Oswalt	1.50
14	Paul Byrd, Carlos Beltran	1.00
15	Shawn Green, Hideo Nomo	1.50
16	Richie Sexson, Ben Sheets	1.00
17	Torii Hunter, Kyle Lohse, Johan Santana	1.00
18	Vladimir Guerrero, Tomokazu Ohka, Javier Vazquez	2.00
19	Mike Piazza, Al Leiter	3.00
20	Jason Giambi, David Wells, Roger Clemens	4.00
21	Eric Chavez, Miguel Tejada, Barry Zito	1.50
22	Pat Burrell, Vicente Padilla, Randy Wolf	1.50
23	Brian Giles, Josh Fogg, Kip Wells	1.00
24	Ryan Klesko, Brian Lawrence	1.00
25	Barry Bonds, Russ Ortiz, Jason Schmidt	5.00
26	Mike Cameron, Bret Boone, Freddy Garcia	1.00
27	Albert Pujols, Matt Morris	3.00
28	Aubrey Huff, Randy Winn, Joe Kennedy, Tanyon Sturtze	1.00
29	Alex Rodriguez, Kenny Rogers, Chan Ho Park	5.00
30	Carlos Delgado, Roy Halladay	1.00
31	Greg Maddux	6.00
32	Nick Neugebauer	1.00
33	Larry Walker	1.50
34	Freddy Garcia	1.00
35	Rich Aurilia	1.00
36	Craig Wilson	1.00
37	Jeff Suppan	1.00
38	Joel Pineiro	1.00
39	Pedro Feliz	1.00
40	Bartolo Colon	1.50
41	Pete Walker	1.00
42	Mo Vaughn	1.50
43	Sidney Ponson	1.00
44	Jason Isringhausen	1.00
45	Hideki Irabu	1.00
46	Pedro J. Martinez	4.00
47	Tom Glavine	2.50
48	Matt Lawton	1.00
49	Kyle Lohse	1.00
50	Corey Patterson	1.00
51	Ichiro Suzuki	6.00
52	Wade Miller	1.00
53	Ben Diggins	1.00
54	Jayson Werth	1.00
55	Masato Yoshii	1.00
56	Mark Buehrle	1.00
57	Drew Henson	1.50
58	Dave Williams	1.00
59	Juan Rivera	1.00
60	Scott Schoeneweis	1.00
61	Josh Beckett	1.50
62	Vinny Castilla	1.00
63	Barry Zito	2.00
64	Jose Valentin	1.00
65	Jon Lieber	1.00
66	Jorge Padilla	1.00
67	Luis Aparicio	1.00
68	Boog Powell	1.00
69	Dick Radatz	1.00
70	Frank Malzone	1.00
71	Lou Brock	1.50
72	Billy Williams	1.00
73	Early Wynn	1.00
74	Jim Bunning	1.00
75	Al Kaline	5.00
76	Eddie Mathews	3.00
77	Harmon Killebrew	5.00
78	Gil Hodges	1.00
79	Duke Snider	3.00
80	Yogi Berra	4.00
81	Whitey Ford	3.00
82	Willie Stargell	1.50
83	Willie McCovey	1.50
84	Gaylord Perry	1.00
85	Red Schoendienst	1.00
86	Luis Castillo	1.00
87	Derek Jeter	8.00
88	Orlando Hudson	1.00
89	Bobby Higginson	1.00
90	Brent Butler	1.00
91	Brad Wilkerson	1.00
92	Craig Biggio	1.50
93	Marlon Anderson	1.00
94	Ty Wigginton	1.00
95	Hideo Nomo	3.00
96	Barry Larkin	2.00
97	Roberto Alomar	3.00
98	Omar Vizquel	1.50
99	Andres Galarraga	1.00
100	Shawn Green	1.50
101	Rafael Furcal	.15
102	Bill Selby	.15
103	Brent Abernathy	.15
104	Nomar Garciaparra	1.50
105	Michael Barrett	.15
106	Travis Hafner	.15
107	Carl Crawford	.15
108	Jeff Cirillo	.15
109	Mike Hampton	.15
110	Kip Wells	.15
111	Luis Alicea	.15
112	Ellis Burks	.15
113	Matt Anderson	.15
114	Carlos Beltran	.50
115	Paul LoDuca	.15
116	Lance Berkman	.15
117	Moises Alou	.15
118	Roger Cedeno	.15
119	Brad Fullmer	.15
120	Sean Burroughs	.15
121	Eric Byrnes	.15
122	Milton Bradley	.15
123	Jason Giambi	.75
124	Brook Fordyce	.15
125	Kevin Appier	.15
126	Steve Cox	.15
127	Danny Bautista	.15
128	Edgardo Alfonzo	.15
129	Matt Clement	.15
130	Robb Nen	.15
131	Roy Halladay	.15
132	Brian Jordan	.15
133	A.J. Burnett	.15
134	Aaron Cook	.15
135	Paul Byrd	.15
136	Ramon Ortiz	.15
137	Adam Hyzdu	.15
138	Rafael Soriano	.15
139	Marty Cordova	.15
140	Nelson Cruz	.15
141	Jamie Moyer	.15
142	Raul Mondesi	.15
143	Josh Bard	.15
144	Elmer Dessens	.15
145	Rickey Henderson	.75
146	Joe McEwing	.15
147	Luis Rivas	.15
148	Armando Benitez	.15
149	Keith Foulke	.15
150	Zach Day	.15
151	Troy Lunsford	.15
152	Bobby Abreu	.15
153	Juan Cruz	.15
154	Ramon Hernandez	.15
155	Brandon Duckworth	.15
156	Matt Ginter	.15
157	Robert Mackowiak	.15
158	Josh Pearce	.15
159	Marlon Byrd	.15
160	Todd Walker	.15
161	Chad Hermansen	.15
162	Felix Escalona	.15
163	Ruben Mateo	.15
164	Mark Johnson	.15
165	Juan Pierre	.15
166	Gary Sheffield	.30
167	Edgar Martinez	.15
168	Randy Winn	.15
169	Pokey Reese	.15
170	Kevin Mench	.15
171	Albert Pujols	1.50
172	J.T. Snow	.15
173	Dean Palmer	.15
174	Jay Payton	.15
175	Abraham Nunez	.15
176	Richie Sexson	.15
177	Jose Vidro	.15
178	Geoff Jenkins	.15
179	Dan Wilson	.15
180	John Olerud	.15
181	Javy Lopez	.15
182	Carl Everett	.15
183	Vernon Wells	.15
184	Juan Gonzalez	.75
185	Jorge Posada	.35
186	Mike Sweeney	.15
187	Cesar Izturis	.15
188	Jason Schmidt	.15
189	Chris Richard	.15
190	Jason Phillips	.15
191	Fred McGriff	.15
192	Shea Hillenbrand	.15
193	Ivan Rodriguez	.50
194	Mike Lowell	.15
195	Neifi Perez	.15
196	Kenny Lofton	.15
197	A.J. Pierzynski	.15
198	Larry Bigbie	.15
199	Juan Uribe	.15
200	Jeff Bagwell	.75
201	Timoniel Perez	.15
202	Jeremy Giambi	.15
203	Deivi Cruz	.15
204	Marquis Grissom	.15
205	Chipper Jones	1.00
206	Alex Gonzalez	.15
207	Steve Finley	.15
208	Ben Davis	.15
209	Mike Bordick	.15
210	Casey Fossum	.15
211	Aramis Ramirez	.15
212	Aaron Boone	.15
213	Orlando Cabrera	.15
214	Hee Seop Choi	.15
215	Jeromy Burnitz	.15
216	Todd Hollandsworth	.15
217	Rey Sanchez	.15
218	Jose Cruz Jr.	.15
219	Roosevelt Brown	.15
220	Odalis Perez	.15
221	Carlos Delgado	.40
222	Orlando Hernandez	.15
223	Adam Everett	.15
224	Adrian Beltre	.25
225	Ken Griffey Jr.	1.50
226	Brad Penny	.15
227	Carlos Lee	.15
228	J.C. Romero	.15
229	Ramon Martinez	.15
230	Matt Morris	.15
231	Ben Howard	.15
232	Damon Minor	.15
233	Jason Marquis	.15
234	Paul Wilson	.15
235	Ryan Dempster	.15
236	Jeffrey Hammonds	.15
237	Jaret Wright	.15
238	Carlos Pena	.15
239	Toby Hall	.15
240	Rick Helling	.15
241	Alex Escobar	.15
242	Trevor Hoffman	.15
243	Bernie Williams	.35
244	Jorge Julio	.15
245	Byung-Hyun Kim	.15
246	Mike Redmond	.15
247	Tony Armas	.15
248	Aaron Rowand	.15
249	Rusty Greer	.15
250	Aaron Harang	.15
251	Jeremy Fikac	.15
252	Jay Gibbons	.15
253	Brandon Puffer	.15
254	Dewayne Wise	.15
255	Chan Ho Park	.15
256	David Bell	.15
257	Kenny Rogers	.15
258	Mark Quinn	.15
259	Greg LaRocca	.15
260	Reggie Taylor	.15
261	Brett Tomko	.15
262	Jack Wilson	.15
263	Billy Wagner	.15
264	Greg Norton	.15
265	Tim Salmon	.25
266	Joe Randa	.15
267	Geronimo Gil	.15
268	Johnny Damon	.25
269	Robin Ventura	.15
270	Frank Thomas	.75
271	Terrence Long	.15
272	Mark Redman	.15
273	Mark Kotsay	.15
274	Ben Sheets	.15
275	Reggie Sanders	.15
276	Mark Grace	.25
277	Eddie Guardado	.15
278	Julio Mateo	.15
279	Bengie Molina	.15
280	Bill Hall	.15
281	Eric Chavez	.30
282	Joe Kennedy	.15
283	John Valentin	.15
284	Ray Durham	.15
285	Trot Nixon	.15
286	Rondell White	.15
287	Alex Gonzalez	.15
288	Tomas Perez	.15
289	Jared Sandberg	.15
290	Jacque Jones	.15
291	Cliff Floyd	.15
292	Ryan Klesko	.15
293	Morgan Ensberg	.15
294	Jerry Hairston Jr.	.15
295	Doug Mientkiewicz	.15
296	Darin Erstad	.50
297	Jeff Conine	.15
298	Johnny Estrada	.15
299	Mark Mulder	.15
300	Jeff Kent	.15
301	Roger Clemens	1.25
302	Endy Chavez	.15
303	Joe Crede	.15
304	J.D. Drew	.30
305	David Dellucci	.15
306	Eli Marrero	.15
307	Josh Fogg	.15
308	Mike Crudale	.15
309	Bret Boone	.15
310	Mariano Rivera	.30
311	Mike Piazza	1.50
312	Jason Jennings	.15
313	Jason Varitek	.15
314	Vicente Padilla	.15
315	Kevin Millwood	.15
316	Nick Johnson	.15
317	Shane Reynolds	.15
318	Joe Thurston	.15
319	Mike Lamb	.15

320	Aaron Sele	.15
321	Fernando Tatis	.15
322	Randy Wolf	.15
323	David Justice	.15
324	Andy Pettitte	.30
325	Freddy Sanchez	.15
326	Scott Spiezio	.15
327	Randy Johnson	.75
328	Karim Garcia	.15
329	Eric Milton	.15
330	Jermaine Dye	.15
331	Kevin Brown	.15
332	Adam Pettyjohn	.15
333	Jason Lane	.15
334	Mark Prior	.50
335	Mike Lieberthal	.15
336	Matt White	.15
337	John Patterson	.15
338	Marcus Giles	.15
339	Kazuhisa Ishii	.15
340	Willie Harris	.15
341	Travis Phelps	.15
342	Randall Simon	.15
343	Manny Ramirez	.75
344	Kerry Wood	.50
345	Shannon Stewart	.15
346	Mike Mussina	.40
347	Joe Borchard	.15
348	Tyler Walker	.15
349	Preston Wilson	.15
350	Damian Moss	.15
351	Eric Karros	.15
352	Bobby Kielty	.15
353	Jason LaRue	.15
354	Phil Nevin	.15
355	Tony Graffanino	.15
356	Antonio Alfonseca	.15
357	Eddie Taubensee	.15
358	Luis Ugueto	.15
359	Greg Vaughn	.15
360	Corey Thurman	.15
361	Omar Infante	.15
362	Alex Cintron	.15
363	Esteban Loaiza	.15
364	Tino Martinez	.15
365	David Eckstein	.15
366	David Pember **RC**	.15
367	Damian Rolls	.15
368	Richard Hidalgo	.15
369	Brad Radke	.15
370	Alex Sanchez	.15
371	Ben Grieve	.15
372	Brandon Inge	.15
373	Adam Piatt	.15
374	Charles Johnson	.15
375	Rafael Palmeiro	.50
376	Joe Mays	.15
377	Derrek Lee	.15
378	Fernando Vina	.15
379	Andruw Jones	.75
380	Troy Glaus	.15
381	Bobby Hill	.15
382	C.C. Sabathia	.15
383	Jose Hernandez	.15
384	Al Leiter	.15
385	Jarrod Washburn	.15
386	Cody Ransom	.15
387	Matt Stairs	.15
388	Edgar Renteria	.15
389	Tsuyoshi Shinjo	.15
390	Matt Williams	.15
391	Bubba Trammell	.15
392	Jason Kendall	.15
393	Scott Rolen	.50
394	Chuck Knoblauch	.15
395	Jimmy Rollins	.25
396	Gary Bennett	.15
397	David Wells	.15
398	Ronnie Belliard	.15
399	Austin Kearns	.15
400	Tim Hudson	.30
401	Andy Van Hekken	.15
402	Ray Lankford	.15
403	Todd Helton	.75
404	Jeff Weaver	.15
405	Gabe Kapler	.15
406	Luis Gonzalez	.40
407	Sean Casey	.15
408	Kazuhiro Sasaki	.15
409	Mark Teixeira	.50
410	Brian Giles	.15
411	Robert Fick	.15
412	Wilkin Ruan	.15
413	Jose Rijo	.15
414	Ben Broussard	.15
415	Aubrey Huff	.15
416	Magglio Ordonez	.25
417	Barry Bonds	2.00
418	Miguel Tejada	.40
419	Randy Johnson	.75
420	Barry Zito	.30
421	Jason Jennings	.15
422	Eric Hinske	.15
423	Benito Santiago	.15
424	Adam Kennedy	.15
425	Troy Glaus	.50
426	Brandon Phillips	.15
427	Jake Peavy	.15
428	Jason Romano	.15
429	Jeriome Robertson	.15
430	Aaron Guiel	.15
431	Hank Blalock	.15
432	Brad Lidge	.15
433	Francisco Rodriguez	.15
434	Jaime Cerda	.15

435	Jung Bong	.15
436	Reed Johnson	.15
437	Rene Reyes	.15
438	Chris Snelling	.15
439	Miguel Olivo	.15
440	Brian Banks	.15
441	Eric Junge	.15
442	Kirk Saarloos	.15
443	Jamey Carroll	.15
444	Josh Hancock	.15
445	Michael Restovich	.15
446	William Bloomquist	.15
447	John Lackey	.15
448	Marcus Thames	.15
449	Victor Martinez	.15
450	Brett Myers	.15
451	Wes Obermueller	.15
452	Hansel Izquierdo	.15
453	Brian Tallet	.15
454	Craig Monroe	.15
455	Doug DeVore	.15
456	John Buck	.15
457	Tony Alvarez	.15
458	Wily Mo Pena	.15
459	John Stephens	.15
460	Tony Torcato	.15
461	Adam Kennedy	.15
462	Alex Rodriguez	.15
463	Derek Lowe	.15
464	Garret Anderson	.15
465	Pat Burrell	.50
466	Eric Gagne	.15
467	Tomokazu Ohka	.15
468	Josh Phelps	.15
469	Sammy Sosa	1.50
470	Jim Thome	.15
471	Vladimir Guerrero	.75
472	Jason Simontacchi	.15
473	Adam Dunn	.50
474	Jim Edmonds	.15
475	Barry Bonds	2.00
476	Paul Konerko	.25
477	Alfonso Soriano	.75
478	Curt Schilling	.40
479	John Smoltz	.15
480	Torii Hunter	.15
481	Rodrigo Lopez	.15
482	Miguel Tejada	.35
483	Eric Hinske	.15
484	Roy Oswalt	.25
485	Junior Spivey	.15

Glossy

SP's (1-100):	1-2X
Cards (101-485):	5-10X
Production 100 Sets	
Randomly inserted in Update packs.	

B/W Goudey

Chicago Cubs™

		NM/M
Complete Set (25):		80.00
Common Player:		1.50
Production 1,936 Sets		
Golds:		4-8X
Production 36 Sets		
1BWG	Jim Thome	2.50
2BWG	Derek Jeter	10.00
3BWG	Alex Rodriguez	8.00
4BWG	Mark Prior	1.00
5BWG	Nomar Garciaparra	6.00
6BWG	Curt Schilling	2.00
7BWG	Pat Burrell	2.00
8BWG	Frank Thomas	2.50
9BWG	Roger Clemens	5.00
10BWG	Chipper Jones	5.00
11BWG	Barry Larkin	1.50
12BWG	Hideo Nomo	2.00
13BWG	Pedro J. Martinez	3.00
14BWG	Jeff Bagwell	2.50
15BWG	Greg Maddux	5.00
16BWG	Vladimir Guerrero	5.00
17BWG	Ichiro Suzuki	6.00
18BWG	Mike Piazza	8.00
19BWG	Drew Henson	1.50
20BWG	Albert Pujols	3.00
21BWG	Sammy Sosa	5.00
22BWG	Jason Giambi	3.00
23BWG	Randy Johnson	3.00
24BWG	Ken Griffey Jr.	6.00
25BWG	Barry Bonds	8.00

Checklist

	NM/M
Complete Set (18):	6.00

Common Card:		.50
Inserted 1:4		
1CL-9CL	Derek Jeter	.50
10CL-18CL	Barry Bonds	.50

Game-Used Parallel

FRANK THOMAS
Chicago White Sox® - Designated Hitter
Game-Worn Jersey

	NM/M
Common Player:	5.00
Inserted 1:35	
Golds:	1-2X
Production 100 Sets	
Derek Jeter/Jsy/150	35.00
Craig Biggio/Bat	8.00
Hideo Nomo/Jsy/200	20.00
Barry Larkin/Jsy/200	10.00
Kazuhiro Sasaki/Jsy/200	10.00
Greg Maddux/Jsy	15.00
Mo Vaughn/Jsy/60	10.00
Pedro Martinez/Jsy/200	12.00
Barry Zito/Jsy	10.00
Luis Aparicio/Jsy/150	10.00
Willie Stargell/Pants/150	15.00
Nomar Garciaparra/Jsy/200	20.00
Edgardo Alfonzo/Jsy/200	8.00
John Olerud/Jsy	6.00
Juan Gonzalez/Bat/200	10.00
Jorge Posada/Bat	8.00
Shea Hillenbrand/Bat	10.00
Ivan Rodriguez/Jsy	8.00
Mike Lowell/Bat	5.00
Jeff Bagwell/Jsy/200	12.00
Chipper Jones/Jsy	15.00
Jeromy Burnitz/Jsy/200	6.00
Adrian Beltre/Jsy	8.00
Robin Ventura/Jsy	8.00
Frank Thomas/Jsy	15.00
Mark Grace/Jsy	10.00
Darin Erstad/Jsy	8.00
Roger Clemens/Jsy/150	20.00
J.D. Drew/Jsy	8.00
Mike Piazza/Jsy	20.00
Randy Johnson/Jsy/150	12.00
Mark Prior/Jsy/200	15.00
Kazuhisa Ishii/Jsy	10.00
Manny Ramirez/Jsy/150	10.00
Kerry Wood/Jsy/200	15.00
Mike Mussina/Jsy	10.00
Eric Karros/Jsy	5.00
Rafael Palmeiro/Jsy	5.00
Andruw Jones/Bat/150	10.00
Jason Kendall/Jsy	6.00
Jimmy Rollins/Jsy	8.00
Barry Bonds/Jsy/50	40.00
Miguel Tejada/Bat/150	8.00
Jason Jennings/Jsy	6.00

Hardball Preview

		NM/M
Complete Set (10):		125.00
Common Player:		5.00
Inserted 1:400		
1	Miguel Tejada	5.00
2	Derek Jeter	25.00
3	Mike Piazza	20.00
4	Barry Bonds	20.00
5	Mark Prior	4.00
6	Ichiro Suzuki	20.00
7	Alex Rodriguez	20.00
8	Nomar Garciaparra	15.00
9	Alfonso Soriano	12.00
10	Ken Griffey Jr.	15.00

Milestones

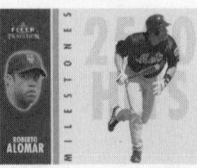

ROBERTO ALOMAR

	NM/M
Complete Set (25):	40.00
Common Player:	1.00
Inserted 1:5	
1	Eddie Mathews	1.50

2	Rickey Henderson	1.50
3	Harmon Killebrew	1.50
4	Al Kaline	2.50
5	Willie McCovey	1.00
6	Tom Seaver	2.00
7	Reggie Jackson	2.00
8	Mike Schmidt	3.00
9	Nolan Ryan	5.00
10	Mike Piazza	4.00
11	Randy Johnson	2.00
12	Bernie Williams	1.50
13	Rafael Palmeiro	1.50
14	Juan Gonzalez	1.50
15	Ken Griffey Jr.	3.00
16	Derek Jeter	5.00
17	Roger Clemens	3.00
18	Roberto Alomar	1.50
19	Manny Ramirez	1.50
20	Luis Gonzalez	1.00
21	Barry Bonds	4.00
22	Nomar Garciaparra	3.00
23	Fred McGriff	1.00
24	Greg Maddux	2.50
25	Barry Bonds	4.00

Milestones Game-Used

PEDRO MARTINEZ

Game-Worn Legacy

	NM/M
Common Player:	8.00
Inserted 1:143	
Golds:	1-2X
Production 100 Sets	
Roberto Alomar/Bat/200	8.00
Barry Bonds/600 HR/Bat/100	30.00
Barry Bonds/5 MVP/Jsy/200	25.00
Roger Clemens/Jsy/150	20.00
Nomar Garciaparra/Jsy/200	20.00
Juan Gonzalez/Bat/250	10.00
Derek Jeter/Jsy/150	35.00
Randy Johnson/Jsy/100	15.00
Greg Maddux	20.00
Fred McGriff	5.00
Rafael Palmeiro/Jsy/200	8.00
Mike Piazza/Jsy/100	20.00
Manny Ramirez/Jsy/150	10.00
Bernie Williams/Jsy/200	10.00

Lumber Company

LUMBER COMPANY

Ichiro

	NM/M
Complete Set (30):	70.00
Common Player:	1.00
Inserted 1:10	
1	Mike Piazza	6.00
2	Derek Jeter	8.00
3	Alex Rodriguez	6.00
4	Miguel Tejada	1.00
5	Nomar Garciaparra	5.00
6	Andruw Jones	1.50
7	Pat Burrell	1.50
8	Albert Pujols	3.00
9	Jeff Bagwell	2.00
10	Chipper Jones	4.00
11	Ichiro Suzuki	6.00
12	Alfonso Soriano	3.00
13	Eric Chavez	1.50
14	Brian Giles	1.00
15	Shawn Green	1.50
16	Jim Thome	2.00
17	Lance Berkman	1.50
18	Bernie Williams	1.50
19	Manny Ramirez	2.00
20	Vladimir Guerrero	3.00
21	Carlos Delgado	1.25
22	Scott Rolen	1.50
23	Sammy Sosa	4.00
24	Ken Griffey Jr.	3.00
25	Barry Bonds	6.00
26	Todd Helton	2.00
27	Jason Giambi	4.00
28	Austin Kearns	1.50
29	Jeff Kent	1.00
30	Magglio Ordonez	1.50

Lumber Company Bat Gold

	NM/M
Numbered to 2002 HR total.	
Lance Berkman/42	25.00

Barry Bonds/46	70.00
Pat Burrell/37	50.00
Eric Chavez/34	20.00
Carlos Delgado/33	35.00
Nomar Garciaparra/24	60.00
Brian Giles/38	25.00
Shawn Green/42	35.00
Todd Helton/30	35.00
Derek Jeter/18	200.00
Andruw Jones/35	25.00
Chipper Jones/26	45.00
Austin Kearns/13	35.00
Jeff Kent/37	20.00
Magglio Ordonez/38	25.00
Mike Piazza/33	65.00
Alex Rodriguez/57	35.00
Miguel Tejada/34	35.00
Jim Thome/52	30.00

Lumber Company Bat

	NM/M
Common Player:	6.00
Inserted 1:108	
Jeff Bagwell/200	15.00
Lance Berkman/200	10.00
Barry Bonds/150	25.00
Pat Burrell/75	25.00
Eric Chavez/125	8.00
Carlos Delgado/200	6.00
Nomar Garciaparra/200	25.00
Brian Giles/200	8.00
Shawn Green/200	8.00
Todd Helton	8.00
Derek Jeter/96	35.00
Andruw Jones	8.00
Chipper Jones	15.00
Austin Kearns/75	18.00
Jeff Kent/200	6.00
Magglio Ordonez	6.00
Mike Piazza/200	20.00
Manny Ramirez	10.00
Alex Rodriguez	15.00
Scott Rolen/80	25.00
Alfonso Soriano/200	12.00
Miguel Tejada	10.00
Jim Thome/200	12.00
Bernie Williams	10.00

Standouts

	NM/M
Complete Set (15):	60.00
Common Player:	1.50
Inserted 1:40	
1SO Greg Maddux	5.00
2SO Derek Jeter	10.00
3SO Alex Rodriguez	8.00
4SO Miguel Tejada	2.00
5SO Nomar Garciaparra	6.00
6SO Barry Bonds	8.00
7SO Pat Burrell	2.00
8SO Ken Griffey Jr.	6.00
9SO Alfonso Soriano	4.00
10SO Mike Piazza	8.00
11SO Sammy Sosa	5.00
12SO Ichiro Suzuki	6.00
13SO Vladimir Guerrero	3.00
14SO Roger Clemens	5.00
15SO Adam Dunn	2.50

2003 Fleer Tradition Update

	NM/M
Complete Set (398):	175.00
Common Player:	.15
Common Rookie (286-398):	.50
Cards (286-299):	
Inserted 1:4	
Pack (10):	2.00
Box (32 + 25 count update box):	50.00
1 Aaron Boone	.15
2 Carl Everett	.15
3 Eduardo Perez	.15
4 Jason Michaels	.15
5 Karim Garcia	.15
6 Rainier Olmedo	.15
7 Scott Williamson	.15
8 Adam Kennedy	.15
9 Carl Pavano	.15
10 Eli Marrero	.15
11 Jason Simontacchi	.15
12 Keith Foulke	.15
13 Preston Wilson	.15

ROOKIE '03

DELMON YOUNG

Tampa Bay Devil Rays™ - Outfield

14 Scott Hatteberg	.15
15 Adam Dunn	.50
16 Carlos Baerga	.15
17 Elmer Dessens	.15
18 Javier Vazquez	.15
19 Kenny Rogers	.15
20 Quinton McCracken	.15
21 Shane Reynolds	.15
22 Adam Eaton	.15
23 Carlos Zambrano	.15
24 Enrique Wilson	.15
25 Jeff DaVanon	.15
26 Kenny Lofton	.25
27 Ramon Castro	.15
28 Shannon Stewart	.15
29 Al Martin	.15
30 Carlos Guillen	.15
31 Eric Karros	.15
32 Tim Worrell	.15
33 Kevin Millwood	.25
34 Randall Simon	.15
35 Shawn Chacon	.15
36 Alex Rodriguez	1.50
37 Casey Blake	.15
38 Eric Munson	.15
39 Jeff Kent	.25
40 Kris Benson	.15
41 Randy Winn	.15
42 Shea Hillenbrand	.15
43 Alfonso Soriano	1.00
44 Chris George	.15
45 Eric Bruntlett	.15
46 Jeromy Burnitz	.15
47 Kyle Farnsworth	.15
48 Torii Hunter	.40
49 Sidney Ponson	.15
50 Andres Galarraga	.25
51 Chris Singleton	.15
52 Eric Gagne	.25
53 Jesse Foppert	.15
54 Lance Carter	.15
55 Ray Durham	.15
56 Tanyon Sturtze	.15
57 Andy Ashby	.15
58 Cliff Floyd	.15
59 Eric Young	.15
60 Jhonny Peralta	.50
61 Livan Hernandez	.15
62 Reggie Sanders	.15
63 Tim Spooneybarger	.15
64 Angel Berroa	.15
65 Coco Crisp	.15
66 Eric Hinske	.15
67 Jim Edmonds	.25
68 Luis Matos	.15
69 Rickey Henderson	.40
70 Todd Walker	.15
71 Antonio Alfonseca	.15
72 Corey Koskie	.15
73 Erubiel Durazo	.15
74 Jim Thome	.50
75 Lyle Overbay	.15
76 Robert Fick	.15
77 Todd Hollandsworth	.15
78 Aramis Ramirez	.15
79 Cristian Guzman	.15
80 Esteban Loaiza	.15
81 Jody Gerut	.15
82 Mark Grudzielanek	.15
83 Roberto Alomar	.40
84 Todd Hundley	.15
85 Mike Hampton	.15
86 Curt Schilling	.40
87 Francisco Rodriguez	.15
88 John Lackey	.15
89 Mark Redman	.15
90 Robin Ventura	.15
91 Todd Zeile	.15
92 B.J. Surhoff	.15
93 Raul Mondesi	.25
94 Frank Catalanotto	.15
95 John Smoltz	.25
96 Mark Ellis	.15
97 Rocco Baldelli	.50
98 Todd Pratt	.15
99 Barry Bonds	2.00
100 Danny Graves	.15
101 Fred McGriff	.25
102 John Burkett	.15
103 Marquis Grissom	.15
104 Rocky Biddle	.15

105 Tom Glavine	.25
106 Bartolo Colon	.25
107 Darren Bragg	.15
108 Gabe Kapler	.15
109 John Franco	.15
110 Matt Mantei	.15
111 Rod Beck	.15
112 Tomokazu Ohka	.15
113 Ben Petrick	.15
114 Darren Dreifort	.15
115 Garret Anderson	.25
116 John Vander Wal	.15
117 Melvin Mora	.15
118 Rodrigo Lopez	.15
119 Raul Ibanez	.15
120 Benito Santiago	.15
121 David Ortiz	.15
122 Gary Bennett	.15
123 Jon Garland	.15
124 Michael Young	.15
125 Rodrigo Rosario	.15
126 Travis Lee	.15
127 Bill Mueller	.15
128 Derek Lowe	.15
129 Gil Meche	.15
130 Jose Guillen	.15
131 Miguel Cabrera	.40
132 Ron Calloway	.15
133 Troy Percival	.15
134 Billy Koch	.15
135 Dmitri Young	.15
136 Glendon Rusch	.15
137 Jose Jimenez	.15
138 Miguel Tejada	.40
139 John Thomson	.15
140 Troy O'Leary	.15
141 Bobby Kielty	.15
142 Dontrelle Willis	.50
143 Greg Myers	.15
144 Jose Vizcaino	.15
145 Mike MacDougal	.15
146 Ronnie Belliard	.15
147 Tyler Houston	.15
148 Brady Clark	.15
149 Edgardo Alfonzo	.15
150 Guillermo Mota	.15
151 Jose Lima	.15
152 Mike Williams	.15
153 Roy Oswalt	.25
154 Scott Podsednik	.25
155 Brandon Lyon	.15
156 Henry Mateo	.15
157 Jose Macias	.15
158 Mike Bordick	.15
159 Royce Clayton	.15
160 Vance Wilson	.15
161 Brent Abernathy	.15
162 Horacio Ramirez	.15
163 Jose Reyes	.50
164 Nick Punto	.15
165 Ruben Sierra	.15
166 Victor Zambrano	.15
167 Brett Tomko	.15
168 Ivan Rodriguez	.75
169 Jose Mesa	.15
170 Octavio Dotel	.15
171 Russ Ortiz	.15
172 Vladimir Guerrero	.75
173 Brian Lawrence	.15
174 Jae Weong Seo	.15
175 Jose Cruz Jr.	.15
176 Pat Burrell	.40
177 Russell Branyan	.15
178 Warren Morris	.15
179 Brian Boehringer	.15
180 Jason Johnson	.15
181 Josh Phelps	.15
182 Paul Konerko	.15
183 Ryan Franklin	.15
184 Wes Helms	.15
185 Brooks Kieschnick	.15
186 Jason Davis	.15
187 Juan Pierre	.15
188 Paul Wilson	.15
189 Sammy Sosa	1.50
190 Wil Cordero	.15
191 Byung-Hyun Kim	.15
192 Juan Encarnacion	.15
193 Placido Polanco	.15
194 Sandy Alomar	.15
195 Julio Lugo	.15
196 Junior Spivey	.15
197 Woody Williams	.15
198 Xavier Nady	.15
199 Mark Loretta	.15
200 Deivi Cruz	.15
201 Jorge Posada	.25
202 Carlos Delgado	.25
203 Alfonso Soriano	.50
204 Alex Rodriguez	1.00
205 Troy Glaus	.25
206 Garret Anderson	.15
207 Hideki Matsui	2.00
208 Ichiro Suzuki	.75
209 Esteban Loaiza	.15
210 Manny Ramirez	.25
211 Roger Clemens	.75
212 Roy Halladay	.15
213 Jason Giambi	.25
214 Edgar Martinez	.15
215 Bret Boone	.15
216 Hank Blalock	.15
217 Nomar Garciaparra	.75
218 Vernon Wells	.15
219 Melvin Mora	.15

220 Magglio Ordonez	.15
221 Mike Sweeney	.15
222 Barry Zito	.25
223 Carl Everett	.15
224 Shigetoshi Hasegawa	.15
225 Jamie Moyer	.15
226 Mark Mulder	.15
227 Eddie Guardado	.15
228 Ramon Hernandez	.15
229 Keith Foulke	.15
230 Javy Lopez	.15
231 Todd Helton	.25
232 Marcus Giles	.15
233 Edgar Renteria	.15
234 Scott Rolen	.25
235 Barry Bonds	1.00
236 Albert Pujols	.75
237 Gary Sheffield	.25
238 Jim Edmonds	.15
239 Jason Schmidt	.15
240 Mark Prior	1.00
241 Dontrelle Willis	.25
242 Kerry Wood	.25
243 Kevin Brown	.15
244 Woody Williams	.15
245 Paul LoDuca	.15
246 Richie Sexson	.15
247 Jose Vidro	.15
248 Luis Castillo	.15
249 Aaron Boone	.15
250 Mike Lowell	.15
251 Rafael Furcal	.15
252 Andruw Jones	.25
253 Preston Wilson	.15
254 John Smoltz	.15
255 Eric Gagne	.15
256 Randy Wolf	.15
257 Billy Wagner	.15
258 Luis Gonzalez	.15
259 Russ Ortiz	.15
260 Jim Thome,	.15
Pedro J. Martinez	.40
261 Alfonso Soriano,	.15
Jeff Bagwell	.50
262 Dontrelle Willis,	.15
Rocco Baldelli	.15
263 Carlos Delgado,	.15
Vladimir Guerrero	.25
264 Sammy Sosa,	.15
Magglio Ordonez	.25
265 Jason Giambi, Adam Dunn	.25
266 Mike Sweeney, Albert Pujols	.50
267 Barry Bonds, Torii Hunter	.75
268 Ichiro Suzuki,	.15
Andruw Jones	.50
269 Chipper Jones,	.15
Hank Blalock	.15
270 Mark Prior, Vernon Wells	.75
271 Nomar Garciaparra,	.15
Scott Rolen	.75
272 Alex Rodriguez,	.15
Lance Berkman	.75
273 Roger Clemens, Kerry Wood	.75
274 Derek Jeter, Jose Reyes	.75
275 Greg Maddux, Barry Zito	.75
276 Carlos Delgado	.25
277 J.D. Drew	.15
278 Barry Bonds	1.00
279 Albert Pujols	.75
280 Jim Thome	.25
281 Sammy Sosa	.75
282 Alfonso Soriano	.50
283 Hideki Matsui	1.00
284 Mike Piazza	.50
285 Vladimir Guerrero	.40
286 Rich Harden	.50
287 Chin-Hui Tsao	.15
288 Edwin Jackson RC	4.00
289 Chien-Ming Wang RC	6.00
290 Josh Willingham RC	2.00
291 Matt Kata RC	2.00
292 Jose Contreras RC	2.00
293 Chris Bootcheck	.50
294 Javier Lopez	1.00
295 Delmon Young RC	8.00
296 Pedro Liriano	.50
297 Noah Lowry	.50
298 Khalil Greene	3.00
299 Rob Bowen	.50
300 Bo Hart RC	2.00
301 Beau Kemp RC	.25
302 Gerald Laird	.15
303 Miguel Ojeda RC	.40
304 Todd Wellemeyer RC	.75
305 Ryan Wagner RC	2.00
306 Jeff Duncan RC	1.50
307 Wilfredo Ledezma RC	1.50
308 Wes Obermueller	.15
309 Bernie Castro RC	.25
310 Tim Olson RC	.25
311 Colin Porter RC	2.00
312 Francisco Cruceta RC	1.50
313 Guillermo Quiroz RC	1.50
314 Brian Stokes RC	.50
315 Robby Hammock RC	.50
316 Lew Ford RC	2.00
317 Todd Linden	.15
318 Mike Gallo RC	.50
319 Francisco Rosario RC	1.50
320 Rosman Garcia RC	.50
321 Felix Sanchez RC	.50
322 Chad Gaudin RC	1.00
323 Phil Seibel RC	.50
324 Jason Gilfillan RC	.50
325 Terrmel Sledge RC	.75

326	Alfredo Gonzalez RC	.50
327	Josh Stewart RC	1.00
328	Jeremy Griffiths	.15
329	Cory Stewart RC	.50
330	Josh Hall RC	1.00
331	Arnie Munoz RC	.50
332	Garrett Atkins	.15
333	Neal Cotts	.15
334	Dan Haren	2.00
335	Shane Victorino RC	.50
336	David Sanders RC	.50
337	Oscar Villarreal RC	.50
338	Michael Hessman RC	.50
339	Andrew Brown RC	.50
340	Kevin Hooper	.15
341	Prentice Redman RC	.50
342	Brandon Webb RC	3.00
343	Jimmy Gobble	.15
344	Pete LaForest RC	.50
345	Chris Waters RC	.75
346	Hideki Matsui RC	8.00
347	Chris Capuano RC	1.00
348	Jon Leicester RC	.50
349	Mike Nicolas RC	.50
350	Nook Logan RC	.50
351	Craig Brazell RC	1.00
352	Aaron Looper RC	.50
353	D.J. Carrasco RC	.50
354	Clint Barmes RC	1.00
355	Doug Waechter RC	.75
356	Julio Manon RC	.50
357	Jeremy Bonderman	3.00
358	Diegomar Markwell RC	.50
359	Dave Matranga RC	.75
360	Luis Ayala RC	.50
361	Jason Stanford	.15
362	Roger Deago RC	.50
363	Geoff Geary RC	.50
364	Edgar Gonzalez RC	.50
365	Michel Hernandez RC	.50
366	Aquilino Lopez RC	.50
367	David Manning RC	1.00
368	Carlos Mendez RC	.50
369	Matt Miller	.15
370	Micheal Nakamura RC	.50
371	Mike Neu RC	.50
372	Ramon Nivar RC	.50
373	Kevin Ohme RC	.50
374	Alex Prieto RC	1.00
375	Stephen Randolph RC	1.00
376	Brian Sweeney RC	1.00
377	Matt Diaz RC	.50
378	Mike Gonzalez	.15
379	Daniel Cabrera RC	2.00
380	Fernando Cabrera RC	.50
381	David DeJesus RC	.50
382	Mike Ryan RC	1.00
383	Rick Roberts RC	.50
384	Seung Jun Song	.15
385	Rickie Weeks RC	5.00
386	Humberto Quintero RC	.50
387	Alexis Rios	.15
388	Aaron Miles RC	2.00
389	Tom Gregorio RC	.50
390	Anthony Ferrari RC	.75
391	Kevin Correia RC	.75
392	Rafael Betancourt RC	.75
393	Rett Johnson RC	.50
394	Richard Fischer RC	.50
395	Greg Aquino RC	.50
396	Daniel Garcia RC	1.00
397	Sergio Mitre RC	1.00
398	Edwin Almonte	.15

Glossy

ELI MARRERO
Cardinals® - Outfield

Stars (1-285): 5-10X
Rookies (286-398): .5-1.5X
Production 100 Sets

Diamond Debuts

		NM/M
Complete Set (25):		40.00
Common Player:		1.00
Inserted 1:10		
1	Dontrelle Willis	4.00
2	Bo Hart	1.00
3	Jose Reyes	4.00
4	Chin-Hui Tsao	1.00
5	Brandon Webb	3.00
6	Rich Harden	2.00
7	Jesse Foppert	1.00

8	Rocco Baldelli	2.00
9	Hideki Matsui	5.00
10	Ron Calloway	1.00
11	Jeremy Bonderman	1.50
12	Mark Teixeira	3.00
13	Ryan Wagner	2.00
14	Jose Contreras	2.00
15	Miguel Cabrera	4.00
16	Lew Ford	1.00
17	Jeff Duncan	1.50
18	Matt Kata	1.00
19	Jeremy Griffiths	1.00
20	Todd Wellemeyer	1.00
21	Robby Hammock	1.00
22	Dave Matranga	1.00
23	Laynce Nix	1.00
24	Jhonny Peralta	1.00
25	Oscar Villarreal	1.00

Long GONE!

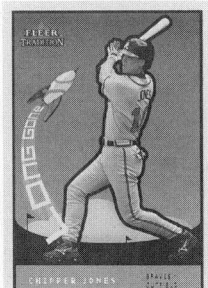

		NM/M
Complete Set (20):		60.00
Common Player:		2.00
Quantity produced listed		
1	Barry Bonds/475	8.00
2	Jason Giambi/440	2.00
3	Albert Pujols/452	6.00
4	Chipper Jones/420	4.00
5	Manny Ramirez/430	2.00
6	Sammy Sosa/536	5.00
7	Alfonso Soriano/440	3.00
8	Alex Rodriguez/430	6.00
9	Jim Thome/445	3.00
10	Vladimir Guerrero/502	3.00
11	Austin Kearns/430	2.00
12	Jeff Bagwell/420	2.00
13	Andruw Jones/430	2.00
14	Carlos Delgado/451	2.00
15	Nomar Garciaparra/440	6.00
16	Adam Dunn/464	2.00
17	Mike Piazza/450	4.00
18	Derek Jeter/410	6.00
19	Ken Griffey Jr./420	4.00
20	Hank Blalock/424	2.00

Milestones

ALFONSO SORIANO

		NM/M
Complete Set (20):		25.00
Common Player:		1.00
Inserted 1:8		
1	Roger Clemens	3.00
2	Rafael Palmeiro	1.00
3	Jeff Bagwell	1.00
4	Barry Bonds	4.00
5	Sammy Sosa	2.50
6	Albert Pujols	3.00
7	Ichiro Suzuki	2.00
8	Alfonso Soriano	1.50
9	Alex Rodriguez	3.00
10	Randy Johnson	1.50
11	Manny Ramirez	1.00
12	Chipper Jones	2.00
13	Todd Helton	1.00
14	Ken Griffey Jr.	2.00
15	Jim Thome	1.00
16	Frank Thomas	1.00
17	Pedro J. Martinez	1.50
18	Hideo Nomo	1.00
19	Jason Schmidt	1.00
20	Carlos Delgado	1.00

Milestones Memorabilia

	NM/M
Common Player:	5.00
Inserted 1:20	
Golds:	1-2X
Production 100 Sets	
Roger Clemens	15.00
Rafael Palmeiro	5.00
Jeff Bagwell	8.00
Sammy Sosa	10.00
Alfonso Soriano	10.00
Alex Rodriguez	10.00
Randy Johnson	8.00
Manny Ramirez	5.00
Chipper Jones	8.00
Todd Helton	6.00
Jim Thome	6.00
Frank Thomas	8.00
Pedro J. Martinez	8.00
Hideo Nomo	8.00
Jason Schmidt	8.00
Carlos Delgado	5.00

Milestones Memorabilia Gold

Complete Set (16): No Pricing

Throwback Threads

AL LEITER

	NM/M
Common Player:	4.00
Inserted 1:64	
Kevin Millwood	6.00
Vladimir Guerrero	8.00
Troy Glaus	6.00
Mike Piazza	10.00
Al Leiter	4.00

Throwback Threads Patch

	NM/M
Common Player:	10.00
Production 100 Sets	
Kevin Millwood	15.00
Vladimir Guerrero	20.00
Troy Glaus	15.00
Mike Piazza	25.00
Al Leiter	10.00

Throwback Threads Dual

	NM/M
Production 100	
Vladimir Guerrero, Troy Glaus	15.00
Mike Piazza, Al Leiter	15.00

Turn Back the Clock

		NM/M
Complete Set (10):		75.00
Common Player:		4.00
Inserted 1:160		
1	Yogi Berra	8.00
2	Mike Schmidt	15.00
3	Tom Seaver	6.00
4	Reggie Jackson	5.00
5	Pee Wee Reese	4.00
6	Phil Rizzuto	4.00
7	Jim Palmer	4.00
8	Robin Yount	15.00
9	Nolan Ryan	20.00
10	Al Kaline	10.00

2004 Fleer America's National Pastime

		NM/M
Common Player (1-60):		.25
Minor Stars (1-60):		.60
Unlisted Stars (1-60):		.75
Common Card (61-90):		3.00
Production 699 Sets		
Pack (5):		10.00
Box (10):		100.00
1	Hideki Matsui	2.50
2	Khalil Greene	1.00
3	Pedro J. Martinez	1.00
4	Sammy Sosa	2.00
5	Mark Teixeira	.40

MIGUEL CABRERA / FLORIDA MARLINS®

6	Orlando Cabrera	.25
7	Scott Podsednik	.25
8	Miguel Tejada	.60
9	Andruw Jones	.75
10	Manny Ramirez	.75
11	Jose Reyes	.25
12	Bobby Abreu	.40
13	Alex Rodriguez	2.50
14	Ivan Rodriguez	.60
15	Jason Schmidt	.40
16	Mike Piazza	1.50
17	Eric Chavez	.40
18	Mark Prior	1.50
19	Adam Dunn	.60
20	Richard Hidalgo	.25
21	Todd Helton	.75
22	Rocco Baldelli	.60
23	Roy Oswalt	.40
24	Angel Berroa	.25
25	Jason Giambi	1.00
26	Jim Thome	1.00
27	Javy Lopez	.40
28	Derek Jeter	3.00
29	Tom Glavine	.40
30	Magglio Ordonez	.40
31	Austin Kearns	.60
32	Scott Rolen	1.00
33	Miguel Cabrera	.75
34	Vernon Wells	.40
35	Frank Thomas	.75
36	Jeff Bagwell	.75
37	Shannon Stewart	.25
38	Richie Sexson	.60
39	Hideo Nomo	.40
40	Nomar Garciaparra	2.50
41	C.C. Sabathia	.25
42	Albert Pujols	2.50
43	Barry Zito	.60
44	Hank Blalock	.60
45	Carlos Delgado	.75
46	Greg Maddux	1.50
47	Randy Johnson	1.00
48	Josh Beckett	.75
49	Kerry Wood	.75
50	Roger Clemens	1.50
51	Garret Anderson	.40
52	Ichiro Suzuki	2.00
53	Kip Wells	.25
54	Vladimir Guerrero	1.00
55	Shawn Green	.40
56	Chipper Jones	1.50
57	Aubrey Huff	.25
58	Ken Griffey Jr.	1.50
59	Torii Hunter	.60
60	Alfonso Soriano	1.00
61	Chris Shelton RC	8.00
62	Graham Koonce	4.00
63	Kazuo Matsui RC	8.00
64	Alfredo Simon RC	4.00
65	Mike Gosling	3.00
66	Mike Rouse	4.00
67	Mariano Gomez RC	3.00
68	Justin Leone RC	3.00
69	Jose Capellan RC	3.00
70	Donald Kelly RC	4.00
71	Merkin Valdez RC	4.00
72	Greg Dobbs RC	4.00
73	Shingo Takatsu RC	4.00
74	Chris Aguila RC	3.00
75	Jerome Gamble RC	4.00
76	Onil Joseph RC	4.00
77	Ramon Ramirez RC	4.00
78	Angel Chavez RC	3.00
79	Hector Gimenez RC	3.00
80	Ivan Ochoa RC	4.00
81	Aarom Baldiris RC	3.00
82	Akinori Otsuka RC	4.00
83	Ruddy Yan RC	3.00
84	Jerry Gil RC	3.00
85	Shawn Hill RC	3.00
86	John Gall RC	4.00
87	Jason Bartlett RC	4.00
88	Jorge Sequea RC	4.00
89	Luis Gonzalez RC	4.00
90	Sean Henn	3.00

Red

(1-60):	1-4X
(61-90):	.75-1.25X
Production 150 Sets	

White

(1-60):	2-6X
(61-90):	.75-2X
Production 50 Sets	

Blue

No Pricing
Production One Set

American GAME

		NM/M
Common Player:		1.00
Inserted 1:10 (Hobby)		
Inserted 1:12 (Retail)		
1	Greg Maddux	2.50
2	Randy Johnson	2.00
3	Roger Clemens	4.00
4	Mark Prior	3.00
5	Mike Piazza	2.50
6	Alex Rodriguez	4.00
7	Adam Dunn	1.00
8	Jim Thome	2.00
9	Derek Jeter	5.00
10	Scott Rolen	2.00
11	Nomar Garciaparra	4.00
12	Kerry Wood	1.50
13	Chipper Jones	2.50
14	Frank Thomas	1.50
15	Jeff Bagwell	1.50

American Game - Jersey

		NM/M
Common Player:		8.00
Inserted 1:96		
Patch #'d between 25 & 50:		2-6X
Patch #'d less than 25:		No Pricing
Masterpiece:		No Pricing
Production One Set		
JB	Jeff Bagwell/50	8.00
RCL	Roger Clemens/47	10.00
AD	Adam Dunn/30	8.00
DJ	Derek Jeter/10	15.00
RJO	Randy Johnson/42	8.00
CJ	Chipper Jones/37	10.00
GM	Greg Maddux/46	12.00
MP	Mike Piazza/29	10.00
MPR	Mark Prior/45	10.00
AR	Alex Rodriguez/13	15.00
SR	Scott Rolen/49	8.00

FT	Frank Thomas/35	8.00
JT	Jim Thome/47	8.00
KW	Kerry Wood/43	8.00

American Game - Dual

Numbered between 10 & 25.
No Pricing

American Game - Single

Numbered between 6 & 31.
No Pricing

American Flag Box Topper

No Pricing
Numbered to indicated quantity.

History in the Making

		NM/M
Common Player:		.75
Inserted 1:5 (Hobby)		
Inserted 1:4 (Retail)		
1	Pedro J. Martinez	1.50
2	Alex Rodriguez	3.00
3	Sammy Sosa	2.50
4	Mike Piazza	2.00
5	Jason Giambi	1.50
6	Jim Thome	1.50
7	Derek Jeter	4.00
8	Hideo Nomo	.75
9	Nomar Garciaparra	3.00
10	Albert Pujols	3.00
11	Greg Maddux	2.00
12	Randy Johnson	1.50
13	Roger Clemens	2.00
14	Ichiro Suzuki	2.50
15	Vladimir Guerrero	1.50
16	Chipper Jones	2.00
17	Ken Griffey Jr.	2.00
18	Manny Ramirez	1.00
19	Ivan Rodriguez	.75
20	Mark Prior	2.00
21	Austin Kearns	.75
22	Alfonso Soriano	1.50
23	Barry Zito	.75
24	Josh Beckett	1.00
25	Angel Berroa	.75
26	Jose Reyes	.75
27	Adam Dunn	.75
28	Todd Helton	1.00
29	Hank Blalock	.75
30	Kazuo Matsui	6.00

History in the Making - Jersey

		NM/M
Common Player:		5.00
Inserted 1:36		
Patch:		2-6X
Numbered between 20 & 50.		
Masterpiece:		No Pricing
Production One Set		
JB	Josh Beckett/45	8.00
AB	Angel Berroa/20	5.00
MB	Hank Blalock/48	8.00
RC	Roger Clemens/25	10.00
AD	Adam Dunn/49	8.00
JG	Jason Giambi/24	8.00
VG	Vladimir Guerrero/50	8.00
TH	Todd Helton/32	8.00
DJ	Derek Jeter/22	15.00
RJ	Randy Johnson/50	8.00
CJ	Chipper Jones/48	10.00
AK	Austin Kearns/41	8.00
GM	Greg Maddux/47	12.00
PM	Pedro J. Martinez/45	8.00
KM	Kazuo Matsui/20	20.00
HN	Hideo Nomo/50	5.00
MP	Mike Piazza/42	10.00
MPR	Mark Prior/49	10.00
AP	Albert Pujols/46	15.00
MR	Manny Ramirez/46	8.00
JR	Jose Reyes/37	5.00
AR	Alex Rodriguez/21	15.00
IR	Ivan Rodriguez/48	8.00
AS	Alfonso Soriano/48	8.00
SS	Sammy Sosa/39	12.00
JT	Jim Thome/49	8.00
BZ	Barry Zito/44	8.00

Dual Swatch

No Pricing
Production Five Sets

National Treasures

		NM/M
Common Card:		3.00
Production 500 Sets		
Gold:	Numbered to notable year.	
#75-99:		1-3X
#25-74:		1-5X
Less than 25:		No Pricing
2NT	Kenesaw Landis	3.00
5NT	Leo Durocher	3.00
9NT	Peter Gammons	3.00

10NT	Ernie Harwell	3.00
11NT	Billy Martin	4.00
12NT	John McGraw	3.00
13NT	Red Barber	3.00
15NT	Casey Stengel	3.00
16NT	Sparky Anderson	3.00
17NT	Harry Caray	4.00
18NT	Ban Johnson	3.00
20NT	Ralph Kiner	3.00

National Treasure - Red

		NM/M
Peter Gammons/50		20.00
Ernie Harwell/50		20.00
Ralph Kiner/50		20.00

National Treasures - White

		NM/M
Ernie Harwell/30		15.00

National Treasures - Blue

No Pricing

National Treasures - Masterpiece

No Pricing

Signature Swing - Gold

	NM/M
Numbered to indicated quantity.	
Carlos Beltran/176	25.00
Lance Berkman/173	20.00
Hank Blalock/265	15.00
Joe Carter/95	12.00
Sean Casey/169	12.00
Eric Chavez/138	15.00
David Eckstein/161	10.00
Carlton Fisk/36	40.00
Lew Ford/183	20.00
Luis Gonzalez/61	15.00
Frank Howard/60	20.00
Derek Jeter/35	125.00
Chipper Jones/116	40.00
Al Kaline/76	40.00
Javy Lopez/201	15.00
Edgar Martinez/85	20.00
Bill Mazeroski/63	25.00
Jim Palmer/33	25.00
Dave Parker/57	15.00
Mike Piazza/64	100.00
Albert Pujols/110	125.00
Gary Sheffield/25	60.00
Warren Spahn/188	30.00
Alan Trammell/138	10.00

Signature Swing - Red

	NM/M
Numbered to indicated quantity.	
Carlos Beltran/109	25.00
Lance Berkman/109	25.00
Hank Blalock/109	20.00
George Brett/42	120.00
Sean Casey/108	15.00
Eric Chavez/85	20.00
Bucky Dent/35	20.00
David Eckstein/76	15.00
Carlton Fisk/51	40.00
Lew Ford/109	20.00
Jay Gibbons/33	20.00
Luis Gonzalez/109	20.00
Chipper Jones/88	40.00
Al Kaline/43	50.00
Javy Lopez/65	20.00
Don Mattingly/73	50.00
Bill Mazeroski/56	30.00
Stan Musial/36	60.00
Jim Palmer/25	25.00
Dave Parker/79	15.00
Mike Piazza/31	125.00
Albert Pujols/76	150.00

Gary Sheffield/26	60.00
Bill "Moose" Skowron/59	15.00
Warren Spahn/106	40.00
Alan Trammell/89	15.00

Signature Swing - White

	NM/M
Numbered to indicated quantity.	
Carlos Beltran/29	25.00
Lance Berkman/42	30.00
Hank Blalock/29	30.00
George Brett/30	120.00
Joe Carter/35	20.00
Sean Casey/35	25.00
Eric Chavez/34	25.00
Jim Edmonds/42	20.00
Carlton Fisk/37	40.00
Jay Gibbons/28	20.00
Luis Gonzalez/57	20.00
Vladimir Guerrero/44	30.00
Frank Howard/48	25.00
Aubrey Huff/34	15.00
Chipper Jones/45	50.00
Al Kaline/29	50.00
Javy Lopez/43	20.00
Edgar Martinez/37	30.00
Don Mattingly/35	80.00
Stan Musial/39	60.00
Rafael Palmeiro/47	50.00
Dave Parker/34	15.00
Mike Piazza/40	125.00
Albert Pujols/43	175.00
Cal Ripken Jr./25	200.00
Ivan Rodriguez/35	50.00
Scott Rolen/28	80.00
Gary Sheffield/43	60.00
Bill "Moose" Skowron/28	20.00
Frank Thomas/43	80.00
Alan Trammell/28	20.00

Signature Swing - Blue

	NM/M
Numbered to indicated quantity.	
Sean Casey/37	40.00
Adam Dunn/31	20.00
David Eckstein/44	15.00
Jim Edmonds/37	20.00
Lew Ford/44	40.00
Bill Mazeroski/39	50.00
Jim Palmer/44	25.00
Dave Parker/29	15.00
Scott Podsednik/38	20.00
Warren Spahn/26	50.00

Signature Swing - Masterpiece

No Pricing

Signs of the Future - Gold

	NM/M
Numbered to indicated quantity.	
Jeremy Bonderman/300	8.00
Miguel Cabrera/300	20.00
Bobby Crosby/299	20.00
Adam Everett/285	10.00
Luis Gonzalez/264	8.00
Mike Gosling/195	8.00
Khalil Greene/300	50.00
Rich Harden/304	10.00
Sean Henn/300	8.00
Koyie Hill/340	8.00
Ryan Howard/53	60.00
Tim Hudson/72	20.00
Adam LaRoche/78	8.00
Micheal Nakamura/231	8.00
Alexis Rios/45	15.00
Alfredo Simon/258	8.00
Javier Vazquez/21	20.00
Ryan Wagner/251	10.00
Dontrelle Willis/47	40.00
Kevin Youkilis/317	15.00

Signs of the Future - Red

	NM/M
Numbered to indicated quantity.	
Aarom Baldiris/64	10.00
Jeremy Bonderman/120	10.00
A.J. Burnett/58	20.00
Miguel Cabrera/133	25.00
Bobby Crosby/114	20.00
Adam Everett/106	12.00
Luis Gonzalez/132	10.00
Mike Gosling/132	10.00
Khalil Greene/121	50.00
Rich Harden/133	15.00
Sean Henn/128	10.00
Koyie Hill/58	12.00
Edwin Jackson/52	15.00
Graham Koonce/55	10.00
Josh Labandeira/55	8.00
Adam LaRoche/124	10.00
Justin Leone/68	20.00
Micheal Nakamura/113	10.00
Bubba Nelson/99	10.00
Jose Reyes/93	25.00
Mike Rouse/124	8.00
Alfredo Simon/112	10.00
Ryan Wagner/98	12.00
Kerry Wood/55	30.00
Kevin Youkilis/133	20.00

Signs of the Future - White

NM/M
Numbered to indicated quantity.

Garrett Atkins/25	15.00
Miguel Cabrera/34	40.00
Bobby Crosby/52	30.00
Adam Everett/36	15.00
Luis Gonzalez/50	15.00
Mike Gosling/41	12.00
Khalil Greene/52	80.00
Rich Harden/52	20.00
Sean Henn/48	12.00
Tim Hudson/28	40.00
Adam LaRoche/50	12.00
Micheal Nakamura/33	15.00
Jose Reyes/25	30.00
Alexis Rios/39	15.00
Mike Rouse/40	10.00
Alfredo Simon/28	15.00
Ryan Wagner/46	15.00
Kevin Youkilis/52	25.00

Signs of the Future - Blue

NM/M

Numbered to indicated quantity.

Javier Vazquez/98	15.00
Kerry Wood/98	25.00

Ted Williams Reprint Set

May 16, 1954 – Ted Is Pitched Up

NM/M

Ted Williams Card (1-81):	6.00
Production 406 Sets	
Masterpiece:	No Pricing
Production One Set	
1-80 Ted Williams	6.00

Ted Willams Game-Used

No Pricing
Production Nine Sets

2004 Fleer Authentix

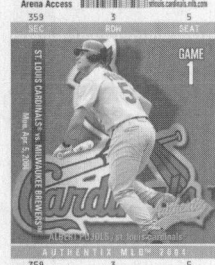

NM/M

Complete Set (130):	
Common Player:	.25
Common SP (101-130):	2.50
Production 999	
Pack (5):	4.00
Box (24):	80.00
1 Albert Pujols	2.50
2 Derek Jeter	3.00
3 Jody Gerut	.25
4 Mark Teixeira	.50
5 Tom Glavine	.50
6 Kerry Wood	1.00
7 Ichiro Suzuki	1.50
8 Jose Vidro	.25
9 Mark Prior	1.50
10 Jim Edmonds	.50
11 Richie Sexson	.25
12 Jay Gibbons	.25
13 Jason Kendall	.25
14 Lance Berkman	.50
15 Andruw Jones	.75
16 Jim Thome	1.00
17 Josh Beckett	.75
18 Troy Glaus	.50
19 Jason Giambi	1.00
20 Sammy Sosa	2.00
21 Bret Boone	.40
22 Eric Gagne	.40
23 Nomar Garciaparra	2.00
24 Geoff Jenkins	.50
25 Ivan Rodriguez	.50
26 Preston Wilson	.40
27 Alex Rodriguez	2.50
28 Jorge Posada	.50
29 Ken Griffey Jr.	1.50
30 Rocco Baldelli	.50
31 Shannon Stewart	.25
32 Frank Thomas	.75
33 Edgar Renteria	.25
34 Torii Hunter	.50
35 Corey Patterson	.25
36 Edgar Martinez	.40
37 Jeff Bagwell	.75
38 Greg Maddux	1.50
39 Mike Lieberthal	.25
40 Craig Biggio	.40
41 Randy Johnson	1.00
42 Marlon Byrd	.25
43 Jay Payton	.25
44 Carlos Delgado	.75
45 Scott Podsednik	.50
46 Pedro J. Martinez	1.00
47 Carlos Beltran	.40
48 Mike Sweeney	.25
49 Gary Sheffield	.50
50 Pat Burrell	.50
51 Shawn Green	.40
52 Tony Batista	.25
53 Brian Giles	.40
54 Roy Oswalt	.40
55 Brandon Webb	.40
56 Miguel Tejada	.50
57 Miguel Cabrera	.75
58 Luis Gonzalez	.40
59 Billy Wagner	.25
60 Craig Monroe	.25
61 Vernon Wells	.40
62 Bernie Williams	.50
63 Austin Kearns	.50
64 Aubrey Huff	.25
65 Mike Piazza	1.50
66 Magglio Ordonez	.50
67 Bo Hart	.25
68 Hideo Nomo	.50
69 Curt Schilling	.50
70 Barry Zito	.50
71 Todd Helton	.75
72 Roy Halladay	.50
73 Alfonso Soriano	1.00
74 Roberto Alomar	.50
75 Scott Rolen	1.00
76 Manny Ramirez	.75
77 Sean Burroughs	.25
78 Angel Berroa	.25
79 Javy Lopez	.40
80 Reggie Sanders	.25
81 Juan Pierre	.25
82 Chipper Jones	1.50
83 Bobby Abreu	.40
84 Dontrelle Willis	.40
85 Tim Salmon	.40
86 Eric Chavez	.40
87 Adam Dunn	.50
88 Rafael Palmeiro	.75
89 Hideki Matsui	2.50
90 Esteban Loaiza	.25
91 Darin Erstad	.40
92 Vladimir Guerrero	1.00
93 David Ortiz	.25
94 Jason Schmidt	.40
95 Dmitri Young	.25
96 Garret Anderson	.50
97 Mark Mulder	.50
98 Omar Vizquel	.25
99 Hank Blalock	.50
100 Jose Reyes	.50
101 Rickie Weeks	8.00
102 Chad Gaudin	2.50
103 Ryan Wagner	3.00
104 Koyie Hill	2.50
105 Rich Harden	2.50
106 Edwin Jackson	4.00
107 Khalil Greene	3.00
108 Chien-Ming Wang	3.00
109 Matt Kata	2.50
110 Chin-Hui Tsao	2.50
111 Dan Haren	2.50
112 Delmon Young	8.00
113 Mike Hessman	2.50
114 Bobby Crosby	2.50
115 Cory Sullivan RC	2.50
116 Brandon Watson	2.50
117 Aaron Miles	2.50
118 Jonny Gomes	2.50
119 Graham Koonce	2.50
120 Shawn Hill RC	2.50
121 Garrett Atkins	2.50
122 John Gall RC	2.50
123 Chad Bentz RC	2.50
124 Alfredo Simon RC	2.50
125 Josh Labandeira RC	3.00
126 Ryan Howard	3.00
127 Jason Bartlett RC	2.50
128 Dallas McPherson	2.50
129 Greg Dobbs RC	2.50
130 Jerry Gil RC	2.50

Balcony

Stars (1-100):	4-8X
SP's (101-130):	1-2X
Production 100 Sets	

Club Box

Stars (1-100):	10-15X
SP's (101-130):	2-4X
Production 25 Sets	

Standing Room Only

No Pricing
Production Five Sets

Autographed Authentix

NM/M

Common Autograph:	15.00
Production 75	
Championship:	No Pricing

Production 25

Rocco Baldelli	40.00
Angel Berroa	15.00
Marlon Byrd	15.00
Miguel Cabrera	40.00
Eric Gagne	40.00
Roy Halladay	20.00
Trot Nixon	35.00
Juan Pierre	15.00
Albert Pujols	120.00
Vernon Wells	20.00

Ballpark Classics

NM/M

Complete Set (10):	15.00
Common Player:	1.00
Inserted 1:12	
1BC Nomar Garciaparra	3.00
2BC Alfonso Soriano	1.50
3BC Chipper Jones	1.50
4BC Albert Pujols	3.00
5BC Jason Giambi	1.00
6BC Mark Prior	2.00
7BC Sammy Sosa	2.50
8BC Derek Jeter	4.00
9BC Greg Maddux	2.00
10BC Alex Rodriguez	3.00

Ballpark Classics Game-Used

NM/M

Common Player:	8.00
Inserted 1:37	
Nomar Garciaparra	10.00
Jason Giambi	8.00
Derek Jeter	15.00
Chipper Jones	8.00
Greg Maddux	10.00
Mark Prior	10.00
Albert Pujols	15.00
Alex Rodriguez	10.00
Alfonso Soriano	8.00
Sammy Sosa	12.00

Jersey Authentix Ripped

NM/M

Common Player:	4.00
Inserted 1:16	
Unripped:	2-3X
Production 50 Sets	
All-Star Unripped:	No Pricing
Production One Set	
Jeff Bagwell	8.00
Josh Beckett	6.00
Miguel Cabrera	8.00
Hee Seop Choi	4.00
Nomar Garciaparra	10.00
Jason Giambi	8.00
Torii Hunter	5.00
Derek Jeter	15.00
Randy Johnson	8.00
Chipper Jones	8.00
Austin Kearns	6.00
Greg Maddux	8.00
Juan Pierre	4.00
Mark Prior	10.00
Albert Pujols	15.00
Jose Reyes	8.00
Alex Rodriguez	10.00
Ivan Rodriguez	6.00
Alfonso Soriano	8.00
Sammy Sosa	12.00
Mark Teixeira	6.00
Jim Thome	8.00
Dontrelle Willis	6.00
Kerry Wood	8.00
Barry Zito	6.00

Jersey Authentix Autograph

NM/M

Common Autograph:	15.00
Production 100	
All-Star Autographs:	1-1.25X
Production 50	
Championship Autos.:	No Pricing
Production 10	
Albert Pujols	125.00
Juan Pierre	15.00
Miguel Cabrera	40.00
Eric Gagne	40.00
Marlon Byrd	15.00
Rocco Baldelli	40.00
Roy Halladay	25.00
Vernon Wells	20.00
Trot Nixon	35.00

Jersey Authentix Game of the Week

NM/M

Common Duo:	10.00
Inserted 1:120	
Unripped:	1-1.5X

Production 50

1 Dontrelle Willis, Kerry Wood	20.00
2 Miguel Cabrera, Mark Teixeira	15.00
3 Nomar Garciaparra, Alfonso Soriano	15.00
4 Jim Thome, Ivan Rodriguez	10.00
5 Josh Beckett, Mark Prior	15.00
6 Alex Rodriguez, Derek Jeter	35.00
7 Jeff Bagwell, Austin Kearns	15.00
8 Jason Giambi, Barry Zito	10.00
9 Jose Reyes, Juan Pierre	10.00
10 Chipper Jones, Albert Pujols	20.00

Ticket for Four

NM/M

Common Quad Jersey:	20.00
Production 100 Sets	
1 Dontrelle Willis, Josh Beckett, Mark Prior, Kerry Wood	20.00
2 Nomar Garciaparra, Alex Rodriguez, Derek Jeter, Jose Reyes	50.00
3 Ivan Rodriguez, Miguel Cabrera, Hee Seop Choi, Juan Pierre	
4 Jason Giambi, Jim Thome, Mark Teixeira, Jeff Bagwell	25.00
5 Chipper Jones, Albert Pujols, Sammy Sosa, Torii Hunter	40.00
6 Greg Maddux, Randy Johnson, Kerry Wood, Barry Zito	20.00
7 Nomar Garciaparra, Alfonso Soriano, Chipper Jones, Albert Pujols	40.00
8 Sammy Sosa, Derek Jeter, Alex Rodriguez, Jim Thome	50.00
9 Mark Prior, Greg Maddux, Austin Kearns, Ivan Rodriguez	15.00
10 Jason Giambi, Randy Johnson, Jeff Bagwell, Torii Hunter	20.00

Ticket Studs

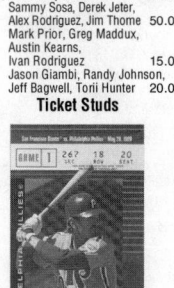

NM/M

Complete Set (15):	20.00
Common Player:	.75
Inserted 1:6	
1TS Nomar Garciaparra	3.00
2TS Josh Beckett	1.00
3TS Derek Jeter	4.00
4TS Mark Prior	2.00
5TS Albert Pujols	3.00
6TS Alfonso Soriano	1.50
7TS Jim Thome	1.50
8TS Ichiro Suzuki	2.00
9TS Hideki Matsui	3.00
10TS Dontrelle Willis	.75
11TS Mike Schmidt	2.00
12TS Nolan Ryan	4.00
13TS Reggie Jackson	1.00
14TS Tom Seaver	1.00
15TS Brooks Robinson	1.00

2004 Fleer Classic Clippings

	NM/M
Common Player (1-75):	.25
Minor Stars (1-75):	.40
Unlisted Stars (1-75):	.60
Common Player (76-110):	5.00
Production 500 Sets	
Pack (5):	5.00
Box (18):	90.00
1 Juan Pierre	.25
2 Derek Jeter	3.00
3 Jose Reyes	.40
4 Eric Chavez	.40
5 Alex Rodriguez	2.50
6 Mark Prior	2.00
7 Carlos Beltran	.40
8 Ichiro Suzuki	2.00
9 Shawn Green	.40
10 Richie Sexson	.60
11 Andruw Jones	.75
12 Geoff Jenkins	.40
13 Luis Gonzalez	.40
14 Garret Anderson	.40
15 Adam Dunn	.60
16 Nomar Garciaparra	2.50
17 Albert Pujols	2.50
18 Jeff Bagwell	.75
19 Rocco Baldelli	.60
20 Preston Wilson	.25
21 Gary Sheffield	.60
22 Magglio Ordonez	.40
23 Kerry Wood	.75
24 Manny Ramirez	.75
25 Randy Johnson	1.00
26 Ken Griffey Jr.	1.50
27 Rafael Palmeiro	.40
28 Vernon Wells	.25
29 Mike Piazza	1.50
30 Hank Blalock	.60
31 Miguel Cabrera	.75
32 Jason Giambi	1.00
33 Troy Glaus	.60
34 Angel Berroa	.25
35 Greg Maddux	1.50
36 Lance Berkman	.40
37 Austin Kearns	.60
38 Hideo Nomo	.40
39 Sammy Sosa	2.00
40 Jose Vidro	.25
41 Curt Schilling	.60
42 Melvin Mora	.25
43 Scott Podsednik	.40
44 Dontrelle Willis	.40
45 Roy Halladay	.40
46 Hideki Matsui	2.50
47 Tom Glavine	.40
48 Torii Hunter	.40
49 Chipper Jones	1.50
50 Barry Zito	.60
51 Vladimir Guerrero	1.00
52 Jim Thome	1.00
53 Shannon Stewart	.25
54 Miguel Tejada	.60
55 Roy Oswalt	.40
56 Jason Kendall	.40
57 Brian Giles	.40
58 Jason Schmidt	.40
59 Pedro J. Martinez	1.00
60 Bret Boone	.40
61 Josh Beckett	.75
62 Scott Rolen	1.00
63 Aubrey Huff	.25
64 Pat Burrell	.40
65 Mark Teixeira	.40
66 Alfonso Soriano	1.00
67 Carlos Delgado	.75
68 Ivan Rodriguez	.60
69 Brandon Webb	.25
70 Eric Gagne	.40
71 Frank Thomas	.75
72 Jody Gerut	.40
73 Todd Helton	.75
74 Andy Pettitte	.60
75 Roger Clemens	1.50
76 Rickie Weeks	6.00
77 Chien-Ming Wang	8.00
78 Edwin Jackson	8.00
79 Dallas McPherson	8.00
80 John Gall RC	5.00
81 Ryan Wagner	6.00
82 Clint Barmes	8.00
83 Khalil Greene	6.00
84 Chin-Hui Tsao	6.00
85 Alexis Rios	8.00
86 Merkin Valdez RC	5.00
87 Aarom Baldiris RC	5.00
88 Onil Joseph RC	5.00
89 Ruddy Yan RC	5.00
90 Chad Bentz RC	5.00
91 Shawn Hill RC	5.00
92 Delmon Young	8.00
93 Hector Gimenez RC	5.00
94 William Bergolla RC	5.00
95 Ronny Cedeno RC	5.00
96 Angel Chavez RC	5.00
97 Justin Leone RC	5.00
98 Ivan Ochoa RC	5.00
99 Ian Snell RC	10.00
100 Rich Harden	6.00
101 Joe Mauer	10.00
102 Akinori Otsuka RC	10.00
103 Bobby Crosby	5.00
104 Garrett Atkins	5.00
105 Dan Haren	5.00
106 Koyie Hill	5.00

107 Kazuo Matsui RC	20.00
108 Adam LaRoche	5.00
109 Terrmel Sledge	5.00
110 Shingo Takatsu RC	5.00

First Edition

(1-75):	1-5X
(76-110):	.5-1.25X
Production 150 Sets	

Press Proof Cyan

(1-100):	No Pricing
Production One Set	

Press Proof Magenta

(1-100):	No Pricing
Production One Set	

Press Proof Yellow

(1-100):	No Pricing
Production One Set	

Press Proof Black

(1-100):	No Pricing
Production One Set	

Press Clippings

	NM/M
Common Player:	1.25
Inserted 1:6	
1PC Josh Beckett	1.75
2PC Albert Pujols	4.00
3PC Derek Jeter	5.00
4PC Alex Rodriguez	5.00
5PC Jim Thome	2.00
6PC Angel Berroa	1.00
7PC Dontrelle Willis	1.25
8PC Roy Halladay	1.25
9PC Kerry Wood	1.75
10PC Mark Prior	3.00
11PC Roger Clemens	3.00
12PC Hideki Matsui	4.00
13PC Ichiro Suzuki	3.50
14PC Eric Gagne	1.25
15PC Miguel Cabrera	1.75
16PC Nomar Garciaparra	4.00
17PC Hank Blalock	1.25
18PC Chipper Jones	3.00
19PC Sammy Sosa	3.50
20PC Alfonso Soriano	2.00

Bat Rack (3 Bat) - Green

	NM/M
Common Card:	10.00
Production 175 Sets	
Red:	.5-1.5X
Production 50 Sets	

Gold:	1-2X
Production 25 Sets	
Derek Jeter, Alex Rodriguez, Gary Sheffield	40.00
Sammy Sosa, Derek Lee, Mark Prior	25.00
Miguel Cabrera, Juan Pierre, Josh Beckett	15.00
Nomar Garciaparra, Manny Ramirez, Curt Schilling	20.00
Alfonso Soriano, Hank Blalock, Mark Teixeira	15.00
Mike Piazza, Jose Reyes, Kazuo Matsui	20.00
Richie Sexson, Brandon Webb, Roberto Alomar	10.00
Mark Prior, Josh Beckett, Curt Schilling	15.00
Carlos Delgado, Aubrey Huff, Jason Giambi	10.00
Albert Pujols, Scott Rolen, Jim Edmonds	30.00
Rocco Baldelli, Aubrey Huff, Carlos Delgado	10.00
Jeff Bagwell, Jim Thome, Todd Helton	15.00
Gary Sheffield, Manny Ramirez, Rocco Baldelli	10.00
Troy Glaus, Scott Rolen, Hank Blalock	15.00
Roberto Alomar, Jose Reyes, Alfonso Soriano	15.00
Alex Rodriguez, Miguel Tejada, Miguel Cabrera	15.00
Vladimir Guerrero, Juan Pierre, Chipper Jones	10.00
Jason Giambi, Jim Thome, Todd Helton	15.00
Vladimir Guerrero, Albert Pujols, Sammy Sosa	25.00
Derek Jeter, Hideki Matsui, Nomar Garciaparra	40.00

Bat Rack (4 Bat) - Green

	NM/M
Common Card:	15.00
Production 75 Sets	
Red:	1-2X
Production 25 Sets	
Gold:	No Pricing
Production 10 Sets	
Derek Jeter, Alex Rodriguez, Gary Sheffield, Jason Giambi	50.00
Sammy Sosa, Mark Prior, Miguel Cabrera, Josh Beckett	30.00
Derek Jeter, Alex Rodriguez, Kazuo Matsui, Nomar Garciaparra	60.00
Juan Pierre, Gary Sheffield, Miguel Cabrera, Rocco Baldelli	15.00
Jim Thome, Jeff Bagwell, Mark Teixeira, Carlos Delgado	20.00
Albert Pujols, Mark Prior, Alex Rodriguez, Curt Schilling	40.00
Todd Helton, Jose Reyes, Kazuo Matsui, Scott Rolen	40.00
Sammy Sosa, Vladimir Guerrero, Jim Edmonds, Chipper Jones	25.00
Alfonso Soriano, Roberto Alomar, Hank Blalock, Troy Glaus	15.00
Rocco Baldelli, Chipper Jones, Juan Pierre, Manny Ramirez	20.00
Jim Thome, Jeff Bagwell, Todd Helton, Derek Lee	20.00
Curt Schilling, Nomar Garciaparra, Brandon Webb, Richie Sexson	25.00
Mike Piazza, Jose Reyes, Albert Pujols, Scott Rolen	30.00
Vladimir Guerrero, Miguel Tejada, Jason Giambi, Mike Piazza	25.00
Jeff Bagwell, Derrek Lee, Aubrey Huff, Carlos Delgado	20.00

Bat Rack Autographs-Bronze

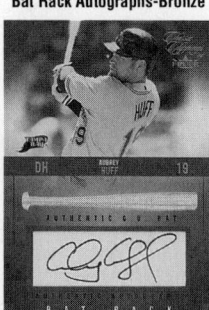

	NM/M
Common Player:	12.00
Production 149 Sets	
Silver Jersey:	.5-1.5X
Production 50 Sets	
Patch Rack Gold:	No Pricing
Production To Player's Jersey No.	
Garret Anderson	15.00
Garrett Atkins	12.00
Rocco Baldelli	20.00
Josh Beckett	20.00
Angel Berroa	15.00
Marlon Byrd	12.00
Miguel Cabrera	40.00
Carlos Delgado	20.00
Jody Gerut	12.00
Roy Halladay	15.00
Dan Haren	12.00
Torii Hunter	15.00
Edwin Jackson	20.00
Barry Larkin	40.00
Mark Mulder	15.00
Mike Mussina	30.00

	NM/M
Common Player:	12.00
Production 75 Sets	
Roberto Alomar	40.00
Josh Beckett	40.00
Hank Blalock	30.00
Miguel Cabrera	40.00
Jim Edmonds	30.00
Aubrey Huff	12.00
Edgar Martinez	25.00
Jose Reyes	25.00
Gary Sheffield	30.00
Mark Teixeira	20.00

C.C. Signature Edition

	NM/M
Common Player:	15.00
Production 50 Sets	
Masterpiece:	No Pricing
Production One Set	
1 Nolan Ryan	125.00
2 Mike Schmidt	75.00
3 Cal Ripken Jr.	175.00
4 Don Mattingly	75.00
5 Albert Pujols	125.00
6 Randy Johnson	60.00
7 Khalil Greene	40.00
8 Rickie Weeks	25.00
9 Edwin Jackson	15.00
10 Rich Harden	15.00
16 Vladimir Guerrero	40.00
17 Mark Prior	40.00

Classic Clippings

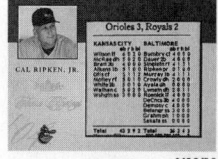

	NM/M
Common Player (1-20):	4.00
Production 750 Sets	
Common Player (21-25):	8.00
Production 100 Sets	
1CC Nolan Ryan	15.00
2CC Mike Schmidt	6.00
3CC Cal Ripken Jr.	10.00
4CC Don Mattingly	8.00
5CC Roger Clemens	5.00
6CC Randy Johnson	4.00
7CC Mark Prior	3.00
8CC Jim Thome	5.00
9CC Sammy Sosa	5.00
10CC Pedro J. Martinez	4.00
11CC Chipper Jones	4.00
12CC Vladimir Guerrero	4.00
13CC Albert Pujols	6.00
14CC Ichiro Suzuki	6.00
15CC Derek Jeter	10.00
16CC Alex Rodriguez	8.00
17CC Greg Maddux	5.00
18CC Nomar Garciaparra	8.00
19CC Mike Piazza	6.00
20CC Ken Griffey Jr.	8.00
21CC Pie Traynor	8.00
22CC Bill Dickey	8.00
23CC George Sisler	10.00
24CC Ted Williams	20.00
25CC Enos Slaughter	8.00

Jersey Rack Auto. - Bronze

Andy Pettitte	40.00
Albert Pujols	120.00
Ivan Rodriguez	50.00
Scott Rolen	50.00
Ryan Wagner	12.00
Brandon Webb	15.00
Dontrelle Willis	20.00
Kerry Wood	30.00

Phenom Lineup Auto. - Red

	NM/M
Common Card:	10.00
Production 150 Sets	
Silver:	.5-1.25X
Production 99 Sets	
Gold:	.5-1.5X
Production 50 Sets	

Cards contain autograph of the first player listed.

Ryan Howard, Jim Thome, Todd Helton	10.00
John Gall, Albert Pujols, Scott Rolen	10.00
Jose Reyes, Kazuo Matsui, Rickie Weeks	15.00
Hank Blalock, Troy Glaus, Alex Rodriguez	20.00
Rich Harden, Roy Halladay, Barry Zito	10.00
Alexis Rios, Carlos Delgado, Vernon Wells	10.00
Laynce Nix, Alex Rodriguez, Garret Anderson	10.00
Khalil Greene, Edgar Renteria, Mike Lowell	25.00
Dontrelle Willis, Mark Prior, Kerry Wood	15.00
Rickie Weeks, Luis Castillo, Jose Reyes	15.00
Dallas McPherson, Troy Glaus, Garret Anderson	15.00
Chien-Ming Wang, Hideki Matsui, Jason Giambi	20.00
Scott Podsednik, Albert Pujols, Andruw Jones	15.00
Bobby Crosby, Nomar Garciaparra, Alex Rodriguez	18.00
Ryan Wagner, Dontrelle Willis, Mark Prior	8.00
Delmon Young, Ichiro Suzuki, Hideki Matsui	30.00
Grady Sizemore, Manny Ramirez, Garret Anderson	20.00
Adam LaRoche, Albert Pujols, Jim Thome	10.00
Edwin Jackson, Mark Prior, Kerry Wood	10.00
Miguel Cabrera, Luis Castillo, Mike Lowell	40.00
Merkin Valdez, Edwin Jackson, Dontrelle Willis	10.00
Angel Berroa, Nomar Garciaparra, Alex Rodriguez	10.00

2004 Fleer EX

	NM/M
Common Player (1-40):	1.50
Minor Stars (1-40):	2.00
Unlisted Stars (1-40):	2.50
Common Player (41-65):	5.00
Production 500 Sets	
Die-Cuts (41-65):	.75-1.25X

First 150 seq. #'d cards are die-cut.

1	Vladimir Guerrero	3.50
2	Randy Johnson	3.50
3	Chipper Jones	4.00
4	Miguel Tejada	2.50
5	Pedro J. Martinez	3.50
6	Nomar Garciaparra	6.00
7	Sammy Sosa	5.00
8	Greg Maddux	4.00
9	Frank Thomas	3.00
10	Ken Griffey Jr.	4.00
11	Omar Vizquel	2.00
12	Todd Helton	3.00
13	Ivan Rodriguez	2.50
14	Miguel Cabrera	3.00
15	Dontrelle Willis	2.00
16	Jeff Bagwell	3.00
17	Roger Clemens	4.00
18	Carlos Beltran	2.00
19	Hideo Nomo	2.00
20	Scott Podsednik	1.50
21	Torii Hunter	2.50
22	Jose Vidro	1.50
23	Mike Piazza	4.00
24	Hideki Matsui	6.00
25	Alex Rodriguez	6.00
26	Derek Jeter	8.00
27	Tim Hudson	2.00
28	Jim Thome	3.50
29	Craig Wilson	1.50
30	Brian Giles	2.00
31	Jason Schmidt	2.00
32	Ichiro Suzuki	5.00
33	Scott Rolen	3.50
34	Albert Pujols	6.00
35	Rocco Baldelli	2.50
36	Alfonso Soriano	3.50
37	Carlos Delgado	3.00
38	Curt Schilling	2.50
39	Mark Prior	4.00
40	Josh Beckett	3.00
41	Merkin Valdez RC	5.00
42	Akinori Otsuka RC	8.00
43	Ian Snell RC	8.00
44	Kazuo Matsui RC	10.00
45	Jason Bartlett RC	8.00
46	Dennis Sarfate RC	5.00
47	Sean Henn	5.00
48	David Aardsma	5.00
49	Casey Kotchman	8.00
50	John Gall RC	5.00
51	William Bergolla RC	5.00
52	Angel Chavez RC	5.00
53	Hector Gimenez RC	5.00
54	Aarom Baldiris RC	5.00
55	Justin Leone RC	8.00
56	Onil Joseph RC	5.00
57	Freddy Guzman RC	5.00
58	Andres Blanco RC	5.00
59	Greg Dobbs RC	5.00
60	Joe Mauer	5.00
61	Luis Gonzalez RC	8.00
62	Chris Saenz RC	5.00
63	Zack Greinke	5.00
64	Jose Capellan RC	8.00
65	Brad Halsey RC	10.00

Essential Credentials Now

Cards 51-65:	1-2X
Cards 41-50:	1.25-2.25X
Cards 25-40:	3-5X
Cards 1-24:	No Pricing
Production 65 - 1 Sets	

Essential Credentials Future

Cards 1-25:	.75-2X
Cards 26-40:	2-4X
Cards 41-65:	No Pricing
Production 65 - 1 Sets	

ConnEXions

		NM/M
Production 25 or 50 Sets		
6	Casey Kotchman, Joe Mauer/50	100.00
7	Shannon Stewart, Torii Hunter/25	90.00
9	Johnny Damon, Trot Nixon/25	90.00
10	Carlos Lee, Magglio Ordonez/25	30.00
12	Scott Podsednik, Lyle Overbay/25	60.00
13	Barry Zito, Tim Hudson/25	125.00
14	Bucky Dent, Mike Torrez/50	40.00
15	Brian Giles, Marcus Giles/25	60.00
17	Dontrelle Willis, Miguel Cabrera/25	60.00
18	Michael Young, Khalil Greene/50	80.00
19	Mark Teixeira, Hank Blalock/25	100.00

Classic ConnEXions Doubles

No Pricing
Production 22 Sets

CLASSIC CONNEXIONS

Emerald:	No Pricing
Production One Set	

Classic ConnEXions Triples

No Pricing
Production 13 Sets

Emerald:	No Pricing
Production One Set	

Clearly Authentics Black Patch

	NM/M
Common Player:	10.00
Production 75 Sets	
Jeff Bagwell	20.00
Rocco Baldelli	15.00
Josh Beckett	20.00
Lance Berkman	15.00
Hank Blalock	15.00
Pat Burrell	15.00
Miguel Cabrera	20.00
Rod Carew	30.00
Roger Clemens	30.00
Adam Dunn	15.00
Eric Gagne	15.00
Jason Giambi	25.00
Brian Giles	15.00
Troy Glaus	15.00
Shawn Green	15.00
Vladimir Guerrero	25.00
Tony Gwynn	30.00
Todd Helton	20.00
Rickey Henderson	30.00
Tim Hudson	15.00
Torii Hunter	15.00
Randy Johnson	25.00
Andruw Jones	20.00
Chipper Jones	30.00
Greg Maddux	30.00
Pedro J. Martinez	25.00
Hideki Matsui	40.00
Kazuo Matsui	40.00
Don Mattingly	40.00
Paul Molitor	30.00
Eddie Murray	50.00
Hideo Nomo	15.00
Magglio Ordonez	15.00
Rafael Palmeiro	20.00
Mike Piazza	30.00
Mark Prior	30.00
Albert Pujols	40.00
Manny Ramirez	20.00
Cal Ripken Jr.	75.00
Alex Rodriguez	40.00
Ivan Rodriguez	15.00
Scott Rolen	25.00
Curt Schilling	15.00
Ozzie Smith	25.00
Alfonso Soriano	25.00
Sammy Sosa	35.00
Mark Teixeira	15.00
Miguel Tejada	15.00
Frank Thomas	20.00
Jim Thome	25.00
Rickie Weeks	15.00
Dontrelle Willis	15.00
Kerry Wood	20.00
Barry Zito	15.00

Clearly Authentics Pewter Patch/Bat

No Pricing
.75-1.5X Black Patch Version
Production 44 Sets

Clearly Authentics Bronze Patch/Jersey

No Pricing
.75-1.5X Black Patch Version
Production 35 Sets

Clearly Authentics Turquoise Nameplate

No Pricing
Sequentially #'d to varying quantities.

Clearly Authentics Tan Double Patch

No Pricing
Production 22 Sets

Clearly Authentics Tan Double Patches

No Pricing
Production 22 Sets

Clearly Authentics Burgundy Triple Patch

No Pricing
Production 13 Sets

Clearly Authentics Royal Patch/Bat/Jersey

No Pricing
Production Eight Sets

Clearly Authentics - Double MLB Logo

No Pricing
Production One Set

Clearly Authentics Signature Black Jersey

	NM/M
Sequentially #'d to varying quantities.	
Burgundy Buttons:	No Pricing
Production 6 Sets	
Emerald MLB Logo:	No Pricing
Production One Set	
Josh Beckett/50	30.00
Hank Blalock/50	50.00
Miguel Cabrera/50	30.00
Roger Clemens/50	150.00
J.D. Drew	30.00
Troy Glaus/50	25.00
Vladimir Guerrero/50	50.00
Todd Helton/50	40.00
Chipper Jones/50	60.00
Roy Oswalt/49	30.00
Rafael Palmeiro/43	60.00
Albert Pujols/50	225.00
Manny Ramirez/50	60.00
Mariano Rivera/50	80.00
Gary Sheffield/50	50.00
Frank Thomas/50	60.00
Bernie Williams/42	75.00
Dontrelle Willis/50	25.00
Kerry Wood/34	50.00

Clearly Authentics Signature Tan Patch

No Pricing
Sequentially #'d to varying quantities.

Clearly Authentics Pewter

No Pricing
Sequentially #'d to varying quantities.

Check Mates

		NM/M
Production 1 or 25 Sets		
1	Albert Pujols, Stan Musial/25	500.00
2	Eddie Murray, Rafael Palmeiro/25	200.00
4	Ernie Banks, Ryne Sandberg/25	300.00
9	Manny Ramirez, Pedro J. Martinez/25	300.00
10	Wade Boggs, Tony Gwynn/25	175.00
11	Reggie Jackson, Don Mattingly/25	200.00
14	Robin Yount, Kirby Puckett/25	150.00

Double Barrel

No Pricing
Production One Set

Signings of the Times Best Year

	NM/M
Sequentially #'d to player's best year.	
Emerald:	No Pricing
Production One Set	
Ernie Banks/58/Bat	60.00
Johnny Bench/72/Jsy	60.00
Wade Boggs/87/Bat	40.00
George Brett/80/Jsy	80.00
Jose Canseco/88/Jsy	30.00
Will Clark/91/Jsy	40.00
Tony Gwynn/94/Jsy	50.00
Rickey Henderson/90/Jsy	75.00
Bo Jackson/89/Jsy	60.00
Don Mattingly/85/Jsy	60.00
Eddie Murray/83/Jsy	60.00
Stan Musial/48/Bat	75.00
Nolan Ryan/73/Jsy	150.00
Ryne Sandberg/90/Bat	60.00
Mike Schmidt/80/Jsy	60.00
Tom Seaver/69/Jsy	75.00
Ozzie Smith/87/Jsy	50.00
Duke Snider/55/Bat	50.00
Carl Yastrzemski/67/Bat	60.00

Signings of the Times HOF Year

NM/M
Sequentially #'d to player's HOF year.

Ernie Banks/77/Bat 60.00
Johnny Bench/89/Jsy 60.00
Yogi Berra/72/Bat 50.00
George Brett/99/Jsy 80.00
Reggie Jackson/93/Jsy 50.00
Stan Musial/69/Bat 75.00
Mike Schmidt/95/Jsy 75.00
Tom Seaver/92/Jsy 50.00
Duke Snider/80/Bat 30.00
Carl Yastrzemski/89/Bat 60.00

Signings of the Times Debut Year

NM/M

Sequentially #'d to player's debut year.

Ernie Banks/53/Bat 60.00
Johnny Bench/67/Jsy 60.00
Yogi Berra/46/Bat 60.00
Wade Boggs/82/Bat 40.00
Jose Canseco/85/Jsy 30.00
Will Clark/86/Jsy 40.00
Tony Gwynn/82/Jsy 50.00
Rickey Henderson/79/Jsy 75.00
Bo Jackson/86/Jsy 50.00
Reggie Jackson/67/Jsy 50.00
Don Mattingly/82/Jsy 80.00
Eddie Murray/77/Jsy 60.00
Stan Musial/41/Bat 75.00
Kirby Puckett/84/Bat 50.00
Nolan Ryan/66/Jsy 150.00
Ryne Sandberg/81/Bat 60.00
Deion Sanders/89/Jsy 40.00
Mike Schmidt/72/Jsy 80.00
Ozzie Smith/78/Jsy 50.00
Duke Snider/47/Bat 50.00
Carl Yastrzemski/61/Bat 75.00
Robin Yount/74/Jsy 40.00

Signings of the Times Pewter

NM/M

Sequentially #'d to varying quantities.

Wade Boggs/32/Bat 50.00
Jose Canseco/27/Jsy 75.00
Rickey Henderson/32/Jsy 75.00
Bo Jackson/60/Jsy 50.00
Don Mattingly/33/Jsy 80.00
Eddie Murray/50/Jsy 80.00
Stan Musial/51/Bat 80.00
Kirby Puckett/31/Bat 50.00
Ryne Sandberg/28/Bat 60.00
Ozzie Smith/36/Jsy 50.00

2004 Fleer Flair

NM/M

Common Player (1-60): 1.00
Minor Star (1-60): 1.25
Unlisted Star (1-60): 1.75
Common Rookie (61-82): 5.00
Rookie Production 799 Sets
Collection Row (1-60): 1-3X
Collection Row (61-82): .5-2X
Row 1 Production 125 Sets
Collection Row 2: No Pricing
Production One Set
Box (1): 100.00

1 Brandon Webb 1.00
2 Todd Helton 2.00
3 Jeff Bagwell 2.00
4 Shawn Green 1.25
5 Vladimir Guerrero 3.00
6 Tom Glavine 1.25
7 Jason Giambi 3.00
8 Barry Zito 1.75
9 Jason Kendall 1.25
10 Carlos Delgado 2.00
11 Curt Schilling 1.75
12 Ken Griffey Jr. 3.50
13 Mike Piazza 3.50
14 Alfonso Soriano 3.00
15 Albert Pujols 5.00
16 Chipper Jones 3.50
17 Alex Rodriguez 5.00
18 Miguel Tejada 1.75
19 Pedro J. Martinez 3.00
20 Mark Prior 4.00
21 Magglio Ordonez 1.25
22 Scott Podsednik 1.75
23 Shannon Stewart 1.00
24 Rocco Baldelli 1.75
25 Darin Erstad 1.25
26 Omar Vizquel 1.00
27 Angel Berroa 1.00
28 Jose Vidro 1.00
29 Rich Harden 1.00
30 Andruw Jones 2.00
31 Troy Glaus 1.75
32 Sammy Sosa 4.00
33 Dontrelle Willis 1.25
34 Ivan Rodriguez 1.75
35 Nomar Garciaparra 3.00
36 Josh Beckett 2.00
37 Jose Reyes 1.00
38 Scott Rolen 3.00
39 Greg Maddux 3.50
40 Andy Pettitte 1.75
41 Jason Schmidt 1.25
42 Edgar Martinez 1.25
43 Manny Ramirez 2.00
44 Torii Hunter 1.75
45 Mark Teixeira 1.25
46 Hideo Nomo 1.00
47 Brian Giles 1.25
48 Adam Dunn 1.75
49 Fernando Vina 1.00
50 Hideki Matsui 5.00
51 Jim Thome 3.00
52 Hank Blalock 1.75
53 Miguel Cabrera 2.00
54 Randy Johnson 3.00
55 Javy Lopez 1.25
56 Frank Thomas 2.00
57 Roger Clemens 3.50
58 Marlon Byrd 1.00
59 Derek Jeter 6.00
60 Ichiro Suzuki 4.00
61 Kazuo Matsui RC 25.00
62 Chad Bentz RC 8.00
63 Greg Dobbs RC 5.00
64 John Gall RC 5.00
65 Cory Sullivan RC 5.00
66 Hector Gimenez RC 5.00
67 Graham Koonce RC 5.00
68 Jason Bartlett RC 5.00
69 Angel Chavez RC 5.00
70 Ronny Cedeno RC 5.00
71 Donald Kelly RC 5.00
72 Ivan Ochoa RC 5.00
73 Ruddy Yan RC 5.00
74 Mike Gosling RC 5.00
75 Alfredo Simon RC 5.00
76 Jerome Gamble RC 5.00
77 Chris Aguila RC 5.00
78 Mike Rouse RC 5.00
79 Justin Leone RC 5.00
80 Merkin Valdez RC 5.00
81 Aarom Baldiris RC 5.00
82 Chris Shelton RC 10.00

Autograph Collection

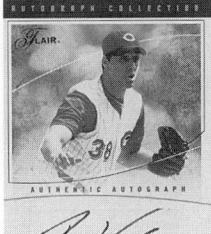

NM/M

Common Player: 10.00
Production between 65-200 Sets
Crown: .5-1X
Production 100 Sets
Parchment: 1-1.75X
Production 25 Sets
Platinum: No Pricing
Production 10 Sets
Masterpiece: No Pricing
Production One Set
Garrett Atkins/195 10.00
Rocco Baldelli/180 25.00
Aarom Baldiris/180 10.00
Jason Bartlett/95 15.00
Josh Beckett/65 40.00
Angel Berroa/178 15.00
Miguel Cabrera/172 40.00
Bobby Crosby/87 30.00
Jim Edmonds/73 25.00
John Gall/94 30.00
Khalil Greene/40 195.00
Dan Haren/195 15.00
Ryan Howard/185 75.00
Edwin Jackson/183 15.00
Andruw Jones/183 25.00
Graham Koonce/175 10.00
Josh Labandeira/166 10.00
Adam LaRoche/280 15.00
Justin Leone/180 15.00
Ryan Meaux/180 10.00
Mike Mussina/69 50.00
Micheal Nakamura/180 10.00
Bubba Nelson/185 10.00
Corey Patterson/172 15.00
Juan Pierre/94 15.00
Scott Podsednik/96 25.00
Mark Prior/60 60.00
Alexis Rios/185 20.00
Michael Rouse/195 10.00
Chris Shelton/170 30.00
Grady Sizemore/197 30.00
Merkin Valdez/179 10.00
Javier Vazquez/187 30.00
Ryan Wagner/175 15.00
Chien-Ming Wang/178 50.00
Brandon Webb/122 15.00
Rickie Weeks/169 20.00
Dontrelle Willis/73 30.00
Kerry Wood/73 40.00
Delmon Young/177 25.00

Cuts and Glory

NM/M

Common Player: 25.00
Production 100 Sets
Silver: .75-1.25X
Production 50 Sets
Gold: No Pricing
Production 15 Sets
Platinum: No Pricing
Production Three Sets
Masterpiece: No Pricing
Production One Set
Garret Anderson 30.00
Hank Blalock 25.00
Marlon Byrd 25.00
Carlos Delgado 30.00
Adam Dunn 40.00
Eric Gagne 40.00
Luis Gonzalez 25.00
Vladimir Guerrero 50.00
Ricky Henderson 100.00
Torii Hunter 25.00
Randy Johnson 60.00
Chipper Jones 60.00
Austin Kearns 25.00
Greg Maddux 75.00
Edgar Martinez 40.00
Magglio Ordonez 25.00
Albert Pujols 150.00
Jose Reyes 30.00
Scott Rolen 40.00
Mark Teixeira 25.00
Frank Thomas 75.00

Diamond Cuts Game-Used Blue

NM/M

Common Player: 5.00
Production 250 Sets
Blue Die-Cut: 1-3X
Production 25 Sets
Red: .5-1.25X
Production 175 Sets
Red Die-Cut: No Pricing
Production 18 Sets
Pewter: .5-1.5X
Production 125 Sets
Pewter Die-Cut: No Pricing
Production 13 Sets
Copper: .5-1.5X
Production 75 Sets
Die-Cut Copper: No Pricing
Production Eight Sets
Silver: .5-1.5X
Production 50 Sets
Silver Die-Cut: No Pricing
Production Five Sets
Gold: 1-5X
Numbered to player's jersey No.
Gold Die-Cut: No Pricing
Production Three Sets
Platinum: 2-5X
Numbered to 2003 HR/Win total.
Platinum Die-Cut: No Pricing
Production One Set
Purple: No Pricing
Production One Set
JB Josh Beckett 8.00
HB Hank Blalock 5.00
RC Roger Clemens 10.00
NG Nomar Garciaparra 12.00
DJ Derek Jeter 15.00
AJ Andruw Jones 8.00
CJ Chipper Jones 8.00
PM Pedro J. Martinez 8.00
HM Hideki Matsui 12.00
ANP Andy Pettitte 8.00
MIP Mike Piazza 8.00
MAP Mark Prior 8.00
ALP Albert Pujols 12.00
JR Jose Reyes 5.00
SR Scott Rolen 8.00
SS Curt Schilling 5.00
SS Sammy Sosa 10.00
IS Ichiro Suzuki 10.00
MT Mark Teixeira 5.00
DW Dontrelle Willis 5.00

Dual Patch

No Pricing
Production 10 Sets

Hot Numbers Game-Used Blue

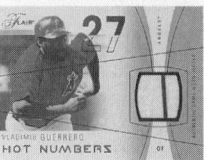

NM/M

Common Player: 5.00
Production 250 Sets
Blue Die-Cut: 1X-3X
Production 25 Sets
Red: .5X-1.25X
Production 175 Sets
Red Die-Cut: No Pricing
Production 18 Sets
Pewter: .5X-1.5X
Production 125 Sets
Pewter Die-Cut: No Pricing
Production 13 Sets
Copper: .5X-1.5X
Production 75 Sets
Die-Cut Copper: No Pricing
Production Eight Sets
Silver: .5X-1.5X
Production 50 Sets
Silver Die-Cut: No Pricing
Production Five Sets
Gold: 1X-5X
Numbered to player's jersey No.
Gold Die-Cut: No Pricing
Production Three Sets
Platinum: 2X-5X
Numbered to 2003 HR/Win total.
Platinum Die-Cut: No Pricing
Production One Set
Purple: No Pricing
Production One Set
Jeff Bagwell 8.00
Rocco Baldelli 5.00
Josh Beckett 8.00
Hank Blalock 5.00
Nomar Garciaparra 12.00
Jason Giambi 8.00
Troy Glaus 5.00
Tom Glavine 5.00
Vladimir Guerrero 8.00
Todd Helton 8.00
Derek Jeter 15.00
Randy Johnson 8.00
Chipper Jones 8.00
Barry Larkin 5.00
Greg Maddux 8.00
Pedro J. Martinez 8.00
Hideo Nomo 5.00
Mike Mussina 5.00
Mike Piazza 8.00
Mark Prior 8.00
Albert Pujols 12.00
Manny Ramirez 8.00
Alex Rodriguez 12.00
Curt Schilling 5.00
Sammy Sosa 10.00
Mark Teixeira 5.00
Frank Thomas 8.00
Jim Thome 8.00
Brandon Webb 5.00
Kerry Wood 8.00

Lettermen

No Pricing
Numbered to number of letters in player's last name.

Power Tools Game-Used Blue

NM/M

Common Player: 5.00
Production 250 Sets
Blue Die-Cut: 1X-3X
Production 25 Sets
Red: .5X-1.25X
Production 175 Sets
Red Die-Cut: No Pricing
Production 18 Sets
Pewter: .5X-1.5X
Production 125 Sets
Pewter Die-Cut: No Pricing
Production 13 Sets

Copper:	.5-1.5X
Production 75 Sets	
Die-Cut Copper:	No Pricing
Production Eight Sets	
Silver:	.5-1.5X
Production 50 Sets	
Silver Die-Cut:	No Pricing
Production Five Sets	
Gold:	1-5X
Numbered to player's jersey No.	
Gold Die-Cut:	No Pricing
Production Three Sets	
Platinum:	2-5X
Numbered to 2003 HR total.	
Platinum Die-Cut:	No Pricing
Production One Set	
Purple:	No Pricing
Production One Set	
Rocco Baldelli	5.00
Adam Dunn	5.00
Nomar Garciaparra	12.00
Jason Giambi	8.00
Vladimir Guerrero	8.00
Derek Jeter	15.00
Chipper Jones	8.00
Mike Piazza	10.00
Jorge Posada	8.00
Albert Pujols	12.00
Manny Ramirez	8.00
Alex Rodriguez	12.00
Alfonso Soriano	8.00
Sammy Sosa	10.00
Jim Thome	8.00

SIGnificant Cuts

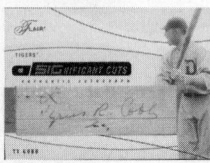

NM/M

Serially Numbered

RA	Roberto Alomar/50	60.00
JB2	Johnny Bench/25	100.00
VC	Vince Carter/200	50.00
TC	Ty Cobb	2,650
DE	Dennis Eckersley/75	30.00
RH	Roy Halladay/50	40.00
BL	Barry Larkin/75	30.00
PM	Paul Molitor/75	50.00
AP1	Andy Pettitte/50	40.00
JR	Jose Reyes/25	40.00
MR	Mariano Rivera/50	75.00
IR	Ivan Rodriguez/50	50.00
NR	Nolan Ryan/25	200.00
MS	Mike Schmidt/25	125.00
GS	Gary Sheffield/50	50.00

2004 Fleer Genuine Insider

NM/M

Common Player (1-90):	.25
Minor Stars:	.40
Unlisted Stars:	.60
Common Rookie Insider (91-100):	4.00
Production 499 Sets	
Common Upside (101-120):	4.00
Production 799 Sets	
Common Mini Rookie:	4.00
Production 350 Sets	
Pack (5):	4.00
Box (18):	75.00
1	Troy Glaus	.60
2	Eric Chavez	.40
3	Lance Berkman	.40
4	Pedro J. Martinez	1.00
5	Jim Edmonds	.40
6	Tom Glavine	.40
7	Ken Griffey Jr.	1.50
8	Vernon Wells	.40
9	Hideki Matsui	2.50
10	Jeff Bagwell	.75
11	Rafael Palmeiro	.40
12	Edgar Martinez	.40
13	Bernie Williams	.60
14	Josh Beckett	.75

15	Javy Lopez	.40
16	Ichiro Suzuki	2.00
17	Scott Podsednik	.40
18	Sammy Sosa	2.00
19	Mark Teixeira	.40
20	Jorge Posada	.60
21	Miguel Cabrera	.75
22	Chipper Jones	1.50
23	Sean Burroughs	.25
24	Dmitri Young	.25
25	Brandon Webb	.25
26	Bobby Abreu	.40
27	Hideo Nomo	.40
28	Frank Thomas	.75
29	Alex Rodriguez	2.50
30	Derek Jeter	3.00
31	Todd Helton	.75
32	Andruw Jones	.75
33	Jason Kendall	.40
34	Eric Gagne	.40
35	Omar Vizquel	.40
36	Vladimir Guerrero	1.00
37	Jim Thome	1.00
38	Mike Sweeney	.40
39	Manny Ramirez	.75
40	Scott Rolen	1.00
41	Jose Vidro	.25
42	Adam Dunn	.60
43	Garret Anderson	.40
44	Mike Lieberthal	.25
45	Roy Oswalt	.40
46	Geoff Jenkins	.40
47	Magglio Ordonez	.40
48	Hank Blalock	.60
49	Barry Zito	.60
50	Dontrelle Willis	1.00
51	Greg Maddux	1.50
52	Brian Giles	.40
53	Shawn Green	.40
54	Carlos Lee	.25
55	Carlos Delgado	.75
56	Alfonso Soriano	1.00
57	Angel Berroa	.25
58	Kerry Wood	.75
59	Rocco Baldelli	.60
60	Gary Sheffield	.60
61	Ivan Rodriguez	.60
62	Richie Sexson	.60
63	Marlon Byrd	.25
64	Carlos Beltran	.40
65	Mark Prior	2.00
66	Aubrey Huff	.25
67	Jason Giambi	1.00
68	Curt Schilling	.60
69	Reggie Sanders	.25
70	Mike Piazza	1.50
71	Craig Monroe	.25
72	Randy Johnson	1.00
73	Pat Burrell	.40
74	Craig Biggio	.40
75	Nomar Garciaparra	2.50
76	Albert Pujols	2.50
77	Jose Reyes	.25
78	Preston Wilson	.25
79	Miguel Tejada	.60
80	Bret Boone	.40
81	Shannon Stewart	.25
82	Jody Gerut	.25
83	Tim Salmon	.25
84	Tim Hudson	.40
85	Juan Pierre	.25
86	Jay Gibbons	.40
87	Jason Schmidt	.40
88	Torii Hunter	.60
89	Austin Kearns	.25
90	Roy Halladay	.40
91	John Gall RC	8.00
92	Hideki Matsui RC	25.00
93	Merkin Valdez RC	8.00
94	William Bergolla RC	4.00
95	Angel Chavez RC	4.00
96	Hector Gimenez RC	4.00
97	Aaron Baldiris RC	4.00
98	Justin Leone RC	6.00
99	Onil Joseph RC	5.00
100	Freddy Guzman RC	4.00
101	Rickie Weeks	5.00
102	Chad Bentz RC	5.00
103	Bobby Crosby	6.00
104	Dallas McPherson	5.00
105	Brandon Watson	5.00
106	Garrett Atkins	6.00
107	Graham Koonce	4.00
108	Chien-Ming Wang	5.00
109	Jonny Gomes	4.00
110	Edwin Jackson	4.00
111	Alfredo Simon RC	5.00
112	Delmon Young	4.00
113	Angel Guzman	4.00
114	Ryan Howard	4.00
115	Scott Hairston	10.00
116	Edwin Encarnacion	5.00
117	Byron Gettis	4.00
118	Kevin Youkilis	8.00
119	Grady Sizemore	4.00
120	Corey Hart	4.00
121	Greg Dobbs RC	4.00
122	Jerry Gil RC	4.00
123	Shawn Hill RC	4.00
124	John Labandeira RC	4.00
125	Jason Bartlett RC	4.00
126	Ronny Cedeno RC	4.00
127	Donald Kelly RC	8.00
128	Ivan Ochoa RC	5.00
129	Mariano Gomez RC	5.00
130	Ruddy Yan RC	5.00

Genuine Reflection

(1-90):	.5-2X
(101-120):	.5-1.25X
Production 99 Sets	

Autograph Insider

NM/M

Common Player:		10.00
Production as indicated.		
RA	Roberto Alomar/150	30.00
MB	Marlon Byrd/550	10.00
MC	Miguel Cabrera/250	40.00
DE	David Eckstein/350	10.00
JG	Jody Gerut/550	10.00
JG2	Jay Gibbons/350	10.00
OH	Orlando Hudson/550	15.00
AH	Aubrey Huff/550	10.00
AK	Austin Kearns/350	10.00
MO	Magglio Ordonez/250	20.00
RP	Rafael Palmeiro/150	50.00
SP	Scott Podsednik/550	15.00
JR	Jose Reyes/350	25.00
MR	Mariano Rivera/150	60.00
IR	Ivan Rodriguez/150	40.00
JR2	Jimmy Rollins/350	15.00
JS	Jason Schmidt/300	300.00
JS2	John Smoltz/150	30.00
MT	Mark Teixeira/350	20.00
BW	Brandon Webb/450	10.00

Autograph Insider - Bat

NM/M

Common Card:		20.00
Production 50 Sets		
RA	Roberto Alomar	40.00
MB	Marlon Byrd	20.00
MC	Miguel Cabrera	60.00
DE	David Eckstein	30.00
JG	Jody Gerut	25.00
JG2	Jay Gibbons	20.00
OH	Orlando Hudson	20.00
AH	Aubrey Huff	25.00
AK	Austin Kearns	20.00
RP	Rafael Palmeiro	50.00
SP	Scott Podsednik	25.00
JR	Jose Reyes	35.00
IR	Ivan Rodriguez	50.00
JR2	Jimmy Rollins	30.00
MT	Mark Teixeira	40.00

Autograph Insider - Ball

No Pricing
Production 10 Sets

Autograph Insider - Jersey

NM/M

Common Player:		10.00
Production 100 Sets		
RA	Roberto Alomar	30.00
MB	Marlon Byrd	10.00
MC	Miguel Cabrera	40.00
DE	David Eckstein	15.00
JG	Jody Gerut	25.00
JG2	Jay Gibbons	20.00
OH	Orlando Hudson	10.00
AH	Aubrey Huff	10.00
AK	Austin Kearns	20.00
MO	Magglio Ordonez	40.00
RP	Rafael Palmeiro	50.00
SP	Scott Podsednik	25.00
AP	Albert Pujols	100.00
JR	Jose Reyes	35.00
MR	Mariano Rivera	50.00
IR	Ivan Rodriguez	50.00
JR2	Jimmy Rollins	20.00
JS	Jason Schmidt	20.00
JS2	John Smoltz	50.00
MT	Mark Teixeira	25.00
BW	Brandon Webb	10.00

Autograph Insider-Cut Sigs

No Pricing

Classic Confrontations

NM/M

Common Card:		3.00
Inserted 1:18		
1CC	Mike Piazza, Roger Clemens	4.00
2CC	Pedro J. Martinez, Derek Jeter	6.00
3CC	Randy Johnson, Jeff Bagwell	3.00
4CC	Mark Prior, Albert Pujols	4.00
5CC	Josh Beckett, Sammy Sosa	4.00
6CC	Eric Gagne, Hank Blalock	3.00
7CC	Mariano Rivera, Nomar Garciaparra	5.00
8CC	Curt Schilling, Chipper Jones	4.00
9CC	Kerry Wood, Jim Edmonds	3.00
10CC	Barry Zito, Alfonso Soriano	3.00
11CC	Randy Johnson, Ken Griffey Jr.	4.00
12CC	Derek Jeter, John Smoltz	6.00
13CC	Roy Oswalt, Ken Griffey Jr.	4.00
14CC	Dontrelle Willis, Hideki Matsui	4.00
15CC	Hideo Nomo, Ichiro Suzuki	4.00

Classic Confrontations Jersey

NM/M

Common Card:		5.00
Production 400 Sets		
JB	Jeff Bagwell with Randy Johnson	6.00
JB2	Josh Beckett with Sammy Sosa	6.00
HB	Hank Blalock with Eric Gagne	8.00
RC	Roger Clemens with Mike Piazza	15.00
JE	Jim Edmonds with Kerry Wood	5.00
EG	Eric Gagne with Hank Blalock	5.00
NG	Nomar Garciaparra with Mariano Rivera	8.00
DJ	Derek Jeter with Pedro J. Martinez	15.00
RJ1	Randy Johnson with Jeff Bagwell	8.00
RJ2	Randy Johnson with Ken Griffey Jr.	8.00
CJ	Chipper Jones with Curt Schilling	8.00
PM	Pedro J. Martinez with Derek Jeter	10.00
HN	Hideo Nomo with Ichiro Suzuki	12.00
RO	Roy Oswalt with Ken Griffey Jr.	5.00
MP	Mike Piazza with Roger Clemens	8.00
MP2	Mark Prior with Albert Pujols	8.00
AP	Albert Pujols with Mark Prior	12.00
MR	Mariano Rivera with Nomar Garciaparra	8.00
CS	Curt Schilling with Chipper Jones	5.00
JS	John Smoltz with Derek Jeter	5.00
AS	Alfonso Soriano with Barry Zito	8.00
SS	Sammy Sosa with Josh Beckett	8.00
DW	Dontrelle Willis with Matsui	5.00
KW	Kerry Wood with Jim Edmonds	8.00
BZ	Barry Zito with Alfonso Soriano	5.00

Classic Conf. Dual Jersey

NM/M

Common Card:		12.00
Production 100 Sets		
Dual Patch:		No Pricing
Production 10 Sets		
	Barry Zito, Alfonso Soriano	12.00

Curt Schilling,	
Chipper Jones	12.00
Eric Gagne, Hank Blalock	12.00
Josh Beckett, Sammy Sosa	12.00
Kerry Wood, Jim Edmonds	15.00
Mark Prior, Albert Pujols	15.00
Mike Piazza,	
Roger Clemens	15.00
Mariano Rivera,	
Nomar Garciaparra	20.00
Pedro J. Martinez,	
Derek Jeter	20.00
Randy Johnson,	
Jeff Bagwell	12.00

Gen. Article Insider-Jersey

		NM/M
Common Player:		5.00
Production 250 Sets		
Bat:		.75-1.25X
Production 100 Sets		
Jersey/Bat:		.75-1.5X
Production 50 Sets		
Jersey Tags:		No Pricing
Production Five Sets		
RB	Rocco Baldelli	5.00
LB	Lance Berkman	5.00
HB	Hank Blalock	8.00
MC	Miguel Cabrera	8.00
CD	Carlos Delgado	6.00
AD	Adam Dunn	5.00
NG	Nomar Garciaparra	12.00
JG	Jason Giambi	6.00
TG	Troy Glaus	5.00
VG	Vladimir Guerrero	8.00
TH	Todd Helton	8.00
DJ	Derek Jeter	18.00
CJ	Chipper Jones	8.00
MO	Magglio Ordonez	5.00
RP	Rafael Palmeiro	5.00
MP	Mike Piazza	8.00
AP	Albert Pujols	12.00
MR	Manny Ramirez	6.00
JR	Jose Reyes	6.00
AR	Alex Rodriguez	15.00
CS	Gary Sheffield	6.00
AS	Alfonso Soriano	8.00
SS	Sammy Sosa	10.00
MT	Mark Teixeira	5.00
JT	Jim Thome	6.00

Tools of the Game

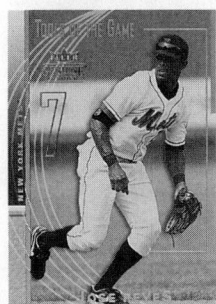

		NM/M
Common Player:		1.00
Inserted 1:6		
1TG	Jason Giambi	1.50
2TG	Torii Hunter	1.00
3TG	Derek Jeter	4.00
4TG	Nomar Garciaparra	3.00
5TG	Albert Pujols	3.00
6TG	Jim Thome	1.50
7TG	Alex Rodriguez	4.00
8TG	Chipper Jones	2.00
9TG	Sammy Sosa	2.50
10TG	Jose Reyes	1.00
11TG	Pedro J. Martinez	1.50
12TG	Greg Maddux	2.00
13TG	Randy Johnson	1.50
14TG	Curt Schilling	1.00
15TG	Mark Prior	2.00
16TG	Ichiro Suzuki	2.50
17TG	Hideki Matsui	3.00
18TG	Kazuo Matsui	2.50
19TG	Kerry Wood Jr.	2.00
20TG	Josh Beckett	1.00

Tools of Game-Game Jersey

	NM/M
Common Player:	5.00
Production 250 Sets	
Jersey/Bat:	.75-2X
Production 125	
Jersey/Bat/Cap:	1-2.5X
Production 75	

NG	Nomar Garciaparra	12.00
JG	Jason Giambi	8.00
TH	Torii Hunter	5.00
DJ	Derek Jeter	15.00
RJ	Randy Johnson	6.00
CJ	Chipper Jones	8.00
GM	Greg Maddux	6.00
PM	Pedro J. Martinez	6.00
MP	Mark Prior	10.00
AP	Albert Pujols	12.00
JR	Jose Reyes	8.00
AR	Alex Rodriguez	15.00
CS	Curt Schilling	5.00
SS	Sammy Sosa	10.00
JT	Jim Thome	6.00

2004 Fleer Greats of the Game

		NM/M
Common Player:		.40
Minor Stars:		.75
Pack (5):		10.00
Box (15):		130.00
1	Lou Gehrig	4.00
2	Ty Cobb	3.00
3	Dizzy Dean	1.50
4	Jimmie Foxx	1.50
5	Hank Greenberg	1.00
6	Babe Ruth	6.00
7	Honus Wagner	1.50
8	Mickey Cochrane	1.50
9	Pepper Martin	.40
10	Charlie Gehringer	.75
11	Carl Hubbell	.40
12	Bill Terry	.40
13	Mel Ott	.75
14	Bill Dickey	1.50
15	Ted Williams	6.00
16	Roger Maris	3.00
17	Thurman Munson	2.00
18	Phil Rizzuto	2.00
19	Stan Musial	3.00
20	Duke Snider	2.50
21	Reggie Jackson	1.50
22	Don Mattingly	1.50
23	Vida Blue	.75
24	Harmon Killebrew	1.50
25	Lou Brock	.75
26	Al Kaline	1.00
27	Dave Parker	.40
28	Nolan Ryan	6.00
29	Jim Rice	.40
30	Paul Molitor	2.00
31	Dwight Evans	.40
32	Brooks Robinson	1.50
33	Jose Canseco	.40
34	Alan Trammell	.40
35	Johnny Bench	2.00
36	Carlton Fisk	1.00
37	Jim Palmer	1.50
38	George Brett	2.00
39	Mike Schmidt	2.00
40	Tony Perez	.75
41	Paul Blair	.40
42	Fred Lynn	.40
43	Carl Yastrzemski	1.50
44	Steve Carlton	1.00
45	Dennis Eckersley	1.50
46	Tom Seaver	1.50
47	Juan Marichal	.75
48	Tony Gwynn	2.00
49	Bill "Moose" Skowron	.40
50	Bob Gibson	1.50
51	Luis Tiant	.75
52	Eddie Murray	1.00
53	Frank Robinson	2.00
54	Rocky Colavito	.75
55	Bobby Shantz	.40
56	Ernie Banks	2.00
57	Rod Carew	1.00
58	Gorman Thomas	.40
59	Bernie Carbo	.40
60	Joe Rudi	.40
61	Graig Nettles	.75
62	Ron Guidry	.75
63	Whitey Ford	1.50
64	George Kell	1.00
65	Cal Ripken Jr.	6.00
66	Willie McCovey	.75
67	Bo Jackson	1.00
68	Kirby Puckett	2.00
69	Ted Kluszewski	.75
70	Johnny Podres	.40
71	Davey Lopes	.40
72	Chris Short	.40
73	Jeff Torborg	.40
74	Bill Freehan	.40
75	Frank Tanana	.40
76	Jack Morris	.75
77	Rick Dempsey	.40
78	Yogi Berra	1.50
79	Tim McCarver	.40
80	Rusty Staub	.40
81	Tony Lazzeri	.40
82	Al Rosen	.40
83	Willie McGee	.75
84	Preacher Roe	.75
85	Dave Kingman	.40
86	Luis Aparicio	1.00
87	John Kruk	.40
88	Bing Miller	.40
89	Joe Charboneau	.40
90	Mark Fidrych	.40
91	Jim "Catfish" Hunter	2.00
92	Nap Lajoie	2.00
93	Eddie Murray	2.00
94	Johnny Pesky	1.00
95	Tom Seaver	2.00
96	Frank Robinson	2.00
97	Enos Slaughter	1.00
98	Cecil Travis	.40
99	Robin Yount	2.00
100	Don Zimmer	.75
101	Babe Herman	.40
102	Ron Santo	.40
103	Willie Stargell	2.00
104	Jimmy Piersall	.75
105	Johnny Sain	.40
106	Joe Pepitone	.75
107	Ryne Sandberg	3.00
108	Jim Thorpe	3.00
109	Steve Garvey	1.50
110	Ray Knight	.75
111	Fernando Valenzuela	1.00
112	Will Clark	1.00
113	Tony Kubek	.75
114	Jim Bouton	.40
115	Jerry Koosman	.75
116	Steve Carlton	3.00
117	Richie Ashburn	.75
118	Roberto Clemente	6.00
119	Paul O'Neill	.40
120	Reggie Jackson	3.00
121	Andre Dawson	1.50
122	Hoyt Wilhelm	1.00
123	Dale Murphy	1.50
124	Dwight Gooden	1.50
125	Roger Maris	1.00
126	Bill Mazeroski	1.00
127	Don Newcombe	.75
128	Robin Roberts	.75
129	Duke Snider	2.00
130	Eddie Mathews	3.00
131	Wade Boggs	2.00
132	Rollie Fingers	1.50
133	Frankie Frisch	.40
134	Billy Williams	.75
135	Rod Carew	1.50
136	Joe DiMaggio	.75
137	Orel Hershiser	.40
138	Gary Carter	1.00
139	Keith Hernandez	.75
140	Bob Lemon	.75
141	Nolan Ryan	6.00
142	Ozzie Smith	1.50
143	Rick Sutcliffe	.40
144	Carlton Fisk	1.50

Blue

Cards 81-145	
Cards #'d to 51-96:	3-5X
Cards #'d to 26-50:	5-10X
Cards #'d to less than 25:	No Pricing

Gold Border Autographs

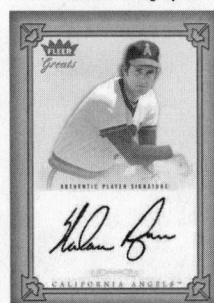

	NM/M
Common Player:	10.00
Randomly Inserted	
Ernie Banks	60.00
Johnny Bench	50.00
Yogi Berra	60.00
Paul Blair	10.00
Vida Blue	10.00
George Brett	125.00
Lou Brock	20.00
Jose Canseco	30.00
Bernie Carbo	10.00
Rod Carew	30.00
Steve Carlton	30.00
Rocky Colavito	100.00
Rick Dempsey	15.00
Dennis Eckersley	50.00
Dwight Evans	15.00
Carlton Fisk	40.00
Whitey Ford	40.00
Bill Freehan	10.00
Bob Gibson	25.00
Ron Guidry	20.00
Tony Gwynn	50.00
Bo Jackson	50.00
Reggie Jackson	100.00
Al Kaline	25.00
George Kell	15.00
Harmon Killebrew	30.00
Davey Lopes	10.00
Fred Lynn	10.00
Juan Marichal	20.00
Don Mattingly	80.00
Tim McCarver	15.00
Willie McCovey	40.00
Paul Molitor	40.00
Jack Morris	10.00
Eddie Murray	80.00
Stan Musial	100.00
Graig Nettles	15.00
Jim Palmer	20.00
Dave Parker	10.00
Tony Perez	30.00
Johnny Podres	10.00
Kirby Puckett	80.00
Jim Rice	20.00
Cal Ripken Jr.	150.00
Phil Rizzuto	40.00
Brooks Robinson	20.00
Frank Robinson	30.00
Joe Rudi	10.00
Nolan Ryan	150.00
Mike Schmidt	60.00
Tom Seaver	80.00
Bobby Shantz	10.00
Bill "Moose" Skowron	10.00
Duke Snider	30.00
Rusty Staub	10.00
Frank Tanana	10.00
Gorman Thomas	10.00
Luis Tiant	10.00
Jeff Torborg	10.00
Alan Trammell	10.00
Carl Yastrzemski	60.00

Gold Border Autograph Series 2

		NM/M
Common Player:		15.00
Inserted 1:75		
LA	Luis Aparicio	20.00
WB	Wade Boggs	40.00
JBO	Jim Bouton	15.00
RC2	Rod Carew/Twins	40.00
SC2	Steve Carlton/Cards	30.00
GC	Gary Carter	25.00
JCH	Joe Charboneau	15.00
WC	Will Clark	40.00
DC	David Cone	15.00
AD	Andre Dawson	20.00
DD	Dom DiMaggio	50.00
RF	Rollie Fingers	15.00
CF2	Carlton Fisk/White Sox	40.00
SG	Steve Garvey	15.00
DG	Dwight Gooden	20.00
KH	Keith Hernandez	15.00
OH	Orel Hershiser	15.00
RJ2	Reggie Jackson/Angels	60.00
DK	Dave Kingman	15.00
RK	Ray Knight	15.00
JK	Jerry Koosman	20.00
JKR	John Kruk	15.00
TK	Tony Kubek	25.00
BM	Bill Mazeroski	30.00
WMG	Willie McGee	25.00
PM2	Paul Molitor/Jays	40.00
DMU	Dale Murphy	25.00
DN	Don Newcombe	15.00

PO	Paul O'Neill	30.00
JPP	Joe Pepitone	15.00
JPS	Johnny Pesky	25.00
JPI	Jimmy Piersall	20.00
RR	Robin Roberts	25.00
FR2	Frank Robinson/O's	30.00
PRO	Preacher Roe	20.00
AR	Al Rosen	15.00
NR2	Nolan Ryan/Angels	120.00
RS	Ryne Sandberg	75.00
DS	Deion Sanders	30.00
RST	Ron Santo	20.00
TS2	Tom Seaver/Reds	75.00
OS	Ozzie Smith	40.00
DS2	Duke Snider	40.00
BW	Billy Williams	20.00
RY	Robin Yount	40.00
DZ	Don Zimmer	25.00

Announcing Greats

NM/M

Common Card: 6.00
Inserted 1:12 Retail

1AG	Harry Kalas, Mike Schmidt	8.00
2AG	Vin Scully, Steve Garvey	12.00
3AG	Harry Caray, Ryne Sandberg	12.00
4AG	Ned Martin, Carlton Fisk	6.00
5AG	Ernie Harwell, Kirk Gibson	6.00
6AG	Ken Harrelson, Carl Yastrzemski	8.00
7AG	Don Mattingly, Phil Rizzuto	10.00
8AG	Yogi Berra, Mel Allen	10.00
9AG	Jonathan Miller, Cal Ripken Jr.	10.00
10AG	Marty Brennaman, Johnny Bench	8.00

Announcing Greats Autographs

NM/M

Sequentially #'d between 1 & 50.

	Ken Harrelson, Carl Yastrzemski/50	75.00
	Phil Rizzuto, Don Mattingly/26	225.00
	Johnny Bench, Marty Brennaman/50	60.00

Battery Mates

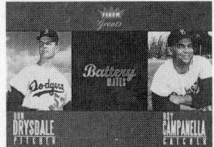

NM/M

Common Card: 5.00
Serially Numbered

1BM	Steve Carlton, Tim McCarver/1972	5.00
2BM	Don Drysdale, Roy Campanella/1957	5.00
3BM	Tom Seaver, Johnny Bench/1979	8.00
4BM	Whitey Ford, Yogi Berra/1956	8.00
5BM	Ron Guidry, Thurman Munson/1978	8.00
6BM	Nolan Ryan, Jeff Torborg/1973	10.00
7BM	Denny McLain, Bill Freehan/1968	5.00
8BM	Lefty Gomez, Bill Dickey/1934	5.00
9BM	Jim Palmer, Rick Dempsey/1977	5.00
10BM	Luis Tiant, Carlton Fisk	5.00

Single Panel: Battery Mates

NM/M

Common Card: 15.00
Serially Numbered

TM	Steve Carlton, Tim McCarver/72	30.00
TS-JB	Tom Seaver, Johnny Bench/79	60.00
WF-YB	Whitey Ford, Yogi Berra/56	40.00
RG-TM	Ron Guidry, Thurman Munson/78	25.00
NR-JT	Nolan Ryan, Jeff Torborg/73	15.00
DM-BF	Denny McLain, Bill Freehan/68	60.00
JP-RD	Jim Palmer, Rick Dempsey/77	25.00

Dual Panel: Battery Mates

No Pricing
Production 10 Sets

Comparison Cuts: Dual Cut

No Pricing
Production One Set

Single Cuts: Etched in Time

NM/M

No Pricing

ET-RC	Roberto Clemente/1 (7/04 Auction)	6,100

Etched In Time Series 2

NM/M

Sequentially #'d to indicated quantity.
Cards #'d 25 or less: No Pricing

EA	Ethan Allen/75	150.00
EAV	Earl Averill/50	125.00
DC	Dolph Camilli/40	250.00
BH	Babe Herman/35	250.00
HK	Harvey Kuenn/32	120.00
SM	Sal Maglie/40	100.00
ER	Edd Roush/95	100.00
PR	Pete Runnels/35	200.00
CS	Chris Short/30	120.00

Forever

NM/M

Common Player: 4.00
Sequentially #'d to player's rookie year

1	Fernando Valenzuela/1980	4.00
2	Steve Garvey/1969	4.00
3	Zach Wheat/1909	4.00
4	Orel Hershiser/1983	4.00
5	Duke Snider/1947	6.00
6	Jim Rice/1974	5.00
7	Carlton Fisk/1969	6.00
8	Wade Boggs/1982	6.00
9	Ted Williams/1939	10.00
10	Carl Yastrzemski/1961	8.00
11	Dom DiMaggio/1940	5.00
12	Ron Santo/1960	4.00
13	Billy Williams/1959	5.00
14	Ryne Sandberg/1981	8.00
15	Ernie Banks/1953	8.00
16	Gabby Hartnett/1922	4.00
17	Hack Wilson/1923	6.00
18	Dwight Gooden/1984	5.00
19	Ray Knight/1974	4.00
20	Tom Seaver/1967	8.00
21	Nolan Ryan/1966	10.00
22	Keith Hernandez/1974	5.00
23	Darryl Strawberry/1983	5.00
24	Bob Gibson/1959	8.00
25	Pepper Martin/1928	4.00
26	Stan Musial/1941	8.00
27	Frankie Frisch/1919	4.00
28	Steve Carlton/1965	8.00
29	Ozzie Smith/1978	6.00

Forever Game-Used Jersey

NM/M

Common Player: 10.00
Production 149 Sets
Jersey: .75-1.5X
Production 99 Sets
Patch Number: 1-2X
Production 49 Sets
Patch Logo: No Pricing
Production 10 Sets

EB	Ernie Banks	20.00
WB	Wade Boggs	12.00
SC	Steve Carlton	12.00
DD	Dom DiMaggio	20.00
CF	Carlton Fisk	15.00
SG	Steve Garvey	10.00
BG	Bob Gibson	15.00
DG	Dwight Gooden	10.00
KH	Keith Hernandez	10.00
OH	Orel Hershiser	10.00
RK	Ray Knight	10.00
SM	Stan Musial	30.00
JR	Jim Rice	12.00
NR	Nolan Ryan	50.00
RS	Ryne Sandberg	25.00
RST	Ron Santo	10.00
TS	Tom Seaver	15.00
OS	Ozzie Smith	10.00
DS	Darryl Strawberry	12.00
FV	Fernando Valenzuela	10.00
BW	Billy Williams	10.00
TW	Ted Williams	75.00
CY	Carl Yastrzemski	20.00

Personality Cuts

No Pricing
Production One Set

Personality Cuts Series 2

No Pricing
Production One or Two Sets

The Glory of Their Time

NM/M

Common Player: 4.00
Serially Numbered

1GOT	Harmon Killebrew/1961	4.00
2GOT	Johnny Bench/1974	4.00
3GOT	George Brett/1980	8.00
4GOT	Tony Gwynn/1987	4.00
5GOT	Paul Molitor/1987	5.00
6GOT	Don Mattingly/1986	5.00
7GOT	Reggie Jackson/1980	8.00
8GOT	Carlton Fisk/1985	5.00
9GOT	Cal Ripken Jr./1983	10.00
10GOT	Brooks Robinson/1964	4.00
11GOT	Eddie Murray/1980	5.00
12GOT	Bill "Moose" Skowron/1960	4.00
13GOT	Lou Brock/1974	5.00
14GOT	Don Drysdale/1962	5.00
15GOT	Tony Gwynn/1997	4.00
16GOT	Mike Schmidt/1984	8.00
17GOT	Carl Yastrzemski/1967	8.00
18GOT	Babe Ruth/1927	10.00
19GOT	Nolan Ryan/1989	10.00
20GOT	Yogi Berra/1950	8.00
21GOT	Al Kaline/1955	5.00
22GOT	Ty Cobb/1911	5.00
23GOT	Duke Snider/1955	5.00
24GOT	Stan Musial/1948	5.00
25GOT	Jose Canseco/1988	5.00
26GOT	Rocky Colavito/1958	5.00
27GOT	Dave Winfield/1979	4.00
28GOT	Nolan Ryan/1982	10.00
29GOT	Thurman Munson/1977	8.00
30GOT	Jackie Robinson/1949	8.00
31GOT	Kirby Puckett/1988	8.00
32GOT	Ted Kluszewski/1954	5.00
33GOT	Warren Spahn/1953	5.00
34GOT	Willie McCovey/1969	4.00
35GOT	Phil Rizzuto/1950	5.00

The Glory/Time: Game-Used

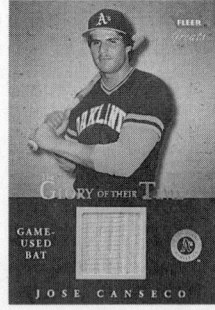

NM/M

Common Player: 10.00
Production 250 Sets
Hobby Only
Gold: 1.5-2X
Retail (Not Numbered)
No Rizzuto Retail Version

JB	Johnny Bench/Jsy	15.00
YB	Yogi Berra/Pants	15.00
GB	George Brett/Jsy	15.00
LB	Lou Brock/Jsy	15.00
JC1	Jose Canseco/Jsy	10.00
JC2	Jose Canseco/Bat	10.00
RC	Rocky Colavito/Jsy	25.00
DD	Don Drysdale/Jsy	15.00
CF1	Carlton Fisk/Jsy	10.00
CF2	Carlton Fisk/Bat	10.00
TG1	Tony Gwynn/Jsy	10.00
TG2	Tony Gwynn/Jsy	10.00
RJ	Reggie Jackson/Pants	20.00
AK	Al Kaline/Pants	15.00
HK	Harmon Killebrew/Bat	10.00
TK	Ted Kluszewski/Pants	15.00
DM	Don Mattingly/Pants	20.00
WM	Willie McCovey/Pants	10.00
PM	Paul Molitor/Jsy	15.00
TM	Thurman Munson/Pants	15.00
EM	Eddie Murray/Jsy	10.00
KP	Kirby Puckett/Bat	20.00
CR	Cal Ripken Jr./Jsy	25.00
PR	Phil Rizzuto/Pants	15.00
BR	Brooks Robinson/Jsy	10.00
NR1	Nolan Ryan/Jsy	20.00
NR2	Nolan Ryan/Bat	20.00
MS	Mike Schmidt/Jsy	15.00
MS	Bill "Moose" Skowron/Pants	10.00
WS	Warren Spahn/Jsy	20.00
DW	Dave Winfield/Jsy	10.00
CY	Carl Yastrzemski/Jsy	20.00

The Glory/Time: G-U Patch

No Pricing
Production 25 Sets

Yankee Clippings

NM/M

Common Player: 25.00
Inserted 1:45

YB	Yogi Berra	60.00
WB	Wade Boggs	40.00
RJ	Reggie Jackson	40.00
LG	Roger Maris	400.00
DM	Don Mattingly	100.00
PO	Paul O'Neill	30.00
PR	Phil Rizzuto	325.00
BS	Bill "Moose" Skowron	25.00

Yankee Clippings Autographs

No Pricing
Sequentially #'d between 3 & 26.

2004 Fleer Hot Prospects Draft Edition

NM/M

Common Player (1-60): .25
Minor Stars (1-60): .40
Unlisted Stars (1-60): .60
Common Rookie (61-70): 3.00
Common Rookie (71-120): 15.00
Production 1,000 Sets
Cards 112 & 113 do not exist.
Production 299 Sets
Pack (5): 7.00
Box (15): 100.00

1	Miguel Tejada	.50
2	Jose Vidro	.25
3	Hideki Matsui	2.00
4	Roger Clemens	2.50
5	Craig Wilson	.25
6	Bobby Crosby	.25
7	Pat Burrell	.40
8	Mike Sweeney	.25
9	Craig Biggio	.40
10	Scott Rolen	1.00
11	Roy Halladay	.40
12	Lyle Overbay	.25
13	Rocco Baldelli	.50
14	Mike Piazza	1.50
15	Rafael Palmeiro	.75
16	Hank Blalock	.50
17	Sammy Sosa	1.50
18	Dontrelle Willis	.40
19	Alfonso Soriano	1.00
20	Gary Sheffield	.75
21	Jim Thome	1.00
22	Ivan Rodriguez	.50
23	Adam Dunn	.50
24	Kerry Wood	.50
25	Khalil Greene	.50
26	Richie Sexson	.50
27	Nomar Garciaparra	1.00
28	Andruw Jones	.75
29	Tom Glavine	.40
30	Carlos Beltran	.75
31	Chipper Jones	1.00
32	Jeff Bagwell	.75
33	Tim Hudson	.40
34	Alex Rodriguez	2.00
35	Omar Vizquel	.40
36	Albert Pujols	2.50
37	Frank Thomas	.75
38	Ben Sheets	.40
39	Jason Schmidt	.40
40	Miguel Cabrera	.75

41 Carlos Delgado .75
42 Ichiro Suzuki 2.00
43 Curt Schilling .75
44 Todd Helton .75
45 Ken Griffey Jr. 1.50
46 Mark Prior .75
47 Vladimir Guerrero 1.00
48 Pedro Martinez 1.00
49 Manny Ramirez 1.00
50 Joe Mauer .50
51 Jorge Posada .75
52 Troy Glaus .50
53 Randy Johnson 1.00
54 Adrian Beltre .40
55 Eric Gagne .40
56 Josh Beckett .50
57 Jason Giambi .75
58 Barry Zito .50
59 Lance Berkman .50
60 Derek Jeter 3.00
61 Kazuo Matsui **RC** 5.00
62 Jason Bartlett **RC** 5.00
63 John Gall **RC** 3.00
64 Chris Saenz **RC** 3.00
65 Merkin Valdez **RC** 3.00
66 Akinori Otsuka **RC** 3.00
67 Joey Gathright **RC** 5.00
68 Brad Halsey **RC** 5.00
69 David Aardsma 3.00
70 Scott Kazmir 10.00
71 Matt Bush/AU **RC** 15.00
72 John Bowker/AU **RC** 30.00
73 Mike Ferris/AU **RC** 10.00
74 Brian Bixler/AU **RC** 15.00
75 Scott Elbert/AU **RC** 20.00
76 Josh Fields/AU **RC** 30.00
77 Bill Bray/AU **RC** 15.00
78 Greg Golson/AU **RC** 30.00
79 Neil Walker/AU **RC** 30.00
80 Phillip Hughes/AU **RC** 100.00
81 Chris Nelson/AU **RC** 15.00
82 Mark Rogers/AU **RC** 20.00
83 Trevor Plouffe/AU **RC** 20.00
84 Christian Garcia/AU **RC** 15.00
85 Thomas Diamond/AU **RC** 20.00
86 B.J. Szymanski/AU **RC** 15.00
87 Richie Robnett/AU **RC** 15.00
88 Seth Smith/AU **RC** 25.00
89 Kyle Waldrop/AU **RC** 15.00
90 Curtis Thigpen/AU **RC** 15.00
91 J.P. Howell/AU **RC** 15.00
92 Blake DeWitt/AU **RC** 35.00
93 Taylor Tankersley/AU **RC** 10.00
94 Zach Jackson/AU **RC** 10.00
95 Justin Orenduff/AU **RC** 15.00
96 Tyler Lumsden/AU **RC** 15.00
97 Danny Putnam **RC** 20.00
98 Jon Poterson/AU **RC** 20.00
99 Matt Fox/AU **RC** 15.00
100 Gio Gonzalez/AU **RC** 35.00
101 Huston Street/AU **RC** 15.00
102 Jay Rainville/AU **RC** 15.00
103 Matt Durkin/AU **RC** 15.00
104 Brett Smith/AU **RC** 15.00
105 Justin Hoyman/AU **RC** 15.00
106 Erick San Pedro/AU **RC** 15.00
107 Jeff Marquez/AU **RC** 15.00
108 Hunter Pence/AU **RC** 120.00
109 Dustin Pedroia/AU **RC** 125.00
110 Kurt Suzuki/AU **RC** 20.00
111 Billy Buckner/AU **RC** 10.00
114 J.C. Holt/AU **RC** 10.00
115 Homer Bailey/AU **RC** 35.00
116 David Purcey/AU **RC** 15.00
117 Jeremy Sowers/AU **RC** 20.00
118 Chris Lambert/AU **RC** 10.00
119 Eric Hurley/AU **RC** 40.00
120 Grant Johnson/AU **RC** 10.00

Red Hot

Veterans (1-60): 2-4X
Rookies (61-70): 1-2X
Production 150
Rookies (71-120): No Pricing
Production 25 Sets

White Hot

Cards (1-120): No Pricing
Production One Set

Alumni Ink

No Pricing
Production 15 Sets
Red Hot: No Pricing
Production Five Sets
White Hot: No Pricing
Production One Set

Double Team Jersey

NM/M

Common Player: 10.00
Production 100 Sets
Red Hot: No Pricing
Production 25 Sets
White Hot: No Pricing
Production One Set
Patch: .75-1.5X
Production 50 Sets
Patch Red Hot: No Pricing
Production 10 Sets
Patch White Hot: No Pricing
Production One Set
CB Carlos Beltran 15.00
RCA Rod Carew 20.00
RCL Roger Clemens 20.00
JG Jason Giambi 12.00
TG Tom Glavine 10.00
VG Vladimir Guerrero 15.00
RH Rickey Henderson 20.00
RJ Reggie Jackson 25.00
GM Greg Maddux 15.00
PM Pedro Martinez 15.00
EM Eddie Murray 20.00
HN Hideo Nomo 15.00
RP Rafael Palmeiro 12.00
MP Mike Piazza 20.00
MR Manny Ramirez 15.00
IR Ivan Rodriguez 10.00
SR Scott Rolen 15.00
NR Nolan Ryan 50.00
AS Alfonso Soriano 12.00
MT Miguel Tejada 10.00

Draft Rewind

NM/M

Common Player: 2.00
Inserted 1:5
1 Joe Mauer 2.00
2 Derek Jeter 6.00
3 Chipper Jones 3.50
4 Greg Maddux 3.50
5 Alex Rodriguez 5.00
6 Nomar Garciaparra 5.00
7 Curt Schilling 3.00
8 Kerry Wood 3.00
9 Troy Glaus 3.00
10 Pat Burrell 2.00
11 Mark Mulder 2.00
12 Josh Beckett 3.00
13 Barry Zito 3.00
14 Mark Prior 4.00
15 Rickie Weeks 2.00
16 Khalil Greene 3.00
17 Ken Griffey Jr. 3.50
18 Gary Sheffield 3.00
19 Todd Helton 3.00
20 Barry Larkin 2.00
21 Kevin Brown 2.00
22 Frank Thomas 3.00
23 Manny Ramirez 3.00
24 Roger Clemens 5.00
25 Lance Berkman 2.00
26 Randy Johnson 3.00
27 Jason Giambi 3.00
28 Ben Sheets 2.00
29 Scott Rolen 3.00
30 Tom Glavine 2.00

Draft Rewind Jersey

NM/M

Common Player: 8.00
Sequentially #'d to indicated quantity.
Red Hot: No Pricing
Production 10 Sets
White Hot: No Pricing
Production One Set
Patch
Cards #'d 41-68: .75-1.5X
Cards #'d 29 or less: No Pricing
Patch Red Hot: No Pricing
Production Five Sets
Patch White Hot: No Pricing
Production One Set
RB Rocco Baldelli/119 8.00
JB Josh Beckett/102 10.00
LB Lance Berkman/116 8.00
KB Kevin Brown/104 8.00
PB Pat Burrell/101 8.00
EC Eric Chavez/110 8.00
RC Roger Clemens/119 15.00
JG Jason Giambi/158 8.00
TG Troy Glaus/103 8.00
TG Tom Glavine/147 8.00
KG Khalil Greene/113 15.00
ZG Zack Greinke/106 8.00
TH Todd Helton/108 10.00
RJ Randy Johnson/136 10.00
CJ Chipper Jones/101 12.00
CK Casey Kotchman/113 8.00
BL Barry Larkin/104 10.00
GM Greg Maddux/131 12.00
JM Joe Mauer/101 10.00
MM Mark Mulder/102 8.00
MP Mark Prior/102 8.00
MR Manny Ramirez/113 10.00
SR Scott Rolen/146 10.00
CS Curt Schilling/139 10.00
BS Ben Sheets/110 8.00
GS Gary Sheffield/106 8.00
FT Frank Thomas/107 15.00
RW Rickie Weeks/102 8.00
KW Kerry Wood/104 10.00
BZ Barry Zito/109 8.00

Hot Tandems

NM/M

Common Card: 3.00
Inserted 1:15

1HT Mark Prior, Greg Maddux 4.00
2HT Jim Thome, Pat Burrell 3.50
3HT Ken Griffey Jr., Adam Dunn 4.00
4HT Mike Piazza, Tom Glavine 4.00
5HT Alex Rodriguez, Derek Jeter 10.00
6HT Roger Clemens, Andy Pettitte 6.00
7HT Hideki Matsui, Jason Giambi 6.00
8HT Hank Blalock, Alfonso Soriano 3.50
9HT Manny Ramirez, David Ortiz 3.50
10HT Miguel Cabrera, Dontrelle Willis 3.50
11HT Hideki Matsui, Ichiro Suzuki 6.00
12HT Albert Pujols, Scott Rolen 6.00
13HT Curt Schilling, Pedro J. Martinez 3.50
14HT Nomar Garciaparra, Sammy Sosa 5.00
15HT Kazuo Matsui, Derek Jeter 8.00

Hot Materials

NM/M

Common Player: 5.00
Production 325 Sets
Red Hot: 1-2X
Production 50 Sets
White Hot Patch: No Pricing
Production One Set
JB Jeff Bagwell/Jsy 6.00
LB Lance Berkman/Jsy 5.00
HB Hank Blalock/Jsy 6.00
MC Miguel Cabrera/Jsy 8.00
RC Roger Clemens/Jsy 12.00
CD Carlos Delgado/Jsy 6.00
JD J.D. Drew/Jsy 6.00
AD Adam Dunn/Jsy 6.00
JE Jim Edmonds/Jsy 5.00
EG Eric Gagne/Jsy 6.00
VG Vladimir Guerrero/Jsy 8.00
THE Todd Helton/Jsy 6.00
THU Tim Hudson/Jsy 5.00
THN Torii Hunter/Jsy 6.00
RJ Randy Johnson/Jsy 8.00
AJ Andruw Jones/Jsy 6.00
CJ Chipper Jones/Jsy 8.00
HM Hideki Matsui/Jsy 20.00
KM Kazuo Matsui/Jsy 10.00
JM Joe Mauer/Jsy 8.00
MM Mike Mussina/Jsy 6.00
HN Hideo Nomo/Jsy 8.00
LO Lyle Overbay/Jsy 5.00
APE Andy Pettitte/Jsy 6.00
MPI Mike Piazza/Jsy 8.00
JP Jorge Posada/Jsy 6.00
MPR Mark Prior/Jsy 8.00
APU Albert Pujols/Jsy 12.00
MR Manny Ramirez/Jsy 8.00
IR Ivan Rodriguez/Jsy 6.00
CS Curt Schilling/Jsy 8.00
JS Jason Schmidt/Jsy 5.00
AS Alfonso Soriano/Jsy 8.00
SS Sammy Sosa/Jsy 10.00
MTX Mark Teixeira/Jsy 6.00
MTJ Miguel Tejada/Jsy 5.00
FT Frank Thomas/Jsy 8.00
JT Jim Thome/Jsy 8.00
DW Dontrelle Willis/Jsy 5.00
KW Kerry Wood/Jsy 8.00

Past, Present, Future Triple Autograph

NM/M

Production 33 Sets
Red Hot: No Pricing
Production Three Sets
White Hot: No Pricing
Production One Set
Matt Durkin, Mookie Wilson, Mike Piazza 150.00
Hideo Nomo, Scott Elbert, Kirk Gibson 250.00
Josh Fields, Carlton Fisk, Ryan Meaux 80.00
Greg Golson, Steve Carlton, Jim Thome 100.00
Jack Wilson, Neil Walker, Ralph Kiner 80.00
Ryne Sandberg, Mark Prior, Grant Johnson 250.00
Homer Bailey, Johnny Bench, Adam Dunn 150.00
Albert Pujols, Chris Lambert, Stan Musial 300.00
Richie Robnett, Reggie Jackson, Eric Chavez 80.00
Dustin Pedroia, Bill Buckner, Manny Ramirez 60.00

Double Team Autograph Patch Red Hot

No Pricing
Production 22 Sets
White Hot: No Pricing
Production One Set

2004 Fleer InScribed

NM/M

Common Player (1-75): .25
Minor Stars (1-75): .40
Unlisted Stars (1-75): .60
Common Player (76-85): 3.00
Production 1,000 Sets
Numbered to 750 3.00
Not all 750 of each card not released.
Pack (5): 10.00
Box (12): 85.00
1 Vladimir Guerrero 1.00
2 Bartolo Colon .40
3 Troy Glaus .60
4 Richie Sexson .60
5 Randy Johnson 1.00
6 Luis Gonzalez .40
7 J.D. Drew .40
8 Chipper Jones 1.50
9 Andruw Jones .75
10 Melvin Mora .25
11 Miguel Tejada .60
12 Curt Schilling .60
13 Pedro J. Martinez 1.00
14 Nomar Garciaparra 2.50
15 Kerry Wood .75
16 Mark Prior 2.00
17 Sammy Sosa 2.00
18 Frank Thomas .75
19 Magglio Ordonez .40
20 Sean Casey .25
21 Ken Griffey Jr. 1.50
22 Adam Dunn .60
23 Jody Gerut .25
24 Omar Vizquel .25
25 Todd Helton .75
26 Vinny Castilla .25
27 Alex Sanchez .25
28 Ivan Rodriguez .60
29 Dontrelle Willis .40
30 Josh Beckett .75
31 Miguel Cabrera .75
32 Roger Clemens 1.50
33 Andy Pettitte .60
34 Jeff Bagwell .75
35 Ken Harvey .25
36 Carlos Beltran .60
37 Shawn Green .40
38 Hideo Nomo .40
39 Scott Podsednik .25
40 Ben Sheets .40
41 Torii Hunter .60
42 Jacque Jones .25
43 Jose Vidro .25
44 Mike Piazza 1.50
45 Tom Glavine .40
46 Derek Jeter 3.00
47 Alex Rodriguez 2.50
48 Jason Giambi 1.00
49 Hideki Matsui 2.50
50 Eric Chavez .40
51 Barry Zito .60
52 Tim Hudson .40
53 Mark Mulder .40
54 Jim Thome 1.00
55 Pat Burrell .40
56 Chase Utley .40
57 Jason Kendall .40
58 Jack Wilson .25
59 Khalil Greene .75
60 Brian Giles .40
61 Jason Schmidt .40
62 Marquis Grissom .25
63 Ichiro Suzuki 2.00
64 Bret Boone .40

65	Albert Pujols	2.50
66	Scott Rolen	1.00
67	Jim Edmonds	.40
68	Tino Martinez	.25
69	Rocco Baldelli	.60
70	Alfonso Soriano	1.00
71	Michael Young	.25
72	Hank Blalock	.40
73	Roy Halladay	.40
74	Carlos Delgado	.75
75	Vernon Wells	.40
76	Johnny Bench	3.00
77	Reggie Jackson	5.00
78	Al Kaline	3.00
79	Nolan Ryan	10.00
80	Tom Seaver	3.00
81	Robin Yount	6.00
82	Mike Schmidt	5.00
83	Jim Palmer	3.00
84	Harmon Killebrew	5.00
85	Joe Morgan	3.00
86	Kazuo Matsui RC	5.00
87	Luis Gonzalez RC	3.00
88	Yadier Molina RC	4.00
89	Jon Knott RC	3.00
90	Kevin Youkilis	5.00
91	Chris Saenz RC	3.00
92	Andres Blanco RC	3.00
93	David Aardsma	3.00
94	Merkin Valdez RC	3.00
95	Jason Bartlett RC	3.00
96	John Gall RC	3.00
97	Zack Greinke	3.00
98	Scott Hairston	3.00
99	Matt Holliday	4.00
100	Casey Kotchman	5.00

Gold
Veterans (1-75): 2-5X
Rookies (76-100): .75-2X
Production 199 Sets

Red
No Pricing
Production Five Sets

Autographs Silver
NM/M
Common Player: 10.00
Numbered to indicated quantity.
Red: No Pricing
Production 25 Sets
Purple: .5-2X
Numbered to jersey number.

RB	Rocco Baldelli/34	25.00
CB	Carlos Beltran/296	25.00
JB	Jeremy Bonderman/287	10.00
EC	Eric Chavez/322	15.00
EG	Eric Gagne/57	40.00
BG	Brian Giles/134	15.00
LG	Luis Gonzalez/55	15.00
RHL	Roy Halladay/139	15.00
RHR	Rich Harden/235	10.00
TH	Trevor Hoffman/174	15.00
BL	Barry Larkin/140	20.00
JL	Javy Lopez/257	15.00
WM	Wade Miller/195	10.00
TN	Trot Nixon/318	10.00
LO	Lyle Overbay/240	10.00
SP	Scott Podsednik/280	10.00
BR	Brad Radke/168	15.00

Award Winners
NM/M
Common Player:
Production 150 Sets

1	Alex Rodriguez	10.00
2	Eric Gagne	3.00
3	Miguel Tejada	4.00
4	Roy Halladay	3.00
5	Randy Johnson	5.00
6	Barry Zito	4.00
7	Chipper Jones	3.00
8	Ivan Rodriguez	4.00
9	Pedro J. Martinez	5.00
10	Barry Larkin	3.00
11	Dontrelle Willis	3.00
12	Angel Berroa	3.00
13	Kerry Wood	5.00
14	Albert Pujols	8.00
15	Hideo Nomo	3.00

Award Winners Autographs
NM/M
Common Player: 15.00
Numbered to Award Year.
All cards not released for some cards.

AB	Angel Berroa/103	15.00
RH	Roy Halladay/102	20.00
BL	Barry Larkin 95/50	30.00
DW	Dontrelle Willis/103	25.00

Award Winners Jersey Silver
NM/M
Common Player:
Production 175 Sets
Copper: .75-1.5X
Production 99 Sets
Purple: 1-3X
Production 49 Sets

AB	Angel Berroa	5.00
EG	Eric Gagne	8.00
RH	Roy Halladay	5.00
RJ	Randy Johnson	10.00
CJ	Chipper Jones	5.00

BL	Barry Larkin	5.00
PM	Pedro J. Martinez	10.00
HN	Hideo Nomo	5.00
AP	Albert Pujols	15.00
IR	Ivan Rodriguez	8.00
MT	Miguel Tejada	8.00
DW	Dontrelle Willis	5.00
KW	Kerry Wood	10.00
BZ	Barry Zito	8.00

Facsimile Signature Gold

Current (1-75): 3-5X
Retired (76-85): 1-2X
Rookies (86-100): .75-1.5X
Production 199 Sets

Induction Ceremony
NM/M
Common Player: 6.00
Numbered to Year of Induction.

1	Carlton Fisk/100	8.00
2	Tony Perez/100	6.00
3	Nolan Ryan/99	20.00
4	Robin Yount/99	10.00
5	Orlando Cepeda/99	8.00
6	Bill Mazeroski/101	8.00
7	Larry Doby/98	6.00
8	Phil Niekro/97	6.00
9	Jim Bunning/96	6.00
10	Sparky Anderson/100	6.00
11	Phil Rizzuto/94	6.00
12	Rollie Fingers/92	6.00
13	Hal Newhouser/92	6.00
14	Rod Carew/91	8.00
15	Reggie Jackson/93	8.00
16	Tom Seaver/90	8.00
17	Bob Gibson/81	6.00
18	Jim Palmer/90	6.00
19	Joe Morgan/90	6.00
20	Al Kaline/80	6.00

Induction Ceremony Autograph Bronze
NM/M
Common Player: 20.00
Numbered to 50
Silver: No Pricing
Production 15 Sets
Gold: No Pricing
Production Five Sets

JB	Jim Bunning	20.00
OC	Orlando Cepeda/40	20.00
RF	Rollie Fingers	30.00
CF	Carlton Fisk	30.00
BG	Bob Gibson	40.00
AK	Al Kaline	50.00
TP	Tony Perez	30.00

Induction Ceremony Material Silver
NM/M
Common Player: 10.00
Numbered (two-digit) to induction year.
Masterpiece: No Pricing
Production One Set

SA	Sparky Anderson/100	10.00
RC	Rod Carew/91	15.00
OC	Orlando Cepeda/99	10.00
LD	Larry Doby/98	20.00
RF	Rollie Fingers/92	15.00
CF	Carlton Fisk/100	15.00
RJ	Reggie Jackson/93	10.00
AK	Al Kaline/80	20.00
BM	Bill Mazeroski/101	10.00
JM	Joe Morgan/90	15.00
PN	Phil Niekro/97	10.00
JP	Jim Palmer/90	10.00
TP	Tony Perez/100	15.00
PR	Phil Rizzuto/94	20.00
NR	Nolan Ryan/99	25.00
TS	Tom Seaver/90	10.00
RY	Robin Yount/99	10.00

Names of the Game
NM/M
Common Player: 2.00
Production 299 Sets

1	Nomar Garciaparra	8.00
2	Randy Johnson	3.00
3	Hideki Matsui	8.00

4	Frank Thomas	2.00
5	Ivan Rodriguez	2.00
6	Roger Clemens	5.00
7	Chipper Jones	5.00
8	Dontrelle Willis	2.00
9	Luis Gonzalez	2.00
10	Alex Rodriguez	8.00
11	Eric Gagne	2.00
12	Juan Gonzalez	2.00
13	Hideo Nomo	2.00
14	Sean Casey	2.00
15	Greg Maddux	5.00
16	Cal Ripken Jr.	15.00
17	Carl Yastrzemski	5.00
18	Tony Perez	3.00
19	Joe Morgan	3.00
20	Carlton Fisk	3.00
21	Willie McCovey	5.00
22	Al Kaline	5.00
23	Dennis Eckersley	3.00
24	Ted Williams	10.00
25	Willie Stargell	5.00
26	Rollie Fingers	3.00
27	Yogi Berra	2.00
28	Reggie Jackson	5.00
29	Harmon Killebrew	5.00
30	Nolan Ryan	10.00

Names of the Game Autograph Silver
NM/M
Common Player: 15.00
Stated Production 99 Sets
All 99 not released for some cards.
Gold: No Pricing
Stated Production 25 Sets.
All 25 not released for some cards.

SC	Sean Casey	20.00
DE	Dennis Eckersley/90	25.00
RF	Rollie Fingers/90	25.00
CF	Carlton Fisk/50	30.00
LG	Luis Gonzalez/75	15.00
CJ	Chipper Jones/40	40.00
AK	Al Kaline/90	40.00
DW	Dontrelle Willis	25.00

Names of the Game Material Copper

NM/M
Common Player: 5.00
Production 250 Sets
Gold: .5-1.25X
Production 150 Sets
Red: .75-1.5X
Production 79 Sets
Purple: 1-2X
Production 33 Sets

YB	Yogi Berra	10.00
SC	Sean Casey	5.00
RC	Roger Clemens	10.00
DE	Dennis Eckersley	8.00
RF	Rollie Fingers	8.00
CF	Carlton Fisk	8.00
EG	Eric Gagne	10.00
JG	Juan Gonzalez	5.00
LG	Luis Gonzalez	5.00
RJA	Reggie Jackson	10.00
RJO	Randy Johnson	8.00
CJ	Chipper Jones	8.00
AK	Al Kaline	10.00
HK	Harmon Killebrew	10.00
GM	Greg Maddux	15.00
HM	Hideki Matsui	15.00
WM	Willie McCovey	8.00
JM	Joe Morgan	8.00
HN	Hideo Nomo	5.00
CR	Cal Ripken Jr.	30.00
IR	Ivan Rodriguez	5.00
NR	Nolan Ryan	20.00
WS	Willie Stargell	10.00
FT	Frank Thomas	5.00
TW	Ted Williams	25.00
DW	Dontrelle Willis	5.00
CY	Carl Yastrzemski	10.00

Rookie Autographs Notation
NM/M
Common Player: 15.00

Stated Production 750 Sets
75 Notation Cards for each player

87	Luis A. Gonzalez 4/6/04	15.00
89	Jon Knott 5/30/04	15.00
90	Kevin Youkilis 5/15/04	20.00
91	Chris Saenz 4/24/04	15.00
92	Andres Blanco 4/17/04	15.00
94	Merkin Valdez Go Giants	20.00
95	Jason Bartlett Go Twins	20.00
96B	John Gall Go Cards/50	20.00
98	Scott Hairston 5/17/04	15.00
100	Casey Kotchman 5/9/04	25.00

2004 Fleer Legacy

NM/M
Common Player (1-60): 1.50
Minor Stars (1-60): 2.00
Unlisted Stars (1-60): 2.50
Common Rookie (61-75): 4.00
Production 599 Sets
Box (1 Pack, 1 Autographed Baseball): 150.00

1	Angel Berroa	1.50
2	Derek Jeter	8.00
3	Jody Gerut	1.50
4	Curt Schilling	2.50
5	Khalil Greene	3.00
6	Manny Ramirez	3.00
7	Rocco Baldelli	2.50
8	Sammy Sosa	5.00
9	Shawn Green	2.00
10	Austin Kearns	2.50
11	Frank Thomas	3.00
12	Alfonso Soriano	4.00
13	Alex Rodriguez	6.00
14	Carlos Delgado	3.00
15	Chipper Jones	4.00
16	Edgar Martinez	2.00
17	Ivan Rodriguez	2.50
18	Mark Prior	4.00
19	Mike Piazza	4.00
20	Orlando Cabrera	1.50
21	Adam Dunn	2.50
22	Andruw Jones	3.00
23	Eric Chavez	2.00
24	Mark Teixeira	2.00
25	Scott Podsednik	1.50
26	Torii Hunter	2.50
27	Miguel Cabrera	3.00
28	Hideki Matsui	6.00
29	Jose Reyes	1.50
30	Vladimir Guerrero	4.00
31	Albert Pujols	6.00
32	Greg Maddux	4.00
33	Jason Giambi	3.00
34	Randy Johnson	4.00
35	Roger Clemens	6.00
36	Casey Kotchman	2.00
37	Ken Griffey Jr.	4.00
38	Todd Helton	3.00
39	Javy Lopez	1.50
40	Jim Thome	3.00
41	Josh Beckett	3.00
42	Kerry Wood	3.00
43	Scott Rolen	3.00
44	Pat Burrell	2.00
45	Pedro J. Martinez	3.00
46	Barry Zito	2.50
47	Hank Blalock	2.50
48	Hideo Nomo	2.00
49	Jeff Bagwell	3.00
50	Magglio Ordonez	2.00
51	Ichiro Suzuki	5.00
52	Joe Mauer	4.00
53	Richie Sexson	2.50
54	Shannon Stewart	1.50
55	Craig Wilson	1.50
56	Miguel Tejada	2.50
57	Sean Casey	1.50
58	Tom Glavine	2.00
59	Jason Schmidt	2.00
60	Nomar Garciaparra	6.00
61	Kazuo Matsui RC	8.00
62	Justin Leone RC	4.00
63	Merkin Valdez RC	6.00
64	Shingo Takatsu RC	6.00
65	Andres Blanco RC	4.00
66	Angel Chavez RC	4.00
67	Hector Gimenez RC	4.00
68	Akinori Otsuka RC	4.00
69	Jason Bartlett RC	4.00
70	Luis Gonzalez RC	4.00
71	Sean Henn	4.00
72	Mike Rouse	4.00
73	Chris Aguila RC	4.00
74	Aarom Baldiris RC	4.00
75	Jerry Gil RC	4.00

Gold Legacy

Veterans (1-60):	2-4X
Rookies (61-75):	.75-1.5X
Production 50 Sets	

Ultimate Legacy

No Pricing
Production One Set

Franchise Legacy Patch

	NM/M
Common Player:	10.00
Production 99 Sets	
Patch 50:	.5-1.5X
Production 50 Sets	
Patch 25:	No Pricing
Production 25 Sets	
Masterpiece:	No Pricing
Production One Set	
JBA Jeff Bagwell	15.00
JBE Josh Beckett	15.00
RC Roger Clemens	25.00
VG Vladimir Guerrero	15.00
RJ Randy Johnson	20.00
CJ Chipper Jones	20.00
JL Javy Lopez	10.00
GM Greg Maddux	30.00
PM Pedro Martinez	15.00
HM Hideki Matsui	60.00
KM Kazuo Matsui	20.00
DM Don Mattingly	40.00
HN Hideo Nomo	25.00
MP Mike Piazza	20.00
MPR Mark Prior	10.00
AP Albert Pujols	50.00
CR Cal Ripken Jr.	60.00
IR Ivan Rodriguez	15.00
NR Nolan Ryan	50.00
SS Sammy Sosa	15.00
MT Miguel Tejada	10.00
JT Jim Thome	15.00
KW Kerry Wood	15.00

Franchise Dual Patch

No Pricing
Sequentially #'d between 5 & 31.

Franchise Legacy Quad Patch

No Pricing
Sequentially #'d between 2 & 22.

Hit Kings Patch Silver

	NM/M
Common Player:	15.00
Production 99 Sets	
Gold:	.5-1.5X
Production 50 Sets	
Masterpiece:	No Pricing
Production One Set	
JB Jeff Bagwell	15.00
LB Lance Berkman	15.00
HB Hank Blalock	20.00
MC Miguel Cabrera	20.00
CD Carlos Delgado	20.00
AD Adam Dunn	30.00
JG Jason Giambi	15.00
VG Vladimir Guerrero	20.00
CJ Chipper Jones	20.00
AK Austin Kearns	15.00
HM Hideki Matsui	50.00
MP Mike Piazza	25.00
AP Albert Pujols	50.00
MR Manny Ramirez	25.00
SR Scott Rolen	20.00
MS Mike Schmidt	40.00
RS Richie Sexson	15.00
GS Gary Sheffield	20.00
SS Sammy Sosa	20.00
MT Mark Teixeira	15.00
FT Frank Thomas	15.00
JT Jim Thome	25.00

Hit Kings Dual Patch

No Pricing
Sequentially numbered between 7 & 21.

2004 Fleer Patchworks

	NM/M
Common Player (1-90):	.15
Minor Stars:	.40

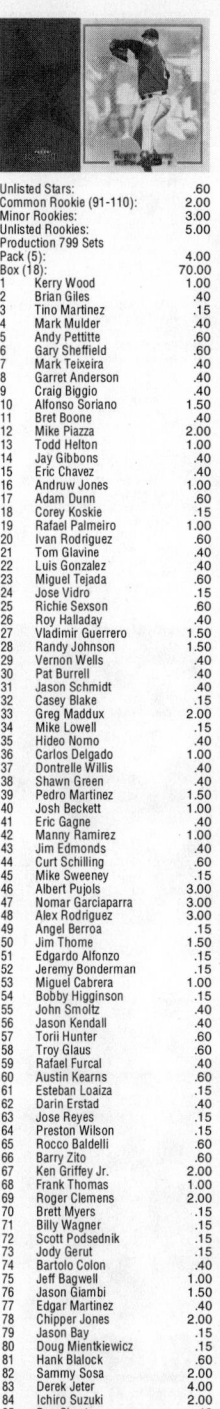

Unlisted Stars:	.60
Common Rookie (91-110):	2.00
Minor Rookies:	3.00
Unlisted Rookies:	5.00
Production 799 Sets	
Pack (5):	4.00
Box (18):	70.00
1 Kerry Wood	1.00
2 Brian Giles	.40
3 Tino Martinez	.15
4 Mark Mulder	.40
5 Andy Pettitte	.60
6 Gary Sheffield	.60
7 Mark Teixeira	.40
8 Garret Anderson	.40
9 Craig Biggio	.40
10 Alfonso Soriano	1.50
11 Bret Boone	.40
12 Mike Piazza	2.00
13 Todd Helton	1.00
14 Jay Gibbons	.40
15 Eric Chavez	.40
16 Andruw Jones	1.00
17 Adam Dunn	.60
18 Corey Koskie	.15
19 Rafael Palmeiro	1.00
20 Ivan Rodriguez	.60
21 Tom Glavine	.40
22 Luis Gonzalez	.40
23 Miguel Tejada	.60
24 Jose Vidro	.15
25 Richie Sexson	.60
26 Roy Halladay	.40
27 Vladimir Guerrero	1.50
28 Randy Johnson	1.50
29 Vernon Wells	.40
30 Pat Burrell	.40
31 Jason Schmidt	.40
32 Casey Blake	.15
33 Greg Maddux	2.00
34 Mike Lowell	.15
35 Hideo Nomo	.40
36 Carlos Delgado	1.00
37 Dontrelle Willis	.40
38 Shawn Green	.40
39 Pedro Martinez	1.50
40 Josh Beckett	1.00
41 Eric Gagne	.40
42 Manny Ramirez	1.00
43 Jim Edmonds	.40
44 Curt Schilling	1.00
45 Mike Sweeney	.15
46 Albert Pujols	3.00
47 Nomar Garciaparra	3.00
48 Alex Rodriguez	3.00
49 Angel Berroa	.15
50 Jim Thome	1.50
51 Edgardo Alfonzo	.15
52 Jeremy Bonderman	.15
53 Miguel Cabrera	1.00
54 Bobby Higginson	.15
55 John Smoltz	.40
56 Jason Kendall	.40
57 Torii Hunter	.60
58 Troy Glaus	.60
59 Rafael Furcal	.40
60 Austin Kearns	.60
61 Esteban Loaiza	.15
62 Darin Erstad	.40
63 Jose Reyes	.60
64 Preston Wilson	.15
65 Rocco Baldelli	.60
66 Barry Zito	.60
67 Ken Griffey Jr.	2.00
68 Frank Thomas	1.00
69 Roger Clemens	2.00
70 Brett Myers	.15
71 Billy Wagner	.15
72 Scott Podsednik	.15
73 Jody Gerut	.15
74 Bartolo Colon	.40
75 Jeff Bagwell	1.00
76 Jason Giambi	1.50
77 Edgar Martinez	.40
78 Chipper Jones	2.00
79 Jason Bay	.15
80 Doug Mientkiewicz	.15
81 Hank Blalock	.60
82 Sammy Sosa	2.00
83 Derek Jeter	4.00
84 Ichiro Suzuki	2.00
85 Ben Sheets	.40
86 Magglio Ordonez	.40
87 Carlos Beltran	.40
88 Mark Prior	2.00
89 Sean Burroughs	.15
90 Tim Hudson	.40
91 Hector Gimenez RC	5.00
92 Khalil Greene RC	5.00
93 Rickie Weeks	8.00
94 Delmon Young	10.00
95 Donald Kelly RC	3.00

96 Chad Bentz RC	3.00
97 Greg Dobbs RC	3.00
98 John Gall RC	3.00
99 Cory Sullivan RC	3.00
100 Kazuo Matsui RC	8.00
101 Graham Koonce RC	3.00
102 Jason Bartlett RC	5.00
103 Angel Chavez RC	2.00
104 Ronny Cedeno RC	3.00
105 Jerry Gil RC	3.00
106 Ivan Ochoa RC	3.00
107 Ruddy Yan RC	4.00
108 Mike Gosling RC	2.00
109 Alfredo Simon RC	2.00
110 Koyie Hill RC	2.00

Ruby

Ruby (1-90):	3-10X
Ruby (91-110):	.5-2X
Production 50 Sets	

Autoworks

	NM/M
Common Player:	10.00
Inserted 1:54	
Parallel:	.5-1.25X
Production 100 Sets	
Patch	
Production 10 Sets	
1 Garret Anderson/145	15.00
2 Josh Beckett/148	30.00
3 Angel Berroa/145	10.00
4 Eric Gagne/193	20.00
5 Jody Gerut/376	10.00
6 Roy Halladay/286	10.00
7 Mark Mulder/190	15.00
8 Andy Pettitte/148	30.00
9 Scott Podsednik/146	20.00
10 Albert Pujols/193	120.00
11 Grady Sizemore/263	25.00
12 Miguel Tejada/164	25.00

By The Numbers

	NM/M
Common Player:	3.00
Inserted 1:24	
Patch:	3-8X
Production 100 Sets	
1 Albert Pujols	8.00
2 Derek Jeter	10.00
3 Mike Piazza	8.00
4 Nomar Garciaparra	8.00
5 Eric Gagne	4.00
6 Sammy Sosa	6.00
7 Josh Beckett	4.00
8 Vladimir Guerrero	5.00
9 Jose Reyes	3.00
10 Bret Boone	3.00
11 Alex Rodriguez	8.00
12 Randy Johnson	6.00
13 Chipper Jones	6.00
14 Tim Hudson	4.00
15 Rocco Baldelli	4.00

Game-Used Level 1

	NM/M
Common Player:	6.00
Production 200 Sets	
Level 2:	1-1.5X
Production 100 Sets	
Patch:	1-2X
Production 50 Sets	
1 Albert Pujols	15.00
2 Andy Pettitte	6.00
3 Dontrelle Willis	6.00
4 Mike Piazza	10.00
5 Barry Zito	6.00
6 Troy Glaus	6.00
7 Carlos Delgado	8.00
8 Torii Hunter	6.00
9 Roy Halladay	6.00
10 Andruw Jones	8.00
11 Garret Anderson	6.00
12 Larry Walker	6.00
13 Shawn Green	6.00
14 Bernie Williams	6.00
15 Alfonso Soriano	10.00
16 Bret Boone	6.00
17 Hank Blalock	6.00
18 Jose Reyes	6.00
19 Mark Prior	10.00

Licensed Apparel

	NM/M
Common Player:	5.00
Production 300 Sets	
Team Name:	1-2X
Production 150 Sets	
Number:	1-2X
Production 100 Sets	
Nameplate:	1-3X
Production 50 Sets	
Jersey Tags:	
Production 10 Sets	
MLB Logo	
Production One Set	
1 Albert Pujols	15.00
2 Derek Jeter	18.00
3 Alex Rodriguez	15.00
4 Jim Thome	8.00
5 Mike Piazza	10.00
6 Dontrelle Willis	5.00
7 Torii Hunter	5.00
8 Tim Hudson	5.00
9 Sammy Sosa	12.00
10 Troy Glaus	5.00
11 Andruw Jones	8.00
12 Austin Kearns	5.00
13 Jeff Bagwell	8.00
14 Mark Prior	10.00
15 Bret Boone	5.00

National Pastime

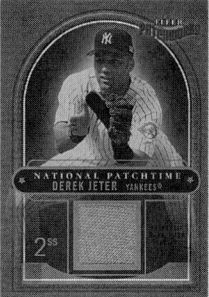

	NM/M
Common Player:	5.00
Production 250 Sets	
Jersey:	1-1.5X
Production 350 Sets	
Gold Jersey:	1-2X
Production 200 Sets	
Patch:	1-3X
Production 100 Sets	
1 Albert Pujols	15.00
2 Alex Rodriguez	15.00
3 Derek Jeter	18.00
4 Nomar Garciaparra	15.00
5 Jim Thome	8.00
6 Chipper Jones	10.00
7 Mark Prior	10.00
8 Ichiro Suzuki	12.00
9 Jeff Bagwell	6.00
10 Troy Glaus	5.00
11 Randy Johnson	8.00
12 Sammy Sosa	12.00
13 Austin Kearns	5.00
14 Miguel Cabrera	6.00
15 Vladimir Guerrero	8.00

Stitches In Time

	NM/M
Common Player:	2.00
Inserted 1:12	
Jersey:	
Production 350 Sets	
Patch:	
Production 150 Sets	
1 Albert Pujols	5.00
2 Alex Rodriguez	5.00
3 Derek Jeter	6.00
4 Nomar Garciaparra	5.00
5 Jim Thome	3.00
6 Chipper Jones	3.00
7 Mark Prior	4.00
8 Eric Gagne	2.00
9 Jeff Bagwell	3.00
10 Troy Glaus	2.00
11 Randy Johnson	3.00
12 Sammy Sosa	4.00
13 Austin Kearns	2.00

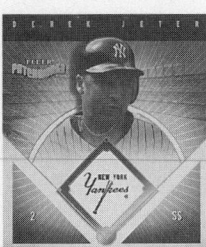

STITCHES IN TIME

NEW YORK YANKEES™

14	Miguel Cabrera	2.00
15	Vladimir Guerrero	3.00
16	Mike Piazza	3.00
17	Jason Giambi	3.00
18	Tim Hudson	2.00
19	Carlos Delgado	3.00
20	Rocco Baldelli	2.00
21	Ichiro Suzuki	4.00
22	Barry Zito	2.00
23	Pedro Martinez	3.00
24	Torii Hunter	2.00
25	Andruw Jones	3.00

2004 Fleer Platinum

Vladimir Guerrero

MONTREAL EXPOS™ • OUTFIELD

	NM/M
Complete Set (200):	35.00
Common Player:	.15
Common SP (136-151):	.50
Inserted 1:3	
Pack (7):	2.00
Jumbo Pack (20):	5.00
Box (18 + 4 Jumbo):	55.00
1	Luis Castillo	.15
2	Preston Wilson	.15
3	Johan Santana	.15
4	Fred McGriff	.25
5	Albert Pujols	1.50
6	Reggie Sanders	.15
7	Ivan Rodriguez	.40
8	Roy Halladay	.25
9	Brian Giles	.25
10	Bernie Williams	.40
11	Barry Larkin	.25
12	Marlon Anderson	.15
13	Ramon Ortiz	.15
14	Luis Matos	.15
15	Esteban Loaiza	.15
16	Orlando Cabrera	.15
17	Jamie Moyer	.15
18	Tino Martinez	.15
19	Josh Beckett	.25
20	Derek Jeter	2.00
21	Derek Lowe	.15
22	Jack Wilson	.15
23	Bret Boone	.25
24	Matt Morris	.15
25	Javier Vazquez	.25
26	Joe Crede	.15
27	Jose Vidro	.15
28	Mike Piazza	1.00
29	Curt Schilling	.40
30	Alex Rodriguez	1.50
31	John Olerud	.25
32	Dontrelle Willis	.25
33	Larry Walker	.25
34	Joe Randa	.15
35	Paul LoDuca	.15
36	Marlon Byrd	.15
37	Bo Hart	.15
38	Rafael Palmeiro	.50
39	Garret Anderson	.40
40	Tom Glavine	.25
41	Ichiro Suzuki	1.25
42	Derek Lee	.25
43	Lance Berkman	.25
44	Nomar Garciaparra	1.50
45	Mike Sweeney	.15
46	A.J. Burnett	.15

47	Sean Casey	.15
48	Eric Gagne	.25
49	Joel Pineiro	.15
50	Russ Ortiz	.15
51	Placido Polanco	.15
52	Sammy Sosa	1.25
53	Mark Teixeira	.25
54	Randy Wolf	.15
55	Vladimir Guerrero	.75
56	Tim Hudson	.25
57	Lew Ford	.15
58	Carlos Delgado	.50
59	Darin Erstad	.25
60	Mike Lieberthal	.15
61	Craig Biggio	.25
62	Ryan Klesko	.25
63	C.C. Sabathia	.15
64	Carlos Lee	.25
65	Al Leiter	.15
66	Brandon Webb	.15
67	Jacque Jones	.15
68	Kerry Wood	.50
69	Omar Vizquel	.25
70	Jeremy Bonderman	.15
71	Kevin Brown	.25
72	Richie Sexson	.40
73	Zach Day	.15
74	Mike Mussina	.40
75	Sidney Ponson	.15
76	Andruw Jones	.50
77	Woody Williams	.15
78	Kazuhiro Sasaki	.15
79	Matt Clement	.15
80	Shea Hillenbrand	.15
81	Bartolo Colon	.25
82	Ken Griffey Jr.	1.00
83	Todd Helton	.50
84	Dmitri Young	.15
85	Richard Hidalgo	.15
86	Carlos Beltran	.25
87	Brad Wilkerson	.15
88	Andy Pettitte	.40
89	Miguel Tejada	.40
90	Edgar Martinez	.25
91	Vernon Wells	.25
92	Magglio Ordonez	.25
93	Tony Batista	.15
94	Jose Reyes	.15
95	Matt Stairs	.15
96	Manny Ramirez	.50
97	Carlos Pena	.15
98	A.J. Pierzynski	.15
99	Jim Thome	.75
100	Aubrey Huff	.15
101	Roberto Alomar	.40
102	Luis Gonzalez	.25
103	Chipper Jones	1.00
104	Jay Gibbons	.25
105	Adam Dunn	.40
106	Jay Payton	.15
107	Scott Podsednik	.40
108	Roy Oswalt	.25
109	Milton Bradley	.15
110	Shawn Green	.25
111	Ryan Wagner	.15
112	Eric Chavez	.25
113	Pat Burrell	.25
114	Frank Thomas	.50
115	Jason Kendall	.25
116	Jake Peavy	.15
117	Mike Cameron	.15
118	Jim Edmonds	.25
119	Hank Blalock	.40
120	Troy Glaus	.40
121	Jeff Kent	.25
122	Jason Schmidt	.25
123	Corey Patterson	.15
124	Austin Kearns	.40
125	Edwin Jackson	.15
126	Alfonso Soriano	.75
127	Bobby Abreu	.25
128	Scott Rolen	.75
129	Jeff Bagwell	.50
130	Shannon Stewart	.15
131	Rich Aurilia	.15
132	Ty Wigginton	.15
133	Randy Johnson	.75
134	Rocco Baldelli	.40
135	Hideo Nomo	.25
136	Greg Maddux	2.00
137	Johnny Damon	1.50
138	Mark Prior	.75
139	Corey Koskie	.50
140	Miguel Cabrera	1.50
141	Hideki Matsui	2.00
142	Jose Cruz	.50
143	Barry Zito	1.00
144	Javy Lopez	.50
145	Jason Varitek	1.00
146	Moises Alou	1.00
147	Torii Hunter	1.00
148	Juan Encarnacion	.50
149	Jorge Posada	1.00
150	Marquis Grissom	.50
151	Rich Harden	1.00
152	Gary Sheffield	4.00
153	Pedro J. Martinez	5.00
154	Brad Radke	3.00
155	Mike Lowell	3.00
156	Jason Giambi	4.00
157	Mark Mulder	4.00
158	Ben Weber	.15
159	Mark DeRosa	.15
160	Melvin Mora	3.00
161	Bill Mueller	.15

162	Jon Garland	.15
163	Jody Gerut	.15
164	Javier Lopez	.15
165	Craig Monroe	.15
166	Juan Pierre	.15
167	Morgan Ensberg	.15
168	Angel Berroa	.25
169	Geoff Jenkins	.25
170	Matt LeCroy	.15
171	Livan Hernandez	.15
172	Jason L. Phillips	.15
173	Mariano Rivera	.25
174	Erubiel Durazo	.15
175	Jason Michaels	.15
176	Kip Wells	.15
177	Ray Durham	.15
178	Randy Winn	.15
179	Edgar Renteria	.15
180	Carl Crawford	.15
181	Laynce Nix	.15
182	Greg Myers	.15
183	Delmon Young, Chad Gaudin	1.00
184	Humberto Quintero, Bernie Castro	.50
185	Craig Brazell, Daniel Garcia	.50
186	Ryan Wing, Francisco Cruceta	.50
187	William Bergolla, Josh Hall	.50
188	Clint Barnes, Garrett Atkins	.50
189	Chris Bootcheck, Richard Fischer	.50
190	Edgar Gonzalez, Matt Kata	.50
191	Andrew Brown, Koyie Hill	.50
192	John Gall, Dan Haren	.50
193	Chad Bentz, Luis Ayala	.50
194	Hector Gimenez, Eric Bruntlett	.50
195	Boof Bonser, Rob Bowen	.50
196	Chris Snelling, Rett Johnson	.50
197	Rickie Weeks, Adam Morrissey	1.00
198	Noah Lowry, Todd Linden	.50
199	Chris Waters, Brett Evert	.50
200	Jorge DePaula, Chien-Ming Wang	.50

Finish

Barry Zito
OAKLAND ATHLETICS™ • PITCHER

Stars (1-200):	4-6X
Production 100 Sets	

Big Signs

RANGERS
RODRIGUEZ
SS 3

	NM/M
Complete Set (15):	25.00
Common Player:	.75
Inserted 1:9	
1	Albert Pujols	3.00
2	Derek Jeter	4.00
3	Mike Piazza	2.00
4	Jason Giambi	1.50
5	Ichiro Suzuki	2.50

6	Nomar Garciaparra	3.00
7	Mark Prior	2.00
8	Randy Johnson	1.50
9	Greg Maddux	2.00
10	Sammy Sosa	2.50
11	Ken Griffey Jr.	2.00
12	Dontrelle Willis	.75
13	Alex Rodriguez	3.00
14	Chipper Jones	2.00
15	Hank Blalock	.75

Big Signs Autographs

	NM/M
Production 100	
Hank Blalock	25.00
Mark Prior	
Albert Pujols	150.00
Dontrelle Willis	25.00

Classic Combinations

	NM/M
Complete Set (10):	50.00
Common Player:	3.00
Inserted 1:108	
1	Ivan Rodriguez, Mike Piazza	6.00
2	Alex Rodriguez, Sammy Sosa	8.00
3	Dontrelle Willis, Angel Berroa	3.00
4	Nomar Garciaparra, Derek Jeter	10.00
5	Ichiro Suzuki, Hideo Nomo	6.00
6	Josh Beckett, Kerry Wood	4.00
7	Albert Pujols, Carlos Delgado	8.00
8	Alfonso Soriano, Joe Morgan	4.00
9	Jason Giambi, Reggie Jackson	4.00
10	Nolan Ryan, Tom Seaver	10.00

Clubhouse Memorabilia

	NM/M
Common Player:	5.00
Inserted 1:24	
Rocco Baldelli	10.00
Josh Beckett	8.00
Hank Blalock	6.00
Nomar Garciaparra	12.00
Jason Giambi	8.00
Vladimir Guerrero	8.00
Todd Helton	6.00
Torii Hunter	5.00
Derek Jeter	15.00
Chipper Jones	8.00
Austin Kearns	6.00
Greg Maddux	10.00
Hideo Nomo	8.00
Mike Piazza	10.00
Mark Prior	10.00
Albert Pujols	12.00
Alex Rodriguez	10.00
Richie Sexson	5.00
Alfonso Soriano	6.00
Sammy Sosa	12.00
Miguel Tejada	5.00
Jim Thome	8.00
Dontrelle Willis	8.00

Clubhouse Memorabilia Dual

	NM/M
Common Player:	10.00
Production 50 Sets	
Hank Blalock	15.00
Nomar Garciaparra	30.00
Jason Giambi	15.00
Vladimir Guerrero	20.00
Todd Helton	20.00
Torii Hunter	15.00
Derek Jeter	35.00
Chipper Jones	15.00
Austin Kearns	10.00
Greg Maddux	30.00
Hideo Nomo	25.00
Mark Prior	30.00
Albert Pujols	30.00
Alex Rodriguez	25.00
Sammy Sosa	20.00
Jim Thome	20.00

Nameplates

	NM/M
Common Player:	8.00

Inserted 1:4 Jumbo
Varying quantities produced

1	Austin Kearns	10.00
2	Juan Pierre	10.00
3	Albert Pujols	30.00
4	Manny Ramirez	15.00
5	Kerry Wood	20.00
6	Alex Rodriguez	20.00
8	Barry Zito	10.00
9	Hee Seop Choi	8.00
10	Kevin Brown	10.00
11	Jose Reyes	15.00
12	Marlon Byrd	10.00
13	Nomar Garciaparra	20.00
14	Josh Beckett	15.00
16	Hideo Nomo	15.00
19	Randy Johnson	15.00
20	Hank Blalock	12.00
21	Tom Glavine/25	25.00
22	Luis Castillo	8.00
23	Mark Teixeira	12.00
24	Gary Sheffield	10.00
25	Richie Sexson	10.00
26	Miguel Cabrera	20.00
27	Sammy Sosa	25.00
28	Curt Schilling	10.00
30	Chipper Jones	20.00

Portraits

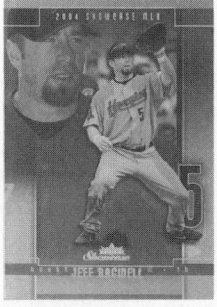

	NM/M
Complete Set (10):	25.00
Common Player:	1.50

Inserted 1:18

1	Jason Giambi	1.50
2	Nomar Garciaparra	4.00
3	Vladimir Guerrero	1.50
4	Mark Prior	3.00
5	Jim Thome	1.50
6	Derek Jeter	5.00
7	Sammy Sosa	3.00
8	Alex Rodriguez	4.00
9	Greg Maddux	2.50
10	Albert Pujols	4.00

Portraits Jersey

	NM/M
Common Player:	8.00

Inserted 1:48

Nomar Garciaparra	15.00
Jason Giambi	8.00
Vladimir Guerrero	8.00
Derek Jeter	15.00
Greg Maddux	8.00
Mark Prior	15.00
Albert Pujols	15.00
Alex Rodriguez	10.00
Sammy Sosa	12.00
Jim Thome	8.00

Portraits Patch

	NM/M
Common Player:	10.00

Production 100 Sets

Nomar Garciaparra	20.00
Jason Giambi	10.00
Vladimir Guerrero	10.00
Derek Jeter	25.00
Mark Prior	20.00
Albert Pujols	30.00
Alex Rodriguez	15.00
Sammy Sosa	20.00
Jim Thome	12.00

Scouting Report

	NM/M
Complete Set (15):	35.00

Common Player:	1.50

Production 400 Sets

1	Josh Beckett	2.00
2	Todd Helton	2.00
3	Rocco Baldelli	2.00
4	Pedro J. Martinez	3.00
5	Jeff Bagwell	2.00
6	Mark Prior	4.00
7	Ichiro Suzuki	4.00
8	Barry Zito	2.00
9	Manny Ramirez	2.00
10	Miguel Cabrera	2.00
11	Richie Sexson	1.50
12	Hideki Matsui	8.00
13	Magglio Ordonez	1.50
14	Brandon Webb	1.50
15	Kerry Wood	2.00

Scouting Report Memorabilia

	NM/M
Common Player:	6.00

Production 250 Sets

Jeff Bagwell	8.00
Rocco Baldelli	8.00
Josh Beckett	8.00
Todd Helton	6.00
Pedro J. Martinez	8.00
Mark Prior	10.00
Manny Ramirez	6.00
Brandon Webb	6.00
Kerry Wood	8.00

2004 Fleer Showcase

	NM/M
Complete Set (130):	
Common Player:	.25
Common SP (101-130):	1.00

Inserted 1:6

Pack (5):	4.50
Box (24):	90.00

1	Corey Patterson	.25
2	Ken Griffey Jr.	1.50
3	Preston Wilson	.40
4	Juan Pierre	.25
5	Jose Reyes	.50
6	Jason Schmidt	.40
7	Rocco Baldelli	.50
8	Carlos Delgado	.75
9	Hideki Matsui	2.50
10	Nomar Garciaparra	2.00
11	Brian Giles	.40
12	Darin Erstad	.40
13	Larry Walker	.40
14	Bernie Williams	.50
15	Laynce Nix	.25
16	Manny Ramirez	.75
17	Magglio Ordonez	.50
18	Khalil Greene	.25
19	Jim Edmonds	.40
20	Troy Glaus	.50
21	Curt Schilling	.50
22	Chipper Jones	1.50
23	Sammy Sosa	2.00
24	Frank Thomas	.75
25	Todd Helton	.75
26	Craig Biggio	.40
27	Shannon Stewart	.25
28	Mark Mulder	.40
29	Mike Lieberthal	.25
30	Reggie Sanders	.25
31	Edgar Martinez	.25
32	Bo Hart	.25
33	Mark Teixeira	.40
34	Jay Gibbons	.25
35	Roberto Alomar	.50
36	Kip Wells	.25
37	J.D. Drew	.25
38	Jason Varitek	.25
39	Craig Monroe	.25
40	Roy Oswalt	.40
41	Edgardo Alfonzo	.25
42	Roy Halladay	.50
43	Gary Sheffield	.50
44	Lance Berkman	.50
45	Torii Hunter	.50
46	Vladimir Guerrero	1.00
47	Marlon Byrd	.25
48	Austin Kearns	.50
49	Angel Berroa	.25
50	Geoff Jenkins	.50
51	Aubrey Huff	.25
52	Dontrelle Willis	.50
53	Tony Batista	.25
54	Shawn Green	.40
55	Jason Kendall	.25
56	Garret Anderson	.50
57	Andruw Jones	.75
58	Dmitri Young	.25
59	Richie Sexson	.25
60	Jorge Posada	.50
61	Bobby Abreu	.40
62	Vernon Wells	.40
63	Javy Lopez	.40
64	Josh Beckett	.75
65	Eric Chavez	.40
66	Tim Salmon	.40
67	Brandon Webb	.40
68	Pedro J. Martinez	1.00
69	Kerry Wood	1.00
70	Jose Vidro	.25
71	Alfonso Soriano	1.00
72	Barry Zito	.50
73	Sean Burroughs	.25
74	Jamie Moyer	.25
75	Luis Gonzalez	.40
76	Adam Dunn	.50
77	Mike Piazza	1.50
78	Pat Burrell	.50
79	Scott Rolen	1.00
80	Milton Bradley	.25
81	Mike Sweeney	.25
82	Hank Blalock	.50
83	Esteban Loaiza	.25
84	Hideo Nomo	.50
85	Derek Jeter	3.00
86	Albert Pujols	2.50
87	Greg Maddux	1.50
88	Mark Prior	1.50
89	Mike Lowell	.25
90	Jeff Bagwell	.75
91	Scott Podsednik	.50
92	Tom Glavine	.50
93	Jason Giambi	1.00
94	Jim Thome	1.00
95	Ichiro Suzuki	2.00
96	Randy Johnson	1.00
97	Omar Vizquel	.25
98	Ivan Rodriguez	.50
99	Miguel Tejada	.50
100	Alex Rodriguez	2.50
101	Rickie Weeks	3.00
102	Chad Gaudin	1.00
103	Rich Harden	1.00
104	Edwin Jackson	1.50
105	Chien-Ming Wang	1.00
106	Matt Kata	1.00
107	Delmon Young	3.00
108	Ryan Wagner	1.00
109	Jeff Duncan	1.00
110	Prentice Redman	1.00
111	Clint Barmes	1.00
112	Jeremy Guthrie	1.00
113	Brian Stokes	1.00
114	David DeJesus	1.00
115	Felix Sanchez	1.00
116	Josh Stewart	1.00
117	Daniel Garcia	1.00
118	Jon Leicester	1.00
119	Francisco Cruceta	1.00
120	Oscar Villarreal	1.00
121	Michael Hessman	1.00
122	Michel Hernandez	1.00
123	Richard Fischer	1.00
124	Robby Hammock	1.00
125	Guillermo Quiroz	1.00
126	Craig Brazell	1.00
127	Wilfredo Ledezma	1.00
128	Josh Willingham	1.00
129	Ramon Nivar	1.00
130	Matt Diaz	1.00

Legacy

Stars (1-100):	4-8X
SP's (101-130):	1-3X

Production 99 Sets

Masterpiece

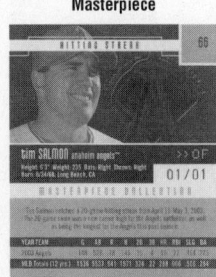

No Pricing
Production One Set

Albert Pujols Legacy Collection Jersey

	NM/M

Varying quantities produced

3	Albert Pujols/30	40.00
4	Albert Pujols/40	30.00
5	Albert Pujols/50	30.00
6	Albert Pujols/60	30.00
7	Albert Pujols/70	25.00
8	Albert Pujols/80	25.00
9	Albert Pujols/90	25.00
10	Albert Pujols/100	25.00

Albert Pujols Legacy Collection Autograph

Varying quantities produced
No Pricing

Albert Pujols Legacy Collection

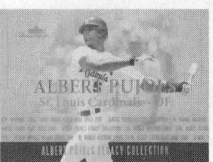

	NM/M
Complete Set (10):	60.00
Common Pujols:	8.00

Production 1,000 Sets

1-10	Albert Pujols	8.00

Baseball's Best

	NM/M
Complete Set (15):	20.00
Common Player:	.75

Inserted 1:24

1	Derek Jeter	4.00
2	Mark Prior	2.00
3	Mike Piazza	2.50
4	Jeff Bagwell	1.00
5	Kerry Wood	1.00
6	Ivan Rodriguez	1.00
7	Albert Pujols	3.00
8	Jim Thome	1.50
9	Sammy Sosa	2.50
10	Vladimir Guerrero	1.50
11	Eric Gagne	.75
12	Randy Johnson	1.50
13	Todd Helton	1.00
14	Chipper Jones	2.00
15	Alex Rodriguez	2.00

Baseball's Best Memorabilia

	NM/M
Common Player:	5.00

Inserted 1:72

Parallel 150:	.75-1.5X

Production 150

Parallel 50:	1.5-2X
Patch Versions:	2-4X

Production 50

Derek Jeter	15.00
Mark Prior	10.00
Mike Piazza	10.00
Jeff Bagwell	8.00
Kerry Wood	8.00
Ivan Rodriguez	5.00
Albert Pujols	15.00
Jim Thome	8.00
Sammy Sosa	10.00
Vladimir Guerrero	8.00
Eric Gagne	8.00
Randy Johnson	8.00
Todd Helton	8.00
Chipper Jones	8.00
Alex Rodriguez	10.00

Grace

	NM/M
Complete Set (20):	20.00

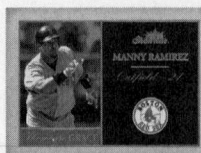

Common Player:		.75
Inserted 1:12		
1	Kerry Wood	1.50
2	Derek Jeter	4.00
3	Nomar Garciaparra	3.00
4	Mike Piazza	2.50
5	Mark Prior	2.00
6	Jose Reyes	1.00
7	Dontrelle Willis	.75
8	Pedro J. Martinez	1.50
9	Tim Hudson	.75
10	Troy Glaus	.75
11	Hank Blalock	1.00
12	Albert Pujols	3.00
13	Juan Pierre	.75
14	Angel Berroa	.75
15	Rocco Baldelli	1.00
16	Carlos Delgado	1.00
17	Manny Ramirez	1.00
18	Alex Rodriguez	3.00
19	Andruw Jones	1.00
20	Luis Gonzalez	.75

Grace Memorabilia

		NM/M
Common Player:		5.00
Inserted 1:48		
Parallel 150:		1-1.5X
Production 150		
Patch:		1.5-2.5X
Production 50		
	Derek Jeter	15.00
	Nomar Garciaparra	10.00
	Mike Piazza	10.00
	Mark Prior	10.00
	Dontrelle Willis	5.00
	Pedro J. Martinez	8.00
	Albert Pujols	15.00
	Rocco Baldelli	8.00
	Manny Ramirez	8.00
	Alex Rodriguez	10.00

Hot Gloves

		NM/M
Common Player:		8.00
Inserted 1:288		
1	Derek Jeter	40.00
2	Nomar Garciaparra	30.00
3	Alex Rodriguez	30.00
4	Chipper Jones	15.00
5	Torii Hunter	8.00
6	Ichiro Suzuki	35.00
7	Mark Prior	20.00
8	Vladimir Guerrero	15.00
9	Albert Pujols	30.00
10	Ivan Rodriguez	10.00
11	Hideki Matsui	30.00
12	Sammy Sosa	25.00
13	Jim Thome	15.00
14	Rocco Baldelli	10.00
15	Jeff Bagwell	10.00

Hot Gloves Memorabilia

		NM/M
Common Player:		20.00
All jerseys unless noted.		
Production 50 Sets		
	Derek Jeter	60.00
	Nomar Garciaparra	50.00
	Alex Rodriguez	40.00
	Chipper Jones	40.00
	Ichiro Suzuki/Base	65.00
	Mark Prior	25.00
	Vladimir Guerrero	30.00
	Albert Pujols	50.00
	Ivan Rodriguez	20.00
	Hideki Matsui/Base	60.00
	Sammy Sosa	40.00
	Jim Thome	20.00
	Rocco Baldelli	20.00
	Jeff Bagwell	20.00

Sweet Sigs

		NM/M
Common Player:		6.00
Inserted 1:24		
Sweet Sigs Game-Used:		No Pricing
Production 5		
	Hank Blalock/824	20.00
	Taylor Bucholz/Redemp.	6.00
	John Gall/Redemp.	8.00
	Bo Hart/667	15.00
	Torii Hunter/294	15.00
	Austin Kearns/224	20.00
	Wilfredo Ledezma/376	6.00
	Mike Lowell/44	15.00
	Corey Patterson/176	15.00
	Carlos Pena/48	10.00
	Albert Pujols/Redemp.	120.00
	Jose Reyes/115	40.00
	Scott Rolen/200	25.00
	Michael Ryan/288	12.00

	Miguel Tejada/52	20.00
	Ryan Wagner/Redemp.	10.00
	Brandon Webb/1,000	15.00
	Rickie Weeks/416	15.00
	Josh Willingham/180	6.00
	Dontrelle Willis/26	60.00
	Delmon Young/1,000	25.00
	Barry Zito/248	25.00

2004 Fleer Sweet Sigs

		NM/M
Common Player (1-75):		.20
Minor Stars (1-75):		.40
Unlisted Star (1-75):		.60
Common Future Sig-cess (76-100):		3.00
Future Sig-cess Production 999 Sets		
Pack (6):		5.00
Box (12):		80.00
1	Manny Ramirez	1.00
2	Frank Thomas	1.00
3	Josh Beckett	1.00
4	Shawn Green	.40
5	Tom Glavine	.40
6	Marquis Grissom	.20
7	Nomar Garciaparra	3.00
8	Magglio Ordonez	.40
9	Alex Rodriguez	3.00
10	Chipper Jones	2.00
11	Jody Gerut	.20
12	Dontrelle Willis	.40
13	Lance Berkman	.40
14	Jose Vidro	.20
15	Barry Zito	.60
16	Jason Kendall	.40
17	Scott Rolen	1.50
18	Troy Glaus	.60
19	Brandon Webb	.20
20	Tim Hudson	.40
21	Shannon Stewart	.20
22	Darin Erstad	.40
23	Curt Schilling	.60
24	Bret Boone	.40
25	Richie Sexson	.60
26	Hideki Matsui	3.00
27	Albert Pujols	3.00
28	Greg Maddux	2.00
29	Austin Kearns	1.00
30	Todd Helton	1.00
31	Miguel Cabrera	1.00
32	Jeff Bagwell	1.00
33	Marlon Byrd	.20
34	Ichiro Suzuki	2.50
35	Rocco Baldelli	.60
36	Garret Anderson	.40
37	Javy Lopez	.40
38	Kerry Wood	1.00
39	Adam Dunn	.60
40	Geoff Jenkins	.40
41	Derek Jeter	4.00
42	Rich Harden	.20
43	Alfonso Soriano	1.50
44	Ken Griffey Jr.	2.00
45	Ivan Rodriguez	.60
46	Pedro J. Martinez	1.50
47	Andy Pettitte	.60
48	Gary Sheffield	.60
49	Brian Giles	.40
50	Carlos Delgado	1.00
51	Mike Piazza	2.00
52	Hank Blalock	.60
53	Roger Clemens	2.00
54	Scott Podsednik	.20
55	Torii Hunter	.60
56	Jose Reyes	.20
57	Jim Thome	1.50
58	Jason Schmidt	.40
59	Jose Cruz	.20
60	Mark Teixeira	.40
61	Randy Johnson	1.50
62	Miguel Tejada	.60
63	Sammy Sosa	2.50
64	Larry Walker	.40
65	Carl Everett	.20
66	Luis Castillo	.20
67	Jason Giambi	1.50
68	Mike Sweeney	.20
69	Andruw Jones	1.00
70	Vladimir Guerrero	1.50
71	J.D. Drew	.40
72	Mark Prior	2.00
73	Angel Berroa	.20

74	Hideo Nomo	.40
75	Roy Halladay	.40
76	John Gall RC	3.00
77	Angel Chavez RC	3.00
78	Alfredo Simon RC	3.00
79	Merkin Valdez RC	3.00
80	Chad Bentz RC	3.00
81	Justin Leone RC	6.00
82	Mike Rouse	3.00
83	Aarom Baldiris RC	3.00
84	Chris Shelton RC	6.00
85	Akinori Otsuka RC	8.00
86	Ruddy Yan RC	3.00
87	Ramon Ramirez RC	3.00
88	Hector Gimenez RC	6.00
89	Mike Gosling	3.00
90	Greg Dobbs RC	3.00
91	Kazuo Matsui RC	8.00
92	Donald Kelly RC	6.00
93	Shingo Takatsu RC	6.00
94	Ivan Ochoa RC	3.00
95	Chris Aguila RC	5.00
96	Jason Bartlett RC	5.00
97	Graham Koonce	5.00
98	Ronny Cedeno RC	6.00
99	Jerome Gamble RC	3.00
100	Onil Joseph RC	3.00

Gold

(1-75):		1-5X
(76-100):		.5-2X
Production 99 Sets		

Black

(1-100):		No Pricing
Production Five Sets		

Ballpark Heroes

		NM/M
Common Player:		1.25
Inserted 1:6		
1	Rocco Baldelli	1.75
2	Adam Dunn	1.75
3	Nomar Garciaparra	5.00
4	Ken Griffey Jr.	3.50
5	Vladimir Guerrero	3.00
6	Torii Hunter	1.75
7	Andruw Jones	2.00
8	Mike Piazza	3.50
9	Alfonso Soriano	3.00
10	Frank Thomas	2.00
11	Dontrelle Willis	1.25
12	Barry Zito	1.75
13	Javy Lopez	1.25
14	Miguel Cabrera	2.00
15	Kazuo Matsui	3.50
16	Josh Beckett	2.00
17	Derek Jeter	6.00
18	Greg Maddux	3.50
19	Pedro J. Martinez	3.00
20	Hideo Nomo	1.25
21	Mark Prior	3.00
22	Albert Pujols	5.00
23	Alex Rodriguez	5.00
24	Scott Rolen	3.00
25	Ichiro Suzuki	4.00

Ballpark Heroes Silver Jersey

		NM/M
Common Player:		4.00
Sequentially Numbered		
RB	Rocco Baldelli/250	4.00
MC	Miguel Cabrera/196	4.00
AD	Adam Dunn/215	4.00
VG	Vladimir Guerrero/200	6.00
GM	Greg Maddux/224	8.00
PM	Pedro J. Martinez/239	6.00
HN	Hideo Nomo/210	4.00
MP	Mike Piazza/163	8.00

AP	Albert Pujols/199	12.00
SR	Scott Rolen/221	6.00
AS	Alfonso Soriano/235	6.00
FT	Frank Thomas/242	5.00
DW	Dontrelle Willis/186	4.00
BZ	Barry Zito/195	4.00

Ballpark Heroes Copper Jersey

		NM/M
Common Player:		5.00
Production 110 Sets		
Gold Patch:		1-3X
Production 50 Sets		
Masterpiece Patch:		No Pricing
Production One Set		
RB	Rocco Baldelli/110	5.00
MC	Miguel Cabrera/110	6.00
AD	Adam Dunn/110	5.00
VG	Vladimir Guerrero/110	8.00
GM	Greg Maddux/110	10.00
PM	Pedro J. Martinez/110	8.00
HN	Hideo Nomo/110	5.00
MP	Mike Piazza/110	10.00
AP	Albert Pujols/110	15.00
SR	Scott Rolen/110	8.00
AS	Alfonso Soriano/110	8.00
FT	Frank Thomas/110	6.00
DW	Dontrelle Willis/110	5.00
BZ	Barry Zito/110	5.00

Ballpark Heroes Black Patch

Sequentially Numbered		
MP	Mike Piazza/31	50.00

Ballpark Heroes Duals

No Pricing	
Sequentially Numbered	

Ballpark Heroes Quad

		NM/M
Sequentially Numbered		
1	Josh Beckett, Greg Maddux, Pedro J. Martinez, Mark Prior/42	150.00
2	Dontrelle Willis, Kazuo Matsui, Miguel Cabrera, Rocco Baldelli/26	75.00
4	Dontrelle Willis, Josh Beckett, Derek Jeter, Alex Rodriguez/32	150.00
5	Albert Pujols, Vladimir Guerrero, Mike Piazza, Alex Rodriguez/37	150.00

Sweet Sigs Copper

		NM/M
Common Player:		10.00
Sequentially Numbered		
Gold:		.75-1.5X
Production 30 Sets		
Hideo Nomo #'d to 10.		
No Roger Clemens or Ted Williams.		
Gold card.		
Masterpiece:		No Pricing
Production One Set		
GA	Garret Anderson/100	20.00
RB	Rocco Baldelli/75	25.00
JB	Josh Beckett/75	30.00
CB	Carlos Beltran/75	20.00
LB	Lance Berkman/150	20.00
AB	Angel Berroa/75	20.00
JB	Jeremy Bonderman/50	15.00
MC	Miguel Cabrera/150	30.00
MC	Mike Cameron/150	20.00
RC	Roger Clemens/52	400.00
CC	Carl Crawford/150	15.00
JD	Johnny Damon/100	30.00
JD	J.D. Drew/98	40.00
DE	Dennis Eckersley/75	40.00
AE	Adam Everett/150	10.00
JF	Julio Franco/150	30.00
LG	Luis Gonzalez/150	15.00
KG	Khalil Greene/75	40.00
VG	Vladimir Guerrero/75	75.00
TH	Torii Hunter/150	15.00
EJ	Edwin Jackson/75	40.00
RJ	Randy Johnson/28	150.00
CJ	Chipper Jones/50	100.00
MK	Matt Kata/150	10.00
BL	Barry Larkin/50	50.00
CL	Carlos Lee/150	15.00
AL	Al Leiter/75	25.00
KL	Kenny Lofton/50	50.00
JL	Javy Lopez/75	25.00
GM	Greg Maddux/50	75.00
PM	Pedro J. Martinez/150	125.00
JM	Joe Mauer/100	40.00
WM	Wade Miller/150	20.00
KM	Kevin Millwood/100	15.00
PM	Paul Molitor/75	40.00
SM	Stan Musial/25	80.00

MM	Mike Mussina/50	40.00
LN	Lance Niekro/150	10.00
JO	John Olerud/75	30.00
MO	Magglio Ordonez/150	20.00
RO	Russ Ortiz/150	15.00
RO	Roy Oswalt/150	20.00
AO	Akinori Otsuka/150	20.00
BP	Brad Penny/150	10.00
AP	Andy Pettitte/50	40.00
MP	Mike Piazza/50	120.00
AP	Albert Pujols/73	300.00
BR	Brad Radke/100	20.00
JR	Jose Reyes/163	30.00
AR	Alexis Rios/150	15.00
NR	Nolan Ryan/50	300.00
CS	C.C. Sabathia/150	20.00
TS	Tim Salmon/100	40.00
DS	Deion Sanders/50	50.00
JS	Johan Santana/150	80.00
MS	Mike Schmidt/50	60.00
SS	Shannon Stewart/75	20.00
FT	Frank Thomas/75	75.00
JV	Jason Varitek/75	40.00
TW	Tim Wakefield/150	30.00
VW	Vernon Wells/150	20.00
BW	Bernie Williams/50	80.00
DW	Dontrelle Willis/150	20.00
KW	Kerry Wood/75	60.00
CY	Carl Yastrzemski/50	100.00
BZ	Barry Zito/44	30.00

Sweet Sigs Jersey Number

NM/M

No. 3-25: 1-3X Copper
No. 26-57: .75-1.5X Copper
Numbered to player's jersey #.
No Hideo Nomo card.

MC	Mike Cameron/44	30.00

Sweet Stitches Silver Jersey

NM/M

Common Player: 5.00
Sequentially Numbered

HB	Hank Blalock/166	5.00
MC	Miguel Cabrera/169	8.00
RC	Roger Clemens/165	8.00
JG	Jason Giambi/125	8.00
VG	Vladimir Guerrero/172	8.00
AJ	Andruw Jones/175	8.00
GM	Greg Maddux/156	8.00
MO	Magglio Ordonez/113	5.00
MP	Mike Piazza/174	8.00
MP	Mark Prior/172	8.00
AP	Albert Pujols/170	12.00
MR	Manny Ramirez/163	8.00
JR	Jose Reyes/171	8.00
SR	Scott Rolen/166	8.00
GS	Gary Sheffield/88	8.00
AS	Alfonso Soriano/162	8.00
SS	Sammy Sosa/158	10.00
MT	Mark Teixeira/158	5.00
MT	Miguel Tejada/162	5.00
FT	Frank Thomas/159	8.00
JT	Jim Thome/8	8.00
KW	Kerry Wood/134	8.00

Sweet Stitches Copper Jersey

NM/M

Common Player: 5.00
Production 125 Sets
Gold Patch: 1-3X
Production 50 Sets
Masterpiece Patch: No Pricing
Production One Set

HB	Hank Blalock/125	5.00
MC	Miguel Cabrera/125	8.00
RC	Roger Clemens/125	8.00
JG	Jason Giambi/125	8.00
VG	Vladimir Guerrero/125	8.00
AJ	Andruw Jones/125	10.00
GM	Greg Maddux/125	8.00
MO	Magglio Ordonez/125	5.00
MP	Mike Piazza/125	8.00
MP;	Mark Prior/125	8.00
AP	Albert Pujols/125	15.00
MR	Manny Ramirez/125	8.00
JR	Jose Reyes/125	8.00
SR	Scott Rolen/125	8.00
GS	Gary Sheffield/125	8.00
AS	Alfonso Soriano/125	8.00
SS	Sammy Sosa/125	10.00
MT	Mark Teixeira/125	5.00
MT	Miguel Tejada/125	5.00
FT	Frank Thomas/125	8.00
JT	Jim Thome/125	8.00
KW	Kerry Wood/125	8.00

Sweet Stitches Black Patch

NM/M

Sequentially Numbered

SS-GM	Greg Maddux/32	25.00

Sweet Stitches Quad Patches

NM/M

Sequentially Numbered
No pricing for quantities less than 25.

4	Andruw Jones/31, Miguel Cabrera/31, Albert Pujols/31, Sammy Sosa/31	80.00
10	Greg Maddux/33, Sammy Sosa/33, Mark Prior/33, Kerry Wood/33	150.00

Sweet Swing

NM/M

Common Player: 2.50
Inserted 1:12

1SS	Sammy Sosa	5.00
2SS	Vladimir Guerrero	3.50
3SS	Jason Giambi	3.50
4SS	Chipper Jones	4.00
5SS	Alfonso Soriano	3.50
6SS	Manny Ramirez	3.00
7SS	Todd Helton	3.00
8SS	Alex Rodriguez	6.00
9SS	Albert Pujols	6.00
10SS	Jeff Bagwell	3.00
11SS	Mike Piazza	4.00
12SS	Hank Blalock	2.50
13SS	Jim Thome	3.50
14SS	Carlos Delgado	3.00
15SS	Nomar Garciaparra	6.00

Sweet Swing Silver Bat

NM/M

Common Player: 5.00
Sequentially Numbered

JG	Jason Giambi/247	6.00
VG	Vladimir Guerrero/250	6.00
CJ	Chipper Jones/235	8.00
MP	Mike Piazza/231	8.00
AP	Albert Pujols/237	12.00
MR	Manny Ramirez/224	5.00
AR	Alex Rodriguez/213	12.00
AS	Alfonso Soriano/216	6.00
SS	Sammy Sosa/221	10.00
JT	Jim Thome/245	6.00

Sweet Swing Copper Jersey

NM/M

Common Player: 4.00
Production 200 Sets
Gold Bat/Jersey: 1.5-4X
Production 50 Sets
Masterpiece Bat/Patch
Production One Set

HB	Hank Blalock/200	4.00
JG	Jason Giambi/200	6.00
VG	Vladimir Guerrero/200	6.00
CJ	Chipper Jones/200	8.00
MP	Mike Piazza/200	8.00
AP	Albert Pujols/200	12.00
MR	Manny Ramirez/200	5.00
AR	Alex Rodriguez/200	12.00
AS	Alfonso Soriano/200	6.00
SS	Sammy Sosa/200	10.00
JT	Jim Thome/200	6.00

Sweet Swing Black Bat/Patch

No Pricing
Numbered to most home runs.

Sweet Swing Quad

NM/M

Sequentially Numbered

1	Jason Giambi, Alex Rodriguez, Jeff Bagwell, Manny Ramirez/35	80.00
3	Mike Piazza, Alfonso Soriano, Todd Helton, Hank Blalock/32	125.00

2004 Fleer Tradition

NM/M

Complete Set (500): 100.00
Common Player: .15
Common SP (401-500): .25
Pack (10): 1.75
Hobby Box (36): 50.00

1	Juan Pierre	.15
2	Josh Beckett	.50
3	Ivan Rodriguez	.50
4	Miguel Cabrera	.50
5	Dontrelle Willis	.25
6	Derek Jeter	2.00
7	Jason Giambi	.75
8	Bernie Williams	.40
9	Alfonso Soriano	.75
10	Hideki Matsui	2.00
11	Garret Anderson, Ramon Ortiz, John Lackey	.15
12	Luis Gonzalez, Brandon Webb, Curt Schilling	.25
13	Javy Lopez, Gary Sheffield, Russ Ortiz	.25
14	Tony Batista, Jay Gibbons, Sidney Ponson, Jason Johnson	.15
15	Manny Ramirez, Nomar Garciaparra, Derek Lowe, Pedro J. Martinez	.50
16	Sammy Sosa, Mark Prior, Kerry Wood	.75
17	Frank Thomas, Carlos Lee, Esteban Loaiza	.25
18	Adam Dunn, Sean Casey, Chris Reitsma, Paul Wilson	.25
19	Jody Gerut, C.C. Sabathia	.15
20	Preston Wilson, Darren Oliver, Jason Jennings	.15
21	Dmitri Young, Mike Maroth, Jeremy Bonderman	.15
22	Mike Lowell, Dontrelle Willis, Josh Beckett	.25
23	Jeff Bagwell, Jeriome Robertson, Wade Miller	.25
24	Carlos Beltran, Darrell May	.15
25	Adrian Beltre, Shawn Green, Hideo Nomo, Kevin Brown	.15
26	Richie Sexson, Ben Sheets	.15
27	Torii Hunter, Brad Radke, Johan Santana	.15
28	Vladimir Guerrero, Orlando Cabrera, Livan Hernandez, Javier Vazquez	.25
29	Cliff Floyd, Ty Wigginton, Steve Trachsel, Al Leiter	.15
30	Jason Giambi, Andy Pettitte, Mike Mussina	.40
31	Eric Chavez, Miguel Tejada, Tim Hudson	.25
32	Jim Thome, Randy Wolf	.25
33	Reggie Sanders, Josh Fogg, Kip Wells	.15
34	Ryan Klesko, Mark Loretta, Jake Peavy	.15
35	Jose Cruz, Edgardo Alfonzo, Jason Schmidt	.15
36	Bret Boone, Jamie Moyer, Joel Pineiro	.15
37	Albert Pujols, Woody Williams	.75
38	Aubrey Huff, Victor Zambrano	.15
39	Alex Rodriguez, John Thomson	.75
40	Carlos Delgado, Roy Halladay	.25
41	Greg Maddux	1.00
42	Ben Grieve	.15
43	Darin Erstad	.25
44	Ruben Sierra	.15
45	Byung-Hyun Kim	.15
46	Freddy Garcia	.15
47	Richard Hidalgo	.15
48	Tike Redman	.15
49	Kevin Millwood	.25
50	Marquis Grissom	.15
51	Jae Weong Seo	.15
52	Wil Cordero	.15
53	LaTroy Hawkins	.15
54	Jolbert Cabrera	.15
55	Kevin Appier	.15
56	John Lackey	.15
57	Garret Anderson	.25
58	R.A. Dickey	.15
59	David Segui	.15
60	Erubiel Durazo	.15
61	Bobby Abreu	.25
62	Travis Hafner	.15
63	Victor Zambrano	.15
64	Randy Johnson	.75
65	Bernie Williams	.40
66	J.T. Snow	.15
67	Sammy Sosa	1.50
68	Al Leiter	.15
69	Jason Jennings	.15
70	Matt Morris	.15
71	Mike Hampton	.15
72	Juan Encarnacion	.15
73	Alex Gonzalez	.15
74	Bartolo Colon	.25
75	Brett Myers	.15
76	Michael Young	.15
77	Ichiro Suzuki	1.50
78	Jason Johnson	.15
79	Brad Ausmus	.15
80	Ted Lilly	.15
81	Ken Griffey Jr.	1.00
82	Chone Figgins	.15
83	Edgar Martinez	.25
84	Adam Eaton	.15
85	Ken Harvey	.15
86	Francisco Rodriguez	.15
87	Bill Mueller	.15
88	Mike Maroth	.15
89	Charles Johnson	.15
90	Jhonny Peralta	.15
91	Kip Wells	.15
92	Cesar Izturis	.15
93	Matt Clement	.15
94	Lyle Overbay	.15
95	Kirk Rueter	.15
96	Cristian Guzman	.15
97	Garrett Stephenson	.15
98	Lance Berkman	.25
99	Brett Tomko	.15
100	Chris Stynes	.15
101	Nate Cornejo	.15
102	Aaron Rowand	.15
103	Javier Vazquez	.15
104	Jason Kendall	.25
105	Mark Redman	.15
106	Benito Santiago	.15
107	C.C. Sabathia	.15
108	David Wells	.15
109	Mark Ellis	.15
110	Casey Blake	.15
111	Sean Burroughs	.15
112	Carlos Beltran	.25
113	Ramon Hernandez	.15
114	Eric Hinske	.15
115	Luis Gonzalez	.25
116	Jarrod Washburn	.15
117	Ronnie Belliard	.15
118	Troy Percival	.15
119	Jose Valentine	.15
120	Chase Utley	.40
121	Odalis Perez	.15
122	Steve Finley	.15
123	Bret Boone	.25
124	Jeff Conine	.15
125	Jason Fogg	.15
126	Neifi Perez	.15
127	Ben Sheets	.25
128	Randy Winn	.15
129	Matt Stairs	.15
130	Carlos Delgado	.50
131	Morgan Ensberg	.15
132	Vinny Castilla	.15
133	Matt Mantei	.15
134	Alex Rodriguez	1.50
135	Matthew LeCroy	.15
136	Woody Williams	.15
137	Frank Catalanotto	.15
138	Rondell White	.15
139	Scott Rolen	.75
140	Cliff Floyd	.15
141	Chipper Jones	.75
142	Robin Ventura	.15
143	Mariano Rivera	.25
144	Brady Clark	.15
145	Ramon Ortiz	.15
146	Omar Infante	.15
147	Mike Matheny	.15
148	Pedro J. Martinez	.75
149	Carlos Baerga	.15
150	Shannon Stewart	.15
151	Travis Lee	.15
152	Eric Byrnes	.15
153	Rafael Furcal	.25
154	B.J. Surhoff	.15
155	Zach Day	.15
156	Marlon Anderson	.15
157	Mark Hendrickson	.15
158	Mike Mussina	.50
159	Randall Simon	.15
160	Jeff DaVanon	.15
161	Joel Pineiro	.15
162	Vernon Wells	.25
163	Adam Kennedy	.15
164	Trot Nixon	.15
165	Rodrigo Lopez	.15
166	Curt Schilling	.50
167	Horacio Ramirez	.15
168	Gerald Laird	.15
169	Magglio Ordonez	.25
170	Scott Schoeneweis	.15
171	Andruw Jones	.50
172	Tino Martinez	.25
173	Moises Alou	.25
174	Kelvim Escobar	.15
175	Xavier Nady	.15
176	Ramon Martinez	.15
177	Pat Hentgen	.15
178	Austin Kearns	.40

179 D'Angelo Jimenez .15
180 Deivi Cruz .15
181 John Smoltz .25
182 Toby Hall .15
183 Mark Buehrle .15
184 Howie Clark .15
185 David Ortiz .15
186 Raul Mondesi .15
187 Milton Bradley .15
188 Jorge Julio .15
189 Victor Martinez .15
190 Gabe Kapler .15
191 Julio Franco .15
192 Ryan Freel .15
193 Brad Fullmer .15
194 Joe Borowski .15
195 Darren Oliver .15
196 Jason Varitek .15
197 Greg Myers .15
198 Eric Munson .15
199 Tim Wakefield .15
200 Kyle Farnsworth .15
201 John Vander Wal .15
202 Alex Escobar .15
203 Sean Casey .15
204 John Thomson .15
205 Carlos Zambrano .15
206 Kenny Lofton .15
207 Marcus Giles .15
208 Wade Miller .15
209 Geoff Blum .15
210 Jason LaRue .15
211 Omar Vizquel .25
212 Carlos Pena .15
213 Adam Dunn .40
214 Oscar Villarreal .15
215 Paul Konerko .15
216 Hideo Nomo .40
217 Mike Sweeney .15
218 Coco Crisp .15
219 Shawn Chacon .15
220 Brook Fordyce .15
221 Josh Beckett .50
222 Paul Wilson .15
223 Josh Towers .15
224 Geoff Jenkins .25
225 Shawn Green .25
226 Derek Lee .15
227 Karim Garcia .15
228 Preston Wilson .15
229 Dane Sardinha .15
230 Aramis Ramirez .15
231 Doug Mientkiewicz .15
232 Jay Gibbons .15
233 Adam Everett .15
234 Brooks Kieschnick .15
235 Dmitri Young .15
236 Brad Penny .15
237 Todd Zeile .15
238 Eric Gagne .25
239 Esteban Loaiza .15
240 Billy Wagner .15
241 Nomar Garciaparra 1.50
242 Desi Relaford .15
243 Luis Rivas .15
244 Andy Pettitte .40
245 Ty Wigginton .15
246 Edgar Gonzalez .15
247 Brian Anderson .15
248 Richie Sexson .40
249 Russell Branyan .15
250 Jose Guillen .15
251 Chin-Hui Tsao .15
252 Jose Hernandez .15
253 Kevin Brown .25
254 Pete LaForest .15
255 Adrian Beltre .15
256 Jacque Jones .15
257 Jimmy Rollins .25
258 Brandon Phillips .15
259 Derek Jeter 2.00
260 Carl Everett .15
261 Wes Helms .15
262 Kyle Lohse .15
263 Jason L. Phillips .15
264 Jake Peavy .15
265 Orlando Hernandez .15
266 Keith Foulke .15
267 Brad Wilkerson .15
268 Corey Koskie .15
269 Josh Hall .15
270 Bobby Higginson .15
271 Andres Galarraga .15
272 Alfonso Soriano .75
273 Carlos Rivera .15
274 Steve Trachsel .15
275 David Bell .15
276 Endy Chavez .15
277 Jay Payton .15
278 Mark Mulder .25
279 Terrence Long .15
280 A.J. Burnett .15
281 Pokey Reese .15
282 Phil Nevin .15
283 Jose Contreras .25
284 Jim Thome .75
285 Pat Burrell .40
286 Luis Castillo .15
287 Juan Uribe .15
288 Raul Ibanez .25
289 Sidney Ponson .15
290 Shane Hatteberg .15
291 Jack Wilson .15
292 Reggie Sanders .15
293 Brian Giles .25
294 Craig Biggio .25
295 Kazuhisa Ishii .15
296 Jim Edmonds .25
297 Trevor Hoffman .15
298 Ray Durham .15
299 Mike Lieberthal .15
300 Todd Worrell .15
301 Chris George .15
302 Jamie Moyer .15
303 Mike Cameron .15
304 Matt Kinney .15
305 Aubrey Huff .15
306 Brian Lawrence .15
307 Carlos Guillen .15
308 J.D. Drew .15
309 Paul LoDuca .15
310 Tim Salmon .25
311 Jason Schmidt .15
312 A.J. Pierzynski .15
313 Lance Carter .15
314 Julio Lugo .15
315 Johan Santana .15
316 Laynce Nix .15
317 John Olerud .25
318 Robb Quinlan .15
319 Scott Spiezio .15
320 Tony Clark .15
321 Jose Vidro .15
322 Shea Hillenbrand .15
323 Doug Glanville .15
324 Orlando Palmeiro .15
325 Juan Gonzalez .40
326 Jason Giambi .75
327 Junior Spivey .15
328 Tom Glavine .25
329 Reed Johnson .15
330 David Eckstein .15
331 Damian Jackson .15
332 Orlando Hudson .15
333 Barry Zito .40
334 Robert Fick .15
335 Aaron Boone .15
336 Rafael Palmeiro .50
337 Bobby Kielty .15
338 Tony Batista .15
339 Ryan Dempster .15
340 Derek Lowe .25
341 Alex Cintron .15
342 Jermaine Dye .15
343 John Burkett .15
344 Javy Lopez .25
345 Eric Karros .15
346 Corey Patterson .25
347 Josh Phelps .15
348 Ryan Klesko .25
349 Craig Wilson .15
350 Brian Roberts .15
351 Roberto Alomar .40
352 Frank Thomas .50
353 Gary Sheffield .40
354 Alex Gonzalez .15
355 Jose Cruz .15
356 Jerome Williams .15
357 Mark Kotsay .15
358 Chris Reitsma .15
359 Carlos Lee .15
360 Todd Helton .50
361 Gil Meche .15
362 Ryan Franklin .15
363 Josh Bard .15
364 Juan Pierre .15
365 Barry Larkin .25
366 Edgar Renteria .15
367 Alex Sanchez .15
368 Jeff Bagwell .50
369 Ben Broussard .15
370 Chan Ho Park .15
371 Darrell May .15
372 Roy Oswalt .25
373 Craig Monroe .15
374 Fred McGriff .25
375 Bengie Molina .15
376 Aaron Guiel .15
377 Jeriome Robertson .15
378 Kenny Rogers .15
379 Colby Lewis .15
380 Jeromy Burnitz .15
381 Orlando Cabrera .15
382 Joe Randa .15
383 Miguel Batista .15
384 Brad Radke .15
385 Jason Giambi .75
386 Vladimir Guerrero .75
387 Melvin Mora .15
388 Royce Clayton .15
389 Danny Garcia .15
390 Manny Ramirez .50
391 Dave McCarty .15
392 Mark Grudzielanek .15
393 Mike Piazza 1.00
394 Jorge Posada .40
395 Tim Hudson .25
396 Placido Polanco .15
397 Mark Loretta .15
398 Jesse Foppert .15
399 Albert Pujols 1.50
400 Jeremi Gonzalez .15
401 Paul Bako .25
402 Luis Matos .25
403 Johnny Damon .50
404 Kerry Wood 1.00
405 Joe Crede .25
406 Jason Davis .25
407 Larry Walker .50
408 Ivan Rodriguez 1.00
409 Nick Johnson .25
410 Jose Lima .25
411 Brian Jordan .25
412 Eddie Guardado .25
413 Ron Calloway .25
414 Aaron Heilman .25
415 Eric Chavez .50
416 Randy Wolf .25
417 Jason Bay .25
418 Edgardo Alfonzo .25
419 Kazuhiro Sasaki .25
420 Eduardo Perez .25
421 Carl Crawford .25
422 Troy Glaus 1.00
423 Joaquin Benoit .25
424 Russ Ortiz .25
425 Larry Bigbie .25
426 Todd Walker .25
427 Kris Benson .25
428 Sandy Alomar .25
429 Jody Gerut .25
430 Rene Reyes .25
431 Mike Lowell .25
432 Jeff Kent .25
433 Mike MacDougal .25
434 Dave Roberts .25
435 Torii Hunter .75
436 Tomokazu Ohka .25
437 Jeremy Griffiths .25
438 Miguel Tejada .75
439 Vicente Padilla .25
440 Bobby Hill .25
441 Rich Aurilia .25
442 Shigetoshi Hasegawa .25
443 So Taguchi .25
444 Damian Rolls .25
445 Roy Halladay .75
446 Rocco Baldelli .75
447 Dontrelle Willis .75
448 Mark Prior 2.00
449 Jason Lane .25
450 Angel Berroa .25
451 Jose Reyes .75
452 Ryan Wagner .25
453 Marlon Byrd .25
454 Hee Seop Choi .25
455 Brandon Webb .50
456 Bo Hart .75
457 Hank Blalock 1.00
458 Mark Teixeira .75
459 Hideki Matsui 4.00
460 Scott Podsednik .25
461 Miguel Cabrera 1.00
462 Josh Beckett 1.00
463 Mariano Rivera .50
464 Ivan Rodriguez 1.00
465 Alex Rodriguez 3.00
466 Albert Pujols 3.00
467 Roy Halladay .75
468 Eric Gagne .50
469 Angel Berroa .25
470 Dontrelle Willis .50
471 Chris Bootcheck, Tom Gregorio, Richard Fischer .25
472 Matt Kata, Tim Olson, Robby Hammock .25
473 Michael Hessman, Chris Waters, Humberto Quintero .25
474 Carlos Mendez, Daniel Cabrera, Jeremy Guthrie .25
475 Edwin Almonte, Phil Seibel, Felix Sanchez .25
476 Todd Wellemeyer, Jon Leicester, Sergio Mitre .25
477 Josh Stewart, Neal Cotts, Aaron Miles .25
478 Termel Sledge, Josh Hall, Brandon Claussen .25
479 Francisco Cruceta, Jason Stanford, Rafael Betancourt .25
480 Javier Lopez, Garrett Atkins, Clint Barmes .25
481 Wilfredo Ledezma, Nook Logan, Jeremy Bonderman .25
482 Josh Willingham, Kevin Hooper, Rick Roberts .25
483 Colin Porter, Mike Gallo, Dave Matranga .25
484 David DeJesus, Jason Gilfillan, Jimmy Gobble .25
485 Koyie Hill, Alfredo Gonzalez, Andrew Brown .25
486 Rickie Weeks, Pedro Liriano, Wes Obermueller 1.00
487 Alex Prieto, Mike Ryan, Lew Ford .25
488 Julio Manon, Luis Ayala, Seung Jun Song .25
489 Jeff Duncan, Prentice Redman, Craig Brazell .25
490 Chien-Ming Wang, Michel Hernandez, Mike Gonzalez .25
491 Rich Harden, Mike Neu, Geoff Geary .25
492 Diegomar Markwell, Chad Gaudin, David Sanders .25
493 Beau Kemp, Micheal Nakamura, D.J. Carrasco .25
494 Khalil Greene, Miguel Ojeda, Bernie Castro .25
495 Noah Lowry, Todd Linden, Kevin Correia .25
496 Aaron Looper, Brian Sweeney, Rett Johnson .25
497 Bo Hart, Dan Haren, Kevin Ohme .50
498 Delmon Young, Doug Waechter, Matt Diaz 1.00
499 Gerald Laird, Rosman Garcia, Ramon Nivar .25
500 Alexis Rios, Guillermo Quiroz, Francisco Rosario .25

Career Tributes

NM/M

Complete Set (10): 30.00
Common Player: 3.00
Numbered to last season.
Die-Cuts: 2-3X
#'d to last two digits of last season
1CT Mike Schmidt/1989 5.00
2CT Nolan Ryan/1993 6.00
3CT Tom Seaver/1986 4.00
4CT Reggie Jackson/1987 3.00
5CT Bob Gibson/1975 4.00
6CT Harmon Killebrew/1975 4.00
7CT Phil Rizzuto/1956 3.00
8CT Lou Brock/1979 3.00
9CT Eddie Mathews/1968 3.00
10CT Al Kaline/1974 4.00

Diamond Tributes

NM/M

Complete Set (20): 18.00
Common Player: .50
Inserted 1:6
1DT Derek Jeter 3.00
2DT Chipper Jones 1.50
3DT Vladimir Guerrero 1.00
4DT Kerry Wood .75
5DT Jim Thome 1.00
6DT Nomar Garciaparra 2.00
7DT Alex Rodriguez 3.00
8DT Mike Piazza 1.50
9DT Jason Giambi 1.00
10DT Barry Zito .50
11DT Dontrelle Willis .50
12DT Albert Pujols 2.50
13DT Todd Helton .75
14DT Richie Sexson .50
15DT Randy Johnson 1.00
16DT Pedro J. Martinez 1.00
17DT Josh Beckett .75
18DT Manny Ramirez .75
19DT Roy Halladay .50
20DT Mark Prior 1.50

Diamond Tributes Game-Used

NM/M

Common Player: 5.00
Inserted 1:36
Patch versions: 2-3X
Production 50 Sets
Josh Beckett 8.00
Nomar Garciaparra 10.00
Jason Giambi 8.00
Vladimir Guerrero 8.00
Roy Halladay 5.00
Todd Helton 8.00

Derek Jeter	15.00
Randy Johnson	8.00
Chipper Jones	8.00
Pedro J. Martinez	10.00
Mike Piazza	8.00
Mark Prior	10.00
Albert Pujols	15.00
Manny Ramirez	8.00
Alex Rodriguez	10.00
Richie Sexson	6.00
Jim Thome	8.00
Dontrelle Willis	8.00
Kerry Wood	8.00
Barry Zito	8.00

Retrospection Collection

	NM/M
Complete Set (10):	60.00
Common Player:	4.00
Inserted 1:360	
1RC Rickie Weeks	8.00
2RC Delmon Young	12.00
3RC Torii Hunter	5.00
4RC Aubrey Huff	4.00
5RC Rocco Baldelli	6.00
6RC Mike Lowell	4.00
7RC Dontrelle Willis	6.00
8RC Albert Pujols	10.00
9RC Bo Hart	8.00
10RC Brandon Webb	8.00

Retrospection Collection Autograph

	NM/M
Common Autograph:	10.00
Production 60	
Hank Blalock	25.00
Bo Hart	25.00
Aubrey Huff	10.00
Torii Hunter	30.00
Austin Kearns	20.00
Corey Patterson	25.00
Albert Pujols	75.00
Jose Reyes	25.00
Scott Rolen	30.00
Mike Ryan	15.00
Ryan Wagner	15.00
Brandon Webb	20.00
Rickie Weeks	25.00
Josh Willingham	20.00
Dontrelle Willis	35.00
Delmon Young	50.00

Retrospection Collection Dual Autograph

No Pricing
Production 19 Sets

Standouts Game-Used

	NM/M
Common Player:	4.00
Inserted 1:41	
Rocco Baldelli	8.00
Angel Berroa	5.00
Hank Blalock	6.00
Marlon Byrd	5.00
Miguel Cabrera	8.00
Hee Seop Choi	4.00
Bo Hart	8.00
Jose Reyes	8.00
Mark Teixeira	6.00
Brandon Webb	5.00
Dontrelle Willis	6.00

Standouts Game-Used Gold

No Pricing
Numbered to player's age.

This Day in History

	NM/M
Complete Set (15):	12.00
Common Player:	.50
Inserted 1:18	
1 Josh Beckett	1.00
2 Carlos Delgado	1.00
3 Javy Lopez	.50
4 Greg Maddux	2.00
5 Rafael Palmeiro	1.00
6 Sammy Sosa	2.50
7 Jeff Bagwell	1.00
8 Frank Thomas	1.00
9 Kevin Millwood	.50
10 Jose Reyes	.75
11 Rafael Furcal	.50
12 Alfonso Soriano	1.50
13 Eric Gagne	.50
14 Hideki Matsui	4.00
15 Hank Blalock	.75

This Day in History Memorabilia

	NM/M
Common Player:	5.00
Inserted 1:288	
Jeff Bagwell	8.00
Carlos Delgado	5.00
Javy Lopez	5.00
Greg Maddux	15.00
Rafael Palmeiro	8.00
Alfonso Soriano	8.00
Sammy Sosa	12.00
Frank Thomas	8.00

This Day/History Dual Memorabilia

	NM/M
Production 25 Sets	
Frank Thomas, Jeff Bagwell	25.00

2005 Fleer

	NM/M
Common Player (1-50):	1.00
Minor Stars (1-50):	1.25
Unlisted Stars (1-50):	1.75
Common Class '05 (51-80):	3.00
Minor Class '05 (51-80):	4.00
Common Veteran (81-90):	5.00
Production 699 Sets	
Box (1):	90.00
Production 699 Sets	
1 Curt Schilling	1.75
2 Jim Thome	3.00
3 Miguel Cabrera	2.00
4 Randy Johnson	3.50
5 David Ortiz	1.75
6 Vladimir Guerrero	3.00
7 Nomar Garciaparra	5.00
8 Ivan Rodriguez	1.75
9 Jason Schmidt	1.25
10 Khalil Greene	2.00
11 Jose Vidro	1.00
12 Lyle Overbay	1.00
13 Todd Helton	2.00
14 Vernon Wells	1.25
15 B.J. Upton	1.25
16 Hideki Matsui	5.00
17 Pedro Martinez	3.00
18 Victor Martinez	1.00
19 Adam Dunn	1.75
20 Andruw Jones	2.00
21 Jeff Bagwell	2.00
22 Mike Sweeney	1.00
23 Mike Piazza	3.50
24 Ben Sheets	1.25
25 Adrian Beltre	1.25
26 Chipper Jones	3.50
27 Greg Maddux	3.50
28 Manny Ramirez	2.00
29 Roger Clemens	5.00
30 Johan Santana	1.25
31 Derek Jeter	6.00
32 Jason Bay	1.00
33 Ken Griffey Jr.	3.50
34 Miguel Tejada	1.75
35 Richie Sexson	1.75
36 Scott Rolen	3.00
37 Alfonso Soriano	3.00
38 Ichiro Suzuki	4.00
39 Sammy Sosa	4.00
40 Barry Zito	1.75
41 Kazuo Matsui	3.00
42 Mark Teixeira	1.25
43 Carlos Beltran	1.75
44 Mark Prior	4.00
45 Travis Hafner	4.00
46 Alex Rodriguez	5.00
47 Lew Ford	1.00
48 Albert Pujols	5.00
49 Frank Thomas	2.00
50 Juan Pierre	1.00
51 David Aardsma	5.00
52 J.D. Durbin	3.00
53 Zack Greinke	4.00
54 Dioner Navarro	4.00
55 Edwin Encarnacion	4.00
56 Luis Hernandez RC	5.00
57 Jeff Baker	4.00
58 Victor Diaz	5.00
59 Joey Gathright	3.00
60 Casey Kotchman	4.00
61 David Wright	5.00
62 Jon Knott	3.00
63 Charlton Jimerson	4.00
64 Nick Swisher	5.00
65 Ryan Raburn	3.00
66 Josh Kroeger	3.00
67 Kelly Johnson	4.00
68 Justin Verlander RC	6.00
69 Taylor Buchholz	3.00
70 Ubaldo Jimenez RC	5.00
71 Russ Adams	4.00
72 Ronny Cedeno	4.00
73 Bobby Jenks	5.00
74 Dan Meyer	4.00
75 Jeff Francis	3.00
76 Scott Kazmir	5.00
77 Sean Burnett	3.00
78 Jose Lopez	4.00
79 Andres Blanco	3.00
80 Gavin Floyd	4.00
81 Tom Seaver	3.00
82 Steve Carlton	3.00
83 Al Kaline	4.00
84 Cal Ripken Jr.	10.00
85 Willie McCovey	5.00
86 Johnny Bench	5.00
87 Nolan Ryan	10.00
88 Mike Schmidt	4.00
89 Carlton Fisk	3.00
90 Don Mattingly	4.00

Row 1

Stars (1-50):	
Class of '05 (51-80):	.5-2X
Veterans:	.5-2X
Production 100 Sets	

Row 2

Cards 1-90:	No Pricing
Production One Set	

Cuts and Glory Jersey

	NM/M
Common Card:	15.00
Production 100 Sets	
Patch:	2-4X
Production 50 Sets	
Jersey and Patch:	No Pricing
Production 15 Sets	
Masterpiece Logo:	No Pricing
Production One Set	
JB Johnny Bench	60.00
CC Carl Crawford	20.00
JL Javy Lopez	20.00
JP Josh Phelps	15.00
BS Ben Sheets	20.00
SS Shannon Stewart	20.00

Cuts and Glory Dual Patch

No Pricing
Production 35 Sets

Diamond Cuts Jersey

	NM/M
Common Player:	5.00
Production 150 Sets	
Die-Cut:	.75-1.5X
Production 75 Sets	
Patch:	1-3X
Production 50 Sets	
Super Patch:	No Pricing
Production 20 Sets	
Die-Cut Patch:	No Pricing
Production 10 Sets	
MLB Logo Masterpiece:	No Pricing
Production One Set	
JB Jeff Bagwell	8.00
CB Carlos Beltran	6.00
HB Hank Blalock	8.00
MC Miguel Cabrera	8.00
RC Roger Clemens	12.00
AD Adam Dunn	6.00
VG Vladimir Guerrero	8.00
TH Todd Helton	8.00
RJ Randy Johnson	8.00
AJ Andruw Jones	8.00
CJ Chipper Jones	8.00
AK Austin Kearns	6.00
PM Pedro Martinez	8.00
VM Victor Martinez	5.00
HM Hideki Matsui	15.00
HN Hideo Nomo	8.00
DO David Ortiz	8.00
MP Mike Piazza	8.00
MP2 Mark Prior	8.00
AP Albert Pujols	12.00
MR Manny Ramirez	8.00
SR Scott Rolen	8.00
CS Curt Schilling	6.00
GS Gary Sheffield	6.00
AS Alfonso Soriano	6.00
SS Sammy Sosa	10.00
MT Mark Teixeira	5.00
JT Jim Thome	8.00
BU B.J. Upton	5.00
KW Kerry Wood	8.00

Diamond Cuts Dual Jersey

	NM/M
Common Card:	8.00
Production 99 Sets	
Die-Cut:	.5-1.5X
Production 50 Sets	
Patch:	No Pricing
Production 15 Sets	

Patch Die-Cut:	No Pricing
Production Five Sets	
BC Jeff Bagwell, Roger Clemens	15.00
BM Carlos Beltran, Pedro Martinez	10.00
BS Hank Blalock, Alfonso Soriano	10.00
CH Miguel Cabrera, Todd Helton	10.00
DK Adam Dunn, Austin Kearns	8.00
JJ Chipper Jones, Andruw Jones	12.00
JS Randy Johnson, Curt Schilling	10.00
MS Hideki Matsui, Gary Sheffield	20.00
MT Victor Martinez, Mark Teixeira	8.00
NU Hideo Nomo, B.J. Upton	10.00
OR David Ortiz, Manny Ramirez	10.00
PR Albert Pujols, Scott Rolen	15.00
PT Mike Piazza, Jim Thome	12.00
PW Mark Prior, Kerry Wood	10.00
SG Sammy Sosa, Vladimir Guerrero	15.00

Dynasty Foundations

	NM/M
Common Card:	6.00
Production 500 Sets	
1DF Rod Carew, Nolan Ryan, Vladimir Guerrero, Garret Anderson, Darin Erstad	8.00
2DF Cal Ripken Jr., Brooks Robinson, Miguel Tejada, Javy Lopez, Jim Palmer	15.00
3DF Ted Williams, Manny Ramirez, Johnny Damon, Carl Yastrzemski, David Ortiz	15.00
4DF Ryne Sandberg, Sammy Sosa, Ernie Banks, Greg Maddux, Mark Prior	8.00
5DF Adam Dunn, Johnny Bench, Tony Perez, Austin Kearns, Joe Morgan	8.00
6DF Victor Martinez, Travis Hafner, Bob Feller, C.C. Sabathia, Larry Doby	6.00
7DF Aaron Miles, Matt Holliday, Todd Helton, Garrett Atkins, Preston Wilson	6.00
8DF Miguel Cabrera, Dontrelle Willis, Juan Pierre, Al Leiter, Josh Beckett	6.00
9DF Lance Berkman, Jeff Bagwell, Craig Biggio, Roger Clemens, Roy Oswalt	8.00
10DF Ben Sheets, Lyle Overbay, Robin Yount, Geoff Jenkins, Paul Molitor	8.00
11DF Johan Santana, Shannon Stewart, Harmon Killebrew, Torii Hunter, Lee Ford	6.00
12DF Tom Glavine, Mike Piazza, Tom Seaver, Nolan Ryan, Pedro Martinez	8.00
13DF Eric Chavez, Reggie Jackson, Bobby Crosby, Dennis Eckersley, Barry Zito	6.00
14DF Jim Thome, Bobby Abreu, Gavin Floyd, Robin Roberts, Mike Schmidt	6.00
15DF Craig Wilson, Willie Stargell, Bill Mazeroski, Jason Bay, Jack Wilson	6.00
16DF Willie McCovey, Jason Schmidt, Juan Marichal, Orlando Cepeda, Ray Durham	6.00
17DF Scott Rolen, Mark Mulder, Albert Pujols, Jim Edmonds, Stan Musial	10.00
18DF Rocco Baldelli, Scott Kazmir, Aubrey Huff, B.J. Upton, Carl Crawford	6.00
19DF Alfonso Soriano, Mark Teixeira, Hank Blalock, Nolan Ryan, Michael Young	10.00
20DF Alexis Rios, Paul Molitor, Roy Halladay, Vernon Wells, Orlando Hudson	6.00

Dynasty Foundations Dual Player Jersey

	NM/M
Common Card:	10.00
Production 150 Sets	
Patch:	1-3X
Production 50 Sets	
BO Miguel Tejada, Javy Lopez	15.00
BR Manny Ramirez, David Ortiz	10.00
CI Victor Martinez, Travis Hafner	10.00
CR1 Adam Dunn, Austin Kearns	12.00
CR2 Todd Helton, Preston Wilson	12.00

FM Miguel Cabrera, Juan Pierre 10.00
HA Jeff Bagwell, Lance Berkman 12.00
LA Vladimir Guerrero, Garret Anderson 12.00
MT Johan Santana, Torii Hunter 12.00
NM Mike Piazza, Tom Glavine 10.00
OA Barry Zito, Eric Chavez 10.00
PP Jim Thome, Bobby Abreu 10.00
SC Scott Rolen, Albert Pujols 25.00
TD B.J. Upton, Scott Kazmir 10.00
TR Mark Teixeira, Michael Young 10.00

Dynasty Foundations Three Player Jersey

NM/M
Common Card: 15.00
Production 99 Sets
Patch: No Pricing
Production 25 Sets
CR1 Adam Dunn, Austin Kearns, Joe Morgan 15.00
FM Miguel Cabrera, Josh Beckett, Juan Pierre 15.00
HA Jeff Bagwell, Lance Berkman, Roger Clemens 40.00
LA Vladimir Guerrero, Garret Anderson, Darin Erstad 20.00
MT Johan Santana, Torii Hunter, Shannon Stewart 15.00
NM Mike Piazza, Pedro Martinez, Tom Glavine 20.00
SC Scott Rolen, Albert Pujols, Jim Edmonds 40.00
TR Alfonso Soriano, Mark Teixeira, Michael Young 15.00

Dynasty Foundations Four Player Jersey

NM/M
Production 40 Sets
Patch: No Pricing
Production 15 Sets
NM Mike Piazza, Nolan Ryan, Pedro Martinez, Tom Glavine 100.00

Dynasty Foundations Five Player Jersey

No Pricing
Production 25 Sets
Patch: No Pricing
Production Nine Sets
MLB Logo Masterpiece: No Pricing
Production One Set

Dynasty Cornerstones Signatures

NM/M
Sequentially Numbered
JB Jeremy Bonderman/75 20.00
DG Dwight Gooden/25 30.00
DO David Ortiz/75 40.00

Dynasty Cornerstones Dual Signatures

No Pricing
Sequentially Numbered

Head of the Class Triple Player Jersey

NM/M
Common Card: 15.00
Numbered to Debut Year.
No pricing for quantities three or less.
Patch: 1-3X
Production 33 Sets
MLB Logo Masterpiece: No Pricing
Production One Set
AGJ Bobby Abreu, Vladimir Guerrero, Andruw Jones/96 20.00
BGB Carlos Beltran, Troy Glaus, Adrian Beltre/98 15.00
BTR Jeff Bagwell, Jim Thome, Ivan Rodriguez/91 15.00
GBH Eric Gagne, A.J. Burnett, Tim Hudson/99 15.00
JDR Chipper Jones, Carlos Delgado, Manny Ramirez/93 20.00
OHS David Ortiz, Torii Hunter, Richie Sexson/97 15.00
SNP Jason Schmidt, Hideo Nomo, Andy Pettitte/95 20.00

Letterman

Sequentially numbered between 4-8.
No Pricing

Significant Dual

NM/M
Common Player: 30.00
Production 40 Sets
Dual Jersey: No Pricing
Production 15 Sets
Dual Patch: No Pricing
Production Five Sets
BR Adrian Beltre, Jeremy Reed 60.00
CF Steve Carlton, Gavin Floyd 40.00
FM Lew Ford, Justin Morneau 40.00
MH Victor Martinez, Travis Hafner 30.00
SR Mike Schmidt, Cal Ripken Jr. 250.00

Significant Signings Blue

NM/M
Common Player: 10.00
Sequentially #'d to indicated quantity.
Silver Die-Cut: 1-3X
Cards #'d 50 or less: .25-1X
Production 50 Sets
Gold Jersey: No Pricing
Production 25 Sets
Patch: No Pricing
Production 15 Sets
Masterpiece Jersey Tag: No Pricing
Production One Set
JB Jason Bay/250 15.00
AB Adrian Beltre/30 50.00
MC Miguel Cabrera/250 20.00
SC Steve Carlton/59 30.00
BC Bobby Crosby/93 15.00
GF Gavin Floyd/221 10.00
LF Lew Ford/230 10.00
ZG Zack Greinke/250 10.00
TH Travis Hafner/250 10.00
SK Scott Kazmir/250 10.00
CK Casey Kotchman/250 10.00
PM Pedro Martinez/101 40.00
VM Victor Martinez/224 10.00
DM Don Mattingly/103 40.00
JM Justin Morneau/225 25.00
JR Jeremy Reed/250 40.00
NR Nolan Ryan/92 100.00
BU B.J. Upton/250 10.00
KW Kerry Wood/200 25.00
DW David Wright/250 40.00

2005 Fleer America's National Pastime

NM/M
Common Player (1-50): .25
Minor Stars (1-50): .40
Unlisted Stars (1-50): .60
Common Player (51-70): 3.00
Production 699 Sets
Common Player (71-80): 3.00
Production 699 Sets
Pack (5): 7.00
Box (10): 60.00
1 Khalil Greene .75
2 Pedro Martinez 1.00
3 Mark Teixeira .40
4 Jim Thome 1.00
5 Jack Wilson .25
6 Johan Santana .40
7 Jason Bay .25
8 Adam Dunn .60
9 Lyle Overbay .25
10 Jason Schmidt .40
11 Bobby Crosby .25
12 J.D. Drew .40
13 Ken Griffey Jr. 1.50
14 Sammy Sosa 2.00
15 Hank Blalock .60
16 Victor Martinez .25
17 Randy Johnson 1.00
18 Vernon Wells .40
19 Todd Helton .75
20 Javy Lopez .40
21 Kazuo Matsui .60
22 Ben Sheets .40
23 Brad Wilkerson .25
24 Miguel Cabrera .75
25 Mike Sweeney .25
26 Roger Clemens 2.50
27 Chipper Jones 1.50
28 Hideki Matsui 2.50
29 Manny Ramirez .75
30 Scott Rolen 1.00
31 Lance Berkman .40
32 Jim Edmonds .40
33 Derek Jeter 3.00
34 B.J. Upton .40
35 Carlos Delgado .75
36 Ichiro Suzuki 2.00
37 Nomar Garciaparra 2.50
38 Albert Pujols 2.50
39 Ivan Rodriguez .60
40 Gary Sheffield .60
41 Alfonso Soriano 1.00
42 Carlos Beltran .60
43 Magglio Ordonez .40
44 Alex Rodriguez 2.50
45 Curt Schilling .60
46 Greg Maddux 1.50
47 Vladimir Guerrero 1.00
48 Mike Piazza 1.50
49 Miguel Tejada .60
50 Adrian Beltre .40
51 Scott Kazmir 5.00
52 Gavin Floyd 4.00
53 Zack Greinke 4.00
54 David Wright 5.00
55 David Aardsma 4.00
56 Ryan Raburn 3.00
57 Joey Gathright 3.00
58 J.D. Durbin 3.00
59 Sean Burnett 3.00
60 Jose Lopez 3.00
61 Nick Swisher 4.00
62 Bobby Jenks 3.00
63 Kelly A. Johnson 3.00
65 Ronny Cedeno 4.00
66 Edwin Encarnacion 3.00
67 Jeff Baker 3.00
68 Taylor Buchholz 3.00
69 Justin Verlander **RC** 5.00
70 Luis Hernandez **RC** 5.00
71 Mike Schmidt 5.00
72 Al Kaline 3.00
73 Yogi Berra 4.00
74 Robin Yount 4.00
75 Nolan Ryan 6.00
76 Johnny Bench 5.00
77 Eddie Murray 4.00
78 Tom Seaver 4.00
79 Willie McCovey 3.00
80 Cal Ripken Jr. 6.00

Red Foil

Cards 1-50: 1-3X
Cards 51-70: .75-1.5X
Cards 71-80: .75-1.5X
Production 150 Sets

White Foil

Cards 1-50 #'d to 41-57: 2-6X
Cards 1-50 #'d to 26-40: 4-8X
Cards 1-50 #'d 25 or less: No Pricing
Cards 71-80 #'d to 26-44: 1-3X
Cards 71-80 #'d 25 or less: No Pricing
Numbered to player's jersey number.

Blue Foil

No Pricing
Production One Set

Beltway Baseball

NM/M
Common Card: 6.00
Production 202 Sets
1 Ed Delahanty 8.00
2 Benjamin Harrison 8.00
3 William Howard Taft 6.00
4 Clark Griffith 6.00
5 Bobby Burke 8.00
6 Roy Seivers 8.00
7 Tom Cheney 8.00
8 Woodrow Wilson 8.00
9 Franklin D. Roosevelt 8.00
10 John F. Kennedy 10.00
11 Frank Howard 8.00
12 Griffith Stadium 10.00
13 RFK Stadium 8.00
14 All-Star Game 6.00
15 Ted Williams 15.00
16 Harmon Killebrew 12.00
17 Jeff Burroughs 8.00
18 All-Star Game 6.00
19 Unveiling the Nationals 10.00
20 New Logo 8.00

First Name Bases Autograph Silver

NM/M
Sequentially #'d to indicated quantity.
Blue: No Pricing
Production One Set
MCAM Mike Cameron/375 10.00
SH Shea Hillenbrand/316 10.00
JL Javy Lopez/158 15.00
MT Mark Teixeira/225 20.00
JV Justin Verlander/401 15.00

First Name Bases Autograph White

NM/M
Cards #'d 25 or less: No Pricing
Sequentially #'d to indicated quantity.
AB Adrian Beltre/48 25.00

First Name Bases Autograph Red

NM/M
Cards #'d 25 or less: No Pricing
Sequentially #'d to indicated quantity.
MCAM Mike Cameron/90 15.00
BL Barry Larkin/27 40.00
MT Mark Teixeira/95 30.00
JV Justin Verlander/99 20.00

First Name Bases Autograph Gold

NM/M
Cards #'d 25 or less: No Pricing
Sequentially #'d to indicated quantity.
AB Adrian Beltre/96 25.00
MCAM Mike Cameron/126 15.00
SH Shea Hillenbrand/99 15.00
JL Javy Lopez/73 15.00
AP Albert Pujols/73 200.00
MT Mark Teixeira/147 25.00
JV Justin Verlander/149 20.00

Grand Old Gamers

NM/M
Common Player: .75
Inserted 1:5
1 Pedro Martinez 1.50
2 Jim Thome 1.50
3 Ken Griffey Jr. 2.00
4 Sammy Sosa 2.50
5 Hank Blalock 1.00
6 Randy Johnson 1.50
7 Roger Clemens 3.00
8 Chipper Jones 2.00
9 Hideki Matsui 3.00
10 Manny Ramirez 1.25
11 Derek Jeter 4.00
12 Ichiro Suzuki 2.50
13 Nomar Garciaparra 3.00
14 Albert Pujols 3.00
15 Gary Sheffield 1.00
16 Alfonso Soriano 1.50
17 Alex Rodriguez 3.00
18 Curt Schilling 1.00
19 Vladimir Guerrero 1.50
20 Mike Piazza 2.00
21 Greg Maddux 2.00
22 Frank Thomas 1.25
23 Adrian Beltre .75
24 Barry Larkin .75
25 Todd Helton 1.25
26 Kerry Wood 1.25
27 Kazuo Matsui 1.00
28 Scott Rolen 1.50
29 Ivan Rodriguez 1.00
30 Miguel Tejada 1.00
31 Mark Teixeira .75
32 Rafael Palmeiro 1.25
33 Andruw Jones 1.25
34 Carlos Beltran 1.00
35 Jeff Bagwell 1.25

Grand Old Gamers Jersey

NM/M
Common Player: 6.00
Inserted 1:36 Retail
JB Jeff Bagwell 8.00
CB Carlos Beltran 8.00
AB Adrian Beltre 6.00
HB Hank Blalock 8.00
RC Roger Clemens/SP/50 15.00
VG Vladimir Guerrero 8.00
TH Todd Helton 8.00
RJ Randy Johnson 8.00
AJ Andruw Jones 8.00
CJ Chipper Jones 8.00
BL Barry Larkin 6.00
GM Greg Maddux/SP/75 12.00
PM Pedro Martinez 8.00
HM Hideki Matsui/SP/50 15.00
KM Kazuo Matsui 8.00
RP Rafael Palmeiro 8.00
MP Mike Piazza 8.00
AP Albert Pujols 12.00
MR Manny Ramirez 8.00
IR Ivan Rodriguez 8.00
SR Scott Rolen 8.00
CS Curt Schilling 8.00
GS Gary Sheffield 8.00
AS Alfonso Soriano 8.00
SS Sammy Sosa 12.00
MT Mark Teixeira 6.00
FT Frank Thomas 8.00
JT Jim Thome 8.00
KW Kerry Wood 8.00

Gamers Patch Blue

NM/M
Numbered to player's jersey number.
Cards numbered 25 or less: No Pricing
Masterpiece: No Pricing
Production One Set
VG Vladimir Guerrero/27 25.00
RJ Randy Johnson/51 20.00
GM Greg Maddux/31 25.00
PM Pedro Martinez/45 20.00
HM Hideki Matsui/55 50.00
MP Mike Piazza/31 25.00
SR Scott Rolen/27 25.00
FT Frank Thomas/35 15.00
KW Kerry Wood/34 20.00

Gamers Dual Patch

NM/M
Cards #'d to 25 or less: No Pricing
Production 5-33 Sets
Ivan Rodriguez, Mike Piazza/31 75.00
Hank Blalock, Mark Teixeira/33 30.00

Historical Record

NM/M
Common Card: 2.00
Inserted 1:6
1 Ichiro Suzuki/2004 2.50
2 Greg Maddux/2004 2.00
3 Alex Rodriguez/1998 3.00
4 Mike Piazza/2004 2.00
5 Nolan Ryan/1991 5.00
6 Albert Pujols/2001 3.00
7 Mike Schmidt/1987 4.00
8 Randy Johnson/2004 2.00
9 Sammy Sosa/2003 2.50
10 Cal Ripken Jr./1996 5.00
11 Roger Clemens/2004 3.00
12 Hideki Matsui/2003 3.00
13 Hideo Nomo/1994 2.00
14 Gene Autry/1961 2.00
15 Walter O'Malley/1944 2.00

Historical Record Jersey

NM/M
Common Player: 6.00

Inserted 1:96 Retail
RC	Roger Clemens	10.00
RJ	Randy Johnson	8.00
GM	Greg Maddux	8.00
HM	Hideki Matsui	12.00
HN	Hideo Nomo	6.00
MP	Mike Piazza	8.00
AP	Albert Pujols	10.00
CR	Cal Ripken Jr.	30.00
NRO	Nolan Ryan	20.00
MS	Mike Schmidt	25.00
SS	Sammy Sosa	10.00

Historical Record Patch Blue
No Pricing
Numbered to player's jersey number.
Masterpiece: No Pricing
Production One Set

Historical Record Dual Patch
No Pricing
Production 8-25 Sets

Signature Swings Silver
		NM/M
Common Player:		10.00
Gold:		.75-1.5X

Sequentially #'d between 50 & 199.
BAY	Jason Bay	20.00
CC	Carl Crawford	10.00
AE	Adam Everett	10.00
CF	Chone Figgins	10.00
LF	Lew Ford	10.00
JG	Joey Gathright	10.00
KG	Khalil Greene	30.00
TH	Travis Hafner	10.00
AH	Aubrey Huff	10.00
CK	Casey Kotchman	10.00
VAL	Val Majewski	10.00
JM	Joe Mauer	25.00
DM	Dallas McPherson	15.00
JMO	Justin Morneau	40.00
WMP	Wily Mo Pena	25.00
JP	Josh Phelps	10.00
RR	Ryan Raburn	10.00
SS	Shannon Stewart	10.00
NS	Nick Swisher	15.00
BJU	B.J. Upton	15.00
CU	Chase Utley	20.00
DW	David Wright	50.00
MY	Michael Young	10.00

Signature Swings Bat Red
		NM/M
Common Player:		20.00

Production 30-99 Sets
BAY	Jason Bay/99	20.00
JB	Johnny Bench/42	80.00
LB	Lance Berkman/99	20.00
CC	Carl Crawford/99	20.00
LF	Lew Ford/76	20.00
CK	Casey Kotchman/99	20.00
BR	Brooks Robinson/49	40.00
MS	Mike Schmidt/30	100.00
SS	Shannon Stewart/99	20.00
DW	David Wright/99	60.00

Signature Swings Jersey White
		NM/M

Production 3-29 Sets
Cards #'d less than 25:		No Pricing
LB	Lance Berkman/29	30.00
CC	Carl Crawford/29	30.00
JP	Josh Phelps/27	15.00

Signature Swings Patch Blue
		NM/M

Numbered to player's jersey number.
Cards #'d less than 25:		No Pricing
Masterpiece:		No Pricing

Production One Set
BAY	Jason Bay/38	60.00
JP	Josh Phelps/45	20.00

2005 Fleer Authentix

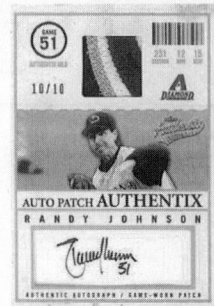

	NM/M
Common Player (1-100):	.25
Minor Stars (1-100):	.40
Unlisted Stars (1-100):	.60

Common Player Autograph (101-125):		10.00
Minor Stars Autograph(101-125):		15.00

Production 250 Sets
Pack (5):		3.00
Box (24):		60.00
1	Albert Pujols	2.50
2	Bernie Williams	.60
3	Vinny Castilla	.25
4	Rocco Baldelli	.60
5	Mike Piazza	1.50
6	Sean Casey	.25
7	Oliver Perez	.25
8	Tony Batista	.25
9	Paul Konerko	.25
10	Scott Rolen	1.00
11	Justin Morneau	.25
12	Nomar Garciaparra	2.50
13	Lance Berkman	.40
14	Mike Sweeney	.25
15	Miguel Tejada	.75
16	Craig Wilson	.25
17	Craig Biggio	.40
18	Shea Hillenbrand	.25
19	Mark Mulder	.40
20	Juan Pierre	.25
21	Troy Glaus	.60
22	Eric Chavez	.40
23	Jeromy Burnitz	.25
24	Carl Crawford	.25
25	Kazuo Matsui	.75
26	Ivan Rodriguez	.60
27	Aubrey Huff	.25
28	Derek Jeter	3.00
29	Casey Blake	.25
30	Mark Teixeira	.40
31	Brad Wilkerson	.25
32	Austin Kearns	.60
33	Jim Edmonds	.40
34	Johan Santana	.40
35	Kerry Wood	.75
36	Ichiro Suzuki	2.00
37	Lyle Overbay	.25
38	Melvin Mora	.25
39	Jason Bay	.25
40	Jake Westbrook	.25
41	Andruw Jones	.75
42	Chase Utley	.50
43	Carl Pavano	.25
44	Luis Gonzalez	.40
45	Bobby Crosby	.25
46	Carlos Guillen	.25
47	Carlos Delgado	.75
48	Alex Rodriguez	2.50
49	Todd Helton	.75
50	Michael Young	.25
51	Geoff Jenkins	.40
52	Pedro Martinez	1.00
53	Brian Giles	.40
54	Ken Harvey	.25
55	Johnny Estrada	.25
56	Billy Wagner	.25
57	Roger Clemens	2.50
58	Chipper Jones	1.50
59	Jim Thome	1.00
60	Miguel Cabrera	.75
61	Vladimir Guerrero	1.00
62	Gary Sheffield	.60
63	Travis Hafner	.25
64	Alfonso Soriano	1.00
65	Richard Hidalgo	.25
66	Adam Dunn	.60
67	Garret Anderson	.40
68	Lew Ford	.25
69	Mark Prior	1.50
70	Bret Boone	.40
71	Ben Sheets	.40
72	David Ortiz	.60
73	Mark Loretta	.25
74	Eric Gagne	.40
75	Curt Schilling	.60
76	Jason Schmidt	.40
77	Adrian Beltre	.40
78	Javy Lopez	.40
79	Jack Wilson	.25
80	Carlos Beltran	.60
81	J.D. Drew	.40
82	Bobby Abreu	.40
83	Jeff Bagwell	.75
84	Randy Johnson	1.00
85	Tim Hudson	.40
86	Carlos Pena	.25
87	Vernon Wells	.40
88	Tom Glavine	.40
89	Victor Martinez	.25
90	Hank Blalock	.60
91	Jose Vidro	.25
92	Magglio Ordonez	.40
93	Jake Peavy	.25
94	Torii Hunter	.60
95	Sammy Sosa	2.00
96	Hideki Matsui	2.50
97	Shawn Green	.40
98	Manny Ramirez	.75
99	Khalil Greene	.75
100	Jason Marquis	.25
101	B.J. Upton/Auto.	20.00
102	Scott Kazmir/Auto.	20.00
103	Gavin Floyd/Auto.	20.00
104	Jeff Francis/Auto.	20.00
105	Russ Adams/Auto. Exch.	10.00
106	Zack Greinke/Auto.	15.00
107	David Wright/Auto.	60.00
108	David Aardsma/Auto.	20.00
109	Josh Kroeger/Auto.	10.00
110	Ryan Raburn/Auto.	30.00
111	Jason Kubel/Auto.	10.00
112	Casey Kotchman/Auto.	20.00
113	Joey Gathright/Auto.	15.00
114	Jon Knott/Auto.	10.00
115	J.D. Durbin/Auto.	25.00
116	Andres Blanco/Auto.	10.00
117	Charlton Jimerson/Auto.	10.00
118	Sean Burnett/Auto.	15.00
119	Joe Mauer/Auto.	30.00
120	Justin Verlander/Auto. RC	30.00
121	Mike Gosling/Auto.	10.00
122	Jeff Keppinger/Auto.	10.00
123	David Krynzel/Auto.	10.00
124	Jose Lopez/Auto.	15.00
125	Ruben Gotay/Auto.	15.00

General Admission
Cards 1-100:	1-2.5X
Cards 101-125:	.75-1.5X

Production 100 Sets

Mezzanine

Cards 1-100:	1-3X
Cards 101-125:	.75-2X

Production 75 Sets

Club Box
Cards 1-100:	1-3.25X
Cards 101-125:	1-2X

Production 50 Sets

Standing Room Only
Cards 1-125:	No Pricing

Production 10 Sets

Autographed General Admission
	NM/M
Common Player:	15.00

Production 100 Sets
Mezzanine:	1-2X

Production 40 Sets
Club Box:	No Pricing

Production Five Sets
Standing Room Only:	No Pricing

Production One Set
JB	Jason Bay	15.00
JE	Johnny Estrada	15.00
CF	Chone Figgins	20.00
LF	Lew Ford	15.00
KG	Khalil Greene	50.00
TH	Travis Hafner	15.00
JM	Justin Morneau	40.00
JS	Johan Santana	25.00
BS	Ben Sheets	20.00
CU	Chase Utley	20.00
JW	Jack Wilson	15.00

Autograph Jersey General Admission
	NM/M
Common Player:	20.00

Production 75 Sets
Mezzanine:	No Pricing

Production 15 Sets
Club Box:	No Pricing

Production Five Sets
Standing Room Only:	No Pricing

Production One Set
JB	Jason Bay	20.00
MC	Miguel Cabrera	30.00
JE	Johnny Estrada	20.00
CF	Chone Figgins	25.00
LF	Lew Ford	20.00
KG	Khalil Greene	60.00
TH	Travis Hafner	20.00
JM	Justin Morneau	50.00
JS	Johan Santana	30.00
MS	Mike Schmidt	75.00
BS	Ben Sheets	25.00
CU	Chase Utley	25.00
JW	Jack Wilson	20.00

Autograph Patch General Admission

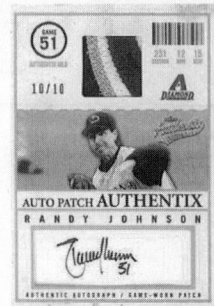

	NM/M

Production 40 Sets
Mezzanine:	No Pricing

Production 10 Sets
Club Box:	No Pricing

Production Five Sets
Standing Room Only
Production One Set
CF	Chone Figgins	25.00
MP	Mike Piazza	150.00
CR	Cal Ripken Jr.	400.00
MS	Mike Schmidt	150.00
JT	Jim Thome	80.00

Hot Ticket

	NM/M
Common Player:	2.00

Inserted 1:12
1	Derek Jeter	6.00
2	Roger Clemens	5.00
3	Vladimir Guerrero	3.00
4	Manny Ramirez	2.00
5	Alex Rodriguez	5.00
6	Albert Pujols	5.00
7	Mike Piazza	3.50
8	Hideki Matsui	5.00
9	Sammy Sosa	4.00
10	Chipper Jones	3.50

Hot Ticket Jersey
	NM/M
Common Player:	8.00

Inserted 1:87
Patch
Cards #'d to 55:	1-3X
Cards #'d to 27:	2-4X
Cards #'d to 25 or less:	No Pricing

Sequentially #'d to player's jersey #.
MLB Logo:	No Pricing

Production One Set
RC	Roger Clemens	15.00
VG	Vladimir Guerrero	8.00
CJ	Chipper Jones	10.00
HM	Hideki Matsui	25.00
MP	Mike Piazza	10.00
AP	Albert Pujols	20.00
MR	Manny Ramirez	8.00
SS	Sammy Sosa	12.00

Jersey General Admission
	NM/M
Common Player:	5.00

Inserted 1:16
Jersey Mezzanine:	1-3X

Production 75 Sets
Jersey Club Box:	No Pricing

Production 25 Sets
Jersey Standing Room Only:	No Pricing

Production One Set
Patch General Admission:	2-4X

Production 75 Sets
Patch Mezzanine:	No Pricing

Production 15 Sets

Patch Club Box: No Pricing
Production Five Sets
Patch Standing Room Only: No Pricing
Production One Set

CB	Carlos Beltran	10.00
AB	Adrian Beltre	5.00
LB	Lance Berkman	5.00
HB	Hank Blalock	5.00
MC	Miguel Cabrera	8.00
RC	Roger Clemens	12.00
AD	Adam Dunn	5.00
EG	Eric Gagne	5.00
KG	Khalil Greene	10.00
VG	Vladimir Guerrero	8.00
TH	Todd Helton	5.00
RJ	Randy Johnson	8.00
CJ	Chipper Jones	8.00
PM	Pedro Martinez	8.00
HM	Hideki Matsui	20.00
KM	Kazuo Matsui	10.00
JM	Joe Mauer	8.00
HN	Hideo Nomo	8.00
DO	David Ortiz	10.00
MP	Mike Piazza	8.00
AP	Albert Pujols	15.00
MR	Manny Ramirez	8.00
MR2	Mariano Rivera	5.00
IR	Ivan Rodriguez	5.00
SR	Scott Rolen	5.00
JS	Johan Santana	5.00
CS	Curt Schilling	5.00
GS	Gary Sheffield	5.00
AS	Alfonso Soriano	5.00
SS	Sammy Sosa	10.00
JT	Jim Thome	8.00
BU	B.J. Upton	8.00
BW	Bernie Williams	5.00
KW	Kerry Wood	8.00
DW	David Wright	15.00

Jersey Game of the Week
NM/M
Common Player: 10.00
Sequentially #'d between 10 & 200.
No pricing for cards #'d to 20 or less.
Patch: No Pricing
Production 10 Sets

BR	Carlos Beltran, Scott Rolen/120	15.00
BT	Tony Batista, Miguel Tejada/170	10.00
CG	Eric Chavez, Troy Glaus/150	12.00
CJ	Roger Clemens, Randy Johnson/70	15.00
CJ2	Miguel Cabrera, Chipper Jones/90	12.00
CP	Carl Crawford, Juan Pierre/190	10.00
DT	Adam Dunn, Jim Thome/110	20.00
GG	Shawn Green, Vladimir Guerrero/180	12.00
GS	Vladimir Guerrero, Alfonso Soriano/100	15.00
KG	Scott Kazmir, Zack Greinke/80	10.00
MM	Kazuo Matsui, Hideki Matsui/30	100.00
MM2	Joe Mauer, Victor Martinez/130	10.00
MR	Pedro Martinez, Mariano Rivera/60	12.00
OP	David Ortiz, Albert Pujols/200	15.00
OS	Magglio Ordonez, Sammy Sosa/160	15.00
RH	Manny Ramirez, Torii Hunter/140	10.00
SS	Johan Santana, Curt Schilling/40	30.00
WO	Kerry Wood, Roy Oswalt/50	30.00

Showstoppers
NM/M
Common Player: 2.00
Inserted 1:8

1	Nomar Garciaparra	4.00
2	Ichiro Suzuki	3.50
3	Ken Griffey Jr.	3.00

4	Alex Rodriguez	4.00
5	Albert Pujols	4.00
6	Derek Jeter	5.00
7	Roger Clemens	4.00
8	Randy Johnson	2.50
9	Hideo Nomo	2.00
10	Jim Thome	2.50
11	Mike Piazza	3.00
12	Hideki Matsui	4.00
13	Sammy Sosa	3.50
14	Kerry Wood	2.00
15	Eric Gagne	2.00

Teammate Trios
NM/M
Common Card: 12.00
Production 75 Sets
Hometown 1: 2-3X
Production 25 Sets
Hometown 2: No Pricing
Production Five Sets

BR	David Ortiz, Manny Ramirez, Pedro Martinez	25.00
NY	Hideki Matsui, Bernie Williams, Gary Sheffield	30.00
AB	J.D. Drew, Chipper Jones, Andruw Jones	15.00
CC	Sammy Sosa, Mark Prior, Nomar Garciaparra	15.00
CI	Victor Martinez, Travis Hafner, Casey Blake	12.00
HA	Lance Berkman, Roger Clemens, Carlos Beltran	25.00
MT	Johan Santana, Torii Hunter, Corey Koskie	12.00
WN	Tony Batista, Jose Vidro, Brad Wilkerson	12.00
NM	Mike Piazza, David Wright, Kazuo Matsui	40.00
OA	Barry Zito, Tim Hudson, Mark Mulder	12.00
PP	Bobby Abreu, Jim Thome, Pat Burrell	15.00
SC	Scott Rolen, Albert Pujols, Jim Edmonds	30.00
TD	Scott Kazmir, Rocco Baldelli, B.J. Upton	25.00
TR	Hank Blalock, Mark Teixeira, Alfonso Soriano	15.00
LD	Shawn Green, Adrian Beltre, Steve Finley	12.00

2005 Fleer Classic Clippings
NM/M
Common Player (1-75): .25
Minor Stars (1-75): .40
Unlisted Stars (1-75): .60
Common Legends (76-105): 2.00
Production 999 Sets
Common Player (106-125): 3.00
Inserted 1:6

1	Frank Thomas	.75
2	Vladimir Guerrero	1.00
3	Ken Griffey Jr.	1.50
4	Derek Jeter	3.00
5	Rafael Palmeiro	.75
6	Adrian Beltre	.40
7	Khalil Greene	.75
8	Richie Sexson	.60
9	Roger Clemens	2.50
10	Mike Piazza	1.50
11	Chipper Jones	1.50
12	Juan Pierre	.25
13	Todd Helton	.75
14	Ben Sheets	.40
15	John Smoltz	.40
16	Steve Finley	.25
17	Jim Thome	1.00
18	Vernon Wells	.40
19	Melvin Mora	.25
20	Dontrelle Willis	.40
21	Eric Gagne	.40
22	Craig Wilson	.25
23	Curt Schilling	.60
24	Justin Morneau	.25
25	Jason Schmidt	.40
26	Kerry Wood	.75
27	Ivan Rodriguez	.60
28	Rocco Baldelli	.60
29	Mark Prior	2.00
30	Josh Beckett	.75
31	Scott Rolen	1.00
32	Nomar Garciaparra	2.50
33	Carl Crawford	.25
34	Paul Konerko	.40
35	Miguel Cabrera	.75
36	Hank Blalock	.60
37	Sammy Sosa	2.00
38	Jim Edmonds	.40
39	David Ortiz	.60
40	Lance Berkman	.40
41	Ichiro Suzuki	2.00

42	Adam Dunn	.60
43	Carlos Guillen	.25
44	Alfonso Soriano	1.00
45	Victor Martinez	.25
46	Torii Hunter	.60
47	Kazuo Matsui	.60
48	Andruw Jones	.75
49	Matt Holliday	.50
50	Eric Chavez	.40
51	Randy Johnson	1.00
52	Lew Ford	.25
53	Hideki Matsui	2.50
54	Manny Ramirez	.75
55	Mark Teixeira	.40
56	Jose Vidro	.25
57	Mike Sweeney	.25
58	Jack Wilson	.25
59	Greg Maddux	1.50
60	Tony Batista	.25
61	Albert Pujols	2.50
62	Miguel Tejada	.60
63	Carlos Beltran	.60
64	Bobby Abreu	.40
65	Carlos Delgado	.75
66	Travis Hafner	.25
67	Scott Podsednik	.25
68	Gary Sheffield	.60
69	Johan Santana	.40
70	Barry Zito	.60
71	Pedro Martinez	1.00
72	Brian Giles	.40
73	Garret Anderson	.40
74	Jeff Bagwell	.75
75	Alex Rodriguez	2.50
76	Johnny Bench	4.00
77	Yogi Berra	3.00
78	Lou Brock	3.00
79	Rod Carew	3.00
80	Orlando Cepeda	2.00
81	Carlton Fisk	3.00
82	Bob Gibson	2.00
83	Reggie Jackson	5.00
84	Al Kaline	4.00
85	Harmon Killebrew	3.00
86	Ralph Kiner	2.00
87	Willie McCovey	2.00
88	Eddie Murray	2.00
89	Phil Rizzuto	4.00
90	Brooks Robinson	3.00
91	Nolan Ryan	5.00
92	Mike Schmidt	4.00
93	Tom Seaver	3.00
94	Willie Stargell	2.00
95	Rollie Fingers	2.00
96	Dennis Eckersley	2.00
97	Enos Slaughter	2.00
98	Jim Palmer	2.00
99	Warren Spahn	3.00
100	Joe Morgan	3.00
101	Richie Ashburn	3.00
102	Robin Yount	3.00
103	Bob Feller	3.00
104	Pee Wee Reese	3.00
105	Eddie Mathews	3.00
106	David Wright	6.00
107	David Aardsma	3.00
108	B.J. Upton	5.00
109	Scott Kazmir	4.00
110	Gavin Floyd	3.00
111	Jeff Francis	3.00
112	Dioner Navarro	3.00
113	Zack Greinke	5.00
114	Nick Swisher	5.00
115	Josh Kroeger	3.00
116	Ryan Raburn	3.00
117	Victor Diaz	4.00
118	Casey Kotchman	4.00
119	Joey Gathright	3.00
120	Jon Knott	3.00
121	J.D. Durbin	3.00
122	Andres Blanco	3.00
123	Charlton Jimerson	3.00
124	Russ Adams	3.00
125	Justin Verlander **RC**	5.00

First Edition
(1-75):	2-5X
(76-105):	1-1.5X
(106-125):	1-2X
Production 150 Sets

Final Edition
No Pricing
Production One Set

Press Clippings
NM/M
Common Player: 2.00
Inserted 1:6
Gold: No Pricing
Production Four Sets

1	Ichiro Suzuki	4.00
2	Manny Ramirez	2.00
3	Albert Pujols	5.00
4	David Ortiz	2.00
5	Greg Maddux	3.00
6	Ken Griffey Jr.	3.00
7	Vladimir Guerrero	3.00
8	Randy Johnson	3.00
9	Johan Santana	2.00
10	Roger Clemens	5.00
11	Bobby Crosby	2.00
12	Jason Bay	2.00

Bat Rack Quad Blue
NM/M
Inserted 1:118
Silver: No Pricing
Production 10 Sets
Purple: No Pricing
Production One Set

Gary Sheffield, Vladimir Guerrero, Manny Ramirez, Sammy Sosa	20.00
Manny Ramirez, Wade Boggs, Carl Yastrzemski, Bobby Doerr	40.00
Kirby Puckett, Jacque Jones, Harmon Killebrew, Torii Hunter	40.00
Brandon Webb, Randy Johnson, Curt Schilling, Roger Clemens	40.00
Willie Stargell, Bill Madlock, Bill Mazeroski, Roberto Clemente	100.00
Al Kaline, Tony Gwynn, Frank Howard, Rocky Colavito	50.00
Jose Reyes, Gary Carter, Mike Piazza, Kazuo Matsui	25.00
Bobby Abreu, Adam Dunn, Rocco Baldelli, Hideki Matsui	30.00
Jim Thome, Albert Pujols, Jeff Bagwell, Todd Helton	40.00
Hank Blalock, Miguel Tejada, Troy Glaus, Ivan Rodriguez	25.00
Carlos Delgado, Jason Giambi, Rafael Palmeiro, Mark Teixeira	25.00

Classic Clippings
NM/M
Common Player: 3.00
Gold: 2-5X
Production 51-95 Sets

1	Nolan Ryan/1991	6.00
2	Cal Ripken Jr./1995	8.00
3	Joe Carter/1993	3.00
4	Bucky Dent/1978	3.00
5	Kirk Gibson/1988	3.00
6	Reggie Jackson/1977	5.00
7	Carlton Fisk/1975	4.00
8	Bobby Thomson/1951	3.00
9	Bill Mazeroski/1960	3.00
10	Don Larsen/1956	4.00

Cut of History Single Jersey Blue
NM/M
Common Player: 6.00
Inserted 1:21
Silver Patch: No Pricing
Production 25 Sets
Purple Patch: No Pricing
Production One Set

SA	Sparky Anderson	6.00
JB	Johnny Bench	15.00
OC	Orlando Cepeda	8.00
CF	Carlton Fisk	10.00
BG	Bob Gibson	8.00
DG	Dwight Gooden	6.00
RJ	Reggie Jackson	12.00
DM	Don Mattingly	15.00
WM	Willie McCovey	6.00
JM	Joe Morgan/SP/82	12.00
EM	Eddie Murray	10.00
CR	Cal Ripken Jr.	20.00
BR	Brooks Robinson	8.00
NR	Nolan Ryan	20.00
MS	Mike Schmidt	12.00
TS	Tom Seaver	10.00
OS	Ozzie Smith	15.00
WS	Willie Stargell	10.00
DS	Darryl Strawberry	6.00
CY	Carl Yastrzemski	10.00

Cut of History Single Autograph Blue
NM/M
Common Player: 20.00
Inserted 1:161
Silver: No Pricing
Production 25 Sets
Purple: No Pricing
Production One Set

JB	Johnny Bench	50.00
BB	Bill Buckner	20.00
BF	Bob Feller	20.00
KG	Kirk Gibson	20.00
DG	Dwight Gooden	30.00
DL	Don Larsen	20.00
DM	Don Mattingly	50.00
JP	Jim Palmer	30.00
BR	Brooks Robinson	40.00
DS	Darryl Strawberry	25.00
MW	Mookie Wilson	20.00

Cut of History Dual Jersey Blue
NM/M
Common Card: 15.00
Inserted 1:112
Silver Patch: No Pricing

Production 15 Sets
Purple Patch: No Pricing
Production One Set

BF	Johnny Bench, Carlton Fisk	20.00
BS	Lou Brock, Mike Schmidt	25.00
CM	Orlando Cepeda, Willie McCovey	15.00
GS	Dwight Gooden, Darryl Strawberry	15.00
JY	Reggie Jackson, Carl Yastrzemski	20.00
RS	Cal Ripken Jr., Ozzie Smith	30.00
RS	Nolan Ryan, Tom Seaver	30.00
SJ	Willie Stargell, Reggie Jackson	20.00

Cut of History Triple Jersey Blue

NM/M

Inserted 1:67
Silver Patch: No Pricing
Production 25 Sets
Purple Patch: No Pricing
Production One Set

ACW	Hank Aaron, Roberto Clemente, Ted Williams	160.00
BSG	Lou Brock, Kirk Gibson, Ozzie Smith	50.00
JKM	Reggie Jackson, Harmon Killebrew, Willie McCovey	40.00
MMC	Eddie Murray, Orlando Cepeda, Willie McCovey	25.00
MRS	Don Mattingly, Cal Ripken Jr., Mike Schmidt	75.00
OJM	Paul O'Neill, Don Mattingly, Reggie Jackson	50.00
RCJ	Nolan Ryan, Roger Clemens, Randy Johnson	50.00

Cut of History Dual Autograph Blue

NM/M

Production 49 Sets
Silver: No Pricing
Production 22 Sets
Purple: No Pricing
Production One Set

GE	Kirk Gibson, Dennis Eckersley	50.00
GS	Dwight Gooden, Darryl Strawberry	40.00
WB	Mookie Wilson, Bill Buckner	40.00

Cut of History Triple Autograph Blue

No Pricing
Production 15 Sets
Silver: No Pricing
Production Five Sets
Purple: No Pricing
Production One Set

Jersey Rack Dual Jersey Blue

NM/M

Common Card: 10.00
Inserted 1:100
Silver Patch: No Pricing
Production 25 Sets
Purple Patch: No Pricing
Production One Set

BW	Josh Beckett, Kerry Wood	10.00
CJ	Miguel Cabrera, Andruw Jones	12.00
DB	Adam Dunn, Lance Berkman	10.00
GS	Vladimir Guerrero, Sammy Sosa	15.00
GT	Khalil Greene, Miguel Tejada	10.00
HB	Todd Helton, Jeff Bagwell	10.00
HE	Torii Hunter, Jim Edmonds	10.00
JC	Randy Johnson, Roger Clemens	20.00
JW	Chipper Jones, David Wright	15.00
MM	Hideki Matsui, Kazuo Matsui	25.00
OG	David Ortiz, Jason Giambi	12.00
RB	Scott Rolen, Adrian Beltre	12.00
RS	Manny Ramirez, Gary Sheffield	12.00
SG	John Smoltz, Eric Gagne	10.00
SM	Jason Schmidt, Pedro Martinez	12.00
SM1	Alfonso Soriano, Kazuo Matsui	10.00
SP	Curt Schilling, Mark Prior	8.00
TP	Jim Thome, Mike Piazza	12.00
WS	Dontrelle Willis, Johan Santana	12.00

Triple Jersey Blue

NM/M

Common Card: 12.00
Inserted 1:54
Silver Patch: No Pricing
Production 25 Sets
Purple Patch: No Pricing

CJS	Roger Clemens, Randy Johnson, Jason Schmidt	20.00
CSJ	Roger Clemens, Curt Schilling, Randy Johnson	20.00
EHJ	Jim Edmonds, Torii Hunter, Andruw Jones	12.00
GRS	Vladimir Guerrero, Manny Ramirez, Gary Sheffield	15.00
GSR	Eric Gagne, John Smoltz, Mariano Rivera	15.00
HSB	Todd Helton, Alfonso Soriano, Adrian Beltre	15.00
MGT	Kazuo Matsui, Khalil Greene, Miguel Tejada	15.00
MRG	Hideki Matsui, Mariano Rivera, Jason Giambi	25.00
ORM	David Ortiz, Manny Ramirez, Pedro Martinez	15.00
PRE	Albert Pujols, Scott Rolen, Jim Edmonds	25.00
PTB	Albert Pujols, Jim Thome, Jeff Bagwell	20.00
RBJ	Scott Rolen, Adrian Beltre, Chipper Jones	15.00
SDC	Sammy Sosa, Adam Dunn, Miguel Cabrera	12.00
SJJ	John Smoltz, Chipper Jones, Andruw Jones	20.00
SPB	Jason Schmidt, Mark Prior, Josh Beckett	10.00
STB	Sammy Sosa, Miguel Tejada, Adrian Beltre	15.00
WPM	David Wright, Mike Piazza, Kazuo Matsui	20.00
WSW	Dontrelle Willis, Johan Santana, Kerry Wood	15.00

Diamond Signings Single Blue

NM/M

Inserted 1:29
Silver: No Pricing
Production 25 Sets
Purple: No Pricing
Production One Set

JB	Jason Bay	20.00
AB	Andres Blanco	15.00
CF	Chone Figgins	15.00
GF	Gavin Floyd	15.00
KG	Khalil Greene/150	25.00
ZG	Zack Greinke	15.00
TH	Travis Hafner	10.00
CJ	Charlton Jimerson	10.00
SK	Scott Kazmir	20.00
CK	Casey Kotchman	10.00
BL	Brad Lidge/97	40.00
JM	Justin Morneau/98	25.00
DN	Dioner Navarro	10.00
JP	Jake Peavy	20.00
NS	Nick Swisher	15.00
BU	B.J. Upton	15.00
JV	Justin Verlander/150	35.00
DW	David Wright/97	50.00

Diamond Signings Dual Blue

NM/M

Production 49 Sets
Silver: No Pricing
Production 22 Sets
Purple: No Pricing
Production One Set

BC	Jason Bay, B. Crosby Exch	30.00
FU	Gavin Floyd, Chase Utley	40.00

Diamond Signings Triple Blue

NM/M

Sequentially Numbered
Silver: No Pricing
Production Five Sets
Purple: No Pricing
Production One Set

Khalil Greene, B.J. Upton, Bobby Crosby/99	50.00
Justin Verlander, Gavin Floyd, Scott Kazmir/99	75.00
Nick Swisher, Charlton Jimerson, Chone Figgins/99	30.00
Casey Kotchman, Justin Morneau, Jason Bay/86	40.00

2005 Fleer Patchworks

NM/M

Complete Set (100):
Common (1-70): .40
Common (71-90): 1.50
Production 499 Sets
Common (91-100): 2.00
Production 999 Sets
Pack (5): 4.00
Box (18): 60.00

1	Bobby Abreu	.50
2	Miguel Cabrera	1.00
3	J.D. Drew	.40
4	Justin Morneau	.40
5	David Ortiz	1.00
6	Ivan Rodriguez	.75
7	Jason Schmidt	.40
8	Frank Thomas	.75
9	Travis Hafner	.50
10	Curt Schilling	1.00
11	Jim Edmonds	.75
12	Randy Johnson	1.00
13	Jose Vidro	.40
14	Vernon Wells	.40
15	Lance Berkman	.50
16	Khalil Greene	.50
17	Andruw Jones	.75
18	Mark Prior	.75
19	Mark Teixeira	.75
20	Jack Wilson	.40
21	Adrian Beltre	.40
22	Lew Ford	.40
23	Shawn Green	.50
24	Juan Pierre	.40
25	Alfonso Soriano	.75
26	Mike Sweeney	.40
27	Chipper Jones	1.00
28	Javy Lopez	.40
29	Victor Martinez	.40
30	Kazuo Matsui	.40
31	Bernie Williams	.50
32	Kerry Wood	.50
33	Barry Zito	.50
34	Austin Kearns	.40
35	Todd Helton	.50
36	B.J. Upton	.40
37	Jeff Bagwell	.75
38	Pedro Martinez	1.00
39	Lyle Overbay	.40
40	Ichiro Suzuki	2.00
41	Jason Bay	.50
42	Bobby Crosby	.40
43	Vladimir Guerrero	1.00
44	Richie Sexson	.50
45	Johan Santana	1.00
46	Magglio Ordonez	.40
47	Derek Jeter	3.00
48	Eric Gagne	.40
49	Albert Pujols	3.00
50	Jim Thome	.75
51	Hideki Matsui	2.00
52	Torii Hunter	.40
53	Greg Maddux	2.00
54	Michael Young	.40
55	Carlos Beltran	.75
56	Carl Crawford	.40
57	Adam Dunn	.75
58	Nomar Garciaparra	1.00
59	Mike Piazza	1.00
60	Alex Rodriguez	3.00
61	Scott Rolen	.75
62	Ben Sheets	.50
63	Sammy Sosa	1.00
64	Hank Blalock	.50
65	Carlos Delgado	.50
66	Ken Griffey Jr.	2.00
67	Manny Ramirez	1.00
68	Miguel Tejada	.75
69	Roger Clemens	3.00
70	Gary Sheffield	.75
71	Jon Knott	1.50
72	Ryan Raburn	1.50
73	Zack Greinke	1.50
74	David Aardsma	1.50
75	Justin Verlander RC	4.00
76	Andres Blanco	1.50
77	David Wright	4.00
78	Jeff Baker	1.50
79	Charlton Jimerson	1.50
80	Sean Burnett	1.50
81	Joey Gathright	1.50
82	Victor Diaz	1.50
83	Scott Kazmir	1.50
84	Edwin Encarnacion	1.50
85	J.D. Durbin	1.50
86	Nick Swisher	1.50
87	Casey Kotchman	1.50
88	Gavin Floyd	1.50
89	Josh Kroeger	1.50
90	Taylor Buchholz	1.50
91	Reggie Jackson	2.00
92	Nolan Ryan	6.00
93	Eddie Murray	2.00
94	Carlton Fisk	2.00
95	Mike Schmidt	4.00
96	Joe Morgan	2.00
97	Rod Carew	2.00
98	Harmon Killebrew	3.00
99	Tom Seaver	3.00
100	Brooks Robinson	3.00

Gold

Gold (1-70): 3-6X
Gold (71-100): 1-2X
Production 99 Sets

Autoworks Copper

NM/M

Production 75-250
Masterpiece: No Pricing
Production One Set

RB	Rocco Baldelli/100	12.00
JB	Jason Bay/150	20.00
JBO	Jeremy Bonderman/100	15.00
SB	Sean Burnett/100	8.00
MC	Miguel Cabrera/75	25.00
CC	Carl Crawford/125	15.00
JD	J.D. Durbin/100	8.00
ZG	Zack Greinke/200	10.00
TH	Travis Hafner/150	15.00
BL	Brad Lidge/75	15.00
VM	Victor Martinez/100	15.00
JM	Justin Morneau/175	20.00
BU	B.J. Upton/150	15.00
JV	Justin Verlander/100	20.00
DW	David Wright/250	50.00

Autoworks Dual

No Pricing
Production 25 Sets

Autoworks Gold

NM/M

Production 49 Sets

HA	Hank Aaron	250.00
RB	Rocco Baldelli	15.00
EB	Ernie Banks	50.00
JB	Jason Bay	20.00
LB	Lance Berkman	20.00
JBO	Jeremy Bonderman	20.00
SB	Sean Burnett	10.00
MC	Miguel Cabrera	30.00
MCA	Mike Cameron	12.00
CC	Carl Crawford	20.00
JD	J.D. Durbin	10.00
GF	Gavin Floyd	10.00
LF	Lew Ford	10.00
ZG	Zack Greinke	12.00
TH	Travis Hafner	20.00
BL	Brad Lidge	20.00
VM	Victor Martinez	20.00
JM	Justin Morneau	25.00
JP	Josh Phelps	10.00
BS	Ben Sheets	20.00
BU	B.J. Upton	20.00
DW	David Wright	60.00
MY	Michael Young	15.00

Autoworks Quad

No Pricing
Production 10 Sets

Autoworks Silver

NM/M

Production 99 Sets

RB	Rocco Baldelli	12.00
JB	Jason Bay	20.00
JBO	Jeremy Bonderman	15.00
SB	Sean Burnett	8.00
MC	Miguel Cabrera	25.00
MCA	Mike Cameron	12.00
CC	Carl Crawford	15.00
JD	J.D. Durbin	8.00
LF	Lew Ford	10.00
ZG	Zack Greinke	10.00
TH	Travis Hafner	15.00
BL	Brad Lidge	15.00
VM	Victor Martinez	15.00
JM	Justin Morneau	20.00
JP	Josh Phelps	10.00
BS	Ben Sheets	15.00
BU	B.J. Upton	15.00
JV	Justin Verlander	20.00
DW	David Wright	60.00

By the Numbers

NM/M

Common Player: 1.00

Inserted 1:18

1	Roy Oswalt	1.00
2	Hideki Matsui	3.00
3	Curt Schilling	1.50
4	Mike Piazza	2.00
5	Alex Rodriguez	4.00
6	Vladimir Guerrero	1.50
7	Victor Martinez	1.00
8	Adrian Beltre	1.00
9	Johnny Estrada	1.00
10	Ken Griffey Jr.	3.00
11	Sammy Sosa	2.00
12	Ichiro Suzuki	3.00
13	Roger Clemens	4.00
14	David Ortiz	1.50
15	Johan Santana	1.50
16	Pedro Martinez	1.50
17	Austin Kearns	1.00
18	Randy Johnson	1.50
19	Nomar Garciaparra	1.50
20	Albert Pujols	4.00

By the Numbers Jersey

		NM/M
Common Player:		4.00
AB	Adrian Beltre	4.00
RC	Roger Clemens/SP	10.00
JE	Johnny Estrada	4.00
VG	Vladimir Guerrero/SP	8.00
RJ	Randy Johnson	8.00
PM	Pedro Martinez	8.00
HM	Hideki Matsui	20.00
RO	Roy Oswalt	4.00
AP	Albert Pujols	15.00
JS	Johan Santana	6.00
CS	Curt Schilling	8.00
SS	Sammy Sosa	8.00

By the Numbers Jersey Die Cut

		NM/M
Production 199 Sets		
Jersey Tag:		No Pricing
Production One Set		
AB	Adrian Beltre	4.00
RC	Roger Clemens	10.00
JE	Johnny Estrada	4.00
VG	Vladimir Guerrero	8.00
RJ	Randy Johnson	8.00
AK	Austin Kearns	4.00
PM	Pedro Martinez	8.00
HM	Hideki Matsui	20.00
DO	David Ortiz	8.00
RO	Roy Oswalt	4.00
MP	Mike Piazza/116	10.00
AP	Albert Pujols	15.00
JS	Johan Santana	6.00
CS	Curt Schilling	8.00
SS	Sammy Sosa	8.00

By the Numbers Patch

		NM/M
Production 99 Sets		
Patch Die-Cut:		No Pricing
Production 25 Sets		
AB	Adrian Beltre	10.00
RC	Roger Clemens	
JE	Johnny Estrada	8.00
VG	Vladimir Guerrero	15.00
AK	Austin Kearns/78	10.00
HM	Hideki Matsui	30.00
DO	David Ortiz/46	15.00
RO	Roy Oswalt	10.00
MP	Mike Piazza	20.00
AP	Albert Pujols	30.00
JS	Johan Santana	15.00
CS	Curt Schilling	15.00
SS	Sammy Sosa	20.00

By the Numbers Patch Autographs

No Pricing
Production 25 Sets

Dual Jersey

		NM/M
Common Duo:		6.00
Die-Cut:		1-1.5X
Production 199 Sets		
Dual MLB Logo:		No Pricing
Production One Set		
Dual Patch:		No Pricing
Production 25 Sets		
Dual Patch Die-Cut:		No Pricing
Production 15 Sets		
DWJB	Dontrelle Willis, Josh Beckett	6.00
DWMP	David Wright, Mike Piazza	15.00
GSBW	Gary Sheffield, Bernie Williams/SP	8.00
KWMP	Kerry Wood, Mark Prior/SP	8.00
MRDO	Manny Ramirez, David Ortiz	15.00
MYAS	Michael Young, Alfonso Soriano	8.00
SSTH	Shannon Stewart, Torii Hunter	6.00

Heart of the Team

		NM/M
Inserted 1:108		
1	Braves/Marlins	8.00

2	Red Sox/Yankees	15.00
3	Cardinals/Astros	15.00
4	Angels/A's	8.00
5	Phillies/Mets	8.00
6	Twins/White Sox	8.00
7	Reds/Cubs	10.00
8	Mariners/Rangers	10.00
9	Orioles/Nationals	8.00
10	Blue Jays/Devil Rays	8.00

Heart of the Team Jersey

Production 199 Sets
Patch: No Pricing
Production 15 Sets

Jersey

		NM/M
Common Player:		4.00
JB	Josh Beckett	4.00
TH	Torii Hunter	4.00
MARK	Mark Prior	4.00
MR	Manny Ramirez	8.00
GS	Gary Sheffield	6.00
AS	Alfonso Soriano	6.00
SS	Shannon Stewart	4.00
BW	Bernie Williams	6.00
DW	Dontrelle Willis	4.00
KW	Kerry Wood	4.00
DWR	David Wright	15.00
MY	Michael Young	4.00

Patch

		NM/M
Production 99 Sets		
Die-Cut:		1-1.5X
Production 49 Sets		
JB	Josh Beckett	8.00
TH	Torii Hunter	10.00
DO	David Ortiz/51	20.00
MIKE	Mike Piazza	20.00
MARK	Mark Prior	15.00
MR	Manny Ramirez	20.00
AS	Alfonso Soriano/73	12.00
SS	Shannon Stewart	10.00
BW	Bernie Williams	12.00
DW	Dontrelle Willis	15.00
KW	Kerry Wood	12.00
DWR	David Wright	35.00
MY	Michael Young	10.00

Property of

		NM/M
Common Player:		1.00
Inserted 1:6		
1	Vladimir Guerrero	1.50
2	Luis Gonzalez	1.00
3	Chipper Jones	1.50
4	Miguel Tejada	1.50
5	David Ortiz	1.50
6	Kerry Wood	1.00
7	Frank Thomas	1.00
8	Adam Dunn	1.00
9	Victor Martinez	1.00
10	Todd Helton	1.00
11	Ivan Rodriguez	1.50
12	Miguel Cabrera	1.50
13	Jeff Bagwell	1.50
14	Mike Sweeney	1.00
15	Eric Gagne	1.00
16	Lyle Overbay	1.00
17	Johan Santana	1.50
18	Mike Piazza	2.00
19	Derek Jeter	5.00
20	Bobby Crosby	1.00
21	Jim Thome	1.50
22	Jason Bay	1.00
23	Khalil Greene	1.00
24	Jason Schmidt	1.00
25	Ichiro Suzuki	3.00
26	Albert Pujols	5.00
27	B.J. Upton	1.00
28	Hank Blalock	1.00
29	Vernon Wells	1.00
30	Jose Vidro	1.00

Property of Jersey

		NM/M
JB	Jeff Bagwell	6.00
JBA	Jason Bay	4.00
HB	Hank Blalock	4.00
MC	Miguel Cabrera	8.00
EG	Eric Gagne	4.00
LG	Luis Gonzalez	4.00
VG	Vladimir Guerrero/SP	8.00
CJ	Chipper Jones	8.00
AP	Albert Pujols	15.00
IR	Ivan Rodriguez	6.00
JS	Johan Santana/SP	8.00
JSC	Jason Schmidt	4.00
MT	Miguel Tejada	6.00
FT	Frank Thomas	6.00
JT	Jim Thome	6.00

BU	B.J. Upton	4.00
VW	Vernon Wells	4.00
KW	Kerry Wood	4.00

Property of Jersey Die Cut

		NM/M
Production 199 Sets		
MLB Logo:		No Pricing
Production One Set		
JB	Jeff Bagwell	6.00
JBA	Jason Bay	4.00
HB	Hank Blalock	4.00
MC	Miguel Cabrera	8.00
EG	Eric Gagne	4.00
LG	Luis Gonzalez	4.00
KG	Khalil Greene	4.00
VG	Vladimir Guerrero	8.00
CJ	Chipper Jones	8.00
DO	David Ortiz	8.00
LO	Lyle Overbay/86 UER	4.00
MP	Mike Piazza	8.00
AP	Albert Pujols	15.00
IR	Ivan Rodriguez	6.00
JS	Johan Santana	4.00
JSC	Jason Schmidt	4.00
MT	Miguel Tejada	6.00
FT	Frank Thomas	6.00
JT	Jim Thome	6.00
BU	B.J. Upton	4.00
VW	Vernon Wells	4.00
KW	Kerry Wood	4.00

Property of Patch

		NM/M
Production 99 Sets		
Die-Cut:		No Pricing
Production 25 Sets		
Nameplate:		1-2X
Production 49 Sets		
JB	Jeff Bagwell	15.00
JBA	Jason Bay/84	10.00
HB	Hank Blalock	12.00
MC	Miguel Cabrera	15.00
AD	Adam Dunn/42	10.00
EG	Eric Gagne	10.00
LG	Luis Gonzalez	10.00
KG	Khalil Greene	10.00
VG	Vladimir Guerrero	15.00
CJ	Chipper Jones	15.00
DO	David Ortiz/45	20.00
MP	Mike Piazza	20.00
AP	Albert Pujols	30.00
IR	Ivan Rodriguez	15.00
JS	Johan Santana/SP	15.00
JSC	Jason Schmidt	12.00
MS	Mike Sweeney/77	10.00
MT	Miguel Tejada	15.00
JT	Jim Thome	15.00
BU	B.J. Upton	10.00
VW	Vernon Wells/30	10.00
KW	Kerry Wood/89	15.00

2005 Fleer Platinum

	NM/M
Common Players (1-100):	.25
Minor Players (1-100):	.40
Unlisted Stars (1-100):	.50
Common Players (101-125):	3.00
Production 1,000 Sets	
Pack (5):	2.00
Box (24):	40.00
1	Nomar Garciaparra	1.50
2	Matt Holliday	.50
3	Rickie Weeks	.25
4	Jim Thome	.75
5	Roy Halladay	.40
6	Paul Konerko	.25
7	Lance Berkman	.40
8	Ichiro Suzuki	1.25
9	Kerry Wood	.60
10	Lew Ford	.25
11	Omar Vizquel	.40
12	Manny Ramirez	.50
13	Carlos Beltran	.50
14	Lyle Overbay	.25
15	Billy Wagner	.40
16	Jose Vidro	.25
17	Vladimir Guerrero	.75
18	Miguel Tejada	.50
19	Alex Rodriguez	1.50
20	Rocco Baldelli	.25
21	David Ortiz	.50

22	Victor Martinez	.25
23	Shawn Green	.40
24	Jason Bay	.25
25	Pedro Martinez	.75
26	Travis Hafner	.25
27	Eric Gagne	.40
28	Jack Wilson	.25
29	Ivan Rodriguez	.50
30	Jody Gerut	.25
31	Adrian Beltre	.40
32	Craig Wilson	.25
33	J.D. Drew	.40
34	Craig Biggio	.40
35	Mark Mulder	.40
36	Mark Teixeira	.50
37	Melvin Mora	.25
38	Ken Griffey Jr.	1.00
39	Mike Sweeney	.25
40	Khalil Greene	.60
41	Rafael Palmeiro	.50
42	Austin Kearns	.50
43	Garret Anderson	.40
44	Trevor Hoffman	.25
45	Andruw Jones	.60
46	Adam Dunn	.50
47	Angel Berroa	.25
48	Ryan Klesko	.40
49	Sean Casey	.25
50	Kazuo Matsui	.50
51	Jim Edmonds	.40
52	Magglio Ordonez	.40
53	Tom Glavine	.40
54	Larry Walker	.40
55	Johnny Estrada	.25
56	Brad Lidge	.25
57	Barry Zito	.50
58	Michael Young	.40
59	Chipper Jones	1.00
60	Andy Pettitte	.50
61	Eric Chavez	.40
62	Carlos Delgado	.60
63	David Eckstein	.25
64	Dmitri Young	.25
65	Mike Piazza	1.00
66	Albert Pujols	1.50
67	Luis Gonzalez	.40
68	Hideki Matsui	1.50
69	Gary Sheffield	.50
70	Carl Crawford	.25
71	Curt Schilling	.50
72	Todd Helton	.60
73	Ben Sheets	.40
74	Bobby Abreu	.40
75	Jose Guillen	.25
76	Richie Sexson	.50
77	Miguel Cabrera	.60
78	Bernie Williams	.50
79	Aubrey Huff	.25
80	John Smoltz	.40
81	Jeff Bagwell	.60
82	Tim Hudson	.40
83	Alfonso Soriano	.75
84	Freddy Garcia	.25
85	Johan Santana	.40
86	Bret Boone	.40
87	Troy Glaus	.50
88	Carlos Guillen	.25
89	Derek Jeter	2.00
90	Scott Rolen	.75
91	Sammy Sosa	1.25
92	Jacque Jones	.25
93	Jason Schmidt	.40
94	Randy Johnson	.75
95	Dontrelle Willis	.40
96	Mariano Rivera	.40
97	Hank Blalock	.50
98	Mark Prior	1.50
99	Torii Hunter	.50
100	Roger Clemens	1.50
101	David Wright	6.00
102	Justin Morneau	4.00
103	Scott Kazmir	4.00
104	Gavin Floyd	3.00
105	Justin Verlander RC	8.00
106	Zack Greinke	4.00
107	David Aardsma	3.00
108	Ryan Raburn	4.00
109	Joey Gathright	3.00
110	J.D. Durbin	3.00
111	Sean Burnett	3.00
112	Jose Lopez	5.00
113	Nick Swisher	4.00
114	Bobby Jenks	8.00
115	Kelly Johnson	8.00
116	B.J. Upton	5.00
117	Ronny Cedeno	3.00
118	Edwin Encarnacion	6.00
119	Jeff Baker	3.00
120	Taylor Buchholz	3.00
121	Livan Hernandez RC	4.00
122	Dioner Navarro	4.00
123	Victor Diaz	4.00
124	Jon Knott	4.00
125	Russ Adams	3.00

Finish

Cards 1-100:	3-6X
Cards 101-125:	.75-1.25X
Production 199 Sets	

Extreme

Cards 1-125:	No Pricing
Production 20 Sets	

Autograph Die Cuts

NM/M

Numbered to indicated quantities.

1	Lew Ford/99	10.00
3	Jason Bay/50	15.00
4	Travis Hafner/99	15.00
6	Brad Lidge/99	30.00
7	Michael Young/99	15.00
8	David Eckstein/99	20.00
9	Carl Crawford/50	15.00
10	Miguel Cabrera/50	25.00
11	David Wright/50	50.00
13	Scott Kazmir/99	15.00
14	Gavin Floyd/99	10.00
15	Justin Verlander/99	40.00
18	Joey Gathright/50	10.00

Decade of Excellence

		NM/M
Common Player:		2.00
Inserted 1:199		
1	Albert Pujols	6.00
2	Derek Jeter	8.00
3	Randy Johnson	4.00
4	Ichiro Suzuki	5.00
5	Alex Rodriguez	6.00
6	Mike Piazza	4.00
7	Greg Maddux	4.00
8	Curt Schilling	3.00
9	Frank Thomas	3.00
10	Torii Hunter	3.00
11	Al Kaline	6.00
12	Travis Hafner	2.00
13	Ivan Rodriguez	3.00
14	Rafael Palmeiro	3.00
15	Mike Schmidt	8.00
16	Johnny Bench	8.00
17	Jim Edmonds	2.00
18	Pedro Martinez	4.00
19	Robin Yount	6.00
20	Sammy Sosa	5.00

Decade of Excellence Jersey Silver

		NM/M
Common Player:		5.00
Inserted 1:54		
Gold:		.75-1.25X
Production 99 Sets		
Patch Platinum:		No Pricing
Production 10 Sets		
JB	Johnny Bench	15.00
JE	Jim Edmonds	5.00
TF	Travis Hafner	5.00
TH	Torii Hunter	5.00
RJ	Randy Johnson	8.00
AK	Al Kaline	10.00
GM	Greg Maddux	8.00
PM	Pedro Martinez	8.00
RP	Rafael Palmeiro	8.00
MP	Mike Piazza	8.00
AP	Albert Pujols	12.00
IR	Ivan Rodriguez	5.00
CS	Curt Schilling	5.00
MS	Mike Schmidt	15.00
SS	Sammy Sosa	10.00
FT	Frank Thomas	8.00
RY	Robin Yount	10.00

Decade of Excellence Autograph Jersey Platinum

No Pricing
Production Five Sets

Diamond Dominators

		NM/M
Common Player:		2.00
Inserted 1:12 Retail		
1	Albert Pujols	6.00
2	Curt Schilling	3.00
3	Adrian Beltre	2.00
4	Randy Johnson	4.00
5	Ivan Rodriguez	3.00
6	Mike Piazza	4.00
7	Chipper Jones	4.00
8	Sammy Sosa	5.00
9	Tim Hudson	2.00
10	Rocco Baldelli	3.00
11	Alfonso Soriano	4.00
12	David Ortiz	3.00
13	Mariano Rivera	2.00
14	Kazuo Matsui	3.00
15	Khalil Greene	3.00
16	Eric Gagne	2.00
17	Vladimir Guerrero	4.00
18	Jason Giambi	4.00
19	Scott Rolen	4.00
20	Miguel Cabrera	3.00

Diamond Dominators Jersey Silver

		NM/M
Common Player:		
Inserted 1:45		
Gold:		.75-1.25X
Production 199 Sets (Hobby)		
Red:		.5-1X
Inserted 1:50 (Retail)		
RB	Rocco Baldelli	5.00
AB	Adrian Beltre	5.00
MC	Miguel Cabrera	8.00
EG	Eric Gagne	5.00
JG	Jason Giambi	8.00
KG	Khalil Greene	8.00
VG	Vladimir Guerrero	8.00
TH	Tim Hudson	5.00

RJ	Randy Johnson	8.00
CJ	Chipper Jones	4.00
KM	Kazuo Matsui	5.00
DO	David Ortiz	5.00
MP	Mike Piazza	8.00
AP	Albert Pujols	12.00
IR	Ivan Rodriguez	5.00
SR	Scott Rolen	8.00
CS	Curt Schilling	5.00
AS	Alfonso Soriano	8.00
SS	Sammy Sosa	10.00

Diamond Dominators Metal

		NM/M
Common Player:		2.00
Inserted 1:18 Hobby		
1	Albert Pujols	6.00
2	Curt Schilling	3.00
3	Adrian Beltre	2.00
4	Randy Johnson	4.00
5	Ivan Rodriguez	3.00
6	Mike Piazza	4.00
7	Chipper Jones	4.00
8	Sammy Sosa	5.00
9	Tim Hudson	2.00
10	Rocco Baldelli	3.00
11	Alfonso Soriano	4.00
12	David Ortiz	3.00
13	Kazuo Matsui	3.00
14	Khalil Greene	3.00
15	Eric Gagne	2.00
16	Vladimir Guerrero	4.00
17	Jason Giambi	4.00
18	Scott Rolen	4.00
19	Miguel Cabrera	3.00

Diamond Dominators Metal Patch

		NM/M
1-2X Diamond Dominators Jersey Silver		
Sequentially #'d to 30.		
HA	Hank Aaron	100.00

Diamond Dominators Metal Autograph

No Pricing
Production 10 Sets

Lumberjacks

		NM/M
Common Player:		.75
Inserted 1:6		
Bat Silver:		2-3X
Inserted 1:9		
Bat Gold:		2-4X
Production 250 Sets		
Bat Patch:		No Pricing
Production 20 Sets		
1	Albert Pujols	2.50
2	Jim Thome	1.25
3	Andruw Jones	1.00
4	Kazuo Matsui	.75
5	Adam Dunn	.75
6	Bernie Williams	.75
7	Hank Blalock	.75
8	Bobby Abreu	.75
9	Rocco Baldelli	.75
10	Jacque Jones	.75
11	Mark Teixeira	.75
12	Ichiro Suzuki	2.00
13	Gary Sheffield	.75
14	Sean Casey	.75
15	Carl Crawford	.75

Lumberjacks Autograph Platinum

No Pricing
Production 20 Sets

Nameplates Patch Platinum

No Pricing
Production 25 Sets
Masterpiece: No Pricing
Production One Set

Nameplates Patch Autograph Platinum

No Pricing
Production 25 Sets

Nameplates Dual Patch Platinum

No Pricing
Production 25 Sets
Masterpiece: No Pricing
Production One Set

Nameplates Dual Patch Autograph Platinum

No Pricing
Production One Set

2005 Fleer Showcase

	NM/M
Common Player (1-100):	.25
Minor Stars (1-100):	.40
Unlisted Stars (1-100):	.60
Common Showcasing Talent (101-110):	2.00
Inserted 1:5	
Common Showcasing History (111-135):	.40
Inserted 1:20	
Pack (5):	3.00
Box (20):	50.00

2	Albert Pujols	2.50
3	Rocco Baldelli	.60
4	Bernie Williams	.60
5	Shawn Green	.40
6	Garret Anderson	.40
7	Paul Konerko	.25
8	Mike Sweeney	.25
9	Jim Thome	1.00
10	Mark Teixeira	.40
11	Mark Prior	2.00
12	Angel Berroa	.25
13	Barry Zito	.60
14	Carlos Delgado	.75
15	Troy Glaus	.60
16	Travis Hafner	.25
17	Lyle Overbay	.25
18	David Ortiz	.60
19	Ivan Rodriguez	.60
20	Jack Wilson	.25
21	Jason Schmidt	.40
22	Mike Piazza	1.50
23	David Eckstein	.25
24	Ben Sheets	.40
25	Randy Johnson	1.00
26	Jacque Jones	.25
27	Jody Gerut	.25
28	Kris Benson	.25
29	Luis Gonzalez	.40
30	Victor Martinez	.25
31	Torii Hunter	.60
32	Gary Sheffield	.60
33	Miguel Tejada	.60
34	Dontrelle Willis	.60
35	Bret Boone	.40
36	Hideki Matsui	.60
37	Shea Hillenbrand	.25
38	Wily Mo Pena	.25
39	Johan Santana	.40
40	Derek Jeter	3.00
41	Chipper Jones	1.50
42	Sean Casey	.25
43	Corey Koskie	.25
44	Alex Rodriguez	2.50
45	Andruw Jones	.75
46	Austin Kearns	.60
47	Jose Vidro	.25
48	Adam Dunn	.60
49	Adrian Beltre	.25
50	Bobby Abreu	.40
51	Michael Young	.25
52	Freddy Garcia	.25
53	Eric Gagne	.40
54	Chase Utley	.50
55	Alfonso Soriano	1.00
56	Nick Johnson	.25
57	Johnny Estrada	.25
58	Jeff Bagwell	.75
59	Randy Winn	.25
60	Roy Halladay	.40
61	J.D. Drew	.40
62	Craig Biggio	.40
63	Scott Rolen	1.00
64	Nomar Garciaparra	2.50
65	Matt Holliday	.50
66	Billy Wagner	.25
67	Carl Crawford	.25
68	Pedro J. Martinez	1.00
69	Jeremy Bonderman	.25
70	Jason Bay	.25
71	A.J. Pierzynski	.25
72	Vladimir Guerrero	1.00
73	Rickie Weeks	.60
74	Mark Loretta	.25
75	Todd Helton	.75
76	Manny Ramirez	.75
77	Carlos Guillen	.25
78	Khalil Greene	.75
79	Javy Lopez	.40
80	Josh Beckett	.75

80	Ichiro Suzuki	2.00
81	Magglio Ordonez	.40
82	Ken Harvey	.25
83	Mark Mulder	.40
84	Hank Blalock	.60
85	Richard Hidalgo	.25
87	Jeromy Burnitz	.25
88	Craig Wilson	.25
89	Aubrey Huff	.25
90	Kerry Wood	.75
91	Andy Pettitte	.60
92	Tim Hudson	.40
93	Jim Edmonds	.40
94	Melvin Mora	.25
95	Miguel Cabrera	.75
96	Trevor Hoffman	.25
97	J.T. Snow	.25
98	Sammy Sosa	2.00
99	Roger Clemens	2.50
100	Eric Chavez	4.00
101	B.J. Upton	5.00
102	Gavin Floyd	3.00
103	Casey Kotchman	3.00
104	David Wright	5.00
105	Dioner Navarro	3.00
106	Scott Kazmir	3.00
107	Andres Blanco	2.00
108	Joey Gathright	2.00
109	Jon Knott	2.00
110	Charlton Jimerson	3.00
111	Larry Doby	.75
112	Reggie Jackson	2.00
113	Enos Slaughter	.60
114	Bill "Moose" Skowron	.60
115	Duke Snider	.75
116	Harmon Killebrew	1.00
117	Willie McCovey	.75
118	Rollie Fingers	1.00
119	Preacher Roe	.40
120	Carlton Fisk	.60
121	Andre Dawson	.60
122	Orlando Cepeda	.60
123	Bucky Dent	.40
124	Cal Ripken Jr.	1.50
125	Nolan Ryan	3.00
126	Tony Perez	.60
127	Mike Schmidt	1.50
128	Johnny Bench	1.50
129	Sparky Anderson	.40
130	Ted Williams	2.50
131	Al Kaline	.75
132	Carl Yastrzemski	1.00
133	Eddie Murray	.75
134	Roberto Clemente	1.50
135	Yogi Berra	1.50

Showtime

Veterans (1-100):	3-6X
Showcasing Talent (101-110):	2-4X
Showcasing History (111-135):	1-3X
Production 99 Sets	
Masterpiece:	No Pricing
Production One Set	

Showdown

Cards (1-135):	No Pricing
Production 15 Sets	
Masterpiece:	No Pricing
Production One Set	

Masterpiece Legacy

Cards (1-135):	No Pricing
Production One Set	

Masterpiece Showpiece Patch

Cards (1-135):	No Pricing
Production One Set	
Autograph Patch:	No Pricing
Production One Set	
Patch Showdown:	No Pricing
Production One Set	
Patch Showtime:	No Pricing
Production One Set	

Autographed Legacy

	NM/M
Common Player:	15.00
Sequentially Numbered	
8	Jim Thome/34	60.00
10	Mark Prior/43	30.00
12	Barry Zito/45	35.00
18	Ivan Rodriguez/217	40.00

AUTOGRAPHED LEGACY

19	Jack Wilson/298	15.00
20	Jason Schmidt/127	15.00
21	Mike Piazza/26	100.00
22	David Eckstein/40	35.00
23	Ben Sheets/427	15.00
40	Chipper Jones/41	60.00
45	Austin Kearns/460	10.00
47	Adam Dunn/52	35.00
48	Adrian Beltre/180	15.00
50	Michael Young/80	15.00
52	Eric Gagne/310	25.00
53	Chase Utley/446	25.00
59	Roy Halladay/99	15.00
68	Jeremy Bonderman/97	20.00
72	Rickie Weeks/453	15.00
75	Manny Ramirez/31	75.00
77	Khalil Greene/299	25.00
88	Craig Wilson/40	20.00
89	Aubrey Huff/453	15.00
90	Kerry Wood/28	25.00
92	Tim Hudson/183	25.00
95	Miguel Cabrera/32	35.00
99	Roger Clemens/64	100.00
100	Eric Chavez/204	15.00
103	Casey Kotchman/454	15.00
104	David Wright/298	40.00
106	Scott Kazmir/458	20.00
107	Andres Blanco/23	15.00
109	Jon Knott/402	10.00
114	Bill "Moose" Skowron/64	20.00
119	Preacher Roe/304	15.00
120	Carlton Fisk/86	30.00
123	Bucky Dent/99	15.00
135	Yogi Berra/25	75.00

Measures of Greatness

	NM/M
Common Player:	.75
Inserted 1:5	
Jersey Red:	2-4X
Production 340 Sets	
Patch:	No Pricing
Production 10 Sets	
Masterpiece:	No Pricing
Production One Set	
1 Albert Pujols	4.00
2 Mike Piazza	2.50
3 Vladimir Guerrero	2.00
4 Jim Thome	2.00
5 Pedro J. Martinez	2.00
6 Rafael Palmeiro	.75
7 Adrian Beltre	.75
8 Sammy Sosa	3.00
9 Todd Helton	1.50
10 Randy Johnson	2.00
11 Jeff Bagwell	1.50
12 Jason Giambi	2.00
13 Scott Rolen	1.00
14 Greg Maddux	2.50
15 Alfonso Soriano	2.00
16 Mariano Rivera	.75
17 Curt Schilling	1.00
18 Derek Jeter	5.00
19 Chipper Jones	2.50
20 Roger Clemens	4.00

Swing Time

	NM/M
Common Player:	2.50
Inserted 1:45	
Jersey Red:	1-3X
Production 610 Sets	
Patch:	2-5X
Production 50 Sets	
Masterpiece:	No Pricing
Production One Set	
1 Ivan Rodriguez	2.50
2 Gary Sheffield	2.50
3 Bernie Williams	2.50
4 Vladimir Guerrero	3.50
5 Jim Edmonds	2.50
6 Manny Ramirez	3.00
7 Todd Helton	3.00
8 Hank Blalock	2.50
9 Hideki Matsui	6.00
10 David Ortiz	2.50
11 Albert Pujols	6.00
12 Miguel Tejada	2.50
13 Miguel Cabrera	3.00
14 Alex Rodriguez	6.00
15 Ichiro Suzuki	5.00

Timepiece Extreme
No Pricing
Production One Set

Timepiece Ink
No Pricing
Production 10 Sets

Timepiece Teammates
No Pricing
Production One Set

Timepiece Unique
No Pricing
Production Five Sets

Wave of the Future

	NM/M
Common Player:	1.00
Inserted 1:15	
Jersey Red:	1-3X
Production 610 Sets	
Patch:	2-5X
Production 50 Sets	
Masterpiece:	No Pricing
Production One Set	
1 Kazuo Matsui	5.00
2 Johan Santana	1.50
3 Khalil Greene	2.00
4 Dontrelle Willis	1.50
5 Mark Teixeira	1.50
6 Travis Hafner	1.00
7 Jason Bay	1.50
8 Angel Berroa	1.00
9 Miguel Cabrera	2.00
10 Joe Mauer	1.50
11 Adam Dunn	2.00
12 B.J. Upton	3.00
13 Victor Martinez	1.00
14 Michael Young	1.00
15 David Wright	3.00

2005 Fleer Tradition

HIDEKI MATSUI

	NM/M
Common Player (1-300):	.15
Minor Stars (1-300):	.25
Unlisted Stars (1-300):	.40
Common Card (301-330):	3.00
Unlisted Card (301-330):	4.00
Inserted 1:2	
Common Player (331-350):	.15
Minor Stars (331-350):	.25
Unlisted Stars (331-350):	.40
Cards 1-12; 331-350 Inserted 1:2	
Pack (10):	1.25
Box (36):	35.00
1 Johan Santana, Curt Schilling, Jake Westbrook	.40
2 Ben Sheets, Jake Peavy, Randy Johnson	.75
3 Johan Santana, Bartolo Colon, Curt Schilling	.40
4 Carl Pavano, Roy Oswalt, Roger Clemens	1.50
5 Johan Santana, Pedro Martinez, Curt Schilling	.75
6 Jason Schmidt, Randy Johnson, Ben Sheets	.75
7 Melvin Mora, Vladimir Guerrero, Ichiro Suzuki	1.25
8 Adrian Beltre, Todd Helton, Mark Loretta	.50
9 Manny Ramirez, Paul Konerko, David Ortiz	.50
10 Albert Pujols, Adrian Beltre, Adam Dunn	.50
11 David Ortiz, Manny Ramirez, Miguel Tejada	.50
12 Albert Pujols, Vinny Castilla, Scott Rolen	1.50
13 Jason Bay	.15
14 Greg Maddux	1.00
15 Melvin Mora	.15
16 Matt Stairs	.15
17 Scott Podsednik	.25
18 Bartolo Colon	.25
19 Roger Clemens	1.50
20 Eric Hinske	.15
21 Johnny Estrada	.15
22 Brett Tomko	.15
23 John Buck	.15
24 Nomar Garciaparra	1.50
25 Milton Bradley	.15
26 Craig Biggio	.25
27 Kyle Denney	.50
28 Brad Penny	.15
29 Todd Helton	.50
30 Luis Gonzalez	.25
31 Bill Hall	.15
32 Ruben Sierra	.15
33 Zack Greinke	.15
34 Sandy Alomar Jr.	.15
35 Jason Giambi	.75
36 Ben Sheets	.25
37 Edgardo Alfonzo	.15
38 Kenny Rogers	.15
39 Coco Crisp	.15
40 Randy Choate	.50
41 Braden Looper	.15
42 Adam Dunn	.50
43 Adam Eaton	.15
44 Luis Castillo	.25
45 Casey Fossum	.15
46 Mike Piazza	1.00
47 Juan Pierre	.15
48 Doug Davis	.15
49 Manny Ramirez	.50
50 Travis Hafner	.15
51 Jack Wilson	.15
52 Mike Maroth	.15
53 Ken Harvey	.15
54 Brooks Kieschnick	.15
55 Brad Fullmer	.15
56 Octavio Dotel	.15
57 Mike Matheny	.15
58 Andruw Jones	.50
59 Alfonso Soriano	.75
60 Royce Clayton	.15
61 Jon Garland	.15
62 John Mabry	.15
63 Rafael Palmeiro	.25
64 Garrett Atkins	.15
65 Brian Meadows	.15
66 Tony Armas Jr.	.15
67 Toby Hall	.15
68 Carlos Baerga	.15
69 Barry Larkin	.25
70 Jody Gerut	.15
71 Brent Mayne	.15
72 Shigetoshi Hasegawa	.15
73 Jose Cruz Jr.	.15
74 Dan Wilson	.15
75 Sidney Ponson	.15
76 Jason Jennings	.15
77 A.J. Burnett	.15
78 Tony Batista	.15
79 Kris Benson	.15
80 Sean Burroughs	.15
81 Eric Young	.15
82 Casey Kotchman	.40
83 Derek Lee	.25
84 Mariano Rivera	.25
85 Julio Franco	.15
86 Corey Patterson	.15
87 Carlos Beltran	.40
88 Trevor Hoffman	.15
89 Danny Garcia	.15

90	Marco Scutaro	.15
91	Marquis Grissom	.15
92	Aubrey Huff	.15
93	Tony Womack	.15
94	Placido Polanco	.15
95	Bengie Molina	.15
96	Roger Cedeno	.15
97	Geoff Jenkins	.25
98	Kip Wells	.15
99	Derek Jeter	2.00
100	Omar Infante	.15
101	Phil Nevin	.15
102	Edgar Renteria	.15
103	B.J. Surhoff	.15
104	David DeJesus	.15
105	Raul Ibanez	.15
106	Hank Blalock	.40
107	Shawn Estes	.15
108	Wily Mo Pena	.15
109	Shawn Green	.25
110	David Wright	.50
111	Kenny Lofton	.15
112	Matt Clement	.15
113	Cesar Izturis	.15
114	John Lackey	.15
115	Torii Hunter	.40
116	Charles Johnson	.15
117	Ray Durham	.15
118	Luke Hudson	.15
119	Jeremy Bonderman	.15
120	Sean Casey	.15
121	Johnny Damon	.25
122	Eric Milton	.15
123	Shea Hillenbrand	.15
124	Jim Edmonds	.25
125	Jim Edmonds	.25
126	Javier Vazquez	.15
127	Jon Adkins	.15
128	Mike Lowell	.15
129	Khalil Greene	.50
130	Quinton McCracken	.15
131	Edgar Martinez	.25
132	Matt Lawton	.15
133	Jeff Weaver	.15
134	Marlon Byrd	.15
135	John Smoltz	.25
136	Grady Sizemore	.15
137	Brian Roberts	.15
138	Dee Brown	.15
139	Joel Pineiro	.15
140	David Dellucci	.15
141	Bobby Higginson	.15
142	Ryan Madson	.15
143	Scott Hatteberg	.15
144	Gregg Zaun	.15
145	Brian Jordan	.15
146	Jason Isringhausen	.15
147	Vinnie Chulk	.15
148	Al Leiter	.15
149	Pedro Martinez	.15
150	Carlos Guillen	.15
151	Randy Wolf	.15
152	Vernon Wells	.25
153	Barry Zito	.40
154	Pedro Feliz	.15
155	Omar Vizquel	.15
156	Chone Figgins	.15
157	David Ortiz	.40
158	Sun-Woo Kim **RC**	1.00
159	Adam Kennedy	.15
160	Carlos Lee	.15
161	Rick Ankiel	.25
162	Roy Oswalt	.25
163	Armando Benitez	.15
164	Erubiel Durazo	.15
165	Adam Hyzdu	.15
166	Esteban Yan	.15
167	Victor Santos	.15
168	Kevin Millwood	.15
169	Andy Pettitte	.60
170	Mike Cameron	.15
171	Scott Rolen	.75
172	Trot Nixon	.15
173	Eric Munson	.15
174	Roy Halladay	.25
175	Juan Encarnacion	.15
176	Eric Chavez	.25
177	Terrmel Sledge	.15
178	Jason Schmidt	.25
179	Endy Chavez	.15
180	Carlos Zambrano	.15
181	Carlos Delgado	.50
182	Dewon Brazelton	.15
183	J.D. Drew	.15
184	Orlando Cabrera	.15
185	Craig Wilson	.15
186	Chin-Hui Tsao	.15
187	Jolbert Cabrera	.15
188	Rod Barajas	.15
189	Craig Monroe	.15
190	Dave Berg	.15
191	Carlos Silva	.15
192	Eric Gagne	.25
193	Marcus Giles	.15
194	Nick Johnson	.15
195	Kelvim Escobar	.15
196	Wade Miller	.15
197	David Bell	.15
198	Rondell White	.15
199	Brian Giles	.25
200	Jeremy Burnitz	.15
201	Carl Pavano	.15
202	Alex Rios	.15
203	Ryan Freel	.15
204	R.A. Dickey	.15

205	Miguel Cairo	.15
206	Kerry Wood	.50
207	C.C. Sabathia	.15
208	Jaime Cerda	.15
209	Jerome Williams	.15
210	Ryan Wagner	.15
211	Javy Lopez	.25
212	Tike Redman	.15
213	Richie Sexson	.40
214	Shannon Stewart	.15
215	Ben Davis	.15
216	Jeff Bagwell	.50
217	David Wells	.15
218	Justin Leone	.15
219	Brad Radke	.15
220	Ramon Santiago	.15
221	Richard Hidalgo	.15
222	Aaron Miles	.15
223	Mark Loretta	.15
224	Aaron Boone	.15
225	Steve Trachsel	.15
226	Geoff Blum	.15
227	Shingo Takatsu	.15
228	Kevin Youkilis	.15
229	Laynce Nix	.15
230	Daniel Cabrera	.15
231	Kyle Lohse	.15
232	Todd Pratt	.15
233	Reed Johnson	.15
234	Lance Berkman	.25
235	Hideki Matsui	1.50
236	Randy Winn	.15
237	Joe Randa	.15
238	Bob Howry	.15
239	Jason LaRue	.15
240	Jose Valentin	.15
241	Livan Hernandez	.15
242	Jamie Moyer	.15
243	Garret Anderson	.25
244	Brad Ausmus	.15
245	Russell Branyan	.15
246	Paul Wilson	.15
247	Tim Wakefield	.15
248	Roberto Alomar	.40
249	Kazuhisa Ishii	.15
250	Tino Martinez	.15
251	Tomokazu Ohka	.15
252	Mark Redman	.15
253	Paul Byrd	.15
254	Greg Aquino	.15
255	Adrian Beltre	.25
256	Ricky Ledee	.15
257	Josh Fogg	.15
258	Derek Lowe	.15
259	Lew Ford	.15
260	Bobby Crosby	.15
261	Jim Thome	.75
262	Jaret Wright	.15
263	Chin-Feng Chen	.15
264	Troy Glaus	.40
265	Jorge Sosa	.15
266	Mike Lamb	.15
267	Russ Ortiz	.15
268	Reggie Sanders	.15
269	Orlando Hudson	.15
270	Rodrigo Lopez	.15
271	Jose Vidro	.15
272	Akinori Otsuka	.15
273	Victor Martinez	.15
274	Carl Crawford	.15
275	Roberto Novoa	.25
276	Brian Lawrence	.15
277	Angel Berroa	.15
278	Josh Beckett	.50
279	Lyle Overbay	.15
280	Dustin Hermanson	.15
281	Jeff Conine	.15
282	Mark Prior	1.00
283	Kevin Brown	.25
284	Magglio Ordonez	.25
285	Dontrelle Willis	.25
286	Dallas McPherson	.25
287	Rafael Furcal	.25
288	Ty Wigginton	.15
289	Moises Alou	.25
290	A.J. Pierzynski	.15
291	Todd Walker	.15
292	Hideo Nomo	.15
293	Larry Walker	.25
294	Choo Freeman	.15
295	Eduardo Perez	.15
296	Miguel Tejada	.40
297	Corey Koskie	.15
298	Jermaine Dye	.15
299	John Riedling	.15
300	John Olerud	.25
301	Tim Bittner, Jake Woods, Bobby Jenks	5.00
302	Josh Kroeger, Casey Daigle, Brandon Medders	5.00
303	Kelly Johnson, Charles Thomas, Dan Meyer	4.00
304	Eddy Rodriguez, Ryan Hannaman, John Maine	6.00
305	Anastacio Martinez, Jerome Gamble, Lenny Dinardo	8.00
306	Ronny Cedeno, Carlos Vasquez, Renyel Pinto	6.00
307	Arnie Munoz, Ryan Wing, Felix Diaz	6.00
308	William Bergolla, Ray Olmedo, Edwin Encarnacion	4.00
309	Mariano Gomez, Ivan Ochoa, Kazuhito Tadano	3.00

310	Toby Miller, Jeff Baker, Matt Holliday	6.00
311	Preston Larrison, Curtis Granderson, Ryan Raburn	8.00
312	Josh Wilson, Logan Kensing, Kevin Cave	5.00
313	Hector Gimenez, Willy Taveras, Taylor Buchholz	3.00
314	Ruben Gotay, Brian Bass, Andres Blanco	4.00
315	Joel Hanrahan, Willy Aybar, Yhency Brazoban	3.00
316	David Krynzel, Ben Hendrickson, Corey Hart	3.00
317	Colby Miller, Jason Kubel, J.D. Durban	5.00
318	Maicer Izturis, Chad Cordero, Brandon Watson	3.00
319	Victor Diaz, Aarom Baldiris, Wayne Lydon	8.00
320	Edwardo Sierra, Dioner Navarro, Sean Henn	3.00
321	Nick Swisher, Joe Blanton, Dan Johnson	6.00
322	Ryan Howard, Gavin Floyd, Keith Bucktrot	6.00
323	Ryan Doumit, Sean Burnett, Bobby Bradley	6.00
324	Justin Germano, Rusty Tucker, Freddy Guzman	3.00
325	David Aardsma, Justin Knoedler, Alfredo Simon	4.00
326	Jose Lopez, Rene Rivera, Cha Sueng Baek	3.00
327	Yadier Molina, Evan Rust, Adam Wainwright	4.00
328	Jorge Cantu, Scott Kazmir, B.J. Upton	5.00
329	Adrian Gonzalez, Ramon Nivar, Jason Bourgeois	6.00
330	Russ Adams, Dustin McGowan, Gustavo Chacin	8.00
331	Alfonso Soriano	.75
332	Albert Pujols	1.50
333	David Ortiz	.40
334	Manny Ramirez	.50
335	Jason Bay	.15
336	Bobby Crosby	.15
337	Roger Clemens	1.50
338	Johan Santana	.25
339	Jim Thome	.75
340	Vladimir Guerrero	.75
341	David Ortiz	.40
342	Alex Rodriguez	1.50
343	Albert Pujols	1.50
344	Carlos Beltran	.40
345	Johnny Damon	.25
346	Scott Rolen	.75
347	Larry Walker	.25
348	Curt Schilling	.40
349	Pedro Martinez	.75
350	David Ortiz	.40

Gray Backs

Cards 13-300:	.75-1.5X
Cards 1-10; 301-350:	.5-1.25X
Inserted 1:2	

Club 3,000/500/300

NM/M

Inserted 1:360

1	Ernie Banks/500	30.00
2	Stan Musial/3,000	40.00
3	Steve Carlton/3,000	15.00
4	Greg Maddux/300	25.00
5	Dave Winfield/3,000	15.00
6	Rafael Palmeiro/500	15.00
7	Rickey Henderson/3,000	15.00
8	Roger Clemens/3,000	30.00
9	Don Sutton/300	10.00
10	George Brett/3,000	25.00
11	Reggie Jackson/500	20.00
12	Wade Boggs/3,000	20.00
13	Bob Gibson/3,000	20.00
14	Eddie Murray/3,000	20.00
15	Tom Seaver/3,000	20.00
16	Willie McCovey/500	20.00
17	Rod Carew/3,000	20.00
18	Fergie Jenkins/300	15.00
19	Phil Niekro/300	10.00
20	Frank Robinson/500	20.00

Cooperstown Tribute

NM/M

Common Player: 4.00
Sequentially #'d to HOF Induction Year.
Gold: .5-1X
Inserted 1:24
Jersey: 1-2X
Inserted 1:200
There are 20 total jersey cards for Joe Morgan & Yogi Berra.
Patch: No Pricing
Production 10 Sets

1	Mike Schmidt/1995	5.00
2	Al Kaline/1980	4.00
3	Yogi Berra/1972	6.00
4	Robin Yount/1999	4.00
5	Joe Morgan/1990	4.00
6	Willie Stargell/1988	4.00
7	Harmon Killebrew/1984	5.00
8	Nolan Ryan/1999	10.00
9	Carlton Fisk/2000	5.00
10	Johnny Bench/1989	6.00

Diamond Tributes

NM/M

Common Player: 2.00
Inserted 1:6

1	Albert Pujols	5.00
2	Alex Rodriguez	5.00
3	Ken Griffey Jr.	3.50
4	Sammy Sosa	4.00
5	Chipper Jones	3.50
6	Johan Santana	2.00
7	Roger Clemens	5.00
8	Pedro Martinez	3.00
9	Jim Thome	3.00
10	Greg Maddux	3.50
11	Alfonso Soriano	3.00
12	Derek Jeter	6.00
13	Randy Johnson	3.00
14	Miguel Cabrera	2.00
15	Adrian Beltre	2.00
16	Ivan Rodriguez	2.00
17	Manny Ramirez	2.00
18	Mark Teixeira	2.00
19	Adam Dunn	2.00
20	Scott Rolen	3.00
21	Mike Piazza	3.50
22	J.D. Drew	2.00
23	Hideki Matsui	5.00
24	Nomar Garciaparra	5.00
25	Kazuo Matsui	5.00

Diamond Tribute Jersey

NM/M

Common Player: 6.00
Inserted 1:30
Patch: 1-3X
Production 50 Sets

AB	Adrian Beltre/Bat	6.00
RC	Roger Clemens/Jsy	12.00
JD	J.D. Drew/Bat	6.00
NG	Nomar Garciaparra/Bat	12.00
RJ	Randy Johnson/Jsy	8.00
CJ	Chipper Jones/Bat	10.00
GM	Greg Maddux/Jsy	10.00
PM	Pedro Martinez/Jsy	8.00
HM	Hideki Matsui/Bat	15.00
KM	Kazuo Matsui/Bat	8.00
MP	Mike Piazza/Bat	10.00
AP	Albert Pujols/Bat	15.00
MR	Manny Ramirez/Bat	6.00
AS	Johan Santana/Jsy	8.00
AS	Alfonso Soriano/Bat	8.00
SS	Sammy Sosa/Bat	10.00
MT	Mark Teixeira/Bat	6.00
JT	Jim Thome/Bat	8.00

Diamond Tributes Dual Patch

NM/M

Common Player: 75.00
Production 50 Sets

APSR	Albert Pujols, Scott Rolen	100.00
ASMT	Alfonso Soriano, Mark Teixeira	75.00
CJJD	Chipper Jones, J.D. Drew	80.00
HMKM	Hideki Matsui, Kazuo Matsui	125.00
JTAB	Jim Thome, Adrian Beltre	75.00
MPIR	Mike Piazza, Ivan Rodriguez	75.00
PMMR	Pedro Martinez, Manny Ramirez	120.00
RCJS	Roger Clemens, Johan Santana	100.00
RJGM	Randy Johnson, Greg Maddux	75.00
SSMC	Miguel Cabrera, Sammy Sosa	80.00

Standouts

NM/M

Common Player: 3.50
Inserted 1:18

1	Albert Pujols	6.00
2	Ichiro Suzuki	5.00
3	Derek Jeter	8.00
4	Randy Johnson	3.50
5	Greg Maddux	4.00
6	Hideki Matsui	6.00
7	Mike Piazza	4.00
8	Vladimir Guerrero	3.50
9	Sammy Sosa	5.00
10	Jim Thome	3.50
11	Chipper Jones	4.00
12	Alex Rodriguez	5.00
13	Roger Clemens	6.00
14	Nomar Garciaparra	6.00
15	Lance Berkman	3.50

Standouts Jersey

Lance Berkman

NM/M

Common Player: 10.00
Inserted 1:18
Patch: 1-3X
Production 50 Sets

LB	Lance Berkman	6.00
RC	Roger Clemens	18.00
VG	Vladimir Guerrero	10.00
RJ	Randy Johnson	10.00
CJ	Chipper Jones	12.00
GM	Greg Maddux	12.00
HM	Hideki Matsui	20.00
MP	Mike Piazza	12.00
AP	Albert Pujols	18.00
SS	Sammy Sosa	15.00
JT	Jim Thome	10.00

2006 Fleer

NM/M

Complete Set (400): 40.00
Complete Factory Set (430): 50.00
#'s 401-430 available in Factory Set
Common Player: .15
Pack (10): 1.50
Box (36): 40.00

1	Adam Kennedy	.15
2	Bartolo Colon	.25
3	Bengie Molina	.15
4	Chone Figgins	.15
5	Dallas McPherson	.15
6	Darin Erstad	.15
7	Francisco Rodriguez	.15
8	Garret Anderson	.25
9	Jarrod Washburn	.15

10 John Lackey .15
11 Orlando Cabrera .15
12 Ryan Theriot **(RC)** .50
13 Steve Finley .15
14 Vladimir Guerrero .75
15 Adam Everett .15
16 Andy Pettitte .40
17 Charlton Jimerson .15
18 Brad Lidge .15
19 Chris Burke .15
20 Craig Biggio .25
21 Jason Lane .15
22 Jeff Bagwell .40
23 Lance Berkman .50
24 Morgan Ensberg .25
25 Roger Clemens 2.00
26 Roy Oswalt .25
27 Willy Taveras .15
28 Barry Zito .25
29 Bobby Crosby .15
30 Bobby Kielty .15
31 Dan Johnson .15
32 Danny Haren .15
33 Eric Chavez .25
34 Huston Street .15
35 Jason Kendall .15
36 Jay Payton .15
37 Joe Blanton .15
38 Mark Kotsay .15
39 Nick Swisher .15
40 Rich Harden .25
41 Ron Flores **RC** .25
42 Alex Rios .15
43 John-Ford Griffin **(RC)** .15
44 David Bush .15
45 Eric Hinske .15
46 Frank Catalanotto .15
47 Gustavo Chacin .15
48 Josh Towers .15
49 Miguel Batista .15
50 Orlando Hudson .15
51 Roy Halladay .25
52 Shea Hillenbrand .15
53 Shaun Marcum **(RC)** .15
54 Vernon Wells .25
55 Adam LaRoche .15
56 Andruw Jones .50
57 Chipper Jones .75
58 Anthony Lerew **(RC)** .15
59 Jeff Francoeur .25
60 John Smoltz .40
61 Johnny Estrada .15
62 Julio Franco .15
63 Joey Devine **RC** 1.00
64 Marcus Giles .15
65 Mike Hampton .15
66 Rafael Furcal .25
67 Chuck James **(RC)** .15
68 Tim Hudson .25
69 Ben Sheets .25
70 Bill Hall .15
71 Brady Clark .15
72 Carlos Lee .25
73 Chris Capuano .15
74 Nelson Cruz **(RC)** .15
75 Derrick Turnbow .15
76 Doug Davis .15
77 Geoff Jenkins .15
78 J.J. Hardy .15
79 Lyle Overbay .15
80 Prince Fielder **(RC)** 1.00
81 Rickie Weeks .25
82 Albert Pujols 2.00
83 Chris Carpenter .25
84 David Eckstein .15
85 Jason Isringhausen .15
86 Tyler Johnson **(RC)** .15
87 Adam Wainwright **(RC)** .15
88 Jim Edmonds .25
89 Chris Duncan .15
90 Mark Grudzielanek .15
91 Mark Mulder .25
92 Matt Morris .15
93 Reggie Sanders .15
94 Scott Rolen .50
95 Yadier Molina .15
96 Aramis Ramirez .40
97 Carlos Zambrano .25
98 Corey Patterson .15
99 Derrek Lee .50
100 Glendon Rusch .15
101 Greg Maddux 1.00
102 Jeromy Burnitz .15
103 Kerry Wood .25
104 Mark Prior .50
105 Michael Barrett .15
106 Geovany Soto **(RC)** .25
107 Nomar Garciaparra .50
108 Ryan Dempster .15
109 Todd Walker .15
110 Alex Gonzalez .15
111 Aubrey Huff .15
112 Victor Diaz .15
113 Carl Crawford .25
114 Danys Baez .15
115 Joey Gathright .15
116 Jonny Gomes .25
117 Jorge Cantu .15
118 Julio Lugo .15
119 Rocco Baldelli .15
120 Scott Kazmir .15
121 Toby Hall .15
122 Tim Corcoran **RC** .40
123 Alex Cintron .15
124 Brandon Webb .15
125 Chad Tracy .15
126 Dustin Nippert **(RC)** .15
127 Claudio Vargas .15
128 Craig Counsell .15
129 Javier Vazquez .15
130 Jose Valverde .15
131 Luis Gonzalez .15
132 Royce Clayton .15
133 Russ Ortiz .15
134 Shawn Green .15
135 Tony Clark .15
136 Troy Glaus .25
137 Brad Penny .15
138 Cesar Izturis .15
139 Derek Lowe .15
140 Eric Gagne .15
141 Hee Seop Choi .15
142 J.D. Drew .15
143 Jason Phillips .15
144 Jayson Werth .15
145 Jeff Kent .25
146 Jeff Weaver .15
147 Milton Bradley .15
148 Odalis Perez .15
149 Hong-Chih Kuo .15
150 Brian Myrow **RC** .25
151 Armando Benitez .15
152 Edgardo Alfonzo .15
153 J.T. Snow .15
154 Jason Schmidt .15
155 Lance Niekro .15
156 Doug Clark .15
157 Daniel Ortmeier **(RC)** .15
158 Moises Alou .25
159 Noah Lowry .15
160 Omar Vizquel .25
161 Pedro Feliz .15
162 Randy Winn .15
163 Jeremy Accardo **RC** .15
164 Aaron Boone .15
165 Ryan Garko **(RC)** .15
166 C.C. Sabathia .15
167 Casey Blake .15
168 Cliff Lee .15
169 Coco Crisp .15
170 Grady Sizemore .40
171 Jake Westbrook .15
172 Jhonny Peralta .15
173 Kevin Millwood .15
174 Scott Elarton .15
175 Travis Hafner .50
176 Victor Martinez .25
177 Adrian Beltre .15
178 Eddie Guardado .15
179 Felix Hernandez .40
180 Gil Meche .15
181 Ichiro Suzuki 1.50
182 Jamie Moyer .15
183 Jeremy Reed .15
184 Jaime Bubela **(RC)** .15
185 Raul Ibanez .15
186 Richie Sexson .40
187 Ryan Franklin .15
188 Jeff Harris **RC** .25
189 A.J. Burnett .15
190 Josh Wilson **(RC)** .15
191 Josh Johnson **(RC)** .15
192 Carlos Delgado .40
193 Dontrelle Willis .25
194 Bernie Castro .15
195 Josh Beckett .25
196 Juan Encarnacion .15
197 Juan Pierre .15
198 Robert Andino **RC** .25
199 Miguel Cabrera .75
200 Ryan Jorgensen **RC** .25
201 Paul LoDuca .15
202 Todd Jones .15
203 Braden Looper .15
204 Carlos Beltran .50
205 Cliff Floyd .15
206 David Wright 1.00
207 Doug Mientkiewicz .15
208 Jae Weong Seo .15
209 Jose Reyes .50
210 Anderson Hernandez **(RC)** .15
211 Miguel Cairo .15
212 Mike Cameron .15
213 Mike Piazza .50
214 Pedro Martinez .75
215 Tom Glavine .25
216 Tim Hamulack .15
217 Brad Wilkerson .15
218 Darrell Rasner **(RC)** .15
219 Chad Cordero .15
220 Cristian Guzman .15
221 Jason Bergmann **RC** .50
222 John Patterson .15
223 Jose Guillen .15
224 Jose Vidro .15
225 Livan Hernandez .15
226 Nick Johnson .15
227 Preston Wilson .15
228 Ryan Zimmerman **(RC)** .25
229 Vinny Castilla .15
230 B.J. Ryan .15
231 B.J. Surhoff .15
232 Brian Roberts .25
233 Walter Young .15
234 Daniel Cabrera .15
235 Erik Bedard .15
236 Javy Lopez .15
237 Jay Gibbons .15
238 Luis Matos .15
239 Melvin Mora .25
240 Miguel Tejada .50
241 Rafael Palmeiro .25
242 Alejandro Freire **RC** .25
243 Sammy Sosa .75
244 Adam Eaton .15
245 Brian Giles .25
246 Brian Lawrence .15
247 Dave Roberts .15
248 Jake Peavy .25
249 Khalil Greene .15
250 Mark Loretta .15
251 Ramon Hernandez .15
252 Ryan Klesko .15
253 Trevor Hoffman .15
254 Woody Williams .15
255 Craig Breslow **RC** .25
256 Billy Wagner .25
257 Bobby Abreu .25
258 Brett Myers .15
259 Chase Utley .50
260 David Bell .15
261 Jim Thome .50
262 Jimmy Rollins .40
263 Jon Lieber .15
264 Danny Sandoval **RC** .25
265 Mike Lieberthal .15
266 Pat Burrell .25
267 Randy Wolf .15
268 Ryan Howard 1.00
269 J.J. Furmaniak **(RC)** .15
270 Ronny Paulino **(RC)** .15
271 Craig Wilson .15
272 Bryan Bullington .15
273 Jack Wilson .15
274 Jason Bay .25
275 Matt Capps **(RC)** .15
276 Oliver Perez .15
277 Robert Mackowiak .15
278 Tom Gorzelanny **(RC)** .15
279 Zachary Duke .15
280 Alfonso Soriano .50
281 Chris Young .15
282 David Dellucci .15
283 Francisco Cordero .15
284 Jason Botts **(RC)** .15
285 Hank Blalock .25
286 Josh Rupe .15
287 Kevin Mench .15
288 Laynce Nix .15
289 Mark Teixeira .50
290 Michael Young .25
291 Richard Hidalgo .15
292 Scott Feldman **RC** .25
293 Bill Mueller .15
294 Hanley Ramirez **(RC)** .40
295 Curt Schilling .75
296 David Ortiz .75
297 Alejandro Machado .15
298 Edgar Renteria .25
299 Jason Varitek .40
300 Johnny Damon .75
301 Keith Foulke .15
302 Manny Ramirez .75
303 Matt Clement .15
304 Craig Hansen **RC** 2.00
305 Tim Wakefield .15
306 Trot Nixon .15
307 Aaron Harang .15
308 Adam Dunn .50
309 Austin Kearns .25
310 Brandon Claussen .15
311 Chris Booker .15
312 Edwin Encarnacion .15
313 Chris Denorfia **(RC)** .15
314 Felipe Lopez .15
315 Miguel Perez **(RC)** .15
316 Ken Griffey Jr. 1.50
317 Ryan Freel .15
318 Sean Casey .15
319 Wily Mo Pena .15
320 Mike Esposito .15
321 Aaron Miles .15
322 Brad Hawpe .15
323 Brian Fuentes .15
324 Clint Barmes .15
325 Cory Sullivan .15
326 Garrett Atkins .15
327 J.D. Closser .15
328 Jeff Francis .15
329 Luis Gonzalez .15
330 Matt Holliday .25
331 Todd Helton .50
332 Angel Berroa .15
333 David DeJesus .15
334 Emil Brown .15
335 Jeremy Affeldt .15
336 Chris Demaria **RC** .50
337 Mark Teahen .15
338 Matt Stairs .15
339 Steve Stemle **RC** .25
340 Mike Sweeney .15
341 Runelvys Hernandez .15
342 Jonah Bayliss **RC** .25
343 Zack Greinke .15
344 Brandon Inge .15
345 Carlos Guillen .15
346 Carlos Pena .15
347 Chris Shelton .25
348 Craig Monroe .15
349 Dmitri Young .15
350 Ivan Rodriguez .40
351 Jeremy Bonderman .15
352 Magglio Ordonez .25
353 Mark Woodyard **(RC)** .15
354 Omar Infante .15
355 Placido Polanco .15
356 Rondell White .15
357 Brad Radke .15
358 Carlos Silva .15
359 Jacque Jones .15
360 Joe Mauer .25
361 Chris Heintz **RC** .25
362 Joe Nathan .15
363 Johan Santana .50
364 Justin Morneau .15
365 Francisco Liriano **(RC)** .50
366 Travis Bowyer .15
367 Michael Cuddyer .15
368 Scott Baker .15
369 Shannon Stewart .15
370 Torii Hunter .25
371 A.J. Pierzynski .15
372 Aaron Rowand .15
373 Carl Everett .15
374 Dustin Hermanson .15
375 Frank Thomas .40
376 Freddy Garcia .15
377 Jermaine Dye .15
378 Joe Crede .15
379 Jon Garland .15
380 Jose Contreras .15
381 Juan Uribe .15
382 Mark Buehrle .25
383 Orlando Hernandez .15
384 Paul Konerko .25
385 Scott Podsednik .15
386 Tadahito Iguchi .25
387 Alex Rodriguez 2.00
388 Bernie Williams .25
389 Chien-Ming Wang .40
390 Derek Jeter 2.00
391 Gary Sheffield .40
392 Hideki Matsui 1.00
393 Jason Giambi .40
394 Jorge Posada .25
395 Michael Vento .15
396 Mariano Rivera .25
397 Mike Mussina .25
398 Randy Johnson .75
399 Robinson Cano .25
400 Tino Martinez .25
401 Alay Soler **RC** .40
402 Boof Bonser **(RC)** .40
403 Cole Hamels **(RC)** 1.50
404 Ian Kinsler **(RC)** .40
405 Jason Kubel **(RC)** .40
406 Joel Zumaya **(RC)** 1.00
407 Jonathan Papelbon **(RC)** 2.50
408 Jered Weaver **(RC)** 2.50
409 Kendry Morales **(RC)** 1.00
410 Lastings Milledge **(RC)** 1.00
411 Matthew Kemp **(RC)** 1.00
412 Taylor Buchholz **(RC)** .40
413 Andre Ethier **(RC)** 2.50
414 Dan Uggla **(RC)** 1.00
415 Jeremy Sowers **(RC)** .40
416 Chad Billingsley **(RC)** .75
417 Josh Barfield **(RC)** .40
418 Matt Cain **(RC)** .75
419 Fausto Carmona **(RC)** .40
420 Josh Willingham **(RC)** .40
421 Jeremy Hermida **(RC)** .75
422 Conor Jackson **(RC)** .75
423 Dave Gassner **(RC)** .40
424 Brian Bannister **(RC)** .40
425 Fernando Nieve **(RC)** .40
426 Justin Verlander **(RC)** 2.50
427 Scott Olsen **(RC)** .40
428 Takashi Saito **RC** .50
429 Willie Eyre **(RC)** .40
430 Travis Ishikawa **(RC)** .40

Glossy

Glossy: 2-3X
Inserted 1:12

Glossy Gold

Glossy Gold: 4-8X
Inserted 1:144

Autographics

		NM/M
Inserted 1:432		
AN	Garret Anderson	15.00
GA	Garrett Atkins	15.00
JB	Joe Blanton	10.00
EC	Eric Chavez	15.00
KG	Ken Griffey Jr.	75.00
TI	Tadahito Iguchi	40.00
CS	Chris Shelton	10.00
NS	Nick Swisher	15.00
KY	Kevin Youkilis	20.00

Award Winners

	NM/M
Complete Set (6):	5.00
Common Player:	.50
1 Albert Pujols	3.00
2 Alex Rodriguez	3.00
3 Chris Carpenter	.50
4 Bartolo Colon	.50
5 Ryan Howard	1.00
6 Huston Street	.50

Fabrics

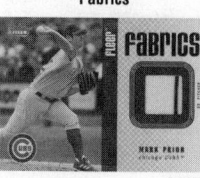

		NM/M
Inserted 1:36		
BA	Bobby Abreu	6.00
CB	Carlos Beltran	8.00
MC	Miguel Cabrera	8.00
EC	Eric Chavez	4.00
RC	Roger Clemens	15.00
JD	Johnny Damon	8.00
JE	Jim Edmonds	6.00
EG	Eric Gagne	4.00
LG	Luis Gonzalez	4.00
GR	Khalil Greene	4.00
KG	Ken Griffey Jr.	15.00
VG	Vladimir Guerrero	8.00
RH	Roy Halladay	4.00
TH	Todd Helton	6.00
DJ	Derek Jeter	20.00
RJ	Randy Johnson	8.00
AJ	Andruw Jones	8.00
CJ	Chipper Jones	8.00
DL	Derrek Lee	8.00
GM	Greg Maddux	15.00
PM	Pedro Martinez	8.00
JM	Joe Mauer	4.00
DO	David Ortiz	8.00
JP	Jake Peavy	6.00
MP	Mark Prior	8.00
AP	Albert Pujols	20.00
AR	Aramis Ramirez	6.00
MR	Manny Ramirez	8.00
IR	Ivan Rodriguez	6.00
SR	Scott Rolen	8.00
JS	Johan Santana	8.00
CS	Curt Schilling	8.00
GS	Gary Sheffield/SP	10.00
SM	John Smoltz	8.00
AS	Alfonso Soriano	6.00
MT	Mark Teixeira	8.00
TE	Miguel Tejada	6.00
JT	Jim Thome	6.00
RW	Rickie Weeks	4.00
DW	Dontrelle Willis/SP	8.00
WR	David Wright	12.00
MY	Michael Young	4.00

Lumber Company

		NM/M
1	Adam Dunn	1.00
2	Albert Pujols	3.00
3	Alex Rodriguez	3.00
4	Alfonso Soriano	.75
5	Andruw Jones	.75
6	Aramis Ramirez	.75
7	Bobby Abreu	.75
8	Carlos Delgado	.75
9	Carlos Lee	.50
10	David Ortiz	1.00
11	David Wright	1.50
12	Derrek Lee	1.00
13	Eric Chavez	.50
14	Gary Sheffield	.75
15	Jeff Kent	.50
16	Ken Griffey Jr.	2.00
17	Manny Ramirez	1.00
18	Mark Teixeira	1.00
19	Miguel Cabrera	1.00
20	Miguel Tejada	.75
21	Paul Konerko	.75
22	Richie Sexson	.50
23	Todd Helton	.75
24	Troy Glaus	.50
25	Vladimir Guerrero	1.00

Smoke 'n Heat

		NM/M
1	Carlos Zambrano	.50
2	Chris Carpenter	.50
3	Curt Schilling	1.00
4	Dontrelle Willis	.50
5	Felix Hernandez	1.00
6	Jake Peavy	.75
7	Johan Santana	1.00
8	John Smoltz	.75
9	Mark Prior	.75
10	Pedro Martinez	1.00
11	Randy Johnson	1.00
12	Roger Clemens	3.00
13	Roy Halladay	.50
14	Roy Oswalt	.50
15	Scott Kazmir	.50

Smooth Leather

		NM/M
Complete Set (14):		10.00
Common Player:		.50
1	Alex Rodriguez	3.00
2	Andruw Jones	1.00
3	Derek Jeter	3.00
4	Derrek Lee	1.00
5	Eric Chavez	.50
6	Greg Maddux	2.00
7	Ichiro Suzuki	2.00
8	Ivan Rodriguez	.75
9	Jim Edmonds	.75
10	Mike Mussina	.75
11	Omar Vizquel	.50
12	Scott Rolen	1.00
13	Todd Helton	.75
14	Torii Hunter	.50

Stars of Tomorrow

		NM/M
Complete Set (10):		5.00
Common Player:		.50
Inserted 1:10		
1	David Wright	1.50
2	Ryan Howard	1.00
3	Felix Hernandez	1.00
4	Jeff Francoeur	.50
5	Joe Mauer	.50
6	Mark Prior	.75
7	Mark Teixeira	1.00
8	Miguel Cabrera	1.00
9	Prince Fielder (RC)	1.00
10	Rickie Weeks	.50

Team Fleer

		NM/M
Inserted 1:Case		
1	Albert Pujols	40.00
2	Alex Rodriguez	30.00
3	Alfonso Soriano	10.00
4	Andruw Jones	10.00
5	Bobby Abreu	10.00
6	David Ortiz	15.00
7	David Wright	25.00
8	Eric Gagne	8.00
9	Ichiro Suzuki	30.00
10	Jason Varitek	15.00
11	Jeff Kent	8.00
12	Johan Santana	15.00
13	Jose Reyes	15.00
14	Manny Ramirez	15.00
15	Mariano Rivera	10.00
16	Miguel Cabrera	15.00
17	Miguel Tejada	10.00
18	Mike Piazza	15.00
19	Roger Clemens	30.00
20	Torii Hunter	8.00

Team Leaders

		NM/M
Complete Set (30):		15.00
Common Player:		.50
1	Troy Glaus, Brandon Webb	.50
2	John Smoltz, Andruw Jones	.50
3	Miguel Tejada, Erik Bedard	.50
4	David Ortiz, Curt Schilling	.75
5	Derrek Lee, Mark Prior	.75
6	Mark Buehrle, Paul Konerko	.50
7	Ken Griffey Jr., Aaron Harang	1.50
8	Cliff Lee, Travis Hafner	.50
9	Todd Helton, Jeff Francis	.50
10	Jeremy Bonderman, Ivan Rodriguez	.50
11	Miguel Cabrera, Dontrelle Willis	.75
12	Lance Berkman, Roger Clemens	2.00
13	Mike Sweeney, Zack Greinke	.50
14	Derek Lowe, Jeff Kent	.50
15	Carlos Lee, Ben Sheets	.50
16	Johan Santana, Torii Hunter	.50
17	Pedro Martinez, David Wright	1.00
18	Derek Jeter, Randy Johnson	2.00
19	Barry Zito, Eric Chavez	.50
20	Bobby Abreu, Brett Myers	.50
21	Jason Bay, Zachary Duke	.50
22	Jake Peavy, Brian Giles	.50
23	Moises Alou, Jason Schmidt	.50
24	Felix Hernandez, Ichiro Suzuki	1.00
25	Chris Carpenter, Albert Pujols	2.00
26	Scott Kazmir, Carl Crawford	.50
27	Mark Teixeira, Kenny Rogers	.50
28	Vernon Wells, Roy Halladay	.50
29	Livan Hernandez, Jose Guillen	.50
30	Bartolo Colon, Vladimir Guerrero	.50

Top 40

		NM/M
Common Player:		.50
Inserted 2:1 Fat Pack		
1	Ken Griffey Jr.	3.00
2	Derek Jeter	4.00
3	Albert Pujols	4.00
4	Alex Rodriguez	4.00
5	Vladimir Guerrero	1.50
6	Roger Clemens	3.00
7	Derrek Lee	1.00
8	David Ortiz	1.50
9	Miguel Cabrera	1.50
10	Bobby Abreu	.50
11	Mark Teixeira	1.00
12	Johan Santana	1.50
13	Hideki Matsui	2.50
14	Ichiro Suzuki	3.00
15	Andruw Jones	1.00
16	Eric Chavez	.50
17	Roy Oswalt	.75
18	Curt Schilling	1.00
19	Randy Johnson	1.50
20	Ivan Rodriguez	1.00
21	Chipper Jones	1.50
22	Mark Prior	.50
23	Jason Bay	.75
24	Pedro Martinez	1.50
25	David Wright	2.50
26	Carlos Beltran	1.00
27	Jim Edmonds	.50
28	Chris Carpenter	.75
29	Roy Halladay	.75
30	Jake Peavy	1.00
31	Paul Konerko	.75
32	Travis Hafner	.75
33	Barry Zito	.50
34	Miguel Tejada	.75
35	Josh Beckett	1.00
36	Todd Helton	1.00
37	Dontrelle Willis	.50
38	Manny Ramirez	1.50
39	Mariano Rivera	1.00
40	Jeff Kent	.50

2006 Fleer Greats of the Game

Kirby Puckett
MINNESOTA TWINS

		NM/M
Complete Set (100):		35.00
Common Player:		.40
Pack (5):		8.00
Box (15):		100.00
1	Al Kaline	1.50
2	Alan Trammell	.50
3	Andre Dawson	.75
4	Barry Larkin	.75
5	Bill Buckner	.40
6	Bill Freehan	.40
7	Bill Madlock	.40
8	Bill Mazeroski	.40
9	Billy Williams	.50
10	Bo Jackson	1.00
11	Bob Feller	1.00
12	Bob Gibson	.50
13	Bobby Doerr	.50
14	Bobby Murcer	.50
15	Boog Powell	.40
16	Brooks Robinson	1.50
17	Bruce Sutter	.40
18	Bucky Dent	.40
19	Cal Ripken Jr.	4.00
20	Rico Petrocelli	.40
21	Carlton Fisk	.75
22	Chris Chambliss	.40
23	Dave Concepcion	.40
24	Dave Parker	.50
25	Dave Winfield	1.00
26	David Cone	.50
27	Denny McLain	.50
28	Don Mattingly	3.00
29	Don Newcombe	.50
30	Don Sutton	.50
31	Dusty Baker	.50
32	Dwight Evans	.50
33	Eric Davis	.50
34	Ernie Banks	2.00
35	Fergie Jenkins	.75
36	Frank Robinson	1.00
37	Fred Lynn	.40
38	Fred McGriff	.50
39	Andre Thornton	.40
40	Garry Maddox	.40
41	Gary Matthews	.40
42	Gaylord Perry	.40
43	George Foster	.40
44	George Kell	.40
45	Graig Nettles	.40
46	Greg Luzinski	.40
47	Harmon Killebrew	1.50
48	Jack Clark	.50
49	Jack Morris	.50
50	Jim Palmer	.75
51	Jim Rice	.75
52	Joe Morgan	.75
53	John Kruk	.50
54	Johnny Bench	2.00
55	Jose Canseco	.75
56	Kirby Puckett	2.00
57	Kirk Gibson	.50
58	Lee Mazzilli	.40
59	Lou Brock	.75
60	Lou Piniella	.50
61	Luis Aparicio	.50
62	Luis Tiant	.50
63	Mark Fidrych	.50
64	Mark Grace	.75
65	Maury Wills	.50
66	Mike Schmidt	2.00
67	Nolan Ryan	3.00
68	Ozzie Smith	1.00
69	Paul Molitor	1.00
70	Paul O'Neill	.50
71	Phil Niekro	.50
72	Ralph Kiner	.75
73	Randy Hundley	.40

#	Player	Price
74	Red Schoendienst	.50
75	Reggie Jackson	1.00
76	Robin Yount	1.00
77	Rod Carew	.75
78	Rollie Fingers	.50
79	Ron Cey	.50
80	Ron Guidry	.50
81	Ron Santo	.75
82	Rusty Staub	.40
83	Ryne Sandberg	2.00
84	Sparky Lyle	.40
85	Stan Musial	2.00
86	Steve Carlton	.75
87	Steve Garvey	.50
88	Steve Sax	.40
89	Tommy Herr	.40
90	Tim McCarver	.50
91	Tim Raines	.50
92	Tom Seaver	1.00
93	Tony Gwynn	1.00
94	Tony Perez	.75
95	Wade Boggs	.75
96	Whitey Ford	1.00
97	Will Clark	.75
98	Willie Horton	.40
99	Willie McCovey	1.00
100	Yogi Berra	1.50

Copper

Copper: 2-4X
Production 299 Sets

Pewter

Pewter: 2X
Inserted 1:15

AUTOGRAPHics

NM/M

Inserted 1:180
Cards are not serial numbered.

		NM/M
LA	Luis Aparicio/25	20.00
LB	Lou Brock/25	25.00
RC	Rod Carew/25	30.00
SC	Steve Carlton/50	25.00
WC	Will Clark/25	40.00
AD	Andre Dawson/99	25.00
BF	Bob Feller/75	30.00
GF	George Foster/50	20.00
SG	Steve Garvey/50	25.00
BG	Bob Gibson/25	40.00
KG	Kirk Gibson/25	25.00
MG	Mark Grace/50	30.00
RG	Ron Guidry/99	50.00
BJ	Bo Jackson/25	75.00
FJ	Fergie Jenkins/25	30.00
AK	Al Kaline/50	35.00
HK	Harmon Killebrew/25	50.00
BL	Barry Larkin/50	40.00
BI	Bill Mazeroski/25	35.00
FM	Fred McGriff/99	30.00
PM	Paul Molitor/50	25.00
JM	Joe Morgan/25	35.00
BM	Bobby Murcer/99	30.00
DN	Don Newcombe/99	15.00
PN	Phil Niekro/50	20.00
JP	Jim Palmer/99	20.00
DP	Dave Parker/99	20.00
TP	Tony Perez/99	30.00
JR	Jim Rice/99	20.00
BR	Brooks Robinson/50	40.00
RS	Ron Santo/99	30.00
OS	Ozzie Smith/25	60.00
BS	Bruce Sutter/50	15.00
SU	Don Sutton/50	20.00
BW	Billy Williams/50	25.00
MW	Maury Wills/99	20.00

Autographs

NM/M

Common Autograph: 10.00

#	Player	Price
1	Al Kaline	25.00
2	Alan Trammell	15.00
3	Andre Dawson	20.00
4	Barry Larkin	35.00
5	Bill Buckner	12.00
6	Bill Freehan	12.00
7	Bill Madlock	15.00
8	Bill Mazeroski	35.00
9	Billy Williams	20.00
10	Bo Jackson	60.00
11	Bob Feller	25.00
12	Bob Gibson	40.00
13	Bobby Doerr	20.00
14	Bobby Murcer	15.00
15	Boog Powell	15.00
16	Brooks Robinson	25.00
17	Bruce Sutter	15.00
18	Bucky Dent	10.00
19	Cal Ripken Jr./SP	140.00
20	Rico Petrocelli	10.00
21	Carlton Fisk	30.00
22	Chris Chambliss	15.00
23	Dave Concepcion	15.00
24	Dave Parker	20.00
25	Dave Winfield	30.00
26	David Cone	15.00
27	Denny McLain	20.00
28	Don Mattingly	60.00
29	Don Newcombe	20.00
30	Don Sutton	15.00
31	Dusty Baker	25.00
32	Dwight Evans	20.00
33	Eric Davis	15.00
34	Ernie Banks	75.00
35	Fergie Jenkins	20.00
36	Frank Robinson	30.00
37	Fred Lynn	15.00
38	Fred McGriff	30.00
39	Andre Thornton	10.00
40	Garry Maddox	20.00
41	Gary Matthews	10.00
42	Gaylord Perry	15.00
43	George Foster	15.00
44	George Kell	15.00
45	Graig Nettles	20.00
46	Greg Luzinski	15.00
47	Harmon Killebrew	35.00
48	Jack Clark/SP/50	20.00
49	Jack Morris	15.00
50	Jim Palmer	20.00
51	Jim Rice	20.00
52	Joe Morgan	25.00
53	John Kruk	20.00
54	Johnny Bench	60.00
55	Kirby Puckett	100.00
56	Kirk Gibson	20.00
57	Lee Mazzilli	15.00
58	Lou Brock	30.00
59	Lou Piniella	15.00
60	Luis Aparicio	15.00
61	Luis Tiant	15.00
62	Mark Fidrych	25.00
63	Mark Grace	25.00
64	Maury Wills	20.00
65	Mike Schmidt	50.00
66	Nolan Ryan/SP/50	100.00
67	Ozzie Smith	40.00
68	Paul Molitor	25.00
69	Paul O'Neill	25.00
70	Phil Niekro	25.00
71	Ralph Kiner	20.00
72	Randy Hundley	15.00
73	Red Schoendienst	25.00
74	Reggie Jackson	35.00
75	Robin Yount	50.00
76	Rod Carew	25.00
77	Rollie Fingers	20.00
78	Ron Cey	10.00
79	Ron Guidry/SP	50.00
80	Ron Santo	25.00
83	Ryne Sandberg/SP	50.00
84	Sparky Lyle	15.00
85	Stan Musial	65.00
86	Steve Carlton	25.00
87	Steve Garvey	25.00
88	Steve Sax	10.00
89	Tommy Herr	15.00
90	Tim McCarver	20.00
91	Tim Raines/SP	20.00
92	Tom Seaver	50.00
93	Tony Gwynn	40.00
94	Tony Perez	25.00
95	Wade Boggs	25.00
96	Whitey Ford	50.00
97	Will Clark/SP	35.00
98	Willie Horton	15.00
99	Willie McCovey	35.00
100	Yogi Berra	60.00

Bat Barrel Autograph

No Pricing
Production 1-5

Cardinals Greats

		NM/M
	Complete Set (10):	8.00
LB	Lou Brock	1.00
SC	Steve Carlton	.50
DD	Dizzy Dean	1.00
BG	Bob Gibson	1.00
TH	Tommy Herr	.25
RH	Rogers Hornsby	1.00
TM	Tim McCarver	.50
SM	Stan Musial	2.00
RS	Red Schoendienst	.50
OS	Ozzie Smith	1.00

Cardinals Greats Memorabila Autograph

		NM/M
	Production 30 Sets	
LB	Lou Brock	50.00
SC	Steve Carlton	35.00
BG	Bob Gibson	60.00
TH	Tommy Herr	20.00
TM	Tim McCarver	30.00
SM	Stan Musial	75.00
RS	Red Schoendienst	30.00
OS	Ozzie Smith	50.00

Cardinals Greats Autograph

		NM/M
	Production 30 Sets	
LB	Lou Brock	40.00
SC	Steve Carlton	30.00
BG	Bob Gibson	50.00
TH	Tommy Herr	20.00
TM	Tim McCarver	30.00
SM	Stan Musial	75.00
RS	Red Schoendienst	25.00
OS	Ozzie Smith	50.00

Cardinals Greats Memorabilia

		NM/M
	Common Player:	5.00
LB	Lou Brock	5.00
SC	Steve Carlton	5.00
DD	Dizzy Dean/SP	50.00
BG	Bob Gibson	15.00
TH	Tommy Herr	5.00
RH	Rogers Hornsby	40.00
TM	Tim McCarver	5.00
SM	Stan Musial	20.00
RS	Red Schoendienst	10.00
OS	Ozzie Smith	15.00

Cubs Greats

		NM/M
	Complete Set (10):	8.00
EB	Ernie Banks	2.00
AD	Andre Dawson	1.00
MG	Mark Grace	1.00
RH	Randy Hundley	.50
FJ	Fergie Jenkins	.50
GM	Gary Mathews	.50
SA	Ryne Sandberg	2.00
RS	Ron Santo	1.00
BS	Bruce Sutter	.50
BW	Billy Williams	.50

Cubs Greats Memorabilia Autograph

		NM/M
	Production 30 Sets	
EB	Ernie Banks	60.00
AD	Andre Dawson	30.00
FJ	Fergie Jenkins	25.00
GM	Gary Matthews	25.00
SA	Ryne Sandberg	60.00
RS	Ron Santo	40.00
BS	Bruce Sutter	30.00
BW	Billy Williams	30.00

Cubs Greats Autograph

		NM/M
	Production 30 Sets	
EB	Ernie Banks	60.00
AD	Andre Dawson	30.00
MG	Mark Grace	30.00
FJ	Fergie Jenkins	25.00
GM	Gary Matthews	25.00
SA	Ryne Sandberg	60.00
RS	Ron Santo	40.00
BS	Bruce Sutter	20.00
BW	Billy Williams	30.00

Cubs Greats Memorabilia

		NM/M
EB	Ernie Banks	20.00
AD	Andre Dawson	8.00
MG	Mark Grace	8.00
FJ	Fergie Jenkins	8.00
GM	Gary Matthews	15.00
SA	Ryne Sandberg	15.00
RS	Ron Santo	10.00
BS	Brian Sutter	5.00
BW	Billy Williams	8.00

Decade Greats

		NM/M
	Complete Set (30):	20.00
EA	Earl Averill	.50
RO	Rod Carew	1.00
SC	Steve Carlton	.75
CC	Chris Chambliss	.50
JC	Jack Clark	.50
WC	Will Clark	1.00
RC	Roberto Clemente	3.00
MC	Mickey Cochrane	.50
BF	Bob Feller	1.00
TG	Tony Gwynn	1.00
BJ	Bo Jackson	1.00
JK	John Kruk	.50
BI	Bill Madlock	.50
EM	Eddie Mathews	1.00
BM	Bill Mazeroski	.50

WM	Willie McCovey	1.00
JM	Johnny Mize	.50
PM	Paul Molitor	1.00
MO	Mel Ott	1.00
DP	Dave Parker	.50
KP	Kirby Puckett	1.00
TR	Tim Raines	.50
CR	Cal Ripken Jr.	3.00
BR	Brooks Robinson	1.00
NR	Nolan Ryan	2.00
TS	Tom Seaver	1.00
MS	Mike Schmidt	1.00
WS	Willie Stargell	1.00
PT	Paul Traynor	.50
RY	Robin Yount	1.00

Decade Greats Memorabilia Autograph

		NM/M
	Production 30 Sets	
RO	Rod Carew	35.00
SC	Steve Carlton	35.00
CC	Chris Chambliss	25.00
JC	Jack Clark	25.00
WC	Will Clark	35.00
BF	Bob Feller	50.00
TG	Tony Gwynn	60.00
BJ	Bo Jackson	65.00
JK	John Kruk	25.00
BI	Bill Madlock	20.00
BM	Bill Mazeroski	35.00
WM	Willie McCovey	40.00
PM	Paul Molitor	35.00
DP	Dave Parker	20.00
KP	Kirby Puckett	100.00
TR	Tim Raines	20.00
CR	Cal Ripken Jr.	150.00
BR	Brooks Robinson	40.00
NR	Nolan Ryan	100.00
MS	Mike Schmidt	75.00
TS	Tom Seaver	50.00
RY	Robin Yount	50.00

Decade Greats Autograph

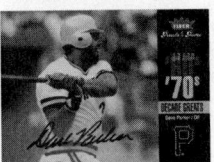

		NM/M
	Production 30 Sets	
RO	Rod Carew	35.00
SC	Steve Carlton	35.00
CC	Chris Chambliss	25.00
JC	Jack Clark	25.00
WC	Will Clark	35.00
BF	Bob Feller	50.00
TG	Tony Gwynn	65.00
BJ	Bo Jackson	65.00
JK	John Kruk	25.00
BI	Bill Madlock	20.00
BM	Bill Mazeroski	35.00
WM	Willie McCovey	40.00
PM	Paul Molitor	35.00
DP	Dave Parker	20.00
KP	Kirby Puckett	100.00
TR	Tim Raines	20.00
CR	Cal Ripken Jr.	150.00
BR	Brooks Robinson	40.00
NR	Nolan Ryan	100.00
MS	Mike Schmidt	75.00
TS	Tom Seaver	50.00
RY	Robin Yount	50.00

Decade Greats Memorabilia

		NM/M
	Common Player:	5.00
EA	Earl Averill	20.00
RO	Rod Carew	8.00
SC	Steve Carlton	5.00
CC	Chris Chambliss	5.00
JC	Jack Clark	5.00
WC	Will Clark	8.00
RC	Roberto Clemente	60.00
BF	Bob Feller	15.00
BJ	Bo Jackson	15.00
JK	John Kruk	8.00
BI	Bill Madlock	5.00
EM	Eddie Matthews	10.00
BM	Bill Mazeroski	8.00
WM	Willie McCovey	10.00
JM	Johnny Mize	15.00
PM	Paul Molitor	8.00
MO	Mel Ott SP	50.00

DP	Dave Parker	5.00
KP	Kirby Puckett	15.00
TR	Tim Raines	5.00
CR	Cal Ripken Jr.	20.00
BR	Brooks Robinson	8.00
NR	Nolan Ryan	15.00
MS	Mike Schmidt	10.00
TS	Tom Seaver	10.00
WS	Willie Stargell	15.00
RY	Robin Yount	8.00

Dodgers Greats

		NM/M
	Complete Set (10):	6.00
DB	Dusty Baker	.50
CA	Roy Campanella	1.00
RC	Ron Cey	.50
DD	Don Drysdale	1.00
SG	Steve Garvey	.50
PR	Pee Wee Reese	.50
JR	Jackie Robinson	2.00
SS	Steve Sax	.50
DS	Don Sutton	.50
MW	Maury Wills	.50

Dodgers Greats Autograph

		NM/M
	Production 30 Sets	
DB	Dusty Baker	40.00
RC	Ron Cey	30.00
SG	Steve Garvey	35.00
SS	Steve Sax	25.00
DS	Don Sutton	35.00
MW	Maury Wills	35.00

Dodgers Greats Memorabilia Autograph

		NM/M
	Production 30 Sets	
DB	Dusty Baker	40.00
RC	Ron Cey	30.00
SG	Steve Garvey	35.00
SS	Steve Sax	20.00
DS	Don Sutton	35.00
MW	Maury Wills	35.00

Dodgers Greats Memorabilia

		NM/M
	Common Player:	5.00
DB	Dusty Baker	8.00
CA	Roy Campanella	35.00
RC	Ron Cey	5.00
DD	Don Drysdale	25.00
SG	Steve Garvey	8.00
PR	Pee Wee Reese	10.00
JR	Jackie Robinson	40.00
SS	Steve Sax	5.00
DS	Don Sutton	5.00
MW	Maury Wills	5.00

Nickname Greats

		NM/M
LA	Luis Aparicio	.50
SB	Steve Balboni	.50
DB	Don Baylor	.50
BE	Steve Bedrosian	.50
JB	Jim Bouton	.50
TB	Tom Brunansky	.50
RC	Ron Cey	.50
CH	Joe Charboneau	.50
JC	Jack Clark	.50
WC	Will Clark	1.00
DD	Darren Daulton	.50
DE	Dwight Evans	.50
BF	Bob Feller	1.00
SF	Sid Fernandez	.50
MF	Mark Fidrych	.50
CF	Carlton Fisk	.75
DF	Dan Ford	.50
GF	George Foster	.50
AG	Andres Galarraga	.50
RG	Ron Guidry	.50
MH	Mike Hargrove	.50
KH	Ken Harrelson	.50
TH	Tom Henke	.50
HE	Tommy Herr	.50
BH	Burt Hooton	.50
AH	Al Hrabosky	.50
GH	Glenn Hubbard	.50
HJ	Howard Johnson	.50
JJ	Jay Johnstone	.50
ML	Mike LaValliere	.50
BL	Bill Lee	.50
SL	Sparky Lyle	.50
GM	Garry Maddox	.50
BM	Bill Madlock	.50
MZ	Dennis Martinez	.50
MA	Gary Matthews	.50
DM	Don Mattingly	2.00
LM	Lee Mazzilli	.50
WM	Willie McCovey	1.00
SM	Sam McDowell	.50
JM	John Montefusco	.50
DP	Dave Parker	.50
JP	Joe Pepitone	.50
LP	Lou Piniella	.50
RA	Doug Rader	.50
TR	Tim Raines	.50
RR	Rick Reuschel	.50
DR	Dave Righetti	.50
MR	Mickey Rivers	.50
FR	Frank Robinson	1.00
GS	George Scott	.50
JS	John Shelby	.50
FS	Fred Stanley	.50
RS	Rusty Staub	.50
AT	Andre Thornton	.50
ST	Steve Trout	.50
EV	Ellis Valentine	.50
MW	Mitch Williams	.50
JW	Jimmy Wynn	.50

Nickname Greats Autograph

"Wild Thing"

		NM/M
SB	Steve Balboni	15.00
BE	Steve Bedrosian	15.00
JB	Jim Bouton	35.00
TB	Tom Brunansky	15.00
RB	Rick Burleson	15.00
CH	Joe Charboneau	20.00
JC	Jack Clark	20.00
WC	Will Clark	30.00
DD	Darren Daulton	20.00
DE	Dwight Evans	20.00
BF	Bob Feller	50.00
SF	Sid Fernandez	15.00
MF	Mark Fidrych	35.00
CF	Carlton Fisk	50.00
DF	Dan Ford	15.00
GF	George Foster	20.00
RG	Ron Guidry	40.00
MH	Mike Hargrove	20.00
TH	Tom Henke	15.00
HE	Tommy Herr	15.00
BH	Burt Hooton	20.00
AH	Al Hrabosky	20.00
GH	Glenn Hubbard	15.00
HJ	Howard Johnson	25.00
JJ	Jay Johnstone	15.00
ML	Mike LaValliere	15.00
BL	Bill Lee	20.00
SL	Sparky Lyle	15.00
GM	Garry Maddox	15.00
BM	Bill Madlock	15.00
MZ	Dennis Martinez	20.00
MA	Gary Matthews	15.00
LM	Lee Mazzilli	15.00
WM	Willie McCovey	50.00
SM	Sam McDowell	20.00
JM	John Montefusco	15.00
DP	Dave Parker	20.00
JP	Joe Pepitone	20.00
LP	Lou Piniella	25.00
RA	Doug Rader	15.00
TR	Tim Raines	15.00
RR	Rick Reuschel	20.00
DR	Dave Righetti	20.00
MR	Mickey Rivers	20.00
FR	Frank Robinson	50.00
GS	George Scott	20.00
JS	John Shelby	15.00
FS	Fred Stanley	20.00
RS	Rusty Staub	20.00
AT	Andre Thornton	15.00
ST	Steve Trout	20.00
EV	Ellis Valentine	15.00
MW	Mitch Williams	15.00
JW	Jimmy Wynn	20.00

Red Sox Greats

		NM/M
	Complete Set (10):	8.00
WB	Wade Boggs	1.00
BD	Bobby Doerr	.50
DE	Dwight Evans	.50
CF	Carlton Fisk	1.00
JF	Jimmie Foxx	2.00
FL	Fred Lynn	.50
RP	Rico Petrocelli	.50
JR	Jim Rice	.75
LT	Luis Tiant	.50
TW	Ted Williams	2.00

Red Sox Greats Memorabilia Autograph

		NM/M
	Production 30 Sets	
WB	Wade Boggs	50.00
BD	Bobby Doerr	20.00
DE	Dwight Evans	25.00
CF	Carlton Fisk	35.00
FL	Fred Lynn	20.00
RP	Rico Petrocelli	20.00
JR	Jim Rice	25.00
LT	Luis Tiant	20.00

Red Sox Greats Autograph

		NM/M
	Production 30 Sets	
WB	Wade Boggs	50.00
BD	Bobby Doerr	20.00
DE	Dwight Evans	25.00
CF	Carlton Fisk	35.00
FL	Fred Lynn	20.00
RP	Rico Petrocelli	20.00
JR	Jim Rice	25.00
LT	Luis Tiant	25.00

Red Sox Greats Memorabilia

		NM/M
	Common Player:	
WB	Wade Boggs	10.00
BD	Bobby Doerr	8.00
DE	Dwight Evans	8.00
CF	Carlton Fisk	8.00
JF	Jimmie Foxx	50.00
FL	Fred Lynn	5.00
RP	Rico Petrocelli	5.00
JR	Jim Rice	8.00
LT	Luis Tiant	5.00
TW	Ted Williams	50.00

Reds Greats

		NM/M
	Complete Set (10):	8.00
JB	Johnny Bench	1.50
DC	Dave Concepcion	.50
ED	Eric Davis	.50
GF	George Foster	.50
KG	Ken Griffey Sr.	.50
BL	Barry Larkin	1.00
JM	Joe Morgan	1.00
TP	Tony Perez	1.00
FR	Frank Robinson	1.00
TS	Tom Seaver	1.00

Reds Greats Autograph

		NM/M
	Production 30 Sets	
JB	Johnny Bench	65.00
DC	Dave Concepcion	25.00
ED	Eric Davis	30.00
GF	George Foster	25.00
KG	Ken Griffey Sr.	30.00
BL	Barry Larkin	40.00
JM	Joe Morgan	40.00
TP	Tony Perez	40.00
FR	Frank Robinson	50.00
TS	Tom Seaver	50.00

Reds Greats Memorabilia

		NM/M
	Common Player:	5.00
JB	Johnny Bench	15.00
DC	Dave Concepcion	5.00
ED	Eric Davis	10.00
GF	George Foster	5.00
KG	Ken Griffey Sr.	5.00
BL	Barry Larkin	8.00
JM	Joe Morgan	8.00
TP	Tony Perez	8.00
FR	Frank Robinson	10.00
TS	Tom Seaver	10.00

Reds Greats Memorabilia Autograph

		NM/M
	Production 30 Sets	
JB	Johnny Bench	65.00
DC	Dave Concepcion	25.00
ED	Eric Davis	30.00
GF	George Foster	25.00
KG	Ken Griffey Sr.	30.00
BL	Barry Larkin	40.00
JM	Joe Morgan	40.00
TP	Tony Perez	40.00
FR	Frank Robinson	50.00
TS	Tom Seaver	50.00

Tigers Greats

		NM/M
	Complete Set (10):	6.00

TC	Ty Cobb	2.00
MF	Mark Fidrych	.50
BF	Bill Freehan	.50
KG	Kirk Gibson	1.00
WH	Willie Horton	.50
AK	Al Kaline	1.00
GK	George Kell	.50
DM	Denny McLain	1.00
JM	Jack Morris	.50
AT	Alan Trammell	.50

Tigers Greats Autograph

		NM/M
	Production 30 Sets	
MF	Mark Fidrych	35.00
BF	Bill Freehan	30.00
KG	Kirk Gibson	35.00
WH	Willie Horton	20.00
AK	Al Kaline	50.00
GK	George Kell	40.00
DM	Denny McLain	35.00
JM	Jack Morris	25.00
AT	Alan Trammell	35.00

Tigers Greats Memorabilia

		NM/M
	Common Player:	5.00
TC	Ty Cobb	85.00
MF	Mark Fidrych	10.00
BF	Bill Freehan	5.00
KG	Kirk Gibson	5.00
WH	Willie Horton	5.00
AK	Al Kaline	12.00
GK	George Kell	8.00
JM	Jack Morris	5.00
AT	Alan Trammell	5.00

Tigers Greats Memorabilia Autograph

		NM/M
	Production 30 Sets	
MF	Mark Fidrych	35.00
BF	Bill Freehan	30.00
KG	Kirk Gibson	35.00
WH	Willie Horton	20.00
AK	Al Kaline	50.00
GK	George Kell	40.00
JM	Jack Morris	25.00
AT	Alan Trammell	35.00

Yankee Clippings

		NM/M
	Complete Set (10):	12.00
YB	Yogi Berra	1.50
JD	Joe DiMaggio	2.00
WF	Whitey Ford	1.00
RG	Ron Guidry	.50
RJ	Reggie Jackson	1.00
DM	Don Mattingly	2.00
TM	Thurman Munson	1.50
BM	Bobby Murcer	.50
GN	Graig Nettles	.50
BR	Babe Ruth	3.00

Yankee Clippings Autograph

		NM/M
	Production 30 Sets	
YB	Yogi Berra	80.00
WF	Whitey Ford	60.00
RG	Ron Guidry	65.00
RJ	Reggie Jackson	50.00
DM	Don Mattingly	100.00
BM	Bobby Murcer	25.00
GN	Graig Nettles	40.00

Yankee Clippings Memorabilia

		NM/M
Common Player:		8.00
YB	Yogi Berra	25.00
JD	Joe DiMaggio	75.00
WF	Whitey Ford	15.00
RG	Ron Guidry	15.00
RJ	Reggie Jackson	12.00
DM	Don Mattingly	15.00
TM	Thurman Munson	20.00
BM	Bobby Murcer	10.00
GN	Graig Nettles	8.00
BR	Babe Ruth	200.00

Yankee Clippings Memorabilia Autograph

		NM/M
Production 30 Sets		
YB	Yogi Berra	80.00
WF	Whitey Ford	60.00
RG	Ron Guidry	65.00
RJ	Reggie Jackson	50.00
DM	Don Mattingly	100.00
BM	Bobby Murcer	25.00
GN	Graig Nettles	40.00

2006 Fleer Tradition

		NM/M
Complete Set (200):		35.00
Common Player:		.15
Hobby Pack (10):		1.50
Hobby Box (36):		50.00
1	Andruw Jones	.50
2	Chipper Jones	.75
3	John Smoltz	.25
4	Tim Hudson	.25
5	Joey Devine RC	.25
6	Chuck James (RC)	.25
7	Alay Soler RC	.50
8	Conor Jackson (RC)	.25
9	Luis Gonzalez	.15
10	Brandon Webb	.15
11	Chad Tracy	.15
12	Orlando Hudson	.15
13	Shawn Green	.15
14	Vladimir Guerrero	.75
15	Bartolo Colon	.15
16	Chone Figgins	.15
17	Garret Anderson	.15
18	Francisco Rodriguez	.15
19	Casey Kotchman	.15
20	Lance Berkman	.25
21	Craig Biggio	.25
22	Andy Pettitte	.25
23	Morgan Ensberg	.15
24	Brad Lidge	.15
25	Jered Weaver (RC)	1.00
26	Roy Oswalt	.25
27	Eric Chavez	.25
28	Rich Harden	.15
29	Cole Hamels (RC)	.25
30	Huston Street	.15
31	Bobby Crosby	.15
32	Nick Swisher	.25
33	Vernon Wells	.25
34	Roy Halladay	.25
35	A.J. Burnett	.15
36	Troy Glaus	.25
37	B.J. Ryan	.15
38	Bengie Molina	.15
39	Alex Rios	.15
40	Prince Fielder (RC)	2.00
41	Jose Capellan (RC)	.25
42	Rickie Weeks	.25
43	Ben Sheets	.25
44	Carlos Lee	.15
45	J.J. Hardy	.15
46	Albert Pujols	2.00
47	Skip Schumaker (RC)	.25
48	Adam Wainwright (RC)	.25
49	Jim Edmonds	.25
50	Scott Rolen	.50
51	Chris Carpenter	.25
52	David Eckstein	.15
53	Derrek Lee	.50
54	Jon Lester (RC)	3.00
55	Mark Prior	.40
56	Aramis Ramirez	.25
57	Juan Pierre	.15
58	Greg Maddux	1.50
59	Michael Barrett	.15
60	Carl Crawford	.15
61	Scott Kazmir	.25
62	Jorge Cantu	.15
63	Jonny Gomes	.15
64	Julio Lugo	.15
65	Aubrey Huff	.15
66	Jeff Kent	.25
67	Nomar Garciaparra	.50
68	Rafael Furcal	.15
69	Tim Hamulack (RC)	.25
70	Chad Billingsley (RC)	.25
71	Hong-Chih Kuo (RC)	.25
72	J.D. Drew	.15
73	Moises Alou	.25
74	Randy Winn	.15
75	Jason Schmidt	.25
76	Jeremy Accardo RC	.25
77	Matt Cain (RC)	.50
78	Joel Zumaya (RC)	.50
79	Travis Hafner	.50
80	Victor Martinez	.25
81	Grady Sizemore	.40
82	C.C. Sabathia	.15
83	Jhonny Peralta	.15
84	Jason Michaels	.15
85	Jeremy Sowers (RC)	.25
86	Ichiro Suzuki	1.50
87	Richie Sexson	.25
88	Adrian Beltre	.25
89	Felix Hernandez	.25
90	Kenji Johjima RC	2.00
91	Jeff Harris RC	.25
92	Taylor Buchholz (RC)	.25
93	Miguel Cabrera	.75
94	Dontrelle Willis	.25
95	Jeremy Hermida (RC)	.25
96	Mike Jacobs (RC)	.25
97	Josh Johnson (RC)	.25
98	Hanley Ramirez (RC)	.40
99	Josh Willingham (RC)	.25
100	Dan Uggla (RC)	1.00
101	David Wright	1.00
102	Jose Reyes	.50
103	Pedro Martinez	.75
104	Carlos Beltran	.50
105	Carlos Delgado	.40
106	Billy Wagner	.25
107	Lastings Milledge (RC)	.50
108	Alfonso Soriano	.75
109	Jose Vidro	.15
110	Livan Hernandez	.15
111	Matthew Kemp (RC)	.25
112	Brandon Watson (RC)	.25
113	Ryan Zimmerman (RC)	2.00
114	Miguel Tejada	.50
115	Ramon Hernandez	.15
116	Brian Roberts	.15
117	Melvin Mora	.15
118	Erik Bedard	.15
119	Jay Gibbons	.15
120	Aaron Rakers (RC)	.25
121	Jake Peavy	.25
122	Brian Giles	.25
123	Khalil Greene	.15
124	Trevor Hoffman	.25
125	Josh Barfield (RC)	.25
126	Ben Johnson (RC)	.25
127	Ryan Howard	1.50
128	Bobby Abreu	.25
129	Chase Utley	.50
130	Pat Burrell	.25
131	Jimmy Rollins	.50
132	Brett Myers	.15
133	Mike Thompson RC	.25
134	Jason Bay	.40
135	Oliver Perez	.15
136	Matt Capps (RC)	.25
137	Paul Maholm (RC)	.25
138	Nate McLouth (RC)	.25
139	John Van Benschoten (RC)	.25
140	Mark Teixeira	.50
141	Michael Young	.25
142	Hank Blalock	.25
143	Kevin Millwood	.15
144	Laynce Nix	.15
145	Francisco Cordero	.15
146	Ian Kinsler (RC)	.25
147	David Ortiz	.75
148	Manny Ramirez	.75
149	Jason Varitek	.25
150	Curt Schilling	.25
151	Josh Beckett	.25
152	Coco Crisp	.15
153	Jonathan Papelbon (RC)	2.00
154	Ken Griffey Jr.	1.50
155	Adam Dunn	.50
156	Felipe Lopez	.15
157	Bronson Arroyo	.15
158	Ryan Freel	.15
159	Chris Denorfia (RC)	.25
160	Todd Helton	.50
161	Garrett Atkins	.15
162	Matt Holliday	.25
163	Clint Barmes	.15
164	Kendry Morales (RC)	.25
165	Ryan Shealy (RC)	.25
166	Josh Wilson (RC)	.25
167	Reggie Sanders	.15
168	Angel Berroa	.15
169	Mike Sweeney	.15
170	Mark Grudzielanek	.15
171	Jeremy Affeldt	.15
172	Steve Stemle RC	.50
173	Justin Verlander (RC)	2.00
174	Ivan Rodriguez	.50
175	Chris Shelton	.15
176	Jeremy Bonderman	.25
177	Magglio Ordonez	.15
178	Carlos Guillen	.15
179	Placido Polanco	.15
180	Johan Santana	.75
181	Torii Hunter	.25
182	Joe Nathan	.15
183	Joe Mauer	.50
184	David Gassner (RC)	.25
185	Jason Kubel (RC)	.25
186	Francisco Liriano (RC)	1.50
187	Jim Thome	.50
188	Paul Konerko	.40
189	Scott Podsednik	.25
190	Tadahito Iguchi	.25
191	A.J. Pierzynski	.15
192	Jose Contreras	.15
193	Brian Anderson (RC)	.25
194	Hideki Matsui	1.50
195	Wilbert Nieves (RC)	.25
196	Alex Rodriguez	1.00
197	Gary Sheffield	.25
198	Randy Johnson	.25
199	Johnny Damon	.40
200	Derek Jeter	1.00

Griffey Jr. 1989 Fleer Buyback Autograph

		NM/M
Production 50		
	Ken Griffey Jr.	250.00

Black & White

B&W (1-200):	2-3X

Printing Plates

No Pricing
Production one set per color.

Sepia Tone

Sepia (1-200):	2-3X

1934 Goudey Greats

		NM/M
Common Player:		2.00
GG-1	Andruw Jones	5.00
GG-2	Chipper Jones	8.00
GG-3	John Smoltz	4.00
GG-4	Tim Hudson	3.00
GG-5	Conor Jackson	2.00
GG-6	Luis Gonzalez	2.00
GG-7	Brandon Webb	2.00
GG-8	Vladimir Guerrero	8.00
GG-9	Bartolo Colon	2.00
GG-10	Lance Berkman	3.00
GG-11	Craig Biggio	3.00
GG-12	Andy Pettitte	3.00
GG-13	Morgan Ensberg	2.00
GG-14	Roy Oswalt	3.00
GG-15	Eric Chavez	3.00
GG-16	Rich Harden	2.00
GG-17	Huston Street	2.00
GG-18	Vernon Wells	3.00
GG-19	Roy Halladay	3.00
GG-20	Troy Glaus	3.00
GG-21	Prince Fielder	10.00
GG-22	Rickie Weeks	3.00
GG-23	Ben Sheets	3.00
GG-24	Carlos Lee	2.00
GG-25	Albert Pujols	20.00
GG-26	Jim Edmonds	4.00
GG-27	Scott Rolen	8.00
GG-28	Chris Carpenter	5.00
GG-29	Derrek Lee	5.00
GG-30	Mark Prior	5.00
GG-31	Greg Maddux	15.00
GG-32	Carl Crawford	4.00
GG-33	Scott Kazmir	3.00
GG-34	Jorge Cantu	2.00
GG-35	Jeff Kent	3.00
GG-36	Nomar Garciaparra	8.00
GG-37	J.D. Drew	2.00
GG-38	Randy Winn	2.00
GG-39	Jason Schmidt	3.00
GG-40	Travis Hafner	5.00
GG-41	Victor Martinez	3.00
GG-42	Grady Sizemore	4.00
GG-43	Jhonny Peralta	2.00
GG-44	Ichiro Suzuki	15.00
GG-45	Richie Sexson	4.00
GG-46	Felix Hernandez	4.00
GG-47	Kenji Johjima	8.00
GG-48	Miguel Cabrera	8.00
GG-49	Dontrelle Willis	4.00
GG-50	Josh Willingham	2.00
GG-51	David Wright	15.00
GG-52	Jose Reyes	5.00
GG-53	Pedro Martinez	8.00
GG-54	Carlos Beltran	5.00
GG-55	Alfonso Soriano	8.00
GG-56	Ryan Zimmerman	8.00
GG-57	Miguel Tejada	4.00
GG-58	Brian Roberts	2.00
GG-59	Jake Peavy	3.00
GG-60	Brian Giles	2.00
GG-61	Khalil Greene	2.00
GG-62	Ryan Howard	15.00
GG-63	Bobby Abreu	4.00
GG-64	Chase Utley	5.00
GG-65	Jimmy Rollins	5.00
GG-66	Jason Bay	4.00
GG-67	Mark Teixeira	5.00
GG-68	Michael Young	3.00
GG-69	Hank Blalock	3.00
GG-70	David Ortiz	8.00
GG-71	Manny Ramirez	8.00
GG-72	Curt Schilling	5.00
GG-73	Josh Beckett	3.00
GG-74	Jonathan Papelbon	10.00
GG-75	Ken Griffey Jr.	15.00
GG-76	Adam Dunn	5.00
GG-77	Todd Helton	4.00
GG-78	Garrett Atkins	2.00
GG-79	Matt Holliday	2.00
GG-80	Reggie Sanders	2.00
GG-81	Justin Verlander	10.00
GG-82	Ivan Rodriguez	5.00
GG-83	Chris Shelton	2.00
GG-84	Jeremy Bonderman	3.00
GG-85	Magglio Ordonez	3.00
GG-86	Johan Santana	6.00
GG-87	Torii Hunter	3.00
GG-88	Joe Nathan	2.00
GG-89	Joe Mauer	5.00
GG-90	Francisco Liriano	8.00
GG-91	Jim Thome	5.00
GG-92	Paul Konerko	4.00
GG-93	Scott Podsednik	3.00
GG-94	Tadahito Iguchi	4.00
GG-95	A.J. Pierzynski	2.00
GG-96	Hideki Matsui	12.00
GG-97	Alex Rodriguez	20.00
GG-98	Gary Sheffield	4.00
GG-99	Derek Jeter	25.00
GG-100	Jason Giambi	6.00

Blue Chip Prospects

		NM/M
Common Player:		.50
BC-1	Ryan Zimmerman	3.00
BC-2	Conor Jackson	.75
BC-3	Jonathan Papelbon	3.00
BC-4	Justin Verlander	3.00
BC-5	Jeremy Hermida	.75
BC-6	Josh Willingham	.50
BC-7	Hanley Ramirez	1.00
BC-8	Prince Fielder	3.00
BC-9	Francisco Liriano	2.00
BC-10	Lastings Milledge	2.00
BC-11	Jon Lester	2.00
BC-12	Matt Cain	1.50
BC-13	Adam Wainwright	.75

BC-14 Chuck James	1.00
BC-15 Kenji Johjima	3.00
BC-16 Josh Johnson	.75
BC-17 Jason Kubel	.50
BC-18 Brian Anderson	.50
BC-19 Cole Hamels	2.00
BC-20 Mike Jacobs	.50
BC-21 Jered Weaver	3.00
BC-22 Kendry Morales	.50
BC-23 Alay Soler	.50
BC-24 Chris Denorfia	.50
BC-25 Chad Billingsley	1.00

Diamond Tribute

Common Player:	NM/M .50
DT-1 Derek Jeter	3.00
DT-2 Ken Griffey Jr.	3.00
DT-3 Vladimir Guerrero	1.50
DT-4 Albert Pujols	3.00
DT-5 Derrek Lee	1.00
DT-6 David Ortiz	1.50
DT-7 Miguel Tejada	1.00
DT-8 Jim Thome	1.00
DT-9 Travis Hafner	1.00
DT-10 Grady Sizemore	1.00
DT-11 Chris Shelton	.50
DT-12 Dontrelle Willis	1.00
DT-13 Craig Biggio	1.00
DT-14 Roy Oswalt	1.00
DT-15 Prince Fielder	2.00
DT-16 David Wright	2.50
DT-17 Jose Reyes	1.00
DT-18 Hideki Matsui	2.00
DT-19 Rich Harden	.75
DT-20 Bobby Abreu	.75
DT-21 Jason Bay	1.00
DT-22 Jake Peavy	.75
DT-23 Felix Hernandez	.75
DT-24 Carl Crawford	.75
DT-25 Vernon Wells	.75

Grass Roots

Common Player:	NM/M .50
GR-1 Ken Griffey Jr.	2.50
GR-2 Albert Pujols	3.00
GR-3 Derek Jeter	3.00
GR-4 Derrek Lee	1.00
GR-5 Vladimir Guerrero	1.00
GR-6 Andruw Jones	1.00
GR-7 Manny Ramirez	1.00
GR-8 Johan Santana	1.00
GR-9 Victor Martinez	.75
GR-10 Todd Helton	1.00
GR-11 Ivan Rodriguez	1.00
GR-12 Miguel Cabrera	1.00
GR-13 Lance Berkman	.75
GR-14 Bartolo Colon	.50
GR-15 Jeff Kent	.50
GR-16 Carlos Lee	.75
GR-17 Torii Hunter	.50
GR-18 Carlos Beltran	.75
GR-19 Alex Rodriguez	3.00
GR-20 Randy Johnson	1.00
GR-21 Eric Chavez	.50
GR-22 Ryan Howard	2.50

GR-23 Ichiro Suzuki	2.00
GR-24 Chris Carpenter	1.00
GR-25 Mark Teixeira	1.00

Signature Tradition

Inserted 1:1,269 Hobby

	NM/M
CH Craig Hansen/SP	35.00
JM Joe Mauer/SP	30.00

Traditional Threads

Common Player:	NM/M 4.00
JB Josh Barfield	4.00
BA Jason Bay	6.00
EB Erik Bedard	4.00
HB Hank Blalock	4.00
SC Sean Casey	4.00
JD Johnny Damon	8.00
ZD Zachary Duke	4.00
PF Prince Fielder	15.00
CF Chone Figgins	4.00
BG Brian Giles	4.00
MG Marcus Giles	4.00
GR Khalil Greene	4.00
KG Ken Griffey Jr.	15.00
VG Vladimir Guerrero	8.00
JH Jeremy Hermida	4.00
FH Felix Hernandez	6.00
LH Livan Hernandez	4.00
GJ Geoff Jenkins	4.00
DJ Derek Jeter	20.00
CK Casey Kotchman/SP	4.00
CL Carlos Lee	6.00
DL Derrek Lee	8.00
JL Javy Lopez	4.00
GM Greg Maddux	10.00
MM Melvin Mora	4.00
DO Dontrelle Willis	10.00
RO Roy Oswalt	6.00
JP Jake Peavy	6.00
AP Albert Pujols	20.00
AR Aramis Ramirez	6.00
AS Alfonso Soriano	8.00
BR Brian Roberts	6.00
BS Ben Sheets	6.00
TE Mark Teixeira	8.00
MT Miguel Tejada	6.00
JV Jose Vidro	4.00
OV Omar Vizquel	6.00
RW Rickie Weeks	6.00
MY Michael Young	6.00
CZ Carlos Zambrano	4.00
RZ Ryan Zimmerman	8.00

Triple Crown Contenders

Common Player:	NM/M .75
TC-1 Albert Pujols	3.00
TC-2 Derrek Lee	.75
TC-3 Manny Ramirez	1.00
TC-4 David Ortiz	1.00
TC-5 Mark Teixeira	.75
TC-6 Alex Rodriguez	3.00
TC-7 Andruw Jones	.75
TC-8 Todd Helton	.75
TC-9 Vladimir Guerrero	1.00
TC-10 Hideki Matsui	2.00
TC-11 Travis Hafner	.75
TC-12 David Wright	2.00
TC-13 Ken Griffey Jr.	2.50
TC-15 Jason Bay	.75

2007 Fleer

	NM/M
Complete Set (400):	75.00
Common Player:	.15
Hobby Pack (10):	1.50
Hobby Box (36):	50.00
Rack Pack (52):	4.50
Rack Box (18):	75.00
1 Chad Cordero	.15
2 Alfonso Soriano	.50
3 Nick Johnson	.15
4 Austin Kearns	.15
5 Ramon Ortiz	.15
6 Brian Schneider	.15
7 Ryan Zimmerman	.40
8 Jose Vidro	.15
9 Felipe Lopez	.15
10 Cristian Guzman	.15
11 B.J. Ryan	.15
12 Alex Rios	.25
13 Vernon Wells	.25
14 Roy Halladay	.25
15 A.J. Burnett	.15
16 Lyle Overbay	.15
17 Troy Glaus	.25
18 Bengie Molina	.15
19 Gustavo Chacin	.15
20 Aaron Hill	.15
21 Vicente Padilla	.15
22 Kevin Millwood	.15
23 Akinori Otsuka	.15
24 Adam Eaton	.15
25 Hank Blalock	.25
26 Mark Teixeira	.40
27 Michael Young	.25
28 Mark DeRosa	.15
29 Gary Matthews	.15
30 Ian Kinsler	.25
31 Carlos Lee	.25
32 James Shields	.15
33 Scott Kazmir	.25
34 Carl Crawford	.25
35 Jonny Gomes	.15
36 Tim Corcoran	.15
37 B.J. Upton	.25
38 Rocco Baldelli	.25
39 Jae Weong Seo	.15
40 Jorge Cantu	.15
41 Ty Wigginton	.15
42 Chris Carpenter	.40
43 Albert Pujols	1.50
44 Scott Rolen	.50
45 Jim Edmonds	.25
46 Jason Isringhausen	.15
47 Yadier Molina	.15
48 Adam Wainwright	.25
49 Mark Mulder	.25
50 Jason Marquis	.15
51 Juan Encarnacion	.15
52 Aaron Miles	.15
53 Ichiro Suzuki	1.00
54 Felix Hernandez	.40
55 Kenji Johjima	.25
56 Richie Sexson	.15
57 Yuniesky Betancourt	.15
58 J.J. Putz	.15
59 Jarrod Washburn	.15
60 Ben Broussard	.15
61 Adrian Beltre	.25
62 Raul Ibanez	.25
63 Jose Lopez	.15
64 Matt Cain	.25
65 Noah Lowry	.15
66 Jason Schmidt	.25
67 Pedro Feliz	.15
68 Matt Morris	.15
69 Ray Durham	.15
70 Steve Finley	.15
71 Randy Winn	.15
72 Moises Alou	.25
73 Eliezer Alfonzo	.15
74 Armando Benitez	.15
75 Omar Vizquel	.25
76 Chris Young	.25
77 Adrian Gonzalez	.25
78 Khalil Greene	.25
79 Mike Piazza	.75
80 Josh Barfield	.25
81 Brian Giles	.25
82 Jake Peavy	.25
83 Trevor Hoffman	.25
84 Mike Cameron	.15
85 Dave Roberts	.15
86 David Wells	.15
87 Zachary Duke	.15
88 Ian Snell	.15
89 Jason Bay	.40
90 Freddy Sanchez	.15
91 Jack Wilson	.15
92 Tom Gorzelanny	.15
93 Chris Duffy	.15
94 Jose Castillo	.15
95 Matt Capps	.15
96 Mike Gonzalez	.15
97 Chase Utley	.50
98 Jimmy Rollins	.50
99 Aaron Rowand	.15
100 Ryan Howard	1.00
101 Cole Hamels	.50
102 Pat Burrell	.25
103 Shane Victorino	.15
104 Jamie Moyer	.15
105 Mike Lieberthal	.15
106 Tom Gordon	.15
107 Brett Myers	.15
108 Nick Swisher	.25
109 Barry Zito	.25
110 Jason Kendall	.15
111 Milton Bradley	.25

112 Bobby Crosby	.15
113 Huston Street	.15
114 Eric Chavez	.25
115 Frank Thomas	.40
116 Danny Haren	.25
117 Jay Payton	.15
118 Randy Johnson	.50
119 Mike Mussina	.40
120 Bobby Abreu	.40
121 Derek Jeter	.40
122 Derek Jeter	1.50
123 Alex Rodriguez	1.50
124 Jorge Posada	.40
125 Robinson Cano	.40
126 Mariano Rivera	.40
127 Chien-Ming Wang	.40
128 Hideki Matsui	1.00
129 Gary Sheffield	.40
130 Lastings Milledge	.25
131 Tom Glavine	.25
132 Billy Wagner	.15
133 Pedro Martinez	.50
134 Paul LoDuca	.15
135 Carlos Delgado	.40
136 Carlos Beltran	.40
137 David Wright	.75
138 Jose Reyes	.50
139 Julio Franco	.15
140 Michael Cuddyer	.15
141 Justin Morneau	.40
142 Johan Santana	.50
143 Francisco Liriano	.25
144 Joe Mauer	.25
145 Torii Hunter	.25
146 Luis Castillo	.15
147 Joe Nathan	.15
148 Carlos Silva	.15
149 Boof Bonser	.15
150 Ben Sheets	.25
151 Prince Fielder	.50
152 Bill Hall	.25
153 Rickie Weeks	.15
154 Geoff Jenkins	.15
155 Kevin Mench	.15
156 Francisco Cordero	.15
157 Chris Capuano	.15
158 Brady Clark	.15
159 Tony Gwynn Jr.	.15
160 Chad Billingsley	.25
161 Russell Martin	.25
162 Wilson Betemit	.15
163 Nomar Garciaparra	.50
164 Kenny Lofton	.15
165 Rafael Furcal	.25
166 Julio Lugo	.15
167 Brad Penny	.15
168 Jeff Kent	.25
169 Greg Maddux	1.00
170 Derek Lowe	.15
171 Andre Ethier	.25
172 Chone Figgins	.15
173 Francisco Rodriguez	.25
174 Garret Anderson	.15
175 Orlando Cabrera	.25
176 Adam Kennedy	.15
177 John Lackey	.25
178 Vladimir Guerrero	.50
179 Bartolo Colon	.25
180 Jered Weaver	.25
181 Juan Rivera	.15
182 Howie Kendrick	.25
183 Ervin Santana	.25
184 Mark Redman	.15
185 David DeJesus	.15
186 Joey Gathright	.15
187 Mike Sweeney	.15
188 Mark Teahen	.15
189 Angel Berroa	.15
190 Ambiorix Burgos	.15
191 Luke Hudson	.15
192 Mark Grudzielanek	.15
193 Roger Clemens	1.50
194 Willy Taveras	.15
195 Craig Biggio	.25
196 Andy Pettitte	.25
197 Roy Oswalt	.40
198 Lance Berkman	.40
199 Morgan Ensberg	.25
200 Brad Lidge	.15
201 Chris Burke	.15
202 Miguel Cabrera	.50
203 Dontrelle Willis	.25
204 Josh Johnson	.15
205 Ricky Nolasco	.15
206 Dan Uggla	.25
207 Jeremy Hermida	.15
208 Scott Olsen	.25
209 Josh Willingham	.15
210 Joe Borowski	.15
211 Hanley Ramirez	.40
212 Mike Jacobs	.15
213 Kenny Rogers	.15
214 Justin Verlander	.40
215 Ivan Rodriguez	.40
216 Magglio Ordonez	.15
217 Todd Jones	.15
218 Joel Zumaya	.25
219 Jeremy Bonderman	.40
220 Nate Robertson	.15
221 Brandon Inge	.15
222 Craig Monroe	.15
223 Carlos Guillen	.15
224 Jeff Francis	.15
225 Brian Fuentes	.15
226 Todd Helton	.40

227	Matt Holliday	.25
228	Garrett Atkins	.25
229	Clint Barmes	.15
230	Jason Jennings	.15
231	Aaron Cook	.15
232	Brad Hawpe	.25
233	Cory Sullivan	.15
234	Aaron Boone	.15
235	C.C. Sabathia	.25
236	Grady Sizemore	.50
237	Travis Hafner	.40
238	Jhonny Peralta	.15
239	Jake Westbrook	.15
240	Jeremy Sowers	.15
241	Andy Marte	.15
242	Victor Martinez	.25
243	Jason Michaels	.15
244	Cliff Lee	.15
245	Bronson Arroyo	.15
246	Aaron Harang	.15
247	Ken Griffey Jr.	1.00
248	Adam Dunn	.40
249	Rich Aurilia	.15
250	Eric Milton	.15
251	David Ross	.15
252	Brandon Phillips	.15
253	Ryan Freel	.15
254	Eddie Guardado	.15
255	Jose Contreras	.15
256	Freddy Garcia	.15
257	Jon Garland	.15
258	Mark Buehrle	.25
259	Bobby Jenks	.15
260	Paul Konerko	.25
261	Jermaine Dye	.25
262	Joe Crede	.25
263	Jim Thome	.40
264	Javier Vazquez	.15
265	A.J. Pierzynski	.15
266	Tadahito Iguchi	.15
267	Carlos Zambrano	.40
268	Derrek Lee	.40
269	Aramis Ramirez	.40
270	Ryan Theriot	.15
271	Juan Pierre	.25
272	Rich Hill	.25
273	Ryan Dempster	.15
274	Jacque Jones	.15
275	Mark Prior	.25
276	Kerry Wood	.25
277	Josh Beckett	.25
278	David Ortiz	.50
279	Kevin Youkilis	.25
280	Jason Varitek	.40
281	Manny Ramirez	.50
282	Curt Schilling	.25
283	Jon Lester	.25
284	Jonathan Papelbon	.50
285	Alex Gonzalez	.15
286	Mike Lowell	.15
287	Kyle Snyder	.15
288	Miguel Tejada	.40
289	Erik Bedard	.25
290	Ramon Hernandez	.15
291	Melvin Mora	.15
292	Nicholas Markakis	.25
293	Brian Roberts	.25
294	Corey Patterson	.15
295	Kris Benson	.15
296	Jay Gibbons	.15
297	Rodrigo Lopez	.15
298	Chris Ray	.15
299	Andruw Jones	.50
300	Brian McCann	.40
301	Jeff Francoeur	.25
302	Chuck James	.15
303	John Smoltz	.40
304	Bob Wickman	.15
305	Edgar Renteria	.25
306	Adam LaRoche	.25
307	Marcus Giles	.15
308	Tim Hudson	.15
309	Chipper Jones	.50
310	Miguel Batista	.15
311	Claudio Vargas	.15
312	Brandon Webb	.25
313	Luis Gonzalez	.15
314	Livan Hernandez	.15
315	Stephen Drew	.15
316	Johnny Estrada	.15
317	Orlando Hudson	.15
318	Conor Jackson	.15
319	Chad Tracy	.15
320	Carlos Quentin	.50
321	Alvin Colina RC	.50
322	Miguel Montero (RC)	.25
323	Jeff Fiorentino (RC)	.25
324	Jeff Baker (RC)	.25
325	Brian Burres (RC)	.25
326	David Murphy (RC)	.25
327	Francisco Cruceta (RC)	.25
328	Beltran Perez (RC)	.25
329	Scott Moore (RC)	.25
330	Sean Henn (RC)	.25
331	Ryan Sweeney (RC)	.25
332	Josh Fields (RC)	.25
333	Jerry Owens (RC)	.25
334	Vinny Rottino (RC)	.25
335	Kevin Kouzmanoff (RC)	.50
336	Alexi Casilla RC	.50
337	Justin Hampson (RC)	.25
338	Troy Tulowitzki (RC)	.50
339	Jose Garcia RC	.50
340	Andrew Miller RC	2.00
341	Glen Perkins (RC)	.25
342	Ubaldo Jimenez (RC)	.50
343	Doug Slaten RC	.50

344	Angel Sanchez RC	.50
345	Mitch Maier RC	.50
346	Ryan Braun (RC)	.50
347	Joselo Diaz (RC)	.25
348	Delwyn Young (RC)	.25
349	Kevin Hooper (RC)	.25
350	Dennis Sarfate (RC)	.25
351	Andy Cannizaro RC	.50
352	Devern Hansack RC	1.00
353	Michael Bourn (RC)	.50
354	Carlos Maldonado (RC)	.25
355	Shane Youman (RC)	.50
356	Philip Humber (RC)	.50
357	Hector Gimenez (RC)	.25
358	Fred Lewis (RC)	.25
359	Ryan Feierabend (RC)	.25
360	Juan Morillo (RC)	.25
361	Travis Chick (RC)	.25
362	Oswaldo Navarro RC	.50
363	Cesar Jimenez RC	.50
364	Brian Stokes (RC)	.50
365	Delmon Young (RC)	.50
366	Juan Salas (RC)	.25
367	Shawn Riggans (RC)	.25
368	Adam Lind (RC)	.25
369	Joaquin Arias (RC)	.25
370	Eric Stults RC	.50
371	Brandon Webb	.25
372	John Smoltz	.50
373	Miguel Tejada	.50
374	David Ortiz	1.00
375	Carlos Zambrano	.50
376	Jermaine Dye	.25
377	Ken Griffey Jr.	1.50
378	Victor Martinez	.50
379	Todd Helton	.50
380	Ivan Rodriguez	.50
381	Miguel Cabrera	.50
382	Lance Berkman	.50
383	Mike Sweeney	.25
384	Vladimir Guerrero	.50
385	Derek Lowe	.25
386	Bill Hall	.25
387	Johan Santana	.75
388	Carlos Beltran	.25
389	Derek Jeter	2.00
390	Nick Swisher	.50
391	Ryan Howard	1.50
392	Jason Bay	.50
393	Trevor Hoffman	.25
394	Omar Vizquel	.25
395	Ichiro Suzuki	1.00
396	Albert Pujols	2.00
397	Carl Crawford	.50
398	Mark Teixeira	.50
399	Roy Halladay	.25
400	Ryan Zimmerman	.50

Printing Plates
No Pricing
Production one set per color

Mini Die-Cuts

Mini:	1.5-2X
Inserted 1:2	
Mini Gold:	No Pricing
Inserted 1:576	

Autographics
No Pricing
Inserted 1:720

Crowning Achievement

		NM/M
Common Player:		.50
Inserted 1:5		
AP	Albert Pujols	3.00
BZ	Barry Zito	.75
CD	Carlos Delgado	.75
CS	Curt Schilling	.75
DJ	Derek Jeter	3.00
DO	David Ortiz	1.00
FT	Frank Thomas	.75
GM	Greg Maddux	2.00
IS	Ichiro Suzuki	2.00
JS	Johan Santana	.75
JT	Jim Thome	.75
KG	Ken Griffey Jr.	2.00
MC	Miguel Cabrera	1.00
MP	Mike Piazza	1.00
MR	Manny Ramirez	1.00
PM	Pedro Martinez	1.00
RC	Roger Clemens	2.50
RH	Ryan Howard	2.00
TG	Tom Glavine	.75
TH	Trevor Hoffman	.50

Fresh Ink

		NM/M
Inserted 1:720		
BB	Brandon Backe	15.00
BW	Brian Wilson	20.00
CB	Clint Barmes	20.00
CC	Craig Counsell	20.00
GQ	Guillermo Quiroz	15.00
JB	Joe Blanton	15.00
JV	John Van Benschoten	10.00
LN	Leo Nunez	10.00
MM	Matt Murton	25.00
SR	Saul Rivera	15.00

Genuine Coverage

		NM/M
Inserted 1:720		
AP	Albert Pujols	25.00
AS	Alfonso Soriano	20.00
BR	Brian Roberts	15.00
DW	Dontrelle Willis	8.00
ES	Johnny Estrada	8.00
JB	Josh Beckett	15.00
JE	Jim Edmonds	15.00
JM	Justin Morneau	15.00
JT	Jim Thome	15.00
LB	Lance Berkman	10.00
RC	Robinson Cano	20.00
SM	John Smoltz	15.00
VG	Vladimir Guerrero	15.00

In the Zone

		NM/M
Common Player:		1.00
Inserted 1:10		
AJ	Andruw Jones	1.00
AP	Albert Pujols	3.00
AR	Alex Rodriguez	2.50
DO	David Ortiz	1.50
DW	David Wright	1.50
KG	Ken Griffey Jr.	2.00
MC	Miguel Cabrera	1.00
MT	Mark Teixeira	1.00
RH	Ryan Howard	2.00
VG	Vladimir Guerrero	1.00

Perfect 10

		NM/M
Common Player:		.50
Inserted 1:5		
CC	Carl Crawford	.75
DO	David Ortiz	1.50
DJ	Derek Jeter	3.00
IR	Ivan Rodriguez	.75
JD	Jermaine Dye	.50
JS	Johan Santana	1.00
MM	Mike Mussina	.75
MY	Michael Young	.75
RH	Roy Halladay	.50
VG	Vladimir Guerrero	1.00
AP	Albert Pujols	3.00
AS	Alfonso Soriano	1.00
BH	Bill Hall	.50
CB	Carlos Beltran	1.00
CJ	Chipper Jones	1.00
CU	Chase Utley	.75
JB	Jason Bay	1.00
MC	Miguel Cabrera	1.00
RC	Roger Clemens	2.50
RH	Ryan Howard	2.00

Rookie Sensations

		NM/M
Common Player:		.50

Inserted 1:1		
BB	Boof Bonser	.50
CB	Chad Billingsley	1.00
CH	Cole Hamels	1.50
CJ	Conor Jackson	.75
DU	Dan Uggla	.50
FL	Francisco Liriano	1.00
HR	Hanley Ramirez	1.00
IK	Ian Kinsler	1.00
JB	Josh Barfield	.75
JH	Jeremy Hermida	.50
JJ	Josh Johnson	.50
JL	Jon Lester	1.00
JP	Jonathan Papelbon	2.00
JS	Jeremy Sowers	.50
JV	Justin Verlander	2.00
JW	Jered Weaver	1.00
KJ	Kenji Johjima	.75
LO	James Loney	.75
MK	Matthew Kemp	.75
NM	Nicholas Markakis	1.00
PF	Prince Fielder	1.50
RG	Matt Garza	1.00
RN	Ricky Nolasco	.50
RZ	Ryan Zimmerman	2.00
SO	Scott Olsen	.75

Soaring Stars

		NM/M
Common Player:		.50
Inserted 1:2 Rack Packs		
AD	Adam Dunn	.75
AJ	Andruw Jones	1.00
AL	Alex Rodriguez	2.50
AP	Albert Pujols	3.00
AR	Alex Rios	.50
AS	Alfonso Soriano	1.00
BW	Brandon Webb	.50
BZ	Barry Zito	.50
CB	Carlos Beltran	1.00
CJ	Chipper Jones	1.00
CU	Chase Utley	1.00
DA	Johnny Damon	1.00
DJ	Derek Jeter	3.00
DL	Derrek Lee	1.00
DO	David Ortiz	1.00
DW	David Wright	1.50
HA	Roy Halladay	.50
IR	Ivan Rodriguez	.75
IS	Ichiro Suzuki	2.00
JB	Jason Bay	.75
JD	Jermaine Dye	.50
JG	Jon Garland	.50
JM	Joe Mauer	.75
JS	Johan Santana	1.00
JV	Justin Verlander	1.00
KG	Ken Griffey Jr.	2.00
LB	Lance Berkman	.75
MC	Miguel Cabrera	1.00
MP	Mike Piazza	1.50
MR	Manny Ramirez	1.00
MT	Mark Teixeira	.75
NG	Nomar Garciaparra	1.00
PF	Prince Fielder	1.00
PM	Pedro Martinez	1.00
RH	Ryan Howard	2.00
RI	Mariano Rivera	.75
RO	Roy Oswalt	.75
TE	Miguel Tejada	.75
TG	Tom Glavine	.75
TH	Travis Hafner	.75
VG	Vladimir Guerrero	1.00
WI	Dontrelle Willis	.75

Year in Review

		NM/M
Common Player:		.50
Inserted 1:5		
AP	Albert Pujols	3.00
AR	Alex Rodriguez	2.50
AS	Alfonso Soriano	1.00
BA	Bobby Abreu	1.00
CU	Chase Utley	1.00
DJ	Derek Jeter	3.00
DO	David Ortiz	1.00
FL	Francisco Liriano	.75
FS	Freddy Sanchez	.50
HO	Ryan Howard	2.00
JD	Jermaine Dye	.50
JM	Joe Mauer	.75
JR	Jose Reyes	1.00
JV	Justin Verlander	1.00
JW	Jered Weaver	1.00
KG	Ken Griffey Jr.	2.00
MD	Mark DeRosa	.50
MO	Justin Morneau	1.00
RH	Roy Halladay	.50
TH	Travis Hafner	.75

L

1990 Leaf

	NM/M
Complete Set (528):	75.00
Series 1 (264):	50.00
Series 2 (264):	25.00
Common Player:	.10
Series 1 Foil Pack (15):	4.00
Series 1 Foil Box (36):	80.00
Series 2 Foil Pack (15):	2.50
Series 2 Foil Box (36):	60.00
1 Introductory Card	.10

2	Mike Henneman	.10
3	Steve Bedrosian	.10
4	Mike Scott	.10
5	Allan Anderson	.10
6	Rick Sutcliffe	.10
7	Gregg Olson	.10
8	Kevin Elster	.10
9	Pete O'Brien	.10
10	Carlton Fisk	1.00
11	Joe Magrane	.10
12	Roger Clemens	2.50
13	Tom Glavine	.35
14	Tom Gordon	.10
15	Todd Benzinger	.10
16	Hubie Brooks	.10
17	Roberto Kelly	.10
18	Barry Larkin	.10
19	Mike Boddicker	.10
20	Roger McDowell	.10
21	Nolan Ryan	5.00
22	John Farrell	.10
23	Bruce Hurst	.10
24	Wally Joyner	.10
25	Greg Maddux	2.00
26	Chris Bosio	.10
27	John Cerutti	.10
28	Tim Burke	.10
29	Dennis Eckersley	.75
30	Glenn Davis	.10
31	Jim Abbott	.10
32	Mike LaValliere	.10
33	Andres Thomas	.10
34	Lou Whitaker	.10
35	Alvin Davis	.10
36	Melido Perez	.10
37	Craig Biggio	.10
38	Rick Aguilera	.10
39	Pete Harnisch	.10
40	David Cone	.10
41	Scott Garrelts	.10
42	Jay Howell	.10
43	Eric King	.10
44	Pedro Guerrero	.10
45	Mike Bielecki	.10
46	Bob Boone	.10
47	Kevin Brown	.10
48	Jerry Browne	.10
49	Mike Scioscia	.10
50	Chuck Cary	.10
51	Wade Boggs	2.00
52	Von Hayes	.10
53	Tony Fernandez	.10
54	Dennis Martinez	.10
55	Tom Candiotti	.10
56	Andy Benes	.10
57	Rob Dibble	.10
58	Chuck Crim	.10
59	John Smoltz	.10
60	Mike Heath	.10
61	Kevin Gross	.10
62	Mark McGwire	3.50
63	Bert Blyleven	.10
64	Bob Walk	.10
65	Mickey Tettleton	.10
66	Sid Fernandez	.10
67	Terry Kennedy	.10
68	Fernando Valenzuela	.10
69	Don Mattingly	2.50
70	Paul O'Neill	.10
71	Robin Yount	1.00
72	Bret Saberhagen	.10
73	Geno Petralli	.10
74	Brook Jacoby	.10
75	Roberto Alomar	.25
76	Devon White	.10
77	Jose Lind	.10
78	Pat Combs	.10
79	Dave Steib	.10
80	Tim Wallach	.10
81	Dave Stewart	.10
82	Eric Anthony **RC**	.10
83	Randy Bush	.10
84	Checklist	.10
85	Jaime Navarro	.10
86	Tommy Gregg	.10
87	Frank Tanana	.10
88	Omar Vizquel	.10
89	Ivan Calderon	.10
90	Vince Coleman	.10
91	Barry Bonds	5.00
92	Randy Milligan	.10
93	Frank Viola	.10
94	Matt Williams	.10
95	Alfredo Griffin	.10
96	Steve Sax	.10
97	Gary Gaetti	.10
98	Ryne Sandberg	2.00
99	Danny Tartabull	.10
100	Rafael Palmeiro	1.00
101	Jesse Orosco	.10
102	Garry Templeton	.10
103	Frank DiPino	.10
104	Tony Pena	.10
105	Dickie Thon	.10
106	Kelly Gruber	.10
107	Marquis Grissom **RC**	2.00
108	Jose Canseco	.60
109	Mike Blowers	.10
110	Tom Browning	.10
111	Greg Vaughn	.10
112	Oddibe McDowell	.10
113	Gary Ward	.10
114	Jay Buhner	.10
115	Eric Show	.10
116	Bryan Harvey	.10
117	Andy Van Slyke	.10
118	Jeff Ballard	.10
119	Barry Lyons	.10
120	Kevin Mitchell	.10
121	Mike Gallego	.10
122	Dave Smith	.10
123	Kirby Puckett	2.00
124	Jerome Walton	.10
125	Bo Jackson	.20
126	Harold Baines	.10
127	Scott Bankhead	.10
128	Ozzie Guillen	.10
129	Jose Oquendo	.10
130	John Dopson	.10
131	Charlie Hayes	.10
132	Fred McGriff	.10
133	Chet Lemon	.10
134	Gary Carter	1.00
135	Rafael Ramirez	.10
136	Shane Mack	.10
137	Mark Grace	.10
138	Phil Bradley	.10
139	Dwight Gooden	.10
140	Harold Reynolds	.10
141	Scott Fletcher	.10
142	Ozzie Smith	2.00
143	Mike Greenwell	.10
144	Pete Smith	.10
145	Mark Gubicza	.10
146	Chris Sabo	.10
147	Ramon Martinez	.10
148	Tim Leary	.10
149	Randy Myers	.10
150	Jody Reed	.10
151	Bruce Ruffin	.10
152	Jeff Russell	.10
153	Doug Jones	.10
154	Tony Gwynn	2.00
155	Mark Langston	.10
156	Mitch Williams	.10
157	Gary Sheffield	.60
158	Tom Henke	.10
159	Oil Can Boyd	.10
160	Rickey Henderson	1.00
161	Bill Doran	.10
162	Chuck Finley	.10
163	Jeff King	.10
164	Nick Esasky	.10
165	Cecil Fielder	.10
166	Dave Valle	.10
167	Robin Ventura	.10
168	Jim Deshaies	.10
169	Juan Berenguer	.10
170	Craig Worthington	.10
171	Gregg Jefferies	.10
172	Will Clark	.10
173	Kirk Gibson	.10
174	Checklist	.10
175	Bobby Thigpen	.10
176	John Tudor	.10
177	Andre Dawson	.35
178	George Brett	2.50
179	Steve Buechele	.10
180	Albert Belle	.10
181	Eddie Murray	1.00
182	Bob Geren	.10
183	Rob Murphy	.10
184	Tom Herr	.10
185	George Bell	.10
186	Spike Owen	.10
187	Cory Snyder	.10
188	Fred Lynn	.10
189	Eric Davis	.10
190	Dave Parker	.10
191	Jeff Blauser	.10
192	Matt Nokes	.10
193	Delino DeShields **RC**	.50
194	Scott Sanderson	.10
195	Lance Parrish	.10
196	Bobby Bonilla	.10
197	Cal Ripken, Jr.	5.00
198	Kevin McReynolds	.10
199	Robby Thompson	.10
200	Tim Belcher	.10
201	Jesse Barfield	.10
202	Mariano Duncan	.10
203	Bill Spiers	.10
204	Frank White	.10
205	Julio Franco	.10
206	Greg Swindell	.10
207	Benito Santiago	.10
208	Johnny Ray	.10
209	Gary Redus	.10
210	Jeff Parrett	.10
211	Jimmy Key	.10
212	Tim Raines	.10
213	Carney Lansford	.10
214	Gerald Young	.10
215	Gene Larkin	.10
216	Dan Plesac	.10
217	Lonnie Smith	.10
218	Alan Trammell	.10
219	Jeffrey Leonard	.10
220	Sammy Sosa **RC**	20.00
221	Todd Zeile	.10
222	Bill Landrum	.10
223	Mike Devereaux	.10
224	Mike Marshall	.10
225	Jose Uribe	.10
226	Juan Samuel	.10
227	Mel Hall	.10
228	Kent Hrbek	.10
229	Shawon Dunston	.10
230	Kevin Seitzer	.10
231	Pete Incaviglia	.10
232	Sandy Alomar	.10
233	Bip Roberts	.10
234	Scott Terry	.10
235	Dwight Evans	.10
236	Ricky Jordan	.10
237	John Olerud **RC**	5.00
238	Zane Smith	.10
239	Walt Weiss	.10
240	Alvaro Espinoza	.10
241	Billy Hatcher	.10
242	Paul Molitor	1.00
243	Dale Murphy	.30
244	Dave Bergman	.10
245	Ken Griffey Jr.	3.00
246	Ed Whitson	.10
247	Kirk McCaskill	.10
248	Jay Bell	.10
249	Ben McDonald **RC**	.50
250	Darryl Strawberry	.10
251	Brett Butler	.10
252	Terry Steinbach	.10
253	Ken Caminiti	.10
254	Dan Gladden	.10
255	Dwight Smith	.10
256	Kurt Stillwell	.10
257	Ruben Sierra	.10
258	Mike Schooler	.10
259	Lance Johnson	.10
260	Terry Pendleton	.10
261	Ellis Burks	.10
262	Len Dykstra	.10
263	Mookie Wilson	.10
264	Checklist (Nolan Ryan)	.10
265	Nolan Ryan (No-Hit King)	2.00
266	Brian DuBois	.10
267	Don Robinson	.10
268	Glenn Wilson	.10
269	Kevin Tapani **RC**	.25
270	Marvell Wynne	.10
271	Billy Ripken	.10
272	Howard Johnson	.10
273	Brian Holman	.10
274	Dan Pasqua	.10
275	Ken Dayley	.10
276	Jeff Reardon	.10
277	Jim Presley	.10
278	Jim Eisenreich	.10
279	Danny Jackson	.10
280	Orel Hershiser	.10
281	Andy Hawkins	.10
282	Jose Rijo	.10
283	Luis Rivera	.10
284	John Kruk	.10
285	Jeff Huson	.10
286	Joel Skinner	.10
287	Jack Clark	.10
288	Chili Davis	.10
289	Joe Girardi	.10
290	B.J. Surhoff	.10
291	Luis Sojo	.10
292	Tom Foley	.10
293	Mike Moore	.10
294	Ken Oberkfell	.10
295	Luis Polonia	.10
296	Doug Drabek	.10
297	Dave Justice **RC**	2.00
298	Paul Gibson	.10
299	Edgar Martinez	.10
300	Frank Thomas **RC**	20.00
301	Eric Yelding	.10
302	Greg Gagne	.10
303	Brad Komminsk	.10
304	Ron Darling	.10
305	Kevin Bass	.10
306	Jeff Hamilton	.10
307	Ron Karkovice	.10
308	Milt Thompson	.10
309	Mike Harkey	.10
310	Mel Stottlemyre	.10
311	Kenny Rogers	.10
312	Mitch Webster	.10
313	Kal Daniels	.10
314	Matt Nokes	.10
315	Dennis Lamp	.10
316	Ken Howell	.10
317	Glenallen Hill	.10
318	Dave Martinez	.10
319	Chris James	.10
320	Mike Pagliarulo	.10
321	Hal Morris	.10
322	Rob Deer	.10
323	Greg Olson	.10
324	Tony Phillips	.10
325	Larry Walker **RC**	8.00
326	Ron Hassey	.10
327	Jack Howell	.10
328	John Smiley	.10
329	Steve Finley	.10
330	Dave Magadan	.10
331	Greg Litton	.10
332	Mickey Hatcher	.10
333	Lee Guetterman	.10
334	Norm Charlton	.10
335	Edgar Diaz	.10
336	Willie Wilson	.10
337	Bobby Witt	.10
338	Candy Maldonado	.10
339	Craig Lefferts	.10
340	Dante Bichette	.10
341	Wally Backman	.10
342	Dennis Cook	.10
343	Pat Borders	.10
344	Wallace Johnson	.10
345	Willie Randolph	.10
346	Danny Darwin	.10
347	Al Newman	.10
348	Mark Knudson	.10
349	Joe Boever	.10
350	Larry Sheets	.10
351	Mike Jackson	.10
352	Wayne Edwards	.10
353	Bernard Gilkey **RC**	.50
354	Don Slaught	.10
355	Joe Orsulak	.10
356	John Franco	.10
357	Jeff Brantley	.10
358	Mike Morgan	.10
359	Deion Sanders	.10
360	Terry Leach	.10
361	Les Lancaster	.10
362	Storm Davis	.10
363	Scott Coolbaugh	.10
364	Checklist	.10
365	Cecilio Guante	.10
366	Joey Cora	.10
367	Willie McGee	.10
368	Jerry Reed	.10
369	Darren Daulton	.10
370	Manny Lee	.10
371	Mark Gardner	.10
372	Rick Honeycutt	.10
373	Steve Balboni	.10
374	Jack Armstrong	.10
375	Charlie O'Brien	.10
376	Ron Gant	.10
377	Lloyd Moseby	.10
378	Gene Harris	.10
379	Joe Carter	.10
380	Scott Bailes	.10
381	R.J. Reynolds	.10
382	Bob Melvin	.10
383	Tim Teufel	.10
384	John Burkett	.10
385	Felix Jose	.10
386	Larry Andersen	.10
387	David West	.10
388	Luis Salazar	.10
389	Mike Macfarlane	.10
390	Charlie Hough	.10
391	Greg Briley	.10
392	Donn Pall	.10
393	Bryn Smith	.10
394	Carlos Quintana	.10
395	Steve Lake	.10
396	Mark Whiten **RC**	.15
397	Edwin Nunez	.10
398	Rick Parker	.10
399	Mark Portugal	.10
400	Roy Smith	.10
401	Hector Villanueva	.10
402	Bob Milacki	.10
403	Alejandro Pena	.10
404	Scott Bradley	.10
405	Ron Kittle	.10
406	Bob Tewksbury	.10
407	Wes Gardner	.10
408	Ernie Whitt	.10
409	Terry Shumpert	.10
410	Tim Layana	.10
411	Chris Gwynn	.10
412	Jeff Robinson	.10
413	Scott Scudder	.10
414	Kevin Romine	.10
415	Jose DeJesus	.10
416	Mike Jeffcoat	.10
417	Rudy Seanez	.10
418	Mike Dunne	.10
419	Dick Schofield	.10
420	Steve Wilson	.10
421	Bill Krueger	.10
422	Junior Felix	.10
423	Drew Hall	.10
424	Curt Young	.10
425	Franklin Stubbs	.10
426	Dave Winfield	1.00
427	Rick Reed	.10
428	Charlie Leibrandt	.10
429	Jeff Robinson	.10
430	Erik Hanson	.10
431	Barry Jones	.10
432	Alex Trevino	.10
433	John Moses	.10
434	Dave Johnson	.10
435	Mackey Sasser	.10
436	Rick Leach	.10
437	Lenny Harris	.10

438	Carlos Martinez	.10
439	Rex Hudler	.10
440	Domingo Ramos	.10
441	Gerald Perry	.10
442	John Russell	.10
443	Carlos Baerga **RC**	.50
444	Checklist	.10
445	Stan Javier	.10
446	Kevin Maas **RC**	.10
447	Tom Brunansky	.10
448	Carmelo Martinez	.10
449	Willie Blair **RC**	.10
450	Andres Galarraga	.10
451	Bud Black	.10
452	Greg Harris	.10
453	Joe Oliver	.10
454	Greg Brock	.10
455	Jeff Treadway	.10
456	Lance McCullers	.10
457	Dave Schmidt	.10
458	Todd Burns	.10
459	Max Venable	.10
460	Neal Heaton	.10
461	Mark Williamson	.10
462	Keith Miller	.10
463	Mike LaCoss	.10
464	Jose Offerman **RC**	.25
465	Jim Leyritz **RC**	.50
466	Glenn Braggs	.10
467	Ron Robinson	.10
468	Mark Davis	.10
469	Gary Pettis	.10
470	Keith Hernandez	.10
471	Dennis Rasmussen	.10
472	Mark Eichhorn	.10
473	Ted Power	.10
474	Terry Mulholland	.10
475	Todd Stottlemyre	.10
476	Jerry Goff	.10
477	Gene Nelson	.10
478	Rich Gedman	.10
479	Brian Harper	.10
480	Mike Felder	.10
481	Steve Avery	.10
482	Jack Morris	.10
483	Randy Johnson	1.00
484	Scott Radinsky	.10
485	Jose DeLeon	.10
486	Stan Belinda **RC**	.10
487	Brian Holton	.10
488	Mark Carreon	.10
489	Trevor Wilson	.10
490	Mike Sharperson	.10
491	Alan Mills **RC**	.10
492	John Candelaria	.10
493	Paul Assenmacher	.10
494	Steve Crawford	.10
495	Brad Arnsberg	.10
496	Sergio Valdez	.10
497	Mark Parent	.10
498	Tom Pagnozzi	.10
499	Greg Harris	.10
500	Randy Ready	.10
501	Duane Ward	.10
502	Nelson Santovenia	.10
503	Joe Klink	.10
504	Eric Plunk	.10
505	Jeff Reed	.10
506	Ted Higuera	.10
507	Joe Hesketh	.10
508	Dan Petry	.10
509	Matt Young	.10
510	Jerald Clark	.10
511	John Orton **RC**	.10
512	Scott Ruskin	.10
513	Chris Hoiles **RC**	.50
514	Daryl Boston	.10
515	Francisco Oliveras	.10
516	Ozzie Canseco	.10
517	Xavier Hernandez **RC**	.10
518	Fred Manrique	.10
519	Shawn Boskie	.10
520	Jeff Montgomery	.10
521	Jack Daugherty	.10
522	Keith Comstock	.10
523	Greg Hibbard **RC**	.10
524	Lee Smith	.10
525	Dana Kiecker	.10
526	Darrel Akerfelds	.10
527	Greg Myers	.10
528	Checklist	.10

1990 Leaf Previews

		NM/M
Complete Set (12):		275.00
Common Player:		12.50
1	Steve Sax	12.50
2	Joe Carter	12.50
3	Dennis Eckersley	20.00
4	Ken Griffey Jr.	200.00
5	Barry Larkin	12.50
6	Mark Langston	12.50
7	Eric Anthony	12.50
8	Robin Ventura	12.50
9	Greg Vaughn	12.50
10	Bobby Bonilla	12.50
11	Gary Gaetti	12.50
12	Ozzie Smith	75.00

1991 Leaf

		NM/M
Complete Set (528):		8.00
Common Player:		.05
Series 1 or 2 Pack (15):		.50
Series 1 or 2 Box (36):		12.50

1	The Leaf Card	.05
2	Kurt Stillwell	.05
3	Bobby Witt	.05
4	Tony Phillips	.05
5	Scott Garrelts	.05
6	Greg Swindell	.05
7	Billy Ripken	.05
8	Dave Martinez	.05
9	Kelly Gruber	.05
10	Juan Samuel	.05
11	Brian Holman	.05
12	Craig Biggio	.05
13	Lonnie Smith	.05
14	Ron Robinson	.05
15	Mike LaValliere	.05
16	Mark Davis	.05
17	Jack Daugherty	.05
18	Mike Henneman	.05
19	Mike Greenwell	.05
20	Dave Magadan	.05
21	Mark Williamson	.05
22	Marquis Grissom	.05
23	Pat Borders	.05
24	Mike Scioscia	.05
25	Shawon Dunston	.05
26	Randy Bush	.05
27	John Smoltz	.05
28	Chuck Crim	.05
29	Don Slaught	.05
30	Mike Macfarlane	.05
31	Wally Joyner	.05
32	Pat Combs	.05
33	Tony Pena	.05
34	Howard Johnson	.05
35	Leo Gomez	.05
36	Spike Owen	.05
37	Eric Davis	.05
38	Roberto Kelly	.05
39	Jerome Walton	.05
40	Shane Mack	.05
41	Kent Mercker	.05
42	B.J. Surhoff	.05
43	Jerry Browne	.05
44	Lee Smith	.05
45	Chuck Finley	.05
46	Terry Mulholland	.05
47	Tom Bolton	.05
48	Tom Herr	.05
49	Jim Deshaies	.05
50	Walt Weiss	.05
51	Hal Morris	.05
52	Lee Guetterman	.05
53	Paul Assenmacher	.05
54	Brian Harper	.05
55	Paul Gibson	.05
56	John Burkett	.05
57	Doug Jones	.05
58	Jose Oquendo	.05
59	Dick Schofield	.05
60	Dickie Thon	.05
61	Ramon Martinez	.05
62	Jay Buhner	.05
63	Mark Portugal	.05
64	Bob Welch	.05
65	Chris Sabo	.05
66	Chuck Cary	.05
67	Mark Langston	.05
68	Joe Boever	.05
69	Jody Reed	.05
70	Alejandro Pena	.05
71	Jeff King	.05
72	Tom Pagnozzi	.05
73	Joe Oliver	.05
74	Mike Witt	.05
75	Hector Villanueva	.05
76	Dan Gladden	.05
77	Dave Justice	.05
78	Mike Gallego	.05
79	Tom Candiotti	.05
80	Ozzie Smith	.60
81	Luis Polonia	.05
82	Randy Ready	.05
83	Greg Harris	.05
84	Dave Justice Checklist	.05
85	Kevin Mitchell	.05
86	Mark McLemore	.05
87	Terry Steinbach	.05
88	Tom Browning	.05
89	Matt Nokes	.05
90	Mike Harkey	.05
91	Omar Vizquel	.05
92	Dave Bergman	.05
93	Matt Williams	.05
94	Steve Olin	.05
95	Craig Wilson	.05
96	Dave Stieb	.05
97	Ruben Sierra	.05
98	Jay Howell	.05
99	Scott Bradley	.05
100	Eric Yelding	.05
101	Rickey Henderson	.45
102	Jeff Reed	.05
103	Jimmy Key	.05
104	Terry Shumpert	.05
105	Kenny Rogers	.05
106	Cecil Fielder	.05
107	Robby Thompson	.05
108	Alex Cole	.05
109	Randy Milligan	.05
110	Andres Galarraga	.05
111	Bill Spiers	.05
112	Kal Daniels	.05
113	Henry Cotto	.05
114	Casy Candaele	.05
115	Jeff Blauser	.05
116	Robin Yount	.45
117	Ben McDonald	.05
118	Bret Saberhagen	.05
119	Juan Gonzalez	.35
120	Lou Whitaker	.05
121	Ellis Burks	.05
122	Charlie O'Brien	.05
123	John Smiley	.05
124	Tim Burke	.05
125	John Olerud	.05
126	Eddie Murray	.45
127	Greg Maddux	.60
128	Kevin Tapani	.05
129	Ron Gant	.05
130	Jay Bell	.05
131	Chris Hoiles	.05
132	Tom Gordon	.05
133	Kevin Seitzer	.05
134	Jeff Huson	.05
135	Jerry Don Gleaton	.05
136	Jeff Brantley	.05
137	Felix Fermin	.05
138	Mike Devereaux	.05
139	Delino DeShields	.05
140	David Wells	.05
141	Tim Crews	.05
142	Erik Hanson	.05
143	Mark Davidson	.05
144	Tommy Gregg	.05
145	Jim Gantner	.05
146	Jose Lind	.05
147	Danny Tartabull	.05
148	Geno Petralli	.05
149	Travis Fryman	.05
150	Tim Naehring	.05
151	Kevin McReynolds	.05
152	Joe Orsulak	.05
153	Steve Frey	.05
154	Duane Ward	.05
155	Stan Javier	.05
156	Damon Berryhill	.05
157	Gene Larkin	.05
158	Greg Olson	.05
159	Mark Knudson	.05
160	Carmelo Martinez	.05
161	Storm Davis	.05
162	Jim Abbott	.05
163	Len Dykstra	.05
164	Tom Brunansky	.05
165	Dwight Gooden	.05
166	Jose Mesa	.05
167	Oil Can Boyd	.05
168	Barry Larkin	.05
169	Scott Sanderson	.05
170	Mark Grace	.05
171	Mark Guthrie	.05
172	Tom Glavine	.15
173	Gary Sheffield	.30
174	Roger Clemens Checklist	.25
175	Chris James	.05
176	Milt Thompson	.05
177	Donnie Hill	.05
178	Wes Chamberlain	.05
179	John Marzano	.05
180	Frank Viola	.05
181	Eric Anthony	.05
182	Jose Canseco	.30
183	Scott Scudder	.05
184	Dave Eiland	.05
185	Luis Salazar	.05
186	Pedro Munoz	.05
187	Steve Searcy	.05
188	Don Robinson	.05
189	Sandy Alomar	.05
190	Jose DeLeon	.05
191	John Orton	.05
192	Darren Daulton	.05
193	Mike Morgan	.05
194	Greg Briley	.05
195	Karl Rhodes	.05
196	Harold Baines	.05
197	Bill Doran	.05
198	Alvaro Espinoza	.05
199	Kirk McCaskill	.05
200	Jose DeJesus	.05
201	Jack Clark	.05
202	Daryl Boston	.05
203	Randy Tomlin	.05
204	Pedro Guerrero	.05
205	Billy Hatcher	.05
206	Tim Leary	.05
207	Ryne Sandberg	.60
208	Kirby Puckett	.60
209	Charlie Leibrandt	.05
210	Rick Honeycutt	.05
211	Joel Skinner	.05
212	Rex Hudler	.05
213	Bryan Harvey	.05
214	Charlie Hayes	.05
215	Matt Young	.05
216	Terry Kennedy	.05
217	Carl Nichols	.05
218	Mike Moore	.05
219	Paul O'Neill	.05
220	Steve Sax	.05
221	Shawn Boskie	.05
222	Rich DeLucia	.05
223	Lloyd Moseby	.05
224	Mike Kingery	.05
225	Carlos Baerga	.05
226	Bryn Smith	.05
227	Todd Stottlemyre	.05
228	Julio Franco	.05
229	Jim Gott	.05
230	Mike Schooler	.05
231	Steve Finley	.05
232	Dave Henderson	.05
233	Luis Quinones	.05
234	Mark Whiten	.05
235	Brian McRae	.05
236	Rich Gossage	.05
237	Rob Deer	.05
238	Will Clark	.10
239	Albert Belle	.05
240	Bob Melvin	.05
241	Larry Walker	.05
242	Dante Bichette	.05
243	Orel Hershiser	.05
244	Pete O'Brien	.05
245	Pete Harnisch	.05
246	Jeff Treadway	.05
247	Julio Machado	.05
248	Dave Johnson	.05
249	Kirk Gibson	.05
250	Kevin Brown	.05
251	Milt Cuyler	.05
252	Jeff Reardon	.05
253	David Cone	.05
254	Gary Redus	.05
255	Junior Noboa	.05
256	Greg Myers	.05
257	Dennis Cook	.05
258	Joe Girardi	.05
259	Allan Anderson	.05
260	Paul Marak	.05
261	Barry Bonds	2.00
262	Juan Bell	.05
263	Russ Morman	.05
264	George Brett Checklist	.25
265	Jerald Clark	.05
266	Dwight Evans	.05
267	Roberto Alomar	.15
268	Danny Jackson	.05
269	Brian Downing	.05
270	John Cerutti	.05
271	Robin Ventura	.05
272	Gerald Perry	.05
273	Wade Boggs	.60
274	Dennis Martinez	.05
275	Andy Benes	.05
276	Tony Fossas	.05
277	Franklin Stubbs	.05
278	John Kruk	.05
279	Kevin Gross	.05
280	Von Hayes	.05
281	Frank Thomas	.45
282	Rob Dibble	.05
283	Mel Hall	.05
284	Rick Mahler	.05
285	Dennis Eckersley	.35
286	Bernard Gilkey	.05
287	Dan Plesac	.05
288	Jason Grimsley	.05
289	Mark Lewis	.05
290	Tony Gwynn	.60
291	Jeff Russell	.05
292	Curt Schilling	.25
293	Pascual Perez	.05
294	Jack Morris	.05
295	Hubie Brooks	.05
296	Alex Fernandez	.05
297	Harold Reynolds	.05
298	Craig Worthington	.05
299	Willie Wilson	.05
300	Mike Maddux	.05
301	Dave Righetti	.05
302	Paul Molitor	.45
303	Gary Gaetti	.05
304	Terry Pendleton	.05
305	Kevin Elster	.05
306	Scott Fletcher	.05
307	Jeff Robinson	.05
308	Jesse Barfield	.05
309	Mike LaCoss	.05
310	Andy Van Slyke	.05
311	Glenallen Hill	.05
312	Bud Black	.05
313	Kent Hrbek	.05
314	Tim Teufel	.05
315	Tony Fernandez	.05
316	Beau Allred	.05
317	Curtis Wilkerson	.05
318	Bill Sampen	.05
319	Randy Johnson	.45
320	Mike Heath	.05
321	Sammy Sosa	1.00

322	Mickey Tettleton	.05
323	Jose Vizcaino	.05
324	John Candelaria	.05
325	David Howard	.05
326	Jose Rijo	.05
327	Todd Zeile	.05
328	Gene Nelson	.05
329	Dwayne Henry	.05
330	Mike Boddicker	.05
331	Ozzie Guillen	.05
332	Sam Horn	.05
333	Wally Whitehurst	.05
334	Dave Parker	.05
335	George Brett	.75
336	Bobby Thigpen	.05
337	Ed Whitson	.05
338	Ivan Calderon	.05
339	Mike Pagliarulo	.05
340	Jack McDowell	.05
341	Dana Kiecker	.05
342	Fred McGriff	.05
343	Mark Lee	.05
344	Alfredo Griffin	.05
345	Scott Bankhead	.05
346	Darrin Jackson	.05
347	Rafael Palmeiro	.35
348	Steve Farr	.05
349	Hensley Meulens	.05
350	Danny Cox	.05
351	Alan Trammell	.05
352	Edwin Nunez	.05
353	Joe Carter	.05
354	Eric Show	.05
355	Vance Law	.05
356	Jeff Gray	.05
357	Bobby Bonilla	.05
358	Ernest Riles	.05
359	Ron Hassey	.05
360	Willie McGee	.05
361	Mackey Sasser	.05
362	Glenn Braggs	.05
363	Mario Diaz	.05
364	Barry Bonds Checklist	.35
365	Kevin Bass	.05
366	Pete Incaviglia	.05
367	Luis Sojo	.05
368	Lance Parrish	.05
369	Mark Leonard	.05
370	Heathcliff Slocumb	.05
371	Jimmy Jones	.05
372	Ken Griffey Jr.	1.00
373	Chris Hammond	.05
374	Chili Davis	.05
375	Joey Cora	.05
376	Ken Hill	.05
377	Darryl Strawberry	.05
378	Ron Darling	.05
379	Sid Bream	.05
380	Bill Swift	.05
381	Shawn Abner	.05
382	Eric King	.05
383	Mickey Morandini	.05
384	Carlton Fisk	.45
385	Steve Lake	.05
386	Mike Jeffcoat	.05
387	Darren Holmes	.05
388	Tim Wallach	.05
389	George Bell	.05
390	Craig Lefferts	.05
391	Ernie Whitt	.05
392	Felix Jose	.05
393	Kevin Maas	.05
394	Devon White	.05
395	Otis Nixon	.05
396	Chuck Knoblauch	.05
397	Scott Coolbaugh	.05
398	Glenn Davis	.05
399	Manny Lee	.05
400	Andre Dawson	.20
401	Scott Chiamparino	.05
402	Bill Gullickson	.05
403	Lance Johnson	.05
404	Juan Agosto	.05
405	Danny Darwin	.05
406	Barry Jones	.05
407	Larry Andersen	.05
408	Luis Rivera	.05
409	Jaime Navarro	.05
410	Roger McDowell	.05
411	Brett Butler	.05
412	Dale Murphy	.15
413	Tim Raines	.05
414	Norm Charlton	.05
415	Greg Cadaret	.05
416	Chris Nabholz	.05
417	Dave Stewart	.05
418	Rich Gedman	.05
419	Willie Randolph	.05
420	Mitch Williams	.05
421	Brook Jacoby	.05
422	Greg Harris	.05
423	Nolan Ryan	2.00
424	Dave Rohde	.05
425	Don Mattingly	.75
426	Greg Gagne	.05
427	Vince Coleman	.05
428	Dan Pasqua	.05
429	Alvin Davis	.05
430	Cal Ripken, Jr.	2.00
431	Jamie Quirk	.05
432	Benito Santiago	.05
433	Jose Uribe	.05
434	Candy Maldonado	.05
435	Junior Felix	.05
436	Deion Sanders	.05
437	John Franco	.05
438	Greg Hibbard	.05
439	Floyd Bannister	.05
440	Steve Howe	.05
441	Steve Decker	.05
442	Vicente Palacios	.05
443	Pat Tabler	.05
444	Darryl Strawberry Checklist	.05
445	Mike Felder	.05
446	Al Newman	.05
447	Chris Donnels	.05
448	Rich Rodriguez	.05
449	Turner Ward	.05
450	Bob Walk	.05
451	Gilberto Reyes	.05
452	Mike Jackson	.05
453	Rafael Belliard	.05
454	Wayne Edwards	.05
455	Andy Allanson	.05
456	Dave Smith	.05
457	Gary Carter	.45
458	Warren Cromartie	.05
459	Jack Armstrong	.05
460	Bob Tewksbury	.05
461	Joe Klink	.05
462	Xavier Hernandez	.05
463	Scott Radinsky	.05
464	Jeff Robinson	.05
465	Gregg Jefferies	.05
466	Denny Neagle	.05
467	Carmelo Martinez	.05
468	Donn Pall	.05
469	Bruce Hurst	.05
470	Eric Bullock	.05
471	Rick Aguilera	.05
472	Charlie Hough	.05
473	Carlos Quintana	.05
474	Marty Barrett	.05
475	Kevin Brown	.05
476	Bobby Ojeda	.05
477	Edgar Martinez	.05
478	Bip Roberts	.05
479	Mike Flanagan	.05
480	John Habyan	.05
481	Larry Casian	.05
482	Wally Backman	.05
483	Doug Dascenzo	.05
484	Rick Dempsey	.05
485	Ed Sprague	.05
486	Steve Chitren	.05
487	Mark McGwire	1.50
488	Roger Clemens	.75
489	Orlando Merced	.05
490	Rene Gonzales	.05
491	Mike Stanton	.05
492	Al Osuna	.05
493	Rick Cerone	.05
494	Mariano Duncan	.05
495	Zane Smith	.05
496	John Morris	.05
497	Frank Tanana	.05
498	Junior Ortiz	.05
499	Dave Winfield	.45
500	Gary Varsho	.05
501	Chico Walker	.05
502	Ken Caminiti	.05
503	Ken Griffey Sr.	.05
504	Randy Myers	.05
505	Steve Bedrosian	.05
506	Cory Snyder	.05
507	Cris Carpenter	.05
508	Tim Belcher	.05
509	Jeff Hamilton	.05
510	Steve Avery	.05
511	Dave Valle	.05
512	Tom Lampkin	.05
513	Shawn Hillegas	.05
514	Reggie Jefferson	.05
515	Ron Karkovice	.05
516	Doug Drabek	.05
517	Tom Henke	.05
518	Chris Bosio	.05
519	Gregg Olson	.05
520	Bob Scanlan	.05
521	Alonzo Powell	.05
522	Jeff Ballard	.05
523	Ray Lankford	.05
524	Tommy Greene	.05
525	Mike Timlin	.05
526	Juan Berenguer	.05
527	Scott Erickson	.05
528	Sandy Alomar Jr. Checklist	.05

Gold Rookies

MO VAUGHN 1B

		NM/M
Complete Set (26):		10.00
Common Player:		.10
1	Scott Leius	.10
2	Luis Gonzalez	.40
3	Wil Cordero	.10
4	Gary Scott	.10
5	Willie Banks	.10
6	Arthur Rhodes	.10
7	Mo Vaughn	.25
8	Henry Rodriguez	.10
9	Todd Van Poppel	.10
10	Reggie Sanders	.10
11	Rico Brogna	.10
12	Mike Mussina	2.00
13	Kirk Dressendorfer	.10
14	Jeff Bagwell	6.00
15	Pete Schourek	.10
16	Wade Taylor	.10
17	Pat Kelly	.10
18	Tim Costo	.10
19	Roger Salkeld	.10
20	Andujar Cedeno	.10
21	Ryan Klesko	.10
22	Mike Huff	.10
23	Anthony Young	.10
24	Eddie Zosky	.10
25	Nolan Ryan (7th no-hitter)	.50
26	Rickey Henderson (Record Steal)	.25
	Babe Ruth Plooey	.01
265	Scott Leius	4.00
266	Luis Gonzalez	6.00
267	Wil Cordero	4.00
268	Gary Scott	4.00
269	Willie Banks	4.00
270	Arthur Rhodes	4.00
271	Mo Vaughn	10.00
272	Henry Rodriguez	4.00
273	Todd Van Poppel	4.00
274	Reggie Sanders	4.00
275	Rico Brogna	4.00
276	Mike Mussina	30.00

1992 Leaf

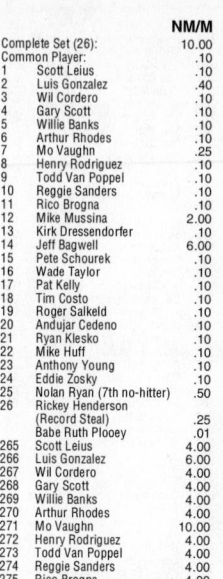

TRAVIS FRYMAN 3B

		NM/M
Complete Set (528):		7.50
Common Player:		.05
Series 1 or 2 Pack:		.40
Series 1 or 2 Wax Box:		7.50
1	Jim Abbott	.05
2	Cal Eldred	.05
3	Bud Black	.05
4	Dave Howard	.05
5	Luis Sojo	.05
6	Gary Scott	.05
7	Joe Oliver	.05
8	Chris Gardner	.05
9	Sandy Alomar	.05
10	Greg Harris	.05
11	Doug Drabek	.05
12	Darryl Hamilton	.05
13	Mike Mussina	.30
14	Kevin Tapani	.05
15	Ron Gant	.05
16	Mark McGwire	1.00
17	Robin Ventura	.05
18	Pedro Guerrero	.05
19	Roger Clemens	.65
20	Steve Farr	.05
21	Frank Tanana	.05
22	Joe Hesketh	.05
23	Erik Hanson	.05
24	Greg Cadaret	.05
25	Rex Hudler	.05
26	Mark Grace	.05
27	Kelly Gruber	.05
28	Jeff Bagwell	.45
29	Darryl Strawberry	.05
30	Dave Smith	.05
31	Kevin Appier	.05
32	Steve Chitren	.05
33	Kevin Gross	.05
34	Rick Aguilera	.05
35	Juan Guzman	.05
36	Joe Orsulak	.05
37	Tim Raines	.05
38	Harold Reynolds	.05
39	Charlie Hough	.05
40	Tony Phillips	.05
41	Nolan Ryan	1.50
42	Vince Coleman	.05
43	Andy Van Slyke	.05
44	Tim Burke	.05
45	Luis Polonia	.05
46	Tom Browning	.05
47	Willie McGee	.05
48	Gary DiSarcina	.05
49	Mark Lewis	.05
50	Phil Plantier	.05
51	Doug Dascenzo	.05
52	Cal Ripken, Jr.	1.50
53	Pedro Munoz	.05
54	Carlos Hernandez	.05
55	Jerald Clark	.05
56	Jeff Brantley	.05
57	Don Mattingly	.65
58	Roger McDowell	.05
59	Steve Avery	.05
60	John Olerud	.05
61	Bill Gullickson	.05
62	Juan Gonzalez	.30
63	Felix Jose	.05
64	Robin Yount	.45
65	Greg Briley	.05
66	Steve Finley	.05
67	Checklist	.05
68	Tom Gordon	.05
69	Rob Dibble	.05
70	Glenallen Hill	.05
71	Calvin Jones	.05
72	Joe Girardi	.05
73	Barry Larkin	.05
74	Andy Benes	.05
75	Milt Cuyler	.05
76	Kevin Bass	.05
77	Pete Harnisch	.05
78	Wilson Alvarez	.05
79	Mike Devereaux	.05
80	Doug Henry	.05
81	Orel Hershiser	.05
82	Shane Mack	.05
83	Mike Macfarlane	.05
84	Thomas Howard	.05
85	Alex Fernandez	.05
86	Reggie Jefferson	.05
87	Leo Gomez	.05
88	Mel Hall	.05
89	Mike Greenwell	.05
90	Jeff Russell	.05
91	Steve Buechele	.05
92	David Cone	.05
93	Kevin Reimer	.05
94	Mark Lemke	.05
95	Bob Tewksbury	.05
96	Zane Smith	.05
97	Mark Eichhorn	.05
98	Kirby Puckett	.60
99	Paul O'Neill	.05
100	Dennis Eckersley	.35
101	Duane Ward	.05
102	Matt Nokes	.05
103	Mo Vaughn	.05
104	Pat Kelly	.05
105	Ron Karkovice	.05
106	Bill Spiers	.05
107	Gary Gaetti	.05
108	Mackey Sasser	.05
109	Robby Thompson	.05
110	Marvin Freeman	.05
111	Jimmy Key	.05
112	Dwight Gooden	.05
113	Charlie Leibrandt	.05
114	Devon White	.05
115	Charles Nagy	.05
116	Rickey Henderson	.45
117	Paul Assenmacher	.05
118	Junior Felix	.05
119	Julio Franco	.05
120	Norm Charlton	.05
121	Scott Servais	.05
122	Gerald Perry	.05
123	Brian McRae	.05
124	Don Slaught	.05
125	Juan Samuel	.05
126	Harold Baines	.05
127	Scott Livingstone	.05
128	Jay Buhner	.05
129	Darrin Jackson	.05
130	Luis Mercedes	.05
131	Brian Harper	.05
132	Howard Johnson	.05
133	Checklist	.05
134	Dante Bichette	.05
135	Dave Righetti	.05
136	Jeff Montgomery	.05
137	Joe Grahe	.05
138	Delino DeShields	.05
139	Jose Rijo	.05
140	Ken Caminiti	.05
141	Steve Olin	.05
142	Kurt Stillwell	.05
143	Jay Bell	.05
144	Jaime Navarro	.05
145	Ben McDonald	.05
146	Greg Gagne	.05
147	Jeff Blauser	.05
148	Carney Lansford	.05
149	Ozzie Guillen	.05
150	Milt Thompson	.05
151	Jeff Reardon	.05
152	Scott Sanderson	.05
153	Cecil Fielder	.05
154	Greg Harris	.05
155	Rich DeLucia	.05
156	Roberto Kelly	.05
157	Bryn Smith	.05
158	Chuck McElroy	.05
159	Tom Henke	.05
160	Luis Gonzalez	.25

161 Steve Wilson .05
162 Shawn Boskie .05
163 Mark Davis .05
164 Mike Moore .05
165 Mike Scioscia .05
166 Scott Erickson .05
167 Todd Stottlemyre .05
168 Alvin Davis .05
169 Greg Hibbard .05
170 David Valle .05
171 Dave Winfield .45
172 Alan Trammell .05
173 Kenny Rogers .05
174 John Franco .05
175 Jose Lind .05
176 Pete Schourek .05
177 Von Hayes .05
178 Chris Hammond .05
179 John Burkett .05
180 Dickie Thon .05
181 Joel Skinner .05
182 Scott Cooper .05
183 Andre Dawson .25
184 Billy Ripken .05
185 Kevin Mitchell .05
186 Brett Butler .05
187 Tony Fernandez .05
188 Cory Snyder .05
189 John Habyan .05
190 Dennis Martinez .05
191 John Smoltz .05
192 Greg Myers .05
193 Rob Deer .05
194 Ivan Rodriguez .45
195 Ray Lankford .05
196 Bill Wegman .05
197 Edgar Martinez .05
198 Darryl Kile .05
199 Checklist .05
200 Brent Mayne .05
201 Larry Walker .05
202 Carlos Baerga .05
203 Russ Swan .05
204 Mike Morgan .05
205 Hal Morris .05
206 Tony Gwynn .60
207 Mark Leiter .05
208 Kirt Manwaring .05
209 Al Osuna .05
210 Bobby Thigpen .05
211 Chris Hoiles .05
212 B.J. Surhoff .05
213 Lenny Harris .05
214 Scott Leius .05
215 Gregg Jefferies .05
216 Bruce Hurst .05
217 Steve Sax .05
218 Dave Otto .05
219 Sam Horn .05
220 Charlie Hayes .05
221 Frank Viola .05
222 Jose Guzman .05
223 Gary Redus .05
224 Dave Gallagher .05
225 Dean Palmer .05
226 Greg Olson .05
227 Jose DeLeon .05
228 Mike LaValliere .05
229 Mark Langston .05
230 Chuck Knoblauch .05
231 Bill Doran .05
232 Dave Henderson .05
233 Roberto Alomar .20
234 Scott Fletcher .05
235 Tim Naehring .05
236 Mike Gallego .05
237 Lance Johnson .05
238 Paul Molitor .45
239 Dan Gladden .05
240 Willie Randolph .05
241 Will Clark .10
242 Sid Bream .05
243 Derek Bell .05
244 Bill Pecota .05
245 Terry Pendleton .05
246 Randy Ready .05
247 Jack Armstrong .05
248 Todd Van Poppel .05
249 Shawon Dunston .05
250 Bobby Rose .05
251 Jeff Huson .05
252 Bip Roberts .05
253 Doug Jones .05
254 Lee Smith .05
255 George Brett .65
256 Randy Tomlin .05
257 Todd Benzinger .05
258 Dave Stewart .05
259 Mark Carreon .05
260 Pete O'Brien .05
261 Tim Teufel .05
262 Bob Milacki .05
263 Mark Guthrie .05
264 Darrin Fletcher .05
265 Omar Vizquel .05
266 Chris Bosio .05
267 Jose Canseco .30
268 Mike Boddicker .05
269 Lance Parrish .05
270 Jose Vizcaino .05
271 Chris Sabo .05
272 Royce Clayton .05
273 Marquis Grissom .05
274 Fred McGriff .05
275 Barry Bonds 1.50
276 Greg Vaughn .05
277 Gregg Olson .05
278 Dave Hollins .05
279 Tom Glavine .25
280 Bryan Hickerson .05
281 Scott Radinsky .05
282 Omar Olivares .05
283 Ivan Calderon .05
284 Kevin Maas .05
285 Mickey Tettleton .05
286 Wade Boggs .60
287 Stan Belinda .05
288 Bret Barberie .05
289 Jose Oquendo .05
290 Frank Castillo .05
291 Dave Stieb .05
292 Tommy Greene .05
293 Eric Karros .05
294 Greg Maddux .60
295 Jim Eisenreich .05
296 Rafael Palmeiro .35
297 Ramon Martinez .05
298 Tim Wallach .05
299 Jim Thome .45
300 Chito Martinez .05
301 Mitch Williams .05
302 Randy Johnson .45
303 Carlton Fisk .45
304 Travis Fryman .05
305 Bobby Witt .05
306 Dave Magadan .05
307 Alex Cole .05
308 Bobby Bonilla .05
309 Bryan Harvey .05
310 Rafael Belliard .05
311 Mariano Duncan .05
312 Chuck Crim .05
313 John Kruk .05
314 Ellis Burks .05
315 Craig Biggio .05
316 Glenn Davis .05
317 Ryne Sandberg .60
318 Mike Sharperson .05
319 Rich Rodriguez .05
320 Lee Guetterman .05
321 Benito Santiago .05
322 Jose Offerman .05
323 Tony Pena .05
324 Pat Borders .05
325 Mike Henneman .05
326 Kevin Brown .05
327 Chris Nabholz .05
328 Franklin Stubbs .05
329 Tino Martinez .05
330 Mickey Morandini .05
331 Checklist .05
332 Mark Gubicza .05
333 Bill Landrum .05
334 Mark Whiten .05
335 Darren Daulton .05
336 Rick Wilkins .05
337 Brian Jordan **RC** .25
338 Kevin Ward .05
339 Ruben Amaro .05
340 Trevor Wilson .05
341 Andujar Cedeno .05
342 Michael Huff .05
343 Brady Anderson .05
344 Craig Grebeck .05
345 Bobby Ojeda .05
346 Mike Pagliarulo .05
347 Terry Shumpert .05
348 Dann Bilardello .05
349 Frank Thomas .45
350 Albert Belle .05
351 Jose Mesa .05
352 Rich Monteleone .05
353 Bob Walk .05
354 Monty Fariss .05
355 Luis Rivera .05
356 Anthony Young .05
357 Geno Petralli .05
358 Otis Nixon .05
359 Tom Pagnozzi .05
360 Reggie Sanders .05
361 Lee Stevens .05
362 Kent Hrbek .05
363 Orlando Merced .05
364 Mike Bordick .05
365 Dion James .05
366 Jack Clark .05
367 Mike Stanley .05
368 Randy Velarde .05
369 Dan Pasqua .05
370 Pat Listach .05
371 Mike Fitzgerald .05
372 Tom Foley .05
373 Matt Williams .05
374 Brian Hunter .05
375 Joe Carter .05
376 Bret Saberhagen .05
377 Mike Stanton .05
378 Hubie Brooks .05
379 Eric Bell .05
380 Walt Weiss .05
381 Danny Jackson .05
382 Manuel Lee .05
383 Ruben Sierra .05
384 Greg Swindell .05
385 Ryan Bowen .05
386 Kevin Ritz .05
387 Curtis Wilkerson .05
388 Gary Varsho .05
389 Dave Hansen .05
390 Bob Welch .05
391 Lou Whitaker .05
392 Ken Griffey Jr. .75
393 Mike Maddux .05
394 Arthur Rhodes .05
395 Chili Davis .05
396 Eddie Murray .45
397 Checklist .05
398 Dave Cochrane .05
399 Kevin Seitzer .05
400 Ozzie Smith .60
401 Paul Sorrento .05
402 Les Lancaster .05
403 Junior Noboa .05
404 Dave Justice .05
405 Andy Ashby .05
406 Danny Tartabull .05
407 Bill Swift .05
408 Craig Lefferts .05
409 Tom Candiotti .05
410 Lance Blankenship .05
411 Jeff Tackett .05
412 Sammy Sosa .65
413 Jody Reed .05
414 Bruce Ruffin .05
415 Gene Larkin .05
416 John Vanderwal .05
417 Tim Belcher .05
418 Steve Frey .05
419 Dick Schofield .05
420 Jeff King .05
421 Kim Batiste .05
422 Jack McDowell .05
423 Damon Berryhill .05
424 Gary Wayne .05
425 Jack Morris .05
426 Moises Alou .05
427 Mark McLemore .05
428 Juan Guerrero .05
429 Scott Scudder .05
430 Eric Davis .05
431 Joe Slusarski .05
432 Todd Zeile .05
433 Dwayne Henry .05
434 Cliff Brantley .05
435 Butch Henry .05
436 Todd Worrell .05
437 Bob Scanlan .05
438 Wally Joyner .05
439 John Flaherty .05
440 Brian Downing .05
441 Darren Lewis .05
442 Gary Carter .45
443 Wally Ritchie .05
444 Chris Jones .05
445 Jeff Kent .05
446 Gary Sheffield .30
447 Ron Darling .05
448 Deion Sanders .05
449 Andres Galarraga .05
450 Chuck Finley .05
451 Derek Lilliquist .05
452 Carl Willis .05
453 Wes Chamberlain .05
454 Roger Mason .05
455 Spike Owen .05
456 Thomas Howard .05
457 Dave Martinez .05
458 Pete Incaviglia .05
459 Keith Miller .05
460 Mike Fetters .05
461 Paul Gibson .05
462 George Bell .05
463 Checklist .05
464 Terry Mulholland .05
465 Storm Davis .05
466 Gary Pettis .05
467 Randy Bush .05
468 Ken Hill .05
469 Rheal Cormier .05
470 Andy Stankiewicz .05
471 Dave Burba .05
472 Henry Cotto .05
473 Dale Sveum .05
474 Rich Gossage .05
475 William Suero .05
476 Doug Strange .05
477 Bill Krueger .05
478 John Wetteland .05
479 Melido Perez .05
480 Lonnie Smith .05
481 Mike Jackson .05
482 Mike Gardiner .05
483 David Wells .05
484 Barry Jones .05
485 Scott Bankhead .05
486 Terry Leach .05
487 Vince Horsman .05
488 Dave Eiland .05
489 Alejandro Pena .05
490 Julio Valera .05
491 Joe Boever .05
492 Paul Miller .05
493 Arci Cianfrocco **RC** .05
494 Dave Fleming .05
495 Kyle Abbott .05
496 Chad Kreuter .05
497 Chris James .05
498 Donnie Hill .05
499 Jacob Brumfield .05
500 Ricky Bones .05
501 Terry Steinbach .05
502 Bernard Gilkey .05
503 Dennis Cook .05
504 Len Dykstra .05
505 Mike Bielecki .05
506 Bob Kipper .05
507 Jose Melendez .05
508 Rick Sutcliffe .05
509 Ken Patterson .05
510 Andy Allanson .05
511 Al Newman .05
512 Mark Gardner .05
513 Jeff Schaefer .05
514 Jim McNamara .05
515 Peter Hoy .05
516 Curt Schilling .30
517 Kirk McCaskill .05
518 Chris Gwynn .05
519 Sid Fernandez .05
520 Jeff Parrett .05
521 Scott Ruskin .05
522 Kevin McReynolds .05
523 Rick Cerone .05
524 Jesse Orosco .05
525 Troy Afenir .05
526 John Smiley .05
527 Dale Murphy .25
528 Leaf Set Card .05

1992 Leaf Gold Edition

NM/M

Complete Set (528): 35.00
Common Player: .10
Stars/Rookies: 3X
(See 1992 Leaf for checklist and base card values.)

1992 Leaf Gold Previews

NM/M

Complete Set (33): 30.00
Common Player: .50
1 Steve Avery .50
2 Ryne Sandberg 2.00
3 Chris Sabo .50
4 Jeff Bagwell 1.50
5 Darryl Strawberry .50
6 Bret Barbarie .50
7 Howard Johnson .50
8 John Kruk .50
9 Andy Van Slyke .50
10 Felix Jose .50
11 Fred McGriff .50
12 Will Clark .60
13 Cal Ripken, Jr. 4.00
14 Phil Plantier .50
15 Lee Stevens .50
16 Frank Thomas 1.50
17 Mark Whiten .50
18 Cecil Fielder .50
19 George Brett 2.50
20 Robin Yount 1.50
21 Scott Erickson .50
22 Don Mattingly 2.50
23 Jose Canseco 1.00
24 Ken Griffey Jr. 3.00
25 Nolan Ryan 4.00
26 Joe Carter .50
27 Deion Sanders .50
28 Dean Palmer .50
29 Andy Benes .50
30 Gary DiSarcina .50
31 Chris Hoiles .50
32 Mark McGwire 3.00
33 Reggie Sanders .50

Gold Rookies

NM/M

Complete Set (24): 4.00
Common Player: .25
Jumbo: 1.5X

1	Chad Curtis	.25
2	Brent Gates	.25
3	Pedro Martinez	3.00
4	Kenny Lofton	.35
5	Turk Wendell	.25
6	Mark Hutton	.25
7	Todd Hundley	.25
8	Matt Stairs	.25
9	Ed Taubensee	.25
10	David Nied	.25
11	Salomon Torres	.25
12	Bret Boone	.50
13	John Ruffin	.25
14	Ed Martel	.25
15	Rick Trlicek	.25
16	Raul Mondesi	.25
17	Pat Mahomes	.25
18	Dan Wilson	.25
19	Donovan Osborne	.25
20	Dave Silvestri	.25
21	Gary DiSarcina	.25
22	Denny Neagle	.25
23	Steve Hosey	.25
24	John Doherty	.25

1993 Leaf

	NM/M
Complete Set (550):	12.50
Common Player:	.05
Series 1 or 2 Pack (14):	.65
Series 1 or 2 Box (36):	12.50
Update Pack (14):	1.50
Update Box (36):	25.00

1	Ben McDonald	.05
2	Sid Fernandez	.05
3	Juan Guzman	.05
4	Curt Schilling	.40
5	Ivan Rodriguez	.65
6	Don Slaught	.05
7	Terry Steinbach	.05
8	Todd Zeile	.05
9	Andy Stankiewicz	.05
10	Tim Teufel	.05
11	Marvin Freeman	.05
12	Jim Austin	.05
13	Bob Scanlan	.05
14	Rusty Meacham	.05
15	Casey Candaele	.05
16	Travis Fryman	.05
17	Jose Offerman	.05
18	Albert Belle	.05
19	John Vander Wahl (Vander Wal)	.05
20	Dan Pasqua	.05
21	Frank Viola	.05
22	Terry Mulholland	.05
23	Gregg Olson	.05
24	Randy Tomlin	.05
25	Todd Stottlemyre	.05
26	Jose Oquendo	.05
27	Julio Franco	.05
28	Tony Gwynn	1.00
29	Ruben Sierra	.05
30	Robby Thompson	.05
31	Jim Bullinger	.05
32	Rick Aguilera	.05
33	Scott Servais	.05
34	Cal Eldred	.05
35	Mike Piazza	1.50
36	Brent Mayne	.05
37	Wil Cordero	.05
38	Milt Cuyler	.05
39	Howard Johnson	.05
40	Kenny Lofton	.05
41	Alex Fernandez	.05
42	Denny Neagle	.05
43	Tony Pena	.05
44	Bob Tewksbury	.05
45	Glenn Davis	.05
46	Fred McGriff	.05
47	John Olerud	.05
48	Steve Hosey	.05
49	Rafael Palmeiro	.65
50	Dave Justice	.05
51	Pete Harnisch	.05
52	Sam Militello	.05
53	Orel Hershiser	.05
54	Pat Mahomes	.05
55	Greg Colbrunn	.05
56	Greg Vaughn	.05
57	Vince Coleman	.05
58	Brian McRae	.05
59	Len Dykstra	.05
60	Dan Gladden	.05
61	Ted Power	.05
62	Donovan Osborne	.05
63	Ron Karkovice	.05
64	Frank Seminara	.05
65	Bob Zupcic	.05
66	Kirt Manwaring	.05
67	Mike Devereaux	.05
68	Mark Lemke	.05
69	Devon White	.05
70	Sammy Sosa	1.25
71	Pedro Astacio	.05
72	Dennis Eckersley	.60
73	Chris Nabholz	.05
74	Melido Perez	.05
75	Todd Hundley	.05
76	Kent Hrbek	.05
77	Mickey Morandini	.05
78	Tim McIntosh	.05
79	Andy Van Slyke	.05
80	Kevin McReynolds	.05
81	Mike Henneman	.05
82	Greg Harris	.05
83	Sandy Alomar Jr.	.05
84	Mike Jackson	.05
85	Ozzie Guillen	.05
86	Jeff Blauser	.05
87	John Valentin	.05
88	Rey Sanchez	.05
89	Rick Sutcliffe	.05
90	Luis Gonzalez	.25
91	Jeff Fassero	.05
92	Kenny Rogers	.05
93	Bret Saberhagen	.05
94	Bob Welch	.05
95	Darren Daulton	.05
96	Mike Gallego	.05
97	Orlando Merced	.05
98	Chuck Knoblauch	.05
99	Bernard Gilkey	.05
100	Billy Ashley	.05
101	Kevin Appier	.05
102	Jeff Brantley	.05
103	Bill Gullickson	.05
104	John Smoltz	.05
105	Paul Sorrento	.05
106	Steve Buechele	.05
107	Steve Sax	.05
108	Andujar Cedeno	.05
109	Billy Hatcher	.05
110	Checklist	.05
111	Alan Mills	.05
112	John Franco	.05
113	Jack Morris	.05
114	Mitch Williams	.05
115	Nolan Ryan	2.50
116	Jay Bell	.05
117	Mike Bordick	.05
118	Geronimo Pena	.05
119	Danny Tartabull	.05
120	Checklist	.05
121	Steve Avery	.05
122	Ricky Bones	.05
123	Mike Morgan	.05
124	Jeff Montgomery	.05
125	Jeff Bagwell	.75
126	Tony Phillips	.05
127	Lenny Harris	.05
128	Glenallen Hill	.05
129	Marquis Grissom	.05
130	Gerald Williams (Photo, stats actually Bernie Williams.)	.20
131	Greg Harris	.05
132	Tommy Greene	.05
133	Chris Hoiles	.05
134	Bob Walk	.05
135	Duane Ward	.05
136	Tom Pagnozzi	.05
137	Jeff Huson	.05
138	Kurt Stillwell	.05
139	Dave Henderson	.05
140	Darrin Jackson	.05
141	Frank Castillo	.05
142	Scott Erickson	.05
143	Darryl Kile	.05
144	Bill Wegman	.05
145	Steve Wilson	.05
146	George Brett	1.25
147	Moises Alou	.05
148	Lou Whitaker	.05
149	Chico Walker	.05
150	Jerry Browne	.05
151	Kirk McCaskill	.05
152	Zane Smith	.05
153	Matt Young	.05
154	Lee Smith	.05
155	Leo Gomez	.05
156	Dan Walters	.05
157	Pat Borders	.05
158	Matt Williams	.05
159	Dean Palmer	.05
160	John Patterson	.05
161	Doug Jones	.05
162	John Habyan	.05
163	Pedro Martinez	.75
164	Carl Willis	.05
165	Darrin Fletcher	.05
166	B.J. Surhoff	.05
167	Eddie Murray	.75
168	Keith Miller	.05
169	Ricky Jordan	.05
170	Juan Gonzalez	.65
171	Charles Nagy	.05
172	Mark Clark	.05
173	Bobby Thigpen	.05
174	Tim Scott	.05
175	Scott Cooper	.05
176	Royce Clayton	.05
177	Brady Anderson	.05
178	Sid Bream	.05
179	Derek Bell	.05
180	Otis Nixon	.05
181	Kevin Gross	.05
182	Ron Darling	.05
183	John Wetteland	.05
184	Mike Stanley	.05
185	Jeff Kent	.05
186	Brian Harper	.05
187	Mariano Duncan	.05
188	Robin Yount	.75
189	Al Martin	.05
190	Eddie Zosky	.05
191	Mike Munoz	.05
192	Andy Benes	.05
193	Dennis Cook	.05
194	Bill Swift	.05
195	Frank Thomas	.75
196	Damon Berryhill	.05
197	Mike Greenwell	.05
198	Mark Grace	.05
199	Darryl Hamilton	.05
200	Derrick May	.05
201	Ken Hill	.05
202	Kevin Brown	.05
203	Dwight Gooden	.05
204	Bobby Witt	.05
205	Juan Bell	.05
206	Kevin Maas	.05
207	Jeff King	.05
208	Scott Leius	.05
209	Rheal Cormier	.05
210	Darryl Strawberry	.05
211	Tom Gordon	.05
212	Bud Black	.05
213	Mickey Tettleton	.05
214	Pete Smith	.05
215	Felix Fermin	.05
216	Rick Wilkins	.05
217	George Bell	.05
218	Eric Anthony	.05
219	Pedro Munoz	.05
220	Checklist	.05
221	Lance Blankenship	.05
222	Deion Sanders	.10
223	Craig Biggio	.05
224	Ryne Sandberg	1.00
225	Ron Gant	.05
226	Tom Brunansky	.05
227	Chad Curtis	.05
228	Joe Carter	.05
229	Brian Jordan	.05
230	Brett Butler	.05
231	Frank Bolick	.05
232	Rod Beck	.05
233	Carlos Baerga	.05
234	Eric Karros	.05
235	Jack Armstrong	.05
236	Bobby Bonilla	.05
237	Don Mattingly	1.25
238	Jeff Gardner	.05
239	Dave Hollins	.05
240	Steve Cooke	.05
241	Jose Canseco	.35
242	Ivan Calderon	.05
243	Tim Belcher	.05
244	Freddie Benavides	.05
245	Roberto Alomar	.25
246	Rob Deer	.05
247	Will Clark	.10
248	Mike Felder	.05
249	Harold Baines	.05
250	David Cone	.05
251	Mark Guthrie	.05
252	Ellis Burks	.05
253	Jim Abbott	.05
254	Chili Davis	.05
255	Chris Bosio	.05
256	Bret Barberie	.05
257	Hal Morris	.05
258	Dante Bichette	.05
259	Storm Davis	.05
260	Gary DiSarcina	.05
261	Ken Caminiti	.05
262	Paul Molitor	.75
263	Joe Oliver	.05
264	Pat Listach	.05
265	Gregg Jefferies	.05
266	Jose Guzman	.05
267	Eric Davis	.05
268	Delino DeShields	.05
269	Barry Bonds	2.50
270	Mike Bielecki	.05
271	Jay Buhner	.05
272	Scott Pose **RC**	.05
273	Tony Fernandez	.05
274	Chito Martinez	.05
275	Phil Plantier	.05
276	Pete Incaviglia	.05
277	Carlos Garcia	.05
278	Tom Henke	.05
279	Roger Clemens	1.25
280	Rob Dibble	.05
281	Daryl Boston	.05
282	Greg Gagne	.05
283	Cecil Fielder	.05
284	Carlton Fisk	.75
285	Wade Boggs	1.00
286	Damion Easley	.05
287	Norm Charlton	.05
288	Jeff Conine	.05
289	Roberto Kelly	.05
290	Jerald Clark	.05
291	Rickey Henderson	.75
292	Chuck Finley	.05
293	Doug Drabek	.05
294	Dave Stewart	.05
295	Tom Glavine	.35
296	Jaime Navarro	.05
297	Ray Lankford	.05
298	Greg Hibbard	.05
299	Jody Reed	.05
300	Dennis Martinez	.05
301	Dave Martinez	.05
302	Reggie Jefferson	.05
303	John Cummings **RC**	.05
304	Orestes Destrade	.05
305	Mike Maddux	.05
306	David Segui	.05
307	Gary Sheffield	.35
308	Danny Jackson	.05
309	Criag Lefferts	.05
310	Andre Dawson	.20
311	Barry Larkin	.05
312	Alex Cole	.05
313	Mark Gardner	.05
314	Kirk Gibson	.05
315	Shane Mack	.05
316	Bo Jackson	.10
317	Jimmy Key	.05
318	Greg Myers	.05
319	Ken Griffey Jr.	1.50
320	Monty Fariss	.05
321	Kevin Mitchell	.05
322	Andres Galarraga	.05
323	Mark McGwire	2.00
324	Mark Langston	.05
325	Steve Finley	.05
326	Greg Maddux	1.00
327	Dave Nilsson	.05
328	Ozzie Smith	1.00
329	Candy Maldonado	.05
330	Checklist	.05
331	Tim Pugh **RC**	.05
332	Joe Girardi	.05
333	Junior Feliz	.05
334	Greg Swindell	.05
335	Ramon Martinez	.05
336	Sean Berry	.05
337	Joe Orsulak	.05
338	Wes Chamberlain	.05
339	Stan Belinda	.05
340	Checklist	.05
341	Bruce Hurst	.05
342	John Burkett	.05
343	Mike Mussina	.40
344	Scott Fletcher	.05
345	Rene Gonzales	.05
346	Roberto Hernandez	.05
347	Carlos Martinez	.05
348	Bill Krueger	.05
349	Felix Jose	.05
350	John Jaha	.05
351	Willie Banks	.05
352	Matt Nokes	.05
353	Kevin Seitzer	.05
354	Erik Hanson	.05
355	David Hulse **RC**	.05
356	Domingo Martinez **RC**	.05
357	Greg Olson	.05
358	Randy Myers	.05
359	Tom Browning	.05
360	Charlie Hayes	.05
361	Bryan Harvey	.05
362	Eddie Taubensee	.05
363	Tim Wallach	.05
364	Mel Rojas	.05
365	Frank Tanana	.05
366	John Kruk	.05
367	Tim Laker **RC**	.05
368	Rich Rodriguez	.05
369	Darren Lewis	.05
370	Harold Reynolds	.05
371	Jose Melendez	.05
372	Joe Grahe	.05
373	Lance Johnson	.05
374	Jose Mesa	.05
375	Scott Livingstone	.05
376	Wally Joyner	.05
377	Kevin Reimer	.05

378	Kirby Puckett	1.00
379	Paul O'Neill	.05
380	Randy Johnson	.75
381	Manuel Lee	.05
382	Dick Schofield	.05
383	Darren Holmes	.05
384	Charlie Hough	.05
385	John Orton	.05
386	Edgar Martinez	.05
387	Terry Pendleton	.05
388	Dan Plesac	.05
389	Jeff Reardon	.05
390	David Nied	.05
391	Dave Magadan	.05
392	Larry Walker	.05
393	Ben Rivera	.05
394	Lonnie Smith	.05
395	Craig Shipley	.05
396	Willie McGee	.05
397	Arthur Rhodes	.05
398	Mike Stanton	.05
399	Luis Polonia	.05
400	Jack McDowell	.05
401	Mike Moore	.05
402	Jose Lind	.05
403	Bill Spiers	.05
404	Kevin Tapani	.05
405	Spike Owen	.05
406	Tino Martinez	.05
407	Charlie Leibrandt	.05
408	Ed Sprague	.05
409	Bryn Smith	.05
410	Benito Santiago	.05
411	Jose Rijo	.05
412	Pete O'Brien	.05
413	Willie Wilson	.05
414	Bip Roberts	.05
415	Eric Young	.05
416	Walt Weiss	.05
417	Milt Thompson	.05
418	Chris Sabo	.05
419	Scott Sanderson	.05
420	Tim Raines	.05
421	Alan Trammell	.05
422	Mike Macfarlane	.05
423	Dave Winfield	.75
424	Bob Wickman	.05
425	David Valle	.05
426	Gary Redus	.05
427	Turner Ward	.05
428	Reggie Sanders	.05
429	Todd Worrell	.05
430	Julio Valera	.05
431	Cal Ripken, Jr.	2.50
432	Mo Vaughn	.05
433	John Smiley	.05
434	Omar Vizquel	.05
435	Billy Ripken	.05
436	Cory Snyder	.05
437	Carlos Quintana	.05
438	Omar Olivares	.05
439	Robin Ventura	.05
440	Checklist	.05
441	Kevin Higgins	.05
442	Carlos Hernandez	.05
443	Dan Peltier	.05
444	Derek Lilliquist	.05
445	Tim Salmon	.05
446	Sherman Obando RC	.05
447	Pat Kelly	.05
448	Todd Van Poppel	.05
449	Mark Whiten	.05
450	Checklist	.05
451	Pat Meares	.05
452	Tony Tarasco RC	.05
453	Chris Gwynn	.05
454	Armando Reynoso	.05
455	Danny Darwin	.05
456	Willie Greene	.05
457	Mike Blowers	.05
458	Kevin Roberson RC	.05
459	Graeme Lloyd RC	.05
460	David West	.05
461	Joey Cora	.05
462	Alex Arias	.05
463	Chad Kreuter	.05
464	Mike Lansing	.05
465	Mike Timlin	.05
466	Paul Wagner	.05
467	Mark Portugal	.05
468	Jim Leyritz	.05
469	Ryan Klesko	.05
470	Mario Diaz	.05
471	Guillermo Velasquez	.05
472	Fernando Valenzuela	.05
473	Raul Mondesi	.05
474	Mike Pagliarulo	.05
475	Chris Hammond	.05
476	Torey Lovullo	.05
477	Trevor Wilson	.05
478	Marcos Armas RC	.05
479	Dave Gallagher	.05
480	Jeff Treadway	.05
481	Jeff Branson	.05
482	Dickie Thon	.05
483	Eduardo Perez	.05
484	David Wells	.05
485	Brian Williams	.05
486	Domingo Cedeno	.05
487	Tom Candiotti	.05
488	Steve Frey	.05
489	Greg McMichael	.05
490	Marc Newfield	.05
491	Larry Andersen	.05
492	Damon Buford	.05

493	Ricky Gutierrez	.05
494	Jeff Russell	.05
495	Vinny Castilla	.05
496	Wilson Alvarez	.05
497	Scott Bullett	.05
498	Larry Casian	.05
499	Jose Vizcaino	.05
500	J.T. Snow RC	.75
501	Bryan Hickerson	.05
502	Jeremy Hernandez	.05
503	Jeromy Burnitz	.05
504	Steve Farr	.05
505	J. Owens	.05
506	Craig Paquette	.05
507	Jim Eisenreich	.05
508	Matt Whiteside	.05
509	Luis Aquino	.05
510	Mike LaValliere	.05
511	Jim Gott	.05
512	Mark McLemore	.05
513	Randy Milligan	.05
514	Gary Gaetti	.05
515	Lou Frazier	.05
516	Rich Amaral	.05
517	Gene Harris	.05
518	Aaron Sele	.05
519	Mark Wohlers	.05
520	Scott Kamieniecki	.05
521	Kent Mercker	.05
522	Jim Deshaies	.05
523	Kevin Stocker	.05
524	Jason Bere	.05
525	Tim Bogar	.05
526	Brad Pennington	.05
527	Curt Leskanic RC	.05
528	Wayne Kirby	.05
529	Tim Costo	.05
530	Doug Henry	.05
531	Trevor Hoffman	.05
532	Kelly Gruber	.05
533	Mike Harkey	.05
534	John Doherty	.05
535	Erik Pappas	.05
536	Brent Gates	.05
537	Roger McDowell	.05
538	Chris Haney	.05
539	Blas Minor	.05
540	Pat Hentgen	.05
541	Chuck Carr	.05
542	Doug Strange	.05
543	Xavier Hernandez	.05
544	Paul Quantrill	.05
545	Anthony Young	.05
546	Bret Boone	.05
547	Dwight Smith	.05
548	Bobby Munoz	.05
549	Russ Springer	.05
550	Roger Pavlik	.05
----	Dave Winfield (3,000 Hits)	2.00

Fasttrack

NM/M		
Complete Set (20):		15.00
Common Player:		.60
1	Frank Thomas	3.00
2	Tim Wakefield	.60
3	Kenny Lofton	.60
4	Mike Mussina	1.00
5	Juan Gonzalez	2.50
6	Chuck Knoblauch	.60
7	Eric Karros	.60
8	Ray Lankford	.60
9	Juan Guzman	.60
10	Pat Listach	.60
11	Carlos Baerga	.60
12	Felix Jose	.60
13	Steve Avery	.60
14	Robin Ventura	.60
15	Ivan Rodriguez	2.50
16	Cal Eldred	.60
17	Jeff Bagwell	3.00
18	Dave Justice	.60
19	Travis Fryman	.60
20	Marquis Grissom	.60

Gold All-Stars

NM/M		
Complete Set (20):		15.00
Common Player:		.25

1	Ivan Rodriguez, Darren Daulton	.75
2	Don Mattingly, Fred McGriff	1.50
3	Cecil Fielder, Jeff Bagwell	.75
4	Carlos Baerga, Ryne Sandberg	1.00
5	Chuck Knoblauch, Delino DeShields	.25
6	Robin Ventura, Terry Pendleton	.25
7	Ken Griffey Jr., Andy Van Slyke	2.00
8	Joe Carter, Dave Justice	.25
9	Jose Canseco, Tony Gwynn	1.00
10	Dennis Eckersley, Rob Dibble	.60
11	Mark McGwire, Will Clark	2.50
12	Frank Thomas, Mark Grace	.75
13	Roberto Alomar, Craig Biggio	.50
14	Barry Larkin, Cal Ripken, Jr.	3.00
15	Gary Sheffield, Edgar Martinez	.50
16	Juan Gonzalez, Barry Bonds	3.00
17	Kirby Puckett, Marquis Grissom	1.00
18	Jim Abbott, Tom Glavine	.40
19	Nolan Ryan, Greg Maddux	3.00
20	Roger Clemens, Doug Drabek	1.50

Gold Rookies

Darrell Sherman

NM/M		
Complete Set (20):		5.00
Common Player:		.25
1	Kevin Young	.25
2	Wil Cordero	.25
3	Mark Kiefer	.25
4	Gerald Williams	.25
5	Brandon Wilson	.25
6	Greg Gohr	.25
7	Ryan Thompson	.25
8	Tim Wakefield	.25
9	Troy Neel	.25
10	Tim Salmon	.50
11	Kevin Rogers	.25
12	Rod Bolton	.25
13	Ken Ryan	.25
14	Phil Hiatt	.25
15	Rene Arocha	.25
16	Nigel Wilson	.25
17	J.T. Snow	.50
18	Benji Gil	.25
19	Chipper Jones	3.00
20	Darrell Sherman	.25

Heading for the Hall

NM/M		
Complete Set (10):		10.00
Common Player:		1.00
1	Nolan Ryan	2.50
2	Tony Gwynn	1.00
3	Robin Yount	1.00
4	Eddie Murray	1.00
5	Cal Ripken, Jr.	2.50
6	Roger Clemens	2.00
7	George Brett	2.00
8	Ryne Sandberg	1.00

9	Kirby Puckett	1.00
10	Ozzie Smith	1.00

Frank Thomas

NM/M		
Complete Set (10):		4.50
Common Card:		.75
Autographed Card:		30.00
1	Frank Thomas Aggressive	.75
2	Frank Thomas Serious	.75
3	Frank Thomas Intense	.75
4	Frank Thomas Confident	.75
5	Frank Thomas Assertive	.75
6	Frank Thomas Power	.75
7	Frank Thomas Control	.75
8	Frank Thomas Strength	.75
9	Frank Thomas Concentration	.75
10	Frank Thomas Preparation	.75

Update Gold All-Stars

NM/M		
Complete Set (10):		7.50
Common Player:		.25
1	Mark Langston, Terry Mulholland	.25
2	Ivan Rodriguez, Darren Daulton	.50
3	John Olerud, John Kruk	.25
4	Roberto Alomar, Ryne Sandberg	1.00
5	Wade Boggs, Gary Sheffield	.75
6	Cal Ripken, Jr., Barry Larkin	3.00
7	Kirby Puckett, Barry Bonds	2.50
8	Marquis Grissom, Ken Griffey Jr.	2.00
9	Joe Carter, Dave Justice	.25
10	Mark Grace, Paul Molitor	.75

Update Gold Rookies

NM/M		
Complete Set (5):		3.50
Common Player:		.25
Jumbos:		1.5X

1	Allen Watson	.25
2	Jeffrey Hammonds	.25
3	David McCarty	.25
4	Mike Piazza	3.00
5	Roberto Meija	.25

1993 Leaf Update Frank Thomas Autograph

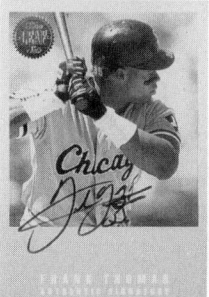

NM/M

FT	Frank Thomas	35.00

Update Frank Thomas Super

NM/M

Complete Set (10):		17.50
Common Card:		2.00
1	Frank Thomas Aggressive	2.00
2	Frank Thomas Serious	2.00
3	Frank Thomas Intense	2.00
4	Frank Thomas Confident	2.00
5	Frank Thomas Assertive	2.00
6	Frank Thomas Power	2.00
7	Frank Thomas Control	2.00
8	Frank Thomas Strength	2.00
9	Frank Thomas Concentration	2.00
10	Frank Thomas Preparation	2.00

1994 Leaf

NM/M

Complete Set (440):		10.00
Common Player:		.05
Series 1 or 2 Pack (12):		.75
Series 1 or 2 Box (36):		12.50
1	Cal Ripken, Jr.	2.50
2	Tony Tarasco	.05
3	Joe Girardi	.05
4	Bernie Williams	.20
5	Chad Kreuter	.05
6	Troy Neel	.05
7	Tom Pagnozzi	.05
8	Kirk Rueter	.05
9	Chris Bosio	.05
10	Dwight Gooden	.05
11	Mariano Duncan	.05
12	Jay Bell	.05

13	Lance Johnson	.05
14	Richie Lewis	.05
15	Dave Martinez	.05
16	Orel Hershiser	.05
17	Rob Butler	.05
18	Glenallen Hill	.05
19	Chad Curtis	.05
20	Mike Stanton	.05
21	Tim Wallach	.05
22	Milt Thompson	.05
23	Kevin Young	.05
24	John Smiley	.05
25	Jeff Montgomery	.05
26	Robin Ventura	.05
27	Scott Lydy	.05
28	Todd Stottlemyre	.05
29	Mark Whiten	.05
30	Robby Thompson	.05
31	Bobby Bonilla	.05
32	Andy Ashby	.05
33	Greg Myers	.05
34	Billy Hatcher	.05
35	Brad Holman	.05
36	Mark McLemore	.05
37	Scott Sanders	.05
38	Jim Abbott	.05
39	David Wells	.05
40	Roberto Kelly	.05
41	Jeff Conine	.05
42	Sean Berry	.05
43	Mark Grace	.05
44	Eric Young	.05
45	Rick Aguilera	.05
46	Chipper Jones	1.00
47	Mel Rojas	.05
48	Ryan Thompson	.05
49	Al Martin	.05
50	Cecil Fielder	.05
51	Pat Kelly	.05
52	Kevin Tapani	.05
53	Tim Costo	.05
54	Dave Hollins	.05
55	Kirt Manwaring	.05
56	Gregg Jefferies	.05
57	Ron Darling	.05
58	Bill Haselman	.05
59	Phil Plantier	.05
60	Frank Viola	.05
61	Todd Zeile	.05
62	Bret Barberie	.05
63	Roberto Mejia	.05
64	Chuck Knoblauch	.05
65	Jose Lind	.05
66	Brady Anderson	.05
67	Ruben Sierra	.05
68	Jose Vizcaino	.05
69	Joe Grahe	.05
70	Kevin Appier	.05
71	Wilson Alvarez	.05
72	Tom Candiotti	.05
73	John Burkett	.05
74	Anthony Young	.05
75	Scott Cooper	.05
76	Nigel Wilson	.05
77	John Valentin	.05
78	Dave McCarty	.05
79	Archi Cianfrocco	.05
80	Lou Whitaker	.05
81	Dante Bichette	.05
82	Mark Dewey	.05
83	Danny Jackson	.05
84	Harold Baines	.05
85	Todd Benzinger	.05
86	Damion Easley	.05
87	Danny Cox	.05
88	Jose Bautista	.05
89	Mike Lansing	.05
90	Phil Hiatt	.05
91	Tim Pugh	.05
92	Tino Martinez	.05
93	Raul Mondesi	.05
94	Greg Maddux	1.00
95	Al Leiter	.05
96	Benito Santiago	.05
97	Len Dykstra	.05
98	Sammy Sosa	1.25
99	Tim Bogar	.05
100	Checklist	.05
101	Deion Sanders	.10
102	Bobby Witt	.05
103	Wil Cordero	.05
104	Rich Amaral	.05
105	Mike Mussina	.50
106	Reggie Sanders	.05

107	Ozzie Guillen	.05
108	Paul O'Neill	.05
109	Tim Salmon	.05
110	Rheal Cormier	.05
111	Billy Ashley	.05
112	Jeff Kent	.05
113	Derek Bell	.05
114	Danny Darwin	.05
115	Chip Hale	.05
116	Tim Raines	.05
117	Ed Sprague	.05
118	Darrin Fletcher	.05
119	Darren Holmes	.05
120	Alan Trammell	.05
121	Don Mattingly	1.25
122	Greg Gagne	.05
123	Jose Offerman	.05
124	Joe Orsulak	.05
125	Jack McDowell	.05
126	Barry Larkin	.05
127	Ben McDonald	.05
128	Mike Bordick	.05
129	Devon White	.05
130	Mike Perez	.05
131	Jay Buhner	.05
132	Phil Leftwich	.05
133	Tommy Greene	.05
134	Charlie Hayes	.05
135	Don Slaught	.05
136	Mike Gallego	.05
137	Dave Winfield	.75
138	Steve Avery	.05
139	Derrick May	.05
140	Bryan Harvey	.05
141	Wally Joyner	.05
142	Andre Dawson	.20
143	Andy Benes	.05
144	John Franco	.05
145	Jeff King	.05
146	Joe Oliver	.05
147	Bill Gullickson	.05
148	Armando Reynoso	.05
149	Dave Fleming	.05
150	Checklist	.05
151	Todd Van Poppel	.05
152	Bernard Gilkey	.05
153	Kevin Gross	.05
154	Mike Devereaux	.05
155	Tim Wakefield	.05
156	Andres Galarraga	.05
157	Pat Meares	.05
158	Jim Leyritz	.05
159	Mike Macfarlane	.05
160	Tony Phillips	.05
161	Brent Gates	.05
162	Mark Langston	.05
163	Allen Watson	.05
164	Randy Johnson	.75
165	Doug Brocail	.05
166	Rob Dibble	.05
167	Roberto Hernandez	.05
168	Felix Jose	.05
169	Steve Cooke	.05
170	Darren Daulton	.05
171	Eric Karros	.05
172	Geronimo Pena	.05
173	Gary DiSarcina	.05
174	Marquis Grissom	.05
175	Joey Cora	.05
176	Jim Eisenreich	.05
177	Brad Pennington	.05
178	Terry Steinbach	.05
179	Pat Borders	.05
180	Steve Buechele	.05
181	Jeff Fassero	.05
182	Mike Greenwell	.05
183	Mike Henneman	.05
184	Ron Karkovice	.05
185	Pat Hentgen	.05
186	Jose Guzman	.05
187	Brett Butler	.05
188	Charlie Hough	.05
189	Terry Pendleton	.05
190	Melido Perez	.05
191	Orestes Destrade	.05
192	Mike Morgan	.05
193	Joe Carter	.05
194	Mike Blauser	.05
195	Chris Hoiles	.05
196	Ricky Gutierrez	.05
197	Mike Moore	.05
198	Carl Willis	.05
199	Aaron Sele	.05
200	Checklist	.05
201	Tim Naehring	.05
202	Scott Livingstone	.05
203	Luis Alicea	.05
204	Torey Lovullo RC	.05
205	Jim Gott	.05
206	Bob Wickman	.05
207	Greg McMichael	.05
208	Scott Brosius	.05
209	Chris Gwynn	.05
210	Steve Sax	.05
211	Dick Schofield	.05
212	Robb Nen	.05
213	Ben Rivera	.05
214	Vinny Castilla	.05
215	Jamie Moyer	.05
216	Wally Whitehurst	.05
217	Frank Castillo	.05
218	Mike Blowers	.05
219	Tim Scott	.05
220	Paul Wagner	.05
221	Jeff Bagwell	.75
222	Ricky Bones	.05
223	Sandy Alomar Jr.	.05
224	Rod Beck	.05

225	Roberto Alomar	.20
226	Jack Armstrong	.05
227	Scott Erickson	.05
228	Rene Arocha	.05
229	Eric Anthony	.05
230	Jeromy Burnitz	.05
231	Kevin Brown	.05
232	Tim Belcher	.05
233	Bret Boone	.05
234	Dennis Eckersley	.60
235	Tom Glavine	.30
236	Craig Biggio	.05
237	Pedro Astacio	.05
238	Ryan Bowen	.05
239	Brad Ausmus	.05
240	Vince Coleman	.05
241	Jason Bere	.05
242	Ellis Burks	.05
243	Wes Chamberlain	.05
244	Ken Caminiti	.05
245	Willie Banks	.05
246	Sid Fernandez	.05
247	Carlos Baerga	.05
248	Carlos Garcia	.05
249	Jose Canseco	.50
250	Alex Diaz	.05
251	Albert Belle	.05
252	Moises Alou	.05
253	Bobby Ayala	.05
254	Tony Gwynn	1.00
255	Roger Clemens	1.25
256	Eric Davis	.05
257	Wade Boggs	1.00
258	Chili Davis	.05
259	Rickey Henderson	.75
260	Andujar Cedeno	.05
261	Cris Carpenter	.05
262	Juan Guzman	.05
263	Dave Justice	.05
264	Barry Bonds	2.50
265	Pete Incaviglia	.05
266	Tony Fernandez	.05
267	Cal Eldred	.05
268	Alex Fernandez	.05
269	Kent Hrbek	.05
270	Steve Farr	.05
271	Doug Drabek	.05
272	Brian Jordan	.05
273	Xavier Hernandez	.05
274	David Cone	.05
275	Brian Hunter	.05
276	Mike Harkey	.05
277	Delino DeShields	.05
278	David Hulse	.05
279	Mickey Tettleton	.05
280	Kevin McReynolds	.05
281	Darryl Hamilton	.05
282	Ken Hill	.05
283	Wayne Kirby	.05
284	Chris Hammond	.05
285	Mo Vaughn	.05
286	Ryan Klesko	.05
287	Rick Wilkins	.05
288	Bill Swift	.05
289	Rafael Palmeiro	.65
290	Brian Harper	.05
291	Chris Turner	.05
292	Luis Gonzalez	.25
293	Kenny Rogers	.05
294	Kirby Puckett	1.00
295	Mike Stanley	.05
296	Carlos Reyes	.05
297	Charles Nagy	.05
298	Reggie Jefferson	.05
299	Bip Roberts	.05
300	Darrin Jackson	.05
301	Mike Jackson	.05
302	Dave Nilsson	.05
303	Ramon Martinez	.05
304	Bobby Jones	.05
305	Johnny Ruffin	.05
306	Brian McRae	.05
307	Bo Jackson	.10
308	Dave Stewart	.05
309	John Smoltz	.05
310	Dennis Martinez	.05
311	Dean Palmer	.05
312	David Nied	.05
313	Eddie Murray	.75
314	Darryl Kile	.05
315	Rick Sutcliffe	.05
316	Shawon Dunston	.05
317	John Jaha	.05
318	Salomon Torres	.05
319	Gary Sheffield	.45
320	Curt Schilling	.30
321	Greg Vaughn	.05
322	Jay Howell	.05
323	Todd Hundley	.05
324	Chris Sabo	.05
325	Stan Javier	.05
326	Willie Greene	.05
327	Hipolito Pichardo	.05
328	Doug Strange	.05
329	Dan Wilson	.05
330	Checklist	.05
331	Omar Vizquel	.05
332	Scott Servais	.05
333	Bob Tewksbury	.05
334	Matt Williams	.05
335	Tom Foley	.05
336	Jeff Russell	.05
337	Scott Leius	.05
338	Ivan Rodriguez	.65
339	Kevin Seitzer	.05
340	Jose Rijo	.05

341	Eduardo Perez	.05
342	Kirk Gibson	.05
343	Randy Milligan	.05
344	Edgar Martinez	.05
345	Fred McGriff	.05
346	Kurt Abbott	.05
347	John Kruk	.05
348	Mike Felder	.05
349	Dave Staton	.05
350	Kenny Lofton	.05
351	Graeme Lloyd	.05
352	David Segui	.05
353	Danny Tartabull	.05
354	Bob Welch	.05
355	Duane Ward	.05
356	Tuffy Rhodes	.05
357	Lee Smith	.05
358	Chris James	.05
359	Walt Weiss	.05
360	Pedro Munoz	.05
361	Paul Sorrento	.05
362	Todd Worrell	.05
363	Bob Hamelin	.05
364	Julio Franco	.05
365	Roberto Petagine	.05
366	Willie McGee	.05
367	Pedro Martinez	.75
368	Ken Griffey Jr.	1.50
369	B.J. Surhoff	.05
370	Kevin Mitchell	.05
371	John Doherty	.05
372	Manuel Lee	.05
373	Terry Mulholland	.05
374	Zane Smith	.05
375	Otis Nixon	.05
376	Jody Reed	.05
377	Doug Jones	.05
378	John Olerud	.05
379	Greg Swindell	.05
380	Checklist	.05
381	Royce Clayton	.05
382	Jim Thome	.65
383	Steve Finley	.05
384	Ray Lankford	.05
385	Henry Rodriguez	.05
386	Dave Magadan	.05
387	Gary Redus	.05
388	Orlando Merced	.05
389	Tom Gordon	.05
390	Luis Polonia	.05
391	Mark McGwire	2.00
392	Mark Lemke	.05
393	Doug Henry	.05
394	Chuck Finley	.05
395	Paul Molitor	.75
396	Randy Myers	.05
397	Larry Walker	.05
398	Pete Harnisch	.05
399	Darren Lewis	.05
400	Frank Thomas	.75
401	Jack Morris	.05
402	Greg Hibbard	.05
403	Jeffrey Hammonds	.05
404	Will Clark	.10
405	Travis Fryman	.05
406	Scott Sanderson	.05
407	Gene Harris	.05
408	Chuck Carr	.05
409	Ozzie Smith	1.00
410	Kent Mercker	.05
411	Andy Van Slyke	.05
412	Jimmy Key	.05
413	Pat Mahomes	.05
414	John Wetteland	.05
415	Todd Jones	.05
416	Greg Harris	.05
417	Kevin Stocker	.05
418	Juan Gonzalez	.65
419	Pete Smith	.05
420	Pat Listach	.05
421	Trevor Hoffman	.05
422	Scott Fletcher	.05
423	Mark Lewis	.05
424	Mickey Morandini	.05
425	Ryne Sandberg	1.00
426	Erik Hanson	.05
427	Gary Gaetti	.05
428	Harold Reynolds	.05
429	Mark Portugal	.05
430	David Valle	.05
431	Mitch Williams	.05
432	Howard Johnson	.05
433	Hal Morris	.05
434	Tom Henke	.05
435	Shane Mack	.05
436	Mike Piazza	1.50
437	Bret Saberhagen	.05
438	Jose Mesa	.05
439	Jaime Navarro	.05
440	Checklist	.05

Clean-Up Crew

		NM/M
Complete Set (12):		8.00
Common Player:		1.00
1	Larry Walker	1.00
2	Andres Galarraga	1.00
3	Dave Hollins	1.00
4	Bobby Bonilla	1.00
5	Cecil Fielder	1.00
6	Danny Tartabull	1.00
7	Juan Gonzalez	2.00
8	Joe Carter	1.00
9	Fred McGriff	1.00

10	Matt Williams	1.00
11	Albert Belle	1.00
12	Harold Baines	1.00

5th Anniversary

FRANK THOMAS 1B

		NM/M
300	Frank Thomas	2.50
400	Frank Thomas	5.00

1994 Leaf Frank Thomas Poster

	NM/M
Frank Thomas	15.00

Gamers

		NM/M
Complete Set (12):		30.00
Common Player:		1.00
1	Ken Griffey Jr.	6.00
2	Len Dykstra	1.00
3	Juan Gonzalez	3.00
4	Don Mattingly	6.00
5	Dave Justice	1.00
6	Mark Grace	1.00

7	Frank Thomas	4.00
8	Barry Bonds	7.50
9	Kirby Puckett	4.50
10	Will Clark	1.00
11	John Kruk	1.00
12	Mike Piazza	6.00

Gold Rookies

		NM/M
Complete Set (20):		6.00
Common Player:		.25
1	Javier Lopez	.25
2	Rondell White	.25
3	Butch Huskey	.25
4	Midre Cummings	.25
5	Scott Ruffcorn	.25
6	Manny Ramirez	3.50
7	Danny Bautista	.25
8	Russ Davis	.25
9	Steve Karsay	.25
10	Carlos Delgado	2.50
11	Bob Hamelin	.25
12	Marcus Moore	.25
13	Miguel Jimenez	.25
14	Matt Walbeck	.25
15	James Mouton	.25
16	Rich Becker	.25
17	Brian Anderson	.25
18	Cliff Floyd	.25
19	Steve Trachsel	.25
20	Hector Carrasco	.25

Gold Stars

PAUL MOLITOR
TORONTO BLUE JAYS

		NM/M
Complete Set (15):		60.00
Common Player:		1.00
1	Roberto Alomar	4.00
2	Barry Bonds	12.00
3	Dave Justice	3.00
4	Ken Griffey Jr.	9.00
5	Len Dykstra	3.00
6	Don Mattingly	7.50
7	Andres Galarraga	3.00
8	Greg Maddux	6.00
9	Carlos Baerga	3.00
10	Paul Molitor	5.00
11	Frank Thomas	5.00
12	John Olerud	3.00
13	Juan Gonzalez	4.00
14	Fred McGriff	3.00
15	Jack McDowell	3.00

MVP Contenders

MVP

	NM/M
Complete Set, Silver (30):	20.00
Complete Set, Gold (30):	40.00

Common Player, Silver:		.25
Common Player, Gold:		.50
AMERICAN LEAGUE		2.00
1a	Albert Belle/Silver	.25
1b	Albert Belle/Gold	.50
2a	Jose Canseco/Silver	1.25
2b	Jose Canseco/Gold	2.00
3a	Joe Carter/Silver	.25
3b	Joe Carter/Gold	.50
4a	Will Clark/Silver	.35
4b	Will Clark/Gold	.60
5a	Cecil Fielder/Silver	.25
5b	Cecil Fielder/Gold	.50
6a	Juan Gonzalez/Silver	1.50
6b	Juan Gonzalez/Gold	2.50
7a	Ken Griffey Jr./Silver	4.00
7b	Ken Griffey Jr./Gold	7.50
8a	Paul Molitor/Silver	2.00
8b	Paul Molitor/Gold	4.00
9a	Rafael Palmeiro/Silver	1.50
9b	Rafael Palmeiro/Gold	2.50
10a	Kirby Puckett/Silver	2.50
10b	Kirby Puckett/Gold	5.00
11a	Cal Ripken, Jr./Silver	6.00
11b	Cal Ripken, Jr./Gold	12.50
12a	Frank Thomas/Silver	2.00
12b	Frank Thomas/Gold	4.00
13a	Mo Vaughn/Silver	.25
13b	Mo Vaughn/Gold	.50
14a	Carlos Baerga/Silver	.25
14b	Carlos Baerga/Gold	.50
15	AL Bonus Card/Silver	.60
NATIONAL LEAGUE		
1a	Gary Sheffield/Silver	.35
1b	Gary Sheffield/Gold	.65
2a	Jeff Bagwell/Silver	2.00
2b	Jeff Bagwell/Gold	4.00
3a	Dante Bichette/Silver	.25
3b	Dante Bichette/Gold	.50
4a	Barry Bonds/Silver	6.00
4b	Barry Bonds/Gold	12.50
5a	Darren Daulton/Silver	.25
5b	Darren Daulton/Gold	.50
6a	Andres Galarraga/Silver	.25
6b	Andres Galarraga/Gold	.50
7a	Gregg Jefferies/Silver	.25
7b	Gregg Jefferies/Gold	.50
8a	Dave Justice/Silver	.25
8b	Dave Justice/Gold	.50
9a	Ray Lankford/Silver	.25
9b	Ray Lankford/Gold	.50
10a	Fred McGriff/Silver	.25
10b	Fred McGriff/Gold	.50
11a	Barry Larkin/Silver	.25
11b	Barry Larkin/Gold	.50
12a	Mike Piazza/Silver	4.00
12b	Mike Piazza/Gold	7.50
13a	Deion Sanders/Silver	.25
13b	Deion Sanders/Gold	.50
14a	Matt Williams/Silver	.25
14b	Matt Williams/Gold	.50
15	NL Bonus Card/Silver	.25

Power Brokers

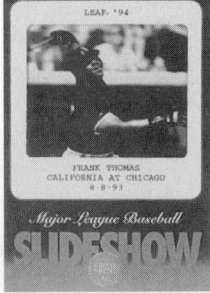

BROKERS
Juan Gonzalez
Rangers

		NM/M
Complete Set (10):		8.00
Common Player:		.40
1	Frank Thomas	.75
2	Dave Justice	.40
3	Barry Bonds	3.00
4	Juan Gonzalez	.65
5	Ken Griffey Jr.	2.00
6	Mike Piazza	2.00
7	Cecil Fielder	.40
8	Fred McGriff	.40
9	Joe Carter	.40
10	Albert Belle	.40

Slide Show

LEAF '94

FRANK THOMAS
CALIFORNIA AT CHICAGO
8-9-93

Major League Baseball
SLIDESHOW

		NM/M
Complete Set (10):		9.00
Common Player:		.25
1	Frank Thomas	1.00
2	Mike Piazza	2.00
3	Darren Daulton	.25
4	Ryne Sandberg	1.50
5	Roberto Alomar	.50
6	Barry Bonds	3.00
7	Juan Gonzalez	.75
8	Tim Salmon	.25
9	Ken Griffey Jr.	2.00
10	Dave Justice	.25

Statistical Standouts

		NM/M
Complete Set (10):		10.00
Common Player:		.40
1	Frank Thomas	.75
2	Barry Bonds	2.50
3	Juan Gonzalez	.65
4	Mike Piazza	2.00
5	Greg Maddux	1.00
6	Ken Griffey Jr.	2.00
7	Joe Carter	.40
8	Dave Winfield	.75
9	Tony Gwynn	1.00
10	Cal Ripken, Jr.	2.50

1994 Leaf/Limited

		NM/M
Complete Set (160):		35.00
Common Player:		.25
Pack (5):		2.50
Wax Box (20):		40.00
1	Jeffrey Hammonds	.25
2	Ben McDonald	.25
3	Mike Mussina	.75
4	Rafael Palmeiro	1.50
5	Cal Ripken, Jr.	6.00
6	Lee Smith	.25
7	Roger Clemens	3.00
8	Scott Cooper	.25
9	Andre Dawson	.40
10	Mike Greenwell	.25
11	Aaron Sele	.25
12	Mo Vaughn	.25
13	Brian Anderson RC	.25
14	Chad Curtis	.25
15	Chili Davis	.25
16	Gary DiSarcina	.25
17	Mark Langston	.25
18	Tim Salmon	.25
19	Wilson Alvarez	.25
20	Jason Bere	.25
21	Julio Franco	.25
22	Jack McDowell	.25
23	Tim Raines	.25
24	Frank Thomas	2.00
25	Robin Ventura	.25
26	Carlos Baerga	.25
27	Albert Belle	.25
28	Kenny Lofton	.25
29	Eddie Murray	2.00
30	Manny Ramirez	2.00
31	Cecil Fielder	.25
32	Travis Fryman	.25
33	Mickey Tettleton	.25
34	Alan Trammell	.25
35	Lou Whitaker	.25
36	David Cone	.25
37	Gary Gaetti	.25
38	Greg Gagne	.25
39	Bob Hamelin	.25
40	Wally Joyner	.25
41	Brian McRae	.25
42	Ricky Bones	.25
43	Brian Harper	.25
44	John Jaha	.25
45	Pat Listach	.25
46	Dave Nilsson	.25
47	Greg Vaughn	.25
48	Kent Hrbek	.25
49	Chuck Knoblauch	.25
50	Shane Mack	.25
51	Kirby Puckett	2.50
52	Dave Winfield	2.00
53	Jim Abbott	.25
54	Wade Boggs	2.50
55	Jimmy Key	.25
56	Don Mattingly	3.00
57	Paul O'Neill	.25
58	Danny Tartabull	.25
59	Dennis Eckersley	1.50
60	Rickey Henderson	2.00
61	Mark McGwire	5.00
62	Troy Neel	.25
63	Ruben Sierra	.25
64	Eric Anthony	.25
65	Jay Buhner	.25
66	Ken Griffey Jr.	4.00
67	Randy Johnson	2.00
68	Edgar Martinez	.25
69	Tino Martinez	.25
70	Jose Canseco	.75
71	Will Clark	.35
72	Juan Gonzalez	1.50
73	Dean Palmer	.25
74	Ivan Rodriguez	1.50
75	Roberto Alomar	.40
76	Joe Carter	.25
77	Carlos Delgado	1.00
78	Paul Molitor	2.00
79	John Olerud	.25
80	Devon White	.25
81	Steve Avery	.25
82	Tom Glavine	.50
83	Dave Justice	.25
84	Roberto Kelly	.25
85	Ryan Klesko	.25
86	Javier Lopez	.25
87	Greg Maddux	2.50
88	Fred McGriff	.25
89	Shawon Dunston	.25
90	Mark Grace	.25
91	Derrick May	.25
92	Sammy Sosa	3.00
93	Rick Wilkins	.25
94	Bret Boone	.25
95	Barry Larkin	.25
96	Kevin Mitchell	.25
97	Hal Morris	.25
98	Deion Sanders	.25
99	Reggie Sanders	.25
100	Dante Bichette	.25
101	Ellis Burks	.25
102	Andres Galarraga	.25
103	Joe Girardi	.25
104	Charlie Hayes	.25
105	Chuck Carr	.25
106	Jeff Conine	.25
107	Bryan Harvey	.25
108	Benito Santiago	.25
109	Gary Sheffield	.60
110	Jeff Bagwell	2.00
111	Craig Biggio	.25
112	Ken Caminiti	.25
113	Andujar Cedeno	.25
114	Doug Drabek	.25
115	Luis Gonzalez	.40
116	Brett Butler	.25
117	Delino DeShields	.25
118	Eric Karros	.25
119	Raul Mondesi	.25
120	Mike Piazza	4.00
121	Henry Rodriguez	.25
122	Tim Wallach	.25
123	Moises Alou	.25
124	Cliff Floyd	.25
125	Marquis Grissom	.25
126	Ken Hill	.25
127	Larry Walker	.25
128	John Wetteland	.25
129	Bobby Bonilla	.25
130	John Franco	.25
131	Jeff Kent	.25
132	Bret Saberhagen	.25
133	Ryan Thompson	.25
134	Darren Daulton	.25
135	Mariano Duncan	.25
136	Len Dykstra	.25
137	Danny Jackson	.25
138	John Kruk	.25
139	Jay Bell	.25
140	Jeff King	.25
141	Al Martin	.25
142	Orlando Merced	.25
143	Andy Van Slyke	.25
144	Bernard Gilkey	.25
145	Gregg Jefferies	.25
146	Ray Lankford	.25
147	Ozzie Smith	2.50
148	Mark Whiten	.25
149	Todd Zeile	.25
150	Derek Bell	.25
151	Andy Benes	.25
152	Tony Gwynn	2.50
153	Phil Plantier	.25
154	Bip Roberts	.25
155	Rod Beck	.25
156	Barry Bonds	6.00
157	John Burkett	.25
158	Royce Clayton	.25
159	Bill Swift	.25
160	Matt Williams	.25

Gold

		NM/M
Complete Set (18):		20.00
Common Player:		.25
1	Frank Thomas	1.50
2	Gregg Jefferies	.25
3	Roberto Alomar	.50
4	Mariano Duncan	.25
5	Wade Boggs	2.00
6	Matt Williams	.25
7	Cal Ripken, Jr.	4.00
8	Ozzie Smith	2.00
9	Kirby Puckett	2.00
10	Barry Bonds	4.00
11	Ken Griffey Jr.	3.00
12	Tony Gwynn	2.00
13	Joe Carter	2.00
14	Dave Justice	.25
15	Ivan Rodriguez	1.25
16	Mike Piazza	3.00
17	Jimmy Key	.25
18	Greg Maddux	2.00

Rookies

		NM/M
Complete Set (80):		17.50
Common Player:		.25
Pack (5):		3.00
Box (20):		60.00
1	Charles Johnson	.25
2	Rico Brogna	.25
3	Melvin Nieves	.25
4	Rich Becker	.25
5	Russ Davis	.25
6	Matt Mieske	.25
7	Paul Shuey	.25
8	Hector Carrasco	.25
9	J.R. Phillips	.25
10	Scott Ruffcorn	.25
11	Kurt Abbott	.25
12	Danny Bautista	.25
13	Rick White	.25
14	Steve Dunn	.25
15	Joe Ausanio	.25
16	Salomon Torres	.25
17	Rick Bottalico	.25
18	Johnny Ruffin	.25
19	Kevin Foster	.25
20	W. Van Landingham RC	.25
21	Troy O'Leary	.25
22	Mark Acre	.25
23	Norberto Martin	.25
24	Jason Jacome RC	.25
25	Steve Trachsel	.25
26	Denny Hocking	.25
27	Mike Lieberthal	.25
28	Gerald Williams	.25
29	John Mabry	.25
30	Greg Blosser	.25
31	Carl Everett	.25
32	Steve Karsay	.25
33	Jose Valentin	.25
34	Jon Lieber	.25
35	Chris Gomez	.25
36	Jesus Tavarez	.25
37	Tony Longmire	.25
38	Luis Lopez	.25
39	Matt Walbeck	.25
40	Rikkert Faneyte	.25
41	Shane Reynolds	.25
42	Joey Hamilton	.25
43	Ismael Valdes	.25
44	Danny Miceli	.25
45	Darren Bragg	.25
46	Alex Gonzalez	.25
47	Rick Helling	.25
48	Jose Oliva	.25
49	Jim Edmonds	4.00
50	Miguel Jimenez	.25
51	Tony Eusebio	.25
52	Shawn Green	4.00
53	Billy Ashley	.25
54	Rondell White	.25
55	Cory Bailey	.25
56	Tim Davis	.25
57	John Hudek	.25
58	Darren Hall	.25
59	Darren Dreifort	.25
60	Mike Kelly	.25
61	Marcus Moore	.25
62	Garret Anderson	.25
63	Brian Hunter	.25
64	Mark Smith	.25
65	Garey Ingram	.25
66	Rusty Greer RC	.25
67	Marc Newfield	.25
68	Gar Finnvold	.25
69	Paul Spoljaric	.25
70	Ray McDavid	.25
71	Orlando Miller	.25
72	Jorge Fabregas	.25
73	Ray Holbert	.25
74	Armando Benitez	.25
75	Ernie Young	.25
76	James Mouton	.25
77	Robert Perez RC	.25
78	Chan Ho Park RC	1.00
79	Roger Salkeld	.25
80	Tony Tarasco	.25

Rookies Rookie Phenoms

		NM/M
Complete Set (10):		260.00
Common Player:		1.00
Production 5,000 Sets		
1	Raul Mondesi	1.00
2	Bob Hamelin	1.00
3	Midre Cummings	1.00
4	Carlos Delgado	8.00
5	Cliff Floyd	1.00
6	Jeffrey Hammonds	1.00
7	Ryan Klesko	1.00
8	Javier Lopez	1.00
9	Manny Ramirez	10.00
10	Alex Rodriguez	250.00

1995 Leaf

		NM/M
Complete Set (400):		12.50
Common Player:		.05
Series 1 or 2 Pack (12):		.75
Series 1 or 2 Wax Box (36):		15.00
1	Frank Thomas	.75
2	Carlos Garcia	.05
3	Todd Hundley	.05
4	Damion Easley	.05
5	Roberto Mejia	.05
6	John Mabry	.05
7	Aaron Sele	.05
8	Kenny Lofton	.05
9	John Doherty	.05
10	Joe Carter	.05
11	Mike Lansing	.05
12	John Valentin	.05

13	Ismael Valdes	.05
14	Dave McCarty	.05
15	Melvin Nieves	.05
16	Bobby Jones	.05
17	Trevor Hoffman	.05
18	John Smoltz	.05
19	Leo Gomez	.05
20	Roger Pavlik	.05
21	Dean Palmer	.05
22	Rickey Henderson	.75
23	Eddie Taubensee	.05
24	Damon Buford	.05
25	Mark Wohlers	.05
26	Jim Edmonds	.05
27	Wilson Alvarez	.05
28	Matt Williams	.05
29	Jeff Montgomery	.05
30	Shawon Dunston	.05
31	Tom Pagnozzi	.05
32	Jose Lind	.05
33	Royce Clayton	.05
34	Cal Eldred	.05
35	Chris Gomez	.05
36	Henry Rodriguez	.05
37	Dave Fleming	.05
38	Jon Lieber	.05
39	Scott Servais	.05
40	Wade Boggs	1.00
41	John Olerud	.05
42	Eddie Williams	.05
43	Paul Sorrento	.05
44	Ron Karkovice	.05
45	Kevin Foster	.05
46	Miguel Jimenez	.05
47	Reggie Sanders	.05
48	Rondell White	.05
49	Scott Leius	.05
50	Jose Valentin	.05
51	William Van Landingham	.05
52	Denny Hocking	.05
53	Jeff Fassero	.05
54	Chris Hoiles	.05
55	Walt Weiss	.05
56	Geronimo Berroa	.05
57	Rich Rowland	.05
58	Dave Weathers	.05
59	Sterling Hitchcock	.05
60	Raul Mondesi	.05
61	Rusty Greer	.05
62	Dave Justice	.05
63	Cecil Fielder	.05
64	Brian Jordan	.05
65	Mike Lieberthal	.05
66	Rick Aguilera	.05
67	Chuck Finley	.05
68	Andy Ashby	.05
69	Alex Fernandez	.05
70	Ed Sprague	.05
71	Steve Buechele	.05
72	Willie Greene	.05
73	Dave Nilsson	.05
74	Bret Saberhagen	.05
75	Jimmy Key	.05
76	Darren Lewis	.05
77	Steve Cooke	.05
78	Kirk Gibson	.05
79	Ray Lankford	.05
80	Paul O'Neill	.05
81	Mike Bordick	.05
82	Wes Chamberlain	.05
83	Rico Brogna	.05
84	Kevin Appier	.05
85	Juan Guzman	.05
86	Kevin Seitzer	.05
87	Mickey Morandini	.05
88	Pedro Martinez	.75
89	Matt Mieske	.05
90	Tino Martinez	.05
91	Paul Shuey	.05
92	Bip Roberts	.05
93	Chili Davis	.05
94	Deion Sanders	.05
95	Darrell Whitmore	.05
96	Joe Orsulak	.05
97	Bret Boone	.05
98	Kent Mercker	.05
99	Scott Livingstone	.05
100	Brady Anderson	.05
101	James Mouton	.05
102	Jose Rijo	.05
103	Bobby Munoz	.05
104	Ramon Martinez	.05
105	Bernie Williams	.10
106	Troy Neel	.05
107	Ivan Rodriguez	.65
108	Salomon Torres	.05
109	Johnny Ruffin	.05
110	Darryl Kile	.05
111	Bobby Ayala	.05
112	Ron Darling	.05
113	Jose Lima	.05
114	Joey Hamilton	.05
115	Greg Maddux	1.00
116	Greg Colbrunn	.05
117	Ozzie Guillen	.05
118	Brian Anderson	.05
119	Jeff Bagwell	.75
120	Pat Listach	.05
121	Sandy Alomar	.05
122	Jose Vizcaino	.05
123	Rick Helling	.05
124	Allen Watson	.05
125	Pedro Munoz	.05
126	Craig Biggio	.05
127	Kevin Stocker	.05
128	Wil Cordero	.05
129	Rafael Palmeiro	.65
130	Gar Finnvold	.05
131	Darren Hall	.05
132	Heath Slocumb	.05
133	Darrin Fletcher	.05
134	Cal Ripken Jr.	2.50
135	Dante Bichette	.05
136	Don Slaught	.05
137	Pedro Astacio	.05
138	Ryan Thompson	.05
139	Greg Gohr	.05
140	Javier Lopez	.05
141	Lenny Dykstra	.05
142	Pat Rapp	.05
143	Mark Kiefer	.05
144	Greg Gagne	.05
145	Eduardo Perez	.05
146	Felix Fermin	.05
147	Jeff Frye	.05
148	Terry Steinbach	.05
149	Jim Eisenreich	.05
150	Brad Ausmus	.05
151	Randy Myers	.05
152	Rick White	.05
153	Mark Portugal	.05
154	Delino DeShields	.05
155	Scott Cooper	.05
156	Pat Hentgen	.05
157	Mark Gubicza	.05
158	Carlos Baerga	.05
159	Joe Girardi	.05
160	Rey Sanchez	.05
161	Todd Jones	.05
162	Luis Polonia	.05
163	Steve Trachsel	.05
164	Roberto Hernandez	.05
165	John Patterson	.05
166	Rene Arocha	.05
167	Will Clark	.10
168	Jim Leyritz	.05
169	Todd Van Poppel	.05
170	Robb Nen	.05
171	Midre Cummings	.05
172	Jay Buhner	.05
173	Kevin Tapani	.05
174	Mark Lemke	.05
175	Marcus Moore	.05
176	Wayne Kirby	.05
177	Rich Amaral	.05
178	Lou Whitaker	.05
179	Jay Bell	.05
180	Rick Wilkins	.05
181	Paul Molitor	.75
182	Gary Sheffield	.35
183	Kirby Puckett	1.00
184	Cliff Floyd	.05
185	Darren Oliver	.05
186	Tim Naehring	.05
187	John Hudek	.05
188	Eric Young	.05
189	Roger Salkeld	.05
190	Kirt Manwaring	.05
191	Kurt Abbott	.05
192	David Nied	.05
193	Todd Zeile	.05
194	Wally Joyner	.05
195	Dennis Martinez	.05
196	Billy Ashley	.05
197	Ben McDonald	.05
198	Bob Hamelin	.05
199	Chris Turner	.05
200	Lance Johnson	.05
201	Willie Banks	.05
202	Juan Gonzalez	.50
203	Scott Sanders	.05
204	Scott Brosius	.05
205	Curt Schilling	.25
206	Alex Gonzalez	.05
207	Travis Fryman	.05
208	Tim Raines	.05
209	Steve Avery	.05
210	Hal Morris	.05
211	Ken Griffey Jr.	1.50
212	Ozzie Smith	1.00
213	Chuck Carr	.05
214	Ryan Klesko	.05
215	Robin Ventura	.05
216	Luis Gonzalez	.20
217	Ken Ryan	.05
218	Mike Piazza	1.50
219	Matt Walbeck	.05
220	Jeff Kent	.05
221	Orlando Miller	.05
222	Kenny Rogers	.05
223	J.T. Snow	.05
224	Alan Trammell	.05
225	John Franco	.05
226	Gerald Williams	.05
227	Andy Benes	.05
228	Dan Wilson	.05
229	Dave Hollins	.05
230	Vinny Castilla	.05
231	Devon White	.05
232	Fred McGriff	.05
233	Quilvio Veras	.05
234	Tom Candiotti	.05
235	Jason Bere	.05
236	Mark Langston	.05
237	Mel Rojas	.05
238	Chuck Knoblauch	.05
239	Bernard Gilkey	.05
240	Mark McGwire	2.00
241	Kirk Rueter	.05
242	Pat Kelly	.05
243	Ruben Sierra	.05
244	Randy Johnson	.75
245	Shane Reynolds	.05
246	Danny Tartabull	.05
247	Darryl Hamilton	.05
248	Danny Bautista	.05
249	Tom Gordon	.05
250	Tom Glavine	.25
251	Orlando Merced	.05
252	Eric Karros	.05
253	Benji Gil	.05
254	Sean Bergman	.05
255	Roger Clemens	1.25
256	Roberto Alomar	.20
257	Benito Santiago	.05
258	Robby Thompson	.05
259	Marvin Freeman	.05
260	Jose Offerman	.05
261	Greg Vaughn	.05
262	David Segui	.05
263	Geronimo Pena	.05
264	Tim Salmon	.05
265	Eddie Murray	.75
266	Mariano Duncan	.05
267	Hideo Nomo **RC**	2.50
268	Derek Bell	.05
269	Mo Vaughn	.05
270	Jeff King	.05
271	Edgar Martinez	.05
272	Sammy Sosa	1.25
273	Scott Ruffcorn	.05
274	Darren Daulton	.05
275	John Jaha	.05
276	Andres Galarraga	.05
277	Mark Grace	.05
278	Mike Moore	.05
279	Barry Bonds	2.50
280	Manny Ramirez	.75
281	Ellis Burks	.05
282	Greg Swindell	.05
283	Barry Larkin	.05
284	Albert Belle	.05
285	Shawn Green	.35
286	John Roper	.05
287	Scott Erickson	.05
288	Moises Alou	.05
289	Mike Blowers	.05
290	Brent Gates	.05
291	Sean Berry	.05
292	Mike Stanley	.05
293	Jeff Conine	.05
294	Tim Wallach	.05
295	Bobby Bonilla	.05
296	Bruce Ruffin	.05
297	Chad Curtis	.05
298	Mike Greenwell	.05
299	Tony Gwynn	1.00
300	Russ Davis	.05
301	Danny Jackson	.05
302	Pete Harnisch	.05
303	Don Mattingly	1.25
304	Rheal Cormier	.05
305	Larry Walker	.05
306	Hector Carrasco	.05
307	Jason Jacome	.05
308	Phil Plantier	.05
309	Harold Baines	.05
310	Mitch Williams	.05
311	Charles Nagy	.05
312	Ken Caminiti	.05
313	Alex Rodriguez	2.00
314	Chris Sabo	.05
315	Gary Gaetti	.05
316	Andre Dawson	.25
317	Mark Clark	.05
318	Vince Coleman	.05
319	Brad Clontz	.05
320	Steve Finley	.05
321	Doug Drabek	.05
322	Mark McLemore	.05
323	Stan Javier	.05
324	Ron Gant	.05
325	Charlie Hayes	.05
326	Carlos Delgado	.50
327	Ricky Bottalico	.05
328	Rod Beck	.05
329	Mark Acre	.05
330	Chris Bosio	.05
331	Tony Phillips	.05
332	Garret Anderson	.05
333	Pat Meares	.05
334	Todd Worrell	.05
335	Marquis Grissom	.05
336	Brent Mayne	.05
337	Lee Tinsley	.05
338	Terry Pendleton	.05
339	David Cone	.05
340	Tony Fernandez	.05
341	Jim Bullinger	.05
342	Armando Benitez	.05
343	John Smiley	.05
344	Dan Miceli	.05
345	Charles Johnson	.05
346	Lee Smith	.05
347	Brian McRae	.05
348	Jim Thome	.65
349	Jose Oliva	.05
350	Terry Mulholland	.05
351	Tom Henke	.05
352	Dennis Eckersley	.65
353	Sid Fernandez	.05
354	Paul Wagner	.05
355	John Dettmer	.05
356	John Wetteland	.05
357	John Burkett	.05
358	Marty Cordova	.05
359	Norm Charlton	.05
360	Mike Devereaux	.05
361	Alex Cole	.05
362	Brett Butler	.05
363	Mickey Tettleton	.05
364	Al Martin	.05
365	Tony Tarasco	.05
366	Pat Mahomes	.05
367	Gary DiSarcina	.05
368	Bill Swift	.05
369	Chipper Jones	1.00
370	Orel Hershiser	.05
371	Kevin Gross	.05
372	Dave Winfield	.75
373	Andujar Cedeno	.05
374	Jim Abbott	.05
375	Glenallen Hill	.05
376	Otis Nixon	.05
377	Roberto Kelly	.05
378	Chris Hammond	.05
379	Mike Macfarlane	.05
380	J.R. Phillips	.05
381	Luis Alicea	.05
382	Bret Barberie	.05
383	Tom Goodwin	.05
384	Mark Whiten	.05
385	Jeffrey Hammonds	.05
386	Omar Vizquel	.05
387	Mike Mussina	.35
388	Rickey Bones	.05
389	Steve Ontiveros	.05
390	Jeff Blauser	.05
391	Jose Canseco	.35
392	Bob Tewksbury	.05
393	Jacob Brumfield	.05
394	Doug Jones	.05
395	Ken Hill	.05
396	Pat Borders	.05
397	Carl Everett	.05
398	Gregg Jefferies	.05
399	Jack McDowell	.05
400	Denny Neagle	.05

Cornerstones

		NM/M
Complete Set (6):		3.50
Common Player:		.40
1	Frank Thomas, Robin Ventura	.75
2	Cecil Fielder, Travis Fryman	.40
3	Don Mattingly, Wade Boggs	2.00
4	Jeff Bagwell, Ken Caminiti	.75
5	Will Clark, Dean Palmer	.40
6	J.R. Phillips, Matt Williams	.40

Frank Thomas

	NM/M
Complete Set (6):	7.50
Common Card:	1.50
1 The Rookie	1.50
2 Sophomore Stardom	1.50
3 Super Star	1.50
4 AL MVP	1.50
5 Back-To-Back	1.50
6 The Big Hurt	1.50

Gold Rookies

	NM/M
Complete Set (16):	3.00
Common Player:	.10
1 Alex Rodriguez	2.50
2 Garret Anderson	.10
3 Shawn Green	.50
4 Armando Benitez	.10
5 Darren Dreifort	.10
6 Orlando Miller	.10
7 Jose Oliva	.10
8 Ricky Bottalico	.10
9 Charles Johnson	.10
10 Brian Hunter	.10
11 Ray McDavid	.10
12 Chan Ho Park	.10
13 Mike Kelly	.10
14 Cory Bailey	.10
15 Alex Gonzalez	.10
16 Andrew Lorraine	.10

Gold Stars

	NM/M
Complete Set (14):	35.00
Common Player:	1.00
1 Jeff Bagwell	2.50
2 Albert Belle	1.00
3 Tony Gwynn	3.50
4 Ken Griffey Jr.	4.50
5 Barry Bonds	6.00
6 Don Mattingly	4.00
7 Raul Mondesi	1.00
8 Joe Carter	1.00
9 Greg Maddux	3.50
10 Frank Thomas	2.50
11 Mike Piazza	4.50
12 Jose Canseco	1.50
13 Kirby Puckett	3.50
14 Matt Williams	1.00

Great Gloves

	NM/M
Complete Set (16):	3.00
Common Player:	.15
1 Jeff Bagwell	.35
2 Roberto Alomar	.20
3 Barry Bonds	1.00
4 Wade Boggs	.45
5 Andres Galarraga	.15
6 Ken Griffey Jr.	.60
7 Marquis Grissom	.15
8 Kenny Lofton	.15
9 Barry Larkin	.15
10 Don Mattingly	.50
11 Greg Maddux	.45
12 Kirby Puckett	.45

13 Ozzie Smith	.45
14 Cal Ripken Jr.	1.00
15 Matt Williams	.15
16 Ivan Rodriguez	.30

Heading For The Hall

	NM/M
Complete Set (8):	50.00
Common Player:	4.50
1 Frank Thomas	4.50
2 Ken Griffey Jr.	9.00
3 Jeff Bagwell	4.50
4 Barry Bonds	15.00
5 Kirby Puckett	6.00
6 Cal Ripken Jr.	15.00
7 Tony Gwynn	6.00
8 Paul Molitor	4.50

Opening Day

	NM/M
Complete Set (8):	6.00
Common Player:	.25
1 Frank Thomas	.50
2 Jeff Bagwell	.50
3 Barry Bonds	2.00
5 Ken Griffey Jr.	1.00
5 Mike Piazza	1.00
6 Cal Ripken Jr.	2.00
7 Jose Canseco	.35
8 Larry Walker	.25

Slideshow

	NM/M
Complete Set (16):	35.00
Complete Series 1 (1a-8a):	20.00
Complete Series 2 (1b-8b):	20.00
Same CL and prices for both series.	
Common Player:	1.50
1a Raul Mondesi	1.50
1b Raul Mondesi	1.50
2a Frank Thomas	3.00
2b Frank Thomas	3.00
3a Fred McGriff	1.50
3b Fred McGriff	1.50
4a Cal Ripken Jr.	6.00
4b Cal Ripken Jr.	6.00
5a Jeff Bagwell	3.00
5b Jeff Bagwell	3.00
6a Will Clark	1.50
6b Will Clark	1.50
7a Matt Williams	1.50
7b Matt Williams	1.50
8a Ken Griffey Jr.	4.50
8b Ken Griffey Jr.	4.50

1995 Leaf Special Edition Jumbos

	NM/M
Complete Set (2):	7.00
1 Frank Thomas	3.00
2 Barry Bonds	5.00

Statistical Standouts

	NM/M
Complete Set (9):	90.00
Common Player:	3.00
Promos: 25-50 Percent	
1 Joe Carter	3.00
2 Ken Griffey Jr.	25.00
3 Don Mattingly	15.00
4 Fred McGriff	3.00
5 Paul Molitor	8.00
6 Kirby Puckett	12.00
7 Cal Ripken Jr.	30.00
8 Frank Thomas	8.00
9 Matt Williams	3.00

300 Club

	NM/M
Complete Set (18):	12.50
Common Player:	.25
1 Frank Thomas	1.00
2 Paul Molitor	1.00
3 Mike Piazza	3.00
4 Moises Alou	.25
5 Mike Greenwell	.25
6 Will Clark	.25
7 Hal Morris	.25
8 Edgar Martinez	.25
9 Carlos Baerga	.25
10 Ken Griffey Jr.	3.00
11 Wade Boggs	1.50
12 Jeff Bagwell	1.00
13 Tony Gwynn	1.50
14 John Kruk	.25
15 Don Mattingly	2.00

16 Mark Grace	.25
17 Kirby Puckett	1.50
18 Kenny Lofton	.25

1995 Leaf/Limited

	NM/M
Complete Set (192):	20.00
Common Player:	.10
Series 1 or 2 Pack (5):	2.00
Series 1 or 2 Wax Box (20):	30.00
1 Frank Thomas	.75
2 Geronimo Berroa	.10
3 Tony Phillips	.10
4 Roberto Alomar	.25
5 Steve Avery	.10
6 Darryl Hamilton	.10
7 Scott Cooper	.10
8 Mark Grace	.10
9 Billy Ashley	.10
10 Wil Cordero	.10
11 Barry Bonds	5.00
12 Kenny Lofton	.10
13 Jay Buhner	.10
14 Alex Rodriguez	3.00
15 Bobby Bonilla	.10
16 Brady Anderson	.10
17 Ken Caminiti	.10
18 Charlie Hayes	.10
19 Jay Bell	.10
20 Will Clark	.15
21 Jose Canseco	.35
22 Bret Boone	.10
23 Dante Bichette	.10
24 Kevin Appier	.10
25 Chad Curtis	.10
26 Marty Cordova	.10
27 Jason Bere	.10
28 Jimmy Key	.10
29 Rickey Henderson	.75
30 Tim Salmon	.10
31 Joe Carter	.10
32 Tom Glavine	.35
33 Pat Listach	.10
34 Brian Jordan	.10
35 Brian McRae	.10
36 Eric Karros	.10
37 Pedro Martinez	.75
38 Royce Clayton	.10
39 Eddie Murray	.75
40 Randy Johnson	.75
41 Jeff Conine	.10
42 Brett Butler	.10
43 Jeffrey Hammonds	.10
44 Andujar Cedeno	.10
45 Dave Hollins	.10
46 Jeff King	.10
47 Benji Gil	.10
48 Roger Clemens	2.00
49 Barry Larkin	.10
50 Joe Girardi	.10
51 Bob Hamelin	.10
52 Travis Fryman	.10
53 Chuck Knoblauch	.10
54 Ray Durham	.10
55 Don Mattingly	2.00
56 Ruben Sierra	.10
57 J.T. Snow	.10

#	Player	Price
58	Derek Bell	.10
59	David Cone	.10
60	Marquis Grissom	.10
61	Kevin Seitzer	.10
62	Ozzie Smith	1.50
63	Rick Wilkins	.10
64	Hideo Nomo RC	3.00
65	Tony Tarasco	.10
66	Manny Ramirez	.75
67	Charles Johnson	.10
68	Craig Biggio	.10
69	Bobby Jones	.10
70	Mike Mussina	.60
71	Alex Gonzalez	.10
72	Gregg Jefferies	.10
73	Rusty Greer	.10
74	Mike Greenwell	.10
75	Hal Morris	.10
76	Paul O'Neill	.10
77	Luis Gonzalez	.25
78	Chipper Jones	1.50
79	Mike Piazza	2.50
80	Rondell White	.10
81	Glenallen Hill	.10
82	Shawn Green	.50
83	Bernie Williams	.10
84	Jim Thome	.65
85	Terry Pendleton	.10
86	Rafael Palmeiro	.65
87	Tony Gwynn	1.50
88	Mickey Tettleton	.10
89	John Valentin	.10
90	Deion Sanders	.10
91	Larry Walker	.10
92	Michael Tucker	.10
93	Alan Trammell	.10
94	Tim Raines	.10
95	Dave Justice	.10
96	Tino Martinez	.10
97	Cal Ripken Jr.	5.00
98	Deion Sanders	.10
99	Darren Daulton	.10
100	Paul Molitor	.75
101	Randy Myers	.10
102	Wally Joyner	.10
103	Carlos Perez	.10
104	Brian Hunter	.10
105	Wade Boggs	1.50
106	Bobby Higginson RC	.50
107	Jeff Kent	.10
108	Jose Offerman	.10
109	Dennis Eckersley	.65
110	Dave Nilsson	.10
111	Chuck Finley	.10
112	Devon White	.10
113	Bip Roberts	.10
114	Ramon Martinez	.10
115	Greg Maddux	1.50
116	Curtis Goodwin	.10
117	John Jaha	.10
118	Ken Griffey Jr.	2.50
119	Geronimo Pena	.10
120	Shawon Dunston	.10
121	Ariel Prieto	.10
122	Kirby Puckett	1.50
123	Carlos Baerga	.10
124	Todd Hundley	.10
125	Tim Naehring	.10
126	Gary Sheffield	.45
127	Dean Palmer	.10
128	Rondell White	.10
129	Greg Gagne	.10
130	Jose Rijo	.10
131	Ivan Rodriguez	.65
132	Jeff Bagwell	.75
133	Greg Vaughn	.10
134	Chili Davis	.10
135	Al Martin	.10
136	Kenny Rogers	.10
137	Aaron Sele	.10
138	Raul Mondesi	.10
139	Cecil Fielder	.10
140	Tim Wallach	.10
141	Andres Galarraga	.10
142	Lou Whitaker	.10
143	Jack McDowell	.10
144	Matt Williams	.10
145	Ryan Klesko	.10
146	Carlos Garcia	.10
147	Albert Belle	.10
148	Ryan Thompson	.10
149	Roberto Kelly	.10
150	Edgar Martinez	.10
151	Robby Thompson	.10
152	Mo Vaughn	.10
153	Todd Zeile	.10
154	Harold Baines	.10
155	Phil Plantier	.10
156	Mike Stanley	.10
157	Ed Sprague	.10
158	Moises Alou	.10
159	Quilvio Veras	.10
160	Reggie Sanders	.10
161	Delino DeShields	.10
162	Rico Brogna	.10
163	Greg Colbrunn	.10
164	Steve Finley	.10
165	Orlando Merced	.10
166	Mark McGwire	3.00
167	Garret Anderson	.10
168	Paul Sorrento	.10
169	Mark Langston	.10
170	Danny Tartabull	.10
171	Vinny Castilla	.10
172	Javier Lopez	.10
173	Bret Saberhagen	.10
174	Eddie Williams	.10
175	Scott Leius	.10
176	Juan Gonzalez	.50
177	Gary Gaetti	.10
178	Jim Edmonds	.10
179	John Olerud	.10
180	Lenny Dykstra	.10
181	Ray Lankford	.10
182	Ron Gant	.10
183	Doug Drabek	.10
184	Fred McGriff	.10
185	Andy Benes	.10
186	Kurt Abbott	.10
187	Bernard Gilkey	.10
188	Sammy Sosa	2.00
189	Lee Smith	.10
190	Dennis Martinez	.10
191	Ozzie Guillen	.10
192	Robin Ventura	.10

Gold

DON MATTINGLY

#	Player	NM/M
	Complete Set (24):	10.00
	Common Player:	.25
1	Frank Thomas	.60
2	Jeff Bagwell	.60
3	Raul Mondesi	.25
4	Barry Bonds	1.50
5	Albert Belle	.25
6	Ken Griffey Jr.	1.00
7	Cal Ripkin (Ripken) Jr.	1.50
8	Will Clark	.25
9	Jose Canseco	.45
10	Larry Walker	.25
11	Kirby Puckett	.75
12	Don Mattingly	1.00
13	Tim Salmon	.25
14	Roberto Alomar	.35
15	Greg Maddux	.75
16	Mike Piazza	1.00
17	Matt Williams	.25
18	Kenny Lofton	.25
19	Alex Rodriquez (Rodriguez)	1.25
20	Tony Gwynn	.75
21	Mo Vaughn	.25
22	Chipper Jones	.75
23	Manny Ramirez	.60
24	Deion Sanders	.25

Lumberjacks

#	Player	NM/M
	Complete Set (16):	55.00
	Common Player:	2.00
1	Albert Belle	2.00
2	Barry Bonds	12.00
3	Juan Gonzalez	3.50
4	Ken Griffey Jr.	7.50
5	Fred McGriff	2.00
6	Mike Piazza	7.50
7	Kirby Puckett	6.00
8	Mo Vaughn	2.00
9	Frank Thomas	4.50
10	Jeff Bagwell	4.50
11	Matt Williams	2.00
12	Jose Canseco	3.00
13	Raul Mondesi	2.00
14	Manny Ramirez	4.50
15	Cecil Fielder	2.00
16	Cal Ripken Jr.	12.00

Bat Patrol

FRED McGRIFF

#	Player	NM/M
	Complete Set (24):	7.50
	Common Player:	.15
1	Frank Thomas	.75
2	Tony Gwynn	1.00
3	Wade Boggs	1.00
4	Larry Walker	.25
5	Ken Griffey Jr.	1.50
6	Jeff Bagwell	.75
7	Manny Ramirez	.75
8	Mark Grace	.25
9	Kenny Lofton	.15
10	Mike Piazza	1.50
11	Will Clark	.25
12	Mo Vaughn	.25
13	Carlos Baerga	.15
14	Rafael Palmeiro	.65
15	Barry Bonds	2.50
16	Kirby Puckett	1.00
17	Roberto Alomar	.35
18	Barry Larkin	.15
19	Eddie Murray	.75
20	Tim Salmon	.25
21	Don Mattingly	1.25
22	Fred McGriff	.15
23	Albert Belle	.25
24	Dante Bichette	.15

1996 Leaf

SAMMY SOSA

#	Player	NM/M
	Complete Set (220):	10.00
	Common Player:	.05
	Complete Gold Set (220):	100.00
	Common Golds:	1.00
	Gold Press Proofs:	15X
	Complete Silver Set (220):	50.00
	Common Silvers:	.50
	Silver Press Proofs:	6X
	Complete Bronze Set (220):	40.00
	Common Bronze:	.25
	Bronze Press Proofs:	4X
	Pack (12):	.25
	Wax Box (30):	25.00
1	John Smoltz	.10
2	Dennis Eckersley	.60
3	Delino DeShields	.05
4	Cliff Floyd	.05
5	Chuck Finley	.05
6	Cecil Fielder	.05
7	Tim Naehring	.05
8	Carlos Perez	.05
9	Brad Ausmus	.05
10	Matt Lawton RC	.15
11	Alan Trammell	.05
12	Steve Finley	.05
13	Paul O'Neill	.05
14	Gary Sheffield	.40
15	Mark McGwire	1.50
16	Bernie Williams	.05
17	Jeff Montgomery	.05
18	Chan Ho Park	.05
19	Greg Vaughn	.05
20	Jeff Kent	.05
21	Cal Ripken Jr.	2.00
22	Charles Johnson	.05
23	Eric Karros	.05
24	Alex Rodriguez	1.50
25	Chris Snopek	.05
26	Jason Isringhausen	.05
27	Chili Davis	.05
28	Chipper Jones	.75
29	Bret Saberhagen	.05
30	Tony Clark	.05
31	Marty Cordova	.05
32	Dwayne Hosey	.05
33	Fred McGriff	.05
34	Deion Sanders	.05
35	Orlando Merced	.05
36	Brady Anderson	.05
37	Ray Lankford	.05
38	Manny Ramirez	.65
39	Alex Fernandez	.05
40	Greg Colbrunn	.05
41	Ken Griffey Jr.	1.00
42	Mickey Morandini	.05
43	Chuck Knoblauch	.05
44	Quinton McCracken	.05
45	Tim Salmon	.05
46	Jose Mesa	.05
47	Marquis Grissom	.05
48	Checklist	.05
49	Raul Mondesi	.05
50	Mark Grudzielanek	.05
51	Ray Durham	.05
52	Matt Williams	.05
53	Bob Hamelin	.05
54	Lenny Dykstra	.05
55	Jeff King	.05
56	LaTroy Hawkins	.05
57	Terry Pendleton	.05
58	Kevin Stocker	.05
59	Ozzie Timmons	.05
60	David Justice	.05
61	Ricky Bottalico	.05
62	Andy Ashby	.05
63	Larry Walker	.05
64	Jose Canseco	.40
65	Bret Boone	.05
66	Shawn Green	.35
67	Chad Curtis	.05
68	Travis Fryman	.05
69	Roger Clemens	1.00
70	David Bell	.05
71	Rusty Greer	.05
72	Bob Higginson	.05
73	Joey Hamilton	.05
74	Kevin Seitzer	.05
75	Julian Tavarez	.05
76	Troy Percival	.05
77	Kirby Puckett	.75
78	Barry Bonds	2.00
79	Michael Tucker	.05
80	Paul Molitor	.65
81	Carlos Garcia	.05
82	Johnny Damon	.35
83	Mike Hampton	.05
84	Ariel Prieto	.05
85	Tony Tarasco	.05
86	Pete Schourek	.05
87	Tom Glavine	.30
88	Rondell White	.05
89	Jim Edmonds	.05
90	Robby Thompson	.05
91	Wade Boggs	.75
92	Pedro Martinez	.65
93	Gregg Jefferies	.05
94	Albert Belle	.05
95	Benji Gil	.05
96	Denny Neagle	.05
97	Mark Langston	.05
98	Sandy Alomar	.05
99	Tony Gwynn	.75
100	Todd Hundley	.05
101	Dante Bichette	.05
102	Eddie Murray	.65
103	Lyle Mouton	.05
104	John Jaha	.05
105	Checklist	.05
106	Jon Nunnally	.05
107	Juan Gonzalez	.50
108	Kevin Appier	.05
109	Brian McRae	.05
110	Lee Smith	.05
111	Tim Wakefield	.05
112	Sammy Sosa	1.00
113	Jay Buhner	.05
114	Garret Anderson	.05
115	Edgar Martinez	.05
116	Edgardo Alfonzo	.05
117	Billy Ashley	.05
118	Joe Carter	.05
119	Javy Lopez	.05
120	Bobby Bonilla	.05
121	Ken Caminiti	.05
122	Barry Larkin	.05
123	Shannon Stewart	.05
124	Orel Hershiser	.05
125	Jeff Conine	.05
126	Mark Grace	.05
127	Kenny Lofton	.05
128	Luis Gonzalez	.25
129	Rico Brogna	.05
130	Mo Vaughn	.05
131	Brad Radke	.05
132	Jose Herrera	.05
133	Rick Aguilera	.05
134	Gary DiSarcina	.05
135	Andres Galarraga	.05

#	Player	Price
136	Carl Everett	.05
137	Steve Avery	.05
138	Vinny Castilla	.05
139	Dennis Martinez	.05
140	John Wetteland	.05
141	Alex Gonzalez	.05
142	Brian Jordan	.05
143	Todd Hollandsworth	.05
144	Terrell Wade	.05
145	Wilson Alvarez	.05
146	Reggie Sanders	.05
147	Will Clark	.10
148	Hideo Nomo	.50
149	J.T. Snow	.05
150	Frank Thomas	.65
151	Ivan Rodriguez	.60
152	Jay Bell	.05
153	Checklist	.05
154	David Cone	.05
155	Roberto Alomar	.20
156	Carlos Delgado	.40
157	Carlos Baerga	.05
158	Geronimo Berroa	.05
159	Joe Vitiello	.05
160	Terry Steinbach	.05
161	Doug Drabek	.05
162	David Segui	.05
163	Ozzie Smith	.75
164	Kurt Abbott	.05
165	Randy Johnson	.65
166	John Valentin	.05
167	Mickey Tettleton	.05
168	Ruben Sierra	.05
169	Jim Thome	.60
170	Mike Greenwell	.05
171	Quilvio Veras	.05
172	Robin Ventura	.05
173	Bill Pulsipher	.05
174	Rafael Palmeiro	.60
175	Hal Morris	.05
176	Ryan Klesko	.05
177	Eric Young	.05
178	Shane Andrews	.05
179	Brian Hunter	.05
180	Brett Butler	.05
181	John Olerud	.05
182	Moises Alou	.05
183	Glenallen Hill	.05
184	Ismael Valdes	.05
185	Andy Pettitte	.25
186	Yamil Benitez	.05
187	Jason Bere	.05
188	Dean Palmer	.05
189	Jimmy Haynes	.05
190	Trevor Hoffman	.05
191	Mike Mussina	.40
192	Greg Maddux	.75
193	Ozzie Guillen	.05
194	Pat Listach	.05
195	Derek Bell	.05
196	Darren Daulton	.05
197	John Mabry	.05
198	Ramon Martinez	.05
199	Jeff Bagwell	.65
200	Mike Piazza	1.00
201	Al Martin	.05
202	Aaron Sele	.05
203	Ed Sprague	.05
204	Rod Beck	.05
205	Checklist	.05
206	Mike Lansing	.05
207	Craig Biggio	.05
208	Jeffrey Hammonds	.05
209	Dave Nilsson	.05
210	Dante Bichette, Albert Belle Checklist, Inserts	.05
211	Derek Jeter	2.00
212	Alan Benes	.05
213	Jason Schmidt	.05
214	Alex Ochoa	.05
215	Ruben Rivera	.05
216	Roger Cedeno	.05
217	Jeff Suppan	.05
218	Billy Wagner	.05
219	Mark Loretta	.05
220	Karim Garcia	.10

1996 Leaf Press Proofs

	NM/M
Complete Set, Gold (220):	200.00
Complete Set, Silver (220):	100.00

Complete Set, Bronze (220):	75.00
Common Player, Gold:	1.00
Common Player, Silver:	.50
Common Player, Bronze:	.25

(Press Proof stars valued as follows in comparison to regular-issue '96 Leaf: Gold - 15X; Silver - 6X; Bronze - 4X.)

All-Star MVP Contenders

		NM/M
Complete Set (20):		12.50
Common Card:		.25
Golds:		1.5X
1	Frank Thomas	.75
2	Mike Piazza	1.50
2c	Mike Piazza (Redeemed and punch-cancelled.)	1.00
3	Sammy Sosa	1.50
4	Cal Ripken Jr.	2.00
5	Jeff Bagwell	.75
6	Reggie Sanders	.25
7	Mo Vaughn	.25
8	Tony Gwynn	1.00
9	Dante Bichette	.25
10	Tim Salmon	.25
11	Chipper Jones	1.00
12	Kenny Lofton	.25
13	Manny Ramirez	.75
14	Barry Bonds	2.00
15	Raul Mondesi	.25
16	Kirby Puckett	1.00
17	Albert Belle	.25
18	Ken Griffey Jr.	1.50
19	Greg Maddux	1.00
20	Bonus Card	.10

Frank Thomas' Greatest Hits

		NM/M
Complete Set (8):		12.50
Common Card:		2.00
1	1990	2.00
2	1991	2.00
3	1992	2.00
4	1993	2.00
5	1994	2.00
6	1995	2.00
7	Career	2.00
8	MVP	2.00

1996 Leaf Frank Thomas The Big Heart

		NM/M
Complete Set (4):		35.00
Common Card:		10.00
(1)	Frank Thomas (Bat on shoulder.)	10.00
(2)	Frank Thomas (Holding glove.)	10.00
(3)	Frank Thomas (Horizontal)	10.00
(4)	Frank Thomas (Seated)	10.00

Gold Leaf Stars

		NM/M
Complete Set (15):		125.00
Common Player:		3.00
1	Frank Thomas	9.00
2	Dante Bichette	3.00
3	Sammy Sosa	15.00
4	Ken Griffey Jr.	15.00
5	Mike Piazza	15.00
6	Tim Salmon	3.00
7	Hideo Nomo	6.00
8	Cal Ripken Jr.	20.00
9	Chipper Jones	12.00
10	Albert Belle	3.00
11	Tony Gwynn	12.00
12	Mo Vaughn	3.00

		NM/M
13	Barry Larkin	3.00
14	Manny Ramirez	9.00
15	Greg Maddux	12.00

Hats Off

		NM/M
Complete Set (8):		30.00
Common Player:		3.00
1	Cal Ripken Jr.	12.00
2	Barry Larkin	3.00
3	Frank Thomas	4.50
4	Mo Vaughn	3.00
5	Ken Griffey Jr.	7.50
6	Hideo Nomo	4.00
7	Albert Belle	3.00
8	Greg Maddux	6.00

Picture Perfect

		NM/M
Complete Set (12):		22.50
Common Player:		1.00
Promos:		2X
1	Frank Thomas	2.00
2	Cal Ripken Jr.	5.00
3	Greg Maddux	2.50
4	Manny Ramirez	2.00
5	Chipper Jones	2.50
6	Tony Gwynn	2.50
7	Ken Griffey Jr.	3.00
8	Albert Belle	1.00
9	Jeff Bagwell	2.00
10	Mike Piazza	3.00
11	Mo Vaughn	1.00
12	Barry Bonds	5.00

Statistical Standouts

		NM/M
Complete Set (8):		60.00
Common Player:		3.00
1	Cal Ripken Jr.	20.00
2	Tony Gwynn	10.00
3	Frank Thomas	7.50
4	Ken Griffey Jr.	13.50
5	Hideo Nomo	6.00

Total Bases

6	Greg Maddux	10.00
7	Albert Belle	3.00
8	Chipper Jones	10.00

		NM/M
Complete Set (12):		25.00
Common Player:		1.00
Promos:		2X
1	Frank Thomas	2.50
2	Albert Belle	1.00
3	Rafael Palmeiro	2.00
4	Barry Bonds	6.00
5	Kirby Puckett	3.00
6	Joe Carter	1.00
7	Paul Molitor	2.50
8	Fred McGriff	1.00
9	Ken Griffey Jr.	4.00
10	Carlos Baerga	1.00
11	Juan Gonzalez	2.00
12	Cal Ripken Jr.	6.00

1996 Leaf/Limited

	NM/M
Complete Set (90):	15.00
Common Player:	.10
Gold Set (90):	50.00
Gold Stars/Rookies:	3X
Pack (5):	1.50
Wax Box (14):	20.00
1 Ivan Rodriguez	.60
2 Roger Clemens	1.50
3 Gary Sheffield	.40
4 Tino Martinez	.10
5 Sammy Sosa	1.50
6 Reggie Sanders	.10
7 Ray Lankford	.10
8 Manny Ramirez	.75
9 Jeff Bagwell	.75
10 Greg Maddux	1.00
11 Ken Griffey Jr.	1.50
12 Rondell White	.10
13 Mike Piazza	1.50
14 Marc Newfield	.10

15	Cal Ripken Jr.	3.00
16	Carlos Delgado	.40
17	Tim Salmon	.10
18	Andres Galarraga	.10
19	Chuck Knoblauch	.10
20	Matt Williams	.10
21	Mark McGwire	2.00
22	Ben McDonald	.10
23	Frank Thomas	.75
24	Johnny Damon	.35
25	Gregg Jefferies	.10
26	Travis Fryman	.10
27	Chipper Jones	1.00
28	David Cone	.10
29	Kenny Lofton	.10
30	Mike Mussina	.30
31	Alex Rodriguez	2.00
32	Carlos Baerga	.10
33	Brian Hunter	.10
34	Juan Gonzalez	.60
35	Bernie Williams	.10
36	Wally Joyner	.10
37	Fred McGriff	.10
38	Randy Johnson	.75
39	Marty Cordova	.10
40	Garret Anderson	.10
41	Albert Belle	.10
42	Edgar Martinez	.10
43	Barry Larkin	.10
44	Paul O'Neill	.10
45	Cecil Fielder	.10
46	Rusty Greer	.10
47	Mo Vaughn	.10
48	Dante Bichette	.10
49	Ryan Klesko	.10
50	Roberto Alomar	.25
51	Raul Mondesi	.10
52	Robin Ventura	.10
53	Tony Gwynn	1.00
54	Mark Grace	.10
55	Jim Thome	.60
56	Jason Giambi	.50
57	Tom Glavine	.25
58	Jim Edmonds	.10
59	Pedro Martinez	.75
60	Charles Johnson	.10
61	Wade Boggs	1.00
62	Orlando Merced	.10
63	Craig Biggio	.10
64	Brady Anderson	.10
65	Hideo Nomo	.60
66	Ozzie Smith	1.00
67	Eddie Murray	.75
68	Will Clark	.15
69	Jay Buhner	.10
70	Kirby Puckett	1.00
71	Barry Bonds	3.00
72	Ray Durham	.10
73	Sterling Hitchcock	.10
74	John Smoltz	.10
75	Andre Dawson	.35
76	Joe Carter	.10
77	Ryne Sandberg	1.00
78	Rickey Henderson	.75
79	Brian Jordan	.10
80	Greg Vaughn	.10
81	Andy Pettitte	.25
82	Dean Palmer	.10
83	Paul Molitor	.75
84	Rafael Palmeiro	.60
85	Henry Rodriguez	.10
86	Larry Walker	.10
87	Ismael Valdes	.10
88	Derek Bell	.10
89	J.T. Snow	.10
90	Jack McDowell	.10

Lumberjacks

Complete Set (10):		40.00
Common Player:		1.50
Lumberjack Blacks (500):		2X
Promos:		2X
1	Ken Griffey Jr.	5.00
2	Sammy Sosa	5.00
3	Cal Ripken Jr.	7.50
4	Frank Thomas	3.00
5	Alex Rodriguez	6.00
6	Mo Vaughn	1.50
7	Chipper Jones	4.00
8	Mike Piazza	5.00

9	Jeff Bagwell	3.00
10	Mark McGwire	6.00

Pennant Craze

Complete Set (10):		20.00
Common Player:		1.00
Promos:		2X
1	Juan Gonzalez	1.25
2	Cal Ripken Jr.	4.00
3	Frank Thomas	1.50
4	Ken Griffey Jr.	2.50
5	Albert Belle	1.00
6	Greg Maddux	2.00
7	Paul Molitor	1.50
8	Alex Rodriguez	3.00
9	Barry Bonds	4.00
10	Chipper Jones	2.00

Rookies

Complete Set (10):		7.50
Common Player:		.50
Limited Gold:		3X
1	Alex Ochoa	.50
2	Darin Erstad	1.00
3	Ruben Rivera	.50
4	Derek Jeter	5.00
5	Jermaine Dye	.50
6	Jason Kendall	.50
7	Mike Grace	.50
8	Andruw Jones	2.50
9	Rey Ordonez	.50
10	George Arias	.50

1996 Leaf/Preferred

Complete Set (150):		15.00
Common Player:		.05
Press Proofs:		12X
Pack (6):		1.00
Wax Box (24):		20.00
1	Ken Griffey Jr.	1.25
2	Rico Brogna	.05
3	Gregg Jefferies	.05
4	Reggie Sanders	.05
5	Manny Ramirez	.75
6	Shawn Green	.40
7	Tino Martinez	.05
8	Jeff Bagwell	.75
9	Marc Newfield	.05
10	Ray Lankford	.05
11	Jay Bell	.05
12	Greg Maddux	1.00
13	Frank Thomas	.75

14	Travis Fryman	.05
15	Mark McGwire	1.50
16	Chuck Knoblauch	.05
17	Sammy Sosa	1.25
18	Matt Williams	.05
19	Roger Clemens	1.25
20	Rondell White	.05
21	Ivan Rodriguez	.65
22	Cal Ripken Jr.	2.00
23	Ben McDonald	.05
24	Kenny Lofton	.05
25	Mike Piazza	1.25
26	David Cone	.05
27	Gary Sheffield	.40
28	Tim Salmon	.05
29	Andres Galarraga	.05
30	Johnny Damon	.35
31	Ozzie Smith	1.00
32	Carlos Baerga	.05
33	Raul Mondesi	.05
34	Moises Alou	.05
35	Alex Rodriguez	1.50
36	Mike Mussina	.40
37	Jason Isringhausen	.05
38	Barry Larkin	.05
39	Bernie Williams	.05
40	Chipper Jones	1.00
41	Joey Hamilton	.05
42	Charles Johnson	.05
43	Juan Gonzalez	.50
44	Greg Vaughn	.05
45	Robin Ventura	.05
46	Albert Belle	.05
47	Rafael Palmeiro	.65
48	Brian Hunter	.05
49	Mo Vaughn	.05
50	Paul O'Neill	.05
51	Mark Grace	.05
52	Randy Johnson	.75
53	Pedro Martinez	.75
54	Marty Cordova	.05
55	Garret Anderson	.05
56	Joe Carter	.05
57	Jim Thome	.60
58	Edgardo Alfonzo	.05
59	Dante Bichette	.05
60	Darryl Hamilton	.05
61	Roberto Alomar	.20
62	Fred McGriff	.05
63	Kirby Puckett	1.00
64	Hideo Nomo	.60
65	Alex Fernandez	.05
66	Ryan Klesko	.05
67	Wade Boggs	1.00
68	Eddie Murray	.75
69	Eric Karros	.05
70	Jim Edmonds	.05
71	Edgar Martinez	.05
72	Andy Pettitte	.30
73	Mark Grudzielanek	.05
74	Tom Glavine	.25
75	Ken Caminiti	.05
76	Will Clark	.10
77	Craig Biggio	.05
78	Brady Anderson	.05
79	Tony Gwynn	1.00
80	Larry Walker	.05
81	Brian Jordan	.05
82	Lenny Dykstra	.05
83	Butch Huskey	.05
84	Jack McDowell	.05
85	Cecil Fielder	.05
86	Jose Canseco	.40
87	Jason Giambi	.50
88	Rickey Henderson	.75
89	Kevin Seitzer	.05
90	Carlos Delgado	.40
91	Ryne Sandberg	1.00
92	Dwight Gooden	.05
93	Michael Tucker	.05
94	Barry Bonds	2.00
95	Eric Young	.05
96	Dean Palmer	.05
97	Henry Rodriguez	.05
98	John Mabry	.05
99	J.T. Snow	.05
100	Andre Dawson	.25
101	Ismael Valdes	.05
102	Charles Nagy	.05
103	Jay Buhner	.05
104	Derek Bell	.05
105	Paul Molitor	.75
106	Hal Morris	.05
107	Ray Durham	.05
108	Bernard Gilkey	.05
109	John Valentin	.05
110	Melvin Nieves	.05
111	John Smoltz	.05
112	Terrell Wade	.05
113	Chad Mottola	.05
114	Tony Clark	.05
115	John Wasdin	.05
116	Derek Jeter	2.00
117	Rey Ordonez	.05
118	Jason Thompson	.05
119	Robin Jennings RC	.05
120	Rocky Coppinger RC	.05
121	Billy Wagner	.05
122	Steve Gibralter	.05
123	Jermaine Dye	.05
124	Jason Kendall	.05
125	Mike Grace RC	.05
126	Jason Schmidt	.05
127	Paul Wilson	.05
128	Alan Benes	.05

129	Justin Thompson	.05
130	Brooks Kieschnick	.05
131	George Arias	.05
132	Osvaldo Fernandez RC	.20
133	Todd Hollandsworth	.05
134	Eric Owens	.05
135	Chan Ho Park	.05
136	Mark Loretta	.05
137	Ruben Rivera	.05
138	Jeff Suppan	.05
139	Ugueth Urbina	.05
140	LaTroy Hawkins	.05
141	Chris Snopek	.05
142	Edgar Renteria	.05
143	Raul Casanova	.05
144	Jose Herrera	.05
145	Matt Lawton RC	.05
146	Ralph Milliard RC	.05
147	Frank Thomas Checklist	.05
148	Jeff Bagwell Checklist	.05
149	Ken Griffey Jr. Checklist	.05
150	Mike Piazza Checklist	.05

1996 Leaf/Preferred Press Proofs

Complete Set (150):		100.00
Common Player:		.50
Stars/Rookies:		12X

(See 1996 Leaf Preferred for checklist and base card values.)

Leaf Steel

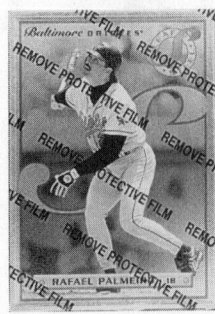

Complete Set (77):		25.00
Common Player:		.15
Gold:		2X
1	Frank Thomas	1.00
2	Paul Molitor	1.00
3	Kenny Lofton	.15
4	Travis Fryman	.15
5	Jeff Conine	.15
6	Barry Bonds	3.00
7	Gregg Jefferies	.15
8	Alex Rodriguez	2.50
9	Wade Boggs	1.50
10	David Justice	.15
11	Hideo Nomo	.75
12	Roberto Alomar	.30
13	Todd Hollandsworth	.15
14	Mark McGwire	2.50
15	Rafael Palmeiro	.75
16	Will Clark	.25
17	Cal Ripken Jr.	3.00
18	Derek Bell	.15
19	Gary Sheffield	.50
20	Juan Gonzalez	.65
21	Garret Anderson	.15
22	Mo Vaughn	.15
23	Robin Ventura	.15
24	Carlos Baerga	.15
25	Tim Salmon	.15
26	Matt Williams	.15
27	Fred McGriff	.15
28	Rondell White	.15
29	Ray Lankford	.15

30	Lenny Dykstra	.15
31	J.T. Snow	.15
32	Sammy Sosa	2.00
33	Chipper Jones	1.50
34	Bobby Bonilla	.15
35	Paul Wilson	.15
36	Darren Daulton	.15
37	Larry Walker	.15
38	Raul Mondesi	.15
39	Jeff Bagwell	1.00
40	Derek Jeter	3.00
41	Kirby Puckett	1.50
42	Jason Isringhausen	.15
43	Vinny Castilla	.15
44	Jim Edmonds	.15
45	Ron Gant	.15
46	Carlos Delgado	.50
47	Jose Canseco	.40
48	Tony Gwynn	1.50
49	Mike Mussina	.50
50	Charles Johnson	.15
51	Mike Piazza	2.00
52	Ken Griffey Jr.	2.00
53	Greg Maddux	1.50
54	Mark Grace	.15
55	Ryan Klesko	.15
56	Dennis Eckersley	.75
57	Rickey Henderson	1.00
58	Michael Tucker	.15
59	Joe Carter	.15
60	Randy Johnson	1.00
61	Brian Jordan	.15
62	Shawn Green	.50
63	Roger Clemens	2.00
64	Andres Galarraga	.15
65	Johnny Damon	.40
66	Ryne Sandberg	1.50
67	Alan Benes	.15
68	Albert Belle	.15
69	Barry Larkin	.15
70	Marty Cordova	.15
71	Dante Bichette	.15
72	Craig Biggio	.15
73	Reggie Sanders	.15
74	Moises Alou	.15
75	Chuck Knoblauch	.15
76	Cecil Fielder	.15
77	Manny Ramirez	1.00

Staremaster

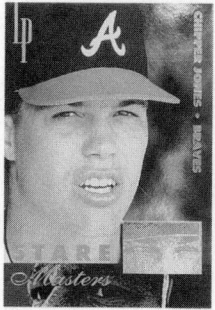

		NM/M
Complete Set (12):		50.00
Common Player:		3.00
1	Chipper Jones	5.00
2	Alex Rodriguez	7.50
3	Derek Jeter	10.00
4	Tony Gwynn	5.00
5	Frank Thomas	4.00
6	Ken Griffey Jr.	6.00
7	Cal Ripken Jr.	10.00
8	Greg Maddux	5.00
9	Albert Belle	3.00
10	Barry Bonds	10.00
11	Jeff Bagwell	4.00
12	Mike Piazza	6.00

Steel Power

1996 Leaf/Signature Series

		NM/M
Complete Set (8):		17.50
Common Player:		1.00
1	Albert Belle	1.00
2	Mo Vaughn	1.00
3	Ken Griffey Jr.	3.50
4	Cal Ripken Jr.	5.00
5	Mike Piazza	3.50
6	Barry Bonds	5.00
7	Jeff Bagwell	2.50
8	Frank Thomas	2.50

1996 Leaf/Signature Series

Derek Jeter

		NM/M
Complete Set (150):		30.00
Complete 1st Series (100):		20.00
Complete Extended Series (50):		10.00
Common Player:		.05
Gold PP Stars/Rookies:		8X
Platinum PP Stars/Rookies:		20X
Pack (4):		5.00
Wax Box (12):		50.00
1	Mike Piazza	1.25
2	Juan Gonzalez	.65
3	Greg Maddux	1.00
4	Marc Newfield	.05
5	Wade Boggs	1.00
6	Ray Lankford	.05
7	Frank Thomas	.75
8	Rico Brogna	.05
9	Tim Salmon	.05
10	Ken Griffey Jr.	1.25
11	Manny Ramirez	.75
12	Cecil Fielder	.05
13	Gregg Jefferies	.05
14	Rondell White	.05
15	Cal Ripken Jr.	2.00
16	Alex Rodriguez	1.50
17	Bernie Williams	.05
18	Andres Galarraga	.05
19	Mike Mussina	.50
20	Chuck Knoblauch	.05
21	Joe Carter	.05
22	Jeff Bagwell	.75
23	Mark McGwire	1.50
24	Sammy Sosa	1.00
25	Reggie Sanders	.05
26	Chipper Jones	1.00
27	Jeff Cirillo	.05
28	Roger Clemens	1.25
29	Craig Biggio	.05
30	Gary Sheffield	.45
31	Paul O'Neill	.05
32	Johnny Damon	.35
33	Jason Isringhausen	.05
34	Jay Bell	.05
35	Henry Rodriguez	.05
36	Matt Williams	.05
37	Randy Johnson	.75
38	Fred McGriff	.05
39	Jason Giambi	.60
40	Ivan Rodriguez	.65
41	Raul Mondesi	.05
42	Barry Larkin	.05
43	Ryan Klesko	.05
44	Joey Hamilton	.05
45	Todd Hundley	.05
46	Jim Edmonds	.05
47	Dante Bichette	.05
48	Roberto Alomar	.20
49	Mark Grace	.05
50	Brady Anderson	.05
51	Hideo Nomo	.65
52	Ozzie Smith	1.00
53	Robin Ventura	.05
54	Andy Pettitte	.35
55	Kenny Lofton	.05
56	John Mabry	.05
57	Paul Molitor	.75
58	Rey Ordonez	.05
59	Albert Belle	.05
60	Charles Johnson	.05
61	Edgar Martinez	.05
62	Derek Bell	.05
63	Carlos Delgado	.50
64	Raul Casanova	.05
65	Ismael Valdes	.05
66	J.T. Snow	.05
67	Derek Jeter	2.00
68	Jason Kendall	.05
69	John Smoltz	.05
70	Chad Mottola	.05
71	Jim Thome	.60
72	Will Clark	.10
73	Mo Vaughn	.05
74	John Wasdin	.05
75	Rafael Palmeiro	.65
76	Mark Grudzielanek	.05
77	Larry Walker	.05
78	Alan Benes	.05
79	Michael Tucker	.05
80	Billy Wagner	.05
81	Paul Wilson	.05
82	Greg Vaughn	.05
83	Dean Palmer	.05
84	Ryne Sandberg	1.00
85	Eric Young	.05
86	Jay Buhner	.05
87	Tony Clark	.05
88	Jermaine Dye	.05
89	Barry Bonds	2.00
90	Ugueth Urbina	.05
91	Charles Nagy	.05
92	Ruben Rivera	.05
93	Todd Hollandsworth	.05
94	Darin Erstad RC	1.50
95	Brooks Kieschnick	.05
96	Edgar Renteria	.05
97	Lenny Dykstra	.05
98	Tony Gwynn	1.00
99	Kirby Puckett	1.00
100	Checklist	.05
101	Andruw Jones	.75
102	Alex Ochoa	.05
103	David Cone	.05
104	Rusty Greer	.05
105	Jose Canseco	.45
106	Ken Caminiti	.05
107	Mariano Rivera	.15
108	Ron Gant	.05
109	Darryl Strawberry	.05
110	Vladimir Guerrero	.75
111	George Arias	.05
112	Jeff Conine	.05
113	Bobby Higginson	.05
114	Eric Karros	.05
115	Brian Hunter	.05
116	Eddie Murray	.75
117	Todd Walker	.05
118	Chan Ho Park	.05
119	John Jaha	.05
120	David Justice	.05
121	Makoto Suzuki	.05
122	Scott Rolen	.65
123	Tino Martinez	.05
124	Kimera Bartee	.05
125	Garret Anderson	.05
126	Brian Jordan	.05
127	Andre Dawson	.30
128	Javier Lopez	.05
129	Bill Pulsipher	.05
130	Dwight Gooden	.05
131	Al Martin	.05
132	Terrell Wade	.05
133	Steve Gibralter	.05
134	Tom Glavine	.35
135	Kevin Appier	.05
136	Tim Raines	.05
137	Curtis Pride	.05
138	Todd Greene	.05
139	Bobby Bonilla	.05
140	Trey Beamon	.05
141	Marty Cordova	.05
142	Rickey Henderson	.75
143	Ellis Burks	.05
144	Dennis Eckersley	.65
145	Kevin Brown	.05
146	Carlos Baerga	.05
147	Brett Butler	.05
148	Marquis Grissom	.05
149	Karim Garcia	.05
150	Checklist	.05

Press Proofs

	NM/M
Common Gold:	2.00
Gold Stars:	8X
Common Platinum:	4.00
Platinum Stars:	20X

(See 1996 Leaf/Signature Series for checklist and base card values.)

1996 Leaf/Signature Series Autographs Promos

	NM/M
Frank Thomas (Facsimile signature.)	4.00
Frank Thomas (Genuine autograph.)	50.00

Autographs

		NM/M
Common Bronze Player:		4.00
Silver:		1.5X
Gold:		2X
SPs: 100 Gold, 200 Silver, 700 Bronze		
(1)	Kurt Abbott	4.00
(2)	Juan Acevedo	4.00
(3)	Terry Adams	4.00
(4)	Manny Alexander	4.00
(5)	Roberto Alomar/SP	35.00
(6)	Moises Alou	12.00
(7)	Wilson Alvarez	4.00
(8)	Garret Anderson	10.00
(9)	Shane Andrews	4.00
(10)	Andy Ashby	4.00
(11)	Pedro Astacio	4.00
(12)	Brad Ausmus	4.00
(13)	Bobby Ayala	4.00
(14)	Carlos Baerga	4.00
(15)	Harold Baines	10.00
(16)	Jason Bates	4.00
(17)	Allen Battle	4.00
(18)	Rich Becker	4.00
(19)	David Bell	4.00
(20)	Rafael Belliard	4.00
(21)	Andy Benes	4.00
(22)	Armando Benitez	4.00
(23)	Jason Bere	4.00
(24)	Geronimo Berroa	4.00
(25)	Willie Blair	4.00
(26)	Mike Blowers	4.00
(27)	Wade Boggs/SP	50.00
(28)	Ricky Bones	4.00
(29)	Mike Bordick	4.00
(30)	Toby Borland	4.00
(31)	Ricky Bottalico	4.00
(32)	Darren Bragg	4.00
(33)	Jeff Branson	4.00
(34)	Tilson Brito	4.00
(35)	Rico Brogna	4.00
(36)	Scott Brosius	7.50
(37)	Damon Buford	4.00
(38)	Mike Busby	4.00
(39)	Tom Candiotti	4.00
(40)	Frank Castillo	4.00
(41)	Andujar Cedeno	4.00
(42)	Domingo Cedeno	4.00
(43)	Roger Cedeno	4.00
(44)	Norm Charlton	4.00
(45)	Jeff Cirillo	4.00
(46)	Will Clark	10.00
(47)	Jeff Conine	4.00
(48)	Steve Cooke	4.00
(49)	Joey Cora	4.00
(50)	Marty Cordova	4.00
(51)	Rheal Cormier	4.00
(52)	Felipe Crespo	4.00

(53)	Chad Curtis	4.00
(54)	Johnny Damon	15.00
(55)	Russ Davis	4.00
(56)	Andre Dawson	10.00
(57a)	Carlos Delgado (Black autograph.)	15.00
(57b)	Carlos Delgado (Blue autograph.)	15.00
(58)	Doug Drabek	4.00
(59)	Darren Dreifort	4.00
(60)	Shawon Dunston	4.00
(61)	Ray Durham	4.00
(62)	Jim Edmonds	12.00
(63)	Joey Eischen	4.00
(64)	Jim Eisenreich	4.00
(65)	Sal Fasano	4.00
(66)	Jeff Fassero	4.00
(67)	Alex Fernandez	4.00
(68)	Darrin Fletcher	4.00
(69)	Chad Fonville	4.00
(70)	Kevin Foster	4.00
(71)	John Franco	4.00
(72)	Julio Franco	10.00
(73)	Marvin Freeman	4.00
(74)	Travis Fryman	4.00
(75)	Gary Gaetti	4.00
(76)	Carlos Garcia	4.00
(77)	Jason Giambi	10.00
(78)	Benji Gil	4.00
(79)	Greg Gohr	4.00
(80)	Chris Gomez	4.00
(81)	Leo Gomez	4.00
(82)	Tom Goodwin	4.00
(83)	Mike Grace	4.00
(84)	Mike Greenwell	6.00
(85)	Rusty Greer	4.00
(86)	Mark Grudzielanek	4.00
(87)	Mark Gubicza	4.00
(88)	Juan Guzman	4.00
(89)	Darryl Hamilton	4.00
(90)	Joey Hamilton	4.00
(91)	Chris Hammond	4.00
(92)	Mike Hampton	7.50
(93)	Chris Haney	4.00
(94)	Todd Haney	4.00
(95)	Erik Hanson	4.00
(96)	Pete Harnisch	4.00
(97)	LaTroy Hawkins	4.00
(98)	Charlie Hayes	4.00
(99)	Jimmy Haynes	4.00
(100)	Roberto Hernandez	4.00
(101)	Bobby Higginson	4.00
(102)	Glenallen Hill	4.00
(103)	Ken Hill	4.00
(104)	Sterling Hitchcock	4.00
(105)	Trevor Hoffman	10.00
(106)	Dave Hollins	4.00
(107)	Dwayne Hosey	4.00
(108)	Thomas Howard	4.00
(109)	Steve Howe	6.00
(110)	John Hudek	4.00
(111)	Rex Hudler	4.00
(112)	Brian Hunter	4.00
(113)	Butch Huskey	4.00
(114)	Mark Hutton	4.00
(115)	Jason Jacome	4.00
(116)	John Jaha	4.00
(117)	Reggie Jefferson	4.00
(118)	Derek Jeter/SP	150.00
(119)	Bobby Jones	4.00
(120)	Todd Jones	4.00
(121)	Brian Jordan	5.00
(122)	Kevin Jordan	4.00
(123)	Jeff Juden	4.00
(124)	Ron Karkovice	4.00
(125)	Roberto Kelly	4.00
(126)	Mark Kiefer	4.00
(127)	Brooks Kieschnick	4.00
(128)	Jeff King	4.00
(129)	Mike Lansing	4.00
(130)	Matt Lawton	7.50
(131)	Al Leiter	6.00
(132)	Mark Leiter	4.00
(133)	Curtis Leskanic	4.00
(134)	Darren Lewis	4.00
(135)	Mark Lewis	4.00
(136)	Felipe Lira	4.00
(137)	Pat Listach	4.00
(138)	Keith Lockhart	4.00
(139)	Kenny Lofton/SP	25.00
(140)	John Mabry	4.00
(141)	Mike Macfarlane	4.00
(142)	Kirt Manwaring	4.00
(143)	Al Martin	4.00
(144)	Norberto Martin	4.00
(145)	Dennis Martinez	5.00
(146)	Pedro Martinez	40.00
(147)	Sandy Martinez	4.00
(148)	Mike Matheny	4.00
(149)	T.J. Mathews	4.00
(150)	David McCarty	4.00
(151)	Ben McDonald	4.00
(152)	Pat Meares	4.00
(153)	Orlando Merced	4.00
(154)	Jose Mesa	4.00
(155)	Matt Mieske	4.00
(156)	Orlando Miller	4.00
(157)	Mike Mimbs	4.00
(158)	Paul Molitor/SP	40.00
(159)	Raul Mondesi/SP	20.00
(160)	Jeff Montgomery	4.00
(161)	Mickey Morandini	4.00
(162)	Lyle Mouton	4.00
(163)	James Mouton	4.00
(164)	Jamie Moyer	4.00
(165)	Rodney Myers	4.00
(166)	Denny Neagle	4.00
(167)	Robb Nen	4.00
(168)	Marc Newfield	4.00
(169)	Dave Nilsson	4.00
(170)	Jon Nunnally	4.00
(171)	Chad Ogea	4.00
(172)	Troy O'Leary	4.00
(173)	Rey Ordonez	4.00
(174)	Jayhawk Owens	4.00
(175)	Tom Pagnozzi	4.00
(176)	Dean Palmer	4.00
(177)	Roger Pavlik	4.00
(178)	Troy Percival	4.00
(179)	Carlos Perez	4.00
(180)	Robert Perez	4.00
(181)	Andy Pettitte	30.00
(182)	Phil Plantier	4.00
(183)	Mike Potts	4.00
(184)	Curtis Pride	4.00
(185)	Ariel Prieto	4.00
(186)	Bill Pulsipher	4.00
(187)	Brad Radke	4.00
(188)	Manny Ramirez/SP	35.00
(189)	Joe Randa	4.00
(190)	Pat Rapp	4.00
(191)	Bryan Rekar	4.00
(192)	Shane Reynolds	4.00
(193)	Arthur Rhodes	4.00
(194)	Mariano Rivera	45.00
(195a)	Alex Rodriguez/SP (Black autograph.)	120.00
(195b)	Alex Rodriguez/SP (Blue autograph.)	120.00
(196)	Frank Rodriguez	4.00
(197)	Mel Rojas	4.00
(198)	Ken Ryan	4.00
(199)	Bret Saberhagen	4.00
(200)	Tim Salmon	5.00
(201)	Rey Sanchez	4.00
(202)	Scott Sanders	4.00
(203)	Steve Scarsone	4.00
(204)	Curt Schilling	25.00
(205)	Jason Schmidt	20.00
(206)	David Segui	4.00
(207)	Kevin Seitzer	4.00
(208)	Scott Servais	4.00
(209)	Don Slaught	4.00
(210)	Zane Smith	4.00
(211)	Paul Sorrento	4.00
(212)	Scott Stahoviak	4.00
(213)	Mike Stanley	4.00
(214)	Terry Steinbach	4.00
(215)	Kevin Stocker	4.00
(216)	Jeff Suppan	4.00
(217)	Bill Swift	4.00
(218)	Greg Swindell	4.00
(219)	Kevin Tapani	4.00
(220)	Danny Tartabull	4.00
(221)	Julian Tavarez	4.00
(222a)	Frank Thomas/SP (Blue autograph.)	40.00
(222b)	Frank Thomas/SP (Black autograph.)	40.00
(223)	Jim Thome/SP (Silver)	40.00
(224)	Ozzie Timmons	4.00
(225a)	Michael Tucker (Black autograph.)	4.00
(225b)	Michael Tucker (Blue autograph.)	4.00
(226)	Ismael Valdez	4.00
(227)	Jose Valentin	4.00
(228)	Todd Van Poppel	4.00
(229)	Mo Vaughn/SP	15.00
(230)	Quilvio Veras	4.00
(231)	Fernando Vina	4.00
(232)	Joe Vitiello	4.00
(233)	Jose Vizcaino	4.00
(234)	Omar Vizquel	12.00
(235)	Terrell Wade	4.00
(236)	Paul Wagner	4.00
(237)	Matt Walbeck	4.00
(238)	Jerome Walton	4.00
(239)	Turner Ward	4.00
(240)	Allen Watson	4.00
(241)	David Weathers	4.00
(242)	Walt Weiss	4.00
(244)	Turk Wendell	4.00
(244)	Rondell White	5.00
(245)	Brian Williams	4.00
(246)	George Williams	4.00
(247)	Paul Wilson	4.00
(248)	Bobby Witt	4.00
(249)	Bob Wolcott	4.00
(250)	Eric Young	4.00
(251)	Ernie Young	4.00
(252)	Gregg Zaun	4.00
---	Frank Thomas (Autographed jumbo edition of 1,500.)	25.00

Extended Autographs

		NM/M
	Common Player:	4.00
	Extended Pack:	20.00
	Extended Box:	150.00
(1)	Scott Aldred	4.00
(2)	Mike Aldrete	4.00
(3)	Rich Amaral	4.00
(4)	Alex Arias	4.00
(5)	Paul Assenmacher	4.00
(6)	Roger Bailey	4.00
(7)	Erik Bennett	4.00
(8)	Sean Bergman	4.00
(9)	Doug Bochtler	4.00
(10)	Tim Bogar	4.00

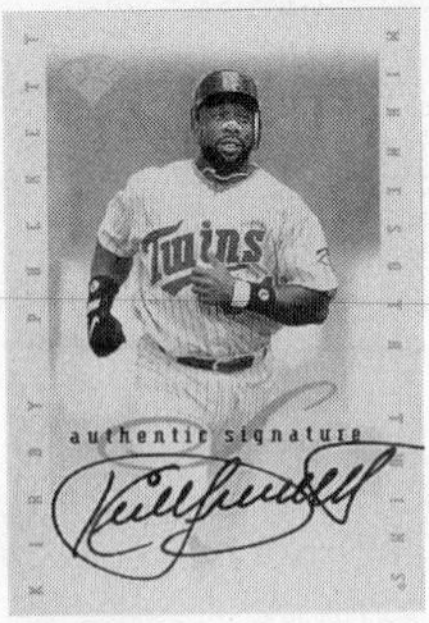

(11)	Pat Borders	4.00
(12)	Pedro Borbon	4.00
(13)	Shawn Boskie	4.00
(14)	Rafael Bournigal	4.00
(15)	Mark Brandenburg	4.00
(16)	John Briscoe	4.00
(17)	Jorge Brito	4.00
(18)	Doug Brocail	4.00
(19)	Jay Buhner/SP/1,000	17.50
(20)	Scott Bullett	4.00
(21)	Dave Burba	4.00
(22)	Ken Caminiti/SP/1,000	25.00
(23)	John Cangelosi	4.00
(24)	Cris Carpenter	4.00
(25)	Chuck Carr	4.00
(26)	Larry Casian	4.00
(27)	Tony Castillo	4.00
(28)	Jason Christiansen	4.00
(29)	Archi Cianfrocco	4.00
(30)	Mark Clark	4.00
(31)	Terry Clark	4.00
(32)	Roger Clemens/SP/1,000	150.00
(33)	Jim Converse	4.00
(34)	Dennis Cook	4.00
(35)	Francisco Cordova	4.00
(36)	Jim Corsi	4.00
(37)	Tim Crabtree	4.00
(38)	Doug Creek/SP/1,950	8.00
(39)	John Cummings	4.00
(40)	Omar Daal	4.00
(41)	Rich DeLucia	4.00
(42)	Mark Dewey	4.00
(43)	Alex Diaz	4.00
(44)	Jermaine Dye/SP/2,500	12.00
(45)	Ken Edenfield	4.00
(46)	Mark Eichhorn	4.00
(47)	John Ericks	4.00
(48)	Darin Erstad	10.00
(49)	Alvaro Espinoza	4.00
(50)	Jorge Fabregas	4.00
(51)	Mike Fetters	4.00
(52)	John Flaherty	4.00
(53)	Bryce Florie	4.00
(54)	Tony Fossas	4.00
(55)	Lou Frazier	4.00
(56)	Mike Gallego	4.00
(57)	Karim Garcia/SP/2,500	6.00
(58)	Jason Giambi	12.00
(59)	Ed Giovanola	4.00
(60)	Tom Glavine/SP/1,250	40.00
(61)	Juan Gonzalez/SP/1,000	30.00
(61)	Juan Gonzalez (Redemption card.)	5.00
(62)	Craig Grebeck	4.00
(63)	Buddy Groom	4.00
(64)	Kevin Gross	4.00
(65)	Eddie Guardado	4.00
(66)	Mark Guthrie	4.00
(67)	Tony Gwynn/SP/1,000	60.00
(68)	Chip Hale	4.00
(69)	Darren Hall	4.00
(70)	Lee Hancock	4.00
(71)	Dave Hansen	4.00
(72)	Bryan Harvey	4.00
(73)	Bill Haselman	4.00
(74)	Mike Henneman	4.00
(75)	Doug Henry	4.00
(76)	Gil Heredia	4.00
(77)	Carlos Hernandez	4.00
(78)	Jose Hernandez	4.00
(79)	Darren Holmes	4.00
(80)	Mark Holzemer	4.00
(81)	Rick Honeycutt	4.00
(82)	Chris Hook	4.00
(83)	Chris Howard	4.00
(84)	Jack Howell	4.00
(85)	David Hulse	4.00
(86)	Edwin Hurtado	4.00
(87)	Jeff Huson	4.00
(88)	Mike James	4.00
(89)	Derek Jeter/SP/1,000	160.00
(90)	Brian Johnson	4.00
(91)	Randy Johnson/ SP/1,000	125.00
(92)	Mark Johnson	4.00
(93)	Andruw Jones/SP/2,000	30.00
(93)	Andruw Jones (Redemption card.)	5.00
(94)	Chris Jones	4.00
(95)	Ricky Jordan	4.00
(96)	Matt Karchner	4.00
(97)	Scott Karl	4.00
(98)	Jason Kendall/SP/2,500	10.00
(99)	Brian Keyser	4.00
(100)	Mike Kingery	4.00
(101)	Wayne Kirby	4.00
(102)	Ryan Klesko/SP/1,000	17.50
(103)	Chuck Knoblauch/SP/1,000	15.00
(104)	Chad Kreuter	4.00
(105)	Tom Lampkin	4.00
(106)	Scott Leius	4.00
(107)	Jon Lieber	4.00
(108)	Nelson Liriano	4.00
(109)	Scott Livingstone	4.00
(110)	Graeme Lloyd	4.00
(111)	Kenny Lofton/SP/1,000	10.00
(112)	Luis Lopez	4.00
(113)	Torey Lovullo	4.00
(114)	Greg Maddux/SP/500	250.00
(115)	Mike Maddux	4.00
(116)	Dave Magadan	4.00
(117)	Mike Magnante	4.00
(118)	Joe Magrane	4.00
(119)	Pat Mahomes	4.00
(120)	Matt Mantei	4.00
(121)	John Marzano	4.00
(122)	Terry Matthews	4.00
(123)	Chuck McElroy	4.00
(124)	Fred McGriff/SP/1,000	35.00
(125)	Mark McLemore	4.00
(126)	Greg McMichael	4.00
(127)	Blas Minor	4.00
(128)	Dave Mlicki	4.00
(129)	Mike Mohler	4.00
(130)	Paul Molitor/SP/1,000	25.00
(131)	Steve Montgomery	4.00
(132)	Mike Mordecai	4.00
(133)	Mike Morgan	4.00
(134)	Mike Munoz	4.00
(135)	Greg Myers	4.00
(136)	Jimmy Myers	4.00
(137)	Mike Myers	4.00
(138)	Bob Natal	4.00
(139)	Dan Naulty	4.00
(140)	Jeff Nelson	4.00
(141)	Warren Newson	4.00
(142)	Chris Nichting	4.00
(143)	Melvin Nieves	4.00
(144)	Charlie O'Brien	4.00
(145)	Alex Ochoa	4.00
(146)	Omar Olivares	4.00
(147)	Joe Oliver	4.00
(148)	Lance Painter	4.00
(149)	Rafael Palmeiro/SP/2,000	35.00
(150)	Mark Parent	4.00
(151)	Steve Parris/SP/1,800	7.50
(152)	Bob Patterson	4.00
(153)	Tony Pena	7.50
(154)	Eddie Perez	4.00
(155)	Yorkis Perez	4.00
(156)	Robert Person	4.00
(157)	Mark Petkovsek	4.00
(158)	Andy Pettitte/SP/1,000	60.00
(159)	J.R. Phillips	4.00
(160)	Hipolito Pichardo	4.00
(161)	Eric Plunk	4.00
(162)	Jimmy Poole	4.00
(163)	Kirby Puckett/SP/1,000	80.00
(164)	Paul Quantrill	4.00
(165)	Tom Quinlan	4.00
(166)	Jeff Reboulet	4.00
(167)	Jeff Reed	4.00
(168)	Steve Reed	4.00
(169)	Carlos Reyes	4.00
(170)	Bill Risley	4.00
(171)	Kevin Ritz	4.00
(172)	Kevin Roberson	4.00
(173)	Rich Robertson	4.00
(174)	Alex Rodriguez/SP/500	180.00
(174)	Alex Rodriguez (Redemption card.)	15.00
(175)	Ivan Rodriguez/SP/1,250	40.00
(176)	Bruce Ruffin	4.00
(177)	Juan Samuel	4.00
(178)	Tim Scott	4.00
(179)	Kevin Sefcik	4.00
(180)	Jeff Shaw	4.00
(181)	Danny Sheaffer	4.00
(182)	Craig Shipley	4.00
(183)	Dave Silvestri	4.00
(184)	Aaron Small	4.00
(185)	John Smoltz/SP/1,000	90.00
(186)	Luis Sojo	4.00
(187)	Sammy Sosa/SP/1,000	160.00
(188)	Steve Sparks	4.00
(189)	Tim Spehr	4.00
(190)	Russ Springer	4.00
(191)	Matt Stairs	4.00
(192)	Andy Stankiewicz	4.00
(193)	Mike Stanton	4.00
(194)	Kelly Stinnett	4.00
(195)	Doug Strange	4.00
(196)	Mark Sweeney	4.00
(197)	Jeff Tabaka	4.00
(198)	Jesus Tavarez	4.00
(199)	Frank Thomas/SP/1,000	45.00
(200)	Larry Thomas	4.00
(201)	Mark Thompson	4.00
(202)	Mike Timlin	4.00
(203)	Steve Trachsel	4.00
(204)	Tom Urbani	4.00
(205)	Julio Valera	4.00
(206)	Dave Valle	4.00
(207)	William Van Landingham	4.00
(208)	Mo Vaughn/SP/1,000	10.00
(209)	Dave Veres	4.00

(210) Ed Vosberg 4.00
(211) Don Wengert 4.00
(212) Matt Whiteside 4.00
(213) Bob Wickman 4.00
(214) Matt Williams/SP/1,250 12.00
(215) Mike Williams 4.00
(216) Woody Williams 4.00
(217) Craig Worthington 4.00
--- Frank Thomas (Autographed jumbo edition of 1,500.) 30.00

Extended Autographs - Century Marks

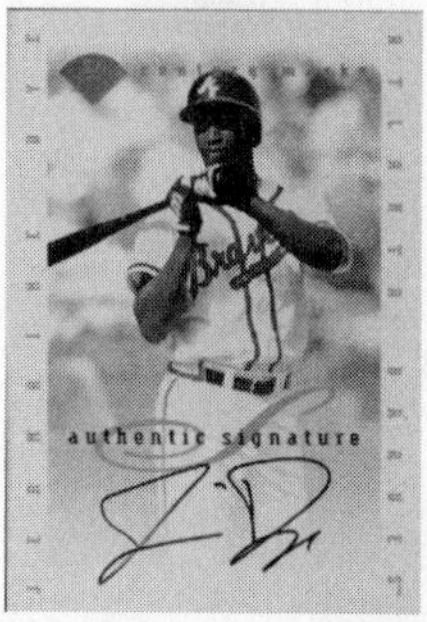

	NM/M
Common Player:	15.00
(1) Jay Buhner	30.00
(2) Ken Caminiti	30.00
(3) Roger Clemens	250.00
(4) Jermaine Dye	30.00
(5) Darin Erstad	45.00
(6) Karim Garcia	30.00
(7) Jason Giambi	75.00
(8) Tom Glavine	90.00
(9) Juan Gonzalez	90.00
(9) Juan Gonzalez (Redemption card.)	7.50
(10) Tony Gwynn	150.00
(11) Derek Jeter	350.00
(11) Derek Jeter (Redemption card.)	15.00
(12) Randy Johnson	185.00
(13) Andruw Jones	150.00
(13) Andruw Jones (Redemption card.)	7.50
(14) Jason Kendall	30.00
(15) Ryan Klesko	30.00
(16) Chuck Knoblauch	30.00
(17) Kenny Lofton	30.00
(18) Greg Maddux	200.00
(19) Fred McGriff	30.00
(20) Paul Molitor	110.00
(21) Alex Ochoa	15.00
(22) Rafael Palmeiro	110.00
(22) Rafael Palmeiro (Redemption card.)	7.50
(23) Andy Pettitte	75.00
(24) Kirby Puckett	185.00
(25) Alex Rodriguez	350.00
(25) Alex Rodriguez (Redemption card.)	15.00
(26) Ivan Rodriguez	100.00
(27) John Smoltz	100.00
(28) Sammy Sosa	350.00
(29) Frank Thomas	135.00
(30) Mo Vaughn	30.00
(31) Matt Williams	30.00

1997 Leaf

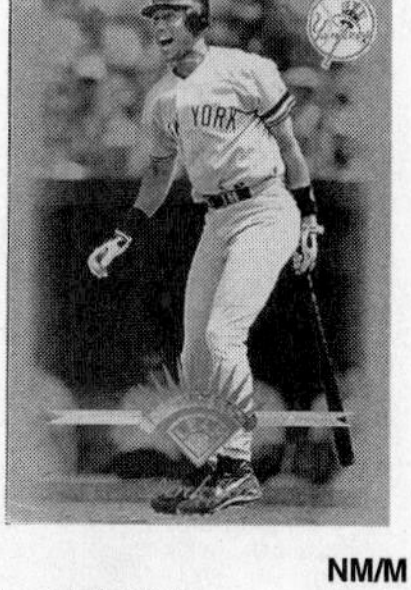

	NM/M
Complete Set (400):	25.00
Common Player:	.05
Jackie Robinson 1948 Leaf Reprint:	10.00
Series 1 Pack (12):	2.00
Series 1 Wax Box (18):	30.00
Series 2 Pack (12):	1.50
Series 2 Wax Box (24):	30.00
1 Wade Boggs	1.50
2 Brian McRae	.05
3 Jeff D'Amico	.05
4 George Arias	.05
5 Billy Wagner	.05
6 Ray Lankford	.05
7 Will Clark	.10
8 Edgar Renteria	.05
9 Alex Ochoa	.05
10 Roberto Hernandez	.05
11 Joe Carter	.05
12 Gregg Jefferies	.05
13 Mark Grace	.05
14 Roberto Alomar	.10
15 Joe Randa	.05
16 Alex Rodriguez	2.50
17 Tony Gwynn	1.50
18 Steve Gibralter	.05
19 Scott Stahoviak	.05
20 Matt Williams	.05
21 Quinton McCracken	.05
22 Ugueth Urbina	.05
23 Jermaine Allensworth	.05
24 Paul Molitor	.75
25 Carlos Delgado	.50
26 Bob Abreu	.05
27 John Jaha	.05
28 Rusty Greer	.05
29 Kimera Bartee	.05
30 Ruben Rivera	.05
31 Jason Kendall	.05
32 Lance Johnson	.05
33 Robin Ventura	.05
34 Kevin Appier	.05
35 John Mabry	.05
36 Ricky Otero	.05
37 Mike Lansing	.05
38 Mark McGwire	2.50
39 Tim Naehring	.05
40 Tom Glavine	.30
41 Rey Ordonez	.05
42 Tony Clark	.05
43 Rafael Palmeiro	.65
44 Pedro Martinez	.75
45 Keith Lockhart	.05
46 Dan Wilson	.05
47 John Wetteland	.05
48 Chan Ho Park	.05
49 Gary Sheffield	.40
50 Shawn Estes	.05
51 Royce Clayton	.05
52 Jaime Navarro	.05
53 Raul Casanova	.05
54 Jeff Bagwell	1.00
55 Barry Larkin	.05
56 Charles Nagy	.05
57 Ken Caminiti	.05
58 Todd Hollandsworth	.05
59 Pat Hentgen	.05
60 Jose Valentin	.05
61 Frank Rodriguez	.05
62 Mickey Tettleton	.05
63 Marty Cordova	.05
64 Cecil Fielder	.05
65 Barry Bonds	3.00
66 Scott Servais	.05
67 Ernie Young	.05
68 Wilson Alvarez	.05
69 Mike Grace	.05
70 Shane Reynolds	.05
71 Henry Rodriguez	.05
72 Eric Karros	.05
73 Mark Langston	.05
74 Scott Karl	.05
75 Trevor Hoffman	.05
76 Orel Hershiser	.05
77 John Smoltz	.05
78 Raul Mondesi	.05
79 Jeff Brantley	.05
80 Donne Wall	.05
81 Joey Cora	.05
82 Mel Rojas	.05
83 Chad Mottola	.05
84 Omar Vizquel	.05
85 Greg Maddux	1.50
86 Jamey Wright	.05
87 Chuck Finley	.05
88 Brady Anderson	.05
89 Alex Gonzalez	.05
90 Andy Benes	.05
91 Reggie Jefferson	.05
92 Paul O'Neill	.05
93 Javier Lopez	.05
94 Mark Grudzielanek	.05
95 Marc Newfield	.05
96 Kevin Ritz	.05
97 Fred McGriff	.05
98 Dwight Gooden	.05
99 Hideo Nomo	.65
100 Steve Finley	.05
101 Juan Gonzalez	.65
102 Jay Buhner	.05
103 Paul Wilson	.05
104 Alan Benes	.05
105 Manny Ramirez	1.00
106 Kevin Elster	.05
107 Frank Thomas	1.00
108 Orlando Miller	.05
109 Ramon Martinez	.05
110 Kenny Lofton	.05
111 Bernie Williams	.05
112 Robby Thompson	.05
113 Bernard Gilkey	.05
114 Ray Durham	.05
115 Jeff Cirillo	.05
116 Brian Jordan	.05
117 Rich Becker	.05
118 Al Leiter	.05
119 Mark Johnson	.05
120 Ellis Burks	.05
121 Sammy Sosa	2.00
122 Willie Greene	.05
123 Michael Tucker	.05
124 Eddie Murray	.75
125 Joey Hamilton	.05
126 Antonio Osuna	.05
127 Bobby Higginson	.05
128 Tomas Perez	.05
129 Tim Salmon	.05
130 Mark Wohlers	.05
131 Charles Johnson	.05
132 Randy Johnson	.75
133 Brooks Kieschnick	.05
134 Al Martin	.05
135 Dante Bichette	.05
136 Andy Pettitte	.30
137 Jason Giambi	.60
138 James Baldwin	.05
139 Ben McDonald	.05
140 Shawn Green	.35
141 Geronimo Berroa	.05
142 Jose Offerman	.05
143 Curtis Pride	.05
144 Terrell Wade	.05
145 Ismael Valdes	.05
146 Mike Mussina	.40
147 Mariano Rivera	.15
148 Ken Hill	.05
149 Darin Erstad	.25
150 Jay Bell	.05
151 Mo Vaughn	.05
152 Ozzie Smith	1.50
153 Jose Mesa	.05
154 Osvaldo Fernandez	.05
155 Vinny Castilla	.05
156 Jason Isringhausen	.05
157 B.J. Surhoff	.05
158 Robert Perez	.05
159 Ron Coomer	.05
160 Darren Oliver	.05
161 Mike Mohler	.05
162 Russ Davis	.05
163 Bret Boone	.05
164 Ricky Bottalico	.05
165 Derek Jeter	3.00
166 Orlando Merced	.05
167 John Valentin	.05
168 Andruw Jones	1.00
169 Angel Echevarria	.05
170 Todd Walker	.05
171 Desi Relaford	.05
172 Trey Beamon	.05
173 Brian Giles **RC**	.75
174 Scott Rolen	.60
175 Shannon Stewart	.05
176 Dmitri Young	.05
177 Justin Thompson	.05
178 Trot Nixon	.05
179 Josh Booty	.05
180 Robin Jennings	.05
181 Marvin Benard	.05
182 Luis Castillo	.05
183 Wendell Magee	.05
184 Vladimir Guerrero	1.00
185 Nomar Garciaparra	2.00
186 Ryan Hancock	.05
187 Mike Cameron	.05
188 Cal Ripken Jr. (Legacy)	1.50
189 Chipper Jones (Legacy)	.75
190 Albert Belle (Legacy)	.05
191 Mike Piazza (Legacy)	1.00
192 Chuck Knoblauch (Legacy)	.05
193 Ken Griffey Jr. (Legacy)	1.00
194 Ivan Rodriguez (Legacy)	.30
195 Jose Canseco (Legacy)	.25
196 Ryne Sandberg (Legacy)	.75
197 Jim Thome (Legacy)	.30
198 Andy Pettitte (Checklist)	.05
199 Andruw Jones (Checklist)	.50
200 Derek Jeter (Checklist)	1.50
201 Chipper Jones	1.50
202 Albert Belle	.05
203 Mike Piazza	2.00
204 Ken Griffey Jr.	2.00
205 Ryne Sandberg	1.50
206 Jose Canseco	.40
207 Chili Davis	.05
208 Roger Clemens	2.00
209 Deion Sanders	.05
210 Darryl Hamilton	.05
211 Jermaine Dye	.05
212 Matt Williams	.05
213 Kevin Elster	.05
214 John Wetteland	.05
215 Garret Anderson	.05
216 Kevin Brown	.05
217 Matt Lawton	.05
218 Cal Ripken Jr.	3.00
219 Moises Alou	.05
220 Chuck Knoblauch	.05
221 Ivan Rodriguez	.65
222 Travis Fryman	.05
223 Jim Thome	.65
224 Eddie Murray	.75
225 Eric Young	.05
226 Ron Gant	.05
227 Tony Phillips	.05
228 Reggie Sanders	.05
229 Johnny Damon	.35
230 Bill Pulsipher	.05
231 Jim Edmonds	.05
232 Melvin Nieves	.05
233 Ryan Klesko	.05
234 David Cone	.05
235 Derek Bell	.05
236 Julio Franco	.05
237 Juan Guzman	.05
238 Larry Walker	.05
239 Delino DeShields	.05
240 Troy Percival	.05
241 Andres Galarraga	.05
242 Rondell White	.05
243 John Burkett	.05
244 J.T. Snow	.05
245 Alex Fernandez	.05
246 Edgar Martinez	.05
247 Craig Biggio	.05
248 Todd Hundley	.05
249 Jimmy Key	.05
250 Cliff Floyd	.05
251 Jeff Conine	.05
252 Curt Schilling	.35
253 Jeff King	.05
254 Tino Martinez	.05
255 Carlos Baerga	.05
256 Jeff Fassero	.05
257 Dean Palmer	.05
258 Robb Nen	.05
259 Sandy Alomar Jr.	.05
260 Carlos Perez	.05
261 Rickey Henderson	.75
262 Bobby Bonilla	.05
263 Darren Daulton	.05
264 Jim Leyritz	.05
265 Dennis Martinez	.05
266 Butch Huskey	.05
267 Joe Vitiello	.05
268 Steve Trachsel	.05
269 Glenallen Hill	.05
270 Terry Steinbach	.05
271 Mark McLemore	.05
272 Devon White	.05
273 Jeff Kent	.05
274 Tim Raines	.05
275 Carlos Garcia	.05
276 Hal Morris	.05
277 Gary Gaetti	.05
278 John Olerud	.05
279 Wally Joyner	.05
280 Brian Hunter	.05
281 Steve Karsay	.05
282 Denny Neagle	.05
283 Jose Herrera	.05
284 Todd Stottlemyre	.05
285 Bip Roberts	.05
286 Kevin Seitzer	.05
287 Benji Gil	.05
288 Dennis Eckersley	.65
289 Brad Ausmus	.05
290 Otis Nixon	.05
291 Darryl Strawberry	.05
292 Marquis Grissom	.05
293 Darryl Kile	.05
294 Quilvio Veras	.05
295 Tom Goodwin	.05
296 Benito Santiago	.05
297 Mike Bordick	.05
298 Roberto Kelly	.05
299 David Justice	.05
300 Carl Everett	.05
301 Mark Whiten	.05
302 Aaron Sele	.05
303 Darren Dreifort	.05
304 Bobby Jones	.05
305 Fernando Vina	.05
306 Ed Sprague	.05
307 Andy Ashby	.05
308 Tony Fernandez	.05
309 Roger Pavlik	.05
310 Mark Clark	.05
311 Mariano Duncan	.05
312 Tyler Houston	.05
313 Eric Davis	.05
314 Greg Vaughn	.05
315 David Segui	.05
316 Dave Nilsson	.05
317 F.P. Santangelo	.05
318 Wilton Guerrero	.05
319 Jose Guillen	.05
320 Kevin Orie	.05
321 Derrek Lee	.05
322 Bubba Trammell **RC**	.50
323 Pokey Reese	.05
324 Hideki Irabu **RC**	.25
325 Scott Spiezio	.05
326 Bartolo Colon	.05
327 Damon Mashore	.05
328 Ryan McGuire	.05
329 Chris Carpenter	.05
330 Jose Cruz Jr. **RC**	.50
331 Todd Greene	.05
332 Brian Moehler	.05
333 Mike Sweeney	.05
334 Neifi Perez	.05
335 Matt Morris	.05
336 Marvin Benard	.05
337 Karim Garcia	.05
338 Jason Dickson	.05
339 Brant Brown	.05
340 Jeff Suppan	.05
341 Deivi Cruz **RC**	.25
342 Antone Williamson	.05
343 Curtis Goodwin	.05
344 Brooks Kieschnick	.05
345 Tony Womack **RC**	.25
346 Rudy Pemberton	.05

347	Todd Dunwoody	.05
348	Frank Thomas (Legacy)	.50
349	Andruw Jones (Legacy)	.50
350	Alex Rodriguez (Legacy)	1.25
351	Greg Maddux (Legacy)	.75
352	Jeff Bagwell (Legacy)	.50
353	Juan Gonzalez (Legacy)	.35
354	Barry Bonds (Legacy)	1.50
355	Mark McGwire (Legacy)	1.25
356	Tony Gwynn (Legacy)	.75
357	Gary Sheffield (Legacy)	.25
358	Derek Jeter (Legacy)	1.50
359	Manny Ramirez (Legacy)	.50
360	Hideo Nomo (Legacy)	.30
361	Sammy Sosa (Legacy)	1.00
362	Paul Molitor (Legacy)	.40
363	Kenny Lofton (Legacy)	.05
364	Eddie Murray (Legacy)	.40
365	Barry Larkin (Legacy)	.05
366	Roger Clemens (Legacy)	1.00
367	John Smoltz (Legacy)	.05
368	Alex Rodriguez (Gamers)	1.50
369	Frank Thomas (Gamers)	.40
370	Cal Ripken Jr. (Gamers)	1.50
371	Ken Griffey Jr. (Gamers)	1.50
372	Greg Maddux (Gamers)	1.00
373	Mike Piazza (Gamers)	1.25
374	Chipper Jones (Gamers)	1.00
375	Albert Belle (Gamers)	.05
376	Chuck Knoblauch (Gamers)	.05
377	Brady Anderson (Gamers)	.05
378	David Justice (Gamers)	.05
379	Randy Johnson (Gamers)	.40
380	Wade Boggs (Gamers)	.75
381	Kevin Brown (Gamers)	.05
382	Tom Glavine (Gamers)	.05
383	Raul Mondesi (Gamers)	.05
384	Ivan Rodriguez (Gamers)	.30
385	Larry Walker (Gamers)	.05
386	Bernie Williams (Gamers)	.05
387	Rusty Greer (Gamers)	.05
388	Rafael Palmeiro (Gamers)	.05
389	Matt Williams (Gamers)	.05
390	Eric Young (Gamers)	.05
391	Fred McGriff (Gamers)	.05
392	Ken Caminiti (Gamers)	.05
393	Roberto Alomar (Gamers)	.05
394	Brian Jordan (Gamers)	.05
395	Mark Grace (Gamers)	.05
396	Jim Edmonds (Gamers)	.05
397	Deion Sanders (Gamers)	.05
398	Vladimir Guerrero Checklist	.50
399	Darin Erstad Checklist	.10
400	Nomar Garciaparra Checklist	1.00

Banner Season

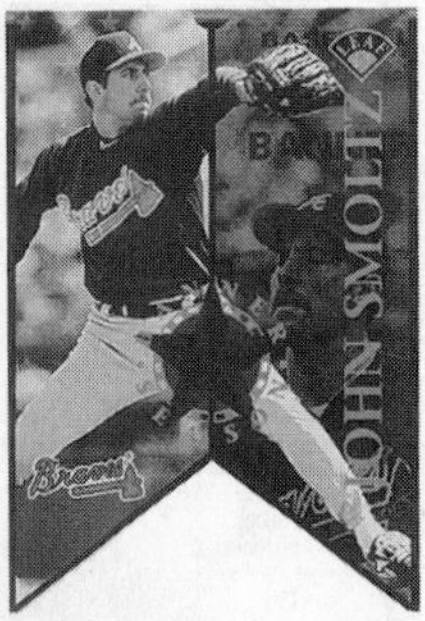

		NM/M
Complete Set (15):		30.00
Common Player:		.50
1	Jeff Bagwell	2.50
2	Ken Griffey Jr.	5.00
3	Juan Gonzalez	1.50
4	Frank Thomas	2.50
5	Alex Rodriguez	6.00
6	Kenny Lofton	.50
7	Chuck Knoblauch	.50
8	Mo Vaughn	.50
9	Chipper Jones	4.00
10	Ken Caminiti	.50
11	Craig Biggio	.50
12	John Smoltz	.50
13	Pat Hentgen	.50
14	Derek Jeter	7.50
15	Todd Hollandsworth	.50

Dress for Success

		NM/M
Complete Set (18):		17.50
Common Player:		.25
1	Greg Maddux	1.50
2	Cal Ripken Jr.	3.00
3	Albert Belle	.25
4	Frank Thomas	1.00
5	Dante Bichette	.25
6	Gary Sheffield	.50
7	Jeff Bagwell	1.00
8	Mike Piazza	2.00
9	Mark McGwire	2.25
10	Ken Caminiti	.25
11	Alex Rodriguez	2.50
12	Ken Griffey Jr.	2.00

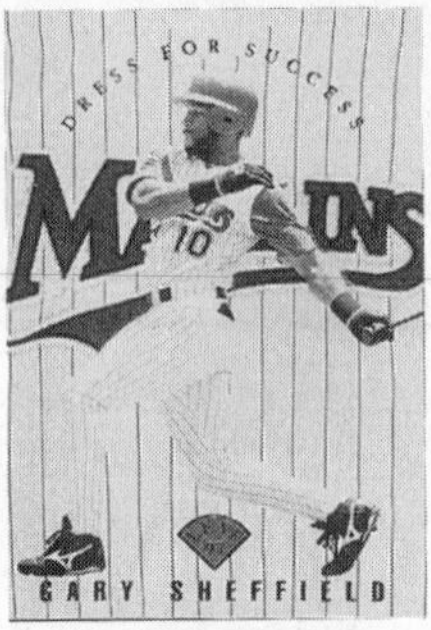

13	Juan Gonzalez	.75
14	Brian Jordan	.25
15	Mo Vaughn	.25
16	Ivan Rodriguez	.75
17	Andruw Jones	1.00
18	Chipper Jones	1.50

Fractal Matrix

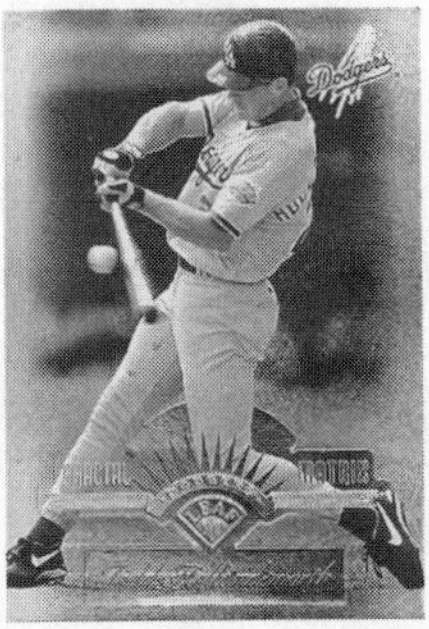

		NM/M
Common Bronze:		.35
Common Silver:		.50
Common Gold:		1.25
1	Wade Boggs G/Y	8.00
2	Brian McRae B/Y	.35
3	Jeff D'Amico B/Y	.35
4	George Arias S/Y	.50
5	Billy Wagner S/Y	.50
6	Ray Lankford B/Z	.35
7	Will Clark S/Y	.60
8	Edgar Renteria S/Y	.50
9	Alex Ochoa S/Y	.50
10	Roberto Hernandez B/X	.35
11	Joe Carter S/Y	.50
12	Gregg Jefferies B/Y	.35
13	Mark Grace S/Y	.75
14	Roberto Alomar G/Y	2.00
15	Joe Randa B/X	.35
16	Alex Rodriguez G/Z	10.00
17	Tony Gwynn G/Z	6.00
18	Steve Gibralter B/Y	.35
19	Scott Stahoviak B/X	.35
20	Matt Williams S/Z	.50
21	Quinton McCracken B/Y	.35
22	Ugueth Urbina B/X	.35
23	Jermaine Allensworth S/X	.50
24	Paul Molitor G/X	5.00
25	Carlos Delgado S/Y	1.00
26	Bob Abreu S/Y	.50
27	John Jaha S/Y	.50
28	Rusty Greer S/Z	.50
29	Kimera Bartee B/X	.35
30	Ruben Rivera S/Y	.50
31	Jason Kendall S/Y	.50
32	Lance Johnson B/X	.35
33	Robin Ventura B/Y	.35
34	Kevin Appier S/X	.50
35	John Mabry S/Y	.50
36	Ricky Otero B/X	.35
37	Mike Lansing B/X	.35
38	Mark McGwire G/Z	10.00
39	Tim Naehring B/X	.35
40	Tom Glavine S/Z	1.00
41	Rey Ordonez S/Y	.50
42	Tony Clark S/Y	.50
43	Rafael Palmeiro S/Z	2.00
44	Pedro Martinez B/X	2.00
45	Keith Lockhart B/X	.35
46	Dan Wilson B/Y	.35
47	John Wetteland B/Y	.35
48	Chan Ho Park B/X	.35
49	Gary Sheffield G/Z	3.00
50	Shawn Estes B/X	.35
51	Royce Clayton B/X	.35
52	Jaime Navarro B/X	.35
53	Raul Casanova B/X	.35
54	Jeff Bagwell G/Z	5.00
55	Barry Larkin G/X	1.25
56	Charles Nagy B/Y	.35
57	Ken Caminiti G/Y	1.25
58	Todd Hollandsworth S/Z	.50
59	Pat Hentgen S/X	.50
60	Jose Valentin B/X	.35
61	Frank Rodriguez B/X	.35
62	Mickey Tettleton B/X	.35
63	Marty Cordova G/X	1.25
64	Cecil Fielder S/X	.50
65	Barry Bonds G/Z	13.50
66	Scott Servais B/X	.35
67	Ernie Young B/X	.35
68	Wilson Alvarez B/X	.35
69	Mike Grace B/X	.35
70	Shane Reynolds S/X	.50
71	Henry Rodriguez S/Y	.50
72	Eric Karros B/X	.35
73	Mark Langston B/X	.35
74	Scott Karl B/X	.35
75	Trevor Hoffman B/X	.35
76	Orel Hershiser S/X	.50
77	John Smoltz G/Y	1.50
78	Raul Mondesi G/Z	1.25
79	Jeff Brantley B/X	.35
80	Donne Wall B/X	.35
81	Joey Cora B/X	.35
82	Mel Rojas B/X	.35
83	Chad Mottola B/X	.35
84	Omar Vizquel B/X	.35
85	Greg Maddux G/Z	6.00
86	Jamey Wright S/Y	.50
87	Chuck Finley B/X	.35
88	Brady Anderson G/Y	1.25
89	Alex Gonzalez S/X	.50
90	Andy Benes B/X	.35
91	Reggie Jefferson B/X	.35
92	Paul O'Neill B/Y	.35
93	Javier Lopez S/X	.50
94	Mark Grudzielanek S/X	.50
95	Marc Newfield B/X	.35
96	Kevin Ritz B/X	.35
97	Fred McGriff G/Y	1.25
98	Dwight Gooden S/X	.50
99	Hideo Nomo S/Y	1.50
100	Steve Finley B/X	.35
101	Juan Gonzalez G/Z	4.00
102	Jay Buhner S/Z	.50
103	Paul Wilson S/Y	.50
104	Alan Benes B/Y	.35
105	Manny Ramirez G/Z	5.00
106	Kevin Elster B/X	.35
107	Frank Thomas G/Z	5.00
108	Orlando Miller B/X	.35
109	Ramon Martinez B/X	.35
110	Kenny Lofton G/Z	1.25
111	Bernie Williams G/Y	1.25
112	Robby Thompson B/X	.35
113	Bernard Gilkey B/Z	.35
114	Ray Durham B/X	.35
115	Jeff Cirillo S/Z	.50
116	Brian Jordan G/Z	1.25
117	Rich Becker S/Y	.50
118	Al Leiter B/X	.35
119	Mark Johnson B/X	.35
120	Ellis Burks B/Y	.35
121	Sammy Sosa G/Z	7.50
122	Willie Greene B/X	.35
123	Michael Tucker B/X	.35
124	Eddie Murray G/Y	6.00
125	Joey Hamilton S/Y	.50
126	Antonio Osuna B/X	.35
127	Bobby Higginson S/Y	.50
128	Tomas Perez B/X	.35
129	Tim Salmon G/Z	1.25
130	Mark Wohlers B/X	.35
131	Charles Johnson S/X	.50
132	Randy Johnson S/Y	2.00
133	Brooks Kieschnick S/X	.50
134	Al Martin S/Y	.50
135	Dante Bichette B/X	.35
136	Andy Pettitte G/Z	2.00
137	Jason Giambi G/Y	4.00
138	James Baldwin S/X	.50
139	Ben McDonald B/X	.35
140	Shawn Green S/X	1.00
141	Geronimo Berroa B/Y	.35
142	Jose Offerman B/X	.35
143	Curtis Pride B/X	.35
144	Terrell Wade B/X	.35
145	Ismael Valdes S/X	.50
146	Mike Mussina S/Y	1.25
147	Mariano Rivera S/X	.75
148	Ken Hill B/Y	.35
149	Darin Erstad G/Z	4.00
150	Jay Bell B/X	.35
151	Mo Vaughn G/Z	1.25
152	Ozzie Smith G/Y	8.00
153	Jose Mesa B/X	.35
154	Osvaldo Fernandez B/X	.35
155	Vinny Castilla B/Y	.35
156	Jason Isringhausen S/Y	.50
157	B.J. Surhoff B/X	.35
158	Robert Perez B/X	.35
159	Ron Coomer B/X	.35
160	Darren Oliver B/X	.35
161	Mike Mohler B/X	.35
162	Russ Davis B/X	.35
163	Bret Boone B/X	.35
164	Ricky Bottalico B/X	.35
165	Derek Jeter G/Z	13.50
166	Orlando Merced B/X	.35
167	John Valentin B/X	.35
168	Andruw Jones G/Z	5.00
169	Angel Echevarria B/X	.35
170	Todd Walker G/Z	1.25
171	Desi Relaford B/Y	.35
172	Trey Beamon S/X	.50
173	Brian Giles S/Y	.50
174	Scott Rolen G/Z	3.50
175	Shannon Stewart S/Z	.50
176	Dmitri Young G/Z	1.25
177	Justin Thompson B/X	.35
178	Trot Nixon S/Y	.50
179	Josh Booty S/Y	.50
180	Robin Jennings B/X	.35
181	Marvin Benard B/X	.35
182	Luis Castillo B/Y	.35
183	Wendell Magee B/X	.35
184	Vladimir Guerrero G/X	5.00
185	Nomar Garciaparra G/X	12.50
186	Ryan Hancock B/X	.35
187	Mike Cameron S/X	.50
188	Cal Ripken Jr. B/Z	5.00
189	Chipper Jones S/Z	4.00
190	Albert Belle S/Z	1.00
191	Mike Piazza B/Z	4.00
192	Chuck Knoblauch S/Y	.50
193	Ken Griffey Jr. B/Z	3.50
194	Ivan Rodriguez G/Z	4.00
195	Jose Canseco S/X	1.25
196	Ryne Sandberg S/X	3.00
197	Jim Thome G/Y	1.50
198	Andy Pettitte B/Y Checklist	.75
199	Andruw Jones B/Y Checklist	2.00
200	Derek Jeter S/Y Checklist	2.00
201	Chipper Jones G/X	10.00
202	Albert Belle G/Y	1.25
203	Mike Piazza G/Y	12.00
204	Ken Griffey Jr. G/X	15.00
205	Ryne Sandberg G/Z	6.00
206	Jose Canseco S/Y	.75
207	Chili Davis B/X	.35
208	Roger Clemens G/Z	6.50
209	Deion Sanders G/Z	1.50
210	Darryl Hamilton B/X	.35
211	Jermaine Dye S/X	.50
212	Matt Williams G/Y	1.25
213	Kevin Elster B/Y	.35
214	John Wetteland S/X	.50
215	Garret Anderson G/Z	1.25
216	Kevin Brown G/Y	1.25
217	Matt Lawton S/Y	.50
218	Cal Ripken Jr. G/X	16.50
219	Moises Alou G/Y	1.25
220	Chuck Knoblauch G/Z	1.25
221	Ivan Rodriguez G/Y	5.50
222	Travis Fryman B/Y	.35
223	Jim Thome G/Z	2.00
224	Eddie Murray S/Z	3.00
225	Eric Young G/Z	1.25
226	Ron Gant S/X	.50
227	Tony Phillips B/X	.35
228	Reggie Sanders B/Y	.35
229	Johnny Damon S/Z	1.00
230	Bill Pulsipher B/X	.35
231	Jim Edmonds G/Z	1.25
232	Melvin Nieves B/X	.35
233	Ryan Klesko G/Z	1.25
234	David Cone S/X	.50
235	Derek Bell B/Y	.35
236	Julio Franco S/X	.50
237	Juan Guzman B/X	.35
238	Larry Walker G/Z	1.25
239	Delino DeShields B/X	.35
240	Troy Percival B/Y	.35
241	Andres Galarraga G/Z	1.25
242	Rondell White G/Z	1.25
243	John Burkett B/X	.35
244	J.T. Snow B/Y	.35
245	Alex Fernandez S/Y	.50
246	Edgar Martinez G/Z	1.25
247	Craig Biggio G/Z	1.25
248	Todd Hundley G/Y	1.25
249	Jimmy Key S/X	.50
250	Cliff Floyd B/Y	.35
251	Jeff Conine B/Y	.35
252	Curt Schilling B/X	.65
253	Jeff King B/X	.35
254	Tino Martinez G/Z	1.25
255	Carlos Baerga S/Y	.50
256	Jeff Fassero B/Y	.35
257	Dean Palmer S/Y	.50
258	Robb Nen B/X	.35
259	Sandy Alomar Jr. S/Y	.50
260	Carlos Perez B/X	.35
261	Rickey Henderson S/Y	2.00
262	Bobby Bonilla S/Y	.50
263	Darren Daulton B/X	.35
264	Jim Leyritz B/X	.35
265	Dennis Martinez B/X	.35
266	Butch Huskey B/X	.35
267	Joe Vitiello S/Y	.50
268	Steve Trachsel B/X	.35
269	Glenallen Hill B/X	.35
270	Terry Steinbach B/X	.35
271	Mark McLemore B/X	.35
272	Devon White B/X	.35
273	Jeff Kent B/X	.35
274	Tim Raines B/X	.35
275	Carlos Garcia B/X	.35
276	Hal Morris B/X	.35
277	Gary Gaetti B/X	.35
278	John Olerud S/Y	.50
279	Wally Joyner B/X	.35
280	Brian Hunter S/X	.50
281	Steve Karsay B/X	.35
282	Denny Neagle S/X	.50
283	Jose Herrera B/X	.35
284	Todd Stottlemyre B/X	.35
285	Bip Roberts S/X	.50

286	Kevin Seitzer B/X	.35
287	Benji Gil B/X	.35
288	Dennis Eckersley S/X	.50
289	Brad Ausmus B/X	.35
290	Otis Nixon B/X	.35
291	Darryl Strawberry B/X	.35
292	Marquis Grissom S/Y	.50
293	Darryl Kile B/X	.35
294	Quilvio Veras B/X	.35
295	Tom Goodwin B/X	.35
296	Benito Santiago B/X	.35
297	Mike Bordick B/X	.35
298	Roberto Kelly B/X	.35
299	David Justice G/Z	1.25
300	Carl Everett B/X	.35
301	Mark Whiten B/X	.35
302	Aaron Sele B/X	.35
303	Darren Dreifort B/X	.35
304	Bobby Jones B/X	.35
305	Fernando Vina B/X	.35
306	Ed Sprague B/X	.35
307	Andy Ashby S/X	.50
308	Tony Fernandez B/X	.35
309	Roger Pavlik B/X	.35
310	Mark Clark B/X	.35
311	Mariano Duncan B/X	.35
312	Tyler Houston B/X	.35
313	Eric Davis S/Y	.50
314	Greg Vaughn B/Y	.35
315	David Segui S/Y	.50
316	Dave Nilsson S/X	.50
317	F.P. Santangelo S/X	.50
318	Wilton Guerrero G/Z	1.25
319	Jose Guillen G/Z	1.25
320	Kevin Orie S/Y	.50
321	Derrek Lee G/Z	2.50
322	Bubba Trammell S/Y	.50
323	Pokey Reese G/Z	1.25
324	Hideki Irabu G/X	1.25
325	Scott Spiezio S/Y	.50
326	Bartolo Colon G/Z	1.25
327	Damon Mashore S/Y	.50
328	Ryan McGuire S/Y	.50
329	Chris Carpenter B/X	.35
330	Jose Cruz, Jr. G/X	1.25
331	Todd Greene S/Z	.50
332	Brian Moehler B/X	.35
333	Mike Sweeney B/Y	.35
334	Neifi Perez G/Z	1.25
335	Matt Morris S/Y	.50
336	Marvin Benard B/Y	.35
337	Karim Garcia S/Z	.75
338	Jason Dickson S/Y	.50
339	Brant Brown S/Y	.50
340	Jeff Suppan S/Z	.50
341	Delvi Cruz B/X	.35
342	Antone Williamson G/Z	1.25
343	Curtis Goodwin B/X	.35
344	Brooks Kieschnick S/Y	.50
345	Tony Womack S/Y	.35
346	Rudy Pemberton B/X	.35
347	Todd Dunwoody B/X	.35
348	Frank Thomas B/Y	2.25
349	Andruw Jones S/X	2.00
350	Alex Rodriguez B/X	4.00
351	Greg Maddux S/Y	3.00
352	Jeff Bagwell B/Y	2.25
353	Juan Gonzalez S/Y	1.50
354	Barry Bonds B/Y	5.00
355	Mark McGwire B/Y	4.00
356	Tony Gwynn B/Y	3.00
357	Gary Sheffield B/X	.75
358	Derek Jeter S/X	4.00
359	Manny Ramirez S/Y	2.00
360	Hideo Nomo G/Z	4.00
361	Sammy Sosa B/X	3.50
362	Paul Molitor S/Y	3.00
363	Kenny Lofton B/Y	.35
364	Eddie Murray B/X	2.00
365	Barry Larkin S/Z	.50
366	Roger Clemens S/Y	3.50
367	John Smoltz B/Z	.35
368	Alex Rodriguez S/X	3.25
369	Frank Thomas B/X	2.25
370	Cal Ripken Jr. S/Y	4.00
371	Ken Griffey Jr. B/Y	3.25
372	Greg Maddux B/X	3.00
373	Mike Piazza S/X	3.25
374	Chipper Jones B/Y	3.00
375	Albert Belle B/X	.50
376	Chuck Knoblauch B/X	.35
377	Brady Anderson B/Z	.35
378	David Justice S/X	.50
379	Randy Johnson B/Z	2.00
380	Wade Boggs B/X	3.00
381	Kevin Brown B/Y	.35
382	Tom Glavine G/Y	3.00
383	Raul Mondesi S/X	.50
384	Ivan Rodriguez S/X	1.25
385	Larry Walker B/Y	.35
386	Bernie Williams B/Z	.45
387	Rusty Greer G/Y	1.25
388	Rafael Palmeiro G/Y	4.50
389	Matt Williams B/X	.35
390	Eric Young B/X	.35
391	Fred McGriff B/X	.35
392	Ken Caminiti B/X	.35
393	Roberto Alomar B/Z	.75
394	Brian Jordan B/X	.35
395	Mark Grace G/Z	.35
396	Jim Edmonds B/Y	.35
397	Deion Sanders S/Y	.50
398	Vladimir Guerrero S/Z Checklist	
399	Darin Erstad S/Y Checklist	1.00
400	Nomar Garciaparra S/Z Checklist	2.00

Get-A-Grip

		NM/M
Complete Set (16):		30.00
Common Card:		1.00
1	Ken Griffey Jr., Greg Maddux	3.00
2	John Smoltz, Frank Thomas	1.50
3	Mike Piazza, Andy Pettitte	3.00
4	Randy Johnson, Chipper Jones	2.50
5	Tom Glavine, Alex Rodriguez	4.00
6	Pat Hentgen, Jeff Bagwell	1.50
7	Kevin Brown, Juan Gonzalez	1.25
8	Barry Bonds, Mike Mussina	5.00
9	Hideo Nomo, Albert Belle	1.25
10	Troy Percival, Andruw Jones	1.50
11	Roger Clemens, Brian Jordan	3.00
12	Paul Wilson, Ivan Rodriguez	1.25
13	Andy Benes, Mo Vaughn	1.00
14	Al Leiter, Derek Jeter	5.00
15	Bill Pulsipher, Cal Ripken Jr.	5.00
16	Mariano Rivera, Ken Caminiti	1.00

Knot-Hole Gang

		NM/M
Complete Set (12):		18.00
Common Player:		.50
Promos:		2X
1	Chuck Knoblauch	.50
2	Ken Griffey Jr.	3.50
3	Frank Thomas	1.50
4	Tony Gwynn	2.50
5	Mike Piazza	3.50
6	Jeff Bagwell	1.50
7	Rusty Greer	.50
8	Cal Ripken Jr.	5.00
9	Chipper Jones	2.50
10	Ryan Klesko	.50
11	Barry Larkin	.50
12	Paul Molitor	1.50

Leagues of the Nation

	NM/M
Complete Set (18):	40.00

Complete Set (15):		60.00
Common Card:		1.50
1	Juan Gonzalez, Barry Bonds	10.00
2	Cal Ripken Jr., Chipper Jones	10.00
3	Mark McGwire, Ken Caminiti	7.00
4	Derek Jeter, Kenny Lofton	10.00
5	Ivan Rodriguez, Mike Piazza	6.00
6	Ken Griffey Jr., Larry Walker	6.00
7	Frank Thomas, Sammy Sosa	5.00
8	Paul Molitor, Barry Larkin	3.00
9	Albert Belle, Deion Sanders	1.50
10	Matt Williams, Jeff Bagwell	3.00
11	Mo Vaughn, Gary Sheffield	1.50
12	Alex Rodriguez, Tony Gwynn	7.50
13	Tino Martinez, Scott Rolen	2.00
14	Darin Erstad, Wilton Guerrero	2.00
15	Tony Clark, Vladimir Guerrero	3.00

Statistical Standouts

		NM/M
Complete Set (15):		175.00
Common Player:		4.00
1	Albert Belle	4.00
2	Juan Gonzalez	9.00
3	Ken Griffey Jr.	20.00
4	Alex Rodriguez	25.00
5	Frank Thomas	12.00
6	Chipper Jones	15.00
7	Greg Maddux	15.00
8	Mike Piazza	20.00
9	Cal Ripken Jr.	30.00
10	Mark McGwire	25.00
11	Barry Bonds	30.00
12	Derek Jeter	30.00
13	Ken Caminiti	4.00
14	John Smoltz	4.00
15	Paul Molitor	12.00

Thomas Collection

		NM/M
Complete Set (6):		360.00
Common Card:		60.00
1	Frank Thomas/Hat	60.00
2	Frank Thomas/Home Jsy	60.00
3	Frank Thomas/Btg Glv	60.00
4	Frank Thomas/Bat	60.00
5	Frank Thomas/Sweatband	60.00
6	Frank Thomas/Away Jsy	80.00

Warning Track

	NM/M
Complete Set (18):	40.00

Common Player:		1.00
1	Ken Griffey Jr.	6.00
2	Albert Belle	1.00
3	Barry Bonds	7.50
4	Andruw Jones	4.00
5	Kenny Lofton	1.00
6	Tony Gwynn	5.00
7	Manny Ramirez	4.00
8	Rusty Greer	1.00
9	Bernie Williams	1.00
10	Gary Sheffield	2.00
11	Juan Gonzalez	2.50
12	Raul Mondesi	1.00
13	Brady Anderson	1.00
14	Rondell White	1.00
15	Sammy Sosa	6.00
16	Deion Sanders	1.00
17	David Justice	1.00
18	Jim Edmonds	1.00

22kt Gold Stars

		NM/M
Complete Set (36):		115.00
Common Player:		1.00
1	Frank Thomas	4.00
2	Alex Rodriguez	8.00
3	Ken Griffey Jr.	6.50
4	Andruw Jones	4.00
5	Chipper Jones	6.00
6	Jeff Bagwell	4.00
7	Derek Jeter	10.00
8	Deion Sanders	1.00
9	Ivan Rodriguez	3.50
10	Juan Gonzalez	3.00
11	Greg Maddux	5.50
12	Andy Pettitte	2.50
13	Roger Clemens	6.00
14	Hideo Nomo	3.00
15	Tony Gwynn	5.50
16	Barry Bonds	10.00
17	Kenny Lofton	1.00
18	Paul Molitor	4.00
19	Jim Thome	3.00
20	Albert Belle	1.00
21	Cal Ripken Jr.	10.00
22	Mark McGwire	8.00
23	Barry Larkin	4.00
24	Mike Piazza	6.50
25	Darin Erstad	2.00
26	Chuck Knoblauch	1.00
27	Vladimir Guerrero	4.00
28	Tony Clark	1.00
29	Scott Rolen	3.00
30	Nomar Garciaparra	6.50
31	Eric Young	1.00
32	Ryne Sandberg	5.50
33	Roberto Alomar	2.00
34	Eddie Murray	4.00
35	Rafael Palmeiro	3.50
36	Jose Guillen	1.00

1998 Leaf

	NM/M
Complete Set (200):	40.00
Common Player:	.05
Common SP (#148-197):	.40
Pack (10):	2.00

Wax Box (24): 40.00
1 Rusty Greer .05
2 Tino Martinez .05
3 Bobby Bonilla .05
4 Jason Giambi .50
5 Matt Morris .05
6 Craig Counsell .05
7 Reggie Jefferson .05
8 Brian Rose .05
9 Ruben Rivera .05
10 Shawn Estes .05
11 Tony Gwynn 1.00
12 Jeff Abbott .05
13 Jose Cruz Jr. .05
14 Francisco Cordova .05
15 Ryan Klesko .05
16 Tim Salmon .05
17 Brett Tomko .05
18 Matt Williams .05
19 Joe Carter .05
20 Harold Baines .05
21 Gary Sheffield .50
22 Charles Johnson .05
23 Aaron Boone .05
24 Eddie Murray .75
25 Matt Stairs .05
26 David Cone .05
27 Jon Nunnally .05
28 Chris Stynes .05
29 Enrique Wilson .05
30 Randy Johnson .75
31 Garret Anderson .05
32 Manny Ramirez .75
33 Jeff Suppan .05
34 Rickey Henderson .75
35 Scott Spiezio .05
36 Rondell White .05
37 Todd Greene .05
38 Delino DeShields .05
39 Kevin Brown .05
40 Chili Davis .05
41 Jimmy Key .05
42 Not Issued
43 Mike Mussina .40
44 Joe Randa .05
45 Chan Ho Park .05
46 Brad Radke .05
47 Geronimo Berroa .05
48 Wade Boggs 1.00
49 Kevin Appier .05
50 Moises Alou .05
51 David Justice .05
52 Ivan Rodriguez .65
53 J.T. Snow .05
54 Brian Giles .05
55 Will Clark .10
56 Justin Thompson .05
57 Javier Lopez .05
58 Hideki Irabu .05
59 Mark Grudzielanek .05
60 Abraham Nunez .05
61 Todd Hollandsworth .05
62 Jay Bell .05
63 Nomar Garciaparra 1.25
64 Vinny Castilla .05
65 Lou Collier .05
66 Kevin Orie .05
67 John Valentin .05
68 Robin Ventura .05
69 Denny Neagle .05
70 Tony Womack .05
71 Dennis Reyes .05
72 Wally Joyner .05
73 Kevin Brown .05
74 Ray Durham .05
75 Mike Cameron .05
76 Dante Bichette .05
77 Jose Guillen .05
78 Carlos Delgado .50
79 Paul Molitor .75
80 Jason Kendall .05
81 Mark Belhorn .05
82 Damian Jackson .05
83 Bill Mueller .05
84 Kevin Young .05
85 Curt Schilling .25
86 Jeffrey Hammonds .05
87 Sandy Alomar Jr. .05
88 Bartolo Colon .05
89 Wilton Guerrero .05
90 Bernie Williams .05
91 Deion Sanders .05
92 Mike Piazza 1.25
93 Butch Huskey .05
94 Edgardo Alfonzo .05
95 Alan Benes .05
96 Craig Biggio .05
97 Mark Grace .05
98 Shawn Green .25
99 Derrek Lee .60
100 Ken Griffey Jr. 1.25
101 Tim Raines .05
102 Pokey Reese .05
103 Lee Stevens .05
104 Shannon Stewart .05
105 John Smoltz .05
106 Frank Thomas .75
107 Jeff Fassero .05
108 Jay Buhner .05
109 Jose Canseco .50
110 Omar Vizquel .05
111 Travis Fryman .05
112 Dave Nilsson .05
113 John Olerud .05
114 Larry Walker .05
115 Jim Edmonds .05
116 Bobby Higginson .05
117 Todd Hundley .05
118 Paul O'Neill .05
119 Bip Roberts .05
120 Ismael Valdes .05
121 Pedro Martinez .75
122 Jeff Cirillo .05
123 Andy Benes .05
124 Bobby Jones .05
125 Brian Hunter .05
126 Darryl Kile .05
127 Pat Hentgen .05
128 Marquis Grissom .05
129 Eric Davis .05
130 Chipper Jones 1.00
131 Edgar Martinez .05
132 Andy Pettitte .20
133 Cal Ripken Jr. 2.00
134 Scott Rolen .65
135 Ron Coomer .05
136 Luis Castillo .05
137 Fred McGriff .05
138 Neifi Perez .05
139 Eric Karros .05
140 Alex Fernandez .05
141 Jason Dickson .05
142 Lance Johnson .05
143 Ray Lankford .05
144 Sammy Sosa 1.25
145 Eric Young .05
146 Bubba Trammell .05
147 Todd Walker .05
148 Mo Vaughn/CC .40
149 Jeff Bagwell/CC 1.00
150 Kenny Lofton/CC .40
151 Raul Mondesi/CC .40
152 Mike Piazza/CC 2.00
153 Chipper Jones/CC 1.50
154 Larry Walker/CC .40
155 Greg Maddux/CC 1.50
156 Ken Griffey Jr./CC 2.00
157 Frank Thomas/CC 1.00
158 Darin Erstad/GLS .75
159 Roberto Alomar/GLS .60
160 Albert Belle/GLS .40
161 Jim Thome/GLS .75
162 Tony Clark/GLS .40
163 Chuck Knoblauch/GLS .40
164 Derek Jeter/GLS 3.00
165 Alex Rodriguez/GLS 2.50
166 Tony Gwynn/GLS 1.50
167 Roger Clemens/GLS 2.00
168 Barry Larkin/GLS .40
169 Andres Galarraga/GLS .40
170 Vladimir Guerrero/GLS 1.00
171 Mark McGwire/GLS 2.50
172 Barry Bonds/GLS 3.00
173 Juan Gonzalez/GLS .75
174 Andruw Jones/GLS 1.00
175 Paul Molitor/GLS 1.00
176 Hideo Nomo/GLS .75
177 Cal Ripken Jr./GLS 3.00
178 Brad Fullmer/GLR .40
179 Jaret Wright/GLR .40
180 Bobby Estalella/GLR .40
181 Ben Grieve/GLR .40
182 Paul Konerko/GLR .60
183 David Ortiz /GLR .75
184 Todd Helton/GLR 1.00
185 Juan Encarnacion/GLR .40
186 Miguel Tejada/GLR .60
187 Jacob Cruz /GLR .40
188 Mark Kotsay/GLR .40
189 Fernando Tatis/GLR .40
190 Ricky Ledee/GLR .40
191 Richard Hidalgo/GLR .40
192 Richie Sexson/GLR .40
193 Luis Ordaz /GLR .40
194 Eli Marrero/GLR .40
195 Livan Hernandez/GLR .40
196 Homer Bush/GLR .40
197 Raul Ibanez/GLR .40
198 Nomar Garciaparra Checklist .60
199 Scott Rolen Checklist .30
200 Jose Cruz Jr. Checklist .05
201 Al Martin .05

Crusade

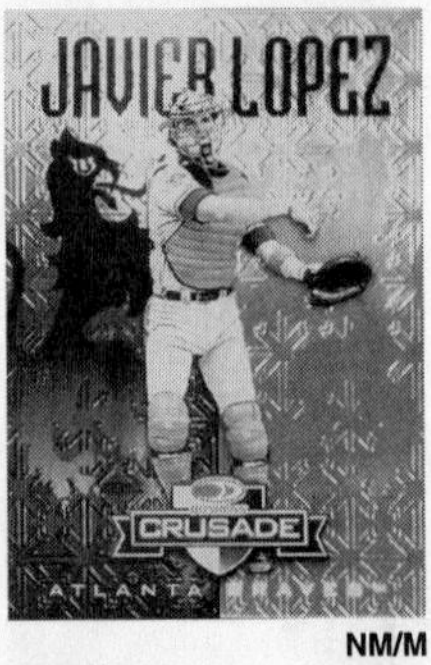

NM/M
Complete Set (30): 400.00
Common Player: 6.00
Purples: 3X
Reds: 12X
3 Jim Edmonds 7.50
4 Darin Erstad 7.50
11 Mike Mussina 15.00
15 Albert Belle 6.00
18 Manny Ramirez 25.00
19 Jim Thome 20.00
24 Bubba Trammell 6.00
26 Bobby Higginson 6.00
28 Paul Molitor 25.00
30 Todd Walker 6.00
34 Andy Pettitte 10.00
35 Wade Boggs 30.00
40 Alex Rodriguez 60.00
41 Randy Johnson 25.00
46 Ivan Rodriguez 20.00
48 Roger Clemens 40.00
54 John Smoltz 6.00
56 Andruw Jones 25.00
58 Javier Lopez 6.00
59 Fred McGriff 6.00
64 Pokey Reese 6.00
66 Andres Galarraga 6.00
70 Eric Young 6.00
73 Moises Alou 6.00
76 Ben Grieve 6.00
79 Mike Piazza 50.00
91 Jason Kendall 6.00
95 Alan Benes 6.00
97 Tony Gwynn 30.00
98 Ken Caminiti 6.00

Heading for the Hall

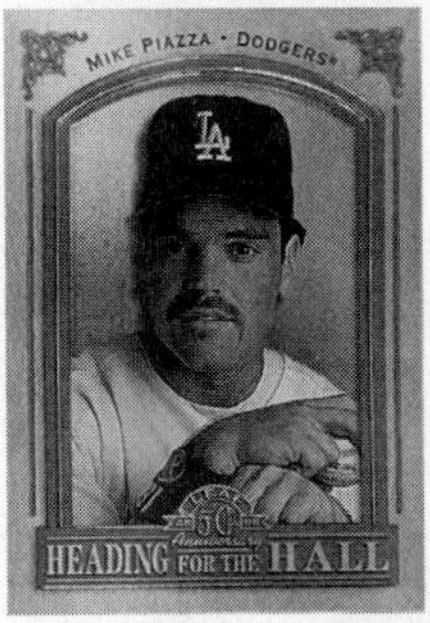

NM/M
Complete Set (20): 35.00
Common Player: .75
Samples: 1X
1 Roberto Alomar 1.00
2 Jeff Bagwell 1.50
3 Albert Belle .75
4 Wade Boggs 2.00
5 Barry Bonds 5.00
6 Roger Clemens 2.50
7 Juan Gonzalez 1.50
8 Ken Griffey Jr. 3.00
9 Tony Gwynn 2.00
10 Barry Larkin .75
11 Kenny Lofton .75
12 Greg Maddux 2.00
13 Mark McGwire 4.00
14 Paul Molitor 1.50
15 Eddie Murray 1.50
16 Mike Piazza 3.00
17 Cal Ripken Jr. 5.00
18 Ivan Rodriguez 1.25
19 Ryne Sandberg 2.00
20 Frank Thomas 1.50

Statistical Standouts

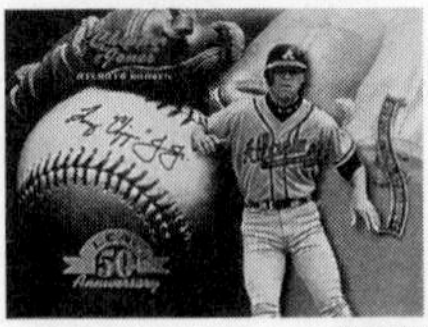

NM/M
Complete Set (24): 55.00
Common Player: 1.00
Die-Cuts: 2X
1 Frank Thomas 2.50
2 Ken Griffey Jr. 4.00
3 Alex Rodriguez 5.00
4 Mike Piazza 4.00
5 Greg Maddux 3.00
6 Cal Ripken Jr. 6.00
7 Chipper Jones 3.00
8 Juan Gonzalez 2.00
9 Jeff Bagwell 2.50
10 Mark McGwire 5.00
11 Tony Gwynn 3.00
12 Mo Vaughn 1.00
13 Nomar Garciaparra 4.00
14 Jose Cruz Jr. 1.00
15 Vladimir Guerrero 2.50
16 Scott Rolen 2.00
17 Andy Pettitte 1.50
18 Randy Johnson 2.50
19 Larry Walker 1.00
20 Kenny Lofton 1.00
21 Tony Clark 1.00
22 David Justice 1.00
23 Derek Jeter 6.00
24 Barry Bonds 6.00

Fractal Matrix

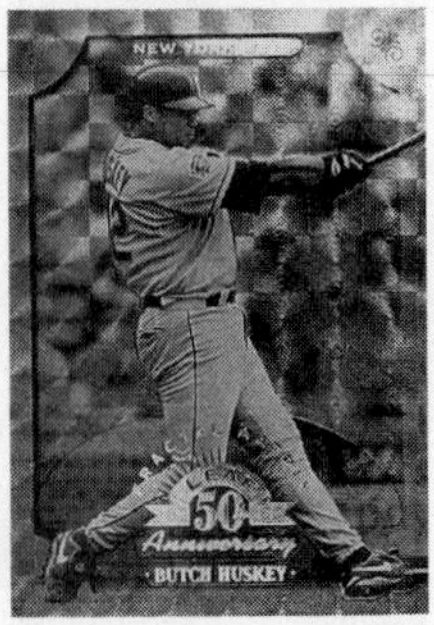

NM/M
Complete Set (200): 250.00
Common Bronze: .25
Common Silver: .75
Common Gold: 2.00
1 Rusty Greer G/Z 2.00
2 Tino Martinez G/Z 2.00
3 Bobby Bonilla S/Y .75
4 Jason Giambi S/Y 1.25
5 Matt Morris S/Y .75
6 Craig Counsell B/X .25
7 Reggie Jefferson B/X .25
8 Brian Rose S/Y .75
9 Ruben Rivera B/X .25
10 Shawn Estes S/Y .75
11 Tony Gwynn G/Z 10.00
12 Jeff Abbott B/Y .25
13 Jose Cruz Jr. G/Z 2.00
14 Francisco Cordova B/X .25
15 Ryan Klesko B/X .25
16 Tim Salmon G/Y 2.00
17 Brett Tomko B/X .25
18 Matt Williams S/Y .75
19 Joe Carter B/X .25
20 Harold Baines B/X .25
21 Gary Sheffield S/Z 1.25
22 Charles Johnson S/X .75
23 Aaron Boone B/X .25
24 Eddie Murray G/Y 7.50
25 Matt Stairs B/X .25
26 David Cone B/X .25
27 Jon Nunnally B/X .25
28 Chris Stynes B/X .25
29 Enrique Wilson B/Y .25
30 Randy Johnson S/Z 2.00
31 Garret Anderson S/Y .75
32 Manny Ramirez G/Z 7.50
33 Jeff Suppan S/X .75
34 Rickey Henderson B/X 1.00
35 Scott Spiezio B/X .25
36 Rondell White S/Y .75
37 Todd Greene S/Z .75
38 Delino DeShields B/X .25
39 Kevin Brown S/X .75
40 Chili Davis B/X .25
41 Jimmy Key B/X .25
42 Not Issued
43 Mike Mussina G/Y 5.00
44 Joe Randa B/X .25
45 Chan Ho Park S/Z .75
46 Brad Radke B/X .25
47 Geronimo Berroa B/X .25
48 Wade Boggs S/Y 2.50
49 Kevin Appier B/X .25
50 Moises Alou S/Y .75
51 David Justice G/Y 2.00
52 Ivan Rodriguez G/Z 6.00
53 J.T. Snow B/X .25
54 Brian Giles B/X .25
55 Will Clark B/Y .25
56 Justin Thompson S/Y .75
57 Javier Lopez S/X .75
58 Hideki Irabu B/Z .25
59 Mark Grudzielanek B/X .25
60 Abraham Nunez S/X .75
61 Todd Hollandsworth B/X .25
62 Jay Bell B/X .25
63 Nomar Garciaparra G/Z 10.00
64 Vinny Castilla B/Y .25
65 Lou Collier B/Y .25
66 Kevin Orie S/X .75
67 John Valentin B/X .25
68 Robin Ventura B/X .25
69 Denny Neagle B/X .25
70 Tony Womack S/Y .75
71 Dennis Reyes S/Y .75
72 Wally Joyner B/X .25
73 Kevin Brown B/Y .25
74 Ray Durham B/X .25
75 Mike Cameron S/Z .75
76 Dante Bichette B/X .25
77 Jose Guillen G/Y 2.00
78 Carlos Delgado B/Y .50
79 Paul Molitor G/Z 7.50

80	Jason Kendall B/X	.25
81	Mark Belhorn B/X	.25
82	Damian Jackson B/X	.25
83	Bill Mueller B/X	.25
84	Kevin Young B/X	.25
85	Curt Schilling B/X	.40
86	Jeffrey Hammonds B/X	.25
87	Sandy Alomar Jr. S/Y	.75
88	Bartolo Colon B/Y	.50
89	Wilton Guerrero B/Y	.25
90	Bernie Williams G/Y	2.00
91	Deion Sanders S/Y	.75
92	Mike Piazza G/X	12.50
93	Butch Huskey B/X	.25
94	Edgardo Alfonzo S/X	.75
95	Alan Benes S/Y	.75
96	Craig Biggio S/Y	.75
97	Mark Grace S/Y	.75
98	Shawn Green S/Y	1.50
99	Derrek Lee S/Y	2.00
100	Ken Griffey Jr. G/Z	12.50
101	Tim Raines B/X	.25
102	Pokey Reese S/X	.75
103	Lee Stevens B/X	.25
104	Shannon Stewart S/Y	.75
105	John Smoltz S/Y	.75
106	Frank Thomas G/X	7.50
107	Jeff Fassero B/X	.25
108	Jay Buhner B/Y	.25
109	Jose Canseco B/X	.50
110	Omar Vizquel B/X	.25
111	Travis Fryman B/X	.25
112	Dave Nilsson B/X	.25
113	John Olerud B/X	.25
114	Larry Walker G/Z	2.00
115	Jim Edmonds S/Y	.75
116	Bobby Higginson S/X	.75
117	Todd Hundley S/X	.75
118	Paul O'Neill B/X	.25
119	Bip Roberts B/X	.25
120	Ismael Valdes B/X	.25
121	Pedro Martinez S/Y	2.00
122	Jeff Cirillo B/X	.25
123	Andy Benes B/X	.25
124	Bobby Jones B/X	.25
125	Brian Hunter B/X	.25
126	Darryl Kile B/X	.25
127	Pat Hentgen B/X	.25
128	Marquis Grissom B/X	.25
129	Eric Davis B/X	.25
130	Chipper Jones G/Z	10.00
131	Edgar Martinez S/Z	.75
132	Andy Pettitte G/Z	3.00
133	Cal Ripken Jr. G/X	20.00
134	Scott Rolen G/Z	6.00
135	Ron Coomer B/X	.25
136	Luis Castillo B/Y	.25
137	Fred McGriff B/Y	.25
138	Neifi Perez S/Y	.75
139	Eric Karros B/X	.25
140	Alex Fernandez B/X	.25
141	Jason Dickson B/X	.25
142	Lance Johnson B/X	.25
143	Ray Lankford B/Y	.25
144	Sammy Sosa G/Y	10.00
145	Eric Young B/Y	.25
146	Bubba Trammell S/Y	.75
147	Todd Walker S/Y	.75
148	Mo Vaughn S/X/CC	.75
149	Jeff Bagwell S/X/CC	2.00
150	Kenny Lofton S/X/CC	.75
151	Raul Mondesi S/X/CC	.75
152	Mike Piazza S/X/CC	4.00
153	Chipper Jones S/X/CC	3.00
154	Larry Walker S/X/CC	.75
155	Greg Maddux S/X/CC	3.00
156	Ken Griffey Jr. S/X/CC	4.00
157	Frank Thomas S/X/CC	2.00
158	Darin Erstad B/Z/GLS	.50
159	Roberto Alomar B/Y/GLS	.35
160	Albert Belle G/Y/GLS	2.00
161	Jim Thome G/Y/GLS	4.00
162	Tony Clark G/Y/GLS	2.00
163	Chuck Knoblauch B/Y/GLS	.25
164	Derek Jeter G/Z/GLS	20.00
165	Alex Rodriguez G/Z/GLS	15.00
166	Tony Gwynn B/X/GLS	1.25
167	Roger Clemens G/Z/GLS	12.00
168	Barry Larkin B/Y/GLS	.25
169	Andres Galarraga B/Y/GLS	.25
170	Vladimir Guerrero G/Z/GLS	7.50
171	Mark McGwire B/Z/GLS	2.00
172	Barry Bonds B/Z/GLS	3.00
173	Juan Gonzalez G/Z/GLS	4.00
174	Andruw Jones G/Z/GLS	7.50
175	Paul Molitor B/X/GLS	1.00
176	Hideo Nomo B/Z/GLS	.75
177	Cal Ripken Jr. B/X/GLS	2.25
178	Brad Fullmer S/Z/GLR	.75
179	Jaret Wright G/Z/GLR	2.00
180	Bobby Estalella B/Y/GLR	.25
181	Ben Grieve G/X/GLR	2.00
182	Paul Konerko G/Z/GLR	3.00
183	David Ortiz G/Z/GLR	6.00
184	Todd Helton G/X/GLR	5.00
185	Juan Encarnacion G/Z/GLR	2.00
186	Miguel Tejada G/Z/GLR	4.00
187	Jacob Cruz B/Y/GLR	.25
188	Mark Kotsay G/Z/GLR	2.00
189	Fernando Tatis S/Z/GLR	.75
190	Ricky Ledee S/Y/GLR	.75
191	Richard Hidalgo S/Y/GLR	.75
192	Richie Sexson S/Y/GLR	.75
193	Luis Ordaz B/X/GLR	.25
194	Eli Marrero S/Z/GLR	.75
195	Livan Hernandez S/Z/GLR	.75
196	Homer Bush B/X/GLR	.25
197	Raul Ibanez B/X/GLR	.25
198	Nomar Garciaparra B/X Checklist	.75
199	Scott Rolen B/X Checklist	.35
200	Jose Cruz Jr. B/X Checklist	.25
201	Al Martin B/X	.25

Fractal Matrix Diamond Axis

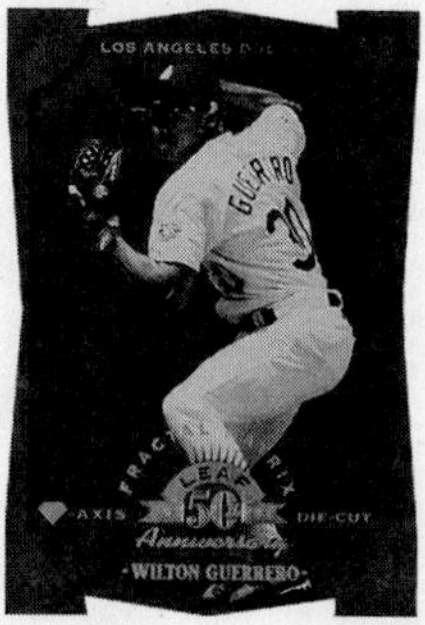

	NM/M
Common Player:	7.50
Stars/Rookies:	20X
SP (148-177):	12X

(See 1998 Leaf for checklist and base card values.)

1998 Leaf Fractal Foundation

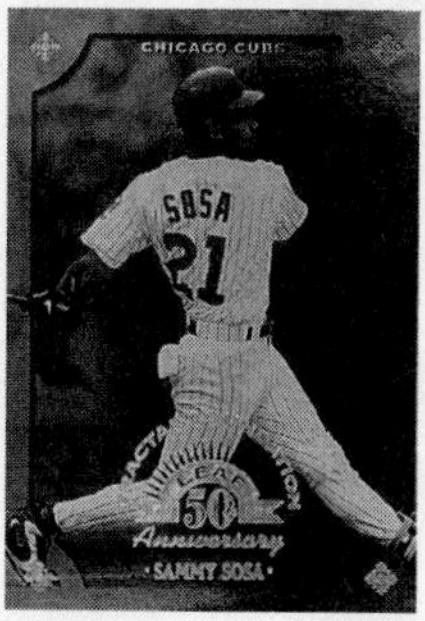

	NM/M
Complete Set (200):	60.00
Common Player:	.20
Semistars:	.60
Unlisted Stars:	1.00
Pack (3):	2.00
Wax Box (18):	35.00

1	Rusty Greer	.20
2	Tino Martinez	.20
3	Bobby Bonilla	.20
4	Jason Giambi	.60
5	Matt Morris	.20
6	Craig Counsell	.20
7	Reggie Jefferson	.20
8	Brian Rose	.20
9	Ruben Rivera	.20
10	Shawn Estes	.20
11	Tony Gwynn	1.50
12	Jeff Abbott	.20
13	Jose Cruz Jr.	.20
14	Francisco Cordova	.20
15	Ryan Klesko	.20
16	Tim Salmon	.20
17	Brett Tomko	.20
18	Matt Williams	.20
19	Joe Carter	.20
20	Harold Baines	.20
21	Gary Sheffield	.50
22	Charles Johnson	.20
23	Aaron Boone	.20
24	Eddie Murray	1.00
25	Matt Stairs	.20
26	David Cone	.20
27	Jon Nunnally	.20
28	Chris Stynes	.20
29	Enrique Wilson	.20
30	Randy Johnson	1.00
31	Garret Anderson	.20
32	Manny Ramirez	1.00
33	Jeff Suppan	.20
34	Rickey Henderson	1.00
35	Scott Spiezio	.20
36	Rondell White	.20
37	Todd Greene	.20
38	Delino DeShields	.20
39	Kevin Brown	.20
40	Chili Davis	.20
41	Jimmy Key	.20
42	Not Issued	
43	Mike Mussina	.40
44	Joe Randa	.20
45	Chan Ho Park	.20
46	Brad Radke	.20
47	Geronimo Berroa	.20
48	Wade Boggs	1.50
49	Kevin Appier	.20
50	Moises Alou	.20
51	David Justice	.20
52	Ivan Rodriguez	.75
53	J.T. Snow	.20
54	Brian Giles	.20
55	Will Clark	.20
56	Justin Thompson	.20
57	Javier Lopez	.20
58	Hideki Irabu	.20
59	Mark Grudzielanek	.20
60	Abraham Nunez	.20
61	Todd Hollandsworth	.20
62	Jay Bell	.20
63	Nomar Garciaparra	1.75
64	Vinny Castilla	.20
65	Lou Collier	.20
66	Kevin Orie	.20
67	John Valentin	.20
68	Robin Ventura	.20
69	Denny Neagle	.20
70	Tony Womack	.20
71	Dennis Reyes	.20
72	Wally Joyner	.20
73	Kevin Brown	.20
74	Ray Durham	.20
75	Mike Cameron	.20
76	Dante Bichette	.20
77	Jose Guillen	.20
78	Carlos Delgado	.50
79	Paul Molitor	1.00
80	Jason Kendall	.20
81	Mark Belhorn	.20
82	Damian Jackson	.20
83	Bill Mueller	.20
84	Kevin Young	.20
85	Curt Schilling	.40
86	Jeffrey Hammonds	.20
87	Sandy Alomar Jr.	.20
88	Bartolo Colon	.20
89	Wilton Guerrero	.20
90	Bernie Williams	.20
91	Deion Sanders	.20
92	Mike Piazza	2.00
93	Butch Huskey	.20
94	Edgardo Alfonzo	.20
95	Alan Benes	.20
96	Craig Biggio	.20
97	Mark Grace	.20
98	Shawn Green	.40
99	Derrek Lee	.50
100	Ken Griffey Jr.	2.00
101	Tim Raines	.20
102	Pokey Reese	.20
103	Lee Stevens	.20
104	Shannon Stewart	.20
105	John Smoltz	.20
106	Frank Thomas	1.00
107	Jeff Fassero	.20
108	Jay Buhner	.20
109	Jose Canseco	.40
110	Omar Vizquel	.20
111	Travis Fryman	.20
112	Dave Nilsson	.20
113	John Olerud	.20
114	Larry Walker	.20
115	Jim Edmonds	.20
116	Bobby Higginson	.20
117	Todd Hundley	.20
118	Paul O'Neill	.20
119	Bip Roberts	.20
120	Ismael Valdes	.20
121	Pedro Martinez	1.00
122	Jeff Cirillo	.20
123	Andy Benes	.20
124	Bobby Jones	.20
125	Brian Hunter	.20
126	Darryl Kile	.20
127	Pat Hentgen	.20
128	Marquis Grissom	.20
129	Eric Davis	.20
130	Chipper Jones	1.50
131	Edgar Martinez	.20
132	Andy Pettitte	.35
133	Cal Ripken Jr.	3.00
134	Scott Rolen	.75
135	Ron Coomer	.20
136	Luis Castillo	.20
137	Fred McGriff	.20
138	Neifi Perez	.20
139	Eric Karros	.20
140	Alex Fernandez	.20
141	Jason Dickson	.20
142	Lance Johnson	.20
143	Ray Lankford	.20
144	Sammy Sosa	1.75
145	Eric Young	.20
146	Bubba Trammell	.20
147	Todd Walker	.20
148	Mo Vaughn/CC	.20
149	Jeff Bagwell/CC	1.00
150	Kenny Lofton/CC	.20
151	Raul Mondesi/CC	.20
152	Mike Piazza/CC	2.00
153	Chipper Jones/CC	1.50
154	Larry Walker/CC	.20
155	Greg Maddux/CC	1.50
156	Ken Griffey Jr./CC	2.00
157	Frank Thomas/CC	1.00
158	Darin Erstad/GLS	.50
159	Roberto Alomar/GLS	.40
160	Albert Belle/GLS	.20
161	Jim Thome/GLS	.75
162	Tony Clark/GLS	.20
163	Chuck Knoblauch/GLS	.20
164	Derek Jeter/GLS	3.00
165	Alex Rodriguez/GLS	2.50
166	Tony Gwynn/GLS	1.50
167	Roger Clemens/GLS	1.75
168	Barry Larkin/GLS	.20
169	Andres Galarraga/GLS	.20
170	Vladimir Guerrero/GLS	1.00
171	Mark McGwire/GLS	2.50
172	Barry Bonds/GLS	3.00
173	Juan Gonzalez /GLS	.75
174	Andruw Jones/GLS	1.00
175	Paul Molitor/GLS	1.00
176	Hideo Nomo/GLS	.75
177	Cal Ripken Jr./GLS	3.00
178	Brad Fullmer/GLR	.20
179	Jaret Wright/GLR	.20
180	Bobby Estalella/GLR	.20
181	Ben Grieve/GLR	.20
182	Paul Konerko/GLR	.40
183	David Ortiz /GLR	.75
184	Todd Helton/GLR	1.00
185	Juan Encarnacion/GLR	.20
186	Miguel Tejada/GLR	.40
187	Jacob Cruz/GLR	.20
188	Mark Kotsay/GLR	.20
189	Fernando Tatis/GLR	.20
190	Ricky Ledee/GLR	.20
191	Richard Hidalgo/GLR	.20
192	Richie Sexson/GLR	.20
193	Luis Ordaz/GLR	.20
194	Eli Marrero/GLR	.20
195	Livan Hernandez/GLR	.20
196	Homer Bush/GLR	.20
197	Raul Ibanez/GLR	.20
198	Nomar Garciaparra Checklist	1.00
199	Scott Rolen Checklist	.30
200	Jose Cruz Jr. Checklist	.20

Leaf Fractal Materials

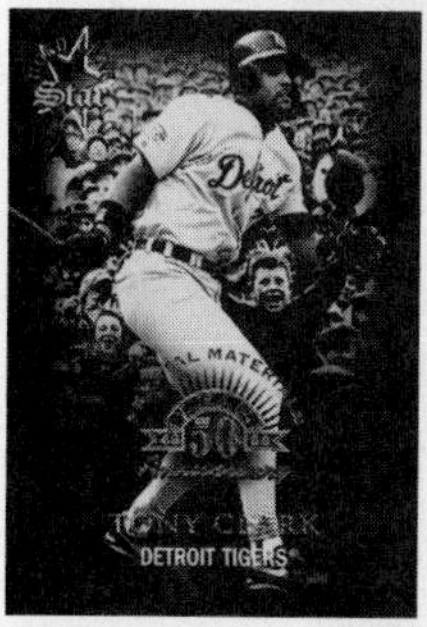

	NM/M
Complete Set (200):	375.00
Complete Plastic Set (100):	65.00
Common Plastic (3,250):	.35
Complete Leather Set (50):	55.00
Common Leather (1,000):	.75
Complete Nylon Set (30):	60.00
Common Nylon (500):	1.25
Complete Wood Set (20):	200.00
Common Wood (250):	5.00
Wax Box:	120.00

1	Rusty Greer/N	1.25
2	Tino Martinez/W	5.00
3	Bobby Bonilla/N	1.25
4	Jason Giambi/N	4.00
5	Matt Morris/L	.75
6	Craig Counsell/P	.35
7	Reggie Jefferson/P	.35
8	Brian Rose/P	.35
9	Ruben Rivera/L	.75
10	Shawn Estes/L	.75
11	Tony Gwynn/W	20.00
12	Jeff Abbott/P	.35
13	Jose Cruz Jr./W	5.00
14	Francisco Cordova/P	.35
15	Ryan Klesko/L	.75
16	Tim Salmon/W	5.00
17	Brett Tomko/L	.75
18	Matt Williams/N	1.25
19	Joe Carter/P	.35
20	Harold Baines/P	.35
21	Gary Sheffield/N	2.50
22	Charles Johnson/L	.75
23	Aaron Boone/P	.35
24	Eddie Murray/N	5.00
25	Matt Stairs/P	.35
26	David Cone/P	.35
27	Jon Nunnally/P	.35
28	Chris Stynes/P	.35
29	Enrique Wilson/P	.35
30	Randy Johnson/W	15.00
31	Garret Anderson/N	1.25
32	Manny Ramirez/W	15.00
33	Jeff Suppan/L	.75
34	Rickey Henderson/N	5.00
35	Scott Spiezio/P	.35
36	Rondell White/L	.75
37	Todd Greene/N	1.25
38	Delino DeShields/P	.35

39 Kevin Brown/L .75
40 Chili Davis/P .35
41 Jimmy Key/P .35
42 Not Issued
43 Mike Mussina/N 4.00
44 Joe Randa/P .35
45 Chan Ho Park/N 1.25
46 Brad Radke/P .35
47 Geronimo Berroa/P .35
48 Wade Boggs/N 6.00
49 Kevin Appier/P .35
50 Moises Alou/N 1.25
51 David Justice/N 1.25
52 Ivan Rodriguez/W 12.50
53 J.T. Snow/L .75
54 Brian Giles/P .35
55 Will Clark/L .75
56 Justin Thompson/N 1.25
57 Javier Lopez/P .35
58 Hideki Irabu/L .75
59 Mark Grudzielanek/P .35
60 Abraham Nunez/P .35
61 Todd Hollandsworth/P .35
62 Jay Bell/P .35
63 Nomar Garciaparra/W 20.00
64 Vinny Castilla/P .35
65 Lou Collier/P .35
66 Kevin Orie/L .75
67 John Valentin/P .35
68 Robin Ventura/P .35
69 Denny Neagle/P .35
70 Tony Womack/L .75
71 Dennis Reyes/L .75
72 Wally Joyner/P .35
73 Kevin Brown/P .35
74 Ray Durham/P .35
75 Mike Cameron/N 1.25
76 Dante Bichette/L .75
77 Jose Guillen/N 1.25
78 Carlos Delgado/L 1.50
79 Paul Molitor/W 15.00
80 Jason Kendall/P .35
81 Mark Belhorn/L .75
82 Damian Jackson/P .35
83 Bill Mueller/P .35
84 Kevin Young/P .35
85 Curt Schilling/P .60
86 Jeffrey Hammonds/P .35
87 Sandy Alomar Jr./L .75
88 Bartolo Colon/P .35
89 Wilton Guerrero/L .75
90 Bernie Williams/N 1.25
91 Deion Sanders/N 1.25
92 Mike Piazza/W 25.00
93 Butch Huskey/L .75
94 Edgardo Alfonzo/L .75
95 Alan Benes/L .75
96 Craig Biggio/N 1.25
97 Mark Grace/L .75
98 Shawn Green/L 1.25
99 Derrek Lee/L 2.00
100 Ken Griffey Jr./W 25.00
101 Tim Raines/P .35
102 Pokey Reese/P .35
103 Lee Stevens/P .35
104 Shannon Stewart/N 1.25
105 John Smoltz/L .75
106 Frank Thomas/W 15.00
107 Jeff Fassero/P .35
108 Jay Buhner/L .75
109 Jose Canseco/L 1.50
110 Omar Vizquel/P .35
111 Travis Fryman/P .35
112 Dave Nilsson/P .35
113 John Olerud/P .35
114 Larry Walker/W 5.00
115 Jim Edmonds/N 1.25
116 Bobby Higginson/L .75
117 Todd Hundley/L .75
118 Paul O'Neill/P .35
119 Bip Roberts/P .35
120 Ismael Valdes/P .35
121 Pedro Martinez/N 5.00
122 Jeff Cirillo/P .35
123 Andy Benes/P .35
124 Bobby Jones/P .35
125 Brian Hunter/P .35
126 Darryl Kile/P .35
127 Pat Hentgen/P .35
128 Marquis Grissom/P .35
129 Eric Davis/P .35
130 Chipper Jones/W 20.00
131 Edgar Martinez/N 1.25
132 Andy Pettitte/W 10.00
133 Cal Ripken Jr./W 35.00
134 Scott Rolen/W 12.50
135 Ron Coomer/P .35
136 Luis Castillo/L .75
137 Fred McGriff/L .75
138 Neifi Perez/L .75
139 Eric Karros/P .35
140 Alex Fernandez/P .35
141 Jason Dickson/P .35
142 Lance Johnson/P .35
143 Ray Lankford/P .35
144 Sammy Sosa/N 7.00
145 Eric Young/P .35
146 Bubba Trammell/L .75
147 Todd Walker/L .75
148 Mo Vaughn/P/CC .35
149 Jeff Bagwell/P/CC 3.00
150 Kenny Lofton/P/CC .35
151 Raul Mondesi/P/CC .35
152 Mike Piazza/P/CC 5.00
153 Chipper Jones/P/CC 4.00
154 Larry Walker/P/CC .35
155 Greg Maddux/P/CC 4.00
156 Ken Griffey Jr./P/CC 5.00
157 Frank Thomas/P/CC 3.00
158 Darin Erstad/L/GLS 2.00
159 Roberto Alomar/P/GLS .65
160 Albert Belle/L/GLS .75
161 Jim Thome/L/GLS 2.00
162 Tony Clark/L/GLS .75
163 Chuck Knoblauch/L/GLS .75
164 Derek Jeter/P/GLS 7.50
165 Alex Rodriguez/P/GLS 6.00
166 Tony Gwynn/P/GLS 4.00
167 Roger Clemens/L/GLS 5.00
168 Barry Larkin/P/GLS .35
169 Andres Galarraga/P/GLS .35
170 Vladimir Guerrero/L/GLS 4.00
171 Mark McGwire/L/GLS 6.00
172 Barry Bonds/L/GLS 7.50
173 Juan Gonzalez/P/GLS 2.00
174 Andruw Jones/P/GLS 3.00
175 Paul Molitor/P/GLS 3.00
176 Hideo Nomo/L/GLS 2.00
177 Cal Ripken Jr./P/GLS 7.50
178 Brad Fullmer/P/GLR .35
179 Jaret Wright/N/GLR 1.25
180 Bobby Estalella/P/GLR .35
181 Ben Grieve/W/GLR 5.00
182 Paul Konerko/W/GLR 6.00
183 David Ortiz/N/GLR 2.50
184 Todd Helton/W/GLR 10.00
185 Juan Encarnacion/N/GLR 1.25
186 Miguel Tejada/N/GLR 1.50
187 Jacob Cruz/P/GLR .35
188 Mark Kotsay/N/GLR 1.25
189 Fernando Tatis/L/GLR .75
190 Ricky Ledee/P/GLR .35
191 Richard Hidalgo/P/GLR .35
192 Richie Sexson/P/GLR .35
193 Luis Ordaz/P/GLR .35
194 Eli Marrero/L/GLR .75
195 Livan Hernandez/L/GLR .75
196 Homer Bush/P/GLR .35
197 Raul Ibanez/P/GLR .35
198 Nomar Garciaparra/P Checklist 3.00
199 Scott Rolen/P Checklist .40
200 Jose Cruz Jr./P Checklist .35
201 Al Martin/L .75

1998 Leaf Rookies & Stars

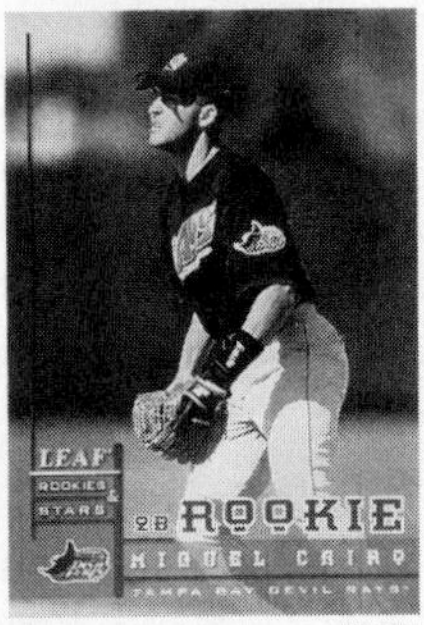

NM/M

Complete Set (339): 200.00
Common Player: .10
Common SP (131-230): .20
Common SP (301-339): .50
Inserted 1:2
True Blues: 12X
SP True Blues: 2X
Production 500 Sets
Longevitys: 50X
SP Longevitys: 15X
Production 50 Sets
Pack (9): 7.50
Wax Box (24): 150.00

1 Andy Pettitte .30
2 Roberto Alomar .20
3 Randy Johnson .75
4 Manny Ramirez .75
5 Paul Molitor .75
6 Mike Mussina .50
7 Jim Thome .65
8 Tino Martinez .10
9 Gary Sheffield .50
10 Chuck Knoblauch .10
11 Bernie Williams .10
12 Tim Salmon .10
13 Sammy Sosa 1.25
14 Wade Boggs 1.00
15 Andres Galarraga .10
16 Pedro Martinez .75
17 David Justice .10
18 Chan Ho Park .10
19 Jay Buhner .10
20 Ryan Klesko .10
21 Barry Larkin .10
22 Will Clark .15
23 Raul Mondesi .10
24 Rickey Henderson .75
25 Jim Edmonds .10
26 Ken Griffey Jr. 1.25
27 Frank Thomas .75
28 Cal Ripken Jr. 2.00
29 Alex Rodriguez 1.50
30 Mike Piazza 1.25
31 Greg Maddux 1.00
32 Chipper Jones 1.00
33 Tony Gwynn 1.00
34 Derek Jeter 2.00
35 Jeff Bagwell .75
36 Juan Gonzalez .50
37 Nomar Garciaparra 1.00
38 Andruw Jones .75
39 Hideo Nomo .60
40 Roger Clemens 1.25
41 Mark McGwire 1.50
42 Scott Rolen .60
43 Vladimir Guerrero .75
44 Barry Bonds 2.00
45 Darin Erstad .25
46 Albert Belle .10
47 Kenny Lofton .10
48 Mo Vaughn .10
49 Ivan Rodriguez .60
50 Jose Cruz Jr. .10
51 Tony Clark .10
52 Larry Walker .10
53 Mark Grace .10
54 Edgar Martinez .10
55 Fred McGriff .10
56 Rafael Palmeiro .60
57 Matt Williams .10
58 Craig Biggio .10
59 Ken Caminiti .10
60 Jose Canseco .40
61 Brady Anderson .10
62 Moises Alou .10
63 Justin Thompson .10
64 John Smoltz .10
65 Carlos Delgado .50
66 J.T. Snow .10
67 Jason Giambi .50
68 Garret Anderson .10
69 Rondell White .10
70 Eric Karros .10
71 Javier Lopez .10
72 Pat Hentgen .10
73 Dante Bichette .10
74 Charles Johnson .10
75 Tom Glavine .30
76 Rusty Greer .10
77 Travis Fryman .10
78 Todd Hundley .10
79 Ray Lankford .10
80 Denny Neagle .10
81 Henry Rodriguez .10
82 Sandy Alomar Jr. .10
83 Robin Ventura .10
84 John Olerud .10
85 Omar Vizquel .10
86 Darren Dreifort .10
87 Kevin Brown .10
88 Curt Schilling .35
89 Francisco Cordova .10
90 Brad Radke .10
91 David Cone .10
92 Paul O'Neill .10
93 Vinny Castilla .10
94 Marquis Grissom .10
95 Brian Hunter .10
96 Kevin Appier .10
97 Bobby Bonilla .10
98 Eric Young .10
99 Jason Kendall .10
100 Shawn Green .40
101 Edgardo Alfonzo .10
102 Alan Benes .10
103 Bobby Higginson .10
104 Todd Greene .10
105 Jose Guillen .15
106 Neifi Perez .10
107 Edgar Renteria .10
108 Chris Stynes .10
109 Todd Walker .10
110 Brian Jordan .10
111 Joe Carter .10
112 Ellis Burks .10
113 Brett Tomko .10
114 Mike Cameron .10
115 Shannon Stewart .10
116 Kevin Orie .10
117 Brian Giles .10
118 Hideki Irabu .10
119 Delino DeShields .10
120 David Segui .10
121 Dustin Hermanson .10
122 Kevin Young .10
123 Jay Bell .10
124 Doug Glanville .10
125 John Roskos **RC** .10
126 Damon Hollins **RC** .10
127 Matt Stairs .10
128 Cliff Floyd .10
129 Derek Bell .10
130 Darryl Strawberry .10
131 Ken Griffey Jr. 1.25
132 Tim Salmon .20
133 Manny Ramirez .75
134 Paul Konerko .30
135 Frank Thomas .75
136 Todd Helton .75
137 Larry Walker .20
138 Mo Vaughn .20
139 Travis Lee .20
140 Ivan Rodriguez .60
141 Ben Grieve .20
142 Brad Fullmer .20
143 Alex Rodriguez 1.50
144 Mike Piazza 1.25
145 Greg Maddux 1.00
146 Chipper Jones 1.00
147 Kenny Lofton .20
148 Albert Belle .20
149 Barry Bonds 2.00
150 Vladimir Guerrero .75
151 Tony Gwynn 1.00
152 Derek Jeter 2.00
153 Jeff Bagwell .75
154 Juan Gonzalez .60
155 Nomar Garciaparra 1.00
156 Andruw Jones .75
157 Hideo Nomo .60
158 Roger Clemens 1.25
159 Mark McGwire 1.50
160 Scott Rolen .60
161 Travis Lee .20
162 Ben Grieve .20
163 Jose Guillen .20
164 John Olerud .20
165 Kevin Appier .20
166 Marquis Grissom .20
167 Rusty Greer .20
168 Ken Caminiti .20
169 Craig Biggio .20
170 Ken Griffey Jr. 1.25
171 Larry Walker .20
172 Barry Larkin .20
173 Andres Galarraga .20
174 Wade Boggs 1.00
175 Sammy Sosa 1.25
176 Mike Piazza 1.50
177 Jim Thome .60
178 Paul Molitor .75
179 Tony Clark .20
180 Jose Cruz Jr. .20
181 Darin Erstad .25
182 Barry Bonds 2.00
183 Vladimir Guerrero .75
184 Scott Rolen .60
185 Mark McGwire 1.50
186 Nomar Garciaparra 1.00
187 Gary Sheffield .50
188 Cal Ripken Jr. 2.00
189 Frank Thomas .75
190 Andy Petitte .30
191 Paul Konerko .35
192 Todd Helton 1.50
193 Mark Kotsay .20
194 Brad Fullmer .20
195 Kevin Millwood **RC** 8.00
196 David Ortiz 3.00
197 Kerry Wood 1.50
198 Miguel Tejada .40
199 Fernando Tatis .20
200 Jaret Wright .20
201 Ben Grieve .20
202 Travis Lee .20
203 Wes Helms .20
204 Geoff Jenkins .20
205 Russell Branyan .20
206 Esteban Yan **RC** .20
207 Ben Ford **RC** .20
208 Rich Butler **RC** .75
209 Ryan Jackson **RC** .50
210 A.J. Hinch .20
211 Maggio Ordonez **RC** 25.00
212 David Dellucci **RC** .50
213 Billy McMillon .20
214 Mike Lowell **RC** 10.00
215 Todd Erdos **RC** .20
216 Carlos Mendoza **RC** .25
217 Frank Catalanotto **RC** .75
218 Julio Ramirez **RC** .20
219 John Halama **RC** .50
220 Wilson Delgado .20
221 Mike Judd **RC** .20
222 Rolando Arrojo **RC** 1.00
223 Jason LaRue **RC** .50
224 Manny Aybar **RC** .50
225 Jorge Velandia .20
226 Mike Kinkade **RC** .75
227 Carlos Lee **RC** 15.00
228 Bobby Hughes .20
229 Ryan Christenson **RC** .50
230 Masato Yoshii **RC** 1.00
231 Richard Hidalgo .10
232 Rafael Medina .10
233 Damian Jackson .10
234 Derek Lowe .15
235 Mario Valdez .10
236 Eli Marrero .10
237 Juan Encarnacion .10
238 Livan Hernandez .10
239 Bruce Chen .10
240 Eric Milton .10
241 Jason Varitek .10
242 Scott Elarton .10
243 Manuel Barrios **RC** .10
244 Mike Caruso .10
245 Tom Evans .10
246 Pat Cline .10
247 Matt Clement .15
248 Karim Garcia .15
249 Richie Sexson .10
250 Sidney Ponson .10
251 Randall Simon .10
252 Tony Saunders .10
253 Javier Valentin .10
254 Danny Clyburn .10
255 Michael Coleman .10
256 Hanley Frias **RC** .10

257	Miguel Cairo	.10
258	Rob Stanifer RC	.10
259	Lou Collier	.10
260	Abraham Nunez	.10
261	Ricky Ledee	.10
262	Carl Pavano	.10
263	Derrek Lee	.50
264	Jeff Abbott	.10
265	Bob Abreu	.10
266	Bartolo Colon	.10
267	Mike Drumright	.10
268	Daryle Ward	.10
269	Gabe Alvarez	.10
270	Josh Booty	.10
271	Damian Moss	.10
272	Brian Rose	.10
273	Jarrod Washburn	.10
274	Bobby Estalella	.10
275	Enrique Wilson	.10
276	Derrick Gibson	.10
277	Ken Cloude	.10
278	Kevin Witt	.10
279	Donnie Sadler	.10
280	Sean Casey	.20
281	Jacob Cruz	.10
282	Ron Wright	.10
283	Jeremi Gonzalez	.10
284	Desi Relaford	.10
285	Bobby Smith	.10
286	Javier Vazquez	.10
287	Steve Woodard RC	.20
288	Greg Norton	.10
289	Cliff Politte	.10
290	Felix Heredia	.10
291	Braden Looper	.10
292	Felix Martinez	.10
293	Brian Meadows	.10
294	Edwin Diaz	.10
295	Pat Watkins	.10
296	Marc Pisciotta RC	.10
297	Rick Gorecki	.10
298	DaRond Stovall	.10
299	Andy Larkin	.10
300	Felix Rodriguez	.10
301	Blake Stein	.50
302	John Rocker RC	1.00
303	Justin Baughman RC	.50
304	Jesus Sanchez RC	.50
305	Randy Winn	.50
306	Lou Merloni	.50
307	Jim Parque RC	1.00
308	Dennis Reyes	.50
309	Orlando Hernandez RC	10.00
310	Jason Johnson	.50
311	Torii Hunter	.50
312	Mike Frank	2.50
313	Mike Frank RC	.50
314	Troy Glaus RC	60.00
315	Jin Cho RC	.75
316	Ruben Mateo RC	1.00
317	Ryan Minor RC	1.00
318	Aramis Ramirez	.75
319	Adrian Beltre	1.00
320	Matt Anderson RC	1.00
321	Gabe Kapler RC	2.00
322	Jeremy Giambi RC	1.00
323	Carlos Beltran	1.00
324	Dermal Brown	.50
325	Ben Davis	.50
326	Eric Chavez	1.50
327	Bob Howry RC	1.00
328	Roy Halladay	1.00
329	George Lombard	.50
330	Michael Barrett	.50
331	Fernando Seguignol RC	1.00
332	J.D. Drew RC	20.00
333	Odalis Perez RC	4.00
334	Alex Cora RC	1.00
335	Placido Polanco RC	8.00
336	Armando Rios RC	.50
337	Sammy Sosa (HR Commemorative)	3.00
338	Mark McGwire (HR Commemorative)	4.00
339	Sammy Sosa, Mark McGwire (Checklist)	4.00

1998 Leaf Rookies & Stars Longevity

	NM/M
Common Player:	3.00

Stars:		50X
SP Stars (131-230):		15X
SP Stars (301-339):		5X

(See 1998 Leaf Rookies & Stars for checklist and base card values.)

True Blue

	NM/M
Common Player:	1.00
Stars:	12X
SP Stars (131-230; 301-339):	2X

(See 1998 Leaf Rookies & Stars for checklist and base card values.)

Cross Training

	NM/M
Complete Set (10):	30.00
Common Player:	1.50
Production 1,000 Sets	
1 Kenny Lofton	1.50
2 Ken Griffey Jr.	6.00
3 Alex Rodriguez	4.00
4 Greg Maddux	4.00
5 Barry Bonds	7.50
6 Ivan Rodriguez	2.50
7 Chipper Jones	4.00
8 Jeff Bagwell	3.00
9 Nomar Garciaparra	4.00
10 Derek Jeter	7.50

Crusade

	NM/M
Complete Green Set (30):	225.00
Common Player:	7.50
Production 250 Sets	
Purples (100 Sets):	3X
Reds (25 Sets):	10X
101 Richard Hidalgo	7.50
102 Paul Konerko	15.00
103 Miguel Tejada	15.00
104 Fernando Tatis	7.50
105 Travis Lee	7.50
106 Wes Helms	7.50

107	Rich Butler	7.50
108	Mark Kotsay	7.50
109	Eli Marrero	7.50
110	David Ortiz	15.00
111	Juan Encarnacion	7.50
112	Jaret Wright	7.50
113	Livan Hernandez	7.50
114	Ron Wright	7.50
115	Ryan Christenson	7.50
116	Eric Milton	7.50
117	Brad Fullmer	7.50
118	Karim Garcia	10.00
119	Abraham Nunez	7.50
120	Ricky Ledee	7.50
121	Carl Pavano	7.50
122	Derrek Lee	15.00
123	A.J. Hinch	7.50
124	Brian Rose	7.50
125	Bobby Estalella	7.50
126	Kevin Millwood	10.00
127	Kerry Wood	30.00
128	Sean Casey	12.50
129	Russell Branyan	7.50
130	Magglio Ordonez	20.00

Extreme Measures

	NM/M
Complete Set (10):	50.00
Common Player:	3.00
1 Ken Griffey Jr./944	7.50
2 Frank Thomas/653	5.00
3 Tony Gwynn/628	6.00
4 Mark McGwire/942	9.00
5 Larry Walker/280	3.00
6 Mike Piazza/960	7.50
7 Roger Clemens/708	6.50
8 Greg Maddux/980	5.00
9 Jeff Bagwell/873	4.50
10 Nomar Garciaparra/989	6.50

Extreme Measures Die-Cuts

	NM/M
Complete Set (10):	375.00
Common Player:	2.50
1 Ken Griffey Jr./56	65.00
2 Frank Thomas/347	11.00
3 Tony Gwynn/372	13.50
4 Mark McGwire/58	80.00
5 Larry Walker/720	2.50
6 Mike Piazza/40	75.00
7 Roger Clemens/292	16.00
8 Greg Maddux/20	100.00
9 Jeff Bagwell/127	20.00
10 Nomar Garciaparra/11	125.00

Freshman Orientation

	NM/M
Complete Set (20):	20.00
Common Player:	.75
Production 5,000 Sets	
Samples:	1X
1 Todd Helton	4.00
2 Ben Grieve	.75
3 Travis Lee	.75
4 Paul Konerko	1.50
5 Jaret Wright	.75
6 Livan Hernandez	.75
7 Brad Fullmer	.75
8 Carl Pavano	.75
9 Richard Hidalgo	.75
10 Miguel Tejada	1.50
11 Mark Kotsay	.75
12 David Ortiz	1.50
13 Juan Encarnacion	.75
14 Fernando Tatis	.75
15 Kevin Millwood	1.50
16 Kerry Wood	2.50

17	Magglio Ordonez	1.50
18	Derrek Lee	1.50
19	Jose Cruz Jr.	.75
20	A.J. Hinch	.75

Great American Heroes

	NM/M
Complete Set (20):	35.00
Common Player:	.75
Production 2,500 Sets	
Samples:	1X
1 Frank Thomas	1.75
2 Cal Ripken Jr.	5.00
3 Ken Griffey Jr.	3.00
4 Alex Rodriguez	4.00
5 Greg Maddux	2.25
6 Mike Piazza	3.00
7 Chipper Jones	3.00
8 Tony Gwynn	2.25
9 Jeff Bagwell	1.75
10 Juan Gonzalez	1.25
11 Hideo Nomo	1.25
12 Roger Clemens	2.50
13 Mark McGwire	4.00
14 Barry Bonds	5.00
15 Kenny Lofton	.75
16 Larry Walker	.75
17 Paul Molitor	1.75
18 Wade Boggs	2.25
19 Barry Larkin	.75
20 Andres Galarraga	.75

Greatest Hits

	NM/M
Complete Set (20):	30.00
Common Player:	.50
Production 2,500 Sets	
1 Ken Griffey Jr.	2.50
2 Frank Thomas	1.50
3 Cal Ripken Jr.	4.00
4 Alex Rodriguez	3.00
5 Ben Grieve	.50
6 Mike Piazza	2.50
7 Chipper Jones	2.00
8 Tony Gwynn	2.00
9 Derek Jeter	4.00
10 Jeff Bagwell	1.50
11 Tino Martinez	.50
12 Juan Gonzalez	.75
13 Nomar Garciaparra	2.00
14 Mark McGwire	3.00
15 Scott Rolen	.75
16 David Justice	.50
17 Darin Erstad	.75
18 Mo Vaughn	.50
19 Ivan Rodriguez	1.00
20 Travis Lee	.50

Home Run Derby

	NM/M
Complete Set (20):	30.00
Common Player:	.75
Production 2,500 Sets	
1 Tino Martinez	.75
2 Jim Thome	1.25
3 Larry Walker	.75

4	Tony Clark	.75
5	Jose Cruz Jr.	.75
6	Barry Bonds	5.00
7	Scott Rolen	1.00
8	Paul Konerko	1.25
9	Travis Lee	.75
10	Todd Helton	1.25
11	Mark McGwire	4.00
12	Andruw Jones	1.50
13	Nomar Garciaparra	2.50
14	Juan Gonzalez	1.00
15	Jeff Bagwell	1.50
16	Chipper Jones	2.50
17	Mike Piazza	3.00
18	Frank Thomas	1.50
19	Ken Griffey Jr.	3.00
20	Albert Belle	.75

ML Hard Drives

NM/M

Complete Set (20): 30.00
Common Player: .75
Production 2,500 Sets
Samples: 1X

1	Jeff Bagwell	1.50
2	Juan Gonzalez	1.00
3	Nomar Garciaparra	2.00
4	Ken Griffey Jr.	3.00
5	Frank Thomas	1.50
6	Cal Ripken Jr.	4.50
7	Alex Rodriguez	3.50
8	Mike Piazza	3.00
9	Chipper Jones	2.00
10	Tony Gwynn	2.00
11	Derek Jeter	4.50
12	Mo Vaughn	.75
13	Ben Grieve	.75
14	Manny Ramirez	1.50
15	Vladimir Guerrero	1.50
16	Scott Rolen	1.00
17	Darin Erstad	.75
18	Kenny Lofton	.75
19	Brad Fullmer	.75
20	David Justice	.75

MVPs

NM/M

Complete Set (20): 35.00
Common Player: .50
Pennant Editions: 2X
Production 500 Sets

1	Frank Thomas	2.00
2	Chuck Knoblauch	.50
3	Cal Ripken Jr.	5.00
4	Alex Rodriguez	4.00
5	Ivan Rodriguez	1.50
6	Albert Belle	.50
7	Ken Griffey Jr.	3.00
8	Juan Gonzalez	1.50
9	Roger Clemens	2.75
10	Mo Vaughn	.50
11	Jeff Bagwell	2.00
12	Craig Biggio	.50
13	Chipper Jones	2.50
14	Barry Larkin	.50
15	Mike Piazza	3.00

16	Barry Bonds	5.00
17	Andruw Jones	2.00
18	Tony Gwynn	2.50
19	Greg Maddux	2.50
20	Mark McGwire	4.00

Standing Ovation

NM/M

Complete Set (10): 12.50
Common Player: .75
Production 5,000 Sets
Samples: 1X

1	Barry Bonds	3.00
2	Mark McGwire	2.50
3	Ken Griffey Jr.	2.00
4	Frank Thomas	1.00
5	Tony Gwynn	1.50
6	Cal Ripken Jr.	3.00
7	Greg Maddux	1.50
8	Roger Clemens	1.75
9	Paul Molitor	1.00
10	Ivan Rodriguez	.75

Ticket Masters

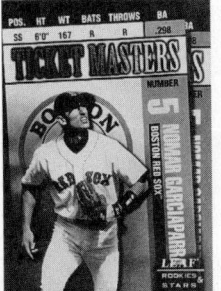

NM/M

Complete Set (20): 32.50
Common Card: .50
Production 2,250 Sets
Die-Cuts: 1.5X
Production 250 Sets

1	Ken Griffey Jr., Alex Rodriguez	4.00
2	Frank Thomas, Albert Belle	1.50
3	Cal Ripken Jr., Roberto Alomar	5.00
4	Greg Maddux, Chipper Jones	2.00
5	Tony Gwynn, Ken Caminiti	2.00
6	Derek Jeter, Andy Pettitte	5.00
7	Jeff Bagwell, Craig Biggio	1.50
8	Juan Gonzalez, Ivan Rodriguez	1.25
9	Nomar Garciaparra, Mo Vaughn	2.00
10	Vladimir Guerrero, Brad Fullmer	1.50
11	Andruw Jones, Andres Galarraga	1.50
12	Tino Martinez, Chuck Knoblauch	.50
13	Raul Mondesi, Paul Konerko	.75
14	Roger Clemens, Jose Cruz Jr.	2.25
15	Mark McGwire, Brian Jordan	4.00
16	Kenny Lofton, Manny Ramirez	
17	Larry Walker, Todd Helton	1.25
18	Darin Erstad, Tim Salmon	.75
19	Travis Lee, Matt Williams	.50
20	Ben Grieve, Jason Giambi	1.00

2001 Leaf Certified Materials

NM/M

Complete Set (160):
Common Player: .40
Common SP (111-160): 10.00

Production 200
Pack (5): 15.00
Box (12): 160.00

1	Alex Rodriguez	5.00
2	Barry Bonds	6.00
3	Cal Ripken Jr.	6.00
4	Chipper Jones	3.00
5	Derek Jeter	6.00
6	Troy Glaus	1.50
7	Frank Thomas	2.00
8	Greg Maddux	4.00
9	Ivan Rodriguez	2.00
10	Jeff Bagwell	2.00
11	Eric Karros	.40
12	Todd Helton	2.00
13	Ken Griffey Jr.	4.00
14	Manny Ramirez	2.00
15	Mark McGwire	4.00
16	Mike Piazza	4.00
17	Nomar Garciaparra	1.50
18	Pedro Martinez	2.00
19	Randy Johnson	2.00
20	Rick Ankiel	1.50
21	Rickey Henderson	1.50
22	Roger Clemens	3.00
23	Sammy Sosa	2.50
24	Tony Gwynn	3.00
25	Vladimir Guerrero	2.00
26	Kazuhiro Sasaki	.40
27	Roberto Alomar	.75
28	Barry Zito	.40
29	Pat Burrell	1.00
30	Harold Baines	.40
31	Carlos Delgado	1.00
32	J.D. Drew	1.00
33	Jim Edmonds	.60
34	Darin Erstad	.50
35	Jason Giambi	1.00
36	Tom Glavine	1.50
37	Juan Gonzalez	1.00
38	Mark Grace	.75
39	Shawn Green	.75
40	Tim Hudson	.75
41	Andruw Jones	.75
42	Jeff Kent	.75
43	Barry Larkin	.75
44	Rafael Furcal	.75
45	Mike Mussina	1.00
46	Hideo Nomo	.75
47	Rafael Palmeiro	1.00
48	Scott Rolen	1.00
49	Gary Sheffield	1.00
50	Bernie Williams	.75
51	Bobby Abreu	.75
52	Edgardo Alfonzo	.40
53	Edgar Martinez	.40
54	Magglio Ordonez	.75
55	Kerry Wood	1.00
56	Adrian Beltre	.75
57	Lance Berkman	1.00
58	Kevin Brown	.40
59	Sean Casey	.60
60	Eric Chavez	.60
61	Bartolo Colon	.40
62	Johnny Damon	1.50
63	Jermaine Dye	.40
64	Juan Encarnacion	.40
65	Carl Everett	.40
66	Brian Giles	.40
67	Mike Hampton	.40
68	Richard Hidalgo	.40
69	Geoff Jenkins	.40
70	Jacque Jones	.40
71	Jason Kendall	.40
72	Ryan Klesko	.40
73	Chan Ho Park	.40
74	Richie Sexson	.40
75	Mike Sweeney	.40
76	Fernando Tatis	.40
77	Miguel Tejada	1.00
78	Jose Vidro	.40
79	Larry Walker	.40
80	Preston Wilson	.40
81	Craig Biggio	.75
82	Fred McGriff	.40
83	Jim Thome	1.50
84	Garret Anderson	.40
85	Russell Branyan	.40
86	Tony Batista	.40
87	Terrence Long	.40
88	Deion Sanders	.40

89	Rusty Greer	.40
90	Orlando Hernandez	.40
91	Gabe Kapler	.40
92	Paul Konerko	.75
93	Carlos Lee	.75
94	Kenny Lofton	.40
95	Raul Mondesi	.40
96	Jorge Posada	.75
97	Tim Salmon	.40
98	Greg Vaughn	.40
99	Mo Vaughn	.40
100	Omar Vizquel	.40
101	Ray Durham	.40
102	Jeff Cirillo	.40
103	Dean Palmer	.40
104	Ryan Dempster	.40
105	Carlos Beltran	1.00
106	Timo Perez	.40
107	Robin Ventura	.40
108	Andy Pettitte	.75
109	Aramis Ramirez	1.00
110	Phil Nevin	.40
111	Alex Escobar	10.00
112	Johnny Estrada RC	15.00
113	Pedro Feliz	10.00
114	Nate Frese RC	10.00
115	Joe Kennedy RC	10.00
116	Brandon Larson RC	10.00
117	Alexis Gomez RC	10.00
118	Jason Hart	10.00
119	Jason Michaels RC	10.00
120	Marcus Giles	10.00
121	Christian Parker RC	10.00
122	Jackson Melian RC	10.00
123	Donaldo Mendez RC	10.00
124	Adrian Hernandez RC	10.00
125	Bud Smith RC	10.00
126	Jose Mieses RC	10.00
127	Roy Oswalt	10.00
128	Eric Munson	10.00
129	Xavier Nady	10.00
130	Horacio Ramirez RC	10.00
131	Abraham Nunez	10.00
132	Jose Ortiz	10.00
133	Jeremy Owens RC	10.00
134	Claudio Vargas RC	10.00
135	Ricardo Rodriguez RC	10.00
136	Aubrey Huff	10.00
137	Ben Sheets	10.00
138	Adam Dunn	15.00
139	Andres Torres RC	10.00
140	Elpidio Guzman RC	10.00
141	Jay Gibbons RC	10.00
142	Wilkin Ruan RC	10.00
143	Tsuyoshi Shinjo RC	10.00
144	Alfonso Soriano	15.00
145	Josh Towers RC	10.00
146	Ichiro Suzuki RC	140.00
147	Juan Uribe RC	10.00
148	Joe Crede	20.00
149	Carlos Valderrama RC	10.00
150	Matt White RC	10.00
151	Dee Brown	10.00
152	Juan Cruz RC	10.00
153	Cory Aldridge RC	10.00
154	Wilmy Caceres	10.00
155	Josh Beckett	15.00
156	Wilson Betemit RC	10.00
157	Corey Patterson	10.00
158	Albert Pujols RC	200.00
159	Rafael Soriano RC	10.00
160	Jack Wilson RC	15.00

Mirror Red/Gold

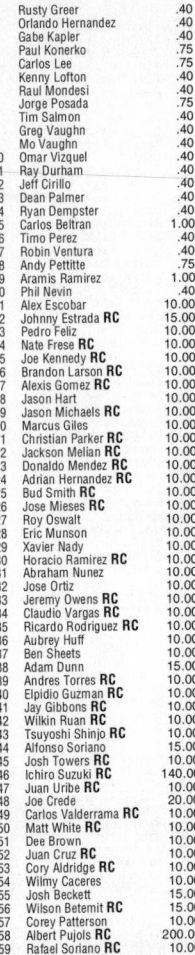

NM/M

Common Mirror Red (1-110):	2.00
Stars (1-110):	3-5X
Common Mirror Red (111-160):	6.00
Stars (111-160):	1-2X
Production 75	
Mirror Gold:	6-8X
Production 25	

(See 2001 Leaf Certified Materials for checklist and base card values.)

Fabric of the Game

NM/M

	Common Player:	5.00
1	Lou Gehrig/184	200.00
1	Lou Gehrig/23	375.00
2	Babe Ruth/136	250.00

2	Babe Ruth/60	400.00
3	Stan Musial/177	40.00
3	Stan Musial/39	100.00
4	Nolan Ryan	40.00
4	Nolan Ryan/61	60.00
4	Nolan Ryan/34	80.00
5	Roberto Clemente/166	100.00
5	Roberto Clemente/29	250.00
6	Al Kaline/137	25.00
7	Brooks Robinson	20.00
7	Brooks Robinson/68	30.00
8	Mel Ott	30.00
8	Mel Ott/72	50.00
9	Dave Winfield/88	15.00
10	Eddie Mathews/115	25.00
10	Eddie Mathews/72	40.00
11	Ernie Banks/50	40.00
11	Ernie Banks/47	40.00
12	Frank Robinson	15.00
13	George Brett/137	40.00
14	Hank Aaron	40.00
14	Hank Aaron/98	50.00
14	Hank Aaron/47	100.00
15	Harmon Killebrew	25.00
15	Harmon Killebrew/49	50.00
16	Joe Morgan	10.00
16	Joe Morgan/96	15.00
17	Johnny Bench	20.00
17	Johnny Bench/68	30.00
18	Kirby Puckett/134	40.00
19	Mike Schmidt	40.00
19	Mike Schmidt/59	60.00
20	Phil Rizzuto/149	15.00
21	Reggie Jackson	15.00
21	Reggie Jackson/44	30.00
22	Catfish Hunter	15.00
22	Catfish Hunter/42	25.00
23	Rod Carew/92	20.00
23	Rod Carew/100	20.00
24	Bob Feller	15.00
24	Bob Feller/44	30.00
25	Lou Brock	10.00
25	Lou Brock/141	15.00
26	Tom Seaver	15.00
26	Tom Seaver/61	30.00
27	Paul Molitor	10.00
27	Paul Molitor/114	25.00
28	Willie McCovey/126	15.00
29	Yogi Berra	20.00
29	Yogi Berra/49	40.00
30	Don Drysdale	15.00
30	Don Drysdale/49	30.00
31	Duke Snider	20.00
31	Duke Snider/99	30.00
33	Orlando Cepeda/46	20.00
34	Casey Stengel	10.00
34	Casey Stengel/103	15.00
35	Robin Yount	20.00
35	Robin Yount/126	40.00
36	Eddie Murray	15.00
36	Eddie Murray/35	40.00
37	Jim Palmer	10.00
38	Juan Marichal	10.00
38	Juan Marichal/52	20.00
39	Willie Stargell	15.00
39	Willie Stargell/55	20.00
40	Ted Williams	150.00
40	Ted Williams/71	100.00
40	Ted Williams/43	150.00
41	Cal Ripken Jr.	30.00
41	Cal Ripken/75	50.00
41	Cal Ripken/277	40.00
42	Vladimir Guerrero/322	15.00
42	Vladimir Guerrero/44	25.00
43	Greg Maddux	15.00
43	Greg Maddux/240	20.00
44	Barry Bonds	30.00
44	Barry Bonds/49	75.00
44	Barry Bonds/289	30.00
45	Pedro Martinez	15.00
45	Pedro Martinez/268	15.00
46	Ivan Rodriguez	10.00
46	Ivan Rodriguez/304	15.00
47	Roger Maris	50.00
47	Roger Maris/275	50.00
48	Randy Johnson	15.00
48	Randy Johnson/179	20.00
49	Roger Clemens	20.00
49	Roger Clemens/260	20.00
50	Todd Helton	10.00
50	Todd Helton/334	10.00
51	Tony Gwynn	15.00
51	Tony Gwynn/119	20.00
51	Tony Gwynn/134	20.00
52	Troy Glaus	8.00
52	Troy Glaus/47	15.00
52	Troy Glaus/256	8.00
53	Phil Niekro	8.00
53	Phil Niekro/245	10.00
54	Don Sutton	8.00
54	Don Sutton/178	10.00
55	Frank Thomas	10.00
55	Frank Thomas/321	15.00
56	Jeff Bagwell	10.00
56	Jeff Bagwell/305	15.00
57	Rickey Henderson	15.00
57	Rickey Henderson/282	15.00
58	Darin Erstad/301	8.00
59	Andruw Jones	10.00
59	Andruw Jones/272	10.00
60	Roberto Alomar	10.00
60	Roberto Alomar/120	15.00
60	Roberto Alomar/170	15.00
61	Mike Piazza	20.00
61	Mike Piazza/328	20.00
62	Chipper Jones	15.00
62	Chipper Jones/189	15.00
63	Shawn Green	8.00
63	Shawn Green/143	8.00
64	Don Mattingly	50.00
64	Don Mattingly/145	50.00
64	Don Mattingly/222	40.00
65	Rafael Palmeiro	10.00
66	Wade Boggs	10.00
66	Wade Boggs/116	15.00
66	Wade Boggs/89	20.00
67	Hoyt Wilhelm	8.00
67	Hoyt Wilhelm/143	10.00
68	Andre Dawson	8.00
68	Andre Dawson/49	15.00
68	Andre Dawson/314	10.00
69	Ryne Sandberg	30.00
69	Ryne Sandberg/282	35.00
70	Nomar Garciaparra/333	25.00
71	Tom Glavine	8.00
71	Tom Glavine/208	10.00
71	Tom Glavine/247	10.00
72	Magglio Ordonez	8.00
72	Magglio Ordonez/301	8.00
72	Magglio Ordonez/126	10.00
73	Bernie Williams	10.00
73	Bernie Williams/304	15.00
74	Jim Edmonds	8.00
74	Jim Edmonds/108	10.00
74	Jim Edmonds/291	10.00
75	Hideo Nomo	20.00
75	Hideo Nomo/69	30.00
76	Barry Larkin	10.00
76	Barry Larkin/300	10.00
77	Scott Rolen	10.00
77	Scott Rolen/284	10.00
78	Miguel Tejada	8.00
78	Miguel Tejada/253	8.00
79	Freddy Garcia	5.00
79	Freddy Garcia/170	5.00
79	Freddy Garcia/249	5.00
80	Edgar Martinez	10.00
80	Edgar Martinez/320	10.00
81	Edgardo Alfonzo	5.00
81	Edgardo Alfonzo/108	5.00
81	Edgardo Alfonzo/296	5.00
82	Steve Garvey	8.00
82	Steve Garvey/272	8.00
83	Larry Walker	5.00
83	Larry Walker/311	5.00
83	Larry Walker/49	10.00
84	A.J. Burnett	5.00
84	A.J. Burnett/90	8.00
85	Richie Sexson	8.00
85	Richie Sexson/242	8.00
85	Richie Sexson/116	8.00
86	Mark Mulder	8.00
86	Mark Mulder/88	10.00
87	Kerry Wood	10.00
87	Kerry Wood/233	10.00
88	Sean Casey	5.00
88	Sean Casey/312	5.00
89	Jermaine Dye	5.00
89	Jermaine Dye/118	5.00
89	Jermaine Dye/286	5.00
90	Kevin Brown	5.00
90	Kevin Brown/170	5.00
90	Kevin Brown/257	5.00
91	Craig Biggio	5.00
91	Craig Biggio/88	8.00
91	Craig Biggio/291	5.00
92	Mike Sweeney	5.00
92	Mike Sweeney/302	5.00
92	Mike Sweeney/144	5.00
93	Jim Thome	10.00
93	Jim Thome/233	10.00
93	Jim Thome/40	20.00
94	Al Leiter	5.00
94	Al Leiter/247	5.00
94	Al Leiter/106	5.00
95	Barry Zito	8.00
95	Barry Zito/272	8.00
95	Barry Zito/78	15.00
96	Rafael Furcal	5.00
96	Rafael Furcal/295	5.00
97	J.D. Drew	5.00
97	J.D. Drew/276	5.00
98	Andres Galarraga	5.00
98	Andres Galarraga/150	5.00
98	Andres Galarraga/291	5.00
99	Kazuhiro Sasaki	5.00
99	Kazuhiro Sasaki/266	5.00
100	Chan Ho Park	5.00
100	Chan Ho Park/65	5.00
100	Chan Ho Park/217	5.00
101	Eric Milton	5.00
101	Eric Milton/163	5.00
102	Carlos Lee	5.00
102	Carlos Lee/297	5.00
103	Preston Wilson	5.00
103	Preston Wilson/266	5.00
104	Adrian Beltre	5.00
104	Adrian Beltre/85	5.00
104	Adrian Beltre/272	5.00
105	Luis Gonzalez	5.00
105	Luis Gonzalez/281	5.00
105	Luis Gonzalez/114	5.00
106	Kenny Lofton	5.00
106	Kenny Lofton/306	5.00
107	Shannon Stewart	5.00
107	Shannon Stewart/297	5.00
108	Javy Lopez	5.00
108	Javy Lopez/290	5.00
108	Javy Lopez/106	5.00
109	Raul Mondesi	5.00
109	Raul Mondesi/286	5.00
110	Mark Grace	10.00
110	Mark Grace/51	20.00
110	Mark Grace/308	15.00
111	Curt Schilling	8.00
111	Curt Schilling/235	8.00
111	Curt Schilling/110	10.00
112	Cliff Floyd	5.00
112	Cliff Floyd/275	5.00
113	Moises Alou	5.00
113	Moises Alou/124	5.00
113	Moises Alou/303	5.00
114	Aaron Sele	5.00
114	Aaron Sele/92	5.00
115	Jose Cruz Jr.	5.00
115	Jose Cruz Jr/245	5.00
116	John Olerud	5.00
116	John Olerud/186	5.00
116	John Olerud/107	5.00
117	Jose Vidro	5.00
117	Jose Vidro/296	5.00
118	John Smoltz	5.00
118	John Smoltz/334	5.00

2001 Leaf Limited

	NM/M
Complete Set (375):	
Common Player:	.75
Common Lumberjack (151-200):	5.00
#'d to 100, 250 or 500	
Common Rk (201-300):	5.00
Production 1,500	
Common Auto.(301-325):	10.00
Production 1,000	
Pack (3):	8.00
Box (18):	125.00

1	Curt Schilling	1.50
2	Craig Biggio	1.00
3	Brian Giles	.75
4	Scott Brosius	.75
5	Barry Larkin	1.00
6	Bartolo Colon	.75
7	John Olerud	.75
8	Cal Ripken Jr.	6.00
9	Moises Alou	.75
10	Barry Zito	.75
11	Ken Griffey Jr.	4.00
12	Garret Anderson	.75
13	Andy Pettitte	1.00
14	Jim Edmonds	1.00
15	Tom Glavine	1.50
16	Jose Canseco	1.00
17	Fred McGriff	.75
18	Robin Ventura	.75
19	Tony Gwynn	3.00
20	Jeff Cirillo	.75
21	Brad Radke	.75
22	Ellis Burks	.75
23	Scott Rolen	1.50
24	Rickey Henderson	1.50
25	Edgar Martinez	.75
26	Kerry Wood	1.00
27	Al Leiter	.75
28	Jose Cruz Jr.	.75
29	Sean Casey	.75
30	Eric Chavez	.75
31	Jarrod Washburn	.75
32	Gary Sheffield	1.00
33	Jermaine Dye	.75
34	Bernie Williams	1.00
35	Tony Armas Jr.	.75
36	Carlos Beltran	1.50
37	Geoff Jenkins	.75
38	Shawn Green	.75
39	Ryan Klesko	.75
40	Richie Sexson	.75
41	Pat Burrell	1.00
42	J.D. Drew	1.00
43	Larry Walker	.75
44	Andres Galarraga	.75
45	Tino Martinez	.75
46	Rafael Furcal	1.00
47	Cristian Guzman	.75
48	Omar Vizquel	.75
49	Bret Boone	.75
50	Wade Miller	.75
51	Eric Milton	.75
52	Gabe Kapler	.75
53	Johnny Damon	1.50
54	Shannon Stewart	.75
55	Kenny Lofton	.75
56	Raul Mondesi	.75
57	Jorge Posada	1.00
58	Mark Grace	1.00
59	Robert Fick	.75
60	Phil Nevin	.75
61	Mike Mussina	1.00
62	Joe Mays	.75
63	Todd Helton	1.50
64	Tim Hudson	1.00
65	Manny Ramirez	2.00
66	Sammy Sosa	3.00
67	Darin Erstad	.75
68	Roberto Alomar	1.00
69	Jeff Bagwell	1.50
70	Mark McGwire	4.00
71	Jason Giambi	1.00
72	Cliff Floyd	.75
73	Barry Bonds	5.00
74	Juan Gonzalez	1.00
75	Jeremy Giambi	.75
76	Carlos Lee	1.00
77	Randy Johnson	2.00
78	Frank Thomas	2.00
79	Carlos Delgado	1.00
80	Pedro Martinez	2.00
81	Rusty Greer	.75
82	Brian Jordan	.75
83	Vladimir Guerrero	2.00
84	Mike Sweeney	.75
85	Jose Vidro	.75
86	Paul LoDuca	.75
87	Matt Morris	.75
88	Adrian Beltre	.75
89	Aramis Ramirez	1.50
90	Derek Jeter	6.00
91	Rich Aurilia	.75
92	Freddy Garcia	.75
93	Preston Wilson	.75
94	Greg Maddux	4.00
95	Miguel Tejada	1.00
96	Luis Gonzalez	.75
97	Torii Hunter	1.00
98	Nomar Garciaparra	1.50
99	Jamie Moyer	.75
100	Javier Vazquez	.75
101	Ben Grieve	.75
102	Mike Piazza	4.00
103	Paul O'Neill	1.00
104	Terrence Long	.75
105	Charles Johnson	.75
106	Rafael Palmeiro	1.00
107	David Cone	.75
108	Alex Rodriguez	5.00
109	John Burkett	.75
110	Chipper Jones	3.00
111	Ryan Dempster	.75
112	Bobby Abreu	1.00
113	Brad Fullmer	.75
114	Kazuhiro Sasaki	.75
115	Mariano Rivera	1.00
116	Edgardo Alfonzo	.75
117	Ray Durham	.75
118	Richard Hidalgo	.75
119	Jeff Weaver	.75
120	Paul Konerko	1.00
121	Jon Lieber	.75
122	Mike Hampton	.75
123	Mike Cameron	.75
124	Kevin Brown	.75
125	Doug Mientkiewicz	.75
126	Jim Thome	1.00
127	Corey Koskie	.75
128	Trot Nixon	.75
129	Darryl Kile	.75
130	Ivan Rodriguez	1.50
131	Carl Everett	.75
132	Jeff Kent	.75
133	Rondell White	.75
134	Chan Ho Park	.75
135	Robert Person	.75
136	Troy Glaus	1.00
137	Aaron Sele	.75
138	Roger Clemens	3.00
139	Tony Clark	.75
140	Mark Buehrle	.75
141	David Justice	.75
142	Magglio Ordonez	1.00
143	Bobby Higginson	.75
144	Hideo Nomo	1.00
145	Tim Salmon	.75
146	Mark Mulder	.75
147	Troy Percival	.75

148	Lance Berkman	1.50
149	Russ Ortiz	.75
150	Andruw Jones	1.00
151	Mike Piazza	15.00
152	Manny Ramirez	10.00
153	Bernie Williams	6.00
154	Nomar Garciaparra	8.00
155	Andres Galarraga	5.00
156	Kenny Lofton	5.00
157	Scott Rolen	8.00
158	Jim Thome	8.00
159	Darin Erstad	5.00
160	Garret Anderson	5.00
161	Andruw Jones	8.00
162	Juan Gonzalez	5.00
163	Rafael Palmeiro	8.00
164	Magglio Ordonez	8.00
165	Jeff Bagwell	8.00
166	Eric Chavez	5.00
167	Brian Giles	5.00
168	Adrian Beltre	5.00
169	Tony Gwynn	15.00
170	Shawn Green	5.00
171	Todd Helton	8.00
172	Troy Glaus	8.00
173	Lance Berkman	10.00
174	Ivan Rodriguez	8.00
175	Sean Casey	5.00
176	Aramis Ramirez	8.00
177	J.D. Drew	5.00
178	Barry Bonds	25.00
179	Barry Larkin	5.00
180	Cal Ripken Jr.	40.00
181	Frank Thomas	8.00
182	Craig Biggio	5.00
183	Carlos Lee	8.00
184	Chipper Jones	10.00
185	Miguel Tejada	8.00
186	Jose Vidro	5.00
187	Terrence Long	5.00
188	Moises Alou	5.00
189	Trot Nixon	5.00
190	Shannon Stewart	5.00
191	Ryan Klesko	5.00
192	Carlos Beltran	10.00
193	Vladimir Guerrero	8.00
194	Edgar Martinez	5.00
195	Luis Gonzalez	5.00
196	Richard Hidalgo	5.00
197	Roberto Alomar	6.00
198	Mike Sweeney	5.00
199	Bobby Abreu	8.00
200	Cliff Floyd	5.00
201	Jackson Melian **RC**	5.00
202	Jason Jennings	5.00
203	Toby Hall	5.00
204	Jason Karnuth **RC**	5.00
205	Jason Smith **RC**	5.00
206	Mike Maroth **RC**	5.00
207	Sean Douglass **RC**	5.00
208	Adam Johnson	5.00
209	Luke Hudson **RC**	5.00
210	Nick Maness **RC**	5.00
211	Les Walrond **RC**	5.00
212	Travis Phelps **RC**	5.00
213	Carlos Garcia **RC**	5.00
214	Bill Ortega	5.00
215	Gene Altman **RC**	5.00
216	Nate Frese	5.00
217	Bob File **RC**	5.00
218	Steve Green **RC**	5.00
219	Kris Keller **RC**	5.00
220	Matt White **RC**	5.00
221	Nate Teut **RC**	5.00
222	Nick Johnson	5.00
223	Jeremy Fikac **RC**	5.00
224	Abraham Nunez	5.00
225	Mike Penney **RC**	5.00
226	Roy Smith **RC**	5.00
227	Tim Christman **RC**	5.00
228	Carlos Pena	5.00
229	Joe Beimel **RC**	5.00
230	Mike Koplove **RC**	5.00
231	Scott MacRae **RC**	5.00
232	Kyle Lohse **RC**	8.00
233	Jerrod Riggan **RC**	5.00
234	Scott Podsednik **RC**	10.00
235	Winston Abreu **RC**	5.00
236	Ryan Freel **RC**	8.00
237	Ken Vining **RC**	5.00
238	Bret Prinz **RC**	5.00
239	Paul Phillips **RC**	5.00
240	Josh Fogg **RC**	5.00
241	Saul Rivera **RC**	5.00
242	Esix Snead **RC**	5.00
243	John Grabow **RC**	5.00
244	Tony Cogan **RC**	5.00
245	Pedro Santana **RC**	5.00
246	Jack Cust	5.00
247	Joe Crede	8.00
248	Juan Moreno **RC**	5.00
249	Kevin Joseph **RC**	5.00
250	Scott Stewart **RC**	5.00
251	Rob Mackowiak **RC**	5.00
252	Luis Pineda **RC**	5.00
253	Bert Snow **RC**	5.00
254	Dustan Mohr **RC**	5.00
255	Justin Kaye **RC**	5.00
256	Chad Paronto **RC**	5.00
257	Nick Punto **RC**	5.00
258	Brian Roberts **RC**	15.00
259	Eric Hinske **RC**	8.00
260	Victor Zambrano **RC**	5.00
261	Juan Pena	5.00
262	Rick Bauer **RC**	5.00
263	Jorge Julio **RC**	5.00
264	Craig Monroe **RC**	5.00
265	Stubby Clapp **RC**	5.00
266	Martin Vargas **RC**	5.00
267	Josue Perez **RC**	5.00
268	Cody Ransom **RC**	5.00
269	Will Ohman **RC**	5.00
270	Juan Diaz **RC**	5.00
271	Ramon Vazquez **RC**	5.00
272	Grant Balfour **RC**	5.00
273	Ryan Jensen **RC**	5.00
274	Benito Baez **RC**	5.00
275	Angel Santos **RC**	5.00
276	Brian Reith **RC**	5.00
277	Brandon Lyon **RC**	5.00
278	Erik Hiljus **RC**	5.00
279	Brandon Knight **RC**	5.00
280	Jose Acevedo **RC**	5.00
281	Cesar Crespo **RC**	5.00
282	Kevin Olsen **RC**	5.00
283	Duaner Sanchez **RC**	5.00
284	Endy Chavez **RC**	5.00
285	Blaine Neal **RC**	5.00
286	Brett Jodie **RC**	5.00
287	Brad Voyles **RC**	5.00
288	Doug Nickle **RC**	5.00
289	Junior Spivey **RC**	5.00
290	Henry Mateo **RC**	5.00
291	Xavier Nady	5.00
292	Lance Davis **RC**	5.00
293	Willie Harris **RC**	5.00
294	Mark Lukasiewicz **RC**	5.00
295	Ryan Drese **RC**	5.00
296	Morgan Ensberg **RC**	5.00
297	Jose Mieses **RC**	5.00
298	Jason Michaels **RC**	5.00
299	Kris Foster **RC**	5.00
300	Justin Duchscherer **RC**	10.00
301	Elpidio Guzman **RC**	5.00
302	Cory Aldridge **RC**	5.00
303	Angel Berroa **RC**	10.00
304	Travis Hafner **RC**	40.00
305	Horacio Ramirez **RC**	10.00
306	Juan Uribe **RC**	10.00
307	Mark Prior **RC**	40.00
308	Brandon Larson **RC**	10.00
309	Nick Neugebauer	10.00
310	Zach Day **RC**	10.00
311	Jeremy Owens **RC**	10.00
312	Dewon Brazelton **RC**	10.00
313	Brandon Duckworth **RC**	10.00
314	Adrian Hernandez **RC**	10.00
315	Mark Teixeira **RC**	100.00
316	Brian Rogers **RC**	10.00
317	David Brous **RC**	10.00
318	Geronimo Gil **RC**	10.00
319	Erick Almonte **RC**	10.00
320	Claudio Vargas **RC**	10.00
321	Wilkin Ruan **RC**	10.00
322	David Williams **RC**	10.00
323	Alexis Gomez **RC**	10.00
324	Mike Rivera **RC**	10.00
325	Brandon Berger **RC**	10.00
326	Keith Ginter	10.00
327	Brandon Inge/700	10.00
328	Brent Abernathy/700	10.00
329	Billy Sylvester/700 **RC**	10.00
330	Bart Miadich/500 **RC**	10.00
331	Tsuyoshi Shinjo/500 **RC**	10.00
332	Eric Valent	10.00
333	Dee Brown/500	10.00
334	Andres Torres/125 **RC**	10.00
335	Timo Perez/700	10.00
336	Cesar Izturis/650	10.00
337	Pedro Feliz	10.00
338	Jason Hart/200	10.00
339	Greg Miller/700 **RC**	10.00
340	Eric Munson/700	10.00
341	Aubrey Huff/450	10.00
342	Wilmy Caceres/700 **RC**	10.00
343	Alex Escobar/650	10.00
344	Brian Lawrence/700 **RC**	10.00
345	Adam Pettyjohn/650 **RC**	10.00
346	Donaldo Mendez/700 **RC**	10.00
347	Carlos Valderrama **RC**	10.00
348	Christian Parker/650 **RC**	10.00
349	Corky Miller/500 **RC**	10.00
350	Michael Cuddyer/500	10.00
351	Adam Dunn/500	10.00
352	Josh Beckett/650	10.00
353	Juan Cruz/500 **RC**	10.00
354	Ben Sheets/400	10.00
355	Roy Oswalt/100	20.00
356	Rafael Soriano/650 **RC**	10.00
357	Ricardo Rodriguez/650 **RC**	10.00
358	Jimmy Rollins/300	20.00
359	C.C. Sabathia	10.00
360	Bud Smith/500 **RC**	10.00
361	Jose Ortiz	10.00
362	Marcus Giles/400	10.00
363	Jack Wilson **RC**	15.00
364	Wilson Betemit/100 **RC**	15.00
365	Corey Patterson/650	10.00
366	Jay Gibbons/Spikes/ 125 **RC**	20.00
367	Albert Pujols/250 **RC**	200.00
368	Joe Kennedy **RC**	10.00
369	Alfonso Soriano/Hat/100	30.00
370	Delvin James/650 **RC**	10.00
371	Josh Towers/500 **RC**	10.00
372	Jeremy Affeldt/650 **RC**	10.00
373	Tim Redding/500	10.00
374	Ichiro Suzuki/100 **RC**	400.00
375	Johnny Estrada/100 **RC**	20.00

2001 Leaf Rookies & Stars

		NM/M
Complete Set (300):		
Common Player:		.15
Common (101-200):		1.50
Inserted 1:4		
Common (201-300):		4.00
Inserted 1:24		8.00
Pack (5):		5.00
Box (24):		100.00
1	Alex Rodriguez	1.50
2	Derek Jeter	2.00
3	Aramis Ramirez	.25
4	Cliff Floyd	.15
5	Nomar Garciaparra	.50
6	Craig Biggio	.25
7	Ivan Rodriguez	.50
8	Cal Ripken Jr.	3.00
9	Fred McGriff	.15
10	Chipper Jones	1.50
11	Roberto Alomar	.40
12	Moises Alou	.25
13	Freddy Garcia	.15
14	Bobby Abreu	.40
15	Shawn Green	.25
16	Jason Giambi	.50
17	Todd Helton	.50
18	Robert Fick	.15
19	Tony Gwynn	1.00
20	Luis Gonzalez	.25
21	Sean Casey	.25
22	Roger Clemens	1.00
23	Brian Giles	.15
24	Manny Ramirez	1.00
25	Barry Bonds	3.00
26	Richard Hidalgo	.15
27	Vladimir Guerrero	1.00
28	Kevin Brown	.15
29	Mike Sweeney	.15
30	Ken Griffey Jr.	1.50
31	Mike Piazza	1.50
32	Richie Sexson	.15
33	Matt Morris	.15
34	Jorge Posada	.40
35	Eric Chavez	.25
36	Mark Buehrle	.15
37	Jeff Bagwell	.50
38	Curt Schilling	.50
39	Bartolo Colon	.15
40	Mark Quinn	.15
41	Tony Clark	.15
42	Brad Radke	.15
43	Gary Sheffield	.40
44	Doug Mientkiewicz	.15
45	Pedro Martinez	.75
46	Carlos Lee	.25
47	Troy Glaus	.50
48	Preston Wilson	.15
49	Phil Nevin	.15
50	Chan Ho Park	.15
51	Randy Johnson	.75
52	Jermaine Dye	.25
53	Terrence Long	.15
54	Joe Mays	.15
55	Scott Rolen	.50
56	Miguel Tejada	.25
57	Jim Thome	.40
58	Jose Vidro	.15
59	Gabe Kapler	.15
60	Darin Erstad	.25
61	Jim Edmonds	.25
62	Jarrod Washburn	.15
63	Tom Glavine	.50
64	Adrian Beltre	.50
65	Sammy Sosa	.75
66	Juan Gonzalez	.40
67	Rafael Furcal	.40
68	Mike Mussina	.50
69	Mark McGwire	1.50
70	Ryan Klesko	.15
71	Raul Mondesi	.15
72	Trot Nixon	.15
73	Barry Larkin	.25
74	Rafael Palmeiro	.50
75	Mark Mulder	.25
76	Carlos Delgado	.40
77	Mike Hampton	.15
78	Carl Everett	.15
79	Paul Konerko	.25
80	Larry Walker	.15
81	Kerry Wood	.40
82	Frank Thomas	1.00
83	Andruw Jones	.40
84	Eric Milton	.15
85	Ben Grieve	.15
86	Carlos Beltran	.50
87	Tim Hudson	.25
88	Hideo Nomo	.50
89	Greg Maddux	1.50
90	Edgar Martinez	.15
91	Lance Berkman	.50
92	Pat Burrell	.40
93	Jeff Kent	.25
94	Magglio Ordonez	.25
95	Cristian Guzman	.15
96	Jose Canseco	.40
97	J.D. Drew	.40
98	Bernie Williams	.40
99	Kazuhiro Sasaki	.15
100	Rickey Henderson	.75
101	Wilson Guzman **RC**	1.50
102	Nick Neugebauer	1.50
103	Lance Davis **RC**	1.50
104	Felipe Lopez	1.50
105	Toby Hall	1.50
106	Jack Cust	1.50
107	Jason Kamuth	1.50
108	Bart Miadich **RC**	1.50
109	Brian Roberts **RC**	8.00
110	Brandon Larson **RC**	1.50
111	Sean Douglass **RC**	1.50
112	Joe Crede	3.00
113	Tim Redding	1.50
114	Adam Johnson	1.50
115	Marcus Giles	1.50
116	Jose Ortiz	1.50
117	Jose Mieses **RC**	1.50
118	Nick Maness **RC**	1.50
119	Les Walrond **RC**	1.50
120	Travis Phelps **RC**	1.50
121	Troy Mattes **RC**	1.50
122	Carlos Garcia	1.50
123	Bill Ortega	1.50
124	Gene Altman **RC**	1.50
125	Nate Frese	1.50
126	Alfonso Soriano	2.00
127	Jose Nunez	1.50
128	Bob File **RC**	1.50
129	Dan Wright	1.50
130	Nick Johnson	1.50
131	Brent Abernathy	1.50
132	Steve Green **RC**	1.50
133	Billy Sylvester **RC**	1.50
134	Scott MacRae **RC**	1.50
135	Kris Keller **RC**	1.50
136	Scott Stewart **RC**	1.50
137	Henry Mateo **RC**	1.50
138	Timoniel Perez	1.50
139	Nate Teut **RC**	1.50
140	Jason Michaels **RC**	1.50
141	Junior Spivey **RC**	2.00
142	Carlos Pena	1.50
143	Wilmy Caceres **RC**	1.50
144	David Lundquist	1.50
145	Jack Wilson **RC**	2.00
146	Jeremy Fikac **RC**	1.50
147	Alex Escobar	1.50
148	Abraham Nunez	1.50
149	Xavier Nady	2.00
150	Michael Cuddyer	1.50
151	Greg Miller **RC**	1.50
152	Eric Munson	1.50
153	Aubrey Huff	1.50
154	Tim Christman **RC**	1.50
155	Erick Almonte **RC**	1.50
156	Mike Penny	1.50
157	Delvin James **RC**	1.50
158	Ben Sheets	1.50
159	Jason Hart	1.50
160	Jose Acevedo **RC**	1.50
161	Will Ohman **RC**	1.50
162	Erik Hiljus **RC**	1.50
163	Juan Moreno **RC**	1.50
164	Mike Koplove **RC**	1.50
165	Pedro Santana **RC**	1.50
166	Jimmy Rollins	3.00
167	Matt White **RC**	1.50
168	Cesar Crespo **RC**	1.50
169	Carlos Hernandez	1.50
170	Chris George	1.50
171	Brad Voyles **RC**	1.50
172	Luis Pineda **RC**	1.50
173	Carlos Zambrano	2.00
174	Nate Comejo	1.50
175	Jason Smith **RC**	1.50
176	Craig Monroe **RC**	1.50
177	Cody Ransom **RC**	1.50
178	John Grabow **RC**	1.50
179	Pedro Feliz	1.50
180	Jeremy Owens **RC**	1.50
181	Kurt Ainsworth	1.50
182	Luis Lopez	1.50
183	Stubby Clapp **RC**	1.50
184	Ryan Freel **RC**	2.00
185	Duaner Sanchez **RC**	1.50
186	Jason Jennings	1.50
187	Kyle Lohse **RC**	3.00
188	Jerrod Riggan **RC**	1.50
189	Joe Beimel **RC**	1.50
190	Nick Punto **RC**	1.50
191	Willie Harris **RC**	1.50
192	Ryan Jensen **RC**	1.50
193	Adam Pettyjohn **RC**	1.50
194	Donaldo Mendez **RC**	1.50
195	Bret Prinz **RC**	1.50

196	Paul Phillips RC	1.50
197	Brian Lawrence RC	1.50
198	Cesar Izturis	1.50
199	Blaine Neal RC	1.50
200	Josh Fogg RC	1.50
201	Josh Towers RC	4.00
202	Tim Spooneybarger RC	4.00
203	Mike Rivera RC	4.00
204	Juan Cruz RC	4.00
205	Albert Pujols RC	200.00
206	Josh Beckett	6.00
207	Roy Oswalt	4.00
208	Elpidio Guzman RC	4.00
209	Horacio Ramirez RC	4.00
210	Corey Patterson	4.00
211	Geronimo Gil RC	4.00
212	Jay Gibbons RC	4.00
213	Orlando Woodwards	4.00
214	David Espinosa	4.00
215	Angel Berroa RC	4.00
216	Brandon Duckworth RC	4.00
217	Brian Reith RC	4.00
218	David Brous RC	4.00
219	Bud Smith RC	4.00
220	Ramon Vazquez RC	4.00
221	Mark Teixeira RC	30.00
222	Justin Atchley RC	4.00
223	Tony Cogan RC	4.00
224	Grant Balfour RC	4.00
225	Ricardo Rodriguez RC	4.00
226	Brian Rogers RC	4.00
227	Adam Dunn	6.00
228	Wilson Betemit RC	4.00
229	Juan Diaz RC	4.00
230	Jackson Melian RC	4.00
231	Claudio Vargas RC	4.00
232	Wilkin Ruan RC	4.00
233	Justin Duchscherer RC	8.00
234	Kevin Olsen RC	4.00
235	Tony Fiore	4.00
236	Jeremy Affeldt RC	4.00
237	Mike Maroth RC	4.00
238	C.C. Sabathia	6.00
239	Cory Aldridge RC	4.00
240	Zach Day RC	6.00
241	Brett Jodie RC	4.00
242	Winston Abreu RC	4.00
243	Travis Hafner RC	10.00
244	Joe Kennedy RC	4.00
245	Rick Bauer RC	4.00
246	Mike Young	6.00
247	Ken Vining RC	4.00
248	Doug Nickle RC	4.00
249	Pablo Ozuno RC	4.00
250	Dustan Mohr RC	4.00
251	Ichiro Suzuki RC	30.00
252	Ryan Drese RC	4.00
253	Morgan Ensberg RC	4.00
254	George Perez RC	4.00
255	Roy Smith RC	4.00
256	Juan Uribe RC	4.00
257	Dewon Brazelton RC	4.00
258	Endy Chavez RC	4.00
259	Kris Foster RC	4.00
260	Eric Knott RC	4.00
261	Corky Miller RC	4.00
262	Larry Bigbie	4.00
263	Andres Torres RC	4.00
264	Adrian Hernandez RC	4.00
265	Johnny Estrada RC	4.00
266	David Williams RC	4.00
267	Steve Lomasney	4.00
268	Victor Zambrano RC	4.00
269	Keith Ginter	4.00
270	Casey Fossum RC	4.00
271	Josue Perez RC	4.00
272	Josh Phelps	4.00
273	Mark Prior RC	10.00
274	Brandon Berger RC	4.00
275	Scott Podsednik RC	6.00
276	Jorge Julio RC	4.00
277	Esix Snead RC	4.00
278	Brandon Knight RC	4.00
279	Saul Rivera RC	4.00
280	Benito Baez RC	4.00
281	Robert Mackowiak RC	4.00
282	Eric Hinske RC	8.00
283	Juan Rivera RC	4.00
284	Kevin Joseph RC	4.00
285	Juan Pena	4.00
286	Brandon Lyon RC	4.00
287	Adam Everett	4.00
288	Eric Valent	4.00
289	Ken Harvey	4.00
290	Bert Snow RC	4.00
291	Wily Mo Pena	4.00
292	Rafael Soriano RC	4.00
293	Carlos Valderrama RC	4.00
294	Christian Parker RC	4.00
295	Tsuyoshi Shinjo RC	4.00
296	Martin Vargas RC	4.00
297	Luke Hudson RC	4.00
298	Dee Brown	4.00
299	Alexis Gomez RC	4.00
300	Angel Santos RC	4.00

Longevity

Stars (1-100): 10-20X
Production 50
#'s 101-300 Production 25

Autographs

		NM/M
Common Player:		8.00
107	Jason Karnuth	8.00

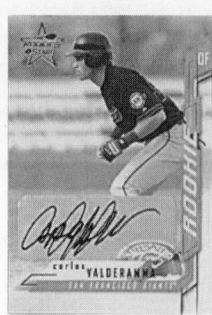

110	Brandon Larson/100	8.00
117	Jose Mieses	8.00
118	Nick Maness	8.00
119	Les Walrond	8.00
122	Carlos Garcia	8.00
123	Bill Ortega	8.00
124	Gene Altman	8.00
125	Nate Frese	8.00
130	Nick Johnson/100	10.00
133	Billy Sylvester	8.00
135	Kris Keller	8.00
139	Nate Teut	8.00
140	Jason Michaels	8.00
143	Wilmy Caceres	8.00
145	Jack Wilson/100	15.00
151	Greg Miller	8.00
155	Erick Almonte	8.00
156	Mike Penney	8.00
157	Delvin James	8.00
161	Will Ohman	8.00
167	Matt White	8.00
180	Jeremy Owens	8.00
184	Ryan Freel	10.00
185	Duaner Sanchez	8.00
193	Adam Pettyjohn/100	8.00
194	Donaldo Mendez/100	8.00
196	Paul Phillips	8.00
197	Brian Lawrence/100	8.00
199	Blaine Neal	8.00
201	Josh Towers/100	8.00
203	Michael Rivera	8.00
204	Juan Cruz/100	10.00
207	Roy Oswalt/50	50.00
208	Elpidio Guzman/100	8.00
209	Horacio Ramirez	10.00
210	Corey Patterson SP	15.00
211	Geronimo Gil	8.00
212	Jay Gibbons/100	10.00
213	Orlando Woodwards	8.00
215	Angel Berroa/100	8.00
216	Brandon Duckworth/100	8.00
218	David Brous	8.00
219	Bud Smith/50	8.00
221	Mark Teixeira/100	200.00
223	Tony Cogan	8.00
225	Ricardo Rodriguez	8.00
226	Brian Rogers	8.00
227	Adam Dunn/50	40.00
228	Wilson Betemit/100	30.00
231	Claudio Vargas	8.00
232	Wilkin Ruan	8.00
234	Kevin Olsen	8.00
236	Jeremy Affeldt	8.00
237	Mike Maroth	8.00
238	C.C. Sabathia/50	35.00
239	Cory Aldridge	8.00
240	Zach Day	8.00
243	Travis Hafner	50.00
244	Joe Kennedy/100	10.00
254	George Perez	10.00
256	Juan Uribe	10.00
257	Dewon Brazelton/100	10.00
261	Corky Miller/100	8.00
263	Andres Torres/100	8.00
265	Johnny Estrada/100	10.00
266	David Williams	10.00
270	Casey Fossum	8.00
273	Mark Prior/50	50.00
274	Brandon Berger	8.00
277	Esix Snead	8.00
282	Eric Hinske	10.00
292	Rafael Soriano	10.00
293	Carlos Valderrama	8.00
299	Alexis Gomez	8.00

Dress For Success

		NM/M
Common Player:		8.00

Inserted 1:96
Prime Cuts: 2X
Numbered to 50 each.

1	Cal Ripken Jr.	40.00
2	Mike Piazza	25.00
3	Barry Bonds	40.00
4	Frank Thomas	15.00
5	Nomar Garciaparra	10.00
6	Richie Sexson	8.00
7	Brian Giles	8.00
8	Todd Helton	15.00
9	Ivan Rodriguez	10.00
10	Andruw Jones	10.00
11	Juan Gonzalez	8.00

12	Vladimir Guerrero	15.00
13	Greg Maddux	25.00
14	Tony Gwynn	20.00
15	Randy Johnson	15.00
16	Jeff Bagwell	10.00
17	Kerry Wood	10.00
18	Roberto Alomar	8.00
19	Chipper Jones	25.00
20	Pedro Martinez	15.00
21	Shawn Green	8.00
22	Magglio Ordonez	10.00
23	Darin Erstad	8.00
24	Rafael Palmeiro	15.00
25	Edgar Martinez	8.00

Dress For Success Autographs

No Pricing

Freshman Orientation

	NM/M
Common Player:	8.00

Inserted 1:96
Class Officers: 2X
Numbered to 50 each.

1	Adam Dunn	15.00
2	Josh Towers	8.00
3	Vernon Wells	10.00
4	Corey Patterson	10.00
5	Ben Sheets	8.00
6	Pedro Feliz	8.00
7	Keith Ginter	8.00
8	Luis Rivas	8.00
9	Andres Torres	8.00
10	Carlos Valderrama	8.00
11	Brandon Inge	8.00
12	Jay Gibbons	15.00
13	Cesar Izturis	8.00
14	Marcus Giles	8.00
15	Tsuyoshi Shinjo	12.00
16	Eric Valent	8.00
17	David Espinosa	8.00
18	Aubrey Huff	8.00
19	Wilmy Caceres	8.00
20	Bud Smith	8.00
21	Ricardo Rodriguez	8.00
22	Wes Helms	8.00
23	Jason Hart	8.00
24	Dee Brown	8.00

Freshman Orientation Autograph

No Pricing

Great American Treasures

	NM/M

Inserted 1:1,120

1	Barry Bonds/Jsy	100.00
2	Magglio Ordonez/Bat	40.00
3	Derek Jeter/Ball	150.00
4	Nolan Ryan/Ball	600.00
5	Sammy Sosa/Ball	125.00
6	Tom Glavine/Jsy	50.00
7	Ivan Rodriguez/Bat	30.00
8	Pedro Martinez/Ball	100.00
9	Mark McGwire/Ball	250.00
10	Ted Williams/Ball	350.00
11	Ryne Sandberg/Bat	60.00
12	Barry Bonds/Ball	300.00
13	Hideo Nomo/Ball	450.00
14	Roger Maris/Ball	300.00
15	Ty Cobb/Ball	750.00
16	Harmon Killebrew/Bat	150.00
17	Magglio Ordonez/Cap	30.00
18	Wade Boggs/Bat	40.00
19	Hank Aaron/Cap	400.00
20	David Cone/Ball	100.00

Great American Treasures Autograph

		NM/M
GT-6	Tom Glavine 96 WS/Jsy	125.00
GT-11	Ryne Sandberg 91 AS/Bat	300.00
GT-16	Harmon Killebrew 570 HR/Bat	200.00
GT-18	Wade Boggs WS/Bat	150.00

Player's Collection

NM/M

Singles #'d to 100.

1	Tony Gwynn/Bat	30.00
2	Tony Gwynn/Jsy	30.00
3	Tony Gwynn/Pants	30.00
4	Tony Gwynn/Shoe	30.00
6	Cal Ripken/Jsy	75.00
7	Cal Ripken/Bat	75.00
8	Cal Ripken/Glove	75.00
9	Cal Ripken/Jsy	75.00
11	Barry Bonds/Jsy	60.00
12	Barry Bonds/Shoe	60.00
13	Barry Bonds/Pants	60.00
14	Barry Bonds/Bat	60.00

Player's Collection Autograph

No Pricing

Slideshow

	NM/M
Common Player:	10.00

Production 100 Sets
View Masters: 1.5X
Numbered to 25 each.

1	Cal Ripken Jr.	40.00
2	Chipper Jones	20.00
3	Jeff Bagwell	15.00
4	Larry Walker	10.00
5	Greg Maddux	25.00
6	Ivan Rodriguez	15.00
7	Andruw Jones	15.00
8	Lance Berkman	10.00
9	Luis Gonzalez	10.00
10	Tony Gwynn	25.00
11	Troy Glaus	15.00
12	Todd Helton	20.00
13	Roberto Alomar	10.00
14	Barry Bonds	40.00
15	Vladimir Guerrero	20.00
16	Sean Casey	10.00
17	Curt Schilling	15.00
18	Frank Thomas	20.00
19	Pedro Martinez	20.00
20	Juan Gonzalez	15.00
21	Randy Johnson	20.00
22	Kerry Wood	10.00
23	Mike Sweeney	10.00
24	Magglio Ordonez	10.00
25	Kazuhiro Sasaki	10.00
26	Manny Ramirez	20.00
27	Roger Clemens	25.00
28	Albert Pujols	120.00
29	Hideo Nomo	25.00
30	Miguel Tejada	10.00

Slideshow Autographs

No Pricing

Statistical Standouts

		NM/M
Common Player:		5.00
Inserted 1:96		
1	Ichiro Suzuki	35.00
2	Barry Bonds	40.00
3	Ivan Rodriguez	10.00
4	Jeff Bagwell	10.00
5	Vladimir Guerrero	10.00
6	Mike Sweeney	5.00
7	Miguel Tejada	5.00
8	Mike Piazza	30.00
9	Darin Erstad	5.00
10	Alex Rodriguez	35.00
11	Jason Giambi	8.00
12	Cal Ripken Jr.	40.00
13	Albert Pujols	35.00
14	Carlos Delgado	8.00
15	Rafael Palmeiro	8.00
16	Lance Berkman	5.00
17	Luis Gonzalez	5.00
18	Sammy Sosa	30.00
19	Andruw Jones	10.00
20	Derek Jeter	40.00
21	Edgar Martinez	5.00
22	Troy Glaus	10.00
23	Magglio Ordonez	5.00
24	Mark McGwire	35.00
25	Manny Ramirez	10.00

Statistical Standouts Auto.

No Pricing

Triple Threads

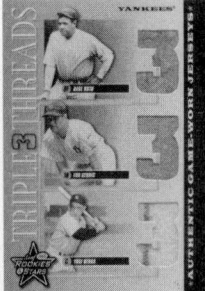

		NM/M
Common Card:		50.00
Numbered to 100.		
TT-1	Pedro Martinez, Manny Ramirez, Nomar Garciaparra	75.00
TT-2	Frank Robinson, Cal Ripken Jr., Brooks Robinson	120.00
TT-3	Yogi Berra, Lou Gehrig, Babe Ruth	500.00
TT-4	Andre Dawson, Ryne Sandberg, Ernie Banks	120.00
TT-5	Warren Spahn, Hank Aaron, Eddie Mathews	150.00
TT-6	Greg Maddux, Chipper Jones, Andruw Jones	75.00
TT-7	Nolan Ryan, Ivan Rodriguez, Juan Gonzalez	100.00

TT-8	Lance Berkman, Jeff Bagwell, Craig Biggio	50.00
TT-9	Rod Carew, Harmon Killebrew, Kirby Puckett	75.00
TT-10	Luis Gonzalez, Curt Schilling, Randy Johnson	60.00

2002 Leaf

		NM/M
Complete Set (1-200):		80.00
Common Player:		.15
Common (151-200):		1.50
Inserted 1:6		
Pack (4):		1.50
Box (24):		30.00
1	Tim Salmon	.25
2	Troy Glaus	.65
3	Curt Schilling	.40
4	Luis Gonzalez	.25
5	Mark Grace	.25
6	Matt Williams	.15
7	Randy Johnson	.65
8	Tom Glavine	.40
9	Brady Anderson	.15
10	Hideo Nomo	.65
11	Pedro Martinez	.65
12	Corey Patterson	.15
13	Paul Konerko	.25
14	Jon Lieber	.15
15	Carlos Lee	.15
16	Magglio Ordonez	.15
17	Adam Dunn	.40
18	Ken Griffey Jr.	1.00
19	C.C. Sabathia	.25
20	Jim Thome	.50
21	Juan Gonzalez	.65
22	Kenny Lofton	.15
23	Juan Encarnacion	.15
24	Tony Clark	.15
25	A.J. Burnett	.15
26	Josh Beckett	.25
27	Lance Berkman	.15
28	Eric Karros	.15
29	Shawn Green	.30
30	Brad Radke	.15
31	Joe Mays	.15
32	Javier Vazquez	.15
33	Alfonso Soriano	.50
34	Jorge Posada	.25
35	Eric Chavez	.25
36	Mark Mulder	.15
37	Miguel Tejada	.25
38	Tim Hudson	.25
39	Bobby Abreu	.15
40	Pat Burrell	.40
41	Ryan Klesko	.15
42	Not Issued	
43	John Olerud	.15
44	Ellis Burks	.15
45	Mike Cameron	.15
46	Jim Edmonds	.15
47	Ben Grieve	.15
48	Carlos Pena	.15
49	Alex Rodriguez	1.50
50	Raul Mondesi	.15
51	Billy Koch	.15
52	Manny Ramirez	.65
53	Darin Erstad	.25
54	Troy Percival	.15
55	Andruw Jones	.65
56	Chipper Jones	.75
57	David Segui	.15
58	Chris Stynes	.15
59	Trot Nixon	.15
60	Sammy Sosa	1.00
61	Kerry Wood	.50
62	Frank Thomas	.65
63	Barry Larkin	.15
64	Bartolo Colon	.15
65	Kazuhiro Sasaki	.25
66	Roberto Alomar	.35
67	Mike Hampton	.15
68	Roger Cedeno	.15
69	Cliff Floyd	.15
70	Mike Lowell	.15
71	Billy Wagner	.15
72	Craig Biggio	.15
73	Jeff Bagwell	.65
74	Carlos Beltran	.50
75	Mark Quinn	.15
76	Mike Sweeney	.15

77	Gary Sheffield	.25
78	Kevin Brown	.15
79	Paul LoDuca	.15
80	Ben Sheets	.15
81	Jeromy Burnitz	.15
82	Richie Sexson	.15
83	Corey Koskie	.15
84	Eric Milton	.15
85	Jose Vidro	.15
86	Mike Piazza	1.00
87	Robin Ventura	.15
88	Andy Pettitte	.25
89	Mike Mussina	.40
90	Orlando Hernandez	.15
91	Roger Clemens	.85
92	Barry Zito	.25
93	Jermaine Dye	.15
94	Jimmy Rollins	.25
95	Jason Kendall	.15
96	Rickey Henderson	.65
97	Andres Galarraga	.15
98	Bret Boone	.15
99	Freddy Garcia	.15
100	J.D. Drew	.25
101	Jose Cruz Jr.	.15
102	Greg Maddux	.75
103	Javy Lopez	.15
104	Nomar Garciaparra	1.00
105	Fred McGriff	.15
106	Keith Foulke	.15
107	Ray Durham	.15
108	Sean Casey	.25
109	Todd Walker	.15
110	Omar Vizquel	.15
111	Travis Fryman	.15
112	Larry Walker	.15
113	Todd Helton	.65
114	Bobby Higginson	.15
115	Charles Johnson	.15
116	Moises Alou	.15
117	Richard Hidalgo	.15
118	Roy Oswalt	.25
119	Neifi Perez	.15
120	Adrian Beltre	.30
121	Chan Ho Park	.15
122	Geoff Jenkins	.15
123	Doug Mientkiewicz	.15
124	Torii Hunter	.15
125	Vladimir Guerrero	.65
126	Matt Lawton	.15
127	Tsuyoshi Shinjo	.15
128	Bernie Williams	.40
129	Derek Jeter	2.00
130	Mariano Rivera	.25
131	Tino Martinez	.15
132	Jason Giambi	.45
133	Scott Rolen	.50
134	Brian Giles	.15
135	Phil Nevin	.15
136	Trevor Hoffman	.15
137	Barry Bonds	2.00
138	Jeff Kent	.15
139	Shannon Stewart	.15
140	Shawn Estes	.15
141	Edgar Martinez	.15
142	Ichiro Suzuki	1.00
143	Albert Pujols	1.50
144	Bud Smith	.15
145	Matt Morris	.15
146	Frank Catalanotto	.15
147	Gabe Kapler	.15
148	Ivan Rodriguez	.45
149	Rafael Palmeiro	.45
150	Carlos Delgado	.40
151	Marlon Byrd	2.00
152	Alex Herrera	1.50
153	Brandon Backe RC	2.00
154	Jorge De La Rosa RC	2.00
155	Corky Miller	1.50
156	Dennis Tankersley	1.50
157	Kyle Kane RC	2.00
158	Justin Duchscherer	1.50
159	Brian Mallette RC	2.00
160	Eric Hinske	1.50
161	Jason Lane	1.50
162	Hee Seop Choi	3.00
163	Juan Cruz	1.50
164	Rodrigo Rosario RC	2.00
165	Matt Guerrier	1.50
166	Anderson Machado RC	2.00
167	Geronimo Gil	1.50
168	Dewon Brazelton	1.50
169	Mark Prior	4.00
170	Bill Hall	1.50
171	Jorge Padilla RC	2.00
172	Josh Pearce	1.50
173	Allan Simpson RC	2.00
174	Doug DeVore RC	2.00
175	Morgan Ensberg	1.50
176	Angel Berroa	1.50
177	Steve Bechler RC	2.00
178	Antonio Perez	1.50
179	Mark Teixeira	3.00
180	Mark Ellis	1.50
181	Michael Cuddyer	1.50
182	Mike Rivera	1.50
183	Raul Chavez RC	2.00
184	Juan Pena	1.50
185	Austin Kearns	2.00
186	Ryan Ludwick	1.50
187	Ed Rogers	1.50
188	Wilson Betemit	1.50
189	Nick Neugebauer	1.50
190	Tom Shearn RC	2.00
191	Eric Cyr RC	2.00

192	Victor Martinez	1.50
193	Brandon Berger	1.50
194	Erik Bedard	1.50
195	Franklin German RC	2.00
196	Joe Thurston	1.50
197	John Buck	1.50
198	Jeff Deardorff RC	2.00
199	Ryan Jamison RC	2.00
200	Alfredo Amezaga	1.50
201	So Taguchi/500 RC	6.00
202	Kazuhisa Ishii/250 RC	8.00

Press Proof Blue

Stars (1-150):	5-10X
Inserted 1:24 Retail	

Press Proof Red

Stars (1-150):	4-6X
Inserted 1:12 Retail	

Lineage

1999 Lineage (1-50):	2-5X
Inserted 1:12	
2000 Lineage (51-100):	2-5X
Inserted 1:12	
2001 Lineage (101-150):	2-5X
Inserted 1:12	
Silver Holofoils:	8-15X
Production 100	

Autograph

No Pricing

Burn n' Turn

		NM/M
Complete Set (10):		50.00
Common Player:		4.00
Inserted 1:96		
1	Fernando Vina, Edgar Renteria	4.00
2	Alex Rodriguez, Mike Young	10.00
3	Derek Jeter, Alfonso Soriano	15.00
4	Carlos Guillen, Bret Boone	4.00
5	Jose Vidro, Orlando Cabrera	4.00
6	Barry Larkin, Todd Walker	4.00
7	Carlos Febles, Neifi Perez	4.00
8	Jeff Kent, Rich Aurilia	4.00
9	Craig Biggio, Julio Lugo	5.00
10	Miguel Tejada, Mark Ellis	4.00

Clean Up Crew

		NM/M
Complete Set (15):		90.00
Common Player:		4.00
Inserted 1:192		
1	Barry Bonds	20.00
2	Sammy Sosa	12.00
3	Luis Gonzalez	4.00
4	Richie Sexson	4.00
5	Jim Thome	6.00
6	Chipper Jones	8.00
7	Alex Rodriguez	15.00
8	Troy Glaus	5.00
9	Rafael Palmeiro	5.00
10	Lance Berkman	4.00
11	Mike Piazza	12.00
12	Jason Giambi	5.00
13	Todd Helton	6.00
14	Shawn Green	5.00
15	Carlos Delgado	5.00

Clubhouse Signatures Bronze

		NM/M
Common Player:		5.00
(1)	Wilson Betemit/150	6.00
(2)	Marlon Byrd/200	6.00
(3)	Joe Crede/200	8.00

(4)	Andre Dawson/100	30.00
(5)	J.D. Drew/25	35.00
(6)	Adam Dunn/200	25.00
(7)	Jermaine Dye/125	10.00
(8)	Mark Ellis/300	8.00
(9)	Johnny Estrada/250	8.00
(10)	Bob Feller/250	15.00
(11)	Robert Fick/300	5.00
(12)	Steve Garvey/200	15.00
(13)	Austin Kearns/300	10.00
(14)	Jason Lane/250	5.00
(15)	Paul LoDuca/300	8.00
(16)	Terrence Long/250	5.00
(17)	Edgar Martinez/50	30.00
(18)	Don Mattingly/25	100.00
(19)	Joe Mays/200	6.00
(20)	Mark Mulder/50	25.00
(21)	Xavier Nady/200	8.00
(22)	Roy Oswalt/300	10.00
(23)	Aramis Ramirez/250	15.00
(24)	Tim Redding/300	5.00
(25)	Phil Rizzuto/25	45.00
(26)	Ryne Sandberg/25	100.00
(27)	Ron Santo/300	15.00
(28)	Bud Smith/200	5.00
(29)	Ozzie Smith/25	85.00
(30)	Alfonso Soriano/75	30.00
(31)	Alan Trammell/75	15.00
(32)	Billy Williams/150	10.00
(33)	Barry Zito/100	25.00

Clubhouse Signatures Silver

NM/M

	Common Player:	10.00
(1)	Rich Aurilia/100	15.00
(2)	Wilson Betemit/100	15.00
(3)	Marlon Byrd/100	15.00
(4)	Sean Casey/100	20.00
(5)	Eric Chavez/100	20.00
(6)	Roger Clemens/25	150.00
(7)	Joe Crede/50	20.00
(8)	Andre Dawson/100	30.00
(9)	Adam Dunn/75	40.00
(10)	Jermaine Dye/100	15.00
(11)	Mark Ellis/100	10.00
(12)	Johnny Estrada/100	15.00
(13)	Bob Feller/100	20.00
(14)	Robert Fick/100	15.00
(15)	Steve Garvey/100	25.00
(16)	Vladimir Guerrero/25	60.00
(17)	Todd Helton/25	50.00
(18)	Austin Kearns/100	20.00
(19)	Jason Lane/100	15.00
(20)	Paul LoDuca/100	15.00
(21)	Terrence Long/100	15.00
(22)	Edgar Martinez/100	25.00
(23)	Joe Mays/50	20.00
(24)	Mark Mulder/100	30.00
(25)	Xavier Nady/100	10.00
(26)	Roy Oswalt/100	15.00
(27)	Aramis Ramirez/100	20.00
(28)	Tim Redding/100	10.00
(29)	Cal Ripken Jr./25	225.00
(30)	Phil Rizzuto/25	50.00
(31)	Ron Santo/100	40.00
(32)	Mike Schmidt/75	75.00
(33)	Bud Smith/100	15.00
(34)	Miguel Tejada/100	30.00
(35)	Javier Vazquez/100	15.00
(36)	Billy Williams/100	20.00
(37)	Barry Zito/100	30.00

Clubhouse Signatures Gold

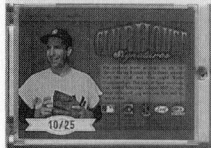

NM/M

	Common Player:	15.00
	Numbered to 25.	
(1)	Rich Aurilia	15.00
(2)	Josh Beckett	60.00
(3)	Wilson Betemit	15.00
(4)	Marlon Byrd	15.00
(5)	Sean Casey	25.00
(6)	Eric Chavez	30.00
(7)	Roger Clemens	150.00
(8)	Joe Crede	50.00
(9)	Andre Dawson	40.00
(10)	J.D. Drew	40.00
(11)	Adam Dunn	65.00
(12)	Jermaine Dye	20.00
(13)	Mark Ellis	15.00
(14)	Johnny Estrada	20.00
(15)	Bob Feller	45.00
(16)	Robert Fick	15.00
(17)	Steve Garvey	40.00
(18)	Luis Gonzalez	35.00
(19)	Vladimir Guerrero	75.00
(20)	Todd Helton	50.00
(21)	Orel Hershiser	35.00
(22)	Austin Kearns	50.00
(23)	Jason Lane	15.00
(24)	Paul LoDuca	25.00
(25)	Terrence Long	15.00
(26)	Edgar Martinez	30.00
(27)	Don Mattingly	125.00
(28)	Joe Mays	25.00
(29)	Mark Mulder	40.00
(30)	Xavier Nady	20.00
(31)	Roy Oswalt	30.00
(32)	Chan Ho Park	15.00
(33)	Kirby Puckett	125.00
(34)	Aramis Ramirez	40.00
(35)	Tim Redding	15.00
(36)	Cal Ripken Jr.	225.00
(37)	Phil Rizzuto	60.00
(38)	Ryne Sandberg	125.00
(39)	Ron Santo	65.00
(40)	Mike Schmidt	90.00
(41)	Bud Smith	20.00
(42)	Ozzie Smith	100.00
(43)	Alfonso Soriano	80.00
(44)	Miguel Tejada	30.00
(45)	Alan Trammell	25.00
(46)	Javier Vazquez	20.00
(47)	Billy Williams	35.00
(48)	Barry Zito	50.00

Cornerstones

NM/M

Production 50 Sets
Some not priced yet

1	Andruw Jones, Chipper Jones	40.00
4	Curt Schilling, Randy Johnson	40.00
6	Larry Walker, Todd Helton	25.00
7	Carlos Delgado, Shannon Stewart	25.00
10	Bernie Williams, Roger Clemens	60.00

Future 500 Club

NM/M

	Complete Set (10):	40.00
	Common Player:	2.00
	Inserted 1:64	
1	Sammy Sosa	8.00
2	Mike Piazza	8.00
3	Alex Rodriguez	10.00
4	Chipper Jones	6.00
5	Jeff Bagwell	4.00
6	Carlos Delgado	2.00
7	Shawn Green	2.00
8	Ken Griffey Jr.	8.00
9	Rafael Palmeiro	3.00
10	Vladimir Guerrero	4.00

Game Collection

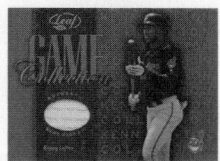

NM/M

	Common Player:	5.00
	Inserted 1:62 R	
	SP's Indicated	
AB B	Adrian Beltre/Bat	5.00
AD BG	Adam Dunn/Btg Glv/25	25.00
AG B	Andres Galarraga/Bat	5.00
AJ B	Andruw Jones/Bat/300	5.00
BG B	Brian Giles/Bat	5.00
BH B	Bobby Higginson/Bat	5.00
BS H	Ben Sheets/Hat/25	35.00
BW S	Bernie Williams/Shoe/25	30.00
BZ FG	Barry Zito/Fldg Glv/25	25.00
CB B	Carlos Beltran/Bat	8.00
CBI B	Craig Biggio/Bat	6.00
CF B	Carlton Fisk/Bat	10.00
CK B	Chuck Knoblauch/Bat	5.00
CP S	Corey Patterson/Shoe/25	25.00
EM B	Eddie Murray/Bat/250	15.00
GJ P	Geoff Jenkins/Pants	5.00
IR BG	Ivan Rodriguez/Btg Glv/25	25.00
JB B	Jeff Bagwell/Bat/100	15.00
JD H	Johnny Damon/Hat/25	25.00
JE B	Juan Encarnacion/Bat	5.00
JG B	Juan Gonzalez/Bat	8.00
KL B	Kenny Lofton/Bat	5.00
KW S	Kerry Wood/Bat Shoe/25	40.00
LB BG	Lance Berkman/Btg Glv/25	25.00
LW B	Larry Walker/Bat/50	15.00
MB BG	Marlon Byrd/Btg Glv/25	20.00
MG B	Mark Grace/Bat/200	5.00
MM FG	Mike Mussina/Fldg Glv/25	55.00
MO B	Magglio Ordonez/Bat/150	6.00
MP B	Mike Piazza/Bat/100	15.00
PB B	Pat Burrell/Bat/100	15.00
RA B	Roberto Alomar/Bat	8.00
RD B	Ray Durham/Bat	8.00
RG B	Rusty Greer/Bat	5.00
RJ FG	Randy Johnson/Fldg Glv	80.00
RP B	Rafael Palmeiro/Bat	10.00
RP BG	Rafael Palmeiro/Btg Glv/25	30.00
RV B	Robin Ventura/Bat	5.00
SC B	Sean Casey/Bat	5.00
SR B	Scott Rolen/Bat/250	15.00
SS H	Shannon Stewart/Hat/25	20.00
TC B	Tony Clark/Bat	5.00
TG BG	Tony Gwynn/Btg Glv/25	90.00
TH B	Todd Helton/Bat	10.00
TN B	Trot Nixon/Bat	5.00
WB B	Wade Boggs/Bat	8.00

Gold Leaf Rookies

NM/M

	Complete Set (10):	20.00
	Common Player:	2.00
	Inserted 1:24	
1	Josh Beckett	4.00
2	Marlon Byrd	2.00
3	Dennis Tankersley	2.00
4	Jason Lane	2.00
5	Dewon Brazelton	2.00
6	Mark Prior	4.00
7	Bill Hall	2.00
8	Angel Berroa	2.00
9	Mark Teixeira	4.00
10	John Buck	2.00

Heading for the Hall

NM/M

	Complete Set (10):	40.00
	Common Player:	2.00
	Inserted 1:64	
1	Greg Maddux	4.00
2	Ozzie Smith	4.00
3	Andre Dawson	2.00
4	Dennis Eckersley	2.00
5	Roberto Alomar	2.00
6	Cal Ripken Jr.	10.00
7	Roger Clemens	5.00
8	Tony Gwynn	4.00
9	Alex Rodriguez	4.00
10	Jeff Bagwell	3.00

Heading for the Hall Autographs

NM/M

	Common Player:	25.00
	Production 50 each.	
1	Greg Maddux	125.00
2	Ozzie Smith	100.00
3	Andre Dawson	40.00
4	Dennis Eckersley	45.00
5	Roberto Alomar	25.00
6	Cal Ripken Jr.	200.00
7	Roger Clemens	150.00
8	Tony Gwynn	100.00
9	Alex Rodriguez	150.00
10	Jeff Bagwell	40.00

League of Nations

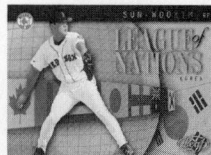

NM/M

	Complete Set (10):	20.00
	Common Player:	2.00
	Inserted 1:60	
1	Ichiro Suzuki	8.00
2	Tsuyoshi Shinjo	2.00
3	Chan Ho Park	2.00
4	Larry Walker	2.00
5	Andruw Jones	4.00
6	Hideo Nomo	4.00
7	Byung-Hyun Kim	2.00
8	Sun-Woo Kim	2.00
9	Orlando Hernandez	2.00
10	Luke Prokopec	2.00

Retired Numbers

#'d to jersey number
No Pricing

Rookie Reprints

FRANK THOMAS 1B

NM/M

	Complete Set (6):	35.00
	Common Player:	3.00
	#'d to year of issue	
1	Roger Clemens/1985	10.00
2	Kirby Puckett/1985	9.00
3	Andres Galarraga/1986	3.00
4	Fred McGriff/1986	3.00
5	Sammy Sosa/1990	10.00
6	Frank Thomas/1990	8.00

Shirt Off My Back

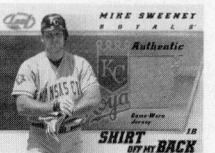

MIKE SWEENEY ROYALS

NM/M

	Common Player:	5.00
	Inserted 1:29	
	Patch Variations:	2-4X
RA	Roberto Alomar	8.00
JB	Jeff Bagwell/SP	20.00
MB	Michael Barrett	5.00
CB	Carlos Beltran	15.00
LB	Lance Berkman	5.00
GB	George Brett/SP	50.00
KB	Kevin Brown	5.00
MB	Mark Buehrle	5.00
AB	A.J. Burnett	5.00
JBU	Jeromy Burnitz	5.00
CD	Carlos Delgado	8.00
RD	Ryan Dempster	5.00
DE	Darin Erstad/SP	15.00
CF	Cliff Floyd	5.00
FG	Freddy Garcia/SP	8.00
NG	Nomar Garciaparra/SP	40.00
TGL	Troy Glaus/SP	20.00
TGL	Tom Glavine	5.00
LG	Luis Gonzalez	5.00
TG	Tony Gwynn	25.00
MH	Mike Hampton	5.00
TH	Todd Helton	20.00
THU	Tim Hudson	6.00
BJA	Bo Jackson/SP	25.00
RJ	Randy Johnson	20.00
CJ	Chipper Jones/SP	30.00
AK	Al Kaline/SP	20.00
EK	Eric Karros	5.00
BL	Barry Larkin	5.00
CL	Carlos Lee	5.00
JL	Javy Lopez	5.00
GM	Greg Maddux/SP	30.00
EM	Edgar Martinez/SP	8.00
PM	Pedro Martinez/SP	20.00
DM	Don Mattingly/SP	50.00
KM	Kevin Millwood	5.00
HN	Hideo Nomo/SP	25.00
JO	John Olerud	5.00
MO	Magglio Ordonez	5.00
RP	Rafael Palmeiro	10.00
CHP	Chan Ho Park/SP	8.00
TP	Troy Percival	5.00

AP	Andy Pettitte/SP	12.00
MP	Mike Piazza	30.00
KP	Kirby Puckett	25.00
BR	Brad Radke	5.00
MR	Manny Ramirez	20.00
CR	Cal Ripken Jr./SP/50	100.00
AR	Alex Rodriguez	35.00
SR	Scott Rolen/SP	15.00
KS	Kazuhiro Sasaki/SP	8.00
CS	Curt Schilling/SP	15.00
RS	Richie Sexson	5.00
TS	Tsuyoshi Shinjo/SP	8.00
JS	John Smoltz	5.00
MS	Mike Sweeney	5.00
MT	Miguel Tejada	6.00
LW	Larry Walker/SP	8.00
MW	Matt Williams	5.00
DW	Dave Winfield/SP	20.00

2002 Leaf Certified

NM/M

Complete Set (200):
Common Player: .50
Common (151-200): 5.00
Production 500
Pack (5): 6.00
Box (16): 75.00

1	Alex Rodriguez	4.00
2	Luis Gonzalez	.65
3	Javier Vazquez	.50
4	Juan Uribe	.50
5	Ben Sheets	.50
6	George Brett	4.00
7	Magglio Ordonez	.50
8	Randy Johnson	1.00
9	Joe Kennedy	.50
10	Richie Sexson	.50
11	Larry Walker	.50
12	Lance Berkman	.50
13	Jose Cruz Jr.	.50
14	Doug Davis	.50
15	Cliff Floyd	.50
16	Ryan Klesko	.50
17	Troy Glaus	1.00
18	Robert Person	.50
19	Bartolo Colon	.50
20	Adam Dunn	.75
21	Kevin Brown	.50
22	John Smoltz	.50
23	Edgar Martinez	.50
24	Eric Karros	.50
25	Tony Gwynn	2.00
26	Mark Mulder	.50
27	Don Mattingly	4.00
28	Brandon Duckworth	.50
29	C.C. Sabathia	.50
30	Nomar Garciaparra	3.00
31	Adam Johnson	.50
32	Miguel Tejada	.65
33	Ryne Sandberg	2.00
34	Roger Clemens	2.50
35	Edgardo Alfonzo	.50
36	Jason Jennings	.50
37	Todd Helton	1.00
38	Nolan Ryan	5.00
39	Paul LoDuca	.50
40	Cal Ripken Jr.	5.00
41	Terrence Long	.50
42	Mike Sweeney	.50
43	Carlos Lee	.50
44	Ben Grieve	.50
45	Tony Armas Jr.	.50
46	Joe Mays	.50
47	Jeff Kent	.50
48	Andy Pettitte	.65
49	Kirby Puckett	2.00
50	Aramis Ramirez	.50
51	Tim Redding	.50
52	Freddy Garcia	.50
53	Javy Lopez	.50
54	Mike Schmidt	4.00
55	Wade Miller	.50
56	Ramon Ortiz	.50
57	Ray Durham	.50
58	J.D. Drew	.75
59	Bret Boone	.50
60	Mark Buehrle	.50
61	Geoff Jenkins	.50
62	Greg Maddux	2.00
63	Mark Grace	.65
64	Toby Hall	.50
65	A.J. Burnett	.50
66	Bernie Williams	.65
67	Roy Oswalt	.65
68	Shannon Stewart	.50
69	Barry Zito	.65
70	Juan Pierre	.50
71	Preston Wilson	.50
72	Rafael Furcal	.50
73	Sean Casey	.50
74	John Olerud	.50
75	Paul Konerko	.75
76	Vernon Wells	.50
77	Juan Gonzalez	1.00
78	Ellis Burks	.50
79	Jim Edmonds	.75
80	Robert Fick	.50
81	Michael Cuddyer	.50
82	Tim Hudson	.65
83	Phil Nevin	.50
84	Curt Schilling	.75
85	Juan Cruz	.50
86	Jeff Bagwell	1.00
87	Raul Mondesi	.50
88	Bud Smith	.50
89	Omar Vizquel	.50
90	Vladimir Guerrero	1.00
91	Garret Anderson	.50
92	Mike Piazza	3.00
93	Josh Beckett	.65
94	Carlos Delgado	.50
95	Kazuhiro Sasaki	.50
96	Chipper Jones	2.00
97	Jacque Jones	.50
98	Pedro J. Martinez	1.00
99	Marcus Giles	.50
100	Craig Biggio	.50
101	Orlando Cabrera	.50
102	Al Leiter	.50
103	Michael Barrett	.50
104	Hideo Nomo	1.00
105	Mike Mussina	.75
106	Jeremy Giambi	.50
107	Cristian Guzman	.50
108	Frank Thomas	1.00
109	Carlos Beltran	1.00
110	Jorge Posada	.65
111	Roberto Alomar	.65
112	Bobby Abreu	.50
113	Robin Ventura	.50
114	Pat Burrell	.75
115	Kenny Lofton	.50
116	Adrian Beltre	.75
117	Gary Sheffield	.75
118	Jermaine Dye	.50
119	Manny Ramirez	1.00
120	Brian Giles	.50
121	Tsuyoshi Shinjo	.50
122	Rafael Palmeiro	.85
123	Mo Vaughn	.50
124	Kerry Wood	.75
125	Moises Alou	.50
126	Rickey Henderson	1.00
127	Corey Patterson	.50
128	Jim Thome	1.00
129	Richard Hidalgo	.50
130	Darin Erstad	.75
131	Johnny Damon	.75
132	Juan Encarnacion	.50
133	Scott Rolen	1.00
134	Tom Glavine	.75
135	Ivan Rodriguez	.85
136	Jay Gibbons	.50
137	Trot Nixon	.50
138	Nick Neugebauer	.50
139	Barry Larkin	.50
140	Andruw Jones	1.00
141	Shawn Green	.75
142	Jose Vidro	.50
143	Derek Jeter	5.00
144	Ichiro Suzuki	3.00
145	Ken Griffey Jr.	3.00
146	Barry Bonds	5.00
147	Albert Pujols	4.00
148	Sammy Sosa	3.00
149	Jason Giambi	.75
150	Alfonso Soriano	.75
151	Drew Henson/Bat	8.00
152	Luis Garcia/Bat	5.00
153	Geronimo Gil/Jsy	5.00
154	Corky Miller/Jsy	5.00
155	Mike Rivera/Bat	5.00
156	Mark Ellis/Jsy	5.00
157	Josh Pearce/Bat	5.00
158	Ryan Ludwick/Bat	5.00
159	So Taguchi/Bat RC	12.00
160	Cody Ransom/Jsy	5.00
161	Jeff Deardorff/Bat RC	5.00
162	Franklyn German/Bat RC	5.00
163	Ed Rogers/Jsy	5.00
164	Eric Cyr/Jsy RC	5.00
165	Victor Alvarez/Jsy RC	5.00
166	Victor Martinez/Jsy	15.00
167	Brandon Berger/Jsy	5.00
168	Juan Diaz/Jsy	5.00
169	Kevin Frederick/Jsy RC	5.00
170	Earl Snyder/Bat RC	5.00
171	Morgan Ensberg/Bat	8.00
172	Ryan Jamison/Jsy RC	5.00
173	Rodrigo Rosario/Jsy RC	5.00
174	Willie Harris/Bat	5.00
175	Ramon Vazquez/Bat	5.00
176	Kazuhisa Ishii/Bat RC	12.00
177	Hank Blalock/Jsy	8.00
178	Mark Prior/Bat	15.00
179	Dewon Brazelton/Jsy	5.00
180	Doug DeVore/Jsy RC	5.00
181	Jorge Padilla/Bat RC	5.00
182	Mark Teixeira/Jsy	10.00
183	Orlando Hudson/Bat	5.00
184	John Buck/Jsy	5.00
185	Erik Bedard/Jsy	5.00
186	Allan Simpson/Jsy RC	5.00
187	Travis Hafner/Jsy	10.00
188	Jason Lane/Jsy	5.00
189	Marlon Byrd/Jsy	5.00
190	Joe Thurston/Jsy	5.00
191	Brandon Backe/Jsy RC	5.00
192	Josh Phelps/Jsy	5.00
193	Bill Hall/Bat	5.00
194	Chris Snelling/Bat RC	8.00
195	Austin Kearns/Jsy	8.00
196	Antonio Perez/Bat	5.00
197	Angel Berroa/Bat	5.00
198	Anderson Machado/Jsy RC	5.00
199	Alfredo Amezaga/Jsy	5.00
200	Eric Hinske/Bat	8.00

Certified Skills

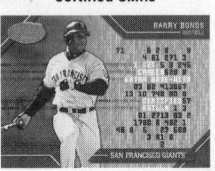

NM/M

Complete Set (20): 65.00
Common Player: 2.00
Inserted 1:17
Mirror Blues: 1.5-2.5X
Production 75 Sets
Mirror Reds: 1-2X
Production 150 Sets
Mirror Golds not priced 25 sets.

1	Barry Bonds	8.00
2	Greg Maddux	4.00
3	Rickey Henderson	2.00
4	Ichiro Suzuki	5.00
5	Pedro J. Martinez	2.00
6	Kazuhisa Ishii	1.50
7	Alex Rodriguez	6.00
8	Mike Piazza	5.00
9	Sammy Sosa	5.00
10	Derek Jeter	8.00
11	Albert Pujols	6.00
12	Roger Clemens	4.50
13	Mark Prior	1.50
14	Chipper Jones	3.00
15	Ken Griffey Jr.	5.00
16	Frank Thomas	5.00
17	Randy Johnson	2.00
18	Vladimir Guerrero	2.00
19	Nomar Garciaparra	5.00
20	Jeff Bagwell	2.00

All Certified Team

NM/M

Complete Set (25): 75.00
Common Player: 1.50
Inserted 1:17
Mirror Blues: 2-4X
Production 50 Sets
Mirror Reds: 1.5-3X
Production 75 Sets
Golds not priced 25 sets produced.

1	Ichiro Suzuki	5.00
2	Alex Rodriguez	6.00
3	Sammy Sosa	5.00
4	Jeff Bagwell	3.00
5	Greg Maddux	4.00
6	Todd Helton	3.00
7	Nomar Garciaparra	5.00
8	Ken Griffey Jr.	5.00
9	Roger Clemens	4.50
10	Adam Dunn	2.00
11	Chipper Jones	4.00
12	Hideo Nomo	3.00
13	Lance Berkman	1.50
14	Barry Bonds	8.00
15	Manny Ramirez	3.00
16	Jason Giambi	2.00
17	Rickey Henderson	3.00
18	Randy Johnson	3.00
19	Derek Jeter	8.00
20	Kazuhisa Ishii	1.50
21	Frank Thomas	3.00
22	Mike Piazza	5.00
23	Albert Pujols	6.00
24	Pedro J. Martinez	3.00
25	Vladimir Guerrero	3.00

Mirror Red

NM/M

Common (1-200): 5.00
Cards (151-200): .5-1X base
Production 150 Sets
Mirror Blues (1-200): .5-1.5X
Production 75 Sets
Mirror Golds not priced.
Production 25 Sets
Mirror Emerald five sets produced.
Mirror Black one set produced.

1	Alex Rodriguez/Jsy	25.00
2	Luis Gonzalez/Jsy	5.00
3	Javier Vazquez/Bat	5.00
4	Juan Uribe/Jsy	5.00
5	Ben Sheets/Jsy	5.00
6	George Brett/Jsy	40.00
7	Magglio Ordonez/Jsy	8.00
8	Randy Johnson/Jsy	15.00
9	Joe Kennedy/Jsy	5.00
10	Richie Sexson/Jsy	10.00
11	Larry Walker/Jsy	8.00
12	Lance Berkman/Jsy	5.00
13	Jose Cruz Jr./Jsy	5.00
14	Doug Davis/Jsy	5.00
15	Cliff Floyd/Jsy	5.00
16	Ryan Klesko/Bat	5.00
17	Troy Glaus/Jsy	10.00
18	Robert Person/Jsy	5.00
19	Bartolo Colon/Jsy	5.00
20	Adam Dunn/Jsy	15.00
21	Kevin Brown/Jsy	8.00
22	John Smoltz/Jsy	8.00
23	Edgar Martinez/Jsy	8.00
24	Eric Karros/Jsy	5.00
25	Tony Gwynn/Jsy	20.00
26	Mark Mulder/Jsy	8.00
27	Don Mattingly/Jsy	40.00
28	Brandon Duckworth/Jsy	5.00
29	C.C. Sabathia/Jsy	5.00
30	Nomar Garciaparra/Jsy	20.00
31	Adam Johnson/Jsy	5.00
32	Miguel Tejada/Jsy	5.00
33	Ryne Sandberg/Jsy	40.00
34	Roger Clemens/Jsy	25.00
35	Edgardo Alfonzo/Jsy	5.00
36	Jason Jennings/Jsy	5.00
37	Todd Helton/Jsy	10.00
38	Nolan Ryan/Jsy	60.00
39	Paul LoDuca/Jsy	5.00
40	Cal Ripken Jr/Jsy	55.00
41	Terrence Long/Jsy	5.00
42	Mike Sweeney/Jsy	5.00
43	Carlos Lee/Jsy	5.00
44	Ben Grieve/Jsy	5.00
45	Tony Armas Jr./Jsy	5.00
46	Joe Mays/Jsy	5.00
47	Jeff Kent/Jsy	8.00
48	Andy Pettitte/Jsy	8.00
49	Kirby Puckett/Jsy	15.00
50	Aramis Ramirez/Jsy	5.00
51	Tim Redding/Jsy	5.00
52	Freddy Garcia/Jsy	5.00
53	Javy Lopez/Jsy	5.00
54	Mike Schmidt/Jsy	35.00
55	Wade Miller/Jsy	5.00
56	Ramon Ortiz/Jsy	5.00
57	Ray Durham/Jsy	5.00
58	J.D. Drew/Jsy	5.00
59	Bret Boone/Jsy	5.00
60	Mark Buehrle/Jsy	5.00
61	Geoff Jenkins/Jsy	5.00
62	Greg Maddux/Jsy	20.00
63	Mark Grace/Jsy	10.00
64	Toby Hall/Jsy	5.00
65	A.J. Burnett/Jsy	5.00
66	Bernie Williams/Jsy	8.00
67	Roy Oswalt/Jsy	8.00
68	Shannon Stewart/Jsy	5.00
69	Barry Zito/Jsy	8.00

70 Juan Pierre/Jsy 5.00
71 Preston Wilson/Jsy 5.00
72 Rafael Furcal/Jsy 5.00
73 Sean Casey/Jsy 5.00
74 John Olerud/Jsy 5.00
75 Paul Konerko/Jsy 5.00
76 Vernon Wells/Jsy 5.00
77 Juan Gonzalez/Jsy 8.00
78 Ellis Burks/Jsy 5.00
79 Jim Edmonds/Jsy 8.00
80 Robert Fick/Jsy 5.00
81 Michael Cuddyer/Jsy 5.00
82 Tim Hudson/Jsy 5.00
83 Phil Nevin/Jsy 5.00
84 Curt Schilling/Jsy 8.00
85 Juan Cruz/Jsy 5.00
86 Jeff Bagwell/Jsy 10.00
87 Raul Mondesi/Jsy 5.00
88 Bud Smith/Jsy 5.00
89 Omar Vizquel/Jsy 5.00
90 Vladimir Guerrero/Jsy 20.00
91 Garret Anderson/Jsy 8.00
92 Mike Piazza/Jsy 15.00
93 Josh Beckett/Jsy 8.00
94 Carlos Delgado/Jsy 8.00
95 Kazuhiro Sasaki/Jsy 5.00
96 Chipper Jones/Jsy 10.00
97 Jacque Jones/Jsy 5.00
98 Pedro Martinez/Jsy 15.00
99 Marcus Giles/Jsy 5.00
100 Craig Biggio/Jsy 6.00
101 Orlando Cabrera/Jsy 5.00
102 Al Leiter/Jsy 5.00
103 Michael Barrett/Jsy 5.00
104 Hideo Nomo/Jsy 15.00
105 Mike Mussina/Jsy 12.00
106 Jeremy Giambi/Jsy 5.00
107 Cristian Guzman/Jsy 5.00
108 Frank Thomas/Jsy 10.00
109 Carlos Beltran/Bat 8.00
110 Jorge Posada/Bat 8.00
111 Roberto Alomar/Bat 12.00
112 Bobby Abreu/Bat 6.00
113 Robin Ventura/Bat 10.00
114 Pat Burrell/Bat 18.00
115 Kenny Lofton/Bat 6.00
116 Adrian Beltre/Bat 8.00
117 Gary Sheffield/Bat 6.00
118 Jermaine Dye/Bat 5.00
119 Manny Ramirez/Bat 8.00
120 Brian Giles/Bat 5.00
121 Tsuyoshi Shinjo/Bat 5.00
122 Rafael Palmeiro/Bat 10.00
123 Mo Vaughn/Bat 5.00
124 Kerry Wood/Bat 15.00
125 Moises Alou/Bat 8.00
126 Rickey Henderson/Bat 15.00
127 Corey Patterson/Bat 8.00
128 Jim Thome/Bat 15.00
129 Richard Hidalgo/Bat 5.00
130 Darin Erstad/Jsy 5.00
131 Johnny Damon/Bat 5.00
132 Juan Encarnacion/Bat 5.00
133 Scott Rolen/Bat 10.00
134 Tom Glavine/Bat 8.00
135 Ivan Rodriguez/Bat 10.00
136 Jay Gibbons/Bat 5.00
137 Trot Nixon/Bat 5.00
138 Nick Neugebauer/Bat 5.00
139 Barry Larkin/Jsy 10.00
140 Andruw Jones/Bat 8.00
141 Shawn Green/Bat 8.00
142 Jose Vidro/Jsy 5.00
143 Derek Jeter/Base 25.00
144 Ichiro Suzuki/Base 20.00
145 Ken Griffey Jr./Base 15.00
146 Barry Bonds/Base 20.00
147 Albert Pujols/Base 15.00
148 Sammy Sosa/Base 15.00
149 Jason Giambi/Base 8.00
150 Alfonso Soriano/Jsy 10.00
151 Drew Henson/Bat 5.00
152 Luis Garcia/Bat 5.00
153 Geronimo Gil/Jsy 5.00
154 Corky Miller/Jsy 5.00
155 Mike Rivera/Bat 5.00
156 Mark Ellis/Jsy 5.00
157 Josh Pearce/Bat 5.00
158 Ryan Ludwick/Bat 5.00
159 So Taguchi/Bat 12.00
160 Cody Ransom/Jsy 5.00
161 Jeff Deardorff/Bat 5.00
162 Franklyn German/Bat 5.00
163 Ed Rogers/Jsy 5.00
164 Eric Cyr/Jsy 5.00
165 Victor Alvarez/Jsy 5.00
166 Victor Martinez/Jsy 10.00
167 Brandon Berger/Jsy 5.00
168 Juan Diaz/Jsy 5.00
169 Kevin Frederick/Jsy 5.00
170 Earl Snyder/Bat 5.00
171 Morgan Ensberg/Bat 5.00
172 Ryan Jamison/Jsy 5.00
173 Rodrigo Rosario/Jsy 5.00
174 Willie Harris/Bat 5.00
175 Ramon Vazquez/Bat 5.00
176 Kazuhisa Ishii/Bat 15.00
177 Hank Blalock/Jsy 10.00
178 Mark Prior/Bat 10.00
179 Dewon Brazelton/Jsy 5.00
180 Doug DeVore/Jsy 5.00
181 Jorge Padilla/Bat 5.00
182 Mark Teixeira/Jsy 10.00
183 Orlando Hudson/Bat 5.00
184 John Buck/Jsy 5.00
185 Erik Bedard/Jsy 5.00
186 Allan Simpson/Jsy 5.00
187 Travis Hafner/Jsy 8.00
188 Jason Lane/Jsy 5.00
189 Marlon Byrd/Jsy 5.00
190 Joe Thurston/Jsy 5.00
191 Brandon Backe/Jsy 5.00
192 Josh Phelps/Jsy 5.00
193 Bill Hall/Bat 5.00
194 Chris Snelling/Bat 5.00
195 Austin Kearns/Jsy 8.00
196 Antonio Perez/Bat 5.00
197 Angel Berroa/Bat 6.00
198 Anderson Machado/Jsy 5.00
199 Alfredo Amezaga/Jsy 5.00
200 Eric Hinske/Bat 6.00

Fabric of the Game

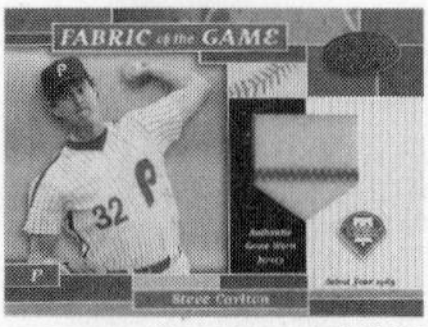

NM/M

Common Player:
1 Bobby Doerr/37 20.00
2 Ozzie Smith/78 40.00
3 Pee Wee Reese/40 35.00
4 Tommy Lasorda/80 8.00
4 Tommy Lasorda/54 15.00
4 Tommy Lasorda/50 15.00
5 Red Schoendienst/45 20.00
7 Harmon Killebrew/54 35.00
8 Roger Maris/A's/57 75.00
10 Mel Ott/26 75.00
11 Paul Molitor/100 20.00
11 Paul Molitor/78 20.00
11 Paul Molitor/50 30.00
12 Duke Snider/47 40.00
13 Brooks Robinson/55 40.00
14 George Brett/40 75.00
14 George Brett/73 50.00
15 Johnny Bench/80 20.00
15 Johnny Bench/67 30.00
15 Johnny Bench/50 30.00
16 Lou Boudreau/38 20.00
17 Stan Musial/41 60.00
18 Al Kaline/53 30.00
19 Steve Garvey/100 8.00
19 Steve Garvey/69 15.00
19 Steve Garvey/45 15.00
20 Nomar Garciaparra/100 25.00
20 Nomar Garciaparra/96 25.00
20 Nomar Garciaparra/50 35.00
21 Joe Morgan/80 10.00
21 Joe Morgan/63 20.00
21 Joe Morgan/50 20.00
22 Willie Stargell/62 25.00
23 Andre Dawson/80 15.00
23 Andre Dawson/76 15.00
23 Andre Dawson/50 20.00
24 Gary Carter/100 10.00
24 Gary Carter/74 20.00
24 Gary Carter/50 20.00
25 Reggie Jackson/A's/67 30.00
27 Phil Rizzuto/41 30.00
28 Luis Aparicio/56 20.00
29 Robin Yount/80 30.00
29 Robin Yount/74 30.00
29 Robin Yount/50 40.00
30 Tony Gwynn/100 20.00
30 Tony Gwynn/82 20.00
30 Tony Gwynn/50 30.00
31 Ernie Banks/53 40.00
32 Joe Torre/50 15.00
32 Joe Torre/60 15.00
33 Bo Jackson/100 20.00
33 Bo Jackson/86 20.00
33 Bo Jackson/35 50.00
34 Alfonso Soriano/80 20.00
34 Alfonso Soriano/99 20.00
34 Alfonso Soriano/50 25.00
35 Cal Ripken Jr./80 60.00
35 Cal Ripken Jr./81 60.00
35 Cal Ripken Jr./50 80.00
36 Miguel Tejada/100 10.00
36 Miguel Tejada/97 10.00
36 Miguel Tejada/50 20.00
37 Alex Rodriguez/M's/100 20.00
37 Alex Rodriguez/M's/94 20.00
37 Alex Rodriguez/M's/50 35.00
38 Mike Schmidt/80 40.00
38 Mike Schmidt/72 40.00
38 Mike Schmidt/50 50.00
39 Lou Brock/61 25.00
40 Don Sutton/80 8.00
40 Don Sutton/66 10.00
40 Don Sutton/50 15.00
41 Roberto Clemente/55 125.00
42 Jim Palmer/65 20.00
43 Don Mattingly/40 75.00
43 Don Mattingly/82 50.00
44 Ryne Sandberg/40 60.00
44 Ryne Sandberg/81 40.00
45 Early Wynn/39 20.00
46 Mike Piazza/Dodgers/100 20.00
46 Mike Piazza/Dodgers/92 20.00
46 Mike Piazza/Dodgers/31 40.00
46 Mike Piazza/Dodgers/50 25.00
47 Wade Boggs/100 15.00
47 Wade Boggs/82 15.00
47 Wade Boggs/26 40.00
47 Wade Boggs/45 30.00
48 Jim "Catfish" Hunter/65 25.00
48 Jim "Catfish" Hunter/27 40.00
49 Juan Marichal/60 20.00
49 Juan Marichal/27 40.00
50 Carlton Fisk/Red Sox/80 25.00
50 Carlton Fisk/Red Sox/69 40.00
50 Carlton Fisk/Red Sox/27 50.00
50 Carlton Fisk/Red Sox/50 30.00
51 Curt Schilling/100 15.00
51 Curt Schilling/88 15.00
51 Curt Schilling/38 25.00
51 Curt Schilling/50 20.00
52 Rod Carew/Angels/80 15.00
52 Rod Carew/Angels/67 25.00
52 Rod Carew/Angels/50 25.00
53 Rod Carew/Twins/67 25.00
54 Joe Carter/100 8.00
54 Joe Carter/83 8.00
54 Joe Carter/29 15.00
54 Joe Carter/50 10.00
55 Nolan Ryan/Angels/66 60.00
56 Orlando Cepeda/80 8.00
56 Orlando Cepeda/55 10.00
56 Orlando Cepeda/30 25.00
56 Orlando Cepeda/50 15.00
57 Dave Winfield/80 15.00
57 Dave Winfield/73 20.00
57 Dave Winfield/31 30.00
57 Dave Winfield/50 20.00
58 Hoyt Wilhelm/80 8.00
58 Hoyt Wilhelm/52 10.00
58 Hoyt Wilhelm/31 20.00
58 Hoyt Wilhelm/50 15.00
59 Steve Carlton/80 15.00
59 Steve Carlton/65 20.00
59 Steve Carlton/32 30.00
59 Steve Carlton/50 20.00
60 Eddie Murray/100 15.00
60 Eddie Murray/77 15.00
60 Eddie Murray/33 30.00
60 Eddie Murray/50 20.00
61 Nolan Ryan/Rangers/40 75.00
61 Nolan Ryan/Rangers/66 60.00
61 Nolan Ryan/Rangers/34 75.00
62 Nolan Ryan/Astros/40 75.00
62 Nolan Ryan/Astros/66 60.00
62 Nolan Ryan/Astros/34 75.00
63 Kirby Puckett/40 40.00
63 Kirby Puckett/84 20.00
63 Kirby Puckett/34 40.00
64 Yogi Berra/46 40.00
64 Yogi Berra/35 40.00
65 Phil Niekro/80 8.00
65 Phil Niekro/64 10.00
65 Phil Niekro/35 15.00
65 Phil Niekro/50 10.00
66 Gaylord Perry/80 8.00
66 Gaylord Perry/62 10.00
66 Gaylord Perry/36 15.00
66 Gaylord Perry/50 10.00
67 Pedro Martinez/Expos/100 15.00
67 Pedro Martinez/Expos/92 15.00
67 Pedro Martinez/Expos/45 25.00
67 Pedro Martinez/Expos/50 20.00
68 Alex Rodriguez/Rgr/100 20.00
68 Alex Rodriguez/Rgr/94 20.00
68 Alex Rodriguez/Rgr/50 30.00
69 Dave Parker/100 8.00
69 Dave Parker/73 10.00
69 Dave Parker/39 15.00
69 Dave Parker/50 10.00
70 Darin Erstad/100 8.00
70 Darin Erstad/96 8.00
70 Darin Erstad/50 15.00
71 Eddie Matthews/52 30.00
71 Eddie Matthews/41 35.00
72 Tom Seaver/Mets/67 30.00
72 Tom Seaver/Mets/41 40.00
73 Tom Seaver/Reds/67 30.00
73 Tom Seaver/Reds/41 40.00
74 Jackie Robinson/47 100.00
74 Jackie Robinson/42 100.00
75 Randy Johnson/M's/80 15.00
75 Randy Johnson/M's/88 15.00
75 Randy Johnson/M's/51 25.00
75 Randy Johnson/M's/50 25.00
76 Reggie Jackson/Yanks/44 40.00
77 Reggie Jackson/Angels/80 20.00
77 Reggie Jackson/Angels/67 30.00
77 Reggie Jackson/Angels/44 40.00
77 Reggie Jackson/Angels/50 40.00
78 Willie McCovey/80 10.00
78 Willie McCovey/59 15.00
78 Willie McCovey/44 20.00
78 Willie McCovey/50 20.00
79 Eric Davis/100 5.00
79 Eric Davis/84 5.00
79 Eric Davis/34 10.00
79 Eric Davis/50 8.00
80 Carlos Delgado/95 6.00
80 Carlos Delgado/93 6.00
81 Dale Murphy/100 20.00
81 Dale Murphy/76 20.00
81 Dale Murphy/50 30.00
82 Brian Giles/100 5.00
82 Brian Giles/95 5.00
82 Brian Giles/50 8.00
83 Kazuhiro Sasaki/100 5.00
83 Kazuhiro Sasaki/100 8.00
83 Kazuhiro Sasaki/50 10.00
84 Phil Nevin/100 5.00
84 Phil Nevin/95 5.00
84 Phil Nevin/50 8.00
85 Frank Thomas/80 15.00
85 Frank Thomas/90 15.00
85 Frank Thomas/35 25.00
85 Frank Thomas/50 15.00
86 Raul Mondesi/100 5.00
86 Raul Mondesi/93 5.00
86 Raul Mondesi/43 8.00
86 Raul Mondesi/50 8.00
87 Don Drysdale/56 25.00
87 Don Drysdale/53 25.00
88 Gary Sheffield/100 6.00
88 Gary Sheffield/88 6.00
88 Gary Sheffield/50 10.00
89 Andy Pettitte/100 15.00
89 Andy Pettitte/95 15.00
89 Andy Pettitte/46 30.00
89 Andy Pettitte/50 20.00
90 Lance Berkman/45 20.00
90 Lance Berkman/99 10.00
91 Paul LoDuca/100 5.00
91 Paul LoDuca/98 5.00
91 Paul LoDuca/50 8.00
92 Kevin Brown/86 5.00
92 Kevin Brown/27 15.00
93 Jim Thome/100 15.00
93 Jim Thome/91 15.00
93 Jim Thome/50 25.00
94 Mike Sweeney/100 5.00
94 Mike Sweeney/95 5.00
94 Mike Sweeney/29 15.00
94 Mike Sweeney/50 10.00
95 Pedro J. Martinez/ Red Sox/100 15.00
95 Pedro J. Martinez/ Red Sox/92 15.00
95 Pedro J. Martinez/ Red Sox/45 25.00
95 Pedro J. Martinez/ Red Sox/45 25.00
96 Cliff Floyd/100 5.00
96 Cliff Floyd/93 5.00
96 Cliff Floyd/30 15.00
96 Cliff Floyd/50 10.00
97 Larry Walker/100 8.00
97 Larry Walker/89 8.00
97 Larry Walker/33 30.00
97 Larry Walker/50 10.00
98 Ivan Rodriguez/80 10.00
98 Ivan Rodriguez/91 10.00
98 Ivan Rodriguez/50 20.00
99 Aramis Ramirez/100 8.00
99 Aramis Ramirez/98 8.00
99 Aramis Ramirez/50 12.00
100 Roberto Alomar/100 10.00
100 Roberto Alomar/88 10.00
100 Roberto Alomar/50 15.00
101 Ben Sheets/100 8.00
101 Ben Sheets/101 8.00
101 Ben Sheets/50 15.00
102 Adam Dunn/101 20.00
102 Adam Dunn/39 40.00
103 Hideo Nomo/95 30.00
104 C.C. Sabathia/50 10.00
104 C.C. Sabathia/101 5.00
104 C.C. Sabathia/52 10.00
104 C.C. Sabathia/50 10.00
105 Rickey Henderson/A's/100 20.00
105 Rickey Henderson/A's/79 20.00
105 Rickey Henderson/A's/30 50.00
105 Rickey Henderson/A's/50 30.00
106 Carlton Fisk/White Sox/80 20.00
106 Carlton Fisk/White Sox/69 30.00
106 Carlton Fisk/White Sox/50 30.00
107 Chan Ho Park/100 5.00
107 Chan Ho Park/94 5.00
107 Chan Ho Park/61 8.00
107 Chan Ho Park/50 8.00
108 Mike Mussina/100 20.00
108 Mike Mussina/91 20.00
108 Mike Mussina/35 50.00
108 Mike Mussina/50 30.00
109 Mark Mulder/100 8.00
109 Mark Mulder/100 8.00
109 Mark Mulder/20 20.00
109 Mark Mulder/35 20.00
110 Tsuyoshi Shinjo/100 5.00
110 Tsuyoshi Shinjo/101 5.00
110 Tsuyoshi Shinjo/30 20.00
111 Pat Burrell/100 10.00
111 Pat Burrell/100 10.00
111 Pat Burrell/50 15.00
112 Edgar Martinez/100 10.00
112 Edgar Martinez/87 10.00
112 Edgar Martinez/50 15.00
113 Barry Larkin/100 10.00
113 Barry Larkin/86 10.00
113 Barry Larkin/50 15.00
114 Jeff Kent/100 6.00
114 Jeff Kent/92 6.00
114 Jeff Kent/50 8.00
115 Chipper Jones/100 15.00
115 Chipper Jones/93 15.00
115 Chipper Jones/50 30.00
116 Magglio Ordonez/100 8.00
116 Magglio Ordonez/97 8.00
116 Magglio Ordonez/30 30.00
116 Magglio Ordonez/50 15.00
117 Jim Edmonds/100 8.00
117 Jim Edmonds/93 8.00
117 Jim Edmonds/50 15.00
118 Andruw Jones/100 10.00

118 Andruw Jones/96 10.00
118 Andruw Jones/45 20.00
119 Jose Canseco/100 15.00
119 Jose Canseco/85 15.00
119 Jose Canseco/50 30.00
120 Manny Ramirez/100 10.00
120 Manny Ramirez/93 10.00
120 Manny Ramirez/50 20.00
121 Sean Casey/100 10.00
121 Sean Casey/97 10.00
121 Sean Casey/50 15.00
122 Bret Boone/100 6.00
122 Bret Boone/92 6.00
122 Bret Boone/29 15.00
122 Bret Boone/50 10.00
123 Tim Hudson/100 8.00
123 Tim Hudson/99 8.00
123 Tim Hudson/50 15.00
124 Craig Biggio/100 10.00
124 Craig Biggio/88 10.00
124 Craig Biggio/50 15.00
125 Mike Piazza Mets/100 20.00
125 Mike Piazza Mets/92 20.00
125 Mike Piazza Mets/31 40.00
125 Mike Piazza Mets/51 25.00
126 Jack Morris/100 5.00
126 Jack Morris/77 5.00
126 Jack Morris/47 10.00
127 Roy Oswalt/100 8.00
127 Roy Oswalt/101 8.00
127 Roy Oswalt/39 15.00
127 Roy Oswalt/50 15.00
128 Shawn Green/100 8.00
128 Shawn Green/93 8.00
128 Shawn Green/50 15.00
129 Carlos Beltran/100 8.00
129 Carlos Beltran/98 8.00
129 Carlos Beltran/50 10.00
130 Todd Helton/100 10.00
130 Todd Helton/97 10.00
130 Todd Helton/50 20.00
131 Barry Zito/75 15.00
131 Barry Zito/100 10.00
131 Barry Zito/75 15.00
131 Barry Zito/30 30.00
132 J.D. Drew/100 15.00
132 J.D. Drew/98 15.00
132 J.D. Drew/50 20.00
133 Mark Grace/100 10.00
133 Mark Grace/88 10.00
133 Mark Grace/17
133 Mark Grace/50 20.00
134 Rickey Henderson/Mets/100 20.00
134 Rickey Henderson/Mets/79 20.00
134 Rickey Henderson/Mets/50 30.00
135 Greg Maddux/100 20.00
135 Greg Maddux/86 20.00
135 Greg Maddux/50 30.00
136 Garret Anderson/100 8.00
136 Garret Anderson/94 8.00
136 Garret Anderson/50 15.00
137 Rafael Palmeiro/100 15.00
137 Rafael Palmeiro/86 15.00
137 Rafael Palmeiro/50 20.00
138 Luis Gonzalez/50 10.00
138 Luis Gonzalez/90 8.00
138 Luis Gonzalez/45 15.00
139 Nick Johnson/100 5.00
139 Nick Johnson/101 5.00
139 Nick Johnson/26 20.00
139 Nick Johnson/50 10.00
140 Vladimir Guerrero/80 15.00
140 Vladimir Guerrero/96 15.00
140 Vladimir Guerrero/50 25.00
141 Mark Buehrle/100 5.00
141 Mark Buehrle/56 8.00
142 Troy Glaus/100 15.00
142 Troy Glaus/98 15.00
142 Troy Glaus/50 25.00
143 Juan Gonzalez/100 10.00
143 Juan Gonzalez/89 10.00
143 Juan Gonzalez/50 15.00
144 Kerry Wood/100 15.00
144 Kerry Wood/98 15.00
144 Kerry Wood/34 40.00
144 Kerry Wood/50 30.00
145 Roger Clemens/80 25.00
145 Roger Clemens/84 25.00
145 Roger Clemens/50 40.00
146 Bob Abreu/100 8.00
146 Bob Abreu/96 8.00
146 Bob Abreu/53 15.00
146 Bob Abreu/50 15.00
147 Bernie Williams/95 10.00
147 Bernie Williams/91 10.00
147 Bernie Williams/51 20.00
148 Tom Glavine/100 10.00
148 Tom Glavine/87 10.00
148 Tom Glavine/47 25.00
148 Tom Glavine/50 25.00
149 Jorge Posada/100 10.00
149 Jorge Posada/95 10.00
149 Jorge Posada/50 25.00
150 Randy Johnson/D'Backs/80 15.00
150 Randy Johnson/D'Backs/88 15.00
150 Randy Johnson/D'Backs/51 30.00
150 Randy Johnson/D'Backs/50 30.00

2002 Leaf Rookies & Stars

NM/M

Complete Set (400):
Common Player: .15
Common SP (1-300): .75
Common (301-400): .40

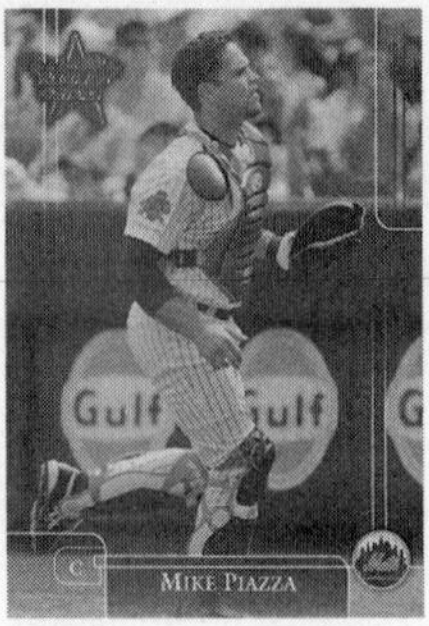

Inserted 1:2
Pack (6): 1.50
Box (24): 30.00
1 Darin Erstad .25
2 Garret Anderson .15
3 Troy Glaus .40
4 David Eckstein .15
5 Adam Kennedy .15
6 Kevin Appier .15
6 Kevin Appier/SP/Mets .75
6 Kevin Appier/SP/Royals .75
7 Jarrod Washburn .15
8 David Segui .15
9 Jay Gibbons .15
10 Tony Batista .15
11 Scott Erickson .15
12 Jeff Conine .15
13 Melvin Mora .15
14 Shea Hillenbrand .15
15 Manny Ramirez .65
15 Manny Ramirez/SP/Indians 2.00
16 Pedro J. Martinez .65
16 Pedro J. Martinez/SP/Dodgers 2.50
16 Pedro J. Martinez/SP/Expos 2.50
17 Nomar Garciaparra 1.00
18 Rickey Henderson .65
18 Rickey Henderson/SP/Angels 3.00
18 Rickey Henderson/SP/A's 3.00
18 Rickey Henderson/SP/Blue Jays 3.00
18 Rickey Henderson/SP/M's 3.00
18 Rickey Henderson/SP/Mets 3.00
18 Rickey Henderson/SP/Padres 3.00
18 Rickey Henderson/SP/Yankees 3.00
19 Johnny Damon .25
19 Johnny Damon/SP/A's 1.00
19 Johnny Damon/SP/Royals 1.00
20 Trot Nixon .15
21 Derek Lowe .15
22 Jason Varitek .15
23 Tim Wakefield .15
24 Frank Thomas .65
25 Kenny Lofton .15
25 Kenny Lofton/SP/Indians .75
26 Magglio Ordonez .15
27 Ray Durham .15
28 Mark Buehrle .15
29 Paul Konerko .25
29 Paul Konerko/SP/Dodgers 1.00
29 Paul Konerko/SP/Reds 1.00
30 Jose Valentin .15
31 C.C. Sabathia .15
32 Ellis Burks .15
32 Ellis Burks/SP/Giants .75
32 Ellis Burks/SP/Red Sox .75
32 Ellis Burks/SP/Rockies .75
33 Omar Vizquel .15
33 Omar Vizquel/SP/Mariners 1.00
34 Jim Thome .50
35 Matt Lawton .15
36 Travis Fryman .15
36 Travis Fryman/SP/Tigers .75
37 Robert Fick .15
38 Bobby Higginson .15
39 Steve Sparks .15
40 Mike Rivera .15
41 Wendell Magee .15
42 Randall Simon .15
43 Carlos Pena .15
43 Carlos Pena/SP/A's .75
43 Carlos Pena/SP/Rangers .75
44 Mike Sweeney .15
45 Chuck Knoblauch .15
46 Carlos Beltran .50
47 Joe Randa .15
48 Paul Byrd .15
49 Mac Suzuki .15
50 Torii Hunter .15
51 Jacque Jones .15
52 David Ortiz .35
53 Corey Koskie .15
54 Brad Radke .15
55 Doug Mientkiewicz .15
56 A.J. Pierzynski .15
57 Dustan Mohr .15
58 Derek Jeter 2.00
59 Bernie Williams .30
60 Roger Clemens .85
60 Roger Clemens/SP/Blue Jays 4.00
60 Roger Clemens/SP/Red Sox 4.00
61 Mike Mussina .40
61 Mike Mussina/SP/Orioles 1.50
62 Jorge Posada .25
63 Alfonso Soriano .50
64 Jason Giambi .40
64 Jason Giambi/SP/A's 2.50
65 Robin Ventura .15
65 Robin Ventura/SP/Mets .75
65 Robin Ventura/SP/White Sox .75
66 Andy Pettitte .25
67 David Wells .15
67 David Wells/SP/Blue Jays .75
67 David Wells/SP/Tigers .75
68 Nick Johnson .15
69 Jeff Weaver .15
69 Jeff Weaver/SP/Tigers .75
70 Raul Mondesi .15
70 Raul Mondesi/SP/Blue Jays .75
70 Raul Mondesi/SP/Dodgers .75
71 Tim Hudson .25
72 Barry Zito .25
73 Mark Mulder .25
74 Miguel Tejada .25
75 Eric Chavez .25
76 Billy Koch .15
76 Billy Koch/SP/Blue Jays .75
77 Jermaine Dye .15
77 Jermaine Dye/SP/Royals .75
78 Scott Hatteberg .15
79 Ichiro Suzuki 1.00
80 Edgar Martinez .15
81 Mike Cameron .15
81 Mike Cameron/SP/White Sox .75
82 John Olerud .15
82 John Olerud/SP/Blue Jays .75
82 John Olerud/SP/Mets .75
83 Bret Boone .15
84 Dan Wilson .15
85 Freddy Garcia .15
86 Jamie Moyer .15
87 Carlos Guillen .15
88 Ruben Sierra .15
89 Kazuhiro Sasaki .15
90 Mark McLemore .15
91 Ben Grieve .15
92 Aubrey Huff .15
93 Steve Cox .15
94 Toby Hall .15
95 Randy Winn .15
96 Brent Abernathy .15
97 Chan Ho Park .15
97 Chan Ho Park/SP/Dodgers .75
98 Alex Rodriguez 1.50
98 Alex Rodriguez/SP/Mariners 4.00
99 Juan Gonzalez .40
99 Juan Gonzalez/SP/Indians 1.50
99 Juan Gonzalez/SP/Tigers 1.50
100 Rafael Palmeiro .60
100 Rafael Palmeiro/SP/Cubs 1.00
100 Rafael Palmeiro/SP/Orioles 1.00
101 Ivan Rodriguez .50
102 Rusty Greer .15
103 Kenny Rogers .15
103 Kenny Rogers/SP/A's .75
103 Kenny Rogers/SP/Yankees .75
104 Hank Blalock .40
105 Mark Teixeira .25
106 Carlos Delgado .40
107 Shannon Stewart .15
108 Eric Hinske .15
109 Roy Halladay .25
110 Felipe Lopez .15
111 Vernon Wells .15
112 Curt Schilling .40
112 Curt Schilling/SP/Phillies 1.50
113 Randy Johnson .65
113 Randy Johnson/SP/Astros 3.00
113 Randy Johnson/SP/Expos 3.00
113 Randy Johnson/SP/Mariners 3.00
114 Luis Gonzalez .25
114 Luis Gonzalez/SP/Astros 1.00
114 Luis Gonzalez/SP/Cubs 1.00
115 Mark Grace .25
115 Mark Grace/SP/Cubs 1.50
116 Junior Spivey .15
117 Tony Womack .15
118 Matt Williams .15
118 Matt Williams/SP/Giants 1.00
118 Matt Williams/SP/Indians 1.00
119 Danny Bautista .15
120 Byung-Hyun Kim .15
121 Craig Counsell .15
122 Greg Maddux .75
122 Greg Maddux/SP/Cubs 4.00
123 Tom Glavine .25
124 John Smoltz .15
124 John Smoltz/SP/Tigers .75
125 Chipper Jones .75
126 Gary Sheffield .25
127 Andruw Jones .65
128 Vinny Castilla .15
129 Damian Moss .15
130 Rafael Furcal .15
131 Kerry Wood .50
132 Fred McGriff .15
132 Fred McGriff/SP/Blue Jays 1.00
132 Fred McGriff/SP/Braves 1.00
132 Fred McGriff/SP/Devil Rays 1.00
132 Fred McGriff/SP/Padres 1.00
133 Sammy Sosa 1.00
133 Sammy Sosa/SP/Rangers 4.00
133 Sammy Sosa/SP/White Sox 4.00
134 Alex Gonzalez .15
135 Corey Patterson .15
136 Moises Alou .15
137 Mark Prior .50
138 Jon Lieber .15
139 Matt Clement .15
140 Ken Griffey Jr. 1.00
140 Ken Griffey Jr./SP/Mariners 4.00
141 Barry Larkin .15
142 Adam Dunn .40
143 Sean Casey .15
143 Sean Casey/SP/Indians .75
144 Jose Rijo .15
145 Elmer Dessens .15
146 Austin Kearns .15
147 Corky Miller .15
148 Todd Walker .15
148 Todd Walker/SP/Rockies .75
148 Todd Walker/SP/Expos .75
149 Chris Reitsma .15
150 Ryan Dempster .15
151 Larry Walker .15
152 Todd Helton .65
153 Juan Uribe .15
154 Juan Pierre .15
155 Mike Hampton .15
156 Todd Zeile .15
157 Josh Beckett .25
158 Mike Lowell .15
158 Mike Lowell/SP/Yankees .75
159 Derrek Lee .15
160 A.J. Burnett .15
161 Luis Castillo .15
162 Tim Raines .15
163 Preston Wilson .15
164 Juan Encarnacion .15
165 Jeff Bagwell .65
166 Craig Biggio .15
167 Lance Berkman .15
168 Wade Miller .15
169 Roy Oswalt .25
170 Richard Hidalgo .15
171 Carlos Hernandez .15
172 Daryle Ward .15
173 Shawn Green .30
173 Shawn Green/SP/Blue Jays 1.00
174 Adrian Beltre .35
175 Paul LoDuca .15
176 Eric Karros .15
177 Kevin Brown .15
178 Hideo Nomo .65
178 Hideo Nomo/SP/Brewers 1.50
178 Hideo Nomo/SP/Mets 1.50
178 Hideo Nomo/SP/Red Sox 1.50
178 Hideo Nomo/SP/Tigers 1.50
179 Odalis Perez .15
180 Eric Gagne .35
181 Brian Jordan .15
182 Cesar Izturis .15
183 Geoff Jenkins .15
184 Richie Sexson .15
184 Richie Sexson/SP/Indians 1.00
185 Jose Hernandez .15
186 Ben Sheets .15
187 Ruben Quevedo .15
188 Jeffrey Hammonds .15
189 Alex Sanchez .15
190 Vladimir Guerrero .65
191 Jose Vidro .15
192 Orlando Cabrera .15
193 Michael Barrett .15
194 Javier Vazquez .15
195 Tony Armas Jr. .15
196 Andres Galarraga .15
197 Tomokazu Ohka .15
198 Bartolo Colon .15
198 Bartolo Colon/SP/Indians .75
199 Cliff Floyd .15
199 Cliff Floyd/SP/Marlins .75
200 Mike Piazza 1.00
200 Mike Piazza/SP/Dodgers 4.00
200 Mike Piazza/SP/Marlins 4.00
201 Jeromy Burnitz .15
202 Roberto Alomar .35
202 Roberto Alomar/SP/Blue Jays 1.50
202 Roberto Alomar/SP/Indians 1.50
202 Roberto Alomar/SP/Orioles 1.50
202 Roberto Alomar/SP/Padres 1.50
203 Mo Vaughn .15
203 Mo Vaughn/SP/Angels 1.00
203 Mo Vaughn/SP/Red Sox 1.00
204 Al Leiter .15
204 Al Leiter/SP/Blue Jays .75
205 Pedro Astacio .15
206 Edgardo Alfonzo .15
207 Armando Benitez .15
208 Scott Rolen .50
209 Pat Burrell .35
210 Bobby Abreu .15
210 Bobby Abreu/SP/Astros 1.00
211 Mike Lieberthal .15
212 Brandon Duckworth .15
213 Jimmy Rollins .40
214 Jeremy Giambi .15
215 Vicente Padilla .15
216 Travis Lee .15
217 Jason Kendall .15
218 Brian Giles .15
218 Brian Giles/SP/Indians 1.00
219 Aramis Ramirez .15
220 Pokey Reese .15
221 Kip Wells .15
222 Josh Fogg .15
222 Josh Fogg/SP/White Sox .75
223 Mike Williams .15
224 Ryan Klesko .15

224	Ryan Klesko/SP/Braves	.75
225	Phil Nevin	.15
225	Phil Nevin/SP/Tigers	.75
226	Brian Lawrence	.15
227	Mark Kotsay	.15
228	Brett Tomko	.15
229	Trevor Hoffman	.15
229	Trevor Hoffman/SP/Marlins	.75
230	Barry Bonds	2.00
230	Barry Bonds/SP/Pirates	6.00
231	Jeff Kent	.15
231	Jeff Kent/SP/Blue Jays	1.00
232	Rich Aurilia	.15
233	Tsuyoshi Shinjo	.15
233	Tsuyoshi Shinjo/SP/Mets	1.00
234	Benito Santiago	.15
234	Benito Santiago/SP/Padres	.75
235	Kirk Rueter	.15
236	Kurt Ainsworth	.15
237	Livan Hernandez	.15
238	Russ Ortiz	.15
239	David Bell	.15
240	Jason Schmidt	.15
241	Reggie Sanders	.15
242	Jim Edmonds	.25
242	Jim Edmonds/SP/Angels	1.00
243	J.D. Drew	.25
244	Albert Pujols	1.50
245	Fernando Vina	.15
246	Tino Martinez	.15
246	Tino Martinez/SP/Mariners	1.00
246	Tino Martinez/SP/Yankees	1.00
247	Edgar Renteria	.15
248	Matt Morris	.15
249	Woody Williams	.15
250	Jason Isringhausen	.15
250	Jason Isringhausen/SP/A's	.75
251	Cal Ripken Jr.	2.00
252	Cal Ripken Jr.	2.00
253	Cal Ripken Jr.	2.00
254	Cal Ripken Jr.	2.00
255	Ryne Sandberg	.75
256	Don Mattingly	1.00
257	Don Mattingly	1.00
258	Roger Clemens	.85
259	Roger Clemens	.85
260	Roger Clemens	.85
261	Roger Clemens	.85
262	Roger Clemens	.85
263	Roger Clemens	.85
264	Roger Clemens	.85
265	Rickey Henderson	.65
266	Rickey Henderson	.65
267	Jose Canseco	.40
268	Barry Bonds	2.00
269	Barry Bonds	2.00
270	Barry Bonds	2.00
271	Barry Bonds	2.00
272	Jeff Bagwell	.65
273	Kirby Puckett	.75
274	Kirby Puckett	.75
275	Greg Maddux	.75
276	Greg Maddux	.75
277	Greg Maddux	.75
278	Greg Maddux	.75
279	Ken Griffey Jr.	1.00
280	Mike Piazza	1.00
281	Kirby Puckett	.75
282	Mike Piazza	1.00
283	Frank Thomas	.65
284	Hideo Nomo	.65
285	Randy Johnson	.65
286	Juan Gonzalez	.65
287	Derek Jeter	2.00
288	Derek Jeter	2.00
289	Derek Jeter	2.00
290	Nomar Garciaparra	1.00
291	Pedro J. Martinez	.65
292	Kerry Wood	.50
293	Sammy Sosa	1.00
294	Chipper Jones	.75
295	Ivan Rodriguez	.50
296	Ivan Rodriguez	.50
297	Albert Pujols	1.50
298	Ichiro Suzuki	1.00
299	Ichiro Suzuki	1.00
300	Ichiro Suzuki	1.00
301	So Taguchi **RC**	1.00
302	Kazuhisa Ishii **RC**	2.00
303	Jeremy Lambert **RC**	.50
304	Sean Burroughs	.40
305	P.J. Bevis **RC**	.50
306	Jon Rauch	.40
307	Scotty Layfield **RC**	.50
308	Miguel Ascencio	.40
309	Franklyn German **RC**	.50
310	Luis Ugueto **RC**	.50
311	Jorge Sosa **RC**	.50
312	Felix Escalona **RC**	.50
313	Jose Valverde **RC**	.50
314	Jeremy Ward **RC**	.50
315	Kevin Gryboski **RC**	.50
316	Francis Beltran **RC**	.50
317	Joe Thurston	.40
318	Cliff Lee **RC**	3.00
319	Takahito Nomura **RC**	.50
320	Bill Hall	.40
321	Marlon Byrd	.50
322	Andy Shibilo **RC**	.50
323	Edwin Almonte **RC**	.50
324	Brandon Backe **RC**	.40
325	Chone Figgins **RC**	1.50
326	Brian Mallette **RC**	.50
327	Rodrigo Rosario **RC**	.50
328	Anderson Machado **RC**	.50
329	Jorge Padilla **RC**	.50
330	Allan Simpson **RC**	.50
331	Doug DeVore **RC**	.50
332	Drew Henson	.50
333	Raul Chavez **RC**	.50
334	Tom Shearn **RC**	.50
335	Ben Howard **RC**	.50
336	Chris Baker **RC**	.50
337	Travis Hughes **RC**	.50
338	Kevin Mench	.40
339	Brian Tallet	.40
340	Mike Moriarty **RC**	.50
341	Corey Thurman **RC**	.50
342	Terry Pearson **RC**	.50
343	Steve Kent **RC**	.50
344	Satoru Komiyama **RC**	.50
345	Jason Lane	.40
346	Freddy Sanchez **RC**	.50
347	Brandon Puffer **RC**	.50
348	Clay Condrey **RC**	.50
349	Rene Reyes **RC**	.50
350	Hee Seop Choi	.50
351	Rodrigo Lopez	.40
352	Colin Young **RC**	.50
353	Jason Simontacchi **RC**	.50
354	Oliver Perez **RC**	2.00
355	Kirk Saarloos	.50
356	Marcus Thames	.40
357	Jeff Austin **RC**	.50
358	Justin Kaye	.40
359	Julio Mateo **RC**	.50
360	Mike Smith **RC**	.50
361	Chris Snelling **RC**	.75
362	Dennis Tankersley	.40
363	Runelvys Hernandez **RC**	.50
364	Aaron Cook **RC**	.50
365	Joe Borchard	.40
366	Earl Snyder **RC**	.50
367	Shane Nance **RC**	.50
368	Aaron Guiel **RC**	.50
369	Steve Bechler **RC**	.50
370	Tim Kalita **RC**	.50
371	Shawn Sedlacek **RC**	.50
372	Eric Good **RC**	.50
373	Eric Junge **RC**	.50
374	Matt Thornton	.40
375	Travis Driskill **RC**	.50
376	Mitch Wylie **RC**	.50
377	John Ennis **RC**	.50
378	Reed Johnson **RC**	.75
379	Juan Brito **RC**	.50
380	Ron Calloway **RC**	.50
381	Adrian Burnside **RC**	.50
382	Josh Bard **RC**	.50
383	Matt Childers **RC**	.50
384	Gustavo Chacin **RC**	.50
385	Luis Martinez **RC**	.50
386	Trey Hodges **RC**	.50
387	Hansel Izquierdo **RC**	.50
388	Jeriome Robertson **RC**	.50
389	Victor Alvarez **RC**	.50
390	David Ross **RC**	.50
391	Ron Chiavacci	.40
392	Adam Walker **RC**	.50
393	Mike Gonzalez **RC**	.50
394	John Foster **RC**	.50
395	Kyle Kane **RC**	.50
396	Cam Esslinger **RC**	.50
397	Kevin Frederick **RC**	.50
398	Franklin Nunez **RC**	.50
399	Todd Donovan **RC**	.50
400	Kevin Cash **RC**	.50

Statistical Standouts

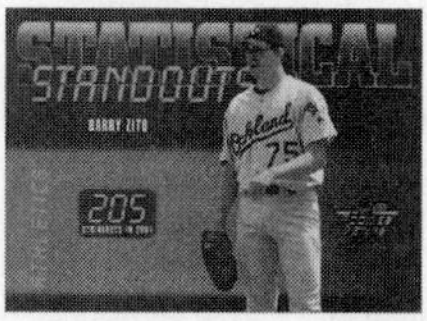

		NM/M
Complete Set (50):		120.00
Common Player:		1.50
Inserted 1:12		
1	Adam Dunn	2.50
2	Alex Rodriguez	8.00
3	Andruw Jones	4.00
4	Brian Giles	1.50
5	Chipper Jones	5.00
6	Cliff Floyd	1.50
7	Craig Biggio	1.50
8	Frank Thomas	4.00
9	Fred McGriff	1.50
10	Garret Anderson	1.50
11	Greg Maddux	5.00
12	Luis Gonzalez	1.50
13	Magglio Ordonez	1.50
14	Ivan Rodriguez	3.00
15	Ken Griffey Jr.	6.00
16	Ichiro Suzuki	6.00
17	Jason Giambi	2.50
18	Derek Jeter	10.00
19	Sammy Sosa	6.00
20	Albert Pujols	8.00
21	J.D. Drew	1.50
22	Jeff Bagwell	4.00
23	Jim Edmonds	1.50
24	Jose Vidro	1.50
25	Juan Encarnacion	1.50
26	Kerry Wood	3.00
27	Al Leiter	1.50
28	Curt Schilling	2.50
29	Manny Ramirez	4.00
30	Lance Berkman	1.50
31	Miguel Tejada	1.50
32	Mike Piazza	6.00
33	Nomar Garciaparra	6.00
34	Omar Vizquel	1.50
35	Pat Burrell	2.00
36	Paul Konerko	1.50
37	Rafael Palmeiro	3.00
38	Randy Johnson	4.00
39	Richie Sexson	1.50
40	Roger Clemens	5.50
41	Shawn Green	2.00
42	Todd Helton	4.00
43	Tom Glavine	1.50
44	Troy Glaus	4.00
45	Vladimir Guerrero	4.00
46	Mike Sweeney	1.50
47	Alfonso Soriano	3.00
48	Barry Zito	1.50
49	John Smoltz	1.50
50	Ellis Burks	1.50

Freshman Orientation

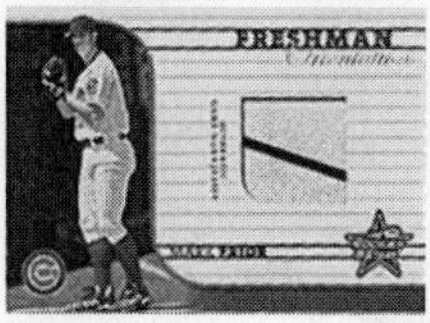

		NM/M
Common Player:		5.00
Inserted 1:142		
Class Officer Parallel:		1.5X
Production 50 Sets		
1	Andres Torres/Bat	8.00
2	Mark Ellis/Jsy	8.00
3	Erik Bedard/Bat	8.00
4	Delvin James/Jsy	5.00
5	Austin Kearns/Bat	10.00
6	Josh Pearce/Bat	5.00
7	Rafael Soriano/Jsy	8.00
8	Jason Lane/Bat	8.00
9	Mark Prior/Jsy	15.00
10	Alfredo Amezaga/Bat	5.00
11	Ryan Ludwick/Bat	5.00
12	So Taguchi/Bat	10.00
13	Duaner Sanchez/Bat	5.00
14	Kazuhisa Ishii/Jsy	15.00
15	Zach Day/Jsy	8.00
16	Eric Cyr/Bat	5.00
17	Francis Beltran/Jsy	5.00
18	Joe Borchard/Jsy	10.00
19	Jeremy Affeldt/Shoe	10.00
20	Alexis Gomez/Jsy	5.00

Dress For Success

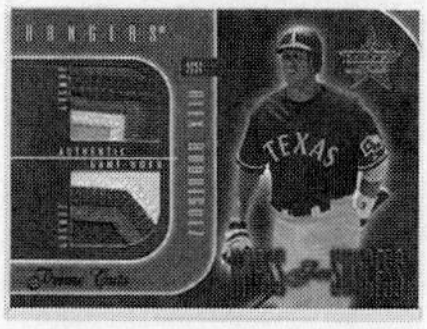

		NM/M
Common Player:		8.00
Production 250 Sets		
Prime Cuts:		Not Priced
Production 25 Sets		
1	Mike Piazza	25.00
2	Cal Ripken Jr.	40.00
3	Carlos Delgado	8.00
4	Chipper Jones	20.00
5	Bernie Williams	8.00
6	Carlos Beltran	10.00
7	Curt Schilling	10.00
8	Greg Maddux	20.00
9	Ivan Rodriguez	12.00
10	Alex Rodriguez	20.00
11	Roger Clemens	20.00
12	Todd Helton	15.00
13	Jim Edmonds	8.00
14	Manny Ramirez	15.00
15	Mark Buehrle	8.00

BLC Homers

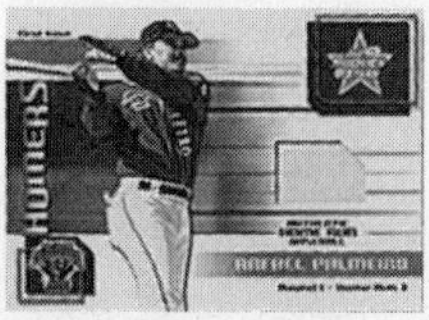

		NM/M
Common Player:		20.00
Production 25 Sets		
1-3	Luis Gonzalez	20.00
4-11	Todd Helton	35.00
12-14	Jim Thome	35.00
15-19	Rafael Palmeiro	30.00
20-22	Troy Glaus	35.00
23-25	Gary Sheffield	20.00
26-30	Mike Piazza	50.00

Triple Threads

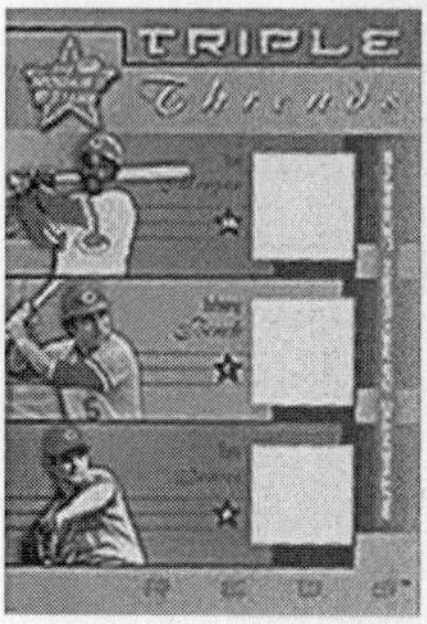

		NM/M
Common Card:		25.00
Production 100 Sets		
1	Reggie Jackson, Alfonso Soriano, Don Mattingly	80.00
2	Alex Rodriguez, Rafael Palmeiro, Ivan Rodriguez	30.00
3	Mike Piazza, Gary Carter, Rickey Henderson	40.00
4	Dale Murphy, Andruw Jones, Chipper Jones	40.00
5	Mike Schmidt, Steve Carlton, Scott Rolen	85.00
6	Rickey Henderson	40.00
7	Johnny Bench, Joe Morgan, Tom Seaver	50.00
8	Randy Johnson, Pedro J. Martinez, Vladimir Guerrero	35.00
9	Nolan Ryan, Rod Carew, Troy Glaus	75.00
10	Lou Brock, J.D. Drew, Stan Musial	65.00

View Masters

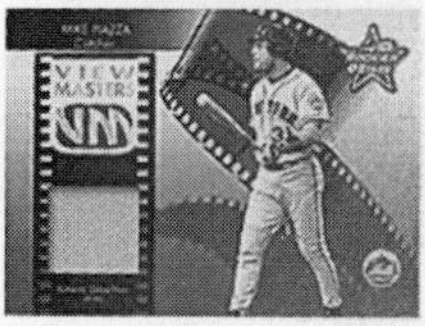

		NM/M
Common Player:		10.00
Production 100 Sets		
Slideshows:		Not Priced
Production 25 Sets		
1	Carlos Delgado	12.00
2	Todd Helton	20.00
3	Tony Gwynn	25.00
4	Bernie Williams	10.00
5	Luis Gonzalez	10.00
6	Larry Walker	10.00
7	Troy Glaus	20.00
8	Alfonso Soriano	15.00
9	Curt Schilling	12.00
10	Chipper Jones	25.00
11	Vladimir Guerrero	20.00
12	Adam Dunn	15.00
13	Rickey Henderson	20.00
14	Miguel Tejada	10.00
15	Kazuhisa Ishii	10.00
16	Greg Maddux	25.00
17	Pedro J. Martinez	20.00
18	Nomar Garciaparra	30.00
19	Mike Piazza	30.00
20	Lance Berkman	10.00

Great American Signings

	NM/M
Common Autograph:	5.00
Inserted 1:56	
Brent Abernathy/175	5.00
Brandon Backe/175	5.00
Chris Baker/175	5.00
Francis Beltran/175	5.00
Raul Chavez/175	5.00
Doug DeVore/175	5.00
Felix Escalona/100	8.00
Franklyn German/175	5.00
Jay Gibbons/150	10.00
Bill Hall/175	8.00
Drew Henson/50	35.00

Eric Hinske/175	8.00
Ben Howard/175	5.00
Aubrey Huff/175	8.00
Travis Hughes/175	5.00
Cesar Izturis/175	8.00
Nick Johnson/175	8.00
Austin Kearns/75	10.00
Satoru Komiyama/75	20.00
Jason Lane/150	8.00
Brian Lawrence/175	5.00
Anderson Machado/175	5.00
Roy Oswalt/100	15.00
Jorge Padilla/175	5.00
Oliver Perez/175	20.00
Rene Reyes/175	5.00
Mike Rivera/175	5.00
Rodrigo Rosario/175	5.00
Tom Shearn/175	5.00
Chris Snelling/175	10.00
Mac Suzuki/100	30.00
So Taguchi/50	40.00
Dennis Tankersley/175	5.00
Corey Thurman/175	5.00
Luis Ugueto/175	5.00
Kip Wells/175	5.00

Stat. Standouts Materials

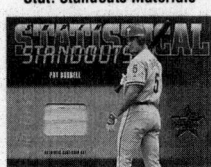

	NM/M
Common Player:	5.00
Inserted 1:69	
Super Materials:	2-3X
Production 25 Sets	
1 Adam Dunn/Bat/200	15.00
2 Alex Rodriguez/Bat/200	15.00
3 Andruw Jones/Bat/200	10.00
4 Brian Giles/Bat	8.00
5 Chipper Jones/Bat/200	15.00
6 Cliff Floyd/Jsy	5.00
7 Craig Biggio/Jsy	8.00
8 Frank Thomas/Jsy/125	12.00
9 Fred McGriff/Bat	10.00
10 Garret Anderson/Bat	8.00
11 Greg Maddux/Jsy/200	20.00
12 Luis Gonzalez/Jsy	8.00
13 Magglio Ordonez/Bat/150	10.00
14 Ivan Rodriguez/Jsy/100	15.00
15 Ken Griffey Jr./Base/100	15.00
16 Ichiro Suzuki/Base/100	30.00
17 Jason Giambi/Base	10.00
18 Derek Jeter/Base/100	25.00
19 Sammy Sosa/Base/100	15.00
20 Albert Pujols/Base/100	15.00
21 J.D. Drew/Bat/150	10.00
22 Jeff Bagwell/Jsy/150	15.00
23 Jim Edmonds/Bat	8.00
24 Jose Vidro/Bat	5.00
25 Juan Encarnacion/Bat	5.00
26 Kerry Wood/Jsy/200	5.00
27 Al Leiter/Jsy	8.00
28 Curt Schilling/Jsy/225	12.00
29 Manny Ramirez/Bat/100	15.00
30 Lance Berkman/Bat/150	10.00
31 Miguel Tejada/Jsy	10.00
32 Mike Piazza/Bat/200	20.00
33 Nomar Garciaparra/Bat/200	20.00
34 Omar Vizquel/Jsy	8.00
35 Pat Burrell/Bat	10.00
36 Paul Konerko/Jsy	6.00
37 Rafael Palmeiro/Bat	8.00
38 Randy Johnson/Jsy/200	15.00
39 Richie Sexson/Jsy	5.00
40 Roger Clemens/Jsy/200	20.00
41 Shawn Green/Jsy	5.00
42 Todd Helton/Jsy/175	15.00
43 Tom Glavine/Jsy/125	10.00
44 Troy Glaus/Jsy	10.00
45 Vladimir Guerrero/Jsy	15.00
46 Mike Sweeney/Bat	5.00
47 Alfonso Soriano/Jsy/200	15.00
48 Barry Zito/Jsy/100	8.00
49 John Smoltz/Jsy	8.00
50 Ellis Burks/Jsy	5.00

Longevity

Stars (1-300):	5-10X
SP's (1-300):	1-3X
Production 100	
Rookies (301-400):	Not Pricing
Production 25	

2003 Leaf

	NM/M
Complete Set (320):	40.00
Common Player:	.15
Pack (10):	1.50
Box (24):	30.00
1 Brad Fullmer	.15
2 Darin Erstad	.25
3 David Eckstein	.15
4 Garret Anderson	.15
5 Jarrod Washburn	.15
6 Kevin Appier	.15
7 Tim Salmon	.25
8 Troy Glaus	.75
9 Troy Percival	.15
10 Buddy Groom	.15
11 Jay Gibbons	.15
12 Jeff Conine	.15
13 Marty Cordova	.15
14 Melvin Mora	.15
15 Rodrigo Lopez	.15
16 Tony Batista	.15
17 Jorge Julio	.15
18 Cliff Floyd	.15
19 Derek Lowe	.15
20 Jason Varitek	.15
21 Johnny Damon	.25
22 Manny Ramirez	.75
23 Nomar Garciaparra	1.25
24 Pedro J. Martinez	.75
25 Rickey Henderson	.75
26 Shea Hillenbrand	.15
27 Trot Nixon	.15
28 Carlos Lee	.15
29 Frank Thomas	.75
30 Jose Valentin	.15
31 Magglio Ordonez	.15
32 Mark Buehrle	.15
33 Paul Konerko	.25
34 C.C. Sabathia	.15
35 Danys Baez	.15
36 Ellis Burks	.15
37 Jim Thome	.75
38 Omar Vizquel	.15
39 Ricky Gutierrez	.15
40 Travis Fryman	.15
41 Bobby Higginson	.15
42 Carlos Pena	.15
43 Juan Acevedo	.15
44 Mark Redman	.15
45 Randall Simon	.15
46 Robert Fick	.15
47 Steve Sparks	.15
48 Carlos Beltran	.50
49 Joe Randa	.15
50 Michael Tucker	.15

51 Mike Sweeney	.15
52 Paul Byrd	.15
53 Raul Ibanez	.15
54 Runelvys Hernandez	.15
55 A.J. Pierzynski	.15
56 Brad Radke	.15
57 Corey Koskie	.15
58 Cristian Guzman	.15
59 David Ortiz	.50
60 Doug Mientkiewicz	.15
61 Dustan Mohr	.15
62 Eddie Guardado	.15
63 Jacque Jones	.15
64 Torii Hunter	.15
65 Alfonso Soriano	.50
66 Andy Pettitte	.35
67 Bernie Williams	.30
68 David Wells	.15
69 Derek Jeter	2.00
70 Jason Giambi	.40
71 Jeff Weaver	.15
72 Jorge Posada	.25
73 Mike Mussina	.30
74 Nick Johnson	.15
75 Raul Mondesi	.15
76 Robin Ventura	.15
77 Roger Clemens	1.00
78 Barry Zito	.25
79 Billy Koch	.15
80 David Justice	.15
81 Eric Chavez	.25
82 Jermaine Dye	.15
83 Mark Mulder	.15
84 Miguel Tejada	.30
85 Ray Durham	.15
86 Scott Hatteberg	.15
87 Ted Lilly	.15
88 Tim Hudson	.25
89 Bret Boone	.15
90 Carlos Guillen	.15
91 Chris Snelling	.15
92 Dan Wilson	.15
93 Edgar Martinez	.15
94 Freddy Garcia	.15
95 Ichiro Suzuki	1.25
96 Jamie Moyer	.15
97 Joel Pineiro	.15
98 John Olerud	.15
99 Mark McLemore	.15
100 Mike Cameron	.15
101 Kazuhiro Sasaki	.15
102 Aubrey Huff	.15
103 Ben Grieve	.15
104 Joe Kennedy	.15
105 Paul Wilson	.15
106 Randy Winn	.15
107 Steve Cox	.15
108 Alex Rodriguez	1.50
109 Chan Ho Park	.15
110 Hank Blalock	.50
111 Herbert Perry	.15
112 Ivan Rodriguez	.65
113 Juan Gonzalez	.75
114 Kenny Rogers	.15
115 Kevin Mench	.15
116 Rafael Palmeiro	.65
117 Carlos Delgado	.40
118 Eric Hinske	.15
119 Jose Cruz	.15
120 Josh Phelps	.15
121 Roy Halladay	.25
122 Shannon Stewart	.15
123 Vernon Wells	.15
124 Curt Schilling	.40
125 Junior Spivey	.15
126 Luis Gonzalez	.25
127 Mark Grace	.25
128 Randy Johnson	.75
129 Steve Finley	.15
130 Tony Womack	.15
131 Andruw Jones	.75
132 Chipper Jones	1.00
133 Gary Sheffield	.30
134 Greg Maddux	1.00
135 John Smoltz	.15
136 Kevin Millwood	.15
137 Rafael Furcal	.15
138 Tom Glavine	.40
139 Alex Gonzalez	.15
140 Corey Patterson	.15
141 Fred McGriff	.15
142 Jon Lieber	.15
143 Kerry Wood	.65
144 Mark Prior	.75
145 Matt Clement	.15
146 Moises Alou	.15
147 Sammy Sosa	1.25
148 Aaron Boone	.15
149 Adam Dunn	.50
150 Austin Kearns	.15
151 Barry Larkin	.15
152 Danny Graves	.15
153 Elmer Dessens	.15
154 Ken Griffey Jr.	1.25
155 Sean Casey	.25
156 Todd Walker	.15
157 Todd Kapler	.15
158 Jason Jennings	.15
159 Jay Payton	.15
160 Larry Walker	.15
161 Mike Hampton	.15
162 Todd Helton	.75
163 Todd Zeile	.15
164 A.J. Burnett	.15
165 Derrek Lee	.15

166 Josh Beckett	.50
167 Juan Encarnacion	.15
168 Luis Castillo	.15
169 Mike Lowell	.15
170 Preston Wilson	.15
171 Billy Wagner	.15
172 Craig Biggio	.25
173 Daryle Ward	.15
174 Jeff Bagwell	.75
175 Lance Berkman	.15
176 Octavio Dotel	.15
177 Richard Hidalgo	.15
178 Roy Oswalt	.25
179 Adrian Beltre	.40
180 Eric Gagne	.40
181 Eric Karros	.15
182 Hideo Nomo	.65
183 Kazuhisa Ishii	.15
184 Kevin Brown	.15
185 Mark Grudzielanek	.15
186 Odalis Perez	.15
187 Paul LoDuca	.15
188 Shawn Green	.40
189 Alex Sanchez	.15
190 Ben Sheets	.15
191 Jeffrey Hammonds	.15
192 Jose Hernandez	.15
193 Takahito Nomura	.15
194 Richie Sexson	.15
195 Andres Galarraga	.15
196 Bartolo Colon	.15
197 Brad Wilkerson	.15
198 Javier Vazquez	.15
199 Jose Vidro	.15
200 Michael Barrett	.15
201 Tomokazu Ohka	.15
202 Vladimir Guerrero	.75
203 Al Leiter	.15
204 Armando Benitez	.15
205 Edgardo Alfonzo	.15
206 Mike Piazza	1.25
207 Mo Vaughn	.15
208 Pedro Astacio	.15
209 Roberto Alomar	.35
210 Roger Cedeno	.15
211 Timoniel Perez	.15
212 Bobby Abreu	.15
213 Jimmy Rollins	.25
214 Mike Lieberthal	.15
215 Pat Burrell	.25
216 Randy Wolf	.15
217 Travis Lee	.15
218 Vicente Padilla	.15
219 Aramis Ramirez	.15
220 Brian Giles	.15
221 Craig Wilson	.15
222 Jason Kendall	.15
223 Josh Fogg	.15
224 Kevin Young	.15
225 Kip Wells	.15
226 Mike Williams	.15
227 Brett Tomko	.15
228 Brian Lawrence	.15
229 Mark Kotsay	.15
230 Oliver Perez	.15
231 Phil Nevin	.15
232 Ryan Klesko	.15
233 Sean Burroughs	.15
234 Trevor Hoffman	.15
235 Barry Bonds	2.00
236 Benito Santiago	.15
237 Jeff Kent	.15
238 Kirk Rueter	.15
239 Livan Hernandez	.15
240 Kenny Lofton	.15
241 Rich Aurilia	.15
242 Russ Ortiz	.15
243 Albert Pujols	1.50
244 Edgar Renteria	.15
245 J.D. Drew	.40
246 Jason Isringhausen	.15
247 Jim Edmonds	.40
248 Matt Morris	.15
249 Tino Martinez	.15
250 Scott Rolen	.75
251 Curt Schilling	.25
252 Ivan Rodriguez	.35
253 Mike Piazza	.75
254 Sammy Sosa	.75
255 Matt Williams	.15
256 Frank Thomas	.25
257 Barry Bonds	1.00
258 Roger Clemens	.65
259 Rickey Henderson	.25
260 Ken Griffey Jr.	.60
261 Greg Maddux	.50
262 Randy Johnson	.40
263 Jeff Bagwell	.25
264 Roberto Alomar	.25
265 Tom Glavine	.25
266 Juan Gonzalez	.25
267 Mark Grace	.25
268 Mike Mussina	.25
269 Ryan Klesko	.15
270 Fred McGriff	.15
271 Joe Borchard	.15
272 Chris Snelling	.15
273 Brian Tallet	.15
274 Cliff Lee	.25
275 Freddy Sanchez	.15
276 Chone Figgins	.15
277 Kevin Cash	.15
278 Josh Bard	.15
279 Jeriome Robertson	.15
280 Jeremy Hill	.15

281	Shane Nance	.15
282	Jeff Baker	.15
283	Trey Hodges	.15
284	Eric Eckenstahler	.15
285	Jim Rushford	.15
286	Carlos Rivera	.15
287	Josh Bonifay	.15
288	Garrett Atkins	.15
289	Nic Jackson	.15
290	Corwin Malone	.15
291	Jimmy Gobble	.15
292	Josh Wilson	.15
293	Clint Barmes **RC**	.50
294	Jon Adkins	.15
295	Tim Kalita	.15
296	Nelson Castro	.15
297	Colin Young	.15
298	Adrian Burnside	.15
299	Luis Martinez	.15
300	Termel Sledge **RC**	.50
301	Todd Donovan	.15
302	Jeremy Ward	.15
303	Wilson Valdez	.15
304	Jose Contreras **RC**	.75
305	Marshall McDougall	.15
306	Mitch Wylie	.15
307	Ron Calloway	.15
308	Jose Valverde	.15
309	Jason Davis	.15
310	Scotty Layfield	.15
311	Matt Thornton	.15
312	Adam Walker	.15
313	Gustavo Chacin	.15
314	Ron Chiavacci	.15
315	Wilbert Nieves	.15
316	Clifford Bartosh	.15
317	Mike Gonzalez	.15
318	Jeremy Guthrie	.15
319	Eric Junge	.15
320	Ben Kozlowski	.15

Red Press Proofs

Stars: 3-5X
Inserted 1:12

Blue Press Proofs

Stars: 8-15X
Production 50 Sets

Green

No Pricing
Production 25 Sets

Clean Up Crew

		NM/M
Complete Set (10):		30.00
Common Card:		1.50
Inserted 1:49		
1	Alex Rodriguez, Rafael Palmeiro, Ivan Rodriguez	6.00
2	Nomar Garciaparra, Manny Ramirez, Cliff Floyd	5.00
3	Jason Giambi, Bernie Williams, Jorge Posada	4.00
4	Rich Aurilia, Jeff Kent, Barry Bonds	6.00
5	Larry Walker, Todd Helton, Jay Payton	1.50
6	Lance Berkman, Jeff Bagwell, Daryle Ward	2.00
7	Scott Rolen, Albert Pujols, Jim Edmonds	5.00
8	Gary Sheffield, Chipper Jones, Andruw Jones	4.00
9	Miguel Tejada, Eric Chavez, Jermaine Dye	1.50
10	Sammy Sosa, Moises Alou, Fred McGriff	4.00

Clean Up Crew Memorabilia

		NM/M
Production 50 Sets		
1	Alex Rodriguez, Rafael Palmeiro, Ivan Rodriguez	30.00
2	Nomar Garciaparra, Manny Ramirez, Cliff Floyd	25.00
3	Jason Giambi, Bernie Williams, Jorge Posada	25.00
4	Rich Aurilia, Jeff Kent, Barry Bonds	35.00
5	Larry Walker, Todd Helton, Jay Payton	20.00
6	Lance Berkman, Jeff Bagwell, Daryle Ward	25.00
7	Scott Rolen, Albert Pujols, Jim Edmonds	40.00
8	Gary Sheffield, Chipper Jones, Andruw Jones	30.00
9	Miguel Tejada, Eric Chavez, Jermaine Dye	30.00
10	Sammy Sosa, Moises Alou, Fred McGriff	30.00

Clubhouse Signatures Bronze

		NM/M
Common Bronze Auto:		8.00
Inserted 1:300		
Silvers:		1-2X
Production 100 Sets		
Golds:		No Pricing
Production 25 Sets		
	Edwin Almonte	8.00
	Jeff Baker	10.00
	Josh Bard	10.00
	Angel Berroa	8.00
	Joe Crede/SP/25	15.00
	Andre Dawson/SP/50	25.00
	Bobby Doerr/SP/100	20.00
	Dwight "Doc" Gooden	25.00
	Drew Henson/SP/50	20.00
	Eric Hinske	10.00
	Torii Hunter/SP/75	35.00
	Omar Infante	8.00
	Brian Lawrence	8.00
	Kevin Mench	8.00
	Jack Morris/SP/100	15.00
	Franklin Nunez	8.00
	Magglio Ordonez/SP/50	25.00
	Corey Patterson/SP/100	15.00
	Jhonny Peralta	20.00
	J.C. Romero	10.00
	Chris Snelling/SP/100	10.00
	Alfonso Soriano/SP/25	40.00
	Brian Tallet/SP/100	8.00

Game Collection

		NM/M
Common Player:		8.00
Production 150 Sets		
1	Miguel Tejada/Cap	10.00
2	Shannon Stewart/Cap	6.00
3	Mike Schmidt/Jkt	40.00
4	Nolan Ryan/Jkt	75.00
5	Rafael Palmeiro/Glv	15.00
6	Andruw Jones/Shoe	10.00
7	Bernie Williams/Shoe	15.00
8	Ivan Rodriguez/Shoe	10.00
9	Lance Berkman/Shoe	10.00
10	Magglio Ordonez/Shoe	10.00
11	Roy Oswalt/Glv	10.00
12	Andy Pettitte/Shoe	10.00
13	Vladimir Guerrero/Glv	30.00
14	Jason Jennings/Glv	8.00
15	Mike Sweeney/Shoe	8.00
16	Joe Borchard/Shoe	10.00
17	Mark Prior/Shoe	10.00
18	Gary Carter/Jkt	10.00
19	Austin Kearns/Glv	10.00
20	Ryan Klesko/Glv	10.00

Gold Leaf Rookies

		NM/M
Complete Set (10):		10.00
Common Player:		1.00
Inserted 1:24		
Mirror Golds:		10-20X
Production 25 Sets		
1	Joe Borchard	1.00
2	Chone Figgins	1.00

3	Alexis Gomez	1.00
4	Chris Snelling	1.00
5	Cliff Lee	1.00
6	Victor Martinez	2.00
7	Hee Seop Choi	1.50
8	Michael Restovich	1.00
9	Anderson Machado	1.00
10	Drew Henson	2.00

Hard Hats

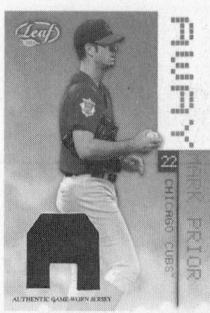

AUTHENTIC GAME-WORN JERSEY

		NM/M
Complete Set (12):		15.00
Common Player:		1.00
Inserted 1:13		
1	Alex Rodriguez	4.00
2	Bernie Williams	1.00
3	Ivan Rodriguez	1.25
4	Jeff Bagwell	1.50
5	Rafael Furcal	1.00
6	Rafael Palmeiro	1.50
7	Tony Gwynn	2.00
8	Vladimir Guerrero	1.50
9	Adrian Beltre	1.00
10	Shawn Green	1.00
11	Andruw Jones	1.50
12	George Brett	5.00

Hard Hats Batting Helmets

		NM/M
Common Player:		15.00
Production 100 Sets		
1	Alex Rodriguez	50.00
2	Bernie Williams	35.00
3	Ivan Rodriguez	30.00
4	Jeff Bagwell	40.00
5	Rafael Furcal	15.00
6	Rafael Palmeiro	35.00
7	Tony Gwynn	35.00
8	Vladimir Guerrero	35.00
9	Adrian Beltre	20.00
10	Shawn Green	20.00
11	Andruw Jones	20.00
12	George Brett	100.00

Home / Away

		NM/M
Complete Set (20):		40.00
Common Player:		1.00
Home Inserted 1:34		
1	Andruw Jones/Home	1.50
2	Cal Ripken Jr./Home	6.00
3	Edgar Martinez/Home	1.00
4	Jim Thome/Home	1.50
5	Larry Walker/Home	1.00
6	Nomar Garciaparra/Home	4.00
7	Mark Prior/Home	1.00
8	Mike Piazza/Home	4.00
9	Vladimir Guerrero/Home	1.50
10	Chipper Jones/Home	3.00
Away Inserted 1:34		
1	Andruw Jones	1.50
2	Cal Ripken Jr.	6.00
3	Edgar Martinez	1.00
4	Jim Thome	2.00
5	Larry Walker	1.00
6	Nomar Garciaparra	4.00
7	Mark Prior	1.00
8	Mike Piazza	4.00
9	Vladimir Guerrero	2.00
10	Chipper Jones	3.00

Home / Away Memorabilia

		NM/M
Common Player:		6.00
Home Production 250		
1	Andruw Jones/Home	8.00
2	Cal Ripken Jr./Home	45.00
3	Edgar Martinez/Home	8.00
4	Jim Thome/Home	10.00
5	Larry Walker/Home	8.00
6	Nomar Garciaparra/Home	20.00
7	Mark Prior/Home	10.00
8	Mike Piazza/Home	15.00
9	Vladimir Guerrero/Home	12.00
10	Chipper Jones/Home	15.00
Away Production 250		
1	Andruw Jones	8.00
2	Cal Ripken Jr.	45.00
3	Edgar Martinez	8.00
4	Jim Thome	10.00
5	Larry Walker	6.00
6	Nomar Garciaparra	20.00
7	Mark Prior	10.00
8	Mike Piazza	15.00
9	Vladimir Guerrero	12.00
10	Chipper Jones	15.00

Maple & Ash

		NM/M
Common Player:		6.00
Production 400 Sets		
1	Jorge Posada	8.00
2	Mike Piazza	12.00
3	Alex Rodriguez	15.00
4	Jeff Bagwell	10.00
5	Joe Borchard	6.00
6	Miguel Tejada	6.00
7	Adam Dunn	8.00
8	Jim Thome	8.00
9	Lance Berkman	6.00
10	Torii Hunter	6.00
11	Carlos Delgado	6.00
12	Reggie Jackson	10.00
13	Juan Gonzalez	6.00
14	Vladimir Guerrero	10.00
15	Richie Sexson	6.00

Number Off My Back

		NM/M
Production 50 Sets		
1	Carlos Delgado	15.00
2	Don Mattingly	100.00
3	Todd Helton	30.00
4	Vernon Wells	10.00
5	Bernie Williams	20.00
6	Luis Gonzalez	20.00
7	Kerry Wood	30.00
8	Eric Chavez	10.00
9	Shawn Green	15.00
10	Roy Oswalt	15.00
11	Nomar Garciaparra	40.00
12	Robin Yount	60.00
13	Troy Glaus	20.00
14	C.C. Sabathia	10.00
15	Alex Rodriguez	50.00
16	Mark Mulder	10.00
17	Will Clark	60.00
18	Alfonso Soriano	30.00
19	Andy Pettitte	20.00
20	Curt Schilling	25.00

Shirt Off My Back

		NM/M
Common Player:		5.00
Production 500 Sets		
Number Off My Back:		2-4X
Production 50 Sets		
1	Carlos Delgado	6.00
2	Don Mattingly	25.00
3	Todd Helton	10.00
4	Vernon Wells	6.00
5	Bernie Williams	6.00
6	Luis Gonzalez	6.00
7	Kerry Wood	8.00
8	Eric Chavez	6.00
9	Shawn Green	6.00
10	Roy Oswalt	5.00
11	Nomar Garciaparra	12.00

12	Robin Yount	15.00
13	Troy Glaus	8.00
14	C.C. Sabathia	5.00
15	Alex Rodriguez	15.00
16	Mark Mulder	5.00
17	Will Clark	10.00
18	Alfonso Soriano	10.00
19	Andy Pettitte	8.00
20	Curt Schilling	8.00

Slick Leather

Slick LEATHER

NM/M
Complete Set (15): 20.00
Common Player: 1.00
Inserted 1:21

1	Omar Vizquel	1.00
2	Roberto Alomar	1.50
3	Ivan Rodriguez	2.00
4	Greg Maddux	3.00
5	Scott Rolen	2.00
6	Todd Helton	2.00
7	Andruw Jones	2.00
8	Jim Edmonds	1.50
9	Barry Bonds	6.00
10	Eric Chavez	1.00
11	Ichiro Suzuki	5.00
12	Mike Mussina	1.50
13	John Olerud	1.00
14	Torii Hunter	1.00
15	Larry Walker	1.00

60

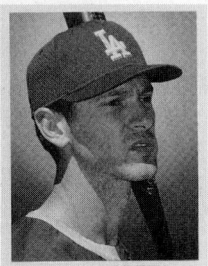

SHAWN GREEN
OUTFIELD—LOS ANGELES DODGERS®

NM/M
Complete Set (50): 80.00
Common Player: .75
Inserted 1:8
Foil Parallels: 3-5X
Production 60 Sets

1	Troy Glaus	3.00
2	Curt Schilling	2.00
3	Randy Johnson	3.00
4	Andruw Jones	3.00
5	Chipper Jones	4.00
6	Greg Maddux	4.00
7	Tom Glavine	1.00
8	Manny Ramirez	3.00
9	Nomar Garciaparra	5.00
10	Pedro J. Martinez	3.00
11	Rickey Henderson	3.00
12	Sammy Sosa	5.00
13	Frank Thomas	3.00
14	Magglio Ordonez	.75
15	Mark Buehrle	.75
16	Adam Dunn	1.50
17	Ken Griffey Jr.	5.00
18	Jim Thome	2.00
19	Omar Vizquel	.75
20	Larry Walker	.75
21	Todd Helton	3.00
22	Lance Berkman	.75
23	Roy Oswalt	.75
24	Mike Sweeney	.75
25	Hideo Nomo	3.00
26	Kazuhisa Ishii	1.00
27	Shawn Green	1.00
28	Torii Hunter	.75
29	Vladimir Guerrero	3.00
30	Mike Piazza	5.00
31	Alfonso Soriano	3.00
32	Bernie Williams	5.00
33	Derek Jeter	8.00
34	Jason Giambi	2.00
35	Roger Clemens	4.00
36	Barry Zito	.75
37	Miguel Tejada	.75
38	Pat Burrell	1.00
39	Ryan Klesko	.75
40	Barry Bonds	8.00
41	Jeff Kent	.75
42	Ichiro Suzuki	5.00
43	John Olerud	.75
44	Albert Pujols	5.00
45	Jim Edmonds	1.00
46	Scott Rolen	2.50
47	Alex Rodriguez	6.00
48	Ivan Rodriguez	2.50
49	Rafael Palmeiro	2.50
50	Roy Halladay	.75

2003 Leaf Certified Materials

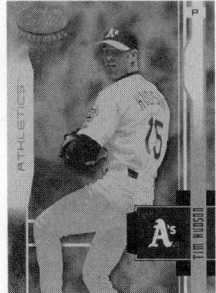

NM/M
Complete Set (250):
Common Player: .50
Common SP Auto. (206-250): .50
Production 400 unless noted.
Mirror Red Auto. SP's (06-250): 1-1.5X
Production 100
Mirror Blue Auto. SP's (206-250): 1-2X
Production 50
Mirror Gold Autos.(206-250): No Pricing
Production 25
Pack (5): 20.00
Box (10): 150.00

1	Troy Glaus	1.00
2	Alfredo Amezaga	.50
3	Garret Anderson	1.00
4	Nolan Ryan	6.00
5	Darin Erstad	.75
6	Junior Spivey	.50
7	Randy Johnson	2.00
8	Curt Schilling	1.50
9	Luis Gonzalez	.75
10	Steve Finley	.50
11	Matt Williams	.75
12	Greg Maddux	3.00
13	Chipper Jones	2.00
14	Gary Sheffield	1.00
15	Adam LaRoche	.50
16	Andruw Jones	1.00
17	Robert Fick	.50
18	John Smoltz	1.00
19	Javy Lopez	.50
20	Jay Gibbons	.50
21	Geronimo Gil	.50
22	Cal Ripken Jr.	6.00
23	Nomar Garciaparra	4.00
24	Pedro J. Martinez	2.00
25	Freddy Sanchez	.50
26	Rickey Henderson	1.00
27	Manny Ramirez	1.50
28	Casey Fossum	.50
29	Sammy Sosa	3.00
30	Kerry Wood	2.00
31	Corey Patterson	1.00
32	Nic Jackson	.50
33	Mark Prior	1.50
34	Juan Cruz	.50
35	Steve Smyth	.50
36	Magglio Ordonez	.75
37	Joe Borchard	.50
38	Frank Thomas	1.50
39	Mark Buehrle	.50
40	Joe Crede	.50
41	Carlos Lee	.50
42	Paul Konerko	.50
43	Adam Dunn	1.50
44	Corky Miller	.50
45	Brandon Larson	.50
46	Ken Griffey Jr.	3.00
47	Barry Larkin	1.00
48	Sean Casey	.50
49	Wily Mo Pena	1.00
50	Austin Kearns	.75
51	Victor Martinez	1.00
52	Brian Tallet	.50
53	Cliff Lee	.50
54	Jeremy Guthrie	.50
55	C.C. Sabathia	.50
56	Ricardo Rodriguez	.50
57	Omar Vizquel	1.00
58	Travis Hafner	.50
59	Todd Helton	1.50
60	Jason Jennings	.50
61	Jeff Baker	.50
62	Larry Walker	.50
63	Travis Chapman	.50
64	Mike Maroth	.50
65	Josh Beckett	1.00
66	Ivan Rodriguez	1.50
67	Brad Penny	.50
68	A.J. Burnett	.50
69	Craig Biggio	1.00
70	Roy Oswalt	1.00
71	Jason Lane	.50
72	Nolan Ryan	6.00
73	Wade Miller	.50
74	Richard Hidalgo	.50
75	Jeff Bagwell	1.00
76	Lance Berkman	1.00
77	Rodrigo Rosario	.50
78	Jeff Kent	1.00
79	John Buck	.50
80	Angel Berroa	.50
81	Mike Sweeney	.50
82	Mac Suzuki	.50
83	Alexis Gomez	.50
84	Carlos Beltran	1.50
85	Runelvys Hernandez	.50
86	Hideo Nomo	1.00
87	Paul LoDuca	.50
88	Cesar Izturis	.50
89	Kazuhisa Ishii	.50
90	Shawn Green	1.00
91	Joe Thurston	.50
92	Adrian Beltre	.50
93	Kevin Brown	1.00
94	Robb Sexson	1.00
95	Ben Sheets	1.00
96	Takahito Nomura	.50
97	Geoff Jenkins	.50
98	Bill Hall	.50
99	Torii Hunter	1.00
100	A.J. Pierzynski	.50
101	Michael Cuddyer	.50
102	Jose Morban	.50
103	Brad Radke	.50
104	Jacque Jones	.50
105	Eric Milton	.50
106	Joe Mays	.50
107	Adam Johnson	.50
108	Javier Vazquez	.50
109	Vladimir Guerrero	2.00
110	Jose Vidro	.50
111	Michael Barrett	.50
112	Orlando Cabrera	.50
113	Tom Glavine	1.00
114	Roberto Alomar	1.00
115	Tsuyoshi Shinjo	.50
116	Cliff Floyd	.50
117	Mike Piazza	3.00
118	Al Leiter	.50
119	Don Mattingly	4.00
120	Roger Clemens	6.00
121	Derek Jeter	6.00
122	Alfonso Soriano	2.00
123	Drew Henson	.50
124	Brandon Claussen	.50
125	Christian Parker	.50
126	Jason Giambi	1.00
127	Mike Mussina	1.00
128	Bernie Williams	1.00
129	Jason Anderson	.50
130	Nick Johnson	.50
131	Jorge Posada	1.00
132	Andy Pettitte	1.00
133	Barry Zito	.50
134	Miguel Tejada	1.00
135	Eric Chavez	1.00
136	Tim Hudson	1.00
137	Mark Mulder	.75
138	Terrence Long	.50
139	Mark Ellis	.50
140	Jim Thome	1.50
141	Pat Burrell	.75
142	Marlon Byrd	.50
143	Bobby Abreu	.75
144	Brandon Duckworth	.50
145	Robert Person	.50
146	Anderson Machado	.50
147	Aramis Ramirez	1.00
148	Jack Wilson	.50
149	Carlos Rivera	.50
150	Jose Castillo	.50
151	Walter Young	.50
152	Brian Giles	.75
153	Jason Kendall	.50
154	Ryan Klesko	.50
155	Mike Rivera	.50
156	Sean Burroughs	.50
157	Brian Lawrence	.50
158	Xavier Nady	.50
159	Dennis Tankersley	.50
160	Phil Nevin	.50
161	Barry Bonds	6.00
162	Kenny Lofton	.50
163	Rich Aurilia	.50
164	Ichiro Suzuki	4.00
165	Edgar Martinez	.75
166	Chris Snelling	.50
167	Rafael Soriano	.50
168	John Olerud	.75
169	Bret Boone	.75
170	Freddy Garcia	.50
171	Aaron Sele	.50
172	Kazuhiro Sasaki	.50
173	Albert Pujols	4.00
174	Scott Rolen	2.00
175	So Taguchi	.50
176	Jim Edmonds	1.00
177	Edgar Renteria	1.00
178	J.D. Drew	1.00
179	Antonio Perez	.50
180	Dewon Brazelton	.50
181	Aubrey Huff	.50
182	Toby Hall	.50
183	Ben Grieve	.50
184	Joe Kennedy	.50
185	Alex Rodriguez	5.00
186	Rafael Palmeiro	1.50
187	Hank Blalock	1.50
188	Mark Teixeira	1.00
189	Juan Gonzalez	1.50
190	Kevin Mench	.50
191	Nolan Ryan	6.00
192	Doug Davis	.50
193	Eric Hinske	.50
194	Vinnie Chulk	.50
195	Alexis Rios	.50
196	Carlos Delgado	1.00
197	Shannon Stewart	.50
198	Josh Phelps	.50
199	Vernon Wells	.75
200	Roy Halladay	.75
201	Babe Ruth	8.00
202	Lou Gehrig	6.00
203	Jackie Robinson	6.00
204	Ty Cobb	6.00
205	Thurman Munson	4.00
206	Prentice Redman RC	5.00
207	Craig Brazell RC	5.00
208	Nook Logan RC	5.00
209	Hong-Chih Kuo RC	75.00
210	Matt Kata RC	5.00
211	Chien-Ming Wang RC	225.00
212	Alejandro Machado RC	5.00
213	Michael Hessman RC	5.00
214	Francisco Rosario RC	5.00
215	Pedro Liriano	5.00
216	Jeremy Bonderman	25.00
217	Oscar Villarreal RC	8.00
218	Arnie Munoz RC	5.00
219	Tim Olson RC	5.00
220	Jose Contreras/100 RC	40.00
221	Francisco Cruceta RC	5.00
222	John Webb	5.00
223	Phil Seibel RC	5.00
224	Aaron Looper RC	5.00
225	Brian Stokes RC	5.00
226	Guillermo Quiroz RC	8.00
227	Fernando Cabrera RC	5.00
228	Josh Hall RC	5.00
229	Diegomar Markwell RC	5.00
230	Andrew Brown RC	5.00
231	Doug Waechter RC	5.00
232	Felix Sanchez RC	5.00
233	Gerardo Garcia RC	5.00
234	Matt Bruback RC	5.00
235	Michel Hernandez RC	5.00
236	Rett Johnson RC	5.00
237	Ryan Cameron RC	5.00
238	Rob Hammock RC	5.00
239	Clint Barmes RC	10.00
240	Brandon Webb RC	65.00
241	Jon Leicester RC	5.00
242	Shane Bazzell RC	5.00
243	Joe Valentine RC	5.00
244	Josh Stewart RC	5.00
245	Pete LaForest RC	5.00
246	Shane Victorino RC	20.00
247	Terrmel Sledge RC	5.00
248	Lew Ford RC	8.00
249	Todd Wellemeyer RC	10.00
250	Hideki Matsui/No Auto. RC	15.00

Mirror Red

NM/M
Stars (1-205): 2-5X
SP's (206-250): .2-.4X
Production 100 Sets
Mirror Blues (1-205): 4-10X
SP's (206-250): .3-.5X
Production 50 Sets
Mirror Golds: No Pricing
Production 25 Sets

Mirror Emeralds: No Pricing
Production Five Sets
Mirror Blacks: One Set Produced

Fabric of the Game

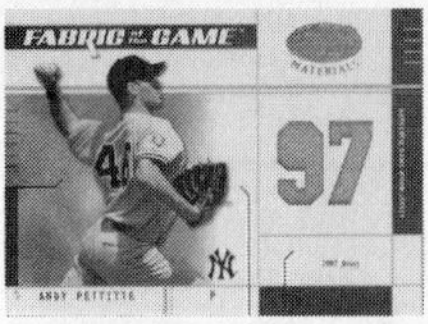

NM/M
Common Player: 4.00
Quantity produced listed

1BA	Bobby Doerr/50	15.00
1JY	Bobby Doerr/39	15.00
1PS	Bobby Doerr/50	15.00
2BA	Ozzie Smith/100	25.00
2IN	Ozzie Smith/50	30.00
2JY	Ozzie Smith/88	20.00
2PS	Ozzie Smith/50	30.00
3DY	Pee Wee Reese/32	30.00
3JY	Pee Wee Reese/58	15.00
4BA	Jeff Bagwell/100	10.00
4DY	Jeff Bagwell/65	10.00
4IN	Jeff Bagwell/50	12.00
4JY	Jeff Bagwell/98	10.00
4PS	Jeff Bagwell/50	12.00
5BA	Tommy Lasorda/100	8.00
5DY	Tommy Lasorda/58	10.00
5JY	Tommy Lasorda/84	8.00
5PS	Tommy Lasorda/50	10.00
6JY	Red Schoendienst/55	10.00
7BA	Harmon Killebrew/50	15.00
7DY	Harmon Killebrew/61	15.00
7IN	Harmon Killebrew/50	15.00
7JY	Harmon Killebrew/71	15.00
7PS	Harmon Killebrew/50	15.00
8DY	Roger Maris/55	40.00
8JY	Roger Maris/58	40.00
8PS	Roger Maris/50	40.00
9BA	Alex Rodriguez/100	15.00
9DY	Alex Rodriguez/77	15.00
9IN	Alex Rodriguez/50	15.00
9JY	Alex Rodriguez/99	15.00
9PS	Alex Rodriguez/50	15.00
10BA	Alex Rodriguez/100	15.00
10DY	Alex Rodriguez/72	15.00
10IN	Alex Rodriguez/50	15.00
10JY	Alex Rodriguez/101	15.00
10PS	Alex Rodriguez/50	15.00
11BA	Dale Murphy/50	15.00
11DY	Dale Murphy/66	15.00
11IN	Dale Murphy/50	15.00
11JY	Dale Murphy/85	15.00
11PS	Dale Murphy/50	15.00
12BA	Alan Trammell/100	10.00
12IN	Alan Trammell/50	10.00
12JY	Alan Trammell/90	10.00
12PS	Alan Trammell/50	10.00
13BA	Babe Ruth/10	250.00
13DY	Babe Ruth/13	250.00
13IN	Babe Ruth/10	250.00
13JY	Babe Ruth/30	200.00
13PS	Babe Ruth/10	250.00
14JY	Lou Gehrig/38	200.00
15JY	Babe Ruth/30	250.00
16JY	Mel Ott/46	30.00
17BA	Paul Molitor/100	15.00
17DY	Paul Molitor/70	15.00
17IN	Paul Molitor/50	15.00
17JY	Paul Molitor/84	15.00
17PS	Paul Molitor/50	15.00
18DY	Duke Snider/58	15.00
18JY	Duke Snider/62	15.00
19BA	Miguel Tejada/50	10.00
19DY	Miguel Tejada/68	8.00
19IN	Miguel Tejada/50	10.00
19JY	Miguel Tejada/99	5.00
19PS	Miguel Tejada/50	10.00
20JY	Lou Gehrig/38	200.00
21DY	Brooks Robinson/54	15.00
21JY	Brooks Robinson/66	15.00
22BA	George Brett/50	30.00
22DY	George Brett/69	25.00
22IN	George Brett/50	30.00
22JY	George Brett/91	25.00
22PS	George Brett/50	30.00
23BA	Johnny Bench/50	15.00
23DY	Johnny Bench/59	15.00
23IN	Johnny Bench/50	15.00
23JY	Johnny Bench/81	15.00
23PS	Johnny Bench/50	15.00
24JY	Lou Boudreau/48	15.00
25BA	Nomar Garciaparra/100	20.00
25IN	Nomar Garciaparra/50	25.00
25JY	Nomar Garciaparra/100	20.00
25PS	Nomar Garciaparra/50	25.00
26BA	Tsuyoshi Shinjo/50	8.00
26DY	Tsuyoshi Shinjo/62	8.00
26JY	Tsuyoshi Shinjo/101	5.00
27BA	Pat Burrell/100	8.00
27DY	Pat Burrell/46	10.00
27JY	Pat Burrell/101	8.00
28BA	Albert Pujols/100	20.00
28IN	Albert Pujols/50	25.00
28JY	Albert Pujols/101	20.00
28PS	Albert Pujols/50	25.00
29JY	Stan Musial/43	30.00
30JY	Al Kaline/64	15.00
31BA	Ivan Rodriguez/100	8.00
31DY	Ivan Rodriguez/72	8.00
31IN	Ivan Rodriguez/50	10.00
31JY	Ivan Rodriguez/101	5.00
32BA	Craig Biggio/100	6.00
32DY	Craig Biggio/65	8.00
32JY	Craig Biggio/101	6.00
32PS	Craig Biggio/50	10.00
33DY	Joe Morgan/59	10.00
33JY	Joe Morgan/74	8.00
34BA	Willie Stargell/50	15.00
34JY	Willie Stargell/68	15.00
34PS	Willie Stargell/50	15.00
35BA	Andre Dawson/100	8.00
35IN	Andre Dawson/50	10.00
35JY	Andre Dawson/87	8.00
35PS	Andre Dawson/50	10.00
36BA	Gary Carter/100	10.00
36DY	Gary Carter/62	10.00
36IN	Gary Carter/50	10.00
36JY	Gary Carter/85	8.00
36PS	Gary Carter/50	10.00
37BA	Cal Ripken Jr./50	50.00
37DY	Cal Ripken Jr./54	50.00
37IN	Cal Ripken Jr./50	50.00
37JY	Cal Ripken Jr./101	40.00
37PS	Cal Ripken Jr./50	50.00
38JY	Enos Slaughter/53	20.00
39BA	Reggie Jackson/50	15.00
39DY	Reggie Jackson/68	15.00
39JY	Reggie Jackson/75	15.00
39PS	Reggie Jackson/50	15.00
40JY	Phil Rizzuto/47	15.00
41BA	Chipper Jones/100	10.00
41DY	Chipper Jones/66	15.00
41IN	Chipper Jones/50	15.00
41JY	Chipper Jones/101	10.00
41PS	Chipper Jones/50	15.00
42BA	Hideo Nomo/100	10.00
42DY	Hideo Nomo/58	15.00
42IN	Hideo Nomo/50	15.00
42JY	Hideo Nomo/95	10.00
42PS	Hideo Nomo/50	15.00
43JY	Luis Aparicio/69	10.00
44BA	Hideo Nomo/100	10.00
44IN	Hideo Nomo/50	15.00
44JY	Hideo Nomo/101	10.00
44PS	Hideo Nomo/50	15.00
45BA	Edgar Martinez/100	8.00
45DY	Edgar Martinez/77	8.00
45JY	Edgar Martinez/100	8.00
45PS	Edgar Martinez/50	10.00
46BA	Barry Larkin/100	6.00
46DY	Barry Larkin/59	10.00
46JY	Barry Larkin/100	6.00
46PS	Barry Larkin/50	10.00
47BA	Alfonso Soriano/100	10.00
47IN	Alfonso Soriano/50	15.00
47JY	Alfonso Soriano/102	10.00
47PS	Alfonso Soriano/50	15.00
48BA	Wade Boggs/100	8.00
48DY	Wade Boggs/98	8.00
48IN	Wade Boggs/50	10.00
48JY	Wade Boggs/99	8.00
48PS	Wade Boggs/50	10.00
49BA	Wade Boggs/50	10.00
49IN	Wade Boggs/50	10.00
49JY	Wade Boggs/94	8.00
49PS	Wade Boggs/50	10.00
50JY	Ernie Banks/68	15.00
51BA	Joe Torre/50	10.00
51DY	Joe Torre/66	10.00
51IN	Joe Torre/50	10.00
51JY	Joe Torre/66	10.00
51PS	Joe Torre/50	10.00
52BA	Tim Hudson/100	4.00
52DY	Tim Hudson/68	6.00
52JY	Tim Hudson/101	4.00
52PS	Tim Hudson/50	6.00
53BA	Shawn Green/100	4.00
53DY	Shawn Green/58	6.00
53JY	Shawn Green/102	4.00
53PS	Shawn Green/50	6.00
54BA	Carlos Beltran/100	6.00
54DY	Carlos Beltran/69	8.00
54JY	Carlos Beltran/101	6.00
54PS	Carlos Beltran/50	8.00
55BA	Bo Jackson/50	15.00
55DY	Bo Jackson/69	15.00
55JY	Bo Jackson/90	10.00
55PS	Bo Jackson/50	15.00
56BA	Hal Newhouser/50	8.00
56JY	Hal Newhouser/55	8.00
56PS	Hal Newhouser/50	8.00
57BA	Jason Giambi/100	6.00
57DY	Jason Giambi/68	8.00
57IN	Jason Giambi/50	8.00
57JY	Jason Giambi/101	6.00
57PS	Jason Giambi/50	8.00
58BA	Lance Berkman/100	6.00
58DY	Lance Berkman/65	8.00
58IN	Lance Berkman/50	8.00
58JY	Lance Berkman/102	6.00
58PS	Lance Berkman/50	8.00
59BA	Todd Helton/100	6.00
59DY	Todd Helton/93	6.00
59JY	Todd Helton/100	6.00
59PS	Todd Helton/50	8.00
60BA	Mark Grace/100	8.00
60JY	Mark Grace/95	8.00
60PS	Mark Grace/50	15.00
61BA	Fred Lynn/100	6.00
61JY	Fred Lynn/75	8.00
61PS	Fred Lynn/50	8.00
62JY	Bob Feller/52	15.00
63BA	Robin Yount/100	20.00
63DY	Robin Yount/70	20.00
63IN	Robin Yount/50	25.00
63JY	Robin Yount/88	20.00
63PS	Robin Yount/50	25.00
64BA	Tony Gwynn/100	15.00
64DY	Tony Gwynn/69	20.00
64IN	Tony Gwynn/50	20.00
64JY	Tony Gwynn/99	20.00
64PS	Tony Gwynn/50	20.00
65BA	Tony Gwynn/100	15.00
65DY	Tony Gwynn/69	15.00
65IN	Tony Gwynn/50	15.00
65JY	Tony Gwynn/99	15.00
65PS	Tony Gwynn/50	15.00
66DY	Frank Robinson/54	10.00
66JY	Frank Robinson/70	10.00
67BA	Mike Schmidt/50	20.00
67DY	Mike Schmidt/46	20.00
67IN	Mike Schmidt/50	20.00
67JY	Mike Schmidt/81	20.00
67PS	Mike Schmidt/50	20.00
68JY	Lou Brock/66	15.00
69BA	Don Sutton/50	8.00
69DY	Don Sutton/58	8.00
69JY	Don Sutton/72	8.00
70BA	Mark Mulder/100	4.00
70DY	Mark Mulder/68	6.00
70JY	Mark Mulder/101	4.00
70PS	Mark Mulder/50	6.00
71BA	Luis Gonzalez/100	4.00
71DY	Luis Gonzalez/98	4.00
71JY	Luis Gonzalez/101	4.00
71PS	Luis Gonzalez/50	6.00
72BA	Jorge Posada/100	6.00
72JY	Jorge Posada/101	6.00
72PS	Jorge Posada/50	8.00
73BA	Sammy Sosa/100	20.00
73IN	Sammy Sosa/50	25.00
73JY	Sammy Sosa/101	20.00
73PS	Sammy Sosa/50	25.00
74BA	Roberto Alomar/100	8.00
74DY	Roberto Alomar/62	10.00
74JY	Roberto Alomar/102	8.00
74PS	Roberto Alomar/50	10.00
75JY	Roberto Clemente/69	80.00
76BA	Jeff Kent/100	4.00
76DY	Jeff Kent/58	6.00
76JY	Jeff Kent/101	4.00
76PS	Jeff Kent/50	6.00
77DY	Sean Casey/59	8.00
77JY	Sean Casey/100	4.00
78BA	Roger Clemens/50	25.00
78IN	Roger Clemens/50	25.00
78JY	Roger Clemens/95	20.00
78PS	Roger Clemens/50	20.00
79DY	Warren Spahn/53	15.00
79JY	Warren Spahn/58	15.00
80BA	Roger Clemens/100	20.00
80IN	Roger Clemens/50	25.00
80JY	Roger Clemens/102	25.00
80PS	Roger Clemens/50	25.00
81BA	Jim Palmer/50	10.00
81DY	Jim Palmer/54	10.00
81JY	Jim Palmer/69	10.00
81PS	Jim Palmer/50	10.00
82BA	Juan Gonzalez/50	10.00
82JY	Juan Gonzalez/101	6.00
82PS	Juan Gonzalez/50	10.00
83BA	Will Clark/100	15.00
83DY	Will Clark/58	15.00
83JY	Will Clark/88	15.00
83PS	Will Clark/50	15.00
84BA	Don Mattingly/50	25.00
84IN	Don Mattingly/50	25.00
84JY	Don Mattingly/93	25.00
84PS	Don Mattingly/50	25.00
85BA	Ryne Sandberg/40	30.00
85IN	Ryne Sandberg/50	30.00
85JY	Ryne Sandberg/85	30.00
85PS	Ryne Sandberg/50	30.00
86JY	Early Wynn/55	8.00
87BA	Manny Ramirez/50	8.00
87JY	Manny Ramirez/102	6.00
87PS	Manny Ramirez/50	8.00
88BA	Rickey Henderson/100	10.00
88DY	Rickey Henderson/62	15.00
88IN	Rickey Henderson/50	15.00
88JY	Rickey Henderson/99	10.00
88PS	Rickey Henderson/50	15.00
89BA	Rickey Henderson/100	10.00
89DY	Rickey Henderson/69	15.00
89PS	Rickey Henderson/50	15.00
90BA	Jason Giambi/100	8.00
90IN	Jason Giambi/50	10.00
90JY	Jason Giambi/102	8.00
90PS	Jason Giambi/50	10.00
91BA	Carlos Delgado/100	4.00
91DY	Carlos Delgado/77	4.00
91JY	Carlos Delgado/100	4.00
91PS	Carlos Delgado/50	6.00
92BA	Jim Thome/100	8.00
92JY	Jim Thome/102	10.00
92PS	Jim Thome/50	10.00
93BA	Andruw Jones/100	6.00
93DY	Andruw Jones/66	8.00
93JY	Andruw Jones/101	6.00
93PS	Andruw Jones/50	8.00
94BA	Rafael Palmeiro/100	8.00
94DY	Rafael Palmeiro/72	8.00
94JY	Rafael Palmeiro/102	8.00
94PS	Rafael Palmeiro/50	8.00
95BA	Troy Glaus/100	6.00
95DY	Troy Glaus/97	6.00
95IN	Troy Glaus/50	6.00
95JY	Troy Glaus/100	6.00
95PS	Troy Glaus/50	8.00
96BA	Wade Boggs/100	8.00
96IN	Wade Boggs/50	10.00
96JN	Wade Boggs/26	25.00
96JY	Wade Boggs/86	8.00
96PS	Wade Boggs/50	10.00
97BA	Jim "Catfish" Hunter/50	10.00
97DY	Jim "Catfish" Hunter/68	10.00
97JN	Jim "Catfish" Hunter/27	15.00
97JY	Jim "Catfish" Hunter/68	10.00
97PS	Jim "Catfish" Hunter/50	10.00
98BA	Juan Marichal/50	10.00
98DY	Juan Marichal/58	10.00
98JN	Juan Marichal/27	20.00
98JY	Juan Marichal/67	10.00
98PS	Juan Marichal/50	10.00
99BA	Carlton Fisk/50	15.00
99JN	Carlton Fisk/27	25.00
99JY	Carlton Fisk/80	10.00
99PS	Carlton Fisk/50	15.00
100BA	Vladimir Guerrero/100	8.00
100DY	Vladimir Guerrero/69	15.00
100JN	Vladimir Guerrero/27	30.00
100JY	Vladimir Guerrero/101	8.00
100PS	Vladimir Guerrero/50	15.00
101BA	Rod Carew/100	10.00
101DY	Rod Carew/65	15.00
101JN	Rod Carew/29	20.00
101JY	Rod Carew/85	10.00
101PS	Rod Carew/50	15.00
102BA	Rod Carew/50	15.00
102DY	Rod Carew/61	15.00
102JN	Rod Carew/29	20.00
102JY	Rod Carew/71	10.00
102PS	Rod Carew/50	15.00
103BA	Joe Carter/50	6.00
103DY	Joe Carter/77	8.00
103JN	Joe Carter/29	15.00
103JY	Joe Carter/94	6.00
104BA	Mike Sweeney/100	4.00
104DY	Mike Sweeney/69	6.00
104JN	Mike Sweeney/29	15.00
104JY	Mike Sweeney/101	4.00
104PS	Mike Sweeney/50	6.00
105DY	Nolan Ryan/65	40.00
105JN	Nolan Ryan/30	50.00
105JY	Nolan Ryan/70	40.00
105PS	Nolan Ryan/50	40.00
106BA	Orlando Cepeda/50	8.00
106DY	Orlando Cepeda/58	8.00
106IN	Orlando Cepeda/50	8.00
106JN	Orlando Cepeda/30	15.00
106JY	Orlando Cepeda/65	8.00
106PS	Orlando Cepeda/50	8.00
107JN	Magglio Ordonez/30	15.00
107JY	Magglio Ordonez/100	4.00
107PS	Magglio Ordonez/50	6.00
108BA	Hoyt Wilhelm/50	8.00
108JN	Hoyt Wilhelm/31	15.00
108JY	Hoyt Wilhelm/68	8.00
108PS	Hoyt Wilhelm/50	8.00
109BA	Mike Piazza/100	15.00
109DY	Mike Piazza/62	20.00
109IN	Mike Piazza/50	25.00
109JN	Mike Piazza/31	30.00
109JY	Mike Piazza/100	15.00
109PS	Mike Piazza/50	20.00
110BA	Greg Maddux/100	10.00
110DY	Greg Maddux/66	15.00
110IN	Greg Maddux/50	15.00
110JN	Greg Maddux/31	30.00
110JY	Greg Maddux/102	10.00
110PS	Greg Maddux/50	15.00
111BA	Mark Prior/100	8.00
111IN	Mark Prior/50	10.00
111JY	Mark Prior/102	8.00
111PS	Mark Prior/50	10.00
112BA	Torii Hunter/100	6.00
112DY	Torii Hunter/61	8.00
112IN	Torii Hunter/50	8.00
112JN	Torii Hunter/48	10.00
112JY	Torii Hunter/101	6.00
112PS	Torii Hunter/50	8.00
113BA	Steve Carlton/100	8.00
113DY	Steve Carlton/46	15.00
113IN	Steve Carlton/50	10.00
113JN	Steve Carlton/32	15.00
113JY	Steve Carlton/81	8.00
113PS	Steve Carlton/50	10.00
114BA	Jose Canseco/100	10.00
114DY	Jose Canseco/68	10.00
114IN	Jose Canseco/50	15.00
114JN	Jose Canseco/33	15.00
114JY	Jose Canseco/89	10.00
114PS	Jose Canseco/50	15.00
115BA	Nolan Ryan/50	30.00
115DY	Nolan Ryan/72	30.00
115IN	Nolan Ryan/50	30.00
115JN	Nolan Ryan/34	40.00
115JY	Nolan Ryan/90	30.00
115PS	Nolan Ryan/50	30.00
116BA	Nolan Ryan/50	30.00
116DY	Nolan Ryan/65	30.00
116JN	Nolan Ryan/34	40.00
116JY	Nolan Ryan/84	30.00
116PS	Nolan Ryan/50	30.00
118BA	Kerry Wood/100	10.00
118JN	Kerry Wood/34	25.00
118JY	Kerry Wood/101	10.00
118PS	Kerry Wood/50	15.00
119BA	Mike Mussina/50	10.00
119JN	Mike Mussina/35	25.00

119JY Mike Mussina/101 8.00
119PS Mike Mussina/50 15.00
120JN Yogi Berra/35 25.00
120JY Yogi Berra/47 25.00
121JY Thurman Munson/79 25.00
122BA Frank Thomas/100 8.00
122JN Frank Thomas/35 15.00
122JY Frank Thomas/94 6.00
122PS Frank Thomas/50 8.00
123BA Rickey Henderson/50 15.00
123DY Rickey Henderson/68 10.00
123JN Rickey Henderson/35 20.00
123JY Rickey Henderson/80 10.00
123PS Rickey Henderson/50 15.00
124BA Mike Mussina/100 6.00
124DY Mike Mussina/54 10.00
124JN Mike Mussina/35 20.00
124JY Mike Mussina/97 6.00
124PS Mike Mussina/50 10.00
125BA Gaylord Perry/100 6.00
125DY Gaylord Perry/77 6.00
125JN Gaylord Perry/36 10.00
125JY Gaylord Perry/82 6.00
125PS Gaylord Perry/50 8.00
126BA Nick Johnson/100 4.00
126JN Nick Johnson/36 6.00
126JY Nick Johnson/102 4.00
126PS Nick Johnson/50 8.00
127BA Curt Schilling/100 8.00
127DY Curt Schilling/98 8.00
127JN Curt Schilling/38 15.00
127JY Curt Schilling/102 8.00
127PS Curt Schilling/50 8.00
128BA Dave Parker/100 6.00
128JN Dave Parker/39 10.00
128JY Dave Parker/80 8.00
128PS Dave Parker/50 8.00
129DY Eddie Mathews/53 15.00
129JN Eddie Mathews/41 25.00
129JY Eddie Mathews/59 20.00
130DY Tom Seaver/62 15.00
130JN Tom Seaver/41 20.00
130JY Tom Seaver/69 15.00
131DY Tom Seaver/59 15.00
131JN Tom Seaver/41 25.00
131JY Tom Seaver/78 15.00
132JN Jackie Robinson/42 80.00
132JY Jackie Robinson/52 60.00
133BA Reggie Jackson/100 10.00
133DY Reggie Jackson/65 15.00
133IN Reggie Jackson/50 15.00
133JN Reggie Jackson/44 20.00
133JY Reggie Jackson/80 10.00
133PS Reggie Jackson/50 15.00
134BA Willie McCovey/100 8.00
134DY Willie McCovey/58 10.00
134JN Willie McCovey/44 10.00
134JY Willie McCovey/77 8.00
134PS Willie McCovey/50 10.00
135BA Eric Davis/100 6.00
135DY Eric Davis/59 8.00
135JN Eddie Davis/44 10.00
135JY Eric Davis/89 6.00
135PS Eric Davis/50 8.00
136BA Adam Dunn/100 8.00
136DY Adam Dunn/59 10.00
136JN Adam Dunn/44 15.00
136JY Adam Dunn/102 8.00
136PS Adam Dunn/50 10.00
137BA Roy Oswalt/100 4.00
137DY Roy Oswalt/65 6.00
137IN Roy Oswalt/50 6.00
137JN Roy Oswalt/44 8.00
137JY Roy Oswalt/102 4.00
137PS Roy Oswalt/50 6.00
138BA Pedro J. Martinez/50 15.00
138DY Pedro J. Martinez/69 15.00
138JN Pedro J. Martinez/45 20.00
138JY Pedro J. Martinez/95 6.00
138PS Pedro J. Martinez/50 10.00
139BA Pedro J. Martinez/100 8.00
139IN Pedro J. Martinez/50 10.00
139JN Pedro J. Martinez/45 15.00
139JY Pedro J. Martinez/102 8.00
139PS Pedro J. Martinez/50 10.00
140BA Andy Pettitte/100 6.00
140JN Andy Pettitte/46 10.00
140JY Andy Pettitte/97 6.00
140PS Andy Pettitte/50 8.00
141BA Jack Morris/100 6.00
141IN Jack Morris/50 8.00
141JN Jack Morris/47 10.00
141JY Jack Morris/85 6.00
141PS Jack Morris/50 8.00
142BA Tom Glavine/100 6.00
142DY Tom Glavine/66 10.00
142JN Tom Glavine/47 15.00
142JY Tom Glavine/100 6.00
142PS Tom Glavine/50 10.00
143BA Randy Johnson/100 10.00
143DY Randy Johnson/77 15.00
143IN Randy Johnson/50 15.00
143JN Randy Johnson/51 15.00
143JY Randy Johnson/98 10.00
143PS Randy Johnson/50 15.00
144BA Bernie Williams/100 8.00
144IN Bernie Williams/50 10.00
144JN Bernie Williams/51 10.00
144JY Bernie Williams/100 8.00
144PS Bernie Williams/50 10.00
145BA Randy Johnson/50 15.00
145DY Randy Johnson/98 10.00
145IN Randy Johnson/50 15.00
145JN Randy Johnson/51 15.00
145JY Randy Johnson/102 15.00
145PS Randy Johnson/50 15.00
146DY Don Drysdale/58 10.00
146JN Don Drysdale/53 10.00
146JY Don Drysdale/64 10.00
147BA Mark Buehrle/100 4.00
147JN Mark Buehrle/56 6.00
147JY Mark Buehrle/101 4.00
147PS Mark Buerhle/50 6.00
148BA Chan Ho Park/100 4.00
148DY Chan Ho Park/58 6.00
148JN Chan Ho Park/61 6.00
148JY Chan Ho Park/101 4.00
148PS Chan Ho Park/50 6.00
149BA Carlton Fisk/100 8.00
149IN Carlton Fisk/50 15.00
149JN Carlton Fisk/72 15.00
149JY Carlton Fisk/92 15.00
149PS Carlton Fisk/50 15.00
150BA Barry Zito/100 6.00
150DY Barry Zito/68 8.00
150JN Barry Zito/75 8.00
150JY Barry Zito/101 6.00
150PS Barry Zito/50 8.00

Mirror Red Materials

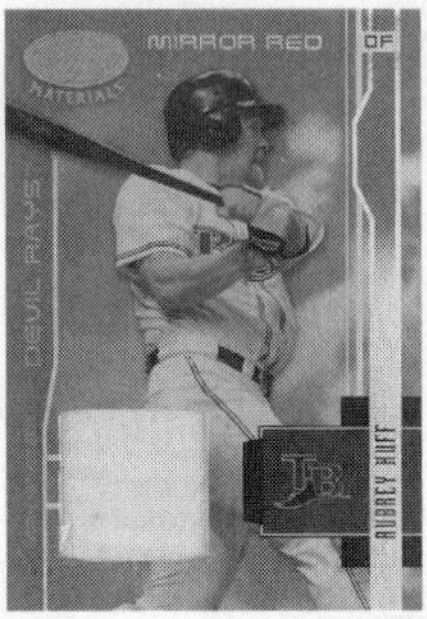

NM/M
Common Player: 4.00
Production 250 unless noted.
Mirror Red SP's (206-250): .5X
Mirror Blues: 1-1.5X
Production 100
Mirror Golds: No Pricing
Production 25 Sets
Mirror Emeralds: No Pricing
Production Five Sets
Mirror Blacks: One Set Produced
1 Troy Glaus 6.00
2 Alfredo Amezaga 4.00
3 Garret Anderson 6.00
4 Nolan Ryan/35 65.00
5 Darin Erstad 5.00
6 Junior Spivey 4.00
7 Randy Johnson 8.00
8 Curt Schilling 8.00
9 Luis Gonzalez 5.00
10 Steve Finley 4.00
11 Matt Williams 5.00
12 Greg Maddux 10.00
13 Chipper Jones 10.00
14 Gary Sheffield/125 6.00
15 Adam LaRoche 4.00
16 Andruw Jones 6.00
17 Robert Fick 4.00
18 John Smoltz 6.00
19 Javy Lopez 6.00
20 Jay Gibbons 4.00
21 Geronimo Gil 4.00
22 Cal Ripken Jr/35 75.00
23 Nomar Garciaparra 15.00
24 Pedro J. Martinez 10.00
25 Freddy Sanchez 4.00
26 Rickey Henderson 10.00
27 Manny Ramirez 8.00
28 Casey Fossum 4.00
29 Sammy Sosa 15.00
30 Kerry Wood 10.00
31 Corey Patterson 6.00
32 Nic Jackson 4.00
33 Mark Prior 8.00
34 Juan Cruz 4.00
35 Steve Smyth 4.00
36 Magglio Ordonez 6.00
37 Joe Borchard 4.00
38 Frank Thomas 10.00
39 Mark Buehrle 5.00
40 Joe Crede/100 8.00
41 Carlos Lee 4.00
42 Paul Konerko 6.00
43 Adam Dunn 8.00
45 Brandon Larson/150 6.00
46 Ken Griffey Jr. 12.00
47 Barry Larkin 8.00
48 Sean Casey 6.00
49 Wily Mo Pena 6.00
50 Austin Kearns 6.00
51 Victor Martinez/100 8.00
55 C.C. Sabathia 4.00
56 Ricardo Rodriguez 4.00
57 Omar Vizquel 6.00
58 Travis Hafner 6.00
59 Todd Helton 8.00
60 Jason Jennings 4.00
62 Larry Walker 6.00
63 Travis Chapman 6.00
64 Mike Maroth 4.00
65 Josh Beckett 6.00
66 Ivan Rodriguez 8.00
67 Brad Penny 4.00
68 A.J. Burnett 4.00
69 Craig Biggio 6.00
70 Roy Oswalt 6.00
71 Jason Lane 4.00
72 Nolan Ryan/35 65.00
73 Wade Miller 5.00
74 Richard Hidalgo 4.00
75 Jeff Bagwell 10.00
76 Lance Berkman 6.00
77 Rodrigo Rosario 4.00
78 Jeff Kent 6.00
79 John Buck 4.00
80 Angel Berroa 4.00
81 Mike Sweeney 6.00
84 Carlos Beltran 8.00
86 Hideo Nomo 15.00
87 Paul LoDuca 6.00
88 Cesar Izturis 4.00
89 Kazuhisa Ishii 5.00
90 Shawn Green 6.00
91 Joe Thurston 4.00
92 Adrian Beltre 6.00
93 Kevin Brown 6.00
94 Richie Sexson 6.00
95 Ben Sheets 6.00
97 Geoff Jenkins 5.00
98 Bill Hall 4.00
99 Torii Hunter 8.00
101 Michael Cuddyer 4.00
102 Jose Morban 4.00
103 Brad Radke 6.00
104 Jacque Jones 6.00
105 Eric Milton 4.00
106 Joe Mays 5.00
107 Adam Johnson 5.00
108 Javier Vazquez 5.00
109 Vladimir Guerrero 10.00
110 Jose Vidro 4.00
111 Michael Barrett/50 6.00
112 Orlando Cabrera 5.00
113 Tom Glavine 8.00
114 Roberto Alomar 10.00
115 Tsuyoshi Shinjo 4.00
116 Cliff Floyd 5.00
117 Mike Piazza 10.00
118 Al Leiter 5.00
119 Don Mattingly/35 60.00
120 Roger Clemens 25.00
121 Derek Jeter 20.00
122 Alfonso Soriano 8.00
123 Drew Henson 6.00
124 Brandon Claussen/50 10.00
125 Christian Parker 4.00
126 Jason Giambi 6.00
127 Mike Mussina 10.00
128 Bernie Williams 8.00
130 Nick Johnson 4.00
131 Jorge Posada 8.00
132 Andy Pettitte 10.00
133 Barry Zito 6.00
134 Miguel Tejada 6.00
135 Eric Chavez 6.00
136 Tim Hudson 6.00
137 Mark Mulder 6.00
138 Terrence Long 4.00
139 Mark Ellis 4.00
140 Jim Thome 8.00
141 Pat Burrell 6.00
142 Marlon Byrd 4.00
143 Bobby Abreu 6.00
144 Brandon Duckworth 4.00
145 Robert Person 4.00
146 Anderson Machado 4.00
147 Aramis Ramirez 6.00
148 Jack Wilson 4.00
150 Jose Castillo 4.00
151 Walter Young 4.00
152 Brian Giles 6.00
153 Jason Kendall 5.00
155 Mike Rivera 4.00
157 Brian Lawrence 4.00
158 Xavier Nady/60 8.00
159 Dennis Tankersley 4.00
160 Phil Nevin 4.00
161 Barry Bonds 20.00
162 Kenny Lofton 6.00
163 Rich Aurilia 5.00
164 Ichiro Suzuki 25.00
165 Edgar Martinez/100 8.00
166 Chris Snelling 4.00
167 Rafael Soriano 4.00
168 John Olerud 4.00
169 Bret Boone 5.00
170 Freddy Garcia 4.00
171 Aaron Sele 4.00
172 Kazuhiro Sasaki 4.00
173 Albert Pujols 25.00
174 Scott Rolen 10.00
175 So Taguchi 4.00
176 Jim Edmonds 6.00
177 Edgar Renteria 8.00
178 J.D. Drew 6.00
179 Antonio Perez 4.00
180 Dewon Brazelton 4.00
181 Aubrey Huff/50 8.00
182 Toby Hall 4.00
183 Ben Grieve 4.00
184 Joe Kennedy 4.00
185 Alex Rodriguez 15.00
186 Rafael Palmeiro 8.00
187 Hank Blalock 8.00
188 Mark Teixeira 8.00
189 Juan Gonzalez 8.00
190 Kevin Mench 4.00
191 Nolan Ryan/35 65.00
192 Doug Davis 4.00
193 Eric Hinske 8.00
196 Carlos Delgado 6.00
197 Shannon Stewart 5.00
198 Josh Phelps 4.00
199 Vernon Wells 5.00
200 Roy Halladay 8.00

Mirror Red Signatures

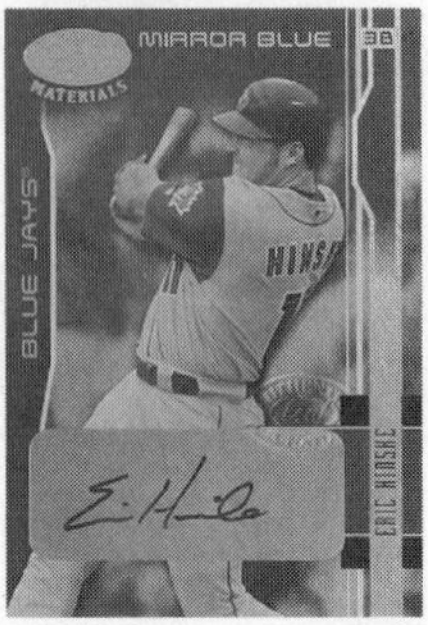

NM/M
Common Player:
Production 100 unless noted.
Mirror Blues: 1-1.5X
Production 50
Mirror Golds: 1.5-2X
Production 25 Sets
Mirror Emeralds: No Pricing
Production Five Sets
Mirror Blacks: One Set Produced
2 Alfredo Amezaga 6.00
15 Adam LaRoche 10.00
17 Robert Fick/15 20.00
20 Jay Gibbons 10.00
21 Geronimo Gil/15 15.00
25 Freddy Sanchez 10.00
28 Casey Fossum/50 10.00
32 Nic Jackson 10.00
34 Juan Cruz/15 15.00
35 Steve Smyth/94 8.00
37 Joe Borchard/50 15.00
39 Mark Buehrle/50 20.00
40 Joe Crede/30 15.00
45 Brandon Larson 10.00
49 Wily Mo Pena 15.00
51 Victor Martinez/50 25.00
53 Cliff Lee/50 20.00
54 Jeremy Guthrie/50 15.00
56 Ricardo Rodriguez 8.00
60 Jason Jennings/50 12.00
61 Jeff Baker/50 8.00
63 Travis Chapman 10.00
64 Mike Maroth 10.00
70 Roy Oswalt/50 20.00
71 Jason Lane 10.00
73 Wade Miller/50 15.00
77 Rodrigo Rosario 10.00
80 Angel Berroa/50 15.00
85 Runelvys Hernandez 10.00
88 Cesar Izturis 6.00
91 Joe Thurston 8.00
98 Bill Hall 10.00
102 Jose Morban 8.00
107 Adam Johnson/50 10.00
117 Mike Piazza/20 150.00
124 Brandon Claussen/60 15.00
125 Christian Parker/50 10.00
129 Jason Anderson 10.00
138 Terrence Long/50 15.00
142 Marlon Byrd 10.00
144 Brandon Duckworth/50 10.00
145 Robert Person/50 10.00
146 Anderson Machado 8.00
149 Carlos Rivera 8.00
150 Jose Castillo 8.00
151 Walter Young 8.00
155 Mike Rivera 8.00
157 Brian Lawrence 8.00
166 Chris Snelling 10.00
167 Rafael Soriano/50 12.00
179 Antonio Perez/50 8.00
180 Dewon Brazelton/50 8.00
181 Aubrey Huff/50 15.00
182 Toby Hall/50 10.00
184 Joe Kennedy/50 12.00
187 Hank Blalock/50 25.00
188 Mark Teixeira/50 40.00
190 Kevin Mench 10.00
193 Eric Hinske 15.00
194 Vinnie Chulk 8.00
195 Alexis Rios 25.00

2003 Leaf Limited

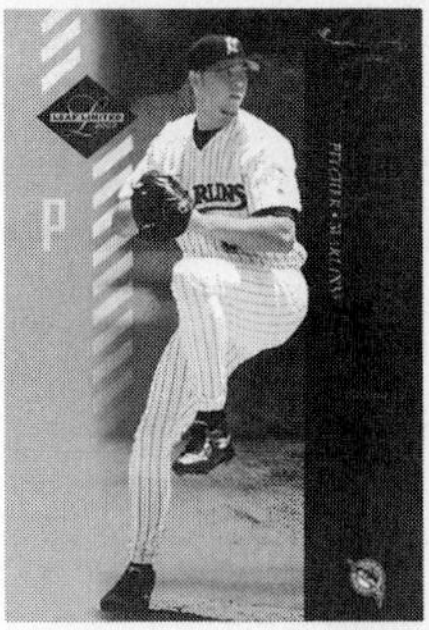

		NM/M
Complete Set (170):		
Common Player (1-151):		1.50
Production 999		
Common (152-170):		4.00
Production 399		
Common Auto. Memor. (171-200):		15.00
Production 99		
Common Auto. (171-200):		8.00
Pack (4):		75.00
Box (4):		250.00
1	Derek Jeter	6.00
2	Eric Chavez	1.50
3	Alex Rodriguez	5.00
4	Miguel Tejada	1.50
5	Nomar Garciaparra	4.00
6	Jeff Bagwell	3.00
7	Jim Thome	2.00
8	Pat Burrell	1.50
9	Albert Pujols	5.00
10	Juan Gonzalez	3.00
11	Shawn Green	1.50
12	Craig Biggio	1.50
13	Chipper Jones	3.00
14	Hideo Nomo	2.00
15	Vernon Wells	1.50
16	Gary Sheffield	2.00
17	Barry Larkin	1.50
18	Josh Beckett	1.50
19	Edgar Martinez	1.50
20	Ivan Rodriguez	2.00
21	Jeff Kent	1.50
22	Roberto Alomar	1.50
23	Alfonso Soriano	3.00
24	Jim Thome	2.00
25	Juan Gonzalez	3.00
26	Carlos Beltran	2.00
27	Shawn Green	1.50
28	Tim Hudson	1.50
29	Deion Sanders	1.50
30	Rafael Palmeiro	2.00
31	Todd Helton	3.00
32	Lance Berkman	1.50
33	Mike Mussina	2.00
34	Kazuhisa Ishii	1.50
35	Bill Burrell	1.50
36	Miguel Tejada	1.50
37	Juan Gonzalez	2.00
38	Roberto Alomar	1.50
39	Roberto Alomar	1.50
40	Luis Gonzalez	1.50
41	Jorge Posada	1.50
42	Mark Mulder	1.50
43	Sammy Sosa	4.00
44	Mark Prior	2.00
45	Roger Clemens	4.00
46	Tom Glavine	1.50
47	Mark Teixeira	1.50
48	Manny Ramirez	2.00
49	Frank Thomas	2.00
50	Troy Glaus	3.00
51	Andruw Jones	3.00
52	Jason Giambi	2.00
53	Jim Thome	2.00
54	Barry Bonds	6.00
55	Rafael Palmeiro	2.00
56	Edgar Martinez	1.50
57	Vladimir Guerrero	3.00
58	Roberto Alomar	1.50
59	Mike Sweeney	1.50
60	Magglio Ordonez	1.50
61	Ken Griffey Jr.	4.00
62	Craig Biggio	1.50
63	Greg Maddux	4.00
64	Mike Piazza	4.00
65	Tom Glavine	1.50
66	Kerry Wood	2.00
67	Frank Thomas	3.00
68	Mike Mussina	2.00
69	Nick Johnson	1.50
70	Bernie Williams	1.50
71	Scott Rolen	2.00
72	Curt Schilling	2.00
73	Adam Dunn	2.00
74	Roy Oswalt	1.50
75	Pedro J. Martinez	3.00
76	Tom Glavine	1.50
77	Torii Hunter	1.50
78	Austin Kearns	1.50
79	Randy Johnson	3.00
80	Bernie Williams	1.50
81	Ichiro Suzuki	4.00
82	Kerry Wood	2.00
83	Kazuhisa Ishii	1.50
84	Randy Johnson	3.00
85	Nick Johnson	1.50
86	Josh Beckett	1.50
87	Curt Schilling	2.00
88	Mike Mussina	2.00
89	Pedro J. Martinez	3.00
90	Barry Zito	1.50
91	Jim Edmonds	1.50
92	Rickey Henderson	3.00
93	Rickey Henderson	3.00
94	Rickey Henderson	3.00
95	Rickey Henderson	3.00
96	Rickey Henderson	3.00
97	Randy Johnson	3.00
98	Mark Grace	1.50
99	Pedro J. Martinez	3.00
100	Hee Seop Choi	1.50
101	Ivan Rodriguez	2.00
102	Jeff Kent	1.50
103	Hideo Nomo	3.00
104	Hideo Nomo	3.00
105	Mike Piazza	4.00
106	Tom Glavine	1.50
107	Roberto Alomar	1.50
108	Roger Clemens	5.00
109	Jason Giambi	2.00
110	Jim Thome	2.00
111	Alex Rodriguez	5.00
112	Juan Gonzalez	2.00
113	Torii Hunter	1.50
114	Roy Oswalt	1.50
115	Curt Schilling	2.00
116	Magglio Ordonez	1.50
117	Rafael Palmeiro	2.00
118	Andruw Jones	3.00
119	Manny Ramirez	3.00
120	Mark Teixeira	1.50
121	Mark Mulder	1.50
122	Garret Anderson	1.50
123	Tim Hudson	1.50
124	Todd Helton	3.00
125	Troy Glaus	3.00
126	Derek Jeter	6.00
127	Barry Bonds	6.00
128	Greg Maddux	4.00
129	Roger Clemens	5.00
130	Nomar Garciaparra	4.00
131	Mike Piazza	4.00
132	Alex Rodriguez	5.00
133	Ichiro Suzuki	4.00
134	Randy Johnson	3.00
135	Sammy Sosa	4.00
136	Ken Griffey Jr.	4.00
137	Alfonso Soriano	3.00
138	Jason Giambi	2.00
139	Albert Pujols	5.00
140	Chipper Jones	3.00
141	Adam Dunn	2.00
142	Pedro J. Martinez	3.00
143	Vladimir Guerrero	3.00
144	Mark Prior	2.00
145	Barry Zito	1.50
146	Jeff Bagwell	3.00
147	Lance Berkman	1.50
148	Shawn Green	1.50
149	Jason Giambi	2.00
150	Randy Johnson	3.00
151	Alex Rodriguez	5.00
152	Babe Ruth	10.00
153	Ty Cobb	6.00
154	Jackie Robinson	6.00
155	Lou Gehrig	8.00
156	Thurman Munson	6.00
157	Roberto Clemente	8.00
158	Nolan Ryan	10.00
159	Nolan Ryan	10.00
160	Nolan Ryan	10.00
161	Cal Ripken Jr.	10.00
162	Don Mattingly	8.00
163	Stan Musial	6.00
164	Tony Gwynn	3.00
165	Yogi Berra	3.00
166	Johnny Bench	5.00
167	Mike Schmidt	8.00
168	George Brett	8.00
169	Ryne Sandberg	4.00
170	Ernie Banks	5.00
171	J. Bonderman/Auto./Jsy	40.00
172	Jose Contreras/Auto. **RC**	40.00
173	Chien-Ming Wang/ Auto. **RC**	300.00
174	Hideki Matsui/Base **RC**	40.00
175	Hong-Chih Kuo/ Auto./Bat **RC**	120.00
176	Brandon Webb/ Auto./Bat **RC**	80.00
177	Richard Fischer/Auto.	8.00
178	Robby Hammock/Auto./Bat	10.00
179	Todd Wellemeyer/ Auto./49 **RC**	20.00
180	Prentice Redman/ Auto./Bat **RC**	10.00
181	Nook Logan/Auto. **RC**	10.00
182	Craig Brazell/Auto. **RC**	10.00
183	Tim Olson/Auto./Bat **RC**	10.00
184	Matt Kata/Auto./Bat **RC**	10.00
185	A. Machado/Auto.	8.00
186	Michael Hessman/Auto. **RC**	10.00
187	Oscar Villarreal/Auto. **RC**	8.00
188	Guillermo Quiroz/ Auto./Bat **RC**	10.00
189	Michel Hernandez/Auto. **RC**	10.00
190	Clint Barmes/Auto./Bat **RC**	20.00
191	Pete LaForest/Auto./Bat **RC**	10.00
192	Adam Loewen/Auto. **RC**	10.00
193	Terrmel Sledge/ Auto./Bat **RC**	10.00
194	Lew Ford/Auto./Bat **RC**	10.00
195	Todd Wellemeyer/ Auto./49 **RC**	20.00
196	Clint Barmes/Auto./Bat **RC**	20.00
197	J. Bonderman/Auto./Jsy	40.00
198	Brandon Webb/ Auto./Jsy **RC**	80.00
199	Hideki Matsui/Base **RC**	30.00
200	Jose Contreras/Auto. **RC**	40.00

Gold Spotlight

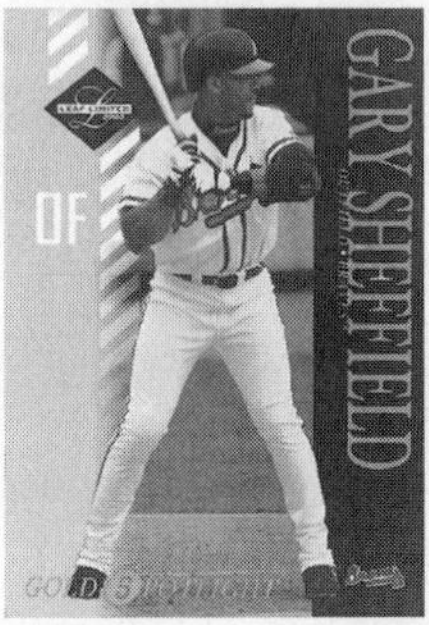

Golds (1-151):	2-4X
Golds (152-170):	1.5-3X
Production 50	
Golds (171-200):	No Pricing
Production 10 to 25	

Silver Spotlight

Silvers (1-170):	1-2X
Production 100	
Silver Auto. Memor. (171-200):	1X
Silver Memor. (171-200):	1X
Silver Auto:	1X
Production 29 to 50	

Jersey Numbers

		NM/M
Common Player:		
Production 5-100		
Some not priced due to scarcity.		
1	Rod Carew/50	20.00
2	Nolan Ryan/50	40.00
3	Reggie Jackson/50	20.00
4	Brooks Robinson/50	25.00
5	Frank Robinson/50	15.00
6	Cal Ripken Jr./100	40.00
7	Carlton Fisk/50	15.00
8	Roger Clemens/100	15.00
10	Lou Boudreau/50	10.00
11	Bob Feller/25	30.00
13	Alan Trammell/50	10.00
14	Harmon Killebrew/50	25.00
15	Rod Carew/50	20.00
16	Kirby Puckett/50	20.00
19	Yogi Berra/50	30.00
20	Thurman Munson/50	30.00
21	Don Mattingly/100	25.00
25	Alex Rodriguez/100	10.00
26	Randy Johnson/50	10.00
27	Nolan Ryan/100	30.00
28	Dale Murphy/50	20.00
29	Warren Spahn/50	20.00
30	Eddie Mathews/50	25.00
32	Ryne Sandberg/100	30.00
33	Johnny Bench/50	30.00
34	Joe Morgan/50	10.00
35	Randy Johnson/50	10.00
36	Nolan Ryan/100	30.00
37	Pee Wee Reese/50	15.00
38	Duke Snider/50	25.00
39	Jackie Robinson/25	65.00
40	Robin Yount/50	30.00
41	Paul Molitor/50	20.00
42	Pedro Martinez/50	10.00
43	Randy Johnson/50	10.00
44	Tom Seaver/25	25.00
45	Gary Carter/50	10.00
46	Mike Schmidt/50	30.00
47	Steve Carlton/50	10.00
48	Willie Stargell/50	20.00
50	Ozzie Smith/50	35.00
51	Stan Musial/100	30.00
52	Enos Slaughter/50	10.00
53	Orlando Cepeda/50	10.00
54	Willie McCovey/50	15.00
57	Harmon Killebrew, Rod Carew/25	50.00
58	Harmon Killebrew, Kirby Puckett/25	50.00
68	Thurman Munson, Yogi Berra/25	50.00
69	Don Mattingly, Yogi Berra/25	60.00
71	Dale Murphy, Warren Spahn/25	50.00
72	Dale Murphy, Eddie Mathews/25	45.00
73	Eddie Mathews, Warren Spahn/25	60.00
74	Joe Morgan, Johnny Bench/25	40.00
75	Duke Snider, Pee Wee Reese/25	40.00
78	Paul Molitor, Robin Yount/25	75.00
81	Ozzie Smith, Stan Musial/25	60.00
82	Enos Slaughter, Stan Musial/25	60.00
83	Orlando Cepeda, Willie McCovey/25	40.00
84	Nolan Ryan, Reggie Jackson/25	60.00
90	Alex Rodriguez, Randy Johnson/25	25.00
91	Pedro J. Martinez, Randy Johnson/25	35.00
94	Reggie Jackson/25	35.00
95	Nolan Ryan/25	60.00
96	Nolan Ryan/25	60.00
97	Nolan Ryan/25	60.00
98	Nolan Ryan/25	60.00
99	Cal Ripken Jr., Rafael Palmeiro/25	90.00
100	Dale Murphy, Deion Sanders/25	50.00

Jersey Numbers Retired

		NM/M
Many not priced due to scarcity.		
1	Rod Carew/29	30.00
2	Nolan Ryan/30	50.00
5	Frank Robinson/20	20.00
7	Carlton Fisk/27	30.00
9	Carlton Fisk/27	15.00
16	Kirby Puckett/34	35.00
21	Don Mattingly/23	50.00
27	Nolan Ryan/34	50.00
30	Eddie Mathews/41	20.00
36	Nolan Ryan/34	50.00
39	Jackie Robinson/42	50.00
44	Tom Seaver/41	20.00
46	Mike Schmidt/20	50.00
47	Steve Carlton/32	15.00
49	Roberto Clemente/21	100.00
53	Orlando Cepeda/30	15.00
54	Willie McCovey/44	10.00

Leather

		NM/M
Common Player:		
Production 10-25		
Golds:		No Pricing
Production 5-10		
Leather & Lace:		No Pricing
Production 10		
Leather & Lace Gold:		No Pricing
Production 5		
1	Alex Rodriguez/25	40.00
2	Chipper Jones/25	30.00
3	Jimmie Foxx/25	65.00
4	Kirby Puckett/25	25.00
5	Mike Schmidt/25	65.00
6	Roger Clemens/25	45.00
8	Tony Gwynn/25	40.00
10	Vladimir Guerrero/25	25.00
11	Adam Dunn/25	20.00
12	Andruw Jones/25	25.00
13	Curt Schilling/25	20.00
14	Randy Johnson/25	25.00
15	Mark Prior/25	40.00

Lineups - Jerseys

		NM/M
Production 5-50		
1	Paul Molitor, Robin Yount/50	35.00
2	Bernie Williams, Don Mattingly/50	40.00
3	Hee Seop Choi, Sammy Sosa/50	30.00
4	Derek Jeter, Hideki Matsui/50/Base	30.00
5	Andre Dawson, Ryne Sandberg/50	35.00
6	Bo Jackson, George Brett/50	50.00
7	Jose Canseco, Reggie Jackson/50	25.00
8	Mark Grace, Ryne Sandberg/50	35.00
9	Jose Canseco, Rickey Henderson/50	25.00
10	Hideo Nomo, Mike Piazza/50	25.00

Lineups - Bats

		NM/M
Common Player:		
Production 25-50		
1	Paul Molitor, Robin Yount/50	35.00
2	Bernie Williams, Don Mattingly/50	40.00
4	Derek Jeter, Hideki Matsui/25	60.00
5	Andre Dawson, Ryne Sandberg/50	40.00

6 Bo Jackson,
George Brett/50 40.00
7 Jose Canseco,
Reggie Jackson/50 25.00
8 Mark Grace,
Ryne Sandberg/50 40.00
9 Jose Canseco,
Rickey Henderson/50 30.00
10 Hideo Nomo,
Mike Piazza/50 30.00

Lineups - Buttons

No Pricing
Production One Set

Lineups Tag Team

No Pricing
Production 5

Lumberjacks

NM/M

Some not priced due to scarcity.
Production 1-25
Black: No Pricing
Production 1-5
Silver: No Pricing
Production 1-10
1 Babe Ruth/25 200.00
2 Lou Gehrig/25 150.00
3 Roberto Clemente/25 120.00
4 Stan Musial/25 40.00
5 Rogers Hornsby/25 50.00
6 Don Mattingly/25 50.00
7 Rickey Henderson/25 20.00
8 Cal Ripken Jr./25 75.00
9 Yogi Berra/25 30.00
10 Reggie Jackson/25 35.00
11 George Brett/25 60.00
12 Mel Ott/25 40.00
13 Roger Maris/25 60.00
14 Ryne Sandberg/25 50.00
16 Richie Ashburn/25 40.00
17 Mike Schmidt/25 40.00
18 Tony Gwynn/25 25.00
19 Ty Cobb/25 110.00
20 Thurman Munson/25 35.00
21 Jimmie Foxx/25 60.00
22 Duke Snider/25 25.00
24 Alex Rodriguez/25 30.00
25 Nomar Garciaparra/25 30.00
26 Hideki Matsui/25/Base 50.00
27 Ichiro Suzuki/25/Base 35.00
28 Barry Bonds/25/Base 35.00
29 Mike Piazza/25 30.00
30 Alfonso Soriano/25 25.00
31 Al Kaline/25 30.00
33 Dale Murphy/25 30.00
34 Orlando Cepeda/25 30.00
35 Willie McCovey/25 30.00
37 Brooks Robinson/25 30.00

Lumberjacks - Barrel

NM/M

1/1 except where indicated
No pricing due to scarcity.
21 Jimmie Foxx (7/05 Auction) 1,525

Lumberjacks Combos

NM/M

Production 1-25
Black: No Pricing
Production 1-5
Silver: No Pricing
Production 1-10
38 Hideki Matsui,
Ichiro Suzuki/25/Base 80.00
40 Don Mattingly,
Lou Gehrig/25 240.00
41 Thurman Munson,
Yogi Berra/25 50.00
42 Mike Schmidt,
Richie Ashburn/25 60.00
43 Rogers Hornsby,
Stan Musial/25 80.00
44 Don Mattingly,
Roger Maris/25 100.00

Lumberjacks Combos - Jerseys

NM/M

Production 1-25
Some not priced due to scarcity.
Black: No Pricing
Production 1-5
Silver: No Pricing
Production 1-10
38 Hideki Matsui,
Ichiro Suzuki/25/Ball 100.00
41 Thurman Munson,
Yogi Berra/25 60.00

Lumberjacks Combos - Jerseys/Bats

NM/M

Production 1-25
Some not priced due to scarcity.
Black: No Pricing
Production 1-5
Silver: No Pricing
Production 1-10
38 Hideki Matsui,
Ichiro Suzuki/25/Ball 100.00
41 Thurman Munson,
Yogi Berra/25 50.00
42 Mike Schmidt,
Richie Ashburn/25 60.00

Lumberjacks - Jerseys

NM/M

Production 1-25
Black: No Pricing
Production 1-5
Silver: No Pricing
Production 1-10
4 Stan Musial/25 40.00
6 Don Mattingly/25 50.00
8 Cal Ripken Jr./25 80.00
9 Yogi Berra/25 25.00
11 George Brett/25 60.00
12 Mel Ott/25 40.00
14 Ryne Sandberg/25 50.00
15 Eddie Mathews/25 25.00
17 Mike Schmidt/25 50.00
18 Tony Gwynn/25 25.00
20 Thurman Munson/25 25.00
22 Duke Snider/25 20.00
24 Alex Rodriguez/25 30.00
25 Nomar Garciaparra/25 30.00
26 Hideki Matsui/25/Ball 50.00
27 Ichiro Suzuki/25/Ball 30.00
28 Barry Bonds/25/Ball 40.00
29 Mike Piazza/25 25.00
30 Alfonso Soriano/25 25.00
32 Harmon Killebrew/25 25.00
33 Dale Murphy/25 25.00
34 Orlando Cepeda/25 15.00
35 Willie McCovey/25 20.00
36 Willie Stargell/25 30.00
37 Brooks Robinson/25 20.00

Lumberjacks - Jerseys/Bats

NM/M

Production 1-25
Some not priced due to scarcity.
Black: No Pricing
Production 1-5
Silver: No Pricing
Production 1-10
4 Stan Musial/25 60.00
6 Don Mattingly/25 75.00
8 Cal Ripken Jr./25 140.00
9 Yogi Berra/25 30.00
13 Roger Maris/25 100.00
14 Ryne Sandberg/25 65.00
15 Eddie Mathews/25 40.00
17 Mike Schmidt/25 65.00
18 Tony Gwynn/25 40.00
20 Thurman Munson/25 40.00
24 Alex Rodriguez/25 40.00
25 Nomar Garciaparra/25 40.00
26 Hideki Matsui/25/Base/Ball 65.00
27 Ichiro Suzuki/25/Base/Ball 60.00
28 Barry Bonds/25/Base/Ball 60.00
29 Mike Piazza/25 40.00
30 Alfonso Soriano/25 25.00
33 Dale Murphy/25 40.00
35 Willie McCovey/25 35.00
36 Willie Stargell/25 30.00
37 Brooks Robinson/25 30.00

Material Monikers Jerseys

NM/M

Common Player:
2 Eric Chavez/25 25.00
4 Miguel Tejada/25 35.00
12 Craig Biggio/25 35.00
15 Vernon Wells/25 25.00
19 Edgar Martinez/25 40.00
26 Carlos Beltran/25 50.00
28 Tim Hudson/25 25.00
44 Mark Prior/25 40.00
47 Mark Teixeira/25 30.00
69 Nick Johnson/25 20.00
73 Adam Dunn/25 40.00
74 Roy Oswalt/25 25.00
77 Torii Hunter/25 25.00
85 Nick Johnson/25 20.00
113 Torii Hunter/25 25.00
114 Roy Oswalt/25 25.00
120 Mark Teixeira/25 40.00

Material Monikers Bats

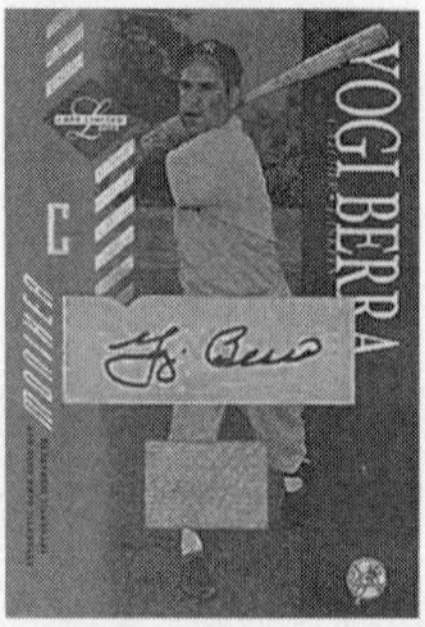

NM/M

Production 1-25
No pricing for many, due to scarcity.
2 Eric Chavez/25 35.00
12 Craig Biggio/25 40.00
15 Vernon Wells/25 30.00
19 Edgar Martinez/25 50.00
26 Carlos Beltran/25 40.00
28 Tim Hudson/25 40.00
44 Mark Prior/25 50.00
47 Mark Teixeira/25 40.00
69 Nick Johnson/25 25.00
73 Adam Dunn/25 40.00
74 Roy Oswalt/25 30.00
77 Torii Hunter/25 30.00
85 Nick Johnson/25 25.00
113 Torii Hunter/25 30.00
114 Roy Oswalt/25 30.00
120 Mark Teixeira/25 40.00

Material Monikers Jersey Numbers

NM/M

Production 1-25
Many not priced due to scarcity.
2 Eric Chavez/25 25.00
4 Miguel Tejada/25 30.00
12 Craig Biggio/25 35.00
15 Vernon Wells/25 20.00
19 Edgar Martinez/25 30.00
26 Carlos Beltran/25 50.00
28 Tim Hudson/25 25.00
44 Mark Prior/25 40.00
47 Mark Teixeira/25 40.00
69 Nick Johnson/25 15.00
73 Adam Dunn/25 40.00
74 Roy Oswalt/25 20.00
77 Torii Hunter/25 25.00
85 Nick Johnson/25 15.00
113 Torii Hunter/25 25.00
114 Roy Oswalt/25 20.00
120 Mark Teixeira/25 40.00

Material Monikers Jersey Position

NM/M

Production 1-25
Many not priced due to scarcity.
2 Eric Chavez/25 25.00
4 Miguel Tejada/25 30.00
12 Craig Biggio/25 35.00
15 Vernon Wells/25 20.00
19 Edgar Martinez/25 40.00
26 Carlos Beltran/25 50.00
28 Tim Hudson/25 25.00
29 Deion Sanders/25 50.00
44 Mark Prior/25 40.00
47 Mark Teixeira/25 40.00
69 Nick Johnson/25 20.00
73 Adam Dunn/25 40.00
74 Roy Oswalt/25 25.00
77 Torii Hunter/25 25.00
85 Nick Johnson/25 20.00
113 Torii Hunter/25 25.00
114 Roy Oswalt/25 25.00
120 Mark Teixeira/25 40.00

Player Threads

NM/M

Production 5-50
Some not priced due to scarcity.
Primes: No Pricing
Production 5-10
1 Roger Clemens/50 15.00
2 Alex Rodriguez/50 15.00
3 Pedro Martinez/50 10.00
4 Randy Johnson/50 10.00
5 Curt Schilling/50 8.00
7 Nolan Ryan/50 35.00
8 Hideo Nomo/50 12.00
9 Mike Piazza/50 15.00
11 Rickey Henderson/50 15.00
12 Ivan Rodriguez/50 10.00
13 Gary Sheffield/50 8.00
14 Jeff Kent/50 8.00
15 Roberto Alomar/50 10.00
16 Rafael Palmeiro/50 10.00
17 Juan Gonzalez/50 8.00
18 Shawn Green/50 8.00
19 Jason Giambi/50 8.00
20 Jim Thome/50 10.00
21 Scott Rolen/50 12.00
22 Mike Mussina/50 10.00
23 Tom Glavine/50 8.00
24 Sammy Sosa/50 15.00

Player Threads Double

NM/M

Production 5-50
Some not priced due to scarcity.
Double Primes: No Pricing
Production 5-10
1 Roger Clemens/50 25.00
2 Alex Rodriguez/50 25.00
3 Pedro Martinez/50 20.00
4 Randy Johnson/50 15.00
5 Curt Schilling/50 10.00
7 Nolan Ryan/50 50.00
8 Hideo Nomo/50 20.00
9 Mike Piazza/50 25.00
11 Rickey Henderson/50 20.00
12 Ivan Rodriguez/50 15.00
13 Gary Sheffield/50 10.00
14 Jeff Kent/50 10.00
15 Roberto Alomar/50 15.00
16 Rafael Palmeiro/50 15.00
17 Juan Gonzalez/50 15.00
18 Shawn Green/50 10.00
19 Jason Giambi/50 15.00
20 Jim Thome/50 15.00
21 Scott Rolen/50 20.00
22 Mike Mussina/50 15.00
23 Tom Glavine/50 10.00
24 Sammy Sosa/50 25.00

Player Threads Triple

NM/M

Production 50
Some not priced due to scarcity.
Triple Primes: No Pricing
Production 5-10
4 Randy Johnson/50 20.00
7 Nolan Ryan/50 75.00
8 Hideo Nomo/50 60.00
11 Rickey Henderson/50 30.00
13 Gary Sheffield/50 15.00
14 Jeff Kent/50 15.00
15 Roberto Alomar/50 25.00

Swatch

No Pricing

Team Threads

NM/M

Production 10-50
Some not priced due to scarcity.
Primes: No Pricing
Production 5-10
26 Alex Rodriguez,
Nolan Ryan/50 50.00
27 Hideo Nomo,
Mike Piazza/50 20.00
28 Cal Ripken Jr.,
Mike Mussina/50 50.00
29 Hideo Nomo,
Kazuhisa Ishii/50 15.00
30 Nolan Ryan,
Randy Johnson/50 40.00

Team Trademarks Threads Jersey Number

NM/M

Some not priced due to scarcity.
Primes: 1-1.5X
Production 1-25
Some not priced due to scarcity.
3 Jim Palmer/22 20.00
12 Eric Davis/44 8.00
15 Jack Morris/47 8.00
17 Deion Sanders/24 25.00
19 Orlando Cepeda/30 10.00
23 Rod Carew/29 20.00
24 Will Clark/22 50.00
25 Willie McCovey/44 10.00
27 Nolan Ryan/34 50.00
31 Rod Carew/29 20.00
32 Nolan Ryan/34 50.00
34 Nolan Ryan/30 50.00
37 Greg Maddux/31 30.00

Team Trademarks Autographs

NM/M

Some not priced due to scarcity.
1 Alan Trammell/25 40.00
3 Jim Palmer/25 30.00
5 Gary Carter/25 40.00
6 Andre Dawson/25 30.00
8 Dale Murphy/25 50.00
10 Bobby Doerr/25 35.00
11 Brooks Robinson/25 50.00
12 Eric Davis/25 35.00
13 Fred Lynn/25 30.00
15 Jack Morris/25 25.00
16 Al Kaline/25 60.00
17 Deion Sanders/25 50.00
18 Luis Aparicio/25 35.00
20 Phil Rizzuto/25 40.00
24 Will Clark/25 70.00

Team Trademarks Jersey Autograph

NM/M

Some not priced due to scarcity.
12 Eric Davis/44 30.00
15 Jack Morris/47 25.00
23 Rod Carew/29 50.00
25 Willie McCovey/44 25.00
27 Nolan Ryan/34 140.00
31 Rod Carew/29 50.00
32 Nolan Ryan/34 140.00
34 Nolan Ryan/30 140.00
37 Greg Maddux/31 150.00

Threads

NM/M

Common Player: 8.00
Varying quantities produced
1 Derek Jeter/Base/50 20.00
2 Eric Chavez/25 10.00
3 Alex Rodriguez/100 15.00
4 Miguel Tejada/50 8.00
5 Nomar Garciaparra/100 15.00
6 Jeff Bagwell/50 10.00
7 Jim Thome/50 10.00
8 Pat Burrell/25 10.00
9 Albert Pujols/100 20.00
10 Juan Gonzalez/25 20.00
11 Shawn Green/50 10.00
12 Craig Biggio/25 10.00

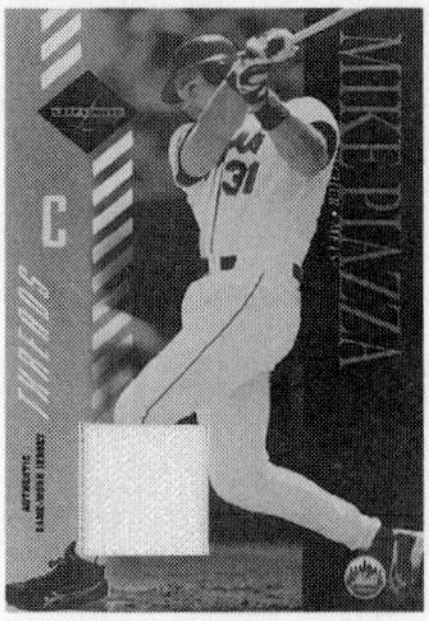

13 Chipper Jones/50 20.00
14 Hideo Nomo/100 12.00
15 Vernon Wells/25 10.00
16 Gary Sheffield/25 10.00
17 Barry Larkin/25 15.00
18 Josh Beckett/25 15.00
19 Edgar Martinez/25 15.00
20 Ivan Rodriguez/25 20.00
21 Jeff Kent/25 10.00
22 Roberto Alomar/25 15.00
23 Alfonso Soriano/100 8.00
24 Jim Thome/50 10.00
25 Juan Gonzalez/25 10.00
26 Carlos Beltran/25 20.00
27 Shawn Green/50 8.00
28 Tim Hudson/25 10.00
29 Deion Sanders/25 20.00
30 Rafael Palmeiro/25 20.00
31 Todd Helton/50 10.00
32 Lance Berkman/25 10.00
33 Mike Mussina/50 10.00
34 Kazuhisa Ishii/50 8.00
35 Pat Burrell/25 10.00
36 Miguel Tejada/50 8.00
37 Juan Gonzalez/25 10.00
38 Roberto Alomar/25 15.00
39 Roberto Alomar/25 15.00
40 Luis Gonzalez/25 10.00
41 Jorge Posada/50 15.00
42 Mark Mulder/25 10.00
43 Sammy Sosa/100 15.00
44 Mark Prior/50 15.00
45 Roger Clemens/100 10.00
46 Tom Glavine/25 15.00
47 Mark Teixeira/25 10.00
48 Manny Ramirez/50 12.00
49 Frank Thomas/25 15.00
50 Troy Glaus/50 8.00
51 Andruw Jones/50 8.00
52 Jason Giambi/100 8.00
53 Jim Thome/50 10.00
54 Barry Bonds/50/Base 25.00
55 Rafael Palmeiro/25 15.00
56 Edgar Martinez/25 10.00
57 Vladimir Guerrero/50 10.00
58 Roberto Alomar/25 15.00
59 Mike Sweeney/25 10.00
60 Magglio Ordonez/25 10.00
62 Craig Biggio/25 10.00
63 Greg Maddux/100 10.00
64 Mike Piazza/100 10.00
65 Tom Glavine/25 15.00
66 Kerry Wood/25 20.00
67 Frank Thomas/25 20.00
68 Mike Mussina/50 10.00
69 Nick Johnson/25 8.00
70 Bernie Williams/50 10.00
71 Scott Rolen/25 20.00
72 Curt Schilling/25 15.00
73 Adam Dunn/50 10.00
74 Roy Oswalt/25 10.00
75 Pedro Martinez/25 20.00
76 Tom Glavine/25 15.00
77 Torii Hunter/25 10.00
78 Austin Kearns/25 10.00
79 Randy Johnson/100 8.00
80 Bernie Williams/50 10.00
81 Ichiro Suzuki/50 25.00
82 Kerry Wood/25 20.00
83 Kazuhisa Ishii/50 8.00
84 Randy Johnson/50 8.00
85 Nick Johnson/25 8.00
86 Josh Beckett/25 10.00
87 Curt Schilling/25 15.00
88 Mike Mussina/50 10.00
89 Pedro Martinez/25 15.00
90 Barry Zito/75 8.00
91 Jim Edmonds/100 6.00
92 Rickey Henderson/100 8.00
93 Rickey Henderson/50 12.00
94 Rickey Henderson/50 12.00
95 Rickey Henderson/50 12.00
96 Rickey Henderson/50 12.00
97 Randy Johnson/50 8.00
98 Mark Grace/50 10.00
99 Pedro Martinez/25 15.00
100 Hee Seop Choi/25 8.00
101 Ivan Rodriguez/25 15.00
102 Jeff Kent/25 10.00
104 Hideo Nomo/50 10.00
105 Mike Piazza/100 10.00
106 Tom Glavine/25 15.00
107 Roberto Alomar/25 15.00
108 Roger Clemens/100 10.00
109 Jason Giambi/25 10.00
110 Jim Thome/25 15.00
111 Alex Rodriguez/100 10.00
112 Juan Gonzalez/25 10.00
113 Torii Hunter/25 10.00
114 Roy Oswalt/25 10.00
115 Curt Schilling/25 15.00
116 Magglio Ordonez/25 10.00
117 Rafael Palmeiro/25 15.00
118 Andruw Jones/50 8.00
119 Manny Ramirez/50 12.00
120 Mark Teixeira/25 10.00
121 Mark Mulder/25 10.00
123 Tim Hudson/25 10.00
124 Todd Helton/50 10.00
125 Troy Glaus/50 6.00
126 Derek Jeter/Base/50 20.00
127 Barry Bonds/Base/50 25.00
128 Greg Maddux/100 10.00
129 Roger Clemens/100 10.00
130 Nomar Garciaparra/100 10.00
131 Mike Piazza/100 10.00
132 Alex Rodriguez/100 10.00
133 Ichiro Suzuki/Base/50 25.00
134 Randy Johnson/100 8.00
135 Sammy Sosa/100 15.00
137 Alfonso Soriano/100 8.00
138 Jason Giambi/100 6.00
139 Albert Pujols/100 20.00
140 Chipper Jones/25 20.00
141 Adam Dunn/50 8.00
142 Pedro Martinez/50 10.00
143 Vladimir Guerrero/50 10.00
144 Mark Prior/50 15.00
145 Barry Zito/50 8.00
146 Jeff Bagwell/50 12.00
147 Lance Berkman/Socks/25 10.00
148 Shawn Green/25 10.00
149 Jason Giambi/25 10.00
150 Randy Johnson/25 20.00
151 Alex Rodriguez/100 10.00
153 Ty Cobb/100 100.00
154 Jackie Robinson/50 50.00
156 Thurman Munson/100 15.00
158 Nolan Ryan/100 30.00
159 Nolan Ryan/100 30.00
160 Nolan Ryan/100 30.00
161 Cal Ripken Jr./100 60.00
162 Don Mattingly/100 25.00
163 Stan Musial/100 25.00
164 Tony Gwynn/100 12.00
165 Yogi Berra/100 12.00
166 Johnny Bench/100 12.00
167 Mike Schmidt/100 25.00
168 George Brett/100 30.00
169 Ryne Sandberg/100 25.00
170 Ernie Banks/50 30.00

Threads Double

NM/M

Common Player:
Production 5 to 25
Some not priced due to scarcity.
Primes: No Pricing
Production 1 to 10
3 Alex Rodriguez/25 40.00
4 Miguel Tejada/25 25.00
10 Juan Gonzalez/25 20.00
12 Craig Biggio/25 25.00
14 Hideo Nomo/25 40.00
15 Vernon Wells/25 15.00
26 Carlos Beltran/25 25.00
28 Tim Hudson/25 20.00
31 Todd Helton/25 25.00
32 Lance Berkman/25 15.00
34 Kazuhisa Ishii/25 20.00
37 Juan Gonzalez/25 20.00
43 Sammy Sosa/25 50.00
44 Mark Prior/25 25.00
51 Andruw Jones/25 20.00
54 Barry Bonds/25 60.00
55 Rafael Palmeiro/25 30.00
60 Magglio Ordonez/25 20.00
73 Adam Dunn/25 20.00
75 Pedro Martinez/25 30.00
78 Austin Kearns/25 20.00
81 Ichiro Suzuki/25 60.00
90 Barry Zito/25 20.00
94 Rickey Henderson/25 25.00
101 Ivan Rodriguez/25 25.00
109 Jason Giambi/25 25.00
116 Magglio Ordonez/25 20.00
117 Rafael Palmeiro/25 30.00
118 Andruw Jones/25 20.00
120 Mark Teixeira/25 20.00
123 Tim Hudson/25 20.00
124 Todd Helton/25 25.00
127 Barry Bonds/25 50.00
132 Alex Rodriguez/25 40.00
133 Ichiro Suzuki/25 60.00
135 Sammy Sosa/25 50.00
141 Adam Dunn/25 30.00
142 Pedro Martinez/25 35.00
144 Mark Prior/25 40.00
145 Barry Zito/25 20.00
146 Jeff Bagwell/25 30.00
147 Lance Berkman/25 15.00
149 Jason Giambi/25 20.00
158 Nolan Ryan/25 80.00
162 Don Mattingly/25 65.00
164 Tony Gwynn/25 40.00
165 Mike Schmidt/25 65.00
168 George Brett/25 75.00
169 Ryne Sandberg/25 65.00

Threads Position

NM/M

Common (2-151): 8.00
#'s 2-151
Production 25
#'s 152-170
Production 5-25
Primes: 1-1.5X
Production 25 for #'s 2-151.
2 Eric Chavez 8.00
3 Alex Rodriguez 25.00
4 Miguel Tejada 10.00
5 Nomar Garciaparra 30.00
6 Jeff Bagwell 15.00
7 Jim Thome 15.00
8 Pat Burrell 10.00
9 Albert Pujols 35.00
10 Juan Gonzalez 10.00
11 Shawn Green 10.00
12 Craig Biggio 8.00
13 Chipper Jones 25.00
14 Hideo Nomo 30.00
15 Vernon Wells 8.00
16 Gary Sheffield 10.00
17 Barry Larkin 10.00
18 Josh Beckett 15.00
19 Edgar Martinez 15.00
20 Ivan Rodriguez 15.00
21 Jeff Kent 8.00
22 Roberto Alomar 15.00
23 Alfonso Soriano 20.00
25 Juan Gonzalez 15.00
26 Carlos Beltran 8.00
27 Shawn Green 10.00
28 Tim Hudson 10.00
29 Deion Sanders 30.00
30 Rafael Palmeiro 15.00
31 Todd Helton 15.00
32 Lance Berkman 10.00
33 Mike Mussina 15.00
34 Kazuhisa Ishii 10.00
35 Pat Burrell 10.00
36 Miguel Tejada 10.00
37 Juan Gonzalez 15.00
38 Roberto Alomar 15.00
39 Roberto Alomar 15.00
40 Luis Gonzalez 10.00
41 Jorge Posada 15.00
42 Mark Mulder 10.00
43 Sammy Sosa 40.00
44 Mark Prior 25.00
45 Roger Clemens 40.00
46 Tom Glavine 15.00
47 Mark Teixeira 10.00
48 Manny Ramirez 15.00
49 Frank Thomas 15.00
50 Troy Glaus 10.00
51 Andruw Jones 15.00
52 Jason Giambi 15.00
53 Jim Thome 15.00
55 Rafael Palmeiro 15.00
56 Edgar Martinez 15.00
57 Vladimir Guerrero 15.00
58 Roberto Alomar 15.00
60 Magglio Ordonez 10.00
62 Craig Biggio 10.00
63 Greg Maddux 30.00
64 Mike Piazza 25.00
65 Tom Glavine 15.00
66 Kerry Wood 15.00
67 Frank Thomas 15.00
68 Mike Mussina 15.00
69 Nick Johnson 10.00
70 Bernie Williams 15.00
71 Scott Rolen 15.00
72 Curt Schilling 15.00
73 Adam Dunn 15.00
74 Roy Oswalt 8.00
75 Pedro J. Martinez 15.00
76 Tom Glavine 15.00
77 Torii Hunter 15.00
78 Austin Kearns 15.00
79 Randy Johnson 15.00
80 Bernie Williams 15.00
82 Kerry Wood 15.00
83 Kazuhisa Ishii 10.00
84 Randy Johnson 15.00
85 Nick Johnson 10.00
86 Josh Beckett 15.00
87 Curt Schilling 15.00
88 Mike Mussina 15.00
89 Pedro J. Martinez 15.00
90 Barry Zito 15.00
91 Jim Edmonds 15.00
93 Rickey Henderson 25.00
94 Rickey Henderson 25.00
95 Rickey Henderson 25.00
96 Rickey Henderson 25.00
97 Randy Johnson 15.00
98 Mark Grace 15.00
99 Pedro J. Martinez 15.00
100 Hee Seop Choi 10.00
101 Ivan Rodriguez 15.00
102 Jeff Kent 10.00
104 Hideo Nomo 30.00
105 Mike Piazza 25.00
106 Tom Glavine 15.00
107 Roberto Alomar 15.00
108 Roger Clemens 40.00
109 Jason Giambi 15.00
110 Jim Thome 15.00
111 Alex Rodriguez 25.00
112 Juan Gonzalez 15.00
113 Torii Hunter 15.00
114 Roy Oswalt 10.00
115 Curt Schilling 15.00
116 Magglio Ordonez 10.00
117 Rafael Palmeiro 15.00
118 Andruw Jones 15.00
119 Manny Ramirez 15.00
120 Mark Teixeira 15.00
121 Mark Mulder 10.00
123 Tim Hudson 10.00
124 Todd Helton 15.00
125 Troy Glaus 10.00
128 Greg Maddux 30.00
129 Roger Clemens 40.00
130 Nomar Garciaparra 30.00
131 Mike Piazza 25.00
132 Alex Rodriguez 25.00
134 Randy Johnson 15.00
135 Sammy Sosa 40.00
137 Alfonso Soriano 20.00
138 Jason Giambi 15.00
139 Albert Pujols 35.00
140 Chipper Jones 25.00
141 Adam Dunn 15.00
142 Pedro J. Martinez 15.00
143 Vladimir Guerrero 15.00
144 Mark Prior 25.00
145 Barry Zito 15.00
146 Jeff Bagwell 15.00
147 Lance Berkman 10.00
148 Shawn Green 10.00
149 Jason Giambi 15.00
150 Randy Johnson 15.00
151 Alex Rodriguez 25.00
153 Ty Cobb 125.00
156 Thurman Munson 30.00
158 Nolan Ryan 50.00
159 Nolan Ryan 50.00
160 Nolan Ryan 50.00
161 Cal Ripken Jr. 85.00
162 Don Mattingly 60.00
163 Stan Musial 60.00
164 Tony Gwynn 30.00
165 Yogi Berra 30.00
168 George Brett 60.00
169 Ryne Sandberg 60.00
170 Ernie Banks/5

Threads Number

NM/M

Common Player:
7 Jim Thome/25 20.00
18 Josh Beckett/61 10.00
24 Jim Thome/25 20.00
29 Deion Sanders/21 35.00
30 Rafael Palmeiro/25 20.00
33 Mike Mussina/35 15.00
40 Luis Gonzalez/20 15.00
41 Jorge Posada/20 25.00
42 Mark Mulder/20 15.00
43 Sammy Sosa/21 50.00
44 Mark Prior/22 25.00
45 Roger Clemens/22 50.00
46 Tom Glavine/47 8.00
47 Mark Teixeira/23 15.00
48 Manny Ramirez/24 30.00
49 Frank Thomas/35 15.00
50 Troy Glaus/25 10.00
51 Andruw Jones/25 15.00
52 Jason Giambi/52 10.00
53 Jim Thome/25 20.00
55 Rafael Palmeiro/25 20.00
57 Vladimir Guerrero/27 20.00
59 Mike Sweeney/29 10.00
60 Magglio Ordonez/30 10.00
63 Greg Maddux/31 25.00
64 Mike Piazza/31 30.00
65 Tom Glavine/47 8.00
66 Kerry Wood/52 15.00
67 Frank Thomas/35 15.00
68 Mike Mussina/35 15.00
69 Nick Johnson/36 8.00
70 Bernie Williams/51 10.00
71 Scott Rolen/27 20.00
72 Curt Schilling/38 10.00
73 Adam Dunn/44 8.00
74 Roy Oswalt/44 6.00
75 Pedro Martinez/45 10.00
76 Tom Glavine/47 8.00
77 Torii Hunter/48 8.00
78 Austin Kearns/28 10.00
79 Randy Johnson/51 10.00
80 Bernie Williams/51 10.00
82 Kerry Wood/34 20.00
84 Randy Johnson/51 10.00
85 Nick Johnson/36 8.00
86 Josh Beckett/61 8.00
87 Curt Schilling/38 10.00
88 Mike Mussina/35 15.00
89 Pedro Martinez/45 10.00
90 Barry Zito/75 8.00
93 Rickey Henderson/24 25.00
94 Rickey Henderson/35 20.00
95 Rickey Henderson/24 25.00
96 Rickey Henderson/24 25.00
97 Randy Johnson/51 10.00
99 Pedro Martinez/45 10.00
105 Mike Piazza/31 30.00
106 Tom Glavine/47 8.00
108 Roger Clemens/21 50.00
110 Jim Thome/25 15.00
112 Juan Gonzalez/22 20.00
113 Torii Hunter/48 8.00
114 Roy Oswalt/44 6.00

115	Curt Schilling/38	10.00
116	Magglio Ordonez/30	8.00
117	Rafael Palmeiro/25	20.00
118	Andruw Jones/25	10.00
119	Manny Ramirez/24	25.00
120	Mark Teixeira/23	20.00
121	Mark Mulder/20	15.00
125	Troy Glaus/25	12.00
128	Greg Maddux/31	25.00
129	Roger Clemens/22	50.00
131	Mike Piazza/31	30.00
134	Randy Johnson/51	12.00
135	Sammy Sosa/21	50.00
138	Jason Giambi/25	10.00
141	Adam Dunn/44	8.00
142	Pedro Martinez/45	10.00
143	Vladimir Guerrero/27	20.00
144	Mark Prior/22	25.00
145	Barry Zito/75	8.00
150	Randy Johnson/51	10.00
154	Jackie Robinson/42	50.00
157	Roberto Clemente/21	140.00
158	Nolan Ryan/34	50.00
159	Nolan Ryan/30	50.00
160	Nolan Ryan/34	50.00
162	Don Mattingly/23	50.00
165	Yogi Berra/42	15.00
167	Mike Schmidt/20	60.00
169	Ryne Sandberg/23	60.00

Threads Button Up

Production 2-6
No Pricing

Timber

		NM/M
Common Player:		10.00
Production 25 Sets		
2	Eric Chavez	10.00
3	Alex Rodriguez	25.00
4	Miguel Tejada	10.00
5	Nomar Garciaparra	30.00
6	Jeff Bagwell	15.00
7	Jim Thome	15.00
8	Pat Burrell	15.00
9	Albert Pujols	35.00
10	Juan Gonzalez	15.00
11	Shawn Green	10.00
12	Craig Biggio	10.00
13	Chipper Jones	25.00
14	Hideo Nomo	30.00
15	Vernon Wells	10.00
16	Gary Sheffield	10.00
17	Barry Larkin	15.00
18	Josh Beckett	15.00
19	Edgar Martinez	15.00
20	Ivan Rodriguez	15.00
21	Jeff Kent	10.00
22	Roberto Alomar	15.00
23	Alfonso Soriano	20.00
24	Jim Thome	15.00
25	Juan Gonzalez	15.00
26	Carlos Beltran	10.00
27	Shawn Green	10.00
28	Tim Hudson	10.00
30	Rafael Palmeiro	15.00
31	Todd Helton	15.00
32	Lance Berkman	10.00
33	Mike Mussina	15.00
34	Kazuhisa Ishii	10.00
35	Pat Burrell	15.00
36	Miguel Tejada	10.00
37	Juan Gonzalez	15.00
38	Roberto Alomar	15.00
39	Roberto Alomar	15.00
40	Luis Gonzalez	10.00
41	Jorge Posada	15.00
42	Mark Mulder	10.00
43	Sammy Sosa	40.00
44	Mark Prior	25.00
45	Roger Clemens	40.00
46	Tom Glavine	15.00
47	Mark Teixeira	15.00
48	Manny Ramirez	15.00
49	Frank Thomas	15.00
50	Troy Glaus	10.00
51	Andruw Jones	15.00
52	Jason Giambi	15.00
53	Jim Thome	15.00
55	Rafael Palmeiro	15.00
56	Edgar Martinez	15.00
57	Vladimir Guerrero	15.00
58	Roberto Alomar	15.00
59	Mike Sweeney	10.00
60	Magglio Ordonez	10.00
62	Craig Biggio	10.00
63	Greg Maddux	30.00
64	Mike Piazza	25.00
65	Tom Glavine	15.00
66	Kerry Wood	15.00
67	Frank Thomas	15.00
68	Mike Mussina	15.00
69	Nick Johnson	10.00
70	Bernie Williams	15.00
71	Scott Rolen	15.00
72	Curt Schilling	15.00
73	Adam Dunn	15.00
74	Roy Oswalt	10.00
75	Pedro J. Martinez	15.00
76	Tom Glavine	15.00
77	Torii Hunter	15.00
78	Austin Kearns	15.00
79	Randy Johnson	15.00
80	Bernie Williams	15.00
82	Kerry Wood	15.00
83	Kazuhisa Ishii	10.00
84	Randy Johnson	15.00
85	Nick Johnson	10.00
86	Josh Beckett	15.00
87	Curt Schilling	15.00
88	Mike Mussina	15.00
89	Pedro J. Martinez	15.00
90	Barry Zito	15.00
91	Jim Edmonds	10.00
92	Rickey Henderson	15.00
93	Rickey Henderson	15.00
94	Rickey Henderson	15.00
95	Rickey Henderson	15.00
96	Rickey Henderson	15.00
97	Randy Johnson	15.00
98	Mark Grace	15.00
99	Pedro J. Martinez	15.00
101	Ivan Rodriguez	15.00
102	Jeff Kent	10.00
103	Hideo Nomo	30.00
104	Hideo Nomo	30.00
105	Mike Piazza	25.00
106	Tom Glavine	15.00
107	Roberto Alomar	15.00
108	Roger Clemens	40.00
109	Jason Giambi	15.00
110	Jim Thome	15.00
111	Alex Rodriguez	25.00
112	Juan Gonzalez	15.00
113	Torii Hunter	15.00
114	Roy Oswalt	10.00
115	Curt Schilling	15.00
116	Magglio Ordonez	10.00
117	Rafael Palmeiro	15.00
118	Andruw Jones	15.00
119	Manny Ramirez	15.00
120	Mark Teixeira	15.00
121	Mark Mulder	10.00
122	Garret Anderson	10.00
123	Tim Hudson	10.00
124	Todd Helton	15.00
125	Troy Glaus	10.00
128	Greg Maddux	30.00
129	Roger Clemens	40.00
130	Nomar Garciaparra	30.00
131	Mike Piazza	25.00
132	Alex Rodriguez	25.00
134	Randy Johnson	15.00
135	Sammy Sosa	40.00
137	Alfonso Soriano	20.00
138	Jason Giambi	15.00
139	Albert Pujols	35.00
140	Chipper Jones	25.00
141	Adam Dunn	15.00
142	Pedro J. Martinez	15.00
143	Vladimir Guerrero	15.00
144	Mark Prior	25.00
145	Barry Zito	15.00
146	Jeff Bagwell	15.00
147	Lance Berkman	10.00
148	Shawn Green	10.00
149	Jason Giambi	15.00
150	Randy Johnson	15.00
151	Alex Rodriguez	25.00
152	Babe Ruth	180.00
153	Ty Cobb	125.00
155	Lou Gehrig	150.00
156	Thurman Munson	30.00
157	Roberto Clemente	140.00
158	Nolan Ryan	50.00
159	Nolan Ryan	50.00
160	Nolan Ryan	50.00
161	Cal Ripken Jr.	85.00
162	Don Mattingly	60.00
163	Stan Musial	60.00
164	Tony Gwynn	30.00
165	Yogi Berra	30.00
166	Johnny Bench	35.00
167	Mike Schmidt	60.00
168	George Brett	60.00
169	Ryne Sandberg	60.00
170	Ernie Banks/1	10.00

TNT

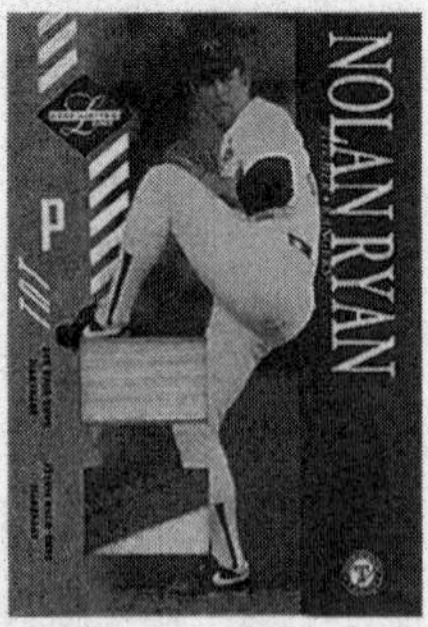

		NM/M
Production 25 unless noted.		
Some not priced due to scarcity.		
Primes:		1X
Production 1-25		
No pricing production 15 or less.		
2	Eric Chavez	15.00
3	Alex Rodriguez	45.00
4	Miguel Tejada	15.00
5	Nomar Garciaparra	45.00
6	Jeff Bagwell	25.00
7	Jim Thome	30.00
8	Pat Burrell	30.00
9	Albert Pujols	60.00
10	Juan Gonzalez	25.00
11	Shawn Green	15.00
12	Craig Biggio	15.00
13	Chipper Jones	40.00
14	Hideo Nomo	50.00
15	Vernon Wells	15.00
16	Gary Sheffield	25.00
17	Barry Larkin	20.00
18	Josh Beckett	25.00
19	Edgar Martinez	25.00
20	Ivan Rodriguez	20.00
21	Jeff Kent	10.00
22	Roberto Alomar	20.00
23	Alfonso Soriano	30.00
24	Jim Thome	30.00
25	Juan Gonzalez	25.00
26	Carlos Beltran	20.00
27	Shawn Green	15.00
28	Tim Hudson	20.00
30	Rafael Palmeiro	20.00
31	Todd Helton	20.00
32	Lance Berkman	20.00
33	Mike Mussina	25.00
34	Kazuhisa Ishii	10.00
35	Pat Burrell	30.00
36	Miguel Tejada	15.00
37	Juan Gonzalez	25.00
38	Roberto Alomar	20.00
39	Roberto Alomar	20.00
40	Luis Gonzalez	15.00
41	Jorge Posada	25.00
42	Mark Mulder	20.00
43	Sammy Sosa	40.00
44	Mark Prior	25.00
45	Roger Clemens	50.00
46	Tom Glavine	20.00
47	Mark Teixeira	20.00
48	Manny Ramirez	25.00
49	Frank Thomas	35.00
50	Troy Glaus	15.00
51	Andruw Jones	20.00
52	Jason Giambi	15.00
53	Jim Thome	30.00
55	Rafael Palmeiro	25.00
56	Edgar Martinez	20.00
57	Vladimir Guerrero	30.00
58	Mike Sweeney	10.00
60	Magglio Ordonez	15.00
62	Craig Biggio	20.00
63	Greg Maddux	40.00
64	Mike Piazza	40.00
65	Tom Glavine	20.00
66	Kerry Wood	30.00
67	Frank Thomas	35.00
68	Mike Mussina	25.00
69	Nick Johnson	15.00
70	Bernie Williams	15.00
71	Scott Rolen	30.00
72	Curt Schilling	20.00
73	Adam Dunn	25.00
74	Roy Oswalt	15.00
75	Pedro J. Martinez	35.00
76	Tom Glavine	20.00
77	Torii Hunter	15.00
78	Austin Kearns	15.00
79	Randy Johnson	30.00
80	Bernie Williams	20.00
82	Kerry Wood	30.00
83	Kazuhisa Ishii	10.00
84	Randy Johnson	30.00
85	Nick Johnson	15.00
86	Josh Beckett	20.00
87	Curt Schilling	25.00
88	Mike Mussina	25.00
89	Pedro J. Martinez	35.00
90	Barry Zito	15.00
91	Jim Edmonds	20.00
92	Rickey Henderson	35.00
93	Rickey Henderson	35.00
94	Rickey Henderson	35.00
95	Rickey Henderson	35.00
96	Rickey Henderson	35.00
97	Randy Johnson	30.00
98	Mark Grace	20.00
99	Pedro J. Martinez	35.00
101	Ivan Rodriguez	20.00
102	Jeff Kent	10.00
103	Hideo Nomo	40.00
104	Hideo Nomo	40.00
105	Mike Piazza	40.00
106	Tom Glavine	20.00
107	Roberto Alomar	25.00
108	Roger Clemens	50.00
109	Jason Giambi	20.00
110	Jim Thome	30.00
111	Alex Rodriguez	45.00
112	Juan Gonzalez	25.00
113	Torii Hunter	15.00
114	Roy Oswalt	15.00
115	Curt Schilling	25.00
116	Magglio Ordonez	15.00
117	Rafael Palmeiro	25.00
118	Andruw Jones	15.00
119	Manny Ramirez	30.00
120	Mark Teixeira	25.00
121	Mark Mulder	20.00
123	Tim Hudson	20.00
124	Todd Helton	20.00
125	Troy Glaus	15.00
128	Greg Maddux	40.00
129	Roger Clemens	50.00
130	Nomar Garciaparra	40.00
131	Mike Piazza	40.00
132	Alex Rodriguez	40.00
134	Randy Johnson	30.00
135	Sammy Sosa	40.00
137	Alfonso Soriano	30.00
138	Jason Giambi	20.00
139	Albert Pujols	60.00
140	Chipper Jones	30.00
141	Adam Dunn	25.00
142	Pedro J. Martinez	35.00
143	Vladimir Guerrero	30.00
144	Mark Prior	25.00
145	Barry Zito	15.00
146	Jeff Bagwell	25.00
147	Lance Berkman	20.00
148	Shawn Green	15.00
149	Jason Giambi	20.00
150	Randy Johnson	30.00
151	Alex Rodriguez	40.00
156	Thurman Munson	50.00
158	Nolan Ryan	65.00
159	Nolan Ryan	65.00
160	Nolan Ryan	65.00
161	Cal Ripken Jr.	100.00
162	Don Mattingly	65.00
163	Stan Musial	65.00
164	Tony Gwynn	40.00
165	Yogi Berra	40.00
166	Johnny Bench	40.00
167	Mike Schmidt	65.00
168	George Brett	75.00
169	Ryne Sandberg	65.00

7th Inning Stretch

		NM/M
Production 50 unless noted.		
1	Alex Rodriguez	20.00
3	Sammy Sosa	25.00
4	Juan Gonzalez	10.00
5	Albert Pujols	30.00
6	Chipper Jones	15.00
7	Alfonso Soriano/40	15.00
8	Jim Thome	15.00
9	Mike Piazza	20.00
10	Rafael Palmeiro	15.00

2004 Leaf

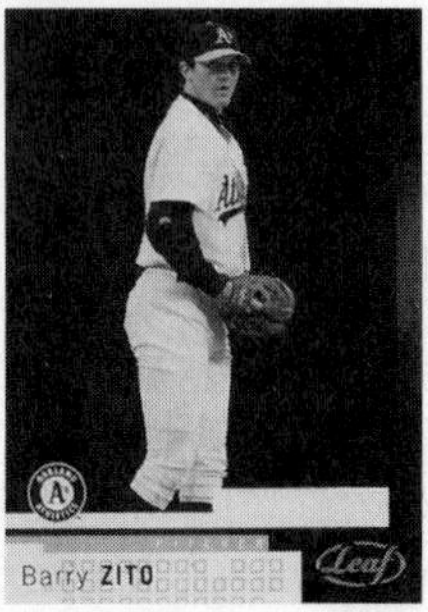

		NM/M
Complete Set (300):		50.00
Common Player:		.15
Common (202-301):		.25
Second Edition (1-301):		1X
Pack (8):		5.00
Box (24):		90.00
1	Darin Erstad	.25
2	Garret Anderson	.25
3	Jarrod Washburn	.15
4	Kevin Appier	.15
5	Tim Salmon	.25
6	Troy Glaus	.40
7	Troy Percival	.15
8	Jason Johnson	.15
9	Jay Gibbons	.25
10	Melvin Mora	.15
11	Sidney Ponson	.15
12	Tony Batista	.15
13	Derek Lowe	.25
14	Robert Person	.15
15	Manny Ramirez	.50
16	Nomar Garciaparra	1.50
17	Pedro J. Martinez	.75
18	Jorge de la Rosa	.15
19	Bartolo Colon	.25
20	Carlos Lee	.15
21	Esteban Loaiza	.15
22	Frank Thomas	.50
23	Joe Crede	.15
24	Magglio Ordonez	.25
25	Ryan Ludwick	.15
26	Luis Garcia	.15
27	Brandon Phillips	.15
28	C.C. Sabathia	.15
29	Jhonny Peralta	.15
30	Josh Bard	.15
31	Omar Vizquel	.25
32	Fernando Rodney	.15
33	Mike Maroth	.15
34	Bobby Higginson	.15

#	Player	Price
35	Omar Infante	.15
36	Dmitri Young	.15
37	Eric Munson	.15
38	Jeremy Bonderman	.15
39	Carlos Beltran	.15
40	Jeremy Affeldt	.15
41	Dee Brown	.15
43	Mike Sweeney	.15
44	Brent Abernathy	.15
45	Runelvys Hernandez	.15
46	A.J. Pierzynski	.15
47	Corey Koskie	.15
48	Cristian Guzman	.15
49	Jacque Jones	.15
50	Kenny Rogers	.15
51	J.C. Romero	.15
52	Torii Hunter	.40
53	Alfonso Soriano	.75
54	Bernie Williams	.50
55	David Wells	.15
56	Derek Jeter	2.00
57	Hideki Matsui	1.50
58	Jason Giambi	.75
59	Jorge Posada	.40
60	Jose Contreras	.25
61	Mike Mussina	.50
62	Nick Johnson	.25
63	Roger Clemens	1.50
64	Barry Zito	.40
65	Justin Duchscherer	.15
66	Eric Chavez	.25
67	Erubiel Durazo	.15
68	Miguel Tejada	.40
69	Mark Mulder	.25
70	Terrence Long	.15
71	Tim Hudson	.25
72	Bret Boone	.25
73	Dan Wilson	.15
74	Edgar Martinez	.25
75	Freddy Garcia	.15
76	Rafael Soriano	.15
77	Ichiro Suzuki	1.25
78	Jamie Moyer	.15
79	John Olerud	.15
80	Kazuhiro Sasaki	.15
81	Aubrey Huff	.15
82	Carl Crawford	.15
83	Joe Kennedy	.15
84	Rocco Baldelli	.40
85	Toby Hall	.15
86	Alex Rodriguez	1.50
87	Kevin Mench	.15
88	Hank Blalock	.25
89	Juan Gonzalez	.50
90	Mark Teixeira	.25
91	Rafael Palmeiro	.50
92	Carlos Delgado	.25
93	Eric Hinske	.15
94	Josh Phelps	.15
95	Brian Bowles	.15
96	Roy Halladay	.40
97	Shannon Stewart	.15
98	Vernon Wells	.25
99	Curt Schilling	.40
100	Junior Spivey	.15
101	Luis Gonzalez	.25
102	Lyle Overbay	.15
103	Mark Grace	.40
104	Randy Johnson	.75
105	Shea Hillenbrand	.15
106	Andruw Jones	.50
107	Chipper Jones	.75
108	Gary Sheffield	.40
109	Greg Maddux	1.00
110	Javy Lopez	.25
111	John Smoltz	.25
112	Marcus Giles	.15
113	Rafael Furcal	.15
114	Corey Patterson	.15
115	Juan Cruz	.15
116	Kerry Wood	.50
117	Mark Prior	1.00
118	Moises Alou	.25
119	Sammy Sosa	1.00
120	Aaron Boone	.15
121	Adam Dunn	.50
122	Austin Kearns	.25
123	Barry Larkin	.40
124	Ken Griffey Jr.	1.00
125	Brian Reith	.15
126	Wily Mo Pena	.15
127	Jason Jennings	.15
128	Jay Payton	.15
129	Larry Walker	.25
130	Preston Wilson	.15
131	Todd Helton	.50
132	Dontrelle Willis	.40
133	Ivan Rodriguez	.50
134	Josh Beckett	.50
135	Juan Encarnacion	.15
136	Mike Lowell	.25
137	Craig Biggio	.25
138	Jeff Bagwell	.50
139	Jeff Kent	.25
140	Lance Berkman	.25
141	Richard Hidalgo	.15
142	Roy Oswalt	.25
143	Eric Gagne	.25
144	Fred McGriff	.25
145	Hideo Nomo	.40
146	Kazuhisa Ishii	.15
147	Kevin Brown	.25
148	Paul LoDuca	.25
149	Shawn Green	.25
150	Ben Sheets	.25

#	Player	Price
151	Geoff Jenkins	.25
152	Rey Sanchez	.15
153	Richie Sexson	.40
154	Wes Helms	.15
155	Shane Nance	.15
156	Fernando Tatis	.15
157	Javier Vazquez	.15
158	Jose Vidro	.15
159	Orlando Cabrera	.15
160	Henry Mateo	.15
161	Vladimir Guerrero	.75
162	Zach Day	.15
163	Edwin Almonte	.15
164	Al Leiter	.15
165	Cliff Floyd	.15
166	Jae Weong Seo	.15
167	Mike Piazza	1.00
168	Roberto Alomar	.50
169	Tom Glavine	.25
170	Bobby Abreu	.25
171	Brandon Duckworth	.15
172	Jim Thome	.75
173	Kevin Millwood	.25
174	Pat Burrell	.25
175	Aramis Ramirez	.15
176	Jack Wilson	.15
177	Brian Giles	.25
178	Jason Kendall	.25
179	Kenny Lofton	.25
180	Kip Wells	.15
181	Kris Benson	.15
182	Albert Pujols	1.50
183	J.D. Drew	.15
184	Jim Edmonds	.25
185	Matt Morris	.15
186	Scott Rolen	.75
187	Woody Williams	.15
188	Clifford Bartosh	.15
189	Brian Lawrence	.15
190	Ryan Klesko	.25
191	Sean Burroughs	.15
192	Xavier Nady	.15
193	Dennis Tankersley	.15
194	Donaldo Mendez	.15
195	Barry Bonds	2.00
196	Benito Santiago	.15
197	Edgardo Alfonzo	.15
198	Cody Ransom	.15
199	Jason Schmidt	.15
200	Rich Aurilia	.15
201	Ken Harvey	.15
202	Adam Loewen	.25
203	Alfredo Gonzalez	.25
204	Arnie Munoz	.25
205	Andrew Brown	.25
206	Josh Hall	.25
207	Josh Stewart	.25
208	Clint Barmes	.25
209	Brandon Webb	.25
210	Chien-Ming Wang	.40
211	Edgar Gonzalez	.25
212	Alejandro Machado	.25
213	Jeremy Griffiths	.25
214	Craig Brazell	.25
215	Daniel Cabrera	.25
216	Fernando Cabrera	.25
217	Terrmel Sledge	.25
218	Rob Hammock	.25
219	Francisco Rosario	.25
220	Francisco Cruceta	.25
221	Rett Johnson	.25
222	Guillermo Quiroz	.25
223	Hong-Chih Kuo	.25
224	Ian Ferguson	.25
225	Tim Olson	.25
226	Todd Wellemeyer	.25
227	Rich Fischer	.25
228	Phil Seibel	.25
229	Joe Valentine	.25
230	Matt Kata	.25
231	Michael Hessman	.25
232	Michel Hernandez	.25
233	Doug Waechter	.25
234	Prentice Redman	.25
235	Nook Logan	.25
236	Oscar Villarreal	.25
237	Pete LaForest	.25
238	Matt Bruback	.25
239	Josh Willingham	.25
240	Greg Aquino	.25
241	Lew Ford	.25
242	Jeff Duncan	.25
243	Chris Waters	.25
244	Miguel Ojeda	.25
245	Rosman Garcia	.25
246	Felix Sanchez	.25
247	Jon Leicester	.25
248	Roger Deago	.25
249	Mike Ryan	.25
250	Chris Capuano	.25
251	Matt White	.25
252	Bernie Williams	.50
253	Mark Grace	.50
254	Chipper Jones	1.00
255	Greg Maddux	1.50
256	Sammy Sosa	2.00
257	Mike Mussina	.75
258	Tim Salmon	.50
259	Barry Larkin	.50
260	Randy Johnson	1.00
261	Jeff Bagwell	.75
262	Roberto Alomar	.50
263	Tom Glavine	.50
264	Roger Clemens	2.50
265	Barry Bonds	3.00

#	Player	Price
266	Ivan Rodriguez	.75
267	Pedro J. Martinez	1.00
268	Ken Griffey Jr.	1.50
269	Jim Thome	1.00
270	Frank Thomas	.75
271	Mike Piazza	1.50
272	Troy Glaus	.40
273	Melvin Mora	.25
274	Nomar Garciaparra	2.00
275	Magglio Ordonez	.40
276	Omar Vizquel	.40
277	Dmitri Young	.25
278	Mike Sweeney	.25
279	Torii Hunter	.50
280	Derek Jeter	2.00
281	Barry Zito	.50
282	Ichiro Suzuki	1.50
283	Rocco Baldelli	.50
284	Alex Rodriguez	2.00
285	Carlos Delgado	.50
286	Randy Johnson	.75
287	Greg Maddux	1.00
288	Sammy Sosa	1.50
289	Ken Griffey Jr.	1.00
290	Todd Helton	.50
291	Ivan Rodriguez	.50
292	Jeff Bagwell	.50
293	Hideo Nomo	.50
294	Richie Sexson	.50
295	Vladimir Guerrero	.75
296	Mike Piazza	1.00
297	Jim Thome	.75
298	Jason Kendall	.40
299	Albert Pujols	1.50
300	Ryan Klesko	.40
301	Barry Bonds	2.00

Blue Press Proof

Josh BECKETT

Stars (1-301):	4-8X
Production 100 Sets	

Black Press Proof

Stars (1-301):	5-10X
Production 50 Sets	
Hot Pack Exclusive	

Gold Press Proof

Cards (1-301):	12-25X
Production 25 Sets	

Red Press Proof

Curt SCHILLING

Stars (1-301):	1-2X
Inserted 1:8	

Autographs

		NM/M
	Common Autograph	6.00
14	Robert Person	6.00
18	Jorge De La Rosa	6.00
25	Ryan Ludwick	10.00
26	Luis Garcia	6.00
29	Jhonny Peralta	6.00
30	Josh Bard	6.00
32	Fernando Rodney	6.00
35	Mike Maroth	6.00
41	Omar Infante	6.00
44	Brent Abernathy/SP	10.00
51	J.C. Romero	6.00

Jorge DE LA ROSA

65	Justin Duchscherer	10.00
70	Terrence Long/SP	15.00
76	Rafael Soriano	8.00
85	Toby Hall/SP	10.00
87	Kevin Mench	6.00
95	Brian Bowles	6.00
115	Juan Cruz	6.00
125	Brian Reith	6.00
126	Wily Mo Pena	6.00
127	Jason Jennings	6.00
155	Shane Nance	6.00
160	Henry Mateo/SP	8.00
163	Edwin Almonte	6.00
171	Brandon Duckworth	6.00
176	Jack Wilson	6.00
180	Kip Wells	6.00
188	Clifford Bartosh	6.00
189	Brian Lawrence	6.00
193	Dennis Tankersley	6.00
194	Donaldo Mendez	6.00
198	Cody Ransom/SP	8.00
247	Jon Leicester/SP	8.00

Away

	NM/M
Complete Set (10):	20.00
Common Player:	1.00
Inserted 1:35	
1 Greg Maddux	2.50
2 Sammy Sosa	3.00
3 Alex Rodriguez	4.00
4 Albert Pujols	4.00
5 Jason Giambi	1.50
6 Chipper Jones	2.00
7 Vladimir Guerrero	1.50
8 Mike Piazza	2.50
9 Nomar Garciaparra	3.00
10 Austin Kearns	1.00

Away Jersey

SAMMY SOSA

	NM/M
Common Player:	5.00
Inserted 1:119	
Prime:	1.5-2X
Production 50	
1 Greg Maddux	8.00
2 Sammy Sosa	12.00
3 Alex Rodriguez	10.00
4 Albert Pujols	15.00
5 Jason Giambi	8.00
6 Chipper Jones	8.00
7 Vladimir Guerrero	8.00
8 Mike Piazza	12.00
9 Nomar Garciaparra	12.00
10 Austin Kearns	5.00

Clean Up Crew

	NM/M
Complete Set (10):	20.00
Common Player:	1.00
Inserted 1:49	
1 Sammy Sosa, Moises Alou, Hee Seop Choi	3.00
2 Jason Giambi, Alfonso Soriano, Hideki Matsui	5.00
3 Vernon Wells, Carlos Delgado, Josh Phelps	1.00

4	Alex Rodriguez, Juan Gonzalez, Hank Blalock	4.00
5	Gary Sheffield, Andruw Jones, Chipper Jones	2.50
6	Ken Griffey Jr., Austin Kearns, Aaron Boone	3.00
7	Albert Pujols, Jim Edmonds, Scott Rolen	4.00
8	Jeff Bagwell, Jeff Kent, Lance Berkman	1.50
9	Todd Helton, Preston Wilson, Larry Walker	1.50
10	Miguel Tejada, Erubiel Durazo, Eric Chavez	1.00

Clean Up Crew Materials

		NM/M
Common Card:		15.00
Production 50 Sets		
1	Sammy Sosa, Moises Alou, Hee Seop Choi	35.00
2	Jason Giambi, Alfonso Soriano, Hideki Matsui	60.00
3	Vernon Wells, Carlos Delgado, Josh Phelps	15.00
4	Alex Rodriguez, Juan Gonzalez, Hank Blalock	35.00
5	Gary Sheffield, Andruw Jones, Chipper Jones	20.00
6	Ken Griffey Jr., Austin Kearns, Aaron Boone	25.00
7	Albert Pujols, Jim Edmonds, Scott Rolen	40.00
8	Jeff Bagwell, Jeff Kent, Lance Berkman	25.00
9	Todd Helton, Preston Wilson, Larry Walker	20.00
10	Miguel Tejada, Erubiel Durazo, Eric Chavez	15.00

Cornerstones

		NM/M
Complete Set (10):		20.00
Common Player:		1.00
Inserted 1:78		
1	Alex Rodriguez, Hank Blalock	3.00
2	Kerry Wood, Mark Prior	1.50
3	Roger Clemens, Alfonso Soriano	4.00
4	Nomar Garciaparra, Manny Ramirez	4.00
5	Austin Kearns, Adam Dunn	1.00
6	Tom Glavine, Mike Piazza	2.50
7	Andruw Jones, Chipper Jones	2.50
8	Albert Pujols, Scott Rolen	4.00
9	Curt Schilling, Randy Johnson	2.00
10	Hideo Nomo, Kazuhisa Ishii	1.00

Cornerstones Materials

		NM/M
Common Duo:		15.00
Production 50 Sets		
1	Alex Rodriguez, Hank Blalock	25.00
2	Kerry Wood, Mark Prior	40.00
3	Roger Clemens, Alfonso Soriano	40.00
4	Nomar Garciaparra, Manny Ramirez	30.00
5	Austin Kearns, Adam Dunn	15.00
7	Andruw Jones, Chipper Jones	20.00
8	Albert Pujols, Scott Rolen	40.00
9	Curt Schilling, Randy Johnson	20.00
10	Hideo Nomo, Kazuhisa Ishii	20.00

Exhibits

		NM/M
Common Player:		2.50
Production 66 Sets		
Variations #'d to 63:		1X
Variations #'d to 46:		1X
Variations #'d 21 to 27:		1.5X
1	Adam Dunn	2.50
2	Albert Pujols	8.00
3	Alex Rodriguez	8.00
4	Alfonso Soriano	4.00
5	Andruw Jones	3.00
6	Barry Bonds	10.00
7	Barry Larkin	2.50
8	Barry Zito	2.50
9	Cal Ripken Jr.	10.00
10	Chipper Jones	5.00
11	Dale Murphy	2.50
12	Derek Jeter	10.00
13	Don Mattingly	8.00
14	Ernie Banks	5.00
15	Frank Thomas	4.00
16	George Brett	6.00
17	Greg Maddux	5.00
18	Hank Blalock	2.00
19	Hideo Nomo	2.50
20	Ichiro Suzuki	6.00
21	Jason Giambi	3.00
22	Jim Thome	4.00
23	Juan Gonzalez	2.50
24	Ken Griffey Jr.	5.00
25	Kirby Puckett	4.00
26	Mark Prior	5.00

27	Mike Mussina	2.50
28	Mike Piazza	5.00
29	Mike Schmidt	6.00
30	Nolan Ryan	8.00
31	Nolan Ryan	8.00
32	Nolan Ryan	8.00
33	Nomar Garciaparra	8.00
34	Ozzie Smith	2.50
35	Pedro J. Martinez	4.00
36	Randy Johnson	3.00
37	Reggie Jackson	2.50
38	Reggie Jackson	2.50
39	Rickey Henderson	2.50
40	Roberto Alomar	2.50
41	Roberto Clemente	8.00
42	Rod Carew	3.00
43	Roger Clemens	8.00
44	Sammy Sosa	6.00
45	Stan Musial	6.00
46	Tom Glavine	2.50
47	Tom Seaver	4.00
48	Tony Gwynn	4.00
49	Vladimir Guerrero	4.00
50	Yogi Berra	4.00

Gamers

		NM/M
Complete Set (20):		40.00
Common Player:		1.00
Quantum:		2-4X
Production 100 Sets		
1	Albert Pujols	4.00
2	Alex Rodriguez	4.00
3	Alfonso Soriano	1.50
4	Barry Bonds	5.00
5	Barry Zito	1.00
6	Chipper Jones	2.00
7	Derek Jeter	5.00
8	Greg Maddux	2.50
9	Ichiro Suzuki	3.00
10	Jason Giambi	1.50
11	Jeff Bagwell	1.50
12	Ken Griffey Jr.	2.50
13	Manny Ramirez	1.50
14	Mark Prior	3.00
15	Mike Piazza	2.50
16	Nomar Garciaparra	3.00
17	Pedro J. Martinez	2.00
18	Randy Johnson	2.00
19	Roger Clemens	3.00
20	Sammy Sosa	3.00

Gold Leaf Rookies

		NM/M
Complete Set (10):		6.00
Common Player:		.50
Inserted 1:23		
Mirror Gold:		No Pricing
Production 25 Sets		
1	Adam Loewen	2.00
2	Rickie Weeks	5.00
3	Khalil Greene	.50
4	Chad Tracy	.50
5	Alexis Rios	.50
6	Craig Brazell	.50
7	Clint Barmes	.50
8	Pete LaForest	.50

9	Alfredo Gonzalez	.50
10	Arnie Munoz	.50

Home

VLADIMIR GUERRERO

		NM/M
Complete Set (10):		20.00
Common Player:		1.00
Inserted 1:35		
1	Greg Maddux	2.50
2	Sammy Sosa	3.00
3	Alex Rodriguez	4.00
4	Albert Pujols	4.00
5	Jason Giambi	1.50
6	Chipper Jones	2.00
7	Vladimir Guerrero	1.50
8	Mike Piazza	2.50
9	Nomar Garciaparra	3.00
10	Austin Kearns	1.00

Home Jersey

		NM/M
Common Player:		5.00
Inserted 1:119		
Primes:		1.5-2X
Production 50		
1	Greg Maddux	8.00
2	Sammy Sosa	12.00
3	Alex Rodriguez	10.00
4	Albert Pujols	15.00
5	Jason Giambi	8.00
6	Chipper Jones	8.00
7	Vladimir Guerrero	8.00
8	Mike Piazza	10.00
9	Nomar Garciaparra	12.00
10	Austin Kearns	5.00

Previews

		NM/M
Common Player:		2.00
Production 999 Sets		
Silver:		1-2X
Production 100 Sets		
Gold:		2-3X
Production 50 Sets		
1	Derek Jeter	8.00
2	Barry Zito	2.00
3	Ichiro Suzuki	6.00
4	Pedro J. Martinez	3.00
5	Alfonso Soriano	3.00
6	Alex Rodriguez	6.00
7	Greg Maddux	4.00
8	Mike Piazza	4.00
9	Mark Prior	2.00
10	Albert Pujols	5.00
11	Sammy Sosa	5.00
12	Ken Griffey Jr.	4.00
13	Nomar Garciaparra	4.00
14	Randy Johnson	3.00
15	Jason Giambi	2.00
16	Barry Bonds	8.00
17	Manny Ramirez	3.00
18	Chipper Jones	4.00
19	Jeff Bagwell	2.00
20	Roger Clemens	6.00

MVP Winners

		NM/M
Complete Set (20):		50.00

Common Player:		1.00
Gold:		1-2X
Production 500 Sets		
1	Stan Musial/1948 NL	3.00
2	Ernie Banks/1958 NL	2.00
3	Roberto Clemente/1966 NL	4.00
4	George Brett/1980 AL	4.00
5	Mike Schmidt/1980 NL	4.00
6	Cal Ripken Jr./1983 AL	5.00
7	Dale Murphy/1983 NL	1.50
8	Ryne Sandberg/1984 NL	3.00
9	Don Mattingly/1985 AL	3.00
10	Roger Clemens/1986 AL	4.00
11	Rickey Henderson/1990 AL	1.00
12	Cal Ripken Jr./1991 AL	5.00
13	Barry Bonds/1992 NL	5.00
14	Barry Bonds/1993 NL	5.00
15	Frank Thomas/1994 AL	1.50
16	Ken Griffey Jr./1997 AL	2.50
17	Sammy Sosa/1998 NL	3.00
18	Chipper Jones/1999 NL	1.50
19	Jason Giambi/2000 AL	1.50
20	Ichiro Suzuki/2001 AL	3.00

Picture Perfect

		NM/M
Complete Set (15):		25.00
Common Player:		1.00
Inserted 1:37		
1	Albert Pujols	5.00
2	Alex Rodriguez	5.00
3	Alfonso Soriano	2.00
4	Austin Kearns	1.00
5	Carlos Delgado	1.50
6	Chipper Jones	2.50
7	Hank Blalock	1.50
8	Jason Giambi	2.00
9	Jeff Bagwell	1.50
10	Jim Thome	2.00
11	Manny Ramirez	1.50
12	Mike Piazza	3.00
13	Nomar Garciaparra	4.00
14	Sammy Sosa	3.00
15	Todd Helton	1.50

Picture Perfect Materials

		NM/M
Common Player:		6.00
Inserted 1:437		
1	Albert Pujols	15.00
2	Alex Rodriguez	10.00
3	Alfonso Soriano	8.00
4	Austin Kearns	6.00
5	Carlos Delgado	6.00
6	Chipper Jones	8.00
7	Hank Blalock	6.00
8	Jason Giambi	8.00
9	Jeff Bagwell	8.00
10	Jim Thome	10.00
11	Manny Ramirez	6.00
12	Mike Piazza	10.00
13	Nomar Garciaparra	10.00
14	Sammy Sosa	10.00
15	Todd Helton	8.00

Recollection Autographs

	NM/M
All are 1990 Leaf cards.	
No Pricing	

Shirt Off My Back

		NM/M
Common Player:		4.00
Inserted 1:47		
1	Shawn Green	4.00
2	Andruw Jones	6.00
3	Ivan Rodriguez	6.00
4	Hideo Nomo	6.00
5	Don Mattingly	20.00
6	Mark Prior	10.00
7	Alfonso Soriano	6.00
8	Richie Sexson	5.00
9	Vernon Wells	4.00
10	Nomar Garciaparra	8.00
11	Jason Giambi	6.00
12	Austin Kearns	5.00
13	Chipper Jones	6.00
14	Rickey Henderson	6.00
15	Alex Rodriguez	12.00
16	Garret Anderson	4.00
17	Vladimir Guerrero	4.00
18	Sammy Sosa	10.00
19	Mike Piazza	8.00
20	David Wells	4.00
21	Scott Rolen	6.00
22	Adam Dunn	5.00
23	Carlos Delgado	5.00
24	Greg Maddux	8.00
25	Hank Blalock	5.00

Shirt Off My Back Team Logo Patch

NM/M

Common Player: 10.00
Autographs: No Pricing
Production Five Sets
Jersey Number Patch: .75-1X
Production 50 Sets
Sosa #'d to 42.
Jersey Number Patch Auto.: No Pricing
Production Five Sets

1	Shawn Green/41	15.00
2	Andruw Jones/75	15.00
3	Ivan Rodriguez/75	15.00
4	Hideo Nomo/74	20.00
6	Mark Prior/46	20.00
7	Alfonso Soriano/28	25.00
8	Richie Sexson/38	15.00
9	Vernon Wells/74	10.00
10	Nomar Garciaparra/75	25.00
11	Jason Giambi/26	20.00
12	Austin Kearns/32	10.00
13	Chipper Jones/75	20.00
14	Rickey Henderson/40	20.00
15	Alex Rodriguez/75	30.00
16	Garret Anderson/71	10.00
17	Vladimir Guerrero/55	20.00
18	Sammy Sosa/39	25.00
19	Mike Piazza/75	20.00
20	David Wells/74	10.00
21	Scott Rolen/29	30.00
22	Adam Dunn/32	15.00
23	Carlos Delgado/56	15.00
24	Greg Maddux/75	20.00
25	Hank Blalock/62	15.00

Sunday Dress

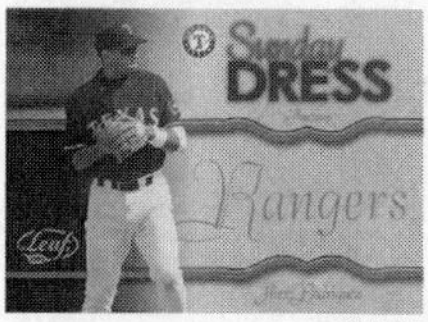

NM/M

Complete Set (10): 10.00
Common Player: .75
Inserted 1:17

1	Frank Thomas	1.00
2	Barry Zito	.75
3	Mike Piazza	2.00
4	Mark Prior	2.00
5	Jeff Bagwell	1.00
6	Roy Oswalt	.75
7	Todd Helton	1.00
8	Magglio Ordonez	.75
9	Alex Rodriguez	3.00
10	Manny Ramirez	1.00

Sunday Dress Jersey

NM/M

Common Player: 5.00
Inserted 1:119
Prime Jersey: 1-1.5X
Production 100

1	Frank Thomas	8.00
2	Barry Zito	6.00
3	Mike Piazza	10.00
4	Mark Prior	10.00
5	Jeff Bagwell	8.00
6	Roy Oswalt	5.00
7	Todd Helton	8.00
8	Magglio Ordonez	6.00
9	Alex Rodriguez	10.00
10	Manny Ramirez	6.00

2004 Leaf Certified Cuts

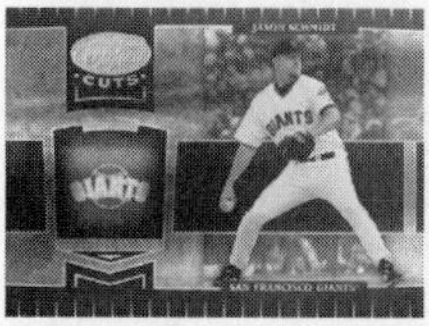

NM/M

Complete Set (300):
Common Player (1-200): .75
Common (201-250): 2.00
Production 599
Common (251-300): 5.00
Production 499
Auto. Production 99-499
Pack (5): 20.00
Box (10): 160.00

1	Vladimir Guerrero	1.50
2	Garret Anderson	.75
3	John Lackey	.75
4	Bartolo Colon	.75
5	Troy Glaus	.75
6	Tim Salmon	.75
7	Shea Hillenbrand	.75
8	Brandon Webb	.75
9	Roberto Alomar	.75
10	Randy Johnson	2.00
11	Alex Cintron	.75
12	Richie Sexson	.75
13	Luis Gonzalez	.75
14	Adam LaRoche	.75
15	Rafael Furcal	.75
16	Chipper Jones	2.00
17	Marcus Giles	.75
18	Andruw Jones	1.00
19	Russ Ortiz	.75
20	Rafael Palmeiro	1.00
21	Melvin Mora	.75
22	Luis Matos	.75
23	Jay Gibbons	.75
24	Adam Loewen	.75
25	Larry Bigbie	.75
26	Rodrigo Lopez	.75
27	Javy Lopez	.75
28	Miguel Tejada	1.00
29	Trot Nixon	.75
30	Curt Schilling	1.00
31	Jason Varitek	.75
32	Manny Ramirez	1.00
33	Keith Foulke	.75
34	Derek Lowe	.75
35	Pedro J. Martinez	1.50
36	Nomar Garciaparra	2.50
37	Bill Mueller	.75
38	Johnny Damon	.75
39	David Ortiz	1.50
40	Mark Prior	1.00
41	Kerry Wood	1.50
42	Sammy Sosa	2.50
43	Derrek Lee	.75
44	Greg Maddux	2.00
45	Aramis Ramirez	.75
46	Matt Clement	.75
47	Carlos Zambrano	.75
48	Todd Walker	.75
49	Moises Alou	.75
50	Corey Patterson	.75
51	Frank Thomas	1.00
52	Magglio Ordonez	.75
53	Carlos Lee	.75
54	Mark Buehrle	.75
55	Esteban Loaiza	.75
56	Joe Crede	.75
57	Paul Konerko	.75
58	Adam Dunn	1.00
59	Austin Kearns	.75
60	Barry Larkin	.75
61	Ryan Wagner	.75
62	Danny Graves	.75
63	Sean Casey	.75
64	Ken Griffey Jr.	2.00
65	Jody Gerut	.75
66	Cliff Lee	.75
67	Victor Martinez	.75
68	C.C. Sabathia	.75
69	Omar Vizquel	.75
70	Travis Hafner	.75
71	Todd Helton	1.00
72	Preston Wilson	.75
73	Jeromy Burnitz	.75
74	Larry Walker	.75
75	Ivan Rodriguez	1.00
76	Rondell White	.75
77	Miguel Cabrera	1.50
78	Luis Castillo	.75
79	Josh Beckett	.75
80	Mike Lowell	.75
81	Dontrelle Willis	.75
82	Brad Penny	.75
83	Hee Seop Choi	.75
84	Juan Pierre	.75
85	Andy Pettitte	.75
86	Jeff Bagwell	1.00
87	Roy Oswalt	.75
88	Lance Berkman	.75
89	Morgan Ensberg	.75
90	Craig Biggio	.75
91	Octavio Dotel	.75
92	Wade Miller	.75
93	Jeff Kent	.75
94	Richard Hidalgo	.75
95	Roger Clemens	3.00
96	Carlos Beltran	1.00
97	Angel Berroa	.75
98	Jeremy Affeldt	.75
99	Juan Gonzalez	.75
100	Mike Sweeney	.75
101	Kazuhisa Ishii	.75
102	Shawn Green	.75
103	Milton Bradley	.75
104	Paul LoDuca	.75
105	Hideo Nomo	.75
106	Eric Gagne	.75
107	Adrian Beltre	.75
108	Scott Podsednik	.75
109	Rickie Weeks	.75
110	Ben Sheets	.75
111	Geoff Jenkins	.75
112	Jacque Jones	.75
113	Johan Santana	1.00
114	Shannon Stewart	.75
115	Corey Koskie	.75
116	Lew Ford	.75
117	Torii Hunter	.75
118	Chad Cordero	.75
119	Orlando Cabrera	.75
120	Jose Vidro	.75
121	Nick Johnson	.75
122	Brad Wilkerson	.75
123	Mike Piazza	2.00
124	Jae Weong Seo	.75
125	Jose Reyes	.75
126	Tom Glavine	.75
127	Jorge Posada	.75
128	Gary Sheffield	1.00
129	Bernie Williams	.75
130	Mike Mussina	1.00
131	Mariano Rivera	.75
132	Bubba Crosby	.75
133	Kevin Brown	.75
134	Javier Vazquez	.75
135	Jason Giambi	.75
136	Derek Jeter	4.00
137	Alex Rodriguez	4.00
138	Hideki Matsui	3.00
139	Mark Mulder	.75
140	Jermaine Dye	.75
141	Tim Hudson	.75
142	Barry Zito	.75
143	Eric Chavez	.75
144	Bobby Crosby	.75
145	Eric Byrnes	.75
146	Marlon Byrd	.75
147	Billy Wagner	.75
148	Mike Lieberthal	.75
149	Jimmy Rollins	1.00
150	Jim Thome	1.50
151	Bobby Abreu	.75
152	Pat Burrell	.75
153	Jose Castillo	.75
154	Craig Wilson	.75
155	Jason Bay	.75
156	Jason Kendall	.75
157	Raul Mondesi	.75
158	Jay Payton	.75
159	Trevor Hoffman	.75
160	Jake Peavy	.75
161	Sean Burroughs	.75
162	Phil Nevin	.75
163	Brian Giles	.75
164	Ryan Klesko	.75
165	Todd Linden	.75
166	Jerome Williams	.75
167	Jason Schmidt	1.00
168	Ray Durham	.75
169	Marquis Grissom	.75
170	Shigetoshi Hasegawa	.75
171	Edgar Martinez	.75
172	Freddy Garcia	.75
173	Bret Boone	.75
174	Raul Ibanez	.75
175	Ichiro Suzuki	3.00
176	Randy Winn	.75
177	Scott Rolen	1.50
178	Jim Edmonds	.75
179	Albert Pujols	3.00
180	Matt Morris	.75
181	Edgar Renteria	.75
182	Aubrey Huff	.75
183	Delmon Young	.75
184	Dewon Brazelton	.75
185	Rocco Baldelli	.75
186	Carl Crawford	.75
187	Mark Teixeira	.75
188	Hank Blalock	1.00
189	Michael Young	.75
190	Laynce Nix	.75
191	Alfonso Soriano	1.50
192	Kevin Mench	.75
193	Adrian Gonzalez	.75
194	Alexis Rios	.75
195	Roy Halladay	.75
196	Vernon Wells	.75
197	Carlos Delgado	.75
198	Bill Hall	.75
199	Jose Guillen	.75
200	Jeremy Bonderman	.75
201	Roger Clemens/SP	6.00
202	Alex Rodriguez/SP	6.00
203	Greg Maddux/SP	4.00
204	Miguel Tejada/SP	2.00
205	Alfonso Soriano/SP	3.00
206	Andy Pettitte/SP	2.00
207	Curt Schilling/SP	2.00
208	Gary Sheffield/SP	2.00
209	Ivan Rodriguez/SP	2.00
210	Jim Thome/SP	2.00
211	Mike Mussina/SP	2.00
212	Mike Piazza/SP	4.00
213	Randy Johnson/SP	3.00
214	Roger Clemens/SP	6.00
215	Sammy Sosa/SP	4.00
216	Alex Rodriguez/SP	6.00
217	Randy Johnson/SP	3.00
218	Vladimir Guerrero/SP	3.00
219	Rafael Palmeiro/SP	2.00
220	Manny Ramirez/SP	2.00
221	Mike Piazza/SP	4.00
222	Cal Ripken Jr.	10.00
223	Ted Williams	8.00
224	Duke Snider	2.00
225	Ernie Banks	4.00
226	Ryne Sandberg	8.00
227	Mark Grace	2.00
228	Andre Dawson	2.00
229	Bob Feller	2.00
230	Bob Feller	6.00
231	George Brett	8.00
232	Bo Jackson	3.00
233	Robin Yount	4.00
234	Harmon Killebrew	4.00
235	Gary Carter	2.00
236	Don Mattingly	8.00
237	Phil Rizzuto	2.00
238	Babe Ruth	8.00
239	Lou Gehrig	8.00
240	Reggie Jackson	3.00
241	Rickey Henderson	3.00
242	Mike Schmidt	8.00
243	Roberto Clemente	8.00
244	Tony Gwynn	3.00
245	Will Clark	3.00
246	Lou Brock	2.00
247	Bob Gibson	3.00
248	Stan Musial	5.00
249	Nolan Ryan	10.00
250	Dale Murphy	2.00
251	Aarom Baldiris/Auto./499 **RC**	8.00
252	Akinori Otsuka/ Auto./99 **RC**	40.00
253	Andres Blanco/ Auto./499 **RC**	8.00
254	Angel Chavez/Auto./499 **RC**	5.00
255	Carlos Hines/Auto./199 **RC**	8.00
256	Carlos Vasquez/ Auto./499 **RC**	10.00
257	Casey Daigle/499 **RC**	10.00
258	Chris Oxspring/ Auto./499 **RC**	8.00
259	Colby Miller/Auto./499 **RC**	5.00
260	David Crouthers/Auto./199	8.00
261	Donald Kelly/Auto./499 **RC**	5.00
262	Eddy Rodriguez/ Auto./499 **RC**	10.00
263	Edwardo Sierra/ Auto./299 **RC**	8.00
264	Edwin Moreno/ Auto./499 **RC**	10.00
265	Fernando Nieve/ Auto./499 **RC**	5.00
266	Freddy Guzman/ Auto./499 **RC**	5.00
267	Greg Dobbs/Auto./499 **RC**	5.00
268	Brad Halsey/Auto./499 **RC**	5.00
269	Hector Gimenez/ Auto./499 **RC**	8.00
270	Ivan Ochoa/Auto./499 **RC**	5.00
271	Jake Woods/Auto./499	8.00
272	Jamie Brown/Auto./499 **RC**	5.00
273	Jason Bartlett/Auto./499 **RC**	8.00
274	Jason Szuminski/ Auto./499 **RC**	5.00
275	John Gall/499 **RC**	5.00
276	Jorge Vasquez/ Auto./499 **RC**	5.00
277	Josh Labandeira/ Auto./499 **RC**	8.00
278	Justin Hampson/ Auto./499 **RC**	5.00
279	Kazuo Matsui/499 **RC**	15.00
280	Kevin Cave/Auto./499 **RC**	8.00
281	Lance Cormier/ Auto./499 **RC**	5.00
282	Lincoln Holdzkom/ Auto./199 **RC**	8.00
283	Merkin Valdez/ Auto./199 **RC**	15.00
284	Mike Wuertz/Auto./499 **RC**	8.00
285	Mike Johnston/Auto./499 **RC**	5.00
286	Mike Rouse/Auto./329	8.00
287	Onil Joseph/Auto./499 **RC**	5.00
288	Phil Stockman/ Auto./499 **RC**	5.00
289	Roberto Novoa/ Auto./499 **RC**	8.00
290	Ronald Belisario/ Auto./499 **RC**	5.00
291	Ronny Cedeno/ Auto./499 **RC**	5.00
292	Ryan Meaux/Auto./499 **RC**	5.00
293	Scott Proctor/499 **RC**	5.00
294	Sean Henn/Auto./499	10.00
295	Shawn Camp/ Auto./499 **RC**	5.00
296	Shawn Hill/Auto./499 **RC**	5.00
297	Shingo Takatsu/ Auto./99 **RC**	40.00
298	Tim Bittner/Auto./199 **RC**	8.00
299	William Bergolla/499 **RC**	5.00
300	Yadier Molina/ Auto./499 **RC**	15.00

Marble Black

No Pricing
Production One Set

Marble Blue

Blue 1-200: 3-5X
Blue 201-250: 2-3X
Blue 251-300: .5-1X
Production 50 Sets

Marble Emerald

No Pricing
Production Five Sets

Marble Gold

Gold 1-200: 6-8X
Gold 201-250: 2-4X
Gold 251-300: No Pricing
Production 25 Sets

Marble Red

Red 1-200: 2-3X
Red 201-250: 1-2X
Red 251-300: .4-1X
Production 100 Sets

Marble Material Black

Production One Set

Marble Material Emerald Prime

No Pricing
Production Five Sets

Marble Signature Black

No Pricing
Production One Set

Marble Signature Emerald

No Pricing
Production 1-5

Marble Signature Gold

No Pricing
Production 1-25

Marble Material Red Position

NM/M

Quantity produced listed
1 Vladimir Guerrero/Jsy/100 10.00
2 Garret Anderson/Jsy/100 4.00
5 Troy Glaus/Jsy/75 4.00
6 Tim Salmon/Jsy/75 6.00
10 Randy Johnson/Jsy/100 8.00
13 Luis Gonzalez/Jsy/100 4.00
15 Rafael Furcal/Jsy/100 4.00
16 Chipper Jones/Jsy/100 8.00
17 Marcus Giles/Jsy/100 4.00
18 Andruw Jones/Jsy/100 6.00
20 Rafael Palmeiro/Jsy/100 8.00
21 Melvin Mora/Jsy/50 6.00
22 Luis Matos/Jsy/50 6.00
23 Jay Gibbons/Jsy/100 4.00
25 Larry Bigbie/Jsy/50 6.00
26 Rodrigo Lopez/Jsy/50 6.00
27 Javy Lopez/Jsy/25 10.00
28 Miguel Tejada/Jsy/100 6.00
30 Curt Schilling/Jsy/50 8.00
31 Jason Varitek/Jsy/100 4.00
32 Manny Ramirez/Jsy/100 8.00
35 Pedro J. Martinez/Jsy/100 10.00
39 David Ortiz/Jsy/100 8.00
40 Mark Prior/Jsy/100 8.00
41 Kerry Wood/Pants/100 10.00
42 Sammy Sosa/Jsy/100 10.00
44 Greg Maddux/Jsy/50 15.00
45 Aramis Ramirez/Jsy/100 6.00
51 Frank Thomas/Jsy/100 8.00
52 Magglio Ordonez/Jsy/100 4.00
53 Carlos Lee/Jsy/100 4.00
54 Mark Buehrle/Jsy/100 4.00
57 Paul Konerko/Jsy/50 6.00
58 Adam Dunn/Jsy/100 8.00
59 Austin Kearns/Jsy/100 4.00
60 Barry Larkin/Jsy/100 6.00
65 Jody Gerut/Jsy/100 4.00
66 Cliff Lee/Jsy/100 4.00
67 Victor Martinez/Jsy/100 6.00
68 C.C. Sabathia/Jsy/100 4.00
69 Omar Vizquel/Jsy/100 4.00
70 Travis Hafner/Jsy/100 4.00
71 Todd Helton/Jsy/100 8.00
72 Preston Wilson/Jsy/100 4.00
75 Ivan Rodriguez/Jsy/50 10.00
77 Miguel Cabrera/Jsy/100 8.00
79 Josh Beckett/Jsy/100 6.00
81 Dontrelle Willis/Jsy/100 4.00
82 Brad Penny/Jsy/100 4.00
86 Jeff Bagwell/Jsy/100 8.00
87 Roy Oswalt/Jsy/100 4.00
88 Lance Berkman/Jsy/100 4.00
89 Morgan Ensberg/Jsy/100 4.00
90 Craig Biggio/Jsy/100 6.00
93 Jeff Kent/Jsy/100 4.00
94 Richard Hidalgo/Pants/100 4.00
95 Roger Clemens/Jsy/25 30.00
96 Carlos Beltran/Jsy/100 6.00
97 Angel Berroa/Pants/100 4.00
100 Mike Sweeney/Jsy/100 4.00
101 Kazuhisa Ishii/Jsy/100 4.00
102 Shawn Green/Jsy/100 4.00
104 Paul LoDuca/Jsy/100 4.00
105 Hideo Nomo/Jsy/100 8.00
107 Adrian Beltre/Jsy/100 8.00
110 Ben Sheets/Jsy/100 6.00
111 Geoff Jenkins/Jsy/100 4.00
112 Jacque Jones/Jsy/100 4.00
113 Johan Santana/Jsy/100 8.00
114 Shannon Stewart/Jsy/100 4.00
117 Torii Hunter/Jsy/75 4.00
123 Mike Piazza/Jsy/100 10.00
125 Jose Reyes/Jsy/75 4.00
126 Tom Glavine/Jsy/75 6.00
127 Jorge Posada/Jsy/100 8.00
129 Bernie Williams/Jsy/100 6.00
130 Mike Mussina/Jsy/25 20.00
131 Mariano Rivera/Jsy/100 8.00
138 Hideki Matsui/Jsy/100 25.00
139 Mark Mulder/Jsy/100 4.00
142 Barry Zito/Jsy/100 4.00
143 Eric Chavez/Jsy/100 4.00
146 Marlon Byrd/Jsy/100 4.00
150 Jim Thome/Jsy/100 8.00
151 Bobby Abreu/Jsy/100 4.00
152 Pat Burrell/Jsy/100 4.00
154 Craig Wilson/Jsy/100 4.00
156 Jason Kendall/Jsy/100 4.00
161 Sean Burroughs/Jsy/100 4.00
164 Ryan Klesko/Jsy/100 4.00
166 Jerome Williams/Jsy/25 10.00
171 Edgar Martinez/Jsy/100 6.00
172 Freddy Garcia/Jsy/100 4.00
177 Scott Rolen/Jsy/100 10.00
178 Jim Edmonds/Jsy/100 6.00
179 Albert Pujols/Jsy/100 20.00
180 Matt Morris/Jsy/75 4.00
181 Edgar Renteria/Jsy/25 10.00
182 Aubrey Huff/Jsy/100 4.00
185 Rocco Baldelli/Jsy/100 4.00
186 Carl Crawford/Jsy/100 4.00
187 Mark Teixeira/Jsy/25 8.00
188 Hank Blalock/Jsy/100 8.00
191 Alfonso Soriano/Jsy/100 8.00
192 Kevin Mench/Jsy/100 4.00
195 Roy Halladay/Jsy/100 4.00
196 Vernon Wells/Jsy/100 4.00
197 Carlos Delgado/Jsy/100 4.00
200 Jeremy Bonderman/Jsy/100 4.00
201 Roger Clemens/Jsy/100 10.00
202 Alex Rodriguez/Jsy/100 10.00
203 Greg Maddux/Jsy/100 10.00
204 Miguel Tejada/Jsy/100 4.00
205 Alfonso Soriano/Jsy/100 8.00
206 Andy Pettitte/Jsy/100 6.00
207 Curt Schilling/Jsy/100 8.00
208 Gary Sheffield/Jsy/50 8.00
209 Ivan Rodriguez/Jsy/100 8.00
210 Jim Thome/Jsy/25 20.00
211 Mike Mussina/Jsy/50 10.00
212 Mike Piazza/Jsy/100 10.00
213 Randy Johnson/Jsy/100 8.00
214 Roger Clemens/Jsy/100 10.00
215 Sammy Sosa/Jsy/50 15.00
216 Alex Rodriguez/Jsy/100 10.00
217 Randy Johnson/Jsy/100 8.00
218 Vladimir Guerrero/Jsy/100 8.00
219 Rafael Palmeiro/Jsy/100 8.00
221 Mike Piazza/Jsy/100 10.00
222 Cal Ripken Jr./Jsy/50 50.00
223 Ted Williams/Jsy/25 100.00
225 Ernie Banks/Jsy/50 15.00
226 Ryne Sandberg/Jsy/100 15.00
227 Mark Grace/Jsy/25 20.00
228 Andre Dawson/Jsy/100 6.00
229 Bob Feller/Jsy/25 20.00
231 George Brett/Jsy/100 15.00
232 Bo Jackson/Jsy/100 10.00
233 Robin Yount/Jsy/100 12.00
234 Harmon Killebrew/Jsy/25 25.00
235 Gary Carter/Jkt/100 6.00
236 Don Mattingly/Jsy/50 25.00
237 Phil Rizzuto/Pants/25 20.00
238 Babe Ruth/Pants/50 200.00
239 Lou Gehrig/Pants/50 150.00
240 Reggie Jackson/Jsy/100 8.00
241 Rickey Henderson/Jsy/100 10.00
242 Mike Schmidt/Jsy/50 25.00
243 Roberto Clemente/Jsy/50 75.00
244 Tony Gwynn/Jsy/100 10.00
245 Will Clark/Jsy/100 10.00
246 Lou Brock/Jsy/25 20.00
247 Bob Gibson/Jsy/25 20.00
248 Stan Musial/Jsy/25 60.00
249 Nolan Ryan/Jsy/50 40.00
250 Dale Murphy/Jsy/100 10.00

Marble Signature Blue

NM/M

Quantity produced listed
2 Garret Anderson/50 20.00
3 John Lackey/75 15.00
7 Shea Hillenbrand/75 15.00
8 Brandon Webb/75 10.00
11 Alex Cintron/75 10.00
14 Adam LaRoche/75 15.00
15 Rafael Furcal/50 20.00
17 Marcus Giles/50 15.00
19 Russ Ortiz/75 10.00
21 Melvin Mora/75 15.00
22 Luis Matos/75 10.00
23 Jay Gibbons/75 15.00
24 Adam Loewen/50 10.00
25 Larry Bigbie/75 15.00
26 Rodrigo Lopez/75 10.00
29 Trot Nixon/50 35.00
33 Keith Foulke/75 8.00
39 David Ortiz/50 40.00
40 Mark Prior/25 40.00
41 Kerry Wood/25 50.00
43 Derrek Lee/25 30.00
45 Aramis Ramirez/75 20.00
46 Matt Clement/25 15.00
47 Carlos Zambrano/75 35.00
48 Todd Walker/75 10.00
52 Magglio Ordonez/25 20.00
53 Carlos Lee/75 15.00
54 Mark Buehrle/50 15.00
55 Esteban Loaiza/25 15.00
58 Adam Dunn/25 40.00
59 Austin Kearns/25 20.00
63 Sean Casey/25 25.00
65 Jody Gerut/75 8.00
66 Cliff Lee/75 15.00
67 Victor Martinez/75 20.00
68 C.C. Sabathia/75 15.00
70 Travis Hafner/75 15.00
72 Preston Wilson/75 15.00
77 Miguel Cabrera/50 35.00
80 Mike Lowell/25 20.00
82 Brad Penny/75 10.00
87 Roy Oswalt/50 15.00
89 Morgan Ensberg/75 12.00
90 Craig Biggio/25 30.00
91 Octavio Dotel/75 15.00
92 Wade Miller/75 10.00
96 Carlos Beltran/50 50.00
97 Angel Berroa/50 10.00
98 Jeremy Affeldt/75 10.00
103 Milton Bradley/75 15.00
104 Paul LoDuca/50 15.00
108 Scott Podsednik/75 15.00
109 Rickie Weeks/25 20.00
112 Jacque Jones/75 10.00
113 Johan Santana/50 50.00
114 Shannon Stewart/50 15.00
116 Lew Ford/75 15.00
117 Torii Hunter/25 25.00
118 Chad Cordero/75 10.00
119 Orlando Cabrera/75 20.00
120 Jose Vidro/50 10.00
125 Jose Reyes/25 30.00
132 Bubba Crosby/75 10.00
139 Mark Mulder/25 25.00
140 Jermaine Dye/75 10.00
144 Bobby Crosby/75 40.00
145 Eric Byrnes/75 10.00
146 Marlon Byrd/75 10.00
148 Mike Lieberthal/75 15.00
153 Jose Castillo/75 10.00
154 Craig Wilson/75 10.00
155 Jason Bay/75 25.00
158 Jay Payton/75 10.00
161 Sean Burroughs/25 15.00
165 Todd Linden/75 8.00
170 Shigetoshi Hasegawa/50 40.00
171 Edgar Martinez/25 40.00
174 Raul Ibanez/75 10.00
177 Scott Rolen/50 35.00
182 Aubrey Huff/75 10.00
183 Delmon Young/25 20.00
184 Dewon Brazelton/75 10.00
186 Carl Crawford/75 20.00
187 Mark Teixeira/25 40.00
188 Hank Blalock/50 25.00
189 Michael Young/75 15.00
190 Laynce Nix/75 15.00
191 Alfonso Soriano/25 50.00
193 Adrian Gonzalez/75 10.00
194 Alexis Rios/75 20.00
196 Vernon Wells/50 15.00
198 Bill Hall/75 10.00
199 Jose Guillen/75 15.00
200 Jeremy Bonderman/75 10.00
222 Cal Ripken Jr./25 150.00
224 Duke Snider/35 35.00
228 Andre Dawson/50 20.00
229 Bob Feller/50 30.00
235 Gary Carter/25 20.00
237 Phil Rizzuto/25 40.00
245 Will Clark/25 50.00
246 Lou Brock/25 35.00
247 Bob Gibson/25 40.00
248 Stan Musial/25 75.00
249 Nolan Ryan/25 150.00
250 Dale Murphy/50 30.00
251 Aarom Baldiris/75 10.00
252 Akinori Otsuka/25 50.00
253 Andres Blanco/75 10.00
254 Angel Chavez/75 8.00
255 Carlos Hines/75 8.00
256 Carlos Vasquez/75 12.00
258 Chris Oxspring/75 10.00
259 Colby Miller/75 8.00
261 Donald Kelly/75 8.00
262 Eddy Rodriguez/75 8.00
263 Edwardo Sierra/65 10.00
264 Edwin Moreno/75 12.00
265 Fernando Nieve/75 8.00
266 Freddy Guzman/75 8.00
267 Greg Dobbs/75 8.00
268 Brad Halsey/75 8.00
269 Hector Gimenez/75 8.00
270 Ivan Ochoa/75 8.00
271 Jake Woods/75 10.00
272 Jamie Brown/75 8.00
273 Jason Bartlett/75 15.00
274 Jason Szuminski/75 8.00
275 John Gall/75 10.00
276 Jorge Vasquez/75 8.00
277 Josh Labandeira/75 8.00
278 Justin Hampson/75 8.00
280 Kevin Cave/75 10.00
281 Lance Cormier/75 8.00
283 Merkin Valdez/75 15.00
284 Mike Wuertz/75 10.00
285 Mike Johnston/75 8.00
287 Onil Joseph/75 8.00
288 Phil Stockman/75 8.00
289 Roberto Novoa/75 10.00
290 Ronald Belisario/75 8.00
291 Ronny Cedeno/75 8.00
292 Ryan Meaux/75 8.00
293 Scott Proctor/75 10.00
295 Shawn Camp/75 8.00
296 Shawn Hill/75 8.00
297 Shingo Takatsu/25 60.00
299 William Bergolla/75 8.00
300 Yadier Molina/75 25.00

Marble Signature Red

NM/M

Quantity produced listed
2 Garret Anderson/50 20.00
3 John Lackey/100 15.00
7 Shea Hillenbrand/100 15.00
8 Brandon Webb/100 10.00
11 Alex Cintron/100 10.00
14 Adam LaRoche/100 15.00
15 Rafael Furcal/50 20.00
17 Marcus Giles/50 15.00
19 Russ Ortiz/100 10.00
21 Melvin Mora/100 15.00
22 Luis Matos/100 10.00
23 Jay Gibbons/100 15.00
25 Larry Bigbie/100 15.00
26 Rodrigo Lopez/100 10.00
29 Trot Nixon/50 35.00
33 Keith Foulke/100 8.00
39 David Ortiz/50 40.00
40 Mark Prior/25 40.00
43 Derrek Lee/50 25.00
45 Aramis Ramirez/100 20.00
46 Matt Clement/25 15.00
47 Carlos Zambrano/100 35.00
48 Todd Walker/100 10.00
53 Carlos Lee/100 15.00
54 Mark Buehrle/50 15.00
55 Esteban Loaiza/100 10.00
58 Adam Dunn/25 40.00
59 Austin Kearns/25 20.00
63 Sean Casey/25 25.00
65 Jody Gerut/100 8.00
66 Cliff Lee/100 15.00
67 Victor Martinez/100 20.00
68 C.C. Sabathia/100 15.00
70 Travis Hafner/100 15.00
72 Preston Wilson/100 15.00
77 Miguel Cabrera/50 35.00
80 Mike Lowell/25 20.00
82 Brad Penny/100 10.00
89 Morgan Ensberg/100 10.00
90 Craig Biggio/25 30.00
91 Octavio Dotel/100 15.00
92 Wade Miller/100 10.00
96 Carlos Beltran/50 50.00
97 Angel Berroa/50 10.00
98 Jeremy Affeldt/100 10.00
103 Milton Bradley/100 15.00
104 Paul LoDuca/50 15.00
108 Scott Podsednik/100 15.00
109 Rickie Weeks/25 20.00
112 Jacque Jones/100 10.00
113 Johan Santana/50 50.00
114 Shannon Stewart/50 15.00
116 Lew Ford/100 15.00
117 Torii Hunter/25 25.00
118 Chad Cordero/100 10.00
119 Orlando Cabrera/100 20.00
120 Jose Vidro/50 10.00
132 Bubba Crosby/100 10.00
139 Mark Mulder/25 25.00
140 Jermaine Dye/100 10.00
144 Bobby Crosby/100 40.00
145 Eric Byrnes/100 10.00
146 Marlon Byrd/100 10.00
148 Mike Lieberthal/100 15.00
153 Jose Castillo/100 10.00
154 Craig Wilson/100 10.00
155 Jason Bay/100 25.00
158 Jay Payton/100 10.00
161 Sean Burroughs/25 15.00
165 Todd Linden/100 8.00
170 Shigetoshi Hasegawa/50 40.00
171 Edgar Martinez/25 40.00
174 Raul Ibanez/100 10.00
177 Scott Rolen/50 35.00
182 Aubrey Huff/100 10.00
183 Delmon Young/25 20.00
184 Dewon Brazelton/100 10.00
186 Carl Crawford/100 20.00
187 Mark Teixeira/25 40.00
188 Hank Blalock/50 25.00
189 Michael Young/100 15.00
190 Laynce Nix/100 15.00
191 Alfonso Soriano/25 50.00
193 Adrian Gonzalez/100 10.00
194 Alexis Rios/100 20.00
196 Vernon Wells/50 15.00
198 Bill Hall/100 10.00
199 Jose Guillen/100 15.00
200 Jeremy Bonderman/100 10.00
222 Cal Ripken Jr./25 150.00
224 Duke Snider/25 40.00
228 Andre Dawson/100 20.00
229 Bob Feller/100 25.00
235 Gary Carter/25 20.00
237 Phil Rizzuto/25 40.00
245 Will Clark/25 50.00
247 Bob Gibson/25 40.00
248 Stan Musial/25 75.00
249 Nolan Ryan/25 150.00
250 Dale Murphy/50 30.00
251 Aarom Baldiris/100 10.00
252 Akinori Otsuka/25 50.00
253 Andres Blanco/100 10.00
254 Angel Chavez/100 8.00
255 Carlos Hines/100 8.00
256 Carlos Vasquez/100 12.00
258 Chris Oxspring/100 10.00
259 Colby Miller/100 8.00
260 David Crouthers/50 8.00
261 Donald Kelly/100 8.00
262 Eddy Rodriguez/100 8.00
263 Edwardo Sierra/100 10.00
264 Edwin Moreno/100 10.00
266 Freddy Guzman/100 8.00
267 Greg Dobbs/100 8.00
268 Brad Halsey/100 8.00
269 Hector Gimenez/100 8.00
270 Ivan Ochoa/100 8.00
271 Jake Woods/100 10.00
272 Jamie Brown/100 8.00
273 Jason Bartlett/100 15.00
274 Jason Szuminski/100 8.00
275 John Gall/100 10.00
276 Jorge Vasquez/100 8.00
277 Josh Labandeira/100 8.00
280 Kevin Cave/100 10.00
281 Lance Cormier/100 8.00

283 Merkin Valdez/100 15.00
284 Mike Wuertz/100 10.00
285 Mike Johnston/100 8.00
287 Onil Joseph/100 8.00
288 Phil Stockman/100 8.00
289 Roberto Novoa/100 10.00
291 Ronny Cedeno/100 8.00
292 Ryan Meaux/100 8.00
293 Scott Proctor/100 10.00
295 Shawn Camp/100 8.00
297 Shingo Takatsu/25 60.00
299 William Bergolla/100 8.00
300 Yadier Molina/100 25.00

Marble Signature Material Gold Position

NM/M

Quantity produced listed
1 Vladimir Guerrero/Jsy/10
2 Garret Anderson/Jsy/50 20.00
8 Brandon Webb/Jsy/50 15.00
15 Rafael Furcal/Jsy/50 20.00
17 Marcus Giles/Jsy/50 20.00
21 Melvin Mora/Jsy/50 20.00
22 Luis Matos/Jsy/50 15.00
23 Jay Gibbons/Jsy/50 15.00
25 Larry Bigbie/Jsy/50 15.00
26 Rodrigo Lopez/Jsy/50 10.00
45 Aramis Ramirez/Jsy/50 30.00
53 Carlos Lee/Jsy/50 20.00
54 Mark Buehrle/Jsy/50 20.00
59 Austin Kearns/Jsy/50 20.00
65 Jody Gerut/Jsy/50 10.00
66 Cliff Lee/Jsy/50 20.00
67 Victor Martinez/Jsy/50 25.00
68 C.C. Sabathia/Jsy/50 20.00
70 Travis Hafner/Jsy/50 20.00
72 Preston Wilson/Jsy/50 20.00
82 Brad Penny/Jsy/50 10.00
89 Morgan Ensberg/Jsy/50 10.00
96 Carlos Beltran/Jsy/50 50.00
97 Angel Berroa/Pants/50 10.00
104 Paul LoDuca/Jsy/25 25.00
112 Jacque Jones/Jsy/50 20.00
113 Johan Santana/Jsy/50 50.00
114 Shannon Stewart/Jsy/50 20.00
117 Torii Hunter/Jsy/25 25.00
119 Orlando Cabrera/Jsy/50 20.00
120 Jose Vidro/Jsy/50 10.00
139 Mark Mulder/Jsy/25 25.00
146 Marlon Byrd/Jsy/50 15.00
154 Craig Wilson/Jsy/50 15.00
161 Sean Burroughs/Jsy/50 15.00
171 Edgar Martinez/Jsy/25 50.00
182 Aubrey Huff/Jsy/50 20.00
186 Carl Crawford/Jsy/50 30.00
188 Hank Blalock/Jsy/25 50.00
200 Jeremy Bonderman/Jsy/50 10.00
228 Andre Dawson/Jsy/50 20.00
229 Bob Feller/Jsy/50 35.00
234 Harmon Killebrew/Jsy/25 65.00

Marble Signature Material Gold Number

NM/M

Quantity produced listed
1 Vladimir Guerrero/Jsy/27 60.00
8 Brandon Webb/Jsy/55 10.00
18 Andruw Jones/Jsy/25 40.00
22 Luis Matos/Jsy/32 15.00
23 Jay Gibbons/Jsy/31 25.00
32 Manny Ramirez/Jsy/24 75.00
39 David Ortiz/Jsy/34 50.00
40 Mark Prior/Jsy/22 50.00
41 Kerry Wood/Pants/34 50.00
42 Sammy Sosa/Jsy/21 150.00
44 Greg Maddux/Jsy/31 100.00
51 Frank Thomas/Jsy/35 50.00
52 Magglio Ordonez/Jsy/30 25.00
53 Carlos Lee/Jsy/45 20.00
54 Mark Buehrle/Jsy/56 20.00
58 Adam Dunn/Jsy/44 40.00
59 Austin Kearns/Jsy/28 25.00
66 Cliff Lee/Jsy/34 20.00
67 Victor Martinez/Jsy/41 25.00
68 C.C. Sabathia/Jsy/52 20.00
70 Travis Hafner/Jsy/48 20.00
71 Todd Helton/Jsy/17 60.00
72 Preston Wilson/Jsy/44 20.00
81 Dontrelle Willis/Jsy/35 30.00
82 Brad Penny/Jsy/31 15.00
85 Andy Pettitte/Jsy/21 50.00
104 Paul LoDuca/Jsy/16 35.00
113 Johan Santana/Jsy/57 50.00
114 Shannon Stewart/Jsy/23 25.00
117 Torii Hunter/Jsy/48 20.00
119 Orlando Cabrera/Jsy/18 30.00
123 Mike Piazza/Jsy/31 100.00
124 Jae Weong/Seo Jsy/26 20.00
127 Jorge Posada/Jsy/20 40.00
130 Mike Mussina/Jsy/35 40.00
139 Mark Mulder/Jsy/20 25.00
141 Tim Hudson/Jsy/15 30.00
146 Marlon Byrd/Jsy/29 15.00
177 Scott Rolen/Jsy/27 50.00
182 Aubrey Huff/Jsy/19 30.00
184 Dewon Brazelton/Jsy/45 15.00
187 Mark Teixeira/Jsy/23 50.00
195 Roy Halladay/Jsy/32 15.00
200 Jeremy Bonderman/Jsy/38 10.00
236 Don Mattingly/Jsy/23 85.00
240 Reggie Jackson/Jsy/44 50.00
241 Rickey Henderson/Jsy/35 50.00
242 Mike Schmidt/Pants/20 100.00
244 Tony Gwynn/Jsy/19 75.00
245 Will Clark/Jsy/22 50.00
246 Lou Brock/Jsy/20 40.00
247 Bob Gibson/Jsy/45 40.00
249 Nolan Ryan/Jsy/34 150.00

Marble Material Blue Number

NM/M

Quanity produced listed
1 Vladimir Guerrero/Jsy/27 25.00
2 Garret Anderson/Jsy/16 15.00
5 Troy Glaus/Jsy/25 10.00
6 Tim Salmon/Jsy/15 20.00
8 Brandon Webb/Jsy/55 5.00
10 Randy Johnson/Jsy/51 12.00
13 Luis Gonzalez/Jsy/20 10.00
17 Marcus Giles/Jsy/22 10.00
18 Andruw Jones/Jsy/25 10.00
20 Rafael Palmeiro/Jsy/25 15.00
22 Luis Matos/Jsy/32 10.00
23 Jay Gibbons/Jsy/31 10.00
26 Rodrigo Lopez/Jsy/19 10.00
27 Javy Lopez/Jsy/18 15.00
30 Curt Schilling/Jsy/38 12.00
31 Jason Varitek/Jsy/33 10.00
32 Manny Ramirez/Jsy/24 20.00
35 Pedro Martinez/Jsy/45 15.00
39 David Ortiz/Jsy/34 20.00
40 Mark Prior/Jsy/22 15.00
41 Kerry Wood/Pants/34 20.00
42 Sammy Sosa/Jsy/21 30.00
44 Greg Maddux/Jsy/31 25.00
45 Aramis Ramirez/Jsy/16 15.00
49 Moises Alou/Jsy/18 15.00
51 Frank Thomas/Jsy/35 20.00
52 Magglio Ordonez/Jsy/30 10.00
53 Carlos Lee/Jsy/45 5.00
54 Mark Buehrle/Jsy/56 5.00
58 Adam Dunn/Jsy/44 12.00
59 Austin Kearns/Jsy/28 10.00
63 Sean Casey/Jsy/21 10.00
66 Cliff Lee/Jsy/34 10.00
67 Victor Martinez/Jsy/41 8.00
68 C.C. Sabathia/Jsy/52 5.00
70 Travis Hafner/Jsy/48 8.00
71 Todd Helton/Jsy/17 20.00
72 Preston Wilson/Jsy/44 5.00
73 Jeromy Burnitz/Jsy/35 5.00
74 Larry Walker/Jsy/33 10.00
77 Miguel Cabrera/Jsy/24 20.00
79 Josh Beckett/Jsy/21 12.00
81 Dontrelle Willis/Jsy/35 10.00
82 Brad Penny/Jsy/31 8.00
85 Andy Pettitte/Jsy/21 15.00
87 Roy Oswalt/Jsy/44 5.00
88 Lance Berkman/Jsy/17 10.00
95 Roger Clemens/Jsy/22 25.00
100 Mike Sweeney/Jsy/29 10.00
101 Kazuhisa Ishii/Jsy/17 15.00
107 Adrian Beltre/Jsy/29 15.00
113 Johan Santana/Jsy/57 15.00
114 Shannon Stewart/Jsy/23 10.00
117 Torii Hunter/Jsy/48 5.00
119 Orlando Cabrera/Jsy/18 20.00
123 Mike Piazza/Jsy/31 30.00
124 Jae Weong/Seo Jsy/26 10.00
126 Tom Glavine/Jsy/47 10.00
127 Jorge Posada/Jsy/20 15.00
129 Bernie Williams/Jsy/51 10.00
130 Mike Mussina/Jsy/35 15.00
131 Mariano Rivera/Jsy/42 10.00
135 Jason Giambi/Jsy/25 10.00
138 Hideki Matsui/Jsy/55 40.00
139 Mark Mulder/Jsy/20 10.00
142 Barry Zito/Jsy/75 5.00
146 Marlon Byrd/Jsy/29 10.00
150 Jim Thome/Jsy/25 20.00
151 Bobby Abreu/Jsy/53 5.00
154 Craig Wilson/Jsy/36 5.00
161 Sean Burroughs/Jsy/32 10.00
163 Brian Giles/Jsy/24 8.00
164 Ryan Klesko/Jsy/30 10.00
166 Jerome Williams/Jsy/57 5.00
172 Freddy Garcia/Jsy/34 8.00
177 Scott Rolen/Jsy/27 20.00
178 Jim Edmonds/Jsy/15 15.00
180 Matt Morris/Jsy/35 10.00
181 Edgar Renteria/Jsy/15 15.00
182 Aubrey Huff/Jsy/19 10.00
184 Dewon Brazelton/Jsy/45 5.00
187 Mark Teixeira/Jsy/23 15.00
192 Kevin Mench/Jsy/28 8.00
195 Roy Halladay/Jsy/32 10.00
197 Carlos Delgado/Jsy/25 10.00
200 Jeremy Bonderman/Jsy/38 5.00
201 Roger Clemens/Jsy/22 30.00
203 Greg Maddux/Jsy/31 25.00
206 Andy Pettitte/Jsy/46 10.00
207 Curt Schilling/Jsy/38 12.00
210 Jim Thome/Jsy/25 20.00
211 Mike Mussina/Jsy/35 15.00
212 Mike Piazza/Jsy/31 30.00
213 Randy Johnson/Jsy/51 15.00
214 Roger Clemens/Jsy/21 30.00
215 Sammy Sosa/Jsy/21 30.00
217 Randy Johnson/Jsy/51 15.00
218 Vladimir Guerrero/Jsy/27 25.00
219 Rafael Palmeiro/Jsy/25 15.00
221 Mike Piazza/Jsy/25 30.00
226 Ryne Sandberg/Jsy/23 40.00
227 Mark Grace/Jsy/17 25.00
229 Bob Feller/Jsy/19 20.00
232 Bo Jackson/Jsy/16 40.00
233 Robin Yount/Jsy/19 40.00
236 Don Mattingly/Jsy/23 40.00
241 Rickey Henderson/Jsy/35 25.00
242 Mike Schmidt/Jsy/20 40.00
243 Roberto Clemente/Jsy/21 100.00
245 Will Clark/Jsy/22 30.00
246 Lou Brock/Jsy/20 20.00
247 Bob Gibson/Jsy/45 15.00
249 Nolan Ryan/Jsy/34 40.00

Check Signature Green

No Pricing
Production 1-15

Check Signature Red

No Pricing

Check Signature Material Red

NM/M

Quantity produced listed
4 Bob Gibson/Hat/25 50.00
5 Bobby Doerr/Jsy/25 30.00
6 Brooks Robinson/Bat/25 65.00
13 Carlton Fisk/Jkt/25 50.00
14 Carlton Fisk/Jsy/25 50.00
16 Dale Murphy/Jsy/25 40.00
17 Dale Murphy/Jsy/25 40.00
22 Duke Snider/Pants/50 40.00
26 Frank Robinson/Bat/25 40.00
27 George Brett/Jsy/15 100.00
28 George Brett/Jsy/15 100.00
29 George Brett/Bat/15 100.00
33 Harmon Killebrew/Shoe/25 65.00
34 Harmon Killebrew/Bat/25 65.00
41 Lou Brock/Jsy/25 40.00
43 Luis Aparicio/Pants/25 25.00
44 Mark Grace/Fld Glve/25 40.00
53 Paul Molitor/Bat/25 40.00
57 Red Schoendienst/Bat/25 25.00
65 Ryne Sandberg/Jsy/25 75.00
73 Tony Gwynn/Jsy/25 70.00
74 Tony Gwynn/Jsy/25 70.00
77 Whitey Ford/Pants/25 60.00
78 Will Clark/Jsy/25 40.00
79 Will Clark/Bat/25 40.00

Check Signature Material Green

NM/M

Quantity produced listed
1 Al Kaline/Bat/33 65.00
2 Andre Dawson/Jsy/33 25.00
4 Bob Gibson/Hat/15 50.00
6 Brooks Robinson/Bat/15 80.00
22 Duke Snider/Pants/25 50.00
26 Frank Robinson/Bat/15 50.00
41 Lou Brock/Jsy/15 50.00
43 Luis Aparicio/Pants/15 30.00
44 Mark Grace/Fld Glv/15 50.00
53 Paul Molitor/Bat/15 40.00
77 Whitey Ford/Pants/15 75.00

Check Signature Blue

NM/M

Quantity produced listed
1 Al Kaline/22 60.00
2 Andre Dawson/22 25.00
22 Duke Snider/20 40.00
31 George Kell/60 35.00

Check Signature Material Blue

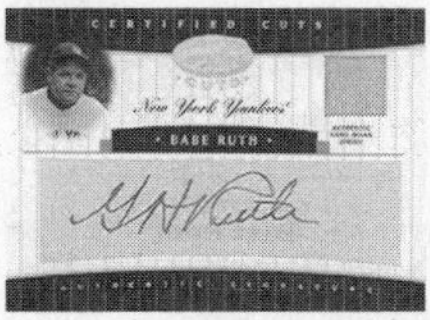

NM/M

Quantity produced listed
1 Al Kaline/Bat/50 50.00
2 Andre Dawson/Jsy/50 20.00
4 Bob Gibson/Hat/50 30.00
5 Bobby Doerr/Jsy/50 20.00
6 Brooks Robinson/Bat/50 50.00
7 Cal Ripken Jr./Jsy/25 200.00
8 Cal Ripken Jr./Jsy/25 200.00
9 Cal Ripken Jr./Bat/25 200.00
10 Cal Ripken Jr./Jkt/25 200.00
13 Carlton Fisk/Jkt/35 40.00
14 Carlton Fisk/Jsy/35 40.00
16 Dale Murphy/Jsy/50 30.00
17 Dale Murphy/Jsy/50 30.00
18 Don Mattingly/Jsy/25 80.00
19 Don Mattingly/Gray Jsy/25 80.00
20 Don Mattingly/Bat/25 80.00
21 Don Mattingly/Jkt/25 80.00
22 Duke Snider/Pants/100 40.00
23 Ozzie Smith/Jsy/40 60.00
24 Ozzie Smith/Jsy/40 60.00
25 Ozzie Smith/Bat/40 60.00
26 Frank Robinson/Bat/50 30.00
27 George Brett/White Jsy/30 80.00
28 George Brett/Blue Jsy/30 80.00
29 George Brett/Bat/30 80.00
32 Hal Newhouser/Jsy/15 30.00
33 Harmon Killebrew/Shoe/35 60.00
34 Harmon Killebrew/Bat/35 60.00
38 Kirby Puckett/Fld Glv/25 60.00
39 Kirby Puckett/Bat/25 60.00
40 Lou Boudreau/Jsy/15 100.00
41 Lou Brock/Jsy/50 30.00
43 Luis Aparicio/Pants/50 20.00
44 Mark Grace/Fld Glv/50 30.00
46 Mike Schmidt/Fld Glv/25 80.00
47 Mike Schmidt/Jsy/25 80.00
48 Mike Schmidt/Jkt/25 80.00
49 Mike Schmidt/Bat/25 80.00
50 Nolan Ryan/Astros Jkt/30 150.00
51 Nolan Ryan/Rgr Pants/30 150.00
52 Nolan Ryan/Angels Jkt/30 150.00
53 Paul Molitor/Bat/50 35.00
57 Red Schoendienst/Bat/50 20.00
63 Ron Santo/Bat/25 40.00
65 Ryne Sandberg/Jsy/50 65.00
67 Stan Musial/White Jsy/30 80.00
68 Stan Musial/Gray Jsy/30 80.00
69 Stan Musial/Bat/30 80.00
70 Steve Carlton/Pants/25 40.00
71 Steve Carlton/Jsy/25 40.00
73 Tony Gwynn/White Jsy/50 50.00
74 Tony Gwynn/Navy Jsy/50 50.00
77 Whitey Ford/Pants/50 30.00
78 Will Clark/Jsy/50 50.00
79 Will Clark/Bat/50 50.00

Hall of Fame Souvenirs

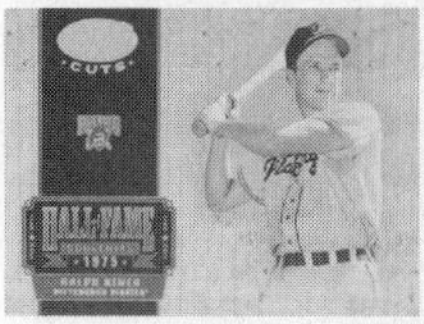

NM/M

Quantity produced listed
1 Ernie Banks/84 8.00
2 Stan Musial/93 15.00
3 Nolan Ryan/99 25.00
4 Duke Snider/87 8.00
5 Bob Feller/94 8.00
6 George Brett/98 20.00
7 Robin Yount/78 15.00
8 Harmon Killebrew/83 10.00
9 Gary Carter/78 4.00
10 Phil Rizzuto/75 8.00
11 Reggie Jackson/94 8.00
12 Mike Schmidt/97 20.00
13 Lou Brock/80 6.00
14 Bob Gibson/84 8.00
15 Bobby Doerr/75 6.00
16 Tony Perez/77 4.00
17 Whitey Ford/78 8.00
18 Juan Marichal/84 4.00
19 Monte Irvin/75 4.00
20 Fergie Jenkins/75 4.00
21 Ralph Kiner/75 8.00
22 Eddie Murray/85 10.00
23 George Kell/75 4.00
24 Hoyt Wilhelm/84 4.00
25 Carlton Fisk/80 6.00
26 Rod Carew/91 8.00
27 Frank Robinson/89 6.00
28 Gaylord Perry/77 4.00
29 Red Schoendienst/75 4.00
30 Brooks Robinson/92 8.00
31 Al Kaline/88 10.00
32 Orlando Cepeda/75 4.00
33 Steve Carlton/96 4.00
34 Luis Aparicio/85 4.00
35 Warren Spahn/83 8.00
36 Kirby Puckett/82 10.00
37 Phil Niekro/80 4.00
38 Jim Bunning/75 4.00
39 Tom Seaver/99 8.00
40 Paul Molitor/85 8.00
41 Johnny Bench/96 8.00
42 Don Sutton/82 4.00
43 Robin Roberts/87 6.00
44 Jim Palmer/93 6.00
45 Joe Morgan/82 4.00
46 Roberto Clemente/93 25.00
47 Lou Gehrig/100 10.00
48 Babe Ruth/95 20.00
49 Ty Cobb/98 10.00
50 Ted Williams/94 20.00

Hall of Fame Souvenirs Signature

NM/M

Quantity produced listed
2 Stan Musial/10
3 Nolan Ryan/34 150.00
4 Duke Snider/50 30.00
5 Bob Feller/50 30.00
8 Harmon Killebrew/25 50.00
9 Gary Carter/50 15.00
10 Phil Rizzuto/50 25.00
12 Mike Schmidt/20 60.00
13 Lou Brock/50 25.00
14 Bob Gibson/45 25.00
15 Bobby Doerr/50 15.00
16 Tony Perez/50 15.00
17 Whitey Ford/16 40.00
18 Juan Marichal/50 15.00
19 Monte Irvin/50 25.00
20 Fergie Jenkins/50 15.00
21 Ralph Kiner/50 25.00

22	Eddie Murray/33	60.00
23	George Kell/50	15.00
24	Hoyt Wilhelm/49	15.00
25	Carlton Fisk/27	30.00
26	Rod Carew/29	30.00
28	Gaylord Perry/50	15.00
29	Red Schoendienst/50	15.00
30	Brooks Robinson/50	40.00
31	Al Kaline/50	40.00
32	Orlando Cepeda/50	15.00
33	Steve Carlton/50	25.00
34	Luis Aparicio/50	15.00
35	Warren Spahn/21	50.00
36	Kirby Puckett/34	50.00
37	Phil Niekro/50	15.00
38	Jim Bunning/50	15.00
40	Paul Molitor/25	30.00
42	Don Sutton/50	15.00
43	Robin Roberts/50	15.00
44	Jim Palmer/22	20.00
45	Joe Morgan/25	20.00

HOF Souvenirs Material

NM/M

Production 25 Sets

1	Ernie Banks/Jsy	30.00
2	Stan Musial/Jsy	50.00
3	Nolan Ryan/Jsy	60.00
4	Duke Snider/Pants	20.00
5	Bob Feller/Jsy	20.00
6	George Brett/Jsy	50.00
7	Robin Yount/Jsy	40.00
8	Harmon Killebrew/Jsy	25.00
9	Gary Carter/Jkt	15.00
10	Phil Rizzuto/Pants	20.00
11	Reggie Jackson/Jsy	25.00
12	Mike Schmidt/Jsy	50.00
13	Lou Brock/Jsy	20.00
14	Bob Gibson/Jsy	20.00
15	Bobby Doerr/Jsy	15.00
16	Tony Perez/Bat	10.00
17	Whitey Ford/Pants	25.00
18	Juan Marichal/Jsy	15.00
20	Fergie Jenkins/Pants	10.00
21	Ralph Kiner/Bat	25.00
22	Eddie Murray/Jsy	25.00
24	Hoyt Wilhelm/Jsy	10.00
25	Carlton Fisk/Jsy	20.00
26	Rod Carew/Jsy	20.00
27	Frank Robinson/Jsy	15.00
29	Red Schoendienst/Jsy	15.00
30	Brooks Robinson/Bat	30.00
31	Al Kaline/Pants	30.00
32	Orlando Cepeda/Bat	10.00
33	Steve Carlton/Pants	15.00
34	Luis Aparicio/Pants	10.00
35	Warren Spahn/Pants	25.00
36	Kirby Puckett/Jsy	25.00
37	Phil Niekro/Jsy	10.00
39	Tom Seaver/Jsy	25.00
40	Paul Molitor/Bat	20.00
41	Johnny Bench/Jsy	25.00
42	Don Sutton/Jsy	10.00
43	Robin Roberts/Hat	15.00
44	Jim Palmer/Jsy	15.00
45	Joe Morgan/Jsy	15.00
46	Roberto Clemente/Jsy	80.00
47	Lou Gehrig/Pants	150.00
48	Babe Ruth/Pants	275.00
49	Ty Cobb/Pants	150.00
50	Ted Williams/Jsy	125.00

HOF Souvenirs Signature Material

NM/M

Quantity produced listed

3	Nolan Ryan/Jsy/34	180.00
5	Bob Feller/Jsy/19	50.00
12	Mike Schmidt/Jsy/20	80.00
13	Lou Brock/Jsy/20	40.00
14	Bob Gibson/Jsy/45	30.00
16	Tony Perez/Bat/24	25.00
17	Whitey Ford/Pants/16	50.00
18	Juan Marichal/Jsy/27	30.00
20	Fergie Jenkins/Pants/31	30.00
22	Eddie Murray/Jsy/33	85.00
25	Carlton Fisk/Jsy/27	50.00
26	Rod Carew/Jsy/29	50.00
32	Orlando Cepeda/Bat/30	30.00
33	Steve Carlton/Pants/32	40.00
35	Warren Spahn/Pants/21	75.00
36	Kirby Puckett/Jsy/34	65.00
37	Phil Niekro/Jsy/35	25.00
42	Don Sutton/Jsy/40	20.00
43	Robin Roberts/Hat/36	25.00
44	Jim Palmer/Jsy/22	30.00
45	Joe Morgan/Jsy/16	35.00

K-Force

NM/M

Quantity produced listed

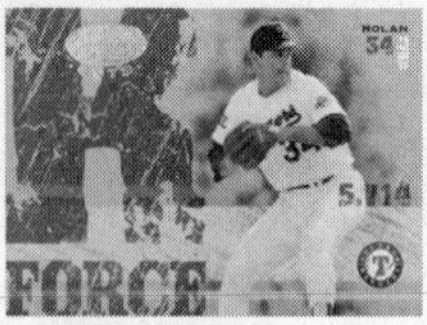

1	Nolan Ryan/500	8.00
2	Steve Carlton/500	2.00
3	Roger Clemens/500	6.00
4	Randy Johnson/500	3.00
5	Bert Blyleven/500	1.50
6	Tom Seaver/500	3.00
7	Don Sutton/500	1.50
8	Gaylord Perry/500	1.50
9	Phil Niekro/500	1.50
10	Fergie Jenkins/500	1.50
11	Bob Gibson/500	3.00
12	Nolan Ryan/383	8.00
13	Randy Johnson/308	3.00
14	Bob Feller/348	3.00
15	Curt Schilling/319	3.00
16	Pedro J. Martinez/313	3.00
17	Dwight Gooden/276	1.50
18	John Smoltz/276	2.00
19	Curt Schilling/316	3.00
20	Randy Johnson/319	3.00
21	Pedro Martinez/305	3.00
22	Roger Clemens/291	6.00
23	Roger Clemens/292	6.00
24	Tom Seaver/289	3.00
25	Hal Newhouser/275	2.00
26	Jim Bunning/201	2.00
27	Robin Roberts/198	3.00
28	Warren Spahn/191	4.00
29	Jack Morris/232	2.00
30	Nolan Ryan/270	8.00
31	Hideo Nomo/236	3.00
32	Barry Zito/205	2.00
33	Mike Mussina/214	3.00
34	Roy Oswalt/208	2.00
35	Mark Prior/245	3.00
36	Kerry Wood/266	4.00
37	Roy Halladay/204	2.00
38	Esteban Loaiza/207	1.50
39	Whitey Ford/94	6.00
40	Bob Gibson/17	12.00
41	Ben Sheets/18	8.00
42	Hoyt Wilhelm/139	3.00
43	Satchel Paige/91	10.00
44	Burleigh Grimes/136	3.00
45	Mark Prior, Kerry Wood/500	3.00
46	Nolan Ryan, Roger Clemens/500	10.00
47	Steve Carlton, Randy Johnson/500	3.00
48	Nolan Ryan, Roger Clemens/500	8.00
49	Nolan Ryan, Steve Carlton/500	8.00
50	Kerry Wood, Roger Clemens/20	30.00

K-Force Material

NM/M

Quantity produced listed

1	Nolan Ryan/Jsy/100	25.00
2	Steve Carlton/Jsy/32	12.00
3	Roger Clemens/Jsy/25	25.00
4	Randy Johnson/Jsy/51	15.00
5	Bert Blyleven/Jsy/28	10.00
6	Tom Seaver/Jsy/25	25.00
8	Gaylord Perry/Jsy/36	8.00
9	Phil Niekro/Jsy/35	10.00
10	Fergie Jenkins/Pants/31	10.00
11	Bob Gibson/Jsy/45	15.00
12	Nolan Ryan/Jkt/100	25.00
13	Randy Johnson/Jsy/51	15.00
14	Bob Feller/Jsy/25	20.00
15	Curt Schilling/Jsy/25	12.00
16	Pedro J. Martinez/Jsy/45	15.00
17	Dwight Gooden/Jsy/25	10.00
18	John Smoltz/Jsy/25	15.00
19	Curt Schilling/Jsy/25	12.00
20	Randy Johnson/Jsy/51	15.00
21	Pedro Martinez/Jsy/45	15.00
22	Roger Clemens/Jsy/100	15.00
25	Hal Newhouser/Jsy/25	20.00
28	Warren Spahn/Jsy/50	15.00
29	Jack Morris/Jsy/47	8.00
30	Nolan Ryan/Jkt/100	25.00
31	Hideo Nomo/Jsy/25	20.00
32	Barry Zito/Jsy/25	10.00
33	Mike Mussina/Jsy/25	20.00
34	Roy Oswalt/Jsy/44	6.00
35	Mark Prior/Jsy/50	10.00
36	Kerry Wood/Jsy/34	20.00
39	Whitey Ford/Jsy/50	15.00
40	Bob Gibson/Jsy/50	10.00
41	Ben Sheets/Jsy/25	10.00
43	Satchel Paige/Jsy/100	60.00
44	Burleigh Grimes/Pants/100	75.00
45	Mark Prior/Jsy, Kerry Wood/Pants/50	15.00
46	Nolan Ryan/Jsy, Roger Clemens/Jsy/50	40.00
47	Steve Carlton/Jsy, Randy Johnson/Jsy/50	25.00
48	Nolan Ryan/Pants, Roger Clemens/Jsy/50	40.00
49	Nolan Ryan/Jsy, Carlton Fisk/Pants/50	35.00
50	Kerry Wood/Jsy, Roger Clemens/Jsy/50	25.00

K-Force Signature

NM/M

Quantity produced listed

2	Steve Carlton/50	30.00
5	Bert Blyleven/50	15.00
7	Don Sutton/50	15.00
8	Gaylord Perry/50	15.00
9	Phil Niekro/50	25.00
10	Fergie Jenkins/50	15.00
14	Bob Feller/50	30.00
17	Dwight Gooden/50	20.00
26	Jim Bunning/50	25.00
27	Robin Roberts/50	20.00
29	Jack Morris/50	15.00
34	Roy Oswalt/50	15.00
38	Esteban Loaiza/50	10.00

K-Force Signature Material

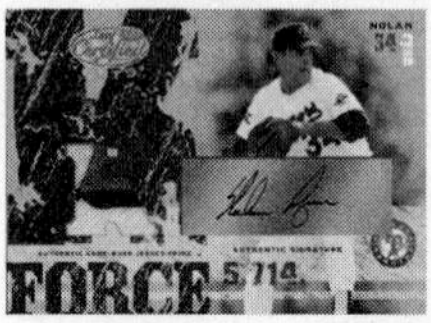

NM/M

Quantity produced listed

1	Nolan Ryan/Jsy/34	150.00
2	Steve Carlton/Jsy/32	50.00
5	Bert Blyleven/Jsy/28	25.00
8	Gaylord Perry/Jsy/36	25.00
9	Phil Niekro/Jsy/35	40.00
10	Fergie Jenkins/Pants/31	25.00
11	Bob Gibson/Jsy/45	40.00
12	Nolan Ryan/Jkt/34	150.00
14	Bob Feller/Jsy/19	50.00
17	Dwight Gooden/Jsy/16	30.00
28	Warren Spahn/Jsy/21	65.00
29	Jack Morris/Jsy/47	20.00
30	Nolan Ryan/Jkt/34	150.00
34	Roy Oswalt/Jsy/44	20.00
36	Kerry Wood/Jsy/34	50.00
37	Roy Halladay/Jsy/32	15.00
39	Whitey Ford/Jsy/16	50.00
40	Bob Gibson/Jsy/45	30.00

Stars

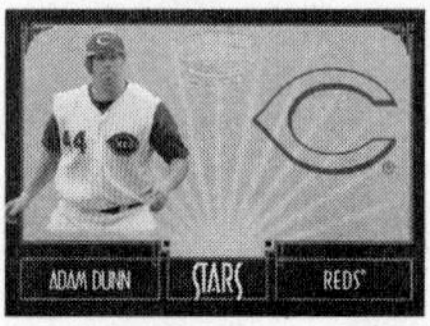

NM/M

Production 599 Sets

1	Ryne Sandberg	6.00
2	Mark Prior	2.00
3	Andre Dawson	2.00
4	Don Mattingly	6.00
5	Vladimir Guerrero	3.00
6	Garret Anderson	2.00
7	Dale Murphy	2.00
8	Cal Ripken Jr.	10.00
9	Mark Grace	3.00
10	Kerry Wood	3.00
11	Frank Thomas	3.00
12	Magglio Ordonez	2.00
13	Adam Dunn	3.00
14	Preston Wilson	2.00
15	Bo Jackson	3.00
16	Carlos Beltran	3.00
17	Tony Gwynn	4.00
18	Will Clark	3.00
19	Edgar Martinez	2.00
20	Scott Rolen	3.00
21	Alfonso Soriano	3.00
22	Randy Johnson	3.00
23	Chipper Jones	3.00
24	Andruw Jones	2.00
25	Javy Lopez	3.00
26	Curt Schilling	3.00
27	Manny Ramirez	5.00
28	Sammy Sosa	4.00
29	Greg Maddux	2.00
30	Todd Helton	3.00
31	Jeff Bagwell	3.00
32	Shawn Green	2.00
33	Mike Piazza	5.00
34	Jorge Posada	2.00
35	Gary Sheffield	3.00
36	Mike Mussina	3.00
37	Miguel Cabrera	3.00
38	Rickey Henderson	3.00
39	Albert Pujols	8.00
40	Vernon Wells	2.00
41	Fred Lynn	2.00
42	Alan Trammell	2.00
43	Lenny Dykstra	2.00
44	Dwight Gooden	2.00
45	Keith Hernandez	2.00
46	Luis Tiant	2.00
47	Orel Hershiser	2.00
48	George Foster	2.00
49	Darryl Strawberry	2.00
50	Marty Marion	2.00

Stars Signature

NM/M

Quantity produced listed

3	Andre Dawson/50	20.00
4	Don Mattingly/25	65.00
6	Garret Anderson/50	20.00
7	Dale Murphy/50	30.00
12	Magglio Ordonez/25	20.00
13	Adam Dunn/25	40.00
14	Preston Wilson/50	15.00
16	Carlos Beltran/50	40.00
18	Will Clark/25	40.00
19	Edgar Martinez/25	40.00
20	Scott Rolen/25	40.00
37	Miguel Cabrera/50	40.00
40	Vernon Wells/25	20.00
41	Fred Lynn/50	10.00
42	Alan Trammell/50	20.00
43	Lenny Dykstra/50	20.00
44	Dwight Gooden/50	20.00
45	Keith Hernandez/50	20.00
46	Luis Tiant/50	15.00
47	Orel Hershiser/50	25.00
48	George Foster/50	10.00
49	Darryl Strawberry/50	20.00

Stars Signature Jersey

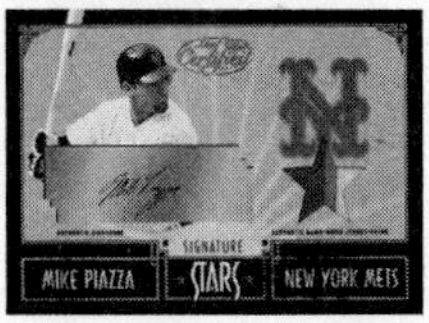

NM/M

Quantity produced listed

1	Ryne Sandberg/23	75.00
2	Mark Prior/22	40.00
4	Don Mattingly/23	75.00
5	Vladimir Guerrero/27	60.00
6	Garret Anderson/16	35.00
9	Mark Grace/17	50.00
10	Kerry Wood/34	50.00
11	Frank Thomas/35	50.00
12	Magglio Ordonez/30	25.00
13	Adam Dunn/44	50.00
14	Preston Wilson/44	20.00
15	Bo Jackson/16	125.00
16	Carlos Beltran/15	75.00
17	Tony Gwynn/19	75.00
18	Will Clark/22	65.00
20	Scott Rolen/27	60.00
24	Andruw Jones/25	40.00
28	Sammy Sosa/21	150.00
29	Greg Maddux/31	100.00
30	Todd Helton/17	50.00
34	Jorge Posada/20	50.00
37	Miguel Cabrera/24	50.00
41	Fred Lynn/19	20.00
45	Keith Hernandez/37	20.00
46	Luis Tiant/25	25.00
48	George Foster/15	25.00
49	Darryl Strawberry/18	35.00
50	Marty Marion/25	25.00

2004 Leaf Certified Materials

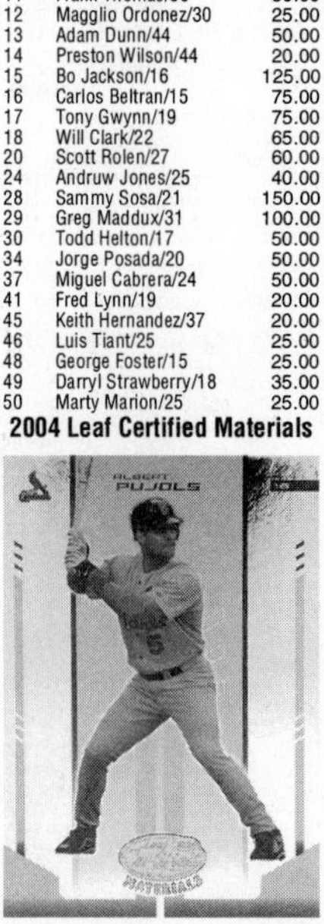

NM/M

Complete Set (300):	
Common Player:	.50
Common (201-211):	4.00
Common (212-240):	4.00
Production 500	
Common Auto. (241-300):	8.00
Pack (5):	10.00

Box (10): 85.00
1 A.J. Burnett .50
2 Adam Dunn 1.00
3 Adam LaRoche .50
4 Adam Loewen .50
5 Adrian Beltre .75
6 Al Leiter .50
7 Albert Pujols 3.00
8 Alex Rodriguez 3.00
9 Alexis Rios .50
10 Alfonso Soriano 1.50
11 Andruw Jones 1.00
12 Andy Pettitte .75
13 Angel Berroa .50
14 Aramis Ramirez .75
15 Aubrey Huff .50
16 Austin Kearns .50
17 Barry Larkin .75
18 Barry Zito .75
19 Ben Sheets .75
20 Bernie Williams .75
21 Bobby Abreu .75
22 Brad Penny .50
23 Brad Wilkerson .50
24 Brandon Webb .50
25 Brendan Harris .50
26 Bret Boone .50
27 Brett Myers .50
28 Bubba Crosby .50
29 Brian Giles .50
30 Chad Cordero .50
31 Bubba Nelson .50
32 Byron Gettis .50
33 C.C. Sabathia .50
34 Carl Crawford .50
35 Carl Everett .50
36 Carlos Beltran .75
37 Carlos Delgado .75
38 Carlos Lee .50
39 Chad Gaudin .50
40 Cliff Lee .50
41 Chipper Jones 1.50
42 Cliff Floyd .50
43 Clint Barmes .50
44 Corey Patterson .75
45 Craig Biggio .75
46 Curt Schilling 1.00
47 Dan Haren .50
48 Darin Erstad .50
49 David Ortiz 1.00
50 Delmon Young .50
51 Derek Jeter 4.00
52 Dewon Brazelton .50
53 Dontrelle Willis .75
54 Edgar Martinez .75
55 Edgar Renteria .75
56 Edwin Almonte .50
57 Edwin Jackson .50
58 Eric Chavez .75
59 Eric Hinske .50
60 Eric Munson .50
61 Erubiel Durazo .50
62 Frank Thomas 1.00
63 Fred McGriff .50
64 Freddy Garcia .50
65 Garret Anderson .75
66 Garrett Atkins .50
67 Gary Sheffield .75
68 Geoff Jenkins .50
69 Greg Maddux 2.00
70 Hank Blalock 1.00
71 Hee Seop Choi .50
72 Hideki Matsui 2.50
73 Hideo Nomo .75
74 Craig Wilson .50
75 Ichiro Suzuki 2.50
76 Ivan Rodriguez 1.00
77 J.D. Drew .50
78 John Lackey .50
79 Jacque Jones .50
80 Jae Weong Seo .50
81 Jamie Moyer .50
82 Jason Giambi 1.00
83 Jason Jennings .50
84 Jason Kendall .50
85 Melvin Mora .50
86 Jason Varitek .75
87 Javier Vazquez .75
88 Javy Lopez .75
89 Jay Gibbons .50
90 Jay Payton .50
91 Jeff Bagwell 1.00
92 Jeff Baker .50
93 Jeff Kent .50
94 Jeremy Bonderman .50
95 Milton Bradley .50
96 Jerome Williams .50
97 Jim Edmonds .75
98 Jim Thome 1.50
99 Jody Gerut .50
100 Joe Borchard .50
101 Joe Crede .50
102 Johan Santana .50
103 John Olerud .50
104 John Smoltz .75
105 Johnny Damon .75
106 Jorge Posada .75
107 Jose Castillo .50
108 Jose Reyes .50
109 Jose Vidro .50
110 Josh Beckett 1.00
111 Josh Phelps .50
112 Juan Encarnacion .50
113 Juan Gonzalez 1.00
114 Junior Spivey .50
115 Kazuhisa Ishii .50
116 Kenny Lofton .50
117 Kerry Wood 1.50
118 Kevin Millwood .50
119 Kevin Youkilis .50
120 Lance Berkman .50
121 Larry Bigbie .50
122 Larry Walker .75
123 Luis Castillo .50
124 Luis Gonzalez .50
125 Luis Matos .50
126 Lyle Overbay .50
127 Magglio Ordonez .75
128 Manny Ramirez 1.00
129 Marcus Giles .50
130 Mariano Rivera .75
131 Mark Buehrle .50
132 Mark Mulder .75
133 Mark Prior 1.00
134 Mark Teixeira .75
135 Marlon Byrd .50
136 Matt Morris .50
137 Miguel Cabrera 1.00
138 Mike Lowell .50
139 Mike Mussina .75
140 Mike Piazza 2.00
141 Mike Sweeney .50
142 Morgan Ensberg .50
143 Nick Johnson .50
144 Nomar Garciaparra 2.00
145 Omar Vizquel .50
146 Orlando Cabrera .50
147 Orlando Hudson .50
148 Pat Burrell .50
149 Paul Konerko .50
150 Paul LoDuca .50
151 Pedro J. Martinez 1.50
152 Jermaine Dye .50
153 Preston Wilson .50
154 Rafael Furcal .50
155 Rafael Palmeiro 1.00
156 Randy Johnson 1.50
157 Rich Aurilia .50
158 Rich Harden .50
159 Richard Hidalgo .50
160 Richie Sexson .75
161 Rickie Weeks .75
162 Roberto Alomar .75
163 Rocco Baldelli .50
164 Roger Clemens 3.00
165 Roy Halladay .50
166 Roy Oswalt .75
167 Ryan Howard 1.50
168 Ryan Klesko .50
169 Rodrigo Lopez .50
170 Sammy Sosa 2.50
171 Scott Podsednik .50
172 Scott Rolen 1.50
173 Sean Burroughs .50
174 Sean Casey .50
175 Shannon Stewart .50
176 Shawn Green .75
177 Shea Hillenbrand .50
178 Shigetoshi Hasegawa .50
179 Steve Finley .50
180 Tim Hudson .75
181 Todd Helton 1.00
182 Tom Glavine .75
183 Torii Hunter .75
184 Trot Nixon .75
185 Troy Glaus .75
186 Vernon Wells .50
187 Victor Martinez .75
188 Vladimir Guerrero 1.50
189 Wade Miller .50
190 Brandon Larson .50
191 Travis Hafner .75
192 Tim Salmon .75
193 Tim Redding .50
194 Runelvys Hernandez .50
195 Ramon Nivar .50
196 Moises Alou .75
197 Michael Young .50
198 Laynce Nix .50
199 Tino Martinez .50
200 Randall Simon .50
201 Roger Clemens/SP 8.00
202 Greg Maddux/SP 8.00
203 Vladimir Guerrero/SP 6.00
204 Miguel Tejada/SP 4.00
205 Kevin Brown/SP 4.00
206 Jason Giambi/SP 5.00
207 Curt Schilling/SP 5.00
208 Alex Rodriguez/SP 8.00
209 Alfonso Soriano/SP 6.00
210 Ivan Rodriguez/SP 6.00
211 Rafael Palmeiro/SP 6.00
212 Gary Carter 4.00
213 Duke Snider 5.00
214 Whitey Ford 4.00
215 Bob Feller 4.00
216 Reggie Jackson 5.00
217 Ryne Sandberg 10.00
218 Dale Murphy 4.00
219 Tony Gwynn 6.00
220 Don Mattingly 10.00
221 Mike Schmidt 10.00
222 Rickey Henderson 5.00
223 Cal Ripken Jr. 20.00
224 Nolan Ryan 15.00
225 George Brett 10.00
226 Bob Gibson 5.00
227 Lou Brock 4.00
228 Andre Dawson 4.00
229 Rod Carew 4.00
230 Wade Boggs 4.00
231 Roberto Clemente 12.00
232 Roy Campanella 5.00
233 Babe Ruth 15.00
234 Lou Gehrig 10.00
235 Ty Cobb 8.00
236 Roger Maris 6.00
237 Satchel Paige 6.00
238 Ernie Banks 6.00
239 Ted Williams 10.00
240 Stan Musial 6.00
241 Hector Gimenez/Auto./500 **RC** 8.00
242 Justin Germano/Auto./500 **RC** 8.00
243 Ian Snell/Auto./500 **RC** 20.00
244 Graham Koonce/Auto./500 8.00
245 Jose Capellan/Auto./500 **RC** 10.00
246 Onil Joseph/Auto./500 **RC** 8.00
247 Shingo Takatsu/Auto./200 **RC** 25.00
248 Carlos Hines/Auto./500 **RC** 8.00
249 Lincoln Holdzkom/Auto./500 **RC** 8.00
250 Mike Gosling/Auto./500 8.00
251 Edwardo Sierra/Auto./500 **RC** 10.00
252 Renyel Pinto/Auto./500 **RC** 10.00
253 Merkin Valdez/Auto./500 **RC** 10.00
254 Angel Chavez/Auto./500 **RC** 8.00
255 Ivan Ochoa/Auto./1,000 **RC** 8.00
256 Greg Dobbs/Auto./300 **RC** 8.00
257 William Bergolla/Auto./500 **RC** 8.00
258 Aarom Baldiris/Auto./500 **RC** 10.00
259 Kazuo Matsui/Auto./500 **RC** 8.00
260 Carlos Vasquez/Auto./500 **RC** 8.00
261 Freddy Guzman/Auto./500 **RC** 8.00
262 Akinori Otsuka/Auto./200 **RC** 25.00
263 Mariano Gomez/Auto./200 **RC** 8.00
264 Nick Regilio/Auto./500 **RC** 8.00
265 Jamie Brown/Auto./500 **RC** 8.00
266 Shawn Hill/Auto./500 **RC** 8.00
267 Roberto Novoa/Auto./500 **RC** 8.00
268 Sean Henn/Auto./500 10.00
269 Ramon Ramirez/Auto./500 **RC** 8.00
270 Ronny Cedeno/Auto./1,000 **RC** 8.00
271 Ryan Wing/Auto./400 8.00
272 Ruddy Yan/Auto./500 **RC** 8.00
273 Fernando Nieve/Auto./500 **RC** 8.00
274 Rusty Tucker/Auto./500 **RC** 8.00
275 Jason Bartlett/Auto./500 **RC** 15.00
276 Mike Rouse/Auto./500 8.00
277 Dennis Sarfate/Auto./500 **RC** 8.00
278 Cory Sullivan/Auto./500 **RC** 8.00
279 Casey Daigle/Auto./250 **RC** 8.00
280 Chris Shelton/Auto./400 **RC** 15.00
281 Jesse Harper/Auto./400 **RC** 8.00
282 Mike Wuertz/Auto./500 **RC** 10.00
283 Tim Bausher/Auto./400 **RC** 8.00
284 Jorge Sequea/Auto./500 **RC** 8.00
285 Josh Labandeira/Auto./100 **RC** 10.00
286 Justin Leone/Auto./500 **RC** 10.00
287 Tim Bittner/Auto./500 **RC** 8.00
288 Andres Blanco/Auto./500 **RC** 8.00
289 Kevin Cave/Auto./1,000 **RC** 8.00
290 Mike Johnston/Auto./1,000 **RC** 8.00
291 Jason Szuminski/Auto./500 **RC** 8.00
292 Shawn Camp/500 **RC** 8.00
293 Colby Miller/Auto./500 **RC** 8.00
294 Jake Woods/Auto./500 8.00
295 Ryan Meaux/Auto./500 **RC** 8.00
296 Donald Kelly/Auto./500 **RC** 8.00
297 Edwin Moreno/Auto./500 **RC** 8.00
298 Phil Stockman/Auto./500 **RC** 8.00
299 Jorge Vasquez/500 **RC** 8.00
300 Kazuhito Tadano/Auto./500 **RC** 15.00

Mirror Black

No Pricing
Production One Set

Mirror Blue

Stars (1-200): 3-5X
Mirror Blue (201-240): 1-2X
Auto. (241-300): .5X
No Auto. (241-300): 1X
Production 50 Sets

Mirror Emerald

No Pricing
Production Five Sets

Mirror Gold

Mirror Gold (1-200): 4-8X
Mirror Gold (201-240): 1.5-2X
Mirror Gold (241-300): No Pricing
Production 25 Sets

Mirror Red

Mirror Red (1-200): 2-4X
Mirror Red (201-240): .5-1X
Mirror Red (241-300): .5X
Production 100 Sets

Mirror White

Mirror White (1-200): 2-4X
Mirror White (201-240): .5-1X
Mirror White (241-300): .5X
Production 100 Sets

Fabric of the Game

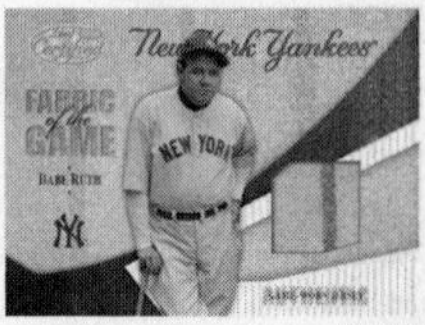

NM/M

Common Player: 6.00
Quantity produced listed
AL/NL: .75-1.5X
Production 1-100
Jersey Number: .75-2X
Production 1-72
Position: .75-2X
Production 1-100
Prime: No Pricing
Production One Set
Game Reward: .75-2X
Production 1-50
Jersey Year: .75-2X
Production 1-99
Game Stats: .75-2X
Production 1-66
No Pricing production 20 or less.

n Ozzie Smith/Jsy/100 20.00
2 Al Kaline/Pants/100 15.00
3 Alan Trammell/Jsy/100 10.00
4 Albert Pujols/Jsy/100 20.00
5 Alex Rodriguez/Jsy/100 12.00
6 Alex Rodriguez/Jsy/100 12.00
7 Andre Dawson/Jsy/100 8.00
8 Andre Dawson/Pants/100 8.00
11 Billy Williams/Jsy/100 10.00
12 Bo Jackson/Jsy/100 20.00
13 Bob Feller/Jsy/50 15.00
14 Bob Gibson/Jsy/50 15.00
15 Bobby Doerr/Jsy/100 8.00
16 Brooks Robinson/Jsy/25 25.00
17 Cal Ripken Jr./Jsy/100 30.00
18 Carl Yastrzemski/Jsy/100 20.00
19 Carlton Fisk/Jsy/100 10.00
20 Dale Murphy/Jsy/100 12.00
21 Darryl Strawberry/Pants/100 10.00
22 Darryl Strawberry/Jsy/100 10.00
23 Dave Parker/Jsy/100 10.00
24 Dave Parker/Jsy/100 10.00
25 Dave Winfield/Jsy/50 10.00
26 Dave Winfield/Jsy/100 10.00
27 Deion Sanders/Jsy/25 25.00
28 Derek Jeter/Jsy/100 20.00
29 Don Drysdale/Jsy/100 15.00
30 Don Mattingly/Jsy/100 20.00
31 Don Mattingly/Jkt/100 20.00
32 Don Sutton/Jsy/100 8.00
33 Duke Snider/Jsy/100 12.00
34 Dwight Gooden/Jsy/100 8.00
35 Early Wynn/Jsy/100 10.00
36 Eddie Mathews/Jsy/50 20.00
37 Eddie Murray/Jsy/100 15.00
38 Eddie Murray/Jsy/100 15.00
39 Enos Slaughter/Jsy/100 10.00
40 Eric Davis/Jsy/50 10.00
41 Ernie Banks/Jsy/100 15.00
42 Fergie Jenkins/Pants/100 10.00
43 Frank Robinson/Jsy/100 10.00
45 Gary Carter/Jsy/100 10.00
46 Gaylord Perry/Jsy/25 15.00
47 George Brett/White Jsy/100 20.00
48 George Foster/Jsy/100 8.00
49 Hal Newhouser/Jsy/100 8.00
50 Harmon Killebrew/Jsy/25 30.00
51 Harmon Killebrew/Pants/25 30.00
52 Harold Baines/Jsy/100 10.00
53 Hoyt Wilhelm/Jsy/50 10.00
54 Jack Morris/Jsy/100 8.00
56 Jim "Catfish" Hunter/Jsy/100 10.00
57 Jim Palmer/Jsy/100 10.00
58 Jim Rice/Jsy/100 10.00
59 Joe Carter/Jsy/100 8.00
60 Joe Morgan/Jsy/100 10.00
61 Tommy Lasorda/Jsy/100 8.00
62 Johnny Mize/Pants/100 12.00
63 Johnny Bench/Jsy/100 15.00
64 Jose Canseco/Jsy/100 10.00
65 Juan Marichal/Jsy/100 10.00
66 Kirby Puckett/Jsy/100 15.00
67 Lou Boudreau/Jsy/100 10.00
68 Lou Brock/Jsy/100 10.00
71 Luis Aparicio/Jsy/100 10.00
72 Luis Aparicio/Pants/100 10.00

73 Mariano Rivera/Jsy/100 10.00
74 Mark Grace/Jsy/100 12.00
75 Mark Prior/Jsy/100 8.00
76 Mel Ott/Jsy/25 60.00
77 Mel Ott/Pants/25 60.00
78 Mike Schmidt/Jsy/100 20.00
79 Mike Schmidt/Pants/100 20.00
80 Mike Schmidt/Jkt/100 20.00
81 Nolan Ryan/Angels Jsy/100 25.00
82 Nolan Ryan/Angels Jkt/100 25.00
83 Nolan Ryan/Astros Jsy/100 25.00
84 Nolan Ryan/Astros Jkt/100 25.00
85 Nolan Ryan/Rgr Jsy/100 25.00
86 Nolan Ryan/Rgr Pants/100 25.00
87 Ty Cobb/Pants/10
88 Ozzie Smith/Jsy/100 15.00
89 Paul Molitor/Jsy/100 12.00
90 Pee Wee Reese/Jsy/100 15.00
91 Phil Niekro/Jsy/100 8.00
92 Phil Rizzuto/Jsy/100 15.00
93 Phil Rizzuto/Pants/100 15.00
94 Red Schoendienst/Jsy/100 10.00
95 Reggie Jackson/Jkt/100 15.00
96 Reggie Jackson/Jsy/100 15.00
97 Richie Ashburn/Jsy/100 20.00
98 Rickey Henderson/Jsy/50 15.00
99 Roberto Clemente/Jsy/50 75.00
100 Robin Yount/Jsy/100 15.00
101 Rod Carew/Jsy/100 10.00
102 Rod Carew/Pants/100 10.00
103 Rod Carew/Jkt/100 10.00
104 Rod Carew/Jsy/100 10.00
105 Roger Clemens/Jsy/100 15.00
106 Roger Clemens/Jsy/100 15.00
107 Roger Maris/Jsy/100 30.00
108 Roger Maris/Pants/100 30.00
109 Roger Maris/Jsy/100 30.00
110 Roy Campanella/Pants/100 15.00
111 Ryne Sandberg/Jsy/100 25.00
112 Stan Musial/Jsy/50 30.00
113 Steve Carlton/Jsy/100 10.00
114 Ted Williams/Jsy/100 75.00
115 Ted Williams/Jkt/100 75.00
116 Thurman Munson/Jsy/100 25.00
117 Thurman Munson/Pants/100 25.00
118 Tony Gwynn/Jsy/100 15.00
119 Wade Boggs/Jsy/100 10.00
120 Wade Boggs/Jsy/100 10.00
121 Warren Spahn/Jsy/100 15.00
122 Warren Spahn/Pants/100 15.00
123 Whitey Ford/Jsy/100 15.00
124 Whitey Ford/Pants/100 15.00
125 Will Clark/Jsy/100 15.00
126 Willie McCovey/Jsy/100 10.00
127 Willie Stargell/Jsy/100 15.00
128 Yogi Berra/Jsy/25 35.00
129 Frankie Frisch/Jkt/100 15.00
130 Marty Marion/Jsy/100 10.00
131 Tommy John/Pants/100 8.00
132 Chipper Jones/Jsy/100 10.00
133 Sammy Sosa/Jsy/100 15.00
134 Rickey Henderson/Jsy/100 10.00
135 Mike Piazza/Jsy/100 12.00
136 Mike Piazza/Jsy/100 12.00
137 Nomar Garciaparra/Jsy/100 15.00
138 Hideo Nomo/Jsy/100 10.00
139 Hideo Nomo/Jsy/50 15.00
140 Randy Johnson/Jsy/100 10.00
141 Randy Johnson/Jsy/100 10.00
142 Randy Johnson/Jsy/100 10.00
143 Jason Giambi/Jsy/100 6.00
144 Jason Giambi/Jsy/100 6.00
145 Curt Schilling/Jsy/100 6.00
146 Dennis Eckersley/Jsy/100 10.00
147 Carlton Fisk/Jkt/100 10.00
148 Tom Seaver/Jsy/25 30.00
149 Joe Torre/Jsy/100 10.00
150 Pedro Martinez/Jsy/100 10.00
151 Albert Pujols/Jsy/100 20.00
152 Andre Dawson/Jsy/50 10.00
153 Bert Blyleven/Jsy/100 8.00
154 Bo Jackson/Jsy/100 15.00
155 Cal Ripken Jr./Pants/100 35.00
156 Carlton Fisk/Jsy/100 10.00
157 Curt Schilling/Jsy/100 6.00
158 Darryl Strawberry/Jsy/100 8.00
159 Dave Concepcion/Jsy/100 8.00
160 Dwight Evans/Jsy/100 8.00
161 Ernie Banks/Pants/100 15.00
163 Gary Carter/Pants/100 8.00
164 Gary Sheffield/Jsy/100 6.00
165 George Brett/Jsy/100 20.00
166 Greg Maddux/Jsy/100 10.00
167 Ivan Rodriguez/Jsy/100 10.00
168 Joe Morgan/Jsy/100 10.00
169 Jose Canseco/Jsy/100 10.00
170 Juan Gonzalez/Jsy/100 8.00
171 Juan Gonzalez/Jsy/100 8.00
172 Keith Hernandez/Jsy/100 10.00
173 Ken Boyer/Jsy/100 20.00
174 Kerry Wood/Jsy/100 10.00
175 Lee Smith/Jsy/100 8.00
176 Luis Tiant/Jsy/100 8.00
177 Manny Ramirez/Jsy/100 8.00
178 Mark Grace/Jsy/100 12.00
179 Matt Williams/Jsy/100 8.00
180 Miguel Tejada/Jsy/100 6.00
181 Mike Mussina/Jsy/100 10.00
182 Mike Piazza/Jsy/100 12.00
183 Nomar Garciaparra/Jsy/100 15.00
184 Pedro Martinez/Jsy/100 10.00
185 Rafael Palmeiro/Jsy/100 8.00
186 Reggie Jackson/Pants/100 12.00
187 Rickey Henderson/Jsy/100 10.00
188 Rickey Henderson/Pants/100 10.00
189 Rickey Henderson/Jsy/100 10.00
190 Sammy Sosa/Jsy/100 15.00
191 Satchel Paige/Jsy/100 60.00
192 Shawn Green/Jsy/100 6.00
193 Stan Musial/Jsy/50 35.00
194 Steve Carlton/Jsy/100 10.00
195 Steve Garvey/Jsy/100 8.00
196 Tom Seaver/Jsy/100 12.00
197 Tony Gwynn/Pants/100 12.00
198 Vladimir Guerrero/Jsy/100 10.00
199 Wade Boggs/Jsy/100 10.00
200 Willie Stargell/Jsy/100 10.00

Fabric of the Game Auto.

No Pricing
Production 1-10
AL/NL Auto.: No Pricing
Production 1-25
Jersey Number Auto.: No Pricing
Production 1-8
Jersey Year Auto.: No Pricing
Production 1-8
Position Auto.: No Pricing
Production 1-8
Reward Auto.: No Pricing
Production 1-8
Stats Auto.: No Pricing
Production 1-8

Mirror Autograph Red

NM/M

Quantity produced listed
3 Adam LaRoche/250 8.00
4 Adam Loewen/250 8.00
9 Alexis Rios/250 15.00
10 Alfonso Soriano/25 50.00
11 Andruw Jones/25 25.00
12 Andy Pettitte/25 35.00
13 Angel Berroa/100 10.00
14 Aramis Ramirez/100 25.00
15 Aubrey Huff/250 10.00
16 Austin Kearns/200 12.00
17 Barry Larkin/25 40.00
22 Brad Penny/25 15.00
24 Brandon Webb/250 8.00
25 Brendan Harris/50 10.00
27 Brett Myers/100 8.00
28 Bubba Crosby/250 8.00
30 Chad Cordero/250 8.00
31 Bubba Nelson/250 8.00
32 Byron Gettis/250 8.00
36 Carlos Beltran/100 25.00
38 Carlos Lee/250 10.00
39 Chad Gaudin/100 8.00
40 Cliff Lee/250 15.00
43 Clint Barmes/100 15.00
47 Dan Haren/250 8.00
49 David Ortiz/250 40.00
50 Delmon Young/50 25.00
52 Dewon Brazelton/250 8.00
53 Dontrelle Willis/100 20.00
56 Edwin Almonte/250 8.00
57 Edwin Jackson/250 8.00
58 Eric Chavez/25 30.00
62 Frank Thomas/50 50.00
65 Garret Anderson/250 15.00
67 Gary Sheffield/50 30.00
70 Hank Blalock/100 30.00
74 Craig Wilson/250 10.00
78 John Lackey/250 8.00
79 Jacque Jones/250 8.00
80 Jae Weong Seo/100 15.00
85 Melvin Mora/250 15.00
86 Jason Varitek/100 40.00
89 Jay Gibbons/250 8.00
90 Jay Payton/250 8.00
91 Jeff Bagwell/50 50.00
92 Jeff Baker/25 20.00
96 Jerome Williams/100 15.00
97 Jim Edmonds/25 35.00
99 Jody Gerut/250 10.00
100 Joe Borchard/250 10.00
101 Joe Crede/50 15.00
102 Johan Santana/250 25.00
106 Jorge Posada/25 50.00
107 Jose Castillo/250 8.00
109 Jose Vidro/250 10.00
113 Juan Gonzalez/25 40.00
114 Junior Spivey/25 15.00
117 Kerry Wood/50 50.00
119 Kevin Youkilis/250 10.00
120 Lance Berkman/25 30.00
121 Larry Bigbie/250 12.00
123 Luis Castillo/25 15.00
125 Luis Matos/250 8.00
127 Magglio Ordonez/250 15.00
129 Marcus Giles/250 12.00
131 Mark Buehrle/250 12.00
132 Mark Mulder/250 20.00
133 Mark Prior/100 40.00
134 Mark Teixeira/100 25.00
135 Marlon Byrd/250 8.00
137 Miguel Cabrera/250 30.00
140 Mike Piazza/25 125.00
142 Morgan Ensberg/250 8.00
146 Orlando Cabrera/25 20.00
150 Paul LoDuca/25 25.00
152 Jermaine Dye/250 10.00
153 Preston Wilson/250 10.00
154 Rafael Furcal/100 12.00
157 Rich Aurilia/25 15.00
158 Rich Harden/203 15.00
165 Roy Halladay/50 15.00
166 Roy Oswalt/50 15.00
167 Ryan Howard/100 80.00
169 Rodrigo Lopez/250 8.00
170 Sammy Sosa/50 100.00
171 Scott Podsednik/250 15.00
172 Scott Rolen/100 40.00
175 Shannon Stewart/100 8.00
176 Shawn Green/25 30.00
177 Shea Hillenbrand/250 10.00
178 Shigetoshi Hasegawa/250 40.00
179 Steve Finley/100 20.00
183 Torii Hunter/250 15.00
184 Trot Nixon/250 20.00
187 Victor Martinez/250 20.00
188 Vladimir Guerrero/50 75.00
190 Brandon Larson/200 10.00
191 Travis Hafner/250 15.00
197 Michael Young/250 15.00
212 Gary Carter/250 15.00
213 Duke Snider/250 25.00
214 Whitey Ford /50 40.00
215 Bob Feller /250 20.00
216 Reggie Jackson/50 50.00
217 Ryne Sandberg/50 60.00
218 Dale Murphy/50 30.00
219 Tony Gwynn/50 50.00
220 Don Mattingly/50 75.00
221 Mike Schmidt/50 75.00
222 Rickey Henderson/50 50.00
223 Cal Ripken Jr./50 180.00
224 Nolan Ryan/50 100.00
225 George Brett/50 75.00
226 Bob Gibson/100 25.00
227 Lou Brock/100 25.00
228 Andre Dawson/250 15.00
229 Rod Carew/50 25.00
230 Wade Boggs/50 25.00
238 Ernie Banks/50 60.00
240 Stan Musial/100 60.00
241 Hector Gimenez/200 8.00
242 Justin Germano/100 8.00
243 Ian Snell/100 25.00
244 Graham Koonce/200 8.00
245 Jose Capellan/100 40.00
246 Onil Joseph/200 8.00
247 Shingo Takatsu/50 50.00
248 Carlos Hines/200 8.00
249 Lincoln Holdzkom/100 8.00
250 Mike Gosling/100 10.00
251 Edwardo Sierra/200 10.00
252 Renyel Pinto/100 10.00
253 Merkin Valdez/200 12.00
254 Angel Chavez/200 8.00
255 Ivan Ochoa/200 8.00
257 William Bergolla/200 8.00
258 Aarom Baldiris/100 10.00
260 Carlos Vasquez/200 8.00
261 Freddy Guzman/200 8.00
262 Akinori Otsuka/50 50.00
264 Nick Regilio/200 8.00
266 Shawn Hill/200 8.00
268 Sean Henn/200 10.00
269 Ramon Ramirez/200 8.00
270 Ronny Cedeno/100 8.00
273 Fernando Nieve/200 8.00
274 Rusty Tucker/200 8.00
275 Jason Bartlett/200 8.00
276 Mike Rouse/200 8.00
277 Dennis Sarfate/200 8.00
278 Cory Sullivan/200 8.00
282 Mike Wuertz/200 8.00
284 Jorge Sequea/100 8.00
287 Tim Bittner/250 8.00
288 Andres Blanco/100 12.00
289 Kevin Cave/100 10.00
290 Mike Johnston/100 8.00
293 Colby Miller/100 8.00
294 Jake Woods/100 10.00
295 Ryan Meaux/200 8.00
296 Donald Kelly/100 8.00
297 Edwin Moreno/100 8.00
298 Phil Stockman/100 8.00

Mirror Autograph Black

No Pricing
Production One Set

Mirror Autograph Blue

Mirror Auto. Blue: .5-1.5X Red Auto.
Production 1-100
No pricing 25 or less.

Mirror Autograph Emerald

No Pricing
Production 1-5

Mirror Autograph Gold

No Pricing
Production 1-25

Mirror Autograph White

White Auto. (1-240): .75-1.5X Red Auto.
White Auto. (241-300): .5-1X Red Auto.
Production 1-100
No pricing 25 or less.

Mirror Bat Red

NM/M

Common Player: 4.00
Quantity produced listed
Black: No Pricing
Production One Set
Emerald: No Pricing
Production Five Sets
2 Adam Dunn/150 6.00
3 Adam LaRoche/250 4.00
5 Adrian Beltre/150 4.00
7 Albert Pujols/150 15.00
8 Alex Rodriguez/250 10.00
9 Alexis Rios/250 4.00
10 Alfonso Soriano/150 8.00
11 Andruw Jones/150 8.00
12 Andy Pettitte/250 6.00
13 Angel Berroa/150 4.00
15 Aubrey Huff/150 4.00
16 Austin Kearns/150 4.00
17 Barry Larkin/150 6.00
20 Bernie Williams/150 6.00
21 Bobby Abreu/150 6.00
24 Brandon Webb/150 4.00
25 Brendan Harris/250 4.00
26 Bret Boone/150 4.00
29 Brian Giles/250 4.00
35 Carl Everett/250 4.00
36 Carlos Beltran/150 6.00
37 Carlos Delgado/150 6.00
38 Carlos Lee/150 4.00
41 Chipper Jones/150 8.00
42 Cliff Floyd/250 4.00
43 Clint Barmes/250 4.00
44 Corey Patterson/250 6.00
45 Craig Biggio/150 4.00
47 Dan Haren/150 4.00
48 Darin Erstad/150 4.00
49 David Ortiz/250 8.00
50 Delmon Young/250 6.00
51 Derek Jeter/150 20.00
54 Edgar Martinez/150 6.00
55 Edgar Renteria/150 6.00
59 Eric Hinske/150 4.00
60 Eric Munson/250 4.00
61 Erubiel Durazo/250 4.00
62 Frank Thomas/150 8.00
63 Fred McGriff/150 4.00
65 Garret Anderson/150 6.00
67 Gary Sheffield/250 6.00
68 Geoff Jenkins/150 4.00
70 Hank Blalock/150 8.00
71 Hee Seop Choi/250 4.00
73 Hideo Nomo/150 8.00
76 Ivan Rodriguez /250 8.00
77 J.D. Drew/250 6.00
79 Jacque Jones/150 4.00
82 Jason Giambi/150 6.00
83 Jason Jennings/150 4.00
86 Jason Varitek/150 6.00
88 Javy Lopez/250 6.00
89 Jay Gibbons/150 4.00
91 Jeff Bagwell/150 8.00
92 Jeff Baker/250 4.00
93 Jeff Kent/150 4.00
97 Jim Edmonds/150 6.00
98 Jim Thome/150 8.00
100 Joe Borchard/150 4.00
101 Joe Crede/250 4.00
103 John Olerud/150 4.00
105 Johnny Damon/250 4.00
106 Jorge Posada/150 6.00
107 Jose Castillo/250 4.00
108 Jose Reyes/150 6.00
109 Jose Vidro/150 4.00
110 Josh Beckett/150 6.00
111 Josh Phelps/150 4.00
112 Juan Encarnacion/250 4.00
113 Juan Gonzalez/250 6.00
114 Junior Spivey/250 4.00
115 Kazuhisa Ishii/150 4.00
116 Kenny Lofton/250 4.00
117 Kerry Wood/150 8.00
119 Kevin Youkilis/250 4.00
120 Lance Berkman/150 4.00
122 Larry Walker/150 4.00
123 Luis Castillo/150 4.00
124 Luis Gonzalez/150 4.00
126 Lyle Overbay/250 4.00
127 Magglio Ordonez/150 4.00
128 Manny Ramirez/150 8.00
129 Marcus Giles/250 4.00
131 Mark Buehrle/150 4.00
132 Mark Mulder/150 6.00
133 Mark Prior/150 8.00
134 Mark Teixeira/150 6.00
135 Marlon Byrd/150 4.00
137 Miguel Cabrera/250 8.00
138 Mike Lowell/150 4.00
140 Mike Piazza/150 10.00
141 Mike Sweeney/150 4.00
143 Nick Johnson/250 4.00
144 Nomar Garciaparra/150 10.00
145 Omar Vizquel/150 4.00
146 Orlando Cabrera/250 4.00
147 Orlando Hudson/150 4.00
148 Pat Burrell/150 4.00
149 Paul Konerko/150 4.00
150 Paul LoDuca/150 4.00
152 Jermaine Dye/250 4.00
153 Preston Wilson/150 4.00
154 Rafael Furcal/150 4.00
155 Rafael Palmeiro/150 8.00
157 Rich Aurilia/250 4.00
159 Richard Hidalgo/150 4.00
160 Richie Sexson/250 6.00
161 Rickie Weeks/250 4.00
162 Roberto Alomar/250 6.00
163 Rocco Baldelli/150 4.00
164 Roger Clemens/250 12.00
168 Ryan Klesko/150 4.00
170 Sammy Sosa/150 12.00

174 Sean Casey/250 4.00
175 Shannon Stewart/150 4.00
176 Shawn Green/150 4.00
181 Todd Helton/150 8.00
183 Torii Hunter/150 6.00
184 Trot Nixon/150 6.00
185 Troy Glaus/150 6.00
186 Vernon Wells/150 4.00
187 Victor Martinez/250 4.00
188 Vladimir Guerrero/250 8.00
189 Wade Miller/250 4.00
190 Brandon Larson/175 4.00
191 Travis Hafner/150 6.00
192 Tim Salmon/150 4.00
195 Ramon Nivar/150 4.00
196 Moises Alou/250 6.00
197 Michael Young/250 4.00
198 Laynce Nix/150 4.00
199 Tino Martinez/250 4.00
200 Randall Simon/250 4.00
201 Roger Clemens/150 12.00
203 Vladimir Guerrero/150 8.00
204 Miguel Tejada/150 6.00
206 Jason Giambi/150 6.00
208 Alex Rodriguez/150 10.00
209 Alfonso Soriano/150 8.00
210 Ivan Rodriguez/150 8.00
211 Rafael Palmeiro/150 8.00
212 Gary Carter/150 8.00
216 Reggie Jackson/150 10.00
220 Don Mattingly/150 20.00
222 Rickey Henderson/150 8.00
227 Lou Brock/150 6.00
228 Andre Dawson/150 6.00
229 Rod Carew /150 8.00
230 Wade Boggs/150 6.00
240 Stan Musial/100 25.00

Mirror Bat Blue

NM/M
Blue Bat: 1-1.5X Red Price
Production 25-100
Cards listed don't have a red version.
217 Ryne Sandberg/50 40.00
219 Tony Gwynn/50 20.00
221 Mike Schmidt/50 25.00
223 Cal Ripken Jr./50 50.00
224 Nolan Ryan/50 35.00
225 George Brett/50 30.00

Mirror Bat Gold

NM/M
Gold Bat: 1.5-3X Red Price
Production 25 Sets
Cards listed don't have a red version.
69 Greg Maddux 25.00
217 Ryne Sandberg 50.00
219 Tony Gwynn 25.00
221 Mike Schmidt 40.00
223 Cal Ripken Jr. 90.00
224 Nolan Ryan 60.00
225 George Brett 40.00
231 Roberto Clemente 90.00
233 Babe Ruth 200.00
234 Lou Gehrig 150.00
235 Ty Cobb 125.00
236 Roger Maris 40.00
239 Ted Williams 80.00

Mirror Bat White

NM/M
White Bat: .75-1X Red Price
Production 25-200
Cards listed don't have a red version.
219 Tony Gwynn/100 15.00
221 Mike Schmidt/100 20.00
223 Cal Ripken Jr./100 40.00
224 Nolan Ryan/100 30.00
225 George Brett/100 20.00
231 Roberto Clemente/50 65.00
233 Babe Ruth/25 200.00
234 Lou Gehrig/25 150.00
235 Ty Cobb/25 125.00
236 Roger Maris/25 40.00
239 Ted Williams/25 80.00

Mirror Combo Red

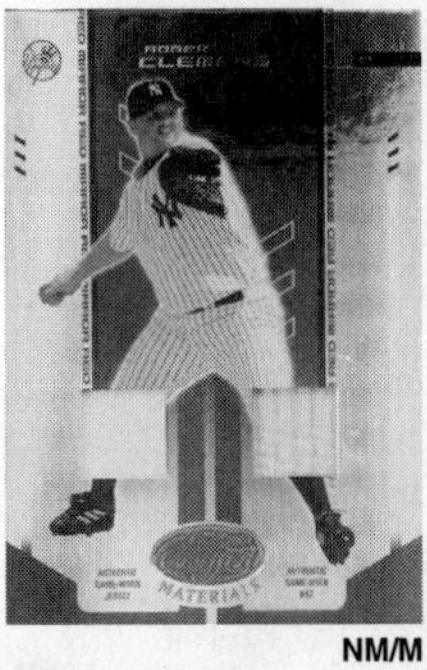

NM/M
Common (2-211): 6.00
Production 250
Common (212-239): 8.00
Production 50-250
Black Prime: No Pricing
Production One Set
2 Adam Dunn/Bat-Jsy 8.00
5 Adrian Beltre/Bat-Jsy 6.00
7 Albert Pujols/Bat-Jsy 25.00
11 Andruw Jones/Bat-Jsy 8.00
13 Angel Berroa/Bat-Pants 6.00
15 Aubrey Huff/Bat-Jsy 6.00
16 Austin Kearns/Bat-Jsy 6.00
17 Barry Larkin/Bat-Jsy 8.00
18 Barry Zito/Bat-Jsy 6.00
19 Ben Sheets/Bat-Jsy 6.00
20 Bernie Williams/Bat-Jsy 10.00
21 Bobby Abreu/Bat-Jsy 8.00
22 Brad Penny/Bat-Jsy 6.00
24 Brandon Webb/Bat-Jsy 6.00
26 Bret Boone/Bat-Jsy 6.00
36 Carlos Beltran/Bat-Jsy 8.00
37 Carlos Delgado/Bat-Jsy 8.00
38 Carlos Lee/Bat-Jsy 6.00
41 Chipper Jones/Bat-Jsy 10.00
45 Craig Biggio/Bat-Pants 6.00
47 Dan Haren/Bat-Jsy 6.00
51 Derek Jeter/Bat-Jsy 30.00
52 Dewon Brazelton/Glv-Jsy 6.00
54 Edgar Martinez/Bat-Jsy 8.00
55 Edgar Renteria/Bat-Jsy 8.00
58 Eric Chavez/Bat-Jsy 8.00
59 Eric Hinske/Bat-Jsy 6.00
62 Frank Thomas/Bat-Jsy 10.00
63 Fred McGriff/Bat-Jsy 6.00
65 Garret Anderson/Bat-Jsy 8.00
68 Geoff Jenkins/Bat-Jsy 6.00
70 Hank Blalock/Bat-Jsy 10.00
73 Hideo Nomo/Bat-Jsy 10.00
79 Jacque Jones/Bat-Jsy 6.00
82 Jason Giambi/Bat-Jsy 10.00
83 Jason Jennings/Bat-Jsy 6.00
86 Jason Varitek/Bat-Jsy 10.00
89 Jay Gibbons/Bat-Jsy 6.00
91 Jeff Bagwell/Bat-Jsy 10.00
93 Jeff Kent/Bat-Jsy 6.00
97 Jim Edmonds/Bat-Jsy 8.00
98 Jim Thome/Bat-Jsy 10.00
100 Joe Borchard/Bat-Jsy 6.00
103 John Olerud/Bat-Jsy 6.00
106 Jorge Posada/Bat-Jsy 8.00
108 Jose Reyes/Bat-Jsy 8.00
109 Jose Vidro/Bat-Jsy 6.00
110 Josh Beckett/Bat-Jsy 8.00
111 Josh Phelps/Bat-Jsy 6.00
115 Kazuhisa Ishii/Bat-Jsy 6.00
117 Kerry Wood/Bat-Jsy 12.00
120 Lance Berkman/Bat-Jsy 6.00
122 Larry Walker/Bat-Jsy 6.00
123 Luis Castillo/Bat-Jsy 6.00
124 Luis Gonzalez/Bat-Jsy 6.00
127 Magglio Ordonez/Bat-Jsy 6.00
128 Manny Ramirez/Bat-Jsy 10.00
131 Mark Buehrle/Bat-Jsy 6.00
132 Mark Mulder/Bat-Jsy 8.00
133 Mark Prior/Bat-Jsy 8.00
134 Mark Teixeira/Bat-Jsy 8.00
135 Marlon Byrd/Bat-Jsy 6.00
138 Mike Lowell/Bat-Jsy 6.00
140 Mike Piazza/Bat-Jsy 12.00
141 Mike Sweeney/Bat-Jsy 6.00
142 Morgan Ensberg/Bat-Jsy 6.00
144 Nomar Garciaparra/Bat-Jsy 12.00
145 Omar Vizquel/Bat-Jsy 6.00
147 Orlando Hudson/Bat-Jsy 6.00
148 Pat Burrell/Bat-Jsy 6.00
149 Paul Konerko/Bat-Jsy 6.00
150 Paul LoDuca/Bat-Jsy 6.00
151 Pedro J. Martinez/Bat-Jsy 10.00
153 Preston Wilson/Bat-Jsy 6.00
154 Rafael Furcal/Bat-Jsy 6.00
155 Rafael Palmeiro/Bat-Jsy 10.00
156 Randy Johnson/Bat-Jsy 12.00
159 Richard Hidalgo/Bat-Pants 6.00
163 Rocco Baldelli/Bat-Jsy 6.00
166 Roy Oswalt/Bat-Jsy 6.00
168 Ryan Klesko/Bat-Jsy 6.00
170 Sammy Sosa/Bat-Jsy 15.00
172 Scott Rolen/Bat-Jsy 10.00
175 Shannon Stewart/Bat-Jsy 6.00
176 Shawn Green/Bat-Jsy 6.00
180 Tim Hudson/Bat-Jsy 8.00
181 Todd Helton/Bat-Jsy 10.00
182 Tom Glavine/Bat-Jsy 8.00
183 Torii Hunter/Bat-Jsy 8.00
184 Trot Nixon/Bat-Jsy 8.00
185 Troy Glaus/Bat-Jsy 8.00
186 Vernon Wells/Bat-Jsy 6.00
191 Travis Hafner/Bat-Jsy 8.00
192 Tim Salmon/Bat-Jsy 6.00
195 Ramon Nivar/Bat-Jsy 6.00
201 Roger Clemens/Bat-Jsy 15.00
203 Vladimir Guerrero/Bat-Jsy 12.00
204 Miguel Tejada/Bat-Jsy 8.00
206 Jason Giambi/Bat-Jsy 8.00
207 Curt Schilling/Bat-Jsy 8.00
208 Alex Rodriguez/Bat-Jsy 12.00
209 Alfonso Soriano/Bat-Jsy 10.00
210 Ivan Rodriguez/Bat-Jsy 10.00
211 Rafael Palmeiro/Bat-Jsy 10.00
212 Gary Carter/Bat-Pants/250 8.00
216 Reggie Jackson/Bat-Jsy/250 12.00
217 Ryne Sandberg/Bat-Jsy/250 25.00
218 Dale Murphy/Bat-Jsy/250 10.00
219 Tony Gwynn/Bat-Jsy/250 12.00
220 Don Mattingly/Bat-Jsy/250 25.00
221 Mike Schmidt/Bat-Pants/250 25.00
222 Rickey Henderson/Bat-Jsy/250 10.00
223 Cal Ripken Jr./Bat-Jsy/250 35.00
224 Nolan Ryan/Bat-Jsy/250 35.00
225 George Brett/Bat-Jsy/250 25.00
227 Lou Brock/Bat-Jsy/250 8.00
228 Andre Dawson/Bat-Jsy/250 8.00
229 Rod Carew/Bat-Jkt/250 10.00
230 Wade Boggs/Bat-Jsy/250 8.00
231 Roberto Clemente/Bat-Jsy/100 100.00
232 Roy Campanella/Bat-Pants/100 15.00
233 Babe Ruth/Bat-Pants/50 350.00
234 Lou Gehrig/Bat-Pants/50 200.00
235 Ty Cobb/Bat-Pants/50 200.00
236 Roger Maris/Bat-Pants/100 50.00
238 Ernie Banks/Bat-Pants/100 15.00
239 Ted Williams/Bat-Jkt/100 85.00

Mirror Fabric Red

NM/M
Common Player: 4.00
Quantity produced listed
1 A.J. Burnett/Jsy/250 4.00
2 Adam Dunn/Jsy/150 6.00
5 Adrian Beltre/Jsy/150 6.00
6 Al Leiter/Jsy/250 4.00
7 Albert Pujols/Jsy/150 15.00
11 Andruw Jones/Jsy/150 6.00
13 Angel Berroa/Pants/150 4.00
15 Aubrey Huff/Jsy/150 4.00
16 Austin Kearns/Jsy/150 4.00
17 Barry Larkin/Jsy/150 6.00
18 Barry Zito/Jsy/150 5.00
19 Ben Sheets/Jsy/150 4.00
20 Bernie Williams/Jsy/150 6.00
21 Bobby Abreu/Jsy/150 6.00
22 Brad Penny/Jsy/150 4.00
27 Brett Myers/Jsy/250 4.00
33 C.C. Sabathia/Jsy/250 4.00
34 Carl Crawford/Jsy/250 4.00
36 Carlos Beltran/Jsy/150 6.00
38 Carlos Lee/Jsy/150 4.00
39 Chad Gaudin/Jsy/250 4.00
41 Chipper Jones/Jsy/150 8.00
45 Craig Biggio/Pants/150 4.00
47 Dan Haren/Jsy/150 4.00
48 Darin Erstad/Jsy/250 4.00
51 Derek Jeter/Jsy/150 20.00
53 Dontrelle Willis/Jsy/250 6.00
54 Edgar Martinez/Jsy/150 6.00
55 Edgar Renteria/Jsy/150 6.00
58 Eric Chavez/Jsy/150 4.00
59 Eric Hinske/Jsy/150 4.00
62 Frank Thomas/Jsy/150 8.00
64 Freddy Garcia/Jsy/250 4.00
66 Garrett Atkins/Jsy/250 4.00
68 Geoff Jenkins/Jsy/150 4.00
70 Hank Blalock/Jsy/150 6.00
72 Hideki Matsui/Base/250 15.00
73 Hideo Nomo/Jsy/150 8.00
75 Ichiro Suzuki/Base/250 15.00
79 Jacque Jones/Jsy/150 4.00
81 Jamie Moyer/Jsy/250 4.00
82 Jason Giambi/Jsy/150 6.00
83 Jason Jennings/Jsy/150 4.00
84 Jason Kendall/Jsy/250 4.00
86 Jason Varitek/Jsy/150 6.00
89 Jay Gibbons/Jsy/150 4.00
91 Jeff Bagwell/Jsy/150 8.00
93 Jeff Kent/Jsy/150 4.00
96 Jerome Williams/Jsy/250 4.00
97 Jim Edmonds/Jsy/150 6.00
98 Jim Thome/Jsy/150 8.00
102 Jose Santana/Jsy/250 4.00
103 John Olerud/Jsy/150 4.00
104 John Smoltz/Jsy/250 4.00
108 Jose Reyes/Jsy/150 6.00
109 Jose Vidro/Jsy/150 4.00
110 Josh Beckett/Jsy/150 6.00
111 Josh Phelps/Jsy/150 4.00
115 Kazuhisa Ishii/Jsy/150 4.00
117 Kerry Wood/Jsy/150 8.00
118 Kevin Millwood/Jsy/250 4.00
120 Lance Berkman/Jsy/150 4.00
121 Larry Bigbie/Jsy/250 4.00
122 Larry Walker/Jsy/150 4.00
123 Luis Castillo/Jsy/150 4.00
124 Luis Gonzalez/Jsy/150 4.00
130 Mariano Rivera/Jsy/250 6.00
131 Mark Buehrle/Jsy/150 4.00
133 Mark Prior/Jsy/150 8.00
135 Marlon Byrd/Jsy/150 4.00
136 Matt Morris/Jsy/250 4.00
139 Mike Mussina/Jsy/250 6.00
140 Mike Piazza/Jsy/150 10.00
141 Mike Sweeney/Jsy/150 4.00
142 Morgan Ensberg/Jsy/150 4.00
144 Nomar Garciaparra/Jsy/150 10.00
145 Omar Vizquel/Jsy/150 4.00
147 Orlando Hudson/Jsy/150 4.00
148 Pat Burrell/Jsy/150 4.00
151 Pedro J. Martinez/Jsy/150 8.00
153 Preston Wilson/Jsy/150 4.00
154 Rafael Furcal/Jsy/150 4.00
156 Randy Johnson/Jsy/150 8.00
158 Rich Harden/Jsy/250 4.00
159 Richard Hidalgo/Pants/150 4.00
163 Rocco Baldelli/Jsy/150 4.00
165 Roy Halladay/Jsy/250 4.00
168 Ryan Klesko/Jsy/150 4.00
170 Sammy Sosa/Jsy/150 12.00
172 Scott Rolen/Jsy/150 8.00
173 Sean Burroughs/Jsy/250 4.00
175 Shannon Stewart/Jsy/150 4.00
176 Shawn Green/Jsy/150 4.00
179 Steve Finley/Jsy/250 4.00
180 Tim Hudson/Jsy/150 6.00
181 Todd Helton/Jsy/150 8.00
182 Tom Glavine/Jsy/150 6.00
185 Troy Glaus/Jsy/150 6.00
186 Vernon Wells/Jsy/150 4.00
191 Travis Hafner/Jsy/150 6.00
192 Tim Salmon/Jsy/150 6.00
193 Tim Redding/Jsy/250 4.00
194 Runelvys Hernandez/Jsy/250 4.00
195 Ramon Nivar/Jsy/150 4.00
201 Roger Clemens/Jsy/150 15.00
202 Greg Maddux/Jsy/250 10.00
203 Vladimir Guerrero/Jsy/150 8.00
204 Miguel Tejada/Jsy/150 6.00
205 Kevin Brown/Jsy/250 4.00
206 Jason Giambi/Jsy/150 6.00
207 Curt Schilling/Jsy/150 6.00
208 Alex Rodriguez/Jsy/150 10.00
209 Alfonso Soriano/Jsy/150 8.00
210 Ivan Rodriguez/Jsy/150 8.00
212 Gary Carter/Pants/150 6.00
226 Bob Gibson/Jsy/250 10.00
237 Satchel Paige/Jsy/100 50.00

Mirror Fabric Blue

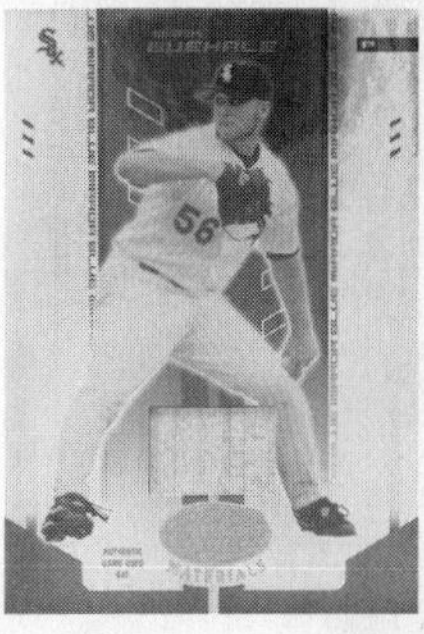

NM/M
Blue: 1-1.5X Red Price
Production 25-100
Cards listed don't have red version.
217 Ryne Sandberg/100 25.00
219 Tony Gwynn/100 15.00
220 Don Mattingly/100 25.00
221 Mike Schmidt/100 20.00
223 Cal Ripken Jr./100 35.00
224 Nolan Ryan/100 25.00
225 George Brett/100 15.00
231 Roberto Clemente/25 90.00
233 Babe Ruth/25 240.00
234 Lou Gehrig/25 150.00
235 Ty Cobb/25 140.00
236 Roger Maris/25 50.00
237 Satchel Paige/25 90.00
239 Ted Williams/25 100.00

Mirror Fabric Gold

NM/M
Gold: 2-3X Red Price
Production 10-25
No pricing 20 or less.
Cards listed don't have red version.
217 Ryne Sandberg/25 45.00
219 Tony Gwynn/25 30.00
220 Don Mattingly/25 60.00
221 Mike Schmidt/25 40.00
223 Cal Ripken Jr./25 90.00
224 Nolan Ryan/25 60.00
225 George Brett/25 50.00

Mirror Fabric White

NM/M
White: .5-1.5X Red Price
Production 25-200
Cards listed don't have red version.
217 Ryne Sandberg/25 45.00
219 Tony Gwynn/25 25.00
220 Don Mattingly/25 50.00
221 Mike Schmidt/25 40.00
223 Cal Ripken Jr./25 90.00
224 Nolan Ryan/25 60.00
225 George Brett/25 50.00
231 Roberto Clemente/25 90.00
233 Babe Ruth/25 240.00
234 Lou Gehrig/25 150.00
235 Ty Cobb/25 140.00
236 Roger Maris/25 50.00

237	Satchel Paige/25	90.00
239	Ted Williams/25	100.00

2004 Leaf Limited

NM/M

Complete Set (275):
Common Player (1-200): 1.50
Common SP (201-229): 3.00
Production 499
Common SP (251-275): 10.00
Production 99
Pack (4): 60.00
Box (4): 200.00

1	Adam Dunn	2.00
2	Adrian Beltre	2.00
3	Albert Pujols	6.00
4	Alex Rodriguez	6.00
5	Alfonso Soriano	2.50
6	Andruw Jones	1.50
7	Andy Pettitte	1.50
8	Angel Berroa	1.50
9	Aramis Ramirez	1.50
10	Aubrey Huff	1.50
11	Aubrey Huff	1.50
12	Barry Larkin	1.50
13	Barry Zito	1.50
14	Bartolo Colon	1.50
15	Ben Sheets	1.50
16	Bernie Williams	1.50
17	Bobby Abreu	1.50
18	Brandon Webb	1.50
19	Brian Giles	1.50
20	C.C. Sabathia	1.50
21	Carlos Beltran	2.00
22	Carlos Delgado	1.50
23	Chipper Jones	3.00
24	Craig Biggio	1.50
25	Curt Schilling	3.00
26	Darin Erstad	1.50
27	Delmon Young	1.50
28	Derek Jeter	6.00
29	Derek Lee	1.50
30	Dontrelle Willis	1.50
31	Edgar Renteria	1.50
32	Eric Chavez	1.50
33	Esteban Loaiza	1.50
34	Frank Thomas	2.00
35	Fred McGriff	1.50
36	Garret Anderson	1.50
37	Gary Sheffield	1.50
38	Geoff Jenkins	1.50
39	Greg Maddux	3.00
40	Hank Blalock	2.00
41	Hideki Matsui	5.00
42	Hideo Nomo	1.50
43	Ichiro Suzuki	5.00
44	Ivan Rodriguez	2.00
45	J.D. Drew	1.50
46	Jacque Jones	1.50
47	Jae Weong Seo	1.50
48	Jake Peavy	1.50
49	Jamie Moyer	1.50
50	Jason Giambi	1.50
51	Jason Kendall	1.50
52	Jason Schmidt	1.50
53	Jason Varitek	1.50
54	Javier Vazquez	1.50

55	Javy Lopez	1.50
56	Jay Gibbons	1.50
57	Jay Payton	1.50
58	Jeff Bagwell	1.50
59	Jeff Kent	1.50
60	Jeremy Bonderman	1.50
61	Jermaine Dye	1.50
62	Jeromy Burnitz	1.50
63	Jim Edmonds	2.00
64	Jim Thome	1.50
65	Jimmy Rollins	1.50
66	Jody Gerut	1.50
67	Johan Santana	2.00
68	John Olerud	1.50
69	John Smoltz	1.50
70	Johnny Damon	2.00
71	Jorge Posada	1.50
72	Jose Contreras	1.50
73	Jose Reyes	1.50
74	Jose Vidro	1.50
75	Josh Beckett	1.50
76	Juan Gonzalez	1.50
77	Juan Pierre	1.50
78	Junior Spivey	1.50
79	Kazuhisa Ishii	1.50
80	Keith Foulke	1.50
81	Ken Griffey Jr.	3.00
82	Ken Harvey	1.50
83	Kenny Rogers	1.50
84	Kerry Wood	2.50
85	Kevin Brown	1.50
86	Kevin Millwood	1.50
87	Kip Wells	1.50
88	Lance Berkman	1.50
89	Larry Bigbie	1.50
90	Larry Walker	1.50
91	Laynce Nix	1.50
92	Luis Castillo	1.50
93	Luis Gonzalez	1.50
94	Luis Matos	1.50
95	Lyle Overbay	1.50
96	Magglio Ordonez	1.50
97	Manny Ramirez	2.00
98	Marcus Giles	1.50
99	Mark Buehrle	1.50
100	Mark Mulder	1.50
101	Mark Prior	2.00
102	Mark Teixeira	1.50
103	Marlon Byrd	1.50
104	Matt Morris	1.50
105	Melvin Mora	1.50
106	Michael Young	1.50
107	Miguel Cabrera	3.00
108	Miguel Tejada	2.00
109	Mike Lowell	1.50
110	Mike Mussina	2.00
111	Mike Piazza	4.00
112	Mike Sweeney	1.50
113	Milton Bradley	1.50
114	Moises Alou	1.50
115	Morgan Ensberg	1.50
116	Nick Johnson	1.50
117	Nomar Garciaparra	4.00
118	Omar Vizquel	1.50
119	Orlando Cabrera	1.50
120	Pat Burrell	1.50
121	Paul Konerko	1.50
122	Paul LoDuca	1.50
123	Pedro J. Martinez	3.00
124	Preston Wilson	1.50
125	Rafael Furcal	1.50
126	Rafael Palmeiro	2.00
127	Randy Johnson	3.00
128	Rich Harden	1.50
129	Richard Hidalgo	1.50
130	Richie Sexson	1.50
131	Rickie Weeks	1.50
132	Roberto Alomar	1.50
133	Robin Ventura	1.50
134	Rocco Baldelli	1.50
135	Roger Clemens	6.00
136	Roy Halladay	1.50
137	Roy Oswalt	1.50
138	Russ Ortiz	1.50
139	Ryan Klesko	1.50
140	Sammy Sosa	5.00
141	Scott Podsednik	1.50
142	Scott Rolen	3.00
143	Sean Burroughs	1.50
144	Sean Casey	1.50
145	Shannon Stewart	1.50
146	Shawn Green	1.50
147	Shigetoshi Hasegawa	1.50
148	Sidney Ponson	1.50
149	Steve Finley	1.50
150	Tim Hudson	1.50
151	Tim Salmon	1.50
152	Tino Martinez	1.50
153	Todd Helton	2.00
154	Tom Glavine	2.00
155	Torii Hunter	1.50
156	Trot Nixon	1.50
157	Troy Glaus	1.50
158	Vernon Wells	1.50
159	Victor Martinez	1.50
160	Vinny Castilla	1.50
161	Vladimir Guerrero	3.00
162	Alex Rodriguez	6.00
163	Alfonso Soriano	2.50
164	Andy Pettitte	1.50
165	Curt Schilling	3.00
166	Gary Sheffield	1.50
167	Greg Maddux	3.00
168	Hideo Nomo	1.50
169	Ivan Rodriguez	2.00

170	Jason Giambi	1.50
171	Jim Thome	2.00
172	Juan Gonzalez	1.50
173	Ken Griffey Jr.	3.00
174	Kevin Brown	1.50
175	Manny Ramirez	2.00
176	Miguel Tejada	2.00
177	Mike Mussina	1.50
178	Mike Piazza	4.00
179	Pedro Martinez	3.00
180	Rafael Palmeiro	2.00
181	Randy Johnson	3.00
182	Roger Clemens	6.00
183	Scott Rolen	3.00
184	Shawn Green	1.50
185	Tom Glavine	1.50
186	Vladimir Guerrero	3.00
187	Alex Rodriguez	6.00
188	Mike Piazza	4.00
189	Randy Johnson	3.00
190	Roger Clemens	6.00
191	Albert Pujols	6.00
192	Barry Zito	1.50
193	Chipper Jones	3.00
194	Garret Anderson	1.50
195	Jeff Bagwell	2.00
196	Josh Beckett	1.50
197	Magglio Ordonez	1.50
198	Mark Prior	2.00
199	Sammy Sosa	5.00
200	Todd Helton	3.00
201	Andre Dawson	3.00
202	Babe Ruth	8.00
203	Bob Feller	4.00
204	Bob Gibson	4.00
205	Bobby Doerr	3.00
206	Cal Ripken Jr.	10.00
207	Dale Murphy	4.00
208	Don Mattingly	8.00
209	Gary Carter	3.00
210	George Brett	8.00
211	Jackie Robinson	5.00
212	Lou Brock	4.00
213	Lou Gehrig	6.00
214	Mark Grace	3.00
215	Maury Wills	3.00
216	Mike Schmidt	8.00
217	Nolan Ryan	8.00
218	Orel Hershiser	4.00
219	Paul Molitor	4.00
220	Roberto Clemente	8.00
221	Rod Carew	4.00
222	Roy Campanella	4.00
223	Ryne Sandberg	8.00
224	Stan Musial	6.00
225	Ted Williams	8.00
226	Tony Gwynn	6.00
227	Ty Cobb	5.00
228	Whitey Ford	4.00
229	Yogi Berra	4.00
230	Carlos Beltran	3.00
231	David Ortiz	3.00
232	David Ortiz	3.00
233	Carlos Zambrano	1.50
234	Carlos Lee	1.50
235	Travis Hafner	1.50
236	Brad Penny	1.50
237	Wade Miller	1.50
238	Edgar Martinez	1.50
239	Carl Crawford	1.50
240	Roy Oswalt	1.50
241	Kazuo Matsui	8.00
242	Carlos Beltran	3.00
243	Carlos Beltran	3.00
244	Miguel Cabrera	2.00
245	Scott Rolen	3.00
246	Hank Blalock	2.00
247	Vernon Wells	1.50
248	Adam Dunn	2.00
249	Preston Wilson	1.50
250	Victor Martinez	1.50
251	Aarom Baldiris **RC**	10.00
252	Akinori Otsuka **RC**	35.00
253	Andres Blanco **RC**	10.00
254	Brad Halsey **RC**	10.00
255	Joey Gathright **RC**	25.00
256	Colby Miller **RC**	10.00
257	Fernando Nieve **RC**	10.00
258	Freddy Guzman **RC**	15.00
259	Hector Gimenez **RC**	10.00
260	Jake Woods **RC**	10.00
261	Jason Bartlett **RC**	10.00
262	John Gall **RC**	15.00
263	Jose Capellan **RC**	35.00
264	Josh Labandeira **RC**	10.00
265	Justin Germano **RC**	10.00
266	Kazuhito Tadano **RC**	40.00
267	Lance Cormier **RC**	10.00
268	Merkin Valdez **RC**	20.00
269	Mike Gosling **RC**	10.00
270	Ramon Ramirez **RC**	10.00
271	Rusty Tucker **RC**	10.00
272	Shawn Hill **RC**	10.00
273	Shingo Takatsu **RC**	40.00
274	William Bergolla **RC**	10.00
275	Yadier Molina **RC**	20.00

Bronze Spotlight

Bronze: 1-2X
Production 100 Sets

Gold Spotlight

Golds (1-250): 3-5X
Production 25 Sets

Platinum Spotlight

No Pricing
Production One Set

Silver Spotlight

Silver (1-250): 2-3X
Production 50 Sets

Barrels

No Pricing
Production 1-5

Cuts

NM/M

Quantity produced listed

1	Nolan Ryan/100	125.00
2	Bob Gibson/50	40.00
3	Harmon Killebrew/100	40.00
4	Duke Snider/100	30.00
5	George Brett/100	75.00
6	Stan Musial/100	80.00
7	Alan Trammell/100	20.00
8	Cal Ripken Jr./100	180.00
9	Steve Carlton/50	40.00
10	Phil Rizzuto/100	30.00
11	Mark Prior/50	40.00
12	Will Clark/100	40.00
13	Lou Brock/100	30.00
14	Ozzie Smith/100	60.00
15	Bob Feller/100	30.00
16	Gary Carter/50	25.00
17	Al Kaline/100	40.00
18	Brooks Robinson/100	40.00
19	Tony Gwynn/100	50.00
20	Mike Schmidt/100	75.00
21	Ralph Kiner/50	40.00
22	Jim Palmer/50	40.00
23	Don Mattingly/100	75.00
24	Paul Molitor/50	40.00
25	Dale Murphy/100	30.00

Cuts Gold

NM/M

Quantity produced listed

1	Nolan Ryan/34	200.00
2	Bob Gibson/45	40.00
9	Steve Carlton/32	50.00
11	Mark Prior/22	60.00
12	Will Clark/22	65.00
13	Lou Brock/20	50.00
15	Bob Feller/28	50.00
19	Tony Gwynn/19	100.00
20	Mike Schmidt/20	100.00
22	Jim Palmer/22	50.00
23	Don Mattingly/23	100.00

Legends Material Autographs Number

NM/M

Quanity produced listed

1	Al Kaline/Pants/50	50.00
3	Bob Feller/Jsy/50	30.00
4	Bob Gibson/Jsy/50	30.00
7	Carl Yastrzemski/Jsy/25	80.00
8	Harmon Killebrew/Jsy/25	65.00
9	Hoyt Wilhelm/Jsy/25	40.00
12	Lou Brock/Jsy/50	30.00
13	Luis Aparicio/Pants/50	20.00
15	Reggie Jackson/Jsy/50	30.00
16	Red Schoendienst/Jsy/50	30.00
19	Stan Musial/Jsy/25	75.00
23	Whitey Ford/Pants/25	50.00
24	Yogi Berra/Jsy/25	75.00

Legends Material Autographs Position

NM/M

Quantity produced listed

1 Al Kaline/Pants/50 50.00
3 Bob Feller/Jsy/50 30.00
4 Bob Gibson/Jsy/50 30.00
7 Carl Yastrzemski/Jsy/25 80.00
8 Harmon Killebrew/Jsy/25 65.00
9 Hoyt Wilhelm/Jsy/50 40.00
12 Lou Brock/Jsy/50 30.00
13 Luis Aparicio/Pants/50 20.00
15 Reggie Jackson/Jsy/50 50.00
16 Red Schoendienst/Jsy/50 30.00
19 Stan Musial/Jsy/50 75.00
23 Whitey Ford/Pants/25 50.00
24 Yogi Berra/Jsy/25 75.00

Legends Material Number
NM/M
Quantity produced listed
1 Al Kaline/Pants/50 15.00
2 Babe Ruth/Pants/50 160.00
3 Bob Feller/Jsy/50 10.00
4 Bob Gibson/Jsy/50 10.00
6 Burleigh Grimes/Pants/100 40.00
7 Carl Yastrzemski/Jsy/100 15.00
8 Harmon Killebrew/Jsy/25 25.00
9 Hoyt Wilhelm/Jsy/100 5.00
10 Johnny Mize/Pants/100 10.00
11 Ernie Banks/Pants/50 15.00
12 Lou Brock/Jsy/50 10.00
13 Luis Aparicio/Pants/100 5.00
14 Pee Wee Reese/Jsy/50 10.00
15 Reggie Jackson/Jsy/100 10.00
16 Red Schoendienst/Jsy/50 8.00
17 Roberto Clemente/Jsy/25 80.00
18 Roger Maris/Pants/100 25.00
19 Stan Musial/Jsy/100 20.00
20 Ted Williams/Jsy/100 75.00
21 Ty Cobb/Pants/50 80.00
22 Warren Spahn/Jsy/100 10.00
23 Whitey Ford/Pants/100 10.00
24 Yogi Berra/Jsy/50 15.00
25 Satchel Paige/CO Jsy/100 50.00

Legends Material Position
NM/M
Quantity produced listed
1 Al Kaline/Pants/50 15.00
2 Babe Ruth/Pants/50 160.00
3 Bob Feller/Jsy/50 10.00
4 Bob Gibson/Jsy/50 10.00
6 Burleigh Grimes/Pants/100 40.00
7 Carl Yastrzemski/Jsy/100 15.00
8 Harmon Killebrew/Jsy/25 25.00
9 Hoyt Wilhelm/Jsy/100 5.00
10 Johnny Mize/Pants/100 10.00
11 Ernie Banks/Pants/50 15.00
12 Lou Brock/Jsy/50 10.00
13 Luis Aparicio/Pants/100 5.00
14 Pee Wee Reese/Jsy/50 10.00
15 Reggie Jackson/Jsy/100 10.00
16 Red Schoendienst/Jsy/50 8.00
17 Roberto Clemente/Pants/25 80.00
18 Roger Maris/Pants/100 25.00
19 Stan Musial/Jsy/100 20.00
20 Ted Williams/Jsy/100 75.00
21 Ty Cobb/Pants/50 80.00
22 Warren Spahn/Jsy/100 10.00
23 Whitey Ford/Pants/100 10.00
24 Yogi Berra/Jsy/50 15.00
25 Satchel Paige/CO Jsy/100 50.00

Lumberjacks

NM/M
Common Player: 2.00
Quantity produced listed
Black: 1-3X
Production 16-100
1 Al Kaline/399 4.00
2 Albert Pujols/114 15.00
3 Andre Dawson/438 2.00
4 Babe Ruth/714 8.00
5 Bo Jackson/141 5.00
6 Bobby Doerr/223 3.00
7 Brooks Robinson/268 4.00
8 Cal Ripken Jr./431 10.00
9 Carlton Fisk/376 2.00
10 Dale Murphy/398 2.00
11 Darryl Strawberry/335 2.00
12 Don Mattingly/222 6.00
13 Duke Snider/407 3.00
14 Eddie Mathews/512 3.00
15 Eddie Murray/504 3.00
16 Frank Robinson/586 3.00
17 Frank Thomas/418 3.00
18 Gary Carter/324 2.00
19 George Brett/317 6.00
20 Harmon Killebrew/573 4.00
22 Lou Gehrig/493 15.00
23 Mark Grace/173 2.00
24 Mike Piazza/358 4.00
25 Mike Schmidt/548 5.00
26 Orlando Cepeda/379 2.00
27 Rafael Palmeiro/528 2.00
28 Ralph Kiner/369 2.00
29 Reggie Jackson/563 3.00
30 Rickey Henderson/297 3.00
31 Roger Maris/275 5.00
32 Ryne Sandberg/282 4.00
33 Sammy Sosa/539 4.00
34 Scott Rolen/192 4.00
35 Stan Musial/475 4.00
36 Ted Williams/521 6.00
37 Thurman Munson/113 5.00
38 Vladimir Guerrero/234 4.00
39 Willie McCovey/521 2.00
40 Willie Stargell/475 2.00
41 Roberto Clemente, Stan Musial 6.00
42 Cal Ripken Jr., Ernie Banks 10.00
43 Babe Ruth, Lou Gehrig 8.00
44 George Brett, Mike Schmidt 8.00
45 Frank Robinson, Jackie Robinson 8.00
46 Don Mattingly, Roger Maris 8.00
47 Nomar Garciaparra, Ted Williams 8.00
48 Johnny Bench, Mike Piazza 4.00
49 Reggie Jackson, Sammy Sosa 4.00
50 Mel Ott, Willie McCovey 4.00

Lumberjacks Autographs
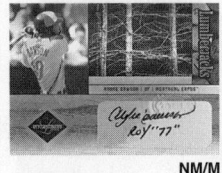

NM/M
Quantity produced listed
1 Al Kaline/100 30.00
2 Albert Pujols/10
3 Andre Dawson/100 15.00
5 Bo Jackson/25 60.00
6 Brooks Robinson/100 50.00
8 Cal Ripken Jr./25 180.00
9 Carlton Fisk/25 30.00
10 Dale Murphy/100 20.00
11 Darryl Strawberry/100 15.00
12 Don Mattingly/100 70.00
13 Duke Snider/100 20.00
16 Frank Robinson/100 20.00
17 Frank Thomas/50 50.00
18 Gary Carter/100 15.00
19 George Brett/100 70.00
20 Harmon Killebrew/100 40.00
23 Mark Grace/25 40.00
25 Mike Schmidt/50 65.00
28 Ralph Kiner/100 20.00
29 Reggie Jackson/25 50.00
32 Ryne Sandberg/25 90.00
34 Scott Rolen/25 40.00
35 Stan Musial/25 65.00
39 Willie McCovey/25 30.00

Lumberjacks Autographs Bat
NM/M
Quantity produced listed
1 Al Kaline/100 40.00
3 Andre Dawson/100 20.00
5 Bo Jackson/25 70.00
6 Bobby Doerr/50 25.00
7 Brooks Robinson/50 60.00
8 Cal Ripken Jr./25 200.00
9 Carlton Fisk/25 40.00
10 Dale Murphy/100 25.00
11 Darryl Strawberry/25 25.00
12 Don Mattingly/25 80.00
17 Frank Thomas/25 70.00
18 Gary Carter/50 20.00
19 George Brett/25 80.00
20 Harmon Killebrew/50 50.00
23 Mark Grace/17 50.00
25 Mike Schmidt/25 50.00
28 Ralph Kiner/100 25.00
29 Reggie Jackson/25 60.00
32 Ryne Sandberg/25 90.00
34 Scott Rolen/25 50.00
35 Stan Musial/50 75.00
39 Willie McCovey/25 40.00

Lumberjacks Autographs Jersey
NM/M
Quantity produced listed
1 Al Kaline Pants/100 40.00
3 Andre Dawson/100 20.00
5 Bo Jackson/25 70.00
6 Bobby Doerr/100 15.00
7 Brooks Robinson/25 75.00
8 Cal Ripken Jr./25 200.00
9 Carlton Fisk/50 30.00
10 Dale Murphy/100 25.00
11 Darryl Strawberry/Pants/25 25.00
12 Don Mattingly/25 80.00
15 Eddie Murray/25 70.00
16 Frank Robinson/50 30.00
17 Frank Thomas/25 70.00
18 Gary Carter/50 20.00
19 George Brett/25 80.00
20 Harmon Killebrew/25 60.00
23 Mark Grace/25 50.00
25 Mike Schmidt/25 80.00
26 Orlando Cepeda/Pants/50 20.00
29 Reggie Jackson/25 60.00
32 Ryne Sandberg/25 90.00
34 Scott Rolen/25 50.00
35 Stan Musial/50 75.00
39 Willie McCovey/25 40.00

Lumberjacks Barrel
Quantity produced listed
No Pricing
Production 1-5

Lumberjacks Bat

NM/M
Quantity produced listed
1 Al Kaline/100 15.00
2 Albert Pujols/100 15.00
3 Andre Dawson/25 15.00
4 Babe Ruth/100 125.00
5 Bo Jackson/50 15.00
6 Bobby Doerr/25 12.00
7 Brooks Robinson/100 20.00
8 Cal Ripken Jr./100 40.00
9 Carlton Fisk/100 15.00
10 Dale Murphy/50 15.00
11 Darryl Strawberry/25 15.00
12 Don Mattingly/100 20.00
14 Eddie Mathews/100 10.00
15 Eddie Murray/100 15.00
16 Frank Robinson/100 8.00
17 Frank Thomas/25 20.00
18 Gary Carter/50 10.00
19 George Brett/100 20.00
20 Harmon Killebrew/100 15.00
21 Hideki Matsui/100 25.00
22 Lou Gehrig/100 100.00
23 Mark Grace/25 15.00
24 Mike Piazza/50 15.00
25 Mike Schmidt/100 10.00
26 Orlando Cepeda/50 8.00
27 Rafael Palmeiro/100 10.00
28 Ralph Kiner/100 8.00
29 Reggie Jackson/100 10.00
30 Rickey Henderson/100 10.00
31 Roger Maris/100 25.00
32 Ryne Sandberg/100 15.00
33 Sammy Sosa/100 15.00
34 Scott Rolen/100 15.00
35 Stan Musial/100 25.00
36 Ted Williams/100 50.00
37 Thurman Munson/100 20.00
38 Vladimir Guerrero/100 15.00
39 Willie McCovey/100 10.00
40 Willie Stargell/50 10.00
41 Roberto Clemente, Stan Musial/100 85.00
42 Cal Ripken Jr., Ernie Banks/50 100.00
43 Babe Ruth, Lou Gehrig/25 250.00
44 George Brett, Mike Schmidt/50 50.00
46 Don Mattingly, Roger Maris/50 40.00
47 Nomar Garciaparra, Ted Williams/100 75.00
48 Johnny Bench, Mike Piazza/25 35.00
49 Reggie Jackson, Sammy Sosa/50 20.00
50 Mel Ott, Willie McCovey/100 40.00

Lumberjacks Combos
NM/M
Quantity produced listed
1 Al Kaline/Bat-Pants/100 20.00
2 Albert Pujols/Bat-Jsy/100 20.00
3 Andre Dawson/Bat-Jsy/25 15.00
4 Babe Ruth/Bat-Jsy/25 400.00
5 Bo Jackson/Bat-Jsy/25 50.00
6 Bobby Doerr/Bat-Jsy/50 12.00
7 Brooks Robinson/Bat-Jsy/25 40.00
8 Cal Ripken Jr./Bat-Jsy/100 50.00
9 Carlton Fisk/Bat-Jsy/15 15.00
10 Dale Murphy/Bat-Jsy/100 15.00
11 Darryl Strawberry/Bat-Pants/25 15.00
12 Don Mattingly/Bat-Jsy/100 25.00
14 Eddie Mathews/Bat-Jsy/50 15.00
15 Eddie Murray/Bat-Jsy/50 20.00
16 Frank Robinson/Bat-Jsy/100 15.00
17 Frank Thomas/Bat-Jsy/50 20.00
18 Gary Carter/Bat-Jsy/50 10.00
19 George Brett/Bat-Jsy/100 25.00
20 Harmon Killebrew/Bat-Jsy/100 30.00
21 Hideki Matsui/Bat-Jsy/100 30.00
22 Lou Gehrig/Bat-Jsy/25 250.00
23 Mark Grace/Bat/17 30.00
24 Mike Piazza/Bat-Jsy/100 15.00
25 Mike Schmidt/Bat-Jsy/100 20.00
26 Orlando Cepeda/Bat-Pants/50 10.00
27 Rafael Palmeiro/Bat-Jsy/50 15.00
29 Reggie Jackson/Bat-Jsy/100 15.00
30 Rickey Henderson/Bat-Jsy/100 10.00
31 Roger Maris/Bat-Jsy/50 25.00
32 Ryne Sandberg/Bat-Jsy/100 15.00
33 Sammy Sosa/Bat-Jsy/100 10.00
34 Scott Rolen/Bat-Jsy/50 10.00
35 Stan Musial/Bat-Jsy/50 30.00
36 Ted Williams/Bat-Jsy/50 50.00
37 Thurman Munson/Bat-Jsy/50 20.00
38 Vladimir Guerrero/Bat-Jsy/50 10.00
39 Willie McCovey/Bat-Jsy/50 10.00
40 Willie Stargell/Bat-Jsy/100 8.00

Lumberjacks Jersey
NM/M
Quantity produced listed
1 Al Kaline/Pants/50 20.00
2 Albert Pujols/50 15.00
3 Andre Dawson/25 15.00
4 Babe Ruth/25 300.00
5 Bo Jackson/50 10.00
6 Bobby Doerr/100 5.00
7 Brooks Robinson/25 30.00
8 Cal Ripken Jr./100 40.00
9 Carlton Fisk/100 10.00
10 Dale Murphy/100 10.00
11 Darryl Strawberry/Pants/50 8.00
12 Don Mattingly/100 20.00
14 Eddie Mathews/100 10.00
15 Eddie Murray/50 20.00
16 Frank Robinson/100 10.00
17 Frank Thomas/50 10.00
18 Gary Carter/50 10.00
19 George Brett/100 20.00
20 Harmon Killebrew/25 30.00
21 Hideki Matsui/25 25.00
22 Lou Gehrig/25 180.00
23 Mark Grace/100 8.00
24 Mike Piazza/100 10.00
25 Mike Schmidt/100 15.00
26 Orlando Cepeda/Pants/100 5.00
27 Rafael Palmeiro/50 10.00
29 Reggie Jackson/100 10.00
30 Rickey Henderson/100 10.00
31 Roger Maris/50 25.00
32 Ryne Sandberg/100 15.00
33 Sammy Sosa/100 10.00
34 Scott Rolen/50 10.00
35 Stan Musial/50 30.00
36 Ted Williams/100 50.00
37 Thurman Munson/100 20.00
38 Vladimir Guerrero/50 10.00
39 Willie McCovey/100 10.00
40 Willie Stargell/100 8.00
41 Roberto Clemente, Stan Musial/50 120.00
42 Cal Ripken Jr., Ernie Banks/100 65.00
43 Babe Ruth, Lou Gehrig/25 400.00
44 George Brett, Mike Schmidt/Jkt/100 30.00
45 Frank Robinson, Jackie Robinson/25 30.00
46 Don Mattingly, Roger Maris/Pants/100 25.00
47 Johnny Bench, Mike Piazza/100 10.00
49 Reggie Jackson, Sammy Sosa/100 15.00
50 Mel Ott Pants, Willie McCovey/25 80.00

Matching Numbers

NM/M
Quantity produced listed
Prime: No Pricing

Production One Set
1 Bobby Doerr/Jsy, Pee Wee Reese/Jsy/100 10.00
2 Lou Gehrig/Pants, Mel Ott/Jsy/50 160.00
3 Albert Pujols/Jsy, George Brett/Jsy/100 30.00
4 Cal Ripken Jr./Jsy, Carl Yastrzemski/Jsy/100 50.00
5 Dwight Gooden/Jsy, Whitey Ford/Pants/50 15.00
6 Mark Grace/Jsy, Todd Helton/Jsy/25 25.00
7 Robin Yount/Jsy, Tony Gwynn/Jsy/50 40.00
8 Frank Robinson/Jsy, Mike Schmidt/Jsy/100 25.00
9 Roberto Clemente/Jsy, Sammy Sosa/Jsy/100 75.00
10 Roger Clemens/Jsy, Warren Spahn/Pant/100 25.00
11 Mark Prior/Jsy, Roger Clemens/Jsy/50 15.00
12 Don Mattingly/Jkt, Ryne Sandberg/Jsy/100 30.00
13 Billy Williams/Jsy, Wade Boggs/Jsy/100 10.00
14 Jim "Catfish" Hunter/Jsy, Juan Marichal/Jsy/50 10.00
15 Fergie Jenkins/Pants, Greg Maddux/Jsy/50 20.00
16 Kerry Wood/Pants, Nolan Ryan/Jsy/100 35.00
17 Rickey Henderson/Jsy, Roger Maris/Pants/100 40.00
18 Dontrelle Willis/Jsy, Mike Mussina/Jsy/50 15.00
19 Reggie Jackson/Jsy, Willie McCovey/Jsy/100 15.00
20 Bob Gibson/Jsy, Pedro Martinez/Jsy/50 15.00
21 Duke Snider/Jsy, Paul Molitor/Jsy/100 10.00
22 Johnny Bench/Jsy, Lou Boudreau/Jsy/100 15.00
23 Andre Dawson/Jsy, Chipper Jones/Jsy/100 15.00
24 Ernie Banks/Jsy, Boyer/Jsy/100 15.00
25 Manny Ramirez/Jsy, Rickey Henderson/Jsy/100 15.00
26 Carlton Fisk/Jsy, Scott Rolen/Jsy/100 15.00
27 Nolan Ryan/Jsy, Orlando Cepeda/Pnt/100 25.00
28 Roy Halladay/Jsy, Steve Carlton/Jsy/100 8.00
29 Eddie Mathews/Jsy, Tom Seaver/Jsy/100 15.00
30 Brandon Webb/Jsy, Orel Hershiser/Jsy/100 10.00

Moniker Bat

NM/M

Quanity produced listed
1 Adam Dunn/50 30.00
5 Alfonso Soriano/25 50.00
6 Andruw Jones/25 40.00
8 Angel Berroa/25 15.00
9 Aramis Ramirez/25 25.00
10 Aubrey Huff/25 25.00
15 Ben Sheets/25 25.00
21 Carlos Beltran/50 40.00
24 Craig Biggio/25 40.00
27 Delmon Young/50 25.00
30 Dontrelle Willis/25 30.00
31 Edgar Renteria/25 25.00
34 Frank Thomas/25 70.00
35 Fred McGriff/50 30.00
36 Garret Anderson/50 20.00
37 Gary Sheffield/25 40.00
40 Hank Blalock/50 35.00
61 Jermaine Dye/25 25.00
71 Jorge Posada/25 50.00
84 Kerry Wood/25 50.00
88 Lance Berkman/25 40.00
100 Mark Mulder/50 20.00
101 Mark Prior/50 40.00
102 Mark Teixeira/25 40.00
106 Michael Young/50 15.00
107 Miguel Cabrera/40 40.00
109 Mike Lowell/25 25.00
122 Paul LoDuca/25 25.00
124 Preston Wilson/25 20.00
131 Rickie Weeks/25 20.00
137 Roy Oswalt/25 20.00
144 Sean Casey/50 20.00
145 Shannon Stewart/25 25.00
155 Torii Hunter/25 25.00
156 Trot Nixon/25 25.00
158 Vernon Wells/50 20.00
159 Victor Martinez/50 25.00
163 Alfonso Soriano/25 50.00
166 Gary Sheffield/25 35.00
194 Garret Anderson/50 20.00
198 Mark Prior/50 40.00
201 Andre Dawson/50 20.00
205 Bobby Doerr/25 25.00
207 Dale Murphy/100 25.00
208 Don Mattingly/50 75.00
209 Gary Carter/100 15.00
212 Lou Brock/50 30.00
214 Mark Grace/25 30.00
216 Mike Schmidt/50 75.00
217 Nolan Ryan/50 150.00
219 Paul Molitor/50 30.00
221 Rod Carew/50 35.00
223 Ryne Sandberg/25 80.00
224 Stan Musial/50 75.00
226 Tony Gwynn/50 50.00
230 Carlos Beltran/50 40.00
231 David Ortiz/50 60.00
232 David Ortiz/50 60.00
234 Carlos Lee/50 20.00
235 Travis Hafner/25 25.00
238 Edgar Martinez/25 40.00
240 Roy Oswalt/25 30.00
242 Carlos Beltran/50 45.00
243 Carlos Beltran/50 45.00
244 Miguel Cabrera/50 40.00
246 Hank Blalock/50 35.00
247 Vernon Wells/50 20.00
248 Adam Dunn/50 35.00
249 Preston Wilson/25 25.00
250 Victor Martinez/25 25.00

Moniker Bronze

NM/M

Quanity produced listed
Silver: .5-1.5X
Production 1-50
No pricing 15 or less.
Platinum: No Pricing
Production One Set
1 Adam Dunn/50 30.00
3 Albert Pujols/25 180.00
5 Alfonso Soriano/100 30.00
6 Andruw Jones/50 30.00
8 Angel Berroa/25 15.00
11 Austin Kearns/50 20.00
18 Brandon Webb/21 15.00
21 Carlos Beltran/50 40.00
23 Chipper Jones/25 65.00
24 Craig Biggio/5 40.00
30 Dontrelle Willis/25 30.00
31 Edgar Renteria/25 25.00
34 Frank Thomas/50 60.00
36 Garret Anderson/50 20.00
37 Gary Sheffield/50 25.00
39 Greg Maddux/25 85.00
40 Hank Blalock/50 35.00
46 Jacque Jones/25 25.00
58 Jeff Bagwell/25 75.00
71 Jorge Posada/25 50.00
76 Juan Gonzalez/25 30.00
79 Kazuhisa Ishii/25 35.00
84 Kerry Wood/25 50.00
88 Lance Berkman/50 30.00
98 Marcus Giles/25 25.00
100 Mark Mulder/100 15.00
101 Mark Prior/50 40.00
102 Mark Teixeira/50 30.00
106 Michael Young/50 15.00
107 Miguel Cabrera/50 40.00
109 Mike Lowell/25 25.00
122 Paul LoDuca/25 25.00
131 Rickie Weeks/25 20.00
137 Roy Oswalt/10 20.00
140 Sammy Sosa/25 85.00
142 Scott Rolen/25 60.00
144 Sean Casey/25 25.00
145 Shannon Stewart/25 20.00
153 Todd Helton/25 40.00
155 Torii Hunter/50 20.00
156 Trot Nixon/25 20.00
158 Vernon Wells/25 25.00
163 Alfonso Soriano/100 30.00
166 Gary Sheffield/10 30.00
167 Greg Maddux/5 80.00
172 Juan Gonzalez/25 40.00
183 Scott Rolen/25 50.00
191 Albert Pujols/5 180.00
193 Chipper Jones/5 65.00
194 Garret Anderson/10 20.00
195 Jeff Bagwell/25 75.00
198 Mark Prior/50 40.00
199 Sammy Sosa/25 80.00
200 Todd Helton/25 40.00
201 Andre Dawson/100 15.00
203 Bob Feller/100 20.00
204 Bob Gibson/100 20.00
205 Bobby Doerr/100 15.00
206 Cal Ripken Jr./25 180.00
207 Dale Murphy/100 25.00
208 Don Mattingly/100 60.00
209 Gary Carter/100 15.00
210 George Brett/25 75.00
212 Lou Brock/100 20.00
214 Mark Grace/100 20.00
215 Maury Wills/100 15.00
216 Mike Schmidt/100 60.00
217 Nolan Ryan/100 120.00
218 Orel Hershiser/25 40.00
219 Paul Molitor/100 25.00
221 Rod Carew/100 25.00
223 Ryne Sandberg/100 50.00
224 Stan Musial/100 60.00
226 Tony Gwynn/100 40.00
230 Carlos Beltran/50 45.00
231 David Ortiz/50 60.00
232 David Ortiz/50 60.00
233 Carlos Zambrano/25 30.00
234 Carlos Lee/25 20.00
238 Edgar Martinez/25 40.00
240 Roy Oswalt/50 20.00
242 Carlos Beltran/50 40.00
243 Carlos Beltran/50 40.00
244 Miguel Cabrera/50 40.00
245 Scott Rolen/25 50.00
246 Hank Blalock/50 35.00
247 Vernon Wells/25 25.00
248 Adam Dunn/50 35.00
250 Victor Martinez/10

Moniker Gold

NM/M

Quanity produced listed
5 Alfonso Soriano/25 40.00
21 Carlos Beltran/25 50.00
100 Mark Mulder/25 25.00
163 Alfonso Soriano/25 40.00
201 Andre Dawson/25 20.00
203 Bob Feller/25 35.00
204 Bob Gibson/25 40.00
205 Bobby Doerr/25 25.00
207 Dale Murphy/25 40.00
208 Don Mattingly/25 90.00
209 Gary Carter/25 25.00
212 Lou Brock/25 30.00
214 Mark Grace/25 30.00
215 Maury Wills/25 25.00
216 Mike Schmidt/25 85.00
217 Nolan Ryan/25 150.00
219 Paul Molitor/25 40.00
221 Rod Carew/25 35.00
223 Ryne Sandberg/25 75.00
224 Stan Musial/25 100.00
226 Tony Gwynn/25 50.00

Moniker Jersey Number

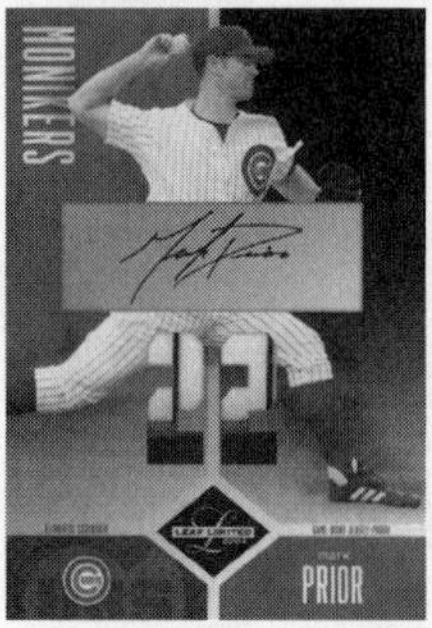

NM/M

Quanity produced listed
Prime: No Pricing
Production One Set
1 Adam Dunn/50 30.00
5 Alfonso Soriano/50 40.00
6 Andruw Jones/25 40.00
8 Angel Berroa Pants/25 15.00
9 Aramis Ramirez/25 25.00
10 Aubrey Huff/25 25.00
11 Austin Kearns/25 25.00
15 Ben Sheets/25 25.00
18 Brandon Webb/25 15.00
20 C.C. Sabathia/25 25.00
21 Carlos Beltran/50 40.00
23 Chipper Jones/25 65.00
24 Craig Biggio/25 40.00
30 Dontrelle Willis/25 30.00
32 Eric Chavez/50 20.00
34 Frank Thomas/25 70.00
35 Fred McGriff/25 40.00
36 Garret Anderson/50 20.00
40 Hank Blalock/50 35.00
46 Jacque Jones/25 25.00
63 Jim Edmonds/25 40.00
66 Jody Gerut/25 15.00
67 Johan Santana/25 40.00
71 Jorge Posada/25 50.00
74 Jose Vidro/25 15.00
84 Kerry Wood/25 50.00
88 Lance Berkman/25 40.00
90 Larry Walker/25 20.00
98 Marcus Giles/25 25.00
99 Mark Buehrle/25 25.00
100 Mark Mulder/75 15.00
101 Mark Prior/50 40.00
102 Mark Teixeira/25 40.00
105 Melvin Mora/25 25.00
107 Miguel Cabrera/50 30.00
109 Mike Lowell/25 25.00
115 Morgan Ensberg/25 15.00
122 Paul LoDuca/25 25.00
124 Preston Wilson/25 25.00
137 Roy Oswalt/25 25.00
140 Sammy Sosa/25 120.00
142 Scott Rolen/25 50.00
143 Sean Burroughs/25 25.00
145 Shannon Stewart/25 25.00
149 Steve Finley/25 25.00
153 Todd Helton/25 40.00
154 Tom Glavine/25 40.00
155 Torii Hunter/25 25.00
156 Trot Nixon/25 25.00
158 Vernon Wells/50 20.00
159 Victor Martinez/50 20.00
163 Alfonso Soriano/50 40.00
166 Gary Sheffield/25 40.00
172 Juan Gonzalez/25 40.00
183 Scott Rolen/50 40.00
185 Tom Glavine/25 40.00
193 Chipper Jones/25 65.00
194 Garret Anderson/50 20.00
199 Sammy Sosa/25 120.00
200 Todd Helton/25 40.00
201 Andre Dawson/50 20.00
204 Bob Gibson/25 40.00
205 Bobby Doerr/50 20.00
207 Dale Murphy/100 25.00
208 Don Mattingly/50 70.00
209 Gary Carter/100 15.00
216 Mike Schmidt/50 75.00
217 Nolan Ryan/100 120.00
218 Orel Hershiser/50 30.00
219 Paul Molitor/50 30.00
221 Rod Carew/50 30.00
223 Ryne Sandberg/25 100.00
224 Stan Musial/25 100.00
226 Tony Gwynn/100 40.00
228 Whitey Ford Pants/25 40.00
229 Yogi Berra/25 75.00
230 Carlos Beltran/50 40.00
231 David Ortiz/50 60.00
232 David Ortiz/50 60.00
234 Carlos Lee/50 20.00
235 Travis Hafner/25 25.00
236 Brad Penny/25 15.00
237 Wade Miller/25 15.00
238 Edgar Martinez/50 40.00
239 Carl Crawford/25 25.00
240 Roy Oswalt/25 25.00
242 Carlos Beltran/50 45.00
243 Carlos Beltran/50 45.00
244 Miguel Cabrera/50 40.00
245 Scott Rolen/50 40.00
246 Hank Blalock/50 35.00
247 Vernon Wells/50 20.00
248 Adam Dunn/50 35.00
249 Preston Wilson/25 25.00
250 Victor Martinez/50 20.00

Moniker Jersey

NM/M

Quanity produced listed
Prime: No Pricing
Production One Set
1 Adam Dunn/50 30.00
5 Alfonso Soriano/50 40.00
6 Andruw Jones/25 40.00
8 Angel Berroa/Pants/25 15.00
9 Aramis Ramirez/25 25.00
10 Aubrey Huff/25 25.00
11 Austin Kearns/25 25.00
15 Ben Sheets/25 25.00
18 Brandon Webb/25 15.00
20 C.C. Sabathia/25 25.00
21 Carlos Beltran/50 40.00
23 Chipper Jones/25 65.00
24 Craig Biggio/25 40.00
30 Dontrelle Willis/25 30.00
32 Eric Chavez/50 20.00
34 Frank Thomas/25 70.00
35 Fred McGriff/25 40.00
36 Garret Anderson/50 20.00
40 Hank Blalock/50 35.00
46 Jacque Jones/25 25.00
63 Jim Edmonds/25 40.00
66 Jody Gerut/25 15.00
67 Johan Santana/25 40.00
71 Jorge Posada/25 50.00
74 Jose Vidro/25 15.00
84 Kerry Wood/25 50.00
88 Lance Berkman/25 40.00
89 Larry Bigbie/25 20.00
98 Marcus Giles/25 25.00
99 Mark Buehrle/25 25.00
100 Mark Mulder/75 15.00
101 Mark Prior/50 40.00
102 Mark Teixeira/25 40.00
105 Melvin Mora/25 25.00
107 Miguel Cabrera/38 40.00
109 Mike Lowell/25 25.00
115 Morgan Ensberg/25 15.00
122 Paul LoDuca/25 25.00
124 Preston Wilson/25 25.00
137 Roy Oswalt/25 25.00
142 Scott Rolen/50 50.00
143 Sean Burroughs/25 25.00
144 Sean Casey/25 25.00
145 Shannon Stewart/25 25.00
149 Steve Finley/25 25.00
153 Todd Helton/25 40.00
154 Tom Glavine/25 40.00
155 Torii Hunter/25 25.00
156 Trot Nixon/25 25.00
158 Vernon Wells/50 20.00
159 Victor Martinez/50 20.00
163 Alfonso Soriano/50 40.00
166 Gary Sheffield/25 40.00
172 Juan Gonzalez/25 40.00
183 Scott Rolen/50 40.00
185 Tom Glavine/25 40.00
193 Chipper Jones/25 65.00
194 Garret Anderson/50 20.00
200 Todd Helton/25 40.00
201 Andre Dawson/50 20.00
204 Bob Gibson/50 30.00
205 Bobby Doerr/50 20.00
207 Dale Murphy/100 25.00
208 Don Mattingly/50 70.00
209 Gary Carter/100 15.00
216 Mike Schmidt/50 75.00
217 Nolan Ryan/100 120.00
218 Orel Hershiser/50 30.00
219 Paul Molitor/50 30.00
221 Rod Carew/50 30.00
223 Ryne Sandberg/25 100.00

224 Stan Musial/25 100.00
226 Tony Gwynn/100 40.00
228 Whitey Ford/Pants/25 40.00
229 Yogi Berra/25 75.00
230 Carlos Beltran/50 40.00
231 David Ortiz/50 60.00
232 David Ortiz/50 60.00
234 Carlos Lee/50 20.00
235 Travis Hafner/25 25.00
236 Brad Penny/25 15.00
237 Wade Miller/25 15.00
238 Edgar Martinez/50 40.00
239 Carl Crawford/25 25.00
240 Roy Oswalt/25 25.00
242 Carlos Beltran/50 45.00
243 Carlos Beltran/50 45.00
244 Miguel Cabrera/50 40.00
245 Scott Rolen/50 40.00
246 Hank Blalock/50 35.00
247 Vernon Wells/50 20.00
248 Adam Dunn/50 35.00
249 Preston Wilson/25 25.00

Player Threads Double

NM/M
Quantity produced listed
1 Mike Piazza/100 15.00
2 Roger Clemens/100 20.00
3 Nolan Ryan/100 30.00
4 Reggie Jackson/100 15.00
5 Wade Boggs/100 10.00
6 Steve Carlton/100 10.00
7 Ivan Rodriguez/100 10.00
8 Pedro Martinez/100 10.00
9 Rickey Henderson/50 25.00
10 Rickey Henderson/100 20.00
11 Randy Johnson/50 20.00
12 Curt Schilling/100 10.00
13 Roger Maris/100 40.00
14 Sammy Sosa/100 15.00
15 Gary Carter/100 8.00
16 Gary Sheffield/50 10.00
17 Eddie Murray/50 20.00
18 Hideo Nomo/50 15.00
19 Rafael Palmeiro/100 10.00
20 Andre Dawson/50 10.00

Player Threads Jersey Number

NM/M
Quantity produced listed
Prime: No Pricing
Production One Set
1 Mike Piazza/100 10.00
3 Nolan Ryan/Jkt/100 20.00
4 Reggie Jackson/100 10.00
5 Wade Boggs/50 10.00
6 Steve Carlton/Pants/100 5.00
7 Ivan Rodriguez/25 15.00
8 Pedro Martinez/50 12.00
10 Rickey Henderson/Pants/100 10.00
11 Randy Johnson/50 10.00
12 Curt Schilling/25 20.00
13 Roger Maris/50 50.00
14 Sammy Sosa/100 10.00
15 Gary Carter/Pants/50 8.00
16 Gary Sheffield/25 10.00
17 Eddie Murray/50 15.00
18 Hideo Nomo/50 10.00
19 Rafael Palmeiro/50 10.00
20 Andre Dawson/50 8.00

Player Threads Triple

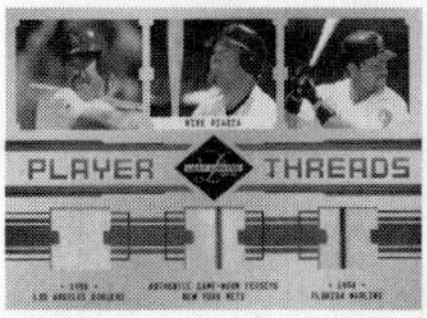

NM/M
Quantity produced listed
1 Mike Piazza/50 30.00
2 Roger Clemens/25 50.00
3 Nolan Ryan/50 70.00
4 Reggie Jackson/25 40.00
5 Wade Boggs/25 30.00
6 Steve Carlton/25 25.00
7 Ivan Rodriguez/25 30.00
8 Pedro Martinez/25 30.00
10 Rickey Henderson/25 50.00
12 Curt Schilling/25 30.00
13 Roger Maris/25 120.00
14 Sammy Sosa/25 40.00
15 Gary Carter/25 20.00
17 Eddie Murray/25 40.00
18 Hideo Nomo/25 30.00
19 Rafael Palmeiro/50 20.00
20 Andre Dawson/25 20.00

Team Threads Jersey Number

NM/M
Common Card: 15.00
Production 100 Sets
Prime: No Pricing
Production One Set
1 Stan Musial, Albert Pujols 40.00
2 Cal Ripken Jr./Jkt, Mike Mussina 40.00
3 Carlton Fisk, Roger Clemens 25.00
4 Dale Murphy, Chipper Jones 15.00
5 Tony Gwynn, Dave Winfield 25.00
6 Don Mattingly, Hideki Matsui 50.00
7 Lou Boudreau, Early Wynn 15.00
8 Ernie Banks, Sammy Sosa 30.00
9 Nolan Ryan/Jkt, Jeff Bagwell 50.00
10 Mike Schmidt, Jim Thome 25.00

Team Trademarks

NM/M
Common Player: 5.00
Production 100 Sets
Gold: No Pricing
Production 10 Sets
1 Bob Gibson 8.00
2 Cal Ripken Jr. 30.00
3 Carl Yastrzemski 10.00
4 Dale Murphy 8.00
5 Gary Carter 5.00
6 George Brett 15.00
7 Tom Seaver 8.00
8 Kerry Wood 8.00
9 Lou Brock 8.00
10 Luis Aparicio 5.00
11 Mike Piazza 10.00
12 Nolan Ryan 15.00
13 Nolan Ryan 15.00
14 Randy Johnson 8.00
15 Reggie Jackson 8.00
16 Ricky Henderson 8.00
17 Robin Yount 10.00
18 Rod Carew 8.00
19 Ryne Sandberg 15.00
20 Steve Carlton 5.00
21 Steve Garvey 5.00
22 Johnny Bench 8.00
23 Tony Gwynn 10.00
24 Whitey Ford 8.00
25 Will Clark 8.00

Team Trademarks Autographs

NM/M
Quantity produced listed
1 Bob Gibson/100 20.00
2 Cal Ripken Jr./25 150.00
3 Carl Yastrzemski/25 60.00
4 Dale Murphy/100 20.00
5 Gary Carter/100 15.00
6 George Brett/25 65.00
7 Tom Seaver/25 50.00
8 Kerry Wood/25 40.00
9 Lou Brock/100 20.00
10 Luis Aparicio/100 15.00
12 Nolan Ryan Astros/25 100.00
13 Nolan Ryan Rgr/25 100.00
15 Reggie Jackson/25 50.00
17 Robin Yount/50 50.00
18 Rod Carew/50 25.00
19 Ryne Sandberg/25 65.00
20 Steve Carlton/100 20.00
21 Steve Garvey/50 15.00
22 Johnny Bench/25 50.00
23 Tony Gwynn/100 30.00
24 Whitey Ford/25 30.00
25 Will Clark/34 50.00

Team Trademarks Autograph Jersey Numbers

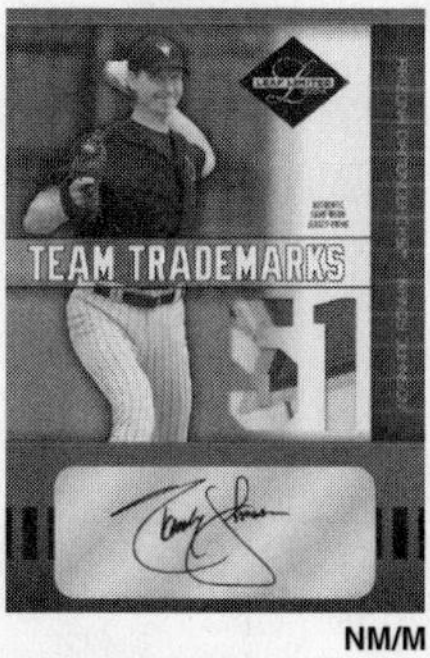

NM/M
Quantity produced listed
Prime: No Pricing
Production One Set
1 Bob Gibson/100 25.00
2 Cal Ripken Jr./Pants/25 200.00
3 Carl Yastrzemski/25 75.00
4 Dale Murphy/100 25.00
5 Gary Carter/100 15.00
6 George Brett/25 80.00
7 Tom Seaver/25 65.00
8 Kerry Wood/Pants/25 50.00
9 Lou Brock/100 25.00
10 Luis Aparicio/Pants/100 15.00
12 Nolan Ryan/Astros/25 120.00
13 Nolan Ryan/Rgr/25 120.00
15 Reggie Jackson/Pants/25 60.00
17 Robin Yount/50 75.00
18 Rod Carew/Jkt/50 30.00
19 Ryne Sandberg/50 65.00
20 Steve Carlton/25 40.00
22 Johnny Bench/50 50.00
23 Tony Gwynn/50 50.00
24 Whitey Ford/50 30.00
25 Will Clark/84 40.00

Team Trademarks Jersey Number

NM/M
Quantity produced listed
Prime: No Pricing
Production One Set
1 Bob Gibson/100 10.00
2 Cal Ripken Jr./Pants/100 40.00
3 Carl Yastrzemski/100 15.00
4 Dale Murphy/100 10.00
5 Gary Carter/100 5.00
6 George Brett/100 15.00
7 Tom Seaver/100 10.00
8 Kerry Wood/Pants/50 10.00
9 Lou Brock/100 10.00
10 Luis Aparicio/Pants/100 5.00
11 Mike Piazza/50 15.00
12 Nolan Ryan/Astros/100 20.00
13 Nolan Ryan/Rgr/100 20.00
14 Randy Johnson/50 10.00
15 Reggie Jackson/Pants/100 8.00
16 Ricky Henderson/100 10.00
17 Robin Yount/100 10.00
18 Rod Carew/Jkt/100 8.00
19 Ryne Sandberg/100 15.00
20 Steve Carlton/50 5.00
22 Johnny Bench/100 10.00
23 Tony Gwynn/100 10.00
24 Whitey Ford/100 10.00
25 Will Clark/50 15.00

Threads Jersey

NM/M
Quanity produced listed
Prime: No Pricing
Production One Set
Button: No Pricing
Production 1-6
1 Adam Dunn/25 15.00
2 Adrian Beltre/5
3 Albert Pujols/50 20.00
5 Alfonso Soriano/25 15.00
6 Andruw Jones/25 10.00
11 Austin Kearns/25 10.00
12 Barry Larkin/25 15.00
13 Barry Zito/25 8.00
16 Bernie Williams/50 8.00
21 Carlos Beltran/25 15.00
22 Carlos Delgado/25 8.00
23 Chipper Jones/50 10.00
24 Craig Biggio/25 15.00
25 Curt Schilling/25 20.00
30 Dontrelle Willis/25 8.00
31 Edgar Renteria/25 10.00
32 Eric Chavez/25 8.00
34 Frank Thomas/25 20.00
36 Garret Anderson/25 10.00
39 Greg Maddux/50 15.00
40 Hank Blalock/25 10.00
41 Hideki Matsui/50 40.00
42 Hideo Nomo/50 10.00
44 Ivan Rodriguez/25 15.00
50 Jason Giambi/50 5.00
55 Javy Lopez/25 10.00
58 Jeff Bagwell/50 10.00
59 Jeff Kent/50 5.00
63 Jim Edmonds/25 10.00
64 Jim Thome/50 10.00
69 John Smoltz/25 15.00
71 Jorge Posada/25 15.00
75 Josh Beckett/25 10.00
76 Juan Gonzalez/25 15.00
84 Kerry Wood/50 12.00
88 Lance Berkman/50 5.00
90 Larry Walker/25 15.00
93 Luis Gonzalez/25 8.00
96 Magglio Ordonez/25 8.00
97 Manny Ramirez/50 10.00
100 Mark Mulder/25 10.00
101 Mark Prior/50 8.00
107 Miguel Cabrera/25 15.00
108 Miguel Tejada/25 10.00
110 Mike Mussina/50 10.00
111 Mike Piazza/50 15.00
112 Mike Sweeney/25 10.00
123 Pedro J. Martinez/50 12.00
126 Rafael Palmeiro/25 15.00
127 Randy Johnson/25 20.00
137 Roy Oswalt/25 10.00
140 Sammy Sosa/50 15.00
142 Scott Rolen/25 20.00
146 Shawn Green/25 8.00
150 Tim Hudson/25 10.00
153 Todd Helton/50 10.00
154 Tom Glavine/25 15.00
155 Torii Hunter/25 10.00
157 Troy Glaus/25 10.00
158 Vernon Wells/25 8.00
161 Vladimir Guerrero/25 20.00
162 Alex Rodriguez/100 10.00
163 Alfonso Soriano/25 10.00
164 Andy Pettitte/25 15.00
165 Curt Schilling/25 10.00
166 Gary Sheffield/25 10.00
167 Greg Maddux/50 15.00
168 Hideo Nomo/25 20.00
169 Ivan Rodriguez/50 12.00
170 Jason Giambi/25 8.00
172 Juan Gonzalez/25 15.00
174 Kevin Brown/25 8.00
176 Miguel Tejada/25 10.00
177 Mike Mussina/50 10.00
178 Mike Piazza/25 25.00
179 Pedro Martinez/25 20.00
180 Rafael Palmeiro/25 15.00
181 Randy Johnson/50 10.00
182 Roger Clemens/100 10.00
183 Scott Rolen/25 20.00
184 Shawn Green/25 8.00
185 Tom Glavine/25 15.00
186 Vladimir Guerrero/25 20.00
187 Alex Rodriguez/100 10.00
189 Randy Johnson/50 10.00
190 Roger Clemens/100 10.00
191 Albert Pujols/50 20.00
192 Barry Zito/25 10.00
193 Chipper Jones/50 10.00
194 Garret Anderson/25 10.00
195 Jeff Bagwell/50 10.00
196 Josh Beckett/25 10.00
197 Magglio Ordonez/25 10.00
198 Mark Prior/50 8.00
199 Sammy Sosa/50 15.00
200 Todd Helton/50 10.00
201 Andre Dawson/50 5.00
202 Babe Ruth/25 350.00
203 Bob Feller/25 20.00
205 Bobby Doerr/50 8.00
206 Cal Ripken Jr./100 40.00
207 Dale Murphy/100 10.00
208 Don Mattingly/50 25.00
209 Gary Carter/50 8.00
210 George Brett/100 15.00
211 Jackie Robinson/50 40.00
212 Lou Brock/25 20.00
213 Lou Gehrig/25 140.00
214 Mark Grace/25 15.00
215 Maury Wills/50 5.00
216 Mike Schmidt/100 15.00
217 Nolan Ryan/100 20.00
218 Orel Hershiser/25 15.00
219 Paul Molitor/50 10.00
220 Roberto Clemente/25 80.00
221 Rod Carew/100 10.00
222 Roy Campanella/Pants/50 15.00
223 Ryne Sandberg/50 25.00
224 Stan Musial/25 40.00
225 Ted Williams/50 75.00
226 Tony Gwynn/100 10.00
227 Ty Cobb Pants/100 75.00
228 Whitey Ford Pants/25 20.00
229 Yogi Berra/25 25.00
230 Carlos Beltran/25 15.00
231 David Ortiz/25 20.00
232 David Ortiz/25 20.00
238 Edgar Martinez/25 10.00
240 Roy Oswalt/25 8.00
242 Carlos Beltran/25 15.00
243 Carlos Beltran/25 15.00
244 Miguel Cabrera/25 15.00
245 Scott Rolen/25 20.00
246 Hank Blalock/25 12.00
247 Vernon Wells/25 8.00
248 Adam Dunn/25 15.00
249 Preston Wilson/5

Threads Jersey Number

NM/M
Quanity produced listed
Prime: No Pricing
Production One Set
MLB Logo: No Pricing
Production One Set
1 Adam Dunn/25 15.00
3 Albert Pujols/50 20.00
5 Alfonso Soriano/25 15.00
6 Andruw Jones/25 10.00
11 Austin Kearns/25 8.00
12 Barry Larkin/25 15.00
13 Barry Zito/25 8.00
16 Bernie Williams/50 10.00
21 Carlos Beltran/25 15.00
22 Carlos Delgado/25 8.00
23 Chipper Jones/50 10.00
24 Craig Biggio/25 10.00
25 Curt Schilling/25 20.00
30 Dontrelle Willis/25 8.00
31 Edgar Renteria/25 10.00
32 Eric Chavez/25 8.00
34 Frank Thomas/25 15.00
36 Garret Anderson/25 10.00
39 Greg Maddux/50 15.00
40 Hank Blalock/25 12.00
41 Hideki Matsui/50 40.00
42 Hideo Nomo/50 10.00
44 Ivan Rodriguez/25 20.00
50 Jason Giambi/50 5.00
55 Javy Lopez/25 8.00
58 Jeff Bagwell/50 10.00
59 Jeff Kent/25 10.00
63 Jim Edmonds/25 10.00
64 Jim Thome/50 15.00
69 John Smoltz/25 15.00
71 Jorge Posada/25 15.00
75 Josh Beckett/25 10.00
76 Juan Gonzalez/25 15.00
84 Kerry Wood/50 12.00
88 Lance Berkman/50 5.00

90 Larry Walker/25 10.00
93 Luis Gonzalez/25 8.00
96 Magglio Ordonez/25 8.00
97 Manny Ramirez/50 12.00
100 Mark Mulder/25 10.00
101 Mark Prior/50 8.00
107 Miguel Cabrera/25 15.00
108 Miguel Tejada/25 10.00
110 Mike Mussina/50 10.00
111 Mike Piazza/50 15.00
112 Mike Sweeney/25 10.00
123 Pedro J. Martinez/50 12.00
126 Rafael Palmeiro/25 15.00
127 Randy Johnson/25 20.00
137 Roy Oswalt/25 10.00
140 Sammy Sosa/50 15.00
142 Scott Rolen/25 20.00
146 Shawn Green/25 8.00
150 Tim Hudson/25 10.00
153 Todd Helton/50 10.00
154 Tom Glavine/25 15.00
155 Torii Hunter/25 10.00
157 Troy Glaus/25 8.00
158 Vernon Wells/25 8.00
161 Vladimir Guerrero/25 20.00
162 Alex Rodriguez/100 10.00
163 Alfonso Soriano/50 10.00
164 Andy Pettitte/25 15.00
165 Curt Schilling/25 10.00
166 Gary Sheffield/25 10.00
167 Greg Maddux/50 15.00
168 Hideo Nomo/25 20.00
169 Ivan Rodriguez/50 12.00
170 Jason Giambi/25 8.00
172 Juan Gonzalez/25 12.00
174 Kevin Brown/25 8.00
176 Miguel Tejada/25 10.00
177 Mike Mussina/50 10.00
178 Mike Piazza/25 25.00
179 Pedro Martinez/25 20.00
180 Rafael Palmeiro/25 15.00
181 Randy Johnson/50 10.00
182 Roger Clemens/100 10.00
183 Scott Rolen/25 20.00
184 Shawn Green/25 8.00
185 Tom Glavine/25 15.00
186 Vladimir Guerrero/25 20.00
187 Alex Rodriguez/100 10.00
189 Randy Johnson/50 10.00
190 Roger Clemens/100 10.00
191 Albert Pujols/50 20.00
192 Barry Zito/25 8.00
193 Chipper Jones/50 10.00
194 Garret Anderson/25 10.00
195 Jeff Bagwell/50 10.00
196 Josh Beckett/25 10.00
197 Magglio Ordonez/25 8.00
198 Mark Prior/50 8.00
199 Sammy Sosa/50 15.00
200 Todd Helton/50 10.00
201 Andre Dawson/50 8.00
202 Babe Ruth/25 300.00
203 Bob Feller/25 20.00
205 Bobby Doerr/50 8.00
206 Cal Ripken Jr./100 40.00
207 Dale Murphy/100 10.00
208 Don Mattingly/50 25.00
209 Gary Carter/50 8.00
210 George Brett/100 15.00
211 Jackie Robinson/100 40.00
212 Lou Brock/25 20.00
213 Lou Gehrig/25 150.00
214 Mark Grace/25 15.00
215 Maury Wills/50 8.00
216 Mike Schmidt/100 15.00
217 Nolan Ryan/100 20.00
218 Orel Hershiser/25 15.00
219 Paul Molitor/50 10.00
220 Roberto Clemente/25 80.00
221 Rod Carew/100 10.00
222 Roy Campanella/Pants/50 15.00
223 Ryne Sandberg/50 25.00
224 Stan Musial/25 40.00
225 Ted Williams/50 75.00
226 Tony Gwynn/100 10.00
227 Ty Cobb/Pants/100 60.00
228 Whitey Ford/Pants/25 20.00
229 Yogi Berra/25 25.00
230 Carlos Beltran/25 15.00
231 David Ortiz/25 20.00
232 David Ortiz/25 20.00
238 Edgar Martinez/25 10.00
240 Roy Oswalt H/25 10.00
242 Carlos Beltran/25 15.00
243 Carlos Beltran/25 15.00
244 Miguel Cabrera/25 15.00
245 Scott Rolen/25 20.00
246 Hank Blalock/25 10.00
247 Vernon Wells/25 10.00
248 Adam Dunn/25 15.00

Timber

NM/M

Quanity produced listed
1 Adam Dunn/25 15.00
4 Alex Rodriguez/100 10.00
5 Alfonso Soriano/25 15.00
6 Andruw Jones/25 10.00
7 Andy Pettitte/25 15.00
11 Austin Kearns/25 8.00
12 Barry Larkin/25 15.00
13 Barry Zito/25 8.00
16 Bernie Williams/25 12.00
21 Carlos Beltran/25 15.00
22 Carlos Delgado/25 10.00
23 Chipper Jones/25 20.00
24 Craig Biggio/25 12.00
25 Curt Schilling/25 20.00
30 Dontrelle Willis/25 8.00
32 Eric Chavez/25 8.00
34 Frank Thomas/25 20.00
35 Fred McGriff/25 12.00
36 Garret Anderson/25 8.00
37 Gary Sheffield/25 10.00
39 Greg Maddux/25 25.00
40 Hank Blalock/25 10.00
41 Hideki Matsui/25 60.00
42 Hideo Nomo/25 20.00
44 Ivan Rodriguez/25 20.00
50 Jason Giambi/25 8.00
55 Javy Lopez/25 8.00
58 Jeff Bagwell/25 15.00
59 Jeff Kent/25 8.00
63 Jim Edmonds/25 10.00
64 Jim Thome/25 20.00
71 Jorge Posada/25 15.00
75 Josh Beckett/25 10.00
76 Juan Gonzalez/25 15.00
84 Kerry Wood/25 20.00
85 Kevin Brown/25 8.00
88 Lance Berkman/25 8.00
90 Larry Walker/25 10.00
93 Luis Gonzalez/25 8.00
96 Magglio Ordonez/25 8.00
97 Manny Ramirez/25 15.00
100 Mark Mulder/25 8.00
101 Mark Prior/25 15.00
102 Mark Teixeira/25 10.00
106 Michael Young/25 8.00
107 Miguel Cabrera/25 15.00
108 Miguel Tejada/25 10.00
109 Mike Lowell/25 8.00
110 Mike Mussina/25 15.00
111 Mike Piazza/25 25.00
112 Mike Sweeney/25 8.00
116 Nick Johnson/25 8.00
117 Nomar Garciaparra/25 20.00
122 Paul LoDuca/25 8.00
123 Pedro J. Martinez/25 20.00
126 Rafael Palmeiro/25 15.00
127 Randy Johnson/25 20.00
130 Richie Sexson/25 10.00
134 Rocco Baldelli/25 8.00
135 Roger Clemens/25 25.00
137 Roy Oswalt/25 8.00
140 Sammy Sosa/50 15.00
142 Scott Rolen/25 20.00
146 Shawn Green/25 8.00
150 Tim Hudson/25 8.00
153 Todd Helton/25 15.00
154 Tom Glavine/25 15.00
155 Torii Hunter/25 8.00
156 Trot Nixon/25 10.00
157 Troy Glaus/25 8.00
158 Vernon Wells/25 8.00
161 Vladimir Guerrero/25 20.00
162 Alex Rodriguez/100 10.00
163 Alfonso Soriano/25 15.00
164 Andy Pettitte/25 15.00
165 Curt Schilling/25 10.00
166 Gary Sheffield/25 10.00
167 Greg Maddux/25 25.00
168 Hideo Nomo/25 15.00
169 Ivan Rodriguez/25 15.00
170 Jason Giambi/25 8.00
171 Jim Thome/25 15.00
172 Juan Gonzalez/25 10.00
174 Kevin Brown/25 8.00
175 Manny Ramirez/25 15.00
176 Miguel Tejada/25 10.00
177 Mike Mussina/25 15.00
178 Mike Piazza/25 25.00
179 Pedro Martinez/25 20.00
180 Rafael Palmeiro/25 15.00
181 Randy Johnson/25 20.00
182 Roger Clemens/25 25.00
183 Scott Rolen/25 20.00
184 Shawn Green/25 8.00
185 Tom Glavine/25 15.00
186 Vladimir Guerrero/25 20.00
187 Alex Rodriguez/100 10.00
188 Mike Piazza/25 25.00
189 Randy Johnson/25 20.00
190 Roger Clemens/25 25.00
191 Albert Pujols/50 20.00
192 Barry Zito/25 8.00
193 Chipper Jones/25 20.00
194 Garret Anderson/25 8.00
195 Jeff Bagwell/25 15.00
196 Josh Beckett/25 8.00
197 Magglio Ordonez/25 8.00
198 Mark Prior/25 15.00
199 Sammy Sosa/50 15.00
200 Todd Helton/25 15.00
201 Andre Dawson/50 8.00
202 Babe Ruth/100 120.00
206 Cal Ripken Jr./100 40.00
207 Dale Murphy/50 15.00
208 Don Mattingly/50 25.00
209 Gary Carter/50 10.00
210 George Brett/50 25.00
212 Lou Brock/25 15.00
213 Lou Gehrig/100 100.00
214 Mark Grace/25 15.00
216 Mike Schmidt/50 25.00
217 Nolan Ryan/50 30.00
219 Paul Molitor/50 10.00
220 Roberto Clemente/100 75.00
221 Rod Carew/25 25.00
222 Roy Campanella/100 10.00
223 Ryne Sandberg/50 25.00
224 Stan Musial/100 20.00
225 Ted Williams/100 50.00
226 Tony Gwynn/50 20.00
227 Ty Cobb/100 75.00
229 Yogi Berra/100 10.00
230 Carlos Beltran/25 15.00
231 David Ortiz/25 20.00
232 David Ortiz/25 20.00
238 Edgar Martinez/25 15.00
240 Roy Oswalt/25 10.00
242 Carlos Beltran/25 15.00
243 Carlos Beltran/25 15.00
244 Miguel Cabrera/25 15.00
245 Scott Rolen/25 20.00
246 Hank Blalock/25 10.00
248 Adam Dunn/25 15.00

TNT

NM/M

Quanity produced listed
Prime: No Pricing
Production One Set
1 Adam Dunn/Bat-Jsy/50 10.00
3 Albert Pujols/Bat-Jsy/100 15.00
5 Alfonso Soriano/Bat-Jsy/50 10.00
6 Andruw Jones/Bat-Jsy/50 8.00
11 Austin Kearns/Bat-Jsy/50 5.00
12 Barry Larkin/Bat-Jsy/25 20.00
13 Barry Zito/Bat-Jsy/50 5.00
16 Bernie Williams/Bat-Jsy/50 10.00
21 Carlos Beltran/Bat-Jsy/50 10.00
22 Carlos Delgado/Bat-Jsy/50 5.00
23 Chipper Jones/Bat-Jsy/50 15.00
24 Craig Biggio/Bat-Jsy/50 8.00
25 Curt Schilling/Bat-Jsy/25 25.00
32 Eric Chavez/Bat-Jsy/25 10.00
34 Frank Thomas/Bat-Jsy/25 20.00
36 Garret Anderson/Bat-Jsy/25 10.00
39 Greg Maddux/Bat-Jsy/50 20.00
40 Hank Blalock/Bat-Jsy/50 8.00
41 Hideki Matsui/Bat-Jsy/50 50.00
42 Hideo Nomo/Bat-Jsy/25 20.00
44 Ivan Rodriguez/Bat-Jsy/25 20.00
50 Jason Giambi/Bat-Jsy/50 8.00
55 Javy Lopez/Bat-Jsy/25 10.00
58 Jeff Bagwell/Bat-Jsy/50 10.00
59 Jeff Kent/Bat-Jsy/25 10.00
63 Jim Edmonds/Bat-Jsy/25 10.00
64 Jim Thome/Bat-Jsy/50 15.00
71 Jorge Posada/Bat-Jsy/25 20.00
75 Josh Beckett/Bat-Jsy/25 10.00
76 Juan Gonzalez/Bat-Jsy/25 20.00
84 Kerry Wood/Bat-Jsy/50 15.00
88 Lance Berkman/Bat-Jsy/50 5.00
90 Larry Walker/Bat-Jsy/25 20.00
93 Luis Gonzalez/Bat-Jsy/25 10.00
96 Magglio Ordonez/
Bat-Jsy/25 10.00
97 Manny Ramirez/Bat-Jsy/50 15.00
100 Mark Mulder/Bat-Jsy/25 10.00
101 Mark Prior/Bat-Jsy/50 10.00
102 Mark Teixeira/Bat-Jsy/25 10.00
107 Miguel Cabrera/Bat-Jsy/25 20.00
108 Miguel Tejada/Bat-Jsy/25 10.00
109 Mike Lowell/Bat-Jsy/25 10.00
110 Mike Mussina/Bat-Jsy/50 10.00
111 Mike Piazza/Bat-Jsy/50 20.00
112 Mike Sweeney/Bat-Jsy/25 10.00
123 Pedro J. Martinez/
Bat-Jsy/50 15.00
126 Rafael Palmeiro/Bat-Jsy/25 20.00
127 Randy Johnson/Bat-Jsy/50 15.00
137 Roy Oswalt/Bat-Jsy/25 10.00
140 Sammy Sosa/Bat-Jsy/50 20.00
142 Scott Rolen/Bat-Jsy/25 25.00
146 Shawn Green/Bat-Jsy/25 10.00
150 Tim Hudson/Bat-Jsy/25 10.00
153 Todd Helton/Bat-Jsy/50 10.00
154 Tom Glavine/Bat-Jsy/25 20.00
155 Torii Hunter/Bat-Jsy/25 10.00
157 Troy Glaus/Bat-Jsy/25 10.00
158 Vernon Wells/Bat-Jsy/25 10.00
161 Vladimir Guerrero/
Bat-Jsy/25 25.00
162 Alex Rodriguez/Bat-Jsy/100 10.00
163 Alfonso Soriano/Bat-Jsy/50 10.00
164 Andy Pettitte/Bat-Jsy/25 20.00
165 Curt Schilling/Bat-Jsy/25 10.00
166 Gary Sheffield/Bat-Jsy/25 10.00
167 Greg Maddux/Bat-Jsy/50 20.00
168 Hideo Nomo/Bat-Jsy/25 20.00
169 Ivan Rodriguez/Bat-Jsy/50 15.00
170 Jason Giambi/Bat-Jsy/25 10.00
172 Juan Gonzalez/Bat-Jsy/25 15.00
174 Kevin Brown/Bat-Jsy/25 10.00
176 Miguel Tejada/Bat-Jsy/25 10.00
177 Mike Mussina/Bat-Jsy/50 10.00
178 Mike Piazza/Bat-Jsy/50 20.00
179 Pedro Martinez/Bat-Jsy/50 15.00
180 Rafael Palmeiro/Bat-Jsy/50 10.00
181 Randy Johnson/Bat-Jsy/50 15.00
182 Roger Clemens/Bat-Jsy/100 10.00
183 Scott Rolen/Bat-Jsy/25 25.00
184 Shawn Green/Bat-Jsy/25 10.00
185 Tom Glavine/Bat-Jsy/25 20.00
186 Vladimir Guerrero/
Bat-Jsy/25 25.00
187 Alex Rodriguez/Bat-Jsy/100 10.00
189 Randy Johnson/Bat-Jsy/50 15.00
190 Roger Clemens/
Bat-Jsy/100 10.00
191 Albert Pujols/Bat-Jsy/50 25.00
192 Barry Zito/Bat-Jsy/25 10.00
193 Chipper Jones/Bat-Jsy/50 15.00
194 Garret Anderson/
Bat-Jsy/25 10.00
195 Jeff Bagwell/Bat-Jsy/50 10.00
196 Josh Beckett/Bat-Jsy/25 10.00
197 Magglio Ordonez/
Bat-Jsy/25 10.00
198 Mark Prior/Bat-Jsy/50 10.00
199 Sammy Sosa/Bat-Jsy/50 20.00
200 Todd Helton/Bat-Jsy/50 10.00
201 Andre Dawson/Bat-Jsy/50 8.00
202 Babe Ruth/Bat-Jsy/25 425.00
206 Cal Ripken Jr./Bat-Jsy/100 60.00
207 Dale Murphy/Bat-Jsy/100 10.00
208 Don Mattingly/Bat-Jsy/100 20.00
209 Gary Carter/Bat-Jsy/50 10.00
210 George Brett/Bat-Jsy/100 20.00
212 Lou Brock/Bat-Jsy/25 25.00
213 Lou Gehrig/Bat-Jsy/25 250.00
214 Mark Grace/Bat-Jsy/25 20.00
216 Mike Schmidt/Bat-Jsy/50 30.00
217 Nolan Ryan/Bat-Jsy/100 25.00
219 Paul Molitor/Bat-Jsy/25 20.00
221 Rod Carew/Bat-Jsy/50 15.00
222 Roy Campanella/
Bat-Pants/50 20.00
223 Ryne Sandberg/Bat-Jsy/50 30.00
224 Stan Musial/Bat-Jsy/25 50.00
225 Ted Williams/Bat-Jsy/50 100.00
226 Tony Gwynn/Bat-Jsy/100 15.00
227 Ty Cobb/Bat-Pants/50 120.00
230 Carlos Beltran/Bat-Jsy/25 20.00
231 David Ortiz/Bat-Jsy/25 25.00
232 David Ortiz/Bat-Jsy/25 25.00
238 Edgar Martinez/Bat-Jsy/25 15.00
240 Roy Oswalt/Bat-Jsy/25 10.00
242 Carlos Beltran/Bat-Jsy/25 20.00
243 Carlos Beltran/Bat-Jsy/25 20.00
244 Miguel Cabrera/Bat-Jsy/25 20.00
245 Scott Rolen/Bat-Jsy/25 20.00
246 Hank Blalock/Bat-Jsy/25 10.00
247 Vernon Wells/Bat-Jsy/25 10.00
248 Adam Dunn/Bat-Jsy/25 20.00

2005 Leaf

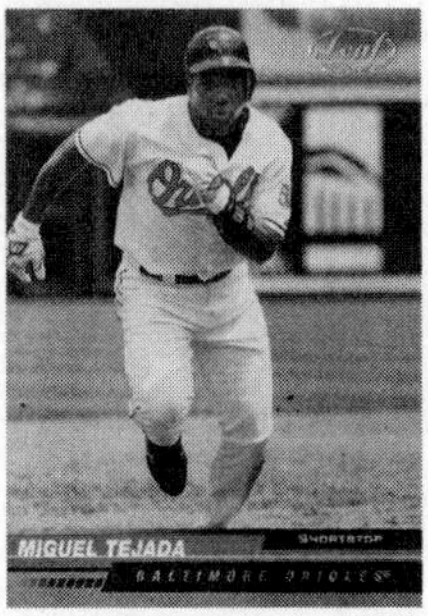
MIGUEL TEJADA
SHORTSTOP
BALTIMORE ORIOLES

NM/M

Complete Set (300):
Common Player (1-200): .15
Common SP (201-250): 1.00
Inserted 1:3
Common SP (251-300): 1.00
#251-270 Inserted 1:6
271-300 Inserted 1:4
Hobby Pack (8): 4.00
Hobby Box (24): 80.00
1 Bartolo Colon .25
2 Casey Kotchman .15
3 Chone Figgins .15
4 Darin Erstad .25
5 Francisco Rodriguez .25
6 Garret Anderson .25
7 Jarrod Washburn .15
8 Troy Glaus .25
9 Vladimir Guerrero .50
10 Brandon Webb .15
11 Casey Fossum .15
12 Luis Gonzalez .25
13 Randy Johnson .50
14 Richie Sexson .25
15 Andruw Jones .25
16 Chipper Jones .50
17 J.D. Drew .25
18 John Smoltz .25
19 Johnny Estrada .15
20 Marcus Giles .15
21 Rafael Furcal .25
22 Russ Ortiz .15
23 Javy Lopez .25
24 Jay Gibbons .15
25 Melvin Mora .15
26 Miguel Tejada .40
27 Rafael Palmeiro .40
28 Sidney Ponson .15
29 Bill Mueller .15
30 Curt Schilling .40
31 David Ortiz .50
32 Doug Mientkiewicz .15
33 Jason Varitek .25
34 Johnny Damon .40
35 Manny Ramirez .50
36 Pedro J. Martinez .50
37 Trot Nixon .15

#	Player	Price
38	Aramis Ramirez	.25
39	Corey Patterson	.25
40	Derrek Lee	.25
41	Greg Maddux	.75
42	Kerry Wood	.50
43	Mark Prior	.50
44	Moises Alou	.25
45	Nomar Garciaparra	1.00
46	Sammy Sosa	1.00
47	Carlos Lee	.15
48	Kip Wells	.15
49	Magglio Ordonez	.25
50	Mark Buehrle	.15
51	Paul Konerko	.25
52	Roberto Alomar	.25
53	Adam Dunn	.40
54	Austin Kearns	.15
55	Barry Larkin	.25
56	Danny Graves	.15
57	Ken Griffey Jr.	1.00
58	Sean Casey	.15
59	C.C. Sabathia	.15
60	Cliff Lee	.15
61	Jody Gerut	.15
62	Omar Vizquel	.25
63	Travis Hafner	.15
64	Victor Martinez	.15
65	Charles Johnson	.15
66	Jason Jennings	.15
67	Jeromy Burnitz	.15
68	Preston Wilson	.15
69	Todd Helton	.40
70	Bobby Higginson	.15
71	Dmitri Young	.15
72	Eric Munson	.15
73	Ivan Rodriguez	.40
74	Jeremy Bonderman	.25
75	Rondell White	.15
76	A.J. Burnett	.15
77	Carl Pavano	.25
78	Dontrelle Willis	.25
79	Hee Seop Choi	.15
80	Josh Beckett	.25
81	Juan Pierre	.15
82	Miguel Cabrera	.50
83	Mike Lowell	.15
84	Paul LoDuca	.15
85	Andy Pettitte	.25
86	Carlos Beltran	.40
87	Craig Biggio	.25
88	Jeff Bagwell	.40
89	Jeff Kent	.25
90	Lance Berkman	.25
91	Roger Clemens	1.50
92	Roy Oswalt	.25
93	Andres Blanco	.15
94	Jeremy Affeldt	.15
95	Juan Gonzalez	.25
96	Ken Harvey	.15
97	Mike Sweeney	.15
98	Zack Greinke	.15
99	Adrian Beltre	.15
100	Brad Penny	.15
101	Eric Gagne	.25
102	Kazuhisa Ishii	.15
103	Milton Bradley	.15
104	Shawn Green	.25
105	Steve Finley	.15
106	Ben Sheets	.15
107	Bill Hall	.15
108	Danny Kolb	.15
109	Geoff Jenkins	.15
110	Junior Spivey	.15
111	Lyle Overbay	.15
112	Scott Podsednik	.15
113	A.J. Pierzynski	.15
114	Brad Radke	.15
115	Corey Koskie	.15
116	Jacque Jones	.15
117	Joe Mauer	.50
118	Joe Nathan	.15
119	Shannon Stewart	.15
120	Torii Hunter	.25
121	Brad Wilkerson	.15
122	Jeff Fassero	.15
123	Jose Vidro	.15
124	Livan Hernandez	.15
125	Nick Johnson	.15
126	Al Leiter	.25
127	Jose Reyes	.25
128	Kazuo Matsui	.25
129	Mike Cameron	.15
130	Mike Piazza	1.00
131	Richard Hidalgo	.15
132	Tom Glavine	.25
133	Alex Rodriguez	1.50
134	Bernie Williams	.25
135	Derek Jeter	1.50
136	Gary Sheffield	.40
137	Jason Giambi	.25
138	Javier Vazquez	.25
139	Jorge Posada	.25
140	Kevin Brown	.15
141	Mariano Rivera	.25
142	Mike Mussina	.25
143	Barry Zito	.25
144	Bobby Crosby	.25
145	Eric Chavez	.25
146	Erubiel Durazo	.15
147	Jermaine Dye	.15
148	Mark Mulder	.25
149	Tim Hudson	.25
150	Bobby Abreu	.25
151	Eric Milton	.15
152	Jim Thome	.50
153	Kevin Millwood	.15
154	Mike Lieberthal	.15
155	Pat Burrell	.25
156	Randy Wolf	.15
157	Craig Wilson	.15
158	Jack Wilson	.15
159	Jason Bay	.25
160	Jason Kendall	.15
161	Kris Benson	.15
162	Brian Giles	.15
163	Jake Peavy	.25
164	Jay Payton	.15
165	Khalil Greene	.25
166	Mark Loretta	.15
167	Ryan Klesko	.15
168	Sean Burroughs	.15
169	David Aardsma	.15
170	Edgardo Alfonzo	.15
171	Jason Schmidt	.25
172	Merkin Valdez	.15
173	Ray Durham	.15
174	Bret Boone	.15
175	Dan Wilson	.15
176	Ichiro Suzuki	1.25
177	Jamie Moyer	.15
178	Rich Aurilia	.15
179	Albert Pujols	1.50
180	Edgar Renteria	.25
181	Jason Isringhausen	.15
182	Jeff Suppan	.15
183	Jim Edmonds	.25
184	Scott Rolen	.50
185	Woody Williams	.15
186	Aubrey Huff	.15
187	Carl Crawford	.15
188	Dewon Brazelton	.15
189	Jose Cruz Jr.	.15
190	Rocco Baldelli	.25
191	Alfonso Soriano	.40
192	Hank Blalock	.25
193	Kenny Rogers	.15
194	Laynce Nix	.15
195	Mark Teixeira	.25
196	Michael Young	.15
197	Alexis Rios	.15
198	Carlos Delgado	.25
199	Roy Halladay	.15
200	Vernon Wells	.15
201	Josh Kroeger	1.00
202	Angel Guzman	1.00
203	Brad Halsey	1.00
204	Bucky Jacobsen	1.00
205	Carlos Hines	1.00
206	Carlos Vasquez	1.00
207	Billy Traber	1.00
208	Bubba Crosby	1.00
209	Chris Oxspring	1.00
210	Chris Shelton	1.00
211	Colby Miller	1.00
212	David Crouthers	1.00
213	Dennis Sarfate	1.00
214	Donald Kelly	1.00
215	Edwardo Sierra	1.00
216	Edwin Moreno	1.00
217	Fernando Nieve	1.00
218	Freddy Guzman	1.00
219	Greg Dobbs	1.00
220	Hector Gimenez	1.00
221	Andy Green	1.00
222	Jason Bartlett	1.00
223	Jerry Gil	1.00
224	Jesse Crain	2.00
225	Joey Gathright	1.00
226	John Gall	1.00
227	Jorge Sequea	1.00
228	Jorge Vasquez	1.00
229	Josh Labandeira	1.00
230	Justin Leone	1.00
231	Lance Cormier	1.00
232	Lincoln Holdzkom	1.00
233	Miguel Olivo	1.00
234	Mike Rouse	1.00
235	Onil Joseph	1.00
236	Phil Stockman	1.00
237	Ramon Ramirez	1.00
238	Robb Quinlan	1.00
239	Roberto Novoa	1.00
240	Ronald Belisario	1.00
241	Ronny Cedeno	1.00
242	Ruddy Yan	1.00
243	Ryan Meaux	1.00
244	Ryan Wing	1.00
245	Scott Proctor	1.00
246	Sean Henn	1.00
247	Tim Bausher	1.00
248	Tim Bittner	1.00
249	William Bergolla	1.00
250	Yadier Molina	1.00
251	Bernie Williams	1.00
252	Craig Biggio	1.00
253	Chipper Jones	2.00
254	Greg Maddux	3.00
255	Sammy Sosa	3.00
256	Mike Mussina	1.50
257	Tim Salmon	1.00
258	Barry Larkin	1.00
259	Randy Johnson	2.00
260	Jeff Bagwell	1.50
261	Roberto Alomar	1.50
262	Tom Glavine	1.00
263	Roger Clemens	4.00
264	Alex Rodriguez	4.00
265	Ivan Rodriguez	1.50
266	Pedro J. Martinez	2.00
267	Ken Griffey Jr.	3.00
268	Jim Thome	2.00
269	Frank Thomas	1.50
270	Mike Piazza	3.00
271	Garret Anderson	1.00
272	Luis Gonzalez	1.00
273	John Smoltz	1.00
274	Rafael Palmeiro	1.50
275	Curt Schilling	1.50
276	Mark Prior	1.50
277	Magglio Ordonez	1.00
278	Adam Dunn	1.50
279	Travis Hafner	1.00
280	Jeromy Burnitz	1.00
281	Carlos Guillen	1.00
282	Dontrelle Willis	1.00
283	Carlos Beltran	1.50
284	Zack Greinke	1.00
285	Adrian Beltre	1.00
286	Ben Sheets	1.00
287	Johan Santana	1.00
288	Livan Hernandez	1.00
289	Kazuo Matsui	1.00
290	Derek Jeter	4.00
291	Tim Hudson	1.00
292	Eric Milton	1.00
293	Jason Kendall	1.00
294	Jake Peavy	1.00
295	Ray Durham	1.00
296	Ichiro Suzuki	3.00
297	Scott Rolen	2.00
298	Carl Crawford	1.00
299	Hank Blalock	1.50
300	Roy Halladay	1.00

Press Proofs Blue

Blue (1-200):	5-10X
Blue (201-250):	1-2X
Blue (251-300):	2-4X
Production 75 Sets	

Press Proofs Gold

Gold (1-200):	10-20X
Gold (201-250):	2-4X
Blue (251-300):	4-8X
Production 25 Sets	

Press Proofs Red

Red (1-200):	2-4X
Red (201-250):	.5-1X
Red (251-300):	1-2X
Inserted 1:8	

4 Star Staffs

	NM/M
Common Card:	2.00
Inserted 1:48	
Die-cut:	1X
Production 250 Sets	

#		
1	Greg Maddux, John Smoltz, Kevin Millwood, Tom Glavine	4.00
2	A.J. Burnett, Carl Pavano, Dontrelle Willis, Josh Beckett	2.00
3	Andy Pettitte, David Wells, Mike Mussina, Roger Clemens	6.00
4	Carlos Zambrano, Greg Maddux, Kerry Wood, Mark Prior	4.00
5	Andy Pettitte, Mariano Rivera, Mike Mussina, Roger Clemens	3.00
6	Curt Schilling, Derek Lowe, Pedro J. Martinez, Tim Wakefield	4.00
7	Barry Zito, Mark Mulder, Rich Harden, Tim Hudson	2.00
8	Brandon Webb, Byung-Hyun Kim, Curt Schilling, Randy Johnson	3.00
9	Jamie Moyer, Kenny Rogers, Kevin Brown, Nolan Ryan	8.00
10	Kelvim Escobar, Roger Clemens, Roy Halladay, Woody Williams	6.00
11	Andy Pettitte, Roger Clemens, Roy Oswalt, Wade Miller	6.00
12	Barry Zito, Billy Koch, Mark Mulder, Tim Hudson	2.00
13	Eric Gagne, Hideo Nomo, Kazuhisa Ishii, Kevin Brown	3.00
14	Greg Maddux, Jason Schmidt, John Smoltz, Tom Glavine	5.00
15	Derek Lowe, Hideo Nomo, Pedro Martinez, Tim Wakefield	4.00

Alternate Threads

	NM/M
Complete Set (25):	30.00
Common Player:	1.00
Inserted 1:18	
Holo:	1-2X
Production 150 Sets	
Holo Die-Cut:	2-4X
Production 50 Sets	
1 Adam Dunn	1.50
2 C.C. Sabathia	1.00
3 Curt Schilling	1.50
4 Dontrelle Willis	1.00
5 Greg Maddux	3.00
6 Hank Blalock	1.50
7 Ichiro Suzuki	4.00
8 Jeff Bagwell	1.50
9 Ken Griffey Jr.	3.00
10 Ken Harvey	1.00
11 Magglio Ordonez	1.00
12 Mark Mulder	1.00
13 Mark Teixeira	1.00
14 Michael Young	1.00
15 Miguel Tejada	1.50
16 Mike Piazza	4.00
17 Pedro Martinez	2.00
18 Randy Johnson	2.00
19 Roger Clemens	6.00
20 Sammy Sosa	4.00
21 Tim Hudson	1.00
22 Todd Helton	1.50
23 Torii Hunter	1.00
24 Travis Hafner	1.00
25 Vernon Wells	1.00

Autographs

	NM/M
Common Autograph:	5.00
201 Josh Kroeger	5.00
202 Angel Guzman	10.00
203 Brad Halsey	5.00
204 Bucky Jacobsen	10.00
205 Carlos Hines	5.00
207 Bill Tucker	5.00
208 Bubba Crosby	10.00
210 Chris Shelton	10.00
211 Colby Miller	5.00
212 David Crouthers	5.00
217 Fernando Nieve	10.00
220 Hector Gimenez	5.00
221 Andy Green	5.00
222 Jason Bartlett	5.00
227 Jorge Sequea/84	10.00
228 Jorge Vasquez	8.00
232 Lincoln Holdzkom	8.00
233 Miguel Olivo	8.00
234 Mike Rouse	8.00
236 Phil Stockman	8.00
237 Ramon Ramirez	8.00
242 Ruddy Yan	8.00
245 Scott Proctor	8.00
247 Tim Bausher	8.00
249 William Bergolla	10.00

Autographs Blue

No Pricing	
Production 15-25	
Golds:	No Pricing

Autographs Red

	NM/M
Common Autograph:	
3 Chone Figgins/100	8.00
19 Johnny Estrada/100	15.00

24	Jay Gibbons/100	10.00
47	Carlos Lee/100	10.00
56	Danny Graves/100	8.00
60	Cliff Lee/100	15.00
63	Travis Hafner/50	15.00
74	Jeremy Bonderman/100	10.00
94	Jeremy Affeldt/100	8.00
96	Ken Harvey/100	8.00
111	Milton Bradley/100	10.00
111	Lyle Overbay/50	15.00
118	Joe Nathan/100	10.00
144	Bobby Crosby/100	25.00
154	Mike Lieberthal/50	15.00
157	Craig Wilson/50	15.00
158	Jack Wilson/100	12.00
163	Jake Peavy/50	25.00
172	Merkin Valdez/100	8.00
182	Jeff Suppan/100	10.00
187	Carl Crawford/50	15.00
188	Dewon Brazelton/50	10.00
194	Laynce Nix/100	10.00
201	Josh Kroeger/100	8.00
202	Angel Guzman/100	15.00
203	Brad Halsey/100	8.00
204	Bucky Jacobsen/100	10.00
205	Carlos Hines/100	8.00
207	Billy Traber/100	8.00
208	Bubba Crosby/100	10.00
210	Chris Shelton/100	8.00
211	Colby Miller/100	8.00
212	David Crouthers/100	8.00
217	Fernando Nieve/100	10.00
218	Freddy Guzman/100	10.00
220	Hector Gimenez/100	8.00
221	Andy Green/100	8.00
222	Jason Bartlett/100	8.00
224	Josh Crain/100	15.00
227	Jorge Sequea/84	10.00
228	Jorge Vasquez/100	8.00
233	Miguel Olivo/100	8.00
234	Mike Rouse/100	8.00
236	Phil Stockman/100	10.00
237	Ramon Ramirez/100	8.00
238	Robb Quinlan/100	8.00
241	Ronny Cedeno/65	10.00
242	Ruddy Yan/100	8.00
243	Ryan Meaux/93	8.00
247	Tim Bausher/100	8.00
249	William Bergolla/100	10.00
250	Yadier Molina/100	15.00

Clean Up Crew

		NM/M
Complete Set (15):		45.00
Common Card:		
Inserted 1:49		
Die-Cut:		1X
Production 250 Sets		
1	Albert Pujols, Jim Edmonds, Scott Rolen	6.00
2	Melvin Mora, Miguel Tejada, Rafael Palmeiro	3.00
3	Alfonso Soriano, Michael Young, Hank Blalock	3.00
4	Gary Sheffield, Alex Rodriguez, Hideki Matsui	5.00
5	Moises Alou, Sammy Sosa, Nomar Garciaparra	5.00
6	Paul LoDuca, Mike Lowell, Miguel Cabrera	3.00
7	Carlos Beltran, Lance Berkman, Jeff Bagwell	3.00
8	Paul Konerko, Magglio Ordonez, Frank Thomas	3.00
9	Sean Casey, Ken Griffey Jr., Adam Dunn	5.00
10	Vladimir Guerrero, Garret Anderson, Troy Glaus	3.00
11	Joe Morgan, Johnny Bench, Tony Perez	3.00
12	Keith Hernandez, Darryl Strawberry, Gary Carter	2.00
13	Jim Rice, Carl Yastrzemski, Dwight Evans	5.00
14	Ryne Sandberg, Andre Dawson, Mark Grace	6.00
15	Cal Ripken Jr., Eddie Murray, Rafael Palmeiro	10.00

Cornerstones

		NM/M
Complete Set (20):		50.00
Common Card:		1.50
Inserted 1:37		
1	Albert Pujols, Scott Rolen	6.00
2	Hideki Matsui, Jorge Posada	5.00
3	Nomar Garciaparra, Sammy Sosa	4.00
4	David Ortiz, Manny Ramirez	3.00
5	Miguel Cabrera, Mike Lowell	3.00

6	Hank Blalock, Mark Teixeira	2.00
7	Chipper Jones, J.D. Drew	3.00
8	Craig Biggio, Jeff Bagwell	3.00
9	Kazuo Matsui, Mike Piazza	4.00
10	Shawn Green, Adrian Beltre	1.50
11	Bobby Abreu, Jim Thome	3.00
12	Mike Schmidt, Steve Carlton	6.00
13	Cal Ripken Jr., Eddie Murray	10.00
14	Carl Yastrzemski, Dwight Evans	5.00
15	Joe Morgan, Johnny Bench	3.00
16	Dale Murphy, Phil Niekro	2.00
17	Alan Trammell, Kirk Gibson	2.00
18	Jose Canseco, Rickey Henderson	3.00
19	Paul Molitor, Robin Yount	4.00
20	Bo Jackson, George Brett	6.00

Cornerstones Bats

		NM/M
Common Dual Bat:		8.00
1	Albert Pujols, Scott Rolen	20.00
2	Hideki Matsui, Jorge Posada	35.00
3	Sammy Sosa, Nomar Garciaparra	15.00
4	Manny Ramirez, David Ortiz	20.00
5	Miguel Cabrera, Mike Lowell	10.00
6	Hank Blalock, Mark Teixeira	10.00
7	Chipper Jones, J.D. Drew	15.00
8	Craig Biggio, Jeff Bagwell	10.00
9	Mike Piazza, Kazuo Matsui	15.00
10	Shawn Green, Adrian Beltre	8.00

Cornerstones Jerseys

		NM/M
Common Dual Jersey:		8.00
1	Albert Pujols, Scott Rolen	20.00
2	Hideki Matsui, Jorge Posada	35.00
4	Manny Ramirez, David Ortiz	20.00
5	Miguel Cabrera, Mike Lowell	10.00
6	Hank Blalock, Mark Teixeira	10.00
8	Craig Biggio, Jeff Bagwell	10.00
9	Mike Piazza, Kazuo Matsui	10.00
10	Shawn Green, Adrian Beltre	8.00

Cy Young Winners

		NM/M
Complete Set (15):		30.00
Common Player:		1.50
Inserted 1:31		
Gold:		1X
Production 350 Sets		
Gold Die-Cut:		1.5-2X
Production 100 Sets		
1	Warren Spahn	3.00
2	Whitey Ford	3.00
3	Bob Gibson	3.00
4	Tom Seaver	3.00
5	Steve Carlton	2.00
6	Jim Palmer	2.00
7	Rollie Fingers	1.50
8	Dwight Gooden	1.50
9	Roger Clemens	6.00
10	Orel Hershiser	1.50
11	Greg Maddux	4.00
12	Dennis Eckersley	2.00
13	Randy Johnson	3.00
14	Pedro Martinez	3.00
15	Eric Gagne	2.00

Fans of the Game

	NM/M
Common Card:	1.50

Inserted 1:24		
1	Sean Astin	1.50
2	Tony Danza	1.50
3	Taye Diggs	1.50

Fans of the Game Autograph

		NM/M
1	Sean Astin	30.00
3	Taye Diggs	30.00

Game Collection

		NM/M
Inserted 1:118		
1	Cal Ripken Jr./Bat	30.00
2	Carl Crawford/Jsy	5.00
3	Dale Murphy/Bat	20.00
4	Don Mattingly/Bat	25.00
5	George Brett/Jsy	25.00
6	Victor Martinez/Bat	8.00
7	Sean Casey/Bat	5.00
8	Torii Hunter/Bat	5.00
9	Magglio Ordonez/Bat	5.00
10	Lance Berkman/Bat	5.00
11	Mike Schmidt/Bat	25.00
12	Nolan Ryan/Jkt	40.00
13	Paul LoDuca/Bat	5.00
14	Preston Wilson/Bat	5.00
15	Rod Carew/Jkt	10.00
16	Reggie Jackson/Bat	10.00
17	Ivan Rodriguez/Bat	10.00
18	Larry Walker/Cards Bat	10.00
19	Miguel Tejada/Bat	8.00
20	Vladimir Guerrero/Bat	10.00

Game Collection Autograph

		NM/M
Production 5-200		
2	Carl Crawford/Jsy/200	15.00
6	Victor Martinez/Bat/200	20.00
7	Sean Casey/Bat/200	20.00
8	Torii Hunter/Bat/50	25.00
13	Paul LoDuca/Bat/100	20.00

Gamers

		NM/M
Complete Set (15):		20.00
Common Player:		1.00
Inserted 1:13		
Quantum:		2-3X
Production 175 Sets		
Quantum Die-Cut:		3-5X
Production 50 Sets		
1	Albert Pujols	4.00
2	Alex Rodriguez	3.00
3	Alfonso Soriano	1.50
4	Chipper Jones	1.50
5	Derek Jeter	4.00
6	Greg Maddux	2.00
7	Ichiro Suzuki	3.00
8	Jim Thome	1.50
9	Ken Griffey Jr.	2.00
10	Lance Berkman	1.00
11	Miguel Tejada	1.00
12	Mike Piazza	2.50
13	Roger Clemens	4.00
14	Scott Rolen	1.50
15	Vladimir Guerrero	1.50

Gold Rookies

		NM/M
Complete Set (10):		15.00
Common Player:		2.00
Inserted 1:24		
Mirror:		3-5X
Production 25 Sets		
1	Dennis Sarfate	2.00
2	Donnie Kelly	2.00
3	Eddy Rodriguez	2.00

Gold Leaf Rookies

4	Edwin Moreno	2.00
5	Greg Dobbs	2.00
6	Josh Labandeira	2.00
7	Kevin Cave	2.00
8	Mariano Gomez	2.00
9	Ronald Belisario	2.00
10	Ruddy Yan	2.00

Gold Rookies Autograph

		NM/M
Common Autograph:		
Mirror:		No Pricing
Production 25 Sets		
1	Dennis Sarfate	10.00
2	Donnie Kelly	8.00
5	Greg Dobbs	8.00
7	Kevin Cave	10.00
9	Ronald Belisario	8.00
10	Ruddy Yan	8.00

Gold Stars

		NM/M
Complete Set (20):		40.00
Common Player:		.75
Inserted 1:27		
Mirror:		4-6X
Production 25 Sets		
1	Albert Pujols	4.00
2	Ichiro Suzuki	3.00
3	Derek Jeter	4.00
4	Alex Rodriguez	3.00
5	Scott Rolen	1.50
6	Randy Johnson	1.50
7	Roger Clemens	4.00
8	Greg Maddux	2.00
9	Alfonso Soriano	1.50
10	Mark Mulder	.75
11	Sammy Sosa	3.00
12	Mike Piazza	3.00
13	Rafael Palmeiro	.75
14	Ivan Rodriguez	.75
15	Miguel Cabrera	.75
16	Stan Musial	3.00
17	Nolan Ryan	6.00
18	Don Mattingly	4.00
19	George Brett	4.00
20	Cal Ripken Jr.	6.00

Home/Road

		NM/M
Common Player:		1.00
Inserted 1:22		
Home & Road price is identical.		
1H	Albert Pujols/H	4.00
1R	Albert Pujols/R	4.00
2H	Alfonso Soriano/H	1.50
2R	Alfonso Soriano/R	1.50
3H	Carlos Beltran/H	1.00
3R	Carlos Beltran/R	1.00
4H	Chipper Jones/H	1.50
4R	Chipper Jones/R	1.50
5H	Frank Thomas/H	1.50
5R	Frank Thomas/R	1.50
6H	Hank Blalock/H	1.00
6R	Hank Blalock/R	1.00
7H	Ivan Rodriguez/H	1.50
7R	Ivan Rodriguez/R	1.50

FLORIDA MARLINS · OUTFIELD
MIGUEL CABRERA

8H	Manny Ramirez/H	1.50
8R	Manny Ramirez/R	1.50
9H	Mark Prior/H	1.50
9R	Mark Prior/R	1.50
10H	Miguel Cabrera/H	1.50
10R	Miguel Cabrera/R	1.50
11H	Miguel Tejada/H	1.00
11R	Miguel Tejada/R	1.00
12H	Mike Piazza/H	2.50
12R	Mike Piazza/R	2.50
13H	Roger Clemens/H	4.00
13R	Roger Clemens/R	4.00
14H	Todd Helton/H	1.50
14R	Todd Helton/R	1.50
15H	Vladimir Guerrero/H	1.50
15R	Vladimir Guerrero/R	1.50

Home/Road Jersey
NM/M

Common Player:
1H	Albert Pujols/H	20.00
1R	Albert Pujols/R	20.00
2H	Alfonso Soriano/H	8.00
3H	Carlos Beltran/H	8.00
3R	Carlos Beltran/R	8.00
4R	Chipper Jones/R	8.00
5H	Frank Thomas/H	8.00
5R	Frank Thomas/R	8.00
6H	Hank Blalock/H	8.00
7H	Ivan Rodriguez/H	8.00
7R	Ivan Rodriguez/R	8.00
8R	Manny Ramirez/R	8.00
9H	Mark Prior/H	8.00
11H	Miguel Tejada/H	5.00
11R	Miguel Tejada/R	5.00
12H	Mike Piazza/H	12.00
13H	Roger Clemens/H	15.00
13R	Roger Clemens/R	15.00
14H	Todd Helton/H	8.00
14R	Todd Helton/R	8.00
15H	Vladimir Guerrero/H	8.00

Patch Off My Back

NM/M
Common Patch: 15.00
Production 50 Sets
1	Adam Dunn	25.00
2	Aubrey Huff	15.00
3	Austin Kearns	15.00
4	Bobby Crosby	25.00
5	C.C. Sabathia	15.00
7	David Ortiz	25.00
8	Dewon Brazelton	15.00
9	Edgar Martinez	20.00
10	Frankie Francisco	15.00
11	Garret Anderson	20.00
12	Hideki Matsui	50.00
13	Hideo Nomo	20.00
14	Jack Wilson	15.00
15	Javy Lopez	15.00
16	Jay Gibbons	15.00
17	Jim Edmonds	20.00
18	Jody Gerut	15.00
19	Joey Gathright	15.00
20	Johan Santana	20.00
21	Jose Reyes	15.00
22	Jose Vidro	15.00
23	Lance Berkman	15.00
24	Mariano Rivera	20.00
25	Mark Teixeira	20.00
26	Michael Young	15.00
27	Mike Cameron	15.00
28	Mike Sweeney	15.00
29	Omar Vizquel	15.00
30	Preston Wilson	15.00
31	Rocco Baldelli	15.00
32	Scott Rolen	25.00
33	Sean Burroughs	15.00
34	Sean Casey	15.00
35	Tim Hudson	20.00
36	Torii Hunter	20.00
37	Trevor Hoffman	20.00
38	Troy Glaus	20.00
39	Vernon Wells	15.00
40	Victor Martinez	20.00

Patch Off My Back Autograph
NM/M

Production 10-75
2	Aubrey Huff/50	35.00
4	Bobby Crosby/75	50.00
5	C.C. Sabathia/75	30.00
7	David Ortiz/50	100.00
8	Dewon Brazelton/75	25.00
14	Jack Wilson/75	30.00
16	Jay Gibbons/50	25.00
18	Jody Gerut/75	20.00
20	Johan Santana/50	60.00
22	Jose Vidro/75	25.00
26	Michael Young/75	35.00
33	Sean Burroughs/25	25.00
40	Victor Martinez/75	35.00

Picture Perfect

Picture Perfect
MARK PRIOR P

NM/M
Complete Set (20):		30.00
Common Player:		1.00
Inserted 1:20		
Die-Cut:		2-3X
Production 100 Sets
1	Albert Pujols	4.00
2	Alex Rodriguez	3.00
3	Alfonso Soriano	1.50
4	Derek Jeter	4.00
5	Greg Maddux	2.00
6	Hideki Matsui	3.00
7	Ichiro Suzuki	3.00
8	Ivan Rodriguez	1.00
9	Jim Thome	1.50
10	Mark Mulder	1.00
11	Mark Prior	1.50
12	Miguel Tejada	1.00
13	Mike Mussina	1.00
14	Mike Piazza	2.50
15	Nomar Garciaparra	2.50
16	Randy Johnson	1.50
17	Roger Clemens	4.00
18	Sammy Sosa	2.50
19	Scott Rolen	1.50
20	Vladimir Guerrero	1.50

Recollection Autographs
No Pricing
Production 1-29

Shirt Off My Back
NM/M

Common Player: 5.00
Inserted 1:48
1	Adam Dunn	15.00
4	Bobby Crosby	15.00
5	C.C. Sabathia	8.00
7	David Ortiz	15.00
8	Dewon Brazelton	5.00
9	Edgar Martinez	5.00
10	Frankie Francisco	5.00
11	Garret Anderson	5.00
12	Hideki Matsui	25.00
13	Hideo Nomo	8.00
14	Jack Wilson	5.00
15	Javy Lopez	8.00
16	Jay Gibbons	5.00
17	Jim Edmonds	15.00
18	Jody Gerut/SP	5.00
19	Joey Gathright	5.00
21	Jose Reyes	10.00
22	Jose Vidro	5.00
23	Lance Berkman	5.00
25	Mark Teixeira	5.00
26	Michael Young	5.00
27	Mike Cameron	5.00
28	Mike Sweeney	5.00
29	Omar Vizquel	8.00
30	Preston Wilson	5.00
31	Rocco Baldelli	8.00
32	Scott Rolen	10.00
33	Sean Burroughs	5.00
34	Sean Casey	5.00
35	Tim Hudson	5.00
36	Torii Hunter	5.00
37	Trevor Hoffman	5.00
38	Troy Glaus	5.00
39	Vernon Wells	5.00
40	Victor Martinez	8.00

Sportscasters 70 Green

Baseball
Steve Carlton

NM/M
Common Player: 2.00
Production 70 Sets
Variations #'d 35-65: 1X
Variations #'d 20-30: 1.5X
No pricing 15 or less.
1	Adam Dunn	3.00
2	Al Kaline	5.00
3	Albert Pujols	8.00
4	Alex Rodriguez	8.00
5	Alfonso Soriano	3.00
6	Bob Gibson	3.00
7	Cal Ripken Jr.	25.00
8	Carl Yastrzemski	8.00
9	Dale Murphy	3.00
10	Derek Jeter	10.00
11	Don Mattingly	10.00
12	Duke Snider	4.00
13	Eric Gagne	3.00
14	Ernie Banks	6.00
15	Frank Robinson	3.00
16	George Brett	10.00
17	Greg Maddux	6.00
18	Harmon Killebrew	5.00
19	Ichiro Suzuki	8.00
20	Ivan Rodriguez	3.00
21	Jim Edmonds	3.00
22	Jim Palmer	2.00
23	Jim Thome	4.00
24	Johnny Bench	5.00
25	Ken Griffey Jr.	6.00
26	Larry Walker	3.00
27	Mark Mulder	2.00
28	Mark Prior	4.00
29	Miguel Tejada	3.00
30	Mike Mussina	3.00
31	Mike Piazza	6.00
32	Mike Schmidt	10.00
33	Nolan Ryan	15.00
34	Nomar Garciaparra	6.00
35	Pedro Martinez	4.00
36	Rafael Palmeiro	3.00
37	Randy Johnson	4.00
38	Reggie Jackson	3.00
39	Rickey Henderson	4.00
40	Roberto Clemente	15.00
41	Rod Carew	3.00
42	Roger Clemens	8.00
43	Ryne Sandberg	4.00
44	Sammy Sosa	4.00
45	Stan Musial	8.00
46	Steve Carlton	2.00
47	Tony Gwynn	5.00
48	Vladimir Guerrero	4.00
49	Warren Spahn	4.00
50	Willie McCovey	3.00

2005 Leaf Century

JOHAN SANTANA
minnesota twins

NM/M
Complete Set (200): 40.00

Common Player: .25
Pack (5): 12.00
Box (10): 100.00
1	Brian Roberts	.25
2	Derek Jeter	2.00
3	Harmon Killebrew	1.00
4	Angel Berroa	.25
5	George Brett	2.00
6	Stan Musial	1.50
7	Ivan Rodriguez	.50
8	Cal Ripken Jr.	3.00
9	Hank Blalock	.50
10	Miguel Tejada	.50
11	Barry Larkin	.40
12	Alfonso Soriano	.75
13	Alex Rodriguez	2.00
14	Paul Konerko	.25
15	Jim Edmonds	.40
16	Garret Anderson	.40
17	Todd Helton	.50
18	Moises Alou	.40
19	Tony Gwynn	.75
20	Mike Schmidt	2.00
21	Sammy Sosa	1.25
22	Roger Clemens	2.00
23	Tony Perez	.25
24	Manny Ramirez	.75
25	Jim Thome	.75
26	Chase Utley	.40
27	Scott Rolen	.75
28	Austin Kearns	.25
29	John Smoltz	.40
30	Ken Griffey Jr.	1.00
31	Mike Piazza	1.00
32	Steve Carlton	.50
33	Larry Walker	.40
34	Nolan Ryan	2.50
35	Mike Mussina	.40
36	Joe Nathan	.25
37	Kenny Rogers	.25
38	Eric Gagne	.40
39	Brett Myers	.25
40	Rich Harden	.25
41	Victor Martinez	.40
42	Mariano Rivera	.50
43	Dennis Eckersley	.50
44	Roy Oswalt	.25
45	Pedro Martinez	.75
46	Jason Bay	.40
47	Tom Glavine	.40
48	Torii Hunter	.25
49	Larry Bigbie	.25
50	Nomar Garciaparra	1.50
51	Ichiro Suzuki	1.50
52	C.C. Sabathia	.25
53	Bobby Abreu	.40
54	Doug Mientkiewicz	.25
55	Hideki Matsui	1.50
56	Mark Buehrle	.25
57	Johan Santana	.50
58	Johnny Damon	.75
59	Edgar Martinez	.25
60	Preston Wilson	.25
61	Livan Hernandez	.25
62	Eric Chavez	.25
63	Lyle Overbay	.40
64	Jason Schmidt	.50
65	Cliff Lee	.25
66	Shingo Takatsu	.25
67	Jeff Bagwell	.50
68	Danny Graves	.25
69	Kip Wells	.25
70	Steve Finley	.25
71	Lew Ford	.25
72	Chone Figgins	.40
73	Delmon Young	.40
74	Esteban Loaiza	.25
75	Barry Zito	.40
76	Carlos Delgado	.25
77	Joe Mauer	.50
78	Ryan Wagner	.25
79	John Lackey	.25
80	Adrian Beltre	.40
81	Vernon Wells	.25
82	Sean Burroughs	.25
83	Francisco Cordero	.25
84	Carlos Guillen	.25
85	Eric Byrnes	.25
86	Jose Reyes	.40
87	Rocco Baldelli	.25
88	Josh Beckett	.40
89	Casey Kotchman	.40
90	Scott Podsednik	.25
91	Mike Sweeney	.25
92	Khalil Greene	.50
93	Trot Nixon	.25
94	Chad Cordero	.25
95	Derek Lowe	.25
96	Jason Giambi	.40
97	Jose Guillen	.25
98	Craig Biggio	.40
99	Pat Burrell	.40
100	Kazuo Matsui	.25
101	Rafael Furcal	.25
102	Jack Wilson	.25
103	Edgar Renteria	.50
104	Carlos Beltran	.75
105	Albert Pujols	2.00
106	Melvin Mora	.25
107	J.D. Drew	.40
108	Andre Dawson	.50
109	Jody Gerut	.25
110	Michael Young	.50
111	Gary Sheffield	.50
112	Wade Boggs	.50
113	Carl Crawford	.40
114	Paul LoDuca	.25

115 Tim Hudson .40
116 Aramis Ramirez .40
117 Lance Berkman .40
118 Javy Lopez .40
119 Robin Yount 1.00
120 Mark Mulder .25
121 Sean Casey .25
122 Will Clark .50
123 Don Mattingly 2.00
124 Miguel Cabrera .75
125 Rafael Palmeiro .50
126 David Ortiz .75
127 Vladimir Guerrero .75
128 Ken Harvey .25
129 Rod Carew .50
130 Magglio Ordonez .25
131 Greg Maddux 1.00
132 Roy Halladay .25
133 Javier Vazquez .25
134 Kerry Wood .75
135 Frank Thomas .50
136 Tom Gordon .25
137 Jake Peavy .25
138 Curt Schilling .75
139 Dewon Brazelton .25
140 Jae Weong Seo .25
141 Danny Kolb .25
142 Jeff Kent .40
143 Juan Encarnacion .25
144 Adam Dunn .50
145 Carlos Lee .25
146 Matt Clement .25
147 Guillermo Mota .25
148 Travis Hafner .40
149 Brad Wilkerson .25
150 Eric Milton .25
151 Randy Johnson .75
152 Joe Crede .25
153 Mark Kotsay .25
154 Jason Varitek .40
155 David Wright .75
156 Brad Penny .25
157 Francisco Rodriguez .25
158 Gary Carter .50
159 Adrian Gonzalez .25
160 Derrek Lee .40
161 Mark Prior .50
162 Carlos Zambrano .40
163 Bobby Crosby .40
164 Jermaine Dye .25
165 Kris Benson .25
166 Dontrelle Willis .40
167 Dallas McPherson .40
168 Johnny Estrada .40
169 Milton Bradley .25
170 Shannon Stewart .25
171 Ben Sheets .40
172 Richard Hidalgo .25
173 Laynce Nix .25
174 B.J. Upton .50
175 Craig Wilson .25
176 Hideo Nomo .40
177 Troy Glaus .40
178 Akinori Otsuka .25
179 Rickie Weeks .40
180 Mike Lowell .40
181 Marcus Giles .25
182 Randy Wolf .25
183 A.J. Burnett .25
184 Aubrey Huff .25
185 Billy Ripken .25
186 Octavio Dotel .25
187 Kazuhisa Ishii .25
188 Mark Teixeira .50
189 Todd Walker .25
190 Dale Murphy .50
191 Alexis Rios .25
192 Reggie Sanders .25
193 Orlando Cabrera .25
194 Shawn Green .40
195 Andy Pettitte .40
196 Chipper Jones .75
197 Jose Vidro .25
198 Jacque Jones .25
199 Brian Giles .25
200 Andruw Jones .40

Post Marks Gold

Golds: 4-8X
Production 50 Sets

Post Marks Silver

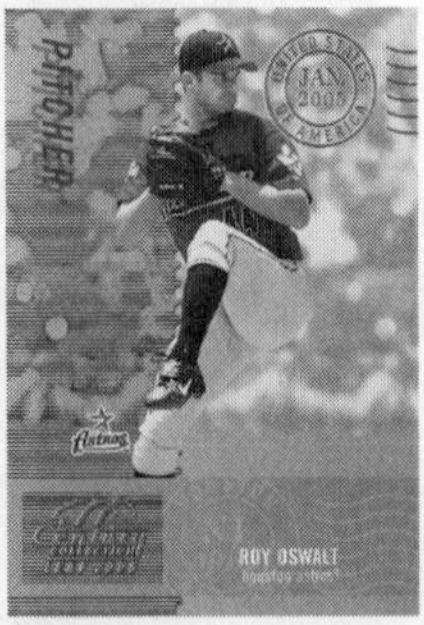
PITCHER
ROY OSWALT

Silvers: 3-6X
Production 100 Sets

Post Marks Platinum

No Pricing
Production One Set

Air Mail Bat

NM/M

Production 50-250
1 Babe Ruth/50 150.00
2 Frank Robinson/250 12.00
3 Harmon Killebrew/100 20.00
4 Sammy Sosa/100 10.00
5 Reggie Jackson/250 15.00
6 Mike Schmidt/100 20.00
7 Rafael Palmeiro/100 8.00
8 Ted Williams/50 80.00
9 Willie McCovey/250 10.00
10 Ernie Banks/100 20.00

Air Mail Bat Signature

NM/M

Production 1-25
2 Frank Robinson/25 40.00
3 Harmon Killebrew/25 60.00
9 Willie McCovey/25 35.00

Material Bat

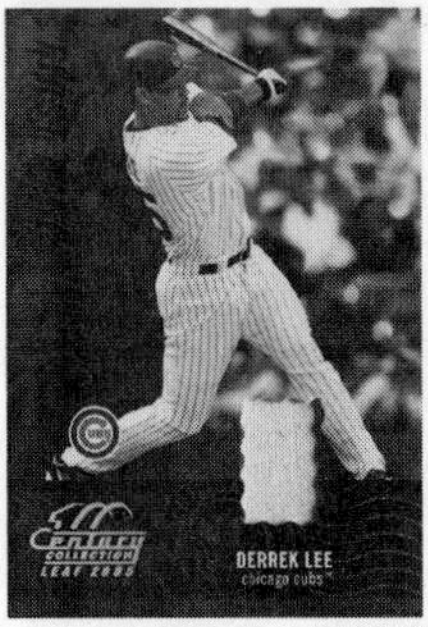
DERREK LEE
chicago cubs

NM/M

Common Player: 5.00
3 Harmon Killebrew/250 12.00
4 Angel Berroa/50 5.00
5 George Brett/250 15.00
6 Stan Musial/250 15.00
7 Ivan Rodriguez/100 8.00
8 Cal Ripken Jr./250 25.00
9 Hank Blalock/100 8.00
10 Miguel Tejada/100 6.00
11 Barry Larkin/100 6.00
12 Alfonso Soriano/100 8.00
14 Paul Konerko/50 5.00
15 Jim Edmonds/100 8.00
16 Garret Anderson/100 5.00
17 Todd Helton/100 8.00
18 Moises Alou/50 6.00
19 Tony Gwynn/50 10.00
20 Mike Schmidt/250 15.00
21 Sammy Sosa/100 10.00
22 Roger Clemens/100 15.00
23 Tony Perez/100 8.00
24 Manny Ramirez/100 10.00
25 Jim Thome/100 12.00
27 Scott Rolen/100 10.00
28 Austin Kearns/50 5.00
31 Mike Piazza/100 12.00
32 Steve Carlton/250 8.00
33 Larry Walker/100 8.00
34 Nolan Ryan/250 20.00
35 Mike Mussina/100 8.00
41 Victor Martinez/50 8.00
44 Roy Oswalt/100 5.00
45 Pedro Martinez/100 8.00
47 Tom Glavine/100 6.00
48 Torii Hunter/100 6.00
50 Nomar Garciaparra/100 15.00
53 Bobby Abreu/25 10.00
54 Doug Mientkiewicz/50 5.00
55 Hideki Matsui/100 25.00
56 Mark Buehrle/50 6.00
58 Johnny Damon/100 12.00
59 Edgar Martinez/100 6.00
60 Preston Wilson/50 6.00
62 Eric Chavez/100 5.00
63 Lyle Overbay/50 8.00
67 Jeff Bagwell/100 8.00
71 Lew Ford/50 5.00
73 Delmon Young/100 8.00
75 Barry Zito/100 5.00
76 Carlos Delgado/100 5.00
80 Adrian Beltre/100 8.00
81 Vernon Wells/100 5.00
86 Jose Reyes/50 8.00
87 Rocco Baldelli/100 5.00
88 Josh Beckett/100 5.00
91 Mike Sweeney/50 5.00
93 Trot Nixon/50 6.00
96 Jason Giambi/100 5.00
98 Craig Biggio/100 6.00
99 Pat Burrell/50 8.00
100 Kazuo Matsui/100 8.00
101 Rafael Furcal/50 6.00
102 Jack Wilson/50 8.00
103 Edgar Renteria/100 6.00
104 Carlos Beltran/100 8.00
105 Albert Pujols/100 15.00
106 Melvin Mora/50 5.00
107 J.D. Drew/100 5.00
108 Andre Dawson/250 6.00
109 Jody Gerut/50 6.00
110 Michael Young/250 5.00
111 Gary Sheffield/100 6.00
112 Wade Boggs/250 8.00
114 Paul LoDuca/100 10.00
115 Tim Hudson/100 5.00
116 Aramis Ramirez/50 8.00
117 Lance Berkman/250 5.00
118 Javy Lopez/50 5.00
119 Robin Yount/250 10.00
120 Mark Mulder/100 5.00
121 Sean Casey/50 5.00
122 Will Clark/250 8.00
123 Don Mattingly/250 15.00
124 Miguel Cabrera/50 12.00
125 Rafael Palmeiro/250 8.00
126 David Ortiz/250 12.00
127 Vladimir Guerrero/250 8.00
128 Ken Harvey/50 5.00
129 Rod Carew/250 8.00
130 Magglio Ordonez/250 5.00
131 Greg Maddux/100 10.00
134 Kerry Wood/100 8.00
135 Frank Thomas/100 8.00
138 Curt Schilling/100 8.00
142 Jeff Kent/250 5.00
143 Juan Encarnacion/50 5.00
144 Adam Dunn/250 8.00
145 Carlos Lee/250 5.00
148 Travis Hafner/50 6.00
149 Brad Wilkerson/100 5.00
151 Randy Johnson/100 10.00
152 Joe Crede/50 6.00
154 Jason Varitek/250 10.00
156 Brad Penny/50 5.00
158 Gary Carter/250 8.00
160 Derrek Lee/250 5.00
161 Mark Prior/100 8.00
164 Jermaine Dye/50 5.00
166 Dontrelle Willis/100 6.00
168 Johnny Estrada/50 6.00
170 Shannon Stewart/100 5.00
171 Ben Sheets/50 8.00
172 Richard Hidalgo/50 5.00
173 Laynce Nix/50 5.00
174 B.J. Upton/50 8.00
175 Craig Wilson/100 5.00
176 Hideo Nomo/100 8.00
177 Troy Glaus/250 5.00
179 Rickie Weeks/25 8.00
180 Mike Lowell/100 5.00
183 A.J. Burnett/100 5.00
184 Aubrey Huff/50 5.00
187 Kazuhisa Ishii/100 5.00
188 Mark Teixeira/250 5.00
190 Dale Murphy/250 8.00
191 Alexis Rios/50 5.00
193 Orlando Cabrera/50 6.00
194 Shawn Green/250 5.00
195 Andy Pettitte/100 6.00
196 Chipper Jones/100 8.00
197 Jose Vidro/250 5.00
198 Jacque Jones/100 5.00
199 Brian Giles/250 5.00
200 Andruw Jones/250 6.00

Material Fabric Number

NM/M

Common Player: 5.00
20 Mike Schmidt/Jsy/20 50.00
21 Sammy Sosa/Jsy/21 20.00
22 Roger Clemens/Jsy/22 40.00
23 Tony Perez/Jsy/24 15.00
24 Manny Ramirez/Jsy/24 20.00
25 Jim Thome/Jsy/25 20.00
27 Scott Rolen/Jsy/27 20.00
28 Austin Kearns/Jsy/28 15.00
29 John Smoltz/Jsy/29 20.00
31 Mike Piazza/Jsy/31 25.00
32 Steve Carlton/Pants/32 15.00
34 Nolan Ryan/Jsy/34 50.00
35 Mike Mussina/Jsy/35 15.00
39 Brett Myers/Jsy/39 8.00
41 Victor Martinez/Jsy/41 8.00
42 Mariano Rivera/Jsy/42 15.00
43 Dennis Eckersley/Jsy/43 10.00
44 Roy Oswalt/Jsy/44 8.00
45 Pedro Martinez/Jsy/45 10.00
47 Tom Glavine/Jsy/47 10.00
48 Torii Hunter/Jsy/48 8.00
52 C.C. Sabathia/Jsy/52 8.00
53 Bobby Abreu/Jsy/53 8.00
55 Hideki Matsui/Jsy/55 35.00
56 Mark Buehrle/Jsy/56 8.00
57 Johan Santana/Jsy/57 15.00
60 Preston Wilson/Jsy/44 8.00
61 Livan Hernandez/Jsy/61 5.00
65 Cliff Lee/Jsy/34 10.00
71 Lew Ford/Jsy/20 10.00
75 Barry Zito/Jsy/75 5.00
76 Carlos Delgado/Jsy/25 10.00
78 Ryan Wagner/Jsy/38 5.00
80 Adrian Beltre/Jsy/29 15.00
82 Sean Burroughs/Jsy/32 8.00
83 Francisco Cordero/Jsy/31 8.00
85 Eric Byrnes/Jsy/22 8.00
91 Mike Sweeney/Jsy/29 8.00
96 Jason Giambi/Jsy/25 10.00
100 Kazuo Matsui/Jsy/25 12.00
118 Javy Lopez/Jsy/18 15.00
119 Robin Yount/Jsy/19 30.00
120 Mark Mulder/Jsy/20 12.00
121 Sean Casey/Jsy/21 10.00
122 Will Clark/Jsy/22 20.00
123 Don Mattingly/Pants/23 40.00
124 Miguel Cabrera/Jsy/24 20.00
125 Rafael Palmeiro/Jsy/25 15.00
126 David Ortiz/Jsy/34 20.00
127 Vladimir Guerrero/Jsy/27 20.00
128 Ken Harvey/Jsy/28 10.00
129 Rod Carew/Jsy/29 20.00
130 Magglio Ordonez/Jsy/30 10.00
131 Greg Maddux/Jsy/31 25.00
132 Roy Halladay/Jsy/32 10.00
134 Kerry Wood/Jsy/34 20.00
135 Frank Thomas/Jsy/35 20.00
138 Curt Schilling/Jsy/34 15.00
139 Dewon Brazelton/Jsy/45 5.00
140 Jae Weong/Seo Jsy/40 5.00
141 Danny Kolb/Jsy/41 5.00
144 Adam Dunn/Jsy/44 15.00
145 Carlos Lee/Jsy/45 8.00
146 Matt Clement/Jsy/30 10.00
148 Travis Hafner/Jsy/48 8.00
151 Randy Johnson/Pants/51 15.00
154 Jason Varitek/Jsy/33 20.00
157 Francisco Rodriguez/Jsy/57 5.00
162 Carlos Zambrano/Jsy/38 8.00
164 Jermaine Dye/Jsy/24 10.00
166 Dontrelle Willis/Jsy/35 12.00
168 Johnny Estrada/Jsy/23 10.00
170 Shannon Stewart/Jsy/23 10.00
175 Craig Wilson/Jsy/36 5.00
177 Troy Glaus/Jsy/25 15.00
180 Mike Lowell/Jsy/19 20.00
183 A.J. Burnett/Jsy/34 10.00
188 Mark Teixeira/Jsy/23 15.00
195 Andy Pettitte/Jsy/21 20.00
200 Andruw Jones/Jsy/5 15.00

Material Fabric Position

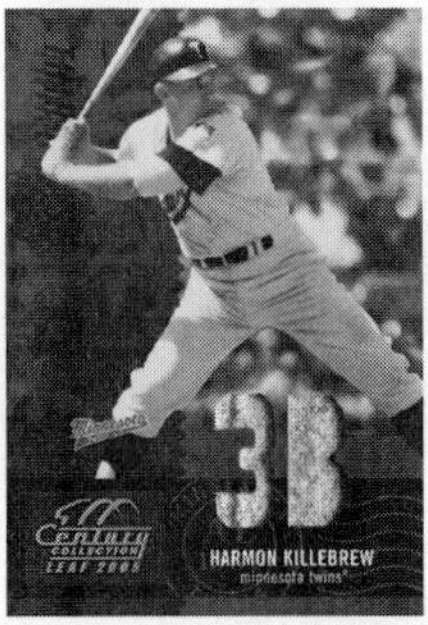
3B
HARMON KILLEBREW
minnesota twins

NM/M

Common Player: 4.00
Prime: No Pricing
Production One Set
1 Brian Roberts/Jsy/250 4.00
3 Harmon Killebrew/Jsy/250 12.00
4 Angel Berroa/Jsy/250 4.00
5 George Brett/Jsy/250 15.00
6 Stan Musial/Pants/100 15.00
7 Ivan Rodriguez/Jsy/250 6.00
8 Cal Ripken Jr./Jkt/250 25.00
9 Hank Blalock/Jsy/250 8.00
10 Miguel Tejada/Jsy/250 6.00
11 Barry Larkin/Jsy/100 6.00
12 Alfonso Soriano/Jsy/250 4.00
14 Paul Konerko/Jsy/250 4.00
15 Jim Edmonds/Jsy/250 6.00
16 Garret Anderson/Jsy/250 4.00
17 Todd Helton/Jsy/250 6.00
19 Tony Gwynn/Jsy/250 10.00
20 Mike Schmidt/Jsy/250 15.00
21 Sammy Sosa/Jsy/250 10.00
22 Roger Clemens/Jsy/250 12.00
23 Tony Perez/Jsy/250 6.00
24 Manny Ramirez/Jsy/250 8.00
25 Jim Thome/Jsy/250 8.00
27 Scott Rolen/Jsy/250 8.00
28 Austin Kearns/Jsy/250 4.00
29 John Smoltz/Jsy/250 6.00
31 Mike Piazza/Jsy/250 10.00
32 Steve Carlton/Pants/250 6.00
34 Nolan Ryan/Jsy/250 20.00
35 Mike Mussina/Jsy/250 6.00
39 Brett Myers/Jsy/250 4.00
41 Victor Martinez/Jsy/250 4.00
42 Mariano Rivera/Jsy/250 6.00
43 Dennis Eckersley/Jsy/250 6.00
44 Roy Oswalt/Jsy/250 4.00
45 Pedro Martinez/Jsy/250 8.00
46 Jason Bay/Jsy/250 4.00
47 Tom Glavine/Jsy/250 6.00
48 Torii Hunter/Jsy/250 4.00
49 Larry Bigbie/Jsy/250 4.00
52 C.C. Sabathia/Jsy/250 4.00
53 Bobby Abreu/Jsy/250 4.00
55 Hideki Matsui/Jsy/250 20.00
56 Mark Buehrle/Jsy/250 4.00

57 Johan Santana/Jsy/250 8.00
59 Edgar Martinez/Jsy/250 6.00
60 Preston Wilson/Jsy/250 4.00
61 Livan Hernandez/Jsy/250 4.00
62 Eric Chavez/Jsy/250 6.00
63 Lyle Overbay/Jsy/250 4.00
65 Cliff Lee/Jsy/250 6.00
67 Jeff Bagwell/Jsy/250 8.00
71 Lew Ford/Jsy/250 4.00
72 Chone Figgins/Jsy/250 4.00
75 Barry Zito/Jsy/250 4.00
76 Carlos Delgado/Jsy/250 4.00
78 Ryan Wagner/Jsy/250 4.00
80 Adrian Beltre/Jsy/250 8.00
81 Vernon Wells/Jsy/250 4.00
82 Sean Burroughs/Jsy/250 4.00
83 Francisco Cordero/Jsy/250 4.00
85 Eric Byrnes/Jsy/250 10.00
86 Jose Reyes/Jsy/250 4.00
87 Rocco Baldelli/Jsy/250 4.00
88 Josh Beckett/Jsy/250 4.00
90 Scott Podsednik/Jsy/250 4.00
91 Mike Sweeney/Jsy/250 4.00
93 Trot Nixon/Jsy/250 4.00
96 Jason Giambi/Jsy/250 4.00
98 Craig Biggio/Jsy/250 6.00
99 Pat Burrell/Jsy/250 4.00
100 Kazuo Matsui/Jsy/250 4.00
101 Rafael Furcal/Jsy/250 4.00
102 Jack Wilson/Jsy/250 4.00
103 Edgar Renteria/Jsy/250 6.00
104 Carlos Beltran/Jsy/250 8.00
105 Albert Pujols/Jsy/250 15.00
106 Melvin Mora/Jsy/100 4.00
108 Andre Dawson/Jsy/250 6.00
109 Jody Gerut/Jsy/250 4.00
110 Michael Young/Jsy/250 4.00
111 Gary Sheffield/Jsy/250 6.00
112 Wade Boggs/Jsy/100 8.00
113 Carl Crawford/Jsy/250 4.00
115 Tim Hudson/Jsy/250 4.00
116 Aramis Ramirez/Jsy/250 6.00
117 Lance Berkman/Jsy/250 4.00
118 Javy Lopez/Jsy/250 4.00
119 Robin Yount/Jsy/250 10.00
120 Mark Mulder/Jsy/250 4.00
121 Sean Casey/Jsy/250 4.00
122 Will Clark/Jsy/250 6.00
123 Don Mattingly/Pants/250 15.00
124 Miguel Cabrera/Jsy/250 8.00
125 Rafael Palmeiro/Jsy/250 8.00
126 David Ortiz/Jsy/250 8.00
127 Vladimir Guerrero/Jsy/250 8.00
128 Ken Harvey/Jsy/250 4.00
129 Rod Carew/Jsy/250 8.00
130 Magglio Ordonez/Jsy/250 4.00
131 Greg Maddux/Jsy/250 10.00
132 Roy Halladay/Jsy/250 4.00
134 Kerry Wood/Jsy/250 8.00
135 Frank Thomas/Jsy/250 8.00
138 Curt Schilling/Jsy/250 8.00
139 Dewon Brazelton/Jsy/100 4.00
140 Jae Weong/Seo Jsy/100 4.00
141 Danny Kolb/Jsy/250 4.00
142 Jeff Kent/Jsy/100 6.00
144 Adam Dunn/Jsy/250 6.00
145 Carlos Lee/Jsy/250 4.00
146 Matt Clement/Jsy/250 4.00
148 Travis Hafner/Jsy/250 4.00
151 Randy Johnson/Pants/250 8.00
154 Jason Varitek/Jsy/100 15.00
157 Francisco Rodriguez/Jsy/100 4.00
158 Gary Carter/Jsy/250 6.00
161 Mark Prior/Jsy/250 8.00
162 Carlos Zambrano/Jsy/100 6.00
163 Bobby Crosby/Jsy/250 8.00
164 Jermaine Dye/Jsy/100 4.00
166 Dontrelle Willis/Jsy/250 4.00
168 Johnny Estrada/Jsy/100 4.00
170 Shannon Stewart/Jsy/100 4.00
171 Ben Sheets/Jsy/250 6.00
173 Laynce Nix/Jsy/100 4.00
175 Craig Wilson/Jsy/100 4.00
176 Hideo Nomo/Jsy/250 8.00
177 Troy Glaus/Jsy/250 4.00
180 Mike Lowell 4.00
183 A.J. Burnett/Jsy/100 4.00
184 Aubrey Huff/Jsy/250 4.00
187 Kazuhisa Ishii/Jsy/250 4.00
188 Mark Teixeira/Jsy/250 6.00
190 Dale Murphy/Jsy/250 8.00
194 Shawn Green/Jsy/250 4.00
195 Andy Pettitte/Jsy/250 6.00
196 Chipper Jones/Jsy/250 8.00
197 Jose Vidro/Jsy/100 4.00
198 Jacque Jones/Jsy/250 4.00
200 Andruw Jones/Jsy/250 6.00

Pennant Patches

NM/M

Production 5-25
1 Ozzie Smith/25 40.00
2 Keith Hernandez/25 20.00
3 Rickey Henderson/25 30.00
4 Paul Molitor/25 25.00
5 George Brett/25 50.00
6 Steve Garvey/25 20.00
7 Randy Johnson/25 25.00
8 Cal Ripken Jr./25 90.00
9 Darryl Strawberry/25 20.00
10 Chipper Jones/25 30.00
11 Steve Carlton/25 20.00
12 Orel Hershiser/25 20.00
13 Carlton Fisk/25 25.00
14 Dave Parker/25 20.00
15 Rollie Fingers/25 20.00
16 Dwight Gooden/25 20.00
18 Dontrelle Willis/25 15.00
19 Dave Righetti/25 15.00

Pennant Patches Signature

NM/M

Production 5-25
2 Keith Hernandez/25 40.00
6 Steve Garvey/25 35.00
9 Darryl Strawberry/25 40.00
11 Steve Carlton/25 40.00
15 Rollie Fingers/25 35.00
16 Dwight Gooden/25 40.00

Shirts

NM/M

Production 25-100
1 Rod Carew/100 10.00
2 Red Schoendienst/50 8.00
3 Harmon Killebrew/50 20.00
4 Joe Cronin/50 35.00
5 Early Wynn/50 8.00
6 Gaylord Perry/100 8.00
7 Willie McCovey/100 10.00
8 Carl Yastrzemski/100 20.00
9 Reggie Jackson/100 10.00
10 Duke Snider/50 15.00
11 Luis Aparicio/100 8.00
12 Bob Gibson/50 15.00
13 Maury Wills/50 8.00
14 Ernie Banks/50 20.00
15 Enos Slaughter/100 10.00
16 Whitey Ford/100 15.00
17 Warren Spahn/100 15.00
18 Roger Maris/100 35.00
19 Hal Newhouser/100 10.00
20 Marty Marion/25 12.00

Shirts Signature

NM/M

Production 5-50
Prime: No Pricing
Production One Set
2 Red Schoendienst/25 25.00
6 Gaylord Perry/50 20.00
7 Willie McCovey/50 30.00
11 Luis Aparicio/50 25.00
13 Maury Wills/50 20.00

Signature Post Marks Gold

NM/M

Production 1-50
36 Joe Nathan/50 20.00
39 Brett Myers/50 12.00
40 Rich Harden/50 15.00
49 Larry Bigbie/50 15.00
61 Livan Hernandez/50 15.00
63 Lyle Overbay/50 15.00
65 Cliff Lee/50 15.00
68 Danny Graves/25 20.00
71 Lew Ford/50 15.00
72 Chone Figgins/50 20.00
74 Esteban Loaiza/50 20.00
78 Ryan Wagner/50 10.00
79 John Lackey/50 15.00
83 Francisco Cordero/25 15.00
85 Eric Byrnes/25 20.00
89 Casey Kotchman/50 25.00
90 Scott Podsednik/50 15.00
94 Chad Cordero/25 15.00
97 Jose Guillen/25 20.00
102 Jack Wilson/50 15.00
106 Melvin Mora/25 20.00
109 Jody Gerut/50 10.00
128 Ken Harvey/50 10.00
136 Tom Gordon/50 15.00
137 Jake Peavy/25 25.00
139 Dewon Brazelton/50 10.00
140 Jae Weong Seo/25 20.00
141 Danny Kolb/50 20.00
145 Carlos Lee/25 20.00
147 Guillermo Mota/50 10.00
148 Travis Hafner/25 20.00
156 Brad Penny/50 10.00
159 Adrian Gonzalez/50 15.00
163 Bobby Crosby/25 30.00
164 Jermaine Dye/25 20.00
168 Johnny Estrada/25 25.00
169 Milton Bradley/25 20.00
170 Shannon Stewart/25 15.00
173 Laynce Nix/50 20.00
175 Craig Wilson/50 15.00
182 Randy Wolf/50 15.00
184 Aubrey Huff/25 20.00
185 Billy Ripken/50 10.00
186 Octavio Dotel/50 15.00
189 Todd Walker/25 20.00
191 Alexis Rios/50 15.00
198 Jacque Jones/25 15.00

Signature Post Marks Silver

NM/M

Production 1-250
Platinum: No Pricing
Production One Set
1 Brian Roberts/250 8.00
4 Angel Berroa/25 15.00
36 Joe Nathan/250 15.00
39 Brett Myers/250 8.00
40 Rich Harden/100 15.00
49 Larry Bigbie/250 10.00
52 C.C. Sabathia/25 20.00
56 Mark Buehrle/50 15.00
61 Livan Hernandez/100 10.00
63 Lyle Overbay/100 15.00
65 Cliff Lee/250 10.00
68 Danny Graves/100 10.00
71 Lew Ford/100 10.00
72 Chone Figgins/250 10.00
74 Esteban Loaiza/250 10.00
78 Ryan Wagner/250 10.00
79 John Lackey/250 10.00
82 Sean Burroughs/25 15.00
83 Francisco Cordero/100 8.00
85 Eric Byrnes/100 10.00
89 Casey Kotchman/250 20.00
90 Scott Podsednik/100 10.00
93 Trot Nixon/25 25.00
94 Chad Cordero/250 8.00
97 Jose Guillen/100 10.00
102 Jack Wilson/100 10.00
106 Melvin Mora/100 10.00
108 Andre Dawson/25 25.00
109 Jody Gerut/250 8.00
116 Aramis Ramirez/25 25.00
128 Ken Harvey/250 8.00
136 Tom Gordon/250 10.00
137 Jake Peavy/100 20.00
139 Dewon Brazelton/250 8.00
140 Jae Weong Seo/100 10.00
141 Danny Kolb/250 12.00
145 Carlos Lee/100 12.00
147 Guillermo Mota/250 8.00
148 Travis Hafner/100 15.00
155 David Wright/25 80.00
156 Brad Penny/250 8.00
157 Francisco Rodriguez/100 15.00
159 Adrian Gonzalez/250 10.00
160 Derrek Lee/25 30.00
162 Carlos Zambrano/25 25.00
163 Bobby Crosby/100 25.00
164 Jermaine Dye/250 10.00
168 Johnny Estrada/200 15.00
169 Milton Bradley/100 15.00
170 Shannon Stewart/50 15.00
173 Laynce Nix/250 10.00
175 Craig Wilson/100 15.00
181 Marcus Giles/25 20.00
182 Randy Wolf/250 12.00
184 Aubrey Huff/100 10.00
185 Billy Ripken/250 8.00
186 Octavio Dotel/250 10.00
189 Todd Walker/100 15.00
191 Alexis Rios/200 10.00
193 Orlando Cabrera/25 20.00
197 Jose Vidro/25 15.00
198 Jacque Jones/100 10.00

Stamps Masterpiece Signature Centenni

No Pricing
Production 1-2

Stamps Material Centennial

NM/M

Production 1-39
1 Pee Wee Reese/Bat/39 20.00
3 Babe Ruth/Jsy/39 275.00
4 George Brett/Jsy/39 40.00
5 Stan Musial/Bat/39 40.00
6 Bob Feller/Pants/39 15.00
7 Cal Ripken Jr./Pants/39 100.00
8 Ted Williams/Jsy/39 100.00
11 Dwight Evans/Jsy/39 25.00
12 Dave Concepcion/Jsy/39 20.00
13 Ernie Banks/Jsy/39 25.00
14 Pedro J. Martinez/Jsy/39 20.00
16 Scott Rolen/Jsy/39 25.00
17 Tony Gwynn/Jsy/39 30.00
18 Mike Schmidt/Jsy/39 60.00
19 Roberto Clemente/Hat/21 200.00
20 Roger Clemens/Jsy/39 35.00
21 Don Mattingly/Jsy/39 50.00
22 Tony Perez/Bat/39 15.00
23 Roger Maris/Jsy/39 75.00
24 Billy Williams/Jsy/39 15.00
25 Juan Marichal/Pants/39 20.00
26 Hank Blalock/Jsy/39 20.00
27 Maury Wills/Jsy/39 15.00
28 Fergie Jenkins/Pants/39 20.00
29 Steve Carlton/Jsy/39 15.00
30 Dale Murphy/Jsy/39 20.00
31 Kerry Wood/Jsy/39 20.00
32 Gaylord Perry/Jsy/39 15.00
33 Fred Lynn/Jsy/39 20.00
34 Tom Seaver/Bat/39 20.00
36 Reggie Jackson/Pants/39 25.00
37 Bob Gibson/Jsy/39 20.00
38 Jack Morris/Jsy/39 20.00
39 Torii Hunter/Jsy/39 15.00
40 Andre Dawson/Jsy/39 20.00
41 Dave Righetti/Jsy/39 15.00
42 Hideki Matsui/Pants/39 65.00
43 Lou Brock/Jkt/39 25.00
44 Yogi Berra/Bat/39 30.00
45 Frankie Frisch/Jkt/39 25.00
46 Sean Casey/Jsy/39 15.00
47 Sammy Sosa/Jsy/39 30.00
48 Ralph Kiner/Bat/39 30.00
49 Hoyt Wilhelm/Jsy/39 15.00
50 Jim Rice/Jsy/39 20.00
51 Duke Snider/Pants/39 25.00
52 Harold Baines/Jsy/39 20.00
53 Willie Stargell/Jsy/39 20.00
54 Johnny Bench/Pants/39 25.00
55 Carlton Fisk/Jsy/39 25.00
56 Jim Palmer/Jsy/39 20.00
57 Bobby Doerr/Jsy/39 20.00
58 Mark Prior/Jsy/39 30.00
60 Lou Boudreau/Jsy/39 25.00
61 Alan Trammell/Bat/39 20.00
62 Al Kaline/Bat/39 25.00
63 Warren Spahn/Pants/39 30.00
64 Bert Blyleven/Jsy/39 20.00
65 Miguel Cabrera/Jsy/39 25.00
66 Luis Tiant/Jsy/39 15.00
67 Harmon Killebrew/Jsy/39 30.00
68 Richie Ashburn/Pants/39 25.00
69 Michael Young/Jsy/39 15.00
70 Tony Oliva/Jsy/39 20.00
71 Mark Mulder/Jsy/39 15.00
72 Nolan Ryan/Jsy/39 75.00
73 Willie McCovey/Jsy/39 25.00
74 Kirk Gibson/Jsy/39 20.00
75 Carl Yastrzemski/Pants/39 40.00

Stamps Material Legendary Fields

NM/M

Production 1-34
1 Pee Wee Reese/Bat/34 30.00
11 Dwight Evans/Jsy/34 25.00
12 Dave Concepcion/Jsy/34 20.00
13 Ernie Banks/Jsy/34 40.00
14 Pedro J. Martinez/Jsy/34 25.00
15 Whitey Ford/Jsy/34 35.00
19 Roberto Clemente/Hat/21 200.00
21 Don Mattingly/Jsy/34 50.00
22 Tony Perez/Bat/34 20.00
23 Roger Maris/Jsy/34 85.00
24 Billy Williams/Jsy/34 30.00
28 Fergie Jenkins/Pants/34 20.00
29 Steve Carlton/Jsy/34 25.00
31 Kerry Wood/Jsy/34 30.00
33 Fred Lynn/Jsy/34 20.00
36 Reggie Jackson/Pants/34 25.00
38 Jack Morris/Jsy/34 25.00
40 Andre Dawson/Jsy/34 20.00
41 Dave Righetti/Jsy/34 20.00
42 Hideki Matsui/Pants/34 80.00
44 Yogi Berra/Bat/34 40.00
47 Sammy Sosa/Jsy/34 40.00
48 Ralph Kiner/Bat/34 20.00
49 Hoyt Wilhelm/Jsy/34 15.00
50 Jim Rice/Jsy/34 20.00
51 Duke Snider/Pants/34 40.00
52 Harold Baines/Jsy/34 15.00
53 Willie Stargell/Jsy/34 30.00
54 Johnny Bench/Pants/34 40.00
55 Carlton Fisk/Jsy/34 25.00
57 Bobby Doerr/Jsy/34 25.00
58 Mark Prior/Jsy/34 40.00
61 Alan Trammell/Bat/34 30.00
62 Al Kaline/Bat/34 40.00
66 Luis Tiant/Jsy/34 25.00
74 Kirk Gibson/Jsy/34 30.00
75 Carl Yastrzemski/Pants/34 50.00

Stamps Material Legendary Players 20

NM/M

Complete Set (2):
19 Roberto Clemente/Hat/21 200.00

Stamps Material Legendary Players 33

NM/M

Complete Set (2):
19 Roberto Clemente/Hat/21 200.00

Stamps Material Olympic

NM/M

Production 1-92
1 Pee Wee Reese/Bat/92 15.00
4 George Brett/Jsy/92 30.00
5 Stan Musial/Bat/92 30.00
6 Bob Feller/Pants/92 15.00
7 Cal Ripken Jr./Pants/92 60.00
11 Dwight Evans/Jsy/24 20.00
13 Ernie Banks/Jsy/92 25.00
14 Pedro J. Martinez/Jsy/45 20.00
16 Scott Rolen/Jsy/27 30.00
17 Tony Gwynn/Jsy/92 30.00
18 Mike Schmidt/Jsy/92 40.00
19 Roberto Clemente/Hat/21 200.00
20 Roger Clemens/Jsy/92 30.00
21 Don Mattingly/Jsy/23 40.00
22 Tony Perez/Bat/24 30.00
24 Billy Williams/Jsy/26 20.00
25 Juan Marichal/Pants/92 15.00
26 Hank Blalock/Jsy/92 15.00
27 Maury Wills/Jsy/30 20.00
28 Fergie Jenkins/Pants/92 15.00
29 Steve Carlton/Jsy/92 15.00
30 Dale Murphy/Jsy/92 20.00
31 Kerry Wood/Jsy/92 20.00
32 Gaylord Perry/Jsy/92 15.00
33 Fred Lynn/Jsy/92 15.00
34 Tom Seaver/Bat/92 20.00
36 Reggie Jackson/Pants/44 20.00
37 Bob Gibson/Jsy/45 25.00
38 Jack Morris/Jsy/92 15.00
39 Torii Hunter/Jsy/48 15.00
41 Dave Righetti/Jsy/92 15.00
42 Hideki Matsui/Pants/92 40.00
43 Lou Brock/Jkt/92 15.00
44 Yogi Berra/Bat/92 25.00
45 Frankie Frisch/Jkt/92 15.00

46 Sean Casey/Jsy/21 25.00
47 Sammy Sosa/Jsy/92 25.00
48 Ralph Kiner/Bat/92 15.00
49 Hoyt Wilhelm/Jsy/92 15.00
50 Jim Rice/Jsy/92 15.00
51 Duke Snider/Pants/92 20.00
52 Harold Baines/Jsy/92 15.00
53 Willie Stargell/Jsy/92 20.00
54 Johnny Bench/Pants/92 20.00
55 Carlton Fisk/Jsy/92 25.00
56 Jim Palmer/Jsy/92 15.00
57 Bobby Doerr/Jsy/92 15.00
58 Mark Prior/Jsy/92 20.00
60 Lou Boudreau/Jsy/92 20.00
61 Alan Trammell/Bat/92 15.00
62 Al Kaline Bat/92 20.00
63 Warren Spahn/Pants/92 25.00
65 Miguel Cabrera/Jsy/92 20.00
66 Luis Tiant/Jsy/23 20.00
67 Harmon Killebrew/Jsy/92 30.00
68 Richie Ashburn/Pants/92 20.00
70 Tony Oliva/Jsy/92 15.00
71 Mark Mulder/Jsy/20 20.00
72 Nolan Ryan/Jsy/30 100.00
73 Willie McCovey/Jsy/92 20.00
74 Kirk Gibson/Jsy/92 15.00
75 Carl Yastrzemski/Pants/92 30.00

Stamps Material Pro Ball

NM/M

Production 1-69
1 Pee Wee Reese/Bat/69 20.00
4 George Brett/Jsy/69 40.00
5 Stan Musial/Bat/69 30.00
6 Bob Feller/Pants/69 20.00
7 Cal Ripken Jr./Pants/69 60.00
11 Dwight Evans/Jsy/24 30.00
13 Ernie Banks/Jsy/69 30.00
14 Pedro J. Martinez/Jsy/45 25.00
16 Scott Rolen/Jsy/27 40.00
17 Tony Gwynn/Jsy/69 35.00
18 Mike Schmidt/Jsy/69 60.00
19 Roberto Clemente/Hat/21 200.00
20 Roger Clemens/Jsy/69 30.00
21 Don Mattingly/Jsy/23 50.00
22 Tony Perez/Bat/24 20.00
24 Billy Williams/Jsy/69 15.00
25 Juan Marichal/Pants/69 15.00
26 Hank Blalock/Jsy/69 15.00
27 Maury Wills/Jsy/69 15.00
28 Fergie Jenkins/Pants/69 20.00
29 Steve Carlton/Jsy/69 15.00
30 Dale Murphy/Jsy/69 15.00
31 Kerry Wood/Jsy/69 20.00
32 Gaylord Perry/Jsy/69 15.00
33 Fred Lynn/Jsy/69 15.00
34 Tom Seaver/Bat/69 20.00
36 Reggie Jackson/Pants/69 15.00
37 Bob Gibson/Jsy/45 25.00
38 Jack Morris/Jsy/69 15.00
39 Torii Hunter/Jsy/48 15.00
40 Andre Dawson/Jsy/69 15.00
41 Dave Righetti/Jsy/69 15.00
42 Hideki Matsui/Pants/69 40.00
43 Lou Brock/Jkt/69 15.00
44 Yogi Berra/Bat/69 25.00
45 Frankie Frisch/Jkt/69 20.00
46 Sean Casey/Jsy/69 15.00
47 Sammy Sosa/Jsy/69 20.00
48 Ralph Kiner/Bat/69 15.00
49 Hoyt Wilhelm/Jsy/69 15.00
50 Jim Rice/Jsy/69 15.00
51 Duke Snider/Pants/69 20.00
52 Harold Baines/Jsy/69 15.00
53 Willie Stargell/Jsy/69 20.00
54 Johnny Bench/Pants/69 20.00
55 Carlton Fisk/Jsy/69 15.00
56 Jim Palmer/Jsy/69 15.00
57 Bobby Doerr/Jsy/69 15.00
58 Mark Prior/Jsy/69 20.00
60 Lou Boudreau/Jsy/69 25.00
61 Alan Trammell/Bat/69 15.00
62 Al Kaline/Bat/69 20.00
63 Warren Spahn/Pants/69 25.00
65 Miguel Cabrera/Jsy/69 15.00
66 Luis Tiant/Jsy/69 15.00
67 Harmon Killebrew/Jsy/69 35.00
68 Richie Ashburn/Pants/69 20.00
69 Michael Young/Jsy/69 15.00
70 Tony Oliva/Jsy/69 20.00
71 Mark Mulder/Jsy/20 25.00
72 Nolan Ryan/Jsy/69 60.00
73 Willie McCovey/Jsy/69 25.00
74 Kirk Gibson/Jsy/69 15.00
75 Carl Yastrzemski/Pants/69 30.00

Stamps Material USA Flag

NM/M

Production 1-100
1 Pee Wee Reese/Bat/100 15.00
4 George Brett/Jsy/100 35.00
5 Stan Musial/Bat/100 25.00
6 Bob Feller/Pants/100 15.00
7 Cal Ripken Jr./Pants/100 65.00
11 Dwight Evans/Jsy/24 30.00
13 Ernie Banks/Jsy/100 30.00
14 Pedro J. Martinez/Jsy/45 25.00
16 Scott Rolen/Jsy/27 40.00
17 Tony Gwynn/Jsy/100 30.00
18 Mike Schmidt/Jsy/100 50.00
19 Roberto Clemente/Hat/21 200.00
20 Roger Clemens/Jsy/100 25.00
21 Don Mattingly/Jsy/100 30.00
22 Tony Perez/Bat/100 15.00
24 Billy Williams/Jsy/100 10.00
25 Juan Marichal/Pants/100 15.00
26 Hank Blalock/Jsy/100 15.00
27 Maury Wills/Jsy/100 10.00
28 Fergie Jenkins/Pants/100 15.00
29 Steve Carlton/Jsy/100 15.00
30 Dale Murphy/Jsy/100 15.00
31 Kerry Wood/Jsy/100 20.00
32 Gaylord Perry/Jsy/100 10.00
33 Fred Lynn/Jsy/100 10.00
34 Tom Seaver/Bat/100 15.00
36 Reggie Jackson/Pants/44 20.00
37 Bob Gibson/Jsy/100 20.00
38 Jack Morris/Jsy/100 10.00
39 Torii Hunter/Jsy/48 15.00
40 Andre Dawson 15.00
41 Dave Righetti/Jsy/100 10.00
42 Hideki Matsui/Pants/100 40.00
43 Lou Brock/Jkt/100 15.00
44 Yogi Berra/Bat/100 20.00
45 Frankie Frisch/Jkt/100 15.00
46 Sean Casey/Jsy/100 10.00
47 Sammy Sosa/Jsy/100 15.00
48 Ralph Kiner/Bat/100 15.00
49 Hoyt Wilhelm/Jsy/100 10.00
50 Jim Rice/Jsy/100 12.00
51 Duke Snider/Pants/100 15.00
52 Harold Baines/Jsy/100 10.00
53 Willie Stargell/Jsy/100 15.00
54 Johnny Bench/Pants/100 20.00
55 Carlton Fisk/Jsy/72 15.00
56 Jim Palmer/Jsy/100 15.00
57 Bobby Doerr/Jsy/100 15.00
58 Mark Prior/Jsy/100 15.00
62 Al Kaline/Bat/100 15.00
63 Warren Spahn/Pants/100 20.00
64 Bert Blyleven/Jsy/28 20.00
65 Miguel Cabrera/Jsy/24 25.00
66 Luis Tiant/Jsy/23 20.00
67 Harmon Killebrew/Jsy/100 30.00
68 Richie Ashburn/Pants/100 15.00
70 Tony Oliva/Jsy/100 15.00
71 Mark Mulder/Jsy/20 25.00
72 Nolan Ryan/Jsy/100 50.00
73 Willie McCovey/Jsy/44 25.00
74 Kirk Gibson/Jsy/100 10.00
75 Carl Yastrzemski/Pants/100 25.00

Stamps Centennial Autograph

NM/M

Production 1-40
2 Red Schoendienst/39 40.00
6 Bob Feller/39 40.00
11 Dwight Evans/39 30.00
15 Whitey Ford/27 50.00
22 Tony Perez/24 40.00
24 Billy Williams/39 30.00
25 Juan Marichal/39 30.00
27 Maury Wills/39 25.00
28 Fergie Jenkins/39 30.00
29 Steve Carlton/39 30.00
30 Dale Murphy/39 50.00
32 Gaylord Perry/39 25.00
33 Fred Lynn/39 30.00
35 Ron Guidry/39 40.00
38 Jack Morris/39 25.00
39 Torii Hunter/39 25.00
40 Andre Dawson/39 30.00
41 Dave Righetti/39 20.00
43 Lou Brock/20 40.00
46 Sean Casey/21 40.00
48 Ralph Kiner/39 30.00
50 Jim Rice/39 35.00
51 Duke Snider/25 50.00
52 Harold Baines/39 25.00
56 Jim Palmer/45 40.00
57 Bobby Doerr/59 30.00
59 Monte Irvin/39 35.00
61 Alan Trammell/40 30.00
62 Al Kaline/39 50.00
64 Bert Blyleven/39 25.00
65 Miguel Cabrera/39 30.00
66 Luis Tiant/39 25.00
69 Michael Young/39 25.00
70 Tony Oliva/39 35.00
71 Mark Mulder/25 40.00

Stamps Legendary Fields Autograph

NM/M

Production 1-34
11 Dwight Evans/34 30.00
22 Tony Perez/34 35.00
24 Billy Williams/34 30.00
28 Fergie Jenkins/34 30.00
29 Steve Carlton/34 30.00
33 Fred Lynn/34 30.00
35 Ron Guidry/34 50.00
38 Jack Morris/34 25.00
40 Andre Dawson/34 30.00
41 Dave Righetti/34 20.00
48 Ralph Kiner/34 30.00
50 Jim Rice/34 35.00
52 Harold Baines/34 25.00
57 Bobby Doerr/34 35.00
59 Monte Irvin/34 35.00
66 Luis Tiant/23 30.00

Stamps Material Centennial Autograph

NM/M

Production 1-39
2 Red Schoendienst/Jsy/39 40.00
6 Bob Feller/Pants/39 40.00
11 Dwight Evans/Jsy/39 30.00
22 Tony Perez/Bat/24 40.00
24 Billy Williams/Jsy/39 35.00
25 Juan Marichal/Pants/39 30.00
27 Maury Wills/Jsy/39 30.00
28 Fergie Jenkins/Pants/39 35.00
29 Steve Carlton/Jsy/39 30.00
30 Dale Murphy/Jsy/39 50.00
32 Gaylord Perry/Jsy/39 30.00
33 Fred Lynn/Jsy/39 30.00
37 Bob Gibson/Jsy/39 40.00
38 Jack Morris/Jsy/39 25.00
40 Andre Dawson/Jsy/39 35.00
43 Lou Brock/Jkt/39 30.00
46 Sean Casey/Jsy/39 30.00
48 Ralph Kiner/Bat/39 30.00
50 Jim Rice/Jsy/39 35.00
51 Duke Snider/Pants/39 50.00
52 Harold Baines/Jsy/39 25.00
56 Jim Palmer/Jsy/22 50.00
57 Bobby Doerr/Jsy/39 35.00
61 Alan Trammell/Bat/39 30.00
62 Al Kaline/Bat/39 50.00
64 Bert Blyleven/Jsy/39 25.00
65 Miguel Cabrera/Jsy/39 50.00
66 Luis Tiant/Jsy/39 30.00
67 Harmon Killebrew/Jsy/39 60.00
70 Tony Oliva/Jsy/39 35.00
71 Mark Mulder/Jsy/20 40.00
74 Kirk Gibson/Jsy/39 30.00

Stamps Material Legendary Fields Autograph

NM/M

Production 1-34
11 Dwight Evans/Jsy/34 30.00
22 Tony Perez/Bat/34 40.00
24 Billy Williams/Jsy/34 30.00
28 Fergie Jenkins/Pants/34 35.00
29 Steve Carlton/Jsy/34 35.00
33 Fred Lynn/Jsy/34 30.00
38 Jack Morris/Jsy/34 30.00
40 Andre Dawson/Jsy/34 30.00
41 Dave Righetti/Jsy/34 20.00
50 Jim Rice/Jsy/33 40.00
66 Luis Tiant/Jsy/23 35.00
74 Kirk Gibson/Jsy/23 30.00

Stamps Material Olympic Autograph

NM/M

Production 1-29
6 Bob Feller/Pants/29 45.00
11 Dwight Evans/Jsy/24 35.00
22 Tony Perez/Bat/29 40.00
24 Billy Williams/Jsy/29 35.00
25 Juan Marichal/Pants/29 35.00
27 Maury Wills/Jsy/29 30.00
28 Fergie Jenkins/Pants/29 35.00
29 Steve Carlton/Jsy/29 35.00
30 Dale Murphy/Jsy/29 50.00
32 Gaylord Perry/Jsy/29 30.00
33 Fred Lynn/Jsy/29 35.00
37 Bob Gibson/Jsy/29 40.00
38 Jack Morris/Jsy/29 30.00
40 Andre Dawson/Jsy/25 35.00
43 Lou Brock/Jkt/20 40.00
46 Sean Casey/Jsy/21 40.00
56 Jim Palmer/Jsy/22 50.00
64 Bert Blyleven/Jsy/28 30.00
65 Miguel Cabrera/Jsy/24 60.00
66 Luis Tiant/Jsy/23 30.00
71 Mark Mulder/Jsy/20 40.00
74 Kirk Gibson/Jsy/23 30.00

Stamps Material Pro Ball Autograph

NM/M

Production 1-69
6 Bob Feller/Pants/69 30.00
11 Dwight Evans/Jsy/24 30.00
22 Tony Perez/Bat/24 40.00
24 Billy Williams/Jsy/26 35.00
25 Juan Marichal/Pants/27 35.00
27 Maury Wills/Jsy/69 20.00
28 Fergie Jenkins/Pants/69 25.00
29 Steve Carlton/Jsy/69 30.00
30 Dale Murphy/Jsy/69 40.00
32 Gaylord Perry/Jsy/69 20.00
33 Fred Lynn/Jsy/69 25.00
37 Bob Gibson/Jsy/45 35.00
43 Lou Brock/Jkt/20 40.00
46 Sean Casey/Jsy/21 40.00
57 Bobby Doerr/Jsy/48 30.00
65 Miguel Cabrera/Jsy/24 50.00
66 Luis Tiant/Jsy/23 30.00
71 Mark Mulder/Jsy/20 40.00
74 Kirk Gibson/Jsy/23 30.00

Stamps Material USA Flag Autograph

NM/M

Production 1-37
2 Red Schoendienst/Jsy/37 40.00
6 Bob Feller/Pants/8 40.00
11 Dwight Evans/Jsy/37 30.00
22 Tony Perez/Bat/37 35.00
24 Billy Williams/Jsy/37 30.00
25 Juan Marichal/Pants/37 30.00
27 Maury Wills/Jsy/37 25.00
28 Fergie Jenkins/Pants/37 30.00
29 Steve Carlton/Jsy/37 30.00
30 Dale Murphy/Jsy/37 50.00
32 Gaylord Perry/Jsy/37 25.00
33 Fred Lynn/Jsy/37 30.00
37 Bob Gibson/Jsy/37 40.00
38 Jack Morris/Jsy/37 25.00
41 Dave Righetti/Jsy/37 20.00
43 Lou Brock/Jkt/37 30.00
46 Sean Casey/Jsy/37 30.00
48 Ralph Kiner/Bat/37 30.00
50 Jim Rice/Jsy/37 30.00
51 Duke Snider/Pants/37 40.00
52 Harold Baines/Jsy/37 25.00
56 Jim Palmer/Jsy/37 35.00
57 Bobby Doerr/Jsy/37 40.00
61 Alan Trammell/Bat/37 30.00
62 Al Kaline/Bat/37 50.00
64 Bert Blyleven/Jsy/37 25.00
65 Miguel Cabrera/Jsy/37 50.00
66 Luis Tiant/Jsy/37 25.00
67 Harmon Killebrew/Jsy/37 60.00
70 Tony Oliva/Jsy/37 35.00
71 Mark Mulder/Jsy/37 30.00
74 Kirk Gibson/Jsy/23 30.00

Stamps Olympic Autograph

NM/M

Production 1-92
2 Red Schoendienst/92 25.00
6 Bob Feller/92 25.00
11 Dwight Evans/92 20.00
22 Tony Perez/24 40.00
24 Billy Williams/26 35.00
25 Juan Marichal/27 35.00
27 Maury Wills/92 20.00
28 Fergie Jenkins/92 25.00
29 Steve Carlton/92 20.00
30 Dale Murphy/92 30.00
32 Gaylord Perry/92 20.00
33 Fred Lynn/92 20.00
35 Ron Guidry/48 35.00
38 Jack Morris/92 20.00
39 Torii Hunter/48 25.00
40 Andre Dawson/92 25.00
46 Sean Casey/21 40.00
50 Jim Rice/92 25.00
52 Harold Baines/92 20.00
56 Jim Palmer/22 50.00
57 Bobby Doerr/92 25.00
59 Monte Irvin/92 40.00
61 Alan Trammell/92 25.00
62 Al Kaline/92 40.00
64 Bert Blyleven/92 20.00
65 Miguel Cabrera/24 60.00
66 Luis Tiant/92 20.00
70 Tony Oliva/91 20.00
71 Mark Mulder/20 40.00

Stamps Pro Ball Autograph

NM/M

Production 1-69
6 Bob Feller/69 30.00
11 Dwight Evans/69 25.00
22 Tony Perez/24 40.00
24 Billy Williams/26 35.00
25 Juan Marichal/27 35.00
27 Maury Wills/69 20.00
28 Fergie Jenkins/69 25.00
29 Steve Carlton/69 30.00
30 Dale Murphy/69 40.00
32 Gaylord Perry/69 20.00
33 Fred Lynn/69 25.00
35 Ron Guidry/49 40.00
38 Jack Morris/47 20.00
39 Torii Hunter/48 25.00
43 Lou Brock/20 40.00
46 Sean Casey/21 40.00
57 Bobby Doerr/69 30.00
59 Monte Irvin/20 40.00
64 Bert Blyleven/28 25.00
65 Miguel Cabrera/24 50.00
66 Luis Tiant/23 30.00
71 Mark Mulder/20 40.00

Stamps USA Flag Autograph

NM/M

Production 1-100
2 Red Schoendienst/100 25.00
6 Bob Feller/100 25.00
11 Dwight Evans/24 35.00
22 Tony Perez/24 40.00
24 Billy Williams/26 35.00
25 Juan Marichal/27 35.00
27 Maury Wills/100 20.00
28 Fergie Jenkins/100 25.00
29 Steve Carlton/100 20.00
30 Dale Murphy/100 30.00
32 Gaylord Perry/100 20.00
33 Fred Lynn/100 20.00
35 Ron Guidry/49 35.00
38 Jack Morris/100 20.00
39 Torii Hunter/48 25.00
40 Andre Dawson/100 25.00
43 Lou Brock/20 40.00
46 Sean Casey/21 40.00
48 Ralph Kiner/100 25.00
51 Duke Snider/25 45.00
52 Harold Baines/100 20.00
56 Jim Palmer/22 50.00
57 Bobby Doerr/100 25.00
59 Monte Irvin/100 40.00
61 Alan Trammell/100 25.00
62 Al Kaline/100 40.00
64 Bert Blyleven/100 20.00
65 Miguel Cabrera/24 60.00

66 Luis Tiant/100 20.00
70 Tony Oliva/100 20.00
71 Mark Mulder/20 40.00

Timeline Threads Jersey Number

NM/M

Production 1-43
6 Orlando Cepeda/Pants/30 10.00
9 Tony Perez/Jsy/24 15.00
11 Tommy John/Jsy/25 15.00
15 Carlton Fisk/Jsy/27 20.00
17 Bert Blyleven/Jsy/28 10.00
20 Lou Brock/Jsy/20 20.00
21 Sammy Sosa/Jsy/21 20.00
22 Roger Clemens/Jsy/22 40.00
23 Don Mattingly/Jsy/23 40.00
24 Rickey Henderson/Jsy/35 15.00
26 Wade Boggs/Jsy/26 20.00
29 Jim "Catfish" Hunter/Jsy/29 15.00
30 Maury Wills/Jsy/30 10.00
31 Hoyt Wilhelm/Jsy/31 10.00
33 Eddie Murray/Pants/33 30.00
34 Nolan Ryan/Pants/34 50.00
35 Phil Niekro/Jsy/35 10.00
38 Curt Schilling/Jsy/38 15.00
40 Sandy Koufax/Jsy/32 500.00
41 Don Sutton/Jsy/20 15.00
42 Randy Johnson/Jsy/51 15.00
43 Dennis Eckersley/Jsy/43 10.00
44 Frank Thomas/Jsy/35 20.00
45 Mike Mussina/Jsy/35 15.00
46 Greg Maddux/Jsy/31 25.00
47 Jim Palmer/Pants/22 15.00
49 Mike Piazza/Jsy/31 25.00

Timeline Threads Position

NM/M

Common Player: 4.00
1 Bobby Doerr/Jsy/39 10.00
2 Burleigh Grimes/Pants/26 50.00
3 Babe Ruth/Pants/30 200.00
4 Joe Cronin/Pants/38 20.00
5 Johnny Bench/Pants/71 15.00
6 Orlando Cepeda/Pants/62 8.00
7 Ivan Rodriguez/Jsy/103 8.00
8 Cal Ripken Jr./Jsy/78 40.00
9 Tony Perez/Jsy/78 8.00
10 Andre Dawson/Jsy/86 8.00
11 Tommy John/Jsy/86 4.00
12 Alfonso Soriano/Jsy/102 8.00
13 Ozzie Smith/Jsy/78 15.00
14 Ernie Banks/Jsy/70 15.00
15 Carlton Fisk/Jsy/80 8.00
16 Bo Jackson/Jsy/89 10.00
17 Bert Blyleven/Jsy/83 4.00
18 Darryl Strawberry/Jsy/88 6.00
19 Bob Feller/Pants/36 8.00
20 Lou Brock/Jsy/74 8.00
21 Sammy Sosa/Jsy/103 12.00
22 Roger Clemens/Jsy/101 15.00
23 Don Mattingly/Jsy/94 20.00
24 Rickey Henderson/Jsy/83 10.00
25 Albert Pujols/Jsy/103 15.00
26 Wade Boggs/Jsy/87 10.00
27 Joe Morgan/Jsy/82 8.00
28 Gary Carter/Jsy/86 8.00
29 Jim "Catfish" Hunter/Jsy/78 6.00
30 Maury Wills/Jsy/65 4.00
31 Hoyt Wilhelm/Jsy/68 4.00
32 Matt Williams/Jsy/95 4.00
33 Eddie Murray/Pants/88 8.00
34 Nolan Ryan/Pants/90 25.00
35 Phil Niekro/Jsy/80 6.00
36 Paul Molitor/Jsy/96 10.00
37 Dale Murphy/Jsy/83 8.00
38 Curt Schilling/Jsy/99 8.00
39 Fred Lynn/Jsy/75 4.00
40 Sandy Koufax/Jsy/64 260.00
41 Don Sutton/Jsy/76 4.00
42 Randy Johnson/Jsy/98 8.00
43 Dennis Eckersley/Jsy/97 6.00
44 Frank Thomas/Jsy/94 8.00
45 Mike Mussina/Jsy/100 6.00
46 Greg Maddux/Jsy/96 10.00
47 Jim Palmer/Pants/76 6.00
48 Harmon Killebrew/Jsy/62 20.00
49 Mike Piazza/Jsy/99 10.00
50 Billy Martin/Jsy/83 15.00

Timeline Threads Number Autograph

Production 1-19
Position Autograph: No Pricing
Production 1-19
Prime: No Pricing
Production One Set

2005 Leaf Certified Materials

NM/M

Complete Set (250):
Common Player: .50
Common Auto. (201-250): 6.00
Production 499 unless noted.
Hobby Pack (5): 10.00
Hobby Box (10): 80.00
1 A.J. Burnett .50
2 Adam Dunn .75
3 Adrian Beltre .75
4 Bret Boone .50
5 Albert Pujols 2.50
6 Alex Rodriguez 2.50

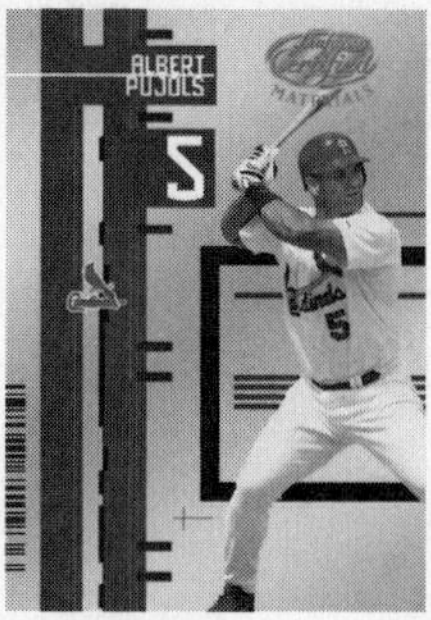

7 Alfonso Soriano 1.00
8 Andruw Jones 1.00
9 Andy Pettitte .75
10 Aramis Ramirez .75
11 Aubrey Huff .50
12 Austin Kearns .50
13 B.J. Upton .50
14 Brandon Webb .50
15 Barry Zito .50
16 Tim Salmon .50
17 Bobby Abreu .50
18 Bobby Crosby .50
19 Brad Penny .50
20 Preston Wilson .50
21 C.C. Sabathia .50
22 Carl Crawford .50
23 Keith Foulke .50
24 Carlos Beltran .75
25 Casey Kotchman .50
26 Chipper Jones 1.00
27 Chone Figgins .50
28 Craig Biggio .75
29 Craig Wilson .50
30 Curt Schilling 1.00
31 Danny Kolb .50
32 David Ortiz 1.00
33 Orlando Hudson .50
34 David Wright 1.50
35 Derek Jeter 2.50
36 Jake Peavy .50
37 Derrek Lee .75
38 Dontrelle Willis .75
39 Edgar Renteria .50
40 Angel Berroa .50
41 Eric Chavez .50
42 Akinori Otsuka .50
43 Francisco Rodriguez .50
44 Garret Anderson .50
45 Gary Sheffield .75
46 Greg Maddux 1.50
47 Hideki Matsui 2.00
48 Hideo Nomo .75
49 Ichiro Suzuki 2.00
50 Ivan Rodriguez .75
51 J.D. Drew .50
52 J.T. Snow .50
53 Jack Wilson .50
54 Jamie Moyer .50
55 Jason Bay .50
56 Jason Giambi .75
57 Trot Nixon .50
58 Jason Schmidt .50
59 Jason Varitek .50
60 Roy Oswalt .50
61 Javy Lopez .50
62 Eric Byrnes .50
63 Jeff Bagwell .75
64 Jeff Kent .50
65 Jeff Suppan .50
66 Jeremy Bonderman .50
67 Jermaine Dye .50
68 Kazuhito Tadano .50
69 Jim Edmonds .75
70 Jim Thome .75
71 Johan Santana 1.00
72 John Smoltz .75
73 Johnny Damon 1.00
74 Johnny Estrada .50
75 Brett Myers .50
76 Jose Guillen .50
77 Jose Vidro .50
78 Josh Beckett .50
79 Edwin Jackson .50
80 Raul Ibanez .50
81 Rich Harden .50
82 Justin Morneau .75
83 Kazuhisa Ishii .50
84 Kazuo Matsui .50
85 Ken Griffey Jr. 1.50
86 Ken Harvey .50
87 Frank Thomas .75
88 Kerry Wood .75
89 Wade Miller .50
90 Kevin Millwood .50
91 Jeremy Affeldt .50
92 Francisco Cordero .50
93 Lance Berkman .50
94 Larry Walker .50
95 Laynce Nix .50
96 Luis Gonzalez .50
97 Lyle Overbay .50
98 Carlos Zambrano .75
99 Manny Ramirez 1.00
100 Marcus Giles .50
101 Mark Buehrle .50
102 Mark Loretta .50
103 Mark Mulder .50
104 Mark Prior 1.00
105 Mark Teixeira .75
106 Marlon Byrd .50
107 Rafael Furcal .50
108 Melvin Mora .50
109 Michael Young .50
110 Miguel Cabrera 1.00
111 Miguel Tejada .75
112 Mike Lowell .50
113 Mike Mussina .75
114 Mike Piazza 1.50
115 Moises Alou .50
116 Livan Hernandez .50
117 Nomar Garciaparra 1.50
118 Omar Vizquel .50
119 Orlando Cabrera .50
120 Pat Burrell .50
121 Paul Konerko .50
122 Paul LoDuca .50
123 Pedro Martinez 1.00
124 Rafael Palmeiro .75
125 Randy Johnson 1.00
126 Richard Hidalgo .50
127 Richie Sexson .50
128 Maggio Ordonez .50
129 Roger Clemens 2.50
130 Russ Ortiz .50
131 Sammy Sosa 1.50
132 Scott Podsednik .50
133 Scott Rolen 1.00
134 Sean Burroughs .50
135 Sean Casey .50
136 Shawn Green .50
137 Jorge Posada .75
138 Roy Halladay .50
139 Steve Finley .50
140 Tim Hudson .75
141 Todd Helton .75
142 Tom Glavine .75
143 Torii Hunter .50
144 Travis Hafner .50
145 Trevor Hoffman .50
146 Troy Glaus .50
147 Vernon Wells .50
148 Victor Martinez .50
149 Vladimir Guerrero 1.00
150 Sammy Sosa 1.50
151 Hank Blalock .75
152 Danny Graves .50
153 Rocco Baldelli .50
154 Carlos Delgado .50
155 Bubba Nelson .50
156 Kevin Youkilis .50
157 Jacque Jones .50
158 Mike Lieberthal .50
159 Ben Sheets .50
160 Lew Ford .50
161 Ervin Santana .50
162 Jody Gerut .50
163 Nick Johnson .50
164 Brian Roberts .50
165 Joe Nathan .50
166 Mike Sweeney .50
167 Ryan Wagner .50
168 David Dellucci .50
169 Jae Weong Seo .50
170 Tom Gordon .50
171 Carlos Lee .50
172 Octavio Dotel .50
173 Jose Castillo .50
174 Troy Percival .50
175 Carlos Delgado .50
176 Curt Schilling 1.00
177 David Ortiz 1.00
178 Greg Maddux 1.50
179 Ivan Rodriguez .75
180 Jeff Kent .50
181 Larry Walker .50
182 Miguel Tejada .75
183 Pedro J. Martinez 1.00
184 Rafael Palmeiro .75
185 Roger Clemens 2.50
186 Shawn Green .50
187 Tim Hudson .75
188 Tom Glavine .75
189 Troy Glaus .50
190 Vladimir Guerrero 1.00
191 Cal Ripken Jr. 4.00
192 Don Mattingly 2.00
193 George Brett 2.00
194 Harmon Killebrew 1.50
195 Mike Schmidt 2.00
196 Nolan Ryan 3.00
197 Stan Musial 2.00
198 Tony Gwynn 1.00
199 Wade Boggs 1.00
200 Willie Mays 2.00
201 Ambiorix Concepcion/Auto. **RC** 10.00
202 Agustin Montero/Auto. **RC** 8.00
203 Carlos Ruiz/Auto. **RC** 10.00
204 Casey Rogowski/Auto. **RC** 6.00
205 Chris Resop/Auto. **RC** 8.00
206 Chris Roberson/Auto. **RC** 6.00
207 Colter Bean **RC** 2.00
208 Danny Rueckel/Auto. **RC** 6.00
209 David Gassner/Auto. **RC** 8.00
210 Devon Lowery/Auto. **RC** 8.00
211 Norihiro Nakamura/Auto./115 **RC** 20.00
212 Erick Threets/Auto./299 **RC** 6.00
213 Garrett Jones/Auto./299 **RC** 8.00
214 Geovany Soto/Auto. **RC** 60.00
215 Jared Gothreaux/Auto./299 **RC** 6.00
216 Jason Hammel/Auto./299 **RC** 10.00
217 Jeff Miller/Auto./299 **RC** 6.00
218 Jeff Niemann/Auto./299 **RC** 20.00
219 Huston Street 2.00
220 John Hattig Jr./Auto. **RC** 6.00
221 Justin Verlander/Auto./299 **RC** 50.00
222 Justin Wechsler/Auto. **RC** 6.00
223 Luke Scott/Auto. **RC** 20.00
224 Mark McLemore/Auto. **RC** 8.00
225 Mark Woodyard/Auto./299 **RC** 6.00
226 Matt Lindstrom/Auto./299 **RC** 8.00
227 Miguel Negron/Auto. **RC** 6.00
228 Mike Morse/Auto. **RC** 10.00
229 Nate McLouth/Auto. **RC** 20.00
230 Paulino Reynoso/Auto./299 **RC** 6.00
231 Philip Humber/Auto./299 **RC** 15.00
232 Tony Pena/Auto. **RC** 6.00
233 Randy Messenger/Auto. **RC** 6.00
234 Raul Tablado/Auto. **RC** 8.00
235 Russel Rohlicek/Auto. **RC** 6.00
236 Ryan Speier/Auto. **RC** 8.00
237 Scott Munter/Auto. **RC** 8.00
238 Sean Thompson/Auto. **RC** 6.00
239 Sean Tracey/Auto./299 **RC** 6.00
240 Marcos Carvajal **RC** 1.50
241 Travis Bowyer/Auto. **RC** 10.00
242 Ubaldo Jimenez/Auto. **RC** 15.00
243 Wladimir Balentien/Auto. **RC** 15.00
244 Eude Brito **RC** 8.00
245 Ambiorix Burgos **RC** 2.00
246 Tadahito Iguchi **RC** 5.00
247 Dae-Sung Koo **RC** 1.00
248 Chris Seddon **RC** 2.00
249 Keiichi Yabu/Auto. **RC** 15.00
250 Yuniesky Betancourt/Auto. **RC** 25.00

Mirror Black

No Pricing
Production One Set

Mirror Blue

Mirror Blue (1-200): 3-6X
Auto. (201-250): .5X
No Auto. (201-250): 1-2X
Production 50 Sets

Mirror Emerald

No Pricing
Production Five Sets

Mirror Gold

Mirror Gold (1-200): 5-10X
Mirror Gold (201-250): No Pricing
Production 25 Sets

Mirror Red

Mirror Red (1-200): 2-4X
Auto. (201-250): .4X
No Auto. (201-250): 1X
Production 100 Sets

Mirror White

Mirror White (1-200): 2-4X
Auto. (201-250): .4X
No Auto. (201-250): 1X
Production 100 Sets

Cuts Blue

NM/M

Production 1-80
3 Willie Mays/26 150.00
7 Jim Palmer/50 25.00
12 Steve Carlton/50 25.00
15 Maury Wills/80 20.00
20 Dale Murphy/50 30.00

Cuts Green

NM/M

Production 3-50
7 Jim Palmer/50 25.00
12 Steve Carlton/50 25.00
15 Maury Wills/80 20.00
20 Dale Murphy/50 30.00

Cuts Red

NM/M

Production 1-60
7 Jim Palmer/50 25.00

12 Steve Carlton/50 25.00
15 Maury Wills/60 20.00
20 Dale Murphy/50 30.00

Cuts Materials Blue

NM/M

Production 4-43
2 Hank Aaron/Bat/43 275.00
3 Willie Mays/Pants/24 175.00
4 Sandy Koufax/Jsy/32 400.00
6 Nolan Ryan/Jsy/34 100.00
9 Rod Carew/Jsy/29 25.00
10 Ryne Sandberg/Jsy/23 120.00
12 Steve Carlton/Pants/32 25.00
14 Mike Schmidt/Jsy/20 65.00
19 Don Mattingly/Jsy/23 75.00

Cuts Materials Green

NM/M

Production 4-32
3 Willie Mays/Pants/24 175.00
9 Rod Carew/Jsy/29 25.00
10 Ryne Sandberg/Jsy/23 120.00
12 Steve Carlton/Pants/32 25.00
14 Mike Schmidt/Jsy/20 65.00

Cuts Materials Red

NM/M

Production 4-32
3 Willie Mays/Pants/24 175.00
9 Rod Carew/Jsy/29 25.00
10 Ryne Sandberg/Jsy/23 120.00
12 Steve Carlton/Pants/32 25.00
14 Mike Schmidt/Jsy/20 65.00

Fabric of the Game

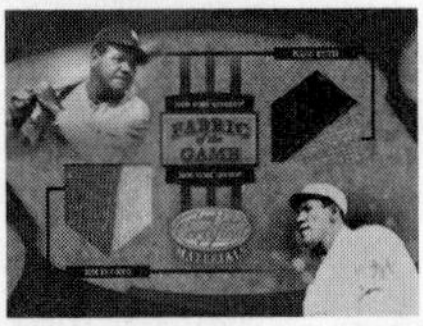

NM/M

Common Player:
Production 5-100
1 Al Oliver/Jsy/50 6.00
2 Alan Trammell/Jsy/100 6.00
3 Andres Galarraga/Jsy/100 4.00
4 Andres Galarraga/Jsy/100 4.00
6 Babe Ruth/Pants/25 240.00
7 Billy Martin/Pants/100 15.00
8 Billy Williams/Jsy/50 6.00
9 Bo Jackson/Jsy/100 10.00
10 Bo Jackson/Jsy/100 10.00
12 Bob Gibson/Jsy/25 12.00
13 Bobby Doerr/Pants/50 10.00
14 Burleigh Grimes/Pants/25 50.00
15 Cal Ripken Jr./Jsy/50 30.00
16 Cal Ripken Jr./Jsy/50 30.00
17 Carl Yastrzemski/Pants/50 15.00
18 Carlton Fisk/Jkt/50 10.00
19 Jim "Catfish" Hunter/Pants/50 8.00
20 Darryl Strawberry/Jsy/25 8.00
21 Darryl Strawberry/Jsy/100 4.00
22 Dave Concepcion/Jsy/50 6.00
23 Dave Righetti/Jsy/50 8.00
24 Dave Winfield/Pants/100 8.00
25 David Cone/Jsy/100 4.00
26 David Justice/Jsy/100 4.00
27 Deion Sanders/Jsy/50 8.00
28 Deion Sanders/Jsy/50 8.00
29 Dennis Eckersley/Jsy/50 8.00
30 Dennis Eckersley/Pants/50 8.00
31 Don Mattingly/Jsy/100 15.00
32 Don Sutton/Jsy/25 8.00
33 Don Sutton/Jsy/50 6.00
37 Dwight Gooden/Jsy/100 6.00
38 Eddie Murray/Jsy/25 15.00
39 Eddie Murray/Pants/50 10.00
40 Edgar Martinez/Jsy/100 4.00
41 Ernie Banks/Jsy/25 15.00
42 Fergie Jenkins/Jsy/50 8.00
43 Frankie Frisch/Jkt/50 20.00
44 Fred Lynn/Jsy/50 4.00
45 Fred McGriff/Jsy/100 6.00
46 Gary Carter/Jsy/50 6.00
47 Gary Carter/Jsy/50 6.00
48 Gaylord Perry/Jsy/50 6.00
49 Gaylord Perry/Jsy/50 6.00
50 George Brett/Jsy/25 20.00
51 Hal Newhouser/Jsy/50 8.00
54 Harmon Killebrew/Jsy/25 15.00
55 Harmon Killebrew/Jsy/50 12.00
56 Harold Baines/Jsy/50 8.00
57 Hoyt Wilhelm/Jsy/100 6.00
58 Jack Morris/Jsy/100 4.00
59 Jim Thorpe/Jsy/25 300.00
60 Jose Cruz/Jsy/100 4.00
61 Jim Rice/Jsy/50 8.00
62 Joe Cronin/Jsy/50 15.00
63 Joe Cronin/Pants/100 15.00
64 Joe Morgan/Jsy/50 8.00
65 Joe Torre/Jsy/50 10.00
66 John Kruk/Jsy/100 10.00
67 Johnny Bench/Jsy/50 10.00
68 Juan Marichal/Pants/100 6.00
71 Kirk Gibson/Jsy/100 4.00
72 Lee Smith/Jsy/100 4.00
73 Lenny Dykstra/Jsy/100 6.00
74 Lou Boudreau/Jsy/25 15.00
75 Luis Aparicio/Jsy/50 6.00
76 Luis Tiant/Pants/100 4.00
77 Mark Grace/Jsy/50 8.00
78 Hoyt Wilhelm/Jsy/100 6.00
79 Matt Williams/Jsy/100 6.00
80 Matt Williams/Jsy/50 6.00
82 Nolan Ryan/Jsy/50 20.00
84 Nolan Ryan/Jsy/25 25.00
85 Nolan Ryan/Jsy/25 25.00
86 Orlando Cepeda/Pants/50 8.00
87 Ozzie Smith/Pants/25 15.00
88 Paul Molitor/Jsy/50 8.00
89 Paul Molitor/Jsy/50 8.00
90 Paul Molitor/Pants/50 8.00
91 Phil Niekro/Jsy/50 8.00
92 Reggie Jackson/Pants/100 8.00
93 Reggie Jackson/Jkt/100 8.00
94 Reggie Jackson/Jsy/50 8.00
95 Reggie Jackson/Jsy/50 8.00
96 Rickey Henderson/Jkt/100 10.00
97 Rickey Henderson/Jsy/50 10.00
98 Rickey Henderson/Jsy/50 10.00
99 Rickey Henderson/Jsy/50 10.00
100 Rickey Henderson/Jsy/50 10.00
101 Rickey Henderson/Pants/50 10.00
102 Robin Ventura/Jsy/100 6.00
103 Robin Ventura/Jsy/100 6.00
104 Robin Yount/Jsy/50 12.00
105 Rod Carew/Jsy/100 8.00
106 Rod Carew/Jsy/100 8.00
107 Roger Maris/Pants/50 40.00
108 Ron Cey/Jsy/50 8.00
109 Ron Guidry/Pants/100 6.00
110 Ryne Sandberg/Jsy/50 15.00
111 Sandy Koufax/Jsy/25 180.00
112 Stan Musial/Jsy/25 25.00
113 Stan Musial/Pants/25 25.00
114 Steve Garvey/Jsy/100 6.00
115 Ted Williams/Jkt/50 50.00
116 Ted Williams/Jsy/25 50.00
117 Tom Seaver/Jsy/50 10.00
118 Tom Seaver/Pants/50 10.00
119 Tommy John/Jsy/100 4.00
120 Tommy John/Pants/100 4.00
121 Tommy Lasorda/Jsy/100 6.00
122 Tony Gwynn/Jsy/100 10.00
123 Tony Gwynn/Pants/100 10.00
124 Tony Perez/Jsy/50 8.00
125 Wade Boggs/Jsy/100 8.00
126 Warren Spahn/Jsy/25 15.00
127 Whitey Ford/Jsy/25 15.00
128 Will Clark/Jsy/50 8.00
129 Willie Mays/Pants/50 40.00
130 Willie McCovey/Pants/100 10.00
131 Roger Clemens/Jsy/50 15.00
132 Roger Clemens/Jsy/50 15.00
133 Roger Clemens/Jsy/50 15.00
134 Randy Johnson/Jsy/50 8.00
135 Randy Johnson/Jsy/50 8.00
136 Cal Ripken Jr./Jsy/50 30.00
137 Don Mattingly/Jsy/100 15.00
138 George Brett/Jsy/25 20.00
139 Harmon Killebrew/Jsy/25 15.00
140 Mike Schmidt/Jsy/50 20.00
141 Nolan Ryan/Jkt/25 25.00
143 Tony Gwynn/Jsy/100 10.00
144 Wade Boggs/Jsy/50 10.00
145 Willie Mays/Jsy/25 50.00
146 Hideo Nomo/Jsy/100 10.00
147 Dale Murphy/Jsy/100 10.00
148 Dale Murphy/Jsy/100 10.00
149 Bo Jackson/Jsy/50 12.00
150 Darryl Strawberry/Jsy/50 6.00
151 Deion Sanders/Jsy/50 8.00
152 Deion Sanders/Pants/50 8.00
153 Dennis Eckersley/Jsy/50 8.00
154 Dwight Gooden/Jsy/100 6.00
155 Edgar Martinez/Jsy/100 4.00
156 Lou Brock/Jsy/50 8.00
157 Steve Carlton/Pants/50 6.00
158 Albert Pujols/Jsy/50 20.00
159 Tom Glavine/Jsy/100 8.00
160 Hideki Matsui/Pants/50 20.00
161 Babe Ruth/Pants, Jim Thorpe/Jsy/25 500.00
162 Ted Williams/Jkt, Bob Gibson/Jsy/50 50.00
164 Whitey Ford/Jsy, Sandy Koufax/Jsy/25 150.00
165 Roger Maris/Pants, Don Mattingly/Jsy/25 50.00
166 Nolan Ryan/Jsy, Tom Seaver/Jsy/50 25.00
167 Cal Ripken Jr./Jsy, George Brett/Jsy/100 40.00
168 Ryne Sandberg/Jsy, Mike Schmidt/Jsy/50 30.00
169 Tony Gwynn/Jsy, Wade Boggs/Jsy/50 15.00
170 Carlton Fisk/Jsy, Johnny Bench/Pants/50 15.00
172 Reggie Jackson/Pants, Darryl Strawberry/Jsy/50 10.00
173 Robin Yount/Jsy, Paul Molitor/Jsy/50 20.00
174 Warren Spahn/Pants, Juan Marichal/Jsy/50 15.00
175 Bo Jackson/Jsy, Deion Sanders/Pants/100 15.00
176 Tony Gwynn/Jsy, Rickey Henderson/Jsy/100 15.00
177 Hideki Matsui/Jsy, Jim Edmonds/Jsy/100 20.00
178 Rickey Henderson/Pants, Lou Brock/Jsy/100 15.00
179 Roger Clemens/Jsy, Albert Pujols/Jsy/100 25.00
180 Hideo Nomo/Jsy, Kazuhisa Ishii/Jsy/100 12.00

Fabric of the Game Auto.

No Pricing
Production One Set

Fabric of the Game Reward

NM/M

Production 3-50
1 Al Oliver/Jsy/50 6.00
2 Alan Trammell/Jsy/50 8.00
3 Andres Galarraga/Jsy/50 6.00
4 Andres Galarraga/Jsy/50 6.00
7 Billy Martin/Pants/50 15.00
9 Bo Jackson/Jsy/50 12.00
10 Bo Jackson/Jsy/50 12.00
13 Bobby Doerr/Pants/25 12.00
17 Carl Yastrzemski/Pants/25 15.00
19 Jim "Catfish" Hunter/Pants/50 8.00
21 Darryl Strawberry/Jsy/50 6.00
23 Dave Righetti/Jsy/25 8.00
44 Fred Lynn/Jsy/50 4.00
45 Fred McGriff/Jsy/5
46 Gary Carter/Jsy/50 6.00
47 Gary Carter/Jsy/25 8.00
48 Gaylord Perry/Jsy/50 6.00
49 Gaylord Perry/Jsy/25 8.00
51 Hal Newhouser/Jsy/25 8.00
58 Jack Morris/Jsy/50 6.00
61 Jim Rice/Jsy/50 8.00
62 Joe Cronin/Jsy/25 20.00
63 Joe Cronin/Pants/25 20.00
64 Joe Morgan/Jsy/25 10.00
66 John Kruk/Jsy/50 10.00
68 Juan Marichal/Pants/25 10.00
71 Kirk Gibson/Jsy/25 8.00
72 Lee Smith/Jsy/50 4.00
75 Luis Aparicio/Jsy/25 8.00
76 Luis Tiant/Pants/25 6.00
78 Hoyt Wilhelm/Jsy/25 10.00
79 Matt Williams/Jsy/25 8.00
82 Nolan Ryan/Jsy/25 25.00
85 Nolan Ryan/Jsy/25 25.00
86 Orlando Cepeda/Pants/25 10.00
87 Ozzie Smith/Pants/25 15.00
88 Paul Molitor/Jsy/50 8.00
89 Paul Molitor/Jsy/50 8.00
90 Paul Molitor/Pants/25 10.00
91 Phil Niekro/Jsy/25 8.00
92 Reggie Jackson/Pants/50 10.00
93 Reggie Jackson/Jkt/25 10.00
95 Reggie Jackson/Js/25 10.00
96 Rickey Henderson/Jkt/50 10.00
97 Rickey Henderson/Jsy/50 10.00
99 Rickey Henderson/Jsy/25 12.00
102 Robin Ventura/Jsy/50 6.00
103 Robin Ventura/Jsy/50 6.00
104 Robin Yount/Jsy/50 12.00
105 Rod Carew/Jsy/25 10.00
106 Rod Carew/Jsy/50 10.00
108 Ron Cey/Jsy/50 8.00
109 Ron Guidry/Pants/50 8.00
110 Ryne Sandberg/Jsy/50 15.00
111 Sandy Koufax/Jsy/25 180.00
113 Stan Musial/Pants/25 25.00
114 Steve Garvey/Jsy/25 8.00
115 Ted Williams/Jkt/25 50.00
118 Tom Seaver/Pants/50 10.00
119 Tommy John/Jsy/50 4.00
120 Tommy John/Pants/50 4.00
121 Tommy Lasorda/Jsy/50 6.00
122 Tony Gwynn/Jsy/50 10.00
123 Tony Gwynn/Pants/50 10.00
124 Tony Perez/Jsy/50 8.00
125 Wade Boggs/Jsy/50 10.00
126 Warren Spahn/Pants/50 12.00
128 Will Clark/Jsy/50 8.00
129 Willie Mays/Pants/25 50.00
130 Willie McCovey/Pants/50 10.00
131 Roger Clemens/Jsy/25 20.00
132 Roger Clemens/Jsy/50 15.00
133 Roger Clemens/Jsy/50 15.00
134 Randy Johnson/Jsy/50 10.00
135 Randy Johnson/Jsy/50 10.00
136 Cal Ripken Jr./Jsy/50 30.00
137 Don Mattingly/Jsy/50 15.00
138 George Brett/Jsy/25 20.00
139 Harmon Killebrew/Jsy/25 15.00
140 Mike Schmidt/Jsy/25 20.00
143 Tony Gwynn/Jsy/50 10.00
144 Wade Boggs/Jsy/25 10.00
145 Willie Mays/Jsy/25 50.00
146 Hideo Nomo/Jsy/50 10.00
147 Dale Murphy/Jsy/50 10.00
148 Dale Murphy/Jsy/50 10.00
150 Darryl Strawberry/Jsy/50 6.00
151 Deion Sanders/Jsy/50 8.00
152 Deion Sanders/Pants/50 8.00
153 Dennis Eckersley/Jsy/50 8.00
154 Dwight Gooden/Jsy/50 6.00
155 Edgar Martinez/Jsy/50 4.00
156 Lou Brock/Jsy/50 8.00
157 Steve Carlton/Pants/50 6.00
158 Albert Pujols/Jsy/50 20.00
159 Tom Glavine/Jsy/50 8.00
160 Hideki Matsui/Pants/50 20.00
161 Babe Ruth/Pants, Jim Thorpe/Jsy/25 500.00
162 Ted Williams/Jkt, Stan Musial/Jsy/25 50.00
163 Willie Mays/Jsy, Bob Gibson/Jsy/25 50.00
164 Whitey Ford/Jsy, Sandy Koufax/Jsy/25 150.00
165 Roger Maris/Pants, Don Mattingly/Jsy/25 50.00
166 Nolan Ryan/Jsy, Tom Seaver/Jsy/50 25.00
167 Cal Ripken Jr./Jsy, George Brett/Jsy/50 40.00
168 Ryne Sandberg/Jsy, Mike Schmidt/Jsy/50 30.00
169 Tony Gwynn/Jsy, Wade Boggs/Jsy/50 15.00
170 Carlton Fisk/Jsy, Johnny Bench/Pants/25 20.00
172 Reggie Jackson/Pants, Darryl Strawberry/Jsy/50 10.00
173 Robin Yount/Jsy, Paul Molitor/Jsy/25 20.00
174 Warren Spahn/Pants, Juan Marichal/Jsy/25 20.00
175 Bo Jackson/Jsy, Deion Sanders/Pants/50 15.00
176 Tony Gwynn/Jsy, Rickey Henderson/Jsy/50 20.00
177 Hideki Matsui/Jsy, Jim Edmonds/Jsy/50 20.00
178 Rickey Henderson/Pants, Lou Brock/Jsy/50 20.00
179 Roger Clemens/Jsy, Albert Pujols/Jsy/50 25.00
180 Hideo Nomo/Jsy, Kazuhisa Ishii/Jsy/50 15.00

Fabric of the Game Stats

NM/M

Production 3-75
1 Al Oliver/Jsy/75 6.00
3 Andres Galarraga/Jsy/75 6.00
4 Andres Galarraga/Jsy/75 6.00
7 Billy Martin/Pants/75 15.00
8 Billy Williams/Jsy/75 6.00
9 Bo Jackson/Jsy/75 10.00
10 Bo Jackson/Jsy/75 10.00
13 Bobby Doerr/Jsy/25 12.00
14 Burleigh Grimes/Pants/25 50.00
15 Cal Ripken Jr./Jsy/75 30.00
16 Cal Ripken Jr./Jsy/75 30.00
17 Carl Yastrzemski/Pants/25 15.00
18 Carlton Fisk/Jkt/75 10.00
19 Jim "Catfish" Hunter/Pants/75 8.00
21 Darryl Strawberry/Jsy/75 6.00
22 Dave Concepcion/Jsy/75 4.00
23 Dave Righetti/Jsy/25 8.00
24 Dave Winfield/Pants/75 8.00
25 David Cone/Jsy/75 4.00
26 David Justice/Jsy/75 4.00
27 Deion Sanders/Jsy/75 8.00
28 Deion Sanders/Jsy/75 8.00
29 Dennis Eckersley/Jsy/75 8.00
30 Dennis Eckersley/Pants/75 8.00
39 Eddie Murray/Pants/75 12.00
40 Edgar Martinez/Jsy/75 4.00
43 Frankie Frisch/Jkt/75 15.00
44 Fred Lynn/Jsy/50 4.00
45 Fred McGriff/Jsy/75 6.00
46 Gary Carter/Jsy/50 6.00
47 Gary Carter/Jsy/25 8.00
48 Gaylord Perry/Jsy/50 6.00
49 Gaylord Perry/Jsy/25 8.00
51 Hal Newhouser/Jsy/25 10.00
54 Harmon Killebrew/Jsy/25 15.00
55 Harmon Killebrew/Jsy/50 12.00
56 Harold Baines/Jsy/50 8.00
57 Hoyt Wilhelm/Jsy/50 6.00
62 Joe Cronin/Jsy/25 20.00
63 Joe Cronin/Pants/25 20.00
64 Joe Morgan/Jsy/25 10.00
66 John Kruk/Jsy/75 10.00
71 Kirk Gibson/Jsy/25 8.00
72 Lee Smith/Jsy/75 4.00
73 Lenny Dykstra/Jsy/75 6.00
75 Luis Aparicio/Jsy/25 8.00
76 Luis Tiant/Pants/25 6.00
78 Hoyt Wilhelm/Jsy/25 10.00
79 Matt Williams/Jsy/25 8.00
82 Nolan Ryan/Jsy/25 25.00
85 Nolan Ryan/Jsy/25 25.00
86 Orlando Cepeda/Pants/25 10.00
87 Ozzie Smith/Pants/25 15.00
88 Paul Molitor/Jsy/50 8.00
89 Paul Molitor/Jsy/50 8.00
90 Paul Molitor/Pants/25 10.00
91 Phil Niekro/Jsy/25 8.00
92 Reggie Jackson/Pants/50 10.00
93 Reggie Jackson/Jkt/25 10.00
94 Reggie Jackson/Jsy/75 10.00
95 Reggie Jackson/Jsy/50 10.00
96 Rickey Henderson/Jkt/75 10.00
97 Rickey Henderson/Jsy/75 10.00
98 Rickey Henderson/Jsy/50 10.00
101 Rickey Henderson/Pants/75 10.00
102 Robin Ventura/Jsy/50 6.00
103 Robin Ventura/Jsy/50 6.00
104 Robin Yount/Jsy/50 12.00
105 Rod Carew/Jsy/25 10.00
106 Rod Carew/Jsy/75 8.00
107 Roger Maris/Pants/50 40.00

108 Ron Cey/Jsy/50 8.00
109 Ron Guidry/Pants/50 8.00
111 Sandy Koufax/Jsy/25 180.00
113 Stan Musial/Pants/25 25.00
114 Steve Garvey/Jsy/25 8.00
115 Ted Williams/Jkt/25 50.00
117 Tom Seaver/Jsy/75 10.00
118 Tom Seaver/Pants/50 10.00
119 Tommy John/Jsy/25 6.00
120 Tommy John/Pants/25 6.00
121 Tommy Lasorda/Jsy/75 6.00
124 Tony Perez/Jsy/75 8.00
125 Wade Boggs/Jsy/75 10.00
126 Warren Spahn/Pants/75 12.00
128 Will Clark/Jsy/50 8.00
129 Willie Mays/Pants/25 50.00
130 Willie McCovey/Pants/75 10.00
131 Roger Clemens/Jsy/25 20.00
140 Mike Schmidt/Jsy/25 20.00
144 Wade Boggs/Jsy/50 10.00
145 Willie Mays/Jsy/25 25.00
146 Hideo Nomo/Jsy/75 10.00
147 Dale Murphy/Jsy/25 10.00
148 Dale Murphy/Jsy/75 10.00
153 Dennis Eckersley/Jsy/75 8.00
154 Dwight Gooden/Jsy/75 6.00
155 Edgar Martinez/Jsy/75 4.00
156 Lou Brock/Jsy/75 8.00
157 Steve Carlton/Pants/75 6.00
159 Tom Glavine/Jsy/75 8.00
160 Hideki Matsui/Pants/75 20.00
161 Babe Ruth/Pants, Jim Thorpe/Jsy/25 500.00
162 Ted Williams/Jkt, Stan Musial/Jsy/25 50.00
163 Willie Mays/Jsy, Bob Gibson/Jsy/25 50.00
164 Whitey Ford/Jsy, Sandy Koufax/Jsy/25 150.00
165 Roger Maris/Pants, Don Mattingly/Jsy/25 50.00
166 Nolan Ryan/Jsy, Tom Seaver/Jsy/50 25.00
167 Cal Ripken Jr./Jsy, George Brett/Jsy/50 40.00
168 Ryne Sandberg/Jsy, Mike Schmidt/Jsy/50 30.00
169 Tony Gwynn/Jsy, Wade Boggs/Jsy/50 15.00
170 Carlton Fisk/Jsy, Johnny Bench/Pants/25 20.00
172 Reggie Jackson/Pants, Darryl Strawberry/Jsy/50 10.00
173 Robin Yount/Jsy, Paul Molitor/Jsy/25 20.00
174 Warren Spahn/Pants, Juan Marichal/Jsy/25 20.00
175 Bo Jackson/Jsy, Deion Sanders/Pants/50 15.00
176 Tony Gwynn/Jsy, Rickey Henderson/Jsy/50 20.00
177 Hideki Matsui/Jsy, Jim Edmonds/Jsy/50 20.00
178 Rickey Henderson/Pants, Lou Brock/Jsy/50 20.00
179 Roger Clemens/Jsy, Albert Pujols/Jsy/50 25.00
180 Hideo Nomo/Jsy, Kazuhisa Ishii/Jsy/50 15.00

Gold Team

NM/M

Complete Set (25):
Common Player: 1.00
Inserted 1:7
Mirror: 2-3X

1 Albert Pujols 4.00
2 Alex Rodriguez 3.00
3 Carlos Beltran 1.00
4 Chipper Jones 1.50
5 Curt Schilling 1.50
6 Derek Jeter 4.00
7 Greg Maddux 2.50
8 Hank Blalock 1.00
9 Ichiro Suzuki 3.00
10 Ivan Rodriguez 1.00
11 Jim Thome 1.00
12 Ken Griffey Jr. 3.00
13 Lyle Overbay 1.00
14 Manny Ramirez 1.50
15 Mark Mulder 1.00
16 Mark Prior 1.50
17 Michael Young 1.00
18 Miguel Cabrera 1.50
19 Mike Piazza 2.00
20 Pedro Martinez 1.50
21 Randy Johnson 1.50
22 Roger Clemens 4.00
23 Sammy Sosa 2.00
24 Tim Hudson 1.00
25 Todd Helton 1.50

Gold Team Autograph

No Pricing
Production 5-10

Gold Team Jersey Number

NM/M

Production 100-250
1 Albert Pujols/100 20.00
3 Carlos Beltran/200 5.00
4 Chipper Jones/100 8.00
5 Curt Schilling/250 8.00
7 Greg Maddux/100 10.00
8 Hank Blalock/250 4.00
10 Ivan Rodriguez/120 6.00
11 Jim Thome/250 6.00
13 Lyle Overbay/250 4.00
14 Manny Ramirez/250 8.00
15 Mark Mulder/250 4.00
16 Mark Prior/100 4.00
17 Michael Young/250 4.00
18 Miguel Cabrera/100 8.00
19 Mike Piazza/250 10.00
20 Pedro Martinez/100 8.00
21 Randy Johnson/250 8.00
22 Roger Clemens/250 10.00
23 Sammy Sosa/250 8.00
24 Tim Hudson/100 4.00
25 Todd Helton/100 6.00

Mirror Autograph Blue

NM/M

Production 1-100
Black: No Pricing
Production One Set
Emerald: No Pricing
Production 1-5
18 Bobby Crosby/25 25.00
25 Casey Kotchman/25 15.00
33 Orlando Hudson/100 10.00
53 Jack Wilson/25 15.00
62 Eric Byrnes/25 12.00
66 Jeremy Bonderman/25 20.00
67 Jermaine Dye/25 15.00
68 Kazuhito Tadano/50 15.00
79 Edwin Jackson/100 8.00
80 Raul Ibanez/25 15.00
86 Ken Harvey/100 8.00
89 Wade Miller/100 10.00
91 Jeremy Affeldt/100 8.00
95 Laynce Nix/50 10.00
106 Marlon Byrd/100 8.00
155 Bubba Nelson/100 8.00
156 Kevin Youkilis/25 25.00
160 Lew Ford/25 15.00
161 Ervin Santana/100 10.00
165 Joe Nathan/25 20.00
167 Ryan Wagner/25 10.00
168 David Dellucci/25 20.00
169 Jae Weong Seo/25 15.00
173 Jose Castillo/100 10.00
223 Luke Scott/49 30.00
229 Nate McLouth/49 20.00
234 Raul Tablado/49 10.00
243 Wladimir Balentien/49 15.00

Mirror Autograph Gold

NM/M

Production 1-25
2 Adam Dunn/25 35.00
11 Aubrey Huff/25 15.00
12 Austin Kearns/25 10.00
13 B.J. Upton/25 15.00
14 Brandon Webb/25 15.00
16 Tim Salmon/25 30.00
18 Bobby Crosby/25 25.00
19 Brad Penny/25 15.00
21 C.C. Sabathia/25 15.00
23 Keith Foulke/25 25.00
25 Casey Kotchman/25 15.00
27 Chone Figgins/25 12.00
29 Craig Wilson/25 10.00
31 Danny Kolb/25 10.00
33 Orlando Hudson/25 10.00
34 David Wright/25 70.00
36 Jake Peavy/25 35.00
37 Derrek Lee/25 40.00
39 Edgar Renteria/25 20.00
40 Angel Berroa/25 10.00
41 Eric Chavez/25 20.00
42 Akinori Otsuka/25 25.00
43 Francisco Rodriguez/25 25.00
44 Garret Anderson/25 20.00
53 Jack Wilson/25 15.00
54 Jamie Moyer/25 15.00
55 Jason Bay/25 25.00
57 Trot Nixon/25 20.00
60 Roy Oswalt/25 25.00
62 Eric Byrnes/25 12.00
63 Jeff Bagwell/25 40.00
65 Jeff Suppan/25 15.00
66 Jeremy Bonderman/25 20.00
67 Jermaine Dye/25 15.00
68 Kazuhito Tadano/25 15.00
75 Brett Myers/25 20.00
76 Jose Guillen/25 15.00
77 Jose Vidro/25 15.00
79 Edwin Jackson/25 10.00
80 Raul Ibanez/25 15.00
81 Rich Harden/25 20.00
86 Ken Harvey/25 10.00
89 Wade Miller/25 15.00
91 Jeremy Affeldt/25 12.00
92 Francisco Cordero/25 15.00
95 Laynce Nix/25 12.00
97 Lyle Overbay/25 15.00
98 Carlos Zambrano/25 30.00
101 Mark Buehrle/25 25.00
102 Mark Loretta/25 15.00
106 Marlon Byrd/25 10.00
107 Rafael Furcal/25 25.00
109 Michael Young/25 25.00
110 Miguel Cabrera/25 40.00
128 Magglio Ordonez/25 15.00
134 Sean Burroughs/25 10.00
135 Sean Casey/25 15.00
139 Steve Finley/25 15.00
143 Torii Hunter/25 20.00
144 Travis Hafner/25 20.00
147 Vernon Wells/25 15.00
152 Danny Graves/25 12.00
155 Bubba Nelson/25 10.00
156 Kevin Youkilis/25 25.00
157 Jacque Jones/25 15.00
158 Mike Lieberthal/25 15.00
160 Lew Ford/25 15.00
161 Ervin Santana/25 15.00
162 Jody Gerut/25 15.00
163 Nick Johnson/25 20.00
164 Brian Roberts/25 30.00
165 Joe Nathan/25 20.00
167 Ryan Wagner/25 10.00
168 David Dellucci/25 20.00
169 Jae Weong Seo/25 15.00
170 Tom Gordon/25 15.00
171 Carlos Lee/25 20.00
172 Octavio Dotel/25 12.00
173 Jose Castillo/25 15.00
174 Troy Percival/25 15.00
194 Harmon Killebrew/25 40.00

Mirror Autograph Red

NM/M

Production 1-250
16 Tim Salmon/25 30.00
18 Bobby Crosby/50 25.00
25 Casey Kotchman/50 12.00
33 Orlando Hudson/250 8.00
53 Jack Wilson/50 12.00
62 Eric Byrnes/50 10.00
66 Jeremy Bonderman/50 15.00
67 Jermaine Dye/50 15.00
68 Kazuhito Tadano/100 12.00
79 Edwin Jackson/250 8.00
80 Raul Ibanez/50 12.00
86 Ken Harvey/250 8.00
89 Wade Miller/250 10.00
91 Jeremy Affeldt/250 8.00
92 Francisco Cordero/25 15.00
95 Laynce Nix/100 8.00
106 Marlon Byrd/250 8.00
155 Bubba Nelson/250 6.00
156 Kevin Youkilis/50 20.00
160 Lew Ford/50 12.00
161 Ervin Santana/250 10.00
162 Jody Gerut/50 15.00
164 Brian Roberts/25 30.00
165 Joe Nathan/50 15.00
167 Ryan Wagner/50 10.00
168 David Dellucci/50 15.00
169 Jae Weong Seo/25 15.00
173 Jose Castillo/250 10.00
202 Agustin Montero/99 10.00
211 Norihiro Nakamura/99 50.00
212 Erick Threets/49 10.00
218 Jeff Niemann/49 25.00
221 Justin Verlander/49 40.00
223 Luke Scott/99 30.00
229 Nate McLouth/25 20.00
230 Paulino Reynoso/49 10.00
231 Philip Humber/49 25.00
234 Raul Tablado/99 12.00
239 Sean Tracey/49 10.00
243 Wladimir Balentien/99 10.00

Mirror Autograph White

NM/M

Production 1-50
18 Bobby Crosby/25 25.00
19 Brad Penny/25 15.00
25 Casey Kotchman/25 15.00
33 Orlando Hudson/50 8.00
53 Jack Wilson/25 15.00
62 Eric Byrnes/25 12.00
67 Jermaine Dye/25 15.00
68 Kazuhito Tadano/50 15.00
79 Edwin Jackson/25 10.00
80 Raul Ibanez/25 15.00
81 Rich Harden/50 15.00
86 Ken Harvey/50 8.00
89 Wade Miller/50 12.00
91 Jeremy Affeldt/50 10.00
95 Laynce Nix/50 10.00
106 Marlon Byrd/50 8.00
155 Bubba Nelson/50 8.00
156 Kevin Youkilis/25 25.00
160 Lew Ford/25 15.00
161 Ervin Santana/50 12.00
162 Jody Gerut/25 15.00
165 Joe Nathan/25 20.00
167 Ryan Wagner/25 10.00
168 David Dellucci/25 20.00
173 Jose Castillo/50 12.00
202 Agustin Montero/49 12.00
211 Norihiro Nakamura/49 60.00
212 Erick Threets/49 10.00
218 Jeff Niemann/49 25.00
221 Justin Verlander/49 40.00
223 Luke Scott/49 40.00
229 Nate McLouth/49 25.00
230 Paulino Reynoso/49 10.00
231 Philip Humber/49 25.00
234 Raul Tablado/49 15.00
239 Sean Tracey/49 10.00
243 Wladimir Balentien/49 15.00

Mirror Bat Blue

NM/M

Production 75-100
Black: No Pricing
Production One Set
Emerald: No Pricing
Production Five Sets
2 Adam Dunn/100 6.00
5 Albert Pujols/100 20.00
8 Andruw Jones/100 8.00
11 Aubrey Huff/100 4.00
13 B.J. Upton/100 6.00
14 Brandon Webb/100 4.00
16 Tim Salmon/100 4.00
25 Casey Kotchman/100 4.00
26 Chipper Jones/100 8.00
32 David Ortiz/100 10.00
37 Derrek Lee/100 8.00
38 Dontrelle Willis/100 6.00
44 Garret Anderson/100 4.00
45 Gary Sheffield/100 6.00
59 Jason Varitek/100 8.00
61 Javy Lopez/100 4.00
63 Jeff Bagwell/100 6.00
77 Jose Vidro/100 4.00
93 Lance Berkman/100 4.00
99 Manny Ramirez/100 8.00
105 Mark Teixeira/100 6.00
109 Michael Young/100 4.00
110 Miguel Cabrera/5 8.00
111 Miguel Tejada/100 8.00
117 Nomar Garciaparra/100 8.00
121 Paul Konerko/100 4.00
124 Rafael Palmeiro/100 6.00
128 Magglio Ordonez/100 4.00
136 Shawn Green/100 4.00
141 Todd Helton/100 6.00
142 Tom Glavine/100 4.00
143 Torii Hunter/100 4.00
144 Travis Hafner/100 4.00
148 Victor Martinez/100 4.00
149 Vladimir Guerrero/100 8.00
150 Sammy Sosa/100 8.00
153 Rocco Baldelli/100 4.00
160 Lew Ford/100 4.00
166 Mike Sweeney/75 4.00
184 Rafael Palmeiro/100 6.00
188 Tom Glavine/100 4.00
190 Vladimir Guerrero/100 8.00

Mirror Bat Red

NM/M

Production 100-250
Gold: 1-2X
Production 25 Sets
2 Adam Dunn/250 6.00
5 Albert Pujols/250 15.00
8 Andruw Jones/250 6.00
11 Aubrey Huff/250 4.00
13 B.J. Upton/250 4.00
14 Brandon Webb/100 4.00
16 Tim Salmon/250 4.00
25 Casey Kotchman/250 4.00
26 Chipper Jones/250 6.00
28 Craig Biggio/50 6.00
29 Craig Wilson/250 4.00
34 David Wright/250 10.00
38 Dontrelle Willis/250 4.00
44 Garret Anderson/250 4.00
45 Gary Sheffield/250 6.00
59 Jason Varitek/250 6.00
61 Javy Lopez/250 4.00
63 Jeff Bagwell/250 6.00
77 Jose Vidro/250 4.00
93 Lance Berkman/250 4.00
99 Manny Ramirez/250 8.00
105 Mark Teixeira/250 6.00
109 Michael Young/250 4.00
110 Miguel Cabrera/250 8.00
111 Miguel Tejada/250 8.00
121 Paul Konerko/250 4.00
124 Rafael Palmeiro/250 6.00
128 Magglio Ordonez/250 4.00
136 Shawn Green/250 4.00
141 Todd Helton/250 6.00
142 Tom Glavine/250 4.00
143 Torii Hunter/200 4.00
148 Victor Martinez/250 4.00
149 Vladimir Guerrero/250 8.00
150 Sammy Sosa/250 8.00
153 Rocco Baldelli/250 4.00
160 Lew Ford/250 4.00
166 Mike Sweeney/100 4.00
184 Rafael Palmeiro/100 6.00
188 Tom Glavine/250 4.00
190 Vladimir Guerrero/250 8.00

Mirror Bat White

NM/M

Production 75-250
2 Adam Dunn/1 6.00
5 Albert Pujols/1 20.00
7 Alfonso Soriano/1 6.00
11 Aubrey Huff/10 4.00
12 Austin Kearns/5 4.00
13 B.J. Upton/5 6.00
14 Brandon Webb/50 4.00
25 Casey Kotchman/250 8.00
26 Chipper Jones/100 6.00
28 Craig Biggio/100 4.00
29 Craig Wilson/250 10.00
34 David Wright/100 6.00
37 Derrek Lee/250 6.00
38 Dontrelle Willis/100 4.00
44 Garret Anderson/100 6.00
45 Gary Sheffield/100 8.00
59 Jason Varitek/100 4.00
61 Javy Lopez/100 6.00
63 Jeff Bagwell/100 4.00
77 Jose Vidro/100 6.00
88 Kerry Wood/100 4.00
93 Lance Berkman/100 6.00
94 Larry Walker/100 8.00

99 Manny Ramirez/250 6.00
105 Mark Teixeira/250 4.00
109 Michael Young/250 8.00
110 Miguel Cabrera/250 8.00
111 Miguel Tejada/250 4.00
121 Paul Konerko/100 4.00
124 Rafael Palmeiro/75 6.00
128 Magglio Ordonez/100 4.00
136 Shawn Green/100 4.00
141 Todd Helton/100 6.00
142 Tom Glavine/100 4.00
143 Torii Hunter/100 4.00
148 Victor Martinez/100 4.00
149 Vladimir Guerrero/100 8.00
150 Sammy Sosa/100 8.00
153 Rocco Baldelli/100 4.00
160 Lew Ford/250 4.00
184 Rafael Palmeiro/250 6.00
188 Tom Glavine/100 4.00
190 Vladimir Guerrero/100 8.00

Mirror Fabric Blue

NM/M

Production 50-100
Black: No Pricing
Production One Set
Emerald: No Pricing
Production Five Sets
2 Adam Dunn/Jsy/100 6.00
5 Albert Pujols/Jsy/100 15.00
7 Alfonso Soriano/Jsy/100 6.00
8 Andruw Jones/Jsy/100 6.00
10 Aramis Ramirez/Jsy/100 6.00
11 Aubrey Huff/Jsy/100 4.00
13 B.J. Upton/Jsy/100 4.00
14 Brandon Webb/Pants/100 4.00
15 Barry Zito/Jsy/100 4.00
17 Bobby Abreu/Jsy/100 4.00
18 Bobby Crosby/Jsy/50 6.00
25 Casey Kotchman/Jsy/100 4.00
26 Chipper Jones/Jsy/100 8.00
28 Craig Biggio/Jsy/100 4.00
30 Curt Schilling/Jsy/100 8.00
32 David Ortiz/Jsy/100 8.00
37 Derrek Lee/Jsy/100 8.00
38 Dontrelle Willis/Jsy/100 4.00
41 Eric Chavez/Jsy/100 4.00
43 Francisco Rodriguez/Jsy/100 4.00
44 Garret Anderson/Jsy/100 4.00
46 Greg Maddux/Jsy/100 10.00
47 Hideki Matsui/Pants/100 15.00
48 Hideo Nomo/Jsy/100 6.00
50 Ivan Rodriguez/Jsy/100 4.00
57 Trot Nixon/Jsy/100 4.00
60 Roy Oswalt/Jsy/50 4.00
61 Javy Lopez/Jsy/100 4.00
63 Jeff Bagwell/Jsy/100 6.00
69 Jim Edmonds/Jsy/100 6.00
70 Jim Thome/Jsy/100 6.00
71 Johan Santana/Jsy/100 6.00
73 Johnny Damon/Jsy/100 8.00
78 Josh Beckett/Jsy/100 4.00
82 Justin Morneau/Jsy/100 6.00
84 Kazuo Matsui/Jsy/100 4.00
87 Frank Thomas/Jsy/100 6.00
88 Kerry Wood/Jsy/100 6.00
92 Francisco Cordero/Jsy/100 4.00
93 Lance Berkman/Jsy/100 4.00
94 Larry Walker/Jsy/100 6.00
96 Luis Gonzalez/Jsy/100 4.00
97 Lyle Overbay/Jsy/100 4.00
98 Carlos Zambrano/Jsy/100 6.00
99 Manny Ramirez/Jsy/100 8.00
104 Mark Prior/Jsy/100 8.00
109 Michael Young/Jsy/100 4.00
110 Miguel Cabrera/Jsy/100 8.00
111 Miguel Tejada/Jsy/100 6.00
113 Mike Mussina/Jsy/50 6.00
114 Mike Piazza/Jsy/100 8.00
121 Paul Konerko/Jsy/100 4.00
124 Rafael Palmeiro/Jsy/100 6.00
129 Roger Clemens/Jsy/100 10.00
131 Sammy Sosa/Jsy/100 8.00
133 Scott Rolen/Jsy/100 6.00
135 Sean Casey/Jsy/100 4.00
138 Roy Halladay/Jsy/100 4.00
141 Todd Helton/Jsy/100 6.00
144 Travis Hafner/Jsy/100 4.00
147 Vernon Wells/Jsy/100 4.00
148 Victor Martinez/Jsy/100 4.00
149 Vladimir Guerrero/Jsy/100 8.00
151 Hank Blalock/Jsy/100 4.00
153 Rocco Baldelli/Jsy/100 4.00
159 Ben Sheets/Jsy/100 4.00
160 Lew Ford/Jsy/100 4.00
166 Mike Sweeney/Jsy/100 4.00
178 Greg Maddux/Jsy/100 10.00
179 Ivan Rodriguez/Jsy/100 4.00
183 Pedro J. Martinez/Jsy/100 8.00
184 Rafael Palmeiro/Pants/100 6.00
185 Roger Clemens/Jsy/100 10.00
188 Tom Glavine/Jsy/100 4.00
190 Vladimir Guerrero/Jsy/100 8.00

Mirror Fabric Red

NM/M

Production 100-250
Gold: 1-2X
Production 25 Sets
2 Adam Dunn/Jsy/250 6.00
5 Albert Pujols/Jsy/250 15.00
7 Alfonso Soriano/Jsy/250 6.00
8 Andruw Jones/Jsy/250 6.00
10 Aramis Ramirez/Jsy/250 4.00
11 Aubrey Huff/Jsy/250 4.00
13 B.J. Upton/Jsy/250 4.00
14 Brandon Webb/Pants/100 4.00
15 Barry Zito/Jsy/250 4.00
17 Bobby Abreu/Jsy/250 4.00
20 Preston Wilson/Jsy/250 4.00
25 Casey Kotchman/Jsy/250 4.00
26 Chipper Jones/Jsy/250 8.00
28 Craig Biggio/Jsy/250 4.00
30 Curt Schilling/Jsy/250 8.00
32 David Ortiz/Jsy/250 8.00
37 Derrek Lee/Jsy/250 8.00
38 Dontrelle Willis/Jsy/225 4.00
41 Eric Chavez/Jsy/250 4.00
43 Francisco Rodriguez/Jsy/250 4.00
44 Garret Anderson/Jsy/250 4.00
45 Gary Sheffield/Jsy/250 6.00
46 Greg Maddux/Jsy/250 10.00
47 Hideki Matsui/Jsy/250 15.00
48 Hideo Nomo/Jsy/250 6.00
50 Ivan Rodriguez/Jsy/250 4.00
57 Trot Nixon/Jsy/250 4.00
60 Roy Oswalt/Jsy/250 4.00
61 Javy Lopez/Jsy/250 4.00
63 Jeff Bagwell/Jsy/250 6.00
69 Jim Edmonds/Jsy/250 6.00
70 Jim Thome/Jsy/250 6.00
71 Johan Santana/Jsy/250 6.00
82 Justin Morneau/Jsy/250 6.00
84 Kazuo Matsui/Jsy/250 4.00
87 Frank Thomas/Jsy/250 6.00
88 Kerry Wood/Jsy/250 6.00
92 Francisco Cordero/Jsy/250 4.00
93 Lance Berkman/Jsy/250 4.00
94 Larry Walker/Jsy/250 6.00
96 Luis Gonzalez/Jsy/250 4.00
97 Lyle Overbay/Jsy/250 4.00
98 Carlos Zambrano/Jsy/250 4.00
99 Manny Ramirez/Jsy/250 8.00
104 Mark Prior/Jsy/250 8.00
109 Michael Young/Jsy/250 4.00
110 Miguel Cabrera/Jsy/250 8.00
111 Miguel Tejada/Jsy/250 6.00
114 Mike Piazza/Jsy/250 8.00
121 Paul Konerko/Jsy/250 4.00
124 Rafael Palmeiro/Jsy/250 6.00
129 Roger Clemens/Jsy/250 10.00
131 Sammy Sosa/Jsy/250 8.00
133 Scott Rolen/Jsy/250 6.00
135 Sean Casey/Jsy/250 4.00
138 Roy Halladay/Jsy/250 4.00
141 Todd Helton/Jsy/250 6.00
144 Travis Hafner/Jsy/250 4.00
147 Vernon Wells/Jsy/250 4.00
148 Victor Martinez/Jsy/250 4.00
149 Vladimir Guerrero/Jsy/250 8.00
153 Rocco Baldelli/Jsy/250 4.00
159 Ben Sheets/Jsy/250 4.00
160 Lew Ford/Jsy/250 4.00
166 Mike Sweeney/Jsy/250 4.00
178 Greg Maddux/Jsy/250 10.00
179 Ivan Rodriguez/Jsy/250 4.00
183 Pedro J. Martinez/Jsy/250 8.00
184 Rafael Palmeiro/Jsy/250 6.00
185 Roger Clemens/Jsy/250 10.00
188 Tom Glavine/Jsy/250 4.00
190 Vladimir Guerrero/Jsy/100 8.00

Mirror Fabric White

NM/M

Production 50-250
2 Adam Dunn/Jsy/250 6.00
5 Albert Pujols/Jsy/100 15.00
7 Alfonso Soriano/Jsy/100 6.00
8 Andruw Jones/Jsy/100 6.00
10 Aramis Ramirez/Jsy/100 6.00
11 Aubrey Huff/Jsy/150 4.00
13 B.J. Upton/Jsy/250 4.00
15 Barry Zito/Jsy/100 4.00
26 Chipper Jones/Jsy/250 8.00
28 Craig Biggio/Pants/250 4.00
30 Curt Schilling/Jsy/100 8.00
32 David Ortiz/Jsy/100 8.00
34 David Wright/Jsy/100 10.00
38 Dontrelle Willis/Jsy/50 4.00
41 Eric Chavez/Jsy/100 4.00
44 Garret Anderson/Jsy/100 4.00
45 Gary Sheffield/Jsy/50 6.00
46 Greg Maddux/Jsy/50 10.00
47 Hideki Matsui/Pants/100 15.00
48 Hideo Nomo/Jsy/100 6.00
57 Trot Nixon/Jsy/100 4.00
60 Roy Oswalt/Jsy/25 6.00
63 Jeff Bagwell/Jsy/100 6.00
69 Jim Edmonds/Jsy/100 6.00
70 Jim Thome/Jsy/100 6.00
71 Johan Santana/Jsy/100 6.00
78 Josh Beckett/Jsy/250 4.00
82 Justin Morneau/Jsy/100 6.00
84 Kazuo Matsui/Jsy/250 4.00
88 Kerry Wood/Jsy/50 6.00
93 Lance Berkman/Jsy/250 4.00
94 Larry Walker/Jsy/100 6.00
95 Laynce Nix/Jsy/100 4.00
96 Luis Gonzalez/Jsy/250 4.00
98 Carlos Zambrano/Jsy/100 6.00
99 Manny Ramirez/Jsy/100 8.00
104 Mark Prior/Jsy/100 8.00
109 Michael Young/Jsy/100 4.00
110 Miguel Cabrera/Jsy/150 8.00
111 Miguel Tejada/Jsy/100 8.00
113 Mike Mussina/Jsy/100 6.00
114 Mike Piazza/Jsy/100 8.00
121 Paul Konerko/Jsy/150 4.00
124 Rafael Palmeiro/Jsy/150 6.00
129 Roger Clemens/Jsy/100 10.00
131 Sammy Sosa/Jsy/150 8.00
133 Scott Rolen/Jsy/100 6.00
135 Sean Casey/Jsy/100 4.00
138 Roy Halladay/Jsy/100 4.00
141 Todd Helton/Jsy/100 6.00
144 Travis Hafner/Jsy/100 4.00
147 Vernon Wells/Jsy/250 4.00
148 Victor Martinez/Jsy/250 4.00
149 Vladimir Guerrero/Jsy/250 8.00
151 Hank Blalock/Jsy/100 4.00
159 Ben Sheets/Jsy/100 4.00
166 Mike Sweeney/Jsy/50 4.00
178 Greg Maddux/Jsy/200 10.00
179 Ivan Rodriguez/Jsy/250 4.00
184 Rafael Palmeiro/Jsy/250 6.00
185 Roger Clemens/Jsy/100 10.00
188 Tom Glavine/Jsy/250 4.00

Skills

NM/M

Common: 1.50
Inserted 1:7
Mirror: 2X-3X
1 Andy Pettitte 1.50
2 Barry Zito 1.50
3 Bobby Crosby 2.00
4 Brandon Webb 1.50
5 Craig Biggio 2.00
6 David Ortiz 3.00
7 Dontrelle Willis 2.00
8 Francisco Rodriguez 1.50
9 Gary Sheffield 2.00
10 Jack Wilson 1.50
11 Jason Bay 1.50
12 Jeff Bagwell 2.00
13 Jim Edmonds 2.00
14 Josh Beckett 1.50
15 Kerry Wood 2.00
16 Lance Berkman 1.50
17 Mark Buehrle 1.50
18 Mark Teixeira 2.00
19 Miguel Tejada 2.00
20 Paul Konerko 1.50
21 Scott Rolen 2.00
22 Sean Burroughs 1.50
23 Vernon Wells 1.50
24 Victor Martinez 1.50
25 Vladimir Guerrero 3.00

Skills Autographs

NM/M

Production 5-25
3 Bobby Crosby/25 25.00
11 Jason Bay/25 25.00

Skills Jersey Position

NM/M

Production 100-250
Prime: No Pricing
Production 5-25
1 Andy Pettitte/250 4.00
2 Barry Zito/250 4.00
3 Bobby Crosby/100 6.00
4 Brandon Webb/Pants/100 4.00
5 Craig Biggio/250 4.00
6 David Ortiz/250 8.00
7 Dontrelle Willis/100 4.00
8 Francisco Rodriguez/250 4.00
9 Gary Sheffield/50 6.00
10 Jack Wilson/50 4.00
11 Jason Bay/100 4.00
12 Jeff Bagwell/250 6.00
13 Jim Edmonds/250 6.00
14 Josh Beckett/250 4.00
15 Kerry Wood/50 6.00
16 Lance Berkman/250 4.00
17 Mark Buehrle/150 4.00
19 Miguel Tejada/250 8.00
20 Paul Konerko/100 4.00
21 Scott Rolen/100 6.00
22 Sean Burroughs/100 4.00
23 Vernon Wells/250 4.00
24 Victor Martinez/250 4.00
25 Vladimir Guerrero/250 8.00

2005 Leaf Limited

NM/M

Complete Set (205):
Common Player (1-150): 1.00
Production 699
Common (151-175, 197): 4.00
Production 99
Commmon Auto. (176-196), (198-200): 12.00
Production 99
Pack (4): 70.00
1 Roger Clemens 5.00
2 Roger Clemens 5.00
3 Ichiro Suzuki 4.00
4 Ichiro Suzuki 4.00
5 Todd Helton 1.50
6 Todd Helton 1.50
7 Vladimir Guerrero 2.00
8 Vladimir Guerrero 2.00
9 Miguel Cabrera 2.00
10 Miguel Cabrera 2.00
11 Albert Pujols 5.00
12 Albert Pujols 5.00
13 Mark Prior 1.50
14 Mark Prior 1.50
15 Chipper Jones 2.00
16 Chipper Jones 2.00
17 Jeff Bagwell 1.50
18 Jeff Bagwell 1.50
19 Kerry Wood 1.00
20 Kerry Wood 1.00
21 Gary Sheffield 1.50
22 Carl Crawford 1.00
23 Mariano Rivera 1.50
24 Curt Schilling 2.00
25 Ben Sheets 1.00
26 Jimmy Rollins 1.00
27 Melvin Mora 1.00
28 Corey Patterson 1.00
29 Rafael Furcal 1.00
30 Jim Thome 1.50
31 Derek Jeter 5.00
32 Jake Peavy 1.50
33 Francisco Cordero 1.00
34 Aramis Ramirez 1.50
35 Javy Lopez 1.00
36 Aaron Rowand 1.00
37 Jason Bay 1.00
38 Michael Young 1.00
39 Ivan Rodriguez 1.50
40 Joe Nathan 1.00
41 Oliver Perez 1.00
42 Adam Dunn 1.50
43 Eric Chavez 1.00
44 Pedro Martinez 2.00
45 Roy Oswalt 1.00
46 Carlos Delgado 1.00
47 Jeff Kent 1.00
48 Johnny Damon 2.00
49 Edgar Renteria 1.00
50 Mark Buehrle 1.00
51 Carl Pavano 1.00
52 J.D. Drew 1.00
53 Hank Blalock 1.00
54 Moises Alou 1.00
55 Brad Radke 1.00
56 Brad Wilkerson 1.00
57 Sean Casey 1.00
58 Mike Lowell 1.00
59 Octavio Dotel 1.00
60 Francisco Rodriguez 1.00
61 Jose Guillen 1.00
62 Greg Maddux 3.00
63 A.J. Burnett 1.00
64 Chris Carpenter 1.50
65 Jose Reyes 1.50
66 Travis Hafner 1.50
67 Rich Harden 1.00
68 Bret Boone 1.00
69 Scott Podsednik 1.00
70 Andruw Jones 1.50
71 Milton Bradley 1.00
72 Zack Greinke 1.00
73 Torii Hunter 1.00
74 Paul Konerko 1.50
75 David Wells 1.00
76 Tim Hudson 1.50
77 Sammy Sosa 2.50
78 Jason Varitek 1.50
79 Lance Berkman 1.50
80 Justin Morneau 1.50
81 Troy Glaus 1.00
82 Jose Vidro 1.00
83 Joe Mauer 1.50
84 Josh Beckett 1.00
85 Craig Biggio 1.00
86 Luis Gonzalez 1.00
87 Larry Walker 1.00
88 Barry Zito 1.00
89 Jacque Jones 1.00
90 Lyle Overbay 1.00
91 Roy Halladay 1.50
92 Orlando Cabrera 1.00
93 Magglio Ordonez 1.00
94 Mike Sweeney 1.00
95 Rafael Palmeiro 1.50
96 Brandon Webb 1.00
97 Preston Wilson 1.00
98 Shannon Stewart 1.00
99 Trot Nixon 1.00
100 Mike Piazza 2.50
101 Dontrelle Willis 1.50
102 Ken Griffey Jr. 3.00
103 Andy Pettitte 1.00
104 Kazuo Matsui 1.00
105 Bobby Crosby 1.00
106 Shawn Green 1.00
107 Alfonso Soriano 2.00
108 Carlos Zambrano 1.00
109 Keith Foulke 1.00
110 Aubrey Huff 1.00
111 Adrian Beltre 1.00
112 Mark Teixeira 1.50
113 Randy Johnson 2.00
114 Miguel Tejada 1.50
115 Alex Rodriguez 4.00
116 Carlos Beltran 1.50
117 Bobby Abreu 1.50
118 Johan Santana 1.50
119 Manny Ramirez 2.00
120 Juan Pierre 1.00
121 Scott Rolen 1.50
122 Livan Hernandez 1.00
123 Carlos Lee 1.00
124 Derrek Lee 1.50
125 Brian Giles 1.00
126 Nomar Garciaparra 2.00
127 John Smoltz 1.50
128 Jim Edmonds 1.50
129 Bartolo Colon 1.00
130 Garret Anderson 1.00
131 Austin Kearns 1.00
132 Shingo Takatsu 1.00

133 Omar Vizquel 1.00
134 Tom Glavine 1.00
135 Mark Mulder 1.50
136 Bernie Williams 1.00
137 Richie Sexson 1.00
138 Mike Mussina 1.50
139 Mark Loretta 1.00
140 Vernon Wells 1.00
141 David Wright 3.00
142 Marcus Giles 1.00
143 David Ortiz 2.00
144 Victor Martinez 1.00
145 Hideki Matsui 4.00
146 C.C. Sabathia 1.00
147 Angel Berroa 1.00
148 Troy Percival 1.00
149 Paul LoDuca 1.00
150 Jorge Posada 1.50
151 Willie Mays 8.00
152 Ryne Sandberg 8.00
153 Rickey Henderson 4.00
154 Ted Williams 10.00
155 Roberto Clemente 10.00
156 George Brett 8.00
157 Whitey Ford 4.00
158 Duke Snider 4.00
159 Don Mattingly 10.00
160 Bob Gibson 4.00
161 Hank Aaron 8.00
162 Al Kaline 6.00
163 Nolan Ryan 10.00
164 Stan Musial 6.00
165 George Kell 4.00
166 Harmon Killebrew 6.00
167 Cal Ripken Jr. 15.00
168 Babe Ruth 10.00
169 Roger Clemens/SP 8.00
170 Curt Schilling/SP 4.00
171 Rafael Palmeiro/SP 4.00
172 Randy Johnson/SP 5.00
173 Mike Piazza/SP 5.00
174 Greg Maddux/SP 6.00
175 Sammy Sosa/SP 5.00
176 Hayden Penn/Auto. **RC** 15.00
177 Ambiorix Concepcion/ Auto. **RC** 15.00
178 Casey Rogowski/Auto. **RC** 15.00
179 Prince Fielder/Auto. 80.00
180 Geovany Soto/Auto. **RC** 50.00
181 Wladimir Balentien/ Auto. **RC** 20.00
182 Jason Hammel/Auto. **RC** 15.00
183 Keiichi Yabu/Auto. **RC** 25.00
184 Brandon McCarthy/ Auto. **RC** 25.00
185 Ubaldo Jimenez/Auto. **RC** 15.00
186 Keiichi Yabu/Auto. **RC** 25.00
187 Miguel Negron/Auto. **RC** 15.00
188 Mike Morse/Auto. **RC** 25.00
189 Nate McLouth/Auto. **RC** 30.00
190 Norihiro Nakamura/ Auto. **RC** 25.00
191 Bill McCarthy/Auto. **RC** 25.00
192 Tony Pena/Auto. **RC** 12.00
193 Ambiorix Concepcion/ Auto. **RC** 15.00
194 Raul Tablado/Auto. **RC** 15.00
195 Hayden Penn/Auto. **RC** 15.00
196 Sean Thompson/Auto. **RC** 15.00
197 Tadahito Iguchi **RC** 15.00
198 Ubaldo Jimenez/Auto. **RC** 15.00
199 Wladimir Balentien/ Auto. **RC** 20.00
200 Prince Fielder/Auto. 80.00
201 Philip Humber/ Auto./99 **RC** 25.00
202 Jeff Niemann/Auto./95 **RC** 40.00
203 Justin Verlander/ Auto./70 **RC** 75.00
205 Yuniesky Betancourt/ Auto./99 **RC** 50.00

Bronze Spotlight

Bronze (1-150): 1-1.5X
Bronze (151-175): 1X
Bronze (176-200): .25X
Production 99 Sets

Gold Spotlight

Gold (1-150): 2-4X
Gold (151-175): 2-3X
Production 25 Sets
Gold (176-205): No Pricing
Production 5-25

Platinum Spotlight

No Pricing
Production One Set

Silver Spotlight

Silver (1-150): 1-2X
Silver (151-175): 1-1.5X
Silver (176-200): .25X
Production 50 Sets

Cuts Silver

NM/M

Production 7-99
Platinum: No Pricing
Production One Set
1 Orlando Cepeda/30 35.00
2 Hank Aaron/44 275.00
3 Willie Mays/24 175.00
4 Sandy Koufax/32 400.00
5 Cal Ripken Jr./25 150.00
6 Nolan Ryan/34 120.00
7 Jim Palmer/22 30.00
8 Tony Gwynn/19 60.00
9 Rod Carew/29 40.00
10 Ryne Sandberg/23 70.00
11 Stan Musial/28 70.00
12 Steve Carlton/32 30.00
14 Mike Schmidt/20 60.00
15 Harmon Killebrew/25 40.00
17 Duke Snider/53 30.00
18 Don Mattingly/25 50.00
19 Dale Murphy/25 35.00
21 Juan Marichal/99 25.00
22 Greg Maddux/37 10.00
24 Paul Molitor/25 35.00
25 Wade Boggs/26 40.00
26 Mark Prior/27 40.00
28 Al Kaline/28 40.00

Cuts Gold

Production 3-30
No Pricing

Legends

NM/M

Common Player:
Production 50 Sets
Foil: No Pricing
Production 10 Sets
1 Billy Martin 4.00
2 Bobby Doerr 3.00
3 Carlton Fisk 4.00
4 Harmon Killebrew 5.00
5 Duke Snider 5.00
6 George Brett 6.00
7 Johnny Bench 5.00
8 Lou Boudreau 3.00
9 Brooks Robinson 4.00
10 Al Kaline 4.00
11 Stan Musial 5.00
12 Burleigh Grimes 3.00
13 Cal Ripken Jr. 10.00
14 Carl Yastrzemski 6.00
15 Willie Stargell 3.00
16 Yogi Berra 4.00
17 Enos Slaughter 3.00
18 Phil Rizzuto 3.00
19 Luis Aparicio 3.00
20 Ernie Banks 5.00
21 Hal Newhouser 3.00
22 Whitey Ford 4.00
23 Tony Gwynn 4.00
24 Bob Feller 4.00
25 Don Sutton 3.00
26 Lou Brock 3.00
27 Jim Palmer 3.00
28 Billy Williams 2.00
29 Juan Marichal 3.00
30 Rod Carew 3.00
31 Jim "Catfish" Hunter 2.00
32 Maury Wills 2.00
33 Joe Cronin 2.00
34 Fergie Jenkins 2.00
35 Sandy Koufax 5.00
36 Steve Carlton 3.00
37 Eddie Murray 3.00
38 Roger Maris 4.00
39 Gaylord Perry 2.00
40 Bob Gibson 3.00
41 Tom Seaver 3.00
42 Dennis Eckersley 2.00
43 Reggie Jackson 3.00
44 Willie McCovey 3.00
45 Willie Mays 6.00
46 Willie Mays 6.00
47 Rickey Henderson 3.00
48 Rickey Henderson 3.00
49 Nolan Ryan 6.00
50 Nolan Ryan 6.00

Legends Jersey Number Prime

NM/M

Production 1-25
3 Carlton Fisk/25 12.00
6 George Brett/25 20.00
13 Cal Ripken Jr./25 50.00
15 Willie Stargell/25 20.00
23 Tony Gwynn/25 25.00
26 Lou Brock/25 20.00
40 Bob Gibson/25 20.00
42 Dennis Eckersley/25 15.00
47 Rickey Henderson/25 20.00
48 Rickey Henderson/25 20.00

Legends Signature Jersey Number Prime

NM/M

42 Dennis Eckersley/25 30.00

Legends Jersey Number

NM/M

Production 1-45
3 Carlton Fisk/50 10.00
25 Don Sutton/20 8.00
26 Lou Brock/20 10.00
27 Jim Palmer/22 8.00
28 Billy Williams/26 8.00
29 Juan Marichal/27 8.00
30 Rod Carew/29 10.00
31 Jim "Catfish" Hunter/ Pants/29 8.00
34 Fergie Jenkins/31 6.00
35 Sandy Koufax/32 250.00
36 Steve Carlton/32 8.00
37 Eddie Murray/33 12.00
39 Gaylord Perry/36 6.00
40 Bob Gibson/45 10.00
41 Tom Seaver/41 10.00
42 Dennis Eckersley/45 5.00
43 Reggie Jackson/Pants/44 8.00
44 Willie McCovey/44 10.00
45 Willie Mays/24 40.00
46 Willie Mays/24 40.00
49 Nolan Ryan/30 25.00
50 Nolan Ryan/30 25.00

Legends Signature

NM/M

Production 2-50
2 Bobby Doerr/50 15.00
4 Harmon Killebrew/50 30.00
5 Duke Snider/25 35.00
9 Brooks Robinson/50 25.00
10 Al Kaline/50 40.00
18 Phil Rizzuto/50 35.00
19 Luis Aparicio/50 20.00
24 Bob Feller/50 25.00
25 Don Sutton/50 15.00
26 Lou Brock/50 30.00
27 Jim Palmer/50 20.00
28 Billy Williams/25 20.00
29 Juan Marichal/50 25.00
30 Rod Carew/25 35.00
32 Maury Wills/50 15.00
34 Fergie Jenkins/50 15.00
36 Steve Carlton/50 25.00
39 Gaylord Perry/50 15.00
40 Bob Gibson/25 40.00
42 Dennis Eckersley/50 20.00

Legends Signature Jersey Number

NM/M

Production 5-30
2 Bobby Doerr/Pants/25 25.00
4 Harmon Killebrew/25 40.00
11 Stan Musial/25 65.00
13 Cal Ripken Jr./25 150.00
18 Phil Rizzuto/Pants/25 40.00
19 Luis Aparicio/25 25.00
23 Tony Gwynn/25 40.00
25 Don Sutton/20 20.00
27 Jim Palmer/22 25.00
34 Fergie Jenkins/25 20.00
36 Steve Carlton/25 30.00
39 Gaylord Perry/25 20.00
40 Bob Gibson/25 40.00
42 Dennis Eckersley/25 25.00
44 Willie McCovey/25 40.00
45 Willie Mays/24 160.00
46 Willie Mays/24 160.00
49 Nolan Ryan/30 90.00
50 Nolan Ryan/30 90.00

Lettermen

NM/M

Production 4-21
DU-H Dale Murphy H/20 150.00
DU-M Dale Murphy M/20 150.00
DU-P Dale Murphy P/20 150.00
DU-R Dale Murphy R/20 150.00
DU-U Dale Murphy U/20 150.00
DU-Y Dale Murphy Y/20 150.00
NR-A Nolan Ryan A/21 200.00
NR-N Nolan Ryan N/21 200.00
NR-R Nolan Ryan R/21 200.00
NR-Y Nolan Ryan Y/21 200.00

Lumberjacks

NM/M

Common Player:
Production 50 Sets
Foil: No Pricing
1 Al Kaline 4.00
2 Albert Pujols 8.00
3 Andre Dawson 3.00
4 Babe Ruth 8.00
5 Cal Ripken Jr. 15.00
6 Chipper Jones 4.00
7 Dale Murphy 3.00
8 Dave Winfield 3.00
9 Don Mattingly 6.00
10 Duke Snider 4.00
11 Eddie Murray 3.00
12 Frank Robinson 4.00
13 Frank Thomas 4.00
14 Gary Carter 3.00
15 Hack Wilson 3.00
16 Hank Aaron 10.00
17 Harmon Killebrew 4.00
18 Joe Morgan 3.00
19 Johnny Bench 4.00
20 Kirby Puckett 4.00
21 Kirk Gibson 3.00
22 Manny Ramirez 4.00
23 Mark Grace 3.00
24 Mike Piazza 5.00
25 Mike Schmidt 6.00
26 Orlando Cepeda 3.00
27 Paul Molitor 4.00
28 Rafael Palmeiro 4.00
29 Ralph Kiner 3.00
30 Reggie Jackson 4.00
31 Richie Ashburn 3.00
32 Rickey Henderson 4.00
33 Robin Yount 5.00
34 Rod Carew 4.00
35 Ryne Sandberg 6.00
36 Stan Musial 5.00
37 Ted Williams 8.00
38 Tony Gwynn 4.00
39 Vladimir Guerrero 4.00
40 Willie Mays 8.00
41 Ernie Banks, Bernie Williams 6.00
42 Ted Williams,Joe Cronin 10.00
43 George Brett, Bo Jackson 8.00
44 John Kruk, Jim Thome 3.00
45 Willie Mays, Jim Thorpe 8.00
46 Wade Boggs, Johnny Damon 6.00
47 M. Williams, W. Clark 3.00
48 Willie Stargell, D. Parker 4.00
49 Ichiro Suzuki, Edgar Martinez 6.00
50 Carl Yastrzemski, Carlton Fisk 6.00

Lumberjacks Barrel

No Pricing
Production 1-5

Lumberjacks Bat

NM/M

Production 1-50
1 Al Kaline/50 10.00
4 Babe Ruth/25 180.00
8 Dave Winfield/50 10.00
11 Eddie Murray/25 15.00
12 Frank Robinson/50 15.00
14 Gary Carter/25 10.00
15 Hack Wilson/50 40.00
16 Hank Aaron/50 40.00
18 Joe Morgan/25 8.00
19 Johnny Bench/50 10.00
20 Kirby Puckett/50 10.00
25 Mike Schmidt/50 15.00
26 Orlando Cepeda/25 8.00
27 Paul Molitor/50 8.00
29 Ralph Kiner/25 15.00
31 Richie Ashburn/25 15.00
33 Robin Yount/25 20.00
35 Ryne Sandberg/25 20.00
36 Stan Musial/50 20.00
37 Ted Williams/50 40.00
40 Willie Mays/50 30.00
43 George Brett, Bo Jackson/50 25.00
47 M. Williams, W. Clark/50 15.00
48 Willie Stargell, D. Parker/50 15.00
50 Carl Yastrzemski, Carlton Fisk/50 20.00

Lumberjacks Combos

NM/M

Production 1-50
2 Albert Pujols/Bat-Jsy/50 30.00
5 Cal Ripken Jr./Bat-Jsy/50 35.00
6 Chipper Jones/Bat-Jsy/25 15.00
7 Dale Murphy/Bat-Jsy/50 12.00
8 Dave Winfield/Bat-Pants/50 8.00
11 Eddie Murray/Bat-Jsy/25 20.00
13 Frank Thomas/Bat-Jsy/25 15.00
16 Hank Aaron/Bat-Jsy/25 60.00
19 Johnny Bench/Bat-Jsy/25 15.00
20 Kirby Puckett/Bat-Jsy/25 15.00
21 Kirk Gibson/Bat-Jsy/50 8.00
22 Manny Ramirez/Bat-Jsy/50 12.00
23 Mark Grace/Bat-Jsy/50 12.00
24 Mike Piazza/Bat-Jsy/50 15.00
25 Mike Schmidt/Bat-Jsy/25 25.00
26 Orlando Cepeda/ Bat-Pants/50 8.00
27 Paul Molitor/Bat-Jsy/50 12.00
31 Richie Ashburn/Bat-Jsy/25 15.00
33 Robin Yount/Bat-Jsy/50 15.00
36 Stan Musial/Bat-Jsy/25 35.00
40 Willie Mays/Bat-Jsy/25 50.00

Lumberjacks Combos Prime

NM/M

Production 1-50
2 Albert Pujols/Bat-Jsy/50 35.00
3 Andre Dawson/Bat-Jsy/50 8.00
5 Cal Ripken Jr./Bat-Jsy/25 50.00
6 Chipper Jones/Bat-Jsy/50 15.00
11 Eddie Murray/Bat-Jsy/25 25.00
12 Frank Robinson/Bat-Jsy/50 12.00
13 Frank Thomas/Bat-Jsy/50 15.00
14 Gary Carter/Bat-Jsy/50 10.00
18 Joe Morgan/Bat-Jsy/25 15.00
21 Kirk Gibson/Bat-Jsy/50 8.00
22 Manny Ramirez/Bat-Jsy/25 20.00
24 Mike Piazza/Bat-Jsy/50 15.00
28 Rafael Palmeiro/Bat-Jsy/50 12.00
32 Rickey Henderson/ Bat-Jsy/25 15.00
33 Robin Yount/Bat-Jsy/50 25.00
34 Rod Carew/Bat-Jsy/50 12.00
39 Vladimir Guerrero/ Bat-Jsy/50 15.00

Lumberjacks Jersey

NM/M

Production 1-50
4 Babe Ruth/25 250.00
8 Dave Winfield/Pants/50 6.00
10 Duke Snider/Pants/50 10.00
11 Eddie Murray/25 15.00
14 Gary Carter/50 5.00
16 Hank Aaron/25 40.00
19 Johnny Bench/25 15.00
20 Kirby Puckett/25 15.00
27 Paul Molitor/50 8.00
30 Reggie Jackson/50 10.00
31 Richie Ashburn/50 10.00

33 Robin Yount/50 12.00
35 Ryne Sandberg/50 12.00
36 Stan Musial/25 25.00
37 Ted Williams/25 50.00
40 Willie Mays/25 35.00
41 Ernie Banks, Bernie Williams/25 30.00
42 Ted Williams, Joe Cronin/25 60.00
43 George Brett, Bo Jackson/50 30.00
44 John Kruk, Jim Thome/25 20.00
45 Willie Mays, Jim Thorpe/25 200.00
46 Wade Boggs, Johnny Damon/50 20.00
47 M. Williams, W. Clark/50 20.00
48 Willie Stargell, D. Parker/25 25.00

Lumberjacks Jersey Prime

NM/M

2 Albert Pujols/25 40.00
3 Andre Dawson/50 10.00
5 Cal Ripken Jr./25 50.00
6 Chipper Jones/50 20.00
11 Eddie Murray/25 25.00
12 Frank Robinson/25 10.00
13 Frank Thomas/50 15.00
14 Gary Carter/50 10.00
21 Kirk Gibson/50 10.00
24 Mike Piazza/50 15.00
25 Mike Schmidt/25 30.00
28 Rafael Palmeiro/50 15.00
32 Rickey Henderson/25 20.00
33 Robin Yount/50 25.00
34 Rod Carew/50 15.00
35 Ryne Sandberg/25 30.00
38 Tony Gwynn/50 20.00
39 Vladimir Guerrero/25 20.00

Lumberjacks Signature

NM/M

Production 1-50
1 Al Kaline/50 40.00
3 Andre Dawson/25 20.00
5 Cal Ripken Jr./21 120.00
7 Dale Murphy/50 25.00
9 Don Mattingly/50 50.00
10 Duke Snider/50 25.00
12 Frank Robinson/50 30.00
13 Frank Thomas/25 50.00
14 Gary Carter/50 20.00
17 Harmon Killebrew/50 35.00
18 Joe Morgan/25 25.00
19 Johnny Bench/50 40.00
20 Kirby Puckett/25 40.00
23 Mark Grace/25 35.00
25 Mike Schmidt/50 40.00
27 Paul Molitor/50 30.00
29 Ralph Kiner/50 30.00
34 Rod Carew/50 25.00
35 Ryne Sandberg/50 40.00
36 Stan Musial/50 50.00
38 Tony Gwynn/50 35.00
40 Willie Mays/25 140.00

Lumberjacks Signature Jersey Prime

NM/M

Production 1-25
3 Andre Dawson/25 30.00
5 Cal Ripken Jr./25 160.00
7 Dale Murphy/25 50.00
12 Frank Robinson/25 35.00
14 Gary Carter/25 30.00

Lumberjacks Signature Combos Prime

Production 1-25
No Pricing

Lumberjacks Signature Bat

NM/M

Production 1-100
1 Al Kaline/50 40.00
3 Andre Dawson/100 20.00
5 Cal Ripken Jr./25 140.00
7 Dale Murphy/100 25.00
9 Don Mattingly/50 50.00
12 Frank Robinson/100 35.00
13 Frank Thomas/25 50.00
14 Gary Carter/25 25.00
18 Joe Morgan/50 25.00
19 Johnny Bench/25 50.00
21 Kirk Gibson/25 25.00
23 Mark Grace/25 40.00
26 Orlando Cepeda/100 20.00
27 Paul Molitor/25 40.00
29 Ralph Kiner/100 30.00
33 Robin Yount/25 50.00
34 Rod Carew/25 30.00
36 Stan Musial/25 65.00
38 Tony Gwynn/50 40.00

Lumberjacks Signature Combos

NM/M

Production 1-100
3 Andre Dawson/Bat-Jsy/100 20.00
5 Cal Ripken Jr./Bat-Jsy/25 140.00
7 Dale Murphy/Bat-Jsy/100 25.00
9 Don Mattingly/Bat-Jsy/50 50.00
13 Frank Thomas/Bat-Jsy/25 50.00
14 Gary Carter/Bat-Jsy/25 25.00
23 Mark Grace/Bat-Jsy/25 40.00
38 Tony Gwynn/Bat-Jsy/25 45.00

Lumberjacks Signature Jersey

NM/M

Production 1-100
3 Andre Dawson/100 20.00
5 Cal Ripken Jr./25 140.00
7 Dale Murphy/100 25.00
9 Don Mattingly/50 50.00
10 Duke Snider/Pants/50 30.00
13 Frank Thomas/25 50.00
14 Gary Carter/50 25.00
17 Harmon Killebrew/25 40.00
19 Johnny Bench/25 50.00
23 Mark Grace/25 40.00
27 Paul Molitor/25 40.00
30 Reggie Jackson/25 40.00
33 Robin Yount/25 50.00
38 Tony Gwynn/50 40.00

Matching Numbers

NM/M

Production 5-50
Prime: No Pricing
Production 1-5
1 Ted Williams, Roger Maris/25 160.00
2 Nolan Ryan, Kerry Wood/50 35.00
3 Cal Ripken Jr., Gary Carter/50 40.00
5 Johnny Bench, Albert Pujols/50 40.00
6 Roger Clemens, W. Clark/50 35.00
7 Willie McCovey, Reggie Jackson/25 20.00
8 Ryne Sandberg, Don Mattingly/50 35.00
9 Duke Snider, Joe Cronin/25 25.00

Monikers Bronze

NM/M

Production 1-100
9 Miguel Cabrera/100 25.00
10 Miguel Cabrera/100 25.00
13 Mark Prior/50 35.00
14 Mark Prior/50 35.00
25 Ben Sheets/100 15.00
27 Melvin Mora/50 15.00
29 Rafael Furcal/25 20.00
32 Jake Peavy/50 25.00
33 Francisco Cordero/25 15.00
38 Michael Young/25 25.00
40 Joe Nathan/25 20.00
43 Eric Chavez/25 25.00
45 Roy Oswalt/50 25.00
49 Edgar Renteria/25 20.00
50 Mark Buehrle/25 30.00
57 Sean Casey/50 15.00
59 Octavio Dotel/25 12.00
60 Francisco Rodriguez/25 30.00
61 Jose Guillen/25 20.00
66 Travis Hafner/50 15.00
67 Rich Harden/50 15.00
71 Milton Bradley/25 15.00
73 Torii Hunter/25 25.00
74 Paul Konerko/50 30.00
76 Tim Hudson/25 25.00
80 Justin Morneau/100 25.00
82 Jose Vidro/25 15.00
84 Josh Beckett/25 30.00
85 Craig Biggio/25 30.00
89 Jacque Jones/50 15.00
91 Roy Halladay/25 15.00
93 Magglio Ordonez/100 15.00
96 Brandon Webb/50 15.00
97 Preston Wilson/50 15.00
98 Shannon Stewart/50 10.00
99 Trot Nixon/50 20.00
105 Bobby Crosby/40 15.00
107 Alfonso Soriano/25 30.00
108 Carlos Zambrano/50 25.00
109 Keith Foulke/25 30.00
110 Aubrey Huff/50 15.00
112 Mark Teixeira/100 25.00
116 Carlos Beltran/25 30.00
118 Johan Santana/100 30.00
121 Scott Rolen/25 30.00
123 Carlos Lee/50 20.00
124 Derrek Lee/50 25.00
130 Garret Anderson/100 15.00
131 Austin Kearns/100 15.00
133 Omar Vizquel/50 20.00
135 Mark Mulder/50 20.00
139 Mark Loretta/25 20.00
141 David Wright/50 60.00
144 Victor Martinez/25 15.00
151 Willie Mays/25 175.00
152 Ryne Sandberg/25 50.00
158 Duke Snider/50 25.00
159 Don Mattingly/25 50.00
160 Bob Gibson/50 50.00
162 Al Kaline/50 30.00
163 Nolan Ryan/25 80.00
164 Stan Musial/25 60.00
165 George Kell/50 15.00
166 Harmon Killebrew/50 30.00
167 Cal Ripken Jr./25 120.00
176 Hayden Penn/50 20.00
177 Ambiorix Concepcion/50 15.00
179 Prince Fielder/50 60.00
181 Wladimir Balentien/50 20.00
182 Jason Hammel/50 15.00
183 Keiichi Yabu/50 25.00
184 Brandon McCarthy/50 50.00
185 Ubaldo Jimenez/50 15.00
186 Keiichi Yabu/50 25.00
187 Miguel Negron/50 10.00
188 Mike Morse/50 30.00
189 Nate McLouth/50 25.00
190 Norihiro Nakamura/50 50.00
191 Brandon McCarthy/50 50.00
192 Tony Pena/50 10.00
193 Ambiorix Concepcion/50 15.00
194 Raul Tablado/50 15.00
195 Hayden Penn/50 20.00
196 Sean Thompson/50 12.00
198 Ubaldo Jimenez/50 15.00
199 Wladimir Balentien/50 20.00
200 Prince Fielder/50 60.00

Monikers Material Bat Bronze

NM/M

Production 1-100
Platinum: No Pricing
Production One Set
9 Miguel Cabrera/50 35.00
10 Miguel Cabrera/50 35.00
13 Mark Prior/25 40.00
14 Mark Prior/25 40.00
29 Rafael Furcal/75 15.00
34 Aramis Ramirez/100 20.00
37 Jason Bay/100 20.00
38 Michael Young/100 20.00
43 Eric Chavez/50 20.00
45 Roy Oswalt/50 25.00
50 Mark Buehrle/50 25.00
57 Sean Casey/25 15.00
66 Travis Hafner/100 15.00
73 Torii Hunter/50 20.00
74 Paul Konerko/50 30.00
80 Justin Morneau/100 25.00
82 Jose Vidro/100 10.00
85 Craig Biggio/25 30.00
93 Magglio Ordonez/50 20.00
97 Preston Wilson/50 15.00
98 Shannon Stewart/50 10.00
107 Alfonso Soriano/25 30.00
110 Aubrey Huff/100 12.00
111 Adrian Beltre/25 20.00
112 Mark Teixeira/50 30.00
116 Carlos Beltran/25 30.00
121 Scott Rolen/25 30.00
123 Carlos Lee/100 15.00
124 Derrek Lee/100 20.00
130 Garret Anderson/100 15.00
131 Austin Kearns/100 15.00
140 Vernon Wells/50 15.00
141 David Wright/50 70.00
143 David Ortiz/50 50.00
144 Victor Martinez/100 15.00
147 Angel Berroa/100 10.00

Monikers Material Button Gold

No Pricing
Production 1-5
Platinum: No Pricing
Production One Set

Monikers Material Jersey Number Silver

NM/M

Production 1-75
Prime Platinum: No Pricing
Production One Set
9 Miguel Cabrera/50 35.00
10 Miguel Cabrera/50 35.00
13 Mark Prior/25 40.00
25 Ben Sheets/Pants/50 20.00
33 Francisco Cordero/25 25.00
34 Aramis Ramirez/75 20.00
38 Michael Young/50 25.00
43 Eric Chavez/75 20.00
45 Roy Oswalt/75 25.00
57 Sean Casey/75 15.00
60 Francisco Rodriguez/75 25.00
66 Travis Hafner/50 20.00
70 Andruw Jones/25 40.00
85 Craig Biggio/25 30.00
89 Jacque Jones/25 15.00
90 Lyle Overbay/75 10.00
98 Shannon Stewart/75 10.00
99 Trot Nixon/50 35.00
101 Dontrelle Willis/24 30.00
107 Alfonso Soriano/50 30.00
112 Mark Teixeira/50 30.00
117 Bobby Abreu/75 20.00
121 Scott Rolen/25 30.00
124 Derrek Lee/25 25.00
128 Jim Edmonds/25 35.00
130 Garret Anderson/50 20.00
131 Austin Kearns/75 15.00
140 Vernon Wells/50 15.00
141 David Wright/75 70.00
143 David Ortiz/75 50.00
144 Victor Martinez/75 15.00
152 Ryne Sandberg/50 40.00
158 Duke Snider/25 40.00
159 Don Mattingly/50 60.00
160 Bob Gibson/50 30.00
163 Nolan Ryan/25 100.00
164 Stan Musial/25 80.00
166 Harmon Killebrew/50 35.00
167 Cal Ripken Jr./25 140.00

Monikers Material Jersey Prime Gold

NM/M

Production 1-100
Platinum: No Pricing
Production One Set
9 Miguel Cabrera/50 40.00
10 Miguel Cabrera/50 40.00
13 Mark Prior/25 50.00
14 Mark Prior/25 50.00
25 Ben Sheets/50 25.00
34 Aramis Ramirez/100 25.00
38 Michael Young/100 25.00
43 Eric Chavez/75 25.00
45 Roy Oswalt/100 30.00
57 Sean Casey/30 20.00
60 Francisco Rodriguez/75 30.00
66 Travis Hafner/100 25.00
70 Andruw Jones/50 40.00
84 Josh Beckett/25 40.00
88 Barry Zito/25 30.00
89 Jacque Jones/50 15.00
98 Shannon Stewart/75 15.00
107 Alfonso Soriano/50 40.00
112 Mark Teixeira/20 50.00
117 Bobby Abreu/100 25.00
121 Scott Rolen/50 35.00
128 Jim Edmonds/25 40.00
130 Garret Anderson/50 25.00
131 Austin Kearns/75 20.00
140 Vernon Wells/50 20.00
152 Ryne Sandberg/25 75.00
159 Don Mattingly/25 85.00
160 Bob Gibson/25 50.00
163 Nolan Ryan/25 120.00
167 Cal Ripken Jr./25 175.00

Monikers Silver

NM/M

Production 1-50
9 Miguel Cabrera/50 30.00
10 Miguel Cabrera/50 30.00
13 Mark Prior/25 40.00
14 Mark Prior/25 40.00
25 Ben Sheets/50 20.00
27 Melvin Mora/25 20.00
29 Rafael Furcal/25 20.00
32 Jake Peavy/50 25.00
33 Francisco Cordero/25 15.00
38 Michael Young/25 25.00
40 Joe Nathan/25 20.00
43 Eric Chavez/25 25.00
45 Roy Oswalt/25 30.00
49 Edgar Renteria/25 25.00
50 Mark Buehrle/25 30.00
57 Sean Casey/25 20.00
59 Octavio Dotel/25 12.00
60 Francisco Rodriguez/25 30.00
61 Jose Guillen/25 20.00
66 Travis Hafner/50 15.00
67 Rich Harden/50 15.00
71 Milton Bradley/25 15.00
80 Justin Morneau/50 25.00
89 Jacque Jones/25 15.00
93 Magglio Ordonez/50 15.00
96 Brandon Webb/25 20.00
97 Preston Wilson/25 20.00
98 Shannon Stewart/25 15.00
99 Trot Nixon/25 25.00
105 Bobby Crosby/29 20.00
108 Carlos Zambrano/50 25.00
109 Keith Foulke/25 30.00
110 Aubrey Huff/25 20.00
112 Mark Teixeira/50 35.00
118 Johan Santana/50 35.00
123 Carlos Lee/50 20.00
130 Garret Anderson/50 20.00
131 Austin Kearns/50 15.00
133 Omar Vizquel/25 25.00
135 Mark Mulder/50 20.00
139 Mark Loretta/25 20.00
141 David Wright/25 70.00
144 Victor Martinez/25 15.00
151 Willie Mays/25 175.00
152 Ryne Sandberg/25 50.00
158 Duke Snider/25 30.00
159 Don Mattingly/25 50.00
162 Al Kaline/25 35.00
163 Nolan Ryan/25 80.00
164 Stan Musial/25 60.00
165 George Kell/50 15.00
166 Harmon Killebrew/25 40.00
167 Cal Ripken Jr./25 120.00

Team Trademarks

NM/M

Common Player: 3.00
Production 50 Sets
Foil: No Pricing
Production 10 Sets
1 Ryne Sandberg 8.00
2 George Brett 8.00
3 Steve Carlton 3.00
4 Reggie Jackson 4.00
5 Edgar Martinez 3.00
6 Barry Larkin 4.00
7 Ozzie Smith 6.00
8 Carlton Fisk 4.00
9 Wade Boggs 5.00
10 Will Clark 4.00
11 Nolan Ryan 8.00
12 Gary Carter 3.00
13 Don Mattingly 8.00

14	Willie Stargell	4.00
15	Don Sutton	3.00
16	Kirk Gibson	3.00
17	Kirby Puckett	5.00
18	Dale Murphy	4.00
19	Rickey Henderson	4.00
20	Willie Mays	8.00
21	Cal Ripken Jr.	10.00
22	Paul Molitor	4.00
23	Tony Gwynn	5.00
24	Andre Dawson	3.00
25	Bob Feller	4.00
26	Alan Trammell	3.00
27	Dave Parker	3.00
28	Dave Righetti	3.00
29	Dwight Gooden	3.00
30	Harold Baines	3.00
31	Jack Morris	3.00
32	John Kruk	3.00
33	Lee Smith	3.00
34	Lenny Dykstra	3.00
35	Luis Tiant	3.00
36	Matt Williams	3.00
37	Ron Guidry	3.00
38	Tony Oliva	3.00

Team Trademarks Jersey Number

		NM/M
Production 1-50		
1	Ryne Sandberg/23	20.00
3	Steve Carlton/Pants/32	8.00
4	Reggie Jackson/44	10.00
8	Carlton Fisk/50	8.00
9	Wade Boggs/26	10.00
11	Nolan Ryan/Pants/34	25.00
20	Willie Mays/24	40.00

Team Trademarks Jersey Number Prime

		NM/M
1	Ryne Sandberg/50	25.00
2	George Brett/50	25.00
3	Steve Carlton/50	10.00
4	Reggie Jackson/50	15.00
5	Edgar Martinez/50	15.00
6	Barry Larkin/50	15.00
7	Ozzie Smith/50	20.00
8	Carlton Fisk/50	15.00
9	Wade Boggs/50	15.00
10	Will Clark/50	15.00
11	Nolan Ryan/50	25.00
12	Gary Carter/50	12.00
13	Don Mattingly/40	25.00
14	Willie Stargell/50	15.00
15	Don Sutton/25	12.00
16	Kirk Gibson/50	12.00
18	Dale Murphy/50	15.00
19	Rickey Henderson/50	15.00
21	Cal Ripken Jr./25	50.00
23	Tony Gwynn/50	20.00
24	Andre Dawson/25	15.00
26	Alan Trammell/25	12.00
27	Dave Parker/50	10.00
29	Dwight Gooden/50	15.00
30	Harold Baines/25	15.00
31	Jack Morris/47	10.00
32	John Kruk/25	15.00
33	Lee Smith/47	10.00
34	Lenny Dykstra/25	15.00
38	Tony Oliva/26	15.00

Team Trademarks Signature

		NM/M
Production 5-50		
1	Ryne Sandberg/25	50.00
3	Steve Carlton/25	25.00
4	Reggie Jackson/25	30.00
5	Edgar Martinez/50	20.00
6	Barry Larkin/50	25.00
7	Ozzie Smith/50	35.00
8	Carlton Fisk/50	25.00
9	Wade Boggs/25	35.00
10	Will Clark/50	25.00
11	Nolan Ryan/50	75.00
12	Gary Carter/50	15.00
13	Don Mattingly/25	50.00
15	Don Sutton/100	12.00
16	Kirk Gibson/50	20.00
17	Kirby Puckett/25	40.00
18	Dale Murphy/100	20.00
20	Willie Mays/25	160.00
21	Cal Ripken Jr./50	90.00
22	Paul Molitor/25	25.00
23	Tony Gwynn/25	40.00
24	Andre Dawson/100	15.00
25	Bob Feller/50	20.00
26	Alan Trammell/25	25.00
27	Dave Parker/50	15.00
28	Dave Righetti/25	20.00
29	Dwight Gooden/50	15.00
30	Harold Baines/50	15.00
31	Jack Morris/50	12.00
32	John Kruk/25	20.00
33	Lee Smith/50	15.00
34	Lenny Dykstra/25	20.00
35	Luis Tiant/50	15.00
36	Matt Williams/50	20.00
37	Ron Guidry/25	25.00
38	Tony Oliva/50	15.00

Team Trade. Sig. Jersey Number Prime

		NM/M
3	Steve Carlton/25	30.00
24	Andre Dawson/25	30.00
27	Dave Parker/39	20.00
31	Jack Morris/47	20.00
33	Lee Smith/47	25.00
38	Tony Oliva/26	35.00

Team Trademarks Sign. Jersey Number

		NM/M
Production 1-72		
4	Reggie Jackson/44	50.00
8	Carlton Fisk/72	35.00
9	Wade Boggs/26	50.00
11	Nolan Ryan/Pants/34	90.00
17	Kirby Puckett/34	60.00
27	Dave Parker/39	25.00
31	Jack Morris/47	20.00
33	Lee Smith/47	20.00
37	Ron Guidry/Pants/49	20.00

Threads Button

No Pricing
Production 1-7

Threads Jersey Number

		NM/M
Production 1-50		
Logo:		No Pricing
Production One Set		
152	Ryne Sandberg/50	15.00
154	Ted Williams/25	60.00
157	Whitey Ford/50	12.00
158	Duke Snider/25	15.00
164	Stan Musial/25	25.00
166	Harmon Killebrew/50	20.00

Threads Jersey Prime

		NM/M
Production 5-100		
1	Roger Clemens/25	25.00
5	Todd Helton/100	10.00
6	Todd Helton/100	10.00
7	Vladimir Guerrero/100	12.00
8	Vladimir Guerrero/Jkt/30	20.00
9	Miguel Cabrera/100	10.00
10	Miguel Cabrera/100	10.00
12	Albert Pujols/50	30.00
13	Mark Prior/100	8.00
14	Mark Prior/25	10.00
15	Chipper Jones/100	10.00
16	Chipper Jones/100	10.00
17	Jeff Bagwell/100	8.00
18	Jeff Bagwell/100	8.00
19	Kerry Wood/100	8.00
22	Carl Crawford/100	5.00
23	Mariano Rivera/60	12.00
25	Ben Sheets/100	8.00
27	Melvin Mora/25	10.00
28	Corey Patterson/100	5.00
29	Rafael Furcal/100	5.00
30	Jim Thome/100	8.00
34	Aramis Ramirez/50	8.00
35	Javy Lopez/100	5.00
38	Michael Young/100	5.00
39	Ivan Rodriguez/100	8.00
42	Adam Dunn/100	8.00
43	Eric Chavez/100	5.00
45	Roy Oswalt/100	5.00
48	Johnny Damon/50	15.00
50	Mark Buehrle/50	8.00
53	Hank Blalock/100	5.00
55	Brad Radke/50	5.00
57	Sean Casey/50	5.00
58	Mike Lowell/100	5.00
60	Francisco Rodriguez/100	5.00
62	Greg Maddux/25	25.00
63	A.J. Burnett/75	5.00
66	Travis Hafner/100	5.00
68	Bret Boone/100	5.00
70	Andruw Jones/100	10.00
73	Torii Hunter/100	5.00
74	Paul Konerko/100	8.00
79	Lance Berkman/100	5.00
80	Justin Morneau/100	10.00
82	Jose Vidro/100	5.00
84	Josh Beckett/100	5.00
86	Luis Gonzalez/100	5.00
88	Barry Zito/100	5.00
91	Roy Halladay/100	5.00
94	Mike Sweeney/100	5.00
95	Rafael Palmeiro/100	8.00
97	Preston Wilson/100	5.00
98	Shannon Stewart/50	5.00
99	Trot Nixon/25	8.00
100	Mike Piazza/100	12.00
101	Dontrelle Willis/100	8.00
103	Andy Pettitte/50	10.00
104	Kazuo Matsui/100	5.00
107	Alfonso Soriano/100	8.00
110	Aubrey Huff/100	5.00
111	Adrian Beltre/50	8.00
112	Mark Teixeira/60	10.00
114	Miguel Tejada/100	8.00
117	Bobby Abreu/100	5.00
119	Manny Ramirez/60	15.00
121	Scott Rolen/100	10.00
124	Derrek Lee/50	10.00
127	John Smoltz/100	8.00
128	Jim Edmonds/100	8.00
130	Garret Anderson/60	8.00
131	Austin Kearns/100	5.00
138	Mike Mussina/50	10.00
140	Vernon Wells/100	5.00
141	David Wright/100	25.00
142	Marcus Giles/100	5.00
144	Victor Martinez/75	5.00
145	Hideki Matsui/100	40.00
146	C.C. Sabathia/100	5.00
150	Jorge Posada/75	10.00
152	Ryne Sandberg/50	25.00
153	Rickey Henderson/25	20.00
156	George Brett/50	25.00
159	Don Mattingly/50	25.00
160	Bob Gibson/25	20.00
161	Hank Aaron/25	75.00
163	Nolan Ryan/100	25.00
167	Cal Ripken Jr./100	30.00
169	Roger Clemens/50	20.00
170	Curt Schilling/100	8.00
171	Rafael Palmeiro/100	8.00
173	Mike Piazza/100	12.00
174	Greg Maddux/100	15.00
175	Sammy Sosa/100	15.00

Timber Barrel

No Pricing
Production 1-3

TNT

		NM/M
Production 1-50		
Prime:		.50X-1.5X
Production 5-100		
7	Vladimir Guerrero/ Bat-Jsy/30	15.00
10	Miguel Cabrera/Bat-Jsy/25	12.00
11	Albert Pujols/Bat-Jsy/25	25.00
12	Albert Pujols/Bat-Jsy/50	25.00
13	Mark Prior/Bat-Jsy/50	8.00
14	Mark Prior/Bat-Jsy/50	8.00
15	Chipper Jones/Bat-Jsy/50	12.00
16	Chipper Jones/Bat-Jsy/50	12.00
39	Ivan Rodriguez/Bat-Jsy/25	12.00
42	Adam Dunn/Bat-Jsy/50	5.00
62	Greg Maddux/Bat-Jsy/25	20.00
100	Mike Piazza/Bat-Jsy/50	12.00
107	Alfonso Soriano/Bat-Jsy/50	12.00
112	Mark Teixeira/Bat-Jsy/50	10.00
119	Manny Ramirez/Bat-Jsy/50	12.00
121	Scott Rolen/Bat-Jsy/50	10.00
124	Derrek Lee/Bat-Jsy/50	8.00
143	David Ortiz/Bat-Jsy/50	15.00
151	Willie Mays/Bat-Jsy/25	50.00
153	Rickey Henderson/ Bat-Jsy/50	15.00
154	Ted Williams/Bat-Jsy/25	85.00
159	Don Mattingly/Bat-Jsy/50	20.00
161	Hank Aaron/Bat-Jsy/25	50.00
163	Nolan Ryan/Bat-Jsy/50	25.00
164	Stan Musial/Bat-Jsy/25	30.00
166	Harmon Killebrew/ Bat-Jsy/25	20.00
167	Cal Ripken Jr./Bat-Jsy/50	30.00
169	Roger Clemens/Bat-Jsy/50	15.00
171	Rafael Palmeiro/Bat-Jsy/50	10.00
172	Randy Johnson/Bat-Jsy/25	15.00
174	Greg Maddux/Bat-Jsy/50	15.00
175	Sammy Sosa/Bat-Jsy/50	15.00

M

1996 Metal Universe

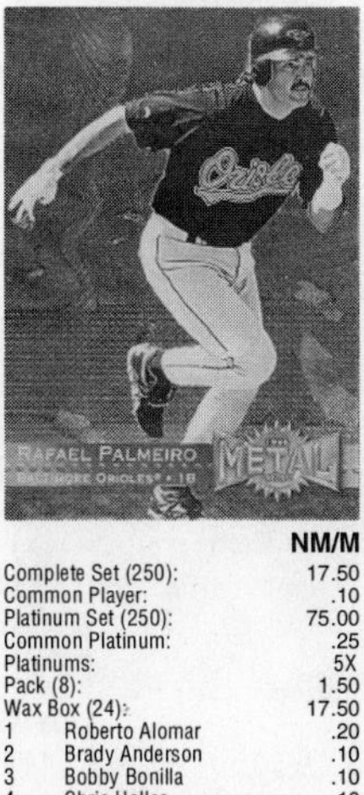

		NM/M
Complete Set (250):		17.50
Common Player:		.10
Platinum Set (250):		75.00
Common Platinum:		.25
Platinums:		5X
Pack (8):		1.50
Wax Box (24):		17.50
1	Roberto Alomar	.20
2	Brady Anderson	.10
3	Bobby Bonilla	.10
4	Chris Holles	.10
5	Ben McDonald	.10
6	Mike Mussina	.40
7	Randy Myers	.10
8	Rafael Palmeiro	.60
9	Cal Ripken Jr.	2.50
10	B.J. Surhoff	.10
11	Luis Alicea	.10
12	Jose Canseco	.50
13	Roger Clemens	1.25
14	Wil Cordero	.10
15	Tom Gordon	.10
16	Mike Greenwell	.10
17	Tim Naehring	.10
18	Troy O'Leary	.10
19	Mike Stanley	.10
20	John Valentin	.10
21	Mo Vaughn	.10
22	Tim Wakefield	.10
23	Garret Anderson	.10
24	Chili Davis	.10
25	Gary DiSarcina	.10
26	Jim Edmonds	.10
27	Chuck Finley	.10
28	Todd Greene	.10
29	Mark Langston	.10
30	Troy Percival	.10
31	Tony Phillips	.10
32	Tim Salmon	.10
33	Lee Smith	.10
34	J.T. Snow	.10
35	Ray Durham	.10
36	Alex Fernandez	.10
37	Ozzie Guillen	.10
38	Roberto Hernandez	.10
39	Lyle Mouton	.10
40	Frank Thomas	.75
41	Robin Ventura	.10
42	Sandy Alomar	.10
43	Carlos Baerga	.10
44	Albert Belle	.10
45	Orel Hershiser	.10
46	Kenny Lofton	.10
47	Dennis Martinez	.10
48	Jack McDowell	.10
49	Jose Mesa	.10
50	Eddie Murray	.75
51	Charles Nagy	.10
52	Manny Ramirez	.75
53	Julian Tavarez	.10
54	Jim Thome	.60
55	Omar Vizquel	.10
56	Chad Curtis	.10
57	Cecil Fielder	.10
58	John Flaherty	.10
59	Travis Fryman	.10
60	Chris Gomez	.10
61	Felipe Lira	.10
62	Kevin Appier	.10
63	Johnny Damon	.35
64	Tom Goodwin	.10
65	Mark Gubicza	.10
66	Jeff Montgomery	.10
67	Jon Nunnally	.10
68	Ricky Bones	.10
69	Jeff Cirillo	.10
70	John Jaha	.10
71	Dave Nilsson	.10
72	Joe Oliver	.10
73	Kevin Seitzer	.10
74	Greg Vaughn	.10
75	Marty Cordova	.10
76	Chuck Knoblauch	.10
77	Pat Meares	.10
78	Paul Molitor	.75
79	Pedro Munoz	.10
80	Kirby Puckett	1.00
81	Brad Radke	.10
82	Scott Stahoviak	.10
83	Matt Walbeck	.10
84	Wade Boggs	1.00
85	David Cone	.10
86	Joe Girardi	.10
87	Derek Jeter	2.50
88	Jim Leyritz	.10
89	Tino Martinez	.10
90	Don Mattingly	1.50
91	Paul O'Neill	.10
92	Andy Pettitte	.25
93	Tim Raines	.10
94	Kenny Rogers	.10
95	Ruben Sierra	.10
96	John Wetteland	.10
97	Bernie Williams	.10
98	Geronimo Berroa	.10
99	Dennis Eckersley	.65
100	Brent Gates	.10
101	Mark McGwire	2.00
102	Steve Ontiveros	.10
103	Terry Steinbach	.10
104	Jay Buhner	.10
105	Vince Coleman	.10
106	Joey Cora	.10
107	Ken Griffey Jr.	1.50
108	Randy Johnson	.75
109	Edgar Martinez	.10
110	Alex Rodriguez	2.00
111	Paul Sorrento	.10
112	Will Clark	.10
113	Juan Gonzalez	.50
114	Rusty Greer	.10
115	Dean Palmer	.10
116	Ivan Rodriguez	.65
117	Mickey Tettleton	.10
118	Joe Carter	.10
119	Alex Gonzalez	.10
120	Shawn Green	.30
121	Erik Hanson	.10
122	Pat Hentgen	.10
123	Sandy Martinez **RC**	.10

124	Otis Nixon	.10
125	John Olerud	.10
126	Steve Avery	.10
127	Tom Glavine	.40
128	Marquis Grissom	.10
129	Chipper Jones	1.00
130	David Justice	.10
131	Ryan Klesko	.10
132	Mark Lemke	.10
133	Javier Lopez	.10
134	Greg Maddux	1.00
135	Fred McGriff	.10
136	John Smoltz	.10
137	Mark Wohlers	.10
138	Frank Castillo	.10
139	Shawon Dunston	.10
140	Luis Gonzalez	.20
141	Mark Grace	.10
142	Brian McRae	.10
143	Jaime Navarro	.10
144	Rey Sanchez	.10
145	Ryne Sandberg	1.00
146	Sammy Sosa	1.25
147	Bret Boone	.10
148	Curtis Goodwin	.10
149	Barry Larkin	.10
150	Hal Morris	.10
151	Reggie Sanders	.10
152	Pete Schourek	.10
153	John Smiley	.10
154	Dante Bichette	.10
155	Vinny Castilla	.10
156	Andres Galarraga	.10
157	Bret Saberhagen	.10
158	Bill Swift	.10
159	Larry Walker	.10
160	Walt Weiss	.10
161	Kurt Abbott	.10
162	John Burkett	.10
163	Greg Colbrunn	.10
164	Jeff Conine	.10
165	Chris Hammond	.10
166	Charles Johnson	.10
167	Al Leiter	.10
168	Pat Rapp	.10
169	Gary Sheffield	.40
170	Quilvio Veras	.10
171	Devon White	.10
172	Jeff Bagwell	.75
173	Derek Bell	.10
174	Sean Berry	.10
175	Craig Biggio	.10
176	Doug Drabek	.10
177	Tony Eusebio	.10
178	Brian Hunter	.10
179	Orlando Miller	.10
180	Shane Reynolds	.10
181	Mike Blowers	.10
182	Roger Cedeno	.10
183	Eric Karros	.10
184	Ramon Martinez	.10
185	Raul Mondesi	.10
186	Hideo Nomo	.60
187	Mike Piazza	1.50
188	Moises Alou	.10
189	Yamil Benitez	.10
190	Darrin Fletcher	.10
191	Cliff Floyd	.10
192	Pedro Martinez	.75
193	Carlos Perez	.10
194	David Segui	.10
195	Tony Tarasco	.10
196	Rondell White	.10
197	Edgardo Alfonzo	.10
198	Rico Brogna	.10
199	Carl Everett	.10
200	Todd Hundley	.10
201	Jason Isringhausen	.10
202	Lance Johnson	.10
203	Bobby Jones	.10
204	Jeff Kent	.10
205	Bill Pulsipher	.10
206	Jose Vizcaino	.10
207	Ricky Bottalico	.10
208	Darren Daulton	.10
209	Lenny Dykstra	.10
210	Jim Eisenreich	.10
211	Gregg Jefferies	.10
212	Mickey Morandini	.10
213	Heathcliff Slocumb	.10
214	Jay Bell	.10
215	Carlos Garcia	.10
216	Jeff King	.10
217	Al Martin	.10
218	Orlando Merced	.10
219	Dan Miceli	.10
220	Denny Neagle	.10
221	Andy Benes	.10
222	Royce Clayton	.10
223	Gary Gaetti	.10
224	Ron Gant	.10
225	Bernard Gilkey	.10
226	Brian Jordan	.10
227	Ray Lankford	.10
228	John Mabry	.10
229	Ozzie Smith	1.00
230	Todd Stottlemyre	.10
231	Andy Ashby	.10
232	Brad Ausmus	.10
233	Ken Caminiti	.10
234	Steve Finley	.10
235	Tony Gwynn	1.00
236	Joey Hamilton	.10
237	Rickey Henderson	.75
238	Trevor Hoffman	.10

239	Wally Joyner	.10
240	Rod Beck	.10
241	Barry Bonds	2.50
242	Glenallen Hill	.10
243	Stan Javier	.10
244	Mark Leiter	.10
245	Deion Sanders	.10
246	William VanLandingham	.10
247	Matt Williams	.10
248	Checklist	.10
249	Checklist	.10
250	Checklist	.10

Platinum Edition

Complete Set (247):	75.00
Common Player:	.25
Stars:	5X

(See 1996 Metal Universe for checklist and base card values.)

Heavy Metal

		NM/M
Complete Set (10):		5.00
Common Player:		.35
1	Albert Belle	.35
2	Barry Bonds	1.50
3	Juan Gonzalez	.50
4	Ken Griffey Jr.	1.00
5	Mark McGwire	1.25
6	Mike Piazza	1.00
7	Sammy Sosa	.90
8	Frank Thomas	.60
9	Mo Vaughn	.35
10	Matt Williams	.35

Mining for Gold

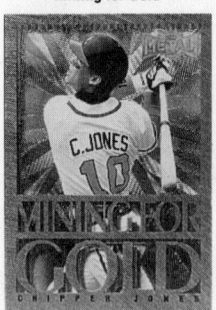

		NM/M
Complete Set (12):		12.50
Common Player:		.75
1	Yamil Benitez	.75
2	Marty Cordova	.75
3	Shawn Green	2.00
4	Todd Greene	.75
5	Brian Hunter	.75

6	Derek Jeter	7.50
7	Charles Johnson	.75
8	Chipper Jones	3.50
9	Hideo Nomo	2.50
10	Alex Ochoa	.75
11	Andy Pettitte	1.00
12	Quilvio Veras	.75

Mother Lode

		NM/M
Complete Set (12):		15.00
Common Player:		.75
1	Barry Bonds	4.50
2	Jim Edmonds	.75
3	Ken Griffey Jr.	3.50
4	Kenny Lofton	.75
5	Raul Mondesi	.75
6	Rafael Palmeiro	1.50
7	Manny Ramirez	2.00
8	Cal Ripken Jr.	4.50
9	Tim Salmon	.75
10	Ryne Sandberg	3.00
11	Frank Thomas	2.00
12	Matt Williams	.75

Platinum Portraits

		NM/M
Complete Set (10):		4.00
Common Player:		.40
1	Garret Anderson	.40
2	Marty Cordova	.40
3	Jim Edmonds	.40
4	Jason Isringhausen	.40
5	Chipper Jones	2.25
6	Ryan Klesko	.40
7	Hideo Nomo	1.00
8	Carlos Perez	.40
9	Manny Ramirez	1.50
10	Rondell White	.40

Titanium

		NM/M
Complete Set (10):		15.00
Common Player:		.50
1	Albert Belle	.50
2	Barry Bonds	4.00
3	Ken Griffey Jr.	2.50
4	Tony Gwynn	1.50
5	Greg Maddux	1.50
6	Mike Piazza	2.50
7	Cal Ripken Jr.	4.00
8	Frank Thomas	1.00
9	Mo Vaughn	.50
10	Matt Williams	.50

1997 Metal Universe

		NM/M
Complete Set (250):		17.50
Common Player:		.10
Pack (8):		1.50
Wax Box (24):		18.00
1	Roberto Alomar	.20
2	Brady Anderson	.10
3	Rocky Coppinger	.10
4	Chris Hoiles	.10
5	Eddie Murray	.60
6	Mike Mussina	.40
7	Rafael Palmeiro	.50
8	Cal Ripken Jr.	2.00
9	B.J. Surhoff	.10
10	Brant Brown	.10
11	Mark Grace	.10
12	Brian McRae	.10
13	Jaime Navarro	.10
14	Ryne Sandberg	.75
15	Sammy Sosa	1.00
16	Amaury Telemaco	.10
17	Steve Trachsel	.10
18	Darren Bragg	.10
19	Jose Canseco	.40
20	Roger Clemens	1.00
21	Nomar Garciaparra	1.00
22	Tom Gordon	.10
23	Tim Naehring	.10
24	Mike Stanley	.10
25	John Valentin	.10
26	Mo Vaughn	.40
27	Jermaine Dye	.10
28	Tom Glavine	.30
29	Marquis Grissom	.10
30	Andruw Jones	.60
31	Chipper Jones	.75
32	Ryan Klesko	.10
33	Greg Maddux	.75
34	Fred McGriff	.10
35	John Smoltz	.10
36	Garret Anderson	.10
37	George Arias	.10
38	Gary DiSarcina	.10
39	Jim Edmonds	.10
40	Darin Erstad	.25
41	Chuck Finley	.10
42	Troy Percival	.10
43	Tim Salmon	.10
44	Bret Boone	.10
45	Jeff Brantley	.10
46	Eric Davis	.10
47	Barry Larkin	.10
48	Hal Morris	.10
49	Mark Portugal	.10
50	Reggie Sanders	.10
51	John Smiley	.10
52	Wilson Alvarez	.10
53	Harold Baines	.10
54	James Baldwin	.10
55	Albert Belle	.10
56	Mike Cameron	.10
57	Ray Durham	.10
58	Alex Fernandez	.10
59	Roberto Hernandez	.10
60	Tony Phillips	.10
61	Frank Thomas	.60
62	Robin Ventura	.10
63	Jeff Cirillo	.10
64	Jeff D'Amico	.10
65	John Jaha	.10
66	Scott Karl	.10
67	Ben McDonald	.10
68	Marc Newfield	.10
69	Dave Nilsson	.10
70	Jose Valentin	.10
71	Dante Bichette	.10
72	Ellis Burks	.10
73	Vinny Castilla	.10
74	Andres Galarraga	.10
75	Kevin Ritz	.10
76	Larry Walker	.10
77	Walt Weiss	.10
78	Jamey Wright	.10
79	Eric Young	.10
80	Julio Franco	.10
81	Orel Hershiser	.10
82	Kenny Lofton	.10
83	Jack McDowell	.10
84	Jose Mesa	.10

85	Charles Nagy	.10
86	Manny Ramirez	.60
87	Jim Thome	.50
88	Omar Vizquel	.10
89	Matt Williams	.10
90	Kevin Appier	.10
91	Johnny Damon	.35
92	Chili Davis	.10
93	Tom Goodwin	.10
94	Keith Lockhart	.10
95	Jeff Montgomery	.10
96	Craig Paquette	.10
97	Jose Rosado	.10
98	Michael Tucker	.10
99	Wilton Guerrero	.10
100	Todd Hollandsworth	.10
101	Eric Karros	.10
102	Ramon Martinez	.10
103	Raul Mondesi	.10
104	Hideo Nomo	.60
105	Mike Piazza	1.25
106	Ismael Valdes	.10
107	Todd Worrell	.10
108	Tony Clark	.10
109	Travis Fryman	.10
110	Bob Higginson	.10
111	Mark Lewis	.10
112	Melvin Nieves	.10
113	Justin Thompson	.10
114	Wade Boggs	.75
115	David Cone	.10
116	Cecil Fielder	.10
117	Dwight Gooden	.10
118	Derek Jeter	2.00
119	Tino Martinez	.10
120	Paul O'Neill	.10
121	Andy Pettitte	.20
122	Mariano Rivera	.20
123	Darryl Strawberry	.10
124	John Wetteland	.10
125	Bernie Williams	.10
126	Tony Batista	.10
127	Geronimo Berroa	.10
128	Scott Brosius	.10
129	Jason Giambi	.50
130	Jose Herrera	.10
131	Mark McGwire	1.50
132	John Wasdin	.10
133	Bob Abreu	.10
134	Jeff Bagwell	.60
135	Derek Bell	.10
136	Craig Biggio	.10
137	Brian Hunter	.10
138	Darryl Kile	.10
139	Orlando Miller	.10
140	Shane Reynolds	.10
141	Billy Wagner	.10
142	Donne Wall	.10
143	Jay Buhner	.10
144	Jeff Fassero	.10
145	Ken Griffey Jr.	1.25
146	Sterling Hitchcock	.10
147	Randy Johnson	.60
148	Edgar Martinez	.10
149	Alex Rodriguez	1.50
149p	Alex Rodriguez ("PROMOTIONAL SAMPLE")	1.50
150	Paul Sorrento	.10
151	Dan Wilson	.10
152	Moises Alou	.10
153	Darrin Fletcher	.10
154	Cliff Floyd	.10
155	Mark Grudzielanek	.10
156	Vladimir Guerrero	.60
157	Mike Lansing	.10
158	Pedro Martinez	.60
159	Henry Rodriguez	.10
160	Rondell White	.10
161	Will Clark	.10
162	Juan Gonzalez	.50
163	Rusty Greer	.10
164	Ken Hill	.10
165	Mark McLemore	.10
166	Dean Palmer	.10
167	Roger Pavlik	.10
168	Ivan Rodriguez	.50
169	Mickey Tettleton	.10
170	Bobby Bonilla	.10
171	Kevin Brown	.10
172	Greg Colbrunn	.10
173	Jeff Conine	.10
174	Jim Eisenreich	.10
175	Charles Johnson	.10
176	Al Leiter	.10
177	Robb Nen	.10
178	Edgar Renteria	.10
179	Gary Sheffield	.40
180	Devon White	.10
181	Joe Carter	.10
182	Carlos Delgado	.40
183	Alex Gonzalez	.10
184	Shawn Green	.35
185	Juan Guzman	.10
186	Pat Hentgen	.10
187	Orlando Merced	.10
188	John Olerud	.10
189	Robert Perez	.10
190	Ed Sprague	.10
191	Mark Clark	.10
192	John Franco	.10
193	Bernard Gilkey	.10
194	Todd Hundley	.10
195	Lance Johnson	.10
196	Bobby Jones	.10
197	Alex Ochoa	.10

198	Rey Ordonez	.10
199	Paul Wilson	.10
200	Ricky Bottalico	.10
201	Gregg Jefferies	.10
202	Wendell Magee Jr.	.10
203	Mickey Morandini	.10
204	Ricky Otero	.10
205	Scott Rolen	.50
206	Benito Santiago	.10
207	Curt Schilling	.25
208	Rich Becker	.10
209	Marty Cordova	.10
210	Chuck Knoblauch	.10
211	Pat Meares	.10
212	Paul Molitor	.60
213	Frank Rodriguez	.10
214	Terry Steinbach	.10
215	Todd Walker	.10
216	Andy Ashby	.10
217	Ken Caminiti	.10
218	Steve Finley	.10
219	Tony Gwynn	.75
220	Joey Hamilton	.10
221	Rickey Henderson	.60
222	Trevor Hoffman	.10
223	Wally Joyner	.10
224	Scott Sanders	.10
225	Fernando Valenzuela	.10
226	Greg Vaughn	.10
227	Alan Benes	.10
228	Andy Benes	.10
229	Dennis Eckersley	.50
230	Ron Gant	.10
231	Brian Jordan	.10
232	Ray Lankford	.10
233	John Mabry	.10
234	Tom Pagnozzi	.10
235	Todd Stottlemyre	.10
236	Jermaine Allensworth	.10
237	Francisco Cordova	.10
238	Jason Kendall	.10
239	Jeff King	.10
240	Al Martin	.10
241	Rod Beck	.10
242	Barry Bonds	2.00
243	Shawn Estes	.10
244	Mark Gardner	.10
245	Glenallen Hill	.10
246	Bill Mueller	.10
247	J.T. Snow	.10
248	Checklist	.10
249	Checklist	.10
250	Checklist	.10

Blast Furnace

		NM/M
Complete Set (12):		40.00
Common Player:		1.50
1	Jeff Bagwell	4.00
2	Albert Belle	1.50
3	Barry Bonds	7.50
4	Andres Galarraga	1.50
5	Juan Gonzalez	2.50
6	Ken Griffey Jr.	5.00
7	Todd Hundley	1.50
8	Mark McGwire	6.00
9	Mike Piazza	5.00
10	Alex Rodriguez	6.00
11	Frank Thomas	4.00
12	Mo Vaughn	1.50

Emerald Autographs

		NM/M
Complete Set (6):		75.00
Common Autograph:		4.00
1	Darin Erstad	6.00
2	Todd Hollandsworth	4.00
3	Alex Ochoa	4.00
4	Alex Rodriguez	60.00
5	Scott Rolen	10.00
6	Todd Walker	4.00

Magnetic Field

		NM/M
Complete Set (10):		15.00
Common Player:		.75
1	Roberto Alomar	.75
2	Jeff Bagwell	1.25
3	Barry Bonds	3.00

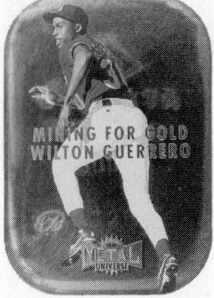

4	Ken Griffey Jr.	2.00
5	Derek Jeter	3.00
6	Kenny Lofton	.75
7	Edgar Renteria	.75
8	Cal Ripken Jr.	3.00
9	Alex Rodriguez	2.50
10	Matt Williams	.75

Mining for Gold

		NM/M
Complete Set (10):		12.00
Common Player:		.75
1	Bob Abreu	.75
2	Kevin Brown	.75
3	Nomar Garciaparra	3.50
4	Vladimir Guerrero	3.00
5	Wilton Guerrero	.75
6	Andruw Jones	3.00
7	Curt Lyons	.75
8	Neifi Perez	.75
9	Scott Rolen	2.00
10	Todd Walker	.75

Mother Lode

		NM/M
Complete Set (12):		80.00
Common Player:		2.00
1	Roberto Alomar	2.50
2	Jeff Bagwell	6.00
3	Barry Bonds	15.00
4	Ken Griffey Jr.	10.00
5	Andruw Jones	6.00
6	Chipper Jones	8.00
7	Kenny Lofton	2.00
8	Mike Piazza	10.00
9	Cal Ripken Jr.	15.00
10	Alex Rodriguez	12.50
11	Frank Thomas	6.00
12	Matt Williams	2.00

Platinum Portraits

		NM/M
Complete Set (10):		10.00
Common Player:		.60
1	James Baldwin	.60
2	Jermaine Dye	.60
3	Todd Hollandsworth	.60
4	Derek Jeter	5.00
5	Chipper Jones	2.00
6	Jason Kendall	.60
7	Rey Ordonez	.60
8	Andy Pettitte	1.00

9	Edgar Renteria	.60
10	Alex Rodriguez	3.25

Titanium

		NM/M
Complete Set (10):		24.00
Common Player:		1.50
1	Jeff Bagwell	2.00
2	Albert Belle	1.50
3	Ken Griffey Jr.	3.00
4	Chipper Jones	2.50
5	Greg Maddux	2.50
6	Mark McGwire	4.00
7	Mike Piazza	3.00
8	Cal Ripken Jr.	5.00
9	Alex Rodriguez	4.00
10	Frank Thomas	2.00

1998 Metal Universe

		NM/M
Complete Set (220):		15.00
Common Player:		.10
Pack (8):		1.50
Wax Box (24):		20.00
1	Jose Cruz Jr.	.10
2	Jeff Abbott	.10
3	Rafael Palmeiro	.65
4	Ivan Rodriguez	.65
5	Jaret Wright	.10
6	Derek Bell	.10
7	Chuck Finley	.10
8	Travis Fryman	.10
9	Randy Johnson	.75
10	Derrek Lee	.50
11	Bernie Williams	.10
12	Carlos Baerga	.10
13	Ricky Bottalico	.10
14	Ellis Burks	.10
15	Russ Davis	.10
16	Nomar Garciaparra	1.00
17	Joey Hamilton	.10
18	Jason Kendall	.10
19	Darryl Kile	.10
20	Edgardo Alfonzo	.10

21	Moises Alou	.10
22	Bobby Bonilla	.10
23	Jim Edmonds	.10
24	Jose Guillen	.10
25	Chuck Knoblauch	.10
26	Javy Lopez	.10
27	Billy Wagner	.10
28	Kevin Appier	.10
29	Joe Carter	.10
30	Todd Dunwoody	.10
31	Gary Gaetti	.10
32	Juan Gonzalez	.60
33	Jeffrey Hammonds	.10
34	Roberto Hernandez	.10
35	Dave Nilsson	.10
36	Manny Ramirez	.75
37	Robin Ventura	.10
38	Rondell White	.10
39	Vinny Castilla	.10
40	Will Clark	.10
41	Scott Hatteberg	.10
42	Russ Johnson	.10
43	Ricky Ledee	.10
44	Kenny Lofton	.10
45	Paul Molitor	.75
46	Justin Thompson	.10
47	Craig Biggio	.10
48	Damion Easley	.10
49	Brad Radke	.10
50	Ben Grieve	.10
51	Mark Bellhorn	.10
52	Henry Blanco RC	.10
53	Mariano Rivera	.20
54	Reggie Sanders	.10
55	Paul Sorrento	.10
56	Terry Steinbach	.10
57	Mo Vaughn	.10
58	Brady Anderson	.10
59	Tom Glavine	.40
60	Sammy Sosa	1.25
61	Larry Walker	.10
62	Rod Beck	.10
63	Jose Canseco	.45
64	Steve Finley	.10
65	Pedro Martinez	.75
66	John Olerud	.10
67	Scott Rolen	.60
68	Ismael Valdes	.10
69	Andrew Vessel	.10
70	Mark Grudzielanek	.10
71	Eric Karros	.10
72	Jeff Shaw	.10
73	Lou Collier	.10
74	Edgar Martinez	.10
75	Vladimir Guerrero	.75
76	Paul Konerko	.25
77	Kevin Orie	.10
78	Kevin Polcovich	.10
79	Brett Tomko	.10
80	Jeff Bagwell	.75
81	Barry Bonds	2.50
82	David Justice	.10
83	Hideo Nomo	.60
84	Ryne Sandberg	1.00
85	Shannon Stewart	.10
86	Derek Wallace	.10
87	Tony Womack	.10
88	Jason Giambi	.50
89	Mark Grace	.10
90	Pat Hentgen	.10
91	Raul Mondesi	.10
92	Matt Morris	.10
93	Matt Perisho	.10
94	Tim Salmon	.10
95	Jeremi Gonzalez	.10
96	Shawn Green	.25
97	Todd Greene	.10
98	Ruben Rivera	.10
99	Deion Sanders	.10
100	Alex Rodriguez	2.00
101	Will Cunnane	.10
102	Ray Lankford	.10
103	Ryan McGuire	.10
104	Charles Nagy	.10
105	Rey Ordonez	.10
106	Mike Piazza	1.50
107	Tony Saunders	.10
108	Curt Schilling	.25
109	Fernando Tatis	.10
110	Mark McGwire	2.00
111	David Dellucci RC	.10
112	Garret Anderson	.10
113	Shane Bowers	.10
114	David Cone	.10
115	Jeff King	.10
116	Matt Williams	.10
117	Aaron Boone	.10
118	Dennis Eckersley	.65
119	Livan Hernandez	.10
120	Richard Hidalgo	.10
121	Bobby Higginson	.10
122	Tino Martinez	.10
123	Tim Naehring	.10
124	Jose Vidro	.10
125	John Wetteland	.10
126	Jay Bell	.10
127	Albert Belle	.10
128	Marty Cordova	.10
129	Chili Davis	.10
130	Jason Dickson	.10
131	Rusty Greer	.10
132	Hideki Irabu	.10
133	Greg Maddux	1.00
134	Billy Taylor	.10
135	Jim Thome	.60

136	Gerald Williams	.10
137	Jeff Cirillo	.10
138	Delino DeShields	.10
139	Andres Galarraga	.10
140	Willie Greene	.10
141	John Jaha	.10
142	Charles Johnson	.10
143	Ryan Klesko	.10
144	Paul O'Neill	.10
145	Robinson Checo	.10
146	Roberto Alomar	.20
147	Wilson Alvarez	.10
148	Bobby Jones	.10
149	Raul Casanova	.10
150	Andruw Jones	.75
151	Mike Lansing	.10
152	Mickey Morandini	.10
153	Neifi Perez	.10
154	Pokey Reese	.10
155	Edgar Renteria	.10
156	Eric Young	.10
157	Darin Erstad	.20
158	Kelvim Escobar	.10
159	Carl Everett	.10
160	Tom Gordon	.10
161	Ken Griffey Jr.	1.50
162	Al Martin	.10
163	Bubba Trammell	.10
164	Carlos Delgado	.30
165	Kevin Brown	.10
166	Ken Caminiti	.10
167	Roger Clemens	1.25
168	Ron Gant	.10
169	Jeff Kent	.10
170	Mike Mussina	.40
171	Dean Palmer	.10
172	Henry Rodriguez	.10
173	Matt Stairs	.10
174	Jay Buhner	.10
175	Frank Thomas	.75
176	Mike Cameron	.10
177	Johnny Damon	.35
178	Tony Gwynn	1.00
179	John Smoltz	.10
180	B.J. Surhoff	.10
181	Antone Williamson	.10
182	Alan Benes	.10
183	Jeromy Burnitz	.10
184	Tony Clark	.10
185	Shawn Estes	.10
186	Todd Helton	.65
187	Todd Hundley	.10
188	Chipper Jones	1.00
189	Mark Kotsay	.10
190	Barry Larkin	.10
191	Mike Lieberthal	.10
192	Andy Pettitte	.25
193	Gary Sheffield	.35
194	Jeff Suppan	.10
195	Mark Wohlers	.10
196	Dante Bichette	.10
197	Trevor Hoffman	.10
198	J.T. Snow	.10
199	Derek Jeter	2.50
200	Cal Ripken Jr.	2.50
201	Steve Woodard RC	.25
202	Ray Durham	.10
203	Barry Bonds	1.50
204	Tony Clark	1.00
205	Roger Clemens	.65
206	Ken Griffey Jr.	.75
207	Tony Gwynn	.50
208	Derek Jeter	1.50
209	Randy Johnson	.40
210	Mark McGwire	1.00
211	Hideo Nomo	.30
212	Mike Piazza	.75
213	Cal Ripken Jr.	1.50
214	Alex Rodriguez	1.00
215	Frank Thomas	.40
216	Mo Vaughn	.10
217	Larry Walker	.10
218	Ken Griffey Jr. Checklist	.50
219	Alex Rodriguez Checklist	.60
220	Frank Thomas Checklist	.30

Precious Metal Gems

CHARLES NAGY

NM/M	
Common Player:	3.00
Stars:	25X

All-Galactic Team

ALL-GALACTIC TEAM
FRANK THOMAS

NM/M		
Complete Set (18):		140.00
Common Player:		3.00
Inserted 1:192		
1	Ken Griffey Jr.	12.50
2	Frank Thomas	7.50
3	Chipper Jones	10.00
4	Albert Belle	3.00
5	Juan Gonzalez	5.00
6	Jeff Bagwell	7.50
7	Andruw Jones	7.50
8	Cal Ripken Jr.	20.00
9	Derek Jeter	20.00
10	Nomar Garciaparra	10.00
11	Darin Erstad	4.00
12	Greg Maddux	10.00
13	Alex Rodriguez	15.00
14	Mike Piazza	12.50
15	Vladimir Guerrero	7.50
16	Jose Cruz Jr.	3.00
17	Mark McGwire	15.00
18	Scott Rolen	5.00

Diamond Heroes

NM/M		
Complete Set (6):		8.00
Common Player:		.50
Inserted 1:18		
1	Ken Griffey Jr.	2.00
2	Frank Thomas	1.50
3	Andruw Jones	1.50
4	Alex Rodriguez	2.50
5	Jose Cruz Jr.	.50
6	Cal Ripken Jr.	3.00

Platinum Portraits

PLATINUM PORTRAITS

NM/M	
Complete Set (12):	90.00

Production 50 Sets
(See 1998 Metal Universe for checklist and base card values.)

Common Player:		4.00
Inserted 1:360		
1	Ken Griffey Jr.	12.00
2	Frank Thomas	7.50
3	Chipper Jones	10.00
4	Jose Cruz Jr.	4.00
5	Andruw Jones	7.50
6	Cal Ripken Jr.	17.50
7	Derek Jeter	17.50
8	Darin Erstad	4.00
9	Greg Maddux	9.00
10	Alex Rodriguez	15.00
11	Mike Piazza	12.00
12	Vladimir Guerrero	7.50

Titanium

NM/M		
Complete Set (15):		50.00
Common Player:		2.00
Inserted 1:96		
1	Ken Griffey Jr.	5.00
2	Frank Thomas	3.00
3	Chipper Jones	4.00
4	Jose Cruz Jr.	2.00
5	Juan Gonzalez	2.50
6	Scott Rolen	2.50
7	Andruw Jones	3.00
8	Cal Ripken Jr.	7.50
9	Derek Jeter	7.50
10	Nomar Garciaparra	4.00
11	Darin Erstad	2.50
12	Greg Maddux	4.00
13	Alex Rodriguez	6.00
14	Mike Piazza	5.00
15	Vladimir Guerrero	3.00

Universal Language

NM/M		
Complete Set (20):		16.00
Common Player:		.40
Inserted 1:6		
1	Ken Griffey Jr.	1.25
2	Frank Thomas	.75
3	Chipper Jones	1.00
4	Albert Belle	.40
5	Juan Gonzalez	.60
6	Jeff Bagwell	.75
7	Andruw Jones	.75
8	Cal Ripken Jr.	2.00
9	Derek Jeter	2.00
10	Nomar Garciaparra	1.00
11	Darin Erstad	.50
12	Greg Maddux	1.00
13	Alex Rodriguez	1.50
14	Mike Piazza	1.25
15	Vladimir Guerrero	.75
16	Jose Cruz Jr.	.40
17	Hideo Nomo	.60
18	Kenny Lofton	.40
19	Tony Gwynn	1.00
20	Scott Rolen	.60

1999 Metal Universe

NM/M	
Complete Set (300):	15.00
Common Player:	.10
Pack (8):	1.00

Wax Box (24):	20.00
1	Mark McGwire	1.50
2	Jim Edmonds	.10
3	Travis Fryman	.10
4	Tom Gordon	.10
5	Jeff Bagwell	.65
6	Rico Brogna	.10
7	Tom Evans	.10
8	John Franco	.10
9	Juan Gonzalez	.50
10	Paul Molitor	.65
11	Roberto Alomar	.20
12	Mike Hampton	.10
13	Orel Hershiser	.10
14	Todd Stottlemyre	.10
15	Robin Ventura	.10
16	Todd Walker	.10
17	Bernie Williams	.10
18	Shawn Estes	.10
19	Richie Sexson	.10
20	Kevin Millwood	.10
21	David Ortiz	.50
22	Mariano Rivera	.15
23	Ivan Rodriguez	.60
24	Mike Sirotka	.10
25	David Justice	.10
26	Carl Pavano	.10
27	Albert Belle	.10
28	Will Clark	.10
29	Jose Cruz Jr.	.10
30	Trevor Hoffman	.10
31	Dean Palmer	.10
32	Edgar Renteria	.10
33	David Segui	.10
34	B.J. Surhoff	.10
35	Miguel Tejada	.15
36	Bob Wickman	.10
37	Charles Johnson	.10
38	Andruw Jones	.65
39	Mike Lieberthal	.10
40	Eli Marrero	.10
41	Neifi Perez	.10
42	Jim Thome	.50
43	Barry Bonds	2.00
44	Carlos Delgado	.30
45	Chuck Finley	.10
46	Brian Meadows	.10
47	Tony Gwynn	.75
48	Jose Offerman	.10
49	Cal Ripken Jr.	2.00
50	Alex Rodriguez	1.50
51	Esteban Yan	.10
52	Matt Stairs	.10
53	Fernando Vina	.10
54	Rondell White	.10
55	Kerry Wood	.30
56	Dmitri Young	.10
57	Ken Caminiti	.10
58	Alex Gonzalez	.10
59	Matt Mantei	.10
60	Tino Martinez	.10
61	Hal Morris	.10
62	Rafael Palmeiro	.60
63	Troy Percival	.10
64	Bobby Smith	.10
65	Ed Sprague	.10
66	Brett Tomko	.10
67	Steve Trachsel	.10
68	Ugueth Urbina	.10
69	Jose Valentin	.10
70	Kevin Brown	.10
71	Shawn Green	.30
72	Dustin Hermanson	.10
73	Livan Hernandez	.10
74	Geoff Jenkins	.10
75	Jeff King	.10
76	Chuck Knoblauch	.10
77	Edgar Martinez	.10
78	Fred McGriff	.10
79	Mike Mussina	.40
80	Dave Nilsson	.10
81	Kenny Rogers	.10
82	Tim Salmon	.10
83	Reggie Sanders	.10
84	Wilson Alvarez	.10
85	Rod Beck	.10
86	Jose Guillen	.10
87	Bob Higginson	.10
88	Gregg Olson	.10
89	Jeff Shaw	.10
90	Masato Yoshii	.10

91	Todd Helton	.50
92	David Dellucci	.10
93	Johnny Damon	.35
94	Cliff Floyd	.10
95	Ken Griffey Jr.	1.00
96	Juan Guzman	.10
97	Derek Jeter	2.00
98	Barry Larkin	.10
99	Quinton McCracken	.10
100	Sammy Sosa	.85
101	Kevin Young	.10
102	Jay Bell	.10
103	Jay Buhner	.10
104	Jeff Conine	.10
105	Ryan Jackson	.10
106	Sidney Ponson	.10
107	Jeromy Burnitz	.10
108	Roberto Hernandez	.10
109	A.J. Hinch	.10
110	Hideki Irabu	.10
111	Paul Konerko	.20
112	Henry Rodriguez	.10
113	Shannon Stewart	.10
114	Tony Womack	.10
115	Wilton Guerrero	.10
116	Andy Benes	.10
117	Jeff Cirillo	.10
118	Chili Davis	.10
119	Eric Davis	.10
120	Vladimir Guerrero	.65
121	Dennis Reyes	.10
122	Rickey Henderson	.65
123	Mickey Morandini	.10
124	Jason Schmidt	.10
125	J.T. Snow	.10
126	Justin Thompson	.10
127	Billy Wagner	.10
128	Armando Benitez	.10
129	Sean Casey	.15
130	Brad Fullmer	.10
131	Ben Grieve	.10
132	Robb Nen	.10
133	Shane Reynolds	.10
134	Todd Zeile	.10
135	Brady Anderson	.10
136	Aaron Boone	.10
137	Orlando Cabrera	.10
138	Jason Giambi	.50
139	Randy Johnson	.65
140	Jeff Kent	.10
141	John Wetteland	.10
142	Rolando Arrojo	.10
143	Scott Brosius	.10
144	Mark Grace	.10
145	Jason Kendall	.10
146	Travis Lee	.10
147	Gary Sheffield	.40
148	David Cone	.10
149	Jose Hernandez	.10
150	Todd Jones	.10
151	Al Martin	.10
152	Ismael Valdes	.10
153	Wade Boggs	.75
154	Garret Anderson	.10
155	Bobby Bonilla	.10
156	Darryl Kile	.10
157	Ryan Klesko	.10
158	Tim Wakefield	.10
159	Kenny Lofton	.10
160	Jose Canseco	.40
161	Doug Glanville	.10
162	Todd Hundley	.10
163	Brian Jordan	.10
164	Steve Finley	.10
165	Tom Glavine	.25
166	Al Leiter	.10
167	Raul Mondesi	.10
168	Desi Relaford	.10
169	Bret Saberhagen	.10
170	Omar Vizquel	.10
171	Larry Walker	.10
172	Bobby Abreu	.10
173	Moises Alou	.10
174	Mike Caruso	.10
175	Royce Clayton	.10
176	Bartolo Colon	.10
177	Marty Cordova	.10
178	Darin Erstad	.30
179	Nomar Garciaparra	.75
180	Andy Ashby	.10
181	Dan Wilson	.10
182	Larry Sutton	.10
183	Tony Clark	.10
184	Andres Galarraga	.10
185	Ray Durham	.10
186	Hideo Nomo	.60
187	Steve Woodard	.10
188	Scott Rolen	.35
189	Mike Stanley	.10
190	Jaret Wright	.10
191	Vinny Castilla	.10
192	Jason Christiansen	.10
193	Paul Bako	.10
194	Carlos Perez	.10
195	Mike Piazza	1.00
196	Fernando Tatis	.10
197	Mo Vaughn	.10
198	Devon White	.10
199	Ricky Gutierrez	.10
200	Charlie Hayes	.10
201	Brad Radke	.10
202	Rick Helling	.10
203	John Smoltz	.10
204	Frank Thomas	.65
205	David Wells	.10

206	Roger Clemens	.85
207	Mark Grudzielanek	.10
208	Chipper Jones	.75
209	Ray Lankford	.10
210	Pedro Martinez	.65
211	Manny Ramirez	.65
212	Greg Vaughn	.10
213	Craig Biggio	.10
214	Rusty Greer	.10
215	Greg Maddux	.75
216	Rick Aguilera	.10
217	Andy Pettitte	.20
218	Dante Bichette	.10
219	Damion Easley	.10
220	Matt Morris	.10
221	John Olerud	.10
222	Chan Ho Park	.10
223	Curt Schilling	.25
224	John Valentin	.10
225	Matt Williams	.10
226	Ellis Burks	.10
227	Tom Goodwin	.10
228	Javy Lopez	.10
229	Eric Milton	.10
230	Paul O'Neill	.10
231	Magglio Ordonez	.15
232	Derrek Lee	.45
233	Ken Griffey Jr.	.60
234	Randy Johnson	.30
235	Alex Rodriguez	.75
236	Darin Erstad	.15
237	Juan Gonzalez	.20
238	Derek Jeter	1.00
239	Tony Gwynn	.40
240	Kerry Wood	.20
241	Cal Ripken Jr.	1.00
242	Sammy Sosa	.50
243	Greg Maddux	.40
244	Mark McGwire	.75
245	Chipper Jones	.40
246	Barry Bonds	1.00
247	Ben Grieve	.10
248	Ben Davis	.10
249	Robert Fick	.10
250	Carlos Guillen	.10
251	Mike Frank	.10
252	Ryan Minor	.10
253	Troy Glaus	.65
254	Matt Anderson	.10
255	Josh Booty	.10
256	Gabe Alvarez	.10
257	Gabe Kapler	.10
258	Enrique Wilson	.10
259	Alex Gonzalez	.10
260	Preston Wilson	.10
261	Eric Chavez	.20
262	Adrian Beltre	.30
263	Corey Koskie	.10
264	Robert Machado RC	.10
265	Orlando Hernandez	.10
266	Matt Clement	.10
267	Luis Ordaz	.10
268	Jeremy Giambi	.10
269	J.D. Drew	.50
269a	J.D. Drew	
	(Building Blocks "Sample" autographed edition of 35.)	30.00
270	Cliff Politte	.10
271	Carlton Loewer	.10
272	Aramis Ramirez	.10
273	Ken Griffey Jr.	.60
274	Randy Johnson	.30
275	Alex Rodriguez	.75
276	Darin Erstad	.20
277	Scott Rolen	.25
278	Juan Gonzalez	.20
279	Jeff Bagwell	.30
280	Mike Piazza	.65
281	Derek Jeter	1.00
282	Travis Lee	.10
283	Tony Gwynn	.40
284	Kerry Wood	.20
285	Albert Belle	.20
286	Sammy Sosa	.50
287	Mo Vaughn	.20
288	Nomar Garciaparra	.45
289	Frank Thomas	.30
290	Cal Ripken Jr.	1.00
291	Greg Maddux	.40
292	Chipper Jones	.40
293	Ben Grieve	.30
294	Andruw Jones	.30
295	Mark McGwire	.75
296	Roger Clemens	.50
297	Barry Bonds	.75
298	Ken Griffey Jr.-Checklist	.60
299	Kerry Wood-Checklist	.20
300	Alex Rodriguez-Checklist	.75

Precious Metal Gems

	NM/M
Common Player:	3.00
Stars:	25X

Gem Master 1 of 1:(Value Undetermined)
(See 1999 Metal Universe for check-list and base card values.)

Boyz With The Wood

	NM/M
Complete Set (15):	17.50
Common Player:	.60
Inserted 1:18	
1	Ken Griffey Jr.	2.00
2	Frank Thomas	1.00
3	Jeff Bagwell	1.00
4	Juan Gonzalez	.75
5	Mark McGwire	2.50
6	Scott Rolen	.60
7	Travis Lee	.60
8	Tony Gwynn	2.00
9	Mike Piazza	2.00
10	Chipper Jones	2.00
11	Nomar Garciaparra	2.00
12	Derek Jeter	3.00
13	Cal Ripken Jr.	3.00
14	Andruw Jones	1.00
15	Alex Rodriguez	2.50

Diamond Soul

	NM/M
Complete Set (15):	60.00
Common Player:	1.50
Inserted 1:72	
1	Cal Ripken Jr.	12.00
2	Alex Rodriguez	9.00
3	Chipper Jones	6.00
4	Derek Jeter	12.00
5	Frank Thomas	4.00
6	Greg Maddux	6.00
7	Juan Gonzalez	3.00
8	Ken Griffey Jr.	7.50
9	Kerry Wood	3.00
10	Mark McGwire	9.00
11	Mike Piazza	7.50
12	Nomar Garciaparra	6.00
13	Scott Rolen	2.50

14	Tony Gwynn	6.00
15	Travis Lee	1.50

Linchpins

		NM/M
Complete Set (10):		75.00
Common Player:		5.00
Inserted 1:360		
1	Mike Piazza	10.00
2	Mark McGwire	12.50
3	Kerry Wood	5.00
4	Ken Griffey Jr.	10.00
5	Greg Maddux	7.50
6	Frank Thomas	6.00
7	Derek Jeter	15.00
8	Chipper Jones	7.50
9	Cal Ripken Jr.	15.00
10	Alex Rodriguez	12.50

Neophytes

		NM/M
Complete Set (15):		7.50
Common Player:		.35
Inserted 1:6		
1	Troy Glaus	3.00
2	Travis Lee	.75
3	Scott Elarton	.35
4	Ricky Ledee	.35
5	Richard Hidalgo	.35
6	J.D. Drew	1.50
7	Paul Konerko	.75
8	Orlando Hernandez	.75
9	Mike Caruso	.35
10	Mike Frank	.35
11	Miguel Tejada	.50
12	Matt Anderson	.35
13	Kerry Wood	1.00
14	Gabe Alvarez	.35
15	Adrian Beltre	.50

Planet Metal

		NM/M
Complete Set (15):		45.00
Common Player:		1.50
Inserted 1:36		
1	Alex Rodriguez	9.00
2	Andruw Jones	3.50
3	Cal Ripken Jr.	12.00
4	Chipper Jones	5.00
5	Darin Erstad	2.00
6	Derek Jeter	12.00
7	Frank Thomas	3.50
8	Travis Lee	1.50
9	Scott Rolen	2.50
10	Nomar Garciaparra	5.00

11	Mike Piazza	6.50
12	Mark McGwire	9.00
13	Ken Griffey Jr.	6.50
14	Juan Gonzalez	2.50
15	Jeff Bagwell	3.50

2000 Metal

		NM/M
Complete Set (250):		20.00
Common Player:		.10
Common Prospect (201-250):		.50
Inserted 1:2		
Pack (10):		1.50
Wax Box (28):		25.00
1	Tony Gwynn	1.00
2	Derek Jeter	2.50
3	Johnny Damon	.35
4	Javy Lopez	.10
5	Preston Wilson	.10
6	Derek Bell	.10
7	Richie Sexson	.10
8	Vinny Castilla	.10
9	Billy Wagner	.10
10	Carlos Beltran	.50
11	Chris Singleton	.10
12	Nomar Garciaparra	1.00
13	Carlos Febles	.10
14	Jason Varitek	.10
15	Luis Gonzalez	.20
16	Jon Lieber	.10
17	Mo Vaughn	.10
18	Dave Burba	.10
19	Brady Anderson	.10
20	Carlos Lee	.20
21	Chuck Finley	.10
22	Alex Gonzalez	.10
23	Matt Williams	.10
24	Chipper Jones	1.00
25	Pokey Reese	.10
26	Todd Helton	.65
27	Mike Mussina	.40
28	Butch Huskey	.10
29	Jeff Bagwell	.75
30	Juan Encarnacion	.10
31	A.J. Burnett	.10
32	Micah Bowie	.10
33	Brian Jordan	.10
34	Scott Erickson	.10
35	Sean Casey	.25
36	John Smoltz	.10
37	Edgard Clemente	.10
38	Mike Hampton	.10
39	Tom Glavine	.35
40	Albert Belle	.10
41	Jim Thome	.60
42	Jermaine Dye	.10
43	Sammy Sosa	1.25
44	Pedro Martinez	.75
45	Paul Konerko	.20
46	Damion Easley	.10
47	Cal Ripken Jr.	2.50
48	Jose Lima	.10
49	Mike Lowell	.10
50	Randy Johnson	.75
51	Dean Palmer	.10
52	Tim Salmon	.10
53	Kevin Millwood	.10
54	Mark Grace	.10
55	Aaron Boone	.10
56	Omar Vizquel	.10
57	Moises Alou	.10
58	Travis Fryman	.10
59	Erubiel Durazo	.10
60	Carl Everett	.10
61	Charles Johnson	.10
62	Trot Nixon	.10
63	Andres Galarraga	.10
64	Magglio Ordonez	.10
65	Pedro Astacio	.10
66	Roberto Alomar	.20
67	Pete Harnisch	.10
68	Scott Williamson	.10
69	Alex Fernandez	.10
70	Robin Ventura	.10
71	Chad Allen	.10
72	Darin Erstad	.20
73	Ron Coomer	.10
74	Ellis Burks	.10
75	Kent Bottenfield	.10
76	Ken Griffey Jr.	1.50
77	Mike Piazza	1.50

78	Jorge Posada	.20
79	Dante Bichette	.10
80	Adrian Beltre	.25
81	Andruw Jones	.75
82	Wilson Alvarez	.10
83	Edgardo Alfonzo	.10
84	Brian Giles	.10
85	Gary Sheffield	.25
86	Matt Stairs	.10
87	Bret Boone	.10
88	Kenny Rogers	.10
89	Barry Bonds	2.50
90	Scott Rolen	.60
91	Edgar Renteria	.10
92	Larry Walker	.10
93	Roger Cedeno	.10
94	Kevin Brown	.10
95	Lee Stevens	.10
96	Brad Radke	.10
97	Andy Pettitte	.25
98	Bobby Higginson	.10
99	Eric Chavez	.25
100	Alex Rodriguez	2.00
100s	Alex Rodriguez/OPS	2.00
101	Shannon Stewart	.10
102	Ryan Rupe	.10
103	Freddy Garcia	.10
104	John Jaha	.10
105	Greg Maddux	1.00
106	Hideki Irabu	.10
107	Rey Ordonez	.10
108	Troy O'Leary	.10
109	Frank Thomas	.75
110	Corey Koskie	.10
111	Bernie Williams	.10
112	Barry Larkin	.10
113	Kevin Appier	.10
114	Curt Schilling	.35
115	Bartolo Colon	.10
116	Edgar Martinez	.10
117	Ray Lankford	.10
118	Todd Walker	.10
119	John Wetteland	.10
120	David Nilsson	.10
121	Tino Martinez	.10
122	Phil Nevin	.10
123	Ben Grieve	.10
124	Ron Gant	.10
125	Jeff Kent	.10
126	Rick Helling	.10
127	Russ Ortiz	.10
128	Troy Glaus	.65
129	Chan Ho Park	.10
130	Jeromy Burnitz	.10
131	Aaron Sele	.10
132	Mike Sirotka	.10
133	Brad Ausmus	.10
134	Jose Rosado	.10
135	Mariano Rivera	.25
136	Jason Giambi	.50
137	Jason Lieberthal	.10
138	Chris Carpenter	.10
139	Henry Rodriguez	.10
140	Mike Sweeney	.10
141	Vladimir Guerrero	.75
142	Charles Nagy	.10
143	Jason Kendall	.10
144	Matt Lawton	.10
145	Michael Barrett	.10
146	David Cone	.10
147	Bobby Abreu	.10
148	Fernando Tatis	.10
149	Jose Canseco	.40
150	Craig Biggio	.10
151	Matt Mantei	.10
152	Jacque Jones	.10
153	John Halama	.10
154	Trevor Hoffman	.10
155	Rondell White	.10
156	Reggie Sanders	.10
157	Steve Finley	.10
158	Roberto Hernandez	.10
159	Geoff Jenkins	.10
160	Chris Widger	.10
161	Orel Hershiser	.10
162	Tim Hudson	.20
163	Kris Benson	.10
164	Kevin Young	.10
165	Rafael Palmeiro	.60
166	David Wells	.10
167	Ben Davis	.10
168	Jamie Moyer	.10
169	Randy Wolf	.10
170	Jeff Cirillo	.10
171	Warren Morris	.10
172	Billy Koch	.10
173	Marquis Grissom	.10
174	Geoff Blum	.10
175	Octavio Dotel	.10
176	Orlando Hernandez	.20
177	J.D. Drew	.25
178	Carlos Delgado	.40
179	Sterling Hitchcock	.10
180	Shawn Green	.25
181	Tony Clark	.10
182	Joe McEwing	.10
183	Fred McGriff	.10
184	Tony Batista	.10
185	Al Leiter	.10
186	Roger Clemens	1.25
187	Al Martin	.10
188	Eric Milton	.10
189	Bobby Smith	.10
190	Rusty Greer	.10
191	Shawn Estes	.10

192	Ken Caminiti	.10
193	Eric Karros	.10
194	Manny Ramirez	.75
195	Jim Edmonds	.10
196	Paul O'Neill	.10
197	Rico Brogna	.10
198	Ivan Rodriguez	.60
199	Doug Glanville	.10
200	Mark McGwire	2.00
201	Mark Quinn	.50
202	Norm Hutchins	.50
203	Ramon Ortiz	.50
204	Brett Laxton	.50
205	Jimmy Anderson	.50
206	Calvin Murray	.50
207	Wilton Veras	.50
208	Chad Hermansen	.50
209	Nick Johnson	.50
210	Kevin Barker	.50
211	Casey Blake	.50
212	Chad Meyers	.50
213	Kip Wells	.50
214	Eric Munson	.50
215	Lance Berkman	.50
216	Wily Pena	.50
217	Gary Matthews Jr.	.50
218	Travis Dawkins	.50
219	Josh Beckett	.75
220	Tony Armas Jr.	.50
221	Alfonso Soriano	1.00
222	Pat Burrell	1.00
223	Danys Baez RC	.50
224	Adam Kennedy	.50
225	Ruben Mateo	.50
226	Vernon Wells	.75
227	Brian Cooper	.50
228	Jeff DaVanon RC	.50
229	Glen Barker	.50
230	Robinson Cancel	.50
231	D'Angelo Jimenez	.50
232	Adam Piatt	.50
233	Buddy Carlyle	.50
234	Chad Hutchinson	.50
235	Matt Riley	.50
236	Cole Liniak	.50
237	Ben Petrick	.50
238	Peter Bergeron	.50
239	Cesar King	.50
240	Aaron Myette	.50
241	Eric Gagne	.60
242	Joe Nathan	.50
243	Bruce Chen	.50
244	Rob Bell	.50
245	Juan Sosa RC	.60
246	Julio Ramirez	.50
247	Wade Miller	.50
248	Trace Coquillette RC	.50
249	Robert Ramsay	.50
250	Rick Ankiel	.60

Emerald

		NM/M
Complete Set (250):		100.00
Common Player:		.25
Stars:		2.5X
Inserted 1:4		
Prospects (201-250):		2.5X
Inserted 1:8		

Autographics

	NM/M
Common Player:	4.00
Bobby Abreu	8.00
Chad Allen	4.00
Marlon Anderson	4.00
Rick Ankiel	10.00
Glen Barker	4.00
Rob Bell	4.00
Mark Bellhorn	5.00
Peter Bergeron	4.00
Lance Berkman	8.00
Wade Boggs	25.00
Barry Bonds	150.00
Kent Bottenfield	4.00
Pat Burrell	10.00
Miguel Cairo	4.00
Mike Cameron	6.00
Chris Carpenter	6.00
Roger Cedeno	4.00
Mike Darr	6.00
Einar Diaz	4.00

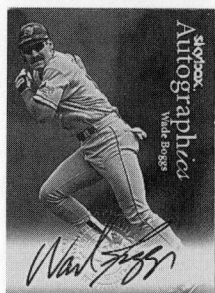

J.D. Drew	15.00
Erubiel Durazo	6.00
Ray Durham	6.00
Damion Easley	4.00
Scott Elarton	4.00
Jeremy Giambi	4.00
Doug Glanville	4.00
Shawn Green	10.00
Jerry Hairston Jr.	4.00
Bob Howry	4.00
Norm Hutchins	4.00
Randy Johnson	40.00
Jacque Jones	4.00
Gabe Kapler	6.00
Cesar King	4.00
Mark Kotsay	4.00
Cole Liniak	4.00
Greg Maddux	50.00
Pedro Martinez	30.00
Ruben Mateo	4.00
Warren Morris	4.00
Heath Murray	4.00
Joe Nathan	4.00
Jim Parque	4.00
Angel Pena	4.00
Cal Ripken Jr.	100.00
Alex Rodriguez	60.00
Ryan Rupe	4.00
Randall Simon	4.00
Chris Singleton	4.00
Mike Sweeney	6.00
Wilton Veras	4.00
Scott Williamson	4.00
Randy Wolf	6.00
Tony Womack	6.00

Base Shredders

	NM/M
Complete Set (18):	160.00
Common Player:	5.00
Inserted 1:288	
(1) Roberto Alomar	7.50
(2) Michael Barrett	5.00
(3) Tony Clark	5.00
(4) Ben Davis	5.00
(5) Erubiel Durazo	5.00
(6) Troy Glaus	12.50
(7) Ben Grieve	5.00
(8) Vladimir Guerrero	15.00
(9) Tony Gwynn	25.00
(10) Todd Helton	12.50
(11) Eric Munson	5.00
(12) Rafael Palmeiro	10.00
(13) Manny Ramirez	20.00
(14) Ivan Rodriguez	10.00
(15) Miguel Tejada	7.50
(16) Mo Vaughn	5.00
(17) Larry Walker	5.00
(18) Matt Williams	5.00

Fusion

	NM/M
Complete Set (15):	12.50
Common Player:	.50
Inserted 1:4	
1 Ken Griffey Jr., Alex Rodriguez	2.00

2	Mark McGwire, Rick Ankiel	2.00
3	Scott Rolen, Curt Schilling	.50
4	Pedro Martinez, Nomar Garciaparra	1.25
5	Carlos Beltran, Carlos Febles	.60
6	Sammy Sosa, Mark Grace	1.50
7	Vladimir Guerrero, Ugueth Urbina	1.00
8	Roger Clemens, Derek Jeter	3.00
9	Jeff Bagwell, Craig Biggio	1.00
10	Chipper Jones, Andruw Jones	1.50
11	Cal Ripken Jr., Mike Mussina	2.50
12	Manny Ramirez, Roberto Alomar	1.00
13	Sean Casey, Barry Larkin	.50
14	Ivan Rodriguez, Rafael Palmeiro	.75
15	Mike Piazza, Robin Ventura	1.50

Heavy Metal

	NM/M
Complete Set (10):	15.00
Common Player:	1.50
Inserted 1:20	
1 Sammy Sosa	2.25
2 Mark McGwire	3.00
3 Ken Griffey Jr.	2.50
4 Mike Piazza	2.50
5 Nomar Garciaparra	2.00
6 Alex Rodriguez	3.00
7 Manny Ramirez	1.50
8 Jeff Bagwell	1.50
9 Chipper Jones	2.00
10 Vladimir Guerrero	1.50

Hit Machines

	NM/M
Complete Set (10):	20.00
Common Player:	1.00
Inserted 1:20	
1 Ken Griffey Jr.	3.00
2 Mark McGwire	4.00
3 Frank Thomas	1.50
4 Tony Gwynn	2.00
5 Rafael Palmeiro	1.25
6 Bernie Williams	1.50
7 Derek Jeter	6.00
8 Sammy Sosa	2.50
9 Mike Piazza	3.00
10 Chipper Jones	2.00

Platinum Portraits

	NM/M
Complete Set (10):	6.00
Common Player:	.25
Inserted 1:8	
1 Carlos Beltran	.50
2 Vladimir Guerrero	.75
3 Manny Ramirez	.75
4 Ivan Rodriguez	.65
5 Sean Casey	.40
6 Alex Rodriguez	1.50
7 Derek Jeter	2.00
8 Nomar Garciaparra	1.00
9 Vernon Wells	.25
10 Shawn Green	.50

Talent Show

	NM/M
Complete Set (15):	6.00
Common Player:	.30
Inserted 1:4	
1 Rick Ankiel	.50
2 Matt Riley	.30
3 Chad Hermansen	.30
4 Ruben Mateo	.30
5 Eric Munson	.30
6 Alfonso Soriano	1.50
7 Wilton Veras	.30
8 Vernon Wells	.75
9 Erubiel Durazo	.30
10 Pat Burrell	1.50
11 Ben Davis	.30
12 A.J. Burnett	.30
13 Peter Bergeron	.30
14 Mark Quinn	.30
15 Ben Petrick	.30

P

1993 Pacific

		NM/M
Complete Set (660):		20.00
Common Player:		.05
1	Rafael Belliard	.05
2	Sid Bream	.05
3	Francisco Cabrera	.05
4	Marvin Freeman	.05
5	Ron Gant	.05
6	Tom Glavine	.25
7	Brian Hunter	.05
8	Dave Justice	.05
9	Ryan Klesko	.05
10	Melvin Nieves	.05
11	Deion Sanders	.05
12	John Smoltz	.25
13	Mark Wohlers	.05
14	Brady Anderson	.05
15	Glenn Davis	.05
16	Mike Devereaux	.05
17	Leo Gomez	.05
18	Chris Hoiles	.05
19	Chito Martinez	.05
20	Ben McDonald	.05
21	Mike Mussina	.40
22	Gregg Olson	.05
23	Joe Orsulak	.05
24	Cal Ripken, Jr.	1.50
25	David Segui	.05
26	Rick Sutcliffe	.05
27	Wade Boggs	.65
28	Tom Brunansky	.05
29	Ellis Burks	.05
30	Roger Clemens	.75
31	John Dopson	.05
32	John Flaherty	.05
33	Mike Greenwell	.05
34	Tony Pena	.05
35	Carlos Quintana	.05
36	Luis Rivera	.05
37	Mo Vaughn	.05
38	Frank Viola	.05
39	Matt Young	.05
40	Scott Bailes	.05
41	Bert Blyleven	.05
42	Chad Curtis	.05
43	Gary DiSarcina	.05
44	Chuck Finley	.05
45	Mike Fitzgerald	.05
46	Gary Gaetti	.05
47	Rene Gonzales	.05
48	Mark Langston	.05
49	Scott Lewis	.05
50	Luis Polonia	.05
51	Tim Salmon	.05
52	Lee Stevens	.05
53	Steve Buechele	.05
54	Frank Castillo	.05
55	Doug Dascenzo	.05
56	Andre Dawson	.25
57	Shawon Dunston	.05
58	Mark Grace	.05
59	Mike Morgan	.05
60	Luis Salazar	.05
61	Rey Sanchez	.05
62	Ryne Sandberg	.65
63	Dwight Smith	.05
64	Jerome Walton	.05
65	Rick Wilkins	.05
66	Wilson Alvarez	.05
67	George Bell	.05
68	Joey Cora	.05
69	Alex Fernandez	.05
70	Carlton Fisk	.50
71	Craig Grebeck	.05
72	Ozzie Guillen	.05
73	Jack McDowell	.05
74	Scott Radinsky	.05
75	Tim Raines	.05
76	Bobby Thigpen	.05
77	Frank Thomas	.50
78	Robin Ventura	.05
79	Tom Browning	.05
80	Jacob Brumfield	.05
81	Rob Dibble	.05
82	Bill Doran	.05
83	Billy Hatcher	.05
84	Barry Larkin	.05
85	Hal Morris	.05
86	Joe Oliver	.05
87	Jeff Reed	.05
88	Jose Rijo	.05
89	Bip Roberts	.05
90	Chris Sabo	.05
91	Sandy Alomar, Jr.	.05
92	Brad Arnsberg	.05
93	Carlos Baerga	.05
94	Albert Belle	.05
95	Felix Fermin	.05
96	Mark Lewis	.05
97	Kenny Lofton	.05
98	Carlos Martinez	.05
99	Rod Nichols	.05
100	Dave Rohde	.05
101	Scott Scudder	.05
102	Paul Sorrento	.05
103	Mark Whiten	.05
104	Mark Carreon	.05
105	Milt Cuyler	.05
106	Rob Deer	.05
107	Cecil Fielder	.05
108	Travis Fryman	.05
109	Dan Gladden	.05
110	Bill Gullickson	.05
111	Les Lancaster	.05

112	Mark Leiter	.05
113	Tony Phillips	.05
114	Mickey Tettleton	.05
115	Alan Trammell	.05
116	Lou Whitaker	.05
117	Jeff Bagwell	.50
118	Craig Biggio	.05
119	Joe Boever	.05
120	Casey Candaele	.05
121	Andujar Cedeno	.05
122	Steve Finley	.05
123	Luis Gonzalez	.05
124	Pete Harnisch	.05
125	Jimmy Jones	.05
126	Mark Portugal	.05
127	Rafael Ramirez	.05
128	Mike Simms	.05
129	Eric Yelding	.05
130	Luis Aquino	.05
131	Kevin Appier	.05
132	Mike Boddicker	.05
133	George Brett	.75
134	Tom Gordon	.05
135	Mark Gubicza	.05
136	David Howard	.05
137	Gregg Jefferies	.05
138	Wally Joyner	.05
139	Brian McRae	.05
140	Jeff Montgomery	.05
141	Terry Shumpert	.05
142	Curtis Wilkerson	.05
143	Brett Butler	.05
144	Eric Davis	.05
145	Kevin Gross	.05
146	Dave Hansen	.05
147	Lenny Harris	.05
148	Carlos Hernandez	.05
149	Orel Hershiser	.05
150	Jay Howell	.05
151	Eric Karros	.05
152	Ramon Martinez	.05
153	Jose Offerman	.05
154	Mike Sharperson	.05
155	Darryl Strawberry	.05
156	Jim Gantner	.05
157	Darryl Hamilton	.05
158	Doug Henry	.05
159	John Jaha	.05
160	Pat Listach	.05
161	Jaime Navarro	.05
162	Dave Nilsson	.05
163	Jesse Orosco	.05
164	Kevin Seitzer	.05
165	B.J. Surhoff	.05
166	Greg Vaughn	.05
167	Robin Yount	.50
168	Rick Aguilera	.05
169	Scott Erickson	.05
170	Mark Guthrie	.05
171	Kent Hrbek	.05
172	Chuck Knoblauch	.05
173	Gene Larkin	.05
174	Shane Mack	.05
175	Pedro Munoz	.05
176	Mike Pagliarulo	.05
177	Kirby Puckett	.65
178	Kevin Tapani	.05
179	Gary Wayne	.05
180	Moises Alou	.05
181	Brian Barnes	.05
182	Archie Cianfrocco	.05
183	Delino DeShields	.05
184	Darrin Fletcher	.05
185	Marquis Grissom	.05
186	Ken Hill	.05
187	Dennis Martinez	.05
188	Bill Sampen	.05
189	John VanderWal	.05
190	Larry Walker	.05
191	Tim Wallach	.05
192	Bobby Bonilla	.05
193	Daryl Boston	.05
194	Vince Coleman	.05
195	Kevin Elster	.05
196	Sid Fernandez	.05
197	John Franco	.05
198	Dwight Gooden	.05
199	Howard Johnson	.05
200	Willie Randolph	.05
201	Bret Saberhagen	.05
202	Dick Schofield	.05
203	Pete Schourek	.05
204	Greg Cadaret	.05
205	John Habyan	.05
206	Pat Kelly	.05
207	Kevin Maas	.05
208	Don Mattingly	.75
209	Matt Nokes	.05
210	Melido Perez	.05
211	Scott Sanderson	.05
212	Andy Stankiewicz	.05
213	Danny Tartabull	.05
214	Randy Velarde	.05
215	Bernie Williams	.05
216	Harold Baines	.05
217	Mike Bordick	.05
218	Scott Brosius	.05
219	Jerry Browne	.05
220	Ron Darling	.05
221	Dennis Eckersley	.40
222	Rickey Henderson	.50
223	Rick Honeycutt	.05
224	Mark McGwire	1.25
225	Ruben Sierra	.05
226	Terry Steinbach	.05
227	Bob Welch	.05
228	Willie Wilson	.05
229	Ruben Amaro	.05
230	Kim Batiste	.05
231	Juan Bell	.05
232	Wes Chamberlain	.05
233	Darren Daulton	.05
234	Mariano Duncan	.05
235	Len Dykstra	.05
236	Dave Hollins	.05
237	Stan Javier	.05
238	John Kruk	.05
239	Mickey Morandini	.05
240	Terry Mulholland	.05
241	Mitch Williams	.05
242	Stan Belinda	.05
243	Jay Bell	.05
244	Carlos Garcia	.05
245	Jeff King	.05
246	Mike LaValliere	.05
247	Lloyd McClendon	.05
248	Orlando Merced	.05
249	Paul Miller	.05
250	Gary Redus	.05
251	Don Slaught	.05
252	Zane Smith	.05
253	Andy Van Slyke	.05
254	Tim Wakefield	.05
255	Andy Benes	.05
256	Dann Bilardello	.05
257	Tony Gwynn	.65
258	Greg Harris	.05
259	Darrin Jackson	.05
260	Mike Maddux	.05
261	Fred McGriff	.05
262	Rich Rodriguez	.05
263	Benito Santiago	.05
264	Gary Sheffield	.35
265	Kurt Stillwell	.05
266	Tim Teufel	.05
267	Bud Black	.05
268	John Burkett	.05
269	Will Clark	.05
270	Royce Calyton	.05
271	Bryan Hickerson	.05
272	Chris James	.05
273	Darren Lewis	.05
274	Willie McGee	.05
275	Jim McNamara	.05
276	Francisco Oliveras	.05
277	Robby Thompson	.05
278	Matt Williams	.05
279	Trevor Wilson	.05
280	Bret Boone	.05
281	Greg Briley	.05
282	Jay Buhner	.05
283	Henry Cotto	.05
284	Rich DeLucia	.05
285	Dave Fleming	.05
286	Ken Griffey Jr.	1.00
287	Erik Hanson	.05
288	Randy Johnson	.50
289	Tino Martinez	.05
290	Edgar Martinez	.05
291	Dave Valle	.05
292	Omar Vizquel	.05
293	Luis Alicea	.05
294	Bernard Gilkey	.05
295	Felix Jose	.05
296	Ray Lankford	.05
297	Omar Olivares	.05
298	Jose Oquendo	.05
299	Tom Pagnozzi	.05
300	Geronimo Pena	.05
301	Gerald Perry	.05
302	Ozzie Smith	.65
303	Lee Smith	.05
304	Bob Tewksbury	.05
305	Todd Zeile	.05
306	Kevin Brown	.05
307	Todd Burns	.05
308	Jose Canseco	.35
309	Hector Fajardo	.05
310	Julio Franco	.05
311	Juan Gonzalez	.25
312	Jeff Huson	.05
313	Rob Maurer	.05
314	Rafael Palmeiro	.45
315	Dean Palmer	.05
316	Ivan Rodriguez	.45
317	Nolan Ryan	1.50
318	Dickie Thon	.05
319	Roberto Alomar	.20
320	Derek Bell	.05
321	Pat Borders	.05
322	Joe Carter	.05
323	Kelly Gruber	.05
324	Juan Guzman	.05
325	Manny Lee	.05
326	Jack Morris	.05
327	John Olerud	.05
328	Ed Sprague	.05
329	Todd Stottlemyre	.05
330	Duane Ward	.05
331	Steve Avery	.05
332	Damon Berryhill	.05
333	Jeff Blauser	.05
334	Mark Lemke	.05
335	Greg Maddux	.65
336	Kent Mercker	.05
337	Otis Nixon	.05
338	Greg Olson	.05
339	Bill Pecota	.05
340	Terry Pendleton	.05
341	Mike Stanton	.05
342	Todd Frohwirth	.05
343	Tim Hulett	.05
344	Mark McLemore	.05
345	Luis Mercedes	.05
346	Alan Mills	.05
347	Sherman Obando	.05
348	Jim Poole	.05
349	Harold Reynolds	.05
350	Arthur Rhodes	.05
351	Jeff Tackett	.05
352	Fernando Valenzuela	.05
353	Scott Bankhead	.05
354	Ivan Calderon	.05
355	Scott Cooper	.05
356	Danny Darwin	.05
357	Scott Fletcher	.05
358	Tony Fossas	.05
359	Greg Harris	.05
360	Joe Hesketh	.05
361	Jose Melendez	.05
362	Paul Quantrill	.05
363	John Valentin	.05
364	Mike Butcher	.05
365	Chuck Crim	.05
366	Chili Davis	.05
367	Damion Easley	.05
368	Steve Frey	.05
369	Joe Grahe	.05
370	Greg Myers	.05
371	John Orton	.05
372	J.T. Snow	.05
373	Ron Tingley	.05
374	Julio Valera	.05
375	Paul Assenmacher	.05
376	Jose Bautista	.05
377	Jose Guzman	.05
378	Greg Hibbard	.05
379	Candy Maldonado	.05
380	Derrick May	.05
381	Dan Plesac	.05
382	Tommy Shields	.05
383	Sammy Sosa	.75
384	Jose Vizcaino	.05
385	Greg Walbeck	.05
386	Ellis Burks	.05
387	Roberto Hernandez	.05
388	Mike Huff	.05
389	Bo Jackson	.10
390	Lance Johnson	.05
391	Ron Karkovice	.05
392	Kirk McCaskill	.05
393	Donn Pall	.05
394	Dan Pasqua	.05
395	Steve Sax	.05
396	Dave Stieb	.05
397	Bobby Ayala	.05
398	Tim Belcher	.05
399	Jeff Branson	.05
400	Cesar Hernandez	.05
401	Roberto Kelly	.05
402	Randy Milligan	.05
403	Kevin Mitchell	.05
404	Juan Samuel	.05
405	Reggie Sanders	.05
406	John Smiley	.05
407	Dan Wilson	.05
408	Mike Christopher	.05
409	Dennis Cook	.05
410	Alvaro Espinoza	.05
411	Glenallen Hill	.05
412	Reggie Jefferson	.05
413	Derek Lilliquist	.05
414	Jose Mesa	.05
415	Charles Nagy	.05
416	Junior Ortiz	.05
417	Eric Plunk	.05
418	Ted Power	.05
419	Scott Aldred	.05
420	Andy Ashby	.05
421	Freddie Benavides	.05
422	Dante Bichette	.05
423	Willie Blair	.05
424	Vinny Castilla	.05
425	Jerald Clark	.05
426	Alex Cole	.05
427	Andres Galarraga	.05
428	Joe Girardi	.05
429	Charlie Hayes	.05
430	Butch Henry	.05
431	Darren Holmes	.05
432	Dale Murphy	.20
433	David Nied	.05
434	Jeff Parrett	.05
435	Steve Reed **RC**	.05
436	Armando Reynoso	.05
437	Bruce Ruffin	.05
438	Bryn Smith	.05
439	Jim Tatum	.05
440	Eric Young	.05
441	Skeeter Barnes	.05
442	Tom Bolton	.05
443	Kirk Gibson	.05
444	Chad Krueter	.05
445	Bill Krueger	.05
446	Scott Livingstone	.05
447	Bob MacDonald	.05
448	Mike Moore	.05
449	Mike Munoz	.05
450	Gary Thurman	.05
451	David Wells	.05
452	Alex Arias	.05
453	Jack Armstrong	.05
454	Bret Barberie	.05
455	Ryan Bowen	.05
456	Cris Carpenter	.05
457	Chuck Carr	.05
458	Jeff Conine	.05
459	Steve Decker	.05
460	Orestes Destrade	.05
461	Monty Fariss	.05
462	Junior Felix	.05
463	Bryan Harvey	.05
464	Trevor Hoffman	.05
465	Charlie Hough	.05
466	Dave Magadan	.05
467	Bob McClure	.05
468	Rob Natal	.05
469	Scott Pose	.05
470	Rich Renteria	.05
471	Benito Santiago	.05
472	Matt Turner	.05
473	Walt Weiss	.05
474	Eric Anthony	.05
475	Chris Donnels	.05
476	Doug Drabek	.05
477	Xavier Hernandez	.05
478	Doug Jones	.05
479	Darryl Kile	.05
480	Scott Servais	.05
481	Greg Swindell	.05
482	Eddie Taubensee	.05
483	Jose Uribe	.05
484	Brian Williams	.05
485	Billy Brewer	.05
486	David Cone	.05
487	Greg Gagne	.05
488	Phil Hiatt	.05
489	Jose Lind	.05
490	Brent Mayne	.05
491	Kevin McReynolds	.05
492	Keith Miller	.05
493	Hipolito Pichardo	.05
494	Harvey Pulliam	.05
495	Rico Rossay	.05
496	Pedro Astacio	.05
497	Tom Candiotti	.05
498	Tom Goodwin	.05
499	Jim Gott	.05
500	Pedro Martinez	.50
501	Roger McDowell	.05
502	Mike Piazza	.75
503	Jody Reed	.05
504	Rick Trlicek	.05
505	Mitch Weber	.05
506	Steve Wilson	.05
507	James Austin	.05
508	Ricky Bones	.05
509	Alex Diaz	.05
510	Mike Fetters	.05
511	Teddy Higuera	.05
512	Graeme Lloyd	.05
513	Carlos Maldonado	.05
514	Josias Manzanillo	.05
515	Kevin Reimer	.05
516	Bill Spiers	.05
517	Bill Wegman	.05
518	Willie Banks	.05
519	J.T. Bruett	.05
520	Brian Harper	.05
521	Terry Jorgensen	.05
522	Scott Leius	.05
523	Pat Mahomes	.05
524	Dave McCarty	.05
525	Jeff Reboulet	.05
526	Mike Trombley	.05
527	Carl Willis	.05
528	Dave Winfield	.50
529	Sean Berry	.05
530	Frank Bolick	.05
531	Kent Bottenfield	.05
532	Wil Cordero	.05
533	Jeff Fassero	.05
534	Tim Laker	.05
535	Mike Lansing	.05
536	Chris Nabholz	.05
537	Mel Rojas	.05
538	John Wetteland	.05
539	Ted Wood (Front photo actually Frank Bollick.)	.05
540	Mike Draper	.05
541	Tony Fernandez	.05
542	Todd Hundley	.05
543	Jeff Innis	.05
544	Jeff McKnight	.05
545	Eddie Murray	.50
546	Charlie O'Brien	.05
547	Frank Tanana	.05
548	Ryan Thompson	.05
549	Chico Walker	.05
550	Anthony Young	.05
551	Jim Abbott	.05
552	Wade Boggs	.75
553	Steve Farr	.05
554	Neal Heaton	.05
555	Steve Howe	.05
556	Dion James	.05
557	Scott Kamieniecki	.05
558	Jimmy Key	.05
559	Jim Leyritz	.05
560	Paul O'Neill	.05
561	Spike Owen	.05
562	Lance Blankenship	.05
563	Joe Boever	.05
564	Storm Davis	.05
565	Kelly Downs	.05
566	Eric Fox	.05
567	Rich Gossage	.05
568	Dave Henderson	.05
569	Shawn Hillegas	.05
570	Mike Mohler **RC**	.05

571	Troy Neel	.05
572	Dale Sveum	.05
573	Larry Anderson	.05
574	Bob Ayrault	.05
575	Jose DeLeon	.05
576	Jim Eisenreich	.05
577	Pete Incaviglia	.05
578	Danny Jackson	.05
579	Ricky Jordan	.05
580	Ben Rivera	.05
581	Curt Schilling	.25
582	Milt Thompson	.05
583	David West	.05
584	John Candelaria	.05
585	Steve Cooke	.05
586	Tom Foley	.05
587	Al Martin	.05
588	Blas Minor	.05
589	Dennis Moeller	.05
590	Denny Neagle	.05
591	Tom Prince	.05
592	Randy Tomlin	.05
593	Bob Walk	.05
594	Kevin Young	.05
595	Pat Gomez	.05
596	Ricky Gutierrez	.05
597	Gene Harris	.05
598	Jeremy Hernandez	.05
599	Phil Plantier	.05
600	Tim Scott	.05
601	Frank Seminara	.05
602	Darrell Sherman	.05
603	Craig Shipley	.05
604	Guillermo Velasquez	.05
605	Dan Walters	.05
606	Mike Benjamin	.05
607	Barry Bonds	1.50
608	Jeff Brantley	.05
609	Dave Burba	.05
610	Craig Colbert	.05
611	Mike Jackson	.05
612	Kirt Manwaring	.05
613	Dave Martinez	.05
614	Dave Righetti	.05
615	Kevin Rogers	.05
616	Bill Swift	.05
617	Rich Amaral	.05
618	Mike Blowers	.05
619	Chris Bosio	.05
620	Norm Charlton	.05
621	John Cummings	.05
622	Mike Felder	.05
623	Bill Haselman	.05
624	Tim Leary	.05
625	Pete O'Brien	.05
626	Russ Swan	.05
627	Fernando Vina	.05
628	Rene Arocha	.05
629	Rod Brewer	.05
630	Ozzie Canseco	.05
631	Rheal Cormier	.05
632	Brian Jordan	.05
633	Joe Magrane	.05
634	Donovan Osborne	.05
635	Mike Perez	.05
636	Stan Royer	.05
637	Hector Villanueva	.05
638	Tracy Woodson	.05
639	Benji Gil	.05
640	Tom Henke	.05
641	David Hulse	.05
642	Charlie Leibrandt	.05
643	Robb Nen	.05
644	Dan Peltier	.05
645	Billy Ripken	.05
646	Kenny Rogers	.05
647	John Russell	.05
648	Dan Smith	.05
649	Matt Whiteside	.05
650	William Canate	.05
651	Darnell Coles	.05
652	Al Leiter	.05
653	Domingo Martinez	.05
654	Paul Molitor	.50
655	Luis Sojo	.05
656	Dave Stewart	.05
657	Mike Timlin	.05
658	Turner Ward	.05
659	Devon White	.05
660	Eddie Zosky	.05

Beisbol Amigos

NM/M

Complete Set (30):		7.50
Common Player:		.50
1	Edgar Martinez	.50
2	Luis Polonia, Stan Javier	.50
3	George Bell, Julio Franco	.50
4	Ozzie Guillen, Ivan Rodriguez	.60
5	Carlos Baerga, Sandy Alomar Jr.	.50
6	Sandy Alomar Jr., Alvaro Espinoza, Paul Sorrento, Carlos Baerga, Felix Fermin, Junior Ortiz, Jose Mesa, Carlos Martinez	.50
7	Sandy Alomar Jr., Roberto Alomar	1.00
8	Jose Lind, Felix Jose	.50
9	Ricky Bones, Jaime Navarro	.50
10	Jaime Navarro, Jesse Orosco	.50
11	Tino Martinez, Edgar Martinez	.50
12	Juan Gonzalez, Ivan Rodriguez	.75
13	Juan Gonzalez, Julio Franco	.60
14	Julio Franco, Jose Canseco, Rafael Palmeiro	.50
15	Juan Gonzalez, Jose Canseco	.65
16	Ivan Rodriguez, Benji Gil	.60
17	Jose Guzman, Frank Castillo	.50
18	Rey Sanchez, Jose Vizcaino	.50
19	Derrick May, Sammy Sosa	2.00
20	Sammy Sosa, Candy Maldonado	2.00
21	Jose Rijo, Juan Samuel	.50
22	Freddie Benavides, Andres Galarraga	.50
23	Guillermo Velasquez, Benito Santiago	.50
24	Luis Gonzalez, Andujar Cedeno	.50
25	Wil Cordero, Dennis Martinez	.50
26	Moises Alou, Wil Cordero	.50
27	Ozzie Canseco, Jose Canseco	.75
28	Jose Oquendo, Luis Alicea	.50
29	Luis Alicea, Rene Arocha	.50
30	Geronimo Pena, Luis Alicea	.50

Estrellas de Beisbol

NM/M

Complete Set (20):		6.00
Common Player:		.50
1	Moises Alou	.50
2	Bobby Bonilla	.50
3	Tony Fernandez	.50
4	Felix Jose	.50
5	Dennis Martinez	.50
6	Orlando Merced	.50
7	Jose Oquendo	.50
8	Geronimo Pena	.50
9	Jose Rijo	.50
10	Benito Santiago	.50
11	Sandy Alomar Jr.	.50
12	Carlos Baerga	.50
13	Jose Canseco	1.50
14	Juan "Igor" Gonzalez	2.00
15	Juan Guzman	.50
16	Edgar Martinez	.50
17	Rafael Palmeiro	2.00
18	Ruben Sierra	.50
19	Danny Tartabull	.50
20	Omar Vizquel	.50

Jugadores Calientes

NM/M

Complete Set (36): 20.00

Common Player:		.50
1	Rich Amaral	.50
2	George Brett	1.75
3	Jay Buhner	.50
4	Roger Clemens	2.00
5	Kirk Gibson	.50
6	Juan Gonzalez	1.00
7	Ken Griffey Jr.	2.00
8	Bo Jackson	.75
9	Kenny Lofton	.50
10	Mark McGwire	2.25
11	Sherman Obando	.50
12	John Olerud	.50
13	Carlos Quintana	.50
14	Ivan Rodriguez	1.00
15	Nolan Ryan	2.50
16	J.T. Snow	.50
17	Fernando Valenzuela	.50
18	Dave Winfield	1.25
19	Moises Alou	.50
20	Jeff Bagwell	1.25
21	Barry Bonds	2.50
22	Bobby Bonilla	.50
23	Vinny Castilla	.50
24	Andujar Cedeno	.50
25	Orestes Destrade	.50
26	Andres Galarraga	.50
27	Mark Grace	.50
28	Tony Gwynn	1.50
29	Roberto Kelly	.50
30	John Kruk	.50
31	Dave Magadan	.50
32	Derrick May	.50
33	Orlando Merced	.50
34	Mike Piazza	2.00
35	Armadno Reynoso	.50
36	Jose Vizcaino	.50

Prism Insert

NM/M

Complete Set (20):		60.00
Common Player:		3.00
1	Francisco Cabrera	3.00
2	Jose Lind	3.00
3	Dennis Martinez	3.00
4	Ramon Martinez	3.00
5	Jose Rijo	3.00
6	Benito Santiago	3.00
7	Roberto Alomar	9.00
8	Sandy Alomar Jr.	3.00
9	Carlos Baerga	3.00
10	George Bell	3.00
11	Jose Canseco	6.00
12	Alex Fernandez	3.00
13	Julio Franco	3.00
14	Igor (Juan) Gonzalez	12.00
15	Ozzie Guillen	3.00
16	Teddy Higuera	3.00
17	Edgar Martinez	3.00
18	Hipolito Pichardo	3.00
19	Luis Polonia	3.00
20	Ivan Rodriguez	7.50

1994 Pacific Crown

NM/M

Complete Set (660): 20.00

Common Player:		.05
Pack (12):		1.00
Wax Box (36):		20.00
1	Steve Avery	.05
2	Steve Bedrosian	.05
3	Damon Beryhill	.05
4	Jeff Blauser	.05
5	Sid Bream	.05
6	Francisco Cabrera	.05
7	Ramon Caraballo	.05
8	Ron Gant	.05
9	Tom Glavine	.25
10	Chipper Jones	.75
11	Dave Justice	.05
12	Ryan Klesko	.05
13	Mark Lemke	.05
14	Javier Lopez	.05
15	Greg Maddux	.75
16	Fred McGriff	.05
17	Greg McMichael	.05
18	Kent Mercker	.05
19	Otis Nixon	.05
20	Terry Pendleton	.05
21	Deion Sanders	.05
22	John Smoltz	.05
23	Tony Tarasco	.05
24	Manny Alexander	.05
25	Brady Anderson	.05
26	Harold Baines	.05
27	Damion Buford (Damon)	.05
28	Paul Carey	.05
29	Mike Devereaux	.05
30	Todd Frohwirth	.05
31	Leo Gomez	.05
32	Jeffrey Hammonds	.05
33	Chris Hoiles	.05
34	Tim Hulett	.05
35	Ben McDonald	.05
36	Mark McLemore	.05
37	Alan Mills	.05
38	Mike Mussina	.35
39	Sherman Obando	.05
40	Gregg Olson	.05
41	Mike Pagliarulo	.05
42	Jim Poole	.05
43	Harold Reynolds	.05
44	Cal Ripken, Jr.	2.00
45	David Segui	.05
46	Fernando Valenzuela	.05
47	Jack Voight	.05
48	Scott Bankhead	.05
49	Roger Clemens	1.00
50	Scott Cooper	.05
51	Danny Darwin	.05
52	Andre Dawson	.20
53	John Dopson	.05
54	Scott Fletcher	.05
55	Tony Fossas	.05
56	Mike Greenwell	.05
57	Billy Hatcher	.05
58	Jeff McNeely	.05
59	Jose Melendez	.05
60	Tim Naehring	.05
61	Tony Pena	.05
62	Carlos Quintana	.05
63	Paul Quantrill	.05
64	Luis Rivera	.05
65	Jeff Russell	.05
66	Aaron Sele	.05
67	John Valentin	.05
68	Mo Vaughn	.05
69	Frank Viola	.05
70	Bob Zupcic	.05
71	Mike Butcher	.05
72	Ron Correia	.05
73	Chad Curtis	.05
74	Chili Davis	.05
75	Gary DiSarcina	.05
76	Damion Easley	.05
77	John Farrell	.05
78	Chuck Finley	.05
79	Joe Grahe	.05
80	Stan Javier	.05
81	Mark Langston	.05
82	Phil Leftwich	.05
83	Torey Lovullo	.05
84	Joe Magrane	.05
85	Greg Myers	.05
86	Eduardo Perez	.05
87	Luis Polonia	.05
88	Tim Salmon	.05
89	J.T. Snow	.05
90	Kurt Stillwell	.05
91	Ron Tingley	.05
92	Chris Turner	.05
93	Julio Valera	.05
94	Jose Bautista	.05
95	Shawn Boskie	.05
96	Steve Buechele	.05
97	Frank Castillo	.05
98	Mark Grace	.05
99	Jose Guzman	.05
100	Mike Harkey	.05
101	Greg Hibbard	.05
102	Doug Jennings	.05
103	Derrick May	.05
104	Mike Morgan	.05
105	Randy Myers	.05
106	Karl Rhodes	.05
107	Kevin Roberson	.05
108	Rey Sanchez	.05
109	Ryne Sandberg	.75
110	Tommy Shields	.05
111	Dwight Smith	.05
112	Sammy Sosa	.75

113	Jose Vizcaino	.05
114	Turk Wendell	.05
115	Rick Wilkins	.05
116	Willie Wilson	.05
117	Eddie Zambrano	.05
118	Wilson Alvarez	.05
119	Tim Belcher	.05
120	Jason Bere	.05
121	Rodney Bolton	.05
122	Ellis Burks	.05
123	Joey Cora	.05
124	Alex Fernandez	.05
125	Ozzie Guillen	.05
126	Craig Grebeck	.05
127	Roberto Hernandez	.05
128	Bo Jackson	.10
129	Lance Johnson	.05
130	Ron Karkovice	.05
131	Mike Lavalliere	.05
132	Norberto Martin	.05
133	Kirk McCaskill	.05
134	Jack McDowell	.05
135	Scott Radinsky	.05
136	Tim Raines	.05
137	Steve Sax	.05
138	Frank Thomas	.60
139	Dan Pasqua	.05
140	Robin Ventura	.05
141	Jeff Branson	.05
142	Tom Browning	.05
143	Jacob Brumfield	.05
144	Tim Costo	.05
145	Rob Dibble	.05
146	Brian Dorsett	.05
147	Steve Foster	.05
148	Cesar Hernandez	.05
149	Roberto Kelly	.05
150	Barry Larkin	.05
151	Larry Luebbers	.05
152	Kevin Mitchell	.05
153	Joe Oliver	.05
154	Tim Pugh	.05
155	Jeff Reardon	.05
156	Jose Rijo	.05
157	Bip Roberts	.05
158	Chris Sabo	.05
159	Juan Samuel	.05
160	Reggie Sanders	.05
161	John Smiley	.05
162	Jerry Spradlin	.05
163	Gary Varsho	.05
164	Sandy Alomar Jr.	.05
165	Carlos Baerga	.05
166	Albert Belle	.05
167	Mark Clark	.05
168	Alvaro Espinoza	.05
169	Felix Fermin	.05
170	Reggie Jefferson	.05
171	Wayne Kirby	.05
172	Tom Kramer	.05
173	Jesse Levis	.05
174	Kenny Lofton	.05
175	Candy Maldonado	.05
176	Carlos Martinez	.05
177	Jose Mesa	.05
178	Jeff Mutis	.05
179	Charles Nagy	.05
180	Bob Ojeda	.05
181	Junior Ortiz	.05
182	Eric Plunk	.05
183	Manny Ramirez	.60
184	Paul Sorrento	.05
185	Jeff Treadway	.05
186	Bill Wertz	.05
187	Freddie Benavides	.05
188	Dante Bichette	.05
189	Willie Blair	.05
190	Daryl Boston	.05
191	Pedro Castellano	.05
192	Vinny Castilla	.05
193	Jerald Clark	.05
194	Alex Cole	.05
195	Andres Galarraga	.05
196	Joe Girardi	.05
197	Charlie Hayes	.05
198	Darren Holmes	.05
199	Chris Jones	.05
200	Curt Leskanic	.05
201	Roberto Mejia	.05
202	David Nied	.05
203	J. Owens	.05
204	Steve Reed	.05
205	Armando Reynoso	.05
206	Bruce Ruffin	.05
207	Keith Shepherd	.05
208	Jim Tatum	.05
209	Eric Young	.05
210	Skeeter Barnes	.05
211	Danny Bautista	.05
212	Tom Bolton	.05
213	Eric Davis	.05
214	Storm Davis	.05
215	Cecil Fielder	.05
216	Travis Fryman	.05
217	Kirk Gibson	.05
218	Dan Gladden	.05
219	John Doherty	.05
220	Chris Gomez	.05
221	David Haas	.05
222	Bill Krueger	.05
223	Chad Kreuter	.05
224	Mark Leiter	.05
225	Bob MacDonald	.05
226	Mike Moore	.05
227	Tony Phillips	.05
228	Rich Rowland	.05
229	Mickey Tettleton	.05
230	Alan Trammell	.05
231	David Wells	.05
232	Lou Whitaker	.05
233	Luis Aquino	.05
234	Alex Arias	.05
235	Jack Armstrong	.05
236	Ryan Bowen	.05
237	Chuck Carr	.05
238	Matias Carrillo	.05
239	Jeff Conine	.05
240	Henry Cotto	.05
241	Orestes Destrade	.05
242	Chris Hammond	.05
243	Bryan Harvey	.05
244	Charlie Hough	.05
245	Richie Lewis	.05
246	Mitch Lyden	.05
247	Dave Magadan	.05
248	Bob Natal	.05
249	Benito Santiago	.05
250	Gary Sheffield	.30
251	Matt Turner	.05
252	David Weathers	.05
253	Walt Weiss	.05
254	Darrell Whitmore	.05
255	Nigel Wilson	.05
256	Eric Anthony	.05
257	Jeff Bagwell	.60
258	Kevin Bass	.05
259	Craig Biggio	.05
260	Ken Caminiti	.05
261	Andujar Cedeno	.05
262	Chris Donnels	.05
263	Doug Drabek	.05
264	Tom Edens	.05
265	Steve Finley	.05
266	Luis Gonzalez	.05
267	Pete Harnisch	.05
268	Xavier Hernandez	.05
269	Todd Jones	.05
270	Darryl Kile	.05
271	Al Osuna	.05
272	Rick Parker	.05
273	Mark Portugal	.05
274	Scott Servais	.05
275	Greg Swindell	.05
276	Eddie Taubensee	.05
277	Jose Uribe	.05
278	Brian Williams	.05
279	Kevin Appier	.05
280	Billy Brewer	.05
281	David Cone	.05
282	Greg Gagne	.05
283	Tom Gordon	.05
284	Chris Gwynn	.05
285	John Habyan	.05
286	Chris Haney	.05
287	Phil Hiatt	.05
288	David Howard	.05
289	Felix Jose	.05
290	Wally Joyner	.05
291	Kevin Koslofski	.05
292	Jose Lind	.05
293	Brent Mayne	.05
294	Mike Mcfarlane	.05
295	Brian McRae	.05
296	Kevin McReynolds	.05
297	Keith Miller	.05
298	Jeff Montgomery	.05
299	Hipolito Pichardo	.05
300	Rico Rossy	.05
301	Curtis Wilkerson	.05
302	Pedro Astacio	.05
303	Rafael Bournigal	.05
304	Brett Butler	.05
305	Tom Candiotti	.05
306	Omar Daal	.05
307	Jim Gott	.05
308	Kevin Gross	.05
309	Dave Hansen	.05
310	Carlos Hernandez	.05
311	Orel Hershiser	.05
312	Eric Karros	.05
313	Pedro Martinez	.60
314	Ramon Martinez	.05
315	Roger McDowell	.05
316	Raul Mondesi	.05
317	Jose Offerman	.05
318	Mike Piazza	1.00
319	Jody Reed	.05
320	Henry Rodriguez	.05
321	Cory Snyder	.05
322	Darryl Strawberry	.05
323	Tim Wallach	.05
324	Steve Wilson	.05
325	Juan Bell	.05
326	Ricky Bones	.05
327	Alex Diaz	.05
328	Cal Eldred	.05
329	Darryl Hamilton	.05
330	Doug Henry	.05
331	John Jaha	.05
332	Pat Listach	.05
333	Graeme Lloyd	.05
334	Carlos Maldonado	.05
335	Angel Miranda	.05
336	Jaime Navarro	.05
337	Dave Nilsson	.05
338	Rafael Novoa	.05
339	Troy O'Leary	.05
340	Jesse Orosco	.05
341	Kevin Seitzer	.05
342	Bill Spiers	.05
343	William Suero	.05
344	B.J. Surhoff	.05
345	Dickie Thon	.05
346	Jose Valentin	.05
347	Greg Vaughn	.05
348	Robin Yount	.60
349	Willie Banks	.05
350	Bernardo Brito	.05
351	Scott Erickson	.05
352	Mark Guthrie	.05
353	Chip Hale	.05
354	Brian Harper	.05
355	Kent Hrbek	.05
356	Terry Jorgenson	.05
357	Chuck Knoblauch	.05
358	Gene Larkin	.05
359	Scott Leius	.05
360	Shane Mack	.05
361	David McCarty	.05
362	Pat Meares	.05
363	Pedro Munoz	.05
364	Derek Parks	.05
365	Kirby Puckett	.75
366	Jeff Reboulet	.05
367	Kevin Tapani	.05
368	Mike Trombley	.05
369	George Tsamis	.05
370	Carl Willis	.05
371	Dave Winfield	.60
372	Moises Alou	.05
373	Brian Barnes	.05
374	Sean Berry	.05
375	Frank Bolick	.05
376	Wil Cordero	.05
377	Delino DeShields	.05
378	Jeff Fassero	.05
379	Darren Fletcher	.05
380	Cliff Floyd	.05
381	Lou Frazier	.05
382	Marquis Grissom	.05
383	Gil Heredia	.05
384	Mike Lansing	.05
385	Oreste Marrero	.05
386	Dennis Martinez	.05
387	Curtis Pride	.05
388	Mel Rojas	.05
389	Kirk Rueter	.05
390	Joe Siddall	.05
391	John Vander Wal	.05
392	Larry Walker	.05
393	John Wetteland	.05
394	Rondell White	.05
395	Tom Bogar	.05
396	Bobby Bonilla	.05
397	Jeromy Burnitz	.05
398	Mike Draper	.05
399	Sid Fernandez	.05
400	John Franco	.05
401	Dave Gallagher	.05
402	Dwight Gooden	.05
403	Eric Hillman	.05
404	Todd Hundley	.05
405	Butch Huskey	.05
406	Jeff Innis	.05
407	Howard Johnson	.05
408	Jeff Kent	.05
409	Ced Landrum	.05
410	Mike Maddux	.05
411	Josias Manzanillo	.05
412	Jeff McKnight	.05
413	Eddie Murray	.60
414	Tito Navarro	.05
415	Joe Orsulak	.05
416	Bret Saberhagen	.05
417	Dave Telgheder	.05
418	Ryan Thompson	.05
419	Chico Walker	.05
420	Jim Abbott	.05
421	Wade Boggs	.75
422	Mike Gallego	.05
423	Mark Hutton	.05
424	Dion James	.05
425	Domingo Jean	.05
426	Pat Kelly	.05
427	Jimmy Key	.05
428	Jim Leyritz	.05
429	Kevin Maas	.05
430	Don Mattingly	1.00
431	Bobby Munoz	.05
432	Matt Nokes	.05
433	Paul O'Neill	.05
434	Spike Owen	.05
435	Melido Perez	.05
436	Lee Smith	.05
437	Andy Stankiewicz	.05
438	Mike Stanley	.05
439	Danny Tartabull	.05
440	Randy Velarde	.05
441	Bernie Williams	.05
442	Gerald Williams	.05
443	Mike Witt	.05
444	Marcos Armas	.05
445	Lance Blankenship	.05
446	Mike Bordick	.05
447	Ron Darling	.05
448	Dennis Eckersley	.45
449	Brent Gates	.05
450	Goose Gossage	.05
451	Scott Hemond	.05
452	Dave Henderson	.05
453	Shawn Hillegas	.05
454	Rick Honeycutt	.05
455	Scott Lydy	.05
456	Mark McGwire	1.50
457	Henry Mercedes	.05
458	Mike Mohler	.05
459	Troy Neel	.05
460	Edwin Nunez	.05
461	Craig Paquette	.05
462	Ruben Sierra	.05
463	Terry Steinbach	.05
464	Todd Van Poppel	.05
465	Bob Welch	.05
466	Bobby Witt	.05
467	Ruben Amaro	.05
468	Larry Anderson	.05
469	Kim Batiste	.05
470	Wes Chamberlain	.05
471	Darren Daulton	.05
472	Mariano Duncan	.05
473	Len Dykstra	.05
474	Jim Eisenreich	.05
475	Tommy Greene	.05
476	Dave Hollins	.05
477	Pete Incaviglia	.05
478	Danny Jackson	.05
479	John Kruk	.05
480	Tony Longmire	.05
481	Jeff Manto	.05
482	Mike Morandini	.05
483	Terry Mulholland	.05
484	Todd Pratt	.05
485	Ben Rivera	.05
486	Curt Schilling	.25
487	Kevin Stocker	.05
488	Milt Thompson	.05
489	David West	.05
490	Mitch Williams	.05
491	Jeff Ballard	.05
492	Jay Bell	.05
493	Scott Bullett	.05
494	Dave Clark	.05
495	Steve Cooke	.05
496	Midre Cummings	.05
497	Mark Dewey	.05
498	Carlos Garcia	.05
499	Jeff King	.05
500	Al Martin	.05
501	Lloyd McClendon	.05
502	Orlando Merced	.05
503	Blas Minor	.05
504	Denny Neagle	.05
505	Tom Prince	.05
506	Don Slaught	.05
507	Zane Smith	.05
508	Randy Tomlin	.05
509	Andy Van Slyke	.05
510	Paul Wagner	.05
511	Tim Wakefield	.05
512	Bob Walk	.05
513	John Wehner	.05
514	Kevin Young	.05
515	Billy Bean	.05
516	Andy Benes	.05
517	Derek Bell	.05
518	Doug Brocail	.05
519	Jarvis Brown	.05
520	Phil Clark	.05
521	Mark Davis	.05
522	Jeff Gardner	.05
523	Pat Gomez	.05
524	Ricky Gutierrez	.05
525	Tony Gwynn	.75
526	Gene Harris	.05
527	Kevin Higgins	.05
528	Trevor Hoffman	.05
529	Luis Lopez	.05
530	Pedro A. Martinez	.05
531	Melvin Nieves	.05
532	Phil Plantier	.05
533	Frank Seminara	.05
534	Craig Shipley	.05
535	Tim Tuefel	.05
536	Guillermo Velasquez	.05
537	Wally Whitehurst	.05
538	Rod Beck	.05
539	Todd Benzinger	.05
540	Barry Bonds	2.00
541	Jeff Brantley	.05
542	Dave Burba	.05
543	John Burkett	.05
544	Will Clark	.05
545	Royce Clayton	.05
546	Brian Hickerson (Bryan)	.05
547	Mike Jackson	.05
548	Darren Lewis	.05
549	Kirt Manwaring	.05
550	Dave Martinez	.05
551	Willie McGee	.05
552	Jeff Reed	.05
553	Dave Righetti	.05
554	Kevin Rogers	.05
555	Steve Scarsone	.05
556	Bill Swift	.05
557	Robby Thompson	.05
558	Salomon Torres	.05
559	Matt Williams	.05
560	Trevor Wilson	.05
561	Rich Amaral	.05
562	Mike Blowers	.05
563	Chris Bosio	.05
564	Jay Buhner	.05
565	Norm Charlton	.05
566	Jim Converse	.05
567	Rich DeLucia	.05
568	Mike Felder	.05
569	Dave Fleming	.05
570	Ken Griffey Jr.	1.00
571	Bill Haselman	.05
572	Dwayne Henry	.05

573	Brad Holman	.05
574	Randy Johnson	.60
575	Greg Litton	.05
576	Edgar Martinez	.05
577	Tino Martinez	.05
578	Jeff Nelson	.05
579	Mark Newfield	.05
580	Roger Salkeld	.05
581	Mackey Sasser	.05
582	Brian Turang	.05
583	Omar Vizquel	.05
584	Dave Valle	.05
585	Luis Alicea	.05
586	Rene Arocha	.05
587	Rheal Cormier	.05
588	Tripp Cromer	.05
589	Bernard Gilkey	.05
590	Lee Guetterman	.05
591	Gregg Jefferies	.05
592	Tim Jones	.05
593	Paul Kilgus	.05
594	Les Lancaster	.05
595	Omar Olivares	.05
596	Jose Oquendo	.05
597	Donovan Osborne	.05
598	Tom Pagnozzi	.05
599	Erik Pappas	.05
600	Geronimo Pena	.05
601	Mike Perez	.05
602	Gerald Perry	.05
603	Stan Royer	.05
604	Ozzie Smith	.75
605	Bob Tewksbury	.05
606	Allen Watson	.05
607	Mark Whiten	.05
608	Todd Zeile	.05
609	Jeff Bronkey	.05
610	Kevin Brown	.05
611	Jose Canseco	.35
612	Doug Dascenzo	.05
613	Butch Davis	.05
614	Mario Diaz	.05
615	Julio Franco	.05
616	Benji Gil	.05
617	Juan Gonzalez	.30
618	Tom Henke	.05
619	Jeff Huson	.05
620	David Hulse	.05
621	Craig Lefferts	.05
622	Rafael Palmeiro	.50
623	Dean Palmer	.05
624	Bob Patterson	.05
625	Roger Pavlik	.05
626	Gary Redus	.05
627	Ivan Rodriguez	.50
628	Kenny Rogers	.05
629	Jon Shave	.05
630	Doug Strange	.05
631	Matt Whiteside	.05
632	Roberto Alomar	.15
633	Pat Borders	.05
634	Scott Brow	.05
635	Rob Butler	.05
636	Joe Carter	.05
637	Tony Castillo	.05
638	Mark Eichhorn	.05
639	Tony Fernandez	.05
640	Huck Flener **RC**	.05
641	Alfredo Griffin	.05
642	Juan Guzman	.05
643	Rickey Henderson	.60
644	Pat Hentgen	.05
645	Randy Knorr	.05
646	Al Leiter	.05
647	Dominigo Martinez	.05
648	Paul Molitor	.60
649	Jack Morris	.05
650	John Olerud	.05
651	Ed Sprague	.05
652	Dave Stewart	.05
653	Devon White	.05
654	Woody Williams	.05
655	Barry Bonds (MVP)	1.00
656	Greg Maddux (CY)	.40
657	Jack McDowell (CY)	.05
658	Mike Piazza (ROY)	.65
659	Tim Salmon (ROY)	.05
660	Frank Thomas (MVP)	1.00

All Latino All-Star Team

		NM/M
	Complete Set (20):	4.00
	Common Player:	.25
1	Benito Santiago	.25
2	Dave Magadan	.25
3	Andres Galarraga	.25
4	Luis Gonzalez	.25
5	Jose Offerman	.25
6	Bobby Bonilla	.25
7	Dennis Martinez	.25
8	Mariano Duncan	.25
9	Orlando Merced	.25
10	Jose Rijo	.25
11	Danny Tartabull	.25
12	Ruben Sierra	.25
13	Ivan Rodriguez	1.00
14	Juan Gonzalez	1.00
15	Jose Canseco	.50
16	Rafael Palmeiro	1.00
17	Roberto Alomar	.50
18	Eduardo Perez	.25
19	Alex Fernandez	.25
20	Omar Vizquel	.25

Homerun Leaders

		NM/M
	Complete Set (20):	25.00
	Common Player:	1.00
1	Juan Gonzalez	1.50
2	Ken Griffey Jr.	3.00
3	Frank Thomas	2.50
4	Albert Belle	1.00
5	Rafael Palmeiro	1.50
6	Joe Carter	1.00
7	Dean Palmer	1.00
8	Mickey Tettleton	1.00
9	Tim Salmon	1.00
10	Danny Tartabull	1.00
11	Barry Bonds	5.00
12	Dave Justice	1.00
13	Matt Williams	1.00
14	Fred McGriff	1.00
15	Ron Gant	1.00
16	Mike Piazza	3.00
17	Bobby Bonilla	1.00
18	Phil Plantier	1.00
19	Sammy Sosa	3.00
20	Rick Wilkins	1.00

Jewels of the Crown

		NM/M
	Complete Set (36):	40.00
	Common Player:	1.00
1	Robin Yount	2.50
2	Juan Gonzalez	1.25
3	Rafael Palmeiro	1.25
4	Paul Molitor	2.50
5	Roberto Alomar	1.25
6	John Olerud	1.00
7	Randy Johnson	2.50
8	Ken Griffey Jr.	4.00
9	Wade Boggs	3.00
10	Don Mattingly	3.50
11	Kirby Puckett	3.00
12	Tim Salmon	1.00
13	Frank Thomas	2.50

14	Fernando Valenzuela (Comeback Player)	1.00
15	Cal Ripken, Jr.	6.00
16	Carlos Baerga	1.00
17	Kenny Lofton	1.00
18	Cecil Fielder	1.00
19	John Burkett	1.00
20	Andres Galarraga (Comeback Player)	1.00
21	Charlie Hayes	1.00
22	Orestes Destrade	1.00
23	Jeff Conine	1.00
24	Jeff Bagwell	2.50
25	Mark Grace	1.00
26	Ryne Sandberg	3.00
27	Gregg Jefferies	1.00
28	Barry Bonds	6.00
29	Mike Piazza	3.50
30	Greg Maddux	3.00
31	Darren Daulton	1.00
32	John Kruk	1.00
33	Len Dykstra	1.00
34	Orlando Merced	1.00
35	Tony Gwynn	3.00
36	Robby Thompson	1.00

Jewels of the Crown - Retail

		NM/M
	Complete Set (36):	40.00
	Common Player:	.75
1	Robin Yount	2.50
2	Juan Gonzalez	1.25
3	Rafael Palmeiro	1.25
4	Paul Molitor	2.50
5	Roberto Alomar	1.00
6	John Olerud	.75
7	Randy Johnson	2.50
8	Ken Griffey Jr.	4.00
9	Wade Boggs	3.00
10	Don Mattingly	3.50
11	Kirby Puckett	3.00
12	Tim Salmon	.75
13	Frank Thomas	2.50
14	Fernando Valenzuela (Comeback Player)	.75
15	Cal Ripken, Jr.	5.00
16	Carlos Baerga	.75
17	Kenny Lofton	.75
18	Cecil Fielder	.75
19	John Burkett	.75
20	Andres Galarraga (Comeback Player)	.75
21	Charlie Hayes	.75
22	Orestes Destrade	.75
23	Jeff Conine	.75
24	Jeff Bagwell	2.50
25	Mark Grace	.75
26	Ryne Sandberg	3.00
27	Gregg Jefferies	.75
28	Barry Bonds	5.00
29	Mike Piazza	3.50
30	Greg Maddux	3.00
31	Darren Daulton	.75
32	John Kruk	.75
33	Len Dykstra	.75
34	Orlando Merced	.75
35	Tony Gwynn	3.00
36	Robby Thompson	.75

1995 Pacific

		NM/M
	Complete Set (450):	20.00
	Common Player:	.05
	Pack (12):	1.00
	Wax Box (36):	20.00
1	Steve Avery	.05
2	Rafael Belliard	.05
3	Jeff Blauser	.05
4	Tom Glavine	.25
5	Dave Justice	.05
6	Mike Kelly	.05
7	Roberto Kelly	.05
8	Ryan Klesko	.05
9	Mark Lemke	.05
10	Javier Lopez	.05
11	Greg Maddux	.75
12	Fred McGriff	.25
13	Greg McMichael	.05
14	Jose Oliva	.05

15	John Smoltz	.05
16	Tony Tarasco	.05
17	Brady Anderson	.05
18	Harold Baines	.05
19	Armando Benitez	.05
20	Mike Devereaux	.05
21	Leo Gomez	.05
22	Jeffrey Hammonds	.05
23	Chris Hoiles	.05
24	Ben McDonald	.05
25	Mark McLemore	.05
26	Jamie Moyer	.05
27	Mike Mussina	.40
28	Rafael Palmeiro	.50
29	Jim Poole	.05
30	Cal Ripken Jr.	2.00
31	Lee Smith	.05
32	Mark Smith	.05
33	Jose Canseco	.35
34	Roger Clemens	1.00
35	Scott Cooper	.05
36	Andre Dawson	.25
37	Tony Fossas	.05
38	Mike Greenwell	.05
39	Chris Howard	.05
40	Jose Melendez	.05
41	Nate Minchey	.05
42	Tim Naehring	.05
43	Otis Nixon	.05
44	Carlos Rodriguez	.05
45	Aaron Sele	.05
46	Lee Tinsley	.05
47	Sergio Valdez	.05
48	John Valentin	.05
49	Mo Vaughn	.05
50	Brian Anderson	.05
51	Garret Anderson	.05
52	Rod Correia	.05
53	Chad Curtis	.05
54	Mark Dalesandro	.05
55	Chili Davis	.05
56	Gary DiSarcina	.05
57	Damion Easley	.05
58	Jim Edmonds	.05
59	Jorge Fabregas	.05
60	Chuck Finley	.05
61	Bo Jackson	.10
62	Mark Langston	.05
63	Eduardo Perez	.05
64	Tim Salmon	.05
65	J.T. Snow	.05
66	Willie Banks	.05
67	Jose Bautista	.05
68	Shawon Dunston	.05
69	Kevin Foster	.05
70	Mark Grace	.05
71	Jose Guzman	.05
72	Jose Hernandez	.05
73	Blaise Ilsley	.05
74	Derrick May	.05
75	Randy Myers	.05
76	Karl Rhodes	.05
77	Kevin Roberson	.05
78	Rey Sanchez	.05
79	Sammy Sosa	.75
80	Steve Trachsel	.05
81	Eddie Zambrano	.05
82	Wilson Alvarez	.05
83	Jason Bere	.05
84	Joey Cora	.05
85	Jose DeLeon	.05
86	Alex Fernandez	.05
87	Julio Franco	.05
88	Ozzie Guillen	.05
89	Joe Hall	.05
90	Roberto Hernandez	.05
91	Darrin Jackson	.05
92	Lance Johnson	.05
93	Norberto Martin	.05
94	Jack McDowell	.05
95	Tim Raines	.05
96	Olmedo Saenz	.05
97	Frank Thomas	.60
98	Robin Ventura	.05
99	Bret Boone	.05
100	Jeff Brantley	.05
101	Jacob Brumfield	.05
102	Hector Carrasco	.05
103	Brian Dorsett	.05
104	Tony Fernandez	.05
105	Willie Greene	.05

106	Erik Hanson	.05
107	Kevin Jarvis	.05
108	Barry Larkin	.05
109	Kevin Mitchell	.05
110	Hal Morris	.05
111	Jose Rijo	.05
112	Johnny Ruffin	.05
113	Deion Sanders	.05
114	Reggie Sanders	.05
115	Sandy Alomar Jr.	.05
116	Ruben Amaro	.05
117	Carlos Baerga	.05
118	Albert Belle	.05
119	Alvaro Espinoza	.05
120	Rene Gonzales	.05
121	Wayne Kirby	.05
122	Kenny Lofton	.05
123	Candy Maldonado	.05
124	Dennis Martinez	.05
125	Eddie Murray	.60
126	Charles Nagy	.05
127	Tony Pena	.05
128	Manny Ramirez	.60
129	Paul Sorrento	.05
130	Jim Thome	.40
131	Omar Vizquel	.05
132	Dante Bichette	.05
133	Ellis Burks	.05
134	Vinny Castilla	.05
135	Marvin Freeman	.05
136	Andres Galarraga	.05
137	Joe Girardi	.05
138	Charlie Hayes	.05
139	Mike Kingery	.05
140	Nelson Liriano	.05
141	Roberto Mejia	.05
142	David Nied	.05
143	Steve Reed	.05
144	Armando Reynoso	.05
145	Bruce Ruffin	.05
146	John Vander Wal	.05
147	Walt Weiss	.05
148	Skeeter Barnes	.05
149	Tim Belcher	.05
150	Junior Felix	.05
151	Cecil Fielder	.05
152	Travis Fryman	.05
153	Kirk Gibson	.05
154	Chris Gomez	.05
155	Buddy Groom	.05
156	Chad Kreuter	.05
157	Mike Moore	.05
158	Tony Phillips	.05
159	Juan Samuel	.05
160	Mickey Tettleton	.05
161	Alan Trammell	.05
162	David Wells	.05
163	Lou Whitaker	.05
164	Kurt Abbott	.05
165	Luis Aquino	.05
166	Alex Arias	.05
167	Bret Barberie	.05
168	Jerry Browne	.05
169	Chuck Carr	.05
170	Matias Carrillo	.05
171	Greg Colbrunn	.05
172	Jeff Conine	.05
173	Carl Everett	.05
174	Robb Nen	.05
175	Yorkis Perez	.05
176	Pat Rapp	.05
177	Benito Santiago	.05
178	Gary Sheffield	.35
179	Darrell Whitmore	.05
180	Jeff Bagwell	.60
181	Kevin Bass	.05
182	Craig Biggio	.05
183	Andujar Cedeno	.05
184	Doug Drabek	.05
185	Tony Eusebio	.05
186	Steve Finley	.05
187	Luis Gonzalez	.05
188	Pete Harnisch	.05
189	John Hudek	.05
190	Orlando Miller	.05
191	James Mouton	.05
192	Roberto Petagine	.05
193	Shane Reynolds	.05
194	Greg Swindell	.05
195	Dave Veres	.05
196	Kevin Appier	.05
197	Stan Belinda	.05
198	Vince Coleman	.05
199	David Cone	.05
200	Gary Gaetti	.05
201	Greg Gagne	.05
202	Mark Gubicza	.05
203	Bob Hamelin	.05
204	Dave Henderson	.05
205	Felix Jose	.05
206	Wally Joyner	.05
207	Jose Lind	.05
208	Mike Macfarlane	.05
209	Brian McRae	.05
210	Jeff Montgomery	.05
211	Hipolito Pichardo	.05
212	Pedro Astacio	.05
213	Brett Butler	.05
214	Omar Daal	.05
215	Delino DeShields	.05
216	Darren Dreifort	.05
217	Carlos Hernandez	.05
218	Orel Hershiser	.05
219	Garey Ingram	.05
220	Eric Karros	.05
221	Ramon Martinez	.05
222	Raul Mondesi	.05
223	Jose Offerman	.05
224	Mike Piazza	1.00
225	Henry Rodriguez	.05
226	Ismael Valdes	.05
227	Tim Wallach	.05
228	Jeff Cirillo	.05
229	Alex Diaz	.05
230	Cal Eldred	.05
231	Mike Fetters	.05
232	Brian Harper	.05
233	Ted Higuera	.05
234	John Jaha	.05
235	Graeme Lloyd	.05
236	Jose Mercedes	.05
237	Jaime Navarro	.05
238	Dave Nilsson	.05
239	Jesse Orosco	.05
240	Jody Reed	.05
241	Jose Valentin	.05
242	Greg Vaughn	.05
243	Turner Ward	.05
244	Rick Aguilera	.05
245	Rich Becker	.05
246	Jim Deshaies	.05
247	Steve Dunn	.05
248	Scott Erickson	.05
249	Kent Hrbek	.05
250	Chuck Knoblauch	.05
251	Scott Leius	.05
252	David McCarty	.05
253	Pat Meares	.05
254	Pedro Munoz	.05
255	Kirby Puckett	.75
256	Carlos Pulido	.05
257	Kevin Tapani	.05
258	Matt Walbeck	.05
259	Dave Winfield	.60
260	Moises Alou	.05
261	Juan Bell	.05
262	Freddie Benavides	.05
263	Sean Berry	.05
264	Wil Cordero	.05
265	Jeff Fassero	.05
266	Darrin Fletcher	.05
267	Cliff Floyd	.05
268	Marquis Grissom	.05
269	Gil Heredia	.05
270	Ken Hill	.05
271	Pedro Martinez	.60
272	Mel Rojas	.05
273	Larry Walker	.05
274	John Wetteland	.05
275	Rondell White	.05
276	Tim Bogar	.05
277	Bobby Bonilla	.05
278	Rico Brogna	.05
279	Jeromy Burnitz	.05
280	John Franco	.05
281	Eric Hillman	.05
282	Todd Hundley	.05
283	Jeff Kent	.05
284	Mike Maddux	.05
285	Joe Orsulak	.05
286	Luis Rivera	.05
287	Bret Saberhagen	.05
288	David Segui	.05
289	Ryan Thompson	.05
290	Fernando Vina	.05
291	Jose Vizcaino	.05
292	Jim Abbott	.05
293	Wade Boggs	.75
294	Russ Davis	.05
295	Mike Gallego	.05
296	Xavier Hernandez	.05
297	Steve Howe	.05
298	Jimmy Key	.05
299	Don Mattingly	1.00
300	Terry Mulholland	.05
301	Paul O'Neill	.05
302	Luis Polonia	.05
303	Mike Stanley	.05
304	Danny Tartabull	.05
305	Randy Velarde	.05
306	Bob Wickman	.05
307	Bernie Williams	.05
308	Mark Acre	.05
309	Geronimo Berroa	.05
310	Mike Bordick	.05
311	Dennis Eckersley	.50
312	Rickey Henderson	.60
313	Stan Javier	.05
314	Miguel Jimenez	.05
315	Francisco Matos	.05
316	Mark McGwire	1.50
317	Troy Neel	.05
318	Steve Ontiveros	.05
319	Carlos Reyes	.05
320	Ruben Sierra	.05
321	Terry Steinbach	.05
322	Bob Welch	.05
323	Bobby Witt	.05
324	Larry Andersen	.05
325	Kim Batiste	.05
326	Darren Daulton	.05
327	Mariano Duncan	.05
328	Lenny Dykstra	.05
329	Jim Eisenreich	.05
330	Danny Jackson	.05
331	John Kruk	.05
332	Tony Longmire	.05
333	Tom Marsh	.05
334	Mickey Morandini	.05
335	Bobby Munoz	.05
336	Todd Pratt	.05
337	Tom Quinlan	.05
338	Kevin Stocker	.05
339	Fernando Valenzuela	.05
340	Jay Bell	.05
341	Dave Clark	.05
342	Steve Cooke	.05
343	Carlos Garcia	.05
344	Jeff King	.05
345	Jon Lieber	.05
346	Ravelo Manzanillo	.05
347	Al Martin	.05
348	Orlando Merced	.05
349	Denny Neagle	.05
350	Alejandro Pena	.05
351	Don Slaught	.05
352	Zane Smith	.05
353	Andy Van Slyke	.05
354	Rick White	.05
355	Kevin Young	.05
356	Andy Ashby	.05
357	Derek Bell	.05
358	Andy Benes	.05
359	Phil Clark	.05
360	Donnie Elliott	.05
361	Ricky Gutierrez	.05
362	Tony Gwynn	.75
363	Trevor Hoffman	.05
364	Tim Hyers	.05
365	Luis Lopez	.05
366	Jose Martinez	.05
367	Pedro A. Martinez	.05
368	Phil Plantier	.05
369	Bip Roberts	.05
370	A.J. Sager	.05
371	Jeff Tabaka	.05
372	Todd Benzinger	.05
373	Barry Bonds	2.00
374	John Burkett	.05
375	Mark Carreon	.05
376	Royce Clayton	.05
377	Pat Gomez	.05
378	Erik Johnson	.05
379	Darren Lewis	.05
380	Kirt Manwaring	.05
381	Dave Martinez	.05
382	John Patterson	.05
383	Mark Portugal	.05
384	Darryl Strawberry	.05
385	Salomon Torres	.05
386	Bill Van Landingham	.05
387	Matt Williams	.05
388	Rich Amaral	.05
389	Bobby Ayala	.05
390	Mike Blowers	.05
391	Chris Bosio	.05
392	Jay Buhner	.05
393	Jim Converse	.05
394	Tim Davis	.05
395	Felix Fermin	.05
396	Dave Fleming	.05
397	Goose Gossage	.05
398	Ken Griffey Jr.	1.00
399	Randy Johnson	.60
400	Edgar Martinez	.05
401	Tino Martinez	.05
402	Alex Rodriguez	1.50
403	Dan Wilson	.05
404	Luis Alicea	.05
405	Rene Arocha	.05
406	Bernard Gilkey	.05
407	Gregg Jefferies	.05
408	Ray Lankford	.05
409	Terry McGriff	.05
410	Omar Olivares	.05
411	Jose Oquendo	.05
412	Vicente Palacios	.05
413	Geronimo Pena	.05
414	Mike Perez	.05
415	Gerald Perry	.05
416	Ozzie Smith	.75
417	Bob Tewksbury	.05
418	Mark Whiten	.05
419	Todd Zeile	.05
420	Esteban Beltre	.05
421	Kevin Brown	.05
422	Cris Carpenter	.05
423	Will Clark	.05
424	Hector Fajardo	.05
425	Jeff Frye	.05
426	Juan Gonzalez	.30
427	Rusty Greer	.05
428	Rick Honeycutt	.05
429	David Hulse	.05
430	Manny Lee	.05
431	Junior Ortiz	.05
432	Dean Palmer	.05
433	Ivan Rodriguez	.50
434	Dan Smith	.05
435	Roberto Alomar	.15
436	Pat Borders	.05
437	Scott Brow	.05
438	Rob Butler	.05
439	Joe Carter	.05
440	Tony Castillo	.05
441	Domingo Cedeno	.05
442	Brad Cornett	.05
443	Carlos Delgado	.35
444	Alex Gonzalez	.05
445	Juan Guzman	.05
446	Darren Hall	.05
447	Paul Molitor	.60
448	John Olerud	.05
449	Robert Perez	.05
450	Devon White	.05

Gold Crown Die-Cut

		NM/M
Complete Set (20):		30.00
Common Player:		.45
1	Greg Maddux	2.50
2	Fred McGriff	.45
3	Rafael Palmeiro	1.50
4	Cal Ripken Jr.	4.50
5	Jose Canseco	1.00
6	Frank Thomas	2.00
7	Albert Belle	.45
8	Manny Ramirez	2.00
9	Andres Galarraga	.45
10	Jeff Bagwell	2.00
11	Chan Ho Park	.45
12	Raul Mondesi	.45
13	Mike Piazza	3.00
14	Kirby Puckett	2.50
15	Barry Bonds	4.50
16	Ken Griffey Jr.	3.00
17	Alex Rodriguez	3.50
18	Juan Gonzalez	1.00
19	Roberto Alomar	1.00
20	Carlos Delgado	1.25

Hot Hispanics

		NM/M
Complete Set (36):		20.00
Common Player:		.25
1	Roberto Alomar	1.25
2	Moises Alou	.25
3	Wilson Alvarez	.25
4	Carlos Baerga	.25
5	Geronimo Berroa	.25
6	Jose Canseco	1.00
7	Hector Carrasco	.25
8	Wil Cordero	.25
9	Carlos Delgado	1.50
10	Damion Easley	.25
11	Tony Eusebio	.25
12	Hector Fajardo	.25
13	Andres Galarraga	.25
14	Carlos Garcia	.25
15	Chris Gomez	.25
16	Alex Gonzalez	.25
17	Juan Gonzalez	1.25
18	Luis Gonzalez	.25
19	Felix Jose	.25
20	Javier Lopez	.25
21	Luis Lopez	.25
22	Dennis Martinez	.25
23	Orlando Miller	.25
24	Raul Mondesi	.25
25	Jose Oliva	.25
26	Rafael Palmeiro	2.00
27	Yorkis Perez	.25
28	Manny Ramirez	2.50
29	Jose Rijo	.25
30	Alex Rodriguez	4.00
31	Ivan Rodriguez	2.00
32	Carlos Rodriguez	.25
33	Sammy Sosa	3.00
34	Tony Tarasco	.25
35	Ismael Valdes	.25
36	Bernie Williams	.25

Mariners Memories

NM/M

Complete Set (50):		10.00
Common Player:		.10
1	Ken Griffey Jr. Griffey slams M's to brink	.50
2	Vince Coleman Mariners clinch tie in Texas	.10
3	Luis Sojo Mariners win the West	.10
4	Randy Johnson At last, something to celebrate	.25
5	Randy Johnson Johnson stands tall	.25
6	Ken Griffey Jr. Griffey has big debut	.50
7	Edgar Martinez, Tino Martinez Tino ignites Mariners	.10
8	Edgar Martinez Mariners tie Yankee series	.10
9	Ken Griffey Jr. Griffey scores winning run	.50
10	Thunder in the Kingdome	.10
11	Series win ends years of futility	.10
12	Bob Wolcott Bob who? beats Cleveland	.10
13	Jay Buhner Buhner rocks Cleveland	.10
14	Randy Johnson Johnson salutes Kingdome crowd	.25
15	Lou Piniella Fans give their all	.10
16	Joey Cora Cora eludes tag	.10
17	Dave Niehaus Voice of M's calls winner	.10
18	Rich Amaral	.10
19	Bobby Ayala	.10
20	Tim Belcher	.10
21	Andy Benes	.10
22	Mike Blowers	.10
23	Chris Bosio	.10
24	Darren Bragg	.10
25	Jay Buhner	.25
26	Rafael Carmona	.10
27	Norm Charlton	.10
28	Vince Coleman	.10
29	Joey Cora	.10
30	Alex Diaz	.10
31	Felix Fermin	.10
32	Ken Griffey Jr.	3.00
33	Lee Guetterman	.10
34	Randy Johnson	3.00
35	Edgar Martinez	.25
36	Tino Martinez	.25
37	Jeff Nelson	.10
38	Warren Newson	.10
39	Greg Pirkl	.10
40	Arquimedez Pozo	.10
41	Bill Risley	.10
42	Alex Rodriguez (Rodriguez)	5.00
43	Luis Sojo	.10
44	Doug Strange	.10
45	Salomon Torres	.10
46	Bob Wells	.10
47	Chris Widger	.10
48	Dan Wilson	.10
49	Bob Wolcott	.10
50	Lou Piniella	.25

Marquee Prism

NM/M

Complete Set (36):		22.50
Common Player:		.35
1	Jose Canseco	.65
2	Gregg Jefferies	.35
3	Fred McGriff	.35
4	Joe Carter	.35
5	Tim Salmon	.35
6	Wade Boggs	1.25
7	Dave Winfield	1.00
8	Bob Hamelin	.35
9	Cal Ripken Jr.	3.00
10	Don Mattingly	1.00
11	Juan Gonzalez	.50
12	Carlos Delgado	.65
13	Barry Bonds	3.00
14	Albert Belle	.35
15	Raul Mondesi	.35
16	Jeff Bagwell	1.00
17	Mike Piazza	1.50

18	Rafael Palmeiro	.75
19	Frank Thomas	1.00
20	Matt Williams	.35
21	Ken Griffey Jr.	2.00
22	Will Clark	.35
23	Bobby Bonilla	.35
24	Kenny Lofton	.35
25	Paul Molitor	1.00
26	Kirby Puckett	1.25
27	Dave Justice	.35
28	Jeff Conine	.35
29	Bret Boone	.35
30	Larry Walker	.35
31	Cecil Fielder	.35
32	Manny Ramirez	1.00
33	Javier Lopez	.35
34	Jimmy Key	.35
35	Andres Galarraga	.35
36	Tony Gwynn	1.25

1995 Pacific Prism

NM/M

Complete Set (144):		65.00
Common Player:		.25
Pack (2):		.60
Wax Box (36):		12.50
1	Dave Justice	.25
2	Ryan Klesko	.25
3	Javier Lopez	.25
4	Greg Maddux	2.00
5	Fred McGriff	.25
6	Tony Tarasco	.25
7	Jeffrey Hammonds	.25
8	Mike Mussina	.75
9	Rafael Palmeiro	1.25
10	Cal Ripken Jr.	5.00
11	Lee Smith	.25
12	Roger Clemens	2.50
13	Scott Cooper	.25
14	Mike Greenwell	.25
15	Carlos Rodriguez	.25
16	Mo Vaughn	.25
17	Chili Davis	.25
18	Jim Edmonds	.25
19	Jorge Fabregas	.25
20	Bo Jackson	.35
21	Tim Salmon	.25
22	Mark Grace	.25
23	Jose Guzman	.25
24	Randy Myers	.25
25	Rey Sanchez	.25
26	Sammy Sosa	2.50
27	Wilson Alvarez	.25
28	Julio Franco	.25
29	Ozzie Guillen	.25
30	Jack McDowell	.25
31	Frank Thomas	1.50
32	Bret Boone	.25
33	Barry Larkin	.25
34	Hal Morris	.25
35	Jose Rijo	.25
36	Deion Sanders	.25
37	Carlos Baerga	.25
38	Albert Belle	.25
39	Kenny Lofton	.25
40	Dennis Martinez	.25
41	Manny Ramirez	1.50

42	Omar Vizquel	.25
43	Dante Bichette	.25
44	Marvin Freeman	.25
45	Andres Galarraga	.25
46	Mike Kingery	.25
47	Danny Bautista	.25
48	Cecil Fielder	.25
49	Travis Fryman	.25
50	Tony Phillips	.25
51	Alan Trammell	.25
52	Lou Whitaker	.25
53	Alex Arias	.25
54	Bret Barberie	.25
55	Jeff Conine	.25
56	Charles Johnson	.25
57	Gary Sheffield	.65
58	Jeff Bagwell	1.50
59	Craig Biggio	.25
60	Doug Drabek	.25
61	Tony Eusebio	.25
62	Luis Gonzalez	.25
63	David Cone	.25
64	Bob Hamelin	.25
65	Felix Jose	.25
66	Wally Joyner	.25
67	Brian McRae	.25
68	Brett Butler	.25
69	Garey Ingram	.25
70	Ramon Martinez	.25
71	Raul Mondesi	.25
72	Mike Piazza	2.50
73	Henry Rodriguez	.25
74	Ricky Bones	.25
75	Pat Listach	.25
76	Dave Nilsson	.25
77	Jose Valentin	.25
78	Rick Aguilera	.25
79	Denny Hocking	.25
80	Shane Mack	.25
81	Pedro Munoz	.25
82	Kirby Puckett	2.00
83	Dave Winfield	1.50
84	Moises Alou	.25
85	Wil Cordero	.25
86	Cliff Floyd	.25
87	Marquis Grissom	.25
88	Pedro Martinez	1.50
89	Larry Walker	.25
90	Bobby Bonilla	.25
91	Jeromy Burnitz	.25
92	John Franco	.25
93	Jeff Kent	.25
94	Jose Vizcaino	.25
95	Wade Boggs	2.00
96	Jimmy Key	.25
97	Don Mattingly	2.50
98	Paul O'Neill	.25
99	Luis Polonia	.25
100	Danny Tartabull	.25
101	Geronimo Berroa	.25
102	Rickey Henderson	1.50
103	Ruben Sierra	.25
104	Terry Steinbach	.25
105	Darren Daulton	.25
106	Mariano Duncan	.25
107	Lenny Dykstra	.25
108	Mike Lieberthal	.25
109	Tony Longmire	.25
110	Tom Marsh	.25
111	Jay Bell	.25
112	Carlos Garcia	.25
113	Orlando Merced	.25
114	Andy Van Slyke	.25
115	Derek Bell	.25
116	Tony Gwynn	2.00
117	Luis Lopez	.25
118	Bip Roberts	.25
119	Rod Beck	.25
120	Barry Bonds	5.00
121	Darryl Strawberry	.25
122	Bill Van Landingham	.25
123	Matt Williams	.25
124	Jay Buhner	.25
125	Felix Fermin	.25
126	Ken Griffey Jr.	3.00
127	Randy Johnson	1.50
128	Edgar Martinez	.25
129	Alex Rodriguez	4.00
130	Rene Arocha	.25
131	Gregg Jefferies	.25
132	Mike Perez	.25
133	Ozzie Smith	2.00
134	Jose Canseco	.65
135	Will Clark	.25
136	Juan Gonzalez	1.00
137	Ivan Rodriguez	1.25
138	Roberto Alomar	.50
139	Joe Carter	.25
140	Carlos Delgado	.75
141	Alex Gonzalez	.25
142	Juan Guzman	.25
143	Paul Molitor	1.50
144	John Olerud	.25

1995 Pacific Prism Team Logos

NM/M

Complete Set (31):		2.00
Common Player:		.10
1	Baltimore Orioles	.10
2	Boston Red Sox	.10
3	California Angels	.10
4	Chicago White Sox	.10
5	Cleveland Indians	.10

6	Detroit Tigers	.10
7	Kansas City Royals	.10
8	Milwaukee Brewers	.10
9	Minnesota Twins	.10
10	New York Yankees	.10
11	Oakland Athletics	.10
12	Seattle Mariners	.10
13	Texas Rangers	.10
14	Toronto Blue Jays	.10
15	Atlanta Braves	.10
16	Chicago Cubs	.10
17	Cincinnati Reds	.10
18	Colorado Rockies	.10
19	Florida Marlins	.10
20	Houston Astros	.10
21	Los Angeles Dodgers	.10
22	Montreal Expos	.10
23	New York Mets	.10
24	Philadelphia Phillies	.10
25	Pittsburgh Pirates	.10
26	St. Louis Cardinals	.10
27	San Diego Padres	.10
28	San Francisco Giants	.10
1	Checklist 1-72	.05
2	Checklist 73-144	.05
---	Pacific Logo Card	.05

1996 Pacific Crown

NM/M

Complete Set (450):		17.50
Common Player:		.05
Pack (12):		1.00
Wax Box (36):		25.00
1	Steve Avery	.05
2	Ryan Klesko	.05
3	Pedro Borbon	.05
4	Chipper Jones	1.00
5	Kent Mercker	.05
6	Greg Maddux	1.00
7	Greg McMichael	.05
8	Mark Wohlers	.05
9	Fred McGriff	.05
10	John Smoltz	.05
11	Rafael Belliard	.05
12	Mark Lemke	.05
13	Tom Glavine	.30
14	Javier Lopez	.05
15	Jeff Blauser	.05
16	Dave Justice	.05
17	Marquis Grissom	.05
18	Greg Maddux (NL Cy Young)	.50
19	Randy Myers	.05
20	Scott Servais	.05
21	Sammy Sosa	1.00
22	Kevin Foster	.05
23	Jose Hernandez	.05
24	Jim Bullinger	.05
25	Mike Perez	.05
26	Shawon Dunston	.05
27	Rey Sanchez	.05
28	Frank Castillo	.05
29	Jaime Navarro	.05
30	Brian McRae	.05
31	Mark Grace	.05
32	Roberto Rivera	.05
33	Luis Gonzalez	.05
34	Hector Carrasco	.05
35	Bret Boone	.05
36	Thomas Howard	.05
37	Hal Morris	.05
38	John Smiley	.05
39	Jeff Brantley	.05
40	Barry Larkin	.05
41	Mariano Duncan	.05
42	Xavier Hernandez	.05
43	Pete Schourek	.05
44	Reggie Sanders	.05
45	Dave Burba	.05

46	Jeff Branson	.05
47	Mark Portugal	.05
48	Ron Gant	.05
49	Benito Santiago	.05
50	Barry Larkin (NL MVP)	.05
51	Steve Reed	.05
52	Kevin Ritz	.05
53	Dante Bichette	.05
54	Darren Holmes	.05
55	Ellis Burks	.05
56	Walt Weiss	.05
57	Armando Reynoso	.05
58	Vinny Castilla	.05
59	Jason Bates	.05
60	Mike Kingery	.05
61	Bryan Rekar	.05
62	Curtis Leskanic	.05
63	Bret Saberhagen	.05
64	Andres Galarraga	.05
65	Larry Walker	.05
66	Joe Girardi	.05
67	Quilvio Veras	.05
68	Robb Nen	.05
69	Mario Diaz	.05
70	Chuck Carr	.05
71	Alex Arias	.05
72	Pat Rapp	.05
73	Rich Garces	.05
74	Kurt Abbott	.05
75	Andre Dawson	.25
76	Greg Colbrunn	.05
77	John Burkett	.05
78	Terry Pendleton	.05
79	Jesus Tavarez	.05
80	Charles Johnson	.05
81	Yorkis Perez	.05
82	Jeff Conine	.05
83	Gary Sheffield	.45
84	Brian Hunter	.05
85	Derrick May	.05
86	Greg Swindell	.05
87	Derek Bell	.05
88	Dave Veres	.05
89	Jeff Bagwell	.75
90	Todd Jones	.05
91	Orlando Miller	.05
92	Pedro A. Martinez	.05
93	Tony Eusebio	.05
94	Craig Biggio	.05
95	Shane Reynolds	.05
96	James Mouton	.05
97	Doug Drabek	.05
98	Dave Magadan	.05
99	Ricky Gutierrez	.05
100	Hideo Nomo	.50
101	Delino DeShields	.05
102	Tom Candiotti	.05
103	Mike Piazza	1.50
104	Ramon Martinez	.05
105	Pedro Astacio	.05
106	Chad Fonville	.05
107	Raul Mondesi	.05
108	Ismael Valdes	.05
109	Jose Offerman	.05
110	Todd Worrell	.05
111	Eric Karros	.05
112	Brett Butler	.05
113	Juan Castro	.05
114	Roberto Kelly	.05
115	Omar Daal	.05
116	Antonio Osuna	.05
117	Hideo Nomo (NL Rookie of Year)	.50
118	Mike Lansing	.05
119	Mel Rojas	.05
120	Sean Berry	.05
121	David Segui	.05
122	Tavo Alvarez	.05
123	Pedro Martinez	.75
124	F.P. Santangelo **RC**	.05
125	Rondell White	.05
126	Cliff Floyd	.05
127	Henry Rodriguez	.05
128	Tony Tarasco	.05
129	Yamil Benitez	.05
130	Carlos Perez	.05
131	Wil Cordero	.05
132	Jeff Fassero	.05
133	Moises Alou	.05
134	John Franco	.05
135	Rico Brogna	.05
136	Dave Mlicki	.05
137	Bill Pulsipher	.05
138	Jose Vizcaino	.05
139	Carl Everett	.05
140	Edgardo Alfonzo	.05
141	Bobby Jones	.05
142	Alberto Castillo	.05
143	Joe Orsulak	.05
144	Jeff Kent	.05
145	Ryan Thompson	.05
146	Jason Isringhausen	.05
147	Todd Hundley	.05
148	Alex Ochoa	.05
149	Charlie Hayes	.05
150	Michael Mimbs	.05
151	Darren Daulton	.05
152	Toby Borland	.05
153	Andy Van Slyke	.05
154	Mickey Morandini	.05
155	Sid Fernandez	.05
156	Tom Marsh	.05
157	Kevin Stocker	.05
158	Paul Quantrill	.05
159	Gregg Jefferies	.05
160	Ricky Bottalico	.05
161	Lenny Dykstra	.05
162	Mark Whiten	.05
163	Tyler Green	.05
164	Jim Eisenreich	.05
165	Heathcliff Slocumb	.05
166	Esteban Loaiza	.05
167	Rich Aude	.05
168	Jason Christiansen	.05
169	Ramon Morel	.05
170	Orlando Merced	.05
171	Paul Wagner	.05
172	Jeff King	.05
173	Jay Bell	.05
174	Jacob Brumfield	.05
175	Nelson Liriano	.05
176	Dan Miceli	.05
177	Carlos Garcia	.05
178	Denny Neagle	.05
179	Angelo Encarnacion	.05
180	Al Martin	.05
181	Midre Cummings	.05
182	Eddie Williams	.05
183	Roberto Petagine	.05
184	Tony Gwynn	1.00
185	Andy Ashby	.05
186	Melvin Nieves	.05
187	Phil Clark	.05
188	Brad Ausmus	.05
189	Bip Roberts	.05
190	Fernando Valenzuela	.05
191	Marc Newfield	.05
192	Steve Finley	.05
193	Trevor Hoffman	.05
194	Andujar Cedeno	.05
195	Jody Reed	.05
196	Ken Caminiti	.05
197	Joey Hamilton	.05
198	Tony Gwynn (NL Batting Champ)	.50
199	Shawn Barton	.05
200	Deion Sanders	.05
201	Rikkert Faneyte	.05
202	Barry Bonds	2.50
203	Matt Williams	.05
204	Jose Bautista	.05
205	Mark Leiter	.05
206	Mark Carreon	.05
207	Robby Thompson	.05
208	Terry Mulholland	.05
209	Rod Beck	.05
210	Royce Clayton	.05
211	J.R. Phillips	.05
212	Kirt Manwaring	.05
213	Glenallen Hill	.05
214	William Van Landingham	.05
215	Scott Cooper	.05
216	Bernard Gilkey	.05
217	Allen Watson	.05
218	Donovan Osborne	.05
219	Ray Lankford	.05
220	Tony Fossas	.05
221	Tom Pagnozzi	.05
222	John Mabry	.05
223	Tripp Cromer	.05
224	Mark Petkovsek	.05
225	Mike Morgan	.05
226	Ozzie Smith	1.00
227	Tom Henke	.05
228	Jose Oquendo	.05
229	Brian Jordan	.05
230	Cal Ripken Jr.	2.50
231	Scott Erickson	.05
232	Harold Baines	.05
233	Jeff Manto	.05
234	Jesse Orosco	.05
235	Jeffrey Hammonds	.05
236	Brady Anderson	.05
237	Manny Alexander	.05
238	Chris Hoiles	.05
239	Rafael Palmeiro	.60
240	Ben McDonald	.05
241	Curtis Goodwin	.05
242	Bobby Bonilla	.05
243	Mike Mussina	.60
244	Kevin Brown	.05
245	Armando Benitez	.05
246	Jose Canseco	.50
247	Erik Hanson	.05
248	Mo Vaughn	.05
249	Tim Naehring	.05
250	Vaughn Eshelman	.05
251	Mike Greenwell	.05
252	Troy O'Leary	.05
253	Tim Wakefield	.05
254	Dwayne Hosey	.05
255	John Valentin	.05
256	Rick Aguilera	.05
257	Mike MacFarlane	.05
258	Roger Clemens	1.50
259	Luis Alicea	.05
260	Mo Vaughn (AL MVP)	.05
261	Mark Langston	.05
262	Jim Edmonds	.05
263	Rod Correia	.05
264	Tim Salmon	.05
265	J.T. Snow	.05
266	Orlando Palmeiro	.05
267	Jorge Fabregas	.05
268	Jim Abbott	.05
269	Eduardo Perez	.05
270	Lee Smith	.05
271	Gary DiSarcina	.05
272	Damion Easley	.05
273	Tony Phillips	.05
274	Garret Anderson	.05
275	Chuck Finley	.05
276	Chili Davis	.05
277	Lance Johnson	.05
278	Alex Fernandez	.05
279	Robin Ventura	.05
280	Chris Snopek	.05
281	Brian Keyser	.05
282	Lyle Mouton	.05
283	Luis Andujar **RC**	.05
284	Tim Raines	.05
285	Larry Thomas	.05
286	Ozzie Guillen	.05
287	Frank Thomas	.75
288	Roberto Hernandez	.05
289	Dave Martinez	.05
290	Ray Durham	.05
291	Ron Karkovice	.05
292	Wilson Alvarez	.05
293	Omar Vizquel	.05
294	Eddie Murray	.75
295	Sandy Alomar	.05
296	Orel Hershiser	.05
297	Jose Mesa	.05
298	Julian Tavarez	.05
299	Dennis Martinez	.05
300	Carlos Baerga	.05
301	Manny Ramirez	.75
302	Jim Thome	.60
303	Kenny Lofton	.05
304	Tony Pena	.05
305	Alvaro Espinoza	.05
306	Paul Sorrento	.05
307	Albert Belle	.05
308	Danny Bautista	.05
309	Chris Gomez	.05
310	Jose Lima	.05
311	Phil Nevin	.05
312	Alan Trammell	.05
313	Chad Curtis	.05
314	John Flaherty	.05
315	Travis Fryman	.05
316	Todd Steverson	.05
317	Brian Bohanon	.05
318	Lou Whitaker	.05
319	Bobby Higginson	.05
320	Steve Rodriguez	.05
321	Cecil Fielder	.05
322	Felipe Lira	.05
323	Juan Samuel	.05
324	Bob Hamelin	.05
325	Tom Goodwin	.05
326	Johnny Damon	.25
327	Hipolito Pichardo	.05
328	Dilson Torres	.05
329	Kevin Appier	.05
330	Mark Gubicza	.05
331	Jon Nunnally	.05
332	Gary Gaetti	.05
333	Brent Mayne	.05
334	Brent Cookson	.05
335	Tom Gordon	.05
336	Wally Joyner	.05
337	Greg Gagne	.05
338	Fernando Vina	.05
339	Joe Oliver	.05
340	John Jaha	.05
341	Jeff Cirillo	.05
342	Pat Listach	.05
343	Dave Nilsson	.05
344	Steve Sparks	.05
345	Ricky Bones	.05
346	David Hulse	.05
347	Scott Karl	.05
348	Darryl Hamilton	.05
349	B.J. Surhoff	.05
350	Angel Miranda	.05
351	Sid Roberson	.05
352	Matt Mieske	.05
353	Jose Valentin **RC**	.05
354	Matt Lawton **RC**	.25
355	Eddie Guardado	.05
356	Brad Radke	.05
357	Pedro Munoz	.05
358	Scott Stahoviak	.05
359	Erik Schullstrom	.05
360	Pat Meares	.05
361	Marty Cordova	.05
362	Scott Leius	.05
363	Matt Walbeck	.05
364	Rich Becker	.05
365	Kirby Puckett	1.00
366	Oscar Munoz	.05
367	Chuck Knoblauch	.05
368	Marty Cordova (AL Rookie of Year)	.05
369	Bernie Williams	.05
370	Mike Stanley	.05
371	Andy Pettitte	.25
372	Jack McDowell	.05
373	Sterling Hitchcock	.05
374	David Cone	.05
375	Randy Velarde	.05
376	Don Mattingly	1.50
377	Melido Perez	.05
378	Wade Boggs	1.00
379	Ruben Sierra	.05
380	Tony Fernandez	.05
381	John Wetteland	.05
382	Mariano Rivera	.15
383	Derek Jeter	2.50
384	Paul O'Neill	.05
385	Mark McGwire	2.00
386	Scott Brosius	.05
387	Don Wengert	.05
388	Terry Steinbach	.05
389	Brent Gates	.05
390	Craig Paquette	.05
391	Mike Bordick	.05
392	Ariel Prieto	.05
393	Dennis Eckersley	.65
394	Carlos Reyes	.05
395	Todd Stottlemyre	.05
396	Rickey Henderson	.75
397	Geronimo Berroa	.05
398	Steve Ontiveros	.05
399	Mike Gallego	.05
400	Stan Javier	.05
401	Randy Johnson	.75
402	Norm Charlton	.05
403	Mike Blowers	.05
404	Tino Martinez	.05
405	Dan Wilson	.05
406	Andy Benes	.05
407	Alex Diaz	.05
408	Edgar Martinez	.05
409	Chris Bosio	.05
410	Ken Griffey Jr.	1.50
411	Luis Sojo	.05
412	Bob Wolcott	.05
413	Vince Coleman	.05
414	Rich Amaral	.05
415	Jay Buhner	.05
416	Alex Rodriguez	2.00
417	Joey Cora	.05
418	Randy Johnson (AL Cy Young)	.25
419	Edgar Martinez (AL Batting Champ)	.05
420	Ivan Rodriguez	.65
421	Mark McLemore	.05
422	Mickey Tettleton	.05
423	Juan Gonzalez	.40
424	Will Clark	.05
425	Kevin Gross	.05
426	Dean Palmer	.05
427	Kenny Rogers	.05
428	Bob Tewksbury	.05
429	Benji Gil	.05
430	Jeff Russell	.05
431	Rusty Greer	.05
432	Roger Pavlik	.05
433	Esteban Beltre	.05
434	Otis Nixon	.05
435	Paul Molitor	.75
436	Carlos Delgado	.50
437	Ed Sprague	.05
438	Juan Guzman	.05
439	Domingo Cedeno	.05
440	Pat Hentgen	.05
441	Tomas Perez	.05
442	John Olerud	.05
443	Shawn Green	.25
444	Al Leiter	.05
445	Joe Carter	.05
446	Robert Perez	.05
447	Devon White	.05
448	Tony Castillo	.05
449	Alex Gonzalez	.05
450	Roberto Alomar	.20
450p	Roberto Alomar (Unmarked promo card, "Games: 128" on back.)	1.50

Cramer's Choice

		NM/M
Complete Set (10):		150.00
Common Player:		6.00
1	Roberto Alomar	7.50
2	Wade Boggs	15.00
3	Cal Ripken Jr.	30.00
4	Greg Maddux	15.00
5	Frank Thomas	12.50
6	Tony Gwynn	15.00
7	Mike Piazza	20.00
8	Ken Griffey Jr.	25.00
9	Manny Ramirez	12.50
10	Edgar Martinez	6.00

Gold Crown Die-Cuts

		NM/M
Complete Set (36):		45.00
Common Player:		.75
1	Roberto Alomar	1.00
2	Will Clark	.75

3	Johnny Damon	1.00
4	Don Mattingly	2.50
5	Edgar Martinez	.75
6	Manny Ramirez	1.50
7	Mike Piazza	2.50
8	Quilvio Veras	.75
9	Rickey Henderson	1.50
10	Jeff Bagwell	1.50
11	Andres Galarraga	.75
12	Tim Salmon	.75
13	Ken Griffey Jr.	2.50
14	Sammy Sosa	2.00
15	Cal Ripken Jr.	4.50
16	Raul Mondesi	.75
17	Jose Canseco	1.00
18	Frank Thomas	1.50
19	Hideo Nomo	1.00
20	Wade Boggs	2.00
21	Reggie Sanders	.75
22	Carlos Baerga	.75
23	Mo Vaughn	.75
24	Ivan Rodriguez	1.25
25	Kirby Puckett	2.00
26	Albert Belle	.75
27	Vinny Castilla	.75
28	Greg Maddux	2.00
29	Dante Bichette	.75
30	Deion Sanders	.75
31	Chipper Jones	2.00
32	Cecil Fielder	.75
33	Randy Johnson	1.50
34	Mark McGwire	3.50
35	Tony Gwynn	2.00
36	Barry Bonds	4.50

Estrellas Latinas

		NM/M
Complete Set (36):		16.00
Common Player:		.25
1	Roberto Alomar	.50
2	Moises Alou	.25
3	Carlos Baerga	.25
4	Geronimo Berroa	.25
5	Ricky Bones	.25
6	Bobby Bonilla	.25
7	Jose Canseco	.65
8	Vinny Castilla	.25
9	Pedro Martinez	1.50
10	John Valentin	.25
11	Andres Galarraga	.25
12	Juan Gonzalez	.75
13	Ozzie Guillen	.25
14	Esteban Loaiza	.25
15	Javier Lopez	.25
16	Dennis Martinez	.25
17	Edgar Martinez	.25
18	Tino Martinez	.25
19	Orlando Merced	.25
20	Jose Mesa	.25
21	Raul Mondesi	.25
22	Jaime Navarro	.25
23	Rafael Palmeiro	.75
24	Carlos Perez	.25
25	Manny Ramirez	1.50
26	Alex Rodriguez	3.50
27	Ivan Rodriguez	1.25
28	David Segui	.25
29	Ruben Sierra	.25

30	Sammy Sosa	2.00
31	Julian Tavarez	.25
32	Ismael Valdes	.25
33	Fernando Valenzuela	.25
34	Quilvio Veras	.25
35	Omar Vizquel	.25
36	Bernie Williams	.25

Hometown of the Players

		NM/M
Complete Set (20):		15.00
Common Player:		.50
1	Mike Piazza	1.50
2	Greg Maddux	1.00
3	Tony Gwynn	1.00
4	Carlos Baerga	.50
5	Don Mattingly	1.50
6	Cal Ripken Jr.	2.50
7	Chipper Jones	1.00
8	Andres Galarraga	.50
9	Manny Ramirez	.75
10	Roberto Alomar	.60
11	Ken Griffey Jr.	1.50
12	Jose Canseco	.60
13	Frank Thomas	.75
14	Vinny Castilla	.50
15	Roberto Kelly	.50
16	Dennis Martinez	.50
17	Kirby Puckett	1.00
18	Raul Mondesi	.50
19	Hideo Nomo	.60
20	Edgar Martinez	.50

Milestones

		NM/M
Complete Set (10):		12.50
Common Player:		.25
1	Albert Belle	.50
2	Don Mattingly	2.25
3	Tony Gwynn	2.00
4	Jose Canseco	1.00
5	Marty Cordova	.50
6	Wade Boggs	2.00
7	Greg Maddux	2.00
8	Eddie Murray	1.50
9	Ken Griffey Jr.	2.50
10	Cal Ripken Jr.	3.00

October Moments

		NM/M
Complete Set (20):		30.00
Common Player:		.60
1	Carlos Baerga	.60
2	Albert Belle	.75
3	Dante Bichette	.60
4	Jose Canseco	1.25
5	Tom Glavine	1.00
6	Ken Griffey Jr.	5.00
7	Randy Johnson	2.50
8	Chipper Jones	3.50
9	Dave Justice	.60
10	Ryan Klesko	.60
11	Kenny Lofton	.60
12	Javier Lopez	.60
13	Greg Maddux	3.50
14	Edgar Martinez	.60
15	Don Mattingly	4.00

16	Hideo Nomo	1.25
17	Mike Piazza	4.00
18	Manny Ramirez	2.50
19	Reggie Sanders	.60
20	Jim Thome	1.50

1996 Pacific Prism

		NM/M
Complete Set (144):		50.00
Common Player:		.35
Golds:		1.5X
Pack (2):		.65
Wax Box (36):		20.00
1	Tom Glavine	.75
2	Chipper Jones	2.00
3	David Justice	.35
4	Ryan Klesko	.35
5	Javier Lopez	.35
6	Greg Maddux	2.00
7	Fred McGriff	.35
8	Frank Castillo	.35
9	Luis Gonzalez	.35
10	Mark Grace	.35
11	Brian McRae	.35
12	Jaime Navarro	.35
13	Sammy Sosa	2.00
14	Bret Boone	.35
15	Ron Gant	.35
16	Barry Larkin	.35
17	Reggie Sanders	.35
18	Benito Santiago	.35
19	Dante Bichette	.35
20	Vinny Castilla	.35
21	Andres Galarraga	.35
22	Bryan Rekar	.35
23	Roberto Alomar	1.00
23p	Roberto Alomar ("Azulejos" rather than "Los Azulajos" on back, unmarked promo card.)	1.00
24	Jeff Conine	.35
25	Andre Dawson	.50
26	Charles Johnson	.35
27	Gary Sheffield	1.00
28	Quilvio Veras	.35
29	Jeff Bagwell	1.50
30	Derek Bell	.35
31	Craig Biggio	.35
32	Tony Eusebio	.35
33	Karim Garcia	.35
34	Eric Karros	.35
35	Ramon Martinez	.35
36	Raul Mondesi	.35
37	Hideo Nomo	1.00
38	Mike Piazza	3.00
39	Ismael Valdes	.35
40	Moises Alou	.35
41	Wil Cordero	.35
42	Pedro Martinez	1.50
43	Mel Rojas	.35
44	David Segui	.35
45	Edgardo Alfonzo	.35
46	Rico Brogna	.35
47	John Franco	.35
48	Jason Isringhausen	.35
49	Jose Vizcaino	.35

50	Ricky Bottalico	.35
51	Darren Daulton	.35
52	Lenny Dykstra	.35
53	Tyler Green	.35
54	Gregg Jefferies	.35
55	Jay Bell	.35
56	Jason Christiansen	.35
57	Carlos Garcia	.35
58	Esteban Loaiza	.35
59	Orlando Merced	.35
60	Andujar Cedeno	.35
61	Tony Gwynn	2.00
62	Melvin Nieves	.35
63	Phil Plantier	.35
64	Fernando Valenzuela	.35
65	Barry Bonds	4.50
66	J.R. Phillips	.35
67	Deion Sanders	.35
68	Matt Williams	.35
69	Bernard Gilkey	.35
70	Tom Henke	.35
71	Brian Jordan	.35
72	Ozzie Smith	2.00
73	Manny Alexander	.35
74	Bobby Bonilla	.35
75	Mike Mussina	1.00
76	Rafael Palmeiro	1.00
77	Cal Ripken Jr.	4.50
78	Jose Canseco	1.00
79	Roger Clemens	2.50
80	John Valentin	.35
81	Mo Vaughn	.35
82	Tim Wakefield	.35
83	Garret Anderson	.35
84	Damion Easley	.35
85	Jim Edmonds	.35
86	Tim Salmon	.35
87	Wilson Alvarez	.35
88	Alex Fernandez	.35
89	Ozzie Guillen	.35
90	Roberto Hernandez	.35
91	Frank Thomas	1.50
92	Robin Ventura	.35
93	Carlos Baerga	.35
94	Albert Belle	.35
95	Kenny Lofton	.35
96	Dennis Martinez	.35
97	Eddie Murray	1.50
98	Manny Ramirez	1.50
99	Omar Vizquel	.35
100	Chad Curtis	.35
101	Cecil Fielder	.35
102	Felipe Lira	.35
103	Alan Trammell	.35
104	Kevin Appier	.35
105	Johnny Damon	.35
106	Gary Gaetti	.35
107	Wally Joyner	.35
108	Ricky Bones	.35
109	John Jaha	.35
110	B.J. Surhoff	.35
111	Jose Valentin	.35
112	Fernando Vina	.35
113	Marty Cordova	.35
114	Chuck Knoblauch	.35
115	Scott Leius	.35
116	Pedro Munoz	.35
117	Kirby Puckett	2.00
118	Wade Boggs	2.00
119	Don Mattingly	2.50
120	Jack McDowell	.35
121	Paul O'Neill	.35
122	Ruben Rivera	.35
123	Bernie Williams	.35
124	Geronimo Berroa	.35
125	Rickey Henderson	1.50
126	Mark McGwire	3.50
127	Terry Steinbach	.35
128	Danny Tartabull	.35
129	Jay Buhner	.35
130	Joey Cora	.35
131	Ken Griffey Jr.	3.00
132	Randy Johnson	1.50
133	Edgar Martinez	.35
134	Tino Martinez	.35
135	Will Clark	.35
136	Juan Gonzalez	.75
137	Dean Palmer	.35
138	Ivan Rodriguez	1.25
139	Mickey Tettleton	.35
140	Larry Walker	.35
141	Joe Carter	.35
142	Carlos Delgado	1.00
143	Alex Gonzalez	.35
144	Paul Molitor	1.50

Gold

	NM/M
Complete Set (144):	100.00
Common Player:	.50

Stars: 1.5X
(See 1996 Pacific Prism for checklist and base card values.)

Fence Busters

		NM/M
Complete Set (19):		50.00
Common Player:		1.50
1	Albert Belle	1.50
2	Dante Bichette	1.50
3	Barry Bonds	7.50
4	Jose Canseco	2.25
5	Ken Griffey Jr.	5.00
6	Chipper Jones	4.00
7	David Justice	1.50
8	Eric Karros	1.50
9	Edgar Martinez	1.50
10	Mark McGwire	6.00
11	Eddie Murray	1.50
12	Mike Piazza	5.00
13	Kirby Puckett	4.00
14	Cal Ripken Jr.	7.50
15	Tim Salmon	1.50
16	Sammy Sosa	4.00
17	Frank Thomas	3.00
18	Mo Vaughn	1.50

Flame Throwers

		NM/M
Complete Set (10):		25.00
Common Player:		1.50
1	Roger Clemens	6.50
2	David Cone	1.50
3	Tom Glavine	2.50
4	Randy Johnson	4.50
5	Greg Maddux	6.00
6	Ramon Martinez	1.50
7	Jose Mesa	1.50
8	Mike Mussina	2.50
9	Hideo Nomo	3.00
10	Jose Rijo	1.50

Red Hot Stars

		NM/M
Complete Set (20):		25.00
Common Player:		.50
1	Roberto Alomar	.75
2	Jeff Bagwell	1.50
3	Albert Belle	.50
4	Wade Boggs	2.00
5	Barry Bonds	4.00
6	Jose Canseco	1.00
7	Ken Griffey Jr.	2.50
8	Tony Gwynn	2.00
9	Randy Johnson	1.50
10	Chipper Jones	2.00
11	Greg Maddux	2.00
12	Edgar Martinez	.50
13	Don Mattingly	2.50
14	Mike Piazza	2.50
15	Kirby Puckett	2.00
16	Manny Ramirez	1.50
17	Cal Ripken Jr.	4.00
18	Tim Salmon	.50
19	Frank Thomas	1.50
20	Mo Vaughn	.50

1997 Pacific Crown

		NM/M
Complete Set (450):		30.00
Common Player:		.05
Silver Stars/RC's:		15X
Light Blue:		1X
Pack (12):		1.25
Wax Box (36):		32.50
1	Garret Anderson	.05
2	George Arias	.05
3	Chili Davis	.05
4	Gary DiSarcina	.05
5	Jim Edmonds	.05
6	Darin Erstad	.15
7	Jorge Fabregas	.05
8	Chuck Finley	.05
9	Rex Hudler	.05
10	Mark Langston	.05
11	Orlando Palmeiro	.05
12	Troy Percival	.05
13	Tim Salmon	.05
14	J.T. Snow	.05
15	Randy Velarde	.05
16	Manny Alexander	.05
17	Roberto Alomar	.25
18	Brady Anderson	.05
19	Armando Benitez	.05
20	Bobby Bonilla	.05
21	Rocky Coppinger	.05
22	Scott Erickson	.05
23	Jeffrey Hammonds	.05
24	Chris Hoiles	.05
25	Eddie Murray	.75
26	Mike Mussina	.60
27	Randy Myers	.05
28	Rafael Palmeiro	.65
29	Cal Ripken Jr.	2.50
30	B.J. Surhoff	.05
31	Tony Tarasco	.05
32	Esteban Beltre	.05
33	Darren Bragg	.05
34	Jose Canseco	.60
35	Roger Clemens	1.50
36	Wil Cordero	.05
37	Alex Delgado	.05
38	Jeff Frye	.05
39	Nomar Garciaparra	1.00
40	Tom Gordon	.05
41	Mike Greenwell	.05
42	Reggie Jefferson	.05
43	Tim Naehring	.05
44	Troy O'Leary	.05
45	Heathcliff Slocumb	.05
46	Lee Tinsley	.05
47	John Valentin	.05
48	Mo Vaughn	.05
49	Wilson Alvarez	.05
50	Harold Baines	.05
51	Ray Durham	.05
52	Alex Fernandez	.05
53	Ozzie Guillen	.05
54	Roberto Hernandez	.05
55	Ron Karkovice	.05
56	Darren Lewis	.05
57	Norberto Martin	.05
58	Dave Martinez	.05
59	Lyle Mouton	.05
60	Jose Munoz	.05
61	Tony Phillips	.05
62	Rich Sauveur	.05
63	Danny Tartabull	.05
64	Frank Thomas	.75
65	Robin Ventura	.05
66	Sandy Alomar Jr.	.05
67	Albert Belle	.05
68	Julio Franco	.05
69	Brian Giles RC	.50
70	Danny Graves	.05
71	Orel Hershiser	.05
72	Jeff Kent	.05
73	Kenny Lofton	.05
74	Dennis Martinez	.05
75	Jack McDowell	.05
76	Jose Mesa	.05
77	Charles Nagy	.05
78	Manny Ramirez	.75
79	Julian Tavarez	.05
80	Jim Thome	.60
81	Jose Vizcaino	.05
82	Omar Vizquel	.05
83	Brad Ausmus	.05
84	Kimera Bartee	.05
85	Raul Casanova	.05
86	Tony Clark	.05
87	Travis Fryman	.05
88	Bobby Higginson	.05
89	Mark Lewis	.05
90	Jose Lima	.05
91	Felipe Lira	.05
92	Phil Nevin	.05
93	Melvin Nieves	.05
94	Curtis Pride	.05
95	Ruben Sierra	.05
96	Alan Trammell	.05
97	Kevin Appier	.05
98	Tim Belcher	.05
99	Johnny Damon	.35
100	Tom Goodwin	.05
101	Bob Hamelin	.05
102	David Howard	.05
103	Jason Jacome	.05
104	Keith Lockhart	.05
105	Mike Macfarlane	.05
106	Jeff Montgomery	.05
107	Jose Offerman	.05
108	Hipolito Pichardo	.05
109	Joe Randa	.05
110	Bip Roberts	.05
111	Chris Stynes	.05
112	Mike Sweeney	.05
113	Joe Vitiello	.05
114	Jeromy Burnitz	.05
115	Chuck Carr	.05
116	Jeff Cirillo	.05
117	Mike Fetters	.05
118	David Hulse	.05
119	John Jaha	.05
120	Scott Karl	.05
121	Jesse Levis	.05
122	Mark Loretta	.05
123	Mike Matheny	.05
124	Ben McDonald	.05
125	Matt Mieske	.05
126	Angel Miranda	.05
127	Dave Nilsson	.05
128	Jose Valentin	.05
129	Fernando Vina	.05
130	Ron Villone	.05
131	Gerald Williams	.05
132	Rick Aguilera	.05
133	Rich Becker	.05
134	Ron Coomer	.05
135	Marty Cordova	.05
136	Eddie Guardado	.05
137	Denny Hocking	.05
138	Roberto Kelly	.05
139	Chuck Knoblauch	.05
140	Matt Lawton	.05
141	Pat Meares	.05
142	Paul Molitor	.75
143	Greg Myers	.05
144	Jeff Reboulet	.05
145	Scott Stahoviak	.05
146	Todd Walker	.05
147	Wade Boggs	1.00
148	David Cone	.05
149	Mariano Duncan	.05
150	Cecil Fielder	.05
151	Dwight Gooden	.05
152	Derek Jeter	2.50
153	Jim Leyritz	.05
154	Tino Martinez	.05
155	Paul O'Neill	.05
156	Andy Pettitte	.25
157	Tim Raines	.05
158	Mariano Rivera	.15
159	Ruben Rivera	.05
160	Kenny Rogers	.05
161	Darryl Strawberry	.05
162	John Wetteland	.05
163	Bernie Williams	.05
164	Tony Batista	.05
165	Geronimo Berroa	.05
166	Mike Bordick	.05
167	Scott Brosius	.05
168	Brent Gates	.05
169	Jason Giambi	.65
170	Jose Herrera	.05
171	Brian Lesher	.05
172	Damon Mashore RC	.05
173	Mark McGwire	2.00
174	Ariel Prieto	.05
175	Carlos Reyes	.05
176	Matt Stairs	.05
177	Terry Steinbach	.05
178	John Wasdin	.05
179	Ernie Young	.05
180	Rich Amaral	.05
181	Bobby Ayala	.05
182	Jay Buhner	.05
183	Rafael Carmona	.05
184	Norm Charlton	.05
185	Joey Cora	.05
186	Ken Griffey Jr.	1.50
187	Sterling Hitchcock	.05
188	Dave Hollins	.05
189	Randy Johnson	.75
190	Edgar Martinez	.05
191	Jamie Moyer	.05
192	Alex Rodriguez	2.00
193	Paul Sorrento	.05
194	Salomon Torres	.05
195	Bob Wells	.05
196	Dan Wilson	.05
197	Will Clark	.05
198	Kevin Elster	.05
199	Rene Gonzales	.05
200	Juan Gonzalez	.40
201	Rusty Greer	.05
202	Darryl Hamilton	.05
203	Mike Henneman	.05
204	Ken Hill	.05
205	Mark McLemore	.05
206	Darren Oliver	.05
207	Dean Palmer	.05
208	Roger Pavlik	.05
209	Ivan Rodriguez	.65
210	Kurt Stillwell	.05
211	Mickey Tettleton	.05
212	Bobby Witt	.05
213	Tilson Brito	.05
214	Jacob Brumfield	.05
215	Miguel Cairo	.05
216	Joe Carter	.05
217	Felipe Crespo	.05
218	Carlos Delgado	.60
219	Alex Gonzalez	.05
220	Shawn Green	.15
221	Juan Guzman	.05
222	Pat Hentgen	.05
223	Charlie O'Brien	.05
224	John Olerud	.05
225	Robert Perez	.05
226	Tomas Perez	.05
227	Juan Samuel	.05
228	Ed Sprague	.05
229	Mike Timlin	.05
230	Rafael Belliard	.05
231	Jermaine Dye	.05
232	Tom Glavine	.25
233	Marquis Grissom	.05
234	Andruw Jones	.75
235	Chipper Jones	1.00
236	David Justice	.05
237	Ryan Klesko	.05
238	Mark Lemke	.05
239	Javier Lopez	.05
240	Greg Maddux	1.00
241	Fred McGriff	.05
242	Denny Neagle	.05
243	Eddie Perez	.05
244	John Smoltz	.05
245	Mark Wohlers	.05
246	Brant Brown	.05
247	Scott Bullett	.05
248	Leo Gomez	.05
249	Luis Gonzalez	.05
250	Mark Grace	.05
251	Jose Hernandez	.05
252	Brooks Kieschnick	.05
253	Brian McRae	.05
254	Jaime Navarro	.05
255	Mike Perez	.05
256	Rey Sanchez	.05
257	Ryne Sandberg	1.00
258	Scott Servais	.05
259	Sammy Sosa	1.00
260	Pedro Valdes RC	.05
261	Turk Wendell	.05
262	Bret Boone	.05
263	Jeff Branson	.05
264	Jeff Brantley	.05
265	Dave Burba	.05
266	Hector Carrasco	.05
267	Eric Davis	.05
268	Willie Greene	.05
269	Lenny Harris	.05
270	Thomas Howard	.05
271	Barry Larkin	.05
272	Hal Morris	.05
273	Joe Oliver	.05
274	Eric Owens	.05
275	Jose Rijo	.05
276	Reggie Sanders	.05
277	Eddie Taubensee	.05
278	Jason Bates	.05
279	Dante Bichette	.05
280	Ellis Burks	.05
281	Vinny Castilla	.05
282	Andres Galarraga	.05
283	Quinton McCracken	.05
284	Jayhawk Owens	.05
285	Jeff Reed	.05
286	Bryan Rekar	.05
287	Armando Reynoso	.05
288	Kevin Ritz	.05
289	Bruce Ruffin	.05

290	John Vander Wal	.05
291	Larry Walker	.05
292	Walt Weiss	.05
293	Eric Young	.05
294	Kurt Abbott	.05
295	Alex Arias	.05
296	Miguel Batista	.05
297	Kevin Brown	.05
298	Luis Castillo	.05
299	Greg Colbrunn	.05
300	Jeff Conine	.05
301	Charles Johnson	.05
302	Al Leiter	.05
303	Robb Nen	.05
304	Joe Orsulak	.05
305	Yorkis Perez	.05
306	Edgar Renteria	.05
307	Gary Sheffield	.30
308	Jesus Tavarez	.05
309	Quilvio Veras	.05
310	Devon White	.05
311	Jeff Bagwell	.75
312	Derek Bell	.05
313	Sean Berry	.05
314	Craig Biggio	.05
315	Doug Drabek	.05
316	Tony Eusebio	.05
317	Ricky Gutierrez	.05
318	Xavier Hernandez	.05
319	Brian L. Hunter	.05
320	Darryl Kile	.05
321	Derrick May	.05
322	Orlando Miller	.05
323	James Mouton	.05
324	Bill Spiers	.05
325	Pedro Astacio	.05
326	Brett Butler	.05
327	Juan Castro	.05
328	Roger Cedeno	.05
329	Delino DeShields	.05
330	Karim Garcia	.10
331	Todd Hollandsworth	.05
332	Eric Karros	.05
333	Oreste Marrero	.05
334	Ramon Martinez	.05
335	Raul Mondesi	.05
336	Hideo Nomo	.50
337	Antonio Osuna	.05
338	Chan Ho Park	.05
339	Mike Piazza	1.50
340	Ismael Valdes	.05
341	Moises Alou	.05
342	Omar Daal	.05
343	Jeff Fassero	.05
344	Cliff Floyd	.05
345	Mark Grudzielanek	.05
346	Mike Lansing	.05
347	Pedro Martinez	.75
348	Sherman Obando	.05
349	Jose Paniagua	.05
350	Henry Rodriguez	.05
351	Mel Rojas	.05
352	F.P. Santangelo	.05
353	Dave Segui	.05
354	Dave Silvestri	.05
355	Ugueth Urbina	.05
356	Rondell White	.05
357	Edgardo Alfonzo	.05
358	Carlos Baerga	.05
359	Tim Bogar	.05
360	Rico Brogna	.05
361	Alvaro Espinoza	.05
362	Carl Everett	.05
363	John Franco	.05
364	Bernard Gilkey	.05
365	Todd Hundley	.05
366	Butch Huskey	.05
367	Jason Isringhausen	.05
368	Bobby Jones	.05
369	Lance Johnson	.05
370	Brent Mayne	.05
371	Alex Ochoa	.05
372	Rey Ordonez	.05
373	Ron Blazier	.05
374	Ricky Bottalico	.05
375	David Doster	.05
376	Lenny Dykstra	.05
377	Jim Eisenreich	.05
378	Bobby Estalella	.05
379	Gregg Jefferies	.05
380	Kevin Jordan	.05
381	Ricardo Jordan	.05
382	Mickey Morandini	.05
383	Ricky Otero	.05
384	Benito Santiago	.05
385	Gene Schall	.05
386	Curt Schilling	.25
387	Kevin Sefcik	.05
388	Kevin Stocker	.05
389	Jermaine Allensworth	.05
390	Jay Bell	.05
391	Jason Christiansen	.05
392	Francisco Cordova	.05
393	Mark Johnson	.05
394	Jason Kendall	.05
395	Jeff King	.05
396	Jon Lieber	.05
397	Nelson Liriano	.05
398	Esteban Loaiza	.05
399	Al Martin	.05
400	Orlando Merced	.05
401	Ramon Morel	.05
402	Luis Alicea	.05
403	Alan Benes	.05
404	Andy Benes	.05
405	Terry Bradshaw	.05
406	Royce Clayton	.05

407	Dennis Eckersley	.65
408	Gary Gaetti	.05
409	Mike Gallego	.05
410	Ron Gant	.05
411	Brian Jordan	.05
412	Ray Lankford	.05
413	John Mabry	.05
414	Willie McGee	.05
415	Tom Pagnozzi	.05
416	Ozzie Smith	1.00
417	Todd Stottlemyre	.05
418	Mark Sweeney	.05
419	Andy Ashby	.05
420	Ken Caminiti	.05
421	Archi Cianfrocco	.05
422	Steve Finley	.05
423	Chris Gomez	.05
424	Tony Gwynn	1.00
425	Joey Hamilton	.05
426	Rickey Henderson	.75
427	Trevor Hoffman	.05
428	Brian Johnson	.05
429	Wally Joyner	.05
430	Scott Livingstone	.05
431	Jody Reed	.05
432	Craig Shipley	.05
433	Fernando Valenzuela	.05
434	Greg Vaughn	.05
435	Rich Aurilia	.05
436	Kim Batiste	.05
437	Jose Bautista	.05
438	Rod Beck	.05
439	Marvin Benard	.05
440	Barry Bonds	2.50
441	Shawon Dunston	.05
442	Shawn Estes	.05
443	Osvaldo Fernandez	.05
444	Stan Javier	.05
445	David McCarty	.05
446	Bill Mueller RC	.15
447	Steve Scarsone	.05
448	Robby Thompson	.05
449	Rick Wilkins	.05
450	Matt Williams	.05

Light Blue

	NM/M
Complete Set (450):	60.00
Common Player:	.25
Stars:	1X

(See 1997 Pacific Crown for checklist and base card values.)

Silver

	NM/M
Common Player:	1.00
Stars/Rookies:	12X

(See 1997 Pacific Crown for checklist and base card values.)

Card-Supials

	NM/M
Complete Set (72):	80.00
Complete Large Set (36):	60.00
Complete Small Set (36):	45.00
Common Large:	.75
Small Cards:	75 Percent
1 Roberto Alomar	1.00
2 Brady Anderson	.75
3 Eddie Murray	2.00
4 Cal Ripken Jr.	5.00
5 Jose Canseco	1.00
6 Mo Vaughn	.75
7 Frank Thomas	2.00
8 Albert Belle	.75
9 Omar Vizquel	.75
10 Chuck Knoblauch	.75
11 Paul Molitor	2.00
12 Wade Boggs	2.50

13	Derek Jeter	5.00
14	Andy Pettitte	1.00
15	Mark McGwire	3.50
16	Jay Buhner	.75
17	Ken Griffey Jr.	3.00
18	Alex Rodriguez	3.50
19	Juan Gonzalez	1.00
20	Ivan Rodriguez	1.50
21	Andruw Jones	2.00
22	Chipper Jones	2.50
23	Ryan Klesko	.75
24	Greg Maddux	2.50
25	Ryne Sandberg	2.50
26	Andres Galarraga	.75
27	Gary Sheffield	1.00
28	Jeff Bagwell	2.00
29	Todd Hollandsworth	.75
30	Hideo Nomo	1.00
31	Mike Piazza	3.00
32	Todd Hundley	.75
33	Dennis Eckersley	1.50
34	Ken Caminiti	.75
35	Tony Gwynn	2.50
36	Barry Bonds	5.00

Cramer's Choice Awards

	NM/M
Complete Set (10):	75.00
Common Player:	4.50
1 Roberto Alomar	5.00
2 Frank Thomas	9.00
3 Albert Belle	4.50
4 Andy Pettitte	4.50
5 Ken Griffey Jr.	17.50
6 Alex Rodriguez	25.00
7 Chipper Jones	12.00
8 John Smoltz	4.50
9 Mike Piazza	15.00
10 Tony Gwynn	12.00

Fireworks Die-Cuts

	NM/M
Complete Set (20):	40.00
Common Player:	.75

1	Roberto Alomar	1.00
2	Brady Anderson	.75
3	Eddie Murray	2.50
4	Cal Ripken Jr.	7.50
5	Frank Thomas	2.50
6	Albert Belle	.75
7	Derek Jeter	7.50
8	Andy Pettitte	1.00
9	Bernie Williams	.75
10	Mark McGwire	6.50
11	Ken Griffey Jr.	5.00
12	Alex Rodriguez	6.50
13	Juan Gonzalez	1.25
14	Andruw Jones	2.50
15	Chipper Jones	3.50
16	Hideo Nomo	1.25
17	Mike Piazza	5.00
18	Henry Rodriguez	.75
19	Tony Gwynn	3.50
20	Barry Bonds	7.50

Gold Crown Die-Cuts

	NM/M
Complete Set (36):	65.00
Common Player:	1.00
1 Roberto Alomar	1.25
2 Brady Anderson	1.00
3 Mike Mussina	1.50
4 Eddie Murray	2.75
5 Cal Ripken Jr.	8.50
6 Jose Canseco	2.00
7 Frank Thomas	2.75
8 Albert Belle	1.00
9 Omar Vizquel	1.00
10 Wade Boggs	3.50
11 Derek Jeter	8.50
12 Andy Pettitte	1.25
13 Mariano Rivera	1.25
14 Bernie Williams	1.00
15 Mark McGwire	6.50
16 Ken Griffey Jr.	5.00
17 Edgar Martinez	1.00
18 Alex Rodriguez	6.50
19 Juan Gonzalez	1.50
20 Ivan Rodriguez	2.50
21 Andruw Jones	2.75
22 Chipper Jones	3.50
23 Ryan Klesko	1.00
24 John Smoltz	1.00
25 Ryne Sandberg	3.50
26 Andres Galarraga	1.00
27 Edgar Renteria	1.00
28 Jeff Bagwell	2.75
29 Todd Hollandsworth	1.00
30 Hideo Nomo	1.50
31 Mike Piazza	5.00
32 Todd Hundley	1.00
33 Brian Jordan	1.00
34 Ken Caminiti	1.00
35 Tony Gwynn	3.50
36 Barry Bonds	8.50

Latinos of the Major Leagues

	NM/M
Complete Set (36):	45.00
Common Player:	1.00
1 George Arias	1.00
2 Roberto Alomar	1.50

3	Rafael Palmeiro	2.50
4	Bobby Bonilla	1.00
5	Jose Canseco	2.00
6	Wilson Alvarez	1.00
7	Dave Martinez	1.00
8	Julio Franco	1.00
9	Manny Ramirez	3.00
10	Omar Vizquel	1.00
11	Marty Cordova	1.00
12	Roberto Kelly	1.00
13	Tino Martinez	1.00
14	Mariano Rivera	1.50
15	Ruben Rivera	1.00
16	Bernie Williams	1.00
17	Geronimo Berroa	1.00
18	Joey Cora	1.00
19	Edgar Martinez	1.00
20	Alex Rodriguez	6.00
21	Juan Gonzalez	2.00
22	Ivan Rodriguez	2.50
23	Andruw Jones	3.00
24	Javier Lopez	1.00
25	Sammy Sosa	4.50
26	Vinny Castilla	1.00
27	Andres Galarraga	1.00
28	Ramon Martinez	1.00
29	Raul Mondesi	1.00
30	Ismael Valdes	1.00
31	Pedro Martinez	3.00
32	Henry Rodriguez	1.00
33	Carlos Baerga	1.00
34	Rey Ordonez	1.00
35	Fernando Valenzuela	1.00
36	Osvaldo Fernandez	1.00

Triple Crown Die-Cuts

		NM/M
Complete Set (20):		75.00
Common Player:		2.00
1	Brady Anderson	2.00
2	Rafael Palmeiro	4.00
3	Mo Vaughn	2.00
4	Frank Thomas	5.00
5	Albert Belle	2.00
6	Jim Thome	4.00
7	Cecil Fielder	2.00
8	Mark McGwire	10.00
9	Ken Griffey Jr.	7.50
10	Alex Rodriguez	10.00
11	Juan Gonzalez	3.00
12	Andruw Jones	5.00
13	Chipper Jones	6.00
14	Dante Bichette	2.00
15	Ellis Burks	2.00
16	Andres Galarraga	2.00
17	Jeff Bagwell	5.00
18	Mike Piazza	7.50
19	Ken Caminiti	2.00
20	Barry Bonds	12.50

1997 Pacific Invincible

		NM/M
Complete Set (150):		30.00
Common Player:		.25
Light Blues:		1X
Platinums:		2X
Pack (3):		1.00
Wax Box (36):		25.00
1	Chili Davis	.25
2	Jim Edmonds	.25
3	Darin Erstad	.50
4	Orlando Palmeiro	.25
5	Tim Salmon	.25
6	J.T. Snow	.25
7	Roberto Alomar	.50
8	Brady Anderson	.25
9	Eddie Murray	1.50
10	Mike Mussina	1.00
11	Rafael Palmeiro	1.25
12	Cal Ripken Jr.	4.00
13	Jose Canseco	1.00
14	Roger Clemens	2.50
15	Nomar Garciaparra	2.00
16	Reggie Jefferson	.25
17	Mo Vaughn	.25
18	Wilson Alvarez	.25
19	Harold Baines	.25
20	Alex Fernandez	.25
21	Danny Tartabull	.25
22	Frank Thomas	1.50
23	Robin Ventura	.25
24	Sandy Alomar Jr.	.25
25	Albert Belle	.25
26	Kenny Lofton	.25
27	Jim Thome	.75
28	Omar Vizquel	.25
29	Raul Casanova	.25
30	Tony Clark	.25
31	Travis Fryman	.25
32	Bobby Higginson	.25
33	Melvin Nieves	.25
34	Justin Thompson	.25
35	Johnny Damon	.50
36	Tom Goodwin	.25
37	Jeff Montgomery	.25
38	Jose Offerman	.25
39	John Jaha	.25
40	Jeff Cirillo	.25
41	Dave Nilsson	.25
42	Jose Valentin	.25
43	Fernando Vina	.25
44	Marty Cordova	.25
45	Roberto Kelly	.25
46	Chuck Knoblauch	.25
47	Paul Molitor	1.50
48	Todd Walker	.25
49	Wade Boggs	2.00
50	Cecil Fielder	.25
51	Derek Jeter	4.00
52	Tino Martinez	.25
53	Andy Pettitte	.40
54	Mariano Rivera	.40
55	Bernie Williams	.25
56	Tony Batista	.25
57	Geronimo Berroa	.25
58	Jason Giambi	.75
59	Mark McGwire	3.00
60	Terry Steinbach	.25
61	Jay Buhner	.25
62	Joey Cora	.25
63	Ken Griffey Jr.	2.50
64	Edgar Martinez	.25
65	Alex Rodriguez	3.00
66	Paul Sorrento	.25
67	Will Clark	.25
68	Juan Gonzalez	.75
69	Rusty Greer	.25
70	Dean Palmer	.25
71	Ivan Rodriguez	1.25
72	Joe Carter	.25
73	Carlos Delgado	.75
74	Juan Guzman	.25
75	Pat Hentgen	.25
76	Ed Sprague	.25
77	Jermaine Dye	.25
78	Andruw Jones	1.50
79	Chipper Jones	2.00
80	Ryan Klesko	.25
81	Javier Lopez	.25
82	Greg Maddux	2.00
83	John Smoltz	.25
84	Mark Grace	.25
85	Luis Gonzalez	.25
86	Brooks Kieschnick	.25
87	Jaime Navarro	.25
88	Ryne Sandberg	2.00
89	Sammy Sosa	2.00
90	Bret Boone	.25
91	Jeff Brantley	.25
92	Eric Davis	.25
93	Barry Larkin	.25
94	Reggie Sanders	.25
95	Ellis Burks	.25
96	Dante Bichette	.25
97	Vinny Castilla	.25
98	Andres Galarraga	.25
99	Eric Young	.25
100	Kevin Brown	.25
101	Jeff Conine	.25
102	Charles Johnson	.25
103	Edgar Renteria	.25
104	Gary Sheffield	.75
105	Jeff Bagwell	1.50
106	Derek Bell	.25
107	Sean Berry	.25
108	Craig Biggio	.25
109	Shane Reynolds	.25
110	Karim Garcia	.25
111	Todd Hollandsworth	.25
112	Ramon Martinez	.25
113	Raul Mondesi	.25
114	Hideo Nomo	.75
115	Mike Piazza	2.50
116	Ismael Valdes	.25
117	Moises Alou	.25
118	Mark Grudzielanek	.25
119	Pedro Martinez	1.50
120	Henry Rodriguez	.25
121	F.P. Santangelo	.25
122	Carlos Baerga	.25
123	Bernard Gilkey	.25
124	Todd Hundley	.25
125	Lance Johnson	.25
126	Alex Ochoa	.25
127	Rey Ordonez	.25
128	Lenny Dykstra	.25
129	Gregg Jefferies	.25
130	Ricky Otero	.25
131	Benito Santiago	.25
132	Jermaine Allensworth	.25
133	Francisco Cordova	.25
134	Carlos Garcia	.25
135	Jason Kendall	.25
136	Al Martin	.25
137	Dennis Eckersley	1.25
138	Ron Gant	.25
139	Brian Jordan	.25
140	John Mabry	.25
141	Ozzie Smith	2.00
142	Ken Caminiti	.25
143	Steve Finley	.25
144	Tony Gwynn	2.00
145	Wally Joyner	.25
146	Fernando Valenzuela	.25
147	Barry Bonds	4.00
148	Jacob Cruz	.25
149	Osvaldo Fernandez	.25
150	Matt Williams	.25

Gate Attractions

		NM/M
Complete Set (32):		80.00
Common Player:		1.00
1	Roberto Alomar	1.00
2	Brady Anderson	1.00
3	Cal Ripken Jr.	8.00
4	Frank Thomas	2.50
5	Kenny Lofton	1.00
6	Omar Vizquel	1.00
7	Paul Molitor	2.50
8	Wade Boggs	3.00
9	Derek Jeter	8.00
10	Andy Pettitte	1.50
11	Bernie Williams	1.00
12	Geronimo Berroa	1.00
13	Mark McGwire	6.00
14	Ken Griffey Jr.	4.50
15	Alex Rodriguez	6.00
16	Juan Gonzalez	1.50
17	Andruw Jones	2.50
18	Chipper Jones	3.00
19	Greg Maddux	3.00
20	Ryne Sandberg	3.00
21	Sammy Sosa	3.00
22	Andres Galarraga	1.00
23	Jeff Bagwell	2.50
24	Todd Hollandsworth	1.00
25	Hideo Nomo	1.50
26	Mike Piazza	4.50
27	Todd Hundley	1.00
28	Lance Johnson	1.00
29	Ozzie Smith	3.00
30	Ken Caminiti	1.00
31	Tony Gwynn	3.00
32	Barry Bonds	8.00

Sizzling Lumber

	NM/M
Complete Set (36):	50.00
Common Player:	.50

1A	Cal Ripken Jr.	6.50
1B	Rafael Palmeiro	2.50
1C	Roberto Alomar	1.00
2A	Frank Thomas	3.00
2B	Robin Ventura	.50
2C	Harold Baines	.50
3A	Albert Belle	.50
3B	Manny Ramirez	3.00
3C	Kenny Lofton	.50
4A	Derek Bell	6.50
4B	Bernie Williams	.50
4C	Wade Boggs	3.50
5A	Mark McGwire	5.00
5B	Jason Giambi	2.00
5C	Geronimo Berroa	.50
6A	Ken Griffey Jr.	4.00
6B	Alex Rodriguez	5.00
6C	Jay Buhner	.50
7A	Juan Gonzalez	1.50
7B	Dean Palmer	.50
7C	Ivan Rodriguez	2.50
8A	Ryan Klesko	.50
8B	Chipper Jones	3.50
8C	Andruw Jones	3.00
9A	Dante Bichette	.50
9B	Andres Galarraga	.50
9C	Vinny Castilla	.50
10A	Jeff Bagwell	3.00
10B	Craig Biggio	.50
10C	Derek Bell	.50
11A	Mike Piazza	4.00
11B	Raul Mondesi	.50
11C	Karim Garcia	.50
12A	Tony Gwynn	3.50
12B	Ken Caminiti	.50
12C	Greg Vaughn	.50

Sluggers & Hurlers

		NM/M
Complete Set (24):		80.00
Common Player:		2.00
SH-1a	Cal Ripken Jr.	10.00
SH-1b	Mike Mussina	2.50
SH-2a	Jose Canseco	2.50
SH-2b	Roger Clemens	6.00
SH-3a	Frank Thomas	3.50
SH-3b	Wilson Alvarez	2.00
SH-4a	Kenny Lofton	2.00
SH-4b	Orel Hershiser	2.00
SH-5a	Derek Jeter	10.00
SH-5b	Andy Pettitte	2.00
SH-6a	Ken Griffey Jr.	6.00
SH-6b	Randy Johnson	3.50
SH-7a	Alex Rodriguez	7.50
SH-7b	Jamie Moyer	2.00
SH-8a	Andruw Jones	3.50
SH-8b	Greg Maddux	4.50
SH-9a	Chipper Jones	4.50
SH-9b	John Smoltz	2.00
SH-10a	Jeff Bagwell	3.50
SH-10b	Shane Reynolds	2.00
SH-11a	Mike Piazza	6.00
SH-11b	Hideo Nomo	2.50
SH-12a	Tony Gwynn	4.50
SH-12b	Fernando Valenzuela	2.00

Gems of the Diamond

NM/M
Complete Set (220): 20.00
Common Player: .10
1 Jim Abbott .10
2 Shawn Boskie .10
3 Gary DiSarcina .10
4 Jim Edmonds .10
5 Todd Greene .10
6 Jack Howell .10
7 Jeff Schmidt .10
8 Shad Williams .10
9 Roberto Alomar .35
10 Cesar Devarez .10
11 Alan Mills .10
12 Eddie Murray .75
13 Jesse Orosco .10
14 Arthur Rhodes .10
15 Bill Ripken .10
16 Cal Ripken Jr. 2.50
17 Mark Smith .10
18 Roger Clemens 1.50
19 Vaughn Eshelman .10
20 Rich Garces .10
21 Bill Haselman .10
22 Dwayne Hosey .10
23 Mike Maddux .10
24 Jose Malave .10
25 Aaron Sele .10
26 James Baldwin .10
27 Pat Borders .10
28 Mike Cameron .10
29 Tony Castillo .10
30 Domingo Cedeno .10
31 Greg Norton .10
32 Frank Thomas .75
33 Albert Belle .10
34 Einar Diaz .10
35 Alan Embree .10
36 Albie Lopez .10
37 Chad Ogea .10
38 Tony Pena .10
39 Joe Roa .10
40 Fausto Cruz .10
41 Joey Eischen .10
42 Travis Fryman .10
43 Mike Myers .10
44 A.J. Sager .10
45 Duane Singleton .10
46 Justin Thompson .10
47 Jeff Granger .10
48 Les Norman .10
49 Jon Nunnally .10
50 Craig Paquette .10
51 Michael Tucker .10
52 Julio Valera .10
53 Kevin Young .10
54 Cal Eldred .10
55 Ramon Garcia .10
56 Marc Newfield .10
57 Al Reyes .10
58 Tim Unroe .10
59 Tim Vanegmond .10
60 Turner Ward .10
61 Bob Wickman .10
62 Chuck Knoblauch .10
63 Paul Molitor .75
64 Kirby Puckett 1.00
65 Tom Quinlan .10
66 Rich Robertson .10
67 Dave Stevens .10
68 Matt Walbeck .10
69 Wade Boggs 1.00
70 Tony Fernandez .10
71 Andy Fox .10
72 Joe Girardi .10
73 Charlie Hayes .10
74 Pat Kelly .10
75 Jeff Nelson .10
76 Melido Perez .10
77 Mark Acre .10
78 Allen Battle .10
79 Rafael Bournigal .10
80 Mark McGwire 2.00
81 Pedro Munoz .10
82 Scott Spiezio .10
83 Don Wengert .10
84 Steve Wojciechowski .10
85 Alex Diaz .10
86 Ken Griffey Jr. 1.50
87 Raul Ibanez .10
88 Mike Jackson .10
89 John Marzano .10
90 Greg McCarthy .10
91 Alex Rodriguez 2.00
92 Andy Sheets .10
93 Makoto Suzuki .10
94 Benji Gil .10
95 Juan Gonzalez .40
96 Kevin Gross .10
97 Gil Heredia .10
98 Luis Ortiz .10
99 Jeff Russell .10
100 Dave Valle .10
101 Marty Janzen .10
102 Sandy Martinez .10
103 Julio Mosquera .10
104 Otis Nixon .10
105 Paul Spoljaric .10
106 Shannon Stewart .10
107 Woody Williams .10
108 Steve Avery .10
109 Mike Bielecki .10
110 Pedro Borbon .10
111 Ed Giovanola .10
112 Chipper Jones 1.00
113 Greg Maddux 1.00
114 Mike Mordecai .10
115 Terrell Wade .10
116 Terry Adams .10
117 Brian Dorsett .10
118 Doug Glanville .10
119 Tyler Houston .10
120 Robin Jennings .10
121 Ryne Sandberg 1.00
122 Terry Shumpert .10
123 Amaury Telemaco .10
124 Steve Trachsel .10
125 Curtis Goodwin .10
126 Mike Kelly .10
127 Chad Mottola .10
128 Mark Portugal .10
129 Roger Salkeld .10
130 John Smiley .10
131 Lee Smith .10
132 Roger Bailey .10
133 Andres Galarraga .10
134 Darren Holmes .10
135 Curtis Leskanic .10
136 Mike Munoz .10
137 Jeff Reed .10
138 Mark Thompson .10
139 Jamey Wright .10
140 Andre Dawson .25
141 Craig Grebeck .10
142 Matt Mantei .10
143 Billy McMillon .10
144 Kurt Miller .10
145 Ralph Milliard .10
146 Bob Natal .10
147 Joe Siddall .10
148 Bob Abreu .25
149 Doug Brocail .10
150 Danny Darwin .10
151 Mike Hampton .10
152 Todd Jones .10
153 Kirt Manwaring .10
154 Alvin Morman .10
155 Billy Ashley .10
156 Tom Candiotti .10
157 Darren Dreifort .10
158 Greg Gagne .10
159 Wilton Guerrero .10
160 Hideo Nomo .40
161 Mike Piazza 1.50
162 Tom Prince .10
163 Todd Worrell .10
164 Moises Alou .10
165 Shane Andrews .10
166 Derek Aucoin .10
167 Raul Chavez .10
168 Darrin Fletcher .10
169 Mark Leiter .10
170 Henry Rodriguez .10
171 Dave Veres .10
172 Paul Byrd .10
173 Alberto Castillo .10
174 Mark Clark .10
175 Rey Ordonez .10
176 Roberto Petagine .10
177 Andy Tomberlin .10
178 Derek Wallace .10
179 Paul Wilson .10
180 Ruben Amaro Jr. .10
181 Toby Borland .10
182 Rich Hunter .10
183 Tony Longmire .10
184 Wendell Magee Jr. .10
185 Bobby Munoz .10
186 Scott Rolen .60
187 Mike Williams .10
188 Trey Beamon .10
189 Jason Christiansen .10
190 Elmer Dessens .10
191 Angelo Encarnacion .10
192 Carlos Garcia .10
193 Mike Kingery .10
194 Chris Peters .10
195 Tony Womack .10
196 Brian Barber .10
197 David Bell .10
198 Tony Fossas .10
199 Rick Honeycutt .10
200 T.J. Mathews .10
201 Miguel Mejia .10
202 Donovan Osborne .10
203 Ozzie Smith 1.00
204 Andres Berumen .10
205 Ken Caminiti .10
206 Chris Gwynn .10
207 Tony Gwynn 1.00
208 Rickey Henderson .75
209 Scott Sanders .10
210 Jason Thompson .10
211 Fernando Valenzuela .10
212 Tim Worrell .10
213 Barry Bonds 2.50
214 Jay Canizaro .10
215 Doug Creek .10
216 Jacob Cruz .10
217 Glenallen Hill .10
218 Tom Lampkin .10
219 Jim Poole .10
220 Desi Wilson .10

1998 Pacific

NM/M
Complete Set (450): 40.00
Common Player: .05
Silvers: 3X

Inserted 1:1 H
Reds: 6X
Inserted 1:1 R
Platinum Blues: 15X
Inserted 1:73
Pack (12): 1.00
Wax Box (36): 20.00
1 Luis Alicea .05
2 Garret Anderson .05
3 Jason Dickson .05
4 Gary DiSarcina .05
5 Jim Edmonds .05
6 Darin Erstad .15
7 Chuck Finley .05
8 Shigetosi Hasegawa .05
9 Rickey Henderson .75
10 Dave Hollins .05
11 Mark Langston .05
12 Orlando Palmeiro .05
13 Troy Percival .05
14 Tony Phillips .05
15 Tim Salmon .05
16 Allen Watson .05
17 Roberto Alomar .25
18 Brady Anderson .05
19 Harold Baines .05
20 Armando Benitez .05
21 Geronimo Berroa .05
22 Mike Bordick .05
23 Eric Davis .05
24 Scott Erickson .05
25 Chris Hoiles .05
26 Jimmy Key .05
27 Aaron Ledesma .05
28 Mike Mussina .50
29 Randy Myers .05
30 Jesse Orosco .05
31 Rafael Palmeiro .65
32 Jeff Reboulet .05
33 Cal Ripken Jr. 2.00
34 B.J. Surhoff .05
35 Steve Avery .05
36 Darren Bragg .05
37 Wil Cordero .05
38 Jeff Frye .05
39 Nomar Garciaparra 1.00
40 Tom Gordon .05
41 Bill Haselman .05
42 Scott Hatteberg .05
43 Butch Henry .05
44 Reggie Jefferson .05
45 Tim Naehring .05
46 Troy O'Leary .05
47 Jeff Suppan .05
48 John Valentin .05
49 Mo Vaughn .05
50 Tim Wakefield .05
51 James Baldwin .05
52 Albert Belle .05
53 Tony Castillo .05
54 Doug Drabek .05
55 Ray Durham .05
56 Jorge Fabregas .05
57 Ozzie Guillen .05
58 Matt Karchner .05
59 Norberto Martin .05
60 Dave Martinez .05
61 Lyle Mouton .05
62 Jaime Navarro .05
63 Frank Thomas .75
64 Mario Valdez .05
65 Robin Ventura .05
66 Sandy Alomar Jr. .05
67 Paul Assenmacher .05
68 Tony Fernandez .05
69 Brian Giles .05
70 Marquis Grissom .05
71 Orel Hershiser .05
72 Mike Jackson .05
73 David Justice .05
74 Albie Lopez .05
75 Jose Mesa .05
76 Charles Nagy .05
77 Chad Ogea .05
78 Manny Ramirez .75
79 Jim Thome .60
80 Omar Vizquel .05
81 Matt Williams .05
82 Jaret Wright .05
83 Willie Blair .05
84 Raul Casanova .05
85 Tony Clark .05
86 Deivi Cruz .05
87 Damion Easley .05
88 Travis Fryman .05
89 Bobby Higginson .05
90 Brian Hunter .05
91 Todd Jones .05
92 Dan Miceli .05
93 Brian Moehler .05
94 Melvin Nieves .05
95 Jody Reed .05
96 Justin Thompson .05
97 Bubba Trammell .05
98 Kevin Appier .05
99 Jay Bell .05
100 Yamil Benitez .05
101 Johnny Damon .35
102 Chili Davis .05
103 Jermaine Dye .05
104 Jed Hansen .05
105 Jeff King .05
106 Mike Macfarlane .05
107 Felix Martinez .05
108 Jeff Montgomery .05
109 Jose Offerman .05
110 Dean Palmer .05
111 Hipolito Pichardo .05
112 Jose Rosado .05
113 Jeromy Burnitz .05
114 Jeff Cirillo .05
115 Cal Eldred .05
116 John Jaha .05
117 Doug Jones .05
118 Scott Karl .05
119 Jesse Levis .05
120 Mark Loretta .05
121 Ben McDonald .05
122 Jose Mercedes .05
123 Matt Mieske .05
124 Dave Nilsson .05
125 Jose Valentin .05
126 Fernando Vina .05
127 Gerald Williams .05
128 Rick Aguilera .05
129 Rich Becker .05
130 Ron Coomer .05
131 Marty Cordova .05
132 Eddie Guardado .05
133 LaTroy Hawkins .05
134 Denny Hocking .05
135 Chuck Knoblauch .05
136 Matt Lawton .05
137 Pat Meares .05
138 Paul Molitor .75
139 David Ortiz .50
140 Brad Radke .05
141 Terry Steinbach .05
142 Bob Tewksbury .05
143 Javier Valentin .05
144 Wade Boggs 1.00
145 David Cone .05
146 Chad Curtis .05
147 Cecil Fielder .05
148 Joe Girardi .05
149 Dwight Gooden .05
150 Hideki Irabu .05
151 Derek Jeter 2.00
152 Tino Martinez .05
153 Ramiro Mendoza .05
154 Paul O'Neill .05
155 Andy Pettitte .20
156 Jorge Posada .05
157 Mariano Rivera .15
158 Rey Sanchez .05
159 Luis Sojo .05
160 David Wells .05
161 Bernie Williams .05
162 Rafael Bournigal .05
163 Scott Brosius .05
164 Jose Canseco .50
165 Jason Giambi .60
166 Ben Grieve .05
167 Dave Magadan .05
168 Brent Mayne .05
169 Jason McDonald .05
170 Izzy Molina .05
171 Ariel Prieto .05
172 Carlos Reyes .05
173 Scott Spiezio .05
174 Matt Stairs .05
175 Bill Taylor .05
176 Dave Telgheder .05
177 Steve Wojciechowski .05
178 Rich Amaral .05
179 Bobby Ayala .05
180 Jay Buhner .05
181 Rafael Carmona .05
182 Ken Cloude .05
183 Joey Cora .05
184 Russ Davis .05
185 Jeff Fassero .05
186 Ken Griffey Jr. 1.25
187 Raul Ibanez .05
188 Randy Johnson .75
189 Roberto Kelly .05
190 Edgar Martinez .05
191 Jamie Moyer .05
192 Omar Olivares .05
193 Alex Rodriguez 1.50
194 Heathcliff Slocumb .05
195 Paul Sorrento .05
196 Dan Wilson .05
197 Scott Bailes .05
198 John Burkett .05
199 Domingo Cedeno .05

200	Will Clark	.05
201	Hanley Frias **RC**	.05
202	Juan Gonzalez	.40
203	Tom Goodwin	.05
204	Rusty Greer	.05
205	Wilson Heredia	.05
206	Darren Oliver	.05
207	Billy Ripken	.05
208	Ivan Rodriguez	.65
209	Lee Stevens	.05
210	Fernando Tatis	.05
211	John Wetteland	.05
212	Bobby Witt	.05
213	Jacob Brumfield	.05
214	Joe Carter	.05
215	Roger Clemens	1.25
216	Felipe Crespo	.05
217	Jose Cruz Jr.	.05
218	Carlos Delgado	.50
219	Mariano Duncan	.05
220	Carlos Garcia	.05
221	Alex Gonzalez	.05
222	Juan Guzman	.05
223	Pat Hentgen	.05
224	Orlando Merced	.05
225	Tomas Perez	.05
226	Paul Quantrill	.05
227	Benito Santiago	.05
228	Woody Williams	.05
229	Rafael Belliard	.05
230	Jeff Blauser	.05
231	Pedro Borbon	.05
232	Tom Glavine	.25
233	Tony Graffanino	.05
234	Andruw Jones	.75
235	Chipper Jones	1.00
236	Ryan Klesko	.05
237	Mark Lemke	.05
238	Kenny Lofton	.05
239	Javier Lopez	.05
240	Fred McGriff	.05
241	Greg Maddux	1.00
242	Denny Neagle	.05
243	John Smoltz	.05
244	Michael Tucker	.05
245	Mark Wohlers	.05
246	Manny Alexander	.05
247	Miguel Batista	.05
248	Mark Clark	.05
249	Doug Glanville	.05
250	Jeremi Gonzalez	.05
251	Mark Grace	.05
252	Jose Hernandez	.05
253	Lance Johnson	.05
254	Brooks Kieschnick	.05
255	Kevin Orie	.05
256	Ryne Sandberg	1.00
257	Scott Servais	.05
258	Sammy Sosa	1.00
259	Kevin Tapani	.05
260	Ramon Tatis	.05
261	Bret Boone	.05
262	Dave Burba	.05
263	Brook Fordyce	.05
264	Willie Greene	.05
265	Barry Larkin	.05
266	Pedro A. Martinez	.05
267	Hal Morris	.05
268	Joe Oliver	.05
269	Eduardo Perez	.05
270	Pokey Reese	.05
271	Felix Rodriguez	.05
272	Deion Sanders	.05
273	Reggie Sanders	.05
274	Jeff Shaw	.05
275	Scott Sullivan	.05
276	Brett Tomko	.05
277	Roger Bailey	.05
278	Dante Bichette	.05
279	Ellis Burks	.05
280	Vinny Castilla	.05
281	Frank Castillo	.05
282	Mike DeJean **RC**	.05
283	Andres Galarraga	.05
284	Darren Holmes	.05
285	Kirt Manwaring	.05
286	Quinton McCracken	.05
287	Neifi Perez	.05
288	Steve Reed	.05
289	John Thomson	.05
290	Larry Walker	.05
291	Walt Weiss	.05
292	Kurt Abbott	.05
293	Antonio Alfonseca	.05
294	Moises Alou	.05
295	Alex Arias	.05
296	Bobby Bonilla	.05
297	Kevin Brown	.05
298	Craig Counsell	.05
299	Darren Daulton	.05
300	Jim Eisenreich	.05
301	Alex Fernandez	.05
302	Felix Heredia	.05
303	Livan Hernandez	.05
304	Charles Johnson	.05
305	Al Leiter	.05
306	Robb Nen	.05
307	Edgar Renteria	.05
308	Gary Sheffield	.45
309	Devon White	.05
310	Bob Abreu	.10
311	Brad Ausmus	.05
312	Jeff Bagwell	.75
313	Derek Bell	.05
314	Sean Berry	.05

315	Craig Biggio	.05
316	Ramon Garcia	.05
317	Luis Gonzalez	.05
318	Ricky Gutierrez	.05
319	Mike Hampton	.05
320	Richard Hidalgo	.05
321	Thomas Howard	.05
322	Darryl Kile	.05
323	Jose Lima	.05
324	Shane Reynolds	.05
325	Bill Spiers	.05
326	Tom Candiotti	.05
327	Roger Cedeno	.05
328	Greg Gagne	.05
329	Karim Garcia	.05
330	Wilton Guerrero	.05
331	Todd Hollandsworth	.05
332	Eric Karros	.05
333	Ramon Martinez	.05
334	Raul Mondesi	.05
335	Otis Nixon	.05
336	Hideo Nomo	.40
337	Antonio Osuna	.05
338	Chan Ho Park	.05
339	Mike Piazza	1.25
340	Dennis Reyes	.05
341	Ismael Valdes	.05
342	Todd Worrell	.05
343	Todd Zeile	.05
344	Darrin Fletcher	.05
345	Mark Grudzielanek	.05
346	Vladimir Guerrero	.75
347	Dustin Hermanson	.05
348	Mike Lansing	.05
349	Pedro Martinez	.75
350	Ryan McGuire	.05
351	Jose Paniagua	.05
352	Carlos Perez	.05
353	Henry Rodriguez	.05
354	F.P. Santangelo	.05
355	David Segui	.05
356	Ugueth Urbina	.05
357	Marc Valdes	.05
358	Jose Vidro	.05
359	Rondell White	.05
360	Juan Acevedo	.05
361	Edgardo Alfonzo	.05
362	Carlos Baerga	.05
363	Carl Everett	.05
364	John Franco	.05
365	Bernard Gilkey	.05
366	Todd Hundley	.05
367	Butch Huskey	.05
368	Bobby Jones	.05
369	Takashi Kashiwada	.05
370	Greg McMichael	.05
371	Brian McRae	.05
372	Alex Ochoa	.05
373	John Olerud	.05
374	Rey Ordonez	.05
375	Turk Wendell	.05
376	Ricky Bottalico	.05
377	Rico Brogna	.05
378	Lenny Dykstra	.05
379	Bobby Estalella	.05
380	Wayne Gomes	.05
381	Tyler Green	.05
382	Gregg Jefferies	.05
383	Mark Leiter	.05
384	Mike Lieberthal	.05
385	Mickey Morandini	.05
386	Scott Rolen	.60
387	Curt Schilling	.25
388	Kevin Stocker	.05
389	Danny Tartabull	.05
390	Jermaine Allensworth	.05
391	Adrian Brown	.05
392	Jason Christiansen	.05
393	Steve Cooke	.05
394	Francisco Cordova	.05
395	Jose Guillen	.05
396	Jason Kendall	.05
397	Jon Lieber	.05
398	Esteban Loaiza	.05
399	Al Martin	.05
400	Kevin Polcovich **RC**	.05
401	Joe Randa	.05
402	Ricardo Rincon	.05
403	Tony Womack	.05
404	Kevin Young	.05
405	Andy Benes	.05
406	Royce Clayton	.05
407	Delino DeShields	.05
408	Mike Difelice	.05
409	Dennis Eckersley	.60
410	John Frascatore	.05
411	Gary Gaetti	.05
412	Ron Gant	.05
413	Brian Jordan	.05
414	Ray Lankford	.05
415	Willie McGee	.05
416	Mark McGwire	1.50
417	Matt Morris	.05
418	Luis Ordaz	.05
419	Todd Stottlemyre	.05
420	Andy Ashby	.05
421	Jim Bruske	.05
422	Ken Caminiti	.05
423	Will Cunnane	.05
424	Steve Finley	.05
425	John Flaherty	.05
426	Chris Gomez	.05
427	Tony Gwynn	1.00
428	Joey Hamilton	.05
429	Carlos Hernandez	.05

430	Sterling Hitchcock	.05
431	Trevor Hoffman	.05
432	Wally Joyner	.05
433	Greg Vaughn	.05
434	Quilvio Veras	.05
435	Wilson Alvarez	.05
436	Rod Beck	.05
437	Barry Bonds	2.00
438	Jacob Cruz	.05
439	Shawn Estes	.05
440	Darryl Hamilton	.05
441	Roberto Hernandez	.05
442	Glenallen Hill	.05
443	Stan Javier	.05
444	Brian Johnson	.05
445	Jeff Kent	.05
446	Bill Mueller	.05
447	Kirk Rueter	.05
448	J.T. Snow	.05
449	Julian Tavarez	.05
450	Jose Vizcaino	.05

Red/Silver/Blue

	NM/M
Common Red:	1.50
Red Stars:	6X
Common Silver:	.75
Silver Stars:	3X
Common Platinum Blue:	3.00
Platinum Blue Stars:	15X
(See 1998 Pacific for checklist and base card values.)	

Cramer's Choice

		NM/M
Complete Set (10):		150.00
Common Player:		7.50
Inserted 1:721		
1	Greg Maddux	15.00
2	Roberto Alomar	7.50
3	Cal Ripken Jr.	30.00
4	Nomar Garciaparra	15.00
5	Larry Walker	7.50
6	Mike Piazza	17.50
7	Mark McGwire	25.00
8	Tony Gwynn	15.00
9	Ken Griffey Jr.	20.00
10	Roger Clemens	17.50

Gold Crown Die-Cuts

		NM/M
Complete Set (36):		85.00
Common Player:		1.50
1	Chipper Jones	4.00
2	Greg Maddux	4.00
3	Denny Neagle	1.50
4	Roberto Alomar	2.00
5	Rafael Palmeiro	2.50
6	Cal Ripken Jr.	8.00
7	Nomar Garciaparra	4.00
8	Mo Vaughn	1.50
9	Frank Thomas	3.00
10	Sandy Alomar Jr.	1.50
11	David Justice	1.50
12	Manny Ramirez	3.00
13	Andres Galarraga	1.50
14	Larry Walker	1.50

Home Run Hitters

15	Moises Alou	1.50
16	Livan Hernandez	1.50
17	Gary Sheffield	2.00
18	Jeff Bagwell	3.00
19	Raul Mondesi	1.50
20	Hideo Nomo	2.00
21	Mike Piazza	4.50
22	Derek Jeter	8.00
23	Tino Martinez	1.50
24	Bernie Williams	1.50
25	Ben Grieve	1.50
26	Mark McGwire	6.50
27	Tony Gwynn	4.00
28	Barry Bonds	8.00
29	Ken Griffey Jr.	5.00
30	Randy Johnson	3.00
31	Edgar Martinez	1.50
32	Alex Rodriguez	6.50
33	Juan Gonzalez	2.00
34	Ivan Rodriguez	2.50
35	Roger Clemens	4.50
36	Jose Cruz Jr.	1.50

		NM/M
Complete Set (20):		50.00
Common Player:		1.00
1	Rafael Palmeiro	3.00
2	Mo Vaughn	1.00
3	Sammy Sosa	4.00
4	Albert Belle	1.00
5	Frank Thomas	3.50
6	David Justice	1.00
7	Jim Thome	3.00
8	Matt Williams	1.00
9	Vinny Castilla	1.00
10	Andres Galarraga	1.00
11	Larry Walker	1.00
12	Jeff Bagwell	3.50
13	Mike Piazza	4.50
14	Tino Martinez	1.00
15	Mark McGwire	6.00
16	Barry Bonds	7.50
17	Jay Buhner	1.00
18	Ken Griffey Jr.	5.00
19	Alex Rodriguez	6.00
20	Juan Gonzalez	2.00

1998 Pacific Home Run Heroes

		NM/M
Complete Set (6):		2.50
Common Player:		.25
1	Mark McGwire	1.00
2	Sammy Sosa	.65
3	Ken Griffey Jr.	.75
4	Greg Vaughn	.25
5	Albert Belle	.25
6	Jose Canseco	.50

In the Cage

		NM/M
Complete Set (20):		175.00
Common Player:		4.00
1	Chipper Jones	12.00
2	Roberto Alomar	4.00
3	Cal Ripken Jr.	25.00
4	Nomar Garciaparra	12.00
5	Frank Thomas	10.00
6	Sandy Alomar Jr.	4.00
7	David Justice	4.00
8	Larry Walker	4.00
9	Bobby Bonilla	4.00
10	Mike Piazza	16.00
11	Tino Martinez	4.00
12	Bernie Williams	4.00
13	Mark McGwire	20.00

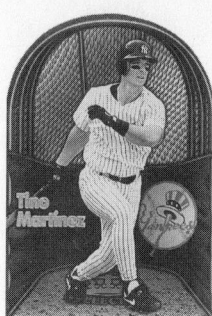

14	Tony Gwynn	12.00
15	Barry Bonds	25.00
16	Ken Griffey Jr.	16.00
17	Edgar Martinez	4.00
18	Alex Rodriguez	20.00
19	Juan Gonzalez	6.00
20	Ivan Rodriguez	7.50

Latinos of the Major Leagues

		NM/M
Complete Set (36):		30.00
Common Player:		.50
Inserted 2:37		
1	Andruw Jones	2.50
2	Javier Lopez	.50
3	Roberto Alomar	1.25
4	Geronimo Berroa	.50
5	Rafael Palmeiro	2.00
6	Nomar Garciaparra	3.00
7	Sammy Sosa	3.00
8	Ozzie Guillen	.50
9	Sandy Alomar Jr.	.50
10	Manny Ramirez	2.50
11	Omar Vizquel	.50
12	Vinny Castilla	.50
13	Andres Galarraga	.50
14	Moises Alou	.50
15	Bobby Bonilla	.50
16	Livan Hernandez	.50
17	Edgar Renteria	.50
18	Wilton Guerrero	.50
19	Raul Mondesi	.50
20	Ismael Valdes	.50
21	Fernando Vina	.50
22	Pedro Martinez	2.50
23	Edgardo Alfonzo	.50
24	Carlos Baerga	.50
25	Rey Ordonez	.50
26	Tino Martinez	.50
27	Mariano Rivera	1.00
28	Bernie Williams	.50
29	Jose Canseco	1.50
30	Joey Cora	.50
31	Roberto Kelly	.50
32	Edgar Martinez	.50
33	Alex Rodriguez	3.50
34	Juan Gonzalez	1.50
35	Manny Ramirez	2.00
36	Jose Cruz Jr.	.50

Team Checklists

		NM/M
Complete Set (30):		60.00
Common Player:		.50
1	Tim Salmon, Jim Edmonds	.50
2	Cal Ripken Jr., Roberto Alomar	6.00
3	Nomar Garciaparra, Mo Vaughn	3.50
4	Frank Thomas, Albert Belle	2.50
5	Sandy Alomar Jr., Manny Ramirez	2.50
6	Justin Thompson, Tony Clark	.50
7	Johnny Damon, Jermaine Dye	.75

8	Dave Nilsson, Jeff Cirillo	.50
9	Paul Molitor, Chuck Knoblauch	2.50
10	Tino Martinez, Derek Jeter	6.00
11	Ben Grieve, Jose Canseco	1.00
12	Ken Griffey Jr., Alex Rodriguez	5.00
13	Juan Gonzalez, Ivan Rodriguez	2.00
14	Jose Cruz Jr., Roger Clemens	4.00
15	Greg Maddux, Chipper Jones	3.50
16	Sammy Sosa, Mark Grace	3.50
17	Barry Larkin, Deion Sanders	.50
18	Larry Walker, Andres Galarraga	.50
19	Moises Alou, Bobby Bonilla	.50
20	Jeff Bagwell, Craig Biggio	2.50
21	Mike Piazza, Hideo Nomo	4.00
22	Pedro Martinez, Henry Rodriguez	2.50
23	Rey Ordonez, Carlos Baerga	.50
24	Curt Schilling, Scott Rolen	1.50
25	Al Martin, Tony Womack	.50
26	Mark McGwire, Dennis Eckersley	5.00
27	Tony Gwynn, Wally Joyner	3.50
28	Barry Bonds, J.T. Snow	6.00
29	Matt Williams, Jay Bell	.50
30	Fred McGriff, Roberto Hernandez	.50

1998 Pacific Aurora

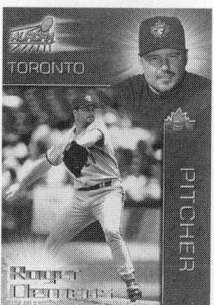

		NM/M
Complete Set (200):		20.00
Common Player:		.05
Pack (6):		1.00
Wax Box (36):		20.00
1	Garret Anderson	.05
2	Jim Edmonds	.05
3	Darin Erstad	.15
4	Cecil Fielder	.05
5	Chuck Finley	.05
6	Todd Greene	.05
7	Ken Hill	.05
8	Tim Salmon	.05
9	Roberto Alomar	.20
10	Brady Anderson	.05
11	Joe Carter	.05
12	Mike Mussina	.35
13	Rafael Palmeiro	.65
14	Cal Ripken Jr.	2.50
15	B.J. Surhoff	.05
16	Steve Avery	.05
17	Nomar Garciaparra	1.00
18	Pedro Martinez	.75
19	John Valentin	.05
20	Jason Varitek	.05
21	Mo Vaughn	.05
22	Albert Belle	.05
23	Ray Durham	.05
24	Magglio Ordonez RC	1.50
25	Frank Thomas	.05
26	Robin Ventura	.05
27	Sandy Alomar Jr.	.05
28	Travis Fryman	.05
29	Dwight Gooden	.05
30	David Justice	.05
31	Kenny Lofton	.05
32	Manny Ramirez	.75
33	Jim Thome	.60
34	Omar Vizquel	.05
35	Enrique Wilson	.05
36	Jaret Wright	.05
37	Tony Clark	.05
38	Bobby Higginson	.05
39	Brian Hunter	.05
40	Bip Roberts	.05
41	Justin Thompson	.05
42	Jeff Conine	.05
43	Johnny Damon	.35
44	Jermaine Dye	.05
45	Jeff King	.05
46	Jeff Montgomery	.05
47	Hal Morris	.05
48	Dean Palmer	.05
49	Terry Pendleton	.05
50	Rick Aguilera	.05
51	Marty Cordova	.05

52	Paul Molitor	.75
53	Otis Nixon	.05
54	Brad Radke	.05
55	Terry Steinbach	.05
56	Todd Walker	.05
57	Chili Davis	.05
58	Derek Jeter	2.50
59	Chuck Knoblauch	.05
60	Tino Martinez	.05
61	Paul O'Neill	.05
62	Andy Pettitte	.20
63	Mariano Rivera	.15
64	Bernie Williams	.05
65	Jason Giambi	.50
66	Ben Grieve	.05
67	Rickey Henderson	.75
68	A.J. Hinch	.05
69	Kenny Rogers	.05
70	Jay Buhner	.05
71	Joey Cora	.05
72	Ken Griffey Jr.	1.50
73	Randy Johnson	.75
74	Edgar Martinez	.05
75	Jamie Moyer	.05
76	Alex Rodriguez	2.00
77	David Segui	.05
78	Rolando Arrojo RC	.35
79	Wade Boggs	1.00
80	Roberto Hernandez	.05
81	Dave Martinez	.05
82	Fred McGriff	.05
83	Paul Sorrento	.05
84	Kevin Stocker	.05
85	Will Clark	.05
86	Juan Gonzalez	.40
87	Tom Goodwin	.05
88	Rusty Greer	.05
89	Ivan Rodriguez	.65
90	John Wetteland	.05
91	Jose Canseco	.40
92	Roger Clemens	1.25
93	Jose Cruz Jr.	.50
94	Carlos Delgado	.50
95	Pat Hentgen	.05
96	Jay Bell	.05
97	Andy Benes	.05
98	Karim Garcia	.05
99	Travis Lee	.05
100	Devon White	.05
101	Matt Williams	.05
102	Andres Galarraga	.05
103	Tom Glavine	.30
104	Andruw Jones	.75
105	Chipper Jones	1.00
106	Ryan Klesko	.05
107	Javy Lopez	.05
108	Greg Maddux	1.00
109	Walt Weiss	.05
110	Rod Beck	.05
111	Jeff Blauser	.05
112	Mark Grace	.05
113	Lance Johnson	.05
114	Mickey Morandini	.05
115	Henry Rodriguez	.05
116	Sammy Sosa	1.00
117	Kerry Wood	.35
118	Lenny Harris	.05
119	Damian Jackson	.05
120	Barry Larkin	.05
121	Reggie Sanders	.05
122	Brett Tomko	.05
123	Dante Bichette	.05
124	Ellis Burks	.05
125	Vinny Castilla	.05
126	Todd Helton	.75
127	Darryl Kile	.05
128	Larry Walker	.05
129	Bobby Bonilla	.05
130	Livan Hernandez	.05
131	Charles Johnson	.05
132	Derrek Lee	.50
133	Edgar Renteria	.05
134	Gary Sheffield	.35
135	Moises Alou	.05
136	Jeff Bagwell	.75
137	Derek Bell	.05
138	Craig Biggio	.05
139	John Halama RC	.15
140	Mike Hampton	.05
141	Richard Hidalgo	.05
142	Wilton Guerrero	.05
143	Todd Hollandsworth	.05
144	Eric Karros	.05
145	Paul Konerko	.05
146	Raul Mondesi	.05
147	Hideo Nomo	.40
148	Chan Ho Park	.05
149	Mike Piazza	1.25
150	Jeromy Burnitz	.05
151	Todd Dunn	.05
152	Marquis Grissom	.05
153	John Jaha	.05
154	Dave Nilsson	.05
155	Fernando Vina	.05
156	Mark Grudzielanek	.05
157	Vladimir Guerrero	.75
158	F.P. Santangelo	.05
159	Jose Vidro	.05
160	Rondell White	.05
161	Edgardo Alfonzo	.05
162	Carlos Baerga	.05
163	John Franco	.05
164	Todd Hundley	.05
165	Brian McRae	.05
166	John Olerud	.05

167	Rey Ordonez	.05
168	Masato Yoshii RC	.25
169	Ricky Bottalico	.05
170	Doug Glanville	.05
171	Gregg Jefferies	.05
172	Desi Relaford	.05
173	Scott Rolen	.60
174	Curt Schilling	.30
175	Jose Guillen	.05
176	Jason Kendall	.05
177	Al Martin	.05
178	Abraham Nunez	.05
179	Kevin Young	.05
180	Royce Clayton	.05
181	Delino DeShields	.05
182	Gary Gaetti	.05
183	Ron Gant	.05
184	Brian Jordan	.05
185	Ray Lankford	.05
186	Willie McGee	.05
187	Mark McGwire	2.00
188	Kevin Brown	.05
189	Ken Caminiti	.05
190	Steve Finley	.05
191	Tony Gwynn	1.00
192	Wally Joyner	.05
193	Ruben Rivera	.05
194	Quilvio Veras	.05
195	Barry Bonds	2.50
196	Shawn Estes	.05
197	Orel Hershiser	.05
198	Jeff Kent	.05
199	Robb Nen	.05
200	J.T. Snow	.05

Cubes

		NM/M
Complete Set (20):		75.00
Common Player:		1.50
Inserted 1:Box		
1	Travis Lee	1.50
2	Chipper Jones	4.00
3	Greg Maddux	4.00
4	Cal Ripken Jr.	10.00
5	Nomar Garciaparra	4.00
6	Frank Thomas	3.00
7	Manny Ramirez	3.00
8	Larry Walker	1.50
9	Hideo Nomo	2.00
10	Mike Piazza	5.00
11	Derek Jeter	10.00
12	Ben Grieve	1.50
13	Mark McGwire	7.50
14	Tony Gwynn	4.00
15	Barry Bonds	10.00
16	Ken Griffey Jr.	6.00
17	Alex Rodriguez	7.50
18	Wade Boggs	4.00
19	Juan Gonzalez	2.00
20	Jose Cruz Jr.	1.50

Hardball Cel-Fusion

		NM/M
Complete Set (20):		60.00
Common Player:		2.00
Inserted 1:73		
1	Travis Lee	2.00
2	Chipper Jones	6.00

3	Greg Maddux	6.00
4	Cal Ripken Jr.	15.00
5	Nomar Garciaparra	6.00
6	Frank Thomas	4.50
7	David Justice	2.00
8	Jeff Bagwell	4.50
9	Hideo Nomo	3.00
10	Mike Piazza	7.50
11	Derek Jeter	15.00
12	Ben Grieve	2.00
13	Scott Rolen	3.00
14	Mark McGwire	12.00
15	Tony Gwynn	6.00
16	Ken Griffey Jr.	9.00
17	Alex Rodriguez	12.00
18	Ivan Rodriguez	3.50
19	Roger Clemens	7.50
20	Jose Cruz Jr.	2.00

Kings of the Major Leagues

		NM/M
Complete Set (10):		75.00
Common Player:		7.50
Inserted 1:361		
1	Chipper Jones	9.00
2	Greg Maddux	9.00
3	Cal Ripken Jr.	20.00
4	Nomar Garciaparra	9.00
5	Frank Thomas	7.50
6	Mike Piazza	10.00
7	Mark McGwire	15.00
8	Tony Gwynn	9.00
9	Ken Griffey Jr.	12.00
10	Alex Rodriguez	15.00

On Deck Laser-Cut

		NM/M
Complete Set (20):		30.00
Common Player:		.60
Inserted 1:9		
1	Travis Lee	.60
2	Chipper Jones	2.25
3	Greg Maddux	2.25
4	Cal Ripken Jr.	6.00
5	Nomar Garciaparra	2.25
6	Frank Thomas	1.50
7	Manny Ramirez	1.50
8	Larry Walker	.60
9	Hideo Nomo	1.00
10	Mike Piazza	2.50
11	Derek Jeter	6.00
12	Ben Grieve	.60
13	Mark McGwire	4.50
14	Tony Gwynn	2.25
15	Barry Bonds	6.00
16	Ken Griffey Jr.	3.00
17	Alex Rodriguez	4.50
18	Wade Boggs	2.25
19	Juan Gonzalez	1.00
20	Jose Cruz Jr.	.60

Pennant Fever

		NM/M
Complete Set (50):		25.00
Common Player:		.20
Inserted 1:1		
Reds (1:4 Retail):		2X

Silvers (250 Sets):		4X
Platinum Blues (100 Sets):		12X
Coppers (20 Sets):		40X
1	Tony Gwynn	1.00
2	Derek Jeter	2.00
3	Alex Rodriguez	1.50
4	Paul Molitor	.75
5	Nomar Garciaparra	1.00
6	Jeff Bagwell	.75
7	Ivan Rodriguez	.65
8	Cal Ripken Jr.	2.00
9	Matt Williams	.20
10	Chipper Jones	1.00
11	Edgar Martinez	.20
12	Wade Boggs	1.00
13	Paul Konerko	.30
14	Ben Grieve	.20
15	Sandy Alomar Jr.	.20
16	Travis Lee	.20
17	Scott Rolen	.65
18	Ryan Klesko	.20
19	Juan Gonzalez	.40
20	Albert Belle	.20
21	Roger Clemens	1.25
22	Javy Lopez	.20
23	Jose Cruz Jr.	.20
24	Ken Griffey Jr.	1.25
25	Mark McGwire	1.50
26	Brady Anderson	.20
27	Jaret Wright	.20
28	Roberto Alomar	.30
29	Joe Carter	.20
30	Hideo Nomo	.40
31	Mike Piazza	1.25
32	Andres Galarraga	.20
33	Larry Walker	.20
34	Tim Salmon	.20
35	Frank Thomas	.75
36	Moises Alou	.20
37	David Justice	.20
38	Manny Ramirez	.75
39	Jim Edmonds	.20
40	Barry Bonds	2.00
41	Jim Thome	.65
42	Mo Vaughn	.20
43	Rafael Palmeiro	.65
44	Darin Erstad	.30
45	Pedro Martinez	.20
46	Greg Maddux	1.00
47	Jose Canseco	.45
48	Vladimir Guerrero	.75
49	Bernie Williams	.20
50	Randy Johnson	.75

1998 Pacific Crown Royale

		NM/M
Complete Set (144):		60.00
Common Player:		.20
Pack (6):		1.00
Wax Box (24):		20.00
1	Garret Anderson	.20
2	Jim Edmonds	.20
3	Darin Erstad	.50
4	Tim Salmon	.20
5	Jarrod Washburn	.20
6	David Dellucci	.20
7	Travis Lee	.20
8	Devon White	.20
9	Matt Williams	.20
10	Andres Galarraga	.20
11	Tom Glavine	.35
12	Andruw Jones	2.00
13	Chipper Jones	3.00
14	Ryan Klesko	.20
15	Javy Lopez	.20
16	Greg Maddux	3.00
17	Walt Weiss	.20
18	Roberto Alomar	.75
19	Harold Baines	.20
20	Eric Davis	.20
21	Mike Mussina	1.00
22	Rafael Palmeiro	1.50
23	Cal Ripken Jr.	5.00
24	Nomar Garciaparra	3.00
25	Pedro Martinez	2.00
26	Troy O'Leary	.20
27	Mo Vaughn	.20
28	Tim Wakefield	.20
29	Mark Grace	.20
30	Mickey Morandini	.20

31	Sammy Sosa	3.00
32	Kerry Wood	.50
33	Albert Belle	.20
34	Mike Caruso	.20
35	Ray Durham	.20
36	Frank Thomas	2.00
37	Robin Ventura	.20
38	Bret Boone	.20
39	Sean Casey	.25
40	Barry Larkin	.20
41	Reggie Sanders	.20
42	Sandy Alomar Jr.	.20
43	David Justice	.20
44	Kenny Lofton	.20
45	Manny Ramirez	2.00
46	Jim Thome	1.00
47	Omar Vizquel	.20
48	Jaret Wright	.20
49	Dante Bichette	.20
50	Ellis Burks	.20
51	Vinny Castilla	.20
52	Todd Helton	2.00
53	Larry Walker	.20
54	Tony Clark	.20
55	Damion Easley	.20
56	Bobby Higginson	.20
57	Cliff Floyd	.20
58	Livan Hernandez	.20
59	Derrek Lee	.75
60	Edgar Renteria	.20
61	Moises Alou	.20
62	Jeff Bagwell	2.00
63	Derek Bell	.20
64	Craig Biggio	.20
65	Johnny Damon	.35
66	Jeff King	.20
67	Hal Morris	.20
68	Dean Palmer	.20
69	Bobby Bonilla	.20
70	Eric Karros	.20
71	Raul Mondesi	.20
72	Gary Sheffield	.75
73	Jeromy Burnitz	.20
74	Jeff Cirillo	.20
75	Marquis Grissom	.20
76	Fernando Vina	.20
77	Marty Cordova	.20
78	Pat Meares	.20
79	Paul Molitor	2.00
80	Terry Steinbach	.20
81	Todd Walker	.20
82	Brad Fullmer	.20
83	Vladimir Guerrero	2.00
84	Carl Pavano	.20
85	Rondell White	.20
86	Carlos Baerga	.20
87	Hideo Nomo	1.00
88	John Olerud	.20
89	Rey Ordonez	.20
90	Mike Piazza	3.00
91	Masato Yoshii **RC**	.75
92	Orlando Hernandez **RC**	1.50
93	Hideki Irabu	.20
94	Derek Jeter	5.00
95	Chuck Knoblauch	.20
96	Ricky Ledee	.20
97	Tino Martinez	.20
98	Paul O'Neill	.20
99	Bernie Williams	.20
100	Jason Giambi	1.25
101	Ben Grieve	.20
102	Rickey Henderson	2.00
103	Matt Stairs	.20
104	Bob Abreu	.25
105	Doug Glanville	.20
106	Scott Rolen	1.50
107	Curt Schilling	.35
108	Jose Guillen	.20
109	Jason Kendall	.20
110	Jason Schmidt	.20
111	Kevin Young	.20
112	Delino DeShields	.20
113	Brian Jordan	.20
114	Ray Lankford	.20
115	Mark McGwire	4.00
116	Tony Gwynn	3.00
117	Wally Joyner	.20
118	Ruben Rivera	.20
119	Greg Vaughn	.20
120	Rich Aurilia	.20
121	Barry Bonds	5.00
122	Bill Mueller	.20
123	Robb Nen	.20
124	Jay Buhner	.20
125	Ken Griffey Jr.	3.50
126	Edgar Martinez	.20
127	Shane Monahan	.20
128	Alex Rodriguez	4.00
129	David Segui	.20
130	Rolando Arrojo **RC**	.75
131	Wade Boggs	3.00
132	Quinton McCracken	.20
133	Fred McGriff	.20
134	Bobby Smith	.20
135	Will Clark	.20
136	Juan Gonzalez	1.00
137	Rusty Greer	.20
138	Ivan Rodriguez	1.50
139	Aaron Sele	.20
140	John Wetteland	.20
141	Jose Canseco	1.00
142	Roger Clemens	3.50
143	Carlos Delgado	1.25
144	Shawn Green	.50

All-Stars

		NM/M
Complete Set (20):		110.00
Common Player:		1.50
Inserted 1:25		
1	Roberto Alomar	2.00
2	Cal Ripken Jr.	15.00
3	Kenny Lofton	1.50
4	Jim Thome	5.00
5	Derek Jeter	15.00
6	David Wells	1.50
7	Ken Griffey Jr.	10.00
8	Alex Rodriguez	12.00
9	Juan Gonzalez	4.00
10	Ivan Rodriguez	5.00
11	Gary Sheffield	2.50
12	Chipper Jones	7.50
13	Greg Maddux	7.50
14	Walt Weiss	1.50
15	Larry Walker	1.50
16	Craig Biggio	1.50
17	Mike Piazza	10.00
18	Mark McGwire	12.00
19	Tony Gwynn	7.50
20	Barry Bonds	15.00

Cramer's Choice Awards

		NM/M
Complete Set (10):		65.00
Common Player:		4.00
Inserted 1:Box		
1	Cal Ripken Jr.	15.00
2	Ken Griffey Jr.	9.00
3	Alex Rodriguez	12.00
4	Juan Gonzalez	5.00
5	Travis Lee	4.00
6	Chipper Jones	7.50
7	Greg Maddux	7.50
8	Kerry Wood	5.00
9	Mark McGwire	12.00
10	Tony Gwynn	7.50

Diamond Knights

		NM/M
Complete Set (25):		20.00
Common Player:		.35
Inserted 1:1		
1	Andres Galarraga	.35
2	Chipper Jones	1.00
3	Greg Maddux	1.00
4	Cal Ripken Jr.	2.50
5	Nomar Garciaparra	1.50
6	Mo Vaughn	.35
7	Kerry Wood	.45
8	Frank Thomas	.75
9	Vinny Castilla	.35
10	Jeff Bagwell	.75
11	Craig Biggio	.35
12	Paul Molitor	.75
13	Mike Piazza	1.50
14	Orlando Hernandez	.35
15	Derek Jeter	2.50
16	Ricky Ledee	.35
17	Mark McGwire	2.00
18	Tony Gwynn	1.00
19	Barry Bonds	2.50
20	Ken Griffey Jr.	1.75
21	Alex Rodriguez	2.00
22	Wade Boggs	1.00
23	Juan Gonzalez	.45
24	Ivan Rodriguez	.65
25	Jose Canseco	.50

Firestone on Baseball

		NM/M
Complete Set (26):		50.00
Common Player:		.35
Firestone Auto. Card:		18.00
Inserted 1:12		
1	Travis Lee	.35
2	Chipper Jones	3.00
3	Greg Maddux	3.00
4	Cal Ripken Jr.	6.00
5	Nomar Garciaparra	3.00
6	Mo Vaughn	.35
7	Kerry Wood	1.00
8	Frank Thomas	2.25
9	Manny Ramirez	2.25
10	Larry Walker	.35
11	Gary Sheffield	1.00
12	Paul Molitor	2.25
13	Hideo Nomo	1.50
14	Mike Piazza	3.50
15	Ben Grieve	.35
16	Mark McGwire	5.00
17	Tony Gwynn	3.00
18	Barry Bonds	6.00
19	Ken Griffey Jr.	4.00
20	Randy Johnson	2.25
21	Alex Rodriguez	5.00
22	Wade Boggs	3.00
23	Juan Gonzalez	1.50
24	Ivan Rodriguez	1.75
25	Roger Clemens	3.50
26	Roy Firestone	.35

Home Run Fever

		NM/M
Complete Set (10):		30.00
Common Player:		1.50
Inserted 1:73		
1	Andres Galarraga	1.50
2	Sammy Sosa	4.50
3	Albert Belle	1.50
4	Jim Thome	3.00
5	Mark McGwire	7.50
6	Greg Vaughn	1.50
7	Ken Griffey Jr.	6.00
8	Alex Rodriguez	7.50
9	Juan Gonzalez	2.50
10	Jose Canseco	2.50

Pillars of the Game

		NM/M
Complete Set (25):		20.00
Common Player:		.35
Inserted 1:1		
1	Jim Edmonds	.35
2	Travis Lee	.35
3	Chipper Jones	1.00
4	Tom Glavine, John Smoltz, Greg Maddux	1.00
5	Cal Ripken Jr.	2.50
6	Nomar Garciaparra	1.00
7	Mo Vaughn	.35
8	Sammy Sosa	1.00
9	Kerry Wood	.40
10	Frank Thomas	.75
11	Jim Thome	.65
12	Larry Walker	.35
13	Moises Alou	.35
14	Raul Mondesi	.35
15	Mike Piazza	1.25
16	Hideki Irabu	.35
17	Bernie Williams	.35
18	Ben Grieve	.35
19	Scott Rolen	.65
20	Mark McGwire	2.00
21	Tony Gwynn	1.00
22	Ken Griffey Jr.	1.50
23	Alex Rodriguez	2.00
24	Juan Gonzalez	.40
25	Roger Clemens	1.25

1998 Pacific Invincible

		NM/M
Complete Set (150):		60.00
Common Player:		.20
Silvers:		4X
Inserted 2:37		
Platinum Blues:		6X
Inserted 1:73		
Pack (5):		1.25
Wax Box (36):		32.50
1	Garret Anderson	.20
2	Jim Edmonds	.20
3	Darin Erstad	.35
4	Chuck Finley	.20
5	Tim Salmon	.35
6	Roberto Alomar	.35
7	Brady Anderson	.20
8	Geronimo Berroa	.20
9	Eric Davis	.20
10	Mike Mussina	.50
11	Rafael Palmeiro	1.00
12	Cal Ripken Jr.	6.00
13	Steve Avery	.20
14	Nomar Garciaparra	2.50
15	John Valentin	.20
16	Mo Vaughn	.20
17	Albert Belle	.20
18	Ozzie Guillen	.20
19	Norberto Martin	.20
20	Frank Thomas	1.50
21	Robin Ventura	.20
22	Sandy Alomar Jr.	.20
23	David Justice	.20
24	Kenny Lofton	.20
25	Manny Ramirez	1.50
26	Jim Thome	1.00
27	Omar Vizquel	.20
28	Matt Williams	.20
29	Jaret Wright	.20
30	Raul Casanova	.20
31	Tony Clark	.20
32	Deivi Cruz	.20
33	Bobby Higginson	.20
34	Justin Thompson	.20
35	Yamil Benitez	.20
36	Johnny Damon	.35
37	Jermaine Dye	.20
38	Jed Hansen	.20
39	Larry Sutton	.20
40	Jeromy Burnitz	.20
41	Jeff Cirillo	.20
42	Dave Nilsson	.20
43	Jose Valentin	.20
44	Fernando Vina	.20
45	Marty Cordova	.20
46	Chuck Knoblauch	.20
47	Paul Molitor	1.50
48	Brad Radke	.20
49	Terry Steinbach	.20
50	Wade Boggs	2.50
51	Hideki Irabu	.20
52	Derek Jeter	6.00
53	Tino Martinez	.20
54	Andy Pettitte	.30
55	Mariano Rivera	.30
56	Bernie Williams	.20
57	Jose Canseco	.75
58	Jason Giambi	.75
59	Ben Grieve	.20
60	Aaron Small	.20
61	Jay Buhner	.20
62	Ken Cloude	.20
63	Joey Cora	.20
64	Ken Griffey Jr.	3.50
65	Randy Johnson	1.50
66	Edgar Martinez	.20
67	Alex Rodriguez	5.00
68	Will Clark	.20
69	Juan Gonzalez	.75
70	Rusty Greer	.20
71	Ivan Rodriguez	1.00
72	Joe Carter	.20
73	Roger Clemens	3.00
74	Jose Cruz Jr.	.20
75	Carlos Delgado	.75
76	Andruw Jones	1.50
77	Chipper Jones	2.50
78	Ryan Klesko	.20
79	Javier Lopez	.20
80	Greg Maddux	2.50
81	Miguel Batista	.20
82	Jeremi Gonzalez	.20
83	Mark Grace	.20
84	Kevin Orie	.20
85	Sammy Sosa	2.50
86	Barry Larkin	.20
87	Deion Sanders	.20
88	Reggie Sanders	.20
89	Chris Stynes	.20
90	Dante Bichette	.20
91	Vinny Castilla	.20
92	Andres Galarraga	.20
93	Neifi Perez	.20
94	Larry Walker	.20
95	Moises Alou	.20
96	Bobby Bonilla	.20
97	Kevin Brown	.20
98	Craig Counsell	.20
99	Livan Hernandez	.20
100	Edgar Renteria	.20
101	Gary Sheffield	.60
102	Jeff Bagwell	1.50
103	Craig Biggio	.20
104	Luis Gonzalez	.20
105	Darryl Kile	.20
106	Wilton Guerrero	.20
107	Eric Karros	.20
108	Ramon Martinez	.20
109	Raul Mondesi	.20
110	Hideo Nomo	.75
111	Chan Ho Park	.20
112	Mike Piazza	3.00
113	Mark Grudzielanek	.20
114	Vladimir Guerrero	1.50
115	Pedro Martinez	1.50
116	Henry Rodriguez	.20
117	David Segui	.20
118	Edgardo Alfonzo	.20
119	Carlos Baerga	.20
120	John Franco	.20
121	John Olerud	.20
122	Rey Ordonez	.20
123	Ricky Bottalico	.20
124	Gregg Jefferies	.20
125	Mickey Morandini	.20
126	Scott Rolen	1.00
127	Curt Schilling	.45
128	Jose Guillen	.20
129	Esteban Loaiza	.20
130	Al Martin	.20
131	Tony Womack	.20
132	Dennis Eckersley	1.00
133	Gary Gaetti	.20
134	Curtis King	.20
135	Ray Lankford	.20
136	Mark McGwire	5.00
137	Ken Caminiti	.20
138	Steve Finley	.20
139	Tony Gwynn	2.50
140	Carlos Hernandez	.20
141	Wally Joyner	.20
142	Barry Bonds	6.00
143	Jacob Cruz	.20
144	Shawn Estes	.20
145	Stan Javier	.20
146	J.T. Snow	.20
147	Nomar Garciaparra (ROY)	1.00
148	Scott Rolen (ROY)	.60
149	Ken Griffey Jr. (MVP)	1.75
150	Larry Walker (MVP)	.20

Cramer's Choice

		NM/M
Complete Green Set (10):		200.00
Common Green (99 Sets):		10.00
Dark Blues (80 Sets):		1X
Light Blues (50 Sets):		1.5X
Reds (25 Sets):		2X
Golds (25 Sets):		3X
Purples (10 Sets):		5X
1	Greg Maddux	20.00
2	Roberto Alomar	10.00

3	Cal Ripken Jr.	40.00
4	Nomar Garciaparra	20.00
5	Larry Walker	10.00
6	Mike Piazza	22.50
7	Mark McGwire	30.00
8	Tony Gwynn	20.00
9	Ken Griffey Jr.	25.00
10	Roger Clemens	22.50

Gems of the Diamond

		NM/M
Complete Set (220):		20.00
Common Player:		.10
1	Jim Edmonds	.10
2	Todd Greene	.10
3	Ken Hill	.10
4	Mike Holtz	.10
5	Mike James	.10
6	Chad Kreuter	.10
7	Tim Salmon	.10
8	Roberto Alomar	.20
9	Brady Anderson	.10
10	David Dellucci	.10
11	Jeffrey Hammonds	.10
12	Mike Mussina	.40
13	Rafael Palmeiro	.65
14	Arthur Rhodes	.10
15	Cal Ripken Jr.	2.50
16	Nerio Rodriguez	.10
17	Tony Tarasco	.10
18	Lenny Webster	.10
19	Mike Benjamin	.10
20	Rich Garces	.10
21	Nomar Garciaparra	1.00
22	Shane Mack	.10
23	Jose Malave	.10
24	Jesus Tavarez	.10
25	Mo Vaughn	.10
26	John Wasdin	.10
27	Jeff Abbott	.10
28	Albert Belle	.10
29	Mike Cameron	.10
30	Al Levine	.10
31	Robert Machado	.10
32	Greg Norton	.10
33	Magglio Ordonez	.20
34	Mike Sirotka	.10
35	Frank Thomas	.75
36	Mario Valdez	.10
37	Sandy Alomar Jr.	.10
38	David Justice	.10
39	Jack McDowell	.10
40	Eric Plunk	.10
41	Manny Ramirez	.75
42	Kevin Seitzer	.10
43	Paul Shuey	.10
44	Omar Vizquel	.10
45	Kimera Bartee	.10
46	Glenn Dishman	.10
47	Orlando Miller	.10
48	Mike Myers	.10
49	Phil Nevin	.10
50	A.J. Sager	.10
51	Ricky Bones	.10
52	Scott Cooper	.10
53	Shane Halter	.10
54	David Howard	.10

55	Glendon Rusch	.10
56	Joe Vitiello	.10
57	Jeff D'Amico	.10
58	Mike Fetters	.10
59	Mike Matheny	.10
60	Jose Mercedes	.10
61	Ron Villone	.10
62	Jack Voigt	.10
63	Brent Brede	.10
64	Chuck Knoblauch	.10
65	Paul Molitor	.75
66	Todd Ritchie	.10
67	Frankie Rodriguez	.10
68	Scott Stahoviak	.10
69	Greg Swindell	.10
70	Todd Walker	.10
71	Wade Boggs	1.00
72	Hideki Irabu	.10
73	Derek Jeter	2.50
74	Pat Kelly	.10
75	Graeme Lloyd	.10
76	Tino Martinez	.10
77	Jeff Nelson	.10
78	Scott Pose	.10
79	Mike Stanton	.10
80	Darryl Strawberry	.10
81	Bernie Williams	.10
82	Tony Batista	.10
83	Mark Bellhorn	.10
84	Ben Grieve	.10
85	Pat Lennon	.10
86	Brian Lesher	.10
87	Miguel Tejada	.20
88	George Williams	.10
89	Joey Cora	.10
90	Rob Ducey	.10
91	Ken Griffey Jr.	1.50
92	Randy Johnson	.75
93	Edgar Martinez	.10
94	John Marzano	.10
95	Greg McCarthy	.10
96	Alex Rodriguez	2.00
97	Andy Sheets	.10
98	Mike Timlin	.10
99	Lee Tinsley	.10
100	Damon Buford	.10
101	Alex Diaz	.10
102	Benji Gil	.10
103	Juan Gonzalez	.40
104	Eric Gunderson	.10
105	Danny Patterson	.10
106	Ivan Rodriguez	.65
107	Mike Simms	.10
108	Luis Andujar	.10
109	Joe Carter	.10
110	Roger Clemens	1.25
111	Jose Cruz Jr.	.10
112	Shawn Green	.30
113	Robert Perez	.10
114	Juan Samuel	.10
115	Ed Sprague	.10
116	Shannon Stewart	.10
117	Danny Bautista	.10
118	Chipper Jones	1.00
119	Ryan Klesko	.10
120	Keith Lockhart	.10
121	Javier Lopez	.10
122	Greg Maddux	1.00
123	Kevin Millwood	.10
124	Mike Mordecai	.10
125	Eddie Perez	.10
126	Randall Simon	.10
127	Miguel Cairo	.10
128	Dave Clark	.10
129	Kevin Foster	.10
130	Mark Grace	.10
131	Tyler Houston	.10
132	Mike Hubbard	.10
133	Kevin Orie	.10
134	Ryne Sandberg	1.00
135	Sammy Sosa	1.00
136	Lenny Harris	.10
137	Kent Mercker	.10
138	Mike Morgan	.10
139	Deion Sanders	.10
140	Chris Stynes	.10
141	Gabe White	.10
142	Jason Bates	.10
143	Vinny Castilla	.10
144	Andres Galarraga	.10
145	Curtis Leskanic	.10
146	Jeff McCurry	.10
147	Mike Munoz	.10
148	Larry Walker	.10
149	Jamey Wright	.10
150	Moises Alou	.10
151	Bobby Bonilla	.10
152	Kevin Brown	.10
153	John Cangelosi	.10
154	Jeff Conine	.10
155	Cliff Floyd	.10
156	Jay Powell	.10
157	Edgar Renteria	.10
158	Tony Saunders	.10
159	Gary Sheffield	.40
160	Jeff Bagwell	.75
161	Tim Bogar	.10
162	Tony Eusebio	.10
163	Chris Holt	.10
164	Ray Montgomery	.10
165	Luis Rivera	.10
166	Eric Anthony	.10
167	Brett Butler	.10
168	Juan Castro	.10
169	Tripp Cromer	.10

170	Raul Mondesi	.10
171	Hideo Nomo	.40
172	Mike Piazza	1.25
173	Tom Prince	.10
174	Adam Riggs	.10
175	Shane Andrews	.10
176	Shayne Bennett	.10
177	Raul Chavez	.10
178	Pedro Martinez	.75
179	Sherman Obando	.10
180	Andy Stankiewicz	.10
181	Alberto Castillo	.10
182	Shawn Gilbert	.10
183	Luis Lopez	.10
184	Roberto Petagine	.10
185	Armando Reynoso	.10
186	Midre Cummings	.10
187	Kevin Jordan	.10
188	Desi Relaford	.10
189	Scott Rolen	.65
190	Ken Ryan	.10
191	Kevin Sefcik	.10
192	Emil Brown	.10
193	Lou Collier	.10
194	Francisco Cordova	.10
195	Kevin Elster	.10
196	Mark Smith	.10
197	Marc Wilkins	.10
198	Manny Aybar	.10
199	Jose Bautista	.10
200	David Bell	.10
201	Rigo Beltran	.10
202	Delino DeShields	.10
203	Dennis Eckersley	.65
204	John Mabry	.10
205	Eli Marrero	.10
206	Willie McGee	.10
207	Mark McGwire	2.00
208	Ken Caminiti	.10
209	Tony Gwynn	1.00
210	Chris Jones	.10
211	Craig Shipley	.10
212	Pete Smith	.10
213	Jorge Velandia	.10
214	Dario Veras	.10
215	Rich Aurilia	.10
216	Damon Berryhill	.10
217	Barry Bonds	2.50
218	Osvaldo Fernandez	.10
219	Dante Powell	.10
220	Rich Rodriguez	.10

Interleague Players

Complete Set (30):		120.00
Common Player:		1.50
Inserted 1:73		
1A	Roberto Alomar	2.50
1N	Craig Biggio	1.50
2A	Cal Ripken Jr.	12.00
2N	Chipper Jones	6.00
3A	Nomar Garciaparra	6.00
3N	Scott Rolen	3.50
4A	Mo Vaughn	1.50
4N	Andres Galarraga	1.50
5A	Frank Thomas	4.50
5N	Tony Gwynn	6.00
6A	Albert Belle	1.50
6N	Barry Bonds	12.00
7A	Hideki Irabu	1.50
7N	Hideo Nomo	2.50
8A	Derek Jeter	12.00
8N	Rey Ordonez	1.50
9A	Tino Martinez	1.50
9N	Mark McGwire	10.00
10A	Alex Rodriguez	10.00
10N	Edgar Renteria	1.50
11A	Ken Griffey Jr.	7.50
11N	Larry Walker	1.50
12A	Randy Johnson	4.50
12N	Greg Maddux	6.00
13A	Ivan Rodriguez	3.50
13N	Mike Piazza	6.50
14A	Roger Clemens	6.50
14N	Pedro Martinez	3.50
15A	Jose Cruz Jr.	1.50
15N	Wilton Guerrero	1.50

Moments in Time

		NM/M
Complete Set (20):		100.00
Common Player:		3.00
Inserted 1:145		
1	Chipper Jones	10.00
2	Cal Ripken Jr.	17.50
3	Frank Thomas	7.50
4	David Justice	3.00
5	Andres Galarraga	3.00
6	Larry Walker	3.00
7	Livan Hernandez	3.00
8	Wilton Guerrero	3.00
9	Hideo Nomo	4.50
10	Mike Piazza	12.00
11	Pedro Martinez	7.50
12	Bernie Williams	3.00
13	Ben Grieve	3.00
14	Scott Rolen	6.00
15	Mark McGwire	15.00
16	Tony Gwynn	10.00
17	Ken Griffey Jr.	13.50
18	Alex Rodriguez	15.00
19	Juan Gonzalez	4.50
20	Jose Cruz Jr.	3.00

Photoengravings

		NM/M
Complete Set (18):		50.00
Common Player:		1.00
Inserted 1:37		
1	Greg Maddux	3.50
2	Cal Ripken Jr.	7.50
3	Nomar Garciaparra	3.50
4	Frank Thomas	2.50
5	Larry Walker	1.00
6	Mike Piazza	4.00
7	Hideo Nomo	2.00
8	Pedro Martinez	2.50
9	Derek Jeter	7.50
10	Tino Martinez	1.00
11	Mark McGwire	6.00
12	Tony Gwynn	3.50
13	Barry Bonds	7.50
14	Ken Griffey Jr.	5.00
15	Alex Rodriguez	6.00
16	Ivan Rodriguez	2.25
17	Roger Clemens	4.00
18	Jose Cruz Jr.	1.00

Team Checklists

		NM/M
Complete Set (30):		60.00
Common Player:		1.00
Inserted 2:37		
1	Jim Edmonds, Tim Salmon, Darin Erstad, Garret Anderson, Rickey Henderson Anaheim Angels	2.50
2	Greg Maddux, Chipper Jones, Javy Lopez, Ryan Klesko, Andruw Jones Atlanta Braves	3.00

3	Cal Ripken Jr., Roberto Alomar, Brady Anderson, Mike Mussina, Rafael Palmeiro Baltimore Orioles	6.00
4	Nomar Garciaparra, Mo Vaughn, Steve Avery, John Valentin Boston Red Sox	3.00
5	Sammy Sosa, Mark Grace, Ryne Sandberg, Jeremi Gonzalez Chicago Cubs	3.00
6	Frank Thomas, Albert Belle, Robin Ventura, Ozzie Guillen Chicago White Sox	2.50
7	Barry Larkin, Deion Sanders, Reggie Sanders, Brett Tomko Cincinnati Reds	1.00
8	Sandy Alomar Jr., Manny Ramirez, David Justice, Jim Thome, Omar Vizquel Cleveland Indians	2.50
9	Andres Galarraga, Larry Walker, Vinny Castilla, Dante Bichette, Ellis Burks Colorado Rockies	1.00
10	Jason Thompson, Tony Clark, Deivi Cruz, Bobby Higginson Detroit Tigers	1.00
11	Gary Sheffield, Edgar Renteria, Livan Hernandez, Charles Johnson, Bobby Bonilla Florida Marlins	1.00
12	Jeff Bagwell, Craig Biggio, Richard Hidalgo, Darryl Kile Houston Astros	2.50
13	Johnny Damon, Jermaine Dye, Chili Davis, Jose Rosado Kansas City Royals	1.00
14	Mike Piazza, Wilton Guerrero, Raul Mondesi, Hideo Nomo, Ramon Martinez Los Angeles Dodgers	4.00
15	David Nilsson, Fernando Vina, Jeromy Burnitz, Julio Franco, Jeff Cirillo Milwaukee Brewers	1.00
16	Paul Molitor, Chuck Knoblauch, Brad Radke, Terry Steinbach, Marty Cordova Minnesota Twins	2.50
17	Henry Rodriguez, Vladimir Guerrero, Pedro Martinez, David Segui, Mark Grudzielanek Montreal Expos	2.50
18	Carlos Baerga, Todd Hundley, Rey Ordonez, John Olerud, Edgardo Alfonzo New York Mets	1.00
19	Derek Jeter, Tino Martinez, Bernie Williams, Andy Pettitte, Mariano Rivera New York Yankees	6.00
20	Jose Canseco, Ben Grieve, Jason Giambi, Matt Stairs Oakland Athletics	1.75
21	Curt Schilling, Scott Rolen, Gregg Jefferies, Lenny Dykstra, Ricky Bottalico Philadelphia Phillies	1.75
22	Al Martin, Tony Womack, Jose Guillen, Esteban Loiaza Pittsburgh Pirates	1.00
23	Mark McGwire, Dennis Eckersley, Delino DeShields, Willie McGee, Ray Lankford St. Louis Cardinals	4.50
24	Tony Gwynn, Ken Caminiti, Wally Joyner, Steve Finley San Diego Padres	3.00
25	Barry Bonds, J.T. Snow, Stan Javier, Rod Beck, Jose Vizcaino San Francisco Giants	6.00
26	Ken Griffey Jr., Alex Rodriguez, Edgar Martinez, Randy Johnson, Jay Buhner Seattle Mariners	4.50
27	Juan Gonzalez, Ivan Rodriguez, Will Clark, John Wetteland, Rusty Greer T exas Rangers	2.00
28	Jose Cruz Jr., Roger Clemens, Pat Hentgen, Joe Carter Toronto Blue Jays	4.00
29	Yamil Benitez, Devon White, Matt Williams, Jay Bell Arizona Diamondbacks	1.00
30	Wade Boggs, Paul Sorrento, Fred McGriff, Roberto Hernandez Tampa Bay Devil Rays	3.00

1998 Pacific Omega

		NM/M
Complete Set (250):		25.00
Common Player:		.10
Reds:		4X
Pack (6):		1.00
Wax Box (36):		15.00
1	Garret Anderson	.10
2	Gary DiSarcina	.10
3	Jim Edmonds	.10
4	Darin Erstad	.20
5	Cecil Fielder	.10
6	Chuck Finley	.10
7	Shigetosi Hasegawa	.10
8	Tim Salmon	.10
9	Brian Anderson	.10
10	Jay Bell	.10
11	Andy Benes	.10
12	Yamil Benitez	.10
13	Jorge Fabregas	.10
14	Travis Lee	.10
15	Devon White	.10
16	Matt Williams	.10
17	Andres Galarraga	.10
18	Tom Glavine	.35
19	Andruw Jones	.75
20	Chipper Jones	1.00
21	Ryan Klesko	.10
22	Javy Lopez	.10
23	Greg Maddux	1.00
24	Kevin Millwood **RC**	.50
25	Denny Neagle	.10
26	John Smoltz	.10
27	Roberto Alomar	.20
28	Brady Anderson	.10
29	Joe Carter	.10
30	Eric Davis	.10
31	Jimmy Key	.10
32	Mike Mussina	.40
33	Rafael Palmeiro	.65
34	Cal Ripken Jr.	2.50
35	B.J. Surhoff	.10
36	Dennis Eckersley	.65
37	Nomar Garciaparra	1.00
38	Reggie Jefferson	.10
39	Derek Lowe	.10
40	Pedro Martinez	.75
41	Brian Rose	.10
42	John Valentin	.10
43	Jason Varitek	.10
44	Mo Vaughn	.10
45	Jeff Blauser	.10
46	Jeremi Gonzalez	.10
47	Mark Grace	.65
48	Lance Johnson	.10
49	Kevin Orie	.10
50	Henry Rodriguez	.10
51	Sammy Sosa	1.00
52	Kerry Wood	.35
53	Albert Belle	.10
54	Mike Cameron	.10
55	Mike Caruso	.10
56	Ray Durham	.10
57	Jaime Navarro	.10
58	Greg Norton	.10
59	Magglio Ordonez **RC**	1.50
60	Frank Thomas	.75
61	Robin Ventura	.10
62	Bret Boone	.10
63	Willie Greene	.10
64	Barry Larkin	.10
65	Jon Nunnally	.10
66	Eduardo Perez	.10
67	Reggie Sanders	.10
68	Brett Tomko	.10
69	Sandy Alomar Jr.	.10
70	Travis Fryman	.10
71	David Justice	.10
72	Kenny Lofton	.10
73	Charles Nagy	.10
74	Manny Ramirez	.75
75	Jim Thome	.65
76	Omar Vizquel	.10
77	Enrique Wilson	.10
78	Jaret Wright	.10
79	Dante Bichette	.10
80	Ellis Burks	.10
81	Vinny Castilla	.10
82	Todd Helton	.75
83	Darryl Kile	.10
84	Mike Lansing	.10
85	Neifi Perez	.10
86	Larry Walker	.65
87	Raul Casanova	.10
88	Tony Clark	.10
89	Luis Gonzalez	.10
90	Bobby Higginson	.10
91	Brian Hunter	.10
92	Bip Roberts	.10
93	Justin Thompson	.10
94	Josh Booty	.10
95	Craig Counsell	.10
96	Livan Hernandez	.10
97	Ryan Jackson **RC**	.10
98	Mark Kotsay	.10
99	Derrek Lee	.50
100	Mike Piazza	1.25
101	Edgar Renteria	.10
102	Cliff Floyd	.10
103	Moises Alou	.10
104	Jeff Bagwell	.75
105	Derrick Bell	.10
106	Sean Berry	.10
107	Craig Biggio	.10
108	John Halama **RC**	.15
109	Richard Hidalgo	.10

110	Shane Reynolds	.10
111	Tim Belcher	.10
112	Brian Bevil	.10
113	Jeff Conine	.10
114	Johnny Damon	.25
115	Jeff King	.10
116	Jeff Montgomery	.10
117	Dean Palmer	.10
118	Terry Pendleton	.10
119	Bobby Bonilla	.10
120	Wilton Guerrero	.10
121	Todd Hollandsworth	.10
122	Charles Johnson	.10
123	Eric Karros	.10
124	Paul Konerko	.20
125	Ramon Martinez	.10
126	Raul Mondesi	.10
127	Hideo Nomo	.40
128	Gary Sheffield	.45
129	Ismael Valdes	.10
130	Jeromy Burnitz	.10
131	Jeff Cirillo	.10
132	Todd Dunn	.10
133	Marquis Grissom	.10
134	John Jaha	.10
135	Scott Karl	.10
136	Dave Nilsson	.10
137	Jose Valentin	.10
138	Fernando Vina	.10
139	Rick Aguilera	.10
140	Marty Cordova	.10
141	Pat Meares	.10
142	Paul Molitor	.75
143	David Ortiz	.50
144	Brad Radke	.10
145	Terry Steinbach	.10
146	Todd Walker	.10
147	Shane Andrews	.10
148	Brad Fullmer	.10
149	Mark Grudzielanek	.10
150	Vladimir Guerrero	.75
151	F.P. Santangelo	.10
152	Jose Vidro	.10
153	Rondell White	.10
154	Carlos Baerga	.10
155	Bernard Gilkey	.10
156	Todd Hundley	.10
157	Butch Huskey	.10
158	Bobby Jones	.10
159	Brian McRae	.10
160	John Olerud	.10
161	Rey Ordonez	.10
162	Masato Yoshii **RC**	.25
163	David Cone	.10
164	Hideki Irabu	.10
165	Derek Jeter	2.50
166	Chuck Knoblauch	.10
167	Tino Martinez	.10
168	Paul O'Neill	.10
169	Andy Pettitte	.30
170	Mariano Rivera	.15
171	Darryl Strawberry	.10
172	David Wells	.10
173	Bernie Williams	.10
174	Ryan Christenson **RC**	.10
175	Jason Giambi	.60
176	Ben Grieve	.10
177	Rickey Henderson	.75
178	A.J. Hinch	.10
179	Kenny Rogers	.10
180	Ricky Bottalico	.10
181	Rico Brogna	.10
182	Doug Glanville	.10
183	Gregg Jefferies	.10
184	Mike Lieberthal	.10
185	Scott Rolen	.65
186	Curt Schilling	.35
187	Jermaine Allensworth	.10
188	Lou Collier	.10
189	Jose Guillen	.10
190	Jason Kendall	.10
191	Al Martin	.10
192	Tony Womack	.10
193	Kevin Young	.10
194	Royce Clayton	.10
195	Delino DeShields	.10
196	Gary Gaetti	.10
197	Ron Gant	.10
198	Brian Jordan	.10
199	Ray Lankford	.10
200	Mark McGwire	2.00
201	Todd Stottlemyre	.10
202	Kevin Brown	.10
203	Ken Caminiti	.10
204	Steve Finley	.10
205	Tony Gwynn	1.00
206	Carlos Hernandez	.10
207	Wally Joyner	.10
208	Greg Vaughn	.10
209	Barry Bonds	2.50
210	Shawn Estes	.10
211	Orel Hershiser	.10
212	Stan Javier	.10
213	Jeff Kent	.10
214	Bill Mueller	.10
215	Robb Nen	.10
216	J.T. Snow	.10
217	Jay Buhner	.10
218	Ken Cloude	.10
219	Joey Cora	.10
220	Ken Griffey Jr.	1.50
221	Glenallen Hill	.10
222	Randy Johnson	.75
223	Edgar Martinez	.10
224	Jamie Moyer	.10
225	Alex Rodriguez	2.00

226	David Segui	.10
227	Dan Wilson	.10
228	Rolando Arrojo **RC**	.25
229	Wade Boggs	1.00
230	Miguel Cairo	.10
231	Roberto Hernandez	.10
232	Quinton McCracken	.10
233	Fred McGriff	.10
234	Paul Sorrento	.10
235	Kevin Stocker	.10
236	Will Clark	.10
237	Juan Gonzalez	.40
238	Rusty Greer	.10
239	Rick Helling	.10
240	Roberto Kelly	.10
241	Ivan Rodriguez	.65
242	Aaron Sele	.10
243	John Wetteland	.10
244	Jose Canseco	.50
245	Roger Clemens	1.25
246	Jose Cruz Jr.	.10
247	Carlos Delgado	.50
248	Alex Gonzalez	.10
249	Ed Sprague	.10
250	Shannon Stewart	.10

Online

		NM/M
Complete Set (36):		35.00
Common Player:		.45
Inserted 1:9		
1	Cal Ripken Jr.	5.00
2	Nomar Garciaparra	2.00
3	Pedro Martinez	1.50
4	Mo Vaughn	.45
5	Frank Thomas	1.50
6	Sandy Alomar Jr.	.45
7	Manny Ramirez	1.50
8	Jaret Wright	.45
9	Paul Molitor	1.50
10	Derek Jeter	5.00
11	Bernie Williams	.45
12	Ben Grieve	.45
13	Ken Griffey Jr.	3.00
14	Edgar Martinez	.45
15	Alex Rodriguez	4.00
16	Wade Boggs	2.00
17	Juan Gonzalez	.75
18	Ivan Rodriguez	1.00
19	Roger Clemens	2.50
20	Travis Lee	.45
21	Matt Williams	.45
22	Andres Galarraga	.45
23	Chipper Jones	2.00
24	Greg Maddux	2.00
25	Sammy Sosa	2.00
26	Kerry Wood	.75
27	Barry Larkin	.45
28	Larry Walker	.45
29	Derrek Lee	1.00
30	Jeff Bagwell	1.50
31	Hideo Nomo	.75
32	Mike Piazza	2.50
33	Scott Rolen	1.00
34	Mark McGwire	4.00
35	Tony Gwynn	2.00
36	Barry Bonds	5.00

Face to Face

		NM/M
Complete Set (10):		50.00
Common Player:		2.00
Inserted 1:145		
1	Alex Rodriguez,	
	Nomar Garciaparra	9.00
2	Mark McGwire,	
	Ken Griffey Jr.	9.00

3	Mike Piazza,	
	Sandy Alomar Jr.	6.00
4	Kerry Wood,	
	Roger Clemens	6.00
5	Cal Ripken Jr., Paul Molitor	10.00
6	Tony Gwynn, Wade Boggs	5.00
7	Frank Thomas,	
	Chipper Jones	5.00
8	Travis Lee, Ben Grieve	2.00
9	Hideo Nomo, Hideki Irabu	3.50
10	Juan Gonzalez,	
	Manny Ramirez	3.50

EO Portraits

MARK McGWIRE St. Louis

		NM/M
Complete Set (20):		70.00
Common Player:		1.25
Inserted 1:73		
1	Cal Ripken Jr.	10.00
2	Nomar Garciaparra	5.00
3	Mo Vaughn	1.25
4	Frank Thomas	4.00
5	Manny Ramirez	4.00
6	Ben Grieve	1.25
7	Ken Griffey Jr.	6.50
8	Alex Rodriguez	7.50
9	Juan Gonzalez	2.00
10	Ivan Rodriguez	3.50
11	Travis Lee	1.25
12	Greg Maddux	5.00
13	Chipper Jones	5.00
14	Kerry Wood	2.00
15	Larry Walker	1.25
16	Jeff Bagwell	4.00
17	Mike Piazza	6.00
18	Mark McGwire	7.50
19	Tony Gwynn	5.00
20	Barry Bonds	10.00

Prism

MIKE PIAZZA

		NM/M
Complete Set (20):		30.00
Common Player:		.75
Inserted 1:37		
1	Cal Ripken Jr.	4.50
2	Nomar Garciaparra	2.50
3	Pedro Martinez	1.50
4	Frank Thomas	1.50
5	Manny Ramirez	1.50
6	Brian Giles	.75
7	Derek Jeter	4.50
8	Ben Grieve	.75
9	Ken Griffey Jr.	3.00
10	Alex Rodriguez	3.50
11	Juan Gonzalez	1.00
12	Travis Lee	.75
13	Chipper Jones	2.50
14	Greg Maddux	2.50
15	Kerry Wood	1.00
16	Larry Walker	.75
17	Hideo Nomo	3.00
18	Mike Piazza	3.00
19	Mark McGwire	3.50
20	Tony Gwynn	2.50

Rising Stars

ROLANDO ARROJO MIGUEL CAIRO ...CARLOS...

	NM/M
Complete Set (30):	15.00
Common Player:	.50
Inserted 1:9	
Tier 1 (# to 100):	3X
Tier 2 (# to 75):	4X
Tier 3 (# to 50):	5X
Tier 4 (# to 25):	10X
Tier 5 (1 of 1):	Value Undetermined

1 Nerio Rodriguez,
  Sidney Ponson .50
2 Frank Catalanotto,
  Roberto Duran, Sean Runyan .50
3 Kevin L. Brown,
  Carlos Almanzar .50
4 Aaron Boone, Pat Watkins,
  Scott Winchester .50
5 Brian Meadows, Andy Larkin,
  Antonio Alfonseca .50
6 DaRond Stovall, Trey Moore,
  Shayne Bennett .50
7 Felix Martinez, Larry Sutton,
  Brian Bevil .50
8 Homer Bush, Mike Buddie .50
9 Rich Butler, Esteban Yan .50
10 Damon Hollins,
  Brian Edmondson .50
11 Lou Collier, Jose Silva,
  Javier Martinez .50
12 Steve Sinclair,
  Mark Dalesandro .50
13 Jason Varitek, Brian Rose,
  Brian Shouse .50
14 Mike Caruso, Jeff Abbott,
  Tom Fordham .50
15 Jason Johnson,
  Bobby Smith .50
16 Dave Berg, Mark Kotsay,
  Jesus Sanchez .50
17 Richard Hidalgo, John Halama,
  Trever Miller .50
18 Geoff Jenkins, Bobby Hughes,
  Steve Woodard .50
19 Eli Marrero, Cliff Politte,
  Mike Busby .50
20 Desi Relaford,
  Darrin Winston .50
21 Todd Helton,
  Bobby Jones 1.50
22 Rolando Arrojo, Miguel Cairo,
  Dan Carlson .50
23 David Ortiz, Javier Valentin,
  Eric Milton 1.25
24 Magglio Ordonez,
  Greg Norton 1.00
25 Brad Fullmer, Javier Vazquez,
  Rick DeHart .50
26 Paul Konerko, Matt Luke 1.00
27 Derrek Lee, Ryan Jackson,
  John Roskos 1.25
28 Ben Grieve, A.J. Hinch,
  Ryan Christenson .50
29 Travis Lee, Karim Garcia,
  David Dellucci .65
30 Kerry Wood, Marc Pisciotta 1.00

1998 Pacific Online

	NM/M
Complete Set (800):	60.00
Common Player:	.50
Web Stars/RC's:	2X
Inserted 1:1	
Pack (9):	.75
Wax Box (36):	20.00

1 Garret Anderson .05
2 Rich DeLucia RC .05
3 Jason Dickson .05
4 Gary DiSarcina .05
5 Jim Edmonds .05
6 Darin Erstad .15
7 Cecil Fielder .05
8 Chuck Finley .05
9 Carlos Garcia .05
10 Shigetosi Hasegawa .05
11 Ken Hill .05
12 Dave Hollins .05
13 Mike Holtz .05
14 Mike James .05
15 Norberto Martin .05
16 Damon Mashore .05
17 Jack McDowell .05
18 Phil Nevin .05
19 Omar Olivares .05
20 Troy Percival .05
21 Rich Robertson .05
22 Tim Salmon .05
23 Craig Shipley .05
24 Matt Walbeck .05
25 Allen Watson .05
26 Jim Edmonds
  (Angels Checklist) .05
27 Brian Anderson .05
28 Tony Batista .05
29 Jay Bell .05
30 Andy Benes .05
31 Yamil Benitez .05
32 Willie Blair .05
33 Brent Brede .05
34 Scott Brow .05
35 Omar Daal .05
36 David Dellucci .05
37 Edwin Diaz .05
38 Jorge Fabregas .05
39 Andy Fox .05
40 Karim Garcia .05
41a Travis Lee/Btg .05
41b Travis Lee/Fldg .05
42 Barry Manuel .05
43 Gregg Olson .05
44 Felix Rodriguez .05
45 Clint Sodowsky .05
46 Russ Springer .05
47 Andy Stankiewicz .05
48 Kelly Stinnett .05
49 Jeff Suppan .05
50 Devon White .05
51 Matt Williams .05
52 Travis Lee
  (Diamondbacks Checklist) .05
53 Danny Bautista .05
54 Rafael Belliard .05
55 Adam Butler RC .10
56 Mike Cather .05
57 Brian Edmondson .05
58 Alan Embree .05
59 Andres Galarraga .05
60 Tom Glavine .35
61 Tony Graffanino .05
62 Andruw Jones .65
63a Chipper Jones/Btg .75
63b Chipper Jones/Fldg .75
64 Ryan Klesko .05
65 Keith Lockhart .05
66 Javy Lopez .05
67a Greg Maddux/Btg .75
67b Greg Maddux/Pitching .75
68 Dennis Martinez .05
69 Kevin Millwood RC .50
70 Denny Neagle .05
71 Eddie Perez .05
72 Curtis Pride .05
73 John Smoltz .05
74 Michael Tucker .05
75 Walt Weiss .05
76 Gerald Williams .05
77 Mark Wohlers .05
78 Chipper Jones
  (Braves Checklist) .40
79 Roberto Alomar .15
80 Brady Anderson .05
81 Harold Baines .05
82 Armando Benitez .05
83 Mike Bordick .05
84 Joe Carter .05
85 Norm Charlton .05
86 Eric Davis .05
87 Doug Drabek .05
88 Scott Erickson .05
89 Jeffrey Hammonds .05
90 Chris Hoiles .05
91 Scott Kamieniecki .05
92 Jimmy Key .05
93 Terry Mathews .05
94 Alan Mills .05
95 Mike Mussina .25
96 Jesse Orosco .05
97 Rafael Palmeiro .60
98 Sidney Ponson .05
99 Jeff Reboulet .05
100 Arthur Rhodes .05
101a Cal Ripken Jr./Btg 2.00
101b Cal Ripken Jr./Btg
  (Close-up.) 2.00
102 Nerio Rodriguez .05
103 B.J. Surhoff .05
104 Lenny Webster .05
105 Cal Ripken Jr.
  (Orioles Checklist) 1.00
106 Steve Avery .05
107 Mike Benjamin .05
108 Darren Bragg .05
109 Damon Buford .05
110 Jim Corsi .05
111 Dennis Eckersley .60
112 Rich Garces .05
113a Nomar Garciaparra/Btg .75
113b Nomar Garciaparra/Fldg .75
114 Tom Gordon .05
115 Scott Hatteberg .05
116 Butch Henry .05
117 Reggie Jefferson .05
118 Mark Lemke .05
119 Darren Lewis .05
120 Jim Leyritz .05
121 Derek Lowe .05
122 Pedro Martinez .65
123 Troy O'Leary .05
124 Brian Rose .05
125 Bret Saberhagen .05
126 Donnie Sadler .05
127 Brian Shouse .05
128 John Valentin .05
129 Jason Varitek .05
130 Mo Vaughn .05
131 Tim Wakefield .05
132 John Wasdin .05
133 Nomar Garciaparra
  (Red Sox Checklist) .45
134 Terry Adams .05
135 Manny Alexander .05
136 Rod Beck .05
137 Jeff Blauser .05
138 Brant Brown .05
139 Mark Clark .05
140 Jeremi Gonzalez .05
141 Mark Grace .05
142 Jose Hernandez .05
143 Tyler Houston .05
144 Lance Johnson .05
145 Sandy Martinez .05
146 Matt Mieske .05
147 Mickey Morandini .05
148 Terry Mulholland .05
149 Kevin Orie .05
150 Bob Patterson .05
151 Marc Pisciotta .05
152 Henry Rodriguez .05
153 Scott Servais .05
154 Sammy Sosa .75
155 Kevin Tapani .05
156 Steve Trachsel .05
157a Kerry Wood/Pitching .30
157b Kerry Wood/Pitching
  (Close-up.) .30
158 Kerry Wood
  (Cubs Checklist) .20
159 Jeff Abbott .05
160 James Baldwin .05
161 Albert Belle .05
162 Jason Bere .05
163 Mike Cameron .05
164 Mike Caruso .05
165 Carlos Castillo .05
166 Tony Castillo .05
167 Ray Durham .05
168 Scott Eyre .05
169 Tom Fordham .05
170 Keith Foulke .05
171 Lou Frazier .05
172 Matt Karchner .05
173 Chad Kreuter .05
174 Jaime Navarro .05
175 Greg Norton .05
176 Charlie O'Brien .05
177 Magglio Ordonez .15
178 Ruben Sierra .05
179 Bill Simas .05
180 Mike Sirotka .05
181 Chris Snopek .05
182a Frank Thomas
  (In batter's box.) .65
182b Frank Thomas/Swinging .05
183 Robin Ventura .05
184 Frank Thomas
  (White Sox Checklist) .40
185 Stan Belinda .05
186 Aaron Boone .05
187 Bret Boone .05
188 Brook Fordyce .05
189 Willie Greene .05
190 Pete Harnisch .05
191 Lenny Harris .05
192 Mark Hutton .05
193 Damian Jackson .05
194 Ricardo Jordan .05
195 Barry Larkin .05
196 Eduardo Perez .05
197 Pokey Reese .05
198 Mike Remlinger .05
199 Reggie Sanders .05
200 Jeff Shaw .05
201 Chris Stynes .05
202 Scott Sullivan .05
203 Eddie Taubensee .05
204 Brett Tomko .05
205 Pat Watkins .05
206 David Weathers .05
207 Gabe White .05
208 Scott Winchester .05
209 Barry Larkin (Reds Checklist) .05
210 Sandy Alomar Jr. .05
211 Paul Assenmacher .05
212 Geronimo Berroa .05
213 Pat Borders .05
214 Jeff Branson .05
215 Dave Burba .05
216 Bartolo Colon .05
217 Shawon Dunston .05
218 Travis Fryman .05
219 Brian Giles .05
220 Dwight Gooden .05
221 Mike Jackson .05
222 David Justice .05
223 Kenny Lofton .05
224 Jose Mesa .05
225 Alvin Morman .05
226 Charles Nagy .05
227 Chad Ogea .05
228 Eric Plunk .05
229 Manny Ramirez .65
230 Paul Shuey .05
231 Jim Thome .65
232 Ron Villone .05
233 Omar Vizquel .05
234 Enrique Wilson .05
235 Jaret Wright .05
236 Manny Ramirez
  (Indians Checklist) .40
237 Pedro Astacio .05
238 Jason Bates .05
239 Dante Bichette .05
240 Ellis Burks .05
241 Vinny Castilla .05
242 Greg Colbrunn .05
243 Mike DeJean .05
244 Jerry Dipoto .05
245 Curtis Goodwin .05
246 Todd Helton .65
247 Bobby Jones .05
248 Darryl Kile .05
249 Mike Lansing .05
250 Curtis Leskanic .05
251 Nelson Liriano .05
252 Kirt Manwaring .05
253 Chuck McElroy .05
254 Mike Munoz .05
255 Neifi Perez .05
256 Jeff Reed .05
257 Mark Thompson .05
258 John Vander Wal .05
259 Dave Veres .05
260a Larry Walker/Btg .05
260b Larry Walker/Btg (Close-up.) .05
261 Jamey Wright .05
262 Larry Walker
  (Rockies Checklist) .05
263 Kimera Bartee .05
264 Doug Brocail .05
265 Raul Casanova .05
266 Frank Castillo .05
267 Frank Catalanotto .05
268 Tony Clark .05
269 Deivi Cruz .05
270 Roberto Duran .05
271 Damion Easley .05
272 Bryce Florie .05
273 Luis Gonzalez .05
274 Bob Higginson .05
275 Brian Hunter .05
276 Todd Jones .05
277 Greg Keagle .05
278 Jeff Manto .05
279 Brian Moehler .05
280 Joe Oliver .05
281 Joe Randa .05
282 Billy Ripken .05
283 Bip Roberts .05
284 Sean Runyan .05
285 A.J. Sager .05
286 Justin Thompson .05
287 Tony Clark
  (Tigers Checklist) .05
288 Antonio Alfonseca .05
289 Dave Berg .05
290 Josh Booty .05
291 John Cangelosi .05
292 Craig Counsell .05
293 Vic Darensbourg .05
294 Cliff Floyd .05
295 Oscar Henriquez .05
296 Felix Heredia .05
297 Ryan Jackson RC .05
298 Mark Kotsay .05
299 Andy Larkin .05
300 Derrek Lee .60
301 Brian Meadows .05
302 Rafael Medina .05
303 Jay Powell .05
304 Edgar Renteria .05
305 Jesus Sanchez RC .05
306 Rob Stanifer .05
307 Gregg Zaun .05
308 Derrek Lee
  (Marlins Checklist) .30
309 Moises Alou .05
310 Brad Ausmus .05
311a Jeff Bagwell/Btg .65
311b Jeff Bagwell/Fldg .65
312 Derek Bell .05
313 Sean Bergman .05
314 Sean Berry .05
315 Craig Biggio .05
316 Tim Bogar .05
317 Jose Cabrera .05
318 Dave Clark .05
319 Tony Eusebio .05
320 Carl Everett .05
321 Ricky Gutierrez .05
322 John Halama .05
323 Mike Hampton .05
324 Doug Henry .05
325 Richard Hidalgo .05
326 Jack Howell .05
327 Jose Lima .05
328 Mike Magnante .05
329 Trever Miller .05
330 C.J. Nitkowski .05
331 Shane Reynolds .05
332 Bill Spiers .05
333 Billy Wagner .05
334 Jeff Bagwell
  (Astros Checklist) .40
335 Tim Belcher .05
336 Brian Bevil .05
337 Johnny Damon .35
338 Jermaine Dye .05

339 Sal Fasano .05
340 Shane Halter .05
341 Chris Haney .05
342 Jed Hansen .05
343 Jeff King .05
344 Jeff Montgomery .05
345 Hal Morris .05
346 Jose Offerman .05
347 Dean Palmer .05
348 Terry Pendleton .05
349 Hipolito Pichardo .05
350 Jim Pittsley .05
351 Pat Rapp .05
352 Jose Rosado .05
353 Glendon Rusch .05
354 Scott Service .05
355 Larry Sutton .05
356 Mike Sweeney .05
357 Joe Vitiello .05
358 Matt Whisenant .05
359 Ernie Young .05
360 Jeff King (Royals Checklist) .05
361 Bobby Bonilla .05
362 Jim Bruske .05
363 Juan Castro .05
364 Roger Cedeno .05
365 Mike Devereaux .05
366 Darren Dreifort .05
367 Jim Eisenreich .05
368 Wilton Guerrero .05
369 Mark Guthrie .05
370 Darren Hall .05
371 Todd Hollandsworth .05
372 Thomas Howard .05
373 Trenidad Hubbard .05
374 Charles Johnson .05
375 Eric Karros .05
376 Paul Konerko .20
377 Matt Luke .05
378 Ramon Martinez .05
379 Raul Mondesi .05
380 Hideo Nomo .35
381 Antonio Osuna .05
382 Chan Ho Park .05
383 Tom Prince .05
384 Scott Radinsky .05
385 Gary Sheffield .40
386 Ismael Valdes .05
387 Jose Vizcaino .05
388 Eric Young .05
389 Gary Sheffield (Dodgers Checklist) .10
390 Jeromy Burnitz .05
391 Jeff Cirillo .05
392 Cal Eldred .05
393 Chad Fox .05
394 Marquis Grissom .05
395 Bob Hamelin .05
396 Bobby Hughes .05
397 Darrin Jackson .05
398 John Jaha .05
399 Geoff Jenkins .05
400 Doug Jones .05
401 Jeff Juden .05
402 Scott Karl .05
403 Jesse Levis .05
404 Mark Loretta .05
405 Mike Matheny .05
406 Jose Mercedes .05
407 Mike Myers .05
408 Marc Newfield .05
409 Dave Nilsson .05
410 Al Reyes .05
411 Jose Valentin .05
412 Fernando Vina .05
413 Paul Wagner .05
414 Bob Wickman .05
415 Steve Woodard .05
416 Marquis Grissom (Brewers Checklist) .05
417 Rick Aguilera .05
418 Ron Coomer .05
419 Marty Cordova .05
420 Brent Gates .05
421 Eddie Guardado .05
422 Denny Hocking .05
423 Matt Lawton .05
424 Pat Meares .05
425 Orlando Merced .05
426 Eric Milton .05
427 Paul Molitor .65
428 Mike Morgan .05
429 Dan Naulty .05
430 Otis Nixon .05
431 Alex Ochoa .05
432 David Ortiz .40
433 Brad Radke .05
434 Todd Ritchie .05
435 Frank Rodriguez .05
436 Terry Steinbach .05
437 Greg Swindell .05
438 Bob Tewksbury .05
439 Mike Trombley .05
440 Javier Valentin .05
441 Todd Walker .05
442 Paul Molitor (Twins Checklist) .40
443 Shane Andrews .05
444 Miguel Batista .05
445 Shayne Bennett .05
446 Rick DeHart .05
447 Brad Fullmer .05
448 Mark Grudzielanek .05
449 Vladimir Guerrero .65
450 Dustin Hermanson .05
451 Steve Kline .05
452 Scott Livingstone .05
453 Mike Maddux .05
454 Derrick May .05
455 Ryan McGuire .05
456 Trey Moore .05
457 Mike Mordecai .05
458 Carl Pavano .05
459 Carlos Perez .05
460 F.P. Santangelo .05
461 DaRond Stovall .05
462 Anthony Telford .05
463 Ugueth Urbina .05
464 Marc Valdes .05
465 Jose Vidro .05
466 Rondell White .05
467 Chris Widger .05
468 Vladimir Guerrero (Expos Checklist) .40
469 Edgardo Alfonzo .05
470 Carlos Baerga .05
471 Rich Becker .05
472 Brian Bohanon .05
473 Alberto Castillo .05
474 Dennis Cook .05
475 John Franco .05
476 Matt Franco .05
477 Bernard Gilkey .05
478 John Hudek .05
479 Butch Huskey .05
480 Bobby Jones .05
481 Al Leiter .05
482 Luis Lopez .05
483 Brian McRae .05
484 Dave Mlicki .05
485 John Olerud .05
486 Rey Ordonez .05
487 Craig Paquette .05
488a Mike Piazza/Btg 1.00
488b Mike Piazza/Btg (Close-up.) 1.00
489 Todd Pratt .05
490 Mel Rojas .05
491 Tim Spehr .05
492 Turk Wendell .05
493 Masato Yoshii **RC** .25
494 Mike Piazza (Mets Checklist) .45
495 Willie Banks .05
496 Scott Brosius .05
497 Mike Buddie .05
498 Homer Bush .05
499 David Cone .05
500 Chad Curtis .05
501 Chili Davis .05
502 Joe Girardi .05
503 Darren Holmes .05
504 Hideki Irabu .05
505a Derek Jeter/Btg 2.00
505b Derek Jeter/Fldg 2.00
506 Chuck Knoblauch .05
507 Graeme Lloyd .05
508 Tino Martinez .05
509 Ramiro Mendoza .05
510 Jeff Nelson .05
511 Paul O'Neill .05
512 Andy Pettitte .20
513 Jorge Posada .05
514 Tim Raines .05
515 Mariano Rivera .15
516 Luis Sojo .05
517 Mike Stanton .05
518 Darryl Strawberry .05
519 Dale Sveum .05
520 David Wells .05
521 Bernie Williams .05
522 Bernie Williams (Yankees Checklist) .05
523 Kurt Abbott .05
524 Mike Blowers .05
525 Rafael Bournigal .05
526 Tom Candiotti .05
527 Ryan Christenson .05
528 Mike Fetters .05
529 Jason Giambi .50
530a Ben Grieve/Btg .05
530b Ben Grieve/Running .05
531 Buddy Groom .05
532 Jimmy Haynes .05
533 Rickey Henderson .65
534 A.J. Hinch .05
535 Mike Macfarlane .05
536 Dave Magadan .05
537 T.J. Mathews .05
538 Jason McDonald .05
539 Kevin Mitchell .05
540 Mike Mohler .05
541 Mike Oquist .05
542 Ariel Prieto .05
543 Kenny Rogers .05
544 Aaron Small .05
545 Scott Spiezio .05
546 Matt Stairs .05
547 Bill Taylor .05
548 Dave Telgheder .05
549 Jack Voigt .05
550 Ben Grieve (A's Checklist) .05
551 Bob Abreu .10
552 Ruben Amaro .05
553 Alex Arias .05
554 Matt Beech .05
555 Ricky Bottalico .05
556 Billy Brewer .05
557 Rico Brogna .05
558 Doug Glanville .05
559 Wayne Gomes .05
560 Mike Grace .05
561 Tyler Green .05
562 Rex Hudler .05
563 Gregg Jefferies .05
564 Kevin Jordan .05
565 Mark Leiter .05
566 Mark Lewis .05
567 Mike Lieberthal .05
568 Mark Parent .05
569 Yorkis Perez .05
570 Desi Relaford .05
571 Scott Rolen .50
572 Curt Schilling .35
573 Kevin Sefcik .05
574 Jerry Spradlin .05
575 Garrett Stephenson .05
576 Darrin Winston .05
577 Scott Rolen (Phillies Checklist) .20
578 Jermaine Allensworth .05
579 Jason Christiansen .05
580 Lou Collier .05
581 Francisco Cordova .05
582 Elmer Dessens .05
583 Freddy Garcia .05
584 Jose Guillen .05
585 Jason Kendall .05
586 Jon Lieber .05
587 Esteban Loaiza .05
588 Al Martin .05
589 Javier Martinez .05
590 Chris Peters **RC** .05
591 Kevin Polcovich .05
592 Ricardo Rincon .05
593 Jason Schmidt .05
594 Jose Silva .05
595 Mark Smith .05
596 Doug Strange .05
597 Turner Ward .05
598 Marc Wilkins .05
599 Mike Williams .05
600 Tony Womack .05
601 Kevin Young .05
602 Tony Womack (Pirates Checklist) .05
603 Manny Aybar .05
604 Kent Bottenfield .05
605 Jeff Brantley .05
606 Mike Busby .05
607 Royce Clayton .05
608 Delino DeShields .05
609 John Frascatore .05
610 Gary Gaetti .05
611 Ron Gant .05
612 David Howard .05
613 Brian Hunter .05
614 Brian Jordan .05
615 Tom Lampkin .05
616 Ray Lankford .05
617 Braden Looper .05
618 John Mabry .05
619 Eli Marrero .05
620 Willie McGee .05
621a Mark McGwire/Btg 1.50
621b Mark McGwire/Fldg 1.50
622 Kent Mercker .05
623 Matt Morris .05
624 Donovan Osborne .05
625 Tom Pagnozzi .05
626 Lance Painter .05
627 Mark Petkovsek .05
628 Todd Stottlemyre .05
629 Mark McGwire (Cardinals Checklist) .75
630 Andy Ashby .05
631 Brian Boehringer .05
632 Kevin Brown .05
633 Ken Caminiti .05
634 Steve Finley .05
635 Ed Giovanola .05
636 Chris Gomez .05
637a Tony Gwynn (Blue jersey.) .75
637b Tony Gwynn (White jersey.) .75
SAMPLE Tony Gwynn (SAMPLE overprint on back.) 1.00
638 Joey Hamilton .05
639 Carlos Hernandez .05
640 Sterling Hitchcock .05
641 Trevor Hoffman .05
642 Wally Joyner .05
643 Dan Miceli .05
644 James Mouton .05
645 Greg Myers .05
646 Carlos Reyes .05
647 Andy Sheets .05
648 Pete Smith .05
649 Mark Sweeney .05
650 Greg Vaughn .05
651 Quilvio Veras .05
652 Tony Gwynn (Padres Checklist) .40
653 Rich Aurilia .05
654 Marvin Benard .05
655a Barry Bonds/Btg 2.00
655b Barry Bonds/Btg (Close-up.) 2.00
656 Danny Darwin .05
657 Shawn Estes .05
658 Mark Gardner .05
659 Darryl Hamilton .05
660 Charlie Hayes .05
661 Orel Hershiser .05
662 Stan Javier .05
663 Brian Johnson .05
664 John Johnstone .05
665 Jeff Kent .05
666 Brent Mayne .05
667 Bill Mueller .05
668 Robb Nen .05
669 Jim Poole .05
670 Steve Reed .05
671 Rich Rodriguez .05
672 Kirk Rueter .05
673 Rey Sanchez .05
674 J.T. Snow .05
675 Julian Tavarez .05
676 Barry Bonds (Giants Checklist) 1.00
677 Rich Amaral .05
678 Bobby Ayala .05
679 Jay Buhner .05
680 Ken Cloude .05
681 Joey Cora .05
682 Russ Davis .05
683 Rob Ducey .05
684 Jeff Fassero .05
685 Tony Fossas .05
686a Ken Griffey Jr./Btg 1.25
686b Ken Griffey Jr./Fldg 1.25
687 Glenallen Hill .05
688 Jeff Huson .05
689 Randy Johnson .65
690 Edgar Martinez .05
691 John Marzano .05
692 Jamie Moyer .05
693a Alex Rodriguez/Btg 1.50
693b Alex Rodriguez/Fldg 1.50
694 David Segui .05
695 Heathcliff Slocumb .05
696 Paul Spoljaric .05
697 Bill Swift .05
698 Mike Timlin .05
699 Bob Wells .05
700 Dan Wilson .05
701 Ken Griffey Jr. (Mariners Checklist) .50
702 Wilson Alvarez .05
703 Rolando Arrojo **RC** .30
704a Wade Boggs/Btg .75
704b Wade Boggs/Fldg .75
705 Rich Butler .05
706 Miguel Cairo .05
707 Mike Difelice .05
708 John Flaherty .05
709 Roberto Hernandez .05
710 Mike Kelly .05
711 Aaron Ledesma .05
712 Albie Lopez .05
713 Dave Martinez .05
714 Quinton McCracken .05
715 Fred McGriff .05
716 Jim Mecir .05
717 Tony Saunders .05
718 Bobby Smith .05
719 Paul Sorrento .05
720 Dennis Springer .05
721 Kevin Stocker .05
722 Ramon Tatis .05
723 Bubba Trammell .05
724 Esteban Yan .05
725 Wade Boggs (Devil Rays Checklist) .40
726 Luis Alicea .05
727 Scott Bailes .05
728 John Burkett .05
729 Domingo Cedeno .05
730 Will Clark .05
731 Kevin Elster .05
732a Juan Gonzalez/Bat .35
732b Juan Gonzalez (No bat.) .35
733 Tom Goodwin .05
734 Rusty Greer .05
735 Eric Gunderson .05
736 Bill Haselman .05
737 Rick Helling .05
738 Roberto Kelly .05
739 Mark McLemore .05
740 Darren Oliver .05
741 Danny Patterson .05
742 Roger Pavlik .05
743a Ivan Rodriguez/Btg .60
743b Ivan Rodriguez/Fldg .60
744 Aaron Sele .05
745 Mike Simms .05
746 Lee Stevens .05
747 Fernando Tatis .05
748 John Wetteland .05
749 Bobby Witt .05
750 Juan Gonzalez (Rangers Checklist) .20
751 Carlos Almanzar .05
752 Kevin Brown .05
753 Jose Canseco .40
754 Chris Carpenter .05
755 Roger Clemens 1.00
756 Felipe Crespo .05
757 Jose Cruz Jr. .05
758 Mark Dalesandro .05
759 Carlos Delgado .50
760 Kelvim Escobar .05
761 Tony Fernandez .05
762 Darrin Fletcher .05
763 Alex Gonzalez .05
764 Craig Grebeck .05
765 Shawn Green .35
766 Juan Guzman .05
767 Erik Hanson .05
768 Pat Hentgen .05
769 Randy Myers .05
770 Robert Person .05
771 Dan Plesac .05

772	Paul Quantrill	.05
773	Bill Risley	.05
774	Juan Samuel	.05
775	Steve Sinclair	.05
776	Ed Sprague	.05
777	Mike Stanley	.05
778	Shannon Stewart	.05
779	Woody Williams	.05
780	Roger Clemens (Blue Jays Checklist)	.45

1998 Pacific Online Web Cards

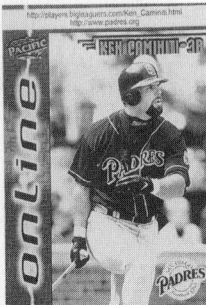

Web Stars/RC's:	2X
Inserted 1:1	

(See 1998 Pacific Online for checklist and base card values.)

1998 Pacific Paramount

	NM/M
Complete Set (250):	20.00
Common Player:	.10
Gold (1:1R):	1X
Copper (1:1H):	1X
Red (1:1 ANCO):	2X
Platinum Blue (1:73):	4X
Holographic Silver:	20X
Production 99 Sets	
Pack (6):	1.00
Wax Box (36):	15.00

1	Garret Anderson	.10
2	Gary DiSarcina	.10
3	Jim Edmonds	.10
4	Darin Erstad	.20
5	Cecil Fielder	.10
6	Chuck Finley	.10
7	Todd Greene	.10
8	Shigetosi Hasegawa	.10
9	Tim Salmon	.10
10	Roberto Alomar	.20
11	Brady Anderson	.10
12	Joe Carter	.10
13	Eric Davis	.10
14	Ozzie Guillen	.10
15	Mike Mussina	.40
16	Rafael Palmeiro	.65
17	Cal Ripken Jr.	2.50
18	B.J. Surhoff	.10
19	Steve Avery	.10
20	Nomar Garciaparra	1.00
21	Reggie Jefferson	.10
22	Pedro Martinez	.75
23	Tim Naehring	.10
24	John Valentin	.10
25	Mo Vaughn	.40
26	James Baldwin	.10
27	Albert Belle	.10
28	Ray Durham	.10
29	Benji Gil	.10
30	Jaime Navarro	.10
31	Magglio Ordonez RC	1.50
32	Frank Thomas	.75
33	Robin Ventura	.10
34	Sandy Alomar Jr.	.10
35	Geronimo Berroa	.10
36	Travis Fryman	.10

37	David Justice	.10
38	Kenny Lofton	.10
39	Charles Nagy	.10
40	Manny Ramirez	.75
41	Jim Thome	.65
42	Omar Vizquel	.10
43	Jaret Wright	.10
44	Raul Casanova	.10
45	Frank Catalanotto RC	.20
46	Tony Clark	.10
47	Bobby Higginson	.10
48	Brian Hunter	.10
49	Todd Jones	.10
50	Bip Roberts	.10
51	Justin Thompson	.10
52	Kevin Appier	.10
53	Johnny Damon	.35
54	Jermaine Dye	.10
55	Jeff King	.10
56	Jeff Montgomery	.10
57	Dean Palmer	.10
58	Jose Rosado	.10
59	Larry Sutton	.10
60	Rick Aguilera	.10
61	Marty Cordova	.10
62	Pat Meares	.10
63	Paul Molitor	.75
64	Otis Nixon	.10
65	Brad Radke	.10
66	Terry Steinbach	.10
67	Todd Walker	.10
68	Hideki Irabu	.10
69	Derek Jeter	2.50
70	Chuck Knoblauch	.10
71	Tino Martinez	.10
72	Paul O'Neill	.10
73	Andy Pettitte	.20
74	Mariano Rivera	.15
75	Bernie Williams	.10
76	Mark Bellhorn	.10
77	Tom Candiotti	.10
78	Jason Giambi	.50
79	Ben Grieve	.10
80	Rickey Henderson	.75
81	Jason McDonald	.10
82	Aaron Small	.10
83	Miguel Tejada	.20
84	Jay Buhner	.10
85	Joey Cora	.10
86	Jeff Fassero	.10
87	Ken Griffey Jr.	1.50
88	Randy Johnson	.75
89	Edgar Martinez	.10
90	Alex Rodriguez	2.00
91	David Segui	.10
92	Dan Wilson	.10
93	Wilson Alvarez	.10
94	Wade Boggs	1.00
95	Miguel Cairo	.10
96	John Flaherty	.10
97	Dave Martinez	.10
98	Quinton McCracken	.10
99	Fred McGriff	.10
100	Paul Sorrento	.10
101	Kevin Stocker	.10
102	John Burkett	.10
103	Will Clark	.10
104	Juan Gonzalez	.40
105	Rusty Greer	.10
106	Roberto Kelly	.10
107	Ivan Rodriguez	.65
108	Fernando Tatis	.10
109	John Wetteland	.10
110	Jose Canseco	.40
111	Roger Clemens	1.25
112	Jose Cruz Jr.	.10
113	Carlos Delgado	.50
114	Alex Gonzalez	.10
115	Pat Hentgen	.10
116	Ed Sprague	.10
117	Shannon Stewart	.10
118	Brian Anderson	.10
119	Jay Bell	.10
120	Andy Benes	.10
121	Yamil Benitez	.10
122	Jorge Fabregas	.10
123	Travis Lee	.10
124	Devon White	.10
125	Matt Williams	.10
126	Bob Wolcott	.10
127	Andres Galarraga	.10
128	Tom Glavine	.35
129	Andruw Jones	.75
130	Chipper Jones	1.00
131	Ryan Klesko	.10
132	Javy Lopez	.10
133	Greg Maddux	1.00
134	Denny Neagle	.10
135	John Smoltz	.10
136	Rod Beck	.10
137	Jeff Blauser	.10
138	Mark Grace	.10
139	Lance Johnson	.10
140	Mickey Morandini	.10
141	Kevin Orie	.10
142	Sammy Sosa	1.00
143	Aaron Boone	.10
144	Bret Boone	.10
145	Dave Burba	.10
146	Lenny Harris	.10
147	Barry Larkin	.10
148	Reggie Sanders	.10
149	Brett Tomko	.10
150	Pedro Astacio	.10
151	Dante Bichette	.10

152	Ellis Burks	.10
153	Vinny Castilla	.10
154	Todd Helton	.75
155	Darryl Kile	.10
156	Jeff Reed	.10
157	Larry Walker	.10
158	Bobby Bonilla	.10
159	Todd Dunwoody	.10
160	Livan Hernandez	.10
161	Charles Johnson	.10
162	Mark Kotsay	.10
163	Derrek Lee	.60
164	Edgar Renteria	.10
165	Gary Sheffield	.50
166	Moises Alou	.10
167	Jeff Bagwell	.75
168	Derek Bell	.10
169	Craig Biggio	.10
170	Mike Hampton	.10
171	Richard Hidalgo	.10
172	Chris Holt	.10
173	Shane Reynolds	.10
174	Wilton Guerrero	.10
175	Eric Karros	.10
176	Paul Konerko	.20
177	Ramon Martinez	.10
178	Raul Mondesi	.10
179	Hideo Nomo	.40
180	Chan Ho Park	.10
181	Mike Piazza	1.25
182	Ismael Valdes	.10
183	Jeromy Burnitz	.10
184	Jeff Cirillo	.10
185	Todd Dunn	.10
186	Marquis Grissom	.10
187	John Jaha	.10
188	Doug Jones	.10
189	Dave Nilsson	.10
190	Jose Valentin	.10
191	Fernando Vina	.10
192	Orlando Cabrera	.10
193	Steve Falteisek	.10
194	Mark Grudzielanek	.10
195	Vladimir Guerrero	.75
196	Carlos Perez	.10
197	F.P. Santangelo	.10
198	Jose Vidro	.10
199	Rondell White	.10
200	Edgardo Alfonzo	.10
201	Carlos Baerga	.10
202	John Franco	.10
203	Bernard Gilkey	.10
204	Todd Hundley	.10
205	Butch Huskey	.10
206	Bobby Jones	.10
207	Brian McRae	.10
208	John Olerud	.10
209	Rey Ordonez	.10
210	Ricky Bottalico	.10
211	Bobby Estalella	.10
212	Doug Glanville	.10
213	Gregg Jefferies	.10
214	Mike Lieberthal	.10
215	Desi Relaford	.10
216	Scott Rolen	.65
217	Curt Schilling	.35
218	Adrian Brown	.10
219	Emil Brown	.10
220	Francisco Cordova	.10
221	Jose Guillen	.10
222	Al Martin	.10
223	Abraham Nunez	.10
224	Tony Womack	.10
225	Kevin Young	.10
226	Alan Benes	.10
227	Royce Clayton	.10
228	Gary Gaetti	.10
229	Ron Gant	.10
230	Brian Jordan	.10
231	Ray Lankford	.10
232	Mark McGwire	2.00
233	Todd Stottlemyre	.10
234	Kevin Brown	.10
235	Ken Caminiti	.10
236	Steve Finley	.10
237	Tony Gwynn	1.00
238	Wally Joyner	.10
239	Ruben Rivera	.10
240	Greg Vaughn	.10
241	Quilvio Veras	.10
242	Barry Bonds	2.50
243	Jacob Cruz	.10
244	Shawn Estes	.10
245	Orel Hershiser	.10
246	Stan Javier	.10
247	Brian Johnson	.10
248	Jeff Kent	.10
249	Robb Nen	.10
250	J.T. Snow	.10

Gold/Copper/Red

	NM/M
Common Gold/Copper Player:	.25
Gold/Copper Stars:	1X
Inserted 1:1	
Common Red Player:	.30
Red Stars:	2X

(See 1998 Pacific Paramount for checklist and base card values.)

Holographic Silver

	NM/M
Common Player:	1.00
Holographic Silver Stars:	20X

Production 99 Sets	

(See 1998 Pacific Paramount for checklist and base card values.)

Platinum Blue

	NM/M
Common Platinum Blue Player:	1.00
Platinum Blue Stars:	4X
Inserted 1:361	

(See 1998 Pacific Paramount for checklist and base card values.)

Cooperstown Bound

		NM/M
Complete Set (10):		60.00
Common Player:		8.00
Inserted 1:361		
Pacific Proofs:		6X
Production 20 Sets		
1	Greg Maddux	10.00
2	Cal Ripken Jr.	15.00
3	Frank Thomas	8.00
4	Mike Piazza	8.00
5	Paul Molitor	8.00
6	Mark McGwire	12.00
7	Tony Gwynn	8.00
8	Barry Bonds	15.00
9	Ken Griffey Jr.	10.00
10	Wade Boggs	8.00

Fielder's Choice

		NM/M
Complete Set (20):		45.00
Common Player:		.75
Inserted 1:73		
1	Chipper Jones	3.00
2	Greg Maddux	3.00
3	Cal Ripken Jr.	6.00
4	Nomar Garciaparra	3.00
5	Frank Thomas	2.50
6	David Justice	.75
7	Larry Walker	.75

8	Jeff Bagwell	2.50
9	Hideo Nomo	1.25
10	Mike Piazza	3.50
11	Derek Jeter	6.00
12	Ben Grieve	.75
13	Mark McGwire	4.50
14	Tony Gwynn	3.00
15	Barry Bonds	6.00
16	Ken Griffey Jr.	4.00
17	Alex Rodriguez	4.50
18	Wade Boggs	3.00
19	Ivan Rodriguez	2.00
20	Jose Cruz Jr.	.75

Inaugural Issue

NM/M

Common Player: 3.00
(Stars and rookies valued at 50-75X regular Paramount version.)

Special Delivery

NM/M

Complete Set (20):		30.00
Common Player:		.50
Inserted 1:37		
1	Chipper Jones	2.50
2	Greg Maddux	2.50
3	Cal Ripken Jr.	5.00
4	Nomar Garciaparra	2.50
5	Pedro Martinez	2.00
6	Frank Thomas	2.00
7	David Justice	.50
8	Larry Walker	.50
9	Jeff Bagwell	2.00
10	Hideo Nomo	1.00
11	Mike Piazza	3.00
12	Vladimir Guerrero	2.00
13	Derek Jeter	5.00
14	Ben Grieve	.50
15	Mark McGwire	4.00
16	Tony Gwynn	2.50
17	Barry Bonds	5.00
18	Ken Griffey Jr.	3.50
19	Alex Rodriguez	4.00
20	Jose Cruz Jr.	.50

Team Checklists

NM/M

Complete Set (30):		25.00
Common Player:		.25
Inserted 1:18		
1	Tim Salmon	.25
2	Cal Ripken Jr.	4.00

3	Nomar Garciaparra	1.50
4	Frank Thomas	1.00
5	Manny Ramirez	1.00
6	Tony Clark	.25
7	Dean Palmer	.25
8	Paul Molitor	1.00
9	Derek Jeter	4.00
10	Ben Grieve	.25
11	Ken Griffey Jr.	2.50
12	Wade Boggs	1.50
13	Ivan Rodriguez	.75
14	Roger Clemens	2.00
15	Matt Williams	.25
16	Chipper Jones	1.50
17	Sammy Sosa	1.50
18	Barry Larkin	.25
19	Larry Walker	.25
20	Livan Hernandez	.25
21	Jeff Bagwell	1.00
22	Mike Piazza	2.00
23	John Jaha	.25
24	Vladimir Guerrero	1.00
25	Todd Hundley	.25
26	Scott Rolen	.75
27	Kevin Young	.25
28	Mark McGwire	3.00
29	Tony Gwynn	1.50
30	Barry Bonds	4.00

1998 Pacific Revolution

NM/M

Complete Set (150):		65.00
Common Player:		.25
Pack (3):		1.00
Wax Box (24):		20.00
1	Garret Anderson	.25
2	Jim Edmonds	.25
3	Darin Erstad	.40
4	Chuck Finley	.25
5	Tim Salmon	.25
6	Jay Bell	.25
7	Travis Lee	.25
8	Devon White	.25
9	Matt Williams	.25
10	Andres Galarraga	.25
11	Tom Glavine	.45
12	Andruw Jones	2.50
13	Chipper Jones	3.50
14	Ryan Klesko	.25
15	Javy Lopez	.25
16	Greg Maddux	3.50
17	Walt Weiss	.25
18	Roberto Alomar	.40
19	Joe Carter	.25
20	Mike Mussina	1.25
21	Rafael Palmeiro	2.00
22	Cal Ripken Jr.	6.00
23	B.J. Surhoff	.25
24	Nomar Garciaparra	3.00
25	Reggie Jefferson	.25
26	Pedro Martinez	2.50
27	Troy O'Leary	.25
28	Mo Vaughn	.25
29	Mark Grace	.25
30	Mickey Morandini	.25
31	Henry Rodriguez	.25
32	Sammy Sosa	3.00
33	Kerry Wood	1.25
34	Albert Belle	.25
35	Ray Durham	.25
36	Magglio Ordonez **RC**	2.00
37	Frank Thomas	2.50
38	Robin Ventura	.25
39	Bret Boone	.25
40	Barry Larkin	.25
41	Reggie Sanders	.25
42	Brett Tomko	.25
43	Sandy Alomar	.25
44	David Justice	.25
45	Kenny Lofton	.25
46	Manny Ramirez	2.50
47	Jim Thome	2.00
48	Omar Vizquel	.25
49	Jaret Wright	.25
50	Dante Bichette	.25
51	Ellis Burks	.25
52	Vinny Castilla	.25
53	Todd Helton	2.50
54	Larry Walker	.25
55	Tony Clark	.25
56	Deivi Cruz	.25

57	Damion Easley	.25
58	Bobby Higginson	.25
59	Brian Hunter	.25
60	Cliff Floyd	.25
61	Livan Hernandez	.25
62	Derrek Lee	1.50
63	Edgar Renteria	.25
64	Moises Alou	.25
65	Jeff Bagwell	2.50
66	Derek Bell	.25
67	Craig Biggio	.25
68	Richard Hidalgo	.25
69	Johnny Damon	.40
70	Jeff King	.25
71	Hal Morris	.25
72	Dean Palmer	.25
73	Bobby Bonilla	.25
74	Charles Johnson	.25
75	Paul Konerko	.35
76	Raul Mondesi	.25
77	Gary Sheffield	.75
78	Jeromy Burnitz	.25
79	Marquis Grissom	.25
80	Dave Nilsson	.25
81	Fernando Vina	.25
82	Marty Cordova	.25
83	Pat Meares	.25
84	Paul Molitor	2.50
85	Brad Radke	.25
86	Terry Steinbach	.25
87	Todd Walker	.25
88	Brad Fullmer	.25
89	Vladimir Guerrero	2.50
90	Carl Pavano	.25
91	Rondell White	.25
92	Bernard Gilkey	.25
93	Hideo Nomo	1.25
94	John Olerud	.25
95	Rey Ordonez	.25
96	Mike Piazza	4.00
97	Masato Yoshii **RC**	.65
98	Hideki Irabu	.25
99	Derek Jeter	6.00
100	Chuck Knoblauch	.25
101	Tino Martinez	.25
102	Paul O'Neill	.25
103	Darryl Strawberry	.25
104	Bernie Williams	.25
105	Jason Giambi	1.50
106	Ben Grieve	.25
107	Rickey Henderson	2.50
108	Matt Stairs	.25
109	Doug Glanville	.25
110	Desi Relaford	.25
111	Scott Rolen	1.50
112	Curt Schilling	.45
113	Jason Kendall	.25
114	Al Martin	.25
115	Jason Schmidt	.25
116	Kevin Young	.25
117	Delino DeShields	.25
118	Gary Gaetti	.25
119	Brian Jordan	.25
120	Ray Lankford	.25
121	Mark McGwire	5.00
122	Kevin Brown	.25
123	Steve Finley	.25
124	Tony Gwynn	3.50
125	Wally Joyner	.25
126	Greg Vaughn	.25
127	Barry Bonds	6.00
128	Orel Hershiser	.25
129	Jeff Kent	.25
130	Bill Mueller	.25
131	Jay Buhner	.25
132	Ken Griffey Jr.	4.50
133	Randy Johnson	2.50
134	Edgar Martinez	.25
135	Alex Rodriguez	5.00
136	David Segui	.25
137	Rolando Arrojo **RC**	.75
138	Wade Boggs	3.50
139	Quinton McCracken	.25
140	Fred McGriff	.25
141	Will Clark	.25
142	Juan Gonzalez	1.25
143	Tom Goodwin	.25
144	Ivan Rodriguez	2.00
145	Aaron Sele	.25
146	John Wetteland	.25
147	Jose Canseco	.50
148	Roger Clemens	4.00
149	Jose Cruz Jr.	.25
150	Carlos Delgado	.65

Shadows

NM/M

Common Player:	2.00
Stars/Rookies:	6X

(See 1998 Pacific Revolution for checklist and base card values.)

Foul Pole

NM/M

Complete Set (20):		100.00
Common Player:		2.00
Inserted 1:49		
1	Cal Ripken Jr.	15.00
2	Nomar Garciaparra	7.50
3	Mo Vaughn	2.00
4	Frank Thomas	6.00
5	Manny Ramirez	6.00
6	Bernie Williams	2.00
7	Ben Grieve	2.00
8	Ken Griffey Jr.	10.00

9	Alex Rodriguez	12.00
10	Juan Gonzalez	3.00
11	Ivan Rodriguez	5.00
12	Travis Lee	2.00
13	Chipper Jones	7.50
14	Sammy Sosa	7.50
15	Vinny Castilla	2.00
16	Moises Alou	2.00
17	Gary Sheffield	3.00
18	Mike Piazza	9.00
19	Mark McGwire	12.00
20	Barry Bonds	15.00

Major League Icons

NM/M

Complete Set (10):		50.00
Common Player:		4.50
Inserted 1:121		
1	Cal Ripken Jr.	15.00
2	Nomar Garciaparra	7.50
3	Frank Thomas	6.00
4	Ken Griffey Jr.	10.00
5	Alex Rodriguez	12.50
6	Chipper Jones	7.50
7	Kerry Wood	4.50
8	Mike Piazza	9.00
9	Mark McGwire	12.50
10	Tony Gwynn	7.50

Prime Time Performers

NM/M

Complete Set (20):		25.00
Common Player:		.50
Inserted 1:25		
1	Cal Ripken Jr.	4.50
2	Nomar Garciaparra	2.00
3	Frank Thomas	1.50
4	Jim Thome	1.25
5	Hideki Irabu	.50
6	Derek Jeter	4.50
7	Ben Grieve	.50
8	Ken Griffey Jr.	3.00
9	Alex Rodriguez	3.50
10	Juan Gonzalez	.75
11	Ivan Rodriguez	1.25
12	Travis Lee	.50
13	Chipper Jones	2.00
14	Greg Maddux	2.00
15	Kerry Wood	.75
16	Larry Walker	.50
17	Jeff Bagwell	1.50
18	Mike Piazza	2.50

19	Mark McGwire	3.50
20	Tony Gwynn	2.00

Rookies and Hardball Heroes

		NM/M
Complete Set (30):		20.00
Common Player:		.25
Inserted 1:6		
Gold (1-20):		10X
Production 50 Sets		
1	Justin Baughman	.25
2	Jarrod Washburn	.25
3	Travis Lee	.25
4	Kerry Wood	.50
5	Magglio Ordonez	.50
6	Todd Helton	1.00
7	Derrek Lee	.25
8	Richard Hidalgo	.25
9	Mike Caruso	.25
10	David Ortiz	.75
11	Brad Fullmer	.25
12	Masato Yoshii	.25
13	Orlando Hernandez	.25
14	Ricky Ledee	.25
15	Ben Grieve	.25
16	Carlton Loewer	.25
17	Desi Relaford	.25
18	Ruben Rivera	.25
19	Rolando Arrojo	.25
20	Matt Perisho	.25
21	Chipper Jones	2.00
22	Greg Maddux	2.00
23	Cal Ripken Jr.	5.00
24	Nomar Garciaparra	2.00
25	Frank Thomas	1.00
26	Mark McGwire	4.00
27	Tony Gwynn	2.00
28	Ken Griffey Jr.	3.00
29	Alex Rodriguez	4.00
30	Juan Gonzalez	.50

Showstoppers

		NM/M
Complete Set (36):		30.00
Common Player:		.45
Inserted 1:12		
1	Cal Ripken Jr.	5.00
2	Nomar Garciaparra	2.50
3	Pedro Martinez	2.00
4	Mo Vaughn	.45
5	Frank Thomas	2.00
6	Manny Ramirez	2.00
7	Jim Thome	1.75
8	Jaret Wright	.45
9	Paul Molitor	2.00
10	Orlando Hernandez	.60
11	Derek Jeter	5.00
12	Bernie Williams	.45
13	Ben Grieve	.45
14	Ken Griffey Jr.	3.50
15	Alex Rodriguez	4.00
16	Wade Boggs	2.50
17	Juan Gonzalez	1.00
18	Ivan Rodriguez	1.75
19	Jose Canseco	.75
20	Roger Clemens	3.00
21	Travis Lee	.45
22	Andres Galarraga	.45
23	Chipper Jones	2.50
24	Greg Maddux	2.50
25	Sammy Sosa	2.50
26	Kerry Wood	.75
27	Vinny Castilla	.45
28	Larry Walker	.45
29	Moises Alou	.45
30	Raul Mondesi	.45
31	Gary Sheffield	.75
32	Hideo Nomo	1.00
33	Mike Piazza	3.00
34	Mark McGwire	4.00
35	Tony Gwynn	2.50
36	Barry Bonds	5.00

1999 Pacific

		NM/M
Complete Set (500):		30.00
Common Player:		.10
Platinum Blues (1:73):		15X
Reds (1:1R):		2.5X
Pack (10):		1.00
Wax Box (36):		35.00
1	Garret Anderson	.10
2	Jason Dickson	.10
3	Gary DiSarcina	.10
4	Jim Edmonds	.10
5	Darin Erstad	.25
6	Chuck Finley	.10
7	Shigetosi Hasegawa	.10
8	Ken Hill	.10
9	Dave Hollins	.10
10	Phil Nevin	.10
11	Troy Percival	.10
12a	Tim Salmon/Action	.10
12b	Tim Salmon/Portrait	.10
13	Brian Anderson	.10
14	Tony Batista	.10
15	Jay Bell	.10
16	Andy Benes	.10
17	Yamil Benitez	.10
18	Omar Daal	.10
19	David Dellucci	.10
20	Karim Garcia	.10
21	Bernard Gilkey	.10
22a	Travis Lee/Action	.10
22b	Travis Lee/Portrait	.10
23	Aaron Small	.10
24	Kelly Stinnett	.10
25	Devon White	.10
26	Matt Williams	.10
27a	Bruce Chen/Action	.10
27b	Bruce Chen/Portrait	.10
28a	Andres Galarraga/Action	.10
28b	Andres Galarraga/Portrait	.10
29	Tom Glavine	.35
30	Ozzie Guillen	.10
31	Andruw Jones	1.00
32a	Chipper Jones/Action	1.50
32b	Chipper Jones/Portrait	1.50
33	Ryan Klesko	.10
34	George Lombard	.10
35	Javy Lopez	.10
36a	Greg Maddux/Action	1.50
36b	Greg Maddux/Portrait	1.50
37a	Marty Malloy/Action	.10
37b	Marty Malloy/Portrait	.10
38	Dennis Martinez	.10
39	Kevin Millwood	.10
40a	Alex Rodriguez/Action	2.50
40b	Alex Rodriguez/Portrait	2.50
41	Denny Neagle	.10
42	John Smoltz	.10
43	Michael Tucker	.10
44	Walt Weiss	.10
45a	Roberto Alomar/Action	.25
45b	Roberto Alomar/Portrait	.25
46	Brady Anderson	.10
47	Harold Baines	.10
48	Mike Bordick	.10
49a	Danny Clyburn/Action	.10
49b	Danny Clyburn/Portrait	.10
50	Eric Davis	.10
51	Scott Erickson	.10
52	Chris Hoiles	.10
53	Jimmy Key	.10
54a	Ryan Minor/Action	.10
54b	Ryan Minor/Portrait	.10
55	Mike Mussina	.40
56	Jesse Orosco	.10
57a	Rafael Palmeiro/Action	.75
57b	Rafael Palmeiro/Portrait	.75
58	Sidney Ponson	.10
59	Arthur Rhodes	.10
60a	Cal Ripken Jr./Action	3.00
60b	Cal Ripken Jr./Portrait	3.00
61	B.J. Surhoff	.10
62	Steve Avery	.10
63	Darren Bragg	.10
64	Dennis Eckersley	.75
65a	Nomar Garciaparra/Action	1.50
65b	Nomar Garciaparra/Portrait	1.50
66a	Sammy Sosa/Action	1.50
66b	Sammy Sosa/Portrait	1.50
67	Tom Gordon	.10
68	Reggie Jefferson	.10
69	Darren Lewis	.10
70a	Mark McGwire/Action	2.50
70b	Mark McGwire/Portrait	2.50
71	Pedro Martinez	1.00
72	Troy O'Leary	.10
73	Bret Saberhagen	.10
74	Mike Stanley	.10
75	John Valentin	.10
76	Jason Varitek	.10
77	Mo Vaughn	.10
78	Tim Wakefield	.10
79	Manny Alexander	.10
80	Rod Beck	.10
81	Brant Brown	.10
82	Mark Clark	.10
83	Gary Gaetti	.10
84	Mark Grace	.10
85	Jose Hernandez	.10
86	Lance Johnson	.10
87a	Jason Maxwell/Action	.10
87b	Jason Maxwell/Portrait	.10
88	Mickey Morandini	.10
89	Terry Mulholland	.10
90	Henry Rodriguez	.10
91	Scott Servais	.10
92	Kevin Tapani	.10
93	Pedro Valdes	.10
94	Kerry Wood	.40
95	Jeff Abbott	.10
96	James Baldwin	.10
97	Albert Belle	.10
98	Mike Cameron	.10
99	Mike Caruso	.10
100	Wil Cordero	.10
101	Ray Durham	.10
102	Jaime Navarro	.10
103	Greg Norton	.10
104	Magglio Ordonez	.25
105	Mike Sirotka	.10
106a	Frank Thomas/Action	1.00
106b	Frank Thomas/Portrait	1.00
107	Robin Ventura	.10
108	Craig Wilson	.10
109	Aaron Boone	.10
110	Bret Boone	.10
111	Sean Casey	.15
112	Pete Harnisch	.10
113	John Hudek	.10
114	Barry Larkin	.10
115	Eduardo Perez	.10
116	Mike Remlinger	.10
117	Reggie Sanders	.10
118	Chris Stynes	.10
119	Eddie Taubensee	.10
120	Brett Tomko	.10
121	Pat Watkins	.10
122	Dmitri Young	.10
123	Sandy Alomar Jr.	.10
124	Dave Burba	.10
125	Bartolo Colon	.10
126	Joey Cora	.10
127	Brian Giles	.10
128	Dwight Gooden	.10
129	Mike Jackson	.10
130	David Justice	.10
131	Kenny Lofton	.10
132	Charles Nagy	.10
133	Chad Ogea	.10
134a	Manny Ramirez/Action	1.00
134b	Manny Ramirez/Portrait	1.00
135	Richie Sexson	.10
136a	Jim Thome/Action	.75
136b	Jim Thome/Portrait	.75
137	Omar Vizquel	.10
138	Jaret Wright	.10
139	Pedro Astacio	.10
140	Jason Bates	.10
141a	Dante Bichette/Action	.10
141b	Dante Bichette/Portrait	.10
142a	Vinny Castilla/Action	.10
142b	Vinny Castilla/Portrait	.10
143a	Edgar Clemente/Action	.10
143b	Edgar Clemente/Portrait	.10
144a	Derrick Gibson/Action	.10
144b	Derrick Gibson/Portrait	.10
145	Curtis Goodwin	.10
146a	Todd Helton/Action	1.00
146b	Todd Helton/Portrait	1.00
147	Bobby Jones	.10
148	Darryl Kile	.10
149	Mike Lansing	.10
150	Chuck McElroy	.10
151	Neifi Perez	.10
152	Jeff Reed	.10
153	John Thomson	.10
154a	Larry Walker/Action	.10
154b	Larry Walker/Portrait	.10
155	Jamey Wright	.10
156	Kimera Bartee	.10
157	Geronimo Berroa	.10
158	Raul Casanova	.10
159	Frank Catalanotto	.10
160	Tony Clark	.10
161	Deivi Cruz	.10
162	Damion Easley	.10
163	Juan Encarnacion	.10
164	Luis Gonzalez	.10
165	Seth Greisinger	.10
166	Bob Higginson	.10
167	Brian Hunter	.10
168	Todd Jones	.10
169	Justin Thompson	.10
170	Antonio Alfonseca	.10
171	Dave Berg	.10
172	John Cangelosi	.10
173	Craig Counsell	.10
174	Todd Dunwoody	.10
175	Cliff Floyd	.10
176	Alex Gonzalez	.10
177	Livan Hernandez	.10
178	Ryan Jackson	.10
179	Mark Kotsay	.10
180	Derrek Lee	.65
181	Matt Mantei	.10
182	Brian Meadows	.10
183	Edgar Renteria	.10
184a	Moises Alou/Action	.10
184b	Moises Alou/Portrait	.10
185	Brad Ausmus	.10
186a	Jeff Bagwell/Action	1.00
186b	Jeff Bagwell/Portrait	1.00
187	Derek Bell	.10
188	Sean Berry	.10
189	Craig Biggio	.10
190	Carl Everett	.10
191	Ricky Gutierrez	.10
192	Mike Hampton	.10
193	Doug Henry	.10
194	Richard Hidalgo	.10
195	Randy Johnson	1.00
196a	Russ Johnson/Action	.10
196b	Russ Johnson/Portrait	.10
197	Shane Reynolds	.10
198	Bill Spiers	.10
199	Kevin Appier	.10
200	Tim Belcher	.10
201	Jeff Conine	.10
202	Johnny Damon	.35
203	Jermaine Dye	.10
204a	Jeremy Giambi (Batting stance.)	.10
204b	Jeremy Giambi (Follow-through.)	.10
205	Jeff King	.10
206	Shane Mack	.10
207	Jeff Montgomery	.10
208	Hal Morris	.10
209	Jose Offerman	.10
210	Dean Palmer	.10
211	Jose Rosado	.10
212	Glendon Rusch	.10
213	Larry Sutton	.10
214	Mike Sweeney	.10
215	Bobby Bonilla	.10
216	Alex Cora	.10
217	Darren Dreifort	.10
218	Mark Grudzielanek	.10
219	Todd Hollandsworth	.10
220	Trenidad Hubbard	.10
221	Charles Johnson	.10
222	Eric Karros	.10
223	Matt Luke	.10
224	Ramon Martinez	.10
225	Raul Mondesi	.10
226	Chan Ho Park	.10
227	Jeff Shaw	.10
228	Gary Sheffield	.40
229	Eric Young	.10
230	Jeromy Burnitz	.10
231	Jeff Cirillo	.10
232	Marquis Grissom	.10
233	Bobby Hughes	.10
234	John Jaha	.10
235	Geoff Jenkins	.10
236	Scott Karl	.10
237	Mark Loretta	.10
238	Mike Matheny	.10
239	Mike Myers	.10
240	Dave Nilsson	.10
241	Bob Wickman	.10
242	Jose Valentin	.10
243	Fernando Vina	.10
244	Rick Aguilera	.10
245	Ron Coomer	.10
246	Marty Cordova	.10
247	Denny Hocking	.10
248	Matt Lawton	.10
249	Pat Meares	.10
250a	Paul Molitor/Action	1.00
250b	Paul Molitor/Portrait	1.00
251	Otis Nixon	.10
252	Alex Ochoa	.10
253	David Ortiz	.65
254	A.J. Pierzynski	.10
255	Brad Radke	.10
256	Terry Steinbach	.10
257	Bob Tewksbury	.10
258	Todd Walker	.10
259	Shane Andrews	.10
260	Shayne Bennett	.10
261	Orlando Cabrera	.10
262	Brad Fullmer	.10
263	Vladimir Guerrero	1.00
264	Wilton Guerrero	.10
265	Dustin Hermanson	.10
266	Terry Jones	.10
267	Steve Kline	.10
268	Carl Pavano	.10
269	F.P. Santangelo	.10
270a	Fernando Seguignol/Action	.10
270b	Fernando Seguignol/Portrait	.10
271	Ugueth Urbina	.10
272	Jose Vidro	.10
273	Chris Widger	.10
274	Edgardo Alfonzo	.10
275	Carlos Baerga	.10

276 John Franco .10
277 Todd Hundley .10
278 Butch Huskey .10
279 Bobby Jones .10
280 Al Leiter .10
281 Greg McMichael .10
282 Brian McRae .10
283 Hideo Nomo .50
284 John Olerud .10
285 Rey Ordonez .10
286a Mike Piazza/Action 1.75
286b Mike Piazza/Portrait 1.75
287 Turk Wendell .10
288 Masato Yoshii .10
289 David Cone .10
290 Chad Curtis .10
291 Joe Girardi .10
292 Orlando Hernandez .10
293a Hideki Irabu/Action .10
293b Hideki Irabu/Portrait .10
294a Derek Jeter/Action 3.00
294b Derek Jeter/Portrait 3.00
295 Chuck Knoblauch .10
296a Mike Lowell/Action .10
296b Mike Lowell/Portrait .10
297 Tino Martinez .10
298 Ramiro Mendoza .10
299 Paul O'Neill .10
300 Andy Pettitte .25
301 Jorge Posada .10
302 Tim Raines .10
303 Mariano Rivera .15
304 David Wells .10
305a Bernie Williams/Action .10
305b Bernie Williams/Portrait .10
306 Mike Blowers .10
307 Tom Candiotti .10
308a Eric Chavez/Action .15
308b Eric Chavez /Portrait .15
309 Ryan Christenson .10
310 Jason Giambi .65
311a Ben Grieve/Action .10
311b Ben Grieve/Portrait .10
312 Rickey Henderson 1.00
313 A.J. Hinch .10
314 Jason McDonald .10
315 Bip Roberts .10
316 Kenny Rogers .10
317 Scott Spiezio .10
318 Matt Stairs .10
319 Miguel Tejada .20
320 Bob Abreu .20
321 Alex Arias .10
322a Gary Bennett RC/Action .10
322b Gary Bennett RC /Portrait .10
323 Ricky Bottalico .10
324 Rico Brogna .10
325 Bobby Estalella .10
326 Doug Glanville .10
327 Kevin Jordan .10
328 Mark Leiter .10
329 Wendell Magee .10
330 Mark Portugal .10
331 Desi Relaford .10
332 Scott Rolen .65
333 Curt Schilling .35
334 Kevin Sefcik .10
335 Adrian Brown .10
336 Emil Brown .10
337 Lou Collier .10
338 Francisco Cordova .10
339 Freddy Garcia .10
340 Jose Guillen .10
341 Jason Kendall .10
342 Al Martin .10
343 Abraham Nunez .10
344 Aramis Ramirez .10
345 Ricardo Rincon .10
346 Jason Schmidt .10
347 Turner Ward .10
348 Tony Womack .10
349 Kevin Young .10
350 Juan Acevedo .10
351 Delino DeShields .10
352a J.D. Drew/Action .40
352b J.D. Drew/Portrait .40
353 Ron Gant .10
354 Brian Jordan .10
355 Ray Lankford .10
356 Eli Marrero .10
357 Kent Mercker .10
358 Matt Morris .10
359 Luis Ordaz .10
360 Donovan Osborne .10
361 Placido Polanco .10
362 Fernando Tatis .10
363 Andy Ashby .10
364 Kevin Brown .10
365 Ken Caminiti .10
366 Steve Finley .10
367 Chris Gomez .10
368a Tony Gwynn/Action 1.50
368b Tony Gwynn/Portrait 1.50
369 Joey Hamilton .10
370 Carlos Hernandez .10
371 Trevor Hoffman .10
372 Wally Joyner .10
373 Jim Leyritz .10
374 Ruben Rivera .10
375 Greg Vaughn .10
376 Quilvio Veras .10
377 Rich Aurilia .10
378a Barry Bonds/Action 3.00
378b Barry Bonds/Portrait 3.00
379 Ellis Burks .10

380 Joe Carter .10
381 Stan Javier .10
382 Brian Johnson .10
383 Jeff Kent .10
384 Jose Mesa .10
385 Bill Mueller .10
386 Robb Nen .10
387a Armando Rios/Action .10
387b Armando Rios/Portrait .10
388 Kirk Rueter .10
389 Rey Sanchez .10
390 J.T. Snow .10
391 David Bell .10
392 Jay Buhner .10
393 Ken Cloude .10
394 Russ Davis .10
395 Jeff Fassero .10
396a Ken Griffey Jr./Action 2.00
396b Ken Griffey Jr./Portrait 2.00
397 Giomar Guevara RC .10
398 Carlos Guillen .10
399 Edgar Martinez .10
400 Shane Monahan .10
401 Jamie Moyer .10
402 David Segui .10
403 Makoto Suzuki .10
404 Mike Timlin .10
405 Dan Wilson .10
406 Wilson Alvarez .10
407 Rolando Arrojo .10
408 Wade Boggs 1.50
409 Miguel Cairo .10
410 Roberto Hernandez .10
411 Mike Kelly .10
412 Aaron Ledesma .10
413 Albie Lopez .10
414 Dave Martinez .10
415 Quinton McCracken .10
416 Fred McGriff .10
417 Bryan Rekar .10
418 Paul Sorrento .10
419 Randy Winn .10
420 John Burkett .10
421 Will Clark .10
422 Royce Clayton .10
423a Juan Gonzalez/Action .50
423b Juan Gonzalez /Portrait .50
424 Tom Goodwin .10
425 Rusty Greer .10
426 Rick Helling .10
427 Roberto Kelly .10
428 Mark McLemore .10
429a Ivan Rodriguez/Action .75
429b Ivan Rodriguez /Portrait .75
430 Aaron Sele .10
431 Lee Stevens .10
432 Todd Stottlemyre .10
433 John Wetteland .10
434 Todd Zeile .10
435 Jose Canseco .50
436a Roger Clemens/Action 1.75
436b Roger Clemens/Portrait 1.75
437 Felipe Crespo .10
438a Jose Cruz Jr./Action .10
438b Jose Cruz Jr./Portrait .10
439 Carlos Delgado .50
440a Tom Evans/Action .10
440b Tom Evans/Portrait .10
441 Tony Fernandez .10
442 Darrin Fletcher .10
443 Alex Gonzalez .10
444 Shawn Green .30
445 Roy Halladay .10
446 Pat Hentgen .10
447 Juan Samuel .10
448 Benito Santiago .10
449 Shannon Stewart .10
450 Woody Williams .10

Cramer's Choice

NM/M
Complete Set (10): 65.00
Common Player: 7.50
Inserted 1:721
1 Cal Ripken Jr. 20.00
2 Nomar Garciaparra 12.50
3 Frank Thomas 10.00
4 Ken Griffey Jr. 15.00
5 Alex Rodriguez 17.50
6 Greg Maddux 12.50
7 Sammy Sosa 12.50
8 Kerry Wood 7.50
9 Mark McGwire 17.50
10 Tony Gwynn 12.50

Dynagon Diamond

NM/M
Complete Set (20): 20.00
Common Player: .40
Inserted 1:9
Titanium (99 Sets): 8X
1 Cal Ripken Jr. 2.50
2 Nomar Garciaparra 1.00
3 Frank Thomas .75
4 Derek Jeter 2.50
5 Ben Grieve .40
6 Ken Griffey Jr. 1.50
7 Alex Rodriguez 2.00
8 Juan Gonzalez .50
9 Travis Lee .40
10 Chipper Jones 1.00
11 Greg Maddux 1.00
12 Sammy Sosa 1.00
13 Kerry Wood .50
14 Jeff Bagwell .75
15 Hideo Nomo .50
16 Mike Piazza 12.50
17 J.D. Drew .50
18 Mark McGwire 2.00
19 Tony Gwynn 1.00
20 Barry Bonds 2.50

Gold Crown Die-Cuts

NM/M
Complete Set (36): 75.00
Common Player: .75
Inserted 1:37
1 Darin Erstad 1.00
2 Cal Ripken Jr. 7.50
3 Nomar Garciaparra 4.00
4 Pedro Martinez 3.00
5 Mo Vaughn .75
6 Frank Thomas 3.00
7 Kenny Lofton .75
8 Manny Ramirez 3.00
9 Paul Molitor 3.00
10 Derek Jeter 7.50
11 Bernie Williams .75
12 Ben Grieve .75
13 Ken Griffey Jr. 5.00
14 Alex Rodriguez 6.00
15 Wade Boggs 4.00
16 Juan Gonzalez 1.50
17 Ivan Rodriguez 2.50
18 Jose Canseco 1.50
19 Roger Clemens 4.50
20 Travis Lee .75
21 Chipper Jones 4.00
22 Greg Maddux 4.00
23 Sammy Sosa 4.00
24 Kerry Wood 1.50
25 Todd Helton 3.00
26 Larry Walker .75
27 Jeff Bagwell 3.00
28 Craig Biggio .75
29 Raul Mondesi .75
30 Vladimir Guerrero 3.00
31 Mike Piazza 4.50
32 Scott Rolen 2.00
33 J.D. Drew 1.50
34 Mark McGwire 6.00
35 Tony Gwynn 4.00
36 Barry Bonds 7.50

Hot Cards

NM/M
Complete Set (10): 75.00
Common Player: 3.00
1 Alex Rodriguez 12.50
2 Tony Gwynn 7.50
3 Ken Griffey Jr. 10.00
4 Sammy Sosa 7.50
5 Ivan Rodriguez 6.00
6 Derek Jeter 15.00
7 Cal Ripken Jr. 15.00
8 Mark McGwire 12.50
9 J.D. Drew 4.50
10 Bernie Williams 3.00

Team Checklists

NM/M
Complete Set (30): 30.00
Common Player: .30
Inserted 1:18
1 Darin Erstad .50
2 Cal Ripken Jr. 3.00
3 Nomar Garciaparra 1.50
4 Frank Thomas 1.00
5 Manny Ramirez 1.00
6 Damion Easley .30
7 Jeff King .30
8 Paul Molitor 1.00
9 Derek Jeter 3.00
10 Ben Grieve .30
11 Ken Griffey Jr. 2.00
12 Wade Boggs 1.50
13 Juan Gonzalez .60
14 Roger Clemens 1.75
15 Travis Lee .30
16 Chipper Jones 1.50
17 Sammy Sosa 1.50
18 Barry Larkin .30
19 Todd Helton 1.00
20 Mark Kotsay .30
21 Jeff Bagwell 1.00
22 Raul Mondesi .30
23 Jeff Cirillo .30
24 Vladimir Guerrero 1.00
25 Mike Piazza 1.75
26 Scott Rolen .75
27 Jason Kendall .30
28 Mark McGwire 2.50
29 Tony Gwynn 1.50
30 Barry Bonds 3.00

Timelines

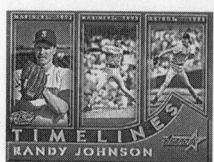

NM/M
Complete Set (20): 200.00
Common Player: 6.00
Inserted 1:181 H
1 Cal Ripken Jr. 30.00
2 Frank Thomas 12.00
3 Jim Thome 10.00
4 Paul Molitor 12.00
5 Bernie Williams 6.00
6 Derek Jeter 30.00
7 Ken Griffey Jr. 20.00
8 Alex Rodriguez 25.00
9 Wade Boggs 15.00
10 Jose Canseco 9.00
11 Roger Clemens 17.50
12 Andres Galarraga 6.00
13 Chipper Jones 15.00
14 Greg Maddux 15.00

15	Sammy Sosa	15.00
16	Larry Walker	6.00
17	Randy Johnson	12.00
18	Mike Piazza	17.50
19	Mark McGwire	25.00
20	Tony Gwynn	15.00

1999 Pacific Aurora

	NM/M
Complete Set (200):	20.00
Common Player:	.10
Opening Days:	20X
Production 31 Sets	
Reds:	2X
Retail Only (1:6)	
Pack (6):	1.50
Wax Box (36):	22.50

1	Garret Anderson	.10
2	Jim Edmonds	.10
3	Darin Erstad	.30
4	Matt Luke	.10
5	Tim Salmon	.10
6	Mo Vaughn	.10
7	Jay Bell	.10
8	David Dellucci	.10
9	Steve Finley	.10
10	Bernard Gilkey	.10
11	Randy Johnson	1.00
12	Travis Lee	.10
13	Matt Williams	.10
14	Andres Galarraga	.10
15	Tom Glavine	.35
16	Andruw Jones	1.00
17	Chipper Jones	1.50
18	Brian Jordan	.10
19	Javy Lopez	.10
20	Greg Maddux	1.50
21	Albert Belle	.10
22	Will Clark	.10
23	Scott Erickson	.10
24	Mike Mussina	.40
25	Cal Ripken Jr.	3.00
26	B.J. Surhoff	.10
27	Nomar Garciaparra	1.50
28	Reggie Jefferson	.10
29	Darren Lewis	.10
30	Pedro Martinez	1.00
31	John Valentin	.10
32	Rod Beck	.10
33	Mark Grace	.10
34	Lance Johnson	.10
35	Mickey Morandini	.10
36	Sammy Sosa	1.50
37	Kerry Wood	.40
38	James Baldwin	.10
39	Mike Caruso	.10
40	Ray Durham	.10
41	Magglio Ordonez	.25
42	Frank Thomas	1.00
43	Aaron Boone	.10
44	Sean Casey	.20
45	Barry Larkin	.10
46	Hal Morris	.10
47	Denny Neagle	.10
48	Greg Vaughn	.10
49	Pat Watkins	.10
50	Roberto Alomar	.25
51	Sandy Alomar Jr.	.10
52	David Justice	.10
53	Kenny Lofton	.10
54	Manny Ramirez	1.00
55	Richie Sexson	.10
56	Jim Thome	.75
57	Omar Vizquel	.10
58	Dante Bichette	.10
59	Vinny Castilla	.10
60	Edgard Clemente RC	.10
61	Derrick Gibson	.10
62	Todd Helton	1.00
63	Darryl Kile	.10
64	Larry Walker	.10
65	Tony Clark	.10
66	Damion Easley	.10
67	Bob Higginson	.10
68	Brian Hunter	.10
69	Dean Palmer	.10
70	Justin Thompson	.10
71	Craig Counsell	.10
72	Todd Dunwoody	.10
73	Cliff Floyd	.10
74	Alex Gonzalez	.10

75	Livan Hernandez	.10
76	Mark Kotsay	.10
77	Derrek Lee	.65
78	Moises Alou	.10
79	Jeff Bagwell	1.00
80	Derek Bell	.10
81	Craig Biggio	.10
82	Ken Caminiti	.10
83	Richard Hidalgo	.10
84	Shane Reynolds	.10
85	Jeff Conine	.10
86	Johnny Damon	.35
87	Jermaine Dye	.10
88	Jeff King	.10
89	Jeff Montgomery	.10
90	Mike Sweeney	.10
91	Kevin Brown	.10
92	Mark Grudzielanek	.10
93	Eric Karros	.10
94	Raul Mondesi	.10
95	Chan Ho Park	.10
96	Gary Sheffield	.40
97	Jeromy Burnitz	.10
98	Jeff Cirillo	.10
99	Marquis Grissom	.10
100	Geoff Jenkins	.10
101	Dave Nilsson	.10
102	Jose Valentin	.10
103	Fernando Vina	.10
104	Marty Cordova	.10
105	Matt Lawton	.10
106	David Ortiz	.60
107	Brad Radke	.10
108	Todd Walker	.10
109	Shane Andrews	.10
110	Orlando Cabrera	.10
111	Brad Fullmer	.10
112	Vladimir Guerrero	1.00
113	Wilton Guerrero	.10
114	Carl Pavano	.10
115	Fernando Seguignol	.10
116	Ugueth Urbina	.10
117	Edgardo Alfonzo	.10
118	Bobby Bonilla	.10
119	Rickey Henderson	1.00
120	Hideo Nomo	.60
121	John Olerud	.10
122	Rey Ordonez	.10
123	Mike Piazza	2.00
124	Masato Yoshii	.10
125	Scott Brosius	.10
126	Orlando Hernandez	.10
127	Hideki Irabu	.10
128	Derek Jeter	3.00
129	Chuck Knoblauch	.10
130	Tino Martinez	.10
131	Jorge Posada	.10
132	Bernie Williams	.10
133	Eric Chavez	.20
134	Ryan Christenson	.10
135	Jason Giambi	.65
136	Ben Grieve	.10
137	A.J. Hinch	.10
138	Matt Stairs	.10
139	Miguel Tejada	.20
140	Bob Abreu	.20
141	Gary Bennett RC	.10
142	Desi Relaford	.10
143	Scott Rolen	.75
144	Curt Schilling	.35
145	Kevin Sefcik	.10
146	Brian Giles	.10
147	Jose Guillen	.10
148	Jason Kendall	.10
149	Aramis Ramirez	.10
150	Tony Womack	.10
151	Kevin Young	.10
152	Eric Davis	.10
153	J.D. Drew	.50
154	Ray Lankford	.10
155	Eli Marrero	.10
156	Mark McGwire	2.50
157	Luis Ordaz	.10
158	Edgar Renteria	.10
159	Andy Ashby	.10
160	Tony Gwynn	1.50
161	Trevor Hoffman	.10
162	Wally Joyner	.10
163	Jim Leyritz	.10
164	Ruben Rivera	.10
165	Reggie Sanders	.10
166	Quilvio Veras	.10
167	Rich Aurilia	.10
168	Marvin Benard	.10
169	Barry Bonds	3.00
170	Ellis Burks	.10
171	Jeff Kent	.10
172	Bill Mueller	.10
173	J.T. Snow	.10
174	Jay Buhner	.10
175	Jeff Fassero	.10
176	Ken Griffey Jr.	2.25
177	Carlos Guillen	.10
178	Edgar Martinez	.10
179	Alex Rodriguez	2.50
180	David Segui	.10
181	Dan Wilson	.10
182	Rolando Arrojo	.10
183	Wade Boggs	1.50
184	Jose Canseco	.40
185	Aaron Ledesma	.10
186	Dave Martinez	.10
187	Quinton McCracken	.10
188	Fred McGriff	.10
189	Juan Gonzalez	.60

190	Tom Goodwin	.10
191	Rusty Greer	.10
192	Roberto Kelly	.10
193	Rafael Palmeiro	.75
194	Ivan Rodriguez	.75
195	Roger Clemens	2.00
196	Jose Cruz Jr.	.10
197	Carlos Delgado	.60
198	Alex Gonzalez	.10
199	Roy Halladay	.10
200	Pat Hentgen	.10

Complete Players

	NM/M
Complete Set (10):	40.00
Common Player:	3.00
Production 299 Sets	

1	Cal Ripken Jr.	9.00
2	Nomar Garciaparra	4.50
3	Sammy Sosa	4.50
4	Kerry Wood	3.00
5	Frank Thomas	4.00
6	Mike Piazza	5.00
7	Mark McGwire	7.50
8	Tony Gwynn	4.50
9	Ken Griffey Jr.	6.00
10	Alex Rodriguez	7.50

Kings of the Major Leagues

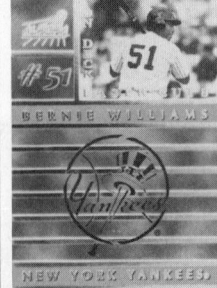

	NM/M
Complete Set (10):	80.00
Common Player:	5.00
Inserted 1:361	

1	Cal Ripken Jr.	17.50
2	Nomar Garciaparra	9.00
3	Sammy Sosa	9.00
4	Kerry Wood	5.00
5	Frank Thomas	7.50
6	Mike Piazza	10.00
7	Mark McGwire	15.00
8	Tony Gwynn	9.00
9	Ken Griffey Jr.	12.50
10	Alex Rodriguez	15.00

On Deck

	NM/M
Complete Set (20):	17.50
Common Player:	.50
Inserted 1:9	

1	Chipper Jones	1.00
2	Cal Ripken Jr.	3.00
3	Nomar Garciaparra	1.00
4	Sammy Sosa	1.00
5	Frank Thomas	.75
6	Manny Ramirez	.75
7	Todd Helton	.75
8	Larry Walker	.50
9	Jeff Bagwell	.75
10	Vladimir Guerrero	.75
11	Mike Piazza	1.50
12	Derek Jeter	3.00
13	Bernie Williams	.50
14	J.D. Drew	.50
15	Mark McGwire	2.50
16	Tony Gwynn	1.00
17	Ken Griffey Jr.	2.00
18	Alex Rodriguez	2.50
19	Juan Gonzalez	.50
20	Ivan Rodriguez	.65

Pennant Fever

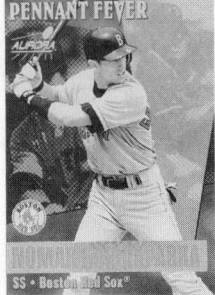

	NM/M
Complete Set (20):	30.00
Common Player:	.75
Silver (250 Sets):	2X
Platinum Blue (100):	6X
Copper (25):	20X
Tony Gwynn Autograph:	25.00

1	Chipper Jones	2.00
2	Greg Maddux	2.00
3	Cal Ripken Jr.	5.00
4	Nomar Garciaparra	2.00
5	Sammy Sosa	2.00
6	Kerry Wood	.75
7	Frank Thomas	1.50
8	Manny Ramirez	1.50
9	Todd Helton	1.50
10	Jeff Bagwell	1.50
11	Mike Piazza	2.50
12	Derek Jeter	5.00
13	Bernie Williams	.75
14	J.D. Drew	.75
15	Mark McGwire	4.00
16	Tony Gwynn	2.00
17	Ken Griffey Jr.	3.00
18	Alex Rodriguez	4.00
19	Juan Gonzalez	.75
20	Ivan Rodriguez	1.25

Styrotechs

	NM/M
Complete Set (20):	35.00
Common Player:	1.00
Inserted 1:37	

1	Chipper Jones	3.00
2	Greg Maddux	3.00
3	Cal Ripken Jr.	6.00
4	Nomar Garciaparra	3.00
5	Sammy Sosa	3.00
6	Kerry Wood	1.25
7	Frank Thomas	2.00
8	Manny Ramirez	2.00

9	Larry Walker	1.00
10	Jeff Bagwell	2.00
11	Mike Piazza	4.00
12	Derek Jeter	6.00
13	Bernie Williams	1.00
14	J.D. Drew	1.25
15	Mark McGwire	5.00
16	Tony Gwynn	3.00
17	Ken Griffey Jr.	4.50
18	Alex Rodriguez	5.00
19	Juan Gonzalez	1.25
20	Ivan Rodriguez	1.50

1999 Pacific Crown Collection

		NM/M
Complete Set (300):		20.00
Common Player:		.10
Red Stars:		6X
Inserted 1:9		
Platinum Blue Stars:		30X
Inserted 1:73		
Pack (12):		1.00
Wax Box (36):		22.50
1	Garret Anderson	.10
2	Gary DiSarcina	.10
3	Jim Edmonds	.10
4	Darin Erstad	.25
5	Shigetosi Hasegawa	.10
6	Norberto Martin	.10
7	Omar Olivares	.10
8	Orlando Palmeiro	.10
9	Tim Salmon	.10
10	Randy Velarde	.10
11	Tony Batista	.10
12	Jay Bell	.10
13	Yamil Benitez	.10
14	Omar Daal	.10
15	David Dellucci	.10
16	Karim Garcia	.10
17	Travis Lee	.10
18	Felix Rodriguez	.10
19	Devon White	.10
20	Matt Williams	.10
21	Andres Galarraga	.10
22	Tom Glavine	.35
23	Ozzie Guillen	.10
24	Andruw Jones	1.00
25	Chipper Jones	1.50
26	Ryan Klesko	.10
27	Javy Lopez	.10
28	Greg Maddux	1.50
29	Dennis Martinez	.10
30	Odaliz Perez	.10
31	Rudy Seanez	.10
32	John Smoltz	.10
33	Roberto Alomar	.25
34	Armando Benitez	.10
35	Scott Erickson	.10
36	Juan Guzman	.10
37	Mike Mussina	.35
38	Jesse Orosco	.10
39	Rafael Palmeiro	.75
40	Sidney Ponson	.10
41	Cal Ripken Jr.	3.00
42	B.J. Surhoff	.10
43	Lenny Webster	.10
44	Dennis Eckersley	.75
45	Nomar Garciaparra	1.50
46	Darren Lewis	.10
47	Pedro Martinez	1.00
48	Troy O'Leary	.10
49	Bret Saberhagen	.10
50	John Valentin	.10
51	Mo Vaughn	.10
52	Tim Wakefield	.10
53	Manny Alexander	.10
54	Rod Beck	.10
55	Gary Gaetti	.10
56	Mark Grace	.10
57	Felix Heredia	.10
58	Jose Hernandez	.10
59	Henry Rodriguez	.10
60	Sammy Sosa	1.50
61	Kevin Tapani	.10
62	Kerry Wood	.45
63	James Baldwin	.10
64	Albert Belle	.10
65	Mike Caruso	.10
66	Carlos Castillo	.10
67	Wil Cordero	.10
68	Jaime Navarro	.10
69	Magglio Ordonez	.25
70	Frank Thomas	1.00
71	Robin Ventura	.10
72	Bret Boone	.10
73	Sean Casey	.20
74	Guillermo Garcia **RC**	.10
75	Barry Larkin	.10
76	Melvin Nieves	.10
77	Eduardo Perez	.10
78	Roberto Petagine	.10
79	Reggie Sanders	.10
80	Eddie Taubensee	.10
81	Brett Tomko	.10
82	Sandy Alomar Jr.	.10
83	Bartolo Colon	.10
84	Joey Cora	.10
85	Einar Diaz	.10
86	David Justice	.10
87	Kenny Lofton	.10
88	Manny Ramirez	1.00
89	Jim Thome	.75
90	Omar Vizquel	.10
91	Enrique Wilson	.10
92	Pedro Astacio	.10
93	Dante Bichette	.10
94	Vinny Castilla	.10
95	Edgard Clemente **RC**	.10
96	Todd Helton	1.00
97	Darryl Kile	.10
98	Mike Munoz	.10
99	Neifi Perez	.10
100	Jeff Reed	.10
101	Larry Walker	.10
102	Gabe Alvarez	.10
103	Kimera Bartee	.10
104	Frank Castillo	.10
105	Tony Clark	.10
106	Deivi Cruz	.10
107	Damion Easley	.10
108	Luis Gonzalez	.10
109	Marino Santana	.10
110	Justin Thompson	.10
111	Antonio Alfonseca	.10
112	Alex Fernandez	.10
113	Cliff Floyd	.10
114	Alex Gonzalez	.10
115	Livan Hernandez	.10
116	Mark Kotsay	.10
117	Derrek Lee	.65
118	Edgar Renteria	.10
119	Jesus Sanchez	.10
120	Moises Alou	.10
121	Jeff Bagwell	1.00
122	Derek Bell	.10
123	Craig Biggio	.10
124	Tony Eusebio	.10
125	Ricky Gutierrez	.10
126	Richard Hidalgo	.10
127	Randy Johnson	1.00
128	Jose Lima	.10
129	Shane Reynolds	.10
130	Johnny Damon	.40
131	Carlos Febles	.10
132	Jeff King	.10
133	Mendy Lopez	.10
134	Hal Morris	.10
135	Jose Offerman	.10
136	Jose Rosado	.10
137	Jose Santiago	.10
138	Bobby Bonilla	.10
139	Roger Cedeno	.10
140	Alex Cora	.10
141	Eric Karros	.10
142	Raul Mondesi	.10
143	Antonio Osuna	.10
144	Chan Ho Park	.10
145	Gary Sheffield	.30
146	Ismael Valdes	.10
147	Jeromy Burnitz	.10
148	Jeff Cirillo	.10
149	Valerio de los Santos	.10
150	Marquis Grissom	.10
151	Scott Karl	.10
152	Dave Nilsson	.10
153	Al Reyes	.10
154	Rafael Roque	.10
155	Jose Valentin	.10
156	Fernando Vina	.10
157	Rick Aguilera	.10
158	Hector Carrasco	.10
159	Marty Cordova	.10
160	Eddie Guardado	.10
161	Paul Molitor	1.00
162	Otis Nixon	.10
163	Alex Ochoa	.10
164	David Ortiz	.45
165	Frank Rodriguez	.10
166	Todd Walker	.10
167	Miguel Batista	.10
168	Orlando Cabrera	.10
169	Vladimir Guerrero	1.00
170	Wilton Guerrero	.10
171	Carl Pavano	.10
172	Robert Perez	.10
173	F.P. Santangelo	.10
174	Fernando Seguignol	.10
175	Ugueth Urbina	.10
176	Javier Vazquez	.10
177	Edgardo Alfonzo	.10
178	Carlos Baerga	.10
179	John Franco	.10
180	Luis Lopez	.10
181	Hideo Nomo	.50
182	John Olerud	.10
183	Rey Ordonez	.10
184	Mike Piazza	1.75
185	Armando Reynoso	.10
186	Masato Yoshii	.10
187	David Cone	.10
188	Orlando Hernandez	.10
189	Hideki Irabu	.10
190	Derek Jeter	3.00
191	Ricky Ledee	.10
192	Tino Martinez	.10
193	Ramiro Mendoza	.10
194	Paul O'Neill	.10
195	Jorge Posada	.10
196	Mariano Rivera	.15
197	Luis Sojo	.10
198	Bernie Williams	.10
199	Rafael Bournigal	.10
200	Eric Chavez	.20
201	Ryan Christenson	.10
202	Jason Giambi	.60
203	Ben Grieve	.10
204	Rickey Henderson	1.00
205	A.J. Hinch	.10
206	Kenny Rogers	.10
207	Miguel Tejada	.20
208	Jorge Velandia	.10
209	Bobby Abreu	.20
210	Marlon Anderson	.10
211	Alex Arias	.10
212	Bobby Estalella	.10
213	Doug Glanville	.10
214	Scott Rolen	.65
215	Curt Schilling	.35
216	Kevin Sefcik	.10
217	Adrian Brown	.10
218	Francisco Cordova	.10
219	Freddy Garcia	.10
220	Jose Guillen	.10
221	Jason Kendall	.10
222	Al Martin	.10
223	Abraham Nunez	.10
224	Aramis Ramirez	.10
225	Ricardo Rincon	.10
226	Kevin Young	.10
227	J.D. Drew	.40
228	Ron Gant	.10
229	Jose Jimenez	.10
230	Brian Jordan	.10
231	Ray Lankford	.10
232	Eli Marrero	.10
233	Mark McGwire	2.50
234	Luis Ordaz	.10
235	Placido Polanco	.10
236	Fernando Tatis	.10
237	Andy Ashby	.10
238	Kevin Brown	.10
239	Ken Caminiti	.10
240	Steve Finley	.10
241	Chris Gomez	.10
242	Tony Gwynn	1.50
243	Carlos Hernandez	.10
244	Trevor Hoffman	.10
245	Wally Joyner	.10
246	Ruben Rivera	.10
247	Greg Vaughn	.10
248	Quilvio Veras	.10
249	Rich Aurilia	.10
250	Barry Bonds	3.00
251	Stan Javier	.10
252	Jeff Kent	.10
253	Ramon Martinez	.10
254	Jose Mesa	.10
255	Armando Rios	.10
256	Rich Rodriguez	.10
257	Rey Sanchez	.10
258	J.T. Snow	.10
259	Julian Tavarez	.10
260	Jeff Fassero	.10
261	Ken Griffey Jr.	2.00
262	Giomar Guevara **RC**	.10
263	Carlos Guillen	.10
264	Raul Ibanez	.10
265	Edgar Martinez	.10
266	Jamie Moyer	.10
267	Alex Rodriguez	2.50
268	David Segui	.10
269	Makoto Suzuki	.10
270	Wilson Alvarez	.10
271	Rolando Arrojo	.10
272	Wade Boggs	1.50
273	Miguel Cairo	.10
274	Roberto Hernandez	.10
275	Aaron Ledesma	.10
276	Albie Lopez	.10
277	Quinton McCracken	.10
278	Fred McGriff	.10
279	Esteban Yan	.10
280	Luis Alicea	.10
281	Will Clark	.10
282	Juan Gonzalez	.50
283	Rusty Greer	.10
284	Rick Helling	.10
285	Xavier Hernandez	.10
286	Roberto Kelly	.10
287	Esteban Loaiza	.10
288	Ivan Rodriguez	.75
289	Aaron Sele	.10
290	John Wetteland	.10
291	Jose Canseco	.40
292	Roger Clemens	1.75
293	Felipe Crespo	.10
294	Jose Cruz Jr.	.10
295	Carlos Delgado	.60
296	Kelvim Escobar	.10
297	Tony Fernandez	.10
298	Alex Gonzalez	.10
299	Tomas Perez	.10
300	Juan Samuel	.10

In The Cage

		NM/M
Complete Set (20):		80.00
Common Player:		2.00
Inserted 1:145		
1	Chipper Jones	7.50
2	Cal Ripken Jr.	15.00
3	Nomar Garciaparra	7.50
4	Sammy Sosa	7.50
5	Frank Thomas	5.00
6	Manny Ramirez	5.00
7	Todd Helton	5.00
8	Moises Alou	2.00
9	Vladimir Guerrero	5.00
10	Mike Piazza	9.00
11	Derek Jeter	15.00
12	Ben Grieve	2.00
13	J.D. Drew	3.00
14	Mark McGwire	12.00
15	Tony Gwynn	7.50
16	Ken Griffey Jr.	10.00
17	Edgar Martinez	2.00
18	Alex Rodriguez	12.00
19	Juan Gonzalez	2.50
20	Ivan Rodriguez	4.00

Latinos/Major Leagues

		NM/M
Complete Set (36):		25.00
Common Player:		.30
Inserted 1:18		
1	Roberto Alomar	.60
2	Rafael Palmeiro	2.00
3	Nomar Garciaparra	3.50
4	Pedro Martinez	2.50
5	Magglio Ordonez	1.50
6	Sandy Alomar Jr.	.30
7	Bartolo Colon	.30
8	Manny Ramirez	2.50
9	Omar Vizquel	.30
10	Enrique Wilson	.30
11	David Ortiz	1.50
12	Orlando Hernandez	.30
13	Tino Martinez	.30
14	Mariano Rivera	.45
15	Bernie Williams	.30
16	Edgar Martinez	.30
17	Alex Rodriguez	5.00
18	David Segui	.30
19	Rolando Arrojo	.30
20	Juan Gonzalez	1.25
21	Ivan Rodriguez	2.00
22	Jose Canseco	1.00
23	Jose Cruz Jr.	.30
24	Andres Galarraga	.30
25	Andruw Jones	2.50
26	Javy Lopez	.30
27	Sammy Sosa	3.50
28	Vinny Castilla	.30
29	Alex Gonzalez	.30
30	Moises Alou	.30
31	Bobby Bonilla	.30
32	Raul Mondesi	.30
33	Fernando Vina	.30
34	Vladimir Guerrero	2.50

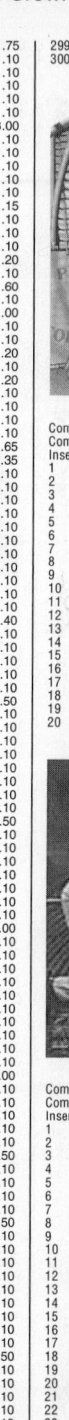

35	Carlos Baerga	.30
36	Rey Ordonez	.30

Pacific Cup

	NM/M
Complete Set (10):	80.00
Common Player:	5.00
Inserted 1:721	

1	Cal Ripken Jr.	20.00
2	Nomar Garciaparra	8.00
3	Frank Thomas	6.00
4	Ken Griffey Jr.	12.00
5	Alex Rodriguez	16.00
6	Greg Maddux	8.00
7	Sammy Sosa	8.00
8	Kerry Wood	5.00
9	Mark McGwire	16.00
10	Tony Gwynn	8.00

Players Choice

	NM/M
Complete Set (6):	55.00
Common Player:	5.00

10	Randy Velarde	5.00
41	Cal Ripken Jr.	30.00
47	Pedro Martinez	12.00
88	Manny Ramirez	12.00
112	Alex Fernandez	5.00
128	Jose Lima	5.00

Tape Measure

IVAN RODRIGUEZ Texas Rangers

	NM/M
Complete Set (20):	20.00
Common Player:	.60
Inserted 1:73	

1	Andres Galarraga	.60
2	Chipper Jones	2.50
3	Nomar Garciaparra	2.50
4	Sammy Sosa	2.50
5	Frank Thomas	1.50
6	Manny Ramirez	1.50
7	Vinny Castilla	.60
8	Moises Alou	.60
9	Jeff Bagwell	1.50
10	Raul Mondesi	.60
11	Vladimir Guerrero	1.50
12	Mike Piazza	2.75
13	J.D. Drew	1.00
14	Mark McGwire	3.50
15	Greg Vaughn	.60
16	Ken Griffey Jr.	3.00
17	Alex Rodriguez	3.50
18	Juan Gonzalez	1.00
19	Ivan Rodriguez	1.25
20	Jose Canseco	1.00

Team Checklists

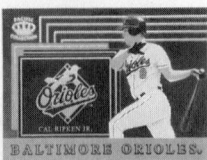

Orioles CAL RIPKEN JR. — BALTIMORE ORIOLES

	NM/M
Complete Set (30):	25.00
Common Player:	.50
Inserted 1:37	

1	Darin Erstad	.60
2	Travis Lee	.50
3	Chipper Jones	2.00
4	Cal Ripken Jr.	4.00
5	Nomar Garciaparra	1.75
6	Sammy Sosa	1.75
7	Frank Thomas	1.25
8	Barry Larkin	.50
9	Manny Ramirez	1.25
10	Larry Walker	.50
11	Bob Higginson	.50
12	Livan Hernandez	.50
13	Moises Alou	.50
14	Jeff King	.50
15	Raul Mondesi	.50
16	Marquis Grissom	.50
17	David Ortiz	1.00
18	Vladimir Guerrero	1.25
19	Mike Piazza	2.00
20	Derek Jeter	4.00
21	Ben Grieve	.50
22	Scott Rolen	.75
23	Jason Kendall	.50
24	Mark McGwire	3.00
25	Tony Gwynn	1.75
26	Barry Bonds	4.00
27	Ken Griffey Jr.	2.50
28	Wade Boggs	1.75
29	Juan Gonzalez	.75
30	Jose Canseco	.60

1999 Pacific Crown Royale

	NM/M
Complete Set (144):	75.00
Common Player:	.25
Common SP:	.25
Limited Series (99 Sets):	6X
SP's:	2X
Opening Day (72 Sets):	12X
SP's:	2X
Pack (6):	2.00
Wax Box (24):	35.00

1	Jim Edmonds	.25
2	Darin Erstad	.50
3	Troy Glaus	2.00
4	Tim Salmon	.25
5	Mo Vaughn	.25
6	Jay Bell	.25
7	Steve Finley	.25
8	Randy Johnson	2.00
9	Travis Lee	.25
10	Matt Williams	.25
11	Andruw Jones	2.00
12	Chipper Jones	3.00
13	Brian Jordan	.25
14	Ryan Klesko	.25
15	Javy Lopez	.25
16	Greg Maddux	3.00
17	Randall Simon/SP	.50
18	Albert Belle	.25
19	Will Clark	.25
20	Delino DeShields	.25
21	Mike Mussina	.50
22	Cal Ripken Jr.	6.00
23	Nomar Garciaparra	3.00
24	Pedro Martinez	2.00
25	Jose Offerman	.25
26	John Valentin	.25
27	Mark Grace	.25
28	Lance Johnson	.25
29	Henry Rodriguez	.25
30	Sammy Sosa	3.00
31	Kerry Wood	1.00
32	Mike Caruso	.25
33	Ray Durham	.25
34	Magglio Ordonez	.40
35	Brian Simmons/SP	.50
36	Frank Thomas	2.00
37	Mike Cameron	.25
38	Barry Larkin	.25
39	Greg Vaughn	.25
40	Dmitri Young	.25
41	Roberto Alomar	.40
42	Sandy Alomar Jr.	.25
43	David Justice	.25
44	Kenny Lofton	.25
45	Manny Ramirez	2.00
46	Jim Thome	1.50
47	Dante Bichette	.25
48	Vinny Castilla	.25
49	Todd Helton	2.00
50	Larry Walker	.50
51	Tony Clark	.25
52	Damion Easley	.25
53	Bob Higginson	.25
54	Brian Hunter	.25
55	Gabe Kapler/SP	.50
56	Jeff Weaver RC/SP	2.50
57	Cliff Floyd	.25
58	Alex Gonzalez/SP	.50
59	Mark Kotsay	.25
60	Derrek Lee	1.00
61	Preston Wilson/SP	.75
62	Moises Alou	.25
63	Jeff Bagwell	2.00
64	Derek Bell	.25
65	Craig Biggio	.25
66	Ken Caminiti	.25
67	Carlos Beltran/SP	2.00
68	Johnny Damon	.45
69	Carlos Febles/SP	.65
70	Jeff King	.25
71	Kevin Brown	.25
72	Todd Hundley	.25
73	Eric Karros	.25
74	Raul Mondesi	.25
75	Gary Sheffield	.75
76	Jeromy Burnitz	.25
77	Jeff Cirillo	.25
78	Marquis Grissom	.25
79	Fernando Vina	.25
80	Chad Allen RC/SP	.50
81	Matt Lawton	.25
82	Doug Mientkiewicz/SP	.75
83	Brad Radke	.25
84	Todd Walker	.25
85	Michael Barrett/SP	.50
86	Brad Fullmer	.25
87	Vladimir Guerrero	2.00
88	Wilton Guerrero	.25
89	Ugueth Urbina	.25
90	Bobby Bonilla	.25
91	Rickey Henderson	2.00
92	Rey Ordonez	.25
93	Mike Piazza	3.50
94	Robin Ventura	.25
95	Roger Clemens	3.50
96	Orlando Hernandez	.25
97	Derek Jeter	6.00
98	Chuck Knoblauch	.25
99	Tino Martinez	.25
100	Bernie Williams	.25
101	Eric Chavez/SP	1.50
102	Jason Giambi	1.00
103	Ben Grieve	.25
104	Tim Raines	.25
105	Marlon Anderson/SP	.65
106	Doug Glanville	.25
107	Scott Rolen	1.25
108	Curt Schilling	.40
109	Brian Giles	.25
110	Jose Guillen	.25
111	Jason Kendall	.25
112	Kevin Young	.25
113	J.D. Drew/SP	2.00
114	Jose Jimenez/SP	.50
115	Ray Lankford	.25
116	Mark McGwire	5.00
117	Fernando Tatis	.25
118	Matt Clement/SP	.75
119	Tony Gwynn	3.00
120	Trevor Hoffman	.25
121	Wally Joyner	.25
122	Reggie Sanders	.25
123	Barry Bonds	6.00
124	Ellis Burks	.25
125	Jeff Kent	.25
126	J.T. Snow	.25
127	Freddy Garcia RC/SP	1.00
128	Ken Griffey Jr.	4.00
129	Edgar Martinez	.25
130	Alex Rodriguez	5.00
131	David Segui	.25
132	Rolando Arrojo	.25
133	Wade Boggs	3.00
134	Jose Canseco	.65
135	Quinton McCracken	.25
136	Fred McGriff	.25
137	Juan Gonzalez	1.00
138	Rusty Greer	.25
139	Rafael Palmeiro	1.50
140	Ivan Rodriguez	1.50
141	Jose Cruz Jr.	.25
142	Carlos Delgado	.75
143	Shawn Green	.75
144	Roy Halladay	1.00

Pivotal Players

CHICAGO CUBS

	NM/M
Complete Set (25):	20.00
Common Player:	.50
Inserted 1:1	

1	Mo Vaughn	.50
2	Chipper Jones	2.00
3	Greg Maddux	2.00
4	Albert Belle	.50
5	Cal Ripken Jr.	4.00
6	Nomar Garciaparra	2.00
7	Sammy Sosa	2.00
8	Frank Thomas	1.50
9	Manny Ramirez	1.50
10	Craig Biggio	.50
11	Raul Mondesi	.50
12	Vladimir Guerrero	1.50
13	Mike Piazza	2.25
14	Roger Clemens	2.50
15	Derek Jeter	4.00
16	Bernie Williams	.50
17	Ben Grieve	.50
18	Scott Rolen	.60
19	J.D. Drew	.75
20	Mark McGwire	3.00
21	Tony Gwynn	2.00
22	Ken Griffey Jr.	2.50
23	Alex Rodriguez	3.00
24	Juan Gonzalez	.75
25	Ivan Rodriguez	1.00

Pillars of the Game

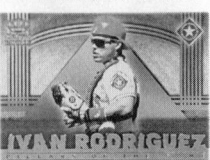

IVAN RODRIGUEZ

	NM/M
Complete Set (25):	30.00
Common Player:	.50
Inserted 1:1	

1	Mo Vaughn	.50
2	Chipper Jones	2.00
3	Greg Maddux	2.00
4	Albert Belle	.50
5	Cal Ripken Jr.	4.00
6	Nomar Garciaparra	2.00
7	Sammy Sosa	2.00
8	Frank Thomas	1.50
9	Manny Ramirez	1.50
10	Jeff Bagwell	1.50
11	Raul Mondesi	.50
12	Vladimir Guerrero	1.50
13	Mike Piazza	2.25
14	Roger Clemens	2.25
15	Derek Jeter	4.00
16	Bernie Williams	.50
17	Ben Grieve	.50
18	J.D. Drew	1.00
19	Mark McGwire	3.00
20	Tony Gwynn	2.00
21	Barry Bonds	4.00
22	Ken Griffey Jr.	2.50
23	Alex Rodriguez	3.00
24	Juan Gonzalez	1.00
25	Ivan Rodriguez	1.25

Master Performers

CAL RIPKEN — ORIOLES — THIRD BASE

	NM/M
Complete Set (20):	40.00
Common Player:	1.00
Inserted 2:25	

1	Chipper Jones	2.50
2	Greg Maddux	2.50
3	Cal Ripken Jr.	5.00
4	Nomar Garciaparra	2.50
5	Sammy Sosa	2.50
6	Frank Thomas	2.00
7	Raul Mondesi	1.00
8	Vladimir Guerrero	2.00
9	Mike Piazza	3.00
10	Roger Clemens	3.00
11	Derek Jeter	5.00
12	Scott Rolen	1.75
13	J.D. Drew	1.50
14	Mark McGwire	4.00
15	Tony Gwynn	2.50
16	Barry Bonds	5.00
17	Ken Griffey Jr.	3.50
18	Alex Rodriguez	4.00
19	Juan Gonzalez	1.50
20	Ivan Rodriguez	1.75

Century 21

		NM/M
	Complete Set (10):	30.00
	Common Player:	2.00
	Inserted 1:25	
1	Cal Ripken Jr.	7.50
2	Nomar Garciaparra	4.00
3	Sammy Sosa	4.00
4	Frank Thomas	3.00
5	Mike Piazza	4.50
6	J.D. Drew	2.00
7	Mark McGwire	6.00
8	Tony Gwynn	4.00
9	Ken Griffey Jr.	5.00
10	Alex Rodriguez	6.00

Cramer's Choice Premiums

		NM/M
	Complete Set (10):	20.00
	Common Player:	2.00
	Inserted 1:Box	
	Dark Blue (35 Sets):	5X
	Green (30):	6X
	Red (25):	8X
	Light Blue (20):	10X
	Gold (10):	15X
	Purple (1):	Value Undetermined
1	Cal Ripken Jr.	6.50
2	Nomar Garciaparra	3.00
3	Sammy Sosa	3.00
4	Frank Thomas	2.50
5	Mike Piazza	3.50
6	Derek Jeter	6.50
7	J.D. Drew	2.00
8	Mark McGwire	5.00
9	Tony Gwynn	3.00
10	Ken Griffey Jr.	4.00

Living Legends

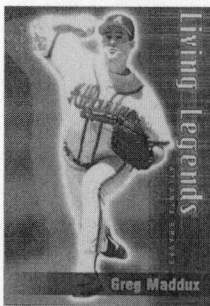

	NM/M
Complete Set (10):	100.00
Common Player:	7.50

	Production 375 Sets	
1	Greg Maddux	10.00
2	Cal Ripken Jr.	20.00
3	Nomar Garciaparra	10.00
4	Sammy Sosa	10.00
5	Frank Thomas	7.50
6	Mike Piazza	12.00
7	Mark McGwire	15.00
8	Tony Gwynn	10.00
9	Ken Griffey Jr.	13.50
10	Alex Rodriguez	15.00

Gold Crown Die-Cut Premiums

		NM/M
	Complete Set (6):	15.00
	Common Player:	2.50
	Inserted 6:10 boxes.	
1	Cal Ripken Jr.	7.00
2	Mike Piazza	4.50
3	Ken Griffey Jr.	5.00
4	Tony Gwynn	3.00
5	Mark McGwire	6.00
6	J.D. Drew	2.50

Pivotal Players Show Cards

	NM/M
Common Card:	5.00
Stars:	6-8X

(See 1999 Pacific Crown Royale Pivotal Players for checklist and base values.)

1999 Pacific Invincible

		NM/M
	Complete Set (150):	60.00
	Common Player:	.25
	Opening Day (69 Sets):	6X
	Platinum Blues (67):	6X
	Pack (3):	1.50
	Wax Box (24):	35.00
1	Jim Edmonds	.25
2	Darin Erstad	.50
3	Troy Glaus	2.50
4	Tim Salmon	.25
5	Mo Vaughn	.25
6	Steve Finley	.25
7	Randy Johnson	2.50
8	Travis Lee	.25
9	Dante Powell	.25
10	Matt Williams	.25
11	Bret Boone	.25
12	Andruw Jones	2.50
13	Chipper Jones	3.00
14	Brian Jordan	.25
15	Ryan Klesko	.25
16	Javy Lopez	.25
17	Greg Maddux	3.00
18	Brady Anderson	.25
19	Albert Belle	.25
20	Will Clark	.25
21	Mike Mussina	.75
22	Cal Ripken Jr.	6.00
23	Nomar Garciaparra	3.00
24	Pedro Martinez	2.50
25	Trot Nixon	.25
26	Jose Offerman	.25
27	Donnie Sadler	.25
28	John Valentin	.25
29	Mark Grace	.25
30	Lance Johnson	.25
31	Henry Rodriguez	.25
32	Sammy Sosa	3.00
33	Kerry Wood	1.25
34	McKay Christensen	.25
35	Ray Durham	.25
36	Jeff Liefer	.25
37	Frank Thomas	2.50
38	Mike Cameron	.25
39	Barry Larkin	.25
40	Greg Vaughn	.25
41	Dmitri Young	.25
42	Roberto Alomar	.50
43	Sandy Alomar Jr.	.25
44	David Justice	.25
45	Kenny Lofton	.25
46	Manny Ramirez	2.50
47	Jim Thome	2.25
48	Dante Bichette	.25
49	Vinny Castilla	.25
50	Darryl Hamilton	.25
51	Todd Helton	2.50
52	Neifi Perez	.25
53	Larry Walker	.25
54	Tony Clark	.25
55	Damion Easley	.25
56	Bob Higginson	.25
57	Brian Hunter	.25
58	Gabe Kapler	.25
59	Cliff Floyd	.25
60	Alex Gonzalez	.25
61	Mark Kotsay	.25
62	Derrek Lee	2.00
63	Braden Looper	.25
64	Moises Alou	.25
65	Jeff Bagwell	2.50
66	Craig Biggio	.25
67	Ken Caminiti	.25
68	Scott Elarton	.25
69	Mitch Meluskey	.25
70	Carlos Beltran	.65
71	Johnny Damon	.50
72	Carlos Febles	.25
73	Jeremy Giambi	.25
74	Kevin Brown	.25
75	Todd Hundley	.25
76	Paul LoDuca	.25
77	Raul Mondesi	.25
78	Gary Sheffield	1.00
79	Geoff Jenkins	.25
80	Jeromy Burnitz	.25
81	Marquis Grissom	.25
82	Jose Valentin	.25
83	Fernando Vina	.25
84	Corey Koskie	.25
85	Matt Lawton	.25
86	Christian Guzman	.25
87	Torii Hunter	.25
88	Doug Mientkiewicz	.25
89	Michael Barrett	.25
90	Brad Fullmer	.25
91	Vladimir Guerrero	2.50
92	Fernando Seguignol	.25
93	Ugueth Urbina	.25
94	Bobby Bonilla	.25
95	Rickey Henderson	2.50
96	Rey Ordonez	.25
97	Mike Piazza	3.50
98	Robin Ventura	.25
99	Roger Clemens	3.50
100	Derek Jeter	6.00
101	Chuck Knoblauch	.25
102	Tino Martinez	.25
103	Paul O'Neill	.25
104	Bernie Williams	.25
105	Eric Chavez	.50
106	Ryan Christenson	.25
107	Jason Giambi	1.25
108	Ben Grieve	.25
109	Miguel Tejada	.50
110	Marlon Anderson	.25
111	Doug Glanville	.25
112	Scott Rolen	2.25
113	Curt Schilling	.50
114	Brian Giles	.25
115	Warren Morris	.25
116	Jason Kendall	.25
117	Kris Benson	.25
118	J.D. Drew	1.25
119	Ray Lankford	.25
120	Mark McGwire	5.00
121	Matt Clement	.25
122	Tony Gwynn	3.00
123	Trevor Hoffman	.25
124	Wally Joyner	.25
125	Reggie Sanders	.25
126	Barry Bonds	6.00
127	Ellis Burks	.25
128	Jeff Kent	.25
129	Stan Javier	.25
130	J.T. Snow	.25
131	Jay Buhner	.25
132	Freddy Garcia RC	2.00
133	Ken Griffey Jr.	4.00
134	Russ Davis	.25
135	Edgar Martinez	.25
136	Alex Rodriguez	5.00
137	David Segui	.25
138	Rolando Arrojo	.25
139	Wade Boggs	3.00
140	Jose Canseco	1.00
141	Quinton McCracken	.25
142	Fred McGriff	.25
143	Juan Gonzalez	1.25
144	Tom Goodwin	.25
145	Rusty Greer	.25
146	Ivan Rodriguez	2.25
147	Jose Cruz Jr.	.25
148	Carlos Delgado	1.00
149	Shawn Green	.75
150	Roy Halladay	.25

Diamond Magic

		NM/M
	Complete Set (10):	35.00
	Common Player:	3.00
	Inserted 1:49	
1	Cal Ripken Jr.	7.50
2	Nomar Garciaparra	4.00
3	Sammy Sosa	4.00
4	Frank Thomas	3.50
5	Mike Piazza	4.50
6	J.D. Drew	3.00
7	Mark McGwire	6.00
8	Tony Gwynn	4.00
9	Ken Griffey Jr.	5.00
10	Alex Rodriguez	6.00

Flash Point

		NM/M
	Complete Set (20):	50.00
	Common Player:	1.25
	Inserted 1:25	
1	Mo Vaughn	1.25
2	Chipper Jones	4.00
3	Greg Maddux	3.50
4	Cal Ripken Jr.	9.00
5	Nomar Garciaparra	3.50
6	Sammy Sosa	3.50
7	Frank Thomas	2.50
8	Manny Ramirez	2.50
9	Vladimir Guerrero	2.50
10	Mike Piazza	4.00
11	Roger Clemens	4.00
12	Derek Jeter	9.00
13	Ben Grieve	1.25
14	Scott Rolen	2.00
15	J.D. Drew	1.50
16	Mark McGwire	7.50
17	Tony Gwynn	3.50
18	Ken Griffey Jr.	5.00
19	Alex Rodriguez	7.50
20	Juan Gonzalez	1.50

Giants of the Game

		NM/M
	Complete Set (10):	300.00
	Common Player:	25.00
	Production 10 Sets	
1	Cal Ripken Jr.	75.00
2	Nomar Garciaparra	35.00
3	Sammy Sosa	35.00
4	Frank Thomas	30.00
5	Mike Piazza	40.00
6	J.D. Drew	25.00
7	Mark McGwire	60.00
8	Tony Gwynn	35.00
9	Ken Griffey Jr.	50.00
10	Alex Rodriguez	60.00

Sandlot Heroes

		NM/M
	Complete Set (20):	15.00
	Common Player:	.50
	Inserted 1:1	
	SportsFest (10 Sets):	25X
1	Mo Vaughn	.50
2	Chipper Jones	1.00
3	Greg Maddux	1.00

4	Cal Ripken Jr.	3.00
5	Nomar Garciaparra	1.00
6	Sammy Sosa	1.00
7	Frank Thomas	.75
8	Manny Ramirez	.75
9	Vladimir Guerrero	.75
10	Mike Piazza	1.25
11	Roger Clemens	1.25
12	Derek Jeter	3.00
13	Eric Chavez	.50
14	Ben Grieve	.50
15	J.D. Drew	.60
16	Mark McGwire	2.00
17	Tony Gwynn	1.00
18	Ken Griffey Jr.	1.50
19	Alex Rodriguez	2.00
20	Juan Gonzalez	.60

Seismic Force

		NM/M
Complete Set (20):		15.00
Common Player:		.50
Inserted 1:1		
SportsFest (20 Sets):		15X
1	Mo Vaughn	.50
2	Chipper Jones	1.00
3	Greg Maddux	1.00
4	Cal Ripken Jr.	3.00
5	Nomar Garciaparra	1.00
6	Sammy Sosa	1.00
7	Frank Thomas	.75
8	Manny Ramirez	.75
9	Vladimir Guerrero	.75
10	Mike Piazza	1.25
11	Bernie Williams	.50
12	Derek Jeter	3.00
13	Ben Grieve	.50
14	J.D. Drew	.60
15	Mark McGwire	2.00
16	Tony Gwynn	1.00
17	Ken Griffey Jr.	1.50
18	Alex Rodriguez	2.00
19	Juan Gonzalez	.50
20	Ivan Rodriguez	.65

Thunder Alley

		NM/M
Complete Set (20):		75.00
Common Player:		2.50
Inserted 1:121		
1	Mo Vaughn	2.50
2	Chipper Jones	6.00
3	Cal Ripken Jr.	12.00
4	Nomar Garciaparra	6.00
5	Sammy Sosa	6.00
6	Frank Thomas	5.00
7	Manny Ramirez	5.00
8	Todd Helton	5.00
9	Vladimir Guerrero	5.00
10	Mike Piazza	7.50
11	Derek Jeter	12.00
12	Ben Grieve	2.50
13	Scott Rolen	4.50
14	J.D. Drew	3.00
15	Mark McGwire	10.00
16	Tony Gwynn	6.00
17	Ken Griffey Jr.	9.00
18	Alex Rodriguez	10.00
19	Juan Gonzalez	3.00
20	Ivan Rodriguez	4.50

1999 Pacific Omega

		NM/M
Complete Set (250):		20.00
Common Player:		.10
Gold (299 Sets):		4X
Copper (99):		10X
Platinum Blue (75):		15X
Premire Date (50):		20X
Wax Pack (6):		1.50
Wax Box (36):		35.00
1	Garret Anderson	.10
2	Jim Edmonds	.10
3	Darin Erstad	.20
4	Chuck Finley	.10
5	Troy Glaus	.75
6	Troy Percival	.10
7	Chris Pritchett	.10
8	Tim Salmon	.10
9	Mo Vaughn	.10
10	Jay Bell	.10
11	Steve Finley	.10
12	Luis Gonzalez	.10
13	Randy Johnson	.75
14	Byung-Hyun Kim RC	.75
15	Travis Lee	.10
16	Matt Williams	.10
17	Tony Womack	.10
18	Bret Boone	.10
19	Mark DeRosa	.10
20	Tom Glavine	.35
21	Andruw Jones	.75
22	Chipper Jones	1.00
23	Brian Jordan	.10
24	Ryan Klesko	.10
25	Javy Lopez	.10
26	Greg Maddux	1.00
27	John Smoltz	.10
28	Bruce Chen, Odalis Perez	.10
29	Brady Anderson	.10
30	Harold Baines	.10
31	Albert Belle	.10
32	Will Clark	.10
33	Delino DeShields	.10
34	Jerry Hairston Jr.	.10
35	Charles Johnson	.10
36	Mike Mussina	.40
37	Cal Ripken Jr.	2.50
38	B.J. Surhoff	.10
39	Jin Ho Cho	.10
40	Nomar Garciaparra	1.00
41	Pedro Martinez	.75
42	Jose Offerman	.10
43	Troy O'Leary	.10
44	John Valentin	.10
45	Jason Varitek	.10
46	Juan Pena, Brian Rose	.10
47	Mark Grace	.10
48	Glenallen Hill	.10
49	Tyler Houston	.10
50	Mickey Morandini	.10
51	Henry Rodriguez	.10
52	Sammy Sosa	1.00
53	Kevin Tapani	.10
54	Mike Caruso	.10
55	Ray Durham	.10
56	Paul Konerko	.20
57	Carlos Lee	.10
58	Magglio Ordonez	.20
59	Mike Sirotka	.10
60	Frank Thomas	.75
61	Mark L. Johnson, Chris Singleton	.10
62	Mike Cameron	.10
63	Sean Casey	.20
64	Pete Harnisch	.10
65	Barry Larkin	.10
66	Pokey Reese	.10
67	Greg Vaughn	.10
68	Scott Williamson	.10
69	Dmitri Young	.10
70	Roberto Alomar	.25
71	Sandy Alomar Jr.	.10
72	Travis Fryman	.10
73	David Justice	.10
74	Kenny Lofton	.10
75	Manny Ramirez	.75
76	Richie Sexson	.10
77	Jim Thome	.65
78	Omar Vizquel	.10
79	Jaret Wright	.10
80	Dante Bichette	.10
81	Vinny Castilla	.10
82	Todd Helton	.75
83	Darryl Hamilton	.10
84	Darryl Kile	.10
85	Neifi Perez	.10
86	Larry Walker	.10
87	Tony Clark	.10
88	Damion Easley	.10
89	Juan Encarnacion	.10
90	Bobby Higginson	.10
91	Gabe Kapler	.10
92	Dean Palmer	.10
93	Justin Thompson	.10
94	Masao Kida, Jeff Weaver RC	1.00
95	Bruce Aven	.10
96	Luis Castillo	.10
97	Alex Fernandez	.10
98	Cliff Floyd	.10
99	Alex Gonzalez	.10
100	Mark Kotsay	.10
101	Preston Wilson	.10
102	Moises Alou	.10
103	Jeff Bagwell	.75
104	Derek Bell	.10
105	Craig Biggio	.10
106	Mike Hampton	.10
107	Richard Hidalgo	.10
108	Jose Lima	.10
109	Billy Wagner	.10
110	Russ Johnson, Daryle Ward	.10
111	Carlos Beltran	.50
112	Johnny Damon	.35
113	Jermaine Dye	.10
114	Carlos Febles	.10
115	Jeremy Giambi	.10
116	Joe Randa	.10
117	Mike Sweeney	.10
118	Orber Moreno, Jose Santiago	.10
119	Kevin Brown	.10
120	Todd Hundley	.10
121	Eric Karros	.10
122	Raul Mondesi	.10
123	Chan Ho Park	.10
124	Angel Pena	.10
125	Gary Sheffield	.45
126	Devon White	.10
127	Eric Young	.10
128	Ron Belliard	.10
129	Jeromy Burnitz	.10
130	Jeff Cirillo	.10
131	Marquis Grissom	.10
132	Geoff Jenkins	.10
133	David Nilsson	.10
134	Hideo Nomo	.40
135	Fernando Vina	.10
136	Ron Coomer	.10
137	Marty Cordova	.10
138	Corey Koskie	.10
139	Brad Radke	.10
140	Todd Walker	.10
141	Chad Allen, Torii Hunter	.10
142	Cristian Guzman, Jacque Jones	.10
143	Michael Barrett	.10
144	Orlando Cabrera	.10
145	Vladimir Guerrero	.75
146	Wilton Guerrero	.10
147	Ugueth Urbina	.10
148	Rondell White	.10
149	Chris Widger	.10
150	Edgardo Alfonzo	.10
151	Roger Cedeno	.10
152	Octavio Dotel	.10
153	Rickey Henderson	.75
154	John Olerud	.10
155	Rey Ordonez	.10
156	Mike Piazza	1.25
157	Robin Ventura	.10
158	Scott Brosius	.10
159	Roger Clemens	1.25
160	David Cone	.10
161	Chili Davis	.10
162	Orlando Hernandez	.10
163	Derek Jeter	2.50
164	Chuck Knoblauch	.10
165	Tino Martinez	.10
166	Paul O'Neill	.10
167	Bernie Williams	.10
168	Jason Giambi	.60
169	Ben Grieve	.10
170	Chad Harville RC	.10
171	Tim Hudson RC	2.00
172	Tony Phillips	.10
173	Kenny Rogers	.10
174	Matt Stairs	.10
175	Miguel Tejada	.25
176	Eric Chavez	.25
177	Bobby Abreu	.20
178	Ron Gant	.10
179	Doug Glanville	.10
180	Mike Lieberthal	.10
181	Desi Relaford	.10
182	Scott Rolen	.65
183	Curt Schilling	.35
184	Marlon Anderson, Randy Wolf	.10
185	Brant Brown	.10
186	Brian Giles	.10
187	Jason Kendall	.10
188	Al Martin	.10
189	Ed Sprague	.10
190	Kevin Young	.10
191	Kris Benson, Warren Morris	.10
192	Kent Bottenfield	.10
193	Eric Davis	.10
194	J.D. Drew	.45
195	Ray Lankford	.10
196	Joe McEwing RC	.25
197	Mark McGwire	2.00
198	Edgar Renteria	.10
199	Fernando Tatis	.10
200	Andy Ashby	.10
201	Ben Davis	.10
202	Tony Gwynn	1.00
203	Trevor Hoffman	.10
204	Wally Joyner	.10
205	Gary Matthews Jr.	.10
206	Ruben Rivera	.10
207	Reggie Sanders	.10
208	Rich Aurilia	.10
209	Marvin Benard	.10
210	Barry Bonds	2.50
211	Ellis Burks	.10
212	Stan Javier	.10
213	Jeff Kent	.10
214	Robb Nen	.10
215	J.T. Snow	.10
216	David Wells	.10
217	Jay Buhner	.10
218	Freddy Garcia RC	.50
219	Ken Griffey Jr.	1.50
220	Brian Hunter	.10
221	Butch Huskey	.10
222	Edgar Martinez	.10
223	Jamie Moyer	.10
224	Alex Rodriguez	2.00
225	David Segui	.10
226	Rolando Arrojo	.10
227	Wade Boggs	1.00
228	Miguel Cairo	.10
229	Jose Canseco	.60
230	Dave Martinez	.10
231	Fred McGriff	.10
232	Kevin Stocker	.10
233	Mike Duvall, David Lamb	.10
234	Royce Clayton	.10
235	Juan Gonzalez	.40
236	Rusty Greer	.10
237	Ruben Mateo	.10
238	Rafael Palmeiro	.65
239	Ivan Rodriguez	.65
240	John Wetteland	.10
241	Todd Zeile	.10
242	Jeff Zimmerman	.10
243	Homer Bush	.10
244	Jose Cruz Jr.	.10
245	Carlos Delgado	.60
246	Tony Fernandez	.10
247	Shawn Green	.35
248	Shannon Stewart	.10
249	David Wells	.10
250	Roy Halladay, Billy Koch	.10

Debut Duos

		NM/M
Complete Set (10):		45.00
Common Player:		2.50
Inserted 1:145		
1	Nomar Garciaparra, Vladimir Guerrero	6.00
2	Derek Jeter, Andy Pettitte	12.00
3	Garret Anderson, Alex Rodriguez	9.00
4	Chipper Jones, Raul Mondesi	6.00
5	Pedro Martinez, Mike Piazza	6.50
6	Mo Vaughn, Bernie Williams	2.50
7	Juan Gonzalez, Ken Griffey Jr.	7.50
8	Sammy Sosa, Larry Walker	6.00
9	Barry Bonds, Mark McGwire	12.00
10	Wade Boggs, Tony Gwynn	6.00

Diamond Masters

1999 Pacific Paramount (Complete Set 36)

		NM/M
	Complete Set (36):	27.50
	Common Player:	.25
	Inserted 1:9	
1	Darin Erstad	.35
2	Mo Vaughn	.25
3	Matt Williams	.25
4	Andruw Jones	.75
5	Chipper Jones	1.00
6	Greg Maddux	1.00
7	Cal Ripken Jr.	3.00
8	Nomar Garciaparra	1.00
9	Pedro Martinez	.75
10	Sammy Sosa	1.00
11	Frank Thomas	.75
12	Kenny Lofton	.25
13	Manny Ramirez	.75
14	Larry Walker	.25
15	Gabe Kapler	.25
16	Jeff Bagwell	.75
17	Craig Biggio	.25
18	Raul Mondesi	.25
19	Vladimir Guerrero	.75
20	Mike Piazza	1.25
21	Roger Clemens	1.25
22	Derek Jeter	3.00
23	Bernie Williams	.25
24	Scott Rolen	.65
25	J.D. Drew	.60
26	Mark McGwire	2.00
27	Fernando Tatis	.25
28	Tony Gwynn	1.00
29	Barry Bonds	3.00
30	Ken Griffey Jr.	1.50
31	Alex Rodriguez	2.00
32	Jose Canseco	.60
33	Juan Gonzalez	.40
34	Ruben Mateo	.25
35	Ivan Rodriguez	.65
36	Rusty Greer	.25

EO Portraits

		NM/M
	Complete Set (20):	60.00
	Common Player:	1.00
	Inserted 1:73	
	1-of-1 Numbered Parallels Exist	
1	Mo Vaughn	1.00
2	Chipper Jones	5.00
3	Greg Maddux	5.00
4	Cal Ripken Jr.	10.00
5	Nomar Garciaparra	5.00
6	Sammy Sosa	5.00
7	Frank Thomas	4.00
8	Manny Ramirez	4.00
9	Jeff Bagwell	4.00
10	Mike Piazza	5.50
11	Roger Clemens	5.50
12	Derek Jeter	10.00
13	Scott Rolen	3.00
14	Mark McGwire	8.00
15	Tony Gwynn	5.00
16	Barry Bonds	10.00
17	Ken Griffey Jr.	6.00
18	Alex Rodriguez	8.00
19	Jose Canseco	2.50
20	Juan Gonzalez	2.00

Hit Machine 3000

		NM/M
	Complete Set (20):	24.00
	Common Card:	1.50
1	The Hitting Machine	1.50
2	The Eyes Have It	1.50
3	The Art of Hitting	1.50
4	Solid as a Rock	1.50
5	Seeing Doubles	1.50
6	Pitcher's Worst Nightmare	1.50

7	Portrait of an All-Star	1.50
8	An American Hero	1.50
9	Fan Favorite	1.50
10	Mr. Batting Title	1.50
11	4-for-5!	1.50
12	Mission Accomplished	1.50
13	One Hit Away	1.50
14	A Tip of the Hat	1.50
15	It's a Base Hit!	1.50
16	2997th - Grand Slam!	1.50
17	2998th Hit	1.50
18	2999th Hit - 2-Run Double	1.50
19	3000th Hit!	1.50
20	3000 Hits, 8874 At-Bats, 18 Years	1.50

HR '99

		NM/M
	Complete Set (20):	20.00
	Common Player:	.25
	Inserted 1:37	
1	Mo Vaughn	.25
2	Matt Williams	.25
3	Chipper Jones	2.00
4	Albert Belle	.25
5	Nomar Garciaparra	2.00
6	Sammy Sosa	2.00
7	Frank Thomas	1.25
8	Manny Ramirez	1.25
9	Jeff Bagwell	1.25
10	Raul Mondesi	.25
11	Vladimir Guerrero	1.25
12	Mike Piazza	2.25
13	Derek Jeter	4.00
14	Mark McGwire	3.00
15	Fernando Tatis	.25
16	Barry Bonds	4.00
17	Ken Griffey Jr.	2.50
18	Alex Rodriguez	3.00
19	Jose Canseco	.75
20	Juan Gonzalez	.65

5-Tool Talents

		NM/M
	Complete Set (30):	40.00
	Common Player:	.40
	Inserted 4:37	
1	Randy Johnson	1.50
2	Greg Maddux	2.00
3	Pedro Martinez	1.50
4	Kevin Brown	.40
5	Roger Clemens	2.50
6	Carlos Lee	.40
7	Gabe Kapler	.40
8	Carlos Beltran	.75
9	J.D. Drew	.75
10	Ruben Mateo	.40
11	Chipper Jones	2.00
12	Sammy Sosa	2.00
13	Manny Ramirez	1.50
14	Vladimir Guerrero	1.50
15	Mark McGwire	4.00
16	Ken Griffey Jr.	3.00
17	Jose Canseco	.75
18	Nomar Garciaparra	2.00
19	Frank Thomas	1.50
20	Larry Walker	.40

21	Jeff Bagwell	1.50
22	Mike Piazza	2.50
23	Tony Gwynn	2.00
24	Juan Gonzalez	.75
25	Cal Ripken Jr.	5.00
26	Derek Jeter	5.00
27	Scott Rolen	1.25
28	Barry Bonds	5.00
29	Alex Rodriguez	4.00
30	Ivan Rodriguez	1.25

5-Tool Talents Tiered

		NM/M
	TIER 1 (BLUE, 100 SETS)	
1	Randy Johnson	4.00
6	Carlos Lee	2.00
11	Chipper Jones	5.00
18	Nomar Garciaparra	5.00
21	Jeff Bagwell	4.00
28	Barry Bonds	7.50
	TIER 2 (RED, 75 SETS)	
2	Greg Maddux	7.50
7	Gabe Kapler	2.00
13	Manny Ramirez	6.00
16	Ken Griffey Jr.	10.00
19	Frank Thomas	6.00
30	Ivan Rodriguez	5.00
	TIER 3 (GREEN, 50 SETS)	
3	Pedro Martinez	12.50
8	Carlos Beltran	6.00
15	Mark McGwire	20.00
20	Larry Walker	2.00
25	Cal Ripken Jr.	30.00
26	Derek Jeter	30.00
	TIER 4 (PURPLE, 25 SETS)	
4	Kevin Brown	7.50
9	J.D. Drew	15.00
12	Sammy Sosa	25.00
17	Jose Canseco	20.00
23	Tony Gwynn	25.00
29	Alex Rodriguez	35.00
	TIER 5 (GOLD, ONE SET)	
5	Roger Clemens	
10	Ruben Mateo	
14	Vladimir Guerrero	
22	Mike Piazza	
24	Juan Gonzalez	
27	Scott Rolen	

1999 Pacific Paramount

		NM/M
	Complete Set (250):	25.00
	Common Player:	.10
	Copper (1:1H):	2X
	Red (1:1R):	2X
	Gold (1:1R):	2X
	Platinum Blue (1:73):	4X
	Holographic Gold (199):	10X
	Holographic Silver (99 Sets):	15X
	Opening Day (74):	15X
	Pack (6):	1.00
	Wax Box (36):	25.00
1	Garret Anderson	.10
2	Gary DiSarcina	.10
3	Jim Edmonds	.10
4	Darin Erstad	.25
5	Chuck Finley	.10
6	Troy Glaus	.75
7	Troy Percival	.10
8	Tim Salmon	.10
9	Mo Vaughn	.10
10	Tony Batista	.10
11	Jay Bell	.10
12	Andy Benes	.10
13	Steve Finley	.10
14	Luis Gonzalez	.10
15	Randy Johnson	.75
16	Travis Lee	.10
17	Todd Stottlemyre	.10
18	Matt Williams	.10
19	David Dellucci	.10
20	Bret Boone	.10
21	Andres Galarraga	.10
22	Tom Glavine	.35
23	Andruw Jones	.10
24	Chipper Jones	1.50
25	Brian Jordan	.10
26	Ryan Klesko	.10
27	Javy Lopez	.10
28	Greg Maddux	1.50
29	John Smoltz	.10

30	Brady Anderson	.10
31	Albert Belle	.10
32	Will Clark	.10
33	Delino DeShields	.10
34	Charles Johnson	.10
35	Mike Mussina	.40
36	Cal Ripken Jr.	3.00
37	B.J. Surhoff	.10
38	Nomar Garciaparra	1.50
39	Reggie Jefferson	.10
40	Darren Lewis	.10
41	Pedro Martinez	.75
42	Troy O'Leary	.10
43	Jose Offerman	.10
44	Donnie Sadler	.10
45	John Valentin	.10
46	Rod Beck	.10
47	Gary Gaetti	.10
48	Mark Grace	.10
49	Lance Johnson	.10
50	Mickey Morandini	.10
51	Henry Rodriguez	.10
52	Sammy Sosa	1.50
53	Kerry Wood	.40
54	Mike Caruso	.10
55	Ray Durham	.10
56	Paul Konerko	.20
57	Jaime Navarro	.10
58	Greg Norton	.10
59	Magglio Ordonez	.30
60	Frank Thomas	.75
61	Aaron Boone	.10
62	Mike Cameron	.10
63	Barry Larkin	.10
64	Hal Morris	.10
65	Pokey Reese	.10
66	Brett Tomko	.10
67	Greg Vaughn	.10
68	Dmitri Young	.10
69	Roberto Alomar	.25
70	Sandy Alomar Jr.	.10
71	Bartolo Colon	.10
72	Travis Fryman	.10
73	David Justice	.10
74	Kenny Lofton	.10
75	Manny Ramirez	.75
76	Richie Sexson	.10
77	Jim Thome	.65
78	Omar Vizquel	.10
79	Dante Bichette	.10
80	Vinny Castilla	.10
81	Darryl Hamilton	.10
82	Todd Helton	.75
83	Darryl Kile	.10
84	Mike Lansing	.10
85	Neifi Perez	.10
86	Larry Walker	.10
87	Tony Clark	.10
88	Damion Easley	.10
89	Bob Higginson	.10
90	Brian Hunter	.10
91	Dean Palmer	.10
92	Justin Thompson	.10
93	Todd Dunwoody	.10
94	Cliff Floyd	.10
95	Alex Gonzalez	.10
96	Livan Hernandez	.10
97	Mark Kotsay	.10
98	Derrek Lee	.60
99	Kevin Orie	.10
100	Moises Alou	.10
101	Jeff Bagwell	.75
102	Derek Bell	.10
103	Craig Biggio	.10
104	Ken Caminiti	.10
105	Ricky Gutierrez	.10
106	Richard Hidalgo	.10
107	Billy Wagner	.10
108	Jeff Conine	.10
109	Johnny Damon	.35
110	Carlos Febles	.10
111	Jeremy Giambi	.10
112	Jeff King	.10
113	Jeff Montgomery	.10
114	Joe Randa	.10
115	Kevin Brown	.10
116	Mark Grudzielanek	.10
117	Todd Hundley	.10
118	Eric Karros	.10
119	Raul Mondesi	.10
120	Chan Ho Park	.10
121	Gary Sheffield	.40
122	Devon White	.10
123	Eric Young	.10
124	Jeromy Burnitz	.10
125	Jeff Cirillo	.10
126	Marquis Grissom	.10
127	Geoff Jenkins	.10
128	Dave Nilsson	.10
129	Jose Valentin	.10
130	Fernando Vina	.10
131	Rick Aguilera	.10
132	Ron Coomer	.10
133	Marty Cordova	.10
134	Matt Lawton	.10
135	David Ortiz	.50
136	Brad Radke	.10
137	Terry Steinbach	.10
138	Javier Valentin	.10
139	Todd Walker	.10
140	Orlando Cabrera	.10
141	Brad Fullmer	.10
142	Vladimir Guerrero	.75
143	Wilton Guerrero	.10
144	Carl Pavano	.10

145	Ugueth Urbina	.10
146	Rondell White	.10
147	Chris Widger	.10
148	Edgardo Alfonzo	.10
149	Bobby Bonilla	.10
150	Rickey Henderson	.75
151	Brian McRae	.10
152	Hideo Nomo	.40
153	John Olerud	.10
154	Rey Ordonez	.10
155	Mike Piazza	1.75
156	Robin Ventura	.10
157	Masato Yoshii	.10
158	Roger Clemens	1.75
159	David Cone	.10
160	Orlando Hernandez	.10
161	Hideki Irabu	.10
162	Derek Jeter	3.00
163	Chuck Knoblauch	.10
164	Tino Martinez	.10
165	Paul O'Neill	.10
166	Darryl Strawberry	.10
167	Bernie Williams	.10
168	Eric Chavez	.20
169	Ryan Christenson	.10
170	Jason Giambi	.50
171	Ben Grieve	.10
172	Tony Phillips	.10
173	Tim Raines	.10
174	Scott Spiezio	.10
175	Miguel Tejada	.20
176	Bobby Abreu	.20
177	Rico Brogna	.10
178	Ron Gant	.10
179	Doug Glanville	.10
180	Desi Relaford	.10
181	Scott Rolen	.65
182	Curt Schilling	.35
183	Brant Brown	.10
184	Brian Giles	.10
185	Jose Guillen	.10
186	Jason Kendall	.10
187	Al Martin	.10
188	Ed Sprague	.10
189	Kevin Young	.10
190	Eric Davis	.10
191	J.D. Drew	.40
192	Ray Lankford	.10
193	Eli Marrero	.10
194	Mark McGwire	2.50
195	Edgar Renteria	.10
196	Fernando Tatis	.10
197	Andy Ashby	.10
198	Tony Gwynn	1.50
199	Carlos Hernandez	.10
200	Trevor Hoffman	.10
201	Wally Joyner	.10
202	Jim Leyritz	.10
203	Ruben Rivera	.10
204	Matt Clement	.10
205	Quivio Veras	.10
206	Rich Aurilia	.10
207	Marvin Benard	.10
208	Barry Bonds	3.00
209	Ellis Burks	.10
210	Jeff Kent	.10
211	Bill Mueller	.10
212	Robb Nen	.10
213	J.T. Snow	.10
214	Jay Buhner	.10
215	Jeff Fassero	.10
216	Ken Griffey Jr.	2.00
217	Carlos Guillen	.10
218	Butch Huskey	.10
219	Edgar Martinez	.10
220	Alex Rodriguez	2.50
221	David Segui	.10
222	Dan Wilson	.10
223	Rolando Arrojo	.10
224	Wade Boggs	1.50
225	Jose Canseco	.50
226	Roberto Hernandez	.10
227	Dave Martinez	.10
228	Quinton McCracken	.10
229	Fred McGriff	.10
230	Kevin Stocker	.10
231	Randy Winn	.10
232	Royce Clayton	.10
233	Juan Gonzalez	.40
234	Tom Goodwin	.10
235	Rusty Greer	.10
236	Rick Helling	.10
237	Rafael Palmeiro	.65
238	Ivan Rodriguez	.65
239	Aaron Sele	.10
240	John Wetteland	.10
241	Todd Zeile	.10
242	Jose Cruz Jr.	.10
243	Carlos Delgado	.50
244	Tony Fernandez	.10
245	Cecil Fielder	.10
246	Alex Gonzalez	.10
247	Shawn Green	.35
248	Roy Halladay	.10
249	Shannon Stewart	.10
250	David Wells	.10

Cooperstown Bound

		NM/M
Complete Set (10):		35.00
Common Player:		3.00
Inserted 1:361		
1	Greg Maddux	4.00
2	Cal Ripken Jr.	10.00
3	Nomar Garciaparra	4.00
4	Sammy Sosa	4.00
5	Frank Thomas	3.00
6	Mike Piazza	5.00
7	Mark McGwire	10.00
8	Tony Gwynn	4.00
9	Ken Griffey Jr.	6.00
10	Alex Rodriguez	8.00

Fielder's Choice

		NM/M
Complete Set (20):		60.00
Common Player:		2.50
Inserted 1:73		
1	Chipper Jones	5.00
2	Greg Maddux	5.00
3	Cal Ripken Jr.	10.00
4	Nomar Garciaparra	5.00
5	Sammy Sosa	5.00
6	Kerry Wood	3.00
7	Frank Thomas	4.00
8	Manny Ramirez	4.00
9	Todd Helton	4.00
10	Jeff Bagwell	4.00
11	Mike Piazza	5.50
12	Derek Jeter	10.00
13	Bernie Williams	2.50
14	J.D. Drew	3.00
15	Mark McGwire	7.50
16	Tony Gwynn	5.00
17	Ken Griffey Jr.	6.00
18	Alex Rodriguez	7.50
19	Juan Gonzalez	2.50
20	Ivan Rodriguez	3.50

Personal Bests

		NM/M
Complete Set (36):		45.00
Common Player:		.50
Inserted 1:37		
1	Darin Erstad	.65
2	Mo Vaughn	.50
3	Travis Lee	.50
4	Chipper Jones	3.00
5	Greg Maddux	3.00
6	Albert Belle	.50
7	Cal Ripken Jr.	6.00
8	Nomar Garciaparra	3.00
9	Sammy Sosa	3.00
10	Kerry Wood	1.00
11	Frank Thomas	2.00
12	Greg Vaughn	.50
13	Manny Ramirez	2.00
14	Todd Helton	2.00
15	Larry Walker	.50
16	Jeff Bagwell	2.00
17	Craig Biggio	.50
18	Raul Mondesi	.50
19	Vladimir Guerrero	2.00
20	Hideo Nomo	1.00
21	Mike Piazza	3.50
22	Roger Clemens	3.50
23	Derek Jeter	6.00
24	Bernie Williams	.50
25	Eric Chavez	.75
26	Ben Grieve	.50
27	Scott Rolen	1.50
28	J.D. Drew	1.25
29	Mark McGwire	4.50
30	Tony Gwynn	3.00
31	Barry Bonds	6.00
32	Ken Griffey Jr.	4.00
33	Alex Rodriguez	4.50
34	Jose Canseco	1.25
35	Juan Gonzalez	1.00
36	Ivan Rodriguez	1.50

Team Checklists

		NM/M
Complete Set (30):		40.00
Common Player:		.50
Inserted 2:37		
1	Mo Vaughn	.50
2	Travis Lee	.50
3	Chipper Jones	3.00
4	Cal Ripken Jr.	6.00
5	Nomar Garciaparra	3.00
6	Sammy Sosa	3.00
7	Frank Thomas	2.50
8	Greg Vaughn	.50
9	Manny Ramirez	.50
10	Larry Walker	.50
11	Damion Easley	.50
12	Mark Kotsay	.50
13	Jeff Bagwell	2.50
14	Jeremy Giambi	.50
15	Raul Mondesi	.50
16	Marquis Grissom	.50
17	Brad Radke	.50
18	Vladimir Guerrero	2.50
19	Mike Piazza	3.50
20	Roger Clemens	3.50
21	Ben Grieve	.50
22	Scott Rolen	2.00
23	Brian Giles	.50
24	Mark McGwire	5.00
25	Tony Gwynn	3.00
26	Barry Bonds	6.00
27	Ken Griffey Jr.	4.00
28	Jose Canseco	1.25
29	Juan Gonzalez	1.25
30	Jose Cruz Jr.	.50

1999 Pacific Prism

	NM/M
Complete Set (150):	50.00
Common Player:	.15
Red (2:25R):	3X
HoloGold (480 Sets):	3X
HoloPurple (320):	4X
HoloMirror (160):	8X
HoloBlue (80):	15X
Retail Pack (3):	1.00
Hobby Pack (5):	1.50

1	Garret Anderson	.15
2	Jim Edmonds	.15
3	Darin Erstad	.30
4	Chuck Finley	.15
5	Tim Salmon	.15
6	Jay Bell	.15
7	David Dellucci	.15
8	Travis Lee	.15
9	Matt Williams	.15
10	Andres Galarraga	.15
11	Tom Glavine	.40
12	Andruw Jones	1.50
13	Chipper Jones	2.00
14	Ryan Klesko	.15
15	Javy Lopez	.15
16	Greg Maddux	2.00
17	Roberto Alomar	.50
18	Ryan Minor	.15
19	Mike Mussina	.40
20	Rafael Palmeiro	1.25
21	Cal Ripken Jr.	4.00
22	Nomar Garciaparra	2.00
23	Pedro Martinez	1.50
24	John Valentin	.15
25	Mo Vaughn	.15
26	Tim Wakefield	.15
27	Rod Beck	.15
28	Mark Grace	.15
29	Lance Johnson	.15
30	Sammy Sosa	2.00
31	Kerry Wood	.50
32	Albert Belle	.15
33	Mike Caruso	.15
34	Magglio Ordonez	.30
35	Frank Thomas	1.50
36	Robin Ventura	.15
37	Aaron Boone	.15
38	Barry Larkin	.15
39	Reggie Sanders	.15
40	Brett Tomko	.15
41	Sandy Alomar Jr.	.15
42	Bartolo Colon	.15
43	David Justice	.15
44	Kenny Lofton	.15
45	Manny Ramirez	1.50
46	Richie Sexson	.15
47	Jim Thome	1.00
48	Omar Vizquel	.15
49	Dante Bichette	.15
50	Vinny Castilla	.15
51	Edgard Clemente **RC**	.15
52	Todd Helton	1.50
53	Quinton McCracken	.15
54	Larry Walker	.15
55	Tony Clark	.15
56	Damion Easley	.15
57	Luis Gonzalez	.15
58	Bob Higginson	.15
59	Brian Hunter	.15
60	Cliff Floyd	.15
61	Alex Gonzalez	.15
62	Livan Hernandez	.15
63	Derrek Lee	.65
64	Edgar Renteria	.15
65	Moises Alou	.15
66	Jeff Bagwell	1.50
67	Derek Bell	.15
68	Craig Biggio	.15
69	Randy Johnson	1.50
70	Johnny Damon	.35
71	Jeff King	.15
72	Hal Morris	.15
73	Dean Palmer	.15
74	Eric Karros	.15
75	Raul Mondesi	.15
76	Chan Ho Park	.15
77	Gary Sheffield	.50
78	Jeromy Burnitz	.15
79	Jeff Cirillo	.15
80	Marquis Grissom	.15
81	Jose Valentin	.15
82	Fernando Vina	.15
83	Paul Molitor	1.50
84	Otis Nixon	.15
85	David Ortiz	.65
86	Todd Walker	.15
87	Vladimir Guerrero	1.50
88	Carl Pavano	.15
89	Fernando Seguignol	.15
90	Ugueth Urbina	.15
91	Carlos Baerga	.15
92	Bobby Bonilla	.15
93	Hideo Nomo	.75
94	John Olerud	.15
95	Rey Ordonez	.15
96	Mike Piazza	2.25
97	David Cone	.15
98	Orlando Hernandez	.15
99	Hideki Irabu	.15
100	Derek Jeter	4.00
101	Tino Martinez	.15
102	Bernie Williams	.15
103	Eric Chavez	.25
104	Jason Giambi	1.00
105	Ben Grieve	.15
106	Rickey Henderson	1.50
107	Bob Abreu	.25
108	Doug Glanville	.15
109	Scott Rolen	1.00
110	Curt Schilling	.40
111	Emil Brown	.15
112	Jose Guillen	.15
113	Jason Kendall	.15
114	Al Martin	.15
115	Aramis Ramirez	.15

116	Kevin Young	.15
117	J.D. Drew	.75
118	Ron Gant	.15
119	Brian Jordan	.15
120	Eli Marrero	.15
121	Mark McGwire	3.00
122	Kevin Brown	.15
123	Tony Gwynn	2.00
124	Trevor Hoffman	.15
125	Wally Joyner	.15
126	Greg Vaughn	.15
127	Barry Bonds	4.00
128	Ellis Burks	.15
129	Jeff Kent	.15
130	Robb Nen	.15
131	J.T. Snow	.15
132	Jay Buhner	.15
133	Ken Griffey Jr.	2.50
134	Edgar Martinez	.15
135	Alex Rodriguez	3.00
136	David Segui	.15
137	Rolando Arrojo	.15
138	Wade Boggs	2.00
139	Aaron Ledesma	.15
140	Fred McGriff	.15
141	Will Clark	.15
142	Juan Gonzalez	.75
143	Rusty Greer	.15
144	Ivan Rodriguez	1.25
145	Aaron Sele	.15
146	Jose Canseco	.40
147	Roger Clemens	2.25
148	Jose Cruz Jr.	.15
149	Carlos Delgado	.50
150	Alex Gonzalez	.15

Ahead of the Game

		NM/M
Complete Set (20):		40.00
Common Player:		1.00
Inserted 1:49		
1	Darin Erstad	1.25
2	Travis Lee	1.00
3	Chipper Jones	3.00
4	Cal Ripken Jr.	6.00
5	Nomar Garciaparra	3.00
6	Sammy Sosa	3.00
7	Kerry Wood	1.25
8	Frank Thomas	2.00
9	Manny Ramirez	2.00
10	Todd Helton	2.00
11	Jeff Bagwell	2.00
12	Mike Piazza	3.50
13	Derek Jeter	6.00
14	Bernie Williams	1.00
15	J.D. Drew	1.25
16	Mark McGwire	5.00
17	Tony Gwynn	3.00
18	Ken Griffey Jr.	4.00
19	Alex Rodriguez	5.00
20	Ivan Rodriguez	1.50

Ballpark Legends

		NM/M
Complete Set (10):		40.00
Common Player:		2.50
Inserted 1:193		
1	Cal Ripken Jr.	10.00
2	Nomar Garciaparra	5.00
3	Frank Thomas	4.00
4	Ken Griffey Jr.	6.00
5	Alex Rodriguez	7.50
6	Greg Maddux	5.00
7	Sammy Sosa	5.00
8	Kerry Wood	2.50
9	Mark McGwire	7.50
10	Tony Gwynn	5.00

Diamond Glory

		NM/M
Complete Set (20):		25.00
Common Player:		.60
Inserted 2:25		
1	Darin Erstad	.60
2	Travis Lee	.60
3	Chipper Jones	2.00
4	Cal Ripken Jr.	3.50
5	Nomar Garciaparra	2.00
6	Sammy Sosa	2.00
7	Kerry Wood	.75
8	Frank Thomas	1.50
9	Todd Helton	1.50
10	Jeff Bagwell	1.50
11	Mike Piazza	2.25
12	Derek Jeter	3.50
13	Bernie Williams	.60
14	J.D. Drew	.75
15	Mark McGwire	3.00
16	Tony Gwynn	2.00
17	Ken Griffey Jr.	2.50
18	Alex Rodriguez	3.00
19	Juan Gonzalez	.75

Epic Performers

		NM/M
Complete Set (10):		60.00
Common Player:		4.00
Inserted 1:97 H		
1	Cal Ripken Jr.	15.00
2	Nomar Garciaparra	7.50
3	Frank Thomas	6.00
4	Ken Griffey Jr.	10.00
5	Alex Rodriguez	12.50
6	Greg Maddux	7.50
7	Sammy Sosa	7.50
8	Kerry Wood	4.00
9	Mark McGwire	12.50
10	Tony Gwynn	7.50

1999 Pacific Private Stock

		NM/M
Complete Set (150):		25.00
Common Player:		.10
Pack (6):		1.50
Wax Box (24):		20.00
Wax Box (36):		25.00
1	Jeff Bagwell	1.00
2	Roger Clemens	1.75
3	J.D. Drew	.60
4	Nomar Garciaparra	1.50
5	Juan Gonzalez	.50
6	Ken Griffey Jr.	2.00
7	Tony Gwynn	1.50
8	Derek Jeter	3.00
9	Chipper Jones	1.50
10	Travis Lee	.10
11	Greg Maddux	1.50
12	Mark McGwire	2.50
13	Mike Piazza	1.75
14	Manny Ramirez	1.00
15	Cal Ripken Jr.	3.00
16	Alex Rodriguez	2.50
17	Ivan Rodriguez	.75
18	Sammy Sosa	1.50
19	Frank Thomas	1.00
20	Kerry Wood	.40
21	Roberto Alomar	.25
22	Moises Alou	.10
23	Albert Belle	.10
24	Craig Biggio	.10
25	Wade Boggs	.25
26	Barry Bonds	3.00
27	Jose Canseco	.50
28	Jim Edmonds	.10
29	Darin Erstad	.25
30	Andres Galarraga	.10
31	Tom Glavine	.35
32	Ben Grieve	.10
33	Vladimir Guerrero	1.00
34	Wilton Guerrero	.10
35	Todd Helton	1.00
36	Andruw Jones	1.00
37	Ryan Klesko	.10
38	Kenny Lofton	.10
39	Javy Lopez	.10
40	Pedro Martinez	1.00
41	Paul Molitor	1.00
42	Raul Mondesi	.10
43	Rafael Palmeiro	.75
44	Tim Salmon	.10
45	Jim Thome	.75
46	Mo Vaughn	.10
47	Larry Walker	.10
48	David Wells	.10
49	Bernie Williams	.10
50	Jaret Wright	.10
51	Bobby Abreu	.15
52	Garret Anderson	.10
53	Rolando Arrojo	.10
54	Tony Batista	.10
55	Rod Beck	.10
56	Derek Bell	.10
57	Marvin Benard	.10
58	Dave Berg	.10
59	Dante Bichette	.10
60	Aaron Boone	.10
61	Bret Boone	.10
62	Scott Brosius	.10
63	Brant Brown	.10
64	Kevin Brown	.10
65	Jeromy Burnitz	.10
66	Ken Caminiti	.10
67	Mike Caruso	.10
68	Sean Casey	.20
69	Vinny Castilla	.10
70	Eric Chavez	.20
71	Ryan Christenson	.10
72	Jeff Cirillo	.10
73	Tony Clark	.10
74	Will Clark	.10
75	Edgard Clemente RC	.10
76	David Cone	.10
77	Marty Cordova	.10
78	Jose Cruz Jr.	.10
79	Eric Davis	.10
80	Carlos Delgado	.50
81	David Dellucci	.10
82	Delino DeShields	.10
83	Gary DiSarcina	.10
84	Damion Easley	.10
85	Dennis Eckersley	.65
86	Cliff Floyd	.10
87	Jason Giambi	.65
88	Doug Glanville	.10
89	Alex Gonzalez	.10
90	Mark Grace	.10
91	Rusty Greer	.10
92	Jose Guillen	.10
93	Carlos Guillen	.10
94	Jeffrey Hammonds	.10
95	Rick Helling	.10
96	Bob Henley	.10
97	Livan Hernandez	.10
98	Orlando Hernandez	.10
99	Bob Higginson	.10
100	Trevor Hoffman	.10
101	Randy Johnson	1.00
102	Brian Jordan	.10
103	Wally Joyner	.10
104	Eric Karros	.10
105	Jason Kendall	.10
106	Jeff Kent	.10
107	Jeff King	.10
108	Mark Kotsay	.10
109	Ray Lankford	.10

110	Barry Larkin	.10
111	Mark Loretta	.10
112	Edgar Martinez	.10
113	Tino Martinez	.10
114	Quinton McCracken	.10
115	Fred McGriff	.10
116	Ryan Minor	.10
117	Hal Morris	.10
118	Bill Mueller	.10
119	Mike Mussina	.40
120	Dave Nilsson	.10
121	Otis Nixon	.10
122	Hideo Nomo	.50
123	Paul O'Neill	.10
124	Jose Offerman	.10
125	John Olerud	.10
126	Rey Ordonez	.10
127	David Ortiz	.50
128	Dean Palmer	.10
129	Chan Ho Park	.10
130	Aramis Ramirez	.10
131	Edgar Renteria	.10
132	Armando Rios	.10
133	Henry Rodriguez	.10
134	Scott Rolen	.75
135	Curt Schilling	.35
136	David Segui	.10
137	Richie Sexson	.10
138	Gary Sheffield	.45
139	John Smoltz	.10
140	Matt Stairs	.10
141	Justin Thompson	.10
142	Greg Vaughn	.10
143	Omar Vizquel	.10
144	Tim Wakefield	.10
145	Todd Walker	.10
146	Devon White	.10
147	Rondell White	.10
148	Matt Williams	.10
149	Enrique Wilson RC	.25
150	Kevin Young	.10

Exclusive Series

		NM/M
Complete Set (20):		50.00
Common Player:		1.00
Production:		299 Sets H
1	Jeff Bagwell	2.00
2	Roger Clemens	3.50
3	J.D. Drew	1.25
4	Nomar Garciaparra	3.00
5	Juan Gonzalez	1.25
6	Ken Griffey Jr.	4.00
7	Tony Gwynn	3.00
8	Derek Jeter	6.00
9	Chipper Jones	3.00
10	Travis Lee	1.00
11	Greg Maddux	5.00
12	Mark McGwire	5.00
13	Mike Piazza	3.50
14	Manny Ramirez	2.00
15	Cal Ripken Jr.	6.00
16	Alex Rodriguez	5.00
17	Ivan Rodriguez	1.50
18	Sammy Sosa	3.00
19	Frank Thomas	2.00
20	Kerry Wood	1.25

Platinum Series

		NM/M
Complete Set (50):		160.00
Common Player:		.75
Production 199 Sets		
1	Jeff Bagwell	5.00
2	Roger Clemens	6.50
3	J.D. Drew	3.00
4	Nomar Garciaparra	6.00
5	Juan Gonzalez	2.50
6	Ken Griffey Jr.	8.00
7	Tony Gwynn	6.00
8	Derek Jeter	12.00
9	Chipper Jones	6.00
10	Travis Lee	.75
11	Greg Maddux	6.00
12	Mark McGwire	10.00
13	Mike Piazza	6.50
14	Manny Ramirez	5.00
15	Cal Ripken Jr.	12.00
16	Alex Rodriguez	10.00
17	Ivan Rodriguez	4.00
18	Sammy Sosa	6.00

19	Frank Thomas	5.00
20	Kerry Wood	2.00
21	Roberto Alomar	1.50
22	Moises Alou	.75
23	Albert Belle	.75
24	Craig Biggio	.75
25	Wade Boggs	6.00
26	Barry Bonds	12.00
27	Jose Canseco	3.00
28	Jim Edmonds	.75
29	Darin Erstad	1.50
30	Andres Galarraga	.75
31	Tom Glavine	2.00
32	Ben Grieve	.75
33	Vladimir Guerrero	5.00
34	Wilton Guerrero	.75
35	Todd Helton	5.00
36	Andruw Jones	5.00
37	Ryan Klesko	.75
38	Kenny Lofton	.75
39	Javy Lopez	.75
40	Pedro Martinez	5.00
41	Paul Molitor	5.00
42	Raul Mondesi	.75
43	Rafael Palmeiro	4.00
44	Tim Salmon	.75
45	Jim Thome	3.50
46	Mo Vaughn	.75
47	Larry Walker	.75
48	David Wells	.75
49	Bernie Williams	.75
50	Jaret Wright	.75

Preferred Series

		NM/M
Complete Set (20):		37.50
Common Player:		.60
Production:		399 Sets
1	Jeff Bagwell	1.50
2	Roger Clemens	2.25
3	J.D. Drew	.75
4	Nomar Garciaparra	2.00
5	Juan Gonzalez	.75
6	Ken Griffey Jr.	2.50
7	Tony Gwynn	2.00
8	Derek Jeter	5.00
9	Chipper Jones	2.00
10	Travis Lee	.60
11	Greg Maddux	2.00
12	Mark McGwire	3.50
13	Mike Piazza	2.25
14	Manny Ramirez	1.50
15	Cal Ripken Jr.	5.00
16	Alex Rodriguez	3.50
17	Ivan Rodriguez	1.25
18	Sammy Sosa	2.00
19	Frank Thomas	1.50
20	Kerry Wood	.75

PS-206

		NM/M
Complete Set (150):		20.00
Common Player:		.15
Inserted 1:1		
Red Parallels:		4X
Inserted 1:25		
1	Jeff Bagwell	.75

2	Roger Clemens	1.25
3	J.D. Drew	.50
4	Nomar Garciaparra	1.00
5	Juan Gonzalez	.40
6	Ken Griffey Jr.	1.50
7	Tony Gwynn	1.00
8	Derek Jeter	3.00
9	Chipper Jones	1.00
10	Travis Lee	.15
11	Greg Maddux	1.00
12	Mark McGwire	2.00
13	Mike Piazza	1.25
14	Manny Ramirez	.75
15	Cal Ripken Jr.	3.00
16	Alex Rodriguez	2.00
17	Ivan Rodriguez	.65
18	Sammy Sosa	1.00
19	Frank Thomas	.75
20	Kerry Wood	.40
21	Roberto Alomar	.30
22	Moises Alou	.15
23	Albert Belle	.15
24	Craig Biggio	.15
25	Wade Boggs	1.00
26	Barry Bonds	3.00
27	Jose Canseco	.50
28	Jim Edmonds	.15
29	Darin Erstad	.30
30	Andres Galarraga	.15
31	Tom Glavine	.35
32	Ben Grieve	.15
33	Vladimir Guerrero	.75
34	Wilton Guerrero	.15
35	Todd Helton	.75
36	Andruw Jones	.75
37	Ryan Klesko	.15
38	Kenny Lofton	.15
39	Javy Lopez	.15
40	Pedro Martinez	.75
41	Paul Molitor	.75
42	Raul Mondesi	.15
43	Rafael Palmeiro	.65
44	Tim Salmon	.15
45	Jim Thome	.65
46	Mo Vaughn	.15
47	Larry Walker	.15
48	David Wells	.15
49	Bernie Williams	.15
50	Jaret Wright	.15
51	Bobby Abreu	.15
52	Garret Anderson	.15
53	Rolando Arrojo	.15
54	Tony Batista	.15
55	Rod Beck	.15
56	Derek Bell	.15
57	Marvin Benard	.15
58	Dave Berg	.15
59	Dante Bichette	.15
60	Aaron Boone	.15
61	Bret Boone	.15
62	Scott Brosius	.15
63	Brant Brown	.15
64	Kevin Brown	.15
65	Jeromy Burnitz	.15
66	Ken Caminiti	.15
67	Mike Caruso	.15
68	Sean Casey	.25
69	Vinny Castilla	.15
70	Eric Chavez	.25
71	Ryan Christenson	.15
72	Jeff Cirillo	.15
73	Tony Clark	.15
74	Will Clark	.15
75	Edgard Clemente	.15
76	David Cone	.15
77	Marty Cordova	.15
78	Jose Cruz Jr.	.15
79	Eric Davis	.15
80	Carlos Delgado	.60
81	David Dellucci	.15
82	Delino DeShields	.15
83	Gary DiSarcina	.15
84	Damion Easley	.15
85	Dennis Eckersley	.65
86	Cliff Floyd	.15
87	Jason Giambi	.60

88	Doug Glanville	.15
89	Alex Gonzalez	.15
90	Mark Grace	.15
91	Rusty Greer	.15
92	Jose Guillen	.15
93	Carlos Guillen	.15
94	Jeffrey Hammonds	.15
95	Rick Helling	.15
96	Bob Henley	.15
97	Livan Hernandez	.15
98	Orlando Hernandez	.15
99	Bob Higginson	.15
100	Trevor Hoffman	.15
101	Randy Johnson	.75
102	Brian Jordan	.15
103	Wally Joyner	.15
104	Eric Karros	.15
105	Jason Kendall	.15
106	Jeff Kent	.15
107	Jeff King	.15
108	Mark Kotsay	.15
109	Ray Lankford	.15
110	Barry Larkin	.15
111	Mark Loretta	.15
112	Edgar Martinez	.15
113	Tino Martinez	.15
114	Quinton McCracken	.15
115	Fred McGriff	.15
116	Ryan Minor	.15
117	Hal Morris	.15
118	Bill Mueller	.15
119	Mike Mussina	.40
120	Dave Nilsson	.15
121	Otis Nixon	.15
122	Hideo Nomo	.40
123	Paul O'Neill	.15
124	Jose Offerman	.15
125	John Olerud	.15
126	Rey Ordonez	.15
127	David Ortiz	.50
128	Dean Palmer	.15
129	Chan Ho Park	.15
130	Aramis Ramirez	.15
131	Edgar Renteria	.15
132	Armando Rios	.15
133	Henry Rodriguez	.15
134	Scott Rolen	.60
135	Curt Schilling	.35
136	David Segui	.15
137	Richie Sexson	.15
138	Gary Sheffield	.50
139	John Smoltz	.15
140	Matt Stairs	.15
141	Justin Thompson	.15
142	Greg Vaughn	.15
143	Omar Vizquel	.15
144	Tim Wakefield	.15
145	Todd Walker	.15
146	Devon White	.15
147	Rondell White	.15
148	Matt Williams	.15
149	Enrique Wilson	.15
150	Kevin Young	.15

Vintage Series

		NM/M
Complete Set (50):		375.00
Common Player:		2.50
Production:		99 Sets
1	Jeff Bagwell	12.50
2	Roger Clemens	17.50
3	J.D. Drew	7.50
4	Nomar Garciaparra	15.00
5	Juan Gonzalez	6.00
6	Ken Griffey Jr.	20.00
7	Tony Gwynn	15.00
8	Derek Jeter	30.00
9	Chipper Jones	15.00
10	Travis Lee	2.50
11	Greg Maddux	15.00
12	Mark McGwire	25.00
13	Mike Piazza	17.50
14	Manny Ramirez	12.50
15	Cal Ripken Jr.	30.00
16	Alex Rodriguez	25.00
17	Ivan Rodriguez	10.00
18	Sammy Sosa	15.00
19	Frank Thomas	12.50
20	Kerry Wood	6.00
21	Roberto Alomar	3.50
22	Moises Alou	2.50
23	Albert Belle	2.50
24	Craig Biggio	2.50
25	Wade Boggs	15.00
26	Barry Bonds	30.00
27	Jose Canseco	5.00
28	Jim Edmonds	2.50
29	Darin Erstad	3.50
30	Andres Galarraga	2.50
31	Tom Glavine	5.00
32	Ben Grieve	2.50
33	Vladimir Guerrero	12.50
34	Wilton Guerrero	2.50
35	Todd Helton	12.50
36	Andruw Jones	12.50
37	Ryan Klesko	2.50
38	Kenny Lofton	2.50
39	Javy Lopez	2.50
40	Pedro Martinez	12.50
41	Paul Molitor	12.50
42	Raul Mondesi	2.50
43	Rafael Palmeiro	10.00
44	Tim Salmon	2.50
45	Jim Thome	10.00
46	Mo Vaughn	2.50
47	Larry Walker	2.50
48	David Wells	2.50
49	Bernie Williams	2.50
50	Jaret Wright	2.50

1999 Pacific Revolution

		NM/M
Complete Set (150):		60.00
Common Player:		.15
Shadow (99 Sets H):		6X
SP:		3X
Red (299 R):		2X
SP:		1.5X
Premiere Date (49 H):		12X
SP:		6X
Wax Pack (3):		2.00
Wax Box (24):		35.00
1	Jim Edmonds	.15
2	Darin Erstad	.30
3	Troy Glaus	1.00
4	Tim Salmon	.15
5	Mo Vaughn	.15
6	Steve Finley	.15
7	Luis Gonzalez	.15
8	Randy Johnson	1.00
9	Travis Lee	.15
10	Matt Williams	.15
11	Andruw Jones	1.00
12	Chipper Jones	1.50
13	Brian Jordan	.15
14	Javy Lopez	.15
15	Greg Maddux	1.50
16	Kevin McGlinchy **RC**/SP	1.00
17	John Smoltz	.15
18	Brady Anderson	.15
19	Albert Belle	.15
20	Will Clark	.15
21	Willis Otanez **RC**/SP	.25
22	Calvin Pickering **RC**/SP	.25
23	Cal Ripken Jr.	4.00
24	Nomar Garciaparra	1.50
25	Pedro Martinez	1.00
26	Troy O'Leary	.15
27	Jose Offerman	.15
28	Mark Grace	.15
29	Mickey Morandini	.15
30	Henry Rodriguez	.15
31	Sammy Sosa	1.50
32	Ray Durham	.15
33	Carlos Lee/SP	.50
34	Jeff Liefer **RC**/SP	.35
35	Magglio Ordonez	.30
36	Frank Thomas	1.00
37	Mike Cameron	.15
38	Sean Casey	.35
39	Barry Larkin	.15
40	Greg Vaughn	.15
41	Roberto Alomar	.35
42	Sandy Alomar Jr.	.15
43	David Justice	.15
44	Kenny Lofton	.15
45	Manny Ramirez	1.00
46	Richie Sexson	.15
47	Jim Thome	.65
48	Dante Bichette	.15
49	Vinny Castilla	.15
50	Darryl Hamilton	.15
51	Todd Helton	1.00
52	Larry Walker	.15
53	Tony Clark	.15
54	Damion Easley	.15
55	Bob Higginson	.15
56	Gabe Kapler/SP	.25
57	Alex Gonzalez **RC**/SP	.35
58	Mark Kotsay	.15
59	Kevin Orie	.15
60	Preston Wilson/SP	1.00
61	Jeff Bagwell	1.00
62	Derek Bell	.15
63	Craig Biggio	.15
64	Ken Caminiti	.15
65	Carlos Beltran/SP	.65
66	Johnny Damon	.35
67	Jermaine Dye	.15
68	Carlos Febles/SP	.35
69	Kevin Brown	.15
70	Todd Hundley	.15
71	Eric Karros	.15
72	Raul Mondesi	.15
73	Gary Sheffield	.45
74	Jeromy Burnitz	.15

75	Jeff Cirillo	.15
76	Marquis Grissom	.15
77	Fernando Vina	.15
78	Chad Allen **RC**/SP	.25
79	Corey Koskie **RC**/SP	1.50
80	Doug Mientkiewicz **RC**/SP	1.00
81	Brad Radke	.15
82	Todd Walker	.15
83	Michael Barrett **RC**/SP	.35
84	Vladimir Guerrero	1.00
85	Wilton Guerrero	.15
86	Guillermo Mota **RC**/SP	.35
87	Rondell White	.15
88	Edgardo Alfonzo	.15
89	Rickey Henderson	1.00
90	John Olerud	.15
91	Mike Piazza	2.00
92	Robin Ventura	.15
93	Roger Clemens	2.00
94	Chili Davis	.15
95	Derek Jeter	4.00
96	Chuck Knoblauch	.15
97	Tino Martinez	.15
98	Paul O'Neill	.15
99	Bernie Williams	.15
100	Eric Chavez/SP	.35
101	Jason Giambi	.65
102	Ben Grieve	.15
103	John Jaha	.15
104	Olmedo Saenz **RC**/SP	.25
105	Bobby Abreu	.25
106	Doug Glanville	.15
107	Desi Relaford	.15
108	Scott Rolen	.75
109	Curt Schilling	.35
110	Brian Giles	.15
111	Jason Kendall	.15
112	Pat Meares	.15
113	Kevin Young	.15
114	J.D. Drew/SP	1.00
115	Ray Lankford	.15
116	Eli Marrero	.15
117	Joe McEwing **RC**/SP	.35
118	Mark McGwire	3.00
119	Fernando Tatis	.15
120	Tony Gwynn	1.50
121	Trevor Hoffman	.15
122	Wally Joyner	.15
123	Reggie Sanders	.15
124	Barry Bonds	4.00
125	Ellis Burks	.15
126	Jeff Kent	.15
127	Ramon Martinez **RC**/SP	.25
128	Joe Nathan **RC**/SP	.25
129	Freddy Garcia **RC**/SP	1.00
130	Ken Griffey Jr.	2.50
131	Brian Hunter	.15
132	Edgar Martinez	.15
133	Alex Rodriguez	3.00
134	David Segui	.15
135	Wade Boggs	1.50
136	Jose Canseco	.45
137	Quinton McCracken	.15
138	Fred McGriff	.15
139	Kelly Dransfeldt **RC**/SP	.25
140	Juan Gonzalez	.50
141	Rusty Greer	.15
142	Rafael Palmeiro	.75
143	Ivan Rodriguez	.75
144	Lee Stevens	.15
145	Jose Cruz Jr.	.15
146	Carlos Delgado	.60
147	Shawn Green	.50
148	Roy Halladay **RC**/SP	1.50
149	Shannon Stewart	.15
150	Kevin Witt **RC**/SP	.35

Shadow

		NM/M
Common Player:		4.00
Stars:		6X
SP's:		3X

(See 1999 Pacific Revolution for checklist and base card values.)

Diamond Legacy

		NM/M
Complete Set (36):		60.00
Common Player:		.50
Inserted 2:25		
1	Troy Glaus	2.00
2	Mo Vaughn	.50

Roger Clemens

3	Matt Williams	.50
4	Chipper Jones	3.00
5	Andruw Jones	2.00
6	Greg Maddux	3.00
7	Albert Belle	.50
8	Cal Ripken Jr.	6.00
9	Nomar Garciaparra	3.00
10	Sammy Sosa	3.00
11	Frank Thomas	2.00
12	Manny Ramirez	2.00
13	Todd Helton	2.00
14	Larry Walker	.50
15	Gabe Kapler	.50
16	Jeff Bagwell	2.00
17	Craig Biggio	.50
18	Raul Mondesi	.50
19	Vladimir Guerrero	2.00
20	Mike Piazza	3.50
21	Roger Clemens	3.50
22	Derek Jeter	6.00
23	Bernie Williams	.50
24	Ben Grieve	.50
25	Scott Rolen	1.75
26	J.D. Drew	1.50
27	Mark McGwire	5.00
28	Fernando Tatis	.50
29	Tony Gwynn	3.00
30	Barry Bonds	6.00
31	Ken Griffey Jr.	4.00
32	Alex Rodriguez	5.00
33	Jose Canseco	1.25
34	Juan Gonzalez	1.00
35	Ivan Rodriguez	1.75
36	Shawn Green	1.50

Foul Pole

		NM/M
Complete Set (20):		100.00
Common Player:		1.50
Inserted 1:49		
1	Chipper Jones	8.00
2	Andruw Jones	6.00
3	Cal Ripken Jr.	16.00
4	Nomar Garciaparra	8.00
5	Sammy Sosa	8.00
6	Frank Thomas	6.00
7	Manny Ramirez	6.00
8	Jeff Bagwell	6.00
9	Raul Mondesi	1.50
10	Vladimir Guerrero	6.00
11	Mike Piazza	9.00
12	Derek Jeter	16.00
13	Bernie Williams	1.50
14	Scott Rolen	5.00
15	J.D. Drew	3.00
16	Mark McGwire	12.00
17	Tony Gwynn	8.00
18	Ken Griffey Jr.	10.00
19	Alex Rodriguez	12.00
20	Juan Gonzalez	3.00

Icons

		NM/M
Complete Set (10):		50.00
Common Player:		4.00
Inserted 1:121		
1	Cal Ripken Jr.	10.00

2	Nomar Garciaparra	5.00
3	Sammy Sosa	5.00
4	Frank Thomas	4.00
5	Mike Piazza	6.50
6	Derek Jeter	10.00
7	Mark McGwire	8.00
8	Tony Gwynn	5.00
9	Ken Griffey Jr.	7.50
10	Alex Rodriguez	8.00

Thorn in the Side

Jeff Bagwell

		NM/M
Complete Set (20):		35.00
Common Player:		1.00
Inserted 1:25		
1	Mo Vaughn	1.00
2	Chipper Jones	3.00
3	Greg Maddux	3.00
4	Cal Ripken Jr.	6.00
5	Nomar Garciaparra	3.00
6	Sammy Sosa	3.00
7	Frank Thomas	2.25
8	Manny Ramirez	2.25
9	Jeff Bagwell	2.25
10	Mike Piazza	3.50
11	Derek Jeter	6.00
12	Bernie Williams	1.00
13	J.D. Drew	1.50
14	Mark McGwire	4.50
15	Tony Gwynn	3.00
16	Barry Bonds	6.00
17	Ken Griffey Jr.	4.00
18	Alex Rodriguez	4.50
19	Juan Gonzalez	1.50
20	Ivan Rodriguez	2.00

Tripleheader

		NM/M
Complete Set (30):		30.00
Common Player:		.25
Inserted 4:25 H		
Tier 1 (1-10)		
Production 99 Sets H		
Tier 2 (11-20)		

Production 199 Sets H
Tier 3 (21-30)
Production 299 Sets H

1	Greg Maddux	1.50
2	Cal Ripken Jr.	3.00
3	Nomar Garciaparra	1.50
4	Sammy Sosa	1.50
5	Frank Thomas	1.00
6	Mike Piazza	1.75
7	Mark McGwire	2.50
8	Tony Gwynn	1.50
9	Ken Griffey Jr.	2.00
10	Alex Rodriguez	2.50
11	Mo Vaughn	.25
12	Chipper Jones	1.50
13	Manny Ramirez	1.00
14	Larry Walker	.25
15	Jeff Bagwell	1.00
16	Vladimir Guerrero	1.00
17	Derek Jeter	3.00
18	J.D. Drew	.60
19	Barry Bonds	3.00
20	Juan Gonzalez	.50
21	Troy Glaus	1.00
22	Andruw Jones	1.00
23	Matt Williams	.25
24	Craig Biggio	.25
25	Raul Mondesi	.25
26	Roger Clemens	1.75
27	Bernie Williams	.25
28	Scott Rolen	.75
29	Jose Canseco	.50
30	Ivan Rodriguez	.75

2000 Pacific

Henry Rodriguez OF · Chicago Cubs™

		NM/M
Complete Set (500):		60.00
Common Player:		.10
Pack (12):		1.50
Wax Box (24):		25.00
1	Garret Anderson	.10
2	Tim Belcher	.10
3	Gary DiSarcina	.10
4	Trent Durrington	.10
5	Jim Edmonds	.15
6a	Darin Erstad/Action	.35
6b	Darin Erstad/Portrait	.35
7	Chuck Finley	.10
8	Troy Glaus	.75
9	Todd Greene	.10
10	Bret Hemphill	.10
11	Ken Hill	.10
12	Ramon Ortiz	.10
13	Troy Percival	.10
14	Mark Petkovsek	.10
15	Tim Salmon	.20
16a	Mo Vaughn	.15
16b	Mo Vaughn/Portrait	.15
17	Jay Bell	.10
18	Omar Daal	.10
19	Erubiel Durazo	.10
20	Steve Finley	.10
21	Bernard Gilkey	.10
22	Luis Gonzalez	.20
23	Randy Johnson	.75
24	Byung-Hyun Kim	.10
25	Travis Lee	.10
26	Matt Mantei	.10
27	Armando Reynoso	.10
28	Rob Ryan	.10
29	Kelly Stinnett	.10
30	Todd Stottlemyre	.10
31a	Matt Williams/Action	.15
31b	Matt Williams/Portrait	.15
32	Tony Womack	.10
33	Bret Boone	.10
34	Andres Galarraga	.15
35	Tom Glavine	.35
36	Ozzie Guillen	.10
37a	Andruw Jones/Action	.75
37b	Andruw Jones/Portrait	.75
38a	Chipper Jones/Action	1.00
38b	Chipper Jones/Portrait	1.00
39	Brian Jordan	.10
40	Ryan Klesko	.15
41	Javy Lopez	.15
42a	Greg Maddux/Action	1.00
42b	Greg Maddux/Portrait	1.00
43	Kevin Millwood	.15
44	John Rocker	.10
45	Randall Simon	.10
46	John Smoltz	.15

47	Gerald Williams	.10
48	Brady Anderson	.15
49a	Albert Belle/Action	.15
49b	Albert Belle/Portrait	.15
50	Mike Bordick	.10
51	Will Clark	.25
52	Jeff Conine	.10
53	Delino DeShields	.10
54	Jerry Hairston Jr.	.10
55	Charles Johnson	.10
56	Eugene Kingsale	.10
57	Ryan Minor	.10
58	Mike Mussina	.35
59	Sidney Ponson	.10
60a	Cal Ripken Jr./Action	2.50
60b	Cal Ripken Jr./Portrait	2.50
61	B.J. Surhoff	.10
62	Mike Timlin	.10
63	Rod Beck	.10
64a	Nomar Garciaparra/Action	1.50
64b	Nomar Garciaparra/Portrait	1.50
65	Tom Gordon	.10
66	Butch Huskey	.10
67	Derek Lowe	.10
68a	Pedro Martinez/Action	.75
68b	Pedro Martinez/Portrait	.75
69	Trot Nixon	.10
70	Jose Offerman	.10
71	Troy O'Leary	.10
72	Pat Rapp	.10
73	Donnie Sadler	.10
74	Mike Stanley	.10
75	John Valentin	.10
76	Jason Varitek	.10
77	Wilton Veras	.15
78	Tim Wakefield	.10
79	Rick Aguilera	.10
80	Manny Alexander	.10
81	Roosevelt Brown	.10
82	Mark Grace	.20
83	Glenallen Hill	.10
84	Lance Johnson	.10
85	Jon Lieber	.10
86	Cole Liniak	.10
87	Chad Meyers	.10
88	Mickey Morandini	.10
89	Jose Nieves	.10
90	Henry Rodriguez	.10
91a	Sammy Sosa/Action	1.50
91b	Sammy Sosa/Portrait	1.50
92	Kevin Tapani	.10
93	Kerry Wood	.50
94	Mike Caruso	.10
95	Ray Durham	.10
96	Brook Fordyce	.10
97	Bobby Howry	.10
98	Paul Konerko	.25
99	Carlos Lee	.10
100	Aaron Myette	.10
101	Greg Norton	.10
102	Magglio Ordonez	.25
103	Jim Parque	.10
104	Liu Rodriguez	.10
105	Chris Singleton	.10
106	Mike Sirotka	.10
107a	Frank Thomas/Action	.75
107b	Frank Thomas/Portrait	.75
108	Kip Wells	.10
109	Aaron Boone	.10
110	Mike Cameron	.10
111a	Sean Casey/Action	.20
111b	Sean Casey/Portrait	.20
112	Jeffrey Hammonds	.10
113	Pete Harnisch	.10
114a	Barry Larkin/Portrait	.15
114b	Barry Larkin/Portrait	.15
115	Jason LaRue	.10
116	Denny Neagle	.10
117	Pokey Reese	.10
118	Scott Sullivan	.10
119	Eddie Taubensee	.10
120	Greg Vaughn	.10
121	Scott Williamson	.10
122	Dmitri Young	.10
123a	Roberto Alomar/Action	.35
123b	Roberto Alomar/Portrait	.35
124	Sandy Alomar Jr.	.10
125	Harold Baines	.10
126	Russell Branyan	.10
127	Dave Burba	.10
128	Bartolo Colon	.10
129	Travis Fryman	.15
130	Mike Jackson	.10
131	David Justice	.15
132a	Kenny Lofton/Action	.15
132b	Kenny Lofton/Portrait	.15
133	Charles Nagy	.10
134a	Manny Ramirez/Action	.75
134b	Manny Ramirez/Portrait	.75
135	Dave Roberts	.10
136	Richie Sexson	.15
137	Jim Thome	.60
138	Omar Vizquel	.15
139	Jaret Wright	.10
140	Pedro Astacio	.10
141	Dante Bichette	.10
142	Brian Bohanon	.10
143a	Vinny Castilla /Action	.10
143b	Vinny Castilla/Portrait	.10
144	Edgard Clemente	.10
145	Derrick Gibson	.10
146	Todd Helton	.75
147	Darryl Kile	.10
148	Mike Lansing	.10
149	Kirt Manwaring	.10
150	Neifi Perez	.10
151	Ben Petrick	.10
152	Juan Sosa **RC**	.20
153	Dave Veres	.10
154a	Larry Walker/Action	.15
154b	Larry Walker/Portrait	.15
155	Brad Ausmus	.10
156	Dave Borkowski	.10
157	Tony Clark	.10
158	Francisco Cordero	.10
159	Deivi Cruz	.10
160	Damion Easley	.10
161	Juan Encarnacion	.10
162	Robert Fick	.10
163	Bobby Higginson	.10
164	Gabe Kapler	.15
165	Brian Moehler	.10
166	Dean Palmer	.10
167	Luis Polonia	.10
168	Justin Thompson	.10
169	Jeff Weaver	.10
170	Antonio Alfonseca	.10
171	Bruce Aven	.10
172	A.J. Burnett	.15
173	Luis Castillo	.10
174	Ramon Castro	.10
175	Ryan Dempster	.10
176	Alex Fernandez	.10
177	Cliff Floyd	.10
178	Amaury Garcia	.10
179	Alex Gonzalez	.10
180	Mark Kotsay	.10
181	Mike Lowell	.15
182	Brian Meadows	.10
183	Kevin Orie	.10
184	Julio Ramirez	.10
185	Preston Wilson	.15
186	Moises Alou	.15
187a	Jeff Bagwell/Action	.75
187b	Jeff Bagwell/Portrait	.75
188	Glen Barker	.10
189	Derek Bell	.10
190a	Craig Biggio/Action	.15
190b	Craig Biggio/Portrait	.15
191	Ken Caminiti	.10
192	Scott Elarton	.10
193	Carl Everett	.10
194	Mike Hampton	.10
195	Carlos Hernandez	.10
196	Richard Hidalgo	.10
197	Jose Lima	.10
198	Shane Reynolds	.15
199	Bill Spiers	.10
200	Billy Wagner	.15
201a	Carlos Beltran/Action	.50
201b	Carlos Beltran/Portrait	.50
202	Dermal Brown	.10
203	Johnny Damon	.25
204	Jermaine Dye	.10
205	Carlos Febles	.10
206	Jeremy Giambi	.10
207	Mark Quinn	.10
208	Joe Randa	.10
209	Dan Reichert	.10
210	Jose Rosado	.10
211	Rey Sanchez	.10
212	Jeff Suppan	.10
213	Mike Sweeney	.10
214a	Kevin Brown/Action	.15
214b	Kevin Brown/Portrait	.15
215	Darren Dreifort	.10
216	Eric Gagne	.10
217	Mark Grudzielanek	.10
218	Todd Hollandsworth	.10
219	Todd Hundley	.10
220	Eric Karros	.15
221	Raul Mondesi	.15
222	Chan Ho Park	.10
223	Jeff Shaw	.10
224a	Gary Sheffield/Action	.30
224b	Gary Sheffield/Portrait	.30
225	Ismael Valdes	.10
226	Devon White	.10
227	Eric Young	.10
228	Kevin Barker	.10
229	Ron Belliard	.10
230a	Jeromy Burnitz/Action	.10
230b	Jeromy Burnitz/Portrait	.10
231	Jeff Cirillo	.10
232	Marquis Grissom	.10
233	Geoff Jenkins	.10
234	Mark Loretta	.10
235	David Nilsson	.10
236	Hideo Nomo	.75
237	Alex Ochoa	.10
238	Kyle Peterson	.10
239	Fernando Vina	.10
240	Bob Wickman	.10
241	Steve Woodard	.10
242	Chad Allen	.10
243	Ron Coomer	.10
244	Marty Cordova	.10
245	Cristian Guzman	.10
246	Denny Hocking	.10
247	Jacque Jones	.10
248	Corey Koskie	.10
249	Matt Lawton	.10
250	Joe Mays	.10
251	Eric Milton	.10
252	Brad Radke	.10
253	Mark Redman	.10
254	Terry Steinbach	.10
255	Todd Walker	.10
256	Tony Armas Jr.	.10
257	Michael Barrett	.10
258	Peter Bergeron	.10
259	Geoff Blum	.10
260	Orlando Cabrera	.10
261	Trace Coquillette **RC**	.15
262	Brad Fullmer	.10
263a	Vladimir Guerrero/Action	.75
263b	Vladimir Guerrero/Portrait	.75
264	Wilton Guerrero	.10
265	Dustin Hermanson	.10
266	Manny Martinez	.10
267	Ryan McGuire	.10
268	Ugueth Urbina	.10
269	Jose Vidro	.10
270	Rondell White	.15
271	Chris Widger	.10
272	Edgardo Alfonzo	.15
273	Armando Benitez	.10
274	Roger Cedeno	.10
275	Dennis Cook	.10
276	Octavio Dotel	.10
277	John Franco	.10
278	Darryl Hamilton	.10
279	Rickey Henderson	.75
280	Orel Hershiser	.10
281	Al Leiter	.15
282a	John Olerud/Action	.15
282b	John Olerud/Portrait	.15
283	Rey Ordonez	.10
284a	Mike Piazza/Action	1.50
284b	Mike Piazza/Portrait	1.50
285	Kenny Rogers	.10
286	Jorge Toca	.10
287	Robin Ventura	.15
288	Scott Brosius	.10
289a	Roger Clemens/Action	1.25
289b	Roger Clemens/Portrait	1.25
290	David Cone	.15
291	Chili Davis	.10
292	Orlando Hernandez	.15
293	Hideki Irabu	.10
294a	Derek Jeter/Action	2.50
294b	Derek Jeter/Portrait	2.50
295	Chuck Knoblauch	.10
296	Ricky Ledee	.10
297	Jim Leyritz	.10
298	Tino Martinez	.15
299	Paul O'Neill	.15
300	Andy Pettitte	.25
301	Jorge Posada	.15
302	Mariano Rivera	.25
303	Alfonso Soriano	.75
304a	Bernie Williams/Action	.20
304b	Bernie Williams/Portrait	.20
305	Ed Yarnall	.10
306	Kevin Appier	.10
307	Rich Becker	.10
308	Eric Chavez	.25
309	Jason Giambi	.60
310	Ben Grieve	.10
311	Ramon Hernandez	.10
312	Tim Hudson	.25
313	John Jaha	.10
314	Doug Jones	.10
315	Omar Olivares	.10
316	Mike Oquist	.10
317	Matt Stairs	.10
318	Miguel Tejada	.25
319	Randy Velarde	.10
320	Bobby Abreu	.15
321	Marlon Anderson	.10
322	Alex Arias	.10
323	Rico Brogna	.10
324	Paul Byrd	.10
325	Ron Gant	.10
326	Doug Glanville	.10
327	Wayne Gomes	.10
328	Mike Lieberthal	.10
329	Robert Person	.10
330	Desi Relaford	.10
331a	Scott Rolen/Action	.60
331b	Scott Rolen/Portrait	.60
332a	Curt Schilling/Action	.35
332b	Curt Schilling/Portrait	.35
333	Kris Benson	.10
334	Adrian Brown	.10
335	Brant Brown	.10
336	Brian Giles	.15
337	Chad Hermansen	.10
338	Jason Kendall	.15
339	Al Martin	.10
340	Pat Meares	.10
341a	Warren Morris/Action	.10
341b	Warren Morris/Portrait	.10
342	Todd Ritchie	.10
343	Jason Schmidt	.10
344	Ed Sprague	.10
345	Mike Williams	.10
346	Kevin Young	.10
347	Rick Ankiel	.25
348	Ricky Bottalico	.10
349	Kent Bottenfield	.10
350	Darren Bragg	.10
351	Eric Davis	.15
352a	J.D. Drew/Action	.35
352b	J.D. Drew/Portrait	.35
353	Adam Kennedy	.10
354	Ray Lankford	.10
355	Joe McEwing	.10
356a	Mark McGwire/Action	2.00
356b	Mark McGwire/Portrait	2.00
357	Matt Morris	.10
358	Darren Oliver	.10
359	Edgar Renteria	.10
360	Fernando Tatis	.10
361	Andy Ashby	.10
362	Ben Davis	.10
363a	Tony Gwynn/Action	1.00
363b	Tony Gwynn/Portrait	1.00
364	Sterling Hitchcock	.10
365	Trevor Hoffman	.10
366	Damian Jackson	.10
367	Wally Joyner	.10
368	Dave Magadan	.10
369	Gary Matthews Jr.	.10
370	Phil Nevin	.10
371	Eric Owens	.10
372	Ruben Rivera	.10
373a	Reggie Sanders/Action	.10
373b	Reggie Sanders/Portrait	.10
374	Quilvio Veras	.10
375	Rich Aurilia	.10
376	Marvin Benard	.10
377a	Barry Bonds/Action	2.50
377b	Barry Bonds/Portrait	2.50
378	Ellis Burks	.10
379	Shawn Estes	.10
380	Livan Hernandez	.10
381a	Jeff Kent/Action	.15
381b	Jeff Kent/Portrait	.15
382	Brent Mayne	.10
383	Bill Mueller	.10
384	Calvin Murray	.10
385	Robb Nen	.10
386	Russ Ortiz	.10
387	Kirk Rueter	.10
388	J.T. Snow	.10
389	David Bell	.10
390	Jay Buhner	.15
391	Russ Davis	.10
392a	Freddy Garcia/Action	.10
392b	Freddy Garcia/Portrait	.10
393a	Ken Griffey Jr./Action	1.50
393b	Ken Griffey Jr./Portrait	1.50
394	Carlos Guillen	.10
395	John Halama	.10
396	Brian Hunter	.10
397	Ryan Jackson	.10
398	Edgar Martinez	.10
399	Gil Meche	.10
400	Jose Mesa	.10
401	Jamie Moyer	.10
402a	Alex Rodriguez/Action	2.00
402b	Alex Rodriguez/Portrait	2.00
403	Dan Wilson	.10
404	Wilson Alvarez	.10
405	Rolando Arrojo	.10
406a	Wade Boggs/Action	1.00
406b	Wade Boggs/Portrait	1.00
407	Miguel Cairo	.10
408a	Jose Canseco/Action	.40
408b	Jose Canseco/Portrait	.40
409	John Flaherty	.10
410	Jose Guillen	.10
411	Roberto Hernandez	.10
412	Terrell Lowery	.10
413	Dave Martinez	.10
414	Quinton McCracken	.10
415a	Fred McGriff/Action	.15
415b	Fred McGriff/Portrait	.15
416	Ryan Rupe	.10
417	Kevin Stocker	.10
418	Bubba Trammell	.10
419	Royce Clayton	.10
420a	Juan Gonzalez /Action	.75
420b	Juan Gonzalez /Portrait	.75
421	Tom Goodwin	.10
422	Rusty Greer	.10
423	Rick Helling	.10
424	Roberto Kelly	.10
425	Ruben Mateo	.10
426	Mark McLemore	.10
427	Mike Morgan	.10
428	Rafael Palmeiro	.65
429a	Ivan Rodriguez/Action	.65
429b	Ivan Rodriguez/Portrait	.65
430	Aaron Sele	.10
431	Lee Stevens	.10
432	John Wetteland	.10
433	Todd Zeile	.10
434	Jeff Zimmerman	.10
435	Tony Batista	.10
436	Casey Blake	.10
437	Homer Bush	.10
438	Chris Carpenter	.10
439	Jose Cruz Jr.	.10
440a	Carlos Delgado/Action	.50
440b	Carlos Delgado/Portrait	.50
441	Tony Fernandez	.10
442	Darrin Fletcher	.10
443	Alex Gonzalez	.10
444a	Shawn Green/Action	.35
444b	Shawn Green/Portrait	.35
445	Roy Halladay	.20
446	Billy Koch	.10
447	David Segui	.10
448	Shannon Stewart	.10
449	David Wells	.10
450	Vernon Wells	.15

Copper

	NM/M
Common Copper:	5.00
Stars:	4-8X
Production 99 Sets	

Platinum Blue

	NM/M
Common Player:	8.00
Stars:	6-10X
Production 75 Sets	

Premiere Date

	NM/M
Common Player:	15.00
Stars:	8-15X
Production 37 Sets	

2000 Pacific Ruby Red (Seven-11)

	NM/M
Complete Set (500):	65.00
Common Player:	.15
Stars/Rookies:	1.5X

(See 2000 Pacific for checklist and base card values.)

Command Performers

		NM/M
Complete Set (20):		45.00
Common Player:		1.00
Inserted 1:24 Retail		
1	Chipper Jones	3.00
2	Greg Maddux	3.00
3	Cal Ripken Jr.	6.00
4	Nomar Garciaparra	4.00
5	Sammy Sosa	4.00
6	Sean Casey	1.00
7	Manny Ramirez	2.00
8	Larry Walker	1.00
9	Jeff Bagwell	2.00
10	Vladimir Guerrero	2.00
11	Mike Piazza	4.00
12	Roger Clemens	3.50
13	Derek Jeter	6.00
14	Mark McGwire	5.00
15	Tony Gwynn	3.00
16	Barry Bonds	6.00
17	Ken Griffey Jr.	4.00
18	Alex Rodriguez	5.00
19	Ivan Rodriguez	1.50
20	Shawn Green	1.25

Cramer's Choice Awards

		NM/M
Complete Set (10):		300.00
Common Player:		25.00
Inserted 1:721		
1	Chipper Jones	25.00
2	Cal Ripken Jr.	50.00
3	Nomar Garciaparra	30.00
4	Sammy Sosa	30.00
5	Mike Piazza	30.00
6	Derek Jeter	50.00
7	Mark McGwire	40.00
8	Tony Gwynn	25.00
9	Ken Griffey Jr.	30.00
10	Alex Rodriguez	40.00

Diamond Leaders

		NM/M
Complete Set (30):		25.00
Common Card:		.50
Inserted 2:25		
1	Garret Anderson, Chuck Finley, Troy Percival, Mo Vaughn Anaheim Angels	.50
2	Albert Belle, Mike Mussina, B.J. Surhoff Baltimore Orioles	.50
3	Nomar Garciaparra, Pedro J. Martinez, Troy O'Leary Boston Red Sox	3.00
4	Ray Durham, Magglio Ordonez, Frank Thomas Chicago White Sox	1.50
5	Bartolo Colon, Manny Ramirez, Omar Vizquel Cleveland Indians	1.50
6	Deivi Cruz, Dave Mlicki, David Palmer Detroit Tigers	.50
7	Johnny Damon, Jermaine Dye, Jose Rosado, Mike Sweeney Kansas City Royals	.50
8	Corey Koskie, Eric Milton, Brad Radke Minnesota Twins	.50
9	Orlando Hernandez, Derek Jeter, Mariano Rivera, Bernie Williams New York Yankees	4.00
10	Jeremy Giambi, Tim Hudson, Matt Stairs Oakland Athletics	1.00
11	Freddy Garcia, Ken Griffey Jr., Edgar Martinez Seattle Mariners	3.00
12	Jose Canseco, Roberto Hernandez, Fred McGriff Tampa Bay Devil Rays	.75
13	Rafael Palmeiro, Ivan Rodriguez, John Wetteland Texas Rangers	1.00
14	Carlos Delgado, Shannon Stewart, David Wells Toronto Blue Jays	1.00
15	Luis Gonzalez, Randy Johnson, Matt Williams Arizona Diamondbacks	1.50
16	Chipper Jones, Brian Jordan, Greg Maddux Atlanta Braves	2.00
17	Mark Grace, Jon Lieber, Sammy Sosa Chicago Cubs	3.00
18	Sean Casey, Pete Harnisch, Greg Vaughn Cincinnati Reds	.50
19	Pedro Astacio, Dante Bichette, Larry Walker Colorado Rockies	.50
20	Luis Castillo, Alex Fernandez, Preston Wilson Florida Marlins	.50
21	Jeff Bagwell, Mike Hampton, Billy Wagner Houston Astros	1.50
22	Kevin Brown, Mark Grudzielanek, Eric Karros Los Angeles Dodgers	.50
23	Jeromy Burnitz, Jeff Cirillo, Marquis Grissom, Hideo Nomo Milwaukee Brewers	1.00
24	Vladimir Guerrero, Dustin Hermanson, Ugueth Urbina Montreal Expos	1.50
25	Roger Cedeno, Rickey Henderson, Mike Piazza New York Mets	3.00
26	Bobby Abreu, Mike Lieberthal, Curt Schilling Philadelphia Phillies	.75
27	Brian Giles, Jason Kendall, Kevin Young Pittsburgh Pirates	.50
28	Kent Bottenfield, Ray Lankford, Mark McGwire St. Louis Cardinals	3.50
29	Tony Gwynn, Trevor Hoffman, Reggie Sanders San Diego Padres	2.00
30	Barry Bonds, Jeff Kent, Russ Ortiz San Francisco Giants	4.00

Gold Crown Die-Cuts

		NM/M
Complete Set (36):		150.00
Common Player:		1.50
Inserted 1:25		
1	Mo Vaughn	1.50
2	Matt Williams	1.50
3	Andruw Jones	6.00
4	Chipper Jones	8.00
5	Greg Maddux	8.00
6	Cal Ripken Jr.	15.00
7	Nomar Garciaparra	10.00

8	Pedro Martinez	6.00
9	Sammy Sosa	10.00
10	Magglio Ordonez	2.50
11	Frank Thomas	6.00
12	Sean Casey	1.50
13	Roberto Alomar	2.50
14	Manny Ramirez	6.00
15	Larry Walker	1.50
16	Jeff Bagwell	6.00
17	Craig Biggio	1.50
18	Carlos Beltran	4.00
19	Vladimir Guerrero	6.00
20	Mike Piazza	10.00
21	Roger Clemens	9.00
22	Derek Jeter	15.00
23	Bernie Williams	2.00
24	Scott Rolen	5.00
25	Warren Morris	1.50
26	J.D. Drew	2.00
27	Mark McGwire	12.00
28	Tony Gwynn	8.00
29	Barry Bonds	15.00
30	Ken Griffey Jr.	10.00
31	Alex Rodriguez	12.00
32	Jose Canseco	2.00
33	Juan Gonzalez	6.00
34	Rafael Palmeiro	5.00
35	Ivan Rodriguez	5.00
36	Shawn Green	3.00

Ornaments

		NM/M
Complete Set (20):		40.00
Common Player:		1.00
Inserted 2:25		
1	Mo Vaughn	1.00
2	Chipper Jones	3.00
3	Greg Maddux	3.00
4	Cal Ripken Jr.	6.00
5	Nomar Garciaparra	4.00
6	Sammy Sosa	4.00
7	Frank Thomas	2.00
8	Manny Ramirez	2.00
9	Larry Walker	1.00
10	Jeff Bagwell	2.00
11	Mike Piazza	4.00
12	Roger Clemens	3.50
13	Derek Jeter	6.00
14	Scott Rolen	1.50
15	J.D. Drew	1.25
16	Mark McGwire	5.00
17	Tony Gwynn	3.00
18	Ken Griffey Jr.	4.00
19	Alex Rodriguez	5.00
20	Ivan Rodriguez	1.50

Past & Present

		NM/M
Complete Set (20):		80.00
Common Player:		1.50
Inserted 1:49 H		
1	Chipper Jones	5.00
2	Greg Maddux	5.00
3	Cal Ripken Jr.	10.00
4	Nomar Garciaparra	6.00
5	Pedro Martinez	4.00
6	Sammy Sosa	6.00
7	Frank Thomas	4.00

8	Manny Ramirez	4.00
9	Larry Walker	1.50
10	Jeff Bagwell	4.00
11	Mike Piazza	8.00
12	Roger Clemens	5.50
13	Derek Jeter	10.00
14	Mark McGwire	8.00
15	Tony Gwynn	5.00
16	Barry Bonds	10.00
17	Ken Griffey Jr.	6.00
18	Alex Rodriguez	8.00
19	Wade Boggs	5.00
20	Ivan Rodriguez	3.00

Reflections

		NM/M
Common Player:		3.00
Inserted 1:97		
1	Andruw Jones	6.00
2	Chipper Jones	8.00
3	Cal Ripken Jr.	20.00
4	Nomar Garciaparra	12.00
5	Sammy Sosa	12.00
6	Frank Thomas	6.00
7	Manny Ramirez	6.00
8	Jeff Bagwell	6.00
9	Vladimir Guerrero	6.00
10	Mike Piazza	12.00
11	Derek Jeter	20.00
12	Bernie Williams	3.00
13	Scott Rolen	5.00
14	J.D. Drew	3.00
15	Mark McGwire	15.00
16	Tony Gwynn	8.00
17	Ken Griffey Jr.	12.00
18	Alex Rodriguez	15.00
19	Juan Gonzalez	6.00
20	Ivan Rodriguez	5.00

2000 Pacific Aurora

		NM/M
Complete Set (151):		25.00
Common Player:		.15
Pack (10):		2.00
Wax Box (24):		30.00
1	Darin Erstad	.25
2	Troy Glaus	.75
3	Tim Salmon	.25
4	Mo Vaughn	.15
5	Jay Bell	.15
6	Erubiel Durazo	.15
7	Luis Gonzalez	.25
8	Randy Johnson	.75
9	Matt Williams	.15
10	Tom Glavine	.35
11	Andruw Jones	.75
12	Chipper Jones	1.00
13	Brian Jordan	.15
14	Greg Maddux	1.00
15	Kevin Millwood	.15
16	Albert Belle	.15
17	Will Clark	.25
18	Mike Mussina	.35
19	Cal Ripken Jr.	2.50
20	B.J. Surhoff	.15
21	Nomar Garciaparra	1.50

22	Pedro Martinez	.75
23	Troy O'Leary	.15
24	Wilton Veras	.15
25	Mark Grace	.25
26	Henry Rodriguez	.15
27	Sammy Sosa	1.50
28	Kerry Wood	.50
29	Ray Durham	.15
30	Paul Konerko	.25
31	Carlos Lee	.15
32	Magglio Ordonez	.25
33	Chris Singleton	.15
34	Frank Thomas	.75
35	Mike Cameron	.15
36	Sean Casey	.25
37	Barry Larkin	.15
38	Pokey Reese	.15
39	Eddie Taubensee	.15
40	Roberto Alomar	.40
41	David Justice	.15
42	Kenny Lofton	.15
43	Manny Ramirez	.75
44	Richie Sexson	.15
45	Jim Thome	.60
46	Omar Vizquel	.15
47	Todd Helton	.75
48	Mike Lansing	.15
49	Neifi Perez	.15
50	Ben Petrick	.15
51	Larry Walker	.15
52	Tony Clark	.15
53	Damion Easley	.15
54	Juan Encarnacion	.15
55	Juan Gonzalez	.75
56	Dean Palmer	.15
57	Luis Castillo	.15
58	Cliff Floyd	.15
59	Alex Gonzalez	.15
60	Mike Lowell	.15
61	Preston Wilson	.15
62	Jeff Bagwell	.75
63	Craig Biggio	.15
64	Ken Caminiti	.15
65	Jose Lima	.15
66	Billy Wagner	.15
67	Carlos Beltran	.50
68	Johnny Damon	.15
69	Jermaine Dye	.15
70	Mark Quinn	.15
71	Mike Sweeney	.15
72	Kevin Brown	.15
73	Shawn Green	.35
74	Eric Karros	.15
75	Chan Ho Park	.15
76	Gary Sheffield	.40
77	Ron Belliard	.15
78	Jeromy Burnitz	.15
79	Marquis Grissom	.15
80	Geoff Jenkins	.15
81	David Nilsson	.15
82	Ron Coomer	.15
83	Jacque Jones	.15
84	Brad Radke	.15
85	Todd Walker	.15
86	Michael Barrett	.15
87	Peter Bergeron	.15
88	Vladimir Guerrero	.75
89	Jose Vidro	.15
90	Rondell White	.15
91	Edgardo Alfonzo	.15
92	Darryl Hamilton	.15
93	Rey Ordonez	.15
94	Mike Piazza	1.50
95	Robin Ventura	.15
96	Roger Clemens	1.25
97	Orlando Hernandez	.15
98	Derek Jeter	2.50
99	Tino Martinez	.15
100	Mariano Rivera	.25
101	Bernie Williams	.25
102	Eric Chavez	.25
103	Jason Giambi	.60
104	Ben Grieve	.15
105	Tim Hudson	.25
106	John Jaha	.15
107	Matt Stairs	.15
108	Bobby Abreu	.15
109	Doug Glanville	.15
110	Mike Lieberthal	.15
111	Scott Rolen	.60
112	Curt Schilling	.40
113	Brian Giles	.15
114	Chad Hermansen	.15
115	Jason Kendall	.15
116	Warren Morris	.15
117	Kevin Young	.15
118	Rick Ankiel	.25
119	J.D. Drew	.25
120	Ray Lankford	.15
121	Mark McGwire	2.00
122	Edgar Renteria	.15
123	Fernando Tatis	.15
124	Ben Davis	.15
125	Tony Gwynn	1.00
126	Trevor Hoffman	.15
127	Phil Nevin	.15
128	Barry Bonds	2.50
129	Ellis Burks	.15
130	Jeff Kent	.15
131	J.T. Snow	.15
132	Freddy Garcia	.15
133	Ken Griffey Jr.	1.50
133a	Ken Griffey Jr. Reds	2.00
134	Edgar Martinez	.15
135	Alex Rodriguez	2.00

136	Dan Wilson	.15
137	Jose Canseco	.40
138	Roberto Hernandez	.15
139	Dave Martinez	.15
140	Fred McGriff	.15
141	Rusty Greer	.15
142	Ruben Mateo	.15
143	Rafael Palmeiro	.65
144	Ivan Rodriguez	.65
145	Jeff Zimmerman	.15
146	Homer Bush	.15
147	Carlos Delgado	.50
148	Raul Mondesi	.15
149	Shannon Stewart	.15
150	Vernon Wells	.15

Copper

Stars:	2-4X
Production 399 Sets	

Silver

Stars:	3-6X
Production 199 Sets	

Platinum Blue

Stars:	5-10X
Production 67 Sets	

Pinstripes

		NM/M
Complete Set (50):		30.00
Common Player:		.25
Premiere Date:		3-6X
Production 51 Sets		
4	Mo Vaughn	.25
8	Randy Johnson	1.50
9	Matt Williams	.25
11	Andruw Jones	1.50
12	Chipper Jones	2.00
14	Greg Maddux	2.00
19	Cal Ripken Jr.	4.00
21	Nomar Garciaparra	2.50
22	Pedro Martinez	1.50
27	Sammy Sosa	2.50
32	Magglio Ordonez	.35
34	Frank Thomas	1.50
36	Sean Casey	.35
37	Barry Larkin	.25
42	Kenny Lofton	.25
43	Manny Ramirez	1.50
45	Jim Thome	1.50
47	Todd Helton	1.50
51	Larry Walker	.25
55	Juan Gonzalez	1.50
62	Jeff Bagwell	1.50
63	Craig Biggio	.25
67	Carlos Beltran	.50
73	Shawn Green	.40
76	Gary Sheffield	.40
78	Jeromy Burnitz	.25
88	Vladimir Guerrero	1.50
91	Edgardo Alfonzo	.25
94	Mike Piazza	2.50
96	Roger Clemens	2.25
97	Orlando Hernandez	.25
98	Derek Jeter	4.00
101	Bernie Williams	.35
102	Eric Chavez	.35
105	Tim Hudson	.35
111	Scott Rolen	1.25
112	Curt Schilling	.50
113	Brian Giles	.25
114	Rick Ankiel	.25
121	Mark McGwire	3.00
125	Tony Gwynn	2.00
128	Barry Bonds	4.00
130	Jeff Kent	.25
133	Ken Griffey Jr.	2.50
135	Alex Rodriguez	3.00
137	Jose Canseco	.50
140	Fred McGriff	.25
143	Rafael Palmeiro	.75
144	Ivan Rodriguez	.75
147	Carlos Delgado	1.00

At-Bat Styrotechs

	NM/M
Complete Set (20):	125.00
Common Player:	2.00
Production 299 Sets	

1	Chipper Jones	7.50
2	Cal Ripken Jr.	15.00
3	Nomar Garciaparra	10.00
4	Sammy Sosa	10.00
5	Frank Thomas	6.00
6	Manny Ramirez	6.00
7	Larry Walker	2.00
8	Jeff Bagwell	6.00
9	Carlos Beltran	2.00
10	Vladimir Guerrero	6.00
11	Mike Piazza	10.00
12	Derek Jeter	15.00
13	Bernie Williams	2.00
14	Mark McGwire	12.00
15	Tony Gwynn	7.50
16	Barry Bonds	15.00
17	Ken Griffey Jr.	10.00
18	Alex Rodriguez	12.00
19	Jose Canseco	3.00
20	Ivan Rodriguez	5.00

Dugout View Net-Fusions

		NM/M
Complete Set (20):		110.00
Common Player:		2.50
Inserted 1:37		
1	Mo Vaughn	2.50
2	Chipper Jones	8.00
3	Cal Ripken Jr.	15.00
4	Nomar Garciaparra	10.00
5	Sammy Sosa	10.00
6	Manny Ramirez	6.00
7	Larry Walker	2.50
8	Juan Gonzalez	6.00
9	Jeff Bagwell	6.00
10	Craig Biggio	2.50
11	Shawn Green	3.00
12	Vladimir Guerrero	6.00
13	Mike Piazza	10.00
14	Derek Jeter	15.00
15	Scott Rolen	5.00
16	Mark McGwire	12.00
17	Tony Gwynn	8.00
18	Ken Griffey Jr.	10.00
19	Alex Rodriguez	12.00
20	Rafael Palmeiro	4.00

Pennant Fever

		NM/M
Complete Set (20):		25.00
Common Player:		1.00
T. Gwynn Auto./147		75.00
Inserted 4:37		
1	Andruw Jones	1.50
2	Chipper Jones	2.00
3	Greg Maddux	2.00
4	Cal Ripken Jr.	4.00
5	Nomar Garciaparra	2.50
6	Pedro Martinez	1.50
7	Sammy Sosa	2.50
8	Manny Ramirez	1.50
9	Jim Thome	1.50
10	Jeff Bagwell	1.50
11	Mike Piazza	2.50
12	Roger Clemens	2.25
13	Derek Jeter	4.00
14	Bernie Williams	1.00
15	Mark McGwire	3.00
16	Tony Gwynn	2.00
17	Ken Griffey Jr.	2.50
18	Alex Rodriguez	3.00
19	Rafael Palmeiro	1.00
20	Ivan Rodriguez	1.00

Star Factor

		NM/M
Complete Set (10):		200.00
Common Player:		20.00
Inserted 1:361		
1	Chipper Jones	20.00
2	Cal Ripken Jr.	40.00
3	Nomar Garciaparra	25.00
4	Sammy Sosa	25.00
5	Mike Piazza	25.00
6	Derek Jeter	40.00
7	Mark McGwire	30.00
8	Tony Gwynn	20.00
9	Ken Griffey Jr.	25.00
10	Alex Rodriguez	30.00

2000 Pacific Crown Collection

		NM/M
Complete Set (300):		25.00
Common Player:		.10
Pack (10):		1.50
Wax Box (36):		30.00
1	Garret Anderson	.10
2	Darin Erstad	.25
3	Ben Molina	.10
4	Ramon Ortiz	.10
5	Orlando Palmeiro	.10
6	Troy Percival	.10
7	Tim Salmon	.15
8	Mo Vaughn	.10
9	Mo Vaughn Checklist	.10
10	Jay Bell	.10
11	Omar Daal	.10
12	Erubiel Durazo	.10
13	Steve Finley	.10
14	Hanley Frias	.10
15	Luis Gonzalez	.25
16	Randy Johnson	.75
17	Matt Williams	.10
18	Matt Williams Checklist	.10
19	Andres Galarraga	.10
20	Tom Glavine	.35
21	Andruw Jones	.75
22	Chipper Jones	1.00
23	Brian Jordan	.10
24	Javy Lopez	.10
25	Greg Maddux	1.00
26	Kevin Millwood	.10
27	Eddie Perez	.10
28	John Smoltz	.15
29	Chipper Jones Checklist	.50
30	Albert Belle	.15
31	Jesse Garcia	.10
32	Jerry Hairston Jr.	.10
33	Charles Johnson	.10
34	Mike Mussina	.30
35	Sidney Ponson	.10
36	Cal Ripken Jr.	2.50
37	B.J. Surhoff	.10
38	Cal Ripken Jr. Checklist	1.00

39	Nomar Garciaparra	1.50
40	Pedro Martinez	.75
41	Ramon Martinez	.10
42	Trot Nixon	.10
43	Jose Offerman	.10
44	Troy O'Leary	.10
45	John Valentin	.10
46	Wilton Veras	.10
47	Nomar Garciaparra Checklist	.75
48	Mark Grace	.15
49	Felix Heredia	.10
50	Jose Molina	.10
51	Jose Nieves	.10
52	Henry Rodriguez	.10
53	Sammy Sosa	1.50
54	Kerry Wood	.65
55	Sammy Sosa Checklist	.60
56	Mike Caruso	.10
57	Carlos Castillo	.10
58	Jason Dellaero	.10
59	Carlos Lee	.10
60	Magglio Ordonez	.25
61	Jesus Pena	.10
62	Liu Rodriguez	.10
63	Frank Thomas	.75
64	Magglio Ordonez Checklist	.15
65	Aaron Boone	.10
66	Mike Cameron	.10
67	Sean Casey	.20
68	Juan Guzman	.10
69	Barry Larkin	.10
70	Pokey Reese	.10
71	Eddie Taubensee	.10
72	Greg Vaughn	.10
73	Sean Casey Checklist	.15
74	Roberto Alomar	.25
75	Sandy Alomar Jr.	.10
76	Bartolo Colon	.10
77	Jacob Cruz	.10
78	Einar Diaz	.10
79	David Justice	.10
80	Kenny Lofton	.10
81	Manny Ramirez	.75
82	Richie Sexson	.10
83	Jim Thome	.75
84	Omar Vizquel	.10
85	Enrique Wilson	.10
86	Manny Ramirez Checklist	.40
87	Pedro Astacio	.10
88	Henry Blanco	.10
89	Vinny Castilla	.10
90	Edgard Clemente	.10
91	Todd Helton	.75
92	Neifi Perez	.10
93	Terry Shumpert	.10
94	Juan Sosa **RC**	.20
95	Larry Walker	.10
96	Vinny Castilla Checklist	.10
97	Tony Clark	.10
98	Deivi Cruz	.10
99	Damion Easley	.10
100	Juan Encarnacion	.10
101	Karim Garcia	.10
102	Luis Garcia	.10
103	Juan Gonzalez	.75
104	Jose Macias	.10
105	Dean Palmer	.10
106	Juan Encarnacion Checklist	.10
107	Antonio Alfonseca	.10
108	Armando Almanza	.10
109	Bruce Aven	.10
110	Luis Castillo	.10
111	Ramon Castro	.10
112	Alex Fernandez	.10
113	Cliff Floyd	.10
114	Alex Gonzalez	.10
115	Michael Tejera **RC**	.10
116	Preston Wilson	.10
117	Luis Castillo Checklist	.10
118	Jeff Bagwell	.75
119	Craig Biggio	.10
120	Jose Cabrera	.10
121	Tony Eusebio	.10
122	Carl Everett	.10
123	Ricky Gutierrez	.10
124	Mike Hampton	.10
125	Richard Hidalgo	.10
126	Jose Lima	.10
127	Billy Wagner	.10
128	Jeff Bagwell Checklist	.40
129	Carlos Beltran	.50
130	Johnny Damon	.25
131	Jermaine Dye	.10
132	Carlos Febles	.10
133	Jeremy Giambi	.10
134	Jose Rosado	.10
135	Rey Sanchez	.10
136	Jose Santiago	.10
137	Carlos Beltran Checklist	.10
138	Kevin Brown	.10
139	Craig Counsell	.10
140	Shawn Green	.40
141	Eric Karros	.10
142	Angel Pena	.10
143	Gary Sheffield	.25
144	Ismael Valdes	.10
145	Jose Vizcaino	.10
146	Devon White	.10
147	Eric Karros Checklist	.10
148	Ron Belliard	.10
149	Jeromy Burnitz	.10
150	Jeff Cirillo	.10
151	Marquis Grissom	.10
152	Geoff Jenkins	.10
153	Dave Nilsson	.10
154	Rafael Roque	.10
155	Jose Valentin	.10
156	Fernando Vina	.10
157	Jeromy Burnitz	.10
158	Chad Allen	.10
159	Ron Coomer	.10
160	Eddie Guardado	.10
161	Cristian Guzman	.10
162	Jacque Jones	.10
163	Javier Valentin	.10
164	Todd Walker	.10
165	Ron Coomer Checklist	.10
166	Michael Barrett	.10
167	Miguel Batista	.10
168	Vladimir Guerrero	.75
169	Wilton Guerrero	.10
170	Fernando Seguignol	.10
171	Ugueth Urbina	.10
172	Javier Vazquez	.10
173	Jose Vidro	.10
174	Rondell White	.10
175	Vladimir Guerrero Checklist	.25
176	Edgardo Alfonzo	.10
177	Armando Benitez	.10
178	Roger Cedeno	.10
179	Octavio Dotel	.10
180	Melvin Mora	.10
181	Rey Ordonez	.10
182	Mike Piazza	1.50
183	Jorge Toca	.10
184	Robin Ventura	.10
185	Edgardo Alfonzo Checklist	.10
186	Roger Clemens	1.25
187	David Cone	.10
188	Orlando Hernandez	.10
189	Derek Jeter	2.50
190	Ricky Ledee	.10
191	Tino Martinez	.10
192	Ramiro Mendoza	.10
193	Jorge Posada	.10
194	Mariano Rivera	.15
195	Alfonso Soriano	.75
196	Bernie Williams	.30
197	Derek Jeter Checklist	1.00
198	Eric Chavez	.15
199	Jason Giambi	.60
200	Ben Grieve	.10
201	Ramon Hernandez	.10
202	Tim Hudson	.25
203	John Jaha	.10
204	Omar Olivares	.10
205	Olmedo Saenz	.10
206	Matt Stairs	.10
207	Miguel Tejada	.20
208	Tim Hudson Checklist	.20
209	Rico Brogna	.10
210	Bobby Abreu	.10
211	Marlon Anderson	.10
212	Alex Arias	.10
213	Doug Glanville	.10
214	Robert Person	.10
215	Scott Rolen	.60
216	Curt Schilling	.35
217	Scott Rolen Checklist	.25
218	Francisco Cordova	.10
219	Brian Giles	.10
220	Jason Kendall	.10
221	Warren Morris	.10
222	Abraham Nunez	.10
223	Aramis Ramirez	.10
224	Jose Silva	.10
225	Kevin Young	.10
226	Brian Giles Checklist	.10
227	Rick Ankiel	.25
228	Ricky Bottalico	.10
229	J.D. Drew	.25
230	Ray Lankford	.10
231	Mark McGwire	2.00
232	Eduardo Perez	.10
233	Placido Polanco	.10
234	Edgar Renteria	.10
235	Fernando Tatis	.10
236	Mark McGwire Checklist	.85
237	Carlos Almanzar	.10
238	Wiki Gonzalez	.10
239	Tony Gwynn	1.00
240	Trevor Hoffman	.10
241	Damian Jackson	.10
242	Wally Joyner	.10
243	Ruben Rivera	.10
244	Reggie Sanders	.10
245	Quilvio Veras	.10
246	Tony Gwynn Checklist	.50
247	Rich Aurilia	.10
248	Marvin Benard	.10
249	Barry Bonds	2.50
250	Ellis Burks	.10
251	Miguel Del Toro	.10
252	Edwards Guzman	.10
253	Livan Hernandez	.10
254	Jeff Kent	.10
255	Russ Ortiz	.10
256	Armando Rios	.10
257	Barry Bonds Checklist	1.00
258	Rafael Bournigal	.10
259	Freddy Garcia	.10
260	Ken Griffey Jr.	15.00
261	Carlos Guillen	.10
262	Raul Ibanez	.10
263	Edgar Martinez	.10
264	Jose Mesa	.10
265	Jamie Moyer	.10
266	John Olerud	.10
267	Jose Paniagua	.10
268	Alex Rodriguez	2.00
269	Alex Rodriguez Checklist	1.00
270	Wilson Alvarez	.10
271	Rolando Arrojo	.10
272	Wade Boggs	1.00
273	Miguel Cairo	.10
274	Jose Canseco	.40
275	Jose Guillen	.10
276	Roberto Hernandez	.10
277	Albie Lopez	.10
278	Fred McGriff	.10
279	Esteban Yan	.10
280	Jose Canseco Checklist	.20
281	Rusty Greer	.10
282	Roberto Kelly	.10
283	Esteban Loaiza	.10
284	Ruben Mateo	.10
285	Rafael Palmeiro	.65
286	Ivan Rodriguez	.65
287	Aaron Sele	.10
288	John Wetteland	.10
289	Ivan Rodriguez Checklist	.25
290	Tony Batista	.10
291	Jose Cruz Jr.	.10
292	Carlos Delgado	.50
293	Kelvim Escobar	.10
294	Tony Fernandez	.10
295	Billy Koch	.10
296	Raul Mondesi	.10
297	Willis Otanez	.10
298	David Segui	.10
299	David Wells	.10
300	Carlos Delgado Checklist	.20

Holographic Purple

Stars:	4-8X
Production 199 Sets	

Platinum Blue

Stars:	8-15X
Production 67 Sets	

In The Cage

		NM/M
Complete Set (20):		250.00
Common Player:		5.00
Inserted 1:145		
1	Mo Vaughn	5.00
2	Chipper Jones	15.00
3	Cal Ripken Jr.	30.00
4	Nomar Garciaparra	20.00
5	Sammy Sosa	20.00
6	Frank Thomas	10.00
7	Roberto Alomar	6.00
8	Manny Ramirez	10.00
9	Larry Walker	5.00
10	Jeff Bagwell	10.00
11	Vladimir Guerrero	10.00
12	Mike Piazza	20.00
13	Derek Jeter	30.00
14	Bernie Williams	5.00
15	Mark McGwire	25.00
16	Tony Gwynn	15.00
17	Ken Griffey Jr.	20.00
18	Alex Rodriguez	25.00
19	Rafael Palmeiro	8.00
20	Ivan Rodriguez	8.00

Latinos of the Major Leagues

		NM/M
Complete Set (36):		20.00
Common Player:		.25
Inserted 2:37		
Parallel:		2-4X
Production 99 Sets		
1	Erubiel Durazo	.25
2	Luis Gonzalez	.25
3	Andruw Jones	1.00
4	Nomar Garciaparra	2.00
5	Pedro Martinez	1.00
6	Sammy Sosa	2.00
7	Carlos Lee	.25
8	Magglio Ordonez	.25
9	Roberto Alomar	.65
10	Manny Ramirez	1.00
11	Omar Vizquel	.25
12	Vinny Castilla	.25
13	Juan Gonzalez	1.00
14	Luis Castillo	.25
15	Jose Lima	.25
16	Carlos Beltran	.75
17	Vladimir Guerrero	1.00
18	Edgardo Alfonzo	.25
19	Roger Cedeno	.25
20	Rey Ordonez	.25
21	Orlando Hernandez	.25
22	Tino Martinez	.25
23	Mariano Rivera	.35
24	Bernie Williams	.50
25	Miguel Tejada	.50
26	Bobby Abreu	.25
27	Fernando Tatis	.25
28	Freddy Garcia	.25
29	Edgar Martinez	.25
30	Alex Rodriguez	3.00
31	Jose Canseco	.65
32	Ruben Mateo	.25
33	Rafael Palmeiro	.75
34	Ivan Rodriguez	.75
35	Carlos Delgado	.65
36	Raul Mondesi	.25

Moment of Truth

		NM/M
Complete Set (30):		50.00
Common Player:		.50
Inserted 1:37		
1	Mo Vaughn	.50
2	Chipper Jones	3.00
3	Greg Maddux	3.00
4	Albert Belle	.50
5	Cal Ripken Jr.	6.00
6	Nomar Garciaparra	4.00
7	Pedro Martinez	2.00
8	Sammy Sosa	4.00
9	Frank Thomas	2.00
10	Barry Larkin	.50
11	Kenny Lofton	.50
12	Manny Ramirez	2.00
13	Larry Walker	.50
14	Juan Gonzalez	2.00
15	Jeff Bagwell	2.00
16	Craig Biggio	.50
17	Carlos Beltran	1.00
18	Vladimir Guerrero	2.00
19	Mike Piazza	4.00
20	Roger Clemens	3.50
21	Derek Jeter	6.00
22	Bernie Williams	.75
23	Mark McGwire	5.00
24	Tony Gwynn	3.00
25	Barry Bonds	6.00
26	Ken Griffey Jr.	4.00
27	Alex Rodriguez	5.00
28	Rafael Palmeiro	1.50
29	Ivan Rodriguez	1.50
30	Carlos Delgado	1.00

Pacific Cup

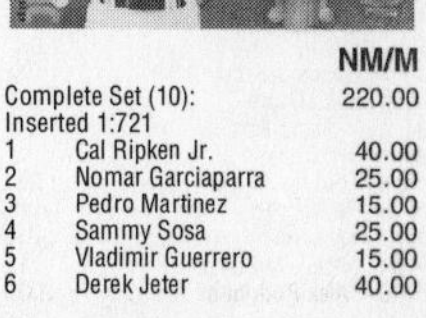

		NM/M
Complete Set (10):		220.00
Inserted 1:721		
1	Cal Ripken Jr.	40.00
2	Nomar Garciaparra	25.00
3	Pedro Martinez	15.00
4	Sammy Sosa	25.00
5	Vladimir Guerrero	15.00
6	Derek Jeter	40.00

7	Mark McGwire	35.00
8	Tony Gwynn	20.00
9	Ken Griffey Jr.	25.00
10	Alex Rodriguez	35.00

Timber 2000

NM/M
Complete Set (20): 100.00
Common Player: 2.00
Inserted 1:73

1	Chipper Jones	8.00
2	Nomar Garciaparra	10.00
3	Sammy Sosa	10.00
4	Magglio Ordonez	6.00
5	Manny Ramirez	6.00
6	Vinny Castilla	2.00
7	Juan Gonzalez	6.00
8	Jeff Bagwell	6.00
9	Shawn Green	3.00
10	Vladimir Guerrero	6.00
11	Mike Piazza	10.00
12	Derek Jeter	15.00
13	Bernie Williams	2.00
14	Mark McGwire	12.00
15	Ken Griffey Jr.	10.00
16	Alex Rodriguez	12.00
17	Jose Canseco	3.00
18	Rafael Palmeiro	5.00
19	Ivan Rodriguez	5.00
20	Carlos Delgado	4.00

2000 Pacific Crown Royale

NM/M
Complete Set (144): 40.00
Common Player: .25
Common SP: 1.00
Pack (6): 2.50
Box (24): 45.00

1	Darin Erstad	.40
2	Troy Glaus	1.00
3	Adam Kennedy/SP	1.00
4	Derrick Turnbow/SP RC	1.00
5	Mo Vaughn	.25
6	Erubiel Durazo	.25
7	Steve Finley	.25
8	Randy Johnson	1.00
9	Travis Lee	.25
10	Matt Williams	.25
11	Rafael Furcal SP	1.00
12	Andres Galarraga	.25
13	Andruw Jones	1.00
14	Chipper Jones	1.50
15	Javy Lopez	.25
16	Greg Maddux	1.50
17	Albert Belle	.25
18	Will Clark	.35
19	Mike Mussina	.40
20	Cal Ripken Jr.	3.00
21	Carl Everett	.25
22	Nomar Garciaparra	2.00
23	Pedro Martinez	1.00
24	Jason Varitek	.25
25	Scott Downs/SP RC	1.00
26	Mark Grace	.35
27	Sammy Sosa	2.00
28	Kerry Wood	.65
29	Ray Durham	.25
30	Paul Konerko	.25
31	Carlos Lee	.25
32	Magglio Ordonez	.40
33	Frank Thomas	1.00
34	Rob Bell/SP	1.00
35	Sean Casey	.25
36	Ken Griffey Jr.	2.00
37	Barry Larkin	.25
38	Pokey Reese	.25
39	Roberto Alomar	.40
40	David Justice	.25
41	Kenny Lofton	.25
42	Manny Ramirez	1.00
43	Richie Sexson	.25
44	Jim Thome	.75
45	Rolando Arrojo	.25
46	Jeff Cirillo	.25
47	Tom Goodwin	.25
48	Todd Helton	1.00
49	Larry Walker	.25
50	Tony Clark	.25
51	Juan Encarnacion	.25
52	Juan Gonzalez	1.00
53	Hideo Nomo	1.00
54	Dean Palmer	.25
55	Cliff Floyd	.25
56	Alex Gonzalez	.25
57	Mike Lowell	.25
58	Brad Penny/SP	1.00
59	Preston Wilson	.25
60	Moises Alou	.25
61	Jeff Bagwell	1.00
62	Craig Biggio	.25
63	Roger Cedeno	.25
64	Julio Lugo/SP	1.00
65	Carlos Beltran	.60
66	Johnny Damon	.40
67	Jermaine Dye	.25
68	Carlos Febles	.25
69	Mark Quinn/SP	1.00
70	Kevin Brown	.25
71	Shawn Green	.50
72	Eric Karros	.25
73	Gary Sheffield	.50
74	Kevin Barker/SP	1.00
75	Ron Belliard	.25
76	Jeromy Burnitz	.25
77	Geoff Jenkins	.25
78	Jacque Jones	.25
79	Corey Koskie	.25
80	Matt LeCroy/SP	1.00
81	Brad Radke	.25
82	Peter Bergeron/SP	1.00
83	Matt Blank/SP	1.00
84	Vladimir Guerrero	1.00
85	Hideki Irabu	.25
86	Rondell White	.25
87	Edgardo Alfonso	.25
88	Mike Hampton	.25
89	Rickey Henderson	1.00
90	Rey Ordonez	.25
91	Jay Payton/SP	1.00
92	Mike Piazza	2.00
93	Roger Clemens	1.75
94	Orlando Hernandez	.25
95	Derek Jeter	3.00
96	Tino Martinez	.25
97	Alfonso Soriano/SP	2.50
98	Bernie Williams	.40
99	Eric Chavez	.40
100	Jason Giambi	.75
101	Ben Grieve	.25
102	Tim Hudson	.50
103	Terrence Long/SP	1.00
104	Mark Mulder/SP	1.00
105	Adam Piatt/SP	1.00
106	Bobby Abreu	.25
107	Doug Glanville	.25
108	Mike Lieberthal	.25
109	Scott Rolen	.75
110	Brian Giles	.25
111	Chad Hermansen/SP	1.00
112	Jason Kendall	.25
113	Warren Morris	.25
114	Rick Ankiel/SP	1.00
115	Justin Brunette/SP RC	1.00
116	J.D. Drew	.40
117	Mark McGwire	2.50
118	Fernando Tatis	.25
119	Wiki Gonzalez/SP	1.00
120	Tony Gwynn	1.50
121	Trevor Hoffman	.25
122	Ryan Klesko	.25
123	Barry Bonds	3.00
124	Ellis Burks	.25
125	Jeff Kent	.25
126	Calvin Murray/SP	1.00
127	J.T. Snow	.25
128	Freddy Garcia	.25
129	John Olerud	.25
130	Alex Rodriguez	2.50
131	Kazuhiro Sasaki/SP RC	3.00
132	Jose Canseco	.50
133	Vinny Castilla	.25
134	Fred McGriff	.25
135	Greg Vaughn	.25
136	Gabe Kapler	.25
137	Mike Lamb/SP RC	1.00
138	Ruben Mateo/SP	1.00
139	Rafael Palmeiro	.75
140	Ivan Rodriguez	.75
141	Tony Batista	.25
142	Carlos Delgado	.75
143	Raul Mondesi	.25
144	Shannon Stewart	.25

Platinum Blue
Stars: 3-6X
Production 75 Sets

Limited Series
Stars: 2-4X
Production 144 Sets

Premiere Date
Stars: 2-4X
Production 121 Sets

Red
All singles: 1X
Base cards in retail packs.

Card-Supials

NM/M
Complete Set (20): 40.00
Common Card: 1.00
Inserted 2:25

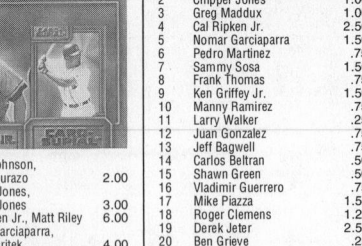

1	Randy Johnson, Erubiel Durazo	2.00
2	Chipper Jones, Andruw Jones	3.00
3	Cal Ripken Jr., Matt Riley	6.00
4	Nomar Garciaparra, Jason Varitek	4.00
5	Sammy Sosa, Kerry Wood	4.00
6	Frank Thomas, Magglio Ordonez	2.00
7	Ken Griffey Jr.,Sean Casey	4.00
8	Manny Ramirez, Richie Sexson	2.00
9	Larry Walker, Ben Petrick	1.00
10	Juan Gonzalez, Juan Encarnacion	2.00
11	Jeff Bagwell, Lance Berkman	2.00
12	Shawn Green, Eric Gagne	1.00
13	Vladimir Guerrero, Peter Bergeron	2.00
14	Mike Piazza, Edgardo Alfonso	4.00
15	Derek Jeter, Alfonso Soriano	5.00
16	Scott Rolen, Bobby Abreu	1.50
17	Mark McGwire, Rick Ankiel	5.00
18	Tony Gwynn, Ben Davis	3.00
19	Alex Rodriguez, Freddy Garcia	5.00
20	Ivan Rodriguez, Ruben Mateo	1.50

Cramer's Choice Jumbo

NM/M
Complete Set (10): 35.00
Common Player: 1.00
Inserted 1:Box H
Aqua: 5-10X
Production 20 Sets
Blue: 2-5X
Production 35 Sets
Gold: 10-20X
Production 10 Sets
Green: 3-6X
Production 30 Sets
Red: 4-8X
Production 25 Sets

1	Cal Ripken Jr.	6.00
2	Nomar Garciaparra	4.00
3	Ken Griffey Jr.	4.00
4	Sammy Sosa	4.00
5	Mike Piazza	4.00
6	Derek Jeter	6.00
7	Rick Ankiel	1.00
8	Mark McGwire	5.00
9	Tony Gwynn	2.00
10	Alex Rodriguez	5.00

Feature Attractions

NM/M
Complete Set (25): 10.00
Common Player: .25
Inserted 1:1
Exclusive Showing: 30-50X
Production 20 Sets

1	Erubiel Durazo	.25
2	Chipper Jones	1.00
3	Greg Maddux	1.50
4	Cal Ripken Jr.	2.50
5	Nomar Garciaparra	1.50
6	Pedro Martinez	.75
7	Sammy Sosa	1.50
8	Frank Thomas	.75
9	Ken Griffey Jr.	1.50
10	Manny Ramirez	.75
11	Larry Walker	.25
12	Juan Gonzalez	.75
13	Jeff Bagwell	.75
14	Carlos Beltran	.50
15	Shawn Green	.50
16	Vladimir Guerrero	.75
17	Mike Piazza	1.50
18	Roger Clemens	1.25
19	Derek Jeter	2.50
20	Ben Grieve	.25
21	Rick Ankiel	.35
22	Mark McGwire	2.00
23	Tony Gwynn	1.00
24	Alex Rodriguez	2.00
25	Ivan Rodriguez	.65

Final Numbers

NM/M
Complete Set (25): 10.00
Common Player: .25
Inserted 1:1

1	Randy Johnson	.75
2	Andruw Jones	.75
3	Chipper Jones	1.00
4	Cal Ripken Jr.	2.50
5	Nomar Garciaparra	1.50
6	Pedro Martinez	.75
7	Sammy Sosa	1.50
8	Ken Griffey Jr.	1.50
9	Sean Casey	.35
10	Manny Ramirez	.75
11	Larry Walker	.25
12	Jeff Bagwell	.75
13	Craig Biggio	.25
14	Shawn Green	.50
15	Vladimir Guerrero	.75
16	Mike Piazza	1.50
17	Derek Jeter	2.50
18	Bernie Williams	.35
19	Scott Rolen	.65
20	Mark McGwire	2.00
21	Tony Gwynn	1.00
22	Barry Bonds	2.50
23	Alex Rodriguez	2.00
24	Jose Canseco	.40
25	Ivan Rodriguez	.65

Jumbo

NM/M
Complete Set (6): 25.00
Inserted 6:10 boxes H

1	Cal Ripken Jr.	6.00
2	Nomar Garciaparra	4.00
3	Ken Griffey Jr.	4.00
4	Derek Jeter	6.00
5	Mark McGwire	5.00
6	Alex Rodriguez	5.00

Proofs

NM/M
Complete Set (36): 90.00
Common Player: 1.00
Inserted 1:25
Proofs: 2-3X

1	Erubiel Durazo	1.50
2	Randy Johnson	3.00
3	Chipper Jones	5.00
4	Greg Maddux	5.00
5	Cal Ripken Jr.	10.00

6	Nomar Garciaparra	8.00
7	Pedro Martinez	3.00
8	Sammy Sosa	5.00
9	Frank Thomas	2.50
10	Sean Casey	1.50
11	Ken Griffey Jr.	5.00
12	Manny Ramirez	2.50
13	Jim Thome	2.50
14	Larry Walker	1.50
15	Juan Gonzalez	2.50
16	Jeff Bagwell	2.50
17	Craig Biggio	1.50
18	Carlos Beltran	2.00
19	Shawn Green	2.00
20	Vladimir Guerrero	2.50
21	Edgardo Alfonzo	1.00
22	Mike Piazza	5.00
23	Roger Clemens	6.00
24	Derek Jeter	10.00
25	Alfonso Soriano	4.00
26	Bernie Williams	2.00
27	Ben Grieve	1.00
28	Rick Ankiel	1.00
29	Mark McGwire	8.00
30	Tony Gwynn	3.00
31	Barry Bonds	8.00
32	Alex Rodriguez	8.00
33	Jose Canseco	2.00
34	Vinny Castilla	1.00
35	Ivan Rodriguez	2.00
36	Rafael Palmeiro	2.00

Sweet Spot Signatures

		NM/M
	Common Player:	5.00
1	Adam Kennedy	5.00
2	Trot Nixon	8.00
3	Magglio Ordonez	10.00
4	Sean Casey	8.00
5	Travis Dawkins	5.00
6	Todd Helton	25.00
7	Ben Petrick	5.00
8	Jeff Weaver	6.00
9	Preston Wilson	5.00
10	Lance Berkman	10.00
11	Roger Cedeno	5.00
12	Eric Gagne	10.00
13	Kevin Barker	5.00
14	Kyle Peterson	5.00
15	Tony Armas Jr.	5.00
16	Peter Bergeron	5.00
17	Alfonso Soriano	40.00
18	Ben Grieve	5.00
19	Ramon Hernandez	5.00
20	Brian Giles	8.00
21	Chad Hermansen	5.00
22	Warren Morris	5.00
23	Ben Davis	5.00
24	Rick Ankiel	15.00
25	Chad Hutchinson	5.00
26	Freddy Garcia	10.00
27	Gabe Kapler	5.00
28	Ruben Mateo	5.00
29	Billy Koch	5.00
30	Vernon Wells	5.00

2000 Pacific Invincible

		NM/M
	Complete Set (150):	75.00
	Common Player:	.25
	Pack (3):	2.00
	Box (36):	50.00
1	Darin Erstad	.50
2	Troy Glaus	1.50
3	Ramon Ortiz	.25
4	Tim Salmon	.35
5	Mo Vaughn	.25
6	Erubiel Durazo	.25
7	Luis Gonzalez	.35
8	Randy Johnson	1.50
9	Matt Williams	.25
10	Rafael Furcal	.25
11	Andres Galarraga	.25
12	Tom Glavine	.40
13	Andruw Jones	1.50
14	Chipper Jones	2.00
15	Greg Maddux	2.00
16	Kevin Millwood	.25
17	Albert Belle	.25
18	Will Clark	.35
19	Mike Mussina	.40
20	Matt Riley	.25
21	Cal Ripken Jr.	4.00
22	Carl Everett	.25
23	Nomar Garciaparra	2.50
24	Steve Lomasney	.25
25	Pedro Martinez	1.50
26	Tomo Ohka RC	.75
27	Wilton Veras	.25
28	Mark Grace	.35
29	Sammy Sosa	2.50
30	Kerry Wood	.75
31	Eric Young	.25
32	Julio Zuleta RC	.25
33	Paul Konerko	.35
34	Carlos Lee	.25
35	Magglio Ordonez	.35
36	Josh Paul	.25
37	Frank Thomas	1.50
38	Rob Bell	.25
39	Dante Bichette	.25
40	Sean Casey	.35
41	Ken Griffey Jr.	2.50
42	Barry Larkin	.25
43	Pokey Reese	.25
44	Roberto Alomar	.40
45	Manny Ramirez	1.50
46	Richie Sexson	.25
47	Jim Thome	1.50
48	Omar Vizquel	.25
49	Jeff Cirillo	.25
50	Todd Helton	1.50
51	Neifi Perez	.25
52	Larry Walker	.25
53	Tony Clark	.25
54	Juan Encarnacion	.25
55	Juan Gonzalez	1.50
56	Hideo Nomo	1.00
57	Luis Castillo	.25
58	Alex Gonzalez	.25
59	Brad Penny	.25
60	Preston Wilson	.25
61	Moises Alou	.25
62	Jeff Bagwell	1.50
63	Lance Berkman	.25
64	Craig Biggio	.25
65	Roger Cedeno	.25
66	Jose Lima	.25
67	Carlos Beltran	.50
68	Johnny Damon	.35
69	Chad Durbin RC	.50
70	Jermaine Dye	.25
71	Carlos Febles	.25
72	Mark Quinn	.25
73	Kevin Brown	.25
74	Eric Gagne	.25
75	Shawn Green	.50
76	Eric Karros	.25
77	Gary Sheffield	.40
78	Kevin Barker	.25
79	Ron Belliard	.25
80	Jeromy Burnitz	.25
81	Geoff Jenkins	.25
82	Jacque Jones	.25
83	Corey Koskie	.25
84	Matt LeCroy	.25
85	David Ortiz	.35
86	Johan Santana RC	20.00
87	Todd Walker	.25
88	Peter Bergeron	.25
89	Vladimir Guerrero	1.50
90	Jose Vidro	.25
91	Rondell White	.25
92	Edgardo Alfonzo	.25
93	Derek Bell	.25
94	Mike Hampton	.25
95	Rey Ordonez	.25
96	Mike Piazza	2.50
97	Robin Ventura	.25
98	Roger Clemens	2.25
99	Orlando Hernandez	.25
100	Derek Jeter	4.00
101	Alfonso Soriano	.75
102	Bernie Williams	.35
103	Eric Chavez	.40
104	Jason Giambi	.75
105	Ben Grieve	.25
106	Tim Hudson	.40
107	Miguel Tejada	.40
108	Bobby Abreu	.25
109	Doug Glanville	.25
110	Mike Lieberthal	.25
111	Scott Rolen	.75
112	Brian Giles	.25
113	Chad Hermansen	.25
114	Jason Kendall	.25
115	Warren Morris	.25
116	Aramis Ramirez	.25
117	Rick Ankiel	.25
118	J.D. Drew	.40
119	Mark McGwire	3.00
120	Fernando Tatis	.25
121	Fernando Vina	.25
122	Bret Boone	.25
123	Ben Davis	.25
124	Tony Gwynn	2.00
125	Trevor Hoffman	.25
126	Ryan Klesko	.25
127	Rich Aurilia	.25
128	Barry Bonds	4.00
129	Ellis Burks	.25
130	Jeff Kent	.25
131	Freddy Garcia	.25
132	Carlos Guillen	.25
133	Edgar Martinez	.25
134	John Olerud	.25
135	Robert Ramsay	.25
136	Alex Rodriguez	3.00
137	Kazuhiro Sasaki RC	3.00
138	Jose Canseco	.50
139	Vinny Castilla	.25
140	Fred McGriff	.25
141	Greg Vaughn (Front photo is Mo Vaughn.)	.25
142	Dan Wheeler	.25
143	Gabe Kapler	.25
144	Ruben Mateo	.25
145	Rafael Palmeiro	.75
146	Ivan Rodriguez	.75
147	Tony Batista	.25
148	Carlos Delgado	.65
149	Raul Mondesi	.25
150	Vernon Wells	.25

Holographic Purple

Stars: 2-3X
Production 299 Sets

Platinum Blue

Stars: 4-8X
Production 67 Sets

Diamond Aces

		NM/M
	Complete Set (20):	5.00
	Common Player:	.25
	Inserted 1:1	
	Edition of 399 Parallel:	2-3X
1	Randy Johnson	.75
2	Greg Maddux	1.00
3	Tom Glavine	.40
4	John Smoltz	.25
5	Mike Mussina	.50
6	Pedro Martinez	.75
7	Kerry Wood	.60
8	Bartolo Colon	.25
9	Brad Penny	.25
10	Billy Wagner	.25
11	Kevin Brown	.25
12	Mike Hampton	.25
13	Roger Clemens	1.50
14	David Cone	.25
15	Orlando Hernandez	.25
16	Mariano Rivera	.40
17	Tim Hudson	.40
18	Trevor Hoffman	.25
19	Rick Ankiel	.25
20	Freddy Garcia	.25

Game Gear

		NM/M
	Common Card:	4.00
1	Jeff Bagwell/Jsy/1,000	8.00
2	Tom Glavine/Jsy/1,000	6.00
3	Mark Grace/Jsy/1,000	8.00
4	Eric Karros/Jsy/1,000	4.00
5	Edgar Martinez/Jsy/800	6.00
6	Manny Ramirez/Jsy/975	8.00
7	Cal Ripken Jr./Jsy/1,000	25.00
8	Alex Rodriguez/Jsy/900	15.00
9	Ken Griffey/Jsy/675	6.00
10	Mo Vaughn Jsy/1,000	4.00
11	Edgar Martinez/Bat-Jsy/200	8.00
12	Manny Ramirez/Jsy/145	15.00
13	Alex Rodriguez/ Bat-Jsy/200	25.00
14	Ivan Rodriguez/ Bat-Jsy/200	10.00
15	Edgar Martinez/Bat/200	10.00
16	Manny Ramirez/Bat/200	15.00
17	Ivan Rodriguez/Bat/200	8.00
18	Alex Rodriguez/Bat/200	20.00
19	Jeff Bagwell/Patch/125	30.00
20	Tom Glavine/Patch/110	25.00
21	Mark Grace/Patch/125	25.00
22	Tony Gwynn/Patch/65	40.00
23	Chipper Jones/Patch/80	40.00
24	Eric Karros/Patch/125	15.00
25	Greg Maddux/Patch/80	50.00
26	Edgar Martinez/Patch/125	20.00
27	Manny Ramirez/Patch/125	30.00
28	Cal Ripken Jr./Patch/125	65.00
29	Alex Rodriguez/Patch/125	50.00
30	Ivan Rodriguez/Patch/125	25.00
31	Frank Thomas/Patch/125	25.00
32	Mo Vaughn/Patch/125	15.00

Eyes of the World

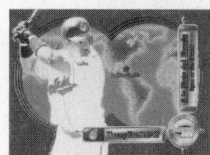

		NM/M
	Complete Set (20):	30.00
	Common Player:	.75
	Inserted 1:25	
1	Erubiel Durazo	.75
2	Andruw Jones	2.00
3	Cal Ripken Jr.	6.00
4	Nomar Garciaparra	4.00
5	Pedro Martinez	2.00
6	Sammy Sosa	4.00
7	Ken Griffey Jr.	4.00
8	Manny Ramirez	2.00
9	Larry Walker	.75
10	Juan Gonzalez	2.00
11	Carlos Beltran	1.25
12	Vladimir Guerrero	2.00
13	Orlando Hernandez	.75
14	Derek Jeter	6.00
15	Mark McGwire	5.00
16	Tony Gwynn	3.00
17	Freddy Garcia	.75
18	Alex Rodriguez	5.00
19	Jose Canseco	1.25
20	Ivan Rodriguez	1.50

Kings of the Diamond

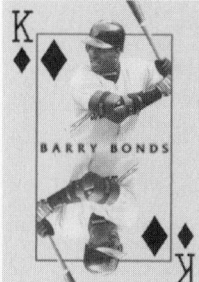

	NM/M
Complete Set (30):	10.00
Common Player:	.20
Inserted 1:1	
1 Mo Vaughn	.20
2 Erubiel Durazo	.20
3 Andruw Jones	.65
4 Chipper Jones	.75
5 Cal Ripken Jr.	1.50
6 Nomar Garciaparra	1.00
7 Sammy Sosa	1.00
8 Frank Thomas	.65
9 Sean Casey	.25
10 Ken Griffey Jr.	1.00
11 Manny Ramirez	.65
12 Larry Walker	.20
13 Juan Gonzalez	.65
14 Jeff Bagwell	.65
15 Craig Biggio	.20
16 Carlos Beltran	.50
17 Shawn Green	.35
18 Vladimir Guerrero	.65
19 Mike Piazza	1.00
20 Derek Jeter	1.50
21 Bernie Williams	.40
22 Ben Grieve	.20
23 Scott Rolen	.40
24 Mark McGwire	1.25
25 Tony Gwynn	.75
26 Barry Bonds	1.50
27 Alex Rodriguez	1.25
28 Jose Canseco	.25
29 Rafael Palmeiro	.50
30 Ivan Rodriguez	.50

Lighting The Fire

	NM/M
Complete Set (20):	120.00
Common Player:	3.00
Inserted 1:49	
1 Chipper Jones	8.00
2 Greg Maddux	8.00
3 Cal Ripken Jr.	15.00
4 Nomar Garciaparra	10.00
5 Pedro Martinez	6.00
6 Ken Griffey Jr.	10.00
7 Sammy Sosa	10.00
8 Manny Ramirez	6.00
9 Juan Gonzalez	6.00
10 Jeff Bagwell	6.00
11 Shawn Green	3.00
12 Vladimir Guerrero	6.00
13 Mike Piazza	10.00
14 Roger Clemens	9.00
15 Derek Jeter	15.00
16 Mark McGwire	12.00
17 Tony Gwynn	8.00
18 Alex Rodriguez	12.00
19 Jose Canseco	3.00
20 Ivan Rodriguez	5.00

Ticket To Stardom

	NM/M
Complete Set (20):	250.00
Common Player:	5.00
Inserted 1:121	
1 Andruw Jones	10.00
2 Chipper Jones	15.00
3 Cal Ripken Jr.	30.00
4 Nomar Garciaparra	20.00
5 Pedro Martinez	10.00
6 Ken Griffey Jr.	20.00
7 Sammy Sosa	20.00
8 Manny Ramirez	10.00
9 Jeff Bagwell	10.00
10 Shawn Green	5.00
11 Vladimir Guerrero	10.00
12 Mike Piazza	20.00
13 Derek Jeter	30.00
14 Alfonso Soriano	8.00
15 Scott Rolen	6.00
16 Rick Ankiel	5.00
17 Mark McGwire	25.00
18 Tony Gwynn	15.00
19 Alex Rodriguez	25.00
20 Ivan Rodriguez	8.00

Wild Vinyl

No Pricing
Production 10 Sets

2000 Pacific Omega

	NM/M
Complete Set (255):	300.00
Common Player:	.10
Common (151-255):	4.00
Production 999 Sets	
1 Garret Anderson	.10
2 Darin Erstad	.25
3 Troy Glaus	.75
4 Tim Salmon	.20
5 Mo Vaughn	.10
6 Jay Bell	.10
7 Steve Finley	.10
8 Luis Gonzalez	.20
9 Randy Johnson	.75
10 Matt Williams	.10
11 Andres Galarraga	.10
12 Andruw Jones	.75
13 Chipper Jones	1.00
14 Brian Jordan	.10
15 Greg Maddux	1.00
16 B.J. Surhoff	.10
17 Brady Anderson	.10
18 Albert Belle	.10
19 Mike Mussina	.40
20 Cal Ripken Jr.	2.50
21 Carl Everett	.10
22 Nomar Garciaparra	1.50
23 Pedro Martinez	.75
24 Jason Varitek	.10
25 Mark Grace	.20
26 Sammy Sosa	1.50
27 Rondell White	.10
28 Kerry Wood	.35
29 Eric Young	.10
30 Ray Durham	.10
31 Carlos Lee	.10
32 Magglio Ordonez	.25
33 Frank Thomas	.75
34 Sean Casey	.20
35 Ken Griffey Jr.	1.50
36 Barry Larkin	.10
37 Pokey Reese	.10
38 Roberto Alomar	.40
39 Kenny Lofton	.10
40 Manny Ramirez	.75
41 David Segui	.10
42 Jim Thome	.60
43 Omar Vizquel	.10
44 Jeff Cirillo	.10
45 Jeffrey Hammonds	.10
46 Todd Helton	.75
47 Todd Hollandsworth	.10
48 Larry Walker	.10
49 Tony Clark	.10
50 Juan Encarnacion	.10
51 Juan Gonzalez	.75
52 Bobby Higginson	.10
53 Hideo Nomo	.75
54 Dean Palmer	.10
55 Luis Castillo	.10
56 Cliff Floyd	.10
57 Derrek Lee	.10
58 Mike Lowell	.10
59 Henry Rodriguez	.10
60 Preston Wilson	.10
61 Moises Alou	.10
62 Jeff Bagwell	.75
63 Craig Biggio	.10
64 Ken Caminiti	.10
65 Richard Hidalgo	.10
66 Carlos Beltran	.40
67 Johnny Damon	.25
68 Jermaine Dye	.10
69 Joe Randa	.10
70 Mike Sweeney	.10
71 Adrian Beltre	.20
72 Kevin Brown	.10
73 Shawn Green	.35
74 Eric Karros	.10
75 Chan Ho Park	.10
76 Gary Sheffield	.30
77 Ron Belliard	.10
78 Jeromy Burnitz	.10
79 Geoff Jenkins	.10
80 Richie Sexson	.10
81 Ron Coomer	.10
82 Jacque Jones	.10
83 Corey Koskie	.10
84 Matt Lawton	.10
85 Vladimir Guerrero	.75
86 Lee Stevens	.10
87 Jose Vidro	.10
88 Edgardo Alfonzo	.10
89 Derek Bell	.10
90 Mike Bordick	.10
91 Mike Piazza	1.50
92 Robin Ventura	.10
93 Jose Canseco	.40
94 Roger Clemens	1.25
95 Orlando Hernandez	.10
96 Derek Jeter	2.50
97 David Justice	.10
98 Tino Martinez	.10
99 Jorge Posada	.10
100 Bernie Williams	.40
101 Eric Chavez	.20
102 Jason Giambi	.50
103 Ben Grieve	.10
104 Miguel Tejada	.25
105 Bobby Abreu	.10
106 Doug Glanville	.10
107 Travis Lee	.10
108 Mike Lieberthal	.10
109 Scott Rolen	.65
110 Brian S. Giles	.10
111 Jason Kendall	.10
112 Warren Morris	.10
113 Kevin Young	.10
114 Will Clark	.20
115 J.D. Drew	.20
116 Jim Edmonds	.10
117 Mark McGwire	2.00
118 Edgar Renteria	.10
119 Fernando Tatis	.10
120 Fernando Vina	.10
121 Bret Boone	.10
122 Tony Gwynn	1.00
123 Trevor Hoffman	.10
124 Phil Nevin	.10
125 Eric Owens	.10
126 Barry Bonds	2.50
127 Ellis Burks	.10
128 Jeff Kent	.10
129 J.T. Snow	.10
130 Jay Buhner	.10
131 Mike Cameron	.10
132 Rickey Henderson	.75
133 Edgar Martinez	.10
134 John Olerud	.10
135 Alex Rodriguez	2.00
136 Kazuhiro Sasaki RC	1.00
137 Fred McGriff	.10
138 Greg Vaughn	.10
139 Gerald Williams	.10
140 Rusty Greer	.10
141 Gabe Kapler	.10
142 Ricky Ledee	.10
143 Rafael Palmeiro	.65
144 Ivan Rodriguez	.65
145 Tony Batista	.10
146 Jose Cruz Jr.	.10
147 Carlos Delgado	.50
148 Brad Fullmer	.10
149 Shannon Stewart	.10
150 David Wells	.10
151 Jose Alvarez, Jeff DaVanon	6.00
152 Seth Etherton, Adam Kennedy	4.00
153 Ramon Ortiz, Lou Pote	4.00
154 Derrick Turnbow, Eric Weaver	4.00
155 Rod Barajas, Jason Conti	4.00
156 Byung-Hyun Kim, Rob Ryan	4.00
157 David Cortes, George Lombard	4.00
158 Ivanon Coffie, Melvin Mora	4.00
159 Ryan Kohlmeier, Luis Matos RC	6.00
160 Willie Morales, John Parrish RC	4.00
161 Chris Richard, Jay Spurgeon RC	5.00
162 Israel Alcantara, Tomokazu Ohka RC	5.00
163 Paxton Crawford, Sang-Hoon Lee RC	4.00
164 Mike Mahoney, Wilton Veras	4.00
165 Daniel Garibay, Ross Gload RC	4.00
166 Gary Matthews Jr., Phil Norton	4.00
167 Roosevelt Brown, Ruben Quevedo	4.00
168 Lorenzo Barcelo, Rocky Biddle RC	4.00
169 Mark Buehrle, John Garland	8.00
170 Aaron Myette, Josh Paul	4.00
171 Kip Wells, Kelly Wunsch	4.00
172 Rob Bell, Travis Dawkins	4.00
173 Hector Mercado, John Riedling RC	4.00
174 Russell Branyan, Sean DePaula	4.00
175 Tim Drew, Mark Watson	4.00
176 Craig House, Ben Petrick	5.00
177 Robert Fick, Jose Macias	4.00
178 Javier Cardona, Brandon Villafuerte	4.00
179 Armando Almanza, A.J. Burnett	4.00
180 Ramon Castro, Pablo Ozuna	4.00
181 Lance Berkman, Jason Green	4.00
182 Julio Lugo, Tony McKnight	4.00
183 Mitch Meluskey, Wade Miller	4.00
184 Chad Durbin, Hector Ortiz RC	5.00
185 Dermal Brown, Mark Quinn	4.00
186 Eric Gagne, Mike Judd	4.00
187 Kane Davis, Valerio de los Santos	4.00
188 Santiago Perez, Paul Rigdon RC	4.00
189 Matt Kinney, Matt LeCroy	4.00
190 Jason Maxwell, A.J. Pierzynski	4.00
191 J.C. Romero, Johan Santana RC	50.00
192 Tony Armas Jr., Peter Bergeron	4.00
193 Matt Blank, Milton Bradley	4.00
194 Tomas De La Rossa, Scott Forster	4.00
195 Yovanny Lara, Talmadge Nunnari RC	4.00
196 Brian Schneider, Andy Tracy	4.00
197 Scott Strickland, T.J. Tucker	4.00
198 Eric Cammack, Jim Mann RC	4.00
199 Grant Roberts, Jorge Toca	4.00
200 Alfonso Soriano, Jay Tessmer	8.00
201 Terrence Long, Mark Mulder	4.00
202 Pat Burrell, Cliff Politte	4.00
203 Jimmy Anderson, Bronson Arroyo	4.00
204 Mike Darr, Kory DeHaan	4.00
205 Adam Eaton, Wiki Gonzalez	4.00
206 Brandon Kolb, Kevin Walker	4.00
207 Damon Minor, Calvin Murray	4.00
208 Kevin Hodges, Joel Pineiro RC	40.00
209 Rob Ramsay, Kazuhiro Sasaki RC	8.00
210 Rick Ankiel, Mike Matthews	4.00
211 Steve Cox, Travis Harper	4.00
212 Kenny Kelly, Damian Rolls RC	4.00
213 Doug Davis, Scott Sheldon	4.00
214 Brian Sikorski, Pedro Valdes	4.00
215 Francisco Cordero, B.J. Waszgis	4.00
216 Matt DeWitt, Josh Phelps RC	8.00
217 Vernon Wells, Dewayne Wise	4.00
218 Geraldo Guzman, Jason Marquis	4.00
219 Rafael Furcal, Steve Sisco RC	4.00
220 B.J. Ryan, Kevin Beirne	4.00
221 Matt Ginter, Brad Penny	4.00
222 Julio Zuleta, Eric Munson	5.00

223	Dan Reichert, Jeff Williams	4.00
224	Jason LaRue, Danny Ardoin	4.00
225	Ray King, Mark Redman	4.00
226	Joe Crede, Mike Bell	4.00
227	Juan Pierre, Jay Payton	6.00
228	Wayne Franklin, Randy Choate **RC**	4.00
229	Chris Truby, Adam Piatt	4.00
230	Kevin Nicholson, Chris Woodward	4.00
231	Barry Zito, Jason Boyd	15.00
232	Brian O'Connor, Miguel Del Toro	4.00
233	Carlos Guillen, Aubrey Huff	4.00
234	Chad Hermansen, Jason Tyner	4.00
235	Aaron Fultz, Ryan Vogelsong	4.00
236	Shawn Wooten, Vance Wilson	4.00
237	Danny Klassen, Mike Lamb **RC**	4.00
238	Chad Bradford, Gene Stechschulte **RC**	4.00
239	Ismael Villegas, Hector Ramirez, Matt T. Williams, Luis Vizcaino **RC**	4.00
240	Mike Garcia, Domingo Guzman, Justin Brunette, Pasqual Coco **RC**	4.00
241	Frank Charles, Keith McDonald **RC**	4.00
242	Carlos Casimiro, Morgan Burkhart **RC**	4.00
243	Raul Gonzalez, Shawn Gilbert	4.00
244	Darrell Einertson, Jeff Sparks **RC**	4.00
245	Augie Ojeda, Brady Clark, Todd Belitz, Eric Byrnes **RC**	6.00
246	Leo Estrella, Charlie Greene	4.00
247	Trace Coquillette, Pedro Feliz **RC**	6.00
248	Tike Redman, David Newhan	4.00
249	Rodrigo Lopez, John Bales	6.00
250	Corey Patterson, Jose Ortiz **RC**	6.00
251	Britt Reames, Oswaldo Mairena **RC**	4.00
252	Xavier Nady, Timoniel Perez **RC**	6.00
253	Tom Jacquez, Vicente Padilla	4.00
254	Elvis Pena, Adam Melhuse **RC**	4.00
255	Ben Weber, Alex Cabrera **RC**	6.00

Copper

Stars (1-150):	8-15X
Production 45 Sets	

Platinum Blue

Stars (1-150):	6-10X
Production 55 Sets	

Premiere Date

Stars (1-150):	4-8X
Production 77 Sets	

Gold

Stars (1-150):	4-8X
Production 120 Sets	
(Retail only, one per box.)	

AL Contenders

		NM/M
Complete Set (18):		20.00
Common Player:		.50
Inserted 2:37		
1	Darin Erstad	.75
2	Troy Glaus	1.50
3	Mo Vaughn	.50
4	Albert Belle	.50
5	Cal Ripken Jr.	4.00
6	Nomar Garciaparra	3.00
7	Pedro Martinez	1.50
8	Frank Thomas	1.50
9	Manny Ramirez	1.50
10	Jim Thome	1.25

11	Juan Gonzalez	1.50
12	Roger Clemens	2.50
13	Derek Jeter	4.00
14	Bernie Williams	.75
15	Jason Giambi	1.00
16	Alex Rodriguez	3.50
17	Edgar Martinez	.50
18	Carlos Delgado	1.00

NL Contenders

		NM/M
Complete Set (18):		20.00
Common Player:		.50
Inserted 2:37		
1	Randy Johnson	1.50
2	Chipper Jones	2.00
3	Greg Maddux	2.00
4	Sammy Sosa	2.50
5	Sean Casey	.50
6	Ken Griffey Jr.	2.50
7	Todd Helton	1.50
8	Jeff Bagwell	1.50
9	Shawn Green	.50
10	Gary Sheffield	.75
11	Vladimir Guerrero	1.50
12	Mike Piazza	2.50
13	Scott Rolen	1.00
14	Barry Bonds	4.00
15	Rick Ankiel	.50
16	J.D. Drew	.50
17	Jim Edmonds	.50
18	Mark McGwire	3.00

EO Portraits

		NM/M
Complete Set (20):		125.00
Common Player:		3.00
Inserted 1:73		
1-of-1 Die-Cut Parallels Exist		
1	Chipper Jones	8.00
2	Greg Maddux	8.00
3	Cal Ripken Jr.	15.00
4	Pedro Martinez	6.00
5	Nomar Garciaparra	10.00
6	Sammy Sosa	10.00
7	Frank Thomas	6.00
8	Ken Griffey Jr.	10.00
9	Gary Sheffield	4.00
10	Mike Piazza	10.00
11	Mike Piazza	10.00
12	Roger Clemens	9.00
13	Derek Jeter	15.00
14	Pat Burrell	4.00
15	Tony Gwynn	8.00
16	Barry Bonds	15.00

17	Alex Rodriguez	12.00
18	Rick Ankiel	3.00
19	Mark McGwire	12.00
20	Ivan Rodriguez	5.00

Full Court

		NM/M
Complete Set (36):		30.00
Common Player:		.50
Inserted 4:37 H		
1	Magglio Ordonez	.50
2	Manny Ramirez	1.50
3	Todd Helton	1.50
4	David Justice	.50
5	Bernie Williams	.50
6	Jason Giambi	1.00
7	Scott Rolen	1.00
8	Jeff Kent	.50
9	Edgar Martinez	.50
10	Randy Johnson	1.50
11	Greg Maddux	2.00
12	Mike Mussina	.60
13	Pedro Martinez	1.50
14	Chuck Finley	.50
15	Kevin Brown	.50
16	Roger Clemens	2.25
17	Tim Hudson	.50
18	Rick Ankiel	.50
19	Troy Glaus	1.50
20	Chipper Jones	2.00
21	Nomar Garciaparra	2.50
22	Jeff Bagwell	1.50
23	Shawn Green	.60
24	Vladimir Guerrero	1.50
25	Mike Piazza	2.50
26	Jim Edmonds	.50
27	Rafael Palmeiro	.75
28	Cal Ripken Jr.	4.00
29	Sammy Sosa	2.50
30	Frank Thomas	1.50
31	Ken Griffey Jr.	2.50
32	Gary Sheffield	.50
33	Barry Bonds	4.00
34	Alex Rodriguez	3.00
35	Mark McGwire	3.00
36	Carlos Delgado	1.00

MLB Generations

		NM/M
Complete Set (20):		100.00
Common Card:		3.00
Inserted 1:145		
1	Mark McGwire, Pat Burrell	12.00
2	Cal Ripken Jr., Alex Rodriguez	15.00
3	Randy Johnson, Rick Ankiel	6.00
4	Tony Gwynn, Darin Erstad	8.00
5	Barry Bonds, Magglio Ordonez	15.00
6	Frank Thomas, Jason Giambi	6.00
7	Roger Clemens, Kerry Wood	10.00
8	Mike Piazza, Mitch Meluskey	10.00
9	Ken Griffey Jr., Andruw Jones	10.00
10	Bernie Williams, J.D. Drew	4.00
11	Chipper Jones, Troy Glaus	8.00
12	Andres Galarraga, Todd Helton	6.00
13	Juan Gonzalez, Vladimir Guerrero	6.00
14	Craig Biggio, Rafael Furcal	3.00
15	Sammy Sosa, Jermaine Dye	10.00
16	Larry Walker, Richard Hidalgo	3.00
17	Greg Maddux, Adam Eaton	8.00
18	Barry Larkin, Derek Jeter	15.00
19	Roberto Alomar, Jose Vidro	4.00
20	Jeff Kent, Edgardo Alfonso	3.00

Signatures

		NM/M
Common Player:		5.00
1	Darin Erstad	10.00
2	Nomar Garciaparra	125.00
3	Cal Eldred	5.00
4	Magglio Ordonez	10.00
5	Frank Thomas	30.00
6	Brady Clark	5.00
7	Richard Hidalgo	5.00
8	Gary Sheffield	10.00

9	Pat Burrell	15.00
10	Jim Edmonds	10.00

Stellar Performers

		NM/M
Complete Set (20):		50.00
Common Player:		1.00
Inserted 1:37		
1	Darin Erstad	1.00
2	Chipper Jones	3.00
3	Greg Maddux	3.00
4	Cal Ripken Jr.	6.00
5	Pedro Martinez	2.00
6	Nomar Garciaparra	4.00
7	Sammy Sosa	4.00
8	Frank Thomas	2.00
9	Ken Griffey Jr.	6.00
10	Todd Helton	2.00
11	Jeff Bagwell	2.00
12	Vladimir Guerrero	2.00
13	Mike Piazza	4.00
14	Derek Jeter	6.00
15	Roger Clemens	3.50
16	Tony Gwynn	3.00
17	Barry Bonds	6.00
18	Alex Rodriguez	5.00
19	Mark McGwire	5.00
20	Ivan Rodriguez	1.50

2000 Pacific Paramount

		NM/M
Complete Set (250):		25.00
Common Player:		.10
Pack (6):		1.50
Wax Box (36):		40.00
1	Garret Anderson	.10
2	Jim Edmonds	.10
3	Darin Erstad	.25
4	Chuck Finley	.10
5	Troy Glaus	.75
6	Troy Percival	.10
7	Tim Salmon	.20
8	Mo Vaughn	.40
9	Jay Bell	.10
10	Erubiel Durazo	.10
11	Steve Finley	.10
12	Luis Gonzalez	.20
13	Randy Johnson	.75
14	Travis Lee	.10
15	Matt Mantei	.10
16	Matt Williams	.10
17	Tony Womack	.10
18	Bret Boone	.10
19	Tom Glavine	.35
20	Andruw Jones	.75

#	Player	Price
21	Chipper Jones	1.00
22	Brian Jordan	.10
23	Javy Lopez	.10
24	Greg Maddux	1.00
25	Kevin Millwood	.10
26	John Rocker	.10
27	John Smoltz	.10
28	Brady Anderson	.10
29	Albert Belle	.10
30	Will Clark	.20
31	Charles Johnson	.10
32	Mike Mussina	.35
33	Cal Ripken Jr.	2.00
34	B.J. Surhoff	.10
35	Nomar Garciaparra	1.25
36	Derek Lowe	.10
37	Pedro Martinez	.75
38	Trot Nixon	.10
39	Troy O'Leary	.10
40	Jose Offerman	.10
41	John Valentin	.10
42	Jason Varitek	.10
43	Mark Grace	.20
44	Glenallen Hill	.10
45	Jon Lieber	.10
46	Cole Liniak	.10
47	Jose Nieves	.10
48	Henry Rodriguez	.10
49	Sammy Sosa	1.25
50	Kerry Wood	.65
51	Jason Dellaero	.10
52	Ray Durham	.10
53	Paul Konerko	.10
54	Carlos Lee	.10
55	Greg Norton	.10
56	Magglio Ordonez	.10
57	Chris Singleton	.10
58	Frank Thomas	.75
59	Aaron Boone	.10
60	Mike Cameron	.10
61	Sean Casey	.20
62	Pete Harnisch	.10
63	Barry Larkin	.10
64	Pokey Reese	.10
65	Greg Vaughn	.10
66	Scott Williamson	.10
67	Roberto Alomar	.35
68	Sean DePaula RC	.20
69	Travis Fryman	.10
70	David Justice	.10
71	Kenny Lofton	.10
72	Manny Ramirez	.75
73	Richie Sexson	.10
74	Jim Thome	.65
75	Omar Vizquel	.10
76	Pedro Astacio	.10
77	Vinny Castilla	.10
78	Derrick Gibson	.10
79	Todd Helton	.75
80	Neifi Perez	.10
81	Ben Petrick	.10
82	Larry Walker	.10
83	Brad Ausmus	.10
84	Tony Clark	.10
85	Deivi Cruz	.10
86	Damion Easley	.10
87	Juan Encarnacion	.10
88	Juan Gonzalez	.75
89	Bobby Higginson	.10
90	Dave Mlicki	.10
91	Dean Palmer	.10
92	Bruce Aven	.10
93	Luis Castillo	.10
94	Ramon Castro	.10
95	Cliff Floyd	.10
96	Alex Gonzalez	.10
97	Mike Lowell	.10
98	Preston Wilson	.10
99	Jeff Bagwell	.75
100	Derek Bell	.10
101	Craig Biggio	.10
102	Ken Caminiti	.10
103	Carl Everett	.10
104	Mike Hampton	.10
105	Jose Lima	.10
106	Billy Wagner	.10
107	Daryle Ward	.10
108	Carlos Beltran	.40
109	Johnny Damon	.25
110	Jermaine Dye	.10
111	Carlos Febles	.10
112	Mark Quinn	.10
113	Joe Randa	.10
114	Jose Rosado	.10
115	Mike Sweeney	.10
116	Kevin Brown	.10
117	Shawn Green	.35
118	Mark Grudzielanek	.10
119	Todd Hollandsworth	.10
120	Eric Karros	.10
121	Chan Ho Park	.10
122	Gary Sheffield	.35
123	Devon White	.10
124	Eric Young	.10
125	Kevin Barker	.10
126	Ron Belliard	.10
127	Jeromy Burnitz	.10
128	Jeff Cirillo	.10
129	Marquis Grissom	.10
130	Geoff Jenkins	.10
131	David Nilsson	.10
132	Chad Allen	.10
133	Ron Coomer	.10
134	Jacque Jones	.10
135	Corey Koskie	.10

#	Player	Price
136	Matt Lawton	.10
137	Brad Radke	.10
138	Todd Walker	.10
139	Michael Barrett	.10
140	Peter Bergeron	.10
141	Brad Fullmer	.10
142	Vladimir Guerrero	.75
143	Ugueth Urbina	.10
144	Jose Vidro	.10
145	Rondell White	.10
146	Edgardo Alfonzo	.10
147	Armando Benitez	.10
148	Roger Cedeno	.10
149	Rickey Henderson	.75
150	Melvin Mora	.10
151	John Olerud	.10
152	Rey Ordonez	.10
153	Mike Piazza	1.25
154	Jorge Toca	.10
155	Robin Ventura	.10
156	Roger Clemens	1.00
157	David Cone	.10
158	Orlando Hernandez	.10
159	Derek Jeter	2.00
160	Chuck Knoblauch	.10
161	Ricky Ledee	.10
162	Tino Martinez	.10
163	Paul O'Neill	.10
164	Mariano Rivera	.20
165	Alfonso Soriano	.75
166	Bernie Williams	.25
167	Eric Chavez	.25
168	Jason Giambi	.50
169	Ben Grieve	.25
170	Tim Hudson	.25
171	John Jaha	.10
172	Matt Stairs	.10
173	Miguel Tejada	.25
174	Randy Velarde	.10
175	Bobby Abreu	.10
176	Marlon Anderson	.10
177	Rico Brogna	.10
178	Ron Gant	.10
179	Doug Glanville	.10
180	Mike Lieberthal	.10
181	Scott Rolen	.65
182	Curt Schilling	.35
183	Brian Giles	.10
184	Chad Hermansen	.10
185	Jason Kendall	.10
186	Al Martin	.10
187	Pat Meares	.10
188	Warren Morris	.10
189	Ed Sprague	.10
190	Kevin Young	.10
191	Rick Ankiel	.25
192	Kent Bottenfield	.10
193	Eric Davis	.10
194	J.D. Drew	.25
195	Adam Kennedy	.10
196	Ray Lankford	.10
197	Joe McEwing	.10
198	Mark McGwire	1.50
199	Edgar Renteria	.10
200	Fernando Tatis	.10
201	Mike Darr	.10
202	Ben Davis	.10
203	Tony Gwynn	1.00
204	Trevor Hoffman	.10
205	Damian Jackson	.10
206	Phil Nevin	.10
207	Reggie Sanders	.10
208	Quilvio Veras	.10
209	Rich Aurilia	.10
210	Marvin Benard	.10
211	Barry Bonds	2.00
212	Ellis Burks	.10
213	Livan Hernandez	.10
214	Jeff Kent	.10
215	Russ Ortiz	.10
216	J.T. Snow	.10
217	Paul Abbott	.10
218	David Bell	.10
219	Freddy Garcia	.10
220	Ken Griffey Jr.	1.50
221	Carlos Guillen	.10
222	Brian Hunter	.10
223	Edgar Martinez	.10
224	Jamie Moyer	.10
225	Alex Rodriguez	1.50
226	Wade Boggs	1.00
227	Miguel Cairo	.10
228	Jose Canseco	.40
229	Roberto Hernandez	.10
230	Dave Martinez	.10
231	Quinton McCracken	.10
232	Fred McGriff	.10
233	Kevin Stocker	.10
234	Royce Clayton	.10
235	Rusty Greer	.10
236	Ruben Mateo	.10
237	Rafael Palmeiro	.65
238	Ivan Rodriguez	.65
239	Aaron Sele	.10
240	John Wetteland	.10
241	Todd Zeile	.10
242	Tony Batista	.10
243	Homer Bush	.10
244	Carlos Delgado	.50
245	Tony Fernandez	.10
246	Billy Koch	.10
247	Raul Mondesi	.10
248	Shannon Stewart	.10
249	David Wells	.10
250	Vernon Wells	.10

Premiere Date

Stars:	8-15X

Production 50 Sets

Copper

Stars:	2X

Inserted 1:1 H

Holographic Silver

Stars:	5-10X

Production 99 Sets

Platinum Blue

Stars:	6-12X

Production 67 Sets

Ruby Red

Stars:	1-2X
RC's:	1X

Inserted 9 per 7-11 pack.

Holographic Gold

Stars:	3-6X

Production 199 Sets

Emerald

Stars:	1-2X
Yng Stars & RC's:	1X

Inserted 1:1 7-11 pack.
Inserted 1:1 R

Stars:	1-2X
Yng Stars & Rc's:	1X

Holographic Green

Stars:	6-10X

Production 99 Sets, 7-11 insert.

Cooperstown Bound

	NM/M
Complete Set (10):	220.00
Common Player:	20.00

Inserted 1:361
Proofs: 2X
Production 20 Sets, hobby only.
Canvas Proofs: Values Undetermined
Production One Set

1	Greg Maddux	20.00
2	Cal Ripken Jr.	40.00
3	Nomar Garciaparra	25.00
4	Sammy Sosa	25.00
5	Roger Clemens	30.00
6	Derek Jeter	40.00
7	Mark McGwire	30.00
8	Tony Gwynn	30.00
9	Ken Griffey Jr.	25.00
10	Alex Rodriguez	30.00

Double Vision

	NM/M
Complete Set (36):	220.00
Common Player:	3.00

Inserted 1:37

1	Chipper Jones	8.00
2	Cal Ripken Jr.	15.00
3	Nomar Garciaparra	10.00
4	Pedro Martinez	6.00
5	Sammy Sosa	10.00
6	Manny Ramirez	6.00
7	Jeff Bagwell	6.00

8	Craig Biggio	3.00
9	Vladimir Guerrero	6.00
10	Mike Piazza	10.00
11	Roger Clemens	9.00
12	Derek Jeter	15.00
13	Mark McGwire	12.00
14	Tony Gwynn	8.00
15	Ken Griffey Jr.	10.00
16	Alex Rodriguez	12.00
17	Rafael Palmeiro	5.00
18	Ivan Rodriguez	5.00
19	Chipper Jones	8.00
20	Cal Ripken Jr.	15.00
21	Nomar Garciaparra	10.00
22	Pedro Martinez	6.00
23	Sammy Sosa	10.00
24	Manny Ramirez	6.00
25	Jeff Bagwell	6.00
26	Craig Biggio	3.00
27	Vladimir Guerrero	6.00
28	Mike Piazza	10.00
29	Roger Clemens	9.00
30	Derek Jeter	15.00
31	Mark McGwire	12.00
32	Tony Gwynn	8.00
33	Ken Griffey Jr.	10.00
34	Alex Rodriguez	12.00
35	Rafael Palmeiro	5.00
36	Ivan Rodriguez	5.00

Fielder's Choice

	NM/M
Complete Set (20):	150.00
Common Player:	3.00

Inserted 1:73
Gold Parallel (10 Sets issued): 6-8X

1	Andruw Jones	5.00
2	Chipper Jones	8.00
3	Greg Maddux	8.00
4	Cal Ripken Jr.	20.00
5	Nomar Garciaparra	10.00
6	Sammy Sosa	10.00
7	Sean Casey	3.00
8	Manny Ramirez	5.00
9	Larry Walker	3.00
10	Jeff Bagwell	5.00
11	Mike Piazza	10.00
12	Derek Jeter	20.00
13	Bernie Williams	3.00
14	Scott Rolen	4.00
15	Mark McGwire	15.00
16	Tony Gwynn	8.00
17	Barry Bonds	20.00
18	Ken Griffey Jr.	10.00
19	Alex Rodriguez	15.00
20	Ivan Rodriguez	4.00

Maximum Impact

	NM/M
Complete Set (20):	25.00
Common Player:	.50

Inserted 2:25 7-11 packs.

1	Chipper Jones	2.00
2	Cal Ripken Jr.	4.00
3	Nomar Garciaparra	2.50
4	Pedro Martinez	1.50
5	Sammy Sosa	2.50
6	Manny Ramirez	1.50

7	Larry Walker	.50
8	Jeff Bagwell	1.50
9	Carlos Beltran	.75
10	Vladimir Guerrero	1.50
11	Mike Piazza	2.50
12	Derek Jeter	4.00
13	Roger Clemens	2.25
14	Mark McGwire	3.00
15	Tony Gwynn	2.00
16	Barry Bonds	4.00
17	Ken Griffey Jr.	2.50
18	Alex Rodriguez	3.00
19	Ivan Rodriguez	1.00
20	Carlos Delgado	.75

Season in Review

		NM/M
Complete Set (30):		25.00
Common Player:		.50
Inserted 2:37		
1	Randy Johnson	1.50
2	Matt Williams	.50
3	Chipper Jones	2.00
4	Greg Maddux	2.00
5	Cal Ripken Jr.	4.00
6	Nomar Garciaparra	2.50
7	Pedro Martinez	1.50
8	Sammy Sosa	2.50
9	Manny Ramirez	1.50
10	Larry Walker	.50
11	Jeff Bagwell	1.50
12	Craig Biggio	.50
13	Carlos Beltran	.75
14	Mark Quinn	.50
15	Vladimir Guerrero	1.50
16	Mike Piazza	2.50
17	Robin Ventura	.50
18	Roger Clemens	2.25
19	David Cone	.50
20	Derek Jeter	4.00
21	Mark McGwire	3.00
22	Fernando Tatis	.50
23	Tony Gwynn	2.00
24	Barry Bonds	4.00
25	Ken Griffey Jr.	2.50
26	Alex Rodriguez	3.00
27	Wade Boggs	2.00
28	Jose Canseco	.65
29	Rafael Palmeiro	1.00
30	Ivan Rodriguez	1.00

2000 Pacific Paramount Update

		NM/M
Complete Set (100):		10.00
Common Player:		.10
Production 12,500 Sets; retail exclusive		
1-U	Adam Kennedy	.10
2-U	Bengie Molina	.10
3-U	Derrick Turnbow	.10
4-U	Randy Johnson	.75
5-U	Danny Klassen	.10
6-U	Vicente Padilla	.10
7-U	Rafael Furcal	.10
8-U	Andres Galarraga	.10
9-U	Chipper Jones	1.00
10-U	Fernando Lunar	.10
11-U	Willie Morales	.10
12-U	Cal Ripken Jr.	2.00
13-U	B.J. Ryan	.10
14-U	Carl Everett	.10
15-U	Nomar Garciaparra	1.25
16-U	Pedro Martinez	.75
17-U	Wilton Veras	.10
18-U	Scott Downs	.10
19-U	Daniel Garibay	.10
20-U	Sammy Sosa	1.25
21-U	Julio Zuleta	.10
22-U	Josh Paul	.10
23-U	Frank Thomas	.75
24-U	Rob Bell	.10
25-U	Dante Bichette	.10
26-U	Travis Dawkins	.10
27-U	Ken Griffey Jr.	1.25
28-U	Chuck Finley	.10
29-U	Manny Ramirez	.75
30-U	Paul Rigdon	.10
31-U	Jeff Cirillo	.10
32-U	Larry Walker	.10
33-U	Masato Yoshii	.10
34-U	Robert Fick	.10
35-U	Jose Macias	.10
36-U	Juan Gonzalez	.75
37-U	Hideo Nomo	.75
38-U	Jason Grilli	.10
39-U	Pablo Ozuna	.10
40-U	Brad Penny	.10
41-U	Jeff Bagwell	.75
42-U	Lance Berkman	.10
43-U	Roger Cedeno	.10
44-U	Octavio Dotel	.10
45-U	Chad Durbin	.10
46-U	Eric Gagne	.10
47-U	Shawn Green	.35
48-U	Jose Hernandez	.10
49-U	Matt LeCroy	.10
50-U	Johan Santana	.10
51-U	Vladimir Guerrero	.75
52-U	Hideki Irabu	.10
53-U	Andrew Tracy	.10
54-U	Derek Bell	.10
55-U	Eric Cammack	.10
56-U	Mike Hampton	.10
57-U	Jay Payton	.10
58-U	Mike Piazza	1.25
59-U	Todd Zeile	.10
60-U	Roger Clemens	1.00
61-U	Darrell Einertson	.10
62-U	Derek Jeter	2.00
63-U	Jason Giambi	.60
64-U	Terrence Long	.10
65-U	Mark Mulder	.10
66-U	Adam Piatt	.10
67-U	Luis Vizcaino	.10
68-U	Pat Burrell	.35
69-U	Scott Rolen	.65
70-U	Chad Hermansen	.10
71-U	Rick Ankiel	.25
72-U	Jim Edmonds	.10
73-U	Mark McGwire	1.50
74-U	Gene Stechschulte	.10
75-U	Fernando Vina	.10
76-U	Bret Boone	.10
77-U	Tony Gwynn	1.00
78-U	Ryan Klesko	.10
79-U	David Newhan	.10
80-U	Kevin Walker	.10
81-U	Barry Bonds	2.00
82-U	Aaron Fultz	.10
83-U	Ben Weber	.10
84-U	Rickey Henderson	.75
85-U	Kevin Hodges	.10
86-U	John Olerud	.10
87-U	Robert Ramsay	.10
88-U	Alex Rodriguez	1.50
89-U	Kazuhiro Sasaki	.15
90-U	Vinny Castilla	.10
91-U	Jeff Sparks	.10
92-U	Greg Vaughn	.10
93-U	Francisco Cordero	.10
94-U	Gabe Kapler	.10
95-U	Mike Lamb	.10
96-U	Ivan Rodriguez	.65
97-U	Clayton Andrews	.10
98-U	Brad Fullmer	.10
99-U	Raul Mondesi	.10
100-U	Dewayne Wise	.10

2000 Pacific Prism

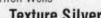

Sammy Sosa - OF

		NM/M
Complete Set (150):		10.00
Common Player:		.10
Pack (5):		1.50
Wax Box (24):		15.00
1	Jeff DaVanon **RC**	.10
2	Troy Glaus	.50
3	Tim Salmon	.15
4	Mo Vaughn	.10
5	Jay Bell	.10
6	Erubiel Durazo	.10
7	Luis Gonzalez	.20
8	Randy Johnson	.50
9	Matt Williams	.10
10	Andres Galarraga	.10
11	Andruw Jones	.50
12	Chipper Jones	.75
13	Brian Jordan	.10
14	Greg Maddux	.65
15	Kevin Millwood	.10
16	John Smoltz	.15
17	Albert Belle	.15
18	Mike Mussina	.25
19	Calvin Pickering	.10
20	Cal Ripken Jr.	1.50
21	B.J. Surhoff	.10
22	Nomar Garciaparra	1.00
23	Pedro Martinez	.50
24	Troy O'Leary	.10
25	John Valentin	.10
26	Jason Varitek	.10
27	Mark Grace	.15
28	Henry Rodriguez	.10
29	Sammy Sosa	1.00
30	Kerry Wood	.25
31	Ray Durham	.10
32	Carlos Lee	.10
33	Magglio Ordonez	.10
34	Chris Singleton	.10
35	Frank Thomas	.50
36	Sean Casey	.10
37	Travis Dawkins	.10
38	Barry Larkin	.10
39	Pokey Reese	.10
40	Scott Williamson	.10
41	Roberto Alomar	.20
42	Bartolo Colon	.10
43	David Justice	.10
44	Manny Ramirez	.50
45	Richie Sexson	.10
46	Jim Thome	.50
47	Omar Vizquel	.10
48	Pedro Astacio	.10
49	Todd Helton	.50
50	Neifi Perez	.10
51	Ben Petrick	.10
52	Larry Walker	.10
53	Tony Clark	.10
54	Damion Easley	.10
55	Juan Gonzalez	.50
56	Dean Palmer	.10
57	A.J. Burnett	.10
58	Luis Castillo	.10
59	Cliff Floyd	.10
60	Alex Gonzalez	.10
61	Preston Wilson	.10
62	Jeff Bagwell	.50
63	Craig Biggio	.10
64	Ken Caminiti	.10
65	Jose Lima	.10
66	Billy Wagner	.10
67	Carlos Beltran	.30
68	Johnny Damon	.25
69	Jermaine Dye	.10
70	Carlos Febles	.10
71	Mike Sweeney	.10
72	Kevin Brown	.10
73	Shawn Green	.25
74	Eric Karros	.10
75	Chan Ho Park	.10
76	Gary Sheffield	.30
77	Ron Belliard	.10
78	Jeromy Burnitz	.10
79	Marquis Grissom	.10
80	Geoff Jenkins	.10
81	Mark Loretta	.10
82	Ron Coomer	.10
83	Jacque Jones	.10
84	Corey Koskie	.10
85	Brad Radke	.10
86	Todd Walker	.10
87	Michael Barrett	.10
88	Peter Bergeron	.10
89	Vladimir Guerrero	.50
90	Jose Vidro	.10
91	Rondell White	.10
92	Edgardo Alfonzo	.10
93	Rickey Henderson	.50
94	Rey Ordonez	.10
95	Mike Piazza	1.00
96	Robin Ventura	.10
97	Roger Clemens	.75
98	Orlando Hernandez	.10
99	Derek Jeter	1.50
100	Tino Martinez	.10
101	Mariano Rivera	.15
102	Alfonso Soriano	.50
103	Bernie Williams	.20
104	Eric Chavez	.15
105	Jason Giambi	.30
106	Ben Grieve	.10
107	Tim Hudson	.20
108	John Jaha	.10
109	Bobby Abreu	.10
110	Doug Glanville	.10
111	Mike Lieberthal	.10
112	Scott Rolen	.40
113	Curt Schilling	.25
114	Brian Giles	.10
115	Jason Kendall	.10
116	Warren Morris	.10
117	Kevin Young	.10
118	Rick Ankiel	.10
119	J.D. Drew	.15
120	Chad Hutchinson	.10
121	Ray Lankford	.10
122	Mark McGwire	1.25
123	Fernando Tatis	.10
124	Bret Boone	.10
125	Ben Davis	.10
126	Tony Gwynn	.65
127	Trevor Hoffman	.10
128	Barry Bonds	1.50
129	Ellis Burks	.10
130	Jeff Kent	.10
131	J.T. Snow	.10
132	Freddy Garcia	.10
133	Ken Griffey Jr.	1.00
134	Edgar Martinez	.10
135	John Olerud	.10
136	Alex Rodriguez	1.25
137	Jose Canseco	.20
138	Vinny Castilla	.10
139	Roberto Hernandez	.10
140	Fred McGriff	.10
141	Rusty Greer	.10
142	Ruben Mateo	.10
143	Rafael Palmeiro	.40
144	Ivan Rodriguez	.40
145	Lee Stevens	.10
146	Tony Batista	.10
147	Carlos Delgado	.35
148	Shannon Stewart	.10
149	David Wells	.10
150	Vernon Wells	.10

Texture Silver

	NM/M
Complete Set (150):	50.00
Common Player:	.50
Stars:	2-3X

(See 2000 Prism for checklist and base card values.)

Woodgrain Silver

	NM/M
Complete Set (150):	50.00
Common Player:	.50
Stars:	2-3X

(See 2000 Prism for checklist and base card values.)

Tinsel Silver

	NM/M
Complete Set (150):	50.00
Common Player:	.50

Stars: 2-3X
(See 2000 Prism for checklist and base card values.)

Rapture Gold

	NM/M
Complete Set (150):	50.00
Common Player:	.50
Stars:	2-3X

(See 2000 Prism for checklist and base card values.)

Holographic Purple

	NM/M
Common Player:	1.00
Stars:	6-8X
Production 99 Sets	

Premiere Date

	NM/M
Common Player:	1.50
Stars:	8-10X
Production 61 Sets	

Rapture Silver

	NM/M
Complete Set (150):	50.00
Common Player:	.50
Stars:	2-3X

(See 2000 Prism for checklist and base values.)

Holographic Blue

	NM/M
Common Player:	1.00
Stars:	4-6X
Production 80 Sets	

Holographic Mirror

	NM/M
Common Player:	1.50
Stars:	4-6X
Production 160 Sets	

Holographic Gold

212/480

	NM/M
Common Player:	.50
Stars:	2-4X
Production 480 Sets	

Diamond Dial-A-Stats

	NM/M
Complete Set (10):	90.00
Common Player:	8.00
Inserted 1:193	
1 Chipper Jones	8.00
2 Greg Maddux	8.00
3 Cal Ripken Jr.	20.00
4 Sammy Sosa	10.00
5 Mike Piazza	10.00
6 Roger Clemens	9.00
7 Mark McGwire	15.00
8 Tony Gwynn	8.00
9 Ken Griffey Jr.	10.00
10 Alex Rodriguez	15.00

A.L. Legends

	NM/M
Complete Set (10):	15.00
Common Player:	.50
Inserted 1:25	
1 Mo Vaughn	.50
2 Cal Ripken Jr.	4.00
3 Nomar Garciaparra	2.50
4 Manny Ramirez	1.50
5 Roger Clemens	2.00
6 Derek Jeter	4.00
7 Ken Griffey Jr.	2.50
8 Alex Rodriguez	3.00
9 Jose Canseco	.75
10 Rafael Palmeiro	1.00

N.L. Legends

	NM/M
Complete Set (10):	15.00
Common Player:	.50
Inserted 1:25	
1 Chipper Jones	2.00
2 Greg Maddux	2.00
3 Sammy Sosa	2.50
4 Larry Walker	.50
5 Jeff Bagwell	1.00
6 Vladimir Guerrero	1.00
7 Mike Piazza	2.50
8 Mark McGwire	3.00

9 Tony Gwynn	2.00
10 Barry Bonds	4.00

Center Stage

	NM/M
Complete Set (20):	40.00
Common Player:	1.00
Inserted 1:25	
1 Chipper Jones	3.00
2 Cal Ripken Jr.	6.00
3 Nomar Garciaparra	4.00
4 Pedro Martinez	2.00
5 Sammy Sosa	4.00
6 Sean Casey	1.00
7 Manny Ramirez	2.00
8 Jim Thome	1.50
9 Jeff Bagwell	2.00
10 Carlos Beltran	1.50
11 Vladimir Guerrero	2.00
12 Mike Piazza	4.00
13 Derek Jeter	6.00
14 Bernie Williams	1.00
15 Scott Rolen	1.50
16 Mark McGwire	5.00
17 Tony Gwynn	3.00
18 Ken Griffey Jr.	4.00
19 Alex Rodriguez	5.00
20 Ivan Rodriguez	1.50

Prospects

Peter Bergeron

	NM/M
Complete Set (10):	12.00
Common Player:	1.00
Inserted 1:97	
1 Erubiel Durazo	1.00
2 Wilton Veras	1.00
3 Ben Petrick	1.00
4 Mark Quinn	1.00
5 Peter Bergeron	1.00
6 Alfonso Soriano	5.00
7 Tim Hudson	2.00
8 Chad Hermansen	1.00
9 Rick Ankiel	1.50
10 Ruben Mateo	1.00

2000 Pacific Private Stock

	NM/M
Complete Set (150):	50.00
Common Player:	.15
Common SP Prospect:	1.00
Inserted 1:4	
Pack (7):	2.00
Wax Box (24):	35.00
1 Darin Erstad	.25
2 Troy Glaus	.75
3 Tim Salmon	.25
4 Mo Vaughn	.15
5 Jay Bell	.15
6 Luis Gonzalez	.25
7 Randy Johnson	.75
8 Matt Williams	.15
9 Andruw Jones	.75
10 Chipper Jones	1.00
11 Brian Jordan	.15
12 Greg Maddux	1.00
13 Kevin Millwood	.15

Seattle Mariners • Shortstop
Alex Rodriguez

14	Albert Belle	.20
15	Mike Mussina	.35
16	Cal Ripken Jr.	2.00
17	B.J. Surhoff	.15
18	Nomar Garciaparra	1.25
19	Butch Huskey	.15
20	Pedro Martinez	.75
21	Troy O'Leary	.15
22	Mark Grace	.25
23	Bo Porter/SP	1.00
24	Henry Rodriguez	.15
25	Sammy Sosa	1.25
26	Kerry Wood	.40
27	Jason Dellaero/SP	1.00
28	Ray Durham	.15
29	Paul Konerko	.20
30	Carlos Lee	.15
31	Magglio Ordonez	.25
32	Frank Thomas	.75
33	Mike Cameron	.15
34	Sean Casey	.25
35	Barry Larkin	.15
36	Greg Vaughn	.15
37	Roberto Alomar	.40
38	Russell Branyan/SP	1.00
39	Kenny Lofton	.15
40	Manny Ramirez	.75
41	Richie Sexson	.15
42	Jim Thome	.75
43	Omar Vizquel	.15
44	Dante Bichette	.15
45	Vinny Castilla	.15
46	Todd Helton	.75
47	Ben Petrick/SP	1.00
48	Juan Sosa/SP	1.00
49	Larry Walker	.15
50	Tony Clark	.15
51	Damion Easley	.15
52	Juan Encarnacion	.15
53	Robert Fick/SP	1.00
54	Dean Palmer	.15
55	A.J. Burnet/SP	1.00
56	Luis Castillo	.15
57	Alex Gonzalez	.15
58	Julio Ramirez/SP	1.00
59	Preston Wilson	.15
60	Jeff Bagwell	.75
61	Craig Biggio	.15
62	Ken Caminiti	.15
63	Carl Everett	.15
64	Mike Hampton	.15
65	Billy Wagner	.15
66	Carlos Beltran	.50
67	Dermal Brown/SP	1.00
68	Jermaine Dye	.15
69	Carlos Febles	.15
70	Mark Quinn/SP	1.00
71	Mike Sweeney	.15
72	Kevin Brown	.15
73	Eric Gagne/SP	1.50
74	Eric Karros	.15
75	Raul Mondesi	.15
76	Gary Sheffield	.40
77	Jeromy Burnitz	.15
78	Jeff Cirillo	.15
79	Geoff Jenkins	.15
80	David Nilsson	.15
81	Ron Coomer	.15
82	Jacque Jones	.15
83	Corey Koskie	.15
84	Brad Radke	.15
85	Tony Armas Jr./SP	1.50
86	Peter Bergeron/SP	1.00
87	Vladimir Guerrero	.75
88	Jose Vidro	.15
89	Rondell White	.15
90	Edgardo Alfonzo	.15
91	Roger Cedeno	.15
92	Rickey Henderson	.75
93	Jay Payton/SP	1.00
94	Mike Piazza	1.25
95	Jorge Toca/SP	1.00
96	Robin Ventura	.15
97	Roger Clemens	1.00
98	David Cone	.15
99	Derek Jeter	2.00
100	D'Angelo Jimenez/SP	1.00
101	Tino Martinez	.15
102	Alfonso Soriano/SP	3.00
103	Bernie Williams	.25
104	Jason Giambi	.50

105	Ben Grieve	.15
106	Tim Hudson	.25
107	Matt Stairs	.15
108	Bobby Abreu	.15
109	Doug Glanville	.15
110	Scott Rolen	.65
111	Curt Schilling	.40
112	Brian Giles	.15
113	Chad Hermansen/SP	1.00
114	Jason Kendall	.15
115	Warren Morris	.15
116	Rick Ankiel/SP	1.00
117	J.D. Drew	.25
118	Adam Kennedy/SP	1.00
119	Ray Lankford	.15
120	Mark McGwire	1.50
121	Fernando Tatis	.15
122	Mike Darr/SP	1.00
123	Ben Davis	.15
124	Tony Gwynn	1.00
125	Trevor Hoffman	.15
126	Reggie Sanders	.15
127	Barry Bonds	2.00
128	Ellis Burks	.15
129	Jeff Kent	.15
130	J.T. Snow	.15
131	Freddy Garcia	.15
132	Ken Griffey Jr.	1.25
133	Carlos Guillen/SP	1.00
134	Edgar Martinez	.15
135	Alex Rodriguez	1.50
136	Miguel Cairo	.15
137	Jose Canseco	.40
138	Steve Cox/SP	1.00
139	Roberto Hernandez	.15
140	Fred McGriff	.15
141	Juan Gonzalez	.75
142	Rusty Greer	.15
143	Ruben Mateo/SP	1.00
144	Rafael Palmeiro	.65
145	Ivan Rodriguez	.65
146	Carlos Delgado	.50
147	Tony Fernandez	.15
148	Shawn Green	.35
149	Shannon Stewart	.15
150	Vernon Wells/SP	1.00

Premiere Date

Stars:	5-10X
Prospects:	1-2X
Inserted 1:24	

Gold Portraits

Stars:	5-10X
Prospects:	1-2X
Production 99 Sets	

Silver Portraits

August 2, 1999 — Derek delivered the Yankees to a 3-1 win over the Blue Jays when he broke a 1-1 tie on his two-run homer off of former teammate David Wells in the eighth inning. It was Jeter's 20th home run of 1999. He is coming off of a July in which he batted .339 with 62 total bases.

Stars:	3-6X
Prospects:	1-2X
Production 199 Sets	

Canvas

	NM/M
Complete Set (20):	120.00
Common Player:	2.00
Inserted 1:49	
1 Chipper Jones	8.00

2	Greg Maddux	8.00
3	Cal Ripken Jr.	15.00
4	Nomar Garciaparra	10.00
5	Sammy Sosa	10.00
6	Frank Thomas	6.00
7	Manny Ramirez	6.00
8	Larry Walker	2.00
9	Jeff Bagwell	6.00
10	Vladimir Guerrero	6.00
11	Mike Piazza	10.00
12	Roger Clemens	9.00
13	Derek Jeter	15.00
14	Mark McGwire	12.00
15	Tony Gwynn	8.00
16	Barry Bonds	15.00
17	Ken Griffey Jr.	10.00
18	Alex Rodriguez	12.00
19	Juan Gonzalez	6.00
20	Ivan Rodriguez	5.00

Extreme Action

	NM/M
Complete Set (20):	25.00
Common Player:	.50
Inserted 2:25	

1	Andruw Jones	1.50
2	Chipper Jones	2.00
3	Cal Ripken Jr.	4.00
4	Nomar Garciaparra	2.50
5	Sammy Sosa	2.50
6	Frank Thomas	1.50
7	Roberto Alomar	.60
8	Manny Ramirez	1.50
9	Larry Walker	.50
10	Jeff Bagwell	1.50
11	Vladimir Guerrero	1.50
12	Mike Piazza	2.50
13	Derek Jeter	4.00
14	Bernie Williams	.50
15	Scott Rolen	1.00
16	Mark McGwire	3.00
17	Tony Gwynn	2.00
18	Ken Griffey Jr.	2.50
19	Alex Rodriguez	3.00
20	Ivan Rodriguez	1.00

PS-2000

	NM/M
Complete Set (60):	15.00
Common Player:	.15
Inserted 2:Pack	

1	Mo Vaughn	.15
2	Greg Maddux	1.00
3	Andruw Jones	.75
4	Chipper Jones	1.00
5	Cal Ripken Jr.	2.50
6	Nomar Garciaparra	1.50
7	Pedro Martinez	.75
8	Sammy Sosa	1.50
9	Jason Dellaero	.15
10	Magglio Ordonez	.15
11	Frank Thomas	.75
12	Sean Casey	.25
13	Russell Branyan	.15
14	Manny Ramirez	.75
15	Richie Sexson	.15
16	Ben Petrick	.15
17	Juan Sosa	.15
18	Larry Walker	.15
19	Robert Fick	.15
20	Craig Biggio	.15
21	Jeff Bagwell	.75
22	Carlos Beltran	.50
23	Dermal Brown	.15
24	Mark Quinn	.15
25	Eric Gagne	.15
26	Jeromy Burnitz	.15
27	Tony Armas Jr.	.15
28	Peter Bergeron	.15
29	Vladimir Guerrero	.75
30	Edgardo Alfonzo	.15
31	Mike Piazza	1.50
32	Jorge Toca	.15
33	Roger Clemens	1.25
34	Alfonso Soriano	.65
35	Bernie Williams	.25
36	Derek Jeter	2.50
37	Tim Hudson	.25
38	Bobby Abreu	.15
39	Scott Rolen	.65
40	Brian Giles	.15
41	Chad Hermansen	.15
42	Warren Morris	.15
43	Rick Ankiel	.25
44	J.D. Drew	.25
45	Adam Kennedy	.15
46	Mark McGwire	2.00
47	Mike Darr	.15
48	Tony Gwynn	1.00
49	Barry Bonds	2.50
50	Ken Griffey Jr.	1.50
51	Carlos Guillen	.15
52	Alex Rodriguez	1.50
53	Juan Gonzalez	.75
54	Ruben Mateo	.15
55	Ivan Rodriguez	.65
56	Rafael Palmeiro	.65
57	Jose Canseco	.40
58	Steve Cox	.15
59	Shawn Green	.30
60	Vernon Wells	.15

PS-2000 Stars

	NM/M
Complete Set (20):	40.00
Common Player:	1.00
Production 299 Sets	

1	Mo Vaughn	1.00
2	Greg Maddux	4.00
3	Cal Ripken Jr.	8.00
4	Pedro Martinez	3.00
5	Sammy Sosa	5.00
6	Frank Thomas	3.00
7	Larry Walker	1.00
8	Craig Biggio	1.00
9	Jeff Bagwell	3.00
10	Mike Piazza	5.00
11	Roger Clemens	4.50
12	Bernie Williams	1.00
13	Mark McGwire	6.00
14	Tony Gwynn	4.00
15	Barry Bonds	8.00
16	Ken Griffey Jr.	5.00
17	Juan Gonzalez	3.00
18	Ivan Rodriguez	2.00
19	Rafael Palmeiro	2.00
20	Jose Canseco	1.50

PS-2000 New Wave

	NM/M
Complete Set (20):	40.00
Common Player:	1.00
Production 199 Sets	

1	Andruw Jones	3.50
2	Chipper Jones	5.00
3	Nomar Garciaparra	6.00
4	Magglio Ordonez	1.00
5	Sean Casey	1.00
6	Manny Ramirez	3.50
7	Richie Sexson	1.00
8	Carlos Beltran	2.00
9	Jeromy Burnitz	1.00

PETER BERGERON
Of Montreal Expos

DEREK JETER
001/199   Shortstop

10	Vladimir Guerrero	3.50
11	Edgardo Alfonzo	1.00
12	Derek Jeter	10.00
13	Tim Hudson	1.00
14	Bobby Abreu	1.00
15	Scott Rolen	2.50
16	Brian Giles	1.00
17	Warren Morris	1.00
18	J.D. Drew	1.25
19	Alex Rodriguez	8.00
20	Shawn Green	1.25

PS-2000 Rookies

	NM/M
Complete Set (20):	20.00
Common Player:	1.00
Inserted 99 Sets	

1	Jason Dellaero	1.00
2	Russell Branyan	1.00
3	Ben Petrick	1.00
4	Juan Sosa	1.00
5	Robert Fick	1.00
6	Dermal Brown	1.00
7	Mark Quinn	1.00
8	Eric Gagne	1.50
9	Tony Armas Jr.	1.00
10	Peter Bergeron	1.00
11	Jorge Toca	1.00
12	Alfonso Soriano	6.00
13	Chad Hermansen	1.00
14	Rick Ankiel	1.50
15	Adam Kennedy	1.00
16	Mike Darr	1.00
17	Carlos Guillen	1.00
18	Steve Cox	1.00
19	Ruben Mateo	1.00
20	Vernon Wells	1.50

Reserve

Jeff Bagwell

	NM/M
Complete Set (20):	50.00
Common Player:	1.00
Inserted 1:25	

1	Chipper Jones	3.00
2	Greg Maddux	3.00
3	Cal Ripken Jr.	6.00
4	Nomar Garciaparra	4.00
5	Sammy Sosa	4.00
6	Frank Thomas	2.00
7	Manny Ramirez	2.00
8	Larry Walker	1.00
9	Jeff Bagwell	2.00
10	Vladimir Guerrero	2.00
11	Mike Piazza	4.00
12	Roger Clemens	3.50
13	Derek Jeter	6.00
14	Mark McGwire	5.00
15	Tony Gwynn	3.00
16	Barry Bonds	6.00
17	Ken Griffey Jr.	4.00
18	Alex Rodriguez	5.00

19	Ivan Rodriguez	1.50
20	Shawn Green	1.25

2000 Pacific Revolution

		NM/M
Complete Set (150):		60.00
Common Player:		.25
Common SP:		1.00
Pack (3):		2.00
Box:		35.00
1	Darin Erstad	.50
2	Troy Glaus	1.00
3	Adam Kennedy/SP	1.50
4	Mo Vaughn	.25
5	Erubiel Durazo	.25
6	Steve Finley	.25
7	Luis Gonzalez	.35
8	Randy Johnson	1.00
9	Travis Lee	.25
10	Vicente Padilla/SP	1.00
11	Matt Williams	.25
12	Rafael Furcal/SP	1.00
13	Andres Galarraga	.25
14	Andruw Jones	1.00
15	Chipper Jones	1.50
16	Greg Maddux	1.50
17	Luis Rivera/SP	1.00
18	Albert Belle	.25
19	Mike Bordick	.25
20	Will Clark	.35
21	Mike Mussina	.40
22	Cal Ripken Jr.	3.00
23	B.J. Surhoff	.25
24	Carl Everett	.25
25	Nomar Garciaparra	2.00
26	Pedro Martinez	1.00
27	Jason Varitek	.25
28	Wilton Veras/SP	1.00
29	Shane Andrews	.25
30	Scott Downs/SP **RC**	1.00
31	Mark Grace	.35
32	Sammy Sosa	2.00
33	Kerry Wood	.50
34	Ray Durham	.25
35	Paul Konerko	.35
36	Carlos Lee	.25
37	Magglio Ordonez	.25
38	Frank Thomas	1.00
39	Rob Bell/SP	1.00
40	Sean Casey	.40
41	Ken Griffey Jr.	2.00
42	Barry Larkin	.25
43	Pokey Reese	.25
44	Roberto Alomar	.40
45	David Justice	.25
46	Kenny Lofton	.25
47	Manny Ramirez	1.00
48	Richie Sexson	.25
49	Jim Thome	1.00
50	Jeff Cirillo	.25
51	Jeffrey Hammonds	.25
52	Todd Helton	1.00
53	Larry Walker	.25
54	Tony Clark	.25
55	Juan Gonzalez	1.00
56	Hideo Nomo	.25
57	Dean Palmer	.25
58	Alex Gonzalez	.25
59	Mike Lowell	.25
60	Pablo Ozuna/SP	1.00
61	Brad Penny/SP	1.00
62	Preston Wilson	.25
63	Moises Alou	.25
64	Jeff Bagwell	1.00
65	Craig Biggio	.25
66	Ken Caminiti	.25
67	Julio Lugo/SP	1.00
68	Carlos Beltran	.60
69	Johnny Damon	.40
70	Jermaine Dye	.25
71	Carlos Febles	.25
72	Mark Quinn/SP	1.00
73	Kevin Brown	.25
74	Shawn Green	.65
75	Chan Ho Park	.25
76	Gary Sheffield	.50
77	Kevin Barker/SP	1.00
78	Ron Belliard	.25
79	Jeromy Burnitz	.25
80	Geoff Jenkins	.25
81	Cristian Guzman	.25

82	Jacque Jones	.25
83	Corey Koskie	.25
84	Matt Lawton	.25
85	Peter Bergeron/SP	1.00
86	Vladimir Guerrero	1.00
87	Andy Tracy/SP	1.00
88	Jose Vidro	.25
89	Rondell White	.25
90	Edgardo Alfonzo	.25
91	Derek Bell	.25
92	Eric Cammack/SP	1.00
93	Mike Piazza	2.00
94	Robin Ventura	.25
95	Roger Clemens	1.75
96	Orlando Hernandez	.25
97	Derek Jeter	3.00
98	Tino Martinez	.25
99	Alfonso Soriano/SP	3.00
100	Bernie Williams	.35
101	Eric Chavez	.35
102	Jason Giambi	.75
103	Ben Grieve	.25
104	Terrence Long/SP	1.00
105	Mark Mulder/SP	1.00
106	Adam Piatt/SP	1.00
107	Bobby Abreu	.25
108	Rico Brogna	.25
109	Doug Glanville	.25
110	Mike Lieberthal	.25
111	Scott Rolen	.75
112	Brian Giles	.25
113	Chad Hermansen/SP	1.00
114	Jason Kendall	.25
115	Warren Morris	.25
116	Rick Ankiel/SP	1.00
117	J.D. Drew	.40
118	Jim Edmonds	.25
119	Mark McGwire	2.50
120	Fernando Tatis	.25
121	Fernando Vina	.25
122	Tony Gwynn	1.50
123	Trevor Hoffman	.25
124	Ryan Klesko	.25
125	Eric Owens	.25
126	Barry Bonds	3.00
127	Ellis Burks	.25
128	Bobby Estalella	.25
129	Jeff Kent	.25
130	Scott Linebrink/SP **RC**	1.00
131	Jay Buhner	.25
132	Stan Javier	.25
133	Edgar Martinez	.25
134	John Olerud	.25
135	Alex Rodriguez	2.50
136	Kazuhiro Sasaki/SP **RC**	2.00
137	Jose Canseco	.40
138	Vinny Castilla	.25
139	Fred McGriff	.25
140	Greg Vaughn	.25
141	Gabe Kapler	.25
142	Mike Lamb/SP **RC**	1.00
143	Ruben Mateo	.25
144	Rafael Palmeiro	.75
145	Ivan Rodriguez	.75
146	Tony Batista	.25
147	Jose Cruz Jr.	.25
148	Carlos Delgado	.75
149	Brad Fullmer	.25
150	Raul Mondesi	.25

Red

Stars:	1-2X
SP's:	1X
Production 299 Sets	

Shadow

Stars:	3-6X
SP's:	1-2X
Production 99 Sets	

Foul Pole Net-Fusions

		NM/M
Complete Set (20):		110.00
Common Player:		2.00
Inserted 1:49		
1	Chipper Jones	8.00
2	Cal Ripken Jr.	15.00
3	Nomar Garciaparra	10.00
4	Pedro Martinez	6.00
5	Sammy Sosa	10.00
6	Frank Thomas	6.00
7	Ken Griffey Jr.	10.00

8	Manny Ramirez	6.00
9	Jeff Bagwell	6.00
10	Shawn Green	3.00
11	Vladimir Guerrero	6.00
12	Mike Piazza	10.00
13	Derek Jeter	15.00
14	Bernie Williams	2.00
15	Rick Ankiel	4.00
16	Mark McGwire	12.00
17	Tony Gwynn	8.00
18	Barry Bonds	15.00
19	Alex Rodriguez	12.00
20	Ivan Rodriguez	6.00

Game-Ball Signatures

		NM/M
Common Player:		5.00
1	Randy Johnson	40.00
2	Greg Maddux	90.00
3	Rafael Furcal	7.50
4	Shane Andrews	5.00
5	Sean Casey	10.00
6	Travis Dawkins	5.00
7	Alex Gonzalez	5.00
8	Shane Reynolds	5.00
9	Eric Gagne	10.00
10	Kevin Barker	5.00
11	Eric Milton	5.00
12	Mark Quinn	5.00
13	Alfonso Soriano	40.00
14	Brian Giles	6.00
15	Mark Mulder	10.00
16	Adam Piatt	5.00
17	Warren Morris	5.00
18	Rick Ankiel	15.00
19	Adam Kennedy	6.00
20	Fernando Tatis	5.00
21	Barry Bonds	100.00
22	Alex Rodriguez	75.00
23	Ruben Mateo	5.00
24	Billy Koch	5.00
25	Brad Penny	5.00

Icons

		NM/M
Complete Set (20):		250.00
Common Player:		8.00
Inserted 1:121		
1	Randy Johnson	10.00
2	Chipper Jones	15.00
3	Greg Maddux	15.00
4	Cal Ripken Jr.	30.00
5	Nomar Garciaparra	20.00
6	Pedro Martinez	10.00
7	Sammy Sosa	20.00

8	Frank Thomas	10.00
9	Ken Griffey Jr.	20.00
10	Juan Gonzalez	10.00
11	Jeff Bagwell	10.00
12	Vladimir Guerrero	10.00
13	Mike Piazza	20.00
14	Roger Clemens	17.50
15	Derek Jeter	30.00
16	Mark McGwire	25.00
17	Tony Gwynn	15.00
18	Barry Bonds	30.00
19	Alex Rodriguez	25.00
20	Ivan Rodriguez	8.00

On Deck

		NM/M
Complete Set (20):		40.00
Common Player:		1.00
Inserted 1:25		
1	Chipper Jones	3.00
2	Cal Ripken Jr.	6.00
3	Nomar Garciaparra	4.00
4	Sammy Sosa	4.00
5	Frank Thomas	2.00
6	Ken Griffey Jr.	4.00
7	Manny Ramirez	2.00
8	Larry Walker	1.00
9	Juan Gonzalez	2.00
10	Jeff Bagwell	2.00
11	Shawn Green	1.50
12	Vladimir Guerrero	2.00
13	Mike Piazza	4.00
14	Derek Jeter	6.00
15	Scott Rolen	1.50
16	Mark McGwire	5.00
17	Tony Gwynn	3.00
18	Alex Rodriguez	5.00
19	Jose Canseco	1.50
20	Ivan Rodriguez	1.75

Season Opener

		NM/M
Complete Set (36):		35.00
Common Player:		.50
Inserted 2:25		
1	Erubiel Durazo	.50
2	Randy Johnson	1.50
3	Andruw Jones	1.50
4	Chipper Jones	2.00
5	Greg Maddux	2.00
6	Cal Ripken Jr.	4.00
7	Nomar Garciaparra	3.00
8	Pedro Martinez	1.50
9	Sammy Sosa	2.50
10	Frank Thomas	1.50
11	Magglio Ordonez	.50
12	Ken Griffey Jr.	2.50
13	Barry Larkin	.50
14	Kenny Lofton	.50
15	Manny Ramirez	1.50
16	Jim Thome	1.50
17	Larry Walker	.50
18	Juan Gonzalez	1.50
19	Jeff Bagwell	1.50
20	Craig Biggio	.50
21	Carlos Beltran	.75
22	Shawn Green	.75
23	Vladimir Guerrero	1.50
24	Mike Piazza	2.50
25	Orlando Hernandez	.50
26	Derek Jeter	4.00
27	Bernie Williams	.50
28	Eric Chavez	.50
29	Scott Rolen	1.00
30	Jim Edmonds	.50
31	Tony Gwynn	2.00
32	Barry Bonds	4.00
33	Alex Rodriguez	3.00

34	Jose Canseco	.65
35	Ivan Rodriguez	1.00
36	Rafael Palmeiro	1.00

Triple Header

	NM/M
Complete Set (30):	25.00
Common Player:	.25
Inserted 4:25	
Parallel (1-10):	3-6X
99 Sets Produced	
Parallel (11-20):	3-6X
99 Sets Produced	
Parallel (21-30):	1-2X
599 Sets Produced	

1	Chipper Jones	1.50
2	Cal Ripken Jr.	3.00
3	Nomar Garciaparra	2.00
4	Frank Thomas	1.00
5	Larry Walker	.25
6	Vladimir Guerrero	1.00
7	Mike Piazza	2.00
8	Derek Jeter	3.00
9	Tony Gwynn	1.50
10	Ivan Rodriguez	.75
11	Sammy Sosa	2.00
12	Ken Griffey Jr.	2.00
13	Manny Ramirez	1.00
14	Jeff Bagwell	1.00
15	Shawn Green	.40
16	Mark McGwire	2.50
17	Barry Bonds	3.00
18	Alex Rodriguez	2.50
19	Jose Canseco	.50
20	Rafael Palmeiro	.75
21	Randy Johnson	1.00
22	Tom Glavine	.40
23	Greg Maddux	1.50
24	Mike Mussina	.40
25	Pedro Martinez	1.00
26	Kerry Wood	.60
27	Chuck Finley	.25
28	Kevin Brown	.25
29	Roger Clemens	1.75
30	Rick Ankiel	.25

2000 Pacific Vanguard

	NM/M
Complete Set (100):	30.00
Common Player:	.15
Pack (4):	2.00
Wax Box (24):	35.00

1	Troy Glaus	1.00
2	Tim Salmon	.25
3	Mo Vaughn	.15
4	Albert Belle	.15
5	Mike Mussina	.35
6	Cal Ripken Jr.	3.00
7	Nomar Garciaparra	2.00
8	Pedro Martinez	1.00
9	Troy O'Leary	.15
10	Wilton Veras	.15
11	Magglio Ordonez	.15
12	Chris Singleton	.15
13	Frank Thomas	1.00
14	Roberto Alomar	.40
15	Russell Branyan	.15
16	Manny Ramirez	1.00

17	Jim Thome	.75
18	Omar Vizquel	.15
19	Tony Clark	.15
20	Juan Gonzalez	1.00
21	Dean Palmer	.15
22	Carlos Beltran	.50
23	Johnny Damon	.30
24	Jermaine Dye	.15
25	Mark Quinn	.15
26	Jacque Jones	.15
27	Corey Koskie	.15
28	Brad Radke	.15
29	Roger Clemens	1.75
30	Derek Jeter	3.00
31	Alfonso Soriano	.75
32	Bernie Williams	.30
33	Eric Chavez	.30
34	Jason Giambi	.75
35	Ben Grieve	.15
36	Tim Hudson	.30
37	Mike Cameron	.15
38	Freddy Garcia	.15
39	Edgar Martinez	.15
40	Alex Rodriguez	2.50
41	Jose Canseco	.50
42	Vinny Castilla	.15
43	Fred McGriff	.15
44	Rusty Greer	.15
45	Ruben Mateo	.15
46	Rafael Palmeiro	.75
47	Ivan Rodriguez	.65
48	Carlos Delgado	.75
49	Shannon Stewart	.15
50	Vernon Wells	.15
51	Erubiel Durazo	.15
52	Randy Johnson	1.00
53	Matt Williams	.15
54	Andruw Jones	1.00
55	Chipper Jones	1.50
56	Greg Maddux	1.50
57	Mark Grace	.25
58	Sammy Sosa	2.00
59	Kerry Wood	.50
60	Sean Casey	.25
61	Ken Griffey Jr.	2.00
62	Barry Larkin	.15
63	Todd Helton	1.00
64	Ben Petrick	.15
65	Larry Walker	.15
66	Luis Castillo	.15
67	Alex Gonzalez	.15
68	Preston Wilson	.15
69	Jeff Bagwell	1.00
70	Craig Biggio	.15
71	Billy Wagner	.15
72	Kevin Brown	.15
73	Shawn Green	.40
74	Gary Sheffield	.40
75	Kevin Barker	.15
76	Ron Belliard	.15
77	Jeromy Burnitz	.15
78	Michael Barrett	.15
79	Peter Bergeron	.15
80	Vladimir Guerrero	1.00
81	Edgardo Alfonzo	.15
82	Rey Ordonez	.15
83	Mike Piazza	2.00
84	Robin Ventura	.15
85	Bobby Abreu	.15
86	Mike Lieberthal	.15
87	Scott Rolen	.75
88	Brian Giles	.15
89	Chad Hermansen	.15
90	Jason Kendall	.15
91	Rick Ankiel	.15
92	J.D. Drew	.25
93	Mark McGwire	2.50
94	Fernando Tatis	.15
95	Ben Davis	.15
96	Tony Gwynn	1.50
97	Trevor Hoffman	.15
98	Barry Bonds	3.00
99	Ellis Burks	.15
100	Jeff Kent	.15

Green

A.L. (1-50):	3-6X
Production 99 Sets	
N.L. (51-100):	2-4X
Production 199 Sets	

Gold

A.L. (1-50):	2-4X
Production 199 Sets R	
N.L. (51-100):	3-6X
Production 99 Sets R	

Premiere Date

Stars:	3-5X
Production 135 Sets H	

Purple

Production 10 Sets	
Values Undetermined	

A.L. Vanguard Press

	NM/M
Complete Set (10):	10.00
Common Player:	.65
Inserted 2:25	

1	Cal Ripken Jr.	3.00
2	Nomar Garciaparra	2.00
3	Pedro Martinez	1.00
4	Manny Ramirez	1.00
5	Carlos Beltran	.65
6	Roger Clemens	1.50
7	Derek Jeter	3.00
8	Alex Rodriguez	2.50
9	Rafael Palmeiro	.75
10	Ivan Rodriguez	.75

N.L. Vanguard Press

Guerrero sets Expos' homer record

Above: The Expos count on Vladimir to drive in the Montreal offense.

	NM/M
Complete Set (10):	10.00
Common Player:	.50
Inserted 2:37	

1	Chipper Jones	1.50
2	Greg Maddux	1.50
3	Sammy Sosa	2.00
4	Ken Griffey Jr.	2.00
5	Larry Walker	.50
6	Jeff Bagwell	1.00
7	Vladimir Guerrero	1.00
8	Mike Piazza	2.00
9	Mark McGwire	2.50
10	Tony Gwynn	1.50

Cosmic Force

	NM/M
Complete Set (10):	30.00
Common Player:	3.00
Inserted 1:73	

1	Chipper Jones	3.00
2	Cal Ripken Jr.	6.00
3	Nomar Garciaparra	4.00
4	Sammy Sosa	4.00
5	Ken Griffey Jr.	4.00
6	Mike Piazza	4.00
7	Derek Jeter	6.00
8	Mark McGwire	5.00
9	Tony Gwynn	3.00
10	Alex Rodriguez	5.00

Diamond Architects

	NM/M
Complete Set (20):	25.00
Common Player:	.50
Inserted 1:25	

1	Chipper Jones	2.00
2	Greg Maddux	2.00
3	Cal Ripken Jr.	4.00
4	Nomar Garciaparra	2.50
5	Sammy Sosa	2.50
6	Ken Griffey Jr.	2.50
7	Manny Ramirez	1.50
8	Larry Walker	.50
9	Jeff Bagwell	1.50
10	Vladimir Guerrero	1.50
11	Mike Piazza	2.50
12	Roger Clemens	2.25
13	Derek Jeter	4.00
14	Bernie Williams	.50
15	Scott Rolen	1.00
16	Mark McGwire	3.00
17	Tony Gwynn	2.00
18	Alex Rodriguez	3.00
19	Rafael Palmeiro	1.00
20	Ivan Rodriguez	.75

Game Worn Jersey

	NM/M
Inserted 1:120	

1	Greg Maddux	10.00
2	Tony Gwynn	10.00
3	Alex Rodriguez	20.00
4	Frank Thomas	8.00
5	Chipper Jones	10.00

High Voltage

	NM/M
Complete Set (36):	10.00
Common Player:	.15
Inserted 1:1	

1	Mo Vaughn	.15
2	Erubiel Durazo	.15
3	Randy Johnson	.60
4	Andruw Jones	.60
5	Chipper Jones	.75
6	Greg Maddux	.75
7	Cal Ripken Jr.	2.00
8	Nomar Garciaparra	1.25
9	Pedro Martinez	.60
10	Sammy Sosa	1.25
11	Frank Thomas	.60
12	Sean Casey	.25
13	Ken Griffey Jr.	1.25
14	Barry Larkin	.15
15	Manny Ramirez	.60
16	Jim Thome	.50
17	Larry Walker	.15
18	Jeff Bagwell	.60
19	Craig Biggio	.15
20	Carlos Beltran	.40
21	Shawn Green	.25
22	Vladimir Guerrero	.60
23	Edgardo Alfonzo	.15
24	Mike Piazza	1.50
25	Roger Clemens	1.00
26	Derek Jeter	2.00
27	Bernie Williams	.25
28	Scott Rolen	.60
29	Brian Giles	.15
30	Rick Ankiel	.15
31	Mark McGwire	1.50
32	Tony Gwynn	.75
33	Barry Bonds	2.00
34	Alex Rodriguez	1.50
35	Rafael Palmeiro	.60
36	Ivan Rodriguez	.60

2001 Pacific

	NM/M
Complete Set (500):	40.00
Common Player:	.10
Pack (12):	1.00
Box (36):	25.00

1	Garret Anderson	.10
2	Gary DiSarcina	.10
3	Darin Erstad	.25
4	Seth Etherton	.10
5	Ron Gant	.10
6	Troy Glaus	.75
7	Shigetosi Hasegawa	.10
8	Adam Kennedy	.10
9	Ben Molina	.10
10	Ramon Ortiz	.10
11	Troy Percival	.10
12	Tim Salmon	.20
13	Scott Schoeneweis	.10
14	Mo Vaughn	.10
15	Jarrod Washburn	.10
16	Brian Anderson	.10
17	Danny Bautista	.10
18	Jay Bell	.10
19	Greg Colbrunn	.10
20	Erubiel Durazo	.10
21	Steve Finley	.10
22	Luis Gonzalez	.20
23	Randy Johnson	.75
24	Byung-Hyun Kim	.10
25	Matt Mantei	.10
26	Armando Reynoso	.10
27	Todd Stottlemyre	.10
28	Matt Williams	.10
29	Tony Womack	.10
30	Andy Ashby	.10
31	Bobby Bonilla	.10
32	Rafael Furcal	.10
33	Andres Galarraga	.10
34	Tom Glavine	.35
35	Andruw Jones	.75
36	Chipper Jones	1.00
37	Brian Jordan	.10
38	Wally Joyner	.10
39	Keith Lockhart	.10
40	Javy Lopez	.10
41	Greg Maddux	1.00
42	Kevin Millwood	.10
43	John Rocker	.10
44	Reggie Sanders	.10
45	John Smoltz	.10
46	B.J. Surhoff	.10
47	Quilvio Veras	.10
48	Walt Weiss	.10
49	Brady Anderson	.10
50	Albert Belle	.15
51	Jeff Conine	.10
52	Delino DeShields	.10
53	Brook Fordyce	.10
54	Jerry Hairston Jr.	.10
55	Mark Lewis	.10
56	Luis Matos	.10
57	Melvin Mora	.10
58	Mike Mussina	.35
59	Chris Richard	.10
60	Cal Ripken Jr.	2.00
61	Manny Alexander	.10
62	Rolando Arrojo	.10
63	Midre Cummings	.10
64	Carl Everett	.10
65	Nomar Garciaparra	1.25
66	Mike Lansing	.10
67	Darren Lewis	.10
68	Derek Lowe	.10
69	Pedro Martinez	.75
70	Ramon Martinez	.10
71	Trot Nixon	.10
72	Troy O'Leary	.10
73	Jose Offerman	.10
74	Tomo Ohka	.10
75	Jason Varitek	.10
76	Rick Aguilera	.10
77	Shane Andrews	.10
78	Brant Brown	.10
79	Damon Buford	.10
80	Joe Girardi	.10
81	Mark Grace	.20
82	Willie Greene	.10
83	Ricky Gutierrez	.10
84	Jon Lieber	.10
85	Sammy Sosa	1.25
86	Kevin Tapani	.10
87	Rondell White	.10
88	Kerry Wood	.50
89	Eric Young	.10
90	Harold Baines	.10
91	James Baldwin	.10
92	Ray Durham	.10
93	Cal Eldred	.10
94	Keith Foulke	.10
95	Charles Johnson	.10
96	Paul Konerko	.20
97	Carlos Lee	.10
98	Magglio Ordonez	.10
99	Jim Parque	.10
100	Herbert Perry	.10
101	Chris Singleton	.10
102	Mike Sirotka	.10
103	Frank Thomas	.75
104	Jose Valentin	.10
105	Rob Bell	.10
106	Aaron Boone	.10
107	Sean Casey	.20
108	Danny Graves	.10
109	Ken Griffey Jr.	1.25
110	Pete Harnisch	.10
111	Brian L. Hunter	.10
112	Barry Larkin	.10
113	Pokey Reese	.10
114	Benito Santiago	.10
115	Chris Stynes	.10
116	Michael Tucker	.10
117	Ron Villone	.10
118	Scott Williamson	.10
119	Dmitri Young	.10
120	Roberto Alomar	.35
121	Sandy Alomar Jr.	.10
122	Russell Branyan	.10
123	Dave Burba	.10
124	Bartolo Colon	.10
125	Wil Cordero	.10
126	Einar Diaz	.10
127	Chuck Finley	.10
128	Travis Fryman	.10
129	Kenny Lofton	.10
130	Charles Nagy	.10
131	Manny Ramirez	.75
132	David Segui	.10
133	Jim Thome	.65
134	Omar Vizquel	.10
135	Brian Bohanon	.10
136	Jeff Cirillo	.10
137	Jeff Frye	.10
138	Jeffrey Hammonds	.10
139	Todd Helton	.75
140	Todd Hollandsworth	.10
141	Jose Jimenez	.10
142	Brent Mayne	.10
143	Neifi Perez	.10
144	Ben Petrick	.10
145	Juan Pierre	.10
146	Larry Walker	.10
147	Todd Walker	.10
148	Masato Yoshii	.10
149	Brad Ausmus	.10
150	Rich Becker	.10
151	Tony Clark	.10
152	Deivi Cruz	.10
153	Damion Easley	.10
154	Juan Encarnacion	.10
155	Robert Fick	.10
156	Juan Gonzalez	.75
157	Bobby Higginson	.10
158	Todd Jones	.10
159	Wendell Magee Jr.	.10
160	Brian Moehler	.10
161	Hideo Nomo	.75
162	Dean Palmer	.10
163	Jeff Weaver	.10
164	Antonio Alfonseca	.10
165	David Berg	.10
166	A.J. Burnett	.10
167	Luis Castillo	.10
168	Ryan Dempster	.10
169	Cliff Floyd	.10
170	Alex Gonzalez	.10
171	Mark Kotsay	.10
172	Derrek Lee	.10
173	Mike Lowell	.10
174	Mike Redmond	.10
175	Henry Rodriguez	.10
176	Jesus Sanchez	.10
177	Preston Wilson	.10
178	Moises Alou	.10
179	Jeff Bagwell	.75
180	Glen Barker	.10
181	Lance Berkman	.10
182	Craig Biggio	.10
183	Tim Bogar	.10
184	Ken Caminiti	.10
185	Roger Cedeno	.10
186	Scott Elarton	.10
187	Tony Eusebio	.10
188	Richard Hidalgo	.10
189	Jose Lima	.10
190	Mitch Meluskey	.10
191	Shane Reynolds	.10
192	Bill Spiers	.10
193	Billy Wagner	.10
194	Daryle Ward	.10
195	Carlos Beltran	.40
196	Ricky Bottalico	.10
197	Johnny Damon	.25
198	Jermaine Dye	.10
199	Jorge Fabregas	.10
200	David McCarty	.10
201	Mark Quinn	.10
202	Joe Randa	.10
203	Jeff Reboulet	.10
204	Rey Sanchez	.10
205	Blake Stein	.10
206	Jeff Suppan	.10
207	Mac Suzuki	.10
208	Mike Sweeney	.10
209	Gregg Zaun	.10
210	Adrian Beltre	.25
211	Kevin Brown	.10
212	Alex Cora	.10
213	Darren Dreifort	.10
214	Tom Goodwin	.10
215	Shawn Green	.30
216	Mark Grudzielanek	.10
217	Todd Hundley	.10
218	Eric Karros	.10
219	Chad Kreuter	.10
220	Jim Leyritz	.10
221	Chan Ho Park	.10
222	Jeff Shaw	.10
223	Gary Sheffield	.25
224	Devon White	.10
225	Ron Belliard	.10
226	Henry Blanco	.10
227	Jeromy Burnitz	.10
228	Jeff D'Amico	.10
229	Marquis Grissom	.10
230	Charlie Hayes	.10
231	Jimmy Haynes	.10
232	Tyler Houston	.10
233	Geoff Jenkins	.10
234	Mark Loretta	.10
235	James Mouton	.10
236	Richie Sexson	.10
237	Jamey Wright	.10
238	Jay Canizaro	.10
239	Ron Coomer	.10
240	Cristian Guzman	.10
241	Denny Hocking	.10
242	Torii Hunter	.10
243	Jacque Jones	.10
244	Corey Koskie	.10
245	Matt Lawton	.10
246	Matt LeCroy	.10
247	Eric Milton	.10
248	David Ortiz	.25
249	Brad Radke	.10
250	Mark Redman	.10
251	Michael Barrett	.10
252	Peter Bergeron	.10
253	Milton Bradley	.10
254	Orlando Cabrera	.10
255	Vladimir Guerrero	.75
256	Wilton Guerrero	.10
257	Dustin Hermanson	.10
258	Hideki Irabu	.10
259	Fernando Seguignol	.10
260	Lee Stevens	.10
261	Andy Tracy	.10
262	Javier Vazquez	.10
263	Jose Vidro	.10
264	Edgardo Alfonzo	.10
265	Derek Bell	.10
266	Armando Benitez	.10
267	Mike Bordick	.10
268	John Franco	.10
269	Darryl Hamilton	.10
270	Mike Hampton	.10
271	Lenny Harris	.10
272	Al Leiter	.10
273	Joe McEwing	.10
274	Rey Ordonez	.10
275	Jay Payton	.10
276	Mike Piazza	1.25
277	Glendon Rusch	.10
278	Bubba Trammell	.10
279	Robin Ventura	.10
280	Todd Zeile	.10
281	Scott Brosius	.10
282	Jose Canseco	.25
283	Roger Clemens	1.00
284	David Cone	.10
285	Dwight Gooden	.10
286	Orlando Hernandez	.10
287	Glenallen Hill	.10
288	Derek Jeter	2.00
289	David Justice	.10
290	Chuck Knoblauch	.10
291	Tino Martinez	.10
292	Denny Neagle	.10
293	Paul O'Neill	.10
294	Andy Pettitte	.20
295	Jorge Posada	.10
296	Mariano Rivera	.20
297	Luis Sojo	.10
298	Jose Vizcaino	.10
299	Bernie Williams	.25
300	Kevin Appier	.10
301	Eric Chavez	.20
302	Ryan Christenson	.10
303	Jason Giambi	.50
304	Jeremy Giambi	.10
305	Ben Grieve	.10
306	Gil Heredia	.10
307	Ramon Hernandez	.10
308	Tim Hudson	.20
309	Jason Isringhausen	.10
310	Terrence Long	.10
311	Mark Mulder	.10
312	Adam Piatt	.10
313	Matt Stairs	.10
314	Miguel Tejada	.25
315	Randy Velarde	.10
316	Alex Arias	.10
317	Pat Burrell	.25
318	Omar Daal	.10
319	Travis Lee	.10
320	Mike Lieberthal	.10
321	Randy Wolf	.10
322	Bobby Abreu	.10
323	Jeff Brantley	.10
324	Bruce Chen	.10
325	Doug Glanville	.10
326	Kevin Jordan	.10
327	Robert Person	.10
328	Scott Rolen	.65
329	Jimmy Anderson	.10
330	Mike Benjamin	.10
331	Kris Benson	.10
332	Adam Brown	.10
333	Brian Giles	.10
334	Jason Kendall	.10
335	Pat Meares	.10
336	Warren Morris	.10
337	Aramis Ramirez	.10
338	Todd Ritchie	.10
339	Jason Schmidt	.10
340	John Vander Wal	.10
341	Mike Williams	.10
342	Enrique Wilson	.10
343	Kevin Young	.10
344	Rick Ankiel	.20
345	Andy Benes	.10
346	Will Clark	.15
347	Eric Davis	.10
348	J.D. Drew	.20
349	Shawon Dunston	.10
350	Jim Edmonds	.10
351	Pat Hentgen	.10
352	Darryl Kile	.10
353	Ray Lankford	.10
354	Mike Matheny	.10
355	Mark McGwire	1.50
356	Craig Paquette	.10
357	Edgar Renteria	.10
358	Garrett Stephenson	.10
359	Fernando Tatis	.10
360	Dave Veres	.10
361	Fernando Vina	.10
362	Bret Boone	.10
363	Matt Clement	.10
364	Ben Davis	.10
365	Adam Eaton	.10
366	Wiki Gonzalez	.10
367	Tony Gwynn	1.00
368	Damian Jackson	.10
369	Ryan Klesko	.10
370	John Mabry	.10
371	Dave Magadan	.10
372	Phil Nevin	.10
373	Eric Owens	.10
374	Desi Relaford	.10
375	Ruben Rivera	.10
376	Woody Williams	.10
377	Rich Aurilia	.10
378	Marvin Bernard	.10
379	Barry Bonds	2.00
380	Ellis Burks	.10
381	Bobby Estalella	.10
382	Shawn Estes	.10
383	Mark Gardner	.10
384	Livan Hernandez	.10
385	Jeff Kent	.10
386	Bill Mueller	.10
387	Robb Nen	.10
388	Russ Ortiz	.10
389	Armando Rios	.10
390	Kirk Rueter	.10
391	J.T. Snow	.10
392	David Bell	.10
393	Jay Buhner	.10
394	Mike Cameron	.10
395	Freddy Garcia	.10
396	Carlos Guillen	.10
397	John Halama	.10
398	Rickey Henderson	.75
399	Al Martin	.10
400	Edgar Martinez	.10
401	Mark McLemore	.10
402	Jamie Moyer	.10
403	John Olerud	.10
404	Joe Oliver	.10
405	Alex Rodriguez	1.50
406	Kazuhiro Sasaki	.15
407	Aaron Sele	.10
408	Dan Wilson	.10
409	Miguel Cairo	.10
410	Vinny Castilla	.10
411	Steve Cox	.10
412	John Flaherty	.10
413	Jose Guillen	.10
414	Roberto Hernandez	.10
415	Russ Johnson	.10
416	Felix Martinez	.10
417	Fred McGriff	.10
418	Greg Vaughn	.10
419	Gerald Williams	.10
420	Luis Alicea	.10
421	Frank Catalanotto	.10
422	Royce Clayton	.10
423	Chad Curtis	.10
424	Rusty Greer	.10
425	Bill Haselman	.10
426	Rick Helling	.10
427	Gabe Kapler	.10
428	Mike Lamb	.10
429	Ricky Ledee	.10
430	Ruben Mateo	.10
431	Rafael Palmeiro	.65
432	Ivan Rodriguez	.65
433	Kenny Rogers	.10
434	John Wetteland	.10
435	Jeff Zimmerman	.10
436	Tony Batista	.10
437	Homer Bush	.10
438	Chris Carpenter	.10
439	Marty Cordova	.10
440	Jose Cruz Jr.	.10
441	Carlos Delgado	.40
442	Darrin Fletcher	.10
443	Brad Fullmer	.10
444	Alex S. Gonzalez	.10
445	Billy Koch	.10
446	Raul Mondesi	.10
447	Mickey Morandini	.10
448	Shannon Stewart	.10
449	Steve Trachsel	.10
450	David Wells	.10
451	Juan Alvarez	.10
452	Shawn Wooten	.10
453	Ismael Villegas	.10
454	Carlos Casimiro	.10
455	Morgan Burkhart	.10
456	Paxton Crawford	.10
457	Dernell Stenson	.10
458	Ross Gload	.10
459	Raul Gonzalez	.10
460	Corey Patterson	.10

461	Julio Zuleta	.10
462	Rocky Biddle	.10
463	Joe Crede	.10
464	Matt Ginter	.10
465	Aaron Myette	.10
466	Mike Bell	.10
467	Travis Dawkins	.10
468	Mark Watson	.10
469	Elvis Pena	.10
470	Eric Munson	.10
471	Pablo Ozuna	.10
472	Frank Charles	.10
473	Mike Judd	.10
474	Hector Ramirez	.10
475	Jack Cressend	.10
476	Talmadge Nunnari	.10
477	Jorge Toca	.10
478	Alfonso Soriano	.65
479	Jay Tessmer	.10
480	Jake Westbrook	.10
481	Todd Belitz	.10
482	Eric Byrnes	.10
483	Jose Ortiz	.10
484	Tike Redman	.10
485	Domingo Guzman	.10
486	Rodrigo Lopez	.10
487	Pedro Feliz	.10
488	Damon Minor	.10
489	Ryan Vogelsong	.10
490	Joel Pineiro	.10
491	Justin Brunette	.10
492	Keith McDonald	.10
493	Aubrey Huff	.10
494	Kenny Kelly	.10
495	Damian Rolls	.10
496	John Bale	.10
497	Pasqual Coco	.10
498	Matt DeWitt	.10
499	Leo Estrella	.10
500	Josh Phelps	.10

Premiere Date

Stars:		20-30X
Production 35 Sets		

Extreme

Stars:		15-25X
Production 45 Sets		

Hobby Limited

Stars:		8-15X
Production 70 Sets		

AL Decade's Best

		NM/M
Complete Set (18):		20.00
Common Player:		.50
Inserted 2:37		
1	Rickey Henderson	1.50
2	Rafael Palmeiro	1.00
3	Cal Ripken Jr.	4.00
4	Jose Canseco	.75
5	Juan Gonzalez	1.50
6	Frank Thomas	1.50
7	Albert Belle	.50
8	Edgar Martinez	.50
9	Mo Vaughn	.50
10	Derek Jeter	4.00

11	Mark McGwire	3.00
12	Alex Rodriguez	3.00
13	Ken Griffey Jr.	2.50
14	Nomar Garciaparra	2.50
15	Roger Clemens	2.00
16	Bernie Williams	.50
17	Ivan Rodriguez	1.00
18	Pedro Martinez	1.50

NL Decade's Best

		NM/M
Complete Set (18):		15.00
Common Player:		.50
Inserted 2:37		
1	Barry Bonds	4.00
2	Jeff Bagwell	1.00
3	Tom Glavine	.65
4	Gary Sheffield	.65
5	Fred McGriff	.50
6	Greg Maddux	1.50
7	Mike Piazza	2.00
8	Tony Gwynn	1.50
9	Hideo Nomo	1.00
10	Andres Galarraga	.50
11	Larry Walker	.50
12	Scott Rolen	.75
13	Pedro Martinez	1.00
14	Sammy Sosa	2.00
15	Mark McGwire	3.00
16	Kerry Wood	.75
17	Chipper Jones	1.50
18	Mark Grace	.75

Cramer's Choice Awards

		NM/M
Complete Set (10):		275.00
Common Player:		15.00
Inserted 1:721		
Styrene & Canvas pricing unavailable.		
1	Cal Ripken Jr.	50.00
2	Nomar Garciaparra	30.00
3	Sammy Sosa	30.00
4	Frank Thomas	15.00
5	Ken Griffey Jr.	30.00
6	Mike Piazza	30.00
7	Derek Jeter	50.00
8	Mark McGwire	40.00
9	Barry Bonds	50.00
10	Alex Rodriguez	40.00

Gold Crown Die-Cuts

		NM/M
Complete Set (36):		100.00
Common Player:		1.50
Inserted 1:73		
1	Darin Erstad	1.50
2	Troy Glaus	4.00
3	Randy Johnson	4.00
4	Rafael Furcal	1.50
5	Andruw Jones	4.00
6	Chipper Jones	5.00
7	Greg Maddux	5.00
8	Cal Ripken Jr.	10.00
9	Nomar Garciaparra	8.00
10	Pedro Martinez	4.00
11	Sammy Sosa	8.00
12	Kerry Wood	2.50
13	Frank Thomas	4.00

14	Ken Griffey Jr.	8.00
15	Manny Ramirez	4.00
16	Todd Helton	4.00
17	Jeff Bagwell	4.00
18	Shawn Green	1.50
19	Gary Sheffield	1.50
20	Vladimir Guerrero	4.00
21	Mike Piazza	8.00
22	Jose Canseco	2.00
23	Roger Clemens	6.00
24	Derek Jeter	10.00
25	Jason Giambi	2.50
26	Pat Burrell	2.00
26	Rick Ankiel (Should be #27.)	1.50
28	Jim Edmonds	1.50
29	Mark McGwire	9.00
30	Tony Gwynn	5.00
31	Barry Bonds	10.00
32	Rickey Henderson	4.00
33	Edgar Martinez	1.50
34	Alex Rodriguez	9.00
35	Ivan Rodriguez	3.00
36	Carlos Delgado	2.00

On The Horizon

		NM/M
Complete Set (10):		20.00
Common Player:		2.00
Inserted 1:145		
1	Rafael Furcal	2.00
2	Corey Patterson	2.50
3	Russell Branyan	2.00
4	Juan Pierre	2.50
5	Mark Quinn	2.00
6	Alfonso Soriano	6.00
7	Adam Piatt	2.00
8	Pat Burrell	4.50
9	Kazuhiro Sasaki	2.50
10	Aubrey Huff	2.00

Ornaments

		NM/M
Complete Set (24):		25.00
Common Player:		.50
Inserted 2:37		
1	Rafael Furcal	.50
2	Chipper Jones	2.00
3	Greg Maddux	2.00
4	Cal Ripken Jr.	4.00
5	Nomar Garciaparra	2.50
6	Pedro Martinez	1.50
7	Sammy Sosa	2.50
8	Frank Thomas	1.50
9	Ken Griffey Jr.	2.50
10	Manny Ramirez	1.50
11	Todd Helton	1.50
12	Vladimir Guerrero	1.50
13	Mike Piazza	2.50
14	Roger Clemens	2.25
15	Derek Jeter	4.00
16	Pat Burrell	1.00
17	Rick Ankiel	.50
18	Mark McGwire	3.00
19	Barry Bonds	4.00
20	Alex Rodriguez	3.00
21	Troy Glaus	1.50
22	Tom Glavine	.50

23	Jim Edmonds	.50
24	Ivan Rodriguez	1.00

2001 Pacific Private Stock

MARK McGWIRE
St. Louis Cardinals First Base

	NM/M
Complete Set (150):	50.00
Common Player:	.25
Common (126-150):	1.00
Inserted 1:4	
Hobby Pack (7):	10.00
Hobby Box (10):	75.00

1	Darin Erstad	.50
2	Troy Glaus	1.00
3	Tim Salmon	.35
4	Mo Vaughn	.25
5	Steve Finley	.25
6	Luis Gonzalez	.35
7	Randy Johnson	1.00
8	Matt Williams	.25
9	Rafael Furcal	.25
10	Andres Galarraga	.25
11	Tom Glavine	.45
12	Andruw Jones	1.00
13	Chipper Jones	1.50
14	Greg Maddux	1.50
15	B.J. Surhoff	.25
16	Brady Anderson	.25
17	Albert Belle	.25
18	Mike Mussina	.45
19	Cal Ripken Jr.	3.00
20	Carl Everett	.25
21	Nomar Garciaparra	2.00
22	Pedro Martinez	1.00
23	Mark Grace	.35
24	Sammy Sosa	2.00
25	Kerry Wood	.50
26	Carlos Lee	.25
27	Magglio Ordonez	.25
28	Frank Thomas	1.00
29	Sean Casey	.35
30	Ken Griffey Jr.	2.00
31	Barry Larkin	.25
32	Pokey Reese	.25
33	Roberto Alomar	.40
34	Kenny Lofton	.25
35	Manny Ramirez	1.00
36	Jim Thome	.75
37	Omar Vizquel	.25
38	Jeff Cirillo	.25
39	Jeffrey Hammonds	.25
40	Todd Helton	1.00
41	Larry Walker	.25
42	Tony Clark	.25
43	Juan Encarnacion	.25
44	Juan Gonzalez	1.00
45	Hideo Nomo	1.00
46	Cliff Floyd	.25
47	Derek Lee	.25
48	Henry Rodriguez	.25
49	Preston Wilson	.25
50	Jeff Bagwell	1.00
51	Craig Biggio	.25
52	Richard Hidalgo	.25
53	Moises Alou	.25
54	Carlos Beltran	.50
55	Johnny Damon	.40
56	Jermaine Dye	.25
57	Mac Suzuki	.25
58	Mike Sweeney	.25
59	Adrian Beltre	.40
60	Kevin Brown	.25
61	Shawn Green	.50
62	Eric Karros	.25
63	Chan Ho Park	.25
64	Gary Sheffield	.40
65	Jeromy Burnitz	.25
66	Geoff Jenkins	.25
67	Richie Sexson	.25
68	Jacque Jones	.25
69	Matt Lawton	.25
70	Eric Milton	.25
71	Vladimir Guerrero	1.00
72	Jose Vidro	.25
73	Edgardo Alfonzo	.25
74	Mike Hampton	.25
75	Mike Piazza	2.00
76	Robin Ventura	.25
77	Jose Canseco	.50
78	Roger Clemens	1.75
79	Derek Jeter	3.00
80	David Justice	.25

81 Jorge Posada .25
82 Bernie Williams .35
83 Jason Giambi .65
84 Ben Grieve .25
85 Tim Hudson .35
86 Terrence Long .25
87 Miguel Tejada .35
88 Bobby Abreu .25
89 Pat Burrell .50
90 Mike Lieberthal .25
91 Scott Rolen .75
92 Kris Benson .25
93 Brian Giles .25
94 Jason Kendall .25
95 Aramis Ramirez .25
96 Rick Ankiel .25
97 Will Clark .35
98 J.D. Drew .25
99 Jim Edmonds .25
100 Mark McGwire 2.50
101 Fernando Tatis .25
102 Adam Eaton .25
103 Tony Gwynn 1.50
104 Phil Nevin .25
105 Eric Owens .25
106 Barry Bonds 3.00
107 Jeff Kent .25
108 J.T. Snow .25
109 Rickey Henderson 1.00
110 Edgar Martinez .25
111 John Olerud .25
112 Alex Rodriguez 2.50
113 Kazuhiro Sasaki .25
114 Vinny Castilla .25
115 Fred McGriff .25
116 Greg Vaughn .25
117 Gabe Kapler .25
118 Ruben Mateo .25
119 Rafael Palmeiro .75
120 Ivan Rodriguez .75
121 Tony Batista .25
122 Jose Cruz Jr. .25
123 Carlos Delgado .75
124 Shannon Stewart .25
125 David Wells .25
126 Shawn Wooten 1.00
127 George Lombard 1.00
128 Morgan Burkhart 1.00
129 Ross Gload 1.00
130 Corey Patterson 1.00
131 Julio Zuleta 1.00
132 Joe Crede 1.00
133 Matt Ginter 1.00
134 Travis Dawkins 1.00
135 Eric Munson 1.00
136 Dee Brown 1.00
137 Luke Prokopec 1.00
138 Timoniel Perez 1.00
139 Alfonso Soriano 2.00
140 Jake Westbrook 1.00
141 Eric Byrnes 1.00
142 Adam Hyzdu 1.00
143 Jimmy Rollins 1.50
144 Xavier Nady 1.00
145 Ryan Vogelsong 1.00
146 Joel Pineiro 2.00
147 Aubrey Huff 1.00
148 Kenny Kelly 1.00
149 Josh Phelps 1.00
150 Vernon Wells 1.00

Silver

Stars: .5-1.5X
SP's: .5-1X
Base cards in retail.

Silver Portraits

Stars: 2-5X
SP's: 1X
Production 290 Sets R

Gold Portraits

Stars: 6-10X
SP's (126-150): 1-2X
Production 75 Sets H

Artist's Canvas

NM/M
Complete Set (20): 50.00
Common Player: 1.00
Inserted 1:21
1 Randy Johnson 2.50
2 Chipper Jones 4.00
3 Greg Maddux 4.00
4 Cal Ripken Jr. 8.00
5 Nomar Garciaparra 5.00
6 Pedro Martinez 2.50
7 Sammy Sosa 5.00
8 Frank Thomas 2.50
9 Ken Griffey Jr. 5.00
10 Manny Ramirez 2.50
11 Vladimir Guerrero 2.50
12 Mike Piazza 5.00
13 Roger Clemens 4.50
14 Derek Jeter 6.00
15 Jason Giambi 2.50
16 Rick Ankiel 1.00
17 Mark McGwire 6.00
18 Barry Bonds 8.00
19 Alex Rodriguez 6.00
20 Ivan Rodriguez 2.00

Premiere Date

Stars: 4-8X
SP's: 1-2X
Production 90 Sets

Game Gear

NM/M
Common Player: 4.00
Inserted 1:1 H
1 Garret Anderson/Bat 6.00
2 Darin Erstad/Jsy 5.00
3 Ron Gant/Bat 4.00
4 Troy Glaus/Jsy 8.00
5 Tim Salmon/Bat 5.00
6 Mo Vaughn/Jsy/Gray 4.00
7 Mo Vaughn/Jsy/White 4.00
8 Mo Vaughn/Bat 4.00
9 Jay Bell/Jsy 4.00
10 Jay Bell/Bat 4.00
11 Erubiel Durazo/Jsy/Black 4.00
12 Erubiel Durazo/Jsy/White 4.00
13 Erubiel Durazo/Bat 4.00
14 Steve Finley/Bat 4.00
15 Randy Johnson/Jsy 10.00
16 Byung-Hyun Kim/Jsy/White 4.00
17 Byung-Hyun Kim/Jsy/Gray 4.00
18 Matt Williams/Jsy/Gray 4.00
19 Matt Williams/Jsy/White 4.00
20 Matt Williams/Jsy/Purple 4.00
21 Bobby Bonilla/Jsy 4.00
22 Rafael Furcal/Bat 5.00
23 Andruw Jones/Bat 8.00
24 Chipper Jones/Jsy 10.00
25 Chipper Jones/Bat 10.00
26 Brian Jordan/Jsy 4.00
27 Javier Lopez/Bat 4.00
28 Greg Maddux/Jsy 15.00
29 Greg Maddux/Bat 15.00
30 Brady Anderson/Bat 4.00
31 Albert Belle/Bat 4.00
32 Nomar Garciaparra/Bat 15.00
33 Pedro Martinez/Bat 10.00
34 Jose Offerman/Bat 4.00
35 Damon Buford/Jsy 4.00
36 Jose Nieves/Bat 4.00
38 Kerry Wood/Bat 8.00
39 James Baldwin/Jsy 4.00
40 Ray Durham/Jsy 4.00
41 Ray Durham/Bat 4.00
42 Carlos Lee/Bat 4.00
43 Magglio Ordonez/Jsy 6.00
44 Magglio Ordonez/Bat 6.00
45 Chris Singleton/Jsy 4.00
46 Aaron Boone/Bat 4.00
47 Sean Casey/Bat 4.00
48 Barry Larkin/Jsy 6.00
49 Pokey Reese/Jsy 4.00
50 Pokey Reese/Bat 4.00
51 Dmitri Young/Bat 4.00
52 Roberto Alomar/Bat 8.00
53 Einar Diaz/Bat 4.00
54 Kenny Lofton/Jsy 4.00
55 David Segui/Bat 4.00
56 Omar Vizquel/Jsy 5.00
57 Luis Castillo/Jsy 4.00
58 Jeff Cirillo/Jsy 4.00
59 Jeff Frye/Bat 4.00
60 Todd Helton/Jsy 8.00
61 Todd Helton/Bat 8.00
62 Neifi Perez/Bat 4.00
63 Larry Walker/Jsy 4.00
64 Larry Walker/Bat 4.00
65 Masato Yoshii/Jsy 4.00
66 Brad Ausmus/Jsy 4.00
67 Rich Becker/Bat 4.00
68 Tony Clark/Bat 4.00
69 Deivi Cruz/Bat 4.00
70 Juan Gonzalez/Bat 6.00
71 Dean Palmer/Bat 4.00
72 Cliff Floyd/Jsy/White 4.00
73 Cliff Floyd/Jsy/Teal 4.00
74 Cliff Floyd/Bat 4.00
75 Alex Gonzalez/Jsy 4.00
76 Alex Gonzalez/Marlins Bat 4.00
77 Mark Kotsay/Bat 4.00
78 Derrek Lee/Bat 4.00
79 Pablo Ozuna/Jsy 4.00
80 Craig Biggio/Bat 4.00
81 Ken Caminiti/Bat 4.00
82 Roger Cedeno/Bat 4.00
83 Ricky Bottalico/Bat 4.00
84 Dee Brown/Bat 4.00
85 Jermaine Dye/Bat 4.00
86 David McCarty/Bat 4.00
87 Hector Ortiz/Bat 4.00
88 Joe Randa/Bat 4.00
89 Adrian Beltre/Jsy 4.00
90 Kevin Brown/Jsy 6.00
91 Alex Cora/Bat 4.00
92 Darren Dreifort/Bat 4.00
93 Shawn Green/Jsy/White 6.00
94 Shawn Green/Jsy/Gray 6.00
95 Shawn Green/Bat 6.00
96 Todd Hundley/Jsy 4.00
97 Eric Karros/Bat 4.00
98 Chan Ho Park/Jsy 4.00
99 Chan Ho Park/Bat 4.00
101 Gary Sheffield/Bat 6.00
102 Ismael Valdes/Bat 4.00
103 Jeromy Burnitz/Bat 4.00
104 Marquis Grissom/Bat 4.00
105 Matt Lawton/Bat 4.00
106 Fernando Seguignol/Bat 4.00
107 Edgardo Alfonzo/White Swing 4.00
108 Edgardo Alfonzo/Jsy/White Drop 4.00
109 Edgardo Alfonzo/Jsy/Black 4.00
110 Derek Bell/Jsy/White 4.00
111 Derek Bell/Jsy/Black 4.00
112 Armando Benitez/Bat 4.00
113 Al Leiter/Bat 4.00
114 Rey Ordonez/Jsy/Gray Field 4.00
115 Rey Ordonez/Jsy/White 4.00
116 Rey Ordonez/Jsy/Gray Bunt 4.00
117 Rey Ordonez/Bat 4.00
118 Jay Payton/Bat 4.00
119 Mike Piazza/Jsy 10.00
120 Robin Ventura/Jsy/Black Hit 4.00
121 Robin Ventura/Jsy/Black Field 4.00
122 Robin Ventura/Jsy White 4.00
123 Luis Polonia/Bat 4.00
124 Bernie Williams/Bat 6.00
125 Eric Chavez/Jsy 4.00
126 Jason Giambi/Jsy 8.00
127 Jason Giambi/Bat 8.00
128 Ben Grieve/Jsy 4.00
129 Ben Grieve/Bat 4.00
130 Ramon Hernandez/Bat 4.00
131 Tim Hudson/Jsy 6.00
132 Terrence Long/Bat 4.00
133 Mark Mulder/Jsy 6.00
134 Adam Piatt/Jsy 4.00
135 Olmedo Saenz/Bat 4.00
136 Matt Stairs/Bat 4.00
137 Mike Stanley/Bat 4.00
138 Miguel Tejada/Bat 6.00
139 Travis Lee/Bat 4.00
140 Brian Giles/Bat 5.00
141 Jason Kendall/Jsy 4.00
142 Will Clark/Bat 6.00
143 J.D. Drew/Bat 4.00
144 Jim Edmonds/Bat 6.00
145 Mark McGwire/Bat 50.00
146 Edgar Renteria/Bat 4.00
147 Garrett Stephenson/Jsy 4.00
148 Tony Gwynn/Jsy 10.00
149 Ruben Rivera/Bat 4.00
150 Barry Bonds/Jsy 40.00
151 Barry Bonds/Bat 40.00
152 Ellis Burks/Jsy 4.00
153 J.T. Snow/Bat 4.00
154 Jay Buhner/Jsy 4.00
155 Jay Buhner/Bat 4.00
156 Carlos Guillen/Jsy 4.00
157 Carlos Guillen/Bat 4.00
158 Rickey Henderson/Bat 15.00
159 Edgar Martinez/Bat 6.00
160 Gil Meche/Jsy 4.00
161 John Olerud/Bat 5.00
162 Joe Oliver/Bat 4.00
163 Alex Rodriguez/Jsy 30.00
164 Kazuhiro Sasaki/Jsy 4.00
165 Dan Wilson/Jsy 4.00
166 Dan Wilson/Bat 4.00
167 Vinny Castilla/Bat 4.00
168 Jose Guillen/Bat 4.00
169 Fred McGriff/Jsy 5.00
170 Rusty Greer/Bat 4.00
171 Mike Lamb/Bat 4.00
172 Ruben Mateo/Jsy 4.00
173 Ruben Mateo/Bat 4.00
174 Rafael Palmeiro/Jsy 8.00
175 Rafael Palmeiro/Bat 8.00
178 Tony Batista/Bat 4.00
179 Marty Cordova/Bat 4.00
180 Jose Cruz Jr./Bat 4.00
181 Alex Gonzalez/Blue Jays Bat 4.00
182 Raul Mondesi/Bat 4.00

Game Jersey Patch

NM/M
Common Player: 8.00
2 Darin Erstad 8.00
4 Troy Glaus 15.00
6 Mo Vaughn/Gray 8.00
7 Mo Vaughn/White 8.00
9 Jay Bell 8.00
11 Erubiel Durazo/Black 8.00
12 Erubiel Durazo/White 8.00
15 Randy Johnson 40.00
16 Byung-Hyun Kim/White 8.00
17 Byung-Hyun Kim/Gray 8.00
18 Matt Williams/Gray 8.00
19 Matt Williams/White 8.00
20 Matt Williams/Purple 8.00
21 Bobby Bonilla 8.00
24 Chipper Jones 25.00
26 Brian Jordan 8.00
28 Greg Maddux 80.00
35 Damon Buford 8.00
39 James Baldwin 8.00
40 Ray Durham 8.00
43 Magglio Ordonez 20.00
45 Chris Singleton 8.00
48 Barry Larkin 15.00
49 Pokey Reese 8.00
54 Kenny Lofton 10.00
56 Omar Vizquel 10.00
57 Luis Castillo 8.00
58 Jeff Cirillo 8.00
60 Todd Helton 20.00
63 Larry Walker 10.00
65 Masato Yoshii 8.00
66 Brad Ausmus 8.00
72 Cliff Floyd/White 8.00
73 Cliff Floyd Teal 8.00
75 Alex Gonzalez 8.00
79 Pablo Ozuna 8.00
89 Adrian Beltre 8.00
90 Kevin Brown 15.00
93 Shawn Green/White 15.00
94 Shawn Green/Gray 15.00
96 Todd Hundley 8.00
98 Chan Ho Park 8.00
107 Edgardo Alfonzo/White Swing 8.00
108 Edgardo Alfonzo/White Drop 8.00
109 Edgardo Alfonzo/Black 8.00
110 Derek Bell/White 8.00
111 Derek Bell/Black 8.00
114 Rey Ordonez/Gray Field 8.00
115 Rey Ordonez/White 8.00
116 Rey Ordonez/Gray Bunt 8.00
119 Mike Piazza 75.00
120 Robin Ventura/Black Hit 10.00
121 Robin Ventura/Black Fld 10.00
122 Robin Ventura/White 10.00
125 Eric Chavez 15.00
126 Jason Giambi 15.00
128 Ben Grieve 8.00
131 Tim Hudson 15.00
133 Mark Mulder 15.00
134 Adam Piatt 8.00
141 Jason Kendall 10.00
147 Garrett Stephenson 8.00
148 Tony Gwynn 40.00
150 Barry Bonds 90.00
152 Ellis Burks 8.00
154 Jay Buhner 8.00
156 Carlos Guillen 8.00
160 Gil Meche 8.00
164 Kazuhiro Sasaki 15.00
165 Dan Wilson 8.00
169 Fred McGriff 10.00
172 Ruben Mateo 8.00
174 Rafael Palmeiro 25.00

Extreme Action

NM/M
Complete Set (20): 20.00
Common Player: .50
Inserted 1:11
1 Troy Glaus 1.00

2	Rafael Furcal	.50
3	Chipper Jones	1.50
4	Cal Ripken Jr.	3.00
5	Nomar Garciaparra	2.00
6	Sammy Sosa	2.00
7	Ken Griffey Jr.	2.00
8	Manny Ramirez	1.00
9	Todd Helton	1.00
10	Jeff Bagwell	1.00
11	Vladimir Guerrero	1.00
12	Derek Jeter	3.00
13	Mike Piazza	2.00
14	Pat Burrell	.75
15	Jim Edmonds	.50
16	Mark McGwire	2.50
17	Barry Bonds	3.00
18	Alex Rodriguez	2.50
19	Ivan Rodriguez	.75
20	Carlos Delgado	.75

PS-206 Stars

		NM/M
Complete Set (20):		50.00
Common Player:		1.00
Inserted 3:Hobby Case		
1	Chipper Jones	3.00
2	Greg Maddux	3.00
3	Cal Ripken Jr.	6.00
4	Nomar Garciaparra	4.00
5	Pedro Martinez	2.00
6	Sammy Sosa	4.00
7	Frank Thomas	2.00
8	Ken Griffey Jr.	4.00
9	Manny Ramirez	2.00
10	Jeff Bagwell	2.00
11	Gary Sheffield	1.00
12	Mike Piazza	4.00
13	Roger Clemens	3.50
14	Derek Jeter	6.00
15	Rick Ankiel	1.00
16	Mark McGwire	5.00
17	Tony Gwynn	3.00
18	Barry Bonds	6.00
19	Alex Rodriguez	5.00
20	Ivan Rodriguez	1.50

PS-206 Action

		NM/M
Complete Set (60):		20.00
Common Player:		.15
Inserted 2:Pack		
1	Darin Erstad	.25
2	Troy Glaus	.65
3	Randy Johnson	.65
4	Rafael Furcal	.15
5	Tom Glavine	.40
6	Andruw Jones	.65
7	Chipper Jones	.75
8	Greg Maddux	.75
9	Albert Belle	.15
10	Mike Mussina	.40
11	Cal Ripken Jr.	1.50
12	Nomar Garciaparra	1.00
13	Pedro Martinez	.65
14	Mark Grace	.25
15	Sammy Sosa	1.00
16	Kerry Wood	.35
17	Magglio Ordonez	.15
18	Frank Thomas	.65
19	Ken Griffey Jr.	1.00
20	Barry Larkin	.15
21	Roberto Alomar	.35
22	Manny Ramirez	.65
23	Jim Thome	.60
24	Jeff Cirillo	.15
25	Todd Helton	.65
26	Larry Walker	.65
27	Juan Gonzalez	.65
28	Hideo Nomo	.65
29	Preston Wilson	.15
30	Jeff Bagwell	.65
31	Craig Biggio	.15
32	Johnny Damon	.25
33	Jermaine Dye	.15
34	Shawn Green	.30
35	Gary Sheffield	.25
36	Vladimir Guerrero	.65
37	Mike Piazza	1.00
38	Jose Canseco	.40
39	Roger Clemens	.85
40	Derek Jeter	1.50

41	Bernie Williams	.30
42	Jason Giambi	.50
43	Ben Grieve	.15
44	Pat Burrell	.40
45	Scott Rolen	.50
46	Rick Ankiel	.15
47	J.D. Drew	.25
48	Jim Edmonds	.15
49	Mark McGwire	1.25
50	Tony Gwynn	.75
51	Barry Bonds	1.50
52	Jeff Kent	.15
53	Edgar Martinez	.15
54	Alex Rodriguez	1.25
55	Kazuhiro Sasaki	.15
56	Fred McGriff	.15
57	Rafael Palmeiro	.50
58	Ivan Rodriguez	.50
59	Tony Batista	.15
60	Carlos Delgado	.45

PS-206 New Wave

		NM/M
Complete Set (20):		30.00
Common Player:		1.00
Inserted 2:Hobby Case		
1	Darin Erstad	1.50
2	Troy Glaus	5.00
3	Rafael Furcal	1.00
4	Andruw Jones	4.00
5	Magglio Ordonez	1.00
6	Carlos Lee	1.00
7	Todd Helton	5.00
8	Johnny Damon	1.50
9	Jermaine Dye	1.00
10	Vladimir Guerrero	5.00
11	Jason Giambi	4.00
12	Ben Grieve	1.00
13	Pat Burrell	3.00
14	Rick Ankiel	1.00
15	J.D. Drew	1.50
16	Adam Eaton	1.00
17	Kazuhiro Sasaki	1.00
18	Ruben Mateo	1.00
19	Tony Batista	1.00
20	Carlos Delgado	3.00

PS-206 Rookies

		NM/M
Complete Set (20):		50.00
Common Player:		3.00
Inserted 1:Case		
1	George Lombard	3.00
2	Morgan Burkhart	3.00
3	Corey Patterson	5.00
4	Julio Zuleta	3.00
5	Joe Crede	3.00
6	Matt Ginter	3.00
7	Aaron Myette	3.00
8	Travis Dawkins	3.00
9	Eric Munson	3.00
10	Dee Brown	3.00
11	Luke Prokopec	3.00
12	Jorge Toca	3.00
13	Alfonso Soriano	7.50
14	Eric Byrnes	3.00
15	Adam Hyzdu	3.00
16	Jimmy Rollins	4.00
17	Joel Pineiro	5.00
18	Aubrey Huff	4.00
19	Kenny Kelly	3.00
20	Vernon Wells	3.00

Reserve

		NM/M
Complete Set (20):		25.00
Common Player:		.50
Inserted 1:21 H		
1	Randy Johnson	1.50
2	Chipper Jones	2.00
3	Greg Maddux	2.00
4	Cal Ripken Jr.	4.00
5	Nomar Garciaparra	2.50
6	Pedro Martinez	1.50
7	Sammy Sosa	2.50
8	Frank Thomas	1.50
9	Ken Griffey Jr.	2.50
10	Todd Helton	1.50
11	Vladimir Guerrero	1.50
12	Mike Piazza	2.50
13	Roger Clemens	2.25
14	Derek Jeter	4.00
15	Rick Ankiel	.50
16	Mark McGwire	3.00
17	Tony Gwynn	2.00
18	Barry Bonds	4.00
19	Alex Rodriguez	3.00
20	Ivan Rodriguez	1.00

1992 Pinnacle

		NM/M
Complete Set (620):		15.00
Common Player:		.05
Foil Pack (16):		.75
Foil Box (36):		17.50
Jumbo Pack (24+3):		1.50
Jumbo Box (12):		22.50
1	Frank Thomas	.75
2	Benito Santiago	.05
3	Carlos Baerga	.05
4	Cecil Fielder	.05
5	Barry Larkin	.05
6	Ozzie Smith	1.00
7	Willie McGee	.05
8	Paul Molitor	.75
9	Andy Van Slyke	.05
10	Ryne Sandberg	1.00
11	Kevin Seitzer	.05
12	Len Dykstra	.05
13	Edgar Martinez	.05
14	Ruben Sierra	.05
15	Howard Johnson	.05
16	Dave Henderson	.05
17	Devon White	.05
18	Terry Pendleton	.05
19	Steve Finley	.05
20	Kirby Puckett	1.00
21	Orel Hershiser	.05
22	Hal Morris	.05
23	Don Mattingly	1.25
24	Delino DeShields	.05
25	Dennis Eckersley	.60
26	Ellis Burks	.05
27	Jay Buhner	.05
28	Matt Williams	.05
29	Lou Whitaker	.05
30	Alex Fernandez	.05
31	Albert Belle	.05
32	Todd Zeile	.05
33	Tony Pena	.05
34	Jay Bell	.05
35	Rafael Palmeiro	.65
36	Wes Chamberlain	.05
37	George Bell	.05
38	Robin Yount	.75
39	Vince Coleman	.05
40	Bruce Hurst	.05
41	Harold Baines	.05
42	Chuck Finley	.05
43	Ken Caminiti	.05
44	Ben McDonald	.05
45	Roberto Alomar	.15
46	Chili Davis	.05
47	Bill Doran	.05
48	Jerald Clark	.05
49	Jose Lind	.05
50	Nolan Ryan	2.00
51	Phil Plantier	.05
52	Gary DiSarcina	.05
53	Kevin Bass	.05
54	Pat Kelly	.05
55	Mark Wohlers	.05
56	Walt Weiss	.05
57	Lenny Harris	.05
58	Ivan Calderon	.05
59	Harold Reynolds	.05
60	George Brett	1.25
61	Gregg Olson	.05
62	Orlando Merced	.05
63	Steve Decker	.05
64	John Franco	.05
65	Greg Maddux	1.00
66	Alex Cole	.05
67	Dave Hollins	.05
68	Kent Hrbek	.05
69	Tom Pagnozzi	.05
70	Jeff Bagwell	.75
71	Jim Gantner	.05
72	Matt Nokes	.05
73	Brian Harper	.05
74	Andy Benes	.05
75	Tom Glavine	.35
76	Terry Steinbach	.05
77	Dennis Martinez	.05
78	John Olerud	.05
79	Ozzie Guillen	.05
80	Darryl Strawberry	.05
81	Gary Gaetti	.05
82	Dave Righetti	.05
83	Chris Hoiles	.05
84	Andujar Cedeno	.05
85	Jack Clark	.05
86	David Howard	.05
87	Bill Gullickson	.05
88	Bernard Gilkey	.05
89	Kevin Elster	.05
90	Kevin Maas	.05
91	Mark Lewis	.05
92	Greg Vaughn	.05
93	Bret Barberie	.05
94	Dave Smith	.05
95	Roger Clemens	1.25
96	Doug Drabek	.05
97	Omar Vizquel	.05
98	Jose Guzman	.05

99	Juan Samuel	.05
100	Dave Justice	.05
101	Tom Browning	.05
102	Mark Gubicza	.05
103	Mickey Morandini	.05
104	Ed Whitson	.05
105	Lance Parrish	.05
106	Scott Erickson	.05
107	Jack McDowell	.05
108	Dave Stieb	.05
109	Mike Moore	.05
110	Travis Fryman	.05
111	Dwight Gooden	.05
112	Fred McGriff	.05
113	Alan Trammell	.05
114	Roberto Kelly	.05
115	Andre Dawson	.25
116	Bill Landrum	.05
117	Brian McRae	.05
118	B.J. Surhoff	.05
119	Chuck Knoblauch	.05
120	Steve Olin	.05
121	Robin Ventura	.05
122	Will Clark	.05
123	Tino Martinez	.05
124	Dale Murphy	.25
125	Pete O'Brien	.05
126	Ray Lankford	.05
127	Juan Gonzalez	.40
128	Ron Gant	.05
129	Marquis Grissom	.05
130	Jose Canseco	.50
131	Mike Greenwell	.05
132	Mark Langston	.05
133	Brett Butler	.05
134	Kelly Gruber	.05
135	Chris Sabo	.05
136	Mark Grace	.05
137	Tony Fernandez	.05
138	Glenn Davis	.05
139	Pedro Munoz	.05
140	Craig Biggio	.05
141	Pete Schourek	.05
142	Mike Boddicker	.05
143	Robby Thompson	.05
144	Mel Hall	.05
145	Bryan Harvey	.05
146	Mike LaValliere	.05
147	John Kruk	.05
148	Joe Carter	.05
149	Greg Olson	.05
150	Julio Franco	.05
151	Darryl Hamilton	.05
152	Felix Fermin	.05
153	Jose Offerman	.05
154	Paul O'Neill	.05
155	Tommy Greene	.05
156	Ivan Rodriguez	.65
157	Dave Stewart	.05
158	Jeff Reardon	.05
159	Felix Jose	.05
160	Doug Dascenzo	.05
161	Tim Wallach	.05
162	Dan Plesac	.05
163	Luis Gonzalez	.05
164	Mike Henneman	.05
165	Mike Devereaux	.05
166	Luis Polonia	.05
167	Mike Sharperson	.05
168	Chris Donnels	.05
169	Greg Harris	.05
170	Deion Sanders	.05
171	Mike Schooler	.05
172	Jose DeJesus	.05
173	Jeff Montgomery	.05
174	Milt Cuyler	.05
175	Wade Boggs	1.00
176	Kevin Tapani	.05
177	Bill Spiers	.05
178	Tim Raines	.05
179	Randy Milligan	.05
180	Rob Dibble	.05
181	Kirt Manwaring	.05
182	Pascual Perez	.05
183	Juan Guzman	.05
184	John Smiley	.05
185	David Segui	.05
186	Omar Olivares	.05
187	Joe Slusarski	.05
188	Erik Hanson	.05
189	Mark Portugal	.05
190	Walt Terrell	.05
191	John Smoltz	.05
192	Wilson Alvarez	.05
193	Jimmy Key	.05
194	Larry Walker	.05
195	Lee Smith	.05
196	Pete Harnisch	.05
197	Mike Harkey	.05
198	Frank Tanana	.05
199	Terry Mulholland	.05
200	Cal Ripken, Jr.	2.00
201	Dave Magadan	.05
202	Bud Black	.05
203	Terry Shumpert	.05
204	Mike Mussina	.40
205	Mo Vaughn	.05
206	Steve Farr	.05
207	Darrin Jackson	.05
208	Jerry Browne	.05
209	Jeff Russell	.05
210	Mike Scioscia	.05
211	Rick Aguilera	.05
212	Jaime Navarro	.05
213	Randy Tomlin	.05

214	Bobby Thigpen	.05
215	Mark Gardner	.05
216	Norm Charlton	.05
217	Mark McGwire	1.75
218	Skeeter Barnes	.05
219	Bob Tewksbury	.05
220	Junior Felix	.05
221	Sam Horn	.05
222	Jody Reed	.05
223	Luis Sojo	.05
224	Jerome Walton	.05
225	Darryl Kile	.05
226	Mickey Tettleton	.05
227	Dan Pasqua	.05
228	Jim Gott	.05
229	Bernie Williams	.05
230	Shane Mack	.05
231	Steve Avery	.05
232	Dave Valle	.05
233	Mark Leonard	.05
234	Spike Owen	.05
235	Gary Sheffield	.20
236	Steve Chitren	.05
237	Zane Smith	.05
238	Tom Gordon	.05
239	Jose Oquendo	.05
240	Todd Stottlemyre	.05
241	Darren Daulton	.05
242	Tim Naehring	.05
243	Tony Phillips	.05
244	Shawon Dunston	.05
245	Manuel Lee	.05
246	Mike Pagliarulo	.05
247	Jim Thome	.65
248	Luis Mercedes	.05
249	Cal Eldred	.05
250	Derek Bell	.05
251	Arthur Rhodes	.05
252	Scott Cooper	.05
253	Roberto Hernandez	.05
254	Mo Sanford	.05
255	Scott Servais	.05
256	Eric Karros	.05
257	Andy Mota	.05
258	Keith Mitchell	.05
259	Joel Johnston	.05
260	John Wehner	.05
261	Gino Minutelli	.05
262	Greg Gagne	.05
263	Stan Royer	.05
264	Carlos Garcia	.05
265	Andy Ashby	.05
266	Kim Batiste	.05
267	Julio Valera	.05
268	Royce Clayton	.05
269	Gary Scott	.05
270	Kirk Dressendorfer	.05
271	Sean Berry	.05
272	Lance Dickson	.05
273	Rob Maurer	.05
274	Scott Brosius	.05
275	Dave Fleming	.05
276	Lenny Webster	.05
277	Mike Humphreys	.05
278	Freddie Benavides	.05
279	Harvey Pulliam	.05
280	Jeff Carter	.05
281	Jim Abbott, Nolan Ryan	.25
282	Wade Boggs, George Brett	.25
283	Ken Griffey Jr., Rickey Henderson	.50
284	Dale Murphy, Wally Joyner	.10
285	Chuck Knoblauch, Ozzie Smith	.20
286	Robin Ventura, Lou Gehrig	.20
287	Robin Yount	.30
288	Bob Tewksbury	.05
289	Kirby Puckett	.50
290	Kenny Lofton	.05
291	Jack McDowell	.05
292	John Burkett	.05
293	Dwight Smith	.05
294	Nolan Ryan	1.00
295	Manny Ramirez **RC**	2.50
296	Cliff Floyd **RC**	.50
297	Al Shirley **RC**	.05
298	Brian Barber **RC**	.05
299	Jon Farrell **RC**	.05
300	Scott Ruffcorn **RC**	.05
301	Tyrone Hill **RC**	.05
302	Benji Gil **RC**	.05
303	Tyler Green **RC**	.05
304	Allen Watson	.05
305	Jay Buhner	.05
306	Roberto Alomar	.05
307	Chuck Knoblauch	.05
308	Darryl Strawberry	.05
309	Danny Tartabull	.05
310	Bobby Bonilla	.05
311	Mike Felder	.05
312	Storm Davis	.05
313	Tim Teufel	.05
314	Tom Brunansky	.05
315	Rex Hudler	.05
316	Dave Otto	.05
317	Jeff King	.05
318	Dan Gladden	.05
319	Bill Pecota	.05
320	Franklin Stubbs	.05
321	Gary Carter	.75
322	Melido Perez	.05
323	Eric Davis	.05
324	Greg Myers	.05
325	Pete Incaviglia	.05
326	Von Hayes	.05
327	Greg Swindell	.05
328	Steve Sax	.05
329	Chuck McElroy	.05
330	Gregg Jefferies	.05
331	Joe Oliver	.05
332	Paul Faries	.05
333	David West	.05
334	Craig Grebeck	.05
335	Chris Hammond	.05
336	Billy Ripken	.05
337	Scott Sanderson	.05
338	Dick Schofield	.05
339	Bob Milacki	.05
340	Kevin Reimer	.05
341	Jose DeLeon	.05
342	Henry Cotto	.05
343	Daryl Boston	.05
344	Kevin Gross	.05
345	Milt Thompson	.05
346	Luis Rivera	.05
347	Al Osuna	.05
348	Rob Deer	.05
349	Tim Leary	.05
350	Mike Stanton	.05
351	Dean Palmer	.05
352	Trevor Wilson	.05
353	Mark Eichhorn	.05
354	Scott Aldred	.05
355	Mark Whiten	.05
356	Leo Gomez	.05
357	Rafael Belliard	.05
358	Carlos Quintana	.05
359	Mark Davis	.05
360	Chris Nabholz	.05
361	Carlton Fisk	.75
362	Joe Orsulak	.05
363	Eric Anthony	.05
364	Greg Hibbard	.05
365	Scott Leius	.05
366	Hensley Meulens	.05
367	Chris Bosio	.05
368	Brian Downing	.05
369	Sammy Sosa	1.00
370	Stan Belinda	.05
371	Joe Grahe	.05
372	Luis Salazar	.05
373	Lance Johnson	.05
374	Kal Daniels	.05
375	Dave Winfield	.75
376	Brook Jacoby	.05
377	Mariano Duncan	.05
378	Ron Darling	.05
379	Randy Johnson	.75
380	Chito Martinez	.05
381	Andres Galarraga	.05
382	Willie Randolph	.05
383	Charles Nagy	.05
384	Tim Belcher	.05
385	Duane Ward	.05
386	Vicente Palacios	.05
387	Mike Gallego	.05
388	Rich DeLucia	.05
389	Scott Radinsky	.05
390	Damon Berryhill	.05
391	Kirk McCaskill	.05
392	Pedro Guerrero	.05
393	Kevin Mitchell	.05
394	Dickie Thon	.05
395	Bobby Bonilla	.05
396	Bill Wegman	.05
397	Dave Martinez	.05
398	Rick Sutcliffe	.05
399	Larry Andersen	.05
400	Tony Gwynn	1.00
401	Rickey Henderson	.75
402	Greg Cadaret	.05
403	Keith Miller	.05
404	Bip Roberts	.05
405	Kevin Brown	.05
406	Mitch Williams	.05
407	Frank Viola	.05
408	Darren Lewis	.05
409	Bob Walk	.05
410	Bob Walk	.05
411	Todd Frohwirth	.05
412	Brian Hunter	.05
413	Ron Karkovice	.05
414	Mike Morgan	.05
415	Joe Hesketh	.05
416	Don Slaught	.05
417	Tom Henke	.05
418	Kurt Stillwell	.05
419	Hector Villanueva	.05
420	Glenallen Hill	.05
421	Pat Borders	.05
422	Charlie Hough	.05
423	Charlie Leibrandt	.05
424	Eddie Murray	.75
425	Jesse Barfield	.05
426	Mark Lemke	.05
427	Kevin McReynolds	.05
428	Gilberto Reyes	.05
429	Ramon Martinez	.05
430	Steve Buechele	.05
431	David Wells	.05
432	Kyle Abbott	.05
433	John Habyan	.05
434	Kevin Appier	.05
435	Gene Larkin	.05
436	Sandy Alomar, Jr.	.05
437	Mike Jackson	.05
438	Todd Benzinger	.05
439	Teddy Higuera	.05
440	Reggie Sanders	.05
441	Mark Carreon	.05
442	Bret Saberhagen	.05
443	Gene Nelson	.05
444	Jay Howell	.05
445	Roger McDowell	.05
446	Sid Bream	.05
447	Mackey Sasser	.05
448	Bill Swift	.05
449	Hubie Brooks	.05
450	David Cone	.05
451	Bobby Witt	.05
452	Brady Anderson	.05
453	Lee Stevens	.05
454	Luis Aquino	.05
455	Carney Lansford	.05
456	Carlos Hernandez	.05
457	Danny Jackson	.05
458	Gerald Young	.05
459	Tom Candiotti	.05
460	Billy Hatcher	.05
461	John Wetteland	.05
462	Mike Bordick	.05
463	Don Robinson	.05
464	Jeff Johnson	.05
465	Lonnie Smith	.05
466	Paul Assenmacher	.05
467	Alvin Davis	.05
468	Jim Eisenreich	.05
469	Brent Mayne	.05
470	Jeff Brantley	.05
471	Tim Burke	.05
472	Pat Mahomes **RC**	.05
473	Ryan Bowen	.05
474	Bryn Smith	.05
475	Mike Flanagan	.05
476	Reggie Jefferson	.05
477	Jeff Blauser	.05
478	Craig Lefferts	.05
479	Todd Worrell	.05
480	Scott Scudder	.05
481	Kirk Gibson	.05
482	Kenny Rogers	.05
483	Jack Morris	.05
484	Russ Swan	.05
485	Mike Huff	.05
486	Ken Hill	.05
487	Geronimo Pena	.05
488	Charlie O'Brien	.05
489	Mike Maddux	.05
490	Scott Livingstone	.05
491	Carl Willis	.05
492	Kelly Downs	.05
493	Dennis Cook	.05
494	Joe Magrane	.05
495	Bob Kipper	.05
496	Jose Mesa	.05
497	Charlie Hayes	.05
498	Joe Girardi	.05
499	Doug Jones	.05
500	Barry Bonds	2.00
501	Bill Krueger	.05
502	Glenn Braggs	.05
503	Eric King	.05
504	Frank Castillo	.05
505	Mike Gardiner	.05
506	Cory Snyder	.05
507	Steve Howe	.05
508	Jose Rijo	.05
509	Sid Fernandez	.05
510	Archi Cianfrocco **RC**	.05
511	Mark Guthrie	.05
512	Bob Ojeda	.05
513	John Doherty	.05
514	Dante Bichette	.05
515	Juan Berenguer	.05
516	Jeff Robinson	.05
517	Mike MacFarlane	.05
518	Matt Young	.05
519	Otis Nixon	.05
520	Brian Holman	.05
521	Chris Haney	.05
522	Jeff Kent **RC**	.75
523	Chad Curtis **RC**	.25
524	Vince Horsman	.05
525	Rod Nichols	.05
526	Peter Hoy **RC**	.05
527	Shawn Boskie	.05
528	Alejandro Pena	.05
529	Dave Burba	.05
530	Ricky Jordan	.05
531	David Silvestri	.05
532	John Patterson	.05
533	Jeff Branson	.05
534	Derrick May	.05
535	Esteban Beltre	.05
536	Jose Melendez	.05
537	Wally Joyner	.05
538	Eddie Taubensee	.05
539	Jim Abbott	.05
540	Brian Williams **RC**	.05
541	Donovan Osborne	.05
542	Patrick Lennon	.05
543	Mike Groppuso **RC**	.05
544	Jarvis Brown **RC**	.05
545	Shawn Livesy **RC**	.05
546	Jeff Ware	.05
547	Danny Tartabull	.05
548	Bobby Jones **RC**	.05
549	Ken Griffey Jr.	1.50
550	Rey Sanchez **RC**	.05
551	Pedro Astacio **RC**	.10
552	Juan Guerrero **RC**	.05
553	Jacob Brumfield **RC**	.05
554	Ben Rivera **RC**	.05
555	Brian Jordan **RC**	.40
556	Denny Neagle	.05
557	Cliff Brantley	.05
558	Anthony Young	.05
559	John VanderWal **RC**	.05
560	Monty Fariss **RC**	.05
561	Russ Springer **RC**	.05
562	Pat Listach **RC**	.05
563	Pat Hentgen	.05
564	Andy Stankiewicz	.05
565	Mike Perez	.05
566	Mike Bielecki	.05
567	Butch Henry	.05
568	Dave Nilsson **RC**	.05
569	Scott Hatteberg **RC**	.05
570	Ruben Amaro Jr.	.05
571	Todd Hundley	.05
572	Moises Alou	.05
573	Hector Fajardo	.05
574	Todd Van Poppel	.05
575	Willie Banks	.05
576	Bob Zupcic	.05
577	J.J. Johnson **RC**	.05
578	John Burkett	.05
579	Trever Miller	.05
580	Scott Bankhead	.05
581	Rich Amaral	.05
582	Kenny Lofton	.05
583	Matt Stairs	.05
584	Don Mattingly, Rod Carew	.25
585	Jack Morris, Steve Avery	.05
586	Roberto Alomar, Sandy Alomar	.10
587	Scott Sanderson, Catfish Hunter	.05
588	Dave Justice, Willie Stargell	.05
589	Rex Hudler, Roger Staubach	.05
590	David Cone, Jackie Gleason	.05
591	Willie Davis, Tony Gwynn	.15
592	Orel Hershiser	.05
593	John Wetteland	.05
594	Tom Glavine	.05
595	Randy Johnson	.25
596	Jim Gott	.05
597	Donald Harris	.05
598	Shawn Hare **RC**	.05
599	Chris Gardner	.05
600	Rusty Meacham	.05
601	Benito Santiago (Shades)	.05
602	Eric Davis (Shades)	.05
603	Jose Lind (Shades)	.05
604	Dave Justice (Shades)	.05
605	Tim Raines (Shades)	.05
606	Randy Tomlin (Grips)	.05
607	Jack McDowell (Grips)	.05
608	Greg Maddux (Grips)	.30
609	Charles Nagy (Grips)	.05
610	Tom Candiotti (Grips)	.05
611	David Cone (Grips)	.05
612	Steve Avery (Grips)	.05
613	Rod Beck **RC**	.10
614	Rickey Henderson	.25
615	Benito Santiago	.05
616	Ruben Sierra	.05
617	Ryne Sandberg	.50
618	Nolan Ryan	1.00
619	Brett Butler	.05
620	Dave Justice	.05

1992 Pinnacle Mickey Mantle

		NM/M
Complete Set (30):		20.00
Common Card:		1.00
1	Father and Son	1.00
2	High School	1.00
3	Commerce Comet	1.00
4	Spring Training	1.00
5	The Beginning	1.00
6	No. 6	1.00
7	The Rookie	1.00
8	Tape-Measure Shots	1.00
9	Shortstop	1.00
10	Outfield	1.00
11	Speed, Speed, Speed	1.00
12	Contracts	1.00
13	Three-time MVP	1.00
14	Triple Crown	1.00
15	Series Slam	1.00
16	Series Star	1.00
17	Switch Hitter	1.00
18	Fan Favorite	1.00
19	Milestones	1.00
20	Enthuiasm	1.00

21	Hitting	1.00
22	First Base	1.00
23	Courage	1.00
24	Mick & Stan (Musial)	1.00
25	Whitey & Yogi	1.00
26	Mick & Billy (Martin)	1.00
27	Mick & Casey (Stengel)	1.00
28	Awards	1.00
29	Retirement	1.00
30	Cooperstown	1.00

Rookies

		NM/M
Complete Set (30):		2.00
Common Player:		.05
1	Luis Mercedes	.05
2	Scott Cooper	.05
3	Kenny Lofton	.25
4	John Doherty	.05
5	Pat Listach	.05
6	Andy Stankiewicz	.05
7	Derek Bell	.25
8	Gary DiSarcina	.05
9	Roberto Hernandez	.15
10	Joel Johnston	.05
11	Pat Mahomes	.05
12	Todd Van Poppel	.05
13	Dave Fleming	.05
14	Monty Fariss	.05
15	Gary Scott	.05
16	Moises Alou	.25
17	Todd Hundley	.25
18	Kim Batiste	.05
19	Denny Neagle	.05
20	Donovan Osborne	.05
21	Mark Wohlers	.05
22	Reggie Sanders	.10
23	Brian Williams	.05
24	Eric Karros	.25
25	Frank Seminara	.05
26	Royce Clayton	.05
27	Dave Nilsson	.05
28	Matt Stairs	.25
29	Chad Curtis	.25
30	Carlos Hernandez	.25

Rookie Idols

		NM/M
Complete Set (18):		20.00
Common Player:		.50
1	Reggie Sanders, Eric Davis	.50
2	Hector Fajardo, Jim Abbott	.50
3	Gary Cooper, George Brett	3.50
4	Mark Wohlers, Roger Clemens	3.50
5	Luis Mercedes, Julio Franco	.50
6	Willie Banks, Dwight Gooden	.50
7	Kenny Lofton, Rickey Henderson	1.50
8	Keith Mitchell, Dave Henderson	.50
9	Kim Batiste, Barry Larkin	.50
10	Thurman Munson, Todd Hundley	1.00
11	Eddie Zosky, Cal Ripken Jr.	4.50
12	Todd Van Poppel, Nolan Ryan	4.50
13	Ryne Sandberg, Jim Thome	2.50
14	Dave Fleming, Bobby Murcer	.50
15	Royce Clayton, Ozzie Smith	2.50
16	Don Harris, Darryl Strawberry	.50
17	Alan Trammell, Chad Curtis	.50
18	Derek Bell, Dave Winfield	1.50

Slugfest

		NM/M
Complete Set (15):		15.00
Common Player:		.30
1	Cecil Fielder	.30

2	Mark McGwire	2.50
3	Jose Canseco	.65
4	Barry Bonds	3.00
5	Dave Justice	.30
6	Bobby Bonilla	.30
7	Ken Griffey Jr.	2.00
8	Ron Gant	.30
9	Ryne Sandberg	1.50
10	Ruben Sierra	.30
11	Frank Thomas	1.00
12	Will Clark	.30
13	Kirby Puckett	1.50
14	Cal Ripken, Jr.	3.00
15	Jeff Bagwell	1.00

Team Pinnacle

		NM/M
Complete Set (12):		40.00
Common Player:		1.50
1	Roger Clemens, Ramon Martinez	8.00
2	Jim Abbott, Steve Avery	1.50
3	Benito Santiago, Ivan Rodriguez	3.00
4	Frank Thomas, Will Clark	3.00
5	Roberto Alomar, Ryne Sandberg	6.00
6	Robin Ventura, Matt Williams	1.50
7	Cal Ripken, Jr., Barry Larkin	10.00
8	Danny Tartabull, Barry Bonds	8.00
9	Brett Butler, Ken Griffey Jr.	8.00
10	Ruben Sierra, Dave Justice	1.50
11	Dennis Eckersley, Rob Dibble	1.50
12	Scott Radinsky, John Franco	1.50

Team 2000

		NM/M
Complete Set (80):		3.00
Common Player:		.05
1	Mike Mussina	.30
2	Phil Plantier	.05
3	Frank Thomas	.50
4	Travis Fryman	.05
5	Kevin Appier	.05
6	Chuck Knoblauch	.05
7	Pat Kelly	.05
8	Ivan Rodriguez	.40
9	Dave Justice	.05
10	Jeff Bagwell	.50
11	Marquis Grissom	.05
12	Andy Benes	.05
13	Gregg Olson	.05
14	Kevin Morton	.05
15	Tim Naehring	.05
16	Dave Hollins	.05
17	Sandy Alomar Jr.	.05
18	Albert Belle	.05
19	Charles Nagy	.05
20	Brian McRae	.05
21	Larry Walker	.05
22	Delino DeShields	.05
23	Jeff Johnson	.05
24	Bernie Williams	.05
25	Jose Offerman	.05
26	Juan Gonzalez	.25
27	Juan Guzman	.05
28	Eric Anthony	.05
29	Brian Hunter	.05
30	John Smoltz	.05
31	Deion Sanders	.05
32	Greg Maddux	.75
33	Andujar Cedeno	.05
34	Royce Clayton	.05
35	Kenny Lofton	.05
36	Cal Eldred	.05
37	Jim Thome	.50
38	Gary DiSarcina	.05
39	Brian Jordan	.05
40	Chad Curtis	.05
41	Ben McDonald	.05
42	Jim Abbott	.05
43	Robin Ventura	.05
44	Milt Cuyler	.05
45	Gregg Jefferies	.05
46	Scott Radinsky	.05
47	Ken Griffey Jr.	1.00
48	Roberto Alomar	.15
49	Ramon Martinez	.05
50	Bret Barberie	.05
51	Ray Lankford	.05
52	Leo Gomez	.05
53	Tommy Greene	.05
54	Mo Vaughn	.05
55	Sammy Sosa	.75
56	Carlos Baerga	.05
57	Mark Lewis	.05
58	Tom Gordon	.05
59	Gary Sheffield	.25
60	Scott Erickson	.05
61	Pedro Munoz	.05
62	Tino Martinez	.05
63	Darren Lewis	.05
64	Dean Palmer	.05
65	John Olerud	.05
66	Steve Avery	.05
67	Pete Harnisch	.05
68	Luis Gonzalez	.05
69	Kim Batiste	.05
70	Reggie Sanders	.05
71	Luis Mercedes	.05
72	Todd Van Poppel	.05
73	Gary Scott	.05
74	Monty Fariss	.05
75	Kyle Abbott	.05
76	Eric Karros	.05
77	Mo Sanford	.05
78	Todd Hundley	.05
79	Reggie Jefferson	.05
80	Pat Mahomes	.05

1993 Pinnacle

		NM/M
Complete Set (620):		17.50
Common Player:		.05
Series 1 Pack (15):		.35
Series 1 Box (36):		8.00
Series 2 Pack (15):		.75
Series 2 Box (36):		20.00
1	Gary Sheffield	.30
2	Cal Eldred	.05
3	Larry Walker	.05
4	Deion Sanders	.05
5	Dave Fleming	.05
6	Carlos Baerga	.05
7	Bernie Williams	.05
8	John Kruk	.05
9	Jimmy Key	.05
10	Jeff Bagwell	.60
11	Jim Abbott	.05
12	Terry Steinbach	.05
13	Bob Tewksbury	.05
14	Eric Karros	.05
15	Ryne Sandberg	.75
16	Will Clark	.05
17	Edgar Martinez	.05
18	Eddie Murray	.60
19	Andy Van Slyke	.05
20	Cal Ripken, Jr.	2.00
21	Ivan Rodriguez	.50
22	Barry Larkin	.05
23	Don Mattingly	.85
24	Gregg Jefferies	.05
25	Roger Clemens	.85
26	Cecil Fielder	.05
27	Kent Hrbek	.05
28	Robin Ventura	.05
29	Rickey Henderson	.60
30	Roberto Alomar	.15
31	Luis Polonia	.05
32	Andujar Cedeno	.05
33	Pat Listach	.05
34	Mark Grace	.05
35	Otis Nixon	.05
36	Felix Jose	.05
37	Mike Sharperson	.05
38	Dennis Martinez	.05
39	Willie McGee	.05
40	Kenny Lofton	.05
41	Randy Johnson	.60
42	Andy Benes	.05
43	Bobby Bonilla	.05
44	Mike Mussina	.50
45	Len Dykstra	.05
46	Ellis Burks	.05
47	Chris Sabo	.05
48	Jay Bell	.05
49	Jose Canseco	.40
50	Craig Biggio	.05
51	Wally Joyner	.05
52	Mickey Tettleton	.05
53	Tim Raines	.05
54	Brian Harper	.05
55	Rene Gonzales	.05
56	Mark Langston	.05
57	Jack Morris	.05
58	Mark McGwire	1.50
59	Ken Caminiti	.05
60	Terry Pendleton	.05
61	Dave Nilsson	.05
62	Tom Pagnozzi	.05
63	Mike Morgan	.05
64	Darryl Strawberry	.05
65	Charles Nagy	.05
66	Ken Hill	.05
67	Matt Williams	.05
68	Jay Buhner	.05
69	Vince Coleman	.05
70	Brady Anderson	.05
71	Fred McGriff	.05
72	Ben McDonald	.05
73	Terry Mulholland	.05
74	Randy Tomlin	.05
75	Nolan Ryan	2.00
76	Frank Viola	.05
77	Jose Rijo	.05
78	Shane Mack	.05
79	Travis Fryman	.05
80	Jack McDowell	.05
81	Mark Gubicza	.05
82	Matt Nokes	.05
83	Bert Blyleven	.05
84	Eric Anthony	.05
85	Mike Bordick	.05
86	John Olerud	.05
87	B.J. Surhoff	.05
88	Bernard Gilkey	.05
89	Shawon Dunston	.05
90	Tom Glavine	.30
91	Brett Butler	.05
92	Moises Alou	.05
93	Albert Belle	.05
94	Darren Lewis	.05
95	Omar Vizquel	.05
96	Dwight Gooden	.05
97	Gregg Olson	.05
98	Tony Gwynn	.75
99	Darren Daulton	.05
100	Dennis Eckersley	.50
101	Rob Dibble	.05
102	Mike Greenwell	.05
103	Jose Lind	.05
104	Julio Franco	.05
105	Tom Gordon	.05
106	Scott Livingstone	.05
107	Chuck Knoblauch	.05
108	Frank Thomas	.60
109	Melido Perez	.05
110	Ken Griffey Jr.	1.00
111	Harold Baines	.05
112	Gary Gaetti	.05
113	Pete Harnisch	.05
114	David Wells	.05
115	Charlie Leibrandt	.05
116	Ray Lankford	.05
117	Kevin Seitzer	.05
118	Robin Yount	.60
119	Lenny Harris	.05
120	Chris James	.05
121	Delino DeShields	.05
122	Kirt Manwaring	.05
123	Glenallen Hill	.05
124	Hensley Meulens	.05
125	Darrin Jackson	.05
126	Todd Hundley	.05
127	Dave Hollins	.05
128	Sam Horn	.05

129	Roberto Hernandez	.05
130	Vicente Palacios	.05
131	George Brett	.85
132	Dave Martinez	.05
133	Kevin Appier	.05
134	Pat Kelly	.05
135	Pedro Munoz	.05
136	Mark Carreon	.05
137	Lance Johnson	.05
138	Devon White	.05
139	Julio Valera	.05
140	Eddie Taubensee	.05
141	Willie Wilson	.05
142	Stan Belinda	.05
143	John Smoltz	.05
144	Darryl Hamilton	.05
145	Sammy Sosa	.75
146	Carlos Hernandez	.05
147	Tom Candiotti	.05
148	Mike Felder	.05
149	Rusty Meacham	.05
150	Ivan Calderon	.05
151	Pete O'Brien	.05
152	Erik Hanson	.05
153	Billy Ripken	.05
154	Kurt Stillwell	.05
155	Jeff Kent	.05
156	Mickey Morandini	.05
157	Randy Milligan	.05
158	Reggie Sanders	.05
159	Luis Rivera	.05
160	Orlando Merced	.05
161	Dean Palmer	.05
162	Mike Perez	.05
163	Scott Erikson	.05
164	Kevin McReynolds	.05
165	Kevin Maas	.05
166	Ozzie Guillen	.05
167	Rob Deer	.05
168	Danny Tartabull	.05
169	Lee Stevens	.05
170	Dave Henderson	.05
171	Derek Bell	.05
172	Steve Finley	.05
173	Greg Olson	.05
174	Geronimo Pena	.05
175	Paul Quantrill	.05
176	Steve Buechele	.05
177	Kevin Gross	.05
178	Tim Wallach	.05
179	Dave Valle	.05
180	Dave Silvestri	.05
181	Bud Black	.05
182	Henry Rodriguez	.05
183	Tim Teufel	.05
184	Mark McLemore	.05
185	Bret Saberhagen	.05
186	Chris Hoiles	.05
187	Ricky Jordan	.05
188	Don Slaught	.05
189	Mo Vaughn	.05
190	Joe Oliver	.05
191	Juan Gonzalez	.30
192	Scott Leius	.05
193	Milt Cuyler	.05
194	Chris Haney	.05
195	Ron Karkovice	.05
196	Steve Farr	.05
197	John Orton	.05
198	Kelly Gruber	.05
199	Ron Darling	.05
200	Ruben Sierra	.05
201	Chuck Finley	.05
202	Mike Moore	.05
203	Pat Borders	.05
204	Sid Bream	.05
205	Todd Zeile	.05
206	Rick Wilkins	.05
207	Jim Gantner	.05
208	Frank Castillo	.05
209	Dave Hansen	.05
210	Trevor Wilson	.05
211	Sandy Alomar, Jr.	.05
212	Sean Berry	.05
213	Tino Martinez	.05
214	Chito Martinez	.05
215	Dan Walters	.05
216	John Franco	.05
217	Glenn Davis	.05
218	Mariano Duncan	.05
219	Mike LaValliere	.05
220	Rafael Palmeiro	.50
221	Jack Clark	.05
222	Hal Morris	.05
223	Ed Sprague	.05
224	John Valentin	.05
225	Sam Militello	.05
226	Bob Wickman	.05
227	Damion Easley	.05
228	John Jaha	.05
229	Bob Ayrault	.05
230	Mo Sanford	.05
231	Walt Weiss	.05
232	Dante Bichette	.05
233	Steve Decker	.05
234	Jerald Clark	.05
235	Bryan Harvey	.05
236	Joe Girardi	.05
237	Dave Magadan	.05
238	David Nied	.05
239	Eric Wedge **RC**	.05
240	Rico Brogna	.05
241	J.T. Bruett	.05
242	Jonathan Hurst	.05
243	Bret Boone	.05
244	Manny Alexander	.05
245	Scooter Tucker	.05
246	Troy Neel	.05
247	Eddie Zosky	.05
248	Melvin Nieves	.05
249	Ryan Thompson	.05
250	Shawn Barton	.05
251	Ryan Klesko	.05
252	Mike Piazza	1.00
253	Steve Hosey	.05
254	Shane Reynolds	.05
255	Dan Wilson	.05
256	Tom Marsh	.05
257	Barry Manuel	.05
258	Paul Miller	.05
259	Pedro Martinez	.60
260	Steve Cooke	.05
261	Johnny Guzman	.05
262	Mike Butcher	.05
263	Bien Figueroa	.05
264	Rich Rowland	.05
265	Shawn Jeter	.05
266	Gerald Williams	.05
267	Derek Parks	.05
268	Henry Mercedes	.05
269	David Hulse **RC**	.05
270	Tim Pugh **RC**	.05
271	William Suero	.05
272	Ozzie Canseco	.05
273	Fernando Ramsey	.05
274	Bernardo Brito	.05
275	Dave Mlicki	.05
276	Tim Salmon	.05
277	Mike Raczka	.05
278	Ken Ryan **RC**	.05
279	Rafael Bournigal	.05
280	Wil Cordero	.05
281	Billy Ashley	.05
282	Paul Wagner	.05
283	Blas Minor	.05
284	Rick Trlicek	.05
285	Willie Greene	.05
286	Ted Wood	.05
287	Phil Clark	.05
288	Jesse Levis	.05
289	Tony Gwynn	.40
290	Nolan Ryan	1.00
291	Dennis Martinez	.05
292	Eddie Murray	.30
293	Robin Yount	.30
294	George Brett	.45
295	Dave Winfield	.30
296	Bert Blyleven	.05
297	Jeff Bagwell	.30
298	John Smoltz	.05
299	Larry Walker	.05
300	Gary Sheffield	.15
301	Ivan Rodriguez	.30
302	Delino DeShields	.05
303	Tim Salmon	.05
304	Bernard Gilkey	.05
305	Cal Ripken, Jr.	1.00
306	Barry Larkin	.05
307	Kent Hrbek	.05
308	Rickey Henderson	.30
309	Darryl Strawberry	.05
310	John Franco	.05
311	Todd Stottlemyre	.05
312	Luis Gonzalez	.05
313	Tommy Greene	.05
314	Randy Velarde	.05
315	Steve Avery	.05
316	Jose Oquendo	.05
317	Rey Sanchez	.05
318	Greg Vaughn	.05
319	Orel Hershiser	.05
320	Paul Sorrento	.05
321	Royce Clayton	.05
322	John Vander Wal	.05
323	Henry Cotto	.05
324	Pete Schourek	.05
325	David Segui	.05
326	Arthur Rhodes	.05
327	Bruce Hurst	.05
328	Wes Chamberlain	.05
329	Ozzie Smith	.75
330	Scott Cooper	.05
331	Felix Fermin	.05
332	Mike Macfarlane	.05
333	Dan Gladden	.05
334	Kevin Tapani	.05
335	Steve Sax	.05
336	Jeff Montgomery	.05
337	Gary DiSarcina	.05
338	Lance Blankenship	.05
339	Brian Williams	.05
340	Duane Ward	.05
341	Chuck McElroy	.05
342	Joe Magrane	.05
343	Jaime Navarro	.05
344	Dave Justice	.05
345	Jose Offerman	.05
346	Marquis Grissom	.05
347	Bill Swift	.05
348	Jim Thome	.50
349	Archi Cianfrocco	.05
350	Anthony Young	.05
351	Leo Gomez	.05
352	Bill Gullickson	.05
353	Alan Trammell	.05
354	Dan Pasqua	.05
355	Jeff King	.05
356	Kevin Brown	.05
357	Tim Belcher	.05
358	Bip Roberts	.05
359	Brent Mayne	.05
360	Rheal Cormier	.05
361	Mark Guthrie	.05
362	Craig Grebeck	.05
363	Andy Stankiewicz	.05
364	Juan Guzman	.05
365	Bobby Witt	.05
366	Mark Portugal	.05
367	Brian McRae	.05
368	Mark Lemke	.05
369	Bill Wegman	.05
370	Donovan Osborne	.05
371	Derrick May	.05
372	Carl Willis	.05
373	Chris Nabholz	.05
374	Mark Lewis	.05
375	John Burkett	.05
376	Luis Mercedes	.05
377	Ramon Martinez	.05
378	Kyle Abbott	.05
379	Mark Wohlers	.05
380	Bob Walk	.05
381	Kenny Rogers	.05
382	Tim Naehring	.05
383	Alex Fernandez	.05
384	Keith Miller	.05
385	Mike Henneman	.05
386	Rick Aguilera	.05
387	George Bell	.05
388	Mike Gallego	.05
389	Howard Johnson	.05
390	Kim Batiste	.05
391	Jerry Browne	.05
392	Damon Berryhill	.05
393	Ricky Bones	.05
394	Omar Olivares	.05
395	Mike Harkey	.05
396	Pedro Astacio	.05
397	John Wetteland	.05
398	Rod Beck	.05
399	Thomas Howard	.05
400	Mike Devereaux	.05
401	Tim Wakefield	.05
402	Curt Schilling	.30
403	Zane Smith	.05
404	Bob Zupcic	.05
405	Tom Browning	.05
406	Tony Phillips	.05
407	John Doherty	.05
408	Pat Mahomes	.05
409	John Habyan	.05
410	Steve Olin	.05
411	Chad Curtis	.05
412	Joe Grahe	.05
413	John Patterson	.05
414	Brian Hunter	.05
415	Doug Henry	.05
416	Lee Smith	.05
417	Bob Scanlan	.05
418	Kent Mercker	.05
419	Mel Rojas	.05
420	Mark Whiten	.05
421	Carlton Fisk	.60
422	Candy Maldonado	.05
423	Doug Drabek	.05
424	Wade Boggs	.75
425	Mark Davis	.05
426	Kirby Puckett	.75
427	Joe Carter	.05
428	Paul Molitor	.60
429	Eric Davis	.05
430	Darryl Kile	.05
431	Jeff Parrett	.05
432	Jeff Blauser	.05
433	Dan Plesac	.05
434	Andres Galarraga	.05
435	Jim Gott	.05
436	Jose Mesa	.05
437	Ben Rivera	.05
438	Dave Winfield	.60
439	Norm Charlton	.05
440	Chris Bosio	.05
441	Wilson Alvarez	.05
442	Dave Stewart	.05
443	Doug Jones	.05
444	Jeff Russell	.05
445	Ron Gant	.05
446	Paul O'Neill	.05
447	Charlie Hayes	.05
448	Joe Hesketh	.05
449	Chris Hammond	.05
450	Hipolito Pichardo	.05
451	Scott Radinsky	.05
452	Bobby Thigpen	.05
453	Xavier Hernandez	.05
454	Lonnie Smith	.05
455	Jamie Arnold **RC**	.05
456	B.J. Wallace	.05
457	Derek Jeter **RC**	10.00
458	Jason Kendall **RC**	.75
459	Rick Helling	.05
460	Derek Wallace **RC**	.05
461	Sean Lowe **RC**	.05
462	Shannon Stewart **RC**	.60
463	Benji Grigsby **RC**	.05
464	Todd Steverson **RC**	.05
465	Dan Serafini **RC**	.05
466	Michael Tucker	.05
467	Chris Roberts	.05
468	Pete Janicki **RC**	.05
469	Jeff Schmidt **RC**	.05
470	Don Mattingly	.45
471	Cal Ripken, Jr.	1.00
472	Jack Morris	.05
473	Terry Pendleton	.05
474	Dennis Eckersley	.25
475	Carlton Fisk	.30
476	Wade Boggs	.35
477	Len Dykstra	.05
478	Danny Tartabull	.05
479	Jeff Conine	.10
480	Gregg Jefferies	.05
481	Paul Molitor	.30
482	John Valentin	.05
483	Alex Arias	.10
484	Barry Bonds	1.00
485	Doug Drabek	.05
486	Dave Winfield	.30
487	Brett Butler	.05
488	Harold Baines	.05
489	David Cone	.05
490	Willie McGee	.05
491	Robby Thompson	.05
492	Pete Incaviglia	.05
493	Manuel Lee	.05
494	Rafael Belliard	.05
495	Scott Fletcher	.05
496	Jeff Frye	.05
497	Andre Dawson	.25
498	Mike Scioscia	.05
499	Spike Owen	.05
500	Sid Fernandez	.05
501	Joe Orsulak	.05
502	Benito Santiago	.05
503	Dale Murphy	.25
504	Barry Bonds	2.00
505	Jose Guzman	.05
506	Tony Pena	.05
507	Greg Swindell	.05
508	Mike Pagliarulo	.05
509	Lou Whitaker	.05
510	Greg Gagne	.05
511	Butch Henry	.05
512	Jeff Brantley	.05
513	Jack Armstrong	.05
514	Danny Jackson	.05
515	Junior Felix	.05
516	Milt Thompson	.05
517	Greg Maddux	.75
518	Eric Young	.05
519	Jody Reed	.05
520	Roberto Kelly	.05
521	Darren Holmes	.05
522	Craig Lefferts	.05
523	Charlie Hough	.05
524	Bo Jackson	.10
525	Bill Spiers	.05
526	Orestes Destrade	.05
527	Greg Hibbard	.05
528	Roger McDowell	.05
529	Cory Snyder	.05
530	Harold Reynolds	.05
531	Kevin Reimer	.05
532	Rick Sutcliffe	.05
533	Tony Fernandez	.05
534	Tom Brunansky	.05
535	Jeff Reardon	.05
536	Chili Davis	.05
537	Bob Ojeda	.05
538	Greg Colbrunn	.05
539	Phil Plantier	.05
540	Brian Jordan	.05
541	Pete Smith	.05
542	Frank Tanana	.05
543	John Smiley	.05
544	David Cone	.05
545	Daryl Boston	.05
546	Tom Henke	.05
547	Bill Krueger	.05
548	Freddie Benavides	.05
549	Randy Myers	.05
550	Reggie Jefferson	.05
551	Kevin Mitchell	.05
552	Dave Stieb	.05
553	Bret Barberie	.05
554	Tim Crews	.05
555	Doug Dascenzo	.05
556	Alex Cole	.05
557	Jeff Innis	.05
558	Carlos Garcia	.05
559	Steve Howe	.05
560	Kirk McCaskill	.05
561	Frank Seminara	.05
562	Cris Carpenter	.05
563	Mike Stanley	.05
564	Carlos Quintana	.05
565	Mitch Williams	.05
566	Juan Bell	.05
567	Eric Fox	.05
568	Al Leiter	.05
569	Mike Stanton	.05
570	Scott Kamieniecki	.05
571	Ryan Bowen	.05
572	Andy Ashby	.05
573	Bob Welch	.05
574	Scott Sanderson	.05
575	Joe Kmak	.05
576	Scott Pose	.05
577	Ricky Gutierrez	.05
578	Mike Trombley	.05
579	Sterling Hitchcock **RC**	.10
580	Rodney Bolton	.05
581	Tyler Green	.05
582	Tim Costo	.05
583	Tim Laker **RC**	.05
584	Steve Reed **RC**	.05
585	Tom Kramer **RC**	.05
586	Robb Nen	.05
587	Jim Tatum **RC**	.05
588	Frank Bolick	.05

589	Kevin Young	.05
590	Matt Whiteside RC	.05
591	Cesar Hernandez	.05
592	Mike Mohler RC	.05
593	Alan Embree	.05
594	Terry Jorgensen	.05
595	John Cummings RC	.05
596	Domingo Martinez	.05
597	Benji Gil	.05
598	Todd Pratt RC	.05
599	Rene Arocha RC	.05
600	Dennis Moeller	.05
601	Jeff Conine	.05
602	Trevor Hoffman	.05
603	Daniel Smith	.05
604	Lee Tinsley	.05
605	Dan Peltier	.05
606	Billy Brewer	.05
607	Matt Walbeck RC	.05
608	Richie Lewis	.05
609	J.T. Snow RC	.40
610	Pat Gomez RC	.05
611	Phil Hiatt	.05
612	Alex Arias	.05
613	Kevin Rogers	.05
614	Al Martin	.05
615	Greg Gohr	.05
616	Grame Lloyd RC	.05
617	Kent Bottenfield	.05
618	Chuck Carr	.05
619	Darrell Sherman RC	.05
620	Mike Lansing RC	.15

1993 Pinnacle Cooperstown

NOLAN RYAN

		NM/M
Complete Set (30):		7.50
Common Player:		.25
Dufex:		25X
Promo:		30X
1	Nolan Ryan	2.00
2	George Brett	.85
3	Robin Yount	.65
4	Carlton Fisk	.65
5	Dale Murphy	.35
6	Dennis Eckersley	.50
7	Rickey Henderson	.65
8	Ryne Sandberg	.75
9	Ozzie Smith	.75
10	Dave Winfield	.65
11	Andre Dawson	.35
12	Kirby Puckett	.75
13	Wade Boggs	.75
14	Don Mattingly	.85
15	Barry Bonds	2.00
16	Will Clark	.25
17	Cal Ripken, Jr.	2.00
18	Roger Clemens	.85
19	Dwight Gooden	.25
20	Tony Gwynn	.75
21	Joe Carter	.25
22	Ken Griffey Jr.	1.00
23	Paul Molitor	.60
24	Frank Thomas	.60
25	Juan Gonzalez	.35
26	Barry Larkin	.25
27	Eddie Murray	.60
28	Cecil Fielder	.25
29	Roberto Alomar	.35
30	Mark McGwire	1.50

1993 Pinnacle Home Run Club

		NM/M
Complete Set (48):		6.00
Common Player:		.10
1	Juan Gonzalez	.40
2	Fred McGriff	.10
3	Cecil Fielder	.10
4	Barry Bonds	1.50
5	Albert Belle	.10
6	Gary Sheffield	.25
7	Joe Carter	.10
8	Mark McGwire	1.25
9	Darren Daulton	.10
10	Jose Canseco	.50
11	Dave Hollins	.10
12	Ryne Sandberg	.85
13	Ken Griffey Jr.	1.00
14	Larry Walker	.10
15	Rob Deer	.10
16	Andre Dawson	.25
17	Frank Thomas	.75

GREG VAUGHN

18	Mickey Tettleton	.10
19	Charlie Hayes	.10
20	Ron Gant	.10
21	Rickey Henderson	.75
22	Matt Williams	.10
23	Kevin Mitchell	.10
24	Robin Ventura	.10
25	Dean Palmer	.10
26	Mike Piazza	1.00
27	J.T. Snow	.10
28	Jeff Bagwell	.75
29	John Olerud	.10
30	Greg Vaughn	.10
31	Dave Justice	.10
32	Dave Winfield	.75
33	Danny Tartabull	.10
34	Eric Anthony	.10
35	Eddie Murray	.75
36	Jay Buhner	.10
37	Derek Bell	.10
38	Will Clark	.10
39	Carlos Baerga	.10
40	Mo Vaughn	.10
41	Bobby Bonilla	.10
42	Tim Salmon	.10
43	Bo Jackson	.10
44	Howard Johnson	.10
45	Kent Hrbek	.10
46	Ruben Sierra	.10
47	Cal Ripken, Jr.	1.50
48	Travis Fryman	.10

Rookie Team Pinnacle

ROOKIE TEAM PINNACLE — MIKE PIAZZA — 3 of 10

		NM/M
Complete Set (10):		20.00
Common Player:		1.50
1	Pedro Martinez, Mike Trombley	6.00
2	Kevin Rogers, Sterling Hitchcock	1.50
3	Mike Piazza, Jesse Levis	10.00
4	Ryan Klesko, J.T. Snow	1.50
5	John Patterson, Bret Boone	1.50
6	Domingo Martinez, Kevin Young	1.50
7	Wil Cordero, Manny Alexander	1.50
8	Steve Hosey, Tim Salmon	1.50
9	Ryan Thompson, Gerald Williams	1.50
10	Melvin Nieves, David Hulse	1.50

Slugfest

		NM/M
Complete Set (30):		12.50
Common Player:		.25
1	Juan Gonzalez	.50
2	Mark McGwire	2.00
3	Cecil Fielder	.25
4	Joe Carter	.25
5	Fred McGriff	.25
6	Barry Bonds	2.50
7	Gary Sheffield	.50
8	Dave Hollins	.25
9	Frank Thomas	1.00
10	Danny Tartabull	.25

RUBEN SIERRA — SLUGFEST

11	Albert Belle	.25
12	Ruben Sierra	.25
13	Larry Walker	.25
14	Jeff Bagwell	1.00
15	Dave Justice	.25
16	Kirby Puckett	1.25
17	John Kruk	.25
18	Howard Johnson	.25
19	Darryl Strawberry	.25
20	Will Clark	.25
21	Kevin Mitchell	.25
22	Mickey Tettleton	.25
23	Don Mattingly	1.50
24	Jose Canseco	.75
25	Sam Militello	.25
26	Andre Dawson	.50
27	Ryne Sandberg	1.25
28	Ken Griffey Jr.	1.75
29	Carlos Baerga	.25
30	Travis Fryman	.25

Team Pinnacle

TEAM PINNACLE — GARY SHEFFIELD • 3B — National League — 6 of 10

		NM/M
Complete Set (11):		40.00
Common Player:		1.50
1	Greg Maddux, Mike Mussina	10.00
2	Tom Glavine, John Smiley	2.00
3	Darren Daulton, Ivan Rodriguez	3.00
4	Fred McGriff, Frank Thomas	4.00
5	Delino DeShields, Carlos Baerga	1.50
6	Gary Sheffield, Edgar Martinez	2.00
7	Ozzie Smith, Pat Listach	8.00
8	Barry Bonds, Juan Gonzalez	15.00
9	Kirby Puckett, Andy Van Slyke	8.00
10	Larry Walker, Joe Carter	1.50
11	Rick Aguilera, Rob Dibble	1.50

Team 2001

		NM/M
Complete Set (30):		5.00
Common Player:		.05
1	Wil Cordero	.05
2	Cal Eldred	.05
3	Mike Mussina	.60
4	Chuck Knoblauch	.05
5	Melvin Nieves	.05
6	Tim Wakefield	.05
7	Carlos Baerga	.05
8	Bret Boone	.05
9	Jeff Bagwell	1.00
10	Travis Fryman	.05
11	Royce Clayton	.05
12	Delino DeShields	.05
13	Juan Gonzalez	.50
14	Pedro Martinez	1.00
15	Bernie Williams	.05
16	Billy Ashley	.05
17	Marquis Grissom	.05
18	Kenny Lofton	.05
19	Ray Lankford	.05

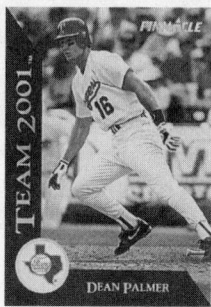

DEAN PALMER — TEAM 2001

20	Tim Salmon	.05
21	Steve Hosey	.05
22	Charles Nagy	.05
23	Dave Fleming	.05
24	Reggie Sanders	.05
25	Sam Militello	.05
26	Eric Karros	.05
27	Ryan Klesko	.05
28	Dean Palmer	.05
29	Ivan Rodriguez	.75
30	Sterling Hitchcock	.05

Tribute

George Brett — TRIBUTE

		NM/M
Complete Set (10):		10.00
George Brett Card (1-5):		1.00
Nolan Ryan Card (6-10):		1.50
1	George Brett Kansas City Royalty	1.00
2	George Brett The Chase for .400	1.00
3	Pine Tar Pandemonium - "The Bat"	1.00
4	George Brett MVP and a World Series, Too	1.00
5	George Brett 3,000 or Bust	1.00
6	Nolan Ryan The Rookie	1.50
7	Nolan Ryan Angel of No Mercy	1.50
8	Nolan Ryan Astronomical Success	1.50
9	Nolan Ryan 5,000 Ks	1.50
10	Nolan Ryan No-Hitter No. 7	1.50

1994 Pinnacle

SANDBERG

		NM/M
Complete Set (540):		15.00
Common Player:		.05
Artist's Proofs:		20X
Museums:		6X
Series 1 or 2 Pack (14):		.75
Series 1 or 2 Box (24):		12.50
1	Frank Thomas	.65
2	Carlos Baerga	.05

3	Sammy Sosa	.75
4	Tony Gwynn	.75
5	John Olerud	.05
6	Ryne Sandberg	.75
7	Moises Alou	.05
8	Steve Avery	.05
9	Tim Salmon	.05
10	Cecil Fielder	.05
11	Greg Maddux	.75
12	Barry Larkin	.05
13	Mike Devereaux	.05
14	Charlie Hayes	.05
15	Albert Belle	.05
16	Andy Van Slyke	.05
17	Mo Vaughn	.05
18	Brian McRae	.05
19	Cal Eldred	.05
20	Craig Biggio	.05
21	Kirby Puckett	.75
22	Derek Bell	.05
23	Don Mattingly	.85
24	John Burkett	.05
25	Roger Clemens	.85
26	Barry Bonds	2.00
27	Paul Molitor	.65
28	Mike Piazza	1.00
29	Robin Ventura	.05
30	Jeff Conine	.05
31	Wade Boggs	.75
32	Dennis Eckersley	.50
33	Bobby Bonilla	.05
34	Len Dykstra	.05
35	Manny Alexander	.05
36	Ray Lankford	.05
37	Greg Vaughn	.05
38	Chuck Finley	.05
39	Todd Benzinger	.05
40	Dave Justice	.05
41	Rob Dibble	.05
42	Tom Henke	.05
43	David Nied	.05
44	Sandy Alomar Jr.	.05
45	Pete Harnisch	.05
46	Jeff Russell	.05
47	Terry Mulholland	.05
48	Kevin Appier	.05
49	Randy Tomlin	.05
50	Cal Ripken, Jr.	2.00
51	Andy Benes	.05
52	Jimmy Key	.05
53	Kirt Manwaring	.05
54	Kevin Tapani	.05
55	Jose Guzman	.05
56	Todd Stottlemyre	.05
57	Jack McDowell	.05
58	Orel Hershiser	.05
59	Chris Hammond	.05
60	Chris Nabholz	.05
61	Ruben Sierra	.05
62	Dwight Gooden	.05
63	John Kruk	.05
64	Omar Vizquel	.05
65	Tim Naehring	.05
66	Dwight Smith	.05
67	Mickey Tettleton	.05
68	J.T. Snow	.05
69	Greg McMichael	.05
70	Kevin Mitchell	.05
71	Kevin Brown	.05
72	Scott Cooper	.05
73	Jim Thome	.60
74	Joe Girardi	.05
75	Eric Anthony	.05
76	Orlando Merced	.05
77	Felix Jose	.05
78	Tommy Greene	.05
79	Bernard Gilkey	.05
80	Phil Plantier	.05
81	Danny Tartabull	.05
82	Trevor Wilson	.05
83	Chuck Knoblauch	.05
84	Rick Wilkins	.05
85	Devon White	.05
86	Lance Johnson	.05
87	Eric Karros	.05
88	Gary Sheffield	.35
89	Wil Cordero	.05
90	Ron Darling	.05
91	Darren Daulton	.05
92	Joe Orsulak	.05
93	Steve Cooke	.05
94	Darryl Hamilton	.05
95	Aaron Sele	.05
96	John Doherty	.05
97	Gary DiSarcina	.05
98	Jeff Blauser	.05
99	John Smiley	.05
100	Ken Griffey Jr.	1.00
101	Dean Palmer	.05
102	Felix Fermin	.05
103	Jerald Clark	.05
104	Doug Drabek	.05
105	Curt Schilling	.30
106	Jeff Montgomery	.05
107	Rene Arocha	.05
108	Carlos Garcia	.05
109	Wally Whitehurst	.05
110	Jim Abbott	.05
111	Royce Clayton	.05
112	Chris Hoiles	.05
113	Mike Morgan	.05
114	Joe Magrane	.05
115	Tom Candiotti	.05
116	Ron Karkovice	.05
117	Ryan Bowen	.05
118	Rod Beck	.05
119	John Wetteland	.05
120	Terry Steinbach	.05
121	Dave Hollins	.05
122	Jeff Kent	.05
123	Ricky Bones	.05
124	Brian Jordan	.05
125	Chad Kreuter	.05
126	John Valentin	.05
127	Billy Hathaway	.05
128	Wilson Alvarez	.05
129	Tino Martinez	.05
130	Rodney Bolton	.05
131	David Segui	.05
132	Wayne Kirby	.05
133	Eric Young	.05
134	Scott Servais	.05
135	Scott Radinsky	.05
136	Bret Barberie	.05
137	John Roper	.05
138	Ricky Gutierrez	.05
139	Bernie Williams	.05
140	Bud Black	.05
141	Jose Vizcaino	.05
142	Gerald Williams	.05
143	Duane Ward	.05
144	Danny Jackson	.05
145	Allen Watson	.05
146	Scott Fletcher	.05
147	Delino DeShields	.05
148	Shane Mack	.05
149	Jim Eisenreich	.05
150	Troy Neel	.05
151	Jay Bell	.05
152	B.J. Surhoff	.05
153	Mark Whiten	.05
154	Mike Henneman	.05
155	Todd Hundley	.05
156	Greg Myers	.05
157	Ryan Klesko	.05
158	Dave Fleming	.05
159	Mickey Morandini	.05
160	Blas Minor	.05
161	Reggie Jefferson	.05
162	David Hulse	.05
163	Greg Swindell	.05
164	Roberto Hernandez	.05
165	Brady Anderson	.05
166	Jack Armstrong	.05
167	Phil Clark	.05
168	Melido Perez	.05
169	Darren Lewis	.05
170	Sam Horn	.05
171	Mike Harkey	.05
172	Juan Guzman	.05
173	Bob Natal	.05
174	Deion Sanders	.05
175	Carlos Quintana	.05
176	Mel Rojas	.05
177	Willie Banks	.05
178	Ben Rivera	.05
179	Kenny Lofton	.05
180	Leo Gomez	.05
181	Roberto Mejia	.05
182	Mike Perez	.05
183	Travis Fryman	.05
184	Ben McDonald	.05
185	Steve Frey	.05
186	Kevin Young	.05
187	Dave Magadan	.05
188	Bobby Munoz	.05
189	Pat Rapp	.05
190	Jose Offerman	.05
191	Vinny Castilla	.05
192	Ivan Calderon	.05
193	Ken Caminiti	.05
194	Benji Gil	.05
195	Chuck Carr	.05
196	Derrick May	.05
197	Pat Kelly	.05
198	Jeff Brantley	.05
199	Jose Lind	.05
200	Steve Buechele	.05
201	Wes Chamberlain	.05
202	Eduardo Perez	.05
203	Bret Saberhagen	.05
204	Gregg Jefferies	.05
205	Darrin Fletcher	.05
206	Kent Hrbek	.05
207	Kim Batiste	.05
208	Jeff King	.05
209	Donovan Osborne	.05
210	Dave Nilsson	.05
211	Al Martin	.05
212	Mike Moore	.05
213	Sterling Hitchcock	.05
214	Geronimo Pena	.05
215	Kevin Higgins	.05
216	Norm Charlton	.05
217	Don Slaught	.05
218	Mitch Williams	.05
219	Derek Lilliquist	.05
220	Armando Reynoso	.05
221	Kenny Rogers	.05
222	Doug Jones	.05
223	Luis Aquino	.05
224	Mike Oquist	.05
225	Darryl Scott	.05
226	Kurt Abbott	.05
227	Andy Tomberlin	.05
228	Norberto Martin	.05
229	Pedro Castellano	.05
230	Curtis Pride **RC**	.05
231	Jeff McNeely	.05
232	Scott Lydy	.05
233	Darren Oliver	.05
234	Danny Bautista	.05
235	Butch Huskey	.05
236	Chipper Jones	.75
237	Eddie Zambrano	.05
238	Jean Domingo	.05
239	Javier Lopez	.05
240	Nigel Wilson	.05
241	Drew Denson **RC**	.05
242	Raul Mondesi	.05
243	Luis Ortiz	.05
244	Manny Ramirez	.65
245	Greg Blosser	.05
246	Rondell White	.05
247	Steve Karsay	.05
248	Scott Stahoviak	.05
249	Jose Valentin	.05
250	Marc Newfield	.05
251	Keith Kessinger	.05
252	Carl Everett	.05
253	John O'Donoghue	.05
254	Turk Wendell	.05
255	Scott Ruffcorn	.05
256	Tony Tarasco	.05
257	Andy Cook	.05
258	Matt Mieske	.05
259	Luis Lopez	.05
260	Ramon Caraballo	.05
261	Salomon Torres	.05
262	Brooks Kieschnick **RC**	.05
263	Daron Kirkreit **RC**	.05
264	Bill Wagner **RC**	.10
265	Matt Drews **RC**	.05
266	Scott Christman	.05
267	Torii Hunter **RC**	1.00
268	Jamey Wright **RC**	.05
269	Jeff Granger	.05
270	Trot Nixon **RC**	1.00
271	Randy Myers	.05
272	Trevor Hoffman	.05
273	Bob Wickman	.05
274	Willie McGee	.05
275	Hipolito Pichardo	.05
276	Bobby Witt	.05
277	Gregg Olson	.05
278	Randy Johnson	.65
279	Robb Nen	.05
280	Paul O'Neill	.05
281	Lou Whitaker	.05
282	Chad Curtis	.05
283	Doug Henry	.05
284	Tom Glavine	.30
285	Mike Greenwell	.05
286	Roberto Kelly	.05
287	Roberto Alomar	.15
288	Charlie Hough	.05
289	Alex Fernandez	.05
290	Jeff Bagwell	.65
291	Wally Joyner	.05
292	Andujar Cedeno	.05
293	Rick Aguilera	.05
294	Darryl Strawberry	.05
295	Mike Mussina	.35
296	Jeff Gardner	.05
297	Chris Gwynn	.05
298	Matt Williams	.05
299	Brent Gates	.05
300	Mark McGwire	1.50
301	Jim Deshaies	.05
302	Edgar Martinez	.05
303	Danny Darwin	.05
304	Pat Meares	.05
305	Benito Santiago	.05
306	Jose Canseco	.40
307	Jim Gott	.05
308	Paul Sorrento	.05
309	Scott Kamieniecki	.05
310	Larry Walker	.05
311	Mark Langston	.05
312	John Jaha	.05
313	Stan Javier	.05
314	Hal Morris	.05
315	Robby Thompson	.05
316	Pat Hentgen	.05
317	Tom Gordon	.05
318	Joey Cora	.05
319	Luis Alicea	.05
320	Andre Dawson	.25
321	Darryl Kile	.05
322	Jose Rijo	.05
323	Luis Gonzalez	.05
324	Billy Ashley	.05
325	David Cone	.05
326	Bill Swift	.05
327	Phil Hiatt	.05
328	Craig Paquette	.05
329	Bob Welch	.05
330	Tony Phillips	.05
331	Archi Cianfrocco	.05
332	Dave Winfield	.65
333	David McCarty	.05
334	Al Leiter	.05
335	Tom Browning	.05
336	Mark Grace	.05
337	Jose Mesa	.05
338	Mike Stanley	.05
339	Roger McDowell	.05
340	Damion Easley	.05
341	Angel Miranda	.05
342	John Smoltz	.05
343	Jay Buhner	.05
344	Bryan Harvey	.05
345	Joe Carter	.05
346	Dante Bichette	.05
347	Jason Bere	.05
348	Frank Viola	.05
349	Ivan Rodriguez	.60
350	Juan Gonzalez	.35
351	Steve Finley	.05
352	Mike Felder	.05
353	Ramon Martinez	.05
354	Greg Gagne	.05
355	Ken Hill	.05
356	Pedro Munoz	.05
357	Todd Van Poppel	.05
358	Marquis Grissom	.05
359	Milt Cuyler	.05
360	Reggie Sanders	.05
361	Scott Erickson	.05
362	Billy Hatcher	.05
363	Gene Harris	.05
364	Rene Gonzales	.05
365	Kevin Rogers	.05
366	Eric Plunk	.05
367	Todd Zeile	.05
368	John Franco	.05
369	Brett Butler	.05
370	Bill Spiers	.05
371	Terry Pendleton	.05
372	Chris Bosio	.05
373	Orestes Destrade	.05
374	Dave Stewart	.05
375	Darren Holmes	.05
376	Doug Strange	.05
377	Brian Turang	.05
378	Carl Willis	.05
379	Mark McLemore	.05
380	Bobby Jones	.05
381	Scott Sanders	.05
382	Kirk Rueter	.05
383	Randy Velarde	.05
384	Fred McGriff	.05
385	Charles Nagy	.05
386	Rich Amaral	.05
387	Geronimo Berroa	.05
388	Eric Davis	.05
389	Ozzie Smith	.75
390	Alex Arias	.05
391	Brad Ausmus	.05
392	Cliff Floyd	.05
393	Roger Salkeld	.05
394	Jim Edmonds	.05
395	Jeromy Burnitz	.05
396	Dave Staton	.05
397	Rob Butler	.05
398	Marcos Armas	.05
399	Darrell Whitmore	.05
400	Ryan Thompson	.05
401	Ross Powell **RC**	.05
402	Joe Oliver	.05
403	Paul Carey	.05
404	Bob Hamelin	.05
405	Chris Turner	.05
406	Nate Minchey	.05
407	Lonnie Maclin **RC**	.05
408	Harold Baines	.05
409	Brian Williams	.05
410	Johnny Ruffin	.05
411	Julian Tavarez **RC**	.05
412	Mark Hutton	.05
413	Carlos Delgado	.50
414	Chris Gomez	.05
415	Mike Hampton	.05
416	Alex Diaz	.05
417	Jeffrey Hammonds	.05
418	Jayhawk Owens	.05
419	J.R. Phillips	.05
420	Cory Bailey **RC**	.05
421	Denny Hocking	.05
422	Jon Shave	.05
423	Damon Buford	.05
424	Troy O'Leary	.05
425	Tripp Cromer	.05
426	Albie Lopez	.05
427	Tony Fernandez	.05
428	Ozzie Guillen	.05
429	Alan Trammell	.05
430	John Wasdin **RC**	.05
431	Marc Valdes	.05
432	Brian Anderson **RC**	.20
433	Matt Brunson **RC**	.05
434	Wayne Gomes **RC**	.05
435	Jay Powell **RC**	.05
436	Kirk Presley **RC**	.05
437	Jon Ratliff **RC**	.05
438	Derrek Lee **RC**	2.00
439	Tom Pagnozzi	.05
440	Kent Mercker	.05
441	Phil Leftwich **RC**	.05
442	Jamie Moyer	.05
443	John Flaherty	.05
444	Mark Wohlers	.05
445	Jose Bautista	.05
446	Andres Galarraga	.05
447	Mark Lemke	.05
448	Tim Wakefield	.05
449	Pat Listach	.05
450	Rickey Henderson	.65
451	Mike Gallego	.05
452	Bob Tewksbury	.05
453	Kirk Gibson	.05
454	Pedro Astacio	.05
455	Mike Lansing	.05
456	Sean Berry	.05
457	Bob Walk	.05
458	Chili Davis	.05
459	Ed Sprague	.05
460	Kevin Stocker	.05
461	Mike Stanton	.05
462	Tim Raines	.05

463	Mike Bordick	.05
464	David Wells	.05
465	Tim Laker	.05
466	Cory Snyder	.05
467	Alex Cole	.05
468	Pete Incaviglia	.05
469	Roger Pavlik	.05
470	Greg W. Harris	.05
471	Xavier Hernandez	.05
472	Erik Hanson	.05
473	Jesse Orosco	.05
474	Greg Colbrunn	.05
475	Harold Reynolds	.05
476	Greg Harris	.05
477	Pat Borders	.05
478	Melvin Nieves	.05
479	Mariano Duncan	.05
480	Greg Hibbard	.05
481	Tim Pugh	.05
482	Bobby Ayala	.05
483	Sid Fernandez	.05
484	Tim Wallach	.05
485	Randy Milligan	.05
486	Walt Weiss	.05
487	Matt Walbeck	.05
488	Mike Macfarlane	.05
489	Jerry Browne	.05
490	Chris Sabo	.05
491	Tim Belcher	.05
492	Spike Owen	.05
493	Rafael Palmeiro	.60
494	Brian Harper	.05
495	Eddie Murray	.65
496	Ellis Burks	.05
497	Karl Rhodes	.05
498	Otis Nixon	.05
499	Lee Smith	.05
500	Bip Roberts	.05
501	Pedro Martinez	.65
502	Brian L. Hunter	.05
503	Tyler Green	.05
504	Bruce Hurst	.05
505	Alex Gonzalez	.05
506	Mark Portugal	.05
507	Bob Ojeda	.05
508	Dave Henderson	.05
509	Bo Jackson	.10
510	Bret Boone	.05
511	Mark Eichhorn	.05
512	Luis Polonia	.05
513	Will Clark	.05
514	Dave Valle	.05
515	Dan Wilson	.05
516	Dennis Martinez	.05
517	Jim Leyritz	.05
518	Howard Johnson	.05
519	Jody Reed	.05
520	Julio Franco	.05
521	Jeff Reardon	.05
522	Willie Greene	.05
523	Shawon Dunston	.05
524	Keith Mitchell	.05
525	Rick Helling	.05
526	Mark Kiefer	.05
527	Chan Ho Park RC	.75
528	Tony Longmire	.05
529	Rich Becker	.05
530	Tim Hyers	.05
531	Darrin Jackson	.05
532	Jack Morris	.05
533	Rick White	.05
534	Mike Kelly	.05
535	James Mouton	.05
536	Steve Trachsel	.05
537	Tony Eusebio	.05
538	Kelly Stinnett	.05
539	Paul Spoljaric	.05
540	Darren Dreifort	.05

Artist's Proof

		NM/M
Complete Set (540):		250.00
Common Player:		1.50
Stars/Rookies:		20X

(See 1994 Pinnacle for checklist and base card values.)

Museum Collection

		NM/M
Complete Set (540):		225.00
Common Player:		1.00

DENNIS ECKERSLEY

Stars/Rookies:		6X

(See 1994 Pinnacle for checklist and base card values.)

1994 Pinnacle New Generation

		NM/M
Complete Set (25):		5.00
Common Player:		.25
1	Tim Salmon	.25
2	Mike Piazza	2.00
3	Jason Bere	.25
4	Jeffrey Hammonds	.25
5	Aaron Sele	.25
6	Salomon Torres	.25
7	Wil Cordero	.25
8	Allen Watson	.25
9	J.T. Snow	.25
10	Cliff Floyd	.25
10a	Cliff Floyd (Overprinted "SAMPLE" card.)	.50
11	Jeff McNeely	.25
12	Butch Huskey	.25
13	J.R. Phillips	.25
14	Bobby Jones	.25
15	Javier Lopez	.25
16	Scott Ruffcorn	.25
17	Manny Ramirez	1.25
18	Carlos Delgado	1.00
19	Rondell White	.25
20	Chipper Jones	1.50
21	Billy Ashley	.25
22	Nigel Wilson	.25
23	Jeromy Burnitz	.25
24	Danny Bautista	.25
25	Darrell Whitmore	.25

1994 Pinnacle Power Surge

		NM/M
Complete Set (25):		4.00
Common Player:		.25
1	Dave Justice	.25
2	Chris Hoiles	.25
3	Mo Vaughn	.25
4	Tim Salmon	.25

5	J.T. Snow	.25
6	Frank Thomas	.65
7	Sammy Sosa	.75
8	Rick Wilkins	.25
9	Robin Ventura	.25
10	Reggie Sanders	.25
11	Albert Belle	.25
12	Carlos Baerga	.25
12a	Carlos Baerga (Overprinted "SAMPLE" card.)	.50
13	Manny Ramirez	.65
14	Travis Fryman	.25
15	Gary Sheffield	.35
16	Jeff Bagwell	.65
17	Mike Piazza	1.00
18	Eric Karros	.25
19	Cliff Floyd	.25
20	Mark Whiten	.25
21	Phil Plantier	.25
22	Derek Bell	.25
23	Ken Griffey Jr.	1.00
24	Juan Gonzalez	.35
25	Dean Palmer	.25

Rookie Team Pinnacle

		NM/M
Complete Set (9):		12.00
Common Player:		.75
1	Carlos Delgado, Javier Lopez	2.50
2	Bob Hamelin, J.R. Phillips	.75
3	Jon Shave, Keith Kessinger	.75
4	Butch Huskey, Luis Ortiz	.75
5	Chipper Jones, Kurt Abbott	5.00
6	Rondell White, Manny Ramirez	3.00
7	Cliff Floyd, Jeffrey Hammonds	.75
8	Marc Newfield, Nigel Wilson	.75
9	Salomon Torres, Mark Hutton	.75

Run Creators

		NM/M
Complete Set (44):		17.50
Common Player:		.25
1	John Olerud	.25
2	Frank Thomas	1.00
3	Ken Griffey Jr.	3.00
4	Paul Molitor	1.00
5	Rafael Palmeiro	.75
6	Roberto Alomar	.35
7	Juan Gonzalez	.50
8	Albert Belle	.25
9	Travis Fryman	.25
10	Rickey Henderson	1.00
11	Tony Phillips	.25
12	Mo Vaughn	.25
13	Tim Salmon	.25
14	Kenny Lofton	.25
15	Carlos Baerga	.25
16	Greg Vaughn	.25
17	Jay Buhner	.25
18	Chris Hoiles	.25
19	Mickey Tettleton	.25
20	Kirby Puckett	1.50
21	Danny Tartabull	.25
22	Devon White	.25
23	Barry Bonds	4.00
24	Lenny Dykstra	.25

25	John Kruk	.25
26	Fred McGriff	.25
27	Gregg Jefferies	.25
28	Mike Piazza	3.00
29	Jeff Blauser	.25
30	Andres Galarraga	.25
31	Darren Daulton	.25
32	Dave Justice	.25
33	Craig Biggio	.25
34	Mark Grace	.25
35	Tony Gwynn	1.50
36	Jeff Bagwell	1.00
37	Jay Bell	.25
38	Marquis Grissom	.25
39	Matt Williams	.25
40	Charlie Hayes	.25
41	Dante Bichette	.25
42	Bernard Gilkey	.25
43	Brett Butler	.25
44	Rick Wilkins	.25

Team Pinnacle

		NM/M
Complete Set (9):		35.00
Common Player:		1.50
1	Jeff Bagwell, Frank Thomas	4.00
2	Carlos Baerga, Robby Thompson	1.50
3	Matt Williams, Dean Palmer	1.50
4	Cal Ripken, Jr., Jay Bell	12.00
5	Ivan Rodriguez, Mike Piazza	6.00
6	Len Dykstra, Ken Griffey Jr.	8.00
7	Juan Gonzalez, Barry Bonds	10.00
8	Tim Salmon, Dave Justice	1.50
9	Greg Maddux, Jack McDowell	8.00

1994 Pinnacle The Naturals

		NM/M
Complete Set (25):		6.00
Common Player:		.15
1	Frank Thomas	.50
2	Barry Bonds	1.50
3	Ken Griffey Jr.	1.00
4	Juan Gonzalez	.25
5	Dave Justice	.15
6	Albert Belle	.15
7	Kenny Lofton	.25
8	Roberto Alomar	.35
9	Tim Salmon	.15
10	Randy Johnson	.50
11	Kirby Puckett	.65
12	Tony Gwynn	.65
13	Fred McGriff	.15
14	Ryne Sandberg	.65
15	Greg Maddux	.65
16	Matt Williams	.15
17	Lenny Dykstra	.15
18	Gary Sheffield	.35
18a	Gary Sheffield (Overprinted "SAMPLE" card.)	.50
19	Mike Piazza	1.00
20	Dean Palmer	.15
21	Travis Fryman	.15
22	Carlos Baerga	.15
23	Cal Ripken, Jr.	1.50
24	John Olerud	.15
25	Roger Clemens	.75

Tribute

	NM/M
Complete Set (18):	15.00
Common Player:	.25
1 Paul Molitor	1.00
2 Jim Abbott	.25
3 Dave Winfield	1.00
4 Bo Jackson	.35
5 Dave Justice	.25
6 Len Dykstra	.25
7 Mike Piazza	2.50
8 Barry Bonds	4.50
9 Randy Johnson	1.00
10 Ozzie Smith	1.50
11 Mark Whiten	.25
12 Greg Maddux	1.50
13 Cal Ripken, Jr.	4.50
14 Frank Thomas	1.00
15 Juan Gonzalez	.45
16 Roberto Alomar	.25
17 Ken Griffey Jr.	3.00
18 Lee Smith	.25

1995 Pinnacle

THOME

	NM/M
Complete Set (450):	15.00
Common Player:	.10
Artist's Proofs:	10X
Museum Collection:	4X
Hobby Pack (12):	1.00
Hobby Wax Box (24):	15.00
Retail Pack (12):	1.00
Retail Wax Box (36):	20.00
1 Jeff Bagwell	.75
2 Roger Clemens	1.25
3 Mark Whiten	.10
4 Shawon Dunston	.10
5 Bobby Bonilla	.10
6 Kevin Tapani	.10
7 Eric Karros	.10
8 Cliff Floyd	.10
9 Pat Kelly	.10
10 Jeffrey Hammonds	.10
11 Jeff Conine	.10
12 Fred McGriff	.10
13 Chris Bosio	.10
14 Mike Mussina	.40
15 Danny Bautista	.10
16 Mickey Morandini	.10
17 Chuck Finley	.10
18 Jim Thome	.65
19 Luis Ortiz	.10
20 Walt Weiss	.10
21 Don Mattingly	1.25
22 Bob Hamelin	.10
23 Melido Perez	.10
24 Kevin Mitchell	.10
25 John Smoltz	.10
26 Hector Carrasco	.10
27 Pat Hentgen	.10
28 Derrick May	.10
29 Mike Kingery	.10
30 Chuck Carr	.10
31 Billy Ashley	.10
32 Todd Hundley	.10
33 Luis Gonzalez	.10

34 Marquis Grissom	.10
35 Jeff King	.10
36 Eddie Williams	.10
37 Tom Pagnozzi	.10
38 Chris Hoiles	.10
39 Sandy Alomar	.10
40 Mike Greenwell	.10
41 Lance Johnson	.10
42 Junior Felix	.10
43 Felix Jose	.10
44 Scott Leius	.10
45 Ruben Sierra	.10
46 Kevin Seitzer	.10
47 Wade Boggs	1.00
48 Reggie Jefferson	.10
49 Jose Canseco	.40
50 Dave Justice	.10
51 John Smiley	.10
52 Joe Carter	.10
53 Rick Wilkins	.10
54 Ellis Burks	.10
55 Dave Weathers	.10
56 Pedro Astacio	.10
57 Ryan Thompson	.10
58 James Mouton	.10
59 Mel Rojas	.10
60 Orlando Merced	.10
61 Matt Williams	.10
62 Bernard Gilkey	.10
63 J.R. Phillips	.10
64 Lee Smith	.10
65 Jim Edmonds	.10
66 Darrin Jackson	.10
67 Scott Cooper	.10
68 Ron Karkovice	.10
69 Chris Gomez	.10
70 Kevin Appier	.10
71 Bobby Jones	.10
72 Doug Drabek	.10
73 Matt Mieske	.10
74 Sterling Hitchcock	.10
75 John Valentin	.10
76 Reggie Sanders	.10
77 Wally Joyner	.10
78 Turk Wendell	.10
79 Wendell Hayes	.10
80 Bret Barberie	.10
81 Troy Neel	.10
82 Ken Caminiti	.10
83 Milt Thompson	.10
84 Paul Sorrento	.10
85 Trevor Hoffman	.10
86 Jay Bell	.10
87 Mark Portugal	.10
88 Sid Fernandez	.10
89 Charles Nagy	.10
90 Jeff Montgomery	.10
91 Chuck Knoblauch	.10
92 Jeff Frye	.10
93 Tony Gwynn	1.00
94 John Olerud	.10
95 David Nied	.10
96 Chris Hammond	.10
97 Edgar Martinez	.10
98 Kevin Stocker	.10
99 Jeff Fassero	.10
100 Curt Schilling	.30
101 Dave Clark	.10
102 Delino DeShields	.10
103 Leo Gomez	.10
104 Dave Hollins	.10
105 Tim Naehring	.10
106 Otis Nixon	.10
107 Ozzie Guillen	.10
108 Jose Lind	.10
109 Stan Javier	.10
110 Greg Vaughn	.10
111 Chipper Jones	1.00
112 Ed Sprague	.10
113 Mike Macfarlane	.10
114 Steve Finley	.10
115 Ken Hill	.10
116 Carlos Garcia	.10
117 Lou Whitaker	.10
118 Todd Zeile	.10
119 Gary Sheffield	.40
120 Ben McDonald	.10
121 Pete Harnisch	.10
122 Ivan Rodriguez	.65
123 Wilson Alvarez	.10
124 Travis Fryman	.10
125 Pedro Munoz	.10
126 Mark Lemke	.10
127 Jose Valentin	.10
128 Ken Griffey, Jr.	1.50
129 Omar Vizquel	.10
130 Milt Cuyler	.10
131 Steve Traschel	.10
132 Alex Rodriguez	2.00
133 Garret Anderson	.10
134 Armando Benitez	.10
135 Shawn Green	.35
136 Jorge Fabregas	.10
137 Orlando Miller	.10
138 Rikkert Faneyte	.10
139 Ismael Valdes	.10
140 Jose Oliva	.10
141 Aaron Small	.10
142 Tim Davis	.10
143 Ricky Bottalacio	.10
144 Mike Matheny	.10
145 Roberto Petagine	.10
146 Fausto Cruz	.10
147 Bryce Florie	.10
148 Jose Lima	.10

149 John Hudek	.10
150 Duane Singleton	.10
151 John Mabry	.10
152 Robert Eenhoorn	.10
153 Jon Lieber	.10
154 Garey Ingram	.10
155 Paul Shuey	.10
156 Mike Lieberthal	.10
157 Steve Dunn	.10
158 Charles Johnson	.10
159 Ernie Young	.10
160 Jose Martinez	.10
161 Kurt Miller	.10
162 Joey Eischen	.10
163 Dave Stevens	.10
164 Brian Hunter	.10
165 Jeff Cirillo	.10
166 Mark Smith	.10
167 McKay Christensen **RC**	.10
168 C.J. Nitkowski	.10
169 Antone Williamson **RC**	.10
170 Paul Konerko	.15
171 Scott Elarton **RC**	.15
172 Jacob Shumate	.10
173 Terrence Long	.10
174 Mark Johnson **RC**	.10
175 Ben Grieve	.10
176 Jayson Peterson **RC**	.10
177 Checklist	.10
178 Checklist	.10
179 Checklist	.10
180 Checklist	.10
181 Brian Anderson	.10
182 Steve Buechele	.10
183 Mark Clark	.10
184 Cecil Fielder	.10
185 Steve Avery	.10
186 Devon White	.10
187 Craig Shipley	.10
188 Brady Anderson	.10
189 Kenny Lofton	.10
190 Alex Cole	.10
191 Brent Gates	.10
192 Dean Palmer	.10
193 Alex Gonzalez	.10
194 Steve Cooke	.10
195 Ray Lankford	.10
196 Mark McGwire	2.00
197 Marc Newfield	.10
198 Pat Rapp	.10
199 Darren Lewis	.10
200 Carlos Baerga	.10
201 Rickey Henderson	.75
202 Kurt Abbott	.10
203 Kirt Manwaring	.10
204 Cal Ripken Jr.	2.50
205 Darren Daulton	.10
206 Greg Colbrunn	.10
207 Darryl Hamilton	.10
208 Bo Jackson	.15
209 Tony Phillips	.10
210 Geronimo Berroa	.10
211 Rich Becker	.10
212 Tony Tarasco	.10
213 Karl Rhodes	.10
214 Phil Plantier	.10
215 J.T. Snow	.10
216 Mo Vaughn	.10
217 Greg Gagne	.10
218 Rickey Bones	.10
219 Mike Bordick	.10
220 Chad Curtis	.10
221 Royce Clayton	.10
222 Roberto Alomar	.15
223 Jose Rijo	.10
224 Ryan Klesko	.10
225 Mark Langston	.10
226 Frank Thomas	.75
227 Juan Gonzalez	.40
228 Ron Gant	.10
229 Javier Lopez	.10
230 Sammy Sosa	1.00
231 Kevin Brown	.10
232 Gary DiSarcina	.10
233 Albert Belle	.10
234 Jay Buhner	.10
235 Pedro Martinez	.75
236 Bob Tewksbury	.10
237 Mike Piazza	1.50
238 Darryl Kile	.10
239 Bryan Harvey	.10
240 Andres Galarraga	.10
241 Jeff Blauser	.10
242 Jeff Kent	.10
243 Bobby Munoz	.10
244 Greg Maddux	1.00
245 Paul O'Neill	.10
246 Lenny Dykstra	.10
247 Todd Van Poppel	.10
248 Bernie Williams	.05
249 Glenallen Hill	.10
250 Duane Ward	.10
251 Dennis Eckersley	.60
252 Pat Mahomes	.10
253 Rusty Greer	.10
(Photo actually Jeff Frye.)	
254 Roberto Kelly	.10
255 Randy Myers	.10
256 Scott Ruffcorn	.10
257 Robin Ventura	.10
258 Eduardo Perez	.10
259 Aaron Sele	.10
260 Paul Molitor	.75
261 Juan Guzman	.10
262 Darren Oliver	.10

263 Mike Stanley	.10
264 Tom Glavine	.30
265 Rico Brogna	.10
266 Craig Biggio	.10
267 Darrell Whitmore	.10
268 Jimmy Key	.10
269 Will Clark	.10
270 David Cone	.10
271 Brian Jordan	.10
272 Barry Bonds	2.50
273 Danny Tartabull	.10
274 Ramon Martinez	.10
275 Al Martin	.10
276 Fred McGriff	.10
277 Carlos Delgado	.25
278 Juan Gonzalez	.20
279 Shawn Green	.20
280 Carlos Baerga	.10
281 Cliff Floyd	.10
282 Ozzie Smith	.50
283 Alex Rodriguez	1.00
284 Kenny Lofton	.10
285 Dave Justice	.10
286 Tim Salmon	.10
287 Manny Ramirez	.40
288 Will Clark	.10
289 Garret Anderson	.10
290 Billy Ashley	.10
291 Tony Gwynn	.50
292 Raul Mondesi	.10
293 Rafael Palmeiro	.30
294 Matt Williams	.10
295 Don Mattingly	.60
296 Kirby Puckett	.50
297 Paul Molitor	.40
298 Albert Belle	.10
299 Barry Bonds	1.25
300 Mike Piazza	.85
301 Jeff Bagwell	.40
302 Frank Thomas	.40
303 Chipper Jones	.50
304 Ken Griffey Jr.	.75
305 Cal Ripken Jr.	1.25
306 Eric Anthony	.10
307 Todd Benzinger	.10
308 Jacob Brumfield	.10
309 Wes Chamberlain	.10
310 Tino Martinez	.10
311 Roberto Mejia	.10
312 Jose Offerman	.10
313 David Segui	.10
314 Eric Young	.10
315 Rey Sanchez	.10
316 Raul Mondesi	.10
317 Bret Boone	.10
318 Andre Dawson	.30
319 Brian McRae	.10
320 Dave Nilsson	.10
321 Moises Alou	.10
322 Don Slaught	.10
323 Dave McCarty	.10
324 Mike Huff	.10
325 Rich Aguilera	.10
326 Rod Beck	.10
327 Kenny Rogers	.10
328 Andy Benes	.10
329 Allen Watson	.10
330 Randy Johnson	.75
331 Willie Greene	.10
332 Hal Morris	.10
333 Ozzie Smith	1.00
334 Jason Bere	.10
335 Scott Erickson	.10
336 Dante Bichette	.10
337 Willie Banks	.10
338 Eric Davis	.10
339 Rondell White	.10
340 Kirby Puckett	1.00
341 Deion Sanders	.10
342 Eddie Murray	.75
343 Mike Harkey	.10
344 Joey Hamilton	.10
345 Roger Salkeld	.10
346 Wil Cordero	.10
347 John Wetteland	.10
348 Geronimo Pena	.10
349 Kirk Gibson	.10
350 Manny Ramirez	.75
351 William Van Landingham	.10
352 B.J. Surhoff	.10
353 Ken Ryan	.10
354 Terry Steinbach	.10
355 Bret Saberhagen	.10
356 John Jaha	.10
357 Joe Girardi	.10
358 Steve Karsay	.10
359 Alex Fernandez	.10
360 Salomon Torres	.10
361 John Burkett	.10
362 Derek Bell	.10
363 Tom Henke	.10
364 Gregg Jefferies	.10
365 Jack McDowell	.10
366 Andujar Cedeno	.10
367 Dave Winfield	.75
368 Carl Everett	.10
369 Danny Jackson	.10
370 Jeromy Burnitz	.10
371 Mark Grace	.10
372 Larry Walker	.10
373 Bill Swift	.10
374 Dennis Martinez	.10
375 Mickey Tettleton	.10
376 Mel Nieves	.10
377 Cal Eldred	.10

#	Player	Price
378	Orel Hershiser	.10
379	David Wells	.10
380	Gary Gaetti	.10
381	Tim Raines	.10
382	Barry Larkin	.10
383	Jason Jacome	.10
384	Tim Wallach	.10
385	Robby Thompson	.10
386	Frank Viola	.10
387	Dave Stewart	.10
388	Bip Roberts	.10
389	Ron Darling	.10
390	Carlos Delgado	.45
391	Tim Salmon	.10
392	Alan Trammell	.10
393	Kevin Foster	.10
394	Jim Abbott	.10
395	John Kruk	.10
396	Andy Van Slyke	.10
397	Dave Magadan	.10
398	Rafael Palmeiro	.65
399	Mike Devereaux	.10
400	Benito Santiago	.10
401	Brett Butler	.10
402	John Franco	.10
403	Matt Walbeck	.10
404	Terry Pendleton	.10
405	Chris Sabo	.10
406	Andrew Lorraine	.10
407	Dan Wilson	.10
408	Mike Lansing	.10
409	Ray McDavid	.10
410	Shane Andrews	.10
411	Tom Gordon	.10
412	Chad Ogea	.10
413	James Baldwin	.10
414	Russ Davis	.10
415	Ray Holbert	.10
416	Ray Durham	.10
417	Matt Nokes	.10
418	Rodney Henderson	.10
419	Gabe White	.10
420	Todd Hollandsworth	.10
421	Midre Cummings	.10
422	Harold Baines	.10
423	Troy Percival	.10
424	Joe Vitiello	.10
425	Andy Ashby	.10
426	Michael Tucker	.10
427	Mark Gubicza	.10
428	Jim Bullinger	.10
429	Jose Malave	.10
430	Pete Schourek	.10
431	Bobby Ayala	.10
432	Marvin Freeman	.10
433	Pat Listach	.10
434	Eddie Taubensee	.10
435	Steve Howe	.10
436	Kent Mercker	.10
437	Hector Fajardo	.10
438	Scott Kamieniecki	.10
439	Robb Nen	.10
440	Mike Kelly	.10
441	Tom Candiotti	.10
442	Albie Lopez	.10
443	Jeff Granger	.10
444	Rich Aude	.10
445	Luis Polonia	.10
446	Frank Thomas A.L. Checklist	.40
447	Ken Griffey Jr. A.L. Checklist	.65
448	Mike Piazza N.L. Checklist	.75
449	Jeff Bagwell N.L. Checklist	.40
450	Frank Thomas, Ken Griffey Jr., Mike Piazza, Jeff Bagwell Insert Checklist	.40

Artist's Proof

	NM/M
Complete Set (450):	300.00
Common Player:	1.00
Stars/Rookies:	10X

(See 1995 Pinnacle for checklist and base card values.)

Museum Collection

	NM/M
Complete Set (450):	200.00
Common Player:	.50

Stars/Rookies:	4X

(See 1995 Pinnacle for checklist and base card values.)

Redemption Card	.25

E.T.A. '95

#	Player	NM/M
	Complete Set (6):	5.00
	Common Player:	.70
1	Ben Grieve	.75
2	Alex Ochoa	.75
3	Joe Vitiello	.75
4	Johnny Damon	3.00
5	Trey Beamon	.75
6	Brooks Kieschnick	.75

FanFest

#	Player	NM/M
	Complete Set (30):	7.50
	Common Player:	.15
1	Cal Ripken Jr.	1.50
2	Roger Clemens	.75
3	Don Mattingly	.75
4	Albert Belle	.15
5	Kirby Puckett	.65
6	Cecil Fielder	.15
7	Kevin Appier	.15
8	Will Clark	.15
9	Juan Gonzalez	.25
10	Ivan Rodriguez	.45
11	Ken Griffey Jr.	1.00
12	Tim Salmon	.15
13	Frank Thomas	.50
14	Roberto Alomar	.20
15	Rickey Henderson	.50
16	Raul Mondesi	.15
17	Matt Williams	.15
18	Ozzie Smith	.65
19	Deion Sanders	.15
20	Tony Gwynn	.65
21	Greg Maddux	.65
22	Sammy Sosa	.65
23	Mike Piazza	1.00
24	Barry Bonds	1.50
25	Jeff Bagwell	.50
26	Len Dykstra	.15
27	Rico Brogna	.15
28	Larry Walker	.15
29	Gary Sheffield	.35
30	Wil Cordero	.15

Gate Attraction

	NM/M
Complete Set (18):	25.00

#	Player	Price
	Common Player:	.50
1	Ken Griffey Jr.	3.50
2	Frank Thomas	1.50
3	Cal Ripken Jr.	5.00
4	Jeff Bagwell	1.50
5	Mike Piazza	3.50
6	Barry Bonds	5.00
7	Kirby Puckett	2.00
8	Albert Belle	.50
9	Tony Gwynn	2.00
10	Raul Mondesi	.50
11	Will Clark	.50
12	Don Mattingly	2.75
13	Roger Clemens	2.75
14	Paul Molitor	1.50
15	Matt Williams	.50
16	Greg Maddux	2.00
17	Kenny Lofton	.50
18	Cliff Floyd	.50

New Blood

#	Player	NM/M
	Complete Set (9):	10.00
	Common Player:	.75
1	Alex Rodriguez	5.00
2	Shawn Green	1.50
3	Brian Hunter	.75
4	Garret Anderson	.75
5	Charles Johnson	.75
6	Chipper Jones	3.00
7	Carlos Delgado	1.50
8	Billy Ashley	.75
9	J.R. Phillips	.75

Performers

#	Player	NM/M
	Complete Set (18):	15.00
	Common Player:	.35
1	Frank Thomas	2.00
2	Albert Belle	.35
3	Barry Bonds	3.50
4	Juan Gonzalez	1.00
5	Andres Galarraga	.35
6	Raul Mondesi	.35

#	Player	Price
7	Paul Molitor	2.00
8	Tim Salmon	.35
9	Mike Piazza	2.50
10	Gregg Jefferies	.35
11	Will Clark	.35
12	Greg Maddux	2.25
13	Manny Ramirez	2.00
14	Kirby Puckett	2.25
15	Shawn Green	1.25
16	Rafael Palmeiro	1.75
17	Paul O'Neill	.35
18	Jason Bere	.35

Team Pinnacle

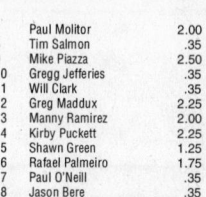

#	Players	NM/M
	Complete Set (9):	35.00
	Common Player:	1.50
1	Mike Mussina, Greg Maddux	8.00
2	Carlos Delgado, Mike Piazza	6.00
3	Frank Thomas, Jeff Bagwell	4.00
4	Roberto Alomar, Craig Biggio	3.00
5	Cal Ripken Jr., Ozzie Smith	12.00
6	Travis Fryman, Matt Williams	1.50
7	Ken Griffey Jr., Barry Bonds	10.00
8	Albert Belle, Dave Justice	1.50
9	Kirby Puckett, Tony Gwynn	8.00

Upstarts

#	Player	NM/M
	Complete Set (30):	10.00
	Common Player:	.15
1	Frank Thomas	1.50
2	Roberto Alomar	.30
3	Mike Piazza	2.50
4	Javier Lopez	.15
5	Albert Belle	.15
6	Carlos Delgado	.75
7	Rusty Greer	.15
8	Tim Salmon	.15
9	Raul Mondesi	.15
10	Juan Gonzalez	.75
11	Manny Ramirez	1.50
12	Sammy Sosa	2.00
13	Jeff Kent	.15
14	Melvin Nieves	.15
15	Rondell White	.15
16	Shawn Green	.75
17	Bernie Williams	.15
18	Aaron Sele	.15
19	Jason Bere	.15
20	Joey Hamilton	.15
21	Mike Kelly	.15
22	Wil Cordero	.15
23	Moises Alou	.15
24	Roberto Kelly	.15
25	Deion Sanders	.15
26	Steve Karsay	.15
27	Bret Boone	.15
28	Willie Greene	.15
29	Billy Ashley	.15
30	Brian Anderson	.15

Red Hot

		NM/M
Complete Set (25):		35.00
Common Player:		.75
1	Cal Ripken Jr.	5.50
2	Ken Griffey Jr.	4.00
3	Frank Thomas	1.50
4	Jeff Bagwell	1.50
5	Mike Piazza	4.00
6	Barry Bonds	5.50
7	Albert Belle	.75
8	Tony Gwynn	2.00
9	Kirby Puckett	2.00
10	Don Mattingly	2.50
11	Matt Williams	.75
12	Greg Maddux	2.00
13	Raul Mondesi	.75
14	Paul Molitor	1.50
15	Manny Ramirez	1.50
16	Joe Carter	.75
17	Will Clark	.75
18	Roger Clemens	2.50
19	Tim Salmon	.75
20	Dave Justice	.75
21	Kenny Lofton	.75
22	Deion Sanders	.75
23	Roberto Alomar	1.00
24	Cliff Floyd	.75
25	Carlos Baerga	.75

White Hot

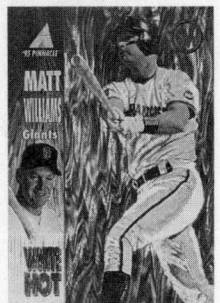

		NM/M
Complete Set (25):		140.00
Common Player:		2.50
1	Cal Ripken Jr.	16.00
2	Ken Griffey Jr.	13.50
3	Frank Thomas	8.00
4	Jeff Bagwell	8.00
5	Mike Piazza	13.50
6	Barry Bonds	16.00
7	Albert Belle	2.50
8	Tony Gwynn	10.00
9	Kirby Puckett	10.00
10	Don Mattingly	12.00
11	Matt Williams	2.50
12	Greg Maddux	10.00
13	Raul Mondesi	2.50
14	Paul Molitor	8.00
15	Manny Ramirez	8.00
16	Joe Carter	2.50
17	Will Clark	2.50
18	Roger Clemens	12.00
19	Tim Salmon	2.50
20	Dave Justice	2.50
21	Kenny Lofton	2.50
22	Deion Sanders	2.50
23	Roberto Alomar	3.50
24	Cliff Floyd	2.50
25	Carlos Baerga	2.50

1996 Pinnacle

	NM/M
Complete Set (400):	15.00
Common Player:	.10
Series 1 or 2 Pack (10):	.75
Series 1 or 2 Box (24):	15.00

RUBEN RIVERA

1	Greg Maddux	1.00
2	Bill Pulsipher	.10
3	Dante Bichette	.10
4	Mike Piazza	1.50
5	Garret Anderson	.10
6	Steve Finley	.10
7	Andy Benes	.10
8	Chuck Knoblauch	.10
9	Tom Gordon	.10
10	Jeff Bagwell	.75
11	Wil Cordero	.10
12	John Mabry	.10
13	Jeff Frye	.10
14	Travis Fryman	.10
15	John Wetteland	.10
16	Jason Bates	.10
17	Danny Tartabull	.10
18	Charles Nagy	.10
19	Robin Ventura	.10
20	Reggie Sanders	.10
21	Dave Clark	.10
22	Jaime Navarro	.10
23	Joey Hamilton	.10
24	Al Leiter	.10
25	Deion Sanders	.10
26	Tim Salmon	.10
27	Tino Martinez	.10
28	Mike Greenwell	.10
29	Phil Plantier	.10
30	Bobby Bonilla	.10
31	Kenny Rogers	.10
32	Chili Davis	.10
33	Joe Carter	.10
34	Mike Mussina	.40
35	Matt Mieske	.10
36	Jose Canseco	.40
37	Brad Radke	.10
38	Juan Gonzalez	.40
39	David Segui	.10
40	Alex Fernandez	.10
41	Jeff Kent	.10
42	Todd Zeile	.10
43	Darryl Strawberry	.10
44	Jose Rijo	.10
45	Ramon Martinez	.10
46	Manny Ramirez	.75
47	Gregg Jefferies	.10
48	Bryan Rekar	.10
49	Jeff King	.10
50	John Olerud	.10
51	Marc Newfield	.10
52	Charles Johnson	.10
53	Robby Thompson	.10
54	Brian Hunter	.10
55	Mike Blowers	.10
56	Keith Lockhart	.10
57	Ray Lankford	.10
58	Tim Wallach	.10
59	Ivan Rodriguez	.65
60	Ed Sprague	.10
61	Paul Molitor	.75
62	Eric Karros	.10
63	Glenallen Hill	.10
64	Jay Bell	.10
65	Tom Pagnozzi	.10
66	Greg Colbrunn	.10
67	Edgar Martinez	.10
68	Paul Sorrento	.10
69	Kirt Manwaring	.10
70	Pete Schourek	.10
71	Orlando Merced	.10
72	Shawon Dunston	.10
73	Ricky Bottalico	.10
74	Brady Anderson	.10
75	Steve Ontiveros	.10
76	Jim Abbott	.10
77	Carl Everett	.10
78	Mo Vaughn	.75
79	Pedro Martinez	.75
80	Harold Baines	.10
81	Alan Trammell	.10
82	Steve Avery	.10
83	Jeff Cirillo	.10
84	John Valentin	.10
85	Bernie Williams	.10
86	Andre Dawson	.30
87	Dave Winfield	.75
88	B.J. Surhoff	.10
89	Jeff Blauser	.10
90	Barry Larkin	.10
91	Cliff Floyd	.10

92	Sammy Sosa	1.00
93	Andres Galarraga	.10
94	Dave Nilsson	.10
95	James Mouton	.10
96	Marquis Grissom	.10
97	Matt Williams	.10
98	John Jaha	.10
99	Don Mattingly	1.25
100	Tim Naehring	.10
101	Kevin Appier	.10
102	Bobby Higginson	.10
103	Andy Pettitte	.25
104	Ozzie Smith	1.00
105	Kenny Lofton	.10
106	Ken Caminiti	.10
107	Walt Weiss	.10
108	Jack McDowell	.10
109	Brian McRae	.10
110	Gary Gaetti	.10
111	Curtis Goodwin	.10
112	Dennis Martinez	.10
113	Omar Vizquel	.10
114	Chipper Jones	1.00
115	Mark Gubicza	.10
116	Ruben Sierra	.10
117	Eddie Murray	.75
118	Chad Curtis	.10
119	Hal Morris	.10
120	Ben McDonald	.10
121	Marty Cordova	.10
122	Ken Griffey Jr.	1.50
123	Gary Sheffield	.40
124	Charlie Hayes	.10
125	Shawn Green	.40
126	Jason Giambi	.50
127	Mark Langston	.10
128	Mark Whiten	.10
129	Greg Vaughn	.10
130	Mark McGwire	1.75
131	Hideo Nomo	.40
132	Eric Karros, Raul Mondesi, Hideo Nomo, Mike Piazza	.50
133	Jason Bere	.10
134	Ken Griffey Jr.	.65
135	Frank Thomas	.40
136	Cal Ripken Jr.	1.00
137	Albert Belle	.10
138	Mike Piazza	.65
139	Dante Bichette	.10
140	Sammy Sosa	.50
141	Mo Vaughn	.10
142	Tim Salmon	.10
143	Reggie Sanders	.10
144	Cecil Fielder	.10
145	Jim Edmonds	.10
146	Rafael Palmeiro	.10
147	Edgar Martinez	.10
148	Barry Bonds	1.00
149	Manny Ramirez	.35
150	Larry Walker	.10
151	Jeff Bagwell	.35
152	Ron Gant	.10
153	Andres Galarraga	.10
154	Eddie Murray	.35
155	Kirby Puckett	.50
156	Will Clark	.10
157	Don Mattingly	.60
158	Mark McGwire	.75
159	Dean Palmer	.10
160	Matt Williams	.10
161	Fred McGriff	.10
162	Joe Carter	.10
163	Juan Gonzalez	.15
164	Alex Ochoa	.10
165	Ruben Rivera	.10
166	Tony Clark	.10
167	Brian Barber	.10
168	Matt Lawton	.10
169	Terrell Wade	.10
170	Johnny Damon	.30
171	Derek Jeter	2.00
172	Phil Nevin	.10
173	Robert Perez	.10
174	C.J. Nitkowski	.10
175	Joe Vitiello	.10
176	Roger Cedeno	.10
177	Ron Coomer	.10
178	Chris Widger	.10
179	Jimmy Haynes	.10
180	Mike Sweeney RC	.50
181	Howard Battle	.10
182	John Wasdin	.10
183	Jim Pittsley	.10
184	Bob Wolcott	.10
185	LaTroy Hawkins	.10
186	Nigel Wilson	.10
187	Dustin Hermanson	.10
188	Chris Snopek	.10
189	Mariano Rivera	.15
190	Jose Herrera	.10
191	Chris Stynes	.10
192	Larry Thomas	.10
193	David Bell	.10
194	Frank Thomas (checklist)	.75
195	Ken Griffey Jr. (checklist)	.65
196	Cal Ripken Jr. (checklist)	.75
197	Jeff Bagwell (checklist)	.35
198	Mike Piazza (checklist)	.60
199	Barry Bonds (checklist)	.75
200	Garret Anderson, Chipper Jones (checklist)	.25
201	Frank Thomas	.75
202	Michael Tucker	.10
203	Kirby Puckett	1.00
204	Alex Gonzalez	.10

205	Tony Gwynn	1.00
206	Moises Alou	.10
207	Albert Belle	.10
208	Barry Bonds	2.00
209	Fred McGriff	.10
210	Dennis Eckersley	.65
211	Craig Biggio	.10
212	David Cone	.10
213	Will Clark	.10
214	Cal Ripken Jr.	2.00
215	Wade Boggs	1.00
216	Pete Schourek	.10
217	Darren Daulton	.10
218	Carlos Baerga	.10
219	Larry Walker	.10
220	Denny Neagle	.10
221	Jim Edmonds	.10
222	Lee Smith	.10
223	Jason Isringhausen	.10
224	Jay Buhner	.10
225	John Olerud	.10
226	Jeff Conine	.10
227	Dean Palmer	.10
228	Jim Abbott	.10
229	Raul Mondesi	.10
230	Tom Glavine	.35
231	Kevin Seitzer	.10
232	Lenny Dykstra	.10
233	Brian Jordan	.10
234	Rondell White	.10
235	Bret Boone	.10
236	Randy Johnson	.75
237	Paul O'Neill	.10
238	Jim Thome	.65
239	Edgardo Alfonzo	.10
240	Terry Pendleton	.10
241	Harold Baines	.10
242	Roberto Alomar	.20
243	Mark Grace	.10
244	Derek Bell	.10
245	Vinny Castilla	.10
246	Cecil Fielder	.10
247	Roger Clemens	1.25
248	Orel Hershiser	.10
249	J.T. Snow	.10
250	Rafael Palmeiro	.65
251	Bret Saberhagen	.10
252	Todd Hollandsworth	.10
253	Ryan Klesko	.10
254	Greg Maddux	.50
255	Ken Griffey Jr.	.65
256	Hideo Nomo	.15
257	Frank Thomas	.40
258	Cal Ripken Jr.	1.00
259	Jeff Bagwell	.35
260	Barry Bonds	1.00
261	Mo Vaughn	.10
262	Albert Belle	.10
263	Sammy Sosa	.50
264	Reggie Sanders	.10
265	Mike Piazza	.65
266	Chipper Jones	.50
267	Tony Gwynn	.50
268	Kirby Puckett	.50
269	Wade Boggs	.45
270	Will Clark	.10
271	Gary Sheffield	.10
272	Dante Bichette	.10
273	Randy Johnson	.35
274	Matt Williams	.10
275	Alex Rodriguez	.75
276	Tim Salmon	.10
277	Johnny Damon	.10
278	Manny Ramirez	.35
279	Derek Jeter	1.00
280	Eddie Murray	.35
281	Ozzie Smith	.50
282	Garret Anderson	.10
283	Raul Mondesi	.10
284	Terry Steinbach	.10
285	Carlos Garcia	.10
286	Dave Justice	.10
287	Eric Anthony	.10
288	Benji Gil	.10
289	Bob Hamelin	.10
290	Dwayne Hosey	.10
291	Andy Pettitte	.25
292	Rod Beck	.10
293	Shane Andrews	.10
294	Julian Tavarez	.10
295	Willie Greene	.10
296	Ismael Valdes	.10
297	Glenallen Hill	.10
298	Troy Percival	.10
299	Ray Durham	.10
300	Jeff Conine	.10
301.8	Ken Griffey Jr.	.75
302	Will Clark	.10
303	Mike Greenwell	.10
304.9	Carlos Baerga	.10
305.3	Paul Molitor	.35
305.6	Jeff Bagwell	.35
306	Mark Grace)	.10
307	Don Mattingly	.60
308	Hal Morris	.10
309	Butch Huskey	.10
310	Ozzie Guillen	.10
311	Erik Hanson	.10
312	Kenny Lofton	.10
313	Edgar Martinez	.10
314	Kurt Abbott	.10
315	John Smoltz	.10
316	Ariel Prieto	.10
317	Mark Carreon	.10
318	Kirby Puckett	.50

319	Carlos Perez	.10
320	Gary DiSarcina	.10
321	Trevor Hoffman	.10
322	Mike Piazza	.65
323	Frank Thomas	.40
324	Juan Acevedo	.10
325	Bip Roberts	.10
326	Javier Lopez	.10
327	Benito Santiago	.10
328	Mark Lewis	.10
329	Royce Clayton	.10
330	Tom Gordon	.10
331	Ben McDonald	.10
332	Dan Wilson	.10
333	Ron Gant	.15
334	Wade Boggs	.45
335	Paul Molitor	.75
336	Tony Gwynn	.50
337	Sean Berry	.10
338	Rickey Henderson	.75
339	Wil Cordero	.10
340	Kent Mercker	.10
341	Kenny Rogers	.10
342	Ryne Sandberg	1.00
343	Charlie Hayes	.10
344	Andy Benes	.10
345	Sterling Hitchcock	.10
346	Bernard Gilkey	.10
347	Julio Franco	.10
348	Ken Hill	.10
349	Russ Davis	.10
350	Mike Blowers	.10
351	B.J. Surhoff	.10
352	Lance Johnson	.10
353	Darryl Hamilton	.10
354	Shawon Dunston	.10
355	Rick Aguilera	.10
356	Danny Tartabull	.10
357	Todd Stottlemyre	.10
358	Mike Bordick	.10
359	Jack McDowell	.10
360	Todd Zeile	.10
361	Tino Martinez	.10
362	Greg Gagne	.10
363	Mike Kelly	.10
364	Tim Raines	.10
365	Ernie Young	.10
366	Mike Stanley	.10
367	Wally Joyner	.10
368	Karim Garcia	.10
369	Paul Wilson	.10
370	Sal Fasano	.10
371	Jason Schmidt	.10
372	Livan Hernandez RC	.25
373	George Arias	.10
374	Steve Gibralter	.10
375	Jermaine Dye	.10
376	Jason Kendall	.10
377	Brooks Kieschnick	.10
378	Jeff Ware	.10
379	Alan Benes	.10
380	Rey Ordonez	.10
381	Jay Powell	.10
382	Osvaldo Fernandez RC	.15
383	Wilton Guerrero RC	.10
384	Eric Owens	.10
385	George Williams	.10
386	Chan Ho Park	.10
387	Jeff Suppan	.10
388	F.P. Santangelo RC	.10
389	Terry Adams	.10
390	Bob Abreu	.10
391	Quinton McCracken RC	.10
392	Mike Busby RC	.10
393	Cal Ripken Jr. (Checklist)	.75
394	Ken Griffey Jr. (Checklist)	.60
395	Frank Thomas (Checklist)	.40
396	Chipper Jones (Checklist)	.50
397	Greg Maddux (Checklist)	.50
398	Mike Piazza (Checklist)	.65
399	Ken Griffey Jr., Frank Thomas, Cal Ripken Jr., Greg Maddux, Chipper Jones, Mike Piazza (Checklist)	.50

Starburst

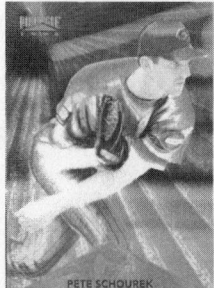

PETE SCHOUREK

	NM/M
Complete Set (200):	150.00
Common Player:	.40
Common Artist's Proof:	.75
Artist's Proofs:	2X

1	Greg Maddux	3.00
2	Bill Pulsipher	.40
3	Dante Bichette	.40
4	Mike Piazza	4.00
5	Garret Anderson	.40
6	Chuck Knoblauch	.40
7	Jeff Bagwell	2.25
8	Wil Cordero	.40
9	Travis Fryman	.40
10	Reggie Sanders	.40
11	Deion Sanders	.40
12	Tim Salmon	.40
13	Tino Martinez	.40
14	Bobby Bonilla	.40
15	Joe Carter	.40
16	Mike Mussina	1.25
17	Jose Canseco	1.25
18	Manny Ramirez	2.25
19	Gregg Jefferies	.40
20	Charles Johnson	.40
21	Brian Hunter	.40
22	Ray Lankford	.40
23	Ivan Rodriguez	2.00
24	Paul Molitor	2.25
25	Eric Karros	.40
26	Edgar Martinez	.40
27	Shawon Dunston	.40
28	Mo Vaughn	.40
29	Pedro Martinez	2.25
30	Marty Cordova	.40
31	Ken Caminiti	.40
32	Gary Sheffield	.75
33	Shawn Green	.75
34	Cliff Floyd	.40
35	Andres Galarraga	.40
36	Matt Williams	.40
37	Don Mattingly	3.50
38	Kevin Appier	.40
39	Ozzie Smith	3.00
40	Kenny Lofton	.40
41	Ken Griffey Jr.	4.00
42	Jack McDowell	.40
43	Gary Gaetti	.40
44	Dennis Martinez	.40
45	Chipper Jones	3.00
46	Eddie Murray	2.25
47	Bernie Williams	.40
48	Andre Dawson	.60
49	Dave Winfield	2.25
50	B.J. Surhoff	.40
51	Barry Larkin	.40
52	Alan Trammell	.40
53	Sammy Sosa	3.00
54	Hideo Nomo	1.00
55	Mark McGwire	4.50
56	Jay Bell	.40
57	Juan Gonzalez	1.00
58	Chili Davis	.40
59	Robin Ventura	.40
60	John Mabry	.40
61	Ken Griffey Jr. (Naturals)	2.00
62	Frank Thomas (Naturals)	1.25
63	Cal Ripken Jr. (Naturals)	3.00
64	Albert Belle (Naturals)	.40
65	Mike Piazza (Naturals)	2.00
66	Dante Bichette (Naturals)	.40
67	Sammy Sosa (Naturals)	1.50
68	Mo Vaughn (Naturals)	.40
69	Tim Salmon (Naturals)	.40
70	Reggie Sanders (Naturals)	.40
71	Cecil Fielder (Naturals)	.40
72	Jim Edmonds (Naturals)	.40
73	Rafael Palmeiro (Naturals)	.75
74	Edgar Martinez (Naturals)	.40
75	Barry Bonds (Naturals)	3.00
76	Manny Ramirez (Naturals)	1.25
77	Larry Walker (Naturals)	.40
78	Jeff Bagwell (Naturals)	1.25
79	Ron Gant (Naturals)	.40
80	Andres Galarraga (Naturals)	.40
81	Eddie Murray (Naturals)	1.25
82	Kirby Puckett (Naturals)	1.50
83	Will Clark (Naturals)	.40
84	Don Mattingly (Naturals)	1.75
85	Mark McGwire (Naturals)	2.25
86	Dean Palmer (Naturals)	.40
87	Matt Williams (Naturals)	.40
88	Fred McGriff (Naturals)	.40
89	Joe Carter (Naturals)	.40
90	Juan Gonzalez (Naturals)	.65
91	Alex Ochoa	.40
92	Ruben Rivera	.40
93	Tony Clark	.40
94	Pete Schourek	.40
95	Terrell Wade	.40
96	Johnny Damon	.65
97	Derek Jeter	6.00
98	Phil Nevin	.40
99	Robert Perez	.40
100	Dustin Hermanson	.40
101	Frank Thomas	2.25
102	Michael Tucker	.40
103	Kirby Puckett	3.00
104	Alex Gonzalez	.40
105	Tony Gwynn	3.00
106	Moises Alou	.40
107	Albert Belle	.40
108	Barry Bonds	6.00
109	Fred McGriff	.40
110	Dennis Eckersley	1.50
111	Craig Biggio	.40
112	David Cone	.40
113	Will Clark	.40
114	Cal Ripken Jr.	6.00
115	Wade Boggs	3.00

116	Pete Schourek	.40
117	Darren Daulton	.40
118	Carlos Baerga	.40
119	Larry Walker	.40
120	Denny Neagle	.40
121	Jim Edmonds	.40
122	Lee Smith	.40
123	Jason Isringhausen	.40
124	Jay Buhner	.40
125	John Olerud	.40
126	Jeff Conine	.40
127	Dean Palmer	.40
128	Jim Abbott	.40
129	Raul Mondesi	.40
130	Tom Glavine	.60
131	Kevin Seitzer	.40
132	Lenny Dykstra	.40
133	Brian Jordan	.40
134	Rondell White	.40
135	Bret Boone	.40
136	Randy Johnson	2.25
137	Paul O'Neill	.40
138	Jim Thome	.75
139	Edgardo Alfonzo	.40
140	Terry Pendleton	.40
141	Harold Baines	.40
142	Roberto Alomar	.45
143	Mark Grace	.40
144	Derek Bell	.40
145	Vinny Castilla	.40
146	Cecil Fielder	.40
147	Roger Clemens	3.50
148	Orel Hershiser	.40
149	J.T. Snow	.40
150	Rafael Palmeiro	1.75
151	Bret Saberhagen	.40
152	Todd Hollandsworth	.40
153	Ryan Klesko	.40
154	Greg Maddux	1.50
155	Ken Griffey Jr.	2.00
156	Hideo Nomo	.65
157	Frank Thomas	1.25
158	Cal Ripken Jr.	3.00
159	Jeff Bagwell	1.25
160	Barry Bonds	3.00
161	Mo Vaughn	.40
162	Albert Belle	.40
163	Sammy Sosa	1.50
164	Reggie Sanders	.40
165	Mike Piazza	2.00
166	Chipper Jones	1.50
167	Tony Gwynn	1.50
168	Kirby Puckett	1.50
169	Wade Boggs	1.25
170	Will Clark	.40
171	Gary Sheffield	.45
172	Dante Bichette	.40
173	Randy Johnson	1.25
174	Matt Williams	.40
175	Alex Rodriguez	4.50
176	Tim Salmon	.40
177	Johnny Damon	.40
178	Manny Ramirez	1.25
179	Derek Jeter	3.00
180	Eddie Murray	1.25
181	Ozzie Smith	1.50
182	Garret Anderson	.40
183	Raul Mondesi	.40
184	Jeff Conine	.40
185	Ken Griffey Jr.	2.00
186	Will Clark	.40
187	Mike Greenwell	.40
188	Carlos Baerga	.40
189	Paul Molitor	1.25
190	Jeff Bagwell	1.25
191	Mark Grace	.40
192	Don Mattingly	1.75
193	Hal Morris	.40
194	Kenny Lofton	.40
195	Edgar Martinez	.40
196	Kirby Puckett	1.50
197	Mike Piazza	2.00
198	Frank Thomas	1.25
199	Wade Boggs	1.25
200	Tony Gwynn	1.50

Artist's Proof

PHIL NEVIN

	NM/M
Common Artist's Proof:	2.00
Stars:	3X

(See 1996 Pinnacle Starburst for checklist and base card values.)

Foil Series 2

	NM/M
Complete Set (200):	15.00
Common Player:	.20
Stars:	1.5X

(See 1996 Pinnacle #201-399 for checklist/base card values.)

Cal Ripken Tribute

	NM/M
1 of 1 Cal Ripken Jr.	5.00

Christie Brinkley Collection

		NM/M
Complete Set (16):		15.00
Common Player:		.75
1	Greg Maddux	3.50
2	Ryan Klesko	.75
3	Dave Justice	.75
4	Tom Glavine	1.50
5	Chipper Jones	4.00
6	Fred McGriff	.75
7	Javier Lopez	.75
8	Marquis Grissom	.75
9	Jason Schmidt	.75
10	Albert Belle	.75
11	Manny Ramirez	2.25
12	Carlos Baerga	.75
13	Sandy Alomar	.75
14	Jim Thome	2.25
15	Julio Franco	.75
16	Kenny Lofton	.75

Essence of the Game

		NM/M
Complete Set (18):		35.00
Common Player:		.75
1	Cal Ripken Jr.	6.00
2	Greg Maddux	3.00
3	Frank Thomas	2.50
4	Matt Williams	.75
5	Chipper Jones	3.00
6	Reggie Sanders	.75

7	Ken Griffey Jr.	4.00
8	Kirby Puckett	3.00
9	Hideo Nomo	1.50
10	Mike Piazza	4.00
11	Jeff Bagwell	2.50
12	Mo Vaughn	.75
13	Albert Belle	.75
14	Tim Salmon	.75
15	Don Mattingly	3.50
16	Will Clark	.75
17	Eddie Murray	2.50
18	Barry Bonds	6.00

First Rate

		NM/M
Complete Set (18):		40.00
Common Player:		1.25
1	Ken Griffey Jr.	5.00
2	Frank Thomas	2.50
3	Mo Vaughn	1.25
4	Chipper Jones	4.00
5	Alex Rodriguez	6.50
6	Kirby Puckett	3.50
7	Gary Sheffield	1.75
8	Matt Williams	1.25
9	Barry Bonds	7.50
10	Craig Biggio	1.25
11	Robin Ventura	1.25
12	Michael Tucker	1.25
13	Derek Jeter	7.50
14	Manny Ramirez	2.50
15	Barry Larkin	1.25
16	Shawn Green	1.75
17	Will Clark	1.25
18	Mark McGwire	6.50

Pinnacle Power

		NM/M
Complete Set (20):		40.00
Common Player:		1.25
1	Frank Thomas	2.50
2	Mo Vaughn	1.25
2p	Mo Vaughn (Promo)	1.50
3	Ken Griffey Jr.	4.50
4	Matt Williams	1.25
5	Barry Bonds	6.00
6	Reggie Sanders	1.25
7	Mike Piazza	4.50
8	Jim Edmonds	1.25
9	Dante Bichette	1.25
10	Sammy Sosa	3.50
11	Jeff Bagwell	2.50
12	Fred McGriff	1.25
13	Albert Belle	1.25
14	Tim Salmon	1.25
15	Joe Carter	1.25
16	Manny Ramirez	2.50
17	Eddie Murray	2.50
18	Cecil Fielder	1.25
19	Larry Walker	1.25
20	Juan Gonzalez	1.75

Project Stardom

		NM/M
Complete Set (18):		35.00
Common Player:		1.00
1	Paul Wilson	1.00

2	Derek Jeter	8.50
3	Karim Garcia	1.00
4	Johnny Damon	2.75
5	Alex Rodriguez	7.50
6	Chipper Jones	8.00
7	Charles Johnson	1.00
8	Bob Abreu	1.25
9	Alan Benes	1.00
10	Richard Hidalgo	1.00
11	Brooks Kieschnick	1.00
12	Garret Anderson	1.00
13	Livan Hernandez	1.00
14	Manny Ramirez	5.00
15	Jermaine Dye	1.00
16	Todd Hollandsworth	1.00
17	Raul Mondesi	1.00
18	Ryan Klesko	1.00

Skylines

		NM/M
Complete Set (18):		375.00
Common Player:		10.00
1	Ken Griffey Jr.	50.00
2	Frank Thomas	30.00
3	Greg Maddux	40.00
4	Cal Ripken Jr.	65.00
5	Albert Belle	10.00
6	Mo Vaughn	10.00
7	Mike Piazza	50.00
8	Wade Boggs	40.00
9	Will Clark	10.00
10	Barry Bonds	65.00
11	Gary Sheffield	10.00
12	Hideo Nomo	25.00
13	Tony Gwynn	40.00
14	Kirby Puckett	40.00
15	Chipper Jones	40.00
16	Jeff Bagwell	30.00
17	Manny Ramirez	30.00
18	Raul Mondesi	10.00

Slugfest

		NM/M
Complete Set (18):		40.00
Common Player:		1.25
1	Frank Thomas	2.75
2	Ken Griffey Jr.	4.00
3	Jeff Bagwell	2.75
4	Barry Bonds	5.00
5	Mo Vaughn	1.25
6	Albert Belle	1.25
7	Mike Piazza	4.00
8	Matt Williams	1.25
9	Dante Bichette	1.25
10	Sammy Sosa	3.00
11	Gary Sheffield	2.00
12	Reggie Sanders	1.25
13	Manny Ramirez	2.75
14	Eddie Murray	2.75
15	Juan Gonzalez	2.25
16	Dean Palmer	1.25
17	Rafael Palmeiro	2.75
18	Cecil Fielder	1.25

Team Pinnacle

		NM/M
Complete Set (9):		35.00
Common Player:		1.50
1	Frank Thomas, Jeff Bagwell	4.00
2	Chuck Knoblauch, Craig Biggio	1.50
3	Jim Thome, Matt Williams	3.00
4	Barry Larkin, Cal Ripken Jr.	12.00
5	Barry Bonds, Tim Salmon	10.00
6	Ken Griffey Jr., Reggie Sanders	8.00
7	Albert Belle, Sammy Sosa	6.00
8	Ivan Rodriguez, Mike Piazza	6.00
9	Greg Maddux, Randy Johnson	8.00

Team Spirit

		NM/M
Complete Set (12):		45.00
Common Player:		1.25
1	Greg Maddux	4.00
2	Ken Griffey Jr.	5.00
3	Derek Jeter	8.00
4	Mike Piazza	5.00
5	Cal Ripken Jr.	8.00
6	Frank Thomas	2.75
7	Jeff Bagwell	2.75
8	Mo Vaughn	1.25
9	Albert Belle	1.25
10	Chipper Jones	4.00
11	Johnny Damon	1.50
12	Barry Bonds	8.00

Team Tomorrow

		NM/M
Complete Set (10):		20.00
Common Player:		.50
1	Ruben Rivera	.50
2	Johnny Damon	1.00
3	Raul Mondesi	.50
4	Manny Ramirez	3.00
5	Hideo Nomo	1.50
6	Chipper Jones	4.00
7	Garret Anderson	.50
8	Alex Rodriguez	5.00
9	Derek Jeter	6.00
10	Karim Garcia	.50

1996 Pinnacle/Aficionado

		NM/M
Complete Set (200):		20.00
Common Player:		.10
Common Artist's Proof:		.50
Artist's Proof Stars:		8X
Pack (5):		1.50
Wax Box (16):		30.00
1	Jack McDowell	.10
2	Jay Bell	.10
3	Rafael Palmeiro	1.25
4	Wally Joyner	.10
5	Ozzie Smith	2.00
6	Mark McGwire	3.00
7	Kevin Seitzer	.10
8	Fred McGriff	.10
9	Roger Clemens	2.25
9s	Roger Clemens (Marked "SAMPLE.")	4.00
10	Randy Johnson	1.50
11	Cecil Fielder	.10
12	David Cone	.10
13	Chili Davis	.10
14	Andres Galarraga	.10
15	Joe Carter	.10
16	Ryne Sandberg	2.00
17	Paul O'Neill	.10
18	Cal Ripken Jr.	4.00
19	Wade Boggs	2.00
20	Greg Gagne	.10
21	Edgar Martinez	.10
22	Greg Maddux	2.00
23	Ken Caminiti	.10
24	Kirby Puckett	2.00
25	Craig Biggio	.10
26	Will Clark	.10
27	Ron Gant	.10
28	Eddie Murray	1.50
29	Lance Johnson	.10
30	Tony Gwynn	2.00
31	Dante Bichette	.10
32	Darren Daulton	.10
33	Danny Tartabull	.10
34	Jeff King	.10
35	Tom Glavine	.40
36	Rickey Henderson	1.50
37	Jose Canseco	1.00
38	Barry Larkin	.10
39	Dennis Martinez	.10
40	Ruben Sierra	.10
41	Bobby Bonilla	.10
42	Jeff Conine	.10
43	Lee Smith	.10
44	Charlie Hayes	.10
45	Walt Weiss	.10
46	Jay Buhner	.10
47	Kenny Rogers	.10
48	Paul Molitor	1.50
49	Hal Morris	.10
50	Todd Stottlemyre	.10
51	Mike Stanley	.10
52	Mark Grace	.10
53	Lenny Dykstra	.10
54	Andre Dawson	.25
55	Dennis Eckersley	1.25
56	Ben McDonald	.10
57	Ray Lankford	.10
58	Mo Vaughn	.10
59	Frank Thomas	1.50
60	Julio Franco	.10
61	Jim Abbott	.10
62	Greg Vaughn	.10
63	Marquis Grissom	.10
64	Tino Martinez	.10
65	Kevin Appier	.10
66	Matt Williams	.10
67	Sammy Sosa	2.00
68	Larry Walker	.10
69	Ivan Rodriguez	1.25
70	Eric Karros	.10
71	Bernie Williams	.10
72	Carlos Baerga	.10
73	Jeff Bagwell	1.50
74	Pete Schourek	.10
75	Ken Griffey Jr.	2.50
76	Bernard Gilkey	.10
77	Albert Belle	.10
78	Chuck Knoblauch	.10
79	John Smoltz	.10
80	Barry Bonds	4.00
81	Vinny Castilla	.10
82	John Olerud	.10
83	Mike Mussina	1.00
84	Alex Fernandez	.10
85	Shawon Dunston	.10
86	Travis Fryman	.10
87	Moises Alou	.10
88	Dean Palmer	.10
89	Gregg Jefferies	.10
90	Jim Thome	1.25
91	Dave Justice	.10

#	Player	Value
92	B.J. Surhoff	.10
93	Ramon Martinez	.10
94	Gary Sheffield	.40
95	Andy Benes	.10
96	Reggie Sanders	.10
97	Roberto Alomar	.35
98	Omar Vizquel	.10
99	Juan Gonzalez	.75
100	Robin Ventura	.10
101	Jason Isringhausen	.10
102	Greg Colbrunn	.10
103	Brian Jordan	.10
104	Shawn Green	.40
105	Brian Hunter	.10
106	Rondell White	.10
107	Ryan Klesko	.10
107s	Ryan Klesko (Marked "SAMPLE.")	1.00
108	Sterling Hitchcock	.10
109	Manny Ramirez	1.50
110	Bret Boone	.10
111	Michael Tucker	.10
112	Julian Tavarez	.10
113	Benji Gil	.10
114	Kenny Lofton	.10
115	Mike Kelly	.10
116	Ray Durham	.10
117	Trevor Hoffman	.10
118	Butch Huskey	.10
119	Phil Nevin	.10
120	Pedro Martinez	1.50
121	Wil Cordero	.10
122	Tim Salmon	.10
123	Jim Edmonds	.10
124	Mike Piazza	2.50
125	Rico Brogna	.10
126	John Mabry	.10
127	Chipper Jones	2.00
128	Johnny Damon	.35
129	Raul Mondesi	.10
130	Denny Neagle	.10
131	Marc Newfield	.10
132	Hideo Nomo	.75
133	Joe Vitiello	.10
134	Garret Anderson	.10
135	Dave Nilsson	.10
136	Alex Rodriguez	3.00
137	Russ Davis	.10
138	Frank Rodriguez	.10
139	Royce Clayton	.10
140	John Valentin	.10
141	Marty Cordova	.10
142	Alex Gonzalez	.10
143	Carlos Delgado	.75
144	Willie Greene	.10
145	Cliff Floyd	.10
146	Bobby Higginson	.10
147	J.T. Snow	.10
148	Derek Bell	.10
149	Edgardo Alfonso	.10
150	Charles Johnson	.10
151	Hideo Nomo	.60
152	Larry Walker	.10
153	Bob Abreu	.10
154	Karim Garcia	.10
155	Dave Nilsson	.10
156	Chan Ho Park	.10
157	Dennis Martinez	.10
158	Sammy Sosa	1.25
159	Rey Ordonez	.10
160	Roberto Alomar	.10
161	George Arias	.10
162	Jason Schmidt	.10
163	Derek Jeter	4.00
164	Chris Snopek	.10
165	Todd Hollandsworth	.10
166	Sal Fasano	.10
167	Jay Powell	.10
168	Paul Wilson	.10
169	Jim Pittsley	.10
170	LaTroy Hawkins	.10
171	Bob Abreu	.10
172	Mike Grace RC	.10
173	Karim Garcia	.10
174	Richard Hidalgo	.10
175	Felipe Crespo	.10
176	Terrell Wade	.10
177	Steve Gibralter	.10
178	Jermaine Dye	.10
179	Alan Benes	.10
180	Wilton Guerrero RC	.10
181	Brooks Kieschnick	.10
182	Roger Cedeno	.10
183	Osvaldo Fernandez RC	.10
184	Matt Lawton RC	.50
185	George Williams	.10
186	Jimmy Haynes	.10
187	Mike Busby RC	.10
188	Chan Ho Park	.10
189	Marc Barcelo	.10
190	Jason Kendall	.10
191	Rey Ordonez	.10
192	Tyler Houston	.10
193	John Wasdin	.10
194	Jeff Suppan	.10
195	Jeff Ware	.10
196	Checklist	.10
197	Checklist	.10
198	Checklist	.10
199	Checklist	.10
200	Checklist	.10

First Pitch Previews

NM/M

Complete Set (200):		250.00
Common Player:		2.00

(Star cards valued at 8-10X regular Aficionado edition.)

Magic Numbers

NM/M

Complete Set (10):		15.50
Common Player:		.75
Samples:		1X
1	Ken Griffey Jr.	3.25
2	Greg Maddux	2.50
3	Frank Thomas	1.50
4	Mo Vaughn	.75
5	Jeff Bagwell	1.50
6	Chipper Jones	2.50
7	Albert Belle	.75
8	Cal Ripken Jr.	4.50
9	Matt Williams	.75
10	Sammy Sosa	2.50

Rivals

NM/M

Complete Set (24):		65.00
Common Player:		2.00
1	Ken Griffey Jr., Frank Thomas	4.00
2	Frank Thomas, Cal Ripken Jr.	4.50
3	Cal Ripken Jr., Mo Vaughn	4.00
4	Mo Vaughn, Ken Griffey Jr.	2.50
5	Ken Griffey Jr., Cal Ripken Jr.	5.00
6	Frank Thomas, Mo Vaughn	2.00
7	Cal Ripken Jr., Ken Griffey Jr.	5.00
8	Mo Vaughn, Frank Thomas	2.00
9	Ken Griffey Jr., Mo Vaughn	2.50
10	Frank Thomas, Ken Griffey Jr.	4.00
11	Cal Ripken Jr., Frank Thomas	4.50
12	Mo Vaughn, Cal Ripken Jr.	4.00
13	Mike Piazza, Jeff Bagwell	2.50
14	Jeff Bagwell, Barry Bonds	4.50
15	Jeff Bagwell, Mike Piazza	2.50
16	Tony Gwynn, Mike Piazza	3.00
17	Mike Piazza, Barry Bonds	5.00
18	Jeff Bagwell, Tony Gwynn	2.00
19	Barry Bonds, Mike Piazza	5.00
20	Tony Gwynn, Jeff Bagwell	2.00
21	Mike Piazza, Tony Gwynn	3.00
22	Barry Bonds, Jeff Bagwell	4.50
23	Tony Gwynn, Barry Bonds	4.50
24	Barry Bonds, Tony Gwynn	4.50

Slick Picks

NM/M

Complete Set (32):		40.00
Common Player:		.50
1	Mike Piazza	2.50
2	Cal Ripken Jr.	4.00
3	Ken Griffey Jr.	2.50
4	Paul Wilson	.50
5	Frank Thomas	1.50
6	Mo Vaughn	.50
7	Barry Bonds	4.00
8	Albert Belle	.50
9	Jeff Bagwell	1.50
10	Dante Bichette	.50
11	Hideo Nomo	.75
12	Raul Mondesi	.50
13	Manny Ramirez	1.50
14	Greg Maddux	2.00
15	Tony Gwynn	2.00
16	Ryne Sandberg	2.00
17	Reggie Sanders	.50
18	Derek Jeter	4.00
19	Johnny Damon	.75
20	Alex Rodriguez	3.00
21	Ryan Klesko	.50
22	Jim Thome	1.50
23	Kenny Lofton	.50
24	Tino Martinez	.50
25	Randy Johnson	1.50
26	Wade Boggs	2.00
27	Juan Gonzalez	.75
28	Kirby Puckett	2.00
29	Tim Salmon	.50
30	Chipper Jones	2.00
31	Garret Anderson	.50
32	Eddie Murray	1.50

1997 Pinnacle

NM/M

Complete Set (200):		10.00
Common Player:		.05
Pack (10):		1.00
Wax Box (24):		12.50
Wax Retail Box (16):		10.00
1	Cecil Fielder	.05
2	Garret Anderson	.05
3	Charles Nagy	.05
4	Darryl Hamilton	.05
5	Greg Myers	.05
6	Eric Davis	.05
7	Jeff Frye	.05
8	Marquis Grissom	.05
9	Curt Schilling	.35
10	Jeff Fassero	.05
11	Alan Benes	.05
12	Orlando Miller	.05
13	Alex Fernandez	.05
14	Andy Pettitte	.25
15	Andre Dawson	.25
16	Mark Grudzielanek	.05
17	Joe Vitiello	.05
18	Juan Gonzalez	.40
19	Mark Whiten	.05
20	Lance Johnson	.05
21	Trevor Hoffman	.05
22	Marc Newfield	.05
23	Jim Eisenreich	.05
24	Joe Carter	.05
25	Jose Canseco	.30
26	Bill Swift	.05
27	Ellis Burks	.05
28	Ben McDonald	.05
29	Edgar Martinez	.05
30	Jamie Moyer	.05

#	Player	Value
31	Chan Ho Park	.05
32	Carlos Delgado	.50
33	Kevin Mitchell	.05
34	Carlos Garcia	.05
35	Darryl Strawberry	.05
36	Jim Thome	.60
37	Jose Offerman	.05
38	Ryan Klesko	.05
39	Ruben Sierra	.05
40	Devon White	.05
41	Brian Jordan	.05
42	Tony Gwynn	.75
43	Rafael Palmeiro	.50
44	Dante Bichette	.05
45	Scott Stahoviak	.05
46	Roger Cedeno	.05
47	Ivan Rodriguez	.50
48	Bob Abreu	.05
49	Darryl Kile	.05
50	Darren Dreifort	.05
51	Shawon Dunston	.05
52	Mark McGwire	1.50
53	Tim Salmon	.05
54	Gene Schall	.05
55	Roger Clemens	.85
56	Rondell White	.05
57	Ed Sprague	.05
58	Craig Paquette	.05
59	David Segui	.05
60	Jaime Navarro	.05
61	Tom Glavine	.35
62	Jeff Brantley	.05
63	Kimera Bartee	.05
64	Fernando Vina	.05
65	Eddie Murray	.65
66	Lenny Dykstra	.05
67	Kevin Elster	.05
68	Vinny Castilla	.05
69	Todd Greene	.05
70	Brett Butler	.05
71	Robby Thompson	.05
72	Reggie Jefferson	.05
73	Todd Hundley	.05
74	Jeff King	.05
75	Ernie Young	.05
76	Jeff Bagwell	.65
77	Dan Wilson	.05
78	Paul Molitor	.65
79	Kevin Seitzer	.05
80	Kevin Brown	.05
81	Ron Gant	.05
82	Dwight Gooden	.05
83	Todd Stottlemyre	.05
84	Ken Caminiti	.05
85	James Baldwin	.05
86	Jermaine Dye	.05
87	Harold Baines	.05
88	Pat Hentgen	.05
89	Frank Rodriguez	.05
90	Mark Johnson	.05
91	Jason Kendall	.05
92	Alex Rodriguez	1.50
93	Alan Trammell	.05
94	Scott Brosius	.05
95	Delino DeShields	.05
96	Chipper Jones	.75
97	Barry Bonds	2.00
98	Brady Anderson	.05
99	Ryne Sandberg	.75
100	Albert Belle	.05
101	Jeff Cirillo	.05
102	Frank Thomas	.65
103	Mike Piazza	1.00
104	Rickey Henderson	.65
105	Rey Ordonez	.05
106	Mark Grace	.05
107	Terry Steinbach	.05
108	Ray Durham	.05
109	Barry Larkin	.05
110	Tony Clark	.05
111	Bernie Williams	.05
112	John Smoltz	.05
113	Moises Alou	.05
114	Alex Gonzalez	.05
115	Rico Brogna	.05
116	Eric Karros	.05
117	Jeff Conine	.05
118	Todd Hollandsworth	.05
119	Troy Percival	.05
120	Paul Wilson	.05
121	Orel Hershiser	.05
122	Ozzie Smith	.75
123	Dave Hollins	.05
124	Ken Hill	.05
125	Rick Wilkins	.05
126	Scott Servais	.05
127	Fernando Valenzuela	.05
128	Mariano Rivera	.15
129	Mark Loretta	.05
130	Shane Reynolds	.05
131	Darren Oliver	.05
132	Steve Trachsel	.05
133	Darren Bragg	.05
134	Jason Dickson	.05
135	Darren Fletcher	.05
136	Gary Gaetti	.05
137	Joey Cora	.05
138	Terry Pendleton	.05
139	Derek Jeter	2.00
140	Danny Tartabull	.05
141	John Flaherty	.05
142	B.J. Surhoff	.05
143	Mark Sweeney	.05
144	Chad Mottola	.05
145	Andujar Cedeno	.05

146	Tim Belcher	.05
147	Mark Thompson	.05
148	Rafael Bournigal	.05
149	Marty Cordova	.05
150	Osvaldo Fernandez	.05
151	Mike Stanley	.05
152	Ricky Bottalico	.05
153	Donnie Wall	.05
154	Omar Vizquel	.05
155	Mike Mussina	.30
156	Brant Brown	.05
157	F.P. Santangelo	.05
158	Ryan Hancock	.05
159	Jeff D'Amico	.05
160	Luis Castillo	.05
161	Darin Erstad	.10
162	Ugueth Urbina	.05
163	Andruw Jones	.65
164	Steve Gibralter	.05
165	Robin Jennings	.05
166	Mike Cameron	.05
167	George Arias	.05
168	Chris Stynes	.05
169	Justin Thompson	.05
170	Jamey Wright	.05
171	Todd Walker	.05
172	Nomar Garciaparra	.75
173	Jose Paniagua	.05
174	Marvin Benard	.05
175	Rocky Coppinger	.05
176	Quinton McCracken	.05
177	Amaury Telemaco	.05
178	Neifi Perez	.05
179	Todd Greene	.05
180	Jason Thompson	.05
181	Wilton Guerrero	.05
182	Edgar Renteria	.05
183	Billy Wagner	.05
184	Alex Ochoa	.05
185	Billy McMillon	.05
186	Kenny Lofton	.05
187	Andres Galarraga (Clout)	.05
188	Chuck Knoblauch (Clout)	.05
189	Greg Maddux (Clout)	.75
190	Mo Vaughn (Clout)	.05
191	Cal Ripken Jr. (Clout)	2.00
192	Hideo Nomo (Clout)	.40
193	Ken Griffey Jr. (Clout)	1.00
194	Sammy Sosa (Clout)	.75
195	Jay Buhner (Clout)	.05
196	Manny Ramirez (Clout)	.65
197	Matt Williams (Clout)	.05
198	Andruw Jones (Checklist)	.30
199	Darin Erstad (Checklist)	.05
200	Trey Beamon (Checklist)	.05

Museum Collection

NM/M
Complete Set (200): 100.00
Common Player: 1.00
Stars/Rookies: 6X
(See 1997 Pinnacle for checklist and regular-issue card values.)

Artist's Proofs

NM/M
Common Bronze (125): 1.00

Bronze Stars: 30X
Common Silver (50): 2.50
Silver Stars: 12X
Common Gold (25): 4.00
Gold Stars: 10X
(See 1997 Pinnacle for checklist and base card values.)

Cardfrontations

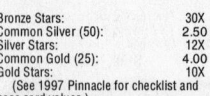

NM/M
Complete Set (20): 35.00
Common Player: .50

1	Greg Maddux, Mike Piazza	3.00
2	Tom Glavine, Ken Caminiti	.75
3	Randy Johnson, Cal Ripken Jr.	5.00
4	Kevin Appier, Mark McGwire	4.00
5	Andy Pettitte, Juan Gonzalez	1.00
6	Pat Hentgen, Albert Belle	.50
7	Hideo Nomo, Chipper Jones	2.00
8	Ismael Valdes, Sammy Sosa	2.50
9	Mike Mussina, Manny Ramirez	1.50
10	David Cone, Jay Buhner	.50
11	Mark Wohlers, Gary Sheffield	.75
12	Alan Benes, Barry Bonds	5.00
13	Roger Clemens, Ivan Rodriguez	2.50
14	Mariano Rivera, Ken Griffey Jr.	3.00
15	Dwight Gooden, Frank Thomas	1.50
16	John Wetteland, Darin Erstad	.50
17	John Smoltz, Brian Jordan	.50
18	Kevin Brown, Jeff Bagwell	1.50
19	Jack McDowell, Alex Rodriguez	4.00
20	Charles Nagy, Bernie Williams	.50

Home/Away

NM/M
Complete Set (12): 65.00
Common Player: 2.00

1	Chipper Jones	5.00
2	Ken Griffey Jr.	6.00
3	Mike Piazza	6.00
4	Frank Thomas	4.00
5	Jeff Bagwell	4.00
6	Alex Rodriguez	8.00
7	Barry Bonds	10.00
8	Mo Vaughn	2.00
9	Derek Jeter	10.00
10	Mark McGwire	8.00
11	Cal Ripken Jr.	10.00
12	Albert Belle	4.00

Passport to the Majors

NM/M
Complete Set (25): 55.00
Common Player: 1.00

1	Greg Maddux	5.00
1s	Greg Maddux ("SAMPLE" overprint.)	4.00
2	Ken Griffey Jr.	6.00
3	Frank Thomas	3.00
4	Cal Ripken Jr.	10.00

5	Mike Piazza	6.00
6	Alex Rodriguez	7.50
7	Mo Vaughn	1.00
8	Chipper Jones	4.00
9	Roberto Alomar	1.00
10	Edgar Martinez	1.00
11	Javier Lopez	1.00
12	Ivan Rodriguez	2.50
13	Juan Gonzalez	1.50
14	Carlos Baerga	1.00
15	Sammy Sosa	4.00
16	Manny Ramirez	3.00
17	Raul Mondesi	1.00
18	Henry Rodriguez	1.00
19	Rafael Palmeiro	2.50
20	Rey Ordonez	1.00
21	Hideo Nomo	1.50
22	Makoto Suzuki	1.00
23	Chan Ho Park	1.00
24	Larry Walker	1.00
25	Ruben Rivera	1.00

Shades

NM/M
Complete Set (10): 15.00
Common Player: .75

1	Ken Griffey Jr.	3.00
2	Juan Gonzalez	1.50
3	John Smoltz	.75
4	Gary Sheffield	1.00
5	Cal Ripken Jr.	5.00
6	Mo Vaughn	.75
7	Brian Jordan	.75
8	Mike Piazza	3.00
9	Frank Thomas	2.25
10	Alex Rodriguez	4.00

Team Pinnacle

NM/M
Complete Set (10): 30.00
Common Player: 1.50

1	Frank Thomas, Jeff Bagwell	4.00
2	Chuck Knoblauch, Eric Young	1.50
3	Ken Caminiti, Jim Thome	3.00
4	Alex Rodriguez, Chipper Jones	6.00
5	Mike Piazza, Ivan Rodriguez	5.00
6	Albert Belle, Barry Bonds	8.00
7	Ken Griffey Jr., Ellis Burks	6.00
8	Juan Gonzalez, Gary Sheffield	3.00
9	John Smoltz, Andy Pettitte	2.00
10	All Players	2.00

1997 Pinnacle Certified

NM/M
Complete Set (150): 30.00
Common Player: .15
Common Certified Red: 1.00
Certified Red Stars: 5X
Common Mirror Red: 3.00
Mirror Red Stars: 12X
Common Mirror Blue: 4.00
Mirror Blue Stars: 15X

Common Mirror Gold: 7.50
Mirror Gold Stars: 35X
Jose Cruz Jr. Redemption: 2.00
Pack (6): 2.00
Wax Box (20): 35.00

1	Barry Bonds	3.00
2	Mo Vaughn	.15
3	Matt Williams	.15
4	Ryne Sandberg	1.25
5	Jeff Bagwell	1.00
6	Alan Benes	.15
7	John Wetteland	.15
8	Fred McGriff	.15
9	Craig Biggio	.15
10	Bernie Williams	.15
11	Brian L. Hunter	.15
12	Sandy Alomar Jr.	.15
13	Ray Lankford	.15
14	Ryan Klesko	.15
15	Jermaine Dye	.15
16	Andy Benes	.15
17	Albert Belle	.15
18	Tony Clark	.15
19	Dean Palmer	.15
20	Bernard Gilkey	.15
21	Ken Caminiti	.15
22	Alex Rodriguez	2.25
23	Tim Salmon	.15
24	Larry Walker	.15
25	Barry Larkin	.15
26	Mike Piazza	1.50
27	Brady Anderson	.15
28	Cal Ripken Jr.	3.00
29	Charles Nagy	.15
30	Paul Molitor	1.00
31	Darin Erstad	.25
32	Rey Ordonez	.15
33	Wally Joyner	.15
34	David Cone	.15
35	Sammy Sosa	1.25
36	Dante Bichette	.15
37	Eric Karros	.15
38	Omar Vizquel	.15
39	Roger Clemens	1.25
40	Joe Carter	.15
41	Frank Thomas	1.00
42	Javier Lopez	.15
43	Mike Mussina	.45
44	Gary Sheffield	.60
45	Tony Gwynn	1.25
46	Jason Kendall	.15
47	Jim Thome	.75
48	Andres Galarraga	.15
49	Mark McGwire	2.25
50	Troy Percival	.15
51	Derek Jeter	3.00
52	Todd Hollandsworth	.15
53	Ken Griffey Jr.	1.50
54	Randy Johnson	1.00
55	Pat Hentgen	.15
56	Rusty Greer	.15
57	John Jaha	.15
58	Kenny Lofton	.15
59	Chipper Jones	1.25
60	Robb Nen	.15
61	Rafael Palmeiro	.75
62	Mariano Rivera	.30
63	Hideo Nomo	.50
64	Greg Vaughn	.15
65	Ron Gant	.15
66	Eddie Murray	1.00
67	John Smoltz	.15
68	Manny Ramirez	1.00
69	Juan Gonzalez	.50
70	F.P. Santangelo	.15
71	Moises Alou	.15
72	Alex Ochoa	.15
73	Chuck Knoblauch	.15
74	Raul Mondesi	.15
75	J.T. Snow	.15
76	Rickey Henderson	1.00
77	Bobby Bonilla	.15
78	Wade Boggs	1.25
79	Ivan Rodriguez	.75
80	Brian Jordan	.15
81	Al Leiter	.15
82	Jay Buhner	.15
83	Greg Maddux	1.25
84	Edgar Martinez	.15
85	Kevin Brown	.15
86	Eric Young	.15
87	Todd Hundley	.15
88	Ellis Burks	.15
89	Marquis Grissom	.15
90	Jose Canseco	.60

91	Henry Rodriguez	.15
92	Andy Pettitte	.45
93	Mark Grudzielanek	.15
94	Dwight Gooden	.15
95	Roberto Alomar	.50
96	Paul Wilson	.15
97	Will Clark	.15
98	Rondell White	.15
99	Charles Johnson	.15
100	Jim Edmonds	.15
101	Jason Giambi	.60
102	Billy Wagner	.15
103	Edgar Renteria	.15
104	Johnny Damon	.45
105	Jason Isringhausen	.15
106	Andruw Jones	1.00
107	Jose Guillen	.15
108	Kevin Orie	.15
109	Brian Giles RC	1.25
110	Danny Patterson	.15
111	Vladimir Guerrero	1.00
112	Scott Rolen	.75
113	Damon Mashore	.15
114	Nomar Garciaparra	1.25
115	Todd Walker	.15
116	Wilton Guerrero	.15
117	Bob Abreu	.25
118	Brooks Kieschnick	.15
119	Pokey Reese	.15
120	Todd Greene	.15
121	Dmitri Young	.15
122	Raul Casanova	.15
123	Glendon Rusch	.15
124	Jason Dickson	.15
125	Jorge Posada	.15
126	Rod Myers RC	.15
127	Bubba Trammell RC	.40
128	Scott Spiezio	.15
129	Hideki Irabu RC	.40
130	Wendell Magee	.15
131	Bartolo Colon	.15
132	Chris Holt	.15
133	Calvin Maduro	.15
134	Ray Montgomery	.15
135	Shannon Stewart	.15
136	Ken Griffey Jr.	1.00
137	Vladimir Guerrero	.50
138	Roger Clemens	.75
139	Mark McGwire	1.25
140	Albert Belle	1.50
141	Derek Jeter	1.50
142	Juan Gonzalez	.25
143	Greg Maddux	.60
144	Alex Rodriguez	1.25
145	Jeff Bagwell	.50
146	Cal Ripken Jr.	1.50
147	Tony Gwynn	.60
148	Frank Thomas	.50
149	Hideo Nomo	.25
150	Andruw Jones	.50

Red

	NM/M
Common Certified Red:	1.00
Certified Red Stars:	5X

(See 1997 Pinnacle Certified for checklist and base values.)

Mirror Red

	NM/M
Common Mirror Red:	3.00
Mirror Red Stars:	12X

(See 1997 Pinnacle Certified for checklist and base values.)

Mirror Blue

	NM/M
Common Mirror Blue:	4.00
Mirror Blue Stars:	15X

(See 1997 Pinnacle Certified for checklist and base values.)

Mirror Gold

	NM/M
Common Mirror Gold:	7.50
Mirror Gold Stars:	35X

(See 1997 Pinnacle Certified for checklist and base values.)

Mirror Black

	NM/M
Common Player:	100.00

(Star cards valued at 150-250X base value.)

Lasting Impression

#	Player	NM/M
	Complete Set (20):	40.00
	Common Player:	1.00
1	Cal Ripken Jr.	7.50
2	Ken Griffey Jr.	5.00
3	Mo Vaughn	1.00
4	Brian Jordan	1.00
5	Mark McGwire	6.00
6	Chuck Knoblauch	1.00
7	Sammy Sosa	3.00
8	Brady Anderson	1.00
9	Frank Thomas	2.00
10	Tony Gwynn	3.00
11	Roger Clemens	4.00
12	Alex Rodriguez	6.00
13	Paul Molitor	2.00
14	Kenny Lofton	1.00
15	John Smoltz	1.00
16	Roberto Alomar	1.50
17	Randy Johnson	2.00
18	Ryne Sandberg	3.00
19	Manny Ramirez	2.00
20	Mike Mussina	1.50

Team

#	Player	NM/M
	Complete Set (20):	30.00
	Common Player:	.50
	Gold:	3X
	Mirror Gold:	15X
	Sample:	1X
1	Frank Thomas	1.50
2	Jeff Bagwell	1.50
3	Derek Jeter	4.00
4	Chipper Jones	2.00
5	Alex Rodriguez	3.00
6	Ken Caminiti	.50
7	Cal Ripken Jr.	4.00
8	Mo Vaughn	.50
9	Ivan Rodriguez	1.00

10	Mike Piazza	2.50
11	Juan Gonzalez	.75
12	Barry Bonds	4.00
13	Ken Griffey Jr.	2.50
14	Andruw Jones	1.50
15	Albert Belle	.50
16	Gary Sheffield	.75
17	Andy Pettitte	.65
18	Hideo Nomo	.75
19	Greg Maddux	2.00
20	John Smoltz	.50

1997 Pinnacle Inside

#	Player	NM/M
	Complete Set (150):	15.00
	Common Player:	.05
	Common Club Edition:	.75
	Club Edition Stars:	5X
	Common Diamond Edition:	5.00
	Diamond Edition Stars:	25X
	Unopened Can (10):	2.00
	Case Cans (48):	60.00
1	David Cone	.05
2	Sammy Sosa	1.00
3	Joe Carter	.05
4	Juan Gonzalez	.40
5	Hideo Nomo	.40
6	Moises Alou	.05
7	Marc Newfield	.05
8	Alex Rodriguez	2.00
9	Kimera Bartee	.05
10	Chuck Knoblauch	.05
11	Jason Isringhausen	.05
12	Jermaine Allensworth	.05
13	Frank Thomas	.75
14	Paul Molitor	.75
15	John Mabry	.05
16	Greg Maddux	1.00
17	Rafael Palmeiro	.65
18	Brian Jordan	.05
19	Ken Griffey Jr.	1.50
20	Brady Anderson	.05
21	Ruben Sierra	.05
22	Travis Fryman	.05
23	Cal Ripken Jr.	2.50
24	Will Clark	.05
25	Todd Hollandsworth	.05
26	Kevin Brown	.05
27	Mike Piazza	1.50
28	Craig Biggio	.05
29	Paul Wilson	.05
30	Andres Galarraga	.05
31	Chipper Jones	1.00
32	Jason Giambi	.65
33	Ernie Young	.05
34	Marty Cordova	.05
35	Albert Belle	.05
36	Roger Clemens	1.25
37	Ryne Sandberg	1.00
38	Henry Rodriguez	.05
39	Jay Buhner	.05
40	Raul Mondesi	.05
41	Jeff Fassero	.05
42	Edgar Martinez	.05
43	Trey Beamon	.05
44	Mo Vaughn	.05
45	Gary Sheffield	.40

46	Ray Durham	.05
47	Brett Butler	.05
48	Ivan Rodriguez	.65
49	Fred McGriff	.05
50	Dean Palmer	.05
51	Rickey Henderson	.75
52	Andy Pettitte	.30
53	Bobby Bonilla	.05
54	Shawn Green	.50
55	Tino Martinez	.05
56	Tony Gwynn	1.00
57	Tom Glavine	.35
58	Eric Young	.05
59	Kevin Appier	.05
60	Barry Bonds	2.50
61	Wade Boggs	1.00
62	Jason Kendall	.05
63	Jeff Bagwell	.75
64	Jeff Conine	.05
65	Greg Vaughn	.05
66	Eric Karros	.05
67	Manny Ramirez	.75
68	John Smoltz	.05
69	Terrell Wade	.05
70	John Wetteland	.05
71	Kenny Lofton	.05
72	Jim Thome	.65
73	Bill Pulsipher	.05
74	Darryl Strawberry	.05
75	Roberto Alomar	.25
76	Bobby Higginson	.05
77	James Baldwin	.05
78	Mark McGwire	2.00
79	Jose Canseco	.40
80	Mark Grudzielanek	.05
81	Ryan Klesko	.05
82	Javier Lopez	.05
83	Ken Caminiti	.05
84	Dave Nilsson	.05
85	Tim Salmon	.05
86	Cecil Fielder	.05
87	Derek Jeter	2.50
88	Garret Anderson	.05
89	Dwight Gooden	.05
90	Carlos Delgado	.50
91	Ugueth Urbina	.05
92	Chan Ho Park	.05
93	Eddie Murray	.75
94	Alex Ochoa	.05
95	Rusty Greer	.05
96	Mark Grace	.05
97	Pat Hentgen	.05
98	John Jaha	.05
99	Charles Johnson	.05
100	Jermaine Dye	.05
101	Quinton McCracken	.05
102	Troy Percival	.05
103	Shane Reynolds	.05
104	Rondell White	.05
105	Charles Nagy	.05
106	Alan Benes	.05
107	Tom Goodwin	.05
108	Ron Gant	.05
109	Dan Wilson	.05
110	Darin Erstad	.10
111	Matt Williams	.05
112	Barry Larkin	.05
113	Mariano Rivera	.15
114	Larry Walker	.05
115	Jim Edmonds	.05
116	Michael Tucker	.05
117	Todd Hundley	.05
118	Alex Fernandez	.05
119	J.T. Snow	.05
120	Ellis Burks	.05
121	Steve Finley	.05
122	Mike Mussina	.40
123	Curtis Pride	.05
124	Derek Bell	.05
125	Dante Bichette	.05
126	Terry Steinbach	.05
127	Randy Johnson	.75
128	Andruw Jones	.75
129	Vladimir Guerrero	.75
130	Ruben Rivera	.05
131	Billy Wagner	.05
132	Scott Rolen	.65
133	Rey Ordonez	.05
134	Karim Garcia	.05
135	George Arias	.05
136	Todd Greene	.05
137	Robin Jennings	.05
138	Raul Casanova	.05
139	Josh Booty	.05
140	Edgar Renteria	.05
141	Chad Mottola	.05
142	Dmitri Young	.05
143	Tony Clark	.05
144	Todd Walker	.05
145	Kevin Brown	.05
146	Nomar Garciaparra	1.00
147	Neifi Perez	.05
148	Derek Jeter, Todd Hollandsworth	.50
149	Pat Hentgen, John Smoltz	.05
150	Juan Gonzalez, Ken Caminiti	.05

Club Edition

	NM/M
Complete Club Edition Set (150):	300.00
Common Club Edition:	.75

Stars: 5X
(See 1997 Pinnacle Inside for check-list and base values.)

Diamond Edition

	NM/M
Common Diamond Edition:	5.00
Stars:	25X

(See 1997 Pinnacle Inside for check-list and base values.)

Cans

		NM/M
Complete Set (24):		10.00
Common Can:		.25
Sealed Cans:		2X
1	Ken Griffey Jr.	.75
2	Juan Gonzalez	.30
3	Frank Thomas	.40
4	Cal Ripken Jr.	1.50
5	Derek Jeter	1.50
6	Andruw Jones	.40
7	Alex Rodriguez	1.00
8	Mike Piazza	.75
9	Mo Vaughn	.25
10	Jeff Bagwell	.40
11	Ken Caminiti	.25
12	Andy Pettitte	.30
13	Barry Bonds	1.50
14	Mark McGwire	1.00
15	Ryan Klesko	.25
16	Manny Ramirez	.40
17	Ivan Rodriguez	.35
18	Chipper Jones	.50
19	Albert Belle	.25
20	Tony Gwynn	.50
21	Kenny Lofton	.25
22	Greg Maddux	.50
23	Hideo Nomo	.40
24	John Smoltz	.25

Dueling Dugouts

		NM/M
Complete Set (20):		65.00
Common Player:		1.25
1	Alex Rodriguez, Cal Ripken Jr.	10.00
2	Jeff Bagwell, Ken Caminiti	3.00
3	Barry Bonds, Albert Belle	10.00
4	Mike Piazza, Ivan Rodriguez	6.00
5	Chuck Knoblauch, Roberto Alomar	1.25
6	Ken Griffey Jr., Andruw Jones	6.00
7	Chipper Jones, Jim Thome	4.00
8	Frank Thomas, Mo Vaughn	3.00
9	Fred McGriff, Mark McGwire	7.50
10	Brian Jordan, Tony Gwynn	4.00
11	Barry Larkin, Derek Jeter	10.00
12	Kenny Lofton, Bernie Williams	1.25
13	Manny Ramirez, Juan Gonzalez	3.00
14	Will Clark, Rafael Palmeiro	2.50
15	Greg Maddux, Roger Clemens	4.50
16	John Smoltz, Andy Pettitte	1.25
17	Mariano Rivera, John Wetteland	1.25
18	Hideo Nomo, Mike Mussina	2.00
19	Todd Hollandsworth, Darin Erstad	1.25
20	Vladimir Guerrero, Karim Garcia	3.00

Fortysomething

		NM/M
Complete Set (16):		50.00
Common Player:		1.00
1	Juan Gonzalez	3.00
2	Barry Bonds	12.00
3	Ken Caminiti	1.00
4	Mark McGwire	10.00
5	Todd Hundley	1.00
6	Albert Belle	1.00
7	Ellis Burks	1.00
8	Jay Buhner	1.00
9	Brady Anderson	1.00
10	Vinny Castilla	1.00
11	Mo Vaughn	1.00
12	Ken Griffey Jr.	7.50
13	Sammy Sosa	6.50
14	Andres Galarraga	1.00
15	Gary Sheffield	2.00
16	Frank Thomas	5.00

1997 Pinnacle Mint Collection

	NM/M
Complete Set (30):	25.00
Common Player:	.25
Silver Cards:	4X
Gold Cards:	6X
Die-Cuts:	50 Percent
Wax Box (24):	25.00

1	Ken Griffey Jr.	2.00
2	Frank Thomas	1.25

3	Alex Rodriguez	2.50
4	Cal Ripken Jr.	3.00
5	Mo Vaughn	.25
6	Juan Gonzalez	.60
7	Mike Piazza	2.00
8	Albert Belle	.25
9	Chipper Jones	1.50
10	Andruw Jones	1.25
11	Greg Maddux	1.50
12	Hideo Nomo	.60
13	Jeff Bagwell	1.25
14	Manny Ramirez	1.25
15	Mark McGwire	2.50
16	Derek Jeter	3.00
17	Sammy Sosa	1.50
18	Barry Bonds	3.00
19	Chuck Knoblauch	.25
20	Dante Bichette	.25
21	Tony Gwynn	1.50
22	Ken Caminiti	.25
23	Gary Sheffield	.60
24	Tim Salmon	.25
25	Ivan Rodriguez	1.00
26	Henry Rodriguez	.25
27	Barry Larkin	.25
28	Ryan Klesko	.25
29	Brian Jordan	.25
30	Jay Buhner	.25

Coins

		NM/M
Complete Set (30):		35.00
Common Brass Coin:		.25
Nickel Coins:		2X
Gold Plated Coins:		6X
Silver Coins:		20X
24K Gold Coins:	Value Undetermined	
1	Ken Griffey Jr.	2.50
2	Frank Thomas	1.50
3	Alex Rodriguez	3.00
4	Cal Ripken Jr.	4.00
5	Mo Vaughn	.25
6	Juan Gonzalez	.75
7	Mike Piazza	2.50
8	Albert Belle	.25
9	Chipper Jones	2.00
10	Andruw Jones	1.50
11	Greg Maddux	2.00
12	Hideo Nomo	.75
13	Jeff Bagwell	1.50
14	Manny Ramirez	1.50
15	Mark McGwire	3.00
16	Derek Jeter	4.00
17	Sammy Sosa	2.00
18	Barry Bonds	4.00
19	Chuck Knoblauch	.25
20	Dante Bichette	.25
21	Tony Gwynn	2.00
22	Ken Caminiti	.25
23	Gary Sheffield	.65
24	Tim Salmon	.25
25	Ivan Rodriguez	1.00
26	Henry Rodriguez	.25
27	Barry Larkin	.25
28	Ryan Klesko	.25
29	Brian Jordan	.25
30	Jay Buhner	.25

1997 Pinnacle X-Press

	NM/M
Complete Set (150):	7.50
Common Player:	.05
Men of Summer:	4X
Pack (8):	.75

Wax Box (24):		10.00
1	Larry Walker	.05
2	Andy Pettitte	.30
3	Matt Williams	.05
4	Juan Gonzalez	.40
5	Frank Thomas	.75
6	Kenny Lofton	.05
7	Ken Griffey Jr.	1.25
8	Andres Galarraga	.05
9	Greg Maddux	1.00
10	Hideo Nomo	.40
11	Cecil Fielder	.05
12	Jose Canseco	.40
13	Tony Gwynn	1.00
14	Eddie Murray	.75
15	Alex Rodriguez	1.50
16	Mike Piazza	1.25
17	Ken Hill	.05
18	Chuck Knoblauch	.05
19	Ellis Burks	.05
20	Rafael Palmeiro	.65
21	Vinny Castilla	.05
22	Rusty Greer	.05
23	Chipper Jones	1.00
24	Rey Ordonez	.05
25	Mariano Rivera	.15
26	Garret Anderson	.05
27	Edgar Martinez	.05
28	Dante Bichette	.05
29	Todd Hundley	.05
30	Barry Bonds	2.00
31	Barry Larkin	.05
32	Derek Jeter	2.00
33	Marquis Grissom	.05
34	David Justice	.05
35	Ivan Rodriguez	.65
36	Jay Buhner	.05
37	Fred McGriff	.05
38	Brady Anderson	.05
39	Tony Clark	.05
40	Eric Young	.05
41	Charles Nagy	.05
42	Mark McGwire	1.50
43	Paul O'Neill	.05
44	Tino Martinez	.05
45	Ryne Sandberg	1.00
46	Bernie Williams	.05
47	Albert Belle	.05
48	Jeff Cirillo	.05
49	Tim Salmon	.05
50	Steve Finley	.05
51	Lance Johnson	.05
52	John Smoltz	.05
53	Javier Lopez	.05
54	Roger Clemens	1.00
55	Kevin Appier	.05
56	Ken Caminiti	.05
57	Cal Ripken Jr.	2.00
58	Moises Alou	.05
59	Marty Cordova	.05
60	David Cone	.05
61	Manny Ramirez	.75
62	Ray Durham	.05
63	Jermaine Dye	.05
64	Craig Biggio	.05
65	Will Clark	.05
66	Omar Vizquel	.05
67	Bernard Gilkey	.05
68	Greg Vaughn	.05
69	Wade Boggs	1.00
70	Dave Nilsson	.05
71	Mark Grace	.05
72	Dean Palmer	.05
73	Sammy Sosa	1.00
74	Mike Mussina	.30
75	Alex Fernandez	.05
76	Henry Rodriguez	.05
77	Travis Fryman	.05
78	Jeff Bagwell	.75
79	Pat Hentgen	.05
80	Gary Sheffield	.40
81	Jim Edmonds	.05
82	Darin Erstad	.10
83	Mark Grudzielanek	.05
84	Jim Thome	.65
85	Bobby Higginson	.05
86	Al Martin	.05
87	Jason Giambi	.50
88	Mo Vaughn	.05
89	Jeff Conine	.05
90	Edgar Renteria	.05
91	Andy Ashby	.05
92	Ryan Klesko	.05
93	John Jaha	.05
94	Paul Molitor	.75
95	Brian Hunter	.05
96	Randy Johnson	.75
97	Joey Hamilton	.05
98	Billy Wagner	.05
99	John Wetteland	.05
100	Jeff Fassero	.05
101	Rondell White	.05

102	Kevin Brown	.05
103	Andy Benes	.05
104	Raul Mondesi	.05
105	Todd Hollandsworth	.05
106	Alex Ochoa	.05
107	Bobby Bonilla	.05
108	Brian Jordan	.05
109	Tom Glavine	.35
110	Ron Gant	.05
111	Jason Kendall	.05
112	Roberto Alomar	.30
113	Troy Percival	.05
114	Michael Tucker	.05
115	Joe Carter	.05
116	Andruw Jones	.75
117	Nomar Garciaparra	1.00
118	Todd Walker	.05
119	Jose Guillen	.05
120	Bubba Trammell RC	.20
121	Wilton Guerrero	.05
122	Bob Abreu	.15
123	Vladimir Guerrero	.75
124	Dmitri Young	.05
125	Kevin Orie	.05
126	Glendon Rusch	.05
127	Brooks Kieschnick	.05
128	Scott Spiezio	.05
129	Brian Giles RC	.75
130	Jason Dickson	.05
131	Damon Mashore	.05
132	Wendell Magee	.05
133	Matt Morris	.05
134	Scott Rolen	.65
135	Shannon Stewart	.05
136	Deivi Cruz RC	.15
137	Hideki Irabu RC	.15
138	Larry Walker (Peak Performers)	.05
139	Ken Griffey Jr.	.65
140	Frank Thomas	.40
141	Ivan Rodriguez	.30
142	Randy Johnson	.40
143	Mark McGwire	.75
144	Tino Martinez	.05
145	Tony Clark	.05
146	Mike Piazza	.50
147	Alex Rodriguez	.75
148	Roger Clemens Checklist	.50
149	Greg Maddux Checklist	.45
150	Hideo Nomo Checklist	.20

Men of Summer

	NM/M
Complete Set (150):	50.00
Common Player:	.25

(See 1997 Pinnacle X-Press for checklist and base card values.)

Stars:	3X

Far & Away

		NM/M
Complete Set (18):		25.00
Common Player:		.50
1	Albert Belle	.50
2	Mark McGwire	4.50
3	Frank Thomas	1.75
4	Mo Vaughn	.50
5	Jeff Bagwell	1.75
6	Juan Gonzalez	1.00
7	Mike Piazza	3.50
8	Andruw Jones	1.75
9	Chipper Jones	2.50
10	Gary Sheffield	1.00
11	Sammy Sosa	2.50
12	Darin Erstad	.75
13	Jay Buhner	.50
14	Ken Griffey Jr.	3.50
15	Ken Caminiti	.50
16	Brady Anderson	.50
17	Manny Ramirez	1.75
18	Alex Rodriguez	4.50

Melting Pot

		NM/M
Complete Set (20):		110.00
Common Player:		1.50
Samples:		1X
1	Jose Guillen	1.50
2	Vladimir Guerrero	8.00
3	Andruw Jones	8.00
4	Larry Walker	1.50
5	Manny Ramirez	8.00
6	Ken Griffey Jr.	10.00
7	Alex Rodriguez	12.00
8	Frank Thomas	8.00
9	Juan Gonzalez	4.00
10	Ivan Rodriguez	6.00
11	Hideo Nomo	4.00
12	Rafael Palmeiro	6.00
13	Dave Nilsson	1.50
14	Nomar Garciaparra	9.00
15	Wilton Guerrero	1.50
16	Sammy Sosa	9.00
17	Edgar Renteria	1.50
18	Cal Ripken Jr.	16.00
19	Derek Jeter	16.00
20	Rey Ordonez	1.50

Metal Works

		NM/M
Complete Set (20):		25.00
Common Player:		.50
Silver:		3X
Gold:		6X
1	Ken Griffey Jr.	2.00
2	Frank Thomas	1.00
3	Andruw Jones	1.00
4	Alex Rodriguez	2.50
5	Derek Jeter	3.00
6	Cal Ripken Jr.	3.00
7	Mike Piazza	2.00
8	Chipper Jones	1.50
9	Juan Gonzalez	.65
10	Greg Maddux	1.50
11	Tony Gwynn	1.50
12	Jeff Bagwell	1.00
13	Albert Belle	.50
14	Mark McGwire	2.50
15	Nomar Garciaparra	1.50
16	Mo Vaughn	.50
17	Andy Pettitte	.65
18	Manny Ramirez	1.00
19	Kenny Lofton	.50
20	Roger Clemens	1.75

Swing for the Fences

		NM/M
Complete Set (60):		20.00
Common Player:		.15
(1)	Sandy Alomar Jr.	.15
(2)	Moises Alou	.15
(3)	Brady Anderson	.15
(4)	Jeff Bagwell	1.00
(5)	Derek Bell	.15
(6)	Jay Bell	.15
(7)	Albert Belle	.15
(8)	Geronimo Berroa	.15
(9)	Dante Bichette	.15
(10)	Barry Bonds	2.50
(11)	Bobby Bonilla	.15
(12)	Jay Buhner	.15
(13)	Ellis Burks	.15
(14)	Ken Caminiti	.15
(15)	Jose Canseco	.40
(16)	Joe Carter	.15
(17)	Vinny Castilla	.15
(18)	Tony Clark	.15
(19)	Carlos Delgado	.50
(20)	Jim Edmonds	.15
(21)	Cecil Fielder	.15
(22)	Andres Galarraga	.15
(23)	Ron Gant	.15
(24)	Bernard Gilkey	.15
(25)	Juan Gonzalez	.50
(26)	Ken Griffey Jr. (AL WINNER)	4.00
(27)	Vladimir Guerrero	1.00
(28)	Todd Hundley	.15
(29)	John Jaha	.15
(30)	Andruw Jones	1.00
(31)	Chipper Jones	1.25
(32)	David Justice	.15
(33)	Jeff Kent	.15
(34)	Ryan Klesko	.15
(35)	Barry Larkin	.15
(36)	Mike Lieberthal	.15
(37)	Javy Lopez	.15
(38)	Edgar Martinez	.15
(39)	Tino Martinez	.15
(40)	Fred McGriff	.15
(41)	Mark McGwire (AL/NL WINNER)	4.00
(42)	Raul Mondesi	.15
(43)	Tim Naehring	.15
(44)	Dave Nillson	.15
(45)	Rafael Palmeiro	.75
(46)	Dean Palmer	.15
(47)	Mike Piazza	1.50
(48)	Cal Ripken Jr.	2.50
(49)	Henry Rodriguez	.15
(50)	Tim Salmon	.15
(51)	Gary Sheffield	.40
(52)	Sammy Sosa	1.25
(53)	Terry Steinbach	.15
(54)	Frank Thomas	1.00
(55)	Jim Thome	.75
(56)	Mo Vaughn	.15
(57)	Larry Walker (NL Winner)	1.25
(58)	Rondell White	.15
(59)	Matt Williams	.15
(60)	Todd Zeile	.15

1998 Pinnacle

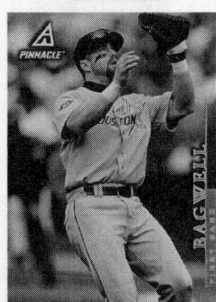

		NM/M
Complete Set (200):		12.50
Common Player:		.05
Pack (10):		1.00
Wax Box (18):		12.00
1	Tony Gwynn/AS	1.00
2	Pedro Martinez/AS	.75
3	Kenny Lofton/AS	.05
4	Curt Schilling/AS	.35
5	Shawn Estes/AS	.05
6	Tom Glavine/AS	.35
7	Mike Piazza/AS	1.50
8	Ray Lankford/AS	.05
9	Barry Larkin/AS	.05
10	Tony Womack/AS	.05
11	Jeff Blauser/AS	.05
12	Rod Beck/AS	.05
13	Larry Walker/AS	.05
14	Greg Maddux/AS	1.00
15	Mark Grace/AS	.05
16	Ken Caminiti/AS	.05
17	Bobby Jones/AS	.05
18	Chipper Jones/AS	1.00
19	Javier Lopez/AS	.05
20	Moises Alou/AS	.05
21	Royce Clayton/AS	.05
22	Darryl Kile/AS	.05
23	Barry Bonds/AS	2.50
24	Steve Finley/AS	.05
25	Andres Galarraga/AS	.05
26	Denny Neagle/AS	.05
27	Todd Hundley/AS	.05
28	Jeff Bagwell	.75
29	Andy Pettitte	.25
30	Darin Erstad	.15
31	Carlos Delgado	.50
32	Matt Williams	.05
33	Will Clark	.05
34	Vinny Castilla	.05
35	Brad Radke	.05
36	John Olerud	.05
37	Andruw Jones	.75
38	Jason Giambi	.50
39	Scott Rolen	.65
40	Gary Sheffield	.40
41	Jimmy Key	.05
42	Kevin Appier	.05
43	Wade Boggs	1.00
44	Hideo Nomo	.40
45	Manny Ramirez	.75
46	Wilton Guerrero	.05
47	Travis Fryman	.05
48	Chili Davis	.05
49	Jeromy Burnitz	.05
50	Craig Biggio	.05
51	Tim Salmon	.05
52	Jose Cruz Jr.	.05
53	Sammy Sosa	1.00
54	Hideki Irabu	.05
55	Chan Ho Park	.05
56	Robin Ventura	.05
57	Jose Guillen	.05
58	Deion Sanders	.05
59	Jose Canseco	.40
60	Jay Buhner	.05
61	Rafael Palmeiro	.65
62	Vladimir Guerrero	.75
63	Mark McGwire	2.00
64	Derek Jeter	2.50
65	Bobby Bonilla	.05
66	Raul Mondesi	.05
67	Paul Molitor	.75
68	Joe Carter	.05
69	Marquis Grissom	.05
70	Juan Gonzalez	.40
71	Kevin Orie	.05
72	Rusty Greer	.05
73	Henry Rodriguez	.05
74	Fernando Tatis	.05
75	John Valentin	.05
76	Matt Morris	.05
77	Ray Durham	.05
78	Geronimo Berroa	.05
79	Scott Brosius	.05
80	Willie Greene	.05
81	Rondell White	.05
82	Doug Drabek	.05
83	Derek Bell	.05
84	Butch Huskey	.05
85	Doug Jones	.05
86	Jeff Kent	.05
87	Jim Edmonds	.05
88	Mark McLemore	.05
89	Todd Zeile	.05
90	Edgardo Alfonzo	.05
91	Carlos Baerga	.05
92	Jorge Fabregas	.05
93	Alan Benes	.05
94	Troy Percival	.05
95	Edgar Renteria	.05
96	Jeff Fassero	.05
97	Reggie Sanders	.05
98	Dean Palmer	.05
99	J.T. Snow	.05
100	Dave Nilsson	.05
101	Dan Wilson	.05
102	Robb Nen	.05
103	Damion Easley	.05
104	Kevin Foster	.05
105	Jose Offerman	.05
106	Steve Cooke	.05
107	Matt Stairs	.05
108	Darryl Hamilton	.05
109	Steve Karsay	.05
110	Gary DiSarcina	.05
111	Dante Bichette	.05
112	Billy Wagner	.05
113	David Segui	.05
114	Bobby Higginson	.05
115	Jeffrey Hammonds	.05
116	Kevin Brown	.05
117	Paul Sorrento	.05
118	Mark Leiter	.05
119	Charles Nagy	.05
120	Danny Patterson	.05

121	Brian McRae	.05
122	Jay Bell	.05
123	Jamie Moyer	.05
124	Carl Everett	.05
125	Greg Colbrunn	.05
126	Jason Kendall	.05
127	Luis Sojo	.05
128	Mike Lieberthal	.05
129	Reggie Jefferson	.05
130	Cal Eldred	.05
131	Orel Hershiser	.05
132	Doug Glanville	.05
133	Willie Blair	.05
134	Neifi Perez	.05
135	Sean Berry	.05
136	Chuck Finley	.05
137	Alex Gonzalez	.05
138	Dennis Eckersley	.65
139	Kenny Rogers	.05
140	Troy O'Leary	.05
141	Roger Bailey	.05
142	Yamil Benitez	.05
143	Wally Joyner	.05
144	Bobby Witt	.05
145	Pete Schourek	.05
146	Terry Steinbach	.05
147	B.J. Surhoff	.15
148	Esteban Loaiza	.05
149	Heathcliff Slocumb	.05
150	Ed Sprague	.05
151	Gregg Jefferies	.05
152	Scott Erickson	.05
153	Jaime Navarro	.05
154	David Wells	.05
155	Alex Fernandez	.05
156	Tim Belcher	.05
157	Mark Grudzielanek	.05
158	Scott Hatteberg	.05
159	Paul Konerko	.15
160	Ben Grieve	.05
161	Abraham Nunez	.05
162	Shannon Stewart	.05
163	Jaret Wright	.05
164	Derrek Lee	.50
165	Todd Dunwoody	.05
166	Steve Woodard RC	.10
167	Ryan McGuire	.05
168	Jeremi Gonzalez	.05
169	Mark Kotsay	.05
170	Brett Tomko	.05
171	Bobby Estalella	.05
172	Livan Hernandez	.05
173	Todd Helton	.75
174	Garrett Stephenson	.05
175	Pokey Reese	.05
176	Tony Saunders	.05
177	Antone Williamson	.05
178	Bartolo Colon	.05
179	Karim Garcia	.05
180	Juan Encarnacion	.05
181	Jacob Cruz	.05
182	Alex Rodriguez	2.00
183	Cal Ripken Jr., Roberto Alomar	1.00
184	Roger Clemens	1.25
185	Derek Jeter	2.00
186	Frank Thomas	.75
187	Ken Griffey Jr.	1.00
188	Mark McGwire	1.00
189	Tino Martinez	.05
190	Larry Walker	.05
191	Brady Anderson	.05
192	Jeff Bagwell	.75
193	Ken Griffey Jr.	1.50
194	Chipper Jones	1.00
195	Ray Lankford	.05
196	Jim Thome	.65
197	Nomar Garciaparra	1.00
198	Checklist	.05
199	Checklist	.05
200	Checklist	.05
9	Ken Griffey Jr./AS (Overprinted "SAMPLE" on back.)	2.00
24	Frank Thomas/AS (Overprinted "SAMPLE" on back.)	2.00

Artist's Proofs

NM/M
Complete Set (100): 375.00
Common Artist's Proof: 1.50

1	Tony Gwynn/AS	12.50
2	Pedro Martinez/AS	10.00
3	Kenny Lofton/AS	1.50
4	Curt Schilling/AS	3.00
5	Shawn Estes/AS	1.50
6	Tom Glavine/AS	3.00
7	Mike Piazza/AS	16.00
8	Ray Lankford/AS	1.50
9	Barry Larkin/AS	1.50
10	Tony Womack/AS	1.50
11	Jeff Blauser/AS	1.50
12	Rod Beck/AS	1.50
13	Larry Walker/AS	1.50
14	Greg Maddux/AS	12.50
15	Mark Grace/AS	1.50
16	Ken Caminiti/AS	1.50
17	Bobby Jones/AS	1.50
18	Chipper Jones/AS	12.50
19	Javier Lopez/AS	1.50
20	Moises Alou/AS	1.50
21	Royce Clayton/AS	1.50
22	Darryl Kile/AS	1.50
23	Barry Bonds/AS	25.00
24	Steve Finley/AS	1.50
25	Andres Galarraga/AS	1.50
26	Denny Neagle/AS	1.50
27	Todd Hundley/AS	1.50
28	Jeff Bagwell	10.00
29	Andy Pettitte	2.50
30	Darin Erstad	2.00
31	Carlos Delgado	4.00
32	Matt Williams	1.50
33	Will Clark	1.50
34	Brad Radke	1.50
35	John Olerud	1.50
36	Andruw Jones	10.00
37	Scott Rolen	7.50
38	Gary Sheffield	3.00
39	Jimmy Key	1.50
40	Wade Boggs	12.50
41	Hideo Nomo	5.00
42	Manny Ramirez	10.00
43	Wilton Guerrero	1.50
44	Travis Fryman	1.50
45	Craig Biggio	1.50
46	Tim Salmon	1.50
47	Jose Cruz Jr.	1.50
48	Sammy Sosa	12.50
49	Hideki Irabu	1.50
50	Jose Guillen	1.50
51	Deion Sanders	1.50
52	Jose Canseco	4.00
53	Jay Buhner	1.50
54	Rafael Palmeiro	7.50
55	Vladimir Guerrero	10.00
56	Mark McGwire	20.00
57	Derek Jeter	25.00
58	Bobby Bonilla	1.50
59	Raul Mondesi	1.50
60	Paul Molitor	10.00
61	Joe Carter	1.50
62	Marquis Grissom	1.50
63	Juan Gonzalez	5.00
64	Dante Bichette	1.50
65	Shannon Stewart (Rookie)	1.50
66	Jaret Wright (Rookie)	1.50
67	Derrek Lee (Rookie)	6.00
68	Todd Dunwoody (Rookie)	1.50
69	Steve Woodard (Rookie)	1.50
70	Ryan McGuire (Rookie)	1.50
71	Jeremi Gonzalez (Rookie)	1.50
72	Mark Kotsay (Rookie)	1.50
73	Brett Tomko (Rookie)	1.50
74	Bobby Estalella (Rookie)	1.50
75	Livan Hernandez (Rookie)	1.50
76	Todd Helton (Rookie)	10.00
77	Garrett Stephenson (Rookie)	1.50
78	Pokey Reese (Rookie)	1.50
79	Tony Saunders (Rookie)	1.50
80	Antone Williamson (Rookie)	1.50
81	Bartolo Colon (Rookie)	1.50
82	Karim Garcia (Rookie)	1.50
83	Juan Encarnacion (Rookie)	1.50
84	Jacob Cruz (Rookie)	1.50
85	Alex Rodriguez	20.00
86	Cal Ripken Jr., Roberto Alomar	15.00
87	Roger Clemens	13.50
88	Derek Jeter	25.00
89	Frank Thomas	10.00
90	Ken Griffey Jr.	16.00
91	Mark McGwire	20.00
92	Tino Martinez	1.50
93	Larry Walker	1.50
94	Brady Anderson	1.50
95	Jeff Bagwell	10.00
96	Ken Griffey Jr.	16.00
97	Chipper Jones	12.50
98	Ray Lankford	1.50
99	Jim Thome	7.50
100	Nomar Garciaparra	12.50

Museum Collection

NM/M
Complete Museum Set (100): 110.00
Common Museum: .50

1	Tony Gwynn/AS	3.00
2	Pedro Martinez/AS	2.50
3	Kenny Lofton/AS	.50
4	Curt Schilling/AS	1.50
5	Shawn Estes/AS	.50
6	Tom Glavine/AS	1.50
7	Mike Piazza/AS	4.00
8	Ray Lankford/AS	.50
9	Barry Larkin/AS	.50
10	Tony Womack/AS	.50
11	Jeff Blauser/AS	.50
12	Rod Beck/AS	.50
13	Larry Walker/AS	.50
14	Greg Maddux/AS	3.00
15	Mark Grace/AS	.50
16	Ken Caminiti/AS	.50
17	Bobby Jones/AS	.50
18	Chipper Jones/AS	3.00
19	Javier Lopez/AS	.50
20	Moises Alou/AS	.50
21	Royce Clayton/AS	.50
22	Darryl Kile/AS	.50
23	Barry Bonds/AS	6.00
24	Steve Finley/AS	.50
25	Andres Galarraga/AS	.50
26	Denny Neagle/AS	.50
27	Todd Hundley/AS	.50
28	Jeff Bagwell	2.50
29	Andy Pettitte	1.00
30	Darin Erstad	1.00
31	Carlos Delgado	1.50
32	Matt Williams	.50
33	Will Clark	.50
34	Brad Radke	.50
35	John Olerud	.50
36	Andruw Jones	2.50
37	Scott Rolen	2.00
38	Gary Sheffield	1.50
39	Jimmy Key	.50
40	Wade Boggs	3.00
41	Hideo Nomo	1.25
42	Manny Ramirez	2.50
43	Wilton Guerrero	.50
44	Travis Fryman	.50
45	Craig Biggio	.50
46	Tim Salmon	.50
47	Jose Cruz Jr.	.50
48	Sammy Sosa	3.00
49	Hideki Irabu	.50
50	Jose Guillen	.50
51	Deion Sanders	.50
52	Jose Canseco	1.50
53	Jay Buhner	.50
54	Rafael Palmeiro	2.00
55	Vladimir Guerrero	2.50
56	Mark McGwire	5.00
57	Derek Jeter	6.00
58	Bobby Bonilla	.50
59	Raul Mondesi	.50
60	Paul Molitor	2.50
61	Joe Carter	.50
62	Marquis Grissom	.50
63	Juan Gonzalez	1.25
64	Dante Bichette	.50
65	Shannon Stewart (Rookie)	.50
66	Jaret Wright (Rookie)	.50
67	Derrek Lee (Rookie)	2.00
68	Todd Dunwoody (Rookie)	.50
69	Steve Woodard (Rookie)	.50
70	Ryan McGuire (Rookie)	.50
71	Jeremi Gonzalez (Rookie)	.50
72	Mark Kotsay (Rookie)	.50
73	Brett Tomko (Rookie)	.50
74	Bobby Estalella (Rookie)	.50
75	Livan Hernandez (Rookie)	.50
76	Todd Helton (Rookie)	2.50
77	Garrett Stephenson (Rookie)	.50
78	Pokey Reese (Rookie)	.50
79	Tony Saunders (Rookie)	.50
80	Antone Williamson (Rookie)	.50
81	Bartolo Colon (Rookie)	.50
82	Karim Garcia (Rookie)	.50
83	Juan Encarnacion (Rookie)	.50
84	Jacob Cruz (Rookie)	.50
85	Alex Rodriguez	5.00
86	Cal Ripken Jr., Roberto Alomar	3.50
87	Roger Clemens	2.50
88	Derek Jeter	6.00
89	Frank Thomas	2.50
90	Ken Griffey Jr.	4.00
91	Mark McGwire	5.00
92	Tino Martinez	.50
93	Larry Walker	.50
94	Brady Anderson	.50
95	Jeff Bagwell	2.50
96	Ken Griffey Jr.	4.00
97	Chipper Jones	3.00
98	Ray Lankford	.50
99	Jim Thome	2.00
100	Nomar Garciaparra	3.00

Press Plates

NM/M
Common Player: 50.00
(See 1998 Pinnacle and inserts for checklists.)

Epix

NM/M
Complete Set (24): 45.00
Common Player: .50
Purples: 2X
Emeralds: 4X

1	Ken Griffey Jr./G	3.00
2	Juan Gonzalez/G	1.25
3	Jeff Bagwell/G	2.00
4	Ivan Rodriguez/G	1.50
5	Nomar Garciaparra/G	2.50
6	Ryne Sandberg/G	2.50
7	Frank Thomas/S	2.00
8	Derek Jeter/S	5.00
9	Tony Gwynn/S	2.50
10	Albert Belle/S	1.00
11	Scott Rolen/S	1.50
12	Barry Larkin/S	1.00
13	Alex Rodriguez/M	4.00
14	Cal Ripken Jr./M	5.00
15	Chipper Jones/M	2.50
16	Roger Clemens/M	2.75
17	Mo Vaughn/M	1.00
18	Mark McGwire/M	4.00
19	Mike Piazza/P	3.00
20	Andruw Jones/P	2.00
21	Greg Maddux/P	2.50
22	Barry Bonds/P	5.00
23	Paul Molitor/P	2.00
24	Eddie Murray/P	2.00

Hit It Here

NM/M
Complete Set (10): 12.00
Common Player: .50
Inserted 1:17

Samples:		1X
1	Larry Walker	.50
2	Ken Griffey Jr.	2.00
3	Mike Piazza	2.00
4	Frank Thomas	1.50
5	Barry Bonds	3.00
6	Albert Belle	.50
7	Tino Martinez	.50
8	Mark McGwire	2.50
9	Juan Gonzalez	.75
10	Jeff Bagwell	1.00

Spellbound

		NM/M
Complete Set (50):		90.00
Common Card:		.75
Inserted 1:17		
1	Mark McGwire/M	3.50
2	Mark McGwire/C	3.50
3	Mark McGwire/G	3.50
4	Mark McGwire/W	3.50
5	Mark McGwire/I	3.50
6	Mark McGwire/R	3.50
7	Mark McGwire/E	3.50
8	Roger Clemens/R	2.50
9	Roger Clemens/O	2.50
10	Roger Clemens/C	2.50
11	Roger Clemens/K	2.50
12	Roger Clemens/E	2.50
13	Roger Clemens/Y	2.50
14	Frank Thomas/B	1.50
15	Frank Thomas/I	1.50
16	Frank Thomas/G	1.50
17	Frank Thomas/H	1.50
18	Frank Thomas/U	1.50
19	Frank Thomas/S	1.50
20	Frank Thomas/T	1.50
21	Scott Rolen/R	1.25
22	Scott Rolen/O	1.25
23	Scott Rolen/L	1.25
24	Scott Rolen/E	1.25
25	Scott Rolen/N	1.25
26	Ken Griffey Jr./G	3.00
27	Ken Griffey Jr./R	3.00
28	Ken Griffey Jr./I	3.00
29	Ken Griffey Jr./F	3.00
30	Ken Griffey Jr./F	3.00
31	Ken Griffey Jr./E	3.00
32	Ken Griffey Jr./Y	3.00
33	Larry Walker/W	.75
34	Larry Walker/A	.75
35	Larry Walker/L	.75
36	Larry Walker/K	.75
37	Larry Walker/E	.75
38	Larry Walker/R	.75
39	Nomar Garciaparra/N	2.25
40	Nomar Garciaparra/O	2.25
41	Nomar Garciaparra/M	2.25
42	Nomar Garciaparra/A	2.25
43	Nomar Garciaparra/R	2.25
44	Cal Ripken Jr./C	4.50
45	Cal Ripken Jr./A	4.50
46	Cal Ripken Jr./L	4.50
47	Tony Gwynn/T	2.25
48	Tony Gwynn/O	2.25
49	Tony Gwynn/N	2.25
50	Tony Gwynn/Y	2.25

1998 Pinnacle Inside

		NM/M
Complete Set (150):		12.00
Common Player:		.05
Club Edition (1:7):		4X
Diamond Edition (1:67):		10X
Can (10):		1.00
Box (48):		45.00
1	Darin Erstad	.15
2	Derek Jeter	2.50
3	Alex Rodriguez	2.00
4	Bobby Higginson	.05
5	Nomar Garciaparra	1.00
6	Kenny Lofton	.05
7	Ivan Rodriguez	.65
8	Cal Ripken Jr.	2.50
9	Todd Hundley	.05
10	Chipper Jones	1.00
11	Barry Larkin	.05
12	Roberto Alomar	.15
13	Mo Vaughn	1.00
14	Sammy Sosa	1.00
15	Sandy Alomar Jr.	.05
16	Albert Belle	.05
17	Scott Rolen	.65
18	Pokey Reese	.05
19	Ryan Klesko	.05
20	Andres Galarraga	.05
21	Justin Thompson	.05
22	Gary Sheffield	.40
23	David Justice	.05
24	Ken Griffey Jr.	1.50
25	Andruw Jones	.75
26	Jeff Bagwell	.75
27	Vladimir Guerrero	.75
28	Mike Piazza	1.50
29	Chuck Knoblauch	.05
30	Rondell White	.05
31	Greg Maddux	1.00
32	Andy Pettitte	.20
33	Larry Walker	.05
34	Bobby Estalella	.05
35	Frank Thomas	.75
36	Tony Womack	.05
37	Tony Gwynn	1.00
38	Barry Bonds	2.50
39	Randy Johnson	.75
40	Mark McGwire	2.00
41	Juan Gonzalez	.40
42	Tim Salmon	.05
43	John Smoltz	.05
44	Rafael Palmeiro	.65
45	Mark Grace	.05
46	Mike Cameron	.05
47	Jim Thome	.65
48	Neifi Perez	.05
49	Kevin Brown	.05
50	Craig Biggio	.05
51	Bernie Williams	.05
52	Hideo Nomo	.40
53	Bob Abreu	.15
54	Edgardo Alfonzo	.05
55	Wade Boggs	1.00
56	Jose Guillen	.05
57	Ken Caminiti	.05
58	Paul Molitor	.75
59	Shawn Estes	.05
60	Edgar Martinez	.05
61	Livan Hernandez	.05
62	Ray Lankford	.05
63	Rusty Greer	.05
64	Jim Edmonds	.35
65	Tom Glavine	.35
66	Alan Benes	.05
67	Will Clark	.05
68	Garret Anderson	.05
69	Javier Lopez	.05
70	Mike Mussina	.35
71	Kevin Orie	.05
72	Matt Williams	.05
73	Bobby Bonilla	.05
74	Ruben Rivera	.05
75	Jason Giambi	.60
76	Todd Walker	.05
77	Tino Martinez	.05
78	Matt Morris	.05
79	Fernando Tatis	.05
80	Todd Greene	.05
81	Fred McGriff	.05
82	Brady Anderson	.05
83	Mark Kotsay	.05
84	Raul Mondesi	.05
85	Moises Alou	.05
86	Roger Clemens	1.25
87	Wilton Guerrero	.05
88	Shannon Stewart	.05
89	Chan Ho Park	.05
90	Carlos Delgado	.60
91	Jose Cruz Jr.	.35
92	Shawn Green	.35
93	Robin Ventura	.05
94	Reggie Sanders	.05
95	Orel Hershiser	.05
96	Dante Bichette	.05
97	Charles Johnson	.05
98	Pedro Martinez	.75
99	Mariano Rivera	.15
100	Joe Randa	.05
101	Jeff Kent	.05
102	Jay Buhner	.05
103	Brian Jordan	.05
104	Jason Kendall	.05
105	Scott Spiezio	.05
106	Desi Relaford	.05
107	Bernard Gilkey	.05
108	Manny Ramirez	.75
109	Tony Clark	.05
110	Eric Young	.05
111	Johnny Damon	.30
112	Glendon Rusch	.05
113	Ben Grieve	.05
114	Homer Bush	.05
115	Miguel Tejada	.25
116	Lou Collier	.05
117	Derrek Lee	.60
118	Jacob Cruz	.05
119	Raul Ibanez	.05
120	Ryan McGuire	.05
121	Antone Williamson	.05
122	Abraham Nunez	.05
123	Jeff Abbott	.05
124	Brett Tomko	.05
125	Richie Sexson	.05
126	Todd Helton	.75
127	Juan Encarnacion	.05
128	Richard Hidalgo	.05
129	Paul Konerko	.10
130	Brad Fullmer	.05
131	Jeremi Gonzalez	.05
132	Jaret Wright	.05
133	Derek Jeter	1.25
134	Frank Thomas	.40
135	Nomar Garciaparra	.50
136	Kenny Lofton	.05
137	Jeff Bagwell	.40
138	Todd Hundley	.05
139	Alex Rodriguez	1.00
140	Ken Griffey Jr.	.75
141	Sammy Sosa	.50
142	Greg Maddux	.50
143	Albert Belle	.05
144	Cal Ripken Jr.	1.25
145	Mark McGwire	1.00
146	Chipper Jones	.50
147	Charles Johnson	.05
148	Ken Griffey Jr. Checklist	.75
149	Jose Cruz Jr. Checklist	.05
150	Larry Walker Checklist	.05

Club Edition

	NM/M
Complete Set (150):	50.00
Common Player:	2.00
Stars:	4X
Inserted 1:7	

(See 1998 Pinnacle Inside for checklist and base card values.)

Diamond Edition

	NM/M
Common Card:	6.00
Stars:	10X
Inserted 1:67	

(See 1998 Pinnacle Inside for checklist and base card values.)

Behind the Numbers

	NM/M
Complete Set (20):	85.00
Common Player:	1.50

Inserted 1:23		
1	Ken Griffey Jr.	7.50
2	Cal Ripken Jr.	12.00
3	Alex Rodriguez	10.00
4	Jose Cruz Jr.	1.50
5	Mike Piazza	7.50
6	Nomar Garciaparra	5.50
7	Scott Rolen	2.50
8	Andruw Jones	4.00
9	Frank Thomas	4.00
10	Mark McGwire	10.00
11	Ivan Rodriguez	3.00
12	Greg Maddux	5.50
13	Roger Clemens	6.50
14	Derek Jeter	12.00
15	Tony Gwynn	5.50
16	Ben Grieve	1.50
17	Jeff Bagwell	4.00
18	Chipper Jones	6.00
19	Hideo Nomo	2.00
20	Sandy Alomar Jr.	1.50

Cans

		NM/M
Complete Set (23):		15.00
Common Can:		.40
Gold Cans:		2X
1	Ken Griffey Jr.	1.25
2	Frank Thomas	.65
3	Alex Rodriguez	1.50
4	Andruw Jones	.65
5	Mike Piazza	1.25
6	Ben Grieve	.40
7	Hideo Nomo	.50
8	Vladimir Guerrero	.65
9	Roger Clemens	1.00
10	Tony Gwynn	.75
11	Mark McGwire	1.50
12	Cal Ripken Jr.	2.00
13	Jose Cruz Jr.	.40
14	Greg Maddux	.75
15	Chipper Jones	.75
16	Derek Jeter	2.00
17	Juan Gonzalez	.50
18	Nomar Garciaparra (AL ROY)	1.00
19	Scott Rolen (NL ROY)	.65
20	Florida Marlins World Series Winner	.40
21	Larry Walker (NL MVP)	.40
22	Tampa Bay Devil Rays	.40
23	Arizona Diamondbacks	.40

Stand Up Guys

		NM/M
Complete Set (50):		35.00
Common Card:		.25
Sample:		3X
1-A/B	Ken Griffey Jr., Cal Ripken Jr.	2.00
1-C/D	Tony Gwynn, Mike Piazza	1.25
2-A/B	Andruw Jones, Alex Rodriguez	1.50

2-C/D	Scott Rolen,	
	Nomar Garciaparra	1.00
3-A/B	Andruw Jones,	
	Greg Maddux	1.00
3-C/D	Javy Lopez,	
	Chipper Jones	1.00
4-A/B	Jay Buhner,	
	Randy Johnson	.75
4-C/D	Ken Griffey Jr.,	
	Alex Rodriguez	1.50
5-A/B	Frank Thomas,	
	Jeff Bagwell	.75
5-C/D	Mark McGwire,	
	Mo Vaughn	1.50
6-A/B	Nomar Garciaparra,	
	Derek Jeter	2.00
6-C/D	Alex Rodriguez,	
	Barry Larkin	1.50
7-A/B	Mike Piazza,	
	Ivan Rodriguez	1.25
7-C/D	Charles Johnson,	
	Javy Lopez	.25
8-A/B	Cal Ripken Jr.,	
	Chipper Jones	2.00
8-C/D	Ken Caminiti,	
	Scott Rolen	.65
9-A/B	Jose Cruz Jr.,	
	Vladimir Guerrero	.75
9-C/D	Andruw Jones,	
	Jose Guillen	.75
10-A/B	Larry Walker,	
	Dante Bichette	.25
10-C/D	Ellis Burks, Neifi Perez	.25
11-A/B	Juan Gonzalez,	
	Sammy Sosa	1.00
11-C/D	Vladimir Guerrero,	
	Manny Ramirez	.75
12-A/B	Greg Maddux,	
	Roger Clemens	1.00
12-C/D	Hideo Nomo,	
	Randy Johnson	.75
13-A/B	Ben Grieve, Paul Konerko	.40
13-C/D	Jose Cruz Jr.,	
	Fernando Tatis	.25
14-A/B	Ryne Sandberg,	
	Chuck Knoblauch	1.00
14-C/D	Roberto Alomar,	
	Craig Biggio	.35
15-A/B	Cal Ripken Jr.,	
	Brady Anderson	2.00
15-C/D	Rafael Palmeiro,	
	Roberto Alomar	.65
16-A/B	Darin Erstad,	
	Jim Edmonds	.35
16-C/D	Tim Salmon,	
	Garret Anderson	.25
17-A/B	Mike Piazza,	
	Hideo Nomo	1.25
17-C/D	Raul Mondesi,	
	Eric Karros	.25
18-A/B	Ivan Rodriguez,	
	Juan Gonzalez	.65
18-C/D	Will Clark, Rusty Greer	.25
19-A/B	Derek Jeter,	
	Bernie Williams	2.00
19-C/D	Tino Martinez,	
	Andy Pettitte	.25
20-A/B	Kenny Lofton,	
	Ken Griffey Jr.	1.25
20-C/D	Brady Anderson,	
	Bernie Williams	.25
21-A/B	Paul Molitor,	
	Eddie Murray	.75
21-C/D	Ryne Sandberg,	
	Rickey Henderson	1.00
22-A/B	Tony Clark,	
	Frank Thomas	.75
22-C/D	Jeff Bagwell,	
	Mark McGwire	1.50
23-A/B	Manny Ramirez,	
	Jim Thome	.75
23-C/D	David Justice,	
	Sandy Alomar Jr.	.25
24-A/B	Barry Bonds,	
	Albert Belle	2.00
24-C/D	Jeff Bagwell,	
	Dante Bichette	.60
25-A/B	Ken Griffey Jr.,	
	Frank Thomas	1.25
25-C/D	Alex Rodriguez,	
	Andruw Jones	1.50

1998 Pinnacle Mint Collection

	NM/M
Complete Set (30):	10.00
Common Die-Cut:	.25
Bronze (1:1H):	2X
Silver (1:15H):	5X
Gold (1:47):	12X
Pack (3+2):	1.00
Wax Box (24):	12.00
1 Jeff Bagwell	.65
2 Albert Belle	.25
3 Barry Bonds	2.00
4 Tony Clark	.25
5 Roger Clemens	1.00
6 Juan Gonzalez	.35
7 Ken Griffey Jr.	1.25
8 Tony Gwynn	.75
9 Derek Jeter	2.00
10 Randy Johnson	.65
11 Chipper Jones	.75
12 Greg Maddux	.75
13 Tino Martinez	.25
14 Mark McGwire	1.50
15 Hideo Nomo	.35
16 Andy Pettitte	.25
17 Mike Piazza	1.25
18 Cal Ripken Jr.	2.00
19 Alex Rodriguez	1.50
20 Ivan Rodriguez	.50
21 Sammy Sosa	.75
22 Frank Thomas	.65
23 Mo Vaughn	.25
24 Larry Walker	.25
25 Jose Cruz Jr.	.25
26 Nomar Garciaparra	.75
27 Vladimir Guerrero	.65
28 Livan Hernandez	.25
29 Andruw Jones	.65
30 Scott Rolen	.50

Coins

	NM/M
Complete Set (30):	20.00
Common Brass Coin:	.50
Brass Proof (500):	5X
Nickel (1:41):	3X
Nickel Proof (250):	12X
Silver:	12X
Inserted 1:288 H, 1:960 R	
Gold Plated (1:199):	15X
Gold Proof (100):	20X
1 Jeff Bagwell	.75
2 Albert Belle	.50
3 Barry Bonds	2.00
4 Tony Clark	.50
5 Roger Clemens	1.50
6 Juan Gonzalez	.50
7 Ken Griffey Jr.	1.50
8 Tony Gwynn	1.00
9 Derek Jeter	2.00
10 Randy Johnson	1.00
11 Chipper Jones	1.00
12 Greg Maddux	1.50
13 Tino Martinez	.50
14 Mark McGwire	1.50
15 Hideo Nomo	.50
16 Andy Pettitte	.75
17 Mike Piazza	1.00
18 Cal Ripken Jr.	2.00
19 Alex Rodriguez	2.00
20 Ivan Rodriguez	.75
21 Sammy Sosa	.75
22 Frank Thomas	.75
23 Mo Vaughn	.50
24 Larry Walker	.50
25 Jose Cruz Jr.	.50
26 Nomar Garciaparra	.75
27 Vladimir Guerrero	.75
28 Livan Hernandez	.50
29 Andruw Jones	.75
30 Scott Rolen	.75

Mint Gems

	NM/M
Complete Set (6)	20.00
Common Player:	2.00
Coins:	1X
1 Ken Griffey Jr.	6.00
2 Larry Walker	2.00
3 Roger Clemens	5.00
4 Pedro Martinez	4.00
5 Nomar Garciaparra	4.50
6 Scott Rolen	3.00

1998 Pinnacle Performers

	NM/M
Complete Set (150):	12.00
Common Player:	.05
Peak Performers (1:7):	2X
Pack (10):	1.00
Wax Box (24):	15.00
1 Ken Griffey Jr.	1.00
2 Frank Thomas	.75
3 Cal Ripken Jr.	1.50
4 Alex Rodriguez	1.25
5 Greg Maddux	.75
6 Mike Piazza	1.00
7 Chipper Jones	.75
8 Tony Gwynn	.75
9 Derek Jeter	1.50
10 Jeff Bagwell	.65
11 Juan Gonzalez	.35
12 Nomar Garciaparra	.75
13 Andruw Jones	.65
14 Hideo Nomo	.35
15 Roger Clemens	.85
16 Mark McGwire	1.25
17 Scott Rolen	.60
18 Vladimir Guerrero	.65
19 Barry Bonds	1.50
20 Darin Erstad	.15
21 Albert Belle	.05
22 Kenny Lofton	.05
23 Mo Vaughn	.05
24 Tony Clark	.05
25 Ivan Rodriguez	.60
26 Jose Cruz Jr.	.05
27 Larry Walker	.05
28 Jaret Wright	.05
29 Andy Pettitte	.05
30 Roberto Alomar	.20
31 Randy Johnson	.65
32 Manny Ramirez	.65
33 Paul Molitor	.65
34 Mike Mussina	.35
35 Jim Thome	.60
36 Tino Martinez	.05
37 Gary Sheffield	.45
38 Chuck Knoblauch	.05
39 Bernie Williams	.05
40 Tim Salmon	.05
41 Sammy Sosa	.75
42 Wade Boggs	.75
43 Will Clark	.05
44 Andres Galarraga	.05
45 Raul Mondesi	.05
46 Rickey Henderson	.65
47 Jose Canseco	.45
48 Pedro Martinez	.65

49	Jay Buhner	.05
50	Ryan Klesko	.05
51	Barry Larkin	.05
52	Charles Johnson	.05
53	Tom Glavine	.35
54	Edgar Martinez	.05
55	Fred McGriff	.05
56	Moises Alou	.05
57	Dante Bichette	.05
58	Jim Edmonds	.05
59	Mark Grace	.05
60	Chan Ho Park	.05
61	Justin Thompson	.05
62	John Smoltz	.05
63	Craig Biggio	.05
64	Ken Caminiti	.05
65	Richard Hidalgo	.05
66	Carlos Delgado	.50
67	David Justice	.05
68	J.T. Snow	.05
69	Jason Giambi	.50
70	Garret Anderson	.05
71	Rondell White	.05
72	Matt Williams	.05
73	Brady Anderson	.05
74	Eric Karros	.05
75	Javier Lopez	.05
76	Pat Hentgen	.05
77	Todd Hundley	.05
78	Ray Lankford	.05
79	Denny Neagle	.05
80	Sandy Alomar Jr.	.05
81	Jason Kendall	.05
82	Omar Vizquel	.05
83	Kevin Brown	.05
84	Kevin Appier	.05
85	Al Martin	.05
86	Rusty Greer	.05
87	Bobby Bonilla	.05
88	Shawn Estes	.05
89	Rafael Palmeiro	.60
90	Edgar Renteria	.05
91	Alan Benes	.05
92	Bobby Higginson	.05
93	Mark Grudzielanek	.05
94	Jose Guillen	.05
95	Neifi Perez	.05
96	Jeff Abbott	.05
97	Todd Walker	.05
98	Eric Young	.05
99	Brett Tomko	.05
100	Mike Cameron	.05
101	Karim Garcia	.05
102	Brian Jordan	.05
103	Jeff Suppan	.05
104	Robin Ventura	.05
105	Henry Rodriguez	.05
106	Shannon Stewart	.05
107	Kevin Orie	.05
108	Bartolo Colon	.05
109	Bob Abreu	.15
110	Vinny Castilla	.05
111	Livan Hernandez	.05
112	Derek Lee	.50
113	Mark Kotsay	.05
114	Todd Greene	.05
115	Edgardo Alfonzo	.05
116	A.J. Hinch	.05
117	Paul Konerko	.15
118	Todd Helton	.65
119	Miguel Tejada	.20
120	Fernando Tatis	.05
121	Ben Grieve	.05
122	Travis Lee	.05
123	Kerry Wood	.25
124	Eli Marrero	.05
125	David Ortiz	.05
126	Juan Encarnacion	.05
127	Brad Fullmer	.05
128	Richie Sexson	.05
129	Aaron Boone	.05
130	Enrique Wilson	.05
131	Javier Valentin	.05
132	Abraham Nunez	.05
133	Ricky Ledee	.05
134	Carl Pavano	.05
135	Bobby Estalella	.05
136	Homer Bush	.05
137	Brian Rose	.05
138	Ken Griffey Jr.	.50
139	Frank Thomas	.35
140	Cal Ripken Jr.	.75
141	Alex Rodriguez	.65
142	Greg Maddux	.40
143	Chipper Jones	.40
144	Mike Piazza	.50
145	Tony Gwynn	.40
146	Derek Jeter	.75
147	Jeff Bagwell	.35
148	Hideo Nomo Checklist	.20
149	Roger Clemens Checklist	.45
150	Greg Maddux Checklist	.35

Big Bang

	NM/M
Complete Set (20):	27.50
Common Player:	.50
Production 2,500 Sets	
Sample:	1X
1 Ken Griffey Jr.	2.50
2 Frank Thomas	1.50
3 Mike Piazza	2.50
4 Chipper Jones	2.00
5 Alex Rodriguez	3.00
6 Nomar Garciaparra	2.00
7 Jeff Bagwell	1.50
8 Cal Ripken Jr.	3.50

9	Albert Belle	.50
10	Mark McGwire	3.00
11	Juan Gonzalez	.75
12	Larry Walker	.50
13	Tino Martinez	.50
14	Jim Thome	1.00
15	Manny Ramirez	1.50
16	Barry Bonds	3.50
17	Mo Vaughn	.50
18	Jose Cruz Jr.	.50
19	Tony Clark	.50
20	Andruw Jones	1.50

Big Bang Seasonal Outburst

		NM/M
Complete Set (20):		500.00
Common Player:		10.00
#'d to player's 1997 HR total		
Unnumbered:		25 Percent
1	Ken Griffey Jr./56	40.00
2	Frank Thomas/35	20.00
3	Mike Piazza/40	40.00
4	Chipper Jones/21	65.00
5	Alex Rodriguez/23	75.00
6	Nomar Garciaparra/30	40.00
7	Jeff Bagwell/43	20.00
8	Cal Ripken Jr./17	80.00
9	Albert Belle/30	10.00
10	Mark McGwire/58	65.00
11	Juan Gonzalez/42	12.50
12	Larry Walker/49	10.00
13	Tino Martinez/44	10.00
14	Jim Thome/40	15.00
15	Manny Ramirez/26	25.00
16	Barry Bonds/40	75.00
17	Mo Vaughn/35	10.00
18	Jose Cruz Jr./26	10.00
19	Tony Clark/32	10.00
20	Andruw Jones/18	25.00

Launching Pad

Peak Performers

	NM/M
Complete Set (150):	100.00
Common Player:	2.00
Stars:	6X
Inserted 1:7	

(See 1998 Pinnacle Performers for checklist and base card values.)

Power Trip

		NM/M
Complete Set (10):		16.00
Common Player:		1.00
Production 10,000 Sets		
1	Frank Thomas	1.00
2	Alex Rodriguez	3.00
3	Nomar Garciaparra	1.50
4	Jeff Bagwell	1.00
5	Cal Ripken Jr.	4.00
6	Mike Piazza	2.00
7	Chipper Jones	1.50
8	Ken Griffey Jr.	2.00
9	Mark McGwire	3.00
10	Juan Gonzalez	1.00

Swing for the Fences

		NM/M
Complete Set (50):		24.00
Common Player:		.25
Inserted 1:1		
1	Brady Anderson	.25
2	Albert Belle	.25
3	Jay Buhner	.25
4	Jose Canseco	.50
5	Tony Clark	.25
6	Jose Cruz Jr.	.25
7	Jim Edmonds	.25
8	Cecil Fielder	.25
9	Travis Fryman	.25
10	Nomar Garciaparra	1.00
11	Juan Gonzalez	.40

12	Ken Griffey Jr.	1.50
13	David Justice	.25
14	Travis Lee	.25
15	Edgar Martinez	.25
16	Tino Martinez	.25
17	Rafael Palmeiro	.65
18	Manny Ramirez	.75
19	Cal Ripken Jr.	2.50
20	Alex Rodriguez	2.00
21	Tim Salmon	.25
22	Frank Thomas	.75
23	Jim Thome	.65
24	Mo Vaughn	.25
25	Bernie Williams	.25
26	Fred McGriff	.25
27	Jeff Bagwell	.75
28	Dante Bichette	.25
29	Barry Bonds	2.50
30	Ellis Burks	.25
31	Ken Caminiti	.25
32	Vinny Castilla	.25
33	Andres Galarraga	.25
34	Vladimir Guerrero	.75
35	Todd Helton	.75
36	Todd Hundley	.25
37	Andruw Jones	.75
38	Chipper Jones	1.00
39	Eric Karros	.25
40	Ryan Klesko	.25
41	Ray Lankford	.25
42	Mark McGwire	2.00
43	Raul Mondesi	.25
44	Mike Piazza	1.50
45	Scott Rolen	.65
46	Gary Sheffield	.50
47	Sammy Sosa	1.00
48	Larry Walker	.25
49	Matt Williams	.25
50	WILDCARD	

1998 Pinnacle Plus

		NM/M
Complete Set (200):		12.00
Common Player:		.05
Pack (10):		1.00
Wax Box (20):		12.00
1	Roberto Alomar/AS	.20
2	Sandy Alomar Jr./AS	.05
3	Brady Anderson/AS	.05
4	Albert Belle/AS	.05
5	Jeff Cirillo/AS	.05
6	Roger Clemens/AS	1.25
7	David Cone/AS	.05
8	Nomar Garciaparra/AS	1.00
9	Ken Griffey Jr./AS	1.50
10	Jason Dickson/AS	.05
11	Edgar Martinez/AS	.05
12	Tino Martinez/AS	.05
13	Randy Johnson/AS	.75
14	Mark McGwire/AS	2.00
15	David Justice/AS	.05
16	Mike Mussina/AS	.40
17	Chuck Knoblauch/AS	.05
18	Joey Cora/AS	.05
19	Pat Hentgen/AS	.05
20	Randy Myers/AS	.05
21	Cal Ripken Jr./AS	2.50
22	Mariano Rivera/AS	.15
23	Jose Rosado/AS	.05
24	Frank Thomas/AS	.75
25	Alex Rodriguez/AS	2.00
26	Justin Thompson/AS	.05
27	Ivan Rodriguez/AS	.65
28	Bernie Williams/AS	.05
29	Pedro Martinez/AS	.05
30	Tony Clark	.05
31	Garret Anderson	.05
32	Travis Fryman	.05
33	Mike Piazza	1.50
34	Carl Pavano	.05
35	Kevin Millwood **RC**	1.00
36	Miguel Tejada	.20
37	Willie Blair	.05
38	Devon White	.05
39	Andres Galarraga	.05
40	Barry Larkin	.05
41	Al Leiter	.05
42	Moises Alou	.05
43	Eric Young	.05
44	John Jaha	.05
45	Bernard Gilkey	.05

46	Freddy Garcia	.05
47	Ruben Rivera	.05
48	Robb Nen	.05
49	Ray Lankford	.05
50	Kenny Lofton	.05
51	Joe Carter	.05
52	Jason McDonald	.05
53	Quinton McCracken	.05
54	Kerry Wood	.50
55	Mike Lansing	.05
56	Chipper Jones	1.00
57	Barry Bonds	2.50
58	Brad Fullmer	.05
59	Jeff Bagwell	.75
60	Rondell White	.05
61	Geronimo Berroa	.05
62	Magglio Ordonez **RC**	1.50
63	Dwight Gooden	.05
64	Brian Hunter	.05
65	Todd Walker	.05
66	Frank Catalanotto **RC**	.05
67	Tony Saunders	.05
68	Travis Lee	.05
69	Michael Tucker	.05
70	Reggie Sanders	.05
71	Derrek Lee	.50
72	Larry Walker	.05
73	Marquis Grissom	.05
74	Craig Biggio	.05
75	Kevin Brown	.05
76	J.T. Snow	.05
77	Eric Davis	.05
78	Jeff Abbott	.05
79	Jermaine Dye	.05
80	Otis Nixon	.05
81	Curt Schilling	.35
82	Enrique Wilson	.05
83	Tony Gwynn	1.00
84	Orlando Cabrera	.05
85	Ramon Martinez	.05
86	Greg Vaughn	.05
87	Alan Benes	.05
88	Dennis Eckersley	.65
89	Jim Thome	.65
90	Juan Encarnacion	.05
91	Jeff King	.05
92	Shannon Stewart	.05
93	Roberto Hernandez	.05
94	Raul Ibanez	.05
95	Darryl Kile	.05
96	Charles Johnson	.05
97	Rich Becker	.05
98	Hal Morris	.05
99	Ismael Valdes	.05
100	Orel Hershiser	.05
101	Mo Vaughn	.05
102	Aaron Boone	.05
103	Jeff Conine	.05
104	Paul O'Neill	.05
105	Tom Candiotti	.05
106	Wilson Alvarez	.05
107	Mike Stanley	.05
108	Carlos Delgado	.50
109	Tony Batista	.05
110	Dante Bichette	.05
111	Henry Rodriguez	.05
112	Karim Garcia	.05
113	Shane Reynolds	.05
114	Ken Caminiti	.05
115	Jose Silva	.05
116	Juan Gonzalez	.40
117	Brian Jordan	.05
118	Jim Leyritz	.05
119	Manny Ramirez	.75
120	Fred McGriff	.05
121	Brooks Kieschnick	.05
122	Sean Casey	.15
123	John Smoltz	.05
124	Rusty Greer	.05
125	Cecil Fielder	.05
126	Mike Cameron	.05
127	Reggie Jefferson	.05
128	Bobby Higginson	.05
129	Kevin Appier	.05
130	Robin Ventura	.05
131	Ben Grieve	.05
132	Wade Boggs	1.00
133	Jose Cruz Jr.	.05
134	Jeff Suppan	.05
135	Vinny Castilla	.05
136	Sammy Sosa	1.00
137	Mark Wohlers	.05
138	Jay Bell	.05
139	Brett Tomko	.05
140	Gary Sheffield	.40
141	Tim Salmon	.05
142	Jaret Wright	.05
143	Kenny Rogers	.05
144	Brian Anderson	.05
145	Darrin Fletcher	.05
146	John Flaherty	.05
147	Dmitri Young	.05
148	Andruw Jones	.75
149	Matt Williams	.05
150	Bobby Bonilla	.05
151	Mike Hampton	.05
152	Al Martin	.05
153	Mark Grudzielanek	.05
154	Dave Nilsson	.05
155	Roger Cedeno	.05
156	Greg Maddux	1.00
157	Mark Kotsay	.05
158	Steve Finley	.05
159	Wilson Delgado	.05
160	Ron Gant	.05

161	Jim Edmonds	.05
162	Jeff Blauser	.05
163	Dave Burba	.05
164	Pedro Astacio	.05
165	Livan Hernandez	.05
166	Neifi Perez	.05
167	Ryan Klesko	.05
168	Fernando Tatis	.05
169	Richard Hidalgo	.05
170	Carlos Perez	.05
171	Bob Abreu	.15
172	Francisco Cordova	.05
173	Todd Helton	.75
174	Doug Glanville	.05
175	Brian Rose	.05
176	Yamil Benitez	.05
177	Darin Erstad	.15
178	Scott Rolen	.60
179	John Wetteland	.05
180	Paul Sorrento	.05
181	Walt Weiss	.05
182	Vladimir Guerrero	.75
183	Ken Griffey Jr.	.75
184	Alex Rodriguez	1.00
185	Cal Ripken Jr.	1.25
186	Frank Thomas	.40
187	Chipper Jones	.50
188	Hideo Nomo	.20
189	Nomar Garciaparra	.60
190	Mike Piazza	1.00
191	Greg Maddux	.50
192	Tony Gwynn	.50
193	Mark McGwire	1.00
194	Roger Clemens	.65
195	Mike Piazza	.75
196	Mark McGwire	1.00
197	Chipper Jones	.50
198	Larry Walker	.05
199	Hideo Nomo	.20
200	Barry Bonds	1.25

Artist's Proofs

		NM/M
Complete Set (60):		150.00
Common Player:		.75
Inserted 1:35		
Golds:		10X
Production 100 Sets		
1	Roberto Alomar/AS	1.50
2	Albert Belle/AS	.75
3	Roger Clemens/AS	8.00
4	Nomar Garciaparra/AS	7.50
5	Ken Griffey Jr./AS	10.00
6	Tino Martinez/AS	.75
7	Randy Johnson/AS	6.00
8	Mark McGwire/AS	12.50
9	David Justice/AS	.75
10	Chuck Knoblauch/AS	.75
11	Cal Ripken Jr./AS	15.00
12	Frank Thomas/AS	6.00
13	Alex Rodriguez/AS	12.50
14	Ivan Rodriguez/AS	5.00
15	Bernie Williams/AS	.75
16	Pedro Martinez	6.00
17	Tony Clark	.75
18	Mike Piazza	10.00
19	Miguel Tejada	1.00
20	Andres Galarraga	.75
21	Barry Larkin	.75
22	Kenny Lofton	.75
23	Chipper Jones	7.50
24	Barry Bonds	15.00
25	Brad Fullmer	.75
26	Jeff Bagwell	6.00
27	Todd Walker	.75
28	Travis Lee	.75
29	Larry Walker	.75
30	Craig Biggio	.75
31	Tony Gwynn	7.50
32	Jim Thome	5.00
33	Juan Encarnacion	.75
34	Mo Vaughn	.75
35	Karim Garcia	.75
36	Ken Caminiti	.75
37	Juan Gonzalez	3.00
38	Manny Ramirez	6.00
39	Fred McGriff	.75
40	Rusty Greer	.75
41	Bobby Higginson	.75
42	Ben Grieve	.75
43	Wade Boggs	7.50

44	Jose Cruz Jr.	.75
45	Sammy Sosa	7.50
46	Gary Sheffield	2.00
47	Tim Salmon	.75
48	Jaret Wright	.75
49	Andruw Jones	6.00
50	Matt Williams	.75
51	Greg Maddux	7.50
52	Jim Edmonds	.75
53	Livan Hernandez	.75
54	Neifi Perez	.75
55	Fernando Tatis	.75
56	Richard Hidalgo	.75
57	Todd Helton	6.00
58	Darin Erstad	1.50
59	Scott Rolen	5.00
60	Vladimir Guerrero	6.00

A Piece of the Game

		NM/M
Complete Set (10):		8.00
Common Player:		.50
Inserted 1:19		
1	Ken Griffey Jr.	1.00
2	Frank Thomas	.65
3	Alex Rodriguez	1.50
4	Chipper Jones	.75
5	Cal Ripken Jr.	2.00
6	Mike Piazza	1.00
7	Greg Maddux	.75
8	Juan Gonzalez	.50
9	Nomar Garciaparra	.75
10	Larry Walker	.50

Epix All-Star Moment

		NM/M
Complete Set (12):		25.00
Common Player:		1.00
Purples:		1.5X
Emeralds:		2.5X
Inserted 1:21		
13	Alex Rodriguez	3.50
14	Cal Ripken Jr.	5.00
15	Chipper Jones	2.50
16	Roger Clemens	2.75
17	Mo Vaughn	1.00
18	Mark McGwire	3.50
19	Mike Piazza	3.00
20	Andruw Jones	2.00
21	Greg Maddux	2.50
22	Barry Bonds	5.00
23	Paul Molitor	2.00
24	Hideo Nomo	1.50

Lasting Memories

		NM/M
Complete Set (30):		16.00
Common Player:		.25
Inserted 1:5		
1	Nomar Garciaparra	.75
2	Ken Griffey Jr.	1.00
3	Livan Hernandez	.25
4	Hideo Nomo	.40
5	Ben Grieve	.25
6	Scott Rolen	.50
7	Roger Clemens	.85
8	Cal Ripken Jr.	2.00
9	Mo Vaughn	.25

10	Frank Thomas	.65
11	Mark McGwire	1.50
12	Barry Larkin	.25
13	Matt Williams	.25
14	Jose Cruz Jr.	.25
15	Andruw Jones	.65
16	Mike Piazza	1.00
17	Jeff Bagwell	.65
18	Chipper Jones	.75
19	Juan Gonzalez	.40
20	Kenny Lofton	.25
21	Greg Maddux	.75
22	Ivan Rodriguez	.50
23	Alex Rodriguez	1.50
24	Derek Jeter	2.00
25	Albert Belle	.25
26	Barry Bonds	2.00
27	Larry Walker	.25
28	Sammy Sosa	.75
29	Tony Gwynn	.75
30	Randy Johnson	.65

Team Pinnacle

		NM/M
Complete Set (15):		50.00
Common Player:		1.50
Inserted 1:71		
Golds:		2X
Inserted 1:199		
1	Mike Piazza, Ivan Rodriguez	6.00
2	Mark McGwire, Mo Vaughn	5.00
3	Roberto Alomar, Craig Biggio	2.00
4	Alex Rodriguez, Barry Larkin	8.00
5	Cal Ripken Jr., Chipper Jones	10.00
6	Ken Griffey Jr., Larry Walker	6.00
7	Juan Gonzalez, Tony Gwynn	4.00
8	Albert Belle, Barry Bonds	3.00
9	Kenny Lofton, Andruw Jones	3.00
10	Tino Martinez, Jeff Bagwell	3.00
11	Frank Thomas, Andres Galarraga	3.00
12	Roger Clemens, Greg Maddux	8.00
13	Pedro Martinez, Hideo Nomo	4.00
14	Nomar Garciaparra, Scott Rolen	5.00
15	Ben Grieve, Paul Konerko	1.50

Yardwork

		NM/M
Complete Set (15):		12.50
Common Player:		.35
Inserted 1:9		
1	Mo Vaughn	.35
2	Frank Thomas	.75
3	Albert Belle	.35
4	Nomar Garciaparra	1.00
5	Tony Clark	.35
6	Tino Martinez	.35
7	Ken Griffey Jr.	1.50
8	Juan Gonzalez	.60
9	Sammy Sosa	1.00
10	Jose Cruz Jr.	.35
11	Jeff Bagwell	.75

12	Mike Piazza	1.50
13	Larry Walker	.35
14	Mark McGwire	2.00
15	Barry Bonds	2.50

2001 Playoff Absolute Memorabilia

		NM/M
Complete Set (200):		
Common Player:		.25
Common SP (151-200):		5.00
Production 700		
Pack (6):		8.00
Box (18) w/baseball:		150.00
1	Alex Rodriguez	2.50
2	Barry Bonds	3.00
3	Cal Ripken Jr.	3.00
4	Chipper Jones	1.50
5	Derek Jeter	3.00
6	Troy Glaus	1.00
7	Frank Thomas	1.00
8	Greg Maddux	1.50
9	Ivan Rodriguez	.75
10	Jeff Bagwell	1.00
11	Ryan Dempster	.25
12	Todd Helton	1.00
13	Ken Griffey Jr.	2.00
14	Manny Ramirez	1.00
15	Mark McGwire	2.50
16	Mike Piazza	2.00
17	Nomar Garciaparra	2.00
18	Pedro Martinez	1.00
19	Randy Johnson	1.00
20	Rick Ankiel	.50
21	Rickey Henderson	1.00
22	Roger Clemens	1.75
23	Sammy Sosa	2.00
24	Tony Gwynn	2.00
25	Vladimir Guerrero	1.00
26	Kazuhiro Sasaki	.25
27	Roberto Alomar	.50
28	Barry Zito	.50
29	Pat Burrell	.50
30	Harold Baines	.25
31	Carlos Delgado	.65
32	J.D. Drew	.50
33	Jim Edmonds	.25
34	Darin Erstad	.50
35	Jason Giambi	.75
36	Tom Glavine	.50
37	Juan Gonzalez	1.00
38	Mark Grace	.35
39	Shawn Green	.50
40	Tim Hudson	.50
41	Andruw Jones	1.00
42	David Justice	.25
43	Jeff Kent	.25
44	Barry Larkin	.25
45	Rafael Furcal	.25
46	Mike Mussina	.50
47	Hideo Nomo	1.00
48	Rafael Palmeiro	.75
49	Adam Piatt	.25
50	Scott Rolen	.75
51	Gary Sheffield	.50
52	Bernie Williams	.35
53	Bob Abreu	.25

54 Edgardo Alfonzo .25
55 Edgar Renteria .25
56 Phil Nevin .25
57 Craig Biggio .25
58 Andres Galarraga .25
59 Edgar Martinez .25
60 Fred McGriff .25
61 Magglio Ordonez .25
62 Jim Thome .75
63 Matt Williams .25
64 Kerry Wood .65
65 Moises Alou .25
66 Brady Anderson .25
67 Garret Anderson .25
68 Russell Branyan .25
69 Tony Batista .25
70 Vernon Wells .25
71 Carlos Beltran .60
72 Adrian Beltre .25
73 Kris Benson .25
74 Lance Berkman .25
75 Kevin Brown .25
76 Dee Brown .25
77 Jeromy Burnitz .25
78 Timoniel Perez .25
79 Sean Casey .40
80 Luis Castillo .25
81 Eric Chavez .35
82 Jeff Cirillo .25
83 Bartolo Colon .25
84 David Cone .25
85 Freddy Garcia .25
86 Johnny Damon .40
87 Ray Durham .25
88 Jermaine Dye .25
89 Juan Encarnacion .25
90 Terrence Long .25
91 Carl Everett .25
92 Steve Finley .25
93 Cliff Floyd .25
94 Brad Fullmer .25
95 Brian Giles .25
96 Luis Gonzalez .35
97 Rusty Greer .25
98 Jeffrey Hammonds .25
99 Mike Hampton .25
100 Orlando Hernandez .25
101 Richard Hidalgo .25
102 Geoff Jenkins .25
103 Jacque Jones .25
104 Brian Jordan .25
105 Gabe Kapler .25
106 Eric Karros .25
107 Jason Kendall .25
108 Adam Kennedy .25
109 Deion Sanders .25
110 Ryan Klesko .25
111 Chuck Knoblauch .25
112 Paul Konerko .25
113 Carlos Lee .25
114 Kenny Lofton .25
115 Javy Lopez .25
116 Tino Martinez .25
117 Ruben Mateo .25
118 Kevin Millwood .25
119 Jimmy Rollins .25
120 Raul Mondesi .25
121 Trot Nixon .25
122 John Olerud .25
123 Paul O'Neill .25
124 Chan Ho Park .25
125 Andy Pettitte .35
126 Jorge Posada .25
127 Mark Quinn .25
128 Aramis Ramirez .25
129 Mariano Rivera .25
130 Tim Salmon .35
131 Curt Schilling .50
132 Richie Sexson .25
133 John Smoltz .25
134 J.T. Snow .25
135 Jay Payton .25
136 Shannon Stewart .25
137 B.J. Surhoff .25
138 Mike Sweeney .25
139 Fernando Tatis .25
140 Miguel Tejada .35
141 Jason Varitek .25
142 Greg Vaughn .25
143 Mo Vaughn .25
144 Robin Ventura .25
145 Jose Vidro .25
146 Omar Vizquel .25
147 Larry Walker .25
148 David Wells .25
149 Rondell White .25
150 Preston Wilson .25
151 Bud Smith **RC** 5.00
152 Cory Aldridge **RC** 5.00
153 Wilmy Caceres **RC** 5.00
154 Josh Beckett 6.00
155 Wilson Betemit **RC** 10.00
156 Jason Michaels **RC** 5.00
157 Albert Pujols **RC** 100.00
158 Andres Torres **RC** 5.00
159 Jack Wilson **RC** 8.00
160 Alex Escobar 5.00
161 Ben Sheets 5.00
162 Rafael Soriano **RC** 10.00
163 Nate Frese **RC** 5.00
164 Carlos Garcia **RC** 5.00
165 Brandon Larson **RC** 5.00
166 Alexis Gomez **RC** 5.00
167 Jason Hart 5.00
168 Nick Johnson 5.00
169 Donaldo Mendez **RC** 5.00
170 Christian Parker **RC** 5.00
171 Jackson Melian **RC** 5.00
172 Jack Cust 5.00
173 Adrian Hernandez **RC** 5.00
174 Joe Crede 8.00
175 Jose Mieses **RC** 5.00
176 Roy Oswalt 5.00
177 Eric Munson 5.00
178 Xavier Nady 5.00
179 Horacio Ramirez **RC** 5.00
180 Abraham Nunez 5.00
181 Jose Ortiz 5.00
182 Jeremy Owens **RC** 5.00
183 Claudio Vargas **RC** 5.00
184 Marcus Giles 5.00
185 Aubrey Huff 5.00
186 C.C. Sabathia 8.00
187 Adam Dunn 5.00
188 Adam Pettyjohn **RC** 5.00
189 Elpidio Guzman **RC** 5.00
190 Jay Gibbons **RC** 5.00
191 Wilkin Ruan **RC** 5.00
192 Tsuyoshi Shinjo **RC** 5.00
193 Alfonso Soriano 8.00
194 Corey Patterson 5.00
195 Ichiro Suzuki **RC** 60.00
196 Billy Sylvester **RC** 5.00
197 Juan Uribe **RC** 5.00
198 Johnny Estrada **RC** 5.00
199 Carlos Valderrama **RC** 5.00
200 Matt White **RC** 5.00

Spectrum

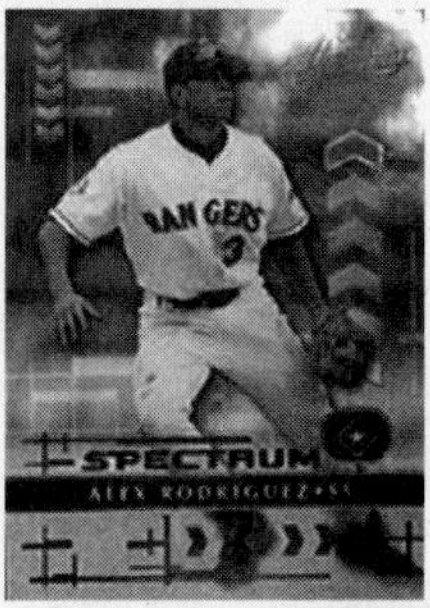

NM/M
Stars (1-150): No Pricing
Production 10
RK's (151-200): 2-4X
Production 25

Ball Hoggs

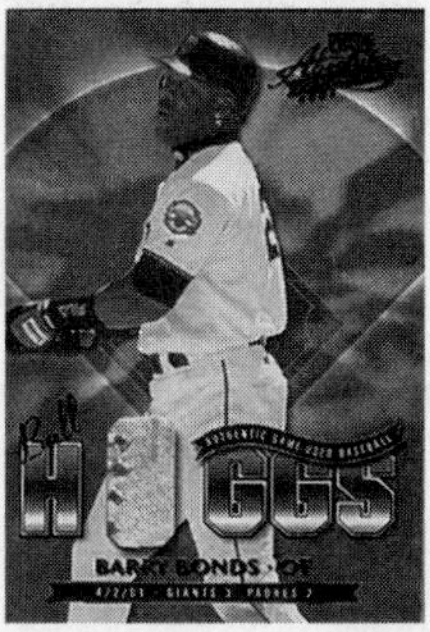

NM/M
Common Player: 8.00
Production 75 unless noted.
1 Vladimir Guerrero 15.00
2 Troy Glaus 10.00
3 Tony Gwynn 20.00
4 Cal Ripken/125 50.00
5 Todd Helton 15.00
6 Jacque Jones/125 8.00
7 Shawn Green/100 8.00
8 Ichiro Suzuki 85.00
9 Scott Rolen 15.00
10 Roger Clemens 30.00
11 Ken Griffey/25 50.00
14 Sammy Sosa 25.00
15 J.D. Drew 10.00
16 Barry Bonds/100 40.00
17 Pat Burrell 15.00
18 Mark McGwire/100 65.00
19 Mike Piazza 20.00
20 Magglio Ordonez/150 10.00
21 Miguel Tejada 10.00
22 Albert Pujols/100 150.00
23 Derek Jeter 40.00
24 Johnny Damon 15.00
25 Mike Sweeney 8.00
26 Ben Grieve 8.00
27 Jeff Kent 8.00
28 Andres Galarraga 8.00
29 Richie Sexson 10.00
30 Juan Encarnacion 8.00
31 Ruben Mateo 8.00
33 Manny Ramirez 15.00
35 Ivan Rodriguez 15.00
36 Darin Erstad 8.00
37 Carlos Delgado 10.00
38 Jeff Bagwell 15.00
39 Jermaine Dye 8.00
40 Jose Ortiz 8.00
41 Gary Sheffield 10.00
42 Eric Chavez 8.00
43 Mark Grace 15.00
44 Rafael Palmeiro 15.00
45 Tsuyoshi Shinjo/100 15.00
46 Terrence Long 8.00
47 Carlos Delgado/25 20.00
48 Frank Thomas 15.00
49 Chipper Jones/25 40.00
50 Jason Giambi 15.00

Ballpark Souvenirs

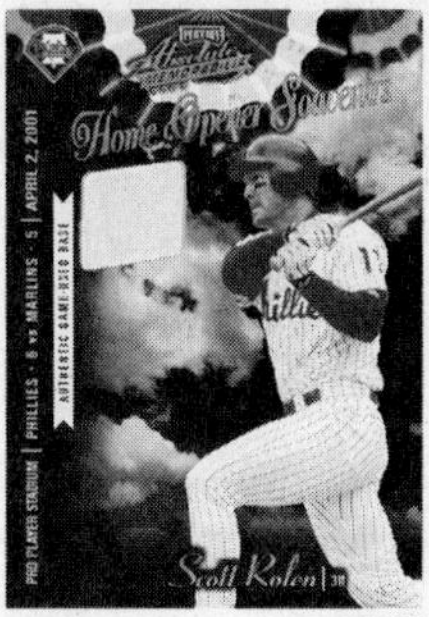

NM/M
Common Player: 4.00
Production 400 Sets
Doubles: 1-1.5X
Production 200 Sets
Triples: 1.5-2X
Production 75 Sets
Home Runs: 2-4X
Production 25 Sets
1 Barry Bonds 20.00
2 Cal Ripken Jr. 25.00
3 Pedro Martinez 10.00
4 Troy Glaus 6.00
5 Frank Thomas 8.00
6 Alex Rodriguez 10.00
7 Ivan Rodriguez 8.00
8 Jeff Bagwell 8.00
9 Mark McGwire 30.00
10 Todd Helton 8.00
11 Gary Sheffield 5.00
12 Manny Ramirez 8.00
13 Mike Piazza 10.00
14 Sammy Sosa 15.00
15 Preston Wilson 4.00
16 Tony Gwynn 8.00
17 Vladimir Guerrero 8.00
18 Carlos Delgado 6.00
19 Roberto Alomar 6.00
20 Todd Helton 8.00
21 Albert Pujols 50.00
22 Jason Giambi 8.00
23 Sammy Sosa 15.00
24 Ken Griffey Jr. 10.00
25 Darin Erstad 4.00
26 Mark McGwire 30.00
27 Carlos Delgado 6.00
28 Juan Gonzalez 8.00
29 Mike Sweeney 4.00
30 Alex Rodriguez 10.00
31 Roger Clemens 15.00
32 Tsuyoshi Shinjo 4.00
33 Ben Grieve 4.00
34 Jeff Kent 4.00
35 Vladimir Guerrero 8.00
36 Shawn Green 6.00
37 Rafael Palmeiro 6.00
38 Tony Gwynn 8.00
39 Scott Rolen 8.00
40 Ken Griffey Jr. 10.00
41 Albert Pujols 50.00
42 Barry Bonds 20.00
43 Mark Grace 8.00
44 Bernie Williams 6.00
45 Frank Thomas 8.00
46 Jermaine Dye 4.00
47 Mike Piazza 10.00
48 Chipper Jones 10.00
49 Richie Sexson 6.00
50 Magglio Ordonez 4.00

Boss Hoggs

NM/M
Production 25 Sets
4 Cal Ripken 80.00
6 Jacque Jones 15.00
7 Shawn Green 15.00
8 Ichiro Suzuki 100.00
9 Scott Rolen 20.00
11 Ken Griffey 50.00
14 Sammy Sosa 50.00
15 J.D. Drew 15.00
16 Barry Bonds 80.00
17 Pat Burrell 20.00
18 Mark McGwire 100.00
19 Mike Piazza 75.00
20 Magglio Ordonez 20.00
21 Miguel Tejada 20.00
23 Derek Jeter 85.00
24 Johnny Damon 15.00
25 Mike Sweeney 15.00
26 Ben Grieve 15.00
27 Jeff Kent 15.00
28 Andres Galarraga 15.00
29 Richie Sexson 20.00
30 Juan Encarnacion 15.00
31 Ruben Mateo 15.00
33 Manny Ramirez 20.00
35 Ivan Rodriguez 20.00
36 Darin Erstad 15.00
37 Carlos Delgado 20.00
38 Jeff Bagwell 20.00
39 Jermaine Dye 15.00
40 Jose Ortiz 15.00
42 Eric Chavez 15.00
43 Mark Grace 30.00
44 Rafael Palmeiro 30.00
45 Tsuyoshi Shinjo 20.00
46 Terrence Long 15.00
47 Carlos Delgado 20.00
48 Frank Thomas 25.00
50 Jason Giambi 25.00

Signing Bonus Baseballs

NM/M
Common Auto. Baseball: 15.00
Inserted 1:Box
Al Oliver/500 15.00
Andre Dawson/550 20.00
Barry Bonds/25 250.00
Bill Madlock/525 15.00
Bill Mazeroski/25 75.00
Billy Williams/325 20.00
Bob Feller/550 20.00
Bob Gibson/25 100.00
Bobby Doerr/300 25.00
Bobby Richardson/500 20.00
Boog Powell/500 20.00
Brian Jordan/25 40.00
Bucky Dent/500 15.00
Charles Johnson/25 40.00
Chipper Jones/25 100.00
Clete Boyer/500 20.00
Dale Murphy/25 80.00
Dave Concepcion/500 15.00
Dave Kingman/500 15.00
Don Larsen/200 40.00
Don Newcombe/500 15.00
Don Zimmer/500 15.00
Duke Snider/25 100.00
Earl Weaver/300 20.00
Enos Slaughter/525 20.00
Fergie Jenkins/1000 20.00
Frank Howard/500 20.00
Frank Robinson/25 100.00
Frank Thomas/25 85.00
Gary Carter/200 30.00
Gaylord Perry/1000 15.00
George Foster/500 15.00
George Kell/300 20.00
Goose Gossage/500 15.00
Greg Maddux/25 100.00
Hank Aaron/25 300.00
Hank Bauer/500 20.00
Harmon Killebrew/200 60.00
Henry Rodriguez/400 15.00
Herb Score/500 15.00
Hoyt Wilhelm/500 15.00
J.D. Drew/75 20.00
Javy Lopez/25 40.00
Jim Edmonds/25 50.00
Jim Palmer/500 20.00
Joe Pepitone/500 20.00
Johnny Bench/25 120.00
Johnny Podres/500 25.00
Juan Marichal/485 20.00
Kirby Puckett/25 100.00
Larry Doby/300 30.00
Lou Brock/25 75.00
Luis Tiant/500 15.00
Magglio Ordonez/200 25.00
Manny Ramirez/25 60.00
Maury Wills/500 20.00
Mike Schmidt/25 150.00
Minnie Minoso/1000 15.00
Monte Irvin/500 25.00
Moose Skowron/500 20.00
Nolan Ryan/25 200.00
Ozzie Smith/25 100.00
Phil Rizzuto/25 75.00
Ralph Kiner/100 40.00
Randy Johnson/25 100.00
Red Schoendienst/500 20.00
Reggie Jackson/25 80.00
Rickey Henderson/25 100.00
Robin Roberts/500 25.00
Roger Clemens/25 125.00
Rollie Fingers/575 20.00
Ryne Sandberg/25 100.00
Sean Casey/25 30.00
Stan Musial/25 100.00
Steve Carlton/25 75.00
Steve Garvey/1000 15.00

Todd Helton/25	50.00	35	Ivan Rodriguez	15.00
Tom Glavine/25	50.00	36	Sean Casey	6.00
Tom Seaver/25	75.00	37	Vladimir Guerrero	20.00
Tommy John/1000	15.00	39	Troy Glaus	8.00
Tony Gwynn/25	75.00	40	Jeff Bagwell	10.00
Tony Perez/400	15.00	41	Barry Bonds	100.00
Wade Boggs/25	75.00	42	Cal Ripken Jr.	125.00
Warren Spahn/500	60.00	43	Roberto Alomar	30.00
Whitey Ford/25	75.00	44	Sean Casey	20.00
Willie Mays/25	150.00	45	Tony Gwynn	40.00
Willie McCovey/25	60.00	46	Bernie Williams	25.00
Willie Stargell/25	75.00	47	Barry Zito	25.00
Yogi Berra/25	75.00	49	Tom Glavine	25.00

Rookie Premiere Autographs

NM/M

Production 25 Sets

151	Bud Smith	15.00
152	Cory Aldridge	15.00
154	Josh Beckett	40.00
155	Wilson Betemit	15.00
157	Albert Pujols	500.00
158	Andres Torres	15.00
160	Alex Escobar	15.00
161	Ben Sheets	30.00
162	Rafael Soriano	25.00
164	Carlos Garcia	15.00
165	Brandon Larson	20.00
167	Jason Hart	15.00
168	Nick Johnson	25.00
169	Donaldo Mendez	15.00
170	Christian Parker	15.00
171	Jackson Melian	15.00
173	Adrian Hernandez	15.00
174	Joe Crede	15.00
175	Jose Mieses	15.00
176	Roy Oswalt	30.00
178	Xavier Nady	20.00
179	Horacio Ramirez	20.00
180	Abraham Nunez	15.00
181	Jose Ortiz	15.00
182	Jeremy Owens	15.00
183	Claudio Vargas	15.00
184	Marcus Giles	20.00
186	C.C. Sabathia	40.00
187	Adam Dunn	50.00
188	Adam Pettyjohn	15.00
190	Jay Gibbons	20.00
191	Wilkin Ruan	15.00
193	Alfonso Soriano	60.00
194	Corey Patterson	20.00
196	Billy Sylvester	15.00
197	Juan Uribe	15.00
198	Johnny Estrada	15.00
199	Carlos Valderrama	15.00
200	Matt White	15.00

Tools Of The Trade

NM/M

Common Player: 5.00
Jerseys (1-20):
Production 300
Bats (21-40):
Production 125
Batting Glove (41-45):
Production 50
Hat (46-50):
Production 100
Autographs: No Pricing
Production 25 Sets

1	Vladimir Guerrero	10.00
2	Troy Glaus	6.00
3	Tony Gwynn	10.00
4	Todd Helton	8.00
5	Scott Rolen	8.00
6	Roger Clemens	20.00
7	Pedro Martinez	10.00
8	Richie Sexson	6.00
9	Magglio Ordonez	5.00
10	Ben Grieve	5.00
11	Jeff Bagwell	8.00
12	Edgar Martinez	5.00
13	Greg Maddux	25.00
14	Frank Thomas	15.00
15	Frank Thomas	15.00
16	Edgardo Alfonzo	5.00
17	Cal Ripken Jr.	40.00
18	Jose Vidro	5.00
19	Andruw Jones	8.00
20	Barry Bonds	50.00
21	Juan Gonzalez	8.00
22	Andruw Jones	8.00
23	Andruw Jones	8.00
24	Cal Ripken Jr.	60.00
25	Greg Maddux	30.00
26	Manny Ramirez	20.00
27	Roberto Alomar	8.00
28	Shawn Green	6.00
29	Edgardo Alfonzo	5.00
30	Rafael Palmeiro	10.00
31	Hideo Nomo	100.00
32	Andres Galarraga	6.00
33	Todd Helton	15.00
34	Darin Erstad	5.00

2002 Playoff Absolute Memorabilia

NM/M

Complete Set (200):
Common Player: .50
Common RK/Prospect (151-200): 3.00
Production 1,000
Pack (6): 3.00
Box + 8 x 10: 140.00

1	David Eckstein	.50
2	Darin Erstad	.75
3	Troy Glaus	1.50
4	Garret Anderson	.50
5	Tim Salmon	.50
6	Curt Schilling	1.00
7	Randy Johnson	1.50
8	Luis Gonzalez	.50
9	Mark Grace	.60
10	Tom Glavine	.75
11	Greg Maddux	2.00
12	Chipper Jones	2.00
13	Gary Sheffield	.75
14	John Smoltz	.50
15	Andruw Jones	1.50
16	Wilson Betemit	.50
17	Tony Batista	.50
18	Javier Vazquez	.50
19	Scott Erickson	.50
20	Josh Towers	.50
21	Pedro J. Martinez	1.50
22	Johnny Damon	.60
23	Manny Ramirez	1.50
24	Rickey Henderson	1.50
25	Trot Nixon	.50
26	Nomar Garciaparra	2.50
27	Juan Cruz	.50
28	Kerry Wood	1.25
29	Fred McGriff	.50
30	Moises Alou	.50
31	Sammy Sosa	2.50
32	Corey Patterson	.50
33	Mark Buehrle	.50
34	Keith Foulke	.50
35	Frank Thomas	1.50
36	Kenny Lofton	.50
37	Magglio Ordonez	.50
38	Barry Larkin	.50
39	Ken Griffey Jr.	2.50
40	Adam Dunn	.75
41	Juan Encarnacion	.50
42	Sean Casey	.60
43	Bartolo Colon	.50
44	C.C. Sabathia	.50
45	Travis Fryman	.50
46	Jim Thome	1.50
47	Omar Vizquel	.50
48	Ellis Burks	.50
49	Russell Branyan	.50
50	Mike Hampton	.50
51	Todd Helton	1.50
52	Jose Ortiz	.50
53	Juan Uribe	.50
54	Juan Pierre	.50
55	Larry Walker	.50
56	Mike Rivera	.50
57	Robert Fick	.50
58	Bobby Higginson	.50
59	Josh Beckett	.50
60	Richard Hidalgo	.50
61	Cliff Floyd	.50
62	Mike Lowell	.50
63	Roy Oswalt	.50
64	Morgan Ensberg	.50
65	Jeff Bagwell	1.50
66	Craig Biggio	.50
67	Lance Berkman	.50
68	Carlos Beltran	.75
69	Mike Sweeney	.50
70	Neifi Perez	.50
71	Kevin Brown	.50
72	Hideo Nomo	1.50
73	Paul LoDuca	.50
74	Adrian Beltre	.60
75	Shawn Green	.75
76	Eric Karros	.50
77	Brad Radke	.50
78	Corey Koskie	.50
79	Doug Mientkiewicz	.50
80	Torii Hunter	.50
81	Jacque Jones	.50
82	Ben Sheets	.50
83	Richie Sexson	.50
84	Geoff Jenkins	.60
85	Tony Armas	.50
86	Michael Barrett	.50
87	Jose Vidro	.50
88	Vladimir Guerrero	1.50
89	Roger Clemens	2.25
90	Derek Jeter	4.00
91	Bernie Williams	.60
92	Jason Giambi	1.25
93	Jorge Posada	.50
94	Mike Mussina	.50
95	Andy Pettitte	.65
96	Nick Johnson	.50
97	Alfonso Soriano	1.25
98	Shawn Estes	.50
99	Al Leiter	.50
100	Mike Piazza	2.50
101	Roberto Alomar	.75
102	Mo Vaughn	.50
103	Jeromy Burnitz	.50
104	Tim Hudson	.65
105	Barry Zito	.50
106	Mark Mulder	.50
107	Eric Chavez	.65
108	Miguel Tejada	.65
109	Jeremy Giambi	.50
110	Jermaine Dye	.50
111	Mike Lieberthal	.50
112	Scott Rolen	1.25
113	Pat Burrell	.75
114	Brandon Duckworth	.50
115	Bobby Abreu	.50
116	Jason Kendall	.50
117	Aramis Ramirez	.50
118	Brian Giles	.50
119	Pokey Reese	.50
120	Phil Nevin	.50
121	Ryan Klesko	.50
122	Carlos Pena	.50
123	Trevor Hoffman	.50
124	Barry Bonds	4.00
125	Rich Aurilia	.50
126	Jeff Kent	.50
127	Tsuyoshi Shinjo	.50
128	Ichiro Suzuki	2.00
129	Edgar Martinez	.50
130	Freddy Garcia	.50
131	Bret Boone	.50
132	Matt Morris	.50
133	Tino Martinez	.50
134	Albert Pujols	3.00
135	J.D. Drew	.75
136	Jim Edmonds	.50
137	Gabe Kapler	.50
138	Paul Wilson	.50
139	Ben Grieve	.50
140	Wade Miller	.50
141	Chan Ho Park	.50
142	Alex Rodriguez	3.00
143	Rafael Palmeiro	1.25
144	Juan Gonzalez	1.50
145	Ivan Rodriguez	1.25
146	Carlos Delgado	.75
147	Jose Cruz Jr.	.50
148	Shannon Stewart	.50
149	Raul Mondesi	.50
150	Vernon Wells	.50
151	So Taguchi RC	8.00
152	Kazuhisa Ishii RC	8.00
153	Hank Blalock	6.00
154	Sean Burroughs	3.00
155	Geronimo Gil	3.00
156	Jon Rauch	3.00
157	Fernando Rodney	3.00
158	Miguel Asencio RC	3.00
159	Franklyn German RC	3.00
160	Luis Ugueto RC	3.00
161	Jorge Sosa RC	3.00
162	Felix Escalona RC	3.00
163	Colby Lewis	3.00
164	Mark Teixeira	5.00
165	Mark Prior	6.00
166	Francis Beltran RC	3.00
167	Joe Thurston	3.00
168	Earl Snyder RC	3.00
169	Takahito Nomura RC	3.00
170	Bill Hall	3.00
171	Marlon Byrd	3.00
172	Dave Williams	3.00
173	Yorvit Torrealba	3.00
174	Brandon Backe RC	3.00
175	Jorge de la Rosa RC	3.00
176	Brian Mallette RC	3.00
177	Rodrigo Rosario RC	3.00
178	Anderson Machado RC	3.00
179	Jorge Padilla RC	3.00
180	Allan Simpson RC	3.00
181	Doug DeVore RC	3.00
182	Steve Bechler RC	3.00
183	Raul Chavez	3.00
184	Tom Shearn RC	3.00
185	Ben Howard RC	3.00
186	Chris Baker RC	3.00
187	Travis Hughes RC	3.00
188	Kevin Mench	3.00
189	Drew Henson	3.00
190	Mike Moriarty RC	3.00
191	Corey Thurman RC	3.00
192	Bobby Hill	3.00
193	Steve Kent RC	3.00
194	Satoru Komiyama RC	3.00
195	Jason Lane	3.00
196	Angel Berroa	3.00
197	Brandon Puffer RC	3.00
198	Brian Fitzgerald RC	3.00
199	Rene Reyes RC	3.00
200	Hee Seop Choi	5.00

Spectrum

Stars (1-150): 3-5X
Production 100
SP's: 1-1.5X
Production 50

Absolutely Ink

NM/M

Common Autograph: 5.00
Inserted 1:27
Gold Parallel #'d to 25 not priced.
Jsy Parallel #'d to Jsy # not priced.

Adrian Beltre	20.00
Alex Rodriguez/50	100.00
Ben Sheets	20.00
Bobby Doerr	15.00
Blaine Neal	5.00
Carlos Beltran	25.00
Carlos Pena	5.00
Corey Patterson/150	15.00
Dave Parker	10.00
David Justice/65	25.00
Don Mattingly/75	65.00
Duaner Sanchez	5.00
Eric Chavez/100	15.00
Freddy Garcia	10.00
Gary Carter	25.00
Ivan Rodriguez/50	40.00
J.D. Drew/100	20.00
Jack Cust	5.00
Jason Michaels	5.00
Jermaine Dye/125	10.00
Jose Vidro	8.00
Josh Towers	6.00
Kerry Wood/50	40.00
Kirby Puckett/50	75.00
Luis Gonzalez/75	25.00
Luis Rivera	5.00
Manny Ramirez/50	40.00
Marcus Giles	10.00
Mark Prior/100	30.00
Mark Teixeira/100	25.00
Marlon Byrd/250	15.00
Matt Ginter	5.00
Moises Alou/150	15.00
Nate Frese	5.00
Nick Johnson	5.00
Pablo Ozuna	5.00
Paul LoDuca/200	20.00
Richie Sexson	15.00
Roberto Alomar/100	40.00
Roy Oswalt/300	15.00
Ryan Klesko/75	15.00
Sean Casey/125	10.00
Shannon Stewart	8.00
So Taguchi	15.00
Terrence Long	8.00
Timoniel Perez	5.00
Tony Gwynn/50	60.00
Troy Glaus/300	15.00
Vladimir Guerrero/225	40.00
Wade Miller	15.00
Wilson Betemit	5.00

Signing Bonus

NM/M

Common Player:
Bobby Abreu/53 40.00
Roberto Alomar/100 50.00

Moises Alou/250	30.00
Carlos Beltran/50	50.00
Adrian Beltre/29	40.00
Adrian Beltre/150	30.00
Angel Berroa/50	20.00
Angel Berroa/100	20.00
Wilson Betemit/250	25.00
Hank Blalock/50	50.00
Lou Brock/100	60.00
Lou Brock/200	50.00
Kevin Brown/27	50.00
Kevin Brown/100	25.00
Kevin Brown/150	25.00
Mark Buehrle/56	60.00
Mark Buehrle/200	40.00
Marlon Byrd/61	25.00
Steve Carlton/100	50.00
Steve Carlton/150	40.00
Sean Casey/100	30.00
Eric Chavez/28	50.00
Juan Cruz/51	25.00
J.D. Drew/100	30.00
Brandon Duckworth/56	25.00
Brandon Duckworth/150	15.00
Adam Dunn/44	60.00
Jermaine Dye/100	40.00
Jermaine Dye/250	30.00
Morgan Ensberg/100	30.00
Cliff Floyd/200	25.00
Freddy Garcia/34	50.00
Freddy Garcia/125	25.00
Troy Glaus/50	65.00
Troy Glaus/100	40.00
Tom Glavine/200	50.00
Luis Gonzalez/125	30.00
Vladimir Guerrero/27	120.00
Vladimir Guerrero/150	80.00
Richard Hidalgo/100	20.00
Richard Hidalgo/135	20.00
Richard Hidalgo/150	20.00
Tim Hudson/50	60.00
Tim Hudson/100	40.00
Reggie Jackson/44	75.00
Nick Johnson/200	30.00
Andruw Jones/75	75.00
Al Kaline/250	60.00
Gabe Kapler/125	25.00
Gabe Kapler/175	25.00
Ryan Klesko/30	40.00
Jason Lane/100	30.00
Barry Larkin/50	60.00
Barry Larkin/100	50.00
Paul LoDuca/50	40.00
Fred Lynn/150	30.00
Fred Lynn/250	30.00
Greg Maddux/31	200.00
Edgar Martinez/150	50.00
Pedro J. Martinez/45	125.00
Don Mattingly/100	140.00
Willie McCovey/190	40.00
Willie McCovey/250	40.00
Wade Miller/52	25.00
Wade Miller/150	25.00
Wade Miller/200	20.00
Paul Molitor/75	50.00
Paul Molitor/100	40.00
Paul Molitor/125	40.00
Mark Mulder/40	35.00
Jose Ortiz/125	15.00
Roy Oswalt/44	40.00
Roy Oswalt/100	40.00
Jim Palmer/150	30.00
Jim Palmer/250	30.00
Dave Parker/150	25.00
Corey Patterson/250	25.00
Carlos Pena/150	15.00
Carlos Pena/250	15.00
Tony Perez/24	40.00
Tony Perez/250	25.00
Juan Pierre/75	25.00
Mark Prior/50	50.00
Mark Prior/75	40.00
Mark Prior/125	40.00
Kirby Puckett/34	125.00
Albert Pujols/100	250.00
Aramis Ramirez/50	50.00
Aramis Ramirez/125	40.00
Phil Rizzuto/10	265.00
Phil Rizzuto/250	70.00
Brooks Robinson/150	70.00
Brooks Robinson/250	60.00
Nolan Ryan/30	200.00
Nolan Ryan/34	200.00
Ryne Sandberg/50	150.00
Mike Schmidt/100	100.00
Richie Sexson/100	30.00
Ben Sheets/100	30.00
Ben Sheets/150	30.00
Alfonso Soriano/100	50.00
Shannon Stewart/100	25.00
Shannon Stewart/150	25.00
Mike Sweeney/100	30.00
So Taguchi/99	40.00
Mark Teixeira/23	65.00
Mark Teixeira/100	60.00
Miguel Tejada/40	60.00
Miguel Tejada/50	60.00
Frank Thomas/35	120.00
Javier Vazquez/125	25.00
Jose Vidro/150	20.00
Kerry Wood/34	75.00
Barry Zito/50	60.00

Team Quads

Curt Schilling

Randy Johnson

	NM/M
Complete Set (20):	75.00
Common Card:	2.00
Inserted 1:18	
Golds:	2X
Inserted 1:72	
1 Troy Glaus, Darin Erstad, Garret Anderson, Troy Percival	2.00
2 Curt Schilling, Randy Johnson, Luis Gonzalez, Mark Grace	4.00
3 Chipper Jones, Andruw Jones, Greg Maddux, Tom Glavine	5.00
4 Nomar Garciaparra, Manny Ramirez, Trot Nixon, Pedro J. Martinez	6.00
5 Kerry Wood, Sammy Sosa, Fred McGriff, Moises Alou	6.00
6 Frank Thomas, Magglio Ordonez, Mark Buehrle, Kenny Lofton	3.00
7 Ken Griffey Jr., Barry Larkin, Juan Encarnacion, Sean Casey	6.00
8 C.C. Sabathia, Jim Thome, Bartolo Colon, Russell Branyan	4.00
9 Todd Helton, Larry Walker, Juan Pierre, Mike Hampton	2.50
10 Jeff Bagwell, Craig Biggio, Lance Berkman, Richard Hidalgo	3.00
11 Shawn Green, Adrian Beltre, Hideo Nomo, Paul LoDuca	2.00
12 Mike Piazza, Roberto Alomar, Mo Vaughn, Roger Cedeno	6.00
13 Roger Clemens, Derek Jeter, Jason Giambi, Mike Mussina	10.00
14 Barry Zito, Tim Hudson, Eric Chavez, Miguel Tejada	2.50
15 Pat Burrell, Scott Rolen, Bobby Abreu, Marlon Byrd	4.00
16 Bernie Williams, Jorge Posada, Alfonso Soriano, Andy Pettitte	3.00
17 Barry Bonds, Rich Aurilia, Tsuyoshi Shinjo, Jeff Kent	8.00
18 Ichiro Suzuki, Kazuhiro Sasaki, Bret Boone, Edgar Martinez	6.00
19 Albert Pujols, J.D. Drew, Jim Edmonds, Tino Martinez	8.00
20 Alex Rodriguez, Ivan Rodriguez, Juan Gonzalez, Rafael Palmeiro	8.00

Team Quads Game Used

	NM/M
Numbered to 100	
Prime:	No Pricing
Production 25	
1 Troy Glaus, Darin Erstad, Garret Anderson, Troy Percival	25.00
2 Curt Schilling, Randy Johnson, Luis Gonzalez, Mark Grace	30.00
3 Chipper Jones, Andruw Jones, Greg Maddux, Tom Glavine	40.00
4 Nomar Garciaparra, Manny Ramirez, Trot Nixon, Pedro J. Martinez	50.00
5 Kerry Wood, Sammy Sosa, Fred McGriff, Moises Alou	35.00
6 Frank Thomas, Magglio Ordonez, Mark Buehrle, Kenny Lofton	25.00
8 C.C. Sabathia, Jim Thome, Bartolo Colon, Russell Branyan	40.00
9 Todd Helton, Larry Walker, Juan Pierre, Mike Hampton	30.00
10 Jeff Bagwell, Craig Biggio, Lance Berkman, Richard Hidalgo	30.00

11 Shawn Green, Adrian Beltre, Hideo Nomo, Paul LoDuca	40.00
12 Mike Piazza, Roberto Alomar, Mo Vaughn, Roger Cedeno	40.00
13 Roger Clemens, Derek Jeter, Jason Giambi, Mike Mussina	75.00
14 Barry Zito, Tim Hudson, Eric Chavez, Miguel Tejada	20.00
15 Pat Burrell, Scott Rolen, Bobby Abreu, Marlon Byrd	35.00
16 Bernie Williams, Jorge Posada, Alfonso Soriano, Andy Pettitte	30.00
17 Barry Bonds, Rich Aurilia, Tsuyoshi Shinjo, Jeff Kent	40.00
18 Ichiro Suzuki, Kazuhiro Sasaki, Bret Boone, Edgar Martinez	50.00
19 Albert Pujols, J.D. Drew, Jim Edmonds, Tino Martinez	40.00
20 Alex Rodriguez, Ivan Rodriguez, Juan Gonzalez, Rafael Palmeiro	40.00

Team Tandems

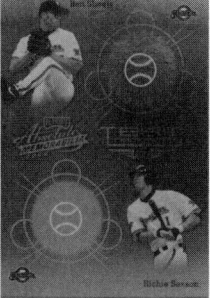

Ben Sheets

Richie Sexson

	NM/M
Complete Set (40):	80.00
Common Card:	1.00
Inserted 1:12	
Golds:	2-3X
Inserted 1:72	
1 Troy Glaus, Darin Erstad	1.50
2 Curt Schilling, Randy Johnson	3.00
3 Chipper Jones, Andruw Jones	3.00
4 Greg Maddux, Tom Glavine	4.00
5 Nomar Garciaparra, Manny Ramirez	6.00
6 Pedro J. Martinez, Trot Nixon	3.00
7 Kerry Wood, Sammy Sosa	5.00
8 Frank Thomas, Magglio Ordonez	5.00
9 Ken Griffey Jr., Barry Larkin	5.00
10 C.C. Sabathia, Jim Thome	2.50
11 Todd Helton, Larry Walker	2.00
12 Bobby Higginson, Shane Halter	1.00
13 Cliff Floyd, Brad Penny	1.00
14 Jeff Bagwell, Craig Biggio	2.00
15 Shawn Green, Adrian Beltre	1.50
16 Ben Sheets, Richie Sexson	1.50
17 Vladimir Guerrero, Jose Vidro	3.00
18 Mike Piazza, Roberto Alomar	8.00
19 Roger Clemens, Mike Mussina	6.00
20 Derek Jeter, Jason Giambi	8.00
21 Barry Zito, Tim Hudson	1.50
22 Eric Chavez, Miguel Tejada	1.50
23 Pat Burrell, Scott Rolen	3.00
24 Brian Giles, Aramis Ramirez	1.50
25 Ryan Klesko, Phil Nevin	1.50
26 Barry Bonds, Rich Aurilia	8.00
27 Ichiro Suzuki, Kazuhiro Sasaki	5.00
28 Albert Pujols, J.D. Drew	6.00
29 Alex Rodriguez, Ivan Rodriguez	6.00
30 Carlos Delgado, Shannon Stewart	1.50
31 Mo Vaughn, Roger Cedeno	1.00
32 Carlos Beltran, Mike Sweeney	1.50
33 Edgar Martinez, Bret Boone	1.50
34 Juan Gonzalez, Rafael Palmeiro	2.00
35 Johnny Damon, Rickey Henderson	1.50
36 Sean Casey, Adam Dunn	2.00
37 Jeff Kent, Tsuyoshi Shinjo	1.50
38 Lance Berkman, Richard Hidalgo	1.50

39 So Taguchi, Tino Martinez	1.50
40 Hideo Nomo, Kazuhisa Ishii	1.50

Team Tandems G-U

Craig Biggio

Jeff Bagwell

	NM/M
Common Card:	5.00
Inserted 1:33	
Golds:	2-3X
Production 50	
1 Troy Glaus, Darin Erstad	8.00
2 Curt Schilling, Randy Johnson	10.00
3 Chipper Jones, Andruw Jones	10.00
4 Greg Maddux, Tom Glavine	20.00
5 Nomar Garciaparra, Manny Ramirez	25.00
6 Pedro J. Martinez, Trot Nixon	15.00
7 Kerry Wood, Sammy Sosa	15.00
8 Frank Thomas, Magglio Ordonez	10.00
9 Ken Griffey Jr., Barry Larkin	15.00
10 C.C. Sabathia, Jim Thome	15.00
11 Todd Helton, Larry Walker	8.00
12 Bobby Higginson, Shane Halter	8.00
13 Cliff Floyd, Brad Penny	5.00
14 Jeff Bagwell, Craig Biggio	15.00
15 Shawn Green, Adrian Beltre	15.00
16 Ben Sheets, Richie Sexson	8.00
17 Vladimir Guerrero, Jose Vidro	12.00
18 Mike Piazza, Roberto Alomar	15.00
19 Roger Clemens, Mike Mussina	50.00
20 Derek Jeter, Jason Giambi	30.00
21 Barry Zito, Tim Hudson	15.00
22 Eric Chavez, Miguel Tejada	10.00
23 Pat Burrell, Scott Rolen	15.00
24 Brian Giles, Aramis Ramirez	10.00
25 Ryan Klesko, Phil Nevin	8.00
26 Barry Bonds, Rich Aurilia	15.00
27 Ichiro Suzuki, Kazuhiro Sasaki	
28 Albert Pujols, J.D. Drew	15.00
29 Alex Rodriguez, Ivan Rodriguez	15.00
30 Carlos Delgado, Shannon Stewart	8.00
31 Mo Vaughn, Roger Cedeno	5.00
32 Carlos Beltran, Mike Sweeney	8.00
33 Edgar Martinez, Bret Boone	8.00
34 Juan Gonzalez, Rafael Palmeiro	12.00
35 Johnny Damon, Rickey Henderson	10.00
36 Sean Casey, Adam Dunn	15.00
37 Jeff Kent, Tsuyoshi Shinjo	10.00
38 Lance Berkman, Richard Hidalgo	8.00
39 So Taguchi, Tino Martinez	15.00
40 Hideo Nomo, Kazuhisa Ishii	35.00

Tools of the Trade

	NM/M
Complete Set (95):	120.00
Common Player:	1.00
Inserted 1:9	
Golds:	2-3X
Inserted 1:45	
1 Mike Mussina	2.00
2 Rickey Henderson	2.00
3 Raul Mondesi	1.00

4 Nomar Garciaparra 6.00
5 Randy Johnson 3.00
6 Roger Clemens 6.00
7 Shawn Green 1.00
8 Todd Helton 2.00
9 Aramis Ramirez 1.50
10 Barry Larkin 1.50
11 Byung-Hyun Kim 1.00
12 C.C. Sabathia 1.00
13 Curt Schilling 2.50
14 Darin Erstad 1.50
15 Eric Karros 1.00
16 Freddy Garcia 1.00
17 Greg Maddux 4.00
18 Jason Kendall 1.00
19 Jim Thome 3.00
20 Juan Gonzalez 2.00
21 Kazuhiro Sasaki 1.00
22 Kerry Wood 3.00
23 Luis Gonzalez 1.50
24 Mark Mulder 1.00
25 Rich Aurilia 1.00
26 Ray Durham 1.00
27 Ben Grieve 1.00
28 Bret Boone 1.00
29 Edgar Martinez 1.00
30 Ivan Rodriguez 2.00
31 Jorge Posada 2.00
32 Mike Piazza 6.00
33 Pat Burrell 1.50
34 Robin Ventura 1.00
35 Trot Nixon 1.00
36 Adrian Beltre 1.00
37 Bernie Williams 1.50
38 Bobby Abreu 1.50
39 Carlos Delgado 1.50
40 Craig Biggio 1.50
41 Garret Anderson 1.50
42 Jermaine Dye 1.00
43 Johnny Damon 1.00
44 Tim Salmon 1.00
45 Tino Martinez 1.00
46 Fred McGriff 1.50
47 Gary Sheffield 1.00
48 Adam Dunn 2.00
49 Joe Mays 1.00
50 Kenny Lofton 1.00
51 Josh Beckett 1.50
52 Bud Smith 1.00
53 Johnny Estrada 1.00
54 Charles Johnson 1.00
55 Craig Wilson 1.00
56 Terrence Long 1.00
57 Andy Pettitte 1.50
58 Brian Giles 1.50
59 Juan Pierre 1.00
60 Cliff Floyd 1.00
61 Ivan Rodriguez 2.00
62 Andruw Jones 2.00
63 Lance Berkman 1.50
64 Mark Buehrle 1.00
65 Miguel Tejada 1.50
66 Wade Miller 1.00
67 Johnny Estrada 1.00
68 Tsuyoshi Shinjo 1.00
69 Scott Rolen 2.50
70 Roberto Alomar 2.00
71 Mark Grace 2.00
72 Larry Walker 1.50
73 Jim Edmonds 1.50
74 Jeff Kent 1.50
75 Frank Thomas 2.50
76 Carlos Beltran 1.50
77 Barry Zito 1.50
78 Alex Rodriguez 8.00
79 Troy Glaus 1.50
80 Ryan Klesko 1.00
81 Tom Glavine 1.50
82 Ben Sheets 1.50
83 Manny Ramirez 2.50
84 Shannon Stewart 1.00
85 Vladimir Guerrero 4.00
86 Chipper Jones 3.00
87 Jeff Bagwell 2.50
88 Richie Sexson 1.50
89 Sean Casey 1.50
90 Tim Hudson 1.50
91 J.D. Drew 1.50
92 Ivan Rodriguez 2.00
93 Magglio Ordonez 1.50
94 John Buck 1.00
95 Paul LoDuca 1.00

Tools of Trade G-U

NM/M

Common Player: 5.00
Jerseys #'d to 300.
Bats #'d to 250.
Shoes #'d to 150.
Shin Guard #'d to 150.
Glove #'d to 125.
Mask #'d to 100.
Hat #'d to 50.
Doubles #'d to 200.
Triples #'d to 75.
Quads #'d to 50.

1 Mike Mussina/Jsy 10.00
2 Rickey Henderson/Jsy 10.00
3 Raul Mondesi/Jsy 8.00
4 Nomar Garciaparra/Jsy 15.00
5 Randy Johnson/Jsy 10.00
6 Roger Clemens/Jsy 15.00
7 Shawn Green/Jsy 8.00
8 Todd Helton/Jsy 8.00
9 Aramis Ramirez/Jsy 8.00
10 Barry Larkin/Jsy 10.00
11 Byung-Hyun Kim/Jsy 5.00
12 C.C. Sabathia/Jsy 5.00
13 Curt Schilling/Jsy 10.00
14 Darin Erstad/Jsy 5.00
15 Eric Karros/Jsy 5.00
16 Freddy Garcia/Jsy 5.00
17 Greg Maddux/Jsy 15.00
18 Jason Kendall/Jsy 5.00
19 Jim Thome/Jsy 10.00
20 Juan Gonzalez/Jsy 8.00
21 Kazuhiro Sasaki/Jsy 5.00
22 Kerry Wood/Jsy 10.00
23 Luis Gonzalez/Jsy 8.00
24 Mark Mulder/Jsy 8.00
25 Rich Aurilia/Jsy 5.00
26 Ray Durham/Jsy 5.00
27 Ben Grieve/Jsy 5.00
28 Bret Boone/Jsy 5.00
29 Edgar Martinez/Jsy 8.00
30 Ivan Rodriguez/Jsy 10.00
31 Jorge Posada/Jsy 10.00
32 Mike Piazza/Jsy 15.00
33 Pat Burrell/Bat 8.00
34 Robin Ventura/Bat 5.00
35 Trot Nixon/Bat 8.00
36 Adrian Beltre/Bat 5.00
37 Bernie Williams/Bat 10.00
38 Bobby Abreu/Bat 8.00
39 Carlos Delgado/Bat 8.00
40 Craig Biggio/Bat 8.00
41 Garret Anderson/Bat 8.00
42 Jermaine Dye/Bat 5.00
43 Johnny Damon/Bat 8.00
44 Tim Salmon/Bat 8.00
45 Tino Martinez/Bat 10.00
46 Fred McGriff/Bat 8.00
47 Gary Sheffield/Bat 5.00
48 Adam Dunn/Shoe 15.00
49 Joe Mays/Shoe 8.00
50 Kenny Lofton/Shoe 10.00
51 Josh Beckett/Shoe 10.00
52 Bud Smith/Shoe 5.00
53 Johnny Estrada/Shin 10.00
54 Charles Johnson/Shin 8.00
55 Craig Wilson/Shin 15.00
56 Terrence Long/Glove 8.00
57 Andy Pettitte/Glove 15.00
58 Brian Giles/Glove 10.00
59 Juan Pierre/Glove 10.00
60 Cliff Floyd/Glove 10.00
61 Ivan Rodriguez/Glove 15.00
62 Andruw Jones/Hat 15.00
63 Lance Berkman/Hat 15.00
64 Mark Buehrle/Hat 15.00
65 Miguel Tejada/Hat 15.00
66 Wade Miller/Hat 10.00
67 Johnny Estrada/Shin 10.00
68 T. Shinjo/Bat/Shoe 15.00
69 S. Rolen/Bat/Shoe 20.00
70 R. Alomar/Bat/Shoe 20.00
71 M. Grace/Glv/Jsy 15.00
72 L. Walker/Jsy/Bat 10.00
73 J. Edmonds/Jsy/Bat 15.00
74 J. Kent/Jsy/Bat 10.00
75 F. Thomas/Jsy/Bat 15.00
76 C. Beltran/Jsy/Bat 10.00
77 B. Zito/Shoe/Jsy 15.00
78 A. Rodriguez/Jsy/Bat 25.00
79 T. Glaus/Dualjsy 15.00
80 R. Klesko/Bat/Glv 10.00
81 T. Glavine/Jsy/Shoe 20.00
82 B. Sheets/Bat/Jsy 10.00
83 M. Ramirez/ Shoe/Glv/Jsy 25.00
84 S. Stewart/Hat/Jsy/Bat 15.00
85 V. Guerrero/Glv/Bat/Jsy 45.00
86 C. Jones/Glv/Bat/Jsy 40.00
87 J. Bagwell/Jsy/Hat/Bat 40.00
88 R. Sexson/Bat/Jsy/Glv/Shoe 40.00
89 S. Casey/Jsy/Hat/Shoe/Bat 30.00
90 T Hudson/Shoe/Hat/Glv/Jsy 30.00
91 JD Drew/Shoe/Jsy/Hat/Bat 40.00
92 I Rodriguez/Jsy/Mask/Chst/Glv 60.00
93 M Ordonez/Hat/Glv/Jsy/Shoe 40.00
94 J Buck/Glv/Chst/Shin/Msk 20.00
95 P LoDuca/Jsy/Chst/Shin/Msk 30.00

2002 Playoff Piece of the Game

NM/M

Complete Set (100):
Common Player: .50
Common SP (51-100): 5.00
Production 500
Pack (5): 15.00

Box (6): 75.00
1 Vladimir Guerrero 1.50
2 Troy Glaus 1.50
3 Ichiro Suzuki 2.50
4 Chipper Jones 2.00
5 Roberto Alomar .75
6 Scott Rolen 1.25
7 Randy Johnson 1.50
8 Roger Clemens 2.25
9 Nomar Garciaparra 2.50
10 Greg Maddux 2.00
11 Barry Bonds 4.00
12 Derek Jeter 4.00
13 Albert Pujols 3.00
14 Kerry Wood 1.25
15 Jim Thome 1.50
16 Manny Ramirez 1.50
17 Carlos Delgado .75
18 Magglio Ordonez .50
19 Torii Hunter .50
20 Garret Anderson .50
21 Eric Chavez .60
22 Rafael Palmeiro 1.25
23 Andruw Jones 1.50
24 Cliff Floyd .50
25 Sammy Sosa 2.50
26 Mike Mussina .60
27 Jeff Bagwell 1.50
28 Miguel Tejada .60
29 Curt Schilling 1.00
30 Tom Glavine .75
31 Frank Thomas 1.50
32 Jim Edmonds .50
33 Juan Gonzalez 1.50
34 Todd Helton 1.50
35 Shawn Green .75
36 Alfonso Soriano 1.25
37 Lance Berkman .50
38 Barry Zito .60
39 Ryan Klesko .50
40 Larry Walker .50
41 Craig Biggio .50
42 Luis Gonzalez .50
43 Ivan Rodriguez 1.25
44 J.D. Drew .75
45 Roy Oswalt .50
46 Jason Giambi 1.25
47 Brian Giles .50
48 Richie Sexson .50
49 Pat Burrell .75
50 Alex Rodriguez 3.00
51 So Taguchi **RC** 8.00
52 Allan Simpson **RC** 5.00
53 Oliver Perez **RC** 10.00
54 Ben Howard **RC** 5.00
55 Kirk Saarloos 5.00
56 Francis Beltran **RC** 5.00
57 Jorge Padilla **RC** 5.00
58 Brandon Puffer **RC** 5.00
59 Brian Mallette **RC** 5.00
60 Kyle Kane **RC** 5.00
61 Travis Driskill **RC** 5.00
62 Jeremy Lambert **RC** 5.00
63 Steve Kent **RC** 5.00
64 Julius Matos **RC** 5.00
65 Julio Mateo **RC** 5.00
66 Kazuhisa Ishii **RC** 8.00
67 Franklyn German **RC** 5.00
68 John Foster **RC** 5.00
69 Luis Ugueto **RC** 5.00
70 Shawn Sedlacek **RC** 5.00
71 Earl Snyder **RC** 5.00
72 Alex Pelaez **RC** 5.00
73 Victor Alvarez **RC** 5.00
74 Tom Shearn **RC** 5.00
75 Corey Thurman **RC** 5.00
76 Eric Junge **RC** 5.00
77 Hansel Izquierdo **RC** 5.00
78 Elio Serrano **RC** 5.00
79 J.J. Trujillo **RC** 5.00
80 Chris Snelling **RC** 6.00
81 Satoru Komiyama **RC** 5.00
82 Brandon Backe **RC** 5.00
83 Anderson Machado **RC** 5.00
84 Doug DeVore **RC** 5.00
85 Steve Bechler **RC** 5.00
86 John Ennis **RC** 5.00
87 Rodrigo Rosario **RC** 5.00
88 Jorge Sosa **RC** 5.00
89 Ken Huckaby **RC** 5.00
90 Mike Moriarty **RC** 5.00
91 Michael Crudale **RC** 5.00
92 Kevin Frederick **RC** 5.00
93 Aaron Guiel **RC** 5.00
94 Jose Rodriguez 5.00
95 Andy Shibilo **RC** 5.00
96 Deivis Santos 5.00
97 Felix Escalona **RC** 5.00
98 Miguel Asencio **RC** 5.00
99 Takahito Nomura **RC** 5.00
100 Cam Esslinger **RC** 5.00

Materials

NM/M

Common Materials (1-90): 4.00
Team Connections (91-95):
Production 500
Superstar Combos (96-100):
Production 250
Bronze Materials (1-90): 1-2X
Production 250
Bronze Team Connect. (91-95): 1.5-2X
Production 100
Bronze Combos (96-100): 2-3X
Production 50
Silver Materials (1-90): 1.5-2.5X
Production 150
Silver Tm. Connect. (91-95): 1.5-3X
Production 50
Silver Combos (96-100): No Pricing
Production 25
Gold Materials (1-90): 2-5X
Production 50
Gold Tm. Connect. (91-95): No Pricing
Production 25
Gold Combos (96-100): No Pricing
Production 10
Platinum Materials (1-90): No Pricing
Production 25
Platinum Tm Connect. (91-95): No Pricing
Production 10
Platinum Combos (96-100): No Pricing
Production 5

1 Adam Dunn/Bat 8.00
2 Adrian Beltre/Bat 4.00
3 Albert Pujols/Base 10.00
4 Alex Rodriguez/Jsy 12.00
5 Alex Rodriguez/Bat 12.00
6 Andruw Jones/Jsy 5.00
7 Andruw Jones/Bat 5.00
8 Barry Bonds/Base 15.00
9 Barry Larkin/Bat 5.00
10 Juan Gonzalez/Jsy 5.00
11 Bernie Williams/Bat 6.00
12 Carlos Delgado/Jsy 5.00
13 Chipper Jones/Jsy 10.00
14 Chipper Jones/Bat 10.00
15 Craig Biggio/Jsy 5.00
16 Craig Biggio/Bat 5.00
17 Cristian Guzman/Jsy 5.00
18 Curt Schilling/Jsy 6.00
19 Derek Jeter/Base 15.00
20 Edgar Martinez/Jsy 5.00
21 Edgardo Alfonzo/Jsy 4.00
22 Ellis Burks/Jsy 4.00
23 Frank Thomas/Bat 6.00
24 Freddy Garcia/Jsy 4.00
25 Greg Maddux/Jsy 10.00
26 Harmon Killebrew/Pants 15.00
27 Hideo Nomo/Jsy 12.00
28 Ichiro Suzuki/Base 15.00
29 Ivan Rodriguez/Jsy 8.00
30 Ivan Rodriguez/Bat 8.00
31 J.D. Drew/Bat 6.00
32 J.D. Drew/Jsy 6.00
33 Javy Lopez/Jsy 6.00
34 Jeff Bagwell/Jsy 6.00
35 Jim Edmonds/Jsy 6.00
36 Jim Edmonds/Bat 6.00
37 John Olerud/Bat 4.00
38 John Smoltz/Jsy 6.00
39 Jose Cruz Jr./Jsy 4.00
40 Jose Vidro/Jsy 4.00
41 Juan Gonzalez/Bat 6.00
42 Juan Pierre/Jsy 4.00
43 Ken Griffey Jr./Base 10.00
44 Kenny Lofton/Bat 4.00
45 Kerry Wood/Bat 8.00
46 Kevin Brown/Jsy 4.00
47 Lance Berkman/Jsy 6.00
48 Lance Berkman/Bat 6.00
49 Larry Walker/Jsy 5.00
50 Luis Gonzalez/Jsy 5.00
51 Magglio Ordonez/Jsy 5.00
52 Magglio Ordonez/Bat 5.00
53 Manny Ramirez/Jsy 8.00
54 Manny Ramirez/Bat 8.00
55 Vladimir Guerrero/Jsy 8.00
56 Mark Grace/Bat 8.00
57 Michael Barrett/Jsy 4.00
58 Miguel Tejada/Jsy 8.00
59 Mike Piazza/Jsy 12.00
60 Mike Piazza/Bat 12.00
61 Mike Schmidt/Bat 15.00
62 Mike Sweeney/Jsy 4.00
63 Nolan Ryan/Jsy 30.00
64 Nomar Garciaparra/Jsy 15.00
65 Paul LoDuca/Jsy 4.00
66 Rafael Palmeiro/Jsy 8.00
67 Rafael Palmeiro/Bat 8.00
68 Jose Canseco/Bat 8.00
69 Raul Mondesi/Jsy 4.00

70 Reggie Jackson/Bat 8.00
71 Rickey Henderson/Bat 8.00
72 Roberto Alomar/Bat 6.00
73 Robin Ventura/Jsy 4.00
74 Rod Carew/Bat 10.00
75 Roger Clemens/Jsy 15.00
76 Sammy Sosa/Base 10.00
77 Sean Casey/Jsy 5.00
78 Shannon Stewart/Jsy 4.00
79 Shawn Green/Jsy 6.00
80 Shawn Green/Bat 6.00
81 Tim Hudson/Jsy 6.00
82 Todd Helton/Bat 8.00
83 Tom Glavine/Jsy 6.00
84 Tony Gwynn/Jsy 10.00
85 Tony Gwynn/Jsy 10.00
86 Tony Gwynn/Bat 10.00
87 Troy Glaus/Jsy 6.00
88 Tsuyoshi Shinjo/Bat 4.00
89 Vladimir Guerrero/Jsy 8.00
90 Vladimir Guerrero/Bat 8.00
91 Nomar Garciaparra, Pedro J. Martinez 30.00
92 Randy Johnson, Curt Schilling 15.00
93 Andruw Jones, Chipper Jones 15.00
94 Todd Helton, Larry Walker 15.00
95 Jeff Bagwell, Craig Biggio 15.00
96 Alex Rodriguez 25.00
97 Greg Maddux 25.00
98 Mike Piazza 25.00
99 Lance Berkman 15.00
100 Vladimir Guerrero 20.00

2003 Playoff Absolute Memorabilia

NM/M

Complete Set (200):
Common Player: .50
Common SP (151-200): 3.00
Production 1,500
Pack (6): 3.00
Box (18 + Glass Plaque): 85.00

1 Nomar Garciaparra 2.50
2 Barry Bonds 4.00
3 Greg Maddux 2.00
4 Roger Clemens 3.00
5 Derek Jeter 4.00
6 Alex Rodriguez 3.00
7 Chipper Jones 2.00
8 Sammy Sosa 2.50
9 Alfonso Soriano 1.00
10 Albert Pujols 3.00
11 Adam Dunn 1.00
12 Tom Glavine .75
13 Pedro J. Martinez 1.50
14 Jim Thome 1.00
15 Hideo Nomo 1.50
16 Roberto Alomar .75
17 Barry Zito .65
18 Troy Glaus 1.50
19 Kerry Wood 1.00
20 Magglio Ordonez .50
21 Todd Helton 1.50
22 Craig Biggio .50
23 Roy Oswalt .50
24 Torii Hunter .50
25 Miguel Tejada .65
26 Tsuyoshi Shinjo .50
27 Scott Rolen 1.00
28 Rafael Palmeiro 1.00
29 Victor Martinez .75
30 Hank Blalock .75
31 Jason Lane .50
32 Junior Spivey .50
33 Gary Sheffield .75
34 Corey Patterson .50
35 Corky Miller .50
36 Brian Tallet .50
37 Cliff Lee 1.00
38 Jason Jennings .50
39 Kirk Saarloos .50
40 Wade Miller .50
41 Angel Berroa .50
42 Mike Sweeney .50
43 Paul LoDuca .50
44 A.J. Pierzynski .50
45 Drew Henson .50
46 Eric Chavez .65
47 Tim Hudson .75
48 Aramis Ramirez .50
49 Jack Wilson .50
50 Ryan Klesko .50
51 Antonio Perez .50
52 Dewon Brazelton .50
53 Mark Teixeira .75
54 Eric Hinske .50
55 Freddy Sanchez .50
56 Mike Rivera .50
57 Alfredo Amezaga .50
58 Cliff Floyd .50
59 Brandon Larson .50
60 Richard Hidalgo .50
61 Cesar Izturis .50
62 Richie Sexson .50
63 Michael Cuddyer .50
64 Javier Vazquez .50
65 Brandon Claussen .50
66 Carlos Rivera .50
67 Vernon Wells .50
68 Kenny Lofton .50
69 Aubrey Huff .50
70 Adam LaRoche .50
71 Jeff Baker .50
72 Jose Castillo .50
73 Joe Borchard .50
74 Walter Young .50
75 Jose Morban .50
76 Vinnie Chulk .50
77 Christian Parker .50
78 Mike Piazza 2.50
79 Ichiro Suzuki 2.50
80 Kazuhisa Ishii .50
81 Rickey Henderson 1.50
82 Ken Griffey Jr. 2.50
83 Jason Giambi .75
84 Randy Johnson 1.50
85 Curt Schilling .75
86 Manny Ramirez 1.50
87 Barry Larkin .50
88 Jeff Bagwell 1.50
89 Vladimir Guerrero 1.50
90 Mike Mussina .65
91 Juan Gonzalez 1.50
92 Andruw Jones 1.50
93 Frank Thomas 1.50
94 Sean Casey .50
95 Josh Beckett .50
96 Lance Berkman .50
97 Shawn Green .75
98 Bernie Williams .65
99 Pat Burrell .75
100 Edgar Martinez .50
101 Ivan Rodriguez 1.00
102 Jeremy Guthrie .50
103 Alexis Rios .50
104 Nic Jackson .50
105 Jason Anderson .50
106 Travis Chapman .50
107 Mac Suzuki .50
108 Toby Hall .50
109 Mark Prior 1.50
110 So Taguchi .50
111 Marlon Byrd .50
112 Garret Anderson .50
113 Luis Gonzalez .50
114 Jay Gibbons .50
115 Mark Buehrle .50
116 Wily Mo Pena .50
117 C.C. Sabathia .50
118 Ricardo Rodriguez .50
119 Robert Fick .50
120 Rodrigo Rosario .50
121 Alexis Gomez .50
122 Carlos Beltran 1.00
123 Joe Thurston .50
124 Ben Sheets .50
125 Jose Vidro .50
126 Nick Johnson .50
127 Mark Mulder .50
128 Bobby Abreu .50
129 Brian Giles .50
130 Brian Lawrence .50
131 Jeff Kent .50
132 Chris Snelling .50
133 Kevin Mench .50
134 Carlos Delgado .75
135 Orlando Hudson .50
136 Juan Cruz .50
137 Jim Edmonds .50
138 Geronimo Gil .50
139 Joe Crede .50
140 Wilson Valdez .50
141 Runelvys Hernandez .50
142 Nick Neugebauer .50
143 Takahito Nomura .50
144 Andres Galarraga .50
145 Mark Grace .65
146 Brandon Duckworth .50
147 Oliver Perez .50
148 Xavier Nady .50
149 Rafael Soriano .50
150 Ben Kozlowski .50
151 Prentice Redman **RC** 3.00
152 Craig Brazell **RC** 3.00
153 Nook Logan **RC** 3.00
154 Greg Aquino **RC** 3.00
155 Matt Kata **RC** 3.00
156 Ian Ferguson **RC** 3.00
157 Chien-Ming Wang **RC** 30.00
158 Beau Kemp **RC** 3.00
159 Alejandro Machado **RC** 3.00
160 Michael Hessman **RC** 3.00
161 Francisco Rosario **RC** 3.00
162 Pedro Liriano 3.00
163 Richard Fischer **RC** 3.00
164 Franklin Perez 3.00
165 Oscar Villarreal **RC** 3.00
166 Arnie Munoz **RC** 3.00
167 Tim Olson **RC** 3.00
168 Jose Contreras **RC** 5.00
169 Francisco Cruceta **RC** 3.00
170 Jeremy Bonderman 8.00
171 Jeremy Griffiths 3.00
172 John Webb 3.00
173 Phil Seibel **RC** 3.00
174 Aaron Looper **RC** 3.00
175 Brian Stokes **RC** 3.00
176 Guillermo Quiroz **RC** 3.00
177 Fernando Cabrera **RC** 3.00
178 Josh Hall **RC** 3.00
179 Diegomar Markwell **RC** 3.00
180 Andrew Brown **RC** 3.00
181 Doug Waechter **RC** 3.00
182 Felix Sanchez **RC** 3.00
183 Gerardo Garcia 3.00
184 Matt Bruback **RC** 3.00
185 Michel Hernandez **RC** 3.00
186 Rett Johnson **RC** 3.00
187 Ryan Cameron **RC** 3.00
188 Rob Hammock **RC** 3.00
189 Clint Barmes **RC** 8.00
190 Brandon Webb **RC** 15.00
191 Jon Leicester **RC** 3.00
192 Shane Bazzell **RC** 3.00
193 Joe Valentine **RC** 3.00
194 Josh Stewart **RC** 3.00
195 Pete LaForest **RC** 3.00
196 Shane Victorino **RC** 8.00
197 Terrmel Sledge **RC** 3.00
198 Lew Ford **RC** 3.00
199 Todd Wellemeyer **RC** 6.00
200 Hideki Matsui **RC** 10.00

Spectrum

Stars (1-150): 3-5X
Rookies (151-200): .75-2X
Production 100 Sets

Spectrum Signatures

NM/M

Common Autograph: 6.00
Varying quantities produced

10 Albert Pujols/10 275.00
16 Roberto Alomar/15 100.00
17 Barry Zito/25 50.00
20 Magglio Ordonez/25 50.00
23 Roy Oswalt/25 30.00
24 Torii Hunter/25 40.00
29 Victor Martinez/100 30.00
30 Hank Blalock/50 30.00
32 Junior Spivey/50 15.00
34 Corey Patterson/50 20.00
35 Corky Miller/100 6.00
36 Brian Tallet/100 6.00
37 Cliff Lee/100 20.00
38 Jason Jennings/100 8.00
39 Kirk Saarloos/100 6.00
40 Wade Miller/50 15.00
41 Angel Berroa/100 10.00
42 Mike Sweeney/50 15.00
43 Paul LoDuca/50 20.00
44 A.J. Pierzynski/100 15.00
45 Drew Henson/50 25.00
47 Tim Hudson/50 40.00
51 Antonio Perez/25 8.00
52 Dewon Brazelton/50 15.00
53 Mark Teixeira/50 40.00
54 Eric Hinske/100 15.00
55 Freddy Sanchez/100 15.00
57 Alfredo Amezaga/100 10.00
59 Brandon Larson/100 8.00
60 Richard Hidalgo/100 10.00
62 Richie Sexson/25 30.00
63 Michael Cuddyer/100 15.00
68 Kenny Lofton/50 30.00
69 Aubrey Huff/100 15.00
70 Adam LaRoche/100 15.00
71 Jeff Baker/100 10.00
72 Jose Castillo/100 10.00
73 Joe Borchard/100 10.00
74 Walter Young/100 8.00
76 Vinnie Chulk/100 8.00
80 Kazuhisa Ishii/25 60.00
87 Barry Larkin/50 50.00
89 Vladimir Guerrero/50 50.00
92 Andruw Jones/25 60.00
95 Josh Beckett/100 25.00
100 Edgar Martinez/50 25.00
102 Jeremy Guthrie/100 15.00
103 Alexis Rios/100 20.00
104 Nic Jackson/100 8.00
105 Jason Anderson/100 8.00
106 Travis Chapman/100 8.00
107 Mac Suzuki/304 15.00
109 Mark Prior/50 30.00
111 Marlon Byrd/100 10.00
114 Jay Gibbons/100 10.00
118 Ricardo Rodriguez/100 10.00
119 Robert Fick/100 10.00
120 Rodrigo Rosario/250 8.00
121 Alexis Gomez/100 10.00
124 Ben Sheets/50 20.00
126 Nick Johnson/50 10.00
127 Mark Mulder/50 40.00
132 Chris Snelling/100 8.00
133 Kevin Mench/100 10.00
135 Orlando Hudson/50 15.00
139 Joe Crede/100 10.00
140 Wilson Valdez/25 10.00
141 Runelvys Hernandez/100 10.00
143 Takahito Nomura/47 15.00
147 Oliver Perez/50 15.00
148 Xavier Nady/100 12.00
150 Ben Kozlowski/100 8.00
151 Prentice Redman/250 10.00
152 Craig Brazell/250 10.00
153 Nook Logan/250 6.00
154 Greg Aquino/250 8.00
155 Matt Kata/250 15.00
156 Ian Ferguson/250 6.00
157 Chien-Ming Wang/250 200.00
158 Beau Kemp/250 6.00
159 Alejandro Machado/250 6.00
160 Michael Hessman/160 6.00
161 Francisco Rosario/250 6.00
162 Pedro Liriano/250 6.00
163 Richard Fischer/250 6.00
164 Franklin Perez/250 6.00
165 Oscar Villarreal/250 10.00
166 Arnie Munoz/250 6.00
167 Tim Olson/250 8.00
168 Jose Contreras/250 25.00
169 Francisco Cruceta/250 8.00
170 Jeremy Bonderman/250 40.00
171 Jeremy Griffiths/250 8.00
172 John Webb/250 6.00
173 Phil Seibel/250 6.00
174 Aaron Looper/250 6.00
175 Brian Stokes/250 6.00
176 Guillermo Quiroz/250 8.00
177 Fernando Cabrera/250 10.00
178 Josh Hall/250 10.00
179 Diegomar Markwell/250 6.00
180 Andrew Brown/250 8.00
181 Doug Waechter/250 8.00
182 Felix Sanchez/250 8.00
183 Gerardo Garcia/250 8.00
184 Matt Bruback/250 6.00
185 Michel Hernandez/250 6.00
186 Rett Johnson/250 10.00
187 Ryan Cameron/250 6.00
188 Rob Hammock/250 15.00
189 Clint Barmes/250 15.00
190 Brandon Webb/250 50.00
191 Jon Leicester/250 6.00
192 Shane Bazzell/250 10.00
193 Joe Valentine/250 8.00
194 Josh Stewart/250 15.00
195 Pete LaForest/250 8.00
196 Shane Victorino/250 8.00
197 Terrmel Sledge/250 6.00
198 Lew Ford/250 15.00
199 Todd Wellemeyer/250 10.00

Absolutely Ink

NM/M

Inserted 1:552
Blues: No Pricing
Production 10-25
Golds: No Pricing
Production 5-10

1 Vladimir Guerrero 50.00
6 Eric Hinske 15.00
8 Jose Vidro 8.00
16 Rodrigo Rosario 8.00
17 Brandon Claussen 20.00
18 Jermaine Dye 8.00
22 Mark Prior 50.00
24 Brian Lawrence 8.00
29 Barry Larkin 50.00
30 Drew Henson 40.00
36 Mark Teixeira 30.00
38 Roberto Alomar 30.00
39 Barry Zito 35.00

Glass Plaques

NM/M

One Per Box:
Roberto Alomar/Bat/Jsy/100 40.00
Roberto Alomar/Jsy/150 30.00
Jeff Bagwell/Bat/Jsy/100 40.00
Jeff Bagwell/Jsy/150 30.00
Ernie Banks/Jsy/150 40.00
Lance Berkman/Bat/Jsy/100 40.00
Lance Berkman/Jsy/150 30.00
Barry Bonds/Ball/Base/50 85.00
Barry Bonds/Ball/Base/100 75.00
Barry Bonds/Base/200 50.00

George Brett/Bat/Jsy/50 125.00
George Brett/Jsy/200 50.00
Pat Burrell/Bat/Jsy/100 35.00
Pat Burrell/Jsy/150 30.00
Steve Carlton/Auto./50 60.00
Steve Carlton/Bat/Jsy/100 40.00
Steve Carlton/Jsy/150 30.00
Roger Clemens/Glv/Jsy/50 150.00
Roger Clemens/Jsy/150 60.00
Roger Clemens/Glv/Jsy/50 150.00
Roger Clemens/Glv/Jsy/200 60.00
Roberto Clemente/
Bat/Jsy/150 80.00
Roberto Clemente/Jsy/200 60.00
Jose Contreras/Jsy/Jsy/100 30.00
Jose Contreras/Jsy/150 25.00
Adam Dunn/Bat/Jsy/100 40.00
Adam Dunn/Jsy/150 30.00
Bob Feller/Auto./50 65.00
Bob Feller/Jsy/150 50.00
Bob Feller/Jsy/150 30.00
Nomar Garciaparra/
Bat/Jsy/100 65.00
Nomar Garciaparra/Jsy/200 55.00
Jason Giambi/Bat/Jsy/100 50.00
Jason Giambi/Jsy/150 40.00
Troy Glaus/Bat/Jsy/100 40.00
Troy Glaus/Jsy/100 35.00
Juan Gonzalez/Bat/Jsy/100 40.00
Juan Gonzalez/Jsy/150 30.00
Luis Gonzalez/Bat/Jsy/100 30.00
Luis Gonzalez/Jsy/150 25.00
Mark Grace/Auto./50 100.00
Mark Grace/Bat/Jsy/100 45.00
Mark Grace/Jsy/150 35.00
Shawn Green/Bat/Jsy/100 30.00
Shawn Green/Jsy/150 25.00
Ken Griffey Jr./
Ball/Base/100 50.00
Ken Griffey Jr./Base/200 40.00
Vladimir Guerrero/
Bat/Jsy/100 40.00
Vladimir Guerrero/Jsy/150 35.00
Tony Gwynn/Bat/Jsy/150 50.00
Tony Gwynn/Jsy/200 40.00
Todd Helton/Bat/Jsy/100 40.00
Todd Helton/Jsy/150 30.00
Rickey Henderson/
Bat/Jsy/150 50.00
Rickey Henderson/Jsy/200 40.00
Tim Hudson/Auto./50 65.00
Tim Hudson/Hat/Jsy/100 30.00
Tim Hudson/Jsy/150 25.00
Torii Hunter/Auto./50 65.00
Torii Hunter/Hat/Jsy/100 40.00
Torii Hunter/Jsy/150 30.00
Kazuhisa Ishii/
Bat/Jsy/100 30.00
Kazuhisa Ishii/Jsy/200 25.00
Derek Jeter/Ball/Base/150 50.00
Derek Jeter/Base/200 50.00
Randy Johnson/
Bat/Jsy/100 50.00
Randy Johnson/Jsy/150 40.00
Andruw Jones/Bat/Jsy/100 35.00
Andruw Jones/Jsy/150 30.00
Chipper Jones/Bat/Jsy/100 40.00
Chipper Jones/Jsy/150 30.00
Al Kaline/Bat/Jsy/100 40.00
Al Kaline/Jsy/150 35.00
Barry Larkin/Auto./50 60.00
Barry Larkin/Bat/Jsy/100 40.00
Barry Larkin/Jsy/150 30.00
Greg Maddux/Bat/Jsy/100 50.00
Greg Maddux/Jsy/200 40.00
Pedro Martinez/Bat/Jsy/100 40.00
Pedro Martinez/Jsy/150 35.00
Hideki Matsui/
Ball/Base/50 110.00
Hideki Matsui/
Ball/Base/150 75.00
Hideki Matsui/Base/200 50.00
Don Mattingly/Bat/Jsy/100 65.00
Don Mattingly/Jsy/200 50.00
Mark Mulder/Auto./50 50.00
Mark Mulder/Jsy/100 25.00
Mark Mulder/Jsy/100 30.00
Stan Musial/Bat/Jsy/100 65.00
Stan Musial/Jsy/200 60.00
Hideo Nomo/Bat/Jsy/100 60.00
Hideo Nomo/Jsy/100 40.00
Hideo Nomo/Jsy/200 30.00
Magglio Ordonez/Auto./50 50.00
Magglio Ordonez/
Bat/Jsy/100 30.00
Magglio Ordonez/Jsy/100 25.00
Roy Oswalt/Auto./50 50.00
Roy Oswalt/Bat/Jsy/100 30.00
Roy Oswalt/Jsy/100 25.00
Rafael Palmeiro/
Bat/Jsy/100 40.00
Rafael Palmeiro/Jsy/150 30.00
Mike Piazza/Bat/Jsy/150 75.00
Mike Piazza/Bat/Jsy/200 50.00
Mike Piazza/Jsy/200 40.00
Mark Prior/Bat/Jsy/100 60.00
Mark Prior/Jsy/150 40.00
Albert Pujols/Bat/Jsy/100 75.00
Albert Pujols/Jsy/150 60.00
Manny Ramirez/
Bat/Jsy/100 40.00
Manny Ramirez/Jsy/150 30.00
Cal Ripken Jr./Bat/Jsy/150 90.00
Cal Ripken Jr./Jsy/200 70.00
Frank Robinson/Auto./50 65.00
Frank Robinson/
Bat/Jsy/100 40.00

Frank Robinson/Jsy/150 30.00
Alex Rodriguez/Bat/Jsy/150 50.00
Alex Rodriguez/Jsy/200 40.00
Nolan Ryan/Jkt/Jsy/150 90.00
Nolan Ryan/Jsy/200 75.00
Nolan Ryan/Jsy/Jsy/100 100.00
Ryne Sandberg/Bat/Jsy/50 100.00
Ryne Sandberg/Jsy/200 65.00
Curt Schilling/Glv/Jsy/50 50.00
Curt Schilling/Jsy/150 50.00
Mike Schmidt/Bat/Jsy/100 70.00
Mike Schmidt/Jsy/200 50.00
Ozzie Smith/Bat/Jsy/100 65.00
Ozzie Smith/Jsy/150 50.00
Alfonso Soriano/
Bat/Jsy/150 60.00
Alfonso Soriano/Jsy/150 50.00
Sammy Sosa/Bat/Jsy/150 50.00
Sammy Sosa/Jsy/200 50.00
Junior Spivey/Auto./50 50.00
Junior Spivey/Bat/Jsy/100 30.00
Junior Spivey/Jsy/150 25.00
Ichiro Suzuki/Ball/Base/50 80.00
Ichiro Suzuki/Ball/Base/150 60.00
Ichiro Suzuki/Base/200 40.00
Mark Teixeira/Bat/Jsy/100 40.00
Mark Teixeira/Jsy/150 30.00
Miguel Tejada/Auto./50 60.00
Miguel Tejada/Bat/Jsy/100 40.00
Miguel Tejada/Jsy/150 30.00
Frank Thomas/Bat/Jsy/100 40.00
Frank Thomas/Jsy/150 30.00
Bernie Williams/
Bat/Jsy/100 40.00
Bernie Williams/Jsy/150 35.00
Kerry Wood/Auto./50 80.00
Kerry Wood/Bat/Jsy/100 45.00
Kerry Wood/Jsy/150 35.00
Barry Zito/Auto./50 75.00
Barry Zito/Hat/Jsy/100 40.00
Barry Zito/Jsy/150 30.00

Player's Collection - Jersey

		NM/M
	Common Player:	4.00
	Production 75 Sets	
1	Adam Dunn	6.00
2	Adrian Beltre	4.00
3	Alex Rodriguez	15.00
4	Alfonso Soriano	12.00
5	Andruw Jones	8.00
6	Andy Pettitte	6.00
7	Barry Larkin	6.00
8	Barry Zito	6.00
9	Ben Grieve	4.00
10	Bernie Williams	8.00
11	Cal Ripken Jr.	40.00
12	Carlos Delgado	6.00
13	C.C. Sabathia	4.00
14	Chipper Jones	10.00
15	Craig Biggio	4.00
16	Curt Schilling	6.00
17	Alex Rodriguez	15.00
18	Frank Thomas	8.00
19	Freddy Garcia	4.00
20	Jay Bell	4.00
21	Roger Clemens	15.00
22	Tony Gwynn	10.00
23	Ivan Rodriguez	8.00
24	Jason Giambi	8.00
25	Jason Jennings	4.00
26	Jay Payton	4.00
27	J.D. Drew	5.00
28	Jeff Bagwell	8.00
29	Jeromy Burnitz	4.00
30	Jim Edmonds	6.00
31	Jim Thome	8.00
32	Joe Borchard	4.00
33	Joe Mays	4.00
34	John Olerud	5.00
35	David Wells	4.00
36	Juan Gonzalez	8.00
37	Kazuhiro Sasaki	4.00
38	Chan Ho Park	4.00
39	Kerry Wood	10.00
40	Kevin Brown	4.00
41	Lance Berkman	6.00
42	Larry Walker	6.00
43	Bret Boone	6.00
44	Magglio Ordonez	8.00
45	Manny Ramirez	8.00
46	Mark Mulder	6.00
47	Mark Prior	10.00
48	Matt Williams	4.00
49	Miguel Tejada	5.00
50	Mike Piazza	12.00
51	Nomar Garciaparra	15.00
52	Doug Davis	4.00
53	Paul Konerko	4.00
54	Paul LoDuca	4.00
55	Pedro J. Martinez	10.00
56	Preston Wilson	4.00
58	Marlon Byrd	4.00
59	Reggie Sanders	4.00
60	Richie Sexson	6.00
62	Rickey Henderson	8.00
63	Robert Person	4.00
65	Roger Clemens	15.00
66	Roy Oswalt	6.00
67	Ryan Klesko	4.00
68	Sammy Sosa	15.00
69	Shawn Green	6.00
70	Steve Finley	4.00
71	Terrence Long	4.00
72	Tim Hudson	6.00
73	Toby Hall	4.00
74	Todd Helton	8.00
75	Travis Lee	4.00
76	Troy Glaus	8.00
77	Tsuyoshi Shinjo	4.00
78	Vernon Wells	6.00
79	Vladimir Guerrero	8.00
80	Wes Helms	4.00

Player's Collection - Bat

		NM/M
	Common Player:	4.00
	Production 75 Sets	
81	Alex Rodriguez	15.00
82	Alfonso Soriano	12.00
83	Barry Larkin	8.00
84	Roberto Alomar	8.00
85	Ivan Rodriguez	8.00
86	Jason Giambi	8.00
87	Jeff Bagwell	8.00
88	Juan Gonzalez	8.00
89	Larry Walker	4.00
90	Luis Gonzalez	4.00
91	Magglio Ordonez	6.00
92	Manny Ramirez	8.00
93	Marlon Byrd	4.00
94	Mike Piazza	12.00
95	Pat Burrell	8.00
96	Todd Helton	8.00
97	Rickey Henderson	8.00
98	Andruw Jones	8.00
99	Craig Biggio	4.00
100	Mark Prior	10.00

Rookie Materials Jersey Number

		NM/M
	Many not priced due to scarcity.	
2	Yogi Berra/35	40.00
3	Vladimir Guerrero/27	35.00
4	Randy Johnson/51	25.00
5	Andruw Jones/25	25.00
10	Alfonso Soriano/33	35.00
13	Rafael Palmeiro/25	20.00

Materials Season

		NM/M
	Common Player:	5.00
	Quantity produced listed	
1	Stan Musial/42	75.00
2	Yogi Berra/47	40.00
3	Vladimir Guerrero/97	15.00
4	Randy Johnson/89	20.00
5	Andruw Jones/96	10.00
7	Jeff Kent/92	5.00
8	Hideo Nomo/95	20.00
9	Ivan Rodriguez/91	10.00
10	Alfonso Soriano/101	20.00
11	Scott Rolen/96	15.00
12	Juan Gonzalez/89	15.00
13	Rafael Palmeiro/86	15.00
14	Mike Schmidt/73	60.00
15	Cal Ripken Jr./82	75.00

Team Tandems

		NM/M
	Common Duo:	2.00
	Inserted 1:48	
	Spectrums:	1-2X
	Production 100 Sets	
1	Mark Prior, Sammy Sosa	5.00
2	Vladimir Guerrero, Jose Vidro	3.00
3	Bernie Williams, Alfonso Soriano	6.00
4	Mike Sweeney, Carlos Beltran	2.00
5	Magglio Ordonez, Paul Konerko	2.00
6	Adam Dunn, Austin Kearns	3.00
7	Randy Johnson, Curt Schilling	4.00
8	Hideo Nomo, Kazuhisa Ishii	2.00
9	Pat Burrell, Bobby Abreu	3.00
10	Todd Helton, Larry Walker	2.00

Team Tandems Material

		NM/M
	Common Duo:	
	Quantity produced listed	
	Spectrums:	No Pricing
	Production 25 or 10	
1	Mark Prior, Sammy Sosa/100	30.00
2	Vladimir Guerrero, Jose Vidro/100	10.00
3	Bernie Williams, Alfonso Soriano/100	20.00
4	Mike Sweeney, Carlos Beltran/100	6.00
5	Magglio Ordonez, Paul Konerko/100	6.00
6	Adam Dunn, Austin Kearns/100	15.00
7	Randy Johnson, Curt Schilling/100	15.00
8	Hideo Nomo, Kazuhisa Ishii/40	50.00
9	Pat Burrell, Bobby Abreu/40	20.00
10	Todd Helton, Larry Walker/100	8.00

Team Trios

		NM/M
	Common Trio:	5.00
	Inserted 1:88	
	Spectrums:	1-2X
	Production 50 Sets	
1	Greg Maddux, Chipper Jones, Andruw Jones	8.00
2	Sammy Sosa, Mark Prior, Kerry Wood	8.00
3	Pedro Martinez, Nomar Garciaparra, Manny Ramirez	8.00
4	Jason Giambi, Roger Clemens, Alfonso Soriano	8.00
5	Alex Rodriguez, Rafael Palmeiro, Mark Teixeira	8.00
6	Mike Piazza, Roberto Alomar, Tsuyoshi Shinjo	6.00
7	Jeff Bagwell, Craig Biggio, Lance Berkman	5.00
8	Troy Glaus, Garret Anderson, Troy Percival	5.00
9	Miguel Tejada, Eric Chavez, Barry Zito	5.00
10	Luis Gonzalez, Randy Johnson, Curt Schilling	6.00

Team Trios Materials

		NM/M
	Quantity produced listed	5.00
	Spectrums:	No Pricing
	Production 10 or 25	
1	Greg Maddux, Chipper Jones, Andruw Jones/100	30.00
2	Sammy Sosa, Mark Prior, Kerry Wood/100	30.00
3	Pedro Martinez, Nomar Garciaparra, Manny Ramirez/50	50.00
4	Jason Giambi, Roger Clemens, Alfonso Soriano/100	40.00
5	Alex Rodriguez, Rafael Palmeiro, Mark Teixeira/100	25.00
6	Mike Piazza, Roberto Alomar, Tsuyoshi Shinjo/40	40.00
7	Jeff Bagwell, Craig Biggio, Lance Berkman/100	20.00
8	Troy Glaus, Garret Anderson, Troy Percival/40	25.00
9	Miguel Tejada, Eric Chavez, Barry Zito/100	20.00
10	Luis Gonzalez, Randy Johnson, Curt Schilling/100	25.00

Tools of the Trade

		NM/M
	Complete Set (110):	125.00
	Common Player:	1.00
	Inserted 1:5	
1	Sammy Sosa	4.00
2	Nomar Garciaparra	5.00
3	Andruw Jones	1.50
4	Troy Glaus	1.00
5	Greg Maddux	4.00
6	Rickey Henderson	1.00

7	Alex Rodriguez	6.00
8	Manny Ramirez	1.50
9	Lance Berkman	1.00
10	Roger Clemens	5.00
11	Ivan Rodriguez	1.00
12	Kazuhisa Ishii	1.00
13	Alfonso Soriano	3.00
14	Austin Kearns	1.00
15	Mike Piazza	3.00
16	Curt Schilling	1.00
17	Jeff Bagwell	1.50
18	Todd Helton	1.50
19	Randy Johnson	2.00
20	Vladimir Guerrero	1.50
21	Kerry Wood	1.00
22	Rafael Palmeiro	1.00
23	Roy Oswalt	1.00
24	Chipper Jones	3.00
25	Pat Burrell	1.00
26	Jason Giambi	2.00
27	Pedro J. Martinez	2.00
28	Roberto Alomar	1.00
29	Shawn Green	1.00
30	Adam Dunn	1.00
31	Juan Gonzalez	1.50
32	Mark Prior	5.00
33	Hideo Nomo	1.00
34	Torii Hunter	1.00
35	Mark Teixeira	1.00
36	Craig Biggio	1.00
37	Rafael Palmeiro	1.00
38	Jeff Bagwell	1.50
39	Albert Pujols	6.00
40	Richie Sexson	1.00
41	Alex Rodriguez	6.00
42	Carlos Delgado	1.50
43	Frank Thomas	1.50
44	Sammy Sosa	4.00
45	Marlon Byrd	1.00
46	Mark Prior	5.00
47	Adrian Beltre	1.00
48	Tom Glavine	1.00
49	So Taguchi	1.00
50	Jeff Bagwell	1.50
51	Mike Sweeney	1.00
52	Luis Gonzalez	1.00
53	Chipper Jones	3.00
54	Jason Giambi	2.00
55	Miguel Tejada	1.00
56	Todd Helton	1.50
57	Andruw Jones	1.50
58	Mike Piazza	3.00
59	Manny Ramirez	1.50
60	Randy Johnson	2.00
61	Carlos Beltran	1.00
62	Victor Martinez	1.00
63	Orlando Hudson	1.00
64	Jeff Kent	1.00
65	Greg Maddux	4.00
66	Garret Anderson	1.00
67	Joe Thurston	1.00
68	Mark Teixeira	1.00
69	Kazuhisa Ishii	1.00
70	Austin Kearns	1.00
71	Pat Burrell	1.00
72	Joe Borchard	1.00
73	Josh Phelps	1.00
74	Travis Hafner	1.00
75	So Taguchi	1.00
76	Victor Martinez	1.00
77	Paul LoDuca	1.00
78	Bernie Williams	1.00
79	Josh Phelps	1.00
80	Marlon Byrd	1.00
81	Manny Ramirez	1.50
82	Jason Giambi	2.00
83	Jeff Bagwell	1.50
84	Sammy Sosa	4.00
85	Josh Phelps	1.00
86	Tim Hudson	1.00
87	Randy Johnson	2.00
88	Troy Glaus	1.00
89	Joe Thurston	1.00
90	Miguel Tejada	1.00
91	Adam Dunn	1.00
92	Magglio Ordonez	1.00
93	Mike Sweeney	1.00
94	Andruw Jones	1.50
95	Carlos Beltran	1.00
96	Joe Borchard	1.00
97	Austin Kearns	1.00
98	Richie Sexson	1.00
99	Mark Prior	5.00
100	Mark Teixeira	1.00
101	Ryan Klesko	1.00
102	Jason Jennings	1.00
103	Travis Hafner	1.00
104	Mark Buehrle	1.00
105	Eric Hinske	1.00
106	Rafael Palmeiro	1.00
107	Roy Oswalt	1.00
108	Kerry Wood	1.00
109	Brian Giles	1.00
110	Ivan Rodriguez	1.00

Tools of the Trade Materials

		NM/M
Common Player:		3.00
Quantity produced listed		
Spectrums:		1-2.5X
Production 10 to 50		
1	Sammy Sosa/250	10.00
2	Nomar Garciaparra/250	10.00
3	Andruw Jones/250	5.00
4	Troy Glaus/250	5.00
5	Greg Maddux/250	10.00
6	Rickey Henderson/40	25.00
7	Alex Rodriguez/250	10.00
8	Manny Ramirez/250	6.00
9	Lance Berkman/250	4.00
10	Roger Clemens/250	10.00
11	Ivan Rodriguez/250	6.00
12	Kazuhisa Ishii/40	5.00
13	Alfonso Soriano/250	10.00
14	Austin Kearns/250	5.00
15	Mike Piazza/250	10.00
16	Curt Schilling/250	5.00
17	Jeff Bagwell/250	6.00
18	Todd Helton/250	6.00
19	Randy Johnson/250	6.00
20	Vladimir Guerrero/250	6.00
21	Kerry Wood/250	6.00
22	Rafael Palmeiro/250	6.00
23	Roy Oswalt/250	3.00
24	Chipper Jones/250	8.00
25	Pat Burrell/40	15.00
26	Jason Giambi/250	8.00
27	Pedro J. Martinez/250	8.00
28	Roberto Alomar/40	15.00
29	Shawn Green/250	3.00
30	Adam Dunn/250	5.00
31	Juan Gonzalez/40	15.00
32	Mark Prior/250	8.00
33	Hideo Nomo/250	8.00
34	Torii Hunter/250	5.00
35	Mark Teixeira/250	5.00
36	Craig Biggio/250	4.00
37	Rafael Palmeiro/250	5.00
38	Jeff Bagwell/250	5.00
39	Albert Pujols/200	12.00
40	Richie Sexson/250	4.00
41	Alex Rodriguez/250	10.00
42	Carlos Delgado/250	3.00
43	Frank Thomas/75	8.00
44	Sammy Sosa/250	10.00
45	Marlon Byrd/250	3.00
46	Mark Prior/250	8.00
47	Adrian Beltre/250	3.00
48	Tom Glavine/250	3.00
49	So Taguchi/250	3.00
50	Jeff Bagwell/250	5.00
51	Mike Sweeney/250	3.00
52	Luis Gonzalez/250	3.00
53	Chipper Jones/100	8.00
54	Jason Giambi/250	6.00
55	Miguel Tejada/250	4.00
56	Todd Helton/250	5.00
57	Andruw Jones/250	5.00
58	Mike Piazza/250	8.00
59	Manny Ramirez/250	6.00
60	Randy Johnson/250	6.00
61	Carlos Beltran/250	3.00
62	Victor Martinez/250	3.00
63	Orlando Hudson/250	3.00
64	Jeff Kent/250	3.00
65	Greg Maddux/250	8.00
66	Garret Anderson/150	4.00
67	Joe Thurston/250	3.00
68	Mark Teixeira/250	3.00
69	Kazuhisa Ishii/250	3.00
70	Austin Kearns/250	4.00
71	Pat Burrell/100	8.00
72	Joe Borchard/250	3.00
73	Josh Phelps/250	3.00
74	Travis Hafner/250	3.00
75	So Taguchi/125	3.00
76	Victor Martinez/125	5.00
77	Paul LoDuca/125	3.00
78	Bernie Williams/125	8.00
79	Josh Phelps/125	5.00
80	Marlon Byrd/125	5.00
81	Manny Ramirez/100	10.00
82	Jason Giambi/125	10.00
83	Jeff Bagwell/50	15.00
84	Sammy Sosa/125	20.00
85	Josh Phelps/125	3.00
86	Tim Hudson/125	5.00
87	Randy Johnson/125	10.00
88	Troy Glaus/125	8.00
89	Joe Thurston/125	4.00
90	Miguel Tejada/125	5.00
91	Adam Dunn/100	15.00
92	Magglio Ordonez/100	10.00
93	Mike Sweeney/100	10.00
94	Andruw Jones/100	15.00
95	Carlos Beltran/100	8.00
96	Joe Borchard/100	8.00
97	Austin Kearns/100	15.00
98	Richie Sexson/50	15.00
99	Mark Prior/50	50.00
100	Mark Teixeira/50	20.00
101	Ryan Klesko/50	10.00
102	Jason Jennings/50	10.00
103	Travis Hafner/50	10.00
104	Mark Buehrle/50	15.00
105	Eric Hinske/50	20.00
106	Rafael Palmeiro/50	40.00
107	Roy Oswalt/50	20.00
108	Kerry Wood/50	40.00
109	Brian Giles/50	15.00
110	Ivan Rodriguez/50	25.00

Total Bases

		NM/M
Complete Set (30):		60.00
Common Player:		1.00
Inserted 1:16		
1	Albert Pujols	6.00
2	Nomar Garciaparra	6.00
3	Jason Giambi	3.00
4	Miguel Tejada	1.00
5	Rafael Palmeiro	1.50
6	Sammy Sosa	5.00
7	Pat Burrell	1.50
8	Lance Berkman	1.00
9	Bernie Williams	1.50
10	Jim Thome	2.00
11	Carlos Beltran	1.00
12	Eric Chavez	1.00
13	Alex Rodriguez	6.00
14	Magglio Ordonez	1.00
15	Brian Giles	1.00
16	Alfonso Soriano	3.00
17	Shawn Green	1.00
18	Vladimir Guerrero	2.00
19	Garret Anderson	1.00
20	Todd Helton	2.00
21	Barry Bonds	8.00
22	Jeff Kent	1.00
23	Torii Hunter	1.00
24	Ichiro Suzuki	4.00
25	Derek Jeter	8.00
26	Chipper Jones	4.00
27	Jeff Bagwell	2.00
28	Mike Piazza	4.00
29	Rickey Henderson	1.50
30	Ken Griffey Jr.	4.00

Bases Materials 1B

		NM/M
Common Player:		4.00
Quantity produced listed		
1	Albert Pujols/109	12.00
2	Nomar Garciaparra/112	12.00
3	Jason Giambi/100	8.00
4	Miguel Tejada/140	4.00
5	Rafael Palmeiro/58	5.00
6	Sammy Sosa/90	15.00
7	Pat Burrell/87	8.00
8	Lance Berkman/90	4.00
9	Bernie Williams/146	6.00
10	Jim Thome/73	8.00
11	Carlos Beltran/94	4.00
12	Eric Chavez/93	4.00
13	Alex Rodriguez/101	15.00
14	Magglio Ordonez/103	4.00
15	Brian Giles/68	4.00
16	Alfonso Soriano/117	10.00
17	Shawn Green/92	4.00
18	Vladimir Guerrero/128	6.00
19	Garret Anderson/107	4.00
20	Todd Helton/109	6.00
21	Barry Bonds/70	20.00
22	Jeff Kent/114	4.00
23	Torii Hunter/92	6.00
24	Ichiro Suzuki/165	25.00
25	Derek Jeter/147	25.00
26	Chipper Jones/117	8.00
27	Jeff Bagwell/100	8.00
28	Mike Piazza/76	10.00
29	Rickey Henderson/28	40.00
30	Ken Griffey Jr./36	40.00

Bases Materials 2B

		NM/M
Quantity produced listed		
1	Albert Pujols/40	40.00
2	Nomar Garciaparra/56	25.00
3	Jason Giambi/34	15.00
4	Miguel Tejada/30	10.00
5	Rafael Palmeiro/34	15.00
7	Pat Burrell/39	10.00
8	Lance Berkman/35	8.00
9	Bernie Williams/37	15.00
11	Carlos Beltran/44	8.00
12	Eric Chavez/31	10.00
13	Alex Rodriguez/27	50.00
14	Magglio Ordonez/47	8.00
15	Brian Giles/37	8.00
16	Alfonso Soriano/51	25.00
17	Shawn Green/31	10.00
18	Vladimir Guerrero/37	15.00
19	Garret Anderson/56	8.00
20	Todd Helton/39	15.00
21	Barry Bonds/31	50.00
22	Jeff Kent/42	8.00
23	Torii Hunter/37	15.00
25	Derek Jeter/26	50.00
26	Chipper Jones/35	25.00
27	Jeff Bagwell/33	25.00
28	Mike Piazza/23	35.00

Bases Materials 3B

No pricing due to scarcity.

Bases Materials HR

		NM/M
Quantity produced listed		
1	Albert Pujols/34	40.00
3	Jason Giambi/41	20.00
4	Miguel Tejada/41	10.00
5	Rafael Palmeiro/43	15.00
6	Sammy Sosa/49	30.00
7	Pat Burrell/37	15.00
8	Lance Berkman/42	10.00
10	Jim Thome/52	15.00
11	Carlos Beltran/29	10.00
12	Eric Chavez/34	12.00
13	Alex Rodriguez/57	25.00
14	Magglio Ordonez/58	8.00
15	Brian Giles/38	8.00
16	Alfonso Soriano/39	30.00
17	Shawn Green/42	8.00
18	Vladimir Guerrero/39	15.00
19	Garret Anderson/29	15.00
20	Todd Helton/30	15.00
21	Barry Bonds/46	40.00
22	Jeff Kent/37	8.00
23	Torii Hunter/29	25.00
26	Chipper Jones/26	35.00
27	Jeff Bagwell/31	20.00
28	Mike Piazza/33	30.00

2003 Playoff Piece of the Game

		NM/M
Common Player:		4.00
Pack (1):		12.00
Box (6):		60.00
1	Adam Dunn/Bat	8.00
2	Adam Dunn/Jsy	8.00
3	Adrian Beltre/Bat	6.00
4	Albert Pujols/Jsy	15.00
5	Albert Pujols/Bat	15.00
6	Alex Rodriguez/Bat	10.00
7	Alex Rodriguez/Blue Jsy	10.00
8	Alex Rodriguez/White Jsy	10.00
9	Alfonso Soriano/Bat	8.00
10	Alfonso Soriano/Gray Jsy	8.00
11	Alfonso Soriano/White Jsy	8.00
12	Brett Myers/Jsy	4.00
13	Andruw Jones/Jsy	6.00
14	Austin Kearns/Jsy	6.00
15	Barry Larkin/Jsy	6.00
16	Barry Zito/Jsy	6.00
17	Bernie Williams/Jsy	6.00
18	Brian Giles/Bat	4.00
19	Zach Day/Jsy	4.00
20	Carlos Beltran/Bat	8.00
21	Brandon Phillips/Bat	4.00
22	Carlos Lee/Bat	4.00
23	Casey Fossum/Jsy	4.00
24	Chipper Jones/Jsy	8.00
25	Marcus Giles/Jsy	4.00
26	Craig Biggio/Jsy	6.00
27	Curt Schilling/Jsy	8.00
28	Derek Jeter/Base	15.00
29	Edgar Martinez/Jsy	6.00
30	Eric Chavez/Jsy	6.00
31	Eric Hinske/Bat	4.00
32	Frank Thomas/190/Bat	8.00
33	Aubrey Huff/Jsy	4.00
34	Gary Carter/Jacket	8.00
35	Greg Maddux/Gray Jsy	8.00
36	Greg Maddux/White Jsy	8.00
37	Hideki Matsui/Base **RC**	15.00
38	Hideo Nomo/White Jsy	8.00
39	Rod Carew/Jacket	8.00
40	Ichiro Suzuki/Base	10.00
41	Ivan Rodriguez/Bat	8.00
42	Jason Giambi/Bat	6.00
43	Jason Giambi/Jsy	6.00
44	J.C. Romero/Jsy	4.00
45	Jason Giambi/White Jsy	6.00
46	Jeff Bagwell/Jsy	6.00
47	Josh Bard/Jsy	4.00
48	Jim Thome/Jsy	8.00
49	Jay Gibbons/Jsy	4.00
50	Jorge Posada/Jsy	6.00

51	Juan Gonzalez/Bat	6.00
52	Kazuhisa Ishii/Bat	4.00
53	George Brett/Bat	15.00
54	Kenny Lofton/Bat	4.00
55	Kerry Wood/Jsy	8.00
56	Kevin Brown/Jsy	4.00
57	Kirk Saarloos/Jsy	4.00
58	Lance Berkman/Jsy	5.00
59	Larry Walker/Jsy	4.00
60	Magglio Ordonez/Jsy	4.00
61	Manny Ramirez/Jsy	8.00
62	Mark Mulder/Jsy	4.00
63	Mark Prior/Jsy	8.00
64	Matt Williams/Jsy	4.00
65	Miguel Tejada/Jsy	6.00
66	Mike Mussina/Jsy	6.00
67	Mike Piazza/Bat	10.00
68	Mike Piazza/Black Jsy	10.00
69	Mike Piazza/White Jsy	10.00
70	Nomar Garciaparra/Bat	10.00
71	Nomar Garciaparra/ Gray Jsy	10.00
72	Nomar Garciaparra/ White Jsy	10.00
73	Paul LoDuca/Jsy	4.00
74	Pedro Martinez/Jsy	8.00
75	Rafael Palmeiro/Jsy	8.00
76	Randy Johnson/Gray Jsy	8.00
77	Randy Johnson/White Jsy	8.00
78	Rickey Henderson/Jsy	8.00
79	Roberto Alomar/Jsy	4.00
80	Rod Carew/Jacket	8.00
81	Roger Clemens/Gray Jsy	15.00
82	Roger Clemens/White Jsy	15.00
83	Cal Ripken Jr./Jsy	25.00
84	Roy Oswalt/Jsy	4.00
85	Jeremy Bonderman/Jsy	8.00
86	Ryne Sandberg/Bat	15.00
87	Sammy Sosa/Bat	12.00
88	Sammy Sosa/Grey Jsy	15.00
89	Sammy Sosa/White Jsy	15.00
90	Scott Rolen/Jsy	8.00
91	Frank Catalanotto/Jsy	4.00
92	Shawn Green/Jsy	5.00
93	Tim Hudson/Jsy	5.00
94	Todd Helton/Jsy	8.00
95	Tony Gwynn/Jsy	8.00
96	Torii Hunter/Jsy	6.00
97	Troy Glaus/Jsy	6.00
98	Runelvys Hernandez/Jsy	4.00
99	Vernon Wells/Jsy	4.00
100	Vladimir Guerrero/Jsy	8.00

Autographs

NM/M
Common Player:
Varying quantities produced
Prime Autos: No Pricing
Production 4-20

12	Brett Myers	10.00
18	Brian Giles/30	30.00
19	Zach Day	8.00
21	Brandon Phillips	10.00
22	Carlos Lee	12.00
23	Casey Fossum	10.00
25	Marcus Giles	15.00
29	Edgar Martinez/100	40.00
30	Eric Chavez/75	25.00
31	Eric Hinske	10.00
33	Aubrey Huff	10.00
41	Ivan Rodriguez/50	50.00
41	Ivan Rodriguez/75	40.00
44	J.C. Romero	8.00
47	Josh Bard	8.00
49	Jay Gibbons	10.00
51	Juan Gonzalez/50	50.00
57	Kirk Saarloos	8.00
62	Mark Mulder/100	25.00
63	Mark Prior/25	75.00
64	Matt Williams	15.00
73	Paul LoDuca	15.00
84	Roy Oswalt/50	25.00
85	Jeremy Bonderman	50.00
86	Ryne Sandberg/40	100.00
90	Scott Rolen/50	40.00
94	Frank Catalanotto	8.00
96	Torii Hunter/140	20.00
98	Runelvys Hernandez	10.00
100	Vladimir Guerrero/150	40.00

Prime Materials

No Pricing
Production 25 Sets

Bronze Materials

Cards (1-100): 1-1.5X
Production 150 Sets

Silver Materials

Cards (1-100): 1-2X
Production 75 Sets

Gold Materials

Cards (1-100): 1.5-2.5X
Production 50 Sets

Platinum Materials

No pricing due to scarcity.
Production 25 Sets

2003 Playoff Portraits

Greg Maddux • Atlanta Braves™

NM/M
Complete Set (144): 40.00
Common Player: .25
Pack (7): 4.00
Box (20): 60.00

1	Vladimir Guerrero	1.50
2	Luis Gonzalez	.35
3	Andruw Jones	.75
4	Manny Ramirez	1.50
5	Derek Jeter	4.00
6	Eric Hinske	.25
7	Curt Schilling	.45
8	Adam Dunn	1.00
9	Jason Jennings	.25
10	Mike Piazza	2.50
11	Jason Giambi	.75
12	Jeff Bagwell	1.00
13	Rickey Henderson	1.50
14	Randy Johnson	1.50
15	Roger Clemens	3.00
16	Troy Glaus	1.00
17	Hideo Nomo	.50
18	Joe Borchard	.25
19	Torii Hunter	.25
20	Lance Berkman	.50
21	Todd Helton	1.50
22	Mike Mussina	.40
23	Vernon Wells	.25
24	Pat Burrell	.35
25	Ichiro Suzuki	2.50
26	Shawn Green	1.00
27	Frank Thomas	1.50
28	Barry Zito	.40
29	Barry Bonds	4.00
30	Ken Griffey Jr.	2.50
31	Albert Pujols	3.00
32	Roberto Alomar	.50
33	Barry Larkin	.25
34	Tony Gwynn	2.00
35	Chipper Jones	2.00
36	Pedro J. Martinez	1.50
37	Juan Gonzalez	.75
38	Greg Maddux	2.00
39	Tim Hudson	.35
40	Sammy Sosa	1.50
41	Victor Martinez	.50
42	Mark Buehrle	.25
43	Austin Kearns	.25
44	Kerry Wood	1.00
45	Nomar Garciaparra	1.00
46	Alfonso Soriano	1.00
47	Mark Prior	.75
48	Richie Sexson	.25
49	Mark Teixeira	.75
50	Craig Biggio	.25
51	Rafael Palmeiro	1.00
52	Carlos Beltran	.75
53	Bernie Williams	.35
54	Eric Chavez	.35
55	Paul Konerko	.35
56	Nolan Ryan	4.00
57	Mark Mulder	.25
58	Miguel Tejada	.35
59	Roy Oswalt	.25
60	Jim Edmonds	.25
61	Ryan Klesko	.25
62	Cal Ripken Jr.	4.00
63	Josh Beckett	.25
64	Kazuhisa Ishii	.25
65	Alex Rodriguez	3.00
66	Mike Sweeney	.25
67	C.C. Sabathia	.25
68	Jose Vidro	.25
69	Magglio Ordonez	.25
70	Carlos Delgado	.75
71	Jorge Posada	.25
72	Bobby Abreu	.25
73	Brian Giles	.25
74	Kirby Puckett	2.00
75	Yogi Berra	1.00
76	Ryne Sandberg	2.00
77	Tom Glavine	.45
78	Jim Thome	1.00
79	Chris Snelling	.25
80	Drew Henson	.25
81	Junior Spivey	.25
82	Mike Schmidt	3.00
83	Jeff Kent	.25
84	Stan Musial	2.00
85	Garret Anderson	.25
86	Jose Contreras RC	3.00
87	Ivan Rodriguez	1.00
88	Hideki Matsui RC	6.00
89	Don Mattingly	3.00
90	Angel Berroa	.25
91	George Brett	3.00
92	Jermaine Dye	.25
93	John Olerud	.25
94	Josh Phelps	.25
95	Sean Casey	.35
96	Larry Walker	.25
97	Jason Lane	.25
98	Travis Hafner	.25
99	Terrence Long	.25
100	Shannon Stewart	.25
101	Richard Hidalgo	.25
102	Joe Thurston	.25
103	Ben Sheets	.25
104	Orlando Cabrera	.25
105	Aramis Ramirez	.25
106	So Taguchi	.25
107	Frank Robinson	.75
108	Phil Nevin	.25
109	Dennis Tankersley	.25
110	J.D. Drew	.50
111	Paul LoDuca	.25
112	Ozzie Smith	2.00
113	Carlos Lee	.25
114	Nick Johnson	.25
115	Edgar Martinez	.25
116	Hank Blalock	.75
117	Orlando Hudson	.25
118	Corey Patterson	.25
119	Steve Carlton	.50
120	Wade Miller	.25
121	Adrian Beltre	.75
122	Scott Rolen	1.00
123	Brian Lawrence	.25
124	Rich Aurilia	.25
125	Tsuyoshi Shinjo	.25
126	John Buck	.25
127	Marlon Byrd	.25
128	Michael Cuddyer	.25
129	Marshall McDougall	.25
130	Travis Chapman	.25
131	Jose Morban	.25
132	Adam LaRoche	.25
133	Jose Castillo	.25
134	Walter Young	.25
135	Jeff Baker	.25
136	Jeremy Guthrie	.25
137	Pedro J. Martinez	.75
138	Randy Johnson	.75
139	Alex Rodriguez	1.50
140	Hideo Nomo	.50
141	Roger Clemens	1.00
142	Rickey Henderson	.50
143	Jason Giambi	.40
144	Mike Piazza	1.00

Gold

No Pricing
Production 10 Sets

Silver

Silver: 4-8X
Production 50 Sets

Beige

Beige: 1-3X
Production 250 Sets

Bronze

Bronze: 2-4X
Production 100 Sets

Bronze Autographs

NM/M
Common Bronze Auto.:
Production 100 or less.
Silvers: 1-1.5X
Production 50 or less.
No Pricing for production 25 or less.
Golds: No Pricing
Production 25 or less.

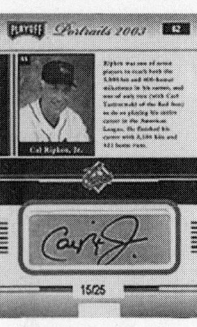

15/25

1	Vladimir Guerrero/100	35.00
3	Andruw Jones/25	50.00
6	Eric Hinske/100	10.00
8	Adam Dunn/50	35.00
9	Jason Jennings/100	8.00
16	Troy Glaus/60	25.00
18	Joe Borchard/100	6.00
19	Torii Hunter/25	40.00
31	Albert Pujols/25	150.00
32	Roberto Alomar/100	35.00
33	Barry Larkin/95	25.00
34	Tony Gwynn/60	75.00
35	Chipper Jones/25	75.00
37	Juan Gonzalez/50	50.00
41	Victor Martinez/100	20.00
42	Mark Buehrle/100	10.00
44	Kerry Wood/40	40.00
47	Mark Prior/25	60.00
48	Richie Sexson/100	20.00
49	Mark Teixeira/25	40.00
50	Craig Biggio/25	40.00
56	Nolan Ryan/25	150.00
57	Mark Mulder/100	20.00
59	Roy Oswalt/40	25.00
61	Ryan Klesko/40	20.00
62	Cal Ripken Jr./150	150.00
67	C.C. Sabathia/50	15.00
72	Bobby Abreu/100	15.00
73	Brian Giles/50	15.00
74	Kirby Puckett/50	60.00
77	Tom Glavine/100	35.00
79	Chris Snelling/100	10.00
80	Drew Henson/25	40.00
81	Junior Spivey/100	10.00
82	Mike Schmidt/50	75.00
83	Jeff Kent/50	25.00
84	Stan Musial/50	65.00
85	Garret Anderson/25	30.00
86	Jose Contreras/50	40.00
89	Don Mattingly/50	90.00
90	Angel Berroa/100	10.00
92	Jermaine Dye/100	10.00
94	Josh Phelps/50	10.00
97	Jason Lane/100	8.00
98	Travis Hafner/100	12.00
99	Terrence Long/100	6.00
100	Shannon Stewart/100	8.00
101	Richard Hidalgo/25	20.00
102	Joe Thurston/100	8.00
103	Ben Sheets/100	15.00
105	Aramis Ramirez/40	15.00
106	So Taguchi/29	30.00
108	Phil Nevin/100	10.00
109	Dennis Tankersley/100	8.00
110	J.D. Drew/25	30.00
111	Paul LoDuca/100	15.00
113	Carlos Lee/100	10.00
114	Nick Johnson/100	10.00
115	Edgar Martinez/100	35.00
117	Orlando Hudson/100	8.00
118	Corey Patterson/100	15.00
119	Steve Carlton/25	40.00
120	Wade Miller/100	6.00
121	Adrian Beltre/25	30.00
122	Scott Rolen/100	30.00
123	Brian Lawrence/100	6.00
126	John Buck/100	6.00
127	Marlon Byrd/100	10.00
128	Michael Cuddyer/100	8.00
129	Marshall McDougall/100	6.00
130	Travis Chapman/100	6.00
131	Jose Morban/100	6.00
132	Adam LaRoche/100	12.00
133	Jose Castillo/100	6.00
134	Walter Young/100	6.00
135	Jeff Baker/100	6.00
136	Jeremy Guthrie/100	10.00

Silver Autographs

Production 50 or less.
No Pricing

Artifacts Bronze

NM/M
Common Player: 4.00
Production 100 or less.
Silvers: 1-1.5X
Production 50 or less.
Golds: No Pricing
Production 25 or less.
Bronze Combos: 1-1.5X

Production 50 or less.
Silver Combos: No Pricing
Production 25 or less.
Gold Combos: No Pricing
Production 10 or less.

1	Vladimir Guerrero/100	8.00
2	Luis Gonzalez/100	5.00
3	Andruw Jones/100	8.00
4	Manny Ramirez/50	10.00
5	Derek Jeter/100	20.00
6	Eric Hinske/100	4.00
7	Curt Schilling/100	8.00
8	Adam Dunn/50	10.00
9	Jason Jennings/100	4.00
10	Mike Piazza/100	12.00
11	Jason Giambi/100	6.00
12	Jeff Bagwell/50	15.00
13	Rickey Henderson/50	20.00
14	Randy Johnson/100	8.00
15	Roger Clemens/100	20.00
16	Troy Glaus/100	6.00
17	Hideo Nomo/100	20.00
18	Joe Borchard	
19	Torii Hunter/100	6.00
20	Lance Berkman/100	6.00
21	Todd Helton/50	15.00
22	Mike Mussina/100	8.00
23	Vernon Wells/100	4.00
24	Pat Burrell/100	6.00
25	Ichiro Suzuki/100	25.00
26	Shawn Green/100	6.00
27	Frank Thomas/100	10.00
28	Barry Zito/100	6.00
29	Barry Bonds/100	20.00
30	Ken Griffey Jr./100	15.00
31	Albert Pujols/100	20.00
32	Roberto Alomar/50	10.00
33	Barry Larkin/50	10.00
34	Tony Gwynn/100	15.00
35	Chipper Jones/100	10.00
36	Pedro Martinez/100	10.00
37	Juan Gonzalez/50	10.00
38	Greg Maddux/100	15.00
39	Tim Hudson/100	6.00
40	Sammy Sosa/100	20.00
41	Victor Martinez/100	8.00
42	Mark Buehrle/50	6.00
43	Austin Kearns/100	6.00
44	Kerry Wood/50	15.00
45	Nomar Garciaparra/100	15.00
46	Alfonso Soriano/100	10.00
47	Mark Prior/100	10.00
48	Richie Sexson/100	6.00
49	Mark Teixeira/50	8.00
50	Craig Biggio/50	8.00
51	Rafael Palmeiro/50	10.00
52	Carlos Beltran/50	10.00
53	Bernie Williams/50	10.00
54	Eric Chavez/100	6.00
55	Paul Konerko/100	4.00
56	Nolan Ryan/100	35.00
57	Mark Mulder/100	6.00
58	Miguel Tejada/100	6.00
59	Roy Oswalt/50	8.00
60	Jim Edmonds/50	8.00
61	Ryan Klesko/50	6.00
62	Cal Ripken Jr/100	40.00
63	Josh Beckett/100	6.00
64	Kazuhisa Ishii/50	6.00
65	Alex Rodriguez/100	15.00
66	Mike Sweeney/100	4.00
67	C.C. Sabathia/100	4.00
68	Jose Vidro/100	4.00
69	Magglio Ordonez/50	6.00
70	Carlos Delgado/50	8.00
71	Jorge Posada/100	8.00
72	Bobby Abreu/100	6.00
74	Kirby Puckett/50	30.00
75	Yogi Berra/50	25.00
76	Ryne Sandberg/50	40.00
77	Tom Glavine/50	8.00
78	Jim Thome/100	10.00
79	Chris Snelling/50	5.00
80	Drew Henson/50	10.00
81	Junior Spivey/50	8.00
82	Mike Schmidt/50	50.00
83	Jeff Kent/50	6.00
84	Stan Musial/100	30.00
85	Garret Anderson/50	8.00
87	Ivan Rodriguez/50	12.00
88	Hideki Matsui/100	25.00
89	Don Mattingly/100	30.00
90	Angel Berroa/100	4.00
91	George Brett/50	50.00
92	Jermaine Dye/50	4.00
93	John Olerud/100	4.00
94	Josh Phelps/50	4.00
95	Sean Casey/50	4.00
96	Larry Walker/50	8.00
97	Jason Lane/50	4.00
98	Travis Hafner/100	6.00
99	Terrence Long/50	4.00
100	Shannon Stewart/50	4.00
101	Richard Hidalgo/50	4.00
102	Joe Thurston/100	4.00
103	Ben Sheets/100	6.00
104	Orlando Cabrera/50	6.00
105	Aramis Ramirez/100	6.00
106	So Taguchi/50	5.00
107	Frank Robinson/50	12.00
109	Dennis Tankersley/100	4.00
110	J.D. Drew/100	6.00
111	Paul LoDuca/50	6.00
112	Ozzie Smith/50	40.00
113	Carlos Lee/100	4.00
114	Nick Johnson/100	4.00
115	Edgar Martinez/100	8.00
116	Hank Blalock/50	15.00
117	Orlando Hudson/100	4.00
118	Corey Patterson/100	6.00
119	Steve Carlton/50	10.00
120	Wade Miller/50	6.00
121	Adrian Beltre/50	8.00
122	Scott Rolen/50	20.00
123	Brian Lawrence/50	4.00
124	Rich Aurilia/50	4.00
125	Tsuyoshi Shinjo/50	8.00
126	John Buck/50	4.00
127	Marlon Byrd/100	4.00
128	Michael Cuddyer/50	4.00
130	Travis Chapman/100	4.00
131	Jose Morban/100	4.00
132	Adam LaRoche/100	4.00
133	Jose Castillo/100	4.00
134	Walter Young/100	4.00

2003 Playoff Prestige

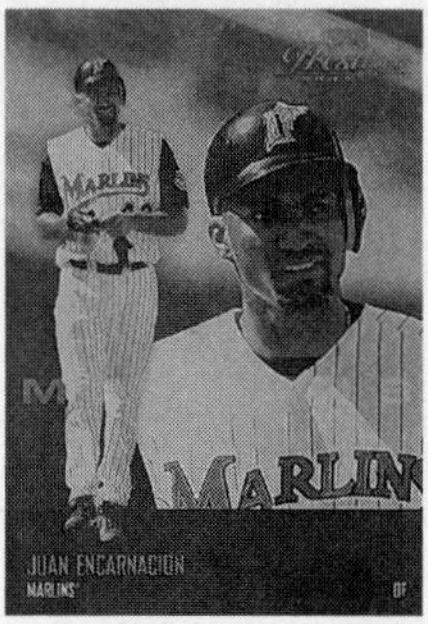

		NM/M
Complete Set (200):		35.00
Common Player:		.15
Pack (6):		2.00
Box (24):		45.00
1	Darin Erstad	.25
2	David Eckstein	.15
3	Garret Anderson	.15
4	Jarrod Washburn	.15
5	Tim Salmon	.25
6	Troy Glaus	.50
7	Jay Gibbons	.15
8	Marty Cordova	.15
9	Melvin Mora	.15
10	Rodrigo Lopez	.15
11	Tony Batista	.15
12	Cliff Floyd	.15
13	Derek Lowe	.15
14	Johnny Damon	.50
15	Manny Ramirez	.75
16	Nomar Garciaparra	.50
17	Pedro J. Martinez	.75
18	Rickey Henderson	.75
19	Shea Hillenbrand	.15
20	Carlos Lee	.15
21	Frank Thomas	.75
22	Magglio Ordonez	.15
23	Mark Buehrle	.15
24	Paul Konerko	.15
25	C.C. Sabathia	.15
26	Danys Baez	.15
27	Ellis Burks	.15
28	Travis Hafner	.15
29	Omar Vizquel	.15
30	Bobby Higginson	.15
31	Carlos Pena	.15
32	Mark Redman	.15
33	Robert Fick	.15
34	Steve Sparks	.15
35	Carlos Beltran	.50
36	Joe Randa	.15
37	Mike Sweeney	.15
38	Paul Byrd	.15
39	Raul Ibanez	.15
40	Runelvys Hernandez	.15
41	Brad Radke	.15
42	Corey Koskie	.15
43	Cristian Guzman	.15
44	David Ortiz	1.00
45	Doug Mientkiewicz	.15
46	Dustan Mohr	.15
47	Jacque Jones	.15
48	Torii Hunter	.15
49	Alfonso Soriano	.75
50	Andy Pettitte	.50
51	Bernie Williams	.40
52	David Wells	.15
53	Derek Jeter	2.00
54	Jason Giambi	.50
55	Jeff Weaver	.15
56	Jorge Posada	.15
57	Mike Mussina	.50
58	Roger Clemens	1.25
59	Barry Zito	.25
60	David Justice	.15
61	Eric Chavez	.25
62	Jermaine Dye	.15
63	Mark Mulder	.15
64	Miguel Tejada	.40
65	Ray Durham	.15
66	Tim Hudson	.40
67	Bret Boone	.15
68	Chris Snelling	.15
69	Edgar Martinez	.15
70	Freddy Garcia	.15
71	Ichiro Suzuki	1.50
72	Jamie Moyer	.15
73	John Olerud	.15
74	Kazuhiro Sasaki	.15
75	Aubrey Huff	.15
76	Joe Kennedy	.15
77	Paul Wilson	.15
78	Alex Rodriguez	1.75
79	Chan Ho Park	.15
80	Hank Blalock	.50
81	Ivan Rodriguez	.50
82	Juan Gonzalez	.50
83	Kevin Mench	.15
84	Rafael Palmeiro	.50
85	Carlos Delgado	.40
86	Eric Hinske	.15
87	Jose Cruz	.15
88	Josh Phelps	.15
89	Roy Halladay	.15
90	Shannon Stewart	.15
91	Vernon Wells	.15
92	Curt Schilling	.40
93	Junior Spivey	.15
94	Luis Gonzalez	.25
95	Mark Grace	.25
96	Randy Johnson	.75
97	Andruw Jones	.40
98	Chipper Jones	1.00
99	Gary Sheffield	.40
100	Greg Maddux	1.00
101	John Smoltz	.15
102	Kevin Millwood	.15
103	Mike Hampton	.15
104	Corey Patterson	.15
105	Fred McGriff	.15
106	Kerry Wood	.50
107	Mark Prior	.40
108	Moises Alou	.15
109	Sammy Sosa	1.00
110	Adam Dunn	.50
111	Austin Kearns	.15
112	Barry Larkin	.15
113	Ken Griffey Jr.	1.50
114	Sean Casey	.25
115	Jason Jennings	.15
116	Jay Payton	.15
117	Larry Walker	.15
118	Todd Helton	.50
119	A.J. Burnett	.15
120	Josh Beckett	.15
121	Juan Encarnacion	.15
122	Mike Lowell	.15
123	Craig Biggio	.15
124	Daryle Ward	.15
125	Jeff Bagwell	.50
126	Lance Berkman	.15
127	Roy Oswalt	.15
128	Adrian Beltre	.40
129	Hideo Nomo	.40
130	Kazuhisa Ishii	.15
131	Kevin Brown	.15
132	Odalis Perez	.15
133	Paul LoDuca	.15
134	Shawn Green	.40
135	Jeff Kent	.15
136	Ben Sheets	.15
137	Jeffrey Hammonds	.15
138	Jose Hernandez	.15
139	Richie Sexson	.15
140	Bartolo Colon	.15
141	Brad Wilkerson	.15
142	Javier Vazquez	.15
143	Jose Vidro	.15
144	Michael Barrett	.15
145	Vladimir Guerrero	.75
146	Al Leiter	.15
147	Mike Piazza	1.50
148	Mo Vaughn	.15
149	Pedro Astacio	.15
150	Roberto Alomar	.40
151	Roger Cedeno	.15
152	Tom Glavine	.40
153	Bobby Abreu	.15
154	Jimmy Rollins	.25
155	Mike Lieberthal	.15
156	Pat Burrell	.40
157	Vicente Padilla	.15
158	Jim Thome	.50
159	Aramis Ramirez	.15
160	Brian Giles	.15
161	Jason Kendall	.15
162	Josh Fogg	.15
163	Kip Wells	.15
164	Mark Kotsay	.15
165	Oliver Perez	.15
166	Phil Nevin	.15
167	Ryan Klesko	.15
168	Sean Burroughs	.15
169	Trevor Hoffman	.15
170	Barry Bonds	2.00
171	Benito Santiago	.15
172	Reggie Sanders	.15
173	Rich Aurilia	.15
174	Russ Ortiz	.15
175	Albert Pujols	1.75
176	J.D. Drew	.25
177	Jim Edmonds	.15
178	Matt Morris	.15
179	Tino Martinez	.15
180	Scott Rolen	.50
181	Joe Borchard	.15
182	Freddy Sanchez	.15
183	Jose Contreras **RC**	3.00
184	Jeff Baker	.15
185	Ryan Church	.15
186	Mario Ramos	.15
187	Corwin Malone	.15
188	Jimmy Gobble	.15
189	Jon Adkins	.15
190	Tim Kalita	.15
191	Nelson Castro	.15
192	Colin Young	.15
193	Luis Martinez	.15
194	Todd Donovan	.15
195	Jeremy Ward	.15
196	Wilson Valdez	.15
197	Hideki Matsui **RC**	6.00
198	Mitch Wylie	.15
199	Adam Walker	.15
200	Clifford Bartosh	.15

X-tra Points

Stars (1-180): 4-8X
Production 150
Prospects (181-200): 4-8X
Production 50

Award Winners

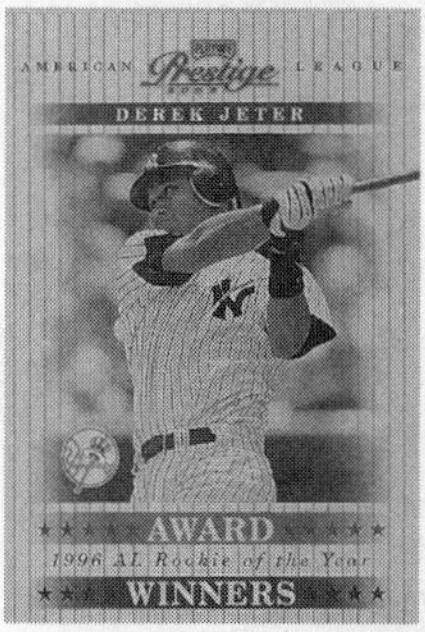

		NM/M
Complete Set (15):		25.00
Common Player:		1.00
#'d to year of award		
1	Barry Zito	1.00
2	Barry Bonds	5.00
3	Randy Johnson	1.50
4	Roger Clemens	2.50
5	Ichiro Suzuki	3.00
6	Chipper Jones	2.00
7	Ken Griffey Jr.	3.00
8	Miguel Tejada	1.00
9	Greg Maddux	2.00
10	Jeff Bagwell	1.50
11	Rickey Henderson	1.50
12	Tom Glavine	1.00
13	Albert Pujols	4.00
14	Nomar Garciaparra	3.00
15	Derek Jeter	5.00

Connections

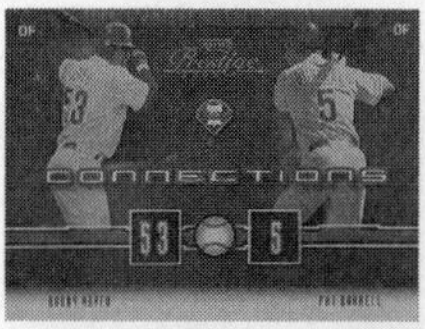

		NM/M
Complete Set (70):		90.00
Common Duo:		1.00
Inserted 1:8		
Century Connections:		3-6X
Production 100 Sets		
1	Troy Glaus, Garret Anderson	1.50
2	Troy Glaus, Tim Salmon	1.50
3	Randy Johnson, Curt Schilling	1.50
4	Matt Williams, Luis Gonzalez	1.00
5	Greg Maddux, John Smoltz	2.00
6	Andruw Jones, Chipper Jones	2.00
7	Greg Maddux, Kevin Millwood	2.00
8	Tony Batista, Geronimo Gil	1.00
9	Pedro J. Martinez, Nomar Garciaparra	3.00
10	Manny Ramirez, Nomar Garciaparra	3.00
11	Nomar Garciaparra, Rickey Henderson	3.00
12	Trot Nixon, Manny Ramirez	1.50
13	Kerry Wood, Mark Prior	1.00
14	Sammy Sosa, Fred McGriff	3.00
15	Sammy Sosa, Corey Patterson	3.00

16	Frank Thomas, Magglio Ordonez	1.50
17	Joe Borchard, Magglio Ordonez	1.00
18	Adam Dunn, Austin Kearns	1.00
19	Barry Larkin, Ken Griffey Jr.	3.00
20	Adam Dunn, Barry Larkin	3.00
21	Adam Dunn, Ken Griffey Jr.	3.00
22	Victor Martinez, Omar Vizquel	1.00
23	C.C. Sabathia, Victor Martinez	1.00
24	Larry Walker, Todd Helton	1.00
25	Carlos Pena, Robert Fick	1.00
26	Josh Beckett, Juan Encarnacion	1.00
27	Jeff Bagwell, Craig Biggio	1.50
28	Lance Berkman, Roy Oswalt	1.00
29	Lance Berkman, Jeff Bagwell	1.50
30	Mike Sweeney, Carlos Beltran	1.00
31	Mike Sweeney, Angel Berroa	1.00
32	Kazuhisa Ishii, Shawn Green	1.00
33	Adrian Beltre, Shawn Green	1.00
34	Kazuhisa Ishii, Hideo Nomo	1.00
35	Richie Sexson, Ben Sheets	1.00
36	Jacque Jones, Torii Hunter	1.00
37	Doug Mientkiewicz, David Ortiz	1.00
38	Vladimir Guerrero, Jose Vidro	1.50
39	Derek Jeter, Jason Giambi	5.00
40	Derek Jeter, Bernie Williams	5.00
41	Roger Clemens, Mike Mussina	2.50
42	Alfonso Soriano, Jorge Posada	1.50
43	Derek Jeter, Alfonso Soriano	5.00
44	Mike Piazza, Roberto Alomar	3.00
45	Mike Piazza, Mo Vaughn	3.00
46	Eric Chavez, Miguel Tejada	1.00
47	Mark Mulder, Barry Zito	1.00
48	Tim Hudson, Barry Zito	1.00
49	Pat Burrell, Bobby Abreu	1.00
50	Jim Thome, Pat Burrell	1.00
51	Jim Thome, Marlon Byrd	1.00
52	Brian Giles, Aramis Ramirez	1.00
53	Ryan Klesko, Phil Nevin	1.00
54	Barry Bonds, Benito Santiago	5.00
55	Jeff Kent, Rich Aurilia	1.00
56	Barry Bonds, Jeff Kent	5.00
57	Ichiro Suzuki, Kazuhiro Sasaki	3.00
58	Edgar Martinez, John Olerud	1.00
59	Albert Pujols, Scott Rolen	4.00
60	Jim Edmonds, J.D. Drew	1.00
61	Albert Pujols, Jim Edmonds	4.00
62	Dewon Brazelton, Joe Kennedy	1.00
63	Alex Rodriguez, Ivan Rodriguez	4.00
64	Juan Gonzalez, Rafael Palmeiro	1.50
65	Mark Teixeira, Hank Blalock	1.00
66	Alex Rodriguez, Juan Gonzalez	4.00
67	Alex Rodriguez, Juan Gonzalez	4.00
68	Shannon Stewart, Carlos Delgado	1.00
69	Josh Phelps, Eric Hinske	1.00
70	Vernon Wells, Roy Halladay	1.00

Diamond Heritage

		NM/M
Complete Set (30):		35.00
Common Player:		1.00
Inserted 1:21		
Golds:		5-10X
Production 50 Sets		
1	Larry Walker	1.00
2	Troy Glaus	1.50
3	Magglio Ordonez	1.00
4	Roy Oswalt	1.00
5	Barry Zito	1.00
6	Nomar Garciaparra	3.00
7	Kerry Wood	1.25

8	Roger Clemens	2.50
9	Pedro J. Martinez	1.50
10	Mark Prior	1.00
11	Sammy Sosa	3.00
12	Randy Johnson	1.50
13	Greg Maddux	2.00
14	Manny Ramirez	1.50
15	Torii Hunter	1.00
16	Alex Rodriguez	4.00
17	Mike Piazza	3.00
18	Vladimir Guerrero	1.50
19	Ivan Rodriguez	1.25
20	Lance Berkman	1.00
21	Miguel Tejada	1.00
22	Chipper Jones	2.00
23	Todd Helton	1.50
24	Shawn Green	1.00
25	Scott Rolen	1.25
26	Adam Dunn	1.25
27	Jim Thome	1.25
28	Rafael Palmeiro	1.25
29	Eric Chavez	1.00
30	Andruw Jones	1.50

Diamond Heritage Materials

	NM/M
Common Player:	5.00
Production 200 unless noted.	
Autographs:	Not Priced
Production 15 to 25	
1 Larry Walker	6.00
2 Troy Glaus	6.00
3 Magglio Ordonez	5.00
4 Roy Oswalt	5.00
5 Barry Zito	8.00
6 Nomar Garciaparra	15.00
7 Kerry Wood	8.00
8 Roger Clemens	15.00
9 Pedro J. Martinez	10.00
10 Mark Prior	6.00
11 Sammy Sosa	15.00
12 Randy Johnson	10.00
13 Greg Maddux	10.00
14 Manny Ramirez	8.00
15 Torii Hunter	6.00
16 Alex Rodriguez/Bat/100	15.00
17 Mike Piazza/Bat/100	15.00
18 V. Guerrero/Bat/100	10.00
19 Ivan Rodriguez/Bat/100	8.00
20 Lance Berkman/Bat/100	8.00
21 Miguel Tejada/Bat/100	8.00
22 Chipper Jones/Bat/100	15.00
23 Todd Helton/Bat/100	10.00
24 Shawn Green/Bat/100	8.00
25 Scott Rolen/Bat/100	15.00
26 Adam Dunn/Bat/100	12.00
27 Jim Thome/Bat/100	10.00
28 Rafael Palmeiro/Bat/100	10.00
29 Eric Chavez/Bat/100	8.00
30 Andruw Jones/Bat/100	8.00

Diamond Heritage Material Autograph

Quantity produced listed
No Pricing

Draft Class Reunion

	NM/M
Complete Set (10):	20.00
Common Player:	1.00
Inserted 1:24	
1 Mike Piazza, John Olerud	3.00
2 Derek Jeter, Shannon Stewart	5.00
3 Alex Rodriguez, Torii Hunter	4.00
4 Nomar Garciaparra, Paul Konerko	3.00
5 Kerry Wood, Todd Helton	1.50
6 Eric Chavez, Billy Koch	1.00
7 Lance Berkman, Troy Glaus	1.50
8 Pat Burrell, Mark Mulder	1.50
9 Barry Zito, Jason Jennings	1.00
10 Mark Prior, Mark Teixeira	1.50

Inside The Numbers

	NM/M
Complete Set (25):	35.00
Common Player:	1.00
Production 2,002 Sets	
Die-Cuts:	10-25X
#'d to jersey number	

1	Roger Clemens	2.50
2	Greg Maddux	2.00
3	Miguel Tejada	1.00
4	Alex Rodriguez	4.00
5	Ichiro Suzuki	2.50
6	Sammy Sosa	3.00
7	Jim Thome	1.50
8	Derek Jeter	5.00
9	Randy Johnson	1.50
10	Barry Zito	1.00
11	Jason Giambi	1.50
12	Shawn Green	1.00
13	Curt Schilling	1.00
14	Albert Pujols	4.00
15	Vladimir Guerrero	1.50
16	Pedro J. Martinez	1.50
17	Alfonso Soriano	1.50
18	Barry Bonds	5.00
19	Magglio Ordonez	1.00
20	Chipper Jones	2.00
21	Pat Burrell	1.00
22	Luis Gonzalez	1.00
23	Jeff Bagwell	1.50
24	Garret Anderson	1.00
25	Larry Walker	1.00

Infield/Outfield Tandems Material

		NM/M
Common Duo:		8.00
Production 100 Sets		
1	Troy Glaus, Garret Anderson	10.00
2	Mark Grace, Luis Gonzalez	10.00
3	Nomar Garciaparra, Manny Ramirez	20.00
4	Alfonso Soriano, Bernie Williams	15.00
5	Jeff Bagwell, Lance Berkman	15.00
6	Alex Rodriguez, Juan Gonzalez	15.00
7	Barry Larkin, Adam Dunn	15.00
8	Scott Rolen, Jim Edmonds	20.00
9	Todd Helton, Larry Walker	10.00
10	Adrian Beltre, Shawn Green	10.00
11	Jose Vidro, Vladimir Guerrero	12.00
12	Mike Sweeney, Carlos Beltran	10.00
13	Josh Phelps, Vernon Wells	8.00
14	Paul Konerko, Magglio Ordonez	10.00
15	Phil Nevin, Ryan Klesko	10.00

League Leaders

		NM/M
Complete Set (15):		25.00
Common Player:		1.00
Production 2,002 Sets		
1	Manny Ramirez	2.00
2	Sammy Sosa	3.00
3	Alex Rodriguez	4.00
4	Alfonso Soriano	2.00
5	Vladimir Guerrero	2.00
6	Nomar Garciaparra	3.00
7	Johnny Damon	1.00
8	Alfonso Soriano	2.00
9	Barry Bonds	5.00
10	Barry Zito	1.00
11	Pedro J. Martinez	2.00
12	John Smoltz	1.00
13	Randy Johnson	2.00
14	Lance Berkman	1.00
15	Randy Johnson	2.00

League Leaders Materials

		NM/M
Common Player:		4.00
Production 250 Sets		
1	Manny Ramirez/Jsy	8.00
2	Sammy Sosa/Base	8.00
3	Alex Rodriguez/Jsy	10.00
4	Alfonso Soriano/Jsy	8.00
5	Vladimir Guerrero/Jsy	8.00
6	Nomar Garciaparra/Jsy	10.00
7	Johnny Damon/Bat	4.00
8	Alfonso Soriano/Jsy	10.00
9	Barry Bonds/Base	12.00
10	Barry Zito/Jsy	6.00
11	Pedro J. Martinez/Jsy	10.00
12	John Smoltz	6.00
13	Randy Johnson/Jsy	10.00
14	Lance Berkman/Jsy	6.00
15	Randy Johnson/Jsy	10.00

Material Connections

		NM/M
Common Duo:		4.00
Production 400 Sets		
1	Troy Glaus, Garret Anderson	8.00
2	Troy Glaus, Tim Salmon	8.00
3	Matt Williams, Luis Gonzalez	6.00
4		
5	Greg Maddux, John Smoltz	12.00
6	Andruw Jones, Chipper Jones	12.00

7	Greg Maddux, Kevin Millwood	12.00
8	Tony Batista, Geronimo Gil	4.00
9	Pedro J. Martinez, Nomar Garciaparra	15.00
10	Manny Ramirez, Nomar Garciaparra	15.00
11	Nomar Garciaparra, Rickey Henderson	15.00
12	Trot Nixon, Manny Ramirez	10.00
13	Kerry Wood, Mark Prior	10.00
14	Sammy Sosa, Fred McGriff	10.00
15	Sammy Sosa, Corey Patterson	10.00
16	Frank Thomas, Magglio Ordonez	8.00
17	Joe Borchard, Magglio Ordonez	6.00
18	Adam Dunn, Austin Kearns	20.00
20	Adam Dunn, Barry Larkin	15.00
22	Victor Martinez, Omar Vizquel	4.00
23	C.C. Sabathia, Victor Martinez	6.00
24	Larry Walker, Todd Helton	8.00
26	Josh Beckett, Juan Encarnacion	8.00
27	Jeff Bagwell, Craig Biggio	10.00
28	Lance Berkman, Roy Oswalt	8.00
29	Lance Berkman, Jeff Bagwell	10.00
30	Mike Sweeney, Carlos Beltran	8.00
31	Mike Sweeney, Angel Berroa	4.00
32	Kazuhisa Ishii, Shawn Green	10.00
33	Adrian Beltre, Shawn Green	6.00
34	Kazuhisa Ishii, Hideo Nomo	25.00
35	Richie Sexson, Ben Sheets	8.00
36	Jacque Jones, Torii Hunter	10.00
37	Doug Mientkiewicz, David Ortiz	6.00
38	Vladimir Guerrero, Jose Vidro	10.00
39	Derek Jeter, Jason Giambi	15.00
40	Derek Jeter, Bernie Williams	15.00
41	Roger Clemens, Mike Mussina	20.00
42	Alfonso Soriano, Jorge Posada	10.00
43	Derek Jeter, Alfonso Soriano	20.00
44	Mike Piazza, Roberto Alomar	15.00
45	Mike Piazza, Mo Vaughn	10.00
46	Eric Chavez, Miguel Tejada	8.00
47	Mark Mulder, Barry Zito	10.00
48	Tim Hudson, Barry Zito	8.00
49	Pat Burrell, Bobby Abreu	8.00
50	Jim Thome, Pat Burrell	10.00
51	Jim Thome, Marlon Byrd	6.00
52	Brian Giles, Aramis Ramirez	6.00
53	Ryan Klesko, Phil Nevin	6.00
54	Barry Bonds, Benito Santiago	12.00
55	Jeff Kent, Rich Aurilia	5.00
56	Barry Bonds, Jeff Kent	12.00
57	Ichiro Suzuki, Kazuhiro Sasaki	25.00
58	Edgar Martinez, John Olerud	6.00
59	Albert Pujols, Scott Rolen	15.00
60	Jim Edmonds, J.D. Drew	8.00
61	Albert Pujols, Jim Edmonds	12.00
62	Dewon Brazelton, Joe Kennedy	8.00
63	Alex Rodriguez, Ivan Rodriguez	12.00
64	Juan Gonzalez, Rafael Palmeiro	8.00
65	Mark Teixeira, Hank Blalock	10.00
66	Alex Rodriguez, Juan Gonzalez	15.00
67	Alex Rodriguez, Juan Gonzalez	12.00
68	Shannon Stewart, Carlos Delgado	6.00
69	Josh Phelps, Eric Hinske	4.00
70	Vernon Wells, Roy Halladay	4.00

Player Collection

	NM/M
Common Player:	4.00
Production 325 Sets	
1 Adam Dunn	8.00
2 Adrian Beltre	6.00

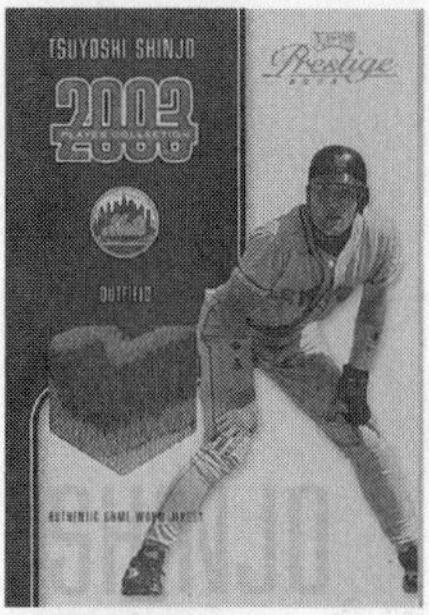

3	Alex Rodriguez	20.00
4	Alfonso Soriano	10.00
5	Andruw Jones	8.00
6	Andy Pettitte	6.00
7	Barry Larkin	4.00
8	Barry Zito	4.00
9	Ben Grieve	4.00
10	Bernie Williams	4.00
11	Cal Ripken Jr.	25.00
12	Carlos Delgado	5.00
13	C.C. Sabathia	4.00
14	Chipper Jones	12.00
15	Craig Biggio	4.00
16	Curt Schilling	5.00
17	Alex Rodriguez	20.00
18	Frank Thomas	8.00
19	Freddy Garcia	4.00
20	Jay Bell	4.00
21	Roger Clemens	15.00
22	Tony Gwynn	12.00
23	Ivan Rodriguez	8.00
24	Jason Giambi	8.00
25	Jason Jennings	4.00
26	Jay Payton	4.00
27	J.D. Drew	6.00
28	Jeff Bagwell	8.00
29	Jeromy Burnitz	4.00
30	Jim Edmonds	4.00
31	Jim Thome	8.00
32	Joe Borchard	4.00
33	Joe Mays	4.00
34	John Olerud	4.00
35	David Wells	4.00
36	Juan Gonzalez	8.00
37	Kazuhiro Sasaki	4.00
38	Chan Ho Park	4.00
39	Kerry Wood	8.00
40	Kevin Brown	4.00
41	Lance Berkman	4.00
42	Larry Walker	4.00
43	Bret Boone	4.00
44	Magglio Ordonez	4.00
45	Manny Ramirez	8.00
46	Mark Mulder	4.00
47	Mark Prior	6.00
48	Matt Williams	4.00
49	Miguel Tejada	4.00
50	Mike Piazza	15.00
51	Nomar Garciaparra	15.00
52	Doug Davis	4.00
53	Paul Konerko	4.00
54	Paul LoDuca	4.00
55	Pedro J. Martinez	8.00
56	Preston Wilson	4.00
57	Rafael Palmeiro	8.00
58	Marlon Byrd	4.00
59	Reggie Sanders	4.00
60	Richie Sexson	4.00
61	Rickey Henderson	10.00
62	Rickey Henderson	10.00
63	Robert Person	4.00
64	Jeff Bagwell	8.00
65	Roger Clemens	15.00
66	Roy Oswalt	4.00
67	Ryan Klesko	4.00
68	Sammy Sosa	15.00
69	Shawn Green	5.00
70	Steve Finley	4.00
71	Terrence Long	4.00
72	Tim Hudson	4.00
73	Toby Hall	4.00
74	Todd Helton	8.00
75	Travis Lee	4.00
76	Troy Glaus	8.00
77	Tsuyoshi Shinjo	4.00
78	Vernon Wells	4.00
79	Vladimir Guerrero	8.00
80	Wes Helms	4.00
81	Alex Rodriguez	20.00
82	Alfonso Soriano	10.00
83	Barry Larkin	4.00
84	Roberto Alomar	5.00
85	Ivan Rodriguez	8.00
86	Jason Giambi	6.00
87	Jeff Bagwell	8.00
88	Juan Gonzalez	8.00
89	Larry Walker	4.00
90	Luis Gonzalez	4.00
91	Magglio Ordonez	4.00
92	Manny Ramirez	8.00
93	Marlon Byrd	4.00
94	Mike Piazza	15.00
95	Pat Burrell	6.00
96	Todd Helton	8.00
97	Rickey Henderson	10.00
98	Andruw Jones	8.00
99	Craig Biggio	4.00
100	Mark Prior	6.00

Signature Impressions

NM/M

Varying quantities produced

1	A.J. Pierzynski/50	20.00
2	Adam Dunn/25	60.00
3	Barry Zito/25	50.00
4	Bobby Abreu/20	30.00
5	Brandon Phillips/25	25.00
7	Don Mattingly/15	250.00
9	Eric Hinske/25	25.00
12	John Candelaria/50	15.00
16	Lance Berkman/25	30.00
18	Miguel Tejada/25	40.00
22	Roy Oswalt/25	30.00
27	Yogi Berra/15	100.00
28	Joe Kennedy/50	10.00
30	Lenny Dykstra/50	25.00
39	Toby Hall/50	10.00
40	Victor Martinez/25	45.00
46	Brian Giles/15	40.00
50	Jeremy Bonderman/100	35.00

Stars of MLB

NM/M

Common Player: 5.00
Production 150 Sets
Patches: 4-8X
Production 25 Sets
Autographs: No Pricing
Production 25
Patch Autographs: No Pricing
Production 5 to 10

1	Roger Clemens	12.00
2	Randy Johnson	8.00
3	Sammy Sosa	12.00
4	Vladimir Guerrero	8.00
5	Lance Berkman	5.00
6	Alfonso Soriano	8.00
7	Alex Rodriguez	15.00
8	Roberto Alomar	6.00
9	Miguel Tejada	5.00
10	Pedro J. Martinez	8.00
11	Greg Maddux	10.00
12	Barry Zito	5.00
13	Magglio Ordonez	5.00
14	Chipper Jones	10.00
15	Manny Ramirez	8.00
16	Troy Glaus	8.00
17	Pat Burrell	6.00
18	Roy Oswalt	5.00
19	Mike Piazza	12.00
20	Nomar Garciaparra	12.00

2004 Playoff Absolute Memorabilia

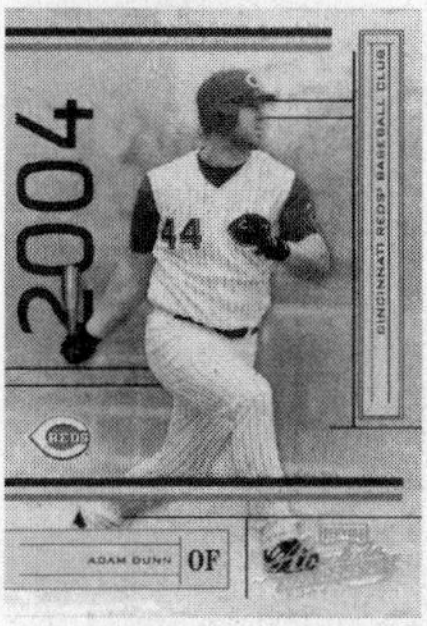

NM/M

Complete Set (250):
Common Player (1-200): 1.50
Production 1,349
Common Non-Auto. (201-250): 2.00
Production 1,000
Common Auto. (201-250): 8.00
Production 500-700
Pack (4): 40.00
Box (6): 185.00

1	Troy Glaus	2.00
2	Garret Anderson	2.00
3	Tim Salmon	2.00
4	Bartolo Colon	1.50
5	Troy Percival	1.50
6	Nolan Ryan Angels	10.00
7	Vladimir Guerrero	4.00
8	Richie Sexson	2.00
9	Shea Hillenbrand	1.50
10	Luis Gonzalez	1.50
11	Brandon Webb	1.50
12	Randy Johnson	4.00
13	Robby Hammock	1.50
14	Edgar Gonzalez	1.50
15	Roberto Alomar	3.00
16	Andruw Jones	3.00
17	Chipper Jones	4.00
18	Dale Murphy	2.00
19	Rafael Furcal	1.50
20	J.D. Drew	2.00
21	Bubba Nelson	1.50
22	Julio Franco	1.50
23	Adam LaRoche	1.50
24	Michael Hessman	1.50
25	Warren Spahn	3.00
26	Jay Gibbons	1.50
27	Cal Ripken Jr.	10.00
28	Miguel Tejada	2.50
29	Adam Loewen	1.50
30	Rafael Palmeiro	3.00
31	Javy Lopez	2.00
32	Luis Matos	1.50
33	Jason Varitek	2.00
34	Carl Yastrzemski	3.00
35	Manny Ramirez	3.00
36	Trot Nixon	2.00
37	Curt Schilling	3.00
38	Pedro J. Martinez	4.00
39	Nomar Garciaparra	5.00
40	Luis Tiant	1.50
41	Kevin Youkilis	1.50
42	Michel Hernandez	1.50
43	Sammy Sosa	5.00
44	Greg Maddux	4.00
45	Kerry Wood	4.00
46	Mark Prior	4.00
47	Ernie Banks	4.00
48	Aramis Ramirez	2.00
49	Brendan Harris	1.50
50	Todd Wellemeyer	1.50
51	Frank Thomas	3.00
52	Magglio Ordonez	2.00
53	Carlos Lee	1.50
54	Joe Crede	1.50
55	Joe Borchard	1.50
56	Mark Buehrle	1.50
57	Sean Casey	2.00
58	Adam Dunn	2.50
59	Austin Kearns	2.00
60	Ken Griffey Jr.	5.00
61	Barry Larkin	2.00
62	Ryan Wagner	1.50
63	Jody Gerut	1.50
64	Jeremy Guthrie	1.50
65	Travis Hafner	2.00
66	Brian Tallet	1.50
67	Todd Helton	3.00
68	Preston Wilson	1.50
69	Jeff Baker	1.50
70	Clint Barmes	1.50
71	Joe Kennedy	1.50
72	Jack Morris	1.50
73	George Kell	1.50
74	Preston Larrison	1.50
75	Dmitri Young	1.50
76	Ivan Rodriguez	3.00
77	Dontrelle Willis	2.00
78	Josh Beckett	2.50
79	Miguel Cabrera	4.00
80	Mike Lowell	2.00
81	Luis Castillo	1.50
82	Juan Pierre	1.50
83	Jeff Bagwell	3.00
84	Jeff Kent	2.00
85	Craig Biggio	2.00
86	Lance Berkman	2.00
87	Andy Pettitte	2.00
88	Roy Oswalt	2.00
89	Chris Burke	1.50
90	Jason Lane	1.50
91	Roger Clemens	6.00
92	Mike Sweeney	1.50
93	Carlos Beltran	2.00
94	Angel Berroa	1.50
95	Juan Gonzalez	2.50
96	Ken Harvey	1.50
97	Byron Gettis	1.50
98	Alexis Gomez	1.50
99	Ian Ferguson	1.50
100	Duke Snider	3.00
101	Shawn Green	2.00
102	Hideo Nomo	2.00
103	Kazuhisa Ishii	1.50
104	Edwin Jackson	1.50
105	Fred McGriff	2.00
106	Hong-Chih Kou	1.50
107	Don Sutton **RC**	2.00
108	Rickey Henderson	2.00
109	Cesar Izturis	1.50
110	Robin Ventura	1.50
111	Paul LoDuca	1.50
112	Rickie Weeks	2.00
113	Scott Podsednik	2.00
114	Junior Spivey	1.50
115	Lyle Overbay	2.00
116	Tony Oliva	1.50
117	Jacque Jones	1.50
118	Shannon Stewart	1.50
119	Torii Hunter	2.00
120	Johan Santana	1.50
121	J.D. Durbin	1.50
122	Jason Kubel	1.50
123	Michael Cuddyer	1.50
124	Nick Johnson	1.50
125	Jose Vidro	1.50
126	Orlando Cabrera	1.50
127	Zach Day	1.50
128	Mike Piazza	5.00
129	Tom Glavine	2.00
130	Jae Weong Seo	1.50
131	Gary Carter	2.00
132	Phil Seibel	1.50
133	Edwin Almonte	1.50
134	Aaron Boone	1.50
135	Kenny Lofton	2.00
136	Don Mattingly	6.00
137	Jason Giambi	3.00
138	Alex Rodriguez Yanks	8.00
139	Jorge Posada	2.00
140	Bernie Williams	2.00
141	Hideki Matsui	5.00
142	Mike Mussina	2.00
143	Mariano Rivera	2.00
144	Gary Sheffield	2.00
145	Derek Jeter	8.00
146	Chien-Ming Wang	1.50
147	Javier Vazquez	1.50
148	Jose Contreras	1.50
149	Whitey Ford	2.00
150	Kevin Brown	2.00
151	Eric Chavez	2.00
152	Barry Zito	2.00
153	Mark Mulder	2.00
154	Tim Hudson	2.00
155	Rich Harden	1.50
156	Eric Byrnes	1.50
157	Jim Thome	4.00
158	Bobby Abreu	2.00
159	Marlon Byrd	1.50
160	Lenny Dykstra	1.50
161	Steve Carlton	2.00
162	Ryan Howard	2.00
163	Bobby Hill	1.50
164	Jose Castillo	1.50
165	Jay Payton	1.50
166	Ryan Klesko	1.50
167	Brian Giles	1.50
168	Henri Stanley	1.50
169	Jason Schmidt	2.00
170	Jerome Williams	1.50
171	J.T. Snow	1.50
172	Bret Boone	2.00
173	Edgar Martinez	2.00
174	Ichiro Suzuki	5.00
175	Jamie Moyer	1.50
176	Rich Aurilia	1.50
177	Chris Snelling	1.50
178	Scott Rolen	4.00
179	Albert Pujols	6.00
180	Jim Edmonds	2.00
181	Stan Musial	4.00
182	Dan Haren	1.50
183	Red Schoendienst	1.50
184	Aubrey Huff	1.50
185	Delmon Young	1.50
186	Rocco Baldelli	2.00
187	Dewon Brazelton	1.50
188	Mark Teixeira	2.50
189	Hank Blalock	3.00
190	Nolan Ryan Ranger	10.00
191	Alfonso Soriano	4.00
192	Michael Young	1.50
193	Vernon Wells	1.50
194	Roy Halladay	2.00
195	Carlos Delgado	2.50
196	Dustin McGowan	1.50
197	Josh Phelps	1.50
198	Alexis Rios	1.50
199	Eric Hinske	1.50
200	Josh Towers	1.50
201	Kazuo Matsui/1,000 **RC**	5.00
202	Fernando Nieve AU/500 **RC**	8.00
203	Mike Rouse/1,000	3.00
204	Dennis Sarfate AU/500 **RC**	8.00
205	Josh Labandeira AU/500 **RC**	8.00
206	Chris Oxspring AU/500 **RC**	8.00
207	Alfredo Simon/1,000 **RC**	2.00
208	Cory Sullivan AU/500 **RC**	8.00
209	Ruddy Yan AU/500 **RC**	8.00
210	Jason Bartlett AU/500 **RC**	8.00
211	Akinori Otsuka/1,000 **RC**	5.00
212	Lincoln Holdzkom/1,000 **RC**	2.00
213	Justin Leone/1,000 **RC**	4.00
214	Jorge Sequea AU/500 **RC**	8.00
215	John Gall/1,000 RC **RC**	3.00
216	Jerome Gamble/ 1,000 RC **RC**	2.00
217	Tim Bittner AU/500 **RC**	8.00
218	Ronny Cedeno AU/500 **RC**	12.00
219	Justin Hampson/ 1,000 RC **RC**	2.00
220	Ryan Wing AU/500	8.00
221	Mariano Gomez AU/500 **RC**	8.00
222	Carlos Vasquez/1,000 **RC**	2.00
223	Casey Daigle AU/500 RC **RC**	8.00
224	Renyel Pinto AU/500 **RC**	8.00
225	Chris Shelton AU/500 **RC**	25.00
226	Mike Gosling AU/700	8.00
227	Aarom Baldiris AU/700 **RC**	8.00
228	Ramon Ramirez AU/700 **RC**	8.00
229	Roberto Novoa AU/500 **RC**	8.00
230	Sean Henn AU/500	10.00
231	Jamie Brown AU/500 **RC**	8.00
232	Nick Regilio AU/500 **RC**	8.00
233	David Crouthers AU/700	8.00
234	Greg Dobbs AU/500 **RC**	8.00
235	Angel Chavez AU/500 **RC**	8.00
236	Willy Taveras AU/500 **RC**	20.00
237	Justin Knoedler AU/500 **RC**	8.00
238	Ian Snell AU/700 **RC**	20.00
239	Jason Frasor AU/500 **RC**	8.00
240	Jerry Gil AU/500 **RC**	8.00
241	Carlos Hines AU/500 **RC**	8.00
242	Ivan Ochoa AU/500 **RC**	8.00
243	Jose Capellan AU/700 **RC**	10.00
244	Onil Joseph AU/700 **RC**	8.00
245	Hector Gimenez AU/700 **RC**	8.00

246 Shawn Hill AU/700 **RC** 8.00
247 Freddy Guzman AU/700 **RC** 8.00
248 Graham Koonce AU/500 8.00
249 Ronald Belisario AU/500 **RC** 8.00
250 Merkin Valdez AU/700 **RC** 8.00

Spectrum Silver

Stars (1-200): 1-2X
Gold Auto. (201-250): .25-.4X
Non-Auto. (201-250): 1X
Production 100 Sets

Spectrum Platinum

No Pricing
Production One Set

Spectrum Gold

Stars (1-200): 2-4X
Gold Auto. (201-250): .5X
Non-Auto. (201-250): 1-2X
Production 50 Sets

Retail

Cards (1-200): .15X
1-200 are not serial numbered

Absolutely Ink

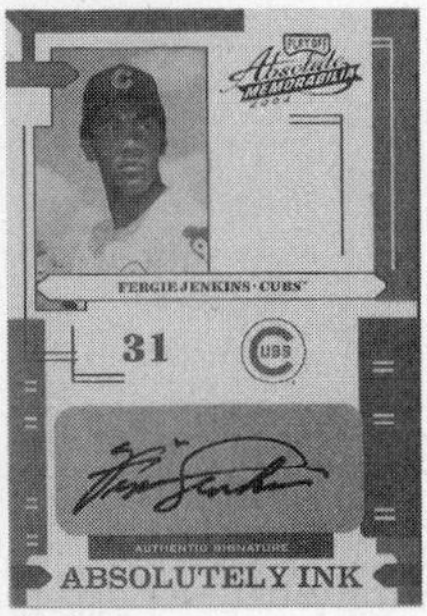

NM/M

Quantity produced listed
Spectrum: .75-1.5X
Production 1-25
No pricing 15 or less.
1 Adam Dunn/100 25.00
2 Al Kaline/100 25.00
3 Alan Trammell/100 15.00
6 Andre Dawson/Cubs/100 15.00
7 Andre Dawson/Expos/100 15.00
8 Andruw Jones/50 25.00
9 Angel Berroa/50 10.00
10 Aramis Ramirez/50 25.00
11 Aubrey Huff/100 12.00
12 Austin Kearns/100 15.00
13 Barry Larkin/50 30.00
16 Bert Blyleven/100 15.00
17 Billy Williams/100 15.00
19 Bob Feller/100 20.00
20 Bob Gibson/25 35.00
21 Bobby Doerr/100 15.00
22 Brandon Webb/100 10.00
23 Brett Myers/50 15.00
24 Brooks Robinson/100 40.00
27 Carlos Beltran/100 30.00
28 Carlos Lee/100 10.00
31 Craig Biggio/50 25.00
33 Dale Murphy/100 25.00
34 Darryl Strawberry/100 15.00
35 Dave Concepcion/50 20.00
36 Dave Parker/50 15.00
38 Don Mattingly/100 60.00
39 Dontrelle Willis/100 20.00
40 Duke Snider/100 30.00
41 Dwight Gooden/100 15.00
42 Edgar Martinez/50 30.00
43 Eric Chavez/50 25.00
44 Ernie Banks/100 50.00
45 Fergie Jenkins/100 15.00
46 Frank Robinson/100 20.00
47 Frank Thomas/25 50.00
48 Fred Lynn/50 15.00
49 Fred McGriff/25 50.00
50 Garret Anderson/100 15.00
51 Gary Carter/Expos/100 15.00
52 Gary Carter/Mets/100 15.00
53 Gary Sheffield/50 25.00
54 Gaylord Perry/100 15.00
57 Hank Blalock/100 25.00
58 Harold Baines/50 25.00
62 Jacque Jones/100 15.00
63 Jae Weong Seo/100 15.00
64 Jamie Moyer/25 25.00
65 Jason Varitek/50 35.00
66 Jay Gibbons/50 15.00
67 Jim Edmonds/25 35.00
68 Jim Palmer/100 20.00
69 Jim Rice/50 20.00
71 Johan Santana/50 40.00
72 Jorge Posada/50 40.00
73 Josh Beckett/25 40.00
74 Juan Gonzalez/25 40.00
75 Keith Hernandez/100 15.00
76 Kirby Puckett/25 60.00
77 Luis Tiant/100 15.00
78 Magglio Ordonez/100 15.00
81 Mark Grace/25 50.00
82 Mark Mulder/100 20.00
83 Mark Prior/100 40.00
84 Mark Teixeira/100 25.00
85 Marty Marion/100 15.00
86 Mike Lowell/25 25.00
90 Nolan Ryan/25 125.00
91 Orel Hershiser/100 30.00
92 Orlando Cepeda/100 15.00
97 Phil Niekro/100 15.00
99 Ralph Kiner/100 20.00
101 Red Schoendienst/100 15.00
103 Robin Roberts/50 25.00
104 Robin Ventura/100 15.00
106 Rocco Baldelli/25 30.00
109 Sammy Sosa/21 150.00
110 Sean Casey/23 25.00
111 Shannon Stewart/50 15.00
113 Stan Musial/100 60.00
114 Steve Carlton/50 40.00
115 Steve Garvey/100 15.00
117 Tommy John/100 15.00
118 Tony Gwynn/25 60.00
119 Tony Oliva/100 15.00
120 Torii Hunter/100 15.00
121 Trot Nixon/50 30.00
122 Troy Glaus/50 20.00
123 Vernon Wells/25 20.00
124 Vladimir Guerrero/100 35.00
125 Will Clark/100 35.00

Absolutely Ink Material

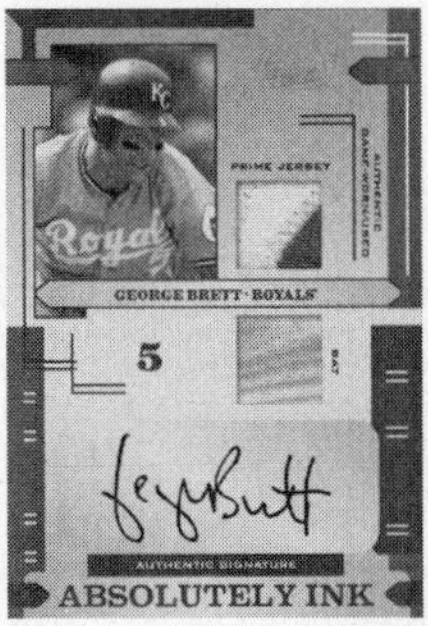

NM/M

Quantity produced listed
Prime: .5-1X
Production 1-25
No pricing 10 or less.
1 Adam Dunn/Jsy/100 30.00
2 Al Kaline/Pants/50 50.00
3 Alan Trammell/Jsy/100 20.00
6 Andre Dawson/ Cubs Jsy/100 20.00
7 Andre Dawson/ Expos Jsy/100 20.00
9 Angel Berroa/Jsy/100 10.00
11 Aubrey Huff/Jsy/100 15.00
12 Austin Kearns/Jsy/100 15.00
16 Bert Blyleven/Jsy/100 15.00
17 Billy Williams/Jsy/100 25.00
19 Bob Feller/Jsy/100 25.00
21 Bobby Doerr/Jsy/100 25.00
22 Brandon Webb/Jsy/50 15.00
23 Brett Myers/Jsy/100 15.00
24 Brooks Robinson/Jsy/100 40.00
27 Carlos Beltran/Jsy/100 40.00
28 Carlos Lee/Jsy/100 15.00
33 Dale Murphy/Jsy/100 30.00
34 Darryl Strawberry/Jsy/100 20.00
35 Dave Concepcion/Jsy/50 20.00
36 Dave Parker/Jsy/100 15.00
38 Don Mattingly/Jsy/50 75.00
39 Dontrelle Willis/Jsy/20 25.00
41 Dwight Gooden/Jsy/60 20.00
42 Edgar Martinez/Jsy/100 30.00
44 Ernie Banks/Jsy/50 50.00
45 Fergie Jenkins/Pants/100 15.00
46 Frank Robinson/Jsy/50 40.00
48 Fred Lynn/Jsy/100 15.00
49 Fred McGriff/Jsy/20 60.00
50 Garret Anderson/Jsy/100 15.00
51 Gary Carter/Expos Jsy/100 20.00
52 Gary Carter/Mets Jkt/100 20.00
53 Gary Sheffield/Jsy/100 20.00
54 Gaylord Perry/Jsy/100 15.00
57 Hank Blalock/Jsy/100 30.00
58 Harold Baines/Jsy/100 20.00
63 Jae Weong Seo/Jsy/100 15.00
64 Jamie Moyer/Jsy/100 20.00
65 Jason Varitek/Jsy/100 30.00
66 Jay Gibbons/Jsy/100 15.00
68 Jim Palmer/Jsy/100 25.00
69 Jim Rice/Jsy/100 20.00
70 Joe Carter/Jsy/50 20.00
71 Johan Santana/Jsy/100 40.00
72 Jorge Posada/Jsy/15 75.00
75 Keith Hernandez/Jsy/100 15.00
77 Luis Tiant Jsy/100 20.00
82 Mark Mulder/Jsy/20 40.00
85 Marty Marion/Jsy/100 15.00
86 Mike Lowell/Jsy/60 20.00
92 Orlando Cepeda/Bat/65 20.00
97 Phil Niekro/Jsy/25 25.00
99 Ralph Kiner/Bat/100 25.00
101 Red Schoendienst/Jsy/60 20.00
103 Robin Roberts/Hat/50 25.00
104 Robin Ventura/Jsy/65 25.00
110 Sean Casey/Jsy/75 20.00
111 Shannon Stewart/Jsy/100 15.00
114 Steve Carlton/Jsy/50 40.00
115 Steve Garvey/Bat/100 20.00
117 Tommy John/Jsy/100 15.00
119 Tony Oliva/Jsy/100 20.00
120 Torii Hunter/Jsy/50 20.00
121 Trot Nixon/Jsy/100 30.00
124 Vladimir Guerrero/Jsy/55 50.00
125 Will Clark/Jsy/100 40.00

Absolutely Ink Triple

No Pricing
Production 1-10
Prime: No Pricing
Production 1-5

Fans of the Game

NM/M

251 Landon Donovan 1.50
252 Jennie Finch 4.00
253 Bonnie Blair 1.50
254 Dan Jansen 2.00
255 Kerri Strug 2.00

Fans of the Game Autograph

NM/M

251 Landon Donovan 25.00
252 Jennie Finch 100.00
253 Bonnie Blair 30.00
254 Dan Jansen 40.00
255 Kerri Strug 75.00

Marks of Fame

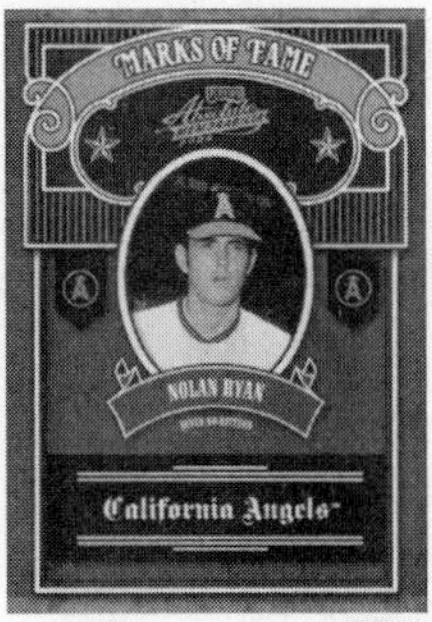

NM/M

Production 100 Sets
Spectrum: 1-2X
Production 25 Sets
1 Nolan Ryan 15.00
2 Ernie Banks 6.00
3 Bob Feller 4.00
4 Duke Snider 5.00
5 Sammy Sosa 10.00
6 Whitey Ford 6.00
7 Steve Carlton 4.00
8 Tony Gwynn 8.00
9 Jim Bunning 4.00
10 Stan Musial 8.00
11 Cal Ripken Jr. 20.00
12 George Brett 15.00
13 Gary Carter 4.00
14 Jim Palmer 4.00
15 Gaylord Perry 4.00

Marks of Fame Signature

NM/M

Quantity produced listed
Spectrum: .75-1.5X
Production 1-25
No pricing 15 or less.
1 Nolan Ryan/50 120.00
2 Ernie Banks/50 50.00
3 Bob Feller/100 25.00
4 Duke Snider/100 25.00
5 Sammy Sosa/21 125.00
6 Whitey Ford/25 50.00
7 Steve Carlton/100 25.00
8 Tony Gwynn/25 75.00
9 Jim Bunning/100 20.00
10 Stan Musial/50 60.00
12 George Brett/25 100.00
13 Gary Carter/100 15.00
14 Jim Palmer/50 25.00
15 Gaylord Perry/100 15.00

Signature Club

NM/M

Quantity produced listed
2 Gary Sheffield/Bat/50 20.00
4 Will Clark/Bat/50 40.00
5 Ernie Banks/Bat/50 50.00

Signature Material

NM/M

Quantity produced listed

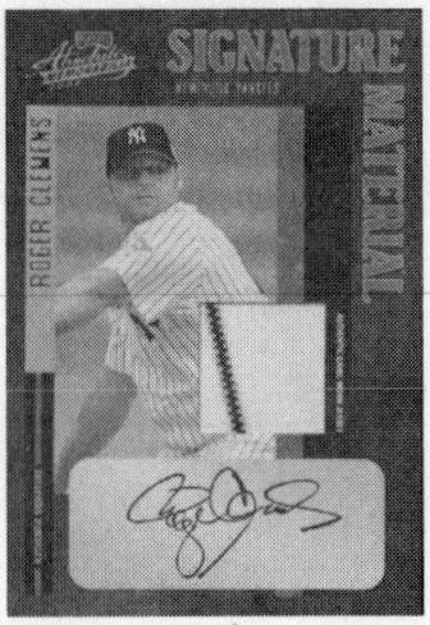

Prime: No Pricing
Production Five Sets
Combo: 1X
Production 25-50
Combo Prime: No Pricing
Production Five Sets
2 Gary Carter/Jsy/50 25.00
3 Dale Murphy/Jsy/50 35.00
4 Don Mattingly/Jsy/25 100.00
5 Stan Musial/Jsy/25 100.00

Signature Spectrum Gold

NM/M

Quantity produced listed
1 Troy Glaus/15 35.00
2 Garret Anderson/100 15.00
7 Vladimir Guerrero/25 60.00
8 Richie Sexson/15 25.00
9 Shea Hillenbrand/100 10.00
11 Brandon Webb/100 10.00
15 Roberto Alomar/25 50.00
18 Dale Murphy/100 25.00
19 Rafael Furcal/100 12.00
22 Julio Franco/25 20.00
23 Adam LaRoche/100 10.00
26 Jay Gibbons/100 10.00
29 Adam Loewen/100 10.00
32 Luis Matos/50 15.00
33 Jason Varitek/25 40.00
36 Trot Nixon/100 20.00
40 Luis Tiant/50 20.00
41 Kevin Youkilis/25 40.00
45 Kerry Wood/25 50.00
46 Mark Prior/100 40.00
47 Ernie Banks/100 40.00
52 Magglio Ordonez/100 15.00
53 Carlos Lee/100 15.00
54 Joe Crede/50 10.00
59 Austin Kearns/100 15.00
61 Barry Larkin/25 40.00
62 Ryan Wagner/50 10.00
63 Jody Gerut/100 10.00
64 Jeremy Guthrie/25 15.00
65 Travis Hafner/25 25.00
68 Preston Wilson/100 10.00
69 Jeff Baker/25 15.00
73 George Kell/100 15.00
79 Miguel Cabrera/100 35.00
81 Luis Castillo/25 15.00
83 Jeff Bagwell/25 50.00
87 Andy Pettitte/25 50.00
93 Carlos Beltran/100 25.00
94 Angel Berroa/100 10.00
100 Duke Snider/100 25.00
104 Edwin Jackson/50 15.00
106 Hong-Chih Kuo/25 75.00
107 Don Sutton/25 25.00
112 Rickie Weeks/24 40.00
113 Scott Podsednik/100 15.00
116 Tony Oliva/50 25.00
117 Jacque Jones/100 15.00
119 Torii Hunter/100 15.00
130 Jae Weong Seo/100 10.00
131 Gary Carter/100 15.00
136 Don Mattingly/100 50.00
139 Jorge Posada/25 50.00
144 Gary Sheffield/25 25.00
146 Chien-Ming Wang/25 180.00
153 Mark Mulder/100 25.00
155 Rich Harden/50 15.00
159 Marlon Byrd/100 10.00
160 Lenny Dykstra/100 15.00
161 Steve Carlton/50 40.00
164 Jose Castillo/50 15.00
165 Jay Payton/100 10.00
170 Jerome Williams/50 25.00
178 Scott Rolen/50 40.00
181 Stan Musial/100 60.00
182 Dan Haren/25 15.00
183 Red Schoendienst/100 15.00
184 Aubrey Huff/100 10.00
185 Delmon Young/100 20.00
187 Dewon Brazelton/25 15.00
188 Mark Teixeira/50 30.00
189 Hank Blalock/25 40.00
192 Michael Young/100 25.00
194 Roy Halladay/25 25.00
198 Alexis Rios/50 25.00
202 Fernando Nieve/100 10.00
205 Josh Labandeira/100 10.00
206 Chris Oxspring/100 15.00

208 Cory Sullivan/100 10.00
209 Ruddy Yan/100 10.00
210 Jason Bartlett/100 15.00
212 Lincoln Holdzkom/100 10.00
213 Justin Leone/100 20.00
214 Jorge Sequea/100 10.00
217 Tim Bittner/100 10.00
219 Justin Hampson/100 10.00
220 Ryan Wing/100 10.00
221 Mariano Gomez/100 10.00
222 Carlos Vasquez/100 10.00
224 Renyel Pinto/100 15.00
225 Chris Shelton/100 35.00
230 Sean Henn/100 10.00
232 Nick Regilio/100 10.00
234 Greg Dobbs/50 15.00
235 Angel Chavez/100 10.00
242 Ivan Ochoa/100 10.00
248 Graham Koonce/100 10.00

Signature Spectrum Silver

NM/M

Quantity produced listed
1 Troy Glaus/34 25.00
2 Garret Anderson/100 15.00
6 Nolan Ryan Angels/25 150.00
7 Vladimir Guerrero/100 40.00
8 Richie Sexson/34 20.00
9 Shea Hillenbrand/100 10.00
11 Brandon Webb/100 10.00
13 Robby Hammock/250 10.00
14 Edgar Gonzalez/104 10.00
15 Roberto Alomar/32 50.00
16 Andruw Jones/50 20.00
18 Dale Murphy/100 25.00
19 Rafael Furcal/100 12.00
21 Bubba Nelson/250 10.00
22 Julio Franco/100 15.00
23 Adam LaRoche/100 10.00
24 Michael Hessman/250 10.00
26 Jay Gibbons/100 10.00
29 Adam Loewen/100 10.00
32 Luis Matos/100 10.00
33 Jason Varitek/50 35.00
36 Trot Nixon/100 20.00
40 Luis Tiant/100 15.00
41 Kevin Youkilis/25 40.00
42 Michel Hernandez/190 10.00
43 Sammy Sosa/21 150.00
45 Kerry Wood/50 40.00
46 Mark Prior/100 40.00
47 Ernie Banks/100 40.00
48 Aramis Ramirez/50 30.00
49 Brendan Harris/250 10.00
50 Todd Wellemeyer/250 10.00
51 Frank Thomas/50 40.00
52 Magglio Ordonez/100 20.00
53 Carlos Lee/100 15.00
54 Joe Crede/100 10.00
55 Joe Borchard/250 10.00
57 Sean Casey/50 20.00
58 Adam Dunn/100 25.00
59 Austin Kearns/100 15.00
61 Barry Larkin/50 30.00
62 Ryan Wagner/100 10.00
63 Jody Gerut/100 10.00
64 Jeremy Guthrie/50 10.00
65 Travis Hafner/50 20.00
66 Brian Tallet/250 10.00
68 Preston Wilson/100 10.00
69 Jeff Baker/50 10.00
70 Clint Barmes/250 10.00
71 Joe Kennedy/250 10.00
73 George Kell/100 15.00
74 Preston Larrison/250 10.00
77 Dontrelle Willis/100 20.00
78 Josh Beckett/25 35.00
79 Miguel Cabrera/100 35.00
80 Mike Lowell/25 25.00
81 Luis Castillo/50 10.00
83 Jeff Bagwell/50 40.00
85 Craig Biggio/50 30.00
86 Lance Berkman/25 40.00
87 Andy Pettitte/25 50.00
88 Roy Oswalt/25 25.00
89 Chris Burke/250 10.00
90 Jason Lane/231 10.00
93 Carlos Beltran/100 25.00
94 Angel Berroa/100 10.00
95 Juan Gonzalez/25 40.00
96 Ken Harvey/200 15.00
97 Byron Gettis/250 10.00
98 Alexis Gomez/250 10.00
99 Ian Ferguson/104 10.00
100 Duke Snider/100 25.00
103 Kazuhisa Ishii/25 40.00
104 Edwin Jackson/100 10.00
105 Fred McGriff/50 15.00
106 Hong-Chih Kuo/50 50.00
107 Don Sutton/100 15.00
109 Cesar Izturis/101 10.00
110 Robin Ventura/25 20.00
111 Paul LoDuca/50 20.00
112 Rickie Weeks/21 40.00
113 Scott Podsednik/100 15.00
114 Junior Spivey/89 10.00
115 Lyle Overbay/89 15.00
116 Tony Oliva/72 15.00
117 Jacque Jones/100 15.00
118 Shannon Stewart/100 10.00
119 Torii Hunter/100 15.00
120 Johan Santana/50 30.00
121 J.D. Durbin/250 10.00
122 Jason Kubel/250 20.00
123 Michael Cuddyer/225 10.00
124 Nick Johnson/25 15.00
125 Jose Vidro/25 15.00
126 Orlando Cabrera/25 20.00
127 Zach Day/100 10.00
130 Jae Weong Seo/100 10.00
131 Gary Carter/100 15.00
132 Phil Seibel/177 10.00
133 Edwin Almonte/250 10.00
136 Don Mattingly/100 50.00
139 Jorge Posada/50 40.00
144 Gary Sheffield/100 15.00
146 Chien-Ming Wang/50 150.00
147 Javier Vazquez/25 40.00
148 Jose Contreras/25 35.00
149 Whitey Ford/50 40.00
151 Eric Chavez/50 25.00
153 Mark Mulder/100 25.00
154 Tim Hudson/50 25.00
155 Rich Harden/100 15.00
156 Eric Byrnes/250 10.00
159 Marlon Byrd/100 10.00
160 Lenny Dykstra/100 15.00
161 Steve Carlton/100 25.00
162 Ryan Howard/250 75.00
163 Bobby Hill/250 10.00
164 Jose Castillo/100 10.00
165 Jay Payton/100 10.00
168 Henri Stanley/112 10.00
170 Jerome Williams/100 15.00
171 J.T. Snow/89 15.00
173 Edgar Martinez/50 30.00
175 Jamie Moyer/19 25.00
176 Rich Aurilia/25 15.00
177 Chris Snelling/177 10.00
178 Scott Rolen/100 30.00
180 Jim Edmonds/50 30.00
181 Stan Musial/100 60.00
182 Dan Haren/200 10.00
183 Red Schoendienst/100 15.00
184 Aubrey Huff/100 10.00
185 Delmon Young/100 20.00
186 Rocco Baldelli/50 20.00
187 Dewon Brazelton/50 15.00
188 Mark Teixeira/100 20.00
189 Hank Blalock/50 30.00
190 Nolan Ryan Rgr/25 125.00
192 Michael Young/100 25.00
194 Roy Halladay/50 20.00
196 Dustin McGowan/250 10.00
197 Josh Phelps/25 15.00
198 Alexis Rios/100 15.00
200 Josh Towers/158 10.00
202 Fernando Nieve/250 10.00
203 Mike Rouse/100 10.00
204 Dennis Sarfate/100 10.00
205 Josh Labandeira/250 10.00
206 Chris Oxspring/250 10.00
207 Alfredo Simon/100 10.00
208 Cory Sullivan/250 10.00
209 Ruddy Yan/250 10.00
210 Jason Bartlett/250 10.00
211 Akinori Otsuka/100 50.00
212 Lincoln Holdzkom/250 10.00
213 Justin Leone/250 20.00
214 Jorge Sequea/250 10.00
215 John Gall/50 25.00
217 Tim Bittner/250 10.00
219 Justin Hampson/250 10.00
220 Ryan Wing/250 10.00
221 Mariano Gomez/250 10.00
222 Carlos Vasquez/250 10.00
223 Casey Daigle/150 10.00
224 Renyel Pinto/250 15.00
225 Chris Shelton/250 35.00
229 Roberto Novoa/225 10.00
230 Sean Henn/250 10.00
231 Jamie Brown/200 10.00
232 Nick Regilio/250 10.00
234 Greg Dobbs/250 10.00
235 Angel Chavez/250 10.00
236 Willy Taveras/225 10.00
237 Justin Knoedler/225 10.00
239 Jason Frasor/225 10.00
240 Jerry Gil/225 10.00
241 Carlos Hines/225 10.00
242 Ivan Ochoa/250 10.00
248 Graham Koonce/250 10.00
249 Ronald Belisario/225 10.00

Team Quad

NM/M

Production 100 Sets
Spectrum: 1.5-2X
Production 25 Sets
1 Jeff Kent, Lance Berkman, Craig Biggio, Jeff Bagwell 6.00
2 Nomar Garciaparra, Manny Ramirez, Pedro Martinez, Trot Nixon 10.00
3 Paul Konerko, Carlos Lee, Magglio Ordonez, Frank Thomas 6.00
4 John Smoltz, Chipper Jones, Andruw Jones, Rafael Furcal 6.00
5 Garret Anderson, Troy Percival, Troy Glaus, Darin Erstad 4.00
6 Steve Finley, Brandon Webb, Randy Johnson, Luis Gonzalez 6.00
7 Paul LoDuca, Hideo Nomo, Shawn Green, Kazuhisa Ishii 6.00
8 Larry Walker, Todd Helton, Jason Jennings, Preston Wilson 6.00
9 Dontrelle Willis, Brad Penny, Josh Beckett 4.00
10 Jose Reyes, Jae Weong Seo, Tom Glavine, Mike Piazza 10.00
11 Bernie Williams, Derek Jeter, Jason Giambi, Alfonso Soriano 15.00
12 Rich Harden, Tim Hudson, Barry Zito, Mark Mulder 4.00
13 Kevin Millwood, Marlon Byrd, Jim Thome, Bobby Abreu 8.00
14 Edgar Renteria, Jim Edmonds, Albert Pujols, Scott Rolen 10.00
15 Roger Clemens, Andy Pettitte, Wade Miller, Roy Oswalt 10.00

Team Quad Material

NM/M

Production 100 Sets
Prime: No Pricing
Production Five Sets
1 Jeff Kent, Lance Berkman, Craig Biggio, Jeff Bagwell 20.00
2 Nomar Garciaparra, Manny Ramirez, Pedro Martinez, Trot Nixon 35.00
3 Paul Konerko, Carlos Lee, Magglio Ordonez, Frank Thomas 20.00
4 John Smoltz, Chipper Jones, Andruw Jones, Rafael Furcal 20.00
5 Garret Anderson, Troy Percival, Troy Glaus, Darin Erstad 10.00
6 Steve Finley, Brandon Webb, Randy Johnson, Luis Gonzalez 20.00
7 Paul LoDuca, Hideo Nomo, Shawn Green, Kazuhisa Ishii 20.00
8 Larry Walker, Todd Helton, Jason Jennings, Preston Wilson 10.00
9 Dontrelle Willis, Brad Penny, Josh Beckett 20.00
10 Jose Reyes, Jae Weong Seo, Tom Glavine, Mike Piazza 20.00
11 Bernie Williams, Derek Jeter, Jason Giambi, Alfonso Soriano 40.00
12 Rich Harden, Tim Hudson, Barry Zito, Mark Mulder 10.00
13 Kevin Millwood, Marlon Byrd, Jim Thome, Bobby Abreu 20.00
14 Edgar Renteria, Jim Edmonds, Albert Pujols, Scott Rolen 40.00
15 Roger Clemens, Andy Pettitte, Wade Miller, Roy Oswalt 30.00

Team Tandem

NM/M

Production 250 Sets
Spectrum: 2-4X
Production 25 Sets
1 Vladimir Guerrero, Reggie Jackson 3.00
2 Dale Murphy, Chipper Jones 3.00
3 Gary Carter, Mike Piazza 4.00
4 Miguel Tejada, Cal Ripken Jr. 8.00
5 Gary Sheffield, Derek Jeter 6.00
6 Curt Schilling, Pedro J. Martinez 3.00
7 Roger Clemens, Andy Pettitte 5.00
8 Mike Sweeney, George Brett 6.00
9 Kazuhisa Ishii, Hideo Nomo 3.00
10 Austin Kearns, Adam Dunn 3.00
11 Miguel Cabrera, Dontrelle Willis 3.00
12 Don Mattingly, Derek Jeter 8.00
13 Barry Zito, Eric Chavez 2.00
14 Jim Thome, Mike Schmidt 4.00
15 Albert Pujols, Stan Musial 4.00
16 Nolan Ryan, Alex Rodriguez 8.00
17 Kerry Wood, Mark Prior 4.00
18 Rafael Palmeiro, Jay Gibbons 3.00
19 Nomar Garciaparra, Manny Ramirez 4.00
20 Ivan Rodriguez, Mike Piazza 4.00

Team Tandem Material

NM/M

Production 250 Sets
Prime: No Pricing
Production Five Sets
1 Reggie Jackson/Bat, Vladimir Guerrero/Bat 10.00
2 Chipper Jones/Jsy, Dale Murphy/Jsy 10.00
3 Gary Carter/Jsy, Mike Piazza/Jsy 10.00
4 Miguel Tejada/Bat, Cal Ripken Jr./Bat 25.00
5 Derek Jeter/Bat, Gary Sheffield/Bat 25.00
6 Curt Schilling/Bat, Pedro J. Martinez/Bat 10.00
7 Roger Clemens/Bat, Andy Pettitte/Bat 15.00
8 Mike Sweeney/Jsy, George Brett/Jsy 15.00
9 Kazuhisa Ishii/Jsy, Hideo Nomo/Jsy 10.00
10 Austin Kearns/Jsy, Adam Dunn/Jsy 10.00
11 Dontrelle Willis/Jsy, Miguel Cabrera/Jsy 10.00
12 Don Mattingly/Jsy, Derek Jeter/Jsy 35.00
13 Barry Zito/Jsy, Eric Chavez/Jsy 8.00
14 Jim Thome/Jsy, Mike Schmidt/Jsy 20.00
15 Albert Pujols/Jsy, Stan Musial/Jsy 40.00
16 Nolan Ryan/Jsy, Alex Rodriguez/Jsy 25.00
17 Mark Prior/Jsy, Kerry Wood/Jsy 15.00
18 Rafael Palmeiro/Jsy, Jay Gibbons/Jsy 10.00
19 Nomar Garciaparra/Jsy, Manny Ramirez/Jsy 15.00
20 Ivan Rodriguez/Jsy, Mike Piazza/Jsy 10.00

Team Trio

NM/M

Production 100 Sets
Spectrum: 1.5-2X
Production 25 Sets
1 Sammy Sosa, Kerry Wood, Mark Prior 10.00
2 Hank Blalock, Mark Teixeira, Alex Rodriguez 10.00
3 Vernon Wells, Roy Halladay, Carlos Delgado 4.00
4 Mike Mussina, Jorge Posada, Mariano Rivera 6.00
5 Shannon Stewart, Torii Hunter, Jacque Jones 4.00
6 Carlos Beltran, Mike Sweeney, Angel Berroa 4.00
7 Dontrelle Willis, Miguel Cabrera, Josh Beckett 6.00
8 Jeff Bagwell, Craig Biggio, Lance Berkman 6.00
9 Nomar Garciaparra, Pedro J. Martinez, Manny Ramirez 10.00
10 Shawn Green, Kazuhisa Ishii, Hideo Nomo 4.00
11 Mark Mulder, Barry Zito, Tim Hudson 4.00
12 Jim Edmonds, Scott Rolen, Albert Pujols 15.00
13 Cal Ripken Jr., Jay Gibbons, Rafael Palmeiro 20.00
14 Sammy Sosa, Mark Grace, Ryne Sandberg 10.00
15 Nolan Ryan, Roger Clemens, Randy Johnson 20.00

Team Trio Material

NM/M

Production 100 Sets
Prime: No Pricing
Production Five Sets
1 Sammy Sosa, Kerry Wood, Mark Prior 25.00
2 Hank Blalock, Mark Teixeira, Alex Rodriguez 15.00
3 Vernon Wells, Roy Halladay, Carlos Delgado 8.00
4 Mike Mussina, Jorge Posada, Mariano Rivera 25.00
5 Shannon Stewart, Torii Hunter, Jacque Jones 8.00
6 Carlos Beltran, Mike Sweeney, Angel Berroa 8.00
7 Dontrelle Willis, Miguel Cabrera, Josh Beckett 15.00
8 Jeff Bagwell, Craig Biggio, Lance Berkman 10.00
9 Nomar Garciaparra, Pedro J. Martinez, Manny Ramirez 20.00
10 Shawn Green, Kazuhisa Ishii, Hideo Nomo 10.00
11 Mark Mulder, Barry Zito, Tim Hudson 8.00
12 Jim Edmonds, Scott Rolen, Albert Pujols 25.00
13 Cal Ripken Jr., Jay Gibbons, Rafael Palmeiro 40.00
14 Sammy Sosa, Mark Grace, Ryne Sandberg 35.00
15 Nolan Ryan, Roger Clemens, Randy Johnson/25 80.00

Tools of Trade Blue

NM/M

Common Player: 1.50
Production 250 Sets
Black: No Pricing
Production One Set
Blue Spectrum: 1-1.5X
Production 125 Sets
Green: 1-1.5X
Production 150 Sets
Green Spectrum: 2-3X
Production 50 Sets
Red: 1X
Production 200 Sets
Red Spectrum: 1-2X
Production 100 Sets
1 Adam Dunn/H 2.50

2 Adam Dunn/A 2.50
3 Alan Trammell 2.00
4 Albert Pujols/H 6.00
5 Albert Pujols/A 6.00
6 Alex Rodriguez 6.00
7 Alex Rodriguez 6.00
8 Alex Rodriguez 6.00
9 Alfonso Soriano 4.00
10 Andre Dawson 2.00
11 Andruw Jones/H 2.00
12 Andruw Jones/A 2.00
13 Andy Pettitte/H 2.00
14 Andy Pettitte/A 2.00
15 Angel Berroa 1.50
16 Aubrey Huff 1.50
17 Austin Kearns 2.00
18 Barry Zito 2.00
19 Barry Zito/A 2.00
20 Bernie Williams 2.00
21 Bobby Abreu 2.00
22 Brandon Webb 1.50
23 Cal Ripken Jr./H 8.00
24 Cal Ripken Jr./A 8.00
25 Cal Ripken Jr. 8.00
26 Carlos Beltran 2.00
27 Carlos Delgado/H 2.00
28 Carlos Delgado/A 2.00
29 Carlos Lee 1.50
30 Chipper Jones/H 3.00
31 Chipper Jones/A 3.00
32 Craig Biggio/H 2.00
33 Craig Biggio/A 2.00
34 Curt Schilling 2.00
35 Curt Schilling 2.00
36 Dale Murphy/H 2.00
37 Dale Murphy/A 2.00
38 Darryl Strawberry 1.50
39 Derek Jeter/H 8.00
40 Derek Jeter/A 8.00
41 Don Mattingly/H 8.00
42 Don Mattingly/A 8.00
43 Dontrelle Willis/H 2.00
44 Dontrelle Willis/A 2.00
45 Dwight Gooden 1.50
46 Edgar Martinez 1.50
47 Eric Chavez 2.00
48 Frank Thomas/A 2.00
49 Frank Thomas 2.00
50 Garret Anderson 2.00
51 Gary Carter 2.00
52 Gary Sheffield 2.00
53 George Brett/H 6.00
54 George Brett/A 6.00
55 Greg Maddux 4.00
56 Hank Blalock 2.00
57 Hideo Nomo 2.00
58 Ivan Rodriguez 2.00
59 Ivan Rodriguez 2.00
60 Jacque Jones 1.50
61 Jae Weong Seo 1.50
62 Jason Giambi 2.00
63 Jason Giambi 2.00
64 Javy Lopez 2.00
65 Jay Gibbons 1.50
66 Jeff Bagwell 2.00
67 Jeff Bagwell 2.00
68 Jeff Kent 1.50
69 Jim Edmonds 2.00
70 Jim Thome 3.00
71 Jorge Posada 2.00
72 Jose Canseco 2.00
73 Jose Reyes 2.00
74 Josh Beckett 2.00
75 Juan Gonzalez 2.00
76 Kazuhisa Ishii 1.50
77 Kerry Wood 3.00
78 Kerry Wood 3.00
79 Kirby Puckett 3.00
80 Lance Berkman 2.00
81 Lou Brock 2.00
82 Luis Castillo 1.50
83 Luis Gonzalez 1.50
84 Magglio Ordonez 1.50
85 Manny Ramirez 2.00
86 Manny Ramirez 2.00
87 Marcus Giles 1.50
88 Mark Grace 2.00
89 Mark Mulder 2.00
90 Mark Prior 4.00
91 Mark Prior 4.00
92 Mark Teixeira 2.00
93 Marlon Byrd 1.50
94 Miguel Cabrera 3.00
95 Miguel Tejada 2.00
96 Mike Lowell 2.00
97 Mike Mussina 2.00
98 Mike Mussina 2.00
99 Mike Piazza 4.00
100 Mike Piazza 4.00
101 Mike Piazza 4.00
102 Mike Schmidt 5.00
103 Mike Schmidt 5.00
104 Mike Sweeney 1.50
105 Nick Johnson 1.50
106 Nolan Ryan 8.00
107 Nolan Ryan 8.00
108 Nolan Ryan 8.00
109 Nomar Garciaparra 5.00
110 Nomar Garciaparra 5.00
111 Pat Burrell 2.00
112 Paul LoDuca 1.50
113 Pedro Martinez 3.00
114 Pedro Martinez 3.00
115 Preston Wilson 1.50
116 Rafael Palmeiro 2.00
117 Rafael Palmeiro 2.00
118 Randy Johnson 4.00
119 Randy Johnson 4.00
120 Richie Sexson 2.00
121 Rickey Henderson 2.00
122 Rickey Henderson 2.00
123 Rickey Henderson 2.00
124 Roberto Alomar 2.00
125 Rocco Baldelli 2.00
126 Rod Carew 2.00
127 Roger Clemens 6.00
128 Roger Clemens 6.00
129 Roy Halladay 2.00
130 Roy Oswalt 1.50
131 Ryne Sandberg 5.00
132 Sammy Sosa 5.00
133 Sammy Sosa 5.00
134 Sammy Sosa 5.00
135 Scott Rolen 4.00
136 Shawn Green 2.00
137 Steve Carlton 2.00
138 Tim Hudson 2.00
139 Todd Helton 2.00
140 Todd Helton 2.00
141 Tom Glavine 2.00
142 Tom Glavine 2.00
143 Tony Gwynn 4.00
144 Tony Gwynn 4.00
145 Torii Hunter 2.00
146 Trot Nixon 2.00
147 Troy Glaus 2.00
148 Vernon Wells 2.00
149 Vladimir Guerrero 4.00
150 Will Clark 3.00

Tools of Trade Material Combo

NM/M

Production 25-250
Single: No Pricing
Production 1-5
Combo Price Single: 2-4X
Production 1-25
Trio: 1-3X
Production 5-100
No pricing 15 or less.
Quad: 2-4X
Production 1-50
No pricing 15 or less.
Five: 3-5X
Production 10-25
Six: 3-6X
Production 5-25

1 Adam Dunn/Bat-Jsy/250 6.00
2 Adam Dunn/Bat-Jsy/250 6.00
3 Alan Trammell/Bat-Jsy/250 4.00
4 Albert Pujols/Bat-Jsy/250 20.00
5 Albert Pujols/Bat-Jsy/250 20.00
6 Alex Rodriguez/Bat-Jsy/250 10.00
7 Alex Rodriguez/Bat-Jsy/250 10.00
8 Alex Rodriguez/Bat-Jsy/250 10.00
9 Alfonso Soriano/ Bat-Jsy/100 10.00
10 Andre Dawson/Bat-Jsy/250 5.00
11 Andruw Jones/Bat-Jsy/100 8.00
12 Andruw Jones/Bat-Jsy/250 8.00
13 Andy Pettitte/Bat-Jsy/100 10.00
14 Andy Pettitte/Bat-Jsy/100 10.00
15 Angel Berroa/Bat-Jsy/250 4.00
16 Aubrey Huff/Bat-Jsy/250 4.00
17 Austin Kearns/Bat-Jsy/250 6.00
18 Barry Zito/Bat-Jsy/250 6.00
19 Barry Zito/Bat-Jsy/250 6.00
20 Bernie Williams/Bat-Jsy/250 8.00
21 Bobby Abreu/Bat-Jsy/250 6.00
22 Brandon Webb/Bat-Jsy/250 4.00
23 Cal Ripken Jr./Bat-Jsy/250 30.00
24 Cal Ripken Jr./Bat-Jsy/250 30.00
25 Cal Ripken Jr./Bat-Jsy/250 30.00
26 Carlos Beltran/Bat-Jsy/250 6.00
27 Carlos Delgado/Bat-Jsy/250 6.00
28 Carlos Delgado/Bat-Jsy/250 6.00
29 Carlos Lee/Bat-Jsy/250 4.00
30 Chipper Jones/Bat-Jsy/250 10.00
31 Chipper Jones/Bat-Jsy/250 10.00
32 Craig Biggio/Bat-Jsy/250 6.00
33 Craig Biggio/Bat-Jsy/100 6.00
34 Curt Schilling/Bat-Jsy/250 8.00
35 Curt Schilling/Bat-Jsy/250 8.00
36 Dale Murphy/Bat-Jsy/250 8.00
37 Dale Murphy/Bat-Jsy/100 8.00
38 Darryl Strawberry/ Bat-Jsy/250 4.00
39 Derek Jeter/Bat-Jsy/100 30.00
40 Derek Jeter/Bat-Jsy/100 30.00
41 Don Mattingly/Bat-Jsy/100 30.00
42 Don Mattingly/Bat-Jsy/100 30.00
43 Dontrelle Willis/Bat-Jsy/250 6.00
44 Dontrelle Willis/Bat-Jsy/250 6.00
45 Dwight Gooden/Bat-Jsy/250 6.00
46 Edgar Martinez/Bat-Jsy/250 6.00
47 Eric Chavez/Bat-Jsy/250 6.00
48 Frank Thomas/Bat-Jsy/250 10.00
49 Frank Thomas/Bat-Jsy/250 10.00
50 Garret Anderson/Bat-Jsy/250 6.00
51 Gary Carter/Bat-Jsy/250 6.00
52 Gary Sheffield/Bat-Jsy/250 6.00
53 George Brett/Bat-Jsy/250 20.00
54 George Brett/Bat-Jsy/250 20.00
55 Greg Maddux/Bat-Jsy/250 10.00
56 Hank Blalock/Bat-Jsy/250 8.00
57 Hideo Nomo/Bat-Jsy/250 10.00
58 Ivan Rodriguez/Bat-Jsy/250 8.00
59 Ivan Rodriguez/Bat-Jsy/250 8.00
60 Jacque Jones/Bat-Jsy/250 4.00
62 Jason Giambi/Bat-Jsy/250 8.00
63 Jason Giambi/Bat-Jsy/250 8.00
64 Javy Lopez/Bat-Jsy/250 6.00
65 Jay Gibbons/Bat-Jsy/250 4.00
66 Jeff Bagwell/Bat-Jsy/250 8.00
67 Jeff Bagwell/Bat-Jsy/250 8.00
68 Jeff Kent/Bat-Jsy/250 5.00
69 Jim Edmonds/Bat-Jsy/250 8.00
70 Jim Thome/Bat-Jsy/250 12.00
71 Jorge Posada/Bat-Jsy/250 8.00
72 Jose Canseco/Bat-Jsy/250 8.00
73 Jose Reyes/Bat-Jsy/250 8.00
74 Josh Beckett/Bat-Jsy/250 8.00
75 Juan Gonzalez/Bat-Jsy/250 8.00
76 Kazuhisa Ishii/Bat-Jsy/250 4.00
77 Kerry Wood/Bat-Jsy/250 10.00
78 Kerry Wood/Bat-Jsy/250 10.00
79 Kirby Puckett/Bat-Jsy/250 10.00
80 Lance Berkman/Bat-Jsy/250 6.00
81 Lou Brock/Bat-Jsy/250 8.00
82 Luis Castillo/Bat-Jsy/250 4.00
83 Luis Gonzalez/Bat-Jsy/250 4.00
84 Magglio Ordonez/ Bat-Jsy/250 6.00
85 Manny Ramirez/Bat-Jsy/250 8.00
86 Manny Ramirez/Bat-Jsy/250 8.00
87 Marcus Giles/Bat-Jsy/25 10.00
88 Mark Grace/Bat-Jsy/250 8.00
89 Mark Mulder/Bat-Jsy/250 8.00
90 Mark Prior/Bat-Jsy/250 10.00
91 Mark Prior/Bat-Jsy/250 10.00
92 Mark Teixeira/Bat-Jsy/250 6.00
93 Marlon Byrd/Bat-Jsy/250 4.00
94 Miguel Cabrera/Bat-Jsy/250 10.00
95 Miguel Tejada/Bat-Jsy/250 6.00
96 Mike Lowell/Bat-Jsy/250 6.00
97 Mike Mussina/Jsy-Pants/250 8.00
98 Mike Mussina/Jsy-Jsy/250 8.00
99 Mike Piazza/Bat-Jsy/250 12.00
100 Mike Piazza/Bat-Jsy/250 12.00
101 Mike Piazza/Bat-Jsy/250 12.00
102 Mike Schmidt/Bat-Jsy/100 20.00
103 Mike Schmidt/Bat-Jsy/100 20.00
104 Mike Sweeney/Bat-Jsy/250 4.00
105 Nick Johnson/Bat-Jsy/250 4.00
106 Nolan Ryan/Jkt-Jsy/250 30.00
107 Nolan Ryan/Jkt-Jsy/250 30.00
108 Nolan Ryan/Jsy-Pants/250 30.00
109 Nomar Garciaparra/ Bat-Jsy/250 15.00
110 Nomar Garciaparra/ Bat-Jsy/250 15.00
111 Pat Burrell/Bat-Jsy/250 6.00
112 Paul LoDuca/Bat-Jsy/250 4.00
113 Pedro J. Martinez/ Bat-Jsy/250 10.00
114 Pedro Martinez/Bat-Jsy/250 10.00
115 Preston Wilson/Bat-Jsy/250 4.00
116 Rafael Palmeiro/Bat-Jsy/250 8.00
117 Rafael Palmeiro/Bat-Jsy/250 8.00
118 Randy Johnson/ Bat-Jsy/250 10.00
119 Randy Johnson/ Bat-Jsy/250 10.00
120 Richie Sexson/Bat-Jsy/250 6.00
121 Rickey Henderson/ Bat-Jsy/250 8.00
122 Rickey Henderson/ Bat-Jsy/250 8.00
123 Rickey Henderson/ Bat-Jsy/250 8.00
124 Roberto Alomar/ Bat-Jsy/250 8.00
125 Rocco Baldelli/Bat-Jsy/250 6.00
126 Rod Carew/Bat-Jsy/250 8.00
127 Roger Clemens/ Bat-Jsy/250 15.00
128 Roger Clemens/Bat-Jsy/250 15.00
129 Roy Halladay/Jsy-Jsy/250 4.00
130 Roy Oswalt/Bat-Jsy/250 6.00
131 Ryne Sandberg/ Bat-Jsy/250 15.00
132 Sammy Sosa/Bat-Jsy/250 15.00
133 Sammy Sosa/Bat-Jsy/250 15.00
134 Sammy Sosa/Bat-Jsy/250 15.00
135 Scott Rolen/Bat-Jsy/250 10.00
136 Shawn Green/Bat-Jsy/250 6.00
137 Steve Carlton/Bat-Jsy/250 6.00
138 Tim Hudson/Bat-Jsy/250 6.00
139 Todd Helton/Bat-Jsy/250 8.00
140 Todd Helton/Bat-Jsy/250 8.00
141 Tom Glavine/Bat-Jsy/250 8.00
142 Tom Glavine/Bat-Jsy/250 8.00
143 Tony Gwynn/Bat-Jsy/250 12.00
144 Tony Gwynn/Bat-Jsy/250 12.00
145 Torii Hunter/Bat-Jsy/250 6.00
146 Trot Nixon/Bat-Jsy/250 8.00
147 Troy Glaus/Bat-Jsy/250 6.00
148 Vernon Wells/Bat-Jsy/250 4.00
149 Vladimir Guerrero/ Bat-Jsy/250 10.00
150 Will Clark/Bat-Jsy/250 10.00

Tools of Trade Material Signature Sing.

NM/M

Quantity produced listed
Combo: 1-2X
Production 1-25
Combo Prime: No Pricing
Production 1-5
Trio: No Pricing
Production 1-10
Quad: No Pricing
Production 1-10

1 Adam Dunn/H/Jsy/25 50.00
2 Adam Dunn/A/Jsy/25 50.00
3 Alan Trammell/Jsy/25 50.00
10 Andre Dawson/Jsy/25 25.00
15 Angel Berroa/Jsy/50 15.00
17 Austin Kearns/Jsy/28 25.00
21 Bobby Abreu/Jsy/25 25.00
22 Brandon Webb/Jsy/25 20.00
26 Carlos Beltran/Jsy/15 50.00
29 Carlos Lee/Jsy/25 25.00
36 Dale Murphy/Jsy/25 40.00
37 Dale Murphy/Jsy/25 40.00
38 Darryl Strawberry/Jsy/39 20.00
43 Dontrelle Willis/Jsy/25 30.00
44 Dontrelle Willis/Jsy/25 30.00
45 Dwight Gooden/Jsy/16 35.00
50 Garret Anderson/Jsy/16 30.00
61 Jae Weong/Seo Jsy/25 20.00
71 Jorge Posada/Jsy/20 60.00
74 Josh Beckett/Jsy/21 40.00
82 Luis Castillo/Jsy/25 20.00
89 Mark Mulder/Jsy/20 40.00
93 Marlon Byrd/Jsy/29 20.00
94 Miguel Cabrera/Jsy/20 50.00
96 Mike Lowell/Jsy/19 30.00
112 Paul LoDuca/Jsy/50 25.00
115 Preston Wilson/Jsy/44 20.00
125 Rocco Baldelli/Jsy/25 30.00
129 Roy Halladay/Jsy/32 25.00
137 Steve Carlton/Jsy/25 50.00
145 Torii Hunter/Jsy/25 25.00
146 Trot Nixon/Jsy/25 50.00

Tools of Trade Signature Blue Spectrum

NM/M

Quantity produced listed
Black: No Pricing
Production One Set
Green: No Pricing
Production 1-10
Red: .75-1.5X
Production 1-50
No pricing 15 or less.

3 Alan Trammell/100 15.00
10 Andre Dawson/100 15.00
15 Angel Berroa/100 8.00
16 Aubrey Huff/100 10.00
17 Austin Kearns/100 15.00
22 Brandon Webb/100 8.00
26 Carlos Beltran/100 20.00
29 Carlos Lee/100 15.00
36 Dale Murphy H/50 30.00
37 Dale Murphy A/50 30.00
38 Darryl Strawberry/50 20.00
41 Don Mattingly H/50 75.00
42 Don Mattingly A/50 75.00
43 Dontrelle Willis H/25 30.00
44 Dontrelle Willis A/25 30.00
45 Dwight Gooden/50 25.00
46 Edgar Martinez/25 50.00
48 Frank Thomas A/25 50.00
49 Frank Thomas/25 50.00
50 Garret Anderson/100 15.00
51 Gary Carter/100 15.00
60 Jacque Jones/50 20.00
61 Jae Weong Seo/25 25.00
65 Jay Gibbons/50 15.00
69 Jim Edmonds/25 35.00
71 Jorge Posada/25 40.00
73 Jose Reyes/25 25.00
75 Juan Gonzalez/20 40.00
77 Kerry Wood H/25 50.00
78 Kerry Wood/25 50.00
81 Lou Brock/100 25.00
84 Magglio Ordonez/50 20.00
87 Marcus Giles/50 20.00
88 Mark Grace/25 40.00
89 Mark Mulder/100 20.00
90 Mark Prior H/50 60.00
91 Mark Prior A/50 60.00
92 Mark Teixeira/50 30.00
93 Marlon Byrd/50 15.00
94 Miguel Cabrera/100 35.00
102 Mike Schmidt H/25 75.00
103 Mike Schmidt A/25 75.00
106 Nolan Ryan/25 125.00
107 Nolan Ryan/25 125.00
108 Nolan Ryan/25 125.00
112 Paul LoDuca/50 25.00
115 Preston Wilson/100 15.00
129 Roy Halladay/25 30.00
130 Roy Oswalt/25 25.00
135 Scott Rolen/50 40.00
137 Steve Carlton/50 30.00
143 Tony Gwynn A/25 60.00
144 Tony Gwynn/25 60.00
145 Torii Hunter/50 25.00
146 Trot Nixon/25 30.00
149 Vladimir Guerrero/25 65.00
150 Will Clark/50 50.00

2004 Playoff Honors

NM/M

Complete Set (250):
Common Player (1-200): .15
Common SP (201-250): 3.00
Production 1,999
Common SP Auto. (226-250): 8.00
Pack (6): 5.00
Box (12): 55.00

1 Bartolo Colon .15
2 Garret Anderson .40
3 Tim Salmon .25

2004 Playoff Honors • 683

4	Troy Glaus	.25
5	Vladimir Guerrero	.75
6	Brandon Webb	.15
7	Brian Bruney	.15
8	Luis Gonzalez	.25
9	Randy Johnson	.75
10	Richie Sexson	.40
11	Robby Hammock	.15
12	Roberto Alomar	.40
13	Shea Hillenbrand	.15
14	Steve Finley	.15
15	Adam LaRoche	.15
16	Andruw Jones	.50
17	Bubba Nelson	.15
18	Chipper Jones	.75
19	Dale Murphy	.50
20	J.D. Drew	.25
21	John Smoltz	.25
22	Marcus Giles	.15
23	Rafael Furcal	.25
24	Warren Spahn	.75
25	Greg Maddux	1.00
26	Adam Loewen	.15
27	Cal Ripken Jr.	3.00
28	Javy Lopez	.25
29	Jay Gibbons	.15
30	Luis Matos	.15
31	Miguel Tejada	.40
32	Rafael Palmeiro	.50
33	Bobby Doerr	.15
34	Curt Schilling	.50
35	Edwin Almonte	.15
36	Jason Varitek	.25
37	Kevin Youkilis	.15
38	Manny Ramirez	.50
39	Nomar Garciaparra	1.00
40	Pedro J. Martinez	.75
41	Trot Nixon	.25
42	Andre Dawson	.25
43	Aramis Ramirez	.40
44	Brendan Harris	.15
45	Derrek Lee	.25
46	Ernie Banks	.75
47	Kerry Wood	.75
48	Mark Prior	1.00
49	Ryne Sandberg	1.00
50	Sammy Sosa	1.50
51	Carlos Lee	.15
52	Frank Thomas	.50
53	Joe Borchard	.15
54	Joe Crede	.15
55	Magglio Ordonez	.25
56	Adam Dunn	.50
57	Austin Kearns	.25
58	Barry Larkin	.40
59	Brandon Larson	.15
60	Ken Griffey Jr.	1.00
61	Ryan Wagner	.15
62	Sean Casey	.25
63	Bob Feller	.25
64	Brian Tallet	.15
65	C.C. Sabathia	.15
66	Jeremy Guthrie	.15
67	Jody Gerut	.15
68	Clint Barmes	.15
69	Jeff Baker	.15
70	Joe Kennedy	.15
71	Larry Walker	.25
72	Preston Wilson	.15
73	Todd Helton	.50
74	Alan Trammell	.25
75	Dmitri Young	.15
76	Ivan Rodriguez	.50
77	Jeremy Bonderman	.15
78	Preston Larrison	.15
79	Dontrelle Willis	.25
80	Josh Beckett	.50
81	Juan Pierre	.15
82	Luis Castillo	.15
83	Miguel Cabrera	.75
84	Mike Lowell	.25
85	Andy Pettitte	.25
86	Chris Burke	.15
87	Craig Biggio	.25
88	Jeff Bagwell	.50
89	Jeff Kent	.25
90	Lance Berkman	.25
91	Morgan Ensberg	.15
92	Richard Hidalgo	.15
93	Roger Clemens	1.50
94	Roy Oswalt	.25
95	Angel Berroa	.15
96	Byron Gettis	.15
97	Carlos Beltran	.40
98	George Brett	2.00
99	Juan Gonzalez	.50
100	Mike Sweeney	.15
101	Duke Snider	.50
102	Edwin Jackson	.15
103	Eric Gagne	.50
104	Hideo Nomo	.40
105	Hong-Chih Kuo	.15
106	Kazuhisa Ishii	.15
107	Paul LoDuca	.15
108	Robin Ventura	.15
109	Shawn Green	.25
110	Junior Spivey	.15
111	Rickie Weeks	.25
112	Scott Podsednik	.25
113	J.D. Durbin	.15
114	Jacque Jones	.15
115	Jason Kubel	.25
116	Johan Santana	.15
117	Shannon Stewart	.15
118	Torii Hunter	.25
119	Brad Wilkerson	.15
120	Jose Vidro	.15
121	Nick Johnson	.15
122	Orlando Cabrera	.15
123	Gary Carter	.25
124	Jae Weong Seo	.15
125	Lenny Dykstra	.15
126	Mike Piazza	1.00
127	Tom Glavine	.25
128	Alex Rodriguez	1.50
129	Bernie Williams	.40
130	Chien-Ming Wang	1.00
131	Derek Jeter	2.00
132	Don Mattingly	1.50
133	Gary Sheffield	.40
134	Hideki Matsui	1.50
135	Jason Giambi	.50
136	Javier Vazquez	.25
137	Jorge Posada	.40
138	Jose Contreras	.15
139	Kevin Brown	.25
140	Mariano Rivera	.40
141	Mike Mussina	.40
142	Whitey Ford	.50
143	Barry Zito	.40
144	Eric Chavez	.25
145	Mark Mulder	.40
146	Rich Harden	.15
147	Tim Hudson	.25
148	Reggie Jackson	.50
149	Rickey Henderson	.50
150	Brett Myers	.15
151	Bobby Abreu	.25
152	Jim Thome	.75
153	Kevin Millwood	.25
154	Marlon Byrd	.15
155	Mike Schmidt	1.50
156	Ryan Howard	3.00
157	Jack Wilson	.15
158	Jason Kendall	.15
159	Brian Giles	.25
160	David Wells	.15
161	Jay Payton	.15
162	Phil Nevin	.15
163	Ryan Klesko	.15
164	Sean Burroughs	.15
165	A.J. Pierzynski	.15
166	J.T. Snow	.15
167	Jason Schmidt	.50
168	Jerome Williams	.15
169	Will Clark	.50
170	Bret Boone	.15
171	Chris Snelling	.15
172	Edgar Martinez	.25
173	Ichiro Suzuki	1.50
174	Randy Winn	.15
175	Rich Aurilia	.15
176	Shigetoshi Hasegawa	.15
177	Albert Pujols	.15
178	Dan Haren	.15
179	Edgar Renteria	.25
180	Jim Edmonds	.40
181	Matt Morris	.15
182	Scott Rolen	.75
183	Stan Musial	1.00
184	Aubrey Huff	.15
185	Chad Gaudin	.15
186	Delmon Young	.25
187	Fred McGriff	.25
188	Rocco Baldelli	.15
189	Alfonso Soriano	.75
190	Hank Blalock	.50
191	Mark Teixeira	.40
192	Nolan Ryan	2.00
193	Alexis Rios	.15
194	Carlos Delgado	.40
195	Dustin McGowan	.15
196	Guillermo Quiroz	.15
197	Josh Phelps	.15
198	Roy Halladay	.25
199	Vernon Wells	.15
200	Vinnie Chulk	.15
201	Jose Capellan/1,999 **RC**	5.00
202	Kazuo Matsui/1,999 **RC**	5.00
203	David Crouthers/1,999	3.00
204	Akinori Otsuka/1,999 **RC**	5.00
205	Nick Regilio/1,999 **RC**	3.00
206	Justin Hampson/1,999 **RC**	3.00
207	Lincoln Holdzkom/1,999 **RC**	3.00
208	Jorge Sequea/1,999 **RC**	3.00
209	Justin Leone/1,999 **RC**	5.00
210	Renyel Pinto/1,999 **RC**	3.00
211	Mariano Gomez/1,999 **RC**	3.00
212	Onil Joseph Auto./1,000 **RC**	8.00
213	Josh Labandeira AU/1,000 **RC**	10.00
214	Cory Sullivan/1,999 **RC**	3.00
215	Carlos Vasquez Auto./675 **RC**	8.00
216	Chris Shelton/1,999 **RC**	8.00
217	Willy Taveras/1,999 **RC**	6.00
218	John Gall/1,999 **RC**	5.00
219	Jerry Gil/1,999 **RC**	3.00
220	Jason Frasor/1,999 **RC**	3.00
221	Justin Knoedler/1,999 **RC**	3.00
222	Ronald Belisario/1,999 **RC**	3.00
223	Mike Rouse/1,999	3.00
224	Dennis Sarfate/1,999 **RC**	3.00
225	Casey Daigle/1,999 **RC**	3.00
226	Shingo Takatsu/ Auto./800 **RC**	10.00
227	Jason Bartlett/ Auto./800 **RC**	8.00
228	Alfredo Simon/ Auto./1,000 **RC**	8.00
229	Chris Oxspring/1,999 **RC**	3.00
230	Fernando Nieve Auto./1,000 **RC**	8.00
231	Ruddy Yan Auto./800 **RC**	8.00
232	Ryan Wing/1,999	3.00
233	Tim Bittner Auto./1,000 **RC**	8.00
234	Ramon Ramirez Auto./1,000 **RC**	8.00
235	Sean Henn Auto./1,000	8.00
236	Roberto Novoa **RC**	4.00
237	Jerome Gamble Auto./800 **RC**	8.00
238	Jamie Brown Auto./800 **RC**	8.00
239	Ian Snell Auto./800 **RC**	30.00
240	Freddy Guzman Auto./800 **RC**	8.00
241	Aarom Baldiris Auto./1,000 **RC**	8.00
242	Greg Dobbs/1,999 **RC**	3.00
243	Ivan Ochoa/1,999 **RC**	3.00
244	Angel Chavez/ Auto./800 **RC**	8.00
245	Merkin Valdez/ Auto./800 **RC**	10.00
246	Mike Gosling/Auto./800	8.00
247	Carlos Hines/ Auto./800 **RC**	8.00
248	Graham Koonce/ Auto./1,000	10.00
249	William Bergolla/ Auto./1,000 **RC**	8.00
250	Hector Gimenez/ Auto./1,000 **RC**	8.00

Credits Bronze

Bronze (1-200): 3-6X
Bronze (201-250): .5-1X
Production 100 Sets

Credits Gold

Gold (1-200): 8-15X
Gold (201-250): No Pricing
Production 25 Sets

Credits Silver

Silver (1-200): 4-8X
Silver (201-250): No Pricing
Production 50 Sets

Credits Platinum

No Pricing
Production One Set

Awards

		NM/M
	Common Player:	2.00
	Quantity produced listed	
1	Phil Rizzuto/1,950	3.00
2	Fred Lynn/1,975	2.00
3	George Brett/1,980	8.00
4	Cal Ripken Jr./1,983	10.00
5	Don Mattingly/1,985	8.00
6	Rickey Henderson/1,990	3.00
7	Stan Musial/1,943	5.00
8	Marty Marion/1,944	3.00
9	Ernie Banks/1,958	5.00
10	Sammy Sosa/1,998	6.00
11	Terry Pendleton/1,991	2.00
12	Ryne Sandberg/1,984	6.00
13	Andre Dawson/1,987	3.00
14	George Foster/1,977	2.00
15	Dave Parker/1,978	2.00
16	Keith Hernandez/1,979	3.00
17	Mike Schmidt/1,980	6.00
18	Dale Murphy/1,982	3.00
19	Whitey Ford/1,961	3.00
20	Roy Halladay/2,003	2.00
21	Orel Hershiser/1,988	2.00
22	Bob Feller/1,940	3.00
23	Dwight Gooden/1,985	2.00
24	Steve Carlton/1,972	3.00
25	Randy Johnson/2,002	4.00

Awards Signature

		NM/M
	Quantity produced listed	
1	Phil Rizzuto/50	25.00
2	Fred Lynn/100	15.00
7	Stan Musial/50	50.00
8	Marty Marion/50	10.00
10	Sammy Sosa/21	125.00
11	Terry Pendleton/100	10.00
13	Andre Dawson/100	15.00
14	George Foster/100	10.00
15	Dave Parker/88	15.00
16	Keith Hernandez/100	20.00
19	Whitey Ford/50	25.00
20	Roy Halladay/25	25.00
21	Orel Hershiser/25	40.00
22	Bob Feller/100	15.00
23	Dwight Gooden/100	10.00

Champions

		NM/M
	Common Player:	2.00
	Quantity produced listed	
1	Stan Musial/1,951	5.00
2	Warren Spahn/1,958	3.00
3	Bob Gibson/1,968	3.00
4	Mike Schmidt/1,980	6.00
5	Dale Murphy/1,982	4.00
6	Steve Carlton/1,983	4.00
7	Will Clark/1,988	4.00
8	Nolan Ryan/1,990	10.00
9	Ryne Sandberg/1,990	6.00
10	Roger Clemens/1,990	8.00
11	George Brett/1,990	8.00
12	Tony Gwynn/1,997	5.00
13	Todd Helton/2,000	3.00
14	Troy Glaus/2,000	2.00
15	Sammy Sosa/2,000	6.00
16	Pedro J. Martinez/2,000	4.00
17	Mark Mulder/2,001	2.00
18	Manny Ramirez/2,002	3.00
19	Lance Berkman/2,002	2.00
20	Alex Rodriguez/Rgr/2,002	6.00

Champions Jersey

		NM/M
	Common Jersey:	5.00
	Quantity produced listed	
1	Stan Musial/100	30.00
2	Warren Spahn/100	10.00
3	Bob Gibson/100	10.00
4	Mike Schmidt/100	20.00
5	Dale Murphy/82	10.00
6	Steve Carlton/100	8.00
7	Will Clark/100	10.00
8	Nolan Ryan/100	25.00
9	Ryne Sandberg/100	20.00
10	Roger Clemens/100	15.00
11	George Brett/100	25.00
12	Tony Gwynn/250	10.00
13	Todd Helton/250	8.00
14	Troy Glaus/250	5.00
15	Sammy Sosa/250	15.00
16	Pedro J. Martinez/250	8.00
17	Mark Mulder/250	5.00
18	Manny Ramirez/250	8.00
19	Lance Berkman/250	5.00
20	Alex Rodriguez/250	10.00

Champions Jersey Signature

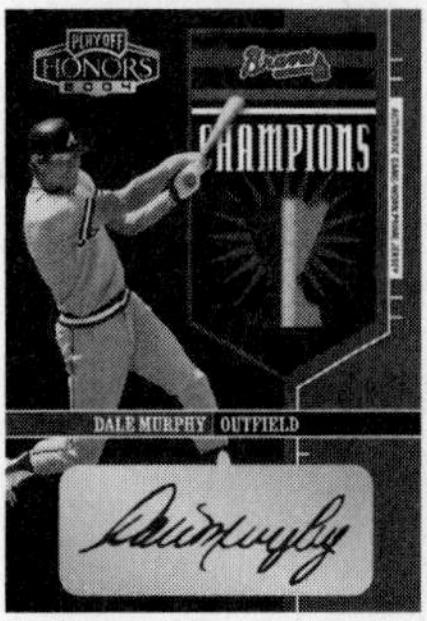
PLAYOFF
HONORS
2004
CHAMPIONS
DALE MURPHY | OUTFIELD

No Pricing
Production Five Sets

Champions Signature

		NM/M
	Quantity produced listed	
1	Stan Musial/50	50.00
3	Bob Gibson/50	25.00
7	Will Clark/50	40.00
8	Nolan Ryan/34	100.00

Class Reunion

		NM/M
	Quantity produced listed	
1	Eddie Murray, Gary Carter/2,003	3.00
2	Carlton Fisk, Tony Perez/2,000	3.00
3	Nolan Ryan, George Brett/1,999	10.00
4	Rod Carew, Fergie Jenkins/1,991	3.00
5	Joe Morgan, Jim Palmer/1,990	3.00
6	Carl Yastrzemski, Johnny Bench/1,989	5.00
7	Harmon Killebrew, Luis Aparicio/1,984	3.00
8	Brooks Robinson, Juan Marichal/1,983	3.00
9	Al Kaline, Duke Snider/1,980	3.00
10	Roberto Clemente, Warren Spahn/1,973	8.00
11	Mark Prior, Mark Teixeira/2,001	3.00
12	Josh Beckett, Barry Zito/1,999	3.00
13	Mark Mulder, Adam Dunn/1,998	3.00
14	Vernon Wells, Lance Berkman/1,997	3.00
15	Eric Chavez, Nick Johnson/1,996	3.00
16	Kerry Wood, Roy Halladay/1,995	4.00
17	Todd Helton, Carlos Beltran/1,995	4.00
18	Derek Jeter, Jason Giambi/1,992	8.00
19	Manny Ramirez, Shawn Green/1,991	4.00
20	Chipper Jones, Mike Mussina/1,990	4.00

Class Reunion Material

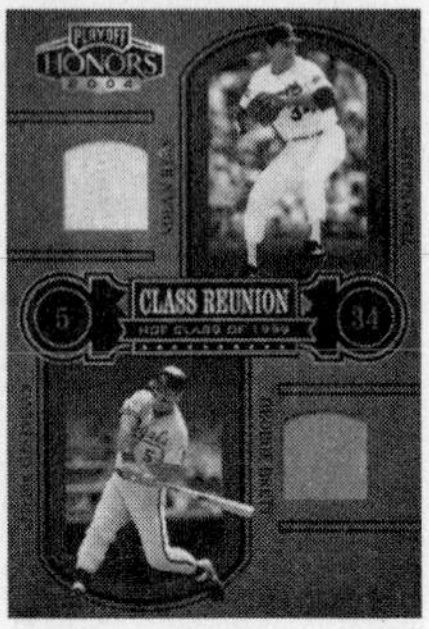

NM/M

Quantity produced listed

1	Eddie Murray/Jsy, Gary Carter/Jsy/100	15.00
2	Carlton Fisk/Jsy, Tony Perez/Bat/250	20.00
3	Nolan Ryan/Jsy, George Brett/Jsy/100	50.00
4	Rod Carew/Jsy, Fergie Jenkins/Pants/250	15.00
5	Joe Morgan/Jsy, Jim Palmer/Jsy/100	10.00
6	Carl Yastrzemski/Jsy, Johnny Bench/Jsy/250	30.00
7	Harmon Killebrew/Jsy, Luis Aparicio/Jsy/250	15.00
8	Brooks Robinson/Jsy, Juan Marichal/Jsy/100	15.00
9	Al Kaline/Jsy, Duke Snider/Jsy/25	35.00
10	Roger Clemens/Jsy, Warren Spahn/Jsy/100	80.00
11	Mark Prior/Jsy, Mark Teixeira/Jsy/250	10.00
12	Josh Beckett/Jsy, Barry Zito/Jsy/250	8.00
13	Mark Mulder/Jsy, Adam Dunn/Jsy/250	10.00
14	Vernon Wells/Jsy, Lance Berkman/Jsy/250	8.00
15	Eric Chavez/Jsy, Nick Johnson/Jsy/250	8.00
16	Kerry Wood/Jsy, Roy Halladay/Jsy/250	12.00
17	Todd Helton/Jsy, Carlos Beltran/Jsy/250	10.00
18	Derek Jeter/Jsy, Jason Giambi/Jsy/250	20.00
19	Manny Ramirez/Jsy, Shawn Green/Jsy/50	10.00
20	Chipper Jones/Jsy, Mike Mussina/Jsy/250	10.00

Fans of the Game

		NM/M
251	Charlie Sheen	3.00
252	Corbin Bernsen	2.00
253	Peter Gammons	3.00
254	Jeff Garlin/SP	2.00
255	Larry King	2.00

Fans of the Game Signature

		NM/M
251	Charlie Sheen	100.00
252	Corbin Bernsen	25.00
253	Peter Gammons	50.00
254	Jeff Garlin/SP	80.00
255	Larry King	45.00

Game Day Souvenir

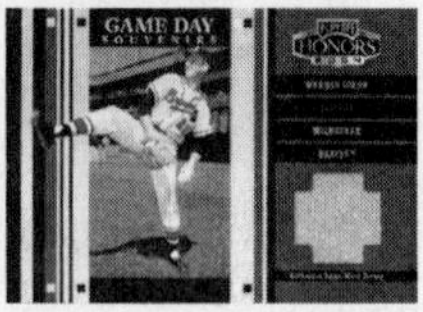

		NM/M
2	Bob Gibson/Jsy/75	15.00
3	Frank Robinson/Bat/61	10.00
4	Tony Gwynn/Pants/99	20.00
5	Warren Spahn/Jsy/53	20.00
6	George Brett/Bat/77	25.00
7	Cal Ripken Jr./Hat/19	100.00
8	Frank Thomas/Bat/93	10.00
9	Sammy Sosa/Jsy/100	15.00
10	Harmon Killebrew/Bat/75	15.00

Game Day Souvenir Signature

No Pricing
Production Five Sets

Piece of the Game Bat

		NM/M
1	Albert Pujols/250	15.00
2	Angel Berroa/250	4.00
3	Aubrey Huff/250	4.00
4	Barry Zito/250	6.00
5	Bobby Abreu/250	4.00
6	Carlos Beltran/250	4.00
7	Chipper Jones/250	8.00
8	Derek Jeter/250	20.00
9	Eric Chavez/150	6.00
10	Eric Hinske/50	6.00
11	Gary Sheffield/250	6.00
12	George Brett/250	15.00
13	Jay Gibbons/250	4.00
14	Jim Edmonds/250	6.00
15	Josh Beckett/250	6.00
16	Manny Ramirez/250	8.00
17	Mark Mulder/250	6.00
18	Marlon Byrd/250	4.00
19	Mike Lowell/250	4.00
20	Mike Schmidt/250	20.00
21	Nolan Ryan/250	20.00
22	Rafael Furcal/250	4.00
23	Randy Johnson/100	10.00
24	Rod Carew/250	8.00
25	Torii Hunter/250	4.00

Piece of the Game Bat Signature

No Pricing
Production 1-10

Piece of the Game Combo

		NM/M
1	Albert Pujols/Bat-Jsy/100	25.00
2	Angel Berroa/Bat-Pants/100	6.00
3	Aubrey Huff/Bat-Jsy/100	6.00
4	Barry Zito/Bat-Jsy/100	8.00
5	Bobby Abreu/Bat-Jsy/100	6.00
6	Carlos Beltran/Bat-Jsy/100	6.00
7	Chipper Jones/Bat-Jsy/100	10.00
8	Derek Jeter/Bat-Jsy/100	40.00
9	Eric Chavez/Bat-Jsy/50	8.00
10	Eric Hinske/Bat-Jsy/25	8.00
12	George Brett/Bat-Jsy/100	25.00
13	Jay Gibbons/Bat-Jsy/100	6.00
14	Jim Edmonds/Bat-Jsy/100	8.00
15	Josh Beckett/Bat-Jsy/100	6.00
16	Manny Ramirez/Bat-Jsy/100	10.00
17	Mark Mulder/Bat-Jsy/25	15.00
18	Marlon Byrd/Bat-Jsy/100	6.00
19	Mike Lowell/Bat-Jsy/100	6.00
20	Mike Schmidt/Bat-Jsy/50	50.00
21	Nolan Ryan/Bat-Jsy/100	35.00
22	Rafael Furcal/Bat-Jsy/100	6.00
23	Randy Johnson/Bat-Jsy/100	15.00
24	Rod Carew/Bat-Jsy/100	15.00
25	Torii Hunter/Bat-Jsy/100	8.00

Piece of the Game Combo Signature

No Pricing
Production 1-10

Piece of the Game Jersey

NM/M

Quantity produced listed

1	Albert Pujols/250	15.00
2	Angel Berroa/250	4.00
3	Aubrey Huff/250	4.00
4	Barry Zito/250	6.00
5	Bobby Abreu/250	4.00
6	Carlos Beltran/250	4.00
7	Chipper Jones/250	8.00
8	Derek Jeter/50	40.00
9	Eric Chavez/250	5.00
10	Eric Hinske/100	4.00
12	George Brett/250	15.00
13	Jay Gibbons/250	4.00
14	Jim Edmonds/250	6.00
15	Josh Beckett/250	4.00
16	Manny Ramirez/250	6.00
17	Mark Mulder/100	6.00
18	Marlon Byrd/250	4.00
19	Mike Lowell/250	4.00
20	Mike Schmidt/50	35.00
21	Nolan Ryan/100	25.00
22	Rafael Furcal/250	4.00
23	Randy Johnson/250	8.00
24	Rod Carew/100	8.00
25	Torii Hunter/250	4.00

Piece of the Game Jersey Signature

Quantity produced listed
No Pricing

Prime Signature Autograph

		NM/M
1	Garret Anderson/100	15.00
2	Rafael Palmeiro/50	40.00
3	Vladimir Guerrero/50	50.00
5	Dontrelle Willis/50	30.00
6	Miguel Cabrera/100	35.00
7	Shannon Stewart/100	10.00
9	Gary Sheffield/100	25.00
12	Tom Glavine/25	40.00
13	Brandon Webb/100	10.00
14	Carlos Lee/100	10.00
17	Maggio Ordonez/100	15.00
19	Andruw Jones/50	20.00
21	Sammy Sosa/50	100.00
22	Juan Gonzalez/50	25.00
23	Jeff Bagwell/25	50.00
24	Rickey Henderson/25	75.00
25	Mike Schmidt/50	60.00
26	Jim Rice/100	15.00
27	Billy Williams/100	15.00
28	Lou Brock/100	20.00
29	Robin Yount/25	75.00
30	Nolan Ryan/50	85.00
31	Darryl Strawberry/100	15.00
32	Cal Ripken Jr./25	200.00
33	Andre Dawson/100	15.00
34	Don Mattingly/50	75.00
35	Paul Molitor/25	50.00
36	Bo Jackson/50	75.00
37	Ernie Banks/50	50.00
38	Orel Hershiser/100	20.00
39	Mark Grace/50	40.00
40	Carlton Fisk/50	25.00

Prime Signature Autograph Bat

Quantity produced listed
No Pricing

Prime Signature Autograph Jersey

NM/M

Quantity produced listed

2	Rafael Palmeiro/25	75.00
6	Miguel Cabrera/20	75.00
7	Shannon Stewart/23	15.00
29	Robin Yount/19	75.00
31	Darryl Strawberry/25	25.00
34	Don Mattingly/23	100.00
39	Mark Grace/17	65.00

Prime Signature Insert

NM/M

Production 2,500 Sets

1	Garret Anderson	2.00
2	Rafael Palmeiro	3.00
3	Vladimir Guerrero	3.00
4	Alex Rodriguez	5.00
5	Dontrelle Willis	2.00
6	Miguel Cabrera	3.00
7	Shannon Stewart	2.00
8	Mike Piazza	4.00
9	Gary Sheffield	2.00
10	Ivan Rodriguez	3.00
11	Randy Johnson	3.00
12	Tom Glavine	2.00
13	Brandon Webb	2.00
14	Carlos Lee	2.00
15	Hideo Nomo	2.00
16	Mike Mussina	3.00
17	Magglio Ordonez	2.00
18	Austin Kearns	2.00
19	Andruw Jones	3.00
20	Mariano Rivera	3.00
21	Sammy Sosa	4.00
22	Juan Gonzalez	3.00
23	Jeff Bagwell	3.00
24	Rickey Henderson	3.00
25	Mike Schmidt	5.00
26	Jim Rice	2.00
27	Billy Williams	2.00
28	Lou Brock	2.00
29	Robin Yount	4.00
30	Nolan Ryan	8.00
31	Darryl Strawberry	2.00
32	Cal Ripken Jr.	10.00
33	Andre Dawson	2.00
34	Don Mattingly	8.00
35	Paul Molitor	3.00
36	Bo Jackson	3.00
37	Ernie Banks	4.00
38	Orel Hershiser	2.00
39	Mark Grace	3.00
40	Carlton Fisk	3.00

Quad Material

NM/M

Quantity produced listed

1	Matt Williams, Mark Grace, Will Clark, Keith Hernandez/100	60.00
2	Jason Giambi, Jim Thome, Carlos Delgado, Rafael Palmeiro/100	20.00
3	Albert Pujols, Ernie Banks, Jeff Bagwell, Jim Thome/100	50.00
4	Paul Molitor, Joe Morgan, Ryne Sandberg, Alfonso Soriano/50	50.00
5	Cal Ripken Jr., Derek Jeter, Alex Rodriguez, Nomar Garciaparra/100	75.00
6	Ozzie Smith, Robin Yount, Alan Trammell, Dave Concepcion/50	50.00
8	Johnny Bench, Carlton Fisk, Gary Carter, Mike Piazza/100	40.00
9	Todd Helton, Brian Giles, Edgar Renteria, Scott Rolen/25	40.00
10	Carlos Delgado, Alfonso Soriano, Alex Rodriguez, Troy Glaus/100	20.00
11	Harmon Killebrew, Reggie Jackson, Mike Schmidt, Sammy Sosa/100	65.00
12	Stan Musial, Rickey Henderson, Tony Gwynn, Lou Brock/25	80.00
13	Cal Ripken Jr., George Brett, Paul Molitor, Rod Carew/100	75.00
14	Sammy Sosa, Vladimir Guerrero, Manny Ramirez, Magglio Ordonez/100	40.00
15	Andruw Jones, Jim Edmonds, Torii Hunter, Vernon Wells/100	20.00
16	Chipper Jones, Shawn Green, Andruw Jones, Lance Berkman/100	20.00
17	Tony Gwynn, Dale Murphy, Kirby Puckett, Andre Dawson/100	40.00
19	Nolan Ryan, Roger Clemens, Kerry Wood, Josh Beckett/100	75.00
21	Dennis Eckersley, John Smoltz, Mariano Rivera, Lee Smith/100	40.00
22	Mike Mussina, Greg Maddux, Jack Morris, Bert Blyleven/100	40.00
23	Steve Carlton, Tom Glavine, Barry Zito, Andy Pettitte/100	20.00
24	Whitey Ford, Warren Spahn, Bob Feller, Juan Marichal/25	80.00
25	Nolan Ryan, Roger Clemens, Steve Carlton, Randy Johnson/100	80.00

Rookie Year Jersey Number

		NM/M
1	Gary Carter/50	10.00
2	Robin Yount/50	30.00
3	Roger Clemens/25	40.00
4	Gary Sheffield/50	8.00
5	Mike Piazza/25	30.00
6	Hideo Nomo/25	30.00
7	Alex Rodriguez/50	20.00
8	Mark Prior/25	15.00
9	Dontrelle Willis/100	10.00
10	Angel Berroa/100	8.00

Rookie Year Jersey Signature

No Pricing
Production 1-10

Signature Bronze

NM/M

Quantity produced listed

2	Garret Anderson/100	15.00
5	Vladimir Guerrero/50	50.00
6	Brandon Webb/100	8.00
7	Brian Bruney/96	8.00
11	Robby Hammock/100	8.00
13	Shea Hillenbrand/100	10.00
15	Adam LaRoche/100	10.00
16	Andruw Jones/25	25.00
17	Bubba Nelson/100	8.00
22	Marcus Giles/100	15.00
23	Rafael Furcal/50	15.00
26	Adam Loewen/100	8.00
27	Cal Ripken Jr./25	150.00
29	Jay Gibbons/100	8.00
30	Luis Matos/100	8.00
33	Bobby Doerr/100	15.00
35	Edwin Almonte/99	8.00
36	Jason Varitek/50	30.00
37	Kevin Youkilis/100	15.00
42	Andre Dawson/100	15.00
43	Aramis Ramirez/25	25.00
44	Brendan Harris/100	8.00
45	Derrek Lee/100	20.00
46	Ernie Banks/25	60.00
47	Kerry Wood/25	50.00
48	Mark Prior/50	40.00
50	Sammy Sosa/50	125.00
51	Carlos Lee/100	10.00
52	Frank Thomas/25	50.00
53	Joe Borchard/100	8.00
54	Joe Crede/50	10.00
55	Magglio Ordonez/50	15.00
58	Barry Larkin/25	40.00
59	Brandon Larson/100	8.00
61	Ryan Wagner/100	8.00
63	Bob Feller/100	20.00
64	Brian Tallet/100	8.00
66	Jeremy Guthrie/100	8.00
67	Jody Gerut/100	10.00
68	Clint Barmes/100	8.00
69	Jeff Baker/25	20.00
72	Preston Wilson/100	15.00
74	Alan Trammell/100	15.00
78	Preston Larrison/100	8.00
79	Dontrelle Willis/25	30.00
83	Miguel Cabrera/100	40.00
85	Andy Pettitte/25	50.00
86	Chris Burke/100	8.00
88	Jeff Bagwell/25	50.00
91	Morgan Ensberg/100	10.00
96	Byron Gettis/100	8.00
97	Carlos Beltran/100	30.00
98	George Brett/25	100.00
101	Duke Snider/100	25.00
102	Edwin Jackson/100	10.00

105	Hong-Chih Kuo/100	25.00
106	Kazuhisa Ishii/25	40.00
107	Paul LoDuca/100	15.00
108	Robin Ventura/50	15.00
110	Junior Spivey/50	10.00
112	Scott Podsednik/100	15.00
113	J.D. Durbin/100	8.00
114	Jacque Jones/100	15.00
116	Johan Santana/100	25.00
117	Shannon Stewart/50	10.00
123	Gary Carter/100	15.00
125	Lenny Dykstra/100	15.00
130	Chien-Ming Wang/100	100.00
132	Don Mattingly/25	80.00
133	Gary Sheffield/50	25.00
137	Jorge Posada/50	25.00
142	Whitey Ford/50	25.00
145	Mark Mulder/100	15.00
146	Rich Harden/100	15.00
147	Tim Hudson/25	40.00
148	Reggie Jackson/25	50.00
149	Rickey Henderson/25	80.00
150	Brett Myers/100	8.00
154	Marlon Byrd/100	8.00
155	Mike Schmidt/50	60.00
156	Ryan Howard/100	80.00
161	Jay Payton/100	10.00
168	Jerome Williams/50	20.00
169	Will Clark/50	50.00
171	Chris Snelling/100	8.00
176	Shigetoshi Hasegawa/100	50.00
178	Dan Haren/100	10.00
180	Jim Edmonds/25	30.00
182	Scott Rolen/50	30.00
183	Stan Musial/50	60.00
184	Aubrey Huff/100	15.00
185	Chad Gaudin/100	8.00
186	Delmon Young/50	30.00
191	Mark Teixeira/50	25.00
192	Nolan Ryan/50	100.00
193	Alexis Rios/100	15.00
195	Dustin McGowan/100	10.00
196	Guillermo Quiroz/50	15.00
197	Josh Phelps/25	15.00
198	Roy Halladay/25	25.00
200	Vinnie Chulk/25	15.00
201	Jose Capellan/100	35.00
203	David Crouthers/100	8.00
204	Akinori Otsuka/100	35.00
205	Nick Regilio/100	8.00
206	Justin Hampson/100	8.00
207	Lincoln Holdzkom/100	8.00
208	Jorge Sequea/100	8.00
209	Justin Leone/100	15.00
210	Renyel Pinto/100	10.00
211	Mariano Gomez/100	8.00
214	Cory Sullivan/100	8.00
216	Chris Shelton/100	40.00
217	Willy Taveras/25	8.00
218	John Gall/100	15.00
222	Ronald Belisario/100	8.00
223	Mike Rouse/100	8.00
224	Dennis Sarfate/100	8.00

Signature Gold

Gold: .75-1.5X Bronze
Production 1-50
No pricing 25 or less.

Signature Silver

Silver: .75-1.5X Bronze
Production 1-100
No pricing 25 or less.

Signature Platinum

No Pricing
Production One Set

Signs of Greatness

		NM/M
Quantity produced listed		
1	Mark Prior/25	50.00
2	Scott Podsednik/25	25.00
4	Dontrelle Willis/25	30.00
5	Rocco Baldelli/20	40.00
6	Brandon Webb/25	20.00
7	Rich Harden/25	25.00
8	Miguel Cabrera/25	50.00
9	Josh Beckett/25	40.00
10	Mark Teixeira/25	50.00

Tandem Material

		NM/M
Common Duo:		10.00
Quantity produced listed		
1	Bo Jackson, Deion Sanders/100	30.00
2	Eddie Murray, Rafael Palmeiro/250	15.00
3	Alex Rodriguez, Dale Murphy/250	15.00
4	Carlton Fisk, Ivan Rodriguez/250	15.00

5	Rickey Henderson, Lou Brock/50	30.00
6	Sammy Sosa, Ernie Banks/250	25.00
7	Warren Spahn, Steve Carlton/100	15.00
8	Carl Yastrzemski, Darrell Evans/250	25.00
9	Keith Hernandez, Lenny Dykstra/250	10.00
10	Pee Wee Reese, Marty Marion/100	15.00
11	Hideo Nomo, Chipper Jones/250	15.00
12	Willie McCovey, Reggie Jackson/100	20.00
13	Mark Prior, Barry Zito/250	10.00
14	Cal Ripken Jr., Miguel Tejada/Bat/100	50.00
15	Roberto Clemente, Vladimir Guerrero/Bat/100	75.00
16	Gary Carter, Mike Piazza/250	15.00
17	Jim Rice, Fred Lynn/50	20.00
18	Willie Stargell, Keith Hernandez/250	15.00
19	Nomar Garciaparra, Mark Teixeira/100	20.00
20	Derek Jeter, Phil Rizzuto/50	50.00
21	Eric Chavez, Hank Blalock/100	10.00
22	Eric Davis, Darryl Strawberry/100	15.00
23	Rickey Henderson, Deion Sanders/100	30.00
24	Dave Parker, Austin Kearns/250	10.00
25	Luis Aparicio, Dave Concepcion/100	15.00
26	Rafael Palmeiro, Will Clark/100	25.00
27	Ryne Sandberg, Ozzie Smith/250	50.00
28	Alex Rodriguez M's, Jose Canseco/250	15.00
29	Sammy Sosa, Juan Gonzalez/250	15.00
30	Pedro J. Martinez, Juan Marichal/50	20.00
32	Dwight Gooden, Gary Sheffield/250	10.00
33	Lou Boudreau, Omar Vizquel/100	15.00
34	Mark Prior, Ron Santo Bat/100	30.00
35	Albert Pujols, Ken Boyer/250	25.00
36	Tom Seaver, Curt Schilling/250	15.00
37	Joe Morgan, Jeff Kent/250	10.00
38	Steve Garvey, Ozzie Smith/250	25.00
39	Mike Piazza, Ivan Rodriguez/250	15.00
40	Mike Schmidt, Jim Thome/100	25.00

2004 Playoff Prestige

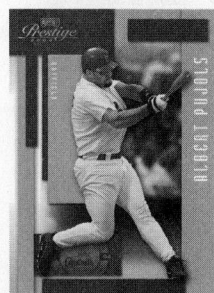

	NM/M
Complete Set (200):	35.00
Common Player:	.15
Pack (6):	3.50
Box (24):	75.00
1 Bengie Molina	.15
2 Garret Anderson	.25
3 Jarrod Washburn	.15
4 Scott Spiezio	.15
5 Tim Salmon	.25
6 Troy Glaus	.40
7 Alex Cintron	.15
8 Brandon Webb	.25
9 Curt Schilling	.50
10 Edgar Gonzalez	.50
11 Luis Gonzalez	.25
12 Randy Johnson	.75
13 Steve Finley	.50
14 Andruw Jones	.50
15 Bubba Nelson	.50

16	Chipper Jones	1.00
17	Gary Sheffield	.40
18	Greg Maddux	1.00
19	Javy Lopez	.40
20	John Smoltz	.25
21	Marcus Giles	.25
22	Rafael Furcal	.25
23	Brian Roberts	.15
24	Jason Johnson	.15
25	Jay Gibbons	.15
26	Luis Matos	.15
27	Melvin Mora	.15
28	Tony Batista	.15
29	Bill Mueller	.25
30	David Ortiz	.40
31	Johnny Damon	.25
32	Kevin Youkilis	1.00
33	Manny Ramirez	.50
34	Nomar Garciaparra	1.50
35	Pedro Martinez	.75
36	Trot Nixon	.25
37	Aramis Ramirez	.25
38	Brendan Harris	.50
39	Carlos Zambrano	.15
40	Corey Patterson	.25
41	Kenny Lofton	.25
42	Kerry Wood	.75
43	Mark Prior	1.50
44	Sammy Sosa	1.50
45	Bartolo Colon	.15
46	Carlos Lee	.25
47	Esteban Loaiza	.15
48	Frank Thomas	.50
49	Joe Crede	.15
50	Magglio Ordonez	.40
51	Roberto Alomar	.40
52	Adam Dunn	.40
53	Austin Kearns	.40
54	Josh Hall	.15
55	Ken Griffey Jr.	1.00
56	Sean Casey	.15
57	Micheal Nakamura	.15
58	C.C. Sabathia	.15
59	Casey Blake	.15
60	Jody Gerut	.15
61	Matt Lawton	.15
62	Milton Bradley	.15
63	Omar Vizquel	.25
64	Jason Jennings	.15
65	Jay Payton	.25
66	Larry Walker	.25
67	Preston Wilson	.25
68	Todd Helton	.50
69	Bobby Higginson	.15
70	Carlos Pena	.15
71	Dmitri Young	.15
72	Jeremy Bonderman	.15
73	Preston Larrison	.50
74	Derek Lee	.25
75	Dontrelle Willis	.40
76	Ivan Rodriguez	.50
77	Josh Beckett	.50
78	Juan Pierre	.15
79	Miguel Cabrera	.75
80	Mike Lowell	.25
81	Chris Burke	.15
82	Craig Biggio	.25
83	Jeff Bagwell	.50
84	Jeff Kent	.25
85	Lance Berkman	.40
86	Richard Hidalgo	.25
87	Roy Oswalt	.25
88	Aaron Guiel	.15
89	Angel Berroa	.15
90	Carlos Beltran	.40
91	Jeremy Affeldt	.15
92	Michael Sweeney	.15
93	Runelvys Hernandez	.15
94	Dave Roberts	.15
95	Eric Gagne	.40
96	Hideo Nomo	.40
97	Kevin Brown	.25
98	Paul Lo Duca	.15
99	Shawn Green	.40
100	Ben Sheets	.25
101	Geoff Jenkins	.40
102	Richie Sexson	.40
103	Rickie Weeks	1.00
104	Scott Podsednik	.50
105	J.D. Durbin	.50
106	Jacque Jones	.15
107	Jason Kubel	.50
108	Shannon Stewart	.15
109	Torii Hunter	.40
110	Chad Cordero	.50
111	Javier Vazquez	.25
112	Jose Vidro	.15
113	Livan Hernandez	.15
114	Orlando Cabrera	.25
115	Tony Armas Jr.	.15
116	Vladimir Guerrero	.75
117	Al Leiter	.15
118	Cliff Floyd	.15
119	Jae Weong So	.15
120	Jose Reyes	.50
121	Mike Piazza	1.00
122	Tom Glavine	.25
123	Aaron Boone	.15
124	Alfonso Soriano	.75
125	Andy Pettitte	.15
126	Derek Jeter	1.50
127	Hideki Matsui	.15
128	Jason Giambi	.15
129	Jorge Posada	.50
130	Jose Contreras	.15

131	Mike Mussina	.50
132	Barry Zito	.40
133	Eric Byrnes	.15
134	Eric Chavez	.40
135	Jose Guillen	.15
136	Mark Mulder	.40
137	Miguel Tejada	.40
138	Ramon Hernandez	.15
139	Rich Harden	.15
140	Tim Hudson	.40
141	Bobby Abreu	.25
142	Brett Myers	.15
143	Jim Thome	.75
144	Kevin Millwood	.40
145	Mike Lieberthal	.15
146	Ryan Howard	1.50
147	Craig Wilson	.15
148	Jack Wilson	.15
149	Jason Kendall	.15
150	Kip Wells	.15
151	Reggie Sanders	.15
152	Albert Pujols	1.50
153	Edgar Renteria	.25
154	Jim Edmonds	.40
155	Matt Morris	.25
156	Scott Rolen	.75
157	Tino Martinez	.15
158	Woody Williams	.15
159	Brian Giles	.25
160	Freddy Guzman RC	.50
161	Jake Peavy	.15
162	Khalil Greene	.50
163	Phil Nevin	.15
164	Ryan Klesko	.25
165	Ray Durham	.15
166	Jason Schmidt	.25
167	Jerome Williams	.50
168	Jesse Foppert	.15
169	Jose Cruz	.15
170	Marquis Grissom	.15
171	Merkin Valdez RC	1.50
172	Rich Aurilia	.15
173	Bret Boone	.25
174	Freddy Garcia	.15
175	Ichiro Suzuki	1.50
176	Jamie Moyer	.15
177	John Olerud	.25
178	Mike Cameron	.15
179	Randy Winn	.15
180	Aubrey Huff	.25
181	Carl Crawford	.50
182	Chad Gaudin	.50
183	Rocco Baldelli	.50
184	Toby Hall	.15
185	Travis Lee	.15
186	Alex Rodriguez	1.50
187	Hank Blalock	.40
188	John Thomson	.15
189	Juan Gonzalez	.40
190	Mark Teixeira	.40
191	Michael Young	.15
192	Rafael Palmeiro	.50
193	Ramon Nivar	.25
194	Carlos Delgado	.50
195	Dustin McGowan	.15
196	Frank Catalanotto	.15
197	Vinnie Chulk	.15
198	Orlando Hudson	.15
199	Roy Halladay	.25
200	Vernon Wells	.25

Xtra Bases Black

Black (1-200): 4-8X
Production 75 Sets

Xtra Bases Purple

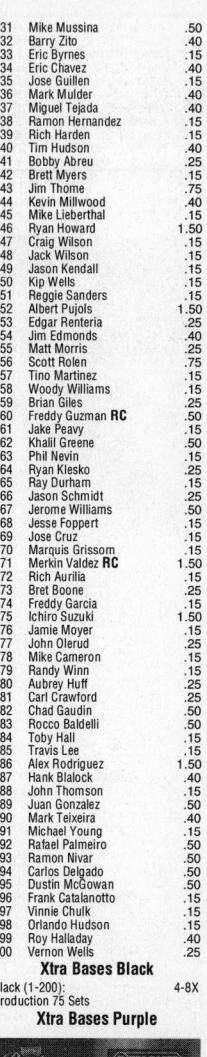

Purple (1-200): 2-5X
Production 150 Sets

Xtra Bases Black Autographs

No Pricing
Production 25 Sets

Xtra Bases Green Autographs

No Pricing

Xtra Bases Purple Autographs

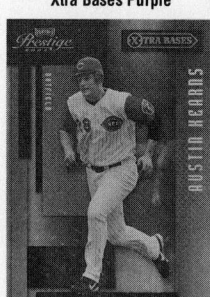

		NM/M
Production 100 Sets		
10	Edgar Gonzalez	6.00
16	Bubba Nelson	8.00
32	Kevin Youkilis	15.00

38	Brendan Harris	8.00
57	Micheal Nakamura	6.00
73	Preston Larrison	6.00
79	Miguel Cabrera	35.00
81	Chris Burke	15.00
105	J.D. Durbin	10.00
107	Jason Kubel	8.00
146	Ryan Howard	75.00
193	Ramon Nivar	8.00
195	Dustin McGowan	10.00
198	Orlando Hudson	8.00

Xtra Bases Red Autographs

No Pricing

Achievements

		NM/M
1	Hideo Nomo/95 ROY	1.50
2	Don Mattingly/85 MVP	6.00
3	Roger Clemens/86 CY/MVP	6.00
4	Greg Maddux/95 CY	4.00
5	Stan Musial/43 MVP	4.00
6	Roberto Clemente/66 MVP	6.00
7	Derek Jeter/96 ROY	6.00
8	Albert Pujols/01 ROY	6.00
9	Cal Ripken Jr./91 MVP	8.00
10	George Brett/80 MVP	8.00
11	Carl Yastrzemski/67 MVP	4.00
12	Rickey Henderson/90 MVP	2.00
13	Sammy Sosa/98 MVP	3.00
14	Randy Johnson/02 CY	3.00
15	Bob Gibson/68 CY/MVP	3.00

Autographs

		NM/M
Quantity produced listed		
8	Brandon Webb/100	20.00
10	Edgar Gonzalez PROS/150	8.00
11	Bubba Nelson PROS/250	10.00
25	Jay Gibbons/50	20.00
32	Kevin Youkilis PROS/100	20.00
36	Trot Nixon/25	40.00
37	Aramis Ramirez/25	25.00
38	Brendan Harris PROS/400	8.00
49	Joe Crede/25	15.00
54	Josh Hall/25	15.00
57	Mike Nakamura/250	8.00
60	Jody Gerut/50	15.00
73	Preston Larrison PROS/250	8.00
75	Dontrelle Willis/25	40.00
79	Miguel Cabrera/100	60.00
81	Chris Burke PROS/250	10.00
93	Runelvys Hernandez/50	8.00
98	Paul Lo Duca/25	15.00
102	Richie Sexson/25	25.00
105	J.D. Durbin PROS/500	10.00
106	Jacque Jones/50	12.00
107	Jason Kubel PROS/400	8.00
108	Shannon Stewart/50	15.00
112	Jose Vidro/25	15.00
114	Orlando Cabrera/25	20.00
119	Jae Weong Seo/25	20.00
133	Eric Byrnes/25	15.00
136	Mark Mulder/25	20.00
139	Rich Harden/50	25.00
146	Ryan Howard PROS/400	75.00
193	Ramon Nivar PROS/100	10.00
195	Dustin McGowan PROS/100	10.00
197	Vinnie Chulk/112	8.00
198	Orlando Hudson/100	10.00

Changing Stripes

	NM/M
Inserted 1:11	
Foil:	1-2X
Production 150 Sets	
Holofoil:	2-3X

Production 50 Sets		
1	Rickey Henderson/ A-s-Yanks	4.00
2	Mike Mussina/O's-Yanks	2.00
3	Jim Thome/Indians-Phils	3.00
4	Hideo Nomo/Sox-Dodgers	1.50
5	Scott Rolen/Phils-Cards	3.00
6	Jason Giambi/A-s-Yanks	3.00
7	Randy Johnson/ Astros-D'backs	3.00
8	Shawn Green/Jays-Dodgers	1.50
9	Curt Schilling/Phils-D'backs	2.00
10	Alex Rodriguez/M's-Rangers	5.00
11	Greg Maddux/Cubs-Braves	4.00
12	Randy Johnson/M's-Astros	3.00
13	Hideo Nomo/Dodgers-Mets	1.50
14	Juan Rodriguez/Rgr-Marlins	2.00
15	Juan Gonzalez/ Indians-Rangers	2.00
16	Manny Ramirez/ Indians-Sox	2.00
17	Mike Piazza/Dodgers-Mets	4.00
18	Nolan Ryan/Angels-Astros	8.00
19	Nolan Ryan/Astros-Rangers	8.00
20	Pedro Martinez/Expos-Sox	3.00
21	Reggie Jackson/ Yanks-Angels	2.00
23	Roberto Alomar/Mets-Sox	1.50
23	Rod Carew/Twins-Angels	2.00
24	Roger Clemens/Sox-Yanks	6.00
25	Sammy Sosa/Sox-Cubs	5.00

Changing Stripes Dual Jersey

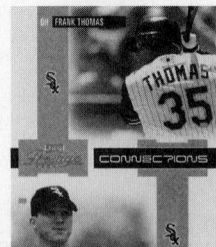

		NM/M
Procdution 150 Sets		
Primes:		No Pricing
Production 25 Sets		
1	Rickey Henderson/ A's-Yanks	10.00
2	Mike Mussina/O's-Yanks	8.00
3	Jim Thome/Indians-Phils	10.00
4	Hideo Nomo/Sox-Dodgers	15.00
5	Scott Rolen/Phils-Cards	10.00
6	Jason Giambi/A's-Yanks	12.00
7	Randy Johnson/ Astros-D'backs	10.00
8	Shawn Green/Jays-Dodgers	6.00
9	Curt Schilling/Phils-D'backs	8.00
10	Alex Rodriguez/ M's-Rangers	15.00
12	Randy Johnson/ M's-Astros	10.00
13	Hideo Nomo/ Dodgers-Mets	15.00
14	Ivan Rodriguez/ Rgr-Marlins	10.00
15	Juan Gonzalez/ Indians-Rangers	8.00
16	Manny Ramirez/ Indians-Sox	8.00
17	Mike Piazza/Dodgers-Mets	10.00
18	Nolan Ryan/Angels-Astros	30.00
19	Nolan Ryan/Astrs-Rangers	30.00
20	Pedro Martinez/Expos-Sox	10.00
22	Roberto Alomar/Mets-Sox	8.00
23	Rod Carew/Twins-Angels	12.00
24	Roger Clemens/Sox-Yanks	15.00
25	Sammy Sosa/Sox-Cubs	15.00

Connections

	NM/M
Inserted 1:9	
Foil:	1.5-2X
Production 100 Sets	
Holofoil:	No Pricing
Production 21 Sets	
1	Derek Jeter, Alfonso Soriano	4.00

2	Greg Maddux, Chipper Jones	2.00
3	Albert Pujols, Scott Rolen	3.00
4	Randy Johnson, Curt Schilling	1.50
5	Nomar Garciaparra, Manny Ramirez	3.00
6	Alex Rodriguez, Mark Teixeira	3.00
7	Barry Zito, Tim Hudson	.75
8	Sammy Sosa, Mark Prior	3.00
9	Derek Jeter, Jason Giambi	4.00
10	Roger Clemens, Mike Mussina	3.00
11	Mark Prior, Kerry Wood	2.00
12	Alex Rodriguez, Hank Blalock	3.00
13	Frank Thomas, Magglio Ordonez	1.00
14	Nomar Garciaparra, Pedro Martinez	3.00
15	Carlos Delgado, Vernon Wells	1.00
16	Miguel Tejada, Eric Chavez	.75
17	Jeff Bagwell, Lance Berkman	1.00
18	Jim Thome, Bobby Abreu	1.50
19	Todd Helton, Preston Wilson	1.00
20	Vladimir Guerrero, Javier Vazquez	1.50

Connections Material

		NM/M
Production 250 Sets		
1	Derek Jeter/Bat, Alfonso Soriano/Bat	20.00
2	Greg Maddux/Bat, Chipper Jones/Jsy	12.00
3	Albert Pujols/Bat, Scott Rolen/Bat	15.00
4	Randy Johnson/Bat, Curt Schilling/Bat	10.00
5	Nomar Garciaparra/Bat, Manny Ramirez/Bat	10.00
6	Alex Rodriguez/Bat, Mark Teixeira/Bat	10.00
7	Barry Zito/Bat, Tim Hudson/Bat	10.00
8	Sammy Sosa/Bat, Mark Prior/Bat	15.00
9	Derek Jeter/Bat, Jason Giambi/Bat	20.00
10	Roger Clemens/Jsy, Mike Mussina/Bat	15.00
11	Mark Prior/Bat, Kerry Wood/Bat	10.00
12	Alex Rodriguez/Bat, Hank Blalock/Bat	10.00
13	Frank Thomas/Bat, Magglio Ordonez/Bat	8.00
14	Nomar Garciaparra/Bat, Pedro Martinez/Bat	15.00
15	Carlos Delgado/Bat, Vernon Wells/Bat	8.00
16	Miguel Tejada/Bat, Eric Chavez/Bat	8.00
17	Jeff Bagwell/Bat, Lance Berkman/Bat	10.00
18	Jim Thome/Jsy, Bobby Abreu/Bat	10.00
19	Todd Helton/Bat, Preston Wilson	8.00
20	Vladimir Guerrero/Bat, Javier Vazquez/Jsy	10.00

Diamond Heritage

		NM/M
Inserted 1:13		
1	Mike Piazza	3.00
2	Greg Maddux	2.50
3	Nomar Garciaparra	3.00
4	Chipper Jones	2.00
5	Albert Pujols	4.00
6	Derek Jeter	5.00
7	Shawn Green	.75
8	Alex Rodriguez	4.00
9	Jim Thome	2.00
10	Jason Giambi	1.50
11	Sammy Sosa	3.00
12	Hank Blalock	1.00
13	Garret Anderson	.75

14	Manny Ramirez	1.50
15	Scott Rolen	1.50
16	Jeff Bagwell	1.50
17	Randy Johnson	2.00
18	Ichiro Suzuki	3.00
19	Ivan Rodriguez	1.50
20	Alfonso Soriano	1.50

Diamond Heritage Material

		NM/M
Inserted 1:92		
1	Mike Piazza/Bat	10.00
2	Greg Maddux/Bat	8.00
3	Nomar Garciaparra/Bat	10.00
4	Chipper Jones/Jsy	8.00
5	Albert Pujols/Bat	15.00
6	Derek Jeter/Jsy	15.00
7	Shawn Green/Bat	5.00
8	Alex Rodriguez/Bat	10.00
9	Jim Thome/Jsy	8.00
10	Jason Giambi/Bat	8.00
11	Sammy Sosa/Bat	12.00
12	Hank Blalock/Bat	6.00
13	Garret Anderson/Bat	5.00
14	Manny Ramirez/Bat	6.00
15	Scott Rolen/Bat	5.00
16	Jeff Bagwell/Bat	6.00
17	Randy Johnson/Bat	6.00
18	Ichiro Suzuki/Bat	6.00
19	Ivan Rodriguez/Bat	6.00
20	Alfonso Soriano/Bat	6.00

League Leaders Double

	NM/M
Production 500 Sets	
Foil:	1-2X
Production 75 Sets	
Holofoil:	No Pricing
Production 10 Sets	
1	Alex Rodriguez, Jim Thome/HR	5.00
2	Mark Prior, Pedro Martinez/ERA	4.00
3	Roger Clemens, Kerry Wood/SO	5.00
4	Nomar Garciaparra, Albert Pujols/Hit	5.00
5	Derek Jeter, Albert Pujols/Avg	5.00

League Leaders Double Material

	NM/M
Production 100 Sets	
1	Alex Rodriguez/Bat, Jim Thome/Bat	20.00
2	Mark Prior/Jsy, Pedro Martinez/Jsy	15.00
3	Roger Clemens/Jsy, Kerry Wood/Jsy	20.00
4	Nomar Garciaparra/Bat, Albert Pujols/Bat	25.00
5	Derek Jeter/Jsy, Albert Pujols/Bat	25.00

League Leaders Quad

	NM/M
Production 250 Sets	
Foil:	1-2X
Production 50 Sets	
Holofoil:	No Pricing
Production Five Sets	
1	Albert Pujols, Todd Helton, Edgar Renteria, Gary Sheffield	10.00
2	Derek Jeter, Manny Ramirez, Ichiro Suzuki, Nomar Garciaparra	10.00
3	Mark Prior, Curt Schilling, Nomar Garciaparra, Kevin Brown	8.00
4	Richie Sexson, Sammy Sosa, Albert Pujols, Jim Thome	10.00
5	Alex Rodriguez, Frank Thomas, Jason Giambi, Carlos Delgado	8.00

League Leaders Quad Material

	NM/M
Production 50 Sets	
1	Albert Pujols, Todd Helton, Edgar Renteria, Gary Sheffield	30.00
3	Mark Prior, Curt Schilling, Hideo Nomo, Kevin Brown	30.00
4	Richie Sexson, Sammy Sosa, Albert Pujols, mJim Thome	40.00
4	Alex Rodriguez, Frank Thomas, Jason Giambi, Carlos Delgado	35.00

League Leaders Single

NM/M

Foil 2-3X
Production 100 Sets
Holofoil: No Pricing
Production 25 Sets

1 Alex Rodriguez/AL HR 3.00
2 Albert Pujols/NL Hit 3.00
3 Albert Pujols/NL Hit 3.00
4 Nomar Garciaparra/AL Hit 2.00
5 Mark Prior/NL ERA 2.00
6 Pedro Martinez/AL ERA 1.00
7 Kerry Wood/NL SO 1.00
8 Derek Jeter/AL Avg 3.00
9 Jason Giambi/AL BB 1.00
10 Roger Clemens/AL SO 2.00

League Leaders Single Material

NM/M

Production 250 Sets

1 Alex Rodriguez/Bat 10.00
2 Albert Pujols/Bat 15.00
3 Albert Pujols/Bat 15.00
4 Nomar Garciaparra/Bat 10.00
5 Mark Prior/Jsy 10.00
6 Pedro Martinez/Jsy 8.00
7 Kerry Wood/Jsy 8.00
8 Derek Jeter/Jsy 15.00
9 Jason Giambi/Jsy 6.00
10 Roger Clemens/Jsy 12.00

Players Collection Jersey

NM/M

Inserted 1:79
Platinum: 1-2X
Production 50

1 Adam Dunn 5.00
2 Adam Dunn 5.00
3 Adam Dunn 5.00
4 Alex Rodriguez 10.00
5 Alex Rodriguez 10.00
6 Alex Rodriguez 10.00
7 Alex Rodriguez 10.00
8 Andruw Jones 6.00
9 Andruw Jones 6.00
10 Austin Kearns 6.00
11 Brandon Webb 4.00
12 C.C. Sabathia 4.00
13 Cal Ripken Jr. 25.00
14 Carlos Beltran 5.00
15 Carlos Delgado 6.00
16 Carlos Lee 4.00
17 Chipper Jones 8.00
18 Chipper Jones 8.00
19 Craig Biggio 4.00
20 Curt Schilling 6.00
21 David Wells 4.00
22 Don Mattingly 15.00
23 Dontrelle Willis 8.00
24 Frank Thomas 8.00
25 Frank Thomas 8.00
26 Fred McGriff 6.00
27 Garret Anderson 6.00
28 Gary Sheffield 6.00
29 Gary Sheffield 6.00
30 Greg Maddux 10.00
31 Hank Blalock 6.00
32 Hank Blalock 6.00
33 Hee Seop Choi 4.00
34 Hideo Nomo 8.00
35 Hideo Nomo 8.00
36 Hideo Nomo 8.00
37 Ivan Rodriguez 6.00
38 Ivan Rodriguez 6.00
39 Jason Giambi 6.00
40 Jim Edmonds 6.00
41 Jim Thome 8.00
42 John Olerud 4.00
43 John Smoltz 6.00
44 Josh Beckett 6.00
45 Josh Phelps 4.00
46 Juan Gonzalez 6.00
47 Juan Gonzalez 6.00
48 Kazuhisa Ishii 4.00
49 Lance Berkman 5.00
50 Larry Walker 5.00
51 Larry Walker 5.00
52 Luis Gonzalez 5.00
53 Magglio Ordonez 6.00
54 Magglio Ordonez 6.00
55 Manny Ramirez 6.00
56 Manny Ramirez 6.00
57 Mark Prior 8.00
58 Mark Prior 8.00
59 Mark Teixeira 6.00
60 Mike Mussina 6.00
61 Mike Piazza 8.00
62 Mike Piazza 8.00
63 Mike Piazza 8.00
64 Nomar Garciaparra 8.00
65 Nomar Garciaparra 8.00
66 Pat Burrell 6.00
67 Paul Konerko 5.00
68 Paul Lo Duca 5.00
69 Pedro Martinez 8.00
70 Rafael Furcal 5.00
71 Rafael Palmeiro 8.00
72 Rafael Palmeiro 8.00
73 Ramon Hernandez 4.00
74 Rickey Henderson 8.00
75 Rickey Henderson 8.00
76 Rickey Henderson 8.00
77 Roberto Alomar 6.00
78 Roberto Alomar 6.00
79 Robin Ventura 5.00
80 Roger Clemens 10.00
81 Roger Clemens 10.00
82 Roy Halladay 6.00
83 Sammy Sosa 12.00
84 Sammy Sosa 12.00
85 Sammy Sosa 12.00
86 Scott Rolen 8.00
87 Shannon Stewart 4.00
88 Shawn Green 5.00
89 Shawn Green 5.00
90 Shawn Green 5.00
91 Terrence Long 4.00
92 Tim Hudson 6.00
93 Todd Helton 8.00
94 Todd Helton 8.00
95 Tom Glavine 6.00
96 Tom Glavine 6.00
97 Torii Hunter 6.00
98 Vernon Wells 4.00
99 Vladimir Guerrero 8.00
100 Vladimir Guerrero 8.00

Prestigious Pros

NM/M

Inserted 1:23

1 Mark Prior 3.00
2 Derek Jeter 5.00
3 Mike Mussina 1.50
4 Nomar Garciaparra 3.00
5 Roger Clemens 4.00
6 Jason Giambi 1.50
7 Randy Johnson 2.00
8 Rafael Palmeiro 1.50
9 Barry Zito 1.00
10 Pat Burrell 1.00

Stars of MLB

NM/M

Foil: 1-2X
Production 100 Sets

Holofoil: No Pricing
Prod. 25 Sets

1 Albert Pujols 6.00
2 Derek Jeter 8.00
3 Mike Piazza 4.00
4 Greg Maddux 4.00
5 Ichiro Suzuki 5.00
6 Nomar Garciaparra 5.00
7 Ivan Rodriguez 2.00
8 Randy Johnson 3.00
9 Alex Rodriguez 6.00
10 Sammy Sosa 5.00
11 Alfonso Soriano 3.00
12 Vladimir Guerrero 3.00
13 Jason Giambi 3.00
14 Mark Prior 4.00
15 Chipper Jones 3.00

Stars of MLB Jersey

NM/M

Production 250 Sets
Prime: 1-2X
Production 50

1 Albert Pujols 15.00
2 Derek Jeter 15.00
3 Mike Piazza 8.00
4 Greg Maddux 10.00
5 Nomar Garciaparra 8.00
6 Ivan Rodriguez 6.00
7 Randy Johnson 8.00
8 Alex Rodriguez 10.00
9 Sammy Sosa 12.00
10 Alfonso Soriano 8.00
11 Vladimir Guerrero 8.00
12 Jason Giambi 6.00
13 Mark Prior 10.00
14 Chipper Jones 8.00

Stars of MLB Jersey Autographs

NM/M

Quantity produced listed

14 Mark Prior/50 75.00

2004 Playoff Prime Cuts

NM/M

Complete Set (50): 150.00
Common Player: 1.50
Production 949 Sets
Box (1): 185.00

1 Roger Clemens 6.00
2 Nomar Garciaparra 6.00
3 Albert Pujols 6.00
4 Sammy Sosa 6.00
5 Greg Maddux 4.00
6 Jason Giambi 4.00
7 Hideo Nomo 1.50
8 Mike Piazza 4.00
9 Ichiro Suzuki 5.00
10 Jeff Bagwell 4.00
11 Derek Jeter 8.00
12 Manny Ramirez 2.00
13 Rickey Henderson 1.50
14 Alex Rodriguez 6.00
15 Troy Glaus 1.50
16 Mike Mussina 1.50
17 Kerry Wood 2.00
18 Kazuhisa Ishii 1.00
19 Hideki Matsui 8.00
20 Frank Thomas 2.00
21 Barry Bonds 8.00
22 Adam Dunn 1.50
23 Randy Johnson 3.00
24 Alfonso Soriano 3.00
25 Pedro J. Martinez 3.00
26 Andruw Jones 2.00
27 Mark Prior 4.00
28 Vladimir Guerrero 3.00
29 Chipper Jones 4.00
30 Todd Helton 2.00
31 Rafael Palmeiro 2.00
32 Mark Grace 2.00
33 Pedro J. Martinez 3.00
34 Randy Johnson 3.00
35 Randy Johnson 3.00
36 Roger Clemens 6.00
37 Roger Clemens 6.00
38 Alex Rodriguez 6.00
39 Greg Maddux 4.00
40 Mike Piazza 4.00
41 Mike Piazza 4.00
42 Hideo Nomo 1.50
43 Rickey Henderson 1.50
44 Rickey Henderson 1.50
45 Barry Bonds 8.00
46 Ivan Rodriguez 2.00
47 George Brett 6.00
48 Cal Ripken Jr. 8.00
49 Nolan Ryan 10.00
50 Don Mattingly 6.00

Century

Cards (1-50): 1-2X
Production 100 Sets
Century Gold: No Pricing
Production 10 Sets
Century Proof: No Pricing
Production One Set

Icons Material

NM/M

Varying quantities produced

4 Johnny Bench/50 35.00
5 Lefty Grove/25 75.00
6 Carlton Fisk/50 25.00
7 Mel Ott/25 75.00
8 Bob Feller/25 30.00
9 Jackie Robinson/25 75.00
10 Ted Williams/50 135.00
11 Roy Campanella/50 40.00
12 Stan Musial/50 40.00
13 Yogi Berra/50 40.00
14 Babe Ruth/25 750.00
15 Roberto Clemente/50 100.00
16 Warren Spahn/50 40.00
17 Ernie Banks/50 40.00
18 Eddie Mathews/50 35.00
19 Ryne Sandberg/50 40.00
20 Rod Carew/50 25.00
21 Duke Snider/50 25.00
22 Jim Palmer/50 20.00
23 Frank Robinson/50 20.00
24 Brooks Robinson/50 25.00
25 Harmon Killebrew/50 40.00
26 Carl Yastrzemski/50 25.00
27 Reggie Jackson/50 25.00
29 Mike Schmidt/50 40.00
30 Robin Yount/50 30.00
31 George Brett/50 40.00
32 Nolan Ryan/50 40.00
33 Kirby Puckett/50 40.00
34 Cal Ripken Jr./50 60.00
35 Don Mattingly/50 35.00
36 Tony Gwynn/19 65.00
37 Deion Sanders/19 45.00
38 Dave Winfield/19 45.00
39 Eddie Murray/19 60.00
40 Tom Seaver/19 50.00
41 Willie Stargell/19 50.00
42 Wade Boggs/19 50.00
43 Ozzie Smith/19 60.00
44 Willie McCovey/19 50.00
45 Reggie Jackson/19 40.00
46 Whitey Ford/19 45.00
47 Lou Brock/19 40.00
48 Lou Boudreau/19 30.00
49 Steve Carlton/19 45.00
50 Rod Carew/19 40.00
51 Bob Gibson/19 35.00
52 Thurman Munson/19 60.00
53 Roger Maris/19 80.00
54 Nolan Ryan/50 40.00
55 Nolan Ryan/50 40.00
56 Bo Jackson/19 50.00
57 Joe Morgan/19 50.00
58 Phil Rizzuto/19 35.00
59 Gary Carter/19 40.00
60 Paul Molitor/19 50.00
61 Don Drysdale/19 50.00
62 Jim "Catfish" Hunter/19 30.00
63 Fergie Jenkins/19 30.00
64 Pee Wee Reese/19 40.00
65 Dave Winfield/19 40.00
66 Wade Boggs/19 40.00
67 Lefty Grove/19 80.00
68 Rickey Henderson/19 45.00
69 Roger Clemens/19 50.00
70 Roger Clemens/19 50.00

Icons Material Combo Prime

NM/M

Varying quantities produced

6	Carlton Fisk/25	50.00
7	Mel Ott/25	85.00
11	Roy Campanella/25	70.00
15	Roberto Clemente/25	200.00
17	Ernie Banks/25	85.00
18	Eddie Mathews/25	50.00
19	Ryne Sandberg/25	80.00
20	Rod Carew/25	50.00
24	Frank Robinson/25	40.00
25	Brooks Robinson/25	50.00
27	Carl Yastrzemski/25	80.00
28	Reggie Jackson/25	50.00
29	Mike Schmidt/25	75.00
30	Robin Yount/25	60.00
31	George Brett/25	75.00
32	Nolan Ryan/25	75.00
33	Kirby Puckett/25	60.00
34	Cal Ripken Jr./25	120.00
35	Don Mattingly/25	70.00
36	Tony Gwynn/19	80.00
37	Deion Sanders/19	60.00
38	Dave Winfield/19	50.00
39	Eddie Murray/19	70.00
41	Willie Stargell/19	60.00
42	Wade Boggs/19	60.00
43	Ozzie Smith/19	70.00
44	Willie McCovey/19	50.00
45	Reggie Jackson/19	50.00
46	Whitey Ford/19	50.00
47	Lou Brock/19	50.00
48	Lou Boudreau/19	40.00
49	Steve Carlton/19	60.00
50	Rod Carew/19	50.00
52	Thurman Munson/19	70.00
53	Roger Maris/19	110.00
54	Nolan Ryan/19	75.00
55	Nolan Ryan/19	75.00
56	Bo Jackson/19	60.00
57	Joe Morgan/19	40.00
58	Phil Rizzuto/19	45.00
59	Gary Carter/19	50.00
60	Paul Molitor/19	60.00
63	Fergie Jenkins/19	40.00
64	Pee Wee Reese/19	50.00
65	Dave Winfield/19	50.00
66	Wade Boggs/19	50.00
69	Roger Clemens/19	50.00
70	Roger Clemens/19	60.00

Icons Material Signature Prime

NM/M

Many not priced due to scarcity.

6	Carlton Fisk/50	60.00
12	Stan Musial/20	120.00
16	Warren Spahn/25	90.00
17	Ernie Banks/50	70.00
19	Ryne Sandberg/50	100.00
20	Rod Carew/50	50.00
22	Jim Palmer/50	40.00
24	Frank Robinson/50	40.00
25	Brooks Robinson/50	60.00
26	Harmon Killebrew/20	100.00
27	Carl Yastrzemski/50	90.00
28	Reggie Jackson/50	60.00
29	Mike Schmidt/20	125.00
30	Robin Yount/50	75.00
31	George Brett/50	100.00
32	Nolan Ryan/50	120.00
33	Kirby Puckett/34	70.00
34	Cal Ripken Jr./50	150.00
35	Don Mattingly/50	100.00
36	Tony Gwynn/50	70.00
37	Deion Sanders/50	50.00
38	Dave Winfield/50	45.00
39	Eddie Murray/50	75.00
42	Wade Boggs/50	60.00
43	Ozzie Smith/50	75.00
44	Willie McCovey/50	50.00
45	Reggie Jackson/50	50.00
46	Whitey Ford/50	50.00
47	Lou Brock/25	50.00
48	Lou Boudreau/50	75.00
49	Steve Carlton/50	50.00
50	Rod Carew/50	40.00
51	Bob Gibson/50	70.00
54	Nolan Ryan/50	125.00
55	Nolan Ryan/50	125.00
56	Bo Jackson/50	60.00
57	Joe Morgan/50	35.00
58	Phil Rizzuto/50	45.00
59	Gary Carter/50	50.00
60	Paul Molitor/50	55.00
63	Fergie Jenkins/50	40.00
65	Dave Winfield/50	45.00
66	Wade Boggs/50	60.00
68	Rickey Henderson/50	85.00
69	Roger Clemens/25	150.00
70	Roger Clemens/50	120.00

Icons Material Signature

NM/M

Varying quantities produced

4	Johnny Bench/18	75.00
8	Bob Feller/45	50.00
12	Stan Musial/30	100.00
13	Yogi Berra/42	65.00
21	Duke Snider/35	50.00
26	Harmon Killebrew/30	100.00
33	Kirby Puckett/16	80.00
69	Roger Clemens/25	150.00

Icons Signature

NM/M

Varying quantities produced

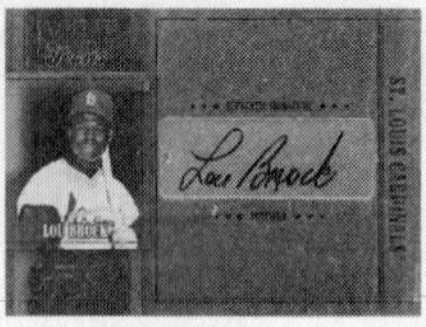

4	Johnny Bench/50	60.00
6	Carlton Fisk/50	40.00
8	Bob Feller/50	40.00
12	Stan Musial/50	65.00
13	Yogi Berra/50	50.00
16	Warren Spahn/25	100.00
17	Ernie Banks/50	60.00
19	Ryne Sandberg/50	70.00
21	Duke Snider/25	50.00
22	Jim Palmer/25	40.00
24	Frank Robinson/50	40.00
25	Brooks Robinson/50	50.00
26	Harmon Killebrew/25	75.00
27	Carl Yastrzemski/50	60.00
28	Reggie Jackson/50	50.00
29	Mike Schmidt/20	75.00
30	Robin Yount/25	65.00
31	George Brett/25	120.00
32	Nolan Ryan/50	110.00
33	Kirby Puckett/25	60.00
34	Cal Ripken Jr./25	200.00
35	Don Mattingly/50	85.00
36	Tony Gwynn/25	70.00
38	Dave Winfield/25	50.00
39	Eddie Murray/25	70.00
42	Wade Boggs/25	60.00
43	Ozzie Smith/25	75.00
44	Willie McCovey/25	50.00
45	Reggie Jackson/25	50.00
47	Lou Brock/25	50.00
48	Lou Boudreau/25	90.00
51	Bob Gibson/25	40.00
56	Bo Jackson/25	65.00
57	Joe Morgan/25	35.00
59	Gary Carter/25	45.00
60	Paul Molitor/25	55.00
65	Dave Winfield/25	50.00
66	Wade Boggs/25	60.00

Material Combos

NM/M

Production 25 Sets

1	Roger Clemens	60.00
2	Nomar Garciaparra	50.00
3	Albert Pujols	80.00
4	Sammy Sosa	50.00
5	Greg Maddux	50.00
6	Jason Giambi	40.00
7	Hideo Nomo	30.00
8	Mike Piazza	40.00
9	Ichiro Suzuki	70.00
10	Jeff Bagwell	40.00
11	Derek Jeter	60.00
12	Manny Ramirez	30.00
13	Rickey Henderson	40.00
14	Alex Rodriguez	70.00
15	Troy Glaus	35.00
16	Mike Mussina	40.00
17	Kerry Wood	50.00
18	Kazuhisa Ishii	35.00
19	Hideki Matsui	75.00
20	Frank Thomas	45.00
21	Barry Bonds	60.00
22	Adam Dunn	35.00
23	Randy Johnson	50.00
24	Alfonso Soriano	40.00
25	Pedro J. Martinez	45.00
26	Andruw Jones	35.00
27	Mark Prior	40.00
28	Vladimir Guerrero	45.00
29	Chipper Jones	45.00
30	Todd Helton	40.00
31	Rafael Palmeiro	45.00
32	Mark Grace	40.00
33	Pedro J. Martinez	45.00
34	Randy Johnson	50.00
35	Randy Johnson	50.00
36	Roger Clemens	60.00
38	Alex Rodriguez	70.00
40	Mike Piazza	40.00
42	Hideo Nomo	25.00
43	Rickey Henderson	40.00
44	Rickey Henderson	40.00
46	Ivan Rodriguez	35.00
47	George Brett	85.00
48	Cal Ripken Jr.	140.00
49	Nolan Ryan	75.00
50	Don Mattingly	75.00

Prime Cut Material Signature

NM/M

Varying quantities produced

1	Roger Clemens/25	185.00
3	Albert Pujols/25	180.00
5	Greg Maddux/25	175.00
10	Jeff Bagwell/25	70.00
12	Manny Ramirez/25	60.00
13	Rickey Henderson/25	100.00
14	Alex Rodriguez/25	180.00
15	Troy Glaus/50	40.00
16	Mike Mussina/25	70.00
17	Kerry Wood/25	90.00
18	Kazuhisa Ishii/50	50.00
20	Frank Thomas/25	80.00
22	Adam Dunn/50	60.00
24	Alfonso Soriano/25	85.00
26	Andruw Jones/25	60.00
27	Mark Prior/50	75.00
28	Vladimir Guerrero/50	75.00
29	Chipper Jones/25	85.00
30	Todd Helton/50	60.00
31	Rafael Palmeiro/25	75.00
32	Mark Grace/50	70.00
36	Roger Clemens/25	185.00
38	Alex Rodriguez/25	180.00
44	Rickey Henderson/25	100.00
46	Ivan Rodriguez/25	60.00
47	George Brett/50	120.00
48	Cal Ripken Jr./50	200.00
49	Nolan Ryan/50	140.00
50	Don Mattingly/50	120.00

Prime Cut Materials

NM/M

Varying quantities produced

1	Roger Clemens/150	40.00
2	Nomar Garciaparra/150	45.00
3	Albert Pujols/150	40.00
4	Sammy Sosa/150	40.00
5	Greg Maddux/150	40.00
6	Jason Giambi/125	40.00
7	Hideo Nomo/150	30.00
8	Mike Piazza/50	30.00
9	Ichiro Suzuki/25	60.00
10	Jeff Bagwell/25	35.00
11	Derek Jeter/25	50.00
12	Manny Ramirez/25	25.00
13	Rickey Henderson/50	30.00
14	Alex Rodriguez/25	60.00
15	Troy Glaus/25	30.00
17	Kerry Wood/25	40.00
18	Kazuhisa Ishii/25	30.00
19	Hideki Matsui/25	65.00
20	Frank Thomas/25	40.00
21	Barry Bonds/25	50.00
22	Adam Dunn/25	30.00
23	Randy Johnson/25	40.00
24	Alfonso Soriano/35	30.00
25	Pedro J. Martinez/25	40.00
26	Andruw Jones/25	30.00
27	Mark Prior/50	30.00
28	Vladimir Guerrero/25	40.00
29	Chipper Jones/25	40.00
30	Todd Helton/25	35.00
31	Rafael Palmeiro/25	40.00
32	Mark Grace/25	35.00
33	Pedro J. Martinez/25	40.00
34	Randy Johnson/25	40.00
35	Randy Johnson/25	40.00
36	Roger Clemens/50	45.00
38	Alex Rodriguez/25	60.00
40	Mike Piazza/50	30.00
42	Hideo Nomo/50	25.00
43	Rickey Henderson/50	30.00
44	Rickey Henderson/50	30.00
46	Ivan Rodriguez/25	30.00
47	George Brett/50	50.00
48	Cal Ripken Jr./50	65.00
49	Nolan Ryan/50	50.00
50	Don Mattingly/50	40.00

Signature

NM/M

Varying quantities produced

1	Roger Clemens/25	150.00
3	Albert Pujols/25	150.00
10	Jeff Bagwell/25	60.00
13	Rickey Henderson/25	80.00
14	Alex Rodriguez/25	150.00
15	Troy Glaus/25	35.00
16	Mike Mussina/25	60.00
17	Kerry Wood/25	80.00
18	Kazuhisa Ishii/25	40.00
20	Frank Thomas/25	70.00
22	Adam Dunn/25	50.00
24	Alfonso Soriano/25	75.00
26	Andruw Jones/25	50.00
27	Mark Prior/25	80.00
28	Vladimir Guerrero/25	60.00
29	Chipper Jones/25	75.00
31	Rafael Palmeiro/25	65.00
32	Mark Grace/25	60.00
36	Roger Clemens/25	150.00
37	Roger Clemens/25	150.00
38	Alex Rodriguez/25	150.00
43	Rickey Henderson/25	80.00
44	Rickey Henderson/25	80.00
46	Ivan Rodriguez/25	50.00
47	George Brett/25	120.00
48	Cal Ripken Jr./25	200.00
49	Nolan Ryan/25	125.00
50	Don Mattingly/25	100.00

Timeline - Material

NM/M

Varying quantities produced

4	Ted Williams/50	140.00
5	Roy Campanella/50	30.00
6	Stan Musial/50	35.00
7	Yogi Berra/50	25.00
9	Roberto Clemente/50	85.00
12	Carl Yastrzemski/50	35.00
13	Mike Schmidt/50	30.00
14	George Brett/50	30.00
15	Nolan Ryan/50	35.00
16	Stan Musial/50	35.00
17	Ted Williams/50	140.00
18	Roberto Clemente/50	90.00
19	Greg Maddux/50	25.00
21	Robin Yount/50	20.00
22	Nolan Ryan/50	35.00
23	Ted Williams/50	140.00
24	George Brett/50	30.00
25	Yogi Berra/50	25.00
26	Rod Carew/50	20.00
27	Dale Murphy/25	40.00

Timeline Dual Achievement Material Combo

No Pricing

Timeline Dual Achievement Material Prime

NM/M

Varying quantities produced

4	George Brett, Mike Schmidt/19	120.00
5	Cal Ripken Jr., Dale Murphy/19	120.00
6	Mike Schmidt, Roger Clemens/19	90.00
10	George Brett, Nolan Ryan/19	140.00

Timeline Dual Achievement Material Signature

NM/M

Varying quantities produced

4	George Brett, Mike Schmidt/24	150.00
5	Cal Ripken Jr., Dale Murphy/25	200.00
6	Mike Schmidt, Roger Clemens/24	220.00
7	Babe Ruth, Ty Cobb/1 (4/04 Auction)	18,000
10	George Brett, Nolan Ryan/25	220.00

Timeline Dual Achievement Material

NM/M

Varying quantities produced

3	Stan Musial, Ted Williams/19	175.00
4	George Brett, Mike Schmidt/19	75.00
5	Cal Ripken Jr., Dale Murphy/19	90.00
6	Mike Schmidt, Roger Clemens/19	65.00
10	George Brett, Nolan Ryan/19	100.00
12	Al Kaline, Duke Snider/19	50.00

Timeline Dual Achievement Signature

NM/M

Production 24 or 25

4	George Brett, Mike Schmidt/24	160.00
5	Cal Ripken Jr., Dale Murphy/25	180.00
6	Mike Schmidt, Roger Clemens/24	220.00
10	George Brett, Nolan Ryan/25	220.00
12	Al Kaline, Duke Snider/25	100.00

Timeline Material Combo

NM/M

Varying quantities produced

10	Will Clark/19	60.00
12	Carl Yastrzemski/19	80.00
13	Mike Schmidt/19	60.00
14	George Brett/19	65.00
15	Nolan Ryan/19	100.00
19	Greg Maddux/19	50.00
21	Robin Yount/19	50.00
22	Nolan Ryan/19	100.00
24	George Brett/19	65.00
26	Rod Carew/19	40.00
27	Dale Murphy/19	50.00

Timeline Material Signature

NM/M

Varying quantities produced

6	Stan Musial/33	100.00
7	Yogi Berra/42	75.00
16	Stan Musial/38	100.00
25	Yogi Berra/42	75.00

Timeline Material Signature Prime

NM/M

Varying quantities produced

10	Will Clark/50	75.00

12	Carl Yastrzemski/50	80.00
13	Mike Schmidt/20	120.00
14	George Brett/25	100.00
15	Nolan Ryan/50	125.00
19	Greg Maddux/50	125.00
21	Robin Yount/50	75.00
22	Nolan Ryan/50	125.00
24	George Brett/25	100.00

Timeline Material Prime

NM/M

Varying quantities produced

5	Roy Campanella/25	40.00
10	Will Clark/25	50.00
12	Carl Yastrzemski/25	75.00
13	Mike Schmidt/25	50.00
14	George Brett/25	50.00
15	Nolan Ryan/25	50.00
19	Greg Maddux/25	40.00
21	Robin Yount/25	40.00
22	Nolan Ryan/25	50.00
24	George Brett/25	50.00
26	Rod Carew/25	40.00
27	Dale Murphy/25	40.00

Timeline Signature

NM/M

Varying quantities produced

6	Stan Musial/50	70.00
7	Yogi Berra/50	50.00
10	Will Clark/25	100.00
12	Carl Yastrzemski/50	80.00
13	Mike Schmidt/20	85.00
14	George Brett/25	90.00
15	Nolan Ryan/50	110.00
16	Stan Musial/50	70.00
19	Greg Maddux/31	120.00
21	Robin Yount/25	75.00
22	Nolan Ryan/50	110.00
24	George Brett/25	90.00
25	Yogi Berra/50	50.00
27	Dale Murphy/25	50.00

Timeline Dual League Leader Material

NM/M

Production 9 or 19

4	Jim Palmer, Steve Carlton/19	40.00
7	Nolan Ryan, Steve Carlton/19	70.00
8	Don Mattingly, Tony Gwynn/19	70.00
9	Nolan Ryan, Roger Clemens/19	80.00

Timeline Dual League Leader Material Prime

NM/M

Production 9 or 19

7	Nolan Ryan, Steve Carlton/19	80.00
8	Don Mattingly, Tony Gwynn/19	80.00
9	Nolan Ryan, Roger Clemens/19	100.00

Timeline Dual League Leader Material Signature

NM/M

Varying quantities produced

4	Jim Palmer, Steve Carlton/50	60.00
7	Nolan Ryan, Steve Carlton/25	200.00
8	Don Mattingly, Tony Gwynn/25	150.00
9	Nolan Ryan, Roger Clemens/25	350.00

Timeline Dual League Leader Signature

NM/M

Production 25 or 50

4	Jim Palmer, Steve Carlton/50	60.00
7	Nolan Ryan, Steve Carlton/25	180.00
8	Don Mattingly, Tony Gwynn/25	140.00
9	Nolan Ryan, Roger Clemens/25	300.00

Timeline Dual League Leader Material Combo

NM/M

Production 9 or 19

7	Nolan Ryan, Steve Carlton/19	80.00
8	Don Mattingly, Tony Gwynn/19	80.00
9	Nolan Ryan, Roger Clemens/19	100.00

2004 Playoff Prime Cuts II

NM/M

Complete Set (100):	
Common (1-91):	1.50
Common (92-100):	3.00
Production 699	
Wood Box (One Pack):	150.00

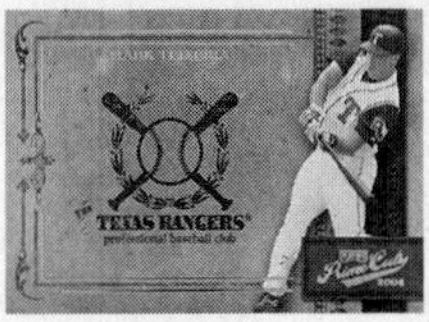

1	Mark Prior	2.00
2	Derek Jeter	8.00
3	Eric Chavez	1.50
4	Carlos Delgado	1.50
5	Albert Pujols	8.00
6	Miguel Cabrera	2.00
7	Ivan Rodriguez	2.00
8	Javy Lopez	1.50
9	Hank Blalock	2.00
10	Chipper Jones	3.00
11	Gary Sheffield	2.00
12	Alfonso Soriano	3.00
13	Alex Rodriguez/Yanks	6.00
14	Edgar Renteria	1.50
15	Jim Edmonds	1.50
16	Garret Anderson	1.50
17	Lance Berkman	1.50
18	Brandon Webb	1.50
19	Mike Lowell	1.50
20	Mark Mulder	1.50
21	Sammy Sosa	5.00
22	Roger Clemens/Astros	8.00
23	Mark Teixeira	1.50
24	Manny Ramirez	3.00
25	Rafael Palmeiro	2.00
26	Ichiro Suzuki	6.00
27	Vladimir Guerrero	3.00
28	Austin Kearns	1.50
29	Troy Glaus	1.50
30	Ken Griffey Jr.	4.00
31	Greg Maddux	4.00
32	Roy Halladay	1.50
33	Roy Oswalt	1.50
34	Kerry Wood	3.00
35	Mike Mussina/Yanks	2.00
36	Michael Young	1.50
37	Juan Gonzalez	1.50
38	Curt Schilling	2.00
39	Shannon Stewart	1.50
40	Todd Helton	2.00
41	Larry Walker/Cards	1.50
42	Mariano Rivera	1.50
43	Nomar Garciaparra	4.00
44	Adam Dunn	2.00
45	Pedro J. Martinez/Sox	3.00
46	Bernie Williams	1.50
47	Tom Glavine	2.00
48	Torii Hunter	1.50
49	David Ortiz	3.00
50	Frank Thomas	2.00
51	Randy Johnson/D'backs	3.00
52	Jason Giambi	1.50
53	Carlos Lee	1.50
54	Mike Sweeney	1.50
55	Hideki Matsui	6.00
56	Dontrelle Willis	1.50
57	Tim Hudson	1.50
58	Jose Vidro	1.50
59	Jeff Bagwell	2.00
60	Rocco Baldelli	1.50
61	Craig Biggio	1.50
62	Mike Piazza/Mets	4.00
63	Magglio Ordonez	1.50
64	Hideo Nomo	1.50
65	Miguel Tejada	2.00
66	Vernon Wells	1.50
67	Barry Larkin	1.50
68	Jacque Jones	1.50
69	Scott Rolen	3.00
70	Jeff Kent	1.50
71	Steve Finley	1.50
72	Kazuo Matsui	6.00
73	Carlos Beltran	2.00
74	Shawn Green	1.50
75	Barry Zito	1.50
76	Aramis Ramirez	1.50
77	Paul LoDuca	1.50
78	Kazuhisa !shii	1.50
79	Aubrey Huff	1.50
80	Jim Thome	3.00
81	Andy Pettitte/Astros	1.50
82	Andruw Jones	1.50
83	Josh Beckett	1.50
84	Sean Casey	1.50
85	Alex Rodriguez/M's	6.00
86	Roger Clemens/Yanks	8.00
87	Mike Mussina/O's	2.00
88	Pedro Martinez/Dgr	3.00
89	Randy Johnson/Astros	3.00
90	Mike Piazza/Dgr	4.00
91	Andy Pettitte/Yanks	1.50
92	Cal Ripken Jr.	15.00
93	Dale Murphy	3.00
94	Don Mattingly	8.00
95	Gary Carter	3.00
96	George Brett	8.00
97	Nolan Ryan	10.00
98	Ozzie Smith	8.00
99	Steve Carlton	3.00
100	Tony Gwynn	6.00

Gold

Gold (1-91):	2-4X
Gold (92-100):	1.5-2X
Production 25 Sets	

Silver

Silver (1-91):	1-2X
Silver (92-100):	1-1.5X
Production 50 Sets	

Platinum

No Pricing
Production One Set

Material Combo

NM/M

Many not priced due to scarcity.

Prime:		No Pricing
Production 1-9		
1	Mark Prior/Hat-Jsy/22	20.00
12	Alfonso Soriano/ Bat-Jsy/25	25.00
15	Jim Edmonds/Bat-Jsy/15	20.00
16	Garret Anderson/ Bat-Jsy/16	15.00
21	Sammy Sosa/Bat-Jsy/21	40.00
22	Roger Clemens/Bat-Jsy/22	50.00
24	Manny Ramirez/Bat-Jsy/24	25.00
25	Rafael Palmeiro/Bat-Jsy/25	20.00
27	Vladimir Guerrero/ Bat-Jsy/27	25.00
31	Greg Maddux/Bat-Jsy/31	40.00
35	Mike Mussina/Bat-Jsy/35	25.00
40	Todd Helton/Bat-Jsy/17	25.00
86	Roger Clemens/ Fld Glv-Jsy/22	50.00
92	Cal Ripken Jr./Bat-Jsy/25	75.00
93	Dale Murphy/Bat-Jsy/25	20.00
94	Don Mattingly/Bat-Jsy/25	50.00
96	George Brett/Bat-Jsy/25	50.00
97	Nolan Ryan/Bat-Jkt/25	60.00
98	Ozzie Smith/Bat-Jsy/25	40.00

Material Number

NM/M

Most not priced.

Prime:		No Pricing
Production 1-10		
86	Roger Clemens/Jsy/25	40.00
92	Cal Ripken Jr./Jsy/25	60.00
93	Dale Murphy/Jsy/25	20.00
94	Don Mattingly/Jsy/25	40.00
96	George Brett/Jsy/25	40.00
97	Nolan Ryan/Jkt/25	50.00
98	Ozzie Smith/Jsy/25	30.00

Icons

NM/M

Common Player:		4.00
Production 50 Sets		
Gold:		No Pricing
Production 10 Sets		
Platinum:		No Pricing
Production One Set		
Silver:		1-1.5X
Production 25 Sets		
1	Dale Murphy	6.00
2	Eddie Mathews	8.00
3	Brooks Robinson	6.00
4	Cal Ripken Jr.	25.00
5	Cal Ripken Jr.	25.00
6	Eddie Murray	8.00
7	Frank Robinson	4.00
8	Jim Palmer	4.00
9	Bobby Doerr	4.00
10	Carl Yastrzemski	10.00
11	Carlton Fisk	6.00
12	Dennis Eckersley	6.00
13	Luis Aparicio	4.00
14	Luis Tiant	4.00
15	Ted Williams	12.00
16	Wade Boggs	4.00
17	Duke Snider	6.00
18	Jackie Robinson	8.00
19	Pee Wee Reese	6.00
20	Burleigh Grimes	4.00
21	Nolan Ryan	20.00
22	Reggie Jackson	6.00
23	Rod Carew	6.00
24	Rod Carew	6.00
25	Billy Williams	4.00
26	Ernie Banks	8.00
27	Mark Grace	6.00
28	Ron Santo	4.00
29	Paul Molitor	6.00
30	Bo Jackson	8.00
31	Carlton Fisk	6.00
32	Johnny Bench	8.00
33	Tom Seaver	6.00
34	Tony Perez	4.00
35	Bob Feller	4.00
36	Lou Boudreau	4.00
37	Al Kaline	8.00
38	Alan Trammell	4.00
39	Ty Cobb	8.00
40	Don Sutton	4.00
41	Nolan Ryan	20.00
42	Roger Maris	8.00
43	Bo Jackson	8.00
44	George Brett	12.00
45	George Brett	12.00
46	Maury Wills	4.00
47	Warren Spahn	6.00
48	Robin Yount	10.00
49	Harmon Killebrew	8.00
50	Kirby Puckett	8.00
51	Paul Molitor	6.00
52	Andre Dawson	4.00
53	Mel Ott	6.00
54	Mel Ott	6.00
55	Duke Snider	6.00
56	Rickey Henderson	8.00
57	Tom Seaver	6.00
58	Babe Ruth	15.00
59	Babe Ruth	15.00
60	Jim "Catfish" Hunter	4.00
61	Dave Righetti	4.00
62	Dave Winfield	4.00
63	Don Mattingly	15.00
64	Don Mattingly	15.00
65	Lou Gehrig	10.00
66	Lou Gehrig	10.00
67	Phil Niekro	4.00
68	Phil Rizzuto	6.00
69	Reggie Jackson	6.00
70	Rickey Henderson	6.00
71	Roger Maris	8.00
72	Thurman Munson	8.00
73	Thurman Munson	8.00
74	Wade Boggs	6.00
75	Whitey Ford	6.00
76	Yogi Berra	8.00
77	Lefty Grove	4.00
78	Mike Schmidt	10.00
79	Mike Schmidt	10.00
80	Steve Carlton	4.00
81	Ralph Kiner	4.00
82	Roberto Clemente	15.00
83	Roberto Clemente	15.00
84	Dave Winfield	4.00
85	Rickey Henderson	6.00
86	Steve Garvey	4.00
87	Tony Gwynn	8.00
88	Tony Gwynn	8.00
89	Gaylord Perry	4.00
90	Joe Morgan	4.00
91	Juan Marichal	4.00
92	Steve Carlton	4.00
93	Will Clark	6.00
94	Willie McCovey	4.00
95	Bob Gibson	6.00
96	Lou Brock	6.00
97	Stan Musial	10.00
98	Fergie Jenkins	4.00
99	Nolan Ryan	20.00
100	Harmon Killebrew	8.00

Icons Material Combo

NM/M

Many not priced.

Prime:		No Pricing
Production 1-10		
4	Cal Ripken Jr./Bat-Jsy/25	75.00
5	Cal Ripken Jr./Jkt-Pants/25	75.00
6	Eddie Murray/Bat-Jsy/25	30.00
7	Frank Robinson/Bat-Jsy/20	20.00
10	Carl Yastrzemski/ Bat-Jsy/25	40.00
11	Carlton Fisk/Bat-Jsy/25	25.00
15	Ted Williams/Bat-Jsy/25	100.00
17	Duke Snider/Jsy-Pants/25	25.00
18	Jackie Robinson/Jkt-Jsy/25	80.00
21	Nolan Ryan/Jkt-Jsy/25	50.00
22	Reggie Jackson/Hat-Jsy/25	25.00
23	Rod Carew/Bat-Jsy/25	25.00
24	Rod Carew/Jkt-Jsy/25	25.00
29	Paul Molitor/Jsy-Pants/25	25.00
31	Carlton Fisk/Bat-Jsy/25	25.00
33	Tom Seaver/Bat-Jsy/25	25.00
39	Ty Cobb/Bat-Pants/25	150.00
41	Nolan Ryan/Bat-Jsy/25	50.00
42	Roger Maris/Jsy-Pants/25	75.00
44	George Brett/Bat-Jsy/25	50.00
45	George Brett/Hat-Jsy/25	50.00
47	Warren Spahn/ Jsy-Pants/25	30.00
48	Robin Yount/Bat-Jsy/19	50.00
49	Harmon Killebrew/ Jsy-Jsy/25	40.00
53	Mel Ott/Bat-Jsy/25	50.00
54	Mel Ott/Bat-Pants/25	50.00
55	Duke Snider/Jsy-Pants/25	25.00
58	Babe Ruth/Bat-Jsy/25	300.00
59	Babe Ruth/Bat-Pants/25	300.00
65	Lou Gehrig/Bat-Jsy/25	200.00
66	Lou Gehrig/Bat-Pants/25	200.00
69	Reggie Jackson/Bat-Jsy/25	25.00
71	Roger Maris/Bat-Pants/25	60.00
72	Thurman Munson/ Bat-Jsy/25	50.00
73	Thurman Munson/ Bat-Pants/25	50.00
75	Whitey Ford/Jsy-Pants/16	40.00
78	Mike Schmidt/Bat-Jsy/20	50.00
79	Mike Schmidt/Hat-Jkt/20	50.00
82	Roberto Clemente/ Bat-Jsy/21	150.00
83	Roberto Clemente/ Bat-Hat/21	150.00
93	Will Clark/Bat-Jsy/22	30.00
94	Willie McCovey/Jsy-Jsy/25	25.00
99	Nolan Ryan/Jsy-Pants/25	50.00
100	Harmon Killebrew/ Bat-Jsy/25	40.00

Icons Material Number

NM/M

Many not priced.

1	Dale Murphy/Jsy/25	20.00
3	Brooks Robinson/Jsy/25	20.00
4	Cal Ripken Jr./Jsy/25	60.00
5	Cal Ripken Jr./Jkt/25	60.00

6 Eddie Murray/Jsy/25 30.00
7 Frank Robinson/Jsy/25 10.00
8 Jim Palmer/Jsy/25 15.00
9 Bobby Doerr/Jsy/25 10.00
10 Carl Yastrzemski/Jsy/25 40.00
11 Carlton Fisk/Jsy/25 20.00
15 Ted Williams/Jsy/50 100.00
17 Duke Snider/Jsy/25 20.00
18 Jackie Robinson/Jkt/50 65.00
19 Pee Wee Reese/Jsy/25 20.00
20 Burleigh Grimes/Pants/25 50.00
21 Nolan Ryan/Jsy/25 40.00
22 Reggie Jackson/Jsy/25 2.00
23 Rod Carew/Jsy/25 20.00
24 Rod Carew/Jkt/25 20.00
25 Billy Williams/Jsy/25 10.00
26 Ernie Banks/Jsy/25 25.00
29 Paul Molitor/Pants/25 25.00
31 Carlton Fisk/Jsy/25 20.00
32 Johnny Bench/Jsy/25 30.00
33 Tom Seaver/Jsy/25 25.00
35 Bob Feller/Jsy/25 15.00
36 Lou Boudreau/Jsy/25 25.00
39 Ty Cobb/Pants/50 100.00
41 Nolan Ryan/Jsy/25 40.00
42 Roger Maris/Jsy/25 50.00
44 George Brett/Jsy/25 40.00
45 George Brett/Jsy/25 40.00
47 Warren Spahn/Jsy/25 25.00
48 Robin Yount/Jsy/25 30.00
49 Harmon Killebrew/Jsy/25 30.00
50 Kirby Puckett/Jsy/25 25.00
51 Paul Molitor/Jsy/25 20.00
53 Mel Ott/Jsy/25 40.00
54 Mel Ott/Pants/25 40.00
55 Duke Snider/Jsy/25 20.00
58 Babe Ruth/Jsy/25 300.00
59 Babe Ruth/Pants/50 180.00
60 Jim "Catfish" Hunter/
Jsy/25 20.00
63 Don Mattingly/Jsy/25 40.00
64 Don Mattingly/Jkt/25 40.00
65 Lou Gehrig/Jsy/25 150.00
66 Lou Gehrig/Pants/50 100.00
68 Phil Rizzuto/Pants/25 20.00
69 Reggie Jackson/Jsy/25 20.00
71 Roger Maris/Pants/25 40.00
72 Thurman Munson/Jsy/50 35.00
73 Thurman Munson/
Pants/50 35.00
77 Lefty Grove/Hat/25 120.00
78 Mike Schmidt/Jsy/20 40.00
79 Mike Schmidt/Jkt/20 40.00
82 Roberto Clemente/Jsy/21 100.00
83 Roberto Clemente/Hat/21 100.00
91 Juan Marichal/Jsy/25 15.00
93 Will Clark/Jsy/22 25.00
94 Willie McCovey/Jsy/25 20.00
95 Bob Gibson/Jsy/25 25.00
96 Lou Brock/Jkt/20 20.00
99 Nolan Ryan/Pants/25 40.00
100 Harmon Killebrew/Jsy/25 35.00

Icons Material Prime

No Pricing
Production 1-10

Icons Signature Century Gold

NM/M

Many not priced.
1 Dale Murphy/25 40.00
3 Brooks Robinson/25 40.00
7 Frank Robinson/20 35.00
8 Jim Palmer/22 35.00
9 Bobby Doerr/25 30.00
17 Duke Snider/25 35.00
32 Johnny Bench/25 50.00
34 Tony Perez/24 40.00
35 Bob Feller/19 40.00
37 Al Kaline/25 50.00
43 Bo Jackson/16 75.00
49 Harmon Killebrew/25 50.00
51 Paul Molitor/25 35.00
55 Duke Snider/25 40.00
63 Don Mattingly/23 75.00
64 Don Mattingly/23 75.00
80 Steve Carlton/25 35.00
81 Ralph Kiner/25 45.00
87 Tony Gwynn/19 50.00
88 Tony Gwynn/19 50.00
92 Steve Carlton/25 35.00
95 Bob Gibson/25 40.00
96 Lou Brock/20 40.00
97 Stan Musial/25 90.00
100 Harmon Killebrew/25 50.00

Icons Signature Century Platinum

No Pricing
Production One Set

Icons Sign. Century Silver

NM/M

1 Dale Murphy/25 40.00
3 Brooks Robinson/50 30.00
4 Cal Ripken Jr./25 180.00
5 Cal Ripken Jr./25 180.00
6 Eddie Murray/25 50.00
7 Frank Robinson/50 30.00
8 Jim Palmer/50 30.00
9 Bobby Doerr/25 30.00
10 Carl Yastrzemski/25 75.00
11 Carlton Fisk/27 40.00
12 Dennis Eckersley/43 30.00
13 Luis Aparicio/25 25.00
16 Wade Boggs/26 40.00
17 Duke Snider/50 30.00
21 Nolan Ryan/30 100.00
22 Reggie Jackson/25 50.00
23 Rod Carew/29 35.00
24 Rod Carew/29 35.00
25 Billy Williams/26 20.00
29 Paul Molitor/25 35.00
30 Bo Jackson/25 50.00
31 Carlton Fisk/25 40.00
32 Johnny Bench/50 30.00
33 Tom Seaver/25 40.00
34 Tony Perez/25 40.00
35 Bob Feller/25 30.00
37 Al Kaline/50 40.00
40 Don Sutton/20 20.00
41 Nolan Ryan/34 100.00
43 Bo Jackson/25 50.00
44 George Brett/25 100.00
45 George Brett/25 100.00
48 Robin Yount/19 65.00
49 Harmon Killebrew/50 40.00
51 Paul Molitor/50 30.00
55 Duke Snider/50 30.00
56 Rickey Henderson/24 60.00
57 Tom Seaver/25 40.00
62 Dave Winfield/31 35.00
63 Don Mattingly/50 60.00
64 Don Mattingly/50 60.00
67 Phil Niekro/35 20.00
68 Phil Rizzuto/25 40.00
69 Reggie Jackson/25 50.00
70 Rickey Henderson/24 60.00
75 Whitey Ford/25 50.00
76 Yogi Berra/25 50.00
78 Mike Schmidt/20 80.00
79 Mike Schmidt/20 80.00
80 Steve Carlton/32 30.00
81 Ralph Kiner/25 45.00
84 Dave Winfield/31 35.00
85 Rickey Henderson/24 60.00
87 Tony Gwynn/50 40.00
88 Tony Gwynn/50 40.00
89 Gaylord Perry/36 20.00
90 Joe Morgan/24 25.00
91 Juan Marichal/27 25.00
92 Steve Carlton/32 30.00
93 Will Clark/22 50.00
94 Willie McCovey/25 30.00
95 Bob Gibson/45 30.00
96 Lou Brock/50 30.00
97 Stan Musial/50 65.00
98 Fergie Jenkins/31 25.00
99 Nolan Ryan/34 100.00
100 Harmon Killebrew/50 40.00

Icons Sign. Material Combo

NM/M

Many not priced.
Prime: No Pricing
Production 1-10
1 Dale Murphy/Bat-Jsy/25 50.00
7 Frank Robinson/
Bat-Jsy/20 45.00
8 Jim Palmer/Hat-Jsy/22 50.00
9 Bobby Doerr/Bat-Jsy/25 40.00
17 Duke Snider/
Jsy-Pants/25 50.00
25 Billy Williams/
Bat-Jsy/26 30.00
29 Paul Molitor/
Jsy-Pants/25 50.00
34 Tony Perez/
Bat-Fld Glv/24 50.00
48 Robin Yount/
Bat-Jsy/19 100.00
49 Harmon Killebrew/
Jsy-Jsy/25 80.00
51 Paul Molitor/Bat-Jsy/25 50.00
63 Don Mattingly/
Bat-Jsy/23 100.00
64 Don Mattingly/
Hat-Jkt/23 100.00
78 Mike Schmidt/
Bat-Jsy/20 100.00
79 Mike Schmidt/
Hat-Jkt/20 100.00
80 Steve Carlton/
Fld Glv-Pants/32 50.00
87 Tony Gwynn/
Fld Glv-Jsy/19 80.00
88 Tony Gwynn/
Jsy-Pants/19 80.00
92 Steve Carlton/Bat-Jsy/32 50.00
93 Will Clark/Bat-Jsy/22 75.00
98 Fergie Jenkins/
Fld Glv-Hat/31 40.00

Icons Signature Material Number

NM/M

Many not priced.
Prime: No Pricing
Production 1-10
7 Frank Robinson/Jsy/20 40.00
8 Jim Palmer/Jsy/22 40.00
9 Bobby Doerr/Jsy/25 30.00
11 Carlton Fisk/Jsy/27 40.00
12 Dennis Eckersley/Jsy/43 30.00
16 Wade Boggs/Jsy/26 40.00
21 Nolan Ryan/Jsy/30 100.00
22 Reggie Jackson/Jsy/44 50.00
25 Billy Williams/Jsy/26 25.00
27 Mark Grace/Jsy/17 45.00
35 Bob Feller/Jsy/19 30.00
40 Don Sutton/Jsy/20 25.00
41 Nolan Ryan/Jsy/34 100.00
43 Bo Jackson/Jsy/16 75.00
48 Robin Yount/Jsy/19 65.00
62 Dave Winfield/Pants/31 40.00
63 Don Mattingly/Jsy/23 80.00
64 Don Mattingly/Jkt/23 80.00
69 Reggie Jackson/Jsy/44 50.00
78 Mike Schmidt/Jsy/20 80.00
79 Mike Schmidt/Jkt/20 80.00
80 Steve Carlton/Pants/32 40.00
84 Dave Winfield/Jsy/31 40.00
87 Tony Gwynn/Jsy/19 75.00
88 Tony Gwynn/Jsy/19 75.00
89 Gaylord Perry/Jsy/36 20.00
91 Juan Marichal/Jsy/27 25.00
92 Steve Carlton/Jsy/32 40.00
93 Will Clark/Jsy/22 65.00
95 Bob Gibson/Jsy/45 35.00
96 Lou Brock/Jkt/20 40.00
98 Fergie Jenkins/Hat/31 25.00
99 Nolan Ryan/Pants/34 100.00

Signature Century Gold

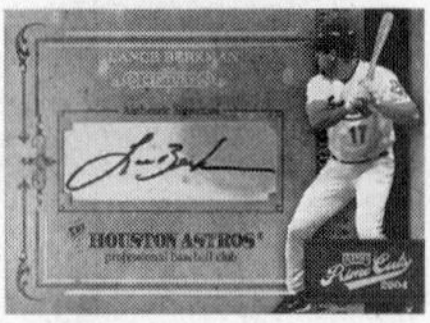

No Pricing
Production 1-17

Signature Century Platinum

No Pricing
Production One Set

Signature Century Silver

NM/M

Many not priced.
1 Mark Prior/22 30.00
6 Miguel Cabrera/24 40.00
9 Hank Blalock/25 40.00
11 Gary Sheffield/25 40.00
15 Jim Edmonds/25 40.00
16 Garret Anderson/25 25.00
17 Lance Berkman/25 30.00
20 Mark Mulder/20 25.00
21 Sammy Sosa/21 125.00
23 Mark Teixeira/40 40.00
24 Manny Ramirez/24 75.00
25 Rafael Palmeiro/25 50.00
31 Greg Maddux/31 100.00
34 Kerry Wood/34 50.00
35 Mike Mussina/35 40.00
37 Juan Gonzalez/22 40.00
44 Adam Dunn/44 30.00
49 David Ortiz/34 50.00
50 Frank Thomas/35 40.00
61 Craig Biggio/25 35.00
63 Magglio Ordonez/30 25.00
66 Vernon Wells/25 20.00
69 Scott Rolen/27 50.00
82 Andruw Jones/25 35.00
83 Josh Beckett/21 25.00
87 Mike Mussina/35 40.00
92 Cal Ripken Jr./25 175.00
93 Dale Murphy/25 40.00
94 Don Mattingly/23 75.00
95 Gary Carter/25 25.00
96 George Brett/10
97 Nolan Ryan/34 100.00
98 Ozzie Smith/10
99 Steve Carlton/32 30.00
100 Tony Gwynn/25 50.00

Signature Material Combo

NM/M

Most not priced.
Prime: No Pricing
Production 1-9
1 Mark Prior/Hat-Jsy/22 50.00
20 Mark Mulder/Jsy-Jsy/20 35.00
40 Todd Helton/Bat-Jsy/17 75.00
83 Josh Beckett/Bat-Jsy/21 35.00
93 Dale Murphy/Bat-Jsy/25 50.00
94 Don Mattingly/Bat-Jsy/25 100.00

Signature Material Number

NM/M

Most not priced.
Prime: No Pricing
Production 1-9
1 Mark Prior/Jsy/22 40.00
17 Lance Berkman/Jsy/17 50.00
20 Mark Mulder/Jsy/20 25.00
40 Todd Helton/Jsy/17 60.00
57 Tim Hudson/Jsy/15 35.00
83 Josh Beckett/Jsy/21 25.00
94 Don Mattingly/Jsy/23 100.00
97 Nolan Ryan/Jkt/34 125.00
99 Steve Carlton/Jsy/32 40.00
100 Tony Gwynn/Jsy/19 80.00

Timeline

NM/M

Common Player: 4.00

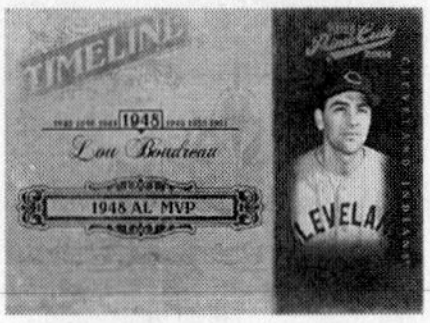

Production 50 Sets
Century Gold: No Pricing
Production 10 Sets
Century Platinum: No Pricing
Production One Set
Century Silver: 1-1.5X
Production 25 Sets
1 Al Kaline 8.00
2 Alex Rodriguez 10.00
3 Andre Dawson 4.00
4 Babe Ruth 15.00
5 Barry Zito 4.00
6 Bob Feller 4.00
7 Bob Gibson 6.00
8 Bobby Doerr 4.00
9 Brooks Robinson 6.00
10 Cal Ripken Jr. 25.00
11 Carl Hubbell 4.00
12 Carl Yastrzemski 10.00
13 Carlton Fisk 6.00
14 Jim "Catfish" Hunter 6.00
15 Chipper Jones 8.00
16 Cy Young 6.00
17 Dale Murphy 6.00
18 Dave Parker 4.00
19 Dennis Eckersley 4.00
20 Don Drysdale 6.00
21 Don Mattingly 15.00
22 Duke Snider 6.00
23 Dwight Gooden 4.00
24 Early Wynn 4.00
25 Eddie Mathews 8.00
26 Eddie Murray 6.00
27 Enos Slaughter 4.00
28 Ernie Banks 8.00
29 Fergie Jenkins 4.00
30 Frank Robinson 6.00
31 Frank Thomas 8.00
32 Frankie Frisch 4.00
33 Fred Lynn 4.00
34 Gary Carter 4.00
35 Gaylord Perry 4.00
36 George Brett 15.00
37 Greg Maddux 10.00
38 Hal Newhouser 4.00
39 Harmon Killebrew 8.00
40 Honus Wagner 6.00
41 Hoyt Wilhelm 4.00
42 Ivan Rodriguez 8.00
43 Jackie Robinson 6.00
44 Jason Giambi 4.00
45 Jeff Bagwell 6.00
46 Jim Palmer 4.00
47 Jimmie Foxx 8.00
48 Joe Morgan 4.00
49 Johnny Bench 8.00
50 Johnny Mize 4.00
51 Jose Canseco 6.00
52 Juan Gonzalez 6.00
53 Juan Marichal 4.00
54 Keith Hernandez 4.00
55 Kirby Puckett 8.00
56 Lefty Grove 4.00
57 Lou Boudreau 4.00
58 Lou Brock 6.00
59 Lou Gehrig 10.00
60 Luis Aparicio 4.00
61 Marty Marion 4.00
62 Mel Ott 6.00
63 Miguel Tejada 6.00
64 Mike Schmidt 10.00
65 Nellie Fox 6.00
66 Nolan Ryan 15.00
67 Orel Hershiser 4.00
68 Orlando Cepeda 4.00
69 Paul Molitor 6.00
70 Pedro Martinez 8.00
71 Pee Wee Reese 6.00
72 Phil Niekro 4.00
73 Phil Rizzuto 6.00
74 Ralph Kiner 4.00
75 Randy Johnson 8.00
76 Red Schoendienst 4.00
77 Reggie Jackson 6.00
78 Rickey Henderson 6.00
79 Roberto Clemente 15.00
80 Robin Yount 10.00
81 Rod Carew 6.00
82 Roger Clemens 10.00
83 Roger Maris 10.00
84 Rogers Hornsby 6.00
85 Roy Campanella 8.00
86 Ozzie Smith 10.00
87 Sammy Sosa 10.00
88 Satchel Paige 6.00
89 Stan Musial 10.00
90 Steve Carlton 4.00
91 Ted Williams 10.00
92 Thurman Munson 8.00
93 Tom Seaver 6.00
94 Ty Cobb 10.00
95 Walter Johnson 6.00

96 Warren Spahn 8.00
97 Whitey Ford 6.00
98 Willie McCovey 6.00
99 Willie Stargell 6.00
100 Yogi Berra 8.00

Timeline Material Combo

NM/M

Quantity produced listed
4 Babe Ruth/Jsy-Jsy/25 350.00
7 Bob Gibson/Hat-Jsy/25 35.00
10 Cal Ripken Jr./Jkt-Jsy/25 75.00
13 Carlton Fisk/Bat-Jsy/27 25.00
14 Jim "Catfish" Hunter/ Jsy-Jsy/27 25.00
17 Dale Murphy/Bat-Jsy/25 25.00
21 Don Mattingly/ Btg Glv-Pants/25 50.00
25 Eddie Mathews/Bat-Jsy/41 40.00
26 Eddie Murray/Bat-Jsy/33 40.00
36 George Brett/Hat-Jsy/25 60.00
39 Harmon Killebrew/ Bat-Jsy/25 50.00
43 Jackie Robinson/ Jkt-Jsy/42 100.00
46 Jim Palmer/Hat-Jsy/22 20.00
47 Jimmie Foxx/ Bat-Fld Glv/25 125.00
49 Johnny Bench/Bat-Jsy/25 40.00
58 Lou Brock/Bat-Jsy/20 25.00
59 Lou Gehrig/Jsy-Pants/25 250.00
62 Mel Ott/Jsy-Pants/25 50.00
64 Mike Schmidt/Bat-Jsy/20 60.00
66 Nolan Ryan/Jsy-Pants/25 60.00
68 Orlando Cepeda/ Bat-Pants/25 20.00
71 Pee Wee Reese/Bat-Jsy/25 30.00
77 Reggie Jackson/ Jsy-Jsy/25 30.00
79 Roberto Clemente/ Hat-Jsy/21 150.00
80 Robin Yount/Bat-Jsy/19 50.00
81 Rod Carew/Bat-Jsy/29 30.00
82 Roger Clemens/Jsy-Jsy/21 40.00
83 Roger Maris/Jsy-Pants/25 75.00
85 Roy Campanella/ Bat-Pants/39 35.00
86 Ozzie Smith/Bat-Jsy/21 40.00
87 Sammy Sosa/Bat-Jsy/21 40.00
90 Steve Carlton/Hat-Jsy/32 20.00
91 Ted Williams/Jsy-Jsy/25 140.00
92 Thurman Munson/ Jsy-Pants/10 50.00
94 Ty Cobb/Bat-Pants/25 160.00
96 Warren Spahn/Jsy-Jsy/21 40.00
98 Willie McCovey/Bat-Jsy/25 25.00

Timeline Material Combo CY

Quantity produced listed
No Pricing

Timeline Material Number

NM/M

Quantity produced listed
4 Babe Ruth/Jsy/25 350.00
6 Bob Feller/Pants/19 25.00
7 Bob Gibson/Jsy/25 30.00
10 Cal Ripken Jr./Jsy/25 60.00
12 Carl Yastrzemski/Jsy/25 40.00
13 Carlton Fisk/Jsy/27 25.00
14 Jim "Catfish" Hunter/ Jsy/27 20.00
20 Don Drysdale/Jsy/25 40.00
22 Duke Snider/Pants/25 25.00
24 Early Wynn/Jsy/24 15.00
25 Eddie Mathews/Jsy/25 30.00
26 Eddie Murray/Jsy/25 25.00
28 Ernie Banks/Jsy/25 35.00
32 Frankie Frisch/Jkt/25 40.00
36 George Brett/Jsy/25 40.00
39 Harmon Killebrew/Jsy/25 35.00
43 Jackie Robinson/Jkt/42 60.00
46 Jim Palmer/Jsy/22 15.00
47 Jimmie Foxx/Fld Glv/25 85.00
49 Johnny Bench/Jsy/25 25.00
53 Juan Marichal/Jsy/25 15.00
55 Kirby Puckett/Jsy/25 30.00
58 Lou Brock/Jsy/20 25.00
59 Lou Gehrig/Jsy/25 180.00
62 Mel Ott/Pants/25 40.00
64 Mike Schmidt/Jsy/20 50.00
66 Nolan Ryan/Jsy/25 50.00
68 Orlando Cepeda/Pants/25 15.00
71 Pee Wee Reese/Jsy/25 25.00
74 Ralph Kiner/Bat/25 25.00
77 Reggie Jackson/Jsy/25 25.00
80 Robin Yount/Jsy/19 40.00
81 Rod Carew/Jsy/25 25.00
82 Roger Clemens/Jsy/21 30.00
83 Roger Maris/Jsy/25 60.00
84 Rogers Hornsby/Bat/25 75.00
85 Roy Campanella/ Pants/25 30.00
86 Ozzie Smith/Jsy/25 35.00
87 Sammy Sosa/Jsy/21 30.00
88 Satchel Paige/Jsy/25 75.00
90 Steve Carlton/Jsy/25 15.00
91 Ted Williams/Jsy/25 100.00
92 Thurman Munson/Jsy/25 40.00
93 Tom Seaver/Pants/25 25.00
94 Ty Cobb/Pants/25 140.00
96 Warren Spahn/Jsy/21 35.00
98 Willie McCovey/Jsy/8 25.00

Timeline Material Position

NM/M

Quantity produced listed
4 Babe Ruth/Jsy/25 350.00
6 Bob Feller/Pants/19 25.00
7 Bob Gibson/Jsy/25 30.00
10 Cal Ripken Jr./Jsy/25 60.00
12 Carl Yastrzemski/Jsy/25 40.00
13 Carlton Fisk/Jsy/27 25.00
14 Jim "Catfish" Hunter/ Jsy/27 20.00
20 Don Drysdale/Jsy/25 40.00
22 Duke Snider/Pants/25 25.00
24 Early Wynn/Jsy/24 15.00
25 Eddie Mathews/Jsy/25 30.00
26 Eddie Murray/Jsy/25 25.00
28 Ernie Banks/Jsy/25 35.00
32 Frankie Frisch/Jkt/25 40.00
36 George Brett/Jsy/25 40.00
39 Harmon Killebrew/Jsy/25 35.00
43 Jackie Robinson/Jkt/42 60.00
46 Jim Palmer/Jsy/22 15.00
47 Jimmie Foxx/Fld Glv/25 85.00
49 Johnny Bench/Jsy/25 25.00
53 Juan Marichal/Jsy/27 15.00
55 Kirby Puckett/Jsy/25 30.00
58 Lou Brock/Jsy/20 25.00
59 Lou Gehrig/Jsy/25 180.00
62 Mel Ott/Pants/25 40.00
64 Mike Schmidt/Jsy/20 50.00
66 Nolan Ryan/Jsy/25 50.00
68 Orlando Cepeda/Pants/25 15.00
71 Pee Wee Reese/Jsy/25 25.00
74 Ralph Kiner/Bat/25 25.00
77 Reggie Jackson/Jsy/25 25.00
80 Robin Yount/Jsy/19 40.00
81 Rod Carew/Jsy/25 25.00
82 Roger Clemens/Jsy/21 30.00
84 Rogers Hornsby/Bat/25 75.00
86 Ozzie Smith/Jsy/25 35.00
87 Sammy Sosa/Jsy/21 30.00
88 Satchel Paige/CO Jsy/25 75.00
90 Steve Carlton/Jsy/25 15.00
92 Thurman Munson/Jsy/15 50.00
93 Tom Seaver/Pants/25 25.00
96 Warren Spahn/Jsy/21 35.00
98 Willie McCovey/Jsy/25 25.00

Timeline Material Prime

No Pricing
Production 1-10

Timeline Material Quad

No Pricing
Production 1-25

Timeline Material Trio

NM/M

Most not priced.
Trio HOF: No Pricing
Production 1-9
Trio MVP: No Pricing
Production 1-10
Trio Stats: No Pricing
Production 1-15
10 Cal Ripken Jr./ Jkt-Jsy-Pants/25 100.00
17 Dale Murphy/ Bat-Jsy-Jsy/25 40.00
21 Don Mattingly/ Bat-Jkt-Pants/25 75.00
26 Eddie Murray/ Bat-Jsy-Shoe/25 85.00
80 Robin Yount/ Bat-Jsy-Jsy/19 70.00
82 Roger Clemens/ Bat-Jsy-Jsy/21 50.00

Timeline Signature Material Combo

NM/M

Most not priced.
7 Bob Gibson/Hat-Jsy/25 50.00
8 Bobby Doerr/Bat-Jsy/25 50.00
58 Lou Brock/Bat-Jsy/20 50.00

Timeline Signature Material Combo CY

NM/M

Most not priced.
7 Bob Gibson/Hat-Jsy/25 50.00
46 Jim Palmer/Hat-Jsy/22 50.00
90 Steve Carlton/Hat-Jsy/32 50.00

Timeline Signature Material Number

NM/M

Most not priced.
6 Bob Feller/Pants/19 40.00
7 Bob Gibson/Jsy/25 50.00
8 Bobby Doerr/Jsy/25 40.00
21 Don Mattingly/Pants/23 80.00
46 Jim Palmer/Jsy/22 40.00
53 Juan Marichal/Jsy/27 40.00
58 Lou Brock/Jsy/20 50.00
66 Nolan Ryan/Jsy/34 150.00
90 Steve Carlton/Jsy/32 40.00

Timeline Signature Material Position

NM/M

Most not priced.
6 Bob Feller/Pants/19 40.00
8 Bobby Doerr/Jsy/25 40.00
21 Don Mattingly/Pants/23 80.00
46 Jim Palmer/Jsy/22 40.00
53 Juan Marichal/Jsy/27 40.00
58 Lou Brock/Jsy/20 50.00
66 Nolan Ryan/Jsy/34 150.00
67 Orel Hershiser/Jsy/25 30.00

Timeline Signature Material Prime

No Pricing
Production 1-9

Timeline Signature Material Quad

NM/M

Most not priced.
21 Don Mattingly/25 180.00

Timeline Signature Material Trio

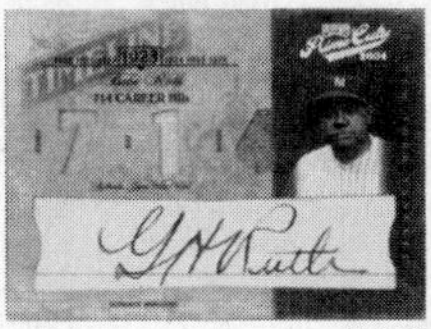

NM/M

No Pricing
Production 1-9
Trio HOF: No Pricing
Production 1-9
Trio MVP: No Pricing
Production 1-8
Trio Stats: No Pricing
Production 1-9
91 Ted Williams/Bat-Jkt-Jsy/1 (2/06 Auction) 1,483

2005 Playoff Absolute Memorabilia

NM/M

Complete Set (100):
Common Player: .50
Retail: .3X
Retail doesn't have foil front.
Pack (4): 40.00
Box (4): 150.00
1 Andruw Jones .75
2 B.J. Upton .75
3 Jim Edmonds .75
4 Johan Santana 1.00
5 Jeff Bagwell .75
6 Derek Jeter 3.00
7 Eric Chavez .75
8 Albert Pujols 3.00
9 Craig Biggio .75
10 Hank Blalock .75
11 Chipper Jones 1.00
12 Jacque Jones .50
13 Alfonso Soriano 1.00
14 Carl Crawford .50
15 Ben Sheets .50
16 Garret Anderson .75
17 Luis Gonzalez .50
18 Andy Pettitte .75
19 Miguel Tejada .75
20 Carlos Delgado .75
21 Austin Kearns .50
22 Adrian Beltre .50
23 Rafael Palmeiro .75
24 Greg Maddux 2.00
25 Jason Bay .50
26 Jason Varitek .75
27 David Ortiz 1.00
28 Dontrelle Willis .75
29 Adam Dunn 1.00
30 Carlos Lee .50
31 Manny Ramirez 1.00
32 Rocco Baldelli .50
33 Jeff Kent .50
34 Jake Peavy .75
35 Vernon Wells .50
36 Ichiro Suzuki 2.00
37 C.C. Sabathia .50
38 Hideki Matsui 2.00
39 Gary Sheffield .75
40 Paul LoDuca .50
41 Vladimir Guerrero 1.00
42 Omar Vizquel .50
43 Lance Berkman .50
44 Shawn Green .50
45 Josh Beckett .50
46 Barry Zito .50
47 Roger Clemens 3.00
48 Sean Casey .50
49 Edgar Renteria .50
50 Mark Teixeira .75
51 Frank Thomas .75
52 Khalil Greene .50
53 Bobby Abreu .75
54 Rafael Furcal .50
55 Jose Vidro .50
56 Nomar Garciaparra 1.00
57 Melvin Mora .50
58 Trot Nixon .50
59 Magglio Ordonez .50
60 Michael Young .50
61 Richie Sexson .50
62 Alex Rodriguez 3.00
63 Tim Hudson .50
64 Todd Helton .75
65 Mike Lowell .50
66 Mark Mulder .50
67 Sammy Sosa 1.50
68 Mark Prior 1.00
69 Shannon Stewart .50
70 Miguel Cabrera 1.00
71 Troy Glaus .50
72 Scott Rolen 1.00
73 Ken Griffey Jr. 2.00
74 Mike Piazza 1.00
75 Roy Halladay .50
76 Larry Walker .75
77 Kerry Wood .75
78 Mike Mussina .75
79 Curt Schilling 1.00
80 Rich Harden .50
81 Victor Martinez .50
82 Roy Oswalt .50
83 Pedro Martinez 1.00
84 Tom Glavine .50
85 Randy Johnson 1.00
86 Ivan Rodriguez 1.00
87 Carlos Beltran .75
88 Torii Hunter .50
89 Hideo Nomo .50
90 Jim Thome 1.00
91 Aramis Ramirez .50
92 J.D. Drew .50
93 Javy Lopez .50
94 David Wright 2.00
95 Bobby Crosby .75
96 Jeff Niemann **RC** 3.00
97 Yuniesky Betancourt **RC** 3.00
98 Tadahito Iguchi **RC** 5.00
99 Philip Humber **RC** 3.00
100 Justin Verlander **RC** 5.00

Black

Black: 2-4X
Inserted 1:18 Retail

Blue

Blue: 1-2X
Inserted 1:3 Retail

Red

Red: 2-3X
Inserted 1:8 Retail

Spectrum Gold

No Pricing
Production 10 Sets

Spectrum Platinum

No Pricing
Production One Set

Spectrum Silver

Silver: 2-3X
Production 100 Sets

Absolutely Ink Swatch Double

NM/M

Production 1-50
1 Rafael Furcal B-J/50 20.00
3 Dale Murphy B-J/50 30.00
7 Bobby Crosby J-J/50 20.00
8 Cal Ripken Jr. J-P/25 150.00
10 Vernon Wells J-J/25 20.00
11 Lyle Overbay J-J/50 15.00
13 Omar Vizquel J-J/50 25.00
16 Aramis Ramirez J-J/25 30.00
18 Travis Hafner BG-J/50 25.00
22 Juan Gonzalez B-J/25 25.00
23 Mark Teixeira FG-J/50 35.00
27 Darryl Strawberry J-J/50 20.00
30 Magglio Ordonez B-J/25 20.00
31 Jay Gibbons B-J/50 15.00
32 Steve Carlton FG-J/25 40.00
37 Keith Hernandez B-J/50 20.00
38 Carlos Zambrano J-J/50 25.00
39 Brett Myers J-J/50 15.00
41 Danny Kolb J-J/50 15.00
42 Mark Prior FG-J/25 40.00
43 Joey Gathright B-J/25 15.00
44 David Cone J-J/50 15.00
45 Carlos Lee FG-J/50 20.00
49 Garret Anderson J-J/25 25.00
51 Dave Parker B-J/25 25.00
52 C.C. Sabathia J-J/50 20.00
53 Dennis Eckersley A's J-P/50 20.00
55 Brandon Webb B-P/50 15.00
56 Sean Casey B-J/50 20.00
57 Johan Santana J-J/25 60.00
58 Miguel Cabrera J-J/50 40.00
59 Bert Blyleven J-J/50 15.00
60 Casey Kotchman B-J/50 20.00
62 Milton Bradley J-J/50 15.00
63 John Kruk J-J/50 25.00
64 Michael Young B-J/50 20.00
69 Lew Ford B-J/50 15.00
70 Jody Gerut B-J/50 15.00
71 Don Sutton J-J/50 15.00
73 Austin Kearns B-J/50 15.00
77 Ryan Wagner J-J/50 15.00
78 Jermaine Dye J-J/50 15.00
80 Al Oliver B-J/50 15.00
81 Angel Berroa B-P/50 15.00

82 Edgar Renteria J-J/50 20.00
84 Roy Oswalt FG-J/25 25.00
86 Dave Righetti J-J/50 20.00
87 Aubrey Huff H-J/25 20.00
89 Jose Vidro B-J/50 15.00
90 Harold Baines J-J/50 15.00
93 Ken Harvey J-J/50 15.00
95 Jason Bay B-J/50 20.00
96 Dwight Evans B-J/50 40.00
99 Brian Roberts J-J/50 40.00

Swatch Double Spectrum

NM/M

Production 1-25
Prime: No Pricing
Production One Set
1 Rafael Furcal B-J/25 20.00
3 Dale Murphy B-J/25 40.00
7 Bobby Crosby J-J/25 25.00
10 Vernon Wells J-J/25 20.00
11 Lyle Overbay J-J/25 15.00
18 Travis Hafner BG-J/25 30.00
27 Darryl Strawberry J-J/25 25.00
31 Jay Gibbons B-J/25 20.00
37 Keith Hernandez B-J/25 25.00
38 Carlos Zambrano J-J/25 30.00
39 Brett Myers J-J/25 15.00
41 Danny Kolb J-J/25 15.00
45 Carlos Lee FG-J/25 20.00
55 Brandon Webb B-P/25 25.00
59 Bert Blyleven J-J/25 15.00
60 Casey Kotchman B-J/25 25.00
62 Milton Bradley J-J/25 20.00
63 John Kruk J-J/25 25.00
64 Michael Young B-J/25 25.00
69 Lew Ford B-J/25 15.00
70 Jody Gerut B-J/25 15.00
71 Don Sutton J-J/25 20.00
73 Austin Kearns B-J/25 20.00
77 Ryan Wagner J-J/25 15.00
78 Jermaine Dye J-J/25 15.00
81 Angel Berroa B-P/25 15.00
89 Jose Vidro B-J/25 15.00
90 Harold Baines J-J/25 20.00
93 Ken Harvey J-J/25 15.00
95 Jason Bay B-J/25 25.00
96 Dwight Evans B-J/25 40.00
99 Brian Roberts J-J/25 40.00

Absolutely Ink Swatch Single

NM/M

Production 5-50
1 Rafael Furcal/Jsy/50 15.00
3 Dale Murphy/Jsy/50 25.00
4 Duke Snider/Pants/25 40.00
5 Bill Madlock/Bat/50 20.00
7 Bobby Crosby/Jsy/50 15.00
8 Cal Ripken Jr./Jsy/25 140.00
9 Hank Blalock/Jsy/25 25.00
10 Vernon Wells/Jsy/50 20.00
11 Lyle Overbay/Jsy/50 15.00
13 Omar Vizquel/Jsy/50 25.00
15 Ben Sheets/Jsy/25 20.00
16 Aramis Ramirez/Jsy/25 30.00
18 Travis Hafner/Jsy/50 20.00
19 Mike Lowell/Jsy/25 15.00
20 Frank Robinson/Bat/50 30.00
22 Juan Gonzalez/Jsy/50 25.00
27 Darryl Strawberry/Jsy/50 20.00
28 Alexis Rios/Bat/50 15.00
30 Magglio Ordonez/Jsy/50 15.00
31 Jay Gibbons/Jsy/50 15.00
32 Steve Carlton/Jsy/25 35.00
34 Kerry Wood/Jsy/25 35.00
36 Eric Chavez/Jsy/25 25.00
37 Keith Hernandez/Jsy/50 15.00
38 Carlos Zambrano/Jsy/50 25.00
39 Brett Myers/Jsy/50 15.00
40 Rich Harden/Jsy/50 20.00
41 Danny Kolb/Jsy/50 15.00
42 Mark Prior/Jsy/25 40.00
43 Joey Gathright/Jsy/25 15.00
44 David Cone/Jsy/50 15.00
45 Carlos Lee/Jsy/50 20.00
47 Jack Morris/Jsy/50 20.00
48 Torii Hunter/Jsy/50 20.00
49 Garret Anderson/Jsy/50 25.00
51 Dave Parker/Bat/50 20.00
52 C.C. Sabathia/Jsy/50 15.00
53 Dennis Eckersley/Jsy/50 20.00
54 Barry Larkin/Jsy/50 40.00
55 Brandon Webb/Pants/50 15.00
56 Sean Casey/Jsy/50 20.00
57 Johan Santana/Jsy/50 40.00
58 Miguel Cabrera/Jsy/50 40.00
59 Bert Blyleven/Jsy/50 15.00
60 Casey Kotchman/Jsy/50 15.00
61 Dwight Gooden/Jsy/50 20.00
62 Milton Bradley/Jsy/50 15.00
63 John Kruk/Jsy/50 25.00
64 Michael Young/Jsy/50 20.00
66 Robin Ventura/Jsy/50 20.00
67 Tim Hudson/Jsy/25 30.00
68 Will Clark/Bat/50 40.00
69 Lew Ford/Jsy/50 15.00
70 Jody Gerut/Jsy/50 15.00
71 Don Sutton/Jsy/50 15.00
72 B.J. Upton/Bat/25 20.00
73 Austin Kearns/Jsy/50 15.00
77 Ryan Wagner/Jsy/50 15.00
78 Jermaine Dye/Jsy/50 15.00
80 Al Oliver/Jsy/50 15.00
81 Angel Berroa/Pants/50 15.00
82 Edgar Renteria/Jsy/50 20.00
83 Dennis Eckersley/Jsy/25 25.00
84 Roy Oswalt/Jsy/50 20.00
86 Dave Righetti/Jsy/50 20.00
87 Aubrey Huff/Jsy/25 20.00
89 Jose Vidro/Jsy/50 15.00
90 Harold Baines/Jsy/50 15.00
93 Ken Harvey/Jsy/50 15.00
95 Jason Bay/Jsy/50 20.00
96 Dwight Evans/Jsy/50 30.00
97 Luis Tiant/Pants/50 15.00
98 Ron Santo/Bat/50 30.00
99 Brian Roberts/Jsy/50 40.00
100 Marty Marion/Jsy/50 15.00

Absolutely Ink Swatch Single Spectrum

NM/M

Production 1-25
Prime: No Pricing
Production One Set
1 Rafael Furcal/Jsy/25 20.00
3 Dale Murphy/Jsy/25 35.00
5 Bill Madlock/Bat/25 25.00
7 Bobby Crosby/Jsy/25 20.00
11 Lyle Overbay/Jsy/25 15.00
13 Omar Vizquel/Jsy/25 25.00
18 Travis Hafner/Jsy/25 25.00
23 Mark Teixeira/Jsy/25 50.00
27 Darryl Strawberry/Jsy/25 20.00
28 Alexis Rios/Bat/25 15.00
30 Magglio Ordonez/Jsy/25 15.00
31 Jay Gibbons/Jsy/25 15.00
37 Keith Hernandez/Jsy/25 20.00
38 Carlos Zambrano/Jsy/25 30.00
39 Brett Myers/Jsy/25 15.00
40 Rich Harden/Jsy/25 25.00
41 Danny Kolb/Jsy/25 15.00
45 Carlos Lee/Jsy/25 20.00
47 Jack Morris/Jsy/25 20.00
51 Dave Parker/Bat/25 20.00
52 C.C. Sabathia/Jsy/25 20.00
55 Brandon Webb/Pants/25 25.00
56 Sean Casey/Jsy/25 20.00
57 Johan Santana/Jsy/25 50.00
58 Miguel Cabrera/Jsy/25 50.00
59 Bert Blyleven/Jsy/25 20.00
60 Casey Kotchman/Jsy/25 25.00
61 Dwight Gooden/Jsy/25 25.00
62 Milton Bradley/Jsy/25 20.00
63 John Kruk/Jsy/25 25.00
64 Michael Young/Jsy/25 25.00
69 Lew Ford/Jsy/25 15.00
70 Jody Gerut/Jsy/25 15.00
71 Don Sutton/Jsy/25 20.00
73 Austin Kearns/Jsy/25 20.00
77 Ryan Wagner/Jsy/25 15.00
78 Jermaine Dye/Jsy/25 15.00
80 Al Oliver/Jsy/25 15.00
81 Angel Berroa/Pants/25 15.00
89 Jose Vidro/Jsy/25 15.00
90 Harold Baines/Jsy/25 20.00
92 Mark Mulder/Jsy/25 25.00
93 Ken Harvey/Jsy/25 15.00
95 Jason Bay/Jsy/25 25.00
96 Dwight Evans/Jsy/25 40.00
97 Luis Tiant/Pants/25 15.00
98 Ron Santo/Bat/25 30.00
99 Brian Roberts/Jsy/25 40.00
100 Marty Marion/Jsy/25 25.00

Absolutely Ink Swatch Triple

NM/M

Production 1-75
1 Rafael Furcal/50 20.00
3 Dale Murphy/50 30.00
8 Cal Ripken Jr./25 160.00
9 Hank Blalock/25 30.00
13 Omar Vizquel/25 30.00
16 Aramis Ramirez/25 35.00
18 Travis Hafner/50 25.00
22 Juan Gonzalez/25 30.00
23 Mark Teixeira/75 40.00
27 Darryl Strawberry/50 20.00
31 Jay Gibbons/25 20.00
37 Keith Hernandez/25 25.00
45 Carlos Lee/50 20.00
49 Garret Anderson/25 30.00
52 C.C. Sabathia/25 20.00
53 Dennis Eckersley/50 25.00
55 Brandon Webb/50 20.00
56 Sean Casey/50 25.00
58 Miguel Cabrera/25 50.00
60 Casey Kotchman/50 25.00
64 Michael Young/75 25.00
69 Lew Ford/50 15.00
70 Jody Gerut/50 15.00
73 Austin Kearns/50 20.00
77 Ryan Wagner/50 15.00
78 Jermaine Dye/50 15.00
81 Angel Berroa/50 15.00
86 Dave Righetti/50 20.00
89 Jose Vidro/50 15.00
90 Harold Baines/50 20.00
95 Jason Bay/25 25.00
96 Dwight Evans/25 40.00

Absolutely Ink Swatch Triple Spectrum

NM/M

Production 1-25
Prime: No Pricing
Production One Set
1 Rafael Furcal/25 20.00
3 Dale Murphy/25 40.00
18 Travis Hafner/25 25.00
23 Mark Teixeira/25 50.00
27 Darryl Strawberry/25 20.00
45 Carlos Lee/25 20.00
60 Casey Kotchman/25 25.00
64 Michael Young/25 30.00
69 Lew Ford/25 15.00
70 Jody Gerut/25 15.00
73 Austin Kearns/25 20.00
77 Ryan Wagner/25 15.00
78 Jermaine Dye/25 15.00
81 Angel Berroa/25 15.00
89 Jose Vidro/25 15.00
90 Harold Baines/25 20.00

Absolute Memorabilia Heroes

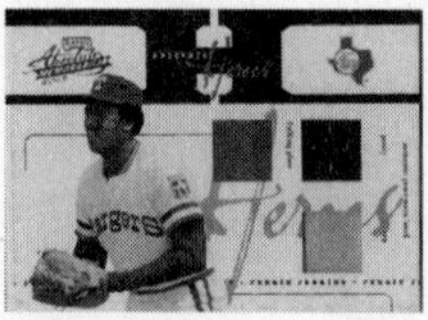

NM/M

Common Player: 1.50
Production 250 Sets
Spectrum: 1-2X
Production 50 Sets
Reverse Spectrum: 2-4X
Production 25 Sets
1 Billy Martin 3.00
2 Rickey Henderson 2.00
3 Alan Trammell 2.00
4 Lenny Dykstra 1.50
5 Jeff Bagwell 2.00
6 Steve Garvey 1.50
7 Jim "Catfish" Hunter 2.00
8 Cal Ripken Jr. 10.00
9 Reggie Jackson 3.00
10 Gary Sheffield 2.00
11 Edgar Martinez 1.50
12 Roberto Alomar 2.00
13 Luis Tiant 1.50
14 Jim Rice 2.00
15 Carlos Beltran 2.00
16 Hideo Nomo 2.00
17 Mark Grace 2.00
18 Joe Cronin 2.00
19 Tony Gwynn 3.00
20 Bo Jackson 3.00
21 Roger Clemens 5.00
22 Roger Clemens 5.00
23 Don Mattingly 5.00
24 Willie Mays 5.00
25 Andruw Jones 2.00
26 Andre Dawson 2.00
27 Carlton Fisk 2.00
28 Robin Yount 3.00
29 Joe Carter 1.50
30 Dale Murphy 2.00
31 Greg Maddux 3.00
32 Ichiro Suzuki 4.00
33 Jose Canseco 2.00
34 Nolan Ryan 8.00
35 Frank Thomas 2.00
36 Fred Lynn 1.50
37 Curt Schilling 2.00
38 Curt Schilling 2.00
39 Dave Parker 1.50
40 Randy Johnson 2.50
41 Randy Johnson 2.50
42 Vladimir Guerrero 2.50
43 Bernie Williams 1.50
44 Wade Boggs 2.00
45 Pedro Martinez 2.50
46 Andy Pettitte 1.50
47 Fergie Jenkins 2.00
48 Darryl Strawberry 1.50
49 Rafael Palmeiro 2.00
50 Albert Pujols 5.00

Heroes Autograph Swatch Double Spectrum Prime

No Pricing
Production 1-15
Triple: No Pricing
Production One Set

Heroes Swatch Double

NM/M

Production 25-50
Spectrum Prime: No Pricing
Production 1-25
1 Billy Martin J-P/50 25.00
2 Rickey Henderson B-J/50 10.00
3 Alan Trammell B-J/50 10.00
4 Lenny Dykstra B-J/50 8.00
5 Jeff Bagwell B-J/50 10.00
6 Steve Garvey B-J/50 8.00
7 Jim "Catfish" Hunter J-J/25 10.00
8 Cal Ripken Jr. J-P/50 40.00
9 Reggie Jackson JK-J/50 10.00
10 Gary Sheffield FG-J/50 8.00
11 Edgar Martinez J-J/50 8.00
12 Roberto Alomar J-J/50 8.00
13 Luis Tiant H-J/25 10.00
14 Jim Rice J-P/50 8.00
15 Carlos Beltran B-J/50 8.00
16 Hideo Nomo B-J/50 10.00
17 Mark Grace FG-J/50 10.00
18 Joe Cronin J-P/50 30.00
19 Tony Gwynn B-J/50 15.00
20 Bo Jackson B-J/50 10.00
21 Roger Clemens J-J/50 25.00
22 Roger Clemens J-J/50 25.00
23 Don Mattingly B-J/50 20.00
24 Willie Mays B-J/50 50.00
25 Andruw Jones B-J/50 8.00
26 Andre Dawson J-P/50 8.00
28 Robin Yount H-J/50 15.00
29 Joe Carter B-J/50 8.00
30 Dale Murphy B-J/50 10.00
31 Greg Maddux J-J/50 15.00
33 Jose Canseco H-J/50 10.00
34 Nolan Ryan B-J/50 30.00
35 Frank Thomas J-P/50 10.00
36 Fred Lynn B-J/50 8.00
37 Curt Schilling J-J/50 10.00
38 Curt Schilling J-J/50 10.00
39 Dave Parker B-J/50 8.00
40 Randy Johnson J-P/50 10.00
41 Randy Johnson B-J/25 10.00
42 Vladimir Guerrero J-J/50 10.00
43 Bernie Williams J-J/50 8.00
44 Wade Boggs B-J/50 10.00
45 Pedro Martinez J-J/50 10.00
46 Andy Pettitte J-J/50 8.00
47 Fergie Jenkins H-J/50 8.00
48 Darryl Strawberry J-P/50 8.00
49 Rafael Palmeiro B-J/50 10.00
50 Albert Pujols J-J/50 30.00

Heroes Swatch Triple

NM/M

Production 1-50
Spectrum Prime: No Pricing
Production 1-15
1 Billy Martin/25 35.00
2 Rickey Henderson/25 15.00
3 Alan Trammell/25 10.00
4 Lenny Dykstra/25 10.00
5 Jeff Bagwell/50 10.00
6 Steve Garvey/25 10.00
8 Cal Ripken Jr./25 50.00
9 Reggie Jackson/25 15.00
10 Gary Sheffield/50 10.00
11 Edgar Martinez/25 10.00
12 Roberto Alomar/50 10.00
14 Jim Rice/25 10.00
15 Carlos Beltran/25 15.00
16 Hideo Nomo/25 20.00
17 Mark Grace/25 15.00
18 Joe Cronin/25 40.00
19 Tony Gwynn/25 25.00
20 Bo Jackson/25 20.00
21 Roger Clemens/50 25.00
22 Roger Clemens/50 25.00
23 Don Mattingly/25 30.00
25 Andruw Jones/50 10.00
26 Andre Dawson/25 10.00
28 Robin Yount/25 60.00
31 Greg Maddux/50 15.00
34 Nolan Ryan/25 40.00
35 Frank Thomas/50 15.00
36 Fred Lynn/25 10.00
37 Curt Schilling/50 15.00
38 Curt Schilling/50 15.00
39 Dave Parker/25 10.00
42 Vladimir Guerrero/50 15.00
43 Bernie Williams/25 10.00
44 Wade Boggs/25 15.00
45 Pedro Martinez/50 15.00
46 Andy Pettitte/50 10.00
47 Fergie Jenkins/25 10.00
48 Darryl Strawberry/25 10.00
49 Rafael Palmeiro/50 15.00
50 Albert Pujols/50 40.00

Marks of Fame

NM/M

Common Player: 2.00
Production 150 Sets
Spectrum: 2-3X
Production 25 Sets
1 Bobby Doerr 2.00
2 Reggie Jackson 3.00
3 Harmon Killebrew 4.00
4 Duke Snider 3.00
5 Brooks Robinson 3.00
6 Al Kaline 4.00
7 Carlton Fisk 3.00
8 Willie Stargell 3.00
9 Enos Slaughter 2.00
10 Nolan Ryan 10.00
11 Luis Aparicio 2.00
12 Hoyt Wilhelm 2.00
13 Orlando Cepeda 2.00
14 Mike Schmidt 6.00
15 Frank Robinson 3.00
16 Whitey Ford 3.00
17 Don Sutton 2.00
18 Joe Morgan 2.00
19 Bob Feller 3.00
20 Lou Brock 3.00
21 Warren Spahn 4.00
22 Jim Palmer 2.00
23 Reggie Jackson 3.00
24 Willie Mays 8.00
25 George Brett 8.00
26 Billy Williams 2.00
27 Juan Marichal 2.00
28 Early Wynn 2.00
29 Rod Carew 3.00
30 Maury Wills 2.00

31 Fergie Jenkins 2.00
32 Steve Carlton 3.00
33 Eddie Murray 3.00
34 Kirby Puckett 3.00
35 Johnny Bench 4.00
36 Gaylord Perry 2.00
37 Gary Carter 2.00
38 Tony Perez 2.00
39 Tony Oliva 2.00
40 Luis Aparicio 2.00
41 Tom Seaver 3.00
42 Paul Molitor 3.00
43 Dennis Eckersley 2.00
44 Willie McCovey 3.00
45 Bob Gibson 3.00
46 Robin Roberts 2.00
47 Carl Yastrzemski 4.00
48 Ozzie Smith 4.00
49 Nolan Ryan 10.00
50 Stan Musial 6.00

Marks of Fame Autograph Swatch Double

NM/M

Production 1-75
Prime: No Pricing
Production 1-10
1 Bobby Doerr B-P/50 25.00
3 Harmon Killebrew B-J/50 40.00
4 Duke Snider J-P/25 40.00
5 Brooks Robinson B-J/25 40.00
7 Carlton Fisk B-JK/25 40.00
10 Nolan Ryan J-P/25 100.00
11 Luis Aparicio B-J/75 20.00
12 Hoyt Wilhelm J-J/25 25.00
13 Orlando Cepeda B-P/25 25.00
14 Mike Schmidt B-J/25 75.00
15 Frank Robinson B-S/25 50.00
16 Whitey Ford J-J/25 50.00
17 Don Sutton J-J/25 20.00
20 Lou Brock B-JK/25 50.00
22 Jim Palmer H-P/25 30.00
27 Juan Marichal J-P/25 25.00
29 Rod Carew B-J/25 40.00
31 Fergie Jenkins FG-P/25 20.00
32 Steve Carlton B-P/25 40.00
35 Johnny Bench B-J/25 50.00
36 Gaylord Perry J-J/25 20.00
37 Gary Carter B-J/25 25.00
38 Tony Perez FG-J/25 25.00
39 Tony Oliva B-J/75 20.00
41 Tom Seaver J-P/25 40.00
42 Paul Molitor B-J/25 35.00
43 Dennis Eckersley J-J/25 25.00
44 Willie McCovey J-P/25 40.00
48 Ozzie Smith H-P/25 50.00
49 Nolan Ryan JK-J/25 100.00
50 Stan Musial B-P/25 80.00

Marks of Fame Autograph Swatch Single

NM/M

Production 5-125
1 Bobby Doerr/Pants/125 20.00
3 Harmon Killebrew/Jsy/50 40.00
4 Duke Snider/Jsy/25 40.00
5 Brooks Robinson/Jsy/125 30.00
6 Al Kaline/Bat/125 35.00
7 Carlton Fisk/Jkt/50 40.00
10 Nolan Ryan/Pants/50 80.00
11 Luis Aparicio/Jsy/125 20.00
13 Orlando Cepeda/Pants/50 25.00
14 Mike Schmidt/Jsy/50 60.00
15 Frank Robinson/Bat/125 30.00
16 Whitey Ford/Jsy/50 50.00
17 Don Sutton/Jsy/125 20.00
19 Bob Feller/Pants/125 30.00
20 Lou Brock/Jkt/125 30.00
22 Jim Palmer/Pants/50 25.00
26 Billy Williams/Jsy/50 25.00
27 Juan Marichal/Pants/125 25.00
29 Rod Carew/Jsy/50 35.00
31 Fergie Jenkins/Pants/125 20.00
32 Steve Carlton/Pants/125 25.00
35 Johnny Bench/Pants/50 50.00
36 Gaylord Perry/Jsy/125 15.00
37 Gary Carter/Pants/50 20.00
38 Tony Perez/Jsy/50 20.00
39 Tony Oliva/Jsy/125 25.00
40 Luis Aparicio/Bat/125 20.00
41 Tom Seaver/Pants/50 35.00
42 Paul Molitor/Pants/50 35.00
43 Dennis Eckersley/Jsy/125 20.00
44 Willie McCovey/Pants/50 35.00
46 Robin Roberts/Hat/50 35.00
48 Ozzie Smith/Pants/50 50.00
49 Nolan Ryan/Jkt/50 80.00
50 Stan Musial/Pants/50 60.00

Marks of Fame Autograph Swatch Triple

No Pricing
Production 1-10
Prime: No Pricing
Production One Set

Marks of Fame Swatch Double

NM/M

Production 1-50
Spectrum Prime: No Pricing
Production 1-25
1 Bobby Doerr/50 10.00
2 Reggie Jackson B-P/50 10.00
3 Harmon Killebrew B-J/50 15.00
4 Duke Snider J-P/25 15.00
5 Brooks Robinson B-J/50 15.00
7 Carlton Fisk B-JK/50 10.00
8 Willie Stargell B-J/50 10.00
9 Enos Slaughter J-J/50 10.00
10 Nolan Ryan J-P/50 25.00
11 Luis Aparicio B-J/50 8.00
12 Hoyt Wilhelm J-J/50 8.00
13 Orlando Cepeda B-P/50 10.00
14 Mike Schmidt B-J/50 20.00
15 Frank Robinson B-S/50 15.00
16 Whitey Ford J-J/25 15.00
17 Don Sutton J-J/50 8.00
18 Joe Morgan B-J/50 8.00
20 Lou Brock B-JK/50 10.00
21 Warren Spahn J-P/50 12.00
22 Jim Palmer H-P/50 10.00
23 Reggie Jackson B-J/50 10.00
24 Willie Mays B-J/25 50.00
26 Billy Williams J-J/50 8.00
27 Juan Marichal J-P/50 8.00
28 Early Wynn J-J/25 10.00
29 Rod Carew B-J/50 10.00
31 Fergie Jenkins FG-P/50 8.00
32 Steve Carlton B-P/50 8.00
33 Eddie Murray B-J/50 15.00
34 Kirby Puckett B-J/50 15.00
35 Johnny Bench B-J/50 15.00
36 Gaylord Perry J-J/50 8.00
37 Gary Carter B-J/50 8.00
39 Tony Oliva B-J/50 8.00
41 Tom Seaver J-P/50 15.00
42 Paul Molitor B-J/50 15.00
43 Dennis Eckersley J-J/50 10.00
44 Willie McCovey J-P/50 10.00
47 Carl Yastrzemski B-J/50 25.00
48 Ozzie Smith H-P/50 20.00
49 Nolan Ryan JK-J/50 25.00
50 Stan Musial B-P/50 30.00

Marks of Fame Swatch Triple

NM/M

Production 1-25
Spectrum Prime: No Pricing
Production 1-15
1 Bobby Doerr/25 15.00
7 Carlton Fisk/25 15.00
8 Willie Stargell/25 15.00
10 Nolan Ryan/25 40.00
11 Luis Aparicio/25 12.00
12 Hoyt Wilhelm/25 10.00
14 Mike Schmidt/25 30.00
18 Joe Morgan/25 12.00
20 Lou Brock/25 15.00
21 Warren Spahn/25 50.00
23 Reggie Jackson/25 15.00
24 Willie Mays/25 60.00
27 Juan Marichal/25 12.00
29 Rod Carew/25 15.00
32 Steve Carlton/25 12.00
33 Eddie Murray/25 20.00
34 Kirby Puckett/25 20.00
35 Johnny Bench/25 20.00
37 Gary Carter/25 12.00
39 Tony Oliva/25 12.00
41 Tom Seaver/25 15.00
42 Paul Molitor/25 15.00
43 Dennis Eckersley/25 12.00
44 Willie McCovey/25 15.00
47 Carl Yastrzemski/25 35.00
48 Ozzie Smith/25 25.00
49 Nolan Ryan/25 40.00
50 Stan Musial/25 40.00

Team Quads

NM/M

Common Quad:
Production 150 Sets
Spectrum: 1X
Production 100 Sets
1 St. Louis Card/Active 6.00
2 Cleveland Indians 2.00
3 California Angels 2.00
4 Boston Red Sox 5.00
5 New York Yanks/Active 6.00
6 Atlanta Braves 3.00
7 Oakland A's 3.00
8 Anaheim Angels 3.00
9 Texas Rangers/Active 2.00
10 Minnesota Twins/Active 3.00
11 New York Mets 4.00
12 Houston Astros 5.00
13 San Diego Padres 4.00
14 Cincinnati Reds 2.00
15 Texas Rangers/Retro 8.00
16 New York Yanks/Retro 8.00
17 St. Louis Cards/Retro 6.00
18 Pittsburgh Pirates 2.00
19 Chicago Cubs 4.00
20 Minnesota Twins/Retro 3.00

Team Quads Swatch Double

NM/M

Production 25-75
1 St. Louis Card/Active/75 25.00
3 California Angels/75 30.00
4 Boston Red Sox/75 30.00
5 New York Yanks/Active/25 75.00
6 Atlanta Braves/25 60.00
7 Oakland A's/75 20.00
8 Anaheim Angels/25 40.00
9 Texas Rangers/Active/75 20.00
10 Minnesota Twins/Active/25 40.00
11 New York Mets/75 30.00
12 Houston Astros/25 75.00
13 San Diego Padres/75 40.00
14 Cincinnati Reds/75 20.00
15 Texas Rangers/Retro/75 50.00
18 Pittsburgh Pirates/75 20.00
20 Minnesota Twins/Retro/75 30.00

Team Quads Swatch Double Spectrum

NM/M

Production 1-25
Prime Black: No Pricing
Production 1-5
1 St. Louis Card/Active/25 40.00
3 California Angels/25 50.00
4 Boston Red Sox/25 60.00
9 Texas Rangers/Active/25 30.00
11 New York Mets/25 50.00
13 San Diego Padres/25 60.00
14 Cincinnati Reds/25 30.00
15 Texas Rangers/Retro/25 70.00

Team Quads Swatch Single

NM/M

Production 25-100
1 St. Louis Card/Active/100 25.00
2 Cleveland Indians/100 30.00
3 California Angels/100 15.00
4 Boston Red Sox/100 20.00
5 New York Yanks/Active/100 30.00
6 Atlanta Braves/100 25.00
7 Oakland A's/100 10.00
8 Anaheim Angels/100 15.00
9 Texas Rangers/Active/100 10.00
10 Minnesota Twins/Active/25 25.00
11 New York Mets/100 20.00
12 Houston Astros/100 30.00
13 San Diego Padres/100 25.00
14 Cincinnati Reds/100 10.00
15 Texas Rangers/Retro/100 30.00
16 New York Yanks/Retro/100 50.00
17 St. Louis Cards/Retro/25 50.00
18 Pittsburgh Pirates/100 15.00
19 Chicago Cubs/100 25.00
20 Minnesota Twins/Retro/100 20.00

Team Quads Swatch Single Spectrum

NM/M

Production 10-35
Prime Black: No Pricing
Production 10 Sets
1 St. Louis Card/Active/35 40.00
2 Cleveland Indians/35 50.00
3 California Angels/35 25.00
4 Boston Red Sox/35 30.00
5 New York Yanks/Active/35 40.00
6 Atlanta Braves/35 40.00
7 Oakland A's/35 20.00
8 Anaheim Angels/35 25.00
9 Texas Rangers/Active/35 20.00
11 New York Mets/35 30.00
12 Houston Astros/35 50.00
13 San Diego Padres/35 40.00
14 Cincinnati Reds/35 20.00
15 Texas Rangers/Retro/35 40.00
16 New York Yanks/Retro/35 75.00
18 Pittsburgh Pirates/35 20.00
19 Chicago Cubs/35 40.00
20 Minnesota Twins/Retro/35 30.00

Team Six

NM/M

Common Card: 1.50
Production 100 Sets
Spectrum: 1-1.5X
Production 50 Sets
1 San Francisco Giants 8.00
2 Houston Astros 6.00
3 Cincinnati Reds 5.00
4 St. Louis Cardinals 8.00
5 New York Yankees 10.00
6 Chicago Cubs 6.00
7 Arizona Diamondbacks 1.50
8 Los Angeles Dodgers 6.00
9 Anaheim Angels 4.00
10 Boston Red Sox 8.00
11 Seattle Mariners 8.00
12 Chicago White Sox 4.00
13 Philadelphia Phillies 10.00
14 New York Mets 10.00
15 Atlanta Braves 4.00

Team Six Swatch Single

NM/M

Production 15-50
1 San Francisco Giants/50 80.00
2 Houston Astros/50 40.00
5 New York Yankees/50 60.00
6 Chicago Cubs/50 40.00
7 Arizona Diamondbacks/50 20.00
8 Los Angeles Dodgers/50 40.00
9 Anaheim Angeles/50 30.00
10 Boston Red Sox/50 50.00
12 Chicago White Sox/50 30.00
13 Philadelphia Phillies/50 40.00
14 New York Mets/50 40.00
15 Atlanta Braves/50 40.00

Team Six Swatch Single Spectrum

NM/M

Production 5-25
Prime Black: No Pricing
Production Five Sets
1 San Francisco Giants/25 100.00
2 Houston Astros/25 50.00
5 New York Yankees/25 75.00
6 Chicago Cubs/25 50.00
7 Arizona Diamondbacks/25 25.00
8 Los Angeles Dodgers/25 50.00
10 Boston Red Sox/25 65.00
12 Chicago White Sox/25 40.00
13 Philadelphia Phillies/25 50.00
14 New York Mets/25 50.00
15 Atlanta Braves/25 50.00

Team Tandems

NM/M

Common Card: 1.50
Production 250 Sets
Spectrum: .75-1.5X
Production 150 Sets
1 Mark Prior, Kerry Wood 2.00
2 Barry Zito, Tim Hudson 1.50
3 Curt Schilling, Pedro Martinez 2.50
4 Will Clark, Matt Williams 2.00
5 Bernie Williams, Jason Giambi 2.00
6 Vernon Wells, Roy Halladay 1.50
7 Josh Beckett, A.J. Burnett 1.50
8 Dale Murphy, Phil Niekro 2.00
9 Mike Schmidt, Steve Carlton 5.00
10 Tony Oliva, Harmon Killebrew 2.00
11 Robin Yount, Paul Molitor 2.50
12 Francisco Rodriguez, Troy Percival 1.50
13 Ben Sheets, Danny Kolb 1.50
14 Andruw Jones, Rafael Furcal 1.50
15 Todd Helton, Preston Wilson 1.50
16 Wade Boggs, Fred McGriff 2.00
17 Manny Ramirez, David Ortiz 2.50
18 Miguel Cabrera, Dontrelle Willis 2.00
19 Edgar Renteria, Scott Rolen 2.00
20 Carlos Beltran, Jeff Kent 2.00
21 Eric Davis, Deion Sanders 2.00
22 Frank Thomas, Paul Konerko 2.00
23 Mike Piazza, Al Leiter 3.00
24 Sean Burroughs, Ryan Klesko 1.50
25 Ken Harvey, Mike Sweeney 1.50
26 David Sanders, Hideki Matsui 4.00
27 Steve Carlton, Mark Buehrle 2.00
28 Gaylord Perry, Randy Johnson 2.00
29 Joe Morgan, Steve Carlton 2.00
30 Vladimir Guerrero, Orlando Cabrera 2.00
31 Scott Rolen, John Kruk 2.00
32 Aaron Boone, Dmitri Young 1.50
33 Rickey Henderson, Vladimir Guerrero 2.00
34 Charles Johnson, Cliff Floyd 1.50
35 Cal Ripken Jr., Rafael Palmeiro 8.00

Team Tandems Swatch Double

NM/M

Production 1-125
Spectrum: 1-2X
Production 1-50
No pricing 20 or less.
1 Mark Prior, Kerry Wood/125 8.00
2 Barry Zito, Tim Hudson/125 8.00
3 Curt Schilling, Pedro Martinez/125 15.00
5 Bernie Williams, Jason Giambi/125 10.00
7 Josh Beckett, A.J. Burnett/125 8.00
8 Dale Murphy, Phil Niekro/125 20.00
10 Tony Oliva, Harmon Killebrew/50 30.00
11 Robin Yount, Paul Molitor/125 20.00
14 Andruw Jones, Rafael Furcal/125 8.00
15 Todd Helton, Preston Wilson/125 10.00
16 Wade Boggs, Fred McGriff/125 15.00
17 Manny Ramirez, David Ortiz/125 15.00
18 Miguel Cabrera, Dontrelle Willis/125 12.00
20 Carlos Beltran, Jeff Kent/50 12.00
21 Eric Davis, Deion Sanders/25 15.00
22 Frank Thomas, Paul Konerko/50 15.00
23 Mike Piazza, Al Leiter/125 20.00
24 Sean Burroughs, Ryan Klesko/50 10.00
26 Deion Sanders, Hideki Matsui/125 35.00
27 Steve Carlton, Mark Buehrle/50 12.00

29	Joe Morgan, Steve Carlton/25	15.00
33	Rickey Henderson, Vladimir Guerrero/50	15.00
34	Charles Johnson, Cliff Floyd/25	8.00
35	Cal Ripken Jr., Rafael Palmeiro/125	40.00

Team Tandems Swatch Single

NM/M

Production 10-125

1	Mark Prior, Kerry Wood/125	6.00
2	Barry Zito, Tim Hudson/125	5.00
3	Curt Schilling, Pedro Martinez/125	8.00
4	Will Clark, Matt Williams/125	8.00
5	Bernie Williams, Jason Giambi/125	8.00
6	Vernon Wells, Roy Halladay/125	5.00
7	Josh Beckett, A.J. Burnett/125	5.00
8	Dale Murphy, Phil Niekro/125	15.00
9	Mike Schmidt, Steve Carlton/125	15.00
10	Tony Oliva, Harmon Killebrew/50	15.00
11	Robin Yount, Paul Molitor/125	15.00
12	Felix Rodriguez, Troy Percival/25	10.00
13	Ben Sheets, Danny Kolb/125	5.00
14	Andruw Jones, Rafael Furcal/125	5.00
15	Todd Helton, Preston Wilson/125	5.00
16	Wade Boggs, Fred McGriff/50	10.00
17	Manny Ramirez, David Ortiz/125	12.00
18	Miguel Cabrera, Dontrelle Willis/125	10.00
19	Edgar Renteria, Scott Rolen/125	10.00
20	Carlos Beltran, Jeff Kent Bat/125	8.00
21	Eric Davis Bat, Deion Sanders/125	8.00
22	Frank Thomas, Paul Konerko/50	10.00
23	Mike Piazza, Al Leiter/125	12.00
24	Sean Burroughs, Ryan Klesko/125	5.00
25	Ken Harvey, Mike Sweeney/125	5.00
26	Deion Sanders, Hideki Matsui/125	25.00
27	Steve Carlton, Mark Buehrle/50	8.00
28	Gaylord Perry, Randy Johnson/125	10.00
29	Joe Morgan, Steve Carlton/25	10.00
31	Scott Rolen, John Kruk/125	10.00
32	Aaron Boone, Dmitri Young/125	5.00
33	Rickey Henderson Hat, Vladimir Guerrero/25	15.00
34	Charles Johnson, Cliff Floyd/25	5.00
35	Cal Ripken Jr., Rafael Palmeiro/125	25.00

Team Tandems Swatch Single Spectrum

NM/M

Production 1-75

1	Mark Prior, Kerry Wood/75	6.00
2	Barry Zito, Tim Hudson/75	5.00
3	Curt Schilling, Pedro Martinez/75	10.00
4	Will Clark, M. Williams/75	8.00
5	Bernie Williams, Jason Giambi/75	5.00
6	Vernon Wells, Roy Halladay/75	5.00
7	Josh Beckett, A.J. Burnett/75	5.00
8	Dale Murphy, Phil Niekro/75	10.00
11	Robin Yount, Paul Molitor/75	15.00
13	Ben Sheets, Danny Kolb/75	5.00
14	Andruw Jones, Rafael Furcal/75	5.00
15	Todd Helton, Preston Wilson/75	5.00
17	Manny Ramirez, David Ortiz/75	10.00
18	Miguel Cabrera, Dontrelle Willis/75	8.00
19	Edgar Renteria, Scott Rolen/75	
20	Carlos Beltran, Jeff Kent Bat/75	8.00
21	Eric Davis Bat, Deion Sanders/75	8.00
23	Mike Piazza, Al Leiter/75	10.00
24	Sean Burroughs, Ryan Klesko/75	5.00
25	Ken Harvey, Mike Sweeney/75	5.00
26	Deion Sanders, Hideki Matsui/75	25.00
28	Gaylord Perry, Randy Johnson/75	8.00
31	Scott Rolen, John Kruk/75	8.00
32	Aaron Boone, D. Young/75	5.00
34	Charles Johnson, Cliff Floyd/75	5.00
35	Cal Ripken Jr., Rafael Palmeiro/75	25.00

Team Trios

NM/M

Common Card:
Production 200 Sets
Spectrum: ... 1X
Production 125 Sets

1	Cal Ripken Jr., Jim Palmer, Eddie Murray	10.00
2	Roger Clemens, Wade Boggs, Evans	5.00
3	Rafael Palmeiro, Miguel Tejada, Javy Lopez	2.00
4	Carl Crawford, Rocco Baldelli, B.J. Upton	1.50
5	Mark Buehrle, Magglio Ordonez, Carlos Lee	1.50
6	Victor Martinez, Travis Hafner, Jody Gerut	1.50
7	Bobby Abreu, Brett Myers, Kevin Millwood	1.50
8	Sammy Sosa, Aramis Ramirez, Carlos Zambrano	3.00
9	Bo, George Brett, Carlos Beltran	5.00
10	Hideo Nomo, Adrian Beltre, Shawn Green	2.00
11	Wilson, Wilson, Jason Bay	1.50
12	Tom Seaver, Nolan Ryan, Dwight Gooden	8.00
13	David Dellucci, Laynce Nix, Kevin Mench	1.50
14	Alan Trammell, Morris, Gibson	2.00
15	M. Will, Grace, Randy Johnson	2.00
16	Dawson, Gary Carter, Tony Perez	2.00
17	Dale Murphy, John Kruk, Lenny Dykstra	2.00
18	B. Roberts, Ian Gibb, Larry Bigbie	1.50
19	Mike Lowell, Ivan Rodriguez, Brad Penny	2.00
20	Murray, Darryl Strawberry, Oliver	2.00
21	Darryl Strawberry, Rickey Henderson, Gary Sheffield	2.00
22	Roberto Alomar, Joe Crede, Durham	2.00
23	Jason Kendall, Giles, Aramis Ramirez	1.50
24	Delmon, Aubrey Huff, Tino	2.00
25	Jeff Bagwell, Cruz, Joe Morgan	2.00
26	Snow, Rich Aurilia, Jeff Kent	1.50
27	Jenkins, Nolan Ryan, Cordero	8.00
28	Lofton, Jim Thome, Roberto Alomar	3.00
29	Atkins, Todd Helton, Jennings	2.00
30	Gary Carter, Pedro, Randy Johnson	2.50

Team Trios Swatch Double

NM/M

Production 25-100
Spectrum: 75-1.5X
Production 5-35
No pricing production 20 or less.
Prime Black: ... No Pricing
Production 5-10

1	Cal Ripken Jr., Jim Palmer, Murray/100	75.00
2	Roger Clemens, Wade Boggs, Evans/100	50.00
3	Rafael Palmeiro, Miguel Tejada, Javy Lopez/50	25.00
5	Mark Buehrle, Magglio Ordonez, Carlos Lee/100	15.00
6	Victor Martinez, Travis Hafner, Jody Gerut/50	20.00
9	Bo, George Brett, Carlos Beltran/100	40.00
10	Hideo Nomo, Adrian Beltre, Shawn Green/100	25.00
11	Wilson, Wilson, Jason Bay/50	15.00
12	Tom Seaver, Nolan Ryan, Dwight Gooden/100	50.00
14	Alan Trammell, Morris, Gibson/50	30.00
15	M. Will, Mark Grace, Randy Johnson/50	30.00
16	Dawson, Gary Carter, Tony Perez/100	20.00
19	Mike Lowell, Ivan Rodriguez, Brad Penny/50	25.00
20	Murray, Darryl Strawberry, Oliver/100	30.00
21	Darryl Strawberry, Rickey Henderson, Gary Sheffield/100	25.00
22	Roberto Alomar, Joe Crede, Durham/100	20.00
28	Lofton, Jim Thome, Roberto Alomar/25	40.00
29	Atkins, Todd Helton, Jennings/100	20.00
30	Gary Carter, Pedro, Randy Johnson/50	30.00

Team Trios Swatch Single

NM/M

Production 50 unless noted.

1	Cal Ripken Jr., Jim Palmer, Murray	40.00
2	Roger Clemens, Wade Boggs, Evans	25.00
3	Rafael Palmeiro, Miguel Tejada, Javy Lopez	12.00
4	Carl Crawford, Rocco Baldelli, B.J. Upton	10.00
5	Mark Buehrle, Magglio Ordonez, Carlos Lee	10.00
6	Victor Martinez, Travis Hafner, Jody Gerut	10.00
7	Bobby Abreu, Brett Myers, Kevin Millwood	10.00
8	Sammy Sosa, Aramis Ramirez, Carlos Zambrano	15.00
9	Bo, George Brett, Carlos Beltran	30.00
10	Hideo Nomo, Adrian Beltre, Shawn Green	15.00
11	Wilson, Wilson, Jason Bay	10.00
12	Tom Seaver, Nolan Ryan, Dwight Gooden	35.00
13	David Dellucci, Laynce Nix, Kevin Mench	8.00
14	Alan Trammell, Morris, Gibson	15.00
15	M. Will, Grace, Randy Johnson	15.00
16	Dawson, Gary Carter, Tony Perez	10.00
17	Dale Murphy, Tomas Kurka, Lenny Dykstra	20.00
18	Roberts, Ian Gibb, Larry Bigbie	15.00
19	Mike Lowell, Ivan Rodriguez, Brad Penny	10.00
20	Murray, Darryl Strawberry, Oliver	20.00
21	Darryl Strawberry, Rickey Henderson, Gary Sheffield	15.00
22	Roberto Alomar, Joe Crede, Durham	10.00
23	Jason Kendall, Giles, Aramis Ramirez	10.00
24	Delmon, Aubrey Huff, Tino	10.00
25	Jeff Bagwell, Cruz, Joe Morgan	12.00
26	Snow, Rich Aurilia, Jeff Kent	8.00
27	Jenkins, Nolan Ryan, Cordero	25.00
28	Lofton, Jim Thome, Roberto Alomar	20.00
29	Atkins, Todd Helton, Jennings	15.00
30	Gary Carter, Pedro, Randy Johnson	15.00

Team Trios Swatch Single Spectrum

NM/M

Production 10-50
Prime Black: ... No Pricing
Production 10 Sets

1	Cal Ripken Jr., Jim Palmer, Murray/50	40.00
2	Roger Clemens, Wade Boggs, Evans/50	30.00
4	Carl Crawford, Rocco Baldelli, B.J. Upton/50	10.00
5	Mark Buehrle, Magglio Ordonez, Carlos Lee/50	10.00
7	Bobby Abreu, Brett Myers, Kevin Millwood/50	15.00
8	Sammy Sosa, Aramis Ramirez, Carlos Zambrano/50	15.00
9	Bo, George Brett, Carlos Beltran/50	25.00
10	Hideo Nomo, Adrian Beltre, Shawn Green/50	15.00
11	Wilson, Wilson, Jason Bay/50	8.00
12	Tom Seaver, Nolan Ryan, Dwight Gooden/50	30.00
13	David Dellucci, Laynce Nix, Kevin Mench/50	10.00
14	Alan Trammell, Morris, Gibson/50	15.00
16	Dawson, Gary Carter, Tony Perez/50	10.00
17	Dale Murphy, Tomas Kurka, Lenny Dykstra/50	15.00
18	Roberts, Ian Gibb, Larry Bigbie/50	10.00
19	Mike Lowell, Ivan Rodriguez, Brad Penny/25	10.00
20	Murray, Darryl Strawberry, Oliver/50	20.00
21	Darryl Strawberry, Rickey Henderson, Gary Sheffield/50	15.00
22	Roberto Alomar, Joe Crede, Durham/50	10.00
24	Delmon, Aubrey Huff, Tino/50	10.00
25	Jeff Bagwell, Cruz, Joe Morgan/50	10.00
26	Snow, Rich Aurilia, Jeff Kent/50	8.00
27	Jenkins, Nolan Ryan, Cordero/50	25.00
28	Lofton, Jim Thome, Roberto Alomar/50	10.00
29	Atkins, Todd Helton, Jennings/50	10.00
30	Gary Carter, Pedro, Randy Johnson/50	15.00

Tools of Trade Autograph Swatch Double

NM/M

Production 1-75
Prime Red: 75-1.5X
Production 1-50
No pricing production 20 or less.
Prime Black: ... No Pricing
Production One Set

1	Ozzie Smith B-P/25	50.00
3	Dale Murphy J-J/50	30.00
4	Paul Molitor J-P/25	40.00
20	Lou Brock B-JK/50	40.00
22	Paul LoDuca B-J/25	25.00
36	Sean Casey J-P/50	20.00
37	Juan Gonzalez J-P/25	30.00
39	Darryl Strawberry B-J/50	25.00
41	Tom Seaver J-P/25	40.00
48	Torii Hunter B-J/40	25.00
56	Brad Penny FG-J/75	10.00
57	Gary Carter J-P/25	30.00
62	Andre Dawson B-J/50	25.00
64	Adrian Beltre B-J/50	25.00
66	Juan Gonzalez B-J/25	30.00
70	Andre Dawson B-J-P/50	25.00
73	Cal Ripken Jr. J-P/25	160.00
88	Magglio Ordonez B-S/25	20.00
91	Gary Carter B-J/25	30.00
96	Bobby Doerr B-P/50	25.00
98	Eric Chavez B-J/25	25.00
100	Harmon Killebrew H-J/25	50.00

Tools of Trade Autograph Swatch Double Reverse

NM/M

Production 1-75

20	Lou Brock B-JK/50	40.00
36	Sean Casey J-P/50	25.00
39	Darryl Strawberry B-J/75	20.00
48	Torii Hunter B-J/50	25.00
56	Brad Penny FG-J/50	12.00
62	Andre Dawson B-J/25	30.00
64	Adrian Beltre B-J/50	20.00
66	Juan Gonzalez B-J/25	30.00
70	Andre Dawson J-P/25	30.00

Tools of Trade Autograph Swatch Quad

NM/M

Production 1-25
Prime Red: ... No Pricing
Production 1-5

3	Dale Murphy/25	60.00
20	Lou Brock/25	80.00
23	Don Mattingly/25	120.00
36	Sean Casey/25	40.00
39	Darryl Strawberry/25	40.00
41	Tom Seaver/25	75.00
42	Mike Schmidt/25	100.00
56	Brad Penny/25	20.00
57	Gary Carter/25	40.00
73	Cal Ripken Jr./25	200.00
78	Tony Gwynn/25	75.00
88	Magglio Ordonez/25	30.00
91	Gary Carter/25	40.00
100	Harmon Killebrew/25	80.00

Tools of Trade Autograph Swatch Quad Reverse

No Pricing
Production 1-15

Tools of Trade Autograph Swatch Triple

NM/M

Production 1-75
Prime Red: ... No Pricing
Production 1-25
Prime Black: ... No Pricing

Production One Set
2 Carlos Beltran/25 40.00
3 Dale Murphy/25 50.00
18 Darryl Strawberry/75 20.00
20 Lou Brock/50 40.00
36 Sean Casey/75 20.00
37 Juan Gonzalez/75 25.00
39 Darryl Strawberry/75 20.00
56 Brad Penny/25 20.00
57 Gary Carter/25 30.00
64 Adrian Beltre/25 25.00
66 Juan Gonzalez/50 25.00
70 Andre Dawson/75 25.00
73 Cal Ripken Jr./25 200.00
82 Carlos Beltran/25 40.00
91 Gary Carter/25 30.00
96 Bobby Doerr/25 30.00
100 Harmon Killebrew/25 60.00

Tools of Trade Autograph Swatch Triple Reverse

NM/M

Production 1-50
18 Darryl Strawberry/50 25.00
36 Sean Casey/25 25.00
37 Juan Gonzalez/25 30.00
39 Darryl Strawberry/50 25.00
70 Andre Dawson/50 25.00

Laundry Tag Prime Red

No Pricing
Production One Set

Tools of the Trade Red

NM/M

Common Player:
Production 250 Sets
Black: 1-1.5X
Production 100 Sets
Blue: 1-1.5X
Production 150 Sets
Rev. Spectrum Red: 1-2X
Production 50 Sets
Rev. Spectrum Blue: No Pricing
Production 10 Sets
1 Ozzie Smith 5.00
2 Carlos Beltran 2.00
3 Dale Murphy 2.00
4 Paul Molitor 2.00
5 George Brett 6.00
6 Stan Musial 5.00
7 Ivan Rodriguez 2.00
8 Carl Yastrzemski 4.00
9 Reggie Jackson 2.00
10 Hideo Nomo 2.00
11 Gary Sheffield 2.00
12 Roberto Alomar 2.00
13 Pedro Martinez 3.00
14 Ernie Banks 3.00
15 Tim Hudson 1.50
16 Dwight Gooden 1.50
17 Lance Berkman 1.50
18 Darryl Strawberry 1.50
19 Larry Walker 1.50
20 Lou Brock 2.00
21 Roger Clemens 6.00
22 Paul LoDuca 1.50
23 Don Mattingly 6.00
24 Willie Mays 6.00
25 Rafael Palmeiro 2.00
26 Roy Oswalt 1.50
27 Vladimir Guerrero 3.00
28 Austin Kearns 1.50
29 Rod Carew 2.00
30 Nolan Ryan 8.00
31 Richie Sexson 2.00
32 Steve Carlton 2.00
33 Eddie Murray 3.00
34 Nolan Ryan 8.00
35 Mike Mussina 2.00
36 Sean Casey 1.50
37 Juan Gonzalez 1.50
38 Curt Schilling 2.00
39 Darryl Strawberry 1.50
40 Alfonso Soriano 3.00
41 Tom Seaver 3.00
42 Mike Schmidt 5.00
43 Todd Helton 2.00
44 Reggie Jackson 2.00
45 Shawn Green 1.50
46 Mike Mussina 2.00
47 Tom Glavine 1.50
48 Torii Hunter 1.50
49 Kerry Wood 2.00
50 Carlos Delgado 2.00
51 Randy Johnson 3.00
52 David Ortiz 3.00
53 Troy Glaus 2.00
54 Rickey Henderson 2.00
55 Craig Biggio 2.00
56 Brad Penny 1.50
57 Gary Carter 2.00
58 Andy Pettitte 1.50
59 Mark Prior 2.00
60 Kirby Puckett 3.00
61 Willie McCovey 3.00
62 Andre Dawson 2.00
63 Greg Maddux 4.00
64 Adrian Beltre 1.50
65 Andruw Jones 2.00
66 Juan Gonzalez 1.50
67 Frank Thomas 2.00
68 Victor Martinez 1.50
69 Randy Johnson 3.00
70 Andre Dawson 2.00
71 Adam Dunn 2.00
72 Carlton Fisk 2.00
73 Cal Ripken Jr. 8.00
74 Kenny Lofton 1.50
75 Barry Zito 1.50
76 Sammy Sosa 4.00
77 Deion Sanders 2.00
78 Tony Gwynn 3.00
79 Mike Piazza 4.00
80 Jeff Bagwell 2.00
81 Manny Ramirez 3.00
82 Carlos Beltran 2.00
83 Mark Grace 2.00
84 Robin Yount 4.00
85 Albert Pujols 6.00
86 Dontrelle Willis 2.00
87 Jim Thome 2.00
88 Magglio Ordonez 1.50
89 Miguel Tejada 2.00
90 Mark Teixeira 2.00
91 Gary Carter 2.00
92 Ivan Rodriguez 2.00
93 Jason Giambi 1.50
94 Rickey Henderson 2.00
95 Curt Schilling 2.00
96 Bobby Doerr 2.00
97 Chipper Jones 3.00
98 Eric Chavez 1.50
99 Johnny Bench 4.00
100 Harmon Killebrew 3.00

Tools of the Trade Swatch Double

NM/M

Production 1-150
Prime Red: No Pricing
Production 1-25
Prime Black: No Pricing
Production 1-25
1 Ozzie Smith B-P/50 15.00
2 Carlos Beltran J-S/50 8.00
3 Dale Murphy J-J/50 8.00
4 Paul Molitor J-P/150 8.00
5 George Brett B-H/25 25.00
6 Stan Musial B-P/25 30.00
7 Ivan Rodriguez J-J/150 8.00
8 Carl Yastrzemski B-J/25 30.00
9 Reggie Jackson J-J/50 10.00
10 Hideo Nomo J-P/150 10.00
11 Gary Sheffield H-J/25 8.00
12 Roberto Alomar B-J/150 8.00
13 Pedro Martinez J-P/150 8.00
15 Tim Hudson H-J/100 5.00
17 Lance Berkman B-J/150 5.00
19 Larry Walker J-J/150 5.00
20 Lou Brock B-JK/150 10.00
21 Roger Clemens B-J/150 15.00
22 Paul LoDuca B-J/50 5.00
23 Don Mattingly BG-P/50 20.00
24 Willie Mays B-P/25 50.00
25 Rafael Palmeiro B-J/150 8.00
27 Vladimir Guerrero B-J/150 8.00
29 Rod Carew JK-JK/150 8.00
30 Nolan Ryan B-JK/150 25.00
31 Richie Sexson H-J/150 8.00
32 Steve Carlton B-H/150 8.00
33 Eddie Murray B-J/150 10.00
34 Nolan Ryan B-J/150 25.00
35 Mike Mussina J-P/125 8.00
36 Sean Casey J-P/150 5.00
38 Curt Schilling J-J/150 8.00
39 Darryl Strawberry B-J/150 5.00
41 Tom Seaver J-P/150 10.00
42 Mike Schmidt B-J/150 15.00
43 Todd Helton B-J/150 8.00
45 Shawn Green B-J/150 5.00
47 Tom Glavine B-J/150 5.00
49 Kerry Wood FG-J/150 8.00
50 Carlos Delgado B-J/100 5.00
51 R. John J-P/150 8.00
52 David Ortiz B-J/150 8.00
53 Troy Glaus J-J/150 5.00
54 Rickey Henderson B-J/150 8.00
55 Craig Biggio B-J/150 5.00
56 Brad Penny FG-J/150 5.00
57 Gary Carter J-P/150 8.00
58 Andy Pettitte J-J/150 5.00
59 Mark Prior FG-J/150 5.00
60 Kirby Puckett B-FG/100 10.00
61 Willie McCovey J-P/150 10.00
63 Greg Maddux B-J/50 15.00
64 Adrian Beltre B-J/150 5.00
65 Andruw Jones B-J/150 8.00
67 Frank Thomas J-J/150 8.00
68 Victor Martinez CP-J/150 5.00
69 R. John J-P/150 8.00
71 Adam Dunn B-J/95 8.00
72 Carlton Fisk B-J/150 8.00
73 Cal Ripken Jr. J-P/150 25.00
74 Kenny Lofton B-H/150 5.00
75 Barry Zito J-J/150 5.00
76 Sammy Sosa B-J/150 10.00
77 Deion Sanders J-P/150 10.00
78 Tony Gwynn J-P/150 10.00
79 Mike Piazza J-P/150 10.00
80 Jeff Bagwell J-P/150 8.00
81 Manny Ramirez B-J/150 8.00
83 Mark Grace B-J/50 8.00
84 Robin Yount B-J/150 12.00
85 Albert Pujols B-J/150 20.00
86 Dontrelle Willis B-J/150 8.00
88 Magglio Ordonez B-S/150 5.00
89 Miguel Tejada H-J/150 8.00
90 Mark Teixeira FG-J/150 8.00
91 Gary Carter B-J/25 10.00
92 Ivan Rodriguez CP-J/150 8.00
93 Jason Giambi H-J/50 5.00
94 Rickey Henderson B-P/150 8.00
95 Curt Schilling J-J/150 8.00
96 Bobby Doerr B-P/150 8.00
97 Chipper Jones B-J/150 8.00
99 Johnny Bench B-P/150 10.00
100 Harmon Killebrew H-J/50 10.00

Tools of the Trade Swatch Five

NM/M

Production 1-50
Prime Red: No Pricing
Production 1-10
Prime Black: No Pricing
Production One Set
Reverse: No Pricing
Production 1-15
4 Paul Molitor/25 35.00
7 Ivan Rodriguez/25 25.00
12 Roberto Alomar/25 20.00
13 Pedro Martinez/25 30.00
15 Tim Hudson/25 25.00
17 Lance Berkman/25 20.00
22 Paul LoDuca/50 15.00
23 Don Mattingly/25 65.00
25 Rafael Palmeiro/25 25.00
26 Roy Oswalt/25 20.00
28 Austin Kearns/25 20.00
29 Rod Carew/25 40.00
31 Richie Sexson/50 15.00
33 Eddie Murray/25 50.00
36 Sean Casey/25 20.00
42 Mike Schmidt/25 70.00
43 Todd Helton/25 25.00
52 David Ortiz/50 35.00
53 Troy Glaus/25 20.00
54 Rickey Henderson/50 25.00
55 Craig Biggio/50 25.00
56 Brad Penny/45 15.00
57 Gary Carter/40 25.00
58 Andy Pettitte/25 25.00
59 Mark Prior/25 25.00
60 Kirby Puckett/25 50.00
64 Adrian Beltre/50 20.00
65 Andruw Jones/25 20.00
67 Frank Thomas/25 25.00
68 Victor Martinez/25 20.00
73 Cal Ripken Jr./50 75.00
76 Sammy Sosa/25 35.00
78 Tony Gwynn/50 40.00
79 Mike Piazza/25 50.00
80 Jeff Bagwell/25 25.00
82 Carlos Beltran/20 25.00
84 Robin Yount/25 40.00
88 Magglio Ordonez/25 20.00
89 Miguel Tejada/50 25.00
90 Mark Teixeira/50 20.00
91 Gary Carter/25 25.00
92 Ivan Rodriguez/25 25.00
94 Rickey Henderson/50 25.00
95 Curt Schilling/50 25.00

Tools of the Trade Swatch Quad

NM/M

Production 1-100
Prime Red: No Pricing
Production 1-10
Prime Black: No Pricing
Production One Set
3 Dale Murphy/50 20.00
4 Paul Molitor/25 30.00
7 Ivan Rodriguez/50 15.00
8 Carl Yastrzemski/25 50.00
9 Reggie Jackson/100 20.00
10 Hideo Nomo/75 15.00
11 Gary Sheffield/30 15.00
12 Roberto Alomar/50 15.00
13 Pedro Martinez/50 20.00
14 Ernie Banks/25 40.00
15 Tim Hudson/50 10.00
17 Lance Berkman/65 10.00
19 Larry Walker/100 10.00
20 Lou Brock/50 20.00
21 Roger Clemens/25 40.00
22 Paul LoDuca/100 10.00
23 Don Mattingly/50 40.00
24 Willie Mays/25 80.00
25 Rafael Palmeiro/100 10.00
26 Roy Oswalt/30 15.00
27 Vladimir Guerrero/50 20.00
29 Rod Carew/75 15.00
31 Richie Sexson/100 10.00
33 Eddie Murray/100 15.00
36 Sean Casey/75 10.00
39 Darryl Strawberry/50 15.00
41 Tom Seaver/35 25.00
42 Mike Schmidt/50 40.00
43 Todd Helton/100 12.00
45 Shawn Green/100 10.00
46 Mike Mussina/25 20.00
50 Carlos Delgado/50 10.00
52 David Ortiz/90 30.00
53 Troy Glaus/50 12.00
54 Rickey Henderson/100 25.00
55 Craig Biggio/100 10.00
56 Brad Penny/25 15.00
57 Gary Carter/50 15.00
58 Andy Pettitte/50 15.00
59 Mark Prior/50 15.00
60 Kirby Puckett/50 25.00
64 Adrian Beltre/50 10.00
65 Andruw Jones/100 10.00
66 Juan Gonzalez/30 20.00
67 Frank Thomas/50 25.00
68 Victor Martinez/50 10.00
70 Andre Dawson/25 15.00
72 Carlton Fisk/25 25.00
73 Cal Ripken Jr./100 50.00
74 Kenny Lofton/100 10.00
75 Barry Zito/50 10.00
76 Sammy Sosa/100 15.00
78 Tony Gwynn/100 20.00
79 Mike Piazza/100 20.00
80 Jeff Bagwell/100 10.00
83 Mark Grace/50 20.00
85 Albert Pujols/50 60.00
86 Dontrelle Willis/50 15.00
88 Magglio Ordonez/50 10.00
89 Miguel Tejada/100 15.00
90 Mark Teixeira/100 15.00
91 Gary Carter/90 15.00
92 Ivan Rodriguez/50 15.00
93 Jason Giambi/25 15.00
94 Rickey Henderson/100 15.00
95 Curt Schilling/100 15.00
100 Harmon Killebrew/25 40.00

Swatch Single Jumbo

NM/M

Production 1-100
Prime Red: No Pricing
Production 1-25
Reverse: 1-2X
Production 1-50
Prime Black: No Pricing
Production One Set
1 Ozzie Smith/25 30.00
2 Carlos Beltran/Jsy/50 10.00
3 Dale Murphy/Jsy/25 20.00
4 Paul Molitor/Jsy/25 25.00
6 Stan Musial/Pants/25 50.00
7 Ivan Rodriguez/Jsy/100 10.00
10 Hideo Nomo/Jsy/100 15.00
11 Gary Sheffield/Jsy/25 15.00
12 Roberto Alomar/Jsy/100 10.00
13 Pedro Martinez/Jsy/50 12.00
15 Tim Hudson/Jsy/100 10.00
17 Lance Berkman/Jsy/75 8.00
19 Larry Walker/Jsy/100 10.00
20 Lou Brock/Jkt/50 20.00
21 Roger Clemens/Jsy/50 30.00
23 Don Mattingly/Jsy/25 40.00
25 Rafael Palmeiro/Jsy/100 10.00
27 Vladimir Guerrero/Jsy/50 15.00
29 Rod Carew/Jsy/50 15.00
30 Nolan Ryan/Jsy/25 50.00
31 Richie Sexson/Jsy/100 10.00
33 Eddie Murray/Jsy/50 20.00
35 Mike Mussina/Jsy/50 12.00
36 Sean Casey/Jsy/100 8.00
37 Juan Gonzalez/Jsy/25 15.00
38 Curt Schilling/Jsy/100 15.00
39 Darryl Strawberry/Jsy/50 10.00
41 Tom Seaver/Jsy/50 15.00
42 Mike Schmidt/Jsy/25 40.00
43 Todd Helton/Jsy/50 10.00
45 Shawn Green/Jsy/100 8.00
47 Tom Glavine/Jsy/100 10.00
49 Kerry Wood/Jsy/50 10.00
51 R. John/Jsy/25 20.00
52 David Ortiz/Jsy/75 15.00
53 Troy Glaus/Jsy/100 10.00
54 Rickey Henderson/Jsy/25 15.00
55 Craig Biggio/Jsy/75 10.00
56 Brad Penny/Jsy/100 8.00
57 Gary Carter/Jsy/25 15.00
58 Andy Pettitte/Jsy/50 10.00
59 Mark Prior/Jsy/50 10.00
60 Kirby Puckett/Jsy/50 20.00
61 Willie McCovey/Jsy/50 15.00
63 Greg Maddux/Jsy/100 20.00
65 Andruw Jones/Jsy/100 10.00
68 Victor Martinez/Jsy/50 8.00
70 Andre Dawson/Jsy/50 10.00
72 Carlton Fisk/Jsy/100 10.00
73 Cal Ripken Jr./Jsy/100 35.00
74 Kenny Lofton/Hat/25 10.00
75 Barry Zito/Jsy/100 8.00
76 Sammy Sosa/Jsy/100 15.00
77 Deion Sanders/Jsy/25 20.00
78 Tony Gwynn/Jsy/100 20.00
79 Mike Piazza/Jsy/100 20.00
80 Jeff Bagwell/Jsy/100 10.00
83 Mark Grace/Jsy/50 15.00
84 Robin Yount/Jsy/50 20.00
85 Albert Pujols/Jsy/100 30.00
86 Dontrelle Willis/Jsy/50 10.00
89 Miguel Tejada/Jsy/100 12.00
90 Mark Teixeira/Jsy/25 15.00
92 Ivan Rodriguez/Jsy/100 10.00
93 Jason Giambi/Jsy/25 10.00
94 Rickey Henderson/Jsy/25 15.00
95 Curt Schilling/Jsy/50 10.00
96 Bobby Doerr/Pants/25 20.00
97 Chipper Jones/Jsy/25 20.00
98 Eric Chavez/Jsy/100 8.00
99 Johnny Bench/Jsy/25 25.00
100 Harmon Killebrew/Jsy/25 40.00

Tools of the Trade Swatch Six

NM/M

Production 1-50
Reverse: No Pricing
Production 1-10
Prime Red: No Pricing

Production 1-5
Prime Black: No Pricing
Production One Set

22	Paul LoDuca/50	20.00
31	Richie Sexson/50	20.00
52	David Ortiz/50	40.00
53	Troy Glaus/50	25.00
57	Gary Carter/25	35.00
59	Mark Prior/50	25.00
73	Cal Ripken Jr./50	85.00
76	Sammy Sosa/25	40.00
78	Tony Gwynn/50	40.00
79	Mike Piazza/50	40.00
80	Jeff Bagwell/50	25.00
90	Mark Teixeira/50	25.00
92	Ivan Rodriguez/25	30.00
94	Rickey Henderson/50	30.00

Tools of the Trade Swatch Triple

NM/M

Production 1-25
Prime Red: No Pricing
Production 1-25
Prime Black: No Pricing
Production 1-15

2	Carlos Beltran/25	15.00
3	Dale Murphy/25	15.00
4	Paul Molitor/25	20.00
5	George Brett/25	35.00
6	Stan Musial/25	40.00
7	Ivan Rodriguez/25	10.00
9	Reggie Jackson/25	15.00
10	Hideo Nomo/25	20.00
12	Roberto Alomar/25	10.00
14	Pedro Martinez/25	15.00
15	Tim Hudson/25	10.00
19	Larry Walker/25	10.00
21	Roger Clemens/25	30.00
22	Paul LoDuca/25	10.00
23	Don Mattingly/25	30.00
25	Rafael Palmeiro/25	15.00
27	Vladimir Guerrero/25	15.00
29	Rod Carew/25	15.00
30	Nolan Ryan/25	40.00
31	Richie Sexson/25	10.00
33	Eddie Murray/25	20.00
34	Nolan Ryan/25	40.00
36	Sean Casey/25	10.00
37	Juan Gonzalez/25	15.00
38	Curt Schilling/25	15.00
43	Todd Helton/25	12.00
45	Shawn Green/25	10.00
47	Tom Glavine/25	10.00
49	Kerry Wood/25	15.00
50	Carlos Delgado/25	10.00
51	R. John/25	15.00
52	David Ortiz/25	15.00
53	Troy Glaus/25	10.00
54	Rickey Henderson/25	15.00
55	Craig Biggio/25	12.00
56	Brad Penny/25	10.00
57	Gary Carter/25	15.00
58	Andy Pettitte/25	10.00
59	Mark Prior/25	10.00
60	Kirby Puckett/25	20.00
63	Greg Maddux/25	30.00
64	Adrian Beltre/25	10.00
65	Andruw Jones/25	12.00
67	Frank Thomas/25	15.00
68	Victor Martinez/25	10.00
70	Andre Dawson/25	12.00
72	Carlton Fisk/25	15.00
73	Cal Ripken Jr./25	40.00
74	Kenny Lofton/25	10.00
75	Barry Zito/25	10.00
76	Sammy Sosa/25	15.00
77	Deion Sanders/25	20.00
78	Tony Gwynn/25	20.00
79	Mike Piazza/25	20.00
80	Jeff Bagwell/25	15.00
81	Manny Ramirez/25	15.00
83	Mark Grace/25	15.00
84	Robin Yount/25	20.00
85	Albert Pujols/25	40.00
86	Dontrelle Willis/25	15.00
88	Magglio Ordonez/25	15.00
89	Miguel Tejada/25	15.00
90	Mark Teixeira/25	12.00
91	Gary Carter/25	15.00
92	Ivan Rodriguez/25	15.00
93	Jason Giambi/25	10.00
94	Rickey Henderson/25	15.00
95	Curt Schilling/25	15.00
96	Bobby Doerr/25	15.00
97	Chipper Jones/25	15.00
98	Eric Chavez/25	10.00
99	Johnny Bench/25	20.00
100	Harmon Killebrew/25	30.00

2005 Playoff Prestige

NM/M

Complete Set (200):		35.00
Common Player:		.25
Hobby Pack (8):		3.00
Hobby Box (24):		65.00
1	Rafael Furcal	.25
2	Derek Jeter	2.00
3	Edgar Renteria	.40
4	Jeff Bagwell	.50
5	Nomar Garciaparra	1.25
6	Melvin Mora	.25
7	Craig Biggio	.40
8	Brad Penny	.25
9	Hank Blalock	.50
10	Vernon Wells	.50
11	Gary Sheffield	.50
12	Jeff Kent	.50
13	Carl Crawford	.25
14	Paul Konerko	.50
15	Carlos Beltran	.50
16	Garret Anderson	.40
17	Todd Helton	.50
18	Javy Lopez	.25
19	Mike Lowell	.25
20	Robb Quinlan	.25
21	Andy Pettitte	.40
22	Roger Clemens	2.00
23	Mark Teixeira	.50
24	Miguel Cabrera	.75
25	Andruw Jones	.40
26	Josh Beckett	.40
27	Scott Rolen	.75
28	J.J. Putz	.25
29	Adrian Beltre	.50
30	Magglio Ordonez	.25
31	Mike Piazza	1.00
32	Danny Graves	.25
33	Larry Walker	.40
34	Kerry Wood	.75
35	Mike Mussina	.50
36	Joe Nathan	.25
37	Chone Figgins	.25
38	Curt Schilling	.75
39	Brett Myers	.25
40	Jae Weong Seo	.25
41	Danny Kolb	.25
42	Mariano Rivera	.50
43	Francisco Cordero	.25
44	Adam Dunn	.50
45	Pedro Martinez	.75
46	Frank Thomas	.50
47	Tom Glavine	.40
48	Torii Hunter	.40
49	Ben Sheets	.25
50	Shawn Green	.25
51	Randy Johnson	.75
52	C.C. Sabathia	.25
53	Bobby Abreu	.40
54	Octavio Dotel	.25
55	Hideki Matsui	1.50
56	Mark Buehrle	.25
57	Johan Santana	.50
58	Brandon Inge	.25
59	Dewon Brazelton	.25
60	Ryan Wagner	.25
61	Kevin Brown	.25
62	Laynce Nix	.25
63	Jason Bay	.40
64	J.D. Drew	.40
65	Jacque Jones	.25
66	Jason Schmidt	.25
67	Joe Kennedy	.25
68	Miguel Tejada	.40
69	Hideo Nomo	.40
70	Michael Young	.50
71	Lyle Overbay	.25
72	Omar Vizquel	.25
73	Johnny Estrada	.25
74	Khalil Greene	.40
75	Barry Zito	.25
76	Wilson Valdez	.25
77	Nick Green	.25
78	Bucky Jacobsen	.25
79	Keith Foulke	.25
80	Sean Burroughs	.25
81	Carlos Zambrano	.25
82	Orlando Cabrera	.25
83	Shigetoshi Hasegawa	.25
84	Troy Glaus	.40
85	Mike Sweeney	.25
86	Jason Giambi	.25
87	Derrek Lee	.40
88	Carlos Delgado	.40
89	Kazuo Matsui	.25
90	Lew Ford	.25
91	Akinori Otsuka	.25
92	Bobby Crosby	.25
93	Jose Reyes	.40
94	Jose Vidro	.25
95	Shingo Takatsu	.25
96	Sean Casey	.25
97	Tim Olson	.25
98	Jeff Suppan	.25
99	Rafael Palmeiro	.50
100	Esteban Loaiza	.25
101	Brian Roberts	.25
102	Jack Wilson	.25
103	Eric Chavez	.40
104	Eric Milton	.25
105	Albert Pujols	2.00
106	Jake Peavy	.25
107	Ivan Rodriguez	.50
108	Chad Cordero	.25
109	Jody Gerut	.25
110	Chipper Jones	.75
111	Barry Larkin	.40
112	Alfonso Soriano	.75
113	Alex Rodriguez	1.50
114	Paul LoDuca	.25
115	Jim Edmonds	.40
116	Aramis Ramirez	.40
117	Lance Berkman	.40
118	Johnny Damon	.75
119	Aubrey Huff	.25
120	Mark Mulder	.40
121	Sammy Sosa	1.50
122	Mark Prior	.75
123	Shannon Stewart	.25
124	Manny Ramirez	.75
125	Jim Thome	.75
126	Doug DeVore	.25
127	Vladimir Guerrero	.75
128	Ken Harvey	.25
129	Jacob Cruz	.25
130	Ken Griffey Jr.	1.00
131	Greg Maddux	1.00
132	Derek Lowe	.25
133	Craig Monroe	.25
134	David Ortiz	.75
135	Dontrelle Willis	.40
136	Tom Gordon	.25
137	David Dellucci	.25
138	Vance Wilson	.25
139	Milton Bradley	.25
140	Ichiro Suzuki	1.50
141	Victor Martinez	.40
142	Wade Miller	.25
143	Francisco Rodriguez	.25
144	Roy Oswalt	.40
145	Carlos Lee	.25
146	Kazuhisa Ishii	.25
147	Tim Hudson	.40
148	Travis Hafner	.25
149	Jermaine Dye	.25
150	Steve Finley	.25
151	Justin Verlander **RC**	1.50
152	Yadier Molina	.25
153	Andy Green	.25
154	Nick Swisher	.25
155	Clint Nageotte	.25
156	Grady Sizemore	.50
157	Gavin Floyd	.25
158	Josh Kroeger	.25
159	Russ Adams	.25
160	Jeff Baker	.25
161	Dioner Navarro	.25
162	Shawn Hill	.25
163	Ryan Howard	1.00
164	Scott Proctor	.25
165	Jason Kubel	.25
166	Jose Lopez	.25
167	Ryan Church	.25
168	Yhency Brazoban	.25
169	Jeff Francis	.25
170	Angel Guzman	.25
171	John Van Benschoten	.25
172	Adrian Gonzalez	.25
173	Casey Kotchman	.25
174	David Wright	.75
175	B.J. Upton	.50
176	Dallas McPherson	.25
177	Rene Rivera	.25
178	Denny Bautista	.25
179	Logan Kensing	.25
180	Matt Peterson	.25
181	Jeremy Reed	.25
182	Jairo Garcia	.25
183	Val Majewski	.25
184	Victor Diaz	.25
185	David Krynzel	.25
186	Ron Cey	.25
187	Bill Madlock	.25
188	Dave Stewart	.25
189	Billy Ripken	.25
190	Gary Carter	.50
191	Darryl Strawberry	.25
192	Dave Parker	.25
193	Ron Guidry	.25
194	Gaylord Perry	.25
195	Fred Lynn	.25
196	Jack Morris	.25
197	Steve Garvey	.25
198	Andre Dawson	.50
199	Nolan Ryan	2.50
200	Paul Molitor	.75

Red Foil

Red Foil:	8-15X

Production 25 Sets

Xtra Bases Black

Black:	8-15X

Production 25 Sets

Xtra Bases Green

Green:	5-10X

Production 50 Sets

Xtra Bases Purple

Purple:	4-8X

Production 100 Sets

Xtra Bases Red

Red:	3-6X

Production 150 Sets

Autographs

NM/M

Common Autograph:		8.00
20	Robb Quinlan	8.00
28	J.J. Putz	8.00
58	Brandon Inge/SP	15.00
67	Joe Kennedy	8.00
76	Wilson Valdez	8.00
77	Nick Green	8.00
78	Bucky Jacobsen	10.00
97	Tim Olson	8.00
98	Jeff Suppan/SP	15.00
126	Doug DeVore	8.00
129	Jacob Cruz	8.00
133	Craig Monroe	10.00
138	Vance Wilson	8.00
153	Andy Green	8.00
164	Scott Proctor	8.00

Signature Xtra Bases Purple

NM/M

Production 5-50

6	Melvin Mora/25	25.00
8	Brad Penny/50	10.00
13	Carl Crawford/25	25.00
20	Robb Quinlan/50	8.00
28	J.J. Putz/50	8.00
32	Danny Graves/50	10.00
36	Joe Nathan/50	25.00
37	Chone Figgins/50	10.00
39	Brett Myers/50	10.00
41	Danny Kolb/50	15.00
43	Francisco Cordero/50	10.00
52	C.C. Sabathia/25	25.00
54	Octavio Dotel/50	15.00
56	Mark Buehrle/50	20.00
58	Brandon Inge/50	15.00
59	Dewon Brazelton/50	10.00
60	Ryan Wagner/50	8.00
62	Laynce Nix/50	15.00
63	Jason Bay/50	15.00
65	Jacque Jones/50	20.00
67	Joe Kennedy/50	8.00
71	Lyle Overbay/50	20.00
73	Johnny Estrada/50	15.00
76	Wilson Valdez/50	8.00
77	Nick Green/50	8.00
78	Bucky Jacobsen/50	10.00
79	Keith Foulke/50	35.00
81	Carlos Zambrano/25	35.00
82	Orlando Cabrera/50	20.00
90	Lew Ford/50	15.00
92	Bobby Crosby/50	20.00
97	Tim Olson/50	8.00
98	Jeff Suppan/50	10.00
100	Esteban Loaiza/50	15.00
101	Brian Roberts/50	35.00
102	Jack Wilson/50	8.00
106	Jake Peavy/50	30.00
108	Chad Cordero/50	10.00
109	Jody Gerut/50	10.00
126	Doug DeVore/50	8.00
128	Ken Harvey/50	10.00
129	Jacob Cruz/50	8.00
133	Craig Monroe/50	10.00
136	Tom Gordon/50	15.00
137	David Dellucci/50	20.00
138	Vance Wilson/50	8.00
139	Milton Bradley/50	15.00
141	Victor Martinez/50	30.00
142	Wade Miller/50	15.00

145	Carlos Lee/25	20.00
148	Travis Hafner/50	15.00
149	Jermaine Dye/50	15.00
152	Yadier Molina/25	20.00
153	Andy Green/50	8.00
161	Dioner Navarro/50	12.00
162	Shawn Hill/50	8.00
164	Scott Proctor/50	10.00
165	Jason Kubel/50	15.00
168	Yhency Brazoban/50	10.00
170	Angel Guzman/50	15.00
172	Adrian Gonzalez/50	12.00
173	Casey Kotchman	15.00
187	Bill Madlock/25	20.00
189	Billy Ripken/25	10.00
190	Gary Carter/25	25.00
191	Darryl Strawberry/25	20.00
192	Dave Parker/25	25.00
195	Fred Lynn/25	20.00
196	Jack Morris/25	25.00
198	Andre Dawson/25	25.00

Signature Xtra Bases Black

No Pricing
Production 3-10

Changing Stripes

	NM/M
Complete Set (25):	25.00
Common Player:	.75
Inserted 1:8	
Foil:	2-3X
Production 100 Sets	
Holo-Foil:	3-6X
Production 25 Sets	
1	Ivan Rodriguez	1.00
2	Roger Clemens	4.00
3	Curt Schilling	1.50
4	Alex Rodriguez	4.00
5	Greg Maddux	2.00
6	Juan Gonzalez	.75
7	Pedro Martinez	1.50
8	Roberto Alomar	.75
9	Randy Johnson	1.50
10	Ken Griffey Jr.	2.00
11	Carlos Beltran	1.00
12	Andy Pettitte	1.00
13	Tom Glavine	.75
14	Miguel Tejada	1.50
15	Alfonso Soriano	1.50
16	Shannon Stewart	.75
17	Nomar Garciaparra	2.00
18	Jeff Kent	.75
19	David Ortiz	1.50
20	Sean Casey	.75
21	Rickey Henderson	1.00
22	Carlton Fisk	1.00
23	Phil Niekro	.75
24	Dale Murphy	1.00
25	Reggie Jackson	1.50

Changing Stripes Material Dual Jersey

	NM/M
Production 12-250	
1	Ivan Rodriguez/250	10.00
2	Roger Clemens/250	20.00
3	Curt Schilling/250	12.00
6	Juan Gonzalez/250	8.00
7	Pedro Martinez/100	15.00
8	Roberto Alomar/250	10.00
9	Randy Johnson/100	15.00
11	Carlos Beltran/100	15.00
12	Andy Pettitte/250	10.00
13	Tom Glavine/50	15.00
14	Miguel Tejada/250	10.00
15	Alfonso Soriano/100	10.00
16	Shannon Stewart/100	8.00
19	David Ortiz/100	15.00
20	Sean Casey/50	20.00
21	Rickey Henderson/250	15.00
22	Carlton Fisk/250	15.00
23	Phil Niekro/250	8.00
24	Dale Murphy/250	15.00
25	Reggie Jackson/100	15.00

Connections

	NM/M
Complete Set (25):	40.00
Common Duo:	1.50

Inserted 1:8	
Foil:	2-3X
Production 100 Sets	
Holo-Foil:	3-6X
Production 25 Sets	
1	Josh Beckett, Dontrelle Willis	1.50
2	Andruw Jones, Chipper Jones	2.00
3	Kazuo Matsui, Jose Reyes	1.50
4	Bobby Abreu, Jim Thome	2.00
5	Jeff Bagwell, Lance Berkman	2.00
6	Roger Clemens, Roy Oswalt	4.00
7	Scott Rolen, Larry Walker	2.00
8	Albert Pujols, Jim Edmonds	4.00
9	Greg Maddux, Sammy Sosa	2.50
10	Mark Prior, Nomar Garciaparra	2.00
11	Barry Larkin, Sean Casey	1.50
12	Adrian Beltre, Shawn Green	1.50
13	Alex Rodriguez, Derek Jeter	6.00
14	Manny Ramirez, Jason Varitek	3.00
15	Miguel Tejada, Javy Lopez	2.00
16	B.J. Upton, Carl Crawford	1.50
17	Frank Thomas, Paul Konerko	2.00
18	Joe Mauer, Justin Morneau	2.00
19	Victor Martinez, Jody Gerut	1.50
20	Bobby Crosby, Barry Zito	1.50
21	Mark Teixeira, Hank Blalock	2.00
22	Reggie Jackson, Rod Carew	2.00
23	Rickey Henderson, Tony Gwynn	2.50
24	Tom Seaver, Johnny Bench	3.00
25	Don Mattingly, Dave Righetti	4.00

Connections Material Dual Bat

	NM/M
Production 25-250	
2	Andruw Jones, Chipper Jones/250	10.00
3	Kazuo Matsui, Jose Reyes/100	10.00
4	Bobby Abreu, Jim Thome/100	12.00
5	Jeff Bagwell, Lance Berkman/250	10.00
6	Roger Clemens, Roy Oswalt/250	15.00
10	Mark Prior, Nomar Garciaparra/100	10.00
11	Barry Larkin, Sean Casey/100	10.00
12	Shawn Green, Adrian Beltre/250	5.00
14	Jason Varitek, Manny Ramirez/100	15.00
15	Miguel Tejada, Javy Lopez/100	10.00
17	Frank Thomas, Paul Konerko/100	10.00
19	Victor Martinez, Jody Gerut/25	12.00
21	Mark Teixeira, Hank Blalock/100	10.00
22	Reggie Jackson, Rod Carew/250	10.00
23	Tony Gwynn, Rickey Henderson/250	15.00
24	Tom Seaver, Johnny Bench/250	15.00

Connections Material Dual Jersey

	NM/M
Production 10-250	
Prime:	1-2X
Production 10-25	
No pricing 20 or less.	

1	Josh Beckett, Dontrelle Willis/250	8.00
2	Andruw Jones, Chipper Jones/250	10.00
3	Kazuo Matsui, Jose Reyes/100	10.00
4	Bobby Abreu, Jim Thome/250	10.00
5	Jeff Bagwell, Lance Berkman/250	10.00
6	Roger Clemens, Roy Oswalt/250	15.00
8	Albert Pujols, Jim Edmonds/250	25.00
11	Barry Larkin, Sean Casey/50	15.00
12	Shawn Green, Adrian Beltre/250	8.00
14	Jason Varitek, Manny Ramirez/50	20.00
15	Miguel Tejada, Javy Lopez/50	12.00
17	Frank Thomas/Pants, Paul Konerko/250	10.00
20	Bobby Crosby, Barry Zito/250	10.00
21	Mark Teixeira, Hank Blalock/100	10.00
22	Reggie Jackson, Rod Carew/Jkt/250	12.00
23	Rickey Henderson, Tony Gwynn/250	15.00
24	Tom Seaver, Johnny Bench/Pants/100	15.00
25	Don Mattingly, Dave Righetti/250	20.00

Diamond Heritage

	NM/M
Complete Set (15):	20.00
Common Player:	.75
Inserted 1:12	
1	Pedro Martinez	1.50
2	Mark Teixeira	1.00
3	Lance Berkman	.75
4	Vladimir Guerrero	1.50
5	Albert Pujols	4.00
6	Roger Clemens	4.00
7	Manny Ramirez	1.50
8	Mike Piazza	2.00
9	Jim Thome	1.50
10	Mark Prior	1.00
11	Gary Sheffield	.75
12	Sammy Sosa	2.50
13	Tim Hudson	.75
14	Hideki Matsui	3.00
15	Jim Edmonds	.75

Diamond Heritage Material Bat

	NM/M
Production 100 Sets	
1	Pedro Martinez	10.00
2	Mark Teixeira	10.00
3	Lance Berkman	5.00
4	Vladimir Guerrero	10.00
7	Roger Clemens	15.00
8	Manny Ramirez	10.00
9	Mike Piazza	10.00
10	Jim Thome	10.00
11	Mark Prior	8.00
12	Gary Sheffield	8.00
13	Sammy Sosa	10.00
14	Tim Hudson	5.00
15	Hideki Matsui	25.00
	Jim Edmonds	8.00

Diamond Heritage Material Jersey

	NM/M
Production 100 Sets	
1	Pedro Martinez	10.00
2	Mark Teixeira	10.00
3	Lance Berkman	5.00
4	Vladimir Guerrero	10.00
5	Albert Pujols	25.00
6	Roger Clemens	15.00
7	Manny Ramirez	10.00
8	Mike Piazza	10.00
9	Jim Thome	10.00
10	Mark Prior	8.00
11	Gary Sheffield	8.00
12	Sammy Sosa	10.00
13	Tim Hudson	5.00
14	Hideki Matsui/Pants	10.00
15	Jim Edmonds	8.00

Fans of the Game

	NM/M
Inserted 1:24	
1	Tony Hawk	3.00

2	Tia Carrere	2.00
3	Mathew Modine	2.00

Fans of the Game Signature Gold

	NM/M
Production 100 Sets	
Platinum:	1X
Production 50 Sets	
1	Tony Hawk	75.00
2	Tia Carrere	85.00
3	Mathew Modine	40.00

Fans of the Game Signature Silver

	NM/M
Common Autograph:	40.00
1	Tony Hawk	75.00
2	Tia Carrere	85.00
3	Mathew Modine	40.00

League Leaders Double

	NM/M
Complete Set (5):	15.00
Inserted 1:39	
Foil:	2-3X
Production 100 Sets	
Holo-Foil:	3-6X
Production 25 Sets	
1	Tim Hudson, Roy Oswalt	2.00
2	Ivan Rodriguez, Todd Helton	3.00
3	Mark Teixeira, Jim Edmonds	2.00
4	Nolan Ryan, Roger Clemens	8.00
5	Sammy Sosa, Troy Glaus	3.00

League Leader Double Material Bat

	NM/M
Production 250 Sets	
1	Tim Hudson, Roy Oswalt	8.00
2	Ivan Rodriguez, Todd Helton	15.00
3	Mark Teixeira, Jim Edmonds	10.00
4	Nolan Ryan, Roger Clemens	25.00
5	Sammy Sosa, Troy Glaus	15.00

League Leaders Double Material Jersey

	NM/M
Production 50-250	
1	Tim Hudson, Roy Oswalt/100	10.00
2	Ivan Rodriguez, Todd Helton/50	15.00
3	Mark Teixeira, Jim Edmonds/250	15.00
4	Nolan Ryan, Roger Clemens/250	25.00
5	Sammy Sosa, Troy Glaus/250	15.00

League Leaders Quad

	NM/M
Inserted 1:39	
Foil:	1-2X
Production 100 Sets	
Holo-Foil:	3-5X
Production 25 Sets	
1	Wade Boggs, Paul Molitor, Alan Trammell, Kirby Puckett	4.00
2	Dale Murphy, Mike Schmidt, Gary Carter, Darryl Strawberry	6.00
3	Jose Canseco, Kirby Puckett, Will Clark, Darryl Strawberry	4.00
4	Pedro Martinez, Kevin Brown, Randy Johnson, Roger Clemens	6.00

5 Don Mattingly, Dave Parker, Eddie Murray, Dale Murphy 4.00

League Leaders Quad Material Bat

NM/M
Production 100 Sets
2 Dale Murphy, Mike Schmidt, Gary Carter, Darryl Strawberry 40.00
4 Pedro Martinez, Kevin Brown, Randy Johnson, Roger Clemens 50.00
5 Don Mattingly, Dave Parker, Eddie Murray, Dale Murphy 50.00

League Leaders Quad Material Jersey

NM/M
Production 100 Sets
1 Wade Boggs, Paul Molitor, Alan Trammell, Kirby Puckett 40.00
2 Dale Murphy, Mike Schmidt, Gary Carter, Darryl Strawberry 40.00
3 Jose Canseco, Kirby Puckett, Will Clark, Darryl Strawberry 40.00
4 Pedro Martinez, Kevin Brown, Randy Johnson, Roger Clemens 50.00
5 Don Mattingly, Dave Parker, Eddie Murray, Dale Murphy 50.00

League Leaders Single

NM/M
Complete Set (10): 25.00
Inserted 1:21
Foil: 2-4X
Production 100 Sets
Holo-Foil: 4-8X
Production 25 Sets
1 Gary Sheffield 2.00
2 Ben Sheets 2.00
3 Adrian Beltre 2.00
4 Scott Rolen 3.00
5 George Brett 4.00
6 Johan Santana 3.00
7 Manny Ramirez 3.00
8 Cal Ripken Jr. 8.00
9 Carlos Zambrano 2.00
10 Tony Gwynn 4.00

League Leader Single Material Bat

NM/M
Production 250 Sets
1 Gary Sheffield 8.00
2 Ben Sheets 5.00
3 Adrian Beltre 5.00
5 George Brett 12.00
7 Manny Ramirez 10.00
8 Cal Ripken Jr. 25.00
10 Tony Gwynn 8.00

League Leaders Single Material Jersey

NM/M
Production 25-250
1 Gary Sheffield/250 8.00
2 Ben Sheets/250 5.00
3 Adrian Beltre/50 8.00
4 Scott Rolen/250 8.00
5 George Brett/250 15.00
6 Johan Santana/25 20.00
7 Manny Ramirez/250 8.00
8 Cal Ripken Jr./250 25.00
9 Carlos Zambrano/250 5.00
10 Tony Gwynn/250 8.00

Playoff Champions Combo Wild Card

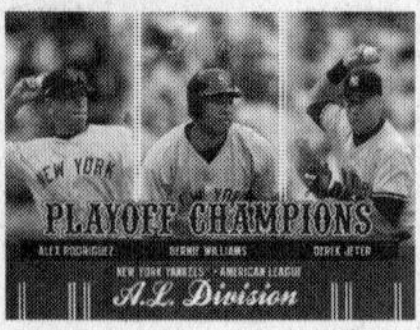

NM/M
Inserted 1:391
Division Combo: .75-1X
League Combo: .75-1X
World Series Combo: .75-1X
Redemption Deadline 4-15-06.
1 Andruw Jones, Johnny Estrada, Chipper Jones 10.00
2 Miguel Cabrera, Josh Beckett, Dontrelle Willis 10.00
3 Chad Cordero, Nick Johnson, Brad Wilkerson 5.00
4 Jim Thome, Bobby Abreu, Chase Utley 10.00
5 Mike Piazza, Kazuo Matsui, David Wright 10.00
6 Albert Pujols, Scott Rolen, Jim Edmonds 15.00
7 Kerry Wood, Mark Prior, Carlos Zambrano 8.00
8 Ben Sheets, Geoff Jenkins, Lyle Overbay 5.00
9 Kip Wells, Jack Wilson, Jason Bay 5.00
10 Austin Kearns, Adam Dunn, Ken Griffey Jr. 10.00
11 Roy Oswalt, Lance Berkman, Jeff Bagwell 10.00
12 Jason Jennings, Matt Holliday, Todd Helton 10.00
13 Eric Gagne, Jayson Werth, Milton Bradley 10.00
14 Alex Cintron, Brandon Webb, Luis Gonzalez 5.00
15 Jason Schmidt, Edgardo Alfonzo, Kirk Rueter 5.00
16 Khalil Greene, Jake Peavy, Trevor Hoffman 10.00
17 Manny Ramirez, Curt Schilling, David Ortiz 15.00
18 Miguel Tejada, Melvin Mora, Javy Lopez 8.00
19 Roy Halladay, Alexis Rios, Gabe Gross 5.00
20 Alex Rodriguez, Derek Jeter, Hideki Matsui 20.00
21 B.J. Upton, Scott Kazmir, Carl Crawford 10.00
22 Frank Thomas, Shingo Takatsu, Aaron Rowand 8.00
23 Victor Martinez, C.C. Sabathia, Travis Hafner 5.00
24 Torii Hunter, Johan Santana, Justin Morneau 10.00
25 Zack Greinke, Mike Sweeney, Ken Harvey 5.00
26 Ivan Rodriguez, Jeremy Bonderman, Carlos Guillen 8.00
27 Rich Harden, Bobby Crosby, Barry Zito 5.00
28 Bret Boone, Ichiro Suzuki, Jeremy Reed 12.00
29 Michael Young, Mark Teixeira, Hank Blalock 10.00
30 Vladimir Guerrero, Darin Erstad, Garret Anderson 10.00

Playoff Game Jersey Collection

Inserted 1:8 Retail
No Pricing

Prestigious Pros Blue

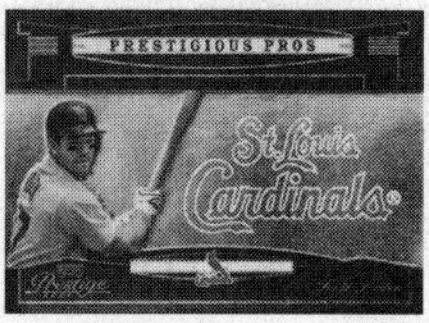

NM/M
Common Player: 1.00
Production 900 Sets
Black: No Pricing
Production 10 Sets
Bronze: 2-3X
Production 100 Sets
Gold: 2-4X
Production 50 Sets
Green: 1-2X
Production 350 Sets
Orange: 1-1.5X
Production 500 Sets
Platinum: 3-5X
Production 25 Sets
Purple: 1-2X
Production 200 Sets
Red: 1X
Production 70 Sets
Silver: 2-3X
Production 75 Sets
1 Ozzie Smith 3.00
2 Derek Jeter 6.00
3 Eric Chavez 1.00
4 Paul Molitor 2.00
5 Jeff Bagwell 1.50
6 Melvin Mora 1.00
7 Craig Biggio 1.00
8 Cal Ripken Jr. 8.00
9 Hank Blalock 1.50
10 Miguel Tejada 2.00
11 Jacque Jones 1.00
12 Alfonso Soriano 2.00
13 Omar Vizquel 1.00
14 Paul Konerko 1.00
15 Tim Hudson 1.00
16 Garret Anderson 1.00
17 Lance Berkman 1.00
18 Randy Johnson 2.00
19 Robin Yount 3.00
20 Mark Mulder 1.00
21 Sean Casey 1.00
22 Jim Palmer 1.50
23 Don Mattingly 5.00
24 Manny Ramirez 2.00
25 Rafael Palmeiro 1.50
26 Vernon Wells 1.00
27 Vladimir Guerrero 2.00
28 Ken Harvey 1.00
29 Rod Carew 1.50
30 Nolan Ryan 8.00
31 Mike Piazza 3.00
32 Steve Carlton 1.50
33 Miguel Cabrera 2.00
34 Kerry Wood 2.00
35 Mike Mussina 1.00
36 Gaylord Perry 1.00
37 Gary Sheffield 1.50
38 Curt Schilling 2.00
39 Don Sutton 1.00
40 Roger Clemens 6.00
41 Victor Martinez 1.00
42 Jason Giambi 1.00
43 Dennis Eckersley 1.00
44 Adam Dunn 1.50
45 Pedro Martinez 2.00
46 Tony Perez 1.00
47 Tom Glavine 1.00
48 Torii Hunter 1.00
49 Hideo Nomo 1.00
50 Scott Rolen 2.00
51 Ichiro Suzuki 5.00
52 C.C. Sabathia 1.00
53 George Brett 5.00
54 David Ortiz 2.00
55 Hideki Matsui 4.00
56 Nomar Garciaparra 4.00
57 Johan Santana 2.00
58 Phil Niekro 1.00
59 Dontrelle Willis 1.00
60 Magglio Ordonez 1.00
61 Livan Hernandez 1.00
62 Edgar Renteria 1.00
63 Todd Helton 1.50
64 Carlos Beltran 1.50
65 Sammy Sosa 4.00
66 Albert Pujols 6.00
67 Mike Lowell 1.00
68 Mark Prior 1.50
69 Ivan Rodriguez 1.50
70 Jake Peavy 1.00
71 Jim Thome 2.00
72 Mark Teixeira 1.50
73 Shawn Green 1.00
74 Rollie Fingers 1.00
75 Barry Zito 1.00
76 Jose Vidro 1.00
77 Ben Sheets 1.00
78 Roy Halladay 1.00
79 Frank Thomas 1.50
80 Chipper Jones 2.00
81 Jason Bay 1.00
82 Tony Gwynn 2.00
83 Shannon Stewart 1.00
84 Carl Crawford 1.00
85 Andruw Jones 1.00
86 Greg Maddux 3.00
87 Barry Larkin 1.00
88 Alex Rodriguez 5.00
89 Rickey Henderson 1.50
90 Troy Glaus 1.00
91 Roy Oswalt 1.00
92 Michael Young 1.00
93 Carlos Lee 1.00
94 Jim Edmonds 1.00
95 Fergie Jenkins 1.00
96 Paul LoDuca 1.00
97 Aubrey Huff 1.00
98 Ken Griffey Jr. 3.00
99 Carlos Delgado 1.50
100 Mike Schmidt 5.00

Prestigious Pros Material Jersey Gold

NM/M
Production 5-50
No pricing 20 or less.
Platinum Patch: No Pricing
Production 5-10
1 Ozzie Smith/50 25.00
3 Eric Chavez/25 10.00
4 Paul Molitor/50 12.00
5 Jeff Bagwell/50 10.00
6 Melvin Mora/25 10.00
7 Craig Biggio/25 15.00
8 Cal Ripken Jr./50 40.00
10 Miguel Tejada/25 12.00
13 Omar Vizquel/25 15.00
14 Paul Konerko/25 8.00
15 Tim Hudson/25 10.00
17 Lance Berkman/50 8.00
18 Randy Johnson/25 20.00
19 Robin Yount/50 15.00
20 Mark Mulder/20 10.00
21 Sean Casey/25 10.00
22 Jim Palmer/50 8.00
23 Don Mattingly/50 25.00
26 Vernon Wells/25 8.00
27 Vladimir Guerrero/25 20.00
28 Ken Harvey/25 8.00
29 Rod Carew/50 10.00
30 Nolan Ryan/50 35.00
31 Mike Piazza/25 20.00
32 Steve Carlton/50 8.00
34 Kerry Wood/25 15.00
35 Mike Mussina/25 15.00
36 Gaylord Perry/50 8.00
37 Gary Sheffield/25 10.00
38 Curt Schilling/25 15.00
39 Don Sutton/50 8.00
40 Roger Clemens/25 25.00
41 Victor Martinez/25 10.00
42 Jason Giambi/25 10.00
43 Dennis Eckersley/50 10.00
45 Pedro Martinez/25 15.00
46 Tony Perez/50 8.00
49 Hideo Nomo/25 25.00
50 Scott Rolen/25 20.00
52 C.C. Sabathia/25 10.00
53 George Brett/50 25.00
55 Hideki Matsui/25 40.00
58 Phil Niekro/50 8.00
59 Dontrelle Willis/25 10.00
60 Magglio Ordonez/25 8.00
61 Livan Hernandez/25 8.00
62 Edgar Renteria/25 10.00
63 Todd Helton/25 15.00
65 Sammy Sosa/25 20.00
66 Albert Pujols/25 35.00
68 Mark Prior/25 10.00
71 Jim Thome/25 15.00
72 Mark Teixeira/25 12.00
73 Shawn Green/25 10.00
74 Rollie Fingers/50 8.00
77 Ben Sheets/25 10.00
78 Roy Halladay/25 10.00
79 Frank Thomas/25 15.00
80 Chipper Jones/25 15.00
81 Jason Bay/25 10.00
82 Tony Gwynn/50 15.00
84 Carl Crawford/25 10.00
85 Andruw Jones/25 10.00
86 Greg Maddux/25 20.00
87 Barry Larkin/25 12.00
89 Rickey Henderson/50 15.00
90 Troy Glaus/25 10.00
92 Michael Young/25 10.00
93 Carlos Lee/25 10.00
94 Jim Edmonds/25 12.00
95 Fergie Jenkins/50 10.00
97 Aubrey Huff/25 10.00
99 Carlos Delgado/25 10.00
100 Mike Schmidt/50 25.00

Prestigious Pros Material Bat Silver

NM/M
Production 5-50
No pricing 20 or less.
1 Ozzie Smith/50 25.00
3 Eric Chavez/25 10.00
4 Paul Molitor/50 12.00
5 Jeff Bagwell/50 10.00
7 Craig Biggio/25 15.00
8 Cal Ripken Jr./50 40.00
9 Hank Blalock/25 12.00
10 Miguel Tejada/25 12.00
14 Paul Konerko/25 8.00
15 Tim Hudson/25 10.00
16 Garret Anderson/25 10.00
17 Lance Berkman/50 8.00
18 Randy Johnson/25 20.00
19 Robin Yount/50 15.00
21 Sean Casey/25 10.00
23 Don Mattingly/50 25.00
25 Rafael Palmeiro/25 15.00
27 Vladimir Guerrero/25 20.00
28 Ken Harvey/25 8.00
29 Rod Carew/50 10.00
30 Nolan Ryan/50 35.00
31 Mike Piazza/25 20.00
32 Steve Carlton/50 8.00
34 Kerry Wood/25 15.00
35 Mike Mussina/25 15.00
37 Gary Sheffield/25 10.00
38 Curt Schilling/25 15.00
40 Roger Clemens/25 25.00
41 Victor Martinez/25 10.00
42 Jason Giambi/25 10.00
44 Adam Dunn/25 12.00
45 Pedro Martinez/25 15.00
46 Tony Perez/50 8.00
47 Tom Glavine/25 12.00
48 Torii Hunter/50 8.00
49 Hideo Nomo/25 25.00
50 Scott Rolen/25 20.00
53 George Brett/50 25.00
54 David Ortiz/50 12.00
55 Hideki Matsui/50 40.00
56 Nomar Garciaparra/25 20.00
58 Phil Niekro/50 8.00
60 Magglio Ordonez/50 8.00
62 Edgar Renteria/25 10.00
63 Todd Helton/25 15.00
64 Carlos Beltran/25 15.00
65 Sammy Sosa/50 15.00
67 Mike Lowell/25 10.00
68 Mark Prior/25 15.00
69 Ivan Rodriguez/50 10.00
71 Jim Thome/50 10.00
72 Mark Teixeira/50 10.00
73 Shawn Green/25 10.00
76 Jose Vidro/25 8.00
77 Ben Sheets/25 10.00
79 Frank Thomas/25 15.00
81 Jason Bay/25 10.00
82 Tony Gwynn/50 15.00
83 Shannon Stewart/25 8.00
85 Andruw Jones/25 10.00
87 Barry Larkin/50 10.00

89 Rickey Henderson/50 15.00
90 Troy Glaus/25 10.00
91 Roy Oswalt/25 10.00
92 Michael Young/25 10.00
93 Carlos Lee/25 10.00
94 Jim Edmonds/50 10.00
96 Paul LoDuca/25 10.00
99 Carlos Delgado/25 10.00
100 Mike Schmidt/50 25.00

Prestigious Pros Signature Black

No Pricing
Production Five Sets

Stars of MLB

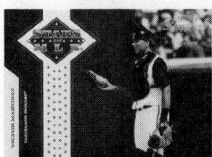

	NM/M
Complete Set (15):	20.00
Common Player:	1.00
Inserted 1:12	
Foil:	2-4X
Production 100 Sets	
Holo-Foil:	4-8X
Production 25 Sets	
1 Randy Johnson	3.00
2 Adrian Beltre	1.00
3 Eric Chavez	1.00
4 Mike Mussina	1.50
5 Todd Helton	2.00
6 Curt Schilling	2.00
7 Miguel Cabrera	3.00
8 Kerry Wood	2.50
9 David Ortiz	3.00
10 Michael Young	1.00
11 Mark Mulder	1.00
12 Victor Martinez	1.00
13 Johan Santana	2.00
14 Scott Rolen	3.00
15 Carlos Beltran	2.00

Stars of MLB Material Bat

	NM/M
Production 50-100	
1 Randy Johnson/100	10.00
2 Adrian Beltre/100	5.00
3 Eric Chavez/100	5.00
4 Mike Mussina/100	8.00
5 Todd Helton/100	8.00
6 Curt Schilling/100	10.00
7 Miguel Cabrera/100	8.00
8 Kerry Wood/100	10.00
9 David Ortiz/100	10.00
10 Michael Young/100	5.00
11 Mark Mulder/50	8.00
14 Scott Rolen/100	10.00
15 Carlos Beltran/100	8.00

Stars of MLB Material Jersey

	NM/M
Production 100 Sets	
Prime:	1-2X
Production 25 Sets	
1 Randy Johnson/Pants	10.00
2 Adrian Beltre	5.00
3 Eric Chavez	5.00
4 Mike Mussina	8.00
5 Todd Helton	8.00
6 Curt Schilling	10.00
7 Miguel Cabrera	10.00
8 Kerry Wood	10.00
9 David Ortiz	12.00
10 Michael Young	5.00
11 Mark Mulder	5.00
12 Victor Martinez	5.00
13 Johan Santana	10.00
14 Scott Rolen	10.00
15 Carlos Beltran	8.00

Stars of MLB Signature Material Bat

	NM/M
Production 10-50	
2 Adrian Beltre/50	25.00
3 Eric Chavez/50	20.00
8 Kerry Wood/25	50.00
9 David Ortiz/50	40.00
10 Michael Young/50	25.00
15 Carlos Beltran/25	50.00

Stars of MLB Signature Material Jersey

	NM/M
Production 10-50	
Prime:	No Pricing
Production Five Sets	
2 Adrian Beltre/50	25.00
3 Eric Chavez/50	20.00
8 Kerry Wood/25	50.00
9 David Ortiz/50	40.00
10 Michael Young/50	25.00
12 Victor Martinez/50	20.00
13 Johan Santana/50	50.00
15 Carlos Beltran/25	50.00

S

1988 Score

MARK McGWIRE

	NM/M
Unopened Fact. Set (660):	9.00
Complete Set (660):	6.00
Common Player:	.05
Pack:	.35
Wax Box:	9.00
Rack Pack (54):	.75
Rack Box (24):	12.00
1 Don Mattingly	.65
2 Wade Boggs	.50
3 Tim Raines	.05
4 Andre Dawson	.25
5 Mark McGwire	.75
6 Kevin Seitzer	.05
7 Wally Joyner	.05
8 Jesse Barfield	.05
9 Pedro Guerrero	.05
10 Eric Davis	.05
11 George Brett	.65
12 Ozzie Smith	.50
13 Rickey Henderson	.40
14 Jim Rice	.15
15 Matt Nokes RC	.05
16 Mike Schmidt	.65
17 Dave Parker	.05
18 Eddie Murray	.40
19 Andres Galarraga	.05
20 Tony Fernandez	.05
21 Kevin McReynolds	.05
22 B.J. Surhoff	.05
23 Pat Tabler	.05
24 Kirby Puckett	.50
25 Benny Santiago	.05
26 Ryne Sandberg	.50
27 Kelly Downs	.05
28 Jose Cruz	.05
29 Pete O'Brien	.05
30 Mark Langston	.05
31 Lee Smith	.05
32 Juan Samuel	.05
33 Kevin Bass	.05
34 R.J. Reynolds	.05
35 Steve Sax	.05
36 John Kruk	.05
37 Alan Trammell	.05
38 Chris Bosio	.05
39 Brook Jacoby	.05
40 Willie McGee	.05
41 Dave Magadan	.05
42 Fred Lynn	.05
43 Kent Hrbek	.05
44 Brian Downing	.05
45 Jose Canseco	.30
46 Jim Presley	.05
47 Mike Stanley	.05
48 Tony Pena	.05

49 David Cone .05
50 Rick Sutcliffe .05
51 Doug Drabek .05
52 Bill Doran .05
53 Mike Scioscia .05
54 Candy Maldonado .05
55 Dave Winfield .40
56 Lou Whitaker .05
57 Tom Henke .05
58 Ken Gerhart .05
59 Glenn Braggs .05
60 Julio Franco .05
61 Charlie Leibrandt .05
62 Gary Gaetti .05
63 Bob Boone .05
64 Luis Polonia RC .05
65 Dwight Evans .05
66 Phil Bradley .05
67 Mike Boddicker .05
68 Vince Coleman .05
69 Howard Johnson .05
70 Tim Wallach .05
71 Keith Moreland .05
72 Barry Larkin .05
73 Alan Ashby .05
74 Rick Rhoden .05
75 Darrell Evans .05
76 Dave Stieb .05
77 Dan Plesac .05
78 Will Clark .05
79 Frank White .05
80 Joe Carter .05
81 Mike Witt .05
82 Terry Steinbach .05
83 Alvin Davis .05
84 Tom Herr .05
85 Vance Law .05
86 Kal Daniels .05
87 Rick Honeycutt .05
88 Alfredo Griffin .05
89 Bret Saberhagen .05
90 Bert Blyleven .05
91 Jeff Reardon .05
92 Cory Snyder .05
93 Greg Walker .05
94 Joe Magrane RC .10
95 Bob Deer .05
96 Ray Knight .05
97 Casey Candaele .05
98 John Cerutti .05
99 Buddy Bell .05
100 Jack Clark .05
101 Eric Bell .05
102 Willie Wilson .05
103 Dave Schmidt .05
104 Dennis Eckersley .35
105 Don Sutton .35
106 Danny Tartabull .05
107 Fred McGriff .05
108 Les Straker RC .05
109 Lloyd Moseby .05
110 Roger Clemens .65
111 Glenn Hubbard .05
112 Ken Williams RC .05
113 Ruben Sierra .05
114 Stan Jefferson .05
115 Milt Thompson .05
116 Bobby Bonilla .05
117 Wayne Tolleson .05
118 Matt Williams .05
119 Chet Lemon .05
120 Dale Sveum .05
121 Dennis Boyd .05
122 Brett Butler .05
123 Terry Kennedy .05
124 Jack Howell .05
125 Curt Young .05
126a Dale Valle (First name incorrect.) .25
126b Dave Valle (Correct spelling.) .05
127 Curt Wilkerson .05
128 Tim Teufel .05
129 Ozzie Virgil .05
130 Brian Fisher .05
131 Lance Parrish .05
132 Tom Browning .05
133a Larry Anderson (Incorrect spelling.) .25
133b Larry Andersen (Correct spelling.) .05
134a Bob Brenley (Incorrect spelling.) .25
134b Bob Brenly (Correct spelling.) .05
135 Mike Marshall .05
136 Gerald Perry .05
137 Bobby Meacham .05
138 Larry Herndon .05
139 Fred Manrique RC .05
140 Charlie Hough .05
141 Ron Darling .05
142 Herm Winningham .05
143 Mike Diaz .05
144 Mike Jackson RC .05
145 Denny Walling .05
146 Rob Thompson .05
147 Franklin Stubbs .05
148 Albert Hall .05
149 Bobby Witt .05
150 Lance McCullers .05
151 Scott Bradley .05
152 Mark McLemore .05
153 Tim Laudner .05
154 Greg Swindell .05

155 Marty Barrett .05
156 Mike Heath .05
157 Gary Ward .05
158a Lee Mazilli (Incorrect spelling.) .25
158b Lee Mazzilli (Correct spelling.) .05
159 Tom Foley .05
160 Robin Yount .40
161 Steve Bedrosian .05
162 Bob Walk .05
163 Nick Esasky .05
164 Ken Caminiti RC .15
165 Jose Uribe .05
166 Dave Anderson .05
167 Ed Whitson .05
168 Ernie Whitt .05
169 Cecil Cooper .05
170 Mike Pagliarulo .05
171 Pat Sheridan .05
172 Chris Bando .05
173 Lee Lacy .05
174 Steve Lombardozzi .05
175 Mike Greenwell .05
176 Greg Minton .05
177 Moose Haas .05
178 Mike Kingery .05
179 Greg Harris .05
180 Bo Jackson .10
181 Carmelo Martinez .05
182 Alex Trevino .05
183 Ron Oester .05
184 Danny Darwin .05
185 Mike Krukow .05
186 Rafael Palmeiro .40
187 Tim Burke .05
188 Roger McDowell .05
189 Garry Templeton .05
190 Terry Pendleton .05
191 Larry Parrish .05
192 Rey Quinones .05
193 Joaquin Andujar .05
194 Tom Brunansky .05
195 Donnie Moore .05
196 Dan Pasqua .05
197 Jim Gantner .05
198 Mark Eichhorn .05
199 John Grubb .05
200 Bill Ripken RC .05
201 Sam Horn RC .05
202 Todd Worrell .05
203 Terry Leach .05
204 Garth Iorg .05
205 Brian Dayett .05
206 Bo Diaz .05
207 Craig Reynolds .05
208 Brian Holton .05
209 Marvelle Wynne (Marvell) .05
210 Dave Concepcion .05
211 Mike Davis .05
212 Devon White .05
213 Mickey Brantley .05
214 Greg Gagne .05
215 Oddibe McDowell .05
216 Jimmy Key .05
217 Dave Bergman .05
218 Calvin Schiraldi .05
219 Larry Sheets .05
220 Mike Easler .05
221 Kurt Stillwell .05
222 Chuck Jackson RC .05
223 Dave Martinez .05
224 Tim Leary .05
225 Steve Garvey .20
226 Greg Mathews .05
227 Doug Sisk .05
228 Dave Henderson .05
229 Jimmy Dwyer .05
230 Larry Owen .05
231 Andre Thornton .05
232 Mark Salas .05
233 Tom Brookens .05
234 Greg Brock .05
235 Rance Mulliniks .05
236 Bob Brower .05
237 Joe Niekro .05
238 Scott Bankhead .05
239 Doug DeCinces .05
240 Tommy John .05
241 Rich Gedman .05
242 Ted Power .05
243 Dave Meads RC .05
244 Jim Sundberg .05
245 Ken Oberkfell .05
246 Jimmy Jones .05
247 Ken Landreaux .05
248 Jose Oquendo .05
249 John Mitchell RC .05
250 Don Baylor .05
251 Scott Fletcher .05
252 Al Newman .05
253 Carney Lansford .05
254 Johnny Ray .05
255 Gary Pettis .05
256 Ken Phelps .05
257 Rick Leach .05
258 Tim Stoddard .05
259 Ed Romero .05
260 Sid Bream .05
261a Tom Neidenfuer (Incorrect spelling.) .25
261b Tom Niedenfuer (Correct spelling.) .05
262 Rick Dempsey .05
263 Lonnie Smith .05

264	Bob Forsch	.05
265	Barry Bonds	1.00
266	Willie Randolph	.05
267	Mike Ramsey	.05
268	Don Slaught	.05
269	Mickey Tettleton	.05
270	Jerry Reuss	.05
271	Marc Sullivan	.05
272	Jim Morrison	.05
273	Steve Balboni	.05
274	Dick Schofield	.05
275	John Tudor	.05
276	Gene Larkin **RC**	.05
277	Harold Reynolds	.05
278	Jerry Browne	.05
279	Willie Upshaw	.05
280	Ted Higuera	.05
281	Terry McGriff	.05
282	Terry Puhl	.05
283	Mark Wasinger **RC**	.05
284	Luis Salazar	.05
285	Ted Simmons	.05
286	John Shelby	.05
287	John Smiley **RC**	.05
288	Curt Ford	.05
289	Steve Crawford	.05
290	Dan Quisenberry	.05
291	Alan Wiggins	.05
292	Randy Bush	.05
293	John Candelaria	.05
294	Tony Phillips	.05
295	Mike Morgan	.05
296	Bill Wegman	.05
297a	Terry Franconia (Incorrect spelling.)	.25
297b	Terry Francona (Correct spelling.)	.05
298	Mickey Hatcher	.05
299	Andres Thomas	.05
300	Bob Stanley	.05
301	Alfredo Pedrique **RC**	.05
302	Jim Lindeman	.05
303	Wally Backman	.05
304	Paul O'Neill	.05
305	Hubie Brooks	.05
306	Steve Buechele	.05
307	Bobby Thigpen	.05
308	George Hendrick	.05
309	John Moses	.05
310	Ron Guidry	.05
311	Bill Schroeder	.05
312	Jose Nunez **RC**	.05
313	Bud Black	.05
314	Joe Sambito	.05
315	Scott McGregor	.05
316	Rafael Santana	.05
317	Frank Williams	.05
318	Mike Fitzgerald	.05
319	Rick Mahler	.05
320	Jim Gott	.05
321	Mariano Duncan	.05
322	Jose Guzman	.05
323	Lee Guetterman	.05
324	Dan Gladden	.05
325	Gary Carter	.40
326	Tracy Jones	.05
327	Floyd Youmans	.05
328	Bill Dawley	.05
329	Paul Noce **RC**	.05
330	Angel Salazar	.05
331	Goose Gossage	.10
332	George Frazier	.05
333	Ruppert Jones	.05
334	Billy Jo Robidoux	.05
335	Mike Scott	.05
336	Randy Myers	.05
337	Bob Sebra	.05
338	Eric Show	.05
339	Mitch Williams	.05
340	Paul Molitor	.40
341	Gus Polidor	.05
342	Steve Trout	.05
343	Jerry Don Gleaton	.05
344	Bob Knepper	.05
345	Mitch Webster	.05
346	John Morris	.05
347	Andy Hawkins	.05
348	Dave Leiper	.05
349	Ernest Riles	.05
350	Dwight Gooden	.05
351	Dave Righetti	.05
352	Pat Dodson	.05
353	John Habyan	.05
354	Jim Deshaies	.05
355	Butch Wynegar	.05
356	Bryn Smith	.05
357	Matt Young	.05
358	Tom Pagnozzi **RC**	.05
359	Floyd Rayford	.05
360	Darryl Strawberry	.05
361	Sal Butera	.05
362	Domingo Ramos	.05
363	Chris Brown	.05
364	Jose Gonzalez	.05
365	Dave Smith	.05
366	Andy McGaffigan	.05
367	Stan Javier	.05
368	Henry Cotto	.05
369	Mike Birkbeck	.05
370	Len Dykstra	.05
371	Dave Collins	.05
372	Spike Owen	.05
373	Geno Petralli	.05
374	Ron Karkovice	.05
375	Shane Rawley	.05
376	DeWayne Buice **RC**	.05
377	Bill Pecota **RC**	.05
378	Leon Durham	.05
379	Ed Olwine	.05
380	Bruce Hurst	.05
381	Bob McClure	.05
382	Mark Thurmond	.05
383	Buddy Biancalana	.05
384	Tim Conroy	.05
385	Tony Gwynn	.50
386	Greg Gross	.05
387	Barry Lyons **RC**	.05
388	Mike Felder	.05
389	Pat Clements	.05
390	Ken Griffey	.05
391	Mark Davis	.05
392	Jose Rijo	.05
393	Mike Young	.05
394	Willie Fraser	.05
395	Dion James	.05
396	Steve Shields **RC**	.05
397	Randy St. Claire	.05
398	Danny Jackson	.05
399	Cecil Fielder	.05
400	Keith Hernandez	.05
401	Don Carman	.05
402	Chuck Crim **RC**	.05
403	Rob Woodward	.05
404	Junior Ortiz	.05
405	Glenn Wilson	.05
406	Ken Howell	.05
407	Jeff Kunkel	.05
408	Jeff Reed	.05
409	Chris James	.05
410	Zane Smith	.05
411	Ken Dixon	.05
412	Ricky Horton	.05
413	Frank DiPino	.05
414	Shane Mack **RC**	.05
415	Danny Cox	.05
416	Andy Van Slyke	.05
417	Danny Heep	.05
418	John Cangelosi	.05
419a	John Christiansen (Incorrect spelling.)	.25
419b	John Christensen (Correct spelling.)	.05
420	Joey Cora **RC**	.05
421	Mike LaValliere	.05
422	Kelly Gruber	.05
423	Bruce Benedict	.05
424	Len Matuszek	.05
425	Kent Tekulve	.05
426	Rafael Ramirez	.05
427	Mike Flanagan	.05
428	Mike Gallego	.05
429	Juan Castillo	.05
430	Neal Heaton	.05
431	Phil Garner	.05
432	Mike Dunne **RC**	.05
433	Wallace Johnson	.05
434	Jack O'Connor	.05
435	Steve Jeltz	.05
436	Donnell Nixon **RC**	.05
437	Jack Lazorko	.05
438	Keith Comstock **RC**	.05
439	Jeff Robinson	.05
440	Graig Nettles	.05
441	Mel Hall	.05
442	Gerald Young **RC**	.05
443	Gary Redus	.05
444	Charlie Moore	.05
445	Bill Madlock	.05
446	Mark Clear	.05
447	Greg Booker	.05
448	Rick Schu	.05
449	Ron Kittle	.05
450	Dale Murphy	.25
451	Bob Dernier	.05
452	Dale Mohorcic	.05
453	Rafael Belliard	.05
454	Charlie Puleo	.05
455	Dwayne Murphy	.05
456	Jim Eisenreich	.05
457	David Palmer	.05
458	Dave Stewart	.05
459	Pascual Perez	.05
460	Glenn Davis	.05
461	Dan Petry	.05
462	Jim Winn	.05
463	Darrell Miller	.05
464	Mike Moore	.05
465	Mike LaCoss	.05
466	Steve Farr	.05
467	Jerry Mumphrey	.05
468	Kevin Gross	.05
469	Bruce Bochy	.05
470	Orel Hershiser	.05
471	Eric King	.05
472	Ellis Burks **RC**	.25
473	Darren Daulton	.05
474	Mookie Wilson	.05
475	Frank Viola	.05
476	Ron Robinson	.05
477	Bob Melvin	.05
478	Jeff Musselman	.05
479	Charlie Kerfeld	.05
480	Richard Dotson	.05
481	Kevin Mitchell	.05
482	Gary Roenicke	.05
483	Tim Flannery	.05
484	Rich Yett	.05
485	Pete Incaviglia	.05
486	Rick Cerone	.05
487	Tony Armas	.05
488	Jerry Reed	.05
489	Davey Lopes	.05
490	Frank Tanana	.05
491	Mike Loynd	.05
492	Bruce Ruffin	.05
493	Chris Speier	.05
494	Tom Hume	.05
495	Jesse Orosco	.05
496	Robby Wine, Jr. **RC**	.05
497	Jeff Montgomery **RC**	.15
498	Jeff Dedmon	.05
499	Luis Aguayo	.05
500	Reggie Jackson (1968-75)	.15
501	Reggie Jackson (1976)	.15
502	Reggie Jackson (1977-81)	.15
503	Reggie Jackson (1982-86)	.15
504	Reggie Jackson (1987)	.15
505	Billy Hatcher	.05
506	Ed Lynch	.05
507	Willie Hernandez	.05
508	Jose DeLeon	.05
509	Joel Youngblood	.05
510	Bob Welch	.05
511	Steve Ontiveros	.05
512	Randy Ready	.05
513	Juan Nieves	.05
514	Jeff Russell	.05
515	Von Hayes	.05
516	Mark Gubicza	.05
517	Ken Dayley	.05
518	Don Aase	.05
519	Rick Reuschel	.05
520	Mike Henneman **RC**	.10
521	Rick Aguilera	.05
522	Jay Howell	.05
523	Ed Correa	.05
524	Manny Trillo	.05
525	Kirk Gibson	.05
526	Wally Ritchie **RC**	.05
527	Al Nipper	.05
528	Atlee Hammaker	.05
529	Shawon Dunston	.05
530	Jim Clancy	.05
531	Tom Paciorek	.05
532	Joel Skinner	.05
533	Scott Garrelts	.05
534	Tom O'Malley	.05
535	John Franco	.05
536	Paul Kilgus **RC**	.05
537	Darrell Porter	.05
538	Walt Terrell	.05
539	Bill Long **RC**	.05
540	George Bell	.05
541	Jeff Sellers	.05
542	Joe Boever **RC**	.05
543	Steve Howe	.05
544	Scott Sanderson	.05
545	Jack Morris	.05
546	Todd Benzinger **RC**	.05
547	Steve Henderson	.05
548	Eddie Milner	.05
549	Jeff Robinson **RC**	.05
550	Cal Ripken, Jr.	1.00
551	Jody Davis	.05
552	Kirk McCaskill	.05
553	Craig Lefferts	.05
554	Darnell Coles	.05
555	Phil Niekro	.35
556	Mike Aldrete	.05
557	Pat Perry	.05
558	Juan Agosto	.05
559	Rob Murphy	.05
560	Dennis Rasmussen	.05
561	Manny Lee	.05
562	Jeff Blauser **RC**	.10
563	Bob Ojeda	.05
564	Dave Dravecky	.05
565	Gene Garber	.05
566	Ron Roenicke	.05
567	Tommy Hinzo **RC**	.05
568	Eric Nolte **RC**	.05
569	Ed Hearn	.05
570	Mark Davidson **RC**	.05
571	Jim Walewander **RC**	.05
572	Donnie Hill	.05
573	Jamie Moyer	.05
574	Ken Schrom	.05
575	Nolan Ryan	1.00
576	Jim Acker	.05
577	Jamie Quirk	.05
578	Jay Aldrich **RC**	.05
579	Claudell Washington	.05
580	Jeff Leonard	.05
581	Carmen Castillo	.05
582	Daryl Boston	.05
583	Jeff DeWillis **RC**	.05
584	John Marzano **RC**	.05
585	Bill Gullickson	.05
586	Andy Allanson	.05
587	Lee Tunnell	.05
588	Gene Nelson	.05
589	Dave LaPoint	.05
590	Harold Baines	.05
591	Bill Buckner	.05
592	Carlton Fisk	.40
593	Rick Manning	.05
594	Doug Jones **RC**	.10
595	Tom Candiotti	.05
596	Steve Lake	.05
597	Jose Lind **RC**	.05
598	Ross Jones **RC**	.05
599	Gary Matthews	.05
600	Fernando Valenzuela	.05
601	Dennis Martinez	.05
602	Les Lancaster **RC**	.05
603	Ozzie Guillen	.05
604	Tony Bernazard	.05
605	Chili Davis	.05
606	Roy Smalley	.05
607	Ivan Calderon	.05
608	Jay Tibbs	.05
609	Guy Hoffman	.05
610	Doyle Alexander	.05
611	Mike Bielecki	.05
612	Shawn Hillegas **RC**	.05
613	Keith Atherton	.05
614	Eric Plunk	.05
615	Sid Fernandez	.05
616	Dennis Lamp	.05
617	Dave Engle	.05
618	Harry Spilman	.05
619	Don Robinson	.05
620	John Farrell **RC**	.05
621	Nelson Liriano **RC**	.05
622	Floyd Bannister	.05
623	Randy Milligan **RC**	.05
624	Kevin Elster **RC**	.10
625	Jody Reed **RC**	.05
626	Shawn Abner **RC**	.05
627	Kirt Manwaring **RC**	.10
628	Pete Stanicek **RC**	.05
629	Rob Ducey **RC**	.05
630	Steve Kiefer	.05
631	Gary Thurman **RC**	.05
632	Darrel Akerfelds **RC**	.05
633	Dave Clark	.05
634	Roberto Kelly **RC**	.05
635	Keith Hughes **RC**	.05
636	John Davis **RC**	.05
637	Mike Devereaux **RC**	.10
638	Tom Glavine **RC**	1.00
639	Keith Miller **RC**	.05
640	Chris Gwynn **RC**	.05
641	Tim Crews **RC**	.05
642	Mackey Sasser **RC**	.05
643	Vicente Palacios **RC**	.05
644	Kevin Romine	.05
645	Gregg Jefferies **RC**	.25
646	Jeff Treadway **RC**	.05
647	Ron Gant **RC**	.25
648	Mark McGwire, Matt Nokes Rookie Sluggers	.35
649	Tim Raines, Eric Davis Speed and Power	.05
650	Jack Clark, Don Mattingly Game Breakers	.25
651	Tony Fernandez, Cal Ripken, Jr., Alan Trammell Super Shortstops	.25
652	Vince Coleman (Highlight)	.05
653	Kirby Puckett (Highlight)	.25
654	Benito Santiago (Highlight)	.05
655	Juan Nieves (Highlight)	.05
656	Steve Bedrosian (Highlight)	.05
657	Mike Schmidt (Highlight)	.30
658	Don Mattingly (Highlight)	.30
659	Mark McGwire (Highlight)	.35
660	Paul Molitor (Highlight)	.20

1988 Score Glossy

	NM/M
Complete Set (660):	65.00
Common Player:	.25
Stars:	15X

(See 1988 Score for checklist and base card values.)

Traded/Rookie

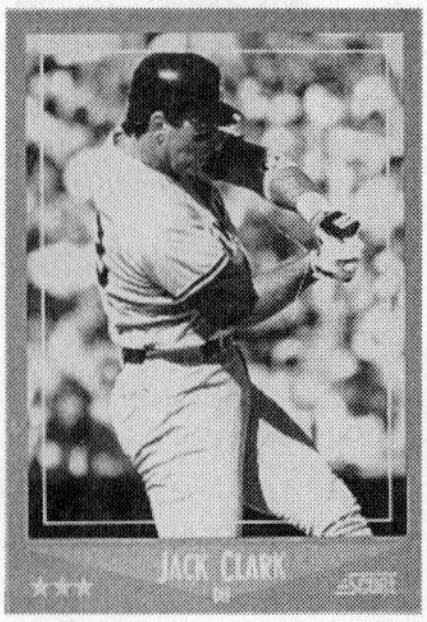

	NM/M
Complete Set (110):	12.00
Common Player:	.05

1	Jack Clark	.05
2	Danny Jackson	.05
3	Brett Butler	.05
4	Kurt Stillwell	.05
5	Tom Brunansky	.05
6	Dennis Lamp	.05
7	Jose DeLeon	.05
8	Tom Herr	.05
9	Keith Moreland	.05
10	Kirk Gibson	.05
11	Bud Black	.05
12	Rafael Ramirez	.05
13	Luis Salazar	.05
14	Goose Gossage	.05
15	Bob Welch	.05
16	Vance Law	.05

17	Ray Knight	.05
18	Dan Quisenberry	.05
19	Don Slaught	.05
20	Lee Smith	.25
21	Rick Cerone	.05
22	Pat Tabler	.05
23	Larry McWilliams	.05
24	Rick Horton	.05
25	Graig Nettles	.05
26	Dan Petry	.05
27	Jose Rijo	.05
28	Chili Davis	.05
29	Dickie Thon	.05
30	Mackey Sasser	.05
31	Mickey Tettleton	.05
32	Rick Dempsey	.05
33	Ron Hassey	.05
34	Phil Bradley	.05
35	Jay Howell	.05
36	Bill Buckner	.05
37	Alfredo Griffin	.05
38	Gary Pettis	.05
39	Calvin Schiraldi	.05
40	John Candelaria	.05
41	Joe Orsulak	.05
42	Willie Upshaw	.05
43	Herm Winningham	.05
44	Ron Kittle	.05
45	Bob Dernier	.05
46	Steve Balboni	.05
47	Steve Shields	.05
48	Henry Cotto	.05
49	Dave Henderson	.05
50	Dave Parker	.05
51	Mike Young	.05
52	Mark Salas	.05
53	Mike Davis	.05
54	Rafael Santana	.05
55	Don Baylor	.05
56	Dan Pasqua	.05
57	Ernest Riles	.05
58	Glenn Hubbard	.05
59	Mike Smithson	.05
60	Richard Dotson	.05
61	Jerry Reuss	.05
62	Mike Jackson	.05
63	Floyd Bannister	.05
64	Jesse Orosco	.05
65	Larry Parrish	.05
66	Jeff Bittiger	.05
67	Ray Hayward	.05
68	Ricky Jordan **RC**	.05
69	Tommy Gregg	.05
70	Brady Anderson **RC**	.50
71	Jeff Montgomery	.05
72	Darryl Hamilton	.05
73	Cecil Espy	.05
74	Greg Briley	.05
75	Joey Meyer	.05
76	Mike Macfarlane **RC**	.05
77	Oswald Peraza	.05
78	Jack Armstrong	.05
79	Don Heinkel	.05
80	Mark Grace **RC**	1.50
81	Steve Curry	.05
82	Damon Berryhill	.05
83	Steve Ellsworth	.05
84	Pete Smith	.05
85	Jack McDowell **RC**	.25
86	Rob Dibble	.05
87	Bryan Harvey	.05
88	John Dopson	.05
89	Dave Gallagher	.05
90	Todd Stottlemyre **RC**	.25
91	Mike Schooler	.05
92	Don Gordon	.05
93	Sil Campusano	.05
94	Jeff Pico	.05
95	Jay Buhner **RC**	.75
96	Nelson Santovenia	.05
97	Al Leiter	.05
98	Luis Alicea	.05
99	Pat Borders	.05
100	Chris Sabo **RC**	.25
101	Tim Belcher	.05
102	Walt Weiss	.05
103	Craig Biggio **RC**	6.00
104	Don August	.05
105	Roberto Alomar **RC**	4.00
106	Todd Burns	.05
107	John Costello	.05
108	Melido Perez	.05
109	Darrin Jackson	.05
110	Orestes Destrade	.05

1988 Score Traded/Rookie Glossy

	NM/M
Complete Set (110):	60.00
Common Player:	.25
Stars:	3X

(See 1988 Score Traded/Rookie for checklist and base card values.)

1989 Score

	NM/M
Unopened Fact. Set (660):	12.00
Complete Set (660):	9.00
Common Player:	.05
Pack (16):	.50
Wax Box (36):	10.00

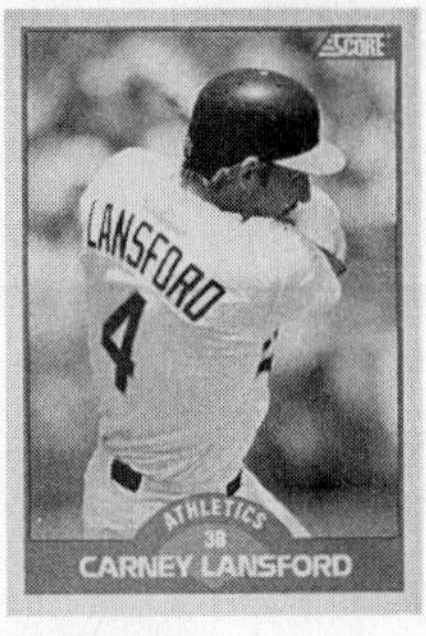

1	Jose Canseco	.25
2	Andre Dawson	.25
3	Mark McGwire	.65
4	Benny Santiago	.05
5	Rick Reuschel	.05
6	Fred McGriff	.05
7	Kal Daniels	.05
8	Gary Gaetti	.05
9	Ellis Burks	.05
10	Darryl Strawberry	.05
11	Julio Franco	.05
12	Lloyd Moseby	.05
13	Jeff Pico **RC**	.05
14	Johnny Ray	.05
15	Cal Ripken, Jr.	.75
16	Dick Schofield	.05
17	Mel Hall	.05
18	Bill Ripken	.05
19	Brook Jacoby	.05
20	Kirby Puckett	.50
21	Bill Doran	.05
22	Pete O'Brien	.05
23	Matt Nokes	.05
24	Brian Fisher	.05
25	Jack Clark	.05
26	Gary Pettis	.05
27	Dave Valle	.05
28	Willie Wilson	.05
29	Curt Young	.05
30	Dale Murphy	.20
31	Barry Larkin	.05
32	Dave Stewart	.05
33	Mike LaValliere	.05
34	Glenn Hubbard	.05
35	Ryne Sandberg	.50
36	Tony Pena	.05
37	Greg Walker	.05
38	Von Hayes	.05
39	Kevin Mitchell	.05
40	Tim Raines	.05
41	Keith Hernandez	.05
42	Keith Moreland	.05
43	Ruben Sierra	.05
44	Chet Lemon	.05
45	Willie Randolph	.05
46	Andy Allanson	.05
47	Candy Maldonado	.05
48	Sid Bream	.05
49	Denny Walling	.05
50	Dave Winfield	.40
51	Alvin Davis	.05
52	Cory Snyder	.05
53	Hubie Brooks	.05
54	Chili Davis	.05
55	Kevin Seitzer	.05
56	Jose Uribe	.05
57	Tony Fernandez	.05
58	Tim Teufel	.05
59	Oddibe McDowell	.05
60	Les Lancaster	.05
61	Billy Hatcher	.05
62	Dan Gladden	.05
63	Marty Barrett	.05
64	Nick Esasky	.05
65	Wally Joyner	.05
66	Mike Greenwell	.05
67	Ken Williams	.05
68	Bob Horner	.05
69	Steve Sax	.05
70	Rickey Henderson	.40
71	Mitch Webster	.05
72	Rob Deer	.05
73	Jim Presley	.05
74	Albert Hall	.05
75a	George Brett ("At age 33 ...")	1.00
75b	George Brett ("At age 35 ...")	.50
76	Brian Downing	.05
77	Dave Martinez	.05
78	Scott Fletcher	.05
79	Phil Bradley	.05
80	Ozzie Smith	.50
81	Larry Sheets	.05
82	Mike Aldrete	.05
83	Darnell Coles	.05
84	Len Dykstra	.05
85	Jim Rice	.15
86	Jeff Treadway	.05
87	Jose Lind	.05
88	Willie McGee	.05
89	Mickey Brantley	.05
90	Tony Gwynn	.50
91	R.J. Reynolds	.05
92	Milt Thompson	.05
93	Kevin McReynolds	.05
94	Eddie Murray	.40
95	Lance Parrish	.05
96	Ron Kittle	.05
97	Gerald Young	.05
98	Ernie Whitt	.05
99	Jeff Reed	.05
100	Don Mattingly	.60
101	Gerald Perry	.05
102	Vance Law	.05
103	John Shelby	.05
104	Chris Sabo	.05
105	Danny Tartabull	.05
106	Glenn Wilson	.05
107	Mark Davidson	.05
108	Dave Parker	.05
109	Eric Davis	.05
110	Alan Trammell	.05
111	Ozzie Virgil	.05
112	Frank Tanana	.05
113	Rafael Ramirez	.05
114	Dennis Martinez	.05
115	Jose DeLeon	.05
116	Bob Ojeda	.05
117	Doug Drabek	.05
118	Andy Hawkins	.05
119	Greg Maddux	.50
120	Cecil Fielder (Reversed negative.)	.05
121	Mike Scioscia	.05
122	Dan Petry	.05
123	Terry Kennedy	.05
124	Kelly Downs	.05
125	Greg Gross	.05
126	Fred Lynn	.05
127	Barry Bonds	.75
128	Harold Baines	.05
129	Doyle Alexander	.05
130	Kevin Elster	.05
131	Mike Heath	.05
132	Teddy Higuera	.05
133	Charlie Leibrandt	.05
134	Tim Laudner	.05
135a	Ray Knight (Photo reversed.)	.40
135b	Ray Knight (Correct photo.)	.05
136	Howard Johnson	.05
137	Terry Pendleton	.05
138	Andy McGaffigan	.05
139	Ken Oberkfell	.05
140	Butch Wynegar	.05
141	Rob Murphy	.05
142	Rich Renteria **RC**	.05
143	Jose Guzman	.05
144	Andres Galarraga	.05
145	Rick Horton	.05
146	Frank DiPino	.05
147	Glenn Braggs	.05
148	John Kruk	.05
149	Mike Schmidt	.60
150	Lee Smith	.05
151	Robin Yount	.40
152	Mark Eichhorn	.05
153	DeWayne Buice	.05
154	B.J. Surhoff	.05
155	Vince Coleman	.05
156	Tony Phillips	.05
157	Willie Fraser	.05
158	Lance McCullers	.05
159	Greg Gagne	.05
160	Jesse Barfield	.05
161	Mark Langston	.05
162	Kurt Stillwell	.05
163	Dion James	.05
164	Glenn Davis	.05
165	Walt Weiss	.05
166	Dave Concepcion	.05
167	Alfredo Griffin	.05
168	Don Heinkel **RC**	.05
169	Luis Rivera	.05
170	Shane Rawley	.05
171	Darrell Evans	.05
172	Robby Thompson	.05
173	Jody Davis	.05
174	Andy Van Slyke	.05
175	Wade Boggs	.50
176	Garry Templeton	.05
177	Gary Redus	.05
178	Craig Lefferts	.05
179	Carney Lansford	.05
180	Ron Darling	.05
181	Kirk McCaskill	.05
182	Tony Armas	.05
183	Steve Farr	.05
184	Tom Brunansky	.05
185	Bryan Harvey **RC**	.05
186	Mike Marshall	.05
187	Bo Diaz	.05
188	Willie Upshaw	.05
189	Mike Pagliarulo	.05
190	Mike Krukow	.05
191	Tommy Herr	.05
192	Jim Pankovits	.05
193	Dwight Evans	.05
194	Kelly Gruber	.05
195	Bobby Bonilla	.05
196	Wallace Johnson	.05
197	Dave Stieb	.05
198	Pat Borders **RC**	.05
199	Rafael Palmeiro	.35
200	Dwight Gooden	.05
201	Pete Incaviglia	.05
202	Chris James	.05
203	Marvell Wynne	.05
204	Pat Sheridan	.05
205	Don Baylor	.05
206	Paul O'Neill	.05
207	Pete Smith	.05
208	Mark McLemore	.05
209	Henry Cotto	.05
210	Kirk Gibson	.05
211	Claudell Washington	.05
212	Randy Bush	.05
213	Joe Carter	.05
214	Bill Buckner	.05
215	Bert Blyleven	.05
216	Brett Butler	.05
217	Lee Mazzilli	.05
218	Spike Owen	.05
219	Bill Swift	.05
220	Tim Wallach	.05
221	David Cone	.05
222	Don Carman	.05
223	Rich Gossage	.05
224	Bob Walk	.05
225	Dave Righetti	.05
226	Kevin Bass	.05
227	Kevin Gross	.05
228	Tim Burke	.05
229	Rick Mahler	.05
230	Lou Whitaker	.05
231	Luis Alicea **RC**	.05
232	Roberto Alomar	.25
233	Bob Boone	.05
234	Dickie Thon	.05
235	Shawon Dunston	.05
236	Pete Stanicek	.05
237	Craig Biggio	.05
238	Dennis Boyd	.05
239	Tom Candiotti	.05
240	Gary Carter	.40
241	Mike Stanley	.05
242	Ken Phelps	.05
243	Chris Bosio	.05
244	Les Straker	.05
245	Dave Smith	.05
246	John Candelaria	.05
247	Joe Orsulak	.05
248	Storm Davis	.05
249	Floyd Bannister	.05
250	Jack Morris	.05
251	Bret Saberhagen	.05
252	Tom Niedenfuer	.05
253	Neal Heaton	.05
254	Eric Show	.05
255	Juan Samuel	.05
256	Dale Sveum	.05
257	Jim Gott	.05
258	Scott Garrelts	.05
259	Larry McWilliams	.05
260	Steve Bedrosian	.05
261	Jack Howell	.05
262	Jay Tibbs	.05
263	Jamie Moyer	.05
264	Doug Sisk	.05
265	Todd Worrell	.05
266	John Farrell	.05
267	Dave Collins	.05
268	Sid Fernandez	.05
269	Tom Brookens	.05
270	Shane Mack	.05
271	Paul Kilgus	.05
272	Chuck Crim	.05
273	Bob Knepper	.05
274	Mike Moore	.05
275	Guillermo Hernandez	.05
276	Dennis Eckersley	.35
277	Graig Nettles	.05
278	Rich Dotson	.05
279	Larry Herndon	.05
280	Gene Larkin	.05
281	Roger McDowell	.05
282	Greg Swindell	.05
283	Juan Agosto	.05
284	Jeff Robinson	.05
285	Mike Dunne	.05
286	Greg Mathews	.05
287	Kent Tekulve	.05
288	Jerry Mumphrey	.05
289	Jack McDowell	.05
290	Frank Viola	.05
291	Mark Gubicza	.05
292	Dave Schmidt	.05
293	Mike Henneman	.05
294	Jimmy Jones	.05
295	Charlie Hough	.05
296	Rafael Santana	.05
297	Chris Speier	.05
298	Mike Witt	.05
299	Pascual Perez	.05
300	Nolan Ryan	.75
301	Mitch Williams	.05
302	Mookie Wilson	.05
303	Mackey Sasser	.05
304	John Cerutti	.05
305	Jeff Reardon	.05
306	Randy Myers	.05
307	Greg Brock	.05
308	Bob Welch	.05
309	Jeff Robinson	.05
310	Harold Reynolds	.05
311	Jim Walewander	.05
312	Dave Magadan	.05
313	Jim Gantner	.05
314	Walt Terrell	.05
315	Wally Backman	.05
316	Luis Salazar	.05
317	Rick Rhoden	.05
318	Tom Henke	.05

319 Mike Macfarlane .05
320 Dan Plesac .05
321 Calvin Schiraldi .05
322 Stan Javier .05
323 Devon White .05
324 Scott Bradley .05
325 Bruce Hurst .05
326 Manny Lee .05
327 Rick Aguilera .05
328 Bruce Ruffin .05
329 Ed Whitson .05
330 Bo Jackson .10
331 Ivan Calderon .05
332 Mickey Hatcher .05
333 Barry Jones .05
334 Ron Hassey .05
335 Bill Wegman .05
336 Damon Berryhill .05
337 Steve Ontiverso .05
338 Dan Pasqua .05
339 Bill Pecota .05
340 Greg Cadaret .05
341 Scott Bankhead .05
342 Ron Guidry .10
343 Danny Heep .05
344 Bob Brower .05
345 Rich Gedman .05
346 Nelson Santovenia **RC** .05
347 George Bell .05
348 Ted Power .05
349 Mark Grant .05
350a Roger Clemens (778 Wins) 2.00
350b Roger Clemens (78 Wins) .60
351 Bill Long .05
352 Jay Bell .05
353 Steve Balboni .05
354 Bob Kipper .05
355 Steve Jeltz .05
356 Jesse Orosco .05
357 Bob Dernier .05
358 Mickey Tettleton .05
359 Duane Ward .05
360 Darrin Jackson .05
361 Rey Quinones .05
362 Mark Grace .05
363 Steve Lake .05
364 Pat Perry .05
365 Terry Steinbach .05
366 Alan Ashby .05
367 Jeff Montgomery .05
368 Steve Buechele .05
369 Chris Brown .05
370 Orel Hershiser .05
371 Todd Benzinger .05
372 Ron Gant .05
373 Paul Assenmacher .05
374 Joey Meyer .05
375 Neil Allen .05
376 Mike Davis .05
377 Jeff Parrett .05
378 Jay Howell .05
379 Rafael Belliard .05
380 Luis Polonia .05
381 Keith Atherton .05
382 Kent Hrbek .05
383 Bob Stanley .05
384 Dave LaPoint .05
385 Rance Mulliniks .05
386 Melido Perez .05
387 Doug Jones .05
388 Steve Lyons .05
389 Alejandro Pena .05
390 Frank White .05
391 Pat Tabler .05
392 Eric Plunk .05
393 Mike Maddux .05
394 Allan Anderson .05
395 Bob Brenly .05
396 Rick Cerone .05
397 Scott Terry .05
398 Mike Jackson .05
399 Bobby Thigpen .05
400 Don Sutton .35
401 Cecil Espy .05
402 Junior Ortiz .05
403 Mike Smithson .05
404 Bud Black .05
405 Tom Foley .05
406 Andres Thomas .05
407 Rick Sutcliffe .05
408 Brian Harper .05
409 John Smiley .05
410 Juan Nieves .05
411 Shawn Abner .05
412 Wes Gardner .05
413 Darren Daulton .05
414 Juan Berenguer .05
415 Charles Hudson .05
416 Rick Honeycutt .05
417 Greg Booker .05
418 Tim Belcher .05
419 Don August .05
420 Dale Mohorcic .05
421 Steve Lombardozzi .05
422 Atlee Hammaker .05
423 Jerry Don Gleaton .05
424 Scott Bailes .05
425 Bruce Sutter .40
426 Randy Ready .05
427 Jerry Reed .05
428 Bryn Smith .05
429 Tim Leary .05
430 Mark Clear .05
431 Terry Leach .05
432 John Moses .05
433 Ozzie Guillen .05
434 Gene Nelson .05
435 Gary Ward .05
436 Luis Aguayo .05
437 Fernando Valenzuela .05
438 Jeff Russell .05
439 Cecilio Guante .05
440 Don Robinson .05
441 Rick Anderson .05
442 Tom Glavine .35
443 Daryl Boston .05
444 Joe Price .05
445 Stewart Cliburn .05
446 Manny Trillo .05
447 Joel Skinner .05
448 Charlie Puleo .05
449 Carlton Fisk .40
450 Will Clark .05
451 Otis Nixon .05
452 Rick Schu .05
453 Todd Stottlemyre .05
454 Tim Birtsas .05
455 Dave Gallagher **RC** .05
456 Barry Lyons .05
457 Fred Manrique .05
458 Ernest Riles .05
459 Doug Jennings **RC** .05
460 Joe Magrane .05
461 Jamie Quirk .05
462 Jack Armstrong **RC** .05
463 Bobby Witt .05
464 Keith Miller .05
465 Todd Burns **RC** .05
466 John Dopson **RC** .05
467 Rich Yett .05
468 Craig Reynolds .05
469 Dave Bergman .05
470 Rex Hudler .05
471 Eric King .05
472 Joaquin Andujar .05
473 Sil Campusano **RC** .05
474 Terry Mulholland .05
475 Mike Flanagan .05
476 Greg Harris .05
477 Tommy John .10
478 Dave Anderson .05
479 Fred Toliver .05
480 Jimmy Key .05
481 Donell Nixon .05
482 Mark Portugal .05
483 Tom Pagnozzi .05
484 Jeff Kunkel .05
485 Frank Williams .05
486 Jody Reed .05
487 Roberto Kelly .05
488 Shawn Hillegas .05
489 Jerry Reuss .05
490 Mark Davis .05
491 Jeff Sellers .05
492 Zane Smith .05
493 Al Newman .05
494 Mike Young .05
495 Larry Parrish .05
496 Herm Winningham .05
497 Carmen Castillo .05
498 Joe Hesketh .05
499 Darrell Miller .05
500 Mike LaCoss .05
501 Charlie Lea .05
502 Bruce Benedict .05
503 Chuck Finley .05
504 Brad Wellman .05
505 Tim Crews .05
506 Ken Gerhart .05
507a Brian Holton (Born: 1/25/65, Denver.) .15
507b Brian Holton (Born: 11/29/59, McKeesport.) .05
508 Dennis Lamp .05
509 Bobby Meacham .05
510 Tracy Jones .05
511 Mike Fitzgerald .05
512 Jeff Bittiger **RC** .05
513 Tim Flannery .05
514 Ray Hayward .05
515 Dave Leiper .05
516 Rod Scurry .05
517 Carmelo Martinez .05
518 Curtis Wilkerson .05
519 Stan Jefferson .05
520 Dan Quisenberry .05
521 Lloyd McClendon .05
522 Steve Trout .05
523 Larry Andersen .05
524 Don Aase .05
525 Bob Forsch .05
526 Geno Petralli .05
527 Angel Salazar .05
528 Mike Schooler **RC** .05
529 Jose Oquendo .05
530 Jay Buhner .05
531 Tom Bolton .05
532 Al Nipper .05
533 Dave Henderson .05
534 John Costello **RC** .05
535 Donnie Moore .05
536 Mike Laga .05
537 Mike Gallego .05
538 Jim Clancy .05
539 Joel Youngblood .05
540 Rick Leach .05
541 Kevin Romine .05
542 Mark Salas .05
543 Greg Minton .05
544 Dave Palmer .05
545 Dwayne Murphy .05
546 Jim Deshaies .05
547 Don Gordon .05
548 Ricky Jordan .05
549 Mike Boddicker .05
550 Mike Scott .05
551 Jeff Ballard .05
552a Jose Rijo (Uniform number #24 on card back.) .15
552b Jose Rijo (Uniform number #27 on card back.) .10
553 Danny Darwin .05
554 Tom Browning .05
555 Danny Jackson .05
556 Rick Dempsey .05
557 Jeffrey Leonard .05
558 Jeff Musselman .05
559 Ron Robinson .05
560 John Tudor .05
561 Don Slaught .05
562 Dennis Rasmussen .05
563 Brady Anderson .05
564 Pedro Guerrero .05
565 Paul Molitor .40
566 Terry Clark **RC** .05
567 Terry Puhl .05
568 Mike Campbell .05
569 Paul Mirabella .05
570 Jeff Hamilton .05
571 Oswald Peraza **RC** .05
572 Bob McClure .05
573 Jose Bautista **RC** .05
574 Alex Trevino .05
575 John Franco .05
576 Mark Parent **RC** .05
577 Nelson Liriano .05
578 Steve Shields .05
579 Odell Jones .05
580 Al Leiter .05
581 Dave Stapleton .05
582 Jose Canseco, Kirk Gibson, Orel Hershiser, Dave Stewart 1988 World Series .10
583 Donnie Hill .05
584 Chuck Jackson .05
585 Rene Gonzales .05
586 Tracy Woodson .05
587 Jim Adduci .05
588 Mario Soto .05
589 Jeff Blauser .05
590 Jim Traber .05
591 Jon Perlman .05
592 Mark Williamson .05
593 Dave Meads .05
594 Jim Eisenreich .05
595a Paul Gibson **RC** (Player in background adjusting cup.) .25
595b Paul Gibson **RC** (Hand airbrushed away.) .05
596 Mike Birkbeck .05
597 Terry Francona .05
598 Paul Zuvella .05
599 Franklin Stubbs .05
600 Gregg Jefferies .05
601 John Cangelosi .05
602 Mike Sharperson .05
603 Mike Diaz .05
604 Gary Varsho **RC** .05
605 Terry Blocker **RC** .05
606 Charlie O'Brien .05
607 Jim Eppard .05
608 John Davis .05
609 Ken Griffey Sr. .05
610 Buddy Bell .05
611 Ted Simmons .05
612 Matt Williams .05
613 Danny Cox .05
614 Al Pedrique .05
615 Ron Oester .05
616 John Smoltz .05
617 Bob Melvin .05
618 Rob Dibble **RC** .10
619 Kirt Manwaring .05
620 Felix Fermin .05
621 Doug Dascenzo **RC** .05
622 Bill Brennan **RC** .05
623 Carlos Quintana **RC** .05
624 Mike Harkey **RC** .05
625 Gary Sheffield **RC** 1.25
626 Tom Prince **RC** .05
627 Steve Searcy **RC** .05
628 Charlie Hayes **RC** .05
629 Felix Jose **RC** .05
630 Sandy Alomar **RC** .50
631 Derek Lilliquist **RC** .05
632 Geronimo Berroa .05
633 Luis Medina **RC** .05
634 Tom Gordon **RC** .10
635 Ramon Martinez **RC** .25
636 Craig Worthington **RC** .05
637 Edgar Martinez .05
638 Chad Krueter **RC** .05
639 Ron Jones **RC** .05
640 Van Snider **RC** .05
641 Lance Blankenship **RC** .05
642 Dwight Smith **RC** .05
643 Cameron Drew **RC** .05
644 Jerald Clark **RC** .05
645 Randy Johnson **RC** 2.00
646 Norm Charlton **RC** .05
647 Todd Frohwirth .05
648 Luis de los Santos **RC** .05
649 Tim Jones **RC** .05
650 Dave West **RC** .05
651 Bob Milacki **RC** .05
652 1988 Highlight (Wrigley Field) .05
653 Orel Hershiser 1988 Highlight .05
654a Wade Boggs 1988 Highlight ("...sixth consecutive seaason..." on back) 2.00
654b Wade Boggs 1988 Highlight ("Season" corrected.) .10
655 Jose Canseco 1988 Highlight .15
656 Doug Jones 1988 Highlight .05
657 Rickey Henderson 1988 Highlight .10
658 Tom Browning 1988 Highlight .05
659 Mike Greenwell 1988 Highlight .05
660 Joe Morgan 1988 Highlight (A.L. Win Streak) .05

Rookie/Traded

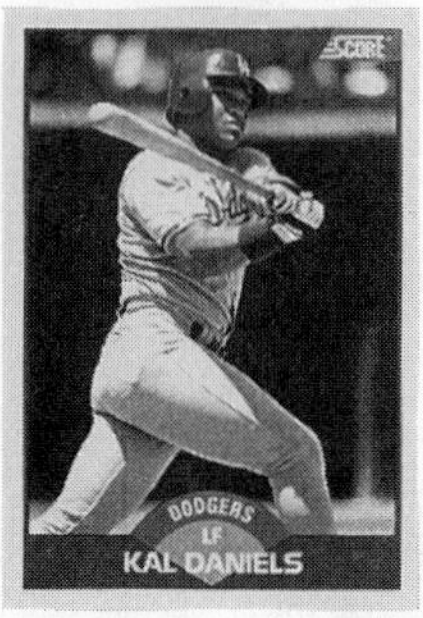

NM/M

Complete Set (110): 10.00
Common Player: .05
1 Rafael Palmeiro .35
2 Nolan Ryan 1.00
3 Jack Clark .05
4 Dave LaPoint .05
5 Mike Moore .05
6 Pete O'Brien .05
7 Jeffrey Leonard .05
8 Rob Murphy .05
9 Tom Herr .05
10 Claudell Washington .05
11 Mike Pagliarulo .05
12 Steve Lake .05
13 Spike Owen .05
14 Andy Hawkins .05
15 Todd Benzinger .05
16 Mookie Wilson .05
17 Bert Blyleven .05
18 Jeff Treadway .05
19 Bruce Hurst .05
20 Steve Sax .05
21 Juan Samuel .05
22 Jesse Barfield .05
23 Carmelo Castillo .05
24 Terry Leach .05
25 Mark Langston .05
26 Eric King .05
27 Steve Balboni .05
28 Len Dykstra .05
29 Keith Moreland .05
30 Terry Kennedy .05
31 Eddie Murray .45
32 Mitch Williams .05
33 Jeff Parrett .05
34 Wally Backman .05
35 Julio Franco .05
36 Lance Parrish .05
37 Nick Esasky .05
38 Luis Polonia .05
39 Kevin Gross .05
40 John Dopson .05
41 Willie Randolph .05
42 Jim Clancy .05
43 Tracy Jones .05
44 Phil Bradley .05
45 Milt Thompson .05
46 Chris James .05
47 Scott Fletcher .05
48 Kal Daniels .05
49 Steve Bedrosian .05
50 Rickey Henderson .45
51 Dion James .05
52 Tim Leary .05
53 Roger McDowell .05
54 Mel Hall .05
55 Dickie Thon .05
56 Zane Smith .05
57 Danny Heep .05
58 Bob McClure .05
59 Brian Holton .05
60 Randy Ready .05
61 Bob Melvin .05
62 Harold Baines .05
63 Lance McCullers .05
64 Jody Davis .05
65 Darrell Evans .05
66 Joel Youngblood .05

67	Frank Viola	.05
68	Mike Aldrete	.05
69	Greg Cadaret	.05
70	John Kruk	.05
71	Pat Sheridan	.05
72	Oddibe McDowell	.05
73	Tom Brookens	.05
74	Bob Boone	.05
75	Walt Terrell	.05
76	Joel Skinner	.05
77	Randy Johnson	1.50
78	Felix Fermin	.05
79	Rick Mahler	.05
80	Rich Dotson	.05
81	Cris Carpenter	.05
82	Bill Spiers	.05
83	Junior Felix	.05
84	Joe Girardi	.05
85	Jerome Walton	.05
86	Greg Litton	.05
87	Greg Harris	.05
88	Jim Abbott	.05
89	Kevin Brown	.05
90	John Wetteland **RC**	.10
91	Gary Wayne	.05
92	Rich Monteleone	.05
93	Bob Geren	.05
94	Clay Parker	.05
95	Steve Finley	.05
96	Gregg Olson	.05
97	Ken Patterson	.05
98	Ken Hill	.05
99	Scott Scudder	.05
100	Ken Griffey Jr. **RC**	6.00
101	Jeff Brantley	.05
102	Donn Pall	.05
103	Carlos Martinez	.05
104	Joe Oliver	.05
105	Omar Vizquel	.25
106	Albert Belle **RC**	1.00
107	Kenny Rogers **RC**	.10
108	Mark Carreon	.05
109	Rolando Roomes	.05
110	Pete Harnisch	.05

1990 Score

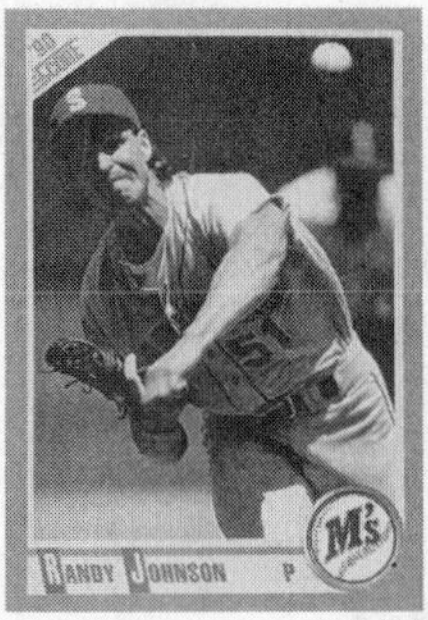

	NM/M
Hobby Factory Set (714):	8.00
Retail Factory Set (704):	7.00
Complete Set (704):	6.00
Common Player:	.05
Plastic Pack (16):	.40
Plastic Wax Box (36):	9.00

1	Don Mattingly	.50
2	Cal Ripken, Jr.	1.00
3	Dwight Evans	.05
4	Barry Bonds	1.00
5	Kevin McReynolds	.05
6	Ozzie Guillen	.05
7	Terry Kennedy	.05
8	Bryan Harvey	.05
9	Alan Trammell	.05
10	Cory Snyder	.05
11	Jody Reed	.05
12	Roberto Alomar	.20
13	Pedro Guerrero	.05
14	Gary Redus	.05
15	Marty Barrett	.05
16	Ricky Jordan	.05
17	Joe Magrane	.05
18	Sid Fernandez	.05
19	Rich Dotson	.05
20	Jack Clark	.05
21	Bob Walk	.05
22	Ron Karkovice	.05
23	Lenny Harris	.05
24	Phil Bradley	.05
25	Andres Galarraga	.05
26	Brian Downing	.05
27	Dave Martinez	.05
28	Eric King	.05
29	Barry Lyons	.05
30	Dave Schmidt	.05
31	Mike Boddicker	.05
32	Tom Foley	.05
33	Brady Anderson	.05
34	Jim Presley	.05
35	Lance Parrish	.05
36	Von Hayes	.05
37	Lee Smith	.05
38	Herm Winningham	.05
39	Alejandro Pena	.05
40	Mike Scott	.05
41	Joe Orsulak	.05
42	Rafael Ramirez	.05
43	Gerald Young	.05
44	Dick Schofield	.05
45	Dave Smith	.05
46	Dave Magadan	.05
47	Dennis Martinez	.05
48	Greg Minton	.05
49	Milt Thompson	.05
50	Orel Hershiser	.05
51	Bip Roberts	.05
52	Jerry Browne	.05
53	Bob Ojeda	.05
54	Fernando Valenzuela	.05
55	Matt Nokes	.05
56	Brook Jacoby	.05
57	Frank Tanana	.05
58	Scott Fletcher	.05
59	Ron Oester	.05
60	Bob Boone	.05
61	Dan Gladden	.05
62	Darnell Coles	.05
63	Gregg Olson	.05
64	Todd Burns	.05
65	Todd Benzinger	.05
66	Dale Murphy	.25
67	Mike Flanagan	.05
68	Jose Oquendo	.05
69	Cecil Espy	.05
70	Chris Sabo	.05
71	Shane Rawley	.05
72	Tom Brunansky	.05
73	Vance Law	.05
74	B.J. Surhoff	.05
75	Lou Whitaker	.05
76	Ken Caminiti	.05
77	Nelson Liriano	.05
78	Tommy Gregg	.05
79	Don Slaught	.05
80	Eddie Murray	.40
81	Joe Boever	.05
82	Charlie Leibrandt	.05
83	Jose Lind	.05
84	Tony Phillips	.05
85	Mitch Webster	.05
86	Dan Plesac	.05
87	Rick Mahler	.05
88	Steve Lyons	.05
89	Tony Fernandez	.05
90	Ryne Sandberg	.45
91	Nick Esasky	.05
92	Luis Salazar	.05
93	Pete Incaviglia	.05
94	Ivan Calderon	.05
95	Jeff Treadway	.05
96	Kurt Stillwell	.05
97	Gary Sheffield	.30
98	Jeffrey Leonard	.05
99	Andres Thomas	.05
100	Roberto Kelly	.05
101	Alvaro Espinoza	.05
102	Greg Gagne	.05
103	John Farrell	.05
104	Willie Wilson	.05
105	Glenn Braggs	.05
106	Chet Lemon	.05
107	Jamie Moyer	.05
108	Chuck Crim	.05
109	Dave Valle	.05
110	Walt Weiss	.05
111	Larry Sheets	.05
112	Don Robinson	.05
113	Danny Heep	.05
114	Carmelo Martinez	.05
115	Dave Gallagher	.05
116	Mike LaValliere	.05
117	Bob McClure	.05
118	Rene Gonzales	.05
119	Mark Parent	.05
120	Wally Joyner	.05
121	Mark Gubicza	.05
122	Tony Pena	.05
123	Carmen Castillo	.05
124	Howard Johnson	.05
125	Steve Sax	.05
126	Tim Belcher	.05
127	Tim Burke	.05
128	Al Newman	.05
129	Dennis Rasmussen	.05
130	Doug Jones	.05
131	Fred Lynn	.05
132	Jeff Hamilton	.05
133	German Gonzalez	.05
134	John Morris	.05
135	Dave Parker	.05
136	Gary Pettis	.05
137	Dennis Boyd	.05
138	Candy Maldonado	.05
139	Rick Cerone	.05
140	George Brett	.50
141	Dave Clark	.05
142	Dickie Thon	.05
143	Junior Ortiz	.05
144	Don August	.05
145	Gary Gaetti	.05
146	Kirt Manwaring	.05
147	Jeff Reed	.05
148	Jose Alvarez	.05
149	Mike Schooler	.05
150	Mark Grace	.05
151	Geronimo Berroa	.05
152	Barry Jones	.05
153	Geno Petralli	.05
154	Jim Deshaies	.05
155	Barry Larkin	.05
156	Alfredo Griffin	.05
157	Tom Henke	.05
158	Mike Jeffcoat	.05
159	Bob Welch	.05
160	Julio Franco	.05
161	Henry Cotto	.05
162	Terry Steinbach	.05
163	Damon Berryhill	.05
164	Tim Crews	.05
165	Tom Browning	.05
166	Frd Manrique	.05
167	Harold Reynolds	.05
168a	Ron Hassey (Uniform #27 on back.)	.05
168b	Ron Hassey (Uniform #24 on back.)	.50
169	Shawon Dunston	.05
170	Bobby Bonilla	.05
171	Tom Herr	.05
172	Mike Heath	.05
173	Rich Gedman	.05
174	Bill Ripken	.05
175	Pete O'Brien	.05
176a	Lloyd McClendon (Uniform number 1 on back.)	.50
176b	Lloyd McClendon (Uniform number 10 on back.)	.05
177	Brian Holton	.05
178	Jeff Blauser	.05
179	Jim Eisenreich	.05
180	Bert Blyleven	.05
181	Rob Murphy	.05
182	Bill Doran	.05
183	Curt Ford	.05
184	Mike Henneman	.05
185	Eric Davis	.05
186	Lance McCullers	.05
187	Steve Davis **RC**	.05
188	Bill Wegman	.05
189	Brian Harper	.05
190	Mike Moore	.05
191	Dale Mohorcic	.05
192	Tim Wallach	.05
193	Keith Hernandez	.05
194	Dave Righetti	.05
195a	Bret Saberhagen ("Joke" on card back.)	.10
195b	Bret Saberhagen ("Joker" on card back.)	.30
196	Paul Kilgus	.05
197	Bud Black	.05
198	Juan Samuel	.05
199	Kevin Seitzer	.05
200	Darryl Strawberry	.05
201	Dave Stieb	.05
202	Charlie Hough	.05
203	Jack Morris	.05
204	Rance Mulliniks	.05
205	Alvin Davis	.05
206	Jack Howell	.05
207	Ken Patterson	.05
208	Terry Pendleton	.05
209	Craig Lefferts	.05
210	Kevin Brown	.05
211	Dan Petry	.05
212	Dave Leiper	.05
213	Daryl Boston	.05
214	Kevin Hickey	.05
215	Mike Krukow	.05
216	Terry Francona	.05
217	Kirk McCaskill	.05
218	Scott Bailes	.05
219	Bob Forsch	.05
220	Mike Aldrete	.05
221	Steve Buechele	.05
222	Jesse Barfield	.05
223	Juan Berenguer	.05
224	Andy McGaffigan	.05
225	Pete Smith	.05
226	Mike Witt	.05
227	Jay Howell	.05
228	Scott Bradley	.05
229	Jerome Walton **RC**	.05
230	Greg Swindell	.05
231	Atlee Hammaker	.05
232a	Mike Devereaux (RF)	.05
232b	Mike Devereaux (CF)	2.00
233	Ken Hill	.05
234	Craig Worthington	.05
235	Scott Terry	.05
236	Brett Butler	.05
237	Doyle Alexander	.05
238	Dave Anderson	.05
239	Bob Milacki	.05
240	Dwight Smith	.05
241	Otis Nixon	.05
242	Pat Tabler	.05
243	Derek Lilliquist	.05
244	Danny Tartabull	.05
245	Wade Boggs	.45
246	Scott Garrelts	.05
247	Spike Owen	.05
248	Norm Charlton	.05
249	Gerald Perry	.05
250	Nolan Ryan	1.00
251	Kevin Gross	.05
252	Randy Milligan	.05
253	Mike LaCoss	.05
254	Dave Bergman	.05
255	Tony Gwynn	.45
256	Felix Fermin	.05
257	Greg Harris	.05
258	Junior Felix **RC**	.05
259	Mark Davis	.05
260	Vince Coleman	.05
261	Paul Gibson	.05
262	Mitch Williams	.05
263	Jeff Russell	.05
264	Omar Vizquel	.05
265	Andre Dawson	.25
266	Storm Davis	.05
267	Guillermo Hernandez	.05
268	Mike Felder	.05
269	Tom Candiotti	.05
270	Bruce Hurst	.05
271	Fred McGriff	.05
272	Glenn Davis	.05
273	John Franco	.05
274	Rich Yett	.05
275	Craig Biggio	.05
276	Gene Larkin	.05
277	Rob Dibble	.05
278	Randy Bush	.05
279	Kevin Bass	.05
280a	Bo Jackson ("Watham" on back.)	.15
280b	Bo Jackson ("Wathan" on back.)	.50
281	Wally Backman	.05
282	Larry Andersen	.05
283	Chris Bosio	.05
284	Juan Agosto	.05
285	Ozzie Smith	.45
286	George Bell	.05
287	Rex Hudler	.05
288	Pat Borders	.05
289	Danny Jackson	.05
290	Carlton Fisk	.40
291	Tracy Jones	.05
292	Allan Anderson	.05
293	Johnny Ray	.05
294	Lee Guetterman	.05
295	Paul O'Neill	.05
296	Carney Lansford	.05
297	Tom Brookens	.05
298	Claudell Washington	.05
299	Hubie Brooks	.05
300	Will Clark	.05
301	Kenny Rogers	.05
302	Darrell Evans	.05
303	Greg Briley	.05
304	Donn Pall	.05
305	Teddy Higuera	.05
306	Dan Pasqua	.05
307	Dave Winfield	.40
308	Dennis Powell	.05
309	Jose DeLeon	.05
310	Roger Clemens	.50
311	Melido Perez	.05
312	Devon White	.05
313	Dwight Gooden	.05
314	Carlos Martinez **RC**	.05
315	Dennis Eckersley	.35
316	Clay Parker	.05
317	Rick Honeycutt	.05
318	Tim Laudner	.05
319	Joe Carter	.05
320	Robin Yount	.40
321	Felix Jose	.05
322	Mickey Tettleton	.05
323	Mike Gallego	.05
324	Edgar Martinez	.05
325	Dave Henderson	.05
326	Chili Davis	.05
327	Steve Balboni	.05
328	Jody Davis	.05
329	Shawn Hillegas	.05
330	Jim Abbott	.05
331	John Dopson	.05
332	Mark Williamson	.05
333	Jeff Robinson	.05
334	John Smiley	.05
335	Bobby Thigpen	.05
336	Garry Templeton	.05
337	Marvell Wynne	.05
338a	Ken Griffey Sr. (Uniform #25 on card back.)	.05
338b	Ken Griffey Sr. (Uniform #30 on card back.)	1.00
339	Steve Finley	.05
340	Ellis Burks	.05
341	Frank Williams	.05
342	Mike Morgan	.05
343	Kevin Mitchell	.05
344	Joel Youngblood	.05
345	Mike Greenwell	.05
346	Glenn Wilson	.05
347	John Costello	.05
348	Wes Gardner	.05
349	Jeff Ballard	.05
350	Mark Thurmond	.05
351	Randy Myers	.05
352	Shawn Abner	.05
353	Jesse Orosco	.05
354	Greg Walker	.05
355	Pete Harnisch	.05
356	Steve Farr	.05
357	Dave LaPoint	.05
358	Willie Fraser	.05
359	Mickey Hatcher	.05
360	Rickey Henderson	.40
361	Mike Fitzgerald	.05
362	Bill Schroeder	.05
363	Mark Carreon	.05
364	Ron Jones	.05
365	Jeff Montgomery	.05
366	Bill Krueger	.05
367	John Cangelosi	.05

368	Jose Gonzalez	.05
369	Greg Hibbard **RC**	.05
370	John Smoltz	.05
371	Jeff Brantley **RC**	.05
372	Frank White	.05
373	Ed Whitson	.05
374	Willie McGee	.05
375	Jose Canseco	.30
376	Randy Ready	.05
377	Don Aase	.05
378	Tony Armas	.05
379	Steve Bedrosian	.05
380	Chuck Finley	.05
381	Kent Hrbek	.05
382	Jim Gantner	.05
383	Mel Hall	.05
384	Mike Marshall	.05
385	Mark McGwire	.75
386	Wayne Tolleson	.05
387	Brian Holton	.05
388	John Wetteland	.05
389	Darren Daulton	.05
390	Rob Deer	.05
391	John Moses	.05
392	Todd Worrell	.05
393	Chuck Cary	.05
394	Stan Javier	.05
395	Willie Randolph	.05
396	Bill Buckner	.05
397	Robby Thompson	.05
398	Mike Scioscia	.05
399	Lonnie Smith	.05
400	Kirby Puckett	.45
401	Mark Langston	.05
402	Danny Darwin	.05
403	Greg Maddux	.45
404	Lloyd Moseby	.05
405	Rafael Palmeiro	.35
406	Chad Kreuter	.05
407	Jimmy Key	.05
408	Tim Birtsas	.05
409	Tim Raines	.05
410	Dave Stewart	.05
411	Eric Yelding **RC**	.05
412	Kent Anderson **RC**	.05
413	Les Lancaster	.05
414	Rick Dempsey	.05
415	Randy Johnson	.40
416	Gary Carter	.40
417	Rolando Roomes	.05
418	Dan Schatzeder	.05
419	Bryn Smith	.05
420	Ruben Sierra	.05
421	Steve Jeltz	.05
422	Ken Oberkfell	.05
423	Sid Bream	.05
424	Jim Clancy	.05
425	Kelly Gruber	.05
426	Rick Leach	.05
427	Len Dykstra	.05
428	Jeff Pico	.05
429	John Cerutti	.05
430	David Cone	.05
431	Jeff Kunkel	.05
432	Luis Aquino	.05
433	Ernie Whitt	.05
434	Bo Diaz	.05
435	Steve Lake	.05
436	Pat Perry	.05
437	Mike Davis	.05
438	Cecilio Guante	.05
439	Duane Ward	.05
440	Andy Van Slyke	.05
441	Gene Nelson	.05
442	Luis Polonia	.05
443	Kevin Elster	.05
444	Keith Moreland	.05
445	Roger McDowell	.05
446	Ron Darling	.05
447	Ernest Riles	.05
448	Mookie Wilson	.05
449a	Bill Spiers **RC** (66 missing for year of birth)	.50
449b	Bill Spiers **RC** (1966 for birth year)	.05
450	Rick Sutcliffe	.05
451	Nelson Santovenia	.05
452	Andy Allanson	.05
453	Bob Melvin	.05
454	Benny Santiago	.05
455	Jose Uribe	.05
456	Bill Landrum	.05
457	Bobby Witt	.05
458	Kevin Romine	.05
459	Lee Mazzilli	.05
460	Paul Molitor	.40
461	Ramon Martinez	.05
462	Frank DiPino	.05
463	Walt Terrell	.05
464	Bob Geren **RC**	.05
465	Rick Reuchel	.05
466	Mark Grant	.05
467	John Kruk	.05
468	Gregg Jefferies	.05
469	R.J. Reynolds	.05
470	Harold Baines	.05
471	Dennis Lamp	.05
472	Tom Gordon	.05
473	Terry Puhl	.05
474	Curtis Wilkerson	.05
475	Dan Quisenberry	.05
476	Oddibe McDowell	.05
477a	Zane Smith (Career ERA 3.93.)	.50
477b	Zane Smith	.05

478	Franklin Stubbs	.05
479	Wallace Johnson	.05
480	Jay Tibbs	.05
481	Tom Glavine	.35
482	Manny Lee	.05
483	Joe Hesketh	.05
484	Mike Bielecki	.05
485	Greg Brock	.05
486	Pascual Perez	.05
487	Kirk Gibson	.05
488	Scott Sanderson	.05
489	Domingo Ramos	.05
490	Kal Daniels	.05
491a	David Wells (Reversed negative on back photo.)	1.50
491b	David Wells (Corrected)	.05
492	Jerry Reed	.05
493	Eric Show	.05
494	Mike Pagliarulo	.05
495	Ron Robinson	.05
496	Brad Komminsk	.05
497	Greg Litton **RC**	.05
498	Chris James	.05
499	Luis Quinones	.05
500	Frank Viola	.05
501	Tim Teufel	.05
502	Terry Leach	.05
503	Matt Williams	.05
504	Tim Leary	.05
505	Doug Drabek	.05
506	Mariano Duncan	.05
507	Charlie Hayes	.05
508	Albert Belle	.05
509	Pat Sheridan	.05
510	Mackey Sasser	.05
511	Jose Rijo	.05
512	Mike Smithson	.05
513	Gary Ward	.05
514	Dion James	.05
515	Jim Gott	.05
516	Drew Hall	.05
517	Doug Bair	.05
518	Scott Scudder **RC**	.05
519	Rick Aguilera	.05
520	Rafael Belliard	.05
521	Jay Buhner	.05
522	Jeff Reardon	.05
523	Steve Rosenberg	.05
524	Randy Velarde	.05
525	Jeff Musselman	.05
526	Bill Long	.05
527	Gary Wayne **RC**	.05
528	Dave Johnson **RC**	.05
529	Ron Kittle	.05
530	Erik Hanson	.05
531	Steve Wilson	.05
532	Joey Meyer	.05
533	Curt Young	.05
534	Kelly Downs	.05
535	Joe Girardi	.05
536	Lance Blankenship	.05
537	Greg Mathews	.05
538	Donell Nixon	.05
539	Mark Knudson	.05
540	Jeff Wetherby **RC**	.05
541	Darrin Jackson	.05
542	Terry Mulholland	.05
543	Eric Hetzel	.05
544	Rick Reed **RC**	.05
545	Dennis Cook	.05
546	Mike Jackson	.05
547	Brian Fisher	.05
548	Gene Harris **RC**	.05
549	Jeff King	.05
550	Dave Dravecky (Salute)	.05
551	Randy Kutcher	.05
552	Mark Portugal	.05
553	Jim Corsi **RC**	.05
554	Todd Stottlemyre	.05
555	Scott Bankhead	.05
556	Ken Dayley	.05
557	Rick Wrona **RC**	.10
558	Sammy Sosa **RC**	3.00
559	Keith Miller	.05
560	Ken Griffey Jr.	.65
561a	Ryne Sandberg (Highlight, 3B on front.)	2.00
561b	Ryne Sandberg (Highlight, no position.)	.25
562	Billy Hatcher	.05
563	Jay Bell	.05
564	Jack Daugherty **RC**	.05
565	Rich Monteleone **RC**	.05
566	Bo Jackson (All-Star MVP)	.10
567	Tony Fossas **RC**	.05
568	Roy Smith **RC**	.05
569	Jaime Navarro **RC**	.05
570	Lance Johnson	.05
571	Mike Dyer **RC**	.05
572	Kevin Ritz **RC**	.05
573	Dave West	.05
574	Gary Mielke **RC**	.05
575	Scott Lusader	.05
576	Joe Oliver	.05
577	Sandy Alomar, Jr.	.05
578	Andy Benes	.05
579	Tim Jones	.05
580	Randy McCament **RC**	.05
581	Curt Schilling	.35
582	John Orton **RC**	.05
583a	Milt Cuyler **RC** (998 games)	1.00
583b	Milt Cuyler **RC** (98 games)	.05
584	Eric Anthony **RC**	.05
585	Greg Vaughn **RC**	.15

586	Deion Sanders	.05
587	Jose DeJesus	.05
588	Chip Hale **RC**	.05
589	John Olerud **RC**	.50
590	Steve Olin **RC**	.05
591	Marquis Grissom **RC**	.40
592	Moises Alou **RC**	.40
593	Mark Lemke	.05
594	Dean Palmer **RC**	.15
595	Robin Ventura	.05
596	Tino Martinez	.05
597	Mike Huff **RC**	.05
598	Scott Hemond **RC**	.05
599	Wally Whitehurst **RC**	.05
600	Todd Zeile **RC**	.15
601	Glenallen Hill	.05
602	Hal Morris	.05
603	Juan Bell	.05
604	Bobby Rose **RC**	.05
605	Matt Merullo **RC**	.05
606	Kevin Maas **RC**	.05
607	Randy Nosek **RC**	.05
608a	Billy Bates **RC** ("12 triples" mentioned in second-last line)	.05
608b	Billy Bates (Triples not mentioned.)	.75
609	Mike Stanton **RC**	.05
610	Goose Gozzo **RC**	.05
611	Charles Nagy **RC**	.40
612	Scott Coolbaugh **RC**	.05
613	Jose Vizcaino **RC**	.10
614	Greg Smith **RC**	.05
615	Jeff Huson **RC**	.05
616	Mickey Weston **RC**	.05
617	John Pawlowski **RC**	.05
618a	Joe Skalski **RC** (Uniform #27 on card back.)	.15
618b	Joe Skalski **RC** (Uniform #67 on card back.)	1.00
619	Bernie Williams **RC**	1.00
620	Shawn Holman **RC**	.05
621	Gary Eave **RC**	.05
622	Darrin Fletcher **RC**	.10
623	Pat Combs **RC**	.05
624	Mike Blowers **RC**	.05
625	Kevin Appier	.05
626	Pat Austin **RC**	.05
627	Kelly Mann **RC**	.05
628	Matt Kinzer **RC**	.05
629	Chris Hammond **RC**	.10
630	Dean Wilkins **RC**	.05
631	Larry Walker **RC**	.50
632	Blaine Beatty **RC**	.05
633a	Tom Barrett (Uniform #29 on card back.)	.05
633b	Tom Barrett (Uniform#14 on card back.)	1.00
634	Stan Belinda **RC**	.05
635	Tex Smith **RC**	.05
636	Hensley Meulens **RC**	.10
637	Juan Gonzalez **RC**	1.50
638	Lenny Webster **RC**	.10
639	Mark Gardner **RC**	.05
640	Tommy Greene **RC**	.05
641	Mike Hartley **RC**	.05
642	Phil Stephenson **RC**	.05
643	Kevin Mmahat **RC**	.05
644	Ed Whited **RC**	.05
645	Delino DeShields **RC**	.15
646	Kevin Blankenship	.05
647	Paul Sorrento **RC**	.05
648	Mike Roesler **RC**	.05
649	Jason Grimsley **RC**	.05
650	Dave Justice **RC**	1.00
651	Scott Cooper **RC**	.05
652	Dave Eiland	.05
653	Mike Munoz **RC**	.05
654	Jeff Fischer **RC**	.05
655	Terry Jorgenson **RC**	.05
656	George Canale **RC**	.05
657	Brian DuBois **RC**	.05
658	Carlos Quintana	.05
659	Luis de los Santos	.05
660	Jerald Clark	.05
661	Donald Harris **RC**	.05
662	Paul Coleman **RC**	.05
663	Frank Thomas **RC**	2.00
664	Brent Mayne **RC**	.10
665	Eddie Zosky **RC**	.05
666	Steve Hosey **RC**	.05
667	Scott Bryant **RC**	.05
668	Tom Goodwin **RC**	.10
669	Cal Eldred **RC**	.10
670	Earl Cunningham **RC**	.05
671	Alan Zinter **RC**	.05
672	Chuck Knoblauch **RC**	.40
672(a)	Chuck Knoblauch (3,000 autographed cards with a special hologram on back were inserted into 1992 rack packs)	10.00
673	Kyle Abbott **RC**	.10
674	Roger Salkeld **RC**	.05
675	Mo Vaughn **RC**	.50
676	Kiki Jones **RC**	.05
677	Tyler Houston **RC**	.10
678	Jeff Jackson **RC**	.05
679	Greg Gohr **RC**	.05
680	Ben McDonald **RC**	.15
681	Greg Blosser **RC**	.05
682	Willie Green **RC** (Greene)	.05
683	Wade Boggs	.25
684	Will Clark	.05
685	Tony Gwynn	.25

686	Rickey Henderson	.20
687	Bo Jackson	.15
688	Mark Langston	.05
689	Barry Larkin	.05
690	Kirby Puckett	.25
691	Ryne Sandberg	.25
692	Mike Scott	.05
693	Terry Steinbach	.05
694	Bobby Thigpen	.05
695	Mitch Williams	.05
696	Nolan Ryan (Highlight)	.40
697	Bo Jackson (FB/BB)	.25
698	Rickey Henderson (ALCS MVP)	.20
699	Will Clark (NLCS MVP)	.05
700	World Series Games 1-2	.05
701	Lights Out: Candlestick	.15
702	World Series Game 3	.05
703	World Series Wrap-up	.05
704	Wade Boggs (Highlight)	.25

Traded

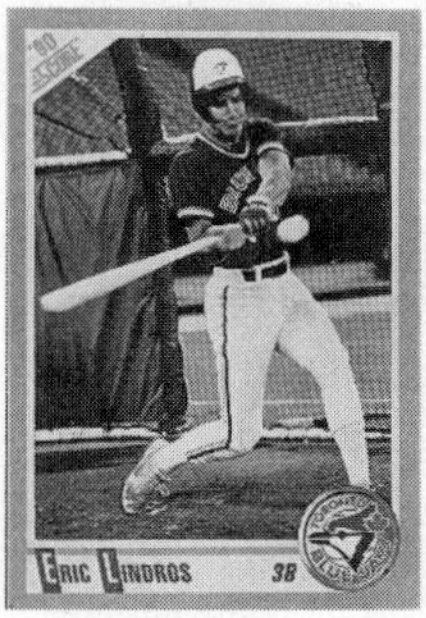
'90 SCORE
ERIC LINDROS
3B

		NM/M
Complete Set (110):		4.00
Common Player:		.05
1	Dave Winfield	.75
2	Kevin Bass	.05
3	Nick Esasky	.05
4	Mitch Webster	.05
5	Pascual Perez	.05
6	Gary Pettis	.05
7	Tony Pena	.05
8	Candy Maldonado	.05
9	Cecil Fielder	.05
10	Carmelo Martinez	.05
11	Mark Langston	.05
12	Dave Parker	.05
13	Don Slaught	.05
14	Tony Phillips	.05
15	John Franco	.05
16	Randy Myers	.05
17	Jeff Reardon	.05
18	Sandy Alomar, Jr.	.05
19	Joe Carter	.05
20	Fred Lynn	.05
21	Storm Davis	.05
22	Craig Lefferts	.05
23	Pete O'Brien	.05
24	Dennis Boyd	.05
25	Lloyd Moseby	.05
26	Mark Davis	.05
27	Tim Leary	.05
28	Gerald Perry	.05
29	Don Aase	.05
30	Ernie Whitt	.05
31	Dale Murphy	.35
32	Alejandro Pena	.05
33	Juan Samuel	.05
34	Hubie Brooks	.05
35	Gary Carter	.75
36	Jim Presley	.05
37	Wally Backman	.05
38	Matt Nokes	.05
39	Dan Petry	.05
40	Franklin Stubbs	.05
41	Jeff Huson	.05
42	Billy Hatcher	.05
43	Terry Leach	.05
44	Phil Bradley	.05
45	Claudell Washington	.05
46	Luis Polonia	.05
47	Daryl Boston	.05
48	Lee Smith	.05
49	Tom Brunansky	.05
50	Mike Witt	.05
51	Willie Randolph	.05
52	Stan Javier	.05
53	Brad Komminsk	.05
54	John Candelaria	.05
55	Bryn Smith	.05
56	Glenn Braggs	.05
57	Keith Hernandez	.05
58	Ken Oberkfell	.05
59	Steve Jeltz	.05
60	Chris James	.05
61	Scott Sanderson	.05
62	Bill Long	.05
63	Rick Cerone	.05
64	Scott Bailes	.05
65	Larry Sheets	.05
66	Junior Ortiz	.05

67	Francisco Cabrera	.05
68	Gary DiSarcina	.05
69	Greg Olson	.05
70	Beau Allred	.05
71	Oscar Azocar	.05
72	Kent Mercker	.05
73	John Burkett	.05
74	Carlos Baerga	.05
75	Dave Hollins	.05
76	Todd Hundley **RC**	.25
77	Rick Parker	.05
78	Steve Cummings	.05
79	Bill Sampen	.05
80	Jerry Kutzler	.05
81	Derek Bell	.05
82	Kevin Tapani	.05
83	Jim Leyritz **RC**	.25
84	Ray Lankford **RC**	.25
85	Wayne Edwards	.05
86	Frank Thomas	2.00
87	Tim Naehring	.05
88	Willie Blair	.05
89	Alan Mills **RC**	.05
90	Scott Radinsky	.05
91	Howard Farmer	.05
92	Julio Machado	.05
93	Rafael Valdez	.05
94	Shawn Boskie **RC**	.05
95	David Segui	.05
96	Chris Hoiles	.05
97	D.J. Dozier	.05
98	Hector Villanueva	.05
99	Eric Gunderson	.05
100	Eric Lindros **RC**	1.00
101	Dave Otto	.05
102	Dana Kiecker	.05
103	Tim Drummond	.05
104	Mickey Pina	.05
105	Craig Grebeck	.05
106	Bernard Gilkey **RC**	.25
107	Tim Layana	.05
108	Scott Chiamparino	.05
109	Steve Avery	.05
110	Terry Shumpert	.05

1991 Score

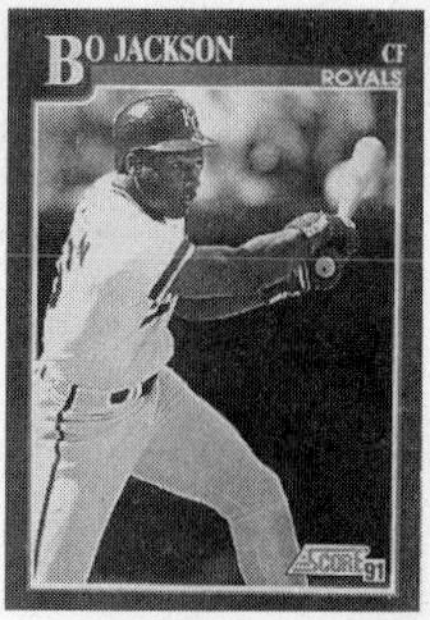

	NM/M
Unopened Fact. Set (900):	10.00
Complete Set (893):	6.00
Common Player:	.05
Series 1 or 2 Pack (16):	.25
Series 1 or 2 Box (36):	6.00

1	Jose Canseco	.25
2	Ken Griffey Jr.	.60
3	Ryne Sandberg	.50
4	Nolan Ryan	.75
5	Bo Jackson	.10
6	Bret Saberhagen	.05
7	Will Clark	.05
8	Ellis Burks	.05
9	Joe Carter	.05
10	Rickey Henderson	.40
11	Ozzie Guillen	.05
12	Wade Boggs	.50
13	Jerome Walton	.05
14	John Franco	.05
15	Ricky Jordan	.05
16	Wally Backman	.05
17	Rob Dibble	.05
18	Glenn Braggs	.05
19	Cory Snyder	.05
20	Kal Daniels	.05
21	Mark Langston	.05
22	Kevin Gross	.05
23	Don Mattingly	.55
24	Dave Righetti	.05
25	Roberto Alomar	.15
26	Robby Thompson	.05
27	Jack McDowell	.05
28	Bip Roberts	.05
29	Jay Howell	.05
30	Dave Steib	.05
31	Johnny Ray	.05
32	Steve Sax	.05
33	Terry Mulholland	.05
34	Lee Guetterman	.05
35	Tim Raines	.05
36	Scott Fletcher	.05
37	Lance Parrish	.05
38	Tony Phillips	.05
39	Todd Stottlemyre	.05
40	Alan Trammell	.05
41	Todd Burns	.05
42	Mookie Wilson	.05
43	Chris Bosio	.05
44	Jeffrey Leonard	.05
45	Doug Jones	.05
46	Mike Scott	.05
47	Andy Hawkins	.05
48	Harold Reynolds	.05
49	Paul Molitor	.40
50	John Farrell	.05
51	Danny Darwin	.05
52	Jeff Blauser	.05
53	John Tudor	.05
54	Milt Thompson	.05
55	Dave Justice	.05
56	Greg Olson **RC**	.05
57	Willie Blair **RC**	.05
58	Rick Parker **RC**	.05
59	Shawn Boskie	.05
60	Kevin Tapani	.05
61	Dave Hollins	.05
62	Scott Radinsky **RC**	.05
63	Francisco Cabrera	.05
64	Tim Layana **RC**	.05
65	Jim Leyritz	.05
66	Wayne Edwards	.05
67	Lee Stevens	.05
68	Bill Sampen **RC**	.05
69	Craig Grebeck **RC**	.05
70	John Burkett	.05
71	Hector Villanueva **RC**	.05
72	Oscar Azocar **RC**	.05
73	Alan Mills	.05
74	Carlos Baerga	.05
75	Charles Nagy	.05
76	Tim Drummond	.05
77	Dana Kiecker **RC**	.05
78	Tom Edens **RC**	.05
79	Kent Mercker	.05
80	Steve Avery	.05
81	Lee Smith	.05
82	Dave Martinez	.05
83	Dave Winfield	.40
84	Bill Spiers	.05
85	Dan Pasqua	.05
86	Randy Milligan	.05
87	Tracy Jones	.05
88	Greg Myers	.05
89	Keith Hernandez	.05
90	Todd Benzinger	.05
91	Mike Jackson	.05
92	Mike Stanley	.05
93	Candy Maldonado	.05
94	John Kruk	.05
95	Cal Ripken, Jr.	.75
96	Willie Fraser	.05
97	Mike Felder	.05
98	Bill Landrum	.05
99	Chuck Crim	.05
100	Chuck Finley	.05
101	Kirt Manwaring	.05
102	Jaime Navarro	.05
103	Dickie Thon	.05
104	Brian Downing	.05
105	Jim Abbott	.05
106	Tom Brookens	.05
107	Darryl Hamilton	.05
108	Bryan Harvey	.05
109	Greg Harris	.05
110	Greg Swindell	.05
111	Juan Berenguer	.05
112	Mike Heath	.05
113	Scott Bradley	.05
114	Jack Morris	.05
115	Barry Jones	.05
116	Kevin Romine	.05
117	Garry Templeton	.05
118	Scott Sanderson	.05
119	Roberto Kelly	.05
120	George Brett	.50
121	Oddibe McDowell	.05
122	Jim Acker	.05
123	Bill Swift	.05
124	Eric King	.05
125	Jay Buhner	.05
126	Matt Young	.05
127	Alvaro Espinoza	.05
128	Greg Hibbard	.05
129	Jeff Robinson	.05
130	Mike Greenwell	.05
131	Dion James	.05
132	Donn Pall	.05
133	Lloyd Moseby	.05
134	Randy Velarde	.05
135	Allan Anderson	.05
136	Mark Davis	.05
137	Eric Davis	.05
138	Phil Stephenson	.05
139	Felix Fermin	.05
140	Pedro Guerrero	.05
141	Charlie Hough	.05
142	Mike Henneman	.05
143	Jeff Montgomery	.05
144	Lenny Harris	.05
145	Bruce Hurst	.05
146	Eric Anthony	.05
147	Paul Assenmacher	.05
148	Jesse Barfield	.05
149	Carlos Quintana	.05
150	Dave Stewart	.05
151	Roy Smith	.05
152	Paul Gibson	.05
153	Mickey Hatcher	.05
154	Jim Eisenreich	.05
155	Kenny Rogers	.05
156	Dave Schmidt	.05
157	Lance Johnson	.05
158	Dave West	.05
159	Steve Balboni	.05
160	Jeff Brantley	.05
161	Craig Biggio	.05
162	Brook Jacoby	.05
163	Dan Gladden	.05
164	Jeff Reardon	.05
165	Mark Carreon	.05
166	Mel Hall	.05
167	Gary Mielke	.05
168	Cecil Fielder	.05
169	Darrin Jackson	.05
170	Rick Aguilera	.05
171	Walt Weiss	.05
172	Steve Farr	.05
173	Jody Reed	.05
174	Mike Jeffcoat	.05
175	Mark Grace	.05
176	Larry Sheets	.05
177	Bill Gullickson	.05
178	Chris Gwynn	.05
179	Melido Perez	.05
180	Sid Fernandez	.05
181	Tim Burke	.05
182	Gary Pettis	.05
183	Rob Murphy	.05
184	Craig Lefferts	.05
185	Howard Johnson	.05
186	Ken Caminiti	.05
187	Tim Belcher	.05
188	Greg Cadaret	.05
189	Matt Williams	.05
190	Dave Magadan	.05
191	Geno Petralli	.05
192	Jeff Robinson	.05
193	Jim Deshaies	.05
194	Willie Randolph	.05
195	George Bell	.05
196	Hubie Brooks	.05
197	Tom Gordon	.05
198	Mike Fitzgerald	.05
199	Mike Pagliarulo	.05
200	Kirby Puckett	.50
201	Shawon Dunston	.05
202	Dennis Boyd	.05
203	Junior Felix	.05
204	Alejandro Pena	.05
205	Pete Smith	.05
206	Tom Glavine	.35
207	Luis Salazar	.05
208	John Smoltz	.05
209	Doug Dascenzo	.05
210	Tim Wallach	.05
211	Greg Gagne	.05
212	Mark Gubicza	.05
213	Mark Parent	.05
214	Ken Oberkfell	.05
215	Gary Carter	.40
216	Rafael Palmeiro	.35
217	Tom Niedenfuer	.05
218	Dave LaPoint	.05
219	Jeff Treadway	.05
220	Mitch Williams	.05
221	Jose DeLeon	.05
222	Mike LaValliere	.05
223	Darrel Akerfelds	.05
224a	Kent Anderson ("Flachy" in first line.)	.05
224b	Kent Anderson ("Flashy" in first line.)	.05
225	Dwight Evans	.05
226	Gary Redus	.05
227	Paul O'Neill	.05
228	Marty Barrett	.05
229	Tom Browning	.05
230	Terry Pendleton	.05
231	Jack Armstrong	.05
232	Mike Boddicker	.05
233	Neal Heaton	.05
234	Marquis Grissom	.05
235	Bert Blyleven	.05
236	Curt Young	.05
237	Don Carman	.05
238	Charlie Hayes	.05
239	Mark Knudson	.05
240	Todd Zeile	.05
241	Larry Walker	.05
242	Jerald Clark	.05
243	Jeff Ballard	.05
244	Jeff King	.05
245	Tom Brunansky	.05
246	Darren Daulton	.05
247	Scott Terry	.05
248	Rob Deer	.05
249	Brady Anderson	.05
250	Len Dykstra	.05
251	Greg Harris	.05
252	Mike Hartley	.05
253	Joey Cora	.05
254	Ivan Calderon	.05
255	Ted Power	.05
256	Sammy Sosa	.50
257	Steve Buechele	.05
258	Mike Devereaux	.05
259	Brad Komminsk	.05
260	Teddy Higuera	.05
261	Shawn Abner	.05
262	Dave Valle	.05
263	Jeff Huson	.05
264	Edgar Martinez	.05
265	Carlton Fisk	.40
266	Steve Finley	.05
267	John Wetteland	.05
268	Kevin Appier	.05
269	Steve Lyons	.05
270	Mickey Tettleton	.05
271	Luis Rivera	.05
272	Steve Jeltz	.05
273	R.J. Reynolds	.05
274	Carlos Martinez	.05
275	Dan Plesac	.05
276	Mike Morgan	.05
277	Jeff Russell	.05
278	Pete Incaviglia	.05
279	Kevin Seitzer	.05
280	Bobby Thigpen	.05
281	Stan Javier	.05
282	Henry Cotto	.05
283	Gary Wayne	.05
284	Shane Mack	.05
285	Brian Holman	.05
286	Gerald Perry	.05
287	Steve Crawford	.05
288	Nelson Liriano	.05
289	Don Aase	.05
290	Randy Johnson	.40
291	Harold Baines	.05
292	Kent Hrbek	.05
293a	Les Lancaster ("Dallas Texas")	.05
293b	Les Lancaster ("Dallas, Texas")	.05
294	Jeff Musselman	.05
295	Kurt Stillwell	.05
296	Stan Belinda	.05
297	Lou Whitaker	.05
298	Glenn Wilson	.05
299	Omar Vizquel	.05
300	Ramon Martinez	.05
301	Dwight Smith	.05
302	Tim Crews	.05
303	Lance Blankenship	.05
304	Sid Bream	.05
305	Rafael Ramirez	.05
306	Steve Wilson	.05
307	Mackey Sasser	.05
308	Franklin Stubbs	.05
309	Jack Daugherty	.05
310	Eddie Murray	.40
311	Bob Welch	.05
312	Brian Harper	.05
313	Lance McCullers	.05
314	Dave Smith	.05
315	Bobby Bonilla	.05
316	Jerry Don Gleaton	.05
317	Greg Maddux	.50
318	Keith Miller	.05
319	Mark Portugal	.05
320	Robin Ventura	.05
321	Bob Ojeda	.05
322	Mike Harkey	.05
323	Jay Bell	.05
324	Mark McGwire	.65
325	Gary Gaetti	.05
326	Jeff Pico	.05
327	Kevin McReynolds	.05
328	Frank Tanana	.05
329	Eric Yelding	.05
330	Barry Bonds	.75
331	Brian McRae **RC**	.05
332	Pedro Munoz **RC**	.05
333	Daryl Irvine **RC**	.05
334	Chris Hoiles	.05
335	Thomas Howard **RC**	.05
336	Jeff Schulz **RC**	.05
337	Jeff Manto	.05
338	Beau Allred	.05
339	Mike Bordick **RC**	.10
340	Todd Hundley	.05
341	Jim Vatcher **RC**	.05
342	Luis Sojo	.05
343	Jose Offerman **RC**	.05
344	Pete Coachman **RC**	.05
345	Mike Benjamin	.05
346	Ozzie Canseco **RC**	.05
347	Tim McIntosh	.05
348	Phil Plantier **RC**	.05
349	Terry Shumpert **RC**	.05
350	Darren Lewis	.05
351	David Walsh **RC**	.05
352a	Scott Chiamparino **RC** (Bats: Left)	.05
352b	Scott Chiamparino **RC** (Bats: Right)	.05
353	Julio Valera **RC**	.05
354	Anthony Telford **RC**	.05
355	Kevin Wickander	.05
356	Tim Naehring **RC**	.05
357	Jim Poole **RC**	.05
358	Mark Whiten **RC**	.05
359	Terry Wells **RC**	.05
360	Rafael Valdez **RC**	.05
361	Mel Stottlemyre **RC**	.05
362	David Segui **RC**	.10
363	Paul Abbott	.05
364	Steve Howard **RC**	.05
365	Karl Rhodes **RC**	.10
366	Rafael Novoa **RC**	.05
367	Joe Grahe **RC**	.05
368	Darren Reed **RC**	.05
369	Jeff McKnight	.05
370	Scott Leius	.05
371	Mark Dewey **RC**	.05
372	Mark Lee **RC**	.05
373	Rosario Rodriguez **RC**	.05
374	Chuck McElroy	.05
375	Mike Bell **RC**	.05
376	Mickey Morandini	.05
377	Bill Haselman **RC**	.05

378	Dave Pavlas **RC**	.05
379	Derrick May	.05
380	Jeromy Burnitz **RC**	.25
381	Donald Peters **RC**	.05
382	Alex Fernandez **RC**	.05
383	Mike Mussina **RC**	1.00
384	Daniel Smith **RC**	.05
385	Lance Dickson **RC**	.10
386	Carl Everett **RC**	.40
387	Thomas Nevers **RC**	.05
388	Adam Hyzdu **RC**	.05
389	Todd Van Poppel **RC**	.10
390	Rondell White **RC**	.30
391	Marc Newfield **RC**	.05
392	Julio Franco/AS	.05
393	Wade Boggs/AS	.25
394	Ozzie Guillen/AS	.05
395	Cecil Fielder/AS	.05
396	Ken Griffey Jr./AS	.30
397	Rickey Henderson/AS	.20
398	Jose Canseco/AS	.15
399	Roger Clemens/AS	.30
400	Sandy Alomar,Jr./AS	.05
401	Bobby Thigpen/AS	.05
402	Bobby Bonilla	.05
403	Eric Davis	.05
404	Fred McGriff	.05
405	Glenn Davis	.05
406	Kevin Mitchell	.05
407	Rob Dibble (K-Man)	.05
408	Ramon Martinez (K-Man)	.05
409	David Cone (K-Man)	.05
410	Bobby Witt (K-Man)	.05
411	Mark Langston (K-Man)	.05
412	Bo Jackson	.10
413	Shawon Dunston	.05
414	Jesse Barfield	.05
415	Ken Caminiti	.05
416	Benito Santiago	.05
417	Nolan Ryan (Highlight)	.40
418	Bobby Thigpen (HL)	.05
419	Ramon Martinez (HL)	.05
420	Bo Jackson (HL)	.10
421	Carlton Fisk (HL)	.20
422	Jimmy Key	.05
423	Junior Noboa	.05
424	Al Newman	.05
425	Pat Borders	.05
426	Von Hayes	.05
427	Tim Teufel	.05
428	Eric Plunk	.05
429	John Moses	.05
430	Mike Witt	.05
431	Otis Nixon	.05
432	Tony Fernandez	.05
433	Rance Mulliniks	.05
434	Dan Petry	.05
435	Bob Geren	.05
436	Steve Frey	.05
437	Jamie Moyer	.05
438	Junior Ortiz	.05
439	Tom O'Malley	.05
440	Pat Combs	.05
441	Jose Canseco/DT	.15
442	Alfredo Griffin	.05
443	Andres Galarraga	.05
444	Bryn Smith	.05
445	Andre Dawson	.25
446	Juan Samuel	.05
447	Mike Aldrete	.05
448	Ron Gant	.05
449	Fernando Valenzuela	.05
450	Vince Coleman	.05
451	Kevin Mitchell	.05
452	Spike Owen	.05
453	Mike Bielecki	.05
454	Dennis Martinez	.05
455	Brett Butler	.05
456	Ron Darling	.05
457	Dennis Rasmussen	.05
458	Ken Howell	.05
459	Steve Bedrosian	.05
460	Frank Viola	.05
461	Jose Lind	.05
462	Chris Sabo	.05
463	Dante Bichette	.05
464	Rick Mahler	.05
465	John Smiley	.05
466	Devon White	.05
467	John Orton	.05
468	Mike Stanton	.05
469	Billy Hatcher	.05
470	Wally Joyner	.05
471	Gene Larkin	.05
472	Doug Drabek	.05
473	Gary Sheffield	.30
474	David Wells	.05
475	Andy Van Slyke	.05
476	Mike Gallego	.05
477	B.J. Surhoff	.05
478	Gene Nelson	.05
479	Mariano Duncan	.05
480	Fred McGriff	.05
481	Jerry Browne	.05
482	Alvin Davis	.05
483	Bill Wegman	.05
484	Dave Parker	.05
485	Dennis Eckersley	.35
486	Erik Hanson	.05
487	Bill Ripken	.05
488	Tom Candiotti	.05
489	Mike Schooler	.05
490	Gregg Olson	.05
491	Chris James	.05
492	Pete Harnisch	.05
493	Julio Franco	.05
494	Greg Briley	.05
495	Ruben Sierra	.05
496	Steve Olin	.05
497	Mike Fetters	.05
498	Mark Williamson	.05
499	Bob Tewksbury	.05
500	Tony Gwynn	.50
501	Randy Myers	.05
502	Keith Comstock	.05
503	Craig Worthington	.05
504	Mark Eichhorn	.05
505	Barry Larkin	.05
506	Dave Johnson	.05
507	Bobby Witt	.05
508	Joe Orsulak	.05
509	Pete O'Brien	.05
510	Brad Arnsberg	.05
511	Storm Davis	.05
512	Bob Milacki	.05
513	Bill Pecota	.05
514	Glenallen Hill	.05
515	Danny Tartabull	.05
516	Mike Moore	.05
517	Ron Robinson	.05
518	Mark Gardner	.05
519	Rick Wrona	.05
520	Mike Scioscia	.05
521	Frank Wills	.05
522	Greg Brock	.05
523	Jack Clark	.05
524	Bruce Ruffin	.05
525	Robin Yount	.40
526	Tom Foley	.05
527	Pat Perry	.05
528	Greg Vaughn	.05
529	Wally Whitehurst	.05
530	Norm Charlton	.05
531	Marvell Wynne	.05
532	Jim Gantner	.05
533	Greg Litton	.05
534	Manny Lee	.05
535	Scott Bailes	.05
536	Charlie Leibrandt	.05
537	Roger McDowell	.05
538	Andy Benes	.05
539	Rick Honeycutt	.05
540	Dwight Gooden	.05
541	Scott Garrelts	.05
542	Dave Clark	.05
543	Lonnie Smith	.05
544	Rick Rueschel	.05
545	Delino DeShields	.05
546	Mike Sharperson	.05
547	Mike Kingery	.05
548	Terry Kennedy	.05
549	David Cone	.05
550	Orel Hershiser	.05
551	Matt Nokes	.05
552	Eddie Williams	.05
553	Frank DiPino	.05
554	Fred Lynn	.05
555	Alex Cole	.05
556	Terry Leach	.05
557	Chet Lemon	.05
558	Paul Mirabella	.05
559	Bill Long	.05
560	Phil Bradley	.05
561	Duane Ward	.05
562	Dave Bergman	.05
563	Eric Show	.05
564	Xavier Hernandez	.05
565	Jeff Parrett	.05
566	Chuck Cary	.05
567	Ken Hill	.05
568	Bob Welch	.05
569	John Mitchell	.05
570	Travis Fryman	.05
571	Derek Lilliquist	.05
572	Steve Lake	.05
573	John Barfield **RC**	.05
574	Randy Bush	.05
575	Joe Magrane	.05
576	Edgar Diaz	.05
577	Casy Candaele	.05
578	Jesse Orosco	.05
579	Tom Henke	.05
580	Rick Cerone	.05
581	Drew Hall	.05
582	Tony Castillo	.05
583	Jimmy Jones	.05
584	Rick Reed	.05
585	Joe Girardi	.05
586	Jeff Gray **RC**	.05
587	Luis Polonia	.05
588	Joe Klink	.05
589	Rex Hudler	.05
590	Kirk McCaskill	.05
591	Juan Agosto	.05
592	Wes Gardner	.05
593	Rich Rodriguez **RC**	.05
594	Mitch Webster	.05
595	Kelly Gruber	.05
596	Dale Mohorcic	.05
597	Willie McGee	.05
598	Bill Krueger	.05
599	Bob Walk	.05
600	Kevin Maas	.05
601	Danny Jackson	.05
602	Craig McMurtry	.05
603	Curtis Wilkerson	.05
604	Adam Peterson	.05
605	Sam Horn	.05
606	Tommy Gregg	.05
607	Ken Dayley	.05
608	Carmelo Castillo	.05
609	John Shelby	.05
610	Don Slaught	.05
611	Calvin Schiraldi	.05
612	Dennis Lamp	.05
613	Andres Thomas	.05
614	Jose Gonzales	.05
615	Randy Ready	.05
616	Kevin Bass	.05
617	Mike Marshall	.05
618	Daryl Boston	.05
619	Andy McGaffigan	.05
620	Joe Oliver	.05
621	Jim Gott	.05
622	Jose Oquendo	.05
623	Jose DeJesus	.05
624	Mike Brumley	.05
625	John Olerud	.05
626	Ernest Riles	.05
627	Gene Harris	.05
628	Jose Uribe	.05
629	Darnell Coles	.05
630	Carney Lansford	.05
631	Tim Leary	.05
632	Tim Hulett	.05
633	Kevin Elster	.05
634	Tony Fossas	.05
635	Francisco Oliveras	.05
636	Bob Patterson	.05
637	Gary Ward	.05
638	Rene Gonzales	.05
639	Don Robinson	.05
640	Darryl Strawberry	.05
641	Dave Anderson	.05
642	Scott Scudder	.05
643	Reggie Harris **RC**	.05
644	Dave Henderson	.05
645	Ben McDonald	.05
646	Bob Kipper	.05
647	Hal Morris	.05
648	Tim Birtsas	.05
649	Steve Searcy	.05
650	Dale Murphy	.20
651	Ron Oester	.05
652	Mike LaCoss	.05
653	Ron Jones	.05
654	Kelly Downs	.05
655	Roger Clemens	.55
656	Herm Winningham	.05
657	Trevor Wilson	.05
658	Jose Rijo	.05
659	Dann Bilardello	.05
660	Gregg Jefferies	.05
661	Doug Drabek/AS	.05
662	Randy Myers/AS	.05
663	Benito Santiago/AS	.05
664	Will Clark/AS	.05
665	Ryne Sandberg/AS	.25
666	Barry Larkin/AS	.05
667	Matt Williams/AS	.05
668	Barry Bonds/AS	.35
669	Eric Davis	.05
670	Bobby Bonilla/AS	.05
671	Chipper Jones **RC**	3.00
672	Eric Christopherson **RC**	.05
673	Robbie Beckett **RC**	.05
674	Shane Andrews **RC**	.15
675	Steve Karsay **RC**	.10
676	Aaron Holbert **RC**	.05
677	Donovan Osborne **RC**	.05
678	Todd Ritchie **RC**	.05
679	Ron Walden **RC**	.05
680	Tim Costo **RC**	.05
681	Dan Wilson **RC**	.10
682	Kurt Miller **RC**	.05
683	Mike Lieberthal **RC**	.25
684	Roger Clemens (K-Man)	.25
685	Dwight Gooden (K-Man)	.05
686	Nolan Ryan (K-Man)	.35
687	Frank Viola (K-Man)	.05
688	Erik Hanson (K-Man)	.05
689	Matt Williams	.05
690	Jose Canseco	.10
691	Darryl Strawberry	.05
692	Bo Jackson	.10
693	Cecil Fielder	.05
694	Sandy Alomar, Jr.	.05
695	Cory Snyder	.05
696	Eric Davis	.05
697	Ken Griffey Jr.	.30
698	Andy Van Slyke	.05
699	Mark Langston, Mike Witt	.05
700	Randy Johnson	.20
701a	Nolan Ryan (White background on stat box.)	2.00
701b	Nolan Ryan (Blue background on stat box.)	.35
702	Dave Stewart	.05
703	Fernando Valenzuela	.05
704	Andy Hawkins	.05
705	Melido Perez	.05
706	Terry Mulholland	.05
707	Dave Stieb	.05
708	Brian Barnes **RC**	.05
709	Bernard Gilkey	.05
710	Steve Decker **RC**	.05
711	Paul Faries **RC**	.05
712	Paul Marak **RC**	.05
713	Wes Chamberlain **RC**	.05
714	Kevin Belcher **RC**	.05
715	Dan Boone	.05
716	Steve Adkins **RC**	.05
717	Geronimo Pena **RC**	.05
718	Howard Farmer **RC**	.05
719	Mark Leonard **RC**	.05
720	Tom Lampkin	.05
721	Mike Gardiner **RC**	.05
722	Jeff Conine **RC**	.25
723	Efrain Valdez **RC**	.05
724	Chuck Malone	.05
725	Leo Gomez **RC**	.05
726	Paul McClellan **RC**	.05
727	Mark Leiter **RC**	.05
728	Rich DeLucia **RC**	.05
729	Mel Rojas	.05
730	Hector Wagner **RC**	.05
731	Ray Lankford	.05
732	Turner Ward **RC**	.05
733	Gerald Alexander **RC**	.05
734	Scott Anderson **RC**	.05
735	Tony Perezchica	.05
736	Jimmy Kremers	.05
737a	American Flag (SCORE 1991 copyright, unmarked promo.)	.25
737b	American Flag (1991 SCORE in copyright)	.25
738	Mike York **RC**	.05
739	Mike Rochford	.05
740	Scott Aldred	.05
741	Rico Brogna **RC**	.05
742	Dave Burba **RC**	.05
743	Ray Stephens **RC**	.05
744	Eric Gunderson **RC**	.05
745	Troy Afenir **RC**	.05
746	Jeff Shaw	.05
747	Orlando Merced **RC**	.10
748	Omar Oliveras **RC**	.05
749	Jerry Kutzler	.05
750	Mo Vaughn	.05
751	Matt Stark **RC**	.05
752	Randy Hennis **RC**	.05
753	Andujar Cedeno **RC**	.05
754	Kelvin Torve	.05
755	Joe Kraemer	.05
756	Phil Clark **RC**	.05
757	Ed Vosberg **RC**	.05
758	Mike Perez **RC**	.05
759	Scott Lewis **RC**	.05
760	Steve Chitren **RC**	.05
761	Ray Young **RC**	.05
762	Andres Santana **RC**	.05
763	Rodney McCray **RC**	.05
764	Sean Berry **RC**	.05
765	Brent Mayne	.05
766	Mike Simms **RC**	.05
767	Glenn Sutko **RC**	.05
768	Gary Disarcina	.05
769	George Brett (HL)	.25
770	Cecil Fielder (HL)	.05
771	Jim Presley	.05
772	John Dopson	.05
773	Bo Jackson (Breaker)	.10
774	Brent Knackert	.05
775	Bill Doran	.05
776	Dick Schofield	.05
777	Nelson Santovenia	.05
778	Mark Guthrie	.05
779	Mark Lemke	.05
780	Terry Steinbach	.05
781	Tom Bolton	.05
782	Randy Tomlin **RC**	.05
783	Jeff Kunkel	.05
784	Felix Jose	.05
785	Rick Sutcliffe	.05
786	John Cerutti	.05
787	Jose Vizcaino	.05
788	Curt Schilling	.35
789	Ed Whitson	.05
790	Tony Pena	.05
791	John Candelaria	.05
792	Carmelo Martinez	.05
793	Sandy Alomar, Jr.	.05
794	Jim Neidlinger **RC**	.05
795	Barry Larkin, Chris Sabo Red's October	.10
796	Paul Sorrento	.05
797	Tom Pagnozzi	.05
798	Tino Martinez	.05
799	Scott Ruskin	.05
800	Kirk Gibson	.05
801	Walt Terrell	.05
802	John Russell	.05
803	Chili Davis	.05
804	Chris Nabholz	.05
805	Juan Gonzalez	.20
806	Ron Hassey	.05
807	Todd Worrell	.05
808	Tommy Greene	.05
809	Joel Skinner	.05
810	Benito Santiago	.05
811	Pat Tabler	.05
812	Scott Erickson **RC**	.05
813	Moises Alou	.05
814	Dale Sveum	.05
815	Ryne Sandberg (Man of the Year)	.25
816	Rick Dempsey	.05
817	Scott Bankhead	.05
818	Jason Grimsley	.05
819	Doug Jennings	.05
820	Tom Herr	.05
821	Rob Ducey	.05
822	Luis Quinones	.05
823	Greg Minton	.05
824	Mark Grant	.05
825	Ozzie Smith	.50
826	Dave Eiland	.05
827	Danny Heep	.05
828	Hensley Meulens	.05

829	Charlie O'Brien	.05
830	Glenn Davis	.05
831	John Marzano	.05
832	Steve Ontiveros	.05
833	Ron Karkovice	.05
834	Jerry Goff	.05
835	Ken Griffey Sr.	.05
836	Kevin Reimer	.05
837	Randy Kutcher	.05
838	Mike Blowers	.05
839	Mike Macfarlane	.05
840	Frank Thomas	.40
841	Ken Griffey Sr., Ken Griffey Jr.	.20
842	Jack Howell	.05
843	Mauro Gozzo	.05
844	Gerald Young	.05
845	Zane Smith	.05
846	Kevin Brown	.05
847	Sil Campusano	.05
848	Larry Andersen	.05
849	Cal Ripken, Jr.	.35
850	Roger Clemens	.30
851	Sandy Alomar, Jr.	.05
852	Alan Trammell	.05
853	George Brett	.25
854	Robin Yount	.25
855	Kirby Puckett	.25
856	Don Mattingly	.30
857	Rickey Henderson	.20
858	Ken Griffey Jr.	.30
859	Ruben Sierra	.05
860	John Olerud	.05
861	Dave Justice	.05
862	Ryne Sandberg	.25
863	Eric Davis	.05
864	Darryl Strawberry	.05
865	Tim Wallach	.05
866	Dwight Gooden	.05
867	Len Dykstra	.05
868	Barry Bonds	.35
869	Todd Zeile	.05
870	Benito Santiago	.05
871	Will Clark	.05
872	Craig Biggio	.05
873	Wally Joyner	.05
874	Frank Thomas	.20
875	Rickey Henderson (MVP)	.20
876	Barry Bonds (MVP)	.35
877	Bob Welch (Cy Young)	.05
878	Doug Drabek (Cy Young)	.05
879	Sandy Alomar, Jr. (ROY)	.05
880	Dave Justice (ROY)	.05
881	Damon Berryhill	.05
882	Frank Viola	.05
883	Dave Stewart	.05
884	Doug Jones	.05
885	Randy Myers	.05
886	Will Clark	.05
887	Roberto Alomar	.10
888	Barry Larkin	.05
889	Wade Boggs	.25
890	Rickey Henderson	.20
891	Kirby Puckett	.25
892	Ken Griffey Jr.	.30
893	Benito Santiago	.05

Cooperstown

COOPERSTOWN CARD®

NOLAN RYAN

		NM/M
Complete Set (7):		3.50
Common Player:		.25
B1	Wade Boggs	.50
B2	Barry Larkin	.25
B3	Ken Griffey Jr.	1.00
B4	Rickey Henderson	.35
B5	George Brett	.75
B6	Will Clark	.50
B7	Nolan Ryan	1.50

Hot Rookies

		NM/M
Complete Set (10):		2.50
Common Player:		.10
1	Dave Justice	.25
2	Kevin Maas	.10
3	Hal Morris	.10
4	Frank Thomas	1.50
5	Jeff Conine	.10
6	Sandy Alomar Jr.	.10
7	Ray Lankford	.10
8	Steve Decker	.10

HOT ROOKIE — HAL MORRIS

9	Juan Gonzalez	.50
10	Jose Offerman	.10

Mickey Mantle

The Rookie

	NM/M
Complete Set (7):	35.00
Common Card:	7.50
Autographed Card:	575.00

1	The Rookie	9.00
2	Triple Crown	7.50
3	World Series	7.50
4	Going, Going, Gone	7.50
5	Speed and Grace	7.50
6	A True Yankee	7.50
7	Twilight	7.50

Traded

	NM/M
Complete Set (110):	4.00
Common Player:	.05

1	Bo Jackson	.10
2	Mike Flanagan	.05
3	Pete Incaviglia	.05
4	Jack Clark	.05
5	Hubie Brooks	.05
6	Ivan Calderon	.05
7	Glenn Davis	.05
8	Wally Backman	.05
9	Dave Smith	.05
10	Tim Raines	.05
11	Joe Carter	.05
12	Sid Bream	.05
13	George Bell	.05
14	Steve Bedrosian	.05
15	Willie Wilson	.05
16	Darryl Strawberry	.05
17	Danny Jackson	.05
18	Kirk Gibson	.05
19	Willie McGee	.05
20	Junior Felix	.05
21	Steve Farr	.05
22	Pat Tabler	.05
23	Brett Butler	.05
24	Danny Darwin	.05

25	Mickey Tettleton	.05
26	Gary Carter	.50
27	Mitch Williams	.05
28	Candy Maldonado	.05
29	Otis Nixon	.05
30	Brian Downing	.05
31	Tom Candiotti	.05
32	John Candelaria	.05
33	Rob Murphy	.05
34	Deion Sanders	.05
35	Willie Randolph	.05
36	Pete Harnisch	.05
37	Dante Bichette	.05
38	Garry Templeton	.05
39	Gary Gaetti	.05
40	John Cerutti	.05
41	Rick Cerone	.05
42	Mike Pagliarulo	.05
43	Ron Hassey	.05
44	Roberto Alomar	.20
45	Mike Boddicker	.05
46	Bud Black	.05
47	Rob Deer	.05
48	Devon White	.05
49	Luis Sojo	.05
50	Terry Pendleton	.05
51	Kevin Gross	.05
52	Mike Huff	.05
53	Dave Righetti	.05
54	Matt Young	.05
55	Ernest Riles	.05
56	Bill Gullickson	.05
57	Vince Coleman	.05
58	Fred McGriff	.05
59	Franklin Stubbs	.05
60	Eric King	.05
61	Cory Snyder	.05
62	Dwight Evans	.05
63	Gerald Perry	.05
64	Eric Show	.05
65	Shawn Hillegas	.05
66	Tony Fernandez	.05
67	Tim Teufel	.05
68	Mitch Webster	.05
69	Mike Heath	.05
70	Chili Davis	.05
71	Larry Andersen	.05
72	Gary Varsho	.05
73	Juan Berenguer	.05
74	Jack Morris	.05
75	Barry Jones	.05
76	Rafael Belliard	.05
77	Steve Buechele	.05
78	Scott Sanderson	.05
79	Bob Ojeda	.05
80	Curt Schilling	.35
81	Brian Drahman	.05
82	Ivan Rodriguez RC	1.00
83	David Howard	.05
84	Heath Slocumb	.05
85	Mike Timlin	.05
86	Darryl Kile	.05
87	Pete Schourek	.05
88	Bruce Walton	.05
89	Al Osuna	.05
90	Gary Scott	.05
91	Doug Simons	.05
92	Chris Jones	.05
93	Chuck Knoblauch	.05
94	Dana Allison	.05
95	Erik Pappas	.05
96	Jeff Bagwell RC	2.50
97	Kirk Dressendorfer	.05
98	Freddie Benavides	.05
99	Luis Gonzalez RC	.50
100	Wade Taylor	.05
101	Ed Sprague	.05
102	Bob Scanlan	.05
103	Rick Wilkins	.05
104	Chris Donnels	.05
105	Joe Slusarski	.05
106	Mark Lewis	.05
107	Pat Kelly	.05
108	John Briscoe	.05
109	Luis Lopez	.05
110	Jeff Johnson	.05

1992 Score

	NM/M
Unopened Fact. Set (910):	7.50
Complete Set (893):	5.00

Common Player:		.05
Wax Pack (16):		.40
Wax Box (36):		7.50
1	Ken Griffey Jr.	.65
2	Nolan Ryan	1.00
3	Will Clark	.05
4	Dave Justice	.05
5	Dave Henderson	.05
6	Bret Saberhagen	.05
7	Fred McGriff	.05
8	Erik Hanson	.05
9	Darryl Strawberry	.05
10	Dwight Gooden	.05
11	Juan Gonzalez	.20
12	Mark Langston	.05
13	Lonnie Smith	.05
14	Jeff Montgomery	.05
15	Roberto Alomar	.20
16	Delino DeShields	.05
17	Steve Bedrosian	.05
18	Terry Pendleton	.05
19	Mark Carreon	.05
20	Mark McGwire	.75
21	Roger Clemens	.60
22	Chuck Crim	.05
23	Don Mattingly	.60
24	Dickie Thon	.05
25	Ron Gant	.05
26	Milt Cuyler	.05
27	Mike Macfarlane	.05
28	Dan Gladden	.05
29	Melido Perez	.05
30	Willie Randolph	.05
31	Albert Belle	.05
32	Dave Winfield	.40
33	Jimmy Jones	.05
34	Kevin Gross	.05
35	Andres Galarraga	.05
36	Mike Devereaux	.05
37	Chris Bosio	.05
38	Mike LaValliere	.05
39	Gary Gaetti	.05
40	Felix Jose	.05
41	Alvaro Espinoza	.05
42	Rick Aguilera	.05
43	Mike Gallego	.05
44	Eric Davis	.05
45	George Bell	.05
46	Tom Brunansky	.05
47	Steve Farr	.05
48	Duane Ward	.05
49	David Wells	.05
50	Cecil Fielder	.05
51	Walt Weiss	.05
52	Todd Zeile	.05
53	Doug Jones	.05
54	Bob Walk	.05
55	Rafael Palmeiro	.35
56	Rob Deer	.05
57	Paul O'Neill	.05
58	Jeff Reardon	.05
59	Randy Ready	.05
60	Scott Erickson	.05
61	Paul Molitor	.40
62	Jack McDowell	.05
63	Jim Acker	.05
64	Jay Buhner	.05
65	Travis Fryman	.05
66	Marquis Grissom	.05
67	Mike Harkey	.05
68	Luis Polonia	.05
69	Ken Caminiti	.05
70	Chris Sabo	.05
71	Gregg Olson	.05
72	Carlton Fisk	.40
73	Juan Samuel	.05
74	Todd Stottlemyre	.05
75	Andre Dawson	.25
76	Alvin Davis	.05
77	Bill Doran	.05
78	B.J. Surhoff	.05
79	Kirk McCaskill	.05
80	Dale Murphy	.25
81	Jose DeLeon	.05
82	Alex Fernandez	.05
83	Ivan Calderon	.05
84	Brent Mayne	.05
85	Jody Reed	.05
86	Randy Tomlin	.05
87	Randy Milligan	.05
88	Pascual Perez	.05
89	Hensley Meulens	.05
90	Joe Carter	.05
91	Mike Moore	.05
92	Ozzie Guillen	.05
93	Shawn Hillegas	.05
94	Chili Davis	.05
95	Vince Coleman	.05
96	Jimmy Key	.05
97	Billy Ripken	.05
98	Dave Smith	.05
99	Tom Bolton	.05
100	Barry Larkin	.05
101	Kenny Rogers	.05
102	Mike Boddicker	.05
103	Kevin Elster	.05
104	Ken Hill	.05
105	Charlie Leibrandt	.05
106	Pat Combs	.05
107	Hubie Brooks	.05
108	Julio Franco	.05
109	Vicente Palacios	.05
110	Kal Daniels	.05
111	Bruce Hurst	.05
112	Willie McGee	.05

113	Ted Power	.05
114	Milt Thompson	.05
115	Doug Drabek	.05
116	Rafael Belliard	.05
117	Scott Garrelts	.05
118	Terry Mulholland	.05
119	Jay Howell	.05
120	Danny Jackson	.05
121	Scott Ruskin	.05
122	Robin Ventura	.05
123	Bip Roberts	.05
124	Jeff Russell	.05
125	Hal Morris	.05
126	Teddy Higuera	.05
127	Luis Sojo	.05
128	Carlos Baerga	.05
129	Jeff Ballard	.05
130	Tom Gordon	.05
131	Sid Bream	.05
132	Rance Mulliniks	.05
133	Andy Benes	.05
134	Mickey Tettleton	.05
135	Rich DeLucia	.05
136	Tom Pagnozzi	.05
137	Harold Baines	.05
138	Danny Darwin	.05
139	Kevin Bass	.05
140	Chris Nabholz	.05
141	Pete O'Brien	.05
142	Jeff Treadway	.05
143	Mickey Morandini	.05
144	Eric King	.05
145	Danny Tartabull	.05
146	Lance Johnson	.05
147	Casey Candaele	.05
148	Felix Fermin	.05
149	Rich Rodriguez	.05
150	Dwight Evans	.05
151	Joe Klink	.05
152	Kevin Reimer	.05
153	Orlando Merced	.05
154	Mel Hall	.05
155	Randy Myers	.05
156	Greg Harris	.05
157	Jeff Brantley	.05
158	Jim Eisenreich	.05
159	Luis Rivera	.05
160	Cris Carpenter	.05
161	Bruce Ruffin	.05
162	Omar Vizquel	.05
163	Gerald Alexander	.05
164	Mark Guthrie	.05
165	Scott Lewis	.05
166	Bill Sampen	.05
167	Dave Anderson	.05
168	Kevin McReynolds	.05
169	Jose Vizcaino	.05
170	Bob Geren	.05
171	Mike Morgan	.05
172	Jim Gott	.05
173	Mike Pagliarulo	.05
174	Mike Jeffcoat	.05
175	Craig Lefferts	.05
176	Steve Finley	.05
177	Wally Backman	.05
178	Kent Mercker	.05
179	John Cerutti	.05
180	Jay Bell	.05
181	Dale Sveum	.05
182	Greg Gagne	.05
183	Donnie Hill	.05
184	Rex Hudler	.05
185	Pat Kelly	.05
186	Jeff Robinson	.05
187	Jeff Gray	.05
188	Jerry Willard	.05
189	Carlos Quintana	.05
190	Dennis Eckersley	.35
191	Kelly Downs	.05
192	Gregg Jefferies	.05
193	Darrin Fletcher	.05
194	Mike Jackson	.05
195	Eddie Murray	.40
196	Billy Landrum	.05
197	Eric Yelding	.05
198	Devon White	.05
199	Larry Walker	.05
200	Ryne Sandberg	.50
201	Dave Magadan	.05
202	Steve Chitren	.05
203	Scott Fletcher	.05
204	Dwayne Henry	.05
205	Scott Coolbaugh	.05
206	Tracy Jones	.05
207	Von Hayes	.05
208	Bob Melvin	.05
209	Scott Scudder	.05
210	Luis Gonzalez	.25
211	Scott Sanderson	.05
212	Chris Donnels	.05
213	Heath Slocumb	.05
214	Mike Timlin	.05
215	Brian Harper	.05
216	Juan Berenguer	.05
217	Mike Henneman	.05
218	Bill Spiers	.05
219	Scott Terry	.05
220	Frank Viola	.05
221	Mark Eichhorn	.05
222	Ernest Riles	.05
223	Ray Lankford	.05
224	Pete Harnisch	.05
225	Bobby Bonilla	.05
226	Mike Scioscia	.05
227	Joel Skinner	.05

228	Brian Holman	.05
229	Gilberto Reyes	.05
230	Matt Williams	.05
231	Jaime Navarro	.05
232	Jose Rijo	.05
233	Atlee Hammaker	.05
234	Tim Teufel	.05
235	John Kruk	.05
236	Kurt Stillwell	.05
237	Dan Pasqua	.05
238	Tim Crews	.05
239	Dave Gallagher	.05
240	Leo Gomez	.05
241	Steve Avery	.05
242	Bill Gullickson	.05
243	Mark Portugal	.05
244	Lee Guetterman	.05
245	Benny Santiago	.05
246	Jim Gantner	.05
247	Robby Thompson	.05
248	Terry Shumpert	.05
249	Mike Bell **RC**	.05
250	Harold Reynolds	.05
251	Mike Felder	.05
252	Bill Pecota	.05
253	Bill Krueger	.05
254	Alfredo Griffin	.05
255	Lou Whitaker	.05
256	Roy Smith	.05
257	Jerald Clark	.05
258	Sammy Sosa	.50
259	Tim Naehring	.05
260	Dave Righetti	.05
261	Paul Gibson	.05
262	Chris James	.05
263	Larry Andersen	.05
264	Storm Davis	.05
265	Jose Lind	.05
266	Greg Hibbard	.05
267	Norm Charlton	.05
268	Paul Kilgus	.05
269	Greg Maddux	.50
270	Ellis Burks	.05
271	Frank Tanana	.05
272	Gene Larkin	.05
273	Ron Hassey	.05
274	Jeff Robinson	.05
275	Steve Howe	.05
276	Daryl Boston	.05
277	Mark Lee	.05
278	Jose Segura **RC**	.05
279	Lance Blankenship	.05
280	Don Slaught	.05
281	Russ Swan	.05
282	Bob Tewksbury	.05
283	Geno Petralli	.05
284	Shane Mack	.05
285	Bob Scanlan	.05
286	Tim Leary	.05
287	John Smoltz	.05
288	Pat Borders	.05
289	Mark Davidson	.05
290	Sam Horn	.05
291	Lenny Harris	.05
292	Franklin Stubbs	.05
293	Thomas Howard	.05
294	Steve Lyons	.05
295	Francisco Oliveras	.05
296	Terry Leach	.05
297	Barry Jones	.05
298	Lance Parrish	.05
299	Wally Whitehurst	.05
300	Bob Welch	.05
301	Charlie Hayes	.05
302	Charlie Hough	.05
303	Gary Redus	.05
304	Scott Bradley	.05
305	Jose Oquendo	.05
306	Pete Incaviglia	.05
307	Marvin Freeman	.05
308	Gary Pettis	.05
309	Joe Slusarski	.05
310	Kevin Seitzer	.05
311	Jeff Reed	.05
312	Pat Tabler	.05
313	Mike Maddux	.05
314	Bob Milacki	.05
315	Eric Anthony	.05
316	Dante Bichette	.05
317	Steve Decker	.05
318	Jack Clark	.05
319	Doug Dascenzo	.05
320	Scott Leius	.05
321	Jim Lindeman	.05
322	Bryan Harvey	.05
323	Spike Owen	.05
324	Roberto Kelly	.05
325	Stan Belinda	.05
326	Joey Cora	.05
327	Jeff Innis	.05
328	Willie Wilson	.05
329	Juan Agosto	.05
330	Charles Nagy	.05
331	Scott Bailes	.05
332	Pete Schourek	.05
333	Mike Flanagan	.05
334	Omar Olivares	.05
335	Dennis Lamp	.05
336	Tommy Greene	.05
337	Randy Velarde	.05
338	Tom Lampkin	.05
339	John Russell	.05
340	Bob Kipper	.05
341	Todd Burns	.05
342	Ron Jones	.05

343	Dave Valle	.05
344	Mike Heath	.05
345	John Olerud	.05
346	Gerald Young	.05
347	Ken Patterson	.05
348	Les Lancaster	.05
349	Steve Crawford	.05
350	John Candelaria	.05
351	Mike Aldrete	.05
352	Mariano Duncan	.05
353	Julio Machado	.05
354	Ken Williams	.05
355	Walt Terrell	.05
356	Mitch Williams	.05
357	Al Newman	.05
358	Bud Black	.05
359	Joe Hesketh	.05
360	Paul Assenmacher	.05
361	Bo Jackson	.05
362	Jeff Blauser	.05
363	Mike Brumley	.05
364	Jim Deshaies	.05
365	Brady Anderson	.05
366	Chuck McElroy	.05
367	Matt Merullo	.05
368	Tim Belcher	.05
369	Luis Aquino	.05
370	Joe Oliver	.05
371	Greg Swindell	.05
372	Lee Stevens	.05
373	Mark Knudson	.05
374	Bill Wegman	.05
375	Jerry Don Gleaton	.05
376	Pedro Guerrero	.05
377	Randy Bush	.05
378	Greg Harris	.05
379	Eric Plunk	.05
380	Jose DeJesus	.05
381	Bobby Witt	.05
382	Curtis Wilkerson	.05
383	Gene Nelson	.05
384	Wes Chamberlain	.05
385	Tom Henke	.05
386	Mark Lemke	.05
387	Greg Briley	.05
388	Rafael Ramirez	.05
389	Tony Fossas	.05
390	Henry Cotto	.05
391	Tim Hulett	.05
392	Dean Palmer	.05
393	Glenn Braggs	.05
394	Mark Salas	.05
395	Rusty Meacham **RC**	.05
396	Andy Ashby **RC**	.10
397	Jose Melendez **RC**	.05
398	Warren Newson **RC**	.05
399	Frank Castillo **RC**	.05
400	Chito Martinez **RC**	.05
401	Bernie Williams	.05
402	Derek Bell	.05
403	Javier Ortiz **RC**	.05
404	Tim Sherrill **RC**	.05
405	Rob MacDonald **RC**	.05
406	Phil Plantier	.05
407	Troy Afenir	.05
408	Gino Minutelli **RC**	.05
409	Reggie Jefferson **RC**	.05
410	Mike Remlinger **RC**	.05
411	Carlos Rodriguez **RC**	.05
412	Joe Redfield **RC**	.05
413	Alonzo Powell	.05
414	Scott Livingstone **RC**	.05
415	Scott Kamieniecki **RC**	.05
416	Tim Spehr **RC**	.05
417	Brian Hunter **RC**	.05
418	Ced Landrum **RC**	.05
419	Bret Barberie **RC**	.05
420	Kevin Morton	.05
421	Doug Henry **RC**	.05
422	Doug Piatt **RC**	.05
423	Pat Rice **RC**	.05
424	Juan Guzman	.05
425	Nolan Ryan (No-Hit)	.50
426	Tommy Greene (No-Hit)	.05
427	Bob Milacki, Mike Flanagan, Mark Williamson, Gregg Olson (No-Hit)	.05
428	Wilson Alvarez (No-Hit)	.05
429	Otis Nixon (Highlight)	.05
430	Rickey Henderson (Highlight)	.20
431	Cecil Fielder/AS	.05
432	Julio Franco/AS	.05
433	Cal Ripken, Jr./AS	.50
434	Wade Boggs/AS	.25
435	Joe Carter/AS	.05
436	Ken Griffey Jr./AS	.35
437	Ruben Sierra/AS	.05
438	Scott Erickson/AS	.05
439	Tom Henkev	.05
440	Terry Steinbach/AS	.05
441	Rickey Henderson (Dream Team)	.20
442	Ryne Sandberg (Dream Team)	.30
443	Otis Nixon	.05
444	Scott Radinsky	.05
445	Mark Grace	.05
446	Tony Pena	.05
447	Billy Hatcher	.05
448	Glenallen Hill	.05
449	Chris Gwynn	.05
450	Tom Glavine	.35
451	John Habyan	.05
452	Al Osuna	.05
453	Tony Phillips	.05
454	Greg Cadaret	.05

455	Rob Dibble	.05
456	Rick Honeycutt	.05
457	Jerome Walton	.05
458	Mookie Wilson	.05
459	Mark Gubicza	.05
460	Craig Biggio	.05
461	Dave Cochrane	.05
462	Keith Miller	.05
463	Alex Cole	.05
464	Pete Smith	.05
465	Brett Butler	.05
466	Jeff Huson	.05
467	Steve Lake	.05
468	Lloyd Moseby	.05
469	Tim McIntosh	.05
470	Dennis Martinez	.05
471	Greg Myers	.05
472	Mackey Sasser	.05
473	Junior Ortiz	.05
474	Greg Olson	.05
475	Steve Sax	.05
476	Ricky Jordan	.05
477	Max Venable	.05
478	Brian McRae	.05
479	Doug Simons	.05
480	Rickey Henderson	.40
481	Gary Varsho	.05
482	Carl Willis	.05
483	Rick Wilkins	.05
484	Donn Pall	.05
485	Edgar Martinez	.05
486	Tom Foley	.05
487	Mark Williamson	.05
488	Jack Armstrong	.05
489	Gary Carter	.40
490	Ruben Sierra	.05
491	Gerald Perry	.05
492	Rob Murphy	.05
493	Zane Smith	.05
494	Darryl Kile	.05
495	Kelly Gruber	.05
496	Jerry Browne	.05
497	Darryl Hamilton	.05
498	Mike Stanton	.05
499	Mark Leonard	.05
500	Jose Canseco	.30
501	Dave Martinez	.05
502	Jose Guzman	.05
503	Terry Kennedy	.05
504	Ed Sprague	.05
505	Frank Thomas	.40
506	Darren Daulton	.05
507	Kevin Tapani	.05
508	Luis Salazar	.05
509	Paul Faries	.05
510	Sandy Alomar, Jr.	.05
511	Jeff King	.05
512	Gary Thurman	.05
513	Chris Hammond	.05
514	Pedro Munoz **RC**	.05
515	Alan Trammell	.05
516	Geronimo Pena	.05
517	Rodney McCray	.05
518	Manny Lee	.05
519	Junior Felix	.05
520	Kirk Gibson	.05
521	Darrin Jackson	.05
522	John Burkett	.05
523	Jeff Johnson	.05
524	Jim Corsi	.05
525	Robin Yount	.40
526	Jamie Quirk	.05
527	Bob Ojeda	.05
528	Mark Lewis	.05
529	Bryn Smith	.05
530	Kent Hrbek	.05
531	Dennis Boyd	.05
532	Ron Karkovice	.05
533	Don August	.05
534	Todd Frohwirth	.05
535	Wally Joyner	.05
536	Dennis Rasmussen	.05
537	Andy Allanson	.05
538	Rich Gossage	.05
539	John Marzano	.05
540	Cal Ripken, Jr.	1.00
541	Bill Swift	.05
542	Kevin Appier	.05
543	Dave Bergman	.05
544	Bernard Gilkey	.05
545	Mike Greenwell	.05
546	Jose Uribe	.05
547	Jesse Orosco	.05
548	Bob Patterson	.05
549	Mike Stanley	.05
550	Howard Johnson	.05
551	Joe Orsulak	.05
552	Dick Schofield	.05
553	Dave Hollins	.05
554	David Segui	.05
555	Barry Bonds	1.00
556	Mo Vaughn	.05
557	Craig Wilson	.05
558	Bobby Rose	.05
559	Rod Nichols	.05
560	Len Dykstra	.05
561	Craig Grebeck	.05
562	Darren Lewis	.05
563	Todd Benzinger	.05
564	Ed Whitson	.05
565	Jesse Barfield	.05
566	Lloyd McClendon	.05
567	Dan Plesac	.05
568	Danny Cox	.05
569	Skeeter Barnes	.05

No.	Player	Price
570	Bobby Thigpen	.05
571	Deion Sanders	.05
572	Chuck Knoblauch	.05
573	Matt Nokes	.05
574	Herm Winningham	.05
575	Tom Candiotti	.05
576	Jeff Bagwell	.40
577	Brook Jacoby	.05
578	Chico Walker	.05
579	Brian Downing	.05
580	Dave Stewart	.05
581	Francisco Cabrera	.05
582	Rene Gonzales	.05
583	Stan Javier	.05
584	Randy Johnson	.40
585	Chuck Finley	.05
586	Mark Gardner	.05
587	Mark Whiten	.05
588	Garry Templeton	.05
589	Gary Sheffield	.30
590	Ozzie Smith	.50
591	Candy Maldonado	.05
592	Mike Sharperson	.05
593	Carlos Martinez	.05
594	Scott Bankhead	.05
595	Tim Wallach	.05
596	Tino Martinez	.05
597	Roger McDowell	.05
598	Cory Snyder	.05
599	Andujar Cedeno	.05
600	Kirby Puckett	.50
601	Rick Parker	.05
602	Todd Hundley	.05
603	Greg Litton	.05
604	Dave Johnson	.05
605	John Franco	.05
606	Mike Fetters	.05
607	Luis Alicea	.05
608	Trevor Wilson	.05
609	Rob Ducey	.05
610	Ramon Martinez	.05
611	Dave Burba	.05
612	Dwight Smith	.05
613	Kevin Maas	.05
614	John Costello	.05
615	Glenn Davis	.05
616	Shawn Abner	.05
617	Scott Hemond	.05
618	Tom Prince	.05
619	Wally Ritchie	.05
620	Jim Abbott	.05
621	Charlie O'Brien	.05
622	Jack Daugherty	.05
623	Tommy Gregg	.05
624	Jeff Shaw	.05
625	Tony Gwynn	.50
626	Mark Leiter	.05
627	Jim Clancy	.05
628	Tim Layana	.05
629	Jeff Schaefer	.05
630	Lee Smith	.05
631	Wade Taylor	.05
632	Mike Simms	.05
633	Terry Steinbach	.05
634	Shawon Dunston	.05
635	Tim Raines	.05
636	Kirt Manwaring	.05
637	Warren Cromartie	.05
638	Luis Quinones	.05
639	Greg Vaughn	.05
640	Kevin Mitchell	.05
641	Chris Hoiles	.05
642	Tom Browning	.05
643	Mitch Webster	.05
644	Steve Olin	.05
645	Tony Fernandez	.05
646	Juan Bell	.05
647	Joe Boever	.05
648	Carney Lansford	.05
649	Mike Benjamin	.05
650	George Brett	.60
651	Tim Burke	.05
652	Jack Morris	.05
653	Orel Hershiser	.05
654	Mike Schooler	.05
655	Andy Van Slyke	.05
656	Dave Stieb	.05
657	Dave Clark	.05
658	Ben McDonald	.05
659	John Smiley	.05
660	Wade Boggs	.50
661	Eric Bullock	.05
662	Eric Show	.05
663	Lenny Webster	.05
664	Mike Huff	.05
665	Rick Sutcliffe	.05
666	Jeff Manto	.05
667	Mike Fitzgerald	.05
668	Matt Young	.05
669	Dave West	.05
670	Mike Hartley	.05
671	Curt Schilling	.35
672	Brian Bohanon	.05
673	Cecil Espy	.05
674	Joe Grahe	.05
675	Sid Fernandez	.05
676	Edwin Nunez	.05
677	Hector Villanueva	.05
678	Sean Berry	.05
679	Dave Eiland	.05
680	David Cone	.05
681	Mike Bordick	.05
682	Tony Castillo	.05
683	John Barfield	.05
684	Jeff Hamilton	.05
685	Ken Dayley	.05
686	Carmelo Martinez	.05
687	Mike Capel	.05
688	Scott Chiamparino	.05
689	Rich Gedman	.05
690	Rich Monteleone	.05
691	Alejandro Pena	.05
692	Oscar Azocar	.05
693	Jim Poole	.05
694	Mike Gardiner	.05
695	Steve Buechele	.05
696	Rudy Seanez	.05
697	Paul Abbott	.05
698	Steve Searcy	.05
699	Jose Offerman	.05
700	Ivan Rodriguez	.35
701	Joe Girardi	.05
702	Tony Perezchica	.05
703	Paul McClellan	.05
704	David Howard RC	.05
705	Dan Petry	.05
706	Jack Howell	.05
707	Jose Mesa	.05
708	Randy St. Claire	.05
709	Kevin Brown	.05
710	Ron Darling	.05
711	Jason Grimsley	.05
712	John Orton	.05
713	Shawn Boskie	.05
714	Pat Clements	.05
715	Brian Barnes	.05
716	Luis Lopez RC	.05
717	Bob McClure	.05
718	Mark Davis	.05
719	Dann Bilardello	.05
720	Tom Edens	.05
721	Willie Fraser	.05
722	Curt Young	.05
723	Neal Heaton	.05
724	Craig Worthington	.05
725	Mel Rojas	.05
726	Daryl Irvine	.05
727	Roger Mason	.05
728	Kirk Dressendorfer	.05
729	Scott Aldred	.05
730	Willie Blair	.05
731	Allan Anderson	.05
732	Dana Kiecker	.05
733	Jose Gonzalez	.05
734	Brian Drahman	.05
735	Brad Komminsk	.05
736	Arthur Rhodes RC	.10
737	Terry Mathews RC	.05
738	Jeff Fassero RC	.05
739	Mike Magnante RC	.05
740	Kip Gross RC	.05
741	Jim Hunter RC	.05
742	Jose Mota RC	.05
743	Joe Bitker	.05
744	Tim Mauser RC	.05
745	Ramon Garcia RC	.05
746	Rod Beck RC	.10
747	Jim Austin RC	.05
748	Keith Mitchell RC	.05
749	Wayne Rosenthal RC	.05
750	Bryan Hickerson RC	.05
751	Bruce Egloff RC	.05
752	John Wehner RC	.05
753	Darren Holmes	.05
754	Dave Hansen	.05
755	Mike Mussina	.30
756	Anthony Young RC	.05
757	Ron Tingley	.05
758	Ricky Bones RC	.05
759	Mark Wohlers RC	.05
760	Wilson Alvarez	.05
761	Harvey Pulliam RC	.05
762	Ryan Bowen RC	.05
763	Terry Bross	.05
764	Joel Johnston RC	.05
765	Terry McDaniel RC	.05
766	Esteban Beltre RC	.05
767	Rob Maurer RC	.05
768	Ted Wood	.05
769	Mo Sanford RC	.05
770	Jeff Carter RC	.05
771	Gil Heredia RC	.05
772	Monty Fariss	.05
773	Will Clark/AS	.05
774	Ryne Sandberg/AS	.25
775	Barry Larkin/AS	.05
776	Howard Johnson/AS	.05
777	Barry Bonds/AS	.50
778	Brett Butler/AS	.05
779	Tony Gwynn/AS	.25
780	Ramon Martinez/AS	.05
781	Lee Smith/AS	.05
782	Mike Scioscia/AS	.05
783	Dennis Martinez (Highlight)	.05
784	Dennis Martinez (No-Hit)	.05
785	Mark Gardner (No-Hit)	.05
786	Bret Saberhagen (No-Hit)	.05
787	Kent Mercker, Mark Wohlers, Alejandro Pena (No-Hit)	.05
788	Cal Ripken (MVP)	.50
789	Terry Pendleton (MVP)	.05
790	Roger Clemens (CY)	.35
791	Tom Glavine (CY)	.05
792	Chuck Knoblauch (ROY)	.05
793	Jeff Bagwell (ROY)	.20
794	Cal Ripken, Jr. (Man of the Year)	.50
795	David Cone (Highlight)	.05
796	Kirby Puckett (Highlight)	.25
797	Steve Avery (Highlight)	.05
798	Jack Morris (Highlight)	.05
799	Allen Watson RC	.05
800	Manny Ramirez RC	2.00
801	Cliff Floyd RC	.50
802	Al Shirley RC	.05
803	Brian Barber RC	.05
804	Jon Farrell RC	.05
805	Brent Gates RC	.05
806	Scott Ruffcorn RC	.05
807	Tyrone Hill RC	.05
808	Benji Gil RC	.05
809	Aaron Sele RC	.25
810	Tyler Green RC	.05
811	Chris Jones	.05
812	Steve Wilson	.05
813	Cliff Young RC	.05
814	Don Wakamatsu RC	.05
815	Mike Humphreys RC	.05
816	Scott Servais RC	.05
817	Rico Rossy RC	.05
818	John Ramos RC	.05
819	Rob Mallicoat	.05
820	Milt Hill RC	.05
821	Carlos Garcia	.05
822	Stan Royer	.05
823	Jeff Plympton RC	.05
824	Braulio Castillo RC	.05
825	David Haas RC	.05
826	Luis Mercedes RC	.05
827	Eric Karros	.05
828	Shawn Hare RC	.05
829	Reggie Sanders	.05
830	Tom Goodwin	.05
831	Dan Gakeler RC	.05
832	Stacy Jones RC	.05
833	Kim Batiste RC	.05
834	Cal Eldred	.05
835	Chris George RC	.05
836	Wayne Housie RC	.05
837	Mike Ignasiak RC	.05
838	Josias Manzanillo RC	.05
839	Jim Olander RC	.05
840	Gary Cooper RC	.05
841	Royce Clayton	.05
842	Hector Fajardo	.05
843	Blaine Beatty	.05
844	Jorge Pedre RC	.05
845	Kenny Lofton	.05
846	Scott Brosius	.05
847	Chris Cron RC	.05
848	Denis Boucher	.05
849	Kyle Abbott	.05
850	Bob Zupcic	.05
851	Rheal Cormier RC	.05
852	Jim Lewis RC	.05
853	Anthony Telford	.05
854	Cliff Brantley RC	.05
855	Kevin Campbell RC	.05
856	Craig Shipley RC	.05
857	Chuck Carr	.05
858	Tony Eusebio RC	.10
859	Jim Thome	.35
860	Vinny Castilla RC	.30
861	Dann Howitt	.05
862	Kevin Ward RC	.05
863	Steve Wapnick RC	.05
864	Rod Brewer	.05
865	Todd Van Poppel	.05
866	Jose Hernandez RC	.05
867	Amalio Carreno RC	.05
868	Calvin Jones RC	.05
869	Jeff Gardner RC	.05
870	Jarvis Brown RC	.05
871	Eddie Taubensee RC	.10
872	Andy Mota RC	.05
873	Chris Haney (Front photo actually Scott Ruskin.)	.05
874	Roberto Hernandez	.05
875	Laddie Renfroe RC	.05
876	Scott Cooper	.05
877	Armando Reynoso RC	.05
878	Ty Cobb	.30
879	Babe Ruth	.30
880	Honus Wagner	.30
881	Lou Gehrig	.25
882	Satchel Paige	.35
883	Will Clark	.05
884	Cal Ripken, Jr.	.50
885	Wade Boggs	.25
886	Kirby Puckett	.30
887	Tony Gwynn	.30
888	Craig Biggio	.05
889	Scott Erickson	.05
890	Tom Glavine	.10
891	Rob Dibble	.05
892	Mitch Williams	.05
893	Frank Thomas	.05

1992 Score Factory Set Inserts - World Series

		NM/M
Complete Set (7):		1.00
Common Card:		.15
1	Greg Gagne World Series Game 1	.15
2	Scott Leius World Series Game 2	.15
3	David Justice, Brian Harper World Series Game 3	.15
4	Lonnie Smith, Brian Harper World Series Game 4	.15
5	David Justice World Series Game 5	.15
6	Kirby Puckett World Series Game 6	1.00
7	Gene Larkin World Series Game 7	.15

Game 6

1992 Score Factory Set Inserts - Cooperstown

COOPERSTOWN CARD
CARLTON FISK

	NM/M
Complete Set (4):	1.50
Common Player:	.50
B8 Carlton Fisk	.50
B9 Ozzie Smith	.75
B10 Dave Winfield	.50
B11 Robin Yount	.50

1992 Score Factory Set Inserts - DiMaggio

JOE DiMAGGIO
The Stylish Fielder

	NM/M
Complete Set (3):	4.00
Common Card:	1.25
B12 Joe DiMaggio (The Hard Hitter)	1.50
B13 Joe DiMaggio (The Stylish Fielder)	1.50
B14 Joe DiMaggio (The Championship Player)	1.50

1992 Score Factory Set Inserts - Yastrzemski

	NM/M
Complete Set (3):	2.00
Common Card:	1.00
B15 Carl Yastrzemski (The Impossible Dream)	1.00
B16 Carl Yastrzemski	1.00
B17 Carl Yastrzemski	1.00

Hot Rookies

	NM/M
Complete Set (10):	4.00
Common Player:	.50
1 Cal Eldred	.50

2	Royce Clayton	.50
3	Kenny Lofton	.75
4	Todd Van Poppel	.50
5	Scott Cooper	.50
6	Todd Hundley	.50
7	Tino Martinez	.75
8	Anthony Telford	.50
9	Derek Bell	.50
10	Reggie Jefferson	.50

Joe DiMaggio

		NM/M
Complete Set (5):		25.00
Common Card:		8.00
Autographed Card:		365.00
1-5	Joe DiMaggio	8.00

The Franchise

		NM/M
Complete Set (4):		5.00
Common Card:		1.25
Musial Autograph:		80.00
Mantle Autograph:		450.00
Yastrzemski Autograph:		80.00
Triple Autograph:		1,100
1	Stan Musial	1.50
2	Mickey Mantle	2.50
3	Carl Yastrzemski	1.25
4	Stan Musial, Mickey Mantle, Carl Yastrzemski	1.50

Rookie & Traded

		NM/M
Complete Set (110):		5.00
Common Player:		.05
1	Gary Sheffield	.20
2	Kevin Seitzer	.05
3	Danny Tartabull	.05
4	Steve Sax	.05
5	Bobby Bonilla	.05
6	Frank Viola	.05
7	Dave Winfield	.60
8	Rick Sutcliffe	.05
9	Jose Canseco	.45

10	Greg Swindell	.05
11	Eddie Murray	.60
12	Randy Myers	.05
13	Wally Joyner	.05
14	Kenny Lofton	.05
15	Jack Morris	.05
16	Charlie Hayes	.05
17	Pete Incaviglia	.05
18	Kevin Mitchell	.05
19	Kurt Stillwell	.05
20	Bret Saberhagen	.05
21	Steve Buechele	.05
22	John Smiley	.05
23	Sammy Sosa	3.00
24	George Bell	.05
25	Curt Schilling	.30
26	Dick Schofield	.05
27	David Cone	.05
28	Dan Gladden	.05
29	Kirk McCaskill	.05
30	Mike Gallego	.05
31	Kevin McReynolds	.05
32	Bill Swift	.05
33	Dave Martinez	.05
34	Storm Davis	.05
35	Willie Randolph	.05
36	Melido Perez	.05
37	Mark Carreon	.05
38	Doug Jones	.05
39	Gregg Jefferies	.05
40	Mike Jackson	.05
41	Dickie Thon	.05
42	Eric King	.05
43	Herm Winningham	.05
44	Derek Lilliquist	.05
45	Dave Anderson	.05
46	Jeff Reardon	.05
47	Scott Bankhead	.05
48	Cory Snyder	.05
49	Al Newman	.05
50	Keith Miller	.05
51	Dave Burba	.05
52	Bill Pecota	.05
53	Chuck Crim	.05
54	Mariano Duncan	.05
55	Dave Gallagher	.05
56	Chris Gwynn	.05
57	Scott Ruskin	.05
58	Jack Armstrong	.05
59	Gary Carter	.60
60	Andres Galarraga	.05
61	Ken Hill	.05
62	Eric Davis	.05
63	Ruben Sierra	.05
64	Darrin Fletcher	.05
65	Tim Belcher	.05
66	Mike Morgan	.05
67	Scott Scudder	.05
68	Tom Candiotti	.05
69	Hubie Brooks	.05
70	Kal Daniels	.05
71	Bruce Ruffin	.05
72	Billy Hatcher	.05
73	Bob Melvin	.05
74	Lee Guetterman	.05
75	Rene Gonzales	.05
76	Kevin Bass	.05
77	Tom Bolton	.05
78	John Wetteland	.05
79	Bip Roberts	.05
80	Pat Listach	.05
81	John Doherty	.05
82	Sam Militello	.05
83	Brian Jordan	.05
84	Jeff Kent	.10
85	Dave Fleming	.05
86	Jeff Tackett	.05
87	Chad Curtis	.05
88	Eric Fox	.05
89	Denny Neagle	.05
90	Donovan Osborne	.05
91	Carlos Hernandez	.05
92	Tim Wakefield	.05
93	Tim Salmon	.05
94	Dave Nilsson	.05
95	Mike Perez	.05
96	Pat Hentgen	.05
97	Frank Seminara	.05
98	Ruben Amaro Jr.	.05
99	Archi Cianfrocco	.05
100	Andy Stankiewicz	.05

101	Jim Bullinger	.05
102	Pat Mahomes	.05
103	Hipolito Pichardo	.05
104	Bret Boone	.05
105	John Vander Wal	.05
106	Vince Horsman	.05
107	James Austin	.05
108	Brian Williams	.05
109	Dan Walters	.05
110	Wil Cordero	.05

1993 Score

	NM/M
Complete Set (660):	15.00
Common Player:	.05
Pack (16):	.75
Wax Box (36):	17.50
1	Ken Griffey Jr.	.65
2	Gary Sheffield	.30
3	Frank Thomas	.40
4	Ryne Sandberg	.45
5	Larry Walker	.05
6	Cal Ripken, Jr.	1.00
7	Roger Clemens	.50
8	Bobby Bonilla	.05
9	Carlos Baerga	.05
10	Darren Daulton	.05
11	Travis Fryman	.05
12	Andy Van Slyke	.05
13	Jose Canseco	.30
14	Roberto Alomar	.15
15	Tom Glavine	.30
16	Barry Larkin	.05
17	Gregg Jefferies	.05
18	Craig Biggio	.05
19	Shane Mack	.05
20	Brett Butler	.05
21	Dennis Eckersley	.35
22	Will Clark	.05
23	Don Mattingly	.50
24	Tony Gwynn	.45
25	Ivan Rodriguez	.35
26	Shawon Dunston	.05
27	Mike Mussina	.30
28	Marquis Grissom	.05
29	Charles Nagy	.05
30	Len Dykstra	.05
31	Cecil Fielder	.05
32	Jay Bell	.05
33	B.J. Surhoff	.05
34	Bob Tewksbury	.05
35	Danny Tartabull	.05
36	Terry Pendleton	.05
37	Jack Morris	.05
38	Hal Morris	.05
39	Luis Polonia	.05
40	Ken Caminiti	.05
41	Robin Ventura	.05
42	Darryl Strawberry	.05
43	Wally Joyner	.05
44	Fred McGriff	.05
45	Kevin Tapani	.05
46	Matt Williams	.05
47	Robin Yount	.40
48	Ken Hill	.05
49	Edgar Martinez	.05
50	Mark Grace	.05
51	Juan Gonzalez	.20
52	Curt Schilling	.30
53	Dwight Gooden	.05
54	Chris Hoiles	.05
55	Frank Viola	.05
56	Ray Lankford	.05
57	George Brett	.50
58	Kenny Lofton	.05
59	Nolan Ryan	1.00
60	Mickey Tettleton	.05
61	John Smoltz	.05
62	Howard Johnson	.05
63	Eric Karros	.05
64	Rick Aguilera	.05
65	Steve Finley	.05
66	Mark Langston	.05
67	Bill Swift	.05
68	John Olerud	.05
69	Kevin McReynolds	.05
70	Jack McDowell	.05
71	Rickey Henderson	.40
72	Brian Harper	.05
73	Mike Morgan	.05

74	Rafael Palmeiro	.40
75	Dennis Martinez	.05
76	Tino Martinez	.05
77	Eddie Murray	.40
78	Ellis Burks	.05
79	John Kruk	.05
80	Gregg Olson	.05
81	Bernard Gilkey	.05
82	Milt Cuyler	.05
83	Mike LaValliere	.05
84	Albert Belle	.05
85	Bip Roberts	.05
86	Melido Perez	.05
87	Otis Nixon	.05
88	Bill Spiers	.05
89	Jeff Bagwell	.40
90	Orel Hershiser	.05
91	Andy Benes	.05
92	Devon White	.05
93	Willie McGee	.05
94	Ozzie Guillen	.05
95	Ivan Calderon	.05
96	Keith Miller	.05
97	Steve Buechele	.05
98	Kent Hrbek	.05
99	Dave Hollins	.05
100	Mike Bordick	.05
101	Randy Tomlin	.05
102	Omar Vizquel	.05
103	Lee Smith	.05
104	Leo Gomez	.05
105	Jose Rijo	.05
106	Mark Whiten	.05
107	Dave Justice	.05
108	Eddie Taubensee	.05
109	Lance Johnson	.05
110	Felix Jose	.05
111	Mike Harkey	.05
112	Randy Milligan	.05
113	Anthony Young	.05
114	Rico Brogna	.05
115	Bret Saberhagen	.05
116	Sandy Alomar, Jr.	.05
117	Terry Mulholland	.05
118	Darryl Hamilton	.05
119	Todd Zeile	.05
120	Bernie Williams	.05
121	Zane Smith	.05
122	Derek Bell	.05
123	Deion Sanders	.05
124	Luis Sojo	.05
125	Joe Oliver	.05
126	Craig Grebeck	.05
127	Andujar Cedeno	.05
128	Brian McRae	.05
129	Jose Offerman	.05
130	Pedro Munoz	.05
131	Bud Black	.05
132	Mo Vaughn	.05
133	Bruce Hurst	.05
134	Dave Henderson	.05
135	Tom Pagnozzi	.05
136	Erik Hanson	.05
137	Orlando Merced	.05
138	Dean Palmer	.05
139	John Franco	.05
140	Brady Anderson	.05
141	Ricky Jordan	.05
142	Jeff Blauser	.05
143	Sammy Sosa	.45
144	Bob Walk	.05
145	Delino DeShields	.05
146	Kevin Brown	.05
147	Mark Lemke	.05
148	Chuck Knoblauch	.05
149	Chris Sabo	.05
150	Bobby Witt	.05
151	Luis Gonzalez	.05
152	Ron Karkovice	.05
153	Jeff Brantley	.05
154	Kevin Appier	.05
155	Darrin Jackson	.05
156	Kelly Gruber	.05
157	Royce Clayton	.05
158	Chuck Finley	.05
159	Jeff King	.05
160	Greg Vaughn	.05
161	Geronimo Pena	.05
162	Steve Farr	.05
163	Jose Oquendo	.05
164	Mark Lewis	.05
165	John Wetteland	.05
166	Mike Henneman	.05
167	Todd Hundley	.05
168	Wes Chamberlain	.05
169	Steve Avery	.05
170	Mike Devereaux	.05
171	Reggie Sanders	.05
172	Jay Buhner	.05
173	Eric Anthony	.05
174	John Burkett	.05
175	Tom Candiotti	.05
176	Phil Plantier	.05
177	Doug Henry	.05
178	Scott Leius	.05
179	Kirt Manwaring	.05
180	Jeff Parrett	.05
181	Don Slaught	.05
182	Scott Radinsky	.05
183	Luis Alicea	.05
184	Tom Gordon	.05
185	Rick Wilkins	.05
186	Todd Stottlemyre	.05
187	Moises Alou	.05
188	Joe Grahe	.05

189	Jeff Kent	.05
190	Bill Wegman	.05
191	Kim Batiste	.05
192	Matt Nokes	.05
193	Mark Wohlers	.05
194	Paul Sorrento	.05
195	Chris Hammond	.05
196	Scott Livingstone	.05
197	Doug Jones	.05
198	Scott Cooper	.05
199	Ramon Martinez	.05
200	Dave Valle	.05
201	Mariano Duncan	.05
202	Ben McDonald	.05
203	Darren Lewis	.05
204	Kenny Rogers	.05
205	Manuel Lee	.05
206	Scott Erickson	.05
207	Dan Gladden	.05
208	Bob Welch	.05
209	Greg Olson	.05
210	Dan Pasqua	.05
211	Tim Wallach	.05
212	Jeff Montgomery	.05
213	Derrick May	.05
214	Ed Sprague	.05
215	David Haas	.05
216	Darrin Fletcher	.05
217	Brian Jordan	.05
218	Jaime Navarro	.05
219	Randy Velarde	.05
220	Ron Gant	.05
221	Paul Quantrill	.05
222	Damion Easley	.05
223	Charlie Hough	.05
224	Brad Brink **RC**	.05
225	Barry Manual **RC**	.05
226	Kevin Koslofski **RC**	.05
227	Ryan Thompson **RC**	.05
228	Mike Munoz **RC**	.05
229	Dan Wilson **RC**	.10
230	Peter Hoy **RC**	.05
231	Pedro Astacio **RC**	.10
232	Matt Stairs **RC**	.10
233	Jeff Reboulet **RC**	.05
234	Manny Alexander **RC**	.05
235	Willie Banks **RC**	.05
236	John Jaha **RC**	.05
237	Scooter Tucker **RC**	.05
238	Russ Springer **RC**	.05
239	Paul Miller **RC**	.05
240	Dan Peltier **RC**	.05
241	Ozzie Canseco **RC**	.05
242	Ben Rivera **RC**	.05
243	John Valentin **RC**	.05
244	Henry Rodriguez	.05
245	Derek Parks **RC**	.05
246	Carlos Garcia **RC**	.10
247	Tim Pugh **RC**	.05
248	Melvin Nieves **RC**	.05
249	Rich Amaral **RC**	.05
250	Willie Greene **RC**	.05
251	Tim Scott **RC**	.05
252	Dave Silvestri **RC**	.05
253	Rob Mallicoat **RC**	.05
254	Donald Harris **RC**	.05
255	Craig Colbert **RC**	.05
256	Jose Guzman	.05
257	Domingo Martinez **RC**	.05
258	William Suero **RC**	.05
259	Juan Guerrero **RC**	.05
260	J.T. Snow **RC**	.45
261	Tony Pena	.05
262	Tim Fortugno **RC**	.05
263	Tom Marsh **RC**	.05
264	Kurt Knudsen **RC**	.05
265	Tim Costo **RC**	.05
266	Steve Shifflett **RC**	.05
267	Billy Ashley **RC**	.05
268	Jerry Nielsen	.05
269	Pete Young **RC**	.05
270	Johnny Guzman **RC**	.05
271	Greg Colbrunn **RC**	.05
272	Jeff Nelson	.05
273	Kevin Young **RC**	.05
274	Jeff Frye	.05
275	J.T. Bruett **RC**	.05
276	Todd Pratt **RC**	.05
277	Mike Butcher **RC**	.05
278	John Flaherty **RC**	.05
279	John Patterson **RC**	.05
280	Eric Hillman **RC**	.05
281	Bien Figueros **RC**	.05
282	Shane Reynolds **RC**	.05
283	Rich Rowland **RC**	.05
284	Steve Foster **RC**	.05
285	Dave Mlicki **RC**	.05
286	Mike Piazza	.65
287	Mike Trombley **RC**	.05
288	Jim Pena **RC**	.05
289	Bob Ayrault **RC**	.05
290	Henry Mercedes **RC**	.05
291	Bob Wickman	.05
292	Jacob Brumfield **RC**	.05
293	David Hulse **RC**	.05
294	Ryan Klesko	.05
295	Doug Linton	.05
296	Steve Cooke	.05
297	Eddie Zosky	.05
298	Gerald Williams **RC**	.05
299	Jonathan Hurst **RC**	.05
300	Larry Carter **RC**	.05
301	William Pennyfeather **RC**	.05
302	Cesar Hernandez **RC**	.05
303	Steve Hosey **RC**	.05
304	Blas Minor **RC**	.05
305	Jeff Grotewold **RC**	.05
306	Bernardo Brito **RC**	.05
307	Rafael Bournigal **RC**	.05
308	Jeff Branson **RC**	.05
309	Tom Quinlan **RC**	.05
310	Pat Gomez **RC**	.05
311	Sterling Hitchcock **RC**	.10
312	Kent Bottenfield	.05
313	Alan Trammell	.05
314	Cris Colon **RC**	.05
315	Paul Wagner **RC**	.05
316	Matt Maysey **RC**	.05
317	Mike Stanton	.05
318	Rick Trlicek **RC**	.05
319	Kevin Rogers **RC**	.05
320	Mark Clark **RC**	.05
321	Pedro Martinez	.40
322	Al Martin **RC**	.05
323	Mike Macfarlane	.05
324	Rey Sanchez **RC**	.10
325	Roger Pavlik **RC**	.05
326	Troy Neel	.05
327	Kerry Woodson **RC**	.05
328	Wayne Kirby **RC**	.05
329	Ken Ryan **RC**	.05
330	Jesse Levis **RC**	.05
331	James Austin	.05
332	Dan Walters	.05
333	Brian Williams	.05
334	Wil Cordero	.05
335	Bret Boone	.05
336	Hipolito Pichardo	.05
337	Pat Mahomes	.05
338	Andy Stankiewicz	.05
339	Jim Bullinger	.05
340	Archi Cianfrocco	.05
341	Ruben Amaro Jr.	.05
342	Frank Seminara	.05
343	Pat Hentgen	.05
344	Dave Nilsson	.05
345	Mike Perez	.05
346	Tim Salmon	.05
347	Tim Wakefield **RC**	.10
348	Carlos Hernandez	.05
349	Donovan Osborne	.05
350	Denny Naegle	.05
351	Sam Militello	.05
352	Eric Fox	.05
353	John Doherty	.05
354	Chad Curtis	.05
355	Jeff Tackett	.05
356	Dave Fleming	.05
357	Pat Listach	.05
358	Kevin Wickander	.05
359	John VanderWal	.05
360	Arthur Rhodes	.05
361	Bob Scanlan	.05
362	Bob Zupcic	.05
363	Mel Rojas	.05
364	Jim Thome	.35
365	Bill Pecota	.05
366	Mark Carreon	.05
367	Mitch Williams	.05
368	Cal Eldred	.05
369	Stan Belinda	.05
370	Pat Kelly	.05
371	Pheal Cormier	.05
372	Juan Guzman	.05
373	Damon Berryhill	.05
374	Gary DiSarcina	.05
375	Norm Charlton	.05
376	Roberto Hernandez	.05
377	Scott Kamieniecki	.05
378	Rusty Meacham	.05
379	Kurt Stillwell	.05
380	Lloyd McClendon	.05
381	Mark Leonard	.05
382	Jerry Browne	.05
383	Glenn Davis	.05
384	Randy Johnson	.40
385	Mike Greenwell	.05
386	Scott Chiamparino	.05
387	George Bell	.05
388	Steve Olin	.05
389	Chuck McElroy	.05
390	Mark Gardner	.05
391	Rod Beck	.05
392	Dennis Rasmussen	.05
393	Charlie Leibrandt	.05
394	Julio Franco	.05
395	Pete Harnisch	.05
396	Sid Bream	.05
397	Milt Thompson	.05
398	Glenallen Hill	.05
399	Chico Walker	.05
400	Alex Cole	.05
401	Trevor Wilson	.05
402	Jeff Conine	.05
403	Kyle Abbott	.05
404	Tom Browning	.05
405	Jerald Clark	.05
406	Vince Horsman	.05
407	Kevin Mitchell	.05
408	Pete Smith	.05
409	Jeff Innis	.05
410	Mike Timlin	.05
411	Charlie Hayes	.05
412	Alex Fernandez	.05
413	Jeff Russell	.05
414	Jody Reed	.05
415	Mickey Morandini	.05
416	Darnell Coles	.05
417	Xavier Hernandez	.05
418	Steve Sax	.05
419	Joe Girardi	.05
420	Mike Fetters	.05
421	Danny Jackson	.05
422	Jim Gott	.05
423	Tim Belcher	.05
424	Jose Mesa	.05
425	Junior Felix	.05
426	Thomas Howard	.05
427	Julio Valera	.05
428	Dante Bichette	.05
429	Mike Sharperson	.05
430	Darryl Kile	.05
431	Lonnie Smith	.05
432	Monty Fariss	.05
433	Reggie Jefferson	.05
434	Bob McClure	.05
435	Craig Lefferts	.05
436	Duane Ward	.05
437	Shawn Abner	.05
438	Roberto Kelly	.05
439	Paul O'Neill	.05
440	Alan Mills	.05
441	Roger Mason	.05
442	Gary Pettis	.05
443	Steve Lake	.05
444	Gene Larkin	.05
445	Larry Anderson	.05
446	Doug Dascenzo	.05
447	Daryl Boston	.05
448	John Candelaria	.05
449	Storm Davis	.05
450	Tom Edens	.05
451	Mike Maddux	.05
452	Tim Naehring	.05
453	John Orton	.05
454	Joey Cora	.05
455	Chuck Crim	.05
456	Dan Plesac	.05
457	Mike Bielecki	.05
458	Terry Jorgensen **RC**	.05
459	John Habyan	.05
460	Pete O'Brien	.05
461	Jeff Treadway	.05
462	Frank Castillo	.05
463	Jimmy Jones	.05
464	Tommy Greene	.05
465	Tracy Woodson	.05
466	Rich Rodriguez	.05
467	Joe Hesketh	.05
468	Greg Myers	.05
469	Kirk McCaskill	.05
470	Ricky Bones	.05
471	Lenny Webster	.05
472	Francisco Cabrera	.05
473	Turner Ward	.05
474	Dwayne Henry	.05
475	Al Osuna	.05
476	Craig Wilson	.05
477	Chris Nabholz	.05
478	Rafael Belliard	.05
479	Terry Leach	.05
480	Tim Teufel	.05
481	Dennis Eckersley	.15
482	Barry Bonds	.50
483	Dennis Eckersley	.15
484	Greg Maddux	.25
485	Pat Listach (ROY)	.05
486	Eric Karros (ROY)	.05
487	Jamie Arnold **RC**	.05
488	B.J. Wallace	.05
489	Derek Jeter **RC**	8.00
490	Jason Kendall **RC**	.45
491	Rick Helling	.05
492	Derek Wallace **RC**	.05
493	Sean Lowe **RC**	.05
494	Shannon Stewart **RC**	.65
495	Benji Grigsby **RC**	.05
496	Todd Steverson **RC**	.05
497	Dan Serafini **RC**	.05
498	Michael Tucker	.05
499	Chris Roberts	.05
500	Pete Janicki **RC**	.05
501	Jeff Schmidt **RC**	.05
502	Edgar Martinez/AS	.05
503	Omar Vizquel/AS	.05
504	Ken Griffey Jr./AS	.35
505	Kirby Puckett/AS	.25
506	Joe Carter/AS	.05
507	Ivan Rodriguez/AS	.15
508	Jack Morris/AS	.05
509	Dennis Eckersley/AS	.15
510	Frank Thomas/AS	.20
511	Roberto Alomar/AS	.10
512	Mickey Morandini	.05
513	Dennis Eckersley	.15
514	Jeff Reardon	.05
515	Danny Tartabull	.05
516	Bip Roberts	.05
517	George Brett	.30
518	Robin Yount	.20
519	Kevin Gross	.05
520	Ed Sprague	.05
521	Dave Winfield	.20
522	Ozzie Smith/AS	.25
523	Barry Bonds/AS	.50
524	Andy Van Slyke/AS	.05
525	Tony Gwynn/AS	.25
526	Darren Daulton/AS	.05
527	Greg Maddux/AS	.25
528	Fred McGriff/AS	.05
529	Lee Smith/AS	.05
530	Ryne Sandberg/AS	.25
531	Gary Sheffield/AS	.10
532	Ozzie Smith	.25
533	Kirby Puckett	.25
534	Gary Sheffield	.10
535	Andy Van Slyke	.05
536	Ken Griffey Jr.	.35
537	Ivan Rodriguez	.15
538	Charles Nagy	.05
539	Tom Glavine	.10
540	Dennis Eckersley	.15
541	Frank Thomas	.20
542	Roberto Alomar	.10
543	Sean Barry	.05
544	Mike Schooler	.05
545	Chuck Carr	.05
546	Lenny Harris	.05
547	Gary Scott	.05
548	Derek Lilliquist	.05
549	Brian Hunter	.05
550	Kirby Puckett (MOY)	.25
551	Jim Eisenreich	.05
552	Andre Dawson	.25
553	David Nied	.05
554	Spike Owen	.05
555	Greg Gagne	.05
556	Sid Fernandez	.05
557	Mark McGwire	.75
558	Bryan Harvey	.05
559	Harold Reynolds	.05
560	Barry Bonds	1.00
561	Eric Wedge **RC**	.05
562	Ozzie Smith	.45
563	Rick Sutcliffe	.05
564	Jeff Reardon	.05
565	Alex Arias **RC**	.05
566	Greg Swindell	.05
567	Brook Jacoby	.05
568	Pete Incaviglia	.05
569	Butch Henry **RC**	.05
570	Eric Davis	.05
571	Kevin Seitzer	.05
572	Tony Fernandez	.05
573	Steve Reed **RC**	.05
574	Cory Snyder	.05
575	Joe Carter	.05
576	Greg Maddux	.45
577	Bert Blyleven	.05
578	Kevin Bass	.05
579	Carlton Fisk	.40
580	Doug Drabek	.05
581	Mark Gubicza	.05
582	Bobby Thigpen	.05
583	Chili Davis	.05
584	Scott Bankhead	.05
585	Harold Baines	.05
586	Eric Young **RC**	.15
587	Lance Parrish	.05
588	Juan Bell	.05
589	Bob Ojeda	.05
590	Joe Orsulak	.05
591	Benito Santiago	.05
592	Wade Boggs	.45
593	Robby Thompson	.05
594	Erik Plunk	.05
595	Hensley Meulens	.05
596	Lou Whitaker	.05
597	Dale Murphy	.25
598	Paul Molitor	.40
599	Greg W. Harris	.05
600	Darren Holmes	.05
601	Dave Martinez	.05
602	Tom Henke	.05
603	Mike Benjamin	.05
604	Rene Gonzales	.05
605	Roger McDowell	.05
606	Kirby Puckett	.45
607	Randy Myers	.05
608	Ruben Sierra	.05
609	Wilson Alvarez	.05
610	Dave Segui	.05
611	Juan Samuel	.05
612	Tom Brunansky	.05
613	Willie Randolph	.05
614	Tony Phillips	.05
615	Candy Maldonado	.05
616	Chris Bosio	.05
617	Bret Barberie	.05
618	Scott Sanderson	.05
619	Ron Darling	.05
620	Dave Winfield	.40
621	Mike Felder	.05
622	Greg Hibbard	.05
623	Mike Scioscia	.05
624	John Smiley	.05
625	Alejandro Pena	.05
626	Terry Steinbach	.05
627	Freddie Benavides	.05
628	Kevin Reimer	.05
629	Braulio Castillo	.05
630	Dave Stieb	.05
631	Dave Magadan	.05
632	Scott Fletcher	.05
633	Cris Carpenter	.05
634	Kevin Maas	.05
635	Todd Worrell	.05
636	Rob Deer	.05
637	Dwight Smith	.05
638	Chito Martinez	.05
639	Jimmy Key	.05
640	Greg Harris	.05
641	Mike Moore	.05
642	Pat Borders	.05
643	Bill Gullickson	.05
644	Gary Gaetti	.05
645	David Howard	.05
646	Jim Abbott	.05
647	Willie Wilson	.05
648	David Wells	.05

649	Andres Galarraga	.05
650	Vince Coleman	.05
651	Rob Dibble	.05
652	Frank Tanana	.05
653	Steve Decker	.05
654	David Cone	.05
655	Jack Armstrong	.05
656	Dave Stewart	.05
657	Billy Hatcher	.05
658	Tim Raines	.05
659	Walt Weiss	.05
660	Jose Lind	.05

Boys of Summer

		NM/M
Complete Set (30):		12.50
Common Player:		.25
1	Billy Ashley	.25
2	Tim Salmon	.50
3	Pedro Martinez	4.00
4	Luis Mercedes	.25
5	Mike Piazza	8.00
6	Troy Neel	.25
7	Melvin Nieves	.25
8	Ryan Klesko	.25
9	Ryan Thompson	.25
10	Kevin Young	.25
11	Gerald Williams	.25
12	Willie Greene	.25
13	John Patterson	.25
14	Carlos Garcia	.25
15	Eddie Zosky	.25
16	Sean Berry	.25
17	Rico Brogna	.25
18	Larry Carter	.25
19	Bobby Ayala	.25
20	Alan Embree	.25
21	Donald Harris	.25
22	Sterling Hitchcock	.25
23	David Nied	.25
24	Henry Mercedes	.25
25	Ozzie Canseco	.25
26	David Hulse	.25
27	Al Martin	.25
28	Dan Wilson	.25
29	Paul Miller	.25
30	Rich Rowland	.25

The Franchise

		NM/M
Complete Set (28):		50.00
Common Player:		.60
1	Cal Ripken, Jr.	12.00
2	Roger Clemens	6.00
3	Mark Langston	.60
4	Frank Thomas	3.50
5	Carlos Baerga	.60
6	Cecil Fielder	.60
7	Gregg Jefferies	.60
8	Robin Yount	3.50
9	Kirby Puckett	5.00
10	Don Mattingly	6.00
11	Dennis Eckersley	3.00
12	Ken Griffey Jr.	9.00
13	Juan Gonzalez	3.50
14	Roberto Alomar	1.50
15	Terry Pendleton	.60

16	Ryne Sandberg	5.00
17	Barry Larkin	.60
18	Jeff Bagwell	3.50
19	Brett Butler	.60
20	Larry Walker	.60
21	Bobby Bonilla	.60
22	Darren Daulton	.60
23	Andy Van Slyke	.60
24	Ray Lankford	.60
25	Gary Sheffield	1.50
26	Will Clark	.60
27	Bryan Harvey	.60
28	David Nied	.60

Dream Team

		NM/M
Complete Set (12):		5.00
Common Player:		.25
1	Ozzie Smith	1.00
2	Kirby Puckett	1.00
3	Gary Sheffield	.35
4	Andy Van Slyke	.25
5	Ken Griffey Jr.	2.00
6	Ivan Rodriguez	.60
7	Charles Nagy	.25
8	Tom Glavine	.35
9	Dennis Eckersley	.60
10	Frank Thomas	.75
11	Roberto Alomar	.30
---	Header Card	.05

1994 Score

		NM/M
Complete Set (660):		15.00
Common Player:		.05
Gold Rush:		2X
Pack (14):		.75
Wax Box (36):		15.00
1	Barry Bonds	1.00
2	John Olerud	.05
3	Ken Griffey Jr.	.65
4	Jeff Bagwell	.40
5	John Burkett	.05
6	Jack McDowell	.05
7	Albert Belle	.50
8	Andres Galarraga	.05
9	Mike Mussina	.30
10	Will Clark	.05
11	Travis Fryman	.05
12	Tony Gwynn	.50
13	Robin Yount	.40
14	Dave Magadan	.05
15	Paul O'Neill	.05
16	Ray Lankford	.05
17	Damion Easley	.05
18	Andy Van Slyke	.05
19	Brian McRae	.05
20	Ryne Sandberg	.50
21	Kirby Puckett	.50
22	Dwight Gooden	.05
23	Don Mattingly	.60
24	Kevin Mitchell	.05
25	Roger Clemens	.60
26	Eric Karros	.05
27	Juan Gonzalez	.20
28	John Kruk	.05
29	Gregg Jefferies	.05

30	Tom Glavine	.30
31	Ivan Rodriguez	.35
32	Jay Bell	.05
33	Randy Johnson	.40
34	Darren Daulton	.05
35	Rickey Henderson	.40
36	Eddie Murray	.40
37	Brian Harper	.05
38	Delino DeShields	.05
39	Jose Lind	.05
40	Benito Santiago	.05
41	Frank Thomas	.40
42	Mark Grace	.05
43	Roberto Alomar	.20
44	Andy Benes	.05
45	Luis Polonia	.05
46	Brett Butler	.05
47	Terry Steinbach	.05
48	Craig Biggio	.05
49	Greg Vaughn	.05
50	Charlie Hayes	.05
51	Mickey Tettleton	.05
52	Jose Rijo	.05
53	Carlos Baerga	.05
54	Jeff Blauser	.05
55	Leo Gomez	.05
56	Bob Tewksbury	.05
57	Mo Vaughn	.05
58	Orlando Merced	.05
59	Tino Martinez	.05
60	Len Dykstra	.05
61	Jose Canseco	.25
62	Tony Fernandez	.05
63	Donovan Osborne	.05
64	Ken Hill	.05
65	Kent Hrbek	.05
66	Bryan Harvey	.05
67	Wally Joyner	.05
68	Derrick May	.05
69	Lance Johnson	.05
70	Willie McGee	.05
71	Mark Langston	.05
72	Terry Pendleton	.05
73	Joe Carter	.05
74	Barry Larkin	.05
75	Jimmy Key	.05
76	Joe Girardi	.05
77	B.J. Surhoff	.05
78	Pete Harnisch	.05
79	Lou Whitaker	.05
80	Cory Snyder	.05
81	Kenny Lofton	.05
82	Fred McGriff	.05
83	Mike Greenwell	.05
84	Mike Perez	.05
85	Cal Ripken, Jr.	1.00
86	Don Slaught	.05
87	Omar Vizquel	.05
88	Curt Schilling	.30
89	Chuck Knoblauch	.05
90	Moises Alou	.05
91	Greg Gagne	.05
92	Bret Saberhagen	.05
93	Ozzie Guillen	.05
94	Matt Williams	.05
95	Chad Curtis	.05
96	Mike Harkey	.05
97	Devon White	.05
98	Walt Weiss	.05
99	Kevin Brown	.05
100	Gary Sheffield	.25
101	Wade Boggs	.50
102	Orel Hershiser	.05
103	Tony Phillips	.05
104	Andujar Cedeno	.05
105	Bill Spiers	.05
106	Otis Nixon	.05
107	Felix Fermin	.05
108	Bip Roberts	.05
109	Dennis Eckersley	.35
110	Dante Bichette	.05
111	Ben McDonald	.05
112	Jim Poole	.05
113	John Dopson	.05
114	Rob Dibble	.05
115	Jeff Treadway	.05
116	Ricky Jordan	.05
117	Mike Henneman	.05
118	Willie Blair	.05
119	Doug Henry	.05
120	Gerald Perry	.05
121	Greg Myers	.05
122	John Franco	.05
123	Roger Mason	.05
124	Chris Hammond	.05
125	Hubie Brooks	.05
126	Kent Mercker	.05
127	Jim Abbott	.05
128	Kevin Bass	.05
129	Rick Aguilera	.05
130	Mitch Webster	.05
131	Eric Plunk	.05
132	Mark Carreon	.05
133	Dave Stewart	.05
134	Willie Wilson	.05
135	Dave Fleming	.05
136	Jeff Tackett	.05
137	Geno Petralli	.05
138	Gene Harris	.05
139	Scott Bankhead	.05
140	Trevor Wilson	.05
141	Alvaro Espinoza	.05
142	Ryan Bowen	.05
143	Mike Moore	.05
144	Bill Pecota	.05

145	Jaime Navarro	.05
146	Jack Daugherty	.05
147	Bob Wickman	.05
148	Chris Jones	.05
149	Todd Stottlemyre	.05
150	Brian Williams	.05
151	Chuck Finley	.05
152	Lenny Harris	.05
153	Alex Fernandez	.05
154	Candy Maldonado	.05
155	Jeff Montgomery	.05
156	David West	.05
157	Mark Williamson	.05
158	Milt Thompson	.05
159	Ron Darling	.05
160	Stan Belinda	.05
161	Henry Cotto	.05
162	Mel Rojas	.05
163	Doug Strange	.05
164	Rene Arocha (1993 Rookie)	.05
165	Tim Hulett	.05
166	Steve Avery	.05
167	Jim Thome	.35
168	Tom Browning	.05
169	Mario Diaz	.05
170	Steve Reed (1993 Rookie)	.05
171	Scott Livingstone	.05
172	Chris Donnels	.05
173	John Jaha	.05
174	Carlos Hernandez	.05
175	Dion James	.05
176	Bud Black	.05
177	Tony Castillo	.05
178	Jose Guzman	.05
179	Torey Lovullo	.05
180	John Vander Wal	.05
181	Mike LaValliere	.05
182	Sid Fernandez	.05
183	Brent Mayne	.05
184	Terry Mulholland	.05
185	Willie Banks	.05
186	Steve Cooke (1993 Rookie)	.05
187	Brent Gates (1993 Rookie)	.05
188	Erik Pappas (1993 Rookie)	.05
189	Bill Haselman (1993 Rookie)	.05
190	Fernando Valenzuela	.05
191	Gary Redus	.05
192	Danny Darwin	.05
193	Mark Portugal	.05
194	Derek Lilliquist	.05
195	Charlie O'Brien	.05
196	Matt Nokes	.05
197	Danny Sheaffer	.05
198	Bill Gullickson	.05
199	Alex Arias (1993 Rookie)	.05
200	Mike Fetters	.05
201	Brian Jordan	.05
202	Joe Grahe	.05
203	Tom Candiotti	.05
204	Jeremy Stanton	.05
205	Mike Stanton	.05
206	David Howard	.05
207	Darren Holmes	.05
208	Rick Honeycutt	.05
209	Danny Jackson	.05
210	Rich Amaral (1993 Rookie)	.05
211	Blas Minor (1993 Rookie)	.05
212	Kenny Rogers	.05
213	Jim Leyritz	.05
214	Mike Morgan	.05
215	Dan Gladden	.05
216	Randy Velarde	.05
217	Mitch Williams	.05
218	Hipolito Pichardo	.05
219	Dave Burba	.05
220	Wilson Alvarez	.05
221	Bob Zupcic	.05
222	Francisco Cabrera	.05
223	Julio Valera	.05
224	Paul Assenmacher	.05
225	Jeff Branson	.05
226	Todd Frohwirth	.05
227	Armando Reynoso	.05
228	Rich Rowland (1993 Rookie)	.05
229	Freddie Benavides	.05
230	Wayne Kirby (1993 Rookie)	.05
231	Darryl Kile	.05
232	Skeeter Barnes	.05
233	Ramon Martinez	.05
234	Tom Gordon	.05
235	Dave Gallagher	.05
236	Ricky Bones	.05
237	Kenny Andersen	.05
238	Pat Meares (1993 Rookie)	.05
239	Zane Smith	.05
240	Tim Leary	.05
241	Phil Clark	.05
242	Danny Cox	.05
243	Mike Jackson	.05
244	Mike Gallego	.05
245	Lee Smith	.05
246	Todd Jones (1993 Rookie)	.05
247	Steve Bedrosian	.05
248	Troy Neel	.05
249	Jose Bautista	.05
250	Steve Frey	.05
251	Jeff Reardon	.05
252	Stan Javier	.05
253	Mo Sanford (1993 Rookie)	.05
254	Steve Sax	.05
255	Luis Aquino	.05
256	Domingo Jean (1993 Rookie)	.05
257	Scott Servais	.05
258	Brad Pennington (1993 Rookie)	.05

259	Dave Hansen	.05
260	Goose Gossage	.05
261	Jeff Fassero	.05
262	Junior Ortiz	.05
263	Anthony Young	.05
264	Chris Bosio	.05
265	Ruben Amaro Jr.	.05
266	Mark Eichhorn	.05
267	Dave Clark	.05
268	Gary Thurman	.05
269	Les Lancaster	.05
270	Jamie Moyer	.05
271	Ricky Gutierrez (1993 Rookie)	.05
272	Greg Harris	.05
273	Mike Benjamin	.05
274	Gene Nelson	.05
275	Damon Berryhill	.05
276	Scott Radinsky	.05
277	Mike Aldrete	.05
278	Jerry DiPoto (1993 Rookie)	.05
279	Chris Haney	.05
280	Richie Lewis (1993 Rookie)	.05
281	Jarvis Brown	.05
282	Juan Bell	.05
283	Joe Klink	.05
284	Graeme Lloyd (1993 Rookie)	.05
285	Casey Candaele	.05
286	Bob MacDonald	.05
287	Mike Sharperson	.05
288	Gene Larkin	.05
289	Brian Barnes	.05
290	David McCarty (1993 Rookie)	.05
291	Jeff Innis	.05
292	Bob Patterson	.05
293	Ben Rivera	.05
294	John Habyan	.05
295	Rich Rodriguez	.05
296	Edwin Nunez	.05
297	Rod Brewer	.05
298	Mike Timlin	.05
299	Jesse Orosco	.05
300	Gary Gaetti	.05
301	Todd Benzinger	.05
302	Jeff Nelson	.05
303	Rafael Belliard	.05
304	Matt Whiteside	.05
305	Vinny Castilla	.05
306	Matt Turner	.05
307	Eduardo Perez	.05
308	Joel Johnston	.05
309	Chris Gomez	.05
310	Pat Rapp	.05
311	Jim Tatum	.05
312	Kirk Rueter	.05
313	John Flaherty	.05
314	Tom Kramer	.05
315	Mark Whiten (Highlights)	.05
316	Chris Bosio (Highlights)	.05
317	Orioles Checklist	.05
318	Red Sox Checklist	.05
319	Angels Checklist	.05
320	White Sox Checklist	.05
321	Indians Checklist	.05
322	Tigers Checklist	.05
323	Royals Checklist	.05
324	Brewers Checklist	.05
325	Twins Checklist	.05
326	Yankees Checklist	.05
327	Athletics Checklist	.05
328	Mariners Checklist	.05
329	Rangers Checklist	.05
330	Blue Jays Checklist	.05
331	Frank Viola	.05
332	Ron Gant	.05
333	Charles Nagy	.05
334	Roberto Kelly	.05
335	Brady Anderson	.05
336	Alex Cole	.05
337	Alan Trammell	.05
338	Derek Bell	.05
339	Bernie Williams	.05
340	Jose Offerman	.05
341	Bill Wegman	.05
342	Ken Caminiti	.05
343	Pat Borders	.05
344	Kirt Manwaring	.05
345	Chili Davis	.05
346	Steve Buechele	.05
347	Robin Ventura	.05
348	Teddy Higuera	.05
349	Jerry Browne	.05
350	Scott Kamieniecki	.05
351	Kevin Tapani	.05
352	Marquis Grissom	.05
353	Jay Buhner	.05
354	Dave Hollins	.05
355	Dan Wilson	.05
356	Bob Walk	.05
357	Chris Hoiles	.05
358	Todd Zeile	.05
359	Kevin Appier	.05
360	Chris Sabo	.05
361	David Segui	.05
362	Jerald Clark	.05
363	Tony Pena	.05
364	Steve Finley	.05
365	Roger Pavlik	.05
366	John Smoltz	.05
367	Scott Fletcher	.05
368	Jody Reed	.05
369	David Wells	.05
370	Jose Vizcaino	.05
371	Pat Listach	.05
372	Orestes Destrade	.05
373	Danny Tartabull	.05
374	Greg W. Harris	.05
375	Juan Guzman	.05
376	Larry Walker	.05
377	Gary DiSarcina	.05
378	Bobby Bonilla	.05
379	Tim Raines	.05
380	Tommy Greene	.05
381	Chris Gwynn	.05
382	Jeff King	.05
383	Shane Mack	.05
384	Ozzie Smith	.50
385	Eddie Zambrano **RC**	.05
386	Mike Devereaux	.05
387	Erik Hanson	.05
388	Scott Cooper	.05
389	Dean Palmer	.05
390	John Wetteland	.05
391	Reggie Jefferson	.05
392	Mark Lemke	.05
393	Cecil Fielder	.05
394	Reggie Sanders	.05
395	Darryl Hamilton	.05
396	Daryl Boston	.05
397	Pat Kelly	.05
398	Joe Orsulak	.05
399	Ed Sprague	.05
400	Eric Anthony	.05
401	Scott Sanderson	.05
402	Jim Gott	.05
403	Ron Karkovice	.05
404	Phil Plantier	.05
405	David Cone	.05
406	Robby Thompson	.05
407	Dave Winfield	.40
408	Dwight Smith	.05
409	Ruben Sierra	.05
410	Jack Armstrong	.05
411	Mike Felder	.05
412	Wil Cordero	.05
413	Julio Franco	.05
414	Howard Johnson	.05
415	Mark McLemore	.05
416	Pete Incaviglia	.05
417	John Valentin	.05
418	Tim Wakefield	.05
419	Jose Mesa	.05
420	Bernard Gilkey	.05
421	Kirk Gibson	.05
422	Dave Justice	.05
423	Tom Brunansky	.05
424	John Smiley	.05
425	Kevin Maas	.05
426	Doug Drabek	.05
427	Paul Molitor	.40
428	Darryl Strawberry	.05
429	Tim Naehring	.05
430	Bill Swift	.05
431	Ellis Burks	.05
432	Greg Hibbard	.05
433	Felix Jose	.05
434	Bret Barberie	.05
435	Pedro Munoz	.05
436	Darrin Fletcher	.05
437	Bobby Witt	.05
438	Wes Chamberlain	.05
439	Mackey Sasser	.05
440	Mark Whiten	.05
441	Harold Reynolds	.05
442	Greg Olson	.05
443	Billy Hatcher	.05
444	Joe Oliver	.05
445	Sandy Alomar Jr.	.05
446	Tim Wallach	.05
447	Karl Rhodes	.05
448	Royce Clayton	.05
449	Cal Eldred	.05
450	Rick Wilkins	.05
451	Mike Stanley	.05
452	Charlie Hough	.05
453	Jack Morris	.05
454	Jon Ratliff **RC**	.05
455	Rene Gonzales	.05
456	Eddie Taubensee	.05
457	Roberto Hernandez	.05
458	Todd Hundley	.05
459	Mike MacFarlane	.05
460	Mickey Morandini	.05
461	Scott Erickson	.05
462	Lonnie Smith	.05
463	Dave Henderson	.05
464	Ryan Klesko	.05
465	Edgar Martinez	.05
466	Tom Pagnozzi	.05
467	Charlie Leibrandt	.05
468	Brian Anderson **RC**	.10
469	Harold Baines	.05
470	Tim Belcher	.05
471	Andre Dawson	.25
472	Eric Young	.05
473	Paul Sorrento	.05
474	Luis Gonzalez	.05
475	Rob Deer	.05
476	Mike Piazza	.65
477	Kevin Reimer	.05
478	Jeff Gardner	.05
479	Melido Perez	.05
480	Darren Lewis	.05
481	Duane Ward	.05
482	Rey Sanchez	.05
483	Mark Lewis	.05
484	Jeff Conine	.05
485	Joey Cora	.05
486	Trot Nixon **RC**	.50
487	Kevin McReynolds	.05
488	Mike Lansing	.05
489	Mike Pagliarulo	.05
490	Mariano Duncan	.05
491	Mike Bordick	.05
492	Kevin Young	.05
493	Dave Valle	.05
494	Wayne Gomes **RC**	.05
495	Rafael Palmeiro	.35
496	Deion Sanders	.05
497	Rick Sutcliffe	.05
498	Randy Milligan	.05
499	Carlos Quintana	.05
500	Chris Turner	.05
501	Thomas Howard	.05
502	Greg Swindell	.05
503	Chad Kreuter	.05
504	Eric Davis	.05
505	Dickie Thon	.05
506	Matt Drews **RC**	.05
507	Spike Owen	.05
508	Rod Beck	.05
509	Pat Hentgen	.05
510	Sammy Sosa	.50
511	J.T. Snow	.05
512	Chuck Carr	.05
513	Bo Jackson	.10
514	Dennis Martinez	.05
515	Phil Hiatt	.05
516	Jeff Kent	.05
517	Brooks Kieschnick **RC**	.05
518	Kirk Presley **RC**	.05
519	Kevin Seitzer	.05
520	Carlos Garcia	.05
521	Mike Blowers	.05
522	Luis Alicea	.05
523	David Hulse	.05
524	Greg Maddux	.50
525	Gregg Olson	.05
526	Hal Morris	.05
527	Daron Kirkreit	.05
528	David Nied	.05
529	Jeff Russell	.05
530	Kevin Gross	.05
531	John Doherty	.05
532	Matt Brunson **RC**	.05
533	Dave Nilsson	.05
534	Randy Myers	.05
535	Steve Farr	.05
536	Billy Wagner **RC**	.10
537	Darnell Coles	.05
538	Frank Tanana	.05
539	Tim Salmon	.05
540	Kim Batiste	.05
541	George Bell	.05
542	Tom Henke	.05
543	Sam Horn	.05
544	Doug Jones	.05
545	Scott Leius	.05
546	Al Martin	.05
547	Bob Welch	.05
548	Scott Christman **RC**	.05
549	Norm Charlton	.05
550	Mark McGwire	.75
551	Greg McMichael	.05
552	Tim Costo	.05
553	Rodney Bolton	.05
554	Pedro Martinez	.40
555	Marc Valdes	.05
556	Darrell Whitmore	.05
557	Tim Bogar	.05
558	Steve Karsay	.05
559	Danny Bautista	.05
560	Jeffrey Hammonds	.05
561	Aaron Sele	.05
562	Russ Springer	.05
563	Jason Bere	.05
564	Billy Brewer	.05
565	Sterling Hitchcock	.05
566	Bobby Munoz	.05
567	Craig Paquette	.05
568	Bret Boone	.05
569	Dan Peltier	.05
570	Jeromy Burnitz	.05
571	John Wasdin **RC**	.05
572	Chipper Jones	.50
573	Jamey Wright **RC**	.05
574	Jeff Granger	.05
575	Jay Powell **RC**	.05
576	Ryan Thompson	.05
577	Lou Frazier	.05
578	Paul Wagner	.05
579	Brad Ausmus	.05
580	Jack Voigt	.05
581	Kevin Rogers	.05
582	Damon Buford	.05
583	Paul Quantrill	.05
584	Marc Newfield	.05
585	Derrek Lee **RC**	1.00
586	Shane Reynolds	.05
587	Cliff Floyd	.05
588	Jeff Schwarz	.05
589	Ross Powell **RC**	.05
590	Gerald Williams	.05
591	Mike Trombley	.05
592	Ken Ryan	.05
593	John O'Donoghue	.05
594	Rod Correia	.05
595	Darrell Sherman	.05
596	Steve Scarsone	.05
597	Sherman Obando	.05
598	Kurt Abbott	.05
599	Dave Telgheder	.05
600	Rick Trlicek	.05
601	Carl Everett	.05
602	Luis Ortiz	.05
603	Larry Luebbers **RC**	.05
604	Kevin Roberson	.05
605	Butch Huskey	.05
606	Benji Gil	.05
607	Todd Van Poppel	.05
608	Mark Hutton	.05
609	Chip Hale	.05
610	Matt Maysey	.05
611	Scott Ruffcorn	.05
612	Hilly Hathaway	.05
613	Allen Watson	.05
614	Carlos Delgado	.30
615	Roberto Mejia	.05
616	Turk Wendell	.05
617	Tony Tarasco	.05
618	Raul Mondesi	.05
619	Kevin Stocker	.05
620	Javier Lopez	.05
621	Keith Kessinger **RC**	.05
622	Bob Hamelin	.05
623	John Roper	.05
624	Len Dykstra (World Series)	.05
625	Joe Carter (World Series)	.05
626	Jim Abbott (Highlight)	.05
627	Lee Smith (Highlight)	.05
628	Ken Griffey Jr. (HL)	.35
629	Dave Winfield (Highlight)	.05
630	Darryl Kile (Highlight)	.05
631	Frank Thomas (MVP)	.25
632	Barry Bonds (MVP)	.50
633	Jack McDowell (Cy Young)	.05
634	Greg Maddux (Cy Young)	.25
635	Tim Salmon (ROY)	.05
636	Mike Piazza (ROY)	.40
637	Brian Turang **RC**	.05
638	Rondell White	.05
639	Nigel Wilson	.05
640	Torii Hunter **RC**	.75
641	Salomon Torres	.05
642	Kevin Higgins	.05
643	Eric Wedge	.05
644	Roger Salkeld	.05
645	Manny Ramirez	.40
646	Jeff McNeely	.05
647	Braves Checklist	.05
648	Cubs Checklist	.05
649	Reds Checklist	.05
650	Rockies Checklist	.05
651	Marlins Checklist	.05
652	Astros Checklist	.05
653	Dodgers Checklist	.05
654	Expos Checklist	.05
655	Mets Checklist	.05
656	Phillies Checklist	.05
657	Pirates Checklist	.05
658	Cardinals Checklist	.05
659	Padres Checklist	.05
660	Giants Checklist	.05

Gold Rush

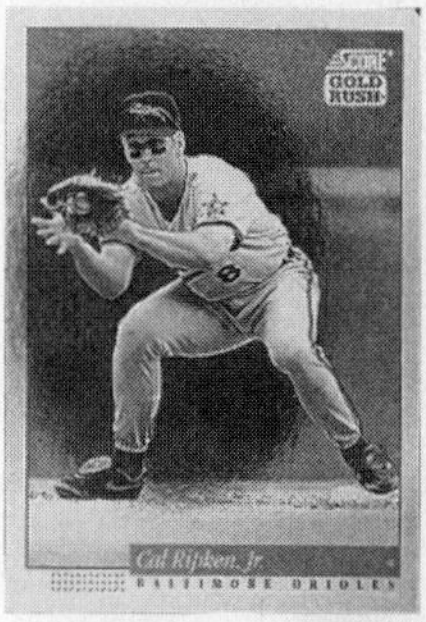

	NM/M
Complete Set (660):	40.00
Common Player:	.15
Stars:	2X

(See 1994 Score for checklist and base card values.)

Boys of Summer

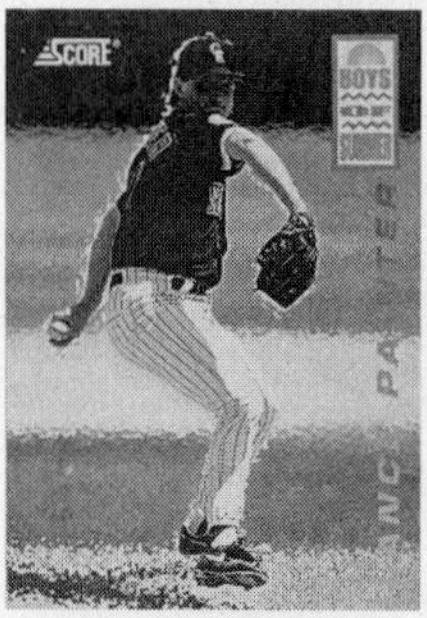

		NM/M
Complete Set (60):		25.00
Common Player:		.25
1	Jeff Conine	.25
2	Aaron Sele	.25
3	Kevin Stocker	.25
4	Pat Meares	.25
5	Jeromy Burnitz	.25
6	Mike Piazza	6.00
7	Allen Watson	.25
8	Jeffrey Hammonds	.25
9	Kevin Roberson	.25
10	Hilly Hathaway	.25
11	Kirk Reuter	.25
12	Eduardo Perez	.25
13	Ricky Gutierrez	.25
14	Domingo Jean	.25
15	David Nied	.25
16	Wayne Kirby	.25
17	Mike Lansing	.25
18	Jason Bere	.25
19	Brent Gates	.25
20	Javier Lopez	.25
21	Greg McMichael	.25
22	David Hulse	.25
23	Roberto Mejia	.25
24	Tim Salmon	.50
25	Rene Arocha	.25
26	Bret Boone	.25
27	David McCarty	.25
28	Todd Van Poppel	.25
29	Lance Painter	.25
30	Erik Pappas	.25
31	Chuck Carr	.25
32	Mark Hutton	.25
33	Jeff McNeely	.25
34	Willie Greene	.25
35	Nigel Wilson	.25
36	Rondell White	.25
37	Brian Turang	.25
38	Manny Ramirez	3.00
39	Salomon Torres	.25
40	Melvin Nieves	.25
41	Ryan Klesko	.25
42	Keith Kessinger	.25
43	Eric Wedge	.25
44	Bob Hamelin	.25
45	Carlos Delgado	2.50
46	Marc Newfield	.25
47	Raul Mondesi	.25
48	Tim Costo	.25
49	Pedro Martinez	3.00
50	Steve Karsay	.25
51	Danny Bautista	.25
52	Butch Huskey	.25
53	Kurt Abbott	.25
54	Darrell Sherman	.25
55	Damon Buford	.25
56	Ross Powell	.25
57	Darrell Whitmore	.25
58	Chipper Jones	5.00
59	Jeff Granger	.25
60	Cliff Floyd	.25

The Cycle

		NM/M
Complete Set (20):		12.00
Common Player:		.50
1	Brett Butler	.50
2	Kenny Lofton	.50
3	Paul Molitor	2.00
4	Carlos Baerga	.50
5	Gregg Jefferies, Tony Phillips	.50
6	John Olerud	.50
7	Charlie Hayes	.50
8	Len Dykstra	.50
9	Dante Bichette	.50
10	Devon White	.50
11	Lance Johnson	.50
12	Joey Cora, Steve Finley	.50
13	Tony Fernandez	.50
14	David Hulse, Brett Butler	.50
15	Jay Bell, Brian McRae, Mickey Morandini	.50
16	Juan Gonzalez, Barry Bonds	4.00
17	Ken Griffey Jr.	4.00
18	Frank Thomas	2.50
19	Dave Justice	.50
20	Matt Williams, Albert Belle	.50

Dream Team

DREAM TEAM

MIKE MUSSINA

		NM/M
Complete Set (10):		15.00
Common Player:		1.00
1	Mike Mussina	2.00
2	Tom Glavine	2.00
3	Don Mattingly	10.00
4	Carlos Baerga	1.00
5	Barry Larkin	1.00
6	Matt Williams	1.00
7	Juan Gonzalez	4.00
8	Andy Van Slyke	1.00
9	Larry Walker	1.00
10	Mike Stanley	1.00

Gold Stars

GOLD STARS

ANDRES GALARRAGA

		NM/M
Complete Set (60):		40.00
Common Player:		.25
1	Barry Bonds	6.00
2	Orlando Merced	.25
3	Mark Grace	.25
4	Darren Daulton	.25
5	Jeff Blauser	.25
6	Deion Sanders	.25
7	John Kruk	.25
8	Jeff Bagwell	2.50
9	Gregg Jefferies	.25
10	Matt Williams	.25
11	Andres Galarraga	.25
12	Jay Bell	.25
13	Mike Piazza	4.50
14	Ron Gant	.25
15	Barry Larkin	.25
16	Tom Glavine	.50
17	Len Dykstra	.25
18	Fred McGriff	.25
19	Andy Van Slyke	.25
20	Gary Sheffield	.75
21	John Burkett	.25
22	Dante Bichette	.25
23	Tony Gwynn	3.50
24	Dave Justice	.25
25	Marquis Grissom	.25
26	Bobby Bonilla	.25
27	Larry Walker	.25
28	Brett Butler	.25
29	Robby Thompson	.25
30	Jeff Conine	.25
31	Joe Carter	.25
32	Ken Griffey Jr.	4.50
33	Juan Gonzalez	1.25
34	Rickey Henderson	2.50
35	Bo Jackson	.35
36	Cal Ripken, Jr.	6.00
37	John Olerud	.25
38	Carlos Baerga	.25
39	Jack McDowell	.25
40	Cecil Fielder	.25
41	Kenny Lofton	.25
42	Roberto Alomar	1.00
43	Randy Johnson	2.50
44	Tim Salmon	.25
45	Frank Thomas	2.50
46	Albert Belle	.25
47	Greg Vaughn	.25

48	Travis Fryman	.25
49	Don Mattingly	4.00
50	Wade Boggs	3.50
51	Mo Vaughn	.25
52	Kirby Puckett	3.50
53	Devon White	.25
54	Tony Phillips	.25
55	Brian Harper	.25
56	Chad Curtis	.25
57	Paul Molitor	2.50
58	Ivan Rodriguez	2.00
59	Rafael Palmeiro	2.00
60	Brian McRae	.25

1994 Score Cal Ripken, Jr.

SCORE '94

CAL RIPKEN JR.

		NM/M
Complete Set (9):		3.00
Complete Set, Gold (9):		6.00
Common Player:		.50
Common Card, Gold:		1.00
Autographed Card:		200.00
1	Double Honors	.50
1a	Double Honors/Gold	1.00
2	Perennial All-Star	.50
2a	Perennial All-Star/Gold	1.00
3	Peerless Power	.50
3a	Peerless Power/Gold	1.00
4	Fitness Fan	.50
4a	Fitness Fan /Gold	1.00
5	Prime Concerns	.50
5a	Prime Concerns/Gold	1.00
6	Home Run Club	.50
6a	Home Run Club/Gold	1.00
7	The Iron Man	.50
7a	The Iron Man/Gold	1.00
8	Heavy Hitter	.50
8a	Heavy Hitter/Gold	1.00
9	Gold Glover	.50
9a	Gold Glover/Gold	1.00

1994 Score Rookie/Traded

TURNER WARD

		NM/M
Complete Set (165):		5.00
Common Player:		.05
Gold Rush:		2X
Pack (10):		.40
Wax Box (36):		9.00
1	Will Clark	.05
2	Lee Smith	.05
3	Bo Jackson	.10
4	Ellis Burks	.05
5	Eddie Murray	1.00
6	Delino DeShields	.05
7	Erik Hanson	.05
8	Rafael Palmeiro	.75
9	Luis Polonia	.05
10	Omar Vizquel	.05
11	Kurt Abbott	.05
12	Vince Coleman	.05
13	Rickey Henderson	1.00
14	Terry Mulholland	.05
15	Greg Hibbard	.05
16	Walt Weiss	.05
17	Chris Sabo	.05
18	Dave Henderson	.05
19	Rick Sutcliffe	.05
20	Harold Reynolds	.05

21	Jack Morris	.05
22	Dan Wilson	.05
23	Dave Magadan	.05
24	Dennis Martinez	.05
25	Wes Chamberlain	.05
26	Otis Nixon	.05
27	Eric Anthony	.05
28	Randy Milligan	.05
29	Julio Franco	.05
30	Kevin McReynolds	.05
31	Anthony Young	.05
32	Brian Harper	.05
33	Lenny Harris	.05
34	Eddie Taubensee	.05
35	David Segui	.05
36	Stan Javier	.05
37	Felix Fermin	.05
38	Darrin Jackson	.05
39	Tony Fernandez	.05
40	Jose Vizcaino	.05
41	Willie Banks	.05
42	Brian Hunter	.05
43	Reggie Jefferson	.05
44	Junior Felix	.05
45	Jack Armstrong	.05
46	Bip Roberts	.05
47	Jerry Browne	.05
48	Marvin Freeman	.05
49	Jody Reed	.05
50	Alex Cole	.05
51	Sid Fernandez	.05
52	Pete Smith	.05
53	Xavier Hernandez	.05
54	Scott Sanderson	.05
55	Turner Ward	.05
56	Rex Hudler	.05
57	Deion Sanders	.05
58	Sid Bream	.05
59	Tony Pena	.05
60	Bret Boone	.05
61	Bobby Ayala	.05
62	Pedro Martinez	1.00
63	Howard Johnson	.05
64	Mark Portugal	.05
65	Roberto Kelly	.05
66	Spike Owen	.05
67	Jeff Treadway	.05
68	Mike Harkey	.05
69	Doug Jones	.05
70	Steve Farr	.05
71	Billy Taylor	.05
72	Manny Ramirez	1.00
73	Bob Hamelin	.05
74	Steve Karsay	.05
75	Ryan Klesko	.05
76	Cliff Floyd	.05
77	Jeffrey Hammonds	.05
78	Javier Lopez	.05
79	Roger Salkeld	.05
80	Hector Carrasco	.05
81	Gerald Williams	.05
82	Raul Mondesi	.05
83	Sterling Hitchcock	.05
84	Danny Bautista	.05
85	Chris Turner	.05
86	Shane Reynolds	.05
87	Rondell White	.05
88	Salomon Torres	.05
89	Turk Wendell	.05
90	Tony Tarasco	.05
91	Shawn Green	.65
92	Greg Colbrunn	.05
93	Eddie Zambrano	.05
94	Rich Becker	.05
95	Chris Gomez	.05
96	John Patterson	.05
97	Derek Parks	.05
98	Rich Rowland	.05
99	James Mouton	.05
100	Tim Hyers	.05
101	Jose Valentin	.05
102	Carlos Delgado	.65
103	Robert Esenhoorn	.05
104	John Hudek	.05
105	Domingo Cedeno	.05
106	Denny Hocking	.05
107	Greg Pirkl	.05
108	Mark Smith	.05
109	Paul Shuey	.05
110	Jorge Fabregas	.05
111	Rikkert Faneyte	.05
112	Rob Butler	.05
113	Darren Oliver	.05
114	Troy O'Leary	.05
115	Scott Brow	.05
116	Tony Eusebio	.05
117	Carlos Reyes	.05
118	J.R. Phillips	.05
119	Alex Diaz	.05
120	Charles Johnson	.05
121	Nate Minchey	.05
122	Scott Sanders	.05
123	Daryl Boston	.05
124	Joey Hamilton	.05
125	Brian Anderson	.05
126	Dan Miceli	.05
127	Tom Brunansky	.05
128	Dave Staton	.05
129	Mike Oquist	.05
130	John Mabry	.05
131	Norberto Martin	.05
132	Hector Fajardo	.05
133	Mark Hutton	.05
134	Fernando Vina	.05
135	Lee Tinsley	.05

136	Chan Ho Park RC	1.50
137	Paul Spoljaric	.05
138	Matias Carrillo	.05
139	Mark Kiefer	.05
140	Stan Royer	.05
141	Bryan Eversgerd	.05
143	Joe Hall	.05
144	Johnny Ruffin	.05
145	Alex Gonzalez	.05
146	Keith Lockhart	.05
147	Tom Marsh	.05
148	Tony Longmire	.05
149	Keith Mitchell	.05
150	Melvin Nieves	.05
151	Kelly Stinnett	.05
152	Miguel Jimenez	.05
153	Jeff Juden	.05
154	Matt Walbeck	.05
155	Marc Newfield	.05
156	Matt Mieske	.05
157	Marcus Moore	.05
158	Jose Lima RC	.25
159	Mike Kelly	.05
160	Jim Edmonds	.05
161	Steve Trachsel	.05
162	Greg Blosser	.05
163	Mark Acre	.05
164	AL Checklist	.05
165	NL Checklist	.05

Changing Places

		NM/M
Complete Set (10):		15.00
Common Player:		1.00
1	Will Clark	1.00
2	Rafael Palmeiro	4.00
3	Roberto Kelly	1.00
4	Bo Jackson	1.25
5	Otis Nixon	1.00
6	Rickey Henderson	5.00
7	Ellis Burks	1.00
8	Lee Smith	1.00
9	Delino DeShields	1.00
10	Deion Sanders	1.00

Rookie/Traded Super Rookies

		NM/M
Complete Set (18):		15.00
Common Player:		1.00
1	Carlos Delgado	5.00
2	Manny Ramirez	5.00
3	Ryan Klesko	1.00
4	Raul Mondesi	1.00
5	Bob Hamelin	1.00
6	Steve Karsay	1.00
7	Jeffrey Hammonds	1.00
8	Cliff Floyd	1.00
9	Kurt Abbott	1.00
10	Marc Newfield	1.00
11	Javier Lopez	1.00
12	Rich Becker	1.00
13	Greg Pirkl	1.00
14	Rondell White	1.00
15	James Mouton	1.00
16	Tony Tarasco	1.00
17	Brian Anderson	1.00
18	Jim Edmonds	1.00

1995 Score

CAL RIPKEN JR.

		NM/M
Complete Set (605):		13.50
Common Player:		.05
Gold Rush:		2X
Platinums:		3X
Series 1 or 2 Pack (12):		.75
Series 1 or 2 Box (36):		12.50
1	Frank Thomas	.50
2	Roberto Alomar	.15
3	Cal Ripken, Jr.	1.50
4	Jose Canseco	.30
5	Matt Williams	.05
6	Esteban Beltre	.05
7	Domingo Cedeno	.05
8	John Valentin	.05
9	Glenallen Hill	.05
10	Rafael Belliard	.05
11	Randy Myers	.05
12	Mo Vaughn	.05
13	Hector Carrasco	.05
14	Chili Davis	.05
15	Dante Bichette	.05
16	Darren Jackson	.05
17	Mike Piazza	.75
18	Junior Felix	.05
19	Moises Alou	.05
20	Mark Gubicza	.05
21	Bret Saberhagen	.05
22	Len Dykstra	.05
23	Steve Howe	.05
24	Mark Dewey	.05
25	Brian Harper	.05
26	Ozzie Smith	.60
27	Scott Erickson	.05
28	Tony Gwynn	.60
29	Bob Welch	.05
30	Barry Bonds	1.50
31	Leo Gomez	.05
32	Greg Maddux	.60
33	Mike Greenwell	.05
34	Sammy Sosa	.60
35	Darnell Coles	.05
36	Tommy Greene	.05
37	Will Clark	.05
38	Steve Ontiveros	.05
39	Stan Javier	.05
40	Bip Roberts	.05
41	Paul O'Neill	.05
42	Bill Haselman	.05
43	Shane Mack	.05
44	Orlando Merced	.05
45	Kevin Seitzer	.05
46	Trevor Hoffman	.05
47	Greg Gagne	.05
48	Jeff Kent	.05
49	Tony Phillips	.05
50	Ken Hill	.05
51	Carlos Baerga	.05
52	Henry Rodriguez	.05
53	Scott Sanderson	.05
54	Jeff Conine	.05
55	Chris Turner	.05
56	Ken Caminiti	.05
57	Harold Baines	.05
58	Charlie Hayes	.05
59	Roberto Kelly	.05
60	John Olerud	.05
61	Tim Davis	.05
62	Rich Rowland	.05
63	Rey Sanchez	.05
64	Junior Ortiz	.05
65	Ricky Gutierrez	.05
66	Rex Hudler	.05
67	Johnny Ruffin	.05
68	Jay Buhner	.05
69	Tom Pagnozzi	.05
70	Julio Franco	.05
71	Eric Young	.05
72	Mike Bordick	.05
73	Don Slaught	.05
74	Goose Gossage	.05
75	Lonnie Smith	.05
76	Jimmy Key	.05
77	Dave Hollins	.05
78	Mickey Tettleton	.05
79	Luis Gonzalez	.05
80	Dave Winfield	.50
81	Ryan Thompson	.05
82	Felix Jose	.05
83	Rusty Meacham	.05
84	Darryl Hamilton	.05
85	John Wetteland	.05
86	Tom Brunansky	.05
87	Mark Lemke	.05
88	Spike Owen	.05
89	Shawon Dunston	.05
90	Wilson Alvarez	.05
91	Lee Smith	.05
92	Scott Kamieniecki	.05
93	Jacob Brumfield	.05
94	Kirk Gibson	.05
95	Joe Girardi	.05
96	Mike Macfarlane	.05
97	Greg Colbrunn	.05
98	Ricky Bones	.05
99	Delino DeShields	.05
100	Pat Meares	.05
101	Jeff Fassero	.05
102	Jim Leyritz	.05
103	Gary Redus	.05
104	Terry Steinbach	.05
105	Kevin McReynolds	.05
106	Felix Fermin	.05
107	Danny Jackson	.05
108	Chris James	.05
109	Jeff King	.05
110	Pat Hentgen	.05
111	Gerald Perry	.05
112	Tim Raines	.05
113	Eddie Williams	.05
114	Jamie Moyer	.05
115	Bud Black	.05
116	Chris Gomez	.05
117	Luis Lopez	.05
118	Roger Clemens	.65
119	Javier Lopez	.05
120	Dave Nilsson	.05
121	Karl Rhodes	.05
122	Rick Aguilera	.05
123	Tony Fernandez	.05
124	Bernie Williams	.05
125	James Mouton	.05
126	Mark Langston	.05
127	Mike Lansing	.05
128	Tino Martinez	.05
129	Joe Orsulak	.05
130	David Hulse	.05
131	Pete Incaviglia	.05
132	Mark Clark	.05
133	Tony Eusebio	.05
134	Chuck Finley	.05
135	Lou Frazier	.05
136	Craig Grebeck	.05
137	Kelly Stinnett	.05
138	Paul Shuey	.05
139	David Nied	.05
140	Billy Brewer	.05
141	Dave Weathers	.05
142	Scott Leius	.05
143	Brian Jordan	.05
144	Melido Perez	.05
145	Tony Tarasco	.05
146	Dan Wilson	.05
147	Rondell White	.05
148	Mike Henneman	.05
149	Brian Johnson	.05
150	Tom Henke	.05
151	John Patterson	.05
152	Bobby Witt	.05
153	Eddie Taubensee	.05
154	Pat Borders	.05
155	Ramon Martinez	.05
156	Mike Kingery	.05
157	Zane Smith	.05
158	Benito Santiago	.05
159	Matias Carrillo	.05
160	Scott Brosius	.05
161	Dave Clark	.05
162	Mark McLemore	.05
163	Curt Schilling	.30
164	J.T. Snow	.05
165	Rod Beck	.05
166	Scott Fletcher	.05
167	Bob Tewksbury	.05
168	Mike LaValliere	.05
169	Dave Hansen	.05
170	Pedro Martinez	.50
171	Kirk Rueter	.05
172	Jose Lind	.05
173	Luis Alicea	.05
174	Mike Moore	.05
175	Andy Ashby	.05
176	Jody Reed	.05
177	Darryl Kile	.05
178	Carl Willis	.05
179	Jeromy Burnitz	.05
180	Mike Gallego	.05
181	W. Van Landingham RC	.05
182	Sid Fernandez	.05
183	Kim Batiste	.05
184	Greg Myers	.05
185	Steve Avery	.05
186	Steve Farr	.05
187	Robb Nen	.05
188	Dan Pasqua	.05
189	Bruce Ruffin	.05
190	Jose Valentin	.05
191	Willie Banks	.05
192	Mike Aldrete	.05
193	Randy Milligan	.05
194	Steve Karsay	.05
195	Mike Stanley	.05
196	Jose Mesa	.05
197	Tom Browning	.05
198	John Vander Wal	.05
199	Kevin Brown	.05
200	Mike Oquist	.05
201	Greg Swindell	.05
202	Eddie Zambrano	.05
203	Joe Boever	.05
204	Gary Varsho	.05
205	Chris Gwynn	.05
206	David Howard	.05
207	Jerome Walton	.05
208	Danny Darwin	.05
209	Darryl Strawberry	.05
210	Todd Van Poppel	.05
211	Scott Livingstone	.05
212	Dave Fleming	.05
213	Todd Worrell	.05
214	Carlos Delgado	.40
215	Bill Pecota	.05
216	Jim Lindeman	.05
217	Rick White	.05
218	Jose Oquendo	.05
219	Tony Castillo	.05
220	Fernando Vina	.05
221	Jeff Bagwell	.50
222	Randy Johnson	.50
223	Albert Belle	.05
224	Chuck Carr	.05
225	Mark Leiter	.05
226	Hal Morris	.05
227	Robin Ventura	.05
228	Mike Munoz	.05
229	Jim Thome	.40
230	Mario Diaz	.05
231	John Doherty	.05
232	Bobby Jones	.05
233	Raul Mondesi	.05
234	Ricky Jordan	.05
235	John Jaha	.05
236	Carlos Garcia	.05
237	Kirby Puckett	.60
238	Orel Hershiser	.05
239	Don Mattingly	.65
240	Sid Bream	.05
241	Brent Gates	.05
242	Tony Longmire	.05
243	Robby Thompson	.05
244	Rick Sutcliffe	.05
245	Dean Palmer	.05
246	Marquis Grissom	.05
247	Paul Molitor	.50
248	Mark Carreon	.05
249	Jack Voight	.05
250	Greg McMichael (Photo on front is Mike Stanton.)	.05
251	Damon Berryhill	.05
252	Brian Dorsett	.05
253	Jim Edmonds	.05
254	Barry Larkin	.05
255	Jack McDowell	.05
256	Wally Joyner	.05
257	Eddie Murray	.50
258	Lenny Webster	.05
259	Milt Cuyler	.05
260	Todd Benzinger	.05
261	Vince Coleman	.05
262	Todd Stottlemyre	.05
263	Turner Ward	.05
264	Ray Lankford	.05
265	Matt Walbeck	.05
266	Deion Sanders	.05
267	Gerald Williams	.05
268	Jim Gott	.05
269	Jeff Frye	.05
270	Jose Rijo	.05
271	Dave Justice	.05
272	Ismael Valdes	.05
273	Ben McDonald	.05
274	Darren Lewis	.05
275	Graeme Lloyd	.05
276	Luis Ortiz	.05
277	Julian Tavarez	.05
278	Mark Dalesandro	.05
279	Brett Merriman	.05
280	Ricky Bottalico	.05
281	Robert Eenhoorn	.05
282	Rikkert Faneyte	.05
283	Mike Kelly	.05
284	Mark Smith	.05
285	Turk Wendell	.05
286	Greg Blosser	.05
287	Garey Ingram	.05
288	Jorge Fabregas	.05
289	Blaise Ilsley	.05
290	Joe Hall	.05
291	Orlando Miller	.05
292	Jose Lima	.05
293	Greg O'Halloran	.05
294	Mark Kiefer	.05
295	Jose Oliva	.05
296	Rich Becker	.05
297	Brian Hunter	.05
298	Dave Silvestri	.05
299	Armando Benitez RC	.10
300	Darren Dreifort	.05
301	John Mabry	.05
302	Greg Pirkl	.05
303	J.R. Phillips	.05
304	Shawn Green	.30
305	Roberto Petagine	.05
306	Keith Lockhart	.05
307	Jonathon Hurst	.05
308	Paul Spoljaric	.05
309	Mike Lieberthal	.05
310	Garret Anderson	.05
311	John Johnston	.05
312	Alex Rodriguez	1.50

313	Kent Mercker	.05
314	John Valentin	.05
315	Kenny Rogers	.05
316	Fred McGriff	.05
317	Atlanta Braves, Baltimore Orioles	.05
318	Chicago Cubs, Boston Red Sox	.05
319	Cincinnati Reds, California Angels	.05
320	Colorado Rockies, Chicago White Sox	.05
321	Cleveland Indians, Florida Marlins	.05
322	Houston Astros, Detroit Tigers	.05
323	Los Angeles Dodgers, Kansas City Royals	.05
324	Montreal Expos, Milwaukee Brewers	.05
325	New York Mets, Minnesota Twins	.05
326	Philadelphia Phillies, New York Yankees	.05
327	Pittsburgh Pirates, Oakland Athletics	.05
328	San Diego Padres, Seattle Mariners	.05
329	San Francisco Giants, Texas Rangers	.05
330	St. Louis Cardinals, Toronto Blue Jays	.05
331	Pedro Munoz	.05
332	Ryan Klesko	.05
333a	Andre Dawson (Red Sox)	.25
333b	Andre Dawson (Marlins)	.35
334	Derrick May	.05
335	Aaron Sele	.05
336	Kevin Mitchell	.05
337	Steve Traschel	.05
338	Andres Galarraga	.05
339a	Terry Pendleton (Braves)	.05
339b	Terry Pendleton (Marlins)	.10
340	Gary Sheffield	.30
341	Travis Fryman	.05
342	Bo Jackson	.10
343	Gary Gaetti	.05
344a	Brett Butler (Dodgers)	.05
344b	Brett Butler (Mets)	.10
345	B. J. Surhoff	.05
346a	Larry Walker (Expos)	.05
346b	Larry Walker (Rockies)	.10
347	Kevin Tapani	.05
348	Rick Wilkins	.05
349	Wade Boggs	.60
350	Mariano Duncan	.05
351	Ruben Sierra	.05
352a	Andy Van Slyke (Pirates)	.05
352b	Andy Van Slyke (Orioles)	.10
353	Reggie Jefferson	.05
354	Gregg Jefferies	.05
355	Tim Naehring	.05
356	John Roper	.05
357	Joe Carter	.05
358	Kurt Abbott	.05
359	Lenny Harris	.05
360	Lance Johnson	.05
361	Brian Anderson	.05
362	Jim Eisenreich	.05
363	Jerry Browne	.05
364	Mark Grace	.05
365	Devon White	.05
366	Reggie Sanders	.05
367	Ivan Rodriguez	.40
368	Kirt Manwaring	.05
369	Pat Kelly	.05
370	Ellis Burks	.05
371	Charles Nagy	.05
372	Kevin Bass	.05
373	Lou Whitaker	.05
374	Rene Arocha	.05
375	Derrick Parks	.05
376	Mark Whiten	.05
377	Mark McGwire	1.00
378	Doug Drabek	.05
379	Greg Vaughn	.05
380	Al Martin	.05
381	Ron Darling	.05
382	Tim Wallach	.05
383	Alan Trammell	.05
384	Randy Velarde	.05
385	Chris Sabo	.05
386	Wil Cordero	.05
387	Darrin Fletcher	.05
388	David Segui	.05
389	Steve Buechele	.05
390	Otis Nixon	.05
391	Jeff Brantley	.05
392a	Chad Curtis (Angels)	.05
392b	Chad Curtis (Tigers)	.10
393	Cal Eldred	.05
394	Jason Bere	.05
395	Bret Barberie	.05
396	Paul Sorrento	.05
397	Steve Finley	.05
398	Cecil Fielder	.05
399	Eric Karros	.05
400	Jeff Montgomery	.05
401	Cliff Floyd	.05
402	Matt Mieske	.05
403	Brian Hunter	.05
404	Alex Cole	.05
405	Kevin Stocker	.05
406	Eric Davis	.05
407	Marvin Freeman	.05
408	Dennis Eckersley	.40
409	Todd Zeile	.05
410	Keith Mitchell	.05
411	Andy Benes	.05
412	Juan Bell	.05
413	Royce Clayton	.05
414	Ed Sprague	.05
415	Mike Mussina	.30
416	Todd Hundley	.05
417	Pat Listach	.05
418	Joe Oliver	.05
419	Rafael Palmeiro	.40
420	Tim Salmon	.05
421	Brady Anderson	.05
422	Kenny Lofton	.05
423	Craig Biggio	.05
424	Bobby Bonilla	.05
425	Kenny Rogers	.05
426	Derek Bell	.05
427a	Scott Cooper (Red Sox)	.05
427b	Scott Cooper (Cardinals)	.10
428	Ozzie Guillen	.05
429	Omar Vizquel	.05
430	Phil Plantier	.05
431	Chuck Knoblauch	.05
432	Darren Daulton	.05
433	Bob Hamelin	.05
434	Tom Glavine	.30
435	Walt Weiss	.05
436	Jose Vizcaino	.05
437	Ken Griffey Jr.	.75
438	Jay Bell	.05
439	Juan Gonzalez	.25
440	Jeff Blauser	.05
441	Rickey Henderson	.50
442	Bobby Ayala	.05
443a	David Cone (Royals)	.05
443b	David Cone (Blue Jays)	.10
444	Pedro Martinez	.05
445	Manny Ramirez	.50
446	Mark Portugal	.05
447	Damion Easley	.05
448	Gary DiSarcina	.05
449	Roberto Hernandez	.05
450	Jeffrey Hammonds	.05
451	Jeff Treadway	.05
452a	Jim Abbott (Yankees)	.05
452b	Jim Abbott (White Sox)	.10
453	Carlos Rodriguez	.05
454	Joey Cora	.05
455	Bret Boone	.05
456	Danny Tartabull	.05
457	John Franco	.05
458	Roger Salkeld	.05
459	Fred McGriff	.05
460	Pedro Astacio	.05
461	Jon Lieber	.05
462	Luis Polonia	.05
463	Geronimo Pena	.05
464	Tom Gordon	.05
465	Brad Ausmus	.05
466	Willie McGee	.05
467	Doug Jones	.05
468	John Smoltz	.05
469	Troy Neel	.05
470	Luis Sojo	.05
471	John Smiley	.05
472	Rafael Bournigal	.05
473	Billy Taylor	.05
474	Juan Guzman	.05
475	Dave Magadan	.05
476	Mike Devereaux	.05
477	Andujar Cedeno	.05
478	Edgar Martinez	.05
479	Troy Neel	.05
480	Allen Watson	.05
481	Ron Karkovice	.05
482	Joey Hamilton	.05
483	Vinny Castilla	.05
484	Kevin Gross	.05
485	Bernard Gilkey	.05
486	John Burkett	.05
487	Matt Nokes	.05
488	Mel Rojas	.05
489	Craig Shipley	.05
490	Chip Hale	.05
491	Bill Swift	.05
492	Pat Rapp	.05
493a	Brian McRae (Royals)	.05
493b	Brian McRae (Cubs)	.10
494	Mickey Morandini	.05
495	Tony Pena	.05
496	Danny Bautista	.05
497	Armando Reynoso	.05
498	Ken Ryan	.05
499	Billy Ripken	.05
500	Pat Mahomes	.05
501	Mark Acre	.05
502	Geronimo Berroa	.05
503	Norberto Martin	.05
504	Chad Kreuter	.05
505	Howard Johnson	.05
506	Eric Anthony	.05
507	Mark Wohlers	.05
508	Scott Sanders	.05
509	Pete Harnisch	.05
510	Wes Chamberlain	.05
511	Tom Candiotti	.05
512	Albie Lopez	.05
513	Denny Neagle	.05
514	Sean Berry	.05
515	Billy Hatcher	.05
516	Todd Jones	.05
517	Wayne Kirby	.05
518	Butch Henry	.05
519	Sandy Alomar Jr.	.05
520	Kevin Appier	.05
521	Robert Mejia	.05
522	Steve Cooke	.05
523	Terry Shumpert	.05
524	Mike Jackson	.05
525	Kent Mercker	.05
526	David Wells	.05
527	Juan Samuel	.05
528	Salomon Torres	.05
529	Duane Ward	.05
530a	Rob Dibble (Reds)	.05
530b	Rob Dibble (White Sox)	.10
531	Mike Blowers	.05
532	Mark Eichhorn	.05
533	Alex Diaz	.05
534	Dan Miceli	.05
535	Jeff Branson	.05
536	Dave Stevens	.05
537	Charlie O'Brien	.05
538	Shane Reynolds	.05
539	Rich Amaral	.05
540	Rusty Greer	.05
541	Alex Arias	.05
542	Eric Plunk	.05
543	John Hudek	.05
544	Kirk McCaskill	.05
545	Jeff Reboulet	.05
546	Sterling Hitchcock	.05
547	Warren Newson	.05
548	Bryan Harvey	.05
549	Mike Huff	.05
550	Lance Parrish	.05
551	Ken Griffey Jr.	.65
552	Matt Williams	.05
553	Roberto Alomar	.10
554	Jeff Bagwell	.25
555	Dave Justice	.05
556	Cal Ripken Jr.	.75
557	Albert Belle	.05
558	Mike Piazza	.45
559	Kirby Puckett	.35
560	Wade Boggs	.30
561	Tony Gwynn	.35
562	Barry Bonds	.75
563	Mo Vaughn	.05
564	Don Mattingly	.40
565	Carlos Baerga	.05
566	Paul Molitor	.25
567	Raul Mondesi	.05
568	Manny Ramirez	.25
569	Alex Rodriguez	.75
570	Will Clark	.05
571	Frank Thomas	.30
572	Moises Alou	.05
573	Jeff Conine	.05
574	Joe Ausanio	.05
575	Charles Johnson	.05
576	Ernie Young	.05
577	Jeff Granger	.05
578	Robert Perez	.05
579	Melvin Nieves	.05
580	Gar Finnvold	.05
581	Duane Singleton	.05
582	Chan Ho Park	.05
583	Fausto Cruz	.05
584	Dave Staton	.05
585	Denny Hocking	.05
586	Nate Minchey	.05
587	Marc Newfield	.05
588	Jayhawk Owens	.05
589	Darren Bragg	.05
590	Kevin King	.05
591	Kurt Miller	.05
592	Aaron Small	.05
593	Troy O'Leary	.05
594	Phil Stidham	.05
595	Steve Dunn	.05
596	Cory Bailey	.05
597	Alex Gonzalez	.05
598	Jim Bowie	.05
599	Jeff Cirillo	.05
600	Mark Hutton	.05
601	Russ Davis	.05
602	Checklist #331-400	.05
603	Checklist #401-469	.05
604	Checklist #470-537	.05
605	Checklist #538-605	.05
----	"You Trade 'em" Redemption Card (Expired Dec. 31, 1995.)	.10

Gold Rush

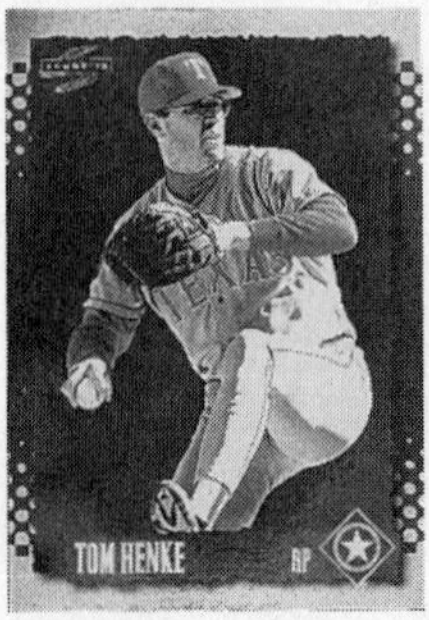

		NM/M
Complete Set (605):		35.00
Common Player:		.10
Gold Rush Stars:		2X

(See 1995 Score for checklist and base card values.)

Airmail

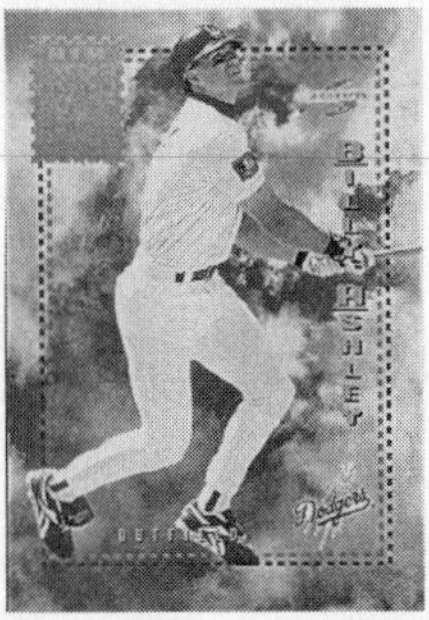

		NM/M
Complete Set (18):		8.00
Common Player:		.25
1	Bob Hamelin	.25
2	John Mabry	.25
3	Marc Newfield	.25
4	Jose Oliva	.25
5	Charles Johnson	.25
6	Russ Davis	.25
7	Ernie Young	.25
8	Billy Ashley	.25
9	Ryan Klesko	.25
10	J.R. Phillips	.25
11	Cliff Floyd	.25
12	Carlos Delgado	1.50
13	Melvin Nieves	.25
14	Raul Mondesi	.25
15	Manny Ramirez	2.00
16	Mike Kelly	.25
17	Alex Rodriguez	5.00
18	Rusty Greer	.25

Double Gold Champions

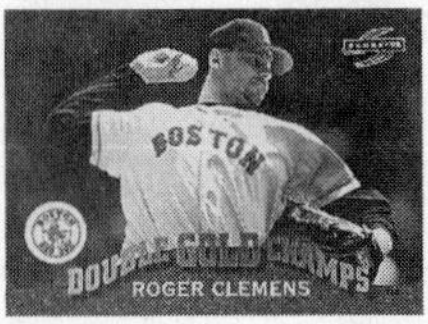

		NM/M
Complete Set (12):		25.00
Common Player:		.40
1	Frank Thomas	2.00
2	Ken Griffey Jr.	3.50
3	Barry Bonds	5.00
4	Tony Gwynn	2.50
5	Don Mattingly	3.00
6	Greg Maddux	2.50
7	Roger Clemens	3.00
8	Kenny Lofton	.40
9	Jeff Bagwell	2.00
10	Matt Williams	.40
11	Kirby Puckett	2.50
12	Cal Ripken Jr.	5.00

Draft Picks

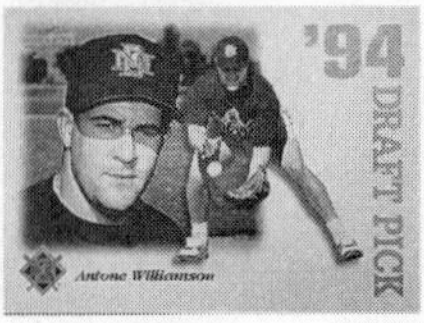

		NM/M
Complete Set (18):		4.00
Common Player:		.50
1	McKay Christensen	.50
2	Brett Wagner	.50
3	Paul Wilson	.50
4	C.J. Nitkowski	.50
5	Josh Booty	.50
6	Antone Williamson	.50
7	Paul Konerko	1.50
8	Scott Elarton	.50
9	Jacob Shumate	.50
10	Terrence Long	.50
11	Mark Johnson	.50
12	Ben Grieve	.50
13	Doug Million	.50
14	Jayson Peterson	.50
15	Dustin Hermanson	.50
16	Matt Smith	.50
17	Kevin Witt	.50
18	Brian Buchanan	.50

Dream Team Gold

		NM/M
Complete Set (12):		12.00
Common Player:		.30
1	Frank Thomas	1.25
2	Roberto Alomar	.50
3	Cal Ripken Jr.	4.00
4	Matt Williams	.30
5	Mike Piazza	2.50
6	Albert Belle	.30
7	Ken Griffey Jr.	2.50
8	Tony Gwynn	1.50
9	Paul Molitor	1.25
10	Jimmy Key	.30
11	Greg Maddux	1.50
12	Lee Smith	.30

Hall of Gold

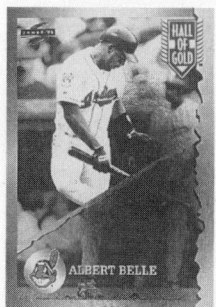

		NM/M
Complete Set (110):		25.00
Common Player:		.10
1	Ken Griffey Jr.	1.25
2	Matt Williams	.10
3	Roberto Alomar	.25
4	Jeff Bagwell	.75
5	Dave Justice	.10
6	Cal Ripken Jr.	2.00
7	Randy Johnson	.75
8	Barry Larkin	.10
9	Albert Belle	.10
10	Mike Piazza	1.25
11	Kirby Puckett	1.00
12	Moises Alou	.10
13	Jose Canseco	.45
14	Tony Gwynn	1.00
15	Roger Clemens	1.00
16	Barry Bonds	2.00
17	Mo Vaughn	.10
18	Greg Maddux	1.00
19	Dante Bichette	.10
20	Will Clark	.10
21	Len Dykstra	.10
22	Don Mattingly	1.00
23	Carlos Baerga	.10
24	Ozzie Smith	1.00
25	Paul Molitor	.75
26	Paul O'Neill	.10
27	Deion Sanders	.10
28	Jeff Conine	.10
29	John Olerud	.10
30	Jose Rijo	.10
31	Sammy Sosa	1.00
32	Robin Ventura	.10
33	Raul Mondesi	.10
34	Eddie Murray	.75
35	Marquis Grissom	.10
36	Darryl Strawberry	.10
37	Dave Nilsson	.10
38	Manny Ramirez	.75
39	Delino DeShields	.10
40	Lee Smith	.10
41	Alex Rodriguez	1.50
42	Julio Franco	.10
43	Bret Saberhagen	.10
44	Ken Hill	.10
45	Roberto Kelly	.10

46	Hal Morris	.10
47	Jimmy Key	.10
48	Terry Steinbach	.10
49	Mickey Tettleton	.10
50	Tony Phillips	.10
51	Carlos Garcia	.10
52	Jim Edmonds	.10
53	Rod Beck	.10
54	Shane Mack	.10
55	Ken Caminiti	.10
56	Frank Thomas	.75
57	Kenny Lofton	.10
58	Jack McDowell	.10
59	Jason Bere	.10
60	Joe Carter	.10
61	Gary Sheffield	.45
62	Andres Galarraga	.10
63	Gregg Jefferies	.10
64	Bobby Bonilla	.10
65	Tom Glavine	.35
66	John Smoltz	.10
67	Fred McGriff	.10
68	Craig Biggio	.10
69	Reggie Sanders	.10
70	Kevin Mitchell	.10
71a	Larry Walker (Expos)	.10
71b	Larry Walker (Rockies)	.10
72	Carlos Delgado	.50
73	Andujar Cedeno	.10
74	Ivan Rodriguez	.65
75	Ryan Klesko	.10
76a	John Kruk (Phillies)	.10
76b	John Kruk (White Sox)	.10
77a	Brian McRae (Royals)	.10
77b	Brian McRae (Cubs)	.10
78	Tim Salmon	.10
79	Travis Fryman	.10
80	Chuck Knoblauch	.10
81	Jay Bell	.10
82	Cecil Fielder	.10
83	Cliff Floyd	.10
84	Ruben Sierra	.10
85	Mike Mussina	.45
86	Mark Grace	.10
87	Dennis Eckersley	.65
88	Dennis Martinez	.10
89	Rafael Palmeiro	.65
90	Ben McDonald	.10
91	Dave Hollins	.10
92	Steve Avery	.10
93a	David Cone (Royals)	.10
93b	David Cone (Blue Jays)	.10
94	Darren Daulton	.10
95	Bret Boone	.10
96	Wade Boggs	1.00
97	Doug Drabek	.10
98	Derek Bell	.10
99	Jim Thome	.65
100	Chili Davis	.10
101	Jeffrey Hammonds	.10
102	Rickey Henderson	.75
103	Brett Butler	.10
104	Tim Wallach	.10
105	Wil Cordero	.10
106	Mark Whiten	.10
107	Bob Hamelin	.10
108	Rondell White	.10
109	Devon White	.10
110a	Tony Tarasco (Braves)	.10
110b	Tony Tarasco (Expos)	.10
----	Redemption Trade Card (Expired Dec. 31, 1995.)	.10

Rookie Dream Team

		NM/M
Complete Set (12):		9.00
Common Player:		.50
1	J.R. Phillips	.50
2	Alex Gonzalez	.50
3	Alex Rodriguez	6.00
4	Jose Oliva	.50
5	Charles Johnson	.50
6	Shawn Green	1.50
7	Brian Hunter	.50
8	Garret Anderson	.50
9	Julian Tavarez	.50
10	Jose Lima	.50
11	Armando Benitez	.50
12	Ricky Bottalico	.50

Rookie Greatness

		NM/M
RG1	Ryan Klesko	1.00
SG1	Ryan Klesko/Auto.	7.50

Score Rules

		NM/M
Complete Set (30):		30.00
Common Player:		.30
1	Ken Griffey Jr.	3.50
2	Frank Thomas	1.50
3	Mike Piazza	3.50
4	Jeff Bagwell	1.50
5	Alex Rodriguez	4.50
6	Albert Belle	.30
7	Matt Williams	.30
8	Roberto Alomar	.45
9	Barry Bonds	5.00
10	Raul Mondesi	.30
11	Jose Canseco	.60
12	Kirby Puckett	2.50
13	Fred McGriff	.30
14	Kenny Lofton	.30
15	Greg Maddux	2.50
16	Juan Gonzalez	.75
17	Cliff Floyd	.30
18	Cal Ripken, Jr.	5.00
19	Will Clark	.30
20	Tim Salmon	.30
21	Paul O'Neill	.30
22	Jason Bere	.30
23	Tony Gwynn	2.50
24	Manny Ramirez	1.50
25	Don Mattingly	3.00
26	Dave Justice	.30
27	Javier Lopez	.30
28	Ryan Klesko	.30
29	Carlos Delgado	.90
30	Mike Mussina	.60

1996 Score

		NM/M
Complete Set (510):		15.00
Common Player:		.05
Wax Pack (10):		.45
Wax Box (36):		10.00
1	Will Clark	.05
2	Rich Becker	.05
3	Ryan Klesko	.05
4	Jim Edmonds	.05
5	Barry Larkin	.05
6	Jim Thome	.40
7	Raul Mondesi	.05
8	Don Mattingly	.65
9	Jeff Conine	.05
10	Rickey Henderson	.50
11	Chad Curtis	.05
12	Darren Daulton	.05
13	Larry Walker	.05
14	Carlos Garcia	.05
15	Carlos Baerga	.05
16	Tony Gwynn	.60
17	Jon Nunally	.05
18	Deion Sanders	.05
19	Mark Grace	.05

20	Alex Rodriguez	1.00
21	Frank Thomas	.50
22	Brian Jordan	.05
23	J.T. Snow	.05
24	Shawn Green	.30
25	Tim Wakefield	.05
26	Curtis Goodwin	.05
27	John Smoltz	.05
28	Devon White	.05
29	Brian Hunter	.05
30	Rusty Greer	.05
31	Rafael Palmeiro	.40
32	Bernard Gilkey	.05
33	John Valentin	.05
34	Randy Johnson	.50
35	Garret Anderson	.05
36	Rikkert Faneyte	.05
37	Ray Durham	.05
38	Bip Roberts	.05
39	Jaime Navarro	.05
40	Mark Johnson	.05
41	Darren Lewis	.05
42	Tyler Green	.05
43	Bill Pulsipher	.05
44	Jason Giambi	.40
45	Kevin Ritz	.05
46	Jack McDowell	.05
47	Felipe Lira	.05
48	Rico Brogna	.05
49	Terry Pendleton	.05
50	Rondell White	.05
51	Andre Dawson	.25
52	Kirby Puckett	.60
53	Wally Joyner	.05
54	B.J. Surhoff	.05
55	Chan Ho Park	.05
56	Greg Vaughn	.05
57	Roberto Alomar	.20
58	Dave Justice	.05
59	Kevin Seitzer	.05
60	Cal Ripken Jr.	1.50
61	Ozzie Smith	.60
62	Mo Vaughn	.05
63	Ricky Bones	.05
64	Gary DiSarcina	.05
65	Matt Williams	.05
66	Wilson Alvarez	.05
67	Lenny Dykstra	.05
68	Brian McRae	.05
69	Todd Stottlemyre	.05
70	Bret Boone	.05
71	Sterling Hitchcock	.05
72	Albert Belle	.05
73	Todd Hundley	.05
74	Vinny Castilla	.05
75	Moises Alou	.05
76	Cecil Fielder	.05
77	Brad Radke	.05
78	Quilvio Veras	.05
79	Eddie Murray	.50
80	James Mouton	.05
81	Pat Listach	.05
82	Mark Gubicza	.05
83	Dave Winfield	.50
84	Fred McGriff	.05
85	Darryl Hamilton	.05
86	Jeffrey Hammonds	.05
87	Pedro Munoz	.05
88	Craig Biggio	.05
89	Cliff Floyd	.05
90	Tim Naehring	.05
91	Brett Butler	.05
92	Kevin Foster	.05
93	Patrick Kelly	.05
94	John Smiley	.05
95	Terry Steinbach	.05
96	Orel Hershiser	.05
97	Darrin Fletcher	.05
98	Walt Weiss	.05
99	John Wetteland	.05
100	Alan Trammell	.05
101	Steve Avery	.05
102	Tony Eusebio	.05
103	Sandy Alomar	.05
104	Joe Girardi	.05
105	Rick Aguilera	.05
106	Tony Tarasco	.05
107	Chris Hammond	.05
108	Mike McFarlane	.05
109	Doug Drabek	.05
110	Derek Bell	.05

111 Ed Sprague .05
112 Todd Hollandsworth .05
113 Otis Nixon .05
114 Keith Lockhart .05
115 Donovan Osborne .05
116 Dave Magadan .05
117 Edgar Martinez .05
118 Chuck Carr .05
119 J.R. Phillips .05
120 Sean Bergman .05
121 Andujar Cedeno .05
122 Eric Young .05
123 Al Martin .05
124 Ken Hill .05
125 Jim Eisenreich .05
126 Benito Santiago .05
127 Ariel Prieto .05
128 Jim Bullinger .05
129 Russ Davis .05
130 Jim Abbott .05
131 Jason Isringhausen .05
132 Carlos Perez .05
133 David Segui .05
134 Troy O'Leary .05
135 Pat Meares .05
136 Chris Hoiles .05
137 Ismael Valdes .05
138 Jose Oliva .05
139 Carlos Delgado .35
140 Tom Goodwin .05
141 Bob Tewksbury .05
142 Chris Gomez .05
143 Jose Oquendo .05
144 Mark Lewis .05
145 Salomon Torres .05
146 Luis Gonzalez .05
147 Mark Carreon .05
148 Lance Johnson .05
149 Melvin Nieves .05
150 Lee Smith .05
151 Jacob Brumfield .05
152 Armando Benitez .05
153 Curt Schilling .30
154 Javier Lopez .05
155 Frank Rodriguez .05
156 Alex Gonzalez .05
157 Todd Worrell .05
158 Benji Gil .05
159 Greg Gagne .05
160 Tom Henke .05
161 Randy Myers .05
162 Joey Cora .05
163 Scott Ruffcorn .05
164 William Van Landingham .05
165 Tony Phillips .05
166 Eddie Williams .05
167 Bobby Bonilla .05
168 Denny Neagle .05
169 Troy Percival .05
170 Billy Ashley .05
171 Andy Van Slyke .05
172 Jose Offerman .05
173 Mark Parent .05
174 Edgardo Alfonzo .05
175 Trevor Hoffman .05
176 David Cone .05
177 Dan Wilson .05
178 Steve Ontiveros .05
179 Dean Palmer .05
180 Mike Kelly .05
181 Jim Leyritz .05
182 Ron Karkovice .05
183 Kevin Brown .05
184 Jose Valentin **RC** .05
185 Jorge Fabregas .05
186 Jose Mesa .05
187 Brent Mayne .05
188 Carl Everett .05
189 Paul Sorrento .05
190 Pete Shourek .05
191 Scott Kamieniecki .05
192 Roberto Hernandez .05
193 Randy Johnson .25
194 Greg Maddux .35
195 Hideo Nomo .15
196 David Cone .05
197 Mike Mussina .15
198 Andy Benes .05
199 Kevin Appier .05
200 John Smoltz .05
201 John Wetteland .05
202 Mark Wohlers .05
203 Stan Belinda .05
204 Brian Anderson .05
205 Mike Devereaux .05
206 Mark Wohlers .05
207 Omar Vizquel .05
208 Jose Rijo .05
209 Willie Blair .05
210 Jamie Moyer .05
211 Craig Shipley .05
212 Shane Reynolds .05
213 Chad Fonville .05
214 Jose Vizcaino .05
215 Sid Fernandez .05
216 Andy Ashby .05
217 Frank Castillo .05
218 Kevin Tapani .05
219 Kent Mercker .05
220 Karim Garcia .05
221 Chris Snopek .05
222 Tim Unroe .05
223 Johnny Damon .25
224 LaTroy Hawkins .05
225 Mariano Rivera .10
226 Jose Alberro .05
227 Angel Martinez .05
228 Jason Schmidt .05
229 Tony Clark .05
230 Kevin Jordan .05
231 Mark Thompson .05
232 Jim Dougherty .05
333 Roger Cedeno .05
234 Ugueth Urbina .05
235 Ricky Otero .05
236 Mark Smith .05
237 Brian Barber .05
238 Marc Kroon .05
239 Joe Rosselli .05
240 Derek Jeter 1.50
241 Michael Tucker .05
242 Joe Borowski **RC** .05
243 Joe Vitiello .05
244 Orlando Palmeiro .05
245 James Baldwin .05
246 Alan Embree .05
247 Shannon Penn .05
248 Chris Stynes .05
249 Oscar Munoz .05
250 Jose Herrera .05
251 Scott Sullivan .05
252 Reggie Williams .05
253 Mark Grudzielanek .05
254 Kevin Jordan .05
255 Terry Bradshaw .05
256 F.P. Santangelo **RC** .05
257 Doug Johns .05
258 George Williams .05
259 Larry Thomas .05
260 Rudy Pemberton .05
261 Jim Pittsley .05
262 Les Norman .05
263 Ruben Rivera .05
264 Cesar Devarez **RC** .05
265 Gregg Zaun .05
266 Eric Owens .05
267 John Frascatore .05
268 Shannon Stewart .05
269 Checklist .05
270 Checklist .05
271 Checklist .05
272 Checklist .05
273 Checklist .05
274 Checklist .05
275 Checklist .05
276 Greg Maddux .60
277 Pedro Martinez .50
278 Bobby Higginson .05
279 Ray Lankford .05
280 Shawon Dunston .05
281 Gary Sheffield .35
282 Ken Griffey Jr. .75
283 Paul Molitor .50
284 Kevin Appier .05
285 Chuck Knoblauch .05
286 Alex Fernandez .05
287 Steve Finley .05
288 Jeff Blauser .05
289 Charles Johnson .05
290 John Franco .05
291 Mark Langston .05
292 Bret Saberhagen .05
293 John Mabry .05
294 Ramon Martinez .05
295 Mike Blowers .05
296 Paul O'Neill .05
297 Dave Nilsson .05
298 Dante Bichette .05
299 Marty Cordova .05
300 Jay Bell .05
301 Mike Mussina .30
302 Ivan Rodriguez .40
303 Jose Canseco .30
304 Jeff Bagwell .50
305 Manny Ramirez .50
306 Dennis Martinez .05
307 Charlie Hayes .05
308 Joe Carter .05
309 Travis Fryman .05
310 Mark McGwire 1.00
311 Reggie Sanders .05
312 Julian Tavarez .05
313 Jeff Montgomery .05
314 Andy Benes .05
315 John Jaha .05
316 Jeff Kent .05
317 Mike Piazza .75
318 Erik Hanson .05
319 Kenny Rogers .05
320 Hideo Nomo .25
321 Gregg Jefferies .05
322 Chipper Jones .75
323 Jay Buhner .05
324 Dennis Eckersley .40
325 Kenny Lofton .05
326 Robin Ventura .05
327 Tom Glavine .35
328 Tim Salmon .05
329 Andres Galarraga .05
330 Hal Morris .05
331 Brady Anderson .05
332 Chili Davis .05
333 Roger Clemens .65
334 Marquis Grissom .05
335 Jeff (Mike) Greenwell .05
336 Sammy Sosa .60
337 Ron Gant .05
338 Ken Caminiti .05
339 Danny Tartabull .05
340 Barry Bonds 1.50
341 Ben McDonald .05
342 Ruben Sierra .05
343 Bernie Williams .05
344 Wil Cordero .05
345 Wade Boggs .60
346 Gary Gaetti .05
347 Greg Colbrunn .05
348 Juan Gonzalez .25
349 Marc Newfield .05
350 Charles Nagy .05
351 Robby Thompson .05
352 Roberto Petagine .05
353 Darryl Strawberry .05
354 Tino Martinez .05
355 Eric Karros .05
356 Cal Ripken Jr. .75
357 Cecil Fielder .05
358 Kirby Puckett .35
359 Jim Edmonds .05
360 Matt Williams .05
361 Alex Rodriguez .50
362 Barry Larkin .05
363 Rafael Palmeiro .20
364 David Cone .05
365 Roberto Alomar .10
366 Eddie Murray .25
367 Randy Johnson .20
368 Ryan Klesko .05
369 Raul Mondesi .05
370 Mo Vaughn .05
371 Will Clark .05
372 Carlos Baerga .05
373 Frank Thomas .30
374 Larry Walker .05
375 Garret Anderson .05
376 Edgar Martinez .05
377 Don Mattingly .40
378 Tony Gwynn .35
379 Albert Belle .05
380 Jason Isringhausen .05
381 Ruben Rivera .05
382 Johnny Damon .05
383 Karim Garcia .05
384 Derek Jeter .75
385 David Justice .05
386 Royce Clayton .05
387 Mark Whiten .05
388 Mickey Tettleton .05
389 Steve Trachsel .05
390 Danny Bautista .05
391 Midre Cummings .05
392 Scott Leius .05
393 Manny Alexander .05
394 Brent Gates .05
395 Rey Sanchez .05
396 Andy Pettitte .20
397 Jeff Cirillo .05
398 Kurt Abbott .05
399 Lee Tinsley .05
400 Paul Assenmacher .05
401 Scott Erickson .05
402 Todd Zeile .05
403 Tom Pagnozzi .05
404 Ozzie Guillen .05
405 Jeff Frye .05
406 Kirt Manwaring .05
407 Chad Ogea .05
408 Harold Baines .05
409 Jason Bere .05
410 Chuck Finley .05
411 Jeff Fassero .05
412 Joey Hamilton .05
413 John Olerud .05
414 Kevin Stocker .05
415 Eric Anthony .05
416 Aaron Sele .05
417 Chris Bosio .05
418 Michael Mimbs .05
419 Orlando Miller .05
420 Stan Javier .05
421 Matt Mieske .05
422 Jason Bates .05
423 Orlando Merced .05
424 John Flaherty .05
425 Reggie Jefferson .05
426 Scott Stahoviak .05
427 John Burkett .05
428 Rod Beck .05
429 Bill Swift .05
430 Scott Cooper .05
431 Mel Rojas .05
432 Todd Van Poppel .05
433 Bobby Jones .05
434 Mike Harkey .05
435 Sean Berry .05
436 Glenallen Hill .05
437 Ryan Thompson .05
438 Luis Alicea .05
439 Esteban Loaiza .05
440 Jeff Reboulet .05
441 Vince Coleman .05
442 Ellis Burks .05
443 Allen Battle .05
444 Jimmy Key .05
445 Ricky Bottalico .05
446 Delino DeShields .05
447 Albie Lopez .05
448 Mark Petkovsek .05
449 Tim Raines .05
450 Bryan Harvey .05
451 Pat Hentgen .05
452 Tim Laker .05
453 Tom Gordon .05
454 Phil Plantier .05
455 Ernie Young .05
456 Pete Harnisch .05
457 Roberto Kelly .05
458 Mark Portugal .05
459 Mark Leiter .05
460 Tony Pena .05
461 Roger Pavlik .05
462 Jeff King .05
463 Bryan Rekar .05
464 Al Leiter .05
465 Phil Nevin .05
466 Jose Lima .05
467 Mike Stanley .05
468 David McCarty .05
469 Herb Perry .05
470 Geronimo Berroa .05
471 David Wells .05
472 Vaughn Eshelman .05
473 Greg Swindell .05
474 Steve Sparks .05
475 Luis Sojo .05
476 Derrick May .05
477 Joe Oliver .05
478 Alex Arias .05
479 Brad Ausmus .05
480 Gabe White .05
481 Pat Rapp .05
482 Damon Buford .05
483 Turk Wendell .05
484 Jeff Brantley .05
485 Curtis Leskanic .05
486 Robb Nen .05
487 Lou Whitaker .05
488 Melido Perez .05
489 Luis Polonia .05
490 Scott Brosius .05
491 Robert Perez .05
492 Mike Sweeney **RC** .50
493 Mark Loretta .05
494 Alex Ochoa .05
495 Matt Lawton **RC** .10
496 Shawn Estes .05
497 John Wasdin .05
498 Marc Kroon .05
499 Chris Snopek .05
500 Jeff Suppan .05
501 Terrell Wade .05
502 Marvin Benard **RC** .10
503 Chris Widger .05
504 Quinton McCracken .05
505 Bob Wolcott .05
506 C.J. Nitkowski .05
507 Aaron Ledesma .05
508 Scott Hatteberg .05
509 Jimmy Haynes .05
510 Howard Battle .05

Dugout Collection

	NM/M
Complete Set (220):	60.00
Complete Series 1 (1-110):	30.00
Complete Series 2 (1-110):	30.00
Common Player:	.20
Artist's Proofs:	4X

SERIES 1

1 Will Clark .20
2 Rich Becker .20
3 Ryan Klesko .20
4 Jim Edmonds .20
5 Barry Larkin .20
6 Jim Thome .65
7 Raul Mondesi .20
8 Don Mattingly 1.25
9 Jeff Conine .20
10 Rickey Henderson .75
11 Chad Curtis .20
12 Darren Daulton .20
13 Larry Walker .20
14 Carlos Baerga .20
15 Tony Gwynn 1.00
16 Jon Nunnally .20
17 Deion Sanders .20
18 Mark Grace .20
19 Alex Rodriguez 2.00
20 Frank Thomas .75
21 Brian Jordan .20
22 J.T. Snow .20
23 Shawn Green .50
24 Tim Wakefield .20
25 Curtis Goodwin .20
26 John Smoltz .20
27 Devon White .20
28 Brian Hunter .20
29 Rusty Greer .20

30	Rafael Palmeiro	.65
31	Bernard Gilkey	.20
32	John Valentin	.20
33	Randy Johnson	.75
34	Garret Anderson	.20
35	Ray Durham	.20
36	Bip Roberts	.20
37	Tyler Green	.20
38	Bill Pulsipher	.20
39	Jason Giambi	.50
40	Jack McDowell	.20
41	Rico Brogna	.20
42	Terry Pendleton	.20
43	Rondell White	.20
44	Andre Dawson	.35
45	Kirby Puckett	1.00
46	Wally Joyner	.20
47	B.J. Surhoff	.20
48	Randy Velarde	.20
49	Greg Vaughn	.20
50	Roberto Alomar	.30
51	David Justice	.20
52	Cal Ripken Jr.	3.00
53	Ozzie Smith	1.00
54	Mo Vaughn	.20
55	Gary DiSarcina	.20
56	Matt Williams	.20
57	Lenny Dykstra	.20
58	Bret Boone	.20
59	Albert Belle	.20
60	Vinny Castilla	.20
61	Moises Alou	.20
62	Cecil Fielder	.20
63	Brad Radke	.20
64	Quilvio Veras	.20
65	Eddie Murray	.75
66	Dave Winfield	.75
67	Fred McGriff	.20
68	Craig Biggio	.20
69	Cliff Floyd	.20
70	Tim Naehring	.20
71	John Wetteland	.20
72	Alan Trammell	.20
73	Steve Avery	.20
74	Rick Aguilera	.20
75	Derek Bell	.20
76	Todd Hollandsworth	.20
77	Edgar Martinez	.20
78	Mark Lemke	.20
79	Ariel Prieto	.20
80	Russ Davis	.20
81	Jim Abbott	.20
82	Jason Isringhausen	.20
83	Carlos Perez	.20
84	David Segui	.20
85	Troy O'Leary	.20
86	Ismael Valdes	.20
87	Carlos Delgado	.50
88	Lee Smith	.20
89	Javy Lopez	.20
90	Frank Rodriguez	.20
91	Alex Gonzalez	.20
92	Benji Gil	.20
93	Greg Gagne	.20
94	Randy Myers	.20
95	Bobby Bonilla	.20
96	Billy Ashley	.20
97	Andy Van Slyke	.20
98	Edgardo Alfonzo	.20
99	David Cone	.20
100	Dean Palmer	.20
101	Jose Mesa	.20
102	Karim Garcia	.20
103	Johnny Damon	.40
104	LaTroy Hawkins	.20
105	Mark Smith	.20
106	Derek Jeter	3.00
107	Michael Tucker	.20
108	Joe Vitiello	.20
109	Ruben Rivera	.20
110	Gregg Zaun	.20

SERIES 2

1	Greg Maddux	1.00
2	Pedro Martinez	.75
3	Bobby Higginson	.20
4	Ray Lankford	.20
5	Shawon Dunston	.20
6	Gary Sheffield	.45
7	Ken Griffey Jr.	1.50
8	Paul Molitor	.75
9	Kevin Appier	.20
10	Chuck Knoblauch	.20
11	Alex Fernandez	.20
12	Steve Finley	.20
13	Jeff Blauser	.20
14	Charles Johnson	.20
15	John Franco	.20
16	Mark Langston	.20
17	Bret Saberhagen	.20
18	John Mabry	.20
19	Ramon Martinez	.20
20	Mike Blowers	.20
21	Paul O'Neill	.20
22	Dave Nilsson	.20
23	Dante Bichette	.20
24	Marty Cordova	.20
25	Jay Bell	.20
26	Mike Mussina	.40
27	Ivan Rodriguez	.65
28	Jose Canseco	.50
29	Jeff Bagwell	.75
30	Manny Ramirez	.75
31	Dennis Martinez	.20
32	Charlie Hayes	.20
33	Joe Carter	.20

34	Travis Fryman	.20
35	Mark McGwire	2.00
36	Reggie Sanders	.20
37	Julian Tavarez	.20
38	Jeff Montgomery	.20
39	Andy Benes	.20
40	John Jaha	.20
41	Jeff Kent	.20
42	Mike Piazza	1.50
43	Erik Hanson	.20
44	Kenny Rogers	.20
45	Hideo Nomo	.50
46	Gregg Jefferies	.20
47	Chipper Jones	1.00
48	Jay Buhner	.20
49	Dennis Eckersley	.65
50	Kenny Lofton	.20
51	Robin Ventura	.20
52	Tom Glavine	.30
53	Tim Salmon	.20
54	Andres Galarraga	.20
55	Hal Morris	.20
56	Brady Anderson	.20
57	Chili Davis	.20
58	Roger Clemens	1.25
59	Marquis Grissom	.20
60	Mike Greenwell	.20
61	Sammy Sosa	1.00
62	Ron Gant	.20
63	Ken Caminiti	.20
64	Danny Tartabull	.20
65	Barry Bonds	3.00
66	Ben McDonald	.20
67	Ruben Sierra	.20
68	Bernie Williams	.20
69	Wil Cordero	.20
70	Wade Boggs	1.00
71	Gary Gaetti	.20
72	Greg Colbrunn	.20
73	Juan Gonzalez	.50
74	Marc Newfield	.20
75	Charles Nagy	.20
76	Robby Thompson	.20
77	Roberto Petagine	.20
78	Darryl Strawberry	.20
79	Tino Martinez	.20
80	Eric Karros	.20
81	Cal Ripken Jr.	1.50
82	Cecil Fielder	.20
83	Kirby Puckett	.50
84	Jim Edmonds	.20
85	Matt Williams	.20
86	Alex Rodriguez	1.00
87	Barry Larkin	.20
88	Rafael Palmeiro	.40
89	David Cone	.20
90	Roberto Alomar	.25
91	Eddie Murray	.40
92	Randy Johnson	.40
93	Ryan Klesko	.20
94	Raul Mondesi	.20
95	Mo Vaughn	.20
96	Will Clark	.20
97	Carlos Baerga	.20
98	Frank Thomas	.45
99	Larry Walker	.20
100	Garret Anderson	.20
101	Edgar Martinez	.20
102	Don Mattingly	.60
103	Tony Gwynn	.50
104	Albert Belle	.20
105	Jason Isringhausen	.20
106	Ruben Rivera	.20
107	Johnny Damon	.35
108	Karim Garcia	.20
109	Derek Jeter	1.50
110	Michael Tucker	.20

Dugout Collection Artist's Proofs

		NM/M
Complete Set (220):		300.00
Common Player:		1.00
Artist's Proof Stars:		4X

(See 1996 Score Dugout Collection for checklist and base card values.)

All-Stars

	NM/M
Complete Set (20):	13.50

Chipper Jones All Stars

Common Player:		.25
1	Frank Thomas	1.25
2	Albert Belle	.25
3	Ken Griffey Jr.	2.00
4	Cal Ripken Jr.	3.00
5	Mo Vaughn	.25
6	Matt Williams	.25
7	Barry Bonds	3.00
8	Dante Bichette	.25
9	Tony Gwynn	1.50
10	Greg Maddux	1.50
11	Randy Johnson	1.25
12	Hideo Nomo	.75
13	Tim Salmon	.25
14	Jeff Bagwell	1.25
15	Edgar Martinez	.25
16	Reggie Sanders	.25
17	Larry Walker	.25
18	Chipper Jones	1.50
19	Manny Ramirez	1.25
20	Eddie Murray	1.25

Big Bats

BIG BATS Tony GWYNN PADRES

		NM/M
Complete Set (20):		12.50
Common Player:		.45
1	Cal Ripken Jr.	3.00
2	Ken Griffey Jr.	2.00
3	Frank Thomas	.75
4	Jeff Bagwell	.75
5	Mike Piazza	2.00
6	Barry Bonds	3.00
7	Matt Williams	.45
8	Raul Mondesi	.45
9	Tony Gwynn	1.25
10	Albert Belle	.45
11	Manny Ramirez	.75
12	Carlos Baerga	.45
13	Mo Vaughn	.45
14	Derek Bell	.45
15	Larry Walker	.45
16	Kenny Lofton	.45
17	Edgar Martinez	.45
18	Reggie Sanders	.45
19	Eddie Murray	.75
20	Chipper Jones	1.25

Diamond Aces

		NM/M
Complete Set (30):		25.00
Common Player:		.35
1	Hideo Nomo	.60
2	Brian Hunter	.35
3	Ray Durham	.35
4	Frank Thomas	1.00
5	Cal Ripken Jr.	3.50
6	Barry Bonds	3.50
7	Greg Maddux	1.25
8	Chipper Jones	1.25
9	Raul Mondesi	.35
10	Mike Piazza	2.00
11	Derek Jeter	3.50
12	Bill Pulsipher	.35
13	Larry Walker	.35
14	Ken Griffey Jr.	2.00
15	Alex Rodriguez	3.00
16	Manny Ramirez	1.00

RAUL MONDESI Los Angeles Dodgers — 1996 Diamond Aces

17	Mo Vaughn	.35
18	Reggie Sanders	.35
19	Derek Bell	.35
20	Jim Edmonds	.35
21	Albert Belle	.35
22	Eddie Murray	1.00
23	Tony Gwynn	1.25
24	Jeff Bagwell	1.00
25	Carlos Baerga	.35
26	Matt Williams	.35
27	Garret Anderson	.35
28	Todd Hollandsworth	.35
29	Johnny Damon	.75
30	Tim Salmon	.35

Dream Team

MIKE PIAZZA Los Angeles Dodgers Dream Team

		NM/M
Complete Set (9):		15.00
Common Player:		.75
1	Cal Ripken Jr.	4.00
2	Frank Thomas	1.50
3	Carlos Baerga	.75
4	Matt Williams	.75
5	Mike Piazza	3.00
6	Barry Bonds	4.00
7	Ken Griffey Jr.	3.00
8	Manny Ramirez	1.50
9	Greg Maddux	2.00

Reserve Collection

	NM/M
Complete Set (221):	250.00
Common Player:	1.00
Reserve Collection Stars:	8X

(See 1997 Score #331-551 for checklist and base card values.)

Gold Stars

		NM/M
Complete Set (30):		20.00
Common Player:		.20
1	Ken Griffey Jr.	2.00
2	Frank Thomas	1.00

3	Reggie Sanders	.20
4	Tim Salmon	.20
5	Mike Piazza	2.00
6	Tony Gwynn	1.50
7	Gary Sheffield	.45
8	Matt Williams	.20
9	Bernie Williams	.20
10	Jason Isringhausen	.20
11	Albert Belle	.20
12	Chipper Jones	1.50
13	Edgar Martinez	.20
14	Barry Larkin	.20
15	Barry Bonds	3.00
16	Jeff Bagwell	1.00
17	Greg Maddux	1.50
18	Mo Vaughn	.20
19	Ryan Klesko	.20
20	Sammy Sosa	1.50
21	Darren Daulton	.20
22	Ivan Rodriguez	.75
23	Dante Bichette	.20
24	Hideo Nomo	.50
25	Cal Ripken Jr.	3.00
26	Rafael Palmeiro	.75
27	Larry Walker	.20
28	Carlos Baerga	.20
29	Randy Johnson	1.00
30	Manny Ramirez	1.00

Future Franchise

	NM/M
Complete Set (16):	20.00
Common Player:	.75
1 Jason Isringhausen	.75
2 Chipper Jones	2.50
3 Derek Jeter	5.00
4 Alex Rodriguez	4.00
5 Alex Ochoa	.75
6 Manny Ramirez	1.50
7 Johnny Damon	1.00
8 Ruben Rivera	.75
9 Karim Garcia	.75
10 Garret Anderson	.75
11 Marty Cordova	.75
12 Bill Pulsipher	.75
13 Hideo Nomo	1.00
14 Marc Newfield	.75
15 Charles Johnson	.75
16 Raul Mondesi	.75

Power Pace

	NM/M
Complete Set (18):	24.00
Common Player:	.50
1 Mark McGwire	4.00

2	Albert Belle	.50
3	Jay Buhner	.50
4	Frank Thomas	1.50
5	Matt Williams	.50
6	Gary Sheffield	.75
7	Mike Piazza	3.00
8	Larry Walker	.50
9	Mo Vaughn	.50
10	Rafael Palmeiro	1.25
11	Dante Bichette	.50
12	Ken Griffey Jr.	3.00
13	Barry Bonds	5.00
14	Manny Ramirez	1.50
15	Sammy Sosa	2.00
16	Tim Salmon	.50
17	Dave Justice	.50
18	Eric Karros	.50

Numbers Game

	NM/M
Complete Set (30):	17.50
Common Player:	.15
1 Cal Ripken Jr.	2.50
2 Frank Thomas	.75
3 Ken Griffey Jr.	1.50
4 Mike Piazza	1.50
5 Barry Bonds	2.50
6 Greg Maddux	1.00
7 Jeff Bagwell	.75
8 Derek Bell	.15
9 Tony Gwynn	1.00
10 Hideo Nomo	.50
11 Raul Mondesi	.15
12 Manny Ramirez	.75
13 Albert Belle	.15
14 Matt Williams	.15
15 Jim Edmonds	.15
16 Edgar Martinez	.15
17 Mo Vaughn	.15
18 Reggie Sanders	.15
19 Chipper Jones	1.00
20 Larry Walker	.15
21 Juan Gonzalez	.50
22 Kenny Lofton	.15
23 Don Mattingly	1.25
24 Ivan Rodriguez	.65
25 Randy Johnson	.75
26 Derek Jeter	2.50
27 J.T. Snow	.15
28 Will Clark	.15
29 Rafael Palmeiro	.65
30 Alex Rodriguez	2.00

Reflexions

	NM/M
Complete Set (20):	35.00
Common Player:	.45
1 Cal Ripken Jr., Chipper Jones	5.00
2 Ken Griffey Jr., Alex Rodriguez	4.50
3 Frank Thomas, Mo Vaughn	2.50
4 Kenny Lofton, Brian Hunter	.45
5 Don Mattingly, J.T. Snow	3.75
6 Manny Ramirez, Raul Mondesi	2.50
7 Tony Gwynn, Garret Anderson	3.75
8 Roberto Alomar, Carlos Baerga	.50
9 Andre Dawson, Larry Walker	.50
10 Barry Larkin, Derek Jeter	5.00
11 Barry Bonds, Reggie Sanders	5.00
12 Mike Piazza, Albert Belle	4.00
13 Wade Boggs, Edgar Martinez	3.75
14 David Cone, John Smoltz	.45

15	Will Clark, Jeff Bagwell	2.50
16	Mark McGwire, Cecil Fielder	4.50
17	Greg Maddux, Mike Mussina	3.75
18	Randy Johnson, Hideo Nomo	2.50
19	Jim Thome, Dean Palmer	2.00
20	Chuck Knoblauch, Craig Biggio	.45

Titantic Taters

	NM/M
Complete Set (18):	25.00
Common Player:	.60
1 Albert Belle	.60
2 Frank Thomas	2.00
3 Mo Vaughn	.60
4 Ken Griffey Jr.	3.00
5 Matt Williams	.60
6 Mark McGwire	3.50
7 Dante Bichette	.60
8 Tim Salmon	.60
9 Jeff Bagwell	2.00
10 Rafael Palmeiro	1.50
11 Mike Piazza	3.00
12 Cecil Fielder	.60
13 Larry Walker	.60
14 Sammy Sosa	2.50
15 Manny Ramirez	2.00
16 Gary Sheffield	.90
17 Barry Bonds	5.00
18 Jay Buhner	.60

1997 Score

	NM/M
Complete Set (551):	16.00
Factory Tin-Box Set (551):	17.50
Common Player:	.05
Showcase:	3X
Artist's Proofs:	10X
Premium Stocks:	3X
Wax Pack (10):	.50
Wax Box (36):	12.00
1 Jeff Bagwell	.50
2 Mickey Tettleton	.05
3 Johnny Damon	.25
4 Jeff Conine	.05
5 Bernie Williams	.05
6 Will Clark	.05
7 Ryan Klesko	.05
8 Cecil Fielder	.05
9 Paul Wilson	.05
10 Gregg Jefferies	.05
11 Chili Davis	.05
12 Albert Belle	.05
13 Ken Hill	.05
14 Cliff Floyd	.05
15 Jaime Navarro	.05
16 Ismael Valdes	.05
17 Jeff King	.05
18 Chris Bosio	.05
19 Reggie Sanders	.05
20 Darren Daulton	.05
21 Ken Caminiti	.05
22 Mike Piazza	.75
23 Chad Mottola	.05

24	Darin Erstad	.15
25	Dante Bichette	.05
26	Frank Thomas	.50
27	Ben McDonald	.05
28	Raul Casanova	.05
29	Kevin Ritz	.05
30	Garret Anderson	.05
31	Jason Kendall	.05
32	Billy Wagner	.05
33	David Justice	.05
34	Marty Cordova	.05
35	Derek Jeter	1.50
36	Trevor Hoffman	.05
37	Geronimo Berroa	.05
38	Walt Weiss	.05
39	Kirt Manwaring	.05
40	Alex Gonzalez	.05
41	Sean Berry	.05
42	Kevin Appier	.05
43	Rusty Greer	.05
44	Pete Incaviglia	.05
45	Rafael Palmeiro	.45
46	Eddie Murray	.50
47	Moises Alou	.05
48	Mark Lewis	.05
49	Hal Morris	.05
50	Edgar Renteria	.05
51	Rickey Henderson	.50
52	Pat Listach	.05
53	John Wasdin	.05
54	James Baldwin	.05
55	Brian Jordan	.05
56	Edgar Martinez	.05
57	Wil Cordero	.05
58	Danny Tartabull	.05
59	Keith Lockhart	.05
60	Rico Brogna	.05
61	Ricky Bottalico	.05
62	Terry Pendleton	.05
63	Bret Boone	.05
64	Charlie Hayes	.05
65	Marc Newfield	.05
66	Sterling Hitchcock	.05
67	Roberto Alomar	.15
68	John Jaha	.05
69	Greg Colbrunn	.05
70	Sal Fasano	.05
71	Brooks Kieschnick	.05
72	Pedro Martinez	.50
73	Kevin Elster	.05
74	Ellis Burks	.05
75	Chuck Finley	.05
76	John Olerud	.05
77	Jay Bell	.05
78	Allen Watson	.05
79	Darryl Strawberry	.05
80	Orlando Miller	.05
81	Jose Herrera	.05
82	Andy Pettitte	.20
83	Juan Guzman	.05
84	Alan Benes	.05
85	Jack McDowell	.05
86	Ugueth Urbina	.05
87	Rocky Coppinger	.05
88	Jeff Cirillo	.05
89	Tom Glavine	.35
90	Robby Thompson	.05
91	Barry Bonds	1.50
92	Carlos Delgado	.40
93	Mo Vaughn	.05
94	Ryne Sandberg	.65
95	Alex Rodriguez	1.00
96	Brady Anderson	.05
97	Scott Brosius	.05
98	Dennis Eckersley	.45
99	Brian McRae	.05
100	Rey Ordonez	.05
101	John Valentin	.05
102	Brett Butler	.05
103	Eric Karros	.05
104	Harold Baines	.05
105	Javier Lopez	.05
106	Alan Trammell	.05
107	Jim Thome	.45
108	Frank Rodriguez	.05
109	Bernard Gilkey	.05
110	Reggie Jefferson	.05
111	Scott Stahoviak	.05
112	Steve Gibralter	.05
113	Todd Hollandsworth	.05
114	Ruben Rivera	.05
115	Dennis Martinez	.05
116	Mariano Rivera	.10
117	John Smoltz	.05
118	John Mabry	.05
119	Tom Gordon	.05
120	Alex Ochoa	.05
121	Jamey Wright	.05
122	Dave Nilsson	.05
123	Bobby Bonilla	.05
124	Al Leiter	.05
125	Rick Aguilera	.05
126	Jeff Brantley	.05
127	Kevin Brown	.05
128	George Arias	.05
129	Darren Oliver	.05
130	Bill Pulsipher	.05
131	Roberto Hernandez	.05
132	Delino DeShields	.05
133	Mark Grudzielanek	.05
134	John Wetteland	.05
135	Carlos Baerga	.05
136	Paul Sorrento	.05
137	Leo Gomez	.05
138	Andy Ashby	.05
139	Julio Franco	.05
140	Brian Hunter	.05

141	Jermaine Dye	.05
142	Tony Clark	.05
143	Ruben Sierra	.05
144	Donovan Osborne	.05
145	Mark McLemore	.05
146	Terry Steinbach	.05
147	Bob Wells	.05
148	Chan Ho Park	.05
149	Tim Salmon	.05
150	Paul O'Neill	.05
151	Cal Ripken Jr.	1.50
152	Wally Joyner	.05
153	Omar Vizquel	.05
154	Mike Mussina	.30
155	Andres Galarraga	.05
156	Ken Griffey Jr.	.75
157	Kenny Lofton	.05
158	Ray Durham	.05
159	Hideo Nomo	.25
160	Ozzie Guillen	.05
161	Roger Pavlik	.05
162	Manny Ramirez	.50
163	Mark Lemke	.05
164	Mike Stanley	.05
165	Chuck Knoblauch	.05
166	Kimera Bartee	.05
167	Wade Boggs	.65
168	Jay Buhner	.05
169	Eric Young	.05
170	Jose Canseco	.30
171	Dwight Gooden	.05
172	Fred McGriff	.05
173	Sandy Alomar Jr.	.05
174	Andy Benes	.05
175	Dean Palmer	.05
176	Larry Walker	.05
177	Charles Nagy	.05
178	David Cone	.05
179	Mark Grace	.05
180	Robin Ventura	.05
181	Roger Clemens	.70
182	Bobby Witt	.05
183	Vinny Castilla	.05
184	Gary Sheffield	.35
185	Dan Wilson	.05
186	Roger Cedeno	.05
187	Mark McGwire	1.00
188	Darren Bragg	.05
189	Quinton McCracken	.05
190	Randy Myers	.05
191	Jeromy Burnitz	.05
192	Randy Johnson	.50
193	Chipper Jones	.75
194	Greg Vaughn	.05
195	Travis Fryman	.05
196	Tim Naehring	.05
197	B.J. Surhoff	.05
198	Juan Gonzalez	.25
199	Terrell Wade	.05
200	Jeff Frye	.05
201	Joey Cora	.05
202	Raul Mondesi	.05
203	Ivan Rodriguez	.45
204	Armando Reynoso	.05
205	Jeffrey Hammonds	.05
206	Darren Dreifort	.05
207	Kevin Seitzer	.05
208	Tino Martinez	.05
209	Jim Bruske	.05
210	Jeff Suppan	.05
211	Mark Carreon	.05
212	Wilson Alvarez	.05
213	John Burkett	.05
214	Tony Phillips	.05
215	Greg Maddux	.65
216	Mark Whiten	.05
217	Curtis Pride	.05
218	Lyle Mouton	.05
219	Todd Hundley	.05
220	Greg Gagne	.05
221	Rich Amaral	.05
222	Tom Goodwin	.05
223	Chris Hoiles	.05
224	Jayhawk Owens	.05
225	Kenny Rogers	.05
226	Mike Greenwell	.05
227	Mark Wohlers	.05
228	Henry Rodriguez	.05
229	Robert Perez	.05
230	Jeff Kent	.05
231	Darryl Hamilton	.05
232	Alex Fernandez	.05
233	Ron Karkovice	.05
234	Jimmy Haynes	.05
235	Craig Biggio	.05
236	Ray Lankford	.05
237	Lance Johnson	.05
238	Matt Williams	.05
239	Chad Curtis	.05
240	Mark Thompson	.05
241	Jason Giambi	.40
242	Barry Larkin	.05
243	Paul Molitor	.50
244	Sammy Sosa	.65
245	Kevin Tapani	.05
246	Marquis Grissom	.05
247	Joe Carter	.05
248	Ramon Martinez	.05
249	Tony Gwynn	.65
250	Andy Fox	.05
251	Troy O'Leary	.05
252	Warren Newson	.05
253	Troy Percival	.05
254	Jamie Moyer	.05
255	Danny Graves	.05
256	David Wells	.05
257	Todd Zeile	.05
258	Raul Ibanez	.05
259	Tyler Houston	.05
260	LaTroy Hawkins	.05
261	Joey Hamilton	.05
262	Mike Sweeney	.05
263	Brant Brown	.05
264	Pat Hentgen	.05
265	Mark Johnson	.05
266	Robb Nen	.05
267	Justin Thompson	.05
268	Ron Gant	.05
269	Jeff D'Amico	.05
270	Shawn Estes	.05
271	Derek Bell	.05
272	Fernando Valenzuela	.05
273	Luis Castillo	.05
274	Ray Montgomery	.05
275	Ed Sprague	.05
276	F.P. Santangelo	.05
277	Todd Greene	.05
278	Butch Huskey	.05
279	Steve Finley	.05
280	Eric Davis	.05
281	Shawn Green	.30
282	Al Martin	.05
283	Michael Tucker	.05
284	Shane Reynolds	.05
285	Matt Mieske	.05
286	Jose Rosado	.05
287	Mark Langston	.05
288	Ralph Milliard	.05
289	Mike Lansing	.05
290	Scott Servais	.05
291	Royce Clayton	.05
292	Mike Grace	.05
293	James Mouton	.05
294	Charles Johnson	.05
295	Gary Gaetti	.05
296	Kevin Mitchell	.05
297	Carlos Garcia	.05
298	Desi Relaford	.05
299	Jason Thompson	.05
300	Osvaldo Fernandez	.05
301	Fernando Vina	.05
302	Jose Offerman	.05
303	Yamil Benitez	.05
304	J.T. Snow	.05
305	Rafael Bournigal	.05
306	Jason Isringhausen	.05
307	Bob Higginson	.05
308	Nerio Rodriguez **RC**	.05
309	Brian Giles **RC**	.50
310	Andruw Jones	.50
311	Billy McMillon	.05
312	Arquimedez Pozo	.05
313	Jermaine Allensworth	.05
314	Luis Andujar	.05
315	Angel Echevarria	.05
316	Karim Garcia	.05
317	Trey Beamon	.05
318	Makoto Suzuki	.05
319	Robin Jennings	.05
320	Dmitri Young	.05
321	Damon Mashore **RC**	.05
322	Wendell Magee	.05
323	Dax Jones **RC**	.05
324	Todd Walker	.05
325	Marvin Benard	.05
326	Brian Raabe **RC**	.05
327	Marcus Jensen	.05
328	Checklist	.05
329	Checklist	.05
330	Checklist	.05
331	Norm Charlton	.05
332	Bruce Ruffin	.05
333	John Wetteland	.05
334	Marquis Grissom	.05
335	Sterling Hitchcock	.05
336	John Olerud	.05
337	David Wells	.05
338	Chili Davis	.05
339	Mark Lewis	.05
340	Kenny Lofton	.05
341	Alex Fernandez	.05
342	Ruben Sierra	.05
343	Delino DeShields	.05
344	John Wasdin	.05
345	Dennis Martinez	.05
346	Kevin Elster	.05
347	Bobby Bonilla	.05
348	Jaime Navarro	.05
349	Chad Curtis	.05
350	Terry Steinbach	.05
351	Ariel Prieto	.05
352	Jeff Kent	.05
353	Carlos Garcia	.05
354	Mark Whiten	.05
355	Todd Zeile	.05
356	Eric Davis	.05
357	Greg Colbrunn	.05
358	Moises Alou	.05
359	Allen Watson	.05
360	Jose Canseco	.30
361	Matt Williams	.05
362	Jeff King	.05
363	Darryl Hamilton	.05
364	Mark Clark	.05
365	J.T. Snow	.05
366	Kevin Mitchell	.05
367	Orlando Miller	.05
368	Rico Brogna	.05
369	Mike James	.05
370	Brad Ausmus	.05
371	Darryl Kile	.05
372	Edgardo Alfonzo	.05
373	Julian Tavarez	.05
374	Darren Lewis	.05
375	Steve Karsay	.05
376	Lee Stevens	.05
377	Albie Lopez	.05
378	Orel Hershiser	.05
379	Lee Smith	.05
380	Rick Helling	.05
381	Carlos Perez	.05
382	Tony Tarasco	.05
383	Melvin Nieves	.05
384	Benji Gil	.05
385	Devon White	.05
386	Armando Benitez	.05
387	Bill Swift	.05
388	John Smiley	.05
389	Midre Cummings	.05
390	Tim Belcher	.05
391	Tim Raines	.05
392	Todd Worrell	.05
393	Quilvio Veras	.05
394	Matt Lawton	.05
395	Aaron Sele	.05
396	Bip Roberts	.05
397	Denny Neagle	.05
398	Tyler Green	.05
399	Hipolito Pichardo	.05
400	Scott Erickson	.05
401	Bobby Jones	.05
402	Jim Edmonds	.05
403	Chad Ogea	.05
404	Cal Eldred	.05
405	Pat Listach	.05
406	Todd Stottlemyre	.05
407	Phil Nevin	.05
408	Otis Nixon	.05
409	Billy Ashley	.05
410	Jimmy Key	.05
411	Mike Timlin	.05
412	Joe Vitiello	.05
413	Rondell White	.05
414	Jeff Fassero	.05
415	Rex Hudler	.05
416	Curt Schilling	.35
417	Rich Becker	.05
418	William Van Landingham	.05
419	Chris Snopek	.05
420	David Segui	.05
421	Eddie Murray	.50
422	Shane Andrews	.05
423	Gary DiSarcina	.05
424	Brian Hunter	.05
425	Willie Greene	.05
426	Felipe Crespo	.05
427	Jason Bates	.05
428	Albert Belle	.05
429	Rey Sanchez	.05
430	Roger Clemens	.70
431	Deion Sanders	.05
432	Ernie Young	.05
433	Jay Bell	.05
434	Jeff Blauser	.05
435	Lenny Dykstra	.05
436	Chuck Carr	.05
437	Russ Davis	.05
438	Carl Everett	.05
439	Damion Easley	.05
440	Pat Kelly	.05
441	Pat Rapp	.05
442	David Justice	.05
443	Graeme Lloyd	.05
444	Damon Buford	.05
445	Jose Valentin	.05
446	Jason Schmidt	.05
447	Dave Martinez	.05
448	Danny Tartabull	.05
449	Jose Vizcaino	.05
450	Steve Avery	.05
451	Mike Devereaux	.05
452	Jim Eisenreich	.05
453	Mark Leiter	.05
454	Roberto Kelly	.05
455	Benito Santiago	.05
456	Steve Trachsel	.05
457	Gerald Williams	.05
458	Pete Schourek	.05
459	Esteban Loaiza	.05
460	Mel Rojas	.05
461	Tim Wakefield	.05
462	Tony Fernandez	.05
463	Doug Drabek	.05
464	Joe Girardi	.05
465	Mike Bordick	.05
466	Jim Leyritz	.05
467	Erik Hanson	.05
468	Michael Tucker	.05
469	Tony Womack **RC**	.10
470	Doug Glanville	.05
471	Rudy Pemberton	.05
472	Keith Lockhart	.05
473	Nomar Garciaparra	.65
474	Scott Rolen	.40
475	Jason Dickson	.05
476	Glendon Rusch	.05
477	Todd Walker	.05
478	Dmitri Young	.05
479	Rod Myers **RC**	.05
480	Wilton Guerrero	.05
481	Jorge Posada	.05
482	Brant Brown	.05
483	Bubba Trammell **RC**	.10
484	Jose Guillen	.05
485	Scott Spiezio	.05
486	Bob Abreu	.10
487	Chris Holt	.05
488	Deivi Cruz **RC**	.15
489	Vladimir Guerrero	.50
490	Julio Santana	.05
491	Ray Montgomery	.05
492	Kevin Orie	.05
493	Todd Hundley	.05
494	Tim Salmon	.05
495	Albert Belle	.05
496	Manny Ramirez	.25
497	Rafael Palmeiro	.20
498	Juan Gonzalez	.15
499	Ken Griffey Jr.	.40
500	Andruw Jones	.25
501	Mike Piazza	.40
502	Jeff Bagwell	.25
503	Bernie Williams	.05
504	Barry Bonds	.65
505	Ken Caminiti	.05
506	Darin Erstad	.10
507	Alex Rodriguez	.50
508	Frank Thomas	.30
509	Chipper Jones	.40
510	Mo Vaughn	.05
511	Mark McGwire	.50
512	Fred McGriff	.05
513	Jay Buhner	.05
514	Jim Thome	.20
515	Gary Sheffield	.20
516	Dean Palmer	.05
517	Henry Rodriguez	.05
518	Andy Pettitte	.10
519	Mike Mussina	.10
520	Greg Maddux	.35
521	John Smoltz	.05
522	Hideo Nomo	.15
523	Troy Percival	.05
524	John Wetteland	.05
525	Roger Clemens	.40
526	Charles Nagy	.05
527	Mariano Rivera	.10
528	Tom Glavine	.15
529	Randy Johnson	.25
530	Jason Isringhausen	.05
531	Alex Fernandez	.05
532	Kevin Brown	.05
533	Chuck Knoblauch	.05
534	Rusty Greer	.05
535	Tony Gwynn	.35
536	Ryan Klesko	.05
537	Ryne Sandberg	.35
538	Barry Larkin	.05
539	Will Clark	.05
540	Kenny Lofton	.05
541	Paul Molitor	.30
542	Roberto Alomar	.10
543	Rey Ordonez	.05
544	Jason Giambi	.25
545	Derek Jeter	.75
546	Cal Ripken Jr.	.75
547	Ivan Rodriguez	.25
548	Ken Griffey Jr. Checklist	.35
549	Frank Thomas Checklist	.25
550	Mike Piazza Checklist	.40
551a	Hideki Irabu/SP **RC** (English on back; factory sets/retailpacks.)	.25
551b	Hideki Irabu/SP **RC** (Japanese back; Hobby Reserve packs.)	.35

Showcase

	NM/M
Complete Set (551):	200.00
Common Player:	.50
Showcase Stars:	3X

(See 1997 Score for checklist and base card values.)

Showcase Artist's Proofs

	NM/M
Common Player:	1.00
Showcase AP Stars:	10X

(See 1997 Score for checklist and base card values.)

Premium Stock

NM/M
Complete Set (330): 17.50
Common Player: .10
Premium Stock Stars: 3X
(See 1997 Score #1-330 for checklist
and base card values.)

White Border Artist's Proofs

NM/M
Complete Set (330): 150.00
Common Player: .50
Artist's Proof Stars: 10X
(See 1997 Score for checklist and base
card values.)

Hobby Reserve

NM/M
Complete Set (221): 35.00
Common Player: .10
Hobby Reserve Stars: 3X
(See 1997 Score #331-551 for
checklist and base card values.)

Blast Masters

NM/M
Complete Set (18): 17.50
Common Player: .25
1 Mo Vaughn .25
2 Mark McGwire 2.25
3 Juan Gonzalez .75
4 Albert Belle .25
5 Barry Bonds 3.00
6 Ken Griffey Jr. 2.00
7 Andruw Jones 1.25
8 Chipper Jones 1.50
9 Mike Piazza 2.00
10 Jeff Bagwell 1.25
11 Dante Bichette .25
12 Alex Rodriguez 2.25
13 Gary Sheffield .60
14 Ken Caminiti .25

15 Sammy Sosa 1.50
16 Vladimir Guerrero 1.25
17 Brian Jordan .25
18 Tim Salmon .25

Heart of the Order

NM/M
Complete Set (36): 35.00
Complete Retail Set (1-18): 20.00
Complete Hobby Set (19-36): 15.00
Common Player: .50
1 Ivan Rodriguez 1.00
2 Will Clark .50
3 Juan Gonzalez .75
4 Frank Thomas 1.25
5 Albert Belle .50
6 Robin Ventura .50
7 Alex Rodriguez 3.00
8 Ken Griffey Jr. 2.50
9 Jay Buhner .50
10 Roberto Alomar .65
11 Rafael Palmeiro 1.00
12 Cal Ripken Jr. 4.00
13 Manny Ramirez 1.25
14 Matt Williams .50
15 Jim Thome .50
16 Derek Jeter 4.00
17 Wade Boggs 2.00
18 Bernie Williams .50
19 Chipper Jones 2.00
20 Andruw Jones 1.25
21 Ryan Klesko .50
22 Wilton Guerrero .50
23 Mike Piazza 2.50
24 Raul Mondesi .50
25 Tony Gwynn 2.00
26 Ken Caminiti .50
27 Greg Vaughn .50
28 Brian Jordan .50
29 Ron Gant .50
30 Dmitri Young .50
31 Darin Erstad .50
32 Jim Edmonds .50
33 Tim Salmon .50
34 Chuck Knoblauch .50
35 Paul Molitor 1.25
36 Todd Walker .50

Highlight Zone

NM/M
Complete Set (18): 30.00
Common Player: .60
1 Frank Thomas 1.50
2 Ken Griffey Jr. 3.00

---

3 Mo Vaughn .60
4 Albert Belle .60
5 Mike Piazza 3.00
6 Barry Bonds 4.50
7 Greg Maddux 2.25
8 Sammy Sosa 2.25
9 Jeff Bagwell 1.50
10 Alex Rodriguez 3.50
11 Chipper Jones 2.50
12 Brady Anderson .60
13 Ozzie Smith 2.25
14 Edgar Martinez .60
15 Cal Ripken Jr. 4.50
16 Ryan Klesko .60
17 Randy Johnson 1.50
18 Eddie Murray 1.50

Pitcher Perfect

NM/M
Complete Set (15): 6.50
Common Player: .15
1 Cal Ripken Jr. 2.00
2 Alex Rodriguez 1.25
3 Cal Ripken Jr.,
   Alex Rodriguez 1.25
4 Edgar Martinez .15
5 Ivan Rodriguez .50
6 Mark McGwire 1.25
7 Tim Salmon .15
8 Chili Davis .15
9 Joe Carter .15
10 Frank Thomas .60
11 Will Clark .15
12 Mo Vaughn .15
13 Wade Boggs .75
14 Ken Griffey Jr. 1.00
15 Randy Johnson .60

Stand & Deliver

NM/M
Complete Set (24): 50.00
Common Player: .50
Gold: 4X
1 Andruw Jones 3.00
2 Greg Maddux 4.00
3 Chipper Jones 4.00
4 John Smoltz .50
5 Ken Griffey Jr. 5.00
6 Alex Rodriguez 6.00
7 Jay Buhner .50
8 Randy Johnson 3.00
9 Derek Jeter 7.50
10 Andy Pettitte .75
11 Bernie Williams .50
12 Mariano Rivera .50
13 Mike Piazza 5.00
14 Hideo Nomo 1.50
15 Raul Mondesi .50
16 Todd Hollandsworth .50
17 Manny Ramirez 3.00
18 Jim Thome 2.00
19 David Justice .50
20 Matt Williams .50
21 Juan Gonzalez 1.50
22 Jeff Bagwell 3.00
23 Cal Ripken Jr. 7.50
24 Frank Thomas 3.00

Stellar Season

NM/M
Complete Set (18): 15.00
Common Player: .50
1 Juan Gonzalez .75
2 Chuck Knoblauch .50
3 Jeff Bagwell 1.50
4 John Smoltz .50
5 Mark McGwire 3.00
6 Ken Griffey Jr. 2.50

STELLAR SEASON

7 Frank Thomas 1.50
8 Alex Rodriguez 3.00
9 Mike Piazza 2.50
10 Albert Belle .50
11 Roberto Alomar .60
12 Sammy Sosa 2.00
13 Mo Vaughn .50
14 Brady Anderson .50
15 Henry Rodriguez .50
16 Eric Young .50
17 Gary Sheffield .75
18 Ryan Klesko .50

The Franchise

NM/M
Complete Set (9): 5.00
Common Player: .15
Glowing: 2.5X
Samples: 2.5X
1 Ken Griffey Jr. 1.00
2 John Smoltz .15
3 Cal Ripken Jr. 2.00
4 Chipper Jones .75
5 Mike Piazza 1.00
6 Albert Belle .15
7 Frank Thomas .60
8 Sammy Sosa .75
9 Roberto Alomar .30

Titanic Taters

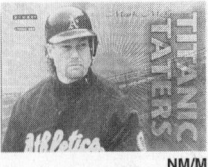

NM/M
Complete Set (18): 25.00
Common Player: .35
1 Mark McGwire 4.00
2 Mike Piazza 3.50
3 Ken Griffey Jr. 3.50
4 Juan Gonzalez 1.00
5 Frank Thomas 1.50
6 Albert Belle .35
7 Sammy Sosa 2.50
8 Jeff Bagwell 1.50
9 Todd Hundley .35
10 Ryan Klesko .35
11 Brady Anderson .35
12 Mo Vaughn .35
13 Jay Buhner .35
14 Chipper Jones 3.00
15 Barry Bonds 6.00
16 Gary Sheffield .75
17 Alex Rodriguez 4.00
18 Cecil Fielder .35

1998 Score

NM/M
Complete Set (270): 12.00
Common Player: .05
Showcases: 3X
Artist's Proofs: 6X
Pack (10): .75
Wax Box (36): .75
All-Star Edition Box (36/10): 10.00
Jumbo Pack (20): 1.00
Jumbo Box (24): 15.00
1 Andruw Jones .50
2 Dan Wilson .05
3 Hideo Nomo .15

No.	Player	Price
4	Chuck Carr	.05
5	Barry Bonds	1.50
6	Jack McDowell	.05
7	Albert Belle	.05
8	Francisco Cordova	.05
9	Greg Maddux	.65
10	Alex Rodriguez	1.00
11	Steve Avery	.05
12	Chuck McElroy	.05
13	Larry Walker	.05
14	Hideki Irabu	.05
15	Roberto Alomar	.20
16	Neifi Perez	.05
17	Jim Thome	.40
18	Rickey Henderson	.50
19	Andres Galarraga	.05
20	Jeff Fassero	.05
21	Kevin Young	.05
22	Derek Jeter	1.50
23	Andy Benes	.05
24	Mike Piazza	.75
25	Todd Stottlemyre	.05
26	Michael Tucker	.05
27	Denny Neagle	.05
28	Javier Lopez	.05
29	Aaron Sele	.05
30	Ryan Klesko	.05
31	Dennis Eckersley	.40
32	Quinton McCracken	.05
33	Brian Anderson	.05
34	Ken Griffey Jr.	.75
35	Shawn Estes	.05
36	Tim Wakefield	.05
37	Jimmy Key	.05
38	Jeff Bagwell	.50
39	Edgardo Alfonzo	.05
40	Mike Cameron	.05
41	Mark McGwire	1.00
42	Tino Martinez	.05
43	Cal Ripken Jr.	1.50
44	Curtis Goodwin	.05
45	Bobby Ayala	.05
46	Sandy Alomar Jr.	.05
47	Bobby Jones	.05
48	Omar Vizquel	.05
49	Roger Clemens	.70
50	Tony Gwynn	.65
51	Chipper Jones	.75
52	Ron Coomer	.05
53	Dmitri Young	.05
54	Brian Giles	.05
55	Steve Finley	.05
56	David Cone	.05
57	Andy Pettitte	.20
58	Wilton Guerrero	.05
59	Deion Sanders	.05
60	Carlos Delgado	.30
61	Jason Giambi	.30
62	Ozzie Guillen	.05
63	Jay Bell	.05
64	Barry Larkin	.05
65	Sammy Sosa	.65
66	Bernie Williams	.05
67	Terry Steinbach	.05
68	Scott Rolen	.40
69	Melvin Nieves	.05
70	Craig Biggio	.05
71	Todd Greene	.05
72	Greg Gagne	.05
73	Shigetosi Hasegawa	.05
74	Mark McLemore	.05
75	Darren Bragg	.05
76	Brett Butler	.05
77	Ron Gant	.05
78	Mike Difelice	.05
79	Charles Nagy	.05
80	Scott Hatteberg	.05
81	Brady Anderson	.05
82	Jay Buhner	.05
83	Todd Hollandsworth	.05
84	Geronimo Berroa	.05
85	Jeff Suppan	.05
86	Ivan Rodriguez	.50
87	Roger Cedeno	.05
88	Ivan Rodriguez	.40
89	Jaime Navarro	.05
90	Chris Hoiles	.05
91	Nomar Garciaparra	.65
92	Rafael Palmeiro	.40
93	Darin Erstad	.15
94	Kenny Lofton	.05
95	Mike Timlin	.05
96	Chris Clemons	.05
97	Vinny Castilla	.05
98	Charlie Hayes	.05
99	Lyle Mouton	.05
100	Jason Dickson	.05
101	Justin Thompson	.05
102	Pat Kelly	.05
103	Chan Ho Park	.05
104	Ray Lankford	.05
105	Frank Thomas	.50
106	Jermaine Allensworth	.05
107	Doug Drabek	.05
108	Todd Hundley	.05
109	Carl Everett	.05
110	Edgar Martinez	.05
111	Robin Ventura	.05
112	John Wetteland	.05
113	Mariano Rivera	.10
114	Jose Rosado	.05
115	Ken Caminiti	.05
116	Paul O'Neill	.05
117	Tim Salmon	.05
118	Eduardo Perez	.05
119	Mike Jackson	.05
120	John Smoltz	.05
121	Brant Brown	.05
122	John Mabry	.05
123	Chuck Knoblauch	.05
124	Reggie Sanders	.05
125	Ken Hill	.05
126	Mike Mussina	.25
127	Chad Curtis	.05
128	Todd Worrell	.05
129	Chris Widger	.05
130	Damon Mashore	.05
131	Kevin Brown	.05
132	Bip Roberts	.05
133	Tim Naehring	.05
134	Dave Martinez	.05
135	Jeff Blauser	.05
136	David Justice	.05
137	Dave Hollins	.05
138	Pat Hentgen	.05
139	Darren Daulton	.05
140	Ramon Martinez	.05
141	Raul Casanova	.05
142	Tom Glavine	.30
143	J.T. Snow	.05
144	Tony Graffanino	.05
145	Randy Johnson	.50
146	Orlando Merced	.05
147	Jeff Juden	.05
148	Darryl Kile	.05
149	Ray Durham	.05
150	Alex Fernandez	.05
151	Joey Cora	.05
152	Royce Clayton	.05
153	Randy Myers	.05
154	Charles Johnson	.05
155	Alan Benes	.05
156	Mike Bordick	.05
157	Heathcliff Slocumb	.05
158	Roger Bailey	.05
159	Reggie Jefferson	.05
160	Ricky Bottalico	.05
161	Scott Erickson	.05
162	Matt Williams	.05
163	Robb Nen	.05
164	Matt Stairs	.05
165	Ismael Valdes	.05
166	Lee Stevens	.05
167	Gary DiSarcina	.05
168	Brad Radke	.05
169	Mike Lansing	.05
170	Armando Benitez	.05
171	Mike James	.05
172	Russ Davis	.05
173	Lance Johnson	.05
174	Joey Hamilton	.05
175	John Valentin	.05
176	David Segui	.05
177	David Wells	.05
178	Delino DeShields	.05
179	Eric Karros	.05
180	Jim Leyritz	.05
181	Raul Mondesi	.05
182	Travis Fryman	.05
183	Todd Zeile	.05
184	Brian Jordan	.05
185	Rey Ordonez	.05
186	Jim Edmonds	.05
187	Terrell Wade	.05
188	Marquis Grissom	.05
189	Chris Snopek	.05
190	Shane Reynolds	.05
191	Jeff Frye	.05
192	Paul Sorrento	.05
193	James Baldwin	.05
194	Brian McRae	.05
195	Fred McGriff	.05
196	Troy Percival	.05
197	Rich Amaral	.05
198	Juan Guzman	.05
199	Willie Blair	.05
200	Chili Davis	.05
201	Gary Gaetti	.05
202	B.J. Surhoff	.05
203	Steve Cooke	.05
204	Chuck Finley	.05
205	Jeff Kent	.05
206	Ben McDonald	.05
207	Jeffrey Hammonds	.05
208	Tom Goodwin	.05
210	Billy Ashley	.05
211	Wil Cordero	.05
212	Shawon Dunston	.05
213	Tony Phillips	.05
214	Jamie Moyer	.05
215	John Jaha	.05
216	Troy O'Leary	.05
217	Brad Ausmus	.05
218	Garret Anderson	.05
219	Wilson Alvarez	.05
220	Kent Mercker	.05
221	Wade Boggs	.65
222	Mark Wohlers	.05
223	Kevin Appier	.05
224	Tony Fernandez	.05
225	Ugueth Urbina	.05
226	Gregg Jefferies	.05
227	Mo Vaughn	.05
228	Arthur Rhodes	.05
229	Jorge Fabregas	.05
230	Mark Gardner	.05
231	Shane Mack	.05
232	Jorge Posada	.05
233	Jose Cruz Jr.	.05
234	Paul Konerko	.15
235	Derrek Lee	.30
236	Steve Woodard **RC**	.15
237	Todd Dunwoody	.05
238	Fernando Tatis	.05
239	Jacob Cruz	.05
240	Pokey Reese **RC**	.25
241	Mark Kotsay	.05
242	Matt Morris	.05
243	Antone Williamson **RC**	.05
244	Ben Grieve	.05
245	Ryan McGuire	.05
246	Lou Collier **RC**	.05
247	Shannon Stewart	.05
248	Brett Tomko **RC**	.10
249	Bobby Estalella	.05
250	Livan Hernandez **RC**	.15
251	Todd Helton	.40
252	Jaret Wright	.05
253	Darryl Hamilton	.05
254	Stan Javier	.05
255	Glenallen Hill	.05
256	Mark Gardner	.05
257	Cal Ripken Jr.	.75
258	Mike Mussina	.15
259	Mike Piazza	.45
260	Sammy Sosa	.35
261	Todd Hundley	.05
262	Eric Karros	.05
263	Denny Neagle	.05
264	Jeromy Burnitz	.05
265	Greg Maddux	.35
266	Tony Clark	.25
267	Vladimir Guerrero	.25
268	Checklist	.05
269	Checklist	.05
270	Checklist	.05

Artist's Proofs

	NM/M
Complete Set (160):	125.00
Common Player:	.50
Inserted 1:35	
1 Andruw Jones	1.25
2 Dan Wilson	.50
3 Hideo Nomo	.75
4 Neifi Perez	.50
5 Jim Thome	1.00
6 Jeff Fassero	.50
7 Derek Jeter	4.00
8 Andy Benes	.50
9 Michael Tucker	.50
10 Ryan Klesko	.50
11 Dennis Eckersley	1.00
12 Jimmy Key	.50
13 Edgardo Alfonzo	.50
14 Mike Cameron	.50
15 Omar Vizquel	.50
16 Ron Coomer	.50
17 Dmitri Young	.50
18 Brian Giles	.50
19 Steve Finley	.50
20 Andy Pettitte	.75
21 Wilton Guerrero	.50
22 Deion Sanders	.50
23 Carlos Delgado	.50
24 Jason Giambi	.75
25 David Cone	.50
26 Jay Bell	.50
27 Sammy Sosa	2.00
28 Barry Larkin	.50
29 Scott Rolen	1.00
30 Todd Greene	.50
31 Bernie Williams	.50
32 Brett Butler	.50
33 Ron Gant	.50
34 Brady Anderson	.50
35 Craig Biggio	.50
36 Charles Nagy	.50
37 Jay Buhner	.50
38 Geronimo Berroa	.50
39 Jeff Suppan	.50
40 Rafael Palmeiro	1.00
41 Darin Erstad	.65
42 Mike Timlin	.50
43 Vinny Castilla	.50
44 Carl Everett	.50
45 Robin Ventura	.50
46 John Wetteland	.50
47 Paul O'Neill	.50
48 Tim Salmon	.50
49 Mike Jackson	.50
50 John Smoltz	.50
51 Brant Brown	.50
52 Reggie Sanders	.50
53 Ken Hill	.50
54 Todd Worrell	.50
55 Bip Roberts	.50
56 Tim Naehring	.50
57 Darren Daulton	.50
58 Ramon Martinez	.50
59 Raul Casanova	.50
60 J.T. Snow	.50
61 Jeff Juden	.50
62 Royce Clayton	.50
63 Charles Johnson	.50
64 Alan Benes	.50
65 Reggie Jefferson	.50
66 Ricky Bottalico	.50
67 Scott Erickson	.50
68 Matt Williams	.50
69 Robb Nen	.50
70 Matt Stairs	.50
71 Ismael Valdes	.50
72 Brad Radke	.50
73 Armando Benitez	.50
74 Russ Davis	.50
75 Lance Johnson	.50
76 Joey Hamilton	.50
77 John Valentin	.50
78 David Segui	.50
79 David Wells	.50
80 Eric Karros	.50
81 Raul Mondesi	.50
82 Travis Fryman	.50
83 Todd Zeile	.50
84 Brian Jordan	.50
85 Rey Ordonez	.50
86 Jim Edmonds	.50
87 Marquis Grissom	.50
88 Shane Reynolds	.50
89 Paul Sorrento	.50
90 Brian McRae	.50
91 Fred McGriff	.50
92 Troy Percival	.50
93 Juan Guzman	.50
94 Cecil Fielder	.50
95 Chili Davis	.50
96 B.J. Surhoff	.50
97 Chuck Finley	.50
98 Jeff Kent	.50
99 Ben McDonald	.50
100 Jeffrey Hammonds	.50
101 Tom Goodwin	.50
102 Wil Cordero	.50
103 Tony Phillips	.50
104 John Jaha	.50
105 Garret Anderson	.50
106 Wilson Alvarez	.50
107 Wade Boggs	2.00
108 Mark Wohlers	.50
109 Kevin Appier	.50
110 Mo Vaughn	.50
111 Ray Durham	.50
112 Alex Fernandez	.50
113 Barry Bonds	4.00
114 Albert Belle	.50
115 Greg Maddux	2.00
116 Alex Rodriguez	3.00
117 Larry Walker	.50
118 Roberto Alomar	.60
119 Andres Galarraga	.50
120 Mike Piazza	2.50
121 Denny Neagle	.50
122 Javier Lopez	.50
123 Ken Griffey Jr.	2.50
124 Shawn Estes	.50
125 Jeff Bagwell	1.25
126 Mark McGwire	3.00
127 Tino Martinez	.50
128 Cal Ripken Jr.	4.00
129 Sandy Alomar Jr.	.50
130 Bobby Jones	.50
131 Roger Clemens	2.25
132 Tony Gwynn	2.00
133 Chipper Jones	2.00
134 Orlando Merced	.50
135 Todd Stottlemyre	.50
136 Delino DeShields	.50
137 Pedro Martinez	1.25
138 Ivan Rodriguez	1.00
139 Nomar Garciaparra	2.00

140	Kenny Lofton	.50
141	Jason Dickson	.50
142	Justin Thompson	.50
143	Ray Lankford	.50
144	Frank Thomas	1.25
145	Todd Hundley	.50
146	Edgar Martinez	.50
147	Mariano Rivera	.50
148	Jose Rosado	.50
149	Ken Caminiti	.50
150	Chuck Knoblauch	.50
151	Mike Mussina	.65
152	Kevin Brown	.50
153	Jeff Blauser	.50
154	David Justice	.50
155	Pat Hentgen	.50
156	Tom Glavine	.65
157	Randy Johnson	1.25
158	Darryl Kile	.50
159	Joey Cora	.50
160	Randy Myers	.50

Showcase Series

	NM/M
Complete Set (160):	40.00
Common Player:	.25
Inserted 1:7	

1	Andruw Jones	.75
2	Dan Wilson	.25
3	Hideo Nomo	.40
4	Neifi Perez	.25
5	Jim Thome	.60
6	Jeff Fassero	.25
7	Derek Jeter	2.00
8	Andy Benes	.25
9	Michael Tucker	.25
10	Ryan Klesko	.25
11	Dennis Eckersley	.65
12	Jimmy Key	.25
13	Edgardo Alfonzo	.25
14	Mike Cameron	.25
15	Omar Vizquel	.25
16	Ron Coomer	.25
17	Dmitri Young	.25
18	Brian Giles	.25
19	Steve Finley	.25
20	Andy Pettitte	.40
21	Wilton Guerrero	.25
22	Deion Sanders	.25
23	Carlos Delgado	.50
24	Jason Giambi	.50
25	David Cone	.25
26	Jay Bell	.25
27	Sammy Sosa	1.00
28	Barry Larkin	.25
29	Scott Rolen	.60
30	Todd Greene	.25
31	Bernie Williams	.25
32	Brett Butler	.25
33	Ron Gant	.25
34	Brady Anderson	.25
35	Craig Biggio	.25
36	Charles Nagy	.25
37	Jay Buhner	.25
38	Geronimo Berroa	.25
39	Jeff Suppan	.25
40	Rafael Palmeiro	.65
41	Darin Erstad	.35
42	Mike Timlin	.25
43	Vinny Castilla	.25
44	Carl Everett	.25
45	Robin Ventura	.25
46	John Wetteland	.25
47	Paul O'Neill	.25
48	Tim Salmon	.25
49	Mike Jackson	.25
50	John Smoltz	.25
51	Brant Brown	.25
52	Reggie Sanders	.25
53	Ken Hill	.25
54	Todd Worrell	.25
55	Bip Roberts	.25
56	Tim Naehring	.25
57	Darren Daulton	.25
58	Ramon Martinez	.25
59	Raul Casanova	.25
60	J.T. Snow	.25
61	Jeff Juden	.25
62	Royce Clayton	.25
63	Charles Johnson	.25
64	Alan Benes	.25

65	Reggie Jefferson	.25
66	Ricky Bottalico	.25
67	Scott Erickson	.25
68	Matt Williams	.25
69	Robb Nen	.25
70	Matt Stairs	.25
71	Ismael Valdes	.25
72	Brad Radke	.25
73	Armando Benitez	.25
74	Russ Davis	.25
75	Lance Johnson	.25
76	Joey Hamilton	.25
77	John Valentin	.25
78	David Segui	.25
79	David Wells	.25
80	Eric Karros	.25
81	Raul Mondesi	.25
82	Travis Fryman	.25
83	Todd Zeile	.25
84	Brian Jordan	.25
85	Rey Ordonez	.25
86	Jim Edmonds	.25
87	Marquis Grissom	.25
88	Shane Reynolds	.25
89	Paul Sorrento	.25
90	Brian McRae	.25
91	Fred McGriff	.25
92	Troy Percival	.25
93	Juan Guzman	.25
94	Cecil Fielder	.25
95	Chili Davis	.25
96	B.J. Surhoff	.25
97	Chuck Finley	.25
98	Jeff Kent	.25
99	Ben McDonald	.25
100	Jeffrey Hammonds	.25
101	Tom Goodwin	.25
102	Wil Cordero	.25
103	Tony Phillips	.25
104	John Jaha	.25
105	Garret Anderson	.25
106	Wilson Alvarez	.25
107	Wade Boggs	1.00
108	Mark Wohlers	.25
109	Kevin Appier	.25
110	Mo Vaughn	.25
111	Ray Durham	.25
112	Alex Fernandez	.25
113	Barry Bonds	2.00
114	Albert Belle	.25
115	Greg Maddux	1.00
116	Alex Rodriguez	1.50
117	Larry Walker	.25
118	Roberto Alomar	.35
119	Andres Galarraga	.25
120	Mike Piazza	1.25
121	Denny Neagle	.25
122	Javier Lopez	.25
123	Ken Griffey Jr.	1.25
124	Shawn Estes	.25
125	Jeff Bagwell	.75
126	Mark McGwire	1.50
127	Tino Martinez	.25
128	Cal Ripken Jr.	2.00
129	Sandy Alomar Jr.	.25
130	Bobby Jones	.25
131	Roger Clemens	1.00
132	Tony Gwynn	1.00
133	Chipper Jones	1.00
134	Orlando Merced	.25
135	Todd Stottlemyre	.25
136	Delino DeShields	.25
137	Pedro Martinez	.75
138	Ivan Rodriguez	.65
139	Nomar Garciaparra	1.00
140	Kenny Lofton	.25
141	Jason Dickson	.25
142	Justin Thompson	.25
143	Ray Lankford	.25
144	Frank Thomas	.75
145	Todd Hundley	.25
146	Edgar Martinez	.25
147	Mariano Rivera	.25
148	Jose Rosado	.25
149	Ken Caminiti	.25
150	Chuck Knoblauch	.25
151	Mike Mussina	.40
152	Kevin Brown	.25
153	Jeff Blauser	.25
154	David Justice	.25
155	Pat Hentgen	.25
156	Tom Glavine	.40
157	Randy Johnson	.75
158	Darryl Kile	.25
159	Joey Cora	.25
160	Randy Myers	.25

All Score Team

	NM/M
Complete Set (20):	15.00
Common Player:	.25
Inserted 1:35	

1	Mike Piazza	1.50
2	Ivan Rodriguez	.65
3	Frank Thomas	.75
4	Mark McGwire	2.00
5	Ryne Sandberg	1.00
6	Roberto Alomar	.35
7	Cal Ripken Jr.	2.50
8	Barry Larkin	.25
9	Paul Molitor	.75
10	Travis Fryman	.25
11	Kirby Puckett	1.00
12	Tony Gwynn	1.00
13	Ken Griffey Jr.	1.50

Roger Clemens   'Blue Jays' P

14	Juan Gonzalez	.45
15	Barry Bonds	2.50
16	Andruw Jones	.75
17	Roger Clemens	1.25
18	Randy Johnson	.75
19	Greg Maddux	1.00
20	Dennis Eckersley	.65

All Score Team Andruw Jones Autograph

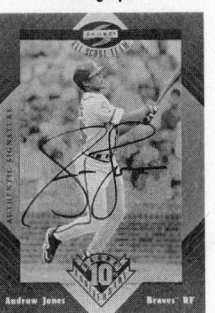

Andruw Jones   Braves' RF

	NM/M
16	Andruw Jones	25.00

Complete Players

	NM/M
Complete Set (30):	75.00
Common Player:	1.00
Inserted 1:23	

Golds:		75 Percent
1A	Ken Griffey Jr.	3.25
1B	Ken Griffey Jr.	3.25
1C	Ken Griffey Jr.	3.25
2A	Mark McGwire	3.75
2B	Mark McGwire	3.75
2C	Mark McGwire	3.75
3A	Derek Jeter	5.00
3B	Derek Jeter	5.00
3C	Derek Jeter	5.00
4A	Cal Ripken Jr.	5.00
4B	Cal Ripken Jr.	5.00
4C	Cal Ripken Jr.	5.00
5A	Mike Piazza	3.25
5B	Mike Piazza	3.25
5C	Mike Piazza	3.25
6A	Darin Erstad	1.00
6B	Darin Erstad	1.00
6C	Darin Erstad	1.00
7A	Frank Thomas	2.00
7B	Frank Thomas	2.00
7C	Frank Thomas	2.00
8A	Andruw Jones	2.00
8B	Andruw Jones	2.00
8C	Andruw Jones	2.00

9A	Nomar Garciaparra	3.00
9B	Nomar Garciaparra	3.00
9C	Nomar Garciaparra	3.00
10A	Manny Ramirez	2.00
10B	Manny Ramirez	2.00
10C	Manny Ramirez	2.00

Epix

	NM/M
Common Card:	.50
Purple:	2X
Emeralds:	3X

1	Ken Griffey Jr./P	2.50
2	Juan Gonzalez/P	.75
3	Jeff Bagwell/P	1.25
4	Ivan Rodriguez/P	1.00
5	Nomar Garciaparra/P	2.00
6	Ryne Sandberg/P	1.50
7	Frank Thomas/G	1.25
8	Derek Jeter/G	3.50
9	Tony Gwynn/G	2.00
10	Albert Belle/G	.50
11	Scott Rolen/G	1.00
12	Barry Larkin/G	.50
13	Alex Rodriguez/S	6.00
14	Cal Ripken Jr./S	7.50
15	Chipper Jones/S	4.00
16	Roger Clemens/S	4.50
17	Mo Vaughn/S	1.50
18	Mark McGwire/S	6.00
19	Mike Piazza/S	8.00
20	Andruw Jones/M	4.00
21	Greg Maddux/M	6.00
22	Barry Bonds/M	12.00
23	Paul Molitor/M	4.00
24	Eddie Murray/M	4.00

First Pitch

	NM/M
Complete Set (20):	25.00
Common Player:	.50
Inserted 1:11 All-Star Edition.	

1	Ken Griffey Jr.	2.00
2	Frank Thomas	1.25
3	Alex Rodriguez	2.50
4	Cal Ripken Jr.	3.25
5	Chipper Jones	1.50
6	Juan Gonzalez	.75
7	Derek Jeter	3.25
8	Mike Piazza	2.00
9	Andruw Jones	1.25
10	Nomar Garciaparra	1.50
11	Barry Bonds	3.25
12	Jeff Bagwell	1.25
13	Scott Rolen	1.00
14	Hideo Nomo	.75
15	Roger Clemens	1.75
16	Mark McGwire	2.50
17	Greg Maddux	1.50
18	Albert Belle	.50
19	Ivan Rodriguez	1.00
20	Mo Vaughn	.50

Loaded Lineup

	NM/M
Complete Set (10):	20.00
Common Player:	

LOADED Lineup

Inserted 1:45 All-Star Edition.

LL1	Chuck Knoblauch	.50
LL2	Tony Gwynn	2.25
LL3	Frank Thomas	1.50
LL4	Ken Griffey Jr.	3.00
LL5	Mike Piazza	3.00
LL6	Barry Bonds	4.50
LL7	Cal Ripken Jr.	4.50
LL8	Paul Molitor	1.50
LL9	Nomar Garciaparra	2.25
LL10	Greg Maddux	2.25

New Season

NEW SEASON

	NM/M
Complete Set (15):	18.00
Common Player:	.50

Inserted 1:23 All-Star Edition.

NS1	Kenny Lofton	.50
NS2	Nomar Garciaparra	2.00
NS3	Todd Helton	1.00
NS4	Miguel Tejada	.75
NS5	Jaret Wright	.50
NS6	Alex Rodriguez	3.00
NS7	Vladimir Guerrero	1.25
NS8	Ken Griffey Jr.	2.50
NS9	Ben Grieve	.50
NS10	Travis Lee	.50
NS11	Jose Cruz Jr.	.50
NS12	Paul Konerko	.75
NS13	Frank Thomas	1.25
NS14	Chipper Jones	2.00
NS15	Cal Ripken Jr.	4.00

1998 Score Rookie & Traded

	NM/M
Complete Set (270):	10.00
Common SP (1-50):	.10
Common Player (51-270):	.05
Artist's Proofs:	4X

Inserted 1:35

Paul Konerko Auto. (500):	15.00
Pack (10):	.65
Wax Box (36):	15.00

Jumbo Pack (20):		1.50
Jumbo Box (24):		25.00
1	Tony Clark	.10
2	Juan Gonzalez	.35
3	Frank Thomas	.60
4	Greg Maddux	.75
5	Barry Larkin	.10
6	Derek Jeter	1.50
7	Randy Johnson	.60
8	Roger Clemens	.85
9	Tony Gwynn	.75
10	Barry Bonds	1.50
11	Jim Edmonds	.10
12	Bernie Williams	.10
13	Ken Griffey Jr.	1.00
14	Tim Salmon	.10
15	Mo Vaughn	.10
16	David Justice	.10
17	Jose Cruz Jr.	.10
18	Andruw Jones	.60
19	Sammy Sosa	.75
20	Jeff Bagwell	.60
21	Scott Rolen	.50
22	Darin Erstad	.30
23	Andy Pettitte	.35
24	Mike Mussina	.40
25	Mark McGwire	1.25
26	Hideo Nomo	.35
27	Chipper Jones	.75
28	Cal Ripken Jr.	1.50
29	Chuck Knoblauch	.10
30	Alex Rodriguez	1.25
31	Jim Thome	.10
32	Mike Piazza	1.00
33	Ivan Rodriguez	.50
34	Roberto Alomar	.40
35	Nomar Garciaparra	.75
36	Albert Belle	.10
37	Vladimir Guerrero	.60
38	Raul Mondesi	.10
39	Larry Walker	.10
40	Manny Ramirez	.60
41	Tino Martinez	.10
42	Craig Biggio	.10
43	Jay Buhner	.10
44	Kenny Lofton	.10
45	Pedro Martinez	.60
46	Edgar Martinez	.10
47	Gary Sheffield	.45
48	Jose Guillen	.10
49	Ken Caminiti	.10
50	Bobby Higginson	.05
51	Alan Benes	.05
52	Shawn Green	.15
53	Ron Coomer	.05
54	Charles Nagy	.05
55	Steve Karsay	.05
56	Matt Morris	.05
57	Bobby Jones	.05
58	Jason Kendall	.05
59	Jeff Conine	.05
60	Joe Girardi	.05
61	Mark Kotsay	.05
62	Eric Karros	.05
63	Bartolo Colon	.05
64	Mariano Rivera	.10
65	Alex Gonzalez	.05
66	Scott Spiezio	.05
67	Luis Castillo	.05
68	Joey Cora	.05
69	Mark McLemore	.05
70	Reggie Jefferson	.05
71	Lance Johnson	.05
72	Damian Jackson	.05
73	Jeff D'Amico	.05
74	David Ortiz	.30
75	J.T. Snow	.05
76	Todd Hundley	.05
77	Billy Wagner	.05
78	Vinny Castilla	.05
79	Ismael Valdes	.05
80	Neifi Perez	.05
81	Derek Bell	.05
82	Ryan Klesko	.05
83	Rey Ordonez	.05
84	Carlos Garcia	.05
85	Curt Schilling	.30
86	Robin Ventura	.05
87	Pat Hentgen	.05
88	Glendon Rusch	.05
89	Hideki Irabu	.05
90	Antone Williamson	.05
91	Denny Neagle	.05
92	Kevin Orie	.05
93	Reggie Sanders	.05
94	Brad Anderson	.05
95	Andy Benes	.05
96	John Valentin	.05
97	Bobby Bonilla	.05
98	Walt Weiss	.05
99	Robin Jennings	.05
100	Marty Cordova	.05
101	Brad Ausmus	.05
102	Brian Rose	.05
103	Calvin Maduro	.05
104	Raul Casanova	.05
105	Jeff King	.05
106	Sandy Alomar	.05
107	Tim Naehring	.05
108	Mike Cameron	.05
109	Omar Vizquel	.05
110	Brad Radke	.05
111	Jeff Fassero	.05
112	Deivi Cruz	.05
113	Dave Hollins	.05

114	Dean Palmer	.05
115	Esteban Loaiza	.05
116	Brian Giles	.05
117	Steve Finley	.05
118	Jose Canseco	.30
119	Al Martin	.05
120	Eric Young	.05
121	Curtis Goodwin	.05
122	Ellis Burks	.05
123	Mike Hampton	.05
124	Lou Collier	.05
125	John Olerud	.05
126	Ramon Martinez	.05
127	Todd Dunwoody	.05
128	Jermaine Allensworth	.05
129	Eduardo Perez	.05
130	Dante Bichette	.05
131	Edgar Renteria	.05
132	Bob Abreu	.10
133	Rondell White	.05
134	Michael Coleman	.05
135	Jason Giambi	.30
136	Brant Brown	.05
137	Michael Tucker	.05
138	Dave Nilsson	.05
139	Benito Santiago	.05
140	Ray Durham	.05
141	Jeff Kent	.05
142	Matt Stairs	.05
143	Kevin Young	.05
144	Eric Davis	.05
145	John Wetteland	.05
146	Esteban Yan	.05
147	Wilton Guerrero	.05
148	Moises Alou	.05
149	Edgardo Alfonzo	.05
150	Andy Ashby	.05
151	Todd Walker	.05
152	Jermaine Dye	.05
153	Brian Hunter	.05
154	Shawn Estes	.05
155	Bernard Gilkey	.05
156	Tony Womack	.05
157	John Smoltz	.05
158	Delino DeShields	.05
159	Jacob Cruz	.05
160	Javier Valentin	.05
161	Chris Hoiles	.05
162	Garret Anderson	.05
163	Dan Wilson	.05
164	Paul O'Neill	.05
165	Matt Williams	.05
166	Travis Fryman	.05
167	Javier Lopez	.05
168	Ray Lankford	.05
169	Bobby Estalella	.05
170	Henry Rodriguez	.05
171	Quinton McCracken	.05
172	Jaret Wright	.05
173	Darryl Kile	.05
174	Wade Boggs	.65
175	Orel Hershiser	.05
176	B.J. Surhoff	.05
177	Fernando Tatis	.05
178	Carlos Delgado	.30
179	Jorge Fabregas	.05
180	Tony Saunders	.05
181	Devon White	.05
182	Dmitri Young	.05
183	Ryan McGuire	.05
184	Mark Bellhorn	.05
185	Joe Carter	.05
186	Kevin Stocker	.05
187	Mike Lansing	.05
188	Jason Dickson	.05
189	Charles Johnson	.05
190	Will Clark	.05
191	Shannon Stewart	.05
192	Johnny Damon	.20
193	Todd Greene	.05
194	Carlos Baerga	.05
195	David Cone	.05
196	Pokey Reese	.05
197	Livan Hernandez	.05
198	Tom Glavine	.25
199	Geronimo Berroa	.05
200	Darryl Hamilton	.05
201	Terry Steinbach	.05
202	Robb Nen	.05
203	Ron Gant	.05
204	Rafael Palmeiro	.40
205	Rickey Henderson	.40
206	Justin Thompson	.05
207	Jeff Suppan	.05
208	Kevin Brown	.05
209	Jimmy Key	.05
210	Brian Jordan	.05
211	Aaron Sele	.05
212	Fred McGriff	.05
213	Jay Bell	.05
214	Andres Galarraga	.05
215	Mark Grace	.05
216	Brett Tomko	.05
217	Francisco Cordova	.05
218	Rusty Greer	.05
219	Bubba Trammell	.05
220	Derrek Lee	.35
221	Brian Anderson	.05
222	Mark Grudzielanek	.05
223	Marquis Grissom	.05
224	Gary DiSarcina	.05
225	Jim Leyritz	.05
226	Jeffrey Hammonds	.05
227	Karim Garcia	.05
228	Chan Ho Park	.05

229	Brooks Kieschnick	.05
230	Trey Beamon	.05
231	Kevin Appier	.05
232	Wally Joyner	.05
233	Richie Sexson	.05
234	Frank Catalanotto **RC**	.15
235	Rafael Medina	.05
236	Travis Lee	.05
237	Eli Marrero	.05
238	Carl Pavano	.05
239	Enrique Wilson	.05
240	Richard Hidalgo	.05
241	Todd Helton	.40
242	Ben Grieve	.05
243	Mario Valdez	.05
244	Magglio Ordonez **RC**	.75
245	Juan Encarnacion	.05
246	Russell Branyan	.05
247	Sean Casey	.10
248	Abraham Nunez	.05
249	Brad Fullmer	.05
250	Paul Konerko	.20
251	Miguel Tejada	.15
252	Mike Lowell **RC**	.50
253	Ken Griffey Jr.	.35
254	Frank Thomas	.25
255	Alex Rodriguez	.45
256	Jose Cruz Jr.	.05
257	Jeff Bagwell	.20
258	Chipper Jones	.30
259	Mo Vaughn	.05
260	Nomar Garciaparra	.30
261	Jim Thome	.05
262	Derek Jeter	.50
263	Mike Piazza	.45
264	Tony Gwynni	.30
265	Scott Rolen	.15
266	Andruw Jones	.20
267	Cal Ripken Jr.	.50
268	Ken Griffey Jr. Checklist	.30
269	Cal Ripken Jr. Checklist	.45
270	Jose Cruz Jr. Checklist	.05

Showcase Series

	NM/M
Complete Set (160):	10.00
Common Player:	.15

1	Tony Clark	.15
2	Juan Gonzalez	.30
3	Frank Thomas	.60
4	Greg Maddux	.75
5	Barry Larkin	.15
6	Derek Jeter	1.50
7	Randy Johnson	.60
8	Roger Clemens	.85
9	Tony Gwynn	.75
10	Barry Bonds	1.50
11	Jim Edmonds	.15
12	Bernie Williams	.15
13	Ken Griffey Jr.	1.00
14	Tim Salmon	.15
15	Mo Vaughn	.15
16	David Justice	.15
17	Jose Cruz Jr.	.15
18	Andruw Jones	.60
19	Sammy Sosa	.75
20	Jeff Bagwell	.60
21	Scott Rolen	.50
22	Darin Erstad	.25
23	Andy Pettitte	.30
24	Mike Mussina	.30
25	Mark McGwire	1.25
26	Hideo Nomo	.30
27	Chipper Jones	.75
28	Cal Ripken Jr.	1.50
29	Chuck Knoblauch	.15
30	Alex Rodriguez	1.25
31	Jim Thome	.15
32	Mike Piazza	1.00
33	Ivan Rodriguez	.50
34	Roberto Alomar	.25
35	Nomar Garciaparra	1.00
36	Albert Belle	.15
37	Vladimir Guerrero	.60
38	Raul Mondesi	.15
39	Larry Walker	.15
40	Manny Ramirez	.60
41	Tino Martinez	.15
42	Craig Biggio	.15
43	Jay Buhner	.15
44	Kenny Lofton	.15

45	Pedro Martinez	.60
46	Edgar Martinez	.15
47	Gary Sheffield	.40
48	Jose Guillen	.15
49	Ken Caminiti	.15
50	Bobby Higginson	.15
51	Alan Benes	.15
52	Shawn Green	.35
53	Matt Morris	.15
54	Jason Kendall	.15
55	Mark Kotsay	.15
56	Bartolo Colon	.15
57	Damian Jackson	.15
58	David Ortiz	.35
59	J.T. Snow	.15
60	Todd Hundley	.15
61	Neifi Perez	.15
62	Ryan Klesko	.15
63	Robin Ventura	.15
64	Pat Hentgen	.15
65	Antone Williamson	.15
66	Kevin Orie	.15
67	Brady Anderson	.15
68	Bobby Bonilla	.15
69	Brian Rose	.15
70	Sandy Alomar Jr.	.15
71	Mike Cameron	.15
72	Omar Vizquel	.15
73	Steve Finley	.15
74	Jose Canseco	.40
75	Al Martin	.15
76	Eric Young	.15
77	Ellis Burks	.15
78	Todd Dunwoody	.15
79	Dante Bichette	.15
80	Edgar Renteria	.15
81	Bobby Abreu	.15
82	Rondell White	.15
83	Michael Coleman	.15
84	Jason Giambi	.50
85	Wilton Guerrero	.15
86	Moises Alou	.15
87	Todd Walker	.15
88	Shawn Estes	.15
89	John Smoltz	.15
90	Jacob Cruz	.15
91	Javier Valentin	.15
92	Garret Anderson	.15
93	Paul O'Neill	.15
94	Matt Williams	.15
95	Travis Fryman	.15
96	Javier Lopez	.15
97	Ray Lankford	.15
98	Bobby Estalella	.15
99	Jaret Wright	.15
100	Wade Boggs	.75
101	Fernando Tatis	.50
102	Carlos Delgado	.15
103	Joe Carter	.15
104	Jason Dickson	.15
105	Charles Johnson	.15
106	Will Clark	.15
107	Shannon Stewart	.15
108	Todd Greene	.15
109	Pokey Reese	.15
110	Livan Hernandez	.15
111	Tom Glavine	.35
112	Rafael Palmeiro	.50
113	Justin Thompson	.15
114	Jeff Suppan	.15
115	Kevin Brown	.15
116	Brian Jordan	.15
117	Fred McGriff	.15
118	Andres Galarraga	.15
119	Mark Grace	.15
120	Rusty Greer	.15
121	Bubba Trammell	.15
122	Derrek Lee	.40
123	Brian Anderson	.15
124	Karim Garcia	.15
125	Chan Ho Park	.15
126	Richie Sexson	.15
127	Frank Catalanotto	.15
128	Rafael Medina	.15
129	Travis Lee	.15
130	Eli Marrero	.15
131	Carl Pavano	.15
132	Enrique Wilson	.15
133	Richard Hidalgo	.15
134	Todd Helton	.40
135	Ben Grieve	.15
136	Mario Valdez	.15
137	Magglio Ordonez	.25
138	Juan Encarnacion	.25
139	Russell Branyan	.15
140	Sean Casey	.25
141	Abraham Nunez	.15
142	Brad Fullmer	.15
143	Paul Konerko	.25
144	Miguel Tejada	.30
145	Mike Lowell	.15
146	Ken Griffey Jr.	.50
147	Frank Thomas	.35
148	Alex Rodriguez	.65
149	Jose Cruz Jr.	.15
150	Jeff Bagwell	.35
151	Chipper Jones	.40
152	Mo Vaughn	.15
153	Nomar Garciaparra	.40
154	Jim Thome	.30
155	Derek Jeter	.75
156	Mike Piazza	.50
157	Tony Gwynn	.40
158	Scott Rolen	.25
159	Andruw Jones	.35
160	Cal Ripken Jr.	.75

Artist's Proofs

	NM/M
Common Player:	1.00
AP Stars:	4X

(See 1998 Score Rookie & Traded Showcase for checklist and base card values.)

Complete Players

		NM/M
Complete Set (30):		65.00
Common Player:		1.00
Inserted 1:11		
Samples:		1X
1A-1C	Ken Griffey Jr.	3.50
2A-2C	Larry Walker	1.00
3A-3C	Alex Rodriguez	4.00
4A-4C	Jose Cruz Jr.	1.00
5A-5C	Jeff Bagwell	2.00
6A-6C	Greg Maddux	2.75
7A-7C	Ivan Rodriguez	1.75
8A-8C	Roger Clemens	3.00
9A-9C	Chipper Jones	2.75
10A-10C	Hideo Nomo	1.50

Epix All-Star Moment

		NM/M
Complete Set (12):		25.00
Common Player:		1.00
Purples:		1.5X
Emeralds:		2.5X
1	Ken Griffey Jr.	4.00
2	Juan Gonzalez	1.50
3	Jeff Bagwell	2.50
4	Ivan Rodriguez	2.00
5	Nomar Garciaparra	3.00
6	Ryne Sandberg	3.00
7	Frank Thomas	2.50
8	Derek Jeter	5.00
9	Tony Gwynn	3.00
10	Albert Belle	1.00
11	Scott Rolen	2.00
12	Barry Larkin	1.00

Star Gazing

		NM/M
Complete Set (20):		12.00
Common Player:		.25
Inserted 1:35		
1	Ken Griffey Jr.	1.00
2	Frank Thomas	.60
3	Chipper Jones	.75
4	Mark McGwire	1.25
5	Cal Ripken Jr.	1.50
6	Mike Piazza	1.00
7	Nomar Garciaparra	.75
8	Derek Jeter	1.50
9	Juan Gonzalez	.35
10	Vladimir Guerrero	.60
11	Alex Rodriguez	1.25
12	Tony Gwynn	.75
13	Andruw Jones	.60
14	Scott Rolen	.40
15	Jose Cruz Jr.	.25
16	Mo Vaughn	.25
17	Bernie Williams	.25
18	Greg Maddux	.75
19	Tony Clark	.25
20	Ben Grieve	.25

1993 Select

		NM/M
Complete Set (405):		15.00
Common Player:		.05
Pack (15):		.75
Wax Box (36):		22.50
1	Barry Bonds	1.50
2	Ken Griffey Jr.	1.00
3	Will Clark	.05
4	Kirby Puckett	.75
5	Tony Gwynn	.75
6	Frank Thomas	.65
7	Tom Glavine	.35
8	Roberto Alomar	.25
9	Andre Dawson	.25
10	Ron Darling	.05
11	Bobby Bonilla	.05
12	Danny Tartabull	.05
13	Darren Daulton	.05
14	Roger Clemens	.85
15	Ozzie Smith	.75
16	Mark McGwire	1.25
17	Terry Pendleton	.05
18	Cal Ripken, Jr.	1.50
19	Fred McGriff	.05
20	Cecil Fielder	.05
21	Darryl Strawberry	.05
22	Robin Yount	.65
23	Barry Larkin	.05
24	Don Mattingly	.85
25	Craig Biggio	.05
26	Sandy Alomar Jr.	.05
27	Larry Walker	.05
28	Junior Felix	.05
29	Eddie Murray	.65
30	Robin Ventura	.05
31	Greg Maddux	.75
32	Dave Winfield	.65
33	John Kruk	.05
34	Wally Joyner	.05

35	Andy Van Slyke	.05
36	Chuck Knoblauch	.05
37	Tom Pagnozzi	.05
38	Dennis Eckersley	.60
39	Dave Justice	.05
40	Juan Gonzalez	.35
41	Gary Sheffield	.40
42	Paul Molitor	.65
43	Delino DeShields	.05
44	Travis Fryman	.05
45	Hal Morris	.05
46	Gregg Olson	.05
47	Ken Caminiti	.05
48	Wade Boggs	.75
49	Orel Hershiser	.05
50	Albert Belle	.05
51	Bill Swift	.05
52	Mark Langston	.05
53	Joe Girardi	.05
54	Keith Miller	.05
55	Gary Carter	.65
56	Brady Anderson	.05
57	Dwight Gooden	.05
58	Julio Franco	.05
59	Len Dykstra	.05
60	Mickey Tettleton	.05
61	Randy Tomlin	.05
62	B.J. Surhoff	.05
63	Todd Zeile	.05
64	Roberto Kelly	.05
65	Rob Dibble	.05
66	Leo Gomez	.05
67	Doug Jones	.05
68	Ellis Burks	.05
69	Mike Scioscia	.05
70	Charles Nagy	.05
71	Cory Snyder	.05
72	Devon White	.05
73	Mark Grace	.05
74	Luis Polonia	.05
75	John Smiley	.05
76	Carlton Fisk	.65
77	Luis Sojo	.05
78	George Brett	.85
79	Mitch Williams	.05
80	Kent Hrbek	.05
81	Jay Bell	.05
82	Edgar Martinez	.05
83	Lee Smith	.05
84	Deion Sanders	.05
85	Bill Gullickson	.05
86	Paul O'Neill	.05
87	Kevin Seitzer	.05
88	Steve Finley	.05
89	Mel Hall	.05
90	Nolan Ryan	1.50
91	Eric Davis	.05
92	Mike Mussina	.35
93	Tony Fernandez	.05
94	Frank Viola	.05
95	Matt Williams	.05
96	Joe Carter	.05
97	Ryne Sandberg	.75
98	Jim Abbott	.05
99	Marquis Grissom	.05
100	George Bell	.05
101	Howard Johnson	.05
102	Kevin Appier	.05
103	Dale Murphy	.20
104	Shane Mack	.05
105	Jose Lind	.05
106	Rickey Henderson	.65
107	Bob Tewksbury	.05
108	Kevin Mitchell	.05
109	Steve Avery	.05
110	Candy Maldonado	.05
111	Bip Roberts	.05
112	Lou Whitaker	.05
113	Jeff Bagwell	.65
114	Dante Bichette	.05
115	Brett Butler	.05
116	Melido Perez	.05
117	Andy Benes	.05
118	Randy Johnson	.65
119	Willie McGee	.05
120	Jody Reed	.05
121	Shawon Dunston	.05
122	Carlos Baerga	.05
123	Bret Saberhagen	.05
124	John Olerud	.05
125	Ivan Calderon	.05
126	Bryan Harvey	.05
127	Terry Mulholland	.05
128	Ozzie Guillen	.05
129	Steve Buechele	.05
130	Kevin Tapani	.05
131	Felix Jose	.05
132	Terry Steinbach	.05
133	Ron Gant	.05
134	Harold Reynolds	.05
135	Chris Sabo	.05
136	Ivan Rodriguez	.60
137	Eric Anthony	.05
138	Mike Henneman	.05
139	Robby Thompson	.05
140	Scott Fletcher	.05
141	Bruce Hurst	.05
142	Kevin Maas	.05
143	Tom Candiotti	.05
144	Chris Hoiles	.05
145	Mike Morgan	.05
146	Mark Whiten	.05
147	Dennis Martinez	.05
148	Tony Pena	.05
149	Dave Magadan	.05

150	Mark Lewis	.05
151	Mariano Duncan	.05
152	Gregg Jefferies	.05
153	Doug Drabek	.05
154	Brian Harper	.05
155	Ray Lankford	.05
156	Carney Lansford	.05
157	Mike Sharperson	.05
158	Jack Morris	.05
159	Otis Nixon	.05
160	Steve Sax	.05
161	Mark Lemke	.05
162	Rafael Palmeiro	.60
163	Jose Rijo	.05
164	Omar Vizquel	.05
165	Sammy Sosa	.75
166	Milt Cuyler	.05
167	John Franco	.05
168	Darryl Hamilton	.05
169	Ken Hill	.05
170	Mike Devereaux	.05
171	Don Slaught	.05
172	Steve Farr	.05
173	Bernard Gilkey	.05
174	Mike Fetters	.05
175	Vince Coleman	.05
176	Kevin McReynolds	.05
177	John Smoltz	.05
178	Greg Gagne	.05
179	Greg Swindell	.05
180	Juan Guzman	.05
181	Kal Daniels	.05
182	Rick Sutcliffe	.05
183	Orlando Merced	.05
184	Bill Wegman	.05
185	Mark Gardner	.05
186	Rob Deer	.05
187	Dave Hollins	.05
188	Jack Clark	.05
189	Brian Hunter	.05
190	Tim Wallach	.05
191	Tim Belcher	.05
192	Walt Weiss	.05
193	Kurt Stillwell	.05
194	Charlie Hayes	.05
195	Willie Randolph	.05
196	Jack McDowell	.05
197	Jose Offerman	.05
198	Chuck Finley	.05
199	Darrin Jackson	.05
200	Kelly Gruber	.05
201	John Wetteland	.05
202	Jay Buhner	.05
203	Mike LaValliere	.05
204	Kevin Brown	.05
205	Luis Gonzalez	.05
206	Rick Aguilera	.05
207	Norm Charlton	.05
208	Mike Bordick	.05
209	Charlie Leibrandt	.05
210	Tom Brunansky	.05
211	Tom Henke	.05
212	Randy Milligan	.05
213	Ramon Martinez	.05
214	Mo Vaughn	.05
215	Randy Myers	.05
216	Greg Hibbard	.05
217	Wes Chamberlain	.05
218	Tony Phillips	.05
219	Pete Harnisch	.05
220	Mike Gallego	.05
221	Bud Black	.05
222	Greg Vaughn	.05
223	Milt Thompson	.05
224	Ben McDonald	.05
225	Billy Hatcher	.05
226	Paul Sorrento	.05
227	Mark Gubicza	.05
228	Mike Greenwell	.05
229	Curt Schilling	.35
230	Alan Trammell	.05
231	Zane Smith	.05
232	Bobby Thigpen	.05
233	Joe Olson	.05
234	Joe Orsulak	.05
235	Joe Oliver	.05
236	Tim Raines	.05
237	Juan Samuel	.05
238	Chili Davis	.05
239	Spike Owen	.05
240	Dave Stewart	.05
241	Jim Eisenreich	.05
242	Phil Plantier	.05
243	Sid Fernandez	.05
244	Dan Gladden	.05
245	Mickey Morandini	.05
246	Tino Martinez	.05
247	Kirt Manwaring	.05
248	Dean Palmer	.05
249	Tom Browning	.05
250	Brian McRae	.05
251	Scott Leius	.05
252	Bert Blyleven	.05
253	Scott Erickson	.05
254	Bob Welch	.05
255	Pat Kelly	.05
256	Felix Fermin	.05
257	Harold Baines	.05
258	Chad Ward	.05
259	Bill Spiers	.05
260	Jaime Navarro	.05
261	Scott Sanderson	.05
262	Gary Gaetti	.05
263	Bob Ojeda	.05
264	Jeff Montgomery	.05

265	Scott Bankhead	.05
266	Lance Johnson	.05
267	Rafael Belliard	.05
268	Kevin Reimer	.05
269	Benito Santiago	.05
270	Mike Moore	.05
271	Dave Fleming	.05
272	Moises Alou	.05
273	Pat Listach	.05
274	Reggie Sanders	.05
275	Kenny Lofton	.05
276	Donovan Osborne	.05
277	Rusty Meacham	.05
278	Eric Karros	.05
279	Andy Stankiewicz	.05
280	Brian Jordan	.05
281	Gary DiSarcina	.05
282	Mark Wohlers	.05
283	Dave Nilsson	.05
284	Anthony Young	.05
285	Jim Bullinger	.05
286	Derek Bell	.05
287	Brian Williams	.05
288	Julio Valera	.05
289	Dan Walters	.05
290	Chad Curtis	.05
291	Michael Tucker	.05
292	Bob Zupcic	.05
293	Todd Hundley	.05
294	Jeff Tackett	.05
295	Greg Colbrunn	.05
296	Cal Eldred	.05
297	Chris Roberts	.05
298	John Doherty	.05
299	Denny Neagle	.05
300	Arthur Rhodes	.05
301	Mark Clark	.05
302	Scott Cooper	.05
303	Jamie Arnold RC	.05
304	Jim Thome	.60
305	Frank Seminara	.05
306	Kurt Knudsen	.05
307	Tim Wakefield	.05
308	John Jaha	.05
309	Pat Hentgen	.05
310	B.J. Wallace	.05
311	Roberto Hernandez	.05
312	Hipolito Pichardo	.05
313	Eric Fox	.05
314	Willie Banks	.05
315	Sam Militello	.05
316	Vince Horsman	.05
317	Carlos Hernandez	.05
318	Jeff Kent	.05
319	Mike Perez	.05
320	Scott Livingstone	.05
321	Jeff Conine	.05
322	James Austin	.05
323	John Vander Wal	.05
324	Pat Mahomes	.05
325	Pedro Astacio	.05
326	Bret Boone	.05
327	Matt Stairs	.05
328	Damion Easley	.05
329	Ben Rivera	.05
330	Reggie Jefferson	.05
331	Luis Mercedes	.05
332	Kyle Abbott	.05
333	Eddie Taubensee	.05
334	Tim McIntosh	.05
335	Phil Clark	.05
336	Wil Cordero	.05
337	Russ Springer	.05
338	Craig Colbert	.05
339	Tim Salmon	.05
340	Braulio Castillo	.05
341	Donald Harris	.05
342	Eric Young	.05
343	Bob Wickman	.05
344	John Valentin	.05
345	Dan Wilson	.05
346	Steve Hosey	.05
347	Mike Piazza	1.00
348	Willie Greene	.05
349	Tom Goodwin	.05
350	Eric Hillman	.05
351	Steve Reed RC	.05
352	Dan Serafini RC	.05
353	Todd Steverson RC	.05
354	Benji Grigsby	.05
355	Shannon Stewart RC	1.00
356	Sean Lowe	.05
357	Derek Wallace	.05
358	Rick Helling	.05
359	Jason Kendall RC	1.00
360	Derek Jeter RC	10.00
361	David Cone	.05
362	Jeff Reardon	.05
363	Bobby Witt	.05
364	Jose Canseco	.40
365	Jeff Russell	.05
366	Ruben Sierra	.05
367	Alan Mills	.05
368	Matt Nokes	.05
369	Pat Borders	.05
370	Pedro Munoz	.05
371	Danny Jackson	.05
372	Geronimo Pena	.05
373	Craig Lefferts	.05
374	Joe Grahe	.05
375	Roger McDowell	.05
376	Jimmy Key	.05
377	Steve Olin	.05
378	Glenn Davis	.05
379	Rene Gonzales	.05

380	Manuel Lee	.05
381	Ron Karkovice	.05
382	Sid Bream	.05
383	Gerald Williams	.05
384	Lenny Harris	.05
385	J.T. Snow RC	.75
386	Dave Stieb	.05
387	Kirk McCaskill	.05
388	Lance Parrish	.05
389	Craig Grebeck	.05
390	Rick Wilkins	.05
391	Manny Alexander	.05
392	Mike Schooler	.05
393	Bernie Williams	.05
394	Kevin Koslofski	.05
395	Willie Wilson	.05
396	Jeff Parrett	.05
397	Mike Harkey	.05
398	Frank Tanana	.05
399	Doug Henry	.05
400	Royce Clayton	.05
401	Eric Wedge	.05
402	Derrick May	.05
403	Carlos Garcia	.05
404	Henry Rodriguez	.05
405	Ryan Klesko	.05

1993 Select Dufex Proofs

Select Rookies: 15X
Select Stars: 20X
Select Triple Crown: 20X
(See 1993 Select Rookies, Stars and Triple Crown for checklist and base card values.)

Aces

		NM/M
Complete Set (24):		20.00
Common Player:		1.00
1	Roger Clemens	6.00
2	Tom Glavine	3.00
3	Jack McDowell	1.00
4	Greg Maddux	4.50
5	Jack Morris	1.00
6	Dennis Martinez	1.00
7	Kevin Brown	1.00
8	Dwight Gooden	1.00
9	Kevin Appier	1.00
10	Juan Guzman	1.00
11	John Smiley	1.00
12	Charles Nagy	1.00
13	Ken Hill	1.00
14	Bob Tewksbury	1.00
15	Doug Drabek	1.00
16	John Smoltz	1.00
17	Greg Swindell	1.00
18	Bruce Hurst	1.00
19	Mike Morgan	1.00
20	Mike Mussina	2.00
21	Cal Eldred	1.00
22	Melido Perez	1.00
23	Dave Fleming	1.00
24	Kevin Tapani	1.00

Rookies

		NM/M
Complete Set (21):		4.00
Common Player:		.50
1	Pat Listach	.50
2	Moises Alou	.50
3	Reggie Sanders	.50
4	Kenny Lofton	.50
5	Eric Karros	.50
6	Brian Williams	.50
7	Donovan Osborne	.50
8	Sam Militello	.50
9	Chad Curtis	.50
10	Bob Zupcic	.50
11	Tim Salmon	1.50
12	Jeff Conine	.50
13	Pedro Astacio	.50
14	Arthur Rhodes	.50
15	Cal Eldred	.50
16	Tim Wakefield	.50
17	Andy Stankiewicz	.50
18	Wil Cordero	.50
19	Todd Hundley	.50
20	Dave Fleming	.50
21	Bret Boone	1.00

Stars

		NM/M
Complete Set (24):		40.00
Common Player:		.60
1	Fred McGriff	.60
2	Ryne Sandberg	4.00
3	Ozzie Smith	4.00
4	Gary Sheffield	1.25
5	Darren Daulton	.60
6	Andy Van Slyke	.60
7	Barry Bonds	7.50
8	Tony Gwynn	4.00
9	Greg Maddux	4.00
10	Tom Glavine	1.00
11	John Franco	.60
12	Lee Smith	.60
13	Cecil Fielder	.60
14	Roberto Alomar	1.00
15	Cal Ripken, Jr.	7.50
16	Edgar Martinez	.60
17	Ivan Rodriguez	2.50
18	Kirby Puckett	4.00
19	Ken Griffey Jr.	6.00
20	Joe Carter	.60
21	Roger Clemens	4.50
22	Dave Fleming	.60
(22)	Dave Fleming (Blank-back sample card.)	1.00
23	Paul Molitor	3.00
(23)	Paul Molitor (Blank-back sample card.)	2.75
24	Dennis Eckersley	2.50

1993 Select Stat Leaders

		NM/M
Complete Set (90):		8.00
Common Player:		.05
1	Edgar Martinez	.05
2	Kirby Puckett	.30
3	Frank Thomas	.25
4	Gary Sheffield	.15
5	Andy Van Slyke	.05
6	John Kruk	.05
7	Kirby Puckett	.30

Gary Sheffield Slugging Leaders

8	Carlos Baerga	.05
9	Paul Molitor	.25
10	Andy Van Slyke, Terry Pendleton	.05
11	Ryne Sandberg	.30
12	Mark Grace	.05
13	Frank Thomas	.25
14	Don Mattingly	.35
15	Ken Griffey Jr.	.45
16	Andy Van Slyke	.05
17	Mariano Duncan, Jerald Clark, Ray Lankford	.05
18	Marquis Grissom, Terry Pendleton	.05
19	Lance Johnson	.05
20	Mike Devereaux	.05
21	Brady Anderson	.05
22	Deion Sanders	.05
23	Steve Finley	.05
24	Andy Van Slyke	.05
25	Juan Gonzalez	.15
26	Mark McGwire	.50
27	Cecil Fielder	.05
28	Fred McGriff	.05
29	Barry Bonds	.60
30	Gary Sheffield	.05
31	Cecil Fielder	.05
32	Joe Carter	.05
33	Frank Thomas	.25
34	Darren Daulton	.05
35	Terry Pendleton	.05
36	Fred McGriff	.05
37	Tony Phillips	.05
38	Frank Thomas	.25
39	Roberto Alomar	.15
40	Barry Bonds	.60
41	Dave Hollins	.05
42	Andy Van Slyke	.05
43	Mark McGwire	.50
44	Edgar Martinez	.05
45	Frank Thomas	.25
46	Barry Bonds	.60
47	Gary Sheffield	.05
48	Fred McGriff	.05
49	Frank Thomas	.25
50	Danny Tartabull	.05
51	Roberto Alomar	.15
52	Barry Bonds	.60
53	John Kruk	.05
54	Brett Butler	.05
55	Kenny Lofton	.05
56	Pat Listach	.05
57	Brady Anderson	.05
58	Marquis Grissom	.05
59	Delino DeShields	.05
60	Steve Finley, Bip Roberts	.05
61	Jack McDowell	.05
62	Kevin Brown	.05
63	Melido Perez	.05
64	Terry Mulholland	.05
65	Curt Schilling	.20
66	John Smoltz, Doug Drabek, Greg Maddux	.05
67	Dennis Eckersley	.20
68	Rick Aguilera	.05
69	Jeff Montgomery	.05
70	Lee Smith	.05
71	Randy Myers	.05
72	John Wetteland	.05
73	Randy Johnson	.25
74	Melido Perez	.05
75	Roger Clemens	.35
76	John Smoltz	.05
77	David Cone	.05
78	Greg Maddux	.30
79	Roger Clemens	.35
80	Kevin Appier	.05
81	Mike Mussina	.15
82	Bill Swift	.05
83	Bob Tewksbury	.05
84	Greg Maddux	.30
85	Kevin Brown	.05
86	Jack McDowell	.05
87	Roger Clemens	.35
88	Tom Glavine	.10
89	Ken Hill, Bob Tewksbury	.05
90	Dennis Martinez, Mike Morgan	.05

Triple Crown

	NM/M
Complete Set (3):	35.00

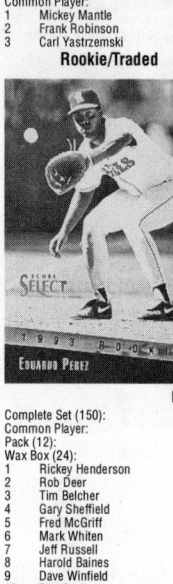

CARL YASTRZEMSKI — Triple Crown

Common Player:		10.00
1	Mickey Mantle	22.50
2	Frank Robinson	10.00
3	Carl Yastrzemski	12.50

Rookie/Traded

Eduardo Perez

		NM/M
Complete Set (150):		11.00
Common Player:		.05
Pack (12):		1.25
Wax Box (24):		20.00
1	Rickey Henderson	.75
2	Rob Deer	.05
3	Tim Belcher	.05
4	Gary Sheffield	.35
5	Fred McGriff	.05
6	Mark Whiten	.05
7	Jeff Russell	.05
8	Harold Baines	.05
9	Dave Winfield	.75
10	Andre Dawson	.25
11	Gregg Jefferies	.05
12	Jimmy Key	.05
13	Harold Reynolds	.05
14	Tom Henke	.05
15	Ellis Burks	.12
16	Paul Molitor	.75
17	Wade Boggs	1.00
18	David Cone	.05
19	Tony Fernandez	.05
20	Roberto Kelly	.05
21	Paul O'Neill	.05
22	Jose Lind	.05
23	Barry Bonds	2.00
24	Dave Stewart	.05
25	Randy Myers	.05
26	Benito Santiago	.05
27	Tom Wallach	.05
28	Greg Gagne	.05
29	Kevin Mitchell	.05
30	Jim Abbott	.05
31	Lee Smith	.05
32	Bobby Munoz RC	.05
33	Mo Sanford RC	.05
34	John Roper	.05
35	Pedro Martinez	.75
36	Dave Hulse RC	.05
37	Chuck Carr RC	.05
38	Armando Reynoso RC	.10
39	Ryan Thompson	.05
40	Carlos Garcia RC	.05
41	Matt Whiteside	.05
42	Benji Gil	.05
43	Rodney Bolton RC	.05
44	J.T. Snow	.05
45	David McCarty	.05
46	Paul Quantrill RC	.05
47	Al Martin	.05
48	Lance Painter	.05
49	Lou Frazier RC	.05
50	Eduardo Perez	.05
51	Kevin Young	.05
52	Mike Trombley	.05
53	Sterling Hitchcock RC	.10
54	Tim Bogar RC	.05
55	Hilly Hathaway RC	.05
56	Wayne Kirby RC	.05

57	Craig Paquette RC	.05
58	Bret Boone	.05
59	Greg McMichael RC	.05
60	Mike Lansing RC	.35
61	Brent Gates	.05
62	Rene Arocha	.05
63	Ricky Gutierrez	.05
64	Kevin Rogers RC	.05
65	Ken Ryan RC	.05
66	Phil Hiatt	.05
67	Pat Meares RC	.05
68	Troy Neel	.05
69	Steve Cooke	.05
70	Sherman Obando RC	.05
71	Blas Minor RC	.05
72	Angel Miranda RC	.05
73	Tom Kramer RC	.05
74	Chip Hale RC	.05
75	Brad Pennington RC	.05
76	Graeme Lloyd RC	.05
77	Darrell Whitmore RC	.05
78	David Nied	.05
79	Todd Van Poppel	.05
80	Chris Gomez RC	.10
81	Jason Bere	.05
82	Jeffrey Hammonds	.05
83	Brad Ausmus RC	.10
84	Kevin Stocker	.05
85	Jeromy Burnitz	.05
86	Aaron Sele	.05
87	Roberto Mejia RC	.05
88	Kirk Rueter RC	.10
89	Kevin Roberson RC	.05
90	Allen Watson RC	.05
91	Charlie Leibrandt	.05
92	Eric Davis	.05
93	Jody Reed	.05
94	Danny Jackson	.05
95	Gary Gaetti	.05
96	Norm Charlton	.05
97	Doug Drabek	.05
98	Scott Fletcher	.05
99	Greg Swindell	.05
100	John Smiley	.05
101	Kevin Reimer	.05
102	Andres Galarraga	.05
103	Greg Hibbard	.05
104	Chris Hammond	.05
105	Darnell Coles	.05
106	Mike Felder	.05
107	Jose Guzman	.05
108	Chris Bosio	.05
109	Spike Owen	.05
110	Felix Jose	.05
111	Cory Snyder	.05
112	Craig Lefferts	.05
113	David Wells	.05
114	Pete Incaviglia	.05
115	Mike Pagliarulo	.05
116	Dave Magadan	.05
117	Charlie Hough	.05
118	Ivan Calderon	.05
119	Manuel Lee	.05
120	Bob Patterson	.05
121	Bob Ojeda	.05
122	Scott Bankhead	.05
123	Greg Maddux	1.00
124	Chili Davis	.05
125	Milt Thompson	.05
126	Dave Martinez	.05
127	Frank Tanana	.05
128	Phil Plantier	.05
129	Juan Samuel	.05
130	Eric Young	.05
131	Joe Orsulak	.05
132	Derek Bell	.05
133	Darrin Jackson	.05
134	Tom Brunansky	.05
135	Jeff Reardon	.05
136	Kevin Higgins RC	.05
137	Joel Johnston RC	.05
138	Rick Trlicek RC	.05
139	Richie Lewis RC	.05
140	Jeff Gardner RC	.05
141	Jack Voigt RC	.05
142	Rod Correia RC	.05
143	Billy Brewer RC	.05
144	Terry Jorgensen RC	.05
145	Rich Amaral RC	.05
146	Sean Berry RC	.05
147	Dan Peltier RC	.05
148	Paul Wagner RC	.05
149	Damon Buford RC	.05
150	Wil Cordero	.05

Rookie/Traded Inserts

		NM/M
Complete Set (3):		60.00
Common Player:		6.00
1NR	Nolan Ryan	40.00
1ROY	Tim Salmon	6.00
2ROY	Mike Piazza	20.00

Rookie/Traded All-Star Rookies

		NM/M
Complete Set (10):		30.00
Common Player:		1.00
1	Jeff Conine	1.00
2	Brent Gates	1.00
3	Mike Lansing	1.00
4	Kevin Stocker	1.00
5	Mike Piazza	25.00
6	Jeffrey Hammonds	1.00

KEVIN STOCKER — '93 ALL-STAR ROOKIE TEAM

7	David Hulse	1.00
8	Tim Salmon	2.00
9	Rene Arocha	1.00
10	Greg McMichael	1.00

1994 Select

	NM/M
Complete Set (420):	12.50
Common Player:	.05
Pack (12):	1.25
Wax Box (24):	16.00
1 Ken Griffey Jr.	1.50
2 Greg Maddux	1.00
3 Paul Molitor	.75
4 Mike Piazza	1.50
5 Jay Bell	.05
6 Frank Thomas	.75
7 Barry Larkin	.05
8 Paul O'Neill	.05
9 Darren Daulton	.05
10 Mike Greenwell	.05
11 Chuck Carr	.05
12 Joe Carter	.05
13 Lance Johnson	.05
14 Jeff Blauser	.05
15 Chris Hoiles	.05
16 Rick Wilkins	.05
17 Kirby Puckett	1.00
18 Larry Walker	.05
19 Randy Johnson	.75
20 Bernard Gilkey	.05
21 Devon White	.05
22 Randy Myers	.05
23 Don Mattingly	1.25
24 John Kruk	.05
25 Ozzie Guillen	.05
26 Jeff Conine	.05
27 Mike Macfarlane	.05
28 Dave Hollins	.05
29 Chuck Knoblauch	.05
30 Ozzie Smith	1.00
31 Harold Baines	.05
32 Ryne Sandberg	1.00
33 Ron Karkovice	.05
34 Terry Pendleton	.05
35 Wally Joyner	.05
36 Mike Mussina	.35
37 Felix Jose	.05
38 Derrick May	.05
39 Scott Cooper	.05
40 Jose Rijo	.05
41 Robin Ventura	.05
42 Charlie Hayes	.05
43 Jimmy Key	.05
44 Eric Karros	.05
45 Ruben Sierra	.05
46 Ryan Thompson	.05
47 Brian McRae	.05
48 Pat Hentgen	.05
49 John Valentin	.05
50 Al Martin	.05
51 Jose Lind	.05
52 Kevin Stocker	.05
53 Mike Gallego	.05
54 Dwight Gooden	.05
55 Brady Anderson	.05
56 Jeff King	.05
57 Mark McGwire	1.75
58 Sammy Sosa	1.00
59 Ryan Bowen	.05
60 Mark Lemke	.05
61 Roger Clemens	1.25
62 Brian Jordan	.05
63 Andres Galarraga	.05
64 Kevin Appier	.05
65 Don Slaught	.05
66 Mike Blowers	.05
67 Wes Chamberlain	.05
68 Troy Neel	.05

#	Player	Price
69	John Wetteland	.05
70	Joe Girardi	.05
71	Reggie Sanders	.05
72	Edgar Martinez	.05
73	Todd Hundley	.05
74	Pat Borders	.05
75	Roberto Mejia	.05
76	David Cone	.05
77	Tony Gwynn	1.00
78	Jim Abbott	.05
79	Jay Buhner	.05
80	Mark McLemore	.05
81	Wil Cordero	.05
82	Pedro Astacio	.05
83	Bob Tewksbury	.05
84	Dave Winfield	.75
85	Jeff Kent	.05
86	Todd Van Poppel	.05
87	Steve Avery	.05
88	Mike Lansing	.05
89	Len Dykstra	.05
90	Jose Guzman	.05
91	Brian Hunter	.05
92	Tim Raines	.05
93	Andre Dawson	.25
94	Joe Orsulak	.05
95	Ricky Jordan	.05
96	Billy Hatcher	.05
97	Jack McDowell	.05
98	Tom Pagnozzi	.05
99	Darryl Strawberry	.05
100	Mike Stanley	.05
101	Bret Saberhagen	.05
102	Willie Greene	.05
103	Bryan Harvey	.05
104	Tim Bogar	.05
105	Jack Voight	.05
106	Brad Ausmus	.05
107	Ramon Martinez	.05
108	Mike Perez	.05
109	Jeff Montgomery	.05
110	Danny Darwin	.05
111	Wilson Alvarez	.05
112	Kevin Mitchell	.05
113	David Nied	.05
114	Rich Amaral	.05
115	Stan Javier	.05
116	Mo Vaughn	.05
117	Ben McDonald	.05
118	Tom Gordon	.05
119	Carlos Garcia	.05
120	Phil Plantier	.05
121	Mike Morgan	.05
122	Pat Meares	.05
123	Kevin Young	.05
124	Jeff Fassero	.05
125	Gene Harris	.05
126	Bob Welch	.05
127	Walt Weiss	.05
128	Bobby Witt	.05
129	Andy Van Slyke	.05
130	Steve Cooke	.05
131	Mike Devereaux	.05
132	Joey Cora	.05
133	Bret Barberie	.05
134	Orel Hershiser	.05
135	Ed Sprague	.05
136	Shawon Dunston	.05
137	Alex Arias	.05
138	Archi Cianfrocco	.05
139	Tim Wallach	.05
140	Bernie Williams	.05
141	Karl Rhodes	.05
142	Pat Kelly	.05
143	Dave Magadan	.05
144	Kevin Tapani	.05
145	Eric Young	.05
146	Derek Bell	.05
147	Dante Bichette	.05
148	Geronimo Pena	.05
149	Joe Oliver	.05
150	Orestes Destrade	.05
151	Tim Naehring	.05
152	Ray Lankford	.05
153	Phil Clark	.05
154	David McCarty	.05
155	Tommy Greene	.05
156	Wade Boggs	1.00
157	Kevin Gross	.05
158	Hal Morris	.05
159	Moises Alou	.05
160	Rick Aguilera	.05
161	Curt Schilling	.35
162	Chip Hale	.05
163	Tino Martinez	.05
164	Mark Whiten	.05
165	Dave Stewart	.05
166	Steve Buechele	.05
167	Bobby Jones	.05
168	Darrin Fletcher	.05
169	John Smiley	.05
170	Cory Snyder	.05
171	Scott Erickson	.05
172	Kirk Rueter	.05
173	Dave Fleming	.05
174	John Smoltz	.05
175	Ricky Gutierrez	.05
176	Mike Bordick	.05
177	Chan Ho Park RC	1.00
178	Alex Gonzalez	.05
179	Steve Karsay	.05
180	Jeffrey Hammonds	.05
181	Manny Ramirez	.75
182	Salomon Torres	.05
183	Raul Mondesi	.05
184	James Mouton	.05
185	Cliff Floyd	.05
186	Danny Bautista	.05
187	Kurt Abbott RC	.05
188	Javier Lopez	.05
189	John Patterson	.05
190	Greg Blosser	.05
191	Bob Hamelin	.05
192	Tony Eusebio	.05
193	Carlos Delgado	.50
194	Chris Gomez	.05
195	Kelly Stinnett	.05
196	Shane Reynolds	.05
197	Ryan Klesko	.05
198	Jim Edmonds	.05
199	James Hurst	.05
200	Dave Staton	.05
201	Rondell White	.05
202	Keith Mitchell	.05
203	Darren Oliver	.05
204	Mike Matheny	.05
205	Chris Turner	.05
206	Matt Mieske	.05
207	N.L. Team Checklist	.05
208	N.L. Team Checklist	.05
209	A.L. Team Checklist	.05
210	A.L. Team Checklist	.05
211	Barry Bonds	2.00
212	Juan Gonzalez	.40
213	Jim Eisenreich	.05
214	Ivan Rodriguez	.65
215	Tony Phillips	.05
216	John Jaha	.05
217	Lee Smith	.05
218	Bip Roberts	.05
219	Dave Hansen	.05
220	Pat Listach	.05
221	Willie McGee	.05
222	Damion Easley	.05
223	Dean Palmer	.05
224	Mike Moore	.05
225	Brian Harper	.05
226	Gary DiSarcina	.05
227	Delino DeShields	.05
228	Otis Nixon	.05
229	Roberto Alomar	.30
230	Mark Grace	.05
231	Kenny Lofton	.05
232	Gregg Jefferies	.05
233	Cecil Fielder	.05
234	Jeff Bagwell	.75
235	Albert Belle	.05
236	Dave Justice	.05
237	Tom Henke	.05
238	Bobby Bonilla	.05
239	John Olerud	.05
240	Robby Thompson	.05
241	Dave Valle	.05
242	Marquis Grissom	.05
243	Greg Swindell	.05
244	Todd Zeile	.05
245	Dennis Eckersley	.65
246	Jose Offerman	.05
247	Greg McMichael	.05
248	Tim Belcher	.05
249	Cal Ripken, Jr.	2.00
250	Tom Glavine	.05
251	Luis Polonia	.05
252	Bill Swift	.05
253	Juan Guzman	.05
254	Rickey Henderson	.75
255	Terry Mulholland	.05
256	Gary Sheffield	.40
257	Terry Steinbach	.05
258	Brett Butler	.05
259	Jason Bere	.05
260	Doug Strange	.05
261	Kent Hrbek	.05
262	Graeme Lloyd	.05
263	Lou Frazier	.05
264	Charles Nagy	.05
265	Bret Boone	.05
266	Kirk Gibson	.05
267	Kevin Brown	.05
268	Matt Williams	.05
269	Greg Gagne	.05
270	Mariano Duncan	.05
271	Jeff Russell	.05
272	Eric Davis	.05
273	Shane Mack	.05
274	Jose Vizcaino	.05
275	Jose Canseco	.45
276	Roberto Hernandez	.05
277	Royce Clayton	.05
278	Carlos Baerga	.05
279	Pete Incaviglia	.05
280	Brent Gates	.05
281	Jeromy Burnitz	.05
282	Chili Davis	.05
283	Pete Harnisch	.05
284	Alan Trammell	.05
285	Anthony Young	.05
286	Ellis Burks	.05
287	Ellis Burks	.05
288	Julio Franco	.05
289	Jack Morris	.05
290	Erik Hanson	.05
291	Chuck Finley	.05
292	Reggie Jefferson	.05
293	Kevin McReynolds	.05
294	Greg Hibbard	.05
295	Travis Fryman	.05
296	Craig Biggio	.05
297	Kenny Rogers	.05
298	Dave Henderson	.05
299	Jim Thome	.50
300	Rene Arocha	.05
301	Pedro Munoz	.05
302	David Hulse	.05
303	Greg Vaughn	.05
304	Darren Lewis	.05
305	Deion Sanders	.05
306	Danny Tartabull	.05
307	Darryl Hamilton	.05
308	Andujar Cedeno	.05
309	Tim Salmon	.05
310	Tony Fernandez	.05
311	Alex Fernandez	.05
312	Roberto Kelly	.05
313	Harold Reynolds	.05
314	Chris Sabo	.05
315	Howard Johnson	.05
316	Mark Portugal	.05
317	Rafael Palmeiro	.65
318	Pete Smith	.05
319	Will Clark	.05
320	Henry Rodriguez	.05
321	Omar Vizquel	.05
322	David Segui	.05
323	Lou Whitaker	.05
324	Felix Fermin	.05
325	Spike Owen	.05
326	Darryl Kile	.05
327	Chad Kreuter	.05
328	Rod Beck	.05
329	Eddie Murray	.75
330	B.J. Surhoff	.05
331	Mickey Tettleton	.05
332	Pedro Martinez	.75
333	Roger Pavlik	.05
334	Eddie Taubensee	.05
335	John Doherty	.05
336	Jody Reed	.05
337	Aaron Sele	.05
338	Leo Gomez	.05
339	Dave Nilsson	.05
340	Rob Dibble	.05
341	John Burkett	.05
342	Wayne Kirby	.05
343	Dan Wilson	.05
344	Armando Reynoso	.05
345	Chad Curtis	.05
346	Dennis Martinez	.05
347	Cal Eldred	.05
348	Luis Gonzalez	.05
349	Doug Drabek	.05
350	Jim Leyritz	.05
351	Mark Langston	.05
352	Darrin Jackson	.05
353	Sid Fernandez	.05
354	Benito Santiago	.05
355	Kevin Seitzer	.05
356	Bo Jackson	.10
357	David Wells	.05
358	Paul Sorrento	.05
359	Ken Caminiti	.05
360	Eduardo Perez	.05
361	Orlando Merced	.05
362	Steve Finley	.05
363	Andy Benes	.05
364	Manuel Lee	.05
365	Todd Benzinger	.05
366	Sandy Alomar Jr.	.05
367	Rex Hudler	.05
368	Mike Henneman	.05
369	Vince Coleman	.05
370	Kirt Manwaring	.05
371	Ken Hill	.05
372	Glenallen Hill	.05
373	Sean Berry	.05
374	Geronimo Berroa	.05
375	Duane Ward	.05
376	Allen Watson	.05
377	Marc Newfield	.05
378	Dan Miceli	.05
379	Denny Hocking	.05
380	Mark Kiefer	.05
381	Tony Tarasco	.05
382	Tony Longmire	.05
383	Brian Anderson RC	.05
384	Fernando Vina	.05
385	Hector Carrasco	.05
386	Mike Kelly	.05
387	Greg Colbrunn	.05
388	Roger Salkeld	.05
389	Steve Trachsel	.05
390	Rich Becker	.05
391	Billy Taylor RC	.05
392	Rich Rowland	.05
393	Carl Everett	.05
394	Johnny Ruffin	.05
395	Keith Lockhart RC	.05
396	J.R. Phillips	.05
397	Sterling Hitchcock	.05
398	Jorge Fabregas	.05
399	Jeff Granger	.05
400	Eddie Zambrano RC	.05
401	Rikkert Faneyte RC	.05
402	Gerald Williams	.05
403	Joey Hamilton	.05
404	Joe Hall RC	.05
405	John Hudek RC	.05
406	Roberto Petagine	.05
407	Charles Johnson	.05
408	Mark Smith	.05
409	Jeff Juden	.05
410	Carlos Pulido RC	.05
411	Paul Shuey	.05
412	Rob Butler	.05
413	Mark Acre	.05
414	Greg Pirkl	.05
415	Melvin Nieves	.05
416	Tim Hyers RC	.05
417	N.L. Checklist	.05
418	N.L. Checklist	.05
419	A.L. Checklist	.05
420	A.L. Checklist	.05

MVP

		NM/M
MVP1	Paul Molitor	5.00

Rookie of the Year

		NM/M
RY1	Carlos Delgado	7.50

Rookie Surge

		NM/M
Complete Set (18):		10.00
Common Player:		.75
1	Cliff Floyd	.75
2	Bob Hamelin	.75
3	Ryan Klesko	.75
4	Carlos Delgado	3.00
5	Jeffrey Hammonds	.75
6	Rondell White	.75
7	Salomon Torres	.75
8	Steve Karsay	.75
9	Javier Lopez	.75
10	Manny Ramirez	3.00
11	Tony Tarasco	.75
12	Kurt Abbott	.75
13	Chan Ho Park	.75
14	Rich Becker	.75
15	James Mouton	.75
16	Alex Gonzalez	.75
17	Raul Mondesi	.75
18	Steve Trachsel	.75

Salute

	NM/M
Complete Set (2):	15.00

| 1 | Cal Ripken, Jr. | 12.50 |
| 2 | Dave Winfield | 5.00 |

Skills

		NM/M
Complete Set (10):		15.00
Common Player:		.75
1	Randy Johnson	3.00
2	Barry Larkin	.75
3	Len Dykstra	.75
4	Kenny Lofton	.75
5	Juan Gonzalez	1.50
6	Barry Bonds	6.00
7	Marquis Grissom	.75
8	Ivan Rodriguez	2.50
9	Larry Walker	.75
10	Travis Fryman	.75

1995 Select

		NM/M
Complete Set (251):		9.00
Common Player:		.05
Artist's Proofs:		10X
Pack (12):		1.50
Wax Box (24):		17.50
1	Cal Ripken Jr.	1.50
2	Robin Ventura	.05
3	Al Martin	.05
4	Jeff Frye	.05
5	Darryl Strawberry	.05
6	Chan Ho Park	.05
7	Steve Avery	.05
8	Bret Boone	.05
9	Danny Tartabull	.05
10	Dante Bichette	.05
11	Rondell White	.05
12	Dave McCarty	.05
13	Bernard Gilkey	.05
14	Mark McGwire	1.25
15	Ruben Sierra	.05
16	Wade Boggs	.75
17	Mike Piazza	1.00
18	Jeffrey Hammonds	.35
19	Mike Mussina	.35
20	Darryl Kile	.05
21	Greg Maddux	.75
22	Frank Thomas	.65
23	Kevin Appier	.05
24	Jay Bell	.05
25	Kirk Gibson	.05
26	Pat Hentgen	.05
27	Joey Hamilton	.05
28	Bernie Williams	.05
29	Aaron Sele	.05
30	Delino DeShields	.05

31	Danny Bautista	.05
32	Jim Thome	.45
33	Rikkert Faneyte	.05
34	Roberto Alomar	.20
35	Paul Molitor	.65
36	Allen Watson	.05
37	Jeff Bagwell	.65
38	Jay Buhner	.05
39	Marquis Grissom	.05
40	Jim Edmonds	.05
41	Ryan Klesko	.05
42	Fred McGriff	.05
43	Tony Tarasco	.05
44	Darren Daulton	.05
45	Marc Newfield	.05
46	Barry Bonds	1.50
47	Bobby Bonilla	.05
48	Greg Pirkl	.05
49	Steve Karsay	.05
50	Bob Hamelin	.05
51	Javier Lopez	.05
52	Barry Larkin	.05
53	Kevin Young	.05
54	Sterling Hitchcock	.05
55	Tom Glavine	.05
56	Carlos Delgado	.40
57	Darren Oliver	.05
58	Cliff Floyd	.05
59	Tim Salmon	.05
60	Albert Belle	.05
61	Salomon Torres	.05
62	Gary Sheffield	.35
63	Ivan Rodriguez	.50
64	Charles Nagy	.05
65	Eduardo Perez	.05
66	Terry Steinbach	.05
67	Dave Justice	.05
68	Jason Bere	.05
69	Dave Nilsson	.05
70	Brian Anderson	.05
71	Billy Ashley	.05
72	Roger Clemens	.85
73	Jimmy Key	.05
74	Wally Joyner	.05
75	Andy Benes	.05
76	Ray Lankford	.05
77	Jeff Kent	.05
78	Moises Alou	.05
79	Kirby Puckett	.75
80	Joe Carter	.05
81	Manny Ramirez	.65
82	J.R. Phillips	.05
83	Matt Mieske	.05
84	John Olerud	.05
85	Andres Galarraga	.05
86	Juan Gonzalez	.35
87	Pedro Martinez	.65
88	Dean Palmer	.05
89	Ken Griffey Jr.	1.00
90	Brian Jordan	.05
91	Hal Morris	.05
92	Lenny Dykstra	.05
93	Wil Cordero	.05
94	Tony Gwynn	.75
95	Alex Gonzalez	.05
96	Cecil Fielder	.05
97	Mo Vaughn	.05
98	John Valentin	.05
99	Will Clark	.05
100	Geronimo Pena	.05
101	Don Mattingly	.85
102	Charles Johnson	.05
103	Raul Mondesi	.05
104	Reggie Sanders	.05
105	Royce Clayton	.05
106	Reggie Jefferson	.05
107	Craig Biggio	.05
108	Jack McDowell	.05
109	James Mouton	.05
110	Mike Greenwell	.05
111	David Cone	.05
112	Matt Williams	.05
113	Garret Anderson	.05
114	Carlos Garcia	.05
115	Alex Fernandez	.05
116	Deion Sanders	.05
117	Chili Davis	.05
118	Mike Kelly	.05
119	Jeff Conine	.05
120	Kenny Lofton	.05
121	Rafael Palmeiro	.50
122	Chuck Knoblauch	.05
123	Ozzie Smith	.75
124	Carlos Baerga	.05
125	Brett Butler	.05
126	Sammy Sosa	.75
127	Ellis Burks	.05
128	Bret Saberhagen	.05
129	Doug Drabek	.05
130	Dennis Martinez	.05
131	Paul O'Neill	.05
132	Travis Fryman	.05
133	Brent Gates	.05
134	Rickey Henderson	.65
135	Randy Johnson	.65
136	Mark Langston	.05
137	Greg Colbrunn	.05
138	Jose Rijo	.05
139	Bryan Harvey	.05
140	Dennis Eckersley	.50
141	Ron Gant	.05
142	Carl Everett	.05
143	Jeff Granger	.05
144	Ben McDonald	.05
145	Kurt Abbott	.05

146	Jim Abbott	.05
147	Jason Jacome	.05
148	Rico Brogna	.05
149	Cal Eldred	.05
150	Rich Becker	.05
151	Pete Harnisch	.05
152	Roberto Petagine	.05
153	Jacob Brumfield	.05
154	Todd Hundley	.05
155	Roger Cedeno	.05
156	Harold Baines	.05
157	Steve Dunn	.05
158	Tim Belk	.05
159	Marty Cordova	.05
160	Russ Davis	.05
161	Jose Malave	.05
162	Brian Hunter	.05
163	Andy Pettitte	.20
164	Brooks Kieschnick	.05
165	Midre Cummings	.05
166	Frank Rodriguez	.05
167	Chad Mottola	.05
168	Brian Barber	.05
169	Tim Unroe	.05
170	Shane Andrews	.05
171	Kevin Flora	.05
172	Ray Durham	.05
173	Chipper Jones	.75
174	Butch Huskey	.05
175	Ray McDavid	.05
176	Jeff Cirillo	.05
177	Terry Pendleton	.05
178	Scott Ruffcorn	.05
179	Ray Holbert	.05
180	Joe Randa	.05
181	Jose Oliva	.05
182	Andy Van Slyke	.05
183	Albie Lopez	.05
184	Chad Curtis	.05
185	Ozzie Guillen	.05
186	Chad Ogea	.05
187	Dan Wilson	.05
188	Tony Fernandez	.05
189	John Smoltz	.05
190	Willie Greene	.05
191	Darren Lewis	.05
192	Orlando Miller	.05
193	Kurt Miller	.05
194	Andrew Lorraine	.05
195	Ernie Young	.05
196	Jimmy Haynes	.05
197	Raul Casanova RC	.05
198	Joe Vitiello	.05
199	Brad Woodall	.05
200	Juan Acevedo	.05
201	Michael Tucker	.05
202	Shawn Green	.35
203	Alex Rodriguez	1.25
204	Julian Tavarez	.05
205	Jose Lima	.05
206	Wilson Alvarez	.05
207	Rich Aude	.05
208	Armando Benitez	.05
209	Dwayne Hosey	.05
210	Gabe White	.05
211	Joey Eischen	.05
212	Bill Pulsipher	.05
213	Robby Thompson	.05
214	Toby Borland	.05
215	Rusty Greer	.05
216	Fausto Cruz	.05
217	Luis Ortiz	.05
218	Duane Singleton	.05
219	Troy Percival	.05
220	Gregg Jefferies	.05
221	Mark Grace	.05
222	Mickey Tettleton	.05
223	Phil Plantier	.05
224	Larry Walker	.05
225	Ken Caminiti	.05
226	Dave Winfield	.65
227	Brady Anderson	.05
228	Kevin Brown	.05
229	Andujar Cedeno	.05
230	Roberto Kelly	.05
231	Jose Canseco	.35
232	Scott Ruffcorn	.05
233	Billy Ashley	.05
234	J.R. Phillips	.05
235	Chipper Jones	.40
236	Charles Johnson	.05
237	Midre Cummings	.05
238	Brian Hunter	.05
239	Garret Anderson	.05
240	Shawn Green	.10
241	Alex Rodriguez	.65
242	Frank Thomas Checklist #1	.35
243	Ken Griffey Jr. Checklist #2	.50
244	Albert Belle Checklist #3	.35
245	Cal Ripken Jr. Checklist #4	.65
246	Barry Bonds Checklist #5	.75
247	Raul Mondesi Checklist #6	.05
248	Mike Piazza Checklist #7	.65
249	Jeff Bagwell Checklist #8	.30
250	Jeff Bagwell, Frank Thomas, Ken Griffey Jr., Mike Piazza Checklist #9	.25
251	Hideo Nomo	.35

1995 Select Artist's Proofs

	NM/M
Complete Set (250):	100.00
Common Player:	1.00

AP Stars: 10X
(See 1995 Select for checklist and base card values.)

Big Sticks

		NM/M
Complete Set (12):		40.00
Common Player:		1.50
1	Frank Thomas	4.00
2	Ken Griffey Jr.	7.50
3	Cal Ripken Jr.	10.00
4	Mike Piazza	7.50
5	Don Mattingly	6.00
6	Will Clark	1.50
7	Tony Gwynn	5.00
8	Jeff Bagwell	4.00
9	Barry Bonds	10.00
10	Paul Molitor	4.00
11	Matt Williams	1.50
12	Albert Belle	1.50

Can't Miss

		NM/M
Complete Set (12):		10.00
Common Player:		.35
1	Cliff Floyd	.35
2	Ryan Klesko	.35
3	Charles Johnson	.35
4	Raul Mondesi	.35
5	Manny Ramirez	2.00
6	Billy Ashley	.35
7	Alex Gonzalez	.35
8	Carlos Delgado	.75
9	Garret Anderson	.35
10	Alex Rodriguez	5.00
11	Chipper Jones	3.00
12	Shawn Green	.75

Sure Shots

		NM/M
Complete Set (10):		10.00
Common Player:		1.00
1	Ben Grieve	1.00
2	Kevin Witt	1.00
3	Mark Farris	1.00
4	Paul Konerko	3.00
5	Dustin Hermanson	1.00
6	Ramon Castro	1.00
7	McKay Christensen	1.00
8	Brian Buchanan	1.00

9	Paul Wilson	1.00
10	Terrence Long	1.00

1995 Select Certified

		NM/M
Complete Set (135):		10.00
Common Player:		.05
Mirror Gold Stars:		5X
Pack (6):		2.00
Wax Box (20):		25.00
1	Barry Bonds	2.50
2	Reggie Sanders	.05
3	Terry Steinbach	.05
4	Eduardo Perez	.05
5	Frank Thomas	.75
6	Wil Cordero	.05
7	John Olerud	.05
8	Deion Sanders	.05
9	Mike Mussina	.40
10	Mo Vaughn	.05
11	Will Clark	.05
12	Chili Davis	.05
13	Jimmy Key	.05
14	Eddie Murray	.75
15	Bernard Gilkey	.05
16	David Cone	.05
17	Tim Salmon	.05
18	(Not issued, see #2131.)	
19	Steve Ontiveros	.05
20	Andres Galarraga	.05
21	Don Mattingly	1.25
22	Kevin Appier	.05
23	Paul Molitor	.75
24	Edgar Martinez	.05
25	Andy Benes	.05
26	Rafael Palmeiro	.65
27	Barry Larkin	.05
28	Gary Sheffield	.25
29	Wally Joyner	.05
30	Wade Boggs	1.00
31	Rico Brogna	.05
32	Eddie Murray (Murray Tribute)	.40
33	Kirby Puckett	1.00
34	Bobby Bonilla	.05
35	Hal Morris	.05
36	Moises Alou	.05
37	Javier Lopez	.05
38	Chuck Knoblauch	.05
39	Mike Piazza	1.50
40	Travis Fryman	.05
41	Rickey Henderson	.75
42	Jim Thome	.60
43	Carlos Baerga	.05
44	Dean Palmer	.05
45	Kirk Gibson	.05
46	Bret Saberhagen	.05
47	Cecil Fielder	.05
48	Manny Ramirez	.75
49	Derek Bell	.05
50	Mark McGwire	2.00
51	Jim Edmonds	.05
52	Robin Ventura	.05
53	Ryan Klesko	.05
54	Jeff Bagwell	.75
55	Ozzie Smith	1.00
56	Albert Belle	.05
57	Darren Daulton	.05

58	Jeff Conine	.05
59	Greg Maddux	1.00
60	Lenny Dykstra	.05
61	Randy Johnson	.75
62	Fred McGriff	.05
63	Ray Lankford	.05
64	Dave Justice	.05
65	Paul O'Neill	.05
66	Tony Gwynn	1.00
67	Matt Williams	.05
68	Dante Bichette	.05
69	Craig Biggio	.05
70	Ken Griffey Jr.	1.50
71	J.T. Snow	.05
72	Cal Ripken Jr.	2.50
73	Jay Bell	.05
74	Joe Carter	.05
75	Roberto Alomar	.30
76	Benji Gil	.05
77	Ivan Rodriguez	.65
78	Raul Mondesi	.05
79	Cliff Floyd	.05
80	Eric Karros, Mike Piazza, Raul Mondesi (Dodger Dynasty)	.30
81	Royce Clayton	.05
82	Billy Ashley	.05
83	Joey Hamilton	.05
84	Sammy Sosa	1.00
85	Jason Bere	.05
86	Dennis Martinez	.05
87	Greg Vaughn	.05
88	Roger Clemens	1.25
89	Larry Walker	.05
90	Mark Grace	.05
91	Kenny Lofton	.05
92	Carlos Perez RC	.05
93	Roger Cedeno	.05
94	Scott Ruffcorn	.05
95	Jim Pittsley	.05
96	Andy Pettitte	.20
97	James Baldwin	.05
98	Hideo Nomo RC	1.50
99	Ismael Valdes	.05
100	Armando Benitez	.05
101	Jose Malave	.05
102	Bobby Higginson RC	.25
103	LaTroy Hawkins	.05
104	Russ Davis	.05
105	Shawn Green	.40
106	Joe Vitiello	.05
107	Chipper Jones	1.00
108	Shane Andrews	.05
109	Jose Oliva	.05
110	Ray Durham	.05
111	Jon Nunnally	.05
112	Alex Gonzalez	.05
113	Vaughn Eshelman	.05
114	Marty Cordova	.05
115	Mark Grudzielanek RC	.25
116	Brian Hunter	.05
117	Charles Johnson	.05
118	Alex Rodriguez	2.00
119	David Bell	.05
120	Todd Hollandsworth	.05
121	Joe Randa	.05
122	Derek Jeter	2.50
123	Frank Rodriguez	.05
124	Curtis Goodwin	.05
125	Bill Pulsipher	.05
126	John Mabry	.05
127	Julian Tavarez	.05
128	Edgardo Alfonzo	.05
129	Orlando Miller	.05
130	Juan Acevedo	.05
131	Jeff Cirillo	.05
132	Roberto Petagine	.05
133	Antonio Osuna	.05
134	Michael Tucker	.05
135	Garret Anderson	.05
2131	Cal Ripken Jr. (Consecutive Game Record)	1.00

Mirror Gold

		NM/M
Complete Set (135):		150.00
Common Player:		1.00
Mirror Gold Stars:		5X
(See 1995 Select Certified for checklist and base card values.)		

Future

Carlos Delgado

		NM/M
Complete Set (10):		10.00
Common Player:		.50
1	Chipper Jones	2.00
2	Curtis Goodwin	.50
3	Hideo Nomo	1.00
4	Shawn Green	1.00
5	Ray Durham	.50
6	Todd Hollandsworth	.50
7	Brian Hunter	.50
8	Carlos Delgado	1.00
9	Michael Tucker	.50
10	Alex Rodriguez	4.00

Gold Team

Barry Bonds

		NM/M
Complete Set (12):		40.00
Common Player:		2.00
1	Ken Griffey Jr.	7.50
2	Frank Thomas	4.00
3	Cal Ripken Jr.	10.00
4	Jeff Bagwell	4.00
5	Mike Piazza	7.50
6	Barry Bonds	10.00
7	Matt Williams	2.00
8	Don Mattingly	6.00
9	Will Clark	5.00
10	Tony Gwynn	5.00
11	Kirby Puckett	5.00
12	Jose Canseco	2.50

Potential Unlimited

RAUL MONDESI

		NM/M
Complete Set (20):		35.00
Common Player:		1.00
903s:		2.5X
1	Cliff Floyd	1.00
2	Manny Ramirez	4.50
3	Raul Mondesi	1.00
4	Scott Ruffcorn	1.00
5	Billy Ashley	1.00

6	Alex Gonzalez	1.00
7	Midre Cummings	1.00
8	Charles Johnson	1.00
9	Garret Anderson	1.00
10	Hideo Nomo	2.00
11	Chipper Jones	8.00
12	Curtis Goodwin	1.00
13	Frank Rodriguez	1.00
14	Shawn Green	2.00
15	Ray Durham	1.00
16	Todd Hollandsworth	1.00
17	Brian Hunter	1.00
18	Carlos Delgado	2.00
19	Michael Tucker	1.00
20	Alex Rodriguez	9.00

1996 Select

		NM/M
Complete Set (200):		9.00
Common Player:		.05
Artist's Proofs:		7X
Pack (10):		1.00
Wax Box (24):		16.00
1	Wade Boggs	1.00
2	Shawn Green	.35
3	Andres Galarraga	.05
4	Bill Pulsipher	.05
5	Chuck Knoblauch	.05
6	Ken Griffey Jr.	1.25
7	Greg Maddux	1.00
8	Manny Ramirez	.75
9	Ivan Rodriguez	.65
10	Tim Salmon	.05
11	Frank Thomas	.75
12	Jeff Bagwell	.75
13	Travis Fryman	.05
14	Kenny Lofton	.05
15	Matt Williams	.05
16	Jay Bell	.05
17	Ken Caminiti	.05
18	Ray Lankford	.05
19	Cal Ripken Jr.	2.00
20	Roger Clemens	1.00
21	Carlos Baerga	.05
22	Mike Piazza	1.25
23	Gregg Jefferies	.05
24	Reggie Sanders	.05
25	Rondell White	.05
26	Sammy Sosa	1.00
27	Kevin Appier	.05
28	Kevin Seitzer	.05
29	Gary Sheffield	.40
30	Mike Mussina	.35
31	Mark McGwire	1.50
32	Barry Larkin	.05
33	Marc Newfield	.05
34	Ismael Valdes	.05
35	Marty Cordova	.05
36	Albert Belle	.05
37	Johnny Damon	.35
38	Garret Anderson	.05
39	Cecil Fielder	.05
40	John Mabry	.05
41	Chipper Jones	1.00
42	Omar Vizquel	.05
43	Jose Rijo	.05
44	Charles Johnson	.05
45	Alex Rodriguez	1.50
46	Rico Brogna	.05
47	Joe Carter	.05
48	Mo Vaughn	.05
49	Moises Alou	.05
50	Raul Mondesi	.05
51	Robin Ventura	.05
52	Jim Thome	.60
53	Dave Justice	.05
54	Jeff King	.05
55	Brian Hunter	.05
56	Juan Gonzalez	.40
57	John Olerud	.05
58	Rafael Palmeiro	.65
59	Tony Gwynn	1.00
60	Eddie Murray	.75
61	Jason Isringhausen	.05
62	Dante Bichette	.05
63	Randy Johnson	.75
64	Kirby Puckett	1.00
65	Jim Edmonds	.05
66	David Cone	.05
67	Ozzie Smith	1.00
68	Fred McGriff	.05
69	Darren Daulton	.05
70	Edgar Martinez	.05
71	J.T. Snow	.05
72	Butch Huskey	.05
73	Hideo Nomo	.40
74	Pedro Martinez	.75
75	Jeff Conine	.05
76	Bobby Bonilla	.05
77	Ryan Klesko	.05
78	Bernie Williams	.05
79	Andre Dawson	.25

80	Trevor Hoffman	.05
81	Mark Grace	.05
82	Benji Gil	.05
83	Eric Karros	.05
84	Pete Schourek	.05
85	Edgardo Alfonzo	.05
86	Jay Buhner	.05
87	Vinny Castilla	.05
88	Bret Boone	.05
89	Ray Durham	.05
90	Brian Jordan	.05
91	Jose Canseco	.40
92	Paul O'Neill	.05
93	Chili Davis	.05
94	Tom Glavine	.30
95	Julian Tavarez	.05
96	Derek Bell	.05
97	Will Clark	.05
98	Larry Walker	.05
99	Denny Neagle	.05
100	Alex Fernandez	.05
101	Barry Bonds	2.00
102	Ben McDonald	.05
103	Andy Pettitte	.25
104	Tino Martinez	.05
105	Sterling Hitchcock	.05
106	Royce Clayton	.05
107	Jim Abbott	.05
108	Rickey Henderson	.75
109	Ramon Martinez	.05
110	Paul Molitor	.75
111	Dennis Eckersley	.65
112	Alex Gonzalez	.05
113	Marquis Grissom	.05
114	Greg Vaughn	.05
115	Lance Johnson	.05
116	Todd Stottlemyre	.05
117	Jack McDowell	.05
118	Ruben Sierra	.05
119	Brady Anderson	.05
120	Julio Franco	.05
121	Brooks Kieshnick	.05
122	Roberto Alomar	.20
123	Greg Gagne	.05
124	Wally Joyner	.05
125	John Smoltz	.05
126	John Valentin	.05
127	Russ Davis	.05
128	Joe Vitiello	.05
129	Shawon Dunston	.05
130	Frank Rodriguez	.05
131	Charlie Hayes	.05
132	Andy Benes	.05
133	B.J. Surhoff	.05
134	Dave Nilsson	.05
135	Carlos Delgado	.50
136	Walt Weiss	.05
137	Mike Stanley	.05
138	Greg Colbrunn	.05
139	Mike Kelly	.05
140	Ryne Sandberg	1.00
141	Lee Smith	.05
142	Dennis Martinez	.05
143	Bernard Gilkey	.05
144	Lenny Dykstra	.05
145	Danny Tartabull	.05
146	Dean Palmer	.05
147	Craig Biggio	.05
148	Juan Acevedo	.05
149	Michael Tucker	.05
150	Bobby Higginson	.05
151	Ken Griffey Jr.	.65
152	Frank Thomas	.45
153	Cal Ripken Jr.	1.00
154	Albert Belle	.05
155	Mike Piazza	.65
156	Barry Bonds	1.00
157	Sammy Sosa	.60
158	Mo Vaughn	.05
159	Greg Maddux	.50
160	Jeff Bagwell	.40
161	Derek Jeter	2.00
162	Paul Wilson	.05
163	Chris Snopek	.05
164	Jason Schmidt	.05
165	Jimmy Haynes	.05
166	George Arias	.05
167	Steve Gibralter	.05
168	Bob Wolcott	.05
169	Jason Kendall	.05
170	Gregg Zaun	.05
171	Quinton McCracken	.05
172	Alan Benes	.05
173	Rey Ordonez	.05
174	Ugueth Urbina	.05
175	Osvaldo Fernandez RC	.10
176	Marc Barcelo	.05
177	Sal Fasano	.05
178	Mike Grace RC	.05
179	Chan Ho Park	.05
180	Robert Perez	.05
181	Todd Hollandsworth	.05
182	Wilton Guerrero RC	.05
183	John Wasdin	.05
184	Jim Pittsley	.05
185	LaTroy Hawkins	.05
186	Jay Powell	.05
187	Felipe Crespo	.05
188	Jermaine Dye	.05
189	Bob Abreu	.05
190	Matt Luke RC	.05
191	Richard Hidalgo	.05
192	Karim Garcia	.05
193	Tavo Alvarez	.05
194	Andy Fox RC	.05
195	Terrell Wade	.05
196	Frank Thomas (Checklist)	.40
197	Ken Griffey Jr. (Checklist)	.65
198	Greg Maddux (Checklist)	.50
199	Mike Piazza (Checklist)	.65
200	Cal Ripken Jr. (Checklist)	.75

Artist's Proofs

	NM/M
Complete Set (200):	200.00
Common Player:	1.00
AP Stars:	7X

(See 1996 Select for checklist and base card values.)

Claim to Fame

		NM/M
Complete Set (20):		45.00
Common Player:		.75
1	Cal Ripken Jr.	7.50
2	Greg Maddux	4.50
3	Ken Griffey Jr.	6.00
4	Frank Thomas	3.50
5	Mo Vaughn	.75
6	Albert Belle	.75
7	Jeff Bagwell	3.50
8	Sammy Sosa	4.50
8s	Sammy Sosa (Overprinted "SAMPLE.")	2.50
9	Reggie Sanders	.75
10	Hideo Nomo	2.00
11	Chipper Jones	4.50
12	Mike Piazza	6.00
13	Matt Williams	.75
14	Tony Gwynn	4.50
15	Johnny Damon	1.50
16	Dante Bichette	.75
17	Kirby Puckett	4.50
18	Barry Bonds	7.50
19	Randy Johnson	3.50
20	Eddie Murray	3.50

En Fuego

		NM/M
Complete Set (25):		35.00
Common Player:		.75
1	Ken Griffey Jr.	3.50
2	Frank Thomas	2.00
3	Cal Ripken Jr.	5.00
4	Greg Maddux	3.00
5	Jeff Bagwell	2.00
6	Barry Bonds	5.00
7	Mo Vaughn	.75
8	Albert Belle	3.00
9	Sammy Sosa	3.00
10	Reggie Sanders	.75
11	Mike Piazza	3.50
12	Chipper Jones	3.00
13	Tony Gwynn	3.00
14	Kirby Puckett	3.00
15	Wade Boggs	3.00
16	Dan Patrick	.75
17	Gary Sheffield	1.25
18	Dante Bichette	.75
19	Randy Johnson	2.00
20	Matt Williams	.75
21	Alex Rodriguez	4.00
22	Tim Salmon	.75
23	Johnny Damon	1.25
24	Manny Ramirez	2.00
25	Hideo Nomo	1.25

Team Nucleus

		NM/M
Complete Set (28):		20.00
Common Player:		.50
1	Albert Belle, Manny Ramirez, Carlos Baerga	1.00
2	Ray Lankford, Brian Jordan, Ozzie Smith	1.25
3	Jay Bell, Jeff King, Denny Neagle	.50
4	Dante Bichette, Andres Galarraga, Larry Walker	.75
5	Mark McGwire, Mike Bordick, Terry Steinbach	1.75
6	Bernie Williams, Wade Boggs, David Cone	1.25
7	Joe Carter, Alex Gonzalez, Shawn Green	.50
8	Roger Clemens, Mo Vaughn, Jose Canseco	1.25
9	Ken Griffey Jr., Edgar Martinez, Randy Johnson	1.50
10	Gregg Jefferies, Darren Daulton, Lenny Dykstra	.50
11	Mike Piazza, Raul Mondesi, Hideo Nomo	1.50
12	Greg Maddux, Chipper Jones, Ryan Klesko	1.25
13	Cecil Fielder, Travis Fryman, Phil Nevin	.50
14	Ivan Rodriguez, Will Clark, Juan Gonzalez	1.00
15	Ryne Sandberg, Sammy Sosa, Mark Grace	1.50
16	Gary Sheffield, Charles Johnson, Andre Dawson	.60
17	Johnny Damon, Michael Tucker, Kevin Appier	.65
18	Barry Bonds, Matt Williams, Rod Beck	2.00
19	Kirby Puckett, Chuck Knoblauch, Marty Cordova	1.50
20	Cal Ripken Jr., Bobby Bonilla, Mike Mussina	2.00
21	Jason Isringhausen, Bill Pulsipher, Rico Brogna	.50
22	Tony Gwynn, Ken Caminiti, Marc Newfield	1.25
23	Tim Salmon, Garret Anderson, Jim Edmonds	.50
24	Moises Alou, Rondell White, Cliff Floyd	.50
25	Barry Larkin, Reggie Sanders, Bret Boone	.50
26	Jeff Bagwell, Craig Biggio, Derek Bell	1.00
27	Frank Thomas, Robin Ventura, Alex Fernandez	1.00
28	John Jaha, Greg Vaughn, Kevin Seitzer	.50

1996 Select Certified

		NM/M
Complete Set (144):		20.00
Common Player:		.15
Pack (6):		2.50
Wax Box (20):		40.00
1	Frank Thomas	1.25
2	Tino Martinez	.15
3	Gary Sheffield	.50
4	Kenny Lofton	.15
5	Joe Carter	.15
6	Alex Rodriguez	2.50
7	Chipper Jones	1.50
8	Roger Clemens	1.75
9	Jay Bell	.15
10	Eddie Murray	1.00
11	Will Clark	.15
12	Mike Mussina	.35
13	Hideo Nomo	.50
14	Andres Galarraga	.15
15	Marc Newfield	.15
16	Jason Isringhausen	.15
17	Randy Johnson	1.00
18	Chuck Knoblauch	.15
19	J.T. Snow	.15
20	Mark McGwire	2.50
21	Tony Gwynn	1.50
22	Albert Belle	.15
23	Gregg Jefferies	.15
24	Reggie Sanders	.15
25	Bernie Williams	.15
26	Ray Lankford	.15
27	Johnny Damon	.40
28	Ryne Sandberg	1.50
29	Rondell White	.15
30	Mike Piazza	2.00
31	Barry Bonds	3.00
32	Greg Maddux	1.50
33	Craig Biggio	.15
34	John Valentin	.15
35	Ivan Rodriguez	.75
36	Rico Brogna	.15
37	Tim Salmon	.15
38	Sterling Hitchcock	.15
39	Charles Johnson	.15
40	Travis Fryman	.15
41	Barry Larkin	.15
42	Tom Glavine	.35
43	Marty Cordova	.15
44	Shawn Green	.40
45	Ben McDonald	.15
46	Robin Ventura	.15
47	Ken Griffey Jr.	2.00
48	Orlando Merced	.15
49	Paul O'Neill	.15
50	Ozzie Smith	1.50
51	Manny Ramirez	1.00
52	Ismael Valdes	.15
53	Cal Ripken Jr.	3.00
54	Jeff Bagwell	1.00
55	Greg Vaughn	.15
56	Juan Gonzalez	.50
57	Raul Mondesi	.15
58	Carlos Baerga	.15
59	Sammy Sosa	1.50
60	Mike Kelly	.15
61	Edgar Martinez	.15
62	Kirby Puckett	1.50
63	Cecil Fielder	.15
64	David Cone	.15
65	Moises Alou	.15
66	Fred McGriff	.15
67	Mo Vaughn	.15
68	Edgardo Alfonzo	.15
69	Jim Thome	.75
70	Rickey Henderson	1.00
71	Dante Bichette	.15
72	Lenny Dykstra	.15
73	Benji Gil	.15
74	Wade Boggs	1.50
75	Jim Edmonds	.15
76	Michael Tucker	.15
77	Carlos Delgado	.65
78	Butch Huskey	.15
79	Billy Ashley	.15
80	Dean Palmer	.15
81	Paul Molitor	1.00
82	Ryan Klesko	.15
83	Brian Hunter	.15
84	Jay Buhner	.15
85	Larry Walker	.15
86	Mike Bordick	.15
87	Matt Williams	.15
88	Jack McDowell	.15
89	Hal Morris	.15
90	Brian Jordan	.15
91	Andy Pettitte	.35
92	Melvin Nieves	.15
93	Pedro Martinez	1.00
94	Mark Grace	.15
95	Garret Anderson	.15
96	Andre Dawson	.30
97	Ray Durham	.15
98	Jose Canseco	.50
99	Roberto Alomar	.30
100	Derek Jeter	3.00
101	Alan Benes	.15
102	Karim Garcia	.15
103	Robin Jennings RC	.15
104	Bob Abreu	.15
105	Sal Fasano (Livan Hernandez' name on front.)	.15
106	Steve Gibralter	.15
107	Jermaine Dye	.15
108	Jason Kendall	.15

109	Mike Grace **RC**	.15
110	Jason Schmidt	.15
111	Paul Wilson	.15
112	Rey Ordonez	.15
113	Wilton Guerrero **RC**	.15
114	Brooks Kieschnick	.15
115	George Arias	.15
116	Osvaldo Fernandez **RC**	.15
117	Todd Hollandsworth	.15
118	John Wasdin	.15
119	Eric Owens	.15
120	Chan Ho Park	.15
121	Mark Loretta	.15
122	Richard Hidalgo	.15
123	Jeff Suppan	.15
124	Jim Pittsley	.15
125	LaTroy Hawkins	.15
126	Chris Snopek	.15
127	Justin Thompson	.15
128	Jay Powell	.15
129	Alex Ochoa	.15
130	Felipe Crespo	.15
131	Matt Lawton **RC**	.15
132	Jimmy Haynes	.15
133	Terrell Wade	.15
134	Ruben Rivera	.15
135	Frank Thomas	.55
136	Ken Griffey Jr.	1.00
137	Greg Maddux	.65
138	Mike Piazza	.75
139	Cal Ripken Jr.	1.50
140	Albert Belle	.15
141	Mo Vaughn	.15
142	Chipper Jones	.75
143	Hideo Nomo	.25
144	Ryan Klesko	.15

Artist's Proofs

	NM/M
Complete Set (144):	200.00
Common Player:	1.00
AP Stars:	7X

(See 1996 Select Certified for checklist and base card values.)

Red, Blue

	NM/M
Common Red:	.50
Red Stars:	3X
Common Blue:	2.50
Blue Stars:	10X

(See 1996 Select Certified for checklist and base card values.)

Mirror Red, Blue, Gold

	NM/M
Common Mirror Red:	6.00
Mirror Red Stars:	20X
Common Mirror Blue:	12.00
Mirror Blue Stars:	30X
Common Mirror Gold:	20.00

Mirror Gold Stars:	100X

(See 1996 Select Certified for checklist and base card values.)

Interleague Preview

		NM/M
Complete Set (25):		45.00
Common Card:		.75
Promos:		1X
1	Ken Griffey Jr., Hideo Nomo	3.50
2	Greg Maddux, Mo Vaughn	3.00
3	Frank Thomas, Sammy Sosa	3.00
4	Mike Piazza, Jim Edmonds	3.50
5	Ryan Klesko, Roger Clemens	3.25
6	Derek Jeter, Rey Ordonez	4.50
7	Johnny Damon, Ray Lankford	1.00
8	Manny Ramirez, Reggie Sanders	2.50
9	Barry Bonds, Jay Buhner	4.50
10	Jason Isringhausen, Wade Boggs	3.00
11	David Cone, Chipper Jones	3.00
12	Jeff Bagwell, Will Clark	2.50
13	Tony Gwynn, Randy Johnson	3.00
14	Cal Ripken Jr., Tom Glavine	4.50
15	Kirby Puckett, Alan Benes	3.00
16	Gary Sheffield, Mike Mussina	1.00
17	Raul Mondesi, Tim Salmon	.75
18	Rondell White, Carlos Delgado	1.00
19	Cecil Fielder, Ryne Sandberg	3.00
20	Kenny Lofton, Brian Hunter	.75
21	Paul Wilson, Paul O'Neill	.75
22	Ismael Valdes, Edgar Martinez	.75
23	Matt Williams, Mark McGwire	4.00
24	Albert Belle, Barry Larkin	.75
25	Brady Anderson, Marquis Grissom	.75

Select Few

	NM/M
Complete Set (18):	40.00
Common Player:	1.00

1	Sammy Sosa	3.00
2	Derek Jeter	5.00
3	Ken Griffey Jr.	3.50
4	Albert Belle	1.00
5	Cal Ripken Jr.	5.00
6	Greg Maddux	3.00
7	Frank Thomas	2.50
8	Mo Vaughn	1.00
9	Chipper Jones	3.00
10	Mike Piazza	3.50
11	Ryan Klesko	1.00
12	Hideo Nomo	1.50
13	Alan Benes	1.00
14	Manny Ramirez	2.50
15	Gary Sheffield	2.00
16	Barry Bonds	5.00
17	Matt Williams	1.00
18	Johnny Damon	2.00

1997 Select

		NM/M
Complete Set (200):		30.00
Series 1 (#1-150):		20.00
Common Red Player:		.10
Common Blue Player:		.25
Registered Golds:		2X
Artist's Proofs:		5X
High Series (#151-200):		10.00
Common High Series:		.25
Pack (6):		1.50
Wax Box (24):		25.00
1	Juan Gonzalez/B	2.00
2	Mo Vaughn/B	.25
3	Tony Gwynn	1.50
4	Manny Ramirez/B	2.00
5	Jose Canseco	.50
6	David Cone	.10
7	Chan Ho Park	.10
8	Frank Thomas/B	2.50
9	Todd Hollandsworth	.10
10	Marty Cordova	.10
11	Gary Sheffield/B	.75
12	John Smoltz/B	.25
13	Mark Grudzielanek	.10
14	Sammy Sosa/B	3.00
15	Paul Molitor	1.00
16	Kevin Brown	.10
17	Albert Belle/B	.25
18	Eric Young	.10
19	John Wetteland	.10
20	Ryan Klesko/B	.25
21	Joe Carter	.10
22	Alex Ochoa	.10
23	Greg Maddux/B	3.00
24	Roger Clemens/B	3.00
25	Ivan Rodriguez/B	1.50
26	Barry Bonds/B	5.00
27	Kenny Lofton/B	.25
28	Javy Lopez	.10
29	Hideo Nomo/B	1.00
30	Rusty Greer	.10
31	Rafael Palmeiro	.75
32	Mike Piazza/B	3.50
33	Ryne Sandberg	1.50
34	Wade Boggs	1.50
35	Jim Thome/B	1.50
36	Ken Caminiti/B	.25
37	Mark Grace	.10
38	Brian Jordan/B	.10
39	Craig Biggio	.10
40	Henry Rodriguez	.10
41	Dean Palmer	.10
42	Jason Kendall	.10
43	Bill Pulsipher	.10
44	Tim Salmon/B	.25
45	Marc Newfield	.10
46	Pat Hentgen	.10
47	Ken Griffey Jr./B	4.00
48	Paul Wilson	.10
49	Jay Buhner/B	.25
50	Rickey Henderson	1.00
51	Jeff Bagwell/B	2.00
52	Cecil Fielder	.10
53	Alex Rodriguez/B	4.00
54	John Jaha	.10
55	Brady Anderson/B	.25
56	Andres Galarraga	.10
57	Raul Mondesi	.10
58	Andy Pettitte	.30
59	Roberto Alomar/B	1.00
60	Derek Jeter/B	5.00

61	Charles Johnson	.10
62	Travis Fryman	.10
63	Chipper Jones/B	3.00
64	Edgar Martinez	.10
65	Bobby Bonilla	.10
66	Greg Vaughn	.10
67	Bobby Higginson	.10
68	Garret Anderson	.10
69	Chuck Knoblauch/B	.25
70	Jermaine Dye	.10
71	Cal Ripken Jr./B	5.00
72	Jason Giambi	.60
73	Trey Beamon	.10
74	Shawn Green	.35
75	Mark McGwire/B	4.00
76	Carlos Delgado	.60
77	Jason Isringhausen	.10
78	Randy Johnson/B	2.00
79	Troy Percival/B	.25
80	Ron Gant	.10
81	Ellis Burks	.10
82	Mike Mussina/B	1.00
83	Todd Hundley	.10
84	Jim Edmonds	.10
85	Charles Nagy	.10
86	Dante Bichette/B	.25
87	Mariano Rivera	.20
88	Matt Williams/B	.25
89	Rondell White	.10
90	Steve Finley	.10
91	Alex Fernandez	.10
92	Barry Larkin	.10
93	Tom Goodwin	.10
94	Will Clark	.10
95	Michael Tucker	.10
96	Derek Bell	.10
97	Larry Walker	.10
98	Alan Benes	.10
99	Tom Glavine	.35
100	Darin Erstad/B	.35
101	Andruw Jones/B	2.00
102	Scott Rolen	.65
103	Todd Walker/B	.25
104	Dmitri Young	.10
105	Vladimir Guerrerov	2.00
106	Nomar Garciaparra	1.50
107	Danny Patterson **RC**	.10
108	Karim Garcia	.10
109	Todd Greene	.10
110	Ruben Rivera	.10
111	Raul Casanova	.10
112	Mike Cameron	.10
113	Bartolo Colon	.10
114	Rod Myers **RC**	.10
115	Todd Dunn	.10
116	Torii Hunter	.10
117	Jason Dickson	.10
118	Gene Kingsale **RC**	.10
119	Rafael Medina	.10
120	Raul Ibanez	.10
121	Bobby Henley **RC**	.10
122	Scott Spiezio	.10
123	Bobby Smith **RC**	.10
124	J.J. Johnson	.10
125	Bubba Trammell **RC**	.50
126	Jeff Abbott	.10
127	Neifi Perez	.10
128	Derrek Lee	.65
129	Kevin Brown **RC**	.10
130	Mendy Lopez	.10
131	Kevin Orie	.10
132	Ryan Jones	.10
133	Juan Encarnacion	.10
134	Jose Guillen/B	.25
135	Greg Norton	.10
136	Richie Sexson	.10
137	Jay Payton	.10
138	Bob Abreu	.15
139	Ronnie Belliard **RC**	.10
140	Wilton Guerrero/B	.25
141	Alex Rodriguez /B	2.00
142	Juan Gonzalez/B	.50
143	Ken Caminiti/B	.25
144	Frank Thomas/B	1.25
145	Ken Griffey Jr./B	1.75
146	John Smoltz/B	.25
147	Mike Piazza/B	1.75
148	Derek Jeter/B	3.00
149	Frank Thomas (Checklist)	.75
150	Ken Griffey Jr. (Checklist)	1.00
151	Jose Cruz Jr. **RC**	1.00
152	Moises Alou	.25
153	Hideki Irabu **RC**	.50
154	Glendon Rusch	.25
155	Ron Coomer	.25
156	Jeremi Gonzalez **RC**	.25
157	Fernando Tatis **RC**	.40
158	John Olerud	.25
159	Rickey Henderson	1.00
160	Shannon Stewart	.25
161	Kevin Polcovich	.25
162	Jose Rosado	.25
163	Ray Lankford	.25
164	David Justice	.25
165	Mark Kotsay **RC**	.25
166	Deivi Cruz **RC**	.50
167	Billy Wagner	.25
168	Jacob Cruz	.25
169	Matt Morris	.25
170	Brian Banks	.25
171	Brett Tomko	.25
172	Todd Helton	.75
173	Eric Young	.25
174	Bernie Williams	.25
175	Jeff Fassero	.25

176	Ryan McGuire	.25
177	Darryl Kile	.25
178	Kelvim Escobar RC	.50
179	Dave Nilsson	.25
180	Geronimo Berroa	.25
181	Livan Hernandez	.25
182	Tony Womack RC	.50
183	Deion Sanders	.25
184	Jeff Kent	.25
185	Brian Hunter	.25
186	Jose Malave	.25
187	Steve Woodard RC	.50
188	Brad Radke	.25
189	Todd Dunwoody	.25
190	Joey Hamilton	.25
191	Denny Naegle	.25
192	Bobby Jones	.25
193	Tony Clark	.25
194	Jaret Wright RC	.50
195	Matt Stairs	.25
196	Francisco Cordova	.25
197	Justin Thompson	.25
198	Pokey Reese	.25
199	Garrett Stephenson	.25
200	Carl Everett	.25

Artist's Proofs

	NM/M
Complete Set (150):	450.00
Common Red:	1.25
Red Stars:	5X
Common Blue:	2.50
Blue Stars:	1.5X

(See 1997 Select #1-150 for checklist and base card values.)

Registered Gold

	NM/M
Complete Set (150):	300.00
Common Red Gold:	.75
Common Blue Gold:	1.50

(See 1997 Select #1-150 for checklist and base card values.)

Registered Gold Stars:	2X

Autographs

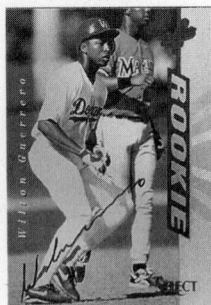

	NM/M
Complete Set (4):	15.00
Common Autograph:	3.00
AU1 Wilton Guerrero	3.00
AU2 Jose Guillen	3.00
AU3 Andruw Jones	10.00
AU4 Todd Walker	3.00

Company

	NM/M
Complete Set (200):	150.00
Common Player:	.50
Red Stars:	3X
Blue Stars:	1.5X
High-Series Stars:	1.5X

Samples:	10X

(See 1997 Select for checklist and base card values.)

Rookie Revolution

ROOKIE REVOLUTION SCOTT ROLEN

		NM/M
Complete Set (20):		21.00
Common Player:		.50
1	Andruw Jones	2.50
2	Derek Jeter	6.00
3	Todd Hollandsworth	.50
4	Edgar Renteria	.50
5	Jason Kendall	.50
6	Rey Ordonez	.50
7	F.P. Santangelo	.50
8	Jermaine Dye	.50
9	Alex Ochoa	.50
10	Vladimir Guerrero	2.50
11	Dmitri Young	.50
12	Todd Walker	.50
13	Scott Rolen	1.50
14	Nomar Garciaparra	3.50
15	Ruben Rivera	.50
16	Darin Erstad	1.00
17	Todd Greene	.50
18	Mariano Rivera	1.00
19	Trey Beamon	.50
20	Karim Garcia	.50

Tools of the Trade

		NM/M
Complete Set (25):		25.00
Common Player:		.40
Mirror Blues:		2.5X
1	Ken Griffey Jr., Andruw Jones	2.00
2	Greg Maddux, Andy Pettitte	1.50
3	Cal Ripken Jr., Chipper Jones	2.50
4	Mike Piazza, Jason Kendall	2.00
5	Albert Belle, Karim Garcia	.40
6	Mo Vaughn, Dmitri Young	.40
7	Juan Gonzalez, Vladimir Guerrero	1.00
8	Tony Gwynn, Jermaine Dye	1.50
9	Barry Bonds, Alex Ochoa	2.50
10	Jeff Bagwell, Jason Giambi	1.00
11	Kenny Lofton, Darin Erstad	.50
12	Gary Sheffield, Manny Ramirez	1.00
13	Tim Salmon, Todd Hollandsworth	.40
14	Sammy Sosa, Ruben Rivera	1.50
15	Paul Molitor, George Arias	1.00
16	Jim Thome, Todd Walker	1.50
17	Wade Boggs, Scott Rolen	1.50
18	Ryne Sandberg, Chuck Knoblauch	1.50
19	Mark McGwire, Frank Thomas	2.25
20	Ivan Rodriguez, Charles Johnson	.75
21	Brian Jordan, Trey Beamon	.40
22	Roger Clemens, Troy Percival	1.75
23	John Smoltz, Mike Mussina	.65
24	Alex Rodriguez, Rey Ordonez	2.25
25	Derek Jeter, Nomar Garciaparra	2.50

1995 SkyBox E-Motion

PRESENCE

		NM/M
Complete Set (200):		15.00
Common Player:		.05
Pack (8):		1.00
Wax Box (36):		20.00
1	Brady Anderson	.05
2	Kevin Brown	.05
3	Curtis Goodwin	.05
4	Jeffrey Hammonds	.05
5	Ben McDonald	.05
6	Mike Mussina	.35
7	Rafael Palmeiro	.65
8	Cal Ripken Jr.	2.00
9	Jose Canseco	.45
10	Roger Clemens	1.00
11	Vaughn Eshelman	.05
12	Mike Greenwell	.05
13	Erik Hanson	.05
14	Tim Naehring	.05
15	Aaron Sele	.05
16	John Valentin	.05
17	Mo Vaughn	.35
18	Chili Davis	.05
19	Gary DiSarcina	.05
20	Chuck Finley	.05
21	Tim Salmon	.05
22	Lee Smith	.05
23	J.T. Snow	.05
24	Jim Abbott	.05
25	Jason Bere	.05
26	Ray Durham	.05
27	Ozzie Guillen	.05
28	Tim Raines	.05
29	Frank Thomas	.75
30	Robin Ventura	.05
31	Carlos Baerga	.05
32	Albert Belle	.05
33	Orel Hershiser	.05
34	Kenny Lofton	.35
35	Dennis Martinez	.05
36	Eddie Murray	.35
37	Manny Ramirez	.75
38	Julian Tavarez	.05
39	Jim Thome	.35
40	Dave Winfield	.75
41	Chad Curtis	.05
42	Cecil Fielder	.05
43	Travis Fryman	.05
44	Kirk Gibson	.05
45	Bob Higginson RC	.25
46	Alan Trammell	.05
47	Lou Whitaker	.05
48	Kevin Appier	.05
49	Gary Gaetti	.05
50	Jeff Montgomery	.05
51	Jon Nunnally	.05
52	Ricky Bones	.05
53	Cal Eldred	.05
54	Joe Oliver	.05
55	Kevin Seitzer	.05
56	Marty Cordova	.05
57	Chuck Knoblauch	.05
58	Kirby Puckett	1.00
59	Wade Boggs	1.00
60	Derek Jeter	2.00
61	Jimmy Key	.05
62	Don Mattingly	1.00
63	Jack McDowell	.05
64	Paul O'Neill	.05
65	Andy Pettitte	.30
66	Ruben Rivera	.05
67	Mike Stanley	.05
68	John Wetteland	.05
69	Geronimo Berroa	.05
70	Dennis Eckersley	.65
71	Rickey Henderson	.75
72	Mark McGwire	1.50
73	Steve Ontiveros	.05
74	Ruben Sierra	.05
75	Terry Steinbach	.05
76	Jay Buhner	.05
77	Ken Griffey Jr.	1.25
78	Randy Johnson	.75
79	Edgar Martinez	.05
80	Tino Martinez	.05
81	Marc Newfield	.05
82	Alex Rodriguez	1.50
83	Will Clark	.05
84	Benji Gil	.05
85	Juan Gonzalez	.40
86	Rusty Greer	.05
87	Dean Palmer	.05
88	Ivan Rodriguez	.65
89	Kenny Rogers	.05
90	Roberto Alomar	.30
91	Joe Carter	.05
92	David Cone	.05
93	Alex Gonzalez	.40
94	Shawn Green	.40
95	Pat Hentgen	.05
96	Paul Molitor	.75
97	John Olerud	.05
98	Devon White	.05
99	Steve Avery	.05
100	Tom Glavine	.35
101	Marquis Grissom	.05
102	Chipper Jones	1.00
103	Dave Justice	.05
104	Ryan Klesko	.05
105	Javier Lopez	.05
106	Greg Maddux	1.00
107	Fred McGriff	.05
108	John Smoltz	.05
109	Shawon Dunston	.05
110	Mark Grace	.05
111	Brian McRae	.05
112	Randy Myers	.05
113	Sammy Sosa	1.00
114	Steve Trachsel	.05
115	Bret Boone	.05
116	Ron Gant	.05
117	Barry Larkin	.05
118	Deion Sanders	.05
119	Reggie Sanders	.05
120	Pete Schourek	.05
121	John Smiley	.05
122	Jason Bates	.05
123	Dante Bichette	.05
124	Vinny Castilla	.05
125	Andres Galarraga	.05
126	Larry Walker	.05
127	Greg Colbrunn	.05
128	Jeff Conine	.05
129	Andre Dawson	.30
130	Chris Hammond	.05
131	Charles Johnson	.05
132	Gary Sheffield	.45
133	Quilvio Veras	.05
134	Jeff Bagwell	.75
135	Derek Bell	.05
136	Craig Biggio	.05
137	Jim Dougherty	.05
138	John Hudek	.05
139	Orlando Miller	.05
140	Phil Plantier	.05
141	Eric Karros	.05
142	Ramon Martinez	.05
143	Raul Mondesi	.05
144	Hideo Nomo RC	2.00
145	Mike Piazza	1.25
146	Ismael Valdes	.05
147	Todd Worrell	.05
148	Moises Alou	.05
149	Yamil Benitez RC	.05
150	Wil Cordero	.05
151	Jeff Fassero	.05
152	Cliff Floyd	.05
153	Pedro Martinez	.75
154	Carlos Perez RC	.05
155	Tony Tarasco	.05
156	Rondell White	.05
157	Edgardo Alfonzo	.05
158	Bobby Bonilla	.05
159	Rico Brogna	.05
160	Bobby Jones	.05
161	Bill Pulsipher	.05
162	Bret Saberhagen	.05
163	Ricky Bottalico	.05
164	Darren Daulton	.05
165	Lenny Dykstra	.05
166	Charlie Hayes	.05
167	Dave Hollins	.05

168	Gregg Jefferies	.05
169	Michael Mimbs **RC**	.05
170	Curt Schilling	.35
171	Heathcliff Slocumb	.05
172	Jay Bell	.05
173	Micah Franklin **RC**	.05
174	Mark Johnson **RC**	.05
175	Jeff King	.05
176	Al Martin	.05
177	Dan Miceli	.05
178	Denny Neagle	.05
179	Bernard Gilkey	.05
180	Ken Hill	.05
181	Brian Jordan	.05
182	Ray Lankford	.05
183	Ozzie Smith	1.00
184	Andy Benes	.05
185	Ken Caminiti	.05
186	Steve Finley	.05
187	Tony Gwynn	1.00
188	Joey Hamilton	.05
189	Melvin Nieves	.05
190	Scott Sanders	.05
191	Rod Beck	.05
192	Barry Bonds	2.00
193	Royce Clayton	.05
194	Glenallen Hill	.05
195	Darren Lewis	.05
196	Mark Portugal	.05
197	Matt Williams	.05
198	Checklist	.05
199	Checklist	.05
200	Checklist	.05

Cal Ripken Jr. Timeless

NM/M

Complete Set (15):		20.00
Common Card:		1.50
1	High School Pitcher	1.50
2	Role Model	1.50
3	Rookie of the Year	1.50
4	1st MVP Season	1.50
5	95 Consecutive Errorless Games	1.50
6	All-Star MVP	1.50
7	Conditioning	1.50
8	Shortstop HR Record	1.50
9	Literacy Work	1.50
10	2000th Consecutive Game	1.50
11	All-Star Selection	2.25
12	Record-tying Game	2.25
13	Record-breaking Game	2.25
14	2,153 and Counting	2.25
15	Birthday	2.25

Masters

NM/M

Complete Set (10):		12.00
Common Player:		.50
1	Barry Bonds	2.50
2	Juan Gonzalez	.65
3	Ken Griffey Jr.	2.00
4	Tony Gwynn	1.50
5	Kenny Lofton	.50
6	Greg Maddux	1.50
7	Raul Mondesi	.50
8	Cal Ripken Jr.	2.50

9	Frank Thomas	1.00
10	Matt Williams	.50

N-Tense

NM/M

Complete Set (12):		16.00
Common Player:		.50
1	Jeff Bagwell	2.00
2	Albert Belle	.50
3	Barry Bonds	4.00
4	Cecil Fielder	.50
5	Ron Gant	.50
6	Ken Griffey Jr.	2.50
7	Mark McGwire	3.00
8	Mike Piazza	2.50
9	Manny Ramirez	2.00
10	Frank Thomas	2.00
11	Mo Vaughn	.50
12	Matt Williams	.50

Rookies

NM/M

Complete Set (10):		6.50
Common Player:		.25
1	Edgardo Alfonzo	.25
2	Jason Bates	.25
3	Marty Cordova	.25
4	Ray Durham	.25
5	Alex Gonzalez	.25
6	Shawn Green	.75
7	Charles Johnson	.25
8	Chipper Jones	1.50
9	Hideo Nomo	1.00
10	Alex Rodriguez	3.00

1996 SkyBox E-Motion XL

NM/M

Complete Set (300):		10.00
Common Player:		.05
Pack (7):		1.00
Wax Box (24):		20.00
1	Roberto Alomar	.15
2	Brady Anderson	.05

3	Bobby Bonilla	.05
4	Jeffrey Hammonds	.05
5	Chris Hoiles	.05
6	Mike Mussina	.30
7	Randy Myers	.05
8	Rafael Palmeiro	.50
9	Cal Ripken Jr.	2.00
10	B.J. Surhoff	.05
11	Jose Canseco	.25
12	Roger Clemens	1.00
13	Wil Cordero	.05
14	Mike Greenwell	.05
15	Dwayne Hosey	.05
16	Tim Naehring	.05
17	Troy O'Leary	.05
18	Mike Stanley	.05
19	John Valentin	.05
20	Mo Vaughn	.05
21	Jim Abbott	.05
22	Garret Anderson	.05
23	George Arias	.05
24	Chili Davis	.05
25	Jim Edmonds	.05
26	Chuck Finley	.05
27	Todd Greene	.05
28	Mark Langston	.05
29	Troy Percival	.05
30	Tim Salmon	.05
31	Lee Smith	.05
32	J.T. Snow	.05
33	Harold Baines	.05
34	Jason Bere	.05
35	Ray Durham	.05
36	Alex Fernandez	.05
37	Ozzie Guillen	.05
38	Darren Lewis	.05
39	Lyle Mouton	.05
40	Tony Phillips	.05
41	Danny Tartabull	.05
42	Frank Thomas	.60
43	Robin Ventura	.05
44	Sandy Alomar	.05
45	Carlos Baerga	.05
46	Albert Belle	.05
47	Julio Franco	.05
48	Orel Hershiser	.05
49	Kenny Lofton	.05
50	Dennis Martinez	.05
51	Jack McDowell	.05
52	Jose Mesa	.05
53	Eddie Murray	.60
54	Charles Nagy	.05
55	Manny Ramirez	.60
55p	Manny Ramirez/OPS	.60
56	Jim Thome	.45
57	Omar Vizquel	.05
58	Chad Curtis	.05
59	Cecil Fielder	.05
60	Travis Fryman	.05
61	Chris Gomez	.05
62	Felipe Lira	.05
63	Alan Trammell	.05
64	Kevin Appier	.05
65	Johnny Damon	.35
66	Tom Goodwin	.05
67	Mark Gubicza	.05
68	Jeff Montgomery	.05
69	Jon Nunnally	.05
70	Bip Roberts	.05
71	Ricky Bones	.05
72	Chuck Carr	.05
73	John Jaha	.05
74	Ben McDonald	.05
75	Matt Mieske	.05
76	Dave Nilsson	.05
77	Kevin Seitzer	.05
78	Greg Vaughn	.05
79	Rick Aguilera	.05
80	Marty Cordova	.05
81	Roberto Kelly	.05
82	Chuck Knoblauch	.05
83	Pat Meares	.05
84	Paul Molitor	.60
85	Kirby Puckett	.75
86	Brad Radke	.05
87	Wade Boggs	.75
88	David Cone	.05
89	Dwight Gooden	.05
90	Derek Jeter	2.00
91	Tino Martinez	.05
92	Paul O'Neill	.05
93	Andy Pettitte	.15
94	Tim Raines	.05
95	Ruben Rivera	.05
96	Kenny Rogers	.05
97	Ruben Sierra	.05
98	John Wetteland	.05
99	Bernie Williams	.05
100	Allen Battle	.05
101	Geronimo Berroa	.05
102	Brent Gates	.05
103	Doug Johns	.05
104	Mark McGwire	1.50
105	Pedro Munoz	.05
106	Ariel Prieto	.05
107	Terry Steinbach	.05
108	Todd Van Poppel	.05
109	Chris Bosio	.05
110	Jay Buhner	.05
111	Joey Cora	.05
112	Russ Davis	.05
113	Ken Griffey Jr.	1.25
114	Sterling Hitchcock	.05
115	Randy Johnson	.60
116	Edgar Martinez	.05

117	Alex Rodriguez	1.50
118	Paul Sorrento	.05
119	Dan Wilson	.05
120	Will Clark	.05
121	Juan Gonzalez	.30
122	Rusty Greer	.05
123	Kevin Gross	.05
124	Ken Hill	.05
125	Dean Palmer	.05
126	Roger Pavlik	.05
127	Ivan Rodriguez	.50
128	Mickey Tettleton	.05
129	Joe Carter	.05
130	Carlos Delgado	.40
131	Alex Gonzalez	.05
132	Shawn Green	.25
133	Erik Hanson	.05
134	Pat Hentgen	.05
135	Otis Nixon	.05
136	John Olerud	.05
137	Ed Sprague	.05
138	Steve Avery	.05
139	Jermaine Dye	.05
140	Tom Glavine	.35
141	Marquis Grissom	.05
142	Chipper Jones	.75
143	David Justice	.05
144	Ryan Klesko	.05
145	Javier Lopez	.05
146	Greg Maddux	.75
147	Fred McGriff	.05
148	Jason Schmidt	.05
149	John Smoltz	.05
150	Mark Wohlers	.05
151	Jim Bullinger	.05
152	Frank Castillo	.05
153	Kevin Foster	.05
154	Luis Gonzalez	.05
155	Mark Grace	.05
156	Brian McRae	.05
157	Jaime Navarro	.05
158	Rey Sanchez	.05
159	Ryne Sandberg	.75
160	Sammy Sosa	.75
161	Bret Boone	.05
162	Jeff Brantley	.05
163	Vince Coleman	.05
164	Steve Gibralter	.05
165	Barry Larkin	.05
166	Hal Morris	.05
167	Mark Portugal	.05
168	Reggie Sanders	.05
169	Pete Schourek	.05
170	John Smiley	.05
171	Jason Bates	.05
172	Dante Bichette	.05
173	Ellis Burks	.05
174	Vinny Castilla	.05
175	Andres Galarraga	.05
176	Kevin Ritz	.05
177	Bill Swift	.05
178	Larry Walker	.05
179	Walt Weiss	.05
180	Eric Young	.05
181	Kurt Abbott	.05
182	Kevin Brown	.05
183	John Burkett	.05
184	Greg Colbrunn	.05
185	Jeff Conine	.05
186	Chris Hammond	.05
187	Charles Johnson	.05
188	Terry Pendleton	.05
189	Pat Rapp	.05
190	Gary Sheffield	.25
191	Quilvio Veras	.05
192	Devon White	.05
193	Jeff Bagwell	.60
194	Derek Bell	.05
195	Sean Berry	.05
196	Craig Biggio	.05
197	Doug Drabek	.05
198	Tony Eusebio	.05
199	Mike Hampton	.05
200	Brian Hunter	.05
201	Derrick May	.05
202	Orlando Miller	.05
203	Shane Reynolds	.05
204	Mike Blowers	.05
205	Tom Candiotti	.05
206	Delino DeShields	.05
207	Greg Gagne	.05
208	Karim Garcia	.05
209	Todd Hollandsworth	.05
210	Eric Karros	.05
211	Ramon Martinez	.05
212	Raul Mondesi	.05
213	Hideo Nomo	.30
214	Chan Ho Park	.05
215	Mike Piazza	1.25
216	Ismael Valdes	.05
217	Todd Worrell	.05
218	Moises Alou	.05
219	Yamil Benitez	.05
220	Jeff Fassero	.05
221	Darrin Fletcher	.05
222	Cliff Floyd	.05
223	Pedro Martinez	.60
224	Carlos Perez	.05
225	Mel Rojas	.05
226	David Segui	.05
227	Rondell White	.05
228	Rico Brogna	.05
229	Carl Everett	.05
230	John Franco	.05
231	Bernard Gilkey	.05

232	Todd Hundley	.05
233	Jason Isringhausen	.05
234	Lance Johnson	.05
235	Bobby Jones	.05
236	Jeff Kent	.05
237	Rey Ordonez	.05
238	Bill Pulsipher	.05
239	Jose Vizcaino	.05
240	Paul Wilson	.05
241	Ricky Bottalico	.05
242	Darren Daulton	.05
243	Lenny Dykstra	.05
244	Jim Eisenreich	.05
245	Sid Fernandez	.05
246	Gregg Jefferies	.05
247	Mickey Morandini	.05
248	Benito Santiago	.05
249	Curt Schilling	.35
250	Mark Whiten	.05
251	Todd Zeile	.05
252	Jay Bell	.05
253	Carlos Garcia	.05
254	Charlie Hayes	.05
255	Jason Kendall	.05
256	Jeff King	.05
257	Al Martin	.05
258	Orlando Merced	.05
259	Dan Miceli	.05
260	Denny Neagle	.05
261	Alan Benes	.05
262	Andy Benes	.05
263	Royce Clayton	.05
264	Dennis Eckersley	.50
265	Gary Gaetti	.05
266	Ron Gant	.05
267	Brian Jordan	.05
268	Ray Lankford	.05
269	John Mabry	.05
270	Tom Pagnozzi	.05
271	Ozzie Smith	.75
272	Todd Stottlemyre	.05
273	Andy Ashby	.05
274	Brad Ausmus	.05
275	Ken Caminiti	.05
276	Steve Finley	.05
277	Tony Gwynn	.75
278	Joey Hamilton	.05
279	Rickey Henderson	.60
280	Trevor Hoffman	.05
281	Wally Joyner	.05
282	Jody Reed	.05
283	Bob Tewksbury	.05
284	Fernando Valenzuela	.05
285	Rod Beck	.05
286	Barry Bonds	2.00
287	Mark Carreon	.05
288	Shawon Dunston	.05
289	Osvaldo Fernandez RC	.10
290	Glenallen Hill	.05
291	Stan Javier	.05
292	Mark Leiter	.05
293	Kirt Manwaring	.05
294	Robby Thompson	.05
295	William Van Landingham	.05
296	Allen Watson	.05
297	Matt Williams	.05
298	Checklist	.05
299	Checklist	.05
300	Checklist	.05

D-Fense

		NM/M
Complete Set (10):		9.00
Common Player:		.50
1	Roberto Alomar	.65
2	Barry Bonds	3.50
3	Mark Grace	.50
4	Ken Griffey Jr.	2.50
5	Kenny Lofton	.50
6	Greg Maddux	1.50
7	Raul Mondesi	.50
8	Cal Ripken Jr.	3.50
9	Ivan Rodriguez	1.00
10	Matt Williams	.50

Legion of Boom

		NM/M
Complete Set (12):		27.50
Common Player:		2.00
1	Albert Belle	2.00
2	Barry Bonds	6.00

3	Juan Gonzalez	2.50
4	Ken Griffey Jr.	4.00
5	Mark McGwire	5.00
6	Mike Piazza	4.00
7	Manny Ramirez	3.00
8	Tim Salmon	2.00
9	Sammy Sosa	3.50
10	Frank Thomas	3.00
11	Mo Vaughn	2.00
12	Matt Williams	2.00

N-Tense

		NM/M
Complete Set (10):		17.50
Common Player:		.50
1	Albert Belle	.50
2	Barry Bonds	3.50
3	Jose Canseco	1.00
4	Ken Griffey Jr.	3.00
5	Tony Gwynn	2.50
6	Randy Johnson	2.00
7	Greg Maddux	2.50
8	Cal Ripken Jr.	3.50
9	Frank Thomas	2.00
10	Matt Williams	.50

Rare Breed

		NM/M
Complete Set (10):		50.00
Common Player:		3.00
1	Garret Anderson	3.00
2	Marty Cordova	3.00
3	Brian Hunter	3.00
4	Jason Isringhausen	3.00
5	Charles Johnson	3.00
6	Chipper Jones	16.00
7	Raul Mondesi	3.00
8	Hideo Nomo	6.00
9	Manny Ramirez	12.00
10	Rondell White	3.00

1997 SkyBox E-X2000

	NM/M
Complete Set (100):	20.00

Common Player:		.15
Credentials Stars:		6X
Essential Credentials:		10X
Pack (2):		1.25
Wax Box (24):		20.00
1	Jim Edmonds	.15
2	Darin Erstad	.25
3	Eddie Murray	1.00
4	Roberto Alomar	.25
5	Brady Anderson	.15
6	Mike Mussina	.45
7	Rafael Palmeiro	.75
8	Cal Ripken Jr.	3.00
9	Steve Avery	.15
10	Nomar Garciaparra	1.50
11	Mo Vaughn	.15
12	Albert Belle	.15
13	Mike Cameron	.15
14	Ray Durham	.15
15	Frank Thomas	1.00
16	Robin Ventura	.15
17	Manny Ramirez	1.00
18	Jim Thome	.65
19	Matt Williams	.15
20	Tony Clark	.15
21	Travis Fryman	.15
22	Bob Higginson	.15
23	Kevin Appier	.15
24	Johnny Damon	.45
25	Jermaine Dye	.15
26	Jeff Cirillo	.15
27	Ben McDonald	.15
28	Chuck Knoblauch	.15
29	Paul Molitor	1.00
30	Todd Walker	.15
31	Wade Boggs	1.50
32	Cecil Fielder	.15
33	Derek Jeter	3.00
34	Andy Pettitte	.25
35	Ruben Rivera	.15
36	Bernie Williams	.15
37	Jose Canseco	.50
38	Mark McGwire	2.50
39	Jay Buhner	.15
40	Ken Griffey Jr.	2.00
41	Randy Johnson	1.00
42	Edgar Martinez	.15
43	Alex Rodriguez	2.50
44	Dan Wilson	.15
45	Will Clark	.40
46	Juan Gonzalez	.50
47	Ivan Rodriguez	.75
48	Joe Carter	.15
49	Roger Clemens	1.75
50	Juan Guzman	.15
51	Pat Hentgen	.15
52	Tom Glavine	.35
53	Andruw Jones	1.00
54	Chipper Jones	1.50
55	Ryan Klesko	.15
56	Kenny Lofton	.15
57	Greg Maddux	1.50
58	Fred McGriff	.15
59	John Smoltz	.15
60	Mark Wohlers	.15
61	Mark Grace	.15
62	Ryne Sandberg	1.50
63	Sammy Sosa	1.50
64	Barry Larkin	.15
65	Deion Sanders	.15
66	Reggie Sanders	.15
67	Dante Bichette	.15
68	Ellis Burks	.15
69	Andres Galarraga	.15
70	Moises Alou	.15
71	Kevin Brown	.15
72	Cliff Floyd	.15
73	Edgar Renteria	.15
74	Gary Sheffield	.50
75	Bob Abreu	.15
76	Jeff Bagwell	1.00
77	Craig Biggio	.15
78	Todd Hollandsworth	.15
79	Eric Karros	.15
80	Raul Mondesi	.15
81	Hideo Nomo	.50
82	Mike Piazza	2.00
83	Vladimir Guerrero	1.00
84	Henry Rodriguez	.15
85	Todd Hundley	.15
86	Rey Ordonez	.15

87	Alex Ochoa	.15
88	Gregg Jefferies	.15
89	Scott Rolen	.65
90	Jermaine Allensworth	.15
91	Jason Kendall	.15
92	Ken Caminiti	.15
93	Tony Gwynn	1.50
94	Rickey Henderson	1.00
95	Barry Bonds	3.00
96	J.T. Snow	.15
97	Dennis Eckersley	.75
98	Ron Gant	.15
99	Brian Jordan	.15
100	Ray Lankford	.15

Credentials

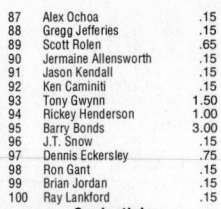

	NM/M
Common Player:	1.00
Credentials Stars:	6X

(See E-X2000 for checklist, base card values)

Essential Credentials

	NM/M
Common Player:	3.00
Essential Credentials Stars:	10X

(See 1997 SkyBox E-X2000 for checklist and base card values.)

A Cut Above

		NM/M
Complete Set (10):		55.00
Common Player:		2.00
1	Frank Thomas	7.50
2	Ken Griffey Jr.	9.00
3	Alex Rodriguez	12.00
4	Albert Belle	2.00
5	Juan Gonzalez	4.00
6	Mark McGwire	10.00
7	Mo Vaughn	2.00
8	Manny Ramirez	7.50
9	Barry Bonds	12.00
10	Fred McGriff	2.00

1997 SkyBox E-X2000
Alex Rodriguez Jumbo

	NM/M
Alex Rodriguez	12.00

Emerald Autographs

	NM/M
Complete Set (6):	75.00
Common Player:	3.00
2 Darin Erstad	12.00
30 Todd Walker	5.00
43 Alex Rodriguez	60.00
78 Todd Hollandsworth	3.00
86 Alex Ochoa	3.00
89 Scott Rolen	25.00

Hall or Nothing

	NM/M
Complete Set (20):	55.00
Common Player:	1.00
1 Frank Thomas	2.50
2 Ken Griffey Jr.	5.00
3 Eddie Murray	2.50
4 Cal Ripken Jr.	7.00
5 Ryne Sandberg	4.00
6 Wade Boggs	4.00
7 Roger Clemens	4.50
8 Tony Gwynn	4.00
9 Alex Rodriguez	6.00
10 Mark McGwire	6.00
11 Barry Bonds	7.00
12 Greg Maddux	4.00
13 Juan Gonzalez	1.25
14 Albert Belle	1.00
15 Mike Piazza	5.00
16 Jeff Bagwell	2.50
17 Dennis Eckersley	1.50
18 Mo Vaughn	1.00
19 Roberto Alomar	1.00
20 Kenny Lofton	1.00

Star Date 2000

1998 SkyBox Dugout Axcess

	NM/M
Complete Set (150):	12.00
Common Player:	.05
Inside Axcess Stars:	25X
Production 50 Sets	
Pack (12):	1.00
Wax Box (36):	20.00
1 Travis Lee	.05
2 Matt Williams	.05
3 Andy Benes	.05
4 Chipper Jones	.75
5 Ryan Klesko	.05
6 Greg Maddux	.75
7 Sammy Sosa	.75
8 Henry Rodriguez	.05
9 Mark Grace	.05
10 Barry Larkin	.05
11 Bret Boone	.05
12 Reggie Sanders	.05
13 Vinny Castilla	.05
14 Larry Walker	.05
15 Darryl Kile	.05
16 Charles Johnson	.05
17 Edgar Renteria	.05
18 Gary Sheffield	.40
19 Jeff Bagwell	.65
20 Craig Biggio	.05
21 Moises Alou	.05
22 Mike Piazza	1.00
23 Hideo Nomo	.35
24 Raul Mondesi	.05
25 John Jaha	.05
26 Jeff Cirillo	.05
27 Jeromy Burnitz	.05
28 Mark Grudzielanek	.05
29 Vladimir Guerrero	.65
30 Rondell White	.05
31 Edgardo Alfonzo	.05
32 Rey Ordonez	.05
33 Bernard Gilkey	.05
34 Scott Rolen	.50
35 Curt Schilling	.35
36 Ricky Bottalico	.05
37 Tony Womack	.05
38 Al Martin	.05
39 Jason Kendall	.05
40 Ron Gant	.05
41 Mark McGwire	1.25
42 Ray Lankford	.05
43 Tony Gwynn	.75
44 Ken Caminiti	.05
45 Kevin Brown	.05
46 Barry Bonds	1.50
47 J.T. Snow	.05
48 Shawn Estes	.05
49 Jim Edmonds	.05
50 Tim Salmon	.05
51 Jason Dickson	.05
52 Cal Ripken Jr.	1.50
53 Mike Mussina	.35
54 Roberto Alomar	.20
55 Mo Vaughn	.05
56 Pedro Martinez	.65
57 Nomar Garciaparra	.75
58 Albert Belle	.05
59 Frank Thomas	.65
60 Robin Ventura	.05
61 Jim Thome	.60
62 Sandy Alomar Jr.	.05
63 Jaret Wright	.05
64 Bobby Higginson	.05
65 Tony Clark	.05
66 Justin Thompson	.05
67 Dean Palmer	.05
68 Kevin Appier	.05
69 Johnny Damon	.35
70 Paul Molitor	.65
71 Marty Cordova	.05
72 Brad Radke	.05
73 Derek Jeter	1.50
74 Bernie Williams	.05
75 Andy Pettitte	.25
76 Matt Stairs	.05
77 Ben Grieve	.05
78 Jason Giambi	.50
79 Randy Johnson	.65
80 Ken Griffey Jr.	1.00
81 Alex Rodriguez	1.25
82 Fred McGriff	.05
83 Wade Boggs	.75
84 Wilson Alvarez	.05
85 Juan Gonzalez	.35
86 Ivan Rodriguez	.50
87 Fernando Tatis	.05
88 Roger Clemens	.85
89 Jose Cruz Jr.	.05
90 Shawn Green	.30
91 Jeff Suppan	.05
92 Eli Marrero	.05
93 Mike Lowell **RC**	1.00
94 Ben Grieve	.05
95 Cliff Politte	.05
96 Rolando Arrojo **RC**	.25
97 Mike Caruso	.05
98 Miguel Tejada	.15
99 Rod Myers	.05
100 Juan Encarnacion	.05
101 Enrique Wilson	.05
102 Brian Giles	.05
103 Magglio Ordonez **RC**	1.00
104 Brian Rose	.05
105 Ryan Jackson **RC**	.05
106 Mark Kotsay	.05
107 Desi Relaford	.05
108 A.J. Hinch	.05
109 Eric Milton	.05
110 Ricky Ledee	.05
111 Karim Garcia	.05
112 Derrek Lee	.60
113 Brad Fullmer	.05
114 Travis Lee	.05
115 Greg Norton	.05
116 Rich Butler	.05
117 Masato Yoshii **RC**	.25
118 Paul Konerko	.20
119 Richard Hidalgo	.05
120 Todd Helton	.40
121 Nomar Garciaparra	.60
122 Scott Rolen	.20
123 Cal Ripken Jr.	.75
124 Derek Jeter	.75
125 Mike Piazza	.45
126 Tony Gwynn	.40
127 Mark McGwire	.65
128 Kenny Lofton	.05
129 Greg Maddux	.40
130 Jeff Bagwell	.30
131 Randy Johnson	.30
132 Alex Rodriguez	.65
133 Mo Vaughn	.05
134 Chipper Jones	.40
135 Juan Gonzalez	.15
136 Tony Clark	.05
137 Fred McGriff	.05
138 Roger Clemens	.45
139 Ken Griffey Jr.	.65
140 Ivan Rodriguez	.25
141 Vinny Castilla	.05
142 Livan Hernandez	.05
143 Jose Cruz Jr.	.05
144 Andruw Jones	.30
145 Rafael Palmeiro	.50
146 Chuck Knoblauch	.05
147 Jay Buhner	.05
148 Andres Galarraga	.05
149 Frank Thomas	.35
150 Todd Hundley	.05

Inside Axcess

	NM/M
Common Player:	4.00

Inside Axcess Stars:	25X
(See 1998 SkyBox Dugout Axcess for	
checklist and base card values.)	

Dishwashers

	NM/M
Complete Set (10):	7.00
Common Player:	.50
Inserted 1:8	
D1 Greg Maddux	2.00
D2 Kevin Brown	.50
D3 Pedro Martinez	1.00
D4 Randy Johnson	1.00
D5 Curt Schilling	.75
D6 John Smoltz	.50
D7 Darryl Kile	.50
D8 Roger Clemens	2.25
D9 Andy Pettitte	.60
D10 Mike Mussina	.65

Double Header

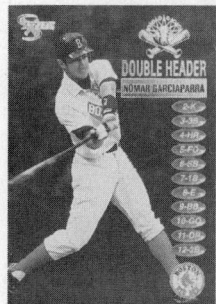

	NM/M
Complete Set (20):	2.00
Common Player:	.05
Inserted 2:1	
DH1 Jeff Bagwell	.15
DH2 Albert Belle	.05
DH3 Barry Bonds	.40
DH4 Derek Jeter	.40
DH5 Tony Clark	.05
DH6 Nomar Garciaparra	.20
DH7 Juan Gonzalez	.10
DH8 Ken Griffey Jr.	.25
DH9 Chipper Jones	.20
DH10 Kenny Lofton	.05
DH11 Mark McGwire	.30
DH12 Mo Vaughn	.05
DH13 Mike Piazza	.25
DH14 Cal Ripken Jr.	.40
DH15 Ivan Rodriguez	.10
DH16 Scott Rolen	.10
DH17 Frank Thomas	.15
DH18 Tony Gwynn	.20
DH19 Travis Lee	.05
DH20 Jose Cruz Jr.	.05

Frequent Flyers

	NM/M
Complete Set (10):	2.50
Common Player:	.25
Inserted 1:4	
FF1 Brian Hunter	.25
FF2 Kenny Lofton	.25
FF3 Chuck Knoblauch	.25

FF4	Tony Womack	.25
FF5	Marquis Grissom	.25
FF6	Craig Biggio	.25
FF7	Barry Bonds	2.00
FF8	Tom Goodwin	.25
FF9	Delino DeShields	.25
FF10	Eric Young	.25

Gronks

		NM/M
Complete Set (10):		30.00
Common Player:		1.50
Inserted 1:72		
G1	Jeff Bagwell	3.50
G2	Albert Belle	1.50
G3	Juan Gonzalez	2.00
G4	Ken Griffey Jr.	6.00
G5	Mark McGwire	7.50
G6	Mike Piazza	6.00
G7	Frank Thomas	3.50
G8	Mo Vaughn	1.50
G9	Ken Caminiti	1.50
G10	Tony Clark	1.50

SuperHeroes

		NM/M
Complete Set (10):		10.00
Common Player:		.50
Inserted 1:20		
SH1	Barry Bonds	3.00
SH2	Andres Galarraga	.50
SH3	Ken Griffey Jr.	1.50
SH4	Chipper Jones	1.00
SH5	Andruw Jones	.75
SH6	Hideo Nomo	.60
SH7	Cal Ripken Jr.	3.00
SH8	Alex Rodriguez	2.00
SH9	Frank Thomas	.75
SH10	Mo Vaughn	.50

1998 SkyBox Dugout Axcess
Todd Helton Autograph

		NM/M
120	Todd Helton	15.00

1998 SkyBox E-X2001

		NM/M
Complete Set (100):		25.00
Common Player:		.15
Pack (2):		1.50
Wax Box (24):		25.00
1	Alex Rodriguez	2.50
2	Barry Bonds	3.00
3	Greg Maddux	1.50
4	Roger Clemens	1.75
5	Juan Gonzalez	1.50
6	Chipper Jones	1.50
7	Derek Jeter	3.00
8	Frank Thomas	1.00
9	Cal Ripken Jr.	3.00
10	Ken Griffey Jr.	2.00
11	Mark McGwire	2.50
12	Hideo Nomo	.50
13	Tony Gwynn	1.50
14	Ivan Rodriguez	.75
15	Mike Piazza	2.00
16	Roberto Alomar	.30
17	Jeff Bagwell	1.00
18	Andruw Jones	1.00
19	Albert Belle	.15
20	Mo Vaughn	.15
21	Kenny Lofton	.15
22	Gary Sheffield	.40
23	Tony Clark	.30
24	Mike Mussina	.30
25	Barry Larkin	.15
26	Moises Alou	.15
27	Brady Anderson	.15
28	Andy Pettitte	.25
29	Sammy Sosa	1.50
30	Raul Mondesi	.15
31	Andres Galarraga	.15
32	Chuck Knoblauch	.15
33	Jim Thome	.65
34	Craig Biggio	.15
35	Jay Buhner	.15
36	Rafael Palmeiro	.75
37	Curt Schilling	.35
38	Tino Martinez	.15
39	Pedro Martinez	1.00
40	Jose Canseco	.50
41	Jeff Cirillo	.15
42	Dean Palmer	.15
43	Tim Salmon	.15
44	Jason Giambi	.50
45	Bobby Higginson	.15
46	Jim Edmonds	.15
47	David Justice	.15
48	John Olerud	.15
49	Ray Lankford	.15
50	Al Martin	.15
51	Mike Lieberthal	.15
52	Henry Rodriguez	.15
53	Edgar Renteria	.15
54	Eric Karros	.15
55	Marquis Grissom	.15
56	Wilson Alvarez	.15
57	Darryl Kile	.15
58	Jeff King	.15
59	Shawn Estes	.15
60	Tony Womack	.15
61	Willie Greene	.15
62	Ken Caminiti	.15
63	Vinny Castilla	.15
64	Mark Grace	.15
65	Ryan Klesko	.15
66	Robin Ventura	.15
67	Todd Hundley	.15
68	Travis Fryman	.15
69	Edgar Martinez	.15
70	Matt Williams	.15
71	Paul Molitor	1.00
72	Kevin Brown	.15
73	Randy Johnson	1.00
74	Bernie Williams	.10
75	Manny Ramirez	1.00
76	Fred McGriff	.15
77	Tom Glavine	.35
78	Carlos Delgado	.60
79	Larry Walker	.15
80	Hideki Irabu	.15
81	Ryan McGuire	.15
82	Justin Thompson	.15
83	Kevin Orie	.15
84	Jon Nunnally	.15
85	Mark Kotsay	.15
86	Todd Walker	.15
87	Jason Dickson	.15
88	Fernando Tatis	.15
89	Karim Garcia	.15
90	Ricky Ledee	.15
91	Paul Konerko	.25
92	Jaret Wright	.15
93	Darin Erstad	.30
94	Livan Hernandez	.15
95	Nomar Garciaparra	1.50
96	Jose Cruz Jr.	.15
97	Scott Rolen	.65
98	Ben Grieve	.15
99	Vladimir Guerrero	1.00
100	Travis Lee	.15

Essential Credentials Now

		NM/M
Common Player:		5.00
21	Kenny Lofton/21	10.00
22	Gary Sheffield/22	20.00
23	Tony Clark/23	10.00
24	Mike Mussina/24	30.00
25	Barry Larkin/25	10.00
26	Moises Alou/26	10.00
27	Brady Anderson/27	10.00
28	Andy Pettitte/28	15.00
29	Sammy Sosa/29	30.00
30	Raul Mondesi/30	10.00
31	Andres Galarraga/31	10.00
32	Chuck Knoblauch/32	10.00
33	Jim Thome/33	25.00
34	Craig Biggio/34	10.00
35	Jay Buhner/35	10.00
36	Rafael Palmeiro/36	25.00
37	Curt Schilling/37	20.00
38	Tino Martinez/38	10.00
39	Pedro Martinez/39	30.00
40	Jose Canseco/40	20.00
41	Jeff Cirillo/41	5.00
42	Dean Palmer/42	5.00
43	Tim Salmon/43	5.00
44	Jason Giambi/44	15.00
45	Bobby Higginson/45	5.00
46	Jim Edmonds/46	5.00
47	David Justice/47	5.00
48	John Olerud/48	5.00
49	Ray Lankford/49	5.00
50	Al Martin/50	5.00
51	Mike Lieberthal/51	5.00
52	Henry Rodriguez/52	5.00
53	Edgar Renteria/53	5.00
54	Eric Karros/54	5.00
55	Marquis Grissom/55	5.00
56	Wilson Alvarez/56	5.00
57	Darryl Kile/57	5.00
58	Jeff King/58	5.00
59	Shawn Estes/59	5.00
60	Tony Womack/60	5.00
61	Willie Greene/61	5.00
62	Ken Caminiti/62	5.00
63	Vinny Castilla/63	5.00
64	Mark Grace/64	5.00
65	Ryan Klesko/65	5.00
66	Robin Ventura/66	5.00
67	Todd Hundley/67	5.00
68	Travis Fryman/68	5.00
69	Edgar Martinez/69	5.00
70	Matt Williams/70	5.00
71	Paul Molitor/71	15.00
72	Kevin Brown/72	5.00
73	Randy Johnson/73	20.00
74	Bernie Williams/74	5.00
75	Manny Ramirez/75	20.00
76	Fred McGriff/76	5.00
77	Tom Glavine/77	12.00
78	Carlos Delgado/78	10.00
79	Larry Walker/79	5.00
80	Hideki Irabu/80	5.00
81	Ryan McGuire/81	5.00
82	Justin Thompson/82	5.00
83	Kevin Orie/83	5.00
84	Jon Nunnally/84	5.00
85	Mark Kotsay/85	5.00
86	Todd Walker/86	5.00
87	Jason Dickson/87	5.00
88	Fernando Tatis/88	5.00
89	Karim Garcia/89	5.00
90	Ricky Ledee/90	5.00
91	Paul Konerko/91	7.50
92	Jaret Wright/92	5.00
93	Darin Erstad/93	5.00
94	Livan Hernandez/94	5.00
95	Nomar Garciaparra/95	20.00
96	Jose Cruz Jr./96	5.00
97	Scott Rolen/97	10.00
98	Ben Grieve/98	5.00
99	Vladimir Guerrero/99	12.00
100	Travis Lee/100	5.00

Essential Credentials Future

		NM/M
Common Player:		5.00
1	Alex Rodriguez/100	55.00
2	Barry Bonds/99	60.00
3	Greg Maddux/98	40.00
4	Roger Clemens/97	45.00
5	Juan Gonzalez/96	15.00
6	Chipper Jones/95	40.00
7	Derek Jeter/94	55.00
8	Frank Thomas/93	35.00
9	Cal Ripken Jr./92	65.00
10	Ken Griffey Jr./91	45.00
11	Mark McGwire/90	55.00

12	Hideo Nomo/89	15.00
13	Tony Gwynn/88	25.00
14	Ivan Rodriguez/87	25.00
15	Mike Piazza/86	40.00
16	Roberto Alomar/85	15.00
17	Jeff Bagwell/84	25.00
18	Andruw Jones/83	25.00
19	Albert Belle/82	5.00
20	Mo Vaughn/81	5.00
21	Kenny Lofton/80	5.00
22	Gary Sheffield/79	12.00
23	Tony Clark/78	5.00
24	Mike Mussina/77	25.00
25	Barry Larkin/76	5.00
26	Moises Alou/75	5.00
27	Brady Anderson/74	5.00
28	Andy Pettitte/73	7.50
29	Sammy Sosa/72	40.00
30	Raul Mondesi/71	6.00
31	Andres Galarraga/70	6.00
32	Chuck Knoblauch/69	6.00
33	Jim Thome/68	20.00
34	Craig Biggio/67	6.00
35	Jay Buhner/66	6.00
36	Rafael Palmeiro/65	30.00
37	Curt Schilling/64	20.00
38	Tino Martinez/63	6.00
39	Pedro Martinez/62	32.50
40	Jose Canseco/61	30.00
41	Jeff Cirillo/60	6.00
42	Dean Palmer/59	6.00
43	Tim Salmon/58	7.50
44	Jason Giambi/57	25.00
45	Bobby Higginson/56	6.00
46	Jim Edmonds/55	6.00
47	David Justice/54	6.00
48	John Olerud/53	6.00
49	Ray Lankford/52	6.00
50	Al Martin/51	6.00
51	Mike Lieberthal/50	6.00
52	Henry Rodriguez/49	6.00
53	Edgar Renteria/48	6.00
54	Eric Karros/47	6.00
55	Marquis Grissom/46	6.00
56	Wilson Alvarez/45	6.00
57	Darryl Kile/44	6.00
58	Jeff King/43	6.00
59	Shawn Estes/42	6.00
60	Tony Womack/41	6.00
61	Willie Greene/40	6.00
62	Ken Caminiti/39	6.00
63	Vinny Castilla/38	6.00
64	Mark Grace/37	6.00
65	Ryan Klesko/36	6.00
66	Robin Ventura/35	6.00
67	Todd Hundley/34	6.00
68	Travis Fryman/33	6.00
69	Edgar Martinez/32	7.50
70	Matt Williams/31	7.50
71	Paul Molitor/30	45.00
72	Kevin Brown/29	7.50
73	Randy Johnson/28	40.00
74	Bernie Williams/27	21.00
75	Manny Ramirez/26	45.00
76	Fred McGriff/25	20.00
77	Tom Glavine/24	35.00
78	Carlos Delgado/23	35.00
79	Larry Walker/22	9.00
80	Hideki Irabu/21	9.00
81	Ryan McGuire/20	9.00
82	Justin Thompson/19	9.00
83	Kevin Orie/18	9.00
84	Jon Nunnally/17	9.00
85	Mark Kotsay/16	9.00

Cheap Seat Treats

		NM/M
Complete Set (20):		30.00
Common Player:		1.00
Inserted 1:24		
1	Frank Thomas	2.00
2	Ken Griffey Jr.	3.00
3	Mark McGwire	4.00
4	Tino Martinez	1.00
5	Larry Walker	1.00
6	Juan Gonzalez	1.50
7	Mike Piazza	3.00
8	Jeff Bagwell	2.00
9	Tony Clark	1.00
10	Albert Belle	1.00
11	Andres Galarraga	1.00

12	Jim Thome	1.50
13	Mo Vaughn	1.00
14	Barry Bonds	5.00
15	Vladimir Guerrero	2.00
16	Scott Rolen	1.25
17	Travis Lee	1.00
18	David Justice	1.00
19	Jose Cruz Jr.	1.00
20	Andruw Jones	2.00

Destination: Cooperstown

		NM/M
Complete Set (15):		375.00
Common Player:		8.00
Inserted 1:720		
1	Alex Rodriguez	40.00
2	Frank Thomas	20.00
3	Cal Ripken Jr.	50.00
4	Roger Clemens	30.00
5	Greg Maddux	25.00
6	Chipper Jones	25.00
7	Ken Griffey Jr.	35.00
8	Mark McGwire	40.00
9	Tony Gwynn	25.00
10	Mike Piazza	35.00
11	Jeff Bagwell	20.00
12	Jose Cruz Jr.	8.00
13	Derek Jeter	50.00
14	Hideo Nomo	10.00
15	Ivan Rodriguez	15.00

Kerry Wood

		NM/M
Complete Set (2):		2.00
---	Kerry Wood (Cardboard trade card.)	1.00
101	Kerry Wood (Plastic redemption card.)	4.00

Signature 2001

	NM/M
Complete Set (17):	100.00

Common Player:		3.00
Inserted 1:60		
1	Ricky Ledee	3.00
2	Derrick Gibson	3.00
3	Mark Kotsay	3.00
4	Kevin Millwood	10.00
5	Brad Fullmer	3.00
6	Todd Walker	4.00
7	Ben Grieve	4.00
8	Tony Clark	3.00
9	Jaret Wright	4.00
10	Randall Simon	3.00
11	Paul Konerko	15.00
12	Todd Helton	15.00
13	David Ortiz	30.00
14	Alex Gonzalez	4.00
15	Bobby Estalella	3.00
16	Alex Rodriguez	50.00
17	Mike Lowell	10.00

Star Date 2001

		NM/M
Complete Set (15):		5.00
Common Player:		.25
Inserted 1:12		
1	Travis Lee	.25
2	Jose Cruz Jr.	.25
3	Paul Konerko	1.00
4	Bobby Estalella	1.00
5	Magglio Ordonez	.25
6	Juan Encarnacion	.25
7	Richard Hidalgo	.25
8	Abraham Nunez	.25
9	Sean Casey	.50
10	Todd Helton	1.50
11	Brad Fullmer	.25
12	Ben Grieve	.25
13	Livan Hernandez	.25
14	Jaret Wright	.25
15	Todd Dunwoody	.25

1999 SkyBox E-X Century

		NM/M
Complete Set (120):		35.00
Common Player:		.15
Common SP (91-120):		.60
Inserted 1:2		
Pack (3):		3.00
Wax Box (18):		40.00
1	Scott Rolen	.75
2	Nomar Garciaparra	1.50
3	Mike Piazza	2.00
4	Tony Gwynn	1.50
5	Sammy Sosa	1.50
6	Alex Rodriguez	2.50
7	Vladimir Guerrero	1.00
8	Chipper Jones	1.50
9	Derek Jeter	3.00
10	Kerry Wood	.50
11	Juan Gonzalez	.50
12	Frank Thomas	1.00
13	Mo Vaughn	.15
14	Greg Maddux	1.50
15	Jeff Bagwell	1.00
16	Mark McGwire	2.50
17	Ken Griffey Jr.	2.00
18	Roger Clemens	1.75
19	Cal Ripken Jr.	3.00
20	Travis Lee	.15
21	Todd Helton	.75
22	Darin Erstad	.30
23	Pedro Martinez	1.00
24	Barry Bonds	3.00
25	Andruw Jones	1.00
26	Larry Walker	.15
27	Albert Belle	.15
28	Ivan Rodriguez	.75
29	Magglio Ordonez	.25
30	Andres Galarraga	.15
31	Mike Mussina	.35
32	Randy Johnson	1.00
33	Tom Glavine	.35
34	Barry Larkin	.15
35	Jim Thome	.75
36	Gary Sheffield	.45
37	Bernie Williams	.15
38	Carlos Delgado	.60
39	Rafael Palmeiro	.75
40	Edgar Renteria	.15
41	Brad Fullmer	.15
42	David Wells	.15
43	Dante Bichette	.15
44	Jaret Wright	.15
45	Ricky Ledee	.15
46	Ray Lankford	.15
47	Mark Grace	.15
48	Jeff Cirillo	.15
49	Rondell White	.15
50	Jeromy Burnitz	.15
51	Sean Casey	.25
52	Rolando Arrojo	.15
53	Jason Giambi	.65
54	John Olerud	.15
55	Will Clark	.15
56	Raul Mondesi	.15
57	Scott Brosius	.15
58	Bartolo Colon	.15
59	Steve Finley	.15
60	Javy Lopez	.15
61	Tim Salmon	.15
62	Roberto Alomar	.30
63	Vinny Castilla	.15
64	Craig Biggio	.15
65	Jose Guillen	.15
66	Greg Vaughn	.15
67	Jose Canseco	.40
68	Shawn Green	.50
69	Curt Schilling	.35
70	Orlando Hernandez	.15
71	Jose Cruz Jr.	.15
72	Alex Gonzalez	.15
73	Tino Martinez	.15
74	Todd Hundley	.15
75	Brian Giles	.15
76	Cliff Floyd	.15
77	Paul O'Neill	.15
78	Ken Caminiti	.15
79	Ron Gant	.15
80	Juan Encarnacion	.15
81	Ben Grieve	.15
82	Brian Jordan	.15
83	Rickey Henderson	1.00
84	Tony Clark	.15
85	Shannon Stewart	.15
86	Robin Ventura	.15
87	Todd Walker	.15
88	Kevin Brown	.15
89	Moises Alou	.15
90	Manny Ramirez	1.00
91	Gabe Alvarez	.60
92	Jeremy Giambi	.60
93	Adrian Beltre	.75
94	George Lombard	.60
95	Ryan Minor	.60
96	Kevin Witt	.60
97	Scott Hunter RC	.60
98	Carlos Guillen	.60
99	Derrick Gibson	.60
100	Trot Nixon	.75
101	Troy Glaus	3.00
102	Armando Rios	.60
103	Preston Wilson	.60
104	Pat Burrell RC	3.00
105	J.D. Drew	1.50
106	Bruce Chen	.60
107	Matt Clement	.60
108	Carlos Beltran	1.50
109	Carlos Febles	.60
110	Rob Fick	.60
111	Russell Branyan	.60
112	Roosevelt Brown RC	.60
113	Corey Koskie	.60
114	Mario Encarnacion	.60
115	Peter Tucci RC	.60
116	Eric Chavez	.75
117	Gabe Kapler	.60
118	Marlon Anderson	.60
119	A.J. Burnett RC	.75
120	Ryan Anderson	.60
---	Checklist 1-96	.05
---	Checklist 97-120/Inserts	.05

Essential Credentials Future

		NM/M
Common Player:		5.00
1	Scott Rolen/120	10.00
2	Nomar Garciaparra/119	15.00
3	Mike Piazza/118	25.00
4	Tony Gwynn/117	20.00
5	Sammy Sosa/116	15.00
6	Alex Rodriguez/115	40.00
7	Vladimir Guerrero/114	15.00
8	Chipper Jones/113	20.00
9	Derek Jeter/112	50.00
10	Kerry Wood/111	10.00
11	Juan Gonzalez/110	10.00
12	Frank Thomas/109	25.00
13	Mo Vaughn/108	5.00
14	Greg Maddux/107	25.00
15	Jeff Bagwell/106	15.00
16	Mark McGwire/105	25.00
17	Ken Griffey Jr./104	25.00
18	Roger Clemens/103	15.00
19	Cal Ripken Jr./102	40.00
20	Travis Lee/101	5.00
21	Todd Helton/100	15.00
22	Darin Erstad/99	5.00
23	Pedro Martinez/98	15.00
24	Barry Bonds/97	40.00
25	Andruw Jones/96	10.00
26	Larry Walker/95	5.00
27	Albert Belle/94	5.00
28	Ivan Rodriguez/93	15.00
29	Magglio Ordonez/92	10.00
30	Andres Galarraga/91	5.00
31	Mike Mussina/90	10.00
32	Randy Johnson/89	20.00
33	Tom Glavine/88	15.00
34	Barry Larkin/87	8.00
35	Jim Thome/86	15.00
36	Gary Sheffield/85	15.00
37	Bernie Williams/84	5.00
38	Carlos Delgado/83	15.00
39	Rafael Palmeiro/82	10.00
40	Edgar Renteria/81	5.00
41	Brad Fullmer/80	5.00
42	David Wells/79	5.00
43	Dante Bichette/78	5.00
44	Jaret Wright/77	5.00
45	Ricky Ledee/76	5.00
46	Ray Lankford/75	5.00
47	Mark Grace/74	8.00
48	Jeff Cirillo/73	5.00
49	Rondell White/72	5.00
50	Jeromy Burnitz/71	5.00
51	Sean Casey/70	5.00
52	Rolando Arrojo/69	5.00
53	Jason Giambi/68	10.00
54	John Olerud/67	5.00
55	Will Clark/66	8.00
56	Raul Mondesi/65	5.00
57	Scott Brosius/64	5.00
58	Bartolo Colon/63	5.00
59	Steve Finley/62	5.00
60	Javy Lopez/61	5.00
61	Tim Salmon/60	5.00
62	Roberto Alomar/59	10.00
63	Vinny Castilla/58	5.00
64	Craig Biggio/57	8.00
65	Jose Guillen/56	5.00
66	Greg Vaughn/55	5.00
67	Jose Canseco/54	10.00
68	Shawn Green/53	5.00
69	Curt Schilling/52	15.00
70	Orlando Hernandez/51	5.00
71	Jose Cruz Jr./50	5.00
72	Alex Gonzalez/49	5.00
73	Tino Martinez/48	8.00
74	Todd Hundley/47	5.00
75	Brian Giles/46	5.00
76	Cliff Floyd/45	5.00
77	Paul O'Neill/44	10.00
78	Ken Caminiti/43	5.00
79	Ron Gant/42	5.00
80	Juan Encarnacion/41	8.00
81	Ben Grieve/40	5.00
82	Brian Jordan/39	5.00
83	Rickey Henderson/38	15.00
84	Tony Clark/37	5.00
85	Shannon Stewart/36	5.00
86	Robin Ventura/35	5.00
87	Todd Walker/34	5.00
88	Kevin Brown/33	5.00

89	Moises Alou/32	10.00
90	Manny Ramirez/31	25.00
91	Gabe Alvarez/30	5.00
92	Jeremy Giambi/29	5.00
93	Adrian Beltre/28	8.00
94	George Lombard/27	5.00
95	Ryan Minor/26	5.00
96	Kevin Witt/25	5.00
97	Scott Hunter/24	5.00
98	Carlos Guillen/23	10.00
99	Derrick Gibson/22	5.00
100	Trot Nixon/21	5.00

Essential Credentials Now

		NM/M
Common Player:		5.00
21	Todd Helton/21	15.00
22	Darin Erstad/22	5.00
23	Pedro Martinez/23	20.00
24	Barry Bonds/24	50.00
25	Andruw Jones/25	10.00
26	Larry Walker/26	8.00
27	Albert Belle/27	5.00
28	Ivan Rodriguez/28	10.00
29	Magglio Ordonez/29	10.00
30	Andres Galarraga/30	5.00
31	Mike Mussina/31	10.00
32	Randy Johnson/32	15.00
33	Tom Glavine/33	10.00
34	Barry Larkin/34	10.00
35	Jim Thome/35	10.00
36	Gary Sheffield/36	10.00
37	Bernie Williams/37	10.00
38	Carlos Delgado/38	10.00
39	Rafael Palmeiro/39	10.00
40	Edgar Renteria/40	10.00
41	Brad Fullmer/41	5.00
42	David Wells/42	5.00
43	Dante Bichette/43	5.00
44	Jaret Wright/44	5.00
45	Ricky Ledee/45	5.00
46	Ray Lankford/46	5.00
47	Mark Grace/47	8.00
48	Jeff Cirillo/48	5.00
49	Rondell White/49	5.00
50	Jeromy Burnitz/50	5.00
51	Sean Casey/51	5.00
52	Rolando Arrojo/52	5.00
53	Jason Giambi/53	10.00
54	John Olerud/54	5.00
55	Will Clark/55	8.00
56	Raul Mondesi/56	5.00
57	Scott Brosius/57	5.00
58	Bartolo Colon/58	5.00
59	Steve Finley/59	5.00
60	Javy Lopez/60	5.00
61	Tim Salmon/61	5.00
62	Roberto Alomar/62	8.00
63	Vinny Castilla/63	5.00
64	Craig Biggio/64	8.00
65	Jose Guillen/65	5.00
66	Greg Vaughn/66	5.00
67	Jose Canseco/67	10.00
68	Shawn Green/68	5.00
69	Curt Schilling/69	15.00
70	Orlando Hernandez/70	5.00
71	Jose Cruz Jr./71	5.00
72	Alex Gonzalez/72	5.00
73	Tino Martinez/73	8.00
74	Todd Hundley/74	5.00
75	Brian Giles/75	5.00
76	Cliff Floyd/76	5.00
77	Paul O'Neill/77	8.00
78	Ken Caminiti/78	5.00
79	Ron Gant/79	5.00
80	Juan Encarnacion/80	5.00
81	Ben Grieve/81	5.00
82	Brian Jordan/82	5.00
83	Rickey Henderson/83	10.00
84	Tony Clark/84	5.00
85	Shannon Stewart/85	5.00
86	Robin Ventura/86	5.00
87	Todd Walker/87	5.00
88	Kevin Brown/88	8.00
89	Moises Alou/89	5.00
90	Manny Ramirez/90	15.00
91	Gabe Alvarez/91	5.00
92	Jeremy Giambi/92	5.00
93	Adrian Beltre/93	5.00
94	George Lombard/94	5.00
95	Ryan Minor/95	5.00

96	Kevin Witt/96	5.00
97	Scott Hunter/97	5.00
98	Carlos Guillen/98	8.00
99	Derrick Gibson/99	5.00
100	Trot Nixon/100	5.00
101	Troy Glaus/101	8.00
102	Armando Rios/102	5.00
103	Preston Wilson/103	5.00
104	Pat Burrell/104	5.00
105	J.D. Drew/105	5.00
106	Bruce Chen/106	5.00
107	Matt Clement/107	5.00
108	Carlos Beltran/108	10.00
109	Carlos Febles/109	5.00
110	Rob Fick/110	5.00
111	Russell Branyan/111	5.00
112	Roosevelt Brown/112	5.00
113	Corey Koskie/113	5.00
114	Mario Encarnacion/114	5.00
115	Peter Tucci/115	5.00
116	Eric Chavez/116	8.00
117	Gabe Kapler/117	5.00
118	Marlon Anderson/118	5.00
119	A.J. Burnett/119	5.00
120	Ryan Bradley/120	5.00

Authen-Kicks

		NM/M
Common Player:		4.00
(1)	J.D. Drew/160	8.00
(1ab)	J.D. Drew/8 (Autographed black.)	75.00
(1ar)	J.D. Drew/8 (Autographed red.)	75.00
(2)	Travis Lee/175	4.00
(3)	Kevin Millwood/160	6.00
(4)	Bruce Chen/205	4.00
(5)	Troy Glaus/205	10.00
(6)	Todd Helton/205	15.00
(7)	Ricky Ledee/180	4.00
(8)	Scott Rolen/205	15.00
(9)	Jeremy Giambi/205	4.00

E-X Quisite

		NM/M
Complete Set (15):		15.00
Common Player:		.50
Inserted 1:18		
1	Troy Glaus	3.00
2	J.D. Drew	2.00
3	Pat Burrell	2.00
4	Russell Branyan	.50
5	Kerry Wood	1.50
6	Eric Chavez	1.00
7	Ben Grieve	.50
8	Gabe Kapler	.50
9	Adrian Beltre	1.00
10	Todd Helton	4.00
11	Roosevelt Brown	.50
12	Marlon Anderson	.50
13	Jeremy Giambi	.50
14	Magglio Ordonez	1.50
15	Travis Lee	.50

Favorites for Fenway

	NM/M
Complete Set (20):	45.00
Common Player:	1.00
Inserted 1:36	
1	Mo Vaughn	1.00
2	Nomar Garciaparra	2.00
3	Frank Thomas	2.00
4	Ken Griffey Jr.	3.00
5	Roger Clemens	2.50
6	Alex Rodriguez	4.00
7	Derek Jeter	5.00
8	Juan Gonzalez	1.50
9	Cal Ripken Jr.	5.00
10	Ivan Rodriguez	1.50
11	J.D. Drew	1.50
12	Barry Bonds	5.00
13	Tony Gwynn	2.00
14	Vladimir Guerrero	2.00
15	Chipper Jones	2.00
16	Kerry Wood	1.50
17	Mike Piazza	3.00
18	Sammy Sosa	2.00
19	Scott Rolen	1.50
20	Mark McGwire	4.00

Milestones of the Century

		NM/M
Common Player:		5.00
Numbered to featured milestone.		
1	Kerry Wood/20	15.00
2	Mark McGwire/70	20.00
3	Sammy Sosa/66	15.00
4	Ken Griffey Jr./350	15.00
5	Roger Clemens/98	25.00
6	Cal Ripken Jr./17	100.00
7	Alex Rodriguez/40	40.00
8	Barry Bonds/400	25.00
9	N.Y. Yankees/114	15.00
10	Travis Lee/98	5.00

1999 SkyBox Molten Metal

	NM/M
Complete Set (150):	35.00
Common Metalsmiths (1-100):	.15
Inserted 4:1	
Common Heavy Metal (101-130):	.25
Inserted 1:1	
Common Supernatural (131-150):	.50
Inserted 1:2	
Pack (6):	1.00
Wax Box (24):	20.00
1	Larry Walker	.15
2	Jose Canseco	.50
3	Brian Jordan	.15
4	Rafael Palmeiro	.65
5	Edgar Renteria	.15
6	Dante Bichette	.15
7	Mark Kotsay	.15
8	Denny Neagle	.15
9	Ellis Burks	.15
10	Paul O'Neill	.15
11	Miguel Tejada	.30
12	Ken Caminiti	.15
13	David Cone	.15
14	Jason Kendall	.15
15	Ruben Rivera	.15
16	Todd Walker	.15

17	Bobby Higginson	.15
18	Derrek Lee	.60
19	Rondell White	.15
20	Pedro J. Martinez	.75
21	Jeff Kent	.15
22	Randy Johnson	.75
23	Matt Williams	.15
24	Sean Casey	.25
25	Eric Davis	.15
26	Ryan Klesko	.15
27	Curt Schilling	.35
28	Geoff Jenkins	.15
29	Armand Abreu	.15
30	Vinny Castilla	.15
31	Will Clark	.15
32	Ray Durham	.15
33	Ray Lankford	.15
34	Richie Sexson	.15
35	Derrick Gibson	.15
36	Mark Grace	.15
37	Greg Vaughn	.15
38	Bartolo Colon	.15
39	Steve Finley	.15
40	Chuck Knoblauch	.15
41	Ricky Ledee	.15
42	John Smoltz	.15
43	Moises Alou	.15
44	Jim Edmonds	.15
45	Cliff Floyd	.15
46	Javy Lopez	.15
47	Jim Thome	.65
48	J.T. Snow	.15
49	Sandy Alomar Jr.	.15
50	Andy Pettitte	.25
51	Juan Encarnacion	.15
52	Travis Fryman	.15
53	Eli Marrero	.15
54	Jeff Cirillo	.15
55	Brady Anderson	.15
56	Jose Cruz Jr.	.15
57	Edgar Martinez	.15
58	Garret Anderson	.15
59	Paul Konerko	.30
60	Eric Milton	.15
61	Jason Giambi	.45
62	Tom Glavine	.35
63	Justin Thompson	.15
64	Brad Fullmer	.15
65	Marquis Grissom	.15
66	Fernando Tatis	.15
67	Carlos Beltran	.45
68	Charles Johnson	.15
69	Raul Mondesi	.15
70	Richard Hidalgo	.15
71	Barry Larkin	.15
72	David Wells	.15
73	Jay Buhner	.15
74	Matt Clement	.15
75	Eric Karros	.15
76	Carl Pavano	.15
77	Mariano Rivera	.25
78	Livan Hernandez	.15
79	A.J. Hinch	.15
80	Tino Martinez	.15
81	Rusty Greer	.15
82	Jose Guillen	.15
83	Robin Ventura	.15
84	Kevin Brown	.15
85	Chan Ho Park	.15
86	John Olerud	.15
87	Johnny Damon	.35
88	Todd Hundley	.15
89	Fred McGriff	.15
90	Wade Boggs	1.00
91	Mike Cameron	.15
92	Gary Sheffield	.50
93	Rickey Henderson	.75
94	Pat Hentgen	.15
95	Omar Vizquel	.15
96	Craig Biggio	.15
97	Mike Caruso	.15
98	Neifi Perez	.15
99	Mike Mussina	.50
100	Carlos Delgado	.45
101	Andruw Jones	1.00
102	Pat Burrell RC	3.00
103	Orlando Hernandez	.25
104	Darin Erstad	.40
105	Roberto Alomar	.35
106	Tim Salmon	.25
107	Albert Belle	.25
108	Chad Allen RC	.25
109	Travis Lee	.25
110	Jesse Garcia RC	.25
111	Tony Clark	.25
112	Ivan Rodriguez	.75
113	Troy Glaus	1.00
114	A.J. Burnett RC	1.50
115	David Justice	.25
116	Adrian Beltre	.50
117	Eric Chavez	.35
118	Kenny Lofton	.25
119	Michael Barrett	.25
120	Jeff Weaver RC	1.50
121	Manny Ramirez	1.00
122	Barry Bonds	2.00
123	Bernie Williams	.25
124	Freddy Garcia RC	1.50
125	Scott Hunter RC	.25
126	Jeremy Giambi	.25
127	Masao Kida RC	.25
128	Todd Helton	1.00
129	Mike Figga	.25
130	Mo Vaughn	.25
131	J.D. Drew	.65

132	Cal Ripken Jr.	3.00
133	Ken Griffey Jr.	1.50
134	Mark McGwire	2.00
135	Nomar Garciaparra	1.00
136	Greg Maddux	1.00
137	Mike Piazza	1.50
138	Alex Rodriguez	2.00
139	Frank Thomas	.85
140	Juan Gonzalez	.65
141	Tony Gwynn	1.00
142	Derek Jeter	3.00
143	Chipper Jones	1.00
144	Scott Rolen	.65
145	Sammy Sosa	1.00
146	Kerry Wood	.50
147	Roger Clemens	1.25
148	Jeff Bagwell	.75
149	Vladimir Guerrero	.75
150	Ben Grieve	.50

Xplosion

Complete Set (150):	300.00
Common Player:	1.00
Stars:	3X
Inserted 1:2	

(See 1999 SkyBox Molten Metal for checklist and base card values.)

Fusion

Complete Set (50):	100.00
Common Heavy Metal (1-30):	1.00
Inserted 1:12	
Common Supernatural (31-50):	2.50
Inserted 1:24	
Sterling (31-50):	1.5X
Production 500 Sets	
Titanium (31-50):	6X
Production 50 Sets	

1	Andruw Jones	4.00
2	Pat Burrell	2.00
3	Orlando Hernandez	1.00
4	Darin Erstad	1.50
5	Roberto Alomar	1.50
6	Tim Salmon	1.00
7	Albert Belle	1.00
8	Chad Allen	1.00
9	Travis Lee	1.00
10	Jesse Garcia	1.00
11	Tony Clark	1.00
12	Ivan Rodriguez	3.00
13	Troy Glaus	3.00
14	A.J. Burnett	1.00
15	David Justice	1.00
16	Adrian Beltre	1.50
17	Eric Chavez	1.50
18	Kenny Lofton	1.00
19	Michael Barrett	1.00
20	Jeff Weaver	1.00
21	Manny Ramirez	4.00
22	Barry Bonds	10.00
23	Bernie Williams	1.00
24	Freddy Garcia	1.00
25	Scott Hunter	1.00
26	Jeremy Giambi	1.00
27	Masao Kida	1.00
28	Todd Helton	3.00

29	Mike Figga	1.00
30	Mo Vaughn	1.00
31	J.D. Drew	2.00
32	Cal Ripken Jr.	10.00
33	Ken Griffey Jr.	6.00
34	Mark McGwire	7.50
35	Nomar Garciaparra	5.00
36	Greg Maddux	5.00
37	Mike Piazza	6.00
38	Alex Rodriguez	7.50
39	Frank Thomas	4.00
40	Juan Gonzalez	1.50
41	Tony Gwynn	5.00
42	Derek Jeter	10.00
43	Chipper Jones	5.00
44	Scott Rolen	3.00
45	Sammy Sosa	5.00
46	Kerry Wood	2.00
47	Roger Clemens	5.50
48	Jeff Bagwell	4.00
49	Vladimir Guerrero	4.00
50	Ben Grieve	1.00

Fusion - Sterling

	NM/M
Common Player:	1.50
Sterling Stars:	1.5X

(See 1999 Molten Metal Fusion for checklist and base card values.)

Fusion - Titanium

	NM/M
Common Player:	4.00
Titanium Stars:	6X

(See 1999 SkyBox Molten Metal Fusion for checklist and base card values.)

Oh Atlanta!

	NM/M
Complete Set (30):	30.00
Common Player:	.60
Inserted 1:1	

1	Kenny Lofton	.60

2	Kevin Millwood	.60
3	Bret Boone	.60
4	Otis Nixon	.60
5	Vinny Castilla	.60
6	Brian Jordan	.60
7	Chipper Jones	8.00
8	Dave Justice	.60
9	Micah Bowie	.60
10	Fred McGriff	.60
11	Ron Gant	.60
12	Andruw Jones	4.00
13	Kent Mercker	.60
14	Greg McMichael	.60
15	Steve Avery	.60
16	Marquis Grissom	.60
17	Jason Schmidt	.60
18	Ryan Klesko	.60
19	Charlie O'Brien	.60
20	Terry Pendleton	.60
21	Denny Neagle	.60
22	Greg Maddux	8.00
23	Tom Glavine	1.50
24	Javy Lopez	.60
25	John Rocker	.60
26	Walt Weiss	.60
27	John Smoltz	.60
28	Michael Tucker	.60
29	Odalis Perez	.60
30	Andres Galarraga	.60

1999 SkyBox Premium

	NM/M
Complete Set (300):	20.00
Complete Set w/SP's (350):	40.00
Common Player:	.10
Common SP (223-272):	.60
SP's inserted 1:8	
Star Rubies:	50X
Production 50 Sets	
SP Star Rubies:	15X
Production 15 Sets	
Pack (8):	1.50
Wax Box (24):	25.00

1	Alex Rodriguez	2.00
2	Sidney Ponson	.10
3	Shawn Green	.35
4	Dan Wilson	.10
5	Rolando Arrojo	.10
6	Roberto Alomar	.30
7	Matt Anderson	.10
8	David Segui	.10
9	Alex Gonzalez	.10
10	Edgar Renteria	.10
11	Benito Santiago	.10
12	Todd Stottlemyre	.10
13	Rico Brogna	.10
14	Troy Glaus	.65
15	Al Leiter	.10
16	Pedro J. Martinez	.75
17	Paul O'Neill	.10
18	Manny Ramirez	.75
19	Scott Brosius	.65
20	Curt Schilling	.35
21	Bobby Abreu	.15
22	Robb Nen	.10
23	Andy Pettitte	.25
24	John Wetteland	.10
25	Bobby Bonilla	.20
26	Darin Erstad	.20
27	Shawn Estes	.10
28	John Franco	.10
29	Nomar Garciaparra	1.00
30	Rick Helling	.10
31	David Justice	.10
32	Chuck Knoblauch	.10
33	Quinton McCracken	.10
34	Kenny Rogers	.10
35	Brian Giles	.10
36	Armando Benitez	.10
37	Trevor Hoffman	.10
38	Charles Johnson	.10
39	Travis Lee	.10
40	Tom Glavine	.35
41	Rondell White	.10
42	Orlando Hernandez	.10
43	Mickey Morandini	.10
44	Darryl Kile	.10
45	Greg Vaughn	.10
46	Gregg Jefferies	.10
47	Mark McGwire	2.00
48	Kerry Wood	.40

49	Jeromy Burnitz	.10
50	Ron Gant	.10
51	Vinny Castilla	.10
52	Doug Glanville	.10
53	Juan Guzman	.10
54	Dustin Hermanson	.10
55	Jose Hernandez	.10
56	Bob Higginson	.10
57	A.J. Hinch	.10
58	Randy Johnson	.75
59	Eli Marrero	.10
60	Rafael Palmeiro	.65
61	Carl Pavano	.10
62	Brett Tomko	.10
63	Jose Guillen	.10
64	Mike Lieberthal	.10
65	Jim Abbott	.10
66	Dante Bichette	.10
67	Jeff Cirillo	.10
68	Eric Davis	.10
69	Delino DeShields	.10
70	Steve Finley	.10
71	Mark Grace	.10
72	Jason Kendall	.10
73	Jeff Kent	.10
74	Desi Relaford	.10
75	Ivan Rodriguez	.65
76	Shannon Stewart	.10
77	Geoff Jenkins	.10
78	Ben Grieve	.10
79	Cliff Floyd	.10
80	Jason Giambi	.50
81	Rod Beck	.10
82	Derek Bell	.10
83	Will Clark	.10
84	David Dellucci	.10
85	Joey Hamilton	.10
86	Livan Hernandez	.10
87	Barry Larkin	.10
88	Matt Mantei	.10
89	Dean Palmer	.10
90	Chan Ho Park	.10
91	Jim Thome	.65
92	Miguel Tejada	.20
93	Justin Thompson	.10
94	David Wells	.10
95	Bernie Williams	.10
96	Jeff Bagwell	.75
97	Derrek Lee	.50
98	Devon White	.10
99	Jeff Shaw	.10
100	Brad Radke	.10
101	Mark Grudzielanek	.10
102	Javy Lopez	.10
103	Mike Sirotka	.10
104	Robin Ventura	.10
105	Andy Ashby	.10
106	Juan Gonzalez	.40
107	Albert Belle	.10
108	Andy Benes	.10
109	Jay Buhner	.10
110	Ken Caminiti	.10
111	Roger Clemens	1.25
112	Mike Hampton	.10
113	Pete Harnisch	.10
114	Mike Piazza	1.50
115	J.T. Snow	.10
116	John Olerud	.10
117	Tony Womack	.10
118	Todd Zeile	.10
119	Tony Gwynn	1.00
120	Brady Anderson	.10
121	Sean Casey	.20
122	Jose Cruz Jr.	.10
123	Carlos Delgado	.50
124	Edgar Martinez	.10
125	Jose Mesa	.10
126	Shane Reynolds	.10
127	John Valentin	.10
128	Mo Vaughn	.10
129	Kevin Young	.10
130	Jay Bell	.10
131	Aaron Boone	.10
132	John Smoltz	.10
133	Mike Stanley	.10
134	Bret Saberhagen	.10
135	Tim Salmon	.10
136	Mariano Rivera	.10
137	Ken Griffey Jr.	1.50
138	Jose Offerman	.10
139	Troy Percival	.10
140	Greg Maddux	1.00
141	Frank Thomas	.75
142	Steve Avery	.10
143	Kevin Millwood	.10
144	Sammy Sosa	1.00
145	Larry Walker	.10
146	Matt Williams	.10
147	Mike Caruso	.10
148	Todd Helton	.65
149	Andruw Jones	.75
150	Ray Lankford	.10
151	Craig Biggio	.10
152	Ugueth Urbina	.10
153	Wade Boggs	1.00
154	Derek Jeter	2.50
155	Wally Joyner	.10
156	Mike Mussina	.30
157	Gregg Olson	.10
158	Henry Rodriguez	.10
159	Reggie Sanders	.10
160	Fernando Tatis	.10
161	Dmitri Young	.10
162	Rick Aguilera	.10
163	Marty Cordova	.10

164	Johnny Damon	.30
165	Ray Durham	.10
166	Brad Fullmer	.10
167	Chipper Jones	1.00
168	Bobby Smith	.10
169	Omar Vizquel	.10
170	Todd Hundley	.10
171	David Cone	.10
172	Royce Clayton	.10
173	Ryan Klesko	.10
174	Jeff Montgomery	.10
175	Magglio Ordonez	.10
176	Billy Wagner	.10
177	Masato Yoshii	.10
178	Jason Christiansen	.10
179	Chuck Finley	.10
180	Tom Gordon	.10
181	Wilton Guerrero	.10
182	Rickey Henderson	.75
183	Sterling Hitchcock	.10
184	Kenny Lofton	.10
185	Tino Martinez	.10
186	Fred McGriff	.10
187	Matt Stairs	.10
188	Neifi Perez	.10
189	Bob Wickman	.10
190	Barry Bonds	2.50
191	Jose Canseco	.40
192	Damion Easley	.10
193	Jim Edmonds	.10
194	Juan Encarnacion	.10
195	Travis Fryman	.10
196	Tom Goodwin	.10
197	Rusty Greer	.10
198	Roberto Hernandez	.10
199	B.J. Surhoff	.10
200	Scott Brosius	.10
201	Brian Jordan	.10
202	Paul Konerko	.20
203	Ismael Valdes	.10
204	Eric Milton	.10
205	Adrian Beltre	.25
206	Tony Clark	.10
207	Bartolo Colon	.10
208	Cal Ripken Jr.	2.50
209	Moises Alou	.10
210	Wilson Alvarez	.10
211	Kevin Brown	.10
212	Orlando Cabrera	.10
213	Vladimir Guerrero	.75
214	Jose Rosado	.10
215	Raul Mondesi	.10
216	Dave Nilsson	.10
217	Carlos Perez	.10
218	Jason Schmidt	.10
219	Richie Sexson	.10
220	Gary Sheffield	.40
221	Fernando Vina	.10
222	Todd Walker	.10
223	Scott Sauerbeck RC	.10
223	Scott Sauerbeck/SP RC	.60
224	Pascual Matos RC	.10
224	Pascual Matos/SP RC	.60
225	Kyle Farnsworth RC	.15
225	Kyle Farnsworth/SP RC	.60
226	Freddy Garcia RC	.75
226	Freddy Garcia/SP RC	1.50
227	David Lundquist RC	.10
227	David Lundquist/SP RC	.60
228	Jolbert Cabrera RC	.10
228	Jolbert Cabrera/SP RC	.60
229	Dan Perkins RC	.10
229	Dan Perkins/SP RC	.60
230	Warren Morris	.10
230	Warren Morris/SP	.60
231	Carlos Febles	.10
231	Carlos Febles/SP	.60
232	Brett Hinchliffe RC	.10
232	Brett Hinchliffe/SP RC	.60
233	Jason Phillips RC	.10
233	Jason Phillips/SP RC	.60
234	Glen Barker RC	.10
234	Glen Barker/SP RC	.60
235	Jose Macias RC	.25
235	Jose Macias/SP RC	1.00
236	Joe Mays RC	.10
236	Joe Mays/SP RC	.60
237	Chad Allen RC	.10
237	Chad Allen/SP RC	.60
238	Miguel Del Toro RC	.10
238	Miguel Del Toro/SP RC	.60
239	Chris Singleton	.10
239	Chris Singleton/SP	.60
240	Jesse Garcia RC	.10
240	Jesse Garcia/SP RC	.60
241	Kris Benson	.10
241	Kris Benson/SP	.60
242	Clay Bellinger RC	.10
242	Clay Bellinger/SP RC	.60
243	Scott Williamson	.10
243	Scott Williamson/SP	.60
244	Masao Kida RC	.10
244	Masao Kida/SP RC	.60
245	Guillermo Garcia RC	.10
245	Guillermo Garcia/SP RC	.60
246	A.J. Burnett RC	.25
246	A.J. Burnett/SP RC	1.50
247	Bo Porter RC	.10
247	Bo Porter/SP RC	.60
248	Pat Burrell RC	1.50
248	Pat Burrell/SP RC	4.00
249	Carlos Lee	.50
249	Carlos Lee/SP	.50
250	Jeff Weaver RC	.50
250	Jeff Weaver/SP RC	1.50

251	Ruben Mateo	.10
251	Ruben Mateo/SP	.60
252	J.D. Drew	.40
252	J.D. Drew/SP	2.00
253	Jeremy Giambi	.10
253	Jeremy Giambi/SP	.60
254	Gary Bennett RC	.10
254	Gary Bennett/SP RC	.60
255	Edwards Guzman RC	.10
255	Edwards Guzman/SP RC	.60
256	Ramon Martinez	.10
256	Ramon Martinez/SP	.60
257	Giomar Guevara RC	.10
257	Giomar Guevara/SP RC	.60
258	Joe McEwing RC	.10
258	Joe McEwing/SP RC	.60
259	Tom Davey RC	.10
259	Tom Davey/SP RC	.60
260	Gabe Kapler	.10
260	Gabe Kapler/SP	.60
261	Ryan Rupe RC	.10
261	Ryan Rupe/SP RC	.60
262	Kelly Dransfeldt RC	.10
262	Kelly Dransfeldt/SP RC	.60
263	Michael Barrett	.10
263	Michael Barrett/SP	.60
264	Eric Chavez	.25
264	Eric Chavez/SP	1.00
265	Orber Moreno RC	.10
265	Orber Moreno/SP RC	.60
266	Marlon Anderson	.10
266	Marlon Anderson/SP	.60
267	Carlos Beltran	.50
267	Carlos Beltran/SP	1.50
268	Doug Mientkiewicz	.10
268	Doug Mientkiewicz/SP	.60
269	Roy Halladay	.10
269	Roy Halladay/SP	.60
270	Torii Hunter	.10
270	Torii Hunter/SP	.60
271	Stan Spencer	.10
271	Stan Spencer/SP	.60
272	Alex Gonzalez	.10
272	Alex Gonzalez/SP	.60
273	Mark McGwire (Spring Fling)	1.00
274	Scott Rolen	.30
275	Jeff Bagwell	.40
276	Derek Jeter	1.50
277	Tony Gwynn	.50
278	Frank Thomas	.40
279	Sammy Sosa	.50
280	Nomar Garciaparra	.50
281	Cal Ripken Jr.	1.50
282	Albert Belle	.10
283	Kerry Wood	.20
284	Greg Maddux	.50
285	Barry Bonds	1.50
286	Juan Gonzalez)	.25
287	Ken Griffey Jr.	.75
288	Alex Rodriguez	1.00
289	Ben Grieve	.10
290	Travis Lee	.10
291	Mo Vaughn	.10
292	Mike Piazza	.85
293	Roger Clemens	.60
294	J.D. Drew	.20
295	Randy Johnson	.40
296	Chipper Jones	.50
297	Vladimir Guerrero	.40
298	Nomar Garciaparra Checklist	.40
299	Ken Griffey Jr. Checklist	.60
300	Mark McGwire Checklist	.60

Star Rubies

Star Rubies:		50X
Production 50 Sets		
SP Star Rubies:		15X
Production 15 Sets		
(See 1999 SkyBox Premium for		
checklist and base card values.)		

Autographics

	NM/M
Common Player:	3.00
Inserted 1:68	
Blue Ink:	1.5X
Production 50 Sets	
Roberto Alomar	15.00
Paul Bako	3.00
Michael Barrett	8.00
Kris Benson	8.00

Micah Bowie	3.00
Roosevelt Brown	3.00
A.J. Burnett	8.00
Pat Burrell	15.00
Ken Caminiti	15.00
Royce Clayton	3.00
Edgard Clemente	3.00
Bartolo Colon	10.00
J.D. Drew	15.00
Damion Easley	5.00
Derrin Ebert	3.00
Mario Encarnacion	5.00
Juan Encarnacion	5.00
Troy Glaus	15.00
Tom Glavine	20.00
Juan Gonzalez/SP	50.00
Shawn Green	10.00
Wilton Guerrero	3.00
Jose Guillen	8.00
Tony Gwynn	30.00
Mark Harriger	3.00
Bobby Higginson	3.00
Todd Hollandsworth	3.00
Scott Hunter	3.00
Gabe Kapler	3.00
Scott Karl	3.00
Mike Kinkade	3.00
Ray Lankford	3.00
Barry Larkin	15.00
Matt Lawton	5.00
Ricky Ledee	3.00
Travis Lee	3.00
Eli Marrero	3.00
Ruben Mateo	3.00
Joe McEwing	4.00
Doug Mientkiewicz	3.00
Russ Ortiz	5.00
Jim Parque	3.00
Robert Person	3.00
Alex Rodriguez	80.00
Scott Rolen	20.00
Benj Sampson	3.00
Luis Saturria	3.00
Curt Schilling	35.00
David Segui	3.00
Fernando Tatis	3.00
Peter Tucci	3.00
Javier Vasquez	6.00
Robin Ventura	10.00
Checklist	.05

Diamond Debuts

	NM/M
Complete Set (15):	17.50
Common Player:	2.00
Inserted 1:49	

1	Eric Chavez	3.00
2	Kyle Farnsworth	2.00
3	Ryan Rupe	2.00
4	Jeremy Giambi	2.00
5	Marlon Anderson	2.00
6	J.D. Drew	4.00
7	Carlos Febles	2.00
8	Joe McEwing	2.00
9	Jeff Weaver	2.00
10	Alex Gonzalez	2.00
11	Chad Allen	2.00
12	Michael Barrett	2.00

13	Gabe Kapler	2.00
14	Carlos Lee	2.00
15	Edwards Guzman	2.00

Intimidation Nation

	NM/M
Complete Set (15):	280.00
Common Player:	12.00
Production 99 Sets	

1	Cal Ripken Jr.	40.00
2	Tony Gwynn	20.00
3	Nomar Garciaparra	20.00
4	Frank Thomas	15.00
5	Mike Piazza	25.00
6	Mark McGwire	30.00
7	Scott Rolen	12.00
8	Chipper Jones	20.00
9	Greg Maddux	20.00
10	Ken Griffey Jr.	25.00
11	Juan Gonzalez	12.00
12	Derek Jeter	40.00
13	J.D. Drew	12.00
14	Roger Clemens	22.50
15	Alex Rodriguez	30.00

Live Bats

	NM/M
Complete Set (15):	10.00
Common Player:	.25
Inserted 1:7	

1	Juan Gonzalez	.35
2	Mark McGwire	1.50
3	Jeff Bagwell	.50
4	Frank Thomas	.50
5	Mike Piazza	1.00
6	Nomar Garciaparra	.75
7	Alex Rodriguez	1.50
8	Scott Rolen	.40
9	Travis Lee	.25
10	Tony Gwynn	.75
11	Derek Jeter	2.00
12	Ben Grieve	.25
13	Chipper Jones	.75
14	Ken Griffey Jr.	1.00
15	Cal Ripken Jr.	2.00

Show Business

	NM/M
Complete Set (15):	60.00
Common Player:	2.00
Inserted 1:70	

1	Mark McGwire	7.50
2	Tony Gwynn	5.00
3	Nomar Garciaparra	5.00
4	Juan Gonzalez	2.50
5	Roger Clemens	5.00
6	Chipper Jones	5.00
7	Cal Ripken Jr.	10.00
8	Alex Rodriguez	7.50
9	Orlando Hernandez	2.00
10	Greg Maddux	5.00
11	Mike Piazza	6.00
12	Frank Thomas	4.00
13	Ken Griffey Jr.	6.00
14	Scott Rolen	3.00
15	Derek Jeter	10.00

Soul of The Game

		NM/M
Complete Set (15):		15.00
Common Player:		.60
Inserted 1:14		
1	Alex Rodriguez	2.00
2	Vladimir Guerrero	.90
3	Chipper Jones	1.25
4	Derek Jeter	2.50
5	Tony Gwynn	1.25
6	Scott Rolen	.60
7	Juan Gonzalez	.60
8	Mark McGwire	2.00
9	Ken Griffey Jr.	1.50
10	Jeff Bagwell	.90
11	Cal Ripken Jr.	2.50
12	Frank Thomas	.90
13	Mike Piazza	1.50
14	Nomar Garciaparra	1.25
15	Sammy Sosa	1.25

1999 SkyBox Thunder

		NM/M
Complete Set (300):		15.00
Common Player (1-240):		.05
Common Player (241-300):		.15
Raves:		15X
Production 150 Sets		
SuperRaves:		45X
Production 25 Sets		
Rants:		8X
Inserted 1:2 R		
Pack (8):		1.50
Wax Box (36):		25.00
1	John Smoltz	.05
2	Garret Anderson	.05
3	Matt Williams	.05
4	Daryle Ward	.05
5	Andy Ashby	.05
6	Miguel Tejada	.15
7	Dmitri Young	.05
8	Roberto Alomar	.25
9	Kevin Brown	.05
10	Eric Young	.05
11	Odalis Perez	.05
12	Preston Wilson	.05
13	Jeff Abbott	.05
14	Bret Boone	.05
15	Mendy Lopez	.05
16	B.J. Surhoff	.05
17	Steve Woodard	.05
18	Ron Coomer	.05
19	Rondell White	.05
20	Edgardo Alfonzo	.05
21	Kevin Millwood	.05
22	Jose Canseco	.45
23	Blake Stein	.05
24	Quilvio Veras	.05
25	Chuck Knoblauch	.05
26	David Segui	.05
27	Eric Davis	.05
28	Francisco Cordova	.05
29	Randy Winn	.05
30	Will Clark	.05
31	Billy Wagner	.05
32	Kevin Witt	.05
33	Jim Edmonds	.05
34	Todd Stottlemyre	.05

35	Shane Andrews	.05
36	Michael Tucker	.05
37	Sandy Alomar Jr.	.05
38	Neifi Perez	.05
39	Jaret Wright	.05
40	Devon White	.05
41	Edgar Renteria	.05
42	Shane Reynolds	.05
43	Jeff King	.05
44	Darren Dreifort	.05
45	Fernando Vina	.05
46	Marty Cordova	.05
47	Ugueth Urbina	.05
48	Bobby Bonilla	.05
49	Omar Vizquel	.05
50	Tom Gordon	.05
51	Ryan Christenson	.05
52	Aaron Boone	.05
53	Jamie Moyer	.05
54	Brian Giles	.05
55	Kevin Tapani	.05
56	Scott Brosius	.05
57	Ellis Burks	.05
58	Al Leiter	.05
59	Royce Clayton	.05
60	Chris Carpenter	.05
61	Bubba Trammell	.05
62	Tom Glavine	.35
63	Shannon Stewart	.05
64	Todd Zeile	.05
65	J.T. Snow	.05
66	Matt Clement	.05
67	Matt Stairs	.05
68	Ismael Valdes	.05
69	Todd Walker	.05
70	Jose Lima	.05
71	Mike Caruso	.05
72	Brett Tomko	.05
73	Mike Lansing	.05
74	Justin Thompson	.05
75	Damion Easley	.05
76	Derrek Lee	.50
77	Derek Bell	.05
78	Brady Anderson	.05
79	Charles Johnson	.05
80	Rafael Roque RC	.05
81	Corey Koskie	.05
82	Fernando Seguignol	.05
83	Jay Tessmer	.05
84	Jason Giambi	.50
85	Mike Lieberthal	.05
86	Jose Guillen	.05
87	Jim Leyritz	.05
88	Shawn Estes	.05
89	Ray Lankford	.05
90	Paul Sorrento	.05
91	Javy Lopez	.05
92	John Wetteland	.05
93	Sean Casey	.15
94	Chuck Finley	.05
95	Trot Nixon	.05
96	Ray Durham	.05
97	Reggie Sanders	.05
98	Bartolo Colon	.05
99	Henry Rodriguez	.05
100	Rolando Arrojo	.05
101	Geoff Jenkins	.05
102	Darryl Kile	.05
103	Mark Kotsay	.05
104	Craig Biggio	.05
105	Omar Daal	.05
106	Carlos Febles	.05
107	Eric Karros	.05
108	Matt Lawton	.05
109	Carl Pavano	.05
110	Brian McRae	.05
111	Mariano Rivera	.15
112	Jay Buhner	.05
113	Doug Glanville	.05
114	Jason Kendall	.05
115	Wally Joyner	.05
116	Jeff Kent	.05
117	Shane Monahan	.05
118	Eli Marrero	.05
119	Bobby Smith	.05
120	Shawn Green	.20
121	Kirk Rueter	.05
122	Tom Goodwin	.05
123	Andy Benes	.05
124	Ed Sprague	.05
125	Mike Mussina	.25
126	Jose Offerman	.05
127	Mickey Morandini	.05
128	Paul Konerko	.20
129	Denny Neagle	.05
130	Travis Fryman	.05
131	John Rocker	.05
132	Rob Fick RC	.05
133	Livan Hernandez	.05
134	Ken Caminiti	.05
135	Johnny Damon	.30
136	Jeff Kubenka	.05
137	Marquis Grissom	.05
138	Doug Mientkiewicz	.05
139	Dustin Hermanson	.05
140	Carl Everett	.05
141	Hideo Nomo	.40
142	Jorge Posada	.05
143	Rickey Henderson	.75
144	Robb Nen	.05
145	Ron Gant	.05
146	Aramis Ramirez	.05
147	Trevor Hoffman	.05
148	Bill Mueller	.05
149	Edgar Martinez	.05
150	Fred McGriff	.05
151	Rusty Greer	.05

152	Tom Evans	.05
153	Todd Greene	.05
154	Jay Bell	.05
155	Mike Lowell	.05
156	Orlando Cabrera	.05
157	Troy O'Leary	.05
158	Jose Hernandez	.05
159	Magglio Ordonez	.05
160	Barry Larkin	.05
161	David Justice	.05
162	Derrick Gibson	.05
163	Luis Gonzalez	.05
164	Alex Gonzalez	.05
165	Scott Elarton	.05
166	Dermal Brown	.05
167	Eric Milton	.05
168	Raul Mondesi	.05
169	Jeff Cirillo	.05
170	Benj Sampson	.05
171	John Olerud	.05
172	Andy Pettitte	.20
173	A.J. Hinch	.05
174	Rico Brogna	.05
175	Jason Schmidt	.05
176	Dean Palmer	.05
177	Matt Morris	.05
178	Quinton McCracken	.05
179	Rick Helling	.05
180	Walt Weiss	.05
181	Troy Percival	.05
182	Tony Batista	.05
183	Brian Jordan	.05
184	Jerry Hairston Jr.	.05
185	Bret Saberhagen	.05
186	Mark Grace	.05
187	Brian Simmons	.05
188	Pete Harnisch	.05
189	Kenny Lofton	.05
190	Vinny Castilla	.05
191	Bobby Higginson	.05
192	Joey Hamilton	.05
193	Cliff Floyd	.05
194	Andres Galarraga	.05
195	Chan Ho Park	.05
196	Jeromy Burnitz	.05
197	David Ortiz	.35
198	Wilton Guerrero	.05
199	Rey Ordonez	.05
200	Paul O'Neill	.05
201	Kenny Rogers	.05
202	Marlon Anderson	.05
203	Tony Womack	.05
204	Robin Ventura	.05
205	Russ Ortiz	.05
206	Mike Frank	.05
207	Fernando Tatis	.05
208	Miguel Cairo	.05
209	Ivan Rodriguez	.65
210	Carlos Delgado	.50
211	Tim Salmon	.15
212	Brian Anderson	.05
213	Ryan Klesko	.05
214	Scott Erickson	.05
215	Mike Stanley	.05
216	Brant Brown	.05
217	Rod Beck	.05
218	Guillermo Garcia RC	.05
219	David Wells	.05
220	Dante Bichette	.05
221	Armando Benitez	.05
222	Todd Dunwoody	.05
223	Kelvim Escobar	.05
224	Richard Hidalgo	.05
225	Angel Pena	.05
226	Ronnie Belliard	.05
227	Brad Radke	.05
228	Brad Fullmer	.05
229	Jay Payton	.05
230	Tino Martinez	.05
231	Scott Spiezio	.05
232	Bobby Abreu	.05
233	John Valentin	.05
234	Kevin Young	.05
235	Steve Finley	.05
236	David Cone	.05
237	Armando Rios	.05
238	Russ Davis	.05
239	Wade Boggs	1.00
240	Aaron Sele	.05
241	Jose Cruz Jr.	.15
242	George Lombard	.15
243	Todd Helton	.65
244	Andruw Jones	.75
245	Troy Glaus	.65
246	Manny Ramirez	.75
247	Ben Grieve	.15
247p	Ben Grieve	
	("PROMOTIONAL SAMPLE")	1.00
248	Richie Sexson	.15
249	Juan Encarnacion	.15
250	Randy Johnson	.75
251	Gary Sheffield	.45
252	Rafael Palmeiro	.65
253	Roy Halladay	.15
254	Mike Piazza	1.50
255	Tony Gwynn	1.00
256	Juan Gonzalez	.40
257	Jeremy Giambi	.15
258	Ben Davis	.15
259	Russ Branyan	.15
260	Pedro Martinez	.75
261	Frank Thomas	.75
262	Calvin Pickering	.15
263	Chipper Jones	1.00
264	Ryan Minor	.15
265	Roger Clemens	1.25
266	Sammy Sosa	1.00

267	Mo Vaughn	.15
268	Carlos Beltran	.50
269	Jim Thome	.65
270	Mark McGwire	2.00
271	Travis Lee	.15
272	Darin Erstad	.30
273	Derek Jeter	2.50
274	Greg Maddux	1.00
275	Ricky Ledee	.15
276	Alex Rodriguez	2.00
277	Vladimir Guerrero	.75
278	Greg Vaughn	.15
279	Scott Rolen	.60
280	Carlos Guillen	.15
281	Jeff Bagwell	.75
282	Bruce Chen	.15
283	Tony Clark	.15
284	Albert Belle	.05
285	Cal Ripken Jr.	2.50
286	Barry Bonds	2.50
287	Curt Schilling	.35
288	Eric Chavez	.30
289	Larry Walker	.15
290	Orlando Hernandez	.15
291	Moises Alou	.15
292	Ken Griffey Jr.	1.50
293	Kerry Wood	.50
294	Nomar Garciaparra	1.00
295	Gabe Kapler	.15
296	Bernie Williams	.15
297	Matt Anderson	.15
298	Adrian Beltre	.35
299	J.D. Drew	.40
300	Ryan Bradley	.15
--	Checklist 1-230	.05
---	Checklist 231-300 and Inserts	.05
--	Derek Jeter Video Game	
	Sweepstakes Form	.05

Rant

	NM/M
Common Player:	.50
Rant Stars:	8X
(See 1999 SkyBox Thunder for	
checklist and base card values.)	

Dial 1

		NM/M
Complete Set (10):		70.00
Common Player:		2.50
Inserted 1:300		
1D	Nomar Garciaparra	7.50
2D	Juan Gonzalez	3.40
3D	Ken Griffey Jr.	10.00
4D	Chipper Jones	7.50
5D	Mark McGwire	12.50
6D	Mike Piazza	10.00
7D	Manny Ramirez	6.00
8D	Alex Rodriguez	12.50
9D	Sammy Sosa	7.50
10D	Mo Vaughn	2.50

Hip-No-Tized

		NM/M
Complete Set (15):		20.00
Common Player:		1.25
Inserted 1:36		
1H	J.D. Drew	1.25
2H	Nomar Garciaparra	2.00
3H	Juan Gonzalez	1.25

4H	Ken Griffey Jr.	2.50
5H	Derek Jeter	4.00
6H	Randy Johnson	1.50
7H	Chipper Jones	2.00
8H	Mark McGwire	3.00
9H	Mike Piazza	2.50
10H	Cal Ripken Jr.	4.00
11H	Alex Rodriguez	3.00
12H	Sammy Sosa	2.00
13H	Frank Thomas	1.50
14H	Jim Thome	1.25
15H	Kerry Wood	1.25

In Depth

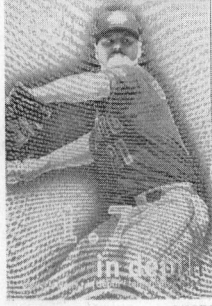

		NM/M
Complete Set (10):		17.50
Common Player:		1.00
Inserted 1:24		
1ID	Albert Belle	1.00
2ID	Barry Bonds	5.00
3ID	Roger Clemens	1.50
4ID	Juan Gonzalez	1.25
5ID	Ken Griffey Jr.	3.00
6ID	Mark McGwire	4.00
7ID	Mike Piazza	3.00
8ID	Sammy Sosa	2.50
9ID	Mo Vaughn	1.00
10ID	Kerry Wood	1.25

Todd Helton Autograph

		NM/M
243	Todd Helton	15.00

Turbo Charged

		NM/M
Complete Set (10):		35.00
Common Player:		2.00
Inserted 1:72		
1TC	Jose Canseco	2.50
2TC	Juan Gonzalez	2.00
3TC	Ken Griffey Jr.	5.00
4TC	Vladimir Guerrero	3.00
5TC	Mark McGwire	6.00
6TC	Mike Piazza	5.00

7TC	Manny Ramirez	3.00
8TC	Alex Rodriguez	6.00
9TC	Sammy Sosa	4.00
10TC	Mo Vaughn	2.00

Unleashed

		NM/M
Complete Set (15):		10.00
Common Player:		.50
Inserted 1:6		
1U	Carlos Beltran	1.50
2U	Adrian Beltre	1.00
3U	Eric Chavez	.75
4U	J.D. Drew	1.00
5U	Juan Encarnacion	.50
6U	Jeremy Giambi	.50
7U	Troy Glaus	2.00
8U	Ben Grieve	.50
9U	Todd Helton	2.00
10U	Orlando Hernandez	.50
11U	Gabe Kapler	.50
12U	Travis Lee	.50
13U	Calvin Pickering	.50
14U	Richie Sexson	.50
15U	Kerry Wood	1.00

www.Batterz.com

		NM/M
Complete Set (10):		12.00
Common Player:		.50
Inserted 1:18		
1WB	J.D. Drew	.60
2WB	Nomar Garciaparra	1.00
3WB	Ken Griffey Jr.	1.50
4WB	Tony Gwynn	1.00
5WB	Derek Jeter	3.00
6WB	Mark McGwire	2.00
7WB	Alex Rodriguez	2.00
8WB	Scott Rolen	.65
9WB	Sammy Sosa	1.00
10WB	Bernie Williams	.50

2000 SkyBox

		NM/M
Complete Set (250):		25.00
Comp. Set w/SPs (300):		60.00
Common Player:		.10
Common SP (201-240):		1.00
Inserted 1:8		
Common SP (241-250):		.50
Inserted 1:12		
Pack (10):		1.50
Wax Box (24):		30.00
1	Cal Ripken Jr.	2.00
2	Ivan Rodriguez	.65
3	Chipper Jones	1.00
4	Dean Palmer	.10
5	Devon White	.10
6	Ugueth Urbina	.10
7	Doug Glanville	.10
8	Damian Jackson	.10
9	Jose Canseco	.40
10	Billy Koch	.10
11	Brady Anderson	.10
12	Vladimir Guerrero	.75
13	Dan Wilson	.10
14	Kevin Brown	.10
15	Eddie Taubensee	.10
16	Jose Lima	.10
17	Greg Maddux	1.00
18	Manny Ramirez	.75
19	Brad Fullmer	.10
20	Ron Gant	.10
21	Edgar Martinez	.10
22	Pokey Reese	.10
23	Jason Varitek	.10
24	Neifi Perez	.10
25	Shane Reynolds	.10
26	Robin Ventura	.10
27	Scott Rolen	.65
28	Trevor Hoffman	.10
29	John Valentin	.10
30	Shannon Stewart	.10
31	Troy Glaus	.75
32	Kerry Wood	.65
33	Jim Thome	.65
34	Rafael Roque	.10
35	Tino Martinez	.10
36	Jeffrey Hammonds	.10
37	Orlando Hernandez	.10
38	Kris Benson	.10
39	Fred McGriff	.10
40	Brian Jordan	.10
41	Trot Nixon	.10
42	Matt Clement	.10
43	Ray Durham	.10
44	Johnny Damon	.30
45	Todd Hollandsworth	.10
46	Edgardo Alfonzo	.10
47	Tim Hudson	.25
48	Tony Gwynn	1.00
49	Barry Bonds	2.00
50	Andruw Jones	.75
51	Pedro Martinez	.75
52	Mike Hampton	.10
53	Miguel Tejada	.25
54	Kevin Young	.10
55	J.T. Snow	.10
56	Carlos Delgado	.50
57	Bobby Howry	.10
58	Andres Galarraga	.10
59	Paul Konerko	.20
60	Mike Cameron	.10
61	Jeremy Giambi	.10
62	Todd Hundley	.10
63	Al Leiter	.10
64	Matt Stairs	.10
65	Edgar Renteria	.10
66	Jeff Kent	.10
67	John Wetteland	.10
68	Nomar Garciaparra	1.25
69	Jeff Weaver	.10
70	Matt Williams	.10
71	Kyle Farnsworth	.10
72	Brad Radke	.10
73	Eric Chavez	.25
74	J.D. Drew	.25
75	Steve Finley	.10
76	Pete Harnisch	.10
77	Chad Kreuter	.10
78	Todd Pratt	.10
79	John Jaha	.10
80	Armando Rios	.10
81	Luis Gonzalez	.25
82	Ryan Minor	.10
83	Juan Gonzalez	.75
84	Rickey Henderson	.75
85	Jason Giambi	.50
86	Shawn Estes	.10
87	Chad Curtis	.10
88	Jeff Cirillo	.10
89	Juan Encarnacion	.10
90	Tony Womack	.10
91	Mike Mussina	.35
92	Jeff Bagwell	.75
93	Rey Ordonez	.10
94	Joe McEwing	.10
95	Robb Nen	.10
96	Will Clark	.10
97	Chris Singleton	.10
98	Jason Kendall	.10
99	Ken Griffey Jr.	1.25
100	Rusty Greer	.10
101	Charles Johnson	.10
102	Carlos Lee	.10
103	Brad Ausmus	.10
104	Preston Wilson	.10
105	Ronnie Belliard	.10
106	Mike Lieberthal	.10
107	Alex Rodriguez	1.50
108	Jay Bell	.10
109	Frank Thomas	.75
110	Adrian Beltre	.30
111	Ron Coomer	.10
112	Ben Grieve	.10
113	Darryl Kile	.10
114	Erubiel Durazo	.10
115	Magglio Ordonez	.10
116	Gary Sheffield	.40
117	Joe Mays	.10
118	Fernando Tatis	.10
119	David Wells	.10
120	Tim Salmon	.20
121	Troy O'Leary	.10
122	Roberto Alomar	.40
123	Damion Easley	.10
124	Brant Brown	.10
125	Carlos Beltran	.45
126	Eric Karros	.10
127	Geoff Jenkins	.10
128	Roger Clemens	1.00
129	Warren Morris	.10
130	Eric Owens	.10
131	Jose Cruz Jr.	.10
132	Mo Vaughn	.10
133	Eric Young	.10
134	Kenny Lofton	.10
135	Marquis Grissom	.10
136	A.J. Burnett	.10
137	Bernie Williams	.25
138	Javy Lopez	.10
139	Jose Offerman	.10
140	Sean Casey	.25
141	Alex Gonzalez	.10
142	Carlos Febles	.10
143	Mike Piazza	1.25
144	Curt Schilling	.35
145	Ben Davis	.10
146	Rafael Palmeiro	.65
147	Scott Williamson	.10
148	Darin Erstad	.25
149	Joe Girardi	.10
150	Gerald Williams	.10
151	Richie Sexson	.10
152	Corey Koskie	.10
153	Paul O'Neill	.10
154	Chad Hermansen	.10
155	Randy Johnson	.75
156	Henry Rodriguez	.10
157	Bartolo Colon	.10
158	Tony Clark	.10
159	Mike Lowell	.10
160	Moises Alou	.10
161	Todd Walker	.10
162	Mariano Rivera	.20
163	Mark McGwire	1.50
164	Roberto Hernandez	.10
165	Larry Walker	.10
166	Albert Belle	.15
167	Barry Larkin	.10
168	Rolando Arrojo	.10
169	Mark Kotsay	.10
170	Ken Caminiti	.10
171	Dermal Brown	.10
172	Michael Barrett	.10
173	Jay Buhner	.10
174	Ruben Mateo	.10
175	Jim Edmonds	.10
176	Sammy Sosa	1.25
177	Omar Vizquel	.10
178	Todd Helton	.75
179	Kevin Barker	.10
180	Derek Jeter	2.00
181	Brian Giles	.10
182	Greg Vaughn	.10
183	Roy Halladay	.10
184	Tom Glavine	.35
185	Craig Biggio	.10
186	Jose Vidro	.10
187	Andy Ashby	.10
188	Freddy Garcia	.10
189	Garret Anderson	.10
190	Mark Grace	.20
191	Travis Fryman	.10
192	Jeromy Burnitz	.10
193	Jacque Jones	.10
194	David Cone	.10

195	Ryan Rupe	.10
196	John Smoltz	.10
197	Daryle Ward	.10
198	Rondell White	.10
199	Bobby Abreu	.10
200	Justin Thompson	.10
201	Norm Hutchins (Prospect)	.10
201	Norm Hutchins/SP	1.00
202	Ramon Ortiz (Prospect)	.10
202	Ramon Ortiz/SP	1.00
203	Dan Wheeler (Prospect)	.10
203	Dan Wheeler/SP	1.00
204	Matt Riley (Prospect)	.10
204	Matt Riley/SP	1.00
205	Steve Lomasney (Prospect)	.10
205	Steve Lomasney/SP	1.00
206	Chad Meyers (Prospect)	.10
206	Chad Meyers/SP	1.00
207	Gary Glover RC (Prospect)	.20
207	Gary Glover/SP	1.00
208	Joe Crede (Prospect)	.10
208	Joe Crede/SP	1.00
209	Kip Wells (Prospect)	.10
209	Kip Wells/SP	1.00
210	Travis Dawkins (Prospect)	.10
210	Travis Dawkins/SP	1.00
211	Denny Stark RC (Prospect)	.20
211	Denny Stark/SP	1.00
212	Ben Petrick (Prospect)	.10
212	Ben Petrick/SP	1.00
213	Eric Munson (Prospect)	.10
213	Eric Munson/SP	1.00
214	Josh Beckett (Prospect)	.25
214	Josh Beckett/SP	1.50
215	Pablo Ozuna (Prospect)	.10
215	Pablo Ozuna/SP	1.00
216	Brad Penny (Prospect)	.10
216	Brad Penny/SP	1.00
217	Julio Ramirez (Prospect)	.10
217	Julio Ramirez/SP	1.00
218	Danny Peoples (Prospect)	.10
218	Danny Peoples/SP	1.00
219	Wilfredo Rodriguez RC (Prospect)	.10
219	Wilfredo Rodriguez/SP RC	1.00
220	Julio Lugo (Prospect)	.10
220	Julio Lugo/SP	1.00
221	Mark Quinn (Prospect)	.10
221	Mark Quinn/SP	1.00
222	Eric Gagne (Prospect)	.10
222	Eric Gagne/SP	1.00
223	Chad Green (Prospect)	.10
223	Chad Green/SP	1.00
224	Tony Armas Jr. (Prospect)	.10
224	Tony Armas Jr./SP	1.00
225	Milton Bradley (Prospect)	.10
225	Milton Bradley/SP	1.00
226	Rob Bell (Prospect)	.10
226	Rob Bell/SP	1.00
227	Alfonso Soriano (Prospect)	.10
227	Alfonso Soriano/SP	4.00
228	Wily Pena (Prospect)	.10
228	Wily Pena/SP	1.00
229	Nick Johnson (Prospect)	.10
229	Nick Johnson/SP	1.50
230	Ed Yarnall (Prospect)	.10
230	Ed Yarnall/SP	1.00
231	Ryan Bradley (Prospect)	.10
231	Ryan Bradley/SP	1.00
232	Adam Piatt (Prospect)	.10
232	Adam Piatt/SP	1.00
233	Chad Harville (Prospect)	.10
233	Chad Harville/SP	1.00
234	Alex Sanchez (Prospect)	.10
234	Alex Sanchez/SP	1.00
235	Michael Coleman (Prospect)	.10
235	Michael Coleman/SP	1.00
236	Pat Burrell (Prospect)	.25
236	Pat Burrell/SP	1.50
237	Wascar Serrano RC (Prospect)	.10
237	Wascar Serrano/SP RC	1.00
238	Rick Ankiel (Prospect)	.25
238	Rick Ankiel/SP	1.00
239	Mike Lamb RC (Prospect)	.10
239	Mike Lamb/SP RC	1.00
240	Vernon Wells (Prospect)	.10
240	Vernon Wells/SP	1.00
241	Jorge Toca, Goefrey Tomlinson (Premium Pairs)	.10
241	Jorge Toca, Goefrey Tomlinson/SP	.50
242	Shea Hillenbrand, Josh Phelps RC (Premium Pairs)	2.00
242	Shea Hillenbrand, Josh Phelps/SP RC	4.00
243	Aaron Myette, Doug Davis (Premium Pairs)	.10
243	Aaron Myette, Doug Davis/SP	.50
244	Brett Laxton, Robert Ramsay (Premium Pairs)	.10
244	Brett Laxton, Robert Ramsay/SP	.50
245	B.J. Ryan, Corey Lee (Premium Pairs)	.10
245	B.J. Ryan, Corey Lee/SP	.50
246	Chris Haas, Wilton Veras (Premium Pairs)	.10
246	Chris Haas, Wilton Veras/SP	.50
247	Jimmy Anderson, Kyle Peterson (Premium Pairs)	.10
247	Jimmy Anderson, Kyle Peterson/SP	.50
248	Jason Dewey, Giuseppe Chiaramonte (Premium Pairs)	.10
248	Jason Dewey, Giuseppe Chiaramonte/SP	.50
249	Guillermo Mota, Orber Moreno (Premium Pairs)	.10
249	Guillermo Mota, Orber Moreno/SP	.50
250	Steve Cox, Julio Zuleta RC (Premium Pairs)	.15
250	Steve Cox, Julio Zuleta/SP RC	.50

Star Rubies

	NM/M
Complete Set (250):	200.00
Common Player (1-200):	.50
Common SP Prospect (201-250):	3.00
Stars:	6X
Star SP's:	3X

(See 2000 SkyBox for checklist and base card values.)

Speed Merchants

	NM/M
Complete Set (10):	12.00
Common Player:	.50

Inserted 1:8
Star Ruby: 3-6X
Production 100 Sets

1	Derek Jeter	3.00
2	Sammy Sosa	1.25
3	Nomar Garciaparra	1.25
4	Alex Rodriguez	2.50
5	Randy Johnson	1.00
6	Ken Griffey Jr.	1.50
7	Pedro Martinez	1.00
8	Pat Burrell	1.00
9	Barry Bonds	3.00
10	Mark McGwire	2.50

Autographics

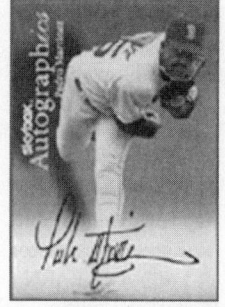

	NM/M
Common Player:	5.00
Rick Ankiel	15.00
Michael Barrett	5.00
Josh Beckett	25.00
Rob Bell	5.00
Adrian Beltre	5.00
Peter Bergeron	5.00
Lance Berkman	20.00
Rico Brogna	5.00
Pat Burrell	20.00
Orlando Cabrera	15.00
Mike Cameron	5.00
Roger Cedeno	5.00
Eric Chavez	15.00
Bruce Chen	5.00
Johnny Damon	20.00
Ben Davis	5.00
Jason Dewey	5.00
Octavio Dotel	6.00
J.D. Drew	15.00
Erubiel Durazo	8.00
Jason Giambi	20.00
Doug Glanville	5.00
Troy Glaus	20.00
Alex Gonzalez	8.00
Shawn Green	15.00
Jason Grilli	5.00
Tony Gwynn	40.00
Mike Hampton	8.00
Tim Hudson	15.00
Norm Hutchins	5.00
John Jaha	5.00
Derek Jeter	100.00
D'Angelo Jimenez	5.00
Randy Johnson	60.00
Andruw Jones	20.00
Gabe Kapler	8.00
Jason Kendall	10.00
Adam Kennedy	8.00
Cesar King	5.00
Paul Konerko	8.00
Mark Kotsay	6.00
Carlos Lee	8.00
Mike Lieberthal	8.00
Steve Lomasney	5.00
Greg Maddux	60.00
Edgar Martinez	15.00
Aaron McNeal	5.00
Kevin Millwood	10.00
Raul Mondesi	8.00
Joe Nathan	5.00
Magglio Ordonez	15.00
Eric Owens	5.00
Rafael Palmeiro	25.00
Angel Pena	5.00
Wily Pena	5.00
Cal Ripken Jr.	85.00
Scott Rolen	20.00
Jimmy Rollins	15.00
B.J. Ryan	5.00
Tim Salmon	10.00
Chris Singleton	5.00
J.T. Snow	6.00
Mike Sweeney	8.00
Jose Vidro	8.00
Rondell White	8.00
Jaret Wright	5.00

E-Ticket

	NM/M
Complete Set (14):	15.00
Common Player:	.50

Inserted 1:4
Star Ruby: 4-8X
Production 100 Sets

1	Alex Rodriguez	2.50
2	Derek Jeter	3.00
3	Nomar Garciaparra	1.50
4	Cal Ripken Jr.	3.00
5	Sean Casey	.50
6	Mark McGwire	2.50
7	Sammy Sosa	1.50
8	Ken Griffey Jr.	2.00
9	Tony Gwynn	1.50
10	Pedro Martinez	1.00
11	Chipper Jones	1.50
12	Vladimir Guerrero	1.00
13	Roger Clemens	1.75
14	Mike Piazza	2.00

Genuine Coverage

	NM/M
Common Player:	8.00

Inserted 1:399

1	Troy Glaus	15.00
2	Cal Ripken Jr.	40.00
3	Alex Rodriguez	25.00
4	Mike Mussina	10.00
5	J.D. Drew	8.00
6	Robin Ventura	8.00
7	Matt Williams	8.00

Genuine Coverage HOBBY

	NM/M
Common Player:	10.00

Inserted 1:144

1	Ivan Rodriguez	12.00
2	Jose Canseco	10.00
3	Frank Thomas	15.00
4	Manny Ramirez	15.00

Higher Level

	NM/M
Complete Set (10):	20.00
Common Player:	1.00

Inserted 1:24
Star Ruby: 5-10X
Production 50 Sets

1	Cal Ripken Jr.	4.00
2	Derek Jeter	4.00
3	Nomar Garciaparra	2.00
4	Chipper Jones	2.00
5	Mike Piazza	2.50
6	Ivan Rodriguez	1.00
7	Ken Griffey Jr.	2.50
8	Sammy Sosa	2.00
9	Alex Rodriguez	3.00
10	Mark McGwire	3.00

2000 SkyBox Hobby Bullpen Embossed

	NM/M
49 Barry Bonds	6.00

Preeminence

	NM/M
Complete Set (10):	15.00
Common Player:	.50

Inserted 1:24
Star Ruby: 5-10X
Production 50 Sets

1	Pedro Martinez	1.25
2	Derek Jeter	4.00
3	Nomar Garciaparra	1.50
4	Alex Rodriguez	3.00
5	Mark McGwire	3.00
6	Sammy Sosa	1.50
7	Sean Casey	.50
8	Mike Piazza	2.00
9	Chipper Jones	1.50
10	Ivan Rodriguez	1.00

SkyLines

	NM/M
Complete Set (10):	10.00
Common Player:	.50

Inserted 1:11
Star Ruby: 10-20X
Production 50 Sets

1	Cal Ripken Jr.	2.00
2	Mark McGwire	1.50
3	Alex Rodriguez	1.50
4	Sammy Sosa	.75
5	Derek Jeter	2.00
6	Mike Piazza	1.00
7	Nomar Garciaparra	.75
8	Chipper Jones	.75
9	Ken Griffey Jr.	1.00
10	Manny Ramirez	.50

The Technique

		NM/M
Complete Set (15):		20.00
Common Player:		.50
Inserted 1:11		
Star Ruby:		3-6X
Production 50 Sets		
1	Alex Rodriguez	3.00
2	Tony Gwynn	1.50
3	Sean Casey	.50
4	Mark McGwire	3.00
5	Sammy Sosa	1.50
6	Ken Griffey Jr.	2.00
7	Mike Piazza	2.00
8	Nomar Garciaparra	1.50
9	Derek Jeter	4.00
10	Vladimir Guerrero	1.00
11	Cal Ripken Jr.	4.00
12	Chipper Jones	1.50
13	Frank Thomas	1.00
14	Manny Ramirez	1.00
15	Jeff Bagwell	1.00

2000 SkyBox Dominion

		NM/M
Complete Set (300):		20.00
Common Player:		.10
Pack (10):		1.50
Wax Box (36):		30.00
1	Mark McGwire, Ken Griffey Jr.	.40
2	Mark McGwire, Manny Ramirez	.40
3	Larry Walker, Nomar Garciaparra	.25
4	Tony Womack, Brian Hunter	.10
5	Mike Hampton, Pedro Martinez	.20
6	Randy Johnson, Pedro Martinez	.20
7	Randy Johnson, Pedro Martinez	.20
8	Ugueth Urbina, Mariano Rivera	.10
9	Vinny Castilla	.10
10	Orioles host Cuban National Team	.10
11	Jose Canseco	.10
12	Fernando Tatis	.10
13	Robin Ventura	.10
14	Roger Clemens	.50
15	Jose Jimenez	.10
16	David Cone	.10
17	Mark McGwire	.65
18	Cal Ripken Jr.	.75
19	Tony Gwynn	.30
20	Wade Boggs	.25
21	Ivan Rodriguez	.20
22	Chuck Finley	.10
23	Eric Milton	.10
24	Adrian Beltre	.10
25	Brad Radke	.10
26	Derek Bell	.10
27	Garret Anderson	.10
28	Ivan Rodriguez	.40
29	Jeff Kent	.10
30	Jeremy Giambi	.10
31	John Franco	.10
32	Jose Hernandez	.10
33	Jose Offerman	.10
34	Jose Rosado	.10
35	Kevin Appier	.10
36	Kris Benson	.10
37	Mark McGwire	1.00
38	Matt Williams	.10
39	Paul O'Neill	.10
40	Rickey Henderson	.50
41	Todd Greene	.10
42	Russ Ortiz	.10
43	Sean Casey	.20
44	Tony Womack	.10
45	Troy O'Leary	.10
46	Ugueth Urbina	.10
47	Tom Glavine	.25
48	Mike Mussina	.30
49	Carlos Febles	.10
50	Jon Lieber	.10
51	Juan Gonzalez	.30
52	Matt Clement	.10
53	Moises Alou	.10
54	Ray Durham	.10
55	Rob Nen	.10
56	Tino Martinez	.10
57	Troy Glaus	.40
58	Curt Schilling	.30
59	Mike Sweeney	.10
60	Steve Finley	.10
61	Roger Cedeno	.10
62	Bobby Jones	.10
63	John Smoltz	.10
64	Darin Erstad	.20
65	Carlos Delgado	.35
66	Ray Lankford	.10
67	Todd Stottlemyre	.10
68	Andy Ashby	.10
69	Bobby Abreu	.15
70	Chuck Finley	.10
71	Damion Easley	.10
72	Dustin Hermanson	.10
73	Frank Thomas	.50
74	Kevin Brown	.10
75	Kevin Millwood	.10
76	Mark Grace	.10
77	Matt Stairs	.10
78	Mike Hampton	.10
79	Omar Vizquel	.10
80	Preston Wilson	.10
81	Robin Ventura	.10
82	Todd Helton	.40
83	Tony Clark	.10
84	Al Leiter	.10
85	Alex Fernandez	.10
86	Bernie Williams	.10
87	Edgar Martinez	.10
88	Edgar Renteria	.10
89	Fred McGriff	.10
90	Jermaine Dye	.10
91	Joe McEwing	.10
92	John Halama	.10
93	Lee Stevens	.10
94	Matt Lawton	.10
95	Mike Piazza	.75
96	Pete Harnisch	.10
97	Scott Karl	.10
98	Tony Fernandez	.10
99	Sammy Sosa	.60
100	Bobby Higginson	.10
101	Tony Gwynn	.60
102	J.D. Drew	.20
103	Roberto Hernandez	.10
104	Rondell White	.10
105	David Nilsson	.10
106	Shane Reynolds	.10
107	Jaret Wright	.10
108	Jeff Bagwell	.50
109	Jay Bell	.10
110	Kevin Tapani	.10
111	Michael Barrett	.10
112	Neifi Perez	.10
113	Pat Hentgen	.10
114	Roger Clemens	.65
115	Travis Fryman	.10
116	Aaron Sele	.10
117	Eric Davis	.10
118	Trevor Hoffman	.10
119	Chris Singleton	.10
120	Ryan Klesko	.10
121	Scott Rolen	.40
122	Jorge Posada	.10
123	Abraham Nunez	.10
124	Alex Gonzalez	.10
125	B.J. Surhoff	.10
126	Barry Bonds	1.50
127	Billy Koch	.10
128	Billy Wagner	.10
129	Brad Ausmus	.10
130	Bret Boone	.10
131	Cal Ripken Jr.	1.50
132	Chad Allen	.10
133	Chris Carpenter	.10
134	Craig Biggio	.10
135	Dante Bichette	.10
136	Dean Palmer	.10
137	Derek Jeter	1.50
138	Ellis Burks	.10
139	Freddy Garcia	.10
140	Gabe Kapler	.10
141	Greg Maddux	.60
142	Greg Vaughn	.10
143	Jason Kendall	.10
144	Jim Parque	.10
145	John Valentin	.10
146	Jose Vidro	.10
147	Ken Griffey Jr.	.75
148	Kenny Lofton	.10
149	Kenny Rogers	.10
150	Kent Bottenfield	.10
151	Chuck Knoblauch	.10
152	Larry Walker	.10
153	Manny Ramirez	.50
154	Mickey Morandini	.10
155	Mike Cameron	.10
156	Mike Lieberthal	.10
157	Mo Vaughn	.10
158	Randy Johnson	.50
159	Rey Ordonez	.10
160	Roberto Alomar	.20
161	Scott Williamson	.10
162	Shawn Estes	.10
163	Tim Wakefield	.10
164	Tony Batista	.10
165	Will Clark	.10
166	Wade Boggs	.60
167	David Cone	.10
168	Doug Glanville	.10
169	Jeff Cirillo	.10
170	John Jaha	.10
171	Mariano Rivera	.20
172	Tom Gordon	.10
173	Wally Joyner	.10
174	Alex Gonzalez	.10
175	Andruw Jones	.50
176	Barry Larkin	.10
177	Bartolo Colon	.10
178	Brian Giles	.10
179	Carlos Lee	.10
180	Darren Dreifort	.10
181	Eric Chavez	.20
182	Henry Rodriguez	.10
183	Ismael Valdes	.10
184	Jason Giambi	.40
185	John Wetteland	.10
186	Juan Encarnacion	.10
187	Luis Gonzalez	.10
188	Reggie Sanders	.10
189	Richard Hidalgo	.10
190	Ryan Rupe	.10
191	Sean Berry	.10
192	Rick Helling	.10
193	Randy Wolf	.10
194	Cliff Floyd	.10
195	Jose Lima	.10
196	Chipper Jones	.60
197	Charles Johnson	.10
198	Nomar Garciaparra	.60
199	Magglio Ordonez	.10
200	Shawn Green	.25
201	Travis Lee	.10
202	Jose Canseco	.35
203	Fernando Tatis	.10
204	Bruce Aven	.10
205	Johnny Damon	.35
206	Gary Sheffield	.25
207	Ken Caminiti	.10
208	Ben Grieve	.10
209	Sidney Ponson	.10
210	Vinny Castilla	.10
211	Alex Rodriguez	1.00
212	Chris Widger	.10
213	Carl Pavano	.10
214	J.T. Snow	.10
215	Jim Thome	.40
216	Kevin Young	.10
217	Mike Sirotka	.10
218	Rafael Palmeiro	.40
219	Rico Brogna	.10
220	Todd Walker	.10
221	Todd Zeile	.10
222	Brian Rose	.10
223	Chris Fussell	.10
224	Corey Koskie	.10
225	Rich Aurilia	.10
226	Geoff Jenkins	.10
227	Pedro Martinez	.50
228	Todd Hundley	.10
229	Brian Jordan	.10
230	Cristian Guzman	.10
231	Raul Mondesi	.10
232	Tim Hudson	.20
233	Albert Belle	.10
234	Andy Pettitte	.25
235	Brady Anderson	.10
236	Brian Bohanon	.10
237	Carlos Beltran	.35
238	Doug Mientkiewicz	.10
239	Jason Schmidt	.10
240	Jeff Zimmerman	.10
241	John Olerud	.10
242	Paul Byrd	.10
243	Vladimir Guerrero	.50
244	Warren Morris	.10
245	Eric Karros	.10
246	Jeff Weaver	.10
247	Jeromy Burnitz	.10
248	David Bell	.10
249	Rusty Greer	.10
250	Kevin Stocker	.10
251	Shea Hillenbrand	.15
252	Alfonso Soriano	.50
253	Micah Bowie	.10
254	Gary Matthews Jr.	.10
255	Lance Berkman	.10
256	Pat Burrell	.25
257	Ruben Mateo	.10
258	Kip Wells	.10
259	Wilton Veras	.10
260	Ben Davis)	.10
261	Eric Munson	.10
262	Ramon Hernandez	.10
263	Tony Armas Jr.	.10
264	Erubiel Durazo	.10
265	Chad Meyers	.10
266	Rick Ankiel	.10
267	Ramon Ortiz	.10
268	Adam Kennedy	.10
269	Vernon Wells	.10
270	Chad Hermansen	.10
271	Norm Hutchins, Trent Durrington	.10
272	Gabe Molina, B.J. Ryan	.10
273	Juan Pena, Tomokazu Ohka RC	.25
274	Pat Daneker, Aaron Myette	.15
275	Jason Rakers, Russell Branyan	.10
276	Beiker Graterol, Dave Borkowski	.10
277	Mark Quinn, Dan Reichert	.10
278	Mark Redman, Jacque Jones	.15
279	Ed Yarnall, Wily Pena	.10
280	Chad Harville, Brett Laxton	.10
281	Aaron Scheffer, Gil Meche	.10
282	Jim Morris, Dan Wheeler	.10
283	Danny Kolb, Kelly Dransfeldt	.10
284	Peter Munro, Casey Blake	.10
285	Rob Ryan, Byung-Hyun Kim	.15
286	Derrin Ebert, Pascual Matos	.10
287	Richard Barker, Kyle Farnsworth	.10
288	Jason LaRue, Travis Dawkins	.10
289	Chris Sexton, Edgard Clemente	.10
290	Amaury Garcia, A.J. Burnett	.10
291	Carlos Hernandez, Daryle Ward	.10
292	Eric Gagne, Jeff Williams	.10
293	Kyle Peterson, Kevin Barker	.10
294	Fernando Seguignol, Guillermo Mota	.10
295	Melvin Mora, Octavio Dotel	.10
296	Anthony Shumaker, Cliff Politte	.10
297	Yamid Haad, Jimmy Anderson	.10
298	Rick Heiserman, Chad Hutchinson	.10
299	Mike Darr, Wiki Gonzalez	.10
300	Joe Nathan, Calvin Murray	.10

Autographics

		NM/M
Common Player:		5.00
Inserted 1:144		
1	Rick Ankiel	15.00
2	Peter Bergeron	5.00
3	Wade Boggs	25.00
4	Barry Bonds	200.00
5	Pat Burrell	20.00
6	Miguel Cairo	5.00
7	Mike Cameron	8.00
8	Ben Davis	5.00
9	Russ Davis	5.00
10	Einar Diaz	5.00
11	Scott Elarton	5.00
12	Jeremy Giambi	5.00
13	Todd Greene	5.00
14	Vladimir Guerrero	25.00
15	Tony Gwynn	30.00
16	Bobby Howry	5.00
17	Tim Hudson	15.00
18	Randy Johnson	50.00
19	Andruw Jones	20.00
20	Jacque Jones	8.00
21	Jason LaRue	5.00
22	Matt Lawton	6.00
23	Greg Maddux	50.00
24	Pedro Martinez	50.00
25	Pokey Reese	5.00
26	Alex Rodriguez	75.00
27	Ryan Rupe	5.00
28	J.T. Snow	6.00
29	Jose Vidro	6.00
30	Tony Womack	6.00
31	Ed Yarnall	5.00
32	Kevin Young	5.00

Eye on October

		NM/M
Complete Set (15):		25.00
Common Player:		1.00
Inserted 1:24		
Plus:		2-4X
Inserted 1:240		
1	Ken Griffey Jr.	2.50
2	Mark McGwire	3.00
3	Derek Jeter	4.00

4	Juan Gonzalez	1.00
5	Chipper Jones	2.00
6	Sammy Sosa	2.00
7	Greg Maddux	2.00
8	Frank Thomas	1.50
9	Nomar Garciaparra	2.00
10	Shawn Green	1.00
11	Cal Ripken Jr.	4.00
12	Manny Ramirez	1.50
13	Scott Rolen	1.25
14	Mike Piazza	2.50
15	Alex Rodriguez	3.00

Double Play

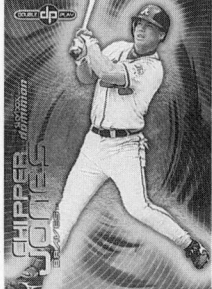

	NM/M
Complete Set (10):	10.00
Common Player:	1.00
Inserted 1:9	
Plus:	2-4X
Inserted 1:90	
WarpTek:	10-20X
Inserted 1:900	

1	Nomar Garciaparra	1.50
2	Pedro Martinez	1.25
3	Chipper Jones	1.50
4	Mark McGwire	2.50
5	Cal Ripken Jr.	3.00
6	Roger Clemens	1.75
7	Juan Gonzalez	1.00
8	Tony Gwynn	1.50
9	Sammy Sosa	1.50
10	Mike Piazza	2.00

Hats Off

	NM/M
Common Player:	15.00
Inserted 1:468 H	

1	Wade Boggs	25.00
2	Barry Bonds	75.00
3	J.D. Drew	15.00
4	Shawn Green	15.00
5	Vladimir Guerrero	25.00
6	Randy Johnson	30.00
7	Andruw Jones	20.00
8	Greg Maddux	40.00
9	Pedro Martinez	25.00
10	Mike Mussina	15.00
11	Rafael Palmeiro	15.00
12	Alex Rodriguez	50.00
13	Scott Rolen	15.00
14	Tim Salmon	15.00
15	Robin Ventura	15.00

Milestones

	NM/M
Common Player:	15.00
Inserted 1:1,999	

1	Mark McGwire	60.00
2	Roger Clemens	40.00
3	Tony Gwynn	25.00
4	Wade Boggs	25.00
5	Cal Ripken Jr.	75.00
6	Jose Canseco	15.00

New Era

	NM/M
Complete Set (20):	5.00
Common Player:	.25
Inserted 1:3	
Plus:	2-4X
Inserted 1:30	
WarpTek:	5-10X
Inserted 1:300	

1	Pat Burrell	.75
2	Ruben Mateo	.25
3	Wilton Veras	.25
4	Eric Munson	.25
5	Jeff Weaver	.25
6	Tim Hudson	.50
7	Carlos Beltran	1.00
8	Chris Singleton	.25
9	Lance Berkman	.25
10	Freddy Garcia	.25
11	Erubiel Durazo	.25
12	Randy Wolf	.25
13	Shea Hillenbrand	.25
14	Kip Wells	.25
15	Alfonso Soriano	1.50
16	Rick Ankiel	.25
17	Ramon Ortiz	.25
18	Adam Kennedy	.25
19	Vernon Wells	.25
20	Chad Hermansen	.25

2004 SkyBox Autographics

	NM/M
Complete Set (100):	.40
Common Player:	.40
Hobby Box (4):	75.00

1	Albert Pujols	2.50
2	Richie Sexson	.75
3	Scott Rolen	1.00
4	Rafael Palmeiro	.75
5	Ichiro Suzuki	2.00
6	Craig Biggio	.50
7	Todd Helton	.75
8	Miguel Cabrera	.75
9	Ken Griffey Jr.	1.50
10	Pat Burrell	.50
11	Jose Reyes	.50
12	Hideki Matsui	2.50
13	Geoff Jenkins	.50
14	Mark Prior	2.00
15	Gary Sheffield	.50
16	Nomar Garciaparra	2.00
17	Luis Gonzalez	.50
18	Troy Glaus	.50
19	Rocco Baldelli	.75
20	Hank Blalock	.50
21	Bret Boone	.50
22	Mike Sweeney	.40
23	Dmitri Young	.40
24	Dontrelle Willis	.50
25	Austin Kearns	.50
26	Jason Kendall	.40
27	Derek Jeter	3.00
28	Miguel Tejada	.50
29	Torii Hunter	.50
30	Sammy Sosa	2.00
31	Chipper Jones	1.50
32	Pedro J. Martinez	1.00
33	Curt Schilling	.75
34	Roy Halladay	.50
35	Jim Edmonds	.50
36	Alex Rodriguez	2.50
37	Jason Schmidt	.50
38	Jeff Bagwell	.75
39	Omar Vizquel	.40
40	Ivan Rodriguez	.75
41	Magglio Ordonez	.50
42	Jim Thome	1.00
43	Mike Piazza	2.00
44	Alfonso Soriano	1.00
45	Hideo Nomo	.50
46	Kerry Wood	1.00
47	Greg Maddux	1.50
48	Tony Batista	.40
49	Randy Johnson	1.00
50	Garret Anderson	.50
51	Mark Teixeira	.50
52	Carlos Delgado	.75
53	Darin Erstad	.50
54	Shawn Green	.50
55	Josh Beckett	.75
56	Lance Berkman	.50
57	Adam Dunn	.50
58	Brian Giles	.50
59	Jason Giambi	1.00
60	Barry Zito	.50
61	Vladimir Guerrero	1.00
62	Frank Thomas	.75
63	Jay Gibbons	.40
64	Manny Ramirez	.75
65	Andruw Jones	.75
66	Rickie Weeks	4.00
67	Chad Bentz RC	4.00
68	Bobby Crosby	4.00
69	Greg Dobbs RC	5.00
70	John Gall RC	5.00
71	Kazuo Matsui RC	20.00
72	Dallas McPherson	3.00
73	Brandon Watson	3.00
74	Jerry Gil RC	3.00
75	Garrett Atkins	3.00
76	Cory Sullivan RC	3.00
77	Khalil Greene	5.00
78	Shawn Hill RC	3.00
79	Graham Koonce	3.00
80	Chien-Ming Wang	3.00
81	Josh Labandeira RC	3.00
82	Jonny Gomes	3.00
83	Edwin Jackson	3.00
84	Alfredo Simon RC	4.00
85	Delmon Young	6.00
86	Jason Bartlett RC	5.00
87	Angel Chavez RC	3.00
88	Angel Guzman	3.00
89	Ryan Howard	3.00
90	Scott Hairston	3.00
91	Ronny Cedeno RC	3.00
92	Donald Kelly RC	3.00
93	Ivan Ochoa RC	3.00
94	Edwin Encarnacion	3.00
95	Byron Gettis	3.00
96	Kevin Youkilis	4.00
97	Grady Sizemore	3.00
98	Mariano Gomez RC	3.00
99	Hector Gimenez RC	3.00
100	Ruddy Yan RC	3.00

Insignia

Cards (1-65):	3-5X
Rookies (66-100):	1-2X
Production 150 Sets	

Royal Insignia

No Pricing
Production 25 Sets

Autoclassics

	NM/M
Complete Set (15):	25.00
Common Player:	1.50
Johnny Bench	4.00
Wade Boggs	2.00
Steve Carlton	2.00
Albert Chandler	1.50
Ty Cobb	4.00
Carlton Fisk	1.50
George Kelly	1.50
Sal Maglie	2.00
Bill Mazeroski	1.50
Jim Palmer	2.00
Nolan Ryan	6.00
Mike Schmidt	3.00
Joe Sewell	2.00
Duke Snider	3.00
Warren Spahn	4.00

Autoclassics Memorabilia

	NM/M
Common Player:	8.00
Johnny Bench	15.00
Wade Boggs	12.00
Steve Carlton	8.00

Carlton Fisk	15.00
Bill Mazeroski	15.00
Jim Palmer	8.00
Nolan Ryan	25.00
Mike Schmidt	15.00
Duke Snider	15.00
Warren Spahn	15.00

Autoclassics Signature

	NM/M
Production 3-50	
Johnny Bench/50	50.00
Wade Boggs/50	40.00
Steve Carlton/50	20.00
Albert Chandler/25	120.00
Carlton Fisk/50	40.00
George Kelly/25	150.00
Sal Maglie/25	150.00
Bill Mazeroski/50	35.00
Jim Palmer/50	20.00
Nolan Ryan/38	150.00
Mike Schmidt/25	100.00
Joe Sewell/25	120.00
Duke Snider/50	40.00
Warren Spahn/50	50.00

Autographics Blue

	NM/M
Common Player:	5.00
Silver:	.75-1.5X
Production 100 Sets	
Gold:	1.5-2X
Production 25 Sets	
Purple:	No Pricing
Production One Set	
Garrett Atkins/175	5.00
Rocco Baldelli/255	15.00
Josh Beckett/100	25.00
Angel Berroa/182	8.00
Hank Blalock/205	15.00
A.J. Burnett/485	10.00
Marlon Byrd/240	8.00
Edwin Encarnacion/188	10.00
Eric Gagne/225	25.00
Jonny Gomes/265	15.00
Khalil Greene/190	25.00
Rich Harden/185	10.00
Dan Haren/176	10.00
Koyie Hill/240	5.00
Shea Hillenbrand/210	10.00
Ryan Howard/170	75.00
Tim Hudson/169	15.00
Aubrey Huff/296	10.00
Torii Hunter/215	10.00
Edwin Jackson/224	10.00
Bobby Jenks/307	10.00
Matt Kata/197	10.00
Austin Kearns/275	8.00
Graham Koonce/190	10.00
Barry Larkin/195	25.00
Dallas McPherson/179	8.00
Aaron Miles/140	10.00
Mark Mulder/186	15.00
Laynce Nix/185	8.00
Trot Nixon/210	15.00
Corey Patterson/220	12.00
Juan Pierre/220	15.00
Scott Podsednik/210	25.00
Albert Pujols/103	160.00
Jose Reyes/195	30.00
Juan Richardson/245	5.00
Gary Sheffield/210	20.00
Chris Snelling/200	5.00
Shannon Stewart/340	10.00
Cory Sullivan/170	5.00
Javier Vazquez/210	15.00
Billy Wagner/180	25.00
Chien-Ming Wang/195	100.00
Brandon Webb/310	12.00
Rickie Weeks/187	15.00
Dontrelle Willis/225	25.00
Kerry Wood/191	25.00
Delmon Young/205	20.00

Autographics Memorabilia

	NM/M
Production 125 Sets	
Patch:	1-2X
Production 25 Sets	
Rocco Baldelli	25.00
Josh Beckett	40.00
Hank Blalock	25.00
Torii Hunter	20.00
Corey Patterson	25.00
Albert Pujols	175.00
Billy Wagner	40.00
Brandon Webb	15.00
Dontrelle Willis	30.00

Jerseygraphics Blue

	NM/M
Common Player:	4.00

Silver:	1-2X
Production 100 Sets	
Gold:	No Pricing
Production 25 Sets	
Bobby Abreu	6.00
Rocco Baldelli	6.00
Josh Beckett	10.00
Lance Berkman	6.00
Craig Biggio	6.00
Hank Blalock	4.00
Pat Burrell	6.00
Miguel Cabrera	10.00
Carlos Delgado	6.00
Adam Dunn	8.00
Jim Edmonds	4.00
Darin Erstad	4.00
Nomar Garciaparra	8.00
Jason Giambi	8.00
Jay Gibbons	4.00
Troy Glaus	6.00
Shawn Green	4.00
Vladimir Guerrero	8.00
Roy Halladay	6.00
Todd Helton	8.00
Torii Hunter	6.00
Derek Jeter	15.00
Andruw Jones	8.00
Chipper Jones	10.00
Austin Kearns	4.00
Greg Maddux	15.00
Pedro J. Martinez	10.00
Kevin Millwood	4.00
Hideo Nomo	8.00
Magglio Ordonez	
David Ortiz	10.00
Rafael Palmeiro	6.00
Mike Piazza	10.00
Mark Prior	6.00
Albert Pujols	15.00
Manny Ramirez	10.00
Jose Reyes	10.00
Alex Rodriguez	15.00
Ivan Rodriguez	6.00
Scott Rolen	8.00
Curt Schilling	6.00
Alfonso Soriano	8.00
Sammy Sosa	8.00
Mark Teixeira	8.00
Miguel Tejada	6.00
Frank Thomas	10.00
Jim Thome	8.00
Dontrelle Willis	4.00
Kerry Wood	4.00
Barry Zito	4.00

Jeter Legacy Collection

Production 25
No Pricing

Prospects Endorsed

		NM/M
Complete Set (15):		10.00
Common Duo:		.50
1	Albert Pujols,	
	Delmon Young	3.00
2	Eric Gagne, Bobby Jenks	.50
3	Barry Larkin,	
	Kazuo Matsui	2.00
4	Andruw Jones,	
	Jonny Gomes	1.00
5	Hideo Nomo,	
	Chien-Ming Wang	.50
6	Gary Sheffield,	
	Cory Sullivan	.75
7	Billy Wagner,	
	Ryan Howard	1.00
8	Jorge Posada, Koyie Hill	.75
9	Curt Schilling,	
	Ryan Wagner	.75
10	Jose Reyes, Rickie Weeks	1.50
11	Alfonso Soriano, Matt Kata	1.50
12	Barry Zito, Rich Harden	.75
13	Randy Johnson,	
	Brandon Webb	1.50
14	Alex Rodriguez,	
	Angel Berroa	1.50
15	Dontrelle Willis,	
	Edwin Jackson	.50

Prospects Endorsed Dual Autograph

		NM/M
Production 50 Sets		.50
APDY	Albert Pujols,	
	Delmon Young	275.00
EGBJ	Eric Gagne, Bobby Jenks	30.00
BLEE	Barry Larkin,	
	Edwin Encarnacion	30.00
AJJG	Andruw Jones,	
	Jonny Gomes	35.00
GSCS	Gary Sheffield,	
	Cory Sullivan	25.00

BWRY	Billy Wagner,	
	Ryan Howard	100.00
JRRW	Jose Reyes,	
	Rickie Weeks	25.00

Prospects Endorsed Dual Jersey

		NM/M
Common Duo:		5.00
APDY	Albert Pujols,	
	Delmon Young	15.00
BLKZ	Barry Larkin,	
	Kazuo Matsui	8.00
HNCW	Hideo Nomo,	
	Chien-Ming Wang	50.00
CSRW	Curt Schilling,	
	Ryan Wagner	8.00
JRRW	Jose Reyes,	
	Rickie Weeks	8.00
ASMK	Alfonso Soriano,	
	Matt Kata	8.00
BZRH	Barry Zito, Rich Harden	5.00
RJBW	Randy Johnson,	
	Brandon Webb	8.00
ARAB	Alex Rodriguez,	
	Angel Berroa	10.00
DWEJ	Dontrelle Willis,	
	Edwin Jackson	8.00

Prospects Endorsed Dual Patch

		NM/M
Common Duo:		25.00
APDY	Albert Pujols,	
	Delmon Young	50.00
HNCW	Hideo Nomo,	
	Chien-Ming Wang	180.00
CSRW	Curt Schilling,	
	Ryan Wagner	25.00
JRRW	Jose Reyes, Rickie Weeks	15.00
ASMK	Alfonso Soriano,	
	Matt Kata	25.00
BZRH	Barry Zito, Rich Harden	25.00
RJBW	Randy Johnson,	
	Brandon Webb	25.00
ARAB	Alex Rodriguez,	
	Angel Berroa	35.00
DWEJ	Dontrelle Willis,	
	Edwin Jackson	25.00

2004 SkyBox LE

		NM/M
Complete Set (160):		
Common Player (1-110):		.25
Common SP (111-160):		4.00
Production 299 unless noted.		
Pack (18):		5.00
Box (18):		80.00
1	Juan Pierre	.25
2	Derek Jeter	3.00
3	Brandon Webb	.25
4	Jeff Bagwell	.75
5	Jason Schmidt	.40
6	Marlon Byrd	.25
7	Garret Anderson	.50
8	Miguel Cabrera	.75
9	Jose Reyes	.50
10	Rocco Baldelli	.50
11	Tony Batista	.25
12	Carlos Beltran	.50
13	Nomar Garciaparra	2.00
14	Shawn Green	.50
15	Albert Pujols	2.50
16	Magglio Ordonez	.50
17	Kip Wells	.25
18	Andruw Jones	.75
19	Ryan Wagner	.25

20	Alex Rodriguez	3.00
21	Vernon Wells	.50
22	Todd Helton	.75
23	David Ortiz	.25
24	Troy Glaus	.50
25	Jim Thome	1.00
26	Greg Maddux	1.50
27	Roberto Alomar	.50
28	Edgardo Alfonzo	.25
29	Hee Seop Choi	.25
30	Ken Griffey Jr.	1.50
31	Tim Hudson	.50
32	Shannon Stewart	.25
33	Ichiro Suzuki	2.00
34	Luis Gonzalez	.50
35	Darin Erstad	.50
36	Dmitri Young	.25
37	Ivan Rodriguez	.75
38	Scott Podsednik	.50
39	Jose Vidro	.25
40	Mark Prior	2.00
41	Mike Mussina	.75
42	Gary Sheffield	.50
43	Manny Ramirez	.75
44	C.C. Sabathia	.40
45	Curt Schilling	.75
46	Scott Rolen	1.00
47	Hideo Nomo	.50
48	Torii Hunter	.50
49	Aubrey Huff	.25
50	Javy Lopez	.50
51	Austin Kearns	.50
52	Mike Piazza	1.50
53	Sean Burroughs	.25
54	Kerry Wood	.75
55	Marquis Grissom	.25
56	Preston Wilson	.25
57	Angel Berroa	.25
58	Jason Kendall	.25
59	Rafael Palmeiro	.75
60	Mike Lowell	.40
61	Eric Chavez	.50
62	Bartolo Colon	.50
63	Adam Dunn	.50
64	Pedro J. Martinez	1.00
65	Lance Berkman	.50
66	Bret Boone	.40
67	Eric Gagne	.40
68	Vladimir Guerrero	1.00
69	Jay Gibbons	.25
70	Larry Walker	.40
71	Orlando Cabrera	.40
72	Jorge Posada	.50
73	Jamie Moyer	.25
74	Carl Crawford	.50
75	Hank Blalock	.50
76	Josh Beckett	.75
77	Jody Gerut	.25
78	Kevin Brown	.50
79	Sammy Sosa	2.00
80	Chipper Jones	1.00
81	Tom Glavine	.50
82	Barry Zito	.50
83	Edgar Renteria	.50
84	Esteban Loaiza	.25
85	Jason Giambi	1.00
86	Miguel Tejada	.50
87	Randy Johnson	1.00
88	A.J. Burnett	.25
89	Richie Sexson	.75
90	Reggie Sanders	.25
91	Carlos Delgado	.75
92	Pat Burrell	.50
93	Jacque Jones	.25
94	Roy Oswalt	.50
95	Frank Thomas	.75
96	Melvin Mora	.25
97	Jeremy Bonderman	.25
98	Mike Sweeney	.25
99	Brian Giles	.50
100	Edgar Martinez	.40
101	Mark Teixeira	.50
102	Sean Casey	.25
103	Javier Vazquez	.50
104	Hideki Matsui	2.50
105	Jim Edmonds	.40
106	Roy Halladay	.50
107	Craig Biggio	.40
108	Geoff Jenkins	.25
109	Alfonso Soriano	1.00
110	Barry Larkin	.50
111	Chris Bootcheck	4.00
112	Dallas McPherson/99	6.00
113	Matt Kata/99	4.00
114	Scott Hairston	4.00
115	Bobby Crosby	8.00
116	Adam Wainright/99	6.00
117	Daniel Cabrera	4.00
118	Kevin Youkilis	8.00
119	Ronny Cedeno RC	6.00
120	Ruddy Yan RC	4.00
121	Ryan Wing	4.00
122	William Bergolla RC	5.00
123	Edwin Encarnacion	6.00
124	Jonny Gomes	4.00
125	Garrett Atkins	4.00
126	Clint Barmes	4.00
127	Wilfredo Ledezma	4.00
128	Cody Ross	6.00
129	Josh Willingham/99	6.00
130	Chin-Hui Tsao	4.00
131	Hector Gimenez RC	6.00
132	David DeJesus	4.00
133	Jimmy Gobble	4.00
134	Edwin Jackson/99	6.00

135	Koyie Hill	4.00
136	Rickie Weeks/99	5.00
137	Graham Koonce	4.00
138	Rob Bowen	6.00
139	Shawn Hill RC	4.00
140	Craig Brazell	4.00
141	Mike Hessman	4.00
142	Jorge DePaula	4.00
143	Chien-Ming Wang/99	6.00
144	Rich Harden	4.00
145	Ryan Howard/99	6.00
146	Alfredo Simon RC	4.00
147	Ian Snell RC	6.00
148	Ryan Doumit	4.00
149	Khalil Greene/99	6.00
150	Angel Chavez RC	4.00
151	Dan Haren	6.00
152	Chris Snelling	4.00
153	Aaron Miles	4.00
154	John Gall RC	4.00
155	Chris Narveson	4.00
156	Delmon Young/99	8.00
157	Chad Gaudin	4.00
158	Gerald Laird	4.00
159	Alexis Rios	8.00
160	Jason Arnold	4.00

Gold Proof

Cards (1-110):	3-5X
SP's (111-160):	1X
Production 150 Sets	

Artist's Proof

Cards (1-110):	3-6X
SP's (110-160):	1-1.5X
Production 50 Sets	

Photographer Proof

Cards (1-110):	6-12X
SP's (110-160):	2-3X
Production 25 Sets	

Executive Proof

No Pricing
Production One Set

History of the Draft Game-Used

	NM/M
Common Player:	4.00
Numbered to last 2 digits of draft yr.	
Silver Proof:	1-1.5X
Production 50 Sets	
Gold Proof:	No Pricing
Production 10 Sets	
Garret Anderson	4.00
Josh Beckett	10.00
Carlos Beltran	8.00
Lance Berkman	6.00
Hank Blalock	4.00
Bret Boone	4.00
A.J. Burnett	4.00
Pat Burrell	4.00
Marlon Byrd	4.00
Eric Chavez	4.00
Adam Dunn	8.00
Darin Erstad	4.00
Nomar Garciaparra	8.00
Jason Giambi	8.00
Shawn Green	4.00
Roy Halladay	6.00
Todd Helton	6.00
Aubrey Huff	4.00
Torii Hunter	6.00
Derek Jeter	15.00
Chipper Jones	10.00
Austin Kearns	4.00
Mike Lowell	5.00
Mike Mussina	8.00
Corey Patterson	4.00
Juan Pierre	4.00
Scott Podsednik	4.00
Jorge Posada	8.00
Albert Pujols	20.00
Manny Ramirez	8.00
Alex Rodriguez	15.00
Scott Rolen	8.00
Jason Schmidt	4.00
Richie Sexson	6.00
Shannon Stewart	4.00
Javier Vazquez	4.00
Vernon Wells	6.00
Kerry Wood	6.00
Barry Zito	6.00

History of the Draft Autographs

	NM/M
Common Autograph:	10.00
Production 199 Sets	
Draft Year:	1-1.25X
#'d to last 2 digits of draft year	
Silver Proof:	1-1.5X
Production 50 Sets	
Gold Proof:	No Pricing
Production 10 Sets	
Hank Blalock	10.00
A.J. Burnett	10.00
Marlon Byrd	10.00
Roy Halladay	20.00
Tim Hudson	15.00
Aubrey Huff	15.00
Torii Hunter	15.00
Austin Kearns	15.00
Mike Lowell	15.00

Corey Patterson		15.00
Juan Pierre		15.00
Scott Podsednik		20.00
Albert Pujols		125.00
Scott Rolen		25.00
Shannon Stewart		10.00
Javier Vazquez		10.00
Vernon Wells		15.00

Jersey Proof

		NM/M
Common Player:		4.00
Production 299 Sets		
Silver Proof:		1.5-2X
Production 50 Sets		
Gold Proof:		No Pricing
Production 10 Sets		
1	Troy Glaus	6.00
2	Curt Schilling	6.00
3	Randy Johnson	8.00
4	Brandon Webb	6.00
5	Gary Sheffield	6.00
6	Greg Maddux	15.00
7	Chipper Jones	10.00
8	David Ortiz	10.00
9	Nomar Garciaparra	15.00
10	Pedro J. Martinez	8.00
11	Manny Ramirez	8.00
12	Kerry Wood	6.00
13	Mark Prior	6.00
14	Sammy Sosa	10.00
15	Frank Thomas	8.00
16	Austin Kearns	4.00
17	Todd Helton	8.00
18	Preston Wilson	4.00
19	Juan Pierre	4.00
20	Josh Beckett	8.00
21	Ivan Rodriguez	6.00
22	Miguel Cabrera	8.00
23	Mike Lowell	6.00
24	Lance Berkman	6.00
25	Jeff Bagwell	8.00
26	Angel Berroa	4.00
27	Hideo Nomo	10.00
28	Eric Gagne	4.00
29	Scott Podsednik	10.00
30	Richie Sexson	6.00
31	Torii Hunter	6.00
32	Mike Piazza	10.00
33	Jose Reyes	10.00
34	Tom Glavine	6.00
35	Derek Jeter	25.00
36	Jorge Posada	6.00
37	Jason Giambi	8.00
38	Alfonso Soriano	8.00
39	Eric Chavez	4.00
40	Miguel Tejada	6.00
41	Jim Thome	8.00
42	Albert Pujols	15.00
43	Scott Rolen	8.00
44	Rocco Baldelli	6.00
45	Alex Rodriguez	15.00
46	Hank Blalock	6.00
47	Mark Teixeira	6.00
48	Rafael Palmeiro	6.00
49	Carlos Delgado	6.00
50	Roy Halladay	6.00

L.E.ague L.E.aders

ALEX RODRIGUEZ/SS

		NM/M
Complete Set (10):		10.00
Common Player:		.50
Inserted 1:18		
1LL	Alex Rodriguez	3.00
2LL	Jim Thome	1.50
3LL	Albert Pujols	3.00
4LL	Pedro J. Martinez	1.50
5LL	Roy Halladay	.75
6LL	Jason Schmidt	.50
7LL	Kerry Wood	1.00
8LL	Juan Pierre	.50
9LL	Preston Wilson	.50
10LL	Carlos Delgado	1.00

L.E.ague L.E.aders Game-Used

		NM/M
Common Player:		4.00
Production 75 Sets		
Silver Proof:		1-1.5X

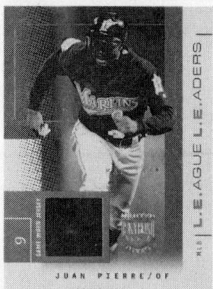

JUAN PIERRE/OF

Production 50 Sets		
Gold Proof:		No Pricing
Production 10 Sets		
	Alex Rodriguez	15.00
	Jim Thome	8.00
	Albert Pujols	20.00
	Pedro J. Martinez	10.00
	Roy Halladay	6.00
	Jason Schmidt	4.00
	Kerry Wood	4.00
	Juan Pierre	4.00
	Preston Wilson	4.00
	Carlos Delgado	6.00

Rare Form

		NM/M
Common Player:		5.00
Inserted 1:288		
1	Albert Pujols	20.00
2	Miguel Cabrera	5.00
3	Jim Thome	10.00
4	Derek Jeter	30.00
5	Nomar Garciaparra	15.00
6	Mike Piazza	15.00
7	Alex Rodriguez	20.00
8	Delmon Young	15.00
9	Chipper Jones	12.00
10	Rickie Weeks	8.00

Rare Form Autographs

		NM/M
Common Autograph:		10.00
Production 299 Sets		
Level 2:		1-1.5X
Production 99 Sets		
Silver Proof:		1.5X
Production 50 Sets		
Gold Proof:		No Pricing
Production 10 Sets		
	Rocco Baldelli	25.00
	Angel Berroa	15.00
	Rich Harden	20.00
	Edwin Jackson	20.00
	Matt Kata	10.00
	Dallas McPherson	15.00
	Brandon Webb	15.00
	Rickie Weeks	20.00
	Delmon Young	25.00

Rare Form Game-Used Silver Proof

		NM/M
Common Player:		5.00
Production 50 Sets		
Gold Proof:		No Pricing
Production 10 Sets		
	Rocco Baldelli	5.00
	Miguel Cabrera	10.00
	Nomar Garciaparra	15.00
	Derek Jeter	25.00
	Chipper Jones	12.00
	Mike Piazza	15.00
	Albert Pujols	25.00
	Alex Rodriguez	15.00
	Jim Thome	10.00

Rare Form Memorabilia Jersey Number

		NM/M
Numbered to jersey number.		
Most not priced due to scarcity.		
Mike Piazza/31		30.00
Jim Thome/25		25.00

Sky's the Limit

		NM/M
Complete Set (20):		20.00
Common Player:		.50
Inserted 1:6		
1SL	Dontrelle Willis	1.00
2SL	Rocco Baldelli	1.00
3SL	Miguel Cabrera	1.00
4SL	Mark Prior	3.00
5SL	Hideki Matsui	4.00
6SL	Kerry Wood	1.50
7SL	Alfonso Soriano	1.50
8SL	Ichiro Suzuki	2.50
9SL	Brandon Webb	.50
10SL	Alex Rodriguez	3.00
11SL	Barry Zito	1.00

BRAVES OF ANDRUW JONES

12SL	Hank Blalock	1.00
13SL	Jose Reyes	.75
14SL	Torii Hunter	.75
15SL	Josh Beckett	1.00
16SL	Manny Ramirez	1.00
17SL	Andruw Jones	1.00
18SL	Vladimir Guerrero	1.50
19SL	Miguel Tejada	.75
20SL	Carlos Delgado	1.00

Sky's the Limit Game-Used

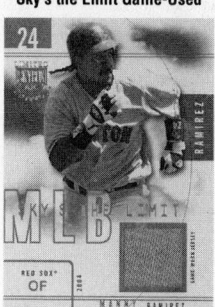

RED SOX OF MANNY RAMIREZ

		NM/M
Common Player:		4.00
Production 99 Sets		
Silver Proof:		1X
Production 50 Sets		
Gold Proof:		No Pricing
Production 10 Sets		
	Rocco Baldelli	4.00
	Josh Beckett	10.00
	Hank Blalock	6.00
	Miguel Cabrera	8.00
	Carlos Delgado	6.00
	Vladimir Guerrero	8.00
	Torii Hunter	6.00
	Andruw Jones	6.00
	Mark Prior	6.00
	Manny Ramirez	8.00
	Jose Reyes	10.00
	Alex Rodriguez	15.00
	Alfonso Soriano	8.00
	Miguel Tejada	6.00
	Brandon Webb	6.00
	Dontrelle Willis	4.00
	Kerry Wood	4.00
	Barry Zito	4.00

2005 SkyBox Autographics

NEW YORK METS OF CARLOS BELTRAN 1S

		NM/M
Complete Set (115):		
Common Player (1-60):		.15
Common (61-115):		1.50
Production 750		
Pack (5):		8.00

Box (12):		85.00
1	Vladimir Guerrero	.75
2	Garret Anderson	.25
3	Troy Glaus	.25
4	Shawn Green	.25
5	Chipper Jones	.75
6	Andruw Jones	.40
7	Miguel Tejada	.50
8	Melvin Mora	.15
9	Manny Ramirez	.75
10	Curt Schilling	.75
11	Nomar Garciaparra	.50
12	Mark Prior	2.00
13	Sammy Sosa	1.00
14	Frank Thomas	.40
15	Paul Konerko	.25
16	Adam Dunn	.50
17	Ken Griffey Jr.	1.50
18	Victor Martinez	.25
19	Travis Hafner	.25
20	Todd Helton	.50
21	Ivan Rodriguez	.50
22	Carlos Guillen	.15
23	Miguel Cabrera	.50
24	Juan Pierre	.15
25	Roger Clemens	2.00
26	Jeff Bagwell	.50
27	Lance Berkman	.25
28	Mike Sweeney	.15
29	Eric Gagne	.15
30	J.D. Drew	.15
31	Ben Sheets	.25
32	Lyle Overbay	.15
33	Johan Santana	.50
34	Torii Hunter	.15
35	Mike Piazza	1.00
36	Pedro Martinez	.75
37	Carlos Beltran	.50
38	Derek Jeter	2.00
39	Alex Rodriguez	2.00
40	Hideki Matsui	1.50
41	Randy Johnson	.75
42	Eric Chavez	.50
43	Jim Thome	.50
44	Craig Wilson	.15
45	Khalil Greene	.25
46	Jake Peavy	.25
47	Jason Schmidt	.15
48	Ichiro Suzuki	1.50
49	Adrian Beltre	.25
50	Albert Pujols	2.00
51	Scott Rolen	.50
52	Carl Crawford	.15
53	Rocco Baldelli	.15
54	Alfonso Soriano	.50
55	Hank Blalock	.25
56	Vernon Wells	.15
57	Jose Vidro	.15
58	David Ortiz	.75
59	Bobby Abreu	.25
60	Gary Sheffield	.40
61	Nolan Ryan	15.00
62	Mike Schmidt	10.00
63	Johnny Bench	8.00
64	Lou Brock	3.00
65	Dennis Eckersley	2.00
66	Carlton Fisk	3.00
67	Bob Gibson	4.00
68	Reggie Jackson	4.00
69	Al Kaline	3.00
70	Bill Mazeroski	2.00
71	Willie McCovey	3.00
72	Jim Palmer	3.00
73	Phil Rizzuto	2.00
74	Warren Spahn	4.00
75	Brooks Robinson	3.00
76	Willie Stargell	3.00
77	Jim "Catfish" Hunter	2.00
78	Tony Perez	2.00
79	George Kell	2.00
80	Robin Yount	4.00
81	Fergie Jenkins	2.00
82	Tom Seaver	3.00
83	Eddie Mathews	2.00
84	Enos Slaughter	2.00
85	Pee Wee Reese	2.00
86	Harmon Killebrew	3.00
87	Eddie Murray	2.00
88	Orlando Cepeda	2.00
89	Billy Williams	2.00
90	Ralph Kiner	2.00
91	Ryan Raburn	1.50
92	Justin Morneau	2.00
93	Zack Greinke	1.50
94	David Aardsma	1.50
95	B.J. Upton	2.00
96	Gavin Floyd	1.50
97	David Wright	8.00
98	Russ Adams	1.50
99	Jose Lopez	2.00
100	Scott Kazmir	2.00
101	Mike Gosling	1.50
102	Jeff Keppinger	1.50
103	David Krynzel	1.50
104	Jeff Niemann **RC**	6.00
105	Ruben Gotay	1.50
106	Dioner Navarro	1.50
107	Nick Swisher	1.50
108	Yadier Molina	1.50
109	Joey Gathright	1.50
110	Jon Knott	1.50
111	J.D. Durbin	1.50
112	Andres Blanco	1.50
113	Charlton Jimerson	1.50
114	Sean Burnett	1.50
115	Justin Verlander **RC**	6.00

Insignia

Insignia (1-60):	2-3X
Insignia (61-115):	1X
Production 150 Sets	

Royal Insignia

Royal Insignia (1-60):	4-6X
Royal Insignia (61-115):	1.5-2X
Production 25 Sets	

Future Signs

		NM/M
Common Player:		.50
Inserted 1:6		
1	Bobby Crosby	.50
2	David Aardsma	.50
3	Russ Adams	.50
4	J.D. Durbin	.50
5	Johnny Estrada	.50
6	Chone Figgins	.50
7	Jason Bay	.75
8	Gavin Floyd	.50
9	Lew Ford	.50
10	Victor Martinez	.50
11	Joe Mauer	.75
12	Justin Morneau	.50
13	Laynce Nix	.50
14	Sean Burnett	.50
15	B.J. Upton	.75
16	Justin Verlander	1.50
17	David Wright	3.00
18	Delmon Young	1.00
19	Michael Young	.50
20	Zack Greinke	.50

Future Signs Autograph Blue

		NM/M
Production 8-505		
Cards not serial numbered.		
JB	Jason Bay/264	15.00
ZG	Zack Greinke/264	10.00
VM	Victor Martinez/500	12.00
JM	Justin Morneau/224	20.00
AO	Akinori Otsuka/639	10.00
JV	Justin Verlander/505	25.00
DW	David Wright/8	

Future Signs Autograph Gold

		NM/M
Production 65 Sets		
JB	Jason Bay	15.00
SB	Sean Burnett	10.00
JD	J.D. Durbin	5.00
EE	Edwin Encarnacion	10.00
ZG	Zack Greinke	8.00
SH	Scott Hairston	8.00
VMJ	Val Majewski	15.00
VM	Victor Martinez	15.00
JM	Justin Morneau	20.00
AO	Akinori Otsuka	10.00
AS	Alfredo Simon	5.00
BU	B.J. Upton	15.00
JV	Justin Verlander	30.00
RW	Rickie Weeks	15.00
DW	David Wright	50.00

Future Signs Auto Gold Embossed

		NM/M
Production 45 Sets		
JB	Jason Bay	15.00
SB	Sean Burnett	10.00
JD	J.D. Durbin	5.00
EE	Edwin Encarnacion	10.00
ZG	Zack Greinke	8.00
SH	Scott Hairston	8.00
VMJ	Val Majewski	15.00
VM	Victor Martinez	15.00
JM	Justin Morneau	20.00
AO	Akinori Otsuka	10.00
AS	Alfredo Simon	5.00
BU	B.J. Upton	30.00
JV	Justin Verlander	30.00
RW	Rickie Weeks	50.00
DW	David Wright	50.00
DY	Delmon Young	20.00

Future Signs Auto. Platinum

		NM/M
Production 25 Sets		
Gold Embossed:		No Pricing
Production 5 Sets		
JB	Jason Bay	20.00
SB	Sean Burnett	10.00
JD	J.D. Durbin	8.00
EE	Edwin Encarnacion	10.00
ZG	Zack Greinke	10.00
SH	Scott Hairston	8.00
VMJ	Val Majewski	15.00
VM	Victor Martinez	20.00
JM	Justin Morneau	25.00
AO	Akinori Otsuka	15.00
AS	Alfredo Simon	8.00
BU	B.J. Upton	20.00
JV	Justin Verlander	35.00
RW	Rickie Weeks	20.00
DW	David Wright	60.00
DY	Delmon Young	20.00

Future Signs Autograph Silver

	NM/M
Production 100 Sets	
Silver Embossed:	1X

J.D. DURBIN
MINNESOTA TWINS

Production 85 Sets		
JB	Jason Bay	15.00
SB	Sean Burnett	10.00
JD	J.D. Durbin	5.00
EE	Edwin Encarnacion	10.00
ZG	Zack Greinke	8.00
VMJ	Val Majewski	15.00
VM	Victor Martinez	15.00
JM	Justin Morneau	20.00
AO	Akinori Otsuka	10.00
AS	Alfredo Simon	5.00
BU	B.J. Upton	15.00
JV	Justin Verlander	30.00
RW	Rickie Weeks	15.00
DW	David Wright	50.00

Jerseygraphics Blue

		NM/M
Common Player:		4.00
Inserted 1:40 Retail		
Gold:		1-2X
Inserted 1:240 Retail		
Silver:		1X
Inserted 1:80 Retail		
GA	Garret Anderson	4.00
JB	Jeff Bagwell	6.00
RB	Rocco Baldelli	4.00
JBE	Josh Beckett	4.00
AB	Adrian Beltre	4.00
HB	Hank Blalock	4.00
MB	Marlon Byrd	4.00
MC	Miguel Cabrera	8.00
CD	Carlos Delgado	4.00
AD	Adam Dunn	6.00
EG	Eric Gagne	4.00
BG	Brian Giles	4.00
TG	Troy Glaus	4.00
TGL	Tom Glavine	4.00
TH	Torii Hunter	6.00
AK	Austin Kearns	4.00
MO	Magglio Ordonez	4.00
JR	Jose Reyes	6.00
BS	Ben Sheets	4.00
MT	Mark Teixeira	6.00

Master Collection

Production 25 Sets	
All are Jsy/Jsy/Patch combos.	
One of a Kind:	No Pricing
Production One Set	

Signature Blue

		NM/M
Print run info provided by UD.		
Cards are not serial #'d.		
Jsy Gold:		1-1.5X
Production 45 Sets		
Jsy Gold Embossed:		1-2X
Production 30 Sets		
Jsy Silver:		1X
Production 100 Sets		
Jsy Silver Embossed:		1X
Production 75 Sets		
EP	Jeremy Bonderman/369	12.00
MC	Miguel Cabrera/250	30.00
MCA	Mike Cameron/200	10.00
CC	Carl Crawford/150	15.00
DE	David Eckstein/546	20.00
AE	Adam Everett/590	6.00
LG	Luis Gonzalez/187	6.00
THA	Travis Hafner/246	15.00
TH	Trevor Hoffman/590	12.00
OH	Orlando Hudson/231	8.00
CK	Casey Kotchman/227	10.00
JK	Jason Kubel/137	8.00
BL	Brad Lidge/164	20.00
JO	John Olerud/446	15.00
CP	Corey Patterson/329	8.00
EP	Eduardo Perez/584	6.00
JS	Jason Santana/200	30.00

Signatures Game Patch Gold

No Pricing	
Production 5 Sets	
Gold Embossed	
Production 15 Sets	
Masterpiece Embossed:	No Pricing
Production One Set	

Signatures Game Patch Silver

	NM/M
Production 25 Sets	

RB	Rocco Baldelli	40.00
JB	Jeremy Bonderman	40.00
SS	Shannon Stewart	20.00

Signature Moments

Signature MOMENTS
REGGIE JACKSON / NEW YORK YANKEES / OF
1977 WORLD SERIES MVP

		NM/M
Complete Set (10):		15.00
Common Player:		1.00
Inserted 1:12		
1	Manny Ramirez	1.50
2	Derek Jeter	4.00
3	Ichiro Suzuki	3.00
4	Roger Clemens	4.00
5	Albert Pujols	4.00
6	Nolan Ryan	4.00
7	Reggie Jackson	1.50
8	Carlton Fisk	1.00
9	Mike Schmidt	1.50
10	Johnny Bench	1.50

1993 SP

TOM GLAVINE

		NM/M
Complete Set (290):		75.00
Common Player:		.10
Pack (12):		10.00
Wax Box (24):		220.00
1	Roberto Alomar	.30
2	Wade Boggs	2.00
3	Joe Carter	.10
4	Ken Griffey Jr.	2.50
5	Mark Langston	.10
6	John Olerud	.10
7	Kirby Puckett	2.00
8	Cal Ripken, Jr.	4.00
9	Ivan Rodriguez	1.25
10	Barry Bonds	4.00
11	Darren Daulton	.10
12	Marquis Grissom	.10
13	Dave Justice	.10
14	John Kruk	.10
15	Barry Larkin	.10
16	Terry Mulholland	.10
17	Ryne Sandberg	2.00
18	Gary Sheffield	.10
19	Chad Curtis	.10
20	Chili Davis	.10
21	Gary DiSarcina	.10
22	Damion Easley	.10
23	Chuck Finley	.10
24	Luis Polonia	.10
25	Tim Salmon	.10
26	J.T. Snow RC	1.00
27	Russ Springer	.10
28	Jeff Bagwell	1.50
29	Craig Biggio	.10
30	Ken Caminiti	.10
31	Andujar Cedeno	.10
32	Doug Drabek	.10
33	Steve Finley	.10
34	Luis Gonzalez	.10
35	Pete Harnisch	.10
36	Darryl Kile	.10
37	Mike Bordick	.10
38	Dennis Eckersley	1.25
39	Brent Gates	.10
40	Rickey Henderson	1.50
41	Mark McGwire	3.00
42	Craig Paquette	.10
43	Ruben Sierra	.10
44	Terry Steinbach	.10
45	Todd Van Poppel	.10
46	Pat Borders	.10
47	Tony Fernandez	.10
48	Juan Guzman	.10
49	Pat Hentgen	.10
50	Paul Molitor	1.50
51	Jack Morris	.10
52	Ed Sprague	.10
53	Duane Ward	.10
54	Devon White	.10
55	Steve Avery	.10
56	Jeff Blauser	.10
57	Ron Gant	.10
58	Tom Glavine	.40
59	Greg Maddux	2.00
60	Fred McGriff	.10
61	Terry Pendleton	.10
62	Deion Sanders	.10
63	John Smoltz	.10
64	Cal Eldred	.10
65	Darryl Hamilton	.10
66	John Jaha	.10
67	Pat Listach	.10
68	Jaime Navarro	.10
69	Kevin Reimer	.10
70	B.J. Surhoff	.10
71	Greg Vaughn	.10
72	Robin Yount	1.50
73	Rene Arocha RC	.10
74	Bernard Gilkey	.10
75	Gregg Jefferies	.10
76	Ray Lankford	.10
77	Tom Pagnozzi	.10
78	Lee Smith	.10
79	Ozzie Smith	2.00
80	Bob Tewksbury	.10
81	Mark Whiten	.10
82	Steve Buechele	.10
83	Mark Grace	.10
84	Jose Guzman	.10
85	Derrick May	.10
86	Mike Morgan	.10
87	Randy Myers	.10
88	Kevin Roberson RC	.10
89	Sammy Sosa	2.00
90	Rick Wilkins	.10
91	Brett Butler	.10
92	Eric Davis	.10
93	Orel Hershiser	.10
94	Eric Karros	.10
95	Ramon Martinez	.10
96	Raul Mondesi	.10
97	Jose Offerman	.10
98	Mike Piazza	2.50
99	Darryl Strawberry	.10
100	Moises Alou	.10
101	Wil Cordero	.10
102	Delino DeShields	.10
103	Darrin Fletcher	.10
104	Ken Hill	.10
105	Mike Lansing RC	.40
106	Dennis Martinez	.10
107	Larry Walker	.10
108	John Wetteland	.10
109	Rod Beck	.10
110	John Burkett	.10
111	Will Clark	.10
112	Royce Clayton	.10
113	Darren Lewis	.10
114	Willie McGee	.10
115	Bill Swift	.10
116	Robby Thompson	.10
117	Matt Williams	.10
118	Sandy Alomar Jr.	.10
119	Carlos Baerga	.10
120	Albert Belle	.10
121	Reggie Jefferson	.10
122	Kenny Lofton	.10
123	Wayne Kirby	.10
124	Carlos Martinez	.10
125	Charles Nagy	.10
126	Paul Sorrento	.10
127	Rich Amaral	.10
128	Jay Buhner	.10
129	Norm Charlton	.10
130	Dave Fleming	.10
131	Erik Hanson	.10
132	Randy Johnson	1.50
133	Edgar Martinez	.10
134	Tino Martinez	.10
135	Omar Vizquel	.10
136	Bret Barberie	.10
137	Chuck Carr	.10
138	Jeff Conine	.10
139	Orestes Destrade	.10
140	Chris Hammond	.10
141	Bryan Harvey	.10
142	Benito Santiago	.10
143	Walt Weiss	.10
144	Darrell Whitmore RC	.10
145	Tim Bolger RC	.10
146	Bobby Bonilla	.10
147	Jeromy Burnitz	.10
148	Vince Coleman	.10
149	Dwight Gooden	.10
150	Todd Hundley	.10
151	Howard Johnson	.10
152	Eddie Murray	1.50
153	Bret Saberhagen	.10
154	Brady Anderson	.10
155	Mike Devereaux	.10
156	Jeffrey Hammonds	.10

157	Chris Hoiles	.10
158	Ben McDonald	.10
159	Mark McLemore	.10
160	Mike Mussina	.50
161	Gregg Olson	.10
162	David Segui	.10
163	Derek Bell	.10
164	Andy Benes	.10
165	Archi Cianfrocco	.10
166	Ricky Gutierrez	.10
167	Tony Gwynn	2.00
168	Gene Harris	.10
169	Trevor Hoffman	.10
170	Ray McDavid RC	.10
171	Phil Plantier	.10
172	Mariano Duncan	.10
173	Len Dykstra	.10
174	Tommy Greene	.10
175	Dave Hollins	.10
176	Pete Incaviglia	.10
177	Mickey Morandini	.10
178	Curt Schilling	.40
179	Kevin Stocker	.10
180	Mitch Williams	.10
181	Stan Belinda	.10
182	Jay Bell	.10
183	Steve Cooke	.10
184	Carlos Garcia	.10
185	Jeff King	.10
186	Orlando Merced	.10
187	Don Slaught	.10
188	Andy Van Slyke	.10
189	Kevin Young	.10
190	Kevin Brown	.10
191	Jose Canseco	.60
192	Julio Franco	.10
193	Benji Gil	.10
194	Juan Gonzalez	.75
195	Tom Henke	.10
196	Rafael Palmeiro	1.25
197	Dean Palmer	.10
198	Nolan Ryan	4.00
199	Roger Clemens	2.25
200	Scott Cooper	.10
201	Andre Dawson	.35
202	Mike Greenwell	.10
203	Carlos Quintana	.10
204	Jeff Russell	.10
205	Aaron Sele	.10
206	Mo Vaughn	.10
207	Frank Viola	.10
208	Rob Dibble	.10
209	Roberto Kelly	.10
210	Kevin Mitchell	.10
211	Hal Morris	.10
212	Joe Oliver	.10
213	Jose Rijo	.10
214	Bip Roberts	.10
215	Chris Sabo	.10
216	Reggie Sanders	.10
217	Dante Bichette	.10
218	Jerald Clark	.10
219	Alex Cole	.10
220	Andres Galarraga	.10
221	Joe Girardi	.10
222	Charlie Hayes	.10
223	Robert Mejia RC	.10
224	Armando Reynoso	.10
225	Eric Young	.10
226	Kevin Appier	.10
227	George Brett	2.25
228	David Cone	.10
229	Phil Hiatt	.10
230	Felix Jose	.10
231	Wally Joyner	.10
232	Mike Macfarlane	.10
233	Brian McRae	.10
234	Jeff Montgomery	.10
235	Rob Deer	.10
236	Cecil Fielder	.10
237	Travis Fryman	.10
238	Mike Henneman	.10
239	Tony Phillips	.10
240	Mickey Tettleton	.10
241	Alan Trammell	.10
242	David Wells	.10
243	Lou Whitaker	.10
244	Rick Aguilera	.10
245	Scott Erickson	.10
246	Brian Harper	.10
247	Kent Hrbek	.10
248	Chuck Knoblauch	.10
249	Shane Mack	.10
250	David McCarty	.10
251	Pedro Munoz	.10
252	Dave Winfield	1.50
253	Alex Fernandez	.10
254	Ozzie Guillen	.10
255	Bo Jackson	.20
256	Lance Johnson	.10
257	Ron Karkovice	.10
258	Jack McDowell	.10
259	Tim Raines	.10
260	Frank Thomas	1.50
261	Robin Ventura	.10
262	Jim Abbott	.10
263	Steve Farr	.10
264	Jimmy Key	.10
265	Don Mattingly	2.25
266	Paul O'Neill	.10
267	Mike Stanley	.10
268	Danny Tartabull	.10
269	Bob Wickman	.10
270	Bernie Williams	.10
271	Jason Bere	.10
272	Roger Cedeno RC	.50
273	Johnny Damon RC	12.00
274	Russ Davis RC	.25
275	Carlos Delgado	.75
276	Carl Everett	.10
277	Cliff Floyd	.10
278	Alex Gonzalez	.10
279	Derek Jeter RC	75.00
280	Chipper Jones	2.00
281	Javier Lopez	.10
282	Chad Mottola RC	.10
283	Marc Newfield	.10
284	Eduardo Perez	.10
285	Manny Ramirez	1.50
286	Todd Steverson RC	.10
287	Michael Tucker	.10
288	Allen Watson	.10
289	Rondell White	.10
290	Dmitri Young	.10

Platinum Power

NM/M

	Complete Set (20):	27.50
	Common Player:	.50
1	Albert Belle	.50
2	Barry Bonds	5.00
3	Joe Carter	.50
4	Will Clark	.50
5	Darren Daulton	.50
6	Cecil Fielder	.50
7	Ron Gant	.50
8	Juan Gonzalez	1.00
9	Ken Griffey Jr.	3.00
10	Dave Hollins	.50
11	Dave Justice	.50
12	Fred McGriff	.50
13	Mark McGwire	5.00
14	Dean Palmer	.50
15	Mike Piazza	3.00
16	Tim Salmon	.50
17	Ryne Sandberg	2.50
18	Gary Sheffield	.75
19	Frank Thomas	2.00
20	Matt Williams	.50

1994 SP

NM/M

	Complete Set (200):	100.00
	Common Player:	.10
	Die-Cut:	1-2X
	Pack (8):	15.00
	Wax Box (32):	450.00
1	Mike Bell RC	.10
2	D.J. Boston	.10
3	Johnny Damon	.45
4	Brad Fullmer RC	.75
5	Joey Hamilton	.10
6	Todd Hollandsworth	.10
7	Brian Hunter	.10
8	LaTroy Hawkins RC	.25
9	Brooks Kieschnick RC	.10
10	Derek Lee RC	15.00
11	Trot Nixon RC	3.00
12	Alex Ochoa	.10
13	Chan Ho Park RC	1.50
14	Kirk Presley RC	.10
15	Alex Rodriguez RC	140.00
16	Jose Silva RC	.10
17	Terrell Wade RC	.10
18	Billy Wagner RC	1.00
19	Glenn Williams RC	.10
20	Preston Wilson	.10
21	Brian Anderson	.10
22	Chad Curtis	.10
23	Chili Davis	.10
24	Bo Jackson	.25
25	Mark Langston	.10
26	Tim Salmon	.10
27	Jeff Bagwell	1.00
28	Craig Biggio	.10
29	Ken Caminiti	.10
30	Doug Drabek	.10
31	John Hudek	.10
32	Greg Swindell	.10
33	Brent Gates	.10
34	Rickey Henderson	1.00
35	Steve Karsay	.10
36	Mark McGwire	2.50
37	Ruben Sierra	.10
38	Terry Steinbach	.10
39	Roberto Alomar	.30
40	Joe Carter	.10
41	Carlos Delgado	.50
42	Alex Gonzalez	.10
43	Juan Guzman	.10
44	Paul Molitor	1.00
45	John Olerud	.10
46	Devon White	.10
47	Steve Avery	.10
48	Jeff Blauser	.10
49	Tom Glavine	.35
50	Dave Justice	.10
51	Roberto Kelly	.10
52	Ryan Klesko	.10
53	Javier Lopez	.10
54	Greg Maddux	1.25
55	Fred McGriff	.10
56	Ricky Bones	.10
57	Cal Eldred	.10
58	Brian Harper	.10
59	Pat Listach	.10
60	B.J. Surhoff	.10
61	Greg Vaughn	.10
62	Bernard Gilkey	.10
63	Gregg Jefferies	.10
64	Ray Lankford	.10
65	Ozzie Smith	1.25
66	Bob Tewksbury	.10
67	Mark Whiten	.10
68	Todd Zeile	.10
69	Mark Grace	.10
70	Randy Myers	.10
71	Ryne Sandberg	1.25
72	Sammy Sosa	1.25
73	Steve Trachsel	.10
74	Rick Wilkins	.10
75	Brett Butler	.10
76	Delino DeShields	.10
77	Orel Hershiser	.10
78	Eric Karros	.10
79	Raul Mondesi	.10
80	Mike Piazza	2.00
81	Tim Wallach	.10
82	Moises Alou	.10
83	Cliff Floyd	.10
84	Marquis Grissom	.10
85	Pedro Martinez	1.00
86	Larry Walker	.10
87	John Wetteland	.10
88	Rondell White	.10
89	Rod Beck	.10
90	Barry Bonds	3.00
91	John Burkett	.10
92	Royce Clayton	.10
93	Billy Swift	.10
94	Robby Thompson	.10
95	Matt Williams	.10
96	Carlos Baerga	.10
97	Albert Belle	.10
98	Kenny Lofton	.10
99	Dennis Martinez	.10
100	Eddie Murray	1.00
101	Manny Ramirez	1.00
102	Eric Anthony	.10
103	Chris Bosio	.10
104	Jay Buhner	.10
105	Ken Griffey Jr.	2.00
106	Randy Johnson	1.00
107	Edgar Martinez	.10
108	Chuck Carr	.10
109	Jeff Conine	.10
110	Carl Everett	.10
111	Chris Hammond	.10
112	Bryan Harvey	.10
113	Charles Johnson	.10
114	Gary Sheffield	.45
115	Bobby Bonilla	.10
116	Dwight Gooden	.10
117	Todd Hundley	.10
118	Bobby Jones	.10
119	Jeff Kent	.10
120	Bret Saberhagen	.10
121	Jeffrey Hammonds	.10
122	Chris Hoiles	.10
123	Ben McDonald	.10
124	Mike Mussina	.40
125	Rafael Palmeiro	.75
126	Cal Ripken, Jr.	3.00
127	Lee Smith	.10
128	Derek Bell	.10
129	Andy Benes	.10
130	Tony Gwynn	1.25
131	Trevor Hoffman	.10
132	Phil Plantier	.10
133	Bip Roberts	.10
134	Darren Daulton	.10
135	Len Dykstra	.10
136	Dave Hollins	.10
137	Danny Jackson	.10
138	John Kruk	.10
139	Kevin Stocker	.10
140	Jay Bell	.10
141	Carlos Garcia	.10
142	Jeff King	.10
143	Orlando Merced	.10
144	Andy Van Slyke	.10
145	Paul Wagner	.10
146	Jose Canseco	.50
147	Will Clark	.10
148	Juan Gonzalez	.50
149	Rick Helling	.10
150	Dean Palmer	.10
151	Ivan Rodriguez	.75
152	Roger Clemens	1.50
153	Scott Cooper	.10
154	Andre Dawson	.30
155	Mike Greenwell	.10
156	Aaron Sele	.10
157	Mo Vaughn	.10
158	Bret Boone	.10
159	Barry Larkin	.10
160	Kevin Mitchell	.10
161	Jose Rijo	.10
162	Deion Sanders	.10
163	Reggie Sanders	.10
164	Dante Bichette	.10
165	Ellis Burks	.10
166	Andres Galarraga	.10
167	Charlie Hayes	.10
168	David Nied	.10
169	Walt Weiss	.10
170	Kevin Appier	.10
171	David Cone	.10
172	Jeff Granger	.10
173	Felix Jose	.10
174	Wally Joyner	.10
175	Brian McRae	.10
176	Cecil Fielder	.10
177	Travis Fryman	.10
178	Mike Henneman	.10
179	Tony Phillips	.10
180	Mickey Tettleton	.10
181	Alan Trammell	.10
182	Rick Aguilera	.10
183	Rich Becker	.10
184	Scott Erickson	.10
185	Chuck Knoblauch	.10
186	Kirby Puckett	1.25
187	Dave Winfield	1.00
188	Wilson Alvarez	.10
189	Jason Bere	.10
190	Alex Fernandez	.10
191	Julio Franco	.10
192	Jack McDowell	.10
193	Frank Thomas	1.00
194	Robin Ventura	.10
195	Jim Abbott	.10
196	Wade Boggs	1.25
197	Jimmy Key	.10
198	Don Mattingly	1.50
199	Paul O'Neill	.10
200	Danny Tartabull	.10

Die-Cut

(Star cards valued at 1-2X corresponding cards in regular SP issue.)

Holoview Blue

NM/M

	Common Player:	1.50
1	Roberto Alomar	2.00
2	Kevin Appier	1.50
3	Jeff Bagwell	3.00
4	Jose Canseco	3.00
5	Roger Clemens	6.00
6	Carlos Delgado	2.00
7	Cecil Fielder	1.50
8	Cliff Floyd	1.50
9	Travis Fryman	1.50
10	Andres Galarraga	1.50
11	Juan Gonzalez	2.00
12	Ken Griffey Jr.	6.00
13	Tony Gwynn	4.00
14	Jeffrey Hammonds	1.50

15	Bo Jackson	3.00
16	Michael Jordan	15.00
17	Dave Justice	1.50
18	Steve Karsay	1.50
19	Jeff Kent	2.00
20	Brooks Kieschnick	1.50
21	Ryan Klesko	1.50
22	John Kruk	1.50
23	Barry Larkin	2.00
24	Pat Listach	1.50
25	Don Mattingly	5.00
26	Mark McGwire	8.00
27	Raul Mondesi	1.50
28	Trot Nixon	1.50
29	Mike Piazza	6.00
30	Kirby Puckett	4.00
31	Manny Ramirez	3.00
32	Cal Ripken, Jr.	10.00
33	Alex Rodriguez	75.00
34	Tim Salmon	1.50
35	Gary Sheffield	2.00
36	Ozzie Smith	4.00
37	Sammy Sosa	4.00
38	Andy Van Slyke	1.50

Holoview Red

		NM/M
Common Player:		12.00
1	Roberto Alomar	15.00
2	Kevin Appier	12.00
3	Jeff Bagwell	30.00
4	Jose Canseco	20.00
5	Roger Clemens	50.00
6	Carlos Delgado	20.00
7	Cecil Fielder	12.00
8	Cliff Floyd	12.00
9	Travis Fryman	12.00
10	Andres Galarraga	12.00
11	Juan Gonzalez	20.00
12	Ken Griffey Jr.	50.00
13	Tony Gwynn	40.00
14	Jeffrey Hammonds	12.00
15	Bo Jackson	20.00
16	Michael Jordan	120.00
17	Dave Justice	12.00
18	Steve Karsay	12.00
19	Jeff Kent	12.00
20	Brooks Kieschnick	12.00
21	Ryan Klesko	12.00
22	John Kruk	12.00
23	Barry Larkin	12.00
24	Pat Listach	12.00
25	Don Mattingly	45.00
26	Mark McGwire	60.00
27	Raul Mondesi	12.00
28	Trot Nixon	20.00
29	Mike Piazza	50.00
30	Kirby Puckett	40.00
31	Manny Ramirez	30.00
32	Cal Ripken, Jr.	80.00
33	Alex Rodriguez	1,200
34	Tim Salmon	12.00
35	Gary Sheffield	15.00
36	Ozzie Smith	40.00
37	Sammy Sosa	40.00
38	Andy Van Slyke	12.00

1994 SP Alex Rodriguez Autographed Jumbo

		NM/M
15	Alex Rodriguez	250.00

1995 SP

		NM/M
Complete Set (207):		12.50
Common Player:		.05
Pack (8):		1.25
Wax Box (32):		25.00
1	Cal Ripken Jr. (Salute)	2.00
2	Nolan Ryan (Salute)	2.00
3	George Brett (Salute)	1.25
4	Mike Schmidt (Salute)	1.25
5	Dustin Hermanson	.05
6	Antonio Osuna	.05
7	Mark Grudzielanek RC	.35
8	Ray Durham	.05
9	Ugueth Urbina	.05
10	Ruben Rivera	.05
11	Curtis Goodwin	.05
12	Jimmy Hurst	.05
13	Jose Malave	.05
14	Hideo Nomo RC	1.50
15	Juan Acevedo	.05
16	Tony Clark	.05
17	Jim Pittsley	.05
18	Freddy Garcia RC	.50
19	Carlos Perez RC	.05
20	Raul Casanova RC	.05
21	Quilvio Veras	.05
22	Edgardo Alfonzo	.05
23	Marty Cordova	.05
24	C.J. Nitkowski	.05
25	Wade Boggs	.05
	Checklist 1-69	.30
26	Dave Winfield	.05
	Checklist 70-138	.25
27	Eddie Murray	.05
	Checklist 139-207	.25
28	Dave Justice	.05
29	Marquis Grissom	.05
30	Fred McGriff	.05
31	Greg Maddux	1.00
32	Tom Glavine	.35
33	Steve Avery	.05
34	Chipper Jones	1.00
35	Sammy Sosa	1.00
36	Jaime Navarro	.05
37	Randy Myers	.05
38	Mark Grace	.05
39	Todd Zeile	.05
40	Brian McRae	.05
41	Reggie Sanders	.05
42	Ron Gant	.05
43	Deion Sanders	.05
44	Barry Larkin	.05
45	Bret Boone	.05
46	Jose Rijo	.05
47	Jason Bates	.05
48	Andres Galarraga	.05
49	Bill Swift	.05
50	Larry Walker	.05
51	Vinny Castilla	.05
52	Dante Bichette	.05
53	Jeff Conine	.05
54	John Burkett	.05
55	Gary Sheffield	.40
56	Andre Dawson	.30
57	Terry Pendleton	.05
58	Charles Johnson	.05
59	Brian L. Hunter	.05
60	Jeff Bagwell	.75
61	Craig Biggio	.05
62	Phil Nevin	.05
63	Doug Drabek	.05
64	Derek Bell	.05
65	Raul Mondesi	.05
66	Eric Karros	.05
67	Roger Cedeno	.05
68	Delino DeShields	.05
69	Ramon Martinez	.05
70	Mike Piazza	1.50
71	Billy Ashley	.05
72	Jeff Fassero	.05
73	Shane Andrews	.05
74	Wil Cordero	.05
75	Tony Tarasco	.05
76	Rondell White	.05
77	Pedro Martinez	.75
78	Moises Alou	.05
79	Rico Brogna	.05
80	Bobby Bonilla	.05
81	Jeff Kent	.05
82	Brett Butler	.05
83	Bobby Jones	.05
84	Bill Pulsipher	.05
85	Bret Saberhagen	.05
86	Gregg Jefferies	.05
87	Lenny Dykstra	.05
88	Dave Hollins	.05
89	Charlie Hayes	.05
90	Darren Daulton	.05
91	Curt Schilling	.35
92	Heathcliff Slocumb	.05
93	Carlos Garcia	.05
94	Denny Neagle	.05
95	Jay Bell	.05
96	Orlando Merced	.05
97	Dave Clark	.05
98	Bernard Gilkey	.05
99	Scott Cooper	.05
100	Ozzie Smith	1.00
100	Ken Griffey Jr. (Promo Card)	2.00
101	Tom Henke	.05
102	Ken Hill	.05
103	Brian Jordan	.05
104	Ray Lankford	.05
105	Tony Gwynn	1.00
106	Andy Benes	.05
107	Ken Caminiti	.05
108	Steve Finley	.05
109	Joey Hamilton	.05
110	Bip Roberts	.05
111	Eddie Williams	.05
112	Rod Beck	.05
113	Matt Williams	.05
114	Glenallen Hill	.05
115	Barry Bonds	2.50
116	Robby Thompson	.05
117	Mark Portugal	.05
118	Brady Anderson	.05
119	Mike Mussina	.35
120	Rafael Palmeiro	.65
121	Chris Hoiles	.05
122	Harold Baines	.05
123	Jeffrey Hammonds	.05
124	Tim Naehring	.05
125	Mo Vaughn	.05
126	Mike Macfarlane	.05
127	Roger Clemens	1.25
128	John Valentin	.05
129	Aaron Sele	.05
130	Jose Canseco	.50
131	J.T. Snow	.05
132	Mark Langston	.05
133	Chili Davis	.05
134	Chuck Finley	.05
135	Tim Salmon	.05
136	Tony Phillips	.05
137	Jason Bere	.05
138	Robin Ventura	.05
139	Tim Raines	.05
140a	Frank Thomas (5-yr. BA .326)	.75
140b	Frank Thomas (5-yr. BA .303)	.75
141	Alex Fernandez	.05
142	Jim Abbott	.05
143	Wilson Alvarez	.05
144	Carlos Baerga	.05
145	Albert Belle	.05
146	Jim Thome	.65
147	Dennis Martinez	.05
148	Eddie Murray	.75
149	Dave Winfield	.75
150	Kenny Lofton	.05
151	Manny Ramirez	.75
152	Chad Curtis	.05
153	Lou Whitaker	.05
154	Alan Trammell	.05
155	Cecil Fielder	.05
156	Kirk Gibson	.05
157	Michael Tucker	.05
158	Jon Nunnally	.05
159	Wally Joyner	.05
160	Kevin Appier	.05
161	Jeff Montgomery	.05
162	Greg Gagne	.05
163	Ricky Bones	.05
164	Cal Eldred	.05
165	Greg Vaughn	.05
166	Kevin Seitzer	.05
167	Jose Valentin	.05
168	Joe Oliver	.05
169	Rick Aguilera	.05
170	Kirby Puckett	1.00
171	Scott Stahoviak	.05
172	Kevin Tapani	.05
173	Chuck Knoblauch	.05
174	Rich Becker	.05
175	Don Mattingly	1.25
176	Jack McDowell	.05
177	Jimmy Key	.05
178	Paul O'Neill	.05
179	John Wetteland	.05
180	Wade Boggs	1.00
181	Derek Jeter	2.50
182	Rickey Henderson	.75
183	Terry Steinbach	.05
184	Ruben Sierra	.05
185	Mark McGwire	2.00
186	Todd Stottlemyre	.05
187	Dennis Eckersley	.65
188	Alex Rodriguez	2.00
189	Randy Johnson	.75
190	Ken Griffey Jr.	1.50
191	Tino Martinez	.05
192	Jay Buhner	.05
193	Edgar Martinez	.05
194	Mickey Tettleton	.05
195	Juan Gonzalez	.40
196	Benji Gil	.05
197	Dean Palmer	.05
198	Ivan Rodriguez	.65
199	Kenny Rogers	.05
200	Will Clark	.05
201	Roberto Alomar	.20
202	David Cone	.05
203	Paul Molitor	.75
204	Shawn Green	.40
205	Joe Carter	.05
206	Alex Gonzalez	.05
207	Pat Hentgen	.05

SuperbaFoil

	NM/M
Complete Set (207):	30.00
Common Player:	.10
SuperbaFoil Stars:	1.5X
(See 1995 SP for checklist and base values.)	

1995 SP Griffey Gold Signature

		NM/M
190	Ken Griffey Jr.	65.00

Platinum Power

		NM/M
Complete Set (20):		10.00
Common Player:		.20
1	Jeff Bagwell	.75
2	Barry Bonds	2.00
3	Ron Gant	.20
4	Fred McGriff	.20
5	Raul Mondesi	.20
6	Mike Piazza	1.25

MIKE PIAZZA • CATCHER • LOS ANGELES DODGERS®

7	Larry Walker	.20
8	Matt Williams	.20
9	Albert Belle	.20
10	Cecil Fielder	.20
11	Juan Gonzalez	.40
12	Ken Griffey Jr.	1.25
13	Mark McGwire	1.50
14	Eddie Murray	.75
15	Manny Ramirez	.75
16	Cal Ripken Jr.	2.00
17	Tim Salmon	.20
18	Frank Thomas	.75
19	Jim Thome	.65
20	Mo Vaughn	.20

Special F/X

		NM/M
Complete Set (48):		200.00
Common Player:		2.00
1	Jose Canseco	6.00
2	Roger Clemens	20.00
3	Mo Vaughn	2.00
4	Tim Salmon	2.00
5	Chuck Finley	2.00
6	Robin Ventura	2.00
7	Jason Bere	2.00
8	Carlos Baerga	2.00
9	Albert Belle	8.00
10	Kenny Lofton	3.00
11	Manny Ramirez	8.00
12	Jeff Montgomery	2.00
13	Kirby Puckett	15.00
14	Wade Boggs	5.00
15	Don Mattingly	15.00
16	Cal Ripken Jr.	25.00
17	Ruben Sierra	2.00
18	Ken Griffey Jr.	20.00
19	Randy Johnson	8.00
20	Alex Rodriguez	25.00
21	Will Clark	5.00
22	Juan Gonzalez	4.00
23	Roberto Alomar	4.00
24	Joe Carter	3.00
25	Alex Gonzalez	2.00
26	Paul Molitor	6.00
27	Ryan Klesko	2.00
28	Fred McGriff	3.00
29	Greg Maddux	15.00
30	Sammy Sosa	10.00
31	Bret Boone	2.00
32	Barry Larkin	5.00
33	Reggie Sanders	2.00
34	Dante Bichette	2.00
35	Andres Galarraga	2.00
36	Charles Johnson	2.00
37	Gary Sheffield	5.00
38	Jeff Bagwell	5.00
39	Craig Biggio	4.00
40	Eric Karros	2.00
41	Billy Ashley	2.00
42	Raul Mondesi	2.00
43	Mike Piazza	10.00
44	Rondell White	2.00
45	Bret Saberhagen	2.00
46	Tony Gwynn	8.00
47	Melvin Nieves	2.00
48	Matt Williams	2.00

1995 SP/Championship

		NM/M
Complete Set (200):		25.00
Common Player:		.05
Die-Cuts:		1.5X
Wax Pack (6):		1.00
Wax Box (44):		30.00
1	Hideo Nomo **RC**	1.50
2	Roger Cedeno	.05
3	Curtis Goodwin	.05
4	Jon Nunnally	.05
5	Bill Pulsipher	.05
6	C.J. Nitkowski	.05
7	Dustin Hermanson	.05
8	Marty Cordova	.05
9	Ruben Rivera	.05
10	Ariel Prieto **RC**	.05
11	Edgardo Alfonzo	.05
12	Ray Durham	.05
13	Quilvio Veras	.05
14	Ugueth Urbina	.05
15	Carlos Perez **RC**	.05
16	Glenn Dishman **RC**	.05
17	Jeff Suppan	.05
18	Jason Bates	.05
19	Jason Isringhausen	.05
20	Derek Jeter	2.00
21	Fred McGriff	.05
22	Marquis Grissom	.05
23	Fred McGriff	.05
24	Tom Glavine	.35
25	Greg Maddux	1.00
26	Chipper Jones	1.00
27	Sammy Sosa	.50
28	Randy Myers	.05
29	Mark Grace	.05
30	Sammy Sosa	1.00
31	Todd Zeile	.05
32	Brian McRae	.05
33	Ron Gant	.05
34	Reggie Sanders	.05
35	Ron Gant	.05
36	Barry Larkin	.05
37	Bret Boone	.05
38	John Smiley	.05
39	Larry Walker	.05
40	Andres Galarraga	.05
41	Bill Swift	.05
42	Larry Walker	.05
43	Vinny Castilla	.05
44	Dante Bichette	.05
45	Jeff Conine	.05
46	Charles Johnson	.05
47	Gary Sheffield	.45
48	Andre Dawson	.25
49	Jeff Conine	.05
50	Jeff Bagwell	.40
51	Phil Nevin	.05
52	Craig Biggio	.05
53	Brian L. Hunter	.05
54	Doug Drabek	.05
55	Jeff Bagwell	.75
56	Derek Bell	.05
57	Mike Piazza	.65
58	Raul Mondesi	.05
59	Eric Karros	.05
60	Mike Piazza	1.25
61	Ramon Martinez	.05
62	Billy Ashley	.05
63	Rondell White	.05
64	Jeff Fassero	.05
65	Moises Alou	.05
66	Tony Tarasco	.05
67	Rondell White	.05
68	Pedro Martinez	.05
69	Bobby Jones	.05
70	Bobby Bonilla	.05
71	Bobby Jones	.05
72	Bret Saberhagen	.05
73	Darren Daulton	.05
74	Darren Daulton	.05
75	Gregg Jefferies	.05
76	Tyler Green	.05
77	Heathcliff Slocumb	.05
78	Lenny Dykstra	.05
79	Will Clark	.05
80	Denny Neagle	.05
81	Orlando Merced	.05
82	Jay Bell	.05
83	Ozzie Smith	.50
84	Ken Hill	.05
85	Ozzie Smith	1.00
86	Bernard Gilkey	.05
87	Ray Lankford	.05
88	Tony Gwynn	.50
89	Ken Caminiti	.05
90	Tony Gwynn	1.00
91	Joey Hamilton	.05
92	Bip Roberts	.05
93	Deion Sanders	.05
94	Glenallen Hill	.05
95	Matt Williams	.05
96	Barry Bonds	2.00
97	Rod Beck	.05
98	Eddie Murray (Checklist)	.35
99	Cal Ripken Jr. (Checklist)	1.00
100	Roberto Alomar	.10
101	George Brett	.60
102	Joe Carter	.05
103	Will Clark	.05
104	Dennis Eckersley	.40
105	Whitey Ford	.40
106	Steve Garvey	.05
107	Kirk Gibson	.05
108	Orel Hershiser	.05
109	Reggie Jackson	.50
110	Paul Molitor	.40
111	Kirby Puckett	.50
112	Mike Schmidt	.60
113	Dave Stewart	.05
114	Alan Trammell	.05
115	Cal Ripken Jr.	1.00
116	Brady Anderson	.05
117	Mike Mussina	.30
118	Rafael Palmeiro	.65
119	Chris Hoiles	.05
120	Cal Ripken Jr.	2.00
121	Mo Vaughn	.05
122	Roger Clemens	1.25
123	Tim Naehring	.05
124	John Valentin	.05
125	Mo Vaughn	.05
126	Tim Wakefield	.05
127	Jose Canseco	.40
128	Rick Aguilera	.05
129	Chili Davis	.05
130	Lee Smith	.05
131	Jim Edmonds	.05
132	Chuck Finley	.05
133	Chili Davis	.05
134	J.T. Snow	.05
135	Tim Salmon	.05
136	Frank Thomas	.45
137	Jason Bere	.05
138	Robin Ventura	.05
139	Tim Raines	.05
140	Frank Thomas	.75
141	Alex Fernandez	.05
142	Eddie Murray	.40
143	Carlos Baerga	.05
144	Eddie Murray	.75
145	Albert Belle	.05
146	Jim Thome	.65
147	Dennis Martinez	.05
148	Dave Winfield	.75
149	Kenny Lofton	.75
150	Manny Ramirez	.75
151	Cecil Fielder	.05
152	Lou Whitaker	.05
153	Alan Trammell	.05
154	Kirk Gibson	.05
155	Cecil Fielder	.05
156	Bobby Higginson **RC**	.25
157	Kevin Appier	.05
158	Wally Joyner	.05
159	Jeff Montgomery	.05
160	Kevin Appier	.05
161	Gary Gaetti	.05
162	Greg Gagne	.05
163	Ricky Bones	.05
164	Greg Vaughn	.05
165	Kevin Seitzer	.05
166	Ricky Bones	.05
167	Kirby Puckett	.50
168	Pedro Munoz	.05
169	Chuck Knoblauch	.05
170	Kirby Puckett	1.00
171	Don Mattingly	.60
172	Wade Boggs	1.00
173	Paul O'Neill	.05
174	John Wetteland	.05
175	Don Mattingly	1.25
176	Jack McDowell	.05
177	Mark McGwire	.75
178	Rickey Henderson	.75
179	Terry Steinbach	.05
180	Ruben Sierra	.05
181	Mark McGwire	1.50
182	Dennis Eckersley	.05
183	Ken Griffey Jr.	.65
184	Alex Rodriguez	1.50
185	Ken Griffey Jr.	1.25
186	Randy Johnson	.75
187	Jay Buhner	.05
188	Edgar Martinez	.05
189	Will Clark	.05
190	Juan Gonzalez	.40
191	Benji Gil	.05
192	Ivan Rodriguez	.65
193	Kenny Rogers	.05
194	Will Clark	.05
195	Paul Molitor	.05
196	Roberto Alomar	.20
197	David Cone	.05
198	Paul Molitor	.75
199	Shawn Green	.30
200	Joe Carter	.05
CR1	Cal Ripken Jr.	
	(2,131 games tribute)	5.00
CR1	Cal Ripken Jr. Die-Cut	7.50

Die-Cuts

		NM/M
Complete Set (200):		50.00
Common Player:		.25
Die-Cut Stars:		1.5X
(See 1995 SP/Championship for checklist and base values.)		

Classic Performances

		NM/M
Complete Set (10):		8.00
Common Player:		.50
Complete Die-Cut Set (10):		16.00
Common Die-Cuts:		1.00
CP1	Reggie Jackson	
	(Game 6 of '77 WS)	.60
CP1	Reggie Jackson (Die-Cut)	2.00
CP2	Nolan Ryan	
	(Game 3 of '69 WS)	4.00
CP2	Nolan Ryan (Die-Cut)	8.00
CP3	Kirk Gibson	
	(Game 1 of '88 WS)	.50
CP3	Kirk Gibson (Die-Cut)	1.00
CP4	Joe Carter	
	(Game 6 of '93 WS)	.50
CP4	Joe Carter (Die-Cut)	1.00
CP5	George Brett	
	(Game 3 of '80 ALCS)	1.25
CP5	George Brett (Die-Cut)	2.50
CP6	Roberto Alomar	
	(Game 4 of '92 ALCS)	.50
CP6	Roberto Alomar (Die-Cut)	1.00
CP7	Ozzie Smith	
	(Game 5 of '85 NLCS)	.75
CP7	Ozzie Smith (Die-Cut)	2.00
CP8	Kirby Puckett	
	(Game 6 of '91 WS)	1.25
CP8	Kirby Puckett (Die-Cut)	2.50
CP9	Bret Saberhagen	
	(Game 7 of '85 WS)	.50
CP9	Bret Saberhagen (Die-Cut)	1.00
CP10	Steve Garvey	
	(Game 4 of '84 NLCS)	.50
CP10	Steve Garvey (Die-Cut)	1.00

Destination: Fall Classic

		NM/M
Complete Set (9):		18.00
Common Player:		1.00
Complete Die-Cut Set (9):		36.00
Common Die-Cut:		2.00
1	Ken Griffey Jr.	3.00
1	Ken Griffey Jr. (Die-Cut)	6.00
2	Frank Thomas	2.00
2	Frank Thomas (Die-Cut)	4.00
3	Albert Belle	1.00
3	Albert Belle (Die-Cut)	2.00
4	Mike Piazza	3.00
4	Mike Piazza (Die-Cut)	6.00
5	Don Mattingly	2.75
5	Don Mattingly (Die-Cut)	5.50

6	Hideo Nomo	1.50
6	Hideo Nomo (Die-Cut)	2.00
7	Greg Maddux	2.50
7	Greg Maddux (Die-Cut)	5.00
8	Fred McGriff	1.00
8	Fred McGriff (Die-Cut)	2.00
9	Barry Bonds	5.00
9	Barry Bonds (Die-Cut)	8.00

Ripken Tribute Jumbo

		NM/M
CR1	Cal Ripken Jr.	12.00

1996 SP

		NM/M
Complete Set (188):		12.50
Common Player:		.05
Pack (8):		1.25
Wax Box (30):		25.00
1	Rey Ordonez	.05
2	George Arias	.05
3	Osvaldo Fernandez **RC**	.25
4	Darin Erstad **RC**	2.00
5	Paul Wilson	.05
6	Richard Hidalgo	.05
7	Bob Wolcott	.05
8	Jimmy Haynes	.05
9	Edgar Renteria	.05
10	Alan Benes	.05
11	Chris Snopek	.05
12	Billy Wagner	.05
13	Mike Grace **RC**	.05
14	Todd Greene	.05
15	Karim Garcia	.05
16	John Wasdin	.05
17	Jason Kendall	.05
18	Bob Abreu	.15
19	Jermaine Dye	.05
20	Jason Schmidt	.05
21	Javy Lopez	.05
22	Ryan Klesko	.05
23	Tom Glavine	.35
24	John Smoltz	.05

25	Greg Maddux	1.00
26	Chipper Jones	1.00
27	Fred McGriff	.05
28	David Justice	.05
29	Roberto Alomar	.20
30	Cal Ripken Jr.	2.00
31	Jeffrey Hammonds	.05
32	Bobby Bonilla	.05
33	Mike Mussina	.30
34	Randy Myers	.05
35	Rafael Palmeiro	.65
36	Brady Anderson	.05
37	Tim Naehring	.05
38	Jose Canseco	.40
39	Roger Clemens	1.00
40	Mo Vaughn	.05
41	Jose Valentin **RC**	.05
42	Kevin Mitchell	.05
43	Chili Davis	.05
44	Garret Anderson	.05
45	Tim Salmon	.05
46	Chuck Finley	.05
47	Mark Langston	.05
48	Jim Abbott	.05
49	J.T. Snow	.05
50	Jim Edmonds	.05
51	Sammy Sosa	1.00
52	Brian McRae	.05
53	Ryne Sandberg	1.00
54	Mark Grace	.05
55	Jaime Navarro	.05
56	Harold Baines	.05
57	Robin Ventura	.05
58	Tony Phillips	.05
59	Alex Fernandez	.05
60	Frank Thomas	.75
61	Ray Durham	.05
62	Bret Boone	.05
63	Barry Larkin	.05
64	Pete Schourek	.05
65	Reggie Sanders	.05
66	John Smiley	.05
67	Carlos Baerga	.05
68	Jim Thome	.65
69	Eddie Murray	.75
70	Albert Belle	.05
71	Dennis Martinez	.05
72	Jack McDowell	.05
73	Kenny Lofton	.05
74	Manny Ramirez	.75
75	Dante Bichette	.05
76	Vinny Castilla	.05
77	Andres Galarraga	.05
78	Walt Weiss	.05
79	Ellis Burks	.05
80	Larry Walker	.05
81	Cecil Fielder	.05
82	Melvin Nieves	.05
83	Travis Fryman	.05
84	Chad Curtis	.05
85	Alan Trammell	.05
86	Gary Sheffield	.45
87	Charles Johnson	.05
88	Andre Dawson	.30
89	Jeff Conine	.05
90	Greg Colbrunn	.05
91	Derek Bell	.05
92	Brian Hunter	.05
93	Doug Drabek	.05
94	Craig Biggio	.05
95	Jeff Bagwell	.75
96	Kevin Appier	.05
97	Jeff Montgomery	.05
98	Michael Tucker	.05
99	Bip Roberts	.05
100	Johnny Damon	.35
101	Eric Karros	.05
102	Raul Mondesi	.05
103	Ramon Martinez	.05
104	Ismael Valdes	.05
105	Mike Piazza	1.25
106	Hideo Nomo	.40
107	Chan Ho Park	.05
108	Ben McDonald	.05
109	Kevin Seitzer	.05
110	Greg Vaughn	.05
111	Jose Valentin	.05
112	Rick Aguilera	.05
113	Marty Cordova	.05
114	Brad Radke	.05
115	Kirby Puckett	1.00
116	Chuck Knoblauch	.05
117	Paul Molitor	.75
118	Pedro Martinez	.75
119	Mike Lansing	.05
120	Rondell White	.05
121	Moises Alou	.05
122	Mark Grudzielanek	.05
123	Jeff Fassero	.05
124	Rico Brogna	.05
125	Jason Isringhausen	.05
126	Jeff Kent	.05
127	Bernard Gilkey	.05
128	Todd Hundley	.05
129	David Cone	.05
130	Andy Pettitte	.25
131	Wade Boggs	1.00
132	Paul O'Neill	.05
133	Ruben Sierra	.05
134	John Wetteland	.05
135	Derek Jeter	2.00
136	Geronimo Pena	.05
137	Terry Steinbach	.05
138	Ariel Prieto	.05
139	Scott Brosius	.05

140	Mark McGwire	1.50
141	Lenny Dykstra	.05
142	Todd Zeile	.05
143	Benito Santiago	.05
144	Mickey Morandini	.05
145	Gregg Jefferies	.05
146	Denny Neagle	.05
147	Orlando Merced	.05
148	Charlie Hayes	.05
149	Carlos Garcia	.05
150	Jay Bell	.05
151	Ray Lankford	.05
152	Alan Benes	.05
153	Dennis Eckersley	.65
154	Gary Gaetti	.05
155	Ozzie Smith	1.00
156	Ron Gant	.05
157	Brian Jordan	.05
158	Ken Caminiti	.05
159	Rickey Henderson	.75
160	Tony Gwynn	1.00
161	Wally Joyner	.05
162	Andy Ashby	.05
163	Steve Finley	.05
164	Glenallen Hill	.05
165	Matt Williams	.05
166	Barry Bonds	2.00
167	William Van Landingham	.05
168	Rod Beck	.05
169	Randy Johnson	.75
170	Ken Griffey Jr.	1.25
170p	Ken Griffey Jr.	
	(Unmarked promo; bio on back	
	says, ". . .against Cleveland"	
	as opposed to ". . .	
	against the Indians.")	4.00
171	Alex Rodriguez	1.50
172	Edgar Martinez	.05
173	Jay Buhner	.05
174	Russ Davis	.05
175	Juan Gonzalez	.40
176	Mickey Tettleton	.05
177	Will Clark	.05
178	Ken Hill	.05
179	Dean Palmer	.05
180	Ivan Rodriguez	.65
181	Carlos Delgado	.50
182	Alex Gonzalez	.05
183	Shawn Green	.30
184	Erik Hanson	.05
185	Joe Carter	.05
186	Hideo Nomo Checklist	.20
187	Cal Ripken Jr. Checklist	1.00
188	Ken Griffey Jr. Checklist	.65

Baseball Heroes

		NM/M
Complete Set (10):		65.00
Common Player:		4.00
81	Ken Griffey Jr. Header	8.00
82	Frank Thomas	6.50
83	Albert Belle	4.00
84	Barry Bonds	12.00
85	Chipper Jones	8.00
86	Hideo Nomo	5.00
87	Mike Piazza	10.00
88	Manny Ramirez	6.50
89	Greg Maddux	8.00
90	Ken Griffey Jr.	10.00

Marquee Matchups Blue

		NM/M
Complete Set (20):		15.00
Common Player:		.50
1	Ken Griffey Jr.	2.00
2	Hideo Nomo	.50
3	Derek Jeter	3.00
4	Rey Ordonez	.50
5	Tim Salmon	.50
6	Mike Piazza	1.50
7	Mark McGwire	1.50
8	Barry Bonds	2.00
9	Cal Ripken Jr.	3.00
10	Greg Maddux	1.50
11	Albert Belle	.50
12	Barry Larkin	1.00
13	Jeff Bagwell	.75
14	Juan Gonzalez	.75
15	Frank Thomas	1.00
16	Sammy Sosa	1.00

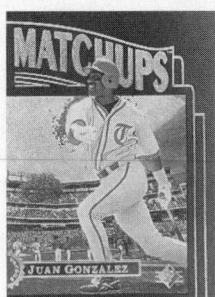

17	Mike Mussina	.75
18	Chipper Jones	1.00
19	Roger Clemens	2.00
20	Fred McGriff	.50

Marquee Matchups Red

		NM/M
Common Player:		1.50
1	Ken Griffey Jr.	10.00
2	Hideo Nomo	2.00
3	Derek Jeter	15.00
4	Rey Ordonez	1.50
5	Tim Salmon	1.50
6	Mike Piazza	8.00
7	Mark McGwire	8.00
8	Barry Bonds	15.00
9	Cal Ripken Jr.	15.00
10	Greg Maddux	10.00
11	Albert Belle	1.50
12	Barry Larkin	4.00
13	Jeff Bagwell	4.00
14	Juan Gonzalez	3.00
15	Frank Thomas	5.00
16	Sammy Sosa	5.00
17	Mike Mussina	4.00
18	Chipper Jones	5.00
19	Roger Clemens	10.00
20	Fred McGriff	3.00

Ripken Collection

		NM/M
Complete Set (5):		25.00
Common Card:		5.00
18-22	Cal Ripken Jr.	5.00

SpecialFX

		NM/M
Complete Set (48):		50.00
Common Player:		.60
1	Greg Maddux	2.50
2	Eric Karros	.60
3	Mike Piazza	3.00
4	Raul Mondesi	.60
5	Hideo Nomo	1.00

6	Jim Edmonds	.60
7	Jason Isringhausen	.60
8	Jay Buhner	.60
9	Barry Larkin	.60
10	Ken Griffey Jr.	3.00
11	Gary Sheffield	1.25
12	Craig Biggio	.60
13	Paul Wilson	.60
14	Rondell White	.60
15	Chipper Jones	2.50
16	Kirby Puckett	2.50
17	Ron Gant	.60
18	Wade Boggs	2.50
19	Fred McGriff	.60
20	Cal Ripken Jr.	5.00
21	Jason Kendall	.60
22	Johnny Damon	.90
23	Kenny Lofton	.60
24	Roberto Alomar	1.00
25	Barry Bonds	5.00
26	Dante Bichette	.60
27	Mark McGwire	4.00
28	Rafael Palmeiro	1.00
29	Juan Gonzalez	1.00
30	Albert Belle	.60
31	Randy Johnson	1.75
32	Jose Canseco	1.25
33	Sammy Sosa	2.50
34	Eddie Murray	1.75
35	Frank Thomas	1.75
36	Tom Glavine	.90
37	Matt Williams	.60
38	Roger Clemens	2.75
39	Paul Molitor	1.75
40	Tony Gwynn	2.50
41	Mo Vaughn	.60
42	Tim Salmon	.60
43	Manny Ramirez	1.75
44	Jeff Bagwell	1.75
45	Edgar Martinez	.60
46	Rey Ordonez	.60
47	Osvaldo Fernandez	.60
48	Derek Jeter	5.00

SpecialFX Red

		NM/M
Common Player:		3.00
Inserted 1:75		
1	Greg Maddux	20.00
2	Eric Karros	3.00
3	Mike Piazza	10.00
4	Raul Mondesi	3.00
5	Hideo Nomo	4.00
6	Jim Edmonds	4.00
7	Jason Isringhausen	3.00
8	Jay Buhner	3.00
9	Barry Larkin	5.00
10	Ken Griffey Jr.	20.00
11	Gary Sheffield	8.00
12	Craig Biggio	5.00
13	Paul Wilson	3.00
14	Rondell White	3.00
15	Chipper Jones	15.00
16	Kirby Puckett	20.00
17	Ron Gant	3.00
18	Wade Boggs	6.00
19	Fred McGriff	4.00
20	Cal Ripken Jr.	25.00
21	Jason Kendall	3.00
22	Johnny Damon	8.00

23	Kenny Lofton	4.00
24	Roberto Alomar	5.00
25	Barry Bonds	25.00
26	Dante Bichette	3.00
27	Mark McGwire	15.00
28	Rafael Palmeiro	6.00
29	Juan Gonzalez	5.00
30	Albert Belle	3.00
31	Randy Johnson	10.00
32	Jose Canseco	5.00
33	Sammy Sosa	10.00
34	Eddie Murray	8.00
35	Frank Thomas	10.00
36	Tom Glavine	10.00
37	Matt Williams	4.00
38	Roger Clemens	20.00
39	Paul Molitor	8.00
40	Tony Gwynn	10.00
41	Mo Vaughn	5.00
42	Tim Salmon	4.00
43	Manny Ramirez	10.00
44	Jeff Bagwell	8.00
45	Edgar Martinez	3.00
46	Rey Ordonez	3.00
47	Osvaldo Fernandez	3.00
48	Derek Jeter	25.00

1996 SPx

		NM/M
Complete Set (60):		17.50
Common Player:		.15
Golds:		1.5X
Pack (1):		1.25
Wax Box (36):		25.00
1	Greg Maddux	1.50
2	Chipper Jones	1.50
3	Fred McGriff	.15
4	Tom Glavine	.50
5	Cal Ripken Jr.	3.00
6	Roberto Alomar	.50
7	Rafael Palmeiro	1.00
8	Jose Canseco	.65
9	Roger Clemens	1.75
10	Mo Vaughn	.15
11	Jim Edmonds	.15
12	Tim Salmon	.15
13	Sammy Sosa	1.50
14	Ryne Sandberg	1.50
15	Mark Grace	.50
16	Frank Thomas	1.25
17	Barry Larkin	.15
18	Kenny Lofton	.15
19	Albert Belle	.15
20	Eddie Murray	1.25
21	Manny Ramirez	1.25
22	Dante Bichette	.15
23	Larry Walker	.15
24	Vinny Castilla	.15
25	Andres Galarraga	.15
26	Cecil Fielder	.15
27	Gary Sheffield	.75
28	Craig Biggio	.15
29	Jeff Bagwell	1.25
30	Derek Bell	.15
31	Johnny Damon	.60
32	Eric Karros	.15
33	Mike Piazza	2.00
34	Raul Mondesi	.15
35	Hideo Nomo	.65
36	Kirby Puckett	1.50
37	Paul Molitor	1.25
38	Marty Cordova	.15
39	Rondell White	.15
40	Jason Isringhausen	.15
41	Paul Wilson	.15
42	Rey Ordonez	.15
43	Derek Jeter	3.00
44	Wade Boggs	1.50
45	Mark McGwire	2.50
46	Jason Kendall	.15
47	Ron Gant	.15
48	Ozzie Smith	1.50
49	Tony Gwynn	1.50
50	Ken Caminiti	.15
51	Barry Bonds	3.00
52	Matt Williams	.15
53	Osvaldo Fernandez RC	.25
54	Jay Buhner	.15
55	Ken Griffey Jr.	2.00
55p	Ken Griffey Jr./OPS	2.00
56	Randy Johnson	1.25
57	Alex Rodriguez	2.50
58	Juan Gonzalez	.65
59	Joe Carter	.15
60	Carlos Delgado	.75

Bound for Glory

		NM/M
Complete Set (10):		18.00
Common Player:		1.00
1	Ken Griffey Jr.	3.00
2	Frank Thomas	1.50
3	Barry Bonds	4.00
4	Cal Ripken Jr.	4.00

5	Greg Maddux	2.00
6	Chipper Jones	2.00
7	Roberto Alomar	1.00
8	Manny Ramirez	1.50
9	Tony Gwynn	2.00
10	Mike Piazza	3.00

Ken Griffey Jr. Commemorative

		NM/M
KG1	Ken Griffey Jr.	2.50
KGA1	Ken Griffey Jr./Auto.	100.00

Mike Piazza Tribute

		NM/M
MP1	Mike Piazza	2.00
MP1	Mike Piazza/Auto.	125.00

1997 SP

		NM/M
Complete Set (184):		12.00
Common Player:		.05
Pack (8):		2.00
Wax Box (30):		45.00
1	Andruw Jones	.75
2	Kevin Orie	.05
3	Nomar Garciaparra	1.00
4	Jose Guillen	.05
5	Todd Walker	.05
6	Derrick Gibson	.05
7	Aaron Boone	.05
8	Bartolo Colon	.05
9	Derek Lee	.05
10	Vladimir Guerrero	.75
11	Wilton Guerrero	.05
12	Luis Castillo	.05
13	Jason Dickson	.05
14	Bubba Trammell RC	.25
15	Jose Cruz Jr. RC	.50
16	Eddie Murray	.75
17	Darin Erstad	.20
18	Garret Anderson	.05
19	Jim Edmonds	.05
20	Tim Salmon	.05
21	Chuck Finley	.05
22	John Smoltz	.05
23	Greg Maddux	1.00
24	Kenny Lofton	.05
25	Chipper Jones	1.00
26	Ryan Klesko	.05
27	Javier Lopez	.05
28	Fred McGriff	.05
29	Roberto Alomar	.20

30	Rafael Palmeiro	.65
31	Mike Mussina	.30
32	Brady Anderson	.05
33	Rocky Coppinger	.05
34	Cal Ripken Jr.	2.00
35	Mo Vaughn	.05
36	Steve Avery	.05
37	Tom Gordon	.05
38	Tim Naehring	.05
39	Troy O'Leary	.05
40	Sammy Sosa	1.00
41	Brian McRae	.05
42	Mel Rojas	.05
43	Ryne Sandberg	1.00
44	Mark Grace	.05
45	Albert Belle	.05
46	Robin Ventura	.05
47	Roberto Hernandez	.05
48	Ray Durham	.05
49	Harold Baines	.05
50	Frank Thomas	.75
51	Bret Boone	.05
52	Reggie Sanders	.05
53	Deion Sanders	.05
54	Hal Morris	.05
55	Barry Larkin	.05
56	Jim Thome	.65
57	Marquis Grissom	.05
58	David Justice	.05
59	Charles Nagy	.05
60	Manny Ramirez	.75
61	Matt Williams	.05
62	Jack McDowell	.05
63	Vinny Castilla	.05
64	Dante Bichette	.05
65	Andres Galarraga	.05
66	Ellis Burks	.05
67	Larry Walker	.05
68	Eric Young	.05
69	Brian L. Hunter	.05
70	Travis Fryman	.05
71	Tony Clark	.05
72	Bobby Higginson	.05
73	Melvin Nieves	.05
74	Jeff Conine	.05
75	Gary Sheffield	.40
76	Moises Alou	.05
77	Edgar Renteria	.05
78	Alex Fernandez	.05
79	Charles Johnson	.05
80	Bobby Bonilla	.05
81	Darryl Kile	.05
82	Derek Bell	.05
83	Shane Reynolds	.05
84	Craig Biggio	.05
85	Jeff Bagwell	.75
86	Billy Wagner	.05
87	Chili Davis	.05
88	Kevin Appier	.05
89	Jay Bell	.05
90	Johnny Damon	.35
91	Jeff King	.05
92	Hideo Nomo	.40
93	Todd Hollandsworth	.05
94	Eric Karros	.05
95	Mike Piazza	1.25
96	Ramon Martinez	.05
97	Todd Worrell	.05
98	Raul Mondesi	.05
99	Dave Nilsson	.05
100	John Jaha	.05
101	Jose Valentin	.05
102	Jeff Cirillo	.05
103	Jeff D'Amico	.05
104	Ben McDonald	.05
105	Paul Molitor	.75
106	Rich Becker	.05
107	Frank Rodriguez	.05
108	Marty Cordova	.05
109	Terry Steinbach	.05
110	Chuck Knoblauch	.05
111	Mark Grudzielanek	.05
112	Mike Lansing	.05
113	Pedro Martinez	.75
114	Henry Rodriguez	.05
115	Rondell White	.05
116	Rey Ordonez	.05
117	Carlos Baerga	.05
118	Lance Johnson	.05
119	Bernard Gilkey	.05
120	Todd Hundley	.05
121	John Franco	.05
122	Bernie Williams	.05
123	David Cone	.05
124	Cecil Fielder	.05
125	Derek Jeter	2.00
126	Tino Martinez	.15
127	Mariano Rivera	.15
128	Andy Pettitte	.15
129	Wade Boggs	1.00
130	Mark McGwire	1.50
131	Jose Canseco	.50
132	Geronimo Berroa	.05
133	Jason Giambi	.45
134	Ernie Young	.05
135	Scott Rolen	.65
136	Ricky Bottalico	.05
137	Curt Schilling	.35
138	Gregg Jefferies	.05
139	Mickey Morandini	.05
140	Jason Kendall	.05
141	Kevin Elster	.05
142	Al Martin	.05
143	Joe Randa	.05
144	Jason Schmidt	.05

145	Ray Lankford	.05
146	Brian Jordan	.05
147	Andy Benes	.05
148	Alan Benes	.05
149	Gary Gaetti	.05
150	Ron Gant	.05
151	Dennis Eckersley	.65
152	Rickey Henderson	.75
153	Joey Hamilton	.05
154	Ken Caminiti	.05
155	Tony Gwynn	1.00
156	Steve Finley	.05
157	Trevor Hoffman	.05
158	Greg Vaughn	.05
159	J.T. Snow	.05
160	Barry Bonds	2.00
161	Glenallen Hill	.05
162	William Van Landingham	.05
163	Jeff Kent	.05
164	Jay Buhner	.05
165	Ken Griffey Jr.	1.25
166	Alex Rodriguez	1.50
167	Randy Johnson	.75
168	Edgar Martinez	.05
169	Dan Wilson	.05
170	Ivan Rodriguez	.65
171	Roger Pavlik	.05
172	Will Clark	.05
173	Dean Palmer	.05
174	Rusty Greer	.05
175	Juan Gonzalez	.40
176	John Wetteland	.05
177	Joe Carter	.05
178	Ed Sprague	.05
179	Carlos Delgado	.45
180	Roger Clemens	1.00
181	Juan Guzman	.05
182	Pat Hentgen	.05
183	Ken Griffey Jr. (Checklist)	.65
184	Hideki Irabu RC	.25

Buy-Back Autographed Inserts

		NM/M
Common Autograph:		7.50
1993 SP		
4	Ken Griffey Jr./16	600.00
28	Jeff Bagwell/7	100.00
167	Tony Gwynn/17	250.00
280	Chipper Jones/34	110.00
1993 SP Platinum Power		
PP9	Ken Griffey Jr./5	800.00
1994 SP		
6	Todd Hollandsworth/167	7.50
15	Alex Rodriguez/94	1,200
105	Ken Griffey Jr./103	125.00
114	Gary Sheffield/130	25.00
130	Tony Gwynn/367	25.00
1994 SP Holoview Blue		
13	Tony Gwynn/31	150.00
1994 SP Holoview Red		
35	Gary Sheffield/4	60.00
1995 SP		
34	Chipper Jones/60	125.00
60	Jeff Bagwell/173	40.00
75	Gary Sheffield/221	20.00
105	Tony Gwynn/64	60.00
188	Alex Rodriguez/63	200.00
190	Ken Griffey Jr./38	200.00
195	Jay Buhner/57	15.00
1996 SP		
1	Rey Ordonez/111	7.50
18	Gary Sheffield/58	30.00
26	Chipper Jones/102	50.00
40	Mo Vaughn/250	15.00
95	Jeff Bagwell/292	20.00
160	Tony Gwynn/20	200.00
170	Ken Griffey Jr./312	65.00
171	Alex Rodriguez/73	125.00
173	Jay Buhner/79	30.00
1996 SP Marquee Matchups		
MM13	Jeff Bagwell/23	65.00
MM4	Rey Ordonez/40	15.00
1996 SP Special F/X		
8	Jay Buhner/27	30.00

Game Film

		NM/M
Complete Set (10):		175.00
Common Player:		12.00
1	Alex Rodriguez	25.00
2	Frank Thomas	12.00

3	Andruw Jones	10.00
4	Cal Ripken Jr.	30.00
5	Mike Piazza	15.00
6	Derek Jeter	30.00
7	Mark McGwire	20.00
8	Chipper Jones	15.00
9	Barry Bonds	30.00
10	Ken Griffey Jr.	20.00

Griffey Baseball Heroes

		NM/M
Complete Set (10):		75.00
Common Griffey Jr.:		10.00
91-100	Ken Griffey Jr.	10.00

Inside Info

		NM/M
Complete Set (25):		75.00
Common Player:		1.00
1	Ken Griffey Jr.	5.00
2	Mark McGwire	6.00
3	Kenny Lofton	1.00
4	Paul Molitor	3.00
5	Frank Thomas	3.00
6	Greg Maddux	3.50
7	Mo Vaughn	1.00
8	Cal Ripken Jr.	7.50
9	Jeff Bagwell	3.00
10	Alex Rodriguez	6.00
11	John Smoltz	1.00
12	Manny Ramirez	3.00
13	Sammy Sosa	3.50
14	Vladimir Guerrero	3.00
15	Albert Belle	1.00
16	Mike Piazza	5.00
17	Derek Jeter	7.50
18	Scott Rolen	2.00
19	Tony Gwynn	3.50
20	Barry Bonds	7.50
21	Ken Caminiti	1.00
22	Chipper Jones	4.00
23	Juan Gonzalez	1.50
24	Roger Clemens	4.00
25	Andruw Jones	3.00

Marquee Matchups

		NM/M
Complete Set (20):		20.00
Common Player:		.25
1	Ken Griffey Jr.	1.50
2	Andres Galarraga	.25
3	Barry Bonds	3.00
4	Mark McGwire	2.00
5	Mike Piazza	1.50
6	Tim Salmon	.25

7	Tony Gwynn	1.00
8	Alex Rodriguez	2.00
9	Chipper Jones	1.00
10	Derek Jeter	3.00
11	Manny Ramirez	.75
12	Jeff Bagwell	.75
13	Greg Maddux	1.00
14	Cal Ripken Jr.	3.00
15	Mo Vaughn	.25
16	Gary Sheffield	.45
17	Jim Thome	.65
18	Barry Larkin	.25
19	Frank Thomas	.75
20	Sammy Sosa	1.00

Special FX

		NM/M
Common Player:		.75
1	Ken Griffey Jr.	6.00
2	Frank Thomas	3.00
3	Barry Bonds	8.00
4	Albert Belle	.75
5	Mike Piazza	4.00
6	Greg Maddux	5.00
7	Chipper Jones	4.00
8	Cal Ripken Jr.	8.00
9	Jeff Bagwell	2.00
10	Alex Rodriguez	8.00
11	Mark McGwire	5.00
12	Kenny Lofton	.75
13	Juan Gonzalez	1.50
14	Mo Vaughn	.75
15	John Smoltz	1.00
16	Derek Jeter	8.00
17	Tony Gwynn	3.00
18	Ivan Rodriguez	2.00
19	Barry Larkin	1.00
20	Sammy Sosa	3.00
21	Mike Mussina	1.50
22	Gary Sheffield	2.00
23	Brady Anderson	.75
24	Roger Clemens	6.00
25	Ken Caminiti	.75
26	Roberto Alomar	1.50
27	Hideo Nomo	1.00
28	Bernie Williams	1.00
29	Todd Hundley	.75
30	Manny Ramirez	3.00
31	Eric Karros	.75
32	Tim Salmon	.75
33	Jay Buhner	.75
34	Andy Pettitte	1.50
35	Jim Thome	2.00
36	Ryne Sandberg	3.00
37	Matt Williams	1.00
38	Ryan Klesko	.75
39	Jose Canseco	1.50
40	Paul Molitor	2.00
41	Eddie Murray	2.00
42	Darin Erstad	.75
43	Todd Walker	.75
44	Wade Boggs	2.50
45	Andruw Jones	2.00
46	Scott Rolen	2.00
47	Vladimir Guerrero	3.00
48	Not issued	
49	Alex Rodriguez (1996 design)	8.00

SPx Force

		NM/M
Complete Set (10):		60.00
Common Player:		6.00
1	Ken Griffey Jr., Jay Buhner, Andres Galarraga, Dante Bichette	7.50
2	Albert Belle, Brady Anderson, Mark McGwire, Cecil Fielder	9.00
3	Mo Vaughn, Ken Caminiti, Frank Thomas, Jeff Bagwell	6.00
4	Gary Sheffield, Sammy Sosa, Barry Bonds, Jose Canseco	12.00
5	Greg Maddux, Roger Clemens, John Smoltz, Randy Johnson	6.00
6	Alex Rodriguez, Derek Jeter, Chipper Jones, Rey Ordonez	12.00
7	Todd Hollandsworth, Mike Piazza, Raul Mondesi, Hideo Nomo	7.50
8	Juan Gonzalez, Manny Ramirez, Roberto Alomar, Ivan Rodriguez	6.00
9	Tony Gwynn, Wade Boggs, Eddie Murray, Paul Molitor	6.00
10	Andruw Jones, Vladimir Guerrero, Todd Walker, Scott Rolen	6.00

SPx Force Autographs

		NM/M
Common Player:		20.00
1	Ken Griffey Jr.	125.00
2	Albert Belle	25.00
3	Mo Vaughn	20.00
4	Gary Sheffield	25.00
5	Greg Maddux	100.00
6	Alex Rodriguez	160.00
7	Todd Hollandsworth	20.00
8	Roberto Alomar	30.00
9	Tony Gwynn	75.00
10	Andruw Jones	40.00

1997 SPx

		NM/M
Complete Set (50):		20.00
Common Player:		.15
Steel:		1.5X
Bronze:		1.5X
Silver:		1.5X
Gold:		3X
Grand Finale:		4X
Pack (3):		2.00
Wax Box (18):		30.00
1	Eddie Murray	1.00
2	Darin Erstad	.35
3	Tim Salmon	.15
4	Andruw Jones	1.00
5	Chipper Jones	1.50
6	John Smoltz	.15
7	Greg Maddux	1.50
8	Kenny Lofton	.30
9	Roberto Alomar	.30
10	Rafael Palmeiro	.75
11	Brady Anderson	.15
12	Cal Ripken Jr.	3.00
13	Nomar Garciaparra	1.50
14	Mo Vaughn	.15
15	Ryne Sandberg	1.50
16	Sammy Sosa	1.50
17	Frank Thomas	1.00
18	Albert Belle	1.50

19	Barry Larkin	.15
20	Deion Sanders	.15
21	Manny Ramirez	1.00
22	Jim Thome	.65
23	Dante Bichette	.15
24	Andres Galarraga	.15
25	Larry Walker	.15
26	Gary Sheffield	.50
27	Jeff Bagwell	1.00
28	Raul Mondesi	.15
29	Hideo Nomo	.50
30	Mike Piazza	2.00
31	Paul Molitor	1.00
32	Todd Walker	.15
33	Vladimir Guerrero	1.00
34	Todd Hundley	.15
35	Andy Pettitte	.25
36	Derek Jeter	3.00
37	Jose Canseco	.50
38	Mark McGwire	2.50
39	Scott Rolen	.65
40	Ron Gant	.15
41	Ken Caminiti	.15
42	Tony Gwynn	1.50
43	Barry Bonds	3.00
44	Jay Buhner	.15
45	Ken Griffey Jr.	2.00
45s	Ken Griffey Jr. (Overprinted "SAMPLE" on back.)	2.00
46	Alex Rodriguez	2.50
47	Jose Cruz Jr. RC	1.00
48	Juan Gonzalez	.50
49	Ivan Rodriguez	.75
50	Roger Clemens	1.75

Bound for Glory

		NM/M
Complete Set (20):		60.00
Common Player:		1.00
1	Andruw Jones	3.00
2	Chipper Jones	4.00
3	Greg Maddux	4.00
4	Kenny Lofton	1.00
5	Cal Ripken Jr.	7.50
6	Mo Vaughn	1.00
7	Frank Thomas	3.00
8	Albert Belle	1.00
9	Manny Ramirez	3.00
10	Gary Sheffield	1.50
11	Jeff Bagwell	3.00
12	Mike Piazza	5.00
13	Derek Jeter	7.50
14	Mark McGwire	6.00
15	Tony Gwynn	4.00
16	Ken Caminiti	1.00
17	Barry Bonds	7.50
18	Alex Rodriguez	6.00
19	Ken Griffey Jr.	5.00
20	Juan Gonzalez	1.50

Bound for Glory Supreme Signatures

		NM/M
Complete Set (5):		250.00
Common Player:		30.00
1	Jeff Bagwell	40.00
2	Ken Griffey Jr.	120.00
3	Andruw Jones	40.00
4	Alex Rodriguez	160.00
5	Gary Sheffield	30.00

Cornerstones of the Game

	NM/M
Complete Set (10):	150.00
Common Player:	12.00

1	Ken Griffey Jr., Barry Bonds	25.00
2	Frank Thomas, Albert Belle	12.00
3	Chipper Jones, Greg Maddux	15.00
4	Tony Gwynn, Paul Molitor	15.00
5	Andruw Jones, Vladimir Guerrero	12.00
6	Jeff Bagwell, Ryne Sandberg	15.00
7	Mike Piazza, Ivan Rodriguez	20.00
8	Cal Ripken Jr., Eddie Murray	25.00
9	Mo Vaughn, Mark McGwire	20.00
10	Alex Rodriguez, Derek Jeter	25.00

1998 SP Authentic

PEDRO MARTINEZ
a Boston Red Sox

		NM/M
Complete Set (198):		15.00
Common Player:		.05
Pack (5):		2.00
Wax Box (24):		35.00
1	Travis Lee	.10
2	Mike Caruso	.05
3	Kerry Wood	.65
4	Mark Kotsay	.05
5	Magglio Ordonez RC	5.00
6	Scott Elarton	.05
7	Carl Pavano	.10
8	A.J. Hinch	.05
9	Rolando Arrojo RC	.40
10	Ben Grieve	.05
11	Gabe Alvarez	.05
12	Mike Kinkade RC	.40
13	Bruce Chen	.05
14	Juan Encarnacion	.05
15	Todd Helton	.75
16	Aaron Boone	.05
17	Sean Casey	.15
18	Ramon Hernandez	.05
19	Daryle Ward	.05
20	Paul Konerko	.15
21	David Ortiz	.50
22	Derrek Lee	.50
23	Brad Fullmer	.05
24	Javier Vazquez	.05
25	Miguel Tejada	.15
26	David Dellucci	.05
27	Alex Gonzalez	.05
28	Matt Clement)	.05
29	Eric Milton	.05
30	Russell Branyan	.05
31	Chuck Finley	.05
32	Jim Edmonds	.05
33	Darin Erstad	.20
34	Jason Dickson	.05
35	Tim Salmon	.05
36	Cecil Fielder	.05
37	Todd Greene	.05
38	Andy Benes	.05
39	Jay Bell	.05
40	Matt Williams	.05
41	Brian Anderson	.05
42	Karim Garcia	.05
43	Javy Lopez	.05
44	Tom Glavine	.35
45	Greg Maddux	1.50
46	Andruw Jones	1.00
47	Chipper Jones	1.50
48	Ryan Klesko	.05
49	John Smoltz	.05
50	Andres Galarraga	.05
51	Rafael Palmeiro	.75
52	Mike Mussina	.30
53	Roberto Alomar	.20
54	Joe Carter	.05
55	Cal Ripken Jr.	3.00
56	Brady Anderson	.05
57	Mo Vaughn	.05
58	John Valentin	.05
59	Dennis Eckersley	.75
60	Nomar Garciaparra	1.50
61	Pedro J. Martinez	1.00
62	Jeff Blauser	.05
63	Kevin Orie	.05
64	Henry Rodriguez	.05
65	Mark Grace	.05
66	Albert Belle	.05
67	Mike Cameron	.05
68	Robin Ventura	.05
69	Frank Thomas	1.00
70	Barry Larkin	.05
71	Brett Tomko	.05
72	Willie Greene	.05
73	Reggie Sanders	.05
74	Sandy Alomar Jr.	.05
75	Kenny Lofton	.05
76	Jaret Wright	.05
77	David Justice	.05
78	Omar Vizquel	.05
79	Manny Ramirez	1.00
80	Jim Thome	.75
81	Travis Fryman	.05
82	Neifi Perez	.05
83	Mike Lansing	.05
84	Vinny Castilla	.05
85	Larry Walker	.05
86	Dante Bichette	.05
87	Darryl Kile	.05
88	Justin Thompson	.05
89	Damion Easley	.05
90	Tony Clark	.05
91	Bobby Higginson	.05
92	Brian L. Hunter	.05
93	Edgar Renteria	.05
94	Craig Counsell	.05
95	Mike Piazza	2.00
96	Livan Hernandez	.05
97	Todd Zeile	.05
98	Richard Hidalgo	.05
99	Moises Alou	.05
100	Jeff Bagwell	1.00
101	Mike Hampton	.05
102	Craig Biggio	.05
103	Dean Palmer	.05
104	Tim Belcher	.05
105	Jeff King	.05
106	Jeff Conine	.05
107	Johnny Damon	.30
108	Hideo Nomo	.50
109	Raul Mondesi	.05
110	Gary Sheffield	.45
111	Ramon Martinez	.05
112	Chan Ho Park	.05
113	Eric Young	.05
114	Charles Johnson	.05
115	Eric Karros	.05
116	Bobby Bonilla	.05
117	Jeromy Burnitz	.05
118	Carl Eldred	.05
119	Jeff D'Amico	.05
120	Marquis Grissom	.05
121	Dave Nilsson	.05
122	Brad Radke	.05
123	Marty Cordova	.05
124	Ron Coomer	.05
125	Paul Molitor	1.00
126	Todd Walker	.05
127	Rondell White	.05
128	Mark Grudzielanek	.05
129	Carlos Perez	.05
130	Vladimir Guerrero	1.00
131	Dustin Hermanson	.05
132	Butch Huskey	.05
133	John Franco	.05
134	Rey Ordonez	.05
135	Todd Hundley	.05
136	Edgardo Alfonzo	.05
137	Bobby Jones	.05
138	John Olerud	.05
139	Chili Davis	.05
140	Tino Martinez	.05
141	Andy Pettitte	.15
142	Chuck Knoblauch	.05
143	Bernie Williams	.05
144	David Cone	.05
145	Derek Jeter	3.00
146	Paul O'Neill	.05
147	Rickey Henderson	1.00
148	Jason Giambi	.50
149	Kenny Rogers	.05
150	Scott Rolen	.75
151	Curt Schilling	.35
152	Ricky Bottalico	.05
153	Mike Lieberthal	.05
154	Francisco Cordova	.05
155	Jose Guillen	.05
156	Jason Schmidt	.05
157	Jason Kendall	.05
158	Kevin Young	.05
159	Delino DeShields	.05
160	Mark McGwire	2.50
161	Ray Lankford	.05
162	Brian Jordan	.05
163	Ron Gant	.05
164	Todd Stottlemyre	.05
165	Ken Caminiti	.05
166	Kevin Brown	.05
167	Trevor Hoffman	.05
168	Steve Finley	.05
169	Wally Joyner	.05
170	Tony Gwynn	1.50
171	Shawn Estes	.05
172	J.T. Snow	.05
173	Jeff Kent	.05
174	Robb Nen	.05
175	Barry Bonds	3.00
176	Randy Johnson	1.00
177	Edgar Martinez	.05
178	Jay Buhner	.05
179	Alex Rodriguez	2.50
180	Ken Griffey Jr.	2.00
181	Ken Cloude	.05
182	Wade Boggs	1.50
183	Tony Saunders	.05
184	Wilson Alvarez	.05
185	Fred McGriff	.05
186	Roberto Hernandez	.05
187	Kevin Stocker	.05
188	Fernando Tatis	.05
189	Will Clark	.05
190	Juan Gonzalez	.50
191	Rusty Greer	.05
192	Ivan Rodriguez	.75
193	Jose Canseco	.45
194	Carlos Delgado	.50
195	Roger Clemens	1.75
196	Pat Hentgen	.05
197	Randy Myers	.05
198	Ken Griffey Jr. Checklist	.85

Chirography

		NM/M
Common Card:		4.00
Inserted 1:25		
RA	Roberto Alomar	15.00
RB	Russell Branyan	4.00
SC	Sean Casey	10.00
TC	Tony Clark	4.00
RC	Roger Clemens/SP/400	80.00
JC	Jose Cruz Jr.	4.00
DE	Darin Erstad	7.50
NG	Nomar Garciaparra/SP/400	30.00
BG	Ben Grieve	4.00
KG	Ken Griffey Jr./SP/400	60.00
VG	Vladimir Guerrero	30.00
TG	Tony Gwynn/SP/850	30.00
TH	Todd Helton	15.00
LH	Livan Hernandez	6.00
CJ	Charles Johnson	6.00
AJ	Andruw Jones	17.50
CHIP	Chipper Jones/SP/800	40.00
PK	Paul Konerko	15.00
MK	Mark Kotsay	6.00
RL	Ray Lankford	6.00
TL	Travis Lee	6.00
PM	Paul Molitor/SP/800	20.00
MM	Mike Mussina	20.00
AR	Alex Rodriguez/SP/800	80.00
IR	Ivan Rodriguez	30.00
SR	Scott Rolen	20.00
GS	Gary Sheffield	15.00
MT	Miguel Tejada	20.00
JW	Jaret Wright	6.00
MV	Mo Vaughn/SP/800	12.50

Jersey Swatch

		NM/M
Complete Set (6):		130.00
Common Player:		7.50
(1)	Jay Buhner/125	7.50
(2)	Ken Griffey Jr./125	50.00
(3)	Tony Gwynn/415	10.00
(4)	Greg Maddux/125	30.00
(5)	Alex Rodriguez/125	60.00
(6)	Gary Sheffield/125	12.00

Ken Griffey Jr. 300th HR Redemption

		NM/M
KG300	Ken Griffey Jr.	30.00

Sheer Dominance

SHEER DOMINANCE
GIANTS
BARRY BONDS

	NM/M
Complete Set (42):	32.50
Common Player:	.25
Inserted 1:3	
Gold (2,000 Sets):	2X
Titanium (100 Sets):	12X
SD1 Ken Griffey Jr.	1.75
SD2 Rickey Henderson	1.00
SD3 Jaret Wright	.25
SD4 Craig Biggio	.25
SD5 Travis Lee	.25
SD6 Kenny Lofton	.25
SD7 Raul Mondesi	.25
SD8 Cal Ripken Jr.	2.50
SD9 Matt Williams	.25
SD10 Mark McGwire	2.00
SD11 Alex Rodriguez	2.00
SD12 Fred McGriff	.25
SD13 Scott Rolen	.75
SD14 Paul Molitor	1.00
SD15 Nomar Garciaparra	1.50
SD16 Vladimir Guerrero	1.00
SD17 Andruw Jones	1.00
SD18 Manny Ramirez	1.00
SD19 Tony Gwynn	1.50
SD20 Barry Bonds	2.50
SD21 Ben Grieve	.25
SD22 Ivan Rodriguez	.75
SD23 Jose Cruz Jr.	.25
SD24 Pedro J. Martinez	1.00
SD25 Chipper Jones	1.50
SD26 Albert Belle	.25
SD27 Todd Helton	.75
SD28 Paul Konerko	.35
SD29 Sammy Sosa	1.50
SD30 Frank Thomas	1.00
SD31 Greg Maddux	1.50
SD32 Randy Johnson	1.00
SD33 Larry Walker	.25
SD34 Roberto Alomar	.45
SD35 Roger Clemens	1.50
SD36 Mo Vaughn	.25
SD37 Jim Thome	.75
SD38 Jeff Bagwell	1.00
SD39 Tino Martinez	.25
SD40 Mike Piazza	1.75
SD41 Derek Jeter	2.50
SD42 Juan Gonzalez	.50

Trade Cards

		NM/M
Common Card:		5.00
(1)	Roberto Alomar/Auto. Ball/100	15.00
(2)	Albert Belle/Auto. Ball/100	7.50
(3)	Jay Buhner/Jsy Card 125	5.00
(4)	Ken Griffey Jr./Auto. Glv/30	200.00
(5)	Ken Griffey Jr./Auto. Jsy/30	200.00
(6)	Ken Griffey Jr./Jsy Card 125	25.00
(7)	Ken Griffey Jr./Standee/200	15.00
(8)	Ken Griffey Jr./300th HR Card 1000	15.00
(9)	Tony Gwynn/Jsy Card 415	15.00
(10)	Brian Jordan/Auto. Ball/50	10.00
(11)	Greg Maddux/Jsy Card/125	20.00
(12)	Raul Mondesi/Auto. Ball/100	5.00
(13)	Alex Rodriguez/Jsy Card/125	40.00
(14)	Gary Sheffield/Jsy Card/125	5.00
(15)	Robin Ventura/Auto. Ball/50	10.00

1998 SPx Finite

	NM/M
Complete Set (360):	200.00
Common Youth Movement: (#1-30, 181-210):	.50
Radiance YM (2,500):	1.5X
Spectrum YM (1,250):	2X
Common Power Explosion:(#31-50):	.50
Radiance PE (1,000):	2X
Spectrum PE (50):	25X

Common Base Card (#51-140, 241-330):	.15
Radiance Base Card (4,500):	1X
Spectrum Base Card (2,250):	2X
Common Star Focus: (#141-170):	.35
Radiance SF (3,500):	1X
Spectrum SF (1,750):	2X
Common Heroes of the Game: (#171-180):	2.50
Radiance HG (100):	15X
Common Power Passion: (#211-240):	.50
Radiance PP (3,500):	1X
Spectrum PP (1,750):	2X
Common Tradewinds: (#331-350):	.75
Radiance TW (1,000):	2X
Spectrum TW (50):	25X
Common Cornerstones/Game: (#351-360):	2.50
Radiance CG (100):	15X
Pack (3):	2.00
Wax Box:	25.00
1 Nomar Garciaparra	3.00
2 Miguel Tejada	.75
3 Mike Cameron	.50
4 Ken Cloude	.50
5 Jaret Wright	.50
6 Mark Kotsay	.50
7 Craig Counsell	.50
8 Jose Guillen	.50
9 Neifi Perez	.50
10 Jose Cruz Jr.	.50
11 Brett Tomko	.50
12 Matt Morris	.50
13 Justin Thompson	.50
14 Jeremi Gonzalez	.50
15 Scott Rolen	1.50
16 Vladimir Guerrero	2.00
17 Brad Fullmer	.50
18 Brian Giles	.50
19 Todd Dunwoody	.50
20 Ben Grieve	.50
21 Juan Encarnacion	.50
22 Aaron Boone	.50
23 Richie Sexson	.50
24 Richard Hidalgo	.50
25 Andruw Jones	2.00
26 Todd Helton	1.50
27 Paul Konerko	.75
28 Dante Powell	.50
29 Elieser Marrero	.50
30 Derek Jeter	5.00
31 Mike Piazza	3.00
32 Tony Clark	.50
33 Larry Walker	.50
34 Jim Thome	1.50
35 Juan Gonzalez	1.00
36 Jeff Bagwell	2.00
37 Jay Buhner	.50
38 Tim Salmon	.50
39 Albert Belle	.50
40 Mark McGwire	4.00
41 Sammy Sosa	2.50
42 Mo Vaughn	.50
43 Manny Ramirez	2.00
44 Tino Martinez	.50
45 Frank Thomas	2.00
46 Nomar Garciaparra	2.50
47 Alex Rodriguez	4.00
48 Chipper Jones	2.50
49 Barry Bonds	5.00
50 Ken Griffey Jr.	3.00
51 Jason Dickson	.15
52 Jim Edmonds	.15
53 Darin Erstad	.35
54 Tim Salmon	.15
55 Chipper Jones	2.00
56 Ryan Klesko	.15
57 Tom Glavine	.35
58 Denny Neagle	.15
59 John Smoltz	.15
60 Javy Lopez	.15
61 Roberto Alomar	.30
62 Rafael Palmeiro	1.25
63 Mike Mussina	.35
64 Cal Ripken Jr.	4.00
65 Mo Vaughn	.15
66 Tim Naehring	.15
67 John Valentin	.15
68 Mark Grace	.15
69 Kevin Orie	.15
70 Sammy Sosa	2.50
71 Albert Belle	.15
72 Frank Thomas	1.50
73 Robin Ventura	.15
74 David Justice	.15
75 Kenny Lofton	.15
76 Omar Vizquel	.15
77 Manny Ramirez	1.50
78 Jim Thome	.65
79 Dante Bichette	.15
80 Larry Walker	.15
81 Vinny Castilla	.15
82 Ellis Burks	.15
83 Bobby Higginson	.15
84 Brian L. Hunter	.15
85 Tony Clark	.15
86 Mike Hampton	.15
87 Jeff Bagwell	1.50
88 Craig Biggio	.15
89 Derek Bell	.15
90 Mike Piazza	3.00
91 Ramon Martinez	.15
92 Raul Mondesi	.15
93 Hideo Nomo	.75
94 Eric Karros	.15
95 Paul Molitor	1.50
96 Marty Cordova	.15
97 Brad Radke	.15
98 Mark Grudzielanek	.15
99 Carlos Perez	.15
100 Rondell White	.15
101 Todd Hundley	.15
102 Edgardo Alfonzo	.15
103 John Franco	.15
104 John Olerud	.15
105 Tino Martinez	.15
106 David Cone	.15
107 Paul O'Neill	.15
108 Andy Pettitte	.25
109 Bernie Williams	.15
110 Rickey Henderson	1.50
111 Jason Giambi	.75
112 Matt Stairs	.15
113 Gregg Jefferies	.15
114 Rico Brogna	.15
115 Curt Schilling	.35
116 Jason Schmidt	.15
117 Jose Guillen	.15
118 Kevin Young	.15
119 Ray Lankford	.15
120 Mark McGwire	3.00
121 Delino DeShields	.15
122 Ken Caminiti	.15
123 Tony Gwynn	2.00
124 Trevor Hoffman	.15
125 Barry Bonds	4.00
126 Jeff Kent	.15
127 Shawn Estes	.15
128 J.T. Snow	.15
129 Jay Buhner	.15
130 Ken Griffey Jr.	2.50
131 Dan Wilson	.15
132 Edgar Martinez	.15
133 Alex Rodriguez	3.00
134 Rusty Greer	.15
135 Juan Gonzalez	.75
136 Fernando Tatis	.15
137 Ivan Rodriguez	1.00
138 Carlos Delgado	.75
139 Pat Hentgen	.15
140 Roger Clemens	2.25
141 Chipper Jones	2.00
142 Greg Maddux	2.00
143 Rafael Palmeiro	1.25
144 Mike Mussina	.65
145 Cal Ripken Jr.	3.00
146 Nomar Garciaparra	2.00
147 Mo Vaughn	.35
148 Sammy Sosa	2.00
149 Albert Belle	.35
150 Frank Thomas	1.50
151 Jim Thome	1.25
152 Kenny Lofton	.35
153 Manny Ramirez	1.50
154 Larry Walker	.35
155 Jeff Bagwell	1.50
156 Craig Biggio	.35
157 Mike Piazza	2.50
158 Paul Molitor	1.50
159 Derek Jeter	4.00
160 Tino Martinez	.35
161 Curt Schilling	.50
162 Mark McGwire	3.00
163 Tony Gwynn	2.00
164 Barry Bonds	4.00
165 Ken Griffey Jr.	2.50
166 Randy Johnson	1.50
167 Alex Rodriguez	3.00
168 Juan Gonzalez	.75
169 Ivan Rodriguez	1.25
170 Roger Clemens	2.25
171 Greg Maddux	2.00
172 Cal Ripken Jr.	6.50
173 Frank Thomas	2.00
174 Jeff Bagwell	2.00
175 Mike Piazza	4.00
176 Mark McGwire	5.00
177 Barry Bonds	6.50
178 Ken Griffey Jr.	5.00
179 Alex Rodriguez	5.00
180 Roger Clemens	3.25
181 Mike Caruso	.15
182 David Ortiz	1.00
183 Gabe Alvarez	.50
184 Gary Matthews Jr.	.50
185 Kerry Wood	1.25
186 Carl Pavano	.50
187 Alex Gonzalez	.50
188 Masato Yoshii	.50
189 Larry Sutton	.50
190 Russell Branyan	.50
191 Bruce Chen	.50
192 Rolando Arrojo	.50
193 Ryan Christenson	.50
194 Cliff Politte	.50
195 A.J. Hinch	.50
196 Kevin Witt	.50
197 Daryle Ward	.50
198 Corey Koskie	.50
199 Mike Lowell RC	3.00
200 Travis Lee	.50
201 Kevin Millwood RC	1.00
202 Robert Smith	.50
203 Magglio Ordonez RC	10.00
204 Eric Milton	.50
205 Geoff Jenkins	.50
206 Rich Butler	.50
207 Mike Kinkade RC	.75
208 Braden Looper	.50
209 Matt Clement	.50
210 Derrek Lee	1.50
211 Randy Johnson	1.50
212 John Smoltz	.50
213 Roger Clemens	2.25
214 Curt Schilling	.75
215 Pedro J. Martinez	1.50
216 Vinny Castilla	.50
217 Jose Cruz Jr.	.50
218 Jim Thome	1.20
219 Alex Rodriguez	3.00
220 Frank Thomas	1.50
221 Tim Salmon	.50
222 Larry Walker	.50
223 Albert Belle	.50
224 Manny Ramirez	1.50
225 Mark McGwire	3.00
226 Mo Vaughn	.50
227 Andres Galarraga	.50
228 Scott Rolen	1.25
229 Travis Lee	.50
230 Mike Piazza	2.50
231 Nomar Garciaparra	2.00
232 Andruw Jones	1.50
233 Barry Bonds	4.00
234 Jeff Bagwell	1.50
235 Juan Gonzalez	.75
236 Tino Martinez	.50
237 Vladimir Guerrero	1.50
238 Rafael Palmeiro	1.25
239 Russell Branyan	.50
240 Ken Griffey Jr.	2.50
241 Cecil Fielder	.15
242 Chuck Finley	.15
243 Jay Bell	.15
244 Andy Benes	.15
245 Matt Williams	.15
246 Brian Anderson	.15
248 David Dellucci	.15
249 Andres Galarraga	.15
250 Greg Maddux	2.00
251 Brady Anderson	.15
252 Joe Carter	.15
253 Eric Davis	.15
254 Pedro J. Martinez	1.50
255 Nomar Garciaparra	2.00
256 Dennis Eckersley	1.25
257 Henry Rodriguez	.15
258 Jeff Blauser	.15
259 Jaime Navarro	.15
260 Ray Durham	.15
261 Chris Stynes	.15
262 Willie Greene	.15
263 Reggie Sanders	.15
264 Bret Boone	.15
265 Barry Larkin	.15
266 Travis Fryman	.15
267 Charles Nagy	.15
268 Sandy Alomar Jr.	.15
269 Darryl Kile	.15
270 Mike Lansing	.15
271 Pedro Astacio	.15
272 Damion Easley	.15
273 Joe Randa	.15
274 Luis Gonzalez	.15
275 Mike Piazza	2.50
276 Todd Zeile	.15
277 Edgar Renteria	.15
278 Livan Hernandez	.15
279 Cliff Floyd	.15
280 Moises Alou	.15
281 Billy Wagner	.15
282 Jeff King	.15
283 Hal Morris	.15
284 Johnny Damon	.35
285 Dean Palmer	.15
286 Tim Belcher	.15
287 Eric Young	.15
288 Bobby Bonilla	.15
289 Gary Sheffield	.60
290 Chan Ho Park	.15
291 Charles Johnson	.15
292 Jeff Cirillo	.15
293 Jeromy Burnitz	.15
294 Jose Valentin	.15
295 Marquis Grissom	.15
296 Todd Walker	.15
297 Terry Steinbach	.15
298 Rick Aguilera	.15
299 Vladimir Guerrero	1.50
300 Rey Ordonez	.15
301 Butch Huskey	.15
302 Bernard Gilkey	.15
303 Mariano Rivera	.25
304 Chuck Knoblauch	.15
305 Derek Jeter	4.00
306 Ricky Bottalico	.15
307 Bob Abreu	.15
308 Scott Rolen	1.25
309 Al Martin	.15
310 Jason Kendall	.15
311 Brian Jordan	.15

312	Ron Gant	.15
313	Todd Stottlemyre	.15
314	Greg Vaughn	.15
315	J. Kevin Brown	.15
316	Wally Joyner	.15
317	Robb Nen	.15
318	Orel Hershiser	.15
319	Russ Davis	.15
320	Randy Johnson	1.50
321	Quinton McCracken	.15
322	Tony Saunders	.15
323	Wilson Alvarez	.15
324	Wade Boggs	2.00
325	Fred McGriff	.15
326	Lee Stevens	.15
327	John Wetteland	.15
328	Jose Canseco	.60
329	Randy Myers	.15
330	Jose Cruz Jr.	.15
331	Matt Williams	.50
332	Andres Galarraga	.50
333	Walt Weiss	.50
334	Joe Carter	.50
335	Pedro J. Martinez	2.00
336	Henry Rodriguez	.50
337	Travis Fryman	.50
338	Darryl Kile	.50
339	Mike Lansing	.50
340	Mike Piazza	4.00
341	Moises Alou	.50
342	Charles Johnson	.50
343	Chuck Knoblauch	.50
344	Rickey Henderson	2.00
345	J. Kevin Brown	.50
346	Orel Hershiser	.50
347	Wade Boggs	3.00
348	Fred McGriff	.50
349	Jose Canseco	1.00
350	Gary Sheffield	1.00
351	Travis Lee	2.50
352	Nomar Garciaparra	5.00
353	Frank Thomas	4.00
354	Cal Ripken Jr.	10.00
355	Mark McGwire	8.00
356	Mike Piazza	6.00
357	Alex Rodriguez	8.00
358	Barry Bonds	10.00
359	Tony Gwynn	5.00
360	Ken Griffey Jr.	6.00

1999 SP Authentic

	NM/M
Complete Set (135):	100.00
Common Player (1-90):	.10
Common Future Watch(91-120):	2.00
Production:	(2,700)
Common Season to Remember (121-135):	2.00
Production:	(2,700)
Pack (5):	3.50
Wax Box (24):	75.00

1	Mo Vaughn	.10
2	Jim Edmonds	.10
3	Darin Erstad	.25
4	Travis Lee	.10
5	Matt Williams	.10
6	Randy Johnson	1.50
7	Chipper Jones	1.75
8	Greg Maddux	1.75
9	Andruw Jones	1.50
10	Andres Galarraga	.10
11	Tom Glavine	.35
12	Cal Ripken Jr.	3.00
13	Brady Anderson	.10
14	Albert Belle	.10
15	Nomar Garciaparra	1.75
16	Donnie Sadler	.10
17	Pedro Martinez	1.50
18	Sammy Sosa	1.75
19	Kerry Wood	.60
20	Mark Grace	.10
21	Mike Caruso	.10
22	Frank Thomas	1.50
23	Paul Konerko	.20
24	Sean Casey	.20
25	Barry Larkin	.10
26	Kenny Lofton	.10
27	Manny Ramirez	1.50
28	Jim Thome	1.25
29	Bartolo Colon	.10
30	Jaret Wright	.10
31	Larry Walker	.10
32	Todd Helton	1.25
33	Tony Clark	.10
34	Dean Palmer	.10
35	Mark Kotsay	.10
36	Cliff Floyd	.10
37	Ken Caminiti	.10
38	Craig Biggio	.10
39	Jeff Bagwell	1.50
40	Moises Alou	.10
41	Johnny Damon	.35
42	Larry Sutton	.10
43	Kevin Brown	.10
44	Gary Sheffield	.40
45	Raul Mondesi	.10
46	Jeromy Burnitz	.10
47	Jeff Cirillo	.10
48	Todd Walker	.10
49	David Ortiz	.50
50	Brad Radtke	.10
51	Vladimir Guerrero	1.50
52	Rondell White	.10
53	Brad Fullmer	.10
54	Mike Piazza	2.00
55	Robin Ventura	.10
56	John Olerud	.10
57	Derek Jeter	3.00
58	Tino Martinez	.10
59	Bernie Williams	.10
60	Roger Clemens	1.75
61	Ben Grieve	.10
62	Miguel Tejada	.20
63	A.J. Hinch	.10
64	Scott Rolen	1.00
65	Curt Schilling	.35
66	Doug Glanville	.10
67	Aramis Ramirez	.10
68	Tony Womack	.10
69	Jason Kendall	.10
70	Tony Gwynn	1.75
71	Wally Joyner	.10
72	Greg Vaughn	.10
73	Barry Bonds	3.00
74	Ellis Burks	.10
75	Jeff Kent	.10
76	Ken Griffey Jr.	2.00
77	Alex Rodriguez	2.50
78	Edgar Martinez	.10
79	Mark McGwire	2.50
80	Eli Marrero	.10
81	Matt Morris	.10
82	Rolando Arrojo	.10
83	Quinton McCracken	.10
84	Jose Canseco	.50
85	Ivan Rodriguez	1.25
86	Juan Gonzalez	.75
87	Royce Clayton	.10
88	Shawn Green	.30
89	Jose Cruz Jr.	.10
90	Carlos Delgado	.60
91	Troy Glaus	6.00
92	George Lombard	2.00
93	Ryan Minor	2.00
94	Calvin Pickering	2.00
95	Jin Ho Cho	2.00
96	Russ Branyon	2.00
97	Derrick Gibson	2.00
98	Gabe Kapler	2.00
99	Matt Anderson	2.00
100	Preston Wilson	2.00
101	Alex Gonzalez	2.00
102	Carlos Beltran	6.00
103	Dee Brown	2.00
104	Jeremy Giambi	2.00
105	Angel Pena	2.00
106	Geoff Jenkins	2.00
107	Corey Koskie	2.00
108	A.J. Pierzynski	2.00
109	Michael Barrett	2.00
110	Fernando Seguignol	2.00
111	Mike Kinkade	2.00
112	Ricky Ledee	2.00
113	Mike Lowell	2.00
114	Eric Chavez	2.50
115	Matt Clement	2.00
116	Shane Monahan	2.00
117	J.D. Drew	4.00
118	Bubba Trammell	2.00
119	Kevin Witt	2.00
120	Roy Halladay	5.00
121	Mark McGwire, Sammy Sosa	4.00
122	Mark McGwire, Sammy Sosa	4.00
123	Sammy Sosa	2.50
124	Ken Griffey Jr.	3.00
125	Cal Ripken Jr.	6.00
126	Juan Gonzalez	2.50
127	Kerry Wood	2.50
128	Trevor Hoffman	2.00
129	Barry Bonds	5.00
130	Alex Rodriguez	4.00
131	Ben Grieve	2.00
132	Tom Glavine	2.00
133	David Wells	2.00
134	Mike Piazza	3.00
135	Scott Brosius	2.00

Chirography

	NM/M
Common Player:	4.00
Inserted 1:24	

EC	Eric Chavez	8.00
GK	Gabe Kapler	4.00
GMj	Gary Matthews Jr.	4.00
CP	Calvin Pickering	4.00

CK	Corey Koskie	6.00
SM	Shane Monahan	4.00
RH	Richard Hidalgo	4.00
MK	Mike Kinkade	4.00
CB	Carlos Beltran	35.00
AG	Alex Gonzalez	4.00
BC	Bruce Chen	4.00
MA	Matt Anderson	4.00
RM	Ryan Minor	4.00
RL	Ricky Ledee	4.00
RR	Ruben Rivera	4.00
BF	Brad Fullmer	4.00
RB	Russ Branyan	4.00
ML	Mike Lowell	15.00
JG	Jeremy Giambi	4.00
GL	George Lombard	4.00
KW	Kevin Witt	4.00
TW	Todd Walker	4.00
SR	Scott Rolen	20.00
KW	Kerry Wood	25.00
BG	Ben Grieve	4.00
JR	Ken Griffey Jr.	75.00
CJ	Chipper Jones	40.00
IR	Ivan Rodriguez	25.00
TGl	Troy Glaus	15.00
TL	Travis Lee	4.00
VG	Vladimir Guerrero	30.00
GV	Greg Vaughn	4.00
JT	Jim Thome	25.00
JD	J.D. Drew	15.00
TH	Todd Helton	15.00
GM	Greg Maddux	75.00
NG	Nomar Garciaparra	40.00
TG	Tony Gwynn	30.00
CR	Cal Ripken Jr.	125.00

Home Run Chronicles

	NM/M
Complete Set (70):	50.00
Common Player:	.15
Inserted 1:1	
Die-Cuts:	10X
Production 70 Sets	

HR01	Mark McGwire	1.50
HR02	Sammy Sosa	1.25
HR03	Ken Griffey Jr.	1.00
HR04	Mark McGwire	1.50
HR05	Mark McGwire	1.50
HR06	Albert Belle	.15
HR07	Jose Canseco	.30
HR08	Juan Gonzalez	.45
HR09	Manny Ramirez	.65
HR10	Rafael Palmeiro	.50
HR11	Mo Vaughn	.15
HR12	Carlos Delgado	.45
HR13	Nomar Garciaparra	.75
HR14	Barry Bonds	1.50
HR15	Alex Rodriguez	1.25
HR16	Tony Clark	.15
HR17	Jim Thome	.50
HR18	Edgar Martinez	.15
HR19	Frank Thomas	.65
HR20	Greg Vaughn	.15
HR21	Vinny Castilla	.15
HR22	Andres Galarraga	.15
HR23	Moises Alou	.15
HR24	Jeromy Burnitz	.15
HR25	Vladimir Guerrero	.65
HR26	Jeff Bagwell	.65
HR27	Chipper Jones	.75
HR28	Javier Lopez	.15
HR29	Mike Piazza	1.00
HR30	Andruw Jones	.65
HR31	Henry Rodriguez	.15
HR32	Jeff Kent	.15
HR33	Ray Lankford	.15
HR34	Scott Rolen	.50
HR35	Raul Mondesi	.15
HR36	Ken Caminiti	.15
HR37	J.D. Drew	.40
HR38	Troy Glaus	.50
HR39	Gabe Kapler	.15
HR40	Alex Rodriguez	1.25
HR41	Ken Griffey Jr.	1.00
HR42	Sammy Sosa	1.25
HR43	Mark McGwire	1.50
HR44	Sammy Sosa	1.25
HR45	Mark McGwire	1.50
HR46	Vinny Castilla	.15
HR47	Sammy Sosa	1.25
HR48	Mark McGwire	1.50
HR49	Sammy Sosa	1.25
HR50	Greg Vaughn	.15
HR51	Sammy Sosa	1.25
HR52	Mark McGwire	1.50
HR53	Sammy Sosa	1.25
HR54	Mark McGwire	1.50
HR55	Sammy Sosa	1.25
HR56	Ken Griffey Jr.	1.00
HR57	Sammy Sosa	1.25
HR58	Mark McGwire	1.50
HR59	Sammy Sosa	1.25
HR60	Mark McGwire	1.50
HR61	Mark McGwire	2.50
HR62	Mark McGwire	2.50
HR63	Mark McGwire	1.50
HR64	Mark McGwire	1.50
HR65	Mark McGwire	1.50
HR66	Sammy Sosa	2.50
HR67	Mark McGwire	1.50
HR68	Mark McGwire	1.50
HR69	Mark McGwire	1.50
HR70	Mark McGwire	4.00

Epic Figures

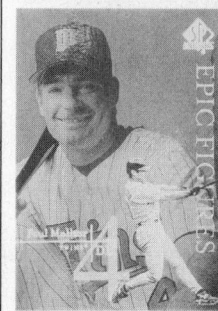

	NM/M
Complete Set (30):	30.00
Common Player:	.50
Inserted 1:7	

E01	Mo Vaughn	.50
E02	Travis Lee	.50
E03	Andres Galarraga	.50
E04	Andruw Jones	1.00
E05	Chipper Jones	1.50
E06	Greg Maddux	1.25
E07	Cal Ripken Jr.	3.00
E08	Nomar Garciaparra	1.25
E09	Sammy Sosa	1.25
E10	Frank Thomas	1.00
E11	Kerry Wood	.60
E12	Kenny Lofton	.50
E13	Manny Ramirez	1.00
E14	Larry Walker	.50
E15	Jeff Bagwell	1.00
E16	Paul Molitor	1.00
E17	Vladimir Guerrero	1.00
E18	Derek Jeter	3.00
E19	Tino Martinez	1.00
E20	Mike Piazza	1.50
E21	Ben Grieve	.50
E22	Scott Rolen	.75
E23	Mark McGwire	2.00
E24	Tony Gwynn	1.25
E25	Barry Bonds	3.00
E26	Ken Griffey Jr.	1.50
E27	Alex Rodriguez	2.00
E28	J.D. Drew	.65
E29	Juan Gonzalez	.60
E30	Kevin Brown	.50

Reflections

	NM/M
Complete Set (30):	60.00
Common Player:	.75
Inserted 1:23	

R01	Mo Vaughn	.75
R02	Travis Lee	.75
R03	Andres Galarraga	.75

R04 Andruw Jones 2.50
R05 Chipper Jones 3.00
R06 Greg Maddux 3.00
R07 Cal Ripken Jr. 6.00
R08 Nomar Garciaparra 3.00
R09 Sammy Sosa 3.00
R10 Frank Thomas 2.50
R11 Kerry Wood 1.50
R12 Kenny Lofton .75
R13 Manny Ramirez 2.50
R14 Larry Walker .75
R15 Jeff Bagwell 2.50
R16 Paul Molitor 2.50
R17 Vladimir Guerrero 2.50
R18 Derek Jeter 6.00
R19 Tino Martinez .75
R20 Mike Piazza 3.50
R21 Ben Grieve .75
R22 Scott Rolen 2.00
R23 Mark McGwire 4.50
R24 Tony Gwynn 3.00
R25 Barry Bonds 6.00
R26 Ken Griffey Jr. 3.50
R27 Alex Rodriguez 4.50
R28 J.D. Drew 1.25
R29 Juan Gonzalez 1.25
R30 Roger Clemens 3.25

SP Authentics

NM/M

Common Card: 10.00
(1) K.Griffey Jr./Auto. Ball/75 60.00
(2) Ken Griffey Jr./Glv/200 20.00
(3) K. Griffey Jr./ HR Cel Card/346 10.00
(4) Ken Griffey Jr./ Auto. Jsy/25 125.00
(5) K. Griffey Jr/ Auto. Mini Helmet/75 80.00
(6) Ken Griffey Jr./ SI Cover/200 15.00
(7) K. Griffey Jr./ SI Cover Auto./75 75.00
(8) Ken Griffey Jr./ Standee/300 10.00

500 Club Piece of History

NM/M

EB Ernie Banks 120.00
EB Ernie Banks/Auto./14 325.00

1999 SP Signature Edition

NM/M

Complete Set (180): 60.00
Common Player: .15
Pack (3): 15.00
Wax Box (12): 150.00
1 Nomar Garciaparra 2.00
2 Ken Griffey Jr. 2.50
3 J.D. Drew .50
4 Alex Rodriguez 3.00
5 Juan Gonzalez .60
6 Mo Vaughn .15
7 Greg Maddux 2.00
8 Chipper Jones 2.00
9 Frank Thomas 1.50
10 Vladimir Guerrero 1.50
11 Mike Piazza 2.50
12 Eric Chavez .25
13 Tony Gwynn 2.00
14 Orlando Hernandez .15
15 Pat Burrell **RC** 6.00
16 Darin Erstad .30
17 Greg Vaughn .15
18 Russ Branyan .15
19 Gabe Kapler .15
20 Craig Biggio .15
21 Troy Glaus 1.25
22 Pedro J. Martinez 1.50
23 Carlos Beltran .50
24 Derrek Lee .50
25 Manny Ramirez 1.50
26 Shea Hillenbrand **RC** 1.00
27 Carlos Lee .15
28 Angel Pena .15
29 Rafael Roque .15
30 Octavio Dotel .15
31 Jeromy Burnitz .15
32 Jeremy Giambi .15
33 Andruw Jones 1.50
34 Todd Helton 1.25
35 Scott Rolen 1.25
36 Jason Kendall .15
37 Trevor Hoffman .15
38 Barry Bonds 4.00
39 Ivan Rodriguez 1.25
40 Roy Halladay .15
41 Rickey Henderson 1.50
42 Ryan Minor .15
43 Brian Jordan .15
44 Alex Gonzalez .15
45 Raul Mondesi .15
46 Corey Koskie .15
47 Paul O'Neill .15
48 Todd Walker .15
49 Carlos Febles .15
50 Travis Fryman .15
51 Albert Belle .15
52 Travis Lee .15
53 Bruce Chen .15
54 Reggie Taylor .15
55 Jerry Hairston Jr. .15
56 Carlos Guillen .15
57 Michael Barrett .15
58 Jason Conti .15
59 Joe Lawrence .15
60 Jeff Cirillo .15
61 Juan Melo .15
62 Chad Hermansen .15
63 Ruben Mateo .15
64 Ben Davis .15
65 Mike Caruso .15
66 Jason Giambi .50
67 Jose Canseco .50
68 Chad Hutchinson **RC** .15
69 Mitch Meluskey .15
70 Adrian Beltre .25
71 Mark Kotsay .15
72 Juan Encarnacion .15
73 Dermal Brown .15
74 Kevin Witt .15
75 Vinny Castilla .15
76 Aramis Ramirez .15
77 Marlon Anderson .15
78 Mike Kinkade .15
79 Kevin Barker .15
80 Ron Belliard .15
81 Chris Haas .15
82 Bob Henley .15
83 Fernando Seguignol .15
84 Damon Minor .15
85 A.J. Burnett **RC** 1.00
86 Calvin Pickering .15
87 Mike Darr .15
88 Cesar King .15
89 Rob Bell .15
90 Derrick Gibson .15
91 Ober Moreno **RC** .15
92 Robert Fick .15
93 Doug Mientkiewicz **RC** .75
94 A.J. Pierzynski .15
95 Orlando Palmeiro .15
96 Sidney Ponson .15
97 Ivanon Coffie **RC** .15
98 Juan Pena **RC** 1.00
99 Mark Karchner .15
100 Carlos Castillo .15
101 Bryan Ward .15
102 Mario Valdez .15
103 Billy Wagner .15
104 Miguel Tejada .25
105 Jose Cruz Jr. .15
106 George Lombard .15
107 Geoff Jenkins .15
108 Ray Lankford .15
109 Todd Stottlemyre .15
110 Mike Lowell .15
111 Matt Clement .15
112 Scott Brosius .15
113 Preston Wilson .15
114 Bartolo Colon .15
115 Rolando Arrojo .15
116 Jose Guillen .15
117 Ron Gant .15
118 Ricky Ledee .15
119 Carlos Delgado .50
120 Abraham Nunez .15
121 John Olerud .15
122 Chan Ho Park .15
123 Brad Radke .15
124 Al Leiter .15
125 Gary Matthews Jr. .15
126 F.P. Santangelo .15
127 Brad Fullmer .15
128 Matt Anderson .15
129 A.J. Hinch .15
130 Sterling Hitchcock .15
131 Edgar Martinez .15
132 Fernando Tatis .15
133 Bobby Smith .15
134 Paul Konerko .25
135 Sean Casey .25
136 Donnie Sadler .15
137 Denny Neagle .15
138 Sandy Alomar .15
139 Mariano Rivera .25
140 Emil Brown .15
141 J.T. Snow .15
142 Eli Marrero .15
143 Rusty Greer .15
144 Johnny Damon .35
145 Damion Easley .15
146 Eric Milton .15
147 Rico Brogna .15
148 Ray Durham .15
149 Wally Joyner .15
150 Royce Clayton .15
151 David Ortiz .50
152 Wade Boggs 2.00
153 Ugueth Urbina .15
154 Richard Hidalgo .15
155 Bobby Abreu .15
156 Robb Nen .15
157 David Segui .15
158 Sean Berry .15
159 Kevin Tapani .15
160 Jason Varitek .15
161 Fernando Vina .15
162 Jim Leyritz .15
163 Enrique Wilson .15
164 Jim Parque .15
165 Doug Glanville .15
166 Jesus Sanchez .15
167 Nolan Ryan 4.00
168 Robin Yount .50
169 Stan Musial 1.00
170 Tom Seaver .50
171 Mike Schmidt 1.00
172 Willie Stargell .50
173 Rollie Fingers .45
174 Willie McCovey .50
175 Harmon Killebrew .50
176 Eddie Mathews .50
177 Reggie Jackson 1.00
178 Frank Robinson .50
179 Ken Griffey Sr. .15
180 Eddie Murray 1.50

Autographs

NM/M

Common Player: 3.00
Inserted 1:1
BA Bobby Abreu 15.00
SA Sandy Alomar 5.00
MA Marlon Anderson 4.00
KB Kevin Barker 3.00
MB Michael Barrett 4.00
RoB Rob Bell 3.00
AB Albert Belle 15.00
RBe Ron Belliard 3.00
CBe Carlos Beltran 50.00
ABe Adrian Beltre 25.00
BB Barry Bonds 180.00
RB Russ Branyan 3.00
SB Scott Brosius/SP 30.00
DB Dermal Brown 3.00
EB Emil Brown 3.00
AJB A.J. Burnett (Exchange Card) 3.00
AJB A.J. Burnett/Auto. 20.00
PB Pat Burrell 25.00
JoC Jose Canseco 30.00
MC Mike Caruso 3.00
SC Sean Casey (Exchange Card) 3.00
SC Sean Casey/Auto. 15.00
VC Vinny Castilla (Exchange Card) 3.00
VC Vinny Castilla/Auto. 8.00
CC Carlos Castillo 3.00
EC Eric Chavez 10.00
BC Bruce Chen 3.00
JCi Jeff Cirillo 3.00
RC Royce Clayton 3.00
MCl Matt Clement 6.00
IC Ivanon Coffie 3.00
BCo Bartolo Colon (Exchange Card) 3.00
BCo Bartolo Colon/Auto. 8.00
JC Jason Conti 3.00
JDa Johnny Damon 25.00
BD Ben Davis 3.00
CD Carlos Delgado 20.00
OD Octavio Dotel 3.00
JD J.D. Drew 15.00
RD Ray Durham 3.00
DEa Damion Easley 3.00
JE Juan Encarnacion 3.00
DE Darin Erstad 8.00
CF Carlos Febles 3.00
Rob Robert Fick 3.00
Rol Rollie Fingers 8.00
BF Brad Fullmer 3.00
RGa Ron Gant 8.00
NG Nomar Garciaparra 30.00
JaG Jason Giambi 20.00
DG Derrick Gibson 3.00
DGl Doug Glanville 3.00
TGl Troy Glaus 15.00
AG Alex Gonzalez 5.00
RGr Rusty Greer 3.00
Jr. Ken Griffey Jr. 80.00
1 Ken Griffey Jr. (Facsimile autographed "SAMPLE.") 15.00
Sr. Ken Griffey Sr. 8.00
VG Vladimir Guerrero 30.00
JG Jose Guillen 10.00
TG Tony Gwynn 35.00
CHa Chris Haas 3.00
JHj Jerry Hairston Jr. 4.00
RH Roy Halladay 15.00
THe Todd Helton 20.00
BH Bob Henley 3.00
ED Orlando Hernandez 40.00
CH Chad Hermansen 3.00
ShH Shea Hillenbrand 8.00
StH Sterling Hitchcock 3.00
THo Trevor Hoffman 8.00
CHu Chad Hutchinson 3.00
RJ Reggie Jackson/SP 40.00
GJ Geoff Jenkins 5.00
AJ Andruw Jones 20.00
CJ Chipper Jones 50.00
WJ Wally Joyner 8.00
GK Gabe Kapler 3.00
MKa Mark Karchner 3.00
JK Jason Kendall 6.00
HK Harmon Killebrew 40.00
CKi Cesar King 3.00
MKi Mike Kinkade 3.00
PK Paul Konerko 15.00
CK Corey Koskie 6.00
MK Mark Kotsay 4.00
RL Ray Lankford 5.00
JLa Joe Lawrence 3.00
CL Carlos Lee 20.00
DL Derrek Lee 25.00
AL Al Leiter 6.00
JLe Jim Leyritz 6.00
GL George Lombard 3.00
GM Greg Maddux 80.00
Eli Eli Marrero 3.00
EM Edgar Martinez 20.00
PM Pedro J. Martinez (Exchange Card) 5.00
PM Pedro J. Martinez/Auto. 100.00
RMa Ruben Mateo (Exchange Card) 3.00
RMa Ruben Mateo/Auto. 8.00
EMa Eddie Mathews 60.00
GMj Gary Matthews Jr. 3.00
WMc Willie McCovey 35.00
JM Juan Melo 3.00
MMe Mitch Meluskey 3.00
DoM Doug Mientkiewicz 6.00
EMi Eric Milton 3.00
DaM Damon Minor 3.00
RM Ryan Minor 3.00
EMu Eddie Murray 20.00
SM Stan Musial 50.00
RN Robb Nen 3.00
AN Abraham Nunez 3.00
JO John Olerud 10.00
PO Paul O'Neill 20.00
DO David Ortiz 40.00
OP Orlando Palmeiro 3.00
JP Jim Parque 3.00
AP Angel Pena 3.00
MP Mike Piazza (Exchange Card) 6.00
MP Mike Piazza/Auto. 150.00
CP Calvin Pickering 3.00
AJP A.J. Pierzynski 5.00
SP Sidney Ponson 8.00
BR Brad Radke 4.00
ARa Aramis Ramirez 20.00
MR Manny Ramirez 50.00
MRi Mariano Rivera 25.00
FR Frank Robinson 25.00
AR Alex Rodriguez 120.00
PG Ivan Rodriguez 25.00
SR Scott Rolen (Exchange Card) 3.00
SR Scott Rolen/Auto. 25.00
RR Rafael Roque 3.00
NR Nolan Ryan 120.00
DS Donnie Sadler 3.00
JS Jesus Sanchez 3.00
MS Mike Schmidt 60.00
TSe Tom Seaver 35.00
DSe David Segui 3.00
FS Fernando Seguignol 3.00
BS Bobby Smith 3.00
JT J.T. Snow (Exchange Card) 3.00
JT J.T. Snow/Auto. 6.00
POP Willie Stargell (Exchange Card) 3.00
POP Willie Stargell/Auto. 60.00
TSt Todd Stottlemyre 3.00
FTa Fernando Tatis 3.00
RT Reggie Taylor 3.00
MT Miguel Tejada 20.00
FT Frank Thomas 50.00
MV Mario Valdez 3.00
JV Jason Varitek 30.00
GV Greg Vaughn 3.00
MO Mo Vaughn 8.00
FV Fernando Vina 3.00

BWa	Billy Wagner	10.00
TW	Todd Walker	3.00
BW	Bryan Ward	3.00
EW	Enrique Wilson	3.00
KW	Kevin Witt	3.00
RY	Robin Yount	40.00

Autographs Gold

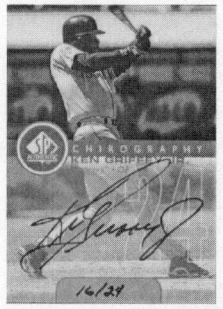

NM/M

Common Player:		12.00
Production 50 Sets		
MA	Marlon Anderson	12.00
KB	Kevin Barker	12.00
MB	Michael Barrett	12.00
RoB	Rob Bell	12.00
AB	Albert Belle	20.00
RBe	Ron Belliard	12.00
CBe	Carlos Beltran	75.00
ABe	Adrian Beltre	40.00
CB	Craig Biggio (Unsigned)	3.00
BB	Barry Bonds	250.00
RB	Russ Branyan	12.00
DB	Dermal Brown	12.00
AJB	A.J. Burnett (Exchange Card)	4.00
AJB	A.J. Burnett (Autographed edition of 20.)	40.00
JB	Jeromy Burnitz (Unsigned)	3.00
PB	Pat Burrell	40.00
JoC	Jose Canseco	50.00
MC	Mike Caruso	12.00
VC	Vinny Castilla (Exchange Card)	3.00
VC	Vinny Castilla/Auto.	20.00
CC	Carlos Castillo	12.00
EC	Eric Chavez	20.00
BC	Bruce Chen	12.00
JCi	Jeff Cirillo	12.00
JC	Jason Conti	12.00
MD	Mike Darr (Unsigned)	3.00
BD	Ben Davis	12.00
OD	Octavio Dotel	12.00
JD	J.D. Drew	30.00
JE	Juan Encarnacion	12.00
DE	Darin Erstad	20.00
CF	Carlos Febles	12.00
TF	Travis Fryman (Unsigned)	3.00
BF	Brad Fullmer	12.00
NG	Nomar Garciaparra	100.00
JaG	Jason Giambi	40.00
JeG	Jeremy Giambi (Unsigned)	3.00
DG	Derrick Gibson	12.00
DGl	Doug Glanville	12.00
TGI	Troy Glaus	30.00
AG	Alex Gonzalez	12.00
JG	Jose Guillen (Unsigned)	6.00
Jr.	Ken Griffey Jr.	150.00
Sr.	Ken Griffey Sr.	12.00
VG	Vladimir Guerrero	75.00
JG	Jose Guillen (Unsigned)	3.00
TG	Tony Gwynn	60.00
CHa	Chris Haas	12.00
JHj	Jerry Hairston Jr.	12.00
RH	Roy Halladay	25.00
THe	Todd Helton	30.00
RH	Rickey Henderson (Unsigned)	6.00
BH	Bob Henley	12.00
ED	Orlando Hernandez	25.00
CH	Chad Hermansen	12.00
ShH	Shea Hillenbrand	20.00
StH	Sterling Hitchcock	12.00
THo	Trevor Hoffman	30.00
CHu	Chad Hutchinson	12.00
GJ	Geoff Jenkins	12.00
AJ	Andruw Jones	40.00
CJ	Chipper Jones	80.00
BJ	Brian Jordan (Unsigned)	12.00
WJ	Wally Joyner	25.00
GK	Gabe Kapler	12.00
MKa	Mark Karchner	12.00
JK	Jason Kendall	20.00
CKi	Cesar King	12.00
MKi	Mike Kinkade	12.00
PK	Paul Konerko	15.00
CK	Corey Koskie	20.00
MK	Mark Kotsay	12.00
RL	Ray Lankford	12.00
JLa	Joe Lawrence	12.00
CL	Carlos Lee	25.00
DL	Derrek Lee	50.00
TL	Travis Lee (Unsigned)	4.00
AL	Al Leiter	12.00
JLe	Jim Leyritz	12.00
GL	George Lombard	12.00
GM	Greg Maddux	150.00
PM	Pedro Martinez (Exchange Card)	6.00
PM	Pedro Martinez/Auto.	200.00

RMa	Ruben Mateo (Exchange Card)	3.00
RMa	Ruben Mateo/Auto.	15.00
GMj	Gary Matthews Jr.	12.00
JM	Juan Melo	12.00
MMe	Mitch Meluskey	12.00
DoM	Doug Mientkiewicz	12.00
EMi	Eric Milton	12.00
DaM	Damon Minor	12.00
RM	Ryan Minor	12.00
PO	Paul O'Neill	30.00
DO	David Ortiz	75.00
OP	Orlando Palmeiro	12.00
AP	Angel Pena	12.00
MP	Mike Piazza (Exchange Card)	10.00
MP	Mike Piazza/Auto.	250.00
CP	Calvin Pickering	12.00
ARa	Aramis Ramirez	30.00
MR	Manny Ramirez	80.00
AR	Alex Rodriguez	185.00
PG	Ivan Rodriguez	45.00
SR	Scott Rolen (Exchange Card)	4.00
SR	Scott Rolen/Auto.	75.00
RR	Rafael Roque	12.00
DSe	David Segui	12.00
FS	Fernando Seguignol	12.00
BS	Bobby Smith	12.00
RT	Reggie Taylor	12.00
FT	Frank Thomas	70.00
MV	Mario Valdez	12.00
GV	Greg Vaughn	12.00
MO	Mo Vaughn	20.00
TW	Todd Walker	12.00
KW	Kevin Witt	12.00

Chirography Gold

NM/M

Common Player:		5.00
Inserted 1:24		
EC	Eric Chavez/30	40.00
GK	Gabe Kapler/51	10.00
GMj	Gary Matthews Jr./68	25.00
CP	Calvin Pickering/6	40.00
CK	Corey Koskie/47	15.00
SM	Shane Monahan/12	20.00
RH	Richard Hidalgo/15	30.00
MK	Mike Kinkade/33	10.00
CB	Carlos Beltran/36	75.00
AG	Alex Gonzalez/22	20.00
BC	Bruce Chen/48	10.00
MA	Matt Anderson/14	20.00
RM	Ryan Minor/10	35.00
RL	Ricky Ledee/38	10.00
RR	Ruben Rivera/28	10.00
BF	Brad Fullmer/20	10.00
RB	Russ Branyon/66	10.00
ML	Mike Lowell/60	15.00
JG	Jeremy Giambi/15	20.00
GL	George Lombard/26	10.00
KW	Kevin Witt/6	20.00
TW	Todd Walker/12	40.00
SR	Scott Rolen/17	75.00
KW	Kerry Wood/34	60.00
BG	Ben Grieve/14	35.00
JR	Ken Griffey Jr./24	250.00
CJ	Chipper Jones/10	200.00
IR	Ivan Rodriguez/7	125.00
TGI	Troy Glaus/14	90.00
TL	Travis Lee/16	35.00
VG	Vladimir Guerrero/27	75.00
GV	Greg Vaughn/23	10.00
JT	Jim Thome/25	40.00
JD	J.D. Drew/8	125.00
TH	Todd Helton/17	75.00
GM	Greg Maddux/31	150.00
NG	Nomar Garciaparra/5	375.00
TG	Tony Gwynn/19	125.00
CR	Cal Ripken Jr./8	650.00

Legendary Cuts

No Pricing
Production One Set

500 Club Piece of History

NM/M

MO	Mel Ott/350	100.00

1999 SPx

Complete Set (120):		100.00
Common Player:		.50
Common SPx Rookie (81-120):		2.00
Production 1,999 Sets		
Radiance (1-80):		7X
Radiance SP (81-120):		1.5X
Spectrum (1-of-1):		Value Undetermined
Pack (3):		3.00
Wax Box (18):		40.00
1	Mark McGwire #61	2.50
2	Mark McGwire #62	1.00
3	Mark McGwire #63	1.00
4	Mark McGwire #64	1.00
5	Mark McGwire #65	1.00
6	Mark McGwire #66	1.00
7	Mark McGwire #67	1.00
8	Mark McGwire #68	1.00
9	Mark McGwire #69	1.00
10	Mark McGwire #70	2.50
11	Mo Vaughn	.50
12	Darin Erstad	.75
13	Travis Lee	.50
14	Randy Johnson	1.50
15	Matt Williams	.50
16	Chipper Jones	2.00
17	Greg Maddux	2.00
18	Andruw Jones	1.50
19	Andres Galarraga	.50
20	Cal Ripken Jr.	4.00
21	Albert Belle	.50
22	Mike Mussina	.75
23	Nomar Garciaparra	2.00
24	Pedro Martinez	1.50
25	John Valentin	.50
26	Kerry Wood	1.00
27	Sammy Sosa	2.00
28	Mark Grace	.50
29	Frank Thomas	1.50
30	Mike Caruso	.50
31	Barry Larkin	.50
32	Sean Casey	.50
33	Jim Thome	1.25
34	Kenny Lofton	.50
35	Manny Ramirez	1.50
36	Larry Walker	.50
37	Todd Helton	1.25
38	Vinny Castilla	.50
39	Tony Clark	.50
40	Derek Lee	1.00
41	Mark Kotsay	.50
42	Jeff Bagwell	1.50
43	Craig Biggio	.50
44	Moises Alou	.50
45	Larry Sutton	.50
46	Johnny Damon	1.00
47	Gary Sheffield	.50
48	Raul Mondesi	.50
49	Jeromy Burnitz	.50
50	Todd Walker	1.00
51	David Ortiz	1.00
52	Vladimir Guerrero	1.50
53	Rondell White	.50
54	Mike Piazza	2.50
55	Derek Jeter	4.00
56	Tino Martinez	.50
57	David Wells	.50
58	Ben Grieve	.50
59	A.J. Hinch	.50
60	Scott Rolen	1.25
61	Doug Glanville	.50
62	Aramis Ramirez	.50
63	Jose Guillen	.50

64	Tony Gwynn	2.00
65	Greg Vaughn	.50
66	Ruben Rivera	.50
67	Barry Bonds	4.00
68	J.T. Snow	.50
69	Alex Rodriguez	3.00
70	Ken Griffey Jr.	2.50
71	Jay Buhner	.50
72	Mark McGwire	3.00
73	Fernando Tatis	.50
74	Quinton McCracken	.50
75	Wade Boggs	2.00
76	Ivan Rodriguez	1.25
77	Juan Gonzalez	1.00
78	Rafael Palmeiro	1.25
79	Jose Cruz Jr.	.50
80	Carlos Delgado	1.00
81	Troy Glaus	5.00
82	Vladimir Nunez	2.00
83	George Lombard	2.00
84	Bruce Chen	2.00
85	Ryan Minor	2.00
86	Calvin Pickering	2.00
87	Jin Ho Cho	2.00
88	Russ Branyan	2.00
89	Derrick Gibson	2.00
90	Gabe Kapler/Auto	6.00
91	Matt Anderson	2.00
92	Robert Fick	2.00
93	Juan Encarnacion	2.00
94	Preston Wilson	2.00
95	Alex Gonzalez	2.00
96	Carlos Beltran	5.00
97	Jeremy Giambi	2.00
98	Dee Brown	2.00
99	Adrian Beltre	4.00
100	Alex Cora	2.00
101	Angel Pena	2.00
102	Geoff Jenkins	2.00
103	Ronnie Belliard	2.00
104	Corey Koskie	2.00
105	A.J. Pierzynski	2.00
106	Michael Barrett	2.00
107	Fernando Seguignol	2.00
108	Mike Kinkade	2.00
109	Mike Lowell	2.00
110	Ricky Ledee	2.00
111	Eric Chavez	3.00
112	Abraham Nunez	2.00
113	Matt Clement	2.00
114	Ben Davis	2.00
115	Mike Darr	2.00
116	Ramon Martinez	2.00
117	Carlos Guillen	2.00
118	Shane Monahan	2.00
119	J.D. Drew/Auto.	15.00
120	Kevin Witt	2.00

Dominance

NM/M

Complete Set (20):		35.00
Common Player:		1.00
Inserted 1:17		
1	Chipper Jones	2.00
2	Greg Maddux	2.00
3	Cal Ripken Jr.	4.00
4	Nomar Garciaparra	2.00
5	Mo Vaughn	1.00
6	Sammy Sosa	2.00
7	Albert Belle	1.00
8	Frank Thomas	1.50
9	Jim Thome	1.25
10	Jeff Bagwell	1.50
11	Vladimir Guerrero	1.50
12	Mike Piazza	2.50
13	Derek Jeter	4.00
14	Tony Gwynn	2.00
15	Barry Bonds	4.00
16	Ken Griffey Jr.	2.50
17	Alex Rodriguez	3.00
18	Mark McGwire	3.00
19	J.D. Drew	1.25
20	Juan Gonzalez	1.25

Power Explosion

NM/M

Complete Set (30):		15.00
Common Player:		.20
Inserted 1:3		
1	Troy Glaus	.65
2	Mo Vaughn	.20
3	Travis Lee	.20

4	Chipper Jones	1.00
5	Andres Galarraga	.20
6	Brady Anderson	.20
7	Albert Belle	.20
8	Nomar Garciaparra	1.00
9	Sammy Sosa	1.00
10	Frank Thomas	.75
11	Jim Thome	.65
12	Manny Ramirez	.75
13	Larry Walker	.20
14	Tony Clark	.20
15	Jeff Bagwell	.75
16	Moises Alou	.20
17	Ken Caminiti	.20
18	Vladimir Guerrero	.75
19	Mike Piazza	1.25
20	Tino Martinez	.20
21	Ben Grieve	.20
22	Scott Rolen	.60
23	Greg Vaughn	.20
24	Barry Bonds	2.00
25	Ken Griffey Jr.	1.25
26	Alex Rodriguez	1.50
27	Mark McGwire	1.50
28	J.D. Drew	.35
29	Juan Gonzalez	.45
30	Ivan Rodriguez	.60

Premier Stars

		NM/M
Complete Set (30):		45.00
Common Player:		1.00
Inserted 1:17		
1	Mark McGwire	3.00
2	Sammy Sosa	2.00
3	Frank Thomas	1.50
4	J.D. Drew	1.25
5	Kerry Wood	1.25
6	Moises Alou	1.00
7	Kenny Lofton	1.00
8	Jeff Bagwell	1.50
9	Tony Clark	1.00
10	Roberto Alomar	1.00
11	Cal Ripken Jr.	4.00
12	Derek Jeter	4.00
13	Mike Piazza	2.50
14	Jose Cruz Jr.	1.00
15	Chipper Jones	2.00
16	Nomar Garciaparra	2.00
17	Greg Maddux	2.00
18	Scott Rolen	1.25
19	Vladimir Guerrero	1.50
20	Albert Belle	1.00
21	Ken Griffey Jr.	2.50
22	Alex Rodriguez	3.00
23	Ben Grieve	1.00
24	Juan Gonzalez	1.25
25	Barry Bonds	4.00
26	Larry Walker	1.00
27	Tony Gwynn	2.00
28	Randy Johnson	1.50
29	Travis Lee	1.00
30	Mo Vaughn	1.00

Star Focus

		NM/M
Complete Set (30):		50.00
Common Player:		.75
Inserted 1:8		
1	Chipper Jones	2.25
2	Greg Maddux	2.25
3	Cal Ripken Jr.	4.50
4	Nomar Garciaparra	2.25
5	Mo Vaughn	.75
6	Sammy Sosa	2.25
7	Albert Belle	.75
8	Frank Thomas	1.50
9	Jim Thome	1.25
10	Kenny Lofton	.75
11	Manny Ramirez	1.50
12	Larry Walker	.75
13	Jeff Bagwell	1.50
14	Craig Biggio	.75
15	Randy Johnson	1.50
16	Vladimir Guerrero	1.50
17	Mike Piazza	3.00
18	Derek Jeter	4.50
19	Tino Martinez	.75
20	Bernie Williams	.75
21	Curt Schilling	1.00
22	Tony Gwynn	2.25
23	Barry Bonds	4.50
24	Ken Griffey Jr.	3.00
25	Alex Rodriguez	4.00
26	Mark McGwire	4.00
27	J.D. Drew	1.00
28	Juan Gonzalez	1.00
29	Ivan Rodriguez	1.25
30	Ben Grieve	.75

Winning Materials

		NM/M
Complete Set (8):		90.00
Common Player:		5.00
Inserted 1:251		
VC	Vinny Castilla	5.00
JD	J.D. Drew	7.50
JR	Ken Griffey Jr.	20.00
VG	Vladimir Guerrero	12.00
TG	Tony Gwynn	15.00
TH	Todd Helton	10.00
TL	Travis Lee	5.00
IR	Ivan Rodriguez	10.00

500 Club Piece of History

		NM/M
WM	Willie Mays/350	275.00
WM	Willie Mays/Auto./24	1,700

2000 SP Authentic

		NM/M
Complete Set (135):		150.00
Common Player:		.15
Common (91-105):		2.00
Production 2,500 Sets		
Common (106-135):		2.00
Production 2,500 Sets		
Pack (5):		3.00
Box (24):		60.00
1	Mo Vaughn	.15
2	Troy Glaus	.50
3	Jason Giambi	.75
4	Tim Hudson	.40
5	Eric Chavez	.25
6	Shannon Stewart	.15
7	Raul Mondesi	.15
8	Carlos Delgado	.50
9	Jose Canseco	.50
10	Vinny Castilla	.15
11	Greg Vaughn	.15
12	Manny Ramirez	1.00
13	Roberto Alomar	.40
14	Jim Thome	.75
15	Richie Sexson	.40
16	Alex Rodriguez	2.50
17	Fred Garcia	.15
18	John Olerud	.15
19	Albert Belle	.25
20	Cal Ripken Jr.	3.00
21	Mike Mussina	.50
22	Ivan Rodriguez	.75
23	Gabe Kapler	.15
24	Rafael Palmeiro	.75
25	Nomar Garciaparra	1.00
26	Pedro Martinez	1.00
27	Carl Everett	.15
28	Carlos Beltran	.50
29	Jermaine Dye	.15
30	Juan Gonzalez	.50
31	Dean Palmer	.15
32	Corey Koskie	.15
33	Jacque Jones	.15
34	Frank Thomas	.75
35	Paul Konerko	.40
36	Magglio Ordonez	.25
37	Bernie Williams	.40
38	Derek Jeter	2.50
39	Roger Clemens	2.00
40	Mariano Rivera	.40
41	Jeff Bagwell	.50
42	Craig Biggio	.40
43	Jose Lima	.15
44	Moises Alou	.25
45	Chipper Jones	1.00
46	Greg Maddux	1.50
47	Andruw Jones	1.00
48	Kevin Millwood	.15
49	Jeromy Burnitz	.15
50	Geoff Jenkins	.15
51	Mark McGwire	1.50
52	Fernando Tatis	.15
53	J.D. Drew	1.00
54	Sammy Sosa	1.00
55	Kerry Wood	.50
56	Mark Grace	.25
57	Matt Williams	.15
58	Randy Johnson	1.00
59	Erubiel Durazo	.15
60	Gary Sheffield	.50
61	Kevin Brown	.15
62	Shawn Green	.40
63	Vladimir Guerrero	1.00
64	Michael Barrett	.15
65	Barry Bonds	2.50
66	Jeff Kent	.25
67	Russ Ortiz	.15
68	Preston Wilson	.15
69	Mike Lowell	.15
70	Mike Piazza	1.00
71	Mike Hampton	.15
72	Robin Ventura	.15
73	Edgardo Alfonzo	.15
74	Tony Gwynn	1.50
75	Ryan Klesko	.15
76	Trevor Hoffman	.15
77	Scott Rolen	1.00
78	Bob Abreu	.40
79	Mike Lieberthal	.15
80	Curt Schilling	.75
81	Jason Kendall	.15
82	Brian Giles	.15
83	Kris Benson	.15
84	Ken Griffey Jr.	2.00
85	Sean Casey	.25
86	Pokey Reese	.15
87	Barry Larkin	.40
88	Larry Walker	.25
89	Todd Helton	.75
90	Jeff Cirillo	.15
91	Ken Griffey Jr.	4.00
92	Mark McGwire	4.00
93	Chipper Jones	3.00
94	Derek Jeter	6.00
95	Shawn Green	2.00
96	Pedro Martinez	4.00
97	Mike Piazza	4.00
98	Alex Rodriguez	5.00
99	Jeff Bagwell	2.50
100	Cal Ripken Jr.	6.00
101	Sammy Sosa	3.00
102	Barry Bonds	5.00
103	Jose Canseco	2.00
104	Nomar Garciaparra	4.00
105	Ivan Rodriguez	2.50
106	Rick Ankiel	2.00
107	Pat Burrell	2.50
108	Vernon Wells	2.50
109	Nick Johnson	2.00
110	Kip Wells	2.00
111	Matt Riley	2.00
112	Alfonso Soriano	8.00
113	Josh Beckett	4.00
114	Danys Baez RC	6.00
115	Travis Dawkins	2.50
116	Eric Gagne	4.00
117	Mike Lamb RC	4.00
118	Eric Munson	2.50
119	Wilfredo Rodriguez RC	2.00
120	Kazuhiro Sasaki RC	3.00
121	Chad Hutchinson	2.00
122	Peter Bergeron	2.00
123	Wascar Serrano RC	2.00
124	Tony Armas Jr.	2.00
125	Ramon Ortiz	2.00
126	Adam Kennedy	2.00
127	Joe Crede	5.00
128	Roosevelt Brown	2.00
129	Mark Mulder	2.50
130	Brad Penny	2.00
131	Terrence Long	2.00
132	Ruben Mateo	2.00
133	Wily Mo Pena	2.00
134	Rafael Furcal	2.00
135	Mario Encarnacion	2.00

Limited

Cards (1-90):	4-8X
Cards (91-105):	2-3X
Cards (106-135):	1-2X
Production 100 Sets	

Chirography

		NM/M
Common Player:		5.00
Inserted 1:23		
RA	Rick Ankiel	25.00
CBe	Carlos Beltran	30.00
BB	Barry Bonds	200.00
PB	Pat Burrell	15.00
JC	Jose Canseco	25.00
SC	Sean Casey	8.00
RC	Roger Clemens	80.00
ED	Erubiel Durazo	5.00
TGI	Troy Glaus	20.00
VG	Vladimir Guerrero	30.00
TG	Tony Gwynn	40.00
DJ	Derek Jeter	120.00
NJ	Nick Johnson	10.00
CJ	Chipper Jones	40.00
AJ	Andruw Jones	20.00
SK	Sandy Koufax	250.00
BP	Ben Petrick	5.00
MQ	Mark Quinn	5.00
MR	Manny Ramirez	40.00
CR	Cal Ripken Jr.	100.00
AR	Alex Rodriguez	90.00
IR	Ivan Rodriguez	25.00
SR	Scott Rolen	25.00
AS	Alfonso Soriano	30.00
MV	Mo Vaughn	8.00
EY	Ed Yarnall	5.00

Chirography Gold

		NM/M
Common Player:		
RA	Rick Ankiel/66 EXCH	50.00
CBe	Carlos Beltran/15	65.00
BB	Barry Bonds/25	300.00
PB	Pat Burrell/33 EXCH	50.00
JC	Jose Canseco/33	75.00
SC	Sean Casey/21	65.00
RC	Roger Clemens/22	300.00
ED	Erubiel Durazo/44	25.00
VG	Vladimir Guerrero/27	100.00

TG	Tony Gwynn/19	200.00
NJ	Nick Johnson/63	15.00
BP	Ben Petrick/15	30.00
MR	Manny Ramirez/24 EXCH	100.00
AS	Alfonso Soriano/53	60.00
MV	Mo Vaughn/42	25.00
EY	Ed Yarnall/41	15.00

Joe DiMaggio Game Jersey

		NM/M
DiMaggio Jersey Card		
JD	Joe DiMaggio/Jsy/500	120.00
JD	Joe DiMaggio/ Jsy Gold/56	200.00

Midsummer Classics

	NM/M
Complete Set (10):	10.00
Common Player:	.50
Inserted 1:12	
1 Cal Ripken Jr.	3.00
2 Roger Clemens	1.75
3 Jeff Bagwell	.75
4 Barry Bonds	3.00
5 Jose Canseco	.50
6 Frank Thomas	.75
7 Mike Piazza	2.00
8 Tony Gwynn	1.50
9 Juan Gonzalez	.75
10 Greg Maddux	1.50

Premier Performers

	NM/M
Complete Set (10):	10.00
Common Player:	.75
Inserted 1:12	
1 Mark McGwire	2.00
2 Alex Rodriguez	2.50
3 Cal Ripken Jr.	3.00
4 Nomar Garciaparra	1.50
5 Ken Griffey Jr.	2.00
6 Chipper Jones	1.50
7 Derek Jeter	3.00
8 Ivan Rodriguez	.75
9 Vladimir Guerrero	.75
10 Sammy Sosa	1.50

SP Buyback

	NM/M
Common Player:	
1 Jeff Bagwell Exch.	50.00
2 Craig Biggio '93/59	50.00
3 Craig Biggio '94/69	50.00
4 Craig Biggio '95/171	40.00
5 Craig Biggio '96/71	50.00

6	Craig Biggio '97/46	50.00
7	Craig Biggio '98/40	50.00
8	Craig Biggio '99/125	40.00
15	Barry Bonds '99/520	150.00
16	Jose Canseco '93/29	60.00
17	Jose Canseco '94/20	60.00
19	Jose Canseco '96/23	60.00
20	Jose Canseco '97/23	60.00
21	Jose Canseco '98/24	60.00
22	Jose Canseco '99/502	30.00
24	Sean Casey '99/139	20.00
25	Roger Clemens '93/68	85.00
26	Roger Clemens '94/60	85.00
27	Roger Clemens '95/68	85.00
28	Roger Clemens '96/68	85.00
30	Roger Clemens '98/25	200.00
31	Roger Clemens '99/534	75.00
32	Jason Giambi '97/34	50.00
33	Jason Giambi '98/25	50.00
34	Tom Glavine '93/99	40.00
35	Tom Glavine '94/107	40.00
36	Tom Glavine '95/97	40.00
37	Tom Glavine '96/42	50.00
38	Tom Glavine '98/40	50.00
39	Tom Glavine '99/138	40.00
40	Shawn Green '96/55	30.00
41	Shawn Green '99/530	20.00
42	Ken Griffey Jr. '96/12	275.00
47	Tony Gwynn '97/24	150.00
49	Tony Gwynn '99/129	50.00
50	Tony Gwynn '99/369	40.00
56	Derek Jeter '99/119	200.00
57	Randy Johnson '93/60	75.00
58	Randy Johnson '94/45	80.00
59	Randy Johnson '95/70	75.00
60	Randy Johnson '96/60	75.00
63	Randy Johnson '99/113	40.00
64	Andruw Jones Exch.	40.00
65	Chipper Jones Exch.	75.00
66	Kenny Lofton '94/100	25.00
67	Kenny Lofton '95/84	25.00
68	Kenny Lofton '96/34	40.00
69	Kenny Lofton '97/82	25.00
70	Kenny Lofton '98/21	40.00
71	Kenny Lofton '99/99	20.00
72	Javy Lopez '93/106	15.00
73	Javy Lopez '94/160	20.00
74	Javy Lopez '96/99	15.00
75	Javy Lopez '97/61	20.00
77	Greg Maddux '93/22	275.00
78	Greg Maddux '94/22	275.00
83	Greg Maddux '99/504	75.00
84	Paul O'Neill '93/110	25.00
85	Paul O'Neill '94/97	30.00
86	Paul O'Neill '95/142	25.00
87	Paul O'Neill '96/70	30.00
88	Paul O'Neill '98/23	40.00
89	Manny Ramirez/Redemp	50.00
91	Cal Ripken Jr. '94/22	300.00
96	Cal Ripken Jr. '99/510	125.00
97	Alex Rodriguez Exch.	150.00
98	Ivan Rodriguez '93/29	100.00
100	Ivan Rodriguez '95/18	125.00
101	Ivan Rodriguez '96/22	125.00
103	Ivan Rodriguez '98/27	125.00
109	Frank Thomas '97/20	75.00
111	Frank Thomas '99/100	50.00
112	Greg Vaughn '93/79	20.00
113	Greg Vaughn '94/75	20.00
114	Greg Vaughn '95/155	15.00
115	Greg Vaughn '96/113	15.00
117	Greg Vaughn '99/527	10.00
118	Mo Vaughn '93/119	20.00
119	Mo Vaughn '94/96	20.00
120	Mo Vaughn '95/121	20.00
121	Mo Vaughn '96/114	20.00
122	Mo Vaughn '97/61	25.00
124	Mo Vaughn '99/537	15.00
125	Robin Ventura '93/59	25.00
126	Robin Ventura '94/49	25.00
127	Robin Ventura '95/125	20.00
128	Robin Ventura '96/55	25.00
129	Robin Ventura '97/44	30.00
130	Robin Ventura '98/28	35.00
131	Robin Ventura '99/370	15.00
133	Matt Williams '94/50	40.00
134	Matt Williams '95/137	40.00
135	Matt Williams '96/77	40.00
136	Matt Williams '97/45	40.00
137	Matt Williams '98/29	60.00
138	Matt Williams '99/55	15.00
139	Preston Wilson '94/249	15.00
140	Preston Wilson '99/195	15.00

SP Cornerstones

	NM/M
Complete Set (7):	15.00
Common Player:	2.00
Inserted 1:23	
1 Ken Griffey Jr.	2.00
2 Cal Ripken Jr.	4.00
3 Mike Piazza	2.00
4 Derek Jeter	4.00
5 Mark McGwire	3.00
6 Nomar Garciaparra	2.00
7 Sammy Sosa	2.00

SP Supremacy

	NM/M
Complete Set (7):	8.00
Common Player:	.75
Inserted 1:23	
1 Alex Rodriguez	3.00
2 Shawn Green	.75
3 Pedro Martinez	1.00
4 Chipper Jones	2.00
5 Tony Gwynn	2.00
6 Ivan Rodriguez	1.00
7 Jeff Bagwell	1.00

United Nations

	NM/M
Complete Set (10):	5.00
Common Player:	.50
Inserted 1:4	
1 Sammy Sosa	1.50
2 Ken Griffey Jr.	2.00
3 Orlando Hernandez	.50
4 Andres Galarraga	.50
5 Kazuhiro Sasaki	.50
6 Larry Walker	.50
7 Vinny Castilla	.50
8 Andruw Jones	.75
9 Ivan Rodriguez	.75
10 Chan Ho Park	.50

3,000 Hit Club

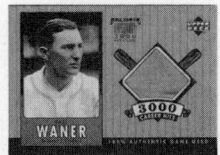

		NM/M
PW	Paul Waner/Bat/350	50.00
TS	Tris Speaker/Bat/350	100.00

2000 SPx

	NM/M
Complete Set (120):	400.00
Common Player:	.15
Common Rookie (91-120):	10.00
Pack (4):	6.00
Box (18):	80.00
1 Troy Glaus	.50
2 Mo Vaughn	.15
3 Ramon Ortiz	.15
4 Jeff Bagwell	.75
5 Moises Alou	.25
6 Craig Biggio	.40
7 Jose Lima	.15
8 Jason Giambi	.75
9 John Jaha	.15
10 Matt Stairs	.15
11 Chipper Jones	1.00
12 Greg Maddux	1.50
13 Andres Galarraga	.15
14 Andruw Jones	1.00
15 Jeromy Burnitz	.15
16 Ron Belliard	.15
17 Carlos Delgado	.75
18 David Wells	.15
19 Tony Batista	.15
20 Shannon Stewart	.15
21 Sammy Sosa	1.00
22 Mark Grace	.50
23 Henry Rodriguez	.15
24 Mark McGwire	2.00
25 J.D. Drew	.25
26 Luis Gonzalez	.25
27 Randy Johnson	1.00
28 Matt Williams	.15
29 Steve Finley	.15
30 Shawn Green	.25
31 Kevin Brown	.15
32 Gary Sheffield	.50
33 Jose Canseco	.50
34 Greg Vaughn	.15
35 Vladimir Guerrero	1.00
36 Michael Barrett	.15
37 Russ Ortiz	.15
38 Barry Bonds	3.00
39 Jeff Kent	.25
40 Richie Sexson	.40
41 Manny Ramirez	1.00
42 Jim Thome	1.00
43 Roberto Alomar	.50
44 Edgar Martinez	.15
45 Alex Rodriguez	2.50
46 John Olerud	.15
47 Alex Gonzalez	.15
48 Cliff Floyd	.15
49 Mike Piazza	1.50
50 Al Leiter	.15
51 Robin Ventura	.15
52 Edgardo Alfonzo	.15
53 Albert Belle	.15
54 Cal Ripken Jr.	3.00
55 B.J. Surhoff	.15
56 Tony Gwynn	1.50
57 Trevor Hoffman	.15
58 Brian Giles	.15
59 Jason Kendall	.15
60 Kris Benson	.15
61 Bob Abreu	.50
62 Scott Rolen	1.00
63 Curt Schilling	.75
64 Mike Lieberthal	.15
65 Sean Casey	.25
66 Dante Bichette	.15
67 Ken Griffey Jr.	2.00
68 Pokey Reese	.15
69 Mike Sweeney	.15
70 Carlos Febles	.15
71 Ivan Rodriguez	1.00
72 Ruben Mateo	.15
73 Rafael Palmeiro	1.00
74 Larry Walker	.40
75 Todd Helton	.75
76 Nomar Garciaparra	1.00
77 Pedro Martinez	1.00
78 Troy O'Leary	.15
79 Jacque Jones	.15
80 Corey Koskie	.15
81 Juan Gonzalez	.50
82 Dean Palmer	.15

83	Juan Encarnacion	.15
84	Frank Thomas	1.00
85	Magglio Ordonez	.25
86	Paul Konerko	.50
87	Bernie Williams	.50
88	Derek Jeter	3.00
89	Roger Clemens	2.50
90	Orlando Hernandez	.15
91	Vernon Wells AU-1,000	25.00
92	Rick Ankiel AU-1,000	60.00
93	Eric Chavez AU-1,000	20.00
94	Alfonso Soriano AU-1,000	50.00
95	Eric Gagne AU-1,000	25.00
96	Rob Bell AU-1,500	10.00
97	Matt Riley AU-1,500	10.00
98	Josh Beckett AU-1,500	80.00
99	Ben Petrick AU-1,500	10.00
100	Rob Ramsay AU-1,500 RC	10.00
101	Scott Williamson AU-1,500	10.00
102	Doug Davis AU-1,500	15.00
103	Eric Munson AU-1,500	10.00
104	Pat Burrell AU-500	30.00
105	Jim Morris AU-1,500	20.00
106	Gabe Kapler AU-500	15.00
107	Lance Berkman AU-1,500	35.00
108	Erubiel Durazo AU-1,500	10.00
109	Tim Hudson AU-1,500	30.00
110	Ben Davis AU-1,500	10.00
111	Nick Johnson AU-1,500	20.00
112	Octavio Dotel AU-1,500	10.00
113	Jerry Hairston Jr. 1,500	10.00
114	Ruben Mateo 1,500	10.00
115	Chris Singleton 1,500	10.00
116	Bruce Chen AU-1,500	10.00
117	Derrick Gibson AU-1,500	10.00
118	Carlos Beltran AU-500	80.00
119	Fred Garcia AU-500	10.00
120	Preston Wilson AU-500	15.00

Radiance

NM/M
Stars (1-90): 4-8X
Common Young Star (91-120): 10.00
Production 100 Sets

Foundations

NM/M
Complete Set (10): 15.00
Common Player: .50
Inserted 1:32.

1	Ken Griffey Jr.	3.00
2	Nomar Garciaparra	3.00
3	Cal Ripken Jr.	4.00
4	Chipper Jones	2.00
5	Mike Piazza	3.00
6	Derek Jeter	4.00
7	Manny Ramirez	1.00
8	Jeff Bagwell	1.00
9	Tony Gwynn	2.00
10	Larry Walker	.50

Heart of the Order

NM/M
Complete Set (20): 10.00
Common Player: .40
Inserted 1:8

1	Bernie Williams	.50
2	Mike Piazza	2.00

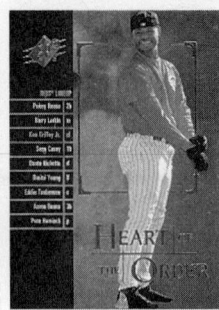

3	Ivan Rodriguez	.75
4	Mark McGwire	2.50
5	Manny Ramirez	1.00
6	Ken Griffey Jr.	2.00
7	Matt Williams	.40
8	Sammy Sosa	2.00
9	Mo Vaughn	.40
10	Carlos Delgado	.75
11	Brian Giles	.40
12	Chipper Jones	1.50
13	Sean Casey	.40
14	Tony Gwynn	1.50
15	Barry Bonds	3.00
16	Carlos Beltran	.65
17	Scott Rolen	.75
18	Juan Gonzalez	1.00
19	Larry Walker	.40
20	Vladimir Guerrero	1.00

Highlight Heroes

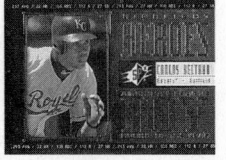

NM/M
Complete Set (10): 10.00
Common Player: .50
Inserted 1:16

1	Pedro Martinez	1.00
2	Ivan Rodriguez	.75
3	Carlos Beltran	.65
4	Nomar Garciaparra	2.00
5	Ken Griffey Jr.	2.00
6	Randy Johnson	1.00
7	Chipper Jones	1.50
8	Scott Williamson	.50
9	Larry Walker	.50
10	Mark McGwire	2.50

Power Brokers

NM/M
Complete Set (20): 10.00
Common Player: .25
Inserted 1:8

1	Rafael Palmeiro	.75
2	Carlos Delgado	.65
3	Ken Griffey Jr.	2.00
4	Matt Stairs	.25
5	Mike Piazza	2.00
6	Vladimir Guerrero	1.00
7	Chipper Jones	1.50
8	Mark McGwire	2.50
9	Matt Williams	.25
10	Juan Gonzalez	1.00
11	Shawn Green	.50
12	Sammy Sosa	2.00
13	Brian Giles	.25
14	Jeff Bagwell	1.00
15	Alex Rodriguez	2.50
16	Frank Thomas	1.00
17	Larry Walker	.25
18	Albert Belle	.25
19	Dean Palmer	.25
20	Mo Vaughn	.25

SPxcitement

NM/M
Complete Set (20): 15.00
Common Player: .25
Inserted 1:4

1	Nomar Garciaparra	1.25
2	Mark McGwire	1.50
3	Derek Jeter	2.00
4	Cal Ripken Jr.	2.00
5	Barry Bonds	2.00
6	Alex Rodriguez	1.50
7	Scott Rolen	.75
8	Pedro Martinez	.75
9	Sean Casey	.25
10	Sammy Sosa	1.25
11	Randy Johnson	.75
12	Ivan Rodriguez	.75
13	Frank Thomas	.75
14	Greg Maddux	1.00
15	Tony Gwynn	1.00
16	Ken Griffey Jr.	1.25
17	Carlos Beltran	.50
18	Mike Piazza	1.25
19	Chipper Jones	1.00
20	Craig Biggio	.25

SPx Signatures

NM/M
Common Player: 10.00
Inserted 1:179

JB	Jeff Bagwell	25.00
BB	Barry Bonds	150.00
JC	Jose Canseco	25.00
SC	Sean Casey	15.00
RC	Roger Clemens	125.00
KG	Ken Griffey Jr.	100.00
VG	Vladimir Guerrero	35.00
TG	Tony Gwynn	40.00
OH	Orlando Hernandez	40.00
DJ	Derek Jeter	125.00
CJ	Chipper Jones	50.00
MR	Manny Ramirez	40.00
CR	Cal Ripken Jr.	125.00
IR	Ivan Rodriguez	25.00
SR	Scott Rolen	30.00

Untouchable Talents

NM/M
Complete Set (10): 30.00
Common Player: 1.50
Inserted 1:96

1	Mark McGwire	8.00
2	Ken Griffey Jr.	6.00
3	Shawn Green	2.00
4	Ivan Rodriguez	2.50
5	Sammy Sosa	6.00
6	Derek Jeter	10.00
7	Sean Casey	1.50
8	Chipper Jones	5.00

9	Pedro Martinez	3.00
10	Vladimir Guerrero	3.00

Winning Materials

NM/M

	Common Bat/Jsy	6.00
AR	Alex Rodriguez/Bat/Jsy	25.00
AR	Alex Rodriguez/Cap/Jsy/100	40.00
DJ	Derek Jeter/Bat/Jsy	40.00
DJ	Derek Jeter/Ball/Jsy/50	75.00
BB	Barry Bonds/Bat/Jersey	30.00
BB	Barry Bonds/Ball/Jsy/100	50.00
BB	Barry Bonds/Ball/Jsy/Auto./25	350.00
JB	Jeff Bagwell/Bat/Jsy	8.00
JB	Jeff Bagwell/Cap/Jsy/100	15.00
JB	Jeff Bagwell/Ball/Jsy/50	25.00
KG	Ken Griffey Jr./Bat/Jsy	20.00
KG	Ken Griffey Jr./Ball/Jsy/50	50.00
KG	Ken Griffey Jr./Jsy/Bat/Auto./24	225.00
TG	Tony Gwynn/Bat/Jsy	10.00
TG	Tony Gwynn/Ball/Jsy/50	15.00
TG	Tony Gwynn/Cap/Jsy/100	30.00
BW	Bernie Williams/Bat/Jsy	8.00
EC	Eric Chavez/Bat/Jsy	8.00
EC	Eric Chavez/Cap/Jsy/100	15.00
GM	Greg Maddux/Bat/Jsy	25.00
IR	Ivan Rodriguez/Bat/Jsy	8.00
JC	Jose Canseco/Bat/Jsy	8.00
JL	Javy Lopez/Bat/Jsy	6.00
JL	Javy Lopez/Cap/Jsy/100	8.00
MM	Mark McGwire/Base/Ball/500	50.00
MR	Manny Ramirez/Bat/Jsy	8.00
MW	Matt Williams/Bat/Jsy	6.00
PM	Pedro Martinez/Cap/Jsy/100	25.00
PO	Paul O'Neill/Bat/Jsy	6.00
VG	Vladimir Guerrero/Bat/Jsy	10.00
VG	Vladimir Guerrero/Cap/Jsy/100	20.00
VG	Vladimir Guerrero/Ball/Jsy/50	30.00
TG	Troy Glaus/Bat/Jersey	8.00

3,000 Hit Club

NM/M
TC-B	Ty Cobb/Bat/350	130.00

2001 SP Authentic

NM/M
Common Player: .25
Common SP (91-135): 4.00
Production 1,250
Common SP (136-180): 2.00
Production 1,250
Pack (5): 12.00
Box (24): 240.00

1	Troy Glaus	.40
2	Darin Erstad	.25
3	Jason Giambi	.75
4	Tim Hudson	.50
5	Eric Chavez	.25

(Houston Astros — Jeff Bagwell)

#	Player	Value
6	Miguel Tejada	.50
7	Jose Ortiz	.25
8	Carlos Delgado	.50
9	Tony Batista	.25
10	Raul Mondesi	.25
11	Aubrey Huff	.25
12	Greg Vaughn	.25
13	Roberto Alomar	.50
14	Juan Gonzalez	.50
15	Jim Thome	.75
16	Omar Vizquel	.25
17	Edgar Martinez	.25
18	Fred Garcia	.25
19	Cal Ripken Jr.	3.00
20	Ivan Rodriguez	.75
21	Rafael Palmeiro	.75
22	Alex Rodriguez	2.00
23	Manny Ramirez	1.00
24	Pedro Martinez	1.00
25	Nomar Garciaparra	.75
26	Mike Sweeney	.25
27	Jermaine Dye	.25
28	Bobby Higginson	.25
29	Dean Palmer	.25
30	Matt Lawton	.25
31	Eric Milton	.25
32	Frank Thomas	.75
33	Magglio Ordonez	.40
34	David Wells	.25
35	Paul Konerko	.50
36	Derek Jeter	3.00
37	Bernie Williams	.50
38	Roger Clemens	2.00
39	Mike Mussina	.50
40	Jorge Posada	.50
41	Jeff Bagwell	.50
42	Richard Hidalgo	.25
43	Craig Biggio	.50
44	Greg Maddux	2.00
45	Chipper Jones	1.00
46	Andruw Jones	.50
47	Rafael Furcal	.40
48	Tom Glavine	.50
49	Jeromy Burnitz	.25
50	Jeffrey Hammonds	.25
51	Mark McGwire	1.50
52	Jim Edmonds	.50
53	Rick Ankiel	.50
54	J.D. Drew	.40
55	Sammy Sosa	.75
56	Corey Patterson	.25
57	Kerry Wood	.50
58	Randy Johnson	1.00
59	Luis Gonzalez	.40
60	Curt Schilling	.75
61	Gary Sheffield	.50
62	Shawn Green	.25
63	Kevin Brown	.25
64	Vladimir Guerrero	.75
65	Jose Vidro	.25
66	Barry Bonds	3.00
67	Jeff Kent	.50
68	Livan Hernandez	.25
69	Preston Wilson	.25
70	Charles Johnson	.25
71	Ryan Dempster	.25
72	Mike Piazza	1.00
73	Al Leiter	.25
74	Edgardo Alfonzo	.25
75	Robin Ventura	.25
76	Tony Gwynn	1.00
77	Phil Nevin	.25
78	Trevor Hoffman	.25
79	Scott Rolen	.50
80	Pat Burrell	.50
81	Bob Abreu	.50
82	Jason Kendall	.25
83	Brian Giles	.25
84	Kris Benson	.25
85	Ken Griffey Jr.	2.00
86	Barry Larkin	.50
87	Sean Casey	.25
88	Todd Helton	.50
89	Mike Hampton	.25
90	Larry Walker	.25
91	Ichiro Suzuki RC	100.00
92	Wilson Betemit RC	6.00
93	Adrian Hernandez RC	4.00
94	Juan Uribe RC	4.00
95	Travis Hafner RC	20.00
96	Morgan Ensberg RC	6.00
97	Sean Douglass RC	4.00
98	Juan Diaz RC	4.00
99	Erick Almonte RC	4.00
100	Ryan Freel RC	8.00
101	Elpidio Guzman RC	4.00
102	Christian Parker RC	4.00
103	Josh Fogg RC	4.00
104	Bert Snow RC	4.00
105	Horacio Ramirez RC	4.00
106	Ricardo Rodriguez RC	4.00
107	Tyler Walker RC	4.00
108	Jose Mieses RC	4.00
109	Billy Sylvester RC	4.00
110	Martin Vargas RC	4.00
111	Andres Torres RC	4.00
112	Greg Miller RC	4.00
113	Alexis Gomez RC	4.00
114	Grant Balfour RC	4.00
115	Henry Mateo RC	4.00
116	Esix Snead RC	4.00
117	Jackson Melian RC	4.00
118	Nate Teut RC	4.00
119	Tsuyoshi Shinjo RC	4.00
120	Carlos Valderrama RC	4.00
121	Johnny Estrada RC	6.00
122	Jason Michaels RC	4.00
123	William Ortega RC	4.00
124	Jason Smith RC	4.00
125	Brian Lawrence RC	4.00
126	Albert Pujols RC	250.00
127	Wilken Ruan RC	4.00
128	Josh Towers RC	4.00
129	Kris Keller RC	4.00
130	Nick Maness RC	4.00
131	Jack Wilson RC	6.00
132	Brandon Duckworth RC	4.00
133	Mike Penney RC	4.00
134	Jay Gibbons RC	4.00
135	Cesar Crespo RC	4.00
136	Ken Griffey Jr.	8.00
137	Mark McGwire	8.00
138	Derek Jeter	10.00
139	Alex Rodriguez	10.00
140	Sammy Sosa	4.00
141	Carlos Delgado	3.00
142	Cal Ripken Jr.	12.00
143	Pedro Martinez	5.00
144	Frank Thomas	4.00
145	Juan Gonzalez	2.00
146	Troy Glaus	3.00
147	Jason Giambi	4.00
148	Ivan Rodriguez	3.00
149	Chipper Jones	5.00
150	Vladimir Guerrero	5.00
151	Mike Piazza	5.00
152	Jeff Bagwell	4.00
153	Randy Johnson	5.00
154	Todd Helton	5.00
155	Gary Sheffield	3.00
156	Tony Gwynn	5.00
157	Barry Bonds	10.00
158	Nomar Garciaparra	3.00
159	Bernie Williams	3.00
160	Greg Vaughn	2.00
161	David Wells	2.00
162	Roberto Alomar	3.00
163	Jermaine Dye	2.00
164	Rafael Palmeiro	4.00
165	Andruw Jones	3.00
166	Preston Wilson	2.00
167	Edgardo Alfonzo	2.00
168	Pat Burrell	3.00
169	Jim Edmonds	3.00
170	Mike Hampton	2.00
171	Jeff Kent	2.00
172	Kevin Brown	2.00
173	Manny Ramirez	5.00
174	Magglio Ordonez	2.00
175	Roger Clemens	8.00
176	Jim Thome	4.00
177	Barry Zito	2.00
178	Brian Giles	2.00
179	Rick Ankiel	2.00
180	Corey Patterson	2.00

Limited

Stars (1-90): 8-15X
SP (91-135): 1-2X
SP (136-180): 1-3X
Production 50 Sets

Buyback Autographs

(Mo Vaughn)

Inserted 1:144
Some not priced due to scarcity.

#	Player	Value
4	Ken Griffey '93 SP/34	125.00
105	Ken Griffey '94 SP/182	80.00
190	Ken Griffey '95 SP/116	80.00
170	Ken Griffey '96 SP/53	100.00
84	Ken Griffey '00 SP/333	70.00
188	Alex Rodriguez '95 SP Red/117	100.00
171	Alex Rodriguez '96 SP/72	120.00
16	Alex Rodriguez '00 SP/332	100.00
260	Frank Thomas '93 SP/79	40.00
193	Frank Thomas '94 SP/165	35.00
50	Frank Thomas '97 SP/34	75.00
34	Frank Thomas '00 SP/302	35.00
34	Chipper Jones '95 SP/118	40.00
26	Chipper Jones '96 SP/72	50.00
45	Chipper Jones '00 SP/303	40.00
132	Randy Johnson '93 SP/97	60.00
106	Randy Johnson '94 SP/146	40.00
189	Randy Johnson '95 SP/121	40.00
169	Randy Johnson '96 SP/78	50.00
58	Randy Johnson '00 SP/213	40.00
41	Carlos Delgado '94 SP/279	15.00
181	Carlos Delgado '96 SP/83	20.00
8	Carlos Delgado '00 SP/174	15.00
50	Jim Edmonds '96 SP/74	20.00
167	Tony Gwynn '93 SP/101	40.00
130	Tony Gwynn '94 SP/88	40.00
105	Tony Gwynn '95 SP/179	30.00
160	Tony Gwynn '97 SP/92	40.00
74	Tony Gwynn '00 SP/95	40.00
3	Jason Giambi '00 SP/290	30.00
9	Ivan Rodriguez '93 SP/89	40.00
180	Ivan Rodriguez '96 SP/64	40.00
22	Ivan Rodriguez '00 SP/163	30.00
47	Andruw Jones '98 SP/336	25.00
10	Barry Bonds '93 SP/75	150.00
90	Barry Bonds '94 SP/103	150.00
166	Barry Bonds '96 SP/49	150.00
65	Barry Bonds '00 SP/146	150.00
18	Gary Sheffield '93 SP/83	20.00
114	Gary Sheffield '94 SP/70	20.00
86	Gary Sheffield '96 SP/69	20.00
60	Gary Sheffield '00 SP/133	15.00
89	Sammy Sosa '93 SP/73	100.00
126	Cal Ripken '94 SP/99	100.00
1	Cal Ripken '95 SP/37	150.00
20	Cal Ripken '00 SP/266	100.00
89	Todd Helton '00 SP/194	25.00
4	Tim Hudson '00 SP/291	20.00
62	Shawn Green '00 SP/340	20.00
52	Fernando Tatis '00 SP/267	6.00
57	Matt Williams '00 SP/340	10.00
72	Robin Ventura '00 SP/340	10.00
2	Troy Glaus '00 SP/340	15.00
39	Roger Clemens '00 SP/145	100.00

Combo Game Jersey

NM/M

Overall jersey odds 1:24

	Players	Value
SD	Sammy Sosa, Andre Dawson	25.00
RS	Alex Rodriguez, Ozzie Smith	35.00
GD	Ken Griffey Jr., Joe DiMaggio/98	120.00
SW	Gary Sheffield, Dave Winfield	15.00
MD	Mickey Mantle, Joe DiMaggio/98	300.00
MG	Mickey Mantle, Ken Griffey /98	160.00

Cooperstown Calling Game Jersey

NM/M

Common Player: 5.00
Overall jersey odds 1:24

	Player	Value
JB	Jeff Bagwell	8.00
WB	Wade Boggs	8.00
GC	Gary Carter	5.00
RC	Roger Clemens	30.00
AD	Andre Dawson	5.00
SG	Steve Garvey	5.00
GG	Goose Gossage	5.00
TG	Tony Gwynn	10.00
RM	Roger Maris/243	75.00
PM	Pedro Martinez/SP	10.00
DM	Don Mattingly	30.00
BM	Bill Mazeroski	5.00
PM	Paul Molitor	5.00
EM	Eddie Murray	5.00
MP	Mike Piazza/SP	25.00
KP	Kirby Puckett	15.00
MR	Manny Ramirez/SP	15.00
CR	Cal Ripken Jr.	30.00
RS	Ryne Sandberg	20.00
OS	Ozzie Smith	10.00
DW	Dave Winfield	5.00

Chirography

NM/M

Common Player: 5.00
Inserted 1:72

	Player	Value
EA	Edgardo Alfonzo	5.00
AB	Albert Belle	15.00
CB	Carlos Beltran	35.00
MB	Milton Bradley	12.00
PB	Pat Burrell	10.00
JC	Jose Canseco	30.00
CD	Carlos Delgado	12.00
DD	Darren Dreifort/206	5.00
JD	J.D. Drew	15.00
JE	Jim Edmonds	20.00
DEr	Darin Erstad	10.00
DEs	David Espinosa	5.00
CF	Cliff Floyd	10.00
RF	Rafael Furcal/222	10.00
JG	Jason Giambi	15.00
TrG	Troy Glaus	15.00
LG	Luis Gonzalez/271	15.00
SG	Shawn Green/82	20.00
KG	Ken Griffey Jr/126	80.00
ToG	Tony Gwynn/76	40.00
RH	Rick Helling/211	5.00
ToH	Todd Helton/152	30.00
TiH	Tim Hudson	15.00
RJ	Randy Johnson/143	50.00
AJ	Andruw Jones	20.00
CJ	Chipper Jones/184	50.00
DJ	David Justice	8.00
MK	Mark Kotsay/228	5.00
TL	Travis Lee/226	5.00
AP	Albert Pujols	400.00
CR	Cal Ripken/109	125.00
AR	Alex Rodriguez/229	100.00
DS	Dane Sardinha	5.00
BS	Ben Sheets	20.00
SS	Sammy Sosa/76	100.00
MS	Mike Sweeney	8.00
MV	Mo Vaughn/103	8.00
RV	Robin Ventura/92	10.00
DW	David Wells	8.00
RW	Rondell White	8.00
MW	Matt Williams	8.00

Chirography Gold

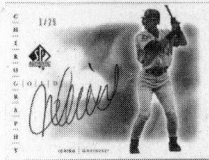

NM/M

Common Player: 15.00

	Player	Value
AB	Albert Belle/88	15.00
CD	Carlos Delgado/25	50.00
DD	Darren Dreifort/37	20.00
DES	David Espinosa/79	15.00
KG	Ken Griffey Jr./30	150.00
RH	Rick Helling/32	15.00
RJ	Randy Johnson/51	65.00
DJ	David Justice/28	30.00
DS	Dane Sardinha/50	15.00
MS	Mike Sweeney/29	20.00
MV	Mo Vaughn/42	15.00
DW	David Wells/33	20.00

Game Jersey

NM/M

Common Player: 5.00
Overall jersey odds 1:24.

	Player	Value
JD	Joe DiMaggio/243	100.00
KG	Ken Griffey Jr.	15.00
MM	Mickey Mantle/243	150.00
AR	Alex Rodriguez	15.00
GS	Gary Sheffield	5.00
SS	Sammy Sosa	10.00

Sultan of Swatch Jersey/Cut

No Pricing
Production One Set

Sultan of Swatch Jersey or Pants

		NM/M
Quantity produced listed		
SOS2	Babe Ruth/29	350.00
SOS3	Babe Ruth/94	300.00
SOS4	Babe Ruth/54	350.00
SOS5	Babe Ruth/59	350.00
SOS6	Babe Ruth/26	350.00
SOS7	Babe Ruth/27	350.00
SOS8	Babe Ruth/32	350.00
SOS9	Babe Ruth/20	350.00
SOS10	Babe Ruth/21	350.00
SOS11	Babe Ruth/23	350.00
SOS12	Babe Ruth/24	350.00
SOS13	Babe Ruth/26	350.00
SOS14	Babe Ruth/27	350.00
SOS15	Babe Ruth/28	350.00
SOS16	Babe Ruth/29	350.00
SOS17	Babe Ruth/30	350.00
SOS18	Babe Ruth/31	350.00
SOS19	Babe Ruth/33	350.00
SOS20	Babe Ruth/36	350.00
SOS21	Babe Ruth/48	350.00

Stars of Japan

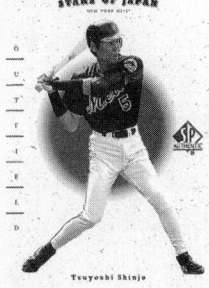

		NM/M
Complete Set (30):		50.00
Common Player:		1.00
One Pack/Hobby Box		
RS1	Ichiro Suzuki, Tsuyoshi Shinjo	5.00
RS2	Shigetosi Hasegawa, Hideki Irabu	1.00
RS3	Tomokazu Ohka, Mac Suzuki	1.00
RS4	Tsuyoshi Shinjo, Hideki Irabu	1.00
RS5	Ichiro Suzuki, Hideo Nomo	5.00
RS6	Tsuyoshi Shinjo, Mac Suzuki	1.00
RS7	Tsuyoshi Shinjo, Kazuhiro Sasaki	1.00
RS8	Hideo Nomo, Tomokazu Ohka	1.50
RS9	Ichiro Suzuki, Mac Suzuki	5.00
RS10	Hideo Nomo, Shigetosi Hasegawa	1.50
RS11	Hideo Nomo, Masato Yoshii	1.50
RS12	Hideo Nomo, Hideki Irabu	1.50
RS13	Shigetosi Hasegawa, Kazuhiro Sasaki	1.00
RS14	Shigetosi Hasegawa, Mac Suzuki	1.00
RS15	Tsuyoshi Shinjo, Hideo Nomo	1.50
RS16	Tsuyoshi Shinjo, Tomokazu Ohka	1.00
RS17	Ichiro Suzuki, Kazuhiro Sasaki	5.00
RS18	Masato Yoshii, Hideki Irabu	1.00
RS19	Ichiro Suzuki, Tomokazu Ohka	5.00
RS20	Hideki Irabu, Kazuhiro Sasaki	1.00
RS21	Tsuyoshi Shinjo, Masato Yoshii	1.00
RS22	Ichiro Suzuki, Shigetosi Hasegawa	5.00
RS23	Mac Suzuki, Kazuhiro Sasaki	1.00
RS24	Ichiro Suzuki, Hideki Irabu	5.00
RS25	Tomokazu Ohka, Kazuhiro Sasaki	1.00
RS26	Tsuyoshi Shinjo, Shigetosi Hasegawa	1.00
RS27	Masato Yoshii, Kazuhiro Sasaki	1.00
RS28	Hideo Nomo, Kazuhiro Sasaki	1.50
RS29	Kazuhiro Sasaki, Masato Yoshii	5.00
RS30	Hideo Nomo, Ichiro Suzuki	5.00

Stars of Japan Game Ball

		NM/M
Common Player:		8.00
SH	Shigetosi Hasegawa/SP/30	8.00
HI	Hideki Irabu	8.00
KS	Kazuhiro Sasaki	10.00
TS	Tsuyoshi Shinjo/SP/50	20.00
IS	Ichiro Suzuki	75.00
MY	Masato Yoshii	10.00

Stars of Japan Game Ball Gold

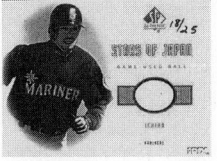

		NM/M
Production 25 Sets		
SH	Shigetosi Hasegawa	40.00
HI	Hideki Irabu	20.00
KS	Kazuhiro Sasaki	40.00

Stars of Japan Game Ball-Base Combos

		NM/M
Inserted 1:576		
HI-KS	Hideki Irabu, Kazuhiro Sasaki/SP/30	25.00
HN-KS	Hideo Nomo, Kazuhiro Sasaki SP/50	75.00
HN-SH	Hideo Nomo, Shigetosi Hasegawa	20.00
IS-KS	Ichiro Suzuki, Kazuhiro Sasaki/SP/30	120.00
IS-MY	Ichiro Suzuki, Masato Yoshii	50.00
IS-SH	Ichiro Suzuki, Shigetosi Hasegawa/SP/72	75.00
IS-TS	Ichiro Suzuki, Tsuyoshi Shinjo/SP/40	125.00
MS-KS	Mac Suzuki, Kazuhiro Sasaki/SP/30	20.00
MY-KS	Masato Yoshii, Kazuhiro Sasaki/SP/30	25.00
SH-KS	Shigetosi Hasegawa, Kazuhiro Sasaki/SP/30	25.00
TO-KS	Tomokazu Ohka, Kazuhiro Sasaki	20.00
TS-HI	Tsuyoshi Shinjo, Hideki Irabu/SP/30	25.00
TS-KS	Tsuyoshi Shinjo, Kazuhiro Sasaki/SP/30	25.00
TS-SH	Tsuyoshi Shinjo, Shigetosi Hasegawa/ SP/30	25.00

Stars of Japan Game Ball-Base Combos Gold

		NM/M
Common Card:		20.00
Production 25 Sets		
HI-KS	Hideki Irabu, Kazuhiro Sasaki	25.00
HN-KS	Hideo Nomo, Kazuhiro Sasaki	65.00
HN-SH	Hideo Nomo, Shigetosi Hasegawa	65.00
IS-KS	Ichiro Suzuki, Kazuhiro Sasaki	150.00
IS-MY	Ichiro Suzuki, Masato Yoshii	150.00
IS-SH	Ichiro Suzuki, Shigetosi Hasegawa	150.00
IS-TS	Ichiro Suzuki, Tsuyoshi Shinjo	150.00
MS-KS	Mac Suzuki, Kazuhiro Sasaki	20.00
MY-KS	Masato Yoshii, Kazuhiro Sasaki	20.00
SH-KS	Shigetosi Hasegawa, Kazuhiro Sasaki	20.00
TO-KS	Tomokazu Ohka, Kazuhiro Sasaki	20.00
TS-HI	Tsuyoshi Shinjo, Hideki Irabu	25.00
TS-KS	Tsuyoshi Shinjo, Kazuhiro Sasaki	25.00
TS-SH	Tsuyoshi Shinjo, Shigetosi Hasegawa	25.00

Stars of Japan Game Ball-Base Trio

		NM/M
Complete Set (1):		
RS	Kazuhiro Sasaki, Ichiro Suzuki, Hideo Nomo	175.00

Stars of Japan Game Ball-Base Trio Gold

Production 25
No Pricing

Stars of Japan Game Base

		NM/M
Common Player:		15.00
SH	Shigetosi Hasegawa/SP/33	20.00
HI	Hideki Irabu/SP/33	15.00
TO	Tomokazu Ohka/SP/33	15.00
KS	Kazuhiro Sasaki/SP/33	25.00
TS	Tsuyoshi Shinjo/SP/33	25.00
MS	Mac Suzuki/SP/23	20.00
MY	Masato Yoshii/SP/33	20.00

Stars of Japan Game Base Gold

		NM/M
Common Player:		25.00
Production 25 Sets		
SH	Shigetosi Hasegawa	25.00
HI	Hideki Irabu	25.00
TO	Tomokazu Ohka	25.00
KS	Kazuhiro Sasaki	30.00
TS	Tsuyoshi Shinjo	35.00
MS	Mac Suzuki	25.00
MY	Masato Yoshii	25.00

Stars of Japan Game Bat

		NM/M
Inserted 1:12		
HN	Hideo Nomo/SP/30	60.00
TS	Tsuyoshi Shinjo/SP/30	20.00
MY	Masato Yoshii	5.00

Stars of Japan Game Bat Gold

		NM/M
Common Player:		10.00
Production 25 Sets		
HN	Hideo Nomo	80.00
TS	Tsuyoshi Shinjo	50.00
MY	Masato Yoshii	10.00

Stars of Japan Game Jersey-Bat Combos

		NM/M
Common Player:		15.00
HS	Shigetosi Hasegawa, Tsuyoshi Shinjo	15.00
NN	Hideo Nomo	60.00
SN	Kazuhiro Sasaki, Hideo Nomo	40.00

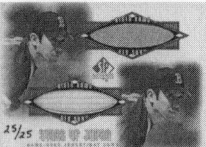

		NM/M
SH	Kazuhiro Sasaki, Shigetosi Hasegawa	15.00

Stars of Japan Game Bat-Jersey Combo Gold

		NM/M
Production 25 Sets		
BB-HS	Shigetosi Hasegawa, Tsuyoshi Shinjo	40.00

Stars of Japan Game Jersey

		NM/M
Common Player:		5.00
Inserted 1:12		
SH	Shigetosi Hasegawa	5.00
HN	Hideo Nomo	40.00
KS	Kazuhiro Sasaki	8.00
TS	Tsuyoshi Shinjo	8.00
IS	Ichiro Suzuki/SP/ 260 EXCH	100.00
MY	Masato Yoshii	5.00

Stars of Japan Game Jersey Gold

		NM/M
Common Player:		10.00
Production 25 Sets		
SH	Shigetosi Hasegawa	10.00
HN	Hideo Nomo	60.00
KS	Kazuhiro Sasaki	15.00
TS	Tsuyoshi Shinjo	15.00
MY	Masato Yoshii	10.00

2001 SP Game Bat

		NM/M
Complete Set (90):		40.00
Common Player:		.25
Pack (4):		10.00
Box (16):		150.00
1	Troy Glaus	.50
2	Darin Erstad	.50
3	Mo Vaughn	.25
4	Jason Giambi	.75
5	Ben Grieve	.25
6	Eric Chavez	.50
7	Carlos Delgado	.75
8	Tony Batista	.25
9	Shannon Stewart	.25
10	Jose Cruz Jr.	.25
11	Fred McGriff	.25
12	Greg Vaughn	.25
13	Roberto Alomar	.50

14	Manny Ramirez	1.00
15	Jim Thome	.75
16	Russ Branyan	.25
17	Alex Rodriguez	2.00
18	John Olerud	.25
19	Edgar Martinez	.25
20	Cal Ripken Jr.	3.00
21	Albert Belle	.25
22	Ivan Rodriguez	.75
23	Rafael Palmeiro	.50
24	Nomar Garciaparra	1.00
25	Carl Everett	.25
26	Dante Bichette	.25
27	Mike Sweeney	.25
28	Jermaine Dye	.25
29	Carlos Beltran	.75
30	Juan Gonzalez	.50
31	Dean Palmer	.25
32	Bobby Higginson	.25
33	Matt Lawton	.25
34	Jacque Jones	.25
35	Frank Thomas	1.00
36	Magglio Ordonez	.25
37	Paul Konerko	.50
38	Carlos Lee	.40
39	Bernie Williams	.50
40	Derek Jeter	3.00
41	Paul O'Neill	.40
42	Jose Canseco	.50
43	Ken Caminiti	.25
44	Jeff Bagwell	.75
45	Craig Biggio	.40
46	Richard Hidalgo	.25
47	Andruw Jones	1.00
48	Chipper Jones	.25
49	Andres Galarraga	.25
50	B.J. Surhoff	.25
51	Jeromy Burnitz	.25
52	Geoff Jenkins	.25
53	Richie Sexson	.40
54	Mark McGwire	2.50
55	Jim Edmonds	.50
56	J.D. Drew	.40
57	Fernando Tatis	.25
58	Sammy Sosa	1.50
59	Mark Grace	.50
60	Eric Young	.25
61	Matt Williams	.25
62	Luis Gonzalez	.25
63	Steve Finley	.25
64	Shawn Green	.40
65	Gary Sheffield	.50
66	Eric Karros	.25
67	Vladimir Guerrero	1.00
68	Jose Vidro	.25
69	Barry Bonds	3.00
70	Jeff Kent	.40
71	Preston Wilson	.25
72	Mike Lowell	.25
73	Luis Castillo	.25
74	Mike Piazza	1.50
75	Robin Ventura	.25
76	Edgardo Alfonzo	.25
77	Tony Gwynn	1.00
78	Eric Owens	.25
79	Ryan Klesko	.25
80	Scott Rolen	.75
81	Bobby Abreu	.50
82	Pat Burrell	.50
83	Brian Giles	.25
84	Jason Kendall	.25
85	Aaron Boone	.25
86	Ken Griffey Jr.	2.00
87	Barry Larkin	.50
88	Todd Helton	1.00
89	Larry Walker	.50
90	Jeffrey Hammonds	.25

Big League Hit Parade

		NM/M
Complete Set (6):		15.00
Common Player:		1.50
Inserted 1:15		
1	Nomar Garciaparra	1.50
2	Ken Griffey Jr.	3.00
3	Sammy Sosa	2.00
4	Alex Rodriguez	4.00
5	Mark McGwire	4.00
6	Ivan Rodriguez	1.50

In the Swing

		NM/M
Complete Set (15):		25.00
Common Player:		1.00
Inserted 1:7		
1	Ken Griffey Jr.	2.50
2	Jim Edmonds	1.00
3	Carlos Delgado	1.00
4	Frank Thomas	1.50
5	Barry Bonds	4.00
6	Nomar Garciaparra	2.00
7	Gary Sheffield	1.00
8	Vladimir Guerrero	1.50
9	Alex Rodriguez	3.00
10	Todd Helton	1.50
11	Darin Erstad	1.00
12	Derek Jeter	4.00
13	Sammy Sosa	2.50
14	Mark McGwire	3.00
15	Jason Giambi	1.00

Lineup Time

	NM/M
Complete Set (11):	20.00

Common Player:		1.00
Inserted 1:8		
1	Mark McGwire	3.00
2	Roberto Alomar	1.00
3	Alex Rodriguez	3.00
4	Chipper Jones	2.00
5	Ivan Rodriguez	1.00
6	Ken Griffey Jr.	2.50
7	Sammy Sosa	2.50
8	Barry Bonds	4.00
9	Frank Thomas	1.50
10	Pedro Martinez	1.50
11	Derek Jeter	4.00

Piece of the Game

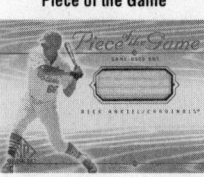

	NM/M
Common Player:	4.00
Inserted 1:1	
SP production 1,500 or fewer	
Golds:	2-5X
Production 25 Sets	

EA	Edgardo Alfonzo/SP	10.00
RA	Roberto Alomar	8.00
SA	Sandy Alomar	4.00
RA	Rick Ankiel	10.00
JB	Jeff Bagwell/SP	15.00
TB	Tony Batista	5.00
CB	Carlos Beltran	5.00
JB	Johnny Bench/SP	25.00
BB	Barry Bonds	25.00
KB	Kevin Brown/SP	10.00
PB	Pat Burrell	8.00
JC	Jose Canseco	6.00
WC	Will Clark	8.00
CD	Carlos Delgado	6.00
JoD	Joe DiMaggio/SP	100.00
JD	J.D. Drew	6.00
JE	Jim Edmonds	6.00
DE	Darin Erstad/SP	10.00
RF	Rafael Furcal	6.00
BG	Bob Gibson/SP	20.00
TGI	Tom Glavine/SP	15.00
MG	Mark Grace	8.00
SG	Shawn Green	6.00
KG	Ken Griffey Jr.	15.00
TGw	Tony Gwynn	10.00
TH	Todd Helton	8.00
TH	Todd Hundley/SP	10.00
RJ	Reggie Jackson/SP	20.00
RJ	Randy Johnson	10.00
AJ	Andruw Jones	8.00
CJ	Chipper Jones	10.00
DJ	David Justice	5.00
KL	Kenny Lofton	4.00
GM	Greg Maddux	15.00
EM	Edgar Martinez	6.00
TM	Tino Martinez	6.00
FM	Fred McGriff/SP	10.00
PN	Phil Nevin/SP	10.00
JO	John Olerud	6.00
PO	Paul O'Neill	6.00
MO	Magglio Ordonez/SP	10.00
MQ	Mark Quinn/SP	10.00
MR	Manny Ramirez	8.00
AR	Cal Ripken Jr./SP	40.00
AR	Alex Rodriguez	10.00
IR	Ivan Rodriguez	8.00
SR	Scott Rolen	8.00
NR	Nolan Ryan/SP	35.00
TS	Tim Salmon/SP	10.00
GS	Gary Sheffield	5.00
SS	Sammy Sosa/SP	25.00
SS	Shannon Stewart	4.00
FT	Frank Thomas	8.00
GV	Greg Vaughn	4.00
MV	Mo Vaughn	4.00
RV	Robin Ventura	4.00
BW	Bernie Williams	6.00
MW	Matt Williams	4.00
PW	Preston Wilson	4.00

Piece of the Game Autograph

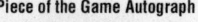

	NM/M
Common Autograph:	30.00
Inserted 1:96	
BB	Barry Bonds	150.00
JC	Jose Canseco	40.00
KG	Ken Griffey Jr.	100.00
TGw	Tony Gwynn	50.00

AJ	Andruw Jones	30.00
AR	Alex Rodriguez	120.00
NR	Nolan Ryan	125.00
FT	Frank Thomas	50.00

The Lumber Yard

	NM/M
Complete Set (10):	15.00
Common Player:	.50
Inserted 1:10	
1	Jason Giambi	1.00
2	Chipper Jones	1.50
3	Carl Everett	.50
4	Alex Rodriguez	3.00
5	Frank Thomas	1.50
6	Barry Bonds	4.00
7	Jeff Bagwell	1.50
8	Sammy Sosa	2.50
9	Carlos Delgado	1.00
10	Mike Piazza	2.50

2001 SP Bat - Milestone

	NM/M
Complete Set (96):	
Common Player:	.40
Common Rookie (91-96):	5.00
Production 500	
Pack (4):	15.00
Box (10):	125.00
1	Troy Glaus	.50
2	Darin Erstad	.50
3	Jason Giambi	.50
4	Jermaine Dye	.40
5	Eric Chavez	.50
6	Carlos Delgado	.50
7	Raul Mondesi	.40
8	Shannon Stewart	.40
9	Greg Vaughn	.40
10	Aubrey Huff	.40
11	Juan Gonzalez	.50
12	Roberto Alomar	.50
13	Jim Thome	.75
14	Omar Vizquel	.40
15	Mike Cameron	.40
16	Edgar Martinez	.40
17	John Olerud	.40
18	Bret Boone	.40
19	Cal Ripken Jr.	3.00
20	Tony Batista	.40
21	Alex Rodriguez	2.50
22	Ivan Rodriguez	.75
23	Rafael Palmeiro	.75
24	Manny Ramirez	1.00
25	Pedro Martinez	1.00
26	Nomar Garciaparra	.50
27	Carl Everett	.40
28	Mike Sweeney	.40
29	Neifi Perez	.40
30	Mark Quinn	.40
31	Bobby Higginson	.40
32	Tony Clark	.40
33	Doug Mientkiewicz	.40
34	Cristian Guzman	.40
35	Joe Mays	.40
36	David Ortiz	1.00
37	Frank Thomas	1.00
38	Magglio Ordonez	.50
39	Carlos Lee	.50
40	Alfonso Soriano	.75
41	Bernie Williams	.50
42	Derek Jeter	3.00
43	Roger Clemens	2.00
44	Jeff Bagwell	.75
45	Richard Hidalgo	.40
46	Moises Alou	.40
47	Chipper Jones	1.00
48	Greg Maddux	.50
49	Rafael Furcal	.50
50	Andruw Jones	.50
51	Jeromy Burnitz	.40
52	Geoff Jenkins	.50
53	Richie Sexson	.50
54	Edgar Renteria	.40
55	Mark McGwire	2.00
56	Jim Edmonds	.50
57	J.D. Drew	.50
58	Sammy Sosa	1.00
59	Bill Mueller	.40
60	Luis Gonzalez	.40
61	Randy Johnson	.50

62	Gary Sheffield	.50
63	Shawn Green	.40
64	Kevin Brown	.40
65	Vladimir Guerrero	1.00
66	Jose Vidro	.40
67	Fernando Tatis	.40
68	Barry Bonds	3.00
69	Jeff Kent	.50
70	Rich Aurilia	.40
71	Preston Wilson	.40
72	Charles Johnson	.40
73	Cliff Floyd	.40
74	Mike Piazza	1.00
75	Matt Lawton	.40
76	Edgardo Alfonzo	.40
77	Tony Gwynn	1.50
78	Phil Nevin	.40
79	Scott Rolen	1.00
80	Pat Burrell	.50
81	Bobby Abreu	.50
82	Brian Giles	.40
83	Jason Kendall	.40
84	Aramis Ramirez	.50
85	Sean Casey	.50
86	Ken Griffey Jr.	2.50
87	Barry Larkin	.50
88	Todd Helton	.75
89	Mike Hampton	.40
90	Larry Walker	.50
91	Ichiro Suzuki RC	50.00
92	Albert Pujols RC	120.00
93	Tsuyoshi Shinjo RC	5.00
94	Jack Wilson RC	8.00
95	Donaldo Mendez RC	5.00
96	Junior Spivey RC	5.00

P.O.A. Milestone Bat

		NM/M
Common Player:		5.00
Golds:		3-5X
Production 35 Sets		
JB	Jeff Bagwell	8.00
BB	Barry Bonds	20.00
RB	Russell Branyan	5.00
JB	Jeromy Burnitz	5.00
RC	Roger Clemens	20.00
DE	Darin Erstad	5.00
LG	Luis Gonzalez	5.00
KG	Ken Griffey Jr.	12.00
TH	Todd Helton	8.00
Chj	Chipper Jones	10.00
MP	Mike Piazza	10.00
CR	Cal Ripken Jr.	30.00
AR	Alex Rodriguez	15.00
GS	Gary Sheffield	5.00
SS	Sammy Sosa	10.00
IS	Ichiro Suzuki/203	80.00
FT	Frank Thomas	8.00
JT	Jim Thome	8.00

P.O.A. Int. Conn. Bat

		NM/M
Common Player:		5.00
Golds:		3-5X
Production 35 Sets		
RA	Roberto Alomar	6.00
AB	Adrian Beltre	5.00
RF	Rafael Furcal	5.00

JG	Juan Gonzalez	6.00
AJ	Andruw Jones	8.00
PM	Pedro Martinez	10.00
HN	Hideo Nomo/203	25.00
MO	Magglio Ordonez	5.00
CP	Chan Ho Park	5.00
JP	Jorge Posada	10.00
AP	Albert Pujols	60.00
MR	Manny Ramirez	8.00
TS	Tsuyoshi Shinjo	8.00
IS	Ichiro Suzuki/273	80.00
MT	Miguel Tejada	6.00
OV	Omar Vizquel	5.00

P.O.A. BFH Bat

NM/M

Common Player:		5.00
Golds:		2-3X
Production 35 Sets		
BB	Barry Bonds	20.00
RC	Roger Clemens/203	25.00
CD	Carlos Delgado	5.00
JG	Jason Giambi	5.00
KG	Ken Griffey Jr.	15.00
TGw	Tony Gwynn	15.00
GM	Greg Maddux	12.00
EM	Edgar Martinez	6.00
FM	Fred McGriff	6.00
RP	Rafael Palmeiro	8.00
MP	Mike Piazza	10.00
CR	Cal Ripken Jr.	30.00
AR	Alex Rodriguez	15.00
IR	Ivan Rodriguez	8.00
SS	Sammy Sosa	10.00

P.O.A. Autograph Bat

NM/M

Common Autograph:		15.00
Inserted 1:100		
RB	Russell Branyan	15.00
CD	Carlos Delgado/97	30.00
JDr	J.D. Drew	20.00
JDy	Jermaine Dye	15.00
LG	Luis Gonzalez	15.00
JK	Jason Kendall	15.00
JK	Jeff Kent/194	30.00
AR	Alex Rodriguez/97	120.00
GS	Gary Sheffield/194	40.00
IS	Ichiro Suzuki/53	800.00
MT	Miguel Tejada	40.00
JV	Jose Vidro	15.00
PW	Preston Wilson	15.00

P.O.A. Triple Bat

NM/M

Common Card:		15.00
Inserted 1:50		
GRS	Ken Griffey Jr., Alex Rodriguez, Sammy Sosa	40.00
JJF	Chipper Jones, Andruw Jones, Rafael Furcal	15.00
RRP	Alex Rodriguez, Ivan Rodriguez, Rafael Palmeiro	35.00
SGB	Gary Sheffield, Shawn Green, Adrian Beltre	15.00
TVA	Jim Thome, Omar Vizquel, Roberto Alomar	15.00

KGR	Jason Kendall, Brian Giles, Aramis Ramirez	15.00
OJC	Paul O'Neill, David Justice, Roger Clemens	15.00
CMG	Roger Clemens, Greg Maddux, Tom Glavine	40.00
VSA	Robin Ventura, Tsuyoshi Shinjo, Edgardo Alfonzo	15.00
OTA	Magglio Ordonez, Frank Thomas, Sandy Alomar	15.00
PWS	Kirby Puckett, Dave Winfield, Ozzie Smith	25.00
GRB	Tony Gwynn, Cal Ripken Jr., Barry Bonds	60.00
GBM	Ken Griffey Jr., Barry Bonds, Fred McGriff	35.00
SFR	Alfonso Soriano, Rafael Furcal, Alex Ramirez	25.00

P.O.A. Quad Bat

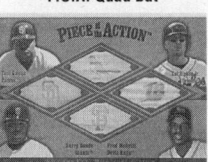

NM/M

Common Card:		15.00
Inserted 1:50		
TVAL	Jim Thome, Omar Vizquel, Roberto Alomar, Kenny Lofton	25.00
RRPM	Alex Rodriguez, Ivan Rodriguez, Rafael Palmeiro, Ruben Mateo	50.00
OJCP	Paul O'Neill, David Justice, Roger Clemens, Jorge Posada	60.00
JJFM	Chipper Jones, Andruw Jones, Rafael Furcal, Greg Maddux	40.00
PWSG	Kirby Puckett, Dave Winfield, Ozzie Smith, Steve Garvey	30.00
GRSB	Ken Griffey Jr., Alex Rodriguez, Sammy Sosa, Barry Bonds	80.00
SGBP	Gary Sheffield, Shawn Green, Adrian Beltre, Chan Ho Park	50.00
GGRR	Ken Griffey Jr., Ken Griffey Jr., Alex Rodriguez, Alex Rodriguez	65.00
GRBM	Tony Gwynn, Cal Ripken Jr., Barry Bonds, Fred McGriff	70.00
TDTA	Frank Thomas, Jermaine Dye, Jim Thome, Roberto Alomar	25.00
GHSK	Luis Gonzalez, Todd Helton, Gary Sheffield, Jeff Kent	20.00
GDBS	Ken Griffey Jr., J.D. Drew, Jeromy Burnitz, Sammy Sosa	50.00
JVBW	Chipper Jones, Robin Ventura, Pat Burrell, Preston Wilson	30.00
RGGM	Alex Rodriguez, Troy Glaus, Jason Giambi, Edgar Martinez	40.00
ONRD	Paul O'Neill, Hideo Nomo, Cal Ripken Jr., Carlos Delgado	80.00

Slugging Sensations

NM/M

Complete Set (12):		12.00
Common Player:		.50
Inserted 1:5		
SS1	Troy Glaus	.50
SS2	Mark McGwire	2.00
SS3	Sammy Sosa	1.50
SS4	Juan Gonzalez	.50

SS5	Barry Bonds	3.00
SS6	Jeff Bagwell	.75
SS7	Jason Giambi	.75
SS8	Ivan Rodriguez	.75
SS9	Mike Piazza	1.50
SS10	Chipper Jones	1.00
SS11	Ken Griffey Jr.	2.00
SS12	Gary Sheffield	.50

The Art of Hitting

NM/M

Complete Set (12):		10.00
Common Player:		.50
Inserted 1:5		
AH1	Tony Gwynn	1.50
AH2	Manny Ramirez	1.00
AH3	Todd Helton	1.00
AH4	Nomar Garciaparra	1.00
AH5	Vladimir Guerrero	1.00
AH6	Ichiro Suzuki	1.50
AH7	Darin Erstad	.50
AH8	Alex Rodriguez	2.50
AH9	Carlos Delgado	.75
AH10	Edgar Martinez	.50
AH11	Luis Gonzalez	.50
AH12	Barry Bonds	3.00

The Trophy Room

NM/M

Complete Set (6):		8.00
Common Player:		1.00
Inserted 1:5		
TR1	Sammy Sosa	1.50
TR2	Jason Giambi	1.00
TR3	Todd Helton	1.00
TR4	Alex Rodriguez	2.50
TR5	Mark McGwire	2.50
TR6	Ken Griffey Jr.	1.50

2001 SP Game-Used Edition

NM/M

Common Player:		.50
Common SP (61-90):		5.00
Production 500		

Pack (3):		30.00
Box (6):		150.00
1	Garret Anderson	.50
2	Troy Glaus	1.00
3	Darin Erstad	.75
4	Jason Giambi	1.50
5	Tim Hudson	.75
6	Johnny Damon	2.00
7	Carlos Delgado	1.00
8	Greg Vaughn	.50
9	Juan Gonzalez	.75
10	Roberto Alomar	1.00
11	Jim Thome	1.50
12	Edgar Martinez	.50
13	Cal Ripken Jr.	5.00
14	Andres Galarraga	.50
15	Alex Rodriguez	4.00
16	Rafael Palmeiro	1.00
17	Ivan Rodriguez	1.50
18	Manny Ramirez	1.50
19	Nomar Garciaparra	1.00
20	Pedro Martinez	2.00
21	Jermaine Dye	.50
22	Dean Palmer	.50
23	Matt Lawton	.50
24	Frank Thomas	1.50
25	David Wells	.50
26	Magglio Ordonez	.50
27	Derek Jeter	5.00
28	Bernie Williams	.50
29	Roger Clemens	3.00
30	Jeff Bagwell	1.50
31	Richard Hidalgo	.50
32	Chipper Jones	2.00
33	Andruw Jones	1.00
34	Greg Maddux	3.00
35	Jeffrey Hammonds	.50
36	Mark McGwire	3.00
37	Jim Edmonds	.75
38	Sammy Sosa	1.50
39	Corey Patterson	.50
40	Randy Johnson	1.50
41	Luis Gonzalez	.50
42	Gary Sheffield	.75
43	Shawn Green	.75
44	Kevin Brown	.50
45	Vladimir Guerrero	1.50
46	Barry Bonds	5.00
47	Jeff Kent	.75
48	Preston Wilson	.50
49	Charles Johnson	.50
50	Mike Piazza	2.00
51	Edgardo Alfonzo	.50
52	Tony Gwynn	2.00
53	Scott Rolen	1.50
54	Pat Burrell	1.00
55	Brian Giles	.50
56	Jason Kendall	.50
57	Ken Griffey Jr.	3.00
58	Mike Hampton	.50
59	Todd Helton	1.50
60	Larry Walker	.75
61	Wilson Betemit **RC**	10.00
62	Travis Hafner **RC**	15.00
63	Ichiro Suzuki **RC**	50.00
64	Juan Diaz **RC**	5.00
65	Morgan Ensberg **RC**	8.00
66	Horacio Ramirez **RC**	8.00
67	Ricardo Rodriguez **RC**	5.00
68	Sean Douglass **RC**	5.00
69	Brandon Duckworth **RC**	5.00
70	Jackson Melian **RC**	5.00
71	Adrian Hernandez **RC**	5.00
72	Kyle Kessel **RC**	5.00
73	Jason Michaels **RC**	5.00
74	Esix Snead **RC**	5.00
75	Jason Smith **RC**	5.00
76	Tyler Walker **RC**	5.00
77	Juan Uribe **RC**	8.00
78	Adam Pettyjohn **RC**	5.00
79	Tsuyoshi Shinjo **RC**	5.00
80	Mike Penney **RC**	5.00
81	Josh Towers **RC**	8.00
82	Erick Almonte **RC**	5.00
83	Ryan Freel **RC**	10.00
84	Juan Pena	5.00
85	Albert Pujols **RC**	200.00
86	Henry Mateo **RC**	5.00
87	Greg Miller **RC**	5.00
88	Jose Mieses **RC**	5.00
89	Jack Wilson **RC**	10.00
90	Carlos Valderrama **RC**	5.00

Authentic Fabric Jersey

NM/M

Common Player:		4.00
Inserted 1:1		
EA	Edgardo Alfonzo	4.00
RA	Roberto Alomar	6.00
RA	Rick Ankiel	8.00
TB	Tony Batista/SP	5.00
BB	Barry Bonds	25.00
KB	Kevin Brown	5.00
JB	Jeromy Burnitz	4.00
PB	Pat Burrell	5.00
JC(B)	Jose Canseco BLC	8.00
JC(H)	Jose Canseco/Yanks	8.00
EC	Eric Chavez	5.00
JCi	Jeff Cirillo	4.00
RC	Roger Clemens	20.00
CD	Carlos Delgado/SP	10.00
JDi	Joe DiMaggio/SP/50	125.00
JDr	J.D. Drew	5.00
JDy	Jermaine Dye/SP	8.00
JE	Jim Edmonds	5.00

DE	Darin Erstad	5.00
JG	Jason Giambi	8.00
BG	Brian Giles/SP	8.00
TGI	Troy Glaus	5.00
ToG	Tom Glavine	6.00
LG	Luis Gonzalez	5.00
MG	Mark Grace	8.00
SG	Shawn Green	6.00
KG(H)	Ken Griffey/Reds	12.00
KG(M)	Ken Griffey/M's	12.00
KG(R)	Ken Griffey/Reds	12.00
TGw	Tony Gwynn	10.00
MH	Mike Hampton	4.00
THe	Todd Helton	8.00
TrH	Trevor Hoffman	4.00
TH	Tim Hudson	6.00
AH	Aubrey Huff	4.00
JI	J. Isringhausen/SP	8.00
CJo	Charles Johnson	4.00
RJ	Randy Johnson	10.00
AJ	Andruw Jones	8.00
CJ	Chipper Jones	10.00
JK	Jason Kendall	4.00
JK	Jeff Kent	5.00
BL	Barry Larkin	6.00
AL	Al Leiter	4.00
KL	Kenny Lofton	4.00
TL	Terrence Long	4.00
GM	Greg Maddux	10.00
MM	Mickey Mantle/SP/50	250.00
RM	Roger Maris/SP	75.00
EM	Edgar Martinez	5.00
TM	Tino Martinez	5.00
FM	Fred McGriff	5.00
KM	Kevin Millwood	4.00
PN	Phil Nevin	4.00
JO	John Olerud	5.00
MO	Magglio Ordonez	5.00
AP	Adam Piatt	4.00
CR	Cal Ripken Jr.	25.00
MR	Mariano Rivera	6.00
AR(H)	Alex Rodriguez/Rangers	10.00
AR(M)	Alex Rodriguez/M's	10.00
IR	Ivan Rodriguez	8.00
SR	Scott Rolen	8.00
NR	Nolan Ryan/SP/50	50.00
TS	Tom Seaver/SP/50	30.00
GS	Gary Sheffield	5.00
SS(H)	Sammy Sosa	15.00
SS(R)	Sammy Sosa	15.00
FTa	Fernando Tatis	4.00
MT	Miguel Tejada	6.00
FTh	Frank Thomas	8.00
JT	Jim Thome	4.00
GV	Greg Vaughn	4.00
RV	Robin Ventura	4.00
JV	Jose Vidro	4.00
DW	David Wells/SP	4.00
MW	Matt Williams	5.00
PW	Preston Wilson	4.00
DY	Dmitri Young	4.00
TZ	Todd Zeile	4.00

Authentic Fabric Jersey Autograph

NM/M

Production 50 Sets

EA	Edgardo Alfonzo	25.00
RA	Rick Ankiel	40.00
BB	Barry Bonds/50	200.00
JC	Jose Canseco	40.00
CD	Carlos Delgado/50	40.00
JDr	J.D. Drew/50	40.00
JG	Jason Giambi/50	40.00
TGI	Troy Glaus/50	50.00
KG	Ken Griffey Jr.	150.00
TH	Tim Hudson/50	50.00
RJ	Randy Johnson	100.00
AJ	Andruw Jones	40.00
CJ	Chipper Jones	80.00
CR	Cal Ripken/50	200.00
AR	Alex Rodriguez	150.00
IR	Ivan Rodriguez	75.00
NR	Nolan Ryan/50	200.00
TS	Tom Seaver/50	80.00
SS	Sammy Sosa/50	120.00
FTh	Frank Thomas	75.00
DW	David Wells/50	25.00

2-Player Auth. Fabric Jersey

NM/M

Common Card: 25.00
Production 50 Sets

R-R	Alex Rodriguez, Ivan Rodriguez	50.00
M-D	Mickey Mantle, Joe DiMaggio	400.00
M-M	Mickey Mantle, Roger Maris	400.00
R-S	Nolan Ryan, Tom Seaver	100.00
B-C	Barry Bonds, Jose Canseco	60.00
S-G	Gary Sheffield, Shawn Green	25.00
J-J	Chipper Jones, Andruw Jones	40.00
C-W	Roger Clemens, Bernie Williams	40.00
J-R	Randy Johnson, Nolan Ryan	75.00
S-T	Sammy Sosa, Frank Thomas	30.00
G-S	Ken Griffey Jr., Sammy Sosa	50.00
G-R	Ken Griffey Jr., Alex Rodriguez	50.00
S-R	Sammy Sosa, Alex Rodriguez	40.00
H-G	Tim Hudson, Jason Giambi	30.00

3-Player Auth. Fabric Jersey

NM/M

Production 25 Sets

GRS	Ken Griffey Jr., Alex Rodriguez, Sammy Sosa	100.00
MJJ	Greg Maddux, Chipper Jones, Andruw Jones	80.00
DMM	Joe DiMaggio, Mickey Mantle, Roger Maris	
JBS	Andruw Jones, Barry Bonds, Sammy Sosa	100.00
JSM	Randy Johnson, Tom Seaver, Greg Maddux	80.00
DGS	Joe DiMaggio, Ken Griffey Jr., Sammy Sosa	

2001 SP Legendary Cuts

NM/M

Complete Set (90):		25.00
Common Player:		.40
Pack (4):		16.00
Box (18):		250.00
1	Al Simmons	.40
2	Jimmie Foxx (Height, weight and birthplace incorrect.)	1.00
3	Mickey Cochrane	.40
4	Phil Niekro	.40
5	Eddie Mathews	1.00
6	Gary Matthews	.40
7	Hank Aaron	2.50
8	Joe Adcock	.40
9	Warren Spahn	.75
10	George Sisler	.40

11	Stan Musial	1.00
12	Dizzy Dean	.75
13	Frankie Frisch	.40
14	Harvey Haddix	.40
15	Johnny Mize	.40
16	Ken Boyer	.40
17	Rogers Hornsby	.40
18	Cap Anson	.40
19	Andre Dawson	.40
20	Billy Williams	.40
21	Billy Herman	.40
22	Hack Wilson	.40
23	Ron Santo	.40
24	Ryne Sandberg	1.50
25	Ernie Banks	1.50
26	Burleigh Grimes	.40
27	Don Drysdale	.75
28	Gil Hodges	.40
29	Jackie Robinson	2.00
30	Tommy Lasorda	.40
31	Pee Wee Reese	.40
32	Roy Campanella	.75
33	Tommy Davis	.40
34	Branch Rickey	.40
35	Leo Durocher	.75
36	Walt Alston	.40
37	Bill Terry	.40
38	Carl Hubbell	.40
39	Eddie Stanky	.40
40	George Kelly	.40
41	Mel Ott	.75
42	Juan Marichal	.40
43	Rube Marquard	.40
44	Travis Jackson	.40
45	Bob Feller	.40
46	Earl Averill	.40
47	Elmer Flick	.40
48	Ken Keltner	.40
49	Lou Boudreau	.40
50	Early Wynn	.40
51	Satchel Paige	1.50
52	Ron Hunt	.40
53	Tom Seaver	1.00
54	Richie Ashburn	.40
55	Mike Schmidt	1.00
56	Honus Wagner	1.00
57	Lloyd Waner	.40
58	Max Carey	.40
59	Paul Waner	.40
60	Roberto Clemente	2.50
61	Nolan Ryan	3.00
62	Bobby Doerr	.40
63	Carlton Fisk	.75
64	Joe Cronin	.40
65	Smokey Joe Wood	.40
66	Tony Conigliaro	.40
67	Edd Roush	.40
68	Johnny Vander Meer	.40
69	Walter Johnson	.75
70	Charlie Gehringer	.40
71	Al Kaline	1.00
72	Ty Cobb	2.00
73	Tony Oliva	.40
74	Luke Appling	.40
75	Minnie Minoso	.40
76	Nellie Fox	.40
77	Shoeless Joe Jackson	2.00
78	Babe Ruth	3.00
79	Bill Dickey	.40
80	Elston Howard	.40
81	Joe DiMaggio	2.50
82	Lefty Gomez	.40
83	Lou Gehrig	2.50
84	Mickey Mantle	3.00
85	Reggie Jackson	1.00
86	Roger Maris	1.00
87	Whitey Ford	.40
88	Waite Hoyt	.40
89	Yogi Berra	1.00
90	Casey Stengel	.40

Bat

NM/M

Common Player:		4.00
Inserted 1:18		
HA	Hank Aaron/SP	40.00
YB	Yogi Berra	10.00
WB	Wade Boggs	8.00
GB	George Brett	15.00
RCa	Roy Campanella/SP	40.00
RC	Rico Carty	4.00
RCl	Roberto Clemente	60.00
TC	Ty Cobb/SP	125.00
KC	Kiki Cuyler	8.00
TD	Tommy Davis/SP	40.00
AD	Andre Dawson	8.00
JD	Joe DiMaggio/SP	100.00
DD	Don Drysdale/SP	25.00
CF	Carlton Fisk	10.00
NF	Nellie Fox	10.00
JF	Jimmie Foxx	40.00
GH	Gil Hodges/SP	40.00

THo	Tommy Holmes (Photo on front is Eddie Mathews.)	8.00
RJ	Reggie Jackson	15.00
DJ	Davey Johnson	4.00
MM	Mickey Mantle/SP	120.00
RM	Roger Maris/SP	60.00
EM	Eddie Mathews	25.00
WMc	Willie McCovey	8.00
PM	Paul Molitor	15.00
MM	Manny Mota	4.00
MO	Mel Ott/SP	50.00
VP	Vada Pinson	4.00
JR	Jackie Robinson/SP	50.00
BR	Babe Ruth/SP	165.00
NR	Nolan Ryan/SP	40.00
RS	Ryne Sandberg	20.00
AS	Al Simmons/SP	25.00
BT	Bill Terry/SP	40.00
MW	Maury Wills	8.00
RY	Robin Yount	15.00

Combo Bat

No pricing due to scarcity.
Production 25 Sets

Debut Bat

NM/M

Common Player:		5.00
Inserted 1:18		
JA	Joe Adcock/SP	15.00
LA	Luke Appling/SP	25.00
RA	Richie Ashburn/SP	25.00
BB	Bobby Bonds	5.00
LB	Lou Boudreau	10.00
KB	Ken Boyer/SP	15.00
BB	Bill Buckner	5.00
MC	Mickey Cochrane	60.00
TC	Tony Conigliaro/SP	15.00
JC	Joe Cronin	15.00
BD	Bobby Doerr/SP	15.00
BF	Bob Feller/SP	15.00
BF	Bill Freehan	5.00
FF	Frankie Frisch/SP	15.00
CG	Charlie Gehringer	15.00
BH	Billy Herman/SP	15.00
WH	Willie Horton	6.00
EH	Elston Howard/SP	15.00
RH	Ron Hunt	5.00
JJ	Joe Jackson	300.00
GL	Greg Luzinski	5.00
GM	Gary Matthews	5.00
MM	Minnie Minoso/SP	15.00
TO	Tony Oliva	8.00
WP	Wes Parker	5.00
BR	Bobby Richardson/SP	15.00
SS	Steve Sax	5.00
GS	George Sisler	20.00
ES	Eddie Stanky	5.00
AT	Alan Trammell	5.00
PW	Paul Waner/SP	60.00
HW	Hack Wilson/SP	70.00
SY	Steve Yeager	5.00

Game Jersey

NM/M

Common Player:		5.00
Inserted 1:18		
YB	Yogi Berra	15.00
WB	Wade Boggs	5.00
RC	Roberto Clemente	80.00
TC	Tony Conigliaro	8.00
BD	Bill Dickey	25.00
JD	Joe DiMaggio/SP	350.00
LD	Leo Durocher	8.00
WF	Whitey Ford	15.00
NF	Nellie Fox	8.00
JF	Jim Fregosi	5.00
GH	Gil Hodges	10.00

THo	Tommy Holmes	5.00
RJ	Reggie Jackson	15.00
TK	Ted Kluszewski	5.00
BL	Bob Lemon	5.00
VL	Vic Lombardi	5.00
MM	Mickey Mantle/SP	275.00
JM	Juan Marichal	10.00
RM	Roger Maris/SP	150.00
WM	Willie McCovey	10.00
JN	Joe Nuxhall	8.00
GP	Gaylord Perry	5.00
BR	Bobby Richardson	5.00
BRo	Brooks Robinson	15.00
BR	Babe Ruth/SP	600.00
NR	Nolan Ryan	40.00
TS	Tom Seaver/SP	100.00
CS	Casey Stengel	15.00
BT	Bobby Thomson	5.00
HW	Honus Wagner/SP	750.00
BW	Billy Williams	6.00
MW	Maury Wills	5.00
RY	Robin Yount	15.00

Signatures

NM/M

Inserted 1:252
WA	Walt Alston/34	175.00
CA	Cap Anson/2 (11/01 Auction)	10,000
LA	Luke Appling/45	205.00
EA	Earl Averill/189	100.00
EB	E.G. Barrow/16	600.00
MC	Max Carey/73	145.00
TC	Ty Cobb/24	2,500
JC	Jocko Conlan/12	1,200
SC	Stanley Coveleski/42	315.00
JC	Joe Cronin/12	1,200
KC	Kiki Cuyler/6	4,000
DDe	Dizzy Dean/56	410.00
BD	Bill Dickey/28	275.00
JD	Joe DiMaggio/25	650.00
JD	Joe DiMaggio/50	400.00
JD	Joe DiMaggio/150	400.00
JD	Joe DiMaggio/275	350.00
DDr	Don Drysdale/12	1,500
LD	Leo Durocher/45	260.00
RF	Rick Ferrell/8	750.00
EF	Elmer Flick/22	400.00
NF	Nellie Fox/9	750.00
JF	Jimmie Foxx/16	2,500
FF	Ford Frick/21	750.00
FF	Frankie Frisch/3	3,500
LGe	Lou Gehrig/7	6,000
WG	Warren Giles/10	800.00
LGo	Lefty Gomez/85	195.00
BG	Burleigh Grimes/18	500.00
LG	Lefty Grove/34	600.00
HH	Harvey Haddix/4	3,000
BH	Bucky Harris/10	500.00
GH	Gabby Hartnett/32	380.00
BH	Billy Herman/88	140.00
GH	Gil Hodges/6	1,050
HH	Harry Hooper/14	800.00
WH	Waite Hoyt/35	245.00
CH	Carl Hubbell/30	375.00
TJ	Travis Jackson/35	225.00
JJ	Judy Johnson/9	650.00
WJ	Walter Johnson/113	510.00
CK	Charlie Keller/16	365.00
GK	George Kelly/52	140.00
KK	Ken Keltner/11	500.00
MK	Mark Koenig/30	275.00
BL	Bob Lemon/23	225.00
EL	Eddie Lopat/22	275.00
TL	Ted Lyons/59	185.00
SM	Sal Maglie/19	400.00
MM	Mickey Mantle/8	5,000
HM	Heinie Manush/50	185.00
RoM	Roger Maris/73	1,675
RuM	Rube Marquard/23	375.00
JMc	Joe McCarthy/40	340.00
JM	Joe Medwick/18	750.00
BM	Bob Meusel/23	250.00
JMi	Johnny Mize/84	160.00
MO	Mel Ott/8	4,000
SP	Satchel Paige/36	900.00
RP	Roger Peckinpaugh/45	200.00
VR	Vic Raschi/29	175.00
BRi	Branch Rickey/16	1,350
JR	Jackie Robinson/147	700.00
ER	Edd Roush/83	170.00
RR	Red Ruffing/5	2,250
BRu	Babe Ruth/7	9,000
GS	George Selkirk/15	450.00
JS	Joe Sewell/55	130.00
RS	Rip Sewell/39	155.00
BS	Bob Shawkey/39	165.00
CS	Satchel Paige/10	1,500
BT	Bill Terry/184	125.00
VM	Johnny Vander Meer/65	125.00
HW	Honus Wagner/24	2,200
BW	Bucky Walters/13	400.00

LW	Lloyd Waner/217	105.00
PW	Paul Waner/4	2,250
HW	Hack Wilson/4	6,000
JW	Smokey Joe Wood/43	215.00

2001 SPx

NM/M

Complete Set (150):
| Common Player: | .25 |
| Common Young Star (91-120): | 4.00 |

Production 2,000
Common Prospect Jersey (121-135):	6.00
Common Prosp. Auto. Jersey (136-150):	10.00
Pack (4):	10.00
Box (18):	160.00

1	Darin Erstad	.50
2	Troy Glaus	.50
3	Mo Vaughn	.25
4	Johnny Damon	1.00
5	Jason Giambi	.75
6	Tim Hudson	.50
7	Miguel Tejada	.50
8	Carlos Delgado	.75
9	Raul Mondesi	.25
10	Tony Batista	.25
11	Ben Grieve	.25
12	Greg Vaughn	.25
13	Juan Gonzalez	.50
14	Jim Thome	.75
15	Roberto Alomar	.50
16	John Olerud	.25
17	Edgar Martinez	.25
18	Albert Belle	.25
19	Cal Ripken Jr.	3.00
20	Ivan Rodriguez	.75
21	Rafael Palmeiro	.75
22	Alex Rodriguez	2.50
23	Nomar Garciaparra	1.00
24	Pedro J. Martinez	1.00
25	Manny Ramirez	.75
26	Jermaine Dye	.25
27	Mark Quinn	.25
28	Carlos Beltran	.75
29	Tony Clark	.25
30	Bobby Higginson	.25
31	Eric Milton	.25
32	Matt Lawton	.25
33	Frank Thomas	1.00
34	Magglio Ordonez	.50
35	Ray Durham	.25
36	David Wells	.25
37	Derek Jeter	3.00
38	Bernie Williams	.50
39	Roger Clemens	2.00
40	David Justice	.25
41	Jeff Bagwell	.75
42	Richard Hidalgo	.25
43	Moises Alou	.40
44	Chipper Jones	1.00
45	Andruw Jones	.50
46	Greg Maddux	2.00
47	Rafael Furcal	.50
48	Jeromy Burnitz	.25
49	Geoff Jenkins	.25
50	Mark McGwire	2.00
51	Jim Edmonds	.50
52	Rick Ankiel	.50
53	Edgar Renteria	.25
54	Sammy Sosa	1.50
55	Kerry Wood	.50
56	Rondell White	.25
57	Randy Johnson	1.00
58	Steve Finley	.25
59	Matt Williams	.25
60	Luis Gonzalez	.25
61	Kevin Brown	.25
62	Gary Sheffield	.50
63	Shawn Green	.50
64	Vladimir Guerrero	1.00
65	Jose Vidro	.25
66	Barry Bonds	3.00
67	Jeff Kent	.40
68	Livan Hernandez	.25
69	Preston Wilson	.25
70	Charles Johnson	.25
71	Cliff Floyd	.25
72	Mike Piazza	1.50
73	Edgardo Alfonzo	.25
74	Jay Payton	.25

75	Robin Ventura	.25
76	Tony Gwynn	1.50
77	Phil Nevin	.25
78	Ryan Klesko	.25
79	Scott Rolen	.75
80	Pat Burrell	.50
81	Bob Abreu	.50
82	Brian Giles	.25
83	Kris Benson	.25
84	Jason Kendall	.25
85	Ken Griffey Jr.	2.00
86	Barry Larkin	.50
87	Sean Casey	.40
88	Todd Helton	.75
89	Larry Walker	.25
90	Mike Hampton	.25
91	Billy Sylvester RC	4.00
92	Josh Towers RC	8.00
93	Zach Day RC	6.00
94	Martin Vargas RC	4.00
95	Adam Pettyjohn RC	4.00
96	Andres Torres RC	4.00
97	Kris Keller RC	4.00
98	Blaine Neal RC	4.00
99	Kyle Kessel RC	4.00
100	Greg Miller RC	4.00
101	Shawn Sonnier	4.00
102	Alexis Gomez RC	4.00
103	Grant Balfour RC	4.00
104	Henry Mateo RC	4.00
105	Wilkin Ruan RC	4.00
106	Nick Maness RC	4.00
107	Jason Michaels RC	4.00
108	Esix Snead RC	4.00
109	William Ortega RC	4.00
110	David Elder RC	4.00
111	Jackson Melian RC	4.00
112	Nate Teut RC	4.00
113	Jason Smith RC	4.00
114	Mike Penney RC	4.00
115	Jose Mieses RC	4.00
116	Juan Pena	4.00
117	Brian Lawrence RC	6.00
118	Jeremy Owens RC	4.00
119	Carlos Valderrama RC	4.00
120	Rafael Soriano RC	6.00
121	Horacio Ramirez RC	10.00
122	Ricardo Rodriguez RC	6.00
123	Juan Diaz RC	6.00
124	Donnie Bridges	6.00
125	Tyler Walker RC	6.00
126	Erick Almonte RC	6.00
127	Jesus Colome	6.00
128	Ryan Freel RC	8.00
129	Elpidio Guzman RC	6.00
130	Jack Cust	8.00
131	Eric Hinske RC	10.00
132	Josh Fogg RC	6.00
133	Juan Uribe RC	10.00
134	Bert Snow RC	6.00
135	Pedro Feliz	6.00
136	Wilson Betemit RC	25.00
137	Sean Douglass RC	10.00
138	Dernell Stenson	10.00
139	Brandon Inge	6.00
140	Morgan Ensberg RC	15.00
141	Brian Cole	10.00
142	Adrian Hernandez RC	10.00
143	Brandon Duckworth RC	10.00
144	Jack Wilson RC	15.00
145	Travis Hafner RC	35.00
146	Carlos Pena	20.00
147	Corey Patterson	10.00
148	Xavier Nady	10.00
149	Jason Hart	10.00
150	Ichiro Suzuki RC	750.00

Spectrum

Stars (1-90):	10-20X
SP's (91-120):	1-1.5X
Production 50 Sets	

Foundations

NM/M

Complete Set (12):	15.00
Common Player:	1.00
Inserted 1:8	
F1	Mark McGwire	3.00
F2	Jeff Bagwell	1.00
F3	Alex Rodriguez	3.00
F4	Ken Griffey Jr.	2.00
F5	Andruw Jones	1.00
F6	Cal Ripken Jr.	4.00
F7	Barry Bonds	4.00
F8	Derek Jeter	4.00
F9	Frank Thomas	1.00
F10	Sammy Sosa	1.50
F11	Tony Gwynn	1.50
F12	Vladimir Guerrero	1.50

SPXcitement

NM/M

Complete Set (12):	15.00
Common Player:	.75
Inserted 1:8	
X1	Alex Rodriguez	3.00
X2	Jason Giambi	.75
X3	Ken Griffey Jr.	2.00
X4	Sammy Sosa	1.50
X5	Frank Thomas	1.00
X6	Todd Helton	1.00
X7	Mark McGwire	2.00
X8	Mike Piazza	1.50
X9	Derek Jeter	4.00
X10	Vladimir Guerrero	1.50
X11	Carlos Delgado	.75
X12	Chipper Jones	1.50

Untouchable Talents

NM/M

Complete Set (6):	10.00
Inserted 1:15	
UT1	Ken Griffey Jr.	2.00
UT2	Mike Piazza	2.00
UT3	Mark McGwire	2.50
UT4	Alex Rodriguez	2.50
UT5	Sammy Sosa	1.50
UT6	Derek Jeter	3.00

Winning Materials Base

NM/M

Common Duo:	40.00
Production 50	
Trios:	No Pricing
Production 25	
MG	Mark McGwire, Ken Griffey Jr.	40.00
MS	Mark McGwire, Sammy Sosa	50.00
MR	Mark McGwire, Alex Rodriguez	40.00
GJ	Nomar Garciaparra, Derek Jeter	50.00
TR	Frank Thomas, Alex Rodriguez	40.00

JG	Derek Jeter, Jason Giambi	40.00
PB	Mike Piazza, Barry Bonds	40.00
RJ	Alex Rodriguez, Derek Jeter	50.00
PM	Mike Piazza, Mark McGwire	40.00
JP	Derek Jeter, Mike Piazza	40.00
MGS	Mark McGwire, Ken Griffey Jr., Sammy Sosa	80.00
JRG	Derek Jeter, Alex Rodriguez, Nomar Garciaparra	100.00
PJW	Mike Piazza, Derek Jeter, Bernie Williams	80.00
BMS	Barry Bonds, Mark McGwire, Sammy Sosa	100.00
GJR	Ken Griffey Jr., Derek Jeter, Alex Rodriguez	100.00

Winning Materials Base/Ball

		NM/M
Common Player:		10.00
Production 250 Sets		
BB	Barry Bonds	50.00
NG	Nomar Garciaparra	20.00
KG	Ken Griffey Jr.	30.00
VG	Vladimir Guerrero	15.00
DJ	Derek Jeter	50.00
AJ	Andruw Jones	10.00
CJ	Chipper Jones	15.00
PM	Pedro Martinez	15.00
MM	Mark McGwire	75.00
MP	Mike Piazza	20.00
AR	Alex Rodriguez	20.00
SS	Sammy Sosa	20.00
FT	Frank Thomas	15.00

Winning Materials Jersey Combo

		NM/M
Common Duo:		25.00
Production 50		
Common Trio:		
Production 25		
KG-AR	Ken Griffey Jr., Alex Rodriguez	50.00
KG-BB	Ken Griffey Jr., Barry Bonds	50.00
KG-RJ	Ken Griffey Jr., Randy Johnson	50.00
CJ-DW	Chipper Jones, David Wells	25.00
BB-SS	Barry Bonds, Sammy Sosa	50.00
KG-JD	Ken Griffey Jr., Joe DiMaggio	180.00
KG-SS	Ken Griffey Jr., Sammy Sosa	50.00
SS-CD	Sammy Sosa, Carlos Delgado	25.00
SS-FT	Sammy Sosa, Frank Thomas	25.00
IR-AR	Ivan Rodriguez, Alex Rodriguez	40.00
AR-CR	Alex Rodriguez, Cal Ripken Jr.	60.00
AJ-CJ	Andruw Jones, Chipper Jones	25.00
KG-KG	Ken Griffey Jr., Ken Griffey Jr.	40.00
G-R-B	Ken Griffey Jr., Alex Rodriguez, Barry Bonds	100.00
S-G-C	Sammy Sosa, Ken Griffey Jr., Chipper Jones	60.00
B-G-J	Barry Bonds, Ken Griffey Jr., Andruw Jones	100.00
R-R-D	Alex Rodriguez, Ivan Rodriguez, Carlos Delgado	60.00
D-G-J	Joe DiMaggio, Ken Griffey Jr., Andruw Jones	60.00
D-B-S	Carlos Delgado, Barry Bonds, Sammy Sosa	60.00
R-J-D	Cal Ripken Jr., Chipper Jones, Carlos Delgado	100.00

Winning Materials Jersey/Bat

	NM/M
Common Player:	8.00

Inserted 1:18		
RA	Rick Ankiel	8.00
BB1	Barry Bonds	25.00
BB2	Barry Bonds	25.00
CD	Carlos Delgado	10.00
JD	Joe DiMaggio	150.00
JE	Jim Edmonds	
KG1	Ken Griffey Jr.	15.00
KG2	Ken Griffey Jr.	15.00
RJ1	Randy Johnson	15.00
RJ2	Randy Johnson	15.00
AJ1	Andruw Jones	10.00
AJ2	Andruw Jones	15.00
CJ1	Chipper Jones	15.00
CJ2	Chipper Jones	15.00
CR	Cal Ripken Jr.	40.00
AR1	Alex Rodriguez	15.00
AR2	Alex Rodriguez	15.00
IR1	Ivan Rodriguez	10.00
IR2	Ivan Rodriguez	10.00
SS	Sammy Sosa	15.00
FT	Frank Thomas	10.00

2002 SP Authentic

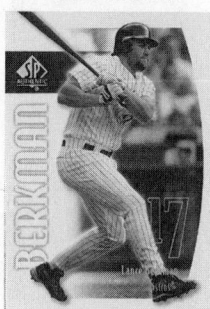

		NM/M
Complete Set (170):		
Common Player:		.25
Common SP (91-135):		4.00
Production 1,999		
Common SP Auto. (136-170):		10.00
Production 999		
Pack (5):		3.50
Box (24):		75.00
1	Troy Glaus	.50
2	Darin Erstad	.40
3	Barry Zito	.40
4	Eric Chavez	.40
5	Tim Hudson	.50
6	Miguel Tejada	.50
7	Carlos Delgado	.60
8	Shannon Stewart	.25
9	Ben Grieve	.25
10	Jim Thome	.75
11	C.C. Sabathia	.50
12	Ichiro Suzuki	2.00
13	Freddy Garcia	.25
14	Edgar Martinez	.25
15	Bret Boone	.25
16	Jeff Conine	.25
17	Alex Rodriguez	.50
18	Juan Gonzalez	.50
19	Ivan Rodriguez	.75
20	Rafael Palmeiro	.25
21	Hank Blalock	.75
22	Pedro J. Martinez	1.00
23	Manny Ramirez	1.00
24	Nomar Garciaparra	1.00
25	Carlos Beltran	.75
26	Mike Sweeney	.25
27	Randall Simon	.25
28	Dmitri Young	.25
29	Bobby Higginson	.25
30	Corey Koskie	.25
31	Eric Milton	.25
32	Torii Hunter	.50
33	Joe Mays	.25
34	Frank Thomas	.75
35	Mark Buehrle	.40
36	Magglio Ordonez	.25
37	Kenny Lofton	.25
38	Roger Clemens	2.00
39	Derek Jeter	2.50
40	Jason Giambi	.75
41	Bernie Williams	.50
42	Alfonso Soriano	.75
43	Lance Berkman	.50
44	Roy Oswalt	.50
45	Jeff Bagwell	.75
46	Craig Biggio	.50
47	Chipper Jones	1.00
48	Greg Maddux	1.50
49	Gary Sheffield	.50
50	Andruw Jones	.75
51	Ben Sheets	.40
52	Richie Sexson	.50
53	Albert Pujols	2.50
54	Matt Morris	.25
55	J.D. Drew	.40
56	Sammy Sosa	1.00
57	Kerry Wood	.50
58	Corey Patterson	.25
59	Mark Prior	.75
60	Randy Johnson	.75
61	Luis Gonzalez	.40
62	Curt Schilling	.75
63	Shawn Green	.50
64	Kevin Brown	.25
65	Hideo Nomo	.75
66	Vladimir Guerrero	.75
67	Jose Vidro	.25
68	Barry Bonds	2.50
69	Jeff Kent	.40
70	Rich Aurilia	.25
71	Preston Wilson	.25
72	Josh Beckett	.40
73	Mike Lowell	.25
74	Roberto Alomar	.40
75	Mo Vaughn	.25
76	Jeromy Burnitz	.25
77	Mike Piazza	1.50
78	Sean Burroughs	.25
79	Phil Nevin	.25
80	Bobby Abreu	.50
81	Pat Burrell	.40
82	Scott Rolen	.75
83	Jason Kendall	.25
84	Brian Giles	.25
85	Ken Griffey Jr.	1.50
86	Adam Dunn	.75
87	Sean Casey	.40
88	Todd Helton	.75
89	Larry Walker	.25
90	Mike Hampton	.25
91	Brandon Puffer RC	4.00
92	Tom Shearn RC	4.00
93	Chris Baker RC	4.00
94	Gustavo Chacin RC	10.00
95	Joe Orloski RC	4.00
96	Mike Smith RC	4.00
97	John Ennis RC	4.00
98	John Foster RC	4.00
99	Kevin Gryboski RC	4.00
100	Brian Mallette RC	4.00
101	Takahito Nomura RC	4.00
102	So Taguchi RC	10.00
103	Jeremy Lambert RC	4.00
104	Jason Simontacchi RC	4.00
105	Jorge Sosa RC	4.00
106	Brandon Backe RC	8.00
107	P.J. Bevis RC	4.00
108	Jeremy Ward RC	4.00
109	Doug DeVore RC	4.00
110	Ron Chiavacci RC	4.00
111	Ron Calloway RC	4.00
112	Nelson Castro RC	4.00
113	Deivis Santos RC	4.00
114	Earl Snyder RC	4.00
115	Julio Mateo RC	4.00
116	J.J. Putz RC	4.00
117	Allan Simpson RC	4.00
118	Satoru Komiyama RC	4.00
119	Adam Walker RC	4.00
120	Oliver Perez RC	10.00
121	Clifford Bartosh RC	4.00
122	Todd Donovan RC	4.00
123	Elio Serrano RC	4.00
124	Peter Zamora RC	4.00
125	Mike Gonzalez RC	4.00
126	Travis Hughes RC	4.00
127	Jorge de la Rosa RC	4.00
128	Anastacio Martinez RC	4.00
129	Colin Young RC	4.00
130	Nate Field RC	4.00
131	Tim Kalita RC	4.00
132	Julius Matos RC	4.00
133	Terry Pearson RC	4.00
134	Kyle Kane RC	4.00
135	Mitch Wylie RC	4.00
136	Rodrigo Rosario RC	10.00
137	Franklyn German RC	10.00
138	Reed Johnson RC	15.00
139	Luis Martinez RC	10.00
140	Michael Crudale RC	10.00
141	Francis Beltran RC	10.00
142	Steve Kent RC	10.00
143	Felix Escalona RC	10.00
144	Jose Valverde RC	15.00
145	Victor Alvarez RC	10.00
146	Kazuhisa Ishii/249 RC	25.00
147	Jorge Nunez RC	10.00
148	Eric Good RC	10.00
149	Luis Ugueto RC	10.00
150	Matt Thornton RC	10.00
151	Wilson Valdez RC	10.00
152	Hansel Izquierdo/249 RC	25.00
153	Jaime Cerda RC	10.00
154	Mark Corey RC	10.00
155	Tyler Yates RC	10.00
156	Steve Bechler RC	10.00
157	Ben Howard/249 RC	20.00
158	Anderson Machado RC	10.00
159	Jorge Padilla RC	15.00
160	Eric Junge RC	10.00
161	Adrian Burnside RC	10.00
162	Josh Hancock RC	10.00
163	Chris Booker RC	10.00
164	Cam Esslinger RC	10.00
165	Rene Reyes RC	10.00
166	Aaron Cook RC	10.00
167	Juan Brito RC	10.00
168	Miguel Ascencio RC	10.00
169	Kevin Frederick RC	10.00
170	Edwin Almonte RC	10.00

Limited

Stars (1-90):	5-10X
Cards (91-135):	.5-1X
Cards (136-170):	.5-1X
Production 125 Sets	
Golds (1-90):	10-20X
Golds (91-135):	.75-1.5X
Golds (136-170):	.75-1.5X
Production 50 Sets	

Big Mac Missing Link

Production 25 Sets
No Pricing

Signed SP Big Mac

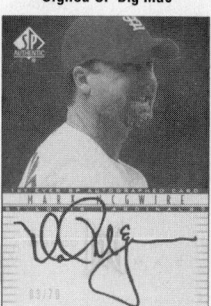

	NM/M
Quantity signed listed	
MM6 Mark McGwire/70	250.00

Chirography

		NM/M
Common Autograph:		10.00
Inserted 1:72		
HB	Hank Blalock/282	25.00
BB	Barry Bonds/112	180.00
BBo	Bret Boone/500	15.00
MB	Milton Bradley/470	15.00
JB	John Buck/427	10.00
MB	Mark Buehrle/438	15.00
SB	Sean Burroughs/275	15.00
AD	Adam Dunn/348	30.00
DE	Darin Erstad/80	15.00
CF	Cliff Floyd/313	10.00
FG	Freddy Garcia/456	15.00
JG	Jason Giambi/244	25.00
TG	Tom Glavine/376	25.00
AG	Alex Graman/418	10.00
KG	Ken Griffey Jr/238	100.00
TG	Tony Gwynn/75	40.00
JL	Jon Lieber/462	15.00
JM	Joe Mays/469	15.00
MM	Mark McGwire/300	300.00
DM	Doug Mientkiewicz/478	15.00
AR	Alex Rodriguez/391	90.00
CS	C.C. Sabathia/442	15.00
RS	Richie Sexson/483	15.00
SS	Sammy Sosa/247	100.00
IS	Ichiro Suzuki/78	350.00
MS	Mike Sweeney/265	15.00
BZ	Barry Zito/419	20.00

Chirography Gold

	NM/M
Quantity produced listed	
MB	Mark Buehrle/56	25.00
AD	Adam Dunn/44	40.00
CF	Cliff Floyd/30	20.00
FG	Freddy Garcia/34	35.00

		50.00
TG	Tom Glavine/47	50.00
AG	Alex Graman/76	15.00
KG	Ken Griffey Jr./30	200.00
JL	Jon Lieber/32	20.00
CS	C.C. Sabathia/52	25.00
MS	Mike Sweeney/29	40.00
BZ	Barry Zito/75	25.00

Excellence

NM/M

Production 25
AE-1 Ken Griffey Jr., Sammy Sosa, Cal Ripken Jr., Jason Giambi, Mark McGwire, Ichiro Suzuki — 1,500

Future USA Watch

		NM/M
Common Player:		5.00
Production 1,999 Sets		
USA1	Chad Cordero	5.00
USA2	Philip Humber	10.00
USA3	Grant Johnson	5.00
USA4	Wes Littleton	5.00
USA5	Kyle Sleeth	10.00
USA6	Huston Street	15.00
USA7	Brad Sullivan	5.00
USA8	Bob Zimmermann	5.00
USA9	Abe Alvarez	5.00
USA10	Kyle Bakker	5.00
USA11	Landon Powell	5.00
USA12	Clint Sammons	5.00
USA13	Michael Aubrey	10.00
USA14	Aaron Hill	5.00
USA15	Conor Jackson	20.00
USA16	Eric Patterson	5.00
USA17	Dustin Pedroia	10.00
USA18	Rickie Weeks	20.00
USA19	Shane Costa	5.00
USA20	Mark Jurich	5.00
USA21	Sam Fuld	5.00
USA22	Carlos Quentin	20.00

Game Jerseys

		NM/M
Common Player:		5.00
Inserted 1:24		
RA	Roberto Alomar	8.00
JB	Jeff Bagwell	10.00
JB	Jeromy Burnitz/SP	5.00
RC	Roger Clemens	15.00
CD	Carlos Delgado	6.00
JE	Jim Edmonds	8.00
DE	Darin Erstad	8.00
JGi	Jason Giambi	8.00
JGo	Juan Gonzalez	8.00
SG	Shawn Green	6.00
KG	Ken Griffey Jr./95	40.00
TH	Todd Helton	8.00
KI	Kazuhisa Ishii	10.00
RJ	Randy Johnson	10.00
AJ	Andruw Jones	8.00
CJ	Chipper Jones	10.00
JK	Jason Kendall	5.00
GM	Greg Maddux	10.00
MM	Mark McGwire/SP	100.00
MO	Magglio Ordonez	10.00
AP	Andy Pettitte	10.00
MP	Mike Piazza	15.00
MR	Manny Ramirez	10.00
AR	Alex Rodriguez	15.00
IR	Ivan Rodriguez	8.00
SR	Scott Rolen	10.00
CC	C.C. Sabathia	5.00
CS	Curt Schilling	10.00
GS	Gary Sheffield	6.00
TS	Tsuyoshi Shinjo	5.00
SS	Sammy Sosa	15.00
IS	Ichiro Suzuki/SP	50.00
JT	Jim Thome	10.00
RV	Robin Ventura	5.00
OV	Omar Vizquel	5.00
BW	Bernie Williams	5.00
PW	Preston Wilson	5.00
BZ	Barry Zito	6.00

Game Jersey Gold

		NM/M
Quantity produced listed		
KG	Ken Griffey Jr./30	65.00
RJ	Randy Johnson/51	25.00
GM	Greg Maddux/31	50.00
MO	Magglio Ordonez/30	15.00
AP	Andy Pettitte/46	20.00
MP	Mike Piazza/31	50.00
CC	C.C. Sabathia/52	10.00
CS	Curt Schilling/38	30.00
IS	Ichiro Suzuki/51	85.00
BW	Bernie Williams/51	25.00
PW	Preston Wilson/44	10.00
BZ	Barry Zito/75	10.00

Prospect Signatures

		NM/M
Common Autograph:		5.00
Inserted 1:36		
JC	Jose Cueto	5.00
JDe	Jeff Deardorff	5.00
JDi	Jose Diaz	8.00
AG	Alex Graman	8.00
MG	Matt Guerrier	5.00
BH	Bill Hall	15.00
KH	Ken Huckaby	5.00
DM	Dustan Mohr	5.00
XN	Xavier Nady	8.00
MS	Marco Scutaro	5.00
ST	Steve Torrealba	6.00
DW	Danny Wright	5.00

Signs of Greatness

NM/M

Babe Ruth, Joe DiMaggio, Mickey Mantle, Ken Griffey Jr., Sammy Sosa (2/03 Auction) — 30,000

2002 SP Legendary Cuts

		NM/M
Complete Set (90):		30.00
Common Player:		.40
Pack (4):		10.00
Box (12):		100.00
1	Al Kaline	.75
2	Alvin Dark	.40
3	Andre Dawson	.75
4	Babe Ruth	3.00
5	Ernie Banks	1.00
6	Bob Lemon	.40
7	Bobby Bonds	.40
8	Carl Erskine	.40
9	Carl Hubbell	.40
10	Casey Stengel	.40
11	Charlie Gehringer	.40
12	Christy Mathewson	.75
13	Dale Murphy	.40
14	Dave Concepcion	.40
15	Dave Parker	.40
16	Dazzy Vance	.40
17	Dizzy Dean	.75
18	Don Baylor	.40
19	Don Drysdale	.75
20	Duke Snider	1.00
21	Earl Averill	.40
22	Early Wynn	.40
23	Edd Roush	.40
24	Elston Howard	.40
25	Ferguson Jenkins	.75
26	Frank Crosetti	.40
27	Frankie Frisch	.40
28	Gaylord Perry	.40
29	George Foster	.40
30	George Kell	.40
31	Gil Hodges	.40
32	Hank Greenberg	.75
33	Phil Niekro	.40
34	Harvey Haddix	.40
35	Harvey Kuenn	.40
36	Honus Wagner	1.50
37	Jackie Robinson	2.00
38	Orlando Cepeda	.40
39	Joe Adcock	.40
40	Joe Cronin	.40
41	Joe DiMaggio	2.50
42	Joe Morgan	.75
43	Johnny Mize	.40
44	Lefty Gomez	.40
45	Lefty Grove	.40
46	Jim Palmer	.75
47	Lou Boudreau	.40
48	Lou Gehrig	2.50
49	Luke Appling	.40
50	Mark McGwire	2.00
51	Mel Ott	.75
52	Mickey Cochrane	.40
53	Mickey Mantle	3.00
54	Minnie Minoso	.40
55	Brooks Robinson	1.00
56	Nellie Fox	.40
57	Nolan Ryan	3.00
58	Rollie Fingers	.40
59	Pee Wee Reese	.40
60	Phil Rizzuto	.75
61	Ralph Kiner	.75
62	Ray Dandridge	.40
63	Richie Ashburn	.40
64	Robin Yount	.75
65	Rocky Colavito	.40
66	Roger Maris	2.00
67	Rogers Hornsby	.75
68	Ron Santo	.40
69	Ryne Sandberg	1.50
70	Stan Musial	1.50
71	Sam McDowell	.40
72	Satchel Paige	.75
73	Willie McCovey	.40
74	Steve Garvey	.40
75	Ted Kluszewski	.40
76	Catfish Hunter	.40
77	Terry Moore	.40
78	Thurman Munson	1.00
79	Tom Seaver	1.00
80	Tommy John	.40
81	Tony Gwynn	1.00
82	Tony Kubek	.40
83	Tony Lazzeri	.40
84	Ty Cobb	2.00
85	Wade Boggs	1.00
86	Waite Hoyt	.40
87	Walter Johnson	1.00
88	Willie Stargell	.75
89	Yogi Berra	.40
90	Zack Wheat	.40

Bat

		NM/M
Common Player:		6.00
Inserted 1:8		
DBa	Don Baylor	6.00
YBe	Yogi Berra/SP	20.00
BBo	Bobby Bonds	6.00
RCo	Rocky Colavito	12.00
ADa	Alvin Dark	6.00
AnD	Andre Dawson	6.00
GFo	George Foster	6.00
NFo	Nellie Fox	15.00
SGa	Steve Garvey	6.00
HGr	Hank Greenberg/SP	40.00
LGr	Lefty Grove	15.00
TGw	Tony Gwynn	12.00
EHo	Elston Howard/SP	15.00
GKe	George Kell	8.00
RKi	Ralph Kiner	10.00
TKu	Tonk (Tony) Kubek	8.00
TLa	Tony Lazzeri	10.00
MMa	Mickey Mantle/SP	120.00
RMa	Roger Maris/SP	50.00
MMc	Mark McGwire	60.00
JMi	Johnny Mize	12.00
TMu	Thurman Munson	25.00
DMu	Dale Murphy	10.00
DPa	Dave Parker	6.00
GPe	Gaylord Perry	8.00
PWe	Pee Wee Reese	10.00
CRi	Cal Ripken Jr.	25.00
JaR	Jackie Robinson/SP	50.00
BRu	Babe Ruth/SP	150.00
NRy	Nolan Ryan	30.00
RSa	Ryne Sandberg	12.00
TSe	Tom Seaver/SP	20.00
DSn	Duke Snider	12.00
WSt	Willie Stargell	8.00
RYo	Robin Yount	10.00
EWy	Early Wynn	8.00

Bat Barrel

		NM/M
Many not priced due to scarcity.		
BB-ADa	Alvin Dark/4	800.00
BB-AnD	Andre Dawson/4	750.00
BB-GFo	George Foster/5	250.00
BB-LGr	Lefty Grove/1 (8/03 Auction)	10,000
BB-TGw	Tony Gwynn/11	650.00
BB-MMa	Mickey Mantle/7 (8/04 Auction)	3,000
BB-RMa	Roger Maris/1	
BB-MMc	Mark McGwire/4	2,000
BB-JMi	Johnny Mize/2	1,275
BB-DMu	Dale Murphy/3	600.00
BB-PWe	Pee Wee Reese/4	1,500
BB-BRu	Babe Ruth/3 (8/05 Auction)	9,500
BB-NRy	Nolan Ryan/9	1,500
BB-RSa	Ryne Sandberg/3	2,250
BB-DSn	Duke Snider/2	1,500
BB-RYo	Robin Yount/8	750.00

Jersey

		NM/M
Common Player:		6.00
Inserted 1:24		
DBa	Don Baylor	6.00
YBe	Yogi Berra	20.00
BBo	Bobby Bonds	6.00
FCr	Frank Crosetti	10.00
AnD	Andre Dawson	8.00
GFo	George Foster	6.00
SGa	Steve Garvey	8.00
MMa	Mickey Mantle/SP	100.00
RMa	Roger Maris	40.00
DPa	Dave Parker	6.00
PWe	Pee Wee Reese	12.00
JRo	Jackie Robinson/SP	45.00
NRy	Nolan Ryan	30.00
RSa	Ryne Sandberg	25.00
TSe	Tom Seaver	10.00

Signatures

		NM/M
Quantity signed listed		
JAd	Joe Adcock/48	150.00
LAp	Luke Appling/53	150.00
RAs	Richie Ashburn/10	550.00
EAv	Earl Averill/22	275.00
JBe	Johnny Berardino/12	450.00
LBo	Lou Boudreau/85	120.00
GBu	Guy Bush/38	125.00
GCa	George Case/36	180.00
HCh	Happy Chandler/96	100.00
SCh	Spud Chandler/17	350.00
TyC	Ty Cobb/2	5,500
MCo	Mickey Cochrane/2	5,000
JCo	Johnny Cooney/64	75.00
SCo	Stan Coveleski/85	150.00
JCr	Joe Cronin/185	120.00
BDa	Babe Dahlgren/51	180.00
RDa	Ray Dandridge/179	85.00
DDe	Dizzy Dean/4	2,000
JDi	Joe DiMaggio/103	175.00
DDo	Dick Donovan/23	200.00
TDo	Taylor Douthit/60	165.00
DDr	Don Drysdale/14	650.00
JDu	Joe Dugan/39	140.00
BFa	Bibb Falk/44	150.00
RFe	Rick Ferrell/19	225.00
NFo	Nellie Fox/1 (12/02 Auction)	3,100
FoF	Ford Frick/1 (10/03 Auction)	4,000
LGe	Lou Gehrig/3 (6/04 Auction)	7,500
CGe	Charlie Gehringer/3	700.00
LGo	Lefty Gomez/3	750.00
BGo	Billy Goodman/53	140.00
HGr	Hank Greenberg/94	425.00
LGr	Lefty Grove/190	240.00
SHa	Stan Hack/36	200.00
HHa	Harvey Haddix/37	250.00
BHa	Buddy Hassett/56	200.00
WHo	Waite Hoyt/62	250.00
CHu	Carl Hubbell/17	475.00
LJa	Larry Jackson/37	125.00
NJa	Newton "Bucky" Jacobs/44	150.00
EJo	Earl Johnson/31	200.00
JJo	Judy Johnson/86	150.00
WJo	Walter Johnson/20	2,000
BKa	Bob Kahle/53	150.00
WKa	Willie Kamm/57	110.00
CKe	Charlie Keller/29	280.00
KKe	Ken Keltner/11	415.00
TKl	Ted Kluszewski/23	300.00
MKo	Mark Koenig/22	260.00
HKu	Harvey Kuenn/23	230.00
CLa	Cookie Lavagetto/22	200.00
BiL	Billy Lee/40	150.00
BoL	Bob Lemon/29	110.00
ELo	Ed Lopat/58	150.00
SMa	Sal Maglie/29	200.00

HMa	Hank Majeski/21	300.00
MMa	Mickey Mantle/2 (10/04 Auction)	6,000
ChrM	Christy Mathewson/2 (5/03 Auction)	2,000
RMc	Roy McMillan/18	250.00
JMi	Johnny Mize/3	2,500
JMo	Johnny Moore/22	250.00
TMo	Terry Moore/86	95.00
ChM	Chet Morgan/27	185.00
HNe	Hal Newhouser/81	135.00
VRa	Vic Raschi/98	110.00
PWe	Pee Wee Reese/23	450.00
PRe	Pete Reiser/73	140.00
RRe	Rip Repulski/19	275.00
LRi	Lance Richbourg/3	1,800
ORo	Oscar Roettger/9	700.00
ERo	Edd Roush/101	100.00
ERo2	Edd Roush/99	100.00
BRu	Babe Ruth/3 (6/04 Auction)	12,500
BSc	Bob Scheffing/19	200.00
WSc	Willard Schmidt/10	350.00
HSc	Hal Schumacher/17	300.00
BSe	Bill Serena/16	275.00
JSe	Joe Sewell/136	125.00
BSh	Bob Shawkey/10	120.00
BSh	Bill Sherdel/10	450.00
BSz	Bill Shantz/17	300.00
WSt	Willie Stargell/153	95.00
CSt	Casey Stengel/8	750.00
BVe	Bill Veeck/11	500.00
HWa	Honus Wagner/6 (2/05 Auction)	5,000
BWa	Bucky Walters/31	165.00
VWe	Vic Wertz/17	300.00
ZWh	Zack Wheat/127	150.00
PWi	Pete Whisenant/13	300.00
EWy	Early Wynn/4	1,650

Swatches

		NM/M
Common Player:		6.00
Inserted 1:24		
DBa	Don Baylor	6.00
WBo	Wade Boggs	8.00
FCr	Frank Crosetti	8.00
DDr	Don Drysdale	20.00
CEr	Carl Erskine	8.00
TGw	Tony Gwynn	10.00
FJe	Ferguson Jenkins	8.00
TJo	Tommy John	6.00
SMc	Sam McDowell	6.00
MMi	Minnie Minoso	8.00
JMo	Joe Morgan	8.00
MOt	Mel Ott	25.00
DPa	Dave Parker	6.00
CRj	Cal Ripken Jr.	25.00
RSa	Ron Santo	10.00

2002 SPx

		NM/M
Common Player:		.25
Common SP (91-120):		4.00
Production 1,800		
Common SP Auto. (121-150):		10.00
Common Star Swatch (151-190):		5.00
Production 800		
Pack (4):		4.00
Box (18):		60.00
1	Troy Glaus	.50
2	Darin Erstad	.40
3	David Justice	.25
4	Tim Hudson	.50
5	Miguel Tejada	.75
6	Barry Zito	.40
7	Carlos Delgado	.50
8	Shannon Stewart	.25
9	Greg Vaughn	.25
10	Toby Hall	.25
11	Jim Thome	.75
12	C.C. Sabathia	.50
13	Ichiro Suzuki	2.00
14	Edgar Martinez	.25
15	Freddy Garcia	.25
16	Mike Cameron	.25
17	Jeff Conine	.25
18	Tony Batista	.25
19	Alex Rodriguez	2.00
20	Rafael Palmeiro	.75
21	Ivan Rodriguez	.75
22	Carl Everett	.25
23	Pedro J. Martinez	1.00
24	Manny Ramirez	1.00
25	Nomar Garciaparra	1.00
26	Johnny Damon	1.00
27	Mike Sweeney	.25
28	Carlos Beltran	.75
29	Dmitri Young	.25
30	Joe Mays	.25
31	Doug Mientkiewicz	.25
32	Cristian Guzman	.25
33	Corey Koskie	.25
34	Frank Thomas	.75
35	Magglio Ordonez	.25
36	Mark Buehrle	.25
37	Bernie Williams	.50
38	Roger Clemens	2.00
39	Derek Jeter	2.50
40	Jason Giambi	.50
41	Mike Mussina	.50
42	Lance Berkman	.50
43	Jeff Bagwell	.75
44	Roy Oswalt	.50
45	Greg Maddux	2.00
46	Chipper Jones	1.00
47	Andruw Jones	.75
48	Gary Sheffield	.50
49	Geoff Jenkins	.25
50	Richie Sexson	.25
51	Ben Sheets	.40
52	Albert Pujols	2.50
53	J.D. Drew	.40
54	Jim Edmonds	.50
55	Sammy Sosa	1.50
56	Moises Alou	.25
57	Kerry Wood	.50
58	Jon Lieber	.25
59	Fred McGriff	.40
60	Randy Johnson	.75
61	Luis Gonzalez	.35
62	Curt Schilling	.75
63	Kevin Brown	.25
64	Hideo Nomo	.50
65	Shawn Green	.40
66	Vladimir Guerrero	1.00
67	Jose Vidro	.25
68	Barry Bonds	2.50
69	Jeff Kent	.40
70	Rich Aurilia	.25
71	Cliff Floyd	.25
72	Josh Beckett	.25
73	Preston Wilson	.25
74	Mike Piazza	1.00
75	Mo Vaughn	.25
76	Jeromy Burnitz	.25
77	Roberto Alomar	.50
78	Phil Nevin	.25
79	Ryan Klesko	.40
80	Scott Rolen	.75
81	Bobby Abreu	.50
82	Jimmy Rollins	.25
83	Brian Giles	.25
84	Aramis Ramirez	.25
85	Ken Griffey Jr.	1.50
86	Sean Casey	.40
87	Barry Larkin	.50
88	Mike Hampton	.25
89	Larry Walker	.40
90	Todd Helton	.75
91	Ron Calloway RC	4.00
92	Joe Orloski RC	4.00
93	Anderson Machado RC	6.00
94	Eric Good RC	4.00
95	Reed Johnson RC	8.00
96	Brendan Donnelly RC	4.00
97	Chris Baker RC	4.00
98	Wilson Valdez RC	4.00
99	Scotty Layfield RC	4.00
100	P.J. Bevis RC	4.00
101	Edwin Almonte RC	4.00
102	Francis Beltran RC	4.00
103	Valentino Pasucci	4.00
104	Nelson Castro RC	4.00
105	Michael Crudale RC	4.00
106	Colin Young RC	4.00
107	Todd Donovan RC	4.00
108	Felix Escalona RC	4.00
109	Brandon Backe RC	8.00
110	Corey Thurman RC	4.00
111	Kyle Kane RC	4.00
112	Allan Simpson RC	4.00
113	Jose Valverde RC	4.00
114	Chris Booker RC	4.00
115	Brandon Puffer RC	4.00
116	John Foster RC	4.00
117	Clifford Bartosh RC	4.00
118	Gustavo Chacin RC	8.00
119	Steve Kent RC	4.00
120	Nate Field RC	4.00
121	Victor Alvarez RC	10.00
122	Steve Bechler RC	10.00
123	Adrian Burnside RC	10.00
124	Marlon Byrd	15.00
125	Jaime Cerda RC	10.00
126	Brandon Claussen	10.00
127	Mark Corey RC	10.00
128	Doug DeVore RC	10.00
129	Kazuhisa Ishii RC	40.00
130	John Ennis RC	10.00
131	Kevin Frederick RC	10.00
132	Josh Hancock RC	10.00
133	Ben Howard RC	10.00
134	Orlando Hudson	15.00
135	Hansel Izquierdo RC	10.00
136	Eric Junge RC	10.00
137	Austin Kearns	15.00
138	Victor Martinez	25.00
139	Luis Martinez RC	10.00
140	Danny Mota RC	10.00
141	Jorge Padilla RC	10.00
142	Andy Pratt RC	10.00
143	Rene Reyes RC	10.00
144	Rodrigo Rosario RC	10.00
145	Tom Shearn RC	10.00
146	So Taguchi RC	30.00
147	Dennis Tankersley	15.00
148	Matt Thornton	10.00
149	Jeremy Ward RC	10.00
150	Mitch Wylie RC	10.00
151	Pedro Martinez	8.00
152	Cal Ripken Jr.	25.00
153	Roger Clemens	15.00
154	Bernie Williams	6.00
155	Jason Giambi	8.00
156	Robin Ventura	5.00
157	Carlos Delgado	6.00
158	Frank Thomas	8.00
159	Magglio Ordonez	5.00
160	Jim Thome	10.00
161	Darin Erstad	5.00
162	Tim Salmon	5.00
163	Tim Hudson	5.00
164	Barry Zito	5.00
165	Ichiro Suzuki	30.00
166	Edgar Martinez	8.00
167	Alex Rodriguez	15.00
168	Ivan Rodriguez	8.00
169	Juan Gonzalez	6.00
170	Greg Maddux	12.00
171	Chipper Jones	10.00
172	Andruw Jones	8.00
173	Tom Glavine	6.00
174	Mike Piazza	15.00
175	Roberto Alomar	8.00
176	Scott Rolen	12.00
177	Sammy Sosa	15.00
178	Moises Alou	8.00
179	Ken Griffey Jr.	15.00
180	Jeff Bagwell	8.00
181	Jim Edmonds	6.00
182	J.D. Drew	5.00
183	Brian Giles	5.00
184	Randy Johnson	10.00
185	Curt Schilling	10.00
186	Luis Gonzalez	5.00
187	Todd Helton	8.00
188	Shawn Green	5.00
189	David Wells	5.00
190	Jeff Kent	5.00

SuperStar Swatch Gold

Jersey (151-190):	.75-1.5X
Production 150	

SuperStar Swatch Silver

Jersey (151-190):	.5-1X
Production 400	

Sweet Spot Bat Barrel

No Pricing

Winning Materials Base Combo

		NM/M
Common Card:		15.00
Production 200		
PE	Mike Piazza, Jim Edmonds	20.00
RJ	Alex Rodriguez, Derek Jeter	40.00
BG	Barry Bonds, Shawn Green	20.00

IM	Ichiro Suzuki, Edgar Martinez	50.00
SG	Sammy Sosa, Luis Gonzalez	25.00
GR	Troy Glaus, Alex Rodriguez	20.00
WJ	Bernie Williams, Derek Jeter	30.00
GS	Ken Griffey Jr., Sammy Sosa	30.00
PI	Albert Pujols, Ichiro Suzuki	60.00
SR	Kazuhiro Sasaki, Mariano Rivera	20.00

Winning Materials Base/Patch Combo

No Pricing
Production 25 Sets

Winning Materials Ball/Patch Combo

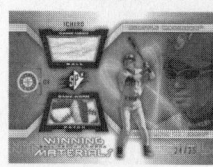

No Pricing
Production 25 Sets

Winning Materials Jersey Combo

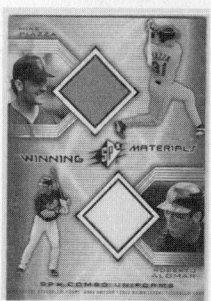

		NM/M
Common Card:		8.00
Inserted 1:18		
AR	Alex Rodriguez, Ivan Rodriguez	20.00
GC	Ken Griffey Jr., Sean Casey/SP	20.00
BR	Jeff Bagwell, Alex Rodriguez	15.00
WG	Bernie Williams, Jason Giambi	10.00
JS	Randy Johnson, Curt Schilling	15.00
MJ	Greg Maddux, Chipper Jones	20.00
MC	Edgar Martinez, Mike Cameron	
SP	Sammy Sosa, Corey Patterson	20.00
ED	Jim Edmonds, J.D. Drew	10.00
PA	Mike Piazza, Roberto Alomar	15.00
DH	Jermaine Dye, Tim Hudson	8.00
RA	Scott Rolen, Bobby Abreu	15.00
TO	Frank Thomas, Magglio Ordonez	15.00
HW	Mike Hampton, Larry Walker	8.00
TS	Jim Thome, C.C. Sabathia	15.00
GK	Shawn Green, Eric Karros	10.00
KG	Jason Kendall, Brian Giles	8.00
WP	David Wells, Jorge Posada	10.00
NM	Hideo Nomo, Pedro Martinez/SP	20.00
RP	Ivan Rodriguez, Chan Ho Park	10.00
LH	Al Leiter, Mike Hampton	8.00
BA	Jeromy Burnitz, Edgardo Alfonzo	8.00
DS	Carlos Delgado, Shannon Stewart	10.00
BG	Jeff Bagwell, Juan Gonzalez	10.00
GR	Juan Gonzalez, Ivan Rodriguez	10.00

VR	Omar Vizquel, Alex Rodriguez	15.00
SE	Aaron Sele, Darin Erstad	8.00
JJ	Chipper Jones, Andruw Jones	15.00
SH	Kazuhiro Sasaki, Shigetoshi Hasegawa	8.00

Winning Materials USA Jersey Combo

		NM/M
Common Card:		10.00
Production 150		
AH	Brent Abernathy, Orlando Hudson	8.00
BT	Sean Burroughs, Mark Teixeira	25.00
GB	Jason Giambi, Sean Burroughs	15.00
HD	Orlando Hudson, Jeff Deardorff	10.00
GT	Jason Giambi, Mark Teixeira	20.00
HOU	Roy Oswalt, Adam Everett	10.00
HP	Dustin Hermanson, Mark Prior	15.00
JC	Jacque Jones, Michael Cuddyer	10.00
KB	Austin Kearns, Sean Burroughs	15.00
KC	Austin Kearns, Michael Cuddyer	15.00
MG	Doug Mientkiewicz, Jason Giambi	15.00
MIN	Doug Mientkiewicz, Michael Cuddyer	10.00
MO	Matt Morris, Roy Oswalt	15.00
MP	Matt Morris, Mark Prior	15.00
AW	Matt Anderson, Jeff Weaver	10.00
MW	Matt Morris, Jeff Weaver	10.00
PB	Mark Prior, Dewon Brazelton	15.00
RE	Brian Roberts, Adam Everett	10.00
SD	Mark Kotsay, Sean Burroughs	10.00
TB	Brent Abernathy, Dewon Brazelton	10.00
TP	Mark Teixeira, Mark Prior	25.00
WB	Jeff Weaver, Dewon Brazelton	10.00
WH	Jeff Weaver, Dustin Hermanson	10.00

2003 SP Authentic

		NM/M
Complete Set (189):		3.50
Common Player:		.25
Common Rk Archives (91-123):		1.00
Production 2,500		
Common Back to '93 (124-150):		4.00
Production 1,993		
Common Future Watch (150-180):		4.00
Production 2,003		
Pack (5):		3.50
Box (24):		70.00
1	Darin Erstad	.40
2	Garret Anderson	.40
3	Troy Glaus	.50
4	Eric Chavez	.40
5	Barry Zito	.50
6	Miguel Tejada	.50
7	Eric Hinske	.25
8	Carlos Delgado	.40
9	Josh Phelps	.25
10	Ben Grieve	.25
11	Carl Crawford	.25
12	Omar Vizquel	.25
13	Matt Lawton	.25
14	C.C. Sabathia	.25
15	Ichiro Suzuki	1.50
16	John Olerud	.40
17	Freddy Garcia	.25
18	Jay Gibbons	.25
19	Tony Batista	.25
20	Melvin Mora	.25
21	Alex Rodriguez	2.00
22	Rafael Palmeiro	.50
23	Hank Blalock	.50
24	Nomar Garciaparra	1.00
25	Pedro J. Martinez	.75
26	Johnny Damon	.25
27	Mike Sweeney	.25
28	Carlos Febles	.25
29	Carlos Beltran	.50
30	Carlos Pena	.25
31	Eric Munson	.25
32	Bobby Higginson	.25
33	Torii Hunter	.40
34	Doug Mientkiewicz	.25
35	Jacque Jones	.25
36	Paul Konerko	.25
37	Bartolo Colon	.25
38	Magglio Ordonez	.40
39	Derek Jeter	2.00
40	Bernie Williams	.50
41	Jason Giambi	.50
42	Alfonso Soriano	.75
43	Roger Clemens	1.50
44	Jeff Bagwell	.50
45	Jeff Kent	.40
46	Lance Berkman	.40
47	Chipper Jones	.75
48	Andruw Jones	.50
49	Gary Sheffield	.50
50	Ben Sheets	.40
51	Richie Sexson	.25
52	Geoff Jenkins	.25
53	Jim Edmonds	.40
54	Albert Pujols	2.00
55	Scott Rolen	.75
56	Sammy Sosa	1.00
57	Kerry Wood	.75
58	Eric Karros	.25
59	Luis Gonzalez	.40
60	Randy Johnson	.75
61	Curt Schilling	.75
62	Fred McGriff	.40
63	Shawn Green	.40
64	Paul LoDuca	.25
65	Vladimir Guerrero	.75
66	Jose Vidro	.25
67	Barry Bonds	2.00
68	Rich Aurilia	.25
69	Edgardo Alfonzo	.25
70	Ivan Rodriguez	.50
71	Mike Lowell	.40
72	Derek Lee	.50
73	Tom Glavine	.50
74	Mike Piazza	1.00
75	Roberto Alomar	.50
76	Ryan Klesko	.25
77	Phil Nevin	.25
78	Mark Kotsay	.25
79	Jim Thome	.75
80	Pat Burrell	.40
81	Bobby Abreu	.40
82	Jason Kendall	.40
83	Brian Giles	.40
84	Aramis Ramirez	.40
85	Austin Kearns	.40
86	Ken Griffey Jr.	1.00
87	Adam Dunn	.50
88	Larry Walker	.40
89	Todd Helton	.50
90	Preston Wilson	.40
91	Derek Jeter	6.00
92	Johnny Damon	3.00
93	Chipper Jones	3.00
94	Manny Ramirez	3.00
95	Trot Nixon	1.00
96	Alex Rodriguez	5.00
97	Chan Ho Park	1.00
98	Brad Fullmer	1.00
99	Billy Wagner	1.00
100	Hideo Nomo	2.00
101	Freddy Garcia	1.00
102	Darin Erstad	1.00
103	Jose Cruz Jr.	1.00
104	Nomar Garciaparra	4.00
105	Magglio Ordonez	1.50
106	Kerry Wood	2.00
107	Troy Glaus	1.50
108	J.D. Drew	1.00
109	Alfonso Soriano	3.00
110	Danys Baez	1.00
111	Kazuhiro Sasaki	1.00
112	Barry Zito	2.00
113	Brent Abernathy	1.00
114	Ben Diggins	1.00
115	Ben Sheets	1.00
116	Brad Wilkerson	1.00
117	Juan Pierre	1.00
118	Jon Rauch	1.00
119	Ichiro Suzuki	5.00
120	Albert Pujols	6.00
121	Mark Prior	2.00
122	Mark Teixeira	2.00
123	Kazuhisa Ishii	1.00
124	Troy Glaus	1.50
125	Randy Johnson	3.00
126	Curt Schilling	3.00
127	Chipper Jones	3.00
128	Greg Maddux	4.00
129	Nomar Garciaparra	3.00
130	Pedro J. Martinez	3.00
131	Sammy Sosa	3.00
132	Mark Prior	2.00
133	Ken Griffey Jr.	4.00
134	Adam Dunn	2.00
135	Jeff Bagwell	2.00
136	Vladimir Guerrero	3.00
137	Mike Piazza	4.00
138	Tom Glavine	1.50
139	Derek Jeter	8.00
140	Roger Clemens	6.00
141	Jason Giambi	2.00
142	Alfonso Soriano	3.00
143	Miguel Tejada	2.00
144	Barry Zito	1.50
145	Jim Thome	3.00
146	Barry Bonds	8.00
147	Ichiro Suzuki	5.00
148	Albert Pujols	8.00
149	Alex Rodriguez	6.00
150	Carlos Delgado	2.00
151	Richard Fischer RC	4.00
152	Brandon Webb RC	35.00
153	Rob Hammock RC	4.00
154	Matt Kata RC	4.00
155	Tim Olson RC	4.00
156	Oscar Villarreal RC	4.00
157	Michael Hessman RC	4.00
158	Daniel Cabrera RC	6.00
159	Jon Leicester RC	4.00
160	Todd Wellemeyer RC	6.00
161	Felix Sanchez RC	4.00
162	David Sanders RC	4.00
163	Josh Stewart RC	4.00
164	Arnie Munoz RC	4.00
165	Ryan Cameron RC	4.00
166	Clint Barmes RC	5.00
167	Josh Willingham RC	10.00
168	Willie Eyre RC	4.00
169	Brent Hoard RC	4.00
170	Termel Sledge RC	4.00
171	Phil Seibel RC	4.00
172	Craig Brazell RC	4.00
173	Jeff Duncan RC	5.00
174	Bernie Castro RC	4.00
177	Mike Nicolas RC	4.00
178	Rett Johnson RC	4.00
179	Bobby Madritsch RC	4.00
180	Chris Capuano RC	15.00
181	Hideki Matsui/ Auto./500 RC	240.00
181	H. Matsui/Bronze/ Auto./75	275.00
182	Jose Contreras/ Auto./500 RC	35.00
183	Lew Ford/Auto./500 RC	10.00
184	Jeremy Griffiths/ Auto./500	10.00
185	Guillermo Quiroz/ Auto./500 RC	10.00
186	Alejandro Machado/ Auto./500 RC	10.00
187	Francisco Cruceta/ Auto./500 RC	10.00
188	Prentice Redman/ Auto./500 RC	10.00
189	Shane Bazzell/ Auto./500 RC	10.00

Chirography

		NM/M
Common Autograph:		10.00
Varying quantities produced		
Bronze Autos.:		1X
Production 100		
Silver Autos.:		1-1.5X
Production 50		
Gold Autos.:		No Pricing
Production 10		
GA1	Garret Anderson/245	15.00
BA	Jeff Bagwell/175	40.00
JD	Johnny Damon/245	35.00
AD	Adam Dunn/170	25.00
JE2	Jim Edmonds/350	12.00
FL	Cliff Floyd/125	12.00
FC	Rafael Furcal/150	15.00
FG	Freddy Garcia/345	15.00
GI	Jason Giambi/250	15.00
GL	Brian Giles/225	15.00
LG1	Luis Gonzalez/195	15.00
GJ	Ken Griffey Jr./350	85.00
JR	Ken Griffey Jr./350	85.00
TO	Torii Hunter/245	15.00
KE	Jason Kendall/145	10.00
MM	Mark McGwire/50	200.00
MP	Mark Prior/150	20.00
CR	Cal Ripken Jr./250	100.00
RO	Scott Rolen/345	30.00
TS	Tim Salmon/350	20.00
RS	Richie Sexson/245	15.00
SA	Sammy Sosa/335	75.00
SO	Sammy Sosa/335	75.00
IC	Ichiro Suzuki/85	350.00
IS	Ichiro Suzuki/85	350.00
SW	Mike Sweeney/125	15.00
JT1	Jim Thome/350	15.00

Chirography Dodger Stars

		NM/M
Common Autograph:		8.00
Bronze Autos.:		1X
Production 100		
Silver Autos.:		1-1.5X
Production 50		
Gold Autos.:		No Pricing
Production 10		
BB	Bill Buckner/245	10.00
CE	Ron Cey/345	15.00
SG	Steve Garvey/320	20.00
JN	Tommy John/170	15.00
DL	Davey Lopes/245	8.00
DN	Don Newcombe/345	15.00
BI	Bill Russell/245	15.00
DS	Duke Snider/345	30.00
SU	Don Sutton/245	15.00
MW	Maury Wills/320	10.00
SY	Steve Yeager/345	15.00

Chirography Double

		NM/M
Common Duo Auto.:		40.00
FB	Yogi Berra, Whitey Ford/75	150.00
FE	Carlton Fisk, Dwight Evans/75	65.00
FM	Carlton Fisk, Bill Mazeroski/75	40.00
GG	Jason Giambi, Ken Griffey Jr.	125.00
GR	Steve Garvey, Ron Cey/75	50.00
JI	Ken Griffey Jr., Ichiro Suzuki	350.00
KR	Tony Kubek, Bobby Richardson/75	80.00
KT	Tom Seaver, Jerry Koosman/75	80.00
MG	Don Mattingly, Jason Giambi/25	150.00
MS	Mark McGwire, Sammy Sosa/15	500.00
SJ	Sammy Sosa, Jason Giambi/25	125.00
WB	Bill Buckner, Mookie Wilson/150	40.00

Chirography Flash Backs

		NM/M
Common Autograph:		8.00
Bronze Autos.:		1X
Production 100		
Silver Autos.:		1-1.5X
Production 50		
Gold Autos.:		No Pricing
No Pricing		
JE1	Jim Edmonds/350	15.00
CF1	Cliff Floyd/350	8.00
JA	Jason Giambi/350	15.00
BN	Brian Giles/245	10.00
LA	Luis Gonzalez/200	15.00
GM	Ken Griffey Jr./350	80.00
MA	Mark McGwire/245	280.00
SR	Sammy Sosa/245	100.00

Chirography Hall of Famers

		NM/M
Common Autograph:		15.00
Bronze Autos.:		1X
Production 100		
Silver Autos.:		1-1.5X
Production 50		
Gold Autos.:		No Pricing
Production 10		
JB1	Johnny Bench/350	40.00
GC1	Gary Carter/350	20.00
OC	Orlando Cepeda/245	20.00
RF	Rollie Fingers/170	15.00
CF	Carlton Fisk/240	35.00
WF	Whitey Ford/150	40.00
BG	Bob Gibson/245	35.00
TP	Tony Perez/320	20.00
RR	Robin Roberts/170	30.00
NR	Nolan Ryan/170	140.00
TS	Tom Seaver/170	30.00
DS	Duke Snider/250	30.00
DW2	Dave Winfield/350	25.00

Chirography Triple

NM/M

Quantity produced listed

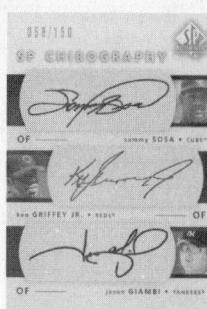

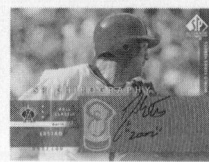

CF	Carlton Fisk/200	40.00
KG	Kirk Gibson/145	15.00
GO	Luis Gonzalez/225	15.00
GS	Ken Griffey Sr./295	10.00
AJ1	Andruw Jones/350	20.00
DJ	David Justice/170	20.00
JK	Jerry Koosman/170	15.00
BM	Bill Mazeroski/245	30.00
TM	Tug McGraw/170	25.00
JP	Jorge Posada/350	35.00
ER	Edgar Renteria/220	15.00
CR	Cal Ripken Jr./295	100.00
TI	Tim Salmon/245	15.00
CS	Curt Schilling/345	30.00

Simply Splendid

		NM/M
Complete Set (30):		200.00
Common Williams:		8.00
Production 406 Sets		
TW1-TW30	Ted Williams	8.00

Splendid Jerseys

		NM/M
Production 406 Sets		
TW	Mickey Mantle, Ted Williams	180.00
SJ-TW	Ted Williams	100.00
TW-IS	Ted Williams, Ichiro Suzuki	100.00
TW-JG	Ted Williams, Jason Giambi	60.00
TW-KG	Ted Williams, Ken Griffey Jr.	75.00
TW-MM	Mark McGwire, Ted Williams	110.00
TW-SS	Ted Williams, Sammy Sosa	80.00
TW-NM1	Ted Williams, Nomar Garciaparra	80.00
TW-NM2	Nomar Garciaparra, Ted Williams	80.00

Splendid Signatures

		NM/M
Hand Numbered to five or three.		
GA	Nomar Garciaparra/406	100.00

BKR	Bobby Richardson, Yogi Berra, Tony Kubek/75	120.00
FCG	Carlton Fisk, Gary Carter, Kirk Gibson/75	75.00
GIS	Sammy Sosa, Ichiro Suzuki, Ken Griffey Jr./75	400.00
GLC	Davey Lopes, Ron Cey, Steve Garvey/75	65.00
GRC	Steve Garvey, Ron Cey, Bill Russell/75	60.00
GSG	Sammy Sosa, Jason Giambi, Ken Griffey Jr./75	250.00
GSJ	Ken Griffey Jr., Jason Giambi, Sammy Sosa/75	250.00
ISG	Sammy Sosa, Jason Giambi, Ichiro Suzuki/75	300.00
SEA	Tim Salmon, Garret Anderson, Darin Erstad/75	100.00
SKM	Tom Seaver, Tug McGraw, Jerry Koosman/75	125.00

Chirography Yankee Stars

	NM/M
Common Autograph:	10.00
Bronze Autos.:	1X
Production 100	
Silver Autos.:	1-1.5X
Production 50	
Gold Autos.:	No Pricing
Production 10	
YB	Yogi Berra/320	35.00
JB	Jim Bouton/345	10.00
RC	Roger Clemens/210	100.00
JG	Jason Giambi/275	15.00
KS	Ken Griffey Sr./350	10.00
TH	Tommy Henrich/345	15.00
HK	Ralph Houk/245	12.00
TJ	Tommy John/245	15.00
TK	Tony Kubek/345	20.00
SL	Sparky Lyle/345	10.00
DM	Don Mattingly/295	60.00
BR	Bobby Richardson/320	20.00
ST	Mel Stottlemyre/345	10.00
DW1	Dave Winfield/350	25.00

Chirography Young Stars

	NM/M
Common Autograph:	6.00
Bronze Autos.:	1X
Production 100	
Silver Autos.:	1-1.5X
Production 50	
Gold Autos.:	No Pricing
Production 10	
HB	Hank Blalock/245	25.00
BO	Joe Borchard/245	8.00
SB	Sean Burroughs/245	8.00
MB	Marlon Byrd/245	8.00
HC	Hee Seop Choi/245	20.00
DI1	Ben Diggins/350	8.00
DH	Drew Henson/245	15.00
EH	Eric Hinske/245	10.00
OH	Orlando Hudson/245	15.00
JJ	Jacque Jones/245	15.00
JJ1	Jimmy Journell/350	10.00
JL	Jason Lane/245	6.00
JO	Joe Mays/245	6.00
MI	Doug Mientkiewicz/245	15.00
MY	Brett Myers/245	10.00
CP	Corey Patterson/245	15.00
PE	Carlos Pena/245	10.00
OP	Oliver Perez/245	10.00
JP	Josh Phelps/245	8.00
BP1	Brandon Phillips/350	10.00
AP	A.J. Pierzynski/245	15.00
FS1	Freddy Sanchez/245	15.00
TX	Mark Teixeira/245	25.00
BZ	Barry Zito/350	15.00

Chirography World Series Heroes

	NM/M
Common Autograph:	10.00
Bronze Autos.:	1X
Production 100	
Silver Autos.:	1-1.5X
Production 50	
Gold Autos.:	No Pricing
Production 10	
GA	Garret Anderson/245	15.00
GC	Gary Carter/345	20.00
DE	Darin Erstad/245	15.00

TW-NM3	Ted Williams, Nomar Garciaparra/3 (10/03 Auction)	2,400

Superstar Flashback

		NM/M
Complete Set (60):		65.00
Common Player:		1.00
Production 2,003 Sets		
SF1	Tim Salmon	1.00
SF2	Darin Erstad	1.00
SF3	Troy Glaus	1.50
SF4	Randy Johnson	2.00
SF5	Curt Schilling	1.50
SF6	Steve Finley	1.00
SF7	Greg Maddux	3.00
SF8	Chipper Jones	3.00
SF9	Andruw Jones	1.50
SF10	Gary Sheffield	1.00
SF11	Manny Ramirez	2.00
SF12	Pedro J. Martinez	2.00
SF13	Nomar Garciaparra	2.50
SF14	Sammy Sosa	3.00
SF15	Frank Thomas	1.50
SF16	Kerry Wood	1.50
SF17	Paul Konerko	1.00
SF18	Corey Patterson	1.00
SF19	Mark Prior	2.00
SF20	Ken Griffey Jr.	3.00
SF21	Adam Dunn	1.50
SF22	Larry Walker	1.00
SF23	Preston Wilson	1.00
SF24	Todd Helton	1.50
SF25	Ivan Rodriguez	1.50
SF26	Josh Beckett	1.00
SF27	Jeff Bagwell	1.50
SF28	Jeff Kent	1.00
SF29	Lance Berkman	1.00
SF30	Carlos Beltran	1.00
SF31	Shawn Green	1.00
SF32	Richie Sexson	1.00
SF33	Vladimir Guerrero	2.00
SF34	Mike Piazza	4.00
SF35	Roberto Alomar	1.50
SF36	Roger Clemens	4.00
SF37	Derek Jeter	6.00
SF38	Jason Giambi	1.50
SF39	Bernie Williams	1.50
SF40	Nick Johnson	1.00
SF41	Alfonso Soriano	3.00
SF42	Miguel Tejada	1.50
SF43	Eric Chavez	1.50
SF44	Barry Zito	1.50
SF45	Jim Thome	1.50
SF46	Pat Burrell	1.00
SF47	Marlon Byrd	1.00
SF48	Jason Kendall	1.00
SF49	Aramis Ramirez	1.50
SF50	Brian Giles	1.00
SF51	Phil Nevin	1.00
SF52	Barry Bonds	6.00
SF53	Ichiro Suzuki	4.00
SF54	Scott Rolen	2.00
SF55	J.D. Drew	1.00
SF56	Albert Pujols	6.00
SF57	Mark Teixeira	1.50
SF58	Hank Blalock	1.50
SF59	Carlos Delgado	1.50
SF60	Roy Halladay	1.00

500 Home Run Club

		NM/M
Production 25		
500HR	Ted Williams, Barry Bonds, Mark McGwire, Sammy Sosa, Mickey Mantle	325.00

2003 SP Legendary Cuts

		NM/M
Complete Set (130):		
Common Player:		.25
Common SP:		3.00
Production 1,299		
Pack (4):		8.00
Box (12):		85.00
1	Luis Aparicio	.25
2	Al Barlick	.25
3	Al Lopez	.25
4	Ernie Banks	1.00
5	Alexander Cartwright	.25
6	Lou Brock	.50
7	Babe Ruth/SP	10.00
8	Bill Dickey	.50
9	Bill Mazeroski	.25
10	Bob Feller	.50
11	Billy Herman	.25
12	Billy Williams	.50
13	Bob Gibson/SP	4.00
14	Bob Lemon	.25
15	Bobby Doerr	.25
16	Branch Rickey	.25
17	Gary Carter	.50
18	Burleigh Grimes	.25
19	Cap Anson	.25
20	Carl Hubbell	.25
21	Carlton Fisk	.50
22	Casey Stengel	.50
23	Charlie Gehringer	.25
24	Chief Bender	.25
25	Christy Mathewson/SP	5.00
26	Cy Young	1.00
27	Dave Winfield	.50
28	Dazzy Vance	.25
29	Dizzy Dean/SP	4.00
30	Don Drysdale/SP	4.00
31	Duke Snider/SP	4.00
32	Earl Averill	.25
33	Earle Combs	.25
34	Edd Roush	.25
35	Earl Weaver	.25
36	Eddie Collins	.25
37	Eddie Plank	.25
38	Elmer Flick	.25
39	Enos Slaughter	.25
40	Ernie Lombardi	.25
41	Ford Frick	.25
42	Jim "Catfish" Hunter	.25
43	Frankie Frisch	.25
44	Gabby Hartnett	.25
45	George Kell	.25
46	Early Wynn	.25
47	Ferguson Jenkins	.25
48	Al Kaline	1.00
49	Harmon Killebrew	1.00
50	Hal Newhouser	.25
51	Hank Greenberg/SP	5.00
52	Harry Caray	.25

53	Tommy Lasorda	.25
54	Honus Wagner/SP	6.00
55	Hoyt Wilhelm/SP	3.00
56	Jackie Robinson/SP	6.00
57	Jim Bottomley	.25
58	Jim Bunning/SP	3.00
59	Jimmie Foxx/SP	6.00
60	Eddie Mathews	1.00
61	Joe Cronin	.25
62	Joe DiMaggio/SP	8.00
63	Joe McCarthy/SP	3.00
64	Joe Morgan/SP	3.00
65	Willie McCovey	.50
66	Joe Tinker	.25
67	Johnny Bench/SP	6.00
68	Johnny Evers/SP	3.00
69	Johnny Mize/SP	3.00
70	Josh Gibson/SP	5.00
71	Juan Marichal	.50
72	Judy Johnson	.25
73	Stan Musial	1.50
74	Kiki Cuyler	.25
75	Larry Doby	.75
76	Nap Lajoie	.25
77	Larry MacPhail	.25
78	Phil Niekro	.25
79	Lefty Gomez/SP	3.00
80	Lefty Grove/SP	3.00
81	Leo Durocher/SP	3.00
82	Leon Day	.25
83	Gaylord Perry/SP	3.00
84	Lou Boudreau	.25
85	Lou Gehrig	3.00
86	Luke Appling	.25
87	Max Carey	.25
88	Mel Allen/SP	3.00
89	Mel Ott/SP	5.00
90	Mickey Cochrane	.50
91	Mickey Mantle	4.00
92	Brooks Robinson	1.00
93	Monte Irvin	.50
94	Nellie Fox	.50
95	Nolan Ryan/SP	10.00
96	Ozzie Smith/SP	6.00
97	Mike Schmidt	2.00
98	Pee Wee Reese/SP	3.00
99	Phil Rizzuto	.75
100	Ralph Kiner	.50
101	Ray Dandridge	.25
102	Richie Ashburn	.25
103	Rick Ferrell	.25
104	Roberto Clemente	2.00
105	Robin Roberts	.25
106	Robin Yount	1.00
107	Rogers Hornsby	.50
108	Rollie Fingers	.25
109	Roy Campanella	.50
110	Rube Marquard	.25
111	Sam Crawford	.25
112	Steve Carlton	.50
113	Satchel Paige/SP	5.00
114	Sparky Anderson	.25
115	Stan Coveleski	.25
116	Red Schoendienst	.25
117	Ted Williams	3.00
118	Tom Seaver	1.00
119	Tom Yawkey	.25
120	Tony Lazzeri	.25
121	Tony Perez	.25
122	Tris Speaker	.25
123	Ty Cobb	2.00
124	Waite Hoyt/SP	3.00
125	Walter Alston	.25
126	Walter Johnson	.75
127	Warren Spahn	1.00
128	Whitey Ford	.75
129	Willie Stargell	.50
130	Yogi Berra	.75

Blue

Non SP's (1-130):	2-4X
SP's:	1-2X

Production 275 Sets

Green

No pricing due to scarcity.
Production 25 Sets

Autographs

	NM/M
Common Player:	1.00

Inserted 1:196
Many not priced due to scarcity.

AL	Alexander Cartwright/1 (6/05 Auction)	7,800
BG	Burleigh Grimes/34	250.00
BI	Billy Herman/30	150.00
BL	Bob Lemon/34	150.00
BL1	Bob Lemon/41	150.00
CH	Carl Hubbell/47	300.00
CH1	Carl Hubbell/63	300.00
EA	Earl Averill/96	125.00
EC	Earle Combs/45	150.00
ES	Enos Slaughter/30	200.00
HC	Harry Caray/29	225.00
HC1	Harry Caray/35	225.00
HG	Hank Greenberg/32	375.00
JD	Joe DiMaggio/50	375.00
JD1	Joe DiMaggio/28	400.00
LB	Lou Boudreau/82	110.00
LB1	Lou Boudreau/49	120.00
LU	Luke Appling/52	150.00
RM	Rube Marquard/40	200.00

Autographs Blue

NM/M

Many not priced due to scarcity.

EA	Earl Averill/50	125.00
HC1	Harry Caray/35	240.00
HN1	Hal Newhouser B2B/29	125.00
JD1	Joe DiMaggio/40	375.00

Combo Cuts

No Pricing
Production One Set

Etched in Time

	NM/M
Common Player:	3.00

Production 400 Sets

Etched 300:	.5-1X

Production 300

Etched 175:	.75-1.5X

Production 175

ME	Mel Allen	3.00
RA	Richie Ashburn	4.00
AB	Al Barlick	3.00
LB	Lou Boudreau	3.00
RO	Roy Campanella	4.00
AC	Alexander Cartwright	3.00
HC	Harry Caray	3.00
RC	Roberto Clemente	10.00
TC	Ty Cobb	6.00
EC	Eddie Collins	3.00
DD	Dizzy Dean	3.00
JD	Joe DiMaggio	8.00
DO	Don Drysdale	3.00
LD	Leo Durocher	3.00
JF	Jimmie Foxx	5.00
LO	Lou Gehrig	8.00
CG	Charlie Gehringer	3.00
JG	Josh Gibson	5.00
LG	Lefty Gomez	3.00
HG	Hank Greenberg	5.00
LE	Lefty Grove	3.00
GH	Gabby Hartnett	3.00
RH	Rogers Hornsby	4.00
CH	Carl Hubbell	3.00
TL	Tony Lazzeri	3.00
EL	Ernie Lombardi	3.00
MM	Mickey Mantle	15.00
CM	Christy Mathewson	8.00
JM	Joe McCarthy	3.00
JO	Johnny Mize	3.00
MO	Mel Ott	4.00
SP	Satchel Paige	5.00
PR	Pee Wee Reese	3.00
JR	Jackie Robinson	5.00
BR	Babe Ruth	10.00
TS	Tris Speaker	3.00
CS	Casey Stengel	5.00
HW	Honus Wagner	5.00
TW	Ted Williams	8.00
CY	Cy Young	5.00

Hall Marks Autographs

NM/M

Inserted 1:196
Many not priced due to scarcity.

Greens:	No Pricing

Production 10

BD1	Bobby Doerr/Black/50	40.00
BM1	Bill Mazeroski/Black/50	40.00
CF1	Carlton Fisk/Black/50	50.00
CY1	Carl Yastrzemski/Black/45	75.00

DS1	Duke Snider/Black/50	40.00
GC1	Gary Carter/Black/50	30.00
GK1	George Kell/Black/50	20.00
JM1	Juan Marichal/Black/50	35.00
JO1	Joe Morgan/Black/75	20.00
LA1	Luis Aparicio/Black/45	30.00
MI1	Monte Irvin/Black/85	30.00
OS1	Ozzie Smith/Black/45	75.00
PR1	Phil Rizzuto/Black/50	40.00
RF1	Rollie Fingers/Black/99	20.00
RK1	Ralph Kiner/Black/50	30.00
RR1	Robin Roberts/Black/55	40.00
RY1	Robin Yount/Black/45	75.00
TP1	Tony Perez/Black/50	30.00
WS1	Warren Spahn/Black/35	70.00
YB1	Yogi Berra/Black/50	60.00

Historic Impressions

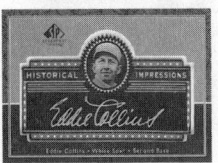

	NM/M
Common Player:	3.00

Production 350 Sets

Golds:	1X

Production 200 Sets

Golds 75:	1.5-2X

Production 75

Silvers:	1X

Production 250 Sets

MA	Mel Allen	3.00
RA	Richie Ashburn	5.00
LB	Lou Boudreau	3.00
RO	Roy Campanella	5.00
AC	Alexander Cartwright	3.00
HC	Harry Caray	4.00
RC	Roberto Clemente	15.00
TY	Ty Cobb	8.00
MC	Mickey Cochrane	5.00
EC	Eddie Collins	3.00
DD	Dizzy Dean	5.00
JD	Joe DiMaggio	8.00
DO	Don Drysdale	3.00
LD	Leo Durocher	3.00
JF	Jimmie Foxx	5.00
LO	Lou Gehrig	10.00
CG	Charlie Gehringer	3.00
LG	Lefty Gomez	3.00
HG	Hank Greenberg	6.00
LE	Lefty Grove	6.00
GH	Gabby Hartnett	3.00
RH	Rogers Hornsby	6.00
CH	Carl Hubbell	6.00
TL	Tony Lazzeri	3.00
MM	Mickey Mantle	25.00
CM	Christy Mathewson	6.00
JO	Joe McCarthy	3.00
JM	Johnny Mize	3.00
MO	Mel Ott	6.00
SP	Satchel Paige	5.00
PR	Pee Wee Reese	3.00
JR	Jackie Robinson	8.00
BR	Babe Ruth	15.00
ES	Enos Slaughter	3.00
TS	Tris Speaker	3.00
CS	Casey Stengel	4.00
HW	Honus Wagner	8.00
HO	Hoyt Wilhelm	3.00
TW	Ted Williams	15.00
CY	Cy Young	8.00

Historic Swatches

	NM/M
Common Player:	5.00

Inserted 1:12

Blues:	.75-1.5X

Production 50 Sets

Greens:	.75-1X

Production 160 to 250

Purples:	.75-1.5X

Production 75 to 150

BG	Bob Gibson CO/Jsy/350	10.00
BM	Bill Mazeroski/Pants/50	15.00
BW	Billy Williams/Jsy/190	5.00
CF	Carlton Fisk/Pants/350	8.00
CM	Christy Mathewson/Pants/300	100.00
CS	Casey Stengel/Jsy/275	10.00
CY	Carl Yastrzemski/Jsy/350	20.00
CY1	Carl Yastrzemski/Pants/350	20.00
DS	Duke Snider/Jsy/350	10.00
DW1	Dave Winfield/Twins Jsy/300	8.00
FR	Frank Robinson/O's Jsy/350	10.00
FR1	Frank Robinson/Angels Jsy/350	5.00
GC	Gary Carter/Mets Jsy/350	5.00
GC1	Gary Carter/Expos Jsy/350	5.00
HW	Honus Wagner/Pants/275	120.00
JB	Johnny Bench/Jsy/150	10.00
JM	Joe Morgan/Jsy/350	5.00
JN	Juan Marichal/Pants/225	5.00
JN1	Juan Marichal/Jsy/48	5.00
LA	Luis Aparicio/Jsy/230	5.00
LB	Lou Boudreau/Jsy/265	5.00
MM	Mickey Mantle/Pants/350	100.00
NR	Nolan Ryan/Rgr. Pants/350	25.00
NR1	Nolan Ryan/Astro Pants/350	25.00
OS	Ozzie Smith/Jsy/85	25.00
RF	Rollie Fingers/Jsy/105	5.00
RY	Robin Yount/Portrait/Jsy/350	10.00
RY1	Robin Yount/Swing/Jsy/350	10.00
SA	Sparky Anderson/Jsy/350	5.00
SC	Steve Carlton/Jsy/350	10.00
SM	Stan Musial/Jsy/350	25.00
TC	Ty Cobb/Pants/350	90.00
TP	Tony Perez/Jsy/350	5.00
TS	Tom Seaver/Jsy/350	10.00
TS1	Tom Seaver/Pants/350	10.00
TW	Ted Williams/Jsy/250	85.00
WA	Walter Alston/Look Left/Jsy/350	
WA1	Walter Alston/Ahead/Jsy/350	5.00
WI	Willie Stargell/Jsy/55	5.00
WS	Warren Spahn/CO/Jsy/350	15.00
YB	Yogi Berra/Jsy/300	10.00

Historic Lumber

	NM/M
Common Player:	6.00

Inserted 1:12

BR	Babe Ruth/Away/150	125.00
BR1	Babe Ruth/Home/150	125.00
CF	Carlton Fisk/R.Sox/50	15.00
CF1	Carlton Fisk/W.Sox/50	15.00
CY	Carl Yastrzemski/w/Bat/300	20.00
CY1	Carl Yastrzemski/w/Cap/350	20.00
CY2	Carl Yastrzemski/w/Helmet/350	20.00
DW	Dave Winfield/Padres/350	10.00
DW1	Dave Winfield/Yanks/350	10.00
FR	Frank Robinson/O's/300	10.00
FR1	Frank Robinson/Reds/350	10.00
FR2	Frank Robinson/Angels/350	10.00
GC	Gary Carter/Mets/300	5.00
GC1	Gary Carter/Helmet/Expos/100	6.00
GC2	Gary Carter/Cap/Expos/100	6.00
HK	Harmon Killebrew/350	10.00

JB	Johnny Bench/w/Bat/350	10.00
JB1	Johnny Bench/Swing/350	10.00
JM	Joe Morgan/Reds/350	6.00
JM1	Joe Morgan/Astros/350	6.00
MM	Mickey Mantle/300	100.00
NR	Nolan Ryan/Rgr./225	25.00
OS	Ozzie Smith/Cards/300	15.00
OS1	Ozzie Smith/Padres/350	15.00
RS	Red Schoendienst/ Look Right/165	6.00
RS1	Red Schoendienst/ Look Left/165	6.00
SC	Steve Carlton/350	8.00
TP	Tony Perez/Swing/350	6.00
TP1	Tony Perez/Portrait/350	6.00
TS	Tom Seaver/100	10.00
TW	Ted Williams/w/3 Bats/150	75.00
TW1	Ted Williams/Portrait/150	75.00
WS	Willie Stargell/ Arms Down/150	8.00
WS1	Willie Stargell/Arms Up/150	8.00
YB	Yogi Berra/Shout/350	10.00
YB1	Yogi Berra w/Bat/350	10.00

Historic Lumber Green

		NM/M
Common Player:		
BR	Babe Ruth/Away/75	140.00
BR1	Babe Ruth/Home/75	140.00
CY	Carl Yastrzemski/w/Bat/125	25.00
CY1	Carl Yastrzemski/ w/Cap/125	25.00
CY2	Carl Yastrzemski/ w/Helmet/125	25.00
DW	Dave Winfield/ Padres/125	10.00
DW1	Dave Winfield/Yanks/125	10.00
FR	Frank Robinson/O's/125	10.00
FR1	Frank Robinson/Reds/125	10.00
FR2	Frank Robinson/Angels/125	10.00
GC	Gary Carter/Mets/125	6.00
GC1	Gary Carter/Helmet/ Expos/125	6.00
GC2	Gary Carter/Cap/Expos/125	6.00
HK	Harmon Killebrew/125	10.00
JB	Johnny Bench/w/Bat/125	10.00
JB1	Johnny Bench/Swing/125	10.00
JM	Joe Morgan/Reds/125	6.00
JM1	Joe Morgan/Astros/125	6.00
MM	Mickey Mantle/75	120.00
NR	Nolan Ryan/Astros/50	50.00
OS	Ozzie Smith/Cards/125	20.00
OS1	Ozzie Smith/Padres/125	20.00
RS	Red Schoendienst/ Look Right/125	8.00
RS1	Red Schoendienst/ Look Left/125	8.00
SC	Steve Carlton/125	10.00
TP	Tony Perez/Swing/125	6.00
TP1	Tony Perez/Portrait/125	6.00
TS	Tom Seaver/50	15.00
TW	Ted Williams/w/3 Bats/75	75.00
TW1	Ted Williams/Portrait/75	75.00
WS	Willie Stargell/ Arms Down/125	10.00
WS1	Willie Stargell/ Arms Up/125	10.00
YB	Yogi Berra/Shout/125	10.00
YB1	Yogi Berra w/Bat/125	10.00

Presidential Cut Signatures

Production between 1-3
No Pricing

2003 SPx

		NM/M
Complete Set (178):		
Common Player:		.25
Common SP (126-160):		4.00
Production 999		
Common Jsy Auto. (161-178):		10.00
Production 1,224 unless noted.		
Pack (4):		6.00
Box (18):		90.00
1	Darin Erstad	.50
2	Garret Anderson	.50
3	Tim Salmon	.50
4	Troy Glaus/SP	2.00
5	Luis Gonzalez	.50
6	Randy Johnson	1.50
7	Curt Schilling	1.00
8	Lyle Overbay	.25
9	Andruw Jones/SP	3.00
10	Gary Sheffield	.75
11	Rafael Furcal	.40
12	Greg Maddux	2.00
13	Chipper Jones/SP	3.00
14	Tony Batista	.25
15	Rodrigo Lopez	.25
16	Jay Gibbons	.25
17	Byung-Hyun Kim	.25
18	Johnny Damon	1.00
19	Derek Lowe	.25
20	Nomar Garciaparra/SP	4.00
21	Pedro J. Martinez	1.50
22	Manny Ramirez/SP	4.00
23	Mark Prior	1.00
24	Kerry Wood	.50
25	Corey Patterson	.50
26	Sammy Sosa/SP	5.00
27	Moises Alou	.50
28	Magglio Ordonez	.50
29	Frank Thomas	1.00
30	Paul Konerko	.50
31	Bartolo Colon	.25
32	Adam Dunn	1.00
33	Austin Kearns	.50
34	Aaron Boone	.25
35	Ken Griffey Jr./SP	5.00
36	Omar Vizquel	.50
37	C.C. Sabathia	.25
38	Jason Davis	.25
39	Travis Hafner	.75
40	Brandon Phillips	.25
41	Larry Walker	.50
42	Preston Wilson	.50
43	Jay Payton	.25
44	Todd Helton	.75
45	Carlos Pena	.25
46	Eric Munson	.25
47	Ivan Rodriguez	1.00
48	Josh Beckett	.50
49	Alex Gonzalez	.25
50	Roy Oswalt	.50
51	Craig Biggio	.50
52	Jeff Bagwell	.75
53	Dontrelle Willis/SP	2.00
54	Mike Sweeney	.25
55	Carlos Beltran	1.00
56	Brent Mayne	.25
57	Hideo Nomo	.75
58	Rickey Henderson	.75
59	Adrian Beltre	.50
60	Miguel Cabrera/SP	4.00
61	Kazuhisa Ishii	.25
62	Ben Sheets	.50
63	Richie Sexson	.50
64	Torii Hunter/SP	2.00
65	Jacque Jones	.25
66	Joe Mays	.25
67	Corey Koskie	.25
68	A.J. Pierzynski	.25
69	Jose Vidro	.25
70	Vladimir Guerrero/SP	4.00
71	Tom Glavine	.50
72	Jose Reyes/SP	4.00
73	Aaron Heilman	.25
74	Mike Piazza	2.00
75	Jorge Posada	.75
76	Mike Mussina	.75
77	Robin Ventura	.25
78	Mariano Rivera	.75
79	Roger Clemens/SP	6.00
80	Jason Giambi	.75
81	Bernie Williams	.75
82	Alfonso Soriano/SP	4.00
83	Derek Jeter	3.00
84	Miguel Tejada/SP	3.00
85	Eric Chavez	.50
86	Tim Hudson	.50
87	Barry Zito	.50
88	Mark Mulder	.50
89	Erubiel Durazo	.25
90	Pat Burrell	.50
91	Jim Thome/SP	3.00
92	Bobby Abreu	.50
93	Brian Giles	.50
94	Reggie Sanders/SP	2.00
95	Kenny Lofton	.50
96	Ryan Klesko	.25
97	Sean Burroughs	.25
98	Edgardo Alfonzo	.25
99	Rich Aurilia	.25
100	Jose Cruz Jr.	.25
101	Barry Bonds/SP	8.00
102	Mike Cameron	.25
103	Kazuhiro Sasaki	.25
104	Bret Boone	.25
105	Ichiro Suzuki/SP	5.00
106	J.D. Drew	.50
107	Jim Edmonds	.50
108	Scott Rolen/SP	3.00
109	Matt Morris	.25
110	Tino Martinez	.25
111	Albert Pujols/SP	8.00
112	Damian Rolls	.25
113	Carl Crawford	.50
114	Rocco Baldelli/SP	2.00
115	Hank Blalock	.50
116	Alex Rodriguez/SP	5.00
117	Kevin Mench	.25
118	Rafael Palmeiro	.75
119	Mark Teixeira	.75
120	Shannon Stewart	.25
121	Vernon Wells	.50
122	Josh Phelps	.25
123	Eric Hinske	.25
124	Orlando Hudson	.25
125	Carlos Delgado/SP	3.00
126	Jason Roach **RC**	4.00
127	Dan Haren	10.00
128	Luis Ayala **RC**	4.00
129	Bo Hart **RC**	4.00
130	Wilfredo Ledezma **RC**	4.00
131	Rick Roberts **RC**	4.00
132	Miguel Ojeda **RC**	4.00
133	Aquilino Lopez **RC**	4.00
134	Roger Deago **RC**	4.00
135	Arnie Munoz **RC**	4.00
136	Brent Hoard **RC**	4.00
137	Terrmel Sledge **RC**	4.00
138	Ryan Cameron **RC**	4.00
139	Prentice Redman **RC**	4.00
140	Clint Barmes **RC**	5.00
141	Jeremy Griffiths	4.00
142	Jon Leicester **RC**	4.00
143	Brandon Webb **RC**	25.00
144	Todd Wellemeyer **RC**	6.00
145	Felix Sanchez **RC**	4.00
146	Anthony Ferrari **RC**	4.00
147	Ian Ferguson **RC**	4.00
148	Micheal Nakamura **RC**	4.00
149	Lew Ford **RC**	8.00
150	Nate Bland **RC**	4.00
151	Dave Matranga **RC**	4.00
152	Edgar Gonzalez **RC**	4.00
153	Carlos Mendez **RC**	4.00
154	Jason Gilfillan **RC**	4.00
155	Mike Neu **RC**	4.00
156	Jason Shiell **RC**	4.00
157	Jeff Duncan **RC**	4.00
158	Oscar Villarreal **RC**	4.00
159	Diegomar Markwell **RC**	4.00
160	Joe Valentine **RC**	4.00
161	Hideki Matsui/864 **RC**	275.00
162	Jose Contreras/800 **RC**	20.00
163	Willie Eyre **RC**	10.00
164	Matt Bruback **RC**	10.00
165	Rett Johnson **RC**	10.00
166	Jeremy Griffiths	10.00
167	Francisco Cruceta **RC**	10.00
168	Fernando Cabrera **RC**	10.00
169	Jhonny Peralta	25.00
170	Shane Bazzell **RC**	10.00
171	Bobby Madritsch **RC**	10.00
172	Phil Seibel **RC**	10.00
173	Josh Willingham **RC**	20.00
174	Robby Hammock **RC**	10.00
175	Alejandro Machado **RC**	10.00
176	David Sanders **RC**	10.00
177	Matt Kata **RC**	10.00
178	Heath Bell **RC**	8.00

Spectrum

Stars (1-125) print run 51-99:	3-6X
Stars (1-125) p/r 26-50:	6-12X
Print run 25 or less not priced.	
Numbered to jersey number.	
SP's (126-160):	.75-1.5X
Production 125	

SPX Combos

		NM/M
Common Duo:		20.00
Quantity produced listed		
MJ	Hideki Matsui, Derek Jeter/90	100.00
RC	Nolan Ryan, Roger Clemens/90	120.00
SJ	Curt Schilling, Randy Johnson/90	30.00
EG	Darin Erstad, Troy Glaus/90	20.00
GC	Greg Maddux, Chipper Jones/90	50.00
GS	Jason Giambi, Alfonso Soriano/90	30.00
BK	Jeff Bagwell, Jeff Kent/90	25.00
GD	Ken Griffey Jr., Adam Dunn/90	50.00
GR	Ken Griffey Jr., Sammy Sosa/90	50.00
SP	Sammy Sosa, Rafael Palmeiro/90	40.00
MG	Pedro Martinez, Nomar Garciaparra/90	40.00
RG	Alex Rodriguez, Nomar Garciaparra/90	40.00
CM	Jose Contreras, Pedro Martinez/90	40.00
FC	Carlton Fisk, Gary Carter/90	30.00
RR	Cal Ripken Jr., Scott Rolen/90	80.00
JJ	Chipper Jones, Andruw Jones/90	30.00
PM	Rafael Palmeiro, Fred McGriff/90	30.00
RT	Alex Rodriguez, Miguel Tejada/90	30.00
SB	Sammy Sosa, Barry Bonds/90	50.00
SN	Ichiro Suzuki, Hideo Nomo/90	175.00
MS	Hideki Matsui, Ichiro Suzuki/50	350.00
MW	Mickey Mantle, Ted Williams/50	300.00
CC	Jose Contreras, Roger Clemens/50	40.00
CL	Cal Ripken Jr., Lou Gehrig/90	300.00
HJ	Hideki Matsui, Jason Giambi/50	75.00
CA	Cal Ripken Jr., Alex Rodriguez/50	150.00
IA	Ichiro Suzuki, Albert Pujols/50	250.00
NI	Hideo Nomo, Kazuhisa Ishii/50	50.00
MD	Mickey Mantle, Derek Jeter/50	180.00
BT	Barry Bonds, Ted Williams/50	180.00
BM	Barry Bonds, Roger Maris/50	80.00
MB	Mickey Mantle, Barry Bonds/50	150.00
PS	Rafael Palmeiro, Sammy Sosa/90	40.00
RS	Nolan Ryan, Tom Seaver/90	110.00

Stars

		NM/M
Common Player:		20.00
Quantity produced listed		
LB	Lance Berkman/590	30.00
PB	Pat Burrell/590	25.00
NM	Nomar Garciaparra/195	80.00
JG	Jason Giambi/315	30.00
TG	Troy Glaus/490	25.00
LG	Luis Gonzalez/790	20.00
KG	Ken Griffey Jr./690	80.00
VG	Vladimir Guerrero/390	50.00
CJ	Chipper Jones/195	50.00
MP	Mark Prior/490	40.00
CS	Curt Schilling/490	40.00

Winning Materials

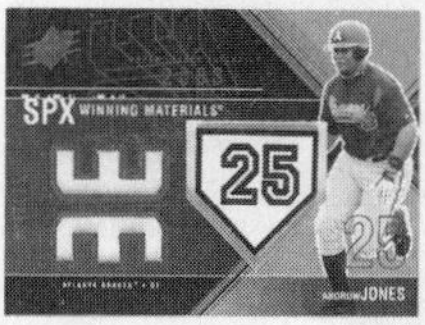

		NM/M
Common Player:		5.00
Version 1 Production 375		
Golds:		1X
Production 250		
Version 2 Production 175		
Golds:		1-2X
Production 50		
RA1	Roberto Alomar	8.00
RA2	Roberto Alomar	10.00
JB1	Jeff Bagwell	6.00
JB2	Jeff Bagwell	8.00
LB1	Lance Berkman	5.00
LB2	Lance Berkman	5.00
PB1	Pat Burrell	6.00
PB2	Pat Burrell	8.00
RC1	Roger Clemens	15.00
RC2	Roger Clemens	15.00
CD1	Carlos Delgado	6.00
CD2	Carlos Delgado	8.00
RF1	Rafael Furcal	6.00
RF2	Rafael Furcal	8.00
JG1	Jason Giambi	8.00
JG2	Jason Giambi	8.00
TR1	Troy Glaus	6.00
TG2	Troy Glaus	8.00
TG1	Tom Glavine	5.00
TG2	Tom Glavine	6.00
LG1	Luis Gonzalez	5.00
LG2	Luis Gonzalez	5.00
SG1	Shawn Green	5.00
SG2	Shawn Green	5.00
KG1	Ken Griffey Jr.	15.00
KG2	Ken Griffey Jr.	15.00
VG1	Vladimir Guerrero	10.00
VG2	Vladimir Guerrero	12.00
TO1	Todd Helton	8.00
TH2	Todd Helton	10.00
TH1	Torii Hunter	8.00
RJ1	Randy Johnson	10.00
RJ2	Randy Johnson	12.00
AJ1	Andruw Jones	8.00
AJ2	Andruw Jones	8.00
CJ1	Chipper Jones	10.00
CJ2	Chipper Jones	15.00
JK1	Jeff Kent	5.00
JK2	Jeff Kent	5.00
GM1	Greg Maddux	15.00
GM2	Greg Maddux	15.00
MM2	Mickey Mantle	120.00
PM1	Pedro Martinez	10.00
PM2	Pedro Martinez	15.00
HM1	Hideki Matsui	30.00
HM2	Hideki Matsui	30.00
HN1	Hideo Nomo	15.00
HN2	Hideo Nomo	20.00
MP1	Mike Piazza	10.00
MP2	Mike Piazza	15.00
MA1	Mark Prior	10.00
MP2	Mark Prior	10.00

AP1	Albert Pujols	20.00
AP2	Albert Pujols	20.00
MR1	Manny Ramirez	10.00
MR2	Manny Ramirez	10.00
AR1	Alex Rodriguez	10.00
AR2	Alex Rodriguez	12.00
IR1	Ivan Rodriguez	8.00
IR2	Ivan Rodriguez	10.00
CS1	Curt Schilling	8.00
CS2	Curt Schilling	10.00
GS1	Gary Sheffield	8.00
GS2	Gary Sheffield	8.00
AS1	Alfonso Soriano	10.00
AS2	Alfonso Soriano	12.00
SS1	Sammy Sosa	10.00
SS2	Sammy Sosa	15.00
IS1	Ichiro Suzuki	25.00
IS2	Ichiro Suzuki	35.00
MT1	Miguel Tejada	6.00
MT2	Miguel Tejada	8.00
FT1	Frank Thomas	8.00
FT2	Frank Thomas	10.00
JT1	Jim Thome	8.00
JT2	Jim Thome	10.00
BW1	Bernie Williams	8.00
BW2	Bernie Williams	10.00
TW2	Ted Williams	80.00
TW2	Ted Williams/Gold/50	200.00
BZ1	Barry Zito	6.00
BZ2	Barry Zito	8.00

Young Stars

		NM/M
Common Player:		8.00
Production 1,295 unless noted.		
KA	Kurt Ainsworth/1,460	8.00
RB	Rocco Baldelli	20.00
JBa	Josh Bard	8.00
HB	Hank Blalock	20.00
SB	Sean Burroughs	8.00
MD	Michael Cuddyer/1,156	10.00
AD	Adam Dunn	20.00
CG	Chris George/1,260	8.00
EH	Eric Hinske	8.00
JA	Jason Jennings	8.00
NJ	Nick Johnson	8.00
JJ	Jacque Jones/1,260	12.00
AK	Austin Kearns/964	15.00
MK	Mike Kinkade	8.00
BM	Brett Myers	8.00
RO	Roy Oswalt	15.00
JP	Josh Phelps	10.00
BP	Brandon Phillips	10.00
KS	Kirk Saarloos	8.00
MT	Mark Teixeira	25.00

2004 SP Authentic

		NM/M
Complete Set (191):		
Common (1-90):		.25
Common RC (91-132, 178-191):		
Production 999		
Common SP (133-177):		2.00
Production 999		
Pack (5):		5.00
Box (24):		100.00
1	Bret Boone	.25
2	Gary Sheffield	.50
3	Rafael Palmeiro	.75
4	Jorge Posada	.50
5	Derek Jeter	3.00
6	Garret Anderson	.50
7	Bartolo Colon	.40
8	Kevin Brown	.40
9	Shea Hillenbrand	.25
10	Ryan Klesko	.25
11	Bobby Abreu	.50
12	Scott Rolen	1.00

13	Alfonso Soriano	.75
14	Jason Giambi	1.00
15	Tom Glavine	.50
16	Hideo Nomo	.50
17	Johan Santana	.75
18	Sammy Sosa	1.00
19	Rickie Weeks	.50
20	Barry Zito	.50
21	Kerry Wood	.50
22	Austin Kearns	.40
23	Shawn Green	.40
24	Miguel Cabrera	1.00
25	Richard Hidalgo	.25
26	Andruw Jones	.75
27	Randy Wolf	.25
28	David Ortiz	1.00
29	Roy Oswalt	.50
30	Vernon Wells	.50
31	Ben Sheets	.50
32	Mike Lowell	.25
33	Todd Helton	.75
34	Jacque Jones	.25
35	Mike Sweeney	.25
36	Hank Blalock	.50
37	Jason Schmidt	.50
38	Jeff Kent	.40
39	Josh Beckett	.50
40	Manny Ramirez	1.00
41	Torii Hunter	.50
42	Brian Giles	.40
43	Javier Vazquez	.25
44	Jim Edmonds	.50
45	Dmitri Young	.25
46	Preston Wilson	.25
47	Jeff Bagwell	.75
48	Pedro J. Martinez	1.00
49	Eric Chavez	.40
50	Ken Griffey Jr.	2.00
51	Shannon Stewart	.25
52	Rafael Furcal	.40
53	Brandon Webb	.50
54	Juan Pierre	.25
55	Roger Clemens	2.00
56	Geoff Jenkins	.25
57	Lance Berkman	.50
58	Albert Pujols	3.00
59	Frank Thomas	.75
60	Edgar Martinez	.40
61	Tim Hudson	.50
62	Eric Gagne	.50
63	Richie Sexson	.50
64	Corey Patterson	.25
65	Nomar Garciaparra	1.00
66	Hideki Matsui	2.00
67	Mark Teixeira	.75
68	Troy Glaus	.50
69	Carlos Lee	.40
70	Mike Mussina	.75
71	Magglio Ordonez	.50
72	Roy Halladay	.50
73	Ichiro Suzuki	2.00
74	Randy Johnson	1.00
75	Luis Gonzalez	.40
76	Mark Prior	.75
77	Carlos Beltran	.50
78	Ivan Rodriguez	.75
79	Alex Rodriguez	2.50
80	Dontrelle Willis	.50
81	Mike Piazza	1.00
82	Curt Schilling	.75
83	Vladimir Guerrero	1.00
84	Greg Maddux	1.50
85	Jim Thome	1.00
86	Miguel Tejada	.50
87	Carlos Delgado	.50
88	Jose Reyes	.75
89	Matt Morris	.25
90	Mark Mulder	.40
91	Angel Chavez RC	4.00
92	Brandon Medders RC	4.00
93	Carlos Vasquez RC	4.00
94	Chris Aguila RC	4.00
95	Colby Miller RC	4.00
96	David Crouthers RC	4.00
97	Dennis Sarfate RC	4.00
98	Donnie Kelly RC	4.00
99	Merkin Valdez RC	6.00
100	Eddy Rodriguez RC	4.00
101	Edwin Moreno RC	4.00
102	Enemencio Pacheco RC	4.00
103	Roberto Novoa RC	4.00
104	Greg Dobbs RC	4.00
105	Hector Gimenez RC	4.00
106	Ian Snell RC	10.00
107	Jake Woods RC	4.00
108	Jamie Brown RC	4.00
109	Jason Frasor RC	4.00
110	Jerome Gamble RC	4.00
111	Jerry Gil RC	6.00
112	Jesse Harper RC	4.00
113	Jorge Vasquez RC	4.00
114	Jose Capellan RC	6.00
115	Josh Labandeira RC	4.00
116	Justin Hampson RC	4.00
117	Justin Huisman RC	4.00
118	Justin Leone RC	6.00
119	Lincoln Holdzkom RC	4.00
120	Lino Urdaneta RC	4.00
121	Mike Gosling RC	4.00
122	Mike Johnston RC	4.00
123	Mike Rouse RC	4.00
124	Scott Proctor RC	4.00
125	Roman Colon RC	4.00
126	Ronny Cedeno RC	6.00
127	Ryan Meaux RC	4.00

128	Scott Dohmann RC	4.00
129	Sean Henn RC	6.00
130	Tim Bausher RC	4.00
131	Tim Bittner RC	4.00
132	William Bergolla RC	6.00
133	Rick Ferrell	2.00
134	Joe DiMaggio	6.00
135	Bob Feller	2.00
136	Ted Williams	6.00
137	Stan Musial	5.00
138	Larry Doby	2.00
139	Red Schoendienst	2.00
140	Enos Slaughter	2.00
141	Stan Musial	5.00
142	Mickey Mantle	6.00
143	Ted Williams	6.00
144	Mickey Mantle	8.00
145	Stan Musial	5.00
146	Tom Seaver	3.00
147	Willie McCovey	2.00
148	Bob Gibson	3.00
149	Frank Robinson	3.00
150	Joe Morgan	2.00
151	Billy Williams	2.00
152	Catfish Hunter	2.00
153	Joe Morgan	2.00
154	Joe Morgan	2.00
155	Mike Schmidt	5.00
156	Tommy Lasorda	2.00
157	Robin Yount	4.00
158	Nolan Ryan	8.00
159	John Franco	2.00
160	Nolan Ryan	8.00
161	Ken Griffey Jr.	4.00
162	Cal Ripken Jr.	8.00
163	Ken Griffey Jr.	5.00
164	Gary Sheffield	2.00
165	Fred McGriff	2.00
166	Hideo Nomo	2.00
167	Mike Piazza	4.00
168	Sandy Alomar Jr.	2.00
169	Roberto Alomar	2.00
170	Ted Williams	6.00
171	Pedro J. Martinez	4.00
172	Derek Jeter	8.00
173	Cal Ripken Jr.	8.00
174	Torii Hunter	2.00
175	Alfonso Soriano	3.00
176	Hank Blalock	2.00
177	Ichiro Suzuki	4.00
178	Orlando Rodriguez RC	4.00
179	Ramon Ramirez RC	4.00
180	Kazuo Matsui RC	6.00
181	Kevin Cave RC	4.00
182	John Gall RC	4.00
183	Freddy Guzman RC	4.00
184	Chris Oxspring RC	4.00
185	Rusty Tucker RC	4.00
186	Jorge Sequea RC	4.00
187	Carlos Hines RC	4.00
188	Luis Gonzalez	4.00
189	Ryan Wing	4.00
190	Jeff Bennett RC	4.00
191	Luis Gonzalez	4.00

Silver

Stars (1-90):		2-4X
Production 499		
SP (91-132, 178-191):		1X
Production 249		

Gold

Stars (1-90):		4-8X
Gold SP (91-132, 178-191):		2X
Production 99		
Gold (133-177):		1-1.5X
Production 499		

Future Watch Autograph

		NM/M
Production 295		
91	Angel Chavez	8.00
92	Brandon Medders	8.00
93	Carlos Vasquez	8.00
94	Chris Aguila	8.00
95	Colby Miller	10.00
96	David Crouthers	10.00
97	Dennis Sarfate	8.00
98	Donnie Kelly	10.00
99	Merkin Valdez	15.00
100	Eddy Rodriguez	15.00
101	Edwin Moreno	10.00

LINCOLN HOLDZKOM
pitcher

102	Enemencio Pacheco	10.00
103	Roberto Novoa	8.00
104	Greg Dobbs	8.00
105	Hector Gimenez	8.00
106	Ian Snell	30.00
107	Jake Woods	10.00
108	Jamie Brown	8.00
109	Jason Frasor	10.00
110	Jerome Gamble	8.00
111	Jerry Gil	12.00
112	Jesse Harper	8.00
113	Jorge Vasquez	12.00
114	Jose Capellan	10.00
115	Josh Labandeira	10.00
116	Justin Hampson	8.00
117	Justin Huisman	8.00
118	Justin Leone	15.00
119	Lincoln Holdzkom	8.00
120	Lino Urdaneta	10.00
121	Mike Gosling	10.00
122	Mike Johnston	10.00
123	Mike Rouse	10.00
124	Scott Proctor	15.00
125	Roman Colon	10.00
126	Ronny Cedeno	15.00
127	Ryan Meaux	8.00
128	Scott Dohmann	8.00
129	Sean Henn	15.00
130	Tim Bausher	10.00
131	Tim Bittner	8.00
132	William Bergolla	10.00
178	Orlando Rodriguez	10.00
179	Ramon Ramirez	10.00
181	Kevin Cave	10.00
182	John Gall	15.00
183	Freddy Guzman	10.00
184	Chris Oxspring	10.00
185	Rusty Tucker	10.00
186	Jorge Sequea	10.00
187	Carlos Hines	8.00
188	Luis Gonzalez	10.00
189	Ryan Wing	10.00
190	Jeff Bennett	10.00
191	Luis Gonzalez	10.00

Chirography

		NM/M
Bronze:		1X
Production 65		
Bronze Duo Tone:		1X
Production 60		
Gold:		1-1.5X
Production 40		
Gold Duo Tone:		No Pricing
Production 20		
Silver:		1X
Production 60		
Silver Duo Tone:		1.5-2X
Production 30		
Duo Tone:		1X
Production 75		
AB	Bobby Abreu	15.00
GA	Garret Anderson	15.00
RB	Rocco Baldelli	20.00
JB	Josh Beckett	20.00
CB	Carlos Beltran	30.00
HB	Hank Blalock	20.00
BB	Bret Boone	20.00
MC	Miguel Cabrera	40.00
EC	Eric Chavez	20.00
DE	Dennis Eckersley	30.00
WE	Willie Eyre	8.00
EG	Eric Gagne	30.00
JG	Juan Gonzalez	20.00
KG	Ken Griffey Jr.	120.00
TH	Travis Hafner	15.00
HY	Roy Halladay	20.00
HA	Robby Hammock	10.00

BH Bo Hart 8.00
HE Runelvys Hernandez 8.00
HI Bobby Hill 10.00
DJ Derek Jeter 150.00
JJ Jacque Jones 15.00
AK Austin Kearns 15.00
CL Cliff Lee 15.00
AL Al Leiter 15.00
PL Paul LoDuca 15.00
JL Javy Lopez 15.00
ML Mike Lowell 15.00
EM Edgar Martinez 25.00
RO Roy Oswalt 20.00
PA Corey Patterson 15.00
PI Mike Piazza 125.00
CP Colin Porter 10.00
JP Jorge Posada 25.00
MP Mark Prior 30.00
HR Horacio Ramirez 15.00
JR Jose Reyes 35.00
CR Cal Ripken Jr. 100.00
JS Jae Weong Seo 15.00
BS Ben Sheets 20.00
SM John Smoltz 60.00
MT Mark Teixeira 25.00
JV Javier Vazquez 20.00
CW Chien-Ming Wang 125.00
RW Rickie Weeks 15.00
BW Brandon Webb 15.00
VW Vernon Wells 15.00
JW Jerome Williams 10.00
DW Dontrelle Willis 30.00
KW Kerry Wood 25.00
DY Delmon Young 20.00
BZ Barry Zito 20.00

Chirography Dual

NM/M

Common Duo: 40.00
Production 50 Sets
BC Bret Boone, Eric Chavez 50.00
BL Mike Lowell, Josh Beckett 50.00
BP Corey Patterson, Carlos Beltran 50.00
BT Hank Blalock, Mark Teixeira 50.00
EG Dennis Eckersley, Eric Gagne 50.00
HW Vernon Wells, Roy Halladay 40.00
JM Johnny Bench, Mike Piazza 200.00
KG Ken Griffey Jr., Austin Kearns 100.00
PB Yogi Berra, Jorge Posada 100.00
RR Alex Rodriguez, Cal Ripken Jr. 400.00
SG Ken Griffey Jr., Ichiro Suzuki 375.00
SM Stan Musial, Ozzie Smith 175.00
WC Miguel Cabrera, Dontrelle Willis 70.00
WJ Chien-Ming Wang, Derek Jeter 350.00
WR Nolan Ryan, Kerry Wood 225.00
WW Dontrelle Willis, Brandon Webb 50.00
YW Delmon Young, Rickie Weeks 40.00
ZC Eric Chavez, Barry Zito 50.00

Chirography Quad

No Pricing
Production 10 Sets

Chirography Triple

NM/M

Production 25 Sets
BWR Kerry Wood, Nolan Ryan, Josh Beckett 250.00
FBB Johnny Bench, Carlton Fisk, Yogi Berra 300.00
GSM Bob Gibson, Stan Musial, Ozzie Smith 220.00
JVB Derek Jeter, Yogi Berra, Javier Vazquez 250.00
PRC Jose Reyes, Miguel Cabrera, Colin Porter 100.00
RBT Hank Blalock, Mark Teixeira, Alex Rodriguez 250.00
RRR Alex Rodriguez, Cal Ripken Jr., Phil Rizzuto 400.00
SJB Rocco Baldelli, Jacque Jones, Ichiro Suzuki 275.00
WLE Chien-Ming Wang, Willie Eyre, Cliff Lee 275.00
WPB Mark Prior, Josh Beckett, Brandon Webb 250.00
YYM Robin Yount, Carl Yastrzemski, Stan Musial 300.00
ZHO Barry Zito, Roy Oswalt, Roy Halladay 200.00

Chirography Hall of Famers

NM/M

Production 40 Sets
Duo Tone: No Pricing
Production 25
LA Luis Aparicio 20.00
JB Johnny Bench 60.00
YB Yogi Berra 50.00
BD Bobby Doerr 30.00
DE Dennis Eckersley 30.00
CF Carlton Fisk 30.00
BG Bob Gibson 40.00
MI Monte Irvin 20.00
AK Al Kaline 50.00
HK Harmon Killebrew 65.00
RK Ralph Kiner 25.00
PM Paul Molitor 30.00
SM Stan Musial 100.00
TP Tony Perez 30.00
KP Kirby Puckett 100.00
PR Phil Rizzuto 40.00
RR Robin Roberts 40.00
BR Brooks Robinson 40.00
NR Nolan Ryan 120.00
MS Mike Schmidt 120.00
TS Tom Seaver 40.00
OS Ozzie Smith 65.00
DS Duke Snider 30.00
CY Carl Yastrzemski 75.00
RY Robin Yount 75.00

USA Signature

NM/M

Production 445 Sets
Reds: 1.5X
Production 50
USA-1 Ernie Young 6.00
USA-2 Chris Burke 12.00
USA-3 Jesse Crain 15.00
USA-4 Justin Duchscherer 15.00
USA-5 J.D. Durbin 10.00
USA-6 Gerald Laird 10.00
USA-7 John Grabow 8.00
USA-8 Gabe Gross 15.00
USA-9 J.J. Hardy 15.00
USA-10 Jeremy Reed 15.00
USA-11 Graham Koonce 10.00
USA-12 Mike Lamb 10.00
USA-13 Justin Leone 15.00
USA-14 Ryan Madson 12.00
USA-15 Joe Mauer 40.00
USA-16 Todd Williams 6.00
USA-17 Horacio Ramirez 15.00
USA-18 Mike Rouse 15.00
USA-19 Jason Stanford 10.00
USA-20 John Van Benschoten 10.00
USA-21 Grady Sizemore 40.00

2004 SP Game-Used Patch

NM/M

Complete Set (119):
Common (1-60): 2.00
Common (61-90): 2.00
Quantity produced listed
Common (91-119): 6.00
Production 375
Box (1:Pack): 125.00
1 Miguel Cabrera 4.00
2 Alex Rodriguez 10.00
3 Edgar Renteria 2.50
4 Juan Gonzalez 2.50
5 Mike Lowell 2.50
6 Andruw Jones 3.00
7 Eric Chavez 2.00
8 Jim Edmonds 2.00
9 Mike Piazza 5.00
10 Angel Berroa 2.00
11 Eric Gagne 3.00
12 Jody Gerut 2.00
13 Orlando Cabrera 2.00
14 Austin Kearns 2.00
15 Frank Thomas 3.00
16 Johan Santana 3.00
17 Randy Johnson 4.00
18 Preston Wilson 2.00
19 Garret Anderson 2.50
20 Jorge Posada 3.00
21 Rich Harden 2.00
22 Barry Zito 2.50
23 Gary Sheffield 3.00
24 Jose Reyes 3.00
25 Roy Halladay 2.00
26 Ben Sheets 2.00
27 Geoff Jenkins 2.00
28 Josh Beckett 3.00
29 Roy Oswalt 2.50
30 Bobby Abreu 2.50
31 Hank Blalock 2.50
32 Kerry Wood 2.50
33 Ryan Klesko 2.00
34 Rafael Furcal 2.00
35 Tom Glavine 2.50
36 Kevin Brown 2.50
37 Scott Rolen 3.00
38 Bret Boone 2.50
39 Ichiro Suzuki 6.00
40 Lance Berkman 3.00
41 Tim Hudson 2.50
42 Carlos Delgado 3.00
43 Ivan Rodriguez 3.00
44 Luis Gonzalez 2.00
45 Torii Hunter 2.00
46 Carlos Lee 2.00
47 Jacque Jones 2.00
48 Manny Ramirez 3.00
49 Troy Glaus 2.50
50 Corey Patterson 2.00
51 Jason Schmidt 2.50
52 Mark Mulder 2.00
53 Vernon Wells 2.00
54 Curt Schilling 4.00
55 Javy Lopez 2.50
56 Mark Prior 3.00
57 Dontrelle Willis 2.50
58 Derek Jeter 10.00
59 Jeff Bagwell 3.00
60 Marlon Byrd 2.00
61 Rafael Palmeiro/500 3.00
62 Kevin Millwood/165 2.00
63 Greg Maddux/273 6.00
64 Adam Dunn/400 3.00
65 Richie Sexson/469 3.00
66 Magglio Ordonez/567 2.00
67 Hideo Nomo/236 2.00
68 Albert Pujols/194 10.00
69 Rocco Baldelli/368 3.00
70 Mark Teixeira/86 4.00
71 Jason Giambi/660 3.00
72 Alfonso Soriano/230 4.00
73 Roger Clemens/300 8.00
74 Miguel Tejada/359 2.00
75 Jeff Kent/684 2.00
76 Bernie Williams/342 3.00
77 Sammy Sosa/470 6.00
78 Mike Mussina/641 3.00
79 Jim Thome/334 4.00
80 Brian Giles/506 2.00
81 Shawn Green/234 2.00
82 Mike Sweeney/340 2.00
83 John Smoltz/262 3.00
84 Carlos Beltran/319 3.00
85 Todd Helton/384 3.00
86 Nomar Garciaparra/372 4.00
87 Ken Griffey Jr./481 8.00
88 Chipper Jones/633 4.00
89 Vladimir Guerrero/226 4.00
90 Pedro Martinez/313 5.00
91 Brandon Medders **RC** 6.00
92 Colby Miller **RC** 6.00
93 David Crouthers 6.00
94 Dennis Sarfate **RC** 8.00
95 Donald Kelly **RC** 6.00
96 Alec Zumwalt **RC** 6.00
97 Chris Aguila **RC** 6.00
98 Greg Dobbs **RC** 6.00
99 Ian Snell **RC** 10.00
100 Jake Woods 6.00
101 Jamie Brown **RC** 6.00
102 Jason Frasor **RC** 6.00
103 Jerome Gamble **RC** 6.00
104 Jesse Harper **RC** 6.00
105 Josh Labandeira **RC** 6.00
106 Justin Hampson **RC** 6.00
107 Justin Huisman **RC** 6.00
108 Justin Leone **RC** 6.00
109 Lincoln Holdzkom **RC** 6.00
110 Mike Bumatay **RC** 6.00
111 Mike Gosling 6.00
112 Mike Johnston **RC** 6.00
113 Mike Rouse 6.00
114 Nick Regilio **RC** 6.00
115 Ryan Meaux **RC** 6.00
116 Scott Dohmann **RC** 6.00
117 Sean Henn 8.00
118 Tim Bausher **RC** 6.00
119 Tim Bittner **RC** 6.00

All-Star Patch Autograph

Production 10 Sets
No Pricing

All-Star Patch Auto-Dual

Production 10 Sets
No Pricing

All-Star Patch Gold

NM/M

Production 50 Sets
AP Albert Pujols 75.00
AR Alex Rodriguez 50.00
AS Alfonso Soriano 25.00
BZ Barry Zito 25.00
CD Carlos Delgado 20.00
CJ Chipper Jones 30.00
CS Curt Schilling 35.00
DJ Derek Jeter 85.00
EC Eric Chavez 20.00
FT Frank Thomas 30.00
GS Gary Sheffield 20.00
HE Todd Helton 25.00
HN Hideo Nomo 50.00
IS Ichiro Suzuki 80.00
JG Juan Gonzalez 20.00
JT Jim Thome 30.00

KG Ken Griffey Jr. 50.00
MP Mark Prior 30.00
SS Sammy Sosa 40.00
TH Tim Hudson 25.00
VW Vernon Wells 20.00

All-Star Patch Number

NM/M

Quantity produced listed
AJ Andruw Jones/25 30.00
AP Andy Pettitte/46 25.00
BZ Barry Zito/50 30.00
CD Carlos Delgado/25 25.00
CS Curt Schilling/38 30.00
FT Frank Thomas/35 40.00
GM Greg Maddux/31 50.00
IS Ichiro Suzuki/50 65.00
JG Juan Gonzalez/19 35.00
JP Jorge Posada/20 30.00
JT Jim Thome/25 30.00
KG Ken Griffey Jr./30 60.00
MM Mike Mussina/35 30.00
MO Magglio Ordonez/30 25.00
PM Pedro Martinez/45 35.00
RC Roger Clemens/22 50.00
RH Roy Halladay/32 25.00
RP Rafael Palmeiro/25 30.00
SG Shawn Green/15 30.00
SR Scott Rolen/27 35.00
SS Sammy Sosa/21 80.00

Famous Nicknames

NM/M

Quantity produced listed
BR Brooks Robinson/23 25.00
CR Cal Ripken Jr./21 140.00
CY Carl Yastrzemski/23 70.00
DM Don Mattingly/14 50.00
DS Darryl Strawberry/17 25.00
ES Duke Snider/18 45.00
FT Frank Thomas/14 40.00
GA Sparky Anderson/27 25.00
GC Gary Carter/19 30.00
HK Harmon Killebrew/22 50.00
JF Nellie Fox/19 120.00
JG Juan Gonzalez/15 35.00
JH "Catfish" Hunter/15 35.00
KG Ken Griffey Jr./15 80.00
LB Yogi Berra/19 50.00
MM Mike Mussina/13 35.00
NR Nolan Ryan/27 60.00
OC Orlando Cepeda/17 25.00
OS Ozzie Smith/19 60.00
PN Phil Niekro/24 25.00
RC Roger Clemens/20 60.00
RI Phil Rizzuto/13 50.00
RJ Randy Johnson/16 40.00
RY Robin Yount/20 40.00
TS Tom Seaver/20 60.00
SM Stan Musial/22 85.00
SS Sammy Sosa/15 50.00
WS Willie Stargell/21 40.00

Famous Nicknames Autograph

NM/M

Production 50 Sets
AD Andre Dawson 45.00
AR Alex Rodriguez 150.00
BM Bill Mazeroski 65.00
BR Brooks Robinson 60.00
DM Don Mattingly 120.00
FT Frank Thomas 70.00
HK Harmon Killebrew 70.00
HM Hideki Matsui 350.00
JB Jeff Bagwell 80.00
JG Juan Gonzalez 50.00
KG Ken Griffey Jr. 160.00
LJ Chipper Jones 80.00
MM Mike Mussina 60.00
NR Nolan Ryan 125.00
OS Ozzie Smith 90.00
PN Phil Niekro 45.00
RC Roger Clemens 150.00
RY Robin Yount 80.00
TS Tom Seaver 65.00
WI Dontrelle Willis 60.00

Hall of Fame Numbers

NM/M

Quantity produced listed
AJ Andruw Jones/25 30.00

BG Bob Gibson/45 35.00
BW Billy Williams/26 20.00
CD Carlos Delgado/25 25.00
CH Jim "Catfish" Hunter/27 40.00
CL Roger Clemens/22 50.00
CS Curt Schilling/38 25.00
DD Don Drysdale/50 35.00
DS Don Sutton/20 25.00
EG Eric Gagne/38 25.00
EM Eddie Mathews/41 50.00
FR Frank Robinson/20 25.00
FT Frank Thomas/35 40.00
GL Tom Glavine/47 25.00
GM Greg Maddux/31 45.00
GO Juan Gonzalez/35 35.00
GP Gaylord Perry/36 25.00
HE Todd Helton/17 35.00
IS Ichiro Suzuki/50 65.00
JC Jose Canseco/33 25.00
JG Jason Giambi/25 30.00
JI Jim Thome/25 30.00
JP Jim Palmer/22 35.00
KG Ken Griffey Jr./30 60.00
MA Juan Marichal/27 25.00
MP Mike Piazza/31 40.00
MR Manny Ramirez/24 30.00
MS Mike Schmidt/20 60.00
MZ Pedro Martinez/45 25.00
NR Nolan Ryan/34 70.00
OC Orlando Cepeda/30 20.00
PI Mark Prior/22 40.00
RC Roberto Clemente/21 200.00
RF Rollie Fingers/34 25.00
RH Rickey Henderson/25 40.00
RP Rafael Palmeiro/25 30.00
RY Robin Yount/19 45.00
SC Steve Carlton/32 30.00
SG Shawn Green/15 25.00
SR Scott Rolen/27 30.00
SS Sammy Sosa/21 50.00
TG Tony Gwynn/19 45.00
TH Tim Hudson/15 25.00
TS Tom Seaver/41 25.00
WB Wade Boggs/26 30.00
WS Warren Spahn/21 65.00

Hall of Fame Numbers Autograph

Production 10 Sets
No Pricing

Hall of Fame Numbers Autograph Dual

Production 10 Sets
No Pricing

Historic Cut Signatures

Production One Set
No Pricing

Legendary Fabrics

NM/M

Production 50 unless noted. 20.00
BE Johnny Bench 25.00
BG Bob Gibson 30.00
BW Billy Williams 25.00
CH "Catfish" Hunter 25.00
CR Cal Ripken Jr. 60.00
CY Carl Yastrzemski/31 45.00
EM Eddie Mathews 35.00
FR Frank Robinson 25.00
GP Gaylord Perry 20.00
HK Harmon Killebrew 40.00
JC Jose Canseco 40.00
JM Joe Morgan 20.00
JT Joe Torre 25.00
LA Luis Aparicio 25.00
LD Leo Durocher 30.00
MS Mike Schmidt 40.00
NR Nolan Ryan 50.00
OC Orlando Cepeda 20.00
OS Ozzie Smith 35.00
PO Paul O'Neill 20.00
RF Rollie Fingers 20.00
RY Robin Yount 35.00
SC Steve Carlton 25.00
TS Tom Seaver 30.00
WS Warren Spahn 40.00

Legendary Fabrics Autograph Dual

NM/M

Production 25 unless noted.
AD Andre Dawson 60.00
BE Johnny Bench 90.00
BR Brooks Robinson 90.00
BW Billy Williams 65.00
CR Cal Ripken Jr. 275.00
CY Carl Yastrzemski/17 125.00
DE Dwight Evans 60.00
DM Don Mattingly 150.00
DS Don Sutton 65.00
FL Fred Lynn 70.00
FR Frank Robinson 75.00
GP Gaylord Perry 40.00
HK Harmon Killebrew 100.00
JC Jose Canseco 100.00
JM Joe Morgan 50.00
JP Jim Palmer 60.00
JT Joe Torre 70.00
KP Kirby Puckett 100.00
LA Luis Aparicio 70.00
LB Lou Brock/13 125.00
NR Nolan Ryan 200.00
OC Orlando Cepeda 50.00
OS Ozzie Smith 100.00
PM Paul Molitor 75.00
PO Paul O'Neill 70.00
RC Roger Clemens 150.00
RF Rollie Fingers 65.00
RY Robin Yount 120.00
SG Steve Garvey 60.00
ST Darryl Strawberry 65.00
TG Tony Gwynn 120.00
TS Tom Seaver 85.00
WB Wade Boggs 100.00
WI Maury Wills 50.00

Legendary Combo Cuts

Production One Set
No Pricing

Logo Threads

No Pricing
Production One Set

Logo Threads Autograph

No Pricing
Production One Set

Masters

NM/M

Quantity produced listed
AJ Andruw Jones/25 25.00
BE Josh Beckett/25 40.00
CD Carlos Delgado/25 25.00
CS Curt Schilling/38 25.00
FT Frank Thomas/35 30.00
GM Greg Maddux/31 45.00
GO Juan Gonzalez/19 30.00
HE Todd Helton/17 35.00
IS Ichiro Suzuki/50 65.00
JG Jason Giambi/25 30.00
JP Jorge Posada/20 30.00
JT Jim Thome/25 30.00
KG Ken Griffey Jr./30 60.00
MO Magglio Ordonez/30 20.00
MP Mark Prior/22 40.00
MR Manny Ramirez/24 25.00
PI Mike Piazza/31 40.00
PM Pedro Martinez/45 25.00
RC Roger Clemens/22 50.00
RH Roy Halladay/32 25.00
SG Shawn Green/15 25.00
SR Scott Rolen/27 30.00
SS Sammy Sosa/21 50.00
TH Tim Hudson/15 25.00

MVP Patch

NM/M

Production 25 Sets
AR Alex Rodriguez 60.00
BR Brooks Robinson 50.00
BW Bernie Williams 35.00
CJ Chipper Jones 40.00
CR Cal Ripken Jr. 90.00
CS Curt Schilling 35.00
DJ Derek Jeter 75.00
FT Frank Thomas 40.00
GA Garret Anderson 30.00
IS Ichiro Suzuki 75.00
IV Ivan Rodriguez 40.00
JB Josh Beckett 30.00
JG Jason Giambi 30.00
KG Ken Griffey Jr. 60.00
MP Mike Piazza 50.00
MT Miguel Tejada 40.00
PM Pedro Martinez 45.00
RC Roger Clemens 60.00
RJ Randy Johnson 40.00
SS Sammy Sosa 40.00
TG Troy Glaus 25.00

Premium Patch

NM/M

Production 50 unless noted.
AD Adam Dunn 30.00
AP Albert Pujols 50.00
AR Alex Rodriguez 50.00
AR1 Alex Rodriguez/Yankees 65.00
AS Alfonso Soriano/34 35.00
BE Josh Beckett 25.00
BW Bernie Williams 25.00
BZ Barry Zito 25.00
CD Carlos Delgado 25.00

CJ Chipper Jones 35.00
CS Curt Schilling 25.00
DJ Derek Jeter 60.00
DW Dontrelle Willis 20.00
EC Eric Chavez 20.00
FT Frank Thomas 40.00
GM Greg Maddux 40.00
GO Juan Gonzalez 25.00
HM Hideki Matsui/17 120.00
IR Ivan Rodriguez 30.00
IS Ichiro Suzuki 65.00
JB Jeff Bagwell 30.00
JG Jason Giambi 30.00
JP Jorge Posada 30.00
JT Jim Thome 30.00
KB Kevin Brown 20.00
KG Ken Griffey Jr. 50.00
MO Magglio Ordonez 20.00
MP Mark Prior 30.00
MR Manny Ramirez 30.00
MT Miguel Tejada 20.00
PI Mike Piazza 35.00
NR Nolan Ryan 50.00
PM Pedro Martinez 30.00
RC Roger Clemens 40.00
RH Roy Halladay 20.00
RI Mariano Rivera 30.00
RJ Randy Johnson 30.00
RP Rafael Palmeiro 30.00
SG Shawn Green 20.00
SR Scott Rolen 30.00
SS Sammy Sosa 35.00
TE Mark Teixeira 20.00
TG Tom Glavine 25.00
TH Tim Hudson 25.00

Premium Patch Autograph

NM/M

Production 50 unless noted.
AK Austin Kearns 45.00
AR Alex Rodriguez 150.00
BZ Barry Zito 60.00
CD Carlos Delgado 50.00
DW Dontrelle Willis 60.00
EC Eric Chavez 40.00
EG Eric Gagne 60.00
HM Hideki Matsui 350.00
IR Ivan Rodriguez 80.00
IS Ichiro Suzuki 300.00
KB Kevin Brown 45.00
KG Ken Griffey Jr. 160.00
MP Mark Prior 60.00
MT Miguel Tejada 50.00
NG Nomar Garciaparra/33 140.00
RC Roger Clemens 150.00
SG Shawn Green 50.00
TH Tim Hudson 50.00
TG Troy Glaus 50.00
VG Vladimir Guerrero 75.00

Significant Numbers

NM/M

Quantity produced listed
CR Cal Ripken Jr./21 120.00
CS Curt Schilling/16 40.00
CY Carl Yastrzemski/23 65.00
DS Darryl Strawberry/17 25.00
EM Eddie Mathews/17 50.00
FT Frank Thomas/14 50.00
GM Greg Maddux/18 50.00
GO Juan Gonzalez/15 40.00
GS Gary Sheffield/16 30.00
JB Jeff Bagwell/13 50.00
KG Ken Griffey Jr./15 75.00
NR Nolan Ryan/27 60.00
PO Paul O'Neill/17 25.00
RC Roger Clemens/20 50.00
RF Rollie Fingers/17 25.00
RJ Randy Johnson/16 35.00
RP Rafael Palmeiro/18 40.00
SN Duke Snider/18 50.00
SS Sammy Sosa/15 60.00
TG Tom Glavine/17 30.00
TS Tom Seaver/20 40.00

Significant Numbers Autograph

NM/M

Production 50 unless noted.
AR Alex Rodriguez 150.00
BA Bobby Abreu 40.00
BG Brian Giles 40.00
BW Bernie Williams 100.00
BZ Barry Zito 60.00
CD Carlos Delgado 50.00
CJ Chipper Jones 90.00
EC Eric Chavez 40.00
EG Eric Gagne 60.00
GM Greg Maddux 110.00
HE Todd Helton 60.00
GO Juan Gonzalez 50.00
HM Hideki Matsui 350.00
KB Kevin Brown 45.00
KG Ken Griffey Jr. 160.00
LB Lou Brock/16 60.00
LG Luis Gonzalez 50.00
MM Mike Mussina 60.00
MP Mike Piazza 185.00
MS Mike Schmidt 90.00
MT Miguel Tejada 50.00
NR Nolan Ryan 140.00
PB Pat Burrell 40.00
PO Paul O'Neill 65.00
PR Mark Prior 60.00
RA Roberto Alomar 60.00
RB Rocco Baldelli 55.00
RF Rollie Fingers 40.00
RO Roy Oswalt 60.00
RP Rafael Palmeiro 70.00
RS Ryne Sandberg 90.00
SG Shawn Green 50.00
TG Tom Glavine 60.00
TH Tim Hudson 50.00
VG Vladimir Guerrero 75.00

Significant Numbers Autograph Dual

NM/M

Production 25 unless noted.
AR Alex Rodriguez 200.00
BA Bobby Abreu 50.00
BG Brian Giles 50.00
BW Bernie Williams 120.00
BZ Barry Zito 80.00
CD Carlos Delgado 70.00
CJ Chipper Jones 100.00
DW Dontrelle Willis 60.00
EC Eric Chavez 65.00
EG Eric Gagne 80.00
GI Bob Gibson 100.00
GL Troy Glaus 70.00
GM Greg Maddux 140.00
HE Todd Helton 85.00
GO Juan Gonzalez 60.00
HM Hideki Matsui 500.00
KB Kevin Brown 65.00
KG Ken Griffey Jr. 200.00
KP Kirby Puckett 100.00
LB Lou Brock/14 85.00
LG Luis Gonzalez 50.00
MM Mike Mussina 80.00
MP Mike Piazza 200.00
MS Mike Schmidt 160.00
MT Miguel Tejada 50.00
NR Nolan Ryan 200.00
PB Pat Burrell 50.00
PO Paul O'Neill 80.00
RA Roberto Alomar 80.00
RF Rollie Fingers 65.00
RP Rafael Palmeiro 100.00
RS Ryne Sandberg 150.00
SG Shawn Green 60.00
TG Tom Glavine 80.00
TH Tim Hudson 75.00
VG Vladimir Guerrero 100.00
TO Tony Gwynn 120.00
TS Tom Seaver 85.00

Star Potential Patch

NM/M

Quantity produced listed
BW Brandon Webb/50 25.00
CP Corey Patterson/20 25.00
DW Dontrelle Willis/35 30.00
HA Roy Halladay/32 30.00
IS Ichiro Suzuki/50 65.00
HB Josh Beckett/21 30.00
LB Lance Berkman/17 30.00
MM Mark Mulder/20 30.00
MP Mark Prior/22 30.00
MT Mark Teixeira/23 25.00
RH Rich Harden/40 25.00
RO Roy Oswalt/44 25.00
RW Rickie Weeks/23 20.00
TG Troy Glaus/25 30.00
TH Tim Hudson/15 30.00

Stellar Combos

NM/M

Production 25 unless noted.

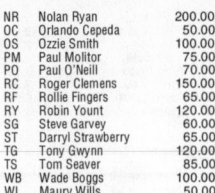

AD	Derek Jeter,	
	Alfonso Soriano,	75.00
AJ	Alex Rodriguez,	
	Juan Gonzalez,	50.00
AT	Jim Thome,	
	Bobby Abreu	40.00
BK	Jeff Bagwell, Jeff Kent	30.00
BT	Mark Teixeira,	
	Hank Blalock	40.00
CA	Roberto Alomar,	
	Joe Carter	60.00
CO	Roger Clemens,	
	Roy Oswalt	40.00
CR	Randy Johnson,	
	Curt Schilling	40.00
DG	Jason Giambi,	
	Carlos Delgado	40.00
DK	Austin Kearns,	
	Adam Dunn	40.00
GH	Eric Gagne,	
	Trevor Hoffman	40.00
GT	Greg Maddux,	
	Tom Glavine	65.00
JJ	Andruw Jones,	
	Chipper Jones	50.00
KR	Nolan Ryan,	
	Jerry Koosman	100.00
LP	Mike Piazza, Al Leiter	50.00
LS	Fred Lynn, Ichiro Suzuki	75.00
MG	Don Mattingly,	
	Jason Giambi	80.00
MT	Frank Thomas,	
	Edgar Martinez	50.00
MY	Paul Molitor,	
	Robin Yount	60.00
NB	Hideo Nomo,	
	Kevin Brown	40.00
NY	Alfonso Soriano,	
	Jose Reyes	40.00
PC	Mark Prior,	
	Roger Clemens	60.00
PE	Albert Pujols,	
	Jim Edmonds	80.00
PM	Mike Mussina,	
	Andy Pettitte	50.00
PP	Mike Piazza,	
	Jorge Posada	60.00
PS	Sammy Sosa,	
	Rafael Palmeiro	50.00
RB	Ivan Rodriguez,	
	Josh Beckett	50.00
RJ	Alex Rodriguez,	
	Derek Jeter	100.00
RR	Alex Rodriguez,	
	Cal Ripken Jr.	180.00
RS	Mike Schmidt,	
	Brooks Robinson	85.00
SG	Shawn Green, Duke Snider	40.00
SJ	Randy Johnson,	
	Gary Sheffield	40.00
SM	Pedro Martinez,	
	Curt Schilling	50.00
SR	Nolan Ryan, Curt Schilling	75.00
TO	Frank Thomas,	
	Magglio Ordonez	60.00
WC	Roger Clemens,	
	David Wells	50.00
WH	Larry Walker, Todd Helton	45.00
WS	Sammy Sosa,	
	Billy Williams	60.00
ZH	Barry Zito, Tim Hudson	50.00
RJ	Alex Rodriguez,	
	Derek Jeter	100.00
RG	Cal Ripken Jr.,	
	Lou Gehrig	350.00
SC	Ty Cobb, Ichiro Suzuki	180.00

Team Threads
Production 10 unless noted.
No Pricing

Triple Authentic
Production 10
No Pricing

World Series Stars
		NM/M
Production 50 unless noted.		
AJ	Andruw Jones	25.00
AP	Andy Pettitte/15	40.00
AS	Alfonso Soriano/15	40.00
BL	Barry Larkin	25.00
BW	Bernie Williams	25.00
CA	Jose Canseco	30.00
CJ	Chipper Jones	30.00
CS	Curt Schilling	25.00
CY	Carl Yastrzemski/31	50.00
DW	Dontrelle Willis	20.00
GA	Garret Anderson	25.00
GL	Troy Glaus	30.00
GM	Greg Maddux	40.00
HM	Hideki Matsui/17	140.00
IR	Ivan Rodriguez	30.00
JB	Josh Beckett	25.00
JE	Derek Jeter	60.00
JM	Joe Morgan	25.00
JP	Jorge Posada	30.00
JT	Jim Thome	25.00
KB	Kevin Brown	20.00
MM	Mike Mussina/43	25.00
MP	Mike Piazza	35.00
MR	Mariano Rivera	30.00
MS	Mike Schmidt	40.00
PM	Paul Molitor	30.00
PO	Paul O'Neill	20.00

RC	Roger Clemens	40.00
RF	Rollie Fingers	25.00
RJ	Randy Johnson	30.00
TG	Tom Glavine	25.00

World Series Stars Autograph
No Pricing
Production One Set

300 Win Club
Production 10 Sets
No Pricing

Autographed 300 Win Club
Production 10 Sets
No Pricing

3000 Hit Club
Production 10 Sets
No Pricing

3000 Hit Club Autograph
Production 10 Sets
No Pricing

500 HR Club
Production 10 Sets
No Pricing

Autographed 500 HR Club
Production 10 Sets
No Pricing

500 HR Club Triple Patches
Production 10 Sets
No Pricing

2004 SP Legendary Cuts

		NM/M
Complete Set (126):		
Common Player:		.40
Pack (4):		12.00
Box (12):		120.00
1	Al Kaline	1.00
2	Al Lopez	.40
3	Alan Trammell	.40
4	Andre Dawson	.40
5	Babe Ruth	3.00
6	Bert Campaneris	.40
7	Bill Mazeroski	.40
8	Bill Russell	.40
9	Billy Williams	.40
10	Bob Feller	.50
11	Bob Gibson	.75
12	Bob Lemon	.40
13	Bobby Doerr	.40
14	Brooks Robinson	1.00
15	Cal Ripken Jr.	3.00
16	Carl Yastrzemski	1.00
17	Carlton Fisk	.40
18	Jim "Catfish" Hunter	.40
19	Dale Murphy	.40
20	Darryl Strawberry	.40
21	Dave Concepcion	.40
22	Dave Winfield	.50
23	Dennis Eckersley	.40
24	Denny McLain	.40
25	Don Drysdale	.50
26	Don Larsen	.50
27	Don Mattingly	2.00
28	Don Sutton	.40
29	Duke Snider	1.00
30	Dusty Baker	.40
31	Dwight Gooden	.40
32	Earl Weaver	.40
33	Early Wynn	.40
34	Eddie Mathews	1.00
35	Eddie Murray	.75
36	Enos Slaughter	.40
37	Ernie Banks	1.50
38	Fergie Jenkins	.40
39	Frank Robinson	.75
40	Fred Lynn	.40
41	Gary Carter	.50
42	Gaylord Perry	.40
43	George Brett	2.00
44	George Foster	.40
45	George Kell	.40
46	Greg Luzinski	.40
47	Hal Newhouser	.40
48	Hank Greenberg	1.00
49	Harmon Killebrew	1.00
50	Honus Wagner	1.00

51	Hoyt Wilhelm	.40
52	Jackie Robinson	1.50
53	Jim Bunning	.40
54	Jim Palmer	.75
55	Jimmie Foxx	1.00
56	Joe Carter	.40
57	Joe DiMaggio	2.00
58	Joe Morgan	.40
59	Joe Torre	.40
60	Johnny Bench	1.00
61	Johnny Podres	.40
62	John Roseboro	.40
63	Johnny Sain	.40
64	Juan Marichal	.50
65	Keith Hernandez	.40
66	Kirby Puckett	.75
67	Kirk Gibson	.40
68	Will Clark	.50
69	Jim Rice	.40
70	Larry Doby	.40
71	Lou Boudreau	.40
72	Lou Brock	.50
73	Lou Gehrig	2.50
74	Lou Piniella	.40
75	Luis Aparicio	.40
76	Mark Grace	.50
77	Mel Ott	.40
78	Mickey Lolich	.40
79	Mickey Mantle	3.00
80	Mike Greenwell	.40
81	Mike Schmidt	2.00
82	Monte Irvin	.40
83	Nellie Fox	.50
84	Nolan Ryan	3.00
85	Orlando Cepeda	.40
86	Ozzie Smith	1.00
87	Paul Molitor	.75
88	Pee Wee Reese	.40
89	Phil Niekro	.40
90	Phil Rizzuto	.75
91	Ralph Kiner	.75
92	Red Rolfe	.40
93	Red Schoendienst	.40
94	Reggie Smith	.40
95	Rich "Goose" Gossage	.40
96	Richie Ashburn	.40
97	Rick Ferrell	.40
98	Elston Howard	.40
99	Roberto Clemente	2.00
100	Robin Roberts	.40
101	Robin Yount	1.00
102	Roger Maris	2.00
103	Rollie Fingers	.40
104	Ron Santo	.40
105	Roy Campanella	.75
106	Ryne Sandberg	1.50
107	Sparky Anderson	.40
108	Sparky Lyle	.40
109	Stan Musial	2.00
110	Steve Carlton	.50
111	Steve Garvey	.40
112	Ted Williams	2.50
113	Thurman Munson	1.00
114	Tom Seaver	1.00
115	Tommy Henrich	.40
116	Tommy Lasorda	.40
117	Tony Gwynn	1.00
118	Tony Perez	.40
119	Ty Cobb	1.50
120	Wade Boggs	.50
121	Warren Spahn	.75
122	Whitey Ford	.75
123	Willie McCovey	.40
124	Willie Randolph	.40
125	Willie Stargell	.75
126	Yogi Berra	.75

All-Time Autographs
		NM/M
Production 50 Sets		
LA	Luis Aparicio	20.00
YB	Yogi Berra	65.00
WB	Wade Boggs	40.00
SC	Steve Carlton	20.00
GC	Gary Carter	25.00
JC	Joe Carter	20.00
OC	Orlando Cepeda	25.00
WC	Will Clark	40.00
BD	Bobby Doerr	20.00
DE	Dennis Eckersley	20.00
RF	Rollie Fingers	20.00
CF	Carlton Fisk	30.00
WF	Whitey Ford	40.00
TG	Tony Gwynn	50.00
MI	Monte Irvin	25.00
FJ	Fergie Jenkins	20.00
AK	Al Kaline	40.00
GK	George Kell	25.00
HK	Harmon Killebrew	25.00
FL	Fred Lynn	15.00
MA	Don Mattingly	60.00
BM	Bill Mazeroski	50.00
MC	Willie McCovey	40.00
MC	Denny McLain	30.00
DM	Dale Murphy	30.00
SM	Stan Musial	80.00
DN	Don Newcombe	25.00
PN	Phil Niekro	20.00
TP	Tony Perez	25.00
GP	Gaylord Perry	20.00
JP	Johnny Podres	20.00
CR	Cal Ripken Jr.	125.00
RR	Robin Roberts	30.00
NR	Nolan Ryan	125.00
SA	Ryne Sandberg	75.00

RS	Red Schoendienst	25.00
TS	Tom Seaver	50.00
DS	Don Sutton	15.00
BW	Billy Williams	20.00
MW	Maury Wills	20.00
RY	Robin Yount	75.00

Game Graphs
		NM/M
Production 25 Sets		
Gold:		No Pricing
Production 10 Sets		
LA	Luis Aparicio	25.00
EB	Ernie Banks	75.00
JB	Johnny Bench	80.00
YB	Yogi Berra	80.00
WB	Wade Boggs	50.00
GB	George Brett	100.00
LB	Lou Brock	40.00
SC	Steve Carlton	30.00
GC	Gary Carter	35.00
JC	Joe Carter	30.00
RF	Rollie Fingers	25.00
CF	Carlton Fisk	50.00
BG	Bob Gibson	40.00
TG	Tony Gwynn	65.00
AK	Al Kaline	50.00
HK	Harmon Killebrew	50.00
JM	Juan Marichal	35.00
MA	Don Mattingly	80.00
BM	Bill Mazeroski	50.00
WM	Willie McCovey	50.00
PM	Paul Molitor	40.00
MO	Joe Morgan	40.00
DM	Dale Murphy	40.00
EM	Eddie Murray	85.00
SM	Stan Musial	100.00
PN	Phil Niekro	30.00
KP	Kirby Puckett	75.00
CR	Cal Ripken Jr.	180.00
PR	Phil Rizzuto	40.00
BR	Brooks Robinson	50.00
FR	Frank Robinson	40.00
NR	Nolan Ryan	175.00
RS	Ryne Sandberg	85.00
MS	Mike Schmidt	80.00
TS	Tom Seaver	50.00
OS	Ozzie Smith	75.00
SN	Duke Snider	50.00
DS	Don Sutton	20.00
BW	Billy Williams	25.00
DW	Dave Winfield	30.00
CY	Carl Yastrzemski	85.00
RY	Robin Yount	85.00

Historic Patches
		NM/M
Production 25 Sets		
EB	Ernie Banks	50.00
GB	George Brett	60.00
DD	Don Drysdale	40.00
BG	Bob Gibson	25.00
TG	Tony Gwynn	50.00
EM	Eddie Mathews	30.00
SM	Stan Musial	60.00
CR	Cal Ripken Jr.	100.00
NR	Nolan Ryan	75.00
TS	Tom Seaver	50.00
DS	Duke Snider	30.00
CY	Carl Yastrzemski	40.00
RY	Robin Yount	50.00

Historic Quads
No Pricing
Production 10 Sets

Historic Swatches

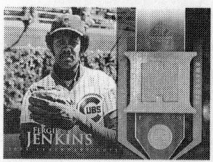

		NM/M
Common Swatch:		4.00
Golds:		2X-3X
Production 25 Sets		
AN	Sparky Anderson	4.00
JB	Johnny Bench/SP	10.00
GB	George Brett	12.00
LB	Lou Brock	8.00
GC	Gary Carter	6.00
JC	Joe Carter	6.00
DC	Dave Concepcion	4.00
DD	Don Drysdale	8.00
RF	Rollie Fingers	6.00
CF	Carlton Fisk	6.00
GF	George Foster	4.00
SG	Steve Garvey	4.00
CH	Jim "Catfish" Hunter	6.00
FJ	Fergie Jenkins	8.00
HK	Harmon Killebrew	10.00
DL	Don Larsen/SP	10.00
ML	Mickey Lolich	4.00
SL	Sparky Lyle	4.00
MA	Eddie Mathews	6.00
DM	Don Mattingly	15.00
PM	Paul Molitor	6.00

JM	Joe Morgan	6.00
TM	Thurman Munson	12.00
MU	Dale Murphy	8.00
EM	Eddie Murray/SP	10.00
SM	Stan Musial	20.00
PN	Phil Niekro	6.00
GP	Gaylord Perry	6.00
JP	Johnny Podres	6.00
KP	Kirby Puckett	10.00
JR	Jim Rice	8.00
CR	Cal Ripken Jr.	20.00
BR	Brooks Robinson	8.00
NR	Nolan Ryan	20.00
TS	Tom Seaver	8.00
OS	Ozzie Smith	10.00
DS	Don Sutton	4.00
HW	Hoyt Wilhelm	4.00
DW	Dave Winfield	6.00
RY	Robin Yount	8.00

Historical Cuts
Quantity Produced Listed
No Pricing

Legendary Cuts
NM/M
Quantity produced listed

WA	Walter Alston/74	200.00
LU	Luke Appling/108	150.00
RA	Richie Ashburn/31	350.00
LB	Lou Boudreau/199	125.00
EC	Earle Combs/27	350.00
ST	Stan Coveleski/102	150.00
RD	Ray Dandridge/199	125.00
DD	Dizzy Dean/33	650.00
BD	Bill Dickey/82	250.00
JD	Joe DiMaggio/111	500.00
DO	Larry Doby/14	400.00
DR	Don Drysdale/66	450.00
LD	Leo Durocher/75	400.00
RF	Rick Ferrell/44	160.00
WF	Wes Ferrell/36	200.00
FF	Frankie Frisch/57	450.00
CG	Charlie Gehringer/171	200.00
LG	Lefty Gomez/98	325.00
HG	Hank Greenberg/37	500.00
BU	Burleigh Grimes/83	200.00
GR	Lefty Grove/75	375.00
GH	Gabby Hartnett/19	475.00
BH	Billy Herman/134	125.00
WH	Waite Hoyt/106	200.00
CH	Carl Hubbell/189	180.00
JH	Jim "Catfish" Hunter/25	220.00
BJ	"Indian" Bob Johnson/32	200.00
HK	Harvey Kuenn/49	150.00
BL	Bob Lemon/199	100.00
EL	Ernie Lombardi/39	450.00
TL	Ted Lyons/199	150.00
RU	Rube Marquard/59	220.00
JM	Joe Medwick/32	450.00
MI	Johnny Mize/118	140.00
HN	Hal Newhouser/51	140.00
KN	Kid Nichols/4	2,500
SP	Satchel Paige/28	1,325
GP	George Pipgras/46	200.00
PR	Pee Wee Reese/35	350.00
SR	Sam Rice/28	500.00
ER	Edd Roush/129	125.00
RR	Red Ruffing/30	500.00
JS	Joe Sewell/199	140.00
GS	George Sisler/32	850.00
ES	Enos Slaughter/147	125.00
WS	Willie Stargell/39	220.00
WM	Hoyt Wilhelm/115	100.00
SW	"Smokey" Joe Wood/79	400.00
EW	Early Wynn/54	200.00

Legendary Duels
NM/M
Production 25 Sets

BG	George Brett, Rich "Goose" Gossage	40.00
DW	Joe DiMaggio, Ted Williams	150.00
EG	Dennis Eckersley, Kirk Gibson	25.00
FM	Joe Morgan, Carlton Fisk	30.00
GL	Bob Gibson, Mickey Lolich	30.00
MW	Mickey Mantle, Ted Williams	200.00
PL	Johnny Podres, Don Larsen	30.00
RM	Juan Marichal, John Roseboro	25.00
RR	Pee Wee Reese, Phil Rizzuto	35.00
SM	Duke Snider, Mickey Mantle	125.00
SS	Ryne Sandberg, Ozzie Smith	80.00
WB	Ernie Banks, Honus Wagner	125.00

Legendary Duels Patch
No Pricing
Production 15 Sets

Legendary Duos
NM/M
Production 25 Sets

CM	Joe Morgan, Dave Concepcion	20.00
DM	Joe DiMaggio, Mickey Mantle	200.00
LB	Yogi Berra, Don Larsen	60.00
MB	Yogi Berra, Mickey Mantle	200.00
MM	Mickey Mantle, Roger Maris	200.00
MY	Paul Molitor, Robin Yount	30.00
PJ	Jackie Robinson, Pee Wee Reese	75.00
RR	Cal Ripken Jr., Brooks Robinson	65.00
RS	Tom Seaver, Nolan Ryan	75.00
SC	Roy Campanella, Duke Snider	40.00
SS	Johnny Sain, Warren Spahn	40.00
WB	Ernie Banks, Billy Williams	40.00

Legendary Duos Patch
No Pricing
Production 15 Sets

Legendary Sigs
NM/M
Production 50 Sets

LA	Luis Aparicio	20.00
EB	Ernie Banks	60.00
JB	Johnny Bench	60.00
WB	Wade Boggs	40.00
GC	Gary Carter	25.00
JC	Joe Carter	20.00
WC	Will Clark	40.00
BD	Bobby Doerr	20.00
DE	Dennis Eckersley	25.00
BF	Bob Feller	30.00
RF	Rollie Fingers	20.00
BG	Bob Gibson	35.00
TG	Tony Gwynn	50.00
MI	Monte Irvin	25.00
AK	Al Kaline	40.00
GK	George Kell	25.00
HK	Harmon Killebrew	40.00
RK	Ralph Kiner	30.00
FL	Fred Lynn	15.00
JM	Juan Marichal	30.00
MA	Don Mattingly	60.00
WM	Willie McCovey	40.00
MC	Denny McLain	30.00
DM	Dale Murphy	30.00
EM	Eddie Murray	80.00
DN	Don Newcombe	25.00
PA	Jim Palmer	30.00
GP	Gaylord Perry	20.00
JP	Johnny Podres	20.00
CR	Cal Ripken Jr.	125.00
PR	Phil Rizzuto	25.00
RR	Robin Roberts	30.00
BR	Brooks Robinson	40.00
SA	Ryne Sandberg	75.00
MS	Mike Schmidt	60.00
RS	Red Schoendienst	25.00
OS	Ozzie Smith	65.00
SN	Duke Snider	40.00
DS	Don Sutton	15.00
MW	Maury Wills	20.00
CY	Carl Yastrzemski	75.00

Legendary Swatches

NM/M
Common Swatch: 4.00
Golds: No Pricing
Production 15 Sets

EB	Ernie Banks SP	15.00
JB	Johnny Bench	10.00
YB	Yogi Berra	12.00
WB	Wade Boggs	6.00
GB	George Brett	12.00
RC	Roy Campanella	10.00
SC	Steve Carlton	6.00
OC	Orlando Cepeda	6.00
BD	Bobby Doerr	8.00
DD	Don Drysdale	8.00
CF	Carlton Fisk	8.00
NF	Nellie Fox	6.00
BG	Bob Gibson	8.00
TG	Tony Gwynn	8.00
EH	Elston Howard	8.00
CH	Jim "Catfish" Hunter	8.00
AK	Al Kaline	10.00
HK	Harmon Killebrew	10.00
MA	Juan Marichal	8.00
EM	Eddie Mathews	10.00
DM	Don Mattingly	15.00
WM	Willie McCovey	6.00
TM	Thurman Munson	12.00
SM	Stan Musial	15.00
TP	Tony Perez	4.00
PO	Johnny Podres	6.00
PR	Pee Wee Reese	8.00
JR	Jim Rice	8.00
CR	Cal Ripken Jr.	20.00
RI	Phil Rizzuto	10.00
FR	Frank Robinson	6.00
NR	Nolan Ryan	20.00
MS	Mike Schmidt	15.00
TS	Tom Seaver	8.00
DS	Duke Snider	10.00
WS	Warren Spahn	10.00
ST	Willie Stargell	8.00
BW	Billy Williams	4.00
DW	Dave Winfield	6.00
CY	Carl Yastrzemski	10.00
RY	Robin Yount	8.00

Marked for the Hall
NM/M
Production 50 Sets

LA	Luis Aparicio	20.00
EB	Ernie Banks	60.00
JB	Johnny Bench	60.00
YB	Yogi Berra	65.00
GB	George Brett	75.00
LB	Lou Brock	30.00
SC	Steve Carlton	20.00
GC	Gary Carter	25.00
OC	Orlando Cepeda	25.00
BD	Bobby Doerr	20.00
BF	Bob Feller	30.00
CF	Carlton Fisk	35.00
WF	Whitey Ford	40.00
BG	Bob Gibson	35.00
AK	Al Kaline	40.00
HK	Harmon Killebrew	40.00
RK	Ralph Kiner	30.00
MA	Juan Marichal	30.00
BM	Bill Mazeroski	50.00
WM	Willie McCovey	40.00
PM	Paul Molitor	40.00
JM	Joe Morgan	35.00
EM	Eddie Murray	80.00
PN	Phil Niekro	20.00
JP	Jim Palmer	30.00
TP	Tony Perez	25.00
GP	Gaylord Perry	20.00
KP	Kirby Puckett	60.00
PR	Phil Rizzuto	25.00
RR	Robin Roberts	30.00
BR	Brooks Robinson	40.00
FR	Frank Robinson	125.00
NR	Nolan Ryan	125.00
MS	Mike Schmidt	60.00
TS	Tom Seaver	50.00
OS	Ozzie Smith	65.00
DS	Duke Snider	40.00
BW	Billy Williams	20.00
DW	Dave Winfield	30.00
CY	Carl Yastrzemski	75.00
RY	Robin Yount	75.00

Marks of Greatness
NM/M
Production 50 Sets

EB	Ernie Banks	60.00
JB	Johnny Bench	60.00
YB	Yogi Berra	65.00
WB	Wade Boggs	40.00
GB	George Brett	75.00
LB	Lou Brock	30.00
SC	Steve Carlton	20.00
JC	Joe Carter	20.00
OC	Orlando Cepeda	25.00
WC	Will Clark	40.00
RF	Rollie Fingers	20.00
CF	Carlton Fisk	35.00
WF	Whitey Ford	40.00
BG	Bob Gibson	35.00
TG	Tony Gwynn	50.00
FJ	Fergie Jenkins	20.00
AK	Al Kaline	40.00
HK	Harmon Killebrew	40.00
FL	Fred Lynn	15.00
MA	Don Mattingly	60.00
MC	Denny McLain	30.00
PM	Paul Molitor	40.00
JM	Joe Morgan	35.00
DM	Dale Murphy	30.00
SM	Stan Musial	80.00
DN	Don Newcombe	25.00
PN	Phil Niekro	20.00
JP	Jim Palmer	30.00
TP	Tony Perez	25.00
KP	Kirby Puckett	60.00
CR	Cal Ripken Jr.	125.00
BR	Brooks Robinson	40.00
FR	Frank Robinson	30.00
NR	Nolan Ryan	125.00
RS	Ryne Sandberg	75.00
MS	Mike Schmidt	60.00
TS	Tom Seaver	50.00
OZ	Ozzie Smith	65.00
DS	Duke Snider	40.00
BW	Billy Williams	20.00
DW	Dave Winfield	30.00
RY	Robin Yount	75.00

Significant Swatches

NM/M
Common Swatch: 4.00
Golds: 2-3X
Production 25 Sets

SA	Sparky Anderson	4.00
EB	Ernie Banks/SP	10.00
LB	Lou Brock/SP	8.00
GC	Gary Carter	4.00
JC	Joe Carter	4.00
OC	Orlando Cepeda	6.00
DC	Dave Concepcion	4.00
BD	Bobby Doerr	8.00
DD	Don Drysdale	8.00
RF	Rollie Fingers	6.00
CF	Carlton Fisk	8.00
GF	George Foster	4.00
SG	Steve Garvey	4.00
CH	Jim "Catfish" Hunter	4.00
FJ	Fergie Jenkins	4.00
SL	Sparky Lyle	4.00
RM	Roger Maris	30.00
ED	Eddie Mathews	10.00
MA	Don Mattingly	15.00
BM	Bill Mazeroski	8.00
WM	Willie McCovey	6.00
PM	Paul Molitor	6.00
TM	Thurman Munson	12.00
DM	Dale Murphy	8.00
EM	Eddie Murray/SP	8.00
PN	Phil Niekro	4.00
TP	Tony Perez	4.00
GP	Gaylord Perry	4.00
JP	Johnny Podres	6.00
CR	Cal Ripken Jr.	20.00
FR	Frank Robinson	6.00
NR	Nolan Ryan	20.00
MS	Mike Schmidt	15.00
TS	Tom Seaver	8.00
SN	Duke Snider	10.00
WS	Warren Spahn	10.00
ST	Willie Stargell	8.00
DS	Don Sutton	4.00
HW	Hoyt Wilhelm	4.00
DW	Dave Winfield	6.00
CY	Carl Yastrzemski	10.00
RY	Robin Yount	8.00

Significant Trips
No Pricing
Production 15 Sets

Significant Trips Patch
No Pricing
Production 10 Sets

Ultimate Autographs

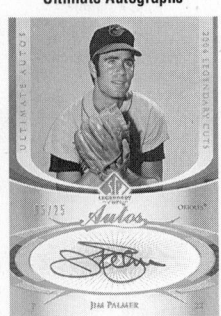

NM/M
Production 25 Sets

EB	Ernie Banks	60.00
JB	Johnny Bench	60.00
YB	Yogi Berra	60.00
GB	George Brett	90.00
LB	Lou Brock	35.00
SC	Steve Carlton	25.00
DE	Dennis Eckersley	25.00
BF	Bob Feller	35.00

WF	Whitey Ford	40.00
BG	Bob Gibson	40.00
MI	Monte Irvin	30.00
FJ	Fergie Jenkins	30.00
AK	Al Kaline	50.00
GK	George Kell	25.00
HK	Harmon Killebrew	50.00
RK	Ralph Kiner	40.00
MA	Juan Marichal	30.00
DM	Don Mattingly	75.00
BM	Bill Mazeroski	40.00
PM	Paul Molitor	40.00
JM	Joe Morgan	35.00
EM	Eddie Murray	80.00
SM	Stan Musial	80.00
PA	Jim Palmer	40.00
JP	Johnny Podres	25.00
KP	Kirby Puckett	70.00
PR	Phil Rizzuto	35.00
BR	Brooks Robinson	40.00
FR	Frank Robinson	40.00
NR	Nolan Ryan	120.00
SA	Ryne Sandberg	80.00
MS	Mike Schmidt	75.00
RS	Red Schoendienst	25.00
TS	Tom Seaver	50.00
OS	Ozzie Smith	60.00
SN	Duke Snider	50.00
DS	Don Sutton	20.00
MW	Maury Willis	25.00
DW	Dave Winfield	30.00
CY	Carl Yastrzemski	80.00
RY	Robin Yount	60.00

Ultimate Swatches

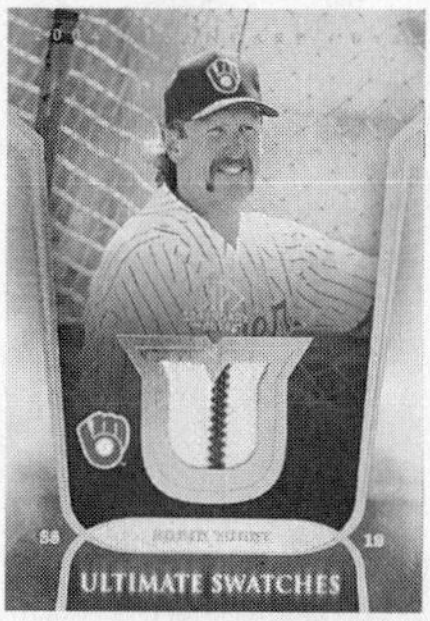

NM/M

Common Swatch: 6.00
Golds: No Pricing
Production 10 Sets

EB	Ernie Banks	12.00
JB	Johnny Bench	10.00
YB	Yogi Berra	12.00
WB	Wade Boggs	6.00
GB	George Brett	12.00
RC	Roy Campanella	10.00
SC	Steve Carlton	6.00
JD	Joe DiMaggio/SP	75.00
DD	Don Drysdale	8.00
NF	Nellie Fox	12.00
BG	Bob Gibson	8.00
HG	Hank Greenberg	20.00
TG	Tony Gwynn	10.00
CH	Jim "Catfish" Hunter	6.00
HK	Harmon Killebrew	10.00
MM	Mickey Mantle/SP	125.00
MA	Juan Marichal	8.00
RM	Roger Maris	30.00
EM	Eddie Mathews	10.00
DM	Don Mattingly	15.00
WM	Willie McCovey	6.00
TM	Thurman Munson	10.00
SM	Stan Musial	15.00
KP	Kirby Puckett	10.00
PR	Pee Wee Reese	8.00
CR	Cal Ripken Jr.	20.00
BR	Brooks Robinson	8.00
FR	Frank Robinson	6.00
JR	Jackie Robinson	40.00
NR	Nolan Ryan	20.00
MS	Mike Schmidt	15.00
TS	Tom Seaver	10.00
OS	Ozzie Smith	10.00
DS	Duke Snider/SP	10.00
WS	Warren Spahn	10.00
HW	Honus Wagner/SP	140.00
BW	Billy Williams	6.00
TW	Ted Williams	60.00
DW	Dave Winfield	6.00
CY	Carl Yastrzemski	10.00
RY	Robin Yount	8.00

2004 SP Prospects

NM/M

Complete Set (447):
Common SP (1-90): .50
1:Pack
Common Rookie (91-290): 1.00
Common Rookie Auto. (291-447): 8.00
Production 400 unless noted.
Overall Autos. 1:5
Pack (5): 8.00

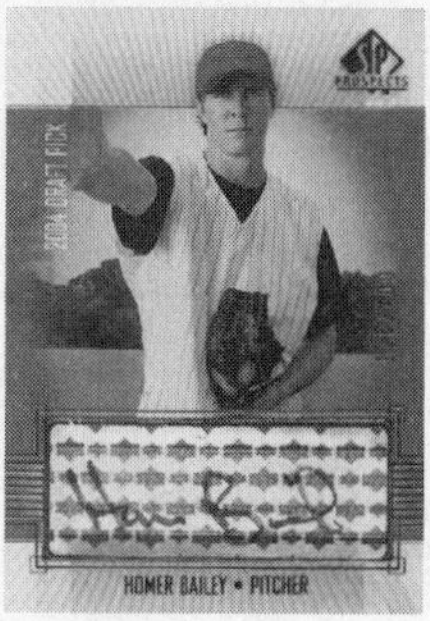

Box (24): 180.00

1	Roger Clemens	3.00
2	Melvin Mora	.50
3	Dontrelle Willis	.50
4	Jose Vidro	.50
5	Oliver Perez	.50
6	Carlos Zambrano	.50
7	Chipper Jones	1.00
8	Greg Maddux	1.50
9	Curt Schilling	1.00
10	Jose Reyes	.75
11	David Ortiz	1.00
12	Mike Piazza	2.00
13	Jason Schmidt	.50
14	Randy Johnson	1.00
15	Magglio Ordonez	.50
16	Mike Mussina	1.00
17	Jake Peavy	.50
18	Jim Edmonds	.75
19	Ken Griffey Jr.	1.50
20	Jason Giambi	.75
21	Mike Sweeney	.50
22	Carlos Lee	.50
23	Craig Wilson	.50
24	Pedro Martinez	1.00
25	Bobby Abreu	.50
26	Mike Lowell	.50
27	Miguel Cabrera	1.00
28	Hank Blalock	.50
29	Frank Thomas	.75
30	Manny Ramirez	1.00
31	Mark Mulder	.50
32	Scott Podsednik	.50
33	Albert Pujols	3.00
34	Preston Wilson	.50
35	Todd Helton	.75
36	Victor Martinez	.50
37	Kerry Wood	.50
38	Carlos Beltran	1.00
39	Vernon Wells	.50
40	Sammy Sosa	1.00
41	Pat Burrell	.50
42	Tim Hudson	.50
43	Eric Gagne	.75
44	Jim Thome	1.00
45	Vladimir Guerrero	1.00
46	Travis Hafner	.75
47	Rickie Weeks	.50
48	Miguel Tejada	.75
49	Ivan Rodriguez	.75
50	J.D. Drew	.50
51	Ben Sheets	.50
52	Garret Anderson	.50
53	Aubrey Huff	.50
54	Nomar Garciaparra	1.00
55	Luis Gonzalez	.50
56	Lance Berkman	.50
57	Ichiro Suzuki	2.00
58	Torii Hunter	.50
59	Adam Dunn	.75
60	Mark Teixeira	.75
61	Bret Boone	.50
62	Roy Oswalt	.50
63	Joe Mauer	.75
64	Scott Rolen	1.00
65	Hideki Matsui	2.00
66	Richie Sexson	.50
67	Jeff Kent	.50
68	Barry Zito	.50
69	C.C. Sabathia	.50
70	Carlos Delgado	.50
71	Gary Sheffield	.75
72	Shawn Green	.50
73	Jason Bay	.50
74	Andruw Jones	.75
75	Jeff Bagwell	.75
76	Rafael Palmeiro	.75
77	Alex Rodriguez	3.00
78	Adrian Beltre	.50
79	Troy Glaus	.50
80	Tom Glavine	.50
81	Paul Konerko	.50
82	Alfonso Soriano	1.00
83	Roy Halladay	.50
84	Derek Jeter	3.00
85	Josh Beckett	.50
86	Delmon Young	.50
87	Brian Giles	.50
88	Eric Chavez	.50
89	Lyle Overbay	.50
90	Mark Prior	.75
91	Shawn Camp **RC**	1.00
92	Travis Smith	1.00
93	Juan Padilla **RC**	1.00
94	Brad Halsey **RC**	1.00
95	Scott Kazmir	6.00
96	Sam Narron **RC**	1.00
97	Frank Francisco **RC**	1.00
98	Mike Johnston **RC**	1.00
99	Sam McConnell **RC**	1.00
100	Josh Labandeira **RC**	1.00
101	Kazuhito Tadano **RC**	1.00
102	Hector Gimenez **RC**	1.00
103	David Aardsma **RC**	1.00
104	Charles Thomas **RC**	2.00
105	Ian Snell **RC**	2.50
106	Jeff Keppinger **RC**	3.00
107	Michael Vento **RC**	2.00
108	Jerry Gil **RC**	1.00
109	Marty McLeary **RC**	1.00
110	Donnie Kelly **RC**	1.00
111	Roman Colon **RC**	1.00
112	Travis Blackley **RC**	1.00
113	Edwardo Sierra **RC**	1.00
114	Chris Shelton **RC**	2.00
115	Bartolome Fortunato **RC**	1.00
116	Brandon Medders **RC**	1.00
117	Merkin Valdez **RC**	2.00
118	Carlos Vasquez **RC**	1.00
119	Shingo Takatsu **RC**	1.50
120	Aarom Baldiris **RC**	1.00
121	Chris Aguila **RC**	1.00
122	Jimmy Serrano **RC**	1.00
123	Mike Gosling	1.00
124	Brian Dallimore **RC**	1.00
125	Ronald Belisario **RC**	1.00
126	George Sherrill **RC**	1.00
127	Fernando Nieve **RC**	1.00
128	Abe Alvarez **RC**	1.50
129	Jeff Bennett **RC**	1.00
130	Ryan Meaux **RC**	1.00
131	Edwin Moreno **RC**	1.00
132	Jesse Crain **RC**	2.00
133	Scott Dohmann **RC**	1.00
134	Ronny Cedeno **RC**	1.00
135	Orlando Rodriguez **RC**	1.00
136	Mike Wuertz **RC**	1.00
137	Justin Hampson **RC**	1.00
138	Matt Treanor **RC**	1.00
139	Andy Green **RC**	1.00
140	Yadier Molina **RC**	2.50
141	Joe Nelson **RC**	1.00
142	Justin Lehr **RC**	1.00
143	Ryan Wing	1.00
144	Kevin Cave **RC**	1.50
145	Evan Rust **RC**	1.00
146	Mike Rouse	1.00
147	Lance Cormier **RC**	1.00
148	Eduardo Villacis **RC**	1.00
149	Justin Knoedler **RC**	1.00
150	Freddy Guzman **RC**	1.00
151	Casey Daigle **RC**	1.00
152	Joey Gathright **RC**	2.00
153	Tim Bittner **RC**	1.00
154	Scott Atchison **RC**	1.00
155	Ivan Ochoa **RC**	1.50
156	Lincoln Holdzkom **RC**	1.00
157	Onil Joseph **RC**	1.00
158	Jason Bartlett **RC**	1.00
159	Jon Knott **RC**	1.00
160	Jake Woods **RC**	1.00
161	Jerome Gamble **RC**	1.00
162	Sean Henn	1.50
163	Kazuo Matsui **RC**	1.50
164	Roberto Novoa **RC**	1.00
165	Eddy Rodriguez **RC**	1.00
166	Ramon Ramirez **RC**	1.00
167	Enemencio Pacheco **RC**	1.00
168	Chad Bentz **RC**	1.00
169	Chris Oxspring **RC**	1.00
170	Justin Leone **RC**	1.00
171	Joe Horgan **RC**	1.00
172	Jose Capellan **RC**	1.50
173	Greg Dobbs **RC**	1.00
174	Jason Frasor **RC**	1.50
175	Shawn Hill **RC**	1.00
176	Carlos Hines **RC**	1.00
177	John Gall **RC**	1.00
178	Steve Andrade **RC**	1.00
179	Scott Proctor **RC**	1.00
180	Rusty Tucker **RC**	1.00
181	David Crouthers	1.00
182	Franklyn Gracesqui **RC**	1.00
183	Justin Germano **RC**	1.00
184	Alfredo Simon **RC**	1.50
185	Jorge Sequea **RC**	1.00
186	Nick Regilio **RC**	1.00
187	Justin Huisman **RC**	1.00
188	Akinori Otsuka **RC**	1.50
189	Luis Gonzalez **RC**	1.00
190	Renyel Pinto **RC**	1.00
191	Josh LeBlanc **RC**	1.50
192	Devin Ivany **RC**	1.00
193	Chad Blackwell **RC**	1.50
194	Brandon Burgess **RC**	1.50
195	Cory Patton **RC**	1.50
196	Daniel Batz **RC**	1.50
197	Adam Russell **RC**	1.00
198	Jarrett Hoffpauir **RC**	1.50
199	Patrick Bryant **RC**	1.00
200	Sean Gamble **RC**	1.50
201	Jermaine Brock **RC**	1.50
202	Benjamin Zobrist **RC**	1.50
203	Cla Meredith **RC**	1.50
204	Derek Tharpe **RC**	1.00
205	Brad McCann **RC**	2.00
206	Justin Hedrick **RC**	1.00
207	Clint Sammons **RC**	2.50
208	Richard Steik **RC**	1.00
209	Fernando Perez **RC**	1.00
210	Mark Jecmen **RC**	1.00
211	Benjamin Harrison **RC**	1.00
212	Jason Quarles **RC**	1.00
213	William Layman **RC**	1.00
214	Koley Kolberg **RC**	1.00
215	Randy Dicken **RC**	1.00
216	Barry Richmond **RC**	1.00
217	Timothy Murphey **RC**	1.50
218	John Hardy **RC**	1.50
219	Sebastien Boucher **RC**	1.00
220	Andrew Alvarado **RC**	1.00
221	Patrick Perry **RC**	1.00
222	Jarod McAuliff **RC**	1.00
223	Jared Gaston **RC**	1.00
224	William Thompson **RC**	1.50
225	Lucas French **RC**	1.00
226	Brandon Parillo **RC**	1.00
227	Greg Goetz **RC**	1.00
228	David Haehnel **RC**	1.50
229	James Miller **RC**	1.00
230	Mark Roberts **RC**	1.00
231	Eric Ridener **RC**	1.00
232	Freddy Sandoval **RC**	1.00
234	Carlos Medero-Stullz **RC**	1.00
235	Matt Shepherd **RC**	1.00
236	Thomas Hubbard **RC**	1.00
238	Kyle Bono **RC**	1.50
239	Craig Moldrem **RC**	1.00
239	Brandon Timm **RC**	1.00
241	Mike Carp **RC**	2.50
242	Joseph Muro **RC**	1.00
243	Derek Decarlo **RC**	1.50
244	Chris Niesel **RC**	1.50
245	Trevor Lawhorn **RC**	1.50
246	Joey Howell **RC**	1.00
247	Dustin Hahn **RC**	1.00
248	Jim Fasano **RC**	2.00
249	Hainley Statia **RC**	1.00
250	Brandon Conway **RC**	1.00
251	Christopher McConnell **RC**	2.00
252	Austin Shappi **RC**	1.50
253	Joey Metropoulos **RC**	2.00
254	David Nicholson **RC**	1.50
255	Ryan McCarthy **RC**	2.00
256	Michael Parisi **RC**	1.00
257	Andrew Macfarlane **RC**	1.00
258	Jeffery Dominguez **RC**	1.50
259	Troy Patton **RC**	4.00
260	Ryan Norwood **RC**	1.50
261	Chad Boyd **RC**	1.00
262	Grant Plumley **RC**	1.00
263	Jeffrey Katz **RC**	2.00
264	Cory Middleton **RC**	1.00
265	Andrew Moffitt **RC**	1.00
266	Jarrett Grube **RC**	1.00
267	Derek Hankins **RC**	1.00
268	Douglas Reinhardt **RC**	1.00
269	Duron Legrande **RC**	1.00
270	Steven Jackson **RC**	1.00
271	Brian Hall **RC**	2.00
272	Cory Wade **RC**	1.50
273	John Grogan **RC**	1.00
274	Robert Asanovich **RC**	1.50
275	Kevin Hart **RC**	1.50
276	Matt Guillory **RC**	1.00
277	Cliff Remole **RC**	1.00
278	David Trahan **RC**	1.00
279	Kristian Bell **RC**	1.00
280	Chris Westervelt **RC**	1.00
281	Garry Bakker **RC**	1.00
282	Jonny Ash **RC**	1.00
283	Ryan Phillips **RC**	1.00
284	Wes Letson **RC**	1.00
285	Jeff Landing **RC**	1.00
286	Mark Worrell **RC**	1.00
287	Sean Gallagher **RC**	5.00
288	Nick Blasi **RC**	1.00
289	Kevin Frandsen **RC**	2.00
290	Richard Mercado **RC**	1.00
291	Matt Bush **RC**	20.00
292	Mark Rogers **RC**	20.00
293	Homer Bailey **RC**	50.00
294	Chris Nelson **RC**	30.00
295	Thomas Diamond **RC**	25.00
296	Neil Walker **RC**	40.00
297	Bill Bray **RC**	15.00
298	David Purcey **RC**	20.00
299	Scott Elbert **RC**	40.00
300	Josh Fields **RC**	50.00
301	Chris Lambert **RC**	20.00
302	Trevor Plouffe **RC**	25.00
303	Greg Golson **RC**	25.00
304	Phillip Hughes **RC**	100.00
305	Kyle Waldrop **RC**	25.00
306	Richie Robnett/350 **RC**	30.00
307	Taylor Tankersley **RC**	20.00
308	Blake Dewitt **RC**	40.00
309	Eric Hurley **RC**	30.00
310	James Howell **RC**	20.00
311	Zachary Jackson **RC**	15.00
312	Justin Orenduff **RC**	20.00
313	Tyler Lumsden **RC**	20.00
314	Matt Fox/600 **RC**	10.00
315	Dan Putnam/450 **RC**	20.00
316	Jon Poterson **RC**	20.00
317	Gio Gonzalez **RC**	60.00
318	Jay Rainville/475 **RC**	20.00
319	Huston Street **RC**	25.00
320	Jeff Marquez **RC**	20.00
321	Eric Beattie/500 **RC**	20.00
322	Reid Brignac/325 **RC**	100.00
323	Yovani Gallardo **RC**	80.00
324	Justin Hoyman **RC**	20.00
325	Brandon Szymanski **RC**	25.00

326	Seth Smith/600 **RC**	35.00
327	Karl Herren/600 **RC**	20.00
328	Brian Bixler/600 **RC**	15.00
329	Wes Whisler/600 **RC**	15.00
330	Erick San Pedro **RC**	10.00
331	Billy Buckner **RC**	20.00
332	Jon Zeringue **RC**	20.00
333	Curtis Thigpen **RC**	20.00
334	Blake Johnson **RC**	15.00
335	Donny Lucy **RC**	10.00
336	Mike Ferris/600 **RC**	15.00
337	Anthony Swarzak/600 **RC**	30.00
338	Jason Jaramillo **RC**	15.00
339	Hunter Pence/600 **RC**	150.00
340	Dustin Pedroia **RC**	160.00
341	Grant Johnson **RC**	15.00
342	Kurt Suzuki **RC**	30.00
343	Jason Vargas/600 **RC**	20.00
344	Ray Liotta **RC**	20.00
346	Eric Campbell **RC**	40.00
347	Jeff Frazier **RC**	15.00
348	Gaby Hernandez **RC**	20.00
349	Wade Davis/600 **RC**	50.00
350	Josh Wahpepah **RC**	15.00
351	Scott Lewis **RC**	20.00
352	Jeff Fiorentino **RC**	15.00
353	Steven Register/600 **RC**	10.00
354	Michael Schlact **RC**	15.00
355	Eddie Prasch **RC**	15.00
356	Adam Lind **RC**	50.00
357	Ian Desmond **RC**	25.00
358	Josh Johnson/575 **RC**	15.00
359	Garrett Mock/600 **RC**	15.00
360	Danny Hill/600 **RC**	10.00
361	Cory Dunlap/600 **RC**	15.00
362	Grant Hansen/600 **RC**	12.00
363	Eric Haberer **RC**	15.00
364	Eduardo Morlan **RC**	20.00
365	James Happ/600 **RC**	15.00
366	Matt Tuiasosopo/600 **RC**	20.00
367	Jordan Parraz **RC**	20.00
368	Andrew Dobies **RC**	20.00
369	Mark Reed **RC**	25.00
370	Jason Windsor **RC**	25.00
371	Gregory Burns/600 **RC**	20.00
372	Christian Garcia/600 **RC**	25.00
373	John Bowker/575 **RC**	35.00
374	John Holt/550 **RC**	15.00
375	Daryl Jones **RC**	25.00
376	Colin Mahoney **RC**	10.00
377	Aaron Hathaway **RC**	15.00
378	Matt Spring **RC**	10.00
379	Josh Baker **RC**	10.00
380	Charles Lofgren **RC**	25.00
381	Rafael Gonzalez **RC**	15.00
382	Bradley Bergesen/575 **RC**	10.00
383	Brandon Boggs **RC**	20.00
384	Joseph Bauserman **RC**	15.00
385	Collin Balester/500 **RC**	40.00
386	James Moore **RC**	10.00
387	Robert Janssen **RC**	20.00
388	Luis Guerra **RC**	15.00
389	Lucas Harrell/550 **RC**	15.00
390	Donnie Smith/500 **RC**	15.00
391	Mark Robinson/525 **RC**	15.00
392	Louis Marson/550 **RC**	20.00
393	Robert Johnson/600 **RC**	10.00
394	Lou Santangelo/600 **RC**	12.00
395	Tommy Hottovy **RC**	10.00
396	Ryan Webb **RC**	15.00
397	Jamar Walton **RC**	15.00
398	Jason Jones **RC**	20.00
399	Clay Timpner/600 **RC**	15.00
400	James Parr **RC**	20.00
401	Sean Kazmar **RC**	20.00
402	Andrew Kown **RC**	15.00
403	Jacob McGee/600 **RC**	50.00
404	Mike Butia/600 **RC**	20.00
405	Paul Janish/500 **RC**	20.00
406	Matt Macri **RC**	25.00
407	Mike Nickeas/500 **RC**	15.00
408	Kyle Bloom/550 **RC**	10.00
409	Luis Rivera/500 **RC**	15.00
410	William Bunn/600 **RC**	15.00
411	Enrique Barrera **RC**	20.00
412	Ryan Klosterman **RC**	15.00
413	John Raglani/515 **RC**	15.00
414	Brandon Allen/500 **RC**	20.00
415	Andy Baldwin/600 **RC**	15.00
416	Mark Lowe **RC**	20.00
417	Mitch Einertson **RC**	20.00
418	Ryan Schroyer/600 **RC**	10.00
419	Brad Davis **RC**	15.00
420	Jesse Hoover/500 **RC**	15.00
421	Garrett Broshuis **RC**	15.00
422	Peter Pope **RC**	25.00
423	Brent Dlugach **RC**	15.00
424	Ryan Coultas **RC**	15.00
425	Ryan Royster **RC**	30.00
426	Stephen Chapman **RC**	15.00
427	Bryce Chamberlin **RC**	25.00
428	Joe Koshansky/550 **RC**	40.00
429	William Susdorf **RC**	15.00
430	A.J. Johnson **RC**	15.00
431	Jeremy Sowers **RC**	20.00
432	Justin Pekarek **RC**	15.00
433	Brett Smith **RC**	15.00
434	Matt Durkin **RC**	15.00
435	Daniel Barone **RC**	15.00
436	Scott Hyde **RC**	15.00
437	Thomas Everidge **RC**	25.00
444	Mark Trumbo **RC**	30.00
446	Eric Patterson **RC**	25.00
447	Mike Rozier **RC**	15.00

Gold

Gold (291-447): No Pricing
Production 10 Sets

Platinum

No Pricing
Production One Set

Draft Class

No Pricing
Production 10 Sets

Draft Duos

NM/M

Common Dual Autograph: 15.00
Production 175 Sets

LK	Adam Lind, Ryan Klosterman	40.00
BB	Bill Bray, Collin Balester	25.00
BI	Bill Bray, Ian Desmond	25.00
BM	William Buckner, James Moore	15.00
JH	James Howell, Josh Johnson	15.00
DB	Blake Dewitt, Daniel Batz	25.00
SJ	Brandon Szymanski, Paul Janish	25.00
SH	Brett Smith, Phillip Hughes	40.00
LS	Chris Lambert, Donnie Smith	15.00
LF	Chris Lambert, Mike Ferris	15.00
NS	Chris Nelson, Seth Smith	25.00
NM	Chris Nelson, Matt Macri	30.00
DG	Cory Dunlap, Luis Guerra	30.00
BN	Matt Bush, Chris Nelson	30.00
TH	Curtis Thigpen, Danny Hill	15.00
PT	Dan Putnam, Derek Tharpe	15.00
PJ	David Purcey, Robert Janssen	15.00
DZ	David Purcey, Zachary Jackson	20.00
LH	Donny Lucy, Grant Hansen	15.00
PD	Dustin Pedroia, Andrew Dobies	30.00
MR	Eduardo Morlan, Mark Robinson	15.00
PB	Eddie Prasch, Joseph Bauserman	20.00
EA	Eric Beattie, Andrew Kown	20.00
EJ	Eric Campbell, John Holt	25.00
EM	Eric Hurley, Mike Nickeas	25.00
PI	Erick San Pedro, Devin Ivany	15.00
HH	Gaby Hernandez, Aaron Hathaway	25.00
SK	Seth Smith, Joe Koshansky	30.00
GM	Gio Gonzalez, Timothy Murphey	25.00
BH	Matt Bush, Phillip Hughes	40.00
JR	Grant Johnson, Mark Reed	25.00
GH	Greg Golson, James Happ	20.00
GG	Greg Golson, Sean Gamble	15.00
BS	Homer Bailey, Brandon Szymanski	40.00
BG	Homer Bailey, Rafael Gonzalez	50.00
HJ	Hunter Pence, Jordan Parraz	80.00
SS	Huston Street, Kurt Suzuki	40.00
SW	Huston Street, Ryan Webb	30.00
HB	James Howell, Chad Blackwell	20.00
JM	Jason Jaramillo, Louis Marson	15.00
RS	Jay Rainville, Anthony Swarzak	20.00
JP	Jay Rainville, Patrick Bryant	20.00
FM	Jeff Frazier, Colin Mahoney	15.00
MS	Jeff Marquez, Brett Smith	20.00
MH	Jeff Marquez, Jesse Hoover	25.00
SL	Jeremy Sowers, Charles Lofgren	35.00
JS	Jeremy Sowers, Scott Lewis	25.00
JJ	Jon Poterson, Jason Jones	25.00
ZM	Jon Zeringue, Garrett Mock	20.00
FH	Josh Fields, Lucas Harrell	30.00
FW	Josh Fields, Wes Whisler	40.00
WB	Josh Wahpepah, Josh Baker	15.00
CL	Justin Hoyman, Jeremy Sowers	25.00
OJ	Justin Orenduff, Blake Johnson	25.00
OG	Justin Orenduff, Luis Guerra	20.00
HS	Karl Herren, Michael Schlact	20.00
WF	Kyle Waldrop, Matt Fox	20.00
KB	Kyle Waldrop, Patrick Bryant	25.00
RW	Richie Robnett, Jason Windsor	25.00
SR	Richie Robnett, Kurt Suzuki	25.00
RB	Mark Rogers, Josh Baker	30.00
RG	Mark Rogers, Yovani Gallardo	50.00
BK	Matt Bush, Sean Kazmar	25.00
WE	William Buckner, Enrique Barrera	15.00
WJ	William Buckner, James Howell	20.00
KH	Matt Durkin, Aaron Hathaway	20.00
NB	Neil Walker, Brian Bixler	25.00
NK	Neil Walker, Kyle Bloom	25.00
HG	Phillip Hughes, Christian Garcia	30.00
HP	Phillip Hughes, Jon Poterson	40.00
LA	Ray Liotta, Brandon Allen	25.00
BR	Reid Brignac, Ryan Royster	40.00
RP	Richie Robnett, Dan Putnam	25.00
RH	Richie Robnett, Huston Street	30.00
CO	Steven Register, Seth Smith	25.00
TD	Taylor Tankersley, Brad Davis	15.00
TV	Taylor Tankersley, Jason Vargas	20.00
BT	Thomas Diamond, Brandon Boggs	30.00
DH	Thomas Diamond, Eric Hurley	30.00
ED	Scott Elbert, Blake Dewitt	35.00
ER	Scott Elbert, John Raglani	25.00
PW	Trevor Plouffe, Kyle Waldrop	30.00
PR	Trevor Plouffe, Mark Robinson	25.00
LR	Tyler Lumsden, Adam Russell	15.00
LG	Tyler Lumsden, Gio Gonzalez	25.00
JB	William Buckner, Josh Johnson	20.00
BJ	Matt Bush, Daryl Jones	30.00
GW	Yovani Gallardo, Josh Wahpepah	40.00
JK	Zachary Jackson, Ryan Klosterman	15.00
DR	Blake Dewitt, John Raglani	25.00
GB	Homer Bailey, Greg Goetz	50.00
WR	Reid Brignac, Wade Davis	40.00
HM	Jeff Marquez, Phillip Hughes	40.00
PZ	Jordan Parraz, Benjamin Zobrist	25.00
RL	Luis Rivera, William Layman	15.00
EC	Eric Beattie, Collin Mahoney	15.00
JE	Jeff Frazier, Eric Beattie	15.00
BP	Matt Bush, Trevor Plouffe	30.00
CH	Ryan Coultas, Aaron Hathaway	15.00
SB	Jeremy Sowers, Homer Bailey	60.00
FB	Jeff Fiorentino, Bradley Bergesen	25.00
CF	Bryce Chamberlin, Jeff Fiorentino	20.00
RD	Cory Dunlap, John Raglani	20.00
ZP	Hunter Pence, Benjamin Zobrist	80.00

Draft Picks Autographs

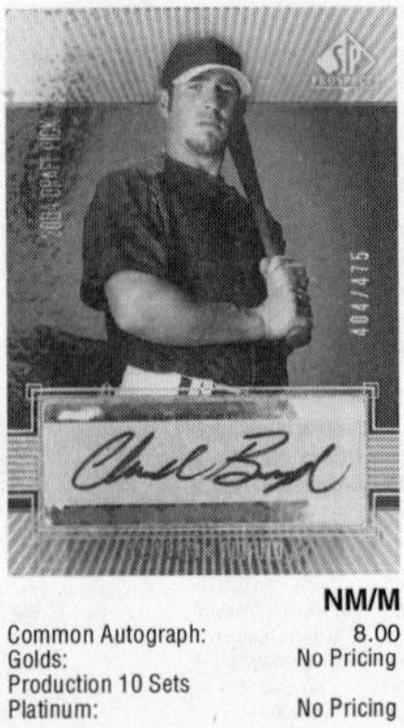

NM/M

Common Autograph: 8.00
Golds: No Pricing
Production 10 Sets
Platinum: No Pricing
Production One Set

AA	Andrew Alvarado/400	8.00
RA	Robert Asanovich/400	15.00
JA	Jonny Ash/400	15.00
GB	Garry Bakker/400	10.00
DB	Daniel Batz/400	10.00
KB	Kristian Bell/400	8.00
BL	Chad Blackwell/400	15.00
NB	Nick Blasi/400	15.00
BO	Kyle Bono/400	10.00
SB	Sebastien Boucher/325	15.00
CB	Chad Boyd/475	8.00
JB	Jermaine Brock/400	8.00
PB	Patrick Bryant/400	10.00
BB	Brandon Burgess/400	10.00
CA	Mike Carp/400	25.00
BC	Brandon Conway/400	8.00
DD	Derek Decarlo/400	10.00
RD	Randy Dicken/475	8.00
JD	Jeffery Dominguez/400	15.00
JF	Jim Fasano/400	15.00
KF	Kevin Frandsen/400	30.00
LF	Lucas French/400	15.00
SE	Sean Gallagher/400	50.00
SG	Sean Gamble/400	10.00
GA	Jared Gaston/400	10.00
GG	Greg Goetz/400	15.00
GR	John Grogan/475	10.00
JG	Jarrett Grube/400	8.00
MG	Matt Guillory/400	10.00
DA	David Haehnel/475	12.00
HA	Dustin Hahn/400	8.00
BH	Brian Hall/400	15.00
DH	Derek Hankins/400	8.00
JO	John Hardy/475	10.00
BE	Benjamin Harrison/387	20.00
KH	Kevin Hart/400	10.00
HE	Justin Hedrick/400	15.00
JH	Jarrett Hoffpauir/400	15.00
HO	Joey Howell/400	15.00
TH	Thomas Hubbard/400	10.00
DI	Devin Ivany/550	10.00
SJ	Steven Jackson/475	15.00
MJ	Mark Jecmen/600	8.00
JK	Jeffrey Katz/400	10.00
KK	Koley Kolberg/400	10.00
LA	Jeff Landing/400	10.00
TL	Trevor Lawhorn/475	10.00
WL	William Layman/400	8.00
JL	Josh LeBlanc/400	10.00
DL	Duron Legrande/400	8.00
LE	Wes Letson/400	10.00
MA	Andrew Macfarlane/400	8.00
MC	Jarod McAuliff/400	15.00
BM	Brad McCann/400	25.00
RM	Ryan McCarthy/400	15.00
CH	Christopher McConnell/400	25.00
ME	Carlos Medero-Stullz/400	8.00
RI	Richard Mercado/475	12.00
CL	Cla Meredith/400	25.00
JM	Joey Metropoulos/400	15.00
CM	Cory Middleton/400	20.00
MI	James Miller/475	12.00
AM	Andrew Moffitt/400	10.00
MO	Craig Molldrem/400	12.00
MU	Joseph Muro/400	8.00
TM	Timothy Murphey/400	10.00
DN	David Nicholson/475	10.00
CN	Chris Niesel/475	15.00
RN	Ryan Norwood/400	25.00
BP	Brandon Parillo/475	15.00
MP	Michael Parisi/475	15.00
CP	Cory Patton/400	15.00
TP	Troy Patton/400	85.00
FP	Fernando Perez/400	20.00
PP	Patrick Perry/475	15.00
RP	Ryan Phillips/400	15.00
GP	Grant Plumley/475	10.00
JQ	Jason Quarles/400	8.00
DR	Douglas Reinhardt/400	8.00
CR	Cliff Remole/400	15.00
BR	Barry Richmond/400	20.00
ER	Eric Ridener/475	10.00
MR	Mark Roberts/400	8.00
AR	Adam Russell/550	8.00
CS	Clint Sammons/400	15.00
FS	Freddy Sandoval/400	10.00
AS	Austin Shappi/475	15.00
MS	Matt Shepherd/400	10.00
HS	Hainley Statia/400	20.00
RS	Richard Steik/400	8.00
DT	Derek Tharpe/400	8.00
WT	William Thompson/475	10.00
BT	Brandon Timm/475	15.00
TR	David Trahan/400	10.00
CW	Cory Wade/400	15.00
WE	Chris Westervelt/400	15.00
MW	Mark Worrell/400	15.00
BZ	Benjamin Zobrist/600	25.00

Draft Generations Triple Autograph

No Pricing
Production 25 Sets

Link to the Future Dual Autograph

NM/M

Common Dual Auto. 10.00
Production 100 Sets

BD	Adrian Beltre, Blake Dewitt	40.00
RF	Scott Rolen, Mike Ferris	40.00

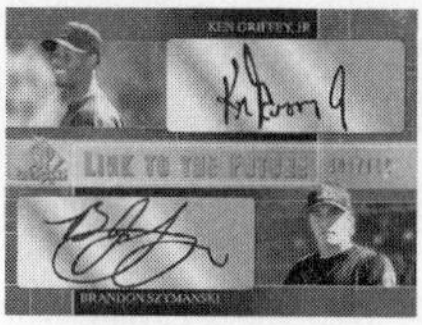

JR	Andruw Jones, Richie Robnett	30.00
KB	Scott Kazmir, Reid Brignac	50.00
JB	Jason Kendall, Brian Bixler	20.00
SR	Ben Sheets, Mark Rogers	40.00
GP	Brian Giles, Dan Putnam	20.00
BG	Carlos Beltran, Greg Golson	30.00
SJ	Johan Santana, Jay Rainville	40.00
WT	Dontrelle Willis, Taylor Tankersley	15.00
JJ	Edwin Jackson, Blake Johnson	15.00
EJ	Eric Chavez, Josh Fields	40.00
QT	Guillermo Quiroz, Curtis Thigpen	10.00
KW	Jason Kendall, Neil Walker	40.00
VM	Javier Vazquez, Jeff Marquez	20.00
MP	Joe Mauer, Trevor Plouffe	50.00
SW	Johan Santana, Kyle Waldrop	40.00
VP	Javier Vazquez, Jon Poterson	20.00
GS	Ken Griffey Jr., Brandon Szymanski	75.00
WB	Kerry Wood, Homer Bailey	50.00
MS	Mike Mussina, Brett Smith	50.00
HS	Todd Helton, Seth Smith	30.00
GZ	Luis Gonzalez, Jon Zeringue	20.00
OH	Magglio Ordonez, Karl Herren	20.00
MB	Mark Mulder, Bill Bray	20.00
PJ	Mark Prior, Grant Johnson	40.00
CF	Matt Clement, Matt Fox	15.00
TN	Miguel Tejada, Chris Nelson	40.00
MH	Mike Mussina, Phillip Hughes	75.00
GB	Nomar Garciaparra, Matt Bush	80.00
PE	Odalis Perez, Scott Elbert	20.00
LS	Paul LoDuca, Erick San Pedro	20.00
HW	Rich Harden, Kyle Waldrop	25.00
CD	Roger Clemens, Thomas Diamond	100.00
RP	Alexis Rios, David Purcey	25.00
RE	Roy Oswalt, Eric Hurley	25.00
RL	Scott Rolen, Chris Lambert	40.00
TS	Tim Hudson, Huston Street	40.00
TJ	Tom Glavine, Jeremy Sowers	35.00
VD	Victor Martinez, Donny Lucy	25.00
BH	Angel Berroa, James Howell	15.00

Link to the Past Dual Autograph

NM/M

Common Dual Autograph
Production 50 Sets

MB	Bill Mazeroski, Brian Bixler	35.00
FL	Carlton Fisk, Tyler Lumsden	35.00
WJ	Dave Winfield, Zachary Jackson	35.00
BW	Johnny Bench, Neil Walker	40.00
JD	Jose Canseco, Dan Putnam	50.00
AS	Billy Williams, Richie Robnett	40.00
RB	Nolan Ryan, Homer Bailey	180.00
PD	Gaylord Perry, Thomas Diamond	50.00
WR	Wade Boggs, Reid Brignac	60.00
WB	Whitey Ford, Brett Smith	30.00
WP	Whitey Ford, Phillip Hughes	60.00

Link to the Future Triple Autograph

NM/M

Common Triple Auto.
Production 50 Sets

BHH	Hank Blalock, Eric Hurley, Benjamin Harrison	40.00
KBS	Scott Kazmir, Reid Brignac, Matt Spring	75.00
SRB	Ben Sheets, Mark Rogers, Josh Baker	50.00
JJB	Edwin Jackson, Blake Johnson, Daniel Batz	20.00
SWM	Johan Santana, Kyle Waldrop, Eduardo Morlan	60.00
VBB	Jose Vidro, Bill Bray, Collin Balester	30.00
GSJ	Ken Griffey Jr., Brandon Szymanski, Paul Janish	60.00
MSH	Mike Mussina, Brett Smith, Jesse Hoover	50.00
OFA	Magglio Ordonez, Josh Fields, Brandon Allen	30.00
PJR	Mark Prior, Grant Johnson, Mark Reed	100.00
GHM	Juan Gonzalez, James Howell, James Moore	40.00
HSW	Rich Harden, Huston Street, Jason Windsor	50.00
GMZ	Luis Gonzalez, Garrett Mock, Jon Zeringue	25.00
HRW	Tim Hudson, Richie Robnett, Ryan Webb	60.00
GTR	Vladimir Guerrero, Mark Trumbo, Luis Rivera	75.00

National Honors

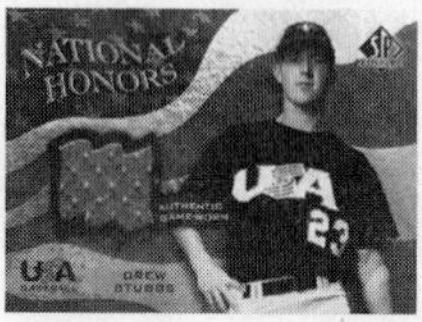

NM/M

Common Player: 4.00
Inserted 1:12

DB	Daniel Bard	8.00
TB	Travis Buck	8.00
JC	Jeff Clement	8.00
BC	Brent Cox	8.00
TC	Trevor Crowe	4.00
JD	Joey Devine	4.00
AG	Alex Gordon	20.00
BH	Brett Hayes	4.00
LH	Luke Hochevar	8.00
SK	Stephen Kahn	4.00
IK	Ian Kennedy	8.00
JL	Jed Lowrie	4.00
JM	John Mayberry Jr.	8.00
MP	Mike Pelfrey	15.00
CR	Cesar Ramos	8.00
MR	Mark Romanczuk	4.00
RR	Ricky Romero	4.00
DS	Drew Stubbs	8.00
TE	Taylor Teagarden	6.00
TT	Troy Tulowitzki	15.00
CV	Chris Valaika	4.00
RZ	Ryan Zimmerman	10.00

2004 SPx

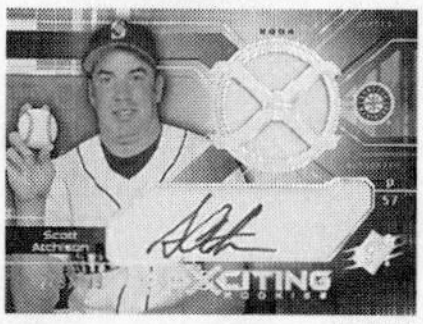

NM/M

Complete Set (202):
Common Player: .25
Common SP (111-145): 3.00
Production 1,599
Common SP (146-154): 5.00
Production 499
Common SP (155-160): 8.00
Production 299
Common Jersey Auto. (161-202): 8.00
Production 799
Pack (4): 5.00
Box (18): 75.00

1	Alfonso Soriano	1.00
2	Todd Helton	.75
3	Andruw Jones	.75
4	Eric Gagne	.50
5	Craig Wilson	.25
6	Brian Giles	.25
7	Miguel Tejada	.50
8	Kevin Brown	.25
9	Shawn Green	.50
10	Ben Sheets	.50
11	John Smoltz	.50
12	Tim Hudson	.50
13	Jason Schmidt	.50
14	Paul Konerko	.50
15	Randy Johnson	1.00
16	Roy Oswalt	.50
17	Mike Lowell	.25
18	Carlos Lee	.50
19	Sean Burroughs	.25
20	Edgar Renteria	.50
21	Michael Young	.25
22	Jose Vidro	.25
23	Scott Rolen	1.00
24	Rafael Furcal	.50
25	Tom Glavine	.75
26	Scott Podsednik	.25
27	Gary Sheffield	.75
28	Eric Chavez	.50
29	Mark Prior	.75
30	Chipper Jones	1.00
31	Frank Thomas	1.00
32	Victor Martinez	.50
33	Jake Peavy	.50
34	Carlos Beltran	1.00
35	Roy Halladay	.50
36	Mark Teixeira	.75
37	Jacque Jones	.25
38	Mike Sweeney	.25
39	Troy Glaus	.50
40	Pat Burrell	.50
41	Ichiro Suzuki	2.00
42	Vladimir Guerrero	1.00
43	Bobby Abreu	.50
44	Jim Edmonds	.50
45	Garret Anderson	.40
46	J.D. Drew	.40
47	C.C. Sabathia	.25
48	Joe Mauer	.50
49	Phil Nevin	.25
50	Hank Blalock	.50
51	Carlos Zambrano	.50
52	Mike Piazza	1.50
53	Manny Ramirez	1.00
54	Lance Berkman	.50
55	Delmon Young	.50
56	Nomar Garciaparra	1.00
57	Alex Rodriguez	2.50
58	Rickie Weeks	.50
59	Adrian Beltre	.50
60	Albert Pujols	2.50
61	Richie Sexson	.50
62	Magglio Ordonez	.50
63	Derrek Lee	.75
64	Sammy Sosa	1.50
65	Jason Giambi	.75
66	Curt Schilling	1.00
67	Jorge Posada	.50
68	Rafael Palmeiro	.75
69	Jeff Kent	.50
70	Jose Reyes	.50
71	David Ortiz	1.00
72	Aubrey Huff	.25
73	Jim Thome	1.00
74	Andy Pettitte	.50
75	Barry Zito	.50
76	Carlos Delgado	.50
77	Hideki Matsui	2.00
78	Sean Casey	.25
79	Luis Gonzalez	.25
80	Marcus Giles	.25
81	Preston Wilson	.25
82	Javy Lopez	.25
83	Mark Mulder	.50
84	Derek Jeter	2.50
85	Miguel Cabrera	1.00
86	Vernon Wells	.50
87	Roger Clemens	2.50
88	Lyle Overbay	.25
89	Bret Boone	.25
90	Melvin Mora	.25
91	Greg Maddux	2.00
92	Kerry Wood	.50
93	Ivan Rodriguez	.75
94	Pedro J. Martinez	1.00
95	Jeff Bagwell	.75
96	Torii Hunter	.50
97	Ken Griffey Jr.	2.00
98	Mike Mussina	.75
99	Oliver Perez	.25
100	Josh Beckett	.50
101	Bob Gibson	4.00
102	Cal Ripken Jr.	8.00
103	Ted Williams	8.00
104	Nolan Ryan	8.00
105	Mickey Mantle	10.00
106	Ernie Banks	5.00
107	Joe DiMaggio	6.00
108	Stan Musial	5.00
109	Tom Seaver	4.00
110	Mike Schmidt	6.00
111	Jerry Gil **RC**	3.00
112	Dioner Navarro **RC**	8.00
113	Bartolome Fortunato **RC**	3.00
114	Carlos Hines **RC**	3.00
115	Franklyn Gracesqui **RC**	3.00
116	Aarom Baldiris **RC**	5.00
117	Casey Daigle **RC**	3.00
118	Joey Gathright **RC**	5.00
119	William Bergolla **RC**	3.00
120	Jeff Bennett **RC**	3.00
121	Lincoln Holdzkom **RC**	3.00
122	Jorge Vasquez **RC**	3.00
123	Donnie Kelly **RC**	3.00
124	Yadier Molina **RC**	8.00
125	Ryan Wing	3.00
126	Justin Germano **RC**	3.00
127	Freddy Guzman **RC**	3.00
128	Onil Joseph **RC**	3.00
129	Roman Colon **RC**	3.00
130	Roberto Novoa **RC**	5.00
131	Renyel Pinto **RC**	5.00
132	Evan Rust **RC**	3.00
133	Orlando Rodriguez **RC**	3.00
134	Edwardo Sierra **RC**	5.00
135	Mike Rose **RC**	3.00
136	Phil Stockman **RC**	3.00
137	Greg Dobbs **RC**	3.00
138	Brad Halsey **RC**	3.00
139	David Aardsma	5.00
140	Joe Hietpas **RC**	3.00
141	Josh Labandeira **RC**	3.00
142	Mariano Gomez **RC**	3.00
143	Jeff Bajenaru **RC**	3.00
144	Travis Blackley **RC**	3.00
145	Abe Alvarez	5.00
146	Ramon Ramirez **RC**	5.00
147	Edwin Moreno **RC**	5.00
148	Ronny Cedeno **RC**	8.00
149	Hector Gimenez **RC**	5.00
150	Carlos Vasquez **RC**	8.00
151	Jesse Crain	8.00
152	Logan Kensing **RC**	5.00
153	Sean Henn	5.00
154	Rusty Tucker **RC**	5.00
155	Justin Lehr **RC**	5.00
156	Ian Snell **RC**	15.00
157	Merkin Valdez **RC**	10.00
158	Scott Proctor **RC**	8.00
159	Jose Capellan **RC**	8.00
160	Kazuo Matsui **RC**	8.00
161	Chris Oxspring **RC**	8.00
162	Jimmy Serrano **RC**	10.00
163	Jeff Keppinger **RC**	35.00
164	Brandon Medders **RC**	8.00
165	Brian Dallimore **RC**	10.00
166	Chad Bentz **RC**	12.00
167	Chris Aguila **RC**	10.00
168	Chris Saenz **RC**	10.00
169	Frank Francisco **RC**	10.00
170	Colby Miller **RC**	12.00
171	David Crouthers	10.00
172	Charles Thomas **RC**	15.00
173	Dennis Sarfate **RC**	12.00
174	Lance Cormier **RC**	10.00
175	Joe Horgan **RC**	10.00
176	Fernando Nieve **RC**	10.00
177	Jake Woods	12.00
178	Matt Treanor **RC**	12.00
179	Jerome Gamble **RC**	15.00
180	John Gall **RC**	15.00
181	Jorge Sequea **RC**	10.00
182	Justin Hampson **RC**	10.00
183	Justin Huisman **RC**	15.00
184	Justin Knoedler **RC**	12.00
185	Justin Leone **RC**	15.00
186	Scott Atchison **RC**	12.00
187	Jon Knott **RC**	15.00
188	Kevin Cave **RC**	10.00
189	Jason Frasor **RC**	10.00
190	George Sherrill **RC**	12.00
191	Mike Gosling	10.00
192	Mike Johnston **RC**	10.00
193	Mike Rouse	10.00
194	Nick Regilio **RC**	10.00
195	Ryan Meaux **RC**	10.00
196	Scott Dohmann **RC**	15.00
197	Shawn Camp **RC**	10.00
198	Shawn Hill **RC**	10.00
199	Shingo Takatsu **RC**	15.00
200	Tim Bausher **RC**	10.00
201	Tim Bittner **RC**	10.00
202	Scott Kazmir	60.00

Spectrum

Stars (1-100): 5-10X
SP's (101-202): 2-3X
Production 25 Sets

Master Player Prints

No Pricing
Production One Set

Superscripts

NM/M

Common Player: 8.00
Inserted 1:18

JB	Josh Beckett	20.00
MC	Miguel Cabrera	25.00
EC	Eric Chavez	15.00
BC	Bobby Crosby	15.00
BF	Bartolome Fortunato	10.00
NG	Nomar Garciaparra/SP	80.00
MG	Mariano Gomez	10.00
KG	Ken Griffey Jr.	75.00
RH	Rich Harden	15.00
SH	Sean Henn	10.00
CH	Carlos Hines	8.00
LH	Lincoln Holdzkom	10.00
EJ	Edwin Jackson	10.00
DJ	Derek Jeter/SP	200.00
DK	Donnie Kelly	8.00
LA	Josh Labandeira	8.00
JL	Justin Lehr	10.00
JM	Joe Mauer	35.00
IO	Ivan Ochoa	8.00
RO	Roy Oswalt	20.00
MP	Mark Prior	40.00
SP	Scott Proctor	10.00
AP	Albert Pujols/SP	240.00
RR	Ramon Ramirez	12.00
JR	Jose Reyes	35.00
CR	Cal Ripken Jr./SP	125.00
RU	Evan Rust	10.00
ES	Edwardo Sierra	10.00
AS	Alfredo Simon	10.00
IS	Ian Snell	25.00
PS	Phil Stockman	10.00
TE	Miguel Tejada	35.00
MT	Mark Teixeira	30.00
MV	Merkin Valdez	12.00
CV	Carlos Vasquez	10.00
VE	Michael Vento	15.00
BW	Brandon Webb	10.00
RW	Rickie Weeks	15.00
DW	Dontrelle Willis	25.00
DY	Delmon Young	20.00

Swatch Supremecy Cut Signatures

No pricing due to scarcity.
No Pricing

Swatch Supremecy Signatures

NM/M
Common Player: 8.00
Production 999 unless noted.
Spectrum: 1.5-3X
Production 25 Sets
GA Garret Anderson/275 20.00
RB Rocco Baldelli 20.00
JB Josh Beckett 15.00
AB Angel Berroa 10.00
HB Hank Blalock 15.00
SB Sean Burroughs 10.00
MC Miguel Cabrera 30.00
EC Eric Chavez/275 20.00
CC Chad Cordero 10.00
BC Bobby Crosby 15.00
AE Adam Eaton 10.00
NG Nomar Garciaparra/275 60.00
MG Marcus Giles 15.00
GR Khalil Greene 25.00
KG Ken Griffey Jr./275 85.00
RH Rich Harden 20.00
DJ Derek Jeter/275 180.00
CK Casey Kotchman 20.00
CL Cliff Lee 15.00
DL Derrek Lee/275 30.00
JM Joe Mauer 40.00
RO Roy Oswalt 20.00
LO Lyle Overbay 15.00
CP Corey Patterson 20.00
JP Jake Peavy 35.00
SP Scott Podsednik 20.00
MP Mark Prior/275 40.00
AP Albert Pujols/275 240.00
HR Horacio Ramirez 10.00
JR Jose Reyes 35.00
CR Cal Ripken Jr./275 140.00
NR Nolan Ryan/275 120.00
BS Ben Sheets 20.00
MT Mark Teixeira 25.00
BW Brandon Webb 15.00
RW Rickie Weeks 15.00
DW Dontrelle Willis 25.00
JW Jerome Williams 15.00
MY Michael Young 15.00

Winning Materials

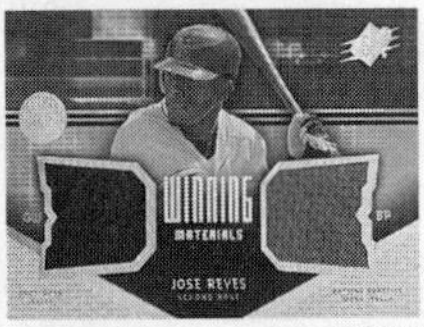

NM/M
Common Player: 8.00
Inserted 1:18
Spectrum: 2-3X
Production 25 Sets
JB Jeff Bagwell 10.00
BE Josh Beckett 10.00
HB Hank Blalock 10.00
KB Kevin Brown 8.00
EC Eric Chavez 8.00
RC Roger Clemens 20.00
CD Carlos Delgado 10.00
JG Jason Giambi 12.00
TG Troy Glaus 8.00
SG Shawn Green 8.00
VG Vladimir Guerrero 12.00
DJ Derek Jeter 35.00
CJ Chipper Jones 10.00
GM Greg Maddux 15.00
HM Hideki Matsui 30.00
MM Mike Mussina 10.00
RP Rafael Palmeiro 10.00
PI Mike Piazza 15.00
JP Jorge Posada 10.00
MP Mark Prior 10.00
AP Albert Pujols 30.00
MR Manny Ramirez 15.00
JR Jose Reyes 15.00
SR Scott Rolen 15.00
GS Gary Sheffield 10.00
SS Sammy Sosa 15.00
IS Ichiro Suzuki 30.00
TE Miguel Tejada 10.00
JT Jim Thome 12.00

2005 SP Collection

NM/M
Complete SPx Set (100): 25.00
Common Player: .25
Pack (5): 6.00
Box (20): 100.00
1 Aaron Harang .25
2 Aaron Rowand .25
3 Aaron Miles .25
4 Adrian Gonzalez .25
5 Alex Rios .25
6 Angel Berroa .25
7 B.J. Upton .25
8 Brandon Claussen .25
9 Andy Marte .25
10 Brandon Webb .25
11 Bronson Arroyo .25
12 Casey Kotchman .25
13 Cesar Izturis .25

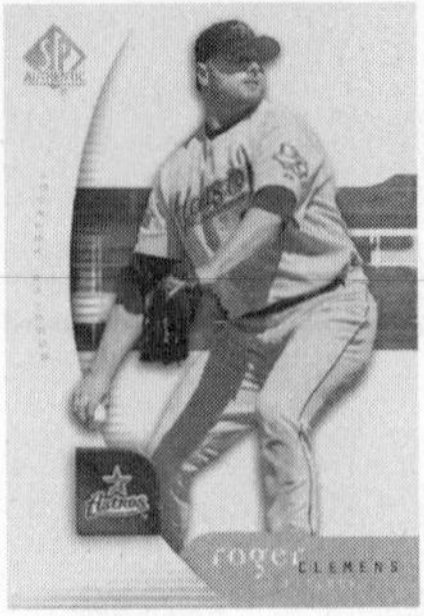

14 Chad Cordero .25
15 Chad Tracy .25
16 Charles Thomas .25
17 Chase Utley .50
18 Chone Figgins .25
19 Chris Burke .25
20 Cliff Lee .25
21 Clint Barmes .25
22 Coco Crisp .25
23 Bill Hall .25
24 Dallas McPherson .25
25 Brad Halsey .25
26 Daniel Cabrera .25
27 Danny Haren .25
28 David Bush .25
29 David DeJesus .25
30 D.J. Houlton .25
31 Derek Jeter 3.00
32 Dewon Brazelton .25
33 Edwin Jackson .25
34 Brad Hawpe .25
35 Brandon Inge .25
36 Brett Myers .25
37 Garrett Atkins .25
38 Gavin Floyd .25
39 Grady Sizemore .50
40 Guillermo Mota .25
41 Carlos Guillen .25
42 Gustavo Chacin .25
43 Huston Street .25
44 Chris Duffy .25
45 J.D. Closser .25
46 J.J. Hardy .25
47 Jason Bartlett .25
48 Jason Dubois .25
49 Chris Shelton .25
50 Jason Lane .25
51 Jayson Werth .25
52 Jeff Baker .25
53 Jeff Francis .25
54 Jeremy Bonderman .25
55 Jeremy Reed .25
56 Jerome Williams .25
57 Jesse Crain .25
58 Chris Young .25
59 Jhonny Peralta .25
60 Joe Blanton .25
61 Joe Crede .25
62 Joel Pineiro .25
63 Joey Gathright .25
64 John Buck .25
65 Jonny Gomes .25
66 Jorge Cantu .25
67 Dan Johnson .25
68 Jose Valverde .25
69 Ervin Santana .25
70 Justin Morneau .50
71 Keiichi Yabu .25
72 Ken Griffey Jr. 2.00
73 Jason Repko .25
74 Kevin Youkilis .25
75 Koyie Hill .25
76 Laynce Nix .25
77 Luke Scott **RC** 1.00
78 Juan Rivera .25
79 Justin Duchscherer .25
80 Mark Teahen .25
81 Lance Niekro .25
82 Michael Cuddyer .25
83 Nick Swisher .25
84 Noah Lowry .25
85 Matt Holliday .50
86 Reed Johnson .25
87 Rich Harden .25
88 Robb Quinlan .25
89 Nick Johnson .25
90 Ryan Howard 1.00
91 Nook Logan .25
92 Steve Schmoll .25
93 Tadahito Iguchi .25
94 Willy Taveras .25
95 Wily Mo Pena .25
96 Xavier Nady .25
97 Yadier Molina .25
98 Yhency Brazoban .25
99 Ryan Freel .25
100 Zack Greinke .25
Complete SP Authentic Set (100): 25.00
Common Player: .25
1 A.J. Burnett .25
2 Aaron Rowand .25
3 Adam Dunn .75
4 Adrian Beltre .50
5 Adrian Gonzalez .25
6 Akinori Otsuka .25
7 Albert Pujols 3.00
8 Andre Dawson .50
9 Andruw Jones .50
10 Aramis Ramirez .50
11 Barry Larkin .50
12 Ben Sheets .50
13 Bo Jackson .50
14 Bobby Abreu .50
15 Bobby Crosby .50
16 Bronson Arroyo .25
17 Cal Ripken Jr. 4.00
18 Carl Crawford .25
19 Carlos Zambrano .50
20 Casey Kotchman .25
21 Cesar Izturis .25
22 Chone Figgins .25
23 Corey Patterson .25
24 Craig Biggio .50
25 Dale Murphy .50
26 Dallas McPherson .25
27 Danny Haren .25
28 Darryl Strawberry .25
29 David Ortiz 1.00
30 David Wright 1.00
31 Derek Jeter 3.00
32 Derrek Lee .50
33 Don Mattingly 1.50
34 Dwight Gooden .25
35 Edgar Renteria .50
36 Eric Chavez .50
37 Eric Gagne .25
38 Gary Sheffield .50
39 Gavin Floyd .25
40 Pedro Martinez 1.00
41 Greg Maddux 2.00
42 Hank Blalock .50
43 Huston Street .25
44 J.D. Drew .25
45 Jake Peavy .50
46 Jake Westbrook .25
47 Jason Bay .25
48 Austin Kearns .25
49 Jeremy Reed .25
50 Jim Rice .50
51 Jimmy Rollins .50
52 Joe Blanton .25
53 Joe Mauer .50
54 Johan Santana 1.00
55 John Smoltz .50
56 Johnny Estrada .25
57 Jose Reyes .50
58 Ken Griffey Jr. 2.00
59 Kerry Wood .50
60 Khalil Greene .50
61 Marcus Giles .25
62 Melvin Mora .25
63 Mark Grace .50
64 Mark Mulder .50
65 Mark Prior 1.00
66 Mark Teixeira .50
67 Matt Clement .25
68 Michael Young .25
69 Miguel Cabrera 1.00
70 Miguel Tejada .75
71 Mike Piazza 1.50
72 Mike Schmidt 2.00
73 Nolan Ryan 3.00
74 Oliver Perez .25
75 Nick Johnson .25
76 Paul Molitor .75
77 Rafael Palmeiro .50
78 Randy Johnson 1.00
79 Reggie Jackson 1.00
80 Rich Harden .25
81 Rickie Weeks .50
82 Robin Yount 1.00
83 Roger Clemens 3.00
84 Roy Oswalt .25
85 Ryan Howard 1.00
86 Ryne Sandberg 2.00
87 Scott Kazmir .25
88 Scott Rolen 1.00
89 Sean Burroughs .25
90 Sean Casey .25
91 Shingo Takatsu .25
92 Tim Hudson .50
93 Tony Gwynn 1.00
94 Torii Hunter .50
95 Travis Hafner .25
96 Victor Martinez .25
97 Vladimir Guerrero 1.00
98 Wade Boggs .50
99 Will Clark .50
100 Yadier Molina .25

SP Authentic Chirography

No Pricing
Production 15 Sets

SP Authentic Chirography Triple

No Pricing
Production Five Sets

SP Authentic Honors

NM/M
Common Player: 1.00
Production 299 Sets
JB Jason Bay 1.50
AB Adrian Beltre 1.50
WB Wade Boggs 1.50
BO Jeremy Bonderman 1.00
CA Miguel Cabrera 2.00
WC Will Clark 1.50
RC Roger Clemens 6.00
CC Carl Crawford 1.00
BC Bobby Crosby 1.50
MG Marcus Giles 1.00
DG Dwight Gooden 1.50
GR Khalil Greene 2.00
ZG Zack Greinke 1.00
KG Ken Griffey Jr. 4.00
TG Tony Gwynn 2.00
TH Travis Hafner 1.00
RH Rich Harden 1.00
BJ Bo Jackson 2.00
DJ Derek Jeter 6.00
SK Scott Kazmir 1.00
BL Barry Larkin 1.50
VM Victor Martinez 1.00
JM Joe Mauer 1.50
MC Dallas McPherson 1.00
PM Paul Molitor 2.00
MO Justin Morneau 1.00
DM Dale Murphy 1.50
DO David Ortiz 2.00
CP Corey Patterson 1.00
JP Jake Peavy 1.50
OP Oliver Perez 1.00
AP Albert Pujols 6.00
AR Aramis Ramirez 1.50
RE Jose Reyes 1.00
CR Cal Ripken Jr. 8.00
JR Jimmy Rollins 1.50
NR Nolan Ryan 6.00
RS Ryne Sandberg 4.00
JS Johan Santana 2.00
MS Mike Schmidt 4.00
BS Ben Sheets 1.50
SM John Smoltz 1.50
ST Shingo Takatsu 1.00
MT Mark Teixeira 1.50
TE Miguel Tejada 2.00
BU B.J. Upton 1.00
JW Jake Westbrook 1.00
DW David Wright 3.00
MY Michael Young 1.00
CZ Carlos Zambrano 1.50

SP Authentic Honors Jersey

NM/M
Common Player: 4.00
Production 130 Sets
JB Jason Bay 4.00
AB Adrian Beltre 6.00
WB Wade Boggs 8.00
BO Jeremy Bonderman 4.00
CA Miguel Cabrera 8.00
WC Will Clark 6.00
RC Roger Clemens 10.00
CC Carl Crawford 4.00
BC Bobby Crosby 4.00
MG Marcus Giles 4.00
DG Dwight Gooden 6.00
GR Khalil Greene 8.00
ZG Zack Greinke 4.00
KG Ken Griffey Jr. 15.00
TG Tony Gwynn 8.00
TH Travis Hafner 4.00
RH Rich Harden 4.00
BJ Bo Jackson 10.00
DJ Derek Jeter 15.00
SK Scott Kazmir 4.00
BL Barry Larkin 6.00
VM Victor Martinez 4.00
JM Joe Mauer 6.00
MC Dallas McPherson 4.00
PM Paul Molitor 8.00
MO Justin Morneau 4.00
DM Dale Murphy 8.00
DO David Ortiz 8.00
CP Corey Patterson 4.00
JP Jake Peavy 6.00
OP Oliver Perez 4.00
AP Albert Pujols 15.00
AR Aramis Ramirez 6.00
RE Jose Reyes 6.00
CR Cal Ripken Jr. 20.00
JR Jimmy Rollins 6.00
NR Nolan Ryan 15.00
RS Ryne Sandberg 10.00
JS Johan Santana 8.00
MS Mike Schmidt 8.00
BS Ben Sheets 4.00
SM John Smoltz 6.00
ST Shingo Takatsu 4.00
MT Mark Teixeira 6.00
TE Miguel Tejada 6.00
BU B.J. Upton 6.00
JW Jake Westbrook 4.00
DW David Wright 15.00
MY Michael Young 4.00
CZ Carlos Zambrano 6.00

SP Authentic Honors Signatures

No Pricing
Production Five Sets

SP Authentic Materials

NM/M
Common Player:
Production 199 Sets
Gold: 1X
Production 99 Sets

1	A.J. Burnett	4.00
2	Aaron Rowand	4.00
3	Adam Dunn	6.00
4	Adrian Beltre	6.00
5	Adrian Gonzalez	4.00
6	Akinori Otsuka	4.00
7	Albert Pujols	15.00
8	Andre Dawson	6.00
9	Andruw Jones	6.00
10	Aramis Ramirez	6.00
11	Barry Larkin	6.00
12	Ben Sheets	4.00
13	Bo Jackson	8.00
14	Bobby Abreu	4.00
15	Bobby Crosby	4.00
16	Bronson Arroyo	6.00
17	Cal Ripken Jr.	20.00
18	Carl Crawford	4.00
19	Carlos Zambrano	4.00
20	Casey Kotchman	4.00
21	Cesar Izturis	4.00
22	Chone Figgins	4.00
23	Corey Patterson	4.00
24	Craig Biggio	6.00
25	Dale Murphy	6.00
26	Dallas McPherson	4.00
27	Danny Haren	4.00
28	Darryl Strawberry	4.00
29	David Ortiz	8.00
30	David Wright	10.00
31	Derek Jeter	15.00
32	Derrek Lee	8.00
33	Don Mattingly	10.00
34	Dwight Gooden	4.00
35	Edgar Renteria	6.00
36	Eric Chavez	4.00
37	Eric Gagne	6.00
38	Gary Sheffield	6.00
39	Gavin Floyd	4.00
40	Pedro Martinez	8.00
41	Greg Maddux	10.00
42	Hank Blalock	4.00
43	Huston Street	6.00
44	J.D. Drew	4.00
45	Jake Peavy	6.00
46	Jake Westbrook	4.00
47	Jason Bay	4.00
48	Austin Kearns	4.00
49	Jeremy Reed	4.00
50	Jim Rice	6.00
51	Jimmy Rollins	6.00
52	Joe Blanton	4.00
53	Joe Mauer	6.00
54	Johan Santana	6.00
55	John Smoltz	6.00
56	Johnny Estrada	4.00
57	Jose Reyes	6.00
58	Ken Griffey Jr.	12.00
59	Kerry Wood	6.00
60	Khalil Greene	6.00
61	Marcus Giles	4.00
62	Melvin Mora	4.00
63	Mark Grace	6.00
64	Mark Mulder	4.00
65	Mark Prior	8.00
66	Mark Teixeira	6.00
67	Matt Clement	4.00
68	Michael Young	4.00
69	Miguel Cabrera	6.00
70	Miguel Tejada	6.00
71	Mike Piazza	8.00
72	Mike Schmidt	8.00
73	Nolan Ryan	15.00
74	Oliver Perez	4.00
75	Nick Johnson	4.00
76	Paul Molitor	8.00
77	Rafael Palmeiro	6.00
78	Randy Johnson	8.00
79	Reggie Jackson	8.00
80	Rich Harden	6.00
81	Rickie Weeks	5.00
82	Robin Yount	8.00
83	Roger Clemens	10.00
84	Roy Oswalt	4.00
85	Ryan Howard	15.00
86	Ryne Sandberg	8.00
87	Scott Kazmir	4.00
88	Scott Rolen	6.00
89	Sean Burroughs	4.00
90	Sean Casey	4.00
91	Shingo Takatsu	4.00
92	Tim Hudson	6.00
93	Tony Gwynn	8.00
94	Torii Hunter	6.00
95	Travis Hafner	4.00
96	Victor Martinez	4.00
97	Vladimir Guerrero	8.00
98	Wade Boggs	6.00
99	Will Clark	6.00
100	Yadier Molina	4.00

SP Authentic Signature Materials

No Pricing
Production 10 Sets

SP Authentic Signatures

		NM/M
Production 25-550		
Gold:		No Pricing
Production 10 Sets		
2	Aaron Rowand/550	20.00
3	Adam Dunn/25	20.00
4	Adrian Beltre/125	15.00
5	Adrian Gonzalez/550	15.00
6	Akinori Otsuka/475	15.00
8	Andre Dawson/125	15.00
10	Aramis Ramirez/475	15.00
11	Barry Larkin/125	20.00
12	Ben Sheets/350	12.00
15	Bobby Crosby/350	10.00
16	Bronson Arroyo/550	15.00
18	Carl Crawford/475	15.00
20	Casey Kotchman/550	10.00
21	Cesar Izturis/550	8.00
22	Chone Figgins/550	15.00
23	Corey Patterson/350	10.00
24	Craig Biggio/125	30.00
25	Dale Murphy/350	20.00
26	Dallas McPherson/550	10.00
27	Danny Haren/550	10.00
28	Darryl Strawberry/125	12.00
30	David Wright/350	60.00
31	Derek Jeter/150	140.00
32	Derrek Lee/350	15.00
34	Dwight Gooden/475	15.00
36	Eric Chavez/75	12.00
39	Gavin Floyd/550	10.00
43	Huston Street/550	25.00
45	Jake Peavy/475	15.00
46	Jake Westbrook/550	10.00
47	Jason Bay/475	12.00
48	Austin Kearns/75	10.00
49	Jeremy Reed/550	15.00
50	Jim Rice/350	15.00
52	Joe Blanton/550	10.00
53	Joe Mauer/350	20.00
57	Jose Reyes/475	35.00
60	Khalil Greene/350	20.00
62	Melvin Mora/475	12.00
64	Mark Mulder/350	15.00
66	Mark Teixeira/125	25.00
67	Matt Clement/350	20.00
68	Michael Young/475	15.00
69	Miguel Cabrera/125	25.00
74	Oliver Perez/475	10.00
75	Nick Johnson/550	10.00
84	Roy Oswalt/125	20.00
85	Ryan Howard/550	70.00
86	Ryne Sandberg/25	125.00
87	Scott Kazmir/475	15.00
89	Sean Burroughs/475	8.00
91	Shingo Takatsu/550	10.00

SP Collection of Stars

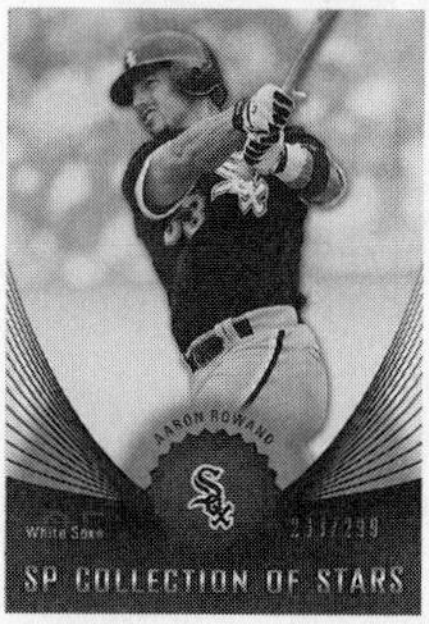

		NM/M
Common Player:		1.00
Production 299 Sets		
BR	Bronson Arroyo	1.00
GA	Garrett Atkins	1.00
JE	Jeff Baker	1.00
BA	Clint Barmes	1.00
JB	Jason Bartlett	1.00
JA	Jason Bay	1.00
BE	Adrian Beltre	1.50
BL	Joe Blanton	1.00
BO	Jeremy Bonderman	1.00
YB	Yhency Brazoban	1.00
CB	Chris Burke	1.50
AB	A.J. Burnett	1.00
DB	David Bush	1.00
DC	Daniel Cabrera	1.00
MC	Miguel Cabrera	2.00
CA	Jorge Cantu	1.00
GC	Gustavo Chacin	1.00
RC	Roger Clemens	6.00
JD	J.D. Closser	1.00
CH	Chad Cordero	1.00
JC	Jesse Crain	1.00
CC	Carl Crawford	1.00
CO	Coco Crisp	1.00
DD	David DeJesus	1.00
DU	Jason Dubois	1.00
CD	Chris Duffy	1.00
CF	Chone Figgins	1.00
GF	Gavin Floyd	1.00
JF	Jeff Francis	1.00
RF	Ryan Freel	1.00
JG	Joey Gathright	1.00
GO	Jonny Gomes	1.00
AG	Adrian Gonzalez	1.00
GR	Khalil Greene	2.00
ZG	Zack Greinke	1.00
KG	Ken Griffey Jr.	4.00
CG	Carlos Guillen	1.00
TR	Travis Hafner	1.00
BH	Bill Hall	1.00
RH	Rich Harden	1.50
DH	Danny Haren	1.00
MH	Matt Holliday	1.00
HO	Ryan Howard	2.00
BI	Brandon Inge	1.00
CI	Cesar Izturis	1.00
EJ	Edwin Jackson	1.00
DJ	Derek Jeter	6.00
NJ	Nick Johnson	1.00
RJ	Reed Johnson	1.00
SK	Scott Kazmir	1.00
CK	Casey Kotchman	1.00
JL	Jason Lane	1.00
LE	Brandon League	1.00
CL	Cliff Lee	1.00
GM	Greg Maddux	4.00
AM	Andy Marte	1.00
JM	Joe Mauer	1.50
DM	Dallas McPherson	1.00
YM	Yadier Molina	1.00
MM	Melvin Mora	1.00
MO	Guillermo Mota	1.00
BM	Brett Myers	1.00
DO	David Ortiz	2.00
CP	Corey Patterson	1.00
JP	Jake Peavy	1.50
WM	Wily Mo Pena	1.00
OP	Oliver Perez	1.00
PI	Joel Pineiro	1.00
MP	Mark Prior	2.00
AP	Albert Pujols	6.00
RQ	Robb Quinlan	1.00
RA	Aramis Ramirez	1.50
JR	Jeremy Reed	1.00
RE	Jose Reyes	1.50
RI	Alex Rios	1.00
CR	Cal Ripken Jr.	8.00
RO	Jimmy Rollins	1.50
AR	Aaron Rowand	1.00
JS	Johan Santana	2.00
MS	Mike Schmidt	4.00
LS	Luke Scott	1.00
CS	Chris Shelton	1.00
GS	Grady Sizemore	1.50
SM	John Smoltz	1.50
HS	Huston Street	1.00
NS	Nick Swisher	1.00
ST	Shingo Takatsu	1.00
WT	Willy Taveras	1.00
MT	Mark Teahen	1.00
TE	Mark Teixeira	1.50
MI	Miguel Tejada	1.50
TH	Charles Thomas	1.00
CT	Chad Tracy	1.00
BU	B.J. Upton	1.50
WE	Jayson Werth	1.00
JW	Jake Westbrook	1.00
DW	David Wright	3.00
KY	Kevin Youkilis	1.00
MY	Michael Young	1.00
CZ	Carlos Zambrano	1.50

SP Collection of Stars Jersey

		NM/M
Production 130 Sets		
BR	Bronson Arroyo	4.00
GA	Garrett Atkins	4.00
JE	Jeff Baker	4.00
BA	Clint Barmes	6.00
JB	Jason Bartlett	4.00
JA	Jason Bay	4.00
BE	Adrian Beltre	6.00
BL	Joe Blanton	4.00
BO	Jeremy Bonderman	4.00
YB	Yhency Brazoban	4.00
CB	Chris Burke	4.00
AB	A.J. Burnett	4.00
DB	David Bush	4.00
DC	Daniel Cabrera	4.00
MC	Miguel Cabrera	8.00
CA	Jorge Cantu	4.00
GC	Gustavo Chacin	4.00
RC	Roger Clemens	10.00
JD	J.D. Closser	4.00
CH	Chad Cordero	4.00
JC	Jesse Crain	4.00
CC	Carl Crawford	4.00
CO	Coco Crisp	4.00
DD	David DeJesus	4.00
DU	Jason Dubois	4.00
CD	Chris Duffy	6.00
CF	Chone Figgins	4.00
GF	Gavin Floyd	4.00
JF	Jeff Francis	4.00
RF	Ryan Freel	4.00
JG	Joey Gathright	4.00
GO	Jonny Gomes	6.00
AG	Adrian Gonzalez	6.00
GR	Khalil Greene	6.00
ZG	Zack Greinke	4.00
KG	Ken Griffey Jr.	15.00
CG	Carlos Guillen	4.00
TR	Travis Hafner	4.00
BH	Bill Hall	4.00
RH	Rich Harden	4.00
DH	Danny Haren	4.00
MH	Matt Holliday	8.00
HO	Ryan Howard	15.00
BI	Brandon Inge	4.00
CI	Cesar Izturis	4.00
EJ	Edwin Jackson	4.00
DJ	Derek Jeter	15.00
NJ	Nick Johnson	4.00
RJ	Reed Johnson	4.00
SK	Scott Kazmir	4.00
CK	Casey Kotchman	4.00
JL	Jason Lane	4.00
LE	Brandon League	4.00
CL	Cliff Lee	4.00
GM	Greg Maddux	10.00
AM	Andy Marte	4.00
JM	Joe Mauer	6.00
DM	Dallas McPherson	4.00
YM	Yadier Molina	4.00
MM	Melvin Mora	4.00
MO	Guillermo Mota	4.00
BM	Brett Myers	4.00
DO	David Ortiz	8.00
CP	Corey Patterson	4.00
JP	Jake Peavy	6.00
WM	Wily Mo Pena	4.00
OP	Oliver Perez	4.00
PI	Joel Pineiro	4.00
MP	Mark Prior	6.00
AP	Albert Pujols	15.00
RQ	Robb Quinlan	4.00
RA	Aramis Ramirez	6.00
JR	Jeremy Reed	4.00
RE	Jose Reyes	6.00
RI	Alex Rios	4.00
CR	Cal Ripken Jr.	20.00
RO	Jimmy Rollins	6.00
AR	Aaron Rowand	6.00
JS	Johan Santana	8.00
MS	Mike Schmidt	10.00
LS	Luke Scott	4.00
CS	Chris Shelton	4.00
GS	Grady Sizemore	6.00
SM	John Smoltz	6.00
HS	Huston Street	6.00
NS	Nick Swisher	4.00
ST	Shingo Takatsu	4.00
WT	Willy Taveras	4.00
MT	Mark Teahen	4.00
TE	Mark Teixeira	6.00
MI	Miguel Tejada	6.00
TH	Charles Thomas	4.00
CT	Chad Tracy	4.00
BU	B.J. Upton	4.00
WE	Jayson Werth	4.00
JW	Jake Westbrook	4.00
DW	David Wright	10.00
KY	Kevin Youkilis	4.00
MY	Michael Young	
CZ	Carlos Zambrano	6.00

SP Collection of Stars Signatures

No Pricing
Production Five Sets

SPx Materials

		NM/M
Common Player:		3.00
Production 199 Sets		
Spectrum:		1X
Production 99 Sets		
1	Aaron Harang	3.00
2	Aaron Rowand	5.00
3	Aaron Miles	3.00
4	Adrian Gonzalez	5.00
5	Alex Rios	3.00
6	Angel Berroa	3.00
7	B.J. Upton	5.00
8	Brandon Claussen	3.00
9	Andy Marte	3.00
10	Brandon Webb	5.00
11	Bronson Arroyo	5.00
12	Casey Kotchman	3.00
13	Cesar Izturis	3.00
14	Chad Cordero	3.00
15	Chad Tracy	3.00
16	Charles Thomas	3.00
17	Chase Utley	8.00
18	Chone Figgins	3.00
19	Chris Burke	5.00
20	Cliff Lee	3.00
21	Clint Barmes	5.00
22	Coco Crisp	3.00
23	Bill Hall	3.00
24	Dallas McPherson	3.00
25	Brad Halsey	3.00
26	Daniel Cabrera	3.00
27	Danny Haren	3.00
28	David Bush	3.00
29	David DeJesus	3.00
30	D.J. Houlton	3.00
31	Derek Jeter	20.00
32	Dewon Brazelton	3.00
33	Edwin Jackson	3.00
34	Brad Hawpe	3.00
35	Brandon Inge	3.00
36	Brett Myers	3.00
37	Garrett Atkins	3.00
38	Gavin Floyd	3.00
39	Grady Sizemore	10.00
40	Guillermo Mota	3.00
41	Carlos Guillen	3.00
42	Gustavo Chacin	3.00
43	Huston Street	5.00
44	Chris Duffy	3.00
45	J.D. Closser	3.00
46	J.J. Hardy	3.00
47	Jason Bartlett	3.00
48	Jason Dubois	3.00
49	Chris Shelton	3.00
50	Jason Lane	3.00

51 Jayson Werth 3.00
52 Jeff Baker 3.00
53 Jeff Francis 3.00
54 Jeremy Bonderman 3.00
55 Jeremy Reed 3.00
56 Jerome Williams 3.00
57 Jesse Crain 3.00
58 Chris Young 3.00
59 Jhonny Peralta 3.00
60 Joe Blanton 3.00
61 Joe Crede 3.00
62 Joel Pineiro 3.00
63 Joey Gathright 3.00
64 John Buck 3.00
65 Jonny Gomes 8.00
66 Jorge Cantu 8.00
67 Dan Johnson 3.00
68 Jose Valverde 3.00
69 Ervin Santana 3.00
70 Justin Morneau 5.00
71 Keiichi Yabu 5.00
72 Ken Griffey Jr. 15.00
73 Jason Repko 5.00
74 Kevin Youkilis 3.00
75 Koyie Hill 3.00
76 Laynce Nix 3.00
77 Luke Scott 3.00
78 Juan Rivera 3.00
79 Justin Duchscherer 3.00
80 Mark Teahen 3.00
81 Lance Niekro 3.00
82 Michael Cuddyer 3.00
83 Nick Swisher 3.00
84 Noah Lowry 3.00
85 Matt Holliday 8.00
86 Reed Johnson 3.00
87 Rich Harden 5.00
88 Robb Quinlan 3.00
89 Nick Johnson 3.00
90 Ryan Howard 20.00
91 Nook Logan 3.00
92 Steve Schmoll 3.00
93 Tadahito Iguchi 20.00
94 Willy Taveras 3.00
95 Wily Mo Pena 3.00
96 Xavier Nady 3.00
97 Yadier Molina 3.00
98 Yhency Brazoban 3.00
99 Ryan Freel 3.00
100 Zack Greinke 3.00

SPx Signatures

NM/M

Production 50-350
Spectrum: No Pricing
Production 10 Sets
Jersey Auto.: No Pricing
Production 10 Sets
1 Aaron Harang/350 8.00
2 Aaron Rowand/150 20.00
4 Adrian Gonzalez/225 15.00
6 Angel Berroa/150 8.00
7 B.J. Upton/50 12.00
8 Brandon Claussen/350 8.00
9 Andy Marte/350 10.00
11 Bronson Arroyo/350 20.00
12 Casey Kotchman/225 8.00
13 Cesar Izturis/150 8.00
14 Chad Cordero/350 10.00
15 Chad Tracy/350 10.00
16 Charles Thomas/350 5.00
17 Chase Utley/50 50.00
18 Chone Figgins/150 8.00
19 Chris Burke/350 15.00
20 Cliff Lee/225 15.00
21 Clint Barmes/350 12.00
22 Coco Crisp/225 15.00
23 Bill Hall/350 8.00
24 Dallas McPherson/150 10.00
25 Brad Halsey/350 8.00
26 Daniel Cabrera/350 15.00
27 Danny Haren/225 10.00
28 David Bush/350 10.00
29 David DeJesus/225 8.00
30 D.J. Houlton/350 8.00
31 Derek Jeter/50 150.00
32 Dewon Brazelton/225 8.00
33 Edwin Jackson/150 8.00
34 Brad Hawpe/350 8.00
35 Brandon Inge/350 10.00
36 Brett Myers/150 8.00
37 Garrett Atkins/350 15.00
38 Gavin Floyd/150 8.00
39 Grady Sizemore/350 40.00
40 Guillermo Mota/225 8.00
41 Carlos Guillen/150 8.00
42 Gustavo Chacin/350 10.00
43 Huston Street/350 25.00
44 Chris Duffy/225 15.00
45 J.D. Closser/350 8.00
46 J.J. Hardy/350 10.00
47 Jason Bartlett/350 8.00
48 Jason Dubois/350 10.00
50 Jason Lane/350 10.00
51 Jayson Werth/350 12.00
52 Jeff Baker/350 8.00
53 Jeff Francis/150 10.00
54 Jeremy Bonderman/50 20.00
55 Jeremy Reed/150 10.00
56 Jerome Williams/50 8.00
57 Jesse Crain/350 10.00
59 Jhonny Peralta/350 15.00
60 Joe Blanton/350 10.00
61 Joe Crede/350 25.00
62 Joel Pineiro/150 12.00
63 Joey Gathright/350 8.00
64 John Buck/350 8.00
65 Jonny Gomes/350 15.00
66 Jorge Cantu/350 15.00
67 Dan Johnson/350 15.00
68 Jose Valverde/350 8.00
69 Ervin Santana/350 15.00
71 Keiichi Yabu/350 25.00
73 Jason Repko/350 25.00
74 Kevin Youkilis/225 12.00
75 Koyie Hill/350 10.00
76 Laynce Nix/150 8.00
77 Luke Scott/350 40.00
78 Juan Rivera/225 8.00
79 Justin Duchscherer/350 10.00
80 Mark Teahen/350 8.00
81 Lance Niekro/350 10.00
82 Michael Cuddyer/350 8.00
84 Noah Lowry/150 15.00
85 Matt Holliday/225 25.00
86 Reed Johnson/350 8.00
88 Robb Quinlan/350 5.00
89 Nick Johnson/150 8.00
90 Ryan Howard/225 80.00
91 Nook Logan/350 8.00
92 Steve Schmoll/350 5.00
93 Tadahito Iguchi/50 150.00
95 Wily Mo Pena/150 8.00
96 Xavier Nady/150 10.00
98 Yhency Brazoban/350 8.00

SPx Superscripts Signatures

No Pricing
Production 15 Sets

SPx Superscripts Triple Signature

No Pricing
Production Five Sets

SPx Winning Materials Dual

No Pricing
Production 20 Sets
Dual Auto.: No Pricing
Production Five Sets

SPXtreme Stats

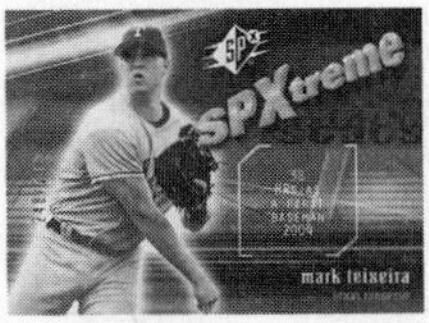

NM/M

Common Player: 1.00
Production 299 Sets
BA Bobby Abreu 1.50
AB Adrian Beltre 1.50
CB Craig Biggio 1.50
HB Hank Blalock 1.50
MC Miguel Cabrera 2.00
SC Sean Casey 1.00
EC Eric Chavez 1.00
RC Roger Clemens 6.00
CC Carl Crawford 1.00
BC Bobby Crosby 1.00
JD J.D. Drew 1.00
AD Adam Dunn 1.50
EG Eric Gagne 1.00
GR Khalil Greene 1.50
KG Ken Griffey Jr. 4.00
VG Vladimir Guerrero 2.00
TH Tim Hudson 1.50
HU Torii Hunter 1.00
DJ Derek Jeter 6.00
RJ Randy Johnson 2.00
AJ Andruw Jones 1.50
DL Derrek Lee 1.50
GM Greg Maddux 4.00
VM Victor Martinez 1.00
JM Joe Mauer 1.50
MO Melvin Mora 1.00
MM Mark Mulder 1.50
DO David Ortiz 2.00
RO Roy Oswalt 1.50
RP Rafael Palmeiro 1.50
CP Corey Patterson 1.00
JP Jake Peavy 1.50
OP Oliver Perez 1.00
PI Mike Piazza 3.00
MP Mark Prior 2.00
AP Albert Pujols 6.00
AR Aramis Ramirez 1.50
ER Edgar Renteria 1.00
JR Jose Reyes 1.00
SR Scott Rolen 2.00
SA Johan Santana 2.00
BS Ben Sheets 1.00
GS Gary Sheffield 1.50
SM John Smoltz 1.50
MT Mark Teixeira 1.50
TE Miguel Tejada 1.50
KW Kerry Wood 1.50
MY Michael Young 1.50
DW David Wright 3.00
CZ Carlos Zambrano 1.50

SPXtreme Stats Jersey

NM/M

BA Bobby Abreu 6.00
AB Adrian Beltre 6.00
CB Craig Biggio 6.00
HB Hank Blalock 4.00
MC Miguel Cabrera 8.00
SC Sean Casey 4.00
EC Eric Chavez 4.00
RC Roger Clemens 10.00
CC Carl Crawford 4.00
BC Bobby Crosby 4.00
JD J.D. Drew 4.00
AD Adam Dunn 6.00
EG Eric Gagne 4.00
GR Khalil Greene 6.00
KG Ken Griffey Jr. 15.00
VG Vladimir Guerrero 8.00
TH Tim Hudson 4.00
HU Torii Hunter 4.00
DJ Derek Jeter 15.00
RJ Randy Johnson 8.00
AJ Andruw Jones 6.00
DL Derrek Lee 6.00
GM Greg Maddux 10.00
VM Victor Martinez 4.00
JM Joe Mauer 6.00
MO Melvin Mora 4.00
MM Mark Mulder 4.00
DO David Ortiz 8.00
RO Roy Oswalt 4.00
RP Rafael Palmeiro 6.00
CP Corey Patterson 4.00
JP Jake Peavy 6.00
OP Oliver Perez 4.00
PI Mike Piazza 8.00
MP Mark Prior 6.00
AP Albert Pujols 15.00
AR Aramis Ramirez 6.00
ER Edgar Renteria 4.00
JR Jose Reyes 66.00
SR Scott Rolen 6.00
SA Johan Santana 8.00
BS Ben Sheets 4.00
GS Gary Sheffield 6.00
SM John Smoltz 6.00
MT Mark Teixeira 6.00
TE Miguel Tejada 6.00
KW Kerry Wood 6.00
DW David Wright 8.00
MY Michael Young 4.00
CZ Carlos Zambrano 6.00

SPXtreme Stats Signatures

No Pricing
Production Five Sets

2005 SP Legendary Cuts

NM/M

Complete Set (90): 25.00
Common Player: .25
Pack (4): 14.00
Box (12): 150.00
1 Al Kaline 1.00
2 Babe Ruth 3.00
3 Bill Mazeroski .25
4 Billy Williams .25
5 Bob Feller .50
6 Bob Gibson 1.00
7 Bob Lemon .25
8 Bobby Doerr .25
9 Brooks Robinson 1.00
10 Carl Yastrzemski 1.50
11 Carlton Fisk .75
12 Casey Stengel .50
13 Jim "Catfish" Hunter .25
14 Christy Mathewson 1.00
15 Cy Young .50
16 Dennis Eckersley .25
17 Dizzy Dean .50
18 Don Drysdale .25
19 Don Sutton .25
20 Duke Snider .75
21 Early Wynn .25
22 Eddie Mathews 1.00
23 Eddie Murray .75
24 Enos Slaughter .25
25 Ernie Banks 1.00
26 Fergie Jenkins .25
27 Frank Robinson 1.00
28 Gary Carter .25
29 Gaylord Perry .25
30 Reggie Jackson 1.00
31 George Kell .25
32 George Sisler .25
33 Hal Newhouser .25
34 Harmon Killebrew 1.00
35 Honus Wagner 1.00
36 Jackie Robinson .50
37 Jim Bunning .25
38 Jim Palmer .50
39 Jimmie Foxx .75
40 Joe DiMaggio 2.00
41 Joe Morgan .50
42 Johnny Bench 1.00
43 Johnny Mize .25
44 Juan Marichal .50
45 Kirby Puckett .75
46 Larry Doby .25
47 Lefty Grove .25
48 Lou Boudreau .25
49 Lou Brock .50
50 Lou Gehrig 2.00
51 Luis Aparicio .25
52 Mel Ott .50
53 Mickey Cochrane .25
54 Mickey Mantle 4.00
55 Mike Schmidt 1.50
56 Monte Irvin .50
57 Nolan Ryan 2.00
58 Orlando Cepeda .25
59 Ozzie Smith 1.00
60 Paul Molitor .50
61 Pee Wee Reese .25
62 Phil Niekro .25
63 Phil Rizzuto .50
64 Ralph Kiner .25
65 Red Schoendienst .25
66 Richie Ashburn .25
67 Rick Ferrell .25
68 Robin Roberts .25
69 Robin Yount 1.00
70 Rod Carew .50
71 Rogers Hornsby .50
72 Rollie Fingers .25
73 Roy Campanella .50
74 Ryne Sandberg 1.00
75 Satchel Paige 1.00
76 Stan Musial 1.00
77 Steve Carlton .25
78 Ted Williams 2.00
79 Thurman Munson 1.00
80 Tom Seaver 1.00
81 Tony Gwynn 1.00
82 Tony Perez .25
83 Ty Cobb 1.50
84 Wade Boggs .50
85 Walter Johnson 1.00
86 Warren Spahn 1.00
87 Whitey Ford 1.00
88 Willie McCovey .50
89 Willie Stargell .75
90 Yogi Berra 1.00

Holofoil

Holofoil: 3-5X
Production 50 Sets

Classic Careers

NM/M

Common Player: 2.00
Production 399 Sets
Gold: 1-2X
Production 75 Sets
Platinum: No Pricing
Production One Set
LA Luis Aparicio 2.00
HB Harold Baines 2.00
JB Jay Buhner 2.00
CA Jose Canseco 3.00
GC Gary Carter 2.00
OC Orlando Cepeda 2.00
JC Jack Clark 2.00
WC Will Clark 3.00
DC David Cone 2.00
AD Andre Dawson 2.00
BD Bobby Doerr 2.00
LD Lenny Dykstra 2.00
CE Carl Erskine 2.00
SF Sid Fernandez 2.00
CF Carlton Fisk 3.00
GF George Foster 2.00
BF Bill Freehan 2.00
DG Dwight Gooden 2.00
GG Rich "Goose" Gossage 2.00
MG Mark Grace 3.00
RG Ron Guidry 2.00
GU Don Gullett 2.00
KH Keith Hernandez 2.00
BH Bob Horner 2.00
FJ Fergie Jenkins 2.00
BL Barry Larkin 3.00
SL Sparky Lyle 2.00
BM Bill Madlock 2.00
DE Dennis Martinez 2.00
GM Gary Mathews 2.00
MA Don Mattingly 5.00
JM Jack Morris 2.00
MU Bobby Murcer 2.00
DM Dale Murphy 3.00
GN Graig Nettles 2.00
PN Phil Niekro 2.00
TO Tony Oliva 2.00
GP Gaylord Perry 2.00
JP Johnny Podres 2.00
TR Tim Raines 2.00
JR Jim Rice 2.00
CR Cal Ripken Jr. 8.00
AR Al Rosen 2.00
ST Dave Stewart 2.00
DS Darryl Strawberry 2.00
SU Bruce Sutter 2.00
DO Don Sutton 2.00
LT Luis Tiant 2.00
AV Andy Van Slyke 2.00
CY Carl Yastrzemski 4.00

Classic Careers Autograph

NM/M

Common Player: 15.00
Production 25 Sets
Gold: No Pricing
Production 10 Sets
Platinum: No Pricing
Production One Set
LA Luis Aparicio 20.00
HB Harold Baines 25.00
JB Jay Buhner 30.00
CA Jose Canseco 40.00
GC Gary Carter 20.00
OC Orlando Cepeda 30.00
JC Jack Clark 20.00
WC Will Clark 25.00

DC David Cone 20.00
AD Andre Dawson 20.00
BD Bobby Doerr 20.00
LD Lenny Dykstra 20.00
CE Carl Erskine 20.00
SF Sid Fernandez 15.00
CF Carlton Fisk 35.00
GF George Foster 25.00
BF Bill Freehan 25.00
DG Dwight Gooden 15.00
GG Rich "Goose" Gossage 20.00
MG Mark Grace 30.00
RG Ron Guidry 35.00
GU Don Gullett 15.00
KH Keith Hernandez 20.00
BH Bob Horner 15.00
FJ Fergie Jenkins 25.00
BL Barry Larkin 40.00
SL Sparky Lyle 20.00
BM Bill Madlock 20.00
DE Dennis Martinez 15.00
GM Gary Mathews 15.00
MA Don Mattingly 60.00
JM Jack Morris 20.00
MU Bobby Murcer 30.00
DM Dale Murphy 35.00
PN Phil Niekro 20.00
GN Graig Nettles 20.00
TO Tony Oliva 20.00
GP Gaylord Perry 20.00
JP Johnny Podres 15.00
TR Tim Raines 20.00
JR Jim Rice 25.00
CR Cal Ripken Jr. 125.00
AR Al Rosen 20.00
ST Dave Stewart 15.00
DS Darryl Strawberry 20.00
SU Bruce Sutter 25.00
DO Don Sutton 20.00
LT Luis Tiant 20.00
AV Andy Van Slyke 30.00
CY Carl Yastrzemski 50.00

Classic Careers Jersey Autograph

NM/M

Production 25 Sets
Gold: No Pricing
Production 10 Sets
Platinum: No Pricing
Production One Set
LA Luis Aparicio 20.00
HB Harold Baines 25.00
JB Jay Buhner 30.00
GC Gary Carter 20.00
OC Orlando Cepeda 30.00
JC Jack Clark 20.00
WC Will Clark 25.00
DC David Cone 20.00
AD Andre Dawson 20.00
BD Bobby Doerr 20.00
LD Lenny Dykstra 20.00
CE Carl Erskine 20.00
SF Sid Fernandez 15.00
GF George Foster 25.00
BF Bill Freehan 25.00
DG Dwight Gooden 15.00
GG Rich "Goose" Gossage 20.00
MG Mark Grace 30.00
RG Ron Guidry 35.00
GU Don Gullett 15.00
KH Keith Hernandez 20.00
BH Bob Horner 15.00
FJ Fergie Jenkins 25.00
BL Barry Larkin 40.00
SL Sparky Lyle 20.00
BM Bill Madlock 20.00
DE Dennis Martinez 15.00
GM Gary Mathews 15.00
MA Don Mattingly 60.00
JM Jack Morris 20.00
MU Bobby Murcer 30.00
DM Dale Murphy 35.00
PN Phil Niekro 20.00
GN Graig Nettles 20.00
TO Tony Oliva 20.00
GP Gaylord Perry 20.00
JP Johnny Podres 15.00
TR Tim Raines 20.00
JR Jim Rice 25.00
CR Cal Ripken Jr. 125.00
AR Al Rosen 20.00
ST Dave Stewart 15.00
DS Darryl Strawberry 20.00
SU Bruce Sutter 25.00
LT Luis Tiant 20.00
AV Andy Van Slyke 30.00
CY Carl Yastrzemski 50.00

Classic Careers Patch Autograph

NM/M

Production 25 Sets
Gold: No Pricing
Production Five Sets
Platinum: No Pricing
Production One Set
HB Harold Baines 40.00
JB Jay Buhner 50.00
JC Jack Clark 35.00
WC Will Clark 40.00
DC David Cone 35.00
AD Andre Dawson 35.00
BD Bobby Doerr 35.00
LD Lenny Dykstra 35.00
SF Sid Fernandez 25.00
GF George Foster 40.00
BF Bill Freehan 40.00
DG Dwight Gooden 25.00
GG Rich "Goose" Gossage 35.00
MG Mark Grace 50.00
GU Don Gullett 25.00
KH Keith Hernandez 35.00
BL Barry Larkin 60.00
DE Dennis Martinez 25.00
GM Gary Mathews 25.00
JM Jack Morris 35.00
GN Graig Nettles 35.00
TO Tony Oliva 35.00
GP Gaylord Perry 30.00
TR Tim Raines 30.00
JR Jim Rice 40.00
CR Cal Ripken Jr. 200.00
ST Dave Stewart 25.00
DS Darryl Strawberry 30.00
AV Andy Van Slyke 40.00

Classic Careers Jersey

NM/M

Common Player: 4.00
Gold: 1X
Production 75 Sets
Platinum: No Pricing
Production One Set
LA Luis Aparicio 6.00
HB Harold Baines 6.00
JB Jay Buhner 6.00
CA Jose Canseco 8.00
GC Gary Carter 4.00
OC Orlando Cepeda 6.00
JC Jack Clark 4.00
WC Will Clark 6.00
DC David Cone 4.00
AD Andre Dawson 6.00
BD Bobby Doerr 6.00
LD Lenny Dykstra 6.00
CE Carl Erskine 6.00
SF Sid Fernandez 4.00
CF Carlton Fisk 6.00
GF George Foster 4.00
BF Bill Freehan 6.00
DG Dwight Gooden 4.00
GG Rich "Goose" Gossage 6.00
MG Mark Grace 8.00
RG Ron Guidry 6.00
GU Don Gullett 4.00
KH Keith Hernandez 4.00
BH Bob Horner 4.00
FJ Fergie Jenkins 6.00
BL Barry Larkin 6.00
SL Sparky Lyle 4.00
BM Bill Madlock 4.00
DE Dennis Martinez 4.00
GM Gary Mathews 4.00
MA Don Mattingly 12.00
JM Jack Morris 4.00
MU Bobby Murcer 4.00
DM Dale Murphy 8.00
PN Phil Niekro 4.00
GN Graig Nettles 4.00
TO Tony Oliva 4.00
GP Gaylord Perry 4.00
JP Johnny Podres 6.00
TR Tim Raines 4.00
JR Jim Rice 6.00
CR Cal Ripken Jr. 20.00
AR Al Rosen 6.00
ST Dave Stewart 4.00
DS Darryl Strawberry 6.00
SU Bruce Sutter 4.00
DO Don Sutton 4.00
LT Luis Tiant 4.00
AV Andy Van Slyke 4.00
CY Carl Yastrzemski 15.00

Classic Careers Patch

NM/M

Production 50 Sets
Gold: No Pricing
Production 10 Sets
Platinum: No Pricing
Production One Set
HB Harold Baines 10.00
JB Jay Buhner
CA Jose Canseco 15.00
JC Jack Clark 10.00
WC Will Clark 20.00
DC David Cone 15.00
AD Andre Dawson 15.00
BD Bobby Doerr 15.00
LD Lenny Dykstra 15.00
SF Sid Fernandez 10.00
GF George Foster 10.00
BF Bill Freehan 12.00
DG Dwight Gooden 15.00
GG Rich "Goose" Gossage 12.00
MG Mark Grace 20.00
KH Keith Hernandez 12.00
BL Barry Larkin 25.00
DE Dennis Martinez 10.00
GM Gary Mathews 10.00
JM Jack Morris 10.00
GN Graig Nettles 10.00
GP Gaylord Perry 12.00
TR Tim Raines 10.00
JR Jim Rice 15.00
CR Cal Ripken Jr. 40.00
AV Andy Van Slyke 15.00
ST Dave Stewart 10.00
DS Darryl Strawberry 12.00

Dual Legendary Cuts

Production 1-10
No Pricing

Glory Days

NM/M

Common Player: 2.00
Production 399 Sets
Gold: 1X-2X
Production 75 Sets
Platinum: No Pricing
Production One Set
HB Harold Baines 2.00
YB Yogi Berra 4.00
LB Lou Brock 2.00
JB Jay Buhner 2.00
CA Jose Canseco 3.00
JC Jack Clark 2.00
WC Will Clark 3.00
DC David Cone 2.00
AD Andre Dawson 2.00
BD Bobby Doerr 2.00
LD Lenny Dykstra 2.00
SF Sid Fernandez 2.00
WF Whitey Ford 3.00
GF George Foster 2.00
BF Bill Freehan 2.00
KG Kirk Gibson 2.00
DG Dwight Gooden 2.00
RG Ron Guidry 3.00
GU Don Gullett 2.00
TG Tony Gwynn 4.00
KH Keith Hernandez 2.00
BH Bob Horner 2.00
FJ Fergie Jenkins 2.00
BL Barry Larkin 3.00
SL Sparky Lyle 2.00
FL Fred Lynn 2.00
BM Bill Madlock 2.00
MA Juan Marichal 3.00
DE Dennis Martinez 2.00
GM Gary Mathews 2.00
PM Paul Molitor 4.00
JM Jack Morris 2.00
MU Bobby Murcer 2.00
DM Dale Murphy 3.00
GN Graig Nettles 2.00
TO Tony Oliva 2.00
JP Jim Palmer 3.00
TR Tim Raines 2.00
JR Jim Rice 2.00
CR Cal Ripken Jr. 8.00
AR Al Rosen 2.00
NR Nolan Ryan 8.00
RS Red Schoendienst 2.00
SN Duke Snider 3.00
ST Dave Stewart 2.00
DS Darryl Strawberry 2.00
BS Bruce Sutter 2.00
LT Luis Tiant 2.00
AV Andy Van Slyke 2.00
RY Robin Yount 4.00

Glory Days Autograph

NM/M

Common Player: 15.00
Production 25 Sets
Gold: No Pricing
Production 10 Sets
Platinum: No Pricing
Production One Set
HB Harold Baines 25.00
YB Yogi Berra 50.00
LB Lou Brock 30.00
JB Jay Buhner 30.00
CA Jose Canseco 40.00
JC Jack Clark 20.00
WC Will Clark 25.00
DC David Cone 20.00
AD Andre Dawson 20.00
BD Bobby Doerr 20.00
LD Lenny Dykstra 20.00
SF Sid Fernandez 15.00
WF Whitey Ford 40.00
GF George Foster 25.00
BF Bill Freehan 25.00
KG Kirk Gibson 20.00
DG Dwight Gooden 15.00
RG Ron Guidry 35.00
GU Don Gullett 15.00
TG Tony Gwynn 40.00
KH Keith Hernandez 20.00
BH Bob Horner 15.00
FJ Fergie Jenkins 25.00
BL Barry Larkin 40.00
SL Sparky Lyle 20.00
FL Fred Lynn 15.00
BM Bill Madlock 20.00
MA Juan Marichal 25.00
DE Dennis Martinez 15.00
GM Gary Mathews 15.00
PM Paul Molitor 40.00
JM Jack Morris 20.00
MU Bobby Murcer 25.00
DM Dale Murphy 35.00
GN Graig Nettles 20.00
TO Tony Oliva 20.00
JP Jim Palmer 25.00
TR Tim Raines 20.00
JR Jim Rice 25.00
CR Cal Ripken Jr. 125.00
AR Al Rosen 20.00
NR Nolan Ryan 100.00
RS Red Schoendienst 20.00
SN Duke Snider 40.00
ST Dave Stewart 15.00
DS Darryl Strawberry 20.00
BS Bruce Sutter 25.00
LT Luis Tiant 20.00
AV Andy Van Slyke 30.00
RY Robin Yount 50.00

Glory Days Patch Autograph

NM/M

Production 25 Sets
Gold: No Pricing
Production Five Sets
Platinum: No Pricing
Production One Set
HB Harold Baines 40.00
JB Jay Buhner 50.00
JC Jack Clark 35.00
DC David Cone 35.00
AD Andre Dawson 35.00
BD Bobby Doerr 35.00
LD Lenny Dykstra 35.00
SF Sid Fernandez 25.00
GF George Foster 40.00
DG Dwight Gooden 25.00
GU Don Gullett
KH Keith Hernandez 35.00
BH Bob Horner 25.00
FJ Fergie Jenkins 40.00
BL Barry Larkin 60.00
BM Bill Madlock 25.00
DE Dennis Martinez 25.00
GM Gary Mathews 25.00
JM Jack Morris 35.00
DM Dale Murphy 40.00
GN Graig Nettles 35.00
TO Tony Oliva 35.00
JP Jim Palmer 40.00
TR Tim Raines 30.00
JR Jim Rice 40.00
RS Red Schoendienst 30.00
DS Darryl Strawberry 30.00
BS Bruce Sutter 25.00
LT Luis Tiant 25.00
AV Andy Van Slyke 40.00

Glory Days Jersey

NM/M

Common Player: 4.00
Gold: 1X
Production 75 Sets
Platinum: No Pricing
Production One Set
HB Harold Baines 6.00
YB Yogi Berra 10.00
LB Lou Brock 6.00
JB Jay Buhner 6.00
CA Jose Canseco 8.00
JC Jack Clark 4.00
WC Will Clark 6.00
DC David Cone 4.00
AD Andre Dawson 6.00
BD Bobby Doerr 6.00
LD Lenny Dykstra 6.00
SF Sid Fernandez 4.00
WF Whitey Ford 10.00
GF George Foster 4.00
BF Bill Freehan 6.00
KG Kirk Gibson 4.00
DG Dwight Gooden 4.00
RG Ron Guidry 6.00
GU Don Gullett 4.00
TG Tony Gwynn 8.00
KH Keith Hernandez 4.00
BH Bob Horner 4.00
FJ Fergie Jenkins 6.00
BL Barry Larkin 6.00
SL Sparky Lyle 4.00
FL Fred Lynn 4.00
BM Bill Madlock 4.00
MA Juan Marichal 6.00
DE Dennis Martinez 4.00
GM Gary Mathews 4.00
PM Paul Molitor 6.00
JM Jack Morris 4.00
MU Bobby Murcer 4.00
DM Dale Murphy 8.00
GN Graig Nettles 4.00
TO Tony Oliva 4.00
JP Jim Palmer 6.00
TR Tim Raines 4.00
JR Jim Rice 6.00
CR Cal Ripken Jr. 20.00
AR Al Rosen 6.00
NR Nolan Ryan 15.00
RS Red Schoendienst 4.00
SN Duke Snider 8.00
ST Dave Stewart 4.00
DS Darryl Strawberry 6.00
BS Bruce Sutter 4.00
LT Luis Tiant 4.00
AV Andy Van Slyke 4.00
RY Robin Yount 10.00

Glory Days Memorabilia Autograph

NM/M

Production 25 Sets
Gold: No Pricing
Production 10 Sets
Platinum: No Pricing
Production One Set
HB Harold Baines 25.00
YB Yogi Berra 50.00

JB	Jay Buhner	30.00
JC	Jack Clark	20.00
WC	Will Clark	25.00
DC	David Cone	20.00
AD	Andre Dawson	20.00
BD	Bobby Doerr	20.00
LD	Lenny Dykstra	20.00
SF	Sid Fernandez	15.00
WF	Whitey Ford	40.00
GF	George Foster	25.00
BF	Bill Freehan	25.00
KG	Kirk Gibson	20.00
DG	Dwight Gooden	15.00
BG	Ron Guidry	35.00
GU	Don Gullett	15.00
TG	Tony Gwynn	40.00
KH	Keith Hernandez	20.00
BH	Bob Horner	15.00
FJ	Fergie Jenkins	25.00
BL	Barry Larkin	40.00
SL	Sparky Lyle	20.00
FL	Fred Lynn	15.00
BM	Bill Madlock	20.00
MA	Juan Marichal	25.00
DE	Dennis Martinez	15.00
GM	Gary Mathews	15.00
PM	Paul Molitor	40.00
JM	Jack Morris	20.00
MU	Bobby Murcer	25.00
DM	Dale Murphy	35.00
GN	Graig Nettles	20.00
TO	Tony Oliva	20.00
JP	Jim Palmer	25.00
TR	Tim Raines	20.00
JR	Jim Rice	25.00
AR	Al Rosen	20.00
NR	Nolan Ryan	100.00
RS	Red Schoendienst	20.00
SN	Duke Snider	40.00
ST	Dave Stewart	15.00
DS	Darryl Strawberry	20.00
BS	Bruce Sutter	25.00
LT	Luis Tiant	20.00
AV	Andy Van Slyke	30.00
RY	Robin Yount	50.00

Glory Days Patch

NM/M

Production 50 Sets
Gold: No Pricing
Production 10 Sets
Platinum: No Pricing
Production One Set

HB	Harold Baines	10.00
JC	Jack Clark	10.00
DC	David Cone	15.00
AD	Andre Dawson	15.00
BD	Bobby Doerr	15.00
LD	Lenny Dykstra	15.00
SF	Sid Fernandez	10.00
GF	George Foster	10.00
DG	Dwight Gooden	15.00
KH	Keith Hernandez	12.00
BH	Bob Horner	10.00
FJ	Fergie Jenkins	15.00
BL	Barry Larkin	25.00
GM	Gary Mathews	10.00
JM	Jack Morris	10.00
DM	Dale Murphy	20.00
GN	Graig Nettles	10.00
JP	Jim Palmer	15.00
TR	Tim Raines	10.00
RS	Red Schoendienst	15.00
DS	Darryl Strawberry	12.00
BS	Bruce Sutter	15.00
LT	Luis Tiant	15.00
AV	Andy Van Slyke	15.00

Historic Cuts

No Pricing
Production One Set

Historic Quads Material

No Pricing
Production Five Sets
Patch: No Pricing
Production One Set

Historic Quads Autograph

No Pricing
Production Five Sets

Lasting Legends

NM/M

Common Player: 2.00
Production 399 Sets
Gold: 1-2X
Production 75 Sets
Platinum: No Pricing
Production One Set

LA	Luis Aparicio	2.00
EB	Ernie Banks	4.00
BE	Johnny Bench	4.00
YB	Yogi Berra	4.00
WB	Wade Boggs	3.00
LB	Lou Brock	3.00
RC	Rod Carew	3.00
SC	Steve Carlton	2.00
GC	Gary Carter	2.00
OC	Orlando Cepeda	2.00
BD	Bobby Doerr	2.00
DE	Dennis Eckersley	2.00
RF	Rollie Fingers	2.00
CF	Carlton Fisk	3.00
WF	Whitey Ford	3.00
BG	Bob Gibson	3.00
DG	Dwight Gooden	2.00
TG	Tony Gwynn	3.00
KH	Keith Hernandez	2.00
FJ	Fergie Jenkins	2.00
AK	Al Kaline	3.00
BL	Barry Larkin	3.00
MA	Juan Marichal	2.00
DM	Don Mattingly	5.00
BM	Bill Mazeroski	2.00
PM	Paul Molitor	3.00
JM	Joe Morgan	2.00
MU	Dale Murphy	3.00
EM	Eddie Murray	3.00
SM	Stan Musial	4.00
PN	Phil Niekro	2.00
GN	Graig Nettles	2.00
JP	Jim Palmer	3.00
TP	Tony Perez	2.00
GP	Gaylord Perry	2.00
KP	Kirby Puckett	3.00
JR	Jim Rice	2.00
CR	Cal Ripken Jr.	8.00
BR	Brooks Robinson	3.00
FR	Frank Robinson	3.00
NR	Nolan Ryan	6.00
SA	Ryne Sandberg	4.00
MS	Mike Schmidt	4.00
RS	Red Schoendienst	3.00
OS	Ozzie Smith	4.00
SN	Duke Snider	3.00
BS	Bruce Sutter	2.00
DS	Don Sutton	2.00
CY	Carl Yastrzemski	4.00
RY	Robin Yount	4.00

Lasting Legends Autograph

NM/M

Common Player:
Production 25 Sets
Gold: No Pricing
Production 10 Sets
Platinum: No Pricing
Production One Set

LA	Luis Aparicio	20.00
EB	Ernie Banks	60.00
BE	Johnny Bench	50.00
YB	Yogi Berra	60.00
WB	Wade Boggs	40.00
LB	Lou Brock	25.00
RC	Rod Carew	35.00
SC	Steve Carlton	25.00
GC	Gary Carter	25.00
OC	Orlando Cepeda	25.00
BD	Bobby Doerr	20.00
DE	Dennis Eckersley	25.00
RF	Rollie Fingers	20.00
CF	Carlton Fisk	35.00
WF	Whitey Ford	40.00
BG	Bob Gibson	40.00
DG	Dwight Gooden	15.00
TG	Tony Gwynn	50.00
KH	Keith Hernandez	20.00
FG	Fergie Jenkins	25.00
AK	Al Kaline	40.00
BL	Barry Larkin	40.00
MA	Juan Marichal	25.00
DM	Don Mattingly	60.00
BM	Bill Mazeroski	35.00
PM	Paul Molitor	40.00
JM	Joe Morgan	25.00
MU	Dale Murphy	40.00
EM	Eddie Murray	50.00
SM	Stan Musial	60.00
GN	Graig Nettles	20.00
PN	Phil Niekro	25.00
JP	Jim Palmer	25.00
TP	Tony Perez	20.00
GP	Gaylord Perry	20.00
KP	Kirby Puckett	50.00
JR	Jerry Rice	25.00
CR	Cal Ripken Jr.	125.00
BR	Brooks Robinson	40.00
FR	Frank Robinson	25.00
NR	Nolan Ryan	100.00
SA	Ryne Sandberg	50.00
MS	Mike Schmidt	50.00
RS	Red Schoendienst	20.00
OS	Ozzie Smith	60.00
SN	Duke Snider	40.00
BS	Bruce Sutter	25.00
DS	Don Sutton	20.00
CY	Carl Yastrzemski	50.00
RY	Robin Yount	50.00

Lasting Legends Jersey Autograph

NM/M

Production 25 Sets
Gold: No Pricing
Production 10 Sets
Platinum: No Pricing
Production One Set

LA	Luis Aparicio	20.00
EB	Ernie Banks	60.00
BE	Johnny Bench	50.00
YB	Yogi Berra	60.00
WB	Wade Boggs	40.00
LB	Lou Brock	25.00
RC	Rod Carew	40.00
SC	Steve Carlton	25.00
GC	Gary Carter	25.00
OC	Orlando Cepeda	25.00
BD	Bobby Doerr	20.00
DE	Dennis Eckersley	25.00
RF	Rollie Fingers	20.00
CF	Carlton Fisk	40.00
WF	Whitey Ford	40.00
BG	Bob Gibson	40.00
DG	Dwight Gooden	15.00
TG	Tony Gwynn	50.00
KH	Keith Hernandez	20.00
FG	Fergie Jenkins	25.00
AK	Al Kaline	50.00
BL	Barry Larkin	40.00
MA	Juan Marichal	25.00
DM	Don Mattingly	60.00
BM	Bill Mazeroski	40.00
PM	Paul Molitor	40.00
JM	Joe Morgan	25.00
MU	Dale Murphy	40.00
SM	Stan Musial	60.00
GN	Graig Nettles	20.00
PN	Phil Niekro	25.00
JP	Jim Palmer	25.00
TP	Tony Perez	20.00
GP	Gaylord Perry	20.00
JR	Jim Rice	25.00
CR	Cal Ripken Jr.	140.00
BR	Brooks Robinson	40.00
FR	Frank Robinson	25.00
NR	Nolan Ryan	100.00
SA	Ryne Sandberg	50.00
MS	Mike Schmidt	50.00
RS	Red Schoendienst	20.00
OS	Ozzie Smith	60.00
SN	Duke Snider	40.00
BS	Bruce Sutter	25.00
CY	Carl Yastrzemski	50.00
RY	Robin Yount	50.00

Lasting Legends Patch Autograph

NM/M

Production 25 Sets
Gold: No Pricing
Production Five Sets
Platinum: No Pricing
Production One Set

WB	Wade Boggs	50.00
LB	Lou Brock	
RC	Rod Carew	50.00
SC	Steve Carlton	35.00
GC	Gary Carter	35.00
OC	Orlando Cepeda	30.00
DE	Dennis Eckersley	35.00
RF	Rollie Fingers	25.00
DG	Dwight Gooden	25.00
KH	Keith Hernandez	25.00
FJ	Fergie Jenkins	35.00
BL	Barry Larkin	50.00
MA	Juan Marichal	35.00
PM	Paul Molitor	50.00
JM	Joe Morgan	35.00
PN	Phil Niekro	35.00
JP	Jim Palmer	40.00
TP	Tony Perez	30.00
GP	Gaylord Perry	30.00
JR	Jim Rice	35.00
BR	Brooks Robinson	50.00
NR	Nolan Ryan	140.00
SA	Ryne Sandberg	80.00
OS	Ozzie Smith	75.00
BS	Bruce Sutter	30.00
RY	Robin Yount	65.00

Lasting Legends Material

NM/M

Common Player: 4.00
Gold: 1-1.5X
Production 75 Sets
Platinum: No Pricing
Production One Set

LA	Luis Aparicio	4.00
EB	Ernie Banks	10.00
BE	Johnny Bench	8.00
YB	Yogi Berra	8.00
WB	Wade Boggs	6.00
LB	Lou Brock	6.00
RC	Rod Carew	6.00
SC	Steve Carlton	4.00
GC	Gary Carter	4.00
OC	Orlando Cepeda	4.00
BD	Bobby Doerr	6.00
DE	Dennis Eckersley	6.00
RF	Rollie Fingers	4.00
CF	Carlton Fisk	6.00
WF	Whitey Ford	6.00
BG	Bob Gibson	8.00
DG	Dwight Gooden	4.00
TG	Tony Gwynn	8.00
KH	Keith Hernandez	4.00
FJ	Fergie Jenkins	4.00
AK	Al Kaline	10.00
BL	Barry Larkin	6.00
MA	Juan Marichal	6.00
DM	Don Mattingly	10.00
BM	Bill Mazeroski	6.00
PM	Paul Molitor	6.00
JM	Joe Morgan	4.00
MU	Dale Murphy	6.00
EM	Eddie Murray	6.00
SM	Stan Musial	10.00
GN	Graig Nettles	4.00
PN	Phil Niekro	4.00
JP	Jim Palmer	6.00
TP	Tony Perez	4.00
GP	Gaylord Perry	4.00
KP	Kirby Puckett	8.00
JR	Jim Rice	4.00
CR	Cal Ripken Jr.	20.00
BR	Brooks Robinson	6.00
FR	Frank Robinson	6.00
NR	Nolan Ryan	15.00
SA	Ryne Sandberg	8.00
MS	Mike Schmidt	10.00
RS	Red Schoendienst	4.00
OS	Ozzie Smith	8.00
SN	Duke Snider	6.00
BS	Bruce Sutter	4.00
DS	Don Sutton	4.00
CY	Carl Yastrzemski	15.00
RY	Robin Yount	8.00

Lasting Legends Patch

NM/M

Production 50 Sets
Gold: No Pricing
Production 10 Sets
Platinum: No Pricing
Production One Set

WB	Wade Boggs	20.00
LB	Lou Brock	15.00
RC	Rod Carew	15.00
SC	Steve Carlton	15.00
GC	Gary Carter	12.00
OC	Orlando Cepeda	15.00
DE	Dennis Eckersley	15.00
RF	Rollie Fingers	10.00
CF	Carlton Fisk	15.00
DG	Dwight Gooden	10.00
KH	Keith Hernandez	10.00
FJ	Fergie Jenkins	15.00
BL	Barry Larkin	25.00
MA	Juan Marichal	15.00
JM	Joe Morgan	15.00
PN	Phil Niekro	15.00
JP	Jim Palmer	15.00
TP	Tony Perez	15.00
GP	Gaylord Perry	12.00
KP	Kirby Puckett	25.00
JR	Jim Rice	15.00
BR	Brooks Robinson	20.00
FR	Frank Robinson	15.00
SA	Ryne Sandberg	25.00
OS	Ozzie Smith	25.00
BS	Bruce Sutter	15.00
DS	Don Sutton	12.00
RY	Robin Yount	25.00

Legendary Battery Cuts

NM/M

Production 6-99

SC	Stan Coveleski/25	140.00
BD	Bill Dickey/22	200.00
DD	Don Drysdale/31	200.00
LG	Lefty Gomez/77	160.00
JH	Jesse Haines/28	200.00
WH	Waite Hoyt/58	125.00
CH	Carl Hubbell/99	140.00
HN	Hal Newhouser/32	140.00
WS	Warren Spahn/43	150.00
EW	Early Wynn/32	125.00

Legendary Cornerstone Cuts

NM/M

Production 1-79

DC	Dolph Camilli/79	120.00
RD	Ray Dandridge/27	125.00
EM	Eddie Mathews/50	150.00
JM	Johnny Mize/44	150.00
WS	Willie Stargell/36	150.00

Legendary Cuts

NM/M

Production 1-108

AN	Cap Anson/1	
LA	Luke Appling/55	125.00
RI	Richie Ashburn/83	150.00
EA	Earl Averill/91	90.00
JB	Cool Papa Bell/78	300.00
LB	Lou Boudreau/99	100.00
MC	Max Carey/84	140.00
HC	Happy Chandler/39	125.00
JC	Jocko Conlan/40	140.00
ST	Stan Coveleski/71	140.00
CR	Joe Cronin/76	140.00
RD	Ray Dandridge/76	100.00
BD	Bill Dickey/95	150.00
JD	Joe DiMaggio/56	500.00
LD	Larry Doby/32	200.00
DD	Don Drysdale/50	200.00
DU	Leo Durocher/57	150.00
FE	Rick Ferrell/80	125.00
CF	Carl Furillo/25	200.00
CG	Charlie Gehringer/97	120.00
GO	Lefty Gomez/68	150.00
HG	Hank Greenberg/44	280.00
BU	Burleigh Grimes/99	125.00
GR	Lefty Grove/41	250.00
HA	Chick Hafey/52	150.00
JH	Jesse Haines/90	150.00
GH	Gabby Hartnett/50	180.00
BH	Billy Herman/99	90.00
WH	Waite Hoyt/99	140.00
CH	Carl Hubbell/99	150.00
HU	Jim "Catfish" Hunter/65	140.00
JJ	Jackie Jensen/48	180.00
JO	Judy Johnson/39	150.00
CK	Charlie Keller/98	140.00
HK	Harvey Kuenn/33	165.00
BL	Bob Lemon/108	100.00

LE	Buck Leonard/71	140.00
LI	Freddie Lindstrom/19	250.00
LO	Ernie Lombardi/29	200.00
HM	Heinie Manush/25	175.00
RU	Rube Marquard/80	150.00
EM	Eddie Mathews/80	150.00
RO	Roy McMillan/23	140.00
MI	Johnny Mize/90	125.00
HN	Hal Newhouser/96	125.00
PR	Pee Wee Reese/69	180.00
SR	Sam Rice/41	180.00
ER	Edd Roush/99	100.00
JS	Joe Sewell/76	140.00
ES	Enos Slaughter/99	100.00
WA	Warren Spahn/92	140.00
WS	Willie Stargell/63	165.00
CS	Casey Stengel/61	250.00
BW	Bucky Walters/34	150.00
JW	Hoyt Wilhelm/48	100.00
EW	Early Wynn/89	120.00

Legendary Cuts Material

NM/M

Production 75 unless noted.
Gold: No Pricing
Production 15 Sets

CA	Roy Campanella	40.00
RC	Roberto Clemente	80.00
TC	Ty Cobb	140.00
CO	Mickey Cochrane	50.00
CR	Joe Cronin	15.00
DE	Dizzy Dean	60.00
BD	Bill Dickey	35.00
JD	Joe DiMaggio	120.00
DD	Don Drysdale	15.00
JF	Jimmie Foxx	60.00
LG	Lou Gehrig	175.00
HG	Hank Greenberg	35.00
HO	Gil Hodges	40.00
RH	Rogers Hornsby	80.00
HU	Jim "Catfish" Hunter	10.00
TK	Ted Kluszewski	20.00
TL	Tony Lazerri	40.00
BL	Bob Lemon	25.00
MM	Mickey Mantle	150.00
RM	Roger Maris	60.00
EM	Eddie Mathews	40.00
CM	Christy Mathewson	125.00
MI	Johnny Mize	25.00
TM	Thurman Munson	35.00
MO	Mel Ott	50.00
SP	Satchel Paige	75.00
PR	Pee Wee Reese	25.00
JR	Jackie Robinson	65.00
BR	Babe Ruth	180.00
SI	George Sisler	35.00
ES	Enos Slaughter	15.00
WA	Warren Spahn	40.00
CS	Casey Stengel	40.00
HW	Honus Wagner/22	140.00
JW	Hoyt Wilhelm	15.00
TW	Ted Williams	75.00
EW	Early Wynn	10.00

Legendary Cuts Quad

No Pricing
Production One Set

Legendary Duels Material

NM/M

Production 25 Sets
Patch: No Pricing
Production 10 Sets

BM	Ernie Banks, Stan Musial	50.00
CC	Jose Canseco, Will Clark	40.00
DM	Paul Molitor, Lenny Dykstra	25.00
EG	Dennis Eckersley, Kirk Gibson	25.00
FB	Carlton Fisk, Johnny Bench	25.00
FR	George Foster, Jim Rice	15.00
JY	Reggie Jackson, Carl Yastrzemski	40.00
MC	Rod Carew, Paul Molitor	25.00
MH	Don Mattingly, Keith Hernandez	35.00
SF	Duke Snider, Whitey Ford	35.00
SG	Ron Guidry, Don Sutton	15.00
SS	Ozzie Smith, Ryne Sandberg	60.00
YS	Mike Schmidt, Robin Yount	35.00

Legendary Duels Autograph

No Pricing
Production 15 Sets

Legendary Duos Material

NM/M

Production 25 Sets
Patch: No Pricing
Production 10 Sets

CO	Tony Oliva, Rod Carew	20.00
ES	Duke Snider, Carl Erskine	15.00
FB	Yogi Berra, Whitey Ford	40.00
GS	Ryne Sandberg, Mark Grace	50.00
JG	Reggie Jackson, Ron Guidry	25.00
MB	Joe Morgan, Johnny Bench	35.00
MY	Robin Yount, Paul Molitor	40.00
RB	Wade Boggs, Jim Rice	20.00
RC	Will Clark, Cal Ripken Jr.	50.00
RM	Cal Ripken Jr., Eddie Murray	50.00
RR	Brooks Robinson, Frank Robinson	25.00
SC	Mike Schmidt, Steve Carlton	30.00
SG	Darryl Strawberry, Dwight Gooden	15.00

Legendary Duos Autograph

No Pricing
Production 15 Sets

Legendary Glovemen Cuts

NM/M

EA	Earl Averill/39	120.00
CP	Cool Papa Bell/29	350.00
MC	Max Carey/50	140.00
JD	Joe DiMaggio/75	400.00
ES	Enos Slaughter/65	120.00

Legendary Lineage

NM/M

Common Player: 2.00
Production 399 Sets
Gold: 1-2X
Production 75 Sets
Platinum: No Pricing
Production One Set

HB	Harold Baines	2.00
JB	Jay Buhner	2.00
CA	Jose Canseco	3.00
SC	Steve Carlton	3.00
JC	Jack Clark	2.00
WC	Will Clark	3.00
DC	David Cone	2.00
AD	Andre Dawson	2.00
BD	Bobby Doerr	2.00
LD	Lenny Dykstra	2.00
EC	Dennis Eckersley	2.00
SF	Sid Fernandez	2.00
BF	Bill Freehan	2.00
DG	Dwight Gooden	2.00
GG	Rich "Goose" Gossage	2.00
MG	Mark Grace	3.00
RG	Ron Guidry	2.00
GU	Don Gullett	2.00
TG	Tony Gwynn	4.00
KH	Keith Hernandez	2.00
BH	Bob Horner	2.00
RJ	Reggie Jackson	3.00
FJ	Fergie Jenkins	2.00
BL	Barry Larkin	3.00
SL	Sparky Lyle	2.00
BM	Bill Madlock	2.00
DE	Dennis Martinez	2.00
GM	Gary Matthews	2.00
MA	Don Mattingly	5.00
PM	Paul Molitor	3.00
JM	Jack Morris	2.00
MU	Bobby Murcer	2.00
DM	Dale Murphy	3.00
GN	Graig Nettles	2.00
TO	Tony Oliva	2.00
JP	Jim Palmer	3.00
KP	Kirby Puckett	4.00
TR	Tim Raines	2.00
JR	Jim Rice	2.00
CR	Cal Ripken Jr.	8.00
BR	Brooks Robinson	3.00
AR	Al Rosen	2.00
MS	Mike Schmidt	5.00
OS	Ozzie Smith	4.00
SN	Duke Snider	3.00
DS	Dave Stewart	2.00
ST	Darryl Strawberry	2.00
SU	Bruce Sutter	2.00
LT	Luis Tiant	2.00
AV	Andy Van Slyke	2.00

Legendary Lineage Autograph

NM/M

Common Player: 15.00
Production 25 Sets
Gold: No Pricing
Production 10 Sets
Platinum: No Pricing
Production One Set

HB	Harold Baines	25.00
JB	Jay Buhner	30.00
CA	Jose Canseco	40.00
SC	Steve Carlton	25.00
JC	Jack Clark	20.00
WC	Will Clark	25.00
DC	David Cone	20.00
AD	Andre Dawson	20.00
BD	Bobby Doerr	20.00
LD	Lenny Dykstra	20.00
EC	Dennis Eckersley	25.00
SF	Sid Fernandez	15.00
BF	Bill Freehan	25.00
DG	Dwight Gooden	15.00
GG	Rich "Goose" Gossage	20.00
MG	Mark Grace	30.00
RG	Ron Guidry	35.00
GU	Don Gullett	15.00
TG	Tony Gwynn	40.00
KH	Keith Hernandez	20.00
BH	Bob Horner	15.00
RJ	Reggie Jackson	40.00
FJ	Fergie Jenkins	25.00
BL	Barry Larkin	40.00
SL	Sparky Lyle	20.00
BM	Bill Madlock	20.00
DE	Dennis Martinez	15.00
GM	Gary Matthews	15.00
MA	Don Mattingly	60.00
PM	Paul Molitor	40.00
JM	Jack Morris	20.00
MU	Bobby Murcer	25.00
DM	Dale Murphy	35.00
GN	Graig Nettles	20.00
TO	Tony Oliva	20.00
JP	Jim Palmer	25.00
KP	Kirby Puckett	50.00
TR	Tim Raines	20.00
JR	Jim Rice	25.00
CR	Cal Ripken Jr.	125.00
BR	Brooks Robinson	40.00
AR	Al Rosen	20.00
MS	Mike Schmidt	60.00
OS	Ozzie Smith	50.00
SN	Duke Snider	40.00
DS	Dave Stewart	15.00
ST	Darryl Strawberry	20.00
SU	Bruce Sutter	25.00
LT	Luis Tiant	20.00
AV	Andy Van Slyke	30.00

Legendary Lineage Jersey Autograph

NM/M

Production 25 Sets
Gold: No Pricing
Production 10 Sets
Platinum: No Pricing
Production One Set

HB	Harold Baines	25.00
JB	Jay Buhner	30.00
CA	Jose Canseco	40.00
SC	Steve Carlton	25.00
JC	Jack Clark	20.00
WC	Will Clark	25.00
DC	David Cone	20.00
AD	Andre Dawson	20.00
BD	Bobby Doerr	25.00
LD	Lenny Dykstra	20.00
EC	Dennis Eckersley	25.00
SF	Sid Fernandez	15.00
BF	Bill Freehan	25.00
DG	Dwight Gooden	15.00
GG	Rich "Goose" Gossage	20.00
MG	Mark Grace	30.00
RG	Ron Guidry	35.00
GU	Don Gullett	15.00
TG	Tony Gwynn	40.00
KH	Keith Hernandez	20.00
BH	Bob Horner	15.00
RJ	Reggie Jackson	40.00
FJ	Fergie Jenkins	25.00
BL	Barry Larkin	40.00
SL	Sparky Lyle	20.00
BM	Bill Madlock	20.00
DE	Dennis Martinez	15.00
GM	Gary Matthews	15.00
MA	Don Mattingly	60.00
PM	Paul Molitor	40.00
JM	Jack Morris	20.00
MU	Bobby Murcer	25.00
DM	Dale Murphy	35.00
GN	Graig Nettles	20.00
TO	Tony Oliva	20.00
JP	Jim Palmer	25.00
KP	Kirby Puckett	50.00
TR	Tim Raines	20.00
JR	Jim Rice	25.00
CR	Cal Ripken Jr.	150.00
BR	Brooks Robinson	40.00
AR	Al Rosen	20.00
MS	Mike Schmidt	60.00
OS	Ozzie Smith	50.00
SN	Duke Snider	40.00
DS	Dave Stewart	20.00
ST	Darryl Strawberry	20.00
SU	Bruce Sutter	25.00
LT	Luis Tiant	20.00
AV	Andy Van Slyke	30.00

Legendary Lineage Patch Autograph

NM/M

Production 25 Sets
Gold: No Pricing
Production Five Sets
Platinum: No Pricing
Production One Set

HB	Harold Baines	40.00
JB	Jay Buhner	50.00
JC	Jack Clark	35.00
WC	Will Clark	40.00
DC	David Cone	35.00
AD	Andre Dawson	35.00
BD	Bobby Doerr	35.00
BF	Bill Freehan	40.00
DG	Dwight Gooden	25.00
GG	Rich "Goose" Gossage	35.00
MG	Mark Grace	50.00
TG	Tony Gwynn	70.00
KH	Keith Hernandez	35.00
BH	Bob Horner	25.00
BL	Barry Larkin	60.00
BM	Bill Madlock	25.00
DE	Dennis Martinez	25.00
PM	Paul Molitor	50.00
JM	Jack Morris	35.00
DM	Dale Murphy	40.00
GN	Graig Nettles	35.00
TR	Tim Raines	30.00
JR	Jim Rice	40.00
CR	Cal Ripken Jr.	200.00
MS	Mike Schmidt	90.00
DS	Dave Stewart	25.00
ST	Darryl Strawberry	30.00
LT	Luis Tiant	25.00
AV	Andy Van Slyke	40.00

Legendary Lineage Jersey

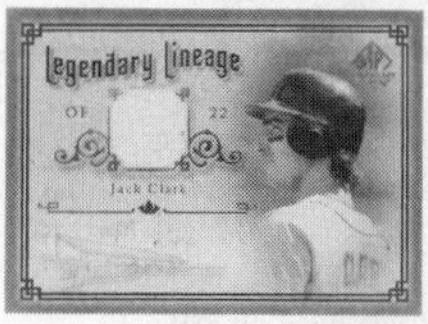

NM/M

Common Player: 4.00
Gold: 1-1.5X
Production 75 Sets
Platinum: No Pricing
Production One Set

HB	Harold Baines	4.00
JB	Jay Buhner	4.00
CA	Jose Canseco	8.00
SC	Steve Carlton	6.00
JC	Jack Clark	4.00
WC	Will Clark	6.00
DC	David Cone	4.00
AD	Andre Dawson	6.00
BD	Bobby Doerr	6.00
LD	Lenny Dykstra	4.00
EC	Dennis Eckersley	6.00
SF	Sid Fernandez	4.00
BF	Bill Freehan	6.00
DG	Dwight Gooden	4.00
GG	Rich "Goose" Gossage	4.00
MG	Mark Grace	8.00
RG	Ron Guidry	4.00
GU	Don Gullett	4.00
TG	Tony Gwynn	8.00
KH	Keith Hernandez	4.00
BH	Bob Horner	4.00
RJ	Reggie Jackson	8.00
FJ	Fergie Jenkins	6.00
BL	Barry Larkin	6.00
SL	Sparky Lyle	4.00
BM	Bill Madlock	4.00
DE	Dennis Martinez	4.00
GM	Gary Matthews	4.00
MA	Don Mattingly	12.00
PM	Paul Molitor	6.00
JM	Jack Morris	4.00
MU	Bobby Murcer	4.00
DM	Dale Murphy	8.00
GN	Graig Nettles	4.00
TO	Tony Oliva	4.00
JP	Jim Palmer	6.00
KP	Kirby Puckett	8.00
TR	Tim Raines	4.00
JR	Jim Rice	6.00
CR	Cal Ripken Jr.	20.00
BR	Brooks Robinson	6.00
AR	Al Rosen	6.00
MS	Mike Schmidt	10.00
OS	Ozzie Smith	8.00
SN	Duke Snider	8.00
DS	Dave Stewart	4.00
ST	Darryl Strawberry	4.00
SU	Bruce Sutter	4.00
LT	Luis Tiant	4.00
AV	Andy Van Slyke	4.00

Legendary Lineage Patch

NM/M

Production 50 Sets
Gold: No Pricing
Production 10 Sets
Platinum: No Pricing
Production One Set

HB	Harold Baines	10.00
JB	Jay Buhner	15.00
JC	Jack Clark	10.00
WC	Will Clark	20.00
DC	David Cone	15.00
AD	Andre Dawson	15.00
BD	Bobby Doerr	15.00
BF	Bill Freehan	12.00
DG	Dwight Gooden	15.00
GG	Rich "Goose" Gossage	12.00
MG	Mark Grace	20.00
TG	Tony Gwynn	20.00
KH	Keith Hernandez	12.00
BH	Bob Horner	10.00
BL	Barry Larkin	25.00
BM	Bill Madlock	10.00
DE	Dennis Martinez	10.00
JM	Jack Morris	10.00
DM	Dale Murphy	20.00
GN	Graig Nettles	10.00
TR	Tim Raines	10.00
CR	Cal Ripken Jr.	40.00
MS	Mike Schmidt	25.00
DS	Dave Stewart	10.00
ST	Darryl Strawberry	12.00
LT	Luis Tiant	10.00
AV	Andy Van Slyke	15.00

Middlemen Cuts

		NM/M
Production 2-99		
LA	Luke Appling/32	150.00
LB	Lou Boudreau/99	100.00
JC	Joe Cronin/30	140.00
CG	Charlie Gehringer/95	140.00
BH	Billy Herman/90	90.00
PW	Pee Wee Reese/39	200.00
JS	Joe Sewell/76	140.00

Significant Tips

No Pricing
Production 10 Sets
Patch: No Pricing
Production Five Sets

Significant Trips Autograph

No Pricing
Production 10 Sets

2006 SP Authentic

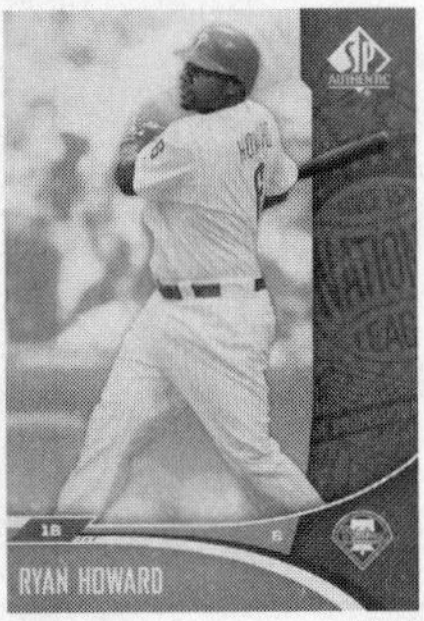

		NM/M
Complete Set (300):		
Common Player (1-100):		.25
Common SP (101-200):		2.00
Production 899		
Common Auto. (201-300):		8.00
Production 125-899		
Pack (5):		5.00
Box (24):		110.00
1	Erik Bedard	.50
2	Corey Patterson	.25
3	Ramon Hernandez	.25
4	Kris Benson	.25
5	Miguel Batista	.25
6	Orlando Hudson	.25
7	Shawn Green	.25
8	Jeff Francoeur	.50
9	Marcus Giles	.25
10	Edgar Renteria	.25
11	Tim Hudson	.50
12	Tim Wakefield	.25
13	Mark Loretta	.25
14	Kevin Youkilis	.50
15	Mike Lowell	.50
16	Coco Crisp	.25
17	Tadahito Iguchi	.25
18	Scott Podsednik	.25
19	Jermaine Dye	.40
20	Jose Contreras	.25
21	Carlos Zambrano	.50
22	Aramis Ramirez	.50
23	Jacque Jones	.25
24	Austin Kearns	.25
25	Felipe Lopez	.25
26	Brandon Phillips	.50
27	Aaron Harang	.40
28	Cliff Lee	.25
29	Jhonny Peralta	.25
30	Jason Michaels	.25
31	Clint Barmes	.25
32	Brad Hawpe	.40
33	Aaron Cook	.25
34	Kenny Rogers	.25
35	Carlos Guillen	.40
36	Brian Moehler	.25
37	Andy Pettitte	.50
38	Wandy Rodriguez	.25
39	Morgan Ensberg	.25
40	Preston Wilson	.25
41	Mark Grudzielanek	.25
42	Angel Berroa	.25
43	Jeremy Affeldt	.25
44	Zack Greinke	.25
45	Orlando Cabrera	.25
46	Garret Anderson	.25
47	Ervin Santana	.40
48	Derek Lowe	.25
49	Nomar Garciaparra	.50
50	J.D. Drew	.25
51	Rafael Furcal	.50
52	Rickie Weeks	.50
53	Geoff Jenkins	.25
54	Bill Hall	.25
55	Chris Capuano	.25
56	Derrick Turnbow	.25
57	Justin Morneau	.50
58	Michael Cuddyer	.25
59	Luis Castillo	.25
60	Hideki Matsui	1.00
61	Jason Giambi	.50
62	Jorge Posada	.50
63	Mariano Rivera	.50
64	Billy Wagner	.25
65	Carlos Delgado	.50
66	Jose Reyes	.75
67	Nick Swisher	.40
68	Bobby Crosby	.25
69	Frank Thomas	.50
70	Ryan Howard	2.00
71	Pat Burrell	.50
72	Jimmy Rollins	.75
73	Craig Wilson	.25
74	Freddy Sanchez	.25
75	Sean Casey	.25
76	Mike Piazza	1.00
77	Dave Roberts	.25
78	Chris Young	.25
79	Noah Lowry	.25
80	Armando Benitez	.25
81	Pedro Feliz	.25
82	Jose Lopez	.25
83	Adrian Beltre	.40
84	Jamie Moyer	.25
85	Jason Isringhausen	.25
86	Jason Marquis	.25
87	David Eckstein	.25
88	Juan Encarnacion	.25
89	Julio Lugo	.25
90	Ty Wigginton	.25
91	Jorge Cantu	.25
92	Akinori Otsuka	.25
93	Hank Blalock	.40
94	Kevin Mench	.25
95	Lyle Overbay	.25
96	Shea Hillenbrand	.25
97	B.J. Ryan	.25
98	Tony Armas	.25
99	Chad Cordero	.25
100	Jose Guillen	.25
101	Miguel Tejada	3.00
102	Brian Roberts	2.00
103	Melvin Mora	2.00
104	Brandon Webb	3.00
105	Chad Tracy	2.00
106	Luis Gonzalez	2.00
107	Andruw Jones	4.00
108	Chipper Jones	5.00
109	John Smoltz	3.00
110	Curt Schilling	4.00
111	Josh Beckett	4.00
112	David Ortiz	5.00
113	Manny Ramirez	4.00
114	Jason Varitek	4.00
115	Jim Thome	4.00
116	Paul Konerko	4.00
117	Javier Vazquez	2.00
118	Mark Prior	3.00
119	Derrek Lee	4.00
120	Greg Maddux	6.00
121	Ken Griffey Jr.	6.00
122	Adam Dunn	3.00
123	Bronson Arroyo	2.00
124	Travis Hafner	3.00
125	Victor Martinez	3.00
126	Grady Sizemore	3.00
127	C.C. Sabathia	3.00
128	Todd Helton	3.00
129	Matt Holliday	3.00
130	Garrett Atkins	3.00
131	Jeff Francis	2.00
132	Jeremy Bonderman	3.00
133	Ivan Rodriguez	3.00
134	Chris Shelton	2.00
135	Magglio Ordonez	2.00
136	Dontrelle Willis	2.00
137	Miguel Cabrera	5.00
138	Roger Clemens	8.00
139	Roy Oswalt	3.00
140	Lance Berkman	3.00
141	Reggie Sanders	2.00
142	Vladimir Guerrero	5.00
143	Bartolo Colon	2.00
144	Chone Figgins	3.00
145	Francisco Rodriguez	2.00
146	Brad Penny	2.00
147	Jeff Kent	3.00
148	Eric Gagne	2.00
149	Carlos Lee	3.00
150	Ben Sheets	2.00
151	Johan Santana	4.00
152	Torii Hunter	2.00
153	Joe Nathan	2.00
154	Alex Rodriguez	6.00
155	Derek Jeter	8.00
156	Randy Johnson	4.00
157	Johnny Damon	3.00
158	Mike Mussina	3.00
159	Pedro Martinez	4.00
160	Tom Glavine	3.00
161	David Wright	5.00
162	Carlos Beltran	4.00
163	Rich Harden	2.00
164	Barry Zito	3.00
165	Eric Chavez	2.00
166	Huston Street	2.00
167	Bobby Abreu	3.00
168	Chase Utley	4.00
169	Brett Myers	2.00
170	Jason Bay	3.00
171	Zachary Duke	2.00
172	Jake Peavy	3.00
173	Brian Giles	2.00
174	Khalil Greene	2.00
175	Trevor Hoffman	2.00
176	Jason Schmidt	2.00
177	Randy Winn	2.00
178	Omar Vizquel	2.00
179	Kenji Johjima	4.00
180	Ichiro Suzuki	6.00
181	Richie Sexson	3.00
182	Felix Hernandez	3.00
183	Albert Pujols	8.00
184	Chris Carpenter	3.00
185	Jim Edmonds	2.00
186	Scott Rolen	4.00
187	Carl Crawford	3.00
188	Scott Kazmir	2.00
189	Jonny Gomes	2.00
190	Mark Teixeira	3.00
191	Michael Young	2.00
192	Kevin Millwood	2.00
193	Vernon Wells	3.00
194	Troy Glaus	3.00
195	Roy Halladay	2.00
196	Alex Rios	3.00
197	Nick Johnson	2.00
198	Livan Hernandez	2.00
199	Alfonso Soriano	4.00
200	Jose Vidro	2.00
201	Aaron Rakers/399 **(RC)**	8.00
202	Angel Pagan/399 **(RC)**	20.00
203	Ben Hendrickson/399 **(RC)**	8.00
204	Bobby Livingston/399 **(RC)**	8.00
205	Darrell Rasner/399 **(RC)**	10.00
206	Brian Bannister/399 **(RC)**	20.00
207	Brian Wilson/899 **RC**	15.00
208	Bobby Keppel/199 **(RC)**	8.00
209	Choo Freeman/399 **(RC)**	8.00
210	Chris Booker/899 **(RC)**	8.00
211	Chris Britton/399 **RC**	10.00
212	Chris Demaria/329 **RC**	8.00
213	Chris Resop/899 **(RC)**	8.00
214	Tony Gwynn Jr./399 **(RC)**	40.00
215	Eric Reed/399 **(RC)**	8.00
216	Fabio Castro/399 **RC**	15.00
217	Fernando Nieve/299 **(RC)**	8.00
218	Freddie Bynum/899 **(RC)**	8.00
219	Guillermo Quiroz/399 **(RC)**	8.00
220	Hong-Chih Kuo/899 **(RC)**	40.00
221	Ryan Theriot/399 **(RC)**	60.00
222	Jack Taschner/899 **(RC)**	8.00
223	Jason Bergmann/899 **RC**	10.00
224	Jason Hammel/899 **(RC)**	8.00
225	Jeff Harris/399 **RC**	8.00
226	Jeremy Accardo/399 **RC**	15.00
227	Ty Taubenheim/399 **RC**	15.00
228	Joel Zumaya/399 **(RC)**	20.00
229	John Koronka/399 **(RC)**	8.00
230	Erick Aybar/399 **(RC)**	15.00
231	Jordan Tata/399 **RC**	8.00
232	Russell Martin/399 **(RC)**	40.00
233	Josh Rupe/399 **(RC)**	8.00
234	Kevin Frandsen/399 **(RC)**	15.00
235	Martin Prado/399 **(RC)**	15.00
236	Matt Capps/399 **(RC)**	15.00
237	Agustin Montero/199 **(RC)**	10.00
238	Mike Thompson/399 **RC**	8.00
239	Nate McLouth/399 **(RC)**	20.00
240	Peter Moylan/399 **RC**	8.00
241	Reggie Abercrombie/ 399 **(RC)**	8.00
242	Carlos Quentin/399 **(RC)**	20.00
243	Ron Flores/399 **RC**	8.00
244	Ryan Shealy/399 **(RC)**	15.00
245	Mike Rouse/399 **(RC)**	10.00
246	Santiago Ramirez/399 **(RC)**	8.00
247	Clay Hensley/899 **(RC)**	8.00
248	Skip Schumaker/399 **(RC)**	20.00
249	Eliezer Alfonzo/899 **RC**	8.00
250	Steve Stemle/399 **RC**	8.00
251	Tim Hamulack/399 **(RC)**	8.00
252	Tony Pena/299 **(RC)**	10.00
253	Emiliano Fruto/899 **RC**	8.00
254	Wilbert Nieves/399 **(RC)**	8.00
255	Joey Devine/399 **RC**	15.00
256	Adam Wainwright/ 399 **(RC)**	25.00
257	Andre Ethier/399 **(RC)**	20.00
258	Ben Johnson/399 **(RC)**	8.00
259	Boone Logan/399 **RC**	10.00
260	Chris Denorfia/899 **(RC)**	8.00
261	Alay Soler/299 **RC**	15.00
262	Cody Ross/899 **(RC)**	8.00
263	Dave Gassner/399 **(RC)**	8.00
264	Fausto Carmona/399 **(RC)**	30.00
265	Jeremy Sowers/299 **(RC)**	15.00
266	Jason Kubel/399 **(RC)**	10.00
267	John Van Benschoten/ 399 **(RC)**	10.00
268	Jose Capellan/399 **(RC)**	8.00
269	Josh Wilson/399 **(RC)**	8.00
270	Kelly Shoppach/399 **(RC)**	8.00
271	Macay McBride/399 **(RC)**	10.00
272	Matt Cain/399 **(RC)**	25.00
273	Mike Jacobs/399 **(RC)**	20.00
274	Paul Maholm/399 **(RC)**	15.00
275	Chad Billingsley/399 **(RC)**	25.00
276	Ruddy Lugo/399 **(RC)**	8.00
277	Jon Lester/399 **(RC)**	40.00
278	Sean Marshall/383 **(RC)**	15.00
279	Melky Cabrera/399 **(RC)**	30.00
280	Yusmeiro Petit/399 **(RC)**	15.00
281	Anderson Hernandez/ 299 **(RC)**	8.00
282	Brian Anderson/699 **(RC)**	8.00
283	Cole Hamels/299 **(RC)**	50.00
284	Boof Bonser/299 **(RC)**	20.00
285	Dan Uggla/199 **(RC)**	50.00
286	Francisco Liriano/299 **(RC)**	25.00
287	Hanley Ramirez/199 **(RC)**	60.00
288	Ian Kinsler/299 **(RC)**	35.00
289	Jeremy Hermida/299 **(RC)**	20.00
290	Jonathan Papelbon/ 199 **(RC)**	60.00
291	Jered Weaver/199 **(RC)**	30.00
292	Josh Johnson/299 **(RC)**	15.00
293	Josh Willingham/199 **(RC)**	15.00
294	Justin Verlander/199 **(RC)**	60.00
295	Stephen Drew/299 **(RC)**	25.00
296	Prince Fielder/125 **(RC)**	100.00
297	Ryan Zimmerman/ 199 **(RC)**	40.00
298	Takashi Saito/283 **RC**	40.00
299	Taylor Buchholz/299 **(RC)**	10.00
300	Conor Jackson/299 **(RC)**	15.00

By The Letter

		NM/M
Production 4-200		
BA	Bronson Arroyo/80	40.00
JB	Jason Bay/110	50.00
JB2	Jason Bay/50	50.00
CB	Craig Biggio/55	100.00
BI	Chad Billingsley/75	40.00
HB	Hank Blalock/50	50.00
AB	A.J. Burnett/50	50.00
MC	Miguel Cabrera/35	85.00
EC	Eric Chavez/75	40.00
AD	Adam Dunn/50	60.00
MG	Marcus Giles/136	30.00
JG	Jonny Gomes/175	30.00
KH	Khalil Greene/75	40.00
KG	Ken Griffey Jr./25	200.00
KG2	Ken Griffey Jr./25	200.00
KG3	Ken Griffey Jr./25	200.00
KG4	Ken Griffey Jr./25	200.00
VG	Vladimir Guerrero/25	120.00
AG	Tony Gwynn Jr./150	50.00
CO	Cole Hamels/120	65.00
CH	Craig Hansen/30	50.00
DH	Danny Haren/180	35.00
JH	Jeremy Hermida/125	35.00
FH	Felix Hernandez/40	50.00
FH2	Felix Hernandez/75	50.00
MH	Matt Holliday/37	60.00
HU	Tim Hudson/50	40.00
TI	Tadahito Iguchi/20	60.00
HK	Howie Kendrick/75	50.00
IK	Ian Kinsler/125	50.00
DL	Derrek Lee/200	65.00
FL	Francisco Liriano/100	50.00
GM	Greg Maddux/25	140.00
GM2	Greg Maddux/25	140.00
VM	Victor Martinez/75	40.00
JM	Joe Mauer/25	60.00
MO	Justin Morneau/75	50.00
MM	Mark Mulder/50	40.00
JN	Joe Nathan/100	35.00
RO	Roy Oswalt/50	50.00
JP	Jonathan Papelbon/100	80.00
PE	Jake Peavy/100	40.00
HR	Hanley Ramirez/125	60.00
JR	Jose Reyes/75	65.00
AR	Alex Rios/100	50.00
CS	C.C. Sabathia/40	40.00
BS	Ben Sheets/125	35.00
SM	John Smoltz/75	75.00
JS	Jeremy Sowers/60	40.00
HS	Huston Street/75	40.00
NS	Nick Swisher/170	35.00
TE	Miguel Tejada/25	50.00
JT	Jim Thome/30	75.00
DU	Dan Uggla/100	50.00
BU	B.J. Upton/20	50.00
CU	Chase Utley/25	100.00
JW	Jered Weaver/40	60.00
RW	Rickie Weeks/100	30.00
WI	Josh Willingham/75	40.00
DW	Dontrelle Willis/150	40.00
MY	Michael Young/50	45.00
CZ	Carlos Zambrano/17	100.00
RZ	Ryan Zimmerman/17	60.00
JZ	Joel Zumaya/25	50.00

Chirography

		NM/M
Production 75 unless noted.		
AN	Brian Anderson	10.00
GA	Garret Anderson	15.00
BB	Brandon Backe	10.00
BA	Brian Bannister	25.00
DB	Denny Bautista	10.00
CB	Craig Biggio	60.00
BI	Chad Billingsley	25.00
HB	Hank Blalock	15.00
JB	Joe Blanton	15.00
BO	Boof Bonser	15.00
TB	Taylor Buchholz	8.00
MC	Matt Cain	30.00
JC	Jose Capellan	8.00
FC	Fausto Carmona	20.00
SC	Sean Casey	25.00
BC	Bobby Crosby	10.00
DD	David DeJesus	10.00
CD	Chris Denorfia	10.00
JD	Joey Devine	10.00
SD	Stephen Drew	30.00
JE	Johnny Estrada	10.00
AE	Andre Ethier	25.00
KF	Keith Foulke	15.00
JF	Jeff Francis	10.00
CF	Choo Freeman	8.00
DG	Dave Gassner	8.00
KG	Khalil Greene	25.00

GR	Ken Griffey Jr.	80.00
CG	Carlos Guillen	15.00
AG	Tony Gwynn Jr.	40.00
TH	Travis Hafner	20.00
CH	Cole Hamels	50.00
RH	Rich Harden	15.00
HA	Jeff Harris	10.00
JH	Jeremy Hermida	15.00
AH	Anderson Hernandez	10.00
FH	Felix Hernandez/25	40.00
CJ	Conor Jackson	15.00
DJ	Derek Jeter	160.00
JJ	Josh Johnson	15.00
JQ	Jacque Jones	10.00
SK	Scott Kazmir/25	20.00
IK	Ian Kinsler	25.00
CK	Casey Kotchman	15.00
JK	Jason Kubel	15.00
HK	Hong-Chih Kuo	60.00
CL	Cliff Lee	15.00
JL	Jon Lester	30.00
LI	Francisco Liriano	25.00
BL	Boone Logan	15.00
FL	Felipe Lopez	15.00
ML	Mark Loretta	10.00
PM	Paul Maholm	15.00
SM	Sean Marshall	10.00
VM	Victor Martinez	15.00
MM	Macay McBride	8.00
KM	Kevin Mench	8.00
JN	Joe Nathan	15.00
LO	Lyle Overbay/40	15.00
VP	Vicente Padilla	8.00
JP	Jonathan Papelbon	40.00
CP	Corey Patterson	10.00
TP	Tony Pena	8.00
WM	Wily Mo Pena	10.00
OP	Oliver Perez	15.00
YP	Yusmeiro Petit	15.00
MP	Mark Prior/55	20.00
HR	Hanley Ramirez	40.00
RE	Eric Reed	10.00
ER	Edgar Renteria	10.00
AR	Alex Rios	15.00
IR	Ivan Rodriguez	25.00
CR	Cody Ross	10.00
JR	Josh Rupe	10.00
CS	C.C. Sabathia	20.00
TS	Takashi Saito	50.00
BS	Ben Sheets	15.00
SH	Chris Shelton	8.00
KS	Kelly Shoppach	8.00
SO	Alay Soler	10.00
AS	Alfonso Soriano	40.00
JS	Jeremy Sowers	10.00
NS	Nick Swisher	20.00
FT	Frank Thomas	65.00
DU	Dan Uggla	25.00
CU	Chase Utley	50.00
VA	John Van Benschoten	10.00
JV	Jason Varitek	50.00
VE	Justin Verlander	40.00
AW	Adam Wainwright	30.00
WE	Jered Weaver	40.00
JW	Josh Willingham	15.00
DW	Dontrelle Willis	15.00
WI	Josh Wilson	8.00
KY	Kevin Youkilis	20.00
RZ	Ryan Zimmerman	30.00

Chirography Dual Signatures

NM/M

Production 25 Sets

CE	Eric Reed, Cody Ross	25.00
FJ	Conor Jackson, Prince Fielder	40.00
GB	Khalil Greene, Josh Barfield	25.00
HA	Jeremy Hermida, Reggie Abercrombie	25.00
HK	Cole Hamels, Scott Kazmir	50.00
KH	Anderson Hernandez, Ian Kinsler	40.00
KS	Takashi Saito, Hong-Chih Kuo	180.00
LB	Francisco Liriano, Boof Bonser	50.00
MH	Rich Hill, Sean Marshall	30.00
MW	Josh Willingham, Victor Martinez	25.00
PB	Freddie Bynum, Angel Pagan	25.00
PG	Ken Griffey Jr., Albert Pujols	350.00
PO	Jake Peavy, Roy Oswalt	40.00
PP	Tony Pena, Martin Prado	25.00
RC	Hanley Ramirez, Miguel Cabrera	60.00
RR	Jose Reyes, Hanley Ramirez	60.00
SC	Jose Capellan, Ben Sheets	25.00
UH	Cole Hamels, Chase Utley	65.00
WS	Josh Wilson, Ryan Shealy	25.00

Chirography Triple Signatures

No Pricing
Production 15 Sets

Heroes

NM/M

Common Player: .50

1	Albert Pujols	3.00
2	Andruw Jones	1.00
3	Aramis Ramirez	.75
4	Brian Roberts	.50
5	Carl Crawford	.75
6	Carlos Lee	.50
7	Vladimir Guerrero	1.00
8	Chris Carpenter	.75
9	Craig Biggio	.75
10	David Ortiz	1.50
11	David Wright	2.00
12	Derrek Lee	.75
13	Dontrelle Willis	.75
14	Felix Hernandez	.75
15	Garrett Atkins	.50
16	Grady Sizemore	.75
17	Huston Street	.50
18	Jake Peavy	.50
19	Jason Bay	.75
20	Joe Mauer	1.00
21	John Smoltz	.75
22	Jonny Gomes	.50
23	Jorge Cantu	.50
24	Ken Griffey Jr.	2.00
25	Marcus Giles	.50
26	Mark Teixeira	.75
27	Matt Cain	.75
28	Michael Young	.50
29	Miguel Cabrera	1.00
30	Johan Santana	1.00
31	Nick Swisher	.50
32	Prince Fielder	1.00
33	Joe Blanton	.50
34	Roy Oswalt	.75
35	Ryan Howard	3.00
36	Scott Kazmir	.50
37	Tadahito Iguchi	.50
38	Travis Hafner	.75
39	Victor Martinez	.50
40	Jose Reyes	1.00
41	Chris Carpenter, Albert Pujols	3.00
42	Albert Pujols, Miguel Cabrera	3.00
43	Andruw Jones, Ken Griffey Jr.	2.00
44	Derrek Lee, Aramis Ramirez	.75
45	Ryan Howard, Prince Fielder	3.00
46	Jake Peavy, Roy Oswalt	.75
47	Morgan Ensberg, Craig Biggio	.75
48	David Ortiz, Travis Hafner	1.50
49	Derek Jeter, David Wright	3.00
50	Derek Jeter, Ken Griffey Jr.	3.00
51	Derek Jeter, Michael Young	3.00
52	Scott Kazmir, Dontrelle Willis	.50
53	Jason Bay, Grady Sizemore	.75
54	Michael Young, Mark Teixeira	.75
55	Brian Roberts, Tadahito Iguchi	.50
56	Matt Cain, Felix Hernandez, Chien-Ming Wang	2.00
57	Mark Teixeira, Derrek Lee, Albert Pujols	3.00
58	Albert Pujols, Ken Griffey Jr., Miguel Cabrera	3.00
59	Marcus Giles, Andruw Jones, John Smoltz	1.00
60	Derrek Lee, Kerry Wood, Aramis Ramirez	1.00
61	Aramis Ramirez, Morgan Ensberg, David Wright	2.00
62	Carl Crawford, Jorge Cantu, Jonny Gomes	.50
63	Jake Peavy, Chris Carpenter, John Smoltz	1.00
64	Travis Hafner, Grady Sizemore, Victor Martinez	.75
65	Ryan Howard, Prince Fielder, David Ortiz	3.00
66	Chris Carpenter, John Smoltz, Jake Peavy, Dontrelle Willis	.75
67	Ken Griffey Jr., Derek Jeter, David Ortiz, Albert Pujols	3.00
68	David Ortiz, Andruw Jones, Derrek Lee, Mark Teixeira	1.50
69	Brian Roberts, Marcus Giles, Craig Biggio, Tadahito Iguchi	.50
70	Jason Bay, David Wright, Mark Teixeira, Miguel Cabrera	2.00

Rookie Signatures Platinum

No Pricing
Production One Set

Sign of the Times

NM/M

Production 75 Sets

RA	Reggie Abercrombie	8.00
BA	Bobby Abreu	35.00
AN	Brian Anderson	10.00
BR	Brian Bannister	15.00
AB	Adrian Beltre	15.00
YB	Yuniesky Betancourt	15.00
BI	Chad Billingsley	25.00
BB	Boof Bonser	15.00
CB	Chris Booker	8.00
TB	Taylor Buchholz	8.00
ME	Melky Cabrera	25.00
MC	Miguel Cabrera	30.00
CA	Matt Cain	30.00
JC	Jose Capellan	8.00
FC	Fausto Carmona	10.00
CC	Carl Crawford	15.00
CD	Chris Demaria	8.00
DE	Chris Denorfia	8.00
JD	J.D. Drew	15.00
SD	Stephen Drew	30.00
AE	Andre Ethier	30.00
FR	Ron Flores	10.00
RF	Rafael Furcal	15.00
EG	Eric Gagne	15.00
DG	Dave Gassner	8.00
ZG	Zack Greinke	15.00
KG	Ken Griffey Jr.	80.00
VG	Vladimir Guerrero	50.00
JG	Jose Guillen	8.00
AG	Tony Gwynn Jr.	35.00
CH	Cole Hamels	50.00
JH	Jason Hammel	8.00
HA	Tim Hamulack	10.00
CY	Clay Hensley	8.00
HE	Jeremy Hermida	15.00
AH	Anderson Hernandez	8.00
RH	Ramon Hernandez	10.00
TH	Tim Hudson	15.00
JA	Conor Jackson	20.00
MJ	Mike Jacobs	15.00
DJ	Derek Jeter	160.00
BJ	Ben Johnson	10.00
JJ	Josh Johnson	10.00
RJ	Randy Johnson	50.00
AJ	Andruw Jones	25.00
JK	Jason Kendall	10.00
IK	Ian Kinsler	25.00
MK	Mark Kotsay	10.00
KU	Jason Kubel	15.00
CL	Carlos Lee	15.00
DL	Derrek Lee	25.00
FL	Francisco Liriano	35.00
BL	Boone Logan	10.00
LO	Derek Lowe	25.00
GM	Greg Maddux	140.00
PM	Paul Maholm	15.00
SM	Sean Marshall	10.00
RM	Russell Martin	20.00
JM	Joe Mauer	20.00
MA	Macay McBride	10.00
MO	Justin Morneau	25.00
MM	Mark Mulder	10.00
PA	Jonathan Papelbon	30.00
JP	Jake Peavy	20.00
TP	Tony Pena	8.00
PE	Joel Peralta	10.00
YP	Yusmeiro Petit	15.00
SP	Scott Podsednik	15.00
AR	Aramis Ramirez	20.00
HR	Hanley Ramirez	35.00
SA	Santiago Ramirez	8.00
ER	Eric Reed	10.00
JR	Jose Reyes	40.00
SR	Scott Rolen	25.00
CR	Cody Ross	10.00
TS	Takashi Saito	50.00
CS	Curt Schilling	50.00
SS	Skip Schumaker	15.00
RS	Ryan Shealy	15.00
JS	John Smoltz	40.00
AS	Alay Soler	10.00
JY	Jeremy Sowers	10.00
ST	Steve Stemle	8.00
MT	Mark Teixeira	20.00
TE	Miguel Tejada	25.00
MI	Mike Thompson	10.00
DU	Dan Uggla	25.00
JV	John Van Benschoten	10.00
VE	Justin Verlander	40.00
AW	Adam Wainwright	30.00
JE	Jered Weaver	40.00
RW	Rickie Weeks	15.00
VW	Vernon Wells	15.00
JW	Josh Willingham	15.00
WI	Josh Wilson	10.00
RZ	Ryan Zimmerman	30.00

Sign of the Times Dual

NM/M

Production 25 Sets

BM	Nate McLouth, Jason Bay	25.00
CH	Jose Capellan, Ben Hendrickson	20.00
FW	Prince Fielder, Rickie Weeks	60.00
GP	Ken Griffey Jr., Albert Pujols	300.00
HD	Tim Hudson, Joey Devine	30.00
HF	Rich Harden, Ron Flores	20.00
KN	Michael Napoli, Howie Kendrick	40.00
LG	Dave Gassner, Francisco Liriano	30.00
MM	Sean Marshall, Greg Maddux	140.00
OB	Roy Oswalt, Taylor Buchholz	30.00
PB	Angel Pagan, Freddie Bynum	20.00
PT	Jake Peavy, Mike Thompson	20.00
RW	Josh Willingham, Hanley Ramirez	40.00
SC	Fausto Carmona, C.C. Sabathia	30.00
WM	Kendry Morales, Jered Weaver	40.00
ZH	Ryan Zimmerman, Brendan Harris	40.00

Signs of the Times Triple

No Pricing
Production 15 Sets

WBC Future Watch

NM/M

Common Player: 3.00
Production 999 Sets

1	Adrian Burnside	3.00
2	Gavin Fingleson	3.00
3	Bradley Harman	3.00
4	Brendan Kingman	3.00
5	Brett Roneberg	3.00
6	Paul Rutgers	3.00
7	Phil Stockman	3.00
8	Stubby Clapp	3.00
9	Steve Green	3.00
10	Pete LaForest	5.00
11	Adam Loewen	5.00
12	Ryan Radmanovich	3.00
13	Chenhao Li	3.00
14	Guangbiao Liu	3.00
15	Guogang Yang	3.00
16	Jingchao Wang	3.00
17	Lei Li	3.00
18	Lingfeng Sun	3.00
19	Nan Wang	3.00
20	Shuo Yang	3.00
21	Tao Bu	3.00
22	Wei Wang	3.00
23	Yi Feng	3.00
24	Chien-Ming Chiang	15.00
25	Yung-Chi Chen	20.00
26	Chia-Hsien Hseih	15.00
27	Chin-Lung Hu	15.00
28	En-Yu Lin	20.00
29	Wei-Lun Pan	10.00
30	Ariel Borrero	3.00
31	Yadel Marti	3.00
32	Yulieski Gourriel	20.00
33	Frederich Cepeda	3.00
34	Yadier Pedroso	3.00
35	Pedro Luis Lazo	3.00
36	Elier Sanchez	3.00
37	Norberto Gonzalez	3.00
38	Carlos Tabares	3.00
39	Eduardo Paret	3.00
40	Osmany Urrutia	3.00
41	Alexei Ramirez	50.00
42	Yoandy Garlobo	3.00
43	Vicyohandry Odelin	3.00
44	Michel Enriquez	3.00
45	Ormari Romero	3.00
46	Ariel Pestano	3.00
47	Francisco Liriano	5.00
48	Dustin Dellucchi	3.00
49	Tony Giarratano	3.00
50	Tom Gregorio	3.00
51	Mark Saccomanno	3.00
52	Takahiro Arai	8.00
53	Akinori Iwamura	20.00
54	Munenori Kawasaki	15.00
55	Nobuhiko Matsunaka	10.00
56	Daisuke Matsuzaka	100.00
57	Shinya Miyamoto	10.00
58	Tsuyoshi Nishioka	15.00
59	Tomoya Satozaki	8.00
60	Koji Uehara	15.00
61	Shunsuke Watanabe	15.00
62	Sadaharu Oh	20.00
63	Byung Kyu Lee	3.00
64	Ji Man Song	3.00
65	Jin Man Park	3.00
66	Jong Beom Lee	3.00
67	Jong Kook Kim	3.00
68	Min Han Son	3.00
69	Min Jae Kim	3.00
70	Seung-Yeop Lee	10.00
71	Luis A. Garcia	3.00
72	Mario Valenzuela	3.00
73	Sharnol Adriana	3.00
74	Rob Cordemans	3.00
75	Michael Duursma	3.00
76	Percy Isenia	3.00
77	Sidney de Jong	3.00
78	Dirk Klooster	3.00
79	Raylinoe Legito	3.00
80	Shairon Martis	5.00
81	Harvey Monte	3.00
82	Hainley Statia	3.00
83	Roger Deago	5.00
84	Audes De Leon	3.00
85	Freddy Herrera	3.00
86	Yoni Lasso	5.00
87	Orlando Miller	3.00
88	Len Picota	5.00
89	Federico Baez	3.00
90	Dicky Gonzalez	3.00
91	Josue Matos	3.00
92	Orlando Roman	3.00
93	Paul Bell	3.00
94	Kyle Botha	3.00
95	Jason Cook	3.00
96	Nicholas Dempsey	3.00
97	Victor Moreno	3.00
98	Ricardo Palma	3.00
99	Huston Street	3.00
100	Chase Utley	3.00

2006 SP Legendary Cuts

NM/M

Complete Set (200):	
Common Player:	.25
Common SP (101-200):	2.00
Production 550	
Pack (4):	10.00
Box (12):	100.00

1	Juan Marichal	.50

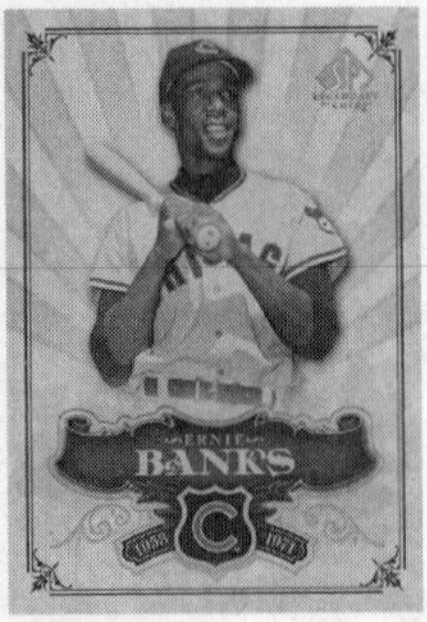

2	Monte Irvin	.75
3	Will Clark	.75
4	Willie McCovey	.75
5	Eddie Gaedel	.25
6	Ken Williams	.25
7	Earl Battey	.25
8	Rick Ferrell	.25
9	Bob Gibson	1.00
10	Elmer Flick	.25
11	Joe Medwick	.25
12	Lou Brock	.75
13	Ozzie Smith	1.00
14	Red Schoendienst	.25
15	Stan Musial	2.00
16	Tony Oliva	.50
17	Phil Niekro	.25
18	Boog Powell	.25
19	Brooks Robinson	1.00
20	Cal Ripken Jr.	3.00
21	Eddie Murray	.75
22	Frank Robinson	1.00
23	Jim Palmer	.50
24	Jocko Conlon	.25
25	Carlton Fisk	.50
26	Dwight Evans	.25
27	Fred Lynn	.25
28	Jim Rice	.50
29	Ted Williams	2.00
30	Wade Boggs	.75
31	Hugh Duffy	.25
32	Kid Nichols	.25
33	Johnny Vander Meer	.25
34	Dolph Camilli	.25
35	Carl Yastrzemski	1.00
36	Chick Hafey	.25
37	Kirby Higbe	.25
38	Pee Wee Reese	.50
39	Pete Reiser	.25
40	Don Sutton	.25
41	Rod Carew	.75
42	Andre Dawson	.50
43	Billy Herman	.25
44	Billy Williams	.25
45	Charlie Root	.25
46	Hack Wilson	.25
47	Ernie Banks	1.00
48	Fergie Jenkins	.50
49	Gabby Hartnett	.25
50	Ken Hubbs	.25
51	Kiki Cuyler	.25
52	Mark Grace	.50
53	Ryne Sandberg	1.50
54	Harold Newhouser	.25
55	Charlie Robertson	.25
56	Harold Baines	.25
57	Luis Aparicio	.25
58	Luke Appling	.25
59	Nellie Fox	.50
60	Ray Schalk	.25
61	Red Faber	.25
62	Sloppy Thurston	.25
63	Freddie Lindstrom	.25
64	Vern Kennedy	.25
65	Barry Larkin	.50
66	Bucky Walters	.25
67	Dolf Luque	.25
68	Al Campanis	.25
69	Ernie Lombardi	.25
70	George Foster	.25
71	Joe Morgan	.75
72	Johnny Bench	1.00
73	Ken Griffey Sr.	.25
74	Ted Kluszewski	.25
75	Tony Perez	.50
76	Wally Post	.25
77	Bob Feller	.50
78	Bob Lemon	.25
79	Earl Averill	.25
80	Joe Sewell	.25
81	Johnny Hodapp	.25
82	Larry Doby	.50
83	Lou Boudreau	.25
84	Rocky Colavito	.25
85	Stan Coveleski	.25
86	Nap Lajoie	.50
87	Al Kaline	1.00
88	Alan Trammell	.50
89	Charlie Gehringer	.25
90	Denny McLain	.50
91	Hank Greenberg	.50
92	Jack Morris	.25
93	Mark Fidrych	.25
94	Ray Boone	.25
95	Rudy York	.25
96	Buck Leonard	.25
97	Bo Jackson	1.00
98	Zoilo Versalles	.25
99	John Kruk	.25
100	Don Drysdale	.50
101	Cecil Cooper	2.00
102	Vic Wertz	2.00
103	Kirk Gibson	2.00
104	Maury Wills	2.00
105	Steve Garvey	2.00
106	Warren Spahn	5.00
107	Paul Molitor	4.00
108	Robin Yount	5.00
109	Rollie Fingers	3.00
110	Bob Allison	2.00
111	Kirby Puckett	6.00
112	Tim Raines	2.00
113	George Pipgras	2.00
114	Eddie Grant	2.00
115	Hoyt Wilhelm	2.00
116	Sal Maglie	2.00
117	Ron Santo	3.00
118	Wally Joyner	2.00
119	Tom Seaver	5.00
120	Tommie Agee	2.00
121	Harmon Killebrew	4.00
122	Bill Dickey	3.00
123	Early Wynn	2.00
124	Bobby Murcer	2.00
125	Bucky Dent	2.00
126	Dave Winfield	4.00
127	Don Larsen	4.00
128	Don Mattingly	8.00
129	Earle Combs	2.00
130	Ed Lopat	2.00
131	Elston Howard	4.00
132	Everett Scott	2.00
133	Rich "Goose" Gossage	2.00
134	Graig Nettles	2.00
135	Joe DiMaggio	8.00
136	Lou Piniella	2.00
137	Bill "Moose" Skowron	2.00
138	Phil Rizzuto	3.00
139	Red Ruffing	2.00
140	Reggie Jackson	4.00
141	Roger Maris	6.00
142	Ron Guidry	3.00
143	Tiny Bonham	2.00
144	Bruce Sutter	2.00
145	Tony Lazzeri	2.00
146	Waite Hoyt	2.00
147	Whitey Ford	4.00
148	Steve Sax	2.00
149	Yogi Berra	5.00
150	Enos Slaughter	2.00
151	Jim "Catfish" Hunter	2.00
152	Dennis Eckersley	3.00
153	Jose Canseco	3.00
154	Al Rosen	2.00
155	Al Simmons	2.00
156	Chief Bender	2.00
157	Cy Williams	2.00
158	Mike Schmidt	5.00
159	Richie Ashburn	2.00
160	Robin Roberts	3.00
161	Steve Carlton	3.00
162	Judy Johnson	2.00
163	Al Oliver	2.00
164	Bill Mazeroski	3.00
165	Dave Parker	3.00
166	Max Carey	2.00
167	Pie Traynor	3.00
168	Ralph Kiner	3.00
169	Roberto Clemente	10.00
170	Willie Stargell	4.00
171	Gaylord Perry	2.00
172	Tony Gwynn	5.00
173	Nolan Ryan	8.00
174	Joe Carter	2.00
175	Frank Howard	2.00
176	George Kell	2.00
177	Heinie Manush	2.00
178	Sam Rice	2.00
179	Babe Ruth	10.00
180	Casey Stengel	3.00
181	Christy Mathewson	4.00
182	Cy Young	4.00
183	Dizzy Dean	4.00
184	Eddie Mathews	5.00
185	George Sisler	3.00
186	Honus Wagner	5.00
187	Jackie Robinson	6.00
188	Jimmie Foxx	5.00
189	Johnny Mize	2.00
190	Lefty Gomez	2.00
191	Lou Gehrig	8.00
192	Mel Ott	3.00
193	Mickey Cochrane	3.00
194	Rogers Hornsby	4.00
195	Roy Campanella	5.00
196	Satchel Paige	5.00
197	Thurman Munson	5.00
198	Ty Cobb	6.00
199	Walter Johnson	3.00
200	Lefty Grove	3.00

Gold

Gold (101-200): 2-4X
Production 99 Sets

Baseball Chronology

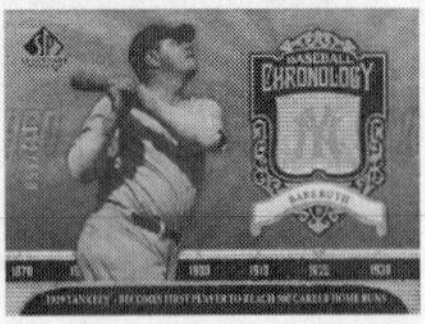

NM/M

Production 550 Sets
Platinum: 1.5-2X
Production 99 Sets

EB	Ernie Banks	5.00
EB2	Ernie Banks	5.00
JB	Johnny Bench	4.00
YB	Yogi Berra	4.00
WB	Wade Boggs	4.00
WB2	Wade Boggs	4.00
LB	Lou Boudreau	2.00
LO	Lou Brock	4.00
RC	Roy Campanella	4.00
CA	Rod Carew	3.00
SC	Steve Carlton	3.00
SC2	Steve Carlton	3.00
JC	Joe Carter	2.00
WC	Will Clark	4.00
CL	Roberto Clemente	10.00
TC	Ty Cobb	6.00
TC2	Ty Cobb	6.00
MC	Mickey Cochrane	3.00
CN	Joe Cronin	2.00
AD	Andre Dawson	3.00
DZ	Dizzy Dean	3.00
BD	Bucky Dent	2.00
JD	Joe DiMaggio	8.00
DD	Don Drysdale	3.00
DE	Dennis Eckersley	3.00
BF	Bob Feller	3.00
MF	Mark Fidrych	2.00
RF	Rollie Fingers	3.00
CF	Carlton Fisk	3.00
WF	Whitey Ford	4.00
JF	Jimmie Foxx	5.00
JF2	Jimmie Foxx	5.00
SG	Steve Garvey	2.00
LG	Lou Gehrig	8.00
LG2	Lou Gehrig	8.00
BG	Bob Gibson	4.00
KG	Kirk Gibson	3.00
HG	Hank Greenberg	3.00
TG	Tony Gwynn	4.00
GH	Gil Hodges	3.00
RH	Rogers Hornsby	4.00
CH	Jim "Catfish" Hunter	2.00
BO	Bo Jackson	4.00
RJ	Reggie Jackson	4.00
WJ	Walter Johnson	4.00
AK	Al Kaline	4.00
RK	Ralph Kiner	2.00
NL	Nap Lajoie	3.00
DL	Don Larsen	3.00
BL	Bob Lemon	2.00
FL	Fred Lynn	2.00
RM	Roger Maris	6.00
CM	Christy Mathewson	4.00
DM	Don Mattingly	6.00
BM	Bill Mazeroski	3.00
WM	Willie McCovey	3.00
JM	Johnny Mize	2.00
PM	Paul Molitor	3.00
JO	Joe Morgan	3.00
TM	Thurman Munson	5.00
EM	Eddie Murray	3.00
SM	Stan Musial	6.00
PN	Phil Niekro	2.00
MO	Mel Ott	3.00
SP	Satchel Paige	5.00
GP	Gaylord Perry	2.00
KP	Kirby Puckett	5.00
PW	Pee Wee Reese	3.00
RI	Jim Rice	3.00
CR	Cal Ripken Jr.	8.00
RO	Brooks Robinson	4.00
FR	Frank Robinson	4.00
JR	Jackie Robinson	6.00
BR	Babe Ruth	10.00
BR2	Babe Ruth	10.00
BR3	Babe Ruth	10.00
NR	Nolan Ryan	8.00
NR2	Nolan Ryan	8.00
NR3	Nolan Ryan	8.00
RS	Ryne Sandberg	5.00
MS	Mike Schmidt	5.00
TS	Tom Seaver	4.00
GS	George Sisler	3.00
ES	Enos Slaughter	2.00
OS	Ozzie Smith	5.00
WS	Warren Spahn	4.00
ST	Willie Stargell	4.00
CS	Casey Stengel	3.00
CS2	Casey Stengel	3.00
DS	Don Sutton	2.00
AT	Alan Trammell	3.00
HW	Honus Wagner	5.00
HY	Hoyt Wilhelm	2.00
BW	Billy Williams	2.00
TW	Ted Williams	8.00
TW2	Ted Williams	8.00
MW	Maury Wills	2.00
YZ	Carl Yastrzemski	4.00
CY	Cy Young	3.00
RY	Robin Yount	4.00

Baseball Chronology Materials

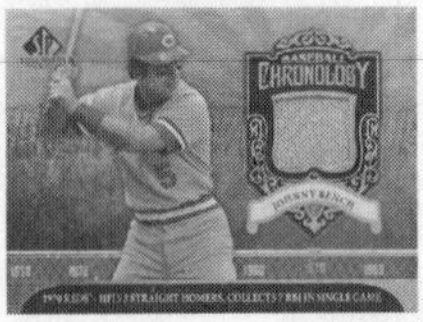

NM/M

Common Player:

EB	Ernie Banks	15.00
EB2	Ernie Banks/SP	20.00
JB	Johnny Bench	15.00
YB	Yogi Berra	20.00
WB	Wade Boggs	10.00
WB2	Wade Boggs	10.00
LB	Lou Boudreau	12.00
LO	Lou Brock	10.00
RC	Roy Campanella	20.00
CA	Rod Carew	10.00
SC	Steve Carlton	8.00
SC2	Steve Carlton	8.00
JC	Joe Carter	6.00
WC	Will Clark	10.00
CL	Roberto Clemente/SP	80.00
TC	Ty Cobb/SP	150.00
TC2	Ty Cobb/SP	150.00
CN	Joe Cronin	15.00
AD	Andre Dawson	8.00
DZ	Dizzy Dean/SP	60.00
BD	Bucky Dent	6.00
JD	Joe DiMaggio/SP	75.00
DD	Don Drysdale/SP	25.00
DE	Dennis Eckersley	10.00
BF	Bob Feller	10.00
MF	Mark Fidrych	10.00
RF	Rollie Fingers	8.00
CF	Carlton Fisk	10.00
JF	Jimmie Foxx/SP	40.00
JF2	Jimmie Foxx/SP	40.00
SG	Steve Garvey	6.00
LG	Lou Gehrig/SP	175.00
LG2	Lou Gehrig	175.00
BG	Bob Gibson	10.00
HG	Hank Greenberg	25.00
TG	Tony Gwynn	12.00
GH	Gil Hodges/SP	40.00
RH	Rogers Hornsby/SP	50.00
CH	Jim "Catfish" Hunter	10.00
BO	Bo Jackson	12.00
RJ	Reggie Jackson	12.00
AK	Al Kaline	15.00
RK	Ralph Kiner	12.00
DL	Don Larsen	12.00
BL	Bob Lemon	10.00
FL	Fred Lynn	8.00
RM	Roger Maris	30.00
CM	Christy Mathewson/SP	240.00
DM	Don Mattingly	15.00
BM	Bill Mazeroski/SP	20.00
WM	Willie McCovey	12.00
JM	Johnny Mize	15.00
PM	Paul Molitor	8.00
JO	Joe Morgan	10.00
TM	Thurman Munson	25.00
EM	Eddie Murray	10.00
SM	Stan Musial	20.00
PN	Phil Niekro	8.00
MO	Mel Ott/SP	35.00
SP	Satchel Paige/SP	75.00
GP	Gaylord Perry	8.00
KP	Kirby Puckett	15.00
PW	Pee Wee Reese	10.00
RI	Jim Rice	8.00
CR	Cal Ripken Jr.	25.00
RO	Brooks Robinson	12.00
FR	Frank Robinson	10.00
JR	Jackie Robinson/SP	60.00
BR	Babe Ruth/SP	250.00
BR2	Babe Ruth/SP	250.00
BR3	Babe Ruth/SP	250.00
NR	Nolan Ryan	20.00
NR2	Nolan Ryan	20.00
NR3	Nolan Ryan	20.00
RS	Ryne Sandberg	15.00
MS	Mike Schmidt	12.00
TS	Tom Seaver	15.00
GS	George Sisler/SP	35.00
ES	Enos Slaughter	15.00
OS	Ozzie Smith	12.00
WS	Warren Spahn	15.00
ST	Willie Stargell	15.00
CS	Casey Stengel	25.00
CS2	Casey Stengel/SP	35.00
DS	Don Sutton	8.00
AT	Alan Trammell	8.00
HW	Honus Wagner/SP	160.00
HY	Hoyt Wilhelm/SP	15.00
BW	Billy Williams	8.00
TW	Ted Williams	40.00
TW2	Ted Williams	40.00
MW	Maury Wills	8.00
YZ	Carl Yastrzemski	15.00
RY	Robin Yount	12.00

Dual Legendary Cuts

Production One Set
No Pricing

Historical Cut Signatures

Production One Set
No Pricing

Legendary Materials

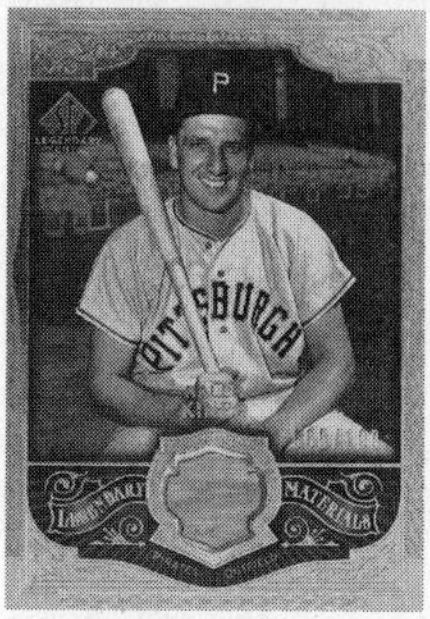

		NM/M
Production 225 unless noted.		
Tier 1:		.75-1.5X
Production 50-199		
Tier 2:		1-2X
Production 25-99		
Tier 3:		No Pricing
Production 5-15		
HB	Harold Baines	6.00
EB	Ernie Banks	20.00
JB	Johnny Bench	15.00
YB	Yogi Berra	15.00
WB	Wade Boggs	10.00
LB	Lou Brock	10.00
LB2	Lou Brock	10.00
JC	Jose Canseco	10.00
CW	Rod Carew	10.00
SC	Steve Carlton	8.00
SC2	Steve Carlton	8.00
WC	Will Clark	10.00
WC2	Will Clark	10.00
RC	Rocky Colavito	20.00
DC	Dave Concepcion	6.00
CC	Cecil Cooper	10.00
AD	Andre Dawson	8.00
BD	Bucky Dent	8.00
JD	Joe DiMaggio/99	75.00
DE	Dennis Eckersley	8.00
DE2	Dennis Eckersley	8.00
EV	Dwight Evans	8.00
BF	Bob Feller	10.00
RF	Rollie Fingers	8.00
CF	Carlton Fisk	10.00
GF	George Foster	6.00
SG	Steve Garvey	6.00
BG	Bob Gibson	10.00
KI	Kirk Gibson	10.00
GG	Rich "Goose" Gossage	8.00
MG	Mark Grace	10.00
KG	Ken Griffey Sr.	6.00
GU	Ron Guidry	10.00
TG	Tony Gwynn	15.00
FH	Frank Howard	8.00
BO	Bo Jackson	15.00
RJ	Reggie Jackson	10.00
FJ	Fergie Jenkins	8.00
WJ	Wally Joyner	10.00
AK	Al Kaline	12.00
RK	Ralph Kiner	10.00
JK	John Kruk	8.00
BL	Barry Larkin	8.00
DL	Don Larsen	12.00
FL	Fred Lynn	6.00
JU	Juan Marichal	10.00
MA	Don Mattingly	20.00
BM	Bill Mazeroski	10.00
WM	Willie McCovey	10.00
PM	Paul Molitor	8.00
JO	Joe Morgan	10.00
JM	Jack Morris	6.00
MU	Bobby Murcer	8.00
EM	Eddie Murray	10.00
SM	Stan Musial	20.00
GN	Graig Nettles	10.00
PN	Phil Niekro	8.00
PN2	Phil Niekro	8.00
TO	Tony Oliva	8.00
AO	Al Oliver	8.00
JP	Jim Palmer	10.00
JP2	Jim Palmer	10.00
DP	Dave Parker	8.00
TP	Tony Perez	8.00
GP	Gaylord Perry	8.00
GP2	Gaylord Perry	8.00
LP	Lou Piniella	8.00
BP	Boog Powell	8.00
KP	Kirby Puckett	15.00
JR	Jim Rice	8.00
CR	Cal Ripken Jr.	25.00
PR	Phil Rizzuto/99	10.00
RR	Robin Roberts	10.00
RO	Brooks Robinson/175	10.00
FR	Frank Robinson	10.00
FR2	Frank Robinson	10.00
AR	Al Rosen	8.00
BR	Babe Ruth/99	225.00
NR	Nolan Ryan	20.00
RS	Ryne Sandberg	15.00
RN	Ron Santo/125	12.00
RN2	Ron Santo/125	12.00
SS	Steve Sax	6.00
MS	Mike Schmidt	15.00
RE	Red Schoendienst/99	12.00
TS	Tom Seaver	12.00
SK	Bill "Moose" Skowron	8.00
OS	Ozzie Smith	15.00
BS	Bruce Sutter	8.00
SU	Don Sutton	8.00
JT	Joe Torre	10.00
BW	Billy Williams	8.00
MW	Maury Wills	6.00
DW	Dave Winfield	8.00
CY	Carl Yastrzemski	15.00
RY	Robin Yount	10.00

Legendary Cuts

		NM/M
Production 1-90		
JA	Joe Adcock/47	120.00
GA	Grover Alexander/1	
MA	Mel Allen/67	175.00
WA	Walter Alston/27	160.00
LA	Luke Appling/84	100.00
RA	Richie Ashburn/22	200.00
EA	Earl Averill/50	100.00
EB	Ed Barrow/35	250.00
RB	Ray Boone/51	120.00
LB	Lou Boudreau/86	100.00
DC	Dolph Camilli/58	100.00
MC	Max Carey/79	140.00
EC	Earle Combs/65	200.00
ST	Stan Coveleski/81	120.00
JO	Joe Cronin/30	125.00
RD	Ray Dandridge/35	100.00
DD	Dizzy Dean/21	600.00
BD	Bill Dickey/34	240.00
DR	Don Drysdale/45	200.00
DU	Joe Dugan/25	160.00
DL	Leo Durocher/22	150.00
CG	Charlie Gehringer/76	100.00
LG	Lefty Gomez/44	125.00
HG	Hank Greenberg/60	250.00
BG	Burleigh Grimes/33	150.00
HE	Billy Herman/87	100.00
WH	Waite Hoyt/49	125.00
CH	Jim "Catfish" Hunter/24	150.00
JJ	Judy Johnson/40	150.00
HK	Harvey Kuenn/89	120.00
BL	Bob Lemon/77	80.00
LO	Ernie Lombardi/25	160.00
EL	Ed Lopat/32	140.00
EM	Eddie Mathews/59	150.00
JM	Joe McCarthy/67	180.00
ME	Joe Medwick/82	180.00
MI	Johnny Mize/90	140.00
WP	Wally Post/66	120.00
PR	Pee Wee Reese/47	160.00
SR	Sam Rice/31	180.00
ER	Edd Roush/90	80.00
RR	Red Ruffing/72	200.00
JS	Joe Sewell/83	120.00
WS	Warren Spahn/52	140.00
CS	Casey Stengel/35	300.00
PT	Pie Traynor/26	500.00
BW	Bucky Walters/52	120.00
WI	Hoyt Wilhelm/47	100.00

Place In History Signatures

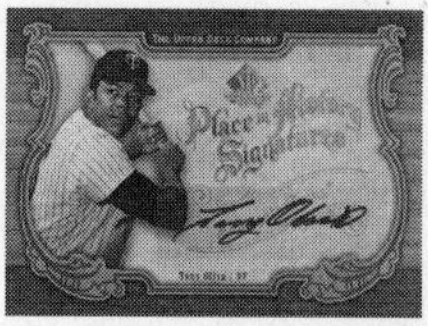

		NM/M
Production 99 unless noted.		
LA	Luis Aparicio	25.00
LA2	Luis Aparicio	25.00
HB	Harold Baines/35	20.00
EB	Ernie Banks/25	75.00
JB	Johnny Bench/42	50.00
WB	Wade Boggs/50	35.00
LB	Lou Brock	25.00
LB2	Lou Brock	25.00
JC	Jose Canseco	40.00
CA	Rod Carew/50	25.00
SC	Steve Carlton	25.00
SC2	Steve Carlton	25.00
WC	Will Clark/92	25.00
WC2	Will Clark	25.00
CC	Cecil Cooper	20.00
AD	Andre Dawson	20.00
BD	Bucky Dent	15.00
DE	Dennis Eckersley	25.00
DE2	Dennis Eckersley	25.00
EV	Dwight Evans	20.00
BF	Bob Feller/35	40.00
RF	Rollie Fingers/77	20.00
CF	Carlton Fisk	30.00
WF	Whitey Ford/35	60.00
GF	George Foster/56	15.00
SG	Steve Garvey	25.00
MG	Mark Grace	25.00
KG	Ken Griffey Sr.	15.00
TG	Tony Gwynn/26	60.00
FH	Frank Howard	25.00
BO	Bo Jackson	50.00
RJ	Reggie Jackson/25	60.00
FJ	Fergie Jenkins	20.00
WJ	Wally Joyner	25.00
BL	Barry Larkin/49	40.00
FL	Fred Lynn	15.00
JU	Juan Marichal/29	35.00
MA	Don Mattingly/50	100.00
BM	Bill Mazeroski	35.00
MC	Denny McLain/31	25.00
PM	Paul Molitor	35.00
JO	Joe Morgan/50	30.00
JM	Jack Morris/82	20.00
SM	Stan Musial/45	70.00
GN	Graig Nettles	20.00
PN	Phil Niekro/52	20.00
PN2	Phil Niekro/52	20.00
TO	Tony Oliva	20.00
TO2	Tony Oliva	20.00
JP	Jim Palmer	25.00
GP	Gaylord Perry	20.00
GP2	Gaylord Perry	20.00
LP	Lou Piniella	20.00
JY	Johnny Podres/38	20.00
BP	Boog Powell	20.00
KP	Kirby Puckett	80.00
TR	Tim Raines	25.00
JR	Jim Rice	20.00
CR	Cal Ripken Jr./50	140.00
PR	Phil Rizzuto	40.00
RR	Robin Roberts/55	25.00
BR	Brooks Robinson/50	40.00
BR2	Brooks Robinson/50	40.00
FR	Frank Robinson	40.00
FR2	Frank Robinson	40.00
AR	Al Rosen	20.00
RO	Ron Santo	60.00
RO2	Ron Santo	60.00
SS	Steve Sax	20.00
MS	Mike Schmidt/25	75.00
RD	Red Schoendienst	35.00
TS	Tom Seaver/55	50.00
SK	Bill "Moose" Skowron	25.00
OS	Ozzie Smith	50.00
BS	Bruce Sutter	20.00
JT	Joe Torre	40.00
BW	Billy Williams	20.00
MW	Maury Wills/96	20.00
CY	Carl Yastrzemski	40.00
RY	Robin Yount	40.00

Place In History Cut Signatures

		NM/M
Production 1-98		
BA	Bob Allison/94	140.00
LA	Luke Appling/94	100.00
EA	Earl Averill/75	80.00
LB	Lou Boudreau/88	100.00
HC	Happy Chandler/61	100.00
CO	Chuck Connors/25	450.00
JC	Joe Cronin/30	125.00
RD	Ray Dandridge/43	120.00
DL	Leo Durocher/42	140.00
DU	Joe Dugan/25	150.00
FF	Ford Frick/30	150.00
CG	Charlie Gehringer/57	120.00
WG	Warren Giles/45	200.00
LG	Lefty Gomez/30	125.00
HG	Hank Greenberg/31	260.00
BG	Burleigh Grimes/43	120.00
HI	Kirby Higbe/59	140.00
JH	Johnny Hodapp/26	125.00
DH	Dick Howser/28	160.00
JJ	Judy Johnson/20	180.00
VK	Vern Kennedy/61	120.00
BL	Bob Lemon/47	90.00
SM	Sal Maglie/73	120.00
EM	Eddie Mathews/34	150.00
JM	Joe McCarthy/58	200.00
ME	Joe Medwick/60	200.00
PR	Pee Wee Reese/57	180.00
RE	Pete Reiser/75	125.00
RO	Charlie Robertson/42	150.00
ER	Edd Roush/98	100.00
JS	Joe Sewell/87	100.00
GS	George Sisler/42	450.00
WS	Warren Spahn/41	140.00
WI	Hoyt Wilhelm/65	100.00
CW	Cy Williams/29	180.00
EW	Early Wynn/36	100.00

Quadruple Legendary Cuts

Production One Set
No Pricing

Memorable Moments Swatch

		NM/M
Common Player:		
Production 225 Sets		
JB	Johnny Bench	15.00
CC	Cesar Cedeno	8.00
RC	Rocky Colavito	20.00
DC	David Cone	8.00
CE	Cecil Cooper	10.00
AD	Andre Dawson	10.00
DE	Dwight Evans	8.00
BF	Bob Feller	12.00
RF	Rollie Fingers	8.00
CF	Carlton Fisk	10.00
GF	George Foster	8.00
SG	Steve Garvey	8.00
KG	Kirk Gibson	10.00
GG	Rich "Goose" Gossage	8.00
RG	Ron Guidry	12.00
TG	Tony Gwynn	12.00
BJ	Bo Jackson	15.00
RJ	Reggie Jackson	10.00
JK	John Kruk	10.00
BL	Barry Larkin	10.00
MA	Juan Marichal	10.00
EM	Eddie Mathews	15.00
DM	Don Mattingly	20.00
JM	Johnny Mize	15.00
MO	Joe Morgan	10.00
BM	Bobby Murcer	8.00
MU	Eddie Murray	10.00
SM	Stan Musial	20.00
PO	Paul O'Neill	10.00
DP	Dave Parker	8.00
GP	Gaylord Perry	8.00
TR	Tim Raines	8.00
PR	Phil Rizzuto	10.00
RS	Ron Santo	10.00
SS	Steve Sax	8.00
MS	Mike Schmidt	15.00
TS	Tom Seaver	12.00
OS	Ozzie Smith	15.00
BS	Bruce Sutter	10.00
DS	Don Sutton	8.00
RY	Robin Yount	12.00

Memorable Moments Autograph

		NM/M
Production 1-99		
CC	Cesar Cedeno/99	20.00
RC	Rocky Colavito/25	80.00
DC	David Cone/99	15.00
CE	Cecil Cooper/99	20.00
AD	Andre Dawson/99	20.00
DE	Dwight Evans/25	20.00
BF	Bob Feller/25	40.00
RF	Rollie Fingers/47	20.00
CF	Carlton Fisk/25	30.00
GF	George Foster/25	20.00
SG	Steve Garvey/25	35.00
KG	Kirk Gibson/25	30.00
TG	Tony Gwynn/25	75.00
BJ	Bo Jackson/25	50.00
JK	John Kruk/99	20.00
BL	Barry Larkin/50	40.00
MA	Juan Marichal/25	30.00
DM	Don Mattingly/50	100.00
MO	Joe Morgan/20	30.00
MU	Eddie Murray/45	20.00
GP	Gaylord Perry/99	20.00
TR	Tim Raines/50	30.00
PR	Phil Rizzuto/99	40.00
RS	Ron Santo/25	65.00
TS	Tom Seaver/44	40.00
OS	Ozzie Smith/25	50.00
RY	Robin Yount/25	60.00

When It Was A Game

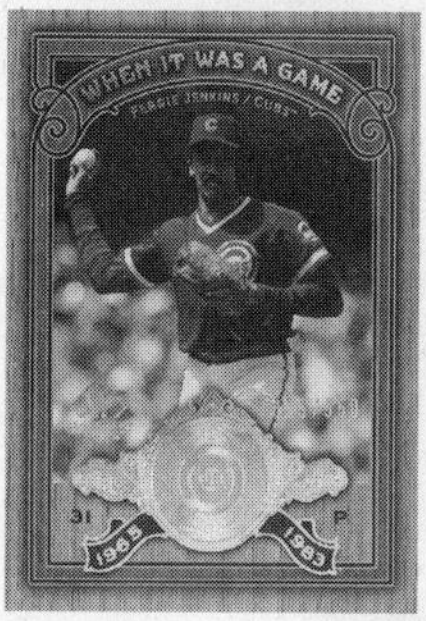

		NM/M
Production 550 Sets		
Gold:		1.5-2X
Production 99 Sets		
LA	Luis Aparicio	2.00
HB	Harold Baines	2.00
EB	Ernie Banks	5.00
JB	Johnny Bench	4.00
YB	Yogi Berra	4.00
WB	Wade Boggs	4.00
LB	Lou Brock	4.00
CA	Rod Carew	3.00
SC	Steve Carlton	3.00
SC2	Steve Carlton	3.00
WC	Will Clark	4.00
RC	Roberto Clemente	10.00
MC	Mickey Cochrane	3.00
CO	Rocky Colavito	3.00
AD	Andre Dawson	3.00
JD	Joe DiMaggio	8.00
DD	Don Drysdale	3.00
DE	Dennis Eckersley	3.00
EV	Dwight Evans	2.00
BF	Bob Feller	3.00

RF Rollie Fingers 3.00
CF Carlton Fisk 3.00
WF Whitey Ford 4.00
JF Jimmie Foxx 5.00
SG Steve Garvey 2.00
LG Lou Gehrig 8.00
BG Bob Gibson 4.00
KI Kirk Gibson 3.00
GG Rich "Goose" Gossage 2.00
HG Hank Greenberg 3.00
KG Ken Griffey Sr. 2.00
GU Ron Guidry 3.00
TG Tony Gwynn 4.00
HO Rogers Hornsby 4.00
FH Frank Howard 2.00
RJ Reggie Jackson 4.00
FJ Fergie Jenkins 3.00
WJ Wally Joyner 2.00
AK Al Kaline 4.00
RK Ralph Kiner 2.00
JK John Kruk 2.00
DL Don Larsen 3.00
FL Fred Lynn 2.00
JU Juan Marichal 3.00
EM Eddie Mathews 3.00
MA Don Mattingly 6.00
BM Bill Mazeroski 3.00
WM Willie McCovey 3.00
DY Denny McLain 3.00
MZ Johnny Mize 2.00
PM Paul Molitor 3.00
JO Joe Morgan 3.00
JM Jack Morris 2.00
TM Thurman Munson 5.00
MU Bobby Murcer 2.00
ED Eddie Murray 3.00
SM Stan Musial 6.00
GN Graig Nettles 2.00
PN Phil Niekro 2.00
TO Tony Oliva 3.00
TO2 Tony Oliva 3.00
MO Mel Ott 3.00
SP Satchel Paige 5.00
JP Jim Palmer 3.00
DP Dave Parker 2.00
TP Tony Perez 2.00
GP Gaylord Perry 2.00
LP Lou Piniella 2.00
PS Johnny Podres 2.00
KP Kirby Puckett 5.00
TR Tim Raines 2.00
RI Jim Rice 3.00
CR Cal Ripken Jr. 8.00
PR Phil Rizzuto 3.00
RR Robin Roberts 2.00
RO Brooks Robinson 4.00
RO2 Brooks Robinson 4.00
FR Frank Robinson 4.00
FR2 Frank Robinson 4.00
JR Jackie Robinson 6.00
AR Al Rosen 2.00
BR Babe Ruth 10.00
NR Nolan Ryan 8.00
SA Ryne Sandberg 5.00
RN Ron Santo 3.00
MS Mike Schmidt 5.00
RS Red Schoendienst 2.00
TS Tom Seaver 4.00
GS George Sisler 3.00
SK Bill "Moose" Skowron 2.00
OS Ozzie Smith 5.00
BS Bruce Sutter 2.00
SU Don Sutton 2.00
JT Joe Torre 3.00
HW Honus Wagner 5.00
BW Billy Williams 2.00
MW Maury Wills 2.00
YZ Carl Yastrzemski 4.00
CY Cy Young 3.00
RY Robin Yount 4.00

When It Was A Game-Used

NM/M

Production 75 unless noted.
LA Luis Aparicio/25 10.00
HB Harold Baines/25 10.00
EB Ernie Banks 20.00
JB Johnny Bench 15.00
YB Yogi Berra 20.00
WB Wade Boggs 10.00
LB Lou Brock/25 12.00
CA Rod Carew 12.00
SC Steve Carlton 10.00
SC2 Steve Carlton 10.00
WC Will Clark 12.00
RC Roberto Clemente 80.00
MC Mickey Cochrane/25 75.00
CO Rocky Colavito 25.00
AD Andre Dawson 10.00
JD Joe DiMaggio 80.00
DD Don Drysdale 15.00
DE Dennis Eckersley 10.00
EV Dwight Evans/25 15.00
BF Bob Feller 10.00
RF Rollie Fingers 10.00
CF Carlton Fisk 12.00
JF Jimmie Foxx 50.00
SG Steve Garvey 8.00
LG Lou Gehrig 140.00
BG Bob Gibson 12.00
KI Kirk Gibson 10.00
GG Rich "Goose" Gossage/25 10.00
HG Hank Greenberg 30.00
KG Ken Griffey Sr. 8.00
GU Ron Guidry 10.00
TG Tony Gwynn 15.00
HO Rogers Hornsby 50.00
FH Frank Howard/25 20.00
RJ Reggie Jackson/25 15.00
FJ Fergie Jenkins 10.00
WJ Wally Joyner 8.00
RK Ralph Kiner 12.00
JK John Kruk 10.00
DL Don Larsen 15.00
FL Fred Lynn 8.00
JU Juan Marichal 10.00
EM Eddie Mathews 15.00
MA Don Mattingly 15.00
BM Bill Mazeroski 25.00
WM Willie McCovey 10.00
MZ Johnny Mize 10.00
PM Paul Molitor 10.00
JO Joe Morgan 10.00
JM Jack Morris/25 10.00
TM Thurman Munson 25.00
MU Bobby Murcer 10.00
ED Eddie Murray 12.00
SM Stan Musial 25.00
GN Graig Nettles 10.00
PN Phil Niekro 10.00
TO Tony Oliva 10.00
TO2 Tony Oliva 10.00
MO Mel Ott 30.00
JP Jim Palmer 10.00
DP Dave Parker 8.00
TP Tony Perez 10.00
GP Gaylord Perry 10.00
LP Lou Piniella 12.00
KP Kirby Puckett 20.00
TR Tim Raines 10.00
RI Jim Rice 10.00
CR Cal Ripken Jr. 25.00
PR Phil Rizzuto/25 25.00
RR Robin Roberts 15.00
RO Brooks Robinson/25 20.00
RO2 Brooks Robinson/25 20.00
FR Frank Robinson 15.00
FR2 Frank Robinson 15.00
JR Jackie Robinson 50.00
AR Al Rosen 10.00
BR Babe Ruth/25 350.00
NR Nolan Ryan/25 30.00
SA Ryne Sandberg/25 20.00
RN Ron Santo 15.00
MS Mike Schmidt 20.00
RS Red Schoendienst 15.00
TS Tom Seaver 15.00
GS George Sisler 30.00
SK Bill "Moose" Skowron 10.00
OS Ozzie Smith 15.00
BS Bruce Sutter 10.00
SU Don Sutton 8.00
JT Joe Torre 10.00
BW Billy Williams 10.00
MW Maury Wills 10.00
YZ Carl Yastrzemski 15.00
RY Robin Yount 12.00

When It Was a Game Cut Signature

NM/M

Production 2-99
JA Joe Adcock/18 150.00
LA Luke Appling/83 100.00
EA Earl Averill/67 80.00
EB Earl Battey/25 175.00
RB Ray Boone/68 120.00
LB Lou Boudreau/50 100.00
AC Al Campanis/30 250.00
MC Max Carey/71 140.00
HC Happy Chandler/64 100.00
SC Stan Coveleski/91 100.00
CR Joe Cronin/34 120.00
JD Joe Dugan/30 150.00
DU Leo Durocher/25 160.00
RF Rick Ferrell/25 150.00
EF Elmer Flick/25 150.00
FF Ford Frick/30 150.00
CG Charlie Gehringer/64 120.00
LG Lefty Gomez/36 125.00
HG Hank Greenberg/21 260.00
BG Burleigh Grimes/56 140.00
HE Billy Herman/99 100.00
WH Waite Hoyt/70 100.00
CH Carl Hubbell/80 140.00
HU Jim "Catfish" Hunter/34 150.00
JJ Judy Johnson/20 180.00
VK Vern Kennedy/58 120.00
TK Ted Kluszewski/50 140.00
BL Bob Lemon/79 90.00
FL Freddie Lindstrom/25 200.00
EL Ernie Lombardi/24 150.00
LO Ed Lopat/28 140.00
SM Sal Maglie/68 120.00
EM Eddie Mathews/33 150.00
JM Joe McCarthy/51 200.00
ME Joe Medwick/57 200.00
MI Johnny Mize/70 120.00
GP George Pipgras/25 180.00
WP Wally Post/66 120.00
PR Pee Wee Reese/52 180.00
SR Sam Rice/33 175.00
ER Edd Roush/98 100.00
RR Red Ruffing/44 180.00
SE George Selkirk/175 175.00
JS Joe Sewell/78 100.00
GS George Sisler/37 450.00
WS Warren Spahn/78 125.00
ST Willie Stargell/27 160.00
JV Johnny Vander Meer/45 150.00
VW Vic Wertz/30 160.00
HW Hoyt Wilhelm/56 100.00
EW Early Wynn/40 100.00

2006 SPx

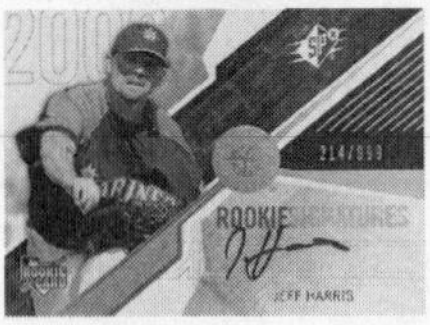

NM/M

Complete Set (160):
Common Player (1-100): .25
Common Auto. (101-160): 10.00
Production 190-999
Pack (4): 7.00
Box (18): 100.00
1 Luis Gonzalez .25
2 Chad Tracy .25
3 Brandon Webb .50
4 Andruw Jones .75
5 Chipper Jones 1.00
6 John Smoltz .75
7 Tim Hudson .50
8 Miguel Tejada .75
9 Brian Roberts .25
10 Ramon Hernandez .25
11 Curt Schilling 1.00
12 David Ortiz 1.50
13 Manny Ramirez 1.00
14 Jason Varitek 1.00
15 Josh Beckett .75
16 Greg Maddux 2.00
17 Derrek Lee .75
18 Mark Prior .50
19 Aramis Ramirez .50
20 Jim Thome .75
21 Paul Konerko .75
22 Scott Podsednik .25
23 Jose Contreras .25
24 Ken Griffey Jr. 2.00
25 Adam Dunn .75
26 Felipe Lopez .25
27 Travis Hafner .75
28 Victor Martinez .50
29 Grady Sizemore .75
30 Jhonny Peralta .25
31 Todd Helton .75
32 Garrett Atkins .50
33 Clint Barmes .25
34 Ivan Rodriguez .75
35 Chris Shelton .25
36 Jeremy Bonderman .50
37 Miguel Cabrera 1.00
38 Dontrelle Willis .50
39 Lance Berkman .50
40 Morgan Ensberg .25
41 Roy Oswalt .50
42 Reggie Sanders .25
43 Mike Sweeney .25
44 Vladimir Guerrero 1.00
45 Bartolo Colon .25
46 Chone Figgins .50
47 Nomar Garciaparra .75
48 Jeff Kent .50
49 J.D. Drew .25
50 Carlos Lee .50
51 Ben Sheets .50
52 Rickie Weeks .50
53 Johan Santana 1.00
54 Torii Hunter .50
55 Joe Mauer .50
56 Pedro Martinez 1.00
57 David Wright 2.00
58 Carlos Beltran .75
59 Carlos Delgado .75
60 Jose Reyes 1.00
61 Derek Jeter 3.00
62 Alex Rodriguez 3.00
63 Randy Johnson 1.00
64 Hideki Matsui 2.00
65 Gary Sheffield .75
66 Rich Harden .50
67 Eric Chavez .25
68 Huston Street .50
69 Bobby Crosby .25
70 Bobby Abreu .50
71 Ryan Howard 2.00
72 Chase Utley .75
73 Pat Burrell .50
74 Jason Bay .50
75 Sean Casey .25
76 Mike Piazza 1.00
77 Jake Peavy .75
78 Brian Giles .25
79 Milton Bradley .25
80 Omar Vizquel .25
81 Jason Schmidt .25
82 Ichiro Suzuki 2.00
83 Felix Hernandez .50
84 Richie Sexson .50
85 Albert Pujols 3.00
86 Chris Carpenter .50
87 Scott Rolen .75
88 Jim Edmonds .25
89 Carl Crawford .50
90 Jonny Gomes .25
91 Scott Kazmir .50
92 Mark Teixeira .75
93 Michael Young .50
94 Phil Nevin .25
95 Vernon Wells .50
96 Roy Halladay .50
97 Troy Glaus .50
98 Alfonso Soriano .75
99 Nick Johnson .25
100 Jose Vidro .25
101 Conor Jackson/999 **(RC)** 15.00
102 Jered Weaver/299 **(RC)** 25.00
103 Macay McBride/999 **(RC)** 10.00
104 Aaron Rakers/499 **(RC)** 10.00
105 Jonathan Papelbon/499 **(RC)** 40.00
106 Jason Bergmann/999 **RC** 10.00
107 Stephen Drew/350 **(RC)** 25.00
108 Chris Denorfia/999 **(RC)** 10.00
109 Kelly Shoppach/999 **(RC)** 10.00
110 Ryan Shealy/999 **(RC)** 10.00
111 Josh Wilson/999 **(RC)** 10.00
112 Brian Anderson/999 **(RC)** 10.00
113 Justin Verlander/749 **(RC)** 40.00
114 Jeremy Hermida/999 **(RC)** 15.00
115 Mike Jacobs/999 **(RC)** 20.00
116 Josh Johnson/999 **(RC)** 10.00
117 Hanley Ramirez/659 **(RC)** 40.00
118 Chris Resop/999 **(RC)** 10.00
119 Josh Willingham/999 **(RC)** 15.00
120 Cole Hamels/499 **(RC)** 40.00
121 Matt Cain/999 **(RC)** 25.00
122 Steve Stemle/999 **RC** 10.00
123 Tim Hamulack/999 **(RC)** 10.00
124 Choo Freeman/999 **(RC)** 10.00
125 Hong-Chih Kuo/999 **(RC)** 30.00
126 Cody Ross/999 **(RC)** 10.00
127 Jose Capellan/999 **(RC)** 10.00
128 Prince Fielder/190 **(RC)** 80.00
129 David Gassner/999 **(RC)** 10.00
130 Jason Kubel/999 **(RC)** 15.00
131 Francisco Liriano/299 **(RC)** 30.00
132 Anderson Hernandez/999 **(RC)** 10.00
133 Joey Devine/499 **RC** 15.00
134 Chris Booker/999 **(RC)** 10.00
135 Matt Capps/999 **(RC)** 15.00
136 Paul Maholm/999 **(RC)** 10.00
137 Nate McLouth/999 **(RC)** 10.00
138 John Van Benschoten/999 **(RC)** 10.00
139 Jeff Harris/999 **RC** 10.00
140 Ben Johnson/999 **(RC)** 10.00
141 Wilbert Nieves/999 **(RC)** 10.00
142 Guillermo Quiroz/999 **(RC)** 10.00
143 Josh Rupe/500 **(RC)** 10.00
144 Skip Schumaker/999 **(RC)** 20.00
145 Jack Taschner/999 **(RC)** 10.00
146 Adam Wainwright/999 **(RC)** 25.00
147 Alay Soler/499 **RC** 15.00
148 Kendry Morales/999 **(RC)** 10.00
149 Ian Kinsler/999 **(RC)** 25.00
150 Jason Hammel/999 **(RC)** 10.00
151 Chad Billingsley/499 **(RC)** 25.00
152 Boof Bonser/999 **(RC)** 15.00
153 Peter Moylan/999 **RC** 10.00
154 Chris Britton/999 **RC** 10.00
155 Takashi Saito/999 **RC** 30.00
156 Scott Dunn **(RC)** 10.00
157 Joel Zumaya/299 **(RC)** 20.00
158 Dan Uggla/999 **(RC)** 35.00
159 Taylor Buchholz/999 **(RC)** 10.00
160 Melky Cabrera/499 **(RC)** 40.00

Spectrum

Stars (1-100): 2-3X
Inserted 1:3

Next in Line

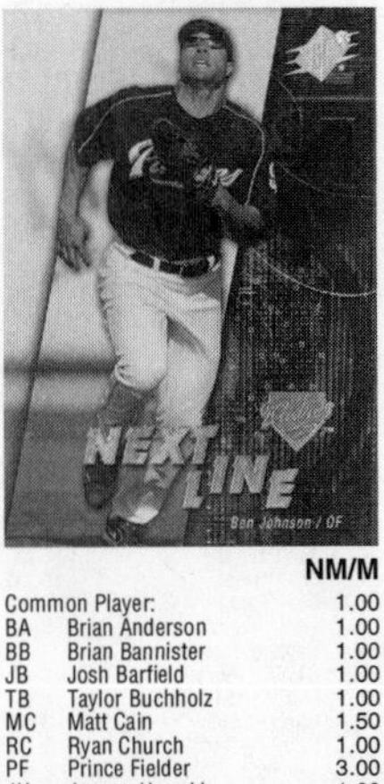

NM/M

Common Player: 1.00
BA Brian Anderson 1.00
BB Brian Bannister 1.00
JB Josh Barfield 1.00
TB Taylor Buchholz 1.00
MC Matt Cain 1.50
RC Ryan Church 1.00
PF Prince Fielder 3.00
JH Jeremy Hermida 1.00
FH Felix Hernandez 1.50
RH Ryan Howard 3.00

TI Travis Ishikawa 1.00
CJ Conor Jackson 1.00
MJ Mike Jacobs 1.00
BJ Ben Johnson 1.00
IK Ian Kinsler 1.00
LE Jon Lester 3.00
FL Francisco Liriano 3.00
JL James Loney 1.00
SO Scott Olsen 1.00
JP Jonathan Papelbon 3.00
HR Hanley Ramirez 1.50
NM Alay Soler 1.00
JS Jeremy Sowers 1.00
HS Huston Street 1.00
DU Dan Uggla 1.00
JV Justin Verlander 3.00
AW Adam Wainwright 1.00
JE Jered Weaver 3.00
JW Josh Willingham 1.00
RZ Ryan Zimmerman 3.00

Rookie Signature Platinum

No Pricing
Production One Set

Rookie Signature Gold

No Pricing
Production Five Sets

Rookie Signature Printing Plates

No Pricing
Production one set per color.

SPxciting Signatures

NM/M

Production 30 unless noted.
JA Jeremy Accardo 10.00
BA Brian Anderson 10.00
BY Jason Bay 20.00
BI Craig Biggio 40.00
CH Chad Billingsley 35.00
HB Hank Blalock 20.00
BR Chris Britton 15.00
MI Miguel Cabrera 40.00
MC Matt Cain 30.00
CA Matt Capps 15.00
RC Roger Clemens 165.00
CW Carl Crawford 30.00
SD Scott Dunn 10.00
EG Eric Gagne 20.00
GR Khalil Greene 25.00
KG Ken Griffey Jr. 100.00
HT Travis Hafner 25.00
HA Jason Hammel 15.00
TH Tim Hamulack 15.00
JH Jeff Harris 12.00
HE Jeremy Hermida 25.00
TR Trevor Hoffman 40.00
CJ Conor Jackson 20.00
KU Jason Kubel 20.00
HK Hong-Chih Kuo 180.00
CL Cliff Lee 15.00
PM Paul Maholm 15.00
VM Victor Martinez 20.00
MM Macay McBride 20.00
NM Nate McLouth 15.00
MU Mark Mulder 20.00
WN Wilbert Nieves 20.00
JP Jonathan Papelbon 100.00
CP Corey Patterson 20.00
PE Jake Peavy 25.00
OP Oliver Perez 10.00
HR Hanley Ramirez 40.00
CR Chris Resop 10.00
RO Cody Ross 20.00
TS Takashi Saito 140.00
SS Skip Schumaker 30.00
RS Ryan Shealy 20.00
KS Kelly Shoppach 25.00
DU Dan Uggla 75.00
JV John Van Benschoten 15.00
VE Justin Verlander 90.00
AW Adam Wainwright 50.00
JW Josh Willingham 20.00
WI Josh Wilson 15.00

SPxtra Info.

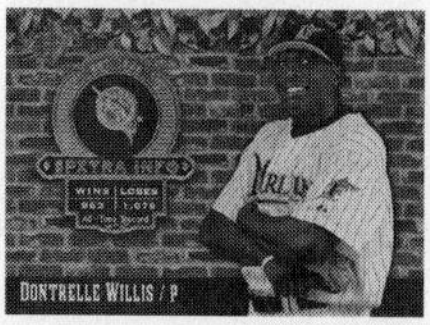

NM/M

Common Player: .50
BA Bobby Abreu .75
JB Jason Bay .75
EC Eric Chavez .50
CC Carl Crawford .75
BG Brian Giles .50
LG Luis Gonzalez .50
KG Ken Griffey Jr. 2.00
VG Vladimir Guerrero 1.00
TH Travis Hafner .75
HE Todd Helton .75
DJ Derek Jeter 3.00
NJ Nick Johnson .50
AJ Andruw Jones 1.00

JK Jeff Kent .50
CL Carlos Lee .75
DL Derrek Lee 1.00
PM Pedro Martinez 1.00
DO David Ortiz 1.50
RO Roy Oswalt .75
AP Albert Pujols 3.00
IR Ivan Rodriguez .75
RS Reggie Sanders .50
JS Johan Santana 1.00
SC Jason Schmidt .50
IS Ichiro Suzuki 2.00
TE Mark Teixeira .75
MT Miguel Tejada .75
JT Jim Thome 1.00
VW Vernon Wells .50
DW Dontrelle Willis .75

SPxtreme Team

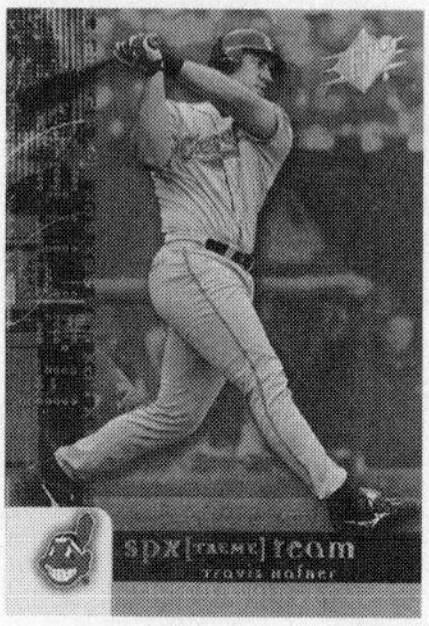

NM/M

Common Player: .50
BA Bobby Abreu .75
JB Jason Bay .75
LB Lance Berkman .75
MC Miguel Cabrera 1.00
CC Chris Carpenter .75
CR Carl Crawford .75
CD Carlos Delgado .75
AD Adam Dunn .75
PF Prince Fielder 3.00
KG Ken Griffey Jr. 2.00
VG Vladimir Guerrero 1.00
HA Travis Hafner .75
RH Rich Harden .50
TH Todd Helton .75
HO Ryan Howard 2.00
DJ Derek Jeter 3.00
AJ Andruw Jones 1.00
JK Jeff Kent .50
PK Paul Konerko .75
CL Carlos Lee .75
DL Derrek Lee 1.00
PM Pedro Martinez 1.00
VM Victor Martinez .50
HM Hideki Matsui 2.00
DO David Ortiz 1.50
JP Jake Peavy .50
AP Albert Pujols 3.00
MR Manny Ramirez 1.00
JR Jose Reyes .75
AR Alex Rodriguez 3.00
JS Johan Santana 1.00
GS Grady Sizemore .75
AS Alfonso Soriano 1.00
IS Ichiro Suzuki 2.00
MT Mark Teixeira .75
TE Miguel Tejada .75
JT Jim Thome 1.00
VW Vernon Wells .50
DW David Wright 2.00
MY Michael Young .50

Winning Materials

NM/M

Common Player: 5.00
BA Bobby Abreu 6.00
JB Jason Bay 10.00
CB Carlos Beltran 10.00
MC Miguel Cabrera 10.00
FC Frederich Cepeda 5.00
HC Hee Seop Choi 10.00
RC Roger Clemens 15.00
JD Johnny Damon 10.00
CD Carlos Delgado 6.00
ME Michel Enriquez 5.00
MF Maikel Folch 5.00
YG Yulieski Gourriel 8.00
KG Ken Griffey Jr. 20.00
AI Akinori Iwamura 20.00
AJ Andruw Jones 8.00
MK Munenori Kawasaki 20.00
PL Pedro Luis Lazo 8.00
DL Derrek Lee 8.00
JL Jong Beom Lee 5.00
VM Victor Martinez 5.00
NM Nobuhiko Matsunaka 20.00
YM Yuneiski Maya 5.00
TN Tsuyoshi Nishioka 25.00
VO Vicyohandry Odelin 5.00
MO Michihiro Ogasawara 20.00
DO David Ortiz 15.00

EP Eduardo Paret 5.00
AP Ariel Pestano 5.00
MP Mike Piazza 15.00
PU Albert Pujols 20.00
AR Alex Rodriguez 20.00
JS Johan Santana 10.00
NS Naoyuki Shimizu 25.00
MS Min Han Son 8.00
AS Alfonso Soriano 10.00
IS Ichiro Suzuki 75.00
HT Hitoshi Tamura 20.00
MT Miguel Tejada 10.00
KU Koji Uehara 20.00
OU Osmany Urrutia 8.00
TW Tsuyoshi Wada 20.00
SW Shunsuke Watanabe 20.00

Winning Big Materials

NM/M

Production 5-55
BA Bobby Abreu/40 75.00
MA Moises Alou/53 50.00
JB Jason Bay/40 80.00
EB Erik Bedard/40 50.00
CB Carlos Beltran/40 75.00
AB Adrian Beltre/40 50.00
MC Miguel Cabrera/40 80.00
FC Frederich Cepeda/30 65.00
HC Hee Seop Choi/32 75.00
JD Johnny Damon/40 100.00
CD Carlos Delgado/40 65.00
ME Michel Enriquez/30 50.00
MF Maikel Folch/30 60.00
JF Jeff Francis/40 50.00
YG Yulieski Gourriel/30 100.00
AI Akinori Iwamura/30 275.00
AJ Andruw Jones/40 80.00
MK Munenori Kawasaki/30 350.00
PL Pedro Luis Lazo/30 80.00
CL Carlos Lee/40 60.00
DL Derrek Lee/40 75.00
JL Jong Beom Lee/20 75.00
WL Wei-Chu Lin/45 350.00
LO Javy Lopez/40 50.00
VM Victor Martinez/40 75.00
NM Nobuhiko Matsunaka/30 300.00
YM Yuneiski Maya/30 60.00
JM Justin Morneau/25 60.00
TN Tsuyoshi Nishioka/30 375.00
VO Vicyohandry Odelin/30 75.00
MO Michihiro Ogasawara/30 350.00
DO David Ortiz/30 150.00
WP Wei-Lun Pan/38 300.00
EP Eduardo Paret/30 50.00
PE Wily Mo Pena/60 50.00
AP Ariel Pestano/30 60.00
MP Mike Piazza/40 100.00
AR Alex Rios/55 50.00
IR Ivan Rodriguez/40 60.00
JS Johan Santana/40 75.00
NS Naoyuki Shimizu/30 250.00
AS Alfonso Soriano/40 90.00
HT Hitoshi Tamura/30 300.00
MT Miguel Tejada/40 60.00
KU Koji Uehara/30 300.00
OU Osmany Urrutia/30 65.00
JV Jason Varitek/40 120.00
TW Tsuyoshi Wada/30 250.00
SW Shunsuke Watanabe/30 260.00
BW Bernie Williams/40 75.00
GY Guogang Yang/52 50.00
CZ Carlos Zambrano/40 50.00

WBC All-World Team

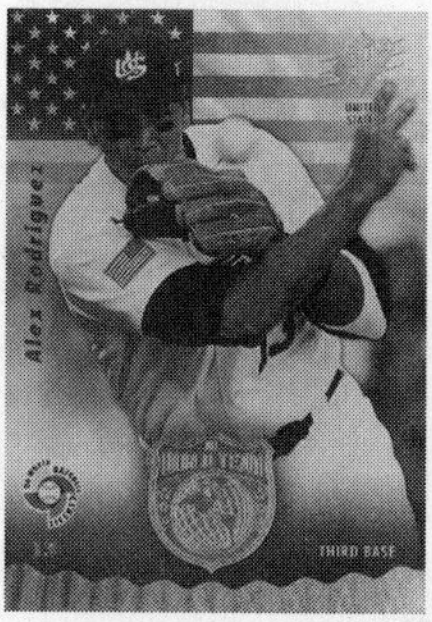

NM/M

Common Player: .50
1 Brett Willemburg .50
2 Bradley Harman .50
3 Adam Stern 1.00
4 Jason Bay 1.00
5 Adam Loewen .50
6 Wei Wang 2.00
7 Yi Feng 1.00
8 Yung-Chi Chen 6.00
9 Chin-Lung Hu 6.00
10 Wei-Lun Pan 5.00
11 Yoandy Garlobo .50
12 Frederich Cepeda .50
13 Osmany Urrutia 1.00
14 Yulieski Gourriel 2.00
15 Yadel Marti .50

16 Pedro Luis Lazo .50
17 Adrian Beltre .50
18 David Ortiz 2.00
19 Albert Pujols 4.00
20 Bartolo Colon .50
21 Miguel Tejada 1.00
22 Mike Piazza 1.50
23 Jason Grilli 1.00
24 Nobuhiko Matsunaka 3.00
25 Tomoya Satozaki 3.00
26 Ichiro Suzuki 3.00
27 Hitoshi Tamura 3.00
28 Daisuke Matsuzaka 8.00
29 Koji Uehara 3.00
30 Jong Beom Lee .50
31 Seung-Yeop Lee .50
32 Jae Weong Seo .50
33 Min Han Son .50
34 Chan Ho Park .50
35 Jorge Cantu .50
36 Miguel Ojeda .50
37 Andruw Jones 1.00
38 Shairon Martis .50
39 Carlos Lee .75
40 Carlos Beltran 1.00
41 Javy Lopez .50
42 Javier Vazquez .50
43 Ken Griffey Jr. 3.00
44 Derek Jeter 4.00
45 Alex Rodriguez 4.00
46 Derrek Lee 1.50
47 Roger Clemens 3.00
48 Miguel Cabrera 1.50
49 Victor Martinez 1.50
50 Johan Santana 1.50

2007 SP Authentic

NM/M

Complete Set (162):
Common Player: .25
Common RC Letter Auto.: 15.00
Pack (5): 5.00
Box (24): 100.00
1 Chipper Jones 1.00
2 Andruw Jones .50
3 John Smoltz .50
4 Carlos Quentin .25
5 Randy Johnson 1.00
6 Brandon Webb .50
7 Alfonso Soriano 1.00
8 Derrek Lee .75
9 Aramis Ramirez .50
10 Carlos Zambrano .50
11 Ken Griffey Jr. 2.00
12 Adam Dunn .50
13 Josh Hamilton .50
14 Todd Helton .50
15 Jeff Francis .25
16 Matt Holliday .50
17 Hanley Ramirez 1.00
18 Dontrelle Willis .25
19 Miguel Cabrera 1.00
20 Lance Berkman .50
21 Roy Oswalt .50
22 Carlos Lee .50
23 Nomar Garciaparra .50
24 Derek Lowe .25
25 Juan Pierre .50
26 Rafael Furcal .50
27 Rickie Weeks .25
28 Prince Fielder 1.50
29 Ben Sheets .50
30 David Wright 1.50
31 Jose Reyes 1.00
32 Tom Glavine .50
33 Carlos Beltran .75
34 Cole Hamels .75
35 Jimmy Rollins .75
36 Ryan Howard 2.00
37 Jason Bay .50
38 Freddy Sanchez .25
39 Ian Snell .25
40 Jake Peavy .50
41 Greg Maddux 2.00
42 Trevor Hoffman .25
43 Matt Cain .50
44 Barry Zito .25
45 Ray Durham .25
46 Albert Pujols 3.00
47 Chris Carpenter .50
48 Jim Edmonds .50
49 Scott Rolen .50
50 Ryan Zimmerman .50
51 Felipe Lopez .25
52 Austin Kearns .25
53 Miguel Tejada .50
54 Erik Bedard .50
55 Daniel Cabrera .25
56 David Ortiz 1.00
57 Curt Schilling .75
58 Manny Ramirez 1.00
59 Jonathan Papelbon .75
60 Jim Thome .75
61 Paul Konerko .50
62 Bobby Jenks .25
63 Grady Sizemore 1.00
64 Victor Martinez .50
65 Travis Hafner .50
66 Ivan Rodriguez .75
67 Justin Verlander .50
68 Joel Zumaya .25
69 Jeremy Bonderman .50
70 Gil Meche .25
71 Mike Sweeney .25
72 Mark Teahen .25

73 Vladimir Guerrero 1.00
74 Howie Kendrick .25
75 Francisco Rodriguez .25
76 Johan Santana 1.00
77 Justin Morneau .50
78 Joe Mauer .50
79 Joe Nathan .25
80 Alex Rodriguez 3.00
81 Derek Jeter 3.00
82 Johnny Damon .75
83 Chien-Ming Wang 1.00
84 Rich Harden .25
85 Mike Piazza 1.00
86 Danny Haren .25
87 Ichiro Suzuki 2.00
88 Felix Hernandez .50
89 Kenji Johjima .50
90 Adrian Beltre .50
91 Carl Crawford .50
92 Scott Kazmir .50
93 Delmon Young .50
94 Michael Young .50
95 Mark Teixeira .50
96 Eric Gagne .25
97 Hank Blalock .25
98 Vernon Wells .50
99 Roy Halladay .50
100 Frank Thomas .75
101 Joaquin Arias/75 **(RC)** 15.00
102 Jeff Baker/Redemp. **(RC)** 15.00
103 Michael Bourn/75 **(RC)** 25.00
104 Brian Burres/75 **(RC)** 20.00
105 Jared Burton/75 **RC** 20.00
106 Ryan Braun/50 **(RC)** 100.00
107 Yovani Gallardo/75 **(RC)** 40.00
107 Yovani Gallardo/35 **(RC)** 40.00
108 Hector Gimenez/75 **(RC)** 15.00
108 Hector Gimenez/50 **(RC)** 15.00
109 Alex Gordon/50 **RC** 50.00
110 Josh Hamilton/50 **(RC)** 50.00
110 Josh Hamilton/35 **(RC)** 50.00
111 Justin Hampson/50 **(RC)** 15.00
111 Justin Hampson/75 **(RC)** 15.00
112 Sean Henn/75 **(RC)** 20.00
113 Phil Hughes/
Redemp. **(RC)** 50.00
114 Kei Igawa/25 **RC** 40.00
115 Akinori Iwamura/20 **RC** 40.00
116 Mark Reynolds/75 **RC** 30.00
116 Mark Reynolds/35 **RC** 35.00
117 Homer Bailey/75 **(RC)** 40.00
117 Homer Bailey/50 **(RC)** 40.00
118 Kevin Kouzmanoff/75 **(RC)** 20.00
118 Kevin Kouzmanoff/40 **(RC)** 20.00
119 Adam Lind/75 **(RC)** 20.00
120 Carlos Gomez/75 **RC** 40.00
120 Carlos Gomez/50 **RC** 40.00
121 Glen Perkins/75 **(RC)** 20.00
121 Glen Perkins/50 **(RC)** 20.00
122 Rick Vanden Hurk/75 **RC** 20.00
122 Rick Vanden Hurk/35 **RC** 20.00
123 Brad Salmon/75 **RC** 15.00
124 Zack Segovia/75 **(RC)** 20.00
124 Zack Segovia/50 **(RC)** 20.00
125 Kurt Suzuki/75 **(RC)** 25.00
125 Kurt Suzuki/50 **(RC)** 25.00
126 Chris Stewart/75 **(RC)** 15.00
126 Chris Stewart/50 **(RC)** 15.00
127 Cesar Jimenez/75 **RC** 15.00
128 Ryan Sweeney/50 **(RC)** 20.00
128 Ryan Sweeney/40 **(RC)** 20.00
129 Troy Tulowitzki/
Redmp. **(RC)** 40.00
130 Chase Wright/75 **RC** 20.00
131 Delmon Young/20 **(RC)** 30.00
132 Tony Abreu/75 **(RC)** 20.00
132 Tony Abreu/50 **(RC)** 20.00
133 Brian Barden/75 **RC** 15.00
134 Curtis Thigpen/75 **(RC)** 20.00
134 Curtis Thigpen/40 **(RC)** 20.00
135 Jon Coutlangus/75 **(RC)** 15.00
135 Jon Coutlangus/55 **(RC)** 15.00
136 Kevin Cameron/75 **RC** 15.00
136 Kevin Cameron/50 **RC** 15.00
137 Billy Butler/75 **(RC)** 30.00
138 Alexi Casilla/75 **RC** 25.00
138 Alexi Casilla/50 **RC** 25.00
139 Kory Casto/75 **(RC)** 20.00
140 Matt Chico/75 **(RC)** 20.00
141 John Danks/75 **(RC)** 30.00
142 Andrew Miller/50 **RC** 40.00
143 Ben Francisco/75 **(RC)** 15.00
143 Ben Francisco/40 **(RC)** 15.00
144 Andy Gonzalez/75 **RC** 15.00
144 Andy Gonzalez/50 **RC** 15.00
145 Devern Hansack/
Redemp. **RC** 20.00
146 Mike Rabelo/75 **RC** 15.00
147 Tim Lincecum/50 **RC** 100.00
147 Tim Lincecum/25 **RC** 100.00
148 Matt Lindstrom/75 **(RC)** 15.00
148 Matt Lindstrom/40 **(RC)** 15.00
149 Jay Marshall/75 **RC** 15.00
149 Jay Marshall/50 **RC** 15.00
150 Daisuke Matsuzaka/
Redemp. **RC** 300.00
151 Miguel Montero/75 **(RC)** 20.00
151 Miguel Montero/50 **(RC)** 20.00
152 Micah Owings/75 **(RC)** 30.00
153 Hunter Pence/75 **(RC)** 40.00
154 Brandon Wood/75 **(RC)** 20.00
155 Felix Pie/75 **(RC)** 20.00
155 Felix Pie/70 **(RC)** 20.00
156 Danny Putnam/75 **(RC)** 15.00
157 Andy LaRoche/50 **(RC)** 20.00
157 Andy LaRoche/40 **(RC)** 20.00
158 Jarrod Saltalamacchia/
75 **(RC)** 30.00
158 Jarrod Saltalamacchia/
25 **(RC)** 30.00
159 Doug Slaten/75 **RC** 20.00
160 Joe Smith/75 **RC** 20.00
161 Justin Upton/120 **RC** 75.00
162 Joba Chamberlain/
60 **RC** 180.00

Autograph Parallel

Production Five Sets

Authentic Power

NM/M

Common Player: .50
1 Adam Dunn 1.00
2 Albert Pujols 4.00
3 Alex Rodriguez 4.00
4 Alfonso Soriano 1.50
5 Andruw Jones .75
6 Aramis Ramirez .75
7 Bill Hall .50
8 Carlos Beltran 1.00
9 Carlos Delgado .75
10 Carlos Lee .75
11 Chase Utley 1.50
12 Chipper Jones 1.50
13 Dan Uggla .50
14 David Ortiz 1.50
15 David Wright 2.00
16 Derrek Lee .75
17 Eric Chavez .50
18 Frank Thomas 1.00
19 Garrett Atkins .50
20 Gary Sheffield 1.00
21 Hideki Matsui 2.50
22 J.D. Drew .50
23 Jason Bay .75
24 Jason Giambi 1.00
25 Jeff Francoeur 1.50
26 Jermaine Dye .50
27 Jim Thome 1.00
28 Justin Morneau 1.00
29 Ken Griffey Jr. 3.00
30 Lance Berkman .75
31 Magglio Ordonez .75
32 Manny Ramirez 1.00
33 Mark Teixeira 1.00
34 Matt Holliday 1.00
35 Miguel Cabrera 1.50
36 Miguel Tejada .75
37 Mike Piazza 1.50
38 Nick Swisher .75
39 Pat Burrell .75
40 Paul Konerko 1.00
41 Prince Fielder 2.00
42 Richie Sexson .75
43 Ryan Howard 2.50
44 Sammy Sosa 1.00
45 Todd Helton 1.00
46 Travis Hafner .75
47 Troy Glaus .75
48 Vernon Wells .75
49 Victor Martinez .75
50 Vladimir Guerrero 1.50

Authentic Speed

NM/M

Common Player: .50
1 Alex Rios .75
2 Alex Rodriguez 4.00
3 Alfonso Soriano 1.50
4 B.J. Upton .75
5 Bobby Abreu .75
6 Brandon Phillips .50
7 Brian Roberts .75
8 Carl Crawford .75
9 Carlos Beltran 1.00
10 Chase Utley 1.50
11 Chone Figgins .75
12 Chris Burke .50
13 Chris Duffy .50
14 Coco Crisp .50
15 Corey Patterson .50
16 Dave Roberts .50
17 David Wright 2.00
18 Derek Jeter 4.00
19 Edgar Renteria .50
20 Eric Byrnes .75
21 Felipe Lopez .50
22 Gary Matthews .50
23 Grady Sizemore 2.00
24 Hanley Ramirez 1.50
25 Ian Kinsler .75
26 Ichiro Suzuki 3.00
27 Jacque Jones .50
28 Jimmy Rollins 1.00
29 Johnny Damon 1.00
30 Jose Reyes 2.00
31 Juan Pierre .50
32 Julio Lugo .50
33 Kenny Lofton .50
34 Luis Castillo .50
35 Marcus Giles .50
36 Melky Cabrera 1.00
37 Mike Cameron .50
38 Orlando Cabrera .75
39 Rafael Furcal .75
40 Randy Winn .50
41 Rickie Weeks .50
42 Rocco Baldelli .50
43 Ryan Freel .50
44 Ryan Theriot 1.00
45 Scott Podsednik .50
46 Shane Victorino .50
47 Tadahito Iguchi .50
48 Torii Hunter .75
49 Vernon Wells .75
50 Willy Taveras .50

By The Letter Signatures

NM/M

Common Player:
1 Derek Jeter/Redemp. 250.00
2 Ken Griffey Jr./25 150.00
2 Ken Griffey Jr./20 150.00
4 Justin Verlander/25 50.00
4 Justin Verlander/15 50.00
5 Adrian Gonzalez/60 25.00
5 Adrian Gonzalez/50 25.00
8 Josh Beckett/15 100.00
10 Aramis Ramirez/25 50.00
11 Austin Kearns/50 15.00
12 B.J. Upton/25 35.00
12 B.J. Upton/15 35.00
13 Boof Bonser/75 15.00
13 Boof Bonser/50 15.00
14 Bronson Arroyo/75 20.00
15 Troy Tulowitzki/Redemp. 40.00
16 Felix Pie/75 25.00
17 Alex Gordon/25 50.00
18 Chris Duffy/Redemp. 15.00
19 Chris Young/75 20.00
19 Chris Young/50 20.00
20 Cliff Lee/75 25.00
20 Cliff Lee/50 25.00
21 Cole Hamels/25 50.00
21 Cole Hamels/15 50.00
22 Adam Lind/75 20.00
23 Akinori Iwamura/25 50.00
23 Akinori Iwamura/15 40.00
24 Dan Uggla/25 30.00
25 Danny Haren/25 30.00
26 David Ortiz/10 125.00
27 Felix Hernandez/10 75.00
28 Tony Gwynn Jr./
Redemp. 25.00
29 Josh Hamilton/75 50.00
29 Josh Hamilton/50 50.00
30 Phil Hughes/Redemp. 60.00
31 Khalil Greene/25 25.00
32 Dontrelle Willis/25 25.00
32 Dontrelle Willis/20 25.00
33 Hanley Ramirez/50 50.00
33 Hanley Ramirez/25 50.00
34 Howie Kendrick/60 20.00
34 Howie Kendrick/50 20.00
35 Huston Street/50 20.00
35 Huston Street/25 20.00
36 Ian Kinsler/Redmp. 30.00
37 Jason Bay/50 25.00
37 Jason Bay/25 25.00
40 Joe Mauer/Redemp. 50.00
41 Jonathan Papelbon/40 50.00
42 Tim Lincecum/50 80.00
42 Tim Lincecum/40 80.00
43 Matt Cain/75 30.00
43 Matt Cain/40 30.00
44 Victor Martinez/25 40.00
46 Ryan Zimmerman/25 50.00
47 Stephen Drew/25 30.00
48 Travis Hafner/25 30.00
49 Josh Willingham/50 15.00
49 Josh Willingham/Redemp. 15.00
50 Torii Hunter/25 30.00
51 Billy Butler/50 30.00
52 Justin Morneau/25 40.00
52 Justin Morneau/15 40.00
53 Andy LaRoche/75 20.00
53 Andy LaRoche/60 20.00
53 Andy LaRoche/50 20.00
54 Brandon Wood/75 20.00
54 Brandon Wood/50 20.00
55 Hunter Pence/50 40.00
56 Devern Hansack/Redemp. 20.00
56 Devern Hansack/75 20.00
58 Derrek Lee/25 40.00
59 Prince Fielder/25 60.00
60 Kevin Kouzmanoff/50 20.00

By The Letter RC Signatures Full Redemption

No Pricing

The Letter Signatures Full Redemption

No Pricing

Chirography Dual Signatures

NM/M

Common Dual Auto: 25.00
CG Eric Chavez,
Alex Gordon/75 50.00
CL Matt Cain,
Tim Lincecum/175 80.00
DR Stephen Drew,
Hanley Ramirez/75 35.00
HD Travis Hafner,
Adam Dunn/75 30.00
HW Danny Haren,
Jered Weaver/175 30.00
KH Scott Kazmir,
Cole Hamels/175 40.00
MI Daisuke Matsuzaka,
Akinori Iwamura/75 300.00
ML Andrew Miller,
Tim Lincecum/175 100.00
MZ Nicholas Markakis,
Ryan Zimmerman/75 40.00
RJ Cal Ripken Jr.,
Derek Jeter/75 200.00
VH Justin Verlander,
Felix Hernandez/175 50.00
WH Vernon Wells,
Torii Hunter/75 25.00
WK Rickie Weeks,
Ian Kinsler/175 20.00

Chirography Quad Signatures

Production Five Sets
No Pricing

Sign of the Times Dual Signatures

NM/M

Common Dual Auto.: 20.00
BP Josh Beckett,
Jonathan Papelbon/75 120.00
CH Eric Chavez,
Rich Harden/75 20.00
CJ Roger Clemens,
Derek Jeter/75 200.00
CL Matt Cain,
Tim Lincecum/175 80.00
FL Rafael Furcal,
Andy LaRoche/175 20.00
GD Ken Griffey Jr.,
Adam Dunn/75 100.00
HM Travis Hafner,
Victor Martinez/75 50.00
SW Ben Sheets,
Rickie Weeks/75 15.00
TK Mark Teixeira,
Ian Kinsler/75 20.00
UY B.J. Upton,
Delmon Young/75 35.00
VM Justin Verlander,
Andrew Miller/75 50.00

Sign of the Times Triple Signatures

No Pricing

Sign of the Times Quad Signatures

Production Five Sets

2007 SP Legendary Cuts

NM/M

Complete Set (200):
Common Player (1-100): .25
Common SP (101-200): 3.00
Production 550 Sets
Pack (4): 10.00
Box (12): 100.00
1 Phil Niekro .25
2 Brooks Robinson 1.00
3 Frank Robinson 1.00
4 Jim Palmer .50
5 Cal Ripken Jr. 3.00
6 Warren Spahn 1.00
7 Cy Young 1.00
8 Carl Yastrzemski 1.00
9 Wade Boggs 1.00
10 Carlton Fisk .50
11 Joe Cronin .25
12 Bobby Doerr .50
13 Roy Campanella 1.00
14 Pee Wee Reese .25
15 Rod Carew .75
16 Ernie Banks 1.00
17 Fergie Jenkins .50
18 Billy Williams .50
19 Gabby Hartnett .25
20 Luis Aparicio .25
21 Nellie Fox .25
22 Luke Appling .25
23 Joe Morgan .50
24 Johnny Bench 1.00
25 Tony Perez .50
26 George Foster .25
27 Johnny Vander Meer .25
28 Bob Feller .50
29 Bob Lemon .25
30 Lou Boudreau .25
31 Early Wynn .25
32 Charlie Gehringer .25
33 George Kell .25
34 Hal Newhouser .25
35 Al Kaline 1.00
36 Ted Kluszewski .25
38 Maury Wills .25
39 Don Drysdale .50
40 Don Sutton .50
41 Eddie Mathews 1.00
42 Joe Adcock .25
43 Paul Molitor .75
44 Kirby Puckett 1.50
45 Harmon Killebrew 1.00
46 Monte Irvin .50
47 Ralph Kiner .50
48 Christy Mathewson 1.00
49 Hoyt Wilhelm .25
50 Tom Seaver 1.00
51 Allie Reynolds .25
52 Joe DiMaggio 2.00
53 Lou Gehrig 2.00
54 Babe Ruth 3.00
55 Casey Stengel 1.00
56 Phil Rizzuto 1.00
57 Thurman Munson 1.00

58	Johnny Mize	.50
59	Yogi Berra	1.00
61	Don Mattingly	1.00
62	Ray Dandridge	.25
63	Rollie Fingers	.50
64	Roberto Clemente	2.00
65	Reggie Jackson	1.00
66	Dennis Eckersley	.50
67	Robin Yount	1.00
68	Jimmie Foxx	1.00
69	Lefty Grove	.50
70	Richie Ashburn	.25
71	Jim Bunning	.25
72	Steve Carlton	.50
73	Robin Roberts	.50
74	Mike Schmidt	1.00
75	Willie Stargell	1.00
76	Ozzie Smith	1.00
77	Bill Mazeroski	.50
78	Honus Wagner	1.00
79	Pie Traynor	.50
80	Tony Gwynn	1.00
81	Willie McCovey	.50
82	Gaylord Perry	.25
83	Juan Marichal	.50
84	Orlando Cepeda	.50
85	Satchel Paige	1.00
86	George Sisler	.50
87	Ken Boyer	.25
88	Joe Medwick	.25
89	Travis Jackson	.25
90	Stan Musial	1.50
91	Dizzy Dean	1.00
92	Bob Gibson	1.00
93	Red Schoendienst	.50
94	Lou Brock	.75
95	Enos Slaughter	.25
96	Nolan Ryan	3.00
97	Smoky Burgess	.25
98	Mickey Vernon	.25
99	Vern Stephens	.25
100	Rick Ferrell	.25
101	Phil Niekro	3.00
102	Brooks Robinson	6.00
103	Frank Robinson	6.00
104	Jim Palmer	5.00
105	Cal Ripken Jr.	15.00
106	Warren Spahn	6.00
107	Cy Young	5.00
108	Nellie Fox	6.00
109	Carl Yastrzemski	6.00
110	Joe Sewell	4.00
111	Wade Boggs	5.00
112	Carlton Fisk	5.00
113	Jackie Robinson	8.00
114	Roy Campanella	6.00
115	Pee Wee Reese	5.00
116	Earl Averill	3.00
117	Rod Carew	5.00
118	Ernie Banks	5.00
119	Fergie Jenkins	3.00
120	Billy Williams	3.00
121	Al Lopez	3.00
122	Luis Aparicio	3.00
123	Luke Appling	3.00
124	Joe Morgan	5.00
125	Johnny Bench	6.00
126	Tony Perez	5.00
127	George Foster	3.00
128	Bob Feller	5.00
129	Bob Lemon	3.00
130	Larry Doby	5.00
132	George Kell	3.00
133	Hal Newhouser	3.00
134	Al Kaline	8.00
135	Ty Cobb	8.00
137	Buck Leonard	5.00
138	Maury Wills	3.00
139	Don Drysdale	5.00
140	Don Sutton	5.00
141	Eddie Mathews	6.00
142	Paul Molitor	5.00
143	Kirby Puckett	8.00
144	Harmon Killebrew	8.00
145	Monte Irvin	5.00
146	Mel Ott	5.00
147	Charlie Gehringer	5.00
148	Hoyt Wilhelm	3.00
149	Tom Seaver	6.00
150	Ted Kluszewski	3.00
151	Joe DiMaggio	8.00
152	Lou Gehrig	8.00
153	Babe Ruth	10.00
154	Casey Stengel	5.00
155	Phil Rizzuto	5.00
156	Thurman Munson	5.00
157	Johnny Mize	3.00
158	Yogi Berra	6.00
159	Roger Maris	6.00
160	Early Wynn	3.00
161	Bobby Doerr	3.00
162	Joe Cronin	5.00
163	Don Mattingly	8.00
164	Ray Dandridge	3.00
165	Rollie Fingers	3.00
166	Christy Mathewson	5.00
167	Reggie Jackson	5.00
168	Dennis Eckersley	3.00
169	Mickey Cochrane	3.00
170	Jimmie Foxx	5.00
171	Lefty Gomez	3.00
172	Jim Bunning	3.00
173	Steve Carlton	3.00
174	Robin Roberts	3.00
175	Richie Ashburn	5.00
176	Mike Schmidt	6.00
177	Ralph Kiner	3.00
178	Willie Stargell	5.00
179	Roberto Clemente	10.00
180	Bill Mazeroski	5.00
181	Honus Wagner	8.00
182	Pie Traynor	3.00
183	Tony Gwynn	5.00
184	Willie McCovey	3.00
185	Gaylord Perry	3.00
186	Juan Marichal	3.00
187	Orlando Cepeda	3.00
188	Satchel Paige	5.00
189	George Sisler	3.00
190	Rogers Hornsby	5.00
191	Stan Musial	8.00
192	Dizzy Dean	5.00
193	Bob Gibson	5.00
194	Red Schoendienst	5.00
195	Lou Brock	5.00
196	Enos Slaughter	3.00
197	Nolan Ryan	8.00
198	Mickey Vernon	3.00
199	Walter Johnson	5.00
200	Rick Ferrell	3.00

A Stitch In Time

		NM/M
Common Player:		5.00
BG	Bob Gibson	8.00
BR	Brooks Robinson	10.00
BW	Billy Williams	5.00
CR	Cal Ripken Jr.	20.00
DE	Dwight Evans	5.00
DM	Don Mattingly	10.00
EM	Eddie Murray	8.00
GP	Gaylord Perry	5.00
HK	Harmon Killebrew	10.00
JB	Johnny Bench	10.00
JR	Jim Rice	5.00
KP	Kirby Puckett	15.00
MS	Mike Schmidt	10.00
PM	Paul Molitor	8.00
RC	Rod Carew	8.00
RJ	Reggie Jackson	10.00
TG	Tony Gwynn	10.00

Cut Signatures

		NM/M
Production 1-133		
AB	Al Barlick/49	75.00
AH	Happy Chandler/44	75.00
AR	Allie Reynolds/40	150.00
BA	Bob Allison/31	90.00
BD	Bill Dickey/50	125.00
BG	Burleigh Grimes/52	125.00
BH	Babe Herman/99	100.00
BV	Bill Veeck/47	250.00
CA	Max Carey/40	80.00
CG	Charlie Gehringer/50	75.00
CH	Carl Hubbell/54	100.00
DC	Dolph Camilli/25	75.00
DI	Joe DiMaggio/52	400.00
DU	Leo Durocher/84	140.00
EA	Earl Averill/62	80.00
EL	Ed Lopat/66	100.00
EM	Eddie Mathews/69	125.00
ER	Edd Roush/50	60.00
ES	Enos Slaughter/47	80.00
EW	Early Wynn/40	100.00
FF	Ford Frick/88	140.00
FL	Freddy Lindstrom/45	200.00
GH	Gabby Hartnett/50	160.00
GP	George Pipgras/70	90.00
GR	Lefty Grove/66	220.00
HG	Hank Greenberg/59	200.00
HO	Gil Hodges/25	450.00
JA	Joe Adcock/49	100.00
JD	Joe Dugan/46	120.00
JO	Judy Johnson/54	150.00
JS	Joe Sewell/110	80.00
JV	Johnny Vander Meer/49	140.00
KB	Ken Boyer/19	275.00
LA	Luke Appling/92	80.00
LD	Larry Doby/50	100.00
MI	Johnny Mize/133	100.00
PR	Pee Wee Reese/39	160.00
RA	Richie Ashburn/50	150.00
RD	Ray Dandridge/50	85.00
RS	Ray Schalk/44	275.00
SC	Stan Coveleski/84	80.00
SW	Warren Spahn/95	100.00
WA	Walter Alston/48	140.00
WH	Waite Hoyt/79	90.00
WI	Hoyt Wilhelm/60	80.00
WS	Willie Stargell/71	180.00

Hall of Fame Cuts

		NM/M
Production 1-86		
AB	Al Barlick/44	100.00
BL	Bob Lemon/53	75.00
CG	Charlie Gehringer/65	85.00
CH	Carl Hubbell/31	100.00
EC	Earle Combs/27	250.00
ER	Edd Roush/65	80.00
GH	Gabby Hartnett/31	180.00
HN	Hal Newhouser/40	80.00
JC	Joe Cronin/86	90.00
LA	Luke Appling/45	80.00
LB	Lou Boudreau/30	80.00
WH	Waite Hoyt/33	100.00
WS	Warren Spahn/35	125.00

Historical Cuts

Production One Set
No Pricing

Inside the Numbers Cuts

		NM/M
Production 4-119		
BD	Bill Dickey/28	150.00
BH	Babe Herman/99	100.00
BL	Bob Lemon/75	75.00
CG	Charlie Gehringer/60	120.00
CH	Carl Hubbell/70	100.00
EA	Earl Averill/57	65.00
EL	Ernie Lombardi/52	200.00
EM	Eddie Mathews/70	125.00
ES	Enos Slaughter/69	80.00
EW	Early Wynn/34	100.00
FS	Fred Snodgrass/75	150.00
GH	Gabby Hartnett/50	160.00
GR	Lefty Grove/73	220.00
HG	Hank Greenberg/25	250.00
JC	Joe Cronin/29	100.00
JM	Joe Medwick/119	140.00
JV	Johnny Vander Meer/39	140.00
LA	Luke Appling/59	80.00
LG	Lefty Gomez/75	125.00
SC	Stan Coveleski/72	65.00
WH	Waite Hoyt/65	100.00
WI	Hoyt Wilhelm/55	80.00
WS	Warren Spahn/55	100.00

Legendary Americana

		NM/M
Common Card:		5.00
Production 550 Sets		
1	George Washington Carver	5.00
3	Frederick Douglass	5.00
4	Crazy Horse	5.00
6	Abraham Lincoln	5.00
7	Thomas Edison	5.00
8	Andrew Carnegie	5.00
9	Eli Whitney	5.00
11	Davy Crockett	5.00
12	Robert E. Lee	5.00
13	John D. Rockefeller	5.00
14	Billy the Kid	5.00
15	Ulysses S. Grant	5.00
18	Kit Carson	5.00
19	Francis Scott Key	5.00
20	Franklin D. Roosevelt	5.00
21	Mark Twain	5.00
24	Alexander Graham Bell	5.00
27	Eleanor Roosevelt	5.00
28	John F. Kennedy	8.00
30	Frank Lloyd Wright	5.00
34	Henry Ford	5.00
35	Dwight D. Eisenhower	5.00
36	Daniel Boone	5.00
38	William Randolph Hearst	5.00
42	Wyatt Earp	5.00
47	Abner Doubleday	5.00
48	Harry S. Truman	5.00
49	Amelia Earhart	5.00
53	Orville Wright	5.00
55	Jack London	5.00
59	Andrew Jackson	5.00
60	Zachary Taylor	5.00
62	Jefferson Davis	5.00
63	Sitting Bull	10.00
64	Clara Barton	5.00
66	Booker T. Washington	5.00
68	Samuel F. B. Morse	5.00
69	Alexander Cartwright	5.00
72	Andrew Johnson	5.00
73	Rutherford B. Hayes	5.00
74	James A. Garfield	5.00
75	Chester Arthur	5.00
76	Grover Cleveland	5.00
78	William McKinley	5.00
79	William H. Taft	5.00
80	Woodrow Wilson	5.00
81	Warren G. Harding	5.00
82	Calvin Coolidge	5.00
83	Herbert Hoover	5.00
84	Lyndon B. Johnson	5.00
85	Richard M. Nixon	5.00
86	Gerald Ford	5.00
88	Ronald Reagan	5.00
92	Babe Ruth	10.00
93	Jackie Robinson	8.00

Legendary Dual Cuts

Production One Set
No Pricing

Legendary Materials

		NM/M
Common Player:		5.00
Production 199 Sets		
AO	Al Oliver	5.00
BJ	Bo Jackson	15.00
BL	Barry Larkin	8.00
BS	Bruce Sutter	5.00
BW	Billy Williams	15.00
CA	Roy Campanella	10.00
DD	Don Drysdale	8.00
DE	Dwight Evans	5.00
DP	Dave Parker	5.00
DS	Don Sutton	5.00
EC	Dennis Eckersley	5.00
FJ	Fergie Jenkins	5.00
FR	Frank Robinson	10.00
GF	George Foster	5.00
GG	Rich "Goose" Gossage	5.00
HB	Harold Baines	5.00
JP	Jim Palmer	8.00
JT	Joe Torre	10.00
KG	Ken Griffey Sr.	5.00
LA	Luis Aparicio	5.00
MA	Bill Madlock	5.00
MG	Mark Grace	10.00
PN	Phil Niekro	5.00
PO	Paul O'Neill	10.00
PW	Pee Wee Reese	10.00
RA	Roberto Alomar	10.00
RC	Roberto Clemente	50.00
RF	Rollie Fingers	8.00
RG	Ron Guidry	20.00
RM	Roger Maris	25.00
RS	Ryne Sandberg	15.00
SC	Red Schoendienst	10.00
TO	Tony Oliva	8.00
TP	Tony Perez	8.00
AD1	Andre Dawson	8.00
AD2	Andre Dawson	8.00
AK1	Al Kaline	15.00
AK2	Al Kaline	15.00
BR1	Brooks Robinson	15.00
BR2	Brooks Robinson	15.00
CF1	Carlton Fisk	10.00
CF2	Carlton Fisk	10.00
CR1	Cal Ripken Jr.	25.00
CR2	Cal Ripken Jr.	25.00
CY1	Carl Yastrzemski	15.00
CY2	Carl Yastrzemski	15.00
DM1	Don Mattingly	20.00
DM2	Don Mattingly	20.00
DW1	Dave Winfield	8.00
DW2	Dave Winfield	8.00
EM1	Eddie Murray	8.00
EM2	Eddie Murray	8.00
FL1	Fred Lynn	5.00
FL2	Fred Lynn	5.00
GP1	Gaylord Perry	5.00
GP2	Gaylord Perry	5.00
HK1	Harmon Killebrew	15.00
HK2	Harmon Killebrew	15.00
JB1	Johnny Bench	15.00
JB2	Johnny Bench	15.00
JM1	Jack Morris	5.00
JM2	Jack Morris	5.00
JR1	Jim Rice	8.00
J2	Jim Rice	8.00
KG1	Kirk Gibson	5.00
KG2	Kirk Gibson	5.00
KP1	Kirby Puckett	25.00
KP2	Kirby Puckett	25.00
LB1	Lou Brock	10.00
LB2	Lou Brock	10.00
MS1	Mike Schmidt	15.00
MS2	Mike Schmidt	15.00
NR1	Nolan Ryan	25.00
NR2	Nolan Ryan	25.00
OS1	Ozzie Smith	20.00
OS2	Ozzie Smith	20.00
PM1	Paul Molitor	8.00
PM2	Paul Molitor	8.00
RC1	Rod Carew	8.00
RC2	Rod Carew	8.00
RJ1	Reggie Jackson	10.00
RJ2	Reggie Jackson	10.00
RY1	Robin Yount	20.00
RY2	Robin Yount	20.00
SC1	Steve Carlton	8.00
SC2	Steve Carlton	8.00
SG1	Steve Garvey	5.00
SG2	Steve Garvey	5.00
TG1	Tony Gwynn	15.00
TG2	Tony Gwynn	15.00
WB1	Wade Boggs	8.00
WB2	Wade Boggs	8.00
WC1	Will Clark	8.00
WC2	Will Clark	8.00

Legendary Quad Cuts

Production One Set
No Pricing

Legendary Signatures

		NM/M
Production 15-199		
JT	Joe Torre/99	40.00
KG	Kirk Gibson/199	15.00
AD1	Andre Dawson/199	20.00
AD2	Andre Dawson/199	20.00
AK1	Al Kaline/199	25.00
AK2	Al Kaline/199	25.00
BF1	Bob Feller/199	20.00
BF2	Bob Feller/199	20.00
BF3	Bob Feller/189	20.00
BG1	Bob Gibson/50	25.00
BG2	Bob Gibson/50	25.00
BG3	Bob Gibson/40	25.00
BJ1	Bo Jackson/100	50.00
BJ2	Bo Jackson/100	50.00
BM1	Bill Mazeroski/189	30.00
BM2	Bill Mazeroski/199	30.00
BR1	Brooks Robinson/150	30.00
BR2	Brooks Robinson/140	30.00
BW1	Billy Williams/199	20.00
BW2	Billy Williams/189	20.00
CF1	Carlton Fisk/75	25.00
CF2	Carlton Fisk/75	25.00
CF3	Carlton Fisk/65	25.00
CR1	Cal Ripken Jr./99	100.00
CR2	Cal Ripken Jr./50	10.00
DM1	Don Mattingly/25	75.00
DM2	Don Mattingly/25	75.00

EB1	Ernie Banks/35	60.00
EB2	Ernie Banks/35	60.00
EM1	Eddie Murray/25	50.00
EM2	Eddie Murray/25	50.00
FJ1	Fergie Jenkins/125	20.00
FJ2	Fergie Jenkins/125	20.00
FJ3	Fergie Jenkins/125	20.00
FR1	Frank Robinson/50	25.00
FR2	Frank Robinson/50	25.00
FR3	Frank Robinson/40	25.00
GP1	Gaylord Perry/199	15.00
GP2	Gaylord Perry/199	15.00
HK1	Harmon Killebrew/100	75.00
HK2	Harmon Killebrew/90	75.00
JM1	Juan Marichal/199	20.00
JM2	Juan Marichal/199	20.00
JM3	Juan Marichal/189	20.00
JP1	Jim Palmer/199	20.00
JP2	Jim Palmer/199	20.00
JP3	Jim Palmer/199	20.00
LA1	Luis Aparicio/199	20.00
LA2	Luis Aparicio/186	20.00
MS1	Mike Schmidt/35	50.00
MS2	Mike Schmidt/35	50.00
MS3	Mike Schmidt/25	60.00
NR1	Nolan Ryan/25	100.00
NR2	Nolan Ryan/25	10.00
OS1	Ozzie Smith/100	40.00
OS2	Ozzie Smith/100	40.00
OS3	Ozzie Smith/100	40.00
PM1	Paul Molitor/100	25.00
PM2	Paul Molitor/90	25.00
RC1	Rod Carew/35	40.00
RC2	Rod Carew/35	40.00
RJ1	Reggie Jackson/25	60.00
RS1	Ryne Sandberg/25	60.00
RS2	Ryne Sandberg/25	60.00
RS3	Ryne Sandberg/25	60.00
RY1	Robin Yount/35	60.00
RY2	Robin Yount/35	60.00
RY3	Robin Yount/25	60.00
SC1	Steve Carlton/199	20.00
SC2	Steve Carlton/199	20.00
SC3	Steve Carlton/189	20.00
TP1	Tony Perez/199	20.00
TP2	Tony Perez/199	20.00
WB1	Wade Boggs/35	50.00
WB2	Wade Boggs/35	50.00
WB3	Wade Boggs/35	50.00
WC1	Will Clark/199	20.00
WC2	Will Clark/199	20.00
WM1	Willie McCovey/25	50.00
WM2	Willie McCovey/25	50.00

Legendary Team Cuts

Production One Set
No Pricing

Masterful Material

NM/M

Common Player:		5.00
AD	Andre Dawson	5.00
BJ	Bo Jackson	10.00
BL	Barry Larkin	8.00
BM	Bill Madlock	5.00
BR	Brooks Robinson	8.00
BS	Bruce Sutter	5.00
CF	Carlton Fisk	8.00
CR	Cal Ripken Jr.	20.00
CY	Carl Yastrzemski	10.00
DE	Dwight Evans	5.00
DM	Don Mattingly	15.00
DP	Dave Parker	5.00
DS	Don Sutton	5.00
DW	Dave Winfield	8.00
EM	Eddie Mathews	10.00
FL	Fred Lynn	5.00
FR	Frank Robinson	8.00
GP	Gaylord Perry	5.00
JB	Johnny Bench	10.00
JR	Jim Rice	5.00
KG	Ken Griffey Sr.	5.00
KP	Kirby Puckett	15.00
MS	Mike Schmidt	10.00
MU	Eddie Murray	8.00
NR	Nolan Ryan	20.00
PM	Paul Molitor	8.00
RJ	Reggie Jackson	10.00
RS	Ryne Sandberg	10.00
RY	Robin Yount	10.00
SC	Steve Carlton	8.00
SG	Steve Garvey	5.00
TG	Tony Gwynn	10.00
WB	Wade Boggs	8.00
WC	Will Clark	8.00
WM	Willie McCovey	8.00
YB	Yogi Berra	15.00

Material Cuts

No Pricing
Production 1-5

Material Signatures

No Pricing
Production 10 Sets

Quotation Cuts

NM/M

Production 1-109

BL	Bob Lemon/80	75.00
CS	Casey Stengel/36	275.00
HC	Happy Chandler/44	75.00
JM	Joe McCarthy/109	140.00
LB	Lou Boudreau/28	60.00
MI	Johnny Mize/45	80.00
RA	Richie Ashburn/48	175.00
RD	Ray Dandridge/72	90.00
SC	Stan Coveleski/71	75.00
WA	Walter Alston/31	80.00
WI	Hoyt Wilhelm/37	90.00
WS	Warren Spahn/60	100.00

Reel History Film Frame

NM/M

Cards are serial numbered 1/1.

BR	Babe Ruth	250.00
LG	Lou Gehrig	200.00

Signature Cuts

Production One Set
No Pricing

When It Was A Game - Memorabilia

NM/M

Common Player:		5.00
AT	Alan Trammell	5.00
BF	Bob Feller	8.00
BG	Bob Gibson	10.00
BM	Bill Mazeroski	8.00
BW	Billy Williams	5.00
CF	Carlton Fisk	8.00
CY	Carl Yastrzemski	10.00
DE	Dennis Eckersley	5.00
DM	Don Mattingly	15.00
DW	Dave Winfield	8.00
EM	Eddie Murray	8.00
FJ	Fergie Jenkins	5.00
FL	Fred Lynn	5.00
FR	Frank Robinson	8.00
GP	Gaylord Perry	5.00
HK	Harmon Killebrew	10.00
JP	Jim Palmer	8.00
JR	Jim Rice	5.00
KG	Kirk Gibson	5.00
KP	Kirby Puckett	15.00
LB	Lou Brock	8.00
MS	Mike Schmidt	10.00
NR	Nolan Ryan	20.00
PM	Paul Molitor	8.00
PW	Pee Wee Reese	10.00
RF	Rollie Fingers	5.00
RJ	Reggie Jackson	10.00
RM	Roger Maris	25.00
RS	Red Schoendienst	8.00
TG	Tony Gwynn	10.00

2007 SPX

NM/M

Complete Set (150):		
Common Player (1-100):		.25
Common RC Auto. (101-150):		10.00
Pack (3):		15.00
Box (10):		140.00
1	Miguel Tejada	.75
2	Brian Roberts	.50
3	Melvin Mora	.25
4	David Ortiz	1.00
5	Manny Ramirez	1.00
6	Jason Varitek	.50
7	Curt Schilling	1.00
8	Jim Thome	.75
9	Paul Konerko	.50
10	Jermaine Dye	.50
11	Travis Hafner	.50
12	Victor Martinez	.50
13	Grady Sizemore	.75
14	C.C. Sabathia	.50
15	Ivan Rodriguez	.75
16	Magglio Ordonez	.50
17	Carlos Guillen	.50
18	Justin Verlander	.75
19	Shane Costa	.25
20	Emil Brown	.25
21	Mark Teahen	.25
22	Vladimir Guerrero	1.00
23	Jered Weaver	.50
24	Juan Rivera	.25
25	Justin Morneau	.75
26	Joe Mauer	.50
27	Torii Hunter	.50
28	Johan Santana	.75
29	Derek Jeter	3.00
30	Alex Rodriguez	3.00
31	Johnny Damon	1.00
32	Jason Giambi	.75
33	Bobby Crosby	.25
34	Nick Swisher	.50
35	Eric Chavez	.25
36	Ichiro Suzuki	2.00
37	Raul Ibanez	.25
38	Richie Sexson	.50
39	Carl Crawford	.50
40	Rocco Baldelli	.25
41	Scott Kazmir	.50
42	Michael Young	.50
43	Mark Teixeira	.75
44	Ian Kinsler	.50
45	Troy Glaus	.50
46	Vernon Wells	.50
47	Roy Halladay	.50
48	Lyle Overbay	.25
49	Brandon Webb	.50
50	Conor Jackson	.25
51	Stephen Drew	.50
52	Chipper Jones	1.00
53	Andruw Jones	.75
54	Adam LaRoche	.25
55	John Smoltz	.50
56	Derrek Lee	.75
57	Aramis Ramirez	.50
58	Carlos Zambrano	.50
59	Ken Griffey Jr.	2.00
60	Adam Dunn	.50
61	Aaron Harang	.25
62	Todd Helton	.75
63	Matt Holliday	.75
64	Garrett Atkins	.50
65	Miguel Cabrera	1.00
66	Hanley Ramirez	1.00
67	Dontrelle Willis	.50
68	Lance Berkman	.50
69	Roy Oswalt	.50
70	Craig Biggio	.50
71	J.D. Drew	.25
72	Nomar Garciaparra	.50
73	Rafael Furcal	.50
74	Jeff Kent	.50
75	Prince Fielder	1.00
76	Bill Hall	.50
77	Rickie Weeks	.50
78	Jose Reyes	1.00
79	David Wright	1.00
80	Carlos Delgado	.75
81	Carlos Beltran	.75
82	Ryan Howard	2.00
83	Chase Utley	1.00
84	Jimmy Rollins	.75
85	Jason Bay	.50
86	Freddy Sanchez	.25
87	Zachary Duke	.25
88	Trevor Hoffman	.25
89	Adrian Gonzalez	.50
90	Chris Young	.50
91	Ray Durham	.25
92	Omar Vizquel	.25
93	Jason Schmidt	.50
94	Albert Pujols	3.00
95	Scott Rolen	.75
96	Jim Edmonds	.50
97	Chris Carpenter	.75
98	Alfonso Soriano	.75
99	Ryan Zimmerman	.50
100	Nick Johnson	.25
101	Delmon Young **(RC)**	20.00
102	Andrew Miller **RC**	20.00
103	Troy Tulowitzki **(RC)**	20.00
104	Jeff Fiorentino **(RC)**	10.00
105	David Murphy **(RC)**	15.00
106	Tim Lincecum **RC**	125.00
107	Phil Hughes **(RC)**	40.00
108	Kevin Kouzmanoff **(RC)**	15.00
109	Adam Lind **(RC)**	15.00
110	Mark Reynolds **RC**	40.00
111	Kevin Hooper **(RC)**	10.00
112	Mitch Maier **RC**	10.00
113	Homer Bailey **(RC)**	20.00
114	Dennis Sarfate **(RC)**	10.00
115	Drew Anderson **(RC)**	10.00
116	Miguel Montero **(RC)**	10.00
117	Glen Perkins **(RC)**	10.00
118	Kevin Slowey **(RC)**	20.00
119	Tim Gradoville **RC**	10.00
120	Ryan Braun **(RC)**	100.00
121	Chris Narveson **(RC)**	10.00
122	Patrick Misch **(RC)**	10.00
123	Juan Salas **(RC)**	10.00
124	Beltran Perez **(RC)**	10.00
125	Joaquin Arias **(RC)**	10.00
126	Philip Humber **(RC)**	15.00
127	Kei Igawa **RC**	20.00
128	Daisuke Matsuzaka **RC**	180.00
129	Andy Cannizaro **RC**	10.00
130	Ubaldo Jimenez **(RC)**	10.00
131	Fred Lewis **(RC)**	15.00
132	Ryan Sweeney **(RC)**	10.00
133	Jeff Baker **(RC)**	10.00
134	Michael Bourn **(RC)**	20.00
135	Akinori Iwamura **RC**	20.00
136	Oswaldo Navarro **RC**	10.00
137	Hunter Pence **(RC)**	30.00
138	Jon Knott **(RC)**	10.00
139	Justin Hampson **(RC)**	10.00
140	Jeff Salazar **(RC)**	10.00
141	Juan Morillo **(RC)**	10.00
142	Delwyn Young **(RC)**	10.00
143	Brian Burres **(RC)**	10.00
144	Chris Stewart **RC**	10.00
145	Eric Stults **RC**	10.00
146	Carlos Maldonado **(RC)**	10.00
147	Angel Sanchez **RC**	10.00
148	Cesar Jimenez **RC**	10.00
149	Shawn Riggans **(RC)**	10.00
150	John Nelson **(RC)**	10.00

Printing Plates

No Pricing
Production one set per color.

Spectrum

Spectrum (101-150): No Pricing
Production 25 Sets

Autofacts Preview

NM/M

Common Autograph:		10.00
1:Hobby Box		
AI	Akinori Iwamura	20.00
AL	Adam Lind	10.00
AM	Andrew Miller/SP	20.00
AS	Angel Sanchez	10.00
BP	Beltran Perez	10.00
BR	Jeremy Brown	10.00
CM	Carlos Maldonado	10.00
CN	Chris Narveson	10.00
CR	Cal Ripken Jr./SP	150.00
DS	Dennis Sarfate	10.00
DW	Dewayne Wise	10.00
DY	Delmon Young	20.00
ES	Eric Stults	10.00
FL	Fred Lewis	15.00
GP	Glen Perkins	10.00
JA	Joaquin Arias	10.00
JB	Jeff Baker	10.00
JH	Justin Hampson	10.00
JK	Jon Knott	15.00
JM	Juan Morillo	10.00
JS	Juan Salas	10.00
JW	Jason Wood	10.00
KG	Ken Griffey Jr./SP	80.00
KH	Kevin Hooper	10.00
KI	Kei Igawa	20.00
KK	Kevin Kouzmanoff	15.00
MB	Michael Bourn	15.00
MM	Miguel Montero	10.00
PH	Philip Humber	15.00
PM	Patrick Misch	10.00
SA	Jeff Salazar	10.00
SR	Shawn Riggans	10.00
ST	Chris Stewart	10.00
TT	Troy Tulowitzki	20.00
YO	Delwyn Young	10.00

Iron Man

NM/M

Common Ripken (1-100):	5.00
Production 699 Sets	
Platinum:	No Pricing
Production One Set	
Printing Plates:	No Pricing
Production One Set	

Iron Man Memorabilia

NM/M

Common Ripken: 40.00
Production 25 Sets

Iron Man Autograph

Production One Set

Young Star Signatures

NM/M

Common Autograph:		10.00
Spectrum:		1-2X
Production 25 Sets		
AE	Andre Ethier	15.00
AG	Adrian Gonzalez	20.00
AS	Anibal Sanchez	10.00
BU	B.J. Upton	20.00
CA	Matt Cain/SP	20.00
CH	Cole Hamels/SP	30.00
CQ	Carlos Quentin	15.00
DJ	Derek Jeter	125.00
DU	Dan Uggla	20.00
DY	Delmon Young	20.00
FH	Felix Hernandez	25.00
FL	Francisco Liriano	20.00
HA	Rich Harden	15.00
HI	Rich Hill/SP	20.00
HK	Howie Kendrick	20.00
HR	Hanley Ramirez	25.00
JB	Jeremy Brown	10.00
JJ	Josh Johnson	10.00
JL	Jon Lester	25.00
JM	Joe Mauer	25.00
JP	Jonathan Papelbon	30.00
JR	Jose Reyes	40.00
JS	Jeremy Sowers	10.00
JV	Justin Verlander	25.00
JW	Jered Weaver/SP	20.00
JZ	Joel Zumaya	20.00
KG	Ken Griffey Jr.	75.00
KU	Hong-Chih Kuo	20.00
LO	James Loney	20.00
MO	Justin Morneau	25.00
NM	Nick Markakis	25.00
PH	Philip Humber	10.00
RW	Rickie Weeks	15.00
RZ	Ryan Zimmerman	20.00
SD	Stephen Drew	20.00
ST	Scott Thorman	10.00
TT	Troy Tulowitzki	20.00
WI	Josh Willingham	15.00

Winning Materials Bronze 199

NM/M

Common Player:		5.00
Gold 199:		1X
Silver 199:		1X
Production 199 Sets		
Blue 175:		1X
Green 175:		1X
Production 175 Sets		
Gold 99:		1-1.5X
Silver 99:		1-1.5X
Production 99 Sets		
Dual Bronze:		No Pricing
Production 25 Sets		
Dual Gold:		1-1.5X
Dual Silver:		1-1.5X
Production 50 Sets		
Dual Green:		No Pricing
Production 15 Sets		
AB	A.J. Burnett	5.00
AD	Adam Dunn	6.00
AE	Andre Ethier	6.00
AJ	Andruw Jones	8.00
AL	Adam LaRoche	5.00
AP	Albert Pujols	20.00

AR Aramis Ramirez 8.00
AS Anibal Sanchez 5.00
BA Bobby Abreu 6.00
BG Brian Giles 5.00
BL Joe Blanton 5.00
BM Brian McCann 5.00
BO Jeremy Bonderman 6.00
BR Brian Roberts 5.00
BS Ben Sheets 5.00
BU B.J. Upton 5.00
CA Miguel Cabrera 8.00
CB Craig Biggio 5.00
CC Chris Carpenter 8.00
CF Chone Figgins 5.00
CH Cole Hamels 10.00
CJ Chipper Jones 8.00
CL Roger Clemens 15.00
CN Robinson Cano 10.00
CR Carl Crawford 5.00
CU Chase Utley 10.00
CW Chien-Ming Wang 35.00
DJ Derek Jeter 20.00
DJ2 Derek Jeter 20.00
DL Derrek Lee 8.00
DO David Ortiz 10.00
DU Dan Uggla 5.00
DW Dontrelle Willis 5.00
EC Eric Chavez 5.00
FH Felix Hernandez 6.00
FL Francisco Liriano 5.00
FS Freddy Sanchez 5.00
FT Frank Thomas 8.00
GA Garrett Atkins 5.00
HA Travis Hafner 6.00
HE Todd Helton 8.00
HK Howie Kendrick 5.00
HN Rich Harden 5.00
HR Hanley Ramirez 8.00
HS Huston Street 5.00
IK Ian Kinsler 5.00
IR Ivan Rodriguez 8.00
JB Jason Bay 6.00
JE Jim Edmonds 5.00
JF Jeff Francoeur 8.00
JJ Josh Johnson 5.00
JL Chad Billingsley 5.00
JM Joe Mauer 8.00
JN Joe Nathan 5.00
JP Jake Peavy 5.00
JR Jose Reyes 10.00
JS Jeremy Sowers 5.00
JT Jim Thome 8.00
JV Justin Verlander 8.00
JW Jered Weaver 8.00
JZ Joel Zumaya 5.00
KG Ken Griffey Jr. 15.00
KG2 Ken Griffey Jr. 15.00
KH Khalil Greene 5.00
KU Hong-Chih Kuo 20.00
LE Jon Lester 8.00
LG Luis Gonzalez 5.00
MC Matt Cain 5.00
ME Melky Cabrera 6.00
MH Matt Holliday 8.00
MO Justin Morneau 8.00
MT Mark Teixeira 8.00
NM Nicholas Markakis 8.00
NS Nick Swisher 5.00
PA Jonathan Papelbon 15.00
PF Prince Fielder 10.00
PL Paul LoDuca 5.00
RC Cal Ripken Jr. 20.00
RI Alex Rios 5.00
RJ Randy Johnson 8.00
RO Roy Oswalt 6.00
RW Rickie Weeks 5.00
RZ Ryan Zimmerman 8.00
SA Alfonso Soriano 8.00
SD Stephen Drew 5.00
SH James Shields 5.00
SK Scott Kazmir 5.00
SM John Smoltz 8.00
SO Scott Olsen 5.00
SR Scott Rolen 8.00
TE Miguel Tejada 6.00
TG Tom Glavine 8.00
TH Trevor Hoffman 5.00
TO Torii Hunter 6.00
VG Vladimir Guerrero 8.00
VM Victor Martinez 5.00
WE David Wells 5.00
WI Josh Willingham 5.00
YB Yuniesky Betancourt 5.00

Winning Materials Patch Gold

NM/M
Common player: 10.00
Production 99 unless noted.
Patch Silver: 1X
Production 3-99
Patch Bronze: 1X
Production 50 Sets
Triple Patch: No Pricing
Production 25 Sets
AB A.J. Burnett 10.00
AD Adam Dunn 15.00
AE Andre Ethier 10.00
AJ Andruw Jones 15.00
AL Adam LaRoche 10.00
AP Albert Pujols 40.00
AR Aramis Ramirez 15.00
AS Anibal Sanchez/54 10.00
BA Bobby Abreu 15.00
BG Brian Giles 10.00
BL Joe Blanton 10.00
BM Brian McCann 10.00
BO Jeremy Bonderman 15.00
BR Brian Roberts 10.00
BS Ben Sheets 10.00
BU B.J. Upton 10.00
CA Miguel Cabrera 20.00
CB Craig Biggio 15.00
CC Chris Carpenter 20.00
CF Chone Figgins 10.00
CH Cole Hamels 20.00
CJ Chipper Jones 20.00
CL Roger Clemens 25.00
CN Robinson Cano 20.00
CR Carl Crawford 10.00
CU Chase Utley 20.00
CW Chien-Ming Wang 60.00
DJ Derek Jeter 40.00
DJ2 Derek Jeter 40.00
DL Derrek Lee 20.00
DO David Ortiz 20.00
DU Dan Uggla 10.00
DW Dontrelle Willis 10.00
EC Eric Chavez 10.00
FH Felix Hernandez 15.00
FL Francisco Liriano 15.00
FS Freddy Sanchez 10.00
FT Frank Thomas 20.00
GA Garrett Atkins 10.00
HA Travis Hafner 15.00
HE Todd Helton 20.00
HK Howie Kendrick/34 15.00
HN Rich Harden 10.00
HR Hanley Ramirez 20.00
HS Huston Street 10.00
IK Ian Kinsler 10.00
IR Ivan Rodriguez 20.00
JB Jason Bay 15.00
JE Jim Edmonds 10.00
JF Jeff Francoeur 20.00
JJ Josh Johnson 10.00
JL Chad Billingsley 10.00
JM Joe Mauer 20.00
JN Joe Nathan 10.00
JP Jake Peavy 10.00
JR Jose Reyes 25.00
JS Jeremy Sowers 10.00
JT Jim Thome 20.00
JW Jered Weaver 20.00
JZ Joel Zumaya 10.00
KG Ken Griffey Jr. 30.00
KG2 Ken Griffey Jr. 30.00
KH Khalil Greene 10.00
KU Hong-Chih Kuo 40.00
LE Jon Lester 20.00
LG Luis Gonzalez 10.00
MC Matt Cain 15.00
ME Melky Cabrera 20.00
MH Matt Holliday 20.00
MO Justin Morneau 15.00
MT Mark Teixeira 15.00
NM Nicholas Markakis 15.00
NS Nick Swisher 10.00
PA Jonathan Papelbon 30.00
PF Prince Fielder 20.00
PL Paul LoDuca 10.00
RC Cal Ripken Jr. 40.00
RI Alex Rios 10.00
RJ Randy Johnson 20.00
RO Roy Oswalt 15.00
RW Rickie Weeks 10.00
RZ Ryan Zimmerman 15.00
SA Alfonso Soriano 20.00
SD Stephen Drew 15.00
SH James Shields 10.00
SK Scott Kazmir 10.00
SM John Smoltz 20.00
SO Scott Olsen 10.00
SR Scott Rolen 15.00
TE Miguel Tejada 15.00
TG Tom Glavine 20.00
TH Trevor Hoffman 10.00
TO Torii Hunter 15.00
VG Vladimir Guerrero 20.00
VM Victor Martinez 10.00
WE David Wells 10.00
WI Josh Willingham 10.00
YB Yuniesky Betancourt 10.00

Winning Materials Triple Signatures

NM/M
Production 15-35 5.00
Platinum: No Pricing
Production 3-10
BR Brian Roberts/35 35.00
EC Eric Chavez/35 30.00
FH Felix Hernandez/35 50.00
GA Garrett Atkins/35 25.00
HA Travis Hafner/35 35.00
HK Howie Kendrick/35 30.00
JJ Josh Johnson/35 20.00
JM Joe Mauer/35 40.00
JP Jake Peavy/35 35.00
JR Jose Reyes/35 75.00
KU Hong-Chih Kuo/35 120.00
LE Jon Lester/35 40.00
TE Miguel Tejada/35 30.00
TG Tom Glavine/35 60.00

Winning Trios Gold

NM/M
Common Trio: 15.00
Production 75 Sets
Silver: 1X
Production 50 Sets
Bronze: 1-1.5X
Production 30 Sets
Patch: No Pricing
Production 8-25
1 Ken Griffey Jr., Derek Jeter, Albert Pujols 40.00
2 Josh Willingham, Hanley Ramirez, Dan Uggla 15.00
3 Josh Johnson, Dontrelle Willis, Anibal Sanchez 15.00
4 Travis Hafner, David Ortiz, Lance Berkman 25.00
5 Ben Sheets, Roy Oswalt, Jake Peavy 15.00
6 Ivan Rodriguez, Jeremy Bonderman, Justin Verlander 25.00
7 Jose Reyes, Stephen Drew, Hanley Ramirez 25.00
8 Miguel Cabrera, Ryan Zimmerman, B.J. Upton 15.00
9 Justin Verlander, Jonathan Papelbon, Jered Weaver 40.00
10 Randy Johnson, Derek Jeter, Bobby Abreu 40.00
11 Craig Biggio, Lance Berkman, Morgan Ensberg 15.00
12 Brian McCann, Jeff Francoeur, Adam LaRoche 30.00
13 Victor Martinez, Joe Mauer, Brian McCann 20.00
14 Carl Crawford, Grady Sizemore, Jose Reyes 30.00
15 Freddy Garcia, Carlos Zambrano, Johan Santana 20.00
16 Vladimir Guerrero, Bobby Abreu, Alfonso Soriano 20.00
17 Justin Morneau, Johan Santana, Joe Mauer 25.00
18 Carlos Delgado, Carlos Beltran, Jose Reyes 25.00
19 Andre Ethier, Chad Billingsley, Matthew Kemp 25.00
20 Jim Thome, Jermaine Dye, Tadahito Iguchi 20.00
21 Jimmy Rollins, Chase Utley, Aaron Rowand 30.00
22 Ivan Rodriguez, Magglio Ordonez, Curtis Granderson 20.00
23 Chris Carpenter, Scott Rolen, Albert Pujols 30.00
24 Carl Crawford, B.J. Upton, James Shields 15.00
25 Howie Kendrick, Mike Napoli, Jered Weaver 15.00
26 Ian Kinsler, Dan Uggla, Howie Kendrick 20.00
27 Miguel Tejada, Brian Roberts, Nicholas Markakis 15.00
28 Justin Verlander, Jered Weaver, Mike Pelfrey 20.00
30 Randy Johnson, Derek Lowe, Anibal Sanchez 15.00
31 Prince Fielder, Ryan Zimmerman, Dan Uggla 20.00
32 Trevor Hoffman, Joe Nathan, Huston Street 15.00
33 Vernon Wells, Alex Rios, A.J. Burnett 15.00
34 Ben Sheets, Rickie Weeks, Prince Fielder 15.00
35 Adrian Beltre, Felix Hernandez, Yuniesky Betancourt 15.00
36 Jeremy Bonderman, Justin Verlander, Joel Zumaya 20.00
37 Billy Wagner, Paul LoDuca, Jose Reyes 20.00
38 Victor Martinez, Jeremy Sowers, C.C. Sabathia 15.00
39 Conor Jackson, Brandon Webb, Stephen Drew 20.00
40 Justin Verlander, Felix Hernandez, Jered Weaver 20.00
41 Ken Griffey Jr., Frank Thomas, Ivan Rodriguez 20.00
42 Cal Ripken Jr., Derek Jeter, Jose Reyes 50.00

2008 SP Authentic

NM/M
Common player (1-100): .25
Common RC Auto.: (101-191): 8.00
Production 149-999
Pack (5): 4.00
Box (24): 80.00
1 Ken Griffey Jr. 2.00
2 Derek Jeter 3.00
3 Albert Pujols 3.00
4 Ichiro Suzuki 2.00
5 Daisuke Matsuzaka 2.00
6 Vladimir Guerrero 1.00
7 Magglio Ordonez .50
8 Eric Chavez .25
9 Randy Johnson 1.00
10 Ryan Braun 1.50
11 Phil Hughes .75
12 Joba Chamberlain 2.00
13 B.J. Upton .50
14 Frank Thomas 1.00
15 Greg Maddux 2.00
16 Delmon Young .25
17 Carlos Beltran .75
18 Derrek Lee .75
19 Aramis Ramirez .50
20 Miguel Tejada .50
21 Manny Ramirez 1.00
22 Justin Upton .75
23 Miguel Cabrera 1.00
24 Prince Fielder 1.00
25 Adam Dunn .75
26 Jose Reyes 1.00
27 Chase Utley 1.00
28 Jimmy Rollins .75
29 Joe Blanton .25
30 Mark Teixeira .50
31 Brian McCann .50
32 Russell Martin .75
33 Ian Kinsler .75
34 Travis Hafner .50
35 Victor Martinez .50
36 Grady Sizemore 1.00
37 Alex Rodriguez 3.00
38 David Wright 2.00
39 Ryan Howard 2.00
40 Carlos Lee .50
41 Lance Berkman .50
42 Hunter Pence .50
43 John Lackey .50
44 C.C. Sabathia .75
45 Michael Young .25
46 Carl Crawford .50
47 Carlos Pena .50
48 Justin Verlander .50
49 Cole Hamels .75
50 Carlos Zambrano .50
51 Jake Peavy .75
52 Khalil Greene .25
53 Chris Young .50
54 Vernon Wells .50
55 Alex Rios .50
56 Roy Halladay .50
57 Roy Oswalt .50
58 Ben Sheets .25
59 J.J. Hardy .25
60 Pedro Martinez .50
61 Nick Swisher .25
62 Curtis Granderson .75
63 Johnny Damon .75
64 Mariano Rivera .50
65 Josh Beckett .75
66 Erik Bedard .25
67 Johan Santana 1.00
68 Joe Mauer .50
69 Justin Morneau .50
70 Torii Hunter .50
71 Alex Gordon .50
72 Jose Guillen .25
73 Jim Thome .75
74 Paul Konerko .50
75 Josh Hamilton 1.00
76 Hanley Ramirez 1.00
77 Dontrelle Willis .25
78 Dan Uggla .50
79 Brandon Phillips .50
80 Rick Ankiel .50
81 Nick Markakis .75
82 Ryan Zimmerman .50
83 Brian Roberts .25
84 Lastings Milledge .25
85 Freddy Sanchez .25
86 Barry Zito .25
87 Matt Cain .50
88 Andruw Jones .25
89 Dan Haren .50
90 Chien-Ming Wang 1.00
91 Jonathan Papelbon .50
92 Felix Hernandez .50
93 David Ortiz 1.00
94 Jason Bay .50
95 Matt Holliday .50
96 Troy Tulowitzki .50
97 Hideki Matsui .75
98 Jeff Francoeur .25
99 Alfonso Soriano .75
100 Curt Schilling .50
101 Alex Romero/Jsy/Auto./799 **(RC)** 10.00
102 Matt Tolbert/Jsy/Auto./699 **RC** 10.00
103 Bobby Wilson/Auto./699 **RC** 10.00
104 Brent Lillibridge/Auto./599 **(RC)** 10.00
105 Brian Barton/Auto./698 **RC** 15.00
106 Brian Bass/Jsy Auto./799 **(RC)** 15.00
107 Brian Bixler/Auto./698 **(RC)** 8.00
108 Brian Bocock/Jsy Auto./599 **RC** 8.00
109 Burke Badenhop/Auto./798 **RC** 8.00
110 Chin-Lung Hu/Jsy Auto./999 **(RC)** 25.00
111 Chris Perez/Auto./699 **RC** 10.00
112 Clay Buchholz/Jsy Auto./999 **(RC)** 15.00
113 Clayton Kershaw/Jsy Auto./699 **RC** 30.00
114 Colt Morton/Jsy Auto./574 **RC** 10.00
115 Daric Barton/Jsy Auto./799 **(RC)** 10.00
116 Darren O'Day/Auto./798 **RC** 8.00
117 David Purcey/Auto./599 **(RC)** 8.00

118 Denard Span/ Jsy Auto./299 **(RC)** 15.00
119 Elliot Johnson/ Auto./798 **(RC)** 8.00
120 Emmanuel Burriss/ Auto./299 **RC** 8.00
121 Evan Longoria/ Jsy Auto./499 **RC** 120.00
122 Evan Meek/ Jsy Auto./649 **RC** 10.00
123 Felipe Paulino/ Jsy Auto./799 **RC** 8.00
124 Carlos Gonzalez/ Jsy Auto./599 **(RC)** 20.00
125 German Duran/ Auto./699 **RC** 8.00
126 Greg Reynolds/ Auto./149 **RC** 8.00
127 Greg Smith/ Jsy Auto./799 **RC** 10.00
128 Harvey Garcia/ Jsy Auto./799 **(RC)** 10.00
129 Hernan Iribarren/ Jsy Auto./799 **(RC)** 10.00
130 Ian Kennedy/ Jsy Auto./669 **RC** 20.00
131 J.R. Towles/ Jsy Auto./499 **RC** 10.00
132 Jay Bruce/ Jsy Auto./549 **(RC)** 40.00
133 Jayson Nix/ Jsy Auto./299 **(RC)** 8.00
134 Jed Lowrie/ Auto./499 **(RC)** 25.00
135 Jeff Clement/ Auto./399 **(RC)** 12.00
136 Jonathan Herrera/ Auto./699 **RC** 8.00
137 Joey Votto/ Jsy Auto./999 **(RC)** 20.00
138 Johnny Cueto/ Jsy Auto./999 **RC** 20.00
139 Jonathan Albaladejo/ Jsy Auto./799 **RC** 10.00
140 Justin Masterson/ Auto./699 **RC** 40.00
141 Justin Ruggiano/ Auto./149 **RC** 8.00
142 Kevin Hart/ Jsy Auto./749 **(RC)** 8.00
143 Kosuke Fukudome/ Jsy/799 **RC** 25.00
144 Luis Mendoza/ Jsy Auto./299 **(RC)** 8.00
145 Luke Carlin/Auto./699 **RC** 15.00
146 Luke Hochevar/ Auto./799 **RC** 12.00
147 Max Scherzer/ Jsy Auto./799 **RC** 25.00
148 Micah Hoffpauir/ Auto./699 **RC** 20.00
149 Mike Parisi/Auto./699 **RC** 15.00
150 Nick Adenhart/ Auto./599 **(RC)** 15.00
151 Nick Blackburn/ Jsy Auto./799 **RC** 20.00
152 Nyjer Morgan/ Jsy Auto./999 **(RC)** 10.00
153 Ramon Troncoso/ Jsy Auto./399 **RC** 10.00
154 Randor Bierd/ Jsy Auto./799 **RC** 10.00
155 Rich Thompson/ Auto./399 **RC** 10.00
156 Rico Washington/ Jsy Auto./799 **(RC)** 8.00
157 Ross Ohlendorf/ Jsy Auto./999 **RC** 10.00
158 Steve Holm/ Jsy Auto./999 **RC** 8.00
159 Wesley Wright/ Jsy Auto./849 **RC** 10.00
160 Wladimir Balentien/ Auto./599 **(RC)** 10.00
161 Alex Hinshaw/ Auto./699 **RC** 15.00
162 Bobby Korecky/ Auto./999 **RC** 15.00
163 Bradley Harman/ Auto./999 **RC** 12.00
164 Brandon Boggs/ Auto./999 **(RC)** 10.00
165 Callix Crabbe/ Auto./325 **(RC)** 10.00
166 Clay Timpner/ Auto./849 **(RC)** 10.00
167 Clete Thomas/ Auto./849 **RC** 15.00
168 Cory Wade/ Auto./999 **(RC)** 8.00
169 Doug Mathis/ Auto./999 **RC** 8.00
170 Eider Torres/ Auto./999 **(RC)** 15.00
171 Gregorio Petit/ Auto./999 **RC** 15.00
172 Michael Aubrey/ Auto./699 **RC** 20.00
173 Jesse Carlson/ Auto./999 **RC** 20.00
174 Billy Buckner/ Auto./999 **(RC)** 10.00
175 Josh Newman/ Auto./699 **RC** 8.00
176 Matt Tupman/Auto./999 **RC** 20.00
177 Matt Joyce/Auto./999 **RC** 25.00
178 Paul Janish/ Auto./999 **(RC)** 15.00
179 Robinzon Diaz/ Auto./999 **(RC)** 8.00
180 Fernando Hernandez/ Auto./999 **RC** 10.00
181 Brandon Jones/ Auto./499 **RC** 10.00
182 Eddie Bonine/ Auto./899 **RC** 15.00
183 Chris Smith/ Auto./385 **(RC)** 10.00
184 Jonathan Van Every/ Auto./999 **RC** 10.00
185 Marino Salas/ Auto./899 **RC** 10.00
186 Mike Aviles/Auto./699 **RC** 20.00
187 Mitch Boggs/ Auto./699 **(RC)** 15.00
188 Chris Carter/ Auto./699 **(RC)** 10.00
189 Travis Denker/Auto./699 **RC** 8.00
190 Carlos Rosa/Auto./699 **RC** 10.00
191 Evan Longoria/ Auto./350 **(RC)** 120.00

Gold

Gold (1-100): 5-10X
Gold RC Auto.: 1-2X
Gold RC Jsy Auto.: 1-2X
Production 50 Sets

Authentic Achievements

NM/M

Common player: .50
Inserted 1:2
1 Derek Jeter 4.00
2 Ken Griffey Jr. 3.00
3 Randy Johnson 1.50
4 Frank Thomas 1.00
5 Tom Glavine 1.00
6 Matt Holliday 1.00
7 Justin Verlander 1.00
8 Manny Ramirez 1.50
9 Scott Rolen 1.00
10 Brandon Webb .75
11 Erik Bedard .50
12 Daisuke Matsuzaka 2.50
13 Johan Santana 1.50
14 Carlos Lee .75
15 Alfonso Soriano 1.00
16 Grady Sizemore 1.50
17 Jose Reyes 1.50
18 Chase Utley 2.00
19 Roy Oswalt .75
20 David Ortiz 1.50
21 Jake Peavy 1.00
22 Hanley Ramirez 1.50
23 Alex Rodriguez 4.00
24 Ryan Howard 2.50
25 David Wright 3.00
26 Trevor Hoffman .50
27 Prince Fielder 1.50
28 Ichiro Suzuki 2.50
29 Jimmy Rollins 1.00
30 Mariano Rivera 1.00
31 Pedro Martinez .75
32 Torii Hunter .75
33 Ivan Rodriguez .75
34 Jim Thome .75
35 Chipper Jones 2.00
36 John Smoltz 1.00
37 Jeff Kent .50
38 Albert Pujols 4.00
39 Lance Berkman 1.00
40 Justin Morneau 1.00
41 Andruw Jones .50
42 Adam Dunn 1.00
43 Greg Maddux 2.50
44 Billy Wagner .50
45 Vladimir Guerrero 1.50
46 C.C. Sabathia 1.50
47 Mark Teixeira 1.00
48 Mark Buehrle .50
49 Miguel Cabrera 1.50
50 Josh Beckett 1.50

By The Letter Autographs

NM/M

Common Letter Auto.: 15.00
Varying numbering for each Letter
AD Adam Dunn/140 25.00
AG Adrian Gonzalez/110 25.00
BH Bill Hall/1570 20.00
BP Brandon Phillips/1259 25.00
BW Billy Wagner/125 50.00
CB Chad Billingsley/1306 25.00
CJ Chipper Jones/100 125.00
CL Carlos Lee/160 40.00
CW Chien-Ming Wang/80 275.00
DA David Murphy/1837 25.00
DJ Derek Jeter/240 150.00
DM Daisuke Matsuzaka/125 250.00
EE Edwin Encarnacion/1570 15.00
FC Fausto Carmona/844 20.00
GA Garrett Atkins/588 25.00
GJ Geoff Jenkins/1200 15.00
GS Grady Sizemore/240 65.00
JB Joe Blanton/580 20.00
JE Jeff Francoeur/275 30.00
JF Jeff Francis/335 25.00
JG Jeremy Guthrie/985 25.00
JL James Loney/1275 20.00
JN Joe Nathan/365 25.00
JO John Lackey/187 25.00
JP Jonathan Papelbon/550 50.00
JS Jon Lester/235 100.00
KE Kevin Youkilis/365 100.00
KG Ken Griffey Jr./275 150.00
KJ Kelly Johnson/1399 15.00
LB Lance Berkman/165 50.00
ME Mark Ellis/995 20.00
MG Matt Garza/235 50.00
MK Matt Kemp/1369 25.00
MM Melvin Mora/490 20.00
NL Noah Lowry/1440 15.00
NS Nick Swisher/1150 20.00
PF Prince Fielder/245 50.00
PH Phil Hughes/385 40.00
PK Paul Konerko/175 30.00
RH Rich Hill/220 25.00
RM Russell Martin/265 100.00
RO Roy Halladay/160 65.00
SB Scott Baker/1248 20.00
TG Tom Gorzelanny/1082 20.00
TT Troy Tulowitzki/252 50.00

Chirography Dual Signatures

NM/M

Production 10-99
GB Chad Billingsley, Tom Gorzelanny/96 20.00
HK Phil Hughes, Ian Kennedy/99 40.00
MK Nick Markakis, Matt Kemp/99 25.00
PE Brandon Phillips, Edwin Encarnacion/99 20.00

Chirography Quad Signatures

Production 5-15
No Pricing

Chirography Triple Signatures

Production 25-50
No Pricing

Marquee Matchups

NM/M

Common Duo: .50
Inserted 1:2
1 Derek Jeter, Curt Schilling 4.00
2 Derek Jeter, Josh Beckett 4.00
3 Albert Pujols, Brad Lidge 4.00
4 Alex Rodriguez, Daisuke Matsuzaka 3.00
5 Ken Griffey Jr., John Smoltz 3.00
6 John Smoltz, David Wright 2.50
7 Gary Sheffield, Jonathan Papelbon 1.00
8 Roy Oswalt, Ryan Braun 2.00
9 Mariano Rivera, David Ortiz 1.50
10 Albert Pujols, Carlos Zambrano 4.00
11 Travis Hafner, Dontrelle Willis .50
12 Victor Martinez, Felix Hernandez 1.00
13 Carlos Lee, Carlos Zambrano .75
14 Manny Ramirez, Chien-Ming Wang 2.50
15 Justin Morneau, Felix Hernandez 1.00
16 Francisco Rodriguez, Ichiro Suzuki 2.50
17 Erik Bedard, Grady Sizemore 1.50
18 Vladimir Guerrero, Justin Verlander 1.50
19 Ichiro Suzuki, Daisuke Matsuzaka 3.00
20 Chris Carpenter, Alfonso Soriano 1.50
21 Pedro Martinez, Hanley Ramirez 1.50
22 Randy Johnson, Chase Utley 2.00
23 Ken Griffey Jr., Roy Oswalt 3.00
24 Ken Griffey Jr., Randy Johnson 3.00
25 Jimmy Rollins, Johan Santana 1.50
26 Andruw Jones, Matt Cain .50
27 Pedro Martinez, Ryan Howard 2.50
39 David Wright, Cole Hamels 2.50
29 Chipper Jones, Johan Santana 2.00
30 Billy Wagner, Mark Teixeira 1.00
31 Magglio Ordonez, C.C. Sabathia 1.00
32 Tom Glavine, Jose Reyes 1.50
33 Derek Jeter, Jonathan Papelbon 4.00
34 Alex Rodriguez, Johan Santana 4.00
35 Alfonso Soriano, Jake Peavy 1.00
36 Ryan Howard, Johan Santana 2.50
37 Jake Peavy, Russell Martin 1.00
38 Carlos Zambrano, Prince Fielder 1.50
39 Carlos Beltran, Cole Hamels 1.50
40 Alex Rodriguez, Josh Beckett 3.00
41 Derek Jeter, Roy Halladay 4.00
42 Hideki Matsui, Daisuke Matsuzaka 2.50
43 Joe Mauer, C.C. Sabathia 1.00
44 Manny Ramirez, Francisco Rodriguez 1.50
45 Miguel Cabrera, Jered Weaver 1.50
46 David Wright, Jake Peavy 3.00
47 Greg Maddux, Ken Griffey Jr. 3.00
48 John Smoltz, Hanley Ramirez 1.50
49 Alex Rodriguez, Pedro Martinez 4.00
50 Trevor Hoffman, Matt Holliday 1.00

Presidential Predictors

NM/M

Both are SP's
15 Sarah Palin 100.00
16 Joseph Biden 125.00

Rookie Exclusives

NM/M

Common player: 2.00
Autographs: No pricing
AH Alex Hinshaw 2.00
AR Alex Romero 2.00
BA Brian Barton 2.00
BB Brandon Boggs 2.00
BH Bradley Harman 2.00
BI Brian Bixler 2.00
BK Bobby Korecky 2.00
BO Brian Bocock 2.00
BR Brian Bass 2.00
BU Burke Badenhop 2.00
BW Bobby Wilson 2.00
CB Clay Buchholz 4.00
CC Callix Crabbe 2.00
CM Colt Morton 3.00
CT Clay Timpner 2.00
CU Johnny Cueto 4.00
CW Cory Wade 2.00
DB Daric Barton 2.00
DM Doug Mathis 2.00
DS Denard Span 3.00
EB Emmanuel Burriss 2.00
EJ Elliot Johnson 2.00
EM Evan Meek 2.00
ET Eider Torres 2.00
FH Fernando Hernandez 2.00
FP Felipe Paulino 2.00
GD German Duran 2.00
GP Gregorio Petit 2.00
GS Greg Smith 2.00
HI Hernan Iribarren 2.00
IK Ian Kennedy 3.00
JA Jonathan Albaladejo 2.00
JB Jay Bruce 5.00
JC Jesse Carlson 3.00
JH Jonathan Herrera 2.00
JL Jed Lowrie 3.00
JN Jayson Nix 2.00
JT J.R. Towles 3.00
KH Kevin Hart 2.00
LC Luke Carlin 2.00
LM Luis Mendoza 2.00
MA Matt Tolbert 2.00
MH Micah Hoffpauir 3.00
MJ Matt Joyce 2.00
MP Mike Parisi 2.00
MT Matt Tupman 2.00
NA Nick Adenhart 2.00
NB Nick Blackburn 3.00
NE Josh Newman 3.00
NM Nyjer Morgan 2.00
RA Alexei Ramirez 15.00
RB Randor Bierd 2.00
RD Robinzon Diaz 2.00
RI Rich Thompson 2.00
RO Ross Ohlendorf 2.00
RT Ramon Troncoso 2.00
RW Rico Washington 2.00
SH Steve Holm 2.00
TH Clete Thomas 2.00
WB Wladimir Balentien 2.00
WW Wesley Wright 2.00

Sign of the Times Dual Signatures

NM/M

Production 10-99
BB Chad Billingsley, Clay Buchholz/99 40.00
GL Yovani Gallardo, Tim Lincecum/99 40.00
NW Billy Wagner, Joe Nathan/74 25.00
PW Josh Willingham, Felix Pie/99 15.00

Sign of the Times Quad Signatures

No Pricing

Sign of the Times Triple Signatures

Production 10-50
No Pricing

USA 18U Jr. Team Jersey Autographs

		NM/M
Production 120 Sets		
Patch:		1.5-2X
Production 50 Sets		
AA	Andrew Aplin	20.00
AM	Austin Maddox	30.00
CC	Colton Cain	8.00
CG	Cameron Garfield	10.00
CT	Cecil Tanner	8.00
DN	David Nick	8.00
DT	Donavan Tate	20.00
FR	Nick Franklin	10.00
HM	Harold Martinez	20.00
JB	Jake Barrett	15.00
MA	Jeff Malm	10.00
ME	Jonathan Meyer	15.00
MP	Matt Purke	15.00
MS	Max Stassi	15.00
TU	Jacob Turner	15.00
WH	Wes Hatton	20.00

USA National Team By the Letter Autograph

		NM/M
Production 50-181		
AG	A.J. Griffin/105	15.00
BS	Blake Smith/105	15.00
CC	Christian Colon/105	20.00
CH	Chris Hernandez/180	25.00
DD	Derek Dietrich/105	25.00
KD	Kentrail Davis/103	40.00
KG	Kyle Gibson/181	20.00
KR	Kevin Rhoderick/171	15.00
KV	Kendal Volz/105	20.00
MD	Matt den Dekker/105	15.00
MG	Micah Gibbs/180	15.00
ML	Mike Leake/180	15.00
MM	Mike Minor/105	20.00
RJ	Ryan Jackson/104	15.00
TL	Tyler Lyons/104	15.00

2008 SP Legendary Cuts

		NM/M
Common Player (1-100):		.25
Common SP (101-200):		4.00
Production 550		
Pack (4):		12.00
Box (12):		110.00
1	Ken Griffey Jr.	1.50
2	Derek Jeter	2.00
3	Albert Pujols	2.00
4	Ichiro Suzuki	1.50
5	Ryan Braun	.75
6	Manny Ramirez	.75
7	David Ortiz	.75
8	Greg Maddux	1.50
9	Roger Clemens	1.00
10	Chase Utley	.75
11	Vladimir Guerrero	.50
12	Johan Santana	.50
13	Chipper Jones	.75
14	Tom Glavine	.50
15	Ryan Howard	.75
16	Hunter Pence	.40
17	Prince Fielder	.75
18	Jeff Francoeur	.40
19	David Wright	.75
20	Carlos Beltran	.50
21	Carlos Lee	.50
22	Cole Hamels	.40
23	Jered Weaver	.40
24	B.J. Upton	.40
25	Akinori Iwamura	.25
26	Daisuke Matsuzaka	1.00
27	Curt Schilling	.50
28	Adam Dunn	.50
29	Jose Reyes	.75
30	Nomar Garciaparra	.40
31	Hideki Matsui	1.00
32	Matt Holliday	.50
33	Jason Bay	.40
34	Grady Sizemore	.75
35	Travis Hafner	.40
36	Victor Martinez	.40
37	C.C. Sabathia	.50
38	Justin Morneau	.40
39	Torii Hunter	.40
40	Joe Mauer	.40
41	Russell Martin	.40
42	Frank Thomas	.75
43	Miguel Tejada	.50
44	Brian Roberts	.40
45	Justin Verlander	.40
46	Gary Sheffield	.40
47	Maggilo Ordonez	.40
48	Alex Rodriguez	2.00
49	Bobby Abreu	.40
50	Mark Teixeira	.50
51	Andruw Jones	.40
52	Derrek Lee	.50
53	Aramis Ramirez	.40
54	Carlos Zambrano	.50
55	Alfonso Soriano	.50
56	Omar Vizquel	.25
57	Lance Berkman	.50
58	Roy Oswalt	.40
59	Jake Peavy	.40
60	Chris Young	.40
61	Khalil Greene	.25
62	Troy Tulowitzki	.40
63	Todd Helton	.50
64	Josh Beckett	.50
65	Miguel Cabrera	.75
66	Hanley Ramirez	.75
67	Dan Uggla	.40
68	Scott Kazmir	.40
69	Delmon Young	.25
70	Erik Bedard	.25
71	Alex Gordon	.40
72	Felix Hernandez	.50
73	Kenji Johjima	.25
74	John Lackey	.40
75	Ryan Zimmerman	.40
76	Jeremy Bonderman	.25
77	Chien-Ming Wang	.75
78	Jim Thome	.40
79	Jimmy Rollins	.75
80	Mariano Rivera	.50
81	Curtis Granderson	.50
82	Nick Markakis	.40
83	Trevor Hoffman	.25
84	Barry Zito	.25
85	Yovani Gallardo	.40
86	Dan Haren	.25
87	Vernon Wells	.40
88	Ian Kennedy **RC**	2.00
89	Phil Hughes	.40
90	Brian McCann	.40
91	J.J. Hardy	.25
92	Roy Halladay	.40
93	Mike Piazza	.75
94	Ivan Rodriguez	.40
95	Dontrelle Willis	.25
96	Brandon Webb	.40
97	Carl Crawford	.40
98	Tim Lincecum	.50
99	Jason Varitek	.40
100	Freddy Sanchez	.25
101	Abraham Lincoln	8.00
102	Ulysses S. Grant	5.00
103	Andrew Johnson	4.00
104	George Washington	8.00
105	Thomas Jefferson	6.00
106	Andrew Jackson	4.00
107	James Madison	5.00
108	James Monroe	4.00
109	Benjamin Franklin	8.00
110	Alexander Graham Bell	4.00
111	Thomas Edison	5.00
112	Red Baron	4.00
113	Robert E. Lee	6.00
114	Mark Twain	5.00
115	Arthur Conan Doyle	4.00
116	Bram Stoker	4.00
117	Jules Verne	4.00
118	Billy the Kid	4.00
119	Harriet Beecher Stowe	4.00
120	Andrew Carnegie	4.00
121	Lewis Carroll	4.00
122	Cornelius Vanderbilt	4.00
123	Brigham Young	4.00
124	Charles Dickens	4.00
125	Vincent Van Gogh	4.00
126	Claude Monet	4.00
127	Jesse James	4.00
128	John D. Rockefeller	4.00
129	Harry Longabaugh	4.00
130	John F. Kennedy	8.00
131	Richard Nixon	4.00
132	Lyndon B. Johnson	4.00
133	Dwight D. Eisenhower	5.00
134	Franklin D. Roosevelt	5.00
135	Harry S. Truman	4.00
136	Ronald Reagan	5.00
137	Bill Clinton	5.00
138	George H.W. Bush	5.00
139	Jimmy Carter	4.00
140	Gerald Ford	4.00
141	Herbert Hoover	4.00
142	Calvin Coolidge	4.00
143	Warren G. Harding	4.00
144	Woodrow Wilson	4.00
145	William Taft	4.00
146	Theodore Roosevelt	5.00
147	Phil Niekro	4.00
148	Brooks Robinson	5.00
149	Cal Ripken Jr.	10.00
150	Eddie Murray	5.00
151	Jim Palmer	4.00
152	Abner Doubleday	4.00
153	Wade Boggs	4.00
154	Carl Yastrzemski	6.00
155	Bobby Doerr	4.00
156	Carlton Fisk	4.00
157	Pee Wee Reese	4.00
158	Ernie Banks	6.00
159	Fergie Jenkins	4.00
160	Billy Williams	4.00
161	Ryne Sandberg	6.00
162	Luis Aparicio	4.00
163	Joe Morgan	5.00
164	Johnny Bench	6.00
165	Tony Perez	4.00
166	Bob Feller	4.00
167	Larry Doby	4.00
168	Bob Lemon	4.00
169	Al Kaline	5.00
170	Warren Spahn	5.00
171	Robin Yount	5.00
172	Rollie Fingers	4.00
173	Harmon Killebrew	5.00
174	Rod Carew	4.00
175	Babe Ruth	12.00
176	Monte Irvin	4.00
177	Tom Seaver	5.00
178	Phil Rizzuto	4.00
179	Jack Chesbro	4.00
180	"Catfish" Hunter	4.00
181	Babe Ruth	12.00
182	Reggie Jackson	5.00
183	Dennis Eckersley	4.00
184	Steve Carlton	4.00
185	Ed Delahanty	4.00
186	Mike Schmidt	6.00
187	Jim Bunning	4.00
188	Robin Roberts	4.00
189	Willie Stargell	5.00
190	Bill Mazeroski	4.00
191	Ralph Kiner	4.00
192	Tony Gwynn	5.00
193	Juan Marichal	4.00
194	Willie McCovey	4.00
195	Orlando Cepeda	4.00
196	Stan Musial	6.00
197	Ozzie Smith	6.00
198	Bob Gibson	5.00
199	Bruce Sutter	4.00
200	Nolan Ryan	8.00

Baseball Headlines Cut Signature

No Pricing

Classic Signatures

		NM/M
Production 25 Sets		
BD	Bucky Dent	15.00
BR	Brooks Robinson	50.00
BT	Bobby Thomson	30.00
BW	Billy Williams	20.00
CF	Carlton Fisk	25.00
DL	Don Larsen	50.00
EB	Ernie Banks	60.00
FL	Fred Lynn	20.00
JB	Johnny Bench	50.00
JC	Joe Carter	20.00
JP	Johnny Pesky	30.00
JP2	Jim Palmer	30.00
JR	Jim Rice	25.00
JR	Lou Brock	40.00
MS	Mike Schmidt	70.00
NR	Nolan Ryan	90.00
OS	Ozzie Smith	50.00
PM	Paul Molitor	35.00
RC	Rod Carew	25.00
RS2	Ron Santo	40.00
RY	Robin Yount	50.00
SC	Steve Carlton	40.00
TG	Tony Gwynn	50.00
TM	Tino Martinez	50.00
TP	Tony Perez	40.00
WB	Wade Boggs	

Destination Stardom Memorabilia

		NM/M
Common Player:		4.00
AG	Alex Gordon	8.00
AI	Akinori Iwamura	4.00
AM	Andrew Miller	4.00
AR	Alex Rios	4.00
BB	Billy Butler	4.00
BM	Brian McCann	6.00
BU	B.J. Upton	6.00
CB	Chad Billingsley	4.00
CD	Chris Duncan	4.00
CG	Curtis Granderson	6.00
CH	Cole Hamels	6.00
DH	Dan Haren	4.00
DM	Daisuke Matsuzaka	15.00
DU	Dan Uggla	6.00
DY	Delmon Young	4.00
FH	Felix Hernandez	6.00
FI	Josh Fields	4.00
GA	Garrett Atkins	4.00
GS	Grady Sizemore	8.00
HA	Corey Hart	8.00
HK	Howie Kendrick	4.00
HP	Hunter Pence	6.00
HR	Hanley Ramirez	8.00
JF	Jeff Francoeur	4.00
JH	J.J. Hardy	4.00
JL	James Loney	6.00
JM	John Maine	4.00
JO	Josh Hamilton	10.00
JP	Jonathan Papelbon	8.00
JV	Justin Verlander	6.00
JW	Jered Weaver	4.00
KG	Khalil Greene	4.00
LE	Jon Lester	8.00
MH	Matt Holliday	6.00
NM	Nick Markakis	6.00
PF	Prince Fielder	8.00
PH	Phil Hughes	8.00
RB	Ryan Braun	8.00
RG	Ryan Garko	4.00
RH	Rich Hill	4.00
RM	Russell Martin	6.00
RZ	Ryan Zimmerman	6.00
SD	Stephen Drew	6.00
TB	Travis Buck	4.00
TL	Tim Lincecum	15.00
TT	Troy Tulowitzki	4.00
YG	Yovani Gallardo	6.00

Destined for History Memorabilia

		NM/M
Common Player:		4.00
AD	Adam Dunn	6.00
AJ	Andruw Jones	4.00
AP	Albert Pujols	15.00
AP	Andy Pettitte	6.00
AR	Alex Rodriguez	15.00
AS	Alfonso Soriano	6.00
BW	Brandon Webb	6.00
CB	Carlos Beltran	6.00
CD	Carlos Delgado	4.00
CJ	Chipper Jones	8.00
CL	Carlos Lee	6.00
CM	Chien-Ming Wang	10.00
CS	Curt Schilling	6.00
CZ	Carlos Zambrano	6.00
DJ	Derek Jeter	20.00
DL	Derrek Lee	6.00
DO	David Ortiz	8.00
DW	Dontrelle Willis	4.00
FT	Frank Thomas	8.00
GM	Greg Maddux	10.00
GS	Gary Sheffield	6.00
HA	Travis Hafner	4.00
IR	Ivan Rodriguez	6.00
JM	Justin Morneau	6.00
JR	Jimmy Rollins	8.00
JS	John Smoltz	8.00
JT	Jim Thome	6.00
MC	Miguel Cabrera	8.00
MO	Magglio Ordonez	4.00
MP	Mike Piazza	10.00
MR	Manny Ramirez	8.00
MT	Mark Teixeira	6.00
MY	Michael Young	4.00
OV	Omar Vizquel	4.00
PM	Pedro Martinez	6.00
RA	Aramis Ramirez	6.00
RC	Roger Clemens	10.00
RE	Jose Reyes	8.00
RH	Roy Halladay	4.00
RJ	Randy Johnson	8.00
RO	Roy Oswalt	4.00
SA	Johan Santana	6.00
SS	Sammy Sosa	6.00
TE	Miguel Tejada	6.00
TG	Tom Glavine	6.00
TH	Todd Helton	6.00
TH	Trevor Hoffman	4.00
VG	Vladimir Guerrero	6.00

Fall Classic Cut Signatures

		NM/M
Production 7-15		
CH	"Catfish" Hunter"/15	60.00
SC	Stan Coveleski/15	60.00

Future Legends Signatures

		NM/M
Production 99 Sets		
BM	Brian McCann	20.00
BU	B.J. Upton	20.00
BW	Brandon Wood	10.00
CB	Clay Buchholz	25.00
CD	Chris Duncan	15.00
CH	Chin-Lung Hu	25.00
CH	Cole Hamels	30.00
CH	Corey Hart	30.00
DB	Daric Barton	10.00
DU	Dan Uggla	15.00
FC	Fausto Carmona	15.00
FH	Felix Hernandez	30.00
GA	Garrett Atkins	10.00
HK	Hong-Chih Kuo	35.00
HR	Hanley Ramirez	25.00
IK	Ian Kennedy	20.00
IK2	Ian Kinsler	20.00
JF	Jeff Francis	10.00
JH	Josh Hamilton	50.00
JL	Jon Lester	25.00
JM	John Maine	15.00
JP	Jonathan Papelbon	20.00
KG	Ken Griffey Jr.	90.00
KY	Kevin Youkilis	20.00
LH	Luke Hochevar	15.00
MC	Matt Cain	15.00
MG	Matt Garza	15.00
NM	Nick Markakis	20.00
PH	Phil Hughes	20.00
RH	Rich Hill	10.00
TH	Travis Hafner	10.00
YG	Yovani Gallardo	15.00

Generations Dual Autographs

		NM/M
Production 75 Sets		
CH	Steve Carlton, Cole Hamels	60.00
GG	Tony Gwynn, Tony Gwynn Jr.	50.00
GM	Ken Griffey Jr., Stan Musial	220.00
MB	Willie McCovey, Lance Berkman	60.00
PC	Gaylord Perry, Fausto Carmona	30.00
PK	Jim Palmer, Ian Kennedy	40.00
RC	Brooks Robinson, Eric Chavez	40.00

Generations Dual Memorabilia

		NM/M
Common Duo:		10.00
AR	Luis Aparicio, Hanley Ramirez	10.00

BC Lou Brock, Carl Crawford 15.00
BL Ernie Banks, Derrek Lee 25.00
BM Johnny Bench, Victor Martinez 10.00
BM Johnny Bench, Joe Mauer 10.00
BP Lance Berkman, Hunter Pence 10.00
BY Wade Boggs, Kevin Youkilis 15.00
CD Cal Ripken Jr., Derek Jeter 30.00
CG Roberto Clemente, Vladimir Guerrero 30.00
CH Roger Clemens, Phil Hughes 15.00
CK Rod Carew, Howie Kendrick 15.00
CM Will Clark, Justin Morneau 10.00
CP Orlando Cepeda, Albert Pujols 20.00
CS Steve Carlton, Johan Santana 10.00
DC Don Sutton, Chad Billingsley 10.00
DD Don Mattingly, Derek Jeter 25.00
DJ Joe DiMaggio, Derek Jeter 80.00
DP Bill Dickey, Jorge Posada 20.00
DS Andre Dawson, Alfonso Soriano 20.00
DT Don Mattingly, Todd Helton 15.00
EA Enos Slaughter, Albert Pujols 25.00
EC Eddie Murray, Chipper Jones 20.00
FF Frank Robinson, Frank Thomas 15.00
FP Carlton Fisk, Mike Piazza 10.00
FS Rollie Fingers, Huston Street 10.00
FV Carlton Fisk, Jason Varitek 15.00
GC Bob Gibson, Chris Carpenter 15.00
GF Tony Gwynn, Prince Fielder 15.00
GG Gaylord Perry, Greg Maddux 15.00
GH Ken Griffey Jr., Josh Hamilton 20.00
GL Tom Glavine, Jon Lester 10.00
GP "Goose" Gossage, Jonathan Papelbon 15.00
GR Rich "Goose" Gossage, Mariano Rivera 15.00
HH "Catfish" Hunter, Phil Hughes 15.00
HU Rogers Hornsby, Chase Utley 30.00
JD Jim Rice, David Ortiz 15.00
JG Frank Robinson, Ken Griffey Jr. 20.00
JG Reggie Jackson, Ken Griffey Jr. 20.00
JH Reggie Jackson, Travis Hafner 10.00
KB Ralph Kiner, Jason Bay 15.00
KD Ted Kluszewski, Adam Dunn 15.00
KH Harmon Killebrew, Travis Hafner 15.00
KK Ken Griffey Jr., Ken Griffey Sr. 15.00
KT Harmon Killebrew, Frank Thomas 15.00
LM Fred Lynn, Nick Markakis 10.00
MA Mike Schmidt, Albert Pujols 20.00
MB Paul Molitor, Ryan Braun 20.00
MG Stan Musial, Ken Griffey Jr. 25.00
MJ Roger Maris, Derek Jeter 35.00
MM Juan Marichal, Pedro Martinez 15.00
MS Bill Mazeroski, Ryne Sandberg 20.00
NW Phil Niekro, Tim Wakefield 10.00
OJ Ozzie Smith, Jose Reyes 15.00
PB Jim Palmer, Erik Bedard 10.00
PH Gaylord Perry, Roy Halladay 10.00
PL Gaylord Perry, Tim Lincecum 15.00
PM Mike Piazza, Russell Martin 10.00
PO Dave Parker, David Ortiz 10.00
PY Gaylord Perry, Chris Young 10.00
RC Nolan Ryan, Roger Clemens 20.00
RD Ryne Sandberg, Dan Uggla 15.00
RJ Phil Rizzuto, Derek Jeter 25.00
RM Cal Ripken Jr., Nick Markakis 20.00
RO Nolan Ryan, Roy Oswalt 20.00
RR Randy Johnson, Rich Hill 10.00
RT Cal Ripken Jr., Troy Tulowitzki 20.00
RV Nolan Ryan, Justin Verlander 15.00
RW Nolan Ryan, Jered Weaver 15.00
SA Stan Musial,Albert Pujols 25.00
SB Mike Schmidt, Ryan Braun 20.00
SC Steve Carlton, Cole Hamels 15.00
SG Ben Sheets, Yovani Gallardo 10.00
SJ Mike Schmidt, Chipper Jones 20.00
SL John Smoltz, Tim Lincecum 15.00
SM Tom Seaver, John Maine 10.00
SP Tom Seaver, Jake Peavy 10.00
SR Ron Santo, Aramis Ramirez 15.00
SU Ryne Sandberg, Chase Utley 15.00
SY Gary Sheffield, Delmon Young 10.00
SZ Mike Schmidt, Ryan Zimmerman 15.00
TM Todd Helton, Matt Holliday 10.00
TR Cal Ripken Jr., Miguel Tejada 15.00
YH Robin Yount, J.J. Hardy 15.00
YJ Robin Yount, Derek Jeter 20.00
YO Carl Yastrzemski, David Ortiz 20.00

Headliners and Heroes Cut Signatures

NM/M

Production 4-122
AB Al Barlick/32 60.00
AL Al Lopez/45 50.00
BH Babe Herman/44 60.00
BH Billy Herman/76 50.00
BL Bob Lemon/39 50.00
BL Buck Leonard/58 50.00
BT Bill Terry/94 70.00
CG Charlie Gehringer/40 60.00
EL Ed Lopat/46 70.00
ER Edd Roush/122 50.00
ES Enos Slaughter/36 60.00
EW Eugene Woodling/72 60.00
GK George Kelly/77 75.00
HC Happy Chandler/75 50.00
HH Harry Hooper/34 350.00
JB James "Cool Papa" Bell/23 225.00
JH Jesse Haines/37 125.00
JJ Judy Johnson/38 70.00
JM Johnny Mize/47 70.00
JM Johnny Mize/50 70.00
JS Joe Sewell/50 50.00
JS Joe Sewell/47 50.00
JS Johnny Sain/59 70.00
LA Luke Appling/45 50.00
MC Max Carey/31 85.00
PR Pee Wee Reese/52 100.00
RC Roy Campanella/37 450.00
TL Ted Lyons/34 65.00

Legendary Cut Signatures

NM/M

Production 2-108
AB Al Barlick/52 60.00
BH Babe Herman/30 60.00
BH Billy Herman/79 50.00
BL Bob Lemon/40 50.00
BL Buck Leonard/62 50.00
CG Charlie Gehringer/45 60.00
CH Carl Hubbell/31 75.00
CK Charlie Keller/34 60.00
EA Earl Averill/44 60.00
ES Enos Slaughter/30 60.00
HC Happy Chandler/55 60.00
HN Hal Newhouser/52 75.00
HW Hoyt Wilhelm/32 60.00
JC Jocko Conlan/40 60.00
JH Jesse Haines/40 125.00
JJ Judy Johnson/29 70.00
JM Johnny Mize/41 70.00
JS Joe Sewell/46 50.00
LB Lou Boudreau/54 50.00
LB Lou Boudreau/50 50.00
LW Lloyd Waner/60 150.00
RC Roy Campanella/26 450.00
RF Rick Ferrell/108 60.00
RM Rube Marquard/40 60.00
SC Stan Coveleski/45 50.00
TL Ted Lyons/32 70.00
WH Waite Hoyt/18 65.00
WS Warren Spahn/39 80.00

Legendary Cut Signatures Dual

No Pricing

Legendary Memorabilia

NM/M

Common Player: 5.00
Production 99 Sets
Parallel 75: 1X
Production 75 Sets
Parallel 50: 1X
Production 50 Sets
Parallel 35: 1-1.5X
Production 35 Sets
Parallel 25: 1-2X
Production 25 Sets
Parallel 15: No Pricing
Production 15 Sets
Parallel 10: No pricing
Production 10 Sets
AD Andre Dawson 6.00
BF Bob Feller 10.00
BL Bob Lemon 5.00
BM Bill Mazeroski 10.00
BR Brooks Robinson 10.00
BS Bruce Sutter 5.00
BW Billy Williams 6.00
CA Rod Carew 6.00
CF2 Carlton Fisk 6.00
CR Cal Ripken Jr. 15.00
CY Carl Yastrzemski 10.00
DM Don Mattingly 10.00
DP Dave Parker 5.00
DP2 Dave Parker 5.00
DS Don Sutton 5.00
DW Dave Winfield 6.00
EB Ernie Banks 10.00
EH Elston Howard 8.00
EW Early Wynn 6.00
FJ Fergie Jenkins 5.00
FL Fred Lynn 5.00
FR Frank Robinson 8.00
GG "Goose" Gossage 5.00
GP Gaylord Perry 5.00
HK Harmon Killebrew 10.00
JB Johnny Bench 10.00
JB Jim Bunning 5.00
JC Joe Carter 5.00
JM Juan Marichal 6.00
JM Joe Morgan 6.00
JT Joe Torre 6.00
LA Luis Aparicio 5.00
MA Edgar Martinez 5.00
MG Mark Grace 6.00
MS Mike Schmidt 10.00
NR Nolan Ryan 15.00
OC Orlando Cepeda 5.00
OS Ozzie Smith 8.00
OS2 Ozzie Smith 8.00
PM Paul Molitor 8.00
PN Phil Niekro 5.00
PO Paul O'Neill 8.00
RC Roberto Clemente 35.00
RF Rollie Fingers 5.00
RG Ron Guidry 15.00
RI Jim Rice 5.00
RM Roger Maris 25.00
RS Red Schoendienst 5.00
RY Robin Yount 8.00
SA Ron Santo 10.00
SM Stan Musial 15.00
ST Steve Carlton 5.00
TG Tony Gwynn 10.00
TP Tony Perez 6.00
TR Tim Raines 5.00
TS Tom Seaver 8.00
WB Wade Boggs 8.00
WC Will Clark 6.00
WF Whitey Ford 10.00

Midsummer Classic Cut Signatures

NM/M

Production 14-16
BD Bill Dickey/15 150.00
EL Ernie Lombardi/14 160.00
LD Larry Doby/14 125.00

Mystery Cut Signatures

No Pricing

2008 SPX

NM/M

Common Player (1-100): .25
Common RC Auto. (101-151): 10.00
Pack (3): 18.00
Box (10): 160.00
1 Brandon Webb .50
2 Chris B. Young .50
3 Eric Byrnes .25
4 Dan Haren .50
5 Mark Teixeira .75
6 Chipper Jones 1.50
7 John Smoltz .50
8 Erik Bedard .50
9 Nick Markakis .50
10 Brian Roberts .50
11 David Ortiz 1.00
12 Curt Schilling .50
13 Manny Ramirez 1.00
14 Daisuke Matsuzaka 1.00
15 Josh Beckett .75
16 Derrek Lee .75
17 Alfonso Soriano 1.00
18 Carlos Zambrano .50
19 Aramis Ramirez .50
20 Jermaine Dye .50
21 Jim Thome .50
22 Nick Swisher .50
23 Ken Griffey Jr. 2.00
24 Adam Dunn .50
25 Brandon Phillips .50
26 Grady Sizemore .75
27 Victor Martinez .50
28 C.C. Sabathia .50
29 Travis Hafner .50
30 Matt Holliday .50
31 Todd Helton .75
32 Troy Tulowitzki .50
33 Magglio Ordonez .50
34 Gary Sheffield .50
35 Justin Verlander .50
36 Curtis Granderson .50
37 Miguel Cabrera .75
38 Hanley Ramirez 1.00
39 Dan Uggla .50
40 Miguel Tejada .50
41 Lance Berkman .75
42 Hunter Pence .50
43 Carlos Lee .50
44 Alex Gordon .50
45 David DeJesus .25
46 Vladimir Guerrero 1.00
47 Jered Weaver .25
48 Torii Hunter .50
49 Andruw Jones .25
50 Rafael Furcal .50
51 Russell Martin .50
52 Brad Penny .25
53 Ryan Braun .75
54 Prince Fielder 1.00
55 J.J. Hardy .25
56 Justin Morneau .50
57 Johan Santana .75
58 Joe Mauer .50
59 Delmon Young .50
60 Jose Reyes .75
61 David Wright 1.00
62 Carlos Beltran .75
63 Pedro Martinez .75
64 Chien-Ming Wang .75
65 Alex Rodriguez 3.00
66 Derek Jeter 3.00
67 Robinson Cano .50
68 Hideki Matsui 1.00
69 Joe Blanton .25
70 Jack Cust .25
71 Cole Hamels .50
72 Jimmy Rollins .75
73 Ryan Howard 1.00
74 Chase Utley 1.00
75 Jason Bay .50
76 Freddy Sanchez .25
77 Jake Peavy .50
78 Greg Maddux 2.00
79 Adrian Gonzalez .50
80 Barry Zito .25
81 Omar Vizquel .25
82 Tim Lincecum .50
83 Ichiro Suzuki 2.00
84 Felix Hernandez .50
85 Kenji Johjima .25
86 Albert Pujols 3.00
87 Scott Rolen .50
88 Chris Carpenter .50
89 Rick Ankiel .50
90 Scott Kazmir .50
91 Carl Crawford .50
92 B.J. Upton .50
93 Michael Young .25
94 Josh Hamilton .50
95 Hank Blalock .25
96 Roy Halladay .50
97 Vernon Wells .50
98 Alex Rios .50
99 Ryan Zimmerman .50
100 Dmitri Young .25
101 Bill Murphy/Auto. **(RC)** 10.00
102 Emilio Bonifacio/Auto. **RC** 10.00
103 Brandon Jones/Auto. **RC** 15.00
104 Clint Sammons/Auto. **(RC)** 10.00
105 Clay Buchholz/Auto. **(RC)** 25.00
106 Kevin Hart/Auto. **(RC)** 10.00
107 Donny Lucy/Auto. **(RC)** 10.00
108 Lance Broadway/Auto. **RC** 10.00
109 Joey Votto/Auto. **(RC)** 30.00
110 Ryan Hanigan/Auto. **RC** 10.00
111 Joe Koshansky/Auto. **(RC)** 10.00
112 Josh Newman/Auto. **RC** 10.00
113 Seth Smith/Auto. **(RC)** 10.00
114 Chris Seddon/Auto. **(RC)** 10.00
115 Harvey Garcia/Auto. **(RC)** 10.00
116 Felipe Paulino/Auto. **RC** 10.00
117 J.R. Towles/Auto. **RC** 10.00
118 Josh Anderson/Auto. **(RC)** 10.00
119 Troy Patton/Auto. **(RC)** 10.00
120 Billy Buckner/Auto. **(RC)** 10.00
121 Luke Hochevar/Auto. **RC** 15.00
122 Chin-Lung Hu/Auto. **(RC)** 15.00
123 Jonathan Meloan/Auto. **RC** 10.00
124 Jose Morales/Auto. **(RC)** 10.00
126 Alberto Gonzalez/Auto. **(RC)** 10.00
127 Bronson Sardinha/Auto. **(RC)** 10.00
128 Ian Kennedy/Auto. **RC** 20.00
129 Ross Ohlendorf/Auto. **RC** 10.00
130 Daric Barton/Auto. **(RC)** 15.00
131 Jerry Blevins/Auto. **RC** 10.00
132 David Davidson/Auto. **RC** 10.00
133 Nyjer Morgan/Auto. **(RC)** 10.00
134 Steve Pearce/Auto. **RC** 15.00
135 Colt Morton/Auto. **RC** 10.00
136 Eugenio Velez/Auto. **RC** 10.00
138 Rob Johnson/Auto. **(RC)** 10.00
139 Wladimir Balentien/Auto. **(RC)** 15.00
140 Justin Ruggiano/Auto. **RC** 10.00
141 Bill White/Auto. **RC** 10.00
142 Luis Mendoza/Auto. **(RC)** 10.00
143 Jonathan Albaladejo/Auto. **RC** 10.00
145 Ross Detwiler/Auto. **RC** 10.00
146 Jay Bruce/Auto. **RC** 60.00
147 Carlos Gonzalez/Auto. **(RC)** 40.00
148 Evan Longoria/Auto. **RC** 150.00
151 Clayton Kershaw/Auto. **RC** 50.00
152 Alexei Ramirez/Auto. **RC** 120.00

Babe Ruth American Legend

Production One Set

Ken Griffey Jr. American Hero

NM/M

Common Griffey (1-100): 5.00
Production 725 Sets
Boxscore: No Pricing
Production One Set

Ken Griffey Jr. American Hero - Memorabilia

NM/M

Common Griffey (1-100): 20.00
Production 25 Sets
Auto.: No Pricing
Production Three Sets

Superstar Signatures

		NM/M
Common Auto.:		15.00
BW	Brandon Webb	25.00
DJ	Derek Jeter	100.00
DM	Daisuke Matsuzaka	150.00
DU	Dan Uggla	20.00
HR	Hanley Ramirez	20.00
KG	Ken Griffey Jr.	80.00
MH	Matt Holliday	20.00
MT	Mark Teixeira	20.00
PF	Prince Fielder	30.00
SR	Scott Rolen	15.00
TG	Tom Glavine	30.00
TH	Travis Hafner	15.00
VG	Vladimir Guerrero	30.00
VM	Victor Martinez	15.00

Winning Materials - Team Letters

No Pricing
Production 15 Sets

Winning Materials

NM/M

Common Player: 5.00
Production 150 Sets
Parallels: 1X
Production 75, 99 or 125
Jersey #: 1.5X
Production 35 Sets
Position: No Pricing
Production 20 Sets
Team Letters: 1.5-2X
Production 25 Sets
Patch 50: 2X
Production 50 Sets
Patch 25: No Pricing
Production 25 Sets
Patch 99: 1.5-2X
Production 99 Sets
Patch 15: No Pricing
Production 15 Sets

AB	A.J. Burnett	5.00
AE	Andre Ethier	5.00
AG	Adrian Gonzalez	8.00
AH	Aaron Harang	5.00
AJ	Andruw Jones	5.00
AK	Austin Kearns	5.00
AL	Adam LaRoche	5.00
AP	Albert Pujols	15.00
AR	Aaron Rowand	5.00
AS	Alfonso Soriano	10.00
AT	Garrett Atkins	8.00
BA	Bobby Abreu	8.00
BC	Bartolo Colon	5.00
BE	Adrian Beltre	5.00
BG	Brian Giles	5.00
BM	Brian McCann	10.00
BS	Ben Sheets	5.00
BU	B.J. Upton	8.00
BW	Billy Wagner	5.00
CA	Chris Carpenter	5.00
CB	Carlos Beltran	8.00
CC	Chad Cordero	5.00
CD	Carlos Delgado	5.00
CG	Carlos Guillen	5.00
CH	Chris Burke	5.00
CJ	Chipper Jones	10.00
CK	Casey Kotchman	5.00
CL	Carlos Lee	5.00
CS	Curt Schilling	8.00
CU	Chase Utley	10.00
CZ	Carlos Zambrano	8.00
DH	Dan Haren	5.00
DJ	Derek Jeter	20.00
DL	Derrek Lee	8.00
DO	David Ortiz	10.00
DU	Dan Uggla	5.00
DW	Dontrelle Willis	5.00
DY	Jermaine Dye	5.00
EC	Eric Chavez	5.00
FH	Felix Hernandez	8.00
FL	Francisco Liriano	5.00
GA	Garret Anderson	5.00
GJ	Geoff Jenkins	5.00
GM	Greg Maddux	10.00
GO	Alex Gordon	8.00
GR	Curtis Granderson	8.00
GS	Grady Sizemore	8.00
HA	Cole Hamels	8.00
HB	Hank Blalock	5.00
HE	Todd Helton	8.00
HO	Trevor Hoffman	5.00
HR	Hanley Ramirez	8.00
HU	Torii Hunter	5.00
IR	Ivan Rodriguez	5.00
J.	J.J. Hardy	5.00
JA	Conor Jackson	5.00
JB	Josh Barfield	5.00
JD	J.D. Drew	5.00
JE	Jim Edmonds	5.00
JF	Jeff Francoeur	8.00
JG	Jason Giambi	5.00
JH	Jhonny Peralta	5.00
JK	Jeff Kent	5.00
JM	Joe Mauer	5.00
JN	Joe Nathan	5.00
JO	Josh Beckett	8.00
JP	Jake Peavy	5.00
JR	Jose Reyes	8.00
JS	Johan Santana	8.00
JT	Jim Thome	5.00
JV	Jason Varitek	8.00
KG	Ken Griffey Jr.	10.00
KJ	Kenji Johjima	5.00
KY	Kevin Youkilis	8.00
LB	Lance Berkman	8.00
LG	Luis Gonzalez	5.00
MC	Miguel Cabrera	8.00
MH	Matt Holliday	8.00
MO	Justin Morneau	8.00
MR	Manny Ramirez	8.00
MT	Mark Teixeira	8.00
MY	Michael Young	5.00
OR	Magglio Ordonez	5.00
PA	Jonathan Papelbon	8.00
PE	Andy Pettitte	5.00
PF	Prince Fielder	10.00
PM	Pedro Martinez	8.00
PO	Jorge Posada	8.00
RA	Aramis Ramirez	8.00
RF	Rafael Furcal	8.00
RH	Roy Halladay	5.00
RJ	Randy Johnson	8.00
RO	Roy Oswalt	5.00
SM	John Smoltz	8.00
TE	Miguel Tejada	5.00
TH	Tim Hudson	5.00
TR	Travis Hafner	5.00
VE	Justin Verlander	8.00
VG	Vladimir Guerrero	8.00
VW	Vernon Wells	5.00

Winning Trios

NM/M

Production 75 Sets
Parallel: 1.5X
Production 25 Sets
Patch: 2X
Production 25 Sets

AGK	Garret Anderson, Vladimir Guerrero, Casey Kotchman	10.00
BHJ	Adrian Beltre, Felix Hernandez, Kenji Johjima	15.00
BSS	Josh Beckett, Johan Santana, C.C. Sabathia	15.00
CRP	Chris Carpenter, Scott Rolen, Albert Pujols	25.00
CRU	Miguel Cabrera, Hanley Ramirez, Dan Uggla	15.00
DBR	Carlos Delgado, Carlos Beltran, Jose Reyes	15.00
DOP	Carlos Delgado, David Ortiz, Albert Pujols	20.00
GHL	Yovani Gallardo, Phil Hughes, Tim Lincecum	15.00
GIB	Alex Gordon, Akinori Iwamura, Ryan Braun	15.00
GJP	Ken Griffey Jr., Derek Jeter, Albert Pujols	35.00
GMW	Tom Glavine, Pedro Martinez, Billy Wagner	20.00
HAH	Todd Helton, Garrett Atkins, Matt Holliday	15.00
HDF	Travis Hafner, Adam Dunn, Prince Fielder	10.00
HFB	J.J. Hardy, Prince Fielder, Ryan Braun	25.00
HRR	J.J. Hardy, Jose Reyes, Hanley Ramirez	15.00
HSS	Travis Hafner, Grady Sizemore, C.C. Sabathia	10.00
JBH	Andruw Jones, Carlos Beltran, Torii Hunter	15.00
JDY	Conor Jackson, Stephen Drew, Chris B. Young	
JRR	Chipper Jones, Scott Rolen, Aramis Ramirez	20.00
JST	Chipper Jones, John Smoltz, Mark Teixeira	15.00
KFE	Jeff Kent, Rafael Furcal, Andre Ethier	10.00
KUY	Scott Kazmir, B.J. Upton, Delmon Young	15.00
LBO	Carlos Lee, Lance Berkman, Roy Oswalt	10.00
LCL	Noah Lowry, Matt Cain, Tim Lincecum	15.00
LSZ	Derrek Lee, Alfonso Soriano, Carlos Zambrano	20.00
MGS	Greg Maddux, Tom Glavine, John Smoltz	20.00
MHP	Greg Maddux, Trevor Hoffman, Jake Peavy	20.00
MPB	Victor Martinez, Jhonny Peralta, Josh Barfield	10.00
MSM	Justin Morneau, Johan Santana, Joe Mauer	15.00
OGV	Magglio Ordonez, Curtis Granderson, Justin Verlander	15.00
PJP	Andy Pettitte, Derek Jeter, Jorge Posada	30.00
RJC	Alex Rodriguez, Derek Jeter, Robinson Cano	40.00
RMM	Ivan Rodriguez, Victor Martinez, Joe Mauer	10.00
SBP	Curt Schilling, Josh Beckett, Jonathan Papelbon	20.00
SOH	Ben Sheets, Roy Oswalt, Aaron Harang	10.00
SRG	Gary Sheffield, Ivan Rodriguez, Carlos Guillen	10.00
TDB	Jim Thome, Jermaine Dye, Mark Buehrle	10.00
UHR	Chase Utley, Cole Hamels, Aaron Rowand	15.00
UKU	Chase Utley, Ian Kinsler, Dan Uggla	15.00
VOY	Jason Varitek, David Ortiz, Kevin Youkilis	20.00
WHB	Vernon Wells, Roy Halladay, A.J. Burnett	10.00
ZPH	Carlos Zambrano, Jake Peavy, Aaron Harang	15.00

Winning Materials - Autograph

Production 20 sets unless noted.
No Pricing

Winning Materials Autograph

No Pricing
Production Five Sets

Young Star Signatures

		NM/M
Common Auto.:		10.00
AC	Alexi Casilla	10.00
AE	Andre Ethier	10.00
BB	Brian Bannister	10.00
BM	Brian McCann	25.00
BU	Brian Burres	10.00
CD	Chris Duncan	15.00
CH	Cole Hamels	20.00
CY	Chris B. Young	15.00
FC	Fausto Carmona	15.00
FL	Francisco Liriano	10.00
IK	Ian Kinsler	15.00
JA	Joaquin Arias	10.00
JD	John Danks	15.00
JJ	Josh Johnson	10.00
JL	James Loney	20.00
JS	Jarrod Saltalamacchia	10.00
JW	Josh Willingham	10.00
JZ	Joel Zumaya	15.00
KK	Kevin Kouzmanoff	10.00
MA	Nick Markakis	20.00
MC	Matt Chico	8.00
MF	Mike Fontenot	15.00
MO	Micah Owings	15.00
MR	Mark Reynolds	15.00
NM	Nate McLouth	15.00
PH	Phil Hughes	25.00
RB	Ryan Braun	35.00
RG	Ryan Garko	10.00
RM	Russell Martin	20.00
SD	Stephen Drew	15.00
SH	James Shields	10.00
TB	Travis Buck	10.00
TG	Tom Gorzelanny	8.00
TT	Troy Tulowitzki	15.00

1997 Sports Illustrated

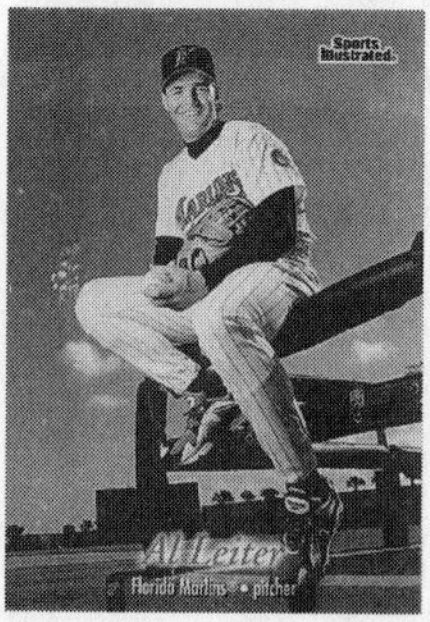

NM/M

Complete Set (180): 20.00
Common Player: .05
Extra Edition Stars: 8X
Pack (6): 1.25
Wax Box (24): 20.00

1	Bob Abreu	.10
2	Jaime Bluma	.05
3	Emil Brown	.05
4	Jose Cruz, Jr.	.05
5	Jason Dickson	.05
6	Nomar Garciaparra	1.00
7	Todd Greene	.05
8	Vladimir Guerrero	.75
9	Wilton Guerrero	.05
10	Jose Guillen	.05
11	Hideki Irabu	.05
12	Russ Johnson	.05
13	Andruw Jones	.75
14	Damon Mashore	.05
15	Jason McDonald	.05
16	Ryan McGuire	.05
17	Matt Morris	.05
18	Kevin Orie	.05
19	Dante Powell	.05
20	Pokey Reese	.05
21	Joe Roa	.05
22	Scott Rolen	.65
23	Glendon Rusch	.05
24	Scott Spiezio	.05
25	Bubba Trammell	.05
26	Todd Walker	.05
27	Jamey Wright	.05
28	Ken Griffey Jr.	.75
29	Tino Martinez	.05
30	Roger Clemens	.65
31	Hideki Irabu	.05
32	Kevin Brown	.05
33	Chipper Jones, Cal Ripken Jr.	.65
34	Sandy Alomar	.05
35	Ken Caminiti	.05
36	Randy Johnson	.40
37	Andy Ashby	.05
38	Jay Buhner	.05
39	Joe Carter	.05
40	Darren Daulton	.05
41	Jeff Fassero	.05
42	Andres Galarraga	.05
43	Rusty Greer	.05
44	Marquis Grissom	.05
45	Joey Hamilton	.05
46	Jimmy Key	.05
47	Ryan Klesko	.05
48	Eddie Murray	.75
49	Charles Nagy	.05
50	Dave Nilsson	.05
51	Ricardo Rincon	.05
52	Billy Wagner	.05
53	Dan Wilson	.05
54	Dmitri Young	.05
55	Roberto Alomar	.30
56	Sandy Alomar Jr.	.05
57	Scott Brosius	.05
58	Tony Clark	.05
59	Carlos Delgado	.45
60	Jermaine Dye	.05
61	Darin Erstad	.20
62	Derek Jeter	1.00
63	Jason Kendall	.05
64	Hideo Nomo	.20
65	Rey Ordonez	.05
66	Andy Pettitte	.10
67	Manny Ramirez	.75
68	Edgar Renteria	.05
69	Shane Reynolds	.05
70	Alex Rodriguez	1.00
71	Ivan Rodriguez	.65
72	Jose Rosado	.05
73	John Smoltz	.05
74	Tom Glavine	.35
75	Greg Maddux	1.00
76	Chipper Jones	1.00
77	Kenny Lofton	.05
78	Fred McGriff	.05
79	Kevin Brown	.05
80	Alex Fernandez	.05
81	Al Leiter	.05
82	Bobby Bonilla	.05
83	Gary Sheffield	.40
84	Moises Alou	.05
85	Henry Rodriguez	.05
86	Mark Grudzielanek	.05
87	Pedro Martinez	.75
88	Todd Hundley	.05
89	Bernard Gilkey	.05
90	Bobby Jones	.05
91	Curt Schilling	.35
92	Ricky Bottalico	.05
93	Mike Lieberthal	.05
94	Sammy Sosa	1.00
95	Ryne Sandberg	1.00
96	Mark Grace	.05
97	Deion Sanders	.05
98	Reggie Sanders	.05
99	Barry Larkin	.05
100	Craig Biggio	.05
101	Jeff Bagwell	.75
102	Derek Bell	.05
103	Brian Jordan	.05
104	Ray Lankford	.05
105	Ron Gant	.05
106	Al Martin	.05
107	Kevin Elster	.05
108	Jermaine Allensworth	.05
109	Vinny Castilla	.05
110	Dante Bichette	.05
111	Larry Walker	.05
112	Mike Piazza	1.25
113	Eric Karros	.05
114	Todd Hollandsworth	.05
115	Raul Mondesi	.05
116	Hideo Nomo	.40
117	Ramon Martinez	.05
118	Ken Caminiti	.05
119	Tony Gwynn	1.00
120	Steve Finley	.05
121	Barry Bonds	2.00
122	J.T. Snow	.05
123	Rod Beck	.05
124	Cal Ripken Jr.	2.00

#	Player	Price
125	Mike Mussina	.30
126	Brady Anderson	.05
127	Bernie Williams	.05
128	Derek Jeter	2.00
129	Tino Martinez	.05
130	Andy Pettitte	.30
131	David Cone	.05
132	Mariano Rivera	.15
133	Roger Clemens	1.00
134	Pat Hentgen	.05
135	Juan Guzman	.05
136	Bob Higginson	.05
137	Tony Clark	.05
138	Travis Fryman	.05
139	Mo Vaughn	.05
140	Tim Naehring	.05
141	John Valentin	.05
142	Matt Williams	.05
143	David Justice	.05
144	Jim Thome	.65
145	Chuck Knoblauch	.05
146	Paul Molitor	.75
147	Marty Cordova	.05
148	Frank Thomas	.85
149	Albert Belle	.05
150	Robin Ventura	.05
151	John Jaha	.05
152	Jeff Cirillo	.05
153	Jose Valentin	.05
154	Jay Bell	.05
155	Jeff King	.05
156	Kevin Appier	.05
157	Ken Griffey Jr.	1.25
158	Alex Rodriguez	1.50
158p	Alex Rodriguez/OPS	1.50
159	Randy Johnson	.75
160	Juan Gonzalez	.40
161	Will Clark	.05
162	Dean Palmer	.05
163	Tim Salmon	.05
164	Jim Edmonds	.05
165	Jim Leyritz	.05
166	Jose Canseco	.40
167	Jason Giambi	.50
168	Mark McGwire	1.50
169	Barry Bonds	1.00
170	Alex Rodriguez	.75
171	Roger Clemens	.65
172	Ken Griffey Jr.	.65
173	Greg Maddux	.50
174	Mike Piazza	.65
175	Will Clark, Mark McGwire	1.00
176	Hideo Nomo	.20
177	Cal Ripken Jr.	1.00
178	Ken Griffey Jr., Frank Thomas	.50
179	Alex Rodriguez, Derek Jeter	1.50
180	John Wetteland	.05
---	Jose Cruz Jr. Checklist	.05

Extra Edition

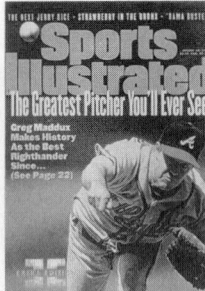

		NM/M
Complete Set (180):		150.00
Common Player:		1.00
Extra Edition Stars:		8X

(See 1997 Sports Illustrated for checklist and base card values.)

Autographed Mini-Covers

	NM/M
Complete Set (6):	300.00
Common Player:	30.00
Alex Rodriguez	100.00
Cal Ripken Jr.	100.00
Kirby Puckett	80.00
Willie Mays	125.00

Frank Robinson	30.00
Hank Aaron	200.00

Box Topper

	NM/M
Alex Rodriguez	4.50

Cooperstown Collection

		NM/M
Complete Set (12):		27.50
Common Player:		2.00
1	Hank Aaron	6.00
2	Yogi Berra	3.00
3	Lou Brock	2.00
4	Rod Carew	2.00
5	Juan Marichal	2.00
6	Al Kaline	2.50
7	Joe Morgan	2.00
8	Brooks Robinson	3.00
9	Willie Stargell	2.00
10	Kirby Puckett	4.00
11	Willie Mays	6.00
12	Frank Robinson	3.00

Great Shots

		NM/M
Complete Set (25):		10.00
Common Player:		.20
(1)	Roberto Alomar	.30
(2)	Andy Ashby	.20
(3)	Albert Belle	.20
(4)	Barry Bonds	2.00
(5)	Jay Buhner	.20
(6)	Vinny Castilla, Andres Galarraga	.20
(7)	Darren Daulton	.20
(8)	Juan Gonzalez	.40
(9)	Ken Griffey Jr.	1.25

(10)	Derek Jeter	2.00
(11)	Randy Johnson	.75
(12)	Chipper Jones	1.00
(13)	Eric Karros	.20
(14)	Ryan Klesko	.20
(15)	Kenny Lofton	.20
(16)	Greg Maddux	1.00
(17)	Mark McGwire	1.50
(18)	Mike Piazza	1.25
(19)	Cal Ripken Jr.	2.00
(20)	Alex Rodriguez	1.50
(21)	Ryne Sandberg	1.00
(22)	Deion Sanders	.30
(23)	John Smoltz	.20
(24)	Frank Thomas	.70
(25)	Mo Vaughn	.20

1998 Sports Illustrated Then & Now

		NM/M
Complete Set (150):		15.00
Common Player:		.05
Extra Edition Stars:		6X
Production 500 Sets		
Pack (5):		1.00
Wax Box (24):		16.00
1	Luis Aparicio	.05
2	Richie Ashburn	.05
3	Ernie Banks	.50
4	Yogi Berra	.50
5	Lou Boudreau	.05
6	Lou Brock	.15
7	Jim Bunning	.05
8	Rod Carew	.15
9	Bob Feller	.25
10	Rollie Fingers	.05
11	Bob Gibson	.25
12	Fergie Jenkins	.05
13	Al Kaline	.25
14	George Kell	.05
15	Harmon Killebrew	.25
16	Ralph Kiner	.05
17	Tommy Lasorda	.05
18	Juan Marichal	.05
19	Eddie Mathews	.25
20	Willie Mays	1.00
21	Willie McCovey	.05
22	Joe Morgan	.15
23	Gaylord Perry	.05
24	Kirby Puckett	1.00
25	Pee Wee Reese	.25
26	Phil Rizzuto	.25
27	Robin Roberts	.05
28	Brooks Robinson	.35
29	Frank Robinson	.35
30	Red Schoendienst	.05
31	Enos Slaughter	.05
32	Warren Spahn	.25
33	Willie Stargell	.15
34	Earl Weaver	.05
35	Billy Williams	.15
36	Early Wynn	.05
37	Rickey Henderson	.75
38	Greg Maddux	1.00
39	Mike Mussina	.25
40	Cal Ripken Jr.	2.00
41	Albert Belle	.05
42	Frank Thomas	.75
43	Jeff Bagwell	.75
44	Paul Molitor	.75
45	Chuck Knoblauch	.05
46	Todd Hundley	.05
47	Bernie Williams	.05
48	Tony Gwynn	1.00
49	Barry Bonds	2.00
50	Ken Griffey Jr.	1.25
51	Randy Johnson	.75
52	Mark McGwire	1.50
53	Roger Clemens	1.00
54	Jose Cruz Jr.	.05
55	Roberto Alomar	.20
56	Sandy Alomar	.05
57	Brady Anderson	.05
58	Kevin Appier	.05
59	Jeff Bagwell	.75
60	Albert Belle	.05
61	Dante Bichette	.05
62	Craig Biggio	.05
63	Barry Bonds	2.00
64	Kevin Brown	.05
65	Jay Buhner	.05
66	Ellis Burks	.05
67	Ken Caminiti	.05
68	Jose Canseco	.50
69	Joe Carter	.05
70	Vinny Castilla	.05
71	Tony Clark	.05
72	Roger Clemens	1.00
73	David Cone	.05
74	Jose Cruz Jr.	.05
75	Jason Dickson	.05
76	Jim Edmonds	.05
77	Scott Erickson	.05
78	Darin Erstad	.20
79	Alex Fernandez	.05
80	Steve Finley	.05
81	Travis Fryman	.05
82	Andres Galarraga	.05
83	Nomar Garciaparra	1.00
84	Tom Glavine	.35
85	Juan Gonzalez	.40
86	Mark Grace	.05
87	Willie Greene	.05
88	Ken Griffey Jr.	1.25
89	Vladimir Guerrero	.75
90	Tony Gwynn	1.00
91	Livan Hernandez	.05
92	Bobby Higginson	.05
93	Charles Johnson	.05
94	Derek Jeter	2.00
95	Randy Johnson	.75
96	Andruw Jones	.75
97	Chipper Jones	1.00
98	David Justice	.05
99	Eric Karros	.05
100	Jason Kendall	.05
101	Jimmy Key	.05
102	Darryl Kile	.05
103	Chuck Knoblauch	.05
104	Ray Lankford	.05
105	Barry Larkin	.05
106	Kenny Lofton	.05
107	Greg Maddux	1.00
108	Al Martin	.05
109	Edgar Martinez	.05
110	Pedro Martinez	.75
111	Ramon Martinez	.05
112	Tino Martinez	.05
113	Mark McGwire	1.50
114	Raul Mondesi	.05
115	Matt Morris	.05
116	Charles Nagy	.05
117	Denny Neagle	.05
118	Hideo Nomo	.40
119	Dean Palmer	.05
120	Andy Pettitte	.25
121	Mike Piazza	1.25
122	Manny Ramirez	.75
123	Edgar Renteria	.05
124	Cal Ripken Jr.	2.00
125	Alex Rodriguez	1.50
126	Henry Rodriguez	.05
127	Ivan Rodriguez	.65
128	Scott Rolen	.65
129	Tim Salmon	.35
130	Curt Schilling	.35
131	Gary Sheffield	.45
132	John Smoltz	.05
133	Sammy Sosa	1.00
134	Frank Thomas	.75
135	Jim Thome	.65
136	Mo Vaughn	.05
137	Robin Ventura	.05
138	Larry Walker	.05
139	Bernie Williams	.05
140	Matt Williams	.05
141	Jaret Wright	.05
142	Michael Coleman	.05
143	Juan Encarnacion	.05
144	Brad Fullmer	.05
145	Ben Grieve	.05
146	Todd Helton	.05
147	Paul Konerko	.20
148	Derek Lee	.50
149	Magglio Ordonez RC	1.50
150	Enrique Wilson	.05
---	Alex Rodriguez	1.00

Extra Edition

	NM/M
Common Extra Edition:	1.00
Extra Edition Stars:	6X

Production 500 Sets
(See 1998 Sports Illustrated Then & Now for checklist and base card values.)

Art of the Game

"Brooks"

		NM/M
Complete Set (8):		11.00
Common Player:		1.00
Inserted 1:9		
1	Ken Griffey Jr. It's Gone	1.50
2	Alex Rodriguez	2.00
3	Mike Piazza	1.50
4	Brooks Robinson	1.00
5	David Justice/AS	1.00
6	Cal Ripken Jr.	3.00
7	The Prospect and the Prospector	1.00
8	Barry Bonds	3.00

Autographs

Scott Rolen

	NM/M
Common Autograph:	15.00
Redemption Cards:	10 Percent
Bob Gibson/500	15.00
Tony Gwynn/250	35.00
Roger Clemens/250	120.00
Scott Rolen/150	20.00
Willie Mays/250	90.00
Harmon Killebrew/500	25.00

Covers

		NM/M
Complete Set (12):		22.00
Common Player:		1.00
Inserted 1:18		
1	Lou Brock (10/16/67)	1.00
2	Kirby Puckett (4/6/92)	2.50
3	Harmon Killebrew (4/8/63 - inside)	1.00
4	Eddie Mathews (8/16/54)	1.00
5	Willie Mays (5/22/72)	2.00
6	Frank Robinson (10/6/69)	1.00
7	Cal Ripken Jr. (9/11/95)	5.00
8	Roger Clemens (5/12/86)	2.50

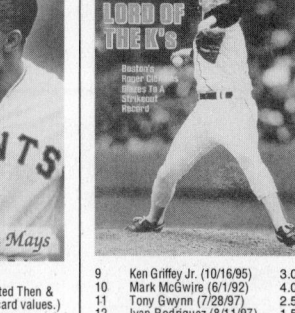

9	Ken Griffey Jr. (10/16/95)	3.00
10	Mark McGwire (6/1/92)	4.00
11	Tony Gwynn (7/28/97)	2.50
12	Ivan Rodriguez (8/11/97)	1.50

Great Shots!

		NM/M
Complete Set (25):		7.50
Common Player:		.10
Inserted 1:1		
1	Ken Griffey Jr.	.65
2	Frank Thomas	.45
3	Alex Rodriguez	.75
4	Andruw Jones	.45
5	Chipper Jones	.50
6	Cal Ripken Jr.	1.00
7	Mark McGwire	.75
8	Derek Jeter	1.00
9	Greg Maddux	.50
10	Jeff Bagwell	.45
11	Mike Piazza	.65
12	Scott Rolen	.35
13	Nomar Garciaparra	.50
14	Jose Cruz Jr.	.10
15	Charles Johnson	.10
16	Fergie Jenkins	.10
17	Lou Brock	.10
18	Bob Gibson	.10
19	Harmon Killebrew	.10
20	Juan Marichal	.10
21	Brooks Robinson	.10
22	Rod Carew	.10
23	Yogi Berra	.25
24	Willie Mays	.50
25	Kirby Puckett	.50

Road to Cooperstown

KEN GRIFFEY, JR.

		NM/M
Complete Set (10):		10.00
Common Player:		.75
Inserted 1:24		
1	Barry Bonds	2.50
2	Roger Clemens	1.25

3	Ken Griffey Jr.	1.50
4	Tony Gwynn	1.00
5	Rickey Henderson	.75
6	Greg Maddux	1.00
7	Paul Molitor	.75
8	Mike Piazza	1.50
9	Cal Ripken Jr.	2.50
10	Frank Thomas	.75

1998 Sports Illustrated

Vladimir Guerrero
Montreal Expos • OF

		NM/M
Complete Set (201):		20.00
Common Player:		.05
Pack (6):		1.50
Wax Box (24):		25.00
1	Edgardo Alfonzo	.05
2	Roberto Alomar	.20
3	Sandy Alomar	.05
4	Moises Alou	.05
5	Brady Anderson	.05
6	Garret Anderson	.05
7	Kevin Appier	.05
8	Jeff Bagwell	.75
9	Jay Bell	.05
10	Albert Belle	.05
11	Dante Bichette	.05
12	Craig Biggio	.05
13	Barry Bonds	2.00
14	Bobby Bonilla	.05
15	Kevin Brown	.05
16	Jay Buhner	.05
17	Ellis Burks	.05
18	Mike Cameron	.05
19	Ken Caminiti	.05
20	Jose Canseco	.45
21	Joe Carter	.05
22	Vinny Castilla	.05
23	Jeff Cirillo	.05
24	Tony Clark	.05
25	Will Clark	.05
26	Roger Clemens	1.00
27	David Cone	.05
28	Jose Cruz Jr.	.05
29	Carlos Delgado	.50
30	Jason Dickson	.05
31	Dennis Eckersley	.65
32	Jim Edmonds	.05
33	Scott Erickson	.05
34	Darin Erstad	.20
35	Shawn Estes	.05
36	Jeff Fassero	.05
37	Alex Fernandez	.05
38	Chuck Finley	.05
39	Steve Finley	.05
40	Travis Fryman	.05
41	Andres Galarraga	.05
42	Ron Gant	.05
43	Nomar Garciaparra	1.00
44	Jason Giambi	.50
45	Tom Glavine	.25
46	Juan Gonzalez	.40
47	Mark Grace	.05
48	Willie Green	.05
49	Rusty Greer	.05
50	Ben Grieve	.05
51	Ken Griffey Jr.	1.25
52	Mark Grudzielanek	.05
53	Vladimir Guerrero	.75
54	Juan Guzman	.05
55	Tony Gwynn	1.00
56	Joey Hamilton	.05
57	Rickey Henderson	.75
58	Pat Hentgen	.05
59	Livan Hernandez	.05
60	Bobby Higginson	.05
61	Todd Hundley	.05
62	Hideki Irabu	.05
63	John Jaha	.05
64	Derek Jeter	2.00
65	Charles Johnson	.05
66	Randy Johnson	.75
67	Andruw Jones	.75
68	Bobby Jones	.05
69	Chipper Jones	1.00
70	Brian Jordan	.05
71	David Justice	.05
72	Eric Karros	.05
73	Jeff Kent	.05
74	Jimmy Key	.05
75	Darryl Kile	.05
76	Jeff King	.05

77	Ryan Klesko	.05
78	Chuck Knoblauch	.05
79	Ray Lankford	.05
80	Barry Larkin	.05
81	Kenny Lofton	.05
82	Greg Maddux	1.00
83	Al Martin	.05
84	Edgar Martinez	.05
85	Pedro Martinez	.75
86	Tino Martinez	.05
87	Mark McGwire	1.50
88	Paul Molitor	.75
89	Raul Mondesi	.05
90	Jamie Moyer	.05
91	Mike Mussina	.30
92	Tim Naehring	.05
93	Charles Nagy	.05
94	Denny Neagle	.05
95	Dave Nilsson	.05
96	Hideo Nomo	.40
97	Rey Ordonez	.05
98	Dean Palmer	.05
99	Rafael Palmeiro	.65
100	Andy Pettitte	.30
101	Mike Piazza	1.25
102	Brad Radke	.05
103	Manny Ramirez	.75
104	Edgar Renteria	.05
105	Cal Ripken Jr.	2.00
106	Alex Rodriguez	1.50
106p	Alex Rodriguez/OPS	1.50
107	Henry Rodriguez	.05
108	Ivan Rodriguez	.65
109	Scott Rolen	.65
110	Tim Salmon	.35
111	Curt Schilling	.45
112	Gary Sheffield	.45
113	John Smoltz	.05
114	J.T. Snow	.05
115	Sammy Sosa	1.00
116	Matt Stairs	.05
117	Shannon Stewart	.05
118	Frank Thomas	.75
119	Jim Thome	.65
120	Justin Thompson	.05
121	Mo Vaughn	.05
122	Robin Ventura	.05
123	Larry Walker	.05
124	Rondell White	.05
125	Bernie Williams	.05
126	Matt Williams	.05
127	Tony Womack	.05
128	Jaret Wright	.05
129	Edgar Renteria	.05
130	Kenny Lofton	.05
131	Tony Gwynn	.50
132	Mark McGwire	.75
133	Craig Biggio	.05
134	Charles Johnson	.05
135	J.T. Snow	.05
136	Ken Caminiti	.05
137	Vladimir Guerrero	.40
138	Jim Edmonds	.05
139	Randy Johnson	.05
140	Darryl Kile	.05
141	John Smoltz	.05
142	Greg Maddux	.50
143	Andy Pettitte	.05
144	Ken Griffey Jr.	.65
145	Mike Piazza	.65
146	Todd Greene	.05
147	Vinny Castilla	.05
148	Derek Jeter	1.00
149	Robert Machado	.05
150	Mike Gulan	.05
151	Randall Simon	.05
152	Michael Coleman	.05
153	Brian Rose	.05
154	Scott Eyre **RC**	.05
155	Magglio Ordonez **RC**	1.50
156	Todd Helton	.65
157	Juan Encarnacion	.05
158	Mark Kotsay	.05
159	Josh Booty	.05
160	Melvin Rosario **RC**	.05
161	Shane Halter	.05
162	Paul Konerko	.25
163	Henry Blanco **RC**	.05
164	Antone Williamson	.05
165	Brad Fullmer	.05
166	Ricky Ledee	.05
167	Ben Grieve	.05
168	Frank Catalanotto **RC**	.25
169	Bobby Estalella	.05
170	Dennis Reyes	.05
171	Kevin Polcovich	.05
172	Jacob Cruz	.05
173	Ken Cloude	.05
174	Eli Marrero	.05
175	Fernando Tatis	.05
176	Tom Evans	.05
177	Carl Everett,	.05
	Nomar Garciaparra	.35
178	Eric Davis	.05
179	Roger Clemens	.60
180	Brett Butler, Eddie Murray	.30
181	Frank Thomas	.45
182	Curt Schilling	.15
183	Jeff Bagwell	.40
184	Mark McGwire,	
	Ken Griffey Jr.	.75
185	Kevin Brown	.05
186	Marty Cordova,	
	Ricardo Rincon	.05
187	Charles Johnson	.05

188	Hideki Irabu	.05
189	Tony Gwynn	.50
190	Sandy Alomar	.05
191	Ken Griffey Jr.	.65
192	Larry Walker	.05
193	Roger Clemens	.60
194	Pedro Martinez	.40
195	Nomar Garciaparra	.60
196	Scott Rolen	.40
197	Brian Anderson	.05
198	Tony Saunders	.05
199	Florida Celebration	.05
200	Livan Hernandez	.05
201	Travis Lee/SP	2.00

Extra Edition

Common Player:	2.00
Extra Edition Stars:	8X

(See 1998 Sports Illustrated for checklist and base card values.)

Autographs

	NM/M
Common Player:	7.50
Lou Brock/500	40.00
Jose Cruz Jr./250	10.00
Rollie Fingers/500	10.00
Ben Grieve/250 (Exchange Card)	3.00
Ben Grieve (Signed Card)	7.50
Paul Konerko/250 (Exchange Card)	3.00
Paul Konerko (Signed Card)	20.00
Brooks Robinson/250	50.00

Covers

		NM/M
Complete Set (10):		15.00
Common Player:		1.00
Inserted 1:9		
1	Ken Griffey Jr., Mike Piazza	2.00
2	Derek Jeter	3.00
3	Ken Griffey Jr.	2.50
4	Cal Ripken Jr.	3.00
5	Manny Ramirez	1.50
6	Jay Buhner	1.00
7	Matt Williams	1.00
8	Randy Johnson	1.50
9	Deion Sanders	1.00
10	Jose Canseco	1.50

Editor's Choice

	NM/M
Complete Set (10):	20.00

EDITOR'S CHOICE

Nomar GARCIAPARRA

Common Player:		1.00
Inserted 1:24		
1	Ken Griffey Jr.	3.00
2	Alex Rodriguez	4.00
3	Frank Thomas	1.50
4	Mark McGwire	4.00
5	Greg Maddux	2.00
6	Derek Jeter	5.00
7	Cal Ripken Jr.	5.00
8	Nomar Garciaparra	2.50
9	Jeff Bagwell	1.50
10	Jose Cruz Jr.	1.00

Mini-Posters

		NM/M
Complete Set (30):		8.00
Common Player:		.10
Inserted 1:1		
1	Tim Salmon	.10
2	Travis Lee	.10
3	John Smoltz, Greg Maddux	.50
4	Cal Ripken Jr.	1.00
5	Nomar Garciaparra	.50
6	Sammy Sosa	.50
7	Frank Thomas	.45
8	Barry Larkin	.10
9	David Justice	.10
10	Larry Walker	.10
11	Tony Clark	.10
12	Livan Hernandez	.10
13	Jeff Bagwell	.45
14	Kevin Appier	.10
15	Mike Piazza	.65
16	Fernando Vina	.10
17	Chuck Knoblauch	.10
18	Vladimir Guerrero	.45
19	Rey Ordonez	.10
20	Bernie Williams	.10
21	Matt Stairs	.10
22	Curt Schilling	.30
23	Tony Womack	.10
24	Mark McGwire	.75
25	Tony Gwynn	.50
26	Barry Bonds	1.00
27	Ken Griffey Jr.	.65
28	Fred McGriff	.10
29	Juan Gonzalez, Alex Rodriguez	.50
30	Roger Clemens	.60

1998 Sports Illustrated World Series Fever

		NM/M
Complete Set (150):		10.00
Common Player:		.05
Pack (6):		1.00
Wax Box (24):		17.50
1	Mickey Mantle	1.50
2	1957 World Series Preview	.15
3	1958 World Series Preview	.15
4	1959 World Series Preview	.15
5	1962 World Series	.10
6	Lou Brock	.10
7	Brooks Robinson	.25
8	Frank Robinson	.25
9	1974 World Series	.10
10	Reggie Jackson	.60
11	1985 World Series	.10

ANDRUW JONES OUTFIELD

12	1987 World Series	.10
13	Orel Hershiser	.05
14	Rickey Henderson	.40
15	1991 World Series	.10
16	1992 World Series	.05
17	Joe Carter	.05
18	1995 World Series	.10
19	1996 World Series	.15
20	Edgar Renteria	.05
21	Bill Mazeroski	.15
22	Joe Carter	.05
23	Carlton Fisk	.40
24	Bucky Dent	.15
25	Mookie Wilson	.05
26	Enos Slaughter	.05
27	Mickey Lolich	.05
28	Bobby Richardson	.05
29	Kirk Gibson	.05
30	Edgar Renteria	.05
31	Albert Belle	.05
32	Kevin Brown	.05
33	Brian Rose	.05
34	Ron Gant	.05
35	Jeromy Burnitz	.05
36	Andres Galarraga	.05
37	Jim Edmonds	.05
38	Jose Cruz Jr.	.05
39	Mark Grudzielanek	.05
40	Shawn Estes	.05
41	Mark Grace	.05
42	Nomar Garciaparra	.50
43	Juan Gonzalez	.20
44	Tom Glavine	.25
45	Brady Anderson	.05
46	Tony Clark	.05
47	Jeff Cirillo	.05
48	Dante Bichette	.05
49	Ben Grieve	.05
50	Ken Griffey Jr.	.65
51	Edgardo Alfonzo	.05
52	Roger Clemens	.60
53	Pat Hentgen	.05
54	Todd Helton	.30
55	Andy Benes	.05
56	Tony Gwynn	.50
57	Andruw Jones	.40
58	Bobby Higginson	.05
59	Bobby Jones	.05
60	Darryl Kile	.05
61	Chan Ho Park	.05
62	Charles Johnson	.05
63	Rusty Greer	.05
64	Travis Fryman	.05
65	Derek Jeter	1.00
66	Jay Buhner	.05
67	Chuck Knoblauch	.05
68	David Justice	.05
69	Brian Hunter	.05
70	Eric Karros	.05
71	Edgar Martinez	.05
72	Chipper Jones	.50
73	Barry Larkin	.05
74	Mike Lansing	.05
75	Craig Biggio	.05
76	Al Martin	.05
77	Barry Bonds	1.00
78	Randy Johnson	.40
79	Ryan Klesko	.05
80	Mark McGwire	.75
81	Fred McGriff	.05
82	Javy Lopez	.05
83	Kenny Lofton	.05
84	Sandy Alomar Jr.	.05
85	Matt Morris	.05
86	Paul Konerko	.10
87	Ray Lankford	.05
88	Kerry Wood	.30
89	Roberto Alomar	.20
90	Greg Maddux	.50
91	Travis Lee	.05
92	Moises Alou	.05
93	Dean Palmer	.05
94	Hideo Nomo	.20
95	Ken Caminiti	.05
96	Pedro Martinez	.40
97	Raul Mondesi	.05
98	Denny Neagle	.05
99	Tino Martinez	.05
100	Mike Mussina	.20
101	Kevin Appier	.05
102	Vinny Castilla	.05
103	Jeff Bagwell	.40
104	Paul O'Neill	.05
105	Rey Ordonez	.05
106	Vladimir Guerrero	.40
107	Rafael Palmeiro	.35
108	Alex Rodriguez	.75
109	Andy Pettitte	.15
110	Carl Pavano	.05
111	Henry Rodriguez	.05
112	Gary Sheffield	.40
113	Curt Schilling	.25
114	John Smoltz	.05
115	Reggie Sanders	.05
116	Scott Rolen	.35
117	Mike Piazza	.65
118	Manny Ramirez	.40
119	Cal Ripken Jr.	1.00
120	Brad Radke	.05
121	Tim Salmon	.05
122	Brett Tomko	.05
123	Robin Ventura	.05
124	Mo Vaughn	.05
125	A.J. Hinch	.05
126	Derek Lee	.45
127	Orlando Hernandez RC	.40
128	Aramis Ramirez	.05
129	Frank Thomas	.40
130	J.T. Snow	.05
131	Magglio Ordonez RC	1.00
132	Bobby Bonilla	.05
133	Marquis Grissom	.05
134	Jim Thome	.45
135	Justin Thompson	.05
136	Matt Williams	.05
137	Matt Stairs	.05
138	Wade Boggs	.50
139	Chuck Finley	.05
140	Jaret Wright	.05
141	Ivan Rodriguez	.35
142	Brad Fullmer	.05
143	Bernie Williams	.05
144	Jason Giambi	.30
145	Larry Walker	.05
146	Tony Womack	.05
147	Sammy Sosa	.50
148	Rondell White	.05
149	Todd Stottlemyre	.05
150	Shane Reynolds	.05

Extra Edition

TINO MARTINEZ FIRST BASE

	NM/M
Common EE Player:	2.00
EE Stars:	15X
Production:	98 Sets
Common FE Player:	100.00
FE Stars:	Values Undetermined
1 of 1	

(See 1998 Sports Illustrated World Series Fever for checklist and base values.)

Autumn Excellence

	NM/M
Complete Set (10):	15.00
Common Player:	.50
Inserted 1:24	
Golds:	2X
Inserted 1:240	
AE1 Willie Mays	2.50

AE2	Kirby Puckett	2.00
AE3	Babe Ruth	4.00
AE4	Reggie Jackson	1.50
AE5	Whitey Ford	.50
AE6	Lou Brock	.50
AE7	Mickey Mantle	4.00
AE8	Yogi Berra	.75
AE9	Bob Gibson	.50
AE10	Don Larsen	1.00

MVP Collection

		NM/M
Complete Set (10):		1.00
Common Player:		.10
Inserted 1:4		
1	Frank Robinson	.25
2	Brooks Robinson	.25
3	Willie Stargell	.10
4	Bret Saberhagen	.10
5	Rollie Fingers	.10
6	Orel Hershiser	.10
7	Paul Molitor	.50
8	Tom Glavine	.15
9	John Wetteland	.10
10	Livan Hernandez	.10

Reggie Jackson Picks

		NM/M
Complete Set (15):		12.50
Common Player:		.25
Inserted 1:12		
1	Paul O'Neill	.25
2	Barry Bonds	2.50
3	Ken Griffey Jr.	1.50
4	Juan Gonzalez	.40
5	Greg Maddux	1.00
6	Mike Piazza	1.50
7	Larry Walker	.25
8	Mo Vaughn	.25
9	Roger Clemens	1.25
10	John Smoltz	.25
11	Alex Rodriguez	2.00
12	Frank Thomas	.75
13	Mark McGwire	2.00
14	Jeff Bagwell	.75
15	Roger Johnson	.75

1999 Sports Illustrated

		NM/M
Complete Set (180):		15.00
Common Player:		.05
Wax Pack (6):		1.00
Hobby Box (24):		15.00
Retail Box (16):		10.00
1	Yankees	.25
2	Scott Brosius	.05
3	David Wells	.05
4	Sterling Hitchcock	.05
5	David Justice	.05
6	David Cone	.05
7	Greg Maddux	.50
8	Jim Leyritz	.05
9	Gary Gaetti	.05
10	Mark McGwire	.75
11	Sammy Sosa	.50
12	Larry Walker	.05
13	Tony Womack	.05

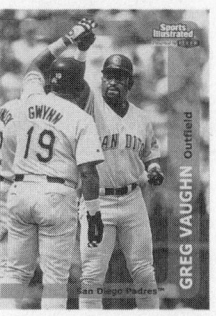

GREG VAUGHN — Outfield — San Diego Padres

14	Tom Glavine	.10
15	Curt Schilling	.10
16	Greg Maddux	.50
17	Trevor Hoffman	.05
18	Kerry Wood	.20
19	Tom Glavine	.10
20	Sammy Sosa	.50
21	Travis Lee	.05
22	Roberto Alomar	.05
23	Roger Clemens	.60
24	Barry Bonds	1.00
25	Paul Molitor	.45
26	Todd Stottlemyre	.05
27	Chris Hoiles	.05
28	Albert Belle	.05
29	Tony Clark	.05
30	Kerry Wood	.05
31	David Wells	.05
32	Dennis Eckersley	.40
33	Mark McGwire	.75
34	Cal Ripken Jr.	1.00
35	Ken Griffey Jr.	.65
36	Alex Rodriguez	.75
37	Craig Biggio	.05
38	Sammy Sosa	.50
39	Dennis Martinez	.05
40	Curt Schilling	.10
41	Orlando Hernandez	.05
42	Troy Glaus, Ben Molina, Todd Greene	.45
43	Mitch Meluskey, Daryle Ward, Mike Grzanich	.05
44	Eric Chavez, Mike Neill, Steve Connelly RC	.10
45	Roy Halladay, Tom Evans, Kevin Witt	.05
46	George Lombard, Adam Butler, Bruce Chen	.05
47	Ronnie Belliard, Valerio de los Santos, Rafael Roque RC	.05
48	J.D. Drew, Placido Polanco, Mark Little RC	.50
49	Jason Maxwell, Jose Nieves, Jeremi Gonzalez	.05
50	Scott McClain, Kerry Robinson, Mike Duvall RC	.05
51	Ben Ford, Bryan Corey, Danny Klassen	.05
52	Angel Pena, Jeff Kubenka, Paul LoDuca	.05
53	Kirk Bullinger, Fernando Seguignol, Tim Young	.05
54	Ramon Martinez, Wilson Delgado, Armando Rios	.05
55	Russ Branyon, Jolbert Cabrera, Jason Rakers	.05
56	Carlos Guillen, David Holdridge, Giomar Guevara RC	.10
57	Alex Gonzalez, Joe Fontenot, Preston Wilson	.05
58	Mike Kinkade, Jay Payton, Masato Yoshii	.05
59	Willis Otanez, Ryan Minor, Calvin Pickering	.05
60	Ben Davis, Matt Clement, Stan Spencer	.05
61	Marlon Anderson, Mike Welch, Gary Bennett RC	.05
62	Abraham Nunez, Sean Lawrence, Aramis Ramirez	.05
63	Jonathan Johnson, Rob Sasser, Scott Sheldon RC	.05
64	Keith Glauber, Guillermo Garcia, Eddie Priest	.05
65	Brian Barkley, Jin Ho Cho, Donnie Sadler	.05
66	Derrick Gibson, Mark Strittmatter, Edgard Clemente RC	.05
67	Jeremy Giambi, Dermal Brown, Chris Hatcher RC	.05
68	Rob Fick, Gabe Kapler, Marino Santana	.10
69	Corey Koskie, A.J. Pierzynski, Benj Sampson	.05
70	Brian Simmons, Mark Johnson, Craig Wilson	.05
71	Ryan Bradley, Mike Lowell, Jay Tessmer	.05
72	Ben Grieve	.05
73	Shawn Green	.45
74	Rafael Palmeiro	.65
75	Juan Gonzalez	.40
76	Mike Piazza	1.25
77	Devon White	.05
78	Jim Thome	.65
79	Barry Larkin	.65
80	Scott Rolen	.65
81	Raul Mondesi	.05
82	Jason Giambi	.50
83	Jose Canseco	.45
84	Tony Gwynn	1.00
85	Cal Ripken Jr.	2.00
86	Andy Pettitte	.15
87	Carlos Delgado	.50
88	Jeff Cirillo	.05
89	Bret Saberhagen	.05
90	John Olerud	.05
91	Ron Coomer	.05
92	Todd Helton	.65
93	Ray Lankford	.05
94	Tim Salmon	.05
95	Fred McGriff	.05
96	Matt Stairs	.05
97	Ken Griffey Jr.	1.25
98	Chipper Jones	1.00
99	Mark Grace	.05
100	Ivan Rodriguez	.65
101	Jeromy Burnitz	.05
102	Kenny Rogers	.05
103	Kevin Millwood	.05
104	Vinny Castilla	.05
105	Jim Edmonds	.05
106	Craig Biggio	.05
107	Andres Galarraga	.05
108	Sammy Sosa	1.00
109	Juan Encarnacion	.05
110	Larry Walker	.05
111	John Smoltz	.05
112	Randy Johnson	.75
113	Bobby Higginson	.05
114	Albert Belle	.05
115	Jaret Wright	.05
116	Edgar Renteria	.05
117	Andruw Jones	.75
118	Barry Bonds	2.00
119	Rondell White	.05
120	Jamie Moyer	.05
121	Darin Erstad	.20
122	Al Leiter	.05
123	Mark McGwire	1.50
124	Mo Vaughn	.05
125	Livan Hernandez	.05
126	Jason Kendall	.05
127	Frank Thomas	.75
128	Denny Neagle	.05
129	Johnny Damon	.35
130	Derek Bell	.05
131	Jeff Kent	.05
132	Tony Womack	.05
133	Trevor Hoffman	.05
134	Gary Sheffield	.40
135	Tino Martinez	.05
136	Travis Fryman	.05
137	Rolando Arrojo	.05
138	Dante Bichette	.05
139	Nomar Garciaparra	1.00
140	Moises Alou	.05
141	Chuck Knoblauch	.05
142	Robin Ventura	.05
143	Scott Erickson	.05
144	David Cone	.05
145	Greg Vaughn	.05
146	Wade Boggs	1.00
147	Mike Mussina	.30
148	Tony Clark	.05
149	Alex Rodriguez	1.50
150	Javy Lopez	.05
151	Bartolo Colon	.05
152	Derek Jeter	2.00
153	Greg Maddux	1.00
154	Ken Brown	.05
155	Curt Schilling	.35
156	Jeff King	.05
157	Bernie Williams	.05
158	Roberto Alomar	.20
159	Travis Lee	.05
160	Kerry Wood	.50
160p	Kerry Wood/OPS	1.00
161	Jeff Bagwell	.75
162	Roger Clemens	1.00
163	Matt Williams	.05
164	Chan Ho Park	.05
165	Damion Easley	.05
166	Manny Ramirez	.75
167	Quinton McCracken	.05
168	Todd Walker	.05
169	Eric Karros	.05
170	Will Clark	.05
171	Edgar Martinez	.05
172	Cliff Floyd	.05
173	Vladimir Guerrero	.75
174	Tom Glavine	.35
175	Pedro Martinez	.75
176	Chuck Finley	.05
177	Dean Palmer	.05
178	Omar Vizquel	.05
179	Checklist	.05
180	Checklist	.05

Diamond Dominators

	NM/M
Complete Set (10):	30.00
Common Player:	1.50
Pitchers inserted 1:90	

Hitters inserted 1:180

1DD	Kerry Wood	1.50
2DD	Roger Clemens	3.00
3DD	Randy Johnson	2.00
4DD	Greg Maddux	2.50
5DD	Pedro Martinez	2.00
6DD	Ken Griffey Jr.	5.00
7DD	Sammy Sosa	2.50
8DD	Nomar Garciaparra	2.50
9DD	Mark McGwire	6.00
10DD	Alex Rodriguez	6.00

Fabulous 40s

		NM/M
Complete Set (13):		9.00
Common Player:		.25
Inserted 1:20		
1FF	Mark McGwire	2.00
2FF	Sammy Sosa	1.25
3FF	Ken Griffey Jr.	1.50
4FF	Greg Vaughn	.25
5FF	Albert Belle	.25
6FF	Jose Canseco	.50
7FF	Vinny Castilla	.25
8FF	Juan Gonzalez	.50
9FF	Manny Ramirez	1.00
10FF	Andres Galarraga	.25
11FF	Rafael Palmeiro	.75
12FF	Alex Rodriguez	2.00
13FF	Mo Vaughn	.25

Fabulous 40s Extra

		NM/M
Common Player:		12.00
Numbered to amount of HRs.		
1FF	Mark McGwire/70	60.00
2FF	Sammy Sosa/66	40.00
3FF	Ken Griffey Jr./56	35.00
4FF	Greg Vaughn/50	12.00
5FF	Albert Belle/49	12.00
6FF	Jose Canseco/46	25.00
7FF	Vinny Castilla/46	12.00
8FF	Juan Gonzalez/45	20.00
9FF	Manny Ramirez/45	30.00

10FF	Andres Galarraga/44	12.00
11FF	Rafael Palmeiro/43	25.00
12FF	Alex Rodriguez/42	45.00
13FF	Mo Vaughn/40	12.00

Headliners

		NM/M
Complete Set (25):		10.00
Common Player:		.25
Inserted 1:4		
1H	Vladimir Guerrero	.40
2H	Randy Johnson	.40
3H	Mo Vaughn	.25
4H	Chipper Jones	.50
5H	Jeff Bagwell	.40
6H	Juan Gonzalez	.30
7H	Mark McGwire	.75
8H	Cal Ripken Jr.	1.00
9H	Frank Thomas	.40
10H	Manny Ramirez	.40
11H	Ken Griffey Jr.	.65
12H	Scott Rolen	.35
13H	Alex Rodriguez	.75
14H	Barry Bonds	1.00
15H	Roger Clemens	.55
16H	Darin Erstad	.30
17H	Nomar Garciaparra	.50
18H	Mike Piazza	.65
19H	Greg Maddux	.50
20H	Ivan Rodriguez	.35
21H	Derek Jeter	1.00
22H	Sammy Sosa	.50
23H	Andruw Jones	.40
24H	Pedro Martinez	.40
25H	Kerry Wood	.35

Ones To Watch

		NM/M
Complete Set (15):		5.00
Common Player:		.25
Inserted 1:12		
10W	J.D. Drew	.65
20W	Marlon Anderson	.25
30W	Roy Halladay	.35
40W	Ben Grieve	.25
50W	Todd Helton	.75
60W	Gabe Kapler	.25
70W	Troy Glaus	.75
80W	Ben Davis	.25
90W	Eric Chavez	.35
100W	Richie Sexson	.25
110W	Fernando Seguignol	.25
120W	Kerry Wood	.50
130W	Bobby Smith	.25
140W	Ryan Minor	.25
150W	Jeremy Giambi	.25
	J.D. Drew/Auto./250	15.00

1999 Sports Illustrated Greats of the Game

		NM/M
Complete Set (90):		12.00
Common Player:		.05
Pack (7):		15.00
Wax Box (12):		150.00
1	Jimmie Foxx	.25
2	Red Schoendienst	.05
3	Babe Ruth	3.00
4	Lou Gehrig	2.00
5	Mel Ott	.05
6	Stan Musial	.25
7	Mickey Mantle	3.00
8	Carl Yastrzemski	.15
9	Enos Slaughter	.05
10	Andre Dawson	.05
11	Luis Aparicio	.05
12	Ferguson Jenkins	.05
13	Christy Mathewson	.25
14	Ernie Banks	.15
15	Johnny Podres	.05
16	George Foster	.05
17	Jerry Koosman	.05
18	Curt Simmons	.05
19	Bob Feller	.05
20	Frank Robinson	.05
21	Gary Carter	.05
22	Frank Thomas	.05
23	Bill Lee	.05
24	Willie Mays	1.00
25	Tommie Agee	.05
26	Boog Powell	.05
27	Jimmy Wynn	.05
28	Sparky Lyle	.05
29	Bo Belinsky	.05
30	Maury Wills	.05
31	Bill Buckner	.05
32	Steve Carlton	.05
33	Harmon Killebrew	.05
34	Nolan Ryan	1.00
35	Randy Jones	.05
36	Robin Roberts	.05
37	Al Oliver	.05
38	Rico Petrocelli	.05
39	Dave Parker	.05
40	Eddie Mathews	.05
41	Earl Weaver	.05
42	Jackie Robinson	1.50
43	Lou Brock	.05
44	Reggie Jackson	.15
45	Bob Gibson	.05
46	Jeff Burroughs	.05
47	Jim Bouton	.05
48	Bob Forsch	.05
49	Ron Guidry	.05
50	Ty Cobb	2.00
51	Roy White	.05
52	Joe Rudi	.05
53	Moose Skowron	.05
54	Goose Gossage	.05
55	Ed Kranepool	.05
56	Paul Blair	.05
57	Kent Hrbek	.05
58	Orlando Cepeda	.05
59	Buck O'Neil	.05
60	Al Kaline	.05
61	Vida Blue	.05
62	Sam McDowell	.05
63	Jesse Barfield	.05
64	Dave Kingman	.05
65	Ron Santo	.05
66	Steve Garvey	.05
67	Gaylord Perry	.05
68	Darrell Evans	.05
69	Rollie Fingers	.05
70	Walter Johnson	.25
71	Al Hrabosky	.05
72	Mickey Rivers	.05
73	Mike Torrez	.05
74	Hank Bauer	.05
75	Tug McGraw	.05
76	David Clyde	.05
77	Jim Lonborg	.05
78	Clete Boyer	.05
79	Harry Walker	.05
80	Cy Young	.25
81	Bud Harrelson	.05
82	Paul Splittorff	.05
83	Bert Campaneris	.05
84	Joe Niekro	.05
85	Bob Horner	.05
86	Jerry Royster	.05
87	Tommy John	.05
88	Mark Fidrych	.05
89	Dick Williams	.05
90	Graig Nettles	.05

Autographs

		NM/M
Common Player:		4.00
Inserted 1:1		
(1)	Tommie Agee	8.00
(2)	Luis Aparicio	12.00
(3)	Ernie Banks	25.00
(4)	Jesse Barfield	6.00
(5)	Hank Bauer	10.00
(6)	Bo Belinsky	6.00
(7)	Paul Blair	6.00
(8)	Vida Blue	10.00
(9)	Jim Bouton	10.00
(10)	Clete Boyer	10.00
(11)	Lou Brock	15.00
(12)	Bill Buckner	10.00
(13)	Jeff Burroughs	5.00
(14)	Bert Campaneris	8.00
(15)	Steve Carlton	20.00
(16)	Gary Carter	10.00
(17)	Orlando Cepeda	12.00
(18)	David Clyde	5.00
(19)	Andre Dawson	10.00
(20)	Darrell Evans	8.00
(21)	Bob Feller	15.00
(22)	Mark Fidrych	15.00
(23)	Rollie Fingers	10.00
(24)	Bob Forsch	6.00
(25)	George Foster	10.00
(26)	Steve Garvey	15.00
(27)	Bob Gibson	15.00
(28)	Goose Gossage	10.00
(29)	Ron Guidry	20.00
(30)	Bud Harrelson	10.00
(31)	Bob Horner	10.00
(32)	Al Hrabosky	8.00
(33)	Kent Hrbek	10.00
(34a)	Reggie Jackson	150.00
(34b)	Reggie Jackson ("Mr. October")	200.00
(34c)	Reggie Jackson ("HoF 93")	200.00
(35)	Ferguson Jenkins	10.00
(36)	Tommy John	8.00
(37)	Randy Jones	4.00
(38)	Al Kaline	25.00
(39)	Harmon Killebrew	25.00
(40)	Dave Kingman	8.00
(41)	Jerry Koosman	8.00
(42)	Ed Kranepool	8.00
(43)	Bill Lee	10.00
(44)	Jim Lonborg	5.00
(45)	Sparky Lyle	8.00
(46)	Eddie Mathews	60.00
(47)	Willie Mays	125.00
(48)	Sam McDowell	8.00
(49)	Tug McGraw	25.00
(50)	Stan Musial	100.00
(51)	Graig Nettles	10.00
(52)	Joe Niekro	8.00
(53)	Buck O'Neil	20.00
(54)	Al Oliver	10.00
(55)	Dave Parker	10.00
(56)	Gaylord Perry	10.00
(57)	Rico Petrocelli	10.00
(58)	Johnny Podres	20.00
(59)	Boog Powell	10.00
(60)	Mickey Rivers	8.00
(61)	Robin Roberts	20.00
(62)	Frank Robinson	20.00
(63)	Jerry Royster	4.00
(64)	Joe Rudi	8.00
(65)	Nolan Ryan	200.00
(66)	Ron Santo	15.00
(67)	Red Schoendienst	12.00
(68)	Curt Simmons	6.00
(69)	Moose Skowron	15.00
(70)	Enos Slaughter	20.00
(71)	Paul Splittorff	6.00
(72)	Frank Thomas	8.00
(73)	Mike Torrez	4.00
(74)	Harry Walker	4.00
(75)	Earl Weaver	10.00
(76)	Roy White	8.00
(77)	Dick Williams	10.00
(78)	Maury Wills	10.00
(79)	Jimmy Wynn	10.00
(80)	Carl Yastrzemski	50.00

Collection

		NM/M
Complete Set (50):		25.00
Common Player:		.50
Inserted 1:1		
1	Johnny Podres	.50
2	Mickey Mantle	5.00
3	Stan Musial	.50
4	Eddie Mathews	.50
5	Frank Thomas	.50
6	Willie Mays	1.00
7	Red Schoendienst	.50
8	Luis Aparicio	.50
9	Mickey Mantle	3.00
10	Al Kaline	.50
11	Maury Wills	.50
12	Sam McDowell	.50
13	Harry Walker	.50
14	Carl Yastrzemski	.50
15	Carl Yastrzemski	.50
16	Lou Brock	.50
17	Ron Santo	.50
18	Reggie Jackson	.50
19	Frank Robinson	.50
20	Jerry Koosman	.50
21	Bud Harrelson	.50
22	Vida Blue	.50
23	Ferguson Jenkins	.50
24	Sparky Lyle	.50
25	Steve Carlton	.50
26	Bert Campaneris	.50
27	Jimmy Wynn	.50
28	Steve Garvey	.50
29	Nolan Ryan	1.00
30	Randy Jones	.50
31	Reggie Jackson	.50
32	Joe Rudi	.50
33	Reggie Jackson	.50
34	Dave Parker	.50
35	Mark Fidrych	.50
36	Earl Weaver	.50
37	Nolan Ryan	1.00
38	Steve Carlton	.50
39	Reggie Jackson	.50
40	Rollie Fingers	.50
41	Gary Carter	.50
42	Graig Nettles	.50
43	Gaylord Perry	.50
44	Kent Hrbek	.50
45	Gary Carter	.50
46	Steve Garvey	.50
47	Steve Carlton	.50
48	Nolan Ryan	1.00
49	Nolan Ryan	1.00
50	Mickey Mantle	3.00

Breakers

		NM/M
Complete Set (10):		40.00
Common Player:		2.00
Inserted 1:12		
Golds:		6X
Inserted 1:120		
1	Mickey Mantle	8.00
2	Stan Musial	3.50
3	Babe Ruth	8.00

4	Christy Mathewson	2.00
5	Cy Young	2.00
6	Nolan Ryan	7.50
7	Jackie Robinson	6.00
8	Lou Gehrig	7.00
9	Ty Cobb	3.50
10	Walter Johnson	2.00

1991 Stadium Club

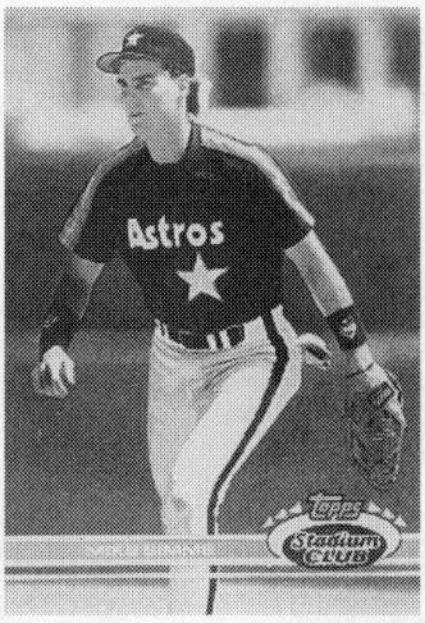

		NM/M
Complete Set (600):		20.00
Common Player:		.05
Series 1 or 2 Pack (13):		.60
Series 1 or 2 Box (36):		15.00
1	Dave Stewart	.05
2	Wally Joyner	.05
3	Shawon Dunston	.05
4	Darren Daulton	.05
5	Will Clark	.05
6	Sammy Sosa	1.00
7	Dan Plesac	.05
8	Marquis Grissom	.05
9	Erik Hanson	.05
10	Geno Petralli	.05
11	Jose Rijo	.05
12	Carlos Quintana	.05
13	Junior Ortiz	.05
14	Bob Walk	.05
15	Mike Macfarlane	.05
16	Eric Yelding	.05
17	Bryn Smith	.05
18	Bip Roberts	.05
19	Mike Scioscia	.05
20	Mark Williamson	.05
21	Don Mattingly	1.00
22	John Franco	.05
23	Chet Lemon	.05
24	Tom Henke	.05
25	Jerry Browne	.05
26	Dave Justice	.05
27	Mark Langston	.05
28	Damon Berryhill	.05
29	Kevin Bass	.05
30	Scott Fletcher	.05
31	Moises Alou	.05
32	Dave Valle	.05
33	Jody Reed	.05
34	Dave West	.05
35	Kevin McReynolds	.05
36	Pat Combs	.05
37	Eric Davis	.05
38	Bret Saberhagen	.05
39	Stan Javier	.05
40	Chuck Cary	.05
41	Tony Phillips	.05
42	Lee Smith	.05
43	Tim Teufel	.05
44	Lance Dickson	.05
45	Greg Litton	.05
46	Teddy Higuera	.05
47	Edgar Martinez	.05
48	Steve Avery	.05
49	Walt Weiss	.05
50	David Segui	.05
51	Andy Benes	.05
52	Karl Rhodes	.05
53	Neal Heaton	.05
54	Dan Gladden	.05
55	Luis Rivera	.05
56	Kevin Brown	.05
57	Frank Thomas	.75
58	Terry Mulholland	.05
59	Dick Schofield	.05
60	Ron Darling	.05
61	Sandy Alomar, Jr.	.05
62	Dave Stieb	.05
63	Alan Trammell	.05
64	Matt Nokes	.05
65	Lenny Harris	.05
66	Milt Thompson	.05
67	Storm Davis	.05
68	Joe Oliver	.05
69	Andres Galarraga	.05
70	Ozzie Guillen	.05
71	Ken Howell	.05
72	Garry Templeton	.05
73	Derrick May	.05
74	Xavier Hernandez	.05
75	Dave Parker	.05
76	Rick Aguilera	.05
77	Robby Thompson	.05
78	Pete Incaviglia	.05
79	Bob Welch	.05
80	Randy Milligan	.05
81	Chuck Finley	.05
82	Alvin Davis	.05
83	Tim Naehring	.05
84	Jay Bell	.05
85	Joe Magrane	.05
86	Howard Johnson	.05
87	Jack McDowell	.05
88	Kevin Seitzer	.05
89	Bruce Ruffin	.05
90	Fernando Valenzuela	.05
91	Terry Kennedy	.05
92	Barry Larkin	.05
93	Larry Walker	.05
94	Luis Salazar	.05
95	Gary Sheffield	.45
96	Bobby Witt	.05
97	Lonnie Smith	.05
98	Bryan Harvey	.05
99	Mookie Wilson	.05
100	Dwight Gooden	.05
101	Lou Whitaker	.05
102	Ron Karkovice	.05
103	Jesse Barfield	.05
104	Jose DeJesus	.05
105	Benito Santiago	.05
106	Brian Holman	.05
107	Rafael Ramirez	.05
108	Ellis Burks	.05
109	Mike Bielecki	.05
110	Kirby Puckett	1.00
111	Terry Shumpert	.05
112	Chuck Crim	.05
113	Todd Benzinger	.05
114	Brian Barnes	.05
115	Carlos Baerga	.05
116	Kal Daniels	.05
117	Dave Johnson	.05
118	Andy Van Slyke	.05
119	John Burkett	.05
120	Rickey Henderson	.75
121	Tim Jones	.05
122	Daryl Irvine	.05
123	Ruben Sierra	.05
124	Jim Abbott	.05
125	Daryl Boston	.05
126	Greg Maddux	1.00
127	Von Hayes	.05
128	Mike Fitzgerald	.05
129	Wayne Edwards	.05
130	Greg Briley	.05
131	Rob Dibble	.05
132	Gene Larkin	.05
133	David Wells	.05
134	Steve Balboni	.05
135	Greg Vaughn	.05
136	Mark Davis	.05
137	Dave Rohde	.05
138	Eric Show	.05
139	Bobby Bonilla	.05
140	Dana Kiecker	.05
141	Gary Pettis	.05
142	Dennis Boyd	.05
143	Mike Benjamin	.05
144	Luis Polonia	.05
145	Doug Jones	.05
146	Al Newman	.05
147	Alex Fernandez	.05
148	Bill Doran	.05
149	Kevin Elster	.05
150	Len Dykstra	.05
151	Mike Gallego	.05
152	Tim Belcher	.05
153	Jay Buhner	.05
154	Ozzie Smith	1.00
155	Jose Canseco	.50
156	Gregg Olson	.05
157	Charlie O'Brien	.05
158	Frank Tanana	.05
159	George Brett	1.00
160	Jeff Huson	.05
161	Kevin Tapani	.05
162	Jerome Walton	.05
163	Charlie Hayes	.05
164	Chris Bosio	.05
165	Chris Sabo	.05
166	Lance Parrish	.05
167	Don Robinson	.05
168	Manuel Lee	.05
169	Dennis Rasmussen	.05
170	Wade Boggs	1.00
171	Bob Geren	.05
172	Mackey Sasser	.05
173	Julio Franco	.05
174	Otis Nixon	.05
175	Bert Blyleven	.05
176	Craig Biggio	.05
177	Eddie Murray	.75
178	Randy Tomlin	.05
179	Tino Martinez	.05
180	Carlton Fisk	.75
181	Dwight Smith	.05
182	Scott Garrelts	.05
183	Jim Gantner	.05
184	Dickie Thon	.05
185	John Farrell	.05
186	Cecil Fielder	.05
187	Glenn Braggs	.05
188	Allan Anderson	.05
189	Kurt Stillwell	.05
190	Joe Oquendo	.05
191	Joe Orsulak	.05
192	Ricky Jordan	.05
193	Kelly Downs	.05
194	Delino DeShields	.05
195	Omar Vizquel	.05
196	Mark Carreon	.05
197	Mike Harkey	.05
198	Jack Howell	.05
199	Lance Johnson	.05
200	Nolan Ryan	2.00
201	John Marzano	.05
202	Doug Drabek	.05
203	Mark Lemke	.05
204	Steve Sax	.05
205	Greg Harris	.05
206	B.J. Surhoff	.05
207	Todd Burns	.05
208	Jose Gonzalez	.05
209	Mike Scott	.05
210	Dave Magadan	.05
211	Dante Bichette	.05
212	Trevor Wilson	.05
213	Hector Villanueva	.05
214	Dan Pasqua	.05
215	Greg Colbrunn	.05
216	Mike Jeffcoat	.05
217	Harold Reynolds	.05
218	Paul O'Neill	.05
219	Mark Guthrie	.05
220	Barry Bonds	2.00
221	Jimmy Key	.05
222	Billy Ripken	.05
223	Tom Pagnozzi	.05
224	Bo Jackson	.10
225	Sid Fernandez	.05
226	Mike Marshall	.05
227	John Kruk	.05
228	Mike Fetters	.05
229	Eric Anthony	.05
230	Ryne Sandberg	1.00
231	Carney Lansford	.05
232	Melido Perez	.05
233	Jose Lind	.05
234	Darryl Hamilton	.05
235	Tom Browning	.05
236	Spike Owen	.05
237	Juan Gonzalez	.40
238	Felix Fermin	.05
239	Keith Miller	.05
240	Mark Gubicza	.05
241	Kent Anderson	.05
242	Alvaro Espinoza	.05
243	Dale Murphy	.20
244	Orel Hershiser	.05
245	Paul Molitor	.75
246	Eddie Whitson	.05
247	Joe Girardi	.05
248	Kent Hrbek	.05
249	Bill Sampen	.05
250	Kevin Mitchell	.05
251	Mariano Duncan	.05
252	Scott Bradley	.05
253	Mike Greenwell	.05
254	Tom Gordon	.05
255	Todd Zeile	.05
256	Bobby Thigpen	.05
257	Gregg Jefferies	.05
258	Kenny Rogers	.05
259	Shane Mack	.05
260	Zane Smith	.05
261	Mitch Williams	.05
262	Jim DeShaies	.05
263	Dave Winfield	.75
264	Ben McDonald	.05
265	Randy Ready	.05
266	Pat Borders	.05
267	Jose Uribe	.05
268	Derek Lilliquist	.05
269	Greg Brock	.05
270	Ken Griffey Jr.	1.25
271	Jeff Gray	.05
272	Danny Tartabull	.05
273	Dennis Martinez	.05
274	Robin Ventura	.05
275	Randy Myers	.05
276	Jack Daugherty	.05
277	Greg Gagne	.05
278	Jay Howell	.05
279	Mike LaValliere	.05
280	Rex Hudler	.05
281	Mike Simms	.05
282	Kevin Maas	.05
283	Jeff Ballard	.05
284	Dave Henderson	.05
285	Pete O'Brien	.05
286	Brook Jacoby	.05
287	Mike Henneman	.05
288	Greg Olson	.05
289	Greg Myers	.05
290	Mark Grace	.05
291	Shawn Abner	.05
292	Frank Viola	.05
293	Lee Stevens	.05
294	Jason Grimsley	.05
295	Matt Williams	.05
296	Ron Robinson	.05
297	Tom Brunansky	.05
298	Checklist	.05
299	Checklist	.05
300	Checklist	.05
301	Darryl Strawberry	.05
302	Bud Black	.05
303	Harold Baines	.05
304	Roberto Alomar	.20
305	Norm Charlton	.05
306	Gary Thurman	.05
307	Mike Felder	.05
308	Tony Gwynn	1.00
309	Roger Clemens	1.00
310	Andre Dawson	.25
311	Scott Radinsky	.05
312	Bob Melvin	.05
313	Kirk McCaskill	.05
314	Pedro Guerrero	.05
315	Walt Terrell	.05
316	Sam Horn	.05
317	Wes Chamberlain **RC**	.05
318	Pedro Munoz **RC**	.05
319	Roberto Kelly	.05
320	Mark Portugal	.05
321	Tim McIntosh	.05
322	Jesse Orosco	.05
323	Gary Green	.05
324	Greg Harris	.05
325	Hubie Brooks	.05
326	Chris Nabholz	.05
327	Terry Pendleton	.05
328	Eric King	.05
329	Chili Davis	.05
330	Anthony Telford	.05
331	Kelly Gruber	.05
332	Dennis Eckersley	.65
333	Mel Hall	.05
334	Bob Kipper	.05
335	Willie McGee	.05
336	Steve Olin	.05
337	Steve Buechele	.05
338	Scott Leius	.05
339	Hal Morris	.05
340	Jose Offerman	.05
341	Kent Mercker	.05
342	Ken Griffey	.05
343	Pete Harnisch	.05
344	Kirk Gibson	.05
345	Dave Smith	.05
346	Dave Martinez	.05
347	Atlee Hammaker	.05
348	Brian Downing	.05
349	Todd Hundley	.05
350	Candy Maldonado	.05
351	Dwight Evans	.05
352	Steve Searcy	.05
353	Gary Gaetti	.05
354	Jeff Reardon	.05
355	Travis Fryman	.05
356	Dave Righetti	.05
357	Fred McGriff	.05
358	Don Slaught	.05
359	Gene Nelson	.05
360	Billy Spiers	.05
361	Lee Guetterman	.05
362	Darren Lewis	.05
363	Duane Ward	.05
364	Lloyd Moseby	.05
365	John Smoltz	.05
366	Felix Jose	.05
367	David Cone	.05
368	Wally Backman	.05
369	Jeff Montgomery	.05
370	Rich Garces	.05
371	Billy Hatcher	.05
372	Bill Swift	.05
373	Jim Eisenreich	.05
374	Rob Ducey	.05
375	Tim Crews	.05
376	Steve Finley	.05
377	Jeff Blauser	.05
378	Willie Wilson	.05
379	Gerald Perry	.05
380	Jose Mesa	.05
381	Pat Kelly	.05
382	Matt Merullo	.05
383	Ivan Calderon	.05
384	Scott Chiamparino	.05
385	Lloyd McClendon	.05
386	Dave Bergman	.05
387	Ed Sprague	.05
388	Jeff Bagwell **RC**	3.00
389	Brett Butler	.05
390	Larry Andersen	.05
391	Glenn Davis	.05
392	Alex Cole (Photo is Otis Nixon.)	.05
393	Mike Heath	.05
394	Danny Darwin	.05
395	Steve Lake	.05
396	Tim Layana	.05
397	Terry Leach	.05
398	Bill Wegman	.05
399	Mark McGwire	1.50
400	Mike Boddicker	.05
401	Steve Howe	.05
402	Bernard Gilkey	.05
403	Thomas Howard	.05
404	Rafael Belliard	.05
405	Tom Candiotti	.05
406	Rene Gonzalez	.05
407	Chuck McElroy	.05
408	Paul Sorrento	.05
409	Randy Johnson	.75
410	Brady Anderson	.05
411	Dennis Cook	.05
412	Mickey Tettleton	.05
413	Mike Stanton	.05
414	Ken Oberkfell	.05
415	Rick Honeycutt	.05
416	Nelson Santovenia	.05
417	Bob Tewksbury	.05
418	Brent Mayne	.05
419	Steve Farr	.05
420	Phil Stephenson	.05
421	Jeff Russell	.05

422	Chris James	.05
423	Tim Leary	.05
424	Gary Carter	.75
425	Glenallen Hill	.05
426	Matt Young	.05
427	Sid Bream	.05
428	Greg Swindell	.05
429	Scott Aldred	.05
430	Cal Ripken, Jr.	2.00
431	Bill Landrum	.05
432	Ernie Riles	.05
433	Danny Jackson	.05
434	Casey Candaele	.05
435	Ken Hill	.05
436	Jaime Navarro	.05
437	Lance Blankenship	.05
438	Randy Velarde	.05
439	Frank DiPino	.05
440	Carl Nichols	.05
441	Jeff Robinson	.05
442	Deion Sanders	.05
443	Vincente Palacios	.05
444	Devon White	.05
445	John Cerutti	.05
446	Tracy Jones	.05
447	Jack Morris	.05
448	Mitch Webster	.05
449	Bob Ojeda	.05
450	Oscar Azocar	.05
451	Luis Aquino	.05
452	Mark Whiten	.05
453	Stan Belinda	.05
454	Ron Gant	.05
455	Jose DeLeon	.05
456	Mark Salas	.05
457	Junior Felix	.05
458	Wally Whitehurst	.05
459	Phil Plantier **RC**	.05
460	Juan Berenguer	.05
461	Franklin Stubbs	.05
462	Joe Boever	.05
463	Tim Wallach	.05
464	Mike Moore	.05
465	Albert Belle	.05
466	Mike Witt	.05
467	Craig Worthington	.05
468	Jerald Clark	.05
469	Scott Terry	.05
470	Milt Cuyler	.05
471	John Smiley	.05
472	Charles Nagy	.05
473	Alan Mills	.05
474	John Russell	.05
475	Bruce Hurst	.05
476	Andujar Cedeno	.05
477	Dave Eiland	.05
478	Brian McRae **RC**	.10
479	Mike LaCoss	.05
480	Chris Gwynn	.05
481	Jamie Moyer	.05
482	John Olerud	.05
483	Efrain Valdez	.05
484	Sil Campusano	.05
485	Pascual Perez	.05
486	Gary Redus	.05
487	Andy Hawkins	.05
488	Cory Snyder	.05
489	Chris Hoiles	.05
490	Ron Hassey	.05
491	Gary Wayne	.05
492	Mark Lewis	.05
493	Scott Coolbaugh	.05
494	Gerald Young	.05
495	Juan Samuel	.05
496	Willie Fraser	.05
497	Jeff Treadway	.05
498	Vince Coleman	.05
499	Cris Carpenter	.05
500	Jack Clark	.05
501	Kevin Appier	.05
502	Rafael Palmeiro	.65
503	Hensley Meulens	.05
504	George Bell	.05
505	Tony Pena	.05
506	Roger McDowell	.05
507	Luis Sojo	.05
508	Mike Schooler	.05
509	Robin Yount	.75
510	Jack Armstrong	.05
511	Rick Cerone	.05
512	Curt Wilkerson	.05
513	Joe Carter	.05
514	Tim Burke	.05
515	Tony Fernandez	.05
516	Ramon Martinez	.05
517	Tim Hulett	.05
518	Terry Steinbach	.05
519	Pete Smith	.05
520	Ken Caminiti	.05
521	Shawn Boskie	.05
522	Mike Pagliarulo	.05
523	Tim Raines	.05
524	Alfredo Griffin	.05
525	Henry Cotto	.05
526	Mike Stanley	.05
527	Charlie Leibrandt	.05
528	Jeff King	.05
529	Eric Plunk	.05
530	Tom Lampkin	.05
531	Steve Bedrosian	.05
532	Tom Herr	.05
533	Craig Lefferts	.05
534	Jeff Reed	.05
535	Mickey Morandini	.05
536	Greg Cadaret	.05
537	Ray Lankford	.05
538	John Candelaria	.05
539	Rob Deer	.05
540	Brad Arnsberg	.05
541	Mike Sharperson	.05
542	Jeff Robinson	.05
543	Mo Vaughn	.05
544	Jeff Parrett	.05
545	Willie Randolph	.05
546	Herm Winningham	.05
547	Jeff Innis	.05
548	Chuck Knoblauch	.05
549	Tommy Greene	.05
550	Jeff Hamilton	.05
551	Barry Jones	.05
552	Ken Dayley	.05
553	Rick Dempsey	.05
554	Greg Smith	.05
555	Mike Devereaux	.05
556	Keith Comstock	.05
557	Paul Faries	.05
558	Tom Glavine	.35
559	Craig Grebeck	.05
560	Scott Erickson	.05
561	Joel Skinner	.05
562	Mike Morgan	.05
563	Dave Gallagher	.05
564	Todd Stottlemyre	.05
565	Rich Rodriguez	.05
566	Craig Wilson **RC**	.05
567	Jeff Brantley	.05
568	Scott Kamieniecki	.05
569	Steve Decker	.05
570	Juan Agosto	.05
571	Tommy Gregg	.05
572	Kevin Wickander	.05
573	Jamie Quirk	.05
574	Jerry Don Gleaton	.05
575	Chris Hammond	.05
576	Luis Gonzalez **RC**	1.00
577	Russ Swan	.05
578	Jeff Conine **RC**	.50
579	Charlie Hough	.05
580	Jeff Kunkel	.05
581	Darrel Akerfelds	.05
582	Jeff Manto	.05
583	Alejandro Pena	.05
584	Mark Davidson	.05
585	Bob MacDonald	.05
586	Paul Assenmacher	.05
587	Dan Wilson	.05
588	Tom Bolton	.05
589	Brian Harper	.05
590	John Habyan	.05
591	John Orton	.05
592	Mark Gardner	.05
593	Turner Ward	.05
594	Bob Patterson	.05
595	Edwin Nunez	.05
596	Gary Scott	.05
597	Scott Bankhead	.05
598	Checklist	.05
599	Checklist	.05
600	Checklist	.05

1991 Stadium Club Nolan Ryan Bronze

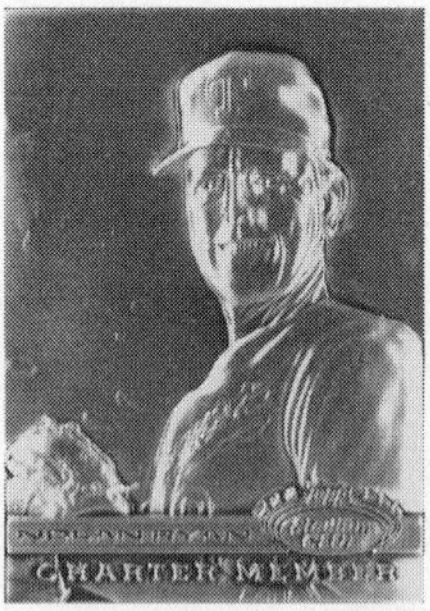

	NM/M
Nolan Ryan/Bronze	15.00

1992 Stadium Club

	NM/M
Complete Set (900):	20.00
Common Player:	.05
Series 1, 2, 3 Pack (15):	.75
Series 1, 2, 3 Box (36):	15.00

1	Cal Ripken, Jr.	1.50
2	Eric Yelding	.05
3	Geno Petralli	.05
4	Wally Backman	.05
5	Milt Cuyler	.05
6	Kevin Bass	.05
7	Dante Bichette	.05
8	Ray Lankford	.05
9	Mel Hall	.05
10	Joe Carter	.05
11	Juan Samuel	.05
12	Jeff Montgomery	.05
13	Glenn Braggs	.05
14	Henry Cotto	.05
15	Deion Sanders	.05

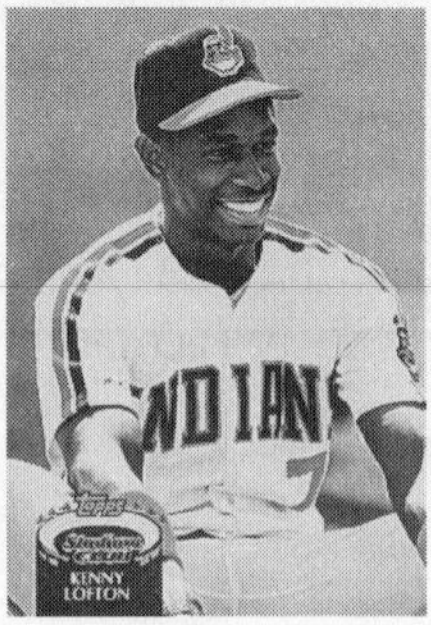

16	Dick Schofield	.05
17	David Cone	.05
18	Chili Davis	.05
19	Tom Foley	.05
20	Ozzie Guillen	.05
21	Luis Salazar	.05
22	Terry Steinbach	.05
23	Chris James	.05
24	Jeff King	.05
25	Carlos Quintana	.05
26	Mike Maddux	.05
27	Tommy Greene	.05
28	Jeff Russell	.05
29	Steve Finley	.05
30	Mike Flanagan	.05
31	Darren Lewis	.05
32	Mark Lee	.05
33	Willie Fraser	.05
34	Mike Henneman	.05
35	Kevin Maas	.05
36	Dave Hansen	.05
37	Erik Hanson	.05
38	Bill Doran	.05
39	Mike Boddicker	.05
40	Vince Coleman	.05
41	Devon White	.05
42	Mark Gardner	.05
43	Scott Lewis	.05
44	Juan Berenguer	.05
45	Carney Lansford	.05
46	Curt Wilkerson	.05
47	Shane Mack	.05
48	Bip Roberts	.05
49	Greg Harris	.05
50	Ryne Sandberg	.75
51	Mark Whiten	.05
52	Jack McDowell	.05
53	Jimmy Jones	.05
54	Steve Lake	.05
55	Bud Black	.05
56	Dave Valle	.05
57	Kevin Reimer	.05
58	Rich Gedman	.05
59	Travis Fryman	.05
60	Steve Avery	.05
61	Francisco de la Rosa	.05
62	Scott Hemond	.05
63	Hal Morris	.05
64	Hensley Meulens	.05
65	Frank Castillo	.05
66	Gene Larkin	.05
67	Jose DeLeon	.05
68	Al Osuna	.05
69	Dave Cochrane	.05
70	Robin Ventura	.05
71	John Cerutti	.05
72	Kevin Gross	.05
73	Ivan Calderon	.05
74	Mike Macfarlane	.05
75	Stan Belinda	.05
76	Shawn Hillegas	.05
77	Pat Borders	.05
78	Jim Vatcher	.05
79	Bobby Rose	.05
80	Roger Clemens	.85
81	Craig Worthington	.05
82	Jeff Treadway	.05
83	Jamie Quirk	.05
84	Randy Bush	.05
85	Anthony Young	.05
86	Trevor Wilson	.05
87	Jaime Navarro	.05
88	Les Lancaster	.05
89	Pat Kelly	.05
90	Alvin Davis	.05
91	Larry Andersen	.05
92	Rob Deer	.05
93	Mike Sharperson	.05
94	Lance Parrish	.05
95	Cecil Espy	.05
96	Tim Spehr	.05
97	Dave Stieb	.05
98	Terry Mulholland	.05
99	Dennis Boyd	.05
100	Barry Larkin	.05
101	Ryan Bowen	.05
102	Felix Fermin	.05
103	Luis Alicea	.05
104	Tim Hulett	.05
105	Rafael Belliard	.05
106	Mike Gallego	.05
107	Dave Righetti	.05
108	Jeff Schaefer	.05
109	Ricky Bones	.05
110	Scott Erickson	.05
111	Matt Nokes	.05
112	Bob Scanlan	.05
113	Tom Candiotti	.05
114	Sean Berry	.05
115	Kevin Morton	.05
116	Scott Fletcher	.05
117	B.J. Surhoff	.05
118	Dave Magadan	.05
119	Bill Gullickson	.05
120	Marquis Grissom	.05
121	Lenny Harris	.05
122	Wally Joyner	.05
123	Kevin Brown	.05
124	Braulio Castillo	.05
125	Eric King	.05
126	Mark Portugal	.05
127	Calvin Jones	.05
128	Mike Heath	.05
129	Todd Van Poppel	.05
130	Benny Santiago	.05
131	Gary Thurman	.05
132	Joe Girardi	.05
133	Dave Eiland	.05
134	Orlando Merced	.05
135	Joe Orsulak	.05
136	John Burkett	.05
137	Ken Dayley	.05
138	Ken Hill	.05
139	Walt Terrell	.05
140	Mike Scioscia	.05
141	Junior Felix	.05
142	Ken Caminiti	.05
143	Carlos Baerga	.05
144	Tony Fossas	.05
145	Craig Grebeck	.05
146	Scott Bradley	.05
147	Kent Mercker	.05
148	Derrick May	.05
149	Jerald Clark	.05
150	George Brett	.85
151	Luis Quinones	.05
152	Mike Pagliarulo	.05
153	Jose Guzman	.05
154	Charlie O'Brien	.05
155	Darren Holmes	.05
156	Joe Boever	.05
157	Rich Monteleone	.05
158	Reggie Harris	.05
159	Roberto Alomar	.20
160	Robby Thompson	.05
161	Chris Hoiles	.05
162	Tom Pagnozzi	.05
163	Omar Vizquel	.05
164	John Candelaria	.05
165	Terry Shumpert	.05
166	Andy Mota	.05
167	Scott Bailes	.05
168	Jeff Blauser	.05
169	Steve Olin	.05
170	Doug Drabek	.05
171	Dave Bergman	.05
172	Eddie Whitson	.05
173	Gilberto Reyes	.05
174	Mark Grace	.05
175	Paul O'Neill	.05
176	Greg Cadaret	.05
177	Mark Williamson	.05
178	Casey Candaele	.05
179	Candy Maldonado	.05
180	Lee Smith	.05
181	Harold Reynolds	.05
182	Dave Justice	.05
183	Lenny Webster	.05
184	Donn Pall	.05
185	Gerald Alexander	.05
186	Jack Clark	.05
187	Stan Javier	.05
188	Ricky Jordan	.05
189	Franklin Stubbs	.05
190	Dennis Eckersley	.60
191	Danny Tartabull	.05
192	Pete O'Brien	.05
193	Mark Lewis	.05
194	Mike Felder	.05
195	Mickey Tettleton	.05
196	Dwight Smith	.05
197	Shawn Abner	.05
198	Jim Leyritz	.05
199	Mike Devereaux	.05
200	Craig Biggio	.05
201	Kevin Elster	.05
202	Rance Mulliniks	.05
203	Tony Fernandez	.05
204	Allan Anderson	.05
205	Herm Winningham	.05
206	Tim Jones	.05
207	Ramon Martinez	.05
208	Teddy Higuera	.05
209	John Kruk	.05
210	Jim Abbott	.05
211	Dean Palmer	.05
212	Mark Davis	.05
213	Jay Buhner	.05
214	Jesse Barfield	.05
215	Kevin Mitchell	.05
216	Mike LaValliere	.05
217	Mark Wohlers	.05
218	Dave Henderson	.05
219	Dave Smith	.05
220	Albert Belle	.05
221	Spike Owen	.05

222	Jeff Gray	.05
223	Paul Gibson	.05
224	Bobby Thigpen	.05
225	Mike Mussina	.30
226	Darrin Jackson	.05
227	Luis Gonzalez	.05
228	Greg Briley	.05
229	Brent Mayne	.05
230	Paul Molitor	.65
231	Al Leiter	.05
232	Andy Van Slyke	.05
233	Ron Tingley	.05
234	Bernard Gilkey	.05
235	Kent Hrbek	.05
236	Eric Karros	.05
237	Randy Velarde	.05
238	Andy Allanson	.05
239	Willie McGee	.05
240	Juan Gonzalez	.35
241	Karl Rhodes	.05
242	Luis Mercedes	.05
243	Billy Swift	.05
244	Tommy Gregg	.05
245	David Howard	.05
246	Dave Hollins	.05
247	Kip Gross	.05
248	Walt Weiss	.05
249	Mackey Sasser	.05
250	Cecil Fielder	.05
251	Jerry Browne	.05
252	Doug Dascenzo	.05
253	Darryl Hamilton	.05
254	Dann Bilardello	.05
255	Luis Rivera	.05
256	Larry Walker	.05
257	Ron Karkovice	.05
258	Bob Tewksbury	.05
259	Jimmy Key	.05
260	Bernie Williams	.05
261	Gary Wayne	.05
262	Mike Simms	.05
263	John Orton	.05
264	Marvin Freeman	.05
265	Mike Jeffcoat	.05
266	Roger Mason	.05
267	Edgar Martinez	.05
268	Henry Rodriguez	.05
269	Sam Horn	.05
270	Brian McRae	.05
271	Kirt Manwaring	.05
272	Mike Bordick	.05
273	Chris Sabo	.05
274	Jim Olander	.05
275	Greg Harris	.05
276	Dan Gakeler	.05
277	Bill Sampen	.05
278	Joel Skinner	.05
279	Curt Schilling	.35
280	Dale Murphy	.25
281	Lee Stevens	.05
282	Lonnie Smith	.05
283	Manuel Lee	.05
284	Shawn Boskie	.05
285	Kevin Seitzer	.05
286	Stan Royer	.05
287	John Dopson	.05
288	Scott Bullett	.05
289	Ken Patterson	.05
290	Todd Hundley	.05
291	Tim Leary	.05
292	Brett Butler	.05
293	Gregg Olson	.05
294	Jeff Brantley	.05
295	Brian Holman	.05
296	Brian Harper	.05
297	Brian Bohanon	.05
298	Checklist 1-100	.05
299	Checklist 101-200	.05
300	Checklist 201-300	.05
301	Frank Thomas	.65
302	Lloyd McClendon	.05
303	Brady Anderson	.05
304	Julio Valera	.05
305	Mike Aldrete	.05
306	Joe Oliver	.05
307	Todd Stottlemyre	.05
308	Rey Sanchez	.05
309	Gary Sheffield	.35
310	Andujar Cedeno	.05
311	Kenny Rogers	.05
312	Bruce Hurst	.05
313	Mike Schooler	.05
314	Mike Benjamin	.05
315	Chuck Finley	.05
316	Mark Lemke	.05
317	Scott Livingstone	.05
318	Chris Nabholz	.05
319	Mike Humphreys	.05
320	Pedro Guerrero	.05
321	Willie Banks	.05
322	Tom Goodwin	.05
323	Hector Wagner	.05
324	Wally Ritchie	.05
325	Mo Vaughn	.05
326	Joe Klink	.05
327	Cal Eldred	.05
328	Daryl Boston	.05
329	Mike Huff	.05
330	Jeff Bagwell	.65
331	Bob Milacki	.05
332	Tom Prince	.05
333	Pat Tabler	.05
334	Ced Landrum	.05
335	Reggie Jefferson	.05
336	Mo Sanford	.05
337	Kevin Ritz	.05
338	Gerald Perry	.05
339	Jeff Hamilton	.05
340	Tim Wallach	.05
341	Jeff Huson	.05
342	Jose Melendez	.05
343	Willie Wilson	.05
344	Mike Stanton	.05
345	Joel Johnston	.05
346	Lee Guetterman	.05
347	Francisco Olivares	.05
348	Dave Burba	.05
349	Tim Crews	.05
350	Scott Leius	.05
351	Danny Cox	.05
352	Wayne Housie	.05
353	Chris Donnels	.05
354	Chris George	.05
355	Gerald Young	.05
356	Roberto Hernandez	.05
357	Neal Heaton	.05
358	Todd Frohwirth	.05
359	Jose Vizcaino	.05
360	Jim Thome	.60
361	Craig Wilson	.05
362	Dave Haas	.05
363	Billy Hatcher	.05
364	John Barfield	.05
365	Luis Aquino	.05
366	Charlie Leibrandt	.05
367	Howard Farmer	.05
368	Bryn Smith	.05
369	Mickey Morandini	.05
370	Jose Canseco (Members Choice, should have been #597.)	.35
371	Jose Uribe	.05
372	Bob MacDonald	.05
373	Luis Sojo	.05
374	Craig Shipley	.05
375	Scott Bankhead	.05
376	Greg Gagne	.05
377	Scott Cooper	.05
378	Jose Offerman	.05
379	Billy Spiers	.05
380	John Smiley	.05
381	Jeff Carter	.05
382	Heathcliff Slocumb	.05
383	Jeff Tackett	.05
384	John Kiely	.05
385	John Vander Wal	.05
386	Omar Olivares	.05
387	Ruben Sierra	.05
388	Tom Gordon	.05
389	Charles Nagy	.05
390	Dave Stewart	.05
391	Pete Harnisch	.05
392	Tim Burke	.05
393	Roberto Kelly	.05
394	Freddie Benavides	.05
395	Tom Glavine	.35
396	Wes Chamberlain	.05
397	Eric Gunderson	.05
398	Dave West	.05
399	Ellis Burks	.05
400	Ken Griffey Jr.	1.00
401	Thomas Howard	.05
402	Juan Guzman	.05
403	Mitch Webster	.05
404	Matt Merullo	.05
405	Steve Buechele	.05
406	Danny Jackson	.05
407	Felix Jose	.05
408	Doug Piatt	.05
409	Jim Eisenreich	.05
410	Bryan Harvey	.05
411	Jim Austin	.05
412	Jim Poole	.05
413	Glenallen Hill	.05
414	Gene Nelson	.05
415	Ivan Rodriguez	.60
416	Frank Tanana	.05
417	Steve Decker	.05
418	Jason Grimsley	.05
419	Tim Layana	.05
420	Don Mattingly	.85
421	Jerome Walton	.05
422	Rob Ducey	.05
423	Andy Benes	.05
424	John Marzano	.05
425	Gene Harris	.05
426	Tim Raines	.05
427	Bret Barberie	.05
428	Harvey Pulliam	.05
429	Cris Carpenter	.05
430	Howard Johnson	.05
431	Orel Hershiser	.05
432	Brian Hunter	.05
433	Kevin Tapani	.05
434	Rick Reed	.05
435	Ron Witmeyer	.05
436	Gary Gaetti	.05
437	Alex Cole	.05
438	Chito Martinez	.05
439	Greg Litton	.05
440	Julio Franco	.05
441	Mike Munoz	.05
442	Erik Pappas	.05
443	Pat Combs	.05
444	Lance Johnson	.05
445	Ed Sprague	.05
446	Mike Greenwell	.05
447	Milt Thompson	.05
448	Mike Magnante	.05
449	Chris Haney	.05
450	Robin Yount	.65
451	Rafael Ramirez	.05
452	Gino Minutelli	.05
453	Tom Lampkin	.05
454	Tony Perezchica	.05
455	Dwight Gooden	.05
456	Mark Guthrie	.05
457	Jay Howell	.05
458	Gary DiSarcina	.05
459	John Smoltz	.05
460	Will Clark	.05
461	Dave Otto	.05
462	Rob Maurer	.05
463	Dwight Evans	.05
464	Tom Brunansky	.05
465	Shawn Hare **RC**	.05
466	Geronimo Pena	.05
467	Alex Fernandez	.05
468	Greg Myers	.05
469	Jeff Fassero	.05
470	Len Dykstra	.05
471	Jeff Johnson	.05
472	Russ Swan	.05
473	Archie Corbin	.05
474	Chuck McElroy	.05
475	Mark McGwire	1.25
476	Wally Whitehurst	.05
477	Tim McIntosh	.05
478	Sid Bream	.05
479	Jeff Juden	.05
480	Carlton Fisk	.65
481	Jeff Plympton	.05
482	Carlos Martinez	.05
483	Jim Gott	.05
484	Bob McClure	.05
485	Tim Teufel	.05
486	Vicente Palacios	.05
487	Jeff Reed	.05
488	Tony Phillips	.05
489	Mel Rojas	.05
490	Ben McDonald	.05
491	Andres Santana	.05
492	Chris Beasley	.05
493	Mike Timlin	.05
494	Brian Downing	.05
495	Kirk Gibson	.05
496	Scott Sanderson	.05
497	Nick Esasky	.05
498	Johnny Guzman **RC**	.05
499	Mitch Williams	.05
500	Kirby Puckett	.75
501	Mike Harkey	.05
502	Jim Gantner	.05
503	Bruce Egloff	.05
504	Josias Manzanillo	.05
505	Delino DeShields	.05
506	Rheal Cormier	.05
507	Jay Bell	.05
508	Rich Rowland	.05
509	Scott Servais	.05
510	Terry Pendleton	.05
511	Rich DeLucia	.05
512	Warren Newson	.05
513	Paul Faries	.05
514	Kal Daniels	.05
515	Jarvis Brown	.05
516	Rafael Palmeiro	.60
517	Kelly Downs	.05
518	Steve Chitren	.05
519	Moises Alou	.05
520	Wade Boggs	.75
521	Pete Schourek	.05
522	Scott Terry	.05
523	Kevin Appier	.05
524	Gary Redus	.05
525	George Bell	.05
526	Jeff Kaiser	.05
527	Alvaro Espinoza	.05
528	Luis Polonia	.05
529	Darren Daulton	.05
530	Norm Charlton	.05
531	John Olerud	.05
532	Dan Plesac	.05
533	Billy Ripken	.05
534	Rod Nichols	.05
535	Joey Cora	.05
536	Harold Baines	.05
537	Bob Ojeda	.05
538	Mark Leonard	.05
539	Danny Darwin	.05
540	Shawon Dunston	.05
541	Pedro Munoz	.05
542	Mark Gubicza	.05
543	Kevin Baez	.05
544	Todd Zeile	.05
545	Don Slaught	.05
546	Tony Eusebio	.05
547	Alonzo Powell	.05
548	Gary Pettis	.05
549	Brian Barnes	.05
550	Lou Whitaker	.05
551	Keith Mitchell	.05
552	Oscar Azocar	.05
553	Stu Cole	.05
554	Steve Wapnick	.05
555	Derek Bell	.05
556	Luis Lopez	.05
557	Anthony Telford	.05
558	Tim Mauser	.05
559	Glenn Sutko	.05
560	Darryl Strawberry	.05
561	Tom Bolton	.05
562	Cliff Young	.05
563	Bruce Walton	.05
564	Chico Walker	.05
565	John Franco	.05
566	Paul McClellan	.05
567	Paul Abbott	.05
568	Gary Varsho	.05
569	Carlos Maldonado	.05
570	Kelly Gruber	.05
571	Jose Oquendo	.05
572	Steve Frey	.05
573	Tino Martinez	.05
574	Bill Haselman	.05
575	Eric Anthony	.05
576	John Habyan	.05
577	Jeffrey McNeely	.05
578	Chris Bosio	.05
579	Joe Grahe	.05
580	Fred McGriff	.05
581	Rick Honeycutt	.05
582	Matt Williams	.05
583	Cliff Brantley	.05
584	Rob Dibble	.05
585	Skeeter Barnes	.05
586	Greg Hibbard	.05
587	Randy Milligan	.05
588	Checklist 301-400	.05
589	Checklist 401-500	.05
590	Checklist 501-600	.05
591	Frank Thomas	.35
592	Dave Justice	.05
593	Roger Clemens	.45
594	Steve Avery	.05
595	Cal Ripken, Jr.	.75
596	Barry Larkin	.05
597	Not issued (See #370)	.05
598	Will Clark	.05
599	Cecil Fielder	.05
600	Ryne Sandberg	.40
601	Chuck Knoblauch	.05
602	Dwight Gooden	.05
603	Ken Griffey Jr.	.65
604	Barry Bonds	.75
605	Nolan Ryan	.75
606	Jeff Bagwell	.35
607	Robin Yount	.30
608	Bobby Bonilla	.05
609	George Brett	.50
610	Howard Johnson	.05
611	Esteban Beltre	.05
612	Mike Christopher	.05
613	Troy Afenir	.05
614	Mariano Duncan	.05
615	Doug Henry	.05
616	Doug Jones	.05
617	Alvin Davis	.05
618	Craig Lefferts	.05
619	Kevin McReynolds	.05
620	Barry Bonds	1.50
621	Turner Ward	.05
622	Joe Magrane	.05
623	Mark Parent	.05
624	Tom Browning	.05
625	John Smiley	.05
626	Steve Wilson	.05
627	Mike Gallego	.05
628	Sammy Sosa	.75
629	Rico Rossy	.05
630	Royce Clayton	.05
631	Clay Parker	.05
632	Pete Smith	.05
633	Jeff McKnight	.05
634	Jack Daugherty	.05
635	Steve Sax	.05
636	Joe Hesketh	.05
637	Vince Horsman	.05
638	Eric King	.05
639	Joe Boever	.05
640	Jack Morris	.05
641	Arthur Rhodes	.05
642	Bob Melvin	.05
643	Rick Wilkins	.05
644	Scott Scudder	.05
645	Bip Roberts	.05
646	Julio Valera	.05
647	Kevin Campbell	.05
648	Steve Searcy	.05
649	Scott Kamieniecki	.05
650	Kurt Stillwell	.05
651	Bob Welch	.05
652	Andres Galarraga	.05
653	Mike Jackson	.05
654	Bo Jackson	.10
655	Sid Fernandez	.05
656	Mike Bielecki	.05
657	Jeff Reardon	.05
658	Wayne Rosenthal	.05
659	Eric Bullock	.05
660	Eric Davis	.05
661	Randy Tomlin	.05
662	Tom Edens	.05
663	Rob Murphy	.05
664	Leo Gomez	.05
665	Greg Maddux	.75
666	Greg Vaughn	.05
667	Wade Taylor	.05
668	Brad Arnsberg	.05
669	Mike Moore	.05
670	Mark Langston	.05
671	Barry Jones	.05
672	Bill Landrum	.05
673	Greg Swindell	.05
674	Wayne Edwards	.05
675	Greg Olson	.05
676	Bill Pulsipher **RC**	.05
677	Bobby Witt	.05
678	Mark Carreon	.05
679	Patrick Lennon	.05

680 Ozzie Smith .75
681 John Briscoe .05
682 Matt Young .05
683 Jeff Conine .05
684 Phil Stephenson .05
685 Ron Darling .05
686 Bryan Hickerson .05
687 Dale Sveum .05
688 Kirk McCaskill .05
689 Rich Amaral .05
690 Danny Tartabull .05
691 Donald Harris .05
692 Doug Davis .05
693 John Farrell .05
694 Paul Gibson .05
695 Kenny Lofton .05
696 Mike Fetters .05
697 Rosario Rodriguez .05
698 Chris Jones .05
699 Jeff Manto .05
700 Rick Sutcliffe .05
701 Scott Bankhead .05
702 Donnie Hill .05
703 Todd Worrell .05
704 Rene Gonzales .05
705 Rick Cerone .05
706 Tony Pena .05
707 Paul Sorrento .05
708 Gary Scott .05
709 Junior Noboa .05
710 Wally Joyner .05
711 Charlie Hayes .05
712 Rich Rodriguez .05
713 Rudy Seanez .05
714 Jim Bullinger .05
715 Jeff Robinson .05
716 Jeff Branson .05
717 Andy Ashby .05
718 Dave Burba .05
719 Rich Gossage .05
720 Randy Johnson .65
721 David Wells .05
722 Paul Kilgus .05
723 Dave Martinez .05
724 Denny Neagle .05
725 Andy Stankiewicz .05
726 Rick Aguilera .05
727 Junior Ortiz .05
728 Storm Davis .05
729 Don Robinson .05
730 Ron Gant .05
731 Paul Assenmacher .05
732 Mark Gardiner .05
733 Milt Hill .05
734 Jeremy Hernandez .05
735 Ken Hill .05
736 Xavier Hernandez .05
737 Gregg Jefferies .05
738 Dick Schofield .05
739 Ron Robinson .05
740 Sandy Alomar .05
741 Mike Stanley .05
742 Butch Henry .05
743 Floyd Bannister .05
744 Brian Drahman .05
745 Dave Winfield .65
746 Bob Walk .05
747 Chris James .05
748 Don Prybylinski .05
749 Dennis Rasmussen .05
750 Rickey Henderson .65
751 Chris Hammond .05
752 Bob Kipper .05
753 Dave Rohde .05
754 Hubie Brooks .05
755 Bret Saberhagen .05
756 Jeff Robinson .05
757 Pat Listach **RC** .05
758 Bill Wegman .05
759 John Wetteland .05
760 Phil Plantier .05
761 Wilson Alvarez .05
762 Scott Aldred .05
763 Armando Reynoso **RC** .05
764 Todd Benzinger .05
765 Kevin Mitchell .05
766 Gary Sheffield .35
767 Allan Anderson .05
768 Rusty Meacham .05
769 Rick Parker .05
770 Nolan Ryan 1.50
771 Jeff Ballard .05
772 Cory Snyder .05
773 Denis Boucher .05
774 Jose Gonzales .05
775 Juan Guerrero .05
776 Ed Nunez .05
777 Scott Ruskin .05
778 Terry Leach .05
779 Carl Willis .05
780 Bobby Bonilla .05
781 Duane Ward .05
782 Joe Slusarski .05
783 David Segui .05
784 Kirk Gibson .05
785 Frank Viola .05
786 Keith Miller .05
787 Mike Morgan .05
788 Kim Batiste .05
789 Sergio Valdez .05
790 Eddie Taubensee .05
791 Jack Armstrong .05
792 Scott Fletcher .05
793 Steve Farr .05
794 Dan Pasqua .05
795 Eddie Murray .65
796 John Morris .05
797 Francisco Cabrera .05
798 Mike Perez .05
799 Ted Wood .05
800 Jose Rijo .05
801 Danny Gladden .05
802 Arci Cianfrocco .05
803 Monty Fariss .05
804 Roger McDowell .05
805 Randy Myers .05
806 Kirk Dressendorfer .05
807 Zane Smith .05
808 Glenn Davis .05
809 Torey Lovullo .05
810 Andre Dawson .25
811 Bill Pecota .05
812 Ted Power .05
813 Willie Blair .05
814 Dave Fleming .05
815 Chris Gwynn .05
816 Jody Reed .05
817 Mark Dewey .05
818 Kyle Abbott .05
819 Tom Henke .05
820 Kevin Seitzer .05
821 Al Newman .05
822 Tim Sherrill .05
823 Chuck Crim .05
824 Darren Reed .05
825 Tony Gwynn .75
826 Steve Foster .05
827 Steve Howe .05
828 Brook Jacoby .05
829 Rodney McCray .05
830 Chuck Knoblauch .05
831 John Wehner .05
832 Scott Garrelts .05
833 Alejandro Pena .05
834 Jeff Parrett .05
835 Juan Bell .05
836 Lance Dickson .05
837 Darryl Kile .05
838 Efrain Valdez .05
839 Bob Zupcic **RC** .05
840 George Bell .05
841 Dave Gallagher .05
842 Tim Belcher .05
843 Jeff Shaw .05
844 Mike Fitzgerald .05
845 Gary Carter .65
846 John Russell .05
847 Eric Hillman **RC** .05
848 Mike Witt .05
849 Curt Wilkerson .05
850 Alan Trammell .05
851 Rex Hudler .05
852 Michael Walkden **RC** .05
853 Kevin Ward .05
854 Tim Naehring .05
855 Bill Swift .05
856 Damon Berryhill .05
857 Mark Eichhorn .05
858 Hector Villanueva .05
859 Jose Lind .05
860 Denny Martinez .05
861 Bill Krueger .05
862 Mike Kingery .05
863 Jeff Innis .05
864 Derek Lilliquist .05
865 Reggie Sanders .05
866 Ramon Garcia .05
867 Bruce Ruffin .05
868 Dickie Thon .05
869 Melido Perez .05
870 Ruben Amaro .05
871 Alan Mills .05
872 Matt Sinatro .05
873 Eddie Zosky .05
874 Pete Incaviglia .05
875 Tom Candiotti .05
876 Bob Patterson .05
877 Neal Heaton .05
878 Terrel Hansen **RC** .05
879 Dave Eiland .05
880 Von Hayes .05
881 Tim Scott .05
882 Otis Nixon .05
883 Herm Winningham .05
884 Dion James .05
885 Dave Wainhouse .05
886 Frank DiPino .05
887 Dennis Cook .05
888 Jose Mesa .05
889 Mark Leiter .05
890 Willie Randolph .05
891 Craig Colbert .05
892 Dwayne Henry .05
893 Jim Lindeman .05
894 Charlie Hough .05
895 Gil Heredia .05
896 Scott Chiamparino .05
897 Lance Blankenship .05
898 Checklist 601-700 .05
899 Checklist 701-800 .05
900 Checklist 801-900 .05

Master Photos

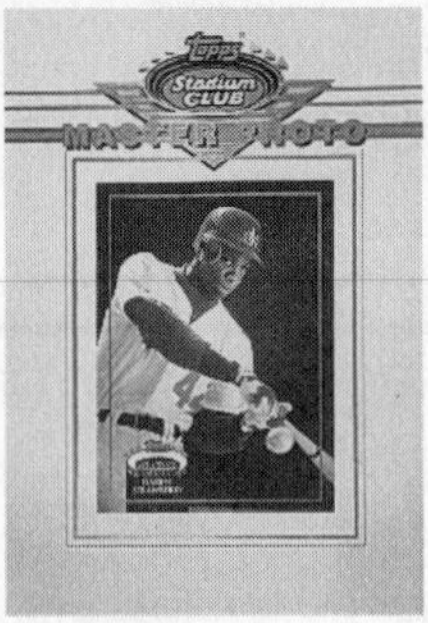

NM/M

Complete Set (15): 20.00
Common Player: .50
(1) Wade Boggs 2.25
(2) Barry Bonds 4.00
(3) Jose Canseco 1.00
(4) Will Clark .50
(5) Cecil Fielder .50
(6) Dwight Gooden .50
(7) Ken Griffey Jr. 3.00
(8) Rickey Henderson 2.00
(9) Lance Johnson .50
(10) Cal Ripken, Jr. 4.00
(11) Nolan Ryan 4.00
(12) Deion Sanders .50
(13) Darryl Strawberry .50
(14) Danny Tartabull .50
(15) Frank Thomas 2.00

SkyDome

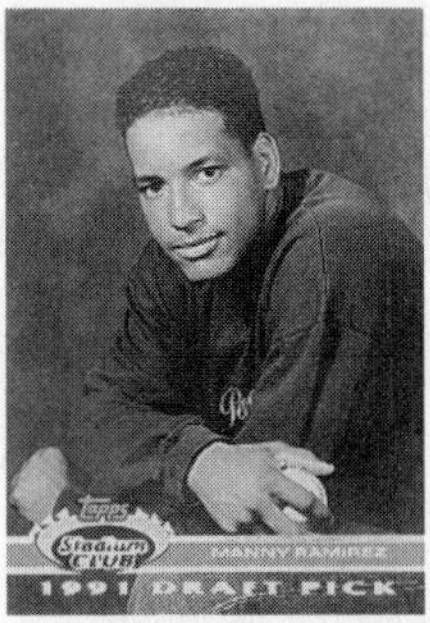

NM/M

Unopened Factory Set (200): 15.00
Complete Set (200): 10.00
Common Player: .05
1 Terry Adams **RC** .05
2 Tommy Adams .05
3 Rick Aguilera .05
4 Ron Allen .05
5 Roberto Alomar/AS .20
6 Sandy Alomar .05
7 Greg Anthony .05
8 James Austin .05
9 Steve Avery .05
10 Harold Baines .05
11 Brian Barber **RC** .05
12 Jon Barnes .05
13 George Bell .05
14 Doug Bennett .05
15 Sean Bergman .05
16 Craig Biggio .05
17 Bill Bliss .05
18 Wade Boggs/AS .60
19 Bobby Bonilla/AS .05
20 Russell Brock .05
21 Tarrik Brock .05
22 Tom Browning .05
23 Brett Butler .05
24 Ivan Calderon .05
25 Joe Carter .05
26 Joe Caruso .05
27 Dan Cholowsky .05
28 Will Clark/AS .05
29 Roger Clemens/AS .65
30 Shawn Curran .05
31 Chris Curtis .05
32 Chili Davis .05
33 Andre Dawson .25
34 Joe DeBerry .05
35 John Dettmer .05
36 Rob Dibble .05
37 John Donati **RC** .05
38 Dave Doorneweerd .05
39 Darren Dreifort .05
40 Mike Durant .05
41 Chris Durkin .05
42 Dennis Eckersley .40
43 Brian Edmondson **RC** .05
44 Vaughn Eshelman **RC** .05
45 Shawn Estes **RC** .50
46 Jorge Fabregas **RC** .10
47 Jon Farrell .05
48 Cecil Fielder/AS .05
49 Carlton Fisk .50
50 Tim Flannelly .05
51 Cliff Floyd **RC** .50
52 Julio Franco .05
53 Greg Gagne .05
54 Chris Gambs **RC** .05
55 Ron Gant .05
56 Brent Gates .05
57 Dwayne Gerald .05
58 Jason Giambi 1.50
59 Benji Gil **RC** .05
60 Mark Gipner .05
61 Danny Gladden .05
62 Tom Glavine .35
63 Jimmy Gonzalez .05
64 Jeff Granger .05
65 Dan Grapenthien .05
66 Dennis Gray .05
67 Shawn Green **RC** 2.00
68 Tyler Green .05
69 Todd Greene .05
70 Ken Griffey Jr./AS .75
71 Kelly Gruber .05
72 Ozzie Guillen .05
73 Tony Gwynn/AS .60
74 Shane Halter .05
75 Jeffrey Hammonds .05
76 Larry Hanlon .05
77 Pete Harnisch .05
78 Mike Harrison .05
79 Bryan Harvey .05
80 Scott Hatteberg .05
81 Rick Helling .05
82 Dave Henderson .05
83 Rickey Henderson/AS .50
84 Tyrone Hill .05
85 Todd Hollandsworth **RC** .10
86 Brian Holliday .05
87 Terry Horn .05
88 Jeff Hostetler .05
89 Kent Hrbek .05
90 Mark Hubbard .05
91 Charles Johnson .05
92 Howard Johnson .05
93 Todd Johnson .05
94 Bobby Jones **RC** .10
95 Dan Jones .05
96 Felix Jose .05
97 Dave Justice .05
98 Jimmy Key .05
99 Marc Kroom **RC** .05
100 John Kruk .05
101 Mark Langston .05
102 Barry Larkin .05
103 Mike LaValliere .05
104a Scott Leius (1991 N.L. All-Star - Error) .05
104b Scott Leius (1991 World Series - Correct) .25
105 Mark Lemke .05
106 Donnie Leshnock .05
107 Jimmy Lewis .05
108 Shawn Livesy .05
109 Ryan Long .05
110 Trevor Mallory .05
111 Denny Martinez .05
112 Justin Mashore .05
113 Jason McDonald .05
114 Jack McDowell .05
115 Tom McKinnon .05
116 Billy McKinnon .05
117 Buck McNabb **RC** .05
118 Jim Mecir .05
119 Dan Melendez .05
120 Shawn Miller **RC** .05
121 Trever Miller .05
122 Paul Molitor .50
123 Vincent Moore .05
124 Mike Morgan .05
125 Jack Morris (World Series) .05
126 Jack Morrisv .05
127 Sean Mulligan .05
128 Eddie Murray .50
129 Mike Neill .05
130 Phil Nevin .05
131 Mark O'Brien .05
132 Alex Ochoa **RC** .05
133 Chad Ogea **RC** .05
134 Greg Olson .05
135 Paul O'Neill .05
136a Jared Osentowski (1991 World Series - Error) .05
136b Jared Osentowski (Draft Pick - Correct) .25
137 Mike Pagliarulo .05
138 Rafael Palmeiro .40
139 Rodney Pedraza .05
140 Tony Phillips .05
141 Scott Pisciotta **RC** .05
142 Chris Pritchett .05
143 Jason Pruitt .05
144a Kirby Puckett (1991 N.L. All-Star - Error) .60
144b Kirby Puckett (1991 World Series - Correct) 3.00
145 Kirby Puckett/AS .60
146 Manny Ramirez **RC** 5.00
147 Eddie Ramos .05
148 Mark Ratekin .05
149 Jeff Reardon .05
150 Sean Rees .05
151 Calvin Reese **RC** .50
152 Desmond Relaford **RC** .10
153 Eric Richardson .05
154 Cal Ripken, Jr./AS 1.50
155 Chris Roberts .05
156 Mike Robertson .05

157	Steve Rodriguez	.05
158	Mike Rossiter	.05
159	Scott Ruffcorn	.05
160a	Chris Sabo (1991 World Series - Error)	.05
160b	Chris Sabo (1991 N.L. All-Star - Correct)	.25
161	Juan Samuel	.05
162	Ryne Sandberg/AS	.60
163	Scott Sanderson	.05
164	Benito Santiago	.05
165	Gene Schall **RC**	.05
166	Chad Schoenvogel	.05
167	Chris Seelbach **RC**	.05
168	Aaron Sele **RC**	.50
169	Basil Shabazz	.05
170	Al Shirley **RC**	.05
171	Paul Shuey	.05
172	Ruben Sierra	.05
173	John Smiley	.05
174	Lee Smith	.05
175	Ozzie Smith	.60
176	Tim Smith	.05
177	Zane Smith	.05
178	John Smoltz	.05
179	Scott Stahoviak	.05
180	Kennie Steenstra	.05
181	Kevin Stocker	.05
182	Chris Stynes **RC**	.05
183	Danny Tartabull	.05
184	Brien Taylor	.05
185	Todd Taylor	.05
186	Larry Thomas	.05
187a	Ozzie Timmons **RC**	.05
187b	David Tuttle (Should be #188.)	.05
188	Not issued	.05
189	Andy Van Slyke	.05
190a	Frank Viola (1991 World Series - Error)	.05
190b	Frank Viola (1991 N.L. All-Star - Correct)	.25
191	Michael Walkden	.05
192	Jeff Ware	.05
193	Allen Watson **RC**	.05
194	Steve Whitaker	.05
195a	Jerry Willard (1991 Draft Pick - Error)	.05
195b	Jerry Willard (1991 World Series - Correct)	.25
196	Craig Wilson	.05
197	Chris Wimmer	.05
198	Steve Wojciechowski **RC**	.05
199	Joel Wolfe	.05
200	Ivan Zweig	.05

1993 Stadium Club

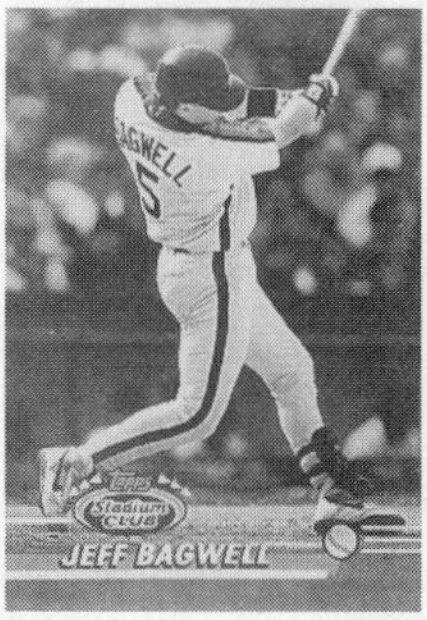

		NM/M
Complete Set (750):		25.00
Common Player:		.05
First Day:		8X
Pack (15):		.75
Wax Box (24):		10.00
1	Pat Borders	.05
2	Greg Maddux	.85
3	Daryl Boston	.05
4	Bob Ayrault	.05
5	Tony Phillips	.05
6	Damion Easley	.05
7	Kip Gross	.05
8	Jim Thome	.65
9	Tim Belcher	.05
10	Gary Wayne	.05
11	Sam Militello	.05
12	Mike Magnante	.05
13	Tim Wakefield	.05
14	Tim Hulett	.05
15	Rheal Cormier	.05
16	Juan Guerrero	.05
17	Rich Gossage	.05
18	Tim Laker	.05
19	Darrin Jackson	.05
20	Jack Clark	.05
21	Roberto Hernandez	.05
22	Dean Palmer	.05
23	Harold Reynolds	.05
24	Dan Plesac	.05
25	Brent Mayne	.05
26	Pat Hentgen	.05
27	Luis Sojo	.05
28	Ron Gant	.05
29	Paul Gibson	.05
30	Bip Roberts	.05
31	Mickey Tettleton	.05
32	Randy Velarde	.05
33	Brian McRae	.05
34	Wes Chamberlain	.05
35	Wayne Kirby	.05
36	Rey Sanchez	.05
37	Jesse Orosco	.05
38	Mike Stanton	.05
39	Royce Clayton	.05
40	Cal Ripken, Jr.	2.50
41	John Dopson	.05
42	Gene Larkin	.05
43	Tim Raines	.05
44	Randy Myers	.05
45	Clay Parker	.05
46	Mike Scioscia	.05
47	Pete Incaviglia	.05
48	Todd Van Poppel	.05
49	Ray Lankford	.05
50	Eddie Murray	.75
51	Barry Bonds	2.50
52	Gary Thurman	.05
53	Bob Wickman	.05
54	Joey Cora	.05
55	Kenny Rogers	.05
56	Mike Devereaux	.05
57	Kevin Seitzer	.05
58	Rafael Belliard	.05
59	David Wells	.05
60	Mark Clark	.05
61	Carlos Baerga	.05
62	Scott Brosius	.05
63	Jeff Grotewold	.05
64	Rick Wrona	.05
65	Kurt Knudsen	.05
66	Lloyd McClendon	.05
67	Omar Vizquel	.05
68	Jose Vizcaino	.05
69	Rob Ducey	.05
70	Casey Candaele	.05
71	Ramon Martinez	.05
72	Todd Hundley	.05
73	John Marzano	.05
74	Derek Parks	.05
75	Jack McDowell	.05
76	Tim Scott	.05
77	Mike Mussina	.40
78	Delino DeShields	.05
79	Chris Bosio	.05
80	Mike Bordick	.05
81	Rod Beck	.05
82	Ted Power	.05
83	John Kruk	.05
84	Steve Shifflett	.05
85	Danny Tartabull	.05
86	Mike Greenwell	.05
87	Jose Melendez	.05
88	Craig Wilson	.05
89	Melvin Nieves	.05
90	Ed Sprague	.05
91	Willie McGee	.05
92	Joe Orsulak	.05
93	Jeff King	.05
94	Dan Pasqua	.05
95	Brian Harper	.05
96	Joe Oliver	.05
97	Shane Turner	.05
98	Lenny Harris	.05
99	Jeff Parrett	.05
100	Luis Polonia	.05
101	Kent Bottenfield	.05
102	Albert Belle	.05
103	Mike Maddux	.05
104	Randy Tomlin	.05
105	Andy Stankiewicz	.05
106	Rico Rossy	.05
107	Joe Hesketh	.05
108	Dennis Powell	.05
109	Derrick May	.05
110	Pete Harnisch	.05
111	Kent Mercker	.05
112	Scott Fletcher	.05
113	Rex Hudler	.05
114	Chico Walker	.05
115	Rafael Palmeiro	.65
116	Mark Leiter	.05
117	Pedro Munoz	.05
118	Jim Bullinger	.05
119	Ivan Calderon	.05
120	Mike Timlin	.05
121	Rene Gonzales	.05
122	Greg Vaughn	.05
123	Mike Flanagan	.05
124	Mike Hartley	.05
125	Jeff Montgomery	.05
126	Mike Gallego	.05
127	Don Slaught	.05
128	Charlie O'Brien	.05
129a	Jose Offerman (Home: (Blank))	2.00
129b	Jose Offerman (Home: S.P. de MACORIS, D.R.)	.05
130	Mark Wohlers	.05
131	Eric Fox	.05
132	Doug Strange	.05
133	Jeff Frye	.05
134	Wade Boggs	.85
135	Lou Whitaker	.05
136	Craig Grebeck	.05
137	Rich Rodriguez	.05
138	Jay Bell	.05
139	Felix Fermin	.05
140	Denny Martinez	.05
141	Eric Anthony	.05
142	Roberto Alomar	.20
143	Darren Lewis	.05
144	Mike Blowers	.05
145	Scott Bankhead	.05
146	Jeff Reboulet	.05
147	Frank Viola	.05
148	Bill Pecota	.05
149	Carlos Hernandez	.05
150	Bobby Witt	.05
151	Sid Bream	.05
152	Todd Zeile	.05
153	Dennis Cook	.05
154	Brian Bohanon	.05
155	Pat Kelly	.05
156	Milt Cuyler	.05
157	Juan Bell	.05
158	Randy Milligan	.05
159	Mark Gardner	.05
160	Pat Tabler	.05
161	Jeff Reardon	.05
162	Ken Patterson	.05
163	Bobby Bonilla	.05
164	Tony Pena	.05
165	Greg Swindell	.05
166	Kirk McCaskill	.05
167	Doug Drabek	.05
168	Franklin Stubbs	.05
169	Ron Tingley	.05
170	Willie Banks	.05
171	Sergio Valdez	.05
172	Mark Lemke	.05
173	Robin Yount	.75
174	Storm Davis	.05
175	Dan Walters	.05
176	Steve Farr	.05
177	Curt Wilkerson	.05
178	Luis Alicea	.05
179	Russ Swan	.05
180	Mitch Williams	.05
181	Wilson Alvarez	.05
182	Carl Willis	.05
183	Craig Biggio	.05
184	Sean Berry	.05
185	Trevor Wilson	.05
186	Jeff Tackett	.05
187	Ellis Burks	.05
188	Jeff Branson	.05
189	Matt Nokes	.05
190	John Smiley	.05
191	Danny Gladden	.05
192	Mike Boddicker	.05
193	Roger Pavlik	.05
194	Paul Sorrento	.05
195	Vince Coleman	.05
196	Gary DiSarcina	.05
197	Rafael Bournigal	.05
198	Mike Schooler	.05
199	Scott Ruskin	.05
200	Frank Thomas	.75
201	Kyle Abbott	.05
202	Mike Perez	.05
203	Andre Dawson	.25
204	Bill Swift	.05
205	Alejandro Pena	.05
206	Dave Winfield	.75
207	Andujar Cedeno	.05
208	Terry Steinbach	.05
209	Chris Hammond	.05
210	Todd Burns	.05
211	Hipolito Pichardo	.05
212	John Kiely	.05
213	Tim Teufel	.05
214	Lee Guetterman	.05
215	Geronimo Pena	.05
216	Brett Butler	.05
217	Bryan Hickerson	.05
218	Rick Trlicek	.05
219	Lee Stevens	.05
220	Roger Clemens	1.25
221	Carlton Fisk	.75
222	Chili Davis	.05
223	Walt Terrell	.05
224	Jim Eisenreich	.05
225	Ricky Bones	.05
226	Henry Rodriguez	.05
227	Ken Hill	.05
228	Rick Wilkins	.05
229	Ricky Jordan	.05
230	Bernard Gilkey	.05
231	Tim Fortugno	.05
232	Geno Petralli	.05
233	Jose Rijo	.05
234	Jim Leyritz	.05
235	Kevin Campbell	.05
236	Al Osuna	.05
237	Pete Smith	.05
238	Pete Schourek	.05
239	Moises Alou	.05
240	Donn Pall	.05
241	Denny Neagle	.05
242	Dan Peltier	.05
243	Scott Scudder	.05
244	Juan Guzman	.05
245	Dave Burba	.05
246	Rick Sutcliffe	.05
247	Tony Fossas	.05
248	Mike Munoz	.05
249	Tim Salmon	.05
250	Rob Murphy	.05
251	Roger McDowell	.05
252	Lance Parrish	.05
253	Cliff Brantley	.05
254	Scott Leius	.05
255	Carlos Martinez	.05
256	Vince Horsman	.05
257	Oscar Azocar	.05
258	Craig Shipley	.05
259	Ben McDonald	.05
260	Jeff Brantley	.05
261	Damon Berryhill	.05
262	Joe Grahe	.05
263	Dave Hansen	.05
264	Rich Amaral	.05
265	Tim Pugh **RC**	.05
266	Dion James	.05
267	Frank Tanana	.05
268	Stan Belinda	.05
269	Jeff Kent	.05
270	Bruce Ruffin	.05
271	Xavier Hernandez	.05
272	Darrin Fletcher	.05
273	Tino Martinez	.05
274	Benny Santiago	.05
275	Scott Radinsky	.05
276	Mariano Duncan	.05
277	Kenny Lofton	.05
278	Dwight Smith	.05
279	Joe Carter	.05
280	Tim Jones	.05
281	Jeff Huson	.05
282	Phil Plantier	.05
283	Kirby Puckett	.85
284	Johnny Guzman	.05
285	Mike Morgan	.05
286	Chris Sabo	.05
287	Matt Williams	.05
288	Checklist 1-100	.05
289	Checklist 101-200	.05
290	Checklist 201-300	.05
291	Dennis Eckersley	.30
292	Eric Karros	.05
293	Pat Listach	.05
294	Andy Van Slyke	.05
295	Robin Ventura	.05
296	Tom Glavine	.05
297	Juan Gonzalez	.20
298	Travis Fryman	.05
299	Larry Walker	.05
300	Gary Sheffield	.20
301	Chuck Finley	.05
302	Luis Gonzalez	.05
303	Darryl Hamilton	.05
304	Bien Figueroa	.05
305	Ron Darling	.05
306	Jonathan Hurst	.05
307	Mike Sharperson	.05
308	Mike Christopher	.05
309	Marvin Freeman	.05
310	Jay Buhner	.05
311	Butch Henry	.05
312	Greg Harris	.05
313	Darren Daulton	.05
314	Chuck Knoblauch	.05
315	Greg Harris	.05
316	John Franco	.05
317	John Wehner	.05
318	Donald Harris	.05
319	Benny Santiago	.05
320	Larry Walker	.05
321	Randy Knorr	.05
322	Ramon D. Martinez **RC**	.05
323	Mike Stanley	.05
324	Bill Wegman	.05
325	Tom Candiotti	.05
326	Glenn Davis	.05
327	Chuck Crim	.05
328	Scott Livingstone	.05
329	Eddie Taubensee	.05
330	George Bell	.05
331	Edgar Martinez	.05
332	Paul Assenmacher	.05
333	Steve Hosey	.05
334	Mo Vaughn	.05
335	Bret Saberhagen	.05
336	Mike Trombley	.05
337	Mark Lewis	.05
338	Terry Pendleton	.05
339	Dave Hollins	.05
340	Jeff Conine	.05
341	Bob Tewksbury	.05
342	Billy Ashley	.05
343	Zane Smith	.05
344	John Wetteland	.05
345	Chris Hoiles	.05
346	Frank Castillo	.05
347	Bruce Hurst	.05
348	Kevin McReynolds	.05
349	Dave Henderson	.05
350	Ryan Bowen	.05
351	Sid Fernandez	.05
352	Mark Whiten	.05
353	Nolan Ryan	2.50
354	Rick Aguilera	.05
355	Mark Langston	.05
356	Jack Morris	.05
357	Rob Deer	.05
358	Dave Fleming	.05
359	Lance Johnson	.05
360	Joe Millette	.05
361	Wil Cordero	.05
362	Chito Martinez	.05
363	Scott Servais	.05
364	Bernie Williams	.05
365	Pedro Martinez	.75
366	Ryne Sandberg	.85
367	Brad Ausmus	.05
368	Scott Cooper	.05
369	Rob Dibble	.05
370	Walt Weiss	.05
371	Mark Davis	.05
372	Orlando Merced	.05
373	Mike Jackson	.05
374	Kevin Appier	.05
375	Esteban Beltre	.05
376	Joe Slusarski	.05
377	William Suero	.05

378	Pete O'Brien	.05
379	Alan Embree	.05
380	Lenny Webster	.05
381	Eric Davis	.05
382	Duane Ward	.05
383	John Habyan	.05
384	Jeff Bagwell	.75
385	Ruben Amaro	.05
386	Julio Valera	.05
387	Robin Ventura	.05
388	Archi Cianfrocco	.05
389	Skeeter Barnes	.05
390	Tim Costo	.05
391	Luis Mercedes	.05
392	Jeremy Hernandez	.05
393	Shawon Dunston	.05
394	Andy Van Slyke	.05
395	Kevin Maas	.05
396	Kevin Brown	.05
397	J.T. Bruett	.05
398	Darryl Strawberry	.05
399	Tom Pagnozzi	.05
400	Sandy Alomar	.05
401	Keith Miller	.05
402	Rich DeLucia	.05
403	Shawn Abner	.05
404	Howard Johnson	.05
405	Mike Benjamin	.05
406	Roberto Mejia **RC**	.05
407	Mike Butcher	.05
408	Deion Sanders	.05
409	Todd Stottlemyre	.05
410	Scott Kamieniecki	.05
411	Doug Jones	.05
412	John Burkett	.05
413	Lance Blankenship	.05
414	Jeff Parrett	.05
415	Barry Larkin	.05
416	Alan Trammell	.05
417	Mark Kiefer	.05
418	Gregg Olson	.05
419	Mark Grace	.05
420	Shane Mack	.05
421	Bob Walk	.05
422	Curt Schilling	.25
423	Erik Hanson	.05
424	George Brett	1.25
425	Reggie Jefferson	.05
426	Mark Portugal	.05
427	Ron Karkovice	.05
428	Matt Young	.05
429	Troy Neel	.05
430	Hector Fajardo	.05
431	Dave Righetti	.05
432	Pat Listach	.05
433	Jeff Innis	.05
434	Bob MacDonald	.05
435	Brian Jordan	.05
436	Jeff Blauser	.05
437	Mike Myers **RC**	.05
438	Frank Seminara	.05
439	Rusty Meacham	.05
440	Greg Briley	.05
441	Derek Lilliquist	.05
442	John Vander Wal	.05
443	Scott Erickson	.05
444	Bob Scanlan	.05
445	Todd Frohwirth	.05
446	Tom Goodwin	.05
447	William Pennyfeather	.05
448	Travis Fryman	.05
449	Mickey Morandini	.05
450	Greg Olson	.05
451	Trevor Hoffman	.05
452	Dave Magadan	.05
453	Shawn Jeter	.05
454	Andres Galarraga	.05
455	Ted Wood	.05
456	Freddie Benavides	.05
457	Junior Felix	.05
458	Alex Cole	.05
459	John Orton	.05
460	Eddie Zosky	.05
461	Dennis Eckersley	.65
462	Lee Smith	.05
463	John Smoltz	.05
464	Ken Caminiti	.05
465	Melido Perez	.05
466	Tom Marsh	.05
467	Jeff Nelson	.05
468	Jesse Levis	.05
469	Chris Nabholz	.05
470	Mike Mcfarlane	.05
471	Reggie Sanders	.05
472	Chuck McElroy	.05
473	Kevin Gross	.05
474	Matt Whiteside **RC**	.05
475	Cal Eldred	.05
476	Dave Gallagher	.05
477	Len Dykstra	.05
478	Mark McGwire	2.00
479	David Segui	.05
480	Mike Henneman	.05
481	Bret Barberie	.05
482	Steve Sax	.05
483	Dave Valle	.05
484	Danny Darwin	.05
485	Devon White	.05
486	Eric Plunk	.05
487	Jim Gott	.05
488	Scooter Tucker	.05
489	Omar Oliveres	.05
490	Greg Myers	.05
491	Brian Hunter	.05
492	Kevin Tapani	.05
493	Rich Monteleone	.05
494	Steve Buechele	.05
495	Bo Jackson	.10
496	Mike LaValliere	.05
497	Mark Leonard	.05
498	Daryl Boston	.05
499	Jose Canseco	.45
500	Brian Barnes	.05
501	Randy Johnson	.75
502	Tim McIntosh	.05
503	Cecil Fielder	.05
504	Derek Bell	.05
505	Kevin Koslofski	.05
506	Darren Holmes	.05
507	Brady Anderson	.05
508	John Valentin	.05
509	Jerry Browne	.05
510	Fred McGriff	.05
511	Pedro Astacio	.05
512	Gary Gaetti	.05
513	John Burke **RC**	.05
514	Dwight Gooden	.05
515	Thomas Howard	.05
516	Darrell Whitmore **RC**	.05
517	Ozzie Guillen	.05
518	Darryl Kile	.05
519	Rich Rowland	.05
520	Carlos Delgado	.50
521	Doug Henry	.05
522	Greg Colbrunn	.05
523	Tom Gordon	.05
524	Ivan Rodriguez	.65
525	Kent Hrbek	.05
526	Eric Young	.05
527	Rod Brewer	.05
528	Eric Karros	.05
529	Marquis Grissom	.05
530	Rico Brogna	.05
531	Sammy Sosa	1.00
532	Bret Boone	.05
533	Luis Rivera	.05
534	Hal Morris	.05
535	Monty Fariss	.05
536	Leo Gomez	.05
537	Wally Joyner	.05
538	Tony Gwynn	.85
539	Mike Williams	.05
540	Juan Gonzalez	.40
541	Ryan Klesko	.05
542	Ryan Thompson	.05
543	Chad Curtis	.05
544	Orel Hershiser	.05
545	Carlos Garcia	.05
546	Bob Welch	.05
547	Vinny Castilla	.05
548	Ozzie Smith	.85
549	Luis Salazar	.05
550	Mark Guthrie	.05
551	Charles Nagy	.05
552	Alex Fernandez	.05
553	Mel Rojas	.05
554	Orestes Destrade	.05
555	Mark Gubicza	.05
556	Steve Finley	.05
557	Don Mattingly	1.25
558	Rickey Henderson	.75
559	Tommy Greene	.05
560	Arthur Rhodes	.05
561	Alfredo Griffin	.05
562	Will Clark	.05
563	Bob Zupcic	.05
564	Chuck Carr	.05
565	Henry Cotto	.05
566	Billy Spiers	.05
567	Jack Armstrong	.05
568	Kurt Stillwell	.05
569	David McCarty	.05
570	Joe Vitiello	.05
571	Gerald Williams	.05
572	Dale Murphy	.25
573	Scott Aldred	.05
574	Bill Gullickson	.05
575	Bobby Thigpen	.05
576	Glenallen Hill	.05
577	Dwayne Henry	.05
578	Calvin Jones	.05
579	Al Martin	.05
580	Ruben Sierra	.05
581	Andy Benes	.05
582	Anthony Young	.05
583	Shawn Boskie	.05
584	Scott Pose **RC**	.05
585	Mike Piazza	1.50
586	Donovan Osborne	.05
587	James Austin	.05
588	Checklist 301-400	.05
589	Checklist 401-500	.05
590	Checklist 501-600	.05
591	Ken Griffey Jr.	.75
592	Ivan Rodriguez	.40
593	Carlos Baerga	.05
594	Fred McGriff	.05
595	Mark McGwire	1.00
596	Roberto Alomar	.10
597	Kirby Puckett	.45
598	Marquis Grissom	.05
599	John Smoltz	.05
600	Ryne Sandberg	.45
601	Wade Boggs	.85
602	Jeff Reardon	.05
603	Billy Ripken	.05
604	Bryan Harvey	.05
605	Carlos Quintana	.05
606	Greg Hibbard	.05
607	Ellis Burks	.05
608	Greg Swindell	.05
609	Dave Winfield	.75
610	Charlie Hough	.05
611	Chili Davis	.05
612	Jody Reed	.05
613	Mark Williamson	.05
614	Phil Plantier	.05
615	Jim Abbott	.05
616	Dante Bichette	.05
617	Mark Eichhorn	.05
618	Gary Sheffield	.45
619	Richie Lewis **RC**	.05
620	Joe Girardi	.05
621	Jaime Navarro	.05
622	Willie Wilson	.05
623	Scott Fletcher	.05
624	Bud Black	.05
625	Tom Brunansky	.05
626	Steve Avery	.05
627	Paul Molitor	.75
628	Gregg Jefferies	.05
629	Dave Stewart	.05
630	Javier Lopez	.05
631	Greg Gagne	.05
632	Bobby Kelly	.05
633	Mike Fetters	.05
634	Ozzie Canseco	.05
635	Jeff Russell	.05
636	Pete Incaviglia	.05
637	Tom Henke	.05
638	Chipper Jones	1.00
639	Jimmy Key	.05
640	Dave Martinez	.05
641	Dave Stieb	.05
642	Milt Thompson	.05
643	Alan Mills	.05
644	Tony Fernandez	.05
645	Randy Bush	.05
646	Joe Magrane	.05
647	Ivan Calderon	.05
648	Jose Guzman	.05
649	John Olerud	.05
650	Tom Glavine	.25
651	Julio Franco	.05
652	Armando Reynoso	.05
653	Felix Jose	.05
654	Ben Rivera	.05
655	Andre Dawson	.25
656	Mike Harkey	.05
657	Kevin Seitzer	.05
658	Lonnie Smith	.05
659	Norm Charlton	.05
660	Dave Justice	.05
661	Fernando Valenzuela	.05
662	Dan Wilson	.05
663	Mark Gardner	.05
664	Doug Dascenzo	.05
665	Greg Maddux	.85
666	Harold Baines	.05
667	Randy Myers	.05
668	Harold Reynolds	.05
669	Candy Maldonado	.05
670	Al Leiter	.05
671	Jerald Clark	.05
672	Doug Drabek	.05
673	Kirk Gibson	.05
674	Steve Reed **RC**	.05
675	Mike Felder	.05
676	Ricky Gutierrez	.05
677	Spike Owen	.05
678	Otis Nixon	.05
679	Scott Sanderson	.05
680	Mark Carreon	.05
681	Troy Percival	.05
682	Kevin Stocker	.05
683	Jim Converse **RC**	.05
684	Barry Bonds	2.50
685	Greg Gohr	.05
686	Tim Wallach	.05
687	Matt Mieske	.05
688	Robby Thompson	.05
689	Brien Taylor	.05
690	Kirt Manwaring	.05
691	Mike Lansing **RC**	.25
692	Steve Decker	.05
693	Mike Moore	.05
694	Kevin Mitchell	.05
695	Phil Hiatt	.05
696	Tony Tarasco **RC**	.05
697	Benji Gil	.05
698	Jeff Juden	.05
699	Kevin Reimer	.05
700	Andy Ashby	.05
701	John Jaha	.05
702	Tim Bogar **RC**	.05
703	David Cone	.05
704	Willie Greene	.05
705	David Hulse **RC**	.05
706	Cris Carpenter	.05
707	Ken Griffey Jr.	1.50
708	Steve Bedrosian	.05
709	Dave Nilsson	.05
710	Paul Wagner	.05
711	B.J. Surhoff	.05
712	Rene Arocha **RC**	.05
713	Manny Lee	.05
714	Brian Williams	.05
715	Sherman Obando **RC**	.05
716	Terry Mulholland	.05
717	Paul O'Neill	.05
718	David Nied	.05
719	J.T. Snow **RC**	.50
720	Nigel Wilson	.05
721	Mike Bielecki	.05
722	Kevin Young	.05
723	Charlie Leibrandt	.05
724	Frank Bolick	.05
725	Jon Shave **RC**	.05
726	Steve Cooke	.05
727	Domingo Martinez **RC**	.05
728	Todd Worrell	.05
729	Jose Lind	.05
730	Jim Tatum **RC**	.05
731	Mike Hampton	.05
732	Mike Draper	.05
733	Henry Mercedes	.05
734	John Johnstone **RC**	.05
735	Mitch Webster	.05
736	Russ Springer	.05
737	Rob Natal	.05
738	Steve Howe	.05
739	Darrell Sherman **RC**	.05
740	Pat Mahomes	.05
741	Alex Arias	.05
742	Damon Buford	.05
743	Charlie Hayes	.05
744	Guillermo Velasquez	.05
745	Checklist 601-750	.05
746	Frank Thomas	.40
747	Barry Bonds	1.50
748	Roger Clemens	.50
749	Joe Carter	.05
750	Greg Maddux	.45

1st Day Production

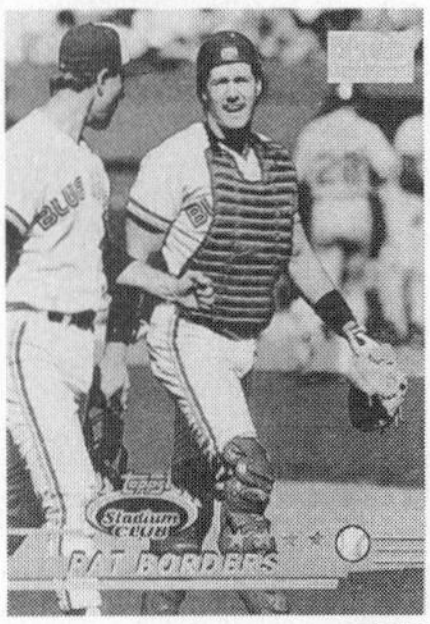

	NM/M
Common Player:	1.00
1st Day Stars:	8X

(See 1993 Stadium Club for checklist and base card values.)

Series 1 Inserts

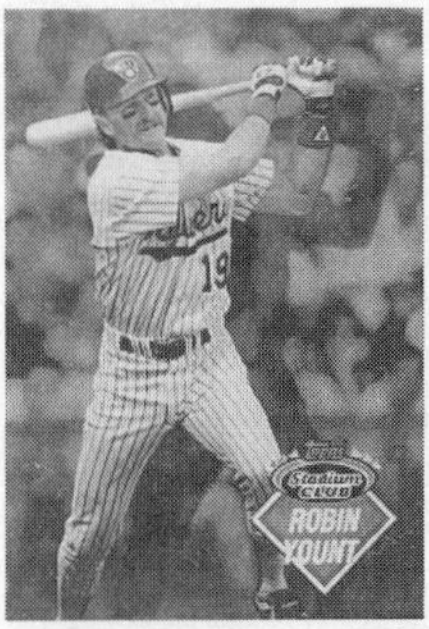

		NM/M
Complete Set (4):		3.00
Common Player:		.25
1	Robin Yount (3,000 hits)	1.00
2	George Brett (3,000 hits)	2.00
3	David Nied (#1 pick)	.25
4	Nigel Wilson (#1 pick)	.25

Series 2 Inserts

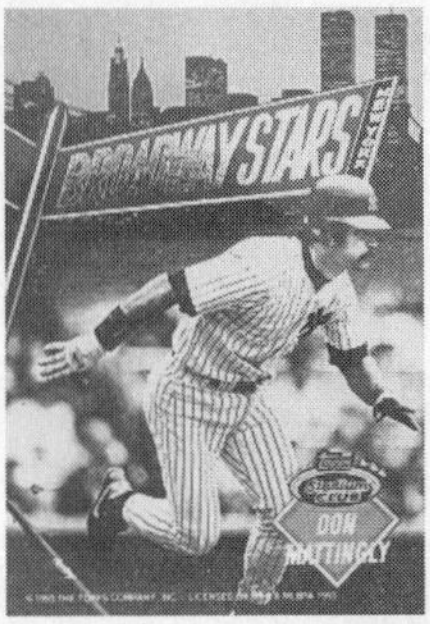

	NM/M
Complete Set (4):	5.00
Common Card:	1.50

1 Will Clark, Mark McGwire
  Pacific Terrific 2.00
2 Dwight Gooden, Don Mattingly
  Broadway Stars 1.50
3 Ryne Sandberg, Frank Thomas
  Second City Sluggers 1.50
4 Ken Griffey Jr., Darryl Strawberry
  Pacific Terrific 1.50

Series 3 Inserts

NM/M
Complete Set (2): .50
Common Player: .25
1 David Nied .25
2 Charlie Hough .25

Master Photos

NM/M
Complete Set (30): 15.00
Common Player: .20
Series 1
(1) Carlos Baerga .20
(2) Delino DeShields .20
(3) Brian McRae .20
(4) Sam Militello .20
(5) Joe Oliver .20
(6) Kirby Puckett 1.50
(7) Cal Ripken Jr. 4.00
(8) Bip Roberts .20
(9) Mike Scioscia .20
(10) Rick Sutcliffe .20
(11) Danny Tartabull .20
(12) Tim Wakefield .20
Series 2
(13) George Brett 3.00
(14) Jose Canseco .50
(15) Will Clark .20
(16) Travis Fryman .20
(17) Dwight Gooden .20
(18) Mark Grace .30
(19) Rickey Henderson 1.00
(20) Mark McGwire 2.50
(21) Nolan Ryan 4.00
(22) Ruben Sierra .20
(23) Darryl Strawberry .20
(24) Larry Walker .20
Series 3
(25) Barry Bonds 5.00
(26) Ken Griffey Jr. 2.50
(27) Greg Maddux 2.00
(28) David Nied .20
(29) J.T. Snow .20
(30) Brien Taylor .20
Redemption Card: 3X

Special

NM/M
Unopened Set (200): 45.00
Complete Set (200): 40.00
Common Player: .05
1 Dave Winfield .75
2 Juan Guzman .05
3 Tony Gwynn .85
4 Chris Roberts .05
5 Benny Santiago .05
6 Sherard Clinkscales .05
7 Jonathan Nunnally RC .05
8 Chuck Knoblauch .05
9 Bob Wolcott RC .05
10 Steve Rodriguez .05
11 Mark Williams RC .05
12 Danny Clyburn RC .05
13 Darren Dreifort .05
14 Andy Van Slyke .05
15 Wade Boggs .85
16 Scott Patton .05
17 Gary Sheffield .45
18 Ron Villone .05
19 Roberto Alomar .20
20 Marc Valdes .05
21 Daron Kirkreit .05
22 Jeff Granger .05
23 Levon Largusa .05
24 Jimmy Key .05
25 Kevin Pearson .05
26 Michael Moore .05
27 Preston Wilson RC 1.00
28 Kirby Puckett .85
29 Tim Crabtree RC .05
30 Bip Roberts .05
31 Kelly Gruber .05
32 Tony Fernandez .05
33 Jason Angel .05
34 Calvin Murray .05
35 Chad McConnell .05
36 Jason Moler .05
37 Mark Lemke .05
38 Tom Knauss .05
39 Larry Mitchell .05
40 Doug Mirabelli .05
41 Everett Stull II .05
42 Chris Wimmer .05
43 Dan Serafini RC .05
44 Ryne Sandberg .85
45 Steve Lyons .05
46 Ryan Freeburg .05
47 Ruben Sierra .05
48 David Mysel .05
49 Joe Hamilton .05
50 Steve Rodriguez .05
51 Tim Wakefield .05
52 Scott Gentile .05
53 Doug Jones .05
54 Willie Brown .05
55 Chad Mottola RC .05
56 Ken Griffey Jr. 1.50
57 Jon Lieber RC .50
58 Denny Martinez .05
59 Joe Petcka .05
60 Benji Simonton .05
61 Brett Backlund .05
62 Damon Berryhill .05
63 Juan Guzman .05
64 Doug Hecker .05
65 Jamie Arnold .05
66 Bob Tewksbury .05
67 Tim Leger .05
68 Todd Etler .05
69 Lloyd McClendon .05
70 Kurt Ehmann .05
71 Rick Magdaleno .05
72 Tom Pagnozzi .05
73 Jeffrey Hammonds .05
74 Joe Carter .05
75 Chris Holt .05
76 Charles Johnson .05
77 Bob Walk .05
78 Fred McGriff .05
79 Tom Evans .05
80 Scott Klingenbeck .05
81 Chad McConnell .05
82 Chris Eddy .05
83 Phil Nevin .05
84 John Kruk .05
85 Tony Sheffield .05
86 John Smoltz .05
87 Trevor Humphry .05
88 Charles Nagy .05
89 Sean Runyan .05
90 Mike Gulan .05
91 Darren Daulton .05
92 Otis Nixon .05
93 Nomar Garciaparra 8.00
94 Larry Walker .05
95 Hut Smith .05
96 Rick Helling .05
97 Roger Clemens 1.00
98 Ron Gant .05
99 Kenny Felder .05
100 Steve Murphy .05
101 Mike Smith .05
102 Terry Pendleton .05
103 Tim Davis .05
104 Jeff Patzke .05
105 Craig Wilson .05
106 Tom Glavine .35
107 Mark Langston .05
108 Mark Thompson .05
109 Eric Owens RC .05
110 Keith Johnson .05

111 Robin Ventura .05
112 Ed Sprague .05
113 Jeff Schmidt RC .05
114 Don Wengert .05
115 Craig Biggio .05
116 Kenny Carlyle .05
117 Derek Jeter RC 30.00
118 Manuel Lee .05
119 Jeff Haas .05
120 Roger Bailey .05
121 Sean Lowe .05
122 Rick Aguilera .05
123 Sandy Alomar .05
124 Derek Wallace .05
125 B.J. Wallace .05
126 Greg Maddux .85
127 Tim Moore .05
128 Lee Smith .05
129 Todd Steverson .05
130 Chris Widger .05
131 Paul Molitor .75
132 Chris Smith .05
133 Chris Gomez RC .05
134 Jimmy Baron .05
135 John Smoltz .05
136 Pat Borders .05
137 Donnie Leshnock .05
138 Gus Gandarillos .05
139 Will Clark .05
140 Ryan Luzinski RC .05
141 Cal Ripken, Jr. 2.50
142 B.J. Wallace .05
143 Trey Beamon RC .05
144 Norm Charlton .05
145 Mike Mussina .30
146 Billy Owens .05
147 Ozzie Smith .85
148 Jason Kendall RC 1.00
149 Mike Matthews RC .05
150 David Spykstra .05
151 Benji Grigsby .05
152 Sean Smith .05
153 Mark McGwire 2.00
154 David Cone .05
155 Shon Walker RC .05
156 Jason Giambi .50
157 Jack McDowell .05
158 Paxton Briley .05
159 Edgar Martinez .05
160 Brian Sackinsky .05
161 Barry Bonds 2.50
162 Roberto Kelly .05
163 Jeff Alkire .05
164 Mike Sharperson .05
165 Jamie Taylor .05
166 John Saffer .05
167 Jerry Browne .05
168 Travis Fryman .05
169 Brady Anderson .05
170 Chris Roberts .05
171 Lloyd Peever .05
172 Francisco Cabrera .05
173 Ramiro Martinez .05
174 Jeff Alkire .05
175 Ivan Rodriguez .65
176 Kevin Brown .05
177 Chad Roper .05
178 Rod Henderson .05
179 Dennis Eckersley .65
180 Shannon Stewart RC 1.00
181 DeShawn Warren .05
182 Lonnie Smith .05
183 Willie Adams .05
184 Jeff Montgomery .05
185 Damon Hollins .05
186 Byron Matthews .05
187 Harold Baines .05
188 Rick Greene .05
189 Carlos Baerga .05
190 Brandon Cromer .05
191 Roberto Alomar .20
192 Rich Ireland .05
193 Steve Montgomery .05
194 Brant Brown .05
195 Ritchie Moody .05
196 Michael Tucker .05
197 Jason Varitek RC 6.00
198 David Manning .05
199 Marquis Riley .05
200 Jason Giambi .60

1994 Stadium Club

NM/M
Complete Set (720): 20.00
Common Player: .05
1st Day: 8X
Golden Rainbow: 2X
Series 1, 2, 3 Pack (12): 1.00
Series 1, 2, 3 Wax Box (24): 15.00
1 Robin Yount .65
2 Rick Wilkins .05
3 Steve Scarsone .05
4 Gary Sheffield .40
5 George Brett 1.00
6 Al Martin .05
7 Joe Oliver .05
8 Stan Belinda .05
9 Denny Hocking .05
10 Roberto Alomar .20
11 Luis Polonia .05
12 Scott Hemond .05
13 Joey Reed .05
14 Mel Rojas .05
15 Junior Ortiz .05
16 Harold Baines .05
17 Brad Pennington .05
18 Jay Bell .05
19 Tom Henke .05
20 Jeff Branson .05
21 Roberto Mejia .05
22 Pedro Munoz .05
23 Matt Nokes .05
24 Jack McDowell .05
25 Cecil Fielder .05
26 Tony Fossas .05
27 Jim Eisenreich .05
28 Anthony Young .05
29 Chuck Carr .05
30 Jeff Treadway .05
31 Chris Nabholz .05
32 Tom Candiotti .05
33 Mike Maddux .05
34 Nolan Ryan 2.00
35 Luis Gonzalez .05
36 Tim Salmon .05
37 Mark Whiten .05
38 Roger McDowell .05
39 Royce Clayton .05
40 Troy Neel .05
41 Mike Harkey .05
42 Darrin Fletcher .05
43 Wayne Kirby .05
44 Rich Amaral .05
45 Robb Nen .05
46 Tim Teufel .05
47 Steve Cooke .05
48 Jeff McNeely .05
49 Jeff Montgomery .05
50 Skeeter Barnes .05
51 Scott Stahoviak .05
52 Pat Kelly .05
53 Brady Anderson .05
54 Mariano Duncan .05
55 Brian Bohanon .05
56 Jerry Spradlin .05
57 Ron Karkovice .05
58 Jeff Gardner .05
59 Bobby Bonilla .05
60 Tino Martinez .05
61 Todd Benzinger .05
62 Steve Trachsel RC .25
63 Brian Jordan .05
64 Steve Bedrosian .05
65 Brent Gates .05
66 Shawn Green .35
67 Sean Berry .05
68 Joe Klink .05
69 Fernando Valenzuela .05
70 Andy Tomberlin .05
71 Tony Pena .05
72 Eric Young .05
73 Chris Gomez .05
74 Paul O'Neill .05
75 Ricky Gutierrez .05
76 Brad Holman .05
77 Lance Painter .05
78 Mike Butcher .05
79 Sid Bream .05
80 Sammy Sosa .75
81 Felix Fermin .05
82 Todd Hundley .05
83 Kevin Higgins .05
84 Todd Pratt .05
85 Ken Griffey Jr. 1.25
86 John O'Donoghue .05
87 Rick Renteria .05
88 John Burkett .05
89 Jose Vizcaino .05
90 Kevin Seitzer .05
91 Bobby Witt .05
92 Chris Turner .05
93 Omar Vizquel .05
94 Dave Justice .05
95 David Segui .05
96 Dave Hollins .05
97 Doug Strange .05
98 Jerald Clark .05
99 Mike Moore .05
100 Joey Cora .05
101 Scott Kamieniecki .05
102 Andy Benes .05
103 Chris Bosio .05
104 Rey Sanchez .05
105 John Jaha .05
106 Otis Nixon .05
107 Rickey Henderson .65

108	Jeff Bagwell	.65
109	Gregg Jefferies	.05
110	Roberto Alomar, Paul Molitor, John Olerud Topps Trios	.25
111	Ron Gant, David Justice, Fred McGriff Topps Trios	.05
112	Juan Gonzalez, Rafael Palmeiro, Dean Palmer Topps Trios	.25
113	Greg Swindell	.05
114	Bill Hasleman	.05
115	Phil Plantier	.05
116	Ivan Rodriguez	.60
117	Kevin Tapani	.05
118	Mike LaValliere	.05
119	Tim Costo	.05
120	Mickey Morandini	.05
121	Brett Butler	.05
122	Tom Pagnozzi	.05
123	Ron Gant	.05
124	Damion Easley	.05
125	Dennis Eckersley	.60
126	Matt Mieske	.05
127	Cliff Floyd	.05
128	Julian Tavarez **RC**	.05
129	Arthur Rhodes	.05
130	Dave West	.05
131	Tim Naehring	.05
132	Freddie Benavides	.05
133	Paul Assenmacher	.05
134	David McCarty	.05
135	Jose Lind	.05
136	Reggie Sanders	.05
137	Don Slaught	.05
138	Andujar Cedeno	.05
139	Rob Deer	.05
140	Mike Piazza	1.25
141	Moises Alou	.05
142	Tom Foley	.05
143	Benny Santiago	.05
144	Sandy Alomar	.05
145	Carlos Hernandez	.05
146	Luis Alicea	.05
147	Tom Lampkin	.05
148	Ryan Klesko	.05
149	Juan Guzman	.05
150	Scott Servais	.05
151	Tony Gwynn	.75
152	Tim Wakefield	.05
153	David Nied	.05
154	Chris Haney	.05
155	Danny Bautista	.05
156	Randy Velarde	.05
157	Darrin Jackson	.05
158	J.R. Phillips **RC**	.05
159	Greg Gagne	.05
160	Luis Aquino	.05
161	John Vander Wal	.05
162	Randy Myers	.05
163	Ted Power	.05
164	Scott Brosius	.05
165	Len Dykstra	.05
166	Jacob Brumfield	.05
167	Bo Jackson	.10
168	Eddie Taubensee	.05
169	Carlos Baerga	.05
170	Tim Bogar	.05
171	Jose Canseco	.50
172	Greg Blosser	.05
173	Chili Davis	.05
174	Randy Knorr	.05
175	Mike Perez	.05
176	Henry Rodriguez	.05
177	Brian Turang **RC**	.05
178	Roger Pavlik	.05
179	Aaron Sele	.05
180	Fred McGriff, Gary Sheffield Tale of 2 Players	.05
181	J.T. Snow, Tim Salmon Tale of 2 Players	.05
182	Roberto Hernandez	.05
183	Jeff Reboulet	.05
184	John Doherty	.05
185	Danny Sheaffer	.05
186	Bip Roberts	.05
187	Denny Martinez	.05
188	Darryl Hamilton	.05
189	Eduardo Perez	.05
190	Pete Harnisch	.05
191	Rick Gossage	.05
192	Mickey Tettleton	.05
193	Lenny Webster	.05
194	Lance Johnson	.05
195	Don Mattingly	1.00
196	Gregg Olson	.05
197	Mark Gubicza	.05
198	Scott Fletcher	.05
199	Jon Shave	.05
200	Tim Mauser	.05
201	Jeromy Burnitz	.05
202	Rob Dibble	.05
203	Will Clark	.05
204	Steve Buechele	.05
205	Brian Williams	.05
206	Carlos Garcia	.05
207	Mark Clark	.05
208	Rafael Palmeiro	.60
209	Eric Davis	.05
210	Pat Meares	.05
211	Chuck Finley	.05
212	Jason Bere	.05
213	Gary DiSarcina	.05
214	Tony Fernandez	.05
215	B.J. Surhoff	.05
216	Lee Guetterman	.05
217	Tim Wallach	.05
218	Kirt Manwaring	.05
219	Albert Belle	.05
220	Dwight Gooden	.05
221	Archi Cianfrocco	.05
222	Terry Mulholland	.05
223	Hipolito Pichardo	.05
224	Kent Hrbek	.05
225	Criag Grebeck	.05
226	Todd Jones	.05
227	Mike Bordick	.05
228	John Olerud	.05
229	Jeff Blauser	.05
230	Alex Arias	.05
231	Bernard Gilkey	.05
232	Denny Neagle	.05
233	Pedro Borbon **RC**	.05
234	Dick Schofield	.05
235	Matias Carrillo	.05
236	Juan Bell	.05
237	Mike Hampton	.05
238	Barry Bonds	2.00
239	Cris Carpenter	.05
240	Eric Karros	.05
241	Greg McMichael	.05
242	Pat Hentgen	.05
243	Tim Pugh	.05
244	Vinny Castilla	.05
245	Charlie Hough	.05
246	Bobby Munoz	.05
247	Kevin Baez	.05
248	Todd Frohwirth	.05
249	Charlie Hayes	.05
250	Mike Macfarlane	.05
251	Danny Darwin	.05
252	Ben Rivera	.05
253	Dave Henderson	.05
254	Steve Avery	.05
255	Tim Belcher	.05
256	Dan Plesac	.05
257	Jim Thome	.60
258	Albert Belle	.05
259	Barry Bonds	1.00
260	Ron Gant	.05
261	Juan Gonzalez	.20
262	Ken Griffey Jr.	.65
263	Dave Justice	.05
264	Fred McGriff	.05
265	Rafael Palmeiro	.20
266	Mike Piazza	.65
267	Frank Thomas	.35
268	Matt Williams	.05
269a	Checklist 1-135	.05
269b	Checklist 271-408	.05
270a	Checklist 136-270	.05
270b	Checklist 409-540	.05
271	Mike Stanley	.05
272	Tony Tarasco	.05
273	Teddy Higuera	.05
274	Ryan Thompson	.05
275	Rick Aguilera	.05
276	Ramon Martinez	.05
277	Orlando Merced	.05
278	Guillermo Velasquez	.05
279	Mark Hutton	.05
280	Larry Walker	.05
281	Kevin Gross	.05
282	Jose Offerman	.05
283	Jim Leyritz	.05
284	Jamie Moyer	.05
285	Frank Thomas	.65
286	Derek Bell	.05
287	Derrick May	.05
288	Dave Winfield	.65
289	Curt Schilling	.35
290	Carlos Quintana	.05
291	Bob Natal	.05
292	David Cone	.05
293	Al Osuna	.05
294	Bob Hamelin	.05
295	Chad Curtis	.05
296	Danny Jackson	.05
297	Bob Welch	.05
298	Felix Jose	.05
299	Jay Buhner	.05
300	Joe Carter	.05
301	Kenny Lofton	.05
302	Kirk Rueter **RC**	.15
303	Kim Batiste	.05
304	Mike Morgan	.05
305	Pat Borders	.05
306	Rene Arocha	.05
307	Ruben Sierra	.05
308	Steve Finley	.05
309	Travis Fryman	.05
310	Zane Smith	.05
311	Willie Wilson	.05
312	Trevor Hoffman	.05
313	Terry Pendleton	.05
314	Salomon Torres	.05
315	Robin Ventura	.05
316	Randy Tomlin	.05
317	Dave Stewart	.05
318	Mike Benjamin	.05
319	Matt Turner	.05
320	Manny Ramirez	.65
321	Kevin Young	.05
322	Ken Caminiti	.05
323	Joe Girardi	.05
324	Jeff McKnight	.05
325	Gene Harris	.05
326	Devon White	.05
327	Darryl Kile	.05
328	Craig Paquette	.05
329	Cal Eldred	.05
330	Bill Swift	.05
331	Alan Trammell	.05
332	Armando Reynoso	.05
333	Brent Mayne	.05
334	Chris Donnels	.05
335	Darryl Strawberry	.05
336	Dean Palmer	.05
337	Frank Castillo	.05
338	Jeff King	.05
339	John Franco	.05
340	Kevin Appier	.05
341	Lance Blankenship	.05
342	Mark McLemore	.05
343	Pedro Astacio	.05
344	Rich Batchelor	.05
345	Ryan Bowen	.05
346	Terry Steinbach	.05
347	Troy O'Leary	.05
348	Willie Blair	.05
349	Wade Boggs	.75
350	Tim Raines	.05
351	Scott Livingstone	.05
352	Rod Carreia	.05
353	Ray Lankford	.05
354	Pat Listach	.05
355	Milt Thompson	.05
356	Miguel Jimenez	.05
357	Marc Newfield	.05
358	Mark McGwire	1.50
359	Kirby Puckett	.75
360	Kent Mercker	.05
361	John Kruk	.05
362	Jeff Kent	.05
363	Hal Morris	.05
364	Edgar Martinez	.05
365	Dave Magadan	.05
366	Dante Bichette	.05
367	Chris Hammond	.05
368	Bret Saberhagen	.05
369	Billy Ripken	.05
370	Bill Gullickson	.05
371	Andre Dawson	.35
372	Bobby Kelly	.05
373	Cal Ripken, Jr.	2.00
374	Craig Biggio	.05
375	Dan Pasqua	.05
376	Dave Nilsson	.05
377	Duane Ward	.05
378	Greg Vaughn	.05
379	Jeff Fassero	.05
380	Jerry Dipoto	.05
381	John Patterson	.05
382	Kevin Brown	.05
383	Kevin Roberson	.05
384	Joe Orsulak	.05
385	Hilly Hathaway	.05
386	Mike Greenwell	.05
387	Orestes Destrade	.05
388	Mike Gallego	.05
389	Ozzie Guillen	.05
390	Raul Mondesi	.05
391	Scott Lydy	.05
392	Tom Urbani	.05
393	Wil Cordero	.05
394	Tony Longmire	.05
395	Todd Zeile	.05
396	Scott Cooper	.05
397	Ryne Sandberg	.75
398	Ricky Bones	.05
399	Phil Clark	.05
400	Orel Hershiser	.05
401	Mike Henneman	.05
402	Mark Lemke	.05
403	Mark Grace	.05
404	Ken Ryan	.05
405	John Smoltz	.05
406	Jeff Conine	.05
407	Greg Harris	.05
408	Doug Drabek	.05
409	Dave Fleming	.05
410	Danny Tartabull	.05
411	Chad Kreuter	.05
412	Brad Ausmus	.05
413	Ben McDonald	.05
414	Barry Larkin	.05
415	Bret Barberie	.05
416	Chuck Knoblauch	.05
417	Ozzie Smith	.75
418	Ed Sprague	.05
419	Matt Williams	.05
420	Jeremy Hernandez	.05
421	Jose Bautista	.05
422	Kevin Mitchell	.05
423	Manuel Lee	.05
424	Mike Devereaux	.05
425	Omar Olivares	.05
426	Rafael Belliard	.05
427	Richie Lewis	.05
428	Ron Darling	.05
429	Shane Mack	.05
430	Tim Hulett	.05
431	Wally Joyner	.05
432	Wes Chamberlain	.05
433	Tom Browning	.05
434	Scott Radinsky	.05
435	Rondell White	.05
436	Rod Beck	.05
437	Rheal Cormier	.05
438	Randy Johnson	.65
439	Pete Schourek	.05
440	Mo Vaughn	.05
441	Mike Timlin	.05
442	Mark Langston	.05
443	Lou Whitaker	.05
444	Kevin Stocker	.05
445	Ken Hill	.05
446	John Wetteland	.05
447	J.T. Snow	.05
448	Erik Pappas	.05
449	David Hulse	.05
450	Darren Daulton	.05
451	Chris Hoiles	.05
452	Bryan Harvey	.05
453	Darren Lewis	.05
454	Andres Galarraga	.05
455	Joe Hesketh	.05
456	Jose Valentin	.05
457	Dan Peltier	.05
458	Joe Boever	.05
459	Kevin Rogers	.05
460	Craig Shipley	.05
461	Alvaro Espinoza	.05
462	Wilson Alvarez	.05
463	Cory Snyder	.05
464	Candy Maldonado	.05
465	Blas Minor	.05
466	Rod Bolton	.05
467	Kenny Rogers	.05
468	Greg Myers	.05
469	Jimmy Key	.05
470	Tony Castillo	.05
471	Mike Stanton	.05
472	Deion Sanders	.05
473	Tito Navarro	.05
474	Mike Gardiner	.05
475	Steve Reed	.05
476	John Roper	.05
477	Mike Trombley	.05
478	Charles Nagy	.05
479	Larry Casian	.05
480	Eric Hillman	.05
481	Bill Wertz	.05
482	Jeff Schwarz	.05
483	John Valentin	.05
484	Carl Willis	.05
485	Gary Gaetti	.05
486	Bill Pecota	.05
487	John Smiley	.05
488	Mike Mussina	.35
489	Mike Ignasiak **RC**	.05
490	Billy Brewer	.05
491	Jack Voigt	.05
492	Mike Munoz	.05
493	Lee Tinsley	.05
494	Bob Wickman	.05
495	Roger Salkeld	.05
496	Thomas Howard	.05
497	Mark Davis	.05
498	Dave Clark	.05
499	Turk Wendell	.05
500	Rafael Bournigal	.05
501	Chip Hale	.05
502	Matt Whiteside	.05
503	Brian Koelling	.05
504	Jeff Reed	.05
505	Paul Wagner	.05
506	Torey Lovullo	.05
507	Curtis Leskanic	.05
508	Derek Lilliquist	.05
509	Joe Magrane	.05
510	Mackey Sasser	.05
511	Lloyd McClendon	.05
512	Jayhawk Owens **RC**	.05
513	Woody Williams **RC**	.05
514	Gary Redus	.05
515	Tim Spehr	.05
516	Jim Abbott	.05
517	Lou Frazier	.05
518	Erik Plantenberg	.05
519	Tim Worrell	.05
520	Brian McRae	.05
521	Chan Ho Park **RC**	1.00
522	Mark Wohlers	.05
523	Geronimo Pena	.05
524	Andy Ashby	.05
525	Tim Raines, Andre Dawson Tale of 2 Players	.05
526	Paul Molitor, Dave Winfield Tale of 2 Players	.40
527	Joe Carter	.05
528	Frank Thomas	.35
529	Ken Griffey Jr.	.65
530	Dave Justice	.05
531	Gregg Jefferies	.05
532	Barry Bonds	1.00
533	John Kruk	.05
534	Roger Clemens	.50
535	Cecil Fielder	.05
536	Ruben Sierra	.05
537	Tony Gwynn	.40
538	Tom Glavine	.10
539	Not Issued, See #269	
540	Not Issued, See #270	
541	Ozzie Smith	.40
542	Eddie Murray	.30
543a	Lee Smith	.05
543b	Lonnie Smith (Should be #643.)	.05
544	Greg Maddux	.75
545	Denis Boucher	.05
546	Mark Gardner	.05
547	Bo Jackson	.10
548	Eric Anthony	.05
549	Delino DeShields	.05
550	Turner Ward	.05
551	Scott Sanderson	.05
552	Hector Carrasco	.05
553	Tony Phillips	.05
554	Melido Perez	.05
555	Mike Felder	.05
556	Jack Morris	.05

557	Rafael Palmeiro	.60
558	Shane Reynolds	.05
559	Pete Incaviglia	.05
560	Greg Harris	.05
561	Matt Walbeck	.05
562	Todd Van Poppel	.05
563	Todd Stottlemyre	.05
564	Ricky Bones	.05
565	Mike Jackson	.05
566	Kevin McReynolds	.05
567	Melvin Nieves	.05
568	Juan Gonzalez	.35
569	Frank Viola	.05
570	Vince Coleman	.05
571	Brian Anderson **RC**	.25
572	Omar Vizquel	.05
573	Bernie Williams	.05
574	Tom Glavine	.35
575	Mitch Williams	.05
576	Shawon Dunston	.05
577	Mike Lansing	.05
578	Greg Pirkl	.05
579	Sid Fernandez	.05
580	Doug Jones	.05
581	Walt Weiss	.05
582	Tim Belcher	.05
583	Alex Fernandez	.05
584	Alex Cole	.05
585	Greg Cadaret	.05
586	Bob Tewksbury	.05
587	Dave Hansen	.05
588	Kurt Abbott **RC**	.25
589	Rick White **RC**	.05
590	Kevin Bass	.05
591	Geronimo Berroa	.05
592	Jaime Navarro	.05
593	Steve Farr	.05
594	Jack Armstrong	.05
595	Steve Howe	.05
596	Jose Rijo	.05
597	Otis Nixon	.05
598	Robby Thompson	.05
599	Kelly Stinnett	.05
600	Carlos Delgado	.50
601	Brian Johnson **RC**	.05
602	Gregg Olson	.05
603	Jim Edmonds	.05
604	Mike Blowers	.05
605	Lee Smith	.05
606	Pat Rapp	.05
607	Mike Magnante	.05
608	Karl Rhodes	.05
609	Jeff Juden	.05
610	Rusty Meacham	.05
611	Pedro Martinez	.65
612	Todd Worrell	.05
613	Stan Javier	.05
614	Mike Hampton	.05
615	Jose Guzman	.05
616	Xavier Hernandez	.05
617	David Wells	.05
618	John Habyan	.05
619	Chris Nabholz	.05
620	Bobby Jones	.05
621	Chris James	.05
622	Ellis Burks	.05
623	Erik Hanson	.05
624	Pat Meares	.05
625	Harold Reynolds	.05
626	Bob Hamelin	.05
627	Manny Ramirez	.30
628	Ryan Klesko	.30
629	Carlos Delgado	.30
630	Javier Lopez	.05
631	Steve Karsay	.05
632	Rick Helling	.05
633	Steve Trachsel	.05
634	Hector Carrasco	.05
635	Andy Stankiewicz	.05
636	Paul Sorrento	.05
637	Scott Erickson	.05
638	Chipper Jones	.75
639	Luis Polonia	.05
640	Howard Johnson	.05
641	John Dopson	.05
642	Jody Reed	.05
643	Not issued, See #543	
644	Mark Portugal	.05
645	Paul Molitor	.65
646	Paul Assenmacher	.05
647	Hubie Brooks	.05
648	Gary Wayne	.05
649	Sean Berry	.05
650	Roger Clemens	1.00
651	Brian Hunter	.05
652	Wally Whitehurst	.05
653	Allen Watson	.05
654	Rickey Henderson	.65
655	Sid Bream	.05
656	Dan Wilson	.05
657	Ricky Jordan	.05
658	Sterling Hitchcock	.05
659	Darrin Jackson	.05
660	Junior Felix	.05
661	Tom Brunansky	.05
662	Jose Vizcaino	.05
663	Mark Leiter	.05
664	Gil Heredia	.05
665	Fred McGriff	.05
666	Will Clark	.05
667	Al Leiter	.05
668	James Mouton	.05
669	Billy Bean	.05
670	Scott Leius	.05
671	Bret Boone	.05

672	Darren Holmes	.05
673	Dave Weathers	.05
674	Eddie Murray	.65
675	Felix Fermin	.05
676	Chris Sabo	.05
677	Billy Spiers	.05
678	Aaron Sele	.05
679	Juan Samuel	.05
680	Julio Franco	.05
681	Heathcliff Slocumb	.05
682	Denny Martinez	.05
683	Jerry Browne	.05
684	Pedro A. Martinez **RC**	.05
685	Rex Hudler	.05
686	Willie McGee	.05
687	Andy Van Slyke	.05
688	Pat Mahomes	.05
689	Dave Henderson	.05
690	Tony Eusebio	.05
691	Rick Sutcliffe	.05
692	Willie Banks	.05
693	Alan Mills	.05
694	Jeff Treadway	.05
695	Alex Gonzalez	.05
696	David Segui	.05
697	Rick Helling	.05
698	Bip Roberts	.05
699	Jeff Cirillo **RC**	.25
700	Terry Mulholland	.05
701	Marvin Freeman	.05
702	Jason Bere	.05
703	Javier Lopez	.05
704	Greg Hibbard	.05
705	Tommy Greene	.05
706	Marquis Grissom	.05
707	Brian Harper	.05
708	Steve Karsay	.05
709	Jeff Brantley	.05
710	Jeff Russell	.05
711	Bryan Hickerson	.05
712	Jim Pittsley **RC**	.05
713	Bobby Ayala	.05
714	John Smoltz	.05
715	Jose Rijo	.05
716	Greg Maddux	.40
717	Matt Williams	.05
718	Frank Thomas	.35
719	Ryne Sandberg	.40
720	Checklist	.05

1st Day Issue

Common Player: 1.00
Stars: 8X
(See 1994 Stadium Club for checklist and base card values.)

Golden Rainbow

NM/M
Complete Set (720): 60.00
Common Player: .25
Stars: 2X
(See 1994 Stadium Club for checklist and base card values.)

Dugout Dirt

NM/M
Complete Set (12): 5.00

Common Player: .25

1	Mike Piazza	1.00
2	Dave Winfield	.65
3	John Kruk	.25
4	Cal Ripken, Jr.	2.00
5	Jack McDowell	.25
6	Barry Bonds	2.00
7	Ken Griffey Jr.	1.00
8	Tim Salmon	.25
9	Frank Thomas	.65
10	Jeff Kent	.25
11	Randy Johnson	.65
12	Darren Daulton	.25

Finest

NM/M
Complete Set (10): 11.00
Common Player: .50

1	Jeff Bagwell	1.25
2	Albert Belle	.50
3	Barry Bonds	3.00
4	Juan Gonzalez	.75
5	Ken Griffey Jr.	2.00
6	Marquis Grissom	.50
7	David Justice	.50
8	Mike Piazza	2.00
9	Tim Salmon	.50
10	Frank Thomas	1.50

1994 Stadium Club Finest Jumbo

NM/M
Complete Set (10): 30.00
Common Player: 2.00

1	Jeff Bagwell	4.00
2	Albert Belle	2.00
3	Barry Bonds	6.50
4	Juan Gonzalez	3.00
5	Ken Griffey Jr.	5.00
6	Marquis Grissom	2.00
7	David Justice	2.00
8	Mike Piazza	5.00
9	Tim Salmon	2.00
10	Frank Thomas	4.00

1994 Stadium Club Super Teams

NM/M
Complete Set (28): 25.00
Common Team: .70
Expired Jan. 31, 1996.

1	Atlanta Braves	5.00
2	Chicago Cubs	.70
3	Cincinnati Reds	1.25
4	Colorado Rockies	1.00
5	Florida Marlins	.70
6	Houston Astros	1.00
7	Los Angeles Dodgers	1.75
8	Montreal Expos	1.00
9	New York Mets	.70
10	Philadelphia Phillies	.70
11	Pittsburgh Pirates	.70
12	St. Louis Cardinals	.70
13	San Diego Padres	.70
14	San Francisco Giants	1.25
15	Baltimore Orioles	1.25
16	Boston Red Sox	1.00
17	California Angels	.70
18	Chicago White Sox	1.50
19	Cleveland Indians	2.00
20	Detroit Tigers	.70
21	Kansas City Royals	1.00
22	Milwaukee Brewers	.70
23	Minnesota Twins	1.00
24	New York Yankees	1.50
25	Oakland Athletics	1.00
26	Seattle Mariners	2.00
27	Texas Rangers	1.00
28	Toronto Blue Jays	1.00

1994 Stadium Club Draft Picks

NM/M
Complete Set (90): 7.50
Common Player: .05
Wax Box (24): 9.00

1	Jacob Shumate	.05
2	C.J. Nitkowski	.05
3	Doug Million	.05
4	Matt Smith	.05
5	Kevin Lovinger	.05
6	Alberto Castillo	.05
7	Mike Russell	.05
8	Dan Lock	.05
9	Tom Szymanski	.05
10	Aaron Boone	.25
11	Jayson Peterson	.05
12	Mark Johnson	.05
13	Cade Gaspar	.05
14	George Lombard	.10
15	Russ Johnson	.10
16	Travis Miller	.10
17	Jay Payton	.50
18	Brian Buchanan	.10
19	Jacob Cruz	.10
20	Gary Rath	.05
21	Ramon Castro	.05
22	Tommy Davis	.05
23	Tony Terry	.05
24	Jerry Whittaker	.05
25	Mike Darr	.05
26	Doug Webb	.05

27 Jason Camilli .05
28 Brad Rigby .05
29 Ryan Nye .05
30 Carl Dale .05
31 Andy Taulbee .05
32 Trey Moore .05
33 John Crowther .05
34 Joe Giuliano .05
35 Brian Rose .05
36 Paul Failla .05
37 Brian Meadows .05
38 Oscar Robles .05
39 Mike Metcalff .05
40 Larry Barnes .05
41 Paul Ottavinia .05
42 Chris McBride .05
43 Ricky Stone .05
44 Billy Blythe .05
45 Eddie Priest .05
46 Scott Forster .05
47 Eric Pickett .05
48 Matt Beaumont .05
49 Darrell Nicolas .05
50 Mike Hampton .05
51 Paul O'Malley .05
52 Steve Shoemaker .05
53 Jason Sikes .05
54 Bryan Farson .05
55 Yates Hall .05
56 Troy Brohawn .05
57 Dan Hower .05
58 Clay Caruthers .05
59 Pepe McNeal .05
60 Ray Ricken .05
61 Scott Shores .05
62 Eddie Brooks .05
63 Dave Kauflin .05
64 David Meyer .05
65 Geoff Blum .05
66 Roy Marsh .05
67 Ryan Beeney .05
68 Derek Dukart .05
69 Nomar Garciaparra 6.00
70 Jason Kelley .05
71 Jesse Ibarra .05
72 Bucky Buckles .05
73 Mark Little .05
74 Heath Murray .05
75 Greg Morris .05
76 Mike Halperin .05
77 Wes Helms .05
78 Ray Brown .05
79 Kevin Brown .05
80 Paul Konerko .50
81 Mike Thurman .05
82 Paul Wilson .10
83 Terrence Long .25
84 Ben Grieve .50
85 Mark Farris .05
86 Bret Wagner .05
87 Dustin Hermanson .05
88 Kevin Witt .05
89 Corey Pointer .05
90 Tim Grieve .05

First Day Issue

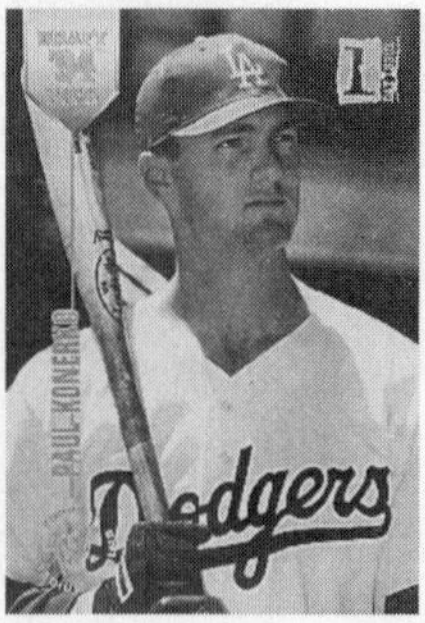

NM/M
Complete Set (90): 150.00
Common Player: 1.00
Stars: 15X
(See 1994 Stadium Club Draft Picks for checklist and base card values.)

1995 Stadium Club

NM/M
Complete Set (630): 25.00
Common Player: .05
Common First Day Production: .50
First Day Stars: 7X
Series 1 or 2 Pack (14): 1.25
Series 1 or 2 Wax Box (24): 20.00
Series 3 Pack (13): 1.25
Series 3 Wax Box (24): 20.00
1 Cal Ripken Jr. 2.50
2 Bo Jackson .10
3 Bryan Harvey .05
4 Curt Schilling .35
5 Bruce Ruffin .05
6 Travis Fryman .05
7 Jim Abbott .05

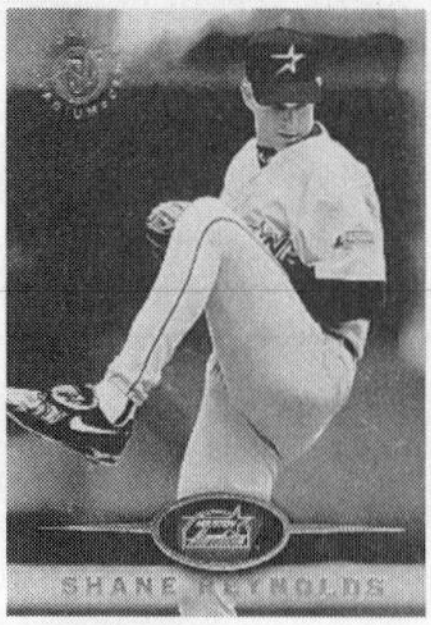

8 David McCarty .05
9 Gary Gaetti .05
10 Roger Clemens 1.25
11 Carlos Garcia .05
12 Lee Smith .05
13 Bobby Ayala .05
14 Charles Nagy .05
15 Lou Frazier .05
16 Rene Arocha .05
17 Carlos Delgado .50
18 Steve Finley .05
19 Ryan Klesko .05
20 Cal Eldred .05
21 Rey Sanchez .05
22 Ken Hill .05
23 Benny Santiago .05
24 Julian Tavarez .05
25 Jose Vizcaino .05
26 Andy Benes .05
27 Mariano Duncan .05
28 Checklist A .05
29 Shawon Dunston .05
30 Rafael Palmeiro .65
31 Dean Palmer .05
32 Andres Galarraga .05
33 Joey Cora .05
34 Mickey Tettleton .05
35 Barry Larkin .05
36 Carlos Baerga .05
37 Orel Hershiser .05
38 Jody Reed .05
39 Paul Molitor .75
40 Jim Edmonds .05
41 Bob Tewksbury .05
42 John Patterson .05
43 Ray McDavid .05
44 Zane Smith .05
45 Bret Saberhagen .05
46 Greg Maddux 1.00
47 Frank Thomas .75
48 Carlos Baerga .05
49 Billy Spiers .05
50 Stan Javier .05
51 Rex Hudler .05
52 Denny Hocking .05
53 Todd Worrell .05
54 Mark Clark .05
55 Hipilito Pichardo .05
56 Bob Wickman .05
57 Raul Mondesi .05
58 Steve Cooke .05
59 Rod Beck .05
60 Tim Davis .05
61 Jeff Kent .05
62 John Valentin .05
63 Alex Arias .05
64 Steve Reed .05
65 Ozzie Smith 1.00
66 Terry Pendleton .05
67 Kenny Rogers .05
68 Vince Coleman .05
69 Tom Pagnozzi .05
70 Roberto Alomar .20
71 Darrin Jackson .05
72 Dennis Eckersley .65
73 Jay Buhner .05
74 Darren Lewis .05
75 Dave Weathers .05
76 Matt Walbeck .05
77 Brad Ausmus .05
78 Danny Bautista .05
79 Bob Hamelin .05
80 Steve Traschel .05
81 Ken Ryan .05
82 Chris Turner .05
83 David Segui .05
84 Ben McDonald .05
85 Wade Boggs 1.00
86 John Vander Wal .05
87 Sandy Alomar .05
88 Ron Karkovice .05
89 Doug Jones .05
90 Gary Sheffield .40
91 Ken Caminiti .05
92 Chris Bosio .05
93 Kevin Tapani .05
94 Walt Weiss .05
95 Erik Hanson .05
96 Ruben Sierra .05
97 Nomar Garciaparra 1.00
98 Terrence Long .05
99 Jacob Shumate .05
100 Paul Wilson .05
101 Kevin Witt .05
102 Paul Konerko .15
103 Ben Grieve .05
104 Mark Johnson **RC** .05
105 Cade Gaspar **RC** .05
106 Mark Farris .05
107 Dustin Hermanson .05
108 Scott Elarton **RC** .15
109 Doug Million .05
110 Matt Smith .05
111 Brian Buchanan **RC** .05
112 Jayson Peterson **RC** .05
113 Bret Wagner .05
114 C.J. Nitkowski .05
115 Ramon Castro **RC** .05
116 Rafael Bournigal .05
117 Jeff Fassero .05
118 Bobby Bonilla .05
119 Ricky Gutierrez .05
120 Roger Pavlik .05
121 Mike Greenwell .05
122 Deion Sanders .05
123 Charlie Hayes .05
124 Paul O'Neill .05
125 Jay Bell .05
126 Royce Clayton .05
127 Willie Banks .05
128 Mark Wohlers .05
129 Todd Jones .05
130 Todd Stottlemyre .05
131 Will Clark .05
132 Wilson Alvarez .05
133 Chili Davis .05
134 Dave Burba .05
135 Chris Hoiles .05
136 Jeff Blauser .05
137 Jeff Reboulet .05
138 Bret Saberhagen .05
139 Kirk Rueter .05
140 Dave Nilsson .05
141 Pat Borders .05
142 Ron Darling .05
143 Derek Bell .05
144 Dave Hollins .05
145 Juan Gonzalez .40
146 Andre Dawson .25
147 Jim Thome .65
148 Larry Walker .05
149 Mike Piazza 1.50
150 Mike Perez .05
151 Steve Avery .05
152 Dan Wilson .05
153 Andy Van Slyke .05
154 Junior Felix .05
155 Jack McDowell .05
156 Danny Tartabull .05
157 Willie Blair .05
158 William Van Landingham .05
159 Robb Nen .05
160 Lee Tinsley .05
161 Ismael Valdes .05
162 Juan Guzman .05
163 Scott Servais .05
164 Cliff Floyd .05
165 Allen Watson .05
166 Eddie Taubensee .05
167 Scott Hemond .05
168 Jeff Tackett .05
169 Chad Curtis .05
170 Rico Brogna .05
171 Luis Polonia .05
172 Checklist B .05
173 Lance Johnson .05
174 Sammy Sosa 1.00
175 Mike MacFarlane .05
176 Darryl Hamilton .05
177 Rick Aguilera .05
178 Dave West .05
179 Mike Gallego .05
180 Marc Newfield .05
181 Steve Buechele .05
182 David Wells .05
183 Tom Glavine .35
184 Joe Girardi .05
185 Craig Biggio .05
186 Eddie Murray .75
187 Kevin Gross .05
188 Sid Fernandez .05
189 John Franco .05
190 Bernard Gilkey .05
191 Matt Williams .05
192 Darrin Fletcher .05
193 Jeff Conine .05
194 Ed Sprague .05
195 Eduardo Perez .05
196 Scott Livingstone .05
197 Ivan Rodriguez .65
198 Orlando Merced .05
199 Ricky Bones .05
200 Javier Lopez .05
201 Miguel Jimenez .05
202 Terry McGriff .05
203 Mike Lieberthal .05
204 David Cone .05
205 Todd Hundley .05
206 Ozzie Guillen .05
207 Alex Cole .05
208 Tony Phillips .05
209 Jim Eisenreich .05
210 Greg Vaughn .05
211 Barry Larkin .05
212 Don Mattingly 1.00
213 Mark Grace .05
214 Jose Canseco .50
215 Joe Carter .05
216 David Cone .05
217 Sandy Alomar .05
218 Al Martin .05
219 Roberto Kelly .05
220 Paul Sorrento .05
221 Tony Fernandez .05
222 Stan Belinda .05
223 Mike Stanley .05
224 Doug Drabek .05
225 Todd Van Poppel .05
226 Matt Mieske .05
227 Tino Martinez .05
228 Andy Ashby .05
229 Midre Cummings .05
230 Jeff Frye .05
231 Hal Morris .05
232 Jose Lind .05
233 Shawn Green .30
234 Rafael Belliard .05
235 Randy Myers .05
236 Frank Thomas .45
237 Darren Daulton .05
238 Sammy Sosa .65
239 Cal Ripken Jr. 1.00
240 Jeff Bagwell .40
241 Ken Griffey Jr. 1.50
242 Brett Butler .05
243 Derrick May .05
244 Pat Listach .05
245 Mike Bordick .05
246 Mark Langston .05
247 Randy Velarde .05
248 Julio Franco .05
249 Chuck Knoblauch .05
250 Bill Gullickson .05
251 Dave Henderson .05
252 Bret Boone .05
253 Al Martin .05
254 Armando Benitez .05
255 Wil Cordero .05
256 Al Leiter .05
257 Luis Gonzalez .05
258 Charlie O'Brien .05
259 Tim Wallach .05
260 Scott Sanders .05
261 Tom Henke .05
262 Otis Nixon .05
263 Darren Daulton .05
264 Manny Ramirez .75
265 Bret Barberie .05
266 Mel Rojas .05
267 John Burkett .05
268 Brady Anderson .05
269 John Roper .05
270 Shane Reynolds .05
271 Barry Bonds 2.50
272 Alex Fernandez .05
273 Brian McRae .05
274 Todd Zeile .05
275 Greg Swindell .05
276 Johnny Ruffin .05
277 Troy Neel .05
278 Eric Karros .05
279 John Hudek .05
280 Thomas Howard .05
281 Joe Carter .05
282 Mike Devereaux .05
283 Butch Henry .05
284 Reggie Jefferson .05
285 Mark Lemke .05
286 Jeff Montgomery .05
287 Ryan Thompson .05
288 Paul Shuey .05
289 Mark McGwire 2.00
290 Bernie Williams .05
291 Mickey Morandini .05
292 Scott Leius .05
293 David Hulse .05
294 Greg Gagne .05
295 Moises Alou .05
296 Geronimo Berroa .05
297 Eddie Zambrano .05
298 Alan Trammell .05
299 Don Slaught .05
300 Jose Rijo .05
301 Joe Ausanio .05
302 Tim Raines .05
303 Melido Perez .05
304 Kent Mercker .05
305 James Mouton .05
306 Luis Lopez .05
307 Mike Kingery .05
308 Willie Greene .05
309 Cecil Fielder .05
310 Scott Kamieniecki .05
311 Mike Greenwell .05
312 Bobby Bonilla .05
313 Andres Galarraga .05
314 Cal Ripken Jr. 1.25
315 Matt Williams .05
316 Tom Pagnozzi .05
317 Len Dykstra .05
318 Frank Thomas .40
319 Kirby Puckett .50
320 Mike Piazza 1.00
321 Jason Jacome .05
322 Brian Hunter .05
323 Brent Gates .05
324 Jim Converse .05
325 Damion Easley .05
326 Dante Bichette .05
327 Kurt Abbott .05
328 Scott Cooper .05

#	Player	Price
329	Mike Henneman	.05
330	Orlando Miller	.05
331	John Kruk	.05
332	Jose Oliva	.05
333	Reggie Sanders	.05
334	Omar Vizquel	.05
335	Devon White	.05
336	Mike Morgan	.05
337	J.R. Phillips	.05
338	Gary DiSarcina	.05
339	Joey Hamilton	.05
340	Randy Johnson	.75
341	Jim Leyritz	.05
342	Bobby Jones	.05
343	Jaime Navarro	.05
344	Bip Roberts	.05
345	Steve Karsay	.05
346	Kevin Stocker	.05
347	Jose Canseco	.50
348	Bill Wegman	.05
349	Rondell White	.05
350	Mo Vaughn	.05
351	Joe Orsulak	.05
352	Pat Meares	.05
353	Albie Lopez	.05
354	Edgar Martinez	.05
355	Brian Jordan	.05
356	Tommy Greene	.05
357	Chuck Carr	.05
358	Pedro Astacio	.05
359	Russ Davis	.05
360	Chris Hammond	.05
361	Gregg Jefferies	.05
362	Shane Mack	.05
363	Fred McGriff	.05
364	Pat Rapp	.05
365	Bill Swift	.05
366	Checklist	.05
367	Robin Ventura	.05
368	Bobby Witt	.05
369	Karl Rhodes	.05
370	Eddie Williams	.05
371	John Jaha	.05
372	Steve Howe	.05
373	Leo Gomez	.05
374	Hector Fajardo	.05
375	Jeff Bagwell	.75
376	Mark Acre	.05
377	Wayne Kirby	.05
378	Mark Portugal	.05
379	Jesus Tavarez	.05
380	Jim Lindeman	.05
381	Don Mattingly	1.25
382	Trevor Hoffman	.05
383	Chris Gomez	.05
384	Garret Anderson	.05
385	Bobby Munoz	.05
386	Jon Lieber	.05
387	Rick Helling	.05
388	Marvin Freeman	.05
389	Juan Castillo	.05
390	Jeff Cirillo	.05
391	Sean Berry	.05
392	Hector Carrasco	.05
393	Mark Grace	.05
394	Pat Kelly	.05
395	Tim Naehring	.05
396	Greg Pirkl	.05
397	John Smoltz	.05
398	Robby Thompson	.05
399	Rick White	.05
400	Frank Thomas	.75
401	Jeff Conine	.05
402	Jose Valentin	.05
403	Carlos Baerga	.05
404	Rick Aguilera	.05
405	Wilson Alvarez	.05
406	Juan Gonzalez	.20
407	Barry Larkin	.05
408	Ken Hill	.05
409	Chuck Carr	.05
410	Tim Raines	.05
411	Bryan Eversgerd	.05
412	Phil Plantier	.05
413	Josias Manzanillo	.05
414	Roberto Kelly	.05
415	Rickey Henderson	.75
416	John Smiley	.05
417	Kevin Brown	.05
418	Jimmy Key	.05
419	Wally Joyner	.05
420	Roberto Hernandez	.05
421	Felix Fermin	.05
422	Checklist	.05
423	Greg Vaughn	.05
424	Ray Lankford	.05
425	Greg Maddux	1.00
426	Mike Mussina	.30
427	Geronimo Pena	.05
428	David Nied	.05
429	Scott Erickson	.05
430	Kevin Mitchell	.05
431	Mike Lansing	.05
432	Brian Anderson	.05
433	Jeff King	.05
434	Ramon Martinez	.05
435	Kevin Seitzer	.05
436	Salomon Torres	.05
437	Brian Hunter	.05
438	Melvin Nieves	.05
439	Mike Kelly	.05
440	Marquis Grissom	.05
441	Chuck Finley	.05
442	Len Dykstra	.05
443	Ellis Burks	.05

#	Player	Price
444	Harold Baines	.05
445	Kevin Appier	.05
446	Dave Justice	.05
447	Darryl Kile	.05
448	John Olerud	.05
449	Greg McMichael	.05
450	Kirby Puckett	1.00
451	Jose Valentin	.05
452	Rick Wilkins	.05
453	Arthur Rhodes	.05
454	Pat Hentgen	.05
455	Tom Gordon	.05
456	Tom Candiotti	.05
457	Jason Bere	.05
458	Wes Chamberlain	.05
459	Greg Colbrunn	.05
460	John Doherty	.05
461	Kevin Foster	.05
462	Mark Whiten	.05
463	Terry Steinbach	.05
464	Aaron Sele	.05
465	Kirt Manwaring	.05
466	Darren Hall	.05
467	Delino DeShields	.05
468	Andujar Cedeno	.05
469	Billy Ashley	.05
470	Kenny Lofton	.05
471	Pedro Munoz	.05
472	John Wetteland	.05
473	Tim Salmon	.05
474	Denny Neagle	.05
475	Tony Gwynn	1.00
476	Vinny Castilla	.05
477	Steve Dreyer	.05
478	Jeff Shaw	.05
479	Chad Ogea	.05
480	Scott Ruffcorn	.05
481	Lou Whitaker	.05
482	J.T. Snow	.05
483	Rich Rowland	.05
484	Dennis Martinez	.05
485	Pedro Martinez	.75
486	Rusty Greer	.05
487	Dave Fleming	.05
488	John Dettmer	.05
489	Albert Belle	.05
490	Ravelo Manzanillo	.05
491	Henry Rodriguez	.05
492	Andrew Lorraine	.05
493	Dwayne Hosey	.05
494	Mike Blowers	.05
495	Turner Ward	.05
496	Fred McGriff	.05
497	Sammy Sosa	.50
498	Barry Larkin	.05
499	Andres Galarraga	.05
500	Gary Sheffield	.15
501	Jeff Bagwell	.40
502	Mike Piazza	1.00
503	Moises Alou	.05
504	Bobby Bonilla	.05
505	Darren Daulton	.05
506	Jeff King	.05
507	Ray Lankford	.05
508	Tony Gwynn	.50
509	Barry Bonds	1.25
510	Cal Ripken Jr.	1.25
511	Mo Vaughn	.05
512	Tim Salmon	.05
513	Frank Thomas	.45
514	Albert Belle	.05
515	Cecil Fielder	.05
516	Kevin Appier	.05
517	Greg Vaughn	.05
518	Kirby Puckett	.50
519	Paul O'Neill	.05
520	Ruben Sierra	.05
521	Ken Griffey Jr.	.75
522	Will Clark	.05
523	Joe Carter	.05
524	Antonio Osuna	.05
525	Glenallen Hill	.05
526	Alex Gonzalez	.05
527	Dave Stewart	.05
528	Ron Gant	.05
529	Jason Bates	.05
530	Mike Macfarlane	.05
531	Esteban Loaiza	.05
532	Joe Randa	.05
533	Dave Winfield	.75
534	Danny Darwin	.05
535	Pete Harnisch	.05
536	Joey Cora	.05
537	Jaime Navarro	.05
538	Marty Cordova	.05
539	Andujar Cedeno	.05
540	Mickey Tettleton	.05
541	Andy Van Slyke	.05
542	Carlos Perez RC	.05
543	Chipper Jones	1.00
544	Tony Fernandez	.05
545	Tom Henke	.05
546	Pat Borders	.05
547	Chad Curtis	.05
548	Ray Durham	.05
549	Joe Oliver	.05
550	Jose Mesa	.05
551	Steve Finley	.05
552	Otis Nixon	.05
553	Jacob Brumfield	.05
554	Bill Swift	.05
555	Quilvio Veras	.05
556	Hideo Nomo RC	1.50
557	Joe Vitiello	.05
558	Mike Perez	.05

#	Player	Price
559	Charlie Hayes	.05
560	Brad Radke RC	.25
561	Darren Bragg	.05
562	Orel Hershiser	.05
563	Edgardo Alfonzo	.05
564	Doug Jones	.05
565	Andy Pettitte	.25
566	Benito Santiago	.05
567	John Burkett	.05
568	Brad Clontz	.05
569	Jim Abbott	.05
570	Joe Rosselli	.05
571	Mark Grudzielanek RC	.25
572	Dustin Hermanson	.05
573	Benji Gil	.05
574	Mark Whiten	.05
575	Mike Ignasiak	.05
576	Kevin Ritz	.05
577	Paul Quantrill	.05
578	Andre Dawson	.25
579	Jerald Clark	.05
580	Frank Rodriguez	.05
581	Mark Kiefer	.05
582	Trevor Wilson	.05
583	Gary Wilson RC	.05
584	Andy Stankiewicz	.05
585	Felipe Lira	.05
586	Mike Mimbs RC	.05
587	Jon Nunnally	.05
588	Tomas Perez RC	.05
589	Checklist	.05
590	Todd Hollandsworth	.05
591	Roberto Petagine	.05
592	Mariano Rivera	.15
593	Mark McLemore	.05
594	Bobby Witt	.05
595	Jose Offerman	.05
596	Jason Christiansen	.05
597	Jeff Manto	.05
598	Jim Dougherty	.05
599	Juan Acevedo	.05
600	Troy O'Leary	.05
601	Ron Villone	.05
602	Tripp Cromer	.05
603	Steve Scarsone	.05
604	Lance Parrish	.05
605	Ozzie Timmons	.05
606	Ray Holbert	.05
607	Tony Phillips	.05
608	Phil Plantier	.05
609	Shane Andrews	.05
610	Heathcliff Slocumb	.05
611	Bobby Higginson RC	.25
612	Bob Tewksbury	.05
613	Terry Pendleton	.05
614	Scott Cooper	.05
615	John Wetteland	.05
616	Ken Hill	.05
617	Marquis Grissom	.05
618	Larry Walker	.05
619	Derek Bell	.05
620	David Cone	.05
621	Ken Caminiti	.05
622	Jack McDowell	.05
623	Vaughn Eshelman	.05
624	Brian McRae	.05
625	Gregg Jefferies	.05
626	Kevin Brown	.05
627	Lee Smith	.05
628	Tony Tarasco	.05
629	Brett Butler	.05
630	Jose Canseco	.35

1995 Stadium Club 1st Day Issue

		NM/M
Common Player:		.50
Stars:		7X

(See 1995 Stadium Club #1-270 for checklist and base card values.)

Clear Cut

		NM/M
Complete Set (28):		20.00
Common Player:		.65
1	Mike Piazza	3.00
2	Ruben Sierra	.65
3	Tony Gwynn	2.50
4	Frank Thomas	2.00
5	Fred McGriff	.65
6	Rafael Palmeiro	1.50
7	Bobby Bonilla	.65
8	Chili Davis	.65
9	Hal Morris	.65
10	Jose Canseco	1.00
11	Jay Bell	.65
12	Kirby Puckett	2.50
13	Gary Sheffield	1.00
14	Bob Hamelin	.65
15	Jeff Bagwell	2.00
16	Albert Belle	.65
17	Sammy Sosa	2.50
18	Ken Griffey Jr.	3.00
19	Todd Zeile	.65
20	Mo Vaughn	.65
21	Moises Alou	.65
22	Paul O'Neill	.65
23	Andres Galarraga	.65
24	Greg Vaughn	.65
25	Len Dykstra	.65
26	Joe Carter	.65
27	Barry Bonds	4.50
28	Cecil Fielder	.65

Crunch Time

		NM/M
Complete Set (20):		15.00
Common Player:		1.00
1	Jeff Bagwell	2.50
2	Kirby Puckett	3.00
3	Frank Thomas	2.50
4	Albert Belle	1.00
5	Julio Franco	1.00
6	Jose Canseco	1.50
7	Paul Molitor	2.50
8	Joe Carter	1.00
9	Ken Griffey Jr.	4.00
10	Larry Walker	1.00
11	Dante Bichette	1.00
12	Carlos Baerga	1.00
13	Fred McGriff	1.00
14	Ruben Sierra	1.00
15	Will Clark	1.00
16	Moises Alou	1.00
17	Rafael Palmeiro	2.00
18	Travis Fryman	1.00
19	Barry Bonds	5.00
20	Cal Ripken Jr.	5.00

Crystal Ball

		NM/M
Complete Set (15):		15.00
Common Player:		.75
1	Chipper Jones	5.00
2	Dustin Hermanson	.75
3	Ray Durham	.75
4	Phil Nevin	.75
5	Billy Ashley	.75
6	Shawn Green	2.50
7	Jason Bates	.75
8	Benji Gil	.75
9	Marty Cordova	.75
10	Quilvio Veras	.75
11	Mark Grudzielanek	.75
12	Ruben Rivera	.75

13	Bill Pulsipher	.75
14	Derek Jeter	7.50
15	LaTroy Hawkins	.75

Power Zone

		NM/M
Complete Set (12):		9.00
Common Player:		.50
1	Jeff Bagwell	1.00
2	Albert Belle	.50
3	Barry Bonds	3.00
4	Joe Carter	.50
5	Cecil Fielder	.50
6	Andres Galarraga	.50
7	Ken Griffey Jr.	2.00
8	Paul Molitor	1.00
9	Fred McGriff	.50
10	Rafael Palmeiro	.75
11	Frank Thomas	1.00
12	Matt Williams	.50

Ring Leaders

		NM/M
Complete Set (40):		70.00
Common Player:		.75
1	Jeff Bagwell	3.00
2	Mark McGwire	7.50
3	Ozzie Smith	4.00
4	Paul Molitor	3.00
5	Darryl Strawberry	.75
6	Eddie Murray	3.00
7	Tony Gwynn	4.00
8	Jose Canseco	2.00
9	Howard Johnson	.75
10	Andre Dawson	1.25
11	Matt Williams	.75
12	Tim Raines	.75
13	Fred McGriff	.75
14	Ken Griffey Jr.	6.00
15	Gary Sheffield	2.00
16	Dennis Eckersley	2.50
17	Kevin Mitchell	.75
18	Will Clark	.75
19	Darren Daulton	.75
20	Paul O'Neill	.75
21	Julio Franco	.75
22	Albert Belle	.75
23	Juan Gonzalez	1.50
24	Kirby Puckett	4.00
25	Joe Carter	.75
26	Frank Thomas	9.00
27	Cal Ripken Jr.	3.00
28	John Olerud	.75
29	Ruben Sierra	.75
30	Barry Bonds	9.00
31	Cecil Fielder	.75
32	Roger Clemens	5.00
33	Don Mattingly	5.00
34	Terry Pendleton	.75
35	Rickey Henderson	3.00
36	Dave Winfield	3.00
37	Edgar Martinez	.75
38	Wade Boggs	4.00
39	Willie McGee	.75
40	Andres Galarraga	.75

Super Skills

		NM/M
Complete Set (20):		30.00
Common Player:		.75
1	Roberto Alomar	1.00
2	Barry Bonds	10.00
3	Jay Buhner	.75
4	Chuck Carr	.75
5	Don Mattingly	5.00
6	Raul Mondesi	.75
7	Tim Salmon	.75
8	Deion Sanders	.75
9	Devon White	.75
10	Mark Whiten	.75
11	Ken Griffey Jr.	7.50
12	Marquis Grissom	.75
13	Paul O'Neill	.75
14	Kenny Lofton	.75
15	Larry Walker	.75
16	Scott Cooper	.75
17	Barry Larkin	.75
18	Matt Williams	.75
19	John Wetteland	.75
20	Randy Johnson	2.50

Virtual Reality

		NM/M
Complete Set (270):		35.00
Common Player:		.10
1	Cal Ripken Jr.	2.50
2	Travis Fryman	.10
3	Jim Abbott	.10
4	Gary Gaetti	.10
5	Roger Clemens	1.25
6	Carlos Garcia	.10
7	Lee Smith	.10
8	Bobby Ayala	.10
9	Charles Nagy	.10
10	Rene Arocha	.10
11	Carlos Delgado	.50
12	Steve Finley	.10
13	Ryan Klesko	.10
14	Cal Eldred	.10
15	Rey Sanchez	.10
16	Ken Hill	.10
17	Jose Vizcaino	.10
18	Andy Benes	.10
19	Shawon Dunston	.10
20	Rafael Palmeiro	.65
21	Dean Palmer	.10
22	Joey Cora	.10
23	Mickey Tettleton	.10
24	Barry Larkin	.10
25	Carlos Baerga	.10
26	Orel Hershiser	.10
27	Jody Reed	.10
28	Paul Molitor	.75
29	Jim Edmonds	.10
30	Bob Tewksbury	.10
31	Ray McDavid	.10
32	Stan Javier	.10
33	Todd Worrell	.10
34	Bob Wickman	.10
35	Raul Mondesi	.10
36	Rod Beck	.10
37	Jeff Kent	.10
38	John Valentin	.10
39	Ozzie Smith	1.00
40	Terry Pendleton	.10
41	Kenny Rogers	.10
42	Vince Coleman	.10
43	Roberto Alomar	.20
44	Darrin Jackson	.10
45	Dennis Eckersley	.65
46	Jay Buhner	.10
47	Dave Weathers	.10
48	Danny Bautista	.10
49	Bob Hamelin	.10
50	Steve Trachsel	.10
51	Ben McDonald	.10
52	Wade Boggs	1.00
53	Sandy Alomar	.10
54	Ron Karkovice	.10
55	Doug Jones	.10
56	Gary Sheffield	.40
57	Ken Caminiti	.10
58	Kevin Tapani	.10
59	Ruben Sierra	.10
60	Bobby Bonilla	.10
61	Deion Sanders	.10
62	Charlie Hayes	.10
63	Paul O'Neill	.10
64	Jay Bell	.10
65	Todd Jones	.10
66	Todd Stottlemyre	.10
67	Will Clark	.10
68	Wilson Alvarez	.10
69	Chili Davis	.10
70	Chris Hoiles	.10
71	Bret Saberhagen	.10
72	Dave Nilsson	.10
73	Derek Bell	.10
74	Juan Gonzalez	.40
75	Andre Dawson	.30
76	Jim Thome	.65
77	Larry Walker	.10
78	Mike Piazza	1.50
79	Dan Wilson	.10
80	Junior Felix	.10
81	Jack McDowell	.10
82	Danny Tartabull	.10
83	William Van Landingham	.10
84	Robb Nen	.10
85	Ismael Valdes	.10
86	Juan Guzman	.10
87	Cliff Floyd	.10
88	Rico Brogna	.10
89	Luis Polonia	.10
90	Lance Johnson	.10
91	Sammy Sosa	1.00
92	Dave West	.10
93	Tom Glavine	.35
94	Joe Girardi	.10
95	Craig Biggio	.10
96	Eddie Murray	.75
97	Kevin Gross	.10
98	John Franco	.10
99	Matt Williams	.10
100	Darrin Fletcher	.10
101	Jeff Conine	.10
102	Ed Sprague	.10
103	Ivan Rodriguez	.65
104	Orlando Merced	.10
105	Ricky Bones	.10
106	David Cone	.10
107	Todd Hundley	.10
108	Alex Cole	.10
109	Tony Phillips	.10
110	Jim Eisenreich	.10
111	Paul Sorrento	.10
112	Mike Stanley	.10
113	Doug Drabek	.10
114	Matt Mieske	.10
115	Tino Martinez	.10
116	Midre Cummings	.10
117	Hal Morris	.10
118	Shawn Green	.40
119	Randy Myers	.10
120	Ken Griffey Jr.	1.50
121	Brett Butler	.10
122	Julio Franco	.10
123	Chuck Knoblauch	.10
124	Bret Boone	.10
125	Wil Cordero	.10
126	Luis Gonzalez	.10
127	Tim Wallach	.10
128	Scott Sanders	.10
129	Tom Henke	.10
130	Otis Nixon	.10
131	Darren Daulton	.10
132	Manny Ramirez	.75
133	Bret Barberie	.10
134	Brady Anderson	.10
135	Shane Reynolds	.10
136	Barry Bonds	2.50
137	Alex Fernandez	.10
138	Brian McRae	.10
139	Todd Zeile	.10
140	Greg Swindell	.10
141	Troy Neel	.10
142	Eric Karros	.10
143	John Hudek	.10
144	Joe Carter	.10
145	Mike Devereaux	.10
146	Butch Henry	.10
147	Mark Lemke	.10
148	Jeff Montgomery	.10
149	Ryan Thompson	.10
150	Bernie Williams	.10
151	Scott Leius	.10
152	Greg Gagne	.10
153	Moises Alou	.10
154	Geronimo Berroa	.10
155	Alan Trammell	.10
156	Don Slaught	.10
157	Jose Rijo	.10
158	Tim Raines	.10
159	Melido Perez	.10
160	Kent Mercker	.10
161	James Mouton	.10
162	Luis Lopez	.10
163	Mike Kingery	.10
164	Cecil Fielder	.10
165	Scott Kamienicki	.10
166	Brent Gates	.10
167	Jason Jacome	.10
168	Dante Bichette	.10
169	Kurt Abbott	.10
170	Mike Henneman	.10
171	John Kruk	.10
172	Jose Oliva	.10
173	Reggie Sanders	.10
174	Omar Vizquel	.10
175	Devon White	.10
176	Mark McGwire	2.00
177	Gary DiSarcina	.10
178	Joey Hamilton	.10
179	Randy Johnson	.75
180	Jim Leyritz	.10
181	Bobby Jones	.10
182	Bip Roberts	.10
183	Jose Canseco	.40
184	Mo Vaughn	.10
185	Edgar Martinez	.10
186	Tommy Greene	.10
187	Chuck Carr	.10
188	Pedro Astacio	.10
189	Shane Mack	.10
190	Fred McGriff	.10
191	Pat Rapp	.10
192	Bill Swift	.10
193	Robin Ventura	.10
194	Bobby Witt	.10
195	Steve Howe	.10
196	Leo Gomez	.10
197	Hector Fajardo	.10
198	Jeff Bagwell	.75
199	Rondell White	.10
200	Don Mattingly	1.25
201	Trevor Hoffman	.10
202	Chris Gomez	.10
203	Bobby Munoz	.10
204	Marvin Freeman	.10
205	Sean Berry	.10
206	Mark Grace	.10
207	Pat Kelly	.10
208	Eddie Williams	.10
209	Frank Thomas	.75
210	Bryan Eversgerd	.10
211	Phil Plantier	.10
212	Roberto Kelly	.10
213	Rickey Henderson	.75
214	John Smiley	.10
215	Kevin Brown	.10
216	Jimmy Key	.10
217	Wally Joyner	.10
218	Roberto Hernandez	.10
219	Felix Fermin	.10
220	Greg Vaughn	.10
221	Ray Lankford	.10
222	Greg Maddux	1.00
223	Mike Mussina	.30
224	David Nied	.10
225	Scott Erickson	.10
226	Kevin Mitchell	.10
227	Brian Anderson	.10
228	Jeff King	.10
229	Ramon Martinez	.10
230	Kevin Seitzer	.10
231	Marquis Grissom	.10
232	Chuck Finley	.10
233	Len Dykstra	.10
234	Ellis Burks	.10
235	Harold Baines	.10
236	Kevin Appier	.10
237	Dave Justice	.10
238	Darryl Kile	.10
239	John Olerud	.10
240	Greg McMichael	.10
241	Kirby Puckett	1.00
242	Jose Valentin	.10
243	Rick Wilkins	.10
244	Pat Hentgen	.10
245	Tom Gordon	.10
246	Tom Candiotti	.10
247	Jason Bere	.10
248	Wes Chamberlain	.10
249	Jeff Cirillo	.10
250	Kevin Foster	.10
251	Mark Whiten	.10
252	Terry Steinbach	.10
253	Aaron Sele	.10
254	Kirt Manwaring	.10
255	Delino DeShields	.10
256	Andujar Cedeno	.10
257	Kenny Lofton	.10
258	John Wetteland	.10
259	Tim Salmon	.10
260	Denny Neagle	.10
261	Tony Gwynn	1.00
262	Lou Whitaker	.10
263	J.T. Snow	.10
264	Dennis Martinez	.10
265	Pedro Martinez	.75
266	Rusty Greer	.10
267	Dave Fleming	.10
268	John Dettmer	.10
269	Albert Belle	.10
270	Henry Rodriguez	.10

VR Extremist

		NM/M
Complete Set (10):		25.00
Common Player:		1.50
1	Barry Bonds	7.50

1995 Stadium Club World Series Winners

#	Player	Price
2	Ken Griffey Jr.	6.00
3	Jeff Bagwell	3.50
4	Albert Belle	1.50
5	Frank Thomas	3.50
6	Tony Gwynn	4.50
7	Kenny Lofton	1.50
8	Deion Sanders	1.50
9	Ken Hill	1.50
10	Jimmy Key	1.50

	NM/M
Complete Set (585):	40.00
Common Player:	.25
Stars:	3X

(See 1995 Stadium Club for checklist and base card values.)

1996 Stadium Club

	NM/M
Complete Set (450):	25.00
Common Player:	.05
Series 1 or 2 Pack (10):	1.00
Series 1 or 2 Wax Box (24):	20.00

#	Player	Price
1	Hideo Nomo	.40
2	Paul Molitor	.75
3	Garret Anderson	.05
4	Jose Mesa	.05
5	Vinny Castilla	.30
6	Mike Mussina	.30
7	Ray Durham	.05
8	Jack McDowell	.05
9	Juan Gonzalez	.40
10	Chipper Jones	1.00
11	Deion Sanders	.05
12	Rondell White	.05
13	Tom Henke	.05
14	Derek Bell	.05
15	Randy Myers	.05
16	Randy Johnson	.75
17	Len Dykstra	.05
18	Bill Pulsipher	.05
19	Greg Colbrunn	.05
20	David Wells	.05
21	Chad Curtis	.05
22	Roberto Hernandez	.05
23	Kirby Puckett	1.00
24	Joe Vitiello	.05
25	Roger Clemens	1.25
26	Al Martin	.05
27	Chad Ogea	.05
28	David Segui	.05
29	Joey Hamilton	.05
30	Dan Wilson	.05
31	Chad Fonville	.05
32	Bernard Gilkey	.05
33	Kevin Seitzer	.05
34	Shawn Green	.35
35	Rick Aguilera	.05
36	Gary DiSarcina	.05
37	Jaime Navarro	.05
38	Doug Jones	.05
39	Brent Gates	.05
40	Dean Palmer	.05
41	Pat Rapp	.05
42	Tony Clark	.05
43	Bill Swift	.05
44	Randy Velarde	.05
45	Matt Williams	.05
46	John Mabry	.05
47	Mike Fetters	.05
48	Orlando Miller	.05
49	Tom Glavine	.35
50	Delino DeShields	.05
51	Scott Erickson	.05
52	Andy Van Slyke	.05
53	Jim Bullinger	.05
54	Lyle Mouton	.05
55	Bret Saberhagen	.05
56	Benito Santiago	.05
57	Dan Miceli	.05
58	Carl Everett	.05
59	Rod Beck	.05
60	Phil Nevin	.05
61	Jason Giambi	.50
62	Paul Menhart	.05
63	Eric Karros	.05
64	Allen Watson	.05
65	Jeff Cirillo	.05
66	Lee Smith	.05
67	Sean Berry	.05
68	Luis Sojo	.05
69	Jeff Montgomery	.05
70	Todd Hundley	.05
71	John Burkett	.05
72	Mark Gubicza	.05
73	Don Mattingly	1.25
74	Jeff Brantley	.05
75	Matt Walbeck	.05
76	Steve Parris	.05
77	Ken Caminiti	.05
78	Kirt Manwaring	.05
79	Greg Vaughn	.05
80	Pedro Martinez	.75
81	Benji Gil	.05
82	Heathcliff Slocumb	.05
83	Joe Girardi	.05
84	Sean Bergman	.05
85	Matt Karchner	.05
86	Butch Huskey	.05
87	Mike Morgan	.05
88	Todd Worrell	.05
89	Mike Bordick	.05
90	Bip Roberts	.05
91	Mike Hampton	.05
92	Troy O'Leary	.05
93	Wally Joyner	.05
94	Dave Stevens	.05
95	Cecil Fielder	.05
96	Wade Boggs	1.00
97	Hal Morris	.05
98	Mickey Tettleton	.05
99	Jeff Kent	.05
100	Denny Martinez	.05
101	Luis Gonzalez	.05
102	John Jaha	.05
103	Javy Lopez	.05
104	Mark McGwire	2.00
105	Ken Griffey Jr.	1.50
106	Darren Daulton	.05
107	Bryan Rekar	.05
108	Mike Macfarlane	.05
109	Gary Gaetti	.05
110	Shane Reynolds	.05
111	Pat Meares	.05
112	Jason Schmidt	.05
113	Otis Nixon	.05
114	John Franco	.05
115	Marc Newfield	.05
116	Andy Benes	.05
117	Ozzie Guillen	.05
118	Brian Jordan	.05
119	Terry Pendleton	.05
120	Chuck Finley	.05
121	Scott Stahoviak	.05
122	Sid Fernandez	.05
123	Derek Jeter	3.00
124	John Smiley	.05
125	David Bell	.05
126	Brett Butler	.05
127	Doug Drabek	.05
128	J.T. Snow	.05
129	Joe Carter	.05
130	Dennis Eckersley	.65
131	Marty Cordova	.05
132	Greg Maddux	1.00
133	Tom Goodwin	.05
134	Andy Ashby	.05
135	Paul Sorrento	.05
136	Ricky Bones	.05
137	Shawon Dunston	.05
138	Moises Alou	.05
139	Mickey Morandini	.05
140	Ramon Martinez	.05
141	Royce Clayton	.05
142	Brad Ausmus	.05
143	Kenny Rogers	.05
144	Tim Naehring	.05
145	Chris Gomez	.05
146	Bobby Bonilla	.05
147	Wilson Alvarez	.05
148	Johnny Damon	.35
149	Pat Hentgen	.05
150	Andres Galarraga	.05
151	David Cone	.05
152	Lance Johnson	.05
153	Carlos Garcia	.05
154	Doug Johns	.05
155	Midre Cummings	.05
156	Steve Sparks	.05
157	Sandy Martinez RC	.05
158	William Van Landingham	.05
159	Dave Justice	.05
160	Mark Grace	.05
161	Robb Nen	.05
162	Mike Greenwell	.05
163	Brad Radke	.05
164	Edgardo Alfonzo	.05
165	Mark Leiter	.05
166	Walt Weiss	.05
167	Mel Rojas	.05
168	Bret Boone	.05
169	Ricky Bottalico	.05
170	Bobby Higginson	.05
171	Trevor Hoffman	.05
172	Jay Bell	.05
173	Gabe White	.05
174	Curtis Goodwin	.05
175	Tyler Green	.05
176	Roberto Alomar	.20
177	Sterling Hitchcock	.05
178	Ryan Klesko	.05
179	Donne Wall RC	.05
180	Brian McRae	.05
181	Will Clark	.05
182	Frank Thomas	.60
183	Jeff Bagwell	.60
184	Mo Vaughn	.05
185	Tino Martinez	.05
186	Craig Biggio	.05
187	Chuck Knoblauch	.05
188	Carlos Baerga	.05
189	Quilvio Veras	.05
190	Luis Alicea	.05
191	Jim Thome	.40
192	Mike Blowers	.05
193	Robin Ventura	.05
194	Jeff King	.05
195	Tony Phillips	.05
196	John Valentin	.05
197	Barry Larkin	.05
198	Cal Ripken Jr.	2.00
199	Omar Vizquel	.05
200	Kurt Abbott	.05
201	Albert Belle	.05
202	Barry Bonds	2.00
203	Ron Gant	.05
204	Dante Bichette	.05
205	Jeff Conine	.05
206	Jim Edmonds	.05
207	Stan Javier	.05
208	Kenny Lofton	.05
209	Ray Lankford	.05
210	Bernie Williams	.05
211	Jay Buhner	.05
212	Paul O'Neill	.05
213	Tim Salmon	.05
214	Reggie Sanders	.05
215	Manny Ramirez	.60
216	Mike Piazza	1.50
217	Mike Stanley	.05
218	Tony Eusebio	.05
219	Chris Hoiles	.05
220	Ron Karkovice	.05
221	Edgar Martinez	.05
222	Chili Davis	.05
223	Jose Canseco	.35
224	Eddie Murray	.60
225	Geronimo Berroa	.05
226	Chipper Jones	.75
227	Garret Anderson	.05
228	Marty Cordova	.05
229	Jon Nunnally	.05
230	Brian Hunter	.05
231	Shawn Green	.20
232	Ray Durham	.05
233	Alex Gonzalez	.05
234	Bobby Higginson	.05
235	Randy Johnson	.60
236	Al Leiter	.05
237	Tom Glavine	.10
238	Kenny Rogers	.05
239	Mike Hampton	.05
240	David Wells	.05
241	Jim Abbott	.05
242	Denny Neagle	.05
243	Wilson Alvarez	.05
244	John Smiley	.05
245	Greg Maddux	.75
246	Andy Ashby	.05
247	Hideo Nomo	.30
248	Pat Rapp	.05
249	Tim Wakefield	.05
250	John Smoltz	.05
251	Joey Hamilton	.05
252	Frank Castillo	.05
253	Denny Martinez	.05
254	Jaime Navarro	.05
255	Karim Garcia	.05
256	Bob Abreu	.05
257	Butch Huskey	.05
258	Ruben Rivera	.05
259	Johnny Damon	.20
260	Derek Jeter	2.00
261	Dennis Eckersley	.50
262	Jose Mesa	.05
263	Tom Henke	.05
264	Rick Aguilera	.05
265	Randy Myers	.05
266	John Franco	.05
267	Jeff Brantley	.05
268	John Wetteland	.05
269	Mark Wohlers	.05
270	Rod Beck	.05
271	Barry Larkin	.05
272	Paul O'Neill	.05
273	Bobby Jones	.05
274	Will Clark	.05
275	Steve Avery	.05
276	Jim Edmonds	.05
277	John Olerud	.05
278	Carlos Perez	.05
279	Chris Hoiles	.05
280	Jeff Conine	.05
281	Jim Eisenreich	.05
282	Jason Jacome	.05
283	Ray Lankford	.05
284	John Wasdin	.05
285	Frank Thomas	.75
286	Jason Isringhausen	.05
287	Glenallen Hill	.05
288	Esteban Loaiza	.05
289	Bernie Williams	.05
290	Curtis Leskanic	.05
291	Scott Cooper	.05
292	Curt Schilling	.35
293	Eddie Murray	.75
294	Rick Krivda	.05
295	Domingo Cedeno	.05
296	Jeff Fassero	.05
297	Albert Belle	.05
298	Craig Biggio	.05
299	Fernando Vina	.05
300	Edgar Martinez	.05
301	Tony Gwynn	1.00
302	Felipe Lira	.05
303	Mo Vaughn	.05
304	Alex Fernandez	.05
305	Keith Lockhart	.05
306	Roger Pavlik	.05
307	Lee Tinsley	.05
308	Omar Vizquel	.05
309	Scott Servais	.05
310	Danny Tartabull	.05
311	Chili Davis	.05
312	Cal Eldred	.05
313	Roger Cedeno	.05
314	Chris Hammond	.05
315	Rusty Greer	.05
316	Brady Anderson	.05
317	Ron Villone	.05
318	Mark Carreon	.05
319	Larry Walker	.05
320	Pete Harnisch	.05
321	Robin Ventura	.05
322	Tim Belcher	.05
323	Tony Tarasco	.05
324	Juan Guzman	.05
325	Kenny Lofton	.05
326	Kevin Foster	.05
327	Wil Cordero	.05
328	Troy Percival	.05
329	Turk Wendell	.05
330	Thomas Howard	.05
331	Carlos Baerga	.05
332	B.J. Surhoff	.05
333	Jay Buhner	.05
334	Andujar Cedeno	.05
335	Jeff King	.05
336	Dante Bichette	.05
337	Alan Trammell	.05
338	Scott Leius	.05
339	Chris Snopek	.05
340	Roger Bailey	.05
341	Jacob Brumfield	.05
342	Jose Canseco	.50
343	Rafael Palmeiro	.65
344	Quilvio Veras	.05
345	Darrin Fletcher	.05
346	Carlos Delgado	.50
347	Tony Eusebio	.05
348	Ismael Valdes	.05
349	Terry Steinbach	.05
350	Orel Hershiser	.05
351	Kurt Abbott	.05
352	Jody Reed	.05
353	David Howard	.05
354	Ruben Sierra	.05
355	John Ericks	.05
356	Buck Showalter	.05
357	Jim Thome	.65
358	Geronimo Berroa	.05
359	Robby Thompson	.05
360	Jose Vizcaino	.05
361	Jeff Frye	.05
362	Kevin Appier	.05
363	Pat Kelly	.05

364	Ron Gant	.05
365	Luis Alicea	.05
366	Armando Benitez	.05
367	Rico Brogna	.05
368	Manny Ramirez	.75
369	Mike Lansing	.05
370	Sammy Sosa	1.00
371	Don Wengert	.05
372	Dave Nilsson	.05
373	Sandy Alomar	.05
374	Joey Cora	.05
375	Larry Thomas	.05
376	John Valentin	.05
377	Kevin Ritz	.05
378	Steve Finley	.05
379	Frank Rodriguez	.05
380	Ivan Rodriguez	.65
381	Alex Ochoa	.05
382	Mark Lemke	.05
383	Scott Brosius	.05
384	James Mouton	.05
385	Mark Langston	.05
386	Ed Sprague	.05
387	Joe Oliver	.05
388	Steve Ontiveros	.05
389	Rey Sanchez	.05
390	Mike Henneman	.05
391	Jose Valentin RC	.05
392	Tom Candiotti	.05
393	Damon Buford	.05
394	Erik Hanson	.05
395	Mark Smith	.05
396	Pete Schourek	.05
397	John Flaherty	.05
398	Dave Martinez	.05
399	Tommy Greene	.05
400	Gary Sheffield	.45
401	Glenn Dishman	.05
402	Barry Bonds	3.00
403	Tom Pagnozzi	.05
404	Todd Stottlemyre	.05
405	Tim Salmon	.05
406	John Hudek	.05
407	Fred McGriff	.05
408	Orlando Merced	.05
409	Brian Barber	.05
410	Ryan Thompson	.05
411	Mariano Rivera	.10
412	Eric Young	.05
413	Chris Bosio	.05
414	Chuck Knoblauch	.05
415	Jamie Moyer	.05
416	Chan Ho Park	.05
417	Mark Portugal	.05
418	Tim Raines	.05
419	Antonio Osuna	.05
420	Todd Zeile	.05
421	Steve Wojciechowski	.05
422	Marquis Grissom	.05
423	Norm Charlton	.05
424	Cal Ripken Jr.	3.00
425	Gregg Jefferies	.05
426	Mike Stanton	.05
427	Tony Fernandez	.05
428	Jose Rijo	.05
429	Jeff Bagwell	.75
430	Raul Mondesi	.05
431	Travis Fryman	.05
432	Ron Karkovice	.05
433	Alan Benes	.05
434	Tony Phillips	.05
435	Reggie Sanders	.05
436	Andy Pettitte	.25
437	Matt Lawton RC	.25
438	Jeff Blauser	.05
439	Michael Tucker	.05
440	Mark Loretta	.05
441	Charlie Hayes	.05
442	Mike Piazza	1.50
443	Shane Andrews	.05
444	Jeff Suppan	.05
445	Steve Rodriguez	.05
446	Mike Matheny	.05
447	Trenidad Hubbard	.05
448	Denny Hocking	.05
449	Mark Grudzielanek	.05
450	Joe Randa	.05

Bash & Burn

Complete Set (10):	10.00

Common Player / Young Guns

	Common Player:	.75
1	Sammy Sosa	3.50
2	Barry Bonds	6.00
3	Reggie Sanders	.75
4	Craig Biggio	.75
5	Raul Mondesi	.75
6	Ron Gant	.75
7	Ray Lankford	.75
8	Glenallen Hill	.75
9	Chad Curtis	.75
10	John Valentin	.75

Mega Heroes

ANDRES GALARRAGA

		NM/M
	Complete Set (10):	10.00
	Common Player:	1.00
1	Frank Thomas	1.50
2	Ken Griffey Jr.	3.00
3	Hideo Nomo	1.25
4	Ozzie Smith	1.75
5	Will Clark	1.00
6	Jack McDowell	1.00
7	Andres Galarraga	1.00
8	Roger Clemens	2.00
9	Deion Sanders	1.00
10	Mo Vaughn	1.00

Metalists

FRANK THOMAS

		NM/M
	Complete Set (8):	12.00
	Common Player:	1.00
1	Jeff Bagwell	1.25
2	Barry Bonds	3.50
3	Jose Canseco	1.00
4	Roger Clemens	2.50
5	Dennis Eckersley	1.00
6	Greg Maddux	2.00
7	Cal Ripken Jr.	3.50
8	Frank Thomas	1.25

Mickey Mantle Retrospective

MICKEY MANTLE

		NM/M
	Complete Set (19):	35.00

	Common Series 1:	4.00
	Common Series 2:	2.00
1	Mickey Mantle/1950 (Minor league)	
2	Mickey Mantle/1951	4.00
3	Mickey Mantle/1951	4.00
4	Mickey Mantle/1953	4.00
5	Mickey Mantle/1954 (W/Yogi Berra.)	4.00
6	Mickey Mantle/1956	4.00
7	Mickey Mantle/1957	4.00
8	Mickey Mantle/1958 (W/Casey Stengel.)	4.00
9	Mickey Mantle/1959	4.00
10	Mickey Mantle/1960 (W/Elston Howard.)	2.00
11	Mickey Mantle/1961	2.00
12	Mickey Mantle/1961 (W/Roger Maris.)	4.00
13	Mickey Mantle/1962	2.00
14	Mickey Mantle/1963	2.00
15	Mickey Mantle/1964	2.00
16	Mickey Mantle	2.00
17	Mickey Mantle/1968	2.00
18	Mickey Mantle/1969	2.00
19	Mickey Mantle (In Memoriam)	3.50

1996 Stadium Club Mickey Mantle "Cereal Box" Set

	NM/M
Unopened Set:	30.00
Common Player:	.10

(See 1996 Stadium Club for checklist and values.)

Midsummer Matchups

		NM/M
	Complete Set (10):	20.00
	Common Player:	1.00
1	Hideo Nomo, Randy Johnson	2.00
2	Mike Piazza, Ivan Rodriguez	4.00
3	Fred McGriff, Frank Thomas	2.00
4	Craig Biggio, Carlos Baerga	1.00
5	Vinny Castilla, Wade Boggs	2.50
6	Barry Larkin, Cal Ripken Jr.	5.00
7	Barry Bonds, Albert Belle	5.00
8	Len Dykstra, Kenny Lofton	1.00
9	Tony Gwynn, Kirby Puckett	3.00
10	Ron Gant, Edgar Martinez	1.00

Power Packed

		NM/M
	Complete Set (15):	15.00
	Common Player:	1.00
1	Albert Belle	1.00
2	Mark McGwire	4.00
3	Jose Canseco	1.75
4	Mike Piazza	3.00
5	Ron Gant	1.00
6	Ken Griffey Jr.	3.00
7	Mo Vaughn	1.00
8	Cecil Fielder	1.00
9	Tim Salmon	1.00
10	Frank Thomas	2.50
11	Juan Gonzalez	1.50
12	Andres Galarraga	1.00
13	Fred McGriff	1.00
14	Jay Buhner	1.00
15	Dante Bichette	1.00

Power Streak

		NM/M
	Complete Set (15):	20.00
	Common Player:	1.00
1	Randy Johnson	2.00
2	Hideo Nomo	1.25
3	Albert Belle	1.00
4	Dante Bichette	1.00
5	Jay Buhner	1.00
6	Frank Thomas	2.00
7	Mark McGwire	4.00
8	Rafael Palmeiro	1.50
9	Mo Vaughn	1.00
10	Sammy Sosa	3.00
11	Larry Walker	1.00
12	Gary Gaetti	1.00
13	Tim Salmon	1.00
14	Barry Bonds	5.00
15	Jim Edmonds	1.00

Prime Cuts

		NM/M
	Complete Set (8):	20.00
	Common Player:	1.50
1	Albert Belle	1.50
2	Barry Bonds	6.00
3	Ken Griffey Jr.	4.00
4	Tony Gwynn	3.00
5	Edgar Martinez	1.50
6	Rafael Palmeiro	2.00
7	Mike Piazza	4.00
8	Frank Thomas	2.50

TSC Awards

		NM/M
	Complete Set (10):	15.00
	Common Player:	.50
1	Cal Ripken Jr.	5.00

2	Albert Belle	.60
3	Tom Glavine	1.00
4	Jeff Conine	.50
5	Ken Griffey Jr.	4.00
6	Hideo Nomo	1.25
7	Greg Maddux	3.00
8	Chipper Jones	3.00
9	Randy Johnson	2.00
10	Jose Mesa	.50

1997 Stadium Club

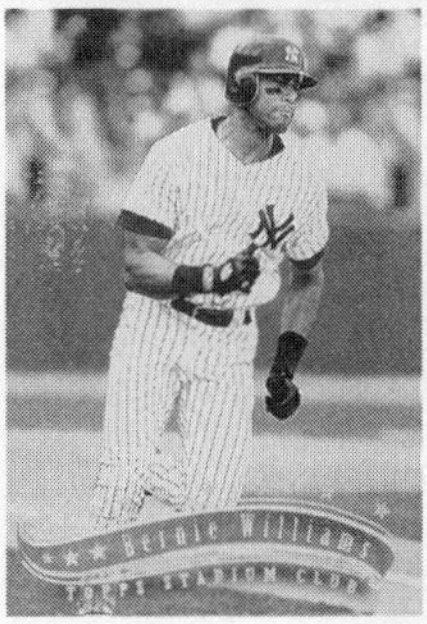

		NM/M
Complete Set (390):		35.00
Common Player:		.05
Series 1 or 2 Pack (9):		1.50
Series 1 or 2 Wax Box (24):		27.50
1	Chipper Jones	1.50
2	Gary Sheffield	.50
3	Kenny Lofton	.05
4	Brian Jordan	.05
5	Mark McGwire	2.50
6	Charles Nagy	.05
7	Tim Salmon	.05
8	Cal Ripken Jr.	3.00
9	Jeff Conine	.05
10	Paul Molitor	1.00
11	Mariano Rivera	.15
12	Pedro Martinez	1.00
13	Jeff Bagwell	1.00
14	Bobby Bonilla	.05
15	Barry Bonds	3.00
16	Ryan Klesko	.05
17	Barry Larkin	.05
18	Jim Thome	.65
19	Jay Buhner	.05
20	Juan Gonzalez	.50
21	Mike Mussina	.30
22	Kevin Appier	.05
23	Eric Karros	.05
24	Steve Finley	.05
25	Ed Sprague	.05
26	Bernard Gilkey	.05
27	Tony Phillips	.05
28	Henry Rodriguez	.05
29	John Smoltz	.05
30	Dante Bichette	.05
31	Mike Piazza	2.00
32	Paul O'Neill	.05
33	Billy Wagner	.05
34	Reggie Sanders	.05
35	John Jaha	.05
36	Eddie Murray	1.00
37	Eric Young	.05
38	Roberto Hernandez	.05
39	Pat Hentgen	.05
40	Sammy Sosa	1.50
41	Todd Hundley	.05
42	Mo Vaughn	.05
43	Robin Ventura	.05
44	Mark Grudzielanek	.05
45	Shane Reynolds	.05
46	Andy Pettitte	.25
47	Fred McGriff	.05
48	Rey Ordonez	.05
49	Will Clark	.05
50	Ken Griffey Jr.	2.00
51	Todd Worrell	.05
52	Rusty Greer	.05
53	Mark Grace	.05
54	Tom Glavine	.35
55	Derek Jeter	3.00
56	Rafael Palmeiro	.75
57	Bernie Williams	.05
58	Marty Cordova	.05
59	Andres Galarraga	.05
60	Ken Caminiti	.05
61	Garret Anderson	.05
62	Denny Martinez	.05
63	Mike Greenwell	.05
64	David Segui	.05
65	Julio Franco	.05
66	Rickey Henderson	1.00
67	Ozzie Guillen	.05
68	Pete Harnisch	.05
69	Chan Ho Park	.05
70	Harold Baines	.05
71	Mark Clark	.05
72	Steve Avery	.05
73	Brian Hunter	.05
74	Pedro Astacio	.05
75	Jack McDowell	.05
76	Gregg Jefferies	.05
77	Jason Kendall	.05
78	Todd Walker	.05
79	B.J. Surhoff	.05
80	Moises Alou	.05
81	Fernando Vina	.05
82	Darryl Strawberry	.05
83	Jose Rosado	.05
84	Chris Gomez	.05
85	Chili Davis	.05
86	Alan Benes	.05
87	Todd Hollandsworth	.05
88	Jose Vizcaino	.05
89	Edgardo Alfonzo	.05
90	Ruben Rivera	.05
91	Donovan Osborne	.05
92	Doug Glanville	.05
93	Gary DiSarcina	.05
94	Brooks Kieschnick	.05
95	Bobby Jones	.05
96	Raul Casanova	.05
97	Jermaine Allensworth	.05
98	Kenny Rogers	.05
99	Mark McLemore	.05
100	Jeff Fassero	.05
101	Sandy Alomar	.05
102	Chuck Finley	.05
103	Eric Owens	.05
104	Billy McMillon	.05
105	Dwight Gooden	.05
106	Sterling Hitchcock	.05
107	Doug Drabek	.05
108	Paul Wilson	.05
109	Chris Snopek	.05
110	Al Leiter	.05
111	Bob Tewksbury	.05
112	Todd Greene	.05
113	Jose Valentin	.05
114	Delino DeShields	.05
115	Mike Bordick	.05
116	Pat Meares	.05
117	Mariano Duncan	.05
118	Steve Trachsel	.05
119	Luis Castillo	.05
120	Andy Benes	.05
121	Donne Wall	.05
122	Alex Gonzalez	.05
123	Dan Wilson	.05
124	Omar Vizquel	.05
125	Devon White	.05
126	Darryl Hamilton	.05
127	Orlando Merced	.05
128	Royce Clayton	.05
129	William Van Landingham	.05
130	Terry Steinbach	.05
131	Jeff Blauser	.05
132	Jeff Cirillo	.05
133	Roger Pavlik	.05
134	Danny Tartabull	.05
135	Jeff Montgomery	.05
136	Bobby Higginson	.05
137	Mike Grace	.05
138	Kevin Elster	.05
139	Brian Giles **RC**	1.00
140	Rod Beck	.05
141	Ismael Valdes	.05
142	Scott Brosius	.05
143	Mike Fetters	.05
144	Gary Gaetti	.05
145	Mike Lansing	.05
146	Glenallen Hill	.05
147	Shawn Green	.35
148	Mel Rojas	.05
149	Joey Cora	.05
150	John Smiley	.05
151	Marvin Benard	.05
152	Curt Schilling	.35
153	Dave Nilsson	.05
154	Edgar Renteria	.05
155	Joey Hamilton	.05
156	Carlos Garcia	.05
157	Nomar Garciaparra	2.00
158	Kevin Ritz	.05
159	Keith Lockhart	.05
160	Justin Thompson	.05
161	Terry Adams	.05
162	Jamey Wright	.05
163	Otis Nixon	.05
164	Michael Tucker	.05
165	Mike Stanley	.05
166	Ben McDonald	.05
167	John Mabry	.05
168	Troy O'Leary	.05
169	Mel Nieves	.05
170	Bret Boone	.05
171	Mike Timlin	.05
172	Scott Rolen	.75
173	Reggie Jefferson	.05
174	Neifi Perez	.05
175	Brian McRae	.05
176	Tom Goodwin	.05
177	Aaron Sele	.05
178	Benny Santiago	.05
179	Frank Rodriguez	.05
180	Eric Davis	.05
181	Andruw Jones	.75
182	Todd Walker	.15
183	Wes Helms	.15
184	Nelson Figueroa **RC**	.15
185	Vladimir Guerrero	.75
186	Billy McMillon	.15
187	Todd Helton	.65
188	Nomar Garciaparra	2.00
189	Katsuhiro Maeda	.15
190	Russell Branyan	.15
191	Glendon Rusch	.15
192	Bartolo Colon	.15
193	Scott Rolen	.50
194	Angel Echevarria	.15
195	Bob Abreu	.20
196	Greg Maddux	1.50
197	Joe Carter	.05
198	Alex Ochoa	.05
199	Ellis Burks	.05
200	Ivan Rodriguez	.75
201	Marquis Grissom	.05
202	Trevor Hoffman	.05
203	Matt Williams	.05
204	Carlos Delgado	.50
205	Ramon Martinez	.05
206	Chuck Knoblauch	.05
207	Juan Guzman	.05
208	Derek Bell	.05
209	Roger Clemens	1.75
210	Vladimir Guerrero	1.00
211	Cecil Fielder	.05
212	Hideo Nomo	.50
213	Frank Thomas	1.00
214	Greg Vaughn	.05
215	Javy Lopez	.05
216	Raul Mondesi	.05
217	Wade Boggs	1.50
218	Carlos Baerga	.05
219	Tony Gwynn	1.50
220	Tino Martinez	.05
221	Vinny Castilla	.05
222	Lance Johnson	.05
223	David Justice	.05
224	Rondell White	.05
225	Dean Palmer	.05
226	Jim Edmonds	.05
227	Albert Belle	.05
228	Alex Fernandez	.05
229	Ryne Sandberg	1.50
230	Jose Mesa	.05
231	David Cone	.05
232	Troy Percival	.05
233	Edgar Martinez	.05
234	Jose Canseco	.50
235	Kevin Brown	.05
236	Ray Lankford	.05
237	Karim Garcia	.05
238	J.T. Snow	.05
239	Dennis Eckersley	.75
240	Roberto Alomar	.35
241	John Valentin	.05
242	Ron Gant	.05
243	Geronimo Berroa	.05
244	Manny Ramirez	1.00
245	Travis Fryman	.05
246	Denny Neagle	.05
247	Randy Johnson	1.00
248	Darin Erstad	.15
249	Mark Wohlers	.05
250	Ken Hill	.05
251	Larry Walker	.05
252	Craig Biggio	.05
253	Brady Anderson	.05
254	John Wetteland	.05
255	Andruw Jones	1.00
256	Turk Wendell	.05
257	Jason Isringhausen	.05
258	Jaime Navarro	.05
259	Sean Berry	.05
260	Albie Lopez	.05
261	Jay Bell	.05
262	Bobby Witt	.05
263	Tony Clark	.05
264	Tim Wakefield	.05
265	Brad Radke	.05
266	Tim Belcher	.05
267	Mark Lewis	.05
268	Roger Cedeno	.05
269	Tim Naehring	.05
270	Kevin Tapani	.05
271	Joe Randa	.05
272	Randy Myers	.05
273	Dave Burba	.05
274a	Mike Sweeney	.05
274b	Tom Pagnozzi (Should be #374.)	.05
275	Danny Graves	.05
276	Chad Mottola	.05
277	Ruben Sierra	.05
278	Norm Charlton	.05
279	Scott Servais	.05
280	Jacob Cruz	.05
281	Mike Macfarlane	.05
282	Rich Becker	.05
283	Shannon Stewart	.05
284	Gerald Williams	.05
285	Jody Reed	.05
286	Jeff D'Amico	.05
287	Walt Weiss	.05
288	Jim Leyritz	.05
289	Francisco Cordova	.05
290	F.P. Santangelo	.05
291	Scott Erickson	.05
292	Hal Morris	.05
293	Ray Durham	.05
294	Andy Ashby	.05
295	Darryl Kile	.05
296	Jose Paniagua	.05
297	Mickey Tettleton	.05
298	Joe Girardi	.05
299	Rocky Coppinger	.05
300	Bob Abreu	.05
301	John Olerud	.05
302	Paul Shuey	.05
303	Jeff Brantley	.05
304	Bob Wells	.05
305	Kevin Seitzer	.05
306	Shawon Dunston	.05
307	Jose Herrera	.05
308	Butch Huskey	.05
309	Jose Offerman	.05
310	Rick Aguilera	.05
311	Greg Gagne	.05
312	John Burkett	.05
313	Mark Thompson	.05
314	Alvaro Espinoza	.05
315	Todd Stottlemyre	.05
316	Al Martin	.05
317	James Baldwin	.05
318	Cal Eldred	.05
319	Sid Fernandez	.05
320	Mickey Morandini	.05
321	Robb Nen	.05
322	Mark Lemke	.05
323	Pete Schourek	.05
324	Marcus Jensen	.05
325	Rich Aurilia	.05
326	Jeff King	.05
327	Scott Stahoviak	.05
328	Ricky Otero	.05
329	Antonio Osuna	.05
330	Chris Hoiles	.05
331	Luis Gonzalez	.05
332	Wil Cordero	.05
333	Johnny Damon	.35
334	Mark Langston	.05
335	Orlando Miller	.05
336	Jason Giambi	.50
337	Damian Jackson	.05
338	David Wells	.05
339	Bip Roberts	.05
340	Matt Ruebel	.05
341	Tom Candiotti	.05
342	Wally Joyner	.05
343	Jimmy Key	.05
344	Tony Batista	.05
345	Paul Sorrento	.05
346	Ron Karkovice	.05
347	Wilson Alvarez	.05
348	John Flaherty	.05
349	Rey Sanchez	.05
350	John Vander Wal	.05
351a	Jermaine Dye	.05
351b	Brant Brown (Should be #361.)	.05
352	Mike Hampton	.05
353	Greg Colbrunn	.05
354	Heathcliff Slocumb	.05
355	Ricky Bottalico	.05
356	Marty Janzen	.05
357	Orel Hershiser	.05
358	Rex Hudler	.05
359	Amaury Telemaco	.05
360	Darrin Fletcher	.05
361	Not Issued - See #351	.05
362	Russ Davis	.05
363	Allen Watson	.05
364	Mike Lieberthal	.05
365	Dave Stevens	.05
366	Jay Powell	.05
367	Tony Fossas	.05
368	Bob Wolcott	.05
369	Mark Loretta	.05
370	Shawn Estes	.05
371	Sandy Martinez	.05
372	Wendell Magee Jr.	.05
373	John Franco	.05
374	Not Issued - See #274	.05
375	Willie Adams	.05
376	Chipper Jones	2.00
377	Mo Vaughn	.15
378	Frank Thomas	1.50
379	Albert Belle	.15
380	Andres Galarraga	.15
381	Gary Sheffield	.85
382	Jeff Bagwell	1.50
383	Mike Piazza	3.00
384	Mark McGwire	3.00
385	Ken Griffey Jr.	2.50
386	Barry Bonds	3.50
387	Juan Gonzalez	.40
388	Brady Anderson	.15
389	Ken Caminiti	.15
390	Jay Buhner	.15

Co-Signers

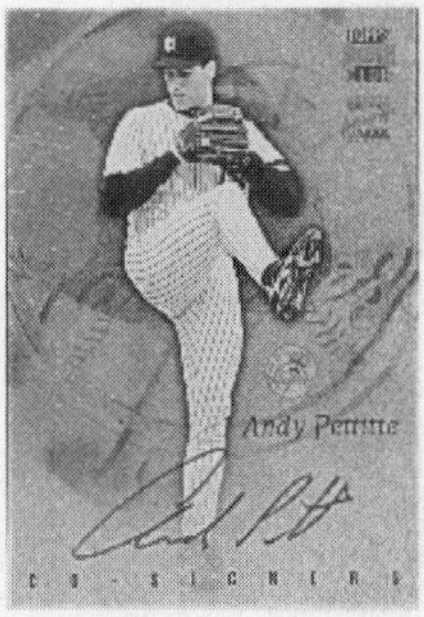

	NM/M
Complete Set (10):	200.00
Common Card:	5.00
C01 Andy Pettitte, Derek Jeter	100.00
C02 Paul Wilson, Todd Hundley	5.00
C03 Jermaine Dye, Mark Wohlers	6.00
C04 Scott Rolen, Gregg Jefferies	15.00
C05 Todd Hollandsworth, Jason Kendall	8.00
C06 Alan Benes, Robin Ventura	8.00
C07 Eric Karros, Raul Mondesi	15.00
C08 Rey Ordonez, Nomar Garciaparra	45.00
C09 Rondell White, Marty Cordova	6.00
C010 Tony Gwynn, Karim Garcia	30.00

Firebrand

	NM/M
Complete Set (12):	25.00
Common Player:	1.00
1 Jeff Bagwell	2.50
2 Albert Belle	1.00
3 Barry Bonds	6.50
4 Andres Galarraga	1.00
5 Ken Griffey Jr.	4.50
6 Brady Anderson	1.00
7 Mark McGwire	5.50
8 Chipper Jones	4.00
9 Frank Thomas	2.50
10 Mike Piazza	4.50
11 Mo Vaughn	1.00
12 Juan Gonzalez	1.50

Instavision

	NM/M
Complete Set (22):	10.00
Common Player:	.35
11 Eddie Murray	.75
12 Paul Molitor	.75
13 Todd Hundley	.35
14 Roger Clemens	1.50
15 Barry Bonds	3.00
16 Mark McGwire	2.00
17 Brady Anderson	.35
18 Barry Larkin	.35
19 Ken Caminiti	.35
110 Hideo Nomo	.45
111 Bernie Williams	.45
112 Juan Gonzalez	.45
113 Andy Pettitte	.45
114 Albert Belle	.35
115 John Smoltz	.35
116 Brian Jordan	.35
117 Derek Jeter	3.00
118 Ken Caminiti	.35
119 John Wetteland	.35
120 Brady Anderson	.35
121 Andruw Jones	.75
122 Jim Leyritz	.35

Millennium

	NM/M
Complete Set (40):	12.50
Common Player:	.25
1 Derek Jeter	5.00
2 Mark Grudzielanek	.25
3 Jacob Cruz	.25
4 Ray Durham	.25
5 Tony Clark	.25
6 Chipper Jones	2.50
7 Luis Castillo	.25
8 Carlos Delgado	.50
9 Brant Brown	.25
10 Jason Kendall	.25
11 Alan Benes	.25
12 Rey Ordonez	.25
13 Justin Thompson	.25
14 Jermaine Allensworth	.25
15 Brian Hunter	.25
16 Marty Cordova	.25
17 Edgar Renteria	.25
18 Karim Garcia	.25
19 Todd Greene	.25
20 Paul Wilson	.25
21 Andruw Jones	1.50
22 Todd Walker	.25
23 Alex Ochoa	.25
24 Bartolo Colon	.25
25 Wendell Magee Jr.	.25
26 Jose Rosado	.25
27 Katsuhiro Maeda	.25
28 Bob Abreu	.25
29 Brooks Kieschnick	.25
30 Derrick Gibson	.25
31 Mike Sweeney	.25
32 Jeff D'Amico	.25
33 Chad Mottola	.25
34 Chris Snopek	.25
35 Jaime Bluma	.25
36 Vladimir Guerrero	1.50
37 Nomar Garciaparra	2.50
38 Scott Rolen	1.25
39 Dmitri Young	.25
40 Neifi Perez	.25

Patent Leather

	NM/M
Complete Set (13):	25.00
Common Player:	1.00
1 Ivan Rodriguez	3.00
2 Ken Caminiti	1.00
3 Barry Bonds	6.00
4 Ken Griffey Jr.	5.00
5 Greg Maddux	4.00
6 Craig Biggio	1.00
7 Andres Galarraga	1.00
8 Kenny Lofton	1.00
9 Barry Larkin	1.00
10 Mark Grace	1.00
11 Rey Ordonez	1.00
12 Roberto Alomar	1.25
13 Derek Jeter	6.00

Pure Gold

	NM/M
Complete Set (20):	60.00
Common Player:	1.25
1 Brady Anderson	1.25
2 Albert Belle	1.25
3 Dante Bichette	1.25
4 Barry Bonds	12.00
5 Jay Buhner	1.25
6 Tony Gwynn	6.00
7 Chipper Jones	6.00
8 Mark McGwire	9.00
9 Gary Sheffield	2.25
10 Frank Thomas	4.50
11 Juan Gonzalez	2.50
12 Ken Caminiti	1.25
13 Kenny Lofton	1.25
14 Jeff Bagwell	5.00
15 Ken Griffey Jr.	7.50
16 Cal Ripken Jr.	12.00
17 Mo Vaughn	1.25
18 Mike Piazza	7.50
19 Derek Jeter	12.00
20 Andres Galarraga	1.25

TSC Matrix

	NM/M
Complete Set (120):	70.00
Common Player:	.50
1 Chipper Jones	2.50
2 Gary Sheffield	1.00
3 Kenny Lofton	.50
4 Brian Jordan	.50
5 Mark McGwire	4.25
6 Charles Nagy	.50
7 Tim Salmon	.50
8 Cal Ripken Jr.	5.00
9 Jeff Conine	.50
10 Paul Molitor	1.75
11 Mariano Rivera	.65
12 Pedro Martinez	1.75
13 Jeff Bagwell	1.75
14 Bobby Bonilla	.50
15 Barry Bonds	5.00
16 Ryan Klesko	.50
17 Barry Larkin	.50
18 Jim Thome	1.50
19 Jay Buhner	.50
20 Juan Gonzalez	1.00
21 Mike Mussina	.75
22 Kevin Appier	.50
23 Eric Karros	.50
24 Steve Finley	.50
25 Ed Sprague	.50
26 Bernard Gilkey	.50
27 Tony Phillips	.50
28 Henry Rodriguez	.50
29 John Smoltz	.50
30 Dante Bichette	.50
31 Mike Piazza	3.25
32 Paul O'Neill	.50
33 Billy Wagner	.50
34 Reggie Sanders	.50
35 John Jaha	.50
36 Eddie Murray	1.75
37 Eric Young	.50
38 Roberto Hernandez	.50
39 Pat Hentgen	.50
40 Sammy Sosa	2.50
41 Todd Hundley	.50
42 Mo Vaughn	.50
43 Robin Ventura	.50
44 Mark Grudzielanek	.50
45 Shane Reynolds	.50
46 Andy Pettitte	.65
47 Fred McGriff	.50
48 Rey Ordonez	.50
49 Will Clark	.50
50 Ken Griffey Jr.	3.25
51 Todd Worrell	.50
52 Rusty Greer	.50
53 Mark Grace	.50
54 Tom Glavine	.75
55 Derek Jeter	5.00
56 Rafael Palmeiro	1.50
57 Bernie Williams	.50
58 Marty Cordova	.50
59 Andres Galarraga	.50
60 Ken Caminiti	.50
196 Greg Maddux	2.50
197 Joe Carter	.50
198 Alex Ochoa	.50
199 Ellis Burks	.50
200 Ivan Rodriguez	1.50
201 Marquis Grissom	.50
202 Trevor Hoffman	.50
203 Matt Williams	.50
204 Carlos Delgado	1.25
205 Ramon Martinez	.50
206 Chuck Knoblauch	.50
207 Juan Guzman	.50
208 Derek Bell	.50
209 Roger Clemens	3.00
210 Vladimir Guerrero	1.75
211 Cecil Fielder	.50
212 Hideo Nomo	1.00
213 Frank Thomas	1.75
214 Greg Vaughn	.50
215 Javy Lopez	.50
216 Raul Mondesi	.50
217 Wade Boggs	2.50
218 Carlos Baerga	.50
219 Tony Gwynn	2.50
220 Tino Martinez	.50
221 Vinny Castilla	.50
222 Lance Johnson	.50
223 David Justice	.50
224 Rondell White	.50
225 Dean Palmer	.50
226 Jim Edmonds	.50
227 Albert Belle	.50
228 Alex Fernandez	.50
229 Ryne Sandberg	2.50
230 Jose Mesa	.50
231 David Cone	.50
232 Troy Percival	.50
233 Edgar Martinez	.50
234 Jose Canseco	1.25
235 Kevin Brown	.50
236 Ray Lankford	.50
237 Karim Garcia	.50
238 J.T. Snow	.50
239 Dennis Eckersley	1.50
240 Roberto Alomar	.75
241 John Valentin	.50
242 Ron Gant	.50
243 Geronimo Berroa	.50
244 Manny Ramirez	1.75
245 Travis Fryman	.50
246 Denny Neagle	.50
247 Randy Johnson	1.75
248 Darin Erstad	.65
249 Mark Wohlers	.50
250 Ken Hill	.50
251 Larry Walker	.50
252 Craig Biggio	.50
253 Brady Anderson	.50
254 John Wetteland	.50
255 Andruw Jones	1.75

1998 Stadium Club

	NM/M
Complete Set (400):	30.00
Common Player:	.05
Hobby Pack (10):	1.50
Retail Pack (7):	1.50
Home Team Adv. Pack (16):	4.00
Hobby Box (24):	30.00
1 Chipper Jones	1.00
2 Frank Thomas	.75
3 Vladimir Guerrero	.75
4 Ellis Burks	.05
5 John Franco	.05
6 Paul Molitor	.75
7 Rusty Greer	.05
8 Todd Hundley	.05
9 Brett Tomko	.05
10 Eric Karros	.05
11 Mike Cameron	.05
12 Jim Edmonds	.05
13 Bernie Williams	.05
14 Denny Neagle	.05
15 Jason Dickson	.05
16 Sammy Sosa	1.00
17 Brian Jordan	.05
18 Jose Vidro	.05
19 Scott Spiezio	.05
20 Jay Buhner	.05
21 Jim Thome	.65
22 Sandy Alomar	.05
23 Devon White	.05
24 Roberto Alomar	.20
25 John Flaherty	.05
26 John Wetteland	.05
27 Willie Greene	.05
28 Gregg Jefferies	.05
29 Johnny Damon	.05

#	Player	Value
30	Barry Larkin	.05
31	Chuck Knoblauch	.05
32	Mo Vaughn	.05
33	Tony Clark	.05
34	Marty Cordova	.05
35	Vinny Castilla	.05
36	Jeff King	.05
37	Reggie Jefferson	.05
38	Mariano Rivera	.15
39	Jermaine Allensworth	.05
40	Livan Hernandez	.05
41	Heathcliff Slocumb	.05
42	Jacob Cruz	.05
43	Barry Bonds	2.50
44	Dave Magadan	.05
45	Chan Ho Park	.05
46	Jeremi Gonzalez	.05
47	Jeff Cirillo	.05
48	Delino DeShields	.05
49	Craig Biggio	.05
50	Benito Santiago	.05
51	Mark Clark	.05
52	Fernando Vina	.05
53	F.P. Santangelo	.05
54	Pep Harris **RC**	.05
55	Edgar Renteria	.05
56	Jeff Bagwell	.75
57	Jimmy Key	.05
58	Bartolo Colon	.05
59	Curt Schilling	.35
60	Steve Finley	.05
61	Andy Ashby	.05
62	John Burkett	.05
63	Orel Hershiser	.05
64	Pokey Reese	.05
65	Scott Servais	.05
66	Todd Jones	.05
67	Javy Lopez	.05
68	Robin Ventura	.05
69	Miguel Tejada	.15
70	Raul Casanova	.05
71	Reggie Sanders	.05
72	Edgardo Alfonzo	.05
73	Dean Palmer	.05
74	Todd Stottlemyre	.05
75	David Wells	.05
76	Troy Percival	.05
77	Albert Belle	.05
78	Pat Hentgen	.05
79	Brian Hunter	.05
80	Richard Hidalgo	.05
81	Darren Oliver	.05
82	Mark Wohlers	.05
83	Cal Ripken Jr.	2.50
84	Hideo Nomo	.40
85	Derrek Lee	.50
86	Stan Javier	.05
87	Rey Ordonez	.05
88	Randy Johnson	.75
89	Jeff Kent	.05
90	Brian McRae	.05
91	Manny Ramirez	.75
92	Trevor Hoffman	.05
93	Doug Glanville	.05
94	Todd Walker	.05
95	Andy Benes	.05
96	Jason Schmidt	.05
97	Mike Matheny	.05
98	Tim Naehring	.05
99	Jeff Blauser	.05
100	Jose Rosado	.05
101	Roger Clemens	1.25
102	Pedro Astacio	.05
103	Mark Bellhorn	.05
104	Paul O'Neill	.05
105	Darin Erstad	.15
106	Mike Lieberthal	.05
107	Wilson Alvarez	.05
108	Mike Mussina	.30
109	George Williams	.05
110	Cliff Floyd	.05
111	Shawn Estes	.05
112	Mark Grudzielanek	.05
113	Tony Gwynn	1.00
114	Alan Benes	.05
115	Terry Steinbach	.05
116	Greg Maddux	1.00
117	Andy Pettitte	.25
118	Dave Nilsson	.05
119	Deivi Cruz	.05
120	Carlos Delgado	.50
121	Scott Hatteberg	.05
122	John Olerud	.05
123	Moises Alou	.05
124	Garret Anderson	.05
125	Royce Clayton	.05
126	Dante Powell	.05
127	Tom Glavine	.35
128	Gary DiSarcina	.05
129	Terry Adams	.05
130	Raul Mondesi	.05
131	Dan Wilson	.05
132	Al Martin	.05
133	Mickey Morandini	.05
134	Rafael Palmeiro	.65
135	Juan Encarnacion	.05
136	Jim Pittsley	.05
137	Magglio Ordonez **RC**	1.00
138	Will Clark	.05
139	Todd Helton	.65
140	Kelvim Escobar	.05
141	Esteban Loaiza	.05
142	John Jaha	.05
143	Jeff Fassero	.05
144	Harold Baines	.05
145	Butch Huskey	.05
146	Pat Meares	.05
147	Brian Giles	.05
148	Ramiro Mendoza	.05
149	John Smoltz	.05
150	Felix Martinez	.05
151	Jose Valentin	.05
152	Brad Rigby	.05
153	Ed Sprague	.05
154	Mike Hampton	.05
155	Mike Lansing	.05
156	Ray Lankford	.05
157	Bobby Bonilla	.05
158	Bill Mueller	.05
159	Jeffrey Hammonds	.05
160	Charles Nagy	.05
161	Rich Loiselle	.05
162	Al Leiter	.05
163	Larry Walker	.05
164	Chris Hoiles	.05
165	Jeff Montgomery	.05
166	Francisco Cordova	.05
167	James Baldwin	.05
168	Mark McLemore	.05
169	Kevin Appier	.05
170	Jamey Wright	.05
171	Nomar Garciaparra	1.00
172	Matt Franco	.05
173	Armando Benitez	.05
174	Jeromy Burnitz	.05
175	Ismael Valdes	.05
176	Lance Johnson	.05
177	Paul Sorrento	.05
178	Rondell White	.05
179	Kevin Elster	.05
180	Jason Giambi	.50
181	Carlos Baerga	.05
182	Russ Davis	.05
183	Ryan McGuire	.05
184	Eric Young	.05
185	Ron Gant	.05
186	Manny Alexander	.05
187	Scott Karl	.05
188	Brady Anderson	.05
189	Randall Simon	.05
190	Tim Belcher	.05
191	Jaret Wright	.05
192	Dante Bichette	.05
193	John Valentin	.05
194	Darren Bragg	.05
195	Mike Sweeney	.05
196	Craig Counsell	.05
197	Jaime Navarro	.05
198	Todd Dunn	.05
199	Ken Griffey Jr.	1.50
200	Juan Gonzalez	.40
201	Billy Wagner	.05
202	Tino Martinez	.05
203	Mark McGwire	2.00
204	Jeff D'Amico	.05
205	Rico Brogna	.05
206	Todd Hollandsworth	.05
207	Chad Curtis	.05
208	Tom Goodwin	.05
209	Neifi Perez	.05
210	Derek Bell	.05
211	Quilvio Veras	.05
212	Greg Vaughn	.05
213	Roberto Hernandez	.05
214	Arthur Rhodes	.05
215	Cal Eldred	.05
216	Bill Taylor	.05
217	Todd Greene	.05
218	Mario Valdes	.05
219	Ricky Bottalico	.05
220	Frank Rodriguez	.05
221	Rich Becker	.05
222	Roberto Duran	.05
223	Ivan Rodriguez	.65
224	Mike Jackson	.05
225	Deion Sanders	.05
226	Tony Womack	.05
227	Mark Kotsay	.05
228	Steve Trachsel	.05
229	Ryan Klesko	.05
230	Ken Cloude	.05
231	Luis Gonzalez	.05
232	Gary Gaetti	.05
233	Michael Tucker	.05
234	Shawn Green	.35
235	Ariel Prieto	.05
236	Kirt Manwaring	.05
237	Omar Vizquel	.05
238	Matt Beech	.05
239	Justin Thompson	.05
240	Bret Boone	.05
241	Derek Jeter	2.50
242	Ken Caminiti	.05
243	Jay Bell	.05
244	Kevin Tapani	.05
245	Jason Kendall	.05
246	Jose Guillen	.05
247	Mike Bordick	.05
248	Dustin Hermanson	.05
249	Darrin Fletcher	.05
250	Dave Hollins	.05
251	Ramon Martinez	.05
252	Hideki Irabu	.05
253	Mark Grace	.05
254	Jason Isringhausen	.05
255	Jose Cruz Jr.	.05
256	Brian Johnson	.05
257	Brad Ausmus	.05
258	Andruw Jones	.75
259	Doug Jones	.05
260	Jeff Shaw	.05
261	Chuck Finley	.05
262	Gary Sheffield	.45
263	David Segui	.05
264	John Smiley	.05
265	Tim Salmon	.05
266	J.T. Snow Jr.	.05
267	Alex Fernandez	.05
268	Matt Stairs	.05
269	B.J. Surhoff	.05
270	Keith Foulke	.05
271	Edgar Martinez	.05
272	Shannon Stewart	.05
273	Eduardo Perez	.05
274	Wally Joyner	.05
275	Kevin Young	.05
276	Eli Marrero	.05
277	Brad Radke	.05
278	Jamie Moyer	.05
279	Joe Girardi	.05
280	Troy O'Leary	.05
281	Aaron Sele	.05
282	Jose Offerman	.05
283	Scott Erickson	.05
284	Sean Berry	.05
285	Shigetoshi Hasegawa	.05
286	Felix Heredia	.05
287	Willie McGee	.05
288	Alex Rodriguez	2.00
289	Ugueth Urbina	.05
290	Jon Lieber	.05
291	Fernando Tatis	.05
292	Chris Stynes	.05
293	Bernard Gilkey	.05
294	Joey Hamilton	.05
295	Matt Karchner	.05
296	Paul Wilson	.05
297	Mel Nieves	.05
298	Kevin Millwood **RC**	.75
299	Quinton McCracken	.05
300	Jerry DiPoto	.05
301	Jermaine Dye	.05
302	Travis Lee	.05
303	Ron Coomer	.05
304	Matt Williams	.05
305	Bobby Higginson	.05
306	Jorge Fabregas	.05
307	Hal Morris	.05
308	Jay Bell	.05
309	Joe Randa	.05
310	Andy Benes	.05
311	Sterling Hitchcock	.05
312	Jeff Suppan	.05
313	Shane Reynolds	.05
314	Willie Blair	.05
315	Scott Rolen	.65
316	Wilson Alvarez	.05
317	David Justice	.05
318	Fred McGriff	.05
319	Bobby Jones	.05
320	Wade Boggs	1.00
321	Tim Wakefield	.05
322	Tony Saunders	.05
323	David Cone	.05
324	Roberto Hernandez	.05
325	Jose Canseco	.45
326	Kevin Stocker	.05
327	Gerald Williams	.05
328	Quinton McCracken	.05
329	Mark Gardner	.05
330	Ben Grieve	.05
331	Kevin Brown	.05
332	Mike Lowell **RC**	1.00
333	Jed Hansen	.05
334	Abraham Nunez	.05
335	John Thomson	.05
336	Derrek Lee	.05
337	Mike Piazza	1.50
338	Brad Fullmer	.05
339	Ray Durham	.05
340	Kerry Wood	.50
341	Neil Polcovich **RC**	.05
342	Russ Johnson	.05
343	Darryl Hamilton	.05
344	David Ortiz	.45
345	Kevin Orie	.05
346	Sean Casey	.25
347	Juan Guzman	.05
348	Ruben Rivera	.05
349	Rick Aguilera	.05
350	Bobby Estalella	.05
351	Bobby Witt	.05
352	Paul Konerko	.25
353	Matt Morris	.05
354	Carl Pavano	.05
355	Todd Zeile	.05
356	Kevin Brown	.05
357	Alex Gonzalez	.05
358	Chuck Knoblauch	.05
359	Joey Cora	.05
360	Mike Lansing	.05
361	Adrian Beltre	.45
362	Dennis Eckersley	.65
363	A.J. Hinch	.05
364	Kenny Lofton	.05
365	Alex Gonzalez	.05
366	Henry Rodriguez	.05
367	Mike Stoner **RC**	.05
368	Darryl Kile	.05
369	Carl Pavano	.05
370	Walt Weiss	.05
371	Kris Benson	.05
372	Cecil Fielder	.05
373	Dermal Brown	.05
374	Rod Beck	.05
375	Eric Milton	.05
376	Travis Fryman	.05
377	Preston Wilson	.10
378	Chili Davis	.05
379	Travis Lee	.10
380	Jim Leyritz	.05
381	Vernon Wells	.05
382	Joe Carter	.05
383	J.J. Davis	.05
384	Marquis Grissom	.05
385	Mike Cuddyer **RC**	.50
386	Rickey Henderson	.75
387	Chris Enochs **RC**	.10
388	Andres Galarraga	.05
389	Jason Dellaero	.05
390	Robb Nen	.05
391	Mark Mangum	.05
392	Jeff Blauser	.05
393	Adam Kennedy	.05
394	Bob Abreu	.05
395	Jack Cust **RC**	1.00
396	Jose Vizcaino	.05
397	Jon Garland	.05
398	Pedro Martinez	.75
399	Aaron Akin	.05
400	Jeff Conine	.05

One of a Kind

NM/M
Common Player: 2.00
Stars: 12X
Production 150 Sets
(See 1998 Stadium Club for checklist and base card values.)

First Day Issue

NM/M
Common Player: 2.00
Stars: 10X
Production 200 Sets
(See 1998 Stadium Club for checklist and base card values.)

Printing Plates

NM/M
Common Player: 25.00
(See 1998 Stadium Club for checklist.)

Bowman Preview

NM/M
Complete Set (10): 10.00
Common Player: .25
Inserted 1:12
BP1 Nomar Garciaparra 1.00
BP2 Scott Rolen .65

FRANK THOMAS

BP3	Ken Griffey Jr.	1.50
BP4	Frank Thomas	.75
BP5	Larry Walker	.25
BP6	Mike Piazza	1.50
BP7	Chipper Jones	1.00
BP8	Tino Martinez	.25
BP9	Mark McGwire	2.00
BP10	Barry Bonds	2.50

Bowman Prospect Preview

		NM/M
Complete Set (10):		3.00
Common Player:		.25
Inserted 1:12		
BP1	Ben Grieve	.25
BP2	Brad Fullmer	.25
BP3	Ryan Anderson	.25
BP4	Mark Kotsay	.25
BP5	Bobby Estalella	.25
BP6	Juan Encarnacion	.25
BP7	Todd Helton	2.00
BP8	Mike Lowell	.50
BP9	A.J. Hinch	.25
BP10	Richard Hidalgo	.25

Co-Signers

		NM/M
Common Card:		10.00
Group A 1:4,372		
Group B 1:1,457		
Group C 1:121		
CS1	Nomar Garciaparra, Scott Rolen/A	120.00
CS2	Nomar Garciaparra, Derek Jeter/B	250.00
CS3	Nomar Garciaparra, Eric Karros/C	60.00
CS4	Scott Rolen, Derek Jeter/C	100.00
CS5	Scott Rolen, Eric Karros/B	40.00
CS6	Derek Jeter, Eric Karros/A	150.00
CS7	Travis Lee, Jose Cruz Jr./B	15.00
CS8	Travis Lee, Mark Kotsay/C	10.00
CS9	Travis Lee, Paul Konerko/A	25.00
CS10	Jose Cruz Jr., Mark Kotsay/A	25.00
CS11	Jose Cruz Jr., Paul Konerko/C	12.00
CS12	Mark Kotsay, Paul Konerko/B	20.00
CS13	Tony Gwynn, Larry Walker/A	120.00
CS14	Tony Gwynn, Mark Grudzielanek/C	30.00
CS15	Tony Gwynn, Andres Galarraga/B	60.00
CS16	Larry Walker, Mark Grudzielanek/B	40.00
CS17	Larry Walker, Andres Galarraga/C	30.00
CS18	Mark Grudzielanek, Andres Galarraga/A	25.00
CS19	Sandy Alomar, Roberto Alomar/A	75.00
CS20	Sandy Alomar, Andy Pettitte/C	20.00
CS21	Sandy Alomar, Tino Martinez/B	40.00
CS22	Roberto Alomar, Andy Pettitte/B	50.00
CS23	Roberto Alomar, Tino Martinez/C	25.00
CS24	Andy Pettitte, Tino Martinez/A	75.00
CS25	Tony Clark, Todd Hundley/A	25.00
CS26	Tony Clark, Tim Salmon/B	30.00
CS27	Tony Clark, Robin Ventura/C	10.00

CS28	Todd Hundley, Tim Salmon/C	15.00
CS29	Todd Hundley, Robin Ventura/B	12.00
CS30	Tim Salmon, Robin Ventura/A	50.00
CS31	Roger Clemens, Randy Johnson/B	175.00
CS32	Roger Clemens, Jaret Wright/A	140.00
CS33	Roger Clemens, Matt Morris/C	100.00
CS34	Randy Johnson, Jaret Wright/C	50.00
CS35	Randy Johnson, Matt Morris/A	85.00
CS36	Jaret Wright, Matt Morris/B	20.00

In the Wings

ELI MARRERO

		NM/M
Complete Set (15):		6.00
Common Player:		.50
Inserted 1:36		
W1	Juan Encarnacion	.50
W2	Brad Fullmer	.50
W3	Ben Grieve	.50
W4	Todd Helton	3.00
W5	Richard Hidalgo	.50
W6	Russ Johnson	.50
W7	Paul Konerko	.75
W8	Mark Kotsay	.50
W9	Derek Lee	1.00
W10	Travis Lee	.50
W11	Eli Marrero	.50
W12	David Ortiz	.75
W13	Randall Simon	.50
W14	Shannon Stewart	.50
W15	Fernando Tatis	.50

Never Compromise

		NM/M
Complete Set (20):		10.00
Common Player:		.15
Inserted 1:12		
NC1	Cal Ripken Jr.	2.00
NC2	Ivan Rodriguez	.50
NC3	Ken Griffey Jr.	1.00
NC4	Frank Thomas	.60
NC5	Tony Gwynn	.75
NC6	Mike Piazza	1.00
NC7	Randy Johnson	.60
NC8	Greg Maddux	.75
NC9	Roger Clemens	.85
NC10	Derek Jeter	2.00
NC11	Chipper Jones	.75
NC12	Barry Bonds	2.00
NC13	Larry Walker	.15
NC14	Jeff Bagwell	.60
NC15	Barry Larkin	.15
NC16	Ken Caminiti	.15
NC17	Mark McGwire	1.50
NC18	Manny Ramirez	.60
NC19	Tim Salmon	.15
NC20	Paul Molitor	.60

Playing with Passion

CRAIG BIGGIO SECOND BASE

PLAYING PASSION

		NM/M
Complete Set (10):		10.00
Common Player:		.35
Inserted 1:12		
P1	Bernie Williams	.35
P2	Jim Edmonds	.35
P3	Chipper Jones	1.00
P4	Cal Ripken Jr.	3.00
P5	Craig Biggio	.35
P6	Juan Gonzalez	.45
P7	Alex Rodriguez	2.25
P8	Tino Martinez	.35
P9	Mike Piazza	1.50
P10	Ken Griffey Jr.	1.50

Royal Court

Frank Thomas

		NM/M
Complete Set (15):		15.00
Common Player:		.50
Inserted 1:36		
RC1	Ken Griffey Jr.	2.00
RC2	Frank Thomas	1.25
RC3	Mike Piazza	2.00
RC4	Chipper Jones	1.50
RC5	Mark McGwire	2.50
RC6	Cal Ripken Jr.	3.00
RC7	Jeff Bagwell	1.25
RC8	Barry Bonds	3.00
RC9	Juan Gonzalez	.85
RC10	Alex Rodriguez	2.50
RC11	Travis Lee	.50
RC12	Paul Konerko	.75
RC13	Todd Helton	1.00
RC14	Ben Grieve	.50
RC15	Mark Kotsay	.50

Screen Plays Sound Chips

SCREEN PLAY

CAL RIPKEN

		NM/M
SC1	Cal Ripken Jr.	5.00

Triumvirate

		NM/M
Complete Set (54):		70.00
Complete Series 1 (24):		30.00
Complete Series 2 (30):		40.00
Common Player:		.50
Luminous 1:48		
Luminescents 1:192:		1.5X
Illuminators 1:384:		2.5X
T1a	Chipper Jones	2.50
T1b	Andruw Jones	2.00
T1c	Kenny Lofton	.50

GIANTS

T2a	Derek Jeter	5.00
T2b	Bernie Williams	.50
T2c	Tino Martinez	.50
T3a	Jay Buhner	.50
T3b	Edgar Martinez	.50
T3c	Ken Griffey Jr.	3.00
T4a	Albert Belle	.50
T4b	Robin Ventura	.50
T4c	Frank Thomas	2.00
T5a	Brady Anderson	.50
T5b	Cal Ripken Jr.	5.00
T5c	Rafael Palmeiro	1.50
T6a	Mike Piazza	3.00
T6b	Raul Mondesi	.50
T6c	Eric Karros	.50
T7a	Vinny Castilla	.50
T7b	Andres Galarraga	.50
T7c	Larry Walker	.50
T8a	Jim Thome	1.50
T8b	Manny Ramirez	2.00
T8c	David Justice	.50
T9a	Mike Mussina	.75
T9b	Greg Maddux	2.50
T9c	Randy Johnson	2.00
T10a	Mike Piazza	3.00
T10b	Sandy Alomar	.50
T10c	Ivan Rodriguez	1.50
T11a	Mark McGwire	4.00
T11b	Tino Martinez	.50
T11c	Frank Thomas	2.00
T12a	Roberto Alomar	.75
T12b	Chuck Knoblauch	.50
T12c	Craig Biggio	.50
T13a	Cal Ripken Jr.	5.00
T13b	Chipper Jones	2.50
T13c	Ken Caminiti	.50
T14a	Derek Jeter	5.00
T14b	Nomar Garciaparra	2.50
T14c	Alex Rodriguez	4.00
T15a	Barry Bonds	5.00
T15b	David Justice	.50
T15c	Albert Belle	.50
T16a	Bernie Williams	.50
T16b	Ken Griffey Jr.	3.00
T16c	Ray Lankford	.50
T17a	Tim Salmon	.50
T17b	Larry Walker	.50
T17c	Tony Gwynn	2.50
T18a	Paul Molitor	2.00
T18b	Edgar Martinez	.50
T18c	Juan Gonzalez	1.00

1999 Stadium Club

		NM/M
Complete Set (355):		40.00
Complete Series 1 (170):		20.00
Complete Series 2 (185):		20.00
Common Player:		.05
Common SP (141-160; 336-355):		.50
Inserted 1:3		
Pack (6):		1.25
Wax Box (24):		25.00
1	Alex Rodriguez	2.00
2	Chipper Jones	1.50
3	Rusty Greer	.05
4	Jim Edmonds	.05
5	Ron Gant	.05

6	Kevin Polcovich	.05
7	Darryl Strawberry	.05
8	Bill Mueller	.05
9	Vinny Castilla	.05
10	Wade Boggs	1.50
11	Jose Lima	.05
12	Darren Dreifort	.05
13	Jay Bell	.05
14	Ben Grieve	.05
15	Shawn Green	.35
16	Andres Galarraga	.05
17	Bartolo Colon	.05
18	Francisco Cordova	.05
19	Paul O'Neill	.05
20	Trevor Hoffman	.05
21	Darren Oliver	.05
22	John Franco	.05
23	Eli Marrero	.05
24	Roberto Hernandez	.05
25	Craig Biggio	.50
26	Brad Fullmer	.05
27	Scott Erickson	.05
28	Tom Gordon	.05
29	Brian Hunter	.05
30	Raul Mondesi	.05
31	Rick Reed	.05
32	Jose Canseco	.50
33	Robb Nen	.05
34	Turner Ward	.05
35	Bret Boone	.05
36	Jose Offerman	.05
37	Matt Lawton	.05
38	David Wells	.05
39	Bob Abreu	.10
40	Jeromy Burnitz	.05
41	Deivi Cruz	.05
42	Mike Cameron	.05
43	Rico Brogna	.05
44	Dmitri Young	.05
45	Chuck Knoblauch	.05
46	Johnny Damon	.35
47	Brian Meadows	.05
48	Jeremi Gonzalez	.05
49	Gary DiSarcina	.05
50	Frank Thomas	1.00
51	F.P. Santangelo	.05
52	Tom Candiotti	.05
53	Shane Reynolds	.05
54	Rod Beck	.05
55	Rey Ordonez	.05
56	Todd Helton	.75
57	Mickey Morandini	.05
58	Jorge Posada	.05
59	Mike Mussina	.30
60	Bobby Bonilla	.05
61	David Segui	.05
62	Brian McRae	.05
63	Fred McGriff	.05
64	Brett Tomko	.05
65	Derek Jeter	2.50
66	Sammy Sosa	1.50
67	Kenny Rogers	.05
68	Dave Nilsson	.05
69	Eric Young	.05
70	Mark McGwire	2.00
71	Kenny Lofton	.05
72	Tom Glavine	.35
73	Joey Hamilton	.05
74	John Valentin	.05
75	Mariano Rivera	.15
76	Ray Durham	.05
77	Tony Clark	.05
78	Livan Hernandez	.05
79	Rickey Henderson	1.00
80	Vladimir Guerrero	1.00
81	J.T. Snow Jr.	.05
82	Juan Guzman	.05
83	Darryl Hamilton	.05
84	Matt Anderson	.05
85	Travis Lee	.05
86	Joe Randa	.05
87	Dave Dellucci	.05
88	Moises Alou	.05
89	Alex Gonzalez	.05
90	Tony Womack	.05
91	Neifi Perez	.05
92	Travis Fryman	.05
93	Masato Yoshii	.05
94	Woody Williams	.05
95	Ray Lankford	.05
96	Roger Clemens	1.50
97	Dustin Hermanson	.05
98	Joe Carter	.05
99	Jason Schmidt	.05
100	Greg Maddux	1.50
101	Kevin Tapani	.05
102	Charles Johnson	.05
103	Derrek Lee	.50
104	Pete Harnisch	.05
105	Dante Bichette	.05
106	Scott Brosius	.05
107	Mike Caruso	.05
108	Eddie Taubensee	.05
109	Jeff Fassero	.05
110	Marquis Grissom	.05
111	Jose Hernandez	.05
112	Chan Ho Park	.05
113	Wally Joyner	.05
114	Bobby Estalella	.05
115	Pedro Martinez	1.00
116	Shawn Estes	.05
117	Walt Weiss	.05
118	John Mabry	.05
119	Brian Johnson	.05
120	Jim Thome	.65
121	Bill Spiers	.05
122	John Olerud	.05
123	Jeff King	.05
124	Tim Belcher	.05
125	John Wetteland	.05
126	Tony Gwynn	1.50
127	Brady Anderson	.05
128	Randy Winn	.05
129	Devon White	.05
130	Eric Karros	.05
131	Kevin Millwood	.05
132	Andy Benes	.05
133	Andy Ashby	.05
134	Ron Comer	.05
135	Juan Gonzalez	.50
136	Randy Johnson	1.00
137	Aaron Sele	.05
138	Edgardo Alfonzo	.05
139	B.J. Surhoff	.05
140	Jose Vizcaino	.05
141	Chad Moeller RC	.75
142	Mike Zwicka RC	.50
143	Angel Pena	.50
144	Nick Johnson RC	2.00
145	Giuseppe Chiaramonte RC	.50
146	Kit Pellow RC	.50
147	Clayton Andrews RC	.50
148	Jerry Hairston Jr. RC	.75
149	Jason Tyner RC	.50
150	Chip Ambres RC	.50
151	Pat Burrell RC	2.00
152	Josh McKinley RC	.75
153	Choo Freeman RC	.75
154	Rick Elder RC	.50
155	Eric Valent RC	.75
156	Jeff Winchester RC	.50
157	Mike Nannini RC	.50
158	Mamon Tucker RC	.50
159	Nate Bump RC	.50
160	Andy Brown RC	.50
161	Troy Glaus	1.00
162	Adrian Beltre	.45
163	Mitch Meluskey	.05
164	Alex Gonzalez	.05
165	George Lombard	.05
166	Eric Chavez	.25
167	Ruben Mateo	.05
168	Calvin Pickering	.05
169	Gabe Kapler	.05
170	Bruce Chen	.05
171	Darin Erstad	.15
172	Sandy Alomar	.05
173	Miguel Cairo	.05
174	Jason Kendall	.05
175	Cal Ripken Jr.	2.50
176	Darryl Kile	.05
177	David Cone	.05
178	Mike Sweeney	.05
179	Royce Clayton	.05
180	Curt Schilling	.25
181	Barry Larkin	.05
182	Eric Milton	.05
183	Ellis Burks	.05
184	A.J. Hinch	.05
185	Garret Anderson	.05
186	Sean Bergman	.05
187	Shannon Stewart	.05
188	Bernard Gilkey	.05
189	Jeff Blauser	.05
190	Andruw Jones	1.00
191	Omar Daal	.05
192	Jeff Kent	.05
193	Mark Kotsay	.05
194	Dave Burba	.05
195	Bobby Higginson	.05
196	Hideki Irabu	.05
197	Jamie Moyer	.05
198	Doug Glanville	.05
199	Quinton McCracken	.05
200	Ken Griffey Jr.	1.75
201	Mike Lieberthal	.05
202	Carl Everett	.05
203	Omar Vizquel	.05
204	Mike Lansing	.05
205	Manny Ramirez	1.00
206	Ryan Klesko	.05
207	Jeff Montgomery	.05
208	Chad Curtis	.05
209	Rick Helling	.05
210	Justin Thompson	.05
211	Tom Goodwin	.05
212	Todd Dunwoody	.05
213	Kevin Young	.05
214	Tony Saunders	.05
215	Gary Sheffield	.45
216	Jaret Wright	.05
217	Quilvio Veras	.05
218	Marty Cordova	.05
219	Tino Martinez	.05
220	Scott Rolen	.75
221	Fernando Tatis	.05
222	Damion Easley	.05
223	Aramis Ramirez	.05
224	Brad Radke	.05
225	Nomar Garciaparra	1.50
226	Magglio Ordonez	.05
227	Andy Pettitte	.20
228	David Ortiz	.45
229	Todd Jones	.05
230	Larry Walker	.05
231	Tim Wakefield	.05
232	Jose Guillen	.05
233	Gregg Olson	.05
234	Ricky Gutierrez	.05
235	Todd Walker	.05
236	Abraham Nunez	.05
237	Sean Casey	.15
238	Greg Norton	.05
239	Bret Saberhagen	.05
240	Bernie Williams	.05
241	Tim Salmon	.05
242	Jason Giambi	.50
243	Fernando Vina	.05
244	Darrin Fletcher	.05
245	Greg Vaughn	.05
246	Dennis Reyes	.05
247	Hideo Nomo	.50
248	Reggie Sanders	.05
249	Mike Hampton	.05
250	Kerry Wood	.50
251	Ismael Valdes	.05
252	Pat Hentgen	.05
253	Scott Spiezio	.05
254	Chuck Finley	.05
255	Troy Glaus	.75
256	Bobby Jones	.05
257	Wayne Gomes	.05
258	Rondell White	.05
259	Todd Zeile	.05
260	Matt Williams	.05
261	Henry Rodriguez	.05
262	Matt Stairs	.05
263	Jose Valentin	.05
264	David Justice	.05
265	Javy Lopez	.05
266	Matt Morris	.05
267	Steve Trachsel	.05
268	Edgar Martinez	.05
269	Al Martin	.05
270	Ivan Rodriguez	.75
271	Carlos Delgado	.50
272	Mark Grace	.05
273	Ugueth Urbina	.05
274	Jay Buhner	.05
275	Mike Piazza	1.75
276	Rick Aguilera	.05
277	Javier Valentin	.05
278	Brian Anderson	.05
279	Cliff Floyd	.05
280	Barry Bonds	2.50
281	Troy O'Leary	.05
282	Seth Greisinger	.05
283	Mark Grudzielanek	.05
284	Jose Cruz Jr.	.05
285	Jeff Bagwell	1.00
286	John Smoltz	.05
287	Jeff Cirillo	.05
288	Richie Sexson	.05
289	Charles Nagy	.05
290	Pedro Martinez	1.00
291	Juan Encarnacion	.05
292	Phil Nevin	.05
293	Terry Steinbach	.05
294	Miguel Tejada	.15
295	Dan Wilson	.05
296	Chris Peters	.05
297	Brian Moehler	.05
298	Jason Christiansen	.05
299	Kelly Stinnett	.05
300	Dwight Gooden	.05
301	Randy Velarde	.05
302	Kirt Manwaring	.05
303	Jeff Abbott	.05
304	Dave Hollins	.05
305	Kerry Ligtenberg	.05
306	Aaron Boone	.05
307	Carlos Hernandez	.05
308	Mike DiFelice	.05
309	Brian Meadows	.05
310	Tim Bogar	.05
311	Greg Vaughn	.05
312	Brant Brown	.05
313	Steve Finley	.05
314	Bret Boone	.05
315	Albert Belle	.05
316	Robin Ventura	.05
317	Eric Davis	.05
318	Todd Hundley	.05
319	Jose Offerman	.05
320	Kevin Brown	.05
321	Denny Neagle	.05
322	Brian Jordan	.05
323	Brian Giles	.05
324	Bobby Bonilla	.05
325	Roberto Alomar	.20
326	Ken Caminiti	.05
327	Todd Stottlemyre	.05
328	Randy Johnson	1.00
329	Luis Gonzalez	.05
330	Rafael Palmeiro	.75
331	Devon White	.05
332	Will Clark	.05
333	Dean Palmer	.05
334	Gregg Jefferies	.05
335	Mo Vaughn	.05
336	Brad Lidge RC	2.00
337	Chris George RC	.75
338	Austin Kearns RC	1.50
339	Matt Belisle RC	.75
340	Nate Cornejo RC	.75
341	Matt Holliday RC	5.00
342	J.M. Gold RC	.50
343	Matt Roney RC	.50
344	Seth Etherton RC	.75
345	Adam Everett RC	.75
346	Marlon Anderson	.50
347	Ron Belliard	.50
348	Fernando Seguignol	.50
349	Michael Barrett	.50
350	Dernell Stenson	.50
351	Ryan Anderson	.50
352	Ramon Hernandez	.50
353	Jeremy Giambi	.50
354	Ricky Ledee	.50
355	Carlos Lee	1.00

First Day Issue

NM/M

Common Player:	2.00
Stars:	8X
SP Stars:	4X

(See 1999 Stadium Club for checklist and base card values.)

One of a Kind

NM/M

Common Player:	2.00
Stars:	8X
SP Stars:	4X

(See 1999 Stadium Club for checklist and base card values.)

Printing Plates

NM/M

Common Player:	25.00

(See 1999 Stadium Club for checklist.)

Autographs

	NM/M
Common Player:	10.00
Inserted 1:1,107	
1 Alex Rodriguez	75.00
2 Chipper Jones	30.00
3 Barry Bonds	150.00
4 Tino Martinez	25.00
5 Ben Grieve	10.00
6 Juan Gonzalez	15.00
7 Vladimir Guerrero	30.00
8 Albert Belle	15.00
9 Kerry Wood	25.00
10 Todd Helton	20.00

Chrome

MANNY RAMIREZ

	NM/M
Complete Set (40):	45.00
Common Player:	.50
Inserted 1:24	
Refractors:	2X
Inserted 1:96	
1 Nomar Garciaparra	2.00
2 Kerry Wood	1.00
3 Jeff Bagwell	1.50
4 Ivan Rodriguez	1.25
5 Albert Belle	.50
6 Gary Sheffield	1.00
7 Andruw Jones	1.50
8 Kevin Brown	.50
9 David Cone	.50
10 Darin Erstad	.75
11 Manny Ramirez	1.50
12 Larry Walker	.50
13 Mike Piazza	2.50
14 Cal Ripken Jr.	4.00
15 Pedro Martinez	1.50
16 Greg Vaughn	.50
17 Barry Bonds	4.00
18 Mo Vaughn	.50
19 Bernie Williams	.50
20 Ken Griffey Jr.	2.50
21 Alex Rodriguez	3.00
22 Chipper Jones	2.00
23 Ben Grieve	.50
24 Frank Thomas	1.50
25 Derek Jeter	4.00
26 Sammy Sosa	2.00
27 Mark McGwire	3.00
28 Vladimir Guerrero	1.50
29 Greg Maddux	2.00
30 Juan Gonzalez	.75
31 Troy Glaus	1.25
32 Adrian Beltre	1.25
33 Mitch Meluskey	.50
34 Alex Gonzalez	.50
35 George Lombard	.50
36 Eric Chavez	.75
37 Ruben Mateo	.50
38 Calvin Pickering	.50
39 Gabe Kapler	.50
40 Bruce Chen	.50

Co-Signers

	NM/M
Common Group A:	90.00
Inserted 1:18,085	
Common Group B:	20.00
Inserted 1:9043	
Common Group C:	9.00
Inserted 1:3014	
Common Group D:	6.00
Inserted 1:254	
CS1 Ben Grieve, Richie Sexson/D	15.00
CS2 Todd Helton, Troy Glaus/D	50.00
CS3 Alex Rodriguez, Scott Rolen/D	85.00

CS4 Derek Jeter, Chipper Jones/D	150.00
CS5 Cliff Floyd, Eli Marrero/D	6.00
CS6 Jay Buhner, Kevin Young/D	8.00
CS7 Ben Grieve, Troy Glaus/C	40.00
CS8 Todd Helton, Richie Sexson/C	40.00
CS9 Alex Rodriguez, Chipper Jones/C	125.00
CS10 Derek Jeter, Scott Rolen/C	125.00
CS11 Cliff Floyd, Kevin Young/C	10.00
CS12 Jay Buhner, Eli Marrero/B	10.00
CS13 Ben Grieve, Todd Helton/B	50.00
CS14 Richie Sexson, Troy Glaus/B	40.00
CS15 Alex Rodriguez, Derek Jeter/B	350.00
CS16 Chipper Jones, Scott Rolen/B	150.00
CS17 Cliff Floyd, Jay Buhner/B	15.00
CS18 Eli Marrero, Kevin Young/B	20.00
CS19 Ben Grieve, Todd Helton, Richie Sexson, Troy Glaus/A	180.00
CS20 Alex Rodriguez, Derek Jeter, Chipper Jones, Scott Rolen/A	2,500
CS21 Cliff Floyd, Jay Buhner, Eli Marrero, Kevin Young/A	100.00
CS22 Edgardo Alfonzo, Jose Guillen/D	15.00
CS23 Mike Lowell, Ricardo Rincon/D	10.00
CS24 Juan Gonzalez, Vinny Castilla/D	20.00
CS25 Moises Alou, Roger Clemens/D	60.00
CS26 Scott Spezio, Tony Womack/D	10.00
CS27 Fernando Vina, Quilvio Veras/D	10.00
CS28 Edgardo Alfonzo, Ricardo Rincon/C	10.00
CS29 Jose Guillen, Mike Lowell/C	10.00
CS30 Juan Gonzalez, Moises Alou/C	25.00
CS31 Roger Clemens, Vinny Castilla/C	85.00
CS32 Scott Spezio, Fernando Vina/C	10.00
CS33 Tony Womack, Quilvio Veras/B	20.00
CS34 Edgardo Alfonzo, Mike Lowell/B	30.00
CS35 Jose Guillen, Ricardo Rincon/B	30.00
CS36 Juan Gonzalez, Roger Clemens/B	135.00
CS37 Moises Alou, Vinny Castilla/B	30.00
CS38 Scott Spezio, Quilvio Veras/B	20.00
CS39 Tony Womack, Fernando Vina/B	20.00
CS40 Edgardo Alfonzo, Jose Guillen, Mike Lowell, Ricardo Rincon/A	90.00
CS41 Juan Gonzalez, Moises Alou, Roger Clemens, Vinny Castilla/A	900.00
CS42 Scott Spezio, Tony Womack, Fernando Vina, Quilvio Veras/A	90.00

Never Compromise

NOMAR GARCIAPARRA
never compromise

	NM/M
Complete Set (20):	10.00
Common Player:	.25
Inserted 1:12	
NC1 Mark McGwire	1.00
NC2 Sammy Sosa	.65
NC3 Barry Bonds	.75
NC4 Greg Maddux	.65
NC5 Barry Bonds	1.50
NC6 Alex Rodriguez	1.00
NC7 Darin Erstad	.35
NC8 Roger Clemens	.65
NC9 Nomar Garciaparra	.65
NC10 Derek Jeter	1.50
NC11 Cal Ripken Jr.	1.50
NC12 Mike Piazza	.75
NC13 Greg Vaughn	.25
NC14 Andres Galarraga	.25
NC15 Vinny Castilla	.25
NC16 Jeff Bagwell	.50
NC17 Chipper Jones	.75
NC18 Eric Chavez	.35
NC19 Orlando Hernandez	.25
NC20 Troy Glaus	.40

Photography

	NM/M
Complete Set (10):	200.00
Common Player:	20.00
1 Alex Rodriguez	20.00
65 Derek Jeter	20.00
66 Sammy Sosa	20.00
135 Juan Gonzalez	20.00
NC1 Mark McGwire	20.00
NC3 Ken Griffey Jr.	20.00
SCA5 Ben Grieve	20.00
SCC1 Nomar Garciaparra	20.00
SCC2 Kerry Wood	20.00
SCC13 Mike Piazza	20.00

Triumvirate

KERRY WOOD

	NM/M
Complete Set (48):	75.00
Common Player:	.50
Inserted 1:36	
Luminescents:	1.5X
Inserted 1:144	
Illuminators:	2.5X
Inserted 1:288	
T1A Greg Vaughn	.50
T1B Ken Caminiti	.50
T1C Tony Gwynn	2.50
T2A Andruw Jones	2.00
T2B Chipper Jones	2.50
T2C Andres Galarraga	.50
T3A Jay Buhner	.50
T3B Ken Griffey Jr.	3.00
T3C Alex Rodriguez	4.00
T4A Derek Jeter	6.00
T4B Tino Martinez	.50
T4C Bernie Williams	.50
T5A Brian Jordan	.50
T5B Ray Lankford	.50
T5C Mark McGwire	4.00
T6A Jeff Bagwell	2.00
T6B Craig Biggio	.50
T6C Randy Johnson	2.00
T7A Nomar Garciaparra	2.50
T7B Pedro Martinez	2.00
T7C Mo Vaughn	.50
T8A Mark Grace	.50
T8B Sammy Sosa	2.50
T8C Kerry Wood	1.00
T9A Alex Rodriguez	4.00
T9B Nomar Garciaparra	2.50
T9C Derek Jeter	6.00
T10A Todd Helton	1.50
T10B Travis Lee	.50
T10C Pat Burrell	1.50
T11A Greg Maddux	2.50
T11B Kerry Wood	1.00
T11C Tom Glavine	.75
T12A Chipper Jones	2.50
T12B Vinny Castilla	.50
T12C Scott Rolen	1.50
T13A Juan Gonzalez	1.00
T13B Ken Griffey Jr.	3.00
T13C Ben Grieve	.50
T14A Sammy Sosa	3.00
T14B Vladimir Guerrero	2.00
T14C Barry Bonds	6.00
T15A Frank Thomas	2.00
T15B Jim Thome	1.50
T15C Tino Martinez	.50
T16A Mark McGwire	4.00
T16B Andres Galarraga	.50
T16C Jeff Bagwell	2.00

Video Replay

	NM/M
Complete Set (5):	4.50
Common Player:	.75
Inserted 1:12	
VR1 Mark McGwire	1.50
VR2 Sammy Sosa	1.00
VR3 Ken Griffey Jr.	1.25
VR4 Kerry Wood	.75
VR5 Alex Rodriguez	1.50

2000 Stadium Club

BARRY LARKIN

	NM/M
Complete Set (250):	80.00
Common Player:	.15
Common SP (201-250):	2.00
Inserted 1:5	
Pack (6):	1.50
Wax Box (24):	30.00
1 Nomar Garciaparra	1.25
2 Brian Jordan	.15
3 Mark Grace	.25
4 Jeromy Burnitz	.15
5 Shane Reynolds	.15
6 Alex Gonzalez	.15
7 Jose Offerman	.15
8 Orlando Hernandez	.15
9 Mike Caruso	.15
10 Tony Clark	.15
11 Sean Casey	.25
12 Johnny Damon	.25
13 Dante Bichette	.15
14 Kevin Young	.15
15 Juan Gonzalez	.75
16 Chipper Jones	1.00
17 Quilvio Veras	.15
18 Trevor Hoffman	.15
19 Roger Cedeno	.15
20 Ellis Burks	.15
21 Richie Sexson	.15
22 Gary Sheffield	.40
23 Delino DeShields	.15
24 Wade Boggs	1.00
25 Ray Lankford	.15
26 Kevin Appier	.15
27 Roy Halladay	.15
28 Harold Baines	.15
29 Todd Zeile	.15
30 Barry Larkin	.15
31 Ron Coomer	.15
32 Jorge Posada	.15
33 Magglio Ordonez	.15
34 Brian Giles	.15
35 Jeff Kent	.15
36 Henry Rodriguez	.15
37 Fred McGriff	.15
38 Shawn Green	.50
39 Derek Bell	.15
40 Ben Grieve	.15
41 Dave Nilsson	.15
42 Mo Vaughn	.15
43 Rondell White	.15
44 Doug Glanville	.15
45 Paul O'Neill	.15
46 Carlos Lee	.15
47 Vinny Castilla	.15
48 Mike Sweeney	.15
49 Rico Brogna	.15
50 Alex Rodriguez	1.50
51 Luis Castillo	.15
52 Kevin Brown	.15
53 Jose Vidro	.15
54 John Smoltz	.15
55 Garret Anderson	.15
56 Matt Stairs	.15
57 Omar Vizquel	.15
58 Tom Goodwin	.15

59	Scott Brosius	.15
60	Robin Ventura	.15
61	B.J. Surhoff	.15
62	Andy Ashby	.15
63	Chris Widger	.15
64	Tim Hudson	.40
65	Javy Lopez	.15
66	Tim Salmon	.25
67	Warren Morris	.15
68	John Wetteland	.15
69	Gabe Kapler	.15
70	Bernie Williams	.30
71	Rickey Henderson	.75
72	Andruw Jones	.75
73	Eric Young	.15
74	Bob Abreu	.15
75	David Cone	.15
76	Rusty Greer	.15
77	Ron Belliard	.15
78	Troy Glaus	.75
79	Mike Hampton	.15
80	Miguel Tejada	.30
81	Jeff Cirillo	.15
82	Todd Hundley	.15
83	Roberto Alomar	.40
84	Charles Johnson	.15
85	Rafael Palmeiro	.65
86	Doug Mientkiewicz	.15
87	Mariano Rivera	.25
88	Neifi Perez	.15
89	Jermaine Dye	.15
90	Ivan Rodriguez	.65
91	Jay Buhner	.15
92	Pokey Reese	.15
93	John Olerud	.15
94	Brady Anderson	.15
95	Manny Ramirez	.75
96	Keith Osik	.15
97	Mickey Morandini	.15
98	Matt Williams	.15
99	Eric Karros	.15
100	Ken Griffey Jr.	1.25
101	Bret Boone	.15
102	Ryan Klesko	.15
103	Craig Biggio	.15
104	John Jaha	.15
105	Vladimir Guerrero	.75
106	Devon White	.15
107	Tony Womack	.15
108	Marvin Benard	.15
109	Kenny Lofton	.15
110	Preston Wilson	.15
111	Al Leiter	.15
112	Reggie Sanders	.15
113	Scott Williamson	.15
114	Deivi Cruz	.15
115	Carlos Beltran	.50
116	Ray Durham	.15
117	Ricky Ledee	.15
118	Torii Hunter	.15
119	John Valentin	.15
120	Scott Rolen	.65
121	Jason Kendall	.15
122	Dave Martinez	.15
123	Jim Thome	.65
124	David Bell	.15
125	Jose Canseco	.45
126	Jose Lima	.15
127	Carl Everett	.15
128	Kevin Millwood	.15
129	Bill Spiers	.15
130	Omar Daal	.15
131	Miguel Cairo	.15
132	Mark Grudzielanek	.15
133	David Justice	.15
134	Russ Ortiz	.15
135	Mike Piazza	1.25
136	Brian Meadows	.15
137	Tony Gwynn	1.00
138	Cal Ripken Jr.	2.00
139	Kris Benson	.15
140	Larry Walker	.15
141	Cristian Guzman	.15
142	Tino Martinez	.25
143	Chris Singleton	.15
144	Lee Stevens	.15
145	Rey Ordonez	.15
146	Russ Davis	.15
147	J.T. Snow Jr.	.15
148	Luis Gonzalez	.25
149	Marquis Grissom	.15
150	Greg Maddux	1.00
151	Fernando Tatis	.15
152	Jason Giambi	.50
153	Carlos Delgado	.50
154	Joe McEwing	.15
155	Raul Mondesi	.15
156	Rich Aurilia	.15
157	Alex Fernandez	.15
158	Albert Belle	.25
159	Pat Meares	.15
160	Mike Lieberthal	.15
161	Mike Cameron	.15
162	Juan Encarnacion	.15
163	Chuck Knoblauch	.15
164	Pedro Martinez	.75
165	Randy Johnson	.75
166	Shannon Stewart	.15
167	Jeff Bagwell	.75
168	Edgar Renteria	.15
169	Barry Bonds	2.00
170	Steve Finley	.15
171	Brian Hunter	.15
172	Tom Glavine	.35
173	Mark Kotsay	.15

174	Tony Fernandez	.15
175	Sammy Sosa	1.25
176	Geoff Jenkins	.15
177	Adrian Beltre	.15
178	Jay Bell	.15
179	Mike Bordick	.15
180	Ed Sprague	.15
181	Dave Roberts	.15
182	Greg Vaughn	.15
183	Brian Daubach	.15
184	Damion Easley	.15
185	Carlos Febles	.15
186	Kevin Tapani	.15
187	Frank Thomas	.75
188	Roger Clemens	1.00
189	Mike Benjamin	.15
190	Curt Schilling	.40
191	Edgardo Alfonzo	.15
192	Mike Mussina	.40
193	Todd Helton	.75
194	Todd Jones	.15
195	Dean Palmer	.15
196	John Flaherty	.15
197	Derek Jeter	2.00
198	Todd Walker	.15
199	Brad Ausmus	.15
200	Mark McGwire	1.50
201	Erubiel Durazo	2.00
202	Nick Johnson	2.50
203	Ruben Mateo	.15
204	Lance Berkman	2.50
205	Pat Burrell	3.00
206	Pablo Ozuna	2.00
207	Roosevelt Brown	2.00
208	Alfonso Soriano	4.00
209	A.J. Burnett	2.00
210	Rafael Furcal	2.00
211	Scott Morgan	2.00
212	Adam Piatt	2.00
213	Dee Brown	2.00
214	Corey Patterson	2.50
215	Mickey Lopez	2.00
216	Rob Ryan	2.00
217	Sean Burroughs	2.00
218	Jack Cust	2.00
219	John Patterson	2.00
220	Kit Pellow	2.00
221	Chad Hermansen	2.00
222	Daryle Ward	2.00
223	Jayson Werth	2.00
224	Jason Standridge	2.00
225	Mark Mulder	2.50
226	Peter Bergeron	2.00
227	Willi Mo Pena	2.00
228	Aramis Ramirez	2.00
229	John Sneed RC	2.00
230	Wilton Veras	2.00
231	Josh Hamilton	2.00
232	Eric Munson	2.00
233	Bobby Bradley RC	2.00
234	Larry Bigbie RC	2.00
235	B.J. Garbe RC	2.00
236	Brett Myers RC	6.00
237	Jason Stumm RC	2.00
238	Corey Myers RC	2.00
239	Ryan Christianson RC	2.00
240	David Walling	2.00
241	Josh Girdley	2.00
242	Omar Ortiz	2.00
243	Jason Jennings	2.00
244	Kyle Snyder RC	2.00
245	Jay Gehrke	2.00
246	Mike Paradis RC	2.00
247	Chance Caple RC	2.00
248	Ben Christiansen RC	2.00
249	Brad Baker RC	2.00
250	Rick Asadoorian RC	2.00
---	Nomar Garciaparra Checklist	.25

One of a Kind

Stars:	5-10X
Short-prints:	2-3X

Production 150 Sets H
(See 2000 Stadium Club for checklist
and base card values.)

First Day Issue

Stars:	5-10X
Short-Prints:	2-3X

Production 150 Sets R
(See 2000 Stadium Club for checklist
and base card values.)

Printing Plates

	NM/M
Common Player:	60.00

(See 2000 Stadium Club for checklist.)

Bats of Brilliance

Alex Rodriguez

	NM/M
Complete Set (10):	10.00
Common Player:	.50
Inserted 1:12	
1	Mark McGwire	2.50
2	Sammy Sosa	1.50
3	Jose Canseco	.50
4	Jeff Bagwell	.75
5	Ken Griffey Jr.	1.50
6	Nomar Garciaparra	1.50
7	Mike Piazza	1.50
8	Alex Rodriguez	2.50
9	Vladimir Guerrero	.75
10	Chipper Jones	1.50

Capture The Action

Ivan Rodriguez

	NM/M
Complete Set (20):	20.00
Common Player:	.50
Inserted 1:12	
Game View Stars:	3-6X
Production 100 Sets H	
1	Josh Hamilton	.50
2	Pat Burrell	.75
3	Erubiel Durazo	.50
4	Alfonso Soriano	1.00
5	A.J. Burnett	.50
6	Alex Rodriguez	3.00
7	Sean Casey	.50
8	Derek Jeter	4.00
9	Vladimir Guerrero	1.00
10	Nomar Garciaparra	2.00
11	Mike Piazza	2.00
12	Ken Griffey Jr.	2.00
13	Sammy Sosa	2.00
14	Luis Gonzalez	1.00
15	Mark McGwire	3.00
16	Ivan Rodriguez	.75
17	Barry Bonds	4.00
18	Wade Boggs	1.50
19	Tony Gwynn	1.50
20	Cal Ripken Jr.	4.00

Chrome Preview

	NM/M
Complete Set (20):	40.00
Common Player:	1.00
Inserted 1:24	
Refractors:	2-3X
Inserted 1:120	
1	Nomar Garciaparra	3.00
2	Juan Gonzalez	1.50
3	Chipper Jones	2.00
4	Alex Rodriguez	4.50
5	Ivan Rodriguez	1.25
6	Manny Ramirez	1.50
7	Ken Griffey Jr.	3.00

Alex Rodriguez

8	Vladimir Guerrero	1.50
9	Mike Piazza	3.00
10	Pedro Martinez	2.00
11	Jeff Bagwell	1.50
12	Barry Bonds	6.00
13	Sammy Sosa	3.00
14	Derek Jeter	6.00
15	Mark McGwire	4.50
16	Erubiel Durazo	1.00
17	Nick Johnson	1.00
18	Pat Burrell	1.00
19	Alfonso Soriano	1.50
20	Adam Piatt	1.00

Co-Signers

	NM/M
Common Card:	15.00
Group A 1:10,184	
Group B 1:5,092	
Group C 1:508	
1	Alex Rodriguez, Derek Jeter	400.00
2	Derek Jeter, Omar Vizquel	150.00
3	Alex Rodriguez, Rey Ordonez	100.00
4	Derek Jeter, Rey Ordonez	150.00
5	Omar Vizquel, Alex Rodriguez	100.00
6	Rey Ordonez, Omar Vizquel	15.00
7	Wade Boggs, Robin Ventura	30.00
8	Randy Johnson, Mike Mussina	90.00
9	Pat Burrell, Magglio Ordonez	40.00
10	Chad Hermansen, Pat Burrell	20.00
11	Magglio Ordonez, Chad Hermansen	20.00
12	Josh Hamilton, Corey Myers	25.00
13	B.J. Garbe, Josh Hamilton	25.00
14	Corey Myers, B.J. Garbe	15.00
15	Tino Martinez, Fred McGriff	60.00

Lone Star Signatures

Derek Jeter

	NM/M
Common Player:	8.00
Group 1 1:1,979	
Group 2 1:2,374	

Group 3 1:1,979
Group 4 1:424

1	Derek Jeter	100.00
2	Alex Rodriguez	100.00
3	Wade Boggs	25.00
4	Robin Ventura	15.00
5	Randy Johnson	60.00
6	Mike Mussina	25.00
7	Tino Martinez	35.00
8	Fred McGriff	25.00
9	Omar Vizquel	15.00
10	Rey Ordonez	8.00
11	Pat Burrell	15.00
12	Chad Hermansen	8.00
13	Magglio Ordonez	10.00
14	Josh Hamilton	35.00
15	Corey Myers	8.00
16	B.J. Garbe	8.00

Onyx Extreme

		NM/M
Complete Set (10):		10.00
Common Player:		.40
Inserted 1:12		
Die-cuts:		2-3X
Inserted 1:60		
1	Ken Griffey Jr.	1.50
2	Derek Jeter	3.00
3	Vladimir Guerrero	1.00
4	Nomar Garciaparra	1.50
5	Barry Bonds	3.00
6	Alex Rodriguez	2.50
7	Sammy Sosa	1.50
8	Ivan Rodriguez	.75
9	Larry Walker	.40
10	Andruw Jones	1.00

Scenes

		NM/M
Complete Set (9):		10.00
Common Player:		.50
Inserted 1:Box		
1	Mark McGwire	2.50
2	Alex Rodriguez	2.50
3	Cal Ripken Jr.	3.00
4	Sammy Sosa	2.00
5	Derek Jeter	3.00
6	Ken Griffey Jr.	2.00
7	Raul Mondesi	.50
8	Chipper Jones	1.50
9	Nomar Garciaparra	2.00

Souvenirs

		NM/M
Complete Set (3):		35.00
Common Player:		8.00
Inserted 2:339		
1	Wade Boggs	20.00
2	Randy Johnson	20.00
3	Robin Ventura	8.00

3 X 3

		NM/M
Complete Set (30):		40.00
Common Player:		.75
Inserted 1:18		
Luminescent:		2X
Inserted 1:72		
Illuminator:		3-4X
Inserted 1:144		
1A	Randy Johnson	1.50
1B	Pedro Martinez	1.50
1C	Greg Maddux	2.00
2A	Mike Piazza	3.00
2B	Ivan Rodriguez	1.25
2C	Mike Lieberthal	.75
3A	Mark McGwire	4.50
3B	Jeff Bagwell	1.50
3C	Sean Casey	.75
4A	Craig Biggio	.75
4B	Roberto Alomar	1.00

ALEX RODRIGUEZ
LUMINOUS

4C	Jay Bell	.75
5A	Chipper Jones	2.00
5B	Matt Williams	.75
5C	Robin Ventura	.75
6A	Alex Rodriguez	4.50
6B	Derek Jeter	6.00
6C	Nomar Garciaparra	3.00
7A	Barry Bonds	6.00
7B	Luis Gonzalez	1.00
7C	Dante Bichette	.75
8A	Ken Griffey Jr.	3.00
8B	Bernie Williams	1.00
8C	Andruw Jones	1.50
9A	Manny Ramirez	1.50
9B	Sammy Sosa	3.00
9C	Juan Gonzalez	1.50
10A	Jose Canseco	1.00
10B	Frank Thomas	1.50
10C	Rafael Palmeiro	1.00

2000 Stadium Club Chrome

STADIUM CLUB
ALFONSO SORIANO

		NM/M
Complete Set (250):		40.00
Common Player:		.15
Pack (11):		1.50
Wax Box (36):		40.00
1	Nomar Garciaparra	1.50
2	Brian Jordan	.15
3	Mark Grace	.25
4	Jeromy Burnitz	.15
5	Shane Reynolds	.15
6	Alex Gonzalez	.15
7	Jose Offerman	.15
8	Orlando Hernandez	.15
9	Mike Caruso	.15
10	Tony Clark	.15
11	Sean Casey	.25
12	Johnny Damon	.25
13	Dante Bichette	.15
14	Kevin Young	.15
15	Juan Gonzalez	.75
16	Chipper Jones	1.00
17	Quivilo Veras	.15
18	Trevor Hoffman	.15
19	Roger Cedeno	.15
20	Ellis Burks	.15
21	Richie Sexson	.15
22	Gary Sheffield	.45
23	Delino DeShields	.15
24	Wade Boggs	1.00
25	Ray Lankford	.15
26	Kevin Appier	.15
27	Roy Halladay	.15
28	Harold Baines	.15
29	Todd Zeile	.15
30	Barry Larkin	.15
31	Ron Coomer	.15
32	Jorge Posada	.15
33	Magglio Ordonez	.15
34	Brian Giles	.15
35	Jeff Kent	.15
36	Henry Rodriguez	.15
37	Fred McGriff	.15
38	Shawn Green	.50
39	Ben Shell	.15
40	Ben Grieve	.15
41	Dave Nilsson	.15
42	Mo Vaughn	.15
43	Rondell White	.15
44	Doug Glanville	.15
45	Paul O'Neill	.15
46	Carlos Lee	.15
47	Vinny Castilla	.15
48	Mike Sweeney	.15
49	Rico Brogna	.15
50	Alex Rodriguez	2.50
51	Luis Castillo	.15
52	Kevin Brown	.15
53	Jose Vidro	.15
54	John Smoltz	.15
55	Garret Anderson	.15
56	Matt Stairs	.15
57	Omar Vizquel	.15
58	Tom Goodwin	.15
59	Scott Brosius	.15
60	Robin Ventura	.15
61	B.J. Surhoff	.15
62	Andy Ashby	.15
63	Chris Widger	.15
64	Tim Hudson	.40
65	Javy Lopez	.25
66	Tim Salmon	.15
67	Warren Morris	.15
68	John Wetteland	.15
69	Gabe Kapler	.15
70	Bernie Williams	.25
71	Rickey Henderson	.75
72	Andruw Jones	.75
73	Eric Young	.15
74	Bobby Abreu	.15
75	David Cone	.15
76	Rusty Greer	.15
77	Ron Belliard	.15
78	Troy Glaus	.75
79	Mike Hampton	.15
80	Miguel Tejada	.30
81	Jeff Cirillo	.15
82	Todd Hundley	.15
83	Roberto Alomar	.35
84	Charles Johnson	.15
85	Rafael Palmeiro	.65
86	Doug Mientkiewicz	.15
87	Mariano Rivera	.25
88	Neifi Perez	.15
89	Jermaine Dye	.15
90	Ivan Rodriguez	.65
91	Jay Buhner	.15
92	Pokey Reese	.15
93	John Olerud	.15
94	Brady Anderson	.15
95	Manny Ramirez	.75
96	Keith Osik	.15
97	Mickey Morandini	.15
98	Matt Williams	.15
99	Eric Karros	.15
100	Ken Griffey Jr.	1.50
101	Bret Boone	.15
102	Ryan Klesko	.15
103	Craig Biggio	.15
104	John Jaha	.15
105	Vladimir Guerrero	.75
106	Devon White	.15
107	Tony Womack	.15
108	Marvin Benard	.15
109	Kenny Lofton	.15
110	Preston Wilson	.15
111	Al Leiter	.15
112	Reggie Sanders	.15
113	Scott Williamson	.15
114	Deivi Cruz	.15
115	Carlos Beltran	.50
116	Ray Durham	.15
117	Ricky Ledee	.15
118	Torii Hunter	.15
119	John Valentin	.15
120	Scott Rolen	.65
121	Jason Kendall	.15
122	Dave Martinez	.15
123	Jim Thome	.65
124	David Bell	.15
125	Jose Canseco	.50
126	Jose Lima	.15
127	Carl Everett	.15
128	Kevin Millwood	.15
129	Bill Spiers	.15
130	Omar Daal	.15
131	Miguel Cairo	.15
132	Mark Grudzielanek	.15
133	David Justice	.15
134	Russ Ortiz	.15
135	Mike Piazza	1.50
136	Brian Meadows	.15
137	Tony Gwynn	1.00
138	Cal Ripken Jr.	3.00
139	Kris Benson	.15
140	Larry Walker	.15
141	Cristian Guzman	.15
142	Tino Martinez	.15
143	Chris Singleton	.15
144	Lee Stevens	.15
145	Rey Ordonez	.15
146	Russ Davis	.15
147	J.T. Snow Jr.	.15
148	Luis Gonzalez	.25
149	Marquis Grissom	.15
150	Greg Maddux	1.00
151	Fernando Tatis	.15
152	Jason Giambi	.50
153	Carlos Delgado	.50
154	Joe McEwing	.15
155	Raul Mondesi	.15
156	Rich Aurilia	.15
157	Alex Fernandez	.15
158	Albert Belle	.25
159	Pat Meares	.15
160	Mike Lieberthal	.15
161	Mike Cameron	.15
162	Juan Encarnacion	.15
163	Chuck Knoblauch	.15
164	Pedro Martinez	.75
165	Randy Johnson	.75
166	Shannon Stewart	.15
167	Jeff Bagwell	.75
168	Edgar Renteria	.15
169	Barry Bonds	3.00
170	Steve Finley	.15
171	Brian Hunter	.15
172	Tom Glavine	.40
173	Mark Kotsay	.15
174	Tony Fernandez	.15
175	Sammy Sosa	1.50
176	Geoff Jenkins	.15
177	Adrian Beltre	.45
178	Jay Bell	.15
179	Mike Bordick	.15
180	Ed Sprague	.15
181	Dave Roberts	.15
182	Greg Vaughn	.15
183	Brian Daubach	.15
184	Damion Easley	.15
185	Carlos Febles	.15
186	Kevin Tapani	.15
187	Frank Thomas	.75
188	Roger Clemens	1.25
189	Mike Benjamin	.15
190	Curt Schilling	.40
191	Edgardo Alfonzo	.15
192	Mike Mussina	.45
193	Todd Helton	.75
194	Todd Jones	.15
195	Dean Palmer	.15
196	John Flaherty	.15
197	Derek Jeter	3.00
198	Todd Walker	.15
199	Brad Ausmus	.15
200	Mark McGwire	2.50
201	Erubiel Durazo	.15
202	Nick Johnson	.15
203	Ruben Mateo	.15
204	Lance Berkman	.15
205	Pat Burrell	.65
206	Pablo Ozuna	.15
207	Roosevelt Brown	.15
208	Alfonso Soriano	1.00
209	A.J. Burnett	.15
210	Rafael Furcal	.15
211	Scott Morgan	.15
212	Adam Piatt	.15
213	Dee Brown	.15
214	Corey Patterson	.15
215	Mickey Lopez	.15
216	Rob Ryan	.15
217	Sean Burroughs	.15
218	Jack Cust	.15
219	John Patterson	.15
220	Kit Pellow	.15
221	Chad Hermansen	.15
222	Daryle Ward	.15
223	Jayson Werth	.15
224	Jason Standridge	.15
225	Mark Mulder	.15
226	Peter Bergeron	.15
227	Willi Mo Pena	.15
228	Aramis Ramirez	.15
229	John Sneed	.15
230	Wilton Veras	.15
231	Josh Hamilton	.50
232	Eric Munson	.15
233	Bobby Bradley RC	1.00
234	Larry Bigbie RC	1.00
235	B.J. Garbe RC	1.00
236	Brett Myers RC	4.00
237	Jason Stumm RC	1.00
238	Corey Myers RC	1.00
239	Ryan Christianson RC	1.00
240	David Walling	.15
241	Josh Girdley	.15
242	Omar Ortiz	.15
243	Jason Jennings	.15
244	Kyle Snyder	.15
245	Jay Gehrke	.15
246	Mike Paradis	.15
247	Chance Caple RC	1.00
248	Ben Christensen RC	1.00
249	Brad Baker RC	1.00
250	Rick Asadoorian RC	1.00

Refractor

Stars:	2-4X
Rookies:	1-2X
Inserted 1:12	

First Day Issue

Stars:	4-8X
Rookies:	1-3X
Production 100 Sets	
Refractor:	25-40X

Rookies: 5-10X
Production 25 Sets

Capture The Action

		NM/M
Complete Set (20):		40.00
Common Player:		1.00
Inserted 1:18		
Refractors:		2-3X
Inserted 1:90		
1	Josh Hamilton	1.00
2	Pat Burrell	1.50
3	Erubiel Durazo	1.00
4	Alfonso Soriano	1.50
5	A.J. Burnett	1.00
6	Alex Rodriguez	5.00
7	Sean Casey	1.00
8	Derek Jeter	6.00
9	Vladimir Guerrero	1.50
10	Nomar Garciaparra	3.00
11	Mike Piazza	3.00
12	Ken Griffey Jr.	3.00
13	Sammy Sosa	3.00
14	Juan Gonzalez	1.50
15	Mark McGwire	5.00
16	Ivan Rodriguez	1.50
17	Barry Bonds	6.00
18	Wade Boggs	2.00
19	Tony Gwynn	2.00
20	Cal Ripken Jr.	6.00

Clear Shots

		NM/M
Complete Set (10):		10.00
Common Player:		.50
Inserted 1:24		
Refractor:		2-3X
Inserted 1:120		
1	Derek Jeter	4.00
2	Bernie Williams	.50
3	Roger Clemens	2.50
4	Chipper Jones	2.00
5	Greg Maddux	2.00
6	Andruw Jones	1.00

7	Juan Gonzalez	1.00
8	Manny Ramirez	1.00
9	Ken Griffey Jr.	3.00
10	Josh Hamilton	.50

Eyes of the Game

		NM/M
Complete Set (10):		10.00
Common Player:		.50
Inserted 1:16		
Refractors:		2-3X
Inserted 1:80		
1	Randy Johnson	1.00
2	Mike Piazza	1.50
3	Nomar Garciaparra	1.50
4	Mark McGwire	2.50
5	Alex Rodriguez	2.50
6	Derek Jeter	3.00
7	Tony Gwynn	1.00
8	Sammy Sosa	1.50
9	Larry Walker	.50
10	Ken Griffey Jr.	1.50

True Colors

		NM/M
Complete Set (10):		15.00
Common Player:		1.00
Inserted 1:32		
Refractors:		2-3X
Inserted 1:160		
1	Sammy Sosa	2.00
2	Nomar Garciaparra	2.00
3	Alex Rodriguez	3.00
4	Derek Jeter	4.00
5	Mark McGwire	3.00
6	Chipper Jones	1.50
7	Mike Piazza	2.00
8	Ken Griffey Jr.	2.00
9	Manny Ramirez	1.00
10	Vladimir Guerrero	1.00

Visionaries

	NM/M
Complete Set (20):	17.50

2001 Stadium Club

		NM/M
Complete Set (200):		65.00
Common Player:		.15
Common SP:		1.50
Inserted 1:6		
Pack (7):		2.00
Box (24):		35.00
1	Nomar Garciaparra	1.25
2	Chipper Jones	1.00
3	Jeff Bagwell	.75
4	Chad Kreuter	.15
5	Randy Johnson	.75
6	Mike Hampton	.15
7	Barry Larkin	.15
8	Bernie Williams	.30
9	Chris Singleton	.15
10	Larry Walker	.15
11	Brad Ausmus	.15
12	Ron Coomer	.15
13	Edgardo Alfonzo	.15
14	Delino DeShields	.15
15	Tony Gwynn	1.00
16	Andruw Jones	.75
17	Raul Mondesi	.15
18	Troy Glaus	.75
19	Ben Grieve	.15
20	Sammy Sosa	1.25
21	Fernando Vina	.15
22	Jeromy Burnitz	.15
23	Jay Bell	.15
24	Pete Harnisch	.15
25	Barry Bonds	2.00
26	Eric Karros	.15
27	Alex Gonzalez	.15
28	Mike Lieberthal	.15
29	Juan Encarnacion	.15
30	Derek Jeter	2.00
31	Bruce Aven	.15
32	Eric Milton	.15
33	Aaron Boone	.15
34	Roberto Alomar	.40
35	John Olerud	.15
36	Orlando Cabrera	.15
37	Shawn Green	.45
38	Roger Cedeno	.15
39	Garret Anderson	.15
40	Jim Thome	.65
41	Gabe Kapler	.15
42	Mo Vaughn	.15
43	Sean Casey	.25
44	Preston Wilson	.15
45	Javy Lopez	.15
46	Ryan Klesko	.15
47	Ray Durham	.15
48	Dean Palmer	.15
49	Jorge Posada	.15
50	Alex Rodriguez	1.50
51	Tom Glavine	.40
52	Ray Lankford	.15
53	Jose Canseco	.40
54	Tim Salmon	.25
55	Cal Ripken Jr.	2.00
56	Bob Abreu	.15
57	Robin Ventura	.15
58	Damion Easley	.15
59	Paul O'Neill	.15
60	Ivan Rodriguez	.65
61	Carl Everett	.15
62	Doug Glanville	.15
63	Jeff Kent	.15
64	Jay Buhner	.15
65	Cliff Floyd	.15
66	Rick Ankiel	.25
67	Mark Grace	.25
68	Brian Jordan	.15
69	Craig Biggio	.15
70	Carlos Delgado	.50
71	Brad Radke	.15
72	Greg Maddux	1.00
73	Al Leiter	.15
74	Pokey Reese	.15
75	Todd Helton	.75
76	Mariano Rivera	.25
77	Shane Spencer	.15
78	Jason Kendall	.15
79	Chuck Knoblauch	.15
80	Scott Rolen	.65
81	Jose Offerman	.15
82	J.T. Snow Jr.	.15
83	Pat Meares	.15
84	Quilvio Veras	.15
85	Edgar Renteria	.15
86	Luis Matos	.15
87	Adrian Beltre	.15
88	Luis Gonzalez	.25
89	Rickey Henderson	.75
90	Brian Giles	.15
91	Carlos Febles	.15
92	Tino Martinez	.15
93	Magglio Ordonez	.15
94	Rafael Furcal	.15
95	Mike Mussina	.30
96	Gary Sheffield	.40
97	Kenny Lofton	.15
98	Fred McGriff	.15
99	Ken Caminiti	.15
100	Mark McGwire	1.50
101	Tom Goodwin	.15
102	Mark Grudzielanek	.15
103	Derek Bell	.15
104	Mike Lowell	.15
105	Jeff Cirillo	.15
106	Orlando Hernandez	.15
107	Jose Valentin	.15
108	Warren Morris	.15
109	Mike Williams	.15
110	Gregg Zaun	.15
111	Jose Vidro	.15
112	Omar Vizquel	.15
113	Vinny Castilla	.15
114	Gregg Jefferies	.15
115	Kevin Brown	.15
116	Shannon Stewart	.15
117	Marquis Grissom	.15
118	Manny Ramirez	.75
119	Albert Belle	.15
120	Bret Boone	.15
121	Johnny Damon	.25
122	Juan Gonzalez	.75
123	David Justice	.15
124	Jeffrey Hammonds	.15
125	Ken Griffey Jr.	1.25
126	Mike Sweeney	.15
127	Tony Clark	.15
128	Todd Zeile	.15
129	Mark Johnson	.15
130	Matt Williams	.15
131	Geoff Jenkins	.15
132	Jason Giambi	.50
133	Steve Finley	.15
134	Derrek Lee	.15
135	Royce Clayton	.15
136	Joe Randa	.15
137	Rafael Palmeiro	.65
138	Kevin Young	.15
139	Curt Schilling	.40
140	Vladimir Guerrero	.75
141	Greg Vaughn	.15
142	Jermaine Dye	.15
143	Roger Clemens	1.00
144	Denny Hocking	.15
145	Frank Thomas	.75
146	Carlos Beltran	.50
147	Eric Young	.15
148	Pat Burrell	.50
149	Pedro Martinez	.75
150	Mike Piazza	1.25
151	Adrian Gonzalez	.50
152	Adam Johnson	.15
153	Luis Montanez RC	1.50
154	Mike Stodolka	.15
155	Phil Dumatrait	.15
156	Sean Burnett	1.50
157	Dominic Rich RC	1.50
158	Adam Wainwright	.50
159	Scott Thorman	.15
160	Scott Heard	.25
161	Chad Petty RC	1.50
162	Matt Wheatland	2.00
163	Brad Digby	.15
164	Rocco Baldelli	1.00
165	Grady Sizemore	1.00
166	Brian Sellier RC	1.50
167	Rick Brosseau RC	1.50
168	Shawn Fagan RC	1.50
169	Sean Smith	1.50
170	Chris Bass RC	1.50
171	Corey Patterson	.25
172	Sean Burroughs	.25
173	Ben Petrick	.15

174	Mike Glendenning	.15
175	Barry Zito	.50
176	Milton Bradley	.15
177	Bobby Bradley	.15
178	Jason Hart	.15
179	Ryan Anderson	.15
180	Ben Sheets	.25
181	Adam Everett	.15
182	Alfonso Soriano	.75
183	Josh Hamilton	.50
184	Eric Munson	.15
185	Chin-Feng Chen	.25
186	Tim Christman RC	1.50
187	J.R. House	2.00
188	Brandon Parker RC	1.50
189	Sean Fesh RC	1.50
190	Joel Pieniero RC	2.00
191	Oscar Ramirez RC	1.50
192	Alex Santos RC	1.50
193	Eddy Reyes RC	1.50
194	Mike Jacobs RC	1.50
195	Erick Almonte RC	2.00
196	Brandon Claussen RC	2.00
197	Kris Keller RC	1.50
198	Wilson Betemit RC	1.50
199	Andy Phillips RC	1.50
200	Adam Pettyjohn RC	1.50
---	Derek Jeter (Checklist)	.25

Beam Team

		NM/M
Complete Set (30):		100.00
Common Player:		1.50
Production 500 Sets		
1	Sammy Sosa	6.00
2	Mark McGwire	8.00
3	Vladimir Guerrero	3.00
4	Chipper Jones	4.50
5	Manny Ramirez	3.00
6	Derek Jeter	10.00
7	Alex Rodriguez	8.00
8	Cal Ripken Jr.	10.00
9	Ken Griffey Jr.	6.00
10	Greg Maddux	4.50
11	Barry Bonds	10.00
12	Pedro Martinez	3.00
13	Nomar Garciaparra	6.00
14	Randy Johnson	3.00
15	Frank Thomas	3.00
16	Ivan Rodriguez	2.50
17	Jeff Bagwell	3.00
18	Mike Piazza	6.00
19	Todd Helton	3.00
20	Shawn Green	2.00
21	Juan Gonzalez	3.00
22	Larry Walker	1.50
23	Tony Gwynn	4.50
24	Pat Burrell	2.00
25	Rafael Furcal	1.50
26	Corey Patterson	1.50
27	Chin-Feng Chen	1.50
28	Sean Burroughs	1.50
29	Ryan Anderson	1.50
30	Josh Hamilton	1.50

Capture The Action

DEREK JETER

		NM/M
Complete Set (15):		15.00
Common Player:		1.00
Inserted 1:8		
1	Cal Ripken Jr.	3.00
2	Alex Rodriguez	2.50
3	Mike Piazza	2.00
4	Mark McGwire	2.50
5	Greg Maddux	1.50
6	Derek Jeter	3.00
7	Chipper Jones	1.00
8	Pedro Martinez	1.00
9	Ken Griffey Jr.	2.00
10	Nomar Garciaparra	2.00
11	Randy Johnson	1.00
12	Sammy Sosa	2.00
13	Vladimir Guerrero	1.00
14	Barry Bonds	3.00
15	Ivan Rodriguez	1.00

Capture The Action Game View

	NM/M
Common Player:	10.00

GAMEVIEW
Barry Bonds

Production 100 Sets		
1	Cal Ripken Jr.	30.00
2	Alex Rodriguez	25.00
3	Mike Piazza	20.00
4	Mark McGwire	25.00
5	Greg Maddux	15.00
6	Derek Jeter	30.00
7	Chipper Jones	15.00
8	Pedro Martinez	10.00
9	Ken Griffey Jr.	20.00
10	Nomar Garciaparra	10.00
11	Randy Johnson	10.00
12	Sammy Sosa	20.00
13	Vladimir Guerrero	10.00
14	Barry Bonds	30.00
15	Ivan Rodriguez	10.00

Co-Signers

CO-SIGNERS

		NM/M
Common Duo:		15.00
Inserted 1:1,117		
1	Nomar Garciaparra, Derek Jeter	400.00
2	Roberto Alomar, Edgardo Alfonzo	50.00
3	Rick Ankiel, Kevin Millwood	15.00
4	Chipper Jones, Troy Glaus	65.00
5	Magglio Ordonez, Bobby Abreu	20.00
6	Adam Piatt, Sean Burroughs	20.00
7	Corey Patterson, Nick Johnson	40.00
8	Adrian Gonzalez, Rocco Baldelli	40.00
9	Adam Johnson, Mike Stodolka	15.00

Diamond Pearls

TODD HELTON

		NM/M
Complete Set (20):		20.00
Common Player:		.65
Inserted 1:8		
1	Ken Griffey Jr.	2.00
2	Alex Rodriguez	2.50
3	Derek Jeter	3.00
4	Chipper Jones	1.50
5	Nomar Garciaparra	2.00
6	Vladimir Guerrero	1.00
7	Jeff Bagwell	1.00
8	Cal Ripken Jr.	3.00
9	Sammy Sosa	2.00
10	Mark McGwire	2.50
11	Frank Thomas	1.00
12	Pedro Martinez	1.00
13	Manny Ramirez	1.00
14	Randy Johnson	1.00
15	Barry Bonds	3.00
16	Ivan Rodriguez	.75
17	Greg Maddux	1.50
18	Mike Piazza	2.00
19	Todd Helton	1.00
20	Shawn Green	.65

Game-Used Cards

PROSPECT PERFORMANCE
BEN SHEETS

		NM/M
Common Player:		5.00
Inserted 1:285		
1	Chin-Feng Chen	20.00
2	Bobby Bradley	5.00
3	Tomokazu Ohka	5.00
4	Kurt Ainsworth	5.00
5	Craig Anderson	5.00
6	Josh Hamilton	10.00
7	Felipe Lopez	5.00
8	Ryan Anderson	5.00
9	Alex Escobar	5.00
10	Ben Sheets	8.00
11	Ntema Ndungidi	5.00
12	Eric Munson	5.00
13	Aaron Myette	5.00
14	Jack Cust	5.00
15	Julio Zuleta	5.00
16	Corey Patterson	10.00
17	Carlos Pena	5.00
18	Marcus Giles	5.00
19	Travis Wilson	5.00
20	Barry Zito	8.00

King of the Hill

		NM/M
Complete Set (5):		30.00
Common Player:		3.00
Inserted 1:21		
1	Pedro Martinez	10.00
2	Randy Johnson	10.00
3	Greg Maddux	15.00
4	Rick Ankiel	3.00
5	Kevin Brown	3.00

Lone Star Signatures

		NM/M
Common Player:		6.00
Inserted 1:196		
1	Nomar Garciaparra	100.00
2	Derek Jeter	120.00
3	Edgardo Alfonzo	20.00
4	Roberto Alomar	40.00
5	Magglio Ordonez	20.00
6	Bobby Abreu	40.00
7	Chipper Jones	50.00
8	Troy Glaus	30.00
9	Nick Johnson	15.00
10	Adam Piatt	6.00
11	Sean Burroughs	8.00
12	Corey Patterson	15.00
13	Rick Ankiel	15.00
14	Kevin Millwood	6.00
15	Adrian Gonzalez	15.00
16	Adam Johnson	6.00
17	Rocco Baldelli	25.00
18	Mike Stodolka	6.00

Play at the Plate

		NM/M
Common Player:		10.00
Inserted 1:11		
1	Mark McGwire	20.00
2	Sammy Sosa	15.00
3	Vladimir Guerrero	8.00
4	Ken Griffey Jr.	15.00
5	Mike Piazza	15.00
6	Chipper Jones	10.00
7	Barry Bonds	25.00
8	Alex Rodriguez	20.00
9	Jeff Bagwell	8.00
10	Nomar Garciaparra	15.00

Souvenirs

	NM/M
Common Player:	4.00

Game-Used Cards

JOSSE VIDRO

1	Scott Rolen/Bat	8.00
2	Larry Walker/Bat	5.00
3	Rafael Furcal/Bat	5.00
4	Darin Erstad/Bat	5.00
5	Mike Sweeney/Jsey	4.00
6	Matt Lawton/Jsy	4.00
7	Jose Vidro/Jsy	4.00
8	Pat Burrell/Jsy	6.00

Super Teams

		NM/M
Common Card:		1.00
STP1	Troy Glaus Anaheim Angels	2.00
STP2	Jeff Bagwell Houston Astros	2.00
STP3	Jason Giambi Oakland A's	1.25
STP4	Carlos Delgado Toronto Blue Jays	1.00
STP5	Chipper Jones Atlanta Braves	2.50
STP6	Geoff Jenkins Milwaukee Brewers	1.00
STP7	Mark McGwire St. Louis Cardinals	4.00
STP8	Sammy Sosa Chicago Cubs	3.00
STP9	Greg Vaughn Tampa Bay Devil Rays	1.00
STP10	Luis Gonzalez Arizona Diamondbacks	1.00
STP11	Shawn Green L.A. Dodgers	1.00
STP12	Vladimir Guerrero Montreal Expos	1.50
STP13	Barry Bonds S.F. Giants	5.00
STP14	Roberto Alomar Cleveland Indians	1.00
STP15	Alex Rodriguez Seattle Mariners	4.00
STP16	Preston Wilson Florida Marlins	1.00
STP17	Mike Piazza N.Y. Mets	3.00
STP18	Mike Mussina Baltimore Orioles	1.00
STP19	Tony Gwynn S.D. Padres	2.00
STP20	Scott Rolen Philadelphia Phillies	1.25
STP21	Jason Kendall Pittsburgh Pirates	1.00
STP22	Ivan Rodriguez Texas Rangers	1.25
STP23	Nomar Garciaparra Boston Red Sox	3.00
STP24	Ken Griffey Jr. Cincinnati Reds	3.00
STP25	Todd Helton Colorado Rockies	1.50
STP26	Mike Sweeney K.C. Royals	1.00
STP27	Juan Gonzalez Detroit Tigers	1.50
STP28	Brad Radke Minnesota Twins	1.00
STP29	Frank Thomas Chicago White Sox	1.50
STP30	Derek Jeter N.Y. Yankees	5.00

2002 Stadium Club Relic Edition

		NM/M
Complete Set (125):		
Common Player:		.15
Common SP (101-125):		5.00
Production 2,999		
Pack (6):		1.50
Box (24):		30.00
1	Pedro Martinez	.75
2	Derek Jeter	2.00
3	Chipper Jones	1.00
4	Roberto Alomar	.40
5	Albert Pujols	1.50
6	Bret Boone	.15
7	Alex Rodriguez	1.50
8	Jose Cruz	.15
9	Mike Hampton	.15
10	Vladimir Guerrero	.75
11	Jim Edmonds	.25
12	Luis Gonzalez	.25
13	Jeff Kent	.15
14	Mike Piazza	1.25
15	Ben Sheets	.15
16	Tsuyoshi Shinjo	.15
17	Pat Burrell	.40
18	Jermaine Dye	.15
19	Rafael Furcal	.15
20	Randy Johnson	.75
21	Carlos Delgado	.50

22	Roger Clemens	1.00
23	Eric Chavez	.25
24	Nomar Garciaparra	1.25
25	Ivan Rodriguez	.65
26	Juan Gonzalez	.15
27	Reggie Sanders	.15
28	Jeff Bagwell	.75
29	Kazuhiro Sasaki	.15
30	Larry Walker	.15
31	Ben Grieve	.15
32	David Justice	.15
33	David Wells	.15
34	Kevin Brown	.15
35	Miguel Tejada	.25
36	Jorge Posada	.15
37	Javy Lopez	.15
38	Cliff Floyd	.15
39	Carlos Lee	.15
40	Manny Ramirez	.75
41	Jim Thome	.65
42	Pokey Reese	.15
43	Scott Rolen	.65
44	Richie Sexson	.15
45	Dean Palmer	.15
46	Rafael Palmeiro	.65
47	Alfonso Soriano	.75
48	Craig Biggio	.15
49	Troy Glaus	.75
50	Andruw Jones	.75
51	Ichiro Suzuki	1.50
52	Kenny Lofton	.15
53	Hideo Nomo	.75
54	Magglio Ordonez	.15
55	Brad Penny	.15
56	Omar Vizquel	.15
57	Mike Sweeney	.15
58	Gary Sheffield	.25
59	Ken Griffey Jr.	1.25
60	Curt Schilling	.40
61	Bobby Higginson	.15
62	Terrence Long	.15
63	Moises Alou	.15
64	Sandy Alomar	.15
65	Cristian Guzman	.15
66	Sammy Sosa	1.25
67	Jose Vidro	.15
68	Edgar Martinez	.15
69	Jason Giambi	.50
70	Mark McGwire	1.50
71	Barry Bonds	2.00
72	Greg Vaughn	.15
73	Phil Nevin	.15
74	Jason Kendall	.15
75	Greg Maddux	1.00
76	Jeromy Burnitz	.15
77	Mike Mussina	.40
78	Johnny Damon	.25
79	Shawn Green	.40
80	Jimmy Rollins	.25
81	Edgardo Alfonzo	.15
82	Barry Larkin	.15
83	Raul Mondesi	.15
84	Preston Wilson	.15
85	Mike Lieberthal	.15
86	J.D. Drew	.40
87	Ryan Klesko	.15
88	David Segui	.15
89	Derek Bell	.15
90	Bernie Williams	.40
91	Doug Mientkiewicz	.15
92	Rich Aurilia	.15
93	Ellis Burks	.15
94	Placido Polanco	.15
95	Darin Erstad	.25
96	Brian Giles	.15
97	Geoff Jenkins	.15
98	Kerry Wood	.65
99	Mariano Rivera	.40
100	Todd Helton	.75
101	Adam Dunn	15.00
102	Grant Balfour	5.00
103	Jae Weong Seo	5.00
104	Hank Blalock	8.00
105	Chris George	5.00
106	Jack Cust	5.00
107	Juan Cruz	5.00
108	Adrian Gonzalez	8.00
109	Nick Johnson	5.00
110	Jeff Devanon RC	5.00
111	Juan Diaz	5.00
112	Brandon Duckworth	5.00
113	Jason Lane	5.00
114	Seung Jun Song	5.00
115	Morgan Ensberg	5.00
116	Marlyn Tisdale RC	5.00
117	Jason Botts RC	5.00
118	Henry Pichardo RC	5.00
119	John Rodriguez RC	5.00
120	Mike Peeples RC	5.00
121	Rob Bowen RC	5.00
122	Jeremy Affeldt RC	5.00
123	Jorge Buret RC	5.00
124	Manny Ravelo RC	5.00
125	Eudy Lajara RC	5.00

All-Star Relics

NM/M

Common Player:		5.00
RA	Roberto Alomar	7.50
MA	Moises Alou	5.00
BB	Barry Bonds	40.00
BRB	Bret Boone	5.00
MC	Mike Cameron	5.00
SC	Sean Casey	7.50
CF	Cliff Floyd	5.00

BG	Brian Giles	5.00
JG	Juan Gonzalez	12.00
LG3	Luis Gonzalez	5.00
CG	Cristian Guzman	5.00
TG	Tony Gwynn	15.00
MH	Mike Hampton	5.00
TH	Todd Helton	12.00
RJ	Randy Johnson	12.00
CJ	Chipper Jones	15.00
JK	Jeff Kent	5.00
RK	Ryan Klesko	5.00
EM	Edgar Martinez	5.00
ERM	Eric Milton	5.00
JO	John Olerud	5.00
MO	Magglio Ordonez	5.00
MP	Mike Piazza	20.00
JP	Jorge Posada	5.00
AP	Albert Pujols	30.00
MR	Manny Ramirez	12.00
CR	Cal Ripken Jr.	
IR	Ivan Rodriguez	10.00
KS	Kazuhiro Sasaki	5.00
MS	Mike Sweeney	5.00
LW	Larry Walker	5.00

Barry Bonds Autograph Ball

NM/M

Inserted as a redemption.

Barry Bonds	200.00

Chasing 500-500

NM/M

Common Player:		5.00
BB1	Barry Bonds/Dual	40.00
BB2	Barry Bonds/Jsy/600	30.00
BB3	Barry Bonds/Mult/200	75.00

Passport to the Majors

NM/M

Common Player:		5.00
Jsy 1:84		
Bat 1:795		
BA	Bobby Abreu/400	6.00
EA	Edgardo Alfonzo	5.00
RA	Roberto Alomar	6.00
WB	Wilson Betemit/325	5.00
BC	Bartolo Colon	5.00
RF	Rafael Furcal	5.00
AG	Andres Galarraga	5.00
JG	Juan Gonzalez	8.00
SH	Shigetoshi Hasegawa	5.00
AJ	Andruw Jones	8.00
CL	Carlos Lee	5.00
JL	Javy Lopez	5.00
PM	Pedro Martinez	10.00
RM	Raul Mondesi	5.00
MO	Magglio Ordonez	5.00
RP	Rafael Palmeiro	8.00
CP	Chan Ho Park	5.00
AP	Albert Pujols/450	40.00
MR	Manny Ramirez	10.00
IR	Ivan Rodriguez	10.00
KS	Kazuhiro Sasaki	5.00
TS	Tsuyoshi Shinjo/400	6.00
AS	Alfonso Soriano/400	10.00
MT	Miguel Tejada/375	6.00
LW	Larry Walker	5.00

Reel Time

NM/M

Complete Set (20):		25.00
Common Player:		.50
Inserted 1:8		
RT1	Luis Gonzalez	.50
RT2	Derek Jeter	4.00
RT3	Ken Griffey Jr.	2.50
RT4	Alex Rodriguez	3.00
RT5	Barry Bonds	4.00
RT6	Ichiro Suzuki	2.50
RT7	Carlos Delgado	1.00
RT8	Manny Ramirez	1.50
RT9	Mike Piazza	2.50
RT10	Mark McGwire	3.00
RT11	Todd Helton	1.50
RT12	Vladimir Guerrero	1.50
RT13	Jim Thome	1.50
RT14	Rich Aurilia	.50
RT15	Bret Boone	.50
RT16	Roberto Alomar	.75
RT17	Jason Giambi	1.00
RT18	Chipper Jones	2.00
RT19	Albert Pujols	3.00
RT20	Sammy Sosa	2.50

Stadium Shots

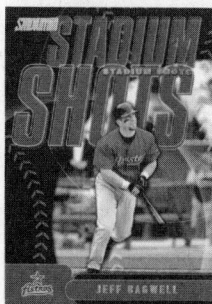

NM/M

Complete Set (10):		15.00
Common Player:		1.00
Inserted 1:12		
SS1	Sammy Sosa	2.00
SS2	Manny Ramirez	1.50
SS3	Jason Giambi	1.00
SS4	Mike Piazza	2.00
SS5	Barry Bonds	4.00
SS6	Ken Griffey Jr.	2.00
SS7	Juan Gonzalez	1.50
SS8	Jeff Bagwell	1.50
SS9	Jim Thome	1.50
SS10	Mark McGwire	3.00

Stadium Slices Handle

NM/M

Common Player:		15.00
BB	Barry Bonds	50.00
LG	Luis Gonzalez	15.00
AP	Albert Pujols	50.00
IR	Ivan Rodriguez	20.00
BW	Bernie Williams	15.00

Stadium Slices Barrel

NM/M

Common Player:		15.00
BB	Barry Bonds	75.00
LG	Luis Gonzalez	15.00
AP	Albert Pujols	75.00
IR	Ivan Rodriguez	35.00
BW	Bernie Williams	15.00

Stadium Slices Trademar

NM/M

Common Player:		15.00
BB	Barry Bonds	60.00
LG	Luis Gonzalez	15.00
AP	Albert Pujols	60.00
IR	Ivan Rodriguez	20.00
BW	Bernie Williams	15.00

World Champions Relics

NM/M

Common Player:		4.00
Jersey 1:106		
Bat 1:94		
Pants 1:795		
Spikes 1:38,400		
RA	Roberto Alomar	15.00
MA	Moises Alou	8.00
DB	Don Baylor	8.00
JB	Johnny Bench	20.00
BB	Bert Blyleven	8.00
WB	Wade Boggs	15.00
BRB	Bob Boone	4.00
GB	George Brett	50.00
SB	Scott Brosius	10.00
AB	Al Bumbry	4.00
JC1	Jose Canseco	15.00
JC2	Jose Canseco	15.00
GC1	Gary Carter	15.00
GC2	Gary Carter	15.00
JC	Joe Carter	10.00
RC	Ron Cey	10.00
CC	Chris Chambliss	8.00
DC	Dave Concepcion	8.00
ED	Eric Davis	10.00
BD	Bucky Dent	8.00
GF	George Foster	8.00
PG	Phil Garner	4.00
KG1	Kirk Gibson	10.00
KG2	Kirk Gibson	10.00
TG	Tom Glavine	15.00
KG	Ken Griffey Sr.	10.00
RH	Rickey Henderson/50	80.00
GH	George Hendrick	6.00
KH	Keith Hernandez	15.00
WH	Willie Hernandez	8.00
OH	Orel Hershiser	10.00
RJ	Reggie Jackson	15.00
CWJ	Chipper Jones	15.00
DJ	David Justice	8.00
CK	Chuck Knoblauch	4.00
AL	Al Leiter	8.00
DL	Davey Lopes	8.00
JL	Javy Lopez	8.00
GL	Greg Luzinski	6.00
GM	Greg Maddux	30.00
BM	Bill Madlock	8.00
TLM	Tino Martinez	15.00
HM	Hal McCrae	8.00
FM	Fred McGriff	10.00
PM	Paul Molitor	15.00
TM	Thurman Munson	50.00
EM1	Eddie Murray	15.00
EM2	Eddie Murray	15.00
JO	John Olerud	6.00
PO	Paul O'Neill	15.00
DP	Dave Parker	10.00
TP	Tony Perez	10.00
LVP	Lou Pinella	8.00
JP	Jorge Posada	10.00
KP	Kirby Puckett	20.00
WR	Willie Randolph	10.00
MJS	Mike Schmidt	50.00
MS	Mike Scoscia	10.00
OS	Ozzie Smith	30.00
JS	John Smoltz	10.00
ES	Ed Sprague	4.00
WS	Willie Stargell	15.00
AT	Alan Trammell	10.00
LW	Lou Whitaker	10.00
BW	Bernie Williams	15.00
MW	Mookie Wilson	10.00
DW	Dave Winfield	10.00
FV	Fernando Valenzuela	8.00
JV	Jose Vizcaino	4.00

2003 Stadium Club

NM/M

Complete Set (125):		30.00
Common Player:		.15
Hobby Pack (6):		1.50
Hobby Box (24):		30.00
1	Rafael Furcal	.15
2	Randy Winn	.15
3	Eric Chavez	.25
4	Fernando Vina	.15
5	Pat Burrell	.25
6	Derek Jeter	2.00
7	Ivan Rodriguez	.65
8	Eric Hinske	.15
9	Roberto Alomar	.40
10	Tony Batista	.15
11	Jacque Jones	.15
12	Alfonso Soriano	.75
13	Omar Vizquel	.15
14	Paul Konerko	.25
15	Shawn Green	.45

16	Garret Anderson	.15
17	Darin Erstad	.25
18	Johnny Damon	.25
19	Juan Gonzalez	.75
20	Luis Gonzalez	.25
21	Sean Burroughs	.15
22	Mark Prior	.75
23	Javier Vazquez	.15
24	Shannon Stewart	.15
25	Jay Gibbons	.15
26	A.J. Pierzynski	.15
27	Vladimir Guerrero	.75
28	Austin Kearns	.25
29	Shea Hillenbrand	.15
30	Magglio Ordonez	.25
31	Mike Cameron	.15
32	Tim Salmon	.25
33	Brian Jordan	.15
34	Moises Alou	.15
35	Rich Aurilia	.15
36	Nick Johnson	.15
37	Junior Spivey	.15
38	Curt Schilling	.40
39	Jose Vidro	.15
40	Orlando Cabrera	.15
41	Jeff Bagwell	.75
42	Mo Vaughn	.15
43	Luis Castillo	.15
44	Vicente Padilla	.15
45	Pedro J. Martinez	.75
46	John Olerud	.15
47	Tom Glavine	.40
48	Torii Hunter	.15
49	J.D. Drew	.25
50	Alex Rodriguez	1.50
51	Randy Johnson	.75
52	Richie Sexson	.15
53	Jimmy Rollins	.25
54	Cristian Guzman	.15
55	Tim Hudson	.25
56	Mark Buehrle	.15
57	Paul LoDuca	.15
58	Aramis Ramirez	.25
59	Todd Helton	.75
60	Lance Berkman	.25
61	Josh Beckett	.25
62	Bret Boone	.15
63	Miguel Tejada	.35
64	Nomar Garciaparra	1.25
65	Albert Pujols	1.50
66	Chipper Jones	1.00
67	Scott Rolen	.65
68	Kerry Wood	.65
69	Jorge Posada	.15
70	Ichiro Suzuki	1.50
71	Jeff Kent	.15
72	David Eckstein	.15
73	Phil Nevin	.15
74	Brian Giles	.15
75	Barry Zito	.25
76	Andruw Jones	.75
77	Jim Thome	.65
78	Robert Fick	.15
79	Rafael Palmeiro	.65
80	Barry Bonds	2.00
81	Gary Sheffield	.40
82	Jim Edmonds	.25
83	Kazuhisa Ishii	.15
84	Jose Hernandez	.15
85	Jason Giambi	.40
86	Mark Mulder	.15
87	Roger Clemens	1.00
88	Troy Glaus	.75
89	Carlos Delgado	.50
90	Mike Sweeney	.15
91	Ken Griffey Jr.	1.25
92	Manny Ramirez	.75
93	Ryan Klesko	.15
94	Larry Walker	.15
95	Adam Dunn	.65
96	Raul Ibanez	.15
97	Preston Wilson	.15
98	Roy Oswalt	.15
99	Sammy Sosa	1.25
100	Mike Piazza	1.25
101	Jose Reyes	.50
102	Ed Rogers	.15
103	Hank Blalock	.75
104	Mark Teixeira	.65
105	Orlando Hudson	.15
106	Drew Henson	.25

107	Joe Mauer	.75
108	Carl Crawford	.15
109	Marlon Byrd	.15
110	Jason Stokes	.15
111	Miguel Cabrera	.50
112	Wilson Betemit	.15
113	Jerome Williams	.15
114	Walter Young	.15
115	Juan Camacho **RC**	.15
116	Chris Duncan **RC**	3.00
117	Franklin Gutierrez **RC**	3.00
118	Adam LaRoche	.50
119	Manuel Ramirez **RC**	.50
120	Il Kim **RC**	.50
121	Wayne Lydon **RC**	.50
122	Daryl Clark **RC**	.50
123	Sean Pierce	.15
124	Andy Marte **RC**	3.00
125	Matthew Peterson **RC**	.75

Beam Team

Complete Set (20):		50.00
Common Player:		1.00
Inserted 1:12		
BT1	Larry Walker	1.00
BT2	Miguel Tejada	1.50
BT3	Ichiro Suzuki	5.00
BT4	Sammy Sosa	5.00
BT5	Ivan Rodriguez	2.50
BT6	Alex Rodriguez	6.00
BT7	Mike Piazza	5.00
BT8	Jeff Kent	1.00
BT9	Chipper Jones	4.00
BT10	Derek Jeter	8.00
BT11	Todd Helton	3.00
BT12	Vladimir Guerrero	3.00
BT13	Shawn Green	1.50
BT14	Brian Giles	1.00
BT15	Jason Giambi	2.00
BT16	Nomar Garciaparra	5.00
BT17	Adam Dunn	2.00
BT18	Carlos Delgado	1.50
BT19	Barry Bonds	8.00
BT20	Lance Berkman	1.00

Born In The USA

Common Player:		5.00
Jerseys Inserted 1:52		
Bats Inserted 1:76		
RA	Rich Aurilia/Jsy	5.00
JB	Jeff Bagwell/Jsy	12.00
CB	Craig Biggio/Jsy	8.00
BB	Bret Boone/Jsy	5.00
AB	A.J. Burnett/Jsy	5.00
JNB	Jeromy Burnitz/Bat	6.00
PB	Pat Burrell/Bat	10.00
SB	Sean Burroughs/Bat	6.00
EC	Eric Chavez/Jsy	6.00
TC	Tony Clark/Bat	5.00
JD	Johnny Damon/Bat	8.00
JDD	J.D. Drew/Bat	6.00
AD	Adam Dunn/Bat	12.00
JE	Jim Edmonds/Jsy	8.00
CF	Cliff Floyd/Bat	5.00
BF	Brad Fullmer/Bat	5.00
NG	Nomar Garciaparra/Bat	20.00
LG	Luis Gonzalez/Bat	6.00
MG	Mark Grace/Jsy	12.00
SG	Shawn Green/Bat	6.00
TJH	Toby Hall	5.00
JH	Josh Hamilton/Bat	10.00
TH	Todd Helton/Bat	8.00
RH	Rickey Henderson/Bat	15.00
RJ	Randy Johnson/Bat	12.00
CJ	Chipper Jones/Jsy	12.00
RK	Ryan Klesko/Bat	5.00

PK	Paul Konerko/Bat	8.00
BL	Barry Larkin/Jsy	5.00
TRL	Travis Lee/Bat	5.00
TL	Terrence Long/Jsy	5.00
GM	Greg Maddux/Jsy	15.00
TM	Tino Martinez/Bat	10.00
WM	Willie Mays/Bat	40.00
EM	Eric Milton/Jsy	6.00
JO	John Olerud/Jsy	6.00
CP	Corey Patterson/Bat	8.00
MP	Mike Piazza/Jsy	15.00
AR	Alex Rodriguez/Bat	15.00
SR	Scott Rolen/Bat	15.00
RS	Richie Sexson/Bat	8.00
GS	Gary Sheffield/Bat	8.00
JS	John Smoltz/Jsy	8.00
FT	Frank Thomas/Bat	8.00
JT	Jim Thome/Jsy	15.00
MV	Mo Vaughn/Bat	6.00
RV	Robin Ventura/Bat	6.00
MW	Matt Williams/Bat	8.00
PW	Preston Wilson/Jsy	5.00
KW	Kerry Wood/Bat	10.00

Co-Signers

HTA Exclusive		
MI	Masanori Murakami, Kazuhisa Ishii	180.00
AM	Hank Aaron, Willie Mays	400.00

Clubhouse Exclusive

Jersey Inserted 1:488		
Jersey & Bat 1:2,073		
Jersey, Bat & Spikes 1:2,750		
CE1	Albert Pujols/Jsy	15.00
CE2	Albert Pujols/Bat/Jsy	35.00
CE3	Albert Pujols/Jsy/ Bat/Spike	100.00

License To Drive

Common Player:		6.00
Inserted 1:98		
RA	Roberto Alomar	8.00
MA	Moises Alou	6.00
AB	Adrian Beltre	8.00
LB	Lance Berkman	6.00
EC	Eric Chavez	6.00
AD	Adam Dunn	8.00
NG	Nomar Garciaparra	15.00
JG	Juan Gonzalez	8.00
LG	Luis Gonzalez	6.00
SG	Shawn Green	8.00
TH	Todd Helton	10.00
AJ	Andruw Jones	10.00
CJ	Chipper Jones	12.00
TM	Tino Martinez	6.00
RP	Rafael Palmeiro	8.00
MP	Mike Piazza	15.00
AP	Albert Pujols	25.00
ANR	Aramis Ramirez	6.00
AR	Alex Rodriguez	20.00
IR	Ivan Rodriguez	8.00
SR	Scott Rolen	10.00
GS	Gary Sheffield	8.00
FT	Frank Thomas	6.00
LW	Larry Walker	6.00
BW	Bernie Williams	6.00

MLB Match-Ups

		NM/M
Inserted 1:485		
BB	Bret Boone	15.00
TH	Todd Helton	15.00

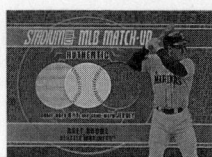

AJ	Andruw Jones	12.00
GM	Greg Maddux	30.00
AP	Albert Pujols	30.00

Photographer's Proof

Stars (1-100):		4-8X
Cards (101-125):		2-4X
Production 299 Sets		

Royal Gold

Stars:		1-3X
Inserted 1:1		

Stadium Shots

Complete Set (10):		25.00
Common Player:		1.00
Inserted 1:24		
SS1	Lance Berkman	1.00
SS2	Barry Bonds	6.00
SS3	Jason Giambi	2.50
SS4	Shawn Green	1.50
SS5	Vladimir Guerrero	3.00
SS6	Paul Konerko	1.00
SS7	Mike Piazza	4.50
SS8	Alex Rodriguez	6.00
SS9	Sammy Sosa	4.50
SS10	Jim Thome	2.00

Stadium Slices Handle

Common Player:		5.00
Inserted 1:237		
Trademarks:		1-1.5X
Inserted 1:415		
Barrels:		1.5-2X
Inserted 1:550		
RA	Roberto Alomar	15.00
CD	Carlos Delgado	8.00
NG	Nomar Garciaparra	20.00
TH	Todd Helton	10.00
AJ	Andruw Jones	8.00
RP	Rafael Palmeiro	10.00
MP	Mike Piazza	15.00
AP	Albert Pujols	20.00
AR	Alex Rodriguez	15.00
GS	Gary Sheffield	10.00

World Stage

		NM/M
Common Player:		5.00
Jerseys Inserted 1:118		
Bats Inserted 1:809		
AB	Adrian Beltre/Jsy	6.00

		NM/M
KI	Kazuhisa Ishii/Jsy	5.00
BK	Byung-Hyun Kim/Jsy	5.00
HN	Hideo Nomo/Bat	20.00
AP	Albert Pujols/Jsy	15.00
IR	Ivan Rodriguez/Jsy	8.00
KS	Kazuhiro Sasaki/Jsy	5.00
TS	Tsuyoshi Shinjo/Bat	5.00
AS	Alfonso Soriano/Bat	15.00
MT	Miguel Tejada/Jsy	8.00

1991 Studio

IVAN CALDERON, LF

		NM/M
Complete Set (264):		7.50
Common Player:		.05
Foil Pack (10):		.50
Foil Box (48):		12.50
1	Glenn Davis	.05
2	Dwight Evans	.05
3	Leo Gomez	.05
4	Chris Hoiles	.05
5	Sam Horn	.05
6	Ben McDonald	.05
7	Randy Milligan	.05
8	Gregg Olson	.05
9	Cal Ripken, Jr.	1.00
10	David Segui	.05
11	Wade Boggs	.40
12	Ellis Burks	.05
13	Jack Clark	.05
14	Roger Clemens	.45
15	Mike Greenwell	.05
16	Tim Naehring	.05
17	Tony Pena	.05
18	Phil Plantier RC	.05
19	Jeff Reardon	.05
20	Mo Vaughn	.05
21	Jimmy Reese	.05
22	Jim Abbott	.05
23	Bert Blyleven	.05
24	Chuck Finley	.05
25	Gary Gaetti	.05
26	Wally Joyner	.05
27	Mark Langston	.05
28	Kirk McCaskill	.05
29	Lance Parrish	.05
30	Dave Winfield	.30
31	Alex Fernandez	.05
32	Carlton Fisk	.30
33	Scott Fletcher	.05
34	Greg Hibbard	.05
35	Charlie Hough	.05
36	Jack McDowell	.05
37	Tim Raines	.05
38	Sammy Sosa	.40
39	Bobby Thigpen	.05
40	Frank Thomas	.30
41	Sandy Alomar	.05
42	John Farrell	.05
43	Glenallen Hill	.05
44	Brook Jacoby	.05
45	Chris James	.05
46	Doug Jones	.05
47	Eric King	.05
48	Mark Lewis	.05
49	Greg Swindell	.05
50	Mark Whiten	.05
51	Milt Cuyler	.05
52	Rob Deer	.05
53	Cecil Fielder	.05
54	Travis Fryman	.05
55	Bill Gullickson	.05
56	Lloyd Moseby	.05
57	Frank Tanana	.05
58	Mickey Tettleton	.05
59	Alan Trammell	.05
60	Lou Whitaker	.05
61	Mike Boddicker	.05
62	George Brett	.45
63	Jeff Conine	.05
64	Warren Cromartie	.05
65	Storm Davis	.05
66	Kirk Gibson	.05
67	Mark Gubicza	.05
68	Brian McRae RC	.05
69	Bret Saberhagen	.05
70	Kurt Stillwell	.05
71	Tim McIntosh	.05
72	Candy Maldonado	.05
73	Paul Molitor	.30
74	Willie Randolph	.05
75	Ron Robinson	.05
76	Gary Sheffield	.20
77	Franklin Stubbs	.05
78	B.J. Surhoff	.05
79	Greg Vaughn	.05
80	Robin Yount	.30
81	Rick Aguilera	.05
82	Steve Bedrosian	.05
83	Scott Erickson	.05
84	Greg Gagne	.05
85	Dan Gladden	.05
86	Brian Harper	.05
87	Kent Hrbek	.05
88	Shane Mack	.05
89	Jack Morris	.05
90	Kirby Puckett	.40
91	Jesse Barfield	.05
92	Steve Farr	.05
93	Steve Howe	.05
94	Roberto Kelly	.05
95	Tim Leary	.05
96	Kevin Maas	.05
97	Don Mattingly	.45
98	Hensley Meulens	.05
99	Scott Sanderson	.05
100	Steve Sax	.05
101	Jose Canseco	.20
102	Dennis Eckersley	.25
103	Dave Henderson	.05
104	Rickey Henderson	.30
105	Rick Honeycutt	.05
106	Mark McGwire	.75
107	Dave Stewart	.05
108	Eric Show	.05
109	Todd Van Poppel RC	.05
110	Bob Welch	.05
111	Alvin Davis	.05
112	Ken Griffey Jr.	.50
113	Ken Griffey Sr.	.05
114	Erik Hanson	.05
115	Brian Holman	.05
116	Randy Johnson	.30
117	Edgar Martinez	.05
118	Tino Martinez	.05
119	Harold Reynolds	.05
120	David Valle	.05
121	Kevin Belcher	.05
122	Scott Chiamparino	.05
123	Julio Franco	.05
124	Juan Gonzalez	.20
125	Rich Gossage	.05
126	Jeff Kunkel	.05
127	Rafael Palmeiro	.25
128	Nolan Ryan	1.00
129	Ruben Sierra	.05
130	Bobby Witt	.05
131	Roberto Alomar	.10
132	Tom Candiotti	.05
133	Joe Carter	.05
134	Ken Dayley	.05
135	Kelly Gruber	.05
136	John Olerud	.05
137	Dave Stieb	.05
138	Turner Ward	.05
139	Devon White	.05
140	Mookie Wilson	.05
141	Steve Avery	.05
142	Sid Bream	.05
143	Nick Esasky	.05
144	Ron Gant	.05
145	Tom Glavine	.20
146	Dave Justice	.05
147	Kelly Mann	.05
148	Terry Pendleton	.05
149	John Smoltz	.05
150	Jeff Treadway	.05
151	George Bell	.05
152	Shawn Boskie	.05
153	Andre Dawson	.20
154	Lance Dickson	.05
155	Shawon Dunston	.05
156	Joe Girardi	.05
157	Mark Grace	.05
158	Ryne Sandberg	.40
159	Gary Scott	.05
160	Dave Smith	.05
161	Tom Browning	.05
162	Eric Davis	.05
163	Rob Dibble	.05
164	Mariano Duncan	.05
165	Chris Hammond	.05
166	Billy Hatcher	.05
167	Barry Larkin	.05
168	Hal Morris	.05
169	Paul O'Neill	.05
170	Chris Sabo	.05
171	Eric Anthony	.05
172	Jeff Bagwell RC	1.50
173	Craig Biggio	.05
174	Ken Caminitti	.05
175	Jim Deshaies	.05
176	Steve Finley	.05
177	Pete Harnisch	.05
178	Darryl Kile	.05
179	Curt Schilling	.20
180	Mike Scott	.05
181	Brett Butler	.05
182	Gary Carter	.30
183	Orel Hershiser	.05
184	Ramon Martinez	.05
185	Eddie Murray	.30
186	Jose Offerman	.05
187	Bob Ojeda	.05
188	Juan Samuel	.05
189	Mike Scioscia	.05
190	Darryl Strawberry	.05
191	Moises Alou	.05
192	Brian Barnes	.05
193	Oil Can Boyd	.05
194	Ivan Calderon	.05
195	Delino DeShields	.05
196	Mike Fitzgerald	.05
197	Andres Galarraga	.05
198	Marquis Grissom	.05
199	Bill Sampen	.05
200	Tim Wallach	.05
201	Daryl Boston	.05
202	Vince Coleman	.05
203	John Franco	.05
204	Dwight Gooden	.05
205	Tom Herr	.05
206	Gregg Jefferies	.05
207	Howard Johnson	.05
208	Dave Magadan	.05
209	Kevin McReynolds	.05
210	Frank Viola	.05
211	Wes Chamberlain	.05
212	Darren Daulton	.05
213	Len Dykstra	.05
214	Charlie Hayes	.05
215	Ricky Jordan	.05
216	Steve Lake	.05
217	Roger McDowell	.05
218	Mickey Morandini	.05
219	Terry Mulholland	.05
220	Dale Murphy	.15
221	Jay Bell	.05
222	Barry Bonds	1.00
223	Bobby Bonilla	.05
224	Doug Drabek	.05
225	Bill Landrum	.05
226	Mike LaValliere	.05
227	Jose Lind	.05
228	Don Slaught	.05
229	John Smiley	.05
230	Andy Van Slyke	.05
231	Bernard Gilkey	.05
232	Pedro Guerrero	.05
233	Rex Hudler	.05
234	Ray Lankford	.05
235	Joe Magrane	.05
236	Jose Oquendo	.05
237	Lee Smith	.05
238	Ozzie Smith	.40
239	Milt Thompson	.05
240	Todd Zeile	.05
241	Larry Andersen	.05
242	Andy Benes	.05
243	Paul Faries	.05
244	Tony Fernandez	.05
245	Tony Gwynn	.40
246	Atlee Hammaker	.05
247	Fred McGriff	.05
248	Bip Roberts	.05
249	Benito Santiago	.05
250	Ed Whitson	.05
251	Dave Anderson	.05
252	Mike Benjamin	.05
253	John Burkett	.05
254	Will Clark	.05
255	Scott Garrelts	.05
256	Willie McGee	.05
257	Kevin Mitchell	.05
258	Dave Righetti	.05
259	Matt Williams	.05
260	Bud Black, Steve Decker Black & Decker	.10
261	Checklist	.03
262	Checklist	.03
263	Checklist	.03
---	Header Card	.03

1991 Studio Preview

GARY PETTIS, CF

		NM/M
Complete Set (18):		5.00
Common Player:		.50
1	Juan Bell	.50
2	Roger Clemens	3.00
3	Dave Parker	.50
4	Tim Raines	.50
5	Kevin Seitzer	.50
6	Teddy Higuera	.50
7	Bernie Williams	.50
8	Harold Baines	.50
9	Gary Pettis	.50
10	Dave Justice	.50
11	Eric Davis	.50
12	Andujar Cedeno	.50
13	Tom Foley	.50
14	Dwight Gooden	.50
15	Doug Drabek	.50
16	Steve Decker	.50
17	Joe Torre	.75
18	Header Card	.10

1992 Studio

PETE HARNISCH RHP
Houston Astros

		NM/M
Complete Set (264):		8.00
Common Player:		.05
Pack (10):		.65
Wax Box (48):		15.00
1	Steve Avery	.05
2	Sid Bream	.05
3	Ron Gant	.05
4	Tom Glavine	.25
5	Dave Justice	.05
6	Mark Lemke	.05
7	Greg Olson	.05
8	Terry Pendleton	.05
9	Deion Sanders	.05
10	John Smoltz	.05
11	Doug Dascenzo	.05
12	Andre Dawson	.25
13	Joe Girardi	.05
14	Mark Grace	.05
15	Greg Maddux	.50
16	Chuck McElroy	.05
17	Mike Morgan	.05
18	Ryne Sandberg	.50
19	Gary Scott	.05
20	Sammy Sosa	.50
21	Norm Charlton	.05
22	Rob Dibble	.05
23	Barry Larkin	.05
24	Hal Morris	.05
25	Paul O'Neill	.05
26	Jose Rijo	.05
27	Bip Roberts	.05
28	Chris Sabo	.05
29	Reggie Sanders	.05
30	Greg Swindell	.05
31	Jeff Bagwell	.45
32	Craig Biggio	.05
33	Ken Caminiti	.05
34	Andujar Cedeno	.05
35	Steve Finley	.05
36	Pete Harnisch	.05
37	Butch Henry	.05
38	Doug Jones	.05
39	Darryl Kile	.05
40	Eddie Taubensee	.05
41	Brett Butler	.05
42	Tom Candiotti	.05
43	Eric Davis	.05
44	Orel Hershiser	.05
45	Eric Karros	.05
46	Ramon Martinez	.05
47	Jose Offerman	.05
48	Mike Scioscia	.05
49	Mike Sharperson	.05
50	Darryl Strawberry	.05
51	Bret Barbarie	.05
52	Ivan Calderon	.05
53	Gary Carter	.45
54	Delino DeShields	.05
55	Marquis Grissom	.05
56	Ken Hill	.05
57	Dennis Martinez	.05
58	Spike Owen	.05
59	Larry Walker	.05
60	Tim Wallach	.05
61	Bobby Bonilla	.05
62	Tim Burke	.05
63	Vince Coleman	.05

64	John Franco	.05
65	Dwight Gooden	.05
66	Todd Hundley	.05
67	Howard Johnson	.05
68	Eddie Murray	.45
69	Bret Saberhagen	.05
70	Anthony Young	.05
71	Kim Batiste	.05
72	Wes Chamberlain	.05
73	Darren Daulton	.05
74	Mariano Duncan	.05
75	Len Dykstra	.05
76	John Kruk	.05
77	Mickey Morandini	.05
78	Terry Mulholland	.05
79	Dale Murphy	.20
80	Mitch Williams	.05
81	Jay Bell	.05
82	Barry Bonds	1.00
83	Steve Buechele	.05
84	Doug Drabek	.05
85	Mike LaValliere	.05
86	Jose Lind	.05
87	Denny Neagle	.05
88	Randy Tomlin	.05
89	Andy Van Slyke	.05
90	Gary Varsho	.05
91	Pedro Guerrero	.05
92	Rex Hudler	.05
93	Brian Jordan	.05
94	Felix Jose	.05
95	Donovan Osborne	.05
96	Tom Pagnozzi	.05
97	Lee Smith	.05
98	Ozzie Smith	.50
99	Todd Worrell	.05
100	Todd Zeile	.05
101	Andy Benes	.05
102	Jerald Clark	.05
103	Tony Fernandez	.05
104	Tony Gwynn	.50
105	Greg Harris	.05
106	Fred McGriff	.05
107	Benito Santiago	.05
108	Gary Sheffield	.30
109	Kurt Stillwell	.05
110	Tim Teufel	.05
111	Kevin Bass	.05
112	Jeff Brantley	.05
113	John Burkett	.05
114	Will Clark	.05
115	Royce Clayton	.05
116	Mike Jackson	.05
117	Darren Lewis	.05
118	Bill Swift	.05
119	Robby Thompson	.05
120	Matt Williams	.05
121	Brady Anderson	.05
122	Glenn Davis	.05
123	Mike Devereaux	.05
124	Chris Hoiles	.05
125	Sam Horn	.05
126	Ben McDonald	.05
127	Mike Mussina	.25
128	Gregg Olson	.05
129	Cal Ripken, Jr.	1.00
130	Rick Sutcliffe	.05
131	Wade Boggs	.50
132	Roger Clemens	.60
133	Greg Harris	.05
134	Tim Naehring	.05
135	Tony Pena	.05
136	Phil Plantier	.05
137	Jeff Reardon	.05
138	Jody Reed	.05
139	Mo Vaughn	.05
140	Frank Viola	.05
141	Jim Abbott	.05
142	Hubie Brooks	.05
143	Chad Curtis RC	.05
144	Gary DiSarcina	.05
145	Chuck Finley	.05
146	Bryan Harvey	.05
147	Von Hayes	.05
148	Mark Langston	.05
149	Lance Parrish	.05
150	Lee Stevens	.05
151	George Bell	.05
152	Alex Fernandez	.05
153	Greg Hibbard	.05
154	Lance Johnson	.05
155	Kirk McCaskill	.05
156	Tim Raines	.05
157	Steve Sax	.05
158	Bobby Thigpen	.05
159	Frank Thomas	.45
160	Robin Ventura	.05
161	Sandy Alomar, Jr.	.05
162	Jack Armstrong	.05
163	Carlos Baerga	.05
164	Albert Belle	.05
165	Alex Cole	.05
166	Glenallen Hill	.05
167	Mark Lewis	.05
168	Kenny Lofton	.05
169	Paul Sorrento	.05
170	Mark Whiten	.05
171	Milt Cuyler (Color photo is Lou Whitaker.)	
172	Rob Deer	.05
173	Cecil Fielder	.05
174	Travis Fryman	.05
175	Mike Henneman	.05
176	Tony Phillips	.05
177	Frank Tanana	.05

178	Mickey Tettleton	.05
179	Alan Trammell	.05
180	Lou Whitaker	.05
181	George Brett	.60
182	Tom Gordon	.05
183	Mark Gubicza	.05
184	Gregg Jefferies	.05
185	Wally Joyner	.05
186	Brent Mayne	.05
187	Brian McRae	.05
188	Kevin McReynolds	.05
189	Keith Miller	.05
190	Jeff Montgomery	.05
191	Dante Bichette	.05
192	Ricky Bones	.05
193	Scott Fletcher	.05
194	Paul Molitor	.45
195	Jaime Navarro	.05
196	Franklin Stubbs	.05
197	B.J. Surhoff	.05
198	Greg Vaughn	.05
199	Bill Wegman	.05
200	Robin Yount	.45
201	Rick Aguilera	.05
202	Scott Erickson	.05
203	Greg Gagne	.05
204	Brian Harper	.05
205	Kent Hrbek	.05
206	Scott Leius	.05
207	Shane Mack	.05
208	Pat Mahomes	.05
209	Kirby Puckett	.50
210	John Smiley	.05
211	Mike Gallego	.05
212	Charlie Hayes	.05
213	Pat Kelly	.05
214	Roberto Kelly	.05
215	Kevin Maas	.05
216	Don Mattingly	.60
217	Matt Nokes	.05
218	Melido Perez	.05
219	Scott Sanderson	.05
220	Danny Tartabull	.05
221	Harold Baines	.05
222	Jose Canseco	.30
223	Dennis Eckersley	.35
224	Dave Henderson	.05
225	Carney Lansford	.05
226	Mark McGwire	.75
227	Mike Moore	.05
228	Randy Ready	.05
229	Terry Steinbach	.05
230	Dave Stewart	.05
231	Jay Buhner	.05
232	Ken Griffey Jr.	.65
233	Erik Hanson	.05
234	Randy Johnson	.45
235	Edgar Martinez	.05
236	Tino Martinez	.05
237	Kevin Mitchell	.05
238	Pete O'Brien	.05
239	Harold Reynolds	.05
240	David Valle	.05
241	Julio Franco	.05
242	Juan Gonzalez	.25
243	Jose Guzman	.05
244	Rafael Palmeiro	.35
245	Dean Palmer	.05
246	Ivan Rodriguez	.35
247	Jeff Russell	.05
248	Nolan Ryan	1.00
249	Ruben Sierra	.05
250	Dickie Thon	.05
251	Roberto Alomar	.20
252	Derek Bell	.05
253	Pat Borders	.05
254	Joe Carter	.05
255	Kelly Gruber	.05
256	Juan Guzman	.05
257	Jack Morris	.05
258	John Olerud	.05
259	Devon White	.05
260	Dave Winfield	.45
261	Checklist	.05
262	Checklist	.05
263	Checklist	.05
264	History Card	.05

1992 Studio Preview

CAL RIPKEN, JR. PREVIEW
Baltimore Orioles

	NM/M
Complete Set (22):	75.00

Common Player:		1.50
1	Ruben Sierra	1.50
2	Kirby Puckett	6.00
3	Ryne Sandberg	6.00
4	John Kruk	1.50
5	Cal Ripken, Jr.	12.00
6	Robin Yount	4.50
7	Dwight Gooden	1.50
8	David Justice	1.50
9	Don Mattingly	7.50
10	Wally Joyner	1.50
11	Will Clark	1.50
12	Rob Dibble	1.50
13	Roberto Alomar	2.50
14	Wade Boggs	6.00
15	Barry Bonds	12.00
16	Jeff Bagwell	4.50
17	Mark McGwire	9.00
18	Frank Thomas	6.00
19	Brett Butler	1.50
20	Ozzie Smith	6.00
21	Jim Abbott	1.50
22	Tony Gwynn	6.00

Heritage

HERITAGE SERIES

RYNE SANDBERG

	NM/M
Complete Set (14):	6.00
Common Player:	.50

1	Ryne Sandberg	1.00
2	Carlton Fisk	.75
3	Wade Boggs	1.00
4	Jose Canseco	.65
5	Don Mattingly	1.25
6	Darryl Strawberry	.50
7	Cal Ripken, Jr.	1.50
8	Will Clark	.50
9	Andre Dawson	.50
10	Andy Van Slyke	.50
11	Paul Molitor	.75
12	Jeff Bagwell	.75
13	Darren Daulton	.50
14	Kirby Puckett	1.00

1993 Studio

	NM/M
Complete Set (220):	15.00
Common Player:	.05
Pack (12):	.75
Wax Box (36):	12.50

1	Dennis Eckersley	.35
2	Chad Curtis	.05
3	Eric Anthony	.05
4	Roberto Alomar	.20
5	Steve Avery	.05
6	Cal Eldred	.05
7	Bernard Gilkey	.05
8	Steve Buechele	.05
9	Brett Butler	.05
10	Terry Mulholland	.05
11	Moises Alou	.05
12	Barry Bonds	1.00
13	Sandy Alomar Jr.	.05
14	Chris Bosio	.05
15	Scott Sanderson	.05
16	Bobby Bonilla	.05
17	Brady Anderson	.05
18	Derek Bell	.05

19	Wes Chamberlain	.05
20	Jay Bell	.05
21	Kevin Brown	.05
22	Roger Clemens	.60
23	Roberto Kelly	.05
24	Dante Bichette	.60
25	George Brett	.60
26	Rob Deer	.05
27	Brian Harper	.05
28	George Bell	.05
29	Jim Abbott	.05
30	Dave Henderson	.05
31	Wade Boggs	.50
32	Chili Davis	.05
33	Ellis Burks	.05
34	Jeff Bagwell	.40
35	Kent Hrbek	.05
36	Pat Borders	.05
37	Cecil Fielder	.05
38	Sid Bream	.05
39	Greg Gagne	.05
40	Darryl Hamilton	.05
41	Jerald Clark	.05
42	Mark Grace	.05
43	Barry Larkin	.05
44	John Burkett	.05
45	Scott Cooper	.05
46	Mike Lansing RC	.25
47	Jose Canseco	.30
48	Will Clark	.05
49	Carlos Garcia	.05
50	Carlos Baerga	.05
51	Darren Daulton	.05
52	Jay Buhner	.05
53	Andy Benes	.05
54	Jeff Conine	.05
55	Mike Devereaux	.05
56	Vince Coleman	.05
57	Terry Steinbach	.05
58	J.T. Snow RC	.40
59	Greg Swindell	.05
60	Devon White	.05
61	John Smoltz	.05
62	Todd Zeile	.05
63	Rick Wilkins	.05
64	Tim Wallach	.05
65	John Wetteland	.05
66	Matt Williams	.05
67	Paul Sorrento	.05
68	David Valle	.05
69	Walt Weiss	.05
70	John Franco	.05
71	Nolan Ryan	1.00
72	Frank Viola	.05
73	Chris Sabo	.05
74	David Nied	.05
75	Kevin McReynolds	.05
76	Lou Whitaker	.05
77	Dave Winfield	.40
78	Robin Ventura	.05
79	Spike Owen	.05
80	Cal Ripken, Jr.	1.00
81	Dan Walter	.05
82	Mitch Williams	.05
83	Tim Wakefield	.05
84	Rickey Henderson	.40
85	Gary DiSarcina	.05
86	Craig Biggio	.05
87	Joe Carter	.05
88	Ron Gant	.05
89	John Jaha	.05
90	Gregg Jefferies	.05
91	Jose Guzman	.05
92	Eric Karros	.05
93	Wil Cordero	.05
94	Royce Clayton	.05
95	Albert Belle	.05
96	Ken Griffey Jr.	.65
97	Orestes Destrade	.05
98	Tony Fernandez	.05
99	Leo Gomez	.05
100	Tony Gwynn	.50
101	Len Dykstra	.05
102	Jeff King	.05
103	Julio Franco	.05
104	Andre Dawson	.25
105	Randy Milligan	.05
106	Alex Cole	.05
107	Phil Hiatt	.05
108	Travis Fryman	.05
109	Chuck Knoblauch	.05
110	Bo Jackson	.10
111	Pat Kelly	.05
112	Bret Saberhagen	.05
113	Ruben Sierra	.05
114	Tim Salmon	.05
115	Doug Jones	.05
116	Ed Sprague	.05
117	Terry Pendleton	.05
118	Robin Yount	.40
119	Mark Whiten	.05
120	Checklist	.05
121	Sammy Sosa	.05
122	Darryl Strawberry	.05
123	Larry Walker	.05
124	Robby Thompson	.05
125	Carlos Martinez	.05
126	Edgar Martinez	.05
127	Benito Santiago	.05
128	Howard Johnson	.05
129	Harold Reynolds	.05
130	Craig Shipley	.05
131	Curt Schilling	.30
132	Andy Van Slyke	.05
133	Ivan Rodriguez	.35

#	Player	Price
134	Mo Vaughn	.05
135	Bip Roberts	.05
136	Charlie Hayes	.05
137	Brian McRae	.05
138	Mickey Tettleton	.05
139	Frank Thomas	.40
140	Paul O'Neill	.05
141	Mark McGwire	.75
142	Damion Easley	.05
143	Ken Caminiti	.05
144	Juan Guzman	.05
145	Tom Glavine	.25
146	Pat Listach	.05
147	Lee Smith	.05
148	Derrick May	.05
149	Ramon Martinez	.05
150	Delino DeShields	.05
151	Kirt Manwaring	.05
152	Reggie Jefferson	.05
153	Randy Johnson	.40
154	Dave Magadan	.05
155	Dwight Gooden	.05
156	Chris Hoiles	.05
157	Fred McGriff	.05
158	Dave Hollins	.05
159	Al Martin	.05
160	Juan Gonzalez	.20
161	Mike Greenwell	.05
162	Kevin Mitchell	.05
163	Andres Galarraga	.05
164	Wally Joyner	.05
165	Kirk Gibson	.05
166	Pedro Munoz	.05
167	Ozzie Guillen	.05
168	Jimmy Key	.05
169	Kevin Seitzer	.05
170	Luis Polonia	.05
171	Luis Gonzalez	.05
172	Paul Molitor	.40
173	Dave Justice	.05
174	B.J. Surhoff	.05
175	Ray Lankford	.05
176	Ryne Sandberg	.50
177	Jody Reed	.05
178	Marquis Grissom	.05
179	Willie McGee	.05
180	Kenny Lofton	.05
181	Junior Felix	.05
182	Jose Offerman	.05
183	John Kruk	.05
184	Orlando Merced	.05
185	Rafael Palmeiro	.35
186	Billy Hatcher	.05
187	Joe Oliver	.05
188	Joe Girardi	.05
189	Jose Lind	.05
190	Harold Baines	.05
191	Mike Pagliarulo	.05
192	Lance Johnson	.05
193	Don Mattingly	.60
194	Doug Drabek	.05
195	John Olerud	.50
196	Greg Maddux	.50
197	Greg Vaughn	.05
198	Tom Pagnozzi	.05
199	Willie Wilson	.05
200	Jack McDowell	.05
201	Mike Piazza	.65
202	Mike Mussina	.30
203	Charles Nagy	.05
204	Tino Martinez	.05
205	Charlie Hough	.05
206	Todd Hundley	.05
207	Gary Sheffield	.30
208	Mickey Morandini	.05
209	Don Slaught	.05
210	Dean Palmer	.05
211	Jose Rijo	.05
212	Vinny Castilla	.05
213	Tony Phillips	.05
214	Kirby Puckett	.50
215	Tim Raines	.05
216	Otis Nixon	.05
217	Ozzie Smith	.50
218	Jose Vizcaino	.05
220	Checklist	.05

Frank Thomas

NM/M
Complete Set (5): 5.00
Common Card: 1.00

#	Subject	Price
1	Childhood	1.00
2	Baseball Memories	1.00
3	Importance of Family	1.00
4	Performance	1.00
5	On Being a Role Model	1.00

Heritage

OZZIE SMITH

NM/M
Complete Set (12): 12.00
Common Player: .50

#	Player	Price
1	George Brett	2.00
2	Juan Gonzalez	.75
3	Roger Clemens	2.00
4	Mark McGwire	4.00
5	Mark Grace	.50
6	Ozzie Smith	1.50
7	Barry Larkin	.50
8	Frank Thomas	1.00
9	Carlos Baerga	.50
10	Eric Karros	.50
11	J.T. Snow	.50
12	John Kruk	.50

Silhouettes

NM/M
Complete Set (10): 7.00
Common Player: .15

#	Player	Price
1	Frank Thomas	.65
2	Barry Bonds	3.00
3	Jeff Bagwell	.65
4	Juan Gonzalez	.40
5	Travis Fryman	.15
6	J.T. Snow	.15
7	John Kruk	.15
8	Jeff Blauser	.15
9	Mike Piazza	2.00
10	Nolan Ryan	3.00

Superstars on Canvas

NM/M
Complete Set (10): 8.00
Common Player: .25

#	Player	Price
1	Ken Griffey Jr.	1.50

1994 Studio

#	Player	Price
2	Jose Canseco	.60
3	Mark McGwire	2.00
4	Mike Mussina	.50
5	Joe Carter	.25
6	Frank Thomas	1.00
7	Darren Daulton	.25
8	Mark Grace	.25
9	Andres Galarraga	.25
10	Barry Bonds	2.50

NM/M
Complete Set (220): 7.50
Common Player: .05
Pack (12): .45
Wax Box (36): 10.00

#	Player	Price
1	Dennis Eckersley	.45
2	Brent Gates	.05
3	Rickey Henderson	.55
4	Mark McGwire	1.00
5	Troy Neel	.05
6	Ruben Sierra	.05
7	Terry Steinbach	.05
8	Chad Curtis	.05
9	Chili Davis	.05
10	Gary DiSarcina	.05
11	Damion Easley	.05
12	Bo Jackson	.10
13	Mark Langston	.05
14	Eduardo Perez	.05
15	Tim Salmon	.05
16	Jeff Bagwell	.55
17	Craig Biggio	.05
18	Ken Caminiti	.05
19	Andujar Cedeno	.05
20	Doug Drabek	.05
21	Steve Finley	.05
22	Luis Gonzalez	.05
23	Darryl Kile	.05
24	Roberto Alomar	.20
25	Pat Borders	.05
26	Joe Carter	.05
27	Carlos Delgado	.40
28	Pat Hentgen	.05
29	Paul Molitor	.55
30	John Olerud	.05
31	Ed Sprague	.05
32	Devon White	.05
33	Steve Avery	.05
34	Tom Glavine	.25
35	David Justice	.05
36	Roberto Kelly	.05
37	Ryan Klesko	.05
38	Javier Lopez	.05
39	Greg Maddux	.60
40	Fred McGriff	.05
41	Terry Pendleton	.05
42	Ricky Bones	.05
43	Darryl Hamilton	.05
44	Brian Harper	.05
45	John Jaha	.05
46	Dave Nilsson	.05
47	Kevin Seitzer	.05
48	Greg Vaughn	.05
49	Turner Ward	.05
50	Bernard Gilkey	.05
51	Gregg Jefferies	.05
52	Ray Lankford	.05
53	Tom Pagnozzi	.05
54	Ozzie Smith	.60
55	Bob Tewksbury	.05
56	Mark Whiten	.05
57	Todd Zeile	.05
58	Steve Buechele	.05
59	Shawon Dunston	.05
60	Mark Grace	.05
61	Derrick May	.05
62	Tuffy Rhodes	.05
63	Ryne Sandberg	.60
64	Sammy Sosa	.60
65	Rick Wilkins	.05
66	Brett Butler	.05
67	Delino DeShields	.05
68	Orel Hershiser	.05
69	Eric Karros	.05
70	Raul Mondesi	.05
71	Jose Offerman	.05
72	Mike Piazza	.75
73	Tim Wallach	.05
74	Moises Alou	.05
75	Sean Berry	.05
76	Wil Cordero	.05
77	Cliff Floyd	.05
78	Marquis Grissom	.05
79	Ken Hill	.05
80	Larry Walker	.05
81	John Wetteland	.05
82	Rod Beck	.05
83	Barry Bonds	1.50
84	Royce Clayton	.05
85	Darren Lewis	.05
86	Willie McGee	.05
87	Bill Swift	.05
88	Robby Thompson	.05
89	Matt Williams	.05
90	Sandy Alomar Jr.	.05
91	Carlos Baerga	.05
92	Albert Belle	.05
93	Kenny Lofton	.05
94	Eddie Murray	.55
95	Manny Ramirez	.55
96	Paul Sorrento	.05
97	Jim Thome	.45
98	Rich Amaral	.05
99	Eric Anthony	.05
100	Jay Buhner	.05
101	Ken Griffey Jr.	.75
102	Randy Johnson	.55
103	Edgar Martinez	.05
104	Tino Martinez	.05
105	Kurt Abbott RC	.05
106	Bret Barberie	.05
107	Chuck Carr	.05
108	Jeff Conine	.05
109	Chris Hammond	.05
110	Bryan Harvey	.05
111	Benito Santiago	.05
112	Gary Sheffield	.30
113	Bobby Bonilla	.05
114	Dwight Gooden	.05
115	Todd Hundley	.05
116	Bobby Jones	.05
117	Jeff Kent	.05
118	Kevin McReynolds	.05
119	Bret Saberhagen	.05
120	Ryan Thompson	.05
121	Harold Baines	.05
122	Mike Devereaux	.05
123	Jeffrey Hammonds	.05
124	Ben McDonald	.05
125	Mike Mussina	.25
126	Rafael Palmeiro	.45
127	Cal Ripken, Jr.	1.50
128	Lee Smith	.05
129	Brad Ausmus	.05
130	Derek Bell	.05
131	Andy Benes	.05
132	Tony Gwynn	.60
133	Trevor Hoffman	.05
134	Scott Livingstone	.05
135	Phil Plantier	.05
136	Darren Daulton	.05
137	Mariano Duncan	.05
138	Len Dykstra	.05
139	Dave Hollins	.05
140	Pete Incaviglia	.05
141	Danny Jackson	.05
142	John Kruk	.05
143	Kevin Stocker	.05
144	Jay Bell	.05
145	Carlos Garcia	.05
146	Jeff King	.05
147	Al Martin	.05
148	Orlando Merced	.05
149	Don Slaught	.05
150	Andy Van Slyke	.05
151	Kevin Brown	.05
152	Jose Canseco	.40
153	Will Clark	.05
154	Juan Gonzalez	.30
155	David Hulse	.05
156	Dean Palmer	.05
157	Ivan Rodriguez	.45
158	Kenny Rogers	.05
159	Roger Clemens	.65
160	Scott Cooper	.05
161	Andre Dawson	.25
162	Mike Greenwell	.05
163	Otis Nixon	.05
164	Aaron Sele	.05
165	John Valentin	.05
166	Mo Vaughn	.05
167	Bret Boone	.05
168	Barry Larkin	.05
169	Kevin Mitchell	.05
170	Hal Morris	.05
171	Jose Rijo	.05
172	Deion Sanders	.05
173	Reggie Sanders	.05
174	John Smiley	.05
175	Dante Bichette	.05
176	Ellis Burks	.05
177	Andres Galarraga	.05
178	Joe Girardi	.05
179	Charlie Hayes	.05
180	Roberto Mejia	.05
181	Walt Weiss	.05
182	David Cone	.05
183	Gary Gaetti	.05
184	Greg Gagne	.05
185	Felix Jose	.05
186	Wally Joyner	.05
187	Mike Macfarlane	.05
188	Brian McRae	.05
189	Eric Davis	.05
190	Cecil Fielder	.05

191	Travis Fryman	.05
192	Tony Phillips	.05
193	Mickey Tettleton	.05
194	Alan Trammell	.05
195	Lou Whitaker	.05
196	Kent Hrbek	.05
197	Chuck Knoblauch	.05
198	Shane Mack	.05
199	Pat Meares	.05
200	Kirby Puckett	.60
201	Matt Walbeck	.05
202	Dave Winfield	.55
203	Wilson Alvarez	.05
204	Alex Fernandez	.05
205	Julio Franco	.05
206	Ozzie Guillen	.05
207	Jack McDowell	.05
208	Tim Raines	.05
209	Frank Thomas	.55
210	Robin Ventura	.05
211	Jim Abbott	.05
212	Wade Boggs	.60
213	Pat Kelly	.05
214	Jimmy Key	.05
215	Don Mattingly	.65
216	Paul O'Neill	.05
217	Mike Stanley	.05
218	Danny Tartabull	.05
219	Checklist	.05
220	Checklist	.05

Gold Stars

		NM/M
Complete Set (10):		80.00
Common Player:		4.50
1	Tony Gwynn	9.00
2	Barry Bonds	16.00
3	Frank Thomas	7.50
4	Ken Griffey Jr.	12.50
5	Joe Carter	4.50
6	Mike Piazza	12.50
7	Cal Ripken, Jr.	16.00
8	Greg Maddux	9.00
9	Juan Gonzalez	5.00
10	Don Mattingly	10.00

Silver Stars

		NM/M
Complete Set (10):		35.00
Common Player:		1.50
1	Tony Gwynn	3.50
2	Barry Bonds	7.50
3	Frank Thomas	2.50
4	Ken Griffey Jr.	4.50
5	Joe Carter	1.50
6	Mike Piazza	4.50
7	Cal Ripken, Jr.	7.50
8	Greg Maddux	3.50
9	Juan Gonzalez	2.00
10	Don Mattingly	4.00

Editor's Choice

		NM/M
Complete Set (8):		12.00
Common Player:		.50
1	Barry Bonds	3.00
2	Frank Thomas	1.50

3	Ken Griffey Jr.	2.50
4	Andres Galarraga	.50
5	Juan Gonzalez	.75
6	Tim Salmon	.50
7	Paul O'Neill	.50
8	Mike Piazza	2.50

Heritage

		NM/M
Complete Set (8):		9.00
Common Player:		.50
1	Barry Bonds	4.00
2	Frank Thomas	1.50
3	Joe Carter	.50
4	Don Mattingly	3.00
5	Ryne Sandberg	2.00
6	Javier Lopez	.50
7	Gregg Jefferies	.50
8	Mike Mussina	.65

1995 Studio

		NM/M
Complete Set (200):		25.00
Common Player:		.05
Pack (5):		1.00
Wax Box (36):		20.00
1	Frank Thomas	.75
2	Jeff Bagwell	.75
3	Don Mattingly	1.25
4	Mike Piazza	1.50
5	Ken Griffey Jr.	1.50
6	Greg Maddux	1.00
7	Barry Bonds	2.50
8	Cal Ripken Jr.	2.50
9	Jose Canseco	.40
10	Paul Molitor	.75
11	Kenny Lofton	.05
12	Will Clark	.05
13	Tim Salmon	.05
14	Joe Carter	.05
15	Albert Belle	.05
16	Roger Clemens	1.25
17	Roberto Alomar	.30
18	Alex Rodriguez	2.00
19	Raul Mondesi	.05
20	Deion Sanders	.05
21	Juan Gonzalez	.40
22	Kirby Puckett	1.00
23	Fred McGriff	.05
24	Matt Williams	.05
25	Tony Gwynn	1.00
26	Cliff Floyd	.05
27	Travis Fryman	.05
28	Shawn Green	.30
29	Mike Mussina	.35
30	Bob Hamelin	.05
31	Dave Justice	.05
32	Manny Ramirez	.75
33	David Cone	.05
34	Marquis Grissom	.05
35	Moises Alou	.05
36	Carlos Baerga	.05
37	Barry Larkin	.05
38	Robin Ventura	.05
39	Mo Vaughn	.05
40	Jeffrey Hammonds	.05
41	Ozzie Smith	1.00
42	Andres Galarraga	.05
43	Carlos Delgado	.50
44	Lenny Dykstra	.05
45	Cecil Fielder	.05
46	Wade Boggs	1.00
47	Gregg Jefferies	.05
48	Randy Johnson	.75
49	Rafael Palmeiro	.65
50	Craig Biggio	.05
51	Steve Avery	.05
52	Ricky Bottalico	.05
53	Chris Gomez	.05
54	Carlos Garcia	.05
55	Brian Anderson	.05
56	Wilson Alvarez	.05
57	Roberto Kelly	.05
58	Larry Walker	.05
59	Dean Palmer	.05
60	Rick Aguilera	.05
61	Javy Lopez	.05
62	Shawon Dunston	.05
63	William Van Landingham	.05
64	Jeff Kent	.05
65	David McCarty	.05
66	Armando Benitez	.05
67	Brett Butler	.05
68	Bernard Gilkey	.05
69	Joey Hamilton	.05
70	Chad Curtis	.05
71	Dante Bichette	.05
72	Chuck Carr	.05
73	Pedro Martinez	.75
74	Ramon Martinez	.05
75	Rondell White	.05
76	Alex Fernandez	.05
77	Dennis Martinez	.05
78	Sammy Sosa	1.00
79	Bernie Williams	.05
80	Lou Whitaker	.05
81	Kurt Abbott	.05
82	Tino Martinez	.05
83	Willie Greene	.05
84	Garret Anderson	.05
85	Jose Rijo	.05
86	Jeff Montgomery	.05
87	Mark Langston	.05
88	Reggie Sanders	.05
89	Rusty Greer	.05
90	Delino DeShields	.05
91	Jason Bere	.05
92	Lee Smith	.05
93	Devon White	.05
94	John Wetteland	.05
95	Luis Gonzalez	.05
96	Greg Vaughn	.05
97	Lance Johnson	.05
98	Alan Trammell	.05
99	Bret Saberhagen	.05
100	Jack McDowell	.05
101	Trevor Hoffman	.05
102	Dave Nilsson	.05
103	Bryan Harvey	.05
104	Chuck Knoblauch	.05
105	Bobby Bonilla	.05
106	Hal Morris	.05
107	Mark Whiten	.05
108	Phil Plantier	.05
109	Ryan Klesko	.05
110	Greg Gagne	.05
111	Ruben Sierra	.05
112	J.R. Phillips	.05
113	Terry Steinbach	.05
114	Jay Buhner	.05
115	Ken Caminiti	.05
116	Gary DiSarcina	.05
117	Ivan Rodriguez	.65
118	Bip Roberts	.05
119	Jay Bell	.05
120	Ken Hill	.05
121	Mike Greenwell	.05
122	Rick Wilkins	.05
123	Rickey Henderson	.75
124	Dave Hollins	.05
125	Terry Pendleton	.05
126	Rich Becker	.05
127	Billy Ashley	.05
128	Derek Bell	.05
129	Dennis Eckersley	.65
130	Andujar Cedeno	.05
131	John Jaha	.05
132	Chuck Finley	.05
133	Steve Finley	.05
134	Danny Tartabull	.05
135	Jeff Conine	.05
136	Jon Lieber	.05
137	Jim Abbott	.05
138	Steve Traschel	.05
139	Bret Boone	.05
140	Charles Johnson	.05
141	Mark McGwire	2.00
142	Eddie Murray	.75
143	Doug Drabek	.05
144	Steve Cooke	.05
145	Kevin Seitzer	.05
146	Rod Beck	.05
147	Eric Karros	.05
148	Tim Raines	.05
149	Joe Girardi	.05
150	Aaron Sele	.05
151	Robby Thompson	.05
152	Chan Ho Park	.05
153	Ellis Burks	.05
154	Brian McRae	.05
155	Jimmy Key	.05
156	Rico Brogna	.05
157	Ozzie Guillen	.05
158	Chili Davis	.05
159	Darren Daulton	.05
160	Chipper Jones	1.00
161	Walt Weiss	.05
162	Paul O'Neill	.05
163	Al Martin	.05
164	John Valentin	.05
165	Tim Wallach	.05
166	Scott Erickson	.05
167	Ryan Thompson	.05
168	Todd Zeile	.05
169	Scott Cooper	.05
170	Matt Mieske	.05
171	Allen Watson	.05
172	Brian Hunter	.05
173	Kevin Stocker	.05
174	Cal Eldred	.05
175	Tony Phillips	.05
176	Ben McDonald	.05
177	Mark Grace	.05
178	Midre Cummings	.05
179	Orlando Merced	.05
180	Jeff King	.05
181	Gary Sheffield	.40
182	Tom Glavine	.35
183	Edgar Martinez	.05
184	Steve Karsay	.05
185	Pat Listach	.05
186	Wil Cordero	.05
187	Brady Anderson	.05
188	Bobby Jones	.05
189	Andy Benes	.05
190	Ray Lankford	.05
191	John Doherty	.05
192	Wally Joyner	.05
193	Jim Thome	.65
194	Royce Clayton	.05
195	John Olerud	.05
196	Steve Buechele	.05
197	Harold Baines	.05
198	Geronimo Berroa	.05
199	Checklist	.05
200	Checklist	.05

Gold

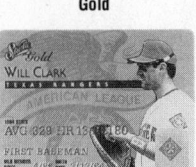

		NM/M
Complete Set (50):		25.00
Common Player:		.15
1	Frank Thomas	1.00
2	Jeff Bagwell	1.00
3	Don Mattingly	1.75
4	Mike Piazza	2.00
5	Ken Griffey Jr.	2.00
6	Greg Maddux	1.50
7	Barry Bonds	3.00
8	Cal Ripken Jr.	3.00
9	Jose Canseco	.50
10	Paul Molitor	1.00
11	Kenny Lofton	.15
12	Will Clark	.15
13	Tim Salmon	.15
14	Joe Carter	.15
15	Albert Belle	.15
16	Roger Clemens	1.75
17	Roberto Alomar	.35
18	Alex Rodriguez	2.50
19	Raul Mondesi	.15
20	Deion Sanders	.15
21	Juan Gonzalez	.50
22	Kirby Puckett	1.50
23	Fred McGriff	.15
24	Matt Williams	.15
25	Tony Gwynn	1.50
26	Cliff Floyd	.15
27	Travis Fryman	.15
28	Shawn Green	.40
29	Mike Mussina	.35
30	Bob Hamelin	.15
31	Dave Justice	.15
32	Manny Ramirez	1.00
33	David Cone	.15
34	Marquis Grissom	.15
35	Moises Alou	.15
36	Carlos Baerga	.15
37	Barry Larkin	.15
38	Robin Ventura	.15
39	Mo Vaughn	.15
40	Jeffrey Hammonds	.15

41	Ozzie Smith	1.50
42	Andres Galarraga	.15
43	Carlos Delgado	.50
44	Lenny Dykstra	.15
45	Cecil Fielder	.15
46	Wade Boggs	1.50
47	Gregg Jefferies	.15
48	Randy Johnson	1.00
49	Rafael Palmeiro	.75
50	Craig Biggio	.15

Platinum

		NM/M
Complete Set (25):		25.00
Common Player:		.50
1	Frank Thomas	2.00
2	Jeff Bagwell	2.00
3	Don Mattingly	3.25
4	Mike Piazza	3.50
5	Ken Griffey Jr.	3.50
6	Greg Maddux	3.00
7	Barry Bonds	5.00
8	Cal Ripken Jr.	5.00
9	Jose Canseco	1.00
10	Paul Molitor	2.00
11	Kenny Lofton	.50
12	Will Clark	.50
13	Tim Salmon	.50
14	Joe Carter	.50
15	Albert Belle	.50
16	Roger Clemens	3.25
17	Roberto Alomar	.75
18	Alex Rodriguez	4.00
19	Raul Mondesi	.50
20	Deion Sanders	.50
21	Juan Gonzalez	1.00
22	Kirby Puckett	3.00
23	Fred McGriff	.50
24	Matt Williams	.50
25	Tony Gwynn	3.00

1996 Studio

		NM/M
Complete Set (150):		9.00
Common Player:		.05
Bronze Press Proofs:		3X
Gold Press Proofs:		7X
Silver Press Proofs:		25X
Pack (7):		1.25
Wax Box (24):		20.00
1	Cal Ripken Jr.	1.50
2	Alex Gonzalez	.05
3	Roger Cedeno	.05
4	Todd Hollandsworth	.05
5	Gregg Jefferies	.05
6	Ryne Sandberg	.65
7	Eric Karros	.05
8	Jeff Conine	.05
9	Rafael Palmeiro	.45
10	Bip Roberts	.05
11	Roger Clemens	.70
12	Tom Glavine	.30
13	Jason Giambi	.40
14	Rey Ordonez	.05
15	Chan Ho Park	.05
16	Vinny Castilla	.05
17	Butch Huskey	.05
18	Greg Maddux	.65
19	Bernard Gilkey	.05
20	Marquis Grissom	.05
21	Chuck Knoblauch	.05
22	Ozzie Smith	.65
23	Garret Anderson	.05
24	J.T. Snow	.05
25	John Valentin	.05
26	Barry Larkin	.05
27	Bobby Bonilla	.05
28	Todd Zeile	.05
29	Roberto Alomar	.20
30	Ramon Martinez	.05
31	Jeff King	.05
32	Dennis Eckersley	.45
33	Derek Jeter	1.50
34	Edgar Martinez	.05
35	Geronimo Berroa	.05
36	Hal Morris	.05
37	Troy Percival	.05
38	Jason Isringhausen	.05
39	Greg Vaughn	.05
40	Robin Ventura	.05
41	Craig Biggio	.05
42	Will Clark	.05
43	Sammy Sosa	.65
44	Bernie Williams	.05
45	Kenny Lofton	.05
46	Wade Boggs	.65
47	Javy Lopez	.05
48	Reggie Sanders	.05
49	Jeff Bagwell	.55
50	Fred McGriff	.05
51	Charles Johnson	.05
52	Darren Daulton	.05
53	Jose Canseco	.40
54	Cecil Fielder	.05
55	Hideo Nomo	.30
56	Tim Salmon	.05
57	Carlos Delgado	.40
58	David Cone	.05
59	Tim Raines	.05
60	Lyle Mouton	.05
61	Wally Joyner	.05
62	Bret Boone	.05
63	Raul Mondesi	.05
64	Gary Sheffield	.35
65	Alex Rodriguez	1.00
66	Russ Davis	.05
67	Checklist	.05
68	Marty Cordova	.05
69	Ruben Sierra	.05
70	Jose Mesa	.05
71	Matt Williams	.05
72	Chipper Jones	.75
73	Randy Johnson	.55
74	Kirby Puckett	.65
75	Jim Edmonds	.05
76	Barry Bonds	1.50
77	David Segui	.05
78	Larry Walker	.05
79	Jason Kendall	.75
80	Mike Piazza	.75
81	Brian Hunter	.05
82	Julio Franco	.05
83	Jay Bell	.05
84	Kevin Seitzer	.05
85	John Smoltz	.05
86	Joe Carter	.05
87	Ray Durham	.05
88	Carlos Baerga	.05
89	Ron Gant	.05
90	Orlando Merced	.05
91	Lee Smith	.05
92	Pedro Martinez	.55
93	Frank Thomas	.55
94	Al Martin	.05
95	Chad Curtis	.05
96	Eddie Murray	.55
97	Rusty Greer	.05
98	Jay Buhner	.05
99	Rico Brogna	.05
100	Todd Hundley	.05
101	Moises Alou	.05
102	Chili Davis	.05
103	Ismael Valdes	.05
104	Mo Vaughn	.30
105	Juan Gonzalez	.30
106	Mark Grudzielanek	.05
107	Derek Bell	.05
108	Shawn Green	.30
109	David Justice	.05
110	Paul O'Neill	.05
111	Kevin Appier	.05
112	Ray Lankford	.05
113	Travis Fryman	.05
114	Manny Ramirez	.55
115	Brooks Kieschnick	.05
116	Ken Griffey Jr.	.75
117	Jeffrey Hammonds	.05
118	Mark McGwire	1.00
119	Denny Neagle	.05
120	Quilvio Veras	.05
121	Alan Benes	.05
122	Rondell White	.05
123	Osvaldo Fernandez RC	.20
124	Andres Galarraga	.05
125	Johnny Damon	.35
126	Lenny Dykstra	.05
127	Jason Schmidt	.05
128	Mike Mussina	.30
129	Ken Caminiti	.05
130	Michael Tucker	.05
131	LaTroy Hawkins	.05
132	Checklist	.05
133	Delino DeShields	.05
134	Dave Nilsson	.05
135	Jack McDowell	.05
136	Joey Hamilton	.05
137	Dante Bichette	.05
138	Paul Molitor	.55
139	Ivan Rodriguez	.45
140	Mark Grace	.05
141	Paul Wilson	.05
142	Orel Hershiser	.05
143	Albert Belle	.05
144	Tino Martinez	.05
145	Tony Gwynn	.65
146	George Arias	.05
147	Brian Jordan	.05
148	Brian McRae	.05
149	Rickey Henderson	.55
150	Ryan Klesko	.05

Press Proofs

	NM/M
Common Player, Bronze:	.50
Bronze Stars:	3X
Common Player, Gold:	1.00
Gold Stars:	7X
Common Player, Silver:	4.00
Silver Stars:	25X

(See 1996 Studio for checklist, base card values.)

Hit Parade

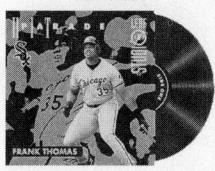

		NM/M
Complete Set (10):		10.00
Common Player:		.75
1	Tony Gwynn	1.50
2	Ken Griffey Jr.	2.00
3	Frank Thomas	1.00
4	Jeff Bagwell	1.00
5	Kirby Puckett	1.50
6	Mike Piazza	2.00
7	Barry Bonds	2.50
8	Albert Belle	.75
9	Tim Salmon	.75
10	Mo Vaughn	.75

Masterstrokes

		NM/M
Complete Set (8):		30.00
Common Player:		4.00
Samples:		75 Percent
1	Tony Gwynn	6.00
2	Mike Piazza	8.00
3	Jeff Bagwell	4.00
4	Manny Ramirez	4.00
5	Cal Ripken Jr.	12.00
6	Frank Thomas	4.00
7	Ken Griffey Jr.	8.00
8	Greg Maddux	6.00

Stained Glass Stars

		NM/M
Complete Set (12):		24.00
Common Player:		1.00
1	Cal Ripken Jr.	5.00
2	Ken Griffey Jr.	3.50

3	Frank Thomas	2.00
4	Greg Maddux	2.50
5	Chipper Jones	2.50
6	Mike Piazza	3.50
7	Albert Belle	1.00
8	Jeff Bagwell	2.00
9	Hideo Nomo	1.50
10	Barry Bonds	5.00
11	Manny Ramirez	2.00
12	Kenny Lofton	1.00

1997 Studio

		NM/M
Complete Set (165):		17.50
Common Player:		.05
Silver Press Proofs:		4X
Gold Press Proofs:		8X
Pack (5):		3.00
Wax Box (18):		40.00
1	Frank Thomas	.65
2	Gary Sheffield	.45
3	Jason Isringhausen	.05
4	Ron Gant	.05
5	Andy Pettitte	.25
6	Todd Hollandsworth	.05
7	Troy Percival	.05
8	Mark McGwire	1.50
9	Barry Larkin	.05
10	Ken Caminiti	.05
11	Paul Molitor	.65
12	Travis Fryman	.05
13	Kevin Brown	.05
14	Robin Ventura	.05
15	Andres Galarraga	.05
16	Ken Griffey Jr.	1.00
17	Roger Clemens	.85
18	Alan Benes	.05
19	David Justice	.05
20	Damon Buford	.05
21	Mike Piazza	1.00
22	Ray Durham	.05
23	Billy Wagner	.05
24	Dean Palmer	.05
25	David Cone	.05
26	Ruben Sierra	.05
27	Henry Rodriguez	.05
28	Ray Lankford	.05
29	Jamey Wright	.05
30	Brady Anderson	.05
31	Tino Martinez	.05
32	Manny Ramirez	.65
33	Jeff Conine	.05
34	Dante Bichette	.05
35	Jose Canseco	.50
36	Mo Vaughn	.05
37	Sammy Sosa	.75
38	Mark Grudzielanek	.05
39	Mike Mussina	.35
40	Bill Pulsipher	.05
41	Ryne Sandberg	.75
42	Rickey Henderson	.65
43	Alex Rodriguez	1.50
44	Eddie Murray	.65
45	Ernie Young	.05
46	Joey Hamilton	.05
47	Wade Boggs	.75
48	Rusty Greer	.05

49	Carlos Delgado	.50
50	Ellis Burks	.05
51	Cal Ripken Jr.	2.00
52	Alex Fernandez	.05
53	Wally Joyner	.05
54	James Baldwin	.05
55	Juan Gonzalez	.35
56	John Smoltz	.05
57	Omar Vizquel	.05
58	Shane Reynolds	.05
59	Barry Bonds	2.00
60	Jason Kendall	.05
61	Marty Cordova	.05
62	Charles Johnson	.05
63	John Jaha	.05
64	Chan Ho Park	.05
65	Jermaine Allensworth	.05
66	Mark Grace	.05
67	Tim Salmon	.05
68	Edgar Martinez	.05
69	Marquis Grissom	.05
70	Craig Biggio	.05
71	Bobby Higginson	.05
72	Kevin Seitzer	.05
73	Hideo Nomo	.35
74	Dennis Eckersley	.60
75	Bobby Bonilla	.05
76	Dwight Gooden	.05
77	Jeff Cirillo	.05
78	Brian McRae	.05
79	Chipper Jones	.75
80	Jeff Fassero	.05
81	Fred McGriff	.05
82	Garret Anderson	.05
83	Eric Karros	.05
84	Derek Bell	.05
85	Kenny Lofton	.05
86	John Mabry	.05
87	Pat Hentgen	.05
88	Greg Maddux	.75
89	Jason Giambi	.45
90	Al Martin	.05
91	Derek Jeter	2.00
92	Rey Ordonez	.05
93	Will Clark	.05
94	Kevin Appier	.05
95	Roberto Alomar	.30
96	Joe Carter	.05
97	Bernie Williams	.05
98	Albert Belle	.05
99	Greg Vaughn	.05
100	Tony Clark	.05
101	Matt Williams	.05
102	Jeff Bagwell	.65
103	Reggie Sanders	.05
104	Mariano Rivera	.15
105	Larry Walker	.05
106	Shawn Green	.30
107	Alex Ochoa	.05
108	Ivan Rodriguez	.60
109	Eric Young	.05
110	Javier Lopez	.05
111	Brian Hunter	.05
112	Raul Mondesi	.05
113	Randy Johnson	.65
114	Tony Phillips	.05
115	Carlos Garcia	.05
116	Moises Alou	.05
117	Paul O'Neill	.05
118	Jim Thome	.60
119	Jermaine Dye	.05
120	Wilson Alvarez	.05
121	Rondell White	.05
122	Michael Tucker	.05
123	Mike Lansing	.05
124	Tony Gwynn	.75
125	Ryan Klesko	.05
126	Jim Edmonds	.05
127	Chuck Knoblauch	.05
128	Rafael Palmeiro	.05
129	Jay Buhner	.05
130	Tom Glavine	.35
131	Julio Franco	.05
132	Cecil Fielder	.05
133	Paul Wilson	.05
134	Deion Sanders	.05
135	Alex Gonzalez	.05
136	Charles Nagy	.05
137	Andy Ashby	.05
138	Edgar Renteria	.05
139	Pedro Martinez	.65
140	Brian Jordan	.05
141	Todd Hundley	.05
142	Marc Newfield	.05
143	Darryl Strawberry	.05
144	Dan Wilson	.05
145	Brian Giles **RC**	.50
146	Bartolo Colon	.05
147	Shannon Stewart	.05
148	Scott Spiezio	.05
149	Andruw Jones	.65
150	Karim Garcia	.05
151	Vladimir Guerrero	.65
152	George Arias	.05
153	Brooks Kieschnick	.05
154	Todd Walker	.05
155	Scott Rolen	.60
156	Todd Greene	.05
157	Dmitri Young	.05
158	Ruben Rivera	.05
159	Trey Beamon	.05
160	Nomar Garciaparra	.75
161	Bob Abreu	.05
162	Darin Erstad	.15
163	Ken Griffey Jr. (Checklist)	.50

164	Frank Thomas (Checklist)	.35
165	Alex Rodriguez (Checklist)	.75

Press Proofs

		NM/M
Common Player, Silver:		.50
Silver Stars:		4X
Common Player, Gold:		1.00
Gold Stars:		8X

(See 1997 Studio for checklist and base card values.)

Hard Hats

		NM/M
Complete Set (24):		50.00
Common Player:		1.50
1	Ivan Rodriguez	3.00
2	Albert Belle	1.50
3	Ken Griffey Jr.	6.00
4	Chuck Knoblauch	1.50
5	Frank Thomas	4.00
6	Cal Ripken Jr.	8.00
7	Todd Walker	1.50
8	Alex Rodriguez	7.00
9	Jim Thome	3.00
10	Mike Piazza	6.00
11	Barry Larkin	1.50
12	Chipper Jones	5.00
13	Derek Jeter	8.00
14	Jermaine Dye	1.50
15	Jason Giambi	2.00
16	Tim Salmon	1.50
17	Brady Anderson	1.50
18	Rondell White	1.50
19	Bernie Williams	1.50
20	Juan Gonzalez	2.00
21	Karim Garcia	1.50
22	Scott Rolen	3.00
23	Darin Erstad	2.00
24	Brian Jordan	1.50

Master Strokes

		NM/M
Complete Set (24):		120.00
Common Player:		2.00
1	Derek Jeter	12.00
2	Jeff Bagwell	4.50
3	Ken Griffey Jr.	8.00
4	Barry Bonds	12.00
5	Frank Thomas	4.50
6	Andy Pettitte	2.25
7	Mo Vaughn	2.00
8	Alex Rodriguez	10.00
9	Andruw Jones	4.50
10	Kenny Lofton	2.00

11	Cal Ripken Jr.	12.00
12	Greg Maddux	6.00
13	Manny Ramirez	4.50
14	Mike Piazza	8.00
14p	Mike Piazza (Promo)	3.50
15	Vladimir Guerrero	4.50
16	Albert Belle	2.00
17	Chipper Jones	6.00
18	Hideo Nomo	2.50
19	Sammy Sosa	6.00
20	Tony Gwynn	6.00
21	Gary Sheffield	2.50
22	Mark McGwire	10.00
23	Juan Gonzalez	2.50
24	Paul Molitor	4.50

Master Strokes 8x10

		NM/M
Complete Set (24):		45.00
Common Player:		.75
1	Derek Jeter	5.00
2	Jeff Bagwell	2.00
3	Ken Griffey Jr.	3.00
4	Barry Bonds	5.00
5	Frank Thomas	2.00
6	Andy Pettitte	1.00
7	Mo Vaughn	.75
8	Alex Rodriguez	4.00
9	Andruw Jones	2.00
10	Kenny Lofton	.75
11	Cal Ripken Jr.	5.00
12	Greg Maddux	2.50
13	Manny Ramirez	2.00
14	Mike Piazza	3.00
15	Vladimir Guerrero	2.00
16	Albert Belle	.75
17	Chipper Jones	2.50
18	Hideo Nomo	1.50
19	Sammy Sosa	2.50
20	Tony Gwynn	2.50
21	Gary Sheffield	1.50
22	Mark McGwire	4.00
23	Juan Gonzalez	1.50
24	Paul Molitor	2.00

Portraits

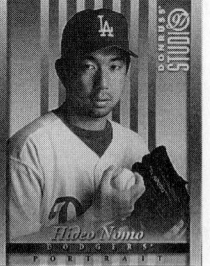

		NM/M
Complete Set (24):		10.00
Common Player:		.25
1	Ken Griffey Jr.	1.00
1s	Frank Thomas (Overprinted "SAMPLE.")	.75
2	Frank Thomas	.65
3	Alex Rodriguez	1.50
4	Andruw Jones	.65
5	Cal Ripken Jr.	2.00
6	Greg Maddux	.75
7	Mike Piazza	1.00
8	Chipper Jones	.75
9	Albert Belle	.25
10	Derek Jeter	2.00
11	Juan Gonzalez	.45
12	Todd Walker	.25
12a	Todd Walker (Autographed edition of 1,250.)	10.00
13	Mark McGwire	1.50
14	Barry Bonds	.65
15	Jeff Bagwell	.65
16	Manny Ramirez	.65
17	Kenny Lofton	.25
18	Mo Vaughn	.25
19	Hideo Nomo	.45

20	Tony Gwynn	.75
21	Vladimir Guerrero	.65
21a	Vladimir Guerrero (Autographed edition of 500.)	30.00
22	Gary Sheffield	.45
23	Ryne Sandberg	.75
24	Scott Rolen	.50
24a	Scott Rolen (Autographed edition of 1,000.)	12.00

1997 Studio Portrait Collection

		NM/M
Complete Set, Studio Portrait (24):		2,850
Complete Set, Master Strokes (24):		5,250
Common Plaque, Studio Portrait:		125.00
Common Plaque, Master Strokes:		225.00
P1	Ken Griffey Jr.	125.00
P2	Frank Thomas	125.00
P3	Alex Rodriguez	125.00
P4	Andruw Jones	125.00
P5	Cal Ripken Jr.	125.00
P6	Greg Maddux	125.00
P7	Mike Piazza	125.00
P8	Chipper Jones	125.00
P9	Albert Belle	125.00
P10	Derek Jeter	125.00
P11	Juan Gonzalez	125.00
P12	Todd Walker	125.00
P13	Mark McGwire	125.00
P14	Barry Bonds	125.00
P15	Jeff Bagwell	125.00
P16	Manny	125.00
P17	Kenny Lofton	125.00
P18	Mo Vaughn	125.00
P19	Hideo Nomo	125.00
P20	Tony Gwynn	125.00
P21	Vladimir Guerrero	125.00
P22	Gary Sheffield	125.00
P23	Ryne Sandberg	125.00
P24	Scott Rolen	125.00
M1	Derek Jeter	225.00
M2	Jeff Bagwell	225.00
M3	Ken Griffey Jr.	225.00
M4	Barry Bonds	225.00
M5	Frank Thomas	225.00
M6	Andy Pettitte	225.00
M7	Mo Vaughn	225.00
M8	Alex Rodriguez	225.00
M9	Andruw Jones	225.00
M10	Kenny Lofton	225.00
M11	Cal Ripken Jr.	225.00
M12	Greg Maddux	225.00
M13	Manny Ramirez	225.00
M14	Mike Piazza	225.00
M15	Vladimir Guerrero	225.00
M16	Albert Belle	225.00
M17	Chipper Jones	225.00
M18	Hideo Nomo	225.00
M19	Sammy Sosa	225.00
M20	Tony Gwynn	225.00
M21	Gary Sheffield	225.00
M22	Mark McGwire	225.00
M23	Juan Gonzalez	225.00
M24	Paul Molitor	225.00

1998 Studio

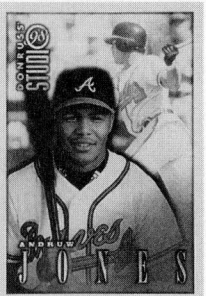

		NM/M
Complete Set (220):		25.00
Common Player:		.05
Silver Proofs:		3X
Gold Proofs:		6X
Pack (7 Cards+8x10):		2.00
Wax Box (18):		20.00
1	Tony Clark	.05
2	Jose Cruz Jr.	.05
3	Ivan Rodriguez	.65
4	Mo Vaughn	.05
5	Kenny Lofton	.05
6	Will Clark	.05
7	Barry Larkin	.05
8	Jay Bell	.05
9	Kevin Young	.05
10	Francisco Cordova	.05
11	Justin Thompson	.05
12	Paul Molitor	.75
13	Jeff Bagwell	.65
14	Jose Canseco	.45
15	Scott Rolen	.65

#	Player	Price
16	Wilton Guerrero	.05
17	Shannon Stewart	.05
18	Hideki Irabu	.05
19	Michael Tucker	.05
20	Joe Carter	.05
21	Gabe Alvarez	.05
22	Ricky Ledee	.05
23	Karim Garcia	.05
24	Eli Marrero	.05
25	Scott Elarton	.05
26	Mario Valdez	.05
27	Ben Grieve	.05
28	Paul Konerko	.15
29	Esteban Yan RC	.05
30	Esteban Loaiza	.05
31	Delino DeShields	.05
32	Bernie Williams	.05
33	Joe Randa	.05
34	Randy Johnson	.75
35	Brett Tomko	.05
36	Todd Erdos RC	.05
37	Bobby Higginson	.05
38	Jason Kendall	.05
39	Ray Lankford	.05
40	Mark Grace	.05
41	Andy Pettitte	.25
42	Alex Rodriguez	2.00
43	Hideo Nomo	.45
44	Sammy Sosa	1.00
45	J.T. Snow	.05
46	Jason Varitek	.05
47	Vinny Castilla	.05
48	Neifi Perez	.05
49	Todd Walker	.05
50	Mike Cameron	.05
51	Jeffrey Hammonds	.05
52	Deivi Cruz	.05
53	Brian Hunter	.05
54	Al Martin	.05
55	Ron Coomer	.05
56	Chan Ho Park	.05
57	Pedro Martinez	.75
58	Darin Erstad	.15
59	Albert Belle	.05
60	Nomar Garciaparra	1.00
61	Tony Gwynn	1.00
62	Mike Piazza	1.50
63	Todd Helton	.65
64	David Ortiz	.45
65	Todd Dunwoody	.05
66	Orlando Cabrera	.05
67	Ken Cloude	.05
68	Andy Benes	.05
69	Mariano Rivera	.15
70	Cecil Fielder	.05
71	Brian Jordan	.05
72	Darryl Kile	.05
73	Reggie Jefferson	.05
74	Shawn Estes	.05
75	Bobby Bonilla	.05
76	Denny Neagle	.05
77	Robin Ventura	.05
78	Omar Vizquel	.05
79	Craig Biggio	.05
80	Moises Alou	.05
81	Garret Anderson	.05
82	Eric Karros	.05
83	Dante Bichette	.05
84	Charles Johnson	.05
85	Rusty Greer	.05
86	Travis Fryman	.05
87	Fernando Tatis	.05
88	Wilson Alvarez	.05
89	Carl Pavano	.05
90	Brian Rose	.05
91	Geoff Jenkins	.05
92	Magglio Ordonez RC	1.50
93	David Segui	.05
94	David Cone	.05
95	John Smoltz	.05
96	Jim Thome	.65
97	Gary Sheffield	.45
98	Brad Fullmer	2.50
99	Andres Galarraga	.05
100	Brad Fullmer	.05
101	Bobby Estalella	.05
102	Enrique Wilson	.05
103	Frank Catalanotto RC	.25
104	Mike Lowell RC	1.00
105	Kevin Orie	.05
106	Matt Morris	.05
107	Pokey Reese	.05
108	Shawn Green	.35
109	Tony Womack	.05
110	Ken Caminiti	.05
111	Roberto Alomar	.20
112	Ken Griffey Jr.	1.50
113	Cal Ripken Jr.	2.50
114	Lou Collier	.05
115	Larry Walker	.05
116	Fred McGriff	.05
117	Jim Edmonds	.05
118	Edgar Martinez	.05
119	Matt Williams	.05
120	Ismael Valdes	.05
121	Bartolo Colon	.05
122	Jeff Cirillo	.05
123	Steve Woodard RC	.25
124	Kevin Millwood RC	1.00
125	Derrick Gibson	.05
126	Jacob Cruz	.05
127	Russell Branyan	.05
128	Sean Casey	.15
129	Derek Lee	.50
130	Paul O'Neill	.05
131	Brad Radke	.05

#	Player	Price
132	Kevin Appier	.05
133	John Olerud	.05
134	Alan Benes	.05
135	Todd Greene	.05
136	Carlos Mendoza RC	.05
137	Wade Boggs	1.00
138	Jose Guillen	.05
139	Tino Martinez	.05
140	Aaron Boone	.05
141	Abraham Nunez	.05
142	Preston Wilson	.05
143	Randall Simon	.05
144	Dennis Reyes	.05
145	Mark Kotsay	.05
146	Richard Hidalgo	.05
147	Travis Lee	.05
148	Hanley Frias RC	.05
149	Ruben Rivera	.05
150	Rafael Medina	.05
151	Dave Nilsson	.05
152	Curt Schilling	.35
153	Brady Anderson	.05
154	Carlos Delgado	.50
155	Jason Giambi	.45
156	Pat Hentgen	.05
157	Tom Glavine	.35
158	Ryan Klesko	.05
159	Chipper Jones	1.00
160	Juan Gonzalez	.45
161	Mark McGwire	2.00
162	Vladimir Guerrero	.75
163	Derek Jeter	2.50
164	Manny Ramirez	.75
165	Mike Mussina	.30
166	Rafael Palmeiro	.65
167	Henry Rodriguez	.05
168	Jeff Suppan	.05
169	Eric Milton	.05
170	Scott Spiezio	.05
171	Wilson Delgado	.05
172	Bubba Trammell	.05
173	Ellis Burks	.05
174	Jason Dickson	.05
175	Butch Huskey	.05
176	Edgardo Alfonzo	.05
177	Eric Young	.05
178	Marquis Grissom	.05
179	Lance Johnson	.05
180	Kevin Brown	.05
181	Sandy Alomar Jr.	.05
182	Todd Hundley	.05
183	Rondell White	.05
184	Javier Lopez	.05
185	Damian Jackson	.05
186	Raul Mondesi	.05
187	Rickey Henderson	.75
188	David Justice	.05
189	Jay Buhner	.05
190	Jaret Wright	.05
191	Miguel Tejada	.25
192	Ron Wright	.05
193	Livan Hernandez	.05
194	A.J. Hinch	.05
195	Richie Sexson	.05
196	Bob Abreu	.05
197	Luis Castillo	.05
198	Michael Coleman	.05
199	Greg Maddux	1.00
200	Frank Thomas	.75
201	Andruw Jones	.75
202	Roger Clemens	1.25
203	Tim Salmon	.05
204	Chuck Knoblauch	.05
205	Wes Helms	.05
206	Juan Encarnacion	.05
207	Russ Davis	.05
208	John Valentin	.05
209	Tony Saunders	.05
210	Mike Sweeney	.05
211	Steve Finley	.05
212	David Dellucci RC	.05
213	Edgar Renteria	.05
214	Jeremi Gonzalez	.05
215	Jeff Bagwell Checklist	.40
216	Mike Piazza Checklist	1.00
217	Greg Maddux Checklist	.50
218	Cal Ripken Jr. Checklist	1.25
219	Frank Thomas Checklist	.45
220	Ken Griffey Jr. Checklist	.75

Gold Proofs

	NM/M
Common Player:	3.00
Stars:	6X

(See 1998 Studio for checklist and base card values.)

Silver Proofs

#	Player	Price
6	Ken Griffey Jr.	3.00
7	Todd Helton	1.50
8	Vladimir Guerrero	2.00
9	Albert Belle	1.00
10	Jeff Bagwell	2.00
11	Juan Gonzalez	1.25
12	Jim Thome	1.50
13	Scott Rolen	1.50
14	Tino Martinez	1.00
15	Mark McGwire	4.00
16	Barry Bonds	5.00
17	Tony Clark	1.00
18	Mo Vaughn	1.00
19	Darin Erstad	1.25
20	Paul Konerko	1.25

	NM/M
Common Player:	1.00
Silver Stars:	3X

(See 1998 Studio for checklist, base cardvalues.)

Autographs

#		NM/M
1	Travis Lee/500	20.00
2	Todd Helton/1,000	20.00
3	Ben Grieve/1,000	10.00

Freeze Frame

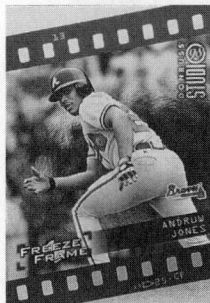

	NM/M
Complete Set (30):	75.00
Common Player:	1.25
Production 4,500 Sets	
Die-Cuts:	1.5X
Production 500 Sets	

#	Player	Price
1	Ken Griffey Jr.	7.50
2	Derek Jeter	7.50
3	Ben Grieve	1.25
4	Cal Ripken Jr.	7.50
5	Alex Rodriguez	6.00
6	Greg Maddux	4.00
7	David Justice	1.25
8	Mike Piazza	5.00
9	Chipper Jones	4.00
10	Randy Johnson	3.00
11	Jeff Bagwell	4.00
12	Nomar Garciaparra	4.00
13	Andruw Jones	3.00
14	Frank Thomas	3.00
15	Scott Rolen	2.50
16	Barry Bonds	7.50
17	Kenny Lofton	1.25
18	Ivan Rodriguez	2.50
19	Chuck Knoblauch	1.25
20	Jose Cruz Jr.	1.25
21	Bernie Williams	1.25
22	Tony Gwynn	4.00
23	Juan Gonzalez	2.00
24	Gary Sheffield	2.25
25	Roger Clemens	4.50
26	Travis Lee	1.25
27	Brad Fullmer	1.25
28	Tim Salmon	1.25
29	Raul Mondesi	1.25
30	Roberto Alomar	2.00

Hit Parade

	NM/M
Complete Set (20):	30.00
Common Player:	1.00
Production 5,000 Sets	

#	Player	Price
1	Tony Gwynn	2.50
2	Larry Walker	1.00
3	Mike Piazza	3.00
4	Frank Thomas	2.00
5	Manny Ramirez	2.00

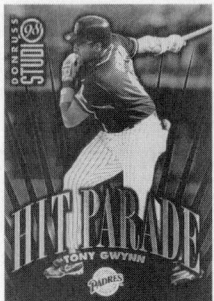

#	Player	Price
6	Ken Griffey Jr.	3.00
7	Todd Helton	1.50
8	Vladimir Guerrero	2.00
9	Albert Belle	1.00
10	Jeff Bagwell	2.00
11	Juan Gonzalez	1.25
12	Jim Thome	1.50
13	Scott Rolen	1.50
14	Tino Martinez	1.00
15	Mark McGwire	4.00
16	Barry Bonds	5.00
17	Tony Clark	1.00
18	Mo Vaughn	1.00
19	Darin Erstad	1.25
20	Paul Konerko	1.25

Masterstrokes

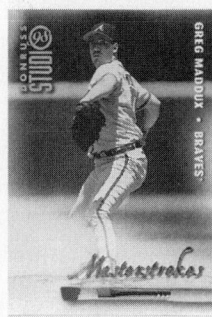

	NM/M
Complete Set (20):	95.00
Common Player:	2.00
Production 1,000 Sets	
Samples:	3X

#	Player	Price
1	Travis Lee	2.00
2	Kenny Lofton	2.00
3	Mo Vaughn	2.00
4	Ivan Rodriguez	3.50
5	Roger Clemens	6.50
6	Mark McGwire	10.00
7	Hideo Nomo	2.50
8	Andruw Jones	4.50
9	Nomar Garciaparra	6.00
10	Juan Gonzalez	2.50
11	Jeff Bagwell	4.50
12	Derek Jeter	12.50
13	Tony Gwynn	6.00
14	Chipper Jones	6.00
15	Mike Piazza	7.50
16	Greg Maddux	6.00
17	Alex Rodriguez	10.00
18	Cal Ripken Jr.	12.50
19	Frank Thomas	4.50
20	Ken Griffey Jr.	7.50

Sony MLB 99

		NM/M
	Complete Set (20):	8.00
	Common Player:	.15
1	Cal Ripken Jr.	1.50
2	Nomar Garciaparra	.75
3	Barry Bonds	1.50
4	Mike Mussina	.35
5	Pedro Martinez	.60
6	Derek Jeter	1.50
7	Andruw Jones	.60
8	Kenny Lofton	.15
9	Gary Sheffield	.45
10	Raul Mondesi	.15
11	Jeff Bagwell	.60
12	Tim Salmon	.15
13	Tom Glavine	.35
14	Ben Grieve	.15
15	Matt Williams	.15
16	Juan Gonzalez	.35
17	Mark McGwire	1.00
18	Bernie Williams	.15
19	Andres Galarraga	.15
20	Jose Cruz Jr.	.15

8x10 Portraits

		NM/M
	Complete Set (36):	65.00
	Common Player:	.50
	Inserted 1:1	
1	Travis Lee	.50
2	Todd Helton	1.50
3	Ben Grieve	.50
4	Paul Konerko	.65
5	Jeff Bagwell	2.00
6	Derek Jeter	7.00
7	Ivan Rodriguez	1.50
8	Cal Ripken Jr.	7.00
9	Mike Piazza	4.00
10	Chipper Jones	3.00
11	Frank Thomas	2.00
12	Tony Gwynn	3.00
13	Nomar Garciaparra	3.00
14	Juan Gonzalez	1.00
15	Greg Maddux	3.00
16	Hideo Nomo	1.00
17	Scott Rolen	1.50
18	Barry Bonds	7.00
19	Ken Griffey Jr.	4.00
20	Alex Rodriguez	5.00
21	Roger Clemens	3.50
22	Mark McGwire	5.00
23	Jose Cruz Jr.	.50
24	Andruw Jones	2.00
25	Tino Martinez	.50
26	Mo Vaughn	.50
27	Vladimir Guerrero	2.00
28	Tony Clark	.50
29	Andy Pettitte	.65
30	Jaret Wright	.50
31	Paul Molitor	2.00
32	Darin Erstad	.65
33	Larry Walker	.50
34	Chuck Knoblauch	.50
35	Barry Larkin	.50
36	Kenny Lofton	.50

8x10 Portraits Gold Proofs

	NM/M
Common Player:	5.00
Stars:	6X

(See 1998 Studio 8X10 Portraits for checklist and base card values.)

1995 Summit

		NM/M
	Complete Set (200):	10.00
	Common Player:	.05
	Pack (7):	1.00
	Wax Box (24):	12.50
1	Ken Griffey Jr.	1.00
2	Alex Fernandez	.05
3	Fred McGriff	.05
4	Ben McDonald	.05
5	Rafael Palmeiro	.60
6	Tony Gwynn	.75
7	Jim Thome	.60
8	Ken Hill	.05
9	Barry Bonds	2.00
10	Barry Larkin	.05
11	Albert Belle	.05
12	Billy Ashley	.05
13	Matt Williams	.05

PAUL MONDESI

14	Andy Benes	.05
15	Midre Cummings	.05
16	J.R. Phillips	.05
17	Edgar Martinez	.05
18	Manny Ramirez	.65
19	Jose Canseco	.40
20	Chili Davis	.05
21	Don Mattingly	.85
22	Bernie Williams	.05
23	Tom Glavine	.35
24	Robin Ventura	.05
25	Jeff Conine	.05
26	Mark Grace	.05
27	Mark McGwire	1.50
28	Carlos Delgado	.45
29	Greg Colbrunn	.05
30	Greg Maddux	.75
31	Craig Biggio	.05
32	Kirby Puckett	.75
33	Derek Bell	.05
34	Lenny Dykstra	.05
35	Tim Salmon	.05
36	Deion Sanders	.05
37	Moises Alou	.05
38	Ray Lankford	.05
39	Willie Greene	.05
40	Ozzie Smith	.75
41	Roger Clemens	.85
42	Andres Galarraga	.05
43	Gary Sheffield	.35
44	Sammy Sosa	.75
45	Larry Walker	.05
46	Kevin Appier	.05
47	Raul Mondesi	.05
48	Kenny Lofton	.05
49	Darryl Hamilton	.05
50	Roberto Alomar	.20
51	Hal Morris	.05
52	Cliff Floyd	.05
53	Brent Gates	.05
54	Rickey Henderson	.65
55	John Olerud	.05
56	Gregg Jefferies	.05
57	Cecil Fielder	.05
58	Paul Molitor	.65
59	Bret Boone	.05
60	Greg Vaughn	.05
61	Wally Joyner	.05
62	Jeffrey Hammonds	.05
63	James Mouton	.05
64	Omar Vizquel	.05
65	Wade Boggs	.75
66	Terry Steinbach	.05
67	Wil Cordero	.05
68	Joey Hamilton	.05
69	Rico Brogna	.05
70	Darren Daulton	.05
71	Chuck Knoblauch	.05
72	Bob Hamelin	.05
73	Carl Everett	.05
74	Joe Carter	.05
75	Dave Winfield	.65
76	Bobby Bonilla	.05
77	Paul O'Neill	.05
78	Javier Lopez	.05
79	Cal Ripken Jr.	2.00
80	David Cone	.05
81	Bernard Gilkey	.05
82	Ivan Rodriguez	.60
83	Dean Palmer	.05
84	Jason Bere	.05
85	Will Clark	.05
86	Scott Cooper	.05
87	Royce Clayton	.05
88	Mike Piazza	1.00
89	Ryan Klesko	.05
90	Juan Gonzalez	.35
91	Travis Fryman	.05
92	Frank Thomas	.65
93	Eduardo Perez	.05
94	Mo Vaughn	.05
95	Jay Bell	.05
96	Jeff Bagwell	.65
97	Randy Johnson	.05
98	Jimmy Key	.05
99	Dennis Eckersley	.60
100	Carlos Baerga	.05
101	Eddie Murray	.65
102	Mike Mussina	.30
103	Brian Anderson	.05
104	Jeff Cirillo	.05

105	Dante Bichette	.05
106	Bret Saberhagen	.05
107	Jeff Kent	.05
108	Ruben Sierra	.05
109	Kirk Gibson	.05
110	Reggie Sanders	.05
111	Dave Justice	.05
112	Benji Gil	.05
113	Vaughn Eshelman	.05
114	Carlos Perez RC	.05
115	Chipper Jones	.75
116	Shane Andrews	.05
117	Orlando Miller	.05
118	Scott Ruffcorn	.05
119	Jose Oliva	.05
120	Joe Vitiello	.05
121	Jon Nunnally	.05
122	Garret Anderson	.05
123	Curtis Goodwin	.05
124	Mark Grudzielanek RC	.25
125	Alex Gonzalez	.05
126	David Bell	.05
127	Dustin Hermanson	.05
128	Dave Nilsson	.05
129	Wilson Heredia	.05
130	Charles Johnson	.05
131	Frank Rodriguez	.05
132	Alex Ochoa	.05
133	Alex Rodriguez	1.50
134	Bobby Higginson RC	.25
135	Edgardo Alfonzo	.05
136	Armando Benitez	.05
137	Rich Aude	.05
138	Tim Naehring	.05
139	Joe Randa	.05
140	Quilvio Veras	.05
141	Hideo Nomo RC	1.00
142	Ray Holbert	.05
143	Michael Tucker	.05
144	Chad Mottola	.05
145	John Valentin	.05
146	James Baldwin	.05
147	Esteban Loaiza	.05
148	Marty Cordova	.05
149	Juan Acevedo RC	.05
150	Tim Unroe RC	.05
151	Brad Clontz	.05
152	Steve Rodriguez	.05
153	Rudy Pemberton	.05
154	Ozzie Timmons	.05
155	Ricky Otero	.05
156	Allen Battle	.05
157	Joe Roselli	.05
158	Roberto Petagine	.05
159	Todd Hollandsworth	.05
160	Shannon Penn	.05
161	Antonio Osuna	.05
162	Russ Davis	.05
163	Jason Giambi	.40
164	Terry Bradshaw	.05
165	Ray Durham	.05
166	Todd Steverson	.05
167	Tim Belk	.05
168	Andy Pettitte	.25
169	Roger Cedeno	.05
170	Jose Parra	.05
171	Scott Sullivan	.05
172	LaTroy Hawkins	.05
173	Jeff McCurry	.05
174	Ken Griffey Jr.	.50
175	Frank Thomas	.30
176	Cal Ripken Jr.	1.00
177	Jeff Bagwell	.30
178	Mike Piazza	.50
179	Barry Bonds	1.00
180	Matt Williams	.05
181	Don Mattingly	.45
182	Will Clark	.05
183	Tony Gwynn	.40
184	Kirby Puckett	.40
185	Jose Canseco	.25
186	Paul Molitor	.30
187	Albert Belle	.05
188	Joe Carter	.05
189	Greg Maddux	.40
190	Roger Clemens	.45
191	David Cone	.05
192	Mike Mussina	.15
193	Randy Johnson	.30
194	Frank Thomas Checklist	.30
195	Ken Griffey Jr. Checklist	.50
196	Cal Ripken Jr. Checklist	.75
197	Jeff Bagwell Checklist	.30
198	Mike Piazza Checklist	.50
199	Barry Bonds Checklist	.75
200	Mo Vaughn, Matt Williams Checklist	.05

Nth Degree

	NM/M
Complete Set (200):	50.00
Common Player:	.25

	NM/M
Stars:	2X

(See 1995 Summit for checklist, base card values.)

Big Bang

		NM/M
	Complete Set (20):	45.00
	Common Player:	1.00
1	Ken Griffey Jr.	6.00
2	Frank Thomas	3.25
3	Cal Ripken Jr.	8.00
4	Jeff Bagwell	3.25
5	Mike Piazza	6.00
6	Barry Bonds	8.00
7	Matt Williams	1.00
8	Don Mattingly	4.50
9	Will Clark	1.00
10	Tony Gwynn	4.00
11	Kirby Puckett	4.00
12	Jose Canseco	2.00
13	Paul Molitor	3.25
14	Albert Belle	1.00
15	Joe Carter	1.00
16	Rafael Palmeiro	3.00
17	Fred McGriff	1.00
18	Dave Justice	1.00
19	Tim Salmon	1.00
20	Mo Vaughn	1.00

New Age

		NM/M
	Complete Set (15):	10.00
	Common Player:	.25
1	Cliff Floyd	.25
2	Manny Ramirez	2.00
3	Raul Mondesi	.25
4	Alex Rodriguez	5.00
5	Billy Ashley	.25
6	Alex Gonzalez	.25
7	Michael Tucker	.25
8	Charles Johnson	.25
9	Carlos Delgado	1.00
10	Benji Gil	.25
11	Chipper Jones	3.00
12	Todd Hollandsworth	.25
13	Frank Rodriguez	.25
14	Shawn Green	.60
15	Ray Durham	.25

21 Club

		NM/M
	Complete Set (9):	4.00
	Common Player:	.50
1	Bob Abreu	.65
2	Pokey Reese	.50

3	Edgardo Alfonzo	.50
4	Jim Pittsley	.50
5	Ruben Rivera	.50
6	Chan Ho Park	.50
7	Julian Tavarez	.50
8	Ismael Valdes	.50
9	Dmitri Young	.50

1996 Summit

MARK McGWIRE

		NM/M
Complete Set (200):		10.00
Common Player:		.05
Pack (7):		1.25
Wax Box (18):		15.00
1	Mike Piazza	1.25
2	Matt Williams	.05
3	Tino Martinez	.05
4	Reggie Sanders	.05
5	Ray Durham	.05
6	Brad Radke	.05
7	Jeff Bagwell	.65
8	Ron Gant	.05
9	Lance Johnson	.05
10	Kevin Seitzer	.05
11	Dante Bichette	.05
12	Ivan Rodriguez	.60
13	Jim Abbott	.05
14	Greg Colbrunn	.05
15	Rondell White	.05
16	Shawn Green	.40
17	Gregg Jefferies	.05
18	Omar Vizquel	.05
19	Cal Ripken Jr.	2.00
20	Mark McGwire	1.50
21	Wally Joyner	.05
22	Chili Davis	.05
23	Jose Canseco	.40
24	Royce Clayton	.05
25	Jay Bell	.05
26	Travis Fryman	.05
27	Jeff King	.05
28	Todd Hundley	.05
29	Joe Vitiello	.05
30	Russ Davis	.05
31	Mo Vaughn	.05
32	Raul Mondesi	.05
33	Ray Lankford	.05
34	Mike Stanley	.05
35	B.J. Surhoff	.05
36	Greg Vaughn	.05
37	Todd Stottlemyre	.05
38	Carlos Delgado	.50
39	Kenny Lofton	.05
40	Hideo Nomo	.35
41	Sterling Hitchcock	.05
42	Pete Schourek	.05
43	Edgardo Alfonzo	.05
44	Ken Hill	.05
45	Ken Caminiti	.05
46	Bobby Higginson	.05
47	Michael Tucker	.05
48	David Cone	.05
49	Cecil Fielder	.05
50	Brian Hunter	.05
51	Charles Johnson	.05
52	Bobby Bonilla	.05
53	Eddie Murray	.65
54	Kenny Rogers	.05
55	Jim Edmonds	.05
56	Trevor Hoffman	.05
57	Kevin Mitchell	.05
58	Ruben Sierra	.05
59	Benji Gil	.05
60	Juan Gonzalez	.35
61	Larry Walker	.05
62	Jack McDowell	.05
63	Shawon Dunston	.05
64	Andy Benes	.05
65	Jay Buhner	.05
66	Rickey Henderson	.65
67	Alex Gonzalez	.05
68	Mike Kelly	.05
69	Fred McGriff	.05
70	Ryne Sandberg	.75
71	Ernie Young	.05
72	Kevin Appier	.05
73	Moises Alou	.05
74	John Jaha	.05
75	J.T. Snow	.05
76	Jim Thome	.60
77	Kirby Puckett	.75
78	Hal Morris	.05
79	Robin Ventura	.05
80	Ben McDonald	.05
81	Tim Salmon	.05
82	Albert Belle	.05
83	Marquis Grissom	.05
84	Alex Rodriguez	1.50
85	Manny Ramirez	.65
86	Ken Griffey Jr.	1.25
87	Sammy Sosa	.75
88	Frank Thomas	.65
89	Lee Smith	.05
90	Marty Cordova	.05
91	Greg Maddux	.75
92	Lenny Dykstra	.05
93	Butch Huskey	.05
94	Garret Anderson	.05
95	Mike Bordick	.05
96	Dave Justice	.05
97	Chad Curtis	.05
98	Carlos Baerga	.05
99	Jason Isringhausen	.05
100	Gary Sheffield	.35
101	Roger Clemens	1.00
102	Ozzie Smith	.75
103	Ramon Martinez	.05
104	Paul O'Neill	.05
105	Will Clark	.05
106	Tom Glavine	.35
107	Barry Bonds	2.00
108	Barry Larkin	.05
109	Derek Bell	.05
110	Randy Johnson	.65
111	Jeff Conine	.05
112	John Mabry	.05
113	Julian Tavarez	.05
114	Gary DiSarcina	.05
115	Andres Galarraga	.05
116	Marc Newfield	.05
117	Frank Rodriguez	.05
118	Brady Anderson	.05
119	Mike Mussina	.30
120	Orlando Merced	.05
121	Melvin Nieves	.05
122	Brian Jordan	.05
123	Rafael Palmeiro	.60
124	Johnny Damon	.35
125	Wil Cordero	.05
126	Chipper Jones	.75
127	Eric Karros	.05
128	Darren Daulton	.05
129	Vinny Castilla	.05
130	Joe Carter	.05
131	Bernie Williams	.05
132	Bernard Gilkey	.05
133	Bret Boone	.05
134	Tony Gwynn	.75
135	Dave Nilsson	.05
136	Ryan Klesko	.05
137	Paul Molitor	.65
138	John Olerud	.05
139	Craig Biggio	.05
140	John Valentin	.05
141	Chuck Knoblauch	.05
142	Edgar Martinez	.05
143	Rico Brogna	.05
144	Dean Palmer	.05
145	Mark Grace	.05
146	Roberto Alomar	.20
147	Alex Fernandez	.05
148	Andre Dawson	.25
149	Wade Boggs	.75
150	Mark Lewis	.05
151	Gary Gaetti	.05
152	Paul Wilson, Roger Clemens	.45
153	Rey Ordonez, Ozzie Smith	.35
154	Derek Jeter, Cal Ripken Jr.	1.00
155	Alan Benes, Andy Benes	.05
156	Jason Kendall, Mike Piazza	.75
157	Ryan Klesko, Frank Thomas	.30
158	Johnny Damon, Ken Griffey Jr.	.65
159	Karim Garcia, Sammy Sosa	.40
160	Raul Mondesi, Tim Salmon	.05
161	Chipper Jones, Matt Williams	.40
162	Rey Ordonez	.05
163	Bob Wolcott	.05
164	Brooks Kieschnick	.05
165	Steve Gibralter	.05
166	Bob Abreu	.05
167	Gregg Zaun	.05
168	Tavo Alvarez	.05
169	Sal Fasano	.05
170	George Arias	.05
171	Derek Jeter	2.00
172	Livan Hernandez RC	.25
173	Alan Benes	.05
174	George Williams	.05
175	John Wasdin	.05
176	Chan Ho Park	.05
177	Paul Wilson	.05
178	Jeff Suppan	.05
179	Quinton McCracken	.05
180	Wilton Guerrero RC	.05
181	Eric Owens	.05
182	Felipe Crespo	.05
183	LaTroy Hawkins	.05
184	Jason Schmidt	.05
185	Terrell Wade	.05
186	Mike Grace RC	.05
187	Chris Snopek	.05
188	Jason Kendall	.05
189	Todd Hollandsworth	.05
190	Jim Pittsley	.05
191	Jermaine Dye	.05
192	Mike Busby RC	.05
193	Richard Hidalgo	.05
194	Tyler Houston	.05
195	Jimmy Haynes	.05
196	Karim Garcia	.05
197	Ken Griffey Jr. (Checklist)	.50
198	Frank Thomas (Checklist)	.30
199	Greg Maddux (Checklist)	.40
200	Cal Ripken Jr. (Checklist)	1.00

Above & Beyond

	NM/M
Complete Set (200):	50.00
Common Player:	.25
Stars:	3X

(See 1996 Summit for checklist, base card values.)

Artist's Proof

MARK McGWIRE

	NM/M
Complete Set (200):	100.00
Common Player:	1.00
Stars:	8X

(See 1996 Summit for checklist, base cardvalues.)

1996 Summit Foil

	NM/M
Complete Set (200):	30.00
Common Player:	.25
Stars:	3X

(See 1996 Summit for checklist and base card values.)

Ballparks

		NM/M
Complete Set (18):		45.00
Common Player:		1.00
1	Cal Ripken Jr.	7.50

2	Albert Belle	1.00
3	Dante Bichette	1.00
4	Mo Vaughn	1.00
5	Ken Griffey Jr.	6.00
6	Derek Jeter	7.50
7	Juan Gonzalez	1.50
8	Greg Maddux	4.00
9	Frank Thomas	3.00
10	Ryne Sandberg	4.00
11	Mike Piazza	6.00
12	Johnny Damon	1.50
13	Barry Bonds	7.50
14	Jeff Bagwell	3.00
15	Paul Wilson	1.00
16	Tim Salmon	1.00
17	Kirby Puckett	4.00
18	Tony Gwynn	4.00

Big Bang

Mike Piazza

		NM/M
Complete Set (16):		60.00
Common Player:		1.50
1	Frank Thomas	4.00
2	Ken Griffey Jr.	7.50
3	Albert Belle	1.50
4	Mo Vaughn	1.50
5	Barry Bonds	12.00
6	Cal Ripken Jr.	12.00
7	Jeff Bagwell	4.00
8	Mike Piazza	7.50
9	Ryan Klesko	1.50
10	Manny Ramirez	4.00
11	Tim Salmon	1.50
12	Dante Bichette	1.50
13	Sammy Sosa	6.00
14	Raul Mondesi	1.50
15	Chipper Jones	6.00
16	Garret Anderson	1.50

Hitters, Inc.

		NM/M
Complete Set (16):		40.00
Common Player:		1.25
1	Tony Gwynn	4.00
2	Mo Vaughn	1.25
3	Tim Salmon	1.25
4	Ken Griffey Jr.	5.00
5	Sammy Sosa	4.00
6	Frank Thomas	3.00
7	Wade Boggs	4.00
8	Albert Belle	1.25
9	Cal Ripken Jr.	8.00
10	Manny Ramirez	3.00
11	Ryan Klesko	1.25
11p	Ryan Klesko (Overprinted "SAMPLE.")	1.25
12	Dante Bichette	1.25
13	Mike Piazza	5.00
14	Chipper Jones	4.00
15	Ryne Sandberg	4.00
16	Matt Williams	1.25

Positions

	NM/M
Complete Set (9):	100.00

Common Card: 6.00
1 Jeff Bagwell, Mo Vaughn, Frank Thomas (First Base) 10.00
2 Roberto Alomar, Craig Biggio, Chuck Knoblauch (Second Base) 6.00
3 Matt Williams, Jim Thome, Chipper Jones (Third Base) 12.50
4 Barry Larkin, Cal Ripken Jr., Alex Rodriguez (Short Stop) 20.00
5 Mike Piazza, Ivan Rodriguez, Charles Johnson (Catcher) 15.00
6 Hideo Nomo, Greg Maddux, Randy Johnson/Picher 12.50
7 Barry Bonds, Albert Belle, Ryan Klesko (Left Field) 20.00
8 Johnny Damon, Jim Edmonds, Ken Griffey Jr. (Center Field) 15.00
9 Manny Ramirez, Gary Sheffield, Sammy Sosa (Right Field) 12.50

T

1981 Topps

NM/M
Complete Set (726): 37.00
Common Player: .08
Wax Pack (15):
Wax Box (36):
Cello Pack (28):
Cello Box (24):
Rack Pack (48):
Rack Box (24):
Vending Box (500):
1 George Brett, Bill Buckner Btg Ldrs. .60
2 Reggie Jackson, Ben Oglivie, Mike Schmidt Home Run Ldrs. .60
3 Cecil Cooper, Mike Schmidt RBI Ldrs. .20
4 Rickey Henderson, Ron LeFlore Stolen Base Ldrs. .40
5 Steve Carlton, Steve Stone Victory Ldrs. .11
6 Len Barker, Steve Carlton Strikeout Ldrs. .11
7 Rudy May, Don Sutton ERA Ldrs. .08
8 Rollie Fingers, Tom Hume, Dan Quisenberry Leading Firemen .08
9 Pete LaCock (DP) .08
10 Mike Flanagan .08
11 Jim Wohlford (DP) .08
12 Mark Clear .08
13 Joe Charboneau RC .40
14 John Tudor RC .15
15 Larry Parrish .08
16 Ron Davis .08
17 Cliff Johnson .08
18 Glenn Adams .08

19 Jim Clancy .08
20 Jeff Burroughs .08
21 Ron Oester .08
22 Danny Darwin .08
23 Alex Trevino .08
24 Don Stanhouse .08
25 Sixto Lezcano .08
26 U.L. Washington .08
27 Champ Summers (DP) .08
28 Enrique Romo .08
29 Gene Tenace .08
30 Jack Clark .08
31 Checklist 1-121 (DP) .08
32 Ken Oberkfell .08
33 Rick Honeycutt .08
34 Aurelio Rodriguez .08
35 Mitchell Page .08
36 Ed Farmer .08
37 Gary Roenicke .08
38 Win Remmerswaal .08
39 Tom Veryzer .08
40 Tug McGraw .08
41 Bob Babcock, John Butcher, Jerry Don Gleaton Rangers Future Stars .08
42 Jerry White (DP) .08
43 Jose Morales .08
44 Larry McWilliams .08
45 Enos Cabell .08
46 Rick Bosetti .08
47 Ken Brett .08
48 Dave Skaggs .08
49 Bob Shirley .08
50 Dave Lopes .08
51 Bill Robinson (DP) .08
52 Hector Cruz .08
53 Kevin Saucier .08
54 Ivan DeJesus .08
55 Mike Norris .08
56 Buck Martinez .08
57 Dave Roberts .08
58 Joel Youngblood .08
59 Dan Petry .08
60 Willie Randolph .08
61 Butch Wynegar .08
62 Joe Pettini .08
63 Steve Renko (DP) .08
64 Brian Asselstine .08
65 Scott McGregor .08
66 Manny Castillo, Tim Ireland, Mike Jones Royals Future Stars .08
67 Ken Kravec .08
68 Matt Alexander (DP) .08
69 Ed Halicki .08
70 Al Oliver (DP) .08
71 Hal Dues .08
72 Barry Evans (DP) .08
73 Doug Bair .08
74 Mike Hargrove .08
75 Reggie Smith .08
76 Mario Mendoza .08
77 Mike Barlow .08
78 Steve Dillard .08
79 Bruce Robbins .08
80 Rusty Staub .11
81 Dave Stapleton .08
82 Danny Heep, Alan Knicely, Bobby Sprowl Astros Future Stars (DP) .08
83 Mike Proly .08
84 Johnnie LeMaster .08
85 Mike Caldwell .08
86 Wayne Gross .08
87 Rick Camp .08
88 Joe Lefebvre .08
89 Darrell Jackson .08
90 Bake McBride .08
91 Tim Stoddard (DP) .08
92 Mike Easler .08
93 Ed Glynn (DP) .08
94 Harry Spilman (DP) .08
95 Jim Sundberg .08
96 Dave Beard, Ernie Camacho, Pat Dempsey A's Future Stars .08
97 Chris Speier .08
98 Clint Hurdle .08
99 Eric Wilkins .08
100 Rod Carew 1.50
101 Benny Ayala .08
102 Dave Tobik .08
103 Jerry Martin .08
104 Terry Forster .08
105 Jose Cruz .08
106 Don Money .08
107 Rich Wortham .08
108 Bruce Benedict .08
109 Mike Scott .08
110 Carl Yastrzemski 1.50
111 Greg Minton .08
112 Rusty Kuntz, Fran Mullins, Leo Sutherland White Sox Future Stars .08
113 Mike Phillips .08
114 Tom Underwood .08
115 Roy Smalley .08
116 Joe Simpson .08
117 Pete Falcone .08
118 Kurt Bevacqua .08
119 Tippy Martinez .08
120 Larry Bowa .08
121 Larry Harlow .08
122 John Denny .08
123 Al Cowens .08
124 Jerry Garvin .08

125 Andre Dawson 1.25
126 Charlie Leibrandt RC .30
127 Rudy Law .08
128 Gary Allenson (DP) .08
129 Art Howe .08
130 Larry Gura .08
131 Keith Moreland RC .15
132 Tommy Boggs .08
133 Jeff Cox .08
134 Steve Mura .08
135 Gorman Thomas .08
136 Doug Capilla .08
137 Hosken Powell .08
138 Rich Dotson RC (DP) .15
139 Oscar Gamble .08
140 Bob Forsch .08
141 Miguel Dilone .08
142 Jackson Todd .08
143 Dan Meyer .08
144 Allen Ripley .08
145 Mickey Rivers .08
146 Bobby Castillo .08
147 Dale Berra .08
148 Randy Niemann .08
149 Joe Nolan .08
150 Mark Fidrych .11
151 Claudell Washington (DP) .08
152 John Urrea .08
153 Tom Poquette .08
154 Rick Langford .08
155 Chris Chambliss .08
156 Bob McClure .08
157 John Wathan .08
158 Fergie Jenkins .70
159 Brian Doyle .08
160 Garry Maddox .08
161 Dan Graham .08
162 Doug Corbett .08
163 Billy Almon .08
164 Lamarr Hoyt (LaMarr) RC .11
165 Tony Scott .08
166 Floyd Bannister .08
167 Terry Whitfield .08
168 Don Robinson (DP) .08
169 John Mayberry .08
170 Ross Grimsley .08
171 Gene Richards .08
172 Gary Woods .08
173 Bump Wills .08
174 Doug Rau .08
175 Dave Collins .08
176 Mike Krukow .08
177 Rick Peters .08
178 Jim Essian (DP) .08
179 Rudy May .08
180 Pete Rose 3.75
181 Elias Sosa .08
182 Bob Grich .08
183 Dick Davis (DP) .08
184 Jim Dwyer .08
185 Dennis Leonard .08
186 Wayne Nordhagen .08
187 Mike Parrott .08
188 Doug DeCinces .08
189 Craig Swan .08
190 Cesar Cedeno .08
191 Rick Sutcliffe .08
192 Terry Harper, Ed Miller, Rafael Ramirez RC Braves Future Stars .08
193 Pete Vuckovich .08
194 Rod Scurry RC .08
195 Rich Murray .08
196 Duffy Dyer .08
197 Jim Kern .08
198 Jerry Dybzinski .08
199 Chuck Rainey .08
200 George Foster .08
201 Johnny Bench .35
202 Steve Carlton .20
203 Bill Gullickson .08
204 Ron LeFlore, Rodney Scott .08
205 Pete Rose 1.25
206 Mike Schmidt .70
207 Ozzie Smith .70
208 Willie Wilson .08
209 Dickie Thon (DP) .08
210 Jim Palmer 1.25
211 Derrel Thomas .08
212 Steve Nicosia .08
213 Al Holland RC .08
214 Ralph Botting, Jim Dorsey, John Harris Angels Future Stars .08
215 Larry Hisle .08
216 John Henry Johnson .08
217 Rich Hebner .08
218 Paul Splittorff .08
219 Ken Landreaux .08
220 Tom Seaver 1.50
221 Bob Davis .08
222 Jorge Orta .08
223 Roy Lee Jackson .08
224 Pat Zachry .08
225 Ruppert Jones .08
226 Manny Sanguillen (DP) .08
227 Fred Martinez .08
228 Tom Paciorek .08
229 Rollie Fingers .70
230 George Hendrick .08
231 Joe Beckwith .08
232 Mickey Klutts .08
233 Skip Lockwood .08
234 Lou Whitaker .08
235 Scott Sanderson .08

236 Mike Ivie .08
237 Charlie Moore .08
238 Willie Hernandez .08
239 Rick Miller (DP) .08
240 Nolan Ryan 3.75
241 Checklist 122-242 (DP) .08
242 Chet Lemon .08
243 Sal Butera .08
244 Tito Landrum, Al Olmsted, Andy Rincon Cardinals Future Stars .08
245 Ed Figueroa .08
246 Ed Ott (DP) .08
247 Glenn Hubbard (DP) .08
248 Joey McLaughlin .08
249 Larry Cox .08
250 Ron Guidry .11
251 Tom Brookens .08
252 Victor Cruz .08
253 Dave Bergman .08
254 Ozzie Smith 2.25
255 Mark Littell .08
256 Bombo Rivera .08
257 Rennie Stennett .08
258 Joe Price RC .08
259 Juan Berenguer, Hubie Brooks, Mookie Wilson RC Mets Future Stars .60
260 Ron Cey .08
261 Rickey Henderson 3.50
262 Sammy Stewart .08
263 Brian Downing .08
264 Jim Norris .08
265 John Candelaria .08
266 Tom Herr .08
267 Stan Bahnsen .08
268 Jerry Royster .08
269 Ken Forsch .08
270 Greg Luzinski .08
271 Bill Castro .08
272 Bruce Kimm .08
273 Stan Papi .08
274 Craig Chamberlain .08
275 Dwight Evans .08
276 Dan Spillner .08
277 Alfredo Griffin .08
278 Rick Sofield .08
279 Bob Knepper .08
280 Ken Griffey .08
281 Fred Stanley .08
282 Rick Anderson, Greg Biercevicz, Rodney Craig Mariners Future Stars .08
283 Billy Sample .08
284 Brian Kingman .08
285 Jerry Turner .08
286 Dave Frost .08
287 Lenn Sakata .08
288 Bob Clark .08
289 Mickey Hatcher .08
290 Bob Boone (DP) .08
291 Aurelio Lopez .08
292 Mike Squires .08
293 Charlie Lea RC .11
294 Mike Tyson (DP) .08
295 Hal McRae .08
296 Bill Nahorodny (DP) .08
297 Bob Bailor .08
298 Buddy Solomon .08
299 Elliott Maddox .08
300 Paul Molitor 1.50
301 Matt Keough .08
302 Jack Perconte, Mike Scioscia, Fernando Valenzuela RC Dodgers Future Stars 1.50
303 Johnny Oates .08
304 John Castino .08
305 Ken Clay .08
306 Juan Beniquez (DP) .08
307 Gene Garber .08
308 Rick Manning .08
309 Luis Salazar RC .08
310 Vida Blue (DP) .08
311 Freddie Patek .08
312 Rick Rhoden .08
313 Luis Pujols .08
314 Rich Dauer .08
315 Kirk Gibson RC 3.75
316 Craig Minetto .08
317 Lonnie Smith .08
318 Steve Yeager .08
319 Rowland Office .08
320 Tom Burgmeier .08
321 Leon Durham RC .11
322 Neil Allen .08
323 Jim Morrison (DP) .08
324 Mike Willis .08
325 Ray Knight .08
326 Biff Pocoroba .08
327 Moose Haas .08
328 Dave Engle, Greg Johnston, Gary Ward Twins Future Stars .11
329 Joaquin Andujar .08
330 Frank White .08
331 Dennis Lamp .08
332 Lee Lacy (DP) .08
333 Sid Monge .08
334 Dane Iorg .08
335 Rick Cerone .08
336 Eddie Whitson .08
337 Lynn Jones .08
338 Checklist 243-363 .08
339 John Ellis .08
340 Bruce Kison .08
341 Dwayne Murphy .08

342 Eric Rasmussen (DP) .08
343 Frank Taveras .08
344 Byron McLaughlin .08
345 Warren Cromartie .08
346 Larry Christenson (DP) .08
347 Harold Baines RC 3.00
348 Bob Sykes .08
349 Glenn Hoffman .08
350 J.R. Richard .08
351 Otto Velez .08
352 Dick Tidrow (DP) .08
353 Terry Kennedy .08
354 Mario Soto .08
355 Bob Horner .08
356 George Stablein, Craig Stimac, Tom Tellmann, Padres Future Stars .08
357 Jim Slaton .08
358 Mark Wagner .08
359 Tom Hausman .08
360 Willie Wilson .08
361 Joe Strain .08
362 Bo Diaz .08
363 Geoff Zahn .08
364 Mike Davis RC .08
365 Graig Nettles (DP) .11
366 Mike Ramsey .08
367 Denny Martinez .08
368 Leon Roberts .08
369 Frank Tanana .08
370 Dave Winfield 1.50
371 Charlie Hough .08
372 Jay Johnstone .08
373 Pat Underwood .08
374 Tom Hutton .08
375 Dave Concepcion .08
376 Ron Reed .08
377 Jerry Morales .08
378 Dave Rader .08
379 Lary Sorensen .08
380 Willie Stargell 1.50
381 Carlos Lezcano, Steve Macko, Randy Martz, Cubs Future Stars .08
382 Paul Mirabella RC .08
383 Eric Soderholm (DP) .08
384 Mike Sadek .08
385 Joe Sambito .08
386 Dave Edwards .08
387 Phil Niekro .70
388 Andre Thornton .08
389 Marty Pattin .08
390 Cesar Geronimo .08
391 Dave Lemanczyk (DP) .08
392 Lance Parrish .08
393 Broderick Perkins .08
394 Woodie Fryman .08
395 Scot Thompson .08
396 Bill Campbell .08
397 Julio Cruz .08
398 Ross Baumgarten .08
399 Mike Boddicker, Mark Corey, Floyd Rayford, Orioles Future Stars .15
400 Reggie Jackson 2.25
401 A.L. Championships (Royals Sweep Yankees) .40
402 N.L. Championships (Phillies Squeak Past Astros) .20
403 World Series (Phillies Beat Royals In 6) .08
404 World Series Summary (Phillies Win First World Series) .20
405 Nino Espinosa .08
406 Dickie Noles .08
407 Ernie Whitt .08
408 Fernando Arroyo .08
409 Larry Herndon .08
410 Bert Campaneris .08
411 Terry Puhl .08
412 Britt Burns RC .08
413 Tony Bernazard .08
414 John Pacella (DP) .08
415 Ben Oglivie .08
416 Gary Alexander .08
417 Dan Schatzeder .08
418 Bobby Brown .08
419 Tom Hume .08
420 Keith Hernandez .08
421 Bob Stanley .08
422 Dan Ford .08
423 Shane Rawley .08
424 Tim Lollar, Bruce Robinson, Dennis Werth, Yankees Future Stars .08
425 Al Bumbry .08
426 Warren Brusstar .08
427 John D'Acquisto .08
428 John Stearns .08
429 Mick Kelleher .08
430 Jim Bibby .08
431 Dave Roberts .08
432 Len Barker .08
433 Rance Mulliniks .08
434 Roger Erickson .08
435 Jim Spencer .08
436 Gary Lucas .08
437 Mike Heath (DP) .08
438 Jim Montefusco .08
439 Denny Walling .08
440 Jerry Reuss .08
441 Ken Reitz .08
442 Ron Pruitt .08
443 Jim Beattie (DP) .08
444 Garth Iorg .08

445 Ellis Valentine .08
446 Checklist 364-484 .08
447 Junior Kennedy (DP) .08
448 Tim Corcoran .08
449 Paul Mitchell .08
450 Dave Kingman (DP) .08
451 Chris Bando, Tom Brennan, Sandy Wihtol, Indians Future Stars .08
452 Renie Martin .08
453 Rob Wilfong (DP) .08
454 Andy Hassler .08
455 Rick Burleson .08
456 Jeff Reardon RC 1.25
457 Mike Lum .08
458 Randy Jones .08
459 Greg Gross .08
460 Rich Gossage .08
461 Dave McKay .08
462 Jack Brohamer .08
463 Milt May .08
464 Adrian Devine .08
465 Bill Russell .08
466 Bob Molinaro .08
467 Dave Stieb .08
468 Johnny Wockenfuss .08
469 Jeff Leonard .08
470 Manny Trillo .08
471 Mike Vail .08
472 Dyar Miller (DP) .08
473 Jose Cardenal .08
474 Mike LaCoss .08
475 Buddy Bell .08
476 Jerry Koosman .08
477 Luis Gomez .08
478 Juan Eichelberger .08
479 Bobby Pate, Tim Raines, Roberto Ramos RC, Expos Future Stars 2.25
480 Carlton Fisk 1.50
481 Bob Lacey (DP) .08
482 Jim Gantner .08
483 Mike Griffin .08
484 Max Venable (DP) .08
485 Garry Templeton .08
486 Marc Hill .08
487 Dewey Robinson .08
488 Damaso Garcia RC .08
489 John Littlefield (Photo actually Mark Riggins.) .08
490 Eddie Murray 1.50
491 Gordy Pladson .08
492 Barry Foote .08
493 Dan Quisenberry .08
494 Bob Walk RC .15
495 Dusty Baker .11
496 Paul Dade .08
497 Fred Norman .08
498 Pat Putnam .08
499 Frank Pastore .08
500 Jim Rice .20
501 Tim Foli (DP) .08
502 Chris Bourjos, Al Hargesheimer, Mike Rowland, Giants Future Stars .08
503 Steve McCatty .08
504 Dale Murphy .60
505 Jason Thompson .08
506 Phil Huffman .08
507 Jamie Quirk .08
508 Rob Dressler .08
509 Pete Mackanin .08
510 Lee Mazzilli .08
511 Wayne Garland .08
512 Gary Thomasson .08
513 Frank LaCorte .08
514 George Riley .08
515 Robin Yount 1.50
516 Doug Bird .08
517 Richie Zisk .08
518 Grant Jackson .08
519 John Tamargo (DP) .08
520 Steve Stone .08
521 Sam Mejias .08
522 Mike Colbern .08
523 John Fulgham .08
524 Willie Aikens .08
525 Mike Torrez .08
526 Marty Bystrom, Jay Loviglio, Jim Wright, Phillies Future Stars .08
527 Danny Goodwin .08
528 Gary Matthews .08
529 Dave LaRoche .08
530 Steve Garvey .60
531 John Curtis .08
532 Bill Stein .08
533 Jesus Figueroa .08
534 Dave Smith RC .08
535 Omar Moreno .08
536 Bob Owchinko (DP) .08
537 Ron Hodges .08
538 Tom Griffin .08
539 Rodney Scott .08
540 Mike Schmidt 2.25
541 Steve Swisher .08
542 Larry Bradford (DP) .08
543 Terry Crowley .08
544 Rich Gale .08
545 Johnny Grubb .08
546 Paul Moskau .08
547 Mario Guerrero .08
548 Dave Goltz .08
549 Jerry Remy .08
550 Tommy John .15

551 Vance Law, Tony Pena, Pascual Perez RC, Pirates Future Stars .60
552 Steve Trout .08
553 Tim Blackwell .08
554 Bert Blyleven .08
555 Cecil Cooper .08
556 Jerry Mumphrey .08
557 Chris Knapp .08
558 Barry Bonnell .08
559 Willie Montanez .08
560 Joe Morgan 1.50
561 Dennis Littlejohn .08
562 Checklist 485-605 .08
563 Jim Kaat .11
564 Ron Hassey (DP) .08
565 Burt Hooton .08
566 Del Unser .08
567 Mark Bomback .08
568 Dave Revering .08
569 Al Williams (DP) .08
570 Ken Singleton .08
571 Todd Cruz .08
572 Jack Morris .08
573 Phil Garner .08
574 Bill Caudill .08
575 Tony Perez .70
576 Reggie Cleveland .08
577 Luis Leal, Brian Milner, Ken Schrom RC, Blue Jays Future Stars .08
578 Bill Gullickson RC .15
579 Tim Flannery .08
580 Don Baylor .11
581 Roy Howell .08
582 Gaylord Perry .70
583 Larry Milbourne .08
584 Randy Lerch .08
585 Amos Otis .08
586 Silvio Martinez .08
587 Jeff Newman .08
588 Gary Lavelle .08
589 Lamar Johnson .08
590 Bruce Sutter .70
591 John Lowenstein .08
592 Steve Comer .08
593 Steve Kemp .08
594 Preston Hanna (DP) .08
595 Butch Hobson .08
596 Jerry Augustine .08
597 Rafael Landestoy .08
598 George Vukovich (DP) .08
599 Dennis Kinney .08
600 Johnny Bench 1.50
601 Don Aase .08
602 Bobby Murcer .08
603 John Verhoeven .08
604 Rob Picciolo .08
605 Don Sutton .70
606 Bruce Berenyi, Geoff Combe, Paul Householder, Reds Future Stars (DP) .08
607 Dave Palmer .08
608 Greg Pryor .08
609 Lynn McGlothen .08
610 Darrell Porter .08
611 Rick Matula (DP) .08
612 Duane Kuiper .08
613 Jim Anderson .08
614 Dave Rozema .08
615 Rick Dempsey .08
616 Rick Wise .08
617 Craig Reynolds .08
618 John Milner .08
619 Steve Henderson .08
620 Dennis Eckersley .70
621 Tom Donohue .08
622 Randy Moffitt .08
623 Sal Bando .08
624 Bob Welch .08
625 Bill Buckner .08
626 Dave Steffen, Jerry Ujdur, Roger Weaver, Tigers Future Stars .08
627 Luis Tiant .08
628 Vic Correll .08
629 Tony Armas .08
630 Steve Carlton 1.50
631 Ron Jackson .08
632 Alan Bannister .08
633 Bill Lee .08
634 Doug Flynn .08
635 Bobby Bonds .08
636 Al Hrabosky .08
637 Jerry Narron .08
638 Checklist 606 .08
639 Carney Lansford .08
640 Dave Parker .08
641 Mark Belanger .08
642 Vern Ruhle .08
643 Lloyd Moseby RC .15
644 Ramon Aviles (DP) .08
645 Rick Reuschel .08
646 Marvis Foley .08
647 Dick Drago .08
648 Darrell Evans .08
649 Manny Sarmiento .08
650 Bucky Dent .08
651 Pedro Guerrero .08
652 John Montague .08
653 Bill Fahey .08
654 Ray Burris .08
655 Dan Driessen .08
656 Jon Matlack .08
657 Mike Cubbage (DP) .08

658 Milt Wilcox .08
659 John Flinn, Ed Romero, Ned Yost, Brewers Future Stars .08
660 Gary Carter 1.50
661 Earl Weaver Orioles Team .20
662 Ralph Houk Red Sox Team .15
663 Jim Fregosi Angels Team .08
664 Tony LaRussa White Sox Team .20
665 Dave Garcia Indians Team .08
666 Sparky Anderson Tigers Team .20
667 Jim Frey Royals Team .08
668 Bob Rodgers Brewers Team .08
669 John Goryl Twins Team .08
670 Gene Michael Yankees Team .11
671 Billy Martin A's Team .20
672 Maury Wills Mariners Team .15
673 Don Zimmer Rangers Team .15
674 Bobby Mattick Blue Jays Team .08
675 Bobby Cox Braves Team .20
676 Joe Amalfitano Cubs Team .08
677 John McNamara Reds Team .08
678 Bill Virdon Astros Team .08
679 Tom Lasorda Dodgers Team .20
680 Dick Williams Expos Team .15
681 Joe Torre Mets Team .20
682 Dallas Green Phillies Team .11
683 Chuck Tanner Pirates Team .08
684 Whitey Herzog Cardinals Team .11
685 Frank Howard Padres Team .15
686 Dave Bristol Giants Team .08
687 Jeff Jones .08
688 Kiko Garcia .08
689 Bruce Hurst, Keith MacWhorter, Reid Nichols RC, Red Sox Future Stars .25
690 Bob Watson .08
691 Dick Ruthven .08
692 Lenny Randle .08
693 Steve Howe RC .15
694 Bud Harrelson (DP) .08
695 Kent Tekulve .08
696 Alan Ashby .08
697 Rick Waits .08
698 Mike Jorgensen .08
699 Glenn Abbott .08
700 George Brett 2.75
701 Joe Rudi .08
702 George Medich .08
703 Alvis Woods .08
704 Bill Travers (DP) .08
705 Ted Simmons .08
706 Dave Ford .08
707 Dave Cash .08
708 Doyle Alexander .08
709 Alan Trammell (DP) .08
710 Ron LeFlore (DP) .08
711 Joe Ferguson .08
712 Bill Bonham .08
713 Bill North .08
714 Pete Redfern .08
715 Bill Madlock .08
716 Glenn Borgmann .08
717 Jim Barr (DP) .08
718 Larry Biittner .08
719 Sparky Lyle .08
720 Fred Lynn .08
721 Toby Harrah .08
722 Joe Niekro .08
723 Bruce Bochte .08
724 Lou Piniella .11
725 Steve Rogers .08
726 Rick Monday .08

Traded

OUTFIELD
EXPOS
TIM RAINES
TOPPS
30

NM/M

Complete Set (132):
Common Player:
727 Danny Ainge 1.50
728 Doyle Alexander .11
729 Gary Alexander .11
730 Billy Almon .11
731 Joaquin Andujar .11
732 Bob Bailor .11
733 Juan Beniquez .11
734 Dave Bergman .11
735 Tony Bernazard .11

736 Larry Biittner .11
737 Doug Bird .11
738 Bert Blyleven .20
739 Mark Bomback .11
740 Bobby Bonds .11
741 Rick Bosetti .11
742 Hubie Brooks .11
743 Rick Burleson .11
744 Ray Burris .11
745 Jeff Burroughs .11
746 Enos Cabell .11
747 Ken Clay .11
748 Mark Clear .11
749 Larry Cox .11
750 Hector Cruz .11
751 Victor Cruz .11
752 Mike Cubbage .11
753 Dick Davis .11
754 Brian Doyle .11
755 Dick Drago .11
756 Leon Durham .11
757 Jim Dwyer .11
758 Dave Edwards .11
759 Jim Essian .11
760 Bill Fahey .11
761 Rollie Fingers .70
762 Carlton Fisk 1.50
763 Barry Foote .11
764 Ken Forsch .11
765 Kiko Garcia .11
766 Cesar Geronimo .11
767 Gary Gray .11
768 Mickey Hatcher .11
769 Steve Henderson .11
770 Marc Hill .11
771 Butch Hobson .11
772 Rick Honeycutt .11
773 Roy Howell .11
774 Mike Ivie .11
775 Roy Lee Jackson .11
776 Cliff Johnson .11
777 Randy Jones .11
778 Ruppert Jones .11
779 Mick Kelleher .11
780 Terry Kennedy .11
781 Dave Kingman .11
782 Bob Knepper .11
783 Ken Kravec .11
784 Bob Lacey .11
785 Dennis Lamp .11
786 Rafael Landestoy .11
787 Ken Landreaux .11
788 Carney Lansford .11
789 Dave LaRoche .11
790 Joe Lefebvre .11
791 Ron LeFlore .11
792 Randy Lerch .11
793 Sixto Lezcano .11
794 John Littlefield .11
795 Mike Lum .11
796 Greg Luzinski .11
797 Fred Lynn .11
798 Jerry Martin .11
799 Buck Martinez .11
800 Gary Matthews .11
801 Mario Mendoza .11
802 Larry Milbourne .11
803 Rick Miller .11
804 John Montefusco .11
805 Jerry Morales .11
806 Jose Morales .11
807 Joe Morgan 1.50
808 Jerry Mumphrey .11
809 Gene Nelson **RC** .11
810 Ed Ott .11
811 Bob Owchinko .11
812 Gaylord Perry .70
813 Mike Phillips .11
814 Darrell Porter .11
815 Mike Proly .11
816 Tim Raines 2.25
817 Lenny Randle .11
818 Doug Rau .11
819 Jeff Reardon .11
820 Ken Reitz .11
821 Steve Renko .11
822 Rick Reuschel .11
823 Dave Revering .11
824 Dave Roberts .11
825 Leon Roberts .11
826 Joe Rudi .11
827 Kevin Saucier .11
828 Tony Scott .11
829 Bob Shirley .11
830 Ted Simmons .11
831 Lary Sorensen .11
832 Jim Spencer .11
833 Harry Spilman .11
834 Fred Stanley .11
835 Rusty Staub .20
836 Bill Stein .11
837 Joe Strain .11
838 Bruce Sutter .70
839 Don Sutton .70
840 Steve Swisher .11
841 Frank Tanana .11
842 Gene Tenace .11
843 Jason Thompson .11
844 Dickie Thon .11
845 Bill Travers .11
846 Tom Underwood .11
847 John Urrea .11
848 Mike Vail .11
849 Ellis Valentine .11
850 Fernando Valenzuela 1.50
851 Pete Vuckovich .11
852 Mark Wagner .11
853 Bob Walk .11
854 Claudell Washington .11
855 Dave Winfield 3.00
856 Geoff Zahn .11
857 Richie Zisk .11
858 Checklist 727-858 .04

1982 Topps

NM/M

Unopened Fact. Set (792): 180.00
Complete Set (792): 70.00
Common Player: .10
Wax Pack (15): 5.00
Wax Box (36): 140.00
Cello Pack (28): 6.00
Cello Box (24): 130.00
Rack Pack (51): 8.00
Rack Box (24): 210.00
Vending Box (500): 60.00

1 Steve Carlton .25
2 Ron Davis .10
3 Tim Raines .10
4 Pete Rose .75
5 Nolan Ryan 3.00
6 Fernando Valenzuela .10
7 Scott Sanderson .10
8 Rich Dauer .10
9 Ron Guidry .15
10 Ron Guidry/IA .10
11 Gary Alexander .10
12 Moose Haas .10
13 Lamar Johnson .10
14 Steve Howe .10
15 Ellis Valentine .10
16 Steve Comer .10
17 Darrell Evans .10
18 Fernando Arroyo .10
19 Ernie Whitt .10
20 Garry Maddox .10
21 Bob Bonner, Cal Ripken, Jr., Jeff Schneider **RC** Orioles Future Stars 50.00
22 Jim Beattie .10
23 Willie Hernandez .10
24 Dave Frost .10
25 Jerry Remy .10
26 Jorge Orta .10
27 Tom Herr .10
28 John Urrea .10
29 Dwayne Murphy .10
30 Tom Seaver 1.50
31 Tom Seaver/IA 1.00
32 Gene Garber .10
33 Jerry Morales .10
34 Joe Sambito .10
35 Willie Aikens .10
36 George Medich, Al Oliver Rangers Btg/Pitch. Ldrs. .10
37 Dan Graham .10
38 Charlie Lea .10
39 Lou Whitaker .10
40 Dave Parker .10
41 Dave Parker/IA .10
42 Rick Sofield .10
43 Mike Cubbage .10
44 Britt Burns .10
45 Rick Cerone .10
46 Jerry Augustine .10
47 Jeff Leonard .10
48 Bobby Castillo .10
49 Alvis Woods .10
50 Buddy Bell .10
51 Jay Howell, Carlos Lezcano, Ty Waller **RC** Chicago Cubs Future Stars .40
52 Larry Andersen .10
53 Greg Gross .10
54 Ron Hassey .10
55 Rick Burleson .10
56 Mark Littell .10
57 Craig Reynolds .10
58 John D'Acquisto .10
59 Rich Gedman **RC** .10
60 Tony Armas .10
61 Tommy Boggs .10
62 Mike Tyson .10
63 Mario Soto .10
64 Lynn Jones .10
65 Terry Kennedy .10
66 Art Howe, Nolan Ryan Astros Btg/Pitch. Ldrs. .75
67 Rich Gale .10
68 Roy Howell .10
69 Al Williams .10
70 Tim Raines .50
71 Roy Lee Jackson .10
72 Rick Auerbach .10
73 Buddy Solomon .10
74 Bob Clark .10
75 Tommy John .20
76 Greg Pryor .10
77 Miguel Dilone .10
78 George Medich .10
79 Bob Bailor .10
80 Jim Palmer 1.00
81 Jim Palmer/IA .30
82 Bob Welch .10
83 Steve Balboni, Andy McGaffigan, Andre Robertson **RC** Yankees Future Stars .15
84 Rennie Stennett .10
85 Lynn McGlothen .10
86 Dane Iorg .10
87 Matt Keough .10
88 Biff Pocoroba .10
89 Steve Henderson .10
90 Nolan Ryan 4.00
91 Carney Lansford .10
92 Brad Havens .10
93 Larry Hisle .10
94 Andy Hassler .10
95 Ozzie Smith 2.00
96 George Brett, Larry Gura Royals Btg/Pitch. Ldrs .35
97 Paul Moskau .10
98 Terry Bulling .10
99 Barry Bonnell .10
100 Mike Schmidt 3.00
101 Mike Schmidt/IA 1.50
102 Dan Briggs .10
103 Bob Lacey .10
104 Rance Mulliniks .10
105 Kirk Gibson .10
106 Enrique Romo .10
107 Wayne Krenchicki .10
108 Bob Sykes .10
109 Dave Revering .10
110 Carlton Fisk 1.50
111 Carlton Fisk/IA .65
112 Billy Sample .10
113 Steve McCatty .10
114 Ken Landreaux .10
115 Gaylord Perry 1.00
116 Jim Wohlford .10
117 Rawly Eastwick .10
118 Terry Francona, Brad Mills, Bryn Smith **RC** Expos Future Stars .20
119 Joe Pittman .10
120 Gary Lucas .10
121 Ed Lynch .10
122 Jamie Easterly .10
123 Danny Goodwin .10
124 Reid Nichols .10
125 Danny Ainge 1.00
126 Rick Mahler, Claudell Washington Braves Btg/Pitch. Ldrs. .10
127 Lonnie Smith .10
128 Frank Pastore .10
129 Checklist 1-132 .10
130 Julio Cruz .10
131 Stan Bahnsen .10
132 Lee May .10
133 Pat Underwood .10
134 Dan Ford .10
135 Andy Rincon .10
136 Lenn Sakata .10
137 George Cappuzzello .10
138 Tony Pena .10
139 Jeff Jones .10
140 Ron LeFlore .10
141 Chris Bando, Tom Brennan, Von Hayes **RC** Indians Future Stars .20
142 Dave LaRoche .10
143 Mookie Wilson .10
144 Fred Breining .10
145 Bob Horner .10
146 Mike Griffin .10
147 Denny Walling .10
148 Mickey Klutts .10
149 Pat Putnam .10
150 Ted Simmons .10
151 Dave Edwards .10
152 Ramon Aviles .10
153 Roger Erickson .10
154 Dennis Werth .10
155 Otto Velez .10
156 Rickey Henderson, Steve McCatty A's Btg/ Pitch. Ldrs. .10
157 Steve Crawford .10
158 Brian Downing .10
159 Larry Biittner .10
160 Luis Tiant .10
161 Carney Lansford, Bill Madlock Btg Ldrs. .10
162 Tony Armas, Dwight Evans, Bobby Grich, Eddie Murray, Mike Schmidt Home Run Ldrs. .25
163 Eddie Murray, Mike Schmidt RBI Ldrs. .40
164 Rickey Henderson, Tim Raines Stolen Base Ldrs. .35
165 Denny Martinez, Steve McCatty, Jack Morris, Tom Seaver, Pete Vuckovich Victory Ldrs. .10
166 Len Barker, Fernando Valenzuela Strikeout Ldrs. .10
167 Steve McCatty, Nolan Ryan ERA Ldrs. 1.50
168 Rollie Fingers, Bruce Sutter Leading Relievers .15
169 Charlie Leibrandt .10
170 Jim Bibby .10
171 Bob Brenly, Chili Davis, Bob Tufts **RC** Giants Future Stars 2.00
172 Bill Gullickson .10
173 Jamie Quirk .10
174 Dave Ford .10
175 Jerry Mumphrey .10
176 Dewey Robinson .10
177 John Ellis .10
178 Dyar Miller .10
179 Steve Garvey .75
180 Steve Garvey/IA .30
181 Silvio Martinez .10
182 Larry Herndon .10
183 Mike Proly .10
184 Mick Kelleher .10
185 Phil Niekro 1.00
186 Bob Forsch, Keith Hernandez Cardinals Btg/Pitch. Ldrs. .10
187 Jeff Newman .10
188 Randy Martz .10
189 Glenn Hoffman .10
190 J.R. Richard .05
191 Tim Wallach **RC** 2.00
192 Broderick Perkins .10
193 Darrell Jackson .10
194 Mike Vail .10
195 Paul Molitor 1.50
196 Willie Upshaw .10
197 Shane Rawley .10
198 Chris Speier .10
199 Don Aase .10
200 George Brett 3.00
201 George Brett/IA 2.00
202 Rick Manning .10
203 Jesse Barfield, Brian Milner, Boomer Wells Blue Jays Future Stars .50
204 Gary Roenicke .10
205 Neil Allen .10
206 Tony Bernazard .10
207 Rod Scurry .10
208 Bobby Murcer .10
209 Gary Lavelle .10
210 Keith Hernandez .10
211 Dan Petry .10
212 Mario Mendoza .10
213 Dave Stewart **RC** 4.00
214 Brian Asselstine .10
215 Mike Krukow .10
216 Dennis Lamp, Chet Lemon White Sox Btg/Pitch. Ldrs. .10
217 Bo McLaughlin .10
218 Dave Roberts .10
219 John Curtis .10
220 Manny Trillo .10
221 Jim Slaton .10
222 Butch Wynegar .10
223 Lloyd Moseby .10
224 Bruce Bochte .10
225 Mike Torrez .10
226 Checklist 133-264 .10
227 Ray Burris .10
228 Sam Mejias .10
229 Geoff Zahn .10
230 Willie Wilson .10
231 Mark Davis, Bob Dernier, Ozzie Virgil **RC** Phillies Future Stars .20
232 Terry Crowley .10
233 Duane Kuiper .10
234 Ron Hodges .10
235 Mike Easler .10
236 John Martin .10
237 Rusty Kuntz .10
238 Kevin Saucier .10
239 Jon Matlack .10
240 Bucky Dent .10
241 Bucky Dent/IA .10
242 Milt May .10
243 Bob Owchinko .10
244 Rufino Linares .10
245 Ken Reitz .10
246 Hubie Brooks, Mike Scott Mets Btg/Pitch. Ldrs. .10
247 Pedro Guerrero .10
248 Frank LaCorte .10
249 Tim Flannery .10
250 Tug McGraw .10
251 Fred Lynn .10
252 Fred Lynn/IA .10
253 Chuck Baker .10
254 George Bell **RC** 1.00
255 Tony Perez 1.00
256 Tony Perez/IA .10
257 Larry Harlow .10
258 Bo Diaz .10
259 Rodney Scott .10
260 Bruce Sutter 1.00
261 Howard Bailey, Marty Castillo, Dave Rucker Tigers Future Stars .10

262	Doug Bair	.10
263	Victor Cruz	.10
264	Dan Quisenberry	.10
265	Al Bumbry	.10
266	Rick Leach	.10
267	Kurt Bevacqua	.10
268	Rickey Keeton	.10
269	Jim Essian	.10
270	Rusty Staub	.15
271	Larry Bradford	.10
272	Bump Wills	.10
273	Doug Bird	.10
274	Bob Ojeda **RC**	.50
275	Bob Watson	.10
276	Rod Carew, Ken Forsch Angels Btg/Pitch. Ldrs.	.25
277	Terry Puhl	.10
278	John Littlefield	.10
279	Bill Russell	.10
280	Ben Oglivie	.10
281	John Verhoeven	.10
282	Ken Macha	.10
283	Brian Allard	.10
284	Bob Grich	.10
285	Sparky Lyle	.10
286	Bill Fahey	.10
287	Alan Bannister	.10
288	Garry Templeton	.10
289	Bob Stanley	.10
290	Ken Singleton	.10
291	Vance Law, Bob Long, Johnny Ray **RC** Pirates Future Stars	.15
292	Dave Palmer	.10
293	Rob Picciolo	.10
294	Mike LaCoss	.10
295	Jason Thompson	.10
296	Bob Walk	.10
297	Clint Hurdle	.10
298	Danny Darwin	.10
299	Steve Trout	.10
300	Reggie Jackson	2.00
301	Reggie Jackson/IA	1.50
302	Doug Flynn	.10
303	Bill Caudill	.10
304	Johnnie LeMaster	.10
305	Don Sutton	1.00
306	Don Sutton/IA	.20
307	Randy Bass	.10
308	Charlie Moore	.10
309	Pete Redfern	.10
310	Mike Hargrove	.10
311	Dusty Baker, Burt Hooton Dodgers Btg/Pitch. Ldrs.	.10
312	Lenny Randle	.10
313	John Harris	.10
314	Buck Martinez	.10
315	Burt Hooton	.10
316	Steve Braun	.10
317	Dick Ruthven	.10
318	Mike Heath	.10
319	Dave Rozema	.10
320	Chris Chambliss	.10
321	Chris Chambliss/IA	.10
322	Garry Hancock	.10
323	Bill Lee	.10
324	Steve Dillard	.10
325	Jose Cruz	.10
326	Pete Falcone	.10
327	Joe Nolan	.10
328	Ed Farmer	.10
329	U.L. Washington	.10
330	Rick Wise	.10
331	Benny Ayala	.10
332	Don Robinson	.10
333	Frank DiPino, Marshall Edwards, Chuck Porter Brewers Future Stars	.10
334	Aurelio Rodriguez	.10
335	Jim Sundberg	.10
336	Glenn Abbott, Tom Paciorek Mariners Btg/Pitch. Ldrs.	.10
337	Pete Rose/AS	1.50
338	Dave Lopes/AS	.10
339	Mike Schmidt/AS	1.00
340	Dave Concepcion/AS	.10
341	Andre Dawson/AS	.25
342a	George Foster (All-Star no autograph)	2.00
342b	George Foster (All-Star autograph on front)	.10
343	Dave Parker/AS	.10
344	Gary Carter/AS	.60
345	Fernando Valenzuela/AS	.10
346	Tom Seaver/AS	.75
347	Bruce Sutter/AS	.50
348	Derrel Thomas	.10
349	George Frazier	.10
350	Thad Bosley	.10
351	Scott Brown, Geoff Combe, Paul Householder Reds Future Stars	.10
352	Dick Davis	.10
353	Jack O'Connor	.10
354	Roberto Ramos	.10
355	Dwight Evans	.10
356	Denny Lewallyn	.10
357	Butch Hobson	.10
358	Mike Parrott	.10
359	Jim Dwyer	.10
360	Len Barker	.10
361	Rafael Landestoy	.10
362	Jim Wright	.10
363	Bob Molinaro	.10
364	Doyle Alexander	.10
365	Bill Madlock	.10
366	Juan Eichelberger, Luis Salazar Padres Btg/Pitch. Ldrs.	.10
367	Jim Kaat	.10
368	Alex Trevino	.10
369	Champ Summers	.10
370	Mike Norris	.10
371	Jerry Don Gleaton	.10
372	Luis Gomez	.10
373	Gene Nelson **RC**	.10
374	Tim Blackwell	.10
375	Dusty Baker	.15
376	Chris Welsh	.10
377	Kiko Garcia	.10
378	Mike Caldwell	.10
379	Rob Wilfong	.10
380	Dave Stieb	.10
381	Bruce Hurst, Dave Schmidt, Julio Valdez Red Sox Future Stars	.25
382	Joe Simpson	.10
383a	Pascual Perez (No position on front.)	20.00
383b	Pascual Perez ("Pitcher" on front)	.10
384	Keith Moreland	.10
385	Ken Forsch	.10
386	Jerry White	.10
387	Tom Veryzer	.10
388	Joe Rudi	.10
389	George Vukovich	.10
390	Eddie Murray	1.50
391	Dave Tobik	.10
392	Rick Bosetti	.10
393	Al Hrabosky	.10
394	Checklist 265-396	.10
395	Omar Moreno	.10
396	Fernando Arroyo, John Castino Twins Btg/Pitch. Ldrs.	.10
397	Ken Brett	.10
398	Mike Squires	.10
399	Pat Zachry	.10
400	Johnny Bench	1.50
401	Johnny Bench/IA	.45
402	Bill Stein	.10
403	Jim Tracy	.10
404	Dickie Thon	.10
405	Rick Reuschel	.10
406	Al Holland	.10
407	Danny Boone	.10
408	Ed Romero	.10
409	Don Cooper	.10
410	Ron Cey	.10
411	Ron Cey/IA	.10
412	Luis Leal	.10
413	Dan Meyer	.10
414	Elias Sosa	.10
415	Don Baylor	.15
416	Marty Bystrom	.10
417	Pat Kelly	.10
418	John Butcher, Bobby Johnson, Dave Schmidt **RC** Rangers Future Stars	.10
419	Steve Stone	.10
420	George Hendrick	.10
421	Mark Clear	.10
422	Cliff Johnson	.10
423	Stan Papi	.10
424	Bruce Benedict	.10
425	John Candelaria	.10
426	Eddie Murray, Sammy Stewart Orioles Btg/Pitch. Ldrs.	.25
427	Ron Oester	.10
428	Lamarr Hoyt (LaMarr)	.10
429	John Wathan	.10
430	Vida Blue	.10
431	Vida Blue/IA	.10
432	Mike Scott	.10
433	Alan Ashby	.10
434	Joe Lefebvre	.10
435	Robin Yount	1.50
436	Joe Strain	.10
437	Juan Berenguer	.10
438	Pete Mackanin	.10
439	Dave Righetti **RC**	.75
440	Jeff Burroughs	.10
441	Danny Heep, Billy Smith, Bobby Sprowl Astros Future Stars	.10
442	Bruce Kison	.10
443	Mark Wagner	.10
444	Terry Forster	.10
445	Larry Parrish	.10
446	Wayne Garland	.10
447	Darrell Porter	.10
448	Darrell Porter/IA	.10
449	Luis Aguayo **RC**	.10
450	Jack Morris	.10
451	Ed Miller	.10
452	Lee Smith **RC**	4.00
453	Art Howe	.10
454	Rick Langford	.10
455	Tom Burgmeier	.10
456	Bill Buckner, Randy Martz Cubs Btg & Pitch. Ldrs.	.10
457	Tim Stoddard	.10
458	Willie Montanez	.10
459	Bruce Berenyi	.10
460	Jack Clark	.10
461	Rich Dotson	.10
462	Dave Chalk	.10
463	Jim Kern	.10
464	Juan Bonilla	.10
465	Lee Mazzilli	.10
466	Randy Lerch	.10
467	Mickey Hatcher	.10
468	Floyd Bannister	.10
469	Ed Ott	.10
470	John Mayberry	.10
471	Atlee Hammaker, Mike Jones, Darryl Motley Royals Future Stars	.15
472	Oscar Gamble	.10
473	Mike Stanton	.10
474	Ken Oberkfell	.10
475	Alan Trammell	.10
476	Brian Kingman	.10
477	Steve Yeager	.10
478	Ray Searage	.10
479	Rowland Office	.10
480	Steve Carlton	1.50
481	Steve Carlton/IA	.40
482	Glenn Hubbard	.10
483	Gary Woods	.10
484	Ivan DeJesus	.10
485	Kent Tekulve	.10
486	Tommy John, Jerry Mumphrey Yankees Btg & Pitch. Ldrs.	.10
487	Bob McClure	.10
488	Ron Jackson	.10
489	Rick Dempsey	.10
490	Dennis Eckersley	1.00
491	Checklist 397-528	.10
492	Joe Price	.10
493	Chet Lemon	.10
494	Hubie Brooks	.10
495	Dennis Leonard	.10
496	Johnny Grubb	.10
497	Jim Anderson	.10
498	Dave Bergman	.10
499	Paul Mirabella	.10
500	Rod Carew	1.50
501	Rod Carew/IA	.40
502	Steve Bedrosian, Brett Butler, Larry Owen Braves Future Stars	2.00
503	Julio Gonzalez	.10
504	Rick Peters	.10
505	Graig Nettles	.10
506	Graig Nettles/IA	.10
507	Terry Harper	.10
508	Jody Davis **RC**	.15
509	Harry Spilman	.10
510	Fernando Valenzuela	.10
511	Ruppert Jones	.10
512	Jerry Dybzinski	.10
513	Rick Rhoden	.10
514	Joe Ferguson	.10
515	Larry Bowa	.10
516	Larry Bowa/IA	.10
517	Mark Brouhard	.10
518	Garth Iorg	.10
519	Glenn Adams	.10
520	Mike Flanagan	.10
521	Billy Almon	.10
522	Chuck Rainey	.10
523	Gary Gray	.10
524	Tom Hausman	.10
525	Ray Knight	.10
526	Warren Cromartie, Bill Gullickson Expos Btg & Pitch. Ldrs.	.10
527	John Henry Johnson	.10
528	Matt Alexander	.10
529	Allen Ripley	.10
530	Dickie Noles	.10
531	Rich Bordi, Mark Budaska, Kelvin Moore A's Future Stars	.10
532	Toby Harrah	.10
533	Joaquin Andujar	.10
534	Dave McKay	.10
535	Lance Parrish	.10
536	Rafael Ramirez	.10
537	Doug Capilla	.10
538	Lou Piniella	.10
539	Vern Ruhle	.10
540	Andre Dawson	.75
541	Barry Evans	.10
542	Ned Yost	.10
543	Bill Robinson	.10
544	Larry Christenson	.10
545	Reggie Smith	.10
546	Reggie Smith/IA	.10
547	Rod Carew/AS	.25
548	Willie Randolph/AS	.10
549	George Brett/AS	1.50
550	Bucky Dent/AS	.10
551	Reggie Jackson/AS	.75
552	Ken Singleton/AS	.10
553	Dave Winfield/AS	.60
554	Carlton Fisk/AS	.25
555	Scott McGregor/AS	.10
556	Jack Morris/AS	.10
557	Rich Gossage/AS	.10
558	John Tudor	.10
559	Bert Blyleven, Mike Hargrove Indians Btg & Pitch. Ldrs.	.10
560	Doug Corbett	.10
561	Glenn Brummer, Luis DeLeon, Gene Roof Cardinals Future Stars	.10
562	Mike O'Berry	.10
563	Ross Baumgarten	.10
564	Doug DeCinces	.10
565	Jackson Todd	.10
566	Mike Jorgensen	.10
567	Bob Babcock	.10
568	Joe Pettini	.10
569	Willie Randolph	.10
570	Willie Randolph/IA	.10
571	Glenn Abbott	.10
572	Juan Beniquez	.10
573	Rick Waits	.10
574	Mike Ramsey	.10
575	Al Cowens	.10
576	Vida Blue, Milt May Giants Btg & Pitch. Ldrs.	.10
577	Rick Monday	.10
578	Shooty Babitt	.10
579	Rick Mahler **RC**	.10
580	Bobby Bonds	.10
581	Ron Reed	.10
582	Luis Pujols	.10
583	Tippy Martinez	.10
584	Hosken Powell	.10
585	Rollie Fingers	1.00
586	Rollie Fingers/IA	.15
587	Tim Lollar	.10
588	Dale Berra	.10
589	Dave Stapleton	.10
590	Al Oliver	.10
591	Al Oliver/IA	.10
592	Craig Swan	.10
593	Billy Smith	.10
594	Renie Martin	.10
595	Dave Collins	.10
596	Damaso Garcia	.10
597	Wayne Nordhagen	.10
598	Bob Galasso	.10
599	Jay Loviglio, Reggie Patterson, Leo Sutherland White Sox Future Stars	.10
600	Dave Winfield	1.50
601	Sid Monge	.10
602	Freddie Patek	.10
603	Rich Hebner	.10
604	Orlando Sanchez	.10
605	Steve Rogers	.10
606	John Mayberry, Dave Stieb Blue Jays Btg & Pitch. Ldrs.	.10
607	Leon Durham	.10
608	Jerry Royster	.10
609	Rick Sutcliffe	.10
610	Rickey Henderson	1.50
611	Joe Niekro	.10
612	Gary Ward	.10
613	Jim Gantner	.10
614	Juan Eichelberger	.10
615	Bob Boone	.10
616	Bob Boone/IA	.10
617	Scott McGregor	.10
618	Tim Foli	.10
619	Bill Campbell	.10
620	Ken Griffey	.10
621	Ken Griffey/IA	.10
622	Dennis Lamp	.10
623	Ron Gardenhire, Terry Leach, Tim Leary **RC** Mets Future Stars	.20
624	Fergie Jenkins	1.00
625	Hal McRae	.10
626	Randy Jones	.10
627	Enos Cabell	.10
628	Bill Travers	.10
629	Johnny Wockenfuss	.10
630	Joe Charboneau	.10
631	Gene Tenace	.10
632	Bryan Clark	.10
633	Mitchell Page	.10
634	Checklist 529-660	.10
635	Ron Davis	.10
636	Steve Carlton, Pete Rose Phillies Btg & Pitch. Ldrs.	.50
637	Rick Camp	.10
638	John Milner	.10
639	Ken Kravec	.10
640	Cesar Cedeno	.10
641	Steve Mura	.10
642	Mike Scioscia	.10
643	Pete Vuckovich	.10
644	John Castino	.10
645	Frank White	.10
646	Frank White/IA	.10
647	Warren Brusstar	.10
648	Jose Morales	.10
649	Ken Clay	.10
650	Carl Yastrzemski	1.50
651	Carl Yastrzemski/IA	.65
652	Steve Nicosia	.10
653	Tom Brunansky, Luis Sanchez, Daryl Sconiers **RC** Angels Future Stars	.40
654	Jim Morrison	.10
655	Joel Youngblood	.10
656	Eddie Whitson	.10
657	Tom Poquette	.10
658	Tito Landrum	.10
659	Fred Martinez	.10
660	Dave Concepcion	.10
661	Dave Concepcion/IA	.10
662	Luis Salazar	.10
663	Hector Cruz	.10
664	Dan Spillner	.10
665	Jim Clancy	.10
666	Steve Kemp, Dan Petry Tigers Btg & Pitch. Ldrs.	.10
667	Jeff Reardon	.15
668	Dale Murphy	.75
669	Larry Milbourne	.10
670	Steve Kemp	.10
671	Mike Davis	.10
672	Bob Knepper	.10
673	Keith Drumright	.10
674	Dave Goltz	.10
675	Cecil Cooper	.10

676	Sal Butera	.10
677	Alfredo Griffin	.10
678	Tom Paciorek	.10
679	Sammy Stewart	.10
680	Gary Matthews	.10
681	Mike Marshall, Ron Roenicke, Steve Sax **RC** Dodgers Future Stars	.75
682	Jesse Jefferson	.10
683	Phil Garner	.10
684	Harold Baines	.05
685	Bert Blyleven	.10
686	Gary Allenson	.10
687	Greg Minton	.10
688	Leon Roberts	.10
689	Lary Sorensen	.10
690	Dave Kingman	.10
691	Dan Schatzeder	.10
692	Wayne Gross	.10
693	Cesar Geronimo	.10
694	Dave Wehrmeister	.10
695	Warren Cromartie	.10
696	Bill Madlock, Buddy Solomon Pirates Btg & Pitch. Ldrs.	.10
697	John Montefusco	.10
698	Tony Scott	.10
699	Dick Tidrow	.10
700	George Foster	.10
701	George Foster/IA	.10
702	Steve Renko	.10
703	Cecil Cooper, Pete Vuckovich Brewers Btg & Pitch. Ldrs.	.10
704	Mickey Rivers	.10
705	Mickey Rivers/IA	.10
706	Barry Foote	.10
707	Mark Bomback	.10
708	Gene Richards	.10
709	Don Money	.10
710	Jerry Reuss	.10
711	Dave Edler, Dave Henderson, Reggie Walton **RC** Mariners Future Stars	.25
712	Denny Martinez	.10
713	Del Unser	.10
714	Jerry Koosman	.10
715	Willie Stargell	1.50
716	Willie Stargell/IA	.30
717	Rick Miller	.10
718	Charlie Hough	.10
719	Jerry Narron	.10
720	Greg Luzinski	.10
721	Greg Luzinski/IA	.10
722	Jerry Martin	.10
723	Junior Kennedy	.10
724	Dave Rosello	.10
725	Amos Otis	.10
726	Amos Otis/IA	.10
727	Sixto Lezcano	.10
728	Aurelio Lopez	.10
729	Jim Spencer	.10
730	Gary Carter	1.50
731	Mike Armstrong, Doug Gwosdz, Fred Kuhaulua Padres Future Stars	.10
732	Mike Lum	.10
733	Larry McWilliams	.10
734	Mike Ivie	.10
735	Rudy May	.10
736	Jerry Turner	.10
737	Reggie Cleveland	.10
738	Dave Engle	.10
739	Joey McLaughlin	.10
740	Dave Lopes	.10
741	Dave Lopes/IA	.10
742	Dick Drago	.10
743	John Stearns	.10
744	Mike Witt **RC**	.25
745	Bake McBride	.10
746	Andre Thornton	.10
747	John Lowenstein	.10
748	Marc Hill	.10
749	Bob Shirley	.10
750	Jim Rice	.20
751	Rick Honeycutt	.10
752	Lee Lacy	.10
753	Tom Brookens	.10
754	Joe Morgan	1.50
755	Joe Morgan/IA	.25
756	Ken Griffey, Tom Seaver Reds Btg & Pitch. Ldrs.	.25
757	Tom Underwood	.10
758	Claudell Washington	.10
759	Paul Splittorff	.10
760	Bill Buckner	.10
761	Dave Smith	.10
762	Mike Phillips	.10
763	Tom Hume	.10
764	Steve Swisher	.10
765	Gorman Thomas	.10
766	Lenny Faedo, Kent Hrbek, Tim Laudner **RC** Twins Future Stars	2.00
767	Roy Smalley	.10
768	Jerry Garvin	.10
769	Richie Zisk	.10
770	Rich Gossage	.10
771	Rich Gossage/IA	.10
772	Bert Campaneris	.10
773	John Denny	.10
774	Jay Johnstone	.10
775	Bob Forsch	.10
776	Mark Belanger	.10
777	Tom Griffin	.10
778	Kevin Hickey	.10
779	Grant Jackson	.10
780	Pete Rose	3.50
781	Pete Rose/IA	2.00
782	Frank Taveras	.10
783	Greg Harris **RC**	.10
784	Milt Wilcox	.10
785	Dan Driessen	.10
786	Carney Lansford, Mike Torrez Red Sox Btg & Pitch. Ldrs.	.10
787	Fred Stanley	.10
788	Woodie Fryman	.10
789	Checklist 661-792	.10
790	Larry Gura	.10
791	Bobby Brown	.10
792	Frank Tanana	.10

Traded

Ozzie Smith
topps
CARDINALS
SHORTSTOP OZZIE SMITH

		NM/M
Complete Set (132):		175.00
Common Player:		.10
1T	Doyle Alexander	.10
2T	Jesse Barfield	.10
3T	Ross Baumgarten	.10
4T	Steve Bedrosian	.10
5T	Mark Belanger	.10
6T	Kurt Bevacqua	.10
7T	Tim Blackwell	.10
8T	Vida Blue	.10
9T	Bob Boone	.30
10T	Larry Bowa	.10
11T	Dan Briggs	.10
12T	Bobby Brown	.10
13T	Tom Brunansky	.10
14T	Jeff Burroughs	.10
15T	Enos Cabell	.10
16T	Bill Campbell	.10
17T	Bobby Castillo	.10
18T	Bill Caudill	.10
19T	Cesar Cedeno	.10
20T	Dave Collins	.10
21T	Doug Corbett	.10
22T	Al Cowens	.10
23T	Chili Davis	.50
24T	Dick Davis	.10
25T	Ron Davis	.10
26T	Doug DeCinces	.10
27T	Ivan DeJesus	.10
28T	Bob Dernier	.10
29T	Bo Diaz	.10
30T	Roger Erickson	.10
31T	Jim Essian	.10
32T	Ed Farmer	.10
33T	Doug Flynn	.10
34T	Tim Foli	.10
35T	Dan Ford	.10
36T	George Foster	.10
37T	Dave Frost	.10
38T	Rich Gale	.10
39T	Ron Gardenhire	.10
40T	Ken Griffey	.10
41T	Greg Harris	.10
42T	Von Hayes	.10
43T	Larry Herndon	.10
44T	Kent Hrbek	2.00
45T	Mike Ivie	.10
46T	Grant Jackson	.10
47T	Reggie Jackson	5.00
48T	Ron Jackson	.10
49T	Fergie Jenkins	2.00
50T	Lamar Johnson	.10
51T	Randy Johnson	.10
52T	Jay Johnstone	.10
53T	Mick Kelleher	.10
54T	Steve Kemp	.10
55T	Junior Kennedy	.10
56T	Jim Kern	.10
57T	Ray Knight	.10
58T	Wayne Krenchicki	.10
59T	Mike Krukow	.10
60T	Duane Kuiper	.10
61T	Mike LaCoss	.10
62T	Chet Lemon	.10
63T	Sixto Lezcano	.10
64T	Dave Lopes	.10
65T	Jerry Martin	.10
66T	Renie Martin	.10
67T	John Mayberry	.10
68T	Lee Mazzilli	.10
69T	Bake McBride	.10
70T	Dan Meyer	.10
71T	Larry Milbourne	.10
72T	Eddie Milner	.10
73T	Sid Monge	.10
74T	John Montefusco	.10
75T	Jose Morales	.10
76T	Keith Moreland	.10
77T	Jim Morrison	.10
78T	Rance Mulliniks	.10
79T	Steve Mura	.10
80T	Gene Nelson	.10
81T	Joe Nolan	.10
82T	Dickie Noles	.10
83T	Al Oliver	.10
84T	Jorge Orta	.10
85T	Tom Paciorek	.10
86T	Larry Parrish	.10
87T	Jack Perconte	.10
88T	Gaylord Perry	2.00
89T	Rob Picciolo	.10
90T	Joe Pittman	.10
91T	Hosken Powell	.10
92T	Mike Proly	.10
93T	Greg Pryor	.10
94T	Charlie Puleo	.10
95T	Shane Rawley	.10
96T	Johnny Ray	.10
97T	Dave Revering	.10
98T	Cal Ripken, Jr.	140.00
99T	Allen Ripley	.10
100T	Bill Robinson	.10
101T	Aurelio Rodriguez	.10
102T	Joe Rudi	.10
103T	Steve Sax	.50
104T	Dan Schatzeder	.10
105T	Bob Shirley	.10
106T	Eric Show	.10
107T	Roy Smalley	.10
108T	Lonnie Smith	.10
109T	Ozzie Smith	20.00
110T	Reggie Smith	.10
111T	Lary Sorensen	.10
112T	Elias Sosa	.10
113T	Mike Stanton	.10
114T	Steve Stroughter	.10
115T	Champ Summers	.10
116T	Rick Sutcliffe	.10
117T	Frank Tanana	.10
118T	Frank Taveras	.10
119T	Garry Templeton	.10
120T	Alex Trevino	.10
121T	Jerry Turner	.10
122T	Ed Vande Berg	.10
123T	Tom Veryzer	.10
124T	Ron Washington	.10
125T	Bob Watson	.10
126T	Dennis Werth	.10
127T	Eddie Whitson	.10
128T	Rob Wilfong	.10
129T	Bump Wills	.10
130T	Gary Woods	.10
131T	Butch Wynegar	.10
132T	Checklist 1-132	.10

1983 Topps

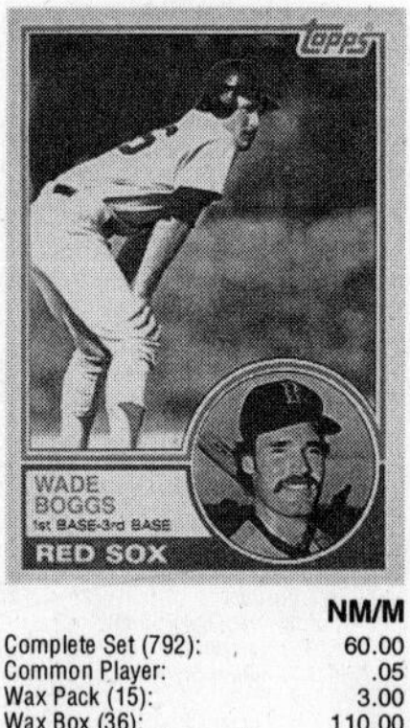
topps
WADE BOGGS
1st BASE-3rd BASE
RED SOX

		NM/M
Complete Set (792):		60.00
Common Player:		.05
Wax Pack (15):		3.00
Wax Box (36):		110.00
Crimp-End Test Pack (15):		4.00
Crimp-end Test Box (36):		110.00
Cello Pack (28):		5.00
Cello Box (24):		125.00
Rack Pack (51):		7.50
Rack Box (24):		175.00
Vending Box (500):		65.00
1	Tony Armas	.05
2	Rickey Henderson	.75
3	Greg Minton	.05
4	Lance Parrish	.05
5	Manny Trillo	.05
6	John Wathan	.05
7	Gene Richards	.05
8	Steve Balboni	.05
9	Joey McLaughlin	.05
10	Gorman Thomas	.05
11	Billy Gardner	.05
12	Paul Mirabella	.05
13	Larry Herndon	.05
14	Frank LaCorte	.05
15	Ron Cey	.05
16	George Vukovich	.05
17	Kent Tekulve	.05
18	Kent Tekulve	.05
19	Oscar Gamble	.05
20	Carlton Fisk	2.00
21	Eddie Murray, Jim Palmer Orioles Btg & Pitch. Ldrs.	.25
22	Randy Martz	.05
23	Mike Heath	.05
24	Steve Mura	.05
25	Hal McRae	.05
26	Jerry Royster	.05
27	Doug Corbett	.05
28	Bruce Bochte	.05
29	Randy Jones	.05
30	Jim Rice	.15
31	Bill Gullickson	.05
32	Dave Bergman	.05
33	Jack O'Connor	.05
34	Paul Householder	.05
35	Rollie Fingers	.75
36	Rollie Fingers)	.15
37	Darrell Johnson	.05
38	Tim Flannery	.05
39	Terry Puhl	.05
40	Fernando Valenzuela	.05
41	Jerry Turner	.05
42	Dale Murray	.05
43	Bob Dernier	.05
44	Don Robinson	.05
45	John Mayberry	.05
46	Richard Dotson	.05
47	Dave McKay	.05
48	Lary Sorensen	.05
49	Willie McGee **RC**	1.50
50	Bob Horner	.05
51	Leon Durham, Fergie Jenkins Cubs Btg & Pitch. Ldrs.	.05
52	Onix Concepcion **RC**	.05
53	Mike Witt	.05
54	Jim Maler	.05
55	Mookie Wilson	.05
56	Chuck Rainey	.05
57	Tim Blackwell	.05
58	Al Holland	.05
59	Benny Ayala	.05
60	Johnny Bench	2.00
61	Johnny Bench	.75
62	Bob McClure	.05
63	Rick Monday	.05
64	Bill Stein	.05
65	Jack Morris	.05
66	Bob Lillis	.05
67	Sal Butera	.05
68	Eric Show **RC**	.15
69	Lee Lacy	.05
70	Steve Carlton	2.00
71	Steve Carlton	.30
72	Tom Paciorek	.05
73	Allen Ripley	.05
74	Julio Gonzalez	.05
75	Amos Otis	.05
76	Rick Mahler	.05
77	Hosken Powell	.05
78	Bill Caudill	.05
79	Mick Kelleher	.05
80	George Foster	.05
81	Jerry Mumphrey, Dave Righetti Yankees Btg & Pitch. Ldrs.	.05
82	Bruce Hurst	.05
83	Ryne Sandberg **RC**	15.00
84	Milt May	.05
85	Ken Singleton	.05
86	Tom Hume	.05
87	Joe Rudi	.05
88	Jim Gantner	.05
89	Leon Roberts	.05
90	Jerry Reuss	.05
91	Larry Milbourne	.05
92	Mike LaCoss	.05
93	John Castino	.05
94	Dave Edwards	.05
95	Alan Trammell	.05
96	Dick Howser	.05
97	Ross Baumgarten	.05
98	Vance Law	.05
99	Dickie Noles	.05
100	Pete Rose	4.00
101	Pete Rose	2.00
102	Dave Beard	.05
103	Darrell Porter	.05
104	Bob Walk	.05
105	Don Baylor	.15
106	Gene Nelson	.05
107	Mike Jorgensen	.05
108	Glenn Hoffman	.05
109	Luis Leal	.05
110	Ken Griffey	.05
111	Al Oliver, Steve Rogers Expos Btg & Pitch. Ldrs.	.05
112	Bob Shirley	.05
113	Ron Roenicke	.05
114	Jim Slaton	.05
115	Chili Davis	.05
116	Dave Schmidt	.05
117	Alan Knicely	.05
118	Chris Welsh	.05
119	Tom Brookens	.05
120	Len Barker	.05
121	Mickey Hatcher	.05
122	Jimmy Smith	.05
123	George Frazier	.05
124	Marc Hill	.05
125	Leon Durham	.05
126	Joe Torre	.25
127	Preston Hanna	.05
128	Mike Ramsey	.05

129	Checklist 1-132	.05
130	Dave Stieb	.05
131	Ed Ott	.05
132	Todd Cruz	.05
133	Jim Barr	.05
134	Hubie Brooks	.05
135	Dwight Evans	.05
136	Willie Aikens	.05
137	Woodie Fryman	.05
138	Rick Dempsey	.05
139	Bruce Berenyi	.05
140	Willie Randolph	.05
141	Toby Harrah, Rick Sutcliffe Indians Btg & Pitch. Ldrs.	.05
142	Mike Caldwell	.05
143	Joe Pettini	.05
144	Mark Wagner	.05
145	Don Sutton	.75
146	Don Sutton	.20
147	Rick Leach	.05
148	Dave Roberts	.05
149	Johnny Ray	.05
150	Bruce Sutter	.75
151	Bruce Sutter	.50
152	Jay Johnstone	.05
153	Jerry Koosman	.05
154	Johnnie LeMaster	.05
155	Dan Quisenberry	.05
156	Billy Martin	.15
157	Steve Bedrosian	.05
158	Rob Wilfong	.05
159	Mike Stanton	.05
160	Dave Kingman	.05
161	Dave Kingman	.05
162	Mark Clear	.05
163	Cal Ripken, Jr.	6.00
164	Dave Palmer	.05
165	Dan Driessen	.05
166	John Pacella	.05
167	Mark Brouhard	.05
168	Juan Eichelberger	.05
169	Doug Flynn	.05
170	Steve Howe	.05
171	Bill Laskey, Joe Morgan Giants Btg & Pitch. Ldrs.	.05
172	Vern Ruhle	.05
173	Jim Morrison	.05
174	Jerry Ujdur	.05
175	Bo Diaz	.05
176	Dave Righetti	.05
177	Harold Baines	.05
178	Luis Tiant	.05
179	Luis Tiant	.05
180	Rickey Henderson	2.00
181	Terry Felton	.05
182	Mike Fischlin	.05
183	Ed Vande Berg **RC**	.05
184	Bob Clark	.05
185	Tim Lollar	.05
186	Whitey Herzog	.05
187	Terry Leach	.05
188	Rick Miller	.05
189	Dan Schatzeder	.05
190	Cecil Cooper	.05
191	Joe Price	.05
192	Floyd Rayford	.05
193	Harry Spilman	.05
194	Cesar Geronimo	.05
195	Bob Stoddard	.05
196	Bill Fahey	.05
197	Jim Eisenreich **RC**	.50
198	Kiko Garcia	.05
199	Marty Bystrom	.05
200	Rod Carew	2.00
201	Rod Carew	.35
202	Damaso Garcia, Dave Stieb Blue Jays Btg & Pitch. Ldrs.	.05
203	Mike Morgan	.05
204	Junior Kennedy	.05
205	Dave Parker	.05
206	Ken Oberkfell	.05
207	Rick Camp	.05
208	Dan Meyer	.05
209	Mike Moore **RC**	.15
210	Jack Clark	.05
211	John Denny	.05
212	John Stearns	.05
213	Tom Burgmeier	.05
214	Jerry White	.05
215	Mario Soto	.05
216	Tony LaRussa	.05
217	Tim Stoddard	.05
218	Roy Howell	.05
219	Mike Armstrong	.05
220	Dusty Baker	.05
221	Joe Niekro	.05
222	Damaso Garcia	.05
223	John Montefusco	.05
224	Mickey Rivers	.05
225	Enos Cabell	.05
226	Enrique Romo	.05
227	Chris Bando	.05
228	Joaquin Andujar	.05
229	Steve Carlton, Bo Diaz Phillies Btg/Pitch. Ldrs.	.15
230	Fergie Jenkins	.75
231	Fergie Jenkins	.20
232	Tom Brunansky	.05
233	Wayne Gross	.05
234	Larry Andersen	.05
235	Claudell Washington	.05
236	Steve Renko	.05
237	Dan Norman	.05
238	Bud Black **RC**	.25
239	Dave Stapleton	.05
240	Rich Gossage	.05
241	Rich Gossage	.05
242	Joe Nolan	.05
243	Duane Walker	.05
244	Dwight Bernard	.05
245	Steve Sax	.05
246	George Bamberger	.05
247	Dave Smith	.05
248	Bake McBride	.05
249	Checklist 133-264	.05
250	Bill Buckner	.05
251	Alan Wiggins **RC**	.05
252	Luis Aguayo	.05
253	Larry McWilliams	.05
254	Rick Cerone	.05
255	Gene Garber	.05
256	Gene Garber	.05
257	Jesse Barfield	.05
258	Manny Castillo	.05
259	Jeff Jones	.05
260	Steve Kemp	.05
261	Larry Herndon, Dan Petry Tigers Btg & Pitch. Ldrs.	.05
262	Ron Jackson	.05
263	Renie Martin	.05
264	Jamie Quirk	.05
265	Joel Youngblood	.05
266	Paul Boris	.05
267	Terry Francona	.05
268	Storm Davis **RC**	.05
269	Ron Oester	.05
270	Dennis Eckersley	.75
271	Ed Romero	.05
272	Frank Tanana	.05
273	Mark Belanger	.05
274	Terry Kennedy	.05
275	Ray Knight	.05
276	Gene Mauch	.05
277	Rance Mulliniks	.05
278	Kevin Hickey	.05
279	Greg Gross	.05
280	Bert Blyleven	.05
281	Andre Robertson	.05
282	Reggie Smith	.05
283	Reggie Smith	.05
284	Jeff Lahti	.05
285	Lance Parrish	.05
286	Rick Langford	.05
287	Bobby Brown	.05
288	Joe Cowley **RC**	.05
289	Jerry Dybzinski	.05
290	Jeff Reardon	.05
291	John Candelaria, Bill Madlock Pirates Btg & Pitch. Ldrs.	.05
292	Craig Swan	.05
293	Glenn Gulliver	.05
294	Dave Engle	.05
295	Jerry Remy	.05
296	Greg Harris	.05
297	Ned Yost	.05
298	Floyd Chiffer	.05
299	George Wright	.05
300	Mike Schmidt	3.00
301	Mike Schmidt	1.50
302	Ernie Whitt	.05
303	Miguel Dilone	.05
304	Dave Rucker	.05
305	Larry Bowa	.05
306	Tom Lasorda	.25
307	Lou Piniella	.05
308	Jesus Vega	.05
309	Jeff Leonard	.05
310	Greg Luzinski	.05
311	Glenn Brummer	.05
312	Brian Kingman	.05
313	Gary Gray	.05
314	Ken Dayley	.05
315	Rick Burleson	.05
316	Paul Splittorff	.05
317	Gary Rajsich	.05
318	John Tudor	.05
319	Lenn Sakata	.05
320	Steve Rogers	.05
321	Pete Vuckovich, Robin Yount Brewers Btg & Pitch. Ldrs.	.10
322	Dave Van Gorder	.05
323	Luis DeLeon	.05
324	Mike Marshall	.05
325	Von Hayes	.05
326	Garth Iorg	.05
327	Bobby Castillo	.05
328	Craig Reynolds	.05
329	Randy Niemann	.05
330	Buddy Bell	.05
331	Mike Krukow	.05
332	Glenn Wilson **RC**	.05
333	Dave LaRoche	.05
334	Dave LaRoche	.05
335	Steve Henderson	.05
336	Rene Lachemann	.05
337	Tito Landrum	.05
338	Bob Owchinko	.05
339	Terry Harper	.05
340	Larry Gura	.05
341	Doug DeCinces	.05
342	Atlee Hammaker	.05
343	Bob Bailor	.05
344	Roger LaFrancois	.05
345	Jim Clancy	.05
346	Joe Pittman	.05
347	Sammy Stewart	.05
348	Alan Bannister	.05
349	Checklist 265-396	.05
350	Robin Yount	2.00
351	Cesar Cedeno, Mario Soto Reds Btg & Pitch. Ldrs.	.05
352	Mike Scioscia	.05
353	Steve Comer	.05
354	Randy S. Johnson	.05
355	Jim Bibby	.05
356	Gary Woods	.05
357	Len Matuszek **RC**	.05
358	Jerry Garvin	.05
359	Dave Collins	.05
360	Nolan Ryan	5.00
361	Nolan Ryan	4.00
362	Bill Almon	.05
363	John Stuper **RC**	.05
364	Brett Butler	.05
365	Dave Lopes	.05
366	Dick Williams	.05
367	Bud Anderson	.05
368	Richie Zisk	.05
369	Jesse Orosco	.05
370	Gary Carter	2.00
371	Mike Richardt	.05
372	Terry Crowley	.05
373	Kevin Saucier	.05
374	Wayne Krenchicki	.05
375	Pete Vuckovich	.05
376	Ken Landreaux	.05
377	Lee May	.05
378	Lee May	.05
379	Guy Sularz	.05
380	Ron Davis	.05
381	Jim Rice, Bob Stanley Red Sox Btg & Pitch. Ldrs.	.05
382	Bob Knepper	.05
383	Ozzie Virgil	.05
384	Dave Dravecky **RC**	.50
385	Mike Easler	.05
386	Rod Carew/AS	.35
387	Bob Grich/AS	.05
388	George Brett/AS	1.50
389	Robin Yount/AS	.60
390	Reggie Jackson/AS	1.00
391	Rickey Henderson/AS	.50
392	Fred Lynn/AS	.05
393	Carlton Fisk/AS	.35
394	Pete Vuckovich/AS	.05
395	Larry Gura/AS	.05
396	Dan Quisenberry/AS	.05
397	Pete Rose/AS	2.00
398	Manny Trillo/AS	.05
399	Mike Schmidt/AS	1.50
400	Dave Concepcion/AS	.05
401	Dale Murphy/AS	.20
402	Andre Dawson/AS	.35
403	Tim Raines/AS	.05
404	Gary Carter/AS	.35
405	Steve Rogers/AS	.05
406	Steve Carlton/AS	.30
407	Bruce Sutter/AS	.25
408	Rudy May	.05
409	Marvis Foley	.05
410	Phil Niekro	.75
411	Phil Niekro	.25
412	Buddy Bell, Charlie Hough Rangers Btg & Pitch. Ldrs.	.05
413	Matt Keough	.05
414	Julio Cruz	.05
415	Bob Forsch	.05
416	Joe Ferguson	.05
417	Tom Hausman	.05
418	Greg Pryor	.05
419	Steve Crawford	.05
420	Al Oliver	.05
421	Al Oliver	.05
422	George Cappuzzello	.05
423	Tom Lawless **RC**	.05
424	Jerry Augustine	.05
425	Pedro Guerrero	.05
426	Earl Weaver	.25
427	Roy Lee Jackson	.05
428	Champ Summers	.05
429	Eddie Whitson	.05
430	Kirk Gibson	.05
431	Gary Gaetti **RC**	.75
432	Porfirio Altamirano	.05
433	Dale Berra	.05
434	Dennis Lamp	.05
435	Tony Armas	.05
436	Bill Campbell	.05
437	Rick Sweet	.05
438	Dave LaPoint **RC**	.05
439	Rafael Ramirez	.05
440	Ron Guidry	.20
441	Ray Knight, Joe Niekro Astros Btg & Pitch. Ldrs.	.05
442	Brian Downing	.05
443	Don Hood	.05
444	Wally Backman	.05
445	Mike Flanagan	.05
446	Reid Nichols	.05
447	Bryn Smith	.05
448	Darrell Evans	.05
449	Eddie Milner **RC**	.05
450	Ted Simmons	.05
451	Ted Simmons	.05
452	Lloyd Moseby	.05
453	Lamar Johnson	.05
454	Bob Welch	.05
455	Sixto Lezcano	.05
456	Lee Elia	.05
457	Milt Wilcox	.05
458	Ron Washington	.05
459	Ed Farmer	.05
460	Roy Smalley	.05
461	Steve Trout	.05
462	Steve Nicosia	.05
463	Gaylord Perry	.75
464	Gaylord Perry	.20
465	Lonnie Smith	.05
466	Tom Underwood	.05
467	Rufino Linares	.05
468	Dave Goltz	.05
469	Ron Gardenhire	.05
470	Greg Minton	.05
471	Vida Blue, Willie Wilson Royals Btg & Pitch. Ldrs.	.05
472	Gary Allenson	.05
473	John Lowenstein	.05
474	Ray Burris	.05
475	Cesar Cedeno	.05
476	Rob Picciolo	.05
477	Tom Niedenfuer	.05
478	Phil Garner	.05
479	Charlie Hough	.05
480	Toby Harrah	.05
481	Scot Thompson	.05
482	Tony Gwynn **RC**	25.00
483	Lynn Jones	.05
484	Dick Ruthven	.05
485	Omar Moreno	.05
486	Clyde King	.05
487	Jerry Hairston Sr.	.05
488	Alfredo Griffin	.05
489	Tom Herr	.05
490	Jim Palmer	1.50
491	Jim Palmer	.20
492	Paul Serna	.05
493	Steve McCatty	.05
494	Bob Brenly	.05
495	Warren Cromartie	.05
496	Tom Veryzer	.05
497	Rick Sutcliffe	.05
498	Wade Boggs **RC**	15.00
499	Jeff Little	.05
500	Reggie Jackson	2.00
501	Reggie Jackson	.75
502	Dale Murphy, Phil Niekro Braves Btg & Pitch. Ldrs.	.20
503	Moose Haas	.05
504	Don Werner	.05
505	Garry Templeton	.05
506	Jim Gott **RC**	.25
507	Tony Scott	.05
508	Tom Filer	.05
509	Lou Whitaker	.05
510	Tug McGraw	.05
511	Tug McGraw	.05
512	Doyle Alexander	.05
513	Fred Stanley	.05
514	Rudy Law	.05
515	Gene Tenace	.05
516	Bill Virdon	.05
517	Gary Ward	.05
518	Bill Laskey	.05
519	Terry Bulling	.05
520	Fred Lynn	.05
521	Bruce Benedict	.05
522	Pat Zachry	.05
523	Carney Lansford	.05
524	Tom Brennan	.05
525	Frank White	.05
526	Checklist 397-528	.05
527	Larry Biittner	.05
528	Jamie Easterly	.05
529	Tim Laudner	.05
530	Eddie Murray	2.00
531	Rickey Henderson, Rick Langford Athletics Btg & Pitch. Ldrs.	.15
532	Dave Stewart	.05
533	Luis Salazar	.05
534	John Butcher	.05
535	Manny Trillo	.05
536	Johnny Wockenfuss	.05
537	Rod Scurry	.05
538	Danny Heep	.05
539	Roger Erickson	.05
540	Ozzie Smith	2.00
541	Britt Burns	.05
542	Jody Davis	.05
543	Alan Fowlkes	.05
544	Larry Whisenton	.05
545	Floyd Bannister	.05
546	Dave Garcia	.05
547	Geoff Zahn	.05
548	Brian Giles	.05
549	Charlie Puleo **RC**	.05
550	Carl Yastrzemski	2.00
551	Carl Yastrzemski	.50
552	Tim Wallach	.05
553	Denny Martinez	.05
554	Mike Vail	.05
555	Steve Yeager	.05
556	Willie Upshaw	.05
557	Rick Honeycutt	.05
558	Dickie Thon	.05
559	Pete Redfern	.05
560	Ron LeFlore	.05
561	Joaquin Andujar, Lonnie Smith Cardinals Btg & Pitch. Ldrs.	.05
562	Dave Rozema	.05
563	Juan Bonilla	.05
564	Sid Monge	.05
565	Bucky Dent	.05
566	Manny Sarmiento	.05
567	Joe Simpson	.05
568	Willie Hernandez	.05
569	Jack Perconte	.05
570	Vida Blue	.05
571	Mickey Klutts	.05
572	Bob Watson	.05

#	Player	Price
573	Andy Hassler	.05
574	Glenn Adams	.05
575	Neil Allen	.05
576	Frank Robinson	.25
577	Luis Aponte	.05
578	David Green	.05
579	Rich Dauer	.05
580	Tom Seaver	2.00
581	Tom Seaver	.50
582	Marshall Edwards	.05
583	Terry Forster	.05
584	Dave Hostetler	.05
585	Jose Cruz	.05
586	Frank Viola RC	1.50
587	Ivan DeJesus	.05
588	Pat Underwood	.05
589	Alvis Woods	.05
590	Tony Pena	.05
591	LaMarr Hoyt, Greg Luzinski White Sox Btg & Pitch. Ldrs.	.05
592	Shane Rawley	.05
593	Broderick Perkins	.05
594	Eric Rasmussen	.05
595	Tim Raines	.05
596	Randy S. Johnson	.05
597	Mike Proly	.05
598	Dwayne Murphy	.05
599	Don Aase	.05
600	George Brett	3.00
601	Ed Lynch	.05
602	Rich Gedman	.05
603	Joe Morgan	2.00
604	Joe Morgan	.35
605	Gary Roenicke	.05
606	Bobby Cox	.05
607	Charlie Leibrandt	.05
608	Don Money	.05
609	Danny Darwin	.05
610	Steve Garvey	.50
611	Bert Roberge	.05
612	Steve Swisher	.05
613	Mike Ivie	.05
614	Ed Glynn	.05
615	Garry Maddox	.05
616	Bill Nahorodny	.05
617	Butch Wynegar	.05
618	LaMarr Hoyt	.05
619	Keith Moreland	.05
620	Mike Norris	.05
621	Craig Swan, Mookie Wilson Mets Btg & Pitch. Ldrs.	.05
622	Dave Edler	.05
623	Luis Sanchez	.05
624	Glenn Hubbard	.05
625	Ken Forsch	.05
626	Jerry Martin	.05
627	Doug Bair	.05
628	Julio Valdez	.05
629	Charlie Lea	.05
630	Paul Molitor	2.00
631	Tippy Martinez	.05
632	Alex Trevino	.05
633	Vicente Romo	.05
634	Max Venable	.05
635	Graig Nettles	.05
636	Graig Nettles	.05
637	Pat Corrales	.05
638	Dan Petry	.05
639	Art Howe	.05
640	Andre Thornton	.05
641	Billy Sample	.05
642	Checklist 529-660	.05
643	Bump Wills	.05
644	Joe Lefebvre	.05
645	Bill Madlock	.05
646	Jim Essian	.05
647	Bobby Mitchell	.05
648	Jeff Burroughs	.05
649	Tommy Boggs	.05
650	George Hendrick	.05
651	Rod Carew, Mike Witt Angels Btg & Pitch. Ldrs.	.05
652	Butch Hobson	.05
653	Ellis Valentine	.05
654	Bob Ojeda	.05
655	Al Bumbry	.05
656	Dave Frost	.05
657	Mike Gates	.05
658	Frank Pastore	.05
659	Charlie Moore	.05
660	Mike Hargrove	.05
661	Bill Russell	.05
662	Joe Sambito	.05
663	Tom O'Malley	.05
664	Bob Molinaro	.05
665	Jim Sundberg	.05
666	Sparky Anderson	.25
667	Dick Davis	.05
668	Larry Christenson	.05
669	Mike Squires	.05
670	Jerry Mumphrey	.05
671	Lenny Faedo	.05
672	Jim Kaat	.10
673	Jim Kaat	.05
674	Kurt Bevacqua	.05
675	Jim Beattie	.05
676	Biff Pocoroba	.05
677	Dave Revering	.05
678	Juan Beniquez	.05
679	Mike Scott	.05
680	Andre Dawson	.60
681	Pedro Guerrero, Fernando Valenzuela Dodgers Btg & Pitch. Ldrs.	.05
682	Bob Stanley	.05
683	Dan Ford	.05
684	Rafael Landestoy	.05
685	Lee Mazzilli	.05
686	Randy Lerch	.05
687	U.L. Washington	.05
688	Jim Wohlford	.05
689	Ron Hassey	.05
690	Kent Hrbek	.05
691	Dave Tobik	.05
692	Denny Walling	.05
693	Sparky Lyle	.05
694	Sparky Lyle	.05
695	Ruppert Jones	.05
696	Chuck Tanner	.05
697	Barry Foote	.05
698	Tony Bernazard	.05
699	Lee Smith	.05
700	Keith Hernandez	.05
701	Al Oliver, Willie Wilson Btg Ldrs.	.05
702	Reggie Jackson, Dave Kingman, Gorman Thomas Home Run Ldrs.	.15
703	Hal McRae, Dale Murphy, Al Oliver Runs Batted In Ldrs.	.05
704	Rickey Henderson, Tim Raines Stolen Base Ldrs.	.10
705	Steve Carlton, LaMarr Hoyt Victory Ldrs.	.05
706	Floyd Bannister, Steve Carlton Strikeout Ldrs.	.05
707	Steve Rogers, Rick Sutcliffe Earned Run Average Ldrs.	.05
708	Dan Quisenberry, Bruce Sutter Leading Firemen	.10
709	Jimmy Sexton	.05
710	Willie Wilson	.05
711	Jim Beattie, Bruce Bochte Mariners Btg & Pitch. Ldrs.	.05
712	Bruce Kison	.05
713	Ron Hodges	.05
714	Wayne Nordhagen	.05
715	Tony Perez	1.50
716	Tony Perez	.05
717	Scott Sanderson	.05
718	Jim Dwyer	.05
719	Rich Gale	.05
720	Dave Concepcion	.05
721	John Martin	.05
722	Jorge Orta	.05
723	Randy Moffitt	.05
724	Johnny Grubb	.05
725	Dan Spillner	.05
726	Harvey Kuenn	.05
727	Chet Lemon	.05
728	Ron Reed	.05
729	Jerry Morales	.05
730	Jason Thompson	.05
731	Al Williams	.05
732	Dave Henderson	.05
733	Buck Martinez	.05
734	Steve Braun	.05
735	Tommy John	.20
736	Tommy John	.05
737	Mitchell Page	.05
738	Tim Foli	.05
739	Rick Ownbey	.05
740	Rusty Staub	.05
741	Rusty Staub	.05
742	Terry Kennedy, Tim Lollar Padres Btg & Pitch. Ldrs.	.05
743	Mike Torrez	.05
744	Brad Mills	.05
745	Scott McGregor	.05
746	John Wathan	.05
747	Fred Breining	.05
748	Derrel Thomas	.05
749	Jon Matlack	.05
750	Ben Oglivie	.05
751	Brad Havens	.05
752	Luis Pujols	.05
753	Elias Sosa	.05
754	Bill Robinson	.05
755	John Candelaria	.05
756	Russ Nixon	.05
757	Rick Manning	.05
758	Aurelio Rodriguez	.05
759	Doug Bird	.05
760	Dale Murphy	.60
761	Gary Lucas	.05
762	Cliff Johnson	.05
763	Al Cowens	.05
764	Pete Falcone	.05
765	Bob Boone	.05
766	Barry Bonnell	.05
767	Duane Kuiper	.05
768	Chris Speier	.05
769	Checklist 661-792	.05
770	Dave Winfield	2.00
771	Bobby Castillo, Kent Hrbek Twins Btg & Pitch. Ldrs.	.05
772	Jim Kern	.05
773	Larry Hisle	.05
774	Alan Ashby	.05
775	Burt Hooton	.05
776	Larry Parrish	.05
777	John Curtis	.05
778	Rich Hebner	.05
779	Rick Waits	.05
780	Gary Matthews	.05
781	Rick Rhoden	.05
782	Bobby Murcer	.05
783	Bobby Murcer	.05
784	Jeff Newman	.05
785	Dennis Leonard	.05
786	Ralph Houk	.05
787	Dick Tidrow	.05
788	Dane Iorg	.05
789	Bryan Clark	.05
790	Bob Grich	.05
791	Gary Lavelle	.05
792	Chris Chambliss	.05

Traded

	NM/M
Complete Set (132):	20.00
Common Player:	.05
1T Neil Allen	.05
2T Bill Almon	.05
3T Joe Altobelli	.05
4T Tony Armas	.05
5T Doug Bair	.05
6T Steve Baker	.05
7T Floyd Bannister	.05
8T Don Baylor	.25
9T Tony Bernazard	.05
10T Larry Biittner	.05
11T Dann Bilardello	.05
12T Doug Bird	.05
13T Steve Boros	.05
14T Greg Brock	.05
15T Mike Brown	.05
16T Tom Burgmeier	.05
17T Randy Bush	.05
18T Bert Campaneris	.05
19T Ron Cey	.05
20T Chris Codiroli	.05
21T Dave Collins	.05
22T Terry Crowley	.05
23T Julio Cruz	.05
24T Mike Davis	.05
25T Frank DiPino	.05
26T Bill Doran	.05
27T Jerry Dybzinski	.05
28T Jamie Easterly	.05
29T Juan Eichelberger	.05
30T Jim Essian	.05
31T Pete Falcone	.05
32T Mike Ferraro	.05
33T Terry Forster	.05
34T Julio Franco RC	3.00
35T Rich Gale	.05
36T Kiko Garcia	.05
37T Steve Garvey	1.00
38T Johnny Grubb	.05
39T Mel Hall	.05
40T Von Hayes	.05
41T Danny Heep	.05
42T Steve Henderson	.05
43T Keith Hernandez	.15
44T Leo Hernandez	.05
45T Willie Hernandez	.05
46T Al Holland	.05
47T Frank Howard	.05
48T Bobby Johnson	.05
49T Cliff Johnson	.05
50T Odell Jones	.05
51T Mike Jorgensen	.05
52T Bob Kearney	.05
53T Steve Kemp	.05
54T Matt Keough	.05
55T Ron Kittle	.05
56T Mickey Klutts	.05
57T Alan Knicely	.05
58T Mike Krukow	.05
59T Rafael Landestoy	.05
60T Carney Lansford	.05
61T Joe Lefebvre	.05
62T Bryan Little	.05
63T Aurelio Lopez	.05
64T Mike Madden	.05
65T Rick Manning	.05
66T Billy Martin	.25
67T Lee Mazzilli	.05
68T Andy McGaffigan	.05
69T Craig McMurtry	.05
70T John McNamara	.05
71T Orlando Mercado	.05
72T Larry Milbourne	.05
73T Randy Moffitt	.05
74T Sid Monge	.05
75T Jose Morales	.05
76T Omar Moreno	.05
77T Joe Morgan	4.00
78T Mike Morgan	.05
79T Dale Murray	.05
80T Jeff Newman	.05
81T Pete O'Brien	.05
82T Jorge Orta	.05
83T Alejandro Pena	.05
84T Pascual Perez	.05
85T Tony Perez	1.00
86T Broderick Perkins	.05
87T Tony Phillips RC	.15
88T Charlie Puleo	.05
89T Pat Putnam	.05
90T Jamie Quirk	.05
91T Doug Rader	.05
92T Chuck Rainey	.05
93T Bobby Ramos	.05
94T Gary Redus	.05
95T Steve Renko	.05
96T Leon Roberts	.05
97T Aurelio Rodriguez	.05
98T Dick Ruthven	.05
99T Daryl Sconiers	.05
100T Mike Scott	.05
101T Tom Seaver	6.00
102T John Shelby	.05
103T Bob Shirley	.05
104T Joe Simpson	.05
105T Doug Sisk	.05
106T Mike Smithson	.05
107T Elias Sosa	.05
108T Darryl Strawberry RC	10.00
109T Tom Tellmann	.05
110T Gene Tenace	.05
111T Gorman Thomas	.05
112T Dick Tidrow	.05
113T Dave Tobik	.05
114T Wayne Tolleson	.05
115T Mike Torrez	.05
116T Manny Trillo	.05
117T Steve Trout	.05
118T Lee Tunnell	.05
119T Mike Vail	.05
120T Ellis Valentine	.05
121T Tom Veryzer	.05
122T George Vukovich	.05
123T Rick Waits	.05
124T Greg Walker	.05
125T Chris Welsh	.05
126T Len Whitehouse	.05
127T Eddie Whitson	.05
128T Jim Wohlford	.05
129T Matt Young	.05
130T Joel Youngblood	.05
131T Pat Zachry	.05
132T Checklist 1-132	.05

1984 Topps

WILLIE McGEE OF

	NM/M
Complete Set (792):	40.00
Common Player:	.05
Wax Pack (15):	2.00
Wax Box (36):	50.00
Cello Pack (28):	2.50
Cello Box (24):	50.00
Rack Pack (54+1):	3.50
Rack Box (24):	60.00
Vending Box (500):	20.00
1 Steve Carlton	.25
2 Rickey Henderson	.25
3 Dan Quisenberry	.05
4 Steve Carlton, Gaylord Perry, Nolan Ryan	.50
5 Bob Forsch, Dave Righetti, Mike Warren	.05
6 Johnny Bench, Gaylord Perry, Carl Yastrzemski	.25
7 Gary Lucas	.05
8 Don Mattingly RC	15.00
9 Jim Gott	.05
10 Robin Yount	1.00
11 Kent Hrbek, Ken Schrom Twins Btg & Pitch. Ldrs.	.05
12 Billy Sample	.05
13 Scott Holman	.05
14 Tom Brookens	.05
15 Burt Hooton	.05
16 Omar Moreno	.05
17 John Denny	.05
18 Dale Berra	.05
19 Ray Fontenot RC	.05
20 Greg Luzinski	.05

21	Joe Altobelli	.05
22	Bryan Clark	.05
23	Keith Moreland	.05
24	John Martin	.05
25	Glenn Hubbard	.05
26	Bud Black	.05
27	Daryl Sconiers	.05
28	Frank Viola	.05
29	Danny Heep	.05
30	Wade Boggs	3.00
31	Andy McGaffigan	.05
32	Bobby Ramos	.05
33	Tom Burgmeier	.05
34	Eddie Milner	.05
35	Don Sutton	.65
36	Denny Walling	.05
37	Buddy Bell, Rick Honeycutt Rangers Btg &Pitch. Ldrs.	.05
38	Luis DeLeon	.05
39	Garth Iorg	.05
40	Dusty Baker	.05
41	Tony Bernazard	.05
42	Johnny Grubb	.05
43	Ron Reed	.05
44	Jim Morrison	.05
45	Jerry Mumphrey	.05
46	Ray Smith	.05
47	Rudy Law	.05
48	Julio Franco	.05
49	John Stuper	.05
50	Chris Chambliss	.05
51	Jim Frey	.05
52	Paul Splittorff	.05
53	Juan Beniquez	.05
54	Jesse Orosco	.05
55	Dave Concepcion	.05
56	Gary Allenson	.05
57	Dan Schatzeder	.05
58	Max Venable	.05
59	Sammy Stewart	.05
60	Paul Molitor	1.00
61	Chris Codiroli **RC**	.05
62	Dave Hostetler	.05
63	Ed Vande Berg	.05
64	Mike Scioscia	.05
65	Kirk Gibson	.05
66	Jose Cruz, Nolan Ryan Astros Btg & Pitch. Ldrs.	.25
67	Gary Ward	.05
68	Luis Salazar	.05
69	Rod Scurry	.05
70	Gary Matthews	.05
71	Leo Hernandez	.05
72	Mike Squires	.05
73	Jody Davis	.05
74	Jerry Martin	.05
75	Bob Forsch	.05
76	Alfredo Griffin	.05
77	Brett Butler	.05
78	Mike Torrez	.05
79	Rob Wilfong	.05
80	Steve Rogers	.05
81	Billy Martin	.15
82	Doug Bird	.05
83	Richie Zisk	.05
84	Lenny Faedo	.05
85	Atlee Hammaker	.05
86	John Shelby **RC**	.05
87	Frank Pastore	.05
88	Rob Picciolo	.05
89	Mike Smithson **RC**	.05
90	Pedro Guerrero	.05
91	Dan Spillner	.05
92	Lloyd Moseby	.05
93	Bob Knepper	.05
94	Mario Ramirez	.05
95	Aurelio Lopez	.05
96	Larry Gura, Hal McRae Royals Btg & Pitch. Ldrs.	.05
97	LaMarr Hoyt	.05
98	Steve Nicosia	.05
99	Craig Lefferts **RC**	.25
100	Reggie Jackson	1.50
101	Porfirio Altamirano	.05
102	Ken Oberkfell	.05
103	Dwayne Murphy	.05
104	Ken Dayley	.05
105	Tony Armas	.05
106	Tim Stoddard	.05
107	Ned Yost	.05
108	Randy Moffitt	.05
109	Brad Wellman	.05
110	Ron Guidry	.05
111	Bill Virdon	.05
112	Tom Niedenfuer	.05
113	Kelly Paris	.05
114	Checklist 1-132	.05
115	Andre Thornton	.05
116	George Bjorkman	.05
117	Tom Veryzer	.05
118	Charlie Hough	.05
119	Johnny Wockenfuss	.05
120	Keith Hernandez	.05
121	Pat Sheridan **RC**	.05
122	Cecilio Guante	.05
123	Butch Wynegar	.05
124	Damaso Garcia	.05
125	Britt Burns	.05
126	Craig McMurtry, Dale Murphy Braves Btg & Pitch. Ldrs.	.05
127	Mike Madden	.05
128	Rick Manning	.05
129	Bill Laskey	.05
130	Ozzie Smith	2.00
131	Wade Boggs, Bill Madlock Btg Ldrs.	.25
132	Jim Rice, Mike Schmidt Home Run Ldrs.	.25
133	Cecil Cooper, Dale Murphy, Jim Rice RBI Ldrs.	.10
134	Rickey Henderson, Tim Raines Stolen Base Ldrs.	.25
135	John Denny, LaMarr Hoyt Victory Ldrs.	.05
136	Steve Carlton, Jack Morris Strikeout Ldrs.	.05
137	Atlee Hammaker, Rick Honeycutt Earned Run Average Ldrs.	.05
138	Al Holland, Dan Quisenberry Leading Firemen	.05
139	Bert Campaneris	.05
140	Storm Davis	.05
141	Pat Corrales	.05
142	Rich Gale	.05
143	Jose Morales	.05
144	Brian Harper **RC**	.20
145	Gary Lavelle	.05
146	Ed Romero	.05
147	Dan Petry	.05
148	Joe Lefebvre	.05
149	Jon Matlack	.05
150	Dale Murphy	.50
151	Steve Trout	.05
152	Glenn Brummer	.05
153	Dick Tidrow	.05
154	Dave Henderson	.05
155	Frank White	.05
156	Tim Conroy, Rickey Henderson Athletics Btg &Pitch. Ldrs.	.15
157	Gary Gaetti	.05
158	John Curtis	.05
159	Darryl Cias	.05
160	Mario Soto	.05
161	Junior Ortiz **RC**	.05
162	Bob Ojeda	.05
163	Lorenzo Gray	.05
164	Scott Sanderson	.05
165	Ken Singleton	.05
166	Jamie Nelson	.05
167	Marshall Edwards	.05
168	Juan Bonilla	.05
169	Larry Parrish	.05
170	Jerry Reuss	.05
171	Frank Robinson	.25
172	Frank DiPino	.05
173	Marvell Wynne **RC**	.05
174	Juan Berenguer	.05
175	Graig Nettles	.05
176	Lee Smith	.05
177	Jerry Hairston Sr.	.05
178	Bill Krueger	.05
179	Buck Martinez	.05
180	Manny Trillo	.05
181	Roy Thomas	.05
182	Darryl Strawberry	.25
183	Al Williams	.05
184	Mike O'Berry	.05
185	Sixto Lezcano	.05
186	Lonnie Smith, John Stuper Cardinals Btg & Pitch. Ldrs.	.05
187	Luis Aponte	.05
188	Bryan Little	.05
189	Tim Conroy **RC**	.05
190	Ben Oglivie	.05
191	Mike Boddicker	.05
192	Nick Esasky **RC**	.05
193	Darrell Brown	.05
194	Domingo Ramos	.05
195	Jack Morris	.05
196	Don Slaught	.05
197	Garry Hancock	.05
198	Bill Doran **RC**	.05
199	Willie Hernandez	.05
200	Andre Dawson	.60
201	Bruce Kison	.05
202	Bobby Cox	.05
203	Matt Keough	.05
204	Bobby Meacham **RC**	.05
205	Greg Minton	.05
206	Andy Van Slyke **RC**	.75
207	Donnie Moore	.05
208	Jose Oquendo **RC**	.05
209	Manny Sarmiento	.05
210	Joe Morgan	1.00
211	Rick Sweet	.05
212	Broderick Perkins	.05
213	Bruce Hurst	.05
214	Paul Householder	.05
215	Tippy Martinez	.05
216	Richard Dotson, Carlton Fisk White Sox Btg & Pitch. Ldrs.	.05
217	Alan Ashby	.05
218	Rick Waits	.05
219	Joe Simpson	.05
220	Fernando Valenzuela	.05
221	Cliff Johnson	.05
222	Rick Honeycutt	.05
223	Wayne Krenchicki	.05
224	Sid Monge	.05
225	Lee Mazzilli	.05
226	Juan Eichelberger	.05
227	Steve Braun	.05
228	John Rabb	.05
229	Paul Owens	.05
230	Rickey Henderson	1.00
231	Gary Woods	.05
232	Tim Wallach	.05
233	Checklist 133-264	.05
234	Rafael Ramirez	.05
235	Matt Young **RC**	.05
236	Ellis Valentine	.05
237	John Castino	.05
238	Reid Nichols	.05
239	Jay Howell	.05
240	Eddie Murray	1.00
241	Billy Almon	.05
242	Alex Trevino	.05
243	Pete Ladd	.05
244	Candy Maldonado	.05
245	Rick Sutcliffe	.05
246	Tom Seaver, Mookie Wilson Mets Btg & Pitch. Ldrs.	.25
247	Onix Concepcion	.05
248	Bill Dawley **RC**	.05
249	Jay Johnstone	.05
250	Bill Madlock	.05
251	Tony Gwynn	4.00
252	Larry Christenson	.05
253	Jim Wohlford	.05
254	Shane Rawley	.05
255	Bruce Benedict	.05
256	Dave Geisel	.05
257	Julio Cruz	.05
258	Luis Sanchez	.05
259	Sparky Anderson	.15
260	Scott McGregor	.05
261	Bobby Brown	.05
262	Tom Candiotti **RC**	.25
263	Jack Fimple	.05
264	Doug Frobel	.05
265	Donnie Hill **RC**	.05
266	Steve Lubratich	.05
267	Carmelo Martinez **RC**	.05
268	Jack O'Connor	.05
269	Aurelio Rodriguez	.05
270	Jeff Russell **RC**	.05
271	Moose Haas	.05
272	Rick Dempsey	.05
273	Charlie Puleo	.05
274	Rick Monday	.05
275	Len Matuszek	.05
276	Rod Carew, Geoff Zahn Angels Btg & Pitch. Ldrs.	.10
277	Eddie Whitson	.05
278	Jorge Bell	.05
279	Ivan DeJesus	.05
280	Floyd Bannister	.05
281	Larry Milbourne	.05
282	Jim Barr	.05
283	Larry Biittner	.05
284	Howard Bailey	.05
285	Darrell Porter	.05
286	Lary Sorensen	.05
287	Warren Cromartie	.05
288	Jim Beattie	.05
289	Randy S. Johnson	.05
290	Dave Dravecky	.05
291	Chuck Tanner	.05
292	Tony Scott	.05
293	Ed Lynch	.05
294	U.L. Washington	.05
295	Mike Flanagan	.05
296	Jeff Newman	.05
297	Bruce Berenyi	.05
298	Jim Gantner	.05
299	John Butcher	.05
300	Pete Rose	5.00
301	Frank LaCorte	.05
302	Barry Bonnell	.05
303	Marty Castillo	.05
304	Warren Brusstar	.05
305	Roy Smalley	.05
306	Pedro Guerrero, Bob Welch Dodgers Btg & Pitch. Ldrs.	.05
307	Bobby Mitchell	.05
308	Ron Hassey	.05
309	Tony Phillips	.05
310	Willie McGee	.05
311	Jerry Koosman	.05
312	Jorge Orta	.05
313	Mike Jorgensen	.05
314	Orlando Mercado	.05
315	Bob Grich	.05
316	Mark Bradley	.05
317	Greg Pryor	.05
318	Bill Gullickson	.05
319	Al Bumbry	.05
320	Bob Stanley	.05
321	Harvey Kuenn	.05
322	Ken Schrom	.05
323	Alan Knicely	.05
324	Alejandro Pena **RC**	.05
325	Darrell Evans	.05
326	Bob Kearney	.05
327	Ruppert Jones	.05
328	Vern Ruhle	.05
329	Pat Tabler	.05
330	John Candelaria	.05
331	Bucky Dent	.05
332	Kevin Gross **RC**	.05
333	Larry Herndon	.05
334	Chuck Rainey	.05
335	Don Baylor	.15
336	Pat Putnam, Matt Young Mariners Btg & Pitch. Ldrs.	.05
337	Kevin Hagen	.05
338	Mike Warren	.05
339	Roy Lee Jackson	.05
340	Hal McRae	.05
341	Dave Tobik	.05
342	Tim Foli	.05
343	Mark Davis	.05
344	Rick Miller	.05
345	Kent Hrbek	.05
346	Kurt Bevacqua	.05
347	Allan Ramirez	.05
348	Toby Harrah	.05
349	Bob L. Gibson	.05
350	George Foster	.05
351	Russ Nixon	.05
352	Dave Stewart	.05
353	Jim Anderson	.05
354	Jeff Burroughs	.05
355	Jason Thompson	.05
356	Glenn Abbott	.05
357	Ron Cey	.05
358	Bob Dernier	.05
359	Jim Acker **RC**	.05
360	Willie Randolph	.05
361	Dave Smith	.05
362	David Green	.05
363	Tim Laudner	.05
364	Scott Fletcher	.05
365	Steve Bedrosian	.05
366	Dave Dravecky, Terry Kennedy Padres Btg & Pitch. Ldrs.	.05
367	Jamie Easterly	.05
368	Hubie Brooks	.05
369	Steve McCatty	.05
370	Tim Raines	.05
371	Dave Gumpert	.05
372	Gary Roenicke	.05
373	Bill Scherrer	.05
374	Don Money	.05
375	Dennis Leonard	.05
376	Dave Anderson **RC**	.05
377	Danny Darwin	.05
378	Bob Brenly	.05
379	Checklist 265-396	.05
380	Steve Garvey	.45
381	Ralph Houk	.05
382	Chris Nyman	.05
383	Terry Puhl	.05
384	Lee Tunnell **RC**	.05
385	Tony Perez	1.00
386	George Hendrick/AS	.05
387	Johnny Ray/AS	.05
388	Mike Schmidt/AS	.75
389	Ozzie Smith/AS	.50
390	Tim Raines/AS	.05
391	Dale Murphy/AS	.20
392	Andre Dawson/AS	.25
393	Gary Carter/AS	.30
394	Steve Rogers/AS	.05
395	Steve Carlton/AS	.25
396	Jesse Orosco/AS	.05
397	Eddie Murray/AS	.40
398	Lou Whitaker/AS	.05
399	George Brett/AS	.75
400	Cal Ripken, Jr./AS	4.00
401	Jim Rice/AS	.05
402	Dave Winfield/AS	.30
403	Lloyd Moseby/AS	.05
404	Ted Simmons/AS	.05
405	LaMarr Hoyt/AS	.05
406	Ron Guidry/AS	.05
407	Dan Quisenberry/AS	.05
408	Lou Piniella	.05
409	Juan Agosto **RC**	.05
410	Claudell Washington	.05
411	Houston Jimenez	.05
412	Doug Rader	.05
413	Spike Owen **RC**	.05
414	Mitchell Page	.05
415	Tommy John	.15
416	Dane Iorg	.05
417	Mike Armstrong	.05
418	Ron Hodges	.05
419	John Henry Johnson	.05
420	Cecil Cooper	.05
421	Charlie Lea	.05
422	Jose Cruz	.05
423	Mike Morgan	.05
424	Dann Bilardello	.05
425	Steve Howe	.05
426	Mike Boddicker, Cal Ripken, Jr. Orioles Btg & Pitch. Ldrs.	.50
427	Rick Leach	.05
428	Fred Breining	.05
429	Randy Bush **RC**	.05
430	Rusty Staub	.05
431	Chris Bando	.05
432	Charlie Hudson **RC**	.05
433	Rich Hebner	.05
434	Harold Baines	.05
435	Neil Allen	.05
436	Rick Peters	.05
437	Mike Proly	.05
438	Biff Pocoroba	.05
439	Bob Stoddard	.05
440	Steve Kemp	.05
441	Bob Lillis	.05
442	Byron McLaughlin	.05
443	Benny Ayala	.05
444	Steve Renko	.05
445	Jerry Remy	.05
446	Luis Pujols	.05
447	Tom Brunansky	.05
448	Ben Hayes	.05
449	Joe Pettini	.05
450	Gary Carter	1.00
451	Bob Jones	.05
452	Chuck Porter	.05
453	Willie Upshaw	.05
454	Joe Beckwith	.05
455	Terry Kennedy	.05
456	Fergie Jenkins, Keith Moreland Cubs Btg & Pitch. Ldrs.	.05
457	Dave Rozema	.05

458	Kiko Garcia	.05
459	Kevin Hickey	.05
460	Dave Winfield	1.00
461	Jim Maler	.05
462	Lee Lacy	.05
463	Dave Engle	.05
464	Jeff Jones	.05
465	Mookie Wilson	.05
466	Gene Garber	.05
467	Mike Ramsey	.05
468	Geoff Zahn	.05
469	Tom O'Malley	.05
470	Nolan Ryan	6.00
471	Dick Howser	.05
472	Mike Brown	.05
473	Jim Dwyer	.05
474	Greg Bargar	.05
475	Gary Redus **RC**	.05
476	Tom Tellmann	.05
477	Rafael Landestoy	.05
478	Alan Bannister	.05
479	Frank Tanana	.05
480	Ron Kittle	.05
481	Mark Thurmond **RC**	.05
482	Enos Cabell	.05
483	Fergie Jenkins	.65
484	Ozzie Virgil	.05
485	Rick Rhoden	.05
486	Don Baylor, Ron Guidry Yankees Btg & Pitch. Ldrs	.05
487	Ricky Adams	.05
488	Jesse Barfield	.05
489	Dave Von Ohlen	.05
490	Cal Ripken, Jr.	6.00
491	Bobby Castillo	.05
492	Tucker Ashford	.05
493	Mike Norris	.05
494	Chili Davis	.05
495	Rollie Fingers	.65
496	Terry Francona	.05
497	Bud Anderson	.05
498	Rich Gedman	.05
499	Mike Witt	.05
500	George Brett	2.00
501	Steve Henderson	.05
502	Joe Torre	.05
503	Elias Sosa	.05
504	Mickey Rivers	.05
505	Pete Vuckovich	.05
506	Ernie Whitt	.05
507	Mike LaCoss	.05
508	Mel Hall	.05
509	Brad Havens	.05
510	Alan Trammell	.05
511	Marty Bystrom	.05
512	Oscar Gamble	.05
513	Dave Beard	.05
514	Floyd Rayford	.05
515	Gorman Thomas	.05
516	Charlie Lea, Al Oliver Expos Btg & Pitch. Ldrs.	.05
517	John Moses	.05
518	Greg Walker **RC**	.05
519	Ron Davis	.05
520	Bob Boone	.05
521	Pete Falcone	.05
522	Dave Bergman	.05
523	Glenn Hoffman	.05
524	Carlos Diaz	.05
525	Willie Wilson	.05
526	Ron Oester	.05
527	Checklist 397-528	.05
528	Mark Brouhard	.05
529	Keith Atherton **RC**	.05
530	Dan Ford	.05
531	Steve Boros	.05
532	Eric Show	.05
533	Ken Landreaux	.05
534	Pete O'Brien	.05
535	Bo Diaz	.05
536	Doug Bair	.05
537	Johnny Ray	.05
538	Kevin Bass	.05
539	George Frazier	.05
540	George Hendrick	.05
541	Dennis Lamp	.05
542	Duane Kuiper	.05
543	Craig McMurtry **RC**	.05
544	Cesar Geronimo	.05
545	Bill Buckner	.05
546	Mike Hargrove, Lary Sorensen Indians Btg & Pitch. Ldrs.	.05
547	Mike Moore	.05
548	Ron Jackson	.05
549	Walt Terrell **RC**	.05
550	Jim Rice	.15
551	Scott Ullger	.05
552	Ray Burris	.05
553	Joe Nolan	.05
554	Ted Power	.05
555	Greg Brock	.05
556	Joey McLaughlin	.05
557	Wayne Tolleson	.05
558	Mike Davis	.05
559	Mike Scott	.05
560	Carlton Fisk	1.00
561	Whitey Herzog	.05
562	Manny Castillo	.05
563	Glenn Wilson	.05
564	Al Holland	.05
565	Leon Durham	.05
566	Jim Bibby	.05
567	Mike Heath	.05
568	Pete Filson	.05
569	Bake McBride	.05
570	Dan Quisenberry	.05
571	Bruce Bochy	.05
572	Jerry Royster	.05
573	Dave Kingman	.05
574	Brian Downing	.05
575	Jim Clancy	.05
576	Atlee Hammaker, Jeff Leonard Giants Btg & Pitch. Ldrs.	.05
577	Mark Clear	.05
578	Lenn Sakata	.05
579	Bob James	.05
580	Lonnie Smith	.05
581	Jose DeLeon **RC**	.05
582	Bob McClure	.05
583	Derrel Thomas	.05
584	Dave Schmidt	.05
585	Dan Driessen	.05
586	Joe Niekro	.05
587	Von Hayes	.05
588	Milt Wilcox	.05
589	Mike Easler	.05
590	Dave Stieb	.05
591	Tony LaRussa	.05
592	Andre Robertson	.05
593	Jeff Lahti	.05
594	Gene Richards	.05
595	Jeff Reardon	.05
596	Ryne Sandberg	3.00
597	Rick Camp	.05
598	Rusty Kuntz	.05
599	Doug Sisk **RC**	.05
600	Rod Carew	1.00
601	John Tudor	.05
602	John Wathan	.05
603	Renie Martin	.05
604	John Lowenstein	.05
605	Mike Caldwell	.05
606	Lloyd Moseby, Dave Stieb Blue Jays Btg & Pitch. Ldrs.	.05
607	Tom Hume	.05
608	Bobby Johnson	.05
609	Dan Meyer	.05
610	Steve Sax	.05
611	Chet Lemon	.05
612	Harry Spilman	.05
613	Greg Gross	.05
614	Len Barker	.05
615	Garry Templeton	.05
616	Don Robinson	.05
617	Rick Cerone	.05
618	Dickie Noles	.05
619	Jerry Dybzinski	.05
620	Al Oliver	.05
621	Frank Howard	.05
622	Al Cowens	.05
623	Ron Washington	.05
624	Terry Harper	.05
625	Larry Gura	.05
626	Bob Clark	.05
627	Dave LaPoint	.05
628	Ed Jurak	.05
629	Rick Langford	.05
630	Ted Simmons	.05
631	Denny Martinez	.05
632	Tom Foley	.05
633	Mike Krukow	.05
634	Mike Marshall	.05
635	Dave Righetti	.05
636	Pat Putnam	.05
637	John Denny, Gary Matthews Phillies Btg & Pitch. Ldrs.	.05
638	George Vukovich	.05
639	Rick Lysander	.05
640	Lance Parrish	.05
641	Mike Richardt	.05
642	Tom Underwood	.05
643	Mike Brown	.05
644	Tim Lollar	.05
645	Tony Pena	.05
646	Checklist 529-660	.05
647	Ron Roenicke	.05
648	Len Whitehouse	.05
649	Tom Herr	.05
650	Phil Niekro	.65
651	John McNamara	.05
652	Rudy May	.05
653	Dave Stapleton	.05
654	Bob Bailor	.05
655	Amos Otis	.05
656	Bryn Smith	.05
657	Thad Bosley	.05
658	Jerry Augustine	.05
659	Duane Walker	.05
660	Ray Knight	.05
661	Steve Yeager	.05
662	Tom Brennan	.05
663	Johnnie LeMaster	.05
664	Dave Stegman	.05
665	Buddy Bell	.05
666	Jack Morris, Lou Whitaker Tigers Btg & Pitch. Ldrs.	.05
667	Vance Law	.05
668	Larry McWilliams	.05
669	Dave Lopes	.05
670	Rich Gossage	.05
671	Jamie Quirk	.05
672	Ricky Nelson	.05
673	Mike Walters	.05
674	Tim Flannery	.05
675	Pascual Perez	.05
676	Brian Giles	.05
677	Doyle Alexander	.05
678	Chris Speier	.05
679	Art Howe	.05
680	Fred Lynn	.05
681	Tom Lasorda	.15
682	Dan Morogiello	.05
683	Marty Barrett **RC**	.05
684	Bob Shirley	.05
685	Willie Aikens	.05
686	Joe Price	.05
687	Roy Howell	.05
688	George Wright	.05
689	Mike Fischlin	.05
690	Jack Clark	.05
691	Steve Lake **RC**	.05
692	Dickie Thon	.05
693	Alan Wiggins	.05
694	Mike Stanton	.05
695	Lou Whitaker	.05
696	Bill Madlock, Rick Rhoden Pirates Btg & Pitch. Ldrs.	.05
697	Dale Murray	.05
698	Marc Hill	.05
699	Dave Rucker	.05
700	Mike Schmidt	2.00
701	Bill Madlock, Dave Parker, Pete Rose NL Active Career Btg Ldrs.	.25
702	Tony Perez, Pete Rose, Rusty Staub NL Active Career Hit Ldrs.	.25
703	Dave Kingman, Tony Perez, Mike Schmidt NL Active Career Home Run Ldrs.	.15
704	Al Oliver, Tony Perez, Rusty Staub NL Active Career RBI Ldrs.	.05
705	Larry Bowa, Cesar Cedeno, Joe Morgan NL Active Career Stolen Bases Ldrs.	.05
706	Steve Carlton, Fergie Jenkins, Tom Seaver NL Active Career Victory Ldrs.	.05
707	Steve Carlton, Nolan Ryan, Tom Seaver NL Active Career Strikeout Ldrs.	.35
708	Steve Carlton, Steve Rogers, Tom Seaver NL Active Career ERA Ldrs.	.05
709	Gene Garber, Tug McGraw, Bruce Sutter NL Active Career Save Ldrs.	.10
710	George Brett, Rod Carew, Cecil Cooper AL Active Career Btg Ldrs.	.25
711	Bert Campaneris, Rod Carew, Reggie Jackson AL Active Career Hit Ldrs.	.15
712	Reggie Jackson, Greg Luzinski, Graig Nettles AL Active Career Home Run Ldrs.	.15
713	Reggie Jackson, Graig Nettles, Ted Simmons AL Active Career RBI Ldrs.	.15
714	Bert Campaneris, Dave Lopes, Omar Moreno AL Active Career Stolen Bases Ldrs.	.05
715	Tommy John, Jim Palmer, Don Sutton AL Active Career Victory Ldrs.	.05
716	Bert Blyleven, Jerry Koosman, Don Sutton AL Active Strikeout Ldrs.	.05
717	Rollie Fingers, Ron Guidry, Jim Palmer AL Active Career ERA Ldrs.	.05
718	Rollie Fingers, Rich Gossage, Dan Quisenberry AL Active Career Save Ldrs.	.05
719	Andy Hassler	.05
720	Dwight Evans	.05
721	Del Crandall	.05
722	Bob Welch	.05
723	Rich Dauer	.05
724	Eric Rasmussen	.05
725	Cesar Cedeno	.05
726	Moose Haas, Ted Simmons Brewers Btg & Pitch. Ldrs.	.05
727	Joel Youngblood	.05
728	Tug McGraw	.05
729	Gene Tenace	.05
730	Bruce Sutter	.75
731	Lynn Jones	.05
732	Terry Crowley	.05
733	Dave Collins	.05
734	Odell Jones	.05
735	Rick Burleson	.05
736	Dick Ruthven	.05
737	Jim Essian	.05
738	Bill Schroeder **RC**	.05
739	Bob Watson	.05
740	Tom Seaver	1.00
741	Wayne Gross	.05
742	Dick Williams	.05
743	Don Hood	.05
744	Jamie Allen	.05
745	Dennis Eckersley	.65
746	Mickey Hatcher	.05
747	Pat Zachry	.05
748	Jeff Leonard	.05
749	Doug Flynn	.05
750a	Jim Palmer	1.00
750b	Jim Palmer (Missing 1980-82 losses on back.)	3.00
750c	Jim Palmer (Missing 1979-83 losses on back.)	4.00
751	Charlie Moore	.05
752	Phil Garner	.05
753	Doug Gwosdz	.05
754	Kent Tekulve	.05
755	Garry Maddox	.05
756	Ron Oester, Mario Soto Reds Btg & Pitch. Ldrs.	.05
757	Larry Bowa	.05
758	Bill Stein	.05
759	Richard Dotson	.05
760	Bob Horner	.05
761	John Montefusco	.05
762	Rance Mulliniks	.05
763	Craig Swan	.05
764	Mike Hargrove	.05
765	Ken Forsch	.05
766	Mike Vail	.05
767	Carney Lansford	.05
768	Champ Summers	.05
769	Bill Caudill	.05
770	Ken Griffey	.05
771	Billy Gardner	.05
772	Jim Slaton	.05
773	Todd Cruz	.05
774	Tom Gorman	.05
775	Dave Parker	.05
776	Craig Reynolds	.05
777	Tom Paciorek	.05
778	Andy Hawkins **RC**	.05
779	Jim Sundberg	.05
780	Steve Carlton	1.00
781	Checklist 661-792	.05
782	Steve Balboni	.05
783	Luis Leal	.05
784	Leon Roberts	.05
785	Joaquin Andujar	.05
786	Wade Boggs, Bob Ojeda Red Sox Btg & Pitch. Ldrs.	.25
787	Bill Campbell	.05
788	Milt May	.05
789	Bert Blyleven	.05
790	Doug DeCinces	.05
791	Terry Forster	.05
792	Bill Russell	.05

1984 Topps Tiffany

	NM/M
Unopened Set (792):	175.00
Complete Set (792):	95.00
Common Player:	.15
Stars:	6X
8 Don Mattingly	80.00

(See 1984 Topps for checklist and base card values.)

Traded

ROYALS
BRET SABERHAGEN P

		NM/M
Complete Set (132):		17.50
Common Player:		.05
1T	Willie Aikens	.05
2T	Luis Aponte	.05
3T	Mike Armstrong	.05
4T	Bob Bailor	.05
5T	Dusty Baker	.15
6T	Steve Balboni	.05
7T	Alan Bannister	.05
8T	Dave Beard	.05
9T	Joe Beckwith	.05
10T	Bruce Berenyi	.05
11T	Dave Bergman	.05
12T	Tony Bernazard	.05
13T	Yogi Berra	.25
14T	Barry Bonnell	.05
15T	Phil Bradley	.05
16T	Fred Breining	.05
17T	Bill Buckner	.05
18T	Ray Burris	.05
19T	John Butcher	.05
20T	Brett Butler	.05
21T	Enos Cabell	.05
22T	Bill Campbell	.05
23T	Bill Caudill	.05
24T	Bob Clark	.05
25T	Bryan Clark	.05
26T	Jaime Cocanower	.05
27T	Ron Darling **RC**	.50
28T	Alvin Davis **RC**	.05
29T	Ken Dayley	.05
30T	Jeff Dedmon	.05
31T	Bob Dernier	.05
32T	Carlos Diaz	.05
33T	Mike Easler	.05
34T	Dennis Eckersley	1.50
35T	Jim Essian	.05
36T	Darrell Evans	.05

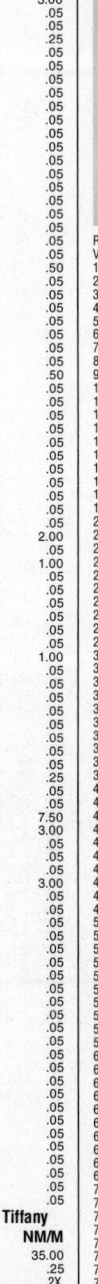

37T	Mike Fitzgerald	.05
38T	Tim Foli	.05
39T	George Frazier	.05
40T	Rich Gale	.05
41T	Barbaro Garbey	.05
42T	Dwight Gooden **RC**	3.00
43T	Rich Gossage	.05
44T	Wayne Gross	.05
45T	Mark Gubicza **RC**	.25
46T	Jackie Gutierrez	.05
47T	Mel Hall	.05
48T	Toby Harrah	.05
49T	Ron Hassey	.05
50T	Rich Hebner	.05
51T	Willie Hernandez	.05
52T	Ricky Horton	.05
53T	Art Howe	.05
54T	Dane Iorg	.05
55T	Brook Jacoby	.05
56T	Mike Jeffcoat	.05
57T	Dave Johnson	.05
58T	Lynn Jones	.05
59T	Ruppert Jones	.05
60T	Mike Jorgensen	.05
61T	Bob Kearney	.05
62T	Jimmy Key **RC**	.50
63T	Dave Kingman	.05
64T	Jerry Koosman	.05
65T	Wayne Krenchicki	.05
66T	Rusty Kuntz	.05
67T	Rene Lachemann	.05
68T	Frank LaCorte	.05
69T	Dennis Lamp	.05
70T	Mark Langston **RC**	.50
71T	Rick Leach	.05
72T	Craig Lefferts	.05
73T	Gary Lucas	.05
74T	Jerry Martin	.05
75T	Carmelo Martinez	.05
76T	Mike Mason	.05
77T	Gary Matthews	.05
78T	Andy McGaffigan	.05
79T	Larry Milbourne	.05
80T	Sid Monge	.05
81T	Jackie Moore	.05
82T	Joe Morgan	2.00
83T	Graig Nettles	.05
84T	Phil Niekro	1.00
85T	Ken Oberkfell	.05
86T	Mike O'Berry	.05
87T	Al Oliver	.05
88T	Jorge Orta	.05
89T	Amos Otis	.05
90T	Dave Parker	.05
91T	Tony Perez	1.00
92T	Gerald Perry	.05
93T	Gary Pettis	.05
94T	Rob Picciolo	.05
95T	Vern Rapp	.05
96T	Floyd Rayford	.05
97T	Randy Ready	.05
98T	Ron Reed	.05
99T	Gene Richards	.05
100T	Jose Rijo **RC**	.25
101T	Jeff Robinson	.05
102T	Ron Romanick	.05
103T	Pete Rose	7.50
104T	Bret Saberhagen **RC**	3.00
105T	Juan Samuel	.05
106T	Scott Sanderson	.05
107T	Dick Schofield	.05
108T	Tom Seaver	3.00
109T	Jim Slaton	.05
110T	Mike Smithson	.05
111T	Lary Sorensen	.05
112T	Tim Stoddard	.05
113T	Champ Summers	.05
114T	Jim Sundberg	.05
115T	Rick Sutcliffe	.05
116T	Craig Swan	.05
117T	Tim Teufel	.05
118T	Derrel Thomas	.05
119T	Gorman Thomas	.05
120T	Alex Trevino	.05
121T	Manny Trillo	.05
122T	John Tudor	.05
123T	Tom Underwood	.05
124T	Mike Vail	.05
125T	Tom Waddell	.05
126T	Gary Ward	.05
127T	Curt Wilkerson	.05
128T	Frank Williams	.05
129T	Glenn Wilson	.05
130T	Johnny Wockenfuss	.05
131T	Ned Yost	.05
132T	Checklist 1-132	.05

1984 Topps Traded Tiffany

	NM/M
Complete Set (132):	35.00
Common Player:	.25
Stars:	2X

(See 1984 Topps Traded for checklist and base card values.)

1985 Topps

	NM/M
Unopened Fact. Set (792):	140.00
Complete Set (792):	70.00
Common Player:	.05
Wax Pack (15):	4.50
Wax Box (36):	150.00
Cello Pack (28):	6.50
Cello Box (24):	150.00
Rack Pack (51+1):	9.00

Rack Box (24):		180.00
Vending Box (500):		60.00
1	Carlton Fisk	.25
2	Steve Garvey	.05
3	Dwight Gooden	.05
4	Cliff Johnson	.05
5	Joe Morgan	.10
6	Pete Rose	.50
7	Nolan Ryan	1.50
8	Juan Samuel	.05
9	Bruce Sutter	.10
10	Don Sutton	.05
11	Ralph Houk	.05
12	Dave Lopes	.05
13	Tim Lollar	.05
14	Chris Bando	.05
15	Jerry Koosman	.05
16	Bobby Meacham	.05
17	Mike Scott	.05
18	Mickey Hatcher	.05
19	George Frazier	.05
20	Chet Lemon	.05
21	Lee Tunnell	.05
22	Duane Kuiper	.05
23	Bret Saberhagen	.05
24	Jesse Barfield	.05
25	Steve Bedrosian	.05
26	Roy Smalley	.05
27	Bruce Berenyi	.05
28	Dann Bilardello	.05
29	Odell Jones	.05
30	Cal Ripken, Jr.	4.00
31	Terry Whitfield	.05
32	Chuck Porter	.05
33	Tito Landrum	.05
34	Ed Nunez	.05
35	Graig Nettles	.05
36	Fred Breining	.05
37	Reid Nichols	.05
38	Jackie Moore	.05
39	Johnny Wockenfuss	.05
40	Phil Niekro	.60
41	Mike Fischlin	.05
42	Luis Sanchez	.05
43	Andre David	.05
44	Dickie Thon	.05
45	Greg Minton	.05
46	Gary Woods	.05
47	Dave Rozema	.05
48	Tony Fernandez	.05
49	Butch Davis	.05
50	John Candelaria	.05
51	Bob Watson	.05
52	Jerry Dybzinski	.05
53	Tom Gorman	.05
54	Cesar Cedeno	.05
55	Frank Tanana	.05
56	Jim Dwyer	.05
57	Pat Zachry	.05
58	Orlando Mercado	.05
59	Rick Waits	.05
60	George Hendrick	.05
61	Curt Kaufman	.05
62	Mike Ramsey	.05
63	Steve McCatty	.05
64	Mark Bailey **RC**	.05
65	Bill Buckner	.05
66	Dick Williams	.05
67	Rafael Santana **RC**	.05
68	Von Hayes	.05
69	Jim Winn **RC**	.05
70	Don Baylor	.10
71	Tim Laudner	.05
72	Rick Sutcliffe	.05
73	Rusty Kuntz	.05
74	Mike Krukow	.05
75	Willie Upshaw	.05
76	Alan Bannister	.05
77	Joe Beckwith	.05
78	Scott Fletcher	.05
79	Rick Mahler	.05
80	Keith Hernandez	.05
81	Lenn Sakata	.05
82	Joe Price	.05
83	Charlie Moore	.05
84	Spike Owen	.05
85	Mike Marshall	.05
86	Don Aase	.05
87	David Green	.05
88	Bryn Smith	.05
89	Jackie Gutierrez	.05
90	Rich Gossage	.05
91	Jeff Burroughs	.05
92	Paul Owens	.05
93	Don Schulze **RC**	.05
94	Toby Harrah	.05
95	Jose Cruz	.05
96	Johnny Ray	.05
97	Pete Filson	.05
98	Steve Lake	.05
99	Milt Wilcox	.05
100	George Brett	3.00
101	Jim Acker	.05
102	Tommy Dunbar	.05
103	Randy Lerch	.05
104	Mike Fitzgerald	.05
105	Ron Kittle	.05
106	Pascual Perez	.05
107	Tom Foley	.05
108	Darnell Coles	.05
109	Gary Roenicke	.05
110	Alejandro Pena	.05
111	Doug DeCinces	.05
112	Tom Tellmann	.05
113	Tom Herr	.05
114	Bob James	.05
115	Rickey Henderson	.75
116	Dennis Boyd	.05
117	Greg Gross	.05
118	Eric Show	.05
119	Pat Corrales	.05
120	Steve Kemp	.05
121	Checklist 1-132	.05
122	Tom Brunansky	.05
123	Dave Smith	.05
124	Rich Hebner	.05
125	Kent Tekulve	.05
126	Ruppert Jones	.05
127	Mark Gubicza	.05
128	Ernie Whitt	.05
129	Gene Garber	.05
130	Al Oliver	.05
131	Buddy Bell, Gus Bell Father - Son	.05
132	Dale Berra, Yogi Berra Father - Son	.10
133	Bob Boone, Ray Boone Father - Son	.05
134	Terry Francona,Tito Francona Father - Son	.05
135	Bob Kennedy, Terry Kennedy Father - Son	.05
136	Bill Kunkel, Jeff Kunkel Father - Son	.05
137	Vance Law, Vern Law Father - Son	.05
138	Dick Schofield, Dick Schofield, Jr. Father - Son	.05
139	Bob Skinner, Joel Skinner Father - Son	.05
140	Roy Smalley, Jr., Roy Smalley III Father - Son	.05
141	Dave Stenhouse, Mike Stenhouse Father - Son	.05
142	Dizzy Trout, Steve Trout Father - Son	.05
143	Ozzie Virgil, Ozzie Virgil Father - Son	.05
144	Ron Gardenhire	.05
145	Alvin Davis	.05
146	Gary Redus	.05
147	Bill Swaggerty	.05
148	Steve Yeager	.05
149	Dickie Noles	.05
150	Jim Rice	.15
151	Moose Haas	.05
152	Steve Braun	.05
153	Frank LaCorte	.05
154	Argenis Salazar	.05
155	Yogi Berra	.10
156	Craig Reynolds	.05
157	Tug McGraw	.05
158	Pat Tabler	.05
159	Carlos Diaz	.05
160	Lance Parrish	.05
161	Ken Schrom	.05
162	Benny Distefano **RC**	.05
163	Dennis Eckersley	.60
164	Jorge Orta	.05
165	Dusty Baker	.05
166	Keith Atherton	.05
167	Rufino Linares	.05
168	Garth Iorg	.05
169	Dan Spillner	.05
170	George Foster	.05
171	Bill Stein	.05
172	Jack Perconte	.05
173	Mike Young	.05
174	Rick Honeycutt	.05
175	Dave Parker	.05
176	Bill Schroeder	.05
177	Dave Von Ohlen	.05
178	Miguel Dilone	.05
179	Tommy John	.10
180	Dave Winfield	.75
181	Roger Clemens	20.00
182	Tim Flannery	.05
183	Larry McWilliams	.05
184	Carmen Castillo	.05
185	Al Holland	.05
186	Bob Lillis	.05
187	Mike Walters	.05
188	Greg Pryor	.05
189	Warren Brusstar	.05
190	Rusty Staub	.05
191	Steve Nicosia	.05
192	Howard Johnson	.05
193	Jimmy Key	.05
194	Dave Stegman	.05
195	Glenn Hubbard	.05
196	Pete O'Brien	.05
197	Mike Warren	.05
198	Eddie Milner	.05
199	Denny Martinez	.05
200	Reggie Jackson	2.00
201	Burt Hooton	.05
202	Gorman Thomas	.05
203	Bob McClure	.05
204	Art Howe	.05
205	Steve Rogers	.05
206	Phil Garner	.05
207	Mark Clear	.05
208	Champ Summers	.05
209	Bill Campbell	.05
210	Gary Matthews	.05
211	Clay Christiansen	.05
212	George Vukovich	.05
213	Billy Gardner	.05
214	John Tudor	.05
215	Bob Brenly	.05
216	Jerry Don Gleaton	.05
217	Leon Roberts	.05
218	Doyle Alexander	.05
219	Gerald Perry	.05
220	Fred Lynn	.05
221	Ron Reed	.05
222	Hubie Brooks	.05
223	Tom Hume	.05
224	Al Cowens	.05
225	Mike Boddicker	.05
226	Juan Beniquez	.05
227	Danny Darwin	.05
228	Dion James	.05
229	Dave LaPoint	.05
230	Gary Carter	.75
231	Dwayne Murphy	.05
232	Dave Beard	.05
233	Ed Jurak	.05
234	Jerry Narron	.05
235	Garry Maddox	.05
236	Mark Thurmond	.05
237	Julio Franco	.05
238	Jose Rijo	.05
239	Tim Teufel	.05
240	Dave Stieb	.05
241	Jim Frey	.05
242	Greg Harris	.05
243	Barbaro Garbey	.05
244	Mike Jones	.05
245	Chili Davis	.05
246	Mike Norris	.05
247	Wayne Tolleson	.05
248	Terry Forster	.05
249	Harold Baines	.05
250	Jesse Orosco	.05
251	Brad Gulden	.05
252	Dan Ford	.05
253	Sid Bream **RC**	.10
254	Pete Vuckovich	.05
255	Lonnie Smith	.05
256	Mike Stanton	.05
257	Brian Little (Bryan)	.05
258	Mike Brown	.05
259	Gary Allenson	.05
260	Dave Righetti	.05
261	Checklist 133-264	.05
262	Greg Booker **RC**	.05
263	Mel Hall	.05
264	Joe Sambito	.05
265	Juan Samuel	.05
266	Frank Viola	.05
267	Henry Cotto **RC**	.05
268	Chuck Tanner	.05
269	Doug Baker **RC**	.05
270	Dan Quisenberry	.05
271	Tim Foli	.05
272	Jeff Burroughs	.05
273	Bill Almon	.05
274	Floyd Bannister	.05
275	Harold Baines	.10
276	Bob Horner	.10
277	Al Chambers	.05
278	Darryl Strawberry	.30
279	Mike Moore	.05
280	Shawon Dunston **RC**	.40
281	Tim Belcher **RC**	.30
282	Shawn Abner **RC**	.05
283	Fran Mullins	.05
284	Marty Bystrom	.05
285	Dan Driessen	.05
286	Rudy Law	.05
287	Walt Terrell	.05
288	Jeff Kunkel **RC**	.05
289	Tom Underwood	.05
290	Cecil Cooper	.05
291	Bob Welch	.05
292	Brad Komminsk	.05
293	Curt Young **RC**	.05
294	Tom Nieto **RC**	.05
295	Joe Niekro	.05
296	Ricky Nelson	.05
297	Gary Lucas	.05
298	Marty Barrett	.05
299	Andy Hawkins	.05
300	Rod Carew	.75
301	John Montefusco	.05
302	Tim Corcoran	.05
303	Mike Jeffcoat **RC**	.05
304	Gary Gaetti	.05
305	Dale Berra	.05
306	Rick Reuschel	.05
307	Sparky Anderson	.10

308	John Wathan	.05
309	Mike Witt	.05
310	Manny Trillo	.05
311	Jim Gott	.05
312	Marc Hill	.05
313	Dave Schmidt	.05
314	Ron Oester	.05
315	Doug Sisk	.05
316	John Lowenstein	.05
317	Jack Lazorko **RC**	.05
318	Ted Simmons	.05
319	Jeff Jones	.05
320	Dale Murphy	.35
321	Ricky Horton **RC**	.05
322	Dave Stapleton	.05
323	Andy McGaffigan	.05
324	Bruce Bochy	.05
325	John Denny	.05
326	Kevin Bass	.05
327	Brook Jacoby	.05
328	Bob Shirley	.05
329	Ron Washington	.05
330	Leon Durham	.05
331	Bill Laskey	.05
332	Brian Harper	.05
333	Willie Hernandez	.05
334	Dick Howser	.05
335	Bruce Benedict	.05
336	Rance Mulliniks	.05
337	Billy Sample	.05
338	Britt Burns	.05
339	Danny Heep	.05
340	Robin Yount	.75
341	Floyd Rayford	.05
342	Ted Power	.05
343	Bill Russell	.05
344	Dave Henderson	.05
345	Charlie Lea	.05
346	Terry Pendleton **RC**	.75
347	Rick Langford	.05
348	Bob Boone	.05
349	Domingo Ramos	.05
350	Wade Boggs	1.00
351	Juan Agosto	.05
352	Joe Morgan	.75
353	Julio Solano	.05
354	Andre Robertson	.05
355	Bert Blyleven	.05
356	Dave Meier	.05
357	Rich Bordi	.05
358	Tony Pena	.05
359	Pat Sheridan	.05
360	Steve Carlton	.75
361	Alfredo Griffin	.05
362	Craig McMurtry	.05
363	Ron Hodges	.05
364	Richard Dotson	.05
365	Danny Ozark	.05
366	Todd Cruz	.05
367	Keefe Cato	.05
368	Dave Bergman	.05
369	R.J. Reynolds **RC**	.05
370	Bruce Sutter	.65
371	Mickey Rivers	.05
372	Roy Howell	.05
373	Mike Moore	.05
374	Brian Downing	.05
375	Jeff Reardon	.05
376	Jeff Newman	.05
377	Checklist 265-396	.05
378	Alan Wiggins	.05
379	Charles Hudson	.05
380	Ken Griffey	.05
381	Roy Smith	.05
382	Denny Walling	.05
383	Rick Lysander	.05
384	Jody Davis	.05
385	Jose DeLeon	.05
386	Dan Gladden **RC**	.30
387	Buddy Biancalana **RC**	.05
388	Bert Roberge	.05
389	Rod Dedeaux	.05
390	Sid Akins	.05
391	Flavio Alfaro	.05
392	Don August	.05
393	Scott Bankhead **RC**	.10
394	Bob Caffrey	.05
395	Mike Dunne	.05
396	Gary Green	.05
397	John Hoover	.05
398	Shane Mack **RC**	.10
399	John Marzano	.05
400	Oddibe McDowell	.05
401	Mark McGwire **RC**	20.00
402	Pat Pacillo	.05
403	Cory Snyder **RC**	.30
404	Billy Swift **RC**	.40
405	Tom Veryzer	.05
406	Len Whitehouse	.05
407	Bobby Ramos	.05
408	Sid Monge	.05
409	Brad Wellman	.05
410	Bob Horner	.05
411	Bobby Cox	.05
412	Bud Black	.05
413	Vance Law	.05
414	Gary Ward	.05
415	Ron Darling	.05
416	Wayne Gross	.05
417	John Franco **RC**	.50
418	Ken Landreaux	.05
419	Mike Caldwell	.05
420	Andre Dawson	.50
421	Dave Rucker	.05
422	Carney Lansford	.05
423	Barry Bonnell	.05
424	Al Nipper **RC**	.05
425	Mike Hargrove	.05
426	Verne Ruhle	.05
427	Mario Ramirez	.05
428	Larry Andersen	.05
429	Rick Cerone	.05
430	Ron Davis	.05
431	U.L. Washington	.05
432	Thad Bosley	.05
433	Jim Morrison	.05
434	Gene Richards	.05
435	Dan Petry	.05
436	Willie Aikens	.05
437	Al Jones	.05
438	Joe Torre	.10
439	Junior Ortiz	.05
440	Fernando Valenzuela	.05
441	Duane Walker	.05
442	Ken Forsch	.05
443	George Wright	.05
444	Tony Phillips	.05
445	Tippy Martinez	.05
446	Jim Sundberg	.05
447	Jeff Lahti	.05
448	Derrel Thomas	.05
449	Phil Bradley **RC**	.10
450	Steve Garvey	.25
451	Bruce Hurst	.05
452	John Castino	.05
453	Tom Waddell	.05
454	Glenn Wilson	.05
455	Bob Knepper	.05
456	Tim Foli	.05
457	Cecilio Guante	.05
458	Randy S. Johnson	.05
459	Charlie Leibrandt	.05
460	Ryne Sandberg	1.00
461	Marty Castillo	.05
462	Gary Lavelle	.05
463	Dave Collins	.05
464	Mike Mason **RC**	.05
465	Bob Grich	.05
466	Tony LaRussa	.10
467	Ed Lynch	.05
468	Wayne Krenchicki	.05
469	Sammy Stewart	.05
470	Steve Sax	.05
471	Pete Ladd	.05
472	Jim Essian	.05
473	Tim Wallach	.05
474	Kurt Kepshire	.05
475	Andre Thornton	.05
476	Jeff Stone **RC**	.05
477	Bob Ojeda	.05
478	Kurt Bevacqua	.05
479	Mike Madden	.05
480	Lou Whitaker	.05
481	Dale Murray	.05
482	Harry Spilman	.05
483	Mike Smithson	.05
484	Larry Bowa	.05
485	Matt Young	.05
486	Steve Balboni	.05
487	Frank Williams **RC**	.05
488	Joel Skinner	.05
489	Bryan Clark	.05
490	Jason Thompson	.05
491	Rick Camp	.05
492	Dave Johnson	.05
493	Orel Hershiser **RC**	2.00
494	Rich Dauer	.05
495	Mario Soto	.05
496	Donnie Scott	.05
497	Gary Pettis	.05
498	Ed Romero	.05
499	Danny Cox	.05
500	Mike Schmidt	2.00
501	Dan Schatzeder	.05
502	Rick Miller	.05
503	Tim Conroy	.05
504	Jerry Willard	.05
505	Jim Beattie	.05
506	Franklin Stubbs **RC**	.05
507	Ray Fontenot	.05
508	John Shelby	.05
509	Milt May	.05
510	Kent Hrbek	.05
511	Lee Smith	.05
512	Tom Brookens	.05
513	Lynn Jones	.05
514	Jeff Cornell	.05
515	Dave Concepcion	.05
516	Roy Lee Jackson	.05
517	Jerry Martin	.05
518	Chris Chambliss	.05
519	Doug Rader	.05
520	LaMarr Hoyt	.05
521	Rick Dempsey	.05
522	Paul Molitor	.75
523	Candy Maldonado	.05
524	Rob Wilfong	.05
525	Darrell Porter	.05
526	Dave Palmer	.05
527	Checklist 397-528	.05
528	Bill Krueger	.05
529	Rich Gedman	.05
530	Dave Dravecky	.05
531	Joe Lefebvre	.05
532	Frank DiPino	.05
533	Tony Bernazard	.05
534	Brian Dayett	.05
535	Pat Putnam	.05
536	Kirby Puckett	10.00
537	Don Robinson	.05
538	Keith Moreland	.05
539	Aurelio Lopez	.05
540	Claudell Washington	.05
541	Mark Davis	.05
542	Don Slaught	.05
543	Mike Squires	.05
544	Bruce Kison	.05
545	Lloyd Moseby	.05
546	Brent Gaff	.05
547	Pete Rose	1.50
548	Larry Parrish	.05
549	Mike Scioscia	.05
550	Scott McGregor	.05
551	Andy Van Slyke	.05
552	Chris Codiroli	.05
553	Bob Clark	.05
554	Doug Flynn	.05
555	Bob Stanley	.05
556	Sixto Lezcano	.05
557	Len Barker	.05
558	Carmelo Martinez	.05
559	Jay Howell	.05
560	Bill Madlock	.05
561	Darryl Motley	.05
562	Houston Jimenez	.05
563	Dick Ruthven	.05
564	Alan Ashby	.05
565	Kirk Gibson	.05
566	Ed Vande Berg	.05
567	Joel Youngblood	.05
568	Cliff Johnson	.05
569	Ken Oberkfell	.05
570	Darryl Strawberry	.10
571	Charlie Hough	.05
572	Tom Paciorek	.05
573	Jay Tibbs **RC**	.05
574	Joe Altobelli	.05
575	Pedro Guerrero	.05
576	Jaime Cocanower	.05
577	Chris Speier	.05
578	Terry Francona	.05
579	Ron Romanick **RC**	.05
580	Dwight Evans	.05
581	Mark Wagner	.05
582	Ken Phelps	.05
583	Bobby Brown	.05
584	Kevin Gross	.05
585	Butch Wynegar	.05
586	Bill Scherrer	.05
587	Doug Frobel	.05
588	Bobby Castillo	.05
589	Bob Dernier	.05
590	Ray Knight	.05
591	Larry Herndon	.05
592	Jeff Robinson **RC**	.05
593	Rick Leach	.05
594	Curt Wilkerson	.05
595	Larry Gura	.05
596	Jerry Hairston Sr.	.05
597	Brad Lesley	.05
598	Jose Oquendo	.05
599	Storm Davis	.05
600	Pete Rose	3.00
601	Tom Lasorda	.10
602	Jeff Dedmon **RC**	.05
603	Rick Manning	.05
604	Daryl Sconiers	.05
605	Ozzie Smith	1.00
606	Rich Gale	.05
607	Bill Almon	.05
608	Craig Lefferts	.05
609	Broderick Perkins	.05
610	Jack Morris	.05
611	Ozzie Virgil	.05
612	Mike Armstrong	.05
613	Terry Puhl	.05
614	Al Williams	.05
615	Marvell Wynne	.05
616	Scott Sanderson	.05
617	Willie Wilson	.05
618	Pete Falcone	.05
619	Jeff Leonard	.05
620	Dwight Gooden	.50
621	Marvis Foley	.05
622	Luis Leal	.05
623	Greg Walker	.05
624	Benny Ayala	.05
625	Mark Langston	.05
626	German Rivera	.05
627	Eric Davis **RC**	1.00
628	Rene Lachemann	.05
629	Dick Schofield	.05
630	Tim Raines	.05
631	Bob Forsch	.05
632	Bruce Bochte	.05
633	Glenn Hoffman	.05
634	Bill Dawley	.05
635	Terry Kennedy	.05
636	Shane Rawley	.05
637	Brett Butler	.05
638	Mike Pagliarulo **RC**	.10
639	Ed Hodge	.05
640	Steve Henderson	.05
641	Rod Scurry	.05
642	Dave Owen	.05
643	Johnny Grubb	.05
644	Mark Huismann	.05
645	Damaso Garcia	.05
646	Scot Thompson	.05
647	Rafael Ramirez	.05
648	Bob Jones	.05
649	Sid Fernandez	.05
650	Greg Luzinski	.05
651	Jeff Russell	.05
652	Joe Nolan	.05
653	Mark Brouhard	.05
654	Dave Anderson	.05
655	Joaquin Andujar	.05
656	Chuck Cottier	.05
657	Jim Slaton	.05
658	Mike Stenhouse	.05
659	Checklist 529-660	.05
660	Tony Gwynn	1.00
661	Steve Crawford	.05
662	Mike Heath	.05
663	Luis Aguayo	.05
664	Steve Farr **RC**	.05
665	Don Mattingly	3.00
666	Mike LaCoss	.05
667	Dave Engle	.05
668	Steve Trout	.05
669	Lee Lacy	.05
670	Tom Seaver	.75
671	Dane Iorg	.05
672	Juan Berenguer	.05
673	Buck Martinez	.05
674	Atlee Hammaker	.05
675	Tony Perez	.75
676	Albert Hall **RC**	.05
677	Wally Backman	.05
678	Joey McLaughlin	.05
679	Bob Kearney	.05
680	Jerry Reuss	.05
681	Ben Oglivie	.05
682	Doug Corbett	.05
683	Whitey Herzog	.05
684	Bill Doran	.05
685	Bill Caudill	.05
686	Mike Easler	.05
687	Bill Gullickson	.05
688	Len Matuszek	.05
689	Luis DeLeon	.05
690	Alan Trammell	.05
691	Dennis Rasmussen	.05
692	Randy Bush	.05
693	Tim Stoddard	.05
694	Joe Carter	.05
695	Rick Rhoden	.05
696	John Rabb	.05
697	Onix Concepcion	.05
698	Jorge Bell	.05
699	Donnie Moore	.05
700	Eddie Murray	.75
701	Eddie Murray/AS	.40
702	Damaso Garcia/AS	.05
703	George Brett/AS	.50
704	Cal Ripken, Jr./AS	1.50
705	Dave Winfield/AS	.40
706	Rickey Henderson/AS	.40
707	Tony Armas/AS	.05
708	Lance Parrish/AS	.05
709	Mike Boddicker/AS	.05
710	Frank Viola/AS	.05
711	Dan Quisenberry/AS	.05
712	Keith Hernandez/AS	.05
713	Ryne Sandberg/AS	.40
714	Mike Schmidt/AS	.75
715	Ozzie Smith/AS	.50
716	Dale Murphy/AS	.15
717	Tony Gwynn/AS	.75
718	Jeff Leonard/AS	.05
719	Gary Carter/AS	.40
720	Rick Sutcliffe/AS	.05
721	Bob Knepper/AS	.05
722	Bruce Sutter/AS	.30
723	Dave Stewart	.05
724	Oscar Gamble	.05
725	Floyd Bannister	.05
726	Al Bumbry	.05
727	Frank Pastore	.05
728	Bob Bailor	.05
729	Don Sutton	.60
730	Dave Kingman	.05
731	Neil Allen	.05
732	John McNamara	.05
733	Tony Scott	.05
734	John Henry Johnson	.05
735	Garry Templeton	.05
736	Jerry Mumphrey	.05
737	Bo Diaz	.05
738	Omar Moreno	.05
739	Ernie Camacho	.05
740	Jack Clark	.05
741	John Butcher	.05
742	Ron Hassey	.05
743	Frank White	.05
744	Doug Bair	.05
745	Buddy Bell	.05
746	Jim Clancy	.05
747	Alex Trevino	.05
748	Lee Mazzilli	.05
749	Julio Cruz	.05
750	Rollie Fingers	.60
751	Kelvin Chapman	.05
752	Bob Owchinko	.05
753	Greg Brock	.05
754	Larry Milbourne	.05
755	Ken Singleton	.05
756	Rob Picciolo	.05
757	Willie McGee	.05
758	Ray Burris	.05
759	Jim Fanning	.05
760	Nolan Ryan	4.00
761	Jerry Remy	.05
762	Eddie Whitson	.05
763	Kiko Garcia	.05
764	Jamie Easterly	.05
765	Willie Randolph	.05
766	Paul Mirabella	.05
767	Darrell Brown	.05

768 Ron Cey .05
769 Joe Cowley .05
770 Carlton Fisk .75
771 Geoff Zahn .05
772 Johnnie LeMaster .05
773 Hal McRae .05
774 Dennis Lamp .05
775 Mookie Wilson .05
776 Jerry Royster .05
777 Ned Yost .05
778 Mike Davis .05
779 Nick Esasky .05
780 Mike Flanagan .05
781 Jim Gantner .05
782 Tom Niedenfuer .05
783 Mike Jorgensen .05
784 Checklist 661-792 .05
785 Tony Armas .05
786 Enos Cabell .05
787 Jim Wohlford .05
788 Steve Comer .05
789 Luis Salazar .05
790 Ron Guidry .10
791 Ivan DeJesus .05
792 Darrell Evans .05

1985 Topps Tiffany

NM/M
Complete Unopened Set (792): 500.00
Complete Set, Opened (792): 325.00
Common Player: .25
Stars: 4X
181 Roger Clemens 150.00
401 Mark McGwire 80.00
(See 1985 Topps for checklist and base card values.)

Traded

NM/M
Complete Set (132): 10.00
Common Player: .05
Wax Test Pack (8): 10.00
Wax Test Wax Box (36): 150.00
1 Don Aase .05
2 Bill Almon .05
3 Benny Ayala .05
4 Dusty Baker .25
5 George Bamberger .05
6 Dale Berra .05
7 Rich Bordi .05
8 Daryl Boston .05
9 Hubie Brooks .05
10 Chris Brown .05
11 Tom Browning .05
12 Al Bumbry .05
13 Ray Burris .05
14 Jeff Burroughs .05
15 Bill Campbell .05
16 Don Carman .05
17 Gary Carter 1.50
18 Bobby Castillo .05
19 Bill Caudill .05
20 Rick Cerone .05
21 Bryan Clark .05
22 Jack Clark .05
23 Pat Clements .05
24 Vince Coleman **RC** .50
25 Dave Collins .05
26 Danny Darwin .05
27 Jim Davenport .05
28 Jerry Davis .05
29 Brian Dayett .05
30 Ivan DeJesus .05
31 Ken Dixon .05
32 Mariano Duncan .05
33 John Felske .05
34 Mike Fitzgerald .05
35 Ray Fontenot .05
36 Greg Gagne .05
37 Oscar Gamble .05
38 Scott Garrelts .05
39 Bob L. Gibson .05
40 Jim Gott .05
41 David Green .05
42 Alfredo Griffin .05
43 Ozzie Guillen **RC** 3.00
44 Eddie Haas .05
45 Terry Harper .05
46 Toby Harrah .05
47 Greg Harris .05
48 Ron Hassey .05
49 Rickey Henderson 2.50
50 Steve Henderson .05
51 George Hendrick .05
52 Joe Hesketh .05
53 Teddy Higuera .05
54 Donnie Hill .05
55 Al Holland .05
56 Burt Hooton .05
57 Jay Howell .05
58 Ken Howell .05
59 LaMarr Hoyt .05
60 Tim Hulett .05
61 Bob James .05
62 Steve Jeltz .05
63 Cliff Johnson .05
64 Howard Johnson .05
65 Ruppert Jones .05
66 Steve Kemp .05
67 Bruce Kison .05
68 Alan Knicely .05
69 Mike LaCoss .05
70 Lee Lacy .05
71 Dave LaPoint .05
72 Gary Lavelle .05
73 Vance Law .05
74 Johnnie LeMaster .05
75 Sixto Lezcano .05
76 Tim Lollar .05
77 Fred Lynn .05
78 Billy Martin .25
79 Ron Mathis .05
80 Len Matuszek .05
81 Gene Mauch .05
82 Oddibe McDowell .05
83 Roger McDowell .05
84 John McNamara .05
85 Donnie Moore .05
86 Gene Nelson .05
87 Steve Nicosia .05
88 Al Oliver .05
89 Joe Orsulak .05
90 Rob Picciolo .05
91 Chris Pittaro .05
92 Jim Presley .05
93 Rick Reuschel .05
94 Bert Roberge .05
95 Bob Rodgers .05
96 Jerry Royster .05
97 Dave Rozema .05
98 Dave Rucker .05
99 Vern Ruhle .05
100 Paul Runge .05
101 Mark Salas .05
102 Luis Salazar .05
103 Joe Sambito .05
104 Rick Schu .05
105 Donnie Scott .05
106 Larry Sheets .05
107 Don Slaught .05
108 Roy Smalley .05
109 Lonnie Smith .05
110 Nate Snell .05
111 Chris Speier .05
112 Mike Stenhouse .05
113 Tim Stoddard .05
114 Jim Sundberg .05
115 Bruce Sutter 1.00
116 Don Sutton .50
117 Kent Tekulve .05
118 Tom Tellmann .05
119 Walt Terrell .05
120 Mickey Tettleton **RC** 1.00
121 Derrel Thomas .05
122 Rich Thompson .05
123 Alex Trevino .05
124 John Tudor .05
125 Jose Uribe .05
126 Bobby Valentine .05
127 Dave Von Ohlen .05
128 U.L. Washington .05
129 Earl Weaver .30
130 Eddie Whitson .05
131 Herm Winningham .05
132 Checklist 1-132 .05

1986 Topps

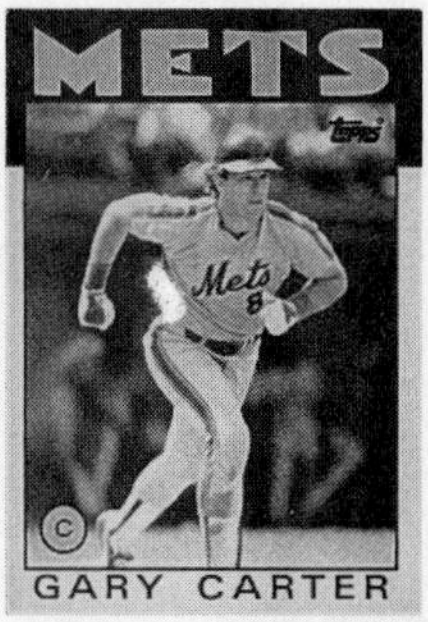

NM/M
Unopened Fact. Set, Retail (792): 65.00
Unopened Fact. Set, Hobby (792): 30.00
Complete Set (792): 25.00
Common Player: .05
Wax Pack (15): .75
Wax Box (36): 20.00
Cello Pack (28): 1.00
Cello Box (24): 20.00
Rack Pack (51): 1.25
Rack Box (24): 25.00
Vending Box (500): 10.00
1 Pete Rose 1.50
2 Pete Rose (Special 1963-66) .50
3 Pete Rose (Special 1967-70) .50
4 Pete Rose (Special 1971-74) .50
5 Pete Rose (Special 1975-78) .50
6 Pete Rose (Special 1972-82) .50
7 Pete Rose (Special 1983-85) .50
8 Dwayne Murphy .05
9 Roy Smith .05
10 Tony Gwynn .75
11 Bob Ojeda .05
12 Jose Uribe **RC** .05
13 Bob Kearney .05
14 Julio Cruz .05
15 Eddie Whitson .05
16 Rick Schu .05
17 Mike Stenhouse .05
18 Brent Gaff .05
19 Rich Hebner .05
20 Lou Whitaker .05
21 George Bamberger .05
22 Duane Walker .05
23 Manny Lee **RC** .05
24 Len Barker .05
25 Willie Wilson .05
26 Frank DiPino .05
27 Ray Knight .05
28 Eric Davis .05
29 Tony Phillips .05
30 Eddie Murray .50
31 Jamie Easterly .05
32 Steve Yeager .05
33 Jeff Lahti .05
34 Ken Phelps .05
35 Jeff Reardon .05
36 Lance Parrish Tigers Ldrs. .05
37 Mark Thurmond .05
38 Glenn Hoffman .05
39 Dave Rucker .05
40 Ken Griffey .05
41 Brad Wellman .05
42 Geoff Zahn .05
43 Dave Engle .05
44 Lance McCullers **RC** .05
45 Damaso Garcia .05
46 Billy Hatcher .05
47 Juan Berenguer .05
48 Bill Almon .05
49 Rick Manning .05
50 Dan Quisenberry .05
51 Not Issued, See #57
52 Chris Welsh .05
53 Len Dykstra **RC** .50
54 John Franco .05
55 Fred Lynn .05
56 Tom Niedenfuer .05
57a Bill Doran .05
57b Bobby Wine (Supposed to be #51.) .05
58 Bill Krueger .05
59 Andre Thornton .05
60 Dwight Evans .05
61 Karl Best .05
62 Bob Boone .05
63 Ron Roenicke .05
64 Floyd Bannister .05
65 Dan Driessen .05
66 Bob Forsch Cardinals Ldrs. .05
67 Carmelo Martinez .05
68 Ed Lynch .05
69 Luis Aguayo .05
70 Dave Winfield .50
71 Ken Schrom .05
72 Shawon Dunston .05
73 Randy O'Neal .05
74 Rance Mulliniks .05
75 Jose DeLeon .05
76 Dion James .05
77 Charlie Leibrandt .05
78 Bruce Benedict .05
79 Dave Schmidt .05
80 Darryl Strawberry .05
81 Gene Mauch .05
82 Tippy Martinez .05
83 Phil Garner .05
84 Curt Young .05
85 Tony Perez .40
86 Tom Waddell .05
87 Candy Maldonado .05
88 Tom Nieto .05
89 Randy St. Claire .05
90 Garry Templeton .05
91 Steve Crawford .05
92 Al Cowens .05
93 Scot Thompson .05
94 Rich Bordi .05
95 Ozzie Virgil .05
96 Jim Clancy Blue Jay Ldrs. .05
97 Gary Gaetti .05
98 Dick Ruthven .05
99 Buddy Biancalana .05
100 Nolan Ryan 2.00
101 Dave Bergman .05
102 Joe Orsulak **RC** .15
103 Luis Salazar .05
104 Sid Fernandez .05
105 Gary Ward .05
106 Ray Burris .05
107 Rafael Ramirez .05
108 Ted Power .05
109 Len Matuszek .05
110 Scott McGregor .05
111 Roger Craig .05
112 Bill Campbell .05
113 U.L. Washington .05
114 Mike Brown .05
115 Jay Howell .05
116 Brook Jacoby .05
117 Bruce Kison .05
118 Jerry Royster .05
119 Barry Bonnell .05
120 Steve Carlton .50
121 Nelson Simmons .05
122 Pete Filson .05
123 Greg Walker .05
124 Luis Sanchez .05
125 Dave Lopes .05
126 Mookie Wilson Mets Ldrs. .05
127 Jack Howell **RC** .05
128 John Wathan .05
129 Jeff Dedmon .05
130 Alan Trammell .05
131 Checklist 1-132 .05
132 Razor Shines .05
133 Andy McGaffigan .05
134 Carney Lansford .05
135 Joe Niekro .05
136 Mike Hargrove .05
137 Charlie Moore .05
138 Mark Davis .05
139 Daryl Boston .05
140 John Candelaria .05
141a Chuck Cottier .05
141b Bob Rodgers (Supposed to be #171.) .05
142 Bob Jones .05
143 Dave Van Gorder .05
144 Doug Sisk .05
145 Pedro Guerrero .05
146 Jack Perconte .05
147 Larry Sheets .05
148 Mike Heath .05
149 Brett Butler .05
150 Joaquin Andujar .05
151 Dave Stapleton .05
152 Mike Morgan .05
153 Ricky Adams .05
154 Bert Roberge .05
155 Bob Grich .05
156 Richard Dotson White Sox Ldrs. .05
157 Ron Hassey .05
158 Derrel Thomas .05
159 Orel Hershiser .05
160 Chet Lemon .05
161 Lee Tunnell .05
162 Greg Gagne .05
163 Pete Ladd .05
164 Steve Balboni .05
165 Mike Davis .05
166 Dickie Thon .05
167 Zane Smith .05
168 Jeff Burroughs .05
169 George Wright .05
170 Gary Carter .50
171 Not Issued, See #141
172 Jerry Reed .05
173 Wayne Gross .05
174 Brian Snyder .05
175 Steve Sax .05
176 Jay Tibbs .05
177 Joel Youngblood .05
178 Ivan DeJesus .05
179 Stu Cliburn **RC** .05
180 Don Mattingly 1.00
181 Al Nipper .05
182 Bobby Brown .05
183 Larry Andersen .05
184 Tim Laudner .05
185 Rollie Fingers .40
186 Jose Cruz Astros Ldrs. .05
187 Scott Fletcher .05
188 Bob Dernier .05
189 Mike Mason .05
190 George Hendrick .05
191 Wally Backman .05
192 Milt Wilcox .05
193 Daryl Sconiers .05
194 Craig McMurtry .05
195 Dave Concepcion .05
196 Doyle Alexander .05
197 Enos Cabell .05
198 Ken Dixon .05
199 Dick Howser .05
200 Mike Schmidt 1.00
201 Vince Coleman .05
202 Dwight Gooden .05
203 Keith Hernandez .05
204 Phil Niekro .05
205 Tony Perez .05
206 Pete Rose .25
207 Fernando Valenzuela .05
208 Ramon Romero .05
209 Randy Ready .05
210 Calvin Schiraldi .05
211 Ed Wojna .05
212 Chris Speier .05

213	Bob Shirley	.05
214	Randy Bush	.05
215	Frank White	.05
216	Dwayne Murphy A's Ldrs.	.05
217	Bill Scherrer	.05
218	Randy Hunt	.05
219	Dennis Lamp	.05
220	Bob Horner	.05
221	Dave Henderson	.05
222	Craig Gerber	.05
223	Atlee Hammaker	.05
224	Cesar Cedeno	.05
225	Ron Darling	.05
226	Lee Lacy	.05
227	Al Jones	.05
228	Tom Lawless	.05
229	Bill Gullickson	.05
230	Terry Kennedy	.05
231	Jim Frey	.05
232	Rick Rhoden	.05
233	Steve Lyons	.05
234	Doug Corbett	.05
235	Butch Wynegar	.05
236	Frank Eufemia	.05
237	Ted Simmons	.05
238	Larry Parrish	.05
239	Joel Skinner	.05
240	Tommy John	.10
241	Tony Fernandez	.05
242	Rich Thompson	.05
243	Johnny Grubb	.05
244	Craig Lefferts	.05
245	Jim Sundberg	.05
246	Steve Carlton Phillies Ldrs.	.10
247	Terry Harper	.05
248	Spike Owen	.05
249	Rob Deer	.05
250	Dwight Gooden	.05
251	Rich Dauer	.05
252	Bobby Castillo	.05
253	Dann Bilardello	.05
254	Ozzie Guillen **RC**	.30
255	Tony Armas	.05
256	Kurt Kepshire	.05
257	Doug DeCinces	.05
258	Tim Burke **RC**	.05
259	Dan Pasqua	.05
260	Tony Pena	.05
261	Bobby Valentine	.05
262	Mario Ramirez	.05
263	Checklist 133-264	.05
264	Darren Daulton	.05
265	Ron Davis	.05
266	Keith Moreland	.05
267	Paul Molitor	.50
268	Mike Scott	.05
269	Dane Iorg	.05
270	Jack Morris	.05
271	Dave Collins	.05
272	Tim Tolman	.05
273	Jerry Willard	.05
274	Ron Gardenhire	.05
275	Charlie Hough	.05
276	Willie Randolph Yankees Ldrs.	.05
277	Jaime Cocanower	.05
278	Sixto Lezcano	.05
279	Al Pardo	.05
280	Tim Raines	.05
281	Steve Mura	.05
282	Jerry Mumphrey	.05
283	Mike Fischlin	.05
284	Brian Dayett	.05
285	Buddy Bell	.05
286	Luis DeLeon	.05
287	John Christensen **RC**	.05
288	Don Aase	.05
289	Johnnie LeMaster	.05
290	Carlton Fisk	.50
291	Tom Lasorda	.10
292	Chuck Porter	.05
293	Chris Chambliss	.05
294	Danny Cox	.05
295	Kirk Gibson	.05
296	Geno Petralli	.05
297	Tim Lollar	.05
298	Craig Reynolds	.05
299	Bryn Smith	.05
300	George Brett	1.00
301	Dennis Rasmussen	.05
302	Greg Gross	.05
303	Curt Wardle	.05
304	Mike Gallego **RC**	.10
305	Phil Bradley	.05
306	Terry Kennedy Padres Ldrs.	.05
307	Dave Sax	.05
308	Ray Fontenot	.05
309	John Shelby	.05
310	Greg Minton	.05
311	Dick Schofield	.05
312	Tom Filer	.05
313	Joe DeSa	.05
314	Frank Pastore	.05
315	Mookie Wilson	.05
316	Sammy Khalifa	.05
317	Ed Romero	.05
318	Terry Whitfield	.05
319	Rick Camp	.05
320	Jim Rice	.15
321	Earl Weaver	.10
322	Bob Forsch	.05
323	Jerry Davis	.05
324	Dan Schatzeder	.05
325	Juan Beniquez	.05
326	Kent Tekulve	.05
327	Mike Pagliarulo	.05
328	Pete O'Brien	.05
329	Kirby Puckett	.75
330	Rick Sutcliffe	.05
331	Alan Ashby	.05
332	Darryl Motley	.05
333	Tom Henke	.05
334	Ken Oberkfell	.05
335	Don Sutton	.40
336	Andre Thornton Indians Ldrs.	.05
337	Darnell Coles	.05
338	Jorge Bell	.05
339	Bruce Berenyi	.05
340	Cal Ripken, Jr.	2.00
341	Frank Williams	.05
342	Gary Redus	.05
343	Carlos Diaz	.05
344	Jim Wohlford	.05
345	Donnie Moore	.05
346	Bryan Little	.05
347	Teddy Higuera **RC**	.10
348	Cliff Johnson	.05
349	Mark Clear	.05
350	Jack Clark	.05
351	Chuck Tanner	.05
352	Harry Spilman	.05
353	Keith Atherton	.05
354	Tony Bernazard	.05
355	Lee Smith	.05
356	Mickey Hatcher	.05
357	Ed Vande Berg	.05
358	Rick Dempsey	.05
359	Mike LaCoss	.05
360	Lloyd Moseby	.05
361	Shane Rawley	.05
362	Tom Paciorek	.05
363	Terry Forster	.05
364	Reid Nichols	.05
365	Mike Flanagan	.05
366	Dave Concepcion Reds Ldrs.	.05
367	Aurelio Lopez	.05
368	Greg Brock	.05
369	Al Holland	.05
370	Vince Coleman **RC**	.35
371	Bill Stein	.05
372	Ben Oglivie	.05
373	Urbano Lugo **RC**	.05
374	Terry Francona	.05
375	Rich Gedman	.05
376	Bill Dawley	.05
377	Joe Carter	.05
378	Bruce Bochte	.05
379	Bobby Meacham	.05
380	LaMarr Hoyt	.05
381	Ray Miller	.05
382	Ivan Calderon **RC**	.05
383	Chris Brown **RC**	.05
384	Steve Trout	.05
385	Cecil Cooper	.05
386	Cecil Fielder **RC**	.75
387	Steve Kemp	.05
388	Dickie Noles	.05
389	Glenn Davis	.05
390	Tom Seaver	.60
391	Julio Franco	.05
392	John Russell	.05
393	Chris Pittaro	.05
394	Checklist 265-396	.05
395	Scott Garrelts	.05
396	Dwight Evans Red Sox Ldrs.	.05
397	Steve Buechele **RC**	.10
398	Earnie Riles **RC**	.05
399	Bill Swift	.05
400	Rod Carew	.50
401	Fernando Valenzuela	.05
402	Tom Seaver	.25
403	Willie Mays	.35
404	Frank Robinson	.10
405	Roger Maris	.30
406	Scott Sanderson	.05
407	Sal Butera	.05
408	Dave Smith	.05
409	Paul Runge **RC**	.05
410	Dave Kingman	.05
411	Sparky Anderson	.10
412	Jim Clancy	.05
413	Tim Flannery	.05
414	Tom Gorman	.05
415	Hal McRae	.05
416	Denny Martinez	.05
417	R.J. Reynolds	.05
418	Alan Knicely	.05
419	Frank Wills	.05
420	Von Hayes	.05
421	Dave Palmer	.05
422	Mike Jorgensen	.05
423	Dan Spillner	.05
424	Rick Miller	.05
425	Larry McWilliams	.05
426	Charlie Moore Brewers Ldrs.	.05
427	Joe Cowley	.05
428	Max Venable	.05
429	Greg Booker	.05
430	Kent Hrbek	.05
431	George Frazier	.05
432	Mark Bailey	.05
433	Chris Codiroli	.05
434	Curt Wilkerson	.05
435	Bill Caudill	.05
436	Doug Flynn	.05
437	Rick Mahler	.05
438	Clint Hurdle	.05
439	Rick Honeycutt	.05
440	Alvin Davis	.05
441	Whitey Herzog	.05
442	Ron Robinson	.05
443	Bill Buckner	.05
444	Alex Trevino	.05
445	Bert Blyleven	.05
446	Lenn Sakata	.05
447	Jerry Don Gleaton	.05
448	Herm Winningham **RC**	.05
449	Rod Scurry	.05
450	Graig Nettles	.05
451	Mark Brown	.05
452	Bob Clark	.05
453	Steve Jeltz	.05
454	Burt Hooton	.05
455	Willie Randolph	.05
456	Dale Murphy Braves Ldrs.	.10
457	Mickey Tettleton	.05
458	Kevin Bass	.05
459	Luis Leal	.05
460	Leon Durham	.05
461	Walt Terrell	.05
462	Domingo Ramos	.05
463	Jim Gott	.05
464	Ruppert Jones	.05
465	Jesse Orosco	.05
466	Tom Foley	.05
467	Bob James	.05
468	Mike Scioscia	.05
469	Storm Davis	.05
470	Bill Madlock	.05
471	Bobby Cox	.05
472	Joe Hesketh	.05
473	Mark Brouhard	.05
474	John Tudor	.05
475	Juan Samuel	.05
476	Ron Mathis	.05
477	Mike Easler	.05
478	Andy Hawkins	.05
479	Bob Melvin **RC**	.05
480	Oddibe McDowell **RC**	.05
481	Scott Bradley	.05
482	Rick Lysander	.05
483	George Vukovich	.05
484	Donnie Hill	.05
485	Gary Matthews	.05
486	Bob Grich Angels Ldrs.	.05
487	Bret Saberhagen	.05
488	Lou Thornton	.05
489	Jim Winn	.05
490	Jeff Leonard	.05
491	Pascual Perez	.05
492	Kelvin Chapman	.05
493	Gene Nelson	.05
494	Gary Roenicke	.05
495	Mark Langston	.05
496	Jay Johnstone	.05
497	John Stuper	.05
498	Tito Landrum	.05
499	Bob L. Gibson	.05
500	Rickey Henderson	.50
501	Dave Johnson	.05
502	Glen Cook	.05
503	Mike Fitzgerald	.05
504	Denny Walling	.05
505	Jerry Koosman	.05
506	Bill Russell	.05
507	Steve Ontiveros **RC**	.05
508	Alan Wiggins	.05
509	Ernie Camacho	.05
510	Wade Boggs	.75
511	Ed Nunez	.05
512	Thad Bosley	.05
513	Ron Washington	.05
514	Mike Jones	.05
515	Darrell Evans	.05
516	Greg Minton Giants Ldrs.	.05
517	Milt Thompson **RC**	.05
518	Buck Martinez	.05
519	Danny Darwin	.05
520	Keith Hernandez	.05
521	Nate Snell	.05
522	Bob Bailor	.05
523	Joe Price	.05
524	Darrell Miller	.05
525	Marvell Wynne	.05
526	Charlie Lea	.05
527	Checklist 397-528	.05
528	Terry Pendleton	.05
529	Marc Sullivan	.05
530	Rich Gossage	.05
531	Tony LaRussa	.05
532	Don Carman **RC**	.05
533	Billy Sample	.05
534	Jeff Calhoun	.05
535	Toby Harrah	.05
536	Jose Rijo	.05
537	Mark Salas	.05
538	Dennis Eckersley	.40
539	Glenn Hubbard	.05
540	Dan Petry	.05
541	Jorge Orta	.05
542	Don Schulze	.05
543	Jerry Narron	.05
544	Eddie Milner	.05
545	Jimmy Key	.05
546	Dave Henderson Mariners Ldrs.	.05
547	Roger McDowell	.05
548	Mike Young	.05
549	Bob Welch	.05
550	Tom Herr	.05
551	Dave LaPoint	.05
552	Marc Hill	.05
553	Jim Morrison	.05
554	Paul Householder	.05
555	Hubie Brooks	.05
556	John Denny	.05
557	Gerald Perry	.05
558	Tim Stoddard	.05
559	Tommy Dunbar	.05
560	Dave Righetti	.05
561	Bob Lillis	.05
562	Joe Beckwith	.05
563	Alejandro Sanchez	.05
564	Warren Brusstar	.05
565	Tom Brunansky	.05
566	Alfredo Griffin	.05
567	Jeff Barkley	.05
568	Donnie Scott	.05
569	Jim Acker	.05
570	Rusty Staub	.10
571	Mike Jeffcoat	.05
572	Paul Zuvella	.05
573	Tom Hume	.05
574	Ron Kittle	.05
575	Mike Boddicker	.05
576	Andre Dawson Expos Ldrs.	.05
577	Jerry Reuss	.05
578	Lee Mazzilli	.05
579	Jim Slaton	.05
580	Willie McGee	.05
581	Bruce Hurst	.05
582	Jim Gantner	.05
583	Al Bumbry	.05
584	Brian Fisher **RC**	.05
585	Garry Maddox	.05
586	Greg Harris	.05
587	Rafael Santana	.05
588	Steve Lake	.05
589	Sid Bream	.05
590	Bob Knepper	.05
591	Jackie Moore	.05
592	Frank Tanana	.05
593	Jesse Barfield	.05
594	Chris Bando	.05
595	Dave Parker	.05
596	Onix Concepcion	.05
597	Sammy Stewart	.05
598	Jim Presley	.05
599	Rick Aguilera **RC**	.25
600	Dale Murphy	.25
601	Gary Lucas	.05
602	Mariano Duncan	.05
603	Bill Laskey	.05
604	Gary Pettis	.05
605	Dennis Boyd	.05
606	Hal McRae Royals Ldrs.	.05
607	Ken Dayley	.05
608	Bruce Bochy	.05
609	Barbaro Garbey	.05
610	Ron Guidry	.05
611	Gary Woods	.05
612	Richard Dotson	.05
613	Roy Smalley	.05
614	Rick Waits	.05
615	Johnny Ray	.05
616	Glenn Brummer	.05
617	Lonnie Smith	.05
618	Jim Pankovits	.05
619	Danny Heep	.05
620	Bruce Sutter	.40
621	John Felske	.05
622	Gary Lavelle	.05
623	Floyd Rayford	.05
624	Steve McCatty	.05
625	Bob Brenly	.05
626	Roy Thomas	.05
627	Ron Oester	.05
628	Kirk McCaskill **RC**	.15
629	Mitch Webster **RC**	.05
630	Fernando Valenzuela	.05
631	Steve Braun	.05
632	Dave Von Ohlen	.05
633	Jackie Gutierrez	.05
634	Roy Lee Jackson	.05
635	Jason Thompson	.05
636	Lee Smith Cubs Ldrs.	.05
637	Rudy Law	.05
638	John Butcher	.05
639	Bo Diaz	.05
640	Jose Cruz	.05
641	Wayne Tolleson	.05
642	Ray Searage	.05
643	Tom Brookens	.05
644	Mark Gubicza	.05
645	Dusty Baker	.05
646	Mike Moore	.05
647	Mel Hall	.05
648	Steve Bedrosian	.05
649	Ronn Reynolds	.05
650	Dave Stieb	.05
651	Billy Martin	.10
652	Tom Browning	.05
653	Jim Dwyer	.05
654	Ken Howell	.05
655	Manny Trillo	.05
656	Brian Harper	.05
657	Juan Agosto	.05
658	Rob Wilfong	.05
659	Checklist 529-660	.05
660	Steve Garvey	.20
661	Roger Clemens	3.00
661	Roger Clemens (Blue streak upper-right.)	7.50
662	Bill Schroeder	.05
663	Neil Allen	.05
664	Tim Corcoran	.05
665	Alejandro Pena	.05
666	Charlie Hough Rangers Ldrs.	.05
667	Tim Teufel	.05
668	Cecilio Guante	.05
669	Ron Cey	.05

#	Player	Price
670	Willie Hernandez	.05
671	Lynn Jones	.05
672	Rob Picciolo	.05
673	Ernie Whitt	.05
674	Pat Tabler	.05
675	Claudell Washington	.05
676	Matt Young	.05
677	Nick Esasky	.05
678	Dan Gladden	.05
679	Britt Burns	.05
680	George Foster	.05
681	Dick Williams	.05
682	Junior Ortiz	.05
683	Andy Van Slyke	.05
684	Bob McClure	.05
685	Tim Wallach	.05
686	Jeff Stone	.05
687	Mike Trujillo	.05
688	Larry Herndon	.05
689	Dave Stewart	.05
690	Ryne Sandberg	.75
691	Mike Madden	.05
692	Dale Berra	.05
693	Tom Tellmann	.05
694	Garth Iorg	.05
695	Mike Smithson	.05
696	Bill Russell Dodgers Ldrs.	.05
697	Bud Black	.05
698	Brad Komminsk	.05
699	Pat Corrales	.05
700	Reggie Jackson	.75
701	Keith Hernandez/AS	.05
702	Tom Herr/AS	.05
703	Tim Wallach/AS	.05
704	Ozzie Smith/AS	.35
705	Dale Murphy/AS	.10
706	Pedro Guerrero/AS	.05
707	Willie McGee/AS	.05
708	Gary Carter/AS	.25
709	Dwight Gooden/AS	.05
710	John Tudor/AS	.05
711	Jeff Reardon/AS	.05
712	Don Mattingly/AS	.50
713	Damaso Garcia/AS	.05
714	George Brett/AS	.45
715	Cal Ripken, Jr./AS	1.00
716	Rickey Henderson/AS	.25
717	Dave Winfield/AS	.25
718	George Bell/AS	.05
719	Carlton Fisk/AS	.20
720	Bret Saberhagen/AS	.05
721	Ron Guidry/AS	.05
722	Dan Quisenberry/AS	.05
723	Marty Bystrom	.05
724	Tim Hulett	.05
725	Mario Soto	.05
726	Rick Dempsey Orioles Ldrs.	.05
727	David Green	.05
728	Mike Marshall	.05
729	Jim Beattie	.05
730	Ozzie Smith	.75
731	Don Robinson	.05
732	Floyd Youmans RC	.05
733	Ron Romanick	.05
734	Marty Barrett	.05
735	Dave Dravecky	.05
736	Glenn Wilson	.05
737	Pete Vuckovich	.05
738	Andre Robertson	.05
739	Dave Rozema	.05
740	Lance Parrish	.05
741	Pete Rose	1.00
742	Frank Viola	.05
743	Pat Sheridan	.05
744	Lary Sorensen	.05
745	Willie Upshaw	.05
746	Denny Gonzalez	.05
747	Rick Cerone	.05
748	Steve Henderson	.05
749	Ed Jurak	.05
750	Gorman Thomas	.05
751	Howard Johnson	.05
752	Mike Krukow	.05
753	Dan Ford	.05
754	Pat Clements RC	.05
755	Harold Baines	.05
756	Rick Rhoden Pirates Ldrs.	.05
757	Darrell Porter	.05
758	Dave Anderson	.05
759	Moose Haas	.05
760	Andre Dawson	.30
761	Don Slaught	.05
762	Eric Show	.05
763	Terry Puhl	.05
764	Kevin Gross	.05
765	Don Baylor	.05
766	Rick Langford	.05
767	Jody Davis	.05
768	Vern Ruhle	.05
769	Harold Reynolds RC	.25
770	Vida Blue	.05
771	John McNamara	.05
772	Brian Downing	.05
773	Greg Pryor	.05
774	Terry Leach	.05
775	Al Oliver	.05
776	Gene Garber	.05
777	Wayne Krenchicki	.05
778	Jerry Hairston Sr.	.05
779	Rick Reuschel	.05
780	Robin Yount	.50
781	Joe Nolan	.05
782	Ken Landreaux	.05
783	Ricky Horton	.05
784	Alan Bannister	.05
785	Bob Stanley	.05
786	Mickey Hatcher Twins Ldrs.	.05
787	Vance Law	.05
788	Marty Castillo	.05
789	Kurt Bevacqua	.05
790	Phil Niekro	.40
791	Checklist 661-792	.05
792	Charles Hudson	.05

1986 Topps Tiffany

	NM/M
Unopened Set (792):	100.00
Complete Set (792):	45.00
Common Player:	.25

(Star cards valued at 4X corresponding cards in regular 1986 Topps issue.)

Traded

JOSE CANSECO

	NM/M
Unopened Set (132):	30.00
Complete Set (132):	25.00
Common Player:	.05

#	Player	Price
1T	Andy Allanson	.05
2T	Neil Allen	.05
3T	Joaquin Andujar	.05
4T	Paul Assenmacher	.05
5T	Scott Bailes	.05
6T	Don Baylor	.15
7T	Steve Bedrosian	.05
8T	Juan Beniquez	.05
9T	Juan Berenguer	.05
10T	Mike Bielecki	.05
11T	Barry Bonds RC	20.00
12T	Bobby Bonilla RC	.50
13T	Juan Bonilla	.05
14T	Rich Bordi	.05
15T	Steve Boros	.05
16T	Rick Burleson	.05
17T	Bill Campbell	.05
18T	Tom Candiotti	.05
19T	John Cangelosi	.05
20T	Jose Canseco RC	4.00
21T	Carmen Castillo	.05
22T	Rick Cerone	.05
23T	John Cerutti	.05
24T	Will Clark RC	1.50
25T	Mark Clear	.05
26T	Darnell Coles	.05
27T	Dave Collins	.05
28T	Tim Conroy	.05
29T	Joe Cowley	.05
30T	Joel Davis	.05
31T	Rob Deer	.05
32T	John Denny	.05
33T	Mike Easler	.05
34T	Mark Eichhorn	.05
35T	Steve Farr	.05
36T	Scott Fletcher	.05
37T	Terry Forster	.05
38T	Terry Francona	.05
39T	Jim Fregosi	.05
40T	Andres Galarraga	.35
41T	Ken Griffey	.05
42T	Bill Gullickson	.05
43T	Jose Guzman	.05
44T	Moose Haas	.05
45T	Billy Hatcher	.05
46T	Mike Heath	.05
47T	Tom Hume	.05
48T	Pete Incaviglia RC	.20
49T	Dane Iorg	.05
50T	Bo Jackson RC	3.00
51T	Wally Joyner RC	.40
52T	Charlie Kerfeld	.05
53T	Eric King	.05
54T	Bob Kipper	.05
55T	Wayne Krenchicki	.05
56T	John Kruk RC	.35
57T	Mike LaCoss	.05
58T	Pete Ladd	.05
59T	Mike Laga	.05
60T	Hal Lanier	.05
61T	Dave LaPoint	.05
62T	Rudy Law	.05
63T	Rick Leach	.05
64T	Tim Leary	.05
65T	Dennis Leonard	.05
66T	Jim Leyland	.05
67T	Steve Lyons	.05
68T	Mickey Mahler	.05
69T	Candy Maldonado	.05
70T	Roger Mason	.05
71T	Bob McClure	.05
72T	Andy McGaffigan	.05
73T	Gene Michael	.05
74T	Kevin Mitchell RC	.25
75T	Omar Moreno	.05
76T	Jerry Mumphrey	.05
77T	Phil Niekro	.25
78T	Randy Niemann	.05
79T	Juan Nieves	.05
80T	Otis Nixon	.05
81T	Bob Ojeda	.05
82T	Jose Oquendo	.05
83T	Tom Paciorek	.05
84T	Dave Palmer	.05
85T	Frank Pastore	.05
86T	Lou Piniella	.05
87T	Dan Plesac	.05
88T	Darrell Porter	.05
89T	Rey Quinones	.05
90T	Gary Redus	.05
91T	Bip Roberts	.05
92T	Billy Jo Robidoux	.05
93T	Jeff Robinson	.05
94T	Gary Roenicke	.05
95T	Ed Romero	.05
96T	Argenis Salazar	.05
97T	Joe Sambito	.05
98T	Billy Sample	.05
99T	Dave Schmidt	.05
100T	Ken Schrom	.05
101T	Tom Seaver	.50
102T	Ted Simmons	.05
103T	Sammy Stewart	.05
104T	Kurt Stillwell	.05
105T	Franklin Stubbs	.05
106T	Dale Sveum	.05
107T	Chuck Tanner	.05
108T	Danny Tartabull	.05
109T	Tim Teufel	.05
110T	Bob Tewksbury	.05
111T	Andres Thomas	.05
112T	Milt Thompson	.05
113T	Robby Thompson	.05
114T	Jay Tibbs	.05
115T	Wayne Tolleson	.05
116T	Alex Trevino	.05
117T	Manny Trillo	.05
118T	Ed Vande Berg	.05
119T	Ozzie Virgil	.05
120T	Bob Walk	.05
121T	Gene Walter	.05
122T	Claudell Washington	.05
123T	Bill Wegman	.05
124T	Dick Williams	.05
125T	Mitch Williams	.05
126T	Bobby Witt	.05
127T	Todd Worrell	.05
128T	George Wright	.05
129T	Ricky Wright	.05
130T	Steve Yeager	.05
131T	Paul Zuvella	.05
132T	Checklist	.05

1986 Topps Traded Tiffany

	NM/M
Unopened Set (132):	700.00
Complete Set (132):	450.00
Common Player:	.25
11T Barry Bonds	200.00

(Star cards valued at 4X corresponding cards in regular Topps Traded.)

1987 Topps

MARIANO DUNCAN

	NM/M
Unopened Factory Set, Retail (792):	30.00
Unopened Factory Set, Hobby (792):	25.00
Complete Set (792):	20.00
Uncut Sheet Set (6):	45.00
Common Player:	.05
Wax Pack (15):	.75
Wax Box (36):	20.00
Cello Pack (31):	1.00
Cello Box (24):	20.00
Rack Pack (49):	1.50
Rack Box (24):	25.00
Vending Box (500):	12.00

#	Player	Price
1	Roger Clemens	.45
2	Jim Deshaies	.05
3	Dwight Evans	.05
4	Dave Lopes	.05
5	Dave Righetti	.05
6	Ruben Sierra	.05
7	Todd Worrell	.05
8	Terry Pendleton	.05
9	Jay Tibbs	.05
10	Cecil Cooper	.05
11	Jack Aker, Chris Bando, Phil Niekro Indians Ldrs.	.05
12	Jeff Sellers RC	.05
13	Nick Esasky	.05
14	Dave Stewart	.05
15	Claudell Washington	.05
16	Pat Clements	.05
17	Pete O'Brien	.05
18	Dick Howser	.05
19	Matt Young	.05
20	Gary Carter	.40
21	Mark Davis	.05
22	Doug DeCinces	.05
23	Lee Smith	.05
24	Tony Walker	.05
25	Bert Blyleven	.05
26	Greg Brock	.05
27	Joe Cowley	.05
28	Rick Dempsey	.05
29	Jimmy Key	.05
30	Tim Raines	.05
31	Glenn Hubbard, Rafael Ramirez Braves Ldrs.	.05
32	Tim Leary	.05
33	Andy Van Slyke	.05
34	Jose Rijo	.05
35	Sid Bream	.05
36	Eric King RC	.05
37	Marvell Wynne	.05
38	Dennis Leonard	.05
39	Marty Barrett	.05
40	Dave Righetti	.05
41	Bo Diaz	.05
42	Gary Redus	.05
43	Gene Michael	.05
44	Greg Harris	.05
45	Jim Presley	.05
46	Danny Gladden	.05
47	Dennis Powell	.05
48	Wally Backman	.05
49	Terry Harper	.05
50	Dave Smith	.05
51	Mel Hall	.05
52	Keith Atherton	.05
53	Ruppert Jones	.05
54	Bill Dawley	.05
55	Tim Wallach	.05
56	Jamie Cocanower, Paul Molitor, Charlie Moore, Herm Starrette Brewers Ldrs.	.10
57	Scott Nielsen RC	.05
58	Thad Bosley	.05
59	Ken Dayley	.05
60	Tony Pena	.05
61	Bobby Thigpen RC	.05
62	Bobby Meacham	.05
63	Fred Toliver	.05
64	Harry Spilman	.05
65	Tom Browning	.05
66	Marc Sullivan	.05
67	Bill Swift	.05
68	Tony LaRussa	.05
69	Lonnie Smith	.05
70	Charlie Hough	.05
71	Mike Aldrete RC	.05
72	Walt Terrell	.05
73	Dave Anderson	.05
74	Dan Pasqua	.05
75	Ron Darling	.05
76	Rafael Ramirez	.05
77	Bryan Oelkers	.05
78	Tom Foley	.05
79	Juan Nieves	.05
80	Wally Joyner RC	.35
81	Andy Hawkins, Terry Kennedy Padres Ldrs.	.05
82	Rob Murphy RC	.05
83	Mike Davis	.05
84	Steve Lake	.05
85	Kevin Bass	.05
86	Nate Snell	.05
87	Mark Salas	.05
88	Ed Wojna	.05
89	Ozzie Guillen	.05
90	Dave Stieb	.05
91	Harold Reynolds	.05
92a	Urbano Lugo (No trademark on front.)	.10
92b	Urbano Lugo (Trademark on front.)	.05
93	Jim Leyland	.05
94	Calvin Schiraldi	.05
95	Oddibe McDowell	.05
96	Frank Williams	.05
97	Glenn Wilson	.05
98	Bill Scherrer	.05
99	Darryl Motley	.05
100	Steve Garvey	.15
101	Carl Willis RC	.05
102	Paul Zuvella	.05
103	Rick Aguilera	.05
104	Billy Sample	.05
105	Floyd Youmans	.05
106	George Bell, Willie Upshaw Blue Jays Ldrs.	.05
107	John Butcher	.05

108	Jim Gantner (Photo reversed.)	.05
109	R.J. Reynolds	.05
110	John Tudor	.05
111	Alfredo Griffin	.05
112	Alan Ashby	.05
113	Neil Allen	.05
114	Billy Beane	.05
115	Donnie Moore	.05
116	Mike Stanley **RC**	.05
117	Jim Beattie	.05
118	Bobby Valentine	.05
119	Ron Robinson	.05
120	Eddie Murray	.40
121	Kevin Romine **RC**	.05
122	Jim Clancy	.05
123	John Kruk	.05
124	Ray Fontenot	.05
125	Bob Brenly	.05
126	Mike Loynd **RC**	.05
127	Vance Law	.05
128	Checklist 1-132	.05
129	Rick Cerone	.05
130	Dwight Gooden	.05
131	Sid Bream, Tony Pena Pirates Ldrs.	.05
132	Paul Assenmacher **RC**	.05
133	Jose Oquendo	.05
134	Rich Yett **RC**	.05
135	Mike Easler	.05
136	Ron Romanick	.05
137	Jerry Willard	.05
138	Roy Lee Jackson	.05
139	Devon White **RC**	.40
140	Bret Saberhagen	.05
141	Herm Winningham	.05
142	Rick Sutcliffe	.05
143	Steve Boros	.05
144	Mike Scioscia	.05
145	Charlie Kerfeld	.05
146	Tracy Jones **RC**	.05
147	Randy Niemann	.05
148	Dave Collins	.05
149	Ray Searage	.05
150	Wade Boggs	.45
151	Mike LaCoss	.05
152	Toby Harrah	.05
153	Duane Ward **RC**	.05
154	Tom O'Malley	.05
155	Eddie Whitson	.05
156	Bob Kearney, Phil Regan, Matt Young Mariners Ldrs.	.05
157	Danny Darwin	.05
158	Tim Teufel	.05
159	Ed Olwine	.05
160	Julio Franco	.05
161	Steve Ontiveros	.05
162	Mike LaValliere **RC**	.10
163	Kevin Gross	.05
164	Sammy Khalifa	.05
165	Jeff Reardon	.05
166	Bob Boone	.05
167	Jim Deshaies **RC**	.10
168	Lou Piniella	.05
169	Ron Washington	.05
170	Bo Jackson	1.50
171	Chuck Cary **RC**	.05
172	Ron Oester	.05
173	Alex Trevino	.05
174	Henry Cotto	.05
175	Bob Stanley	.05
176	Steve Buechele	.05
177	Keith Moreland	.05
178	Cecil Fielder	.05
179	Bill Wegman	.05
180	Chris Brown	.05
181	Mike LaValliere, Ozzie Smith, Ray Soff Cardinals Ldrs.	.10
182	Lee Lacy	.05
183	Andy Hawkins	.05
184	Bobby Bonilla	.05
185	Roger McDowell	.05
186	Bruce Benedict	.05
187	Mark Huismann	.05
188	Tony Phillips	.05
189	Joe Hesketh	.05
190	Jim Sundberg	.05
191	Charles Hudson	.05
192	Cory Snyder	.05
193	Roger Craig	.05
194	Kirk McCaskill	.05
195	Mike Pagliarulo	.05
196	Randy O'Neal	.05
197	Mark Bailey	.05
198	Lee Mazzilli	.05
199	Mariano Duncan	.05
200	Pete Rose	.75
201	John Cangelosi **RC**	.05
202	Ricky Wright	.05
203	Mike Kingery **RC**	.05
204	Sammy Stewart	.05
205	Graig Nettles	.05
206	Tim Laudner, Frank Viola Twins Ldrs.	.05
207	George Frazier	.05
208	John Shelby	.05
209	Rick Schu	.05
210	Lloyd Moseby	.05
211	John Morris	.05
212	Mike Fitzgerald	.05
213	Randy Myers **RC**	.20
214	Omar Moreno	.05
215	Mark Langston	.05
216	B.J. Surhoff **RC**	.20
217	Chris Codiroli	.05
218	Sparky Anderson	.10
219	Cecilio Guante	.05
220	Joe Carter	.05
221	Vern Ruhle	.05
222	Denny Walling	.05
223	Charlie Leibrandt	.05
224	Wayne Tolleson	.05
225	Mike Smithson	.05
226	Max Venable	.05
227	Jamie Moyer **RC**	.05
228	Curt Wilkerson	.05
229	Mike Birkbeck **RC**	.05
230	Don Baylor	.05
231	Bob Brenly, Mike Krukow Giants Ldrs.	.05
232	Reggie Williams **RC**	.05
233	Russ Morman **RC**	.05
234	Pat Sheridan	.05
235	Alvin Davis	.05
236	Tommy John	.10
237	Jim Morrison	.05
238	Bill Krueger	.05
239	Juan Espino	.05
240	Steve Balboni	.05
241	Danny Heep	.05
242	Rick Mahler	.05
243	Whitey Herzog	.05
244	Dickie Noles	.05
245	Willie Upshaw	.05
246	Jim Dwyer	.05
247	Jeff Reed	.05
248	Gene Walter	.05
249	Jim Pankovits	.05
250	Teddy Higuera	.05
251	Rob Wilfong	.05
252	Denny Martinez	.05
253	Eddie Milner	.05
254	Bob Tewksbury **RC**	.20
255	Juan Samuel	.05
256	George Brett, Frank White Royals Ldrs.	.15
257	Bob Forsch	.05
258	Steve Yeager	.05
259	Mike Greenwell **RC**	.25
260	Vida Blue	.05
261	Ruben Sierra	.05
262	Jim Winn	.05
263	Stan Javier	.05
264	Checklist 133-264	.05
265	Darrell Evans	.05
266	Jeff Hamilton **RC**	.05
267	Howard Johnson	.05
268	Pat Corrales	.05
269	Cliff Speck	.05
270	Jody Davis	.05
271	Mike Brown	.05
272	Andres Galarraga	.05
273	Gene Nelson	.05
274	Jeff Hearron **RC**	.05
275	LaMarr Hoyt	.05
276	Jackie Gutierrez	.05
277	Juan Agosto	.05
278	Gary Pettis	.05
279	Dan Plesac **RC**	.05
280	Jeffrey Leonard	.05
281	Bo Diaz, Bill Gullickson, Pete Rose Reds Ldrs.	.10
282	Jeff Calhoun	.05
283	Doug Drabek **RC**	.25
284	John Moses	.05
285	Dennis Boyd	.05
286	Mike Woodard	.05
287	Dave Von Ohlen	.05
288	Tito Landrum	.05
289	Bob Kipper	.05
290	Leon Durham	.05
291	Mitch Williams	.05
292	Franklin Stubbs	.05
293	Bob Rodgers	.05
294	Steve Jeltz	.05
295	Len Dykstra	.05
296	Andres Thomas **RC**	.05
297	Don Schulze	.05
298	Larry Herndon	.05
299	Joel Davis	.05
300	Reggie Jackson	.50
301	Luis Aquino **RC**	.05
302	Bill Schroeder	.05
303	Juan Berenguer	.05
304	Phil Garner	.05
305	John Franco	.05
306	Rich Gedman, John McNamara, Tom Seaver Red Sox Ldrs.	.10
307	Lee Guetterman **RC**	.05
308	Don Slaught	.05
309	Mike Young	.05
310	Frank Viola	.05
311	Rickey Henderson	.10
312	Reggie Jackson	.10
313	Roberto Clemente	.50
314	Carl Yastrzemski	.10
315	Maury Wills	.05
316	Brian Fisher	.05
317	Clint Hurdle	.05
318	Jim Fregosi	.05
319	Greg Swindell **RC**	.10
320	Barry Bonds	8.00
321	Mike Laga	.05
322	Chris Bando	.05
323	Al Newman **RC**	.05
324	Dave Palmer	.05
325	Garry Templeton	.05
326	Mark Gubicza	.05
327	Dale Sveum **RC**	.05
328	Bob Welch	.05
329	Ron Roenicke	.05
330	Mike Scott	.05
331	Gary Carter, Keith Hernandez, Dave Johnson, Darryl Strawberry Mets Ldrs.	.10
332	Joe Price	.05
333	Ken Phelps	.05
334	Ed Correa **RC**	.05
335	Candy Maldonado	.05
336	Allan Anderson **RC**	.05
337	Darrell Miller	.05
338	Tim Conroy	.05
339	Donnie Hill	.05
340	Roger Clemens	.65
341	Mike Brown	.05
342	Bob James	.05
343	Hal Lanier	.05
344a	Joe Niekro (Copyright outside yellow on back.)	.25
344b	Joe Niekro (Copyright inside yellow on back.)	.05
345	Andre Dawson	.25
346	Shawon Dunston	.05
347	Mickey Brantley	.05
348	Carmelo Martinez	.05
349	Storm Davis	.05
350	Keith Hernandez	.05
351	Gene Garber	.05
352	Mike Felder	.05
353	Ernie Camacho	.05
354	Jamie Quirk	.05
355	Don Carman	.05
356	Ed Brinkman, Julio Cruz White Sox Ldrs.	.05
357	Steve Fireovid **RC**	.05
358	Sal Butera	.05
359	Doug Corbett	.05
360	Pedro Guerrero	.05
361	Mark Thurmond	.05
362	Luis Quinones **RC**	.05
363	Jose Guzman	.05
364	Randy Bush	.05
365	Rick Rhoden	.05
366	Mark McGwire	3.00
367	Jeff Lahti	.05
368	John McNamara	.05
369	Brian Dayett	.05
370	Fred Lynn	.05
371	Mark Eichhorn **RC**	.05
372	Jerry Mumphrey	.05
373	Jeff Dedmon	.05
374	Glenn Hoffman	.05
375	Ron Guidry	.10
376	Scott Bradley	.05
377	John Henry Johnson	.05
378	Rafael Santana	.05
379	John Russell	.05
380	Rich Gossage	.05
381	Mike Fitzgerald, Bob Rodgers Expos Ldrs.	.05
382	Rudy Law	.05
383	Ron Davis	.05
384	Johnny Grubb	.05
385	Orel Hershiser	.05
386	Dickie Thon	.05
387	T.R. Bryden **RC**	.05
388	Geno Petralli	.05
389	Jeff Robinson	.05
390	Gary Matthews	.05
391	Jay Howell	.05
392	Checklist 265-396	.05
393	Pete Rose	.60
394	Mike Bielecki	.05
395	Damaso Garcia	.05
396	Tim Lollar	.05
397	Greg Walker	.05
398	Brad Havens	.05
399	Curt Ford	.05
400	George Brett	.50
401	Billy Jo Robidoux	.05
402	Mike Trujillo	.05
403	Jerry Royster	.05
404	Doug Sisk	.05
405	Brook Jacoby	.05
406	Rickey Henderson, Don Mattingly Yankees Ldrs.	.25
407	Jim Acker	.05
408	John Mizerock	.05
409	Milt Thompson	.05
410	Fernando Valenzuela	.05
411	Darnell Coles	.05
412	Eric Davis	.05
413	Moose Haas	.05
414	Joe Orsulak	.05
415	Bobby Witt **RC**	.05
416	Tom Nieto	.05
417	Pat Perry	.05
418	Dick Williams	.05
419	Mark Portugal **RC**	.10
420	Will Clark	.40
421	Jose DeLeon	.05
422	Jack Howell	.05
423	Jaime Cocanower	.05
424	Chris Speier	.05
425	Tom Seaver	.40
426	Floyd Rayford	.05
427	Ed Nunez	.05
428	Bruce Bochy	.05
429	Tim Pyznarski **RC**	.05
430	Mike Schmidt	.50
431	Tom Niedenfuer, Ron Perranoski, Alex Trevino Dodgers Ldrs.	.05
432	Jim Slaton	.05
433	Ed Hearn **RC**	.05
434	Mike Fischlin	.05
435	Bruce Sutter	.35
436	Andy Allanson **RC**	.05
437	Ted Power	.05
438	Kelly Downs **RC**	.05
439	Karl Best	.05
440	Willie McGee	.05
441	Dave Leiper **RC**	.05
442	Mitch Webster	.05
443	John Felske	.05
444	Jeff Russell	.05
445	Dave Lopes	.05
446	Chuck Finley **RC**	.25
447	Bill Almon	.05
448	Chris Bosio **RC**	.10
449	Pat Dodson **RC**	.05
450	Kirby Puckett	.45
451	Joe Sambito	.05
452	Dave Henderson	.05
453	Scott Terry **RC**	.05
454	Luis Salazar	.05
455	Mike Boddicker	.05
456	Carney Lansford, Tony LaRussa, Mickey Tettleton, Dave Von Ohlen A's Ldrs.	.05
457	Len Matuszek	.05
458	Kelly Gruber	.05
459	Dennis Eckersley	.35
460	Darryl Strawberry	.05
461	Craig McMurtry	.05
462	Scott Fletcher	.05
463	Tom Candiotti	.05
464	Butch Wynegar	.05
465	Todd Worrell	.05
466	Kal Daniels	.05
467	Randy St. Claire	.05
468	George Bamberger	.05
469	Mike Diaz **RC**	.05
470	Dave Dravecky	.05
471	Ronn Reynolds	.05
472	Bill Doran	.05
473	Steve Farr	.05
474	Jerry Narron	.05
475	Scott Garrelts	.05
476	Danny Tartabull	.05
477	Ken Howell	.05
478	Tim Laudner	.05
479	Bob Sebra **RC**	.05
480	Jim Rice	.15
481	Von Hayes, Juan Samuel, Glenn Wilson Phillies Ldrs.	.05
482	Daryl Boston	.05
483	Dwight Lowry	.05
484	Jim Traber	.05
485	Tony Fernandez	.05
486	Otis Nixon	.05
487	Dave Gumpert	.05
488	Ray Knight	.05
489	Bill Gullickson	.05
490	Dale Murphy	.20
491	Ron Karkovice **RC**	.05
492	Mike Heath	.05
493	Tom Lasorda	.10
494	Barry Jones **RC**	.05
495	Gorman Thomas	.05
496	Bruce Bochte	.05
497	Dale Mohorcic **RC**	.05
498	Bob Kearney	.05
499	Bruce Ruffin **RC**	.05
500	Don Mattingly	.65
501	Craig Lefferts	.05
502	Dick Schofield	.05
503	Larry Andersen	.05
504	Mickey Hatcher	.05
505	Bryn Smith	.05
506	Rich Bordi, Rick Dempsey, Earl Weaver Orioles Ldrs.	.05
507	Dave Stapleton	.05
508	Scott Bankhead **RC**	.05
509	Enos Cabell	.05
510	Tom Henke	.05
511	Steve Lyons	.05
512	Dave Magadan **RC**	.20
513	Carmen Castillo	.05
514	Orlando Mercado	.05
515	Willie Hernandez	.05
516	Ted Simmons	.05
517	Mario Soto	.05
518	Gene Mauch	.05
519	Curt Young	.05
520	Jack Clark	.05
521	Rick Reuschel	.05
522	Checklist 397-528	.05
523	Earnie Riles	.05
524	Bob Shirley	.05
525	Phil Bradley	.05
526	Roger Mason	.05
527	Jim Wohlford	.05
528	Ken Dixon	.05
529	Alvaro Espinoza **RC**	.05
530	Tony Gwynn	.45
531	Yogi Berra, Hal Lanier, Denis Menke, Gene Tenace Astros Ldrs.	.05
532	Jeff Stone	.05
533	Argenis Salazar	.05
534	Scott Sanderson	.05
535	Tony Armas	.05
536	Terry Mulholland **RC**	.15
537	Rance Mulliniks	.05
538	Tom Niedenfuer	.05
539	Reid Nichols	.05
540	Terry Kennedy	.05
541	Rafael Belliard **RC**	.05
542	Ricky Horton	.05
543	Dave Johnson	.05
544	Zane Smith	.05

545	Buddy Bell	.05
546	Mike Morgan	.05
547	Rob Deer	.05
548	Bill Mooneyham **RC**	.05
549	Bob Melvin	.05
550	Pete Incaviglia	.05
551	Frank Wills	.05
552	Larry Sheets	.05
553	Mike Maddux **RC**	.05
554	Buddy Biancalana	.05
555	Dennis Rasmussen	.05
556	Bob Boone, Marcel Lachemann, Mike Witt Angels Ldrs.	.05
557	John Cerutti **RC**	.05
558	Greg Gagne	.05
559	Lance McCullers	.05
560	Glenn Davis	.05
561	Rey Quinones **RC**	.05
562	Bryan Clutterbuck **RC**	.05
563	John Stefero	.05
564	Larry McWilliams	.05
565	Dusty Baker	.05
566	Tim Hulett	.05
567	Greg Mathews **RC**	.05
568	Earl Weaver	.10
569	Wade Rowdon	.05
570	Sid Fernandez	.05
571	Ozzie Virgil	.05
572	Pete Ladd	.05
573	Hal McRae	.05
574	Manny Lee	.05
575	Pat Tabler	.05
576	Frank Pastore	.05
577	Dann Bilardello	.05
578	Billy Hatcher	.05
579	Rick Burleson	.05
580	Mike Krukow	.05
581	Ron Cey, Steve Trout Cubs Ldrs.	.05
582	Bruce Berenyi	.05
583	Junior Ortiz	.05
584	Ron Kittle	.05
585	Scott Bailes **RC**	.05
586	Ben Oglivie	.05
587	Eric Plunk	.05
588	Wallace Johnson	.05
589	Steve Crawford	.05
590	Vince Coleman	.05
591	Spike Owen	.05
592	Chris Welsh	.05
593	Chuck Tanner	.05
594	Rick Anderson	.05
595	Keith Hernandez/AS	.05
596	Steve Sax/AS	.05
597	Mike Schmidt/AS	.35
598	Ozzie Smith/AS	.30
599	Tony Gwynn/AS	.30
600	Dave Parker/AS	.05
601	Darryl Strawberry/AS	.05
602	Gary Carter/AS	.25
603a	Dwight Gooden/AS (No trademark on front)	.25
603b	Dwight Gooden/AS (Trademark on front)	.05
604	Fernando Valenzuela/AS	.05
605	Todd Worrell/AS	.05
606a	Don Mattingly/AS (No trademark on front.)	.75
606b	Don Mattingly/AS (Trademark on front.)	.35
607	Tony Bernazard/AS	.05
608	Wade Boggs/AS	.30
609	Cal Ripken, Jr./AS	.45
610	Jim Rice/AS	.05
611	Kirby Puckett/AS	.30
612	George Bell/AS	.05
613	Lance Parrish/AS	.05
614	Roger Clemens/AS	.35
615	Teddy Higuera/AS	.05
616	Dave Righetti/AS	.05
617	Al Nipper	.05
618	Tom Kelly	.05
619	Jerry Reed	.05
620	Jose Canseco	.60
621	Danny Cox	.05
622	Glenn Braggs **RC**	.05
623	Kurt Stillwell **RC**	.05
624	Tim Burke	.05
625	Mookie Wilson	.05
626	Joel Skinner	.05
627	Ken Oberkfell	.05
628	Bob Walk	.05
629	Larry Parrish	.05
630	John Candelaria	.05
631	Sparky Anderson, Mike Heath, Willie Hernandez Tigers Ldrs.	.05
632	Rob Woodward	.05
633	Jose Uribe	.05
634	Rafael Palmeiro **RC**	2.00
635	Ken Schrom	.05
636	Darren Daulton	.05
637	Bip Roberts **RC**	.10
638	Rich Bordi	.05
639	Gerald Perry	.05
640	Mark Clear	.05
641	Domingo Ramos	.05
642	Al Pulido	.05
643	Ron Shepherd	.05
644	John Denny	.05
645	Dwight Evans	.05
646	Mike Mason	.05
647	Tom Lawless	.05
648	Barry Larkin **RC**	.60
649	Mickey Tettleton	.05
650	Hubie Brooks	.05
651	Benny Distefano	.05
652	Terry Forster	.05
653	Kevin Mitchell	.05
654	Checklist 529-660	.05
655	Jesse Barfield	.05
656	Bobby Valentine, Rickey Wright Rangers Ldrs.	.05
657	Tom Waddell	.05
658	Robby Thompson **RC**	.05
659	Aurelio Lopez	.05
660	Bob Horner	.05
661	Lou Whitaker	.05
662	Frank DiPino	.05
663	Cliff Johnson	.05
664	Mike Marshall	.05
665	Rod Scurry	.05
666	Von Hayes	.05
667	Ron Hassey	.05
668	Juan Bonilla	.05
669	Bud Black	.05
670	Jose Cruz	.05
671a	Ray Soff (No "D*" before copyright line.)	.20
671b	Ray Soff ("D*" before copyright line.)	.05
672	Chili Davis	.05
673	Don Sutton	.35
674	Bill Campbell	.05
675	Ed Romero	.05
676	Charlie Moore	.05
677	Bob Grich	.05
678	Carney Lansford	.05
679	Kent Hrbek	.05
680	Ryne Sandberg	.45
681	George Bell	.05
682	Jerry Reuss	.05
683	Gary Roenicke	.05
684	Kent Tekulve	.05
685	Jerry Hairston Sr.	.05
686	Doyle Alexander	.05
687	Alan Trammell	.05
688	Juan Beniquez	.05
689	Darrell Porter	.05
690	Dane Iorg	.05
691	Dave Parker	.05
692	Frank White	.05
693	Terry Puhl	.05
694	Phil Niekro	.35
695	Chico Walker	.05
696	Gary Lucas	.05
697	Ed Lynch	.05
698	Ernie Whitt	.05
699	Ken Landreaux	.05
700	Dave Bergman	.05
701	Willie Randolph	.05
702	Greg Gross	.05
703	Dave Schmidt	.05
704	Jesse Orosco	.05
705	Bruce Hurst	.05
706	Rick Manning	.05
707	Bob McClure	.05
708	Scott McGregor	.05
709	Dave Kingman	.05
710	Gary Gaetti	.05
711	Ken Griffey	.05
712	Don Robinson	.05
713	Tom Brookens	.05
714	Dan Quisenberry	.05
715	Bob Dernier	.05
716	Rick Leach	.05
717	Ed Vande Berg	.05
718	Steve Carlton	.40
719	Tom Hume	.05
720	Richard Dotson	.05
721	Tom Herr	.05
722	Bob Knepper	.05
723	Brett Butler	.05
724	Greg Minton	.05
725	George Hendrick	.05
726	Frank Tanana	.05
727	Mike Moore	.05
728	Tippy Martinez	.05
729	Tom Paciorek	.05
730	Eric Show	.05
731	Dave Concepcion	.05
732	Manny Trillo	.05
733	Bill Caudill	.05
734	Bill Madlock	.05
735	Rickey Henderson	.40
736	Steve Bedrosian	.05
737	Floyd Bannister	.05
738	Jorge Orta	.05
739	Chet Lemon	.05
740	Rich Gedman	.05
741	Paul Molitor	.40
742	Andy McGaffigan	.05
743	Dwayne Murphy	.05
744	Roy Smalley	.05
745	Glenn Hubbard	.05
746	Bob Ojeda	.05
747	Johnny Ray	.05
748	Mike Flanagan	.05
749	Ozzie Smith	.45
750	Steve Trout	.05
751	Garth Iorg	.05
752	Dan Petry	.05
753	Rick Honeycutt	.05
754	Dave LaPoint	.05
755	Luis Aguayo	.05
756	Carlton Fisk	.40
757	Nolan Ryan	.75
758	Tony Bernazard	.05
759	Joel Youngblood	.05
760	Mike Witt	.05
761	Greg Pryor	.05
762	Gary Ward	.05
763	Tim Flannery	.05
764	Bill Buckner	.05
765	Kirk Gibson	.05
766	Don Aase	.05
767	Ron Cey	.05
768	Dennis Lamp	.05
769	Steve Sax	.05
770	Dave Winfield	.40
771	Shane Rawley	.05
772	Harold Baines	.05
773	Robin Yount	.40
774	Wayne Krenchicki	.05
775	Joaquin Andujar	.05
776	Tom Brunansky	.05
777	Chris Chambliss	.05
778	Jack Morris	.05
779	Craig Reynolds	.05
780	Andre Thornton	.05
781	Atlee Hammaker	.05
782	Brian Downing	.05
783	Willie Wilson	.05
784	Cal Ripken, Jr.	.75
785	Terry Francona	.05
786	Jimy Williams	.05
787	Alejandro Pena	.05
788	Tim Stoddard	.05
789	Dan Schatzeder	.05
790	Julio Cruz	.05
791	Lance Parrish	.05
792	Checklist 661-792	.05

1987 Topps Tiffany

		NM/M
Unopened Set (792):		90.00
Complete Set (792):		50.00
Common Player:		.15
320	Barry Bonds	35.00

(Star cards valued at 4X corresponding cards in regular 1987 Topps.)

Traded

		NM/M
Complete Set (132):		4.00
Common Player:		.05
1	Bill Almon	.05
2	Scott Bankhead	.05
3	Eric Bell	.05
4	Juan Beniquez	.05
5	Juan Berenguer	.05
6	Greg Booker	.05
7	Thad Bosley	.05
8	Larry Bowa	.05
9	Greg Brock	.05
10	Bob Brower	.05
11	Jerry Browne	.05
12	Ralph Bryant	.05
13	DeWayne Buice	.05
14	Ellis Burks **RC**	.50
15	Ivan Calderon	.05
16	Jeff Calhoun	.05
17	Casey Candaele	.05
18	John Cangelosi	.05
19	Steve Carlton	.25
20	Juan Castillo	.05
21	Rick Cerone	.05
22	Ron Cey	.05
23	John Christensen	.05
24	Dave Cone	.15
25	Chuck Crim	.05
26	Storm Davis	.05
27	Andre Dawson	.25
28	Rick Dempsey	.05
29	Doug Drabek	.05
30	Mike Dunne	.05
31	Dennis Eckersley	.25
32	Lee Elia	.05
33	Brian Fisher	.05
34	Terry Francona	.05
35	Willie Fraser	.05
36	Billy Gardner	.05
37	Ken Gerhart	.05
38	Danny Gladden	.05
39	Jim Gott	.05
40	Cecilio Guante	.05
41	Albert Hall	.05
42	Terry Harper	.05
43	Mickey Hatcher	.05
44	Brad Havens	.05
45	Neal Heaton	.05
46	Mike Henneman **RC**	.20
47	Donnie Hill	.05
48	Guy Hoffman	.05
49	Brian Holton	.05
50	Charles Hudson	.05
51	Danny Jackson	.05
52	Reggie Jackson	.40
53	Chris James	.05
54	Dion James	.05
55	Stan Jefferson	.05
56	Joe Johnson	.05
57	Terry Kennedy	.05
58	Mike Kingery	.05
59	Ray Knight	.05
60	Gene Larkin	.05
61	Mike LaValliere	.05
62	Jack Lazorko	.05
63	Terry Leach	.05
64	Tim Leary	.05
65	Jim Lindeman	.05
66	Steve Lombardozzi	.05
67	Bill Long	.05
68	Barry Lyons	.05
69	Shane Mack **RC**	.05
70	Greg Maddux **RC**	3.00
71	Bill Madlock	.05
72	Joe Magrane	.05
73	Dave Martinez	.05
74	Fred McGriff	.25
75	Mark McLemore	.05
76	Kevin McReynolds	.05
77	Dave Meads	.05
78	Eddie Milner	.05
79	Greg Minton	.05
80	John Mitchell	.05
81	Kevin Mitchell	.05
82	Charlie Moore	.05
83	Jeff Musselman	.05
84	Gene Nelson	.05
85	Graig Nettles	.05
86	Al Newman	.05
87	Reid Nichols	.05
88	Tom Niedenfuer	.05
89	Joe Niekro	.05
90	Tom Nieto	.05
91	Matt Nokes **RC**	.10
92	Dickie Noles	.05
93	Pat Pacillo	.05
94	Lance Parrish	.05
95	Tony Pena	.05
96	Luis Polonia	.05
97	Randy Ready	.05
98	Jeff Reardon	.05
99	Gary Redus	.05
100	Jeff Reed	.05
101	Rick Rhoden	.05
102	Cal Ripken, Sr.	.05
103	Wally Ritchie	.05
104	Jeff Robinson	.05
105	Gary Roenicke	.05
106	Jerry Royster	.05
107	Mark Salas	.05
108	Luis Salazar	.05
109	Benny Santiago	.15
110	Dave Schmidt	.05
111	Kevin Seitzer	.05
112	John Shelby	.05
113	Steve Shields	.05
114	John Smiley **RC**	.20
115	Chris Speier	.05
116	Mike Stanley	.05
117	Terry Steinbach	.15
118	Les Straker	.05
119	Jim Sundberg	.05
120	Danny Tartabull	.05
121	Tom Trebelhorn	.05
122	Dave Valle	.05
123	Ed Vande Berg	.05
124	Andy Van Slyke	.05
125	Gary Ward	.05
126	Alan Wiggins	.05
127	Bill Wilkinson	.05
128	Frank Williams	.05
129	Matt Williams **RC**	.75
130	Jim Winn	.05
131	Matt Young	.05
132	Checklist 1T-132T	.05

1987 Topps Traded Tiffany

	NM/M
Complete Set (132):	30.00
Common Player:	.15

(Star cards valued at 2X corresponding cards in regular Topps Traded.)

1988 Topps

		NM/M
Unopened Factory Set, Retail (792):		15.00
Unopened Factory Set, Hobby (792):		15.00
Complete Set (792):		12.00
Common Player:		.05
Wax Pack (15):		.40
Wax Box (36):		15.00
Cello Pack (28):		.70
Cello Box (24):		13.50
Rack Pack (43):		.75
Rack Box (24):		15.00
Vending Box (500):		7.50
1	Vince Coleman	.05
2	Don Mattingly	.25
3a	Mark McGwire (White triangle by left foot.)	1.00

3b	Mark McGwire (No white triangle.)	.40
4a	Eddie Murray (No mention of record on front.)	.25
4b	Eddie Murray (Record in box on front.)	.20
5	Joe Niekro, Phil Niekro	.05
6	Nolan Ryan	.40
7	Benito Santiago	.05
8	Kevin Elster	.05
9	Andy Hawkins	.05
10	Ryne Sandberg	.50
11	Mike Young	.05
12	Bill Schroeder	.05
13	Andres Thomas	.05
14	Sparky Anderson	.10
15	Chili Davis	.05
16	Kirk McCaskill	.05
17	Ron Oester	.05
18a	Al Leiter **RC** (actually Steve George. Future Stars, no "NY" on shirt, photo)	.40
18b	Al Leiter **RC** (photo. Future Stars, "NY" on shirt, correct)	.20
19	Mark Davidson **RC**	.05
20	Kevin Gross	.05
21	Wade Boggs, Spike Owen Red Sox Ldrs.	.10
22	Greg Swindell	.05
23	Ken Landreaux	.05
24	Jim Deshaies	.05
25	Andres Galarraga	.05
26	Mitch Williams	.05
27	R.J. Reynolds	.05
28	Jose Nunez **RC**	.05
29	Argenis Salazar	.05
30	Sid Fernandez	.05
31	Bruce Bochy	.05
32	Mike Morgan	.05
33	Rob Deer	.05
34	Ricky Horton	.05
35	Harold Baines	.05
36	Jamie Moyer	.05
37	Ed Romero	.05
38	Jeff Calhoun	.05
39	Gerald Perry	.05
40	Orel Hershiser	.05
41	Bob Melvin	.05
42	Bill Landrum **RC**	.05
43	Dick Schofield	.05
44	Lou Piniella	.05
45	Kent Hrbek	.05
46	Darnell Coles	.05
47	Joaquin Andujar	.05
48	Alan Ashby	.05
49	Dave Clark	.05
50	Hubie Brooks	.05
51	Eddie Murray, Cal Ripken, Jr. Orioles Ldrs.	.25
52	Don Robinson	.05
53	Curt Wilkerson	.05
54	Jim Clancy	.05
55	Phil Bradley	.05
56	Ed Hearn	.05
57	Tim Crews **RC**	.05
58	Dave Magadan	.05
59	Danny Cox	.05
60	Rickey Henderson	.40
61	Mark Knudson **RC**	.05
62	Jeff Hamilton	.05
63	Jimmy Jones	.05
64	Ken Caminiti **RC**	.25
65	Leon Durham	.05
66	Shane Rawley	.05
67	Ken Oberkfell	.05
68	Dave Dravecky	.05
69	Mike Hart **RC**	.05
70	Roger Clemens	.60
71	Gary Pettis	.05
72	Dennis Eckersley	.30
73	Randy Bush	.05
74	Tom Lasorda	.05
75	Joe Carter	.05
76	Denny Martinez	.05
77	Tom O'Malley	.05
78	Dan Petry	.05
79	Ernie Whitt	.05
80	Mark Langston	.05
81	John Franco, Ron Robinson Reds Ldrs.	.05
82	Darrel Akerfelds **RC**	.05
83	Jose Oquendo	.05
84	Cecilio Guante	.05
85	Howard Johnson	.05
86	Ron Karkovice	.05
87	Mike Mason	.05
88	Earnie Riles	.05
89	Gary Thurman **RC**	.05
90	Dale Murphy	.20
91	Joey Cora **RC**	.10
92	Len Matuszek	.05
93	Bob Sebra	.05
94	Chuck Jackson **RC**	.05
95	Lance Parrish	.05
96	Todd Benzinger **RC**	.05
97	Scott Garrelts	.05
98	Rene Gonzales **RC**	.05
99	Chuck Finley	.05
100	Jack Clark	.05
101	Allan Anderson	.05
102	Barry Larkin	.05
103	Curt Young	.05
104	Dick Williams	.05
105	Jesse Orosco	.05
106	Jim Walewander **RC**	.05
107	Scott Bailes	.05
108	Steve Lyons	.05
109	Joel Skinner	.05
110	Teddy Higuera	.05
111	Hubie Brooks, Vance Law Expos Ldrs.	.05
112	Les Lancaster **RC**	.05
113	Kelly Gruber	.05
114	Jeff Russell	.05
115	Johnny Ray	.05
116	Jerry Don Gleaton	.05
117	James Steels **RC**	.05
118	Bob Welch	.05
119	Robbie Wine **RC**	.05
120	Kirby Puckett	.50
121	Checklist 1-132	.05
122	Tony Bernazard	.05
123	Tom Candiotti	.05
124	Ray Knight	.05
125	Bruce Hurst	.05
126	Steve Jeltz	.05
127	Jim Gott	.05
128	Johnny Grubb	.05
129	Greg Minton	.05
130	Buddy Bell	.05
131	Don Schulze	.05
132	Donnie Hill	.05
133	Greg Mathews	.05
134	Chuck Tanner	.05
135	Dennis Rasmussen	.05
136	Brian Dayett	.05
137	Chris Bosio	.05
138	Mitch Webster	.05
139	Jerry Browne	.05
140	Jesse Barfield	.05
141	George Brett, Bret Saberhagen Royals Ldrs.	.20
142	Andy Van Slyke	.05
143	Mickey Tettleton	.05
144	Don Gordon **RC**	.05
145	Bill Madlock	.05
146	Donell Nixon **RC**	.05
147	Bill Buckner	.05
148	Carmelo Martinez	.05
149	Ken Howell	.05
150	Eric Davis	.05
151	Bob Knepper	.05
152	Jody Reed **RC**	.10
153	John Habyan	.05
154	Jeff Stone	.05
155	Bruce Sutter	.30
156	Gary Matthews	.05
157	Atlee Hammaker	.05
158	Tim Hulett	.05
159	Brad Arnsberg **RC**	.05
160	Willie McGee	.05
161	Bryn Smith	.05
162	Mark McLemore	.05
163	Dale Mohorcic	.05
164	Dave Johnson	.05
165	Robin Yount	.40
166	Rick Rodriguez **RC**	.05
167	Rance Mulliniks	.05
168	Barry Jones	.05
169	Ross Jones **RC**	.05
170	Rich Gossage	.05
171	Shawon Dunston, Manny Trillo Cubs Ldrs.	.05
172	Lloyd McClendon **RC**	.05
173	Eric Plunk	.05
174	Phil Garner	.05
175	Kevin Bass	.05
176	Jeff Reed	.05
177	Frank Tanana	.05
178	Dwayne Henry	.05
179	Charlie Puleo	.05
180	Terry Kennedy	.05
181	Dave Cone	.05
182	Ken Phelps	.05
183	Tom Lawless	.05
184	Ivan Calderon	.05
185	Rick Rhoden	.05
186	Rafael Palmeiro	.35
187	Steve Kiefer	.05
188	John Russell	.05
189	Wes Gardner **RC**	.05
190	Candy Maldonado	.05
191	John Cerutti	.05
192	Devon White	.05
193	Brian Fisher	.05
194	Tom Kelly	.05
195	Dan Quisenberry	.05
196	Dave Engle	.05
197	Lance McCullers	.05
198	Franklin Stubbs	.05
199	Dave Meads **RC**	.05
200	Wade Boggs	.50
201	Steve Buechele, Pete Incaviglia, Pete O'Brien, Bobby Valentine Rangers Ldrs.	.05
202	Glenn Hoffman	.05
203	Fred Toliver	.05
204	Paul O'Neill	.05
205	Nelson Liriano **RC**	.05
206	Domingo Ramos	.05
207	John Mitchell **RC**	.05
208	Steve Lake	.05
209	Richard Dotson	.05
210	Willie Randolph	.05
211	Frank DiPino	.05
212	Greg Brock	.05
213	Albert Hall	.05
214	Dave Schmidt	.05
215	Von Hayes	.05
216	Jerry Reuss	.05
217	Harry Spilman	.05
218	Dan Schatzeder	.05
219	Mike Stanley	.05
220	Tom Henke	.05
221	Rafael Belliard	.05
222	Steve Farr	.05
223	Stan Jefferson	.05
224	Tom Trebelhorn	.05
225	Mike Scioscia	.05
226	Dave Lopes	.05
227	Ed Correa	.05
228	Wallace Johnson	.05
229	Jeff Musselman	.05
230	Pat Tabler	.05
231	Barry Bonds, Bobby Bonilla Pirates Ldrs.	.50
232	Bob James	.05
233	Rafael Santana	.05
234	Ken Dayley	.05
235	Gary Ward	.05
236	Ted Power	.05
237	Mike Heath	.05
238	Luis Polonia **RC**	.10
239	Roy Smalley	.05
240	Lee Smith	.05
241	Damaso Garcia	.05
242	Tom Niedenfuer	.05
243	Mark Ryal	.05
244	Jeff Robinson	.05
245	Rich Gedman	.05
246	Mike Campbell **RC**	.05
247	Thad Bosley	.05
248	Storm Davis	.05
249	Mike Marshall	.05
250	Nolan Ryan	.75
251	Tom Foley	.05
252	Bob Brower	.05
253	Checklist 133-264	.05
254	Lee Elia	.05
255	Mookie Wilson	.05
256	Ken Schrom	.05
257	Jerry Royster	.05
258	Ed Nunez	.05
259	Ron Kittle	.05
260	Vince Coleman	.05
261	Will Clark, Candy Maldonado, Kevin Mitchell, Robby Thompson, Jose Uribe Giants Ldrs.	.05
262	Drew Hall	.05
263	Glenn Braggs	.05
264	Les Straker **RC**	.05
265	Bo Diaz	.05
266	Paul Assenmacher	.05
267	Billy Bean **RC**	.05
268	Bruce Ruffin	.05
269	Ellis Burks	.05
270	Mike Witt	.05
271	Ken Gerhart	.05
272	Steve Ontiveros	.05
273	Garth Iorg	.05
274	Junior Ortiz	.05
275	Kevin Seitzer	.05
276	Luis Salazar	.05
277	Alejandro Pena	.05
278	Jose Cruz	.05
279	Randy St. Claire	.05
280	Pete Incaviglia	.05
281	Jerry Hairston Sr.	.05
282	Pat Perry	.05
283	Phil Lombardi	.05
284	Larry Bowa	.05
285	Jim Presley	.05
286	Chuck Crim **RC**	.05
287	Manny Trillo	.05
288	Pat Pacillo **RC**	.05
289	Dave Bergman	.05
290	Tony Fernandez	.05
291	Kevin Bass, Billy Hatcher Astros Ldrs.	.05
292	Carney Lansford	.05
293	Doug Jones **RC**	.05
294	Al Pedrique **RC**	.05
295	Bert Blyleven	.05
296	Floyd Rayford	.05
297	Zane Smith	.05
298	Milt Thompson	.05
299	Steve Crawford	.05
300	Don Mattingly	.60
301	Bud Black	.05
302	Jose Uribe	.05
303	Eric Show	.05
304	George Hendrick	.05
305	Steve Sax	.05
306	Billy Hatcher	.05
307	Mike Trujillo	.05
308	Lee Mazzilli	.05
309	Bill Long **RC**	.05
310	Tom Herr	.05
311	Scott Sanderson	.05
312	Joey Meyer	.05
313	Bob McClure	.05
314	Jimy Williams	.05
315	Dave Parker	.05
316	Jose Rijo	.05
317	Tom Nieto	.05
318	Mel Hall	.05
319	Mike Loynd	.05
320	Alan Trammell	.05
321	Harold Baines, Carlton Fisk White Sox Ldrs.	.05
322	Vicente Palacios **RC**	.05
323	Rick Leach	.05
324	Danny Jackson	.05
325	Glenn Hubbard	.05
326	Al Nipper	.05
327	Larry Sheets	.05
328	Greg Cadaret **RC**	.05
329	Chris Speier	.05
330	Eddie Whitson	.05
331	Brian Downing	.05
332	Jerry Reed	.05
333	Wally Backman	.05
334	Dave LaPoint	.05
335	Claudell Washington	.05
336	Ed Lynch	.05
337	Jim Gantner	.05
338	Brian Holton	.05
339	Kurt Stillwell	.05
340	Jack Morris	.05
341	Carmen Castillo	.05
342	Larry Andersen	.05
343	Greg Gagne	.05
344	Tony LaRussa	.05
345	Scott Fletcher	.05
346	Vance Law	.05
347	Joe Johnson	.05
348	Jim Eisenreich	.05
349	Bob Walk	.05
350	Will Clark	.05
351	Tony Pena, Red Schoendienst Cardinals Ldrs.	.05
352	Billy Ripken **RC**	.05
353	Ed Olwine	.05
354	Marc Sullivan	.05
355	Roger McDowell	.05
356	Luis Aguayo	.05
357	Floyd Bannister	.05
358	Rey Quinones	.05
359	Tim Stoddard	.05
360	Tony Gwynn	.50
361	Greg Maddux	.50
362	Juan Castillo	.05
363	Willie Fraser	.05
364	Nick Esasky	.05
365	Floyd Youmans	.05
366	Chet Lemon	.05
367	Tim Leary	.05
368	Gerald Young **RC**	.05
369	Greg Harris	.05
370	Jose Canseco	.25
371	Joe Hesketh	.05
372	Matt Williams	.05
373	Checklist 265-396	.05
374	Doc Edwards	.05
375	Tom Brunansky	.05
376	Bill Wilkinson **RC**	.05
377	Sam Horn **RC**	.05
378	Todd Frohwirth **RC**	.05
379	Rafael Ramirez	.05
380	Joe Magrane **RC**	.05
381	Jack Howell, Wally Joyner Angels Ldrs.	.05
382	Keith Miller **RC**	.05
383	Eric Bell	.05
384	Neil Allen	.05
385	Carlton Fisk	.40
386	Don Mattingly/AS	.30
387	Willie Randolph/AS	.05
388	Wade Boggs/AS	.20
389	Alan Trammell/AS	.05
390	George Bell/AS	.05
391	Kirby Puckett/AS	.25
392	Dave Winfield/AS	.20
393	Matt Nokes/AS	.05
394	Roger Clemens/AS	.35
395	Jimmy Key/AS	.05
396	Tom Henke/AS	.05
397	Jack Clark/AS	.05
398	Juan Samuel/AS	.05
399	Tim Wallach/AS	.05
400	Ozzie Smith/AS	.25
401	Andre Dawson/AS	.15
402	Tony Gwynn/AS	.25
403	Tim Raines/AS	.05
404	Benny Santiago/AS	.05
405	Dwight Gooden/AS	.05
406	Shane Rawley/AS	.05
407	Steve Bedrosian/AS	.05
408	Dion James	.05
409	Joel McKeon	.05
410	Tony Pena	.05
411	Wayne Tolleson	.05
412	Randy Myers	.05

413 John Christensen .05
414 John McNamara .05
415 Don Carman .05
416 Keith Moreland .05
417 Mark Ciardi **RC** .05
418 Joel Youngblood .05
419 Scott McGregor .05
420 Wally Joyner .05
421 Ed Vande Berg .05
422 Dave Concepcion .05
423 John Smiley .05
424 Dwayne Murphy .05
425 Jeff Reardon .05
426 Randy Ready .05
427 Paul Kilgus **RC** .05
428 John Shelby .05
429 Kirk Gibson, Alan Trammell Tigers Ldrs. .05
430 Glenn Davis .05
431 Casey Candaele .05
432 Mike Moore .05
433 Bill Pecota **RC** .05
434 Rick Aguilera .05
435 Mike Pagliarulo .05
436 Mike Bielecki .05
437 Fred Manrique **RC** .05
438 Rob Ducey **RC** .05
439 Dave Martinez .05
440 Steve Bedrosian .05
441 Rick Manning .05
442 Tom Bolton **RC** .05
443 Ken Griffey .05
444 Cal Ripken, Sr. .05
445 Mike Krukow .05
446 Doug DeCinces .05
447 Jeff Montgomery **RC** .20
448 Mike Davis .05
449 Jeff Robinson **RC** .05
450 Barry Bonds .75
451 Keith Atherton .05
452 Willie Wilson .05
453 Dennis Powell .05
454 Marvell Wynne .05
455 Shawn Hillegas **RC** .05
456 Dave Anderson .05
457 Terry Leach .05
458 Ron Hassey .05
459 Willie Randolph, Dave Winfield Yankees Ldrs. .05
460 Ozzie Smith .50
461 Danny Darwin .05
462 Don Slaught .05
463 Fred McGriff .05
464 Jay Tibbs .05
465 Paul Molitor .40
466 Jerry Mumphrey .05
467 Don Aase .05
468 Darren Daulton .05
469 Jeff Dedmon .05
470 Dwight Evans .05
471 Donnie Moore .05
472 Robby Thompson .05
473 Joe Niekro .05
474 Tom Brookens .05
475 Pete Rose .65
476 Dave Stewart .05
477 Jamie Quirk .05
478 Sid Bream .05
479 Brett Butler .05
480 Dwight Gooden .05
481 Mariano Duncan .05
482 Mark Davis .05
483 Rod Booker **RC** .05
484 Pat Clements .05
485 Harold Reynolds .05
486 Pat Keedy **RC** .05
487 Jim Pankovits .05
488 Andy McGaffigan .05
489 Pedro Guerrero, Fernando Valenzuela Dodgers Ldrs. .05
490 Larry Parrish .05
491 B.J. Surhoff .05
492 Doyle Alexander .05
493 Mike Greenwell .05
494 Wally Ritchie **RC** .05
495 Eddie Murray .40
496 Guy Hoffman .05
497 Kevin Mitchell .05
498 Bob Boone .05
499 Eric King .05
500 Andre Dawson .25
501 Tim Birtsas .05
502 Danny Gladden .05
503 Junior Noboa **RC** .05
504 Bob Rodgers .05
505 Willie Upshaw .05
506 John Cangelosi .05
507 Mark Gubicza .05
508 Tim Teufel .05
509 Bill Dawley .05
510 Dave Winfield .40
511 Joel Davis .05
512 Alex Trevino .05
513 Tim Flannery .05
514 Pat Sheridan .05
515 Juan Nieves .05
516 Jim Sundberg .05
517 Ron Robinson .05
518 Greg Gross .05
519 Phil Bradley, Harold Reynolds Mariners Ldrs. .05
520 Dave Smith .05
521 Jim Dwyer .05
522 Bob Patterson **RC** .05
523 Gary Roenicke .05
524 Gary Lucas .05
525 Marty Barrett .05
526 Juan Berenguer .05
527 Steve Henderson .05
528a Checklist 397-528 (#455 is Steve Carlton) .05
528b Checklist 397-528 (#455 is Shawn Hillegas) .05
529 Tim Burke .05
530 Gary Carter .40
531 Rich Yett .05
532 Mike Kingery .05
533 John Farrell **RC** .05
534 John Wathan .05
535 Ron Guidry .05
536 John Morris .05
537 Steve Buechele .05
538 Bill Wegman .05
539 Mike LaValliere .05
540 Bret Saberhagen .05
541 Juan Beniquez .05
542 Paul Noce **RC** .05
543 Kent Tekulve .05
544 Jim Traber .05
545 Don Baylor .05
546 John Candelaria .05
547 Felix Fermin **RC** .05
548 Shane Mack .05
549 Ken Griffey, Dion James, Dale Murphy, Gerald Perry Braves Ldrs. .05
550 Pedro Guerrero .05
551 Terry Steinbach .05
552 Mark Thurmond .05
553 Tracy Jones .05
554 Mike Smithson .05
555 Brook Jacoby .05
556 Stan Clarke **RC** .05
557 Craig Reynolds .05
558 Bob Ojeda .05
559 Ken Williams **RC** .05
560 Tim Wallach .05
561 Rick Cerone .05
562 Jim Lindeman .05
563 Jose Guzman .05
564 Frank Lucchesi .05
565 Lloyd Moseby .05
566 Charlie O'Brien **RC** .05
567 Mike Diaz .05
568 Chris Brown .05
569 Charlie Leibrandt .05
570 Jeffrey Leonard .05
571 Mark Williamson **RC** .05
572 Chris James .05
573 Bob Stanley .05
574 Graig Nettles .05
575 Don Sutton .30
576 Tommy Hinzo **RC** .05
577 Tom Browning .05
578 Gary Gaetti .05
579 Gary Carter, Kevin McReynolds Mets Ldrs. .05
580 Mark McGwire .65
581 Tito Landrum .05
582 Mike Henneman .05
583 Dave Valle .05
584 Steve Trout .05
585 Ozzie Guillen .05
586 Bob Forsch .05
587 Terry Puhl .05
588 Jeff Parrett **RC** .05
589 Geno Petralli .05
590 George Bell .05
591 Doug Drabek .05
592 Dale Sveum .05
593 Bob Tewksbury .05
594 Bobby Valentine .05
595 Frank White .05
596 John Kruk .05
597 Gene Garber .05
598 Lee Lacy .05
599 Calvin Schiraldi .05
600 Mike Schmidt .60
601 Jack Lazorko .05
602 Mike Aldrete .05
603 Rob Murphy .05
604 Chris Bando .05
605 Kirk Gibson .05
606 Moose Haas .05
607 Mickey Hatcher .05
608 Charlie Kerfeld .05
609 Gary Gaetti, Kent Hrbek Twins Ldrs. .05
610 Keith Hernandez .05
611 Tommy John .05
612 Curt Ford .05
613 Bobby Thigpen .05
614 Herm Winningham .05
615 Jody Davis .05
616 Jay Aldrich **RC** .05
617 Oddibe McDowell .05
618 Cecil Fielder .05
619 Mike Dunne **RC** .05
620 Cory Snyder .05
621 Gene Nelson .05
622 Kal Daniels .05
623 Mike Flanagan .05
624 Jim Leyland .05
625 Frank Viola .05
626 Glenn Wilson .05
627 Joe Boever **RC** .05
628 Dave Henderson .05
629 Kelly Downs .05
630 Darrell Evans .05
631 Jack Howell .05
632 Steve Shields **RC** .05
633 Barry Lyons **RC** .05
634 Jose DeLeon .05
635 Terry Pendleton .05
636 Charles Hudson .05
637 Jay Bell **RC** .25
638 Steve Balboni .05
639 Glenn Braggs, Tony Muser Brewers Ldrs. .05
640 Garry Templeton .05
641 Rick Honeycutt .05
642 Bob Dernier .05
643 Rocky Childress **RC** .05
644 Terry McGriff .05
645 Matt Nokes .05
646 Checklist 529-660 .05
647 Pascual Perez .05
648 Al Newman .05
649 DeWayne Buice **RC** .05
650 Cal Ripken, Jr. .75
651 Mike Jackson **RC** .05
652 Bruce Benedict .05
653 Jeff Sellers .05
654 Roger Craig .05
655 Len Dykstra .05
656 Lee Guetterman .05
657 Gary Redus .05
658 Tim Conroy .05
659 Bobby Meacham .05
660 Rick Reuschel .05
661 Nolan Ryan .35
662 Jim Rice .05
663 Ron Blomberg .05
664 Bob Gibson .10
665 Stan Musial .20
666 Mario Soto .05
667 Luis Quinones .05
668 Walt Terrell .05
669 Lance Parrish, Mike Ryan Phillies Ldrs. .05
670 Dan Plesac .05
671 Tim Laudner .05
672 John Davis **RC** .05
673 Tony Phillips .05
674 Mike Fitzgerald .05
675 Jim Rice .20
676 Ken Dixon .05
677 Eddie Milner .05
678 Jim Acker .05
679 Darrell Miller .05
680 Charlie Hough .05
681 Bobby Bonilla .05
682 Jimmy Key .05
683 Julio Franco .05
684 Hal Lanier .05
685 Ron Darling .05
686 Terry Francona .05
687 Mickey Brantley .05
688 Jim Winn .05
689 Tom Pagnozzi **RC** .05
690 Jay Howell .05
691 Dan Pasqua .05
692 Mike Birkbeck .05
693 Benny Santiago .05
694 Eric Nolte **RC** .05
695 Shawon Dunston .05
696 Duane Ward .05
697 Steve Lombardozzi .05
698 Brad Havens .05
699 Tony Gwynn, Benny Santiago Padres Ldrs. .15
700 George Brett .60
701 Sammy Stewart .05
702 Mike Gallego .05
703 Bob Brenly .05
704 Dennis Boyd .05
705 Juan Samuel .05
706 Rick Mahler .05
707 Fred Lynn .05
708 Gus Polidor .05
709 George Frazier .05
710 Darryl Strawberry .05
711 Bill Gullickson .05
712 John Moses .05
713 Willie Hernandez .05
714 Jim Fregosi .05
715 Todd Worrell .05
716 Lenn Sakata .05
717 Jay Baller .05
718 Mike Felder .05
719 Denny Walling .05
720 Tim Raines .05
721 Pete O'Brien .05
722 Manny Lee .05
723 Bob Kipper .05
724 Danny Tartabull .05
725 Mike Boddicker .05
726 Alfredo Griffin .05
727 Greg Booker .05
728 Andy Allanson .05
729 George Bell, Fred McGriff Blue Jays Ldrs. .05
730 John Franco .05
731 Rick Schu .05
732 Dave Palmer .05
733 Spike Owen .05
734 Craig Lefferts .05
735 Kevin McReynolds .05
736 Matt Young .05
737 Butch Wynegar .05
738 Scott Bankhead .05
739 Daryl Boston .05
740 Rick Sutcliffe .05
741 Mike Easler .05
742 Mark Clear .05
743 Larry Herndon .05
744 Whitey Herzog .05
745 Bill Doran .05
746 Gene Larkin **RC** .05
747 Bobby Witt .05
748 Reid Nichols .05
749 Mark Eichhorn .05
750 Bo Jackson .10
751 Jim Morrison .05
752 Mark Grant .05
753 Danny Heep .05
754 Mike LaCoss .05
755 Ozzie Virgil .05
756 Mike Maddux .05
757 John Marzano **RC** .05
758 Eddie Williams **RC** .05
759 Jose Canseco, Mark McGwire A's Ldrs. .35
760 Mike Scott .05
761 Tony Armas .05
762 Scott Bradley .05
763 Doug Sisk .05
764 Greg Walker .05
765 Neal Heaton .05
766 Henry Cotto .05
767 Jose Lind **RC** .10
768 Dickie Noles .05
769 Cecil Cooper .05
770 Lou Whitaker .05
771 Ruben Sierra .05
772 Sal Butera .05
773 Frank Williams .05
774 Gene Mauch .05
775 Dave Stieb .05
776 Checklist 661-792 .05
777 Lonnie Smith .05
778a Keith Comstock **RC** (White team letters.) .40
778b Keith Comstock **RC** (Blue team letters, white name.) .10
778c Keith Comstock **RC** (Blue team letters, yellow name.) 2.00
779 Tom Glavine **RC** 1.50
780 Fernando Valenzuela .05
781 Keith Hughes **RC** .05
782 Jeff Ballard **RC** .05
783 Ron Roenicke .05
784 Joe Sambito .05
785 Alvin Davis .05
786 Joe Price .05
787 Bill Almon .05
788 Ray Searage .05
789 Joe Carter, Cory Snyder Indians Ldrs. .05
790 Dave Righetti .05
791 Ted Simmons .05
792 John Tudor .05

1988 Topps Tiffany

NM/M

Complete Set (792): 40.00
Common Player: .15
(Star cards valued at 3X corresponding cards in regular 1988 Topps issue.)

Traded

NM/M

Complete Set (132): 5.00
Common Player: .05
1 Jim Abbott **RC** (USA) .25
2 Juan Agosto .05
3 Luis Alicea .05
4 Roberto Alomar **RC** 1.50
5 Brady Anderson **RC** .25
6 Jack Armstrong .05
7 Don August .05
8 Floyd Bannister .05
9 Bret Barberie (USA) .05
10 Jose Bautista .05
11 Don Baylor .05
12 Tim Belcher .05
13 Buddy Bell .05
14 Andy Benes **RC** (USA) .25
15 Damon Berryhill .05
16 Bud Black .05
17 Pat Borders .05
18 Phil Bradley .05
19 Jeff Branson (USA) .05
20 Tom Brunansky .05
21 Jay Buhner **RC** .75

22 Brett Butler .05
23 Jim Campanis (USA) .05
24 Sil Campusano .05
25 John Candelaria .05
26 Jose Cecena .05
27 Rick Cerone .05
28 Jack Clark .05
29 Kevin Coffman .05
30 Pat Combs (USA) .05
31 Henry Cotto .05
32 Chili Davis .05
33 Mike Davis .05
34 Jose DeLeon .05
35 Richard Dotson .05
36 Cecil Espy .05
37 Tom Filer .05
38 Mike Fiore (USA) .05
39 Ron Gant **RC** .25
40 Kirk Gibson .05
41 Rich Gossage .05
42 Mark Grace **RC** 1.00
43 Alfredo Griffin .05
44 Ty Griffin (USA) .05
45 Bryan Harvey .05
46 Ron Hassey .05
47 Ray Hayward .05
48 Dave Henderson .05
49 Tom Herr .05
50 Bob Horner .05
51 Ricky Horton .05
52 Jay Howell .05
53 Glenn Hubbard .05
54 Jeff Innis .05
55 Danny Jackson .05
56 Darrin Jackson .05
57 Roberto Kelly .05
58 Ron Kittle .05
59 Ray Knight .05
60 Vance Law .05
61 Jeffrey Leonard .05
62 Mike Macfarlane **RC** .05
63 Scotti Madison .05
64 Kirt Manwaring .05
65 Mark Marquess (USA) .05
66 Tino Martinez **RC** (USA) .75
67 Billy Masse (USA) .05
68 Jack McDowell **RC** .25
69 Jack McKeon .05
70 Larry McWilliams .05
71 Mickey Morandini (USA) .05
72 Keith Moreland .05
73 Mike Morgan .05
74 Charles Nagy (USA) .10
75 Al Nipper .05
76 Russ Nixon .05
77 Jesse Orosco .05
78 Joe Orsulak .05
79 Dave Palmer .05
80 Mark Parent .05
81 Dave Parker .05
82 Dan Pasqua .05
83 Melido Perez .05
84 Steve Peters .05
85 Dan Petry .05
86 Gary Pettis .05
87 Jeff Pico .05
88 Jim Poole (USA) .05
89 Ted Power .05
90 Rafael Ramirez .05
91 Dennis Rasmussen .05
92 Jose Rijo .05
93 Earnie Riles .05
94 Luis Rivera .05
95 Doug Robbins (USA) .05
96 Frank Robinson .15
97 Cookie Rojas .05
98 Chris Sabo **RC** .10
99 Mark Salas .05
100 Luis Salazar .05
101 Rafael Santana .05
102 Nelson Santovenia .05
103 Mackey Sasser .05
104 Calvin Schiraldi .05
105 Mike Schooler .05
106 Scott Servais (USA) .05
107 Dave Silvestri (USA) .05
108 Don Slaught .05
109 Joe Slusarski (USA) .05
110 Lee Smith .05
111 Pete Smith .05
112 Jim Snyder .05
113 Ed Sprague (USA) .05
114 Pete Stanicek .05
115 Kurt Stillwell .05
116 Todd Stottlemyre .05
117 Bill Swift .05
118 Pat Tabler .05
119 Scott Terry .05
120 Mickey Tettleton .05
121 Dickie Thon .05
122 Jeff Treadway .05
123 Willie Upshaw .05
124 Robin Ventura **RC** .25
125 Ron Washington .05
126 Walt Weiss .05
127 Bob Welch .05
128 David Wells .25
129 Glenn Wilson .05
130 Ted Wood (USA) .05
131 Don Zimmer .05
132 Checklist 1T-132T .05

Traded Tiffany

NM/M

Complete Set (132): 25.00
Common Player: .15
(Star cards valued at 3X corresponding cards in regular Topps Traded issue.)

1989 Topps

NM/M

Unopened Factory Set, Retail (792): 25.00
Unopened Factory Set, Hobby (792): 25.00
Complete Set (792): 15.00
Common Player: .05
Wax Pack (15): .75
Wax Box (36): 12.00
Cello Pack (29): 1.00
Cello Box (24): 18.00
Rack Pack (43): .75
Rack Box (24): 15.00
Vending Box (500): 6.00

1 George Bell .05
2 Wade Boggs .25
3 Gary Carter .20
4 Andre Dawson .10
5 Orel Hershiser .05
6 Doug Jones .05
7 Kevin McReynolds .05
8 Dave Eiland **RC** .05
9 Tim Teufel .05
10 Andre Dawson .25
11 Bruce Sutter .35
12 Dale Sveum .05
13 Doug Sisk .05
14 Tom Kelly .05
15 Robby Thompson .05
16 Ron Robinson .05
17 Brian Downing .05
18 Rick Rhoden .05
19 Greg Gagne .05
20 Steve Bedrosian .05
21 Greg Walker White Sox Ldrs. .05
22 Tim Crews .05
23 Mike Fitzgerald .05
24 Larry Andersen .05
25 Frank White .05
26 Dale Mohorcic .05
27 Orestes Destrade **RC** .05
28 Mike Moore .05
29 Kelly Gruber .05
30 Dwight Gooden .05
31 Terry Francona .05
32 Dennis Rasmussen .05
33 B.J. Surhoff .05
34 Ken Williams .05
35 John Tudor .05
36 Mitch Webster .05
37 Bob Stanley .05
38 Paul Runge .05
39 Mike Maddux .05
40 Steve Sax .05
41 Terry Mulholland .05
42 Jim Eppard .05
43 Guillermo Hernandez .05
44 Jim Snyder .05
45 Kal Daniels .05
46 Mark Portugal .05
47 Carney Lansford .05
48 Tim Burke .05
49 Craig Biggio .05
50 George Bell .05
51 Mark McLemore Angels Ldrs. .05
52 Bob Brenly .05
53 Ruben Sierra .05
54 Steve Trout .05
55 Julio Franco .05
56 Pat Tabler .05
57 Alejandro Pena .05
58 Lee Mazzilli .05
59 Mark Davis .05
60 Tom Brunansky .05
61 Neil Allen .05
62 Alfredo Griffin .05
63 Mark Clear .05
64 Alex Trevino .05
65 Rick Reuschel .05
66 Manny Trillo .05
67 Dave Palmer .05
68 Darrell Miller .05
69 Jeff Ballard .05
70 Mark McGwire .65
71 Mike Boddicker .05
72 John Moses .05
73 Pascual Perez .05
74 Nick Leyva .05
75 Tom Henke .05
76 Terry Blocker **RC** .05
77 Doyle Alexander .05
78 Jim Sundberg .05
79 Scott Bankhead .05
80 Cory Snyder .05
81 Tim Raines Expos Ldrs. .05
82 Dave Leiper .05
83 Jeff Blauser .05
84 Bill Bene **RC** .05
85 Kevin McReynolds .05
86 Al Nipper .05
87 Larry Owen .05
88 Darryl Hamilton **RC** .05
89 Dave LaPoint .05
90 Vince Coleman .05
91 Floyd Youmans .05
92 Jeff Kunkel .05
93 Ken Howell .05
94 Chris Speier .05
95 Gerald Young .05
96 Rick Cerone .05
97 Greg Mathews .05
98 Larry Sheets .05
99 Sherman Corbett **RC** .05
100 Mike Schmidt .50
101 Les Straker .05
102 Mike Gallego .05
103 Tim Birtsas .05
104 Dallas Green .05
105 Ron Darling .05
106 Willie Upshaw .05
107 Jose DeLeon .05
108 Fred Manrique .05
109 Hipolito Pena **RC** .05
110 Paul Molitor .40
111 Eric Davis Reds Ldrs. .05
112 Jim Presley .05
113 Lloyd Moseby .05
114 Bob Kipper .05
115 Jody Davis .05
116 Jeff Montgomery .05
117 Dave Anderson .05
118 Checklist 1-132 .05
119 Terry Puhl .05
120 Frank Viola .05
121 Garry Templeton .05
122 Lance Johnson .05
123 Spike Owen .05
124 Jim Traber .05
125 Mike Krukow .05
126 Sid Bream .05
127 Walt Terrell .05
128 Milt Thompson .05
129 Terry Clark **RC** .05
130 Gerald Perry .05
131 Dave Otto .05
132 Curt Ford .05
133 Bill Long .05
134 Don Zimmer .05
135 Jose Rijo .05
136 Joey Meyer .05
137 Geno Petralli .05
138 Wallace Johnson .05
139 Mike Flanagan .05
140 Shawon Dunston .05
141 Brook Jacoby Indians Ldrs. .05
142 Mike Diaz .05
143 Mike Campbell .05
144 Jay Bell .05
145 Dave Stewart .05
146 Gary Pettis .05
147 DeWayne Buice .05
148 Bill Pecota .05
149 Doug Dascenzo **RC** .05
150 Fernando Valenzuela .05
151 Terry McGriff .05
152 Mark Thurmond .05
153 Jim Pankovits .05
154 Don Carman .05
155 Marty Barrett .05
156 Dave Gallagher **RC** .05
157 Tom Glavine .25
158 Mike Aldrete .05
159 Pat Clements .05
160 Jeffrey Leonard .05
161 Gregg Olson **RC** .05
162 John Davis .05
163 Bob Forsch .05
164 Hal Lanier .05
165 Mike Dunne .05
166 Doug Jennings **RC** .05
167 Steve Searcy **RC** .05
168 Willie Wilson .05
169 Mike Jackson .05
170 Tony Fernandez .05
171 Andres Thomas Braves Ldrs. .05
172 Frank Williams .05
173 Mel Hall .05
174 Todd Burns **RC** .05
175 John Shelby .05
176 Jeff Parrett .05
177 Monty Fariss **RC** .05
178 Mark Grant .05
179 Ozzie Virgil .05
180 Mike Scott .05
181 Craig Worthington **RC** .05
182 Bob McClure .05
183 Oddibe McDowell .05
184 John Costello **RC** .05
185 Claudell Washington .05
186 Pat Perry .05
187 Darren Daulton .05
188 Dennis Lamp .05
189 Kevin Mitchell .05
190 Mike Witt .05
191 Sil Campusano **RC** .05
192 Paul Mirabella .05
193 Sparky Anderson .10
194 Greg Harris **RC** .05
195 Ozzie Guillen .05
196 Denny Walling .05
197 Neal Heaton .05
198 Danny Heep .05
199 Mike Schooler **RC** .05
200 George Brett .50
201 Kelly Gruber Blue Jays Ldrs. .05
202 Brad Moore **RC** .05
203 Rob Ducey .05
204 Brad Havens .05
205 Dwight Evans .05
206 Roberto Alomar .35
207 Terry Leach .05
208 Tom Pagnozzi .05
209 Jeff Bittiger **RC** .05
210 Dale Murphy .15
211 Mike Pagliarulo .05
212 Scott Sanderson .05
213 Rene Gonzales .05
214 Charlie O'Brien .05
215 Kevin Gross .05
216 Jack Howell .05
217 Joe Price .05
218 Mike LaValliere .05
219 Jim Clancy .05
220 Gary Gaetti .05
221 Cecil Espy .05
222 Mark Lewis **RC** .05
223 Jay Buhner .05
224 Tony LaRussa .05
225 Ramon Martinez **RC** .25
226 Bill Doran .05
227 John Farrell .05
228 Nelson Santovenia **RC** .05
229 Jimmy Key .05
230 Ozzie Smith .45
231 Roberto Alomar Padres Ldrs. .05
232 Ricky Horton .05
233 Gregg Jefferies .20
234 Tom Browning .05
235 John Kruk .05
236 Charles Hudson .05
237 Glenn Hubbard .05
238 Eric King .05
239 Tim Laudner .05
240 Greg Maddux .45
241 Brett Butler .05
242 Ed Vande Berg .05
243 Bob Boone .05
244 Jim Acker .05
245 Jim Rice .15
246 Rey Quinones .05
247 Shawn Hillegas .05
248 Tony Phillips .05
249 Tim Leary .05
250 Cal Ripken, Jr. .75
251 John Dopson **RC** .05
252 Billy Hatcher .05
253 Jose Alvarez **RC** .05
254 Tom LaSorda .05
255 Ron Guidry .10
256 Benny Santiago .05
257 Rick Aguilera .05
258 Checklist 133-264 .05
259 Larry McWilliams .05
260 Dave Winfield .40
261 Tom Brunansky Cardinals Ldrs. .05
262 Jeff Pico **RC** .05
263 Mike Felder .05
264 Rob Dibble **RC** .10
265 Kent Hrbek .05
266 Luis Aquino .05
267 Jeff Robinson .05
268 Keith Miller .05
269 Tom Bolton .05
270 Wally Joyner .05
271 Jay Tibbs .05
272 Ron Hassey .05
273 Jose Lind .05
274 Mark Eichhorn .05
275 Danny Tartabull .05
276 Paul Kilgus .05
277 Mike Davis .05
278 Andy McGaffigan .05
279 Scott Bradley .05
280 Bob Knepper .05
281 Gary Redus .05
282 Cris Carpenter **RC** .05
283 Andy Allanson .05
284 Jim Leyland .05
285 John Candelaria .05
286 Darrin Jackson .05
287 Juan Nieves .05
288 Pat Sheridan .05
289 Ernie Whitt .05
290 John Franco .05
291 Darryl Strawberry Mets Ldrs. .05
292 Jim Corsi **RC** .05
293 Glenn Wilson .05
294 Juan Berenguer .05
295 Scott Fletcher .05
296 Ron Gant .05
297 Oswald Peraza **RC** .05
298 Chris James .05
299 Steve Ellsworth **RC** .05
300 Darryl Strawberry .05

301	Charlie Leibrandt	.05
302	Gary Ward	.05
303	Felix Fermin	.05
304	Joel Youngblood	.05
305	Dave Smith	.05
306	Tracy Woodson	.05
307	Lance McCullers	.05
308	Ron Karkovice	.05
309	Mario Diaz	.05
310	Rafael Palmeiro	.35
311	Chris Bosio	.05
312	Tom Lawless	.05
313	Denny Martinez	.05
314	Bobby Valentine	.05
315	Greg Swindell	.05
316	Walt Weiss	.05
317	Jack Armstrong **RC**	.05
318	Gene Larkin	.05
319	Greg Booker	.05
320	Lou Whitaker	.05
321	Jody Reed Red Sox Ldrs.	.05
322	John Smiley	.05
323	Gary Thurman	.05
324	Bob Milacki **RC**	.05
325	Jesse Barfield	.05
326	Dennis Boyd	.05
327	Mark Lemke **RC**	.05
328	Rick Honeycutt	.05
329	Bob Melvin	.05
330	Eric Davis	.05
331	Curt Wilkerson	.05
332	Tony Armas	.05
333	Bob Ojeda	.05
334	Steve Lyons	.05
335	Dave Righetti	.05
336	Steve Balboni	.05
337	Calvin Schiraldi	.05
338	Jim Adduci	.05
339	Scott Bailes	.05
340	Kirk Gibson	.05
341	Jim Deshaies	.05
342	Tom Brookens	.05
343	Gary Sheffield **RC**	1.50
344	Tom Trebelhorn	.05
345	Charlie Hough	.05
346	Rex Hudler	.05
347	John Cerutti	.05
348	Ed Hearn	.05
349	Ron Jones **RC**	.05
350	Andy Van Slyke	.05
351	Bob Melvin Giants Ldrs.	.05
352	Rick Schu	.05
353	Marvell Wynne	.05
354	Larry Parrish	.05
355	Mark Langston	.05
356	Kevin Elster	.05
357	Jerry Reuss	.05
358	Ricky Jordan **RC**	.05
359	Tommy John	.10
360	Ryne Sandberg	.45
361	Kelly Downs	.05
362	Jack Lazorko	.05
363	Rich Yett	.05
364	Rob Deer	.05
365	Mike Henneman	.05
366	Herm Winningham	.05
367	Johnny Paredes **RC**	.05
368	Brian Holton	.05
369	Ken Caminiti	.05
370	Dennis Eckersley	.35
371	Manny Lee	.05
372	Craig Lefferts	.05
373	Tracy Jones	.05
374	John Wathan	.05
375	Terry Pendleton	.05
376	Steve Lombardozzi	.05
377	Mike Smithson	.05
378	Checklist 265-396	.05
379	Tim Flannery	.05
380	Rickey Henderson	.40
381	Larry Sheets Orioles Ldrs.	.05
382	John Smoltz	.50
383	Howard Johnson	.05
384	Mark Salas	.05
385	Von Hayes	.05
386	Andres Galarraga/AS	.05
387	Ryne Sandberg/AS	.20
388	Bobby Bonilla/AS	.05
389	Ozzie Smith/AS	.25
390	Darryl Strawberry/AS	.05
391	Andre Dawson/AS	.05
392	Andy Van Slyke/AS	.05
393	Gary Carter/AS	.05
394	Orel Hershiser/AS	.05
395	Danny Jackson/AS	.05
396	Kirk Gibson/AS	.05
397	Don Mattingly/AS	.30
398	Julio Franco/AS	.05
399	Wade Boggs/AS	.20
400	Alan Trammell/AS	.05
401	Jose Canseco/AS	.15
402	Mike Greenwell/AS	.05
403	Kirby Puckett/AS	.25
404	Bob Boone/AS	.05
405	Roger Clemens/AS	.30
406	Frank Viola/AS	.05
407	Dave Winfield/AS	.20
408	Greg Walker	.05
409	Ken Dayley	.05
410	Jack Clark	.05
411	Mitch Williams	.05
412	Barry Lyons	.05
413	Mike Kingery	.05
414	Jim Fregosi	.05
415	Rich Gossage	.05
416	Fred Lynn	.05
417	Mike LaCoss	.05
418	Bob Dernier	.05
419	Tom Filer	.05
420	Joe Carter	.05
421	Kirk McCaskill	.05
422	Bo Diaz	.05
423	Brian Fisher	.05
424	Luis Polonia	.05
425	Jay Howell	.05
426	Danny Gladden	.05
427	Eric Show	.05
428	Craig Reynolds	.05
429	Greg Gagne Twins Ldrs.	.05
430	Mark Gubicza	.05
431	Luis Rivera	.05
432	Chad Kreuter **RC**	.10
433	Albert Hall	.05
434	Ken Patterson **RC**	.05
435	Len Dykstra	.05
436	Bobby Meacham	.05
437	Andy Benes	.05
438	Greg Gross	.05
439	Frank DiPino	.05
440	Bobby Bonilla	.05
441	Jerry Reed	.05
442	Jose Oquendo	.05
443	Rod Nichols **RC**	.05
444	Moose Stubing	.05
445	Matt Nokes	.05
446	Rob Murphy	.05
447	Donell Nixon	.05
448	Eric Plunk	.05
449	Carmelo Martinez	.05
450	Roger Clemens	.50
451	Mark Davidson	.05
452	Israel Sanchez **RC**	.05
453	Tom Prince	.05
454	Paul Assenmacher	.05
455	Johnny Ray	.05
456	Tim Belcher	.05
457	Mackey Sasser	.05
458	Donn Pall **RC**	.05
459	Dave Valle Mariners Ldrs.	.05
460	Dave Stieb	.05
461	Buddy Bell	.05
462	Jose Guzman	.05
463	Steve Lake	.05
464	Bryn Smith	.05
465	Mark Grace	.05
466	Chuck Crim	.05
467	Jim Walewander	.05
468	Henry Cotto	.05
469	Jose Bautista **RC**	.05
470	Lance Parrish	.05
471	Steve Curry **RC**	.05
472	Brian Harper	.05
473	Don Robinson	.05
474	Bob Rodgers	.05
475	Dave Parker	.05
476	Jon Perlman	.05
477	Dick Schofield	.05
478	Doug Drabek	.05
479	Mike Macfarlane	.05
480	Keith Hernandez	.05
481	Chris Brown	.05
482	Steve Peters **RC**	.05
483	Mickey Hatcher	.05
484	Steve Shields	.05
485	Hubie Brooks	.05
486	Jack McDowell	.05
487	Scott Lusader	.05
488	Kevin Coffman	.05
489	Mike Schmidt Phillies Ldrs.	.15
490	Chris Sabo	.05
491	Mike Birkbeck	.05
492	Alan Ashby	.05
493	Todd Benzinger	.05
494	Shane Rawley	.05
495	Candy Maldonado	.05
496	Dwayne Henry	.05
497	Pete Stanicek	.05
498	Dave Valle	.05
499	Don Heinkel **RC**	.05
500	Jose Canseco	.35
501	Vance Law	.05
502	Duane Ward	.05
503	Al Newman	.05
504	Bob Walk	.05
505	Pete Rose	.75
506	Kirt Manwaring	.05
507	Steve Farr	.05
508	Wally Backman	.05
509	Bud Black	.05
510	Bob Horner	.05
511	Richard Dotson	.05
512	Donnie Hill	.05
513	Jesse Orosco	.05
514	Chet Lemon	.05
515	Barry Larkin	.05
516	Eddie Whitson	.05
517	Greg Brock	.05
518	Bruce Ruffin	.05
519	Willie Randolph Yankees Ldrs.	.05
520	Rick Sutcliffe	.05
521	Mickey Tettleton	.05
522	Randy Kramer **RC**	.05
523	Andres Thomas	.05
524	Checklist 397-528	.05
525	Chili Davis	.05
526	Wes Gardner	.05
527	Dave Henderson	.05
528	Luis Medina **RC**	.05
529	Tom Foley	.05
530	Nolan Ryan	.75
531	Dave Hengel	.05
532	Jerry Browne	.05
533	Andy Hawkins	.05
534	Doc Edwards	.05
535	Todd Worrell	.05
536	Joel Skinner	.05
537	Pete Smith	.05
538	Juan Castillo	.05
539	Barry Jones	.05
540	Bo Jackson	.10
541	Cecil Fielder	.05
542	Todd Frohwirth	.05
543	Damon Berryhill	.05
544	Jeff Sellers	.05
545	Mookie Wilson	.05
546	Mark Williamson	.05
547	Mark McLemore	.05
548	Bobby Witt	.05
549	Jamie Moyer Cubs Ldrs.	.05
550	Orel Hershiser	.05
551	Randy Ready	.05
552	Greg Cadaret	.05
553	Luis Salazar	.05
554	Nick Esasky	.05
555	Bert Blyleven	.05
556	Bruce Fields	.05
557	Keith Miller **RC**	.05
558	Dan Pasqua	.05
559	Juan Agosto	.05
560	Tim Raines	.05
561	Luis Aguayo	.05
562	Danny Cox	.05
563	Bill Schroeder	.05
564	Russ Nixon	.05
565	Jeff Russell	.05
566	Al Pedrique	.05
567	David Wells	.05
568	Mickey Brantley	.05
569	German Jimenez **RC**	.05
570	Tony Gwynn	.45
571	Billy Ripken	.05
572	Atlee Hammaker	.05
573	Jim Abbott	.10
574	Dave Clark	.05
575	Juan Samuel	.05
576	Greg Minton	.05
577	Randy Bush	.05
578	John Morris	.05
579	Glenn Davis Astros Ldrs.	.05
580	Harold Reynolds	.05
581	Gene Nelson	.05
582	Mike Marshall	.05
583	Paul Gibson **RC**	.05
584	Randy Velarde	.05
585	Harold Baines	.05
586	Joe Boever	.05
587	Mike Stanley	.05
588	Luis Alicea **RC**	.05
589	Dave Meads	.05
590	Andres Galarraga	.05
591	Jeff Musselman	.05
592	John Cangelosi	.05
593	Drew Hall	.05
594	Jimy Williams	.05
595	Teddy Higuera	.05
596	Kurt Stillwell	.05
597	Terry Taylor **RC**	.05
598	Ken Gerhart	.05
599	Tom Candiotti	.05
600	Wade Boggs	.45
601	Dave Dravecky	.05
602	Devon White	.05
603	Frank Tanana	.05
604	Paul O'Neill	.05
605a	Bob Welch (Missing Complete Major League Pitch. Record line.)	3.00
605b	Bob Welch (Contains Complete Major League Pitch. Record line.)	.05
606	Rick Dempsey	.05
607	Willie Ansley **RC**	.05
608	Phil Bradley	.05
609	Frank Tanana Tigers Ldrs.	.05
610	Randy Myers	.05
611	Don Slaught	.05
612	Dan Quisenberry	.05
613	Gary Varsho **RC**	.05
614	Joe Hesketh	.05
615	Robin Yount	.40
616	Steve Rosenberg **RC**	.05
617	Mark Parent **RC**	.05
618	Rance Mulliniks	.05
619	Checklist 529-660	.05
620	Barry Bonds	.75
621	Rick Mahler	.05
622	Stan Javier	.05
623	Fred Toliver	.05
624	Jack McKeon	.05
625	Eddie Murray	.40
626	Jeff Reed	.05
627	Greg Harris	.05
628	Matt Williams	.05
629	Pete O'Brien	.05
630	Mike Greenwell	.05
631	Dave Bergman	.05
632	Bryan Harvey **RC**	.10
633	Daryl Boston	.05
634	Marvin Freeman	.05
635	Willie Randolph	.05
636	Bill Wilkinson	.05
637	Carmen Castillo	.05
638	Floyd Bannister	.05
639	Walt Weiss Athletics Ldrs.	.05
640	Willie McGee	.05
641	Curt Young	.05
642	Argenis Salazar	.05
643	Louie Meadows **RC**	.05
644	Lloyd McClendon	.05
645	Jack Morris	.05
646	Kevin Bass	.05
647	Randy Johnson **RC**	3.00
648	Sandy Alomar **RC**	.25
649	Stewart Cliburn	.05
650	Kirby Puckett	.45
651	Tom Niedenfuer	.05
652	Rich Gedman	.05
653	Tommy Barrett **RC**	.05
654	Whitey Herzog	.05
655	Dave Magadan	.05
656	Ivan Calderon	.05
657	Joe Magrane	.05
658	R.J. Reynolds	.05
659	Al Leiter	.05
660	Will Clark	.05
661	Dwight Gooden	.05
662	Lou Brock	.05
663	Hank Aaron	.15
664	Gil Hodges	.05
665a	Tony Oliva (No copyright line.)	12.50
665b	Tony Oliva (With copyright line.)	.05
666	Randy St. Claire	.05
667	Dwayne Murphy	.05
668	Mike Bielecki	.05
669	Orel Hershiser Dodgers Ldrs.	.05
670	Kevin Seitzer	.05
671	Jim Gantner	.05
672	Allan Anderson	.05
673	Don Baylor	.05
674	Otis Nixon	.05
675	Bruce Hurst	.05
676	Ernie Riles	.05
677	Dave Schmidt	.05
678	Dion James	.05
679	Willie Fraser	.05
680	Gary Carter	.40
681	Jeff Robinson	.05
682	Rick Leach	.05
683	Jose Cecena **RC**	.05
684	Dave Johnson	.05
685	Jeff Treadway	.05
686	Scott Terry	.05
687	Alvin Davis	.05
688	Zane Smith	.05
689a	Stan Jefferson (Pink triangle at bottom-left photo.)	.05
689b	Stan Jefferson (Pink/purple triangle.)	.05
689c	Stan Jefferson (Purple triangle.)	.05
690	Doug Jones	.05
691	Roberto Kelly	.05
692	Steve Ontiveros	.05
693	Pat Borders **RC**	.05
694	Les Lancaster	.05
695	Carlton Fisk	.40
696	Don August	.05
697	Franklin Stubbs	.05
698	Keith Atherton	.05
699	Al Pedrique Pirates Ldrs.	.05
700	Don Mattingly	.50
701	Storm Davis	.05
702	Jamie Quirk	.05
703	Scott Garrelts	.05
704	Carlos Quintana **RC**	.05
705	Terry Kennedy	.05
706	Pete Incaviglia	.05
707	Steve Jeltz	.05
708	Chuck Finley	.05
709	Tom Herr	.05
710	Dave Cone	.05
711	Candy Sierra **RC**	.05
712	Bill Swift	.05
713	Ty Griffin **RC**	.05
714	Joe M. Morgan	.05
715	Tony Pena	.05
716	Wayne Tolleson	.05
717	Jamie Moyer	.05
718	Glenn Braggs	.05
719	Danny Darwin	.05
720	Tim Wallach	.05
721	Ron Tingley **RC**	.05
722	Todd Stottlemyre	.05
723	Rafael Belliard	.05
724	Jerry Don Gleaton	.05
725	Terry Steinbach	.05
726	Dickie Thon	.05
727	Joe Orsulak	.05
728	Charlie Puleo	.05
729	Steve Buechele Rangers Ldrs.	.05
730	Danny Jackson	.05
731	Mike Young	.05
732	Steve Buechele	.05
733	Randy Bockus **RC**	.05
734	Jody Reed	.05
735	Roger McDowell	.05
736	Jeff Hamilton	.05
737	Norm Charlton **RC**	.05
738	Darnell Coles	.05
739	Brook Jacoby	.05
740	Dan Plesac	.05
741	Ken Phelps	.05
742	Mike Harkey **RC**	.05
743	Mike Heath	.05
744	Roger Craig	.05
745	Fred McGriff	.05
746	German Gonzalez **RC**	.05

747	Wil Tejada	.05
748	Jimmy Jones	.05
749	Rafael Ramirez	.05
750	Bret Saberhagen	.05
751	Ken Oberkfell	.05
752	Jim Gott	.05
753	Jose Uribe	.05
754	Bob Brower	.05
755	Mike Scioscia	.05
756	Scott Medvin **RC**	.05
757	Brady Anderson	.05
758	Gene Walter	.05
759	Rob Deer Brewers Ldrs.	.05
760	Lee Smith	.05
761	Dante Bichette **RC**	.25
762	Bobby Thigpen	.05
763	Dave Martinez	.05
764	Robin Ventura	.25
765	Glenn Davis	.05
766	Cecilio Guante	.05
767	Mike Capel **RC**	.05
768	Bill Wegman	.05
769	Junior Ortiz	.05
770	Alan Trammell	.05
771	Ron Kittle	.05
772	Ron Oester	.05
773	Keith Moreland	.05
774	Frank Robinson	.15
775	Jeff Reardon	.05
776	Nelson Liriano	.05
777	Ted Power	.05
778	Bruce Benedict	.05
779	Craig McMurtry	.05
780	Pedro Guerrero	.05
781	Greg Briley **RC**	.05
782	Checklist 661-792	.05
783	Trevor Wilson **RC**	.05
784	Steve Avery **RC**	.15
785	Ellis Burks	.05
786	Melido Perez	.05
787	Dave West **RC**	.05
788	Mike Morgan	.05
789	Bo Jackson Royals Ldrs.	.05
790	Sid Fernandez	.05
791	Jim Lindeman	.05
792	Rafael Santana	.05

1989 Topps Tiffany

NM/M
Unopened Set (792): 75.00
Complete Set (792): 40.00
Common Player: .10
(Star cards valued at 3X corresponding cards in regular 1989 Topps issue.)

1990 Topps 1989 Major League Debut

MIKE BLOWERS

NM/M
Complete Set (150): 10.00
Common Player: .05

1	Jim Abbott	.05
2	Beau Allred	.05
3	Wilson Alvarez	.05
4	Kent Anderson	.05
5	Eric Anthony	.05
6	Kevin Appier	.05
7	Larry Arndt	.05
8	John Barfield	.05
9	Billy Bates	.05
10	Kevin Batiste	.05
11	Blaine Beatty	.05
12	Stan Belinda	.05
13	Juan Bell	.05
14	Joey Belle	.25
15	Andy Benes	.05
16	Mike Benjamin	.05
17	Geronimo Berroa	.05
18	Mike Blowers	.05
19	Brian Brady	.05
20	Francisco Cabrera	.05
21	George Canale	.05
22	Jose Cano	.05
23	Steve Carter	.05
24	Pat Combs	.05
25	Scott Coolbaugh	.05
26	Steve Cummings	.05
27	Pete Dalena	.05
28	Jeff Datz	.05
29	Bobby Davidson	.05
30	Drew Denson	.05
31	Gary DiSarcina	.05
32	Brian DuBois	.05
33	Mike Dyer	.05
34	Wayne Edwards	.05
35	Junior Felix	.05
36	Mike Fetters	.05
37	Steve Finley	.05
38	Darren Fletcher	.05
39	LaVel Freeman	.05
40	Steve Frey	.05
41	Mark Gardner	.05
42	Joe Girardi	.05
43	Juan Gonzalez	.50
44	Goose Gozzo	.05
45	Tommy Greene	.05
46	Ken Griffey Jr.	3.00
47	Jason Grimsley	.05
48	Marquis Grissom	.05
49	Mark Guthrie	.05
50	Chip Hale	.05
51	John Hardy	.05
52	Gene Harris	.05
53	Mike Hartley	.05
54	Scott Hemond	.05
55	Xavier Hernandez	.05
56	Eric Hetzel	.05
57	Greg Hibbard	.05
58	Mark Higgins	.05
59	Glenallen Hill	.05
60	Chris Hoiles	.05
61	Shawn Holman	.05
62	Dann Howitt	.05
63	Mike Huff	.05
64	Terry Jorgenson	.05
65	Dave Justice	.25
66	Jeff King	.05
67	Matt Kinzer	.05
68	Joe Kraemer	.05
69	Marcus Lawton	.05
70	Derek Lilliquist	.05
71	Scott Little	.05
72	Greg Litton	.05
73	Rick Lueken	.05
74	Julio Machado	.05
75	Tom Magrann	.05
76	Kelly Mann	.05
77	Randy McCament	.05
78	Ben McDonald	.05
79	Chuck McElroy	.05
80	Jeff McKnight	.05
81	Kent Mercker	.05
82	Matt Merullo	.05
83	Hensley Meulens	.05
84	Kevin Mmahat	.05
85	Mike Munoz	.05
86	Dan Murphy	.05
87	Jaime Navarro	.05
88	Randy Nosek	.05
89	John Olerud	.15
90	Steve Olin	.05
91	Joe Oliver	.05
92	Francisco Oliveras	.05
93	Greg Olson	.05
94	John Orton	.05
95	Dean Palmer	.05
96	Ramon Pena	.05
97	Jeff Peterek	.05
98	Marty Pevey	.05
99	Rusty Richards	.05
100	Jeff Richardson	.05
101	Rob Richie	.05
102	Kevin Ritz	.05
103	Rosario Rodriguez	.05
104	Mike Roesler	.05
105	Kenny Rogers	.05
106	Bobby Rose	.05
107	Alex Sanchez	.05
108	Deion Sanders	.25
109	Jeff Schaefer	.05
110	Jeff Schulz	.05
111	Mike Schwabe	.05
112	Dick Scott	.05
113	Scott Scudder	.05
114	Rudy Seanez	.05
115	Joe Skalski	.05
116	Dwight Smith	.05
117	Greg Smith	.05
118	Mike Smith	.05
119	Paul Sorrento	.05
120	Sammy Sosa	3.00
121	Billy Spiers	.05
122	Mike Stanton	.05
123	Phil Stephenson	.05
124	Doug Strange	.05
125	Russ Swan	.05
126	Kevin Tapani	.05
127	Stu Tate	.05
128	Greg Vaughn	.05
129	Robin Ventura	.15
130	Randy Veres	.05
131	Jose Vizcaino	.05
132	Omar Vizquel	.05
133	Larry Walker	.25
134	Jerome Walton	.05
135	Gary Wayne	.05
136	Lenny Webster	.05
137	Mickey Weston	.05
138	Jeff Wetherby	.05
139	John Wetteland	.05
140	Ed Whited	.05
141	Wally Whitehurst	.05
142	Kevin Wickander	.05
143	Dean Wilkins	.05
144	Dana Williams	.05
145	Paul Wilmet	.05
146	Craig Wilson	.05
147	Matt Winters	.05
148	Eric Yelding	.05
149	Clint Zavaras	.05
150	Todd Zeile	.05
----	Checklist (1 of 2)	.05
----	Checklist (2 of 2)	.05

Traded

NM/M
Unopened Set, Retail (132): 12.50
Unopened Set, Hobby (132): 10.00
Complete Set (132): 7.50
Common Player: .05

1T	Don Aase	.05
2T	Jim Abbott	.05
3T	Kent Anderson	.05
4T	Keith Atherton	.05
5T	Wally Backman	.05
6T	Steve Balboni	.05
7T	Jesse Barfield	.05
8T	Steve Bedrosian	.05
9T	Todd Benzinger	.05
10T	Geronimo Berroa	.05
11T	Bert Blyleven	.05
12T	Bob Boone	.05
13T	Phil Bradley	.05
14T	Jeff Brantley **RC**	.05
15T	Kevin Brown	.05
16T	Jerry Browne	.05
17T	Chuck Cary	.05
18T	Carmen Castillo	.05
19T	Jim Clancy	.05
20T	Jack Clark	.05
21T	Bryan Clutterbuck	.05
22T	Jody Davis	.05
23T	Mike Devereaux	.05
24T	Frank DiPino	.05
25T	Benny Distefano	.05
26T	John Dopson	.05
27T	Len Dykstra	.05
28T	Jim Eisenreich	.05
29T	Nick Esasky	.05
30T	Alvaro Espinoza	.05
31T	Darrell Evans	.05
32T	Junior Felix	.05
33T	Felix Fermin	.05
34T	Julio Franco	.05
35T	Terry Francona	.05
36T	Cito Gaston	.05
37T	Bob Geren	.05
	(Photo actually Mike Fennell.)	.05
38T	Tom Gordon **RC**	.10
39T	Tommy Gregg	.05
40T	Ken Griffey	.05
41T	Ken Griffey Jr. **RC**	6.00
42T	Kevin Gross	.05
43T	Lee Guetterman	.05
44T	Mel Hall	.05
45T	Erik Hanson	.05
46T	Gene Harris	.05
47T	Andy Hawkins	.05
48T	Rickey Henderson	.40
49T	Tom Herr	.05
50T	Ken Hill **RC**	.05
51T	Brian Holman	.05
52T	Brian Holton	.05
53T	Art Howe	.05
54T	Ken Howell	.05
55T	Bruce Hurst	.05
56T	Chris James	.05
57T	Randy Johnson	1.50
58T	Jimmy Jones	.05
59T	Terry Kennedy	.05
60T	Paul Kilgus	.05
61T	Eric King	.05
62T	Ron Kittle	.05
63T	John Kruk	.05
64T	Randy Kutcher	.05
65T	Steve Lake	.05
66T	Mark Langston	.05
67T	Dave LaPoint	.05
68T	Rick Leach	.05
69T	Terry Leach	.05
70T	Jim Levebvre	.05
71T	Al Leiter	.05
72T	Jeffrey Leonard	.05
73T	Derek Lilliquist	.05
74T	Rick Mahler	.05
75T	Tom McCarthy	.05
76T	Lloyd McClendon	.05
77T	Lance McCullers	.05
78T	Oddibe McDowell	.05
79T	Roger McDowell	.05
80T	Larry McWilliams	.05
81T	Randy Milligan	.05
82T	Mike Moore	.05
83T	Keith Moreland	.05
84T	Mike Morgan	.05
85T	Jamie Moyer	.05
86T	Rob Murphy	.05
87T	Eddie Murray	.40
88T	Pete O'Brien	.05
89T	Gregg Olson	.05
90T	Steve Ontiveros	.05
91T	Jesse Orosco	.05
92T	Spike Owen	.05
93T	Rafael Palmeiro	.35
94T	Clay Parker	.05
95T	Jeff Parrett	.05
96T	Lance Parrish	.05
97T	Dennis Powell	.05
98T	Rey Quinones	.05
99T	Doug Rader	.05
100T	Willie Randolph	.05
101T	Shane Rawley	.05
102T	Randy Ready	.05
103T	Bip Roberts	.05
104T	Kenny Rogers **RC**	.10
105T	Ed Romero	.05
106T	Nolan Ryan	1.00
107T	Luis Salazar	.05
108T	Juan Samuel	.05
109T	Alex Sanchez	.05
110T	Deion Sanders **RC**	.50
111T	Steve Sax	.05
112T	Rick Schu	.05
113T	Dwight Smith	.05
114T	Lonnie Smith	.05
115T	Billy Spiers	.05
116T	Kent Tekulve	.05
117T	Walt Terrell	.05
118T	Milt Thompson	.05
119T	Dickie Thon	.05
120T	Jeff Torborg	.05
121T	Jeff Treadway	.05
122T	Omar Vizquel **RC**	.50
123T	Jerome Walton	.05
124T	Gary Ward	.05
125T	Claudell Washington	.05
126T	Curt Wilkerson	.05
127T	Eddie Williams	.05
128T	Frank Williams	.05
129T	Ken Williams	.05
130T	Mitch Williams	.05
131T	Steve Wilson	.05
---	Topps Magazine Subscription Offer Card	.05

1989 Topps Traded Tiffany

NM/M
Unopened Set (132): 85.00
Complete Set (132): 50.00
Common Player: .10
(Star cards valued at 3X corresponding cards in regular Topps Traded issue.)

1990 Topps

JOEY BELLE

NM/M
Unopened Factory Set, Retail (792): 25.00
Unopened Factory Set, Hobby (792): 20.00
Complete Set (792): 15.00
Common Player: .05
Wax Pack (16): .60
Wax Box (36): 12.00
Cello Pack (31): 1.00
Cello Box (24): 15.00
Rack Pack (45): 1.00
Rack Box (24): 16.00
Vending Box (500): 7.50

1	Nolan Ryan	.75
2	Nolan Ryan (Mets)	.35
3	Nolan Ryan (Angels)	.25
4	Nolan Ryan (Astros)	.25
5	Nolan Ryan (Rangers)	.25
6	Vince Coleman	.05
7	Rickey Henderson	.20
8	Cal Ripken, Jr.	.40

9	Eric Plunk	.05
10	Barry Larkin	.05
11	Paul Gibson	.05
12	Joe Girardi	.05
13	Mark Williamson	.05
14	Mike Fetters **RC**	.05
15	Teddy Higuera	.05
16	Kent Anderson **RC**	.05
17	Kelly Downs	.05
18	Carlos Quintana	.05
19	Al Newman	.05
20	Mark Gubicza	.05
21	Jeff Torborg	.05
22	Bruce Ruffin	.05
23	Randy Velarde	.05
24	Joe Hesketh	.05
25	Willie Randolph	.05
26	Don Slaught	.05
27	Rick Leach	.05
28	Duane Ward	.05
29	John Cangelosi	.05
30	David Cone	.05
31	Henry Cotto	.05
32	John Farrell	.05
33	Greg Walker	.05
34	Tony Fossas **RC**	.05
35	Benito Santiago	.05
36	John Costello	.05
37	Domingo Ramos	.05
38	Wes Gardner	.05
39	Curt Ford	.05
40	Jay Howell	.05
41	Matt Williams	.05
42	Jeff Robinson	.05
43	Dante Bichette	.05
44	Roger Salkeld **RC**	.10
45	Dave Parker	.05
46	Rob Dibble	.05
47	Brian Harper	.05
48	Zane Smith	.05
49	Tom Lawless	.05
50	Glenn Davis	.05
51	Doug Rader	.05
52	Jack Daugherty **RC**	.05
53	Mike LaCoss	.05
54	Joel Skinner	.05
55	Darrell Evans	.05
56	Franklin Stubbs	.05
57	Greg Vaughn	.05
58	Keith Miller	.05
59	Ted Power	.05
60	George Brett	.50
61	Deion Sanders	.10
62	Ramon Martinez	.05
63	Mike Pagliarulo	.05
64	Danny Darwin	.05
65	Devon White	.05
66	Greg Litton **RC**	.05
67	Scott Sanderson	.05
68	Dave Henderson	.05
69	Todd Frohwirth	.05
70	Mike Greenwell	.05
71	Allan Anderson	.05
72	Jeff Huson **RC**	.05
73	Bob Milacki	.05
74	Jeff Jackson **RC**	.05
75	Doug Jones	.05
76	Dave Valle	.05
77	Dave Bergman	.05
78	Mike Flanagan	.05
79	Ron Kittle	.05
80	Jeff Russell	.05
81	Bob Rodgers	.05
82	Scott Terry	.05
83	Hensley Meulens	.05
84	Ray Searage	.05
85	Juan Samuel	.05
86	Paul Kilgus	.05
87	Rick Luecken **RC**	.05
88	Glenn Braggs	.05
89	Clint Zavaras **RC**	.05
90	Jack Clark	.05
91	Steve Frey **RC**	.05
92	Mike Stanley	.05
93	Shawn Hillegas	.05
94	Herm Winningham	.05
95	Todd Worrell	.05
96	Jody Reed	.05
97	Curt Schilling	.25
98	Jose Gonzalez	.05
99	Rich Monteleone **RC**	.05
100	Will Clark	.05
101	Shane Rawley	.05
102	Stan Javier	.05
103	Marvin Freeman	.05
104	Bob Knepper	.05
105	Randy Myers	.05
106	Charlie O'Brien	.05
107	Fred Lynn	.05
108	Rod Nichols	.05
109	Roberto Kelly	.05
110	Tommy Helms	.05
111	Ed Whited	.05
112	Glenn Wilson	.05
113	Manny Lee	.05
114	Mike Bielecki	.05
115	Tony Pena	.05
116	Floyd Bannister	.05
117	Mike Sharperson	.05
118	Erik Hanson	.05
119	Billy Hatcher	.05
120	John Franco	.05
121	Robin Ventura	.05
122	Shawn Abner	.05
123	Rich Gedman	.05
124	Dave Dravecky	.05
125	Kent Hrbek	.05
126	Randy Kramer	.05
127	Mike Devereaux	.05
128	Checklist 1-132	.05
129	Ron Jones	.05
130	Bert Blyleven	.05
131	Matt Nokes	.05
132	Lance Blankenship	.05
133	Ricky Horton	.05
134	Earl Cunningham **RC**	.05
135	Dave Magadan	.05
136	Kevin Brown	.05
137	Marty Pevey **RC**	.05
138	Al Leiter	.05
139	Greg Brock	.05
140	Andre Dawson	.25
141	John Hart	.05
142	Jeff Wetherby **RC**	.05
143	Rafael Belliard	.05
144	Bud Black	.05
145	Terry Steinbach	.05
146	Rob Richie **RC**	.05
147	Chuck Finley	.05
148	Edgar Martinez	.05
149	Steve Farr	.05
150	Kirk Gibson	.05
151	Rick Mahler	.05
152	Lonnie Smith	.05
153	Randy Milligan	.05
154	Mike Maddux	.05
155	Ellis Burks	.05
156	Ken Patterson	.05
157	Craig Biggio	.05
158	Craig Lefferts	.05
159	Mike Felder	.05
160	Dave Righetti	.05
161	Harold Reynolds	.05
162	Todd Zeile **RC**	.20
163	Phil Bradley	.05
164	Jeff Juden **RC**	.05
165	Walt Weiss	.05
166	Bobby Witt	.05
167	Kevin Appier	.05
168	Jose Lind	.05
169	Richard Dotson	.05
170	George Bell	.05
171	Russ Nixon	.05
172	Tom Lampkin	.05
173	Tim Belcher	.05
174	Jeff Kunkel	.05
175	Mike Moore	.05
176	Luis Quinones	.05
177	Mike Henneman	.05
178	Chris James	.05
179	Brian Holton	.05
180	Rock Raines	.05
181	Juan Agosto	.05
182	Mookie Wilson	.05
183	Steve Lake	.05
184	Danny Cox	.05
185	Ruben Sierra	.05
186	Dave LaPoint	.05
187	Rick Wrona **RC**	.05
188	Mike Smithson	.05
189	Dick Schofield	.05
190	Rick Reuschel	.05
191	Pat Borders	.05
192	Don August	.05
193	Andy Benes	.05
194	Glenallen Hill	.05
195	Tim Burke	.05
196	Gerald Young	.05
197	Doug Drabek	.05
198	Mike Marshall	.05
199	Sergio Valdez **RC**	.05
200	Don Mattingly	.50
201	Cito Gaston	.05
202	Mike Macfarlane	.05
203	Mike Roesler **RC**	.05
204	Bob Dernier	.05
205	Mark Davis	.05
206	Nick Esasky	.05
207	Bob Ojeda	.05
208	Brook Jacoby	.05
209	Greg Mathews	.05
210	Ryne Sandberg	.45
211	John Cerutti	.05
212	Joe Orsulak	.05
213	Scott Bankhead	.05
214	Terry Francona	.05
215	Kirk McCaskill	.05
216	Ricky Jordan	.05
217	Don Robinson	.05
218	Wally Backman	.05
219	Donn Pall	.05
220	Barry Bonds	.75
221	Gary Mielke **RC**	.05
222	Kurt Stillwell	.05
223	Tommy Gregg	.05
224	Delino DeShields **RC**	.15
225	Jim Deshaies	.05
226	Mickey Hatcher	.05
227	Kevin Tapani **RC**	.15
228	Dave Martinez	.05
229	David Wells	.05
230	Keith Hernandez	.05
231	Jack McKeon	.05
232	Darnell Coles	.05
233	Ken Hill	.05
234	Mariano Duncan	.05
235	Jeff Reardon	.05
236	Hal Morris	.05
237	Kevin Ritz **RC**	.05
238	Felix Jose	.05
239	Eric Show	.05
240	Mark Grace	.05
241	Mike Krukow	.05
242	Fred Manrique	.05
243	Barry Jones	.05
244	Bill Schroeder	.05
245	Roger Clemens	.50
246	Jim Eisenreich	.05
247	Jerry Reed	.05
248	Dave Anderson	.05
249	Mike Smith **RC**	.05
250	Jose Canseco	.25
251	Jeff Blauser	.05
252	Otis Nixon	.05
253	Mark Portugal	.05
254	Francisco Cabrera	.05
255	Bobby Thigpen	.05
256	Marvell Wynne	.05
257	Jose DeLeon	.05
258	Barry Lyons	.05
259	Lance McCullers	.05
260	Eric Davis	.05
261	Whitey Herzog	.05
262	Checklist 133-264	.05
263	Mel Stottlemyre, Jr. **RC**	.10
264	Bryan Clutterbuck	.05
265	Pete O'Brien	.05
266	German Gonzalez	.05
267	Mark Davidson	.05
268	Rob Murphy	.05
269	Dickie Thon	.05
270	Dave Stewart	.05
271	Chet Lemon	.05
272	Bryan Harvey	.05
273	Bobby Bonilla	.05
274	Goose Gozzo **RC**	.05
275	Mickey Tettleton	.05
276	Gary Thurman	.05
277	Lenny Harris	.05
278	Pascual Perez	.05
279	Steve Buechele	.05
280	Lou Whitaker	.05
281	Kevin Bass	.05
282	Derek Lilliquist	.05
283	Albert Belle	.15
284	Mark Gardner **RC**	.05
285	Willie McGee	.05
286	Lee Guetterman	.05
287	Vance Law	.05
288	Greg Briley	.05
289	Norm Charlton	.05
290	Robin Yount	.35
291	Dave Johnson	.05
292	Jim Gott	.05
293	Mike Gallego	.05
294	Craig McMurtry	.05
295	Fred McGriff	.05
296	Jeff Ballard	.05
297	Tom Herr	.05
298	Danny Gladden	.05
299	Adam Peterson	.05
300	Bo Jackson	.10
301	Don Aase	.05
302	Marcus Lawton **RC**	.05
303	Rick Cerone	.05
304	Marty Clary	.05
305	Eddie Murray	.35
306	Tom Niedenfuer	.05
307	Bip Roberts	.05
308	Jose Guzman	.05
309	Eric Yelding **RC**	.05
310	Steve Bedrosian	.05
311	Dwight Smith	.05
312	Dan Quisenberry	.05
313	Gus Polidor	.05
314	Donald Harris **RC**	.05
315	Bruce Hurst	.05
316	Carney Lansford	.05
317	Mark Guthrie **RC**	.05
318	Wallace Johnson	.05
319	Dion James	.05
320	Dave Steib	.05
321	Joe M. Morgan	.05
322	Junior Ortiz	.05
323	Willie Wilson	.05
324	Pete Harnisch	.05
325	Robby Thompson	.05
326	Tom McCarthy **RC**	.05
327	Ken Williams	.05
328	Curt Young	.05
329	Oddibe McDowell	.05
330	Ron Darling	.05
331	Juan Gonzalez **RC**	1.50
332	Paul O'Neill	.05
333	Bill Wegman	.05
334	Johnny Ray	.05
335	Andy Hawkins	.05
336	Ken Griffey Jr.	.75
337	Lloyd McClendon	.05
338	Dennis Lamp	.05
339	Dave Clark	.05
340	Fernando Valenzuela	.05
341	Tom Foley	.05
342	Alex Trevino	.05
343	Frank Tanana	.05
344	George Canale **RC**	.05
345	Harold Baines	.05
346	Jim Presley	.05
347	Junior Felix **RC**	.05
348	Gary Wayne **RC**	.05
349	Steve Finley **RC**	.15
350	Bret Saberhagen	.05
351	Roger Craig	.05
352	Bryn Smith	.05
353	Sandy Alomar	.05
354	Stan Belinda **RC**	.05
355	Marty Barrett	.05
356	Randy Ready	.05
357	Dave West	.05
358	Andres Thomas	.05
359	Jimmy Jones	.05
360	Paul Molitor	.35
361	Randy McCament **RC**	.05
362	Damon Berryhill	.05
363	Dan Petry	.05
364	Rolando Roomes	.05
365	Ozzie Guillen	.05
366	Mike Heath	.05
367	Mike Morgan	.05
368	Bill Doran	.05
369	Todd Burns	.05
370	Tim Wallach	.05
371	Jimmy Key	.05
372	Terry Kennedy	.05
373	Alvin Davis	.05
374	Steve Cummings **RC**	.05
375	Dwight Evans	.05
376	Checklist 265-396	.05
377	Mickey Weston **RC**	.05
378	Luis Salazar	.05
379	Steve Rosenberg	.05
380	Dave Winfield	.35
381	Frank Robinson	.10
382	Jeff Musselman	.05
383	John Morris	.05
384	Pat Combs **RC**	.05
385	Fred McGriff/AS	.05
386	Julio Franco/AS	.05
387	Wade Boggs/AS	.20
388	Cal Ripken, Jr./AS	.40
389	Robin Yount/AS	.20
390	Ruben Sierra/AS	.05
391	Kirby Puckett/AS	.25
392	Carlton Fisk/AS	.20
393	Bret Saberhagen/AS	.05
394	Jeff Ballard/AS	.05
395	Jeff Russell/AS	.05
396	A. Bartlett Giamatti	.20
397	Will Clark/AS	.05
398	Ryne Sandberg/AS	.20
399	Howard Johnson/AS	.05
400	Ozzie Smith/AS	.20
401	Kevin Mitchell/AS	.05
402	Eric Davis/AS	.05
403	Tony Gwynn/AS	.25
404	Craig Biggio/AS	.05
405	Mike Scott/AS	.05
406	Joe Magrane/AS	.05
407	Mark Davis/AS	.05
408	Trevor Wilson	.05
409	Tom Brunansky	.05
410	Joe Boever	.05
411	Ken Phelps	.05
412	Jamie Moyer	.05
413	Brian DuBois **RC**	.05
414a	Frank Thomas No Name **RC** (No name on front.)	500.00
414b	Frank Thomas **RC** (Name on front.)	3.00
415	Shawon Dunston	.05
416	Dave Johnson **RC**	.05
417	Jim Gantner	.05
418	Tom Browning	.05
419	Beau Allred **RC**	.05
420	Carlton Fisk	.35
421	Greg Minton	.05
422	Pat Sheridan	.05
423	Fred Toliver	.05
424	Jerry Reuss	.05
425	Bill Landrum	.05
426	Jeff Hamilton	.05
427	Carmem Castillo	.05
428	Steve Davis **RC**	.05
429	Tom Kelly	.05
430	Pete Incaviglia	.05
431	Randy Johnson	.35
432	Damaso Garcia	.05
433	Steve Olin **RC**	.05
434	Mark Carreon	.05
435	Kevin Seitzer	.05
436	Mel Hall	.05
437	Les Lancaster	.05
438	Greg Myers	.05
439	Jeff Parrett	.05
440	Alan Trammell	.05
441	Bob Kipper	.05
442	Jerry Browne	.05
443	Cris Carpenter	.05
444	Kyle Abbott **RC** (FDP)	.10
445	Danny Jackson	.05
446	Dan Pasqua	.05
447	Atlee Hammaker	.05
448	Greg Gagne	.05
449	Dennis Rasmussen	.05
450	Rickey Henderson	.35
451	Mark Lemke	.05
452	Luis de los Santos	.05
453	Jody Davis	.05
454a	Jeff King (No white on back.)	100.00
454b	Jeff King (Correct use of white.)	.05
455	Jeffrey Leonard	.05
456	Chris Gwynn	.05
457	Gregg Jefferies	.05
458	Bob McClure	.05
459	Jim Lefebvre	.05
460	Mike Scott	.05
461	Carlos Martinez **RC**	.05
462	Denny Walling	.05

463	Drew Hall	.05
464	Jerome Walton **RC**	.05
465	Kevin Gross	.05
466	Rance Mulliniks	.05
467	Juan Nieves	.05
468	Billy Ripken	.05
469	John Kruk	.05
470	Frank Viola	.05
471	Mike Brumley	.05
472	Jose Uribe	.05
473	Joe Price	.05
474	Rich Thompson	.05
475	Bob Welch	.05
476	Brad Komminsk	.05
477	Willie Fraser	.05
478	Mike LaValliere	.05
479	Frank White	.05
480	Sid Fernandez	.05
481	Garry Templeton	.05
482	Steve Carter **RC**	.05
483	Alejandro Pena	.05
484	Mike Fitzgerald	.05
485	John Candelaria	.05
486	Jeff Treadway	.05
487	Steve Searcy	.05
488	Ken Oberkfell	.05
489	Nick Leyva	.05
490	Dan Plesac	.05
491	Dave Cochrane **RC**	.05
492	Ron Oester	.05
493	Jason Grimsley **RC**	.05
494	Terry Puhl	.05
495	Lee Smith	.05
496	Cecil Espy	.05
497	Dave Schmidt	.05
498	Rick Schu	.05
499	Bill Long	.05
500	Kevin Mitchell	.05
501	Matt Young	.05
502	Mitch Webster	.05
503	Randy St. Claire	.05
504	Tom O'Malley	.05
505	Kelly Gruber	.05
506	Tom Glavine	.25
507	Gary Redus	.05
508	Terry Leach	.05
509	Tom Pagnozzi	.05
510	Dwight Gooden	.05
511	Clay Parker	.05
512	Gary Pettis	.05
513	Mark Eichhorn	.05
514	Andy Allanson	.05
515	Len Dykstra	.05
516	Tim Leary	.05
517	Roberto Alomar	.15
518	Bill Krueger	.05
519	Bucky Dent	.05
520	Mitch Williams	.05
521	Craig Worthington	.05
522	Mike Dunne	.05
523	Jay Bell	.05
524	Daryl Boston	.05
525	Wally Joyner	.05
526	Checklist 397-528	.05
527	Ron Hassey	.05
528	Kevin Wickander **RC**	.05
529	Greg Harris	.05
530	Mark Langston	.05
531	Ken Caminiti	.05
532	Cecilio Guante	.05
533	Tim Jones	.05
534	Louie Meadows	.05
535	John Smoltz	.05
536	Bob Geren **RC**	.05
537	Mark Grant	.05
538	Billy Spiers **RC**	.05
539	Neal Heaton	.05
540	Danny Tartabull	.05
541	Pat Perry	.05
542	Darren Daulton	.05
543	Nelson Liriano	.05
544	Dennis Boyd	.05
545	Kevin McReynolds	.05
546	Kevin Hickey	.05
547	Jack Howell	.05
548	Pat Clements	.05
549	Don Zimmer	.05
550	Julio Franco	.05
551	Tim Crews	.05
552	Mike Smith **RC**	.05
553	Scott Scudder **RC**	.05
554	Jay Buhner	.05
555	Jack Morris	.05
556	Gene Larkin	.05
557	Jeff Innis **RC**	.05
558	Rafael Ramirez	.05
559	Andy McGaffigan	.05
560	Steve Sax	.05
561	Ken Dayley	.05
562	Chad Kreuter	.05
563	Alex Sanchez	.05
564	Tyler Houston **RC**	.10
565	Scott Fletcher	.05
566	Mark Knudson	.05
567	Ron Gant	.05
568	John Smiley	.05
569	Ivan Calderon	.05
570	Cal Ripken, Jr.	.75
571	Brett Butler	.05
572	Greg Harris	.05
573	Danny Heep	.05
574	Bill Swift	.05
575	Lance Parrish	.05
576	Mike Dyer **RC**	.05
577	Charlie Hayes	.05

578	Joe Magrane	.05
579	Art Howe	.05
580	Joe Carter	.05
581	Ken Griffey	.05
582	Rick Honeycutt	.05
583	Bruce Benedict	.05
584	Phil Stephenson **RC**	.05
585	Kal Daniels	.05
586	Ed Nunez	.05
587	Lance Johnson	.05
588	Rick Rhoden	.05
589	Mike Aldrete	.05
590	Ozzie Smith	.45
591	Todd Stottlemyre	.05
592	R.J. Reynolds	.05
593	Scott Bradley	.05
594	Luis Sojo **RC**	.05
595	Greg Swindell	.05
596	Jose DeJesus	.05
597	Chris Bosio	.05
598	Brady Anderson	.05
599	Frank Williams	.05
600	Darryl Strawberry	.05
601	Luis Rivera	.05
602	Scott Garrelts	.05
603	Tony Armas	.05
604	Ron Robinson	.05
605	Mike Scioscia	.05
606	Storm Davis	.05
607	Steve Jeltz	.05
608	Eric Anthony **RC**	.10
609	Sparky Anderson	.10
610	Pedro Guerrero	.05
611	Walt Terrell	.05
612	Dave Gallagher	.05
613	Jeff Pico	.05
614	Nelson Santovenia	.05
615	Rob Deer	.05
616	Brian Holman	.05
617	Geronimo Berroa	.05
618	Eddie Whitson	.05
619	Rob Ducey	.05
620	Tony Castillo **RC**	.05
621	Melido Perez	.05
622	Sid Bream	.05
623	Jim Corsi	.05
624	Darrin Jackson	.05
625	Roger McDowell	.05
626	Bob Melvin	.05
627	Jose Rijo	.05
628	Candy Maldonado	.05
629	Eric Hetzel	.05
630	Gary Gaetti	.05
631	John Wetteland **RC**	.15
632	Scott Lusader	.05
633	Dennis Cook	.05
634	Luis Polonia	.05
635	Brian Downing	.05
636	Jesse Orosco	.05
637	Craig Reynolds	.05
638	Jeff Montgomery	.05
639	Tony LaRussa	.05
640	Rick Sutcliffe	.05
641	Doug Strange **RC**	.05
642	Jack Armstrong	.05
643	Alfredo Griffin	.05
644	Paul Assenmacher	.05
645	Jose Oquendo	.05
646	Checklist 529-660	.05
647	Rex Hudler	.05
648	Jim Clancy	.05
649	Dan Murphy **RC**	.05
650	Mike Witt	.05
651	Rafael Santana	.05
652	Mike Boddicker	.05
653	John Moses	.05
654	Paul Coleman **RC**	.05
655	Gregg Olson	.05
656	Mackey Sasser	.05
657	Terry Mulholland	.05
658	Donell Nixon	.05
659	Greg Cadaret	.05
660	Vince Coleman	.05
661	Dick Howser	.05
662	Mike Schmidt	.10
663	Fred Lynn	.05
664	Johnny Bench	.05
665	Sandy Koufax	.15
666	Brian Fisher	.05
667	Curt Wilkerson	.05
668	Joe Oliver **RC**	.05
669	Tom Lasorda	.05
670	Dennis Eckersley	.30
671	Bob Boone	.05
672	Roy Smith	.05
673	Joey Meyer	.05
674	Spike Owen	.05
675	Jim Abbott	.05
676	Randy Kutcher	.05
677	Jay Tibbs	.05
678	Kirt Manwaring	.05
679	Gary Ward	.05
680	Howard Johnson	.05
681	Mike Schooler	.05
682	Dann Bilardello	.05
683	Kenny Rogers	.05
684	Julio Machado **RC**	.05
685	Tony Fernandez	.05
686	Carmelo Martinez	.05
687	Tim Birtsas	.05
688	Milt Thompson	.05
689	Rich Yett	.05
690	Mark McGwire	.65
691	Chuck Cary	.05
692	Sammy Sosa **RC**	4.00

693	Calvin Schiraldi	.05
694	Mike Stanton **RC**	.05
695	Tom Henke	.05
696	B.J. Surhoff	.05
697	Mike Davis	.05
698	Omar Vizquel	.05
699	Jim Leyland	.05
700	Kirby Puckett	.45
701	Bernie Williams **RC**	1.00
702	Tony Phillips	.05
703	Jeff Brantley	.05
704	Chip Hale **RC**	.05
705	Claudell Washington	.05
706	Geno Petralli	.05
707	Luis Aquino	.05
708	Larry Sheets	.05
709	Juan Berneguer	.05
710	Von Hayes	.05
711	Rick Aguilera	.05
712	Todd Benzinger	.05
713	Tim Drummond **RC**	.05
714	Marquis Grissom **RC**	.25
715	Greg Maddux	.45
716	Steve Balboni	.05
717	Ron Kakovice	.05
718	Gary Sheffield	.30
719	Wally Whitehurst **RC**	.05
720	Andres Galarraga	.05
721	Lee Mazzilli	.05
722	Felix Fermin	.05
723	Jeff Robinson	.05
724	Juan Bell	.05
725	Terry Pendleton	.05
726	Gene Nelson	.05
727	Pat Tabler	.05
728	Jim Acker	.05
729	Bobby Valentine	.05
730	Tony Gwynn	.45
731	Don Carman	.05
732	Ernie Riles	.05
733	John Dopson	.05
734	Kevin Elster	.05
735	Charlie Hough	.05
736	Rick Dempsey	.05
737	Chris Sabo	.05
738	Gene Harris **RC**	.05
739	Dale Sveum	.05
740	Jesse Barfield	.05
741	Steve Wilson	.05
742	Ernie Whitt	.05
743	Tom Candiotti	.05
744	Kelly Mann **RC**	.05
745	Hubie Brooks	.05
746	Dave Smith	.05
747	Randy Bush	.05
748	Doyle Alexander	.05
749	Mark Parent	.05
750	Dale Murphy	.15
751	Steve Lyons	.05
752	Tom Gordon	.05
753	Chris Speier	.05
754	Bob Walk	.05
755	Rafael Palmeiro	.30
756	Ken Howell	.05
757	Larry Walker **RC**	.75
758	Mark Thurmond	.05
759	Tom Trebelhorn	.05
760	Wade Boggs	.45
761	Mike Jackson	.05
762	Doug Dascenzo	.05
763	Denny Martinez	.05
764	Tim Teufel	.05
765	Chili Davis	.05
766	Brian Meyer	.05
767	Tracy Jones	.05
768	Chuck Crim	.05
769	Greg Hibbard **RC**	.05
770	Cory Snyder	.05
771	Pete Smith	.05
772	Jeff Reed	.05
773	Dave Leiper	.05
774	Ben McDonald **RC**	.20
775	Andy Van Slyke	.05
776	Charlie Leibrandt	.05
777	Tim Laudner	.05
778	Mike Jeffcoat	.05
779	Lloyd Moseby	.05
780	Orel Hershiser	.05
781	Mario Diaz	.05
782	Jose Alvarez	.05
783	Checklist 661-792	.05
784	Scott Bailes	.05
785	Jim Rice	.15
786	Eric King	.05
787	Rene Gonzales	.05
788	Frank DiPino	.05
789	John Wathan	.05
790	Gary Carter	.35
791	Alvaro Espinoza	.05
792	Gerald Perry	.05

1990 Topps Tiffany

	NM/M
Unopened Set (792):	115.00
Complete Set (792):	90.00
Common Player:	.10

(Star cards valued at 5X corresponding cards in regular Topps issue.)

Traded

	NM/M
Complete Set, Retail (132):	6.00
Complete Set, Hobby (132):	4.00
Common Player:	.05
Wax Pack (7):	.75

Wax Box (36):		9.00
1	Darrel Akerfelds	.05
2	Sandy Alomar, Jr.	.05
3	Brad Arnsberg	.05
4	Steve Avery	.05
5	Wally Backman	.05
6	Carlos Baerga **RC**	.10
7	Kevin Bass	.05
8	Willie Blair	.05
9	Mike Blowers	.05
10	Shawn Boskie	.05
11	Daryl Boston	.05
12	Dennis Boyd	.05
13	Glenn Braggs	.05
14	Hubie Brooks	.05
15	Tom Brunansky	.05
16	John Burkett	.05
17	Casey Candaele	.05
18	John Candelaria	.05
19	Gary Carter	.75
20	Joe Carter	.05
21	Rick Cerone	.05
22	Scott Coolbaugh	.05
23	Bobby Cox	.05
24	Mark Davis	.05
25	Storm Davis	.05
26	Edgar Diaz	.05
27	Wayne Edwards	.05
28	Mark Eichhorn	.05
29	Scott Erickson	.05
30	Nick Esasky	.05
31	Cecil Fielder	.05
32	John Franco	.05
33	Travis Fryman **RC**	.25
34	Bill Gullickson	.05
35	Darryl Hamilton	.05
36	Mike Harkey	.05
37	Bud Harrelson	.05
38	Billy Hatcher	.05
39	Keith Hernandez	.05
40	Joe Hesketh	.05
41	Dave Hollins	.05
42	Sam Horn	.05
43	Steve Howard	.05
44	Todd Hundley **RC**	.15
45	Jeff Huson	.05
46	Chris James	.05
47	Stan Javier	.05
48	Dave Justice **RC**	.75
49	Jeff Kaiser	.05
50	Dana Kiecker	.05
51	Joe Klink	.05
52	Brent Knackert	.05
53	Brad Komminsk	.05
54	Mark Langston	.05
55	Tim Layana	.05
56	Rick Leach	.05
57	Terry Leach	.05
58	Tim Leary	.05
59	Craig Lefferts	.05
60	Charlie Leibrandt	.05
61	Jim Leyritz	.05
62	Fred Lynn	.05
63	Kevin Maas	.05
64	Shane Mack	.05
65	Candy Maldonado	.05
66	Fred Manrique	.05
67	Mike Marshall	.05
68	Carmelo Martinez	.05
69	John Marzano	.05
70	Ben McDonald	.05
71	Jack McDowell	.05
72	John McNamara	.05
73	Orlando Mercado	.05
74	Stump Merrill	.05
75	Alan Mills	.05
76	Hal Morris	.05
77	Lloyd Moseby	.05
78	Randy Myers	.05
79	Tim Naehring	.05
80	Junior Noboa	.05
81	Matt Nokes	.05
82	Pete O'Brien	.05
83	John Olerud **RC**	.75
84	Greg Olson	.05
85	Junior Ortiz	.05
86	Dave Parker	.05
87	Rick Parker	.05
88	Bob Patterson	.05
89	Alejandro Pena	.05
90	Tony Pena	.05

#	Player	Price
91	Pascual Perez	.05
92	Gerald Perry	.05
93	Dan Petry	.05
94	Gary Pettis	.05
95	Tony Phillips	.05
96	Lou Pinella	.05
97	Luis Polonia	.05
98	Jim Presley	.05
99	Scott Radinsky	.05
100	Willie Randolph	.05
101	Jeff Reardon	.05
102	Greg Riddoch	.05
103	Jeff Robinson	.05
104	Ron Robinson	.05
105	Kevin Romine	.05
106	Scott Ruskin	.05
107	John Russell	.05
108	Bill Sampen	.05
109	Juan Samuel	.05
110	Scott Sanderson	.05
111	Jack Savage	.05
112	Dave Schmidt	.05
113	Red Schoendienst	.10
114	Terry Shumpert	.05
115	Matt Sinatro	.05
116	Don Slaught	.05
117	Bryn Smith	.05
118	Lee Smith	.05
119	Paul Sorrento	.05
120	Franklin Stubbs	.05
121	Russ Swan	.05
122	Bob Tewksbury	.05
123	Wayne Tolleson	.05
124	John Tudor	.05
125	Randy Veres	.05
126	Hector Villanueva	.05
127	Mitch Webster	.05
128	Ernie Whitt	.05
129	Frank Wills	.05
130	Dave Winfield	.75
131	Matt Young	.05
132	Checklist	.05

1990 Topps Traded Tiffany

NM/M

Complete Set (132): 25.00
Common Player: .15
(Star cards valued at 4X corresponding cards in regular Topps Traded issue.)

1991 Topps 1990 Major League Debut

NM/M

Complete Set (171): 5.00
Common Player: .05

#	Player	Price
1	Paul Abbott	.05
2	Steve Adkins	.05
3	Scott Aldred	.05
4	Gerald Alexander	.05
5	Moises Alou	.25
6	Steve Avery	.05
7	Oscar Azocar	.05
8	Carlos Baerga	.05
9	Kevin Baez	.05
10	Jeff Baldwin	.05
11	Brian Barnes	.05
12	Kevin Bearse	.05
13	Kevin Belcher	.05
14	Mike Bell	.05
15	Sean Berry	.05
16	Joe Bitker	.05
17	Willie Blair	.05
18	Brian Bohanon	.05
19	Mike Bordick	.05
20	Shawn Boskie	.05
21	Rod Brewer	.05
22	Kevin Brown	.10
23	Dave Burba	.05
24	Jim Campbell	.05
25	Ozzie Canseco	.05
26	Chuck Carr	.05
27	Larry Casian	.05
28	Andujar Cedeno	.05
29	Wes Chamberlain	.05
30	Scott Chiamparino	.05
31	Steve Chitren	.05
32	Pete Coachman	.05
33	Alex Cole	.05
34	Jeff Conine	.10
35	Scott Cooper	.05
36	Milt Cuyler	.05
37	Steve Decker	.05
38	Rich DeLucia	.05
39	Delino DeShields	.05
40	Mark Dewey	.05
41	Carlos Diaz	.05
42	Lance Dickson	.05
43	Narciso Elvira	.05
44	Luis Encarnacion	.05
45	Scott Erickson	.05
46	Paul Faries	.05
47	Howard Farmer	.05
48	Alex Fernandez	.05
49	Travis Fryman	.05
50	Rich Garces	.05
51	Carlos Garcia	.05
52	Mike Gardiner	.05
53	Bernard Gilkey	.05
54	Tom Gilles	.05
55	Jerry Goff	.05
56	Leo Gomez	.05
57	Luis Gonzalez	.75
58	Joe Grahe	.05
59	Craig Grebeck	.05
60	Kip Gross	.05
61	Eric Gunderson	.05
62	Chris Hammond	.05
63	Dave Hansen	.05
64	Reggie Harris	.05
65	Bill Haselman	.05
66	Randy Hennis	.05
67	Carlos Hernandez	.05
68	Howard Hilton	.05
69	Dave Hollins	.05
70	Darren Holmes	.05
71	John Hoover	.05
72	Steve Howard	.05
73	Thomas Howard	.05
74	Todd Hundley	.05
75	Daryl Irvine	.05
76	Chris Jelic	.05
77	Dana Kiecker	.05
78	Brent Knackert	.05
79	Jimmy Kremers	.05
80	Jerry Kutzler	.05
81	Ray Lankford	.05
82	Tim Layana	.05
83	Terry Lee	.05
84	Mark Leiter	.05
85	Scott Leius	.05
86	Mark Leonard	.05
87	Darren Lewis	.05
88	Scott Lewis	.05
89	Jim Leyritz	.05
90	Dave Liddell	.05
91	Luis Lopez	.05
92	Kevin Maas	.05
93	Bob MacDonald	.05
94	Carlos Maldonado	.05
95	Chuck Malone	.05
96	Ramon Manon	.05
97	Jeff Manto	.05
98	Paul Marak	.05
99	Tino Martinez	.25
100	Derrick May	.05
101	Brent Mayne	.05
102	Paul McClellan	.05
103	Rodney McCray	.05
104	Tim McIntosh	.05
105	Brian McRae	.05
106	Jose Melendez	.05
107	Orlando Merced	.05
108	Alan Mills	.05
109	Gino Minutelli	.05
110	Mickey Morandini	.05
111	Pedro Munoz	.05
112	Chris Nabholz	.05
113	Tim Naehring	.05
114	Charles Nagy	.05
115	Jim Neidlinger	.05
116	Rafael Novoa	.05
117	Jose Offerman	.05
118	Omar Olivares	.05
119	Javier Ortiz	.05
120	Al Osuna	.05
121	Rick Parker	.05
122	Dave Pavlas	.05
123	Geronimo Pena	.05
124	Mike Perez	.05
125	Phil Plantier	.05
126	Jim Poole	.05
127	Tom Quinlan	.05
128	Scott Radinsky	.05
129	Darren Reed	.05
130	Karl Rhodes	.05
131	Jeff Richardson	.05
132	Rich Rodriguez	.05
133	Dave Rohde	.05
134	Mel Rojas	.05
135	Vic Rosario	.05
136	Rich Rowland	.05
137	Scott Ruskin	.05
138	Bill Sampen	.05
139	Andres Santana	.05
140	David Segui	.05
141	Jeff Shaw	.05
142	Tim Sherrill	.05
143	Terry Shumpert	.05
144	Mike Simms	.05
145	Daryl Smith	.05
146	Luis Sojo	.05
147	Steve Springer	.05
148	Ray Stephens	.05
149	Lee Stevens	.05
150	Mel Stottlemyre, Jr.	.05
151	Glenn Sutko	.05
152	Anthony Telford	.05
153	Frank Thomas	3.00
154	Randy Tomlin	.05
155	Brian Traxler	.05
156	Efrain Valdez	.05
157	Rafael Valdez	.05
158	Julio Valera	.05
159	Jim Vatcher	.05
160	Hector Villanueva	.05
161	Hector Wagner	.05
162	Dave Walsh	.05
163	Steve Wapnick	.05
164	Colby Ward	.05
165	Turner Ward	.05
166	Terry Wells	.05
167	Mark Whiten	.05
168	Mike York	.05
169	Cliff Young	.05
170	Checklist	.05
171	Checklist	.05

1991 Topps

NM/M

Unopened Factory Set, Retail (792): 30.00
Unopened Factory Set, Hobby (792): 25.00
Complete Set (792): 20.00
Common Player: .05
Wax Pack (15): .50
Wax Box (36): 12.50
Cello Pack (34): 1.00
Cello Box (24): 15.00
Rack Pack (45): 1.00
Rack Box (24): 15.00
Vending Box (500): 7.50

#	Player	Price
1	Nolan Ryan	.75
2	George Brett	.25
3	Carlton Fisk	.20
4	Kevin Maas	.05
5	Cal Ripken, Jr.	.40
6	Nolan Ryan	.40
7	Ryne Sandberg	.30
8	Bobby Thigpen	.05
9	Darrin Fletcher	.05
10	Gregg Olson	.05
11	Roberto Kelly	.05
12	Paul Assenmacher	.05
13	Mariano Duncan	.05
14	Dennis Lamp	.05
15	Von Hayes	.05
16	Mike Heath	.05
17	Jeff Brantley	.05
18	Nelson Liriano	.05
19	Jeff Robinson	.05
20	Pedro Guerrero	.05
21	Joe M. Morgan	.05
22	Storm Davis	.05
23	Jim Gantner	.05
24	Dave Martinez	.05
25	Tim Belcher	.05
26	Luis Sojo	.05
27	Bobby Witt	.05
28	Alvaro Espinoza	.05
29	Bob Walk	.05
30	Gregg Jefferies	.05
31	Colby Ward RC	.05
32	Mike Simms RC	.05
33	Barry Jones	.05
34	Atlee Hammaker	.05
35	Greg Maddux	.50
36	Donnie Hill	.05
37	Tom Bolton	.05
38	Scott Bradley	.05
39	Jim Neidlinger RC	.05
40	Kevin Mitchell	.05
41	Ken Dayley	.05
42a	Chris Hoiles RC (White inner photo frame.)	.20
42b	Chris Hoiles (Gray inner photo frame.)	.10
43	Roger McDowell	.05
44	Mike Felder	.05
45	Chris Sabo	.05
46	Tim Drummond	.05
47	Brook Jacoby	.05
48	Dennis Boyd	.05
49a	Pat Borders (40 stolen bases in Kinston 1986)	.20
49b	Pat Borders (0 stolen bases in Kinston 1986)	.10
50	Bob Welch	.05
51	Art Howe	.05
52	Francisco Oliveras RC	.05
53	Mike Sharperson	.05
54	Gary Mielke	.05
55	Jeffrey Leonard	.05
56	Jeff Parrett	.05
57	Jack Howell	.05
58	Mel Stottlemyre	.05
59	Eric Yelding	.05
60	Frank Viola	.05
61	Stan Javier	.05
62	Lee Guetterman	.05
63	Milt Thompson	.05
64	Tom Herr	.05
65	Bruce Hurst	.05
66	Terry Kennedy	.05
67	Rick Honeycutt	.05
68	Gary Sheffield	.25
69	Steve Wilson	.05
70	Ellis Burks	.05
71	Jim Acker	.05
72	Junior Ortiz	.05
73	Craig Worthington	.05
74	Shane Andrews RC	.10
75	Jack Morris	.05
76	Jerry Browne	.05
77	Drew Hall	.05
78	Geno Petralli	.05
79	Frank Thomas	.35
80a	Fernando Valenzuela (No diamond after 104 ER in 1990.)	.25
80b	Fernando Valenzuela (Diamond after 104 ER in 1990.)	.05
81	Cito Gaston	.05
82	Tom Glavine	.20
83	Daryl Boston	.05
84	Bob McClure	.05
85	Jesse Barfield	.05
86	Les Lancaster	.05
87	Tracy Jones	.05
88	Bob Tewksbury	.05
89	Darren Daulton	.05
90	Danny Tartabull	.05
91	Greg Colbrunn RC	.05
92	Danny Jackson	.05
93	Ivan Calderon	.05
94	John Dopson	.05
95	Paul Molitor	.35
96	Trevor Wilson	.05
97a	Brady Anderson (3H, 2RBI in Sept. scoreboard)	.25
97b	Brady Anderson (14H, 3 RBI in Sept. scoreboard)	.05
98	Sergio Valdez	.05
99	Chris Gwynn	.05
100a	Don Mattingly (10 hits 1990)	.50
100b	Don Mattingly (101 hits in 1990)	.50
101	Rob Ducey	.05
102	Gene Larkin	.05
103	Tim Costo RC	.05
104	Don Robinson	.05
105	Kevin McReynolds	.05
106	Ed Nunez	.05
107	Luis Polonia	.05
108	Matt Young	.05
109	Greg Riddoch	.05
110	Tom Henke	.05
111	Andres Thomas	.05
112	Frank DiPino	.05
113	Carl Everett RC	.50
114	Lance Dickson RC	.05
115	Hubie Brooks	.05
116	Mark Davis	.05
117	Dion James	.05
118	Tom Edens RC	.05
119	Carl Nichols	.05
120	Joe Carter	.05
121	Eric King	.05
122	Paul O'Neill	.05
123	Greg Harris	.05
124	Randy Bush	.05
125	Steve Bedrosian	.05
126	Bernard Gilkey RC	.10
127	Joe Price	.05
128	Travis Fryman	.05
129	Mark Eichhorn	.05
130	Ozzie Smith	.50
131a	Checklist 1 (Phil Bradley #727.)	.05
131b	Checklist 1 (Phil Bradley #717.)	.05
132	Jamie Quirk	.05
133	Greg Briley	.05
134	Kevin Elster	.05
135	Jerome Walton	.05
136	Dave Schmidt	.05
137	Randy Ready	.05
138	Jamie Moyer	.05
139	Jeff Treadway	.05
140	Fred McGriff	.05
141	Nick Leyva	.05
142	Curtis Wilkerson	.05
143	John Smiley	.05
144	Dave Henderson	.05
145	Lou Whitaker	.05
146	Dan Plesac	.05
147	Carlos Baerga	.05
148	Rey Palacios	.05
149	Al Osuna RC	.05
150	Cal Ripken, Jr.	.75

151	Tom Browning	.05
152	Mickey Hatcher	.05
153	Bryan Harvey	.05
154	Jay Buhner	.05
155a	Dwight Evans (Diamond after 162 G 1982.)	.10
155b	Dwight Evans (No diamond after 162 G 1982.)	.05
156	Carlos Martinez	.05
157	John Smoltz	.05
158	Jose Uribe	.05
159	Joe Boever	.05
160	Vince Coleman	.05
161	Tim Leary	.05
162	Ozzie Canseco **RC**	.10
163	Dave Johnson	.05
164	Edgar Diaz	.05
165	Sandy Alomar	.05
166	Harold Baines	.05
167a	Randy Tomlin **RC** ("Harriburg" 1989-90.)	.10
167b	Randy Tomlin **RC** ("Harrisburg" 1989-90.)	.05
168	John Olerud	.05
169	Luis Aquino	.05
170	Carlton Fisk	.35
171	Tony LaRussa	.05
172	Pete Incaviglia	.05
173	Jason Grimsley	.05
174	Ken Caminiti	.05
175	Jack Armstrong	.05
176	John Orton	.05
177	Reggie Harris **RC**	.05
178	Dave Valle	.05
179	Pete Harnisch	.05
180	Tony Gwynn	.50
181	Duane Ward	.05
182	Junior Noboa	.05
183	Clay Parker	.05
184	Gary Green	.05
185	Joe Magrane	.05
186	Rod Booker	.05
187	Greg Cadaret	.05
188	Damon Berryhill	.05
189	Daryl Irvine **RC**	.05
190	Matt Williams	.05
191	Willie Blair **RC**	.05
192	Rob Deer	.05
193	Felix Fermin	.05
194	Xavier Hernandez	.05
195	Wally Joyner	.05
196	Jim Vatcher **RC**	.05
197	Chris Nabholz **RC**	.05
198	R.J. Reynolds	.05
199	Mike Hartley	.05
200	Darryl Strawberry	.05
201	Tom Kelly	.05
202	Jim Leyritz **RC**	.20
203	Gene Harris	.05
204	Herm Winningham	.05
205	Mike Perez **RC**	.05
206	Carlos Quintana	.05
207	Gary Wayne	.05
208	Willie Wilson	.05
209	Ken Howell	.05
210	Lance Parrish	.05
211	Brian Barnes **RC**	.05
212	Steve Finley	.05
213	Frank Wills	.05
214	Joe Girardi	.05
215	Dave Smith	.05
216	Greg Gagne	.05
217	Chris Bosio	.05
218	Rick Parker **RC**	.05
219	Jack McDowell	.05
220	Tim Wallach	.05
221	Don Slaught	.05
222	Brian McRae **RC**	.10
223	Allan Anderson	.05
224	Juan Gonzalez	.20
225	Randy Johnson	.35
226	Alfredo Griffin	.05
227	Steve Avery	.05
228	Rex Hudler	.05
229	Rance Mulliniks	.05
230	Sid Fernandez	.05
231	Doug Rader	.05
232	Jose DeJesus	.05
233	Al Leiter	.05
234	Scott Erickson **RC**	.10
235	Dave Parker	.05
236a	Frank Tanana (No diamond after 269 SO 1975.)	.10
236b	Frank Tanana (Diamond after 269 SO 1975.)	.05
237	Rick Cerone	.05
238	Mike Dunne	.05
239	Darren Lewis **RC**	.05
240	Mike Scott	.05
241	Dave Clark	.05
242	Mike LaCoss	.05
243	Lance Johnson	.05
244	Mike Jeffcoat	.05
245	Kal Daniels	.05
246	Kevin Wickander	.05
247	Jody Reed	.05
248	Tom Gordon	.05
249	Bob Melvin	.05
250	Dennis Eckersley	.30
251	Mark Lemke	.05
252	Mel Rojas **RC**	.05
253	Garry Templeton	.05
254	Shawn Boskie **RC**	.05
255	Brian Downing	.05
256	Greg Hibbard	.05
257	Tom O'Malley	.05
258	Chris Hammond	.05
259	Hensley Meulens	.05
260	Harold Reynolds	.05
261	Bud Harrelson	.05
262	Tim Jones	.05
263	Checklist 2	.05
264	Dave Hollins **RC**	.05
265	Mark Gubicza	.05
266	Carmen Castillo	.05
267	Mark Knudson	.05
268	Tom Brookens	.05
269	Joe Hesketh	.05
270a	Mark McGwire (1987 SLG .618)	.75
270b	Mark McGwire (1987 SLG 618)	.75
271	Omar Olivares **RC**	.05
272	Jeff King	.05
273	Johnny Ray	.05
274	Ken Williams	.05
275	Alan Trammell	.05
276	Bill Swift	.05
277	Scott Coolbaugh	.05
278	Alex Fernandez **RC**	.10
279a	Jose Gonzalez (Photo of Billy Bean, left-handed batter.)	.75
279b	Jose Gonzalez (Correct photo, right-handed batter.)	.05
280	Bret Saberhagen	.05
281	Larry Sheets	.05
282	Don Carman	.05
283	Marquis Grissom	.05
284	Bill Spiers	.05
285	Jim Abbott	.05
286	Ken Oberkfell	.05
287	Mark Grant	.05
288	Derrick May	.05
289	Tim Birtsas	.05
290	Steve Sax	.05
291	John Wathan	.05
292	Bud Black	.05
293	Jay Bell	.05
294	Mike Moore	.05
295	Rafael Palmeiro	.30
296	Mark Williamson	.05
297	Manny Lee	.05
298	Omar Vizquel	.05
299	Scott Radinsky **RC**	.05
300	Kirby Puckett	.50
301	Steve Farr	.05
302	Tim Teufel	.05
303	Mike Boddicker	.05
304	Kevin Reimer	.05
305	Mike Scioscia	.05
306a	Lonnie Smith (136 G 1990)	.10
306b	Lonnie Smith (135 G 1990)	.05
307	Andy Benes	.05
308	Tom Pagnozzi	.05
309	Norm Charlton	.05
310	Gary Carter	.35
311	Jeff Pico	.05
312	Charlie Hayes	.05
313	Ron Robinson	.05
314	Gary Pettis	.05
315	Roberto Alomar	.15
316	Gene Nelson	.05
317	Mike Fitzgerald	.05
318	Rick Aguilera	.05
319	Jeff McKnight	.05
320	Tony Fernandez	.05
321	Bob Rodgers	.05
322	Terry Shumpert **RC**	.05
323	Cory Snyder	.05
324a	Ron Kittle ("6 Home Runs" in career summary)	.10
324b	Ron Kittle ("7 Home Runs" in career summary)	.05
325	Brett Butler	.05
326	Ken Patterson	.05
327	Ron Hassey	.05
328	Walt Terrell	.05
329	Dave Justice	.05
330	Dwight Gooden	.05
331	Eric Anthony	.05
332	Kenny Rogers	.05
333	Chipper Jones **RC**	6.00
334	Todd Benzinger	.05
335	Mitch Williams	.05
336	Matt Nokes	.05
337a	Keith Comstock (Mariners logo.)	.05
337b	Keith Comstock (Cubs logo.)	1.50
338	Luis Rivera	.05
339	Larry Walker	.05
340	Ramon Martinez	.05
341	John Moses	.05
342	Mickey Morandini **RC**	.10
343	Jose Oquendo	.05
344	Jeff Russell	.05
345	Len Dykstra	.05
346	Jesse Orosco	.05
347	Greg Vaughn	.05
348	Todd Stottlemyre	.05
349	Dave Gallagher	.05
350	Glenn Davis	.05
351	Joe Torre	.05
352	Frank White	.05
353	Tony Castillo	.05
354	Sid Bream	.05
355	Chili Davis	.05
356	Mike Marshall	.05
357	Jack Savage	.05
358	Mark Parent	.05
359	Chuck Cary	.05
360	Tim Raines	.05
361	Scott Garrelts	.05
362	Hector Villanueva **RC**	.05
363	Rick Mahler	.05
364	Dan Pasqua	.05
365	Mike Schooler	.05
366a	Checklist 3 (Carl Nichols #19.)	.05
366b	Checklist 3 (Carl Nichols #119.)	.05
367	Dave Walsh **RC**	.05
368	Felix Jose	.05
369	Steve Searcy	.05
370	Kelly Gruber	.05
371	Jeff Montgomery	.05
372	Spike Owen	.05
373	Darrin Jackson	.05
374	Larry Casian **RC**	.05
375	Tony Pena	.05
376	Mike Harkey	.05
377	Rene Gonzales	.05
378a	Wilson Alvarez **RC** (No 1989 Port Charlotte stats.)	.50
378b	Wilson Alvarez **RC** (1989 Port Charlotte stats)	.20
379	Randy Velarde	.05
380	Willie McGee	.05
381	Jim Leyland	.05
382	Mackey Sasser	.05
383	Pete Smith	.05
384	Gerald Perry	.05
385	Mickey Tettleton	.05
386	Cecil Fielder/AS	.05
387	Julio Franco/AS	.05
388	Kelly Gruber/AS	.05
389	Alan Trammell/AS	.05
390	Jose Canseco/AS	.15
391	Rickey Henderson/AS	.20
392	Ken Griffey Jr./AS	.35
393	Carlton Fisk/AS	.20
394	Bob Welch/AS	.05
395	Chuck Finley/AS	.05
396	Bobby Thigpen/AS	.05
397	Eddie Murray/AS	.20
398	Ryne Sandberg/AS	.30
399	Matt Williams/AS	.05
400	Barry Larkin/AS	.05
401	Barry Bonds/AS	.40
402	Darryl Strawberry/AS	.05
403	Bobby Bonilla/AS	.05
404	Mike Scoscia/AS	.05
405	Doug Drabek/AS	.05
406	Frank Viola/AS	.05
407	John Franco/AS	.05
408	Ernie Riles	.05
409	Mike Stanley	.05
410	Dave Righetti	.05
411	Lance Blankenship	.05
412	Dave Bergman	.05
413	Terry Mulholland	.05
414	Sammy Sosa	.60
415	Rick Sutcliffe	.05
416	Randy Milligan	.05
417	Bill Krueger	.05
418	Nick Esasky	.05
419	Jeff Reed	.05
420	Bobby Thigpen	.05
421	Alex Cole	.05
422	Rick Rueschel	.05
423	Rafael Ramirez	.05
424	Calvin Schiraldi	.05
425	Andy Van Slyke	.05
426	Joe Grahe **RC**	.05
427	Rick Dempsey	.05
428	John Barfield **RC**	.05
429	Stump Merrill	.05
430	Gary Gaetti	.05
431	Paul Gibson	.05
432	Delino DeShields	.05
433	Pat Tabler	.05
434	Julio Machado	.05
435	Kevin Maas	.05
436	Scott Bankhead	.05
437	Doug Dascenzo	.05
438	Vicente Palacios	.05
439	Dickie Thon	.05
440	George Bell	.05
441	Zane Smith	.05
442	Charlie O'Brien	.05
443	Jeff Innis	.05
444	Glenn Braggs	.05
445	Greg Swindell	.05
446	Craig Grebeck **RC**	.05
447	John Burkett	.05
448	Craig Lefferts	.05
449	Juan Berenguer	.05
450	Wade Boggs	.50
451	Neal Heaton	.05
452	Bill Schroeder	.05
453	Lenny Harris	.05
454a	Kevin Appier (No 1990 Omaha stats.)	.15
454b	Kevin Appier (1990 Omaha stats)	.05
455	Walt Weiss	.05
456	Charlie Leibrandt	.05
457	Todd Hundley	.05
458	Brian Holman	.05
459	Tom Trebelhorn	.05
460	Dave Steib	.05
461a	Robin Ventura (Gray inner photo frame at left.)	.15
461b	Robin Ventura (Red inner photo frame at left.)	.05
462	Steve Frey	.05
463	Dwight Smith	.05
464	Steve Buechele	.05
465	Ken Griffey	.05
466	Charles Nagy	.05
467	Dennis Cook	.05
468	Tim Hulett	.05
469	Chet Lemon	.05
470	Howard Johnson	.05
471	Mike Lieberthal **RC**	.50
472	Kirt Manwaring	.05
473	Curt Young	.05
474	Phil Plantier **RC**	.10
475	Teddy Higuera	.05
476	Glenn Wilson	.05
477	Mike Fetters	.05
478	Kurt Stillwell	.05
479	Bob Patterson	.05
480	Dave Magadan	.05
481	Eddie Whitson	.05
482	Tino Martinez	.05
483	Mike Aldrete	.05
484	Dave LaPoint	.05
485	Terry Pendleton	.05
486	Tommy Greene	.05
487	Rafael Belliard	.05
488	Jeff Manto	.05
489	Bobby Valentine	.05
490	Kirk Gibson	.05
491	Kurt Miller **RC**	.05
492	Ernie Whitt	.05
493	Jose Rijo	.05
494	Chris James	.05
495	Charlie Hough	.05
496	Marty Barrett	.05
497	Ben McDonald	.05
498	Mark Salas	.05
499	Melido Perez	.05
500	Will Clark	.05
501	Mike Bielecki	.05
502	Carney Lansford	.05
503	Roy Smith	.05
504	Julio Valera **RC**	.05
505	Chuck Finley	.05
506	Darnell Coles	.05
507	Steve Jeltz	.05
508	Mike York **RC**	.05
509	Glenallen Hill	.05
510	John Franco	.05
511	Steve Balboni	.05
512	Jose Mesa	.05
513	Jerald Clark	.05
514	Mike Stanton	.05
515	Alvin Davis	.05
516	Karl Rhodes **RC**	.05
517	Joe Oliver	.05
518	Cris Carpenter	.05
519	Sparky Anderson	.10
520	Mark Grace	.05
521	Joe Orsulak	.05
522	Stan Belinda	.05
523	Rodney McCray **RC**	.05
524	Darrel Akerfelds	.05
525	Willie Randolph	.05
526a	Moises Alou (37 R 1990 Pirates)	.20
526b	Moises Alou (0 R 1990 Pirates)	.15
527a	Checklist 4 (Kevin McReynolds #719)	.05
527b	Checklist 4 (Kevin McReynolds #105)	.05
528	Denny Martinez	.05
529	Mark Newfield **RC**	.05
530	Roger Clemens	.60
531	Dave Rhode **RC**	.05
532	Kirk McCaskill	.05
533	Oddibe McDowell	.05
534	Mike Jackson	.05
535	Ruben Sierra	.05
536	Mike Witt	.05
537	Jose Lind	.05
538	Bip Roberts	.05
539	Scott Terry	.05
540	George Brett	.60
541	Domingo Ramos	.05
542	Rob Murphy	.05
543	Junior Felix	.05
544	Alejandro Pena	.05
545	Dale Murphy	.15
546	Jeff Ballard	.05
547	Mike Pagliarulo	.05
548	Jaime Navarro	.05
549	John McNamara	.05
550	Eric Davis	.05
551	Bob Kipper	.05
552	Jeff Hamilton	.05
553	Joe Klink **RC**	.05
554	Brian Harper	.05
555	Turner Ward **RC**	.05
556	Gary Ward	.05
557	Wally Whitehurst	.05
558	Otis Nixon	.05
559	Adam Peterson	.05
560	Greg Smith	.05
561	Tim McIntosh	.05
562	Jeff Kunkel	.05
563	Brent Knackert **RC**	.05
564	Dante Bichette	.05
565	Craig Biggio	.05
566	Craig Wilson **RC**	.05
567	Dwayne Henry	.05
568	Ron Karkovice	.05
569	Curt Schilling	.05
570	Barry Bonds	.75

571 Pat Combs .05
572 Dave Anderson .05
573 Rich Rodriguez **RC** .05
574 John Marzano .05
575 Robin Yount .35
576 Jeff Kaiser .05
577 Bill Doran .05
578 Dave West .05
579 Roger Craig .05
580 Dave Stewart .05
581 Luis Quinones .05
582 Marty Clary .05
583 Tony Phillips .05
584 Kevin Brown .05
585 Pete O'Brien .05
586 Fred Lynn .05
587 Jose Offerman .05
588a Mark Whiten (Hand inside left border.) .05
588b Mark Whiten (Hand over left border.) .20
589 Scott Ruskin **RC** .05
590 Eddie Murray .35
591 Ken Hill .05
592 B.J. Surhoff .05
593a Mike Walker **RC** (No 1990 Canton-Akron stats.) .15
593b Mike Walker **RC** (1990 Canton-Akron stats) .05
594 Rich Garces **RC** .05
595 Bill Landrum .05
596 Ronnie Walden **RC** .05
597 Jerry Don Gleaton .05
598 Sam Horn .05
599a Greg Myers (No 1990 Syracuse stats.) .10
599b Greg Myers (1990 Syracuse stats) .05
600 Bo Jackson .10
601 Bob Ojeda .05
602 Casey Candaele .05
603a Wes Chamberlain **RC** (Photo of Louie Meadows, no bat.) .75
603b Wes Chamberlain **RC** (Correct photo, holding bat.) .05
604 Billy Hatcher .05
605 Jeff Reardon .05
606 Jim Gott .05
607 Edgar Martinez .05
608 Todd Burns .05
609 Jeff Torborg .05
610 Andres Galarraga .05
611 Dave Eiland .05
612 Steve Lyons .05
613 Eric Show .05
614 Luis Salazar .05
615 Bert Blyleven .05
616 Todd Zeile .05
617 Bill Wegman .05
618 Sil Campusano .05
619 David Wells .05
620 Ozzie Guillen .05
621 Ted Power .05
622 Jack Daugherty .05
623 Jeff Blauser .05
624 Tom Candiotti .05
625 Terry Steinbach .05
626 Gerald Young .05
627 Tim Layana **RC** .05
628 Greg Litton .05
629 Wes Gardner .05
630 Dave Winfield .35
631 Mike Morgan .05
632 Lloyd Moseby .05
633 Kevin Tapani .05
634 Henry Cotto .05
635 Andy Hawkins .05
636 Geronimo Pena .05
637 Bruce Ruffin .05
638 Mike Macfarlane .05
639 Frank Robinson .05
640 Andre Dawson .20
641 Mike Henneman .05
642 Hal Morris .05
643 Jim Presley .05
644 Chuck Crim .05
645 Juan Samuel .05
646 Andujar Cedeno **RC** .05
647 Mark Portugal .05
648 Lee Stevens .05
649 Bill Sampen **RC** .05
650 Jack Clark .05
651 Alan Mills **RC** .05
652 Kevin Romine .05
653 Anthony Telford **RC** .05
654 Paul Sorrento .05
655 Erik Hanson .05
656a Checklist 5 (Vincente Palacios #348.) .05
656b Checklist 5 (Palacios #433.) .05
656c Checklist 5 (Palacios #438.) .05
657 Mike Kingery .05
658 Scott Aldred **RC** .05
659 Oscar Azocar **RC** .05
660 Lee Smith .05
661 Steve Lake .05
662 Rob Dibble .05
663 Greg Brock .05
664 John Farrell .05
665 Mike LaValliere .05
666 Danny Darwin .05
667 Kent Anderson .05
668 Bill Long .05
669 Lou Pinella .05
670 Rickey Henderson .35
671 Andy McGaffigan .05
672 Shane Mack .05
673 Greg Olson **RC** .05
674a Kevin Gross (No diamond after 89 BB 1988.) .10
674b Kevin Gross (Diamond after 89 BB 1988.) .05
675 Tom Brunansky .05
676 Scott Chiamparino **RC** .05
677 Billy Ripken .05
678 Mark Davidson .05
679 Bill Bathe .05
680 David Cone .05
681 Jeff Schaefer **RC** .05
682 Ray Lankford **RC** .15
683 Derek Lilliquist .05
684 Milt Cuyler .05
685 Doug Drabek .05
686 Mike Gallego .05
687a John Cerutti (4.46 ERA 1990) .05
687b John Cerutti (4.76 ERA 1990) .05
688 Rosario Rodriguez **RC** .05
689 John Kruk .05
690 Orel Hershiser .05
691 Mike Blowers .05
692a Efrain Valdez **RC** (No text below stats.) .15
692b Efrain Valdez **RC** (Two lines of text below stats.) .05
693 Francisco Cabrera .05
694 Randy Veres .05
695 Kevin Seitzer .05
696 Steve Olin .05
697 Shawn Abner .05
698 Mark Guthrie .05
699 Jim Lefebvre .05
700 Jose Canseco .25
701 Pascual Perez .05
702 Tim Naehring **RC** .05
703 Juan Agosto .05
704 Devon White .05
705 Robby Thompson .05
706a Brad Arnsberg (68.2 IP Rangers 1990) .05
706b Brad Arnsberg (62.2 IP Rangers 1990) .05
707 Jim Eisenreich .05
708 John Mitchell .05
709 Matt Sinatro .05
710 Kent Hrbek .05
711 Jose DeLeon .05
712 Ricky Jordan .05
713 Scott Scudder .05
714 Marvell Wynne .05
715 Tim Burke .05
716 Bob Geren .05
717 Phil Bradley .05
718 Steve Crawford .05
719 Keith Miller .05
720 Cecil Fielder .05
721 Mark Lee **RC** .05
722 Wally Backman .05
723 Candy Maldonado .05
724 David Segui **RC** .10
725 Ron Gant .05
726 Phil Stephenson .05
727 Mookie Wilson .05
728 Scott Sanderson .05
729 Don Zimmer .05
730 Barry Larkin .05
731 Jeff Gray **RC** .05
732 Franklin Stubbs .05
733 Kelly Downs .05
734 John Russell .05
735 Ron Darling .05
736 Dick Schofield .05
737 Tim Crews .05
738 Mel Hall .05
739 Russ Swan **RC** .05
740 Ryne Sandberg .50
741 Jimmy Key .05
742 Tommy Gregg .05
743 Bryn Smith .05
744 Nelson Santovenia .05
745 Doug Jones .05
746 John Shelby .05
747 Tony Fossas .05
748 Al Newman .05
749 Greg Harris .05
750 Bobby Bonilla .05
751 Wayne Edwards **RC** .05
752 Kevin Bass .05
753 Paul Marak **RC** .05
754 Bill Pecota .05
755 Mark Langston .05
756 Jeff Huson .05
757 Mark Gardner .05
758 Mike Devereaux .05
759 Bobby Cox .05
760 Benny Santiago .05
761 Larry Andersen .05
762 Mitch Webster .05
763 Dana Kiecker **RC** .05
764 Mark Carreon .05
765 Shawon Dunston .05
766 Jeff Robinson .05
767 Dan Wilson **RC** .10
768 Donn Pall .05
769 Tim Sherrill **RC** .05
770 Jay Howell .05
771 Gary Redus .05
772 Kent Mercker .05
773 Tom Foley .05
774 Dennis Rasmussen .05
775 Julio Franco .05
776 Brent Mayne .05
777 John Candelaria .05
778 Danny Gladden .05
779 Carmelo Martinez .05
780a Randy Myers (Career losses 15.) .10
780b Randy Myers (Career losses 19.) .05
781 Darryl Hamilton .05
782 Jim Deshaies .05
783 Joel Skinner .05
784 Willie Fraser .05
785 Scott Fletcher .05
786 Eric Plunk .05
787 Checklist 6 .05
788 Bob Milacki .05
789 Tom Lasorda .05
790 Ken Griffey Jr. .60
791 Mike Benjamin .05
792 Mike Greenwell .05

1991 Topps Tiffany

	NM/M
Unopened Set (792):	135.00
Complete Set (792):	85.00
Common Player:	.10

(Star cards valued at 3X corresponding regular issue Topps cards.)

Traded

	NM/M
Unopened Retail or Hobby Set (132):	12.00
Complete Set (132):	10.00
Common Player:	.05
Wax Pack (7):	.65
Wax Box (36):	15.00

1 Juan Agosto .05
2 Roberto Alomar .15
3 Wally Backman .05
4 Jeff Bagwell **RC** 3.00
5 Skeeter Barnes .05
6 Steve Bedrosian .05
7 Derek Bell .05
8 George Bell .05
9 Rafael Belliard .05
10 Dante Bichette .05
11 Bud Black .05
12 Mike Boddicker .05
13 Sid Bream .05
14 Hubie Brooks .05
15 Brett Butler .05
16 Ivan Calderon .05
17 John Candelaria .05
18 Tom Candiotti .05
19 Gary Carter .50
20 Joe Carter .05
21 Rick Cerone .05
22 Jack Clark .05
23 Vince Coleman .05
24 Scott Coolbaugh .05
25 Danny Cox .05
26 Danny Darwin .05
27 Chili Davis .05
28 Glenn Davis .05
29 Steve Decker .05
30 Rob Deer .05
31 Rich DeLucia .05
32 John Dettmer **RC** (USA) .05
33 Brian Downing .05
34 Darren Dreifort **RC** (USA) .25
35 Kirk Dressendorfer .05
36 Jim Essian .05
37 Dwight Evans .05
38 Steve Farr .05
39 Jeff Fassero .05
40 Junior Felix .05
41 Tony Fernandez .05
42 Steve Finley .05
43 Jim Fregosi .05
44 Gary Gaetti .05
45 Jason Giambi **RC** (USA) 4.00
46 Kirk Gibson .05
47 Leo Gomez .05
48 Luis Gonzalez **RC** 1.00
49 Jeff Granger **RC** (USA) .10
50 Todd Greene **RC** (USA) .15
51 Jeffrey Hammonds **RC** (USA) .15
52 Mike Hargrove .05
53 Pete Harnisch .05
54 Rick Helling **RC** (USA) .10
55 Glenallen Hill .05
56 Charlie Hough .05
57 Pete Incaviglia .05
58 Bo Jackson .10
59 Danny Jackson .05
60 Reggie Jefferson .05
61 Charles Johnson **RC** (USA) .15
62 Jeff Johnson .05
63 Todd Johnson **RC** (USA) .05
64 Barry Jones .05
65 Chris Jones .05
66 Scott Kamieniecki .05
67 Pat Kelly **RC** .05
68 Darryl Kile .05
69 Chuck Knoblauch .05
70 Bill Krueger .05
71 Scott Leius .05
72 Donnie Leshnock **RC** (USA) .05
73 Mark Lewis .05
74 Candy Maldonado .05
75 Jason McDonald **RC** (USA) .05
76 Willie McGee .05
77 Fred McGriff .05
78 Billy McMillon **RC** (USA) .05
79 Hal McRae .05
80 Dan Melendez **RC** (USA) .05
81 Orlando Merced .05
82 Jack Morris .05
83 Phil Nevin **RC** (USA) .50
84 Otis Nixon .05
85 Johnny Oates .05
86 Bob Ojeda .05
87 Mike Pagliarulo .05
88 Dean Palmer .05
89 Dave Parker .05
90 Terry Pendleton .05
91 Tony Phillips **RC** (USA) .10
92 Doug Piatt .05
93 Ron Polk (U.S.A.) .05
94 Tim Raines .05
95 Willie Randolph .05
96 Dave Righetti .05
97 Ernie Riles .05
98 Chris Roberts **RC** (USA) .05
99 Jeff Robinson (Angels) .05
100 Jeff Robinson (Orioles) .05
101 Ivan Rodriguez **RC** 3.00
102 Steve Rodriguez **RC** (USA) .05
103 Tom Runnells .05
104 Scott Sanderson .05
105 Bob Scanlan .05
106 Pete Schourek **RC** .10
107 Gary Scott .05
108 Paul Shuey **RC** (USA) .10
109 Doug Simons **RC** .05
110 Dave Smith .05
111 Cory Snyder .05
112 Luis Sojo .05
113 Kennie Steenstra **RC** (USA) .05
114 Darryl Strawberry .05
115 Franklin Stubbs .05
116 Todd Taylor **RC** (USA) .05
117 Wade Taylor .05
118 Garry Templeton .05
119 Mickey Tettleton .05
120 Tim Teufel .05
121 Mike Timlin .05
122 David Tuttle **RC** (USA) .05
123 Mo Vaughn .25
124 Jeff Ware **RC** (USA) .05
125 Devon White .05
126 Mark Whiten .05
127 Mitch Williams .05
128 Craig Wilson **RC** (USA) .05
129 Willie Wilson .05
130 Chris Wimmer **RC** (USA) .05
131 Ivan Zweig **RC** (USA) .05
132 Checklist .05

1991 Topps Traded Tiffany

	NM/M
Unopened Set (132):	165.00
Complete Set (132):	90.00
Common Player:	.25
Stars and Rookies:	4X

(See 1991 Topps Traded for checklist and base card values.)

1992 Topps 1991 Major League Debut

	NM/M
Complete Set (194):	12.50
Common Player:	.05

1 Kyle Abbott .05
2 Dana Allison .05
3 Rich Amaral .05
4 Ruben Amaro .05
5 Andy Ashby .05
6 Jim Austin .05
7 Jeff Bagwell 4.00
8 Jeff Banister .05
9 Willie Banks .05
10 Bret Barberie .05
11 Kim Batiste .05
12 Chris Beasley .05
13 Rod Beck .05
14 Derek Bell .05
15 Esteban Beltre .05
16 Freddie Benavides .05

872 • 1992 Topps 1991 Major League Debut

MIKE MUSSINA
August 4, 1991
Major League Debut

17 Rickey Bones .05
18 Denis Boucher .05
19 Ryan Bowen .05
20 Cliff Brantley .05
21 John Briscoe .05
22 Scott Brosius .05
23 Terry Bross .05
24 Jarvis Brown .05
25 Scott Bullett .05
26 Kevin Campbell .05
27 Amalio Carreno .05
28 Matias Carrillo .05
29 Jeff Carter .05
30 Vinny Castilla .05
31 Braulio Castillo .05
32 Frank Castillo .05
33 Darrin Chapin .05
34 Mike Christopher .05
35 Mark Clark .05
36 Royce Clayton .05
37 Stu Cole .05
38 Gary Cooper .05
39 Archie Corbin .05
40 Rheal Cormier .05
41 Chris Cron .05
42 Mike Dalton .05
43 Mark Davis .05
44 Francisco de la Rosa .05
45 Chris Donnels .05
46 Brian Drahman .05
47 Tom Drees .05
48 Kirk Dressendorfer .05
49 Bruce Egloff .05
50 Cal Eldred .05
51 Jose Escobar .05
52 Tony Eusebio .05
53 Hector Fajardo .05
54 Monty Farriss .05
55 Jeff Fassero .05
56 Dave Fleming .05
57 Kevin Flora .05
58 Steve Foster .05
59 Dan Gakeler .05
60 Ramon Garcia .05
61 Chris Gardner .05
62 Jeff Gardner .05
63 Chris George .05
64 Ray Giannelli .05
65 Tom Goodwin .05
66 Mark Grater .05
67 Johnny Guzman .05
68 Juan Guzman .05
69 Dave Haas .05
70 Chris Haney .05
71 Shawn Hare .05
72 Donald Harris .05
73 Doug Henry .05
74 Pat Hentgen .05
75 Gil Heredia .05
76 Jeremy Hernandez .05
77 Jose Hernandez .05
78 Roberto Hernandez .05
79 Bryan Hickerson .05
80 Milt Hill .05
81 Vince Horsman .05
82 Wayne Housie .05
83 Chris Howard .05
84 David Howard .05
85 Mike Humphreys .05
86 Brian Hunter .05
87 Jim Hunter .05
88 Mike Ignasiak .05
89 Reggie Jefferson .05
90 Jeff Johnson .05
91 Joel Johnson .05
92 Calvin Jones .05
93 Chris Jones .05
94 Stacy Jones .05
95 Jeff Juden .05
96 Scott Kamieniecki .05
97 Eric Karros .05
98 Pat Kelly .05
99 John Kiely .05
100 Darryl Kile .05
101 Wayne Kirby .05
102 Garland Kiser .05
103 Chuck Knoblauch .05
104 Randy Knorr .05
105 Tom Kramer .05
106 Ced Landrum .05
107 Patrick Lennon .05
108 Jim Lewis .05
109 Mark Lewis .05
110 Doug Lindsey .05
111 Scott Livingstone .05
112 Kenny Lofton .10
113 Ever Magallanes .05
114 Mike Magnante .05
115 Barry Manuel .05
116 Josias Manzanillo .05
117 Chito Martinez .05
118 Terry Mathews .05
119 Rob Mauer .05
120 Tim Mauser .05
121 Terry McDaniel .05
122 Rusty Meacham .05
123 Luis Mercedes .05
124 Paul Miller .05
125 Keith Mitchell .05
126 Bobby Moore .05
127 Kevin Morton .05
128 Andy Mota .05
129 Jose Mota .05
130 Mike Mussina 2.00
131 Jeff Mutis .05
132 Denny Neagle .05
133 Warren Newson .05
134 Jim Olander .05
135 Erik Pappas .05
136 Jorge Pedre .05
137 Yorkis Perez .05
138 Mark Petkovsek .05
139 Doug Piatt .05
140 Jeff Plympton .05
141 Harvey Pulliam .05
142 John Ramos .05
143 Mike Remlinger .05
144 Laddie Renfroe .05
145 Armando Reynoso .05
146 Arthur Rhodes .05
147 Pat Rice .05
148 Nikco Riesgo .05
149 Carlos Rodriguez .05
150 Ivan Rodriguez 3.00
151 Wayne Rosenthal .05
152 Rico Rossy .05
153 Stan Royer .05
154 Rey Sanchez .05
155 Reggie Sanders .05
156 Mo Sanford .05
157 Bob Scanlan .05
158 Pete Schourek .05
159 Gary Scott .05
160 Tim Scott .05
161 Tony Scruggs .05
162 Scott Servais .05
163 Doug Simons .05
164 Heathcliff Slocumb .05
165 Joe Slusarski .05
166 Tim Spehr .05
167 Ed Sprague .05
168 Jeff Tackett .05
169 Eddie Taubensee .05
170 Wade Taylor .05
171 Jim Thome 2.50
172 Mike Timlin .05
173 Jose Tolentino .05
174 John Vander Wal .05
175 Todd Van Poppel .05
176 Mo Vaughn .50
177 Dave Wainhouse .05
178 Don Wakamatsu .05
179 Bruce Walton .05
180 Kevin Ward .05
181 Dave Weathers .05
182 Eric Wedge .05
183 John Wehner .05
184 Rick Wilkins .05
185 Bernie Williams .50
186 Brian Williams .05
187 Ron Witmeyer .05
188 Mark Wohlers .05
189 Ted Wood .05
190 Anthony Young .05
191 Eddie Zosky .05
192 Bob Zupcic .05
193 Checklist .05
194 Checklist .05

1992 Topps

NOLAN RYAN
Rangers

NM/M
Unopened Fact. Set (802): 30.00
Complete Set (792): 20.00
Common Player: .05
Golds: 4X
Wax Pack (14): .50
Wax Box (36): 12.50
Cello Pack (34): 1.00
Cello Box (24): 16.00
Vending Box (500): 6.00
1 Nolan Ryan .75
2 Rickey Henderson .20
3 Jeff Reardon .05
4 Nolan Ryan .40
5 Dave Winfield .20
6 Brien Taylor **RC** .05
7 Jim Olander **RC** .05
8 Bryan Hickerson **RC** .05
9 John Farrell .05
10 Wade Boggs .45
11 Jack McDowell .05
12 Luis Gonzalez .05
13 Mike Scioscia .05
14 Wes Chamberlain .05
15 Denny Martinez .05
16 Jeff Montgomery .05
17 Randy Milligan .05
18 Greg Cadaret .05
19 Jamie Quirk .05
20 Bip Roberts .05
21 Buck Rodgers .05
22 Bill Wegman .05
23 Chuck Knoblauch .05
24 Randy Myers .05
25 Ron Gant .05
26 Mike Bielecki .05
27 Juan Gonzalez .20
28 Mike Schooler .05
29 Mickey Tettleton .05
30 John Kruk .05
31 Bryn Smith .05
32 Chris Nabholz .05
33 Carlos Baerga .05
34 Jeff Juden .05
35 Dave Righetti .05
36 Scott Ruffcorn **RC** .05
37 Luis Polonia .05
38 Tom Candiotti .05
39 Greg Olson .05
40 Cal Ripken, Jr. .75
41 Craig Lefferts .05
42 Mike Macfarlane .05
43 Jose Lind .05
44 Rick Aguilera .05
45 Gary Carter .35
46 Steve Farr .05
47 Rex Hudler .05
48 Scott Scudder .05
49 Damon Berryhill .05
50 Ken Griffey Jr. .55
51 Tom Runnells .05
52 Juan Bell .05
53 Tommy Gregg .05
54 David Wells .05
55 Rafael Palmeiro .30
56 Charlie O'Brien .05
57 Donn Pall .05
58 Brad Ausmus, Jim Campanis, Dave Nilsson, Doug Robbins **RC** Top Prospects-Catchers .15
59 Mo Vaughn .05
60 Tony Fernandez .05
61 Paul O'Neill .05
62 Gene Nelson .05
63 Randy Ready .05
64 Bob Kipper .05
65 Willie McGee .05
66 Scott Stahoviak **RC** .05
67 Luis Salazar .05
68 Marvin Freeman .05
69 Kenny Lofton .05
70 Gary Gaetti .05
71 Erik Hanson .05
72 Eddie Zosky .05
73 Brian Barnes .05
74 Scott Leius .05
75 Bret Saberhagen .05
76 Mike Gallego .05
77 Jack Armstrong .05
78 Ivan Rodriguez .35
79 Jesse Orosco .05
80 Dave Justice .05
81 Ced Landrum **RC** .05
82 Doug Simons **RC** .05
83 Tommy Greene .05
84 Leo Gomez .05
85 Jose DeLeon .05
86 Steve Finley .05
87 Bob MacDonald **RC** .05
88 Darrin Jackson .05
89 Neal Heaton .05
90 Robin Yount .35
91 Jeff Reed .05
92 Lenny Harris .05
93 Reggie Jefferson .05
94 Sammy Sosa .45
95 Scott Bailes .05
96 Tom McKinnon **RC** .05
97 Luis Rivera .05
98 Mike Harkey .05
99 Jeff Treadway .05
100 Jose Canseco .25
101 Omar Vizquel .05
102 Scott Kamieniecki **RC** .05
103 Ricky Jordan .05
104 Jeff Ballard .05
105 Felix Jose .05
106 Mike Boddicker .05
107 Dan Pasqua .05
108 Mike Timlin **RC** .10
109 Roger Craig .05
110 Ryne Sandberg .45
111 Mark Carreon .05
112 Oscar Azocar .05
113 Mike Greenwell .05
114 Mark Portugal .05
115 Terry Pendleton .05
116 Willie Randolph .05
117 Scott Terry .05
118 Chili Davis .05
119 Mark Gardner .05
120 Alan Trammell .05
121 Derek Bell .05
122 Gary Varsho .05
123 Bob Ojeda .05
124 Shawn Livsey **RC** .05
125 Chris Hoiles .05
126 Rico Brogna, John Jaha, Ryan Klesko, Dave Staton Top Prospects-1st Baseman .05
127 Carlos Quintana .05
128 Kurt Stillwell .05
129 Melido Perez .05
130 Alvin Davis .05
131 Checklist 1 .05
132 Eric Show .05
133 Rance Mulliniks .05
134 Darryl Kile .05
135 Von Hayes .05
136 Bill Doran .05
137 Jeff Robinson .05
138 Monty Fariss .05
139 Jeff Innis .05
140 Mark Grace .05
141 Jim Leyland .05
142 Todd Van Poppel .05
143 Paul Gibson .05
144 Bill Swift .05
145 Danny Tartabull .05
146 Al Newman .05
147 Cris Carpenter .05
148 Anthony Young **RC** .05
149 Brian Bohanon **RC** .05
150 Roger Clemens .50
151 Jeff Hamilton .05
152 Charlie Leibrandt .05
153 Ron Karkovice .05
154 Hensley Meulens .05
155 Scott Bankhead .05
156 Manny Ramirez **RC** 3.00
157 Keith Miller .05
158 Todd Frohwirth .05
159 Darrin Fletcher .05
160 Bobby Bonilla .05
161 Casey Candaele .05
162 Paul Faries .05
163 Dana Kiecker .05
164 Shane Mack .05
165 Mark Langston .05
166 Geronimo Pena .05
167 Andy Allanson .05
168 Dwight Smith .05
169 Chuck Crim .05
170 Alex Cole .05
171 Bill Plummer .05
172 Juan Berenguer .05
173 Brian Downing .05
174 Steve Frey .05
175 Orel Hershiser .05
176 Ramon Garcia **RC** .05
177 Danny Gladden .05
178 Jim Acker .05
179 Cesar Bernhardt, Bobby DeJardin, Armando Moreno, Andy Stankiewicz **RC** Top Prospects-2nd Baseman .05
180 Kevin Mitchell .05
181 Hector Villanueva .05
182 Jeff Reardon .05
183 Brent Mayne .05
184 Jimmy Jones .05
185 Benny Santiago .05
186 Cliff Floyd **RC** .50
187 Ernie Riles .05
188 Jose Guzman .05
189 Junior Felix .05
190 Glenn Davis .05
191 Charlie Hough .05
192 Dave Fleming **RC** .05
193 Omar Oliveras .05
194 Eric Karros .05
195 David Cone .05
196 Frank Castillo **RC** .05
197 Glenn Braggs .05
198 Scott Aldred .05
199 Jeff Blauser .05
200 Len Dykstra .05
201 Buck Showalter .05
202 Rick Honeycutt .05
203 Greg Myers .05
204 Trevor Wilson .05
205 Jay Howell .05
206 Luis Sojo .05
207 Jack Clark .05
208 Julio Machado .05
209 Lloyd McClendon .05
210 Ozzie Guillen .05
211 Jeremy Hernandez **RC** .05
212 Randy Velarde .05
213 Les Lancaster .05
214 Andy Mota **RC** .05
215 Rich Gossage .05

216	Brent Gates **RC**	.05
217	Brian Harper	.05
218	Mike Flanagan	.05
219	Jerry Browne	.05
220	Jose Rijo	.05
221	Skeeter Barnes	.05
222	Jaime Navarro	.05
223	Mel Hall	.05
224	Brett Barberie **RC**	.05
225	Roberto Alomar	.15
226	Pete Smith	.05
227	Daryl Boston	.05
228	Eddie Whitson	.05
229	Shawn Boskie	.05
230	Dick Schofield	.05
231	Brian Drahman **RC**	.05
232	John Smiley	.05
233	Mitch Webster	.05
234	Terry Steinbach	.05
235	Jack Morris	.05
236	Bill Pecota	.05
237	Jose Hernandez **RC**	.05
238	Greg Litton	.05
239	Brian Holman	.05
240	Andres Galarraga	.05
241	Gerald Young	.05
242	Mike Mussina	.30
243	Alvaro Espinoza	.05
244	Darren Daulton	.05
245	John Smoltz	.05
246	Jason Pruitt **RC**	.05
247	Chuck Finley	.05
248	Jim Gantner	.05
249	Tony Fossas	.05
250	Ken Griffey	.05
251	Kevin Elster	.05
252	Dennis Rasmussen	.05
253	Terry Kennedy	.05
254	Ryan Bowen **RC**	.05
255	Robin Ventura	.05
256	Mike Aldrete	.05
257	Jeff Russell	.05
258	Jim Lindeman	.05
259	Ron Darling	.05
260	Devon White	.05
261	Tom Lasorda	.05
262	Terry Lee	.05
263	Bob Patterson	.05
264	Checklist 2	.05
265	Teddy Higuera	.05
266	Roberto Kelly	.05
267	Steve Bedrosian	.05
268	Brady Anderson	.05
269	Ruben Amaro **RC**	.05
270	Tony Gwynn	.45
271	Tracy Jones	.05
272	Jerry Don Gleaton	.05
273	Craig Grebeck	.05
274	Bob Scanlan **RC**	.05
275	Todd Zeile	.05
276	Shawn Green **RC**	1.50
277	Scott Chiamparino	.05
278	Darryl Hamilton	.05
279	Jim Clancy	.05
280	Carlos Martinez	.05
281	Kevin Appier	.05
282	John Wehner **RC**	.05
283	Reggie Sanders	.05
284	Gene Larkin	.05
285	Bob Welch	.05
286	Gilberto Reyes	.05
287	Pete Schourek	.05
288	Andujar Cedeno	.05
289	Mike Morgan	.05
290	Bo Jackson	.10
291	Phil Garner	.05
292	Ray Lankford	.05
293	Mike Henneman	.05
294	Dave Valle	.05
295	Alonzo Powell	.05
296	Tom Brunansky	.05
297	Kevin Brown	.05
298	Kelly Gruber	.05
299	Charles Nagy	.05
300	Don Mattingly	.50
301	Kirk McCaskill	.05
302	Joey Cora	.05
303	Dan Plesac	.05
304	Joe Oliver	.05
305	Tom Glavine	.25
306	Al Shirley **RC**	.05
307	Bruce Ruffin	.05
308	Craig Shipley **RC**	.05
309	Dave Martinez	.05
310	Jose Mesa	.05
311	Henry Cotto	.05
312	Mike LaValliere	.05
313	Kevin Tapani	.05
314	Jeff Huson	.05
315	Juan Samuel	.05
316	Curt Schilling	.25
317	Mike Bordick	.05
318	Steve Howe	.05
319	Tony Phillips	.05
320	George Bell	.05
321	Lou Pinella	.05
322	Tim Burke	.05
323	Milt Thompson	.05
324	Danny Darwin	.05
325	Joe Orsulak	.05
326	Eric King	.05
327	Jay Buhner	.05
328	Joel Johnston **RC**	.05
329	Franklin Stubbs	.05
330	Will Clark	.05
331	Steve Lake	.05
332	Chris Jones **RC**	.05
333	Pat Tabler	.05
334	Kevin Gross	.05
335	Dave Henderson	.05
336	Greg Anthony **RC**	.05
337	Alejandro Pena	.05
338	Shawn Abner	.05
339	Tom Browning	.05
340	Otis Nixon	.05
341	Bob Geren	.05
342	Tim Spehr **RC**	.05
343	Jon Vander Wal **RC**	.20
344	Jack Daugherty	.05
345	Zane Smith	.05
346	Rheal Cormier **RC**	.05
347	Kent Hrbek	.05
348	Rick Wilkins **RC**	.10
349	Steve Lyons	.05
350	Gregg Olson	.05
351	Greg Riddoch	.05
352	Ed Nunez	.05
353	Braulio Castillo **RC**	.05
354	Dave Bergman	.05
355	Warren Newson **RC**	.05
356	Luis Quinones	.05
357	Mike Witt	.05
358	Ted Wood **RC**	.05
359	Mike Moore	.05
360	Lance Parrish	.05
361	Barry Jones	.05
362	Javier Ortiz **RC**	.05
363	John Candelaria	.05
364	Glenallen Hill	.05
365	Duane Ward	.05
366	Checklist 3	.05
367	Rafael Belliard	.05
368	Bill Krueger	.05
369	Steve Whitaker **RC**	.05
370	Shawon Dunston	.05
371	Dante Bichette	.05
372	Kip Gross **RC**	.05
373	Don Robinson	.05
374	Bernie Williams	.05
375	Bert Blyleven	.05
376	Chris Donnels **RC**	.05
377	Bob Zupcic **RC**	.05
378	Joel Skinner	.05
379	Steve Chitren	.05
380	Barry Bonds	.75
381	Sparky Anderson	.10
382	Sid Fernandez	.05
383	Dave Hollins	.05
384	Mark Lee	.05
385	Tim Wallach	.05
386	Will Clark/AS	.05
387	Ryne Sandberg/AS	.20
388	Howard Johnson/AS	.05
389	Barry Larkin/AS	.05
390	Barry Bonds/AS	.40
391	Ron Gant/AS	.05
392	Bobby Bonilla/AS	.05
393	Craig Biggio/AS	.05
394	Denny Martinez/AS	.05
395	Tom Glavine/AS	.05
396	Lee Smith/AS	.05
397	Cecil Fielder/AS	.05
398	Julio Franco/AS	.05
399	Wade Boggs/AS	.20
400	Cal Ripken, Jr./AS	.40
401	Jose Canseco/AS	.15
402	Joe Carter/AS	.05
403	Ruben Sierra/AS	.05
404	Matt Nokes/AS	.05
405	Roger Clemens/AS	.25
406	Jim Abbott/AS	.05
407	Bryan Harvey/AS	.05
408	Bob Milacki	.05
409	Geno Petralli	.05
410	Dave Stewart	.05
411	Mike Jackson	.05
412	Luis Aquino	.05
413	Tim Teufel	.05
414	Jeff Ware	.05
415	Jim Deshaies	.05
416	Ellis Burks	.05
417	Allan Anderson	.05
418	Alfredo Griffin	.05
419	Wally Whitehurst	.05
420	Sandy Alomar	.05
421	Juan Agosto	.05
422	Sam Horn	.05
423	Jeff Fassero **RC**	.05
424	Paul McClellan **RC**	.05
425	Cecil Fielder	.05
426	Tim Raines	.05
427	Eddie Taubensee **RC**	.05
428	Dennis Boyd	.05
429	Tony LaRussa	.05
430	Steve Sax	.05
431	Tom Gordon	.05
432	Billy Hatcher	.05
433	Cal Eldred	.05
434	Wally Backman	.05
435	Mark Eichhorn	.05
436	Mookie Wilson	.05
437	Scott Servais **RC**	.10
438	Mike Maddux	.05
439	Chico Walker **RC**	.05
440	Doug Drabek	.05
441	Rob Deer	.05
442	Dave West	.05
443	Spike Owen	.05
444	Tyrone Hill **RC**	.05
445	Matt Williams	.05
446	Mark Lewis	.05
447	David Segui	.05
448	Tom Pagnozzi	.05
449	Jeff Johnson **RC**	.05
450	Mark McGwire	.65
451	Tom Henke	.05
452	Wilson Alvarez	.05
453	Gary Redus	.05
454	Darren Holmes	.05
455	Pete O'Brien	.05
456	Pat Combs	.05
457	Hubie Brooks	.05
458	Frank Tanana	.05
459	Tom Kelly	.05
460	Andre Dawson	.25
461	Doug Jones	.05
462	Rich Rodriguez	.05
463	Mike Simms **RC**	.05
464	Mike Jeffcoat	.05
465	Barry Larkin	.05
466	Stan Belinda	.05
467	Lonnie Smith	.05
468	Greg Harris	.05
469	Jim Eisenreich	.05
470	Pedro Guerrero	.05
471	Jose DeJesus	.05
472	Rich Rowland **RC**	.05
473	Frank Bolick, Craig Paquette, Tom Redington, Paul Russo **RC** Top Prospects-3rd Baseman	.05
474	Mike Rossiter **RC**	.05
475	Robby Thompson	.05
476	Randy Bush	.05
477	Greg Hibbard	.05
478	Dale Sveum	.05
479	Chito Martinez **RC**	.05
480	Scott Sanderson	.05
481	Tino Martinez	.05
482	Jimmy Key	.05
483	Terry Shumpert	.05
484	Mike Hartley	.05
485	Chris Sabo	.05
486	Bob Walk	.05
487	John Cerutti	.05
488	Scott Cooper	.05
489	Bobby Cox	.05
490	Julio Franco	.05
491	Jeff Brantley	.05
492	Mike Devereaux	.05
493	Jose Offerman	.05
494	Gary Thurman	.05
495	Carney Lansford	.05
496	Joe Grahe	.05
497	Andy Ashby **RC**	.10
498	Gerald Perry	.05
499	Dave Otto	.05
500	Vince Coleman	.05
501	Rob Mallicoat **RC**	.05
502	Greg Briley	.05
503	Pascual Perez	.05
504	Aaron Sele **RC**	.25
505	Bobby Thigpen	.05
506	Todd Benzinger	.05
507	Candy Maldonado	.05
508	Bill Gullickson	.05
509	Doug Dascenzo	.05
510	Frank Viola	.05
511	Kenny Rogers	.05
512	Mike Heath	.05
513	Kevin Bass	.05
514	Kim Batiste **RC**	.05
515	Delino DeShields	.05
516	Ed Sprague **RC**	.05
517	Jim Gott	.05
518	Jose Melendez **RC**	.05
519	Hal McRae	.05
520	Jeff Bagwell	.35
521	Joe Hesketh	.05
522	Milt Cuyler	.05
523	Shawn Hillegas	.05
524	Don Slaught	.05
525	Randy Johnson	.35
526	Doug Piatt **RC**	.05
527	Checklist 4	.05
528	Steve Foster **RC**	.05
529	Joe Girardi	.05
530	Jim Abbott	.05
531	Larry Walker	.05
532	Mike Huff	.05
533	Mackey Sasser	.05
534	Benji Gil **RC**	.05
535	Dave Stieb	.05
536	Willie Wilson	.05
537	Mark Leiter **RC**	.05
538	Jose Uribe	.05
539	Thomas Howard	.05
540	Ben McDonald	.05
541	Jose Tolentino **RC**	.05
542	Keith Mitchell **RC**	.05
543	Jerome Walton	.05
544	Cliff Brantley **RC**	.05
545	Andy Van Slyke	.05
546	Paul Sorrento	.05
547	Herm Winningham	.05
548	Mark Guthrie	.05
549	Joe Torre	.05
550	Darryl Strawberry	.05
551	Manny Alexander, Alex Arias, Wil Cordero, Chipper Jones Top Prospects-Shortstops	.25
552	Dave Gallagher	.05
553	Edgar Martinez	.05
554	Donald Harris	.05
555	Frank Thomas	.35
556	Storm Davis	.05
557	Dickie Thon	.05
558	Scott Garrelts	.05
559	Steve Olin	.05
560	Rickey Henderson	.35
561	Jose Vizcaino	.05
562	Wade Taylor **RC**	.05
563	Pat Borders	.05
564	Jimmy Gonzalez **RC**	.05
565	Lee Smith	.05
566	Bill Sampen	.05
567	Dean Palmer	.05
568	Bryan Harvey	.05
569	Tony Pena	.05
570	Lou Whitaker	.05
571	Randy Tomlin	.05
572	Greg Vaughn	.05
573	Kelly Downs	.05
574	Steve Avery	.05
575	Kirby Puckett	.45
576	Heathcliff Slocumb **RC**	.05
577	Kevin Seitzer	.05
578	Lee Guetterman	.05
579	Johnny Oates	.05
580	Greg Maddux	.45
581	Stan Javier	.05
582	Vicente Palacios	.05
583	Mel Rojas	.05
584	Wayne Rosenthal **RC**	.05
585	Lenny Webster	.05
586	Rod Nichols	.05
587	Mickey Morandini	.05
588	Russ Swan	.05
589	Mariano Duncan	.05
590	Howard Johnson	.05
591	Jacob Brumfield, Jeromy Burnitz, Alan Cockrell, D.J. Dozier Top Prospects-Outfielders	.25
592	Denny Neagle **RC**	.10
593	Steve Decker	.05
594	Brian Barber **RC**	.05
595	Bruce Hurst	.05
596	Kent Mercker	.05
597	Mike Magnante **RC**	.05
598	Jody Reed	.05
599	Steve Searcy	.05
600	Paul Molitor	.35
601	Dave Smith	.05
602	Mike Fetters	.05
603	Luis Mercedes **RC**	.05
604	Chris Gwynn	.05
605	Scott Erickson	.05
606	Brook Jacoby	.05
607	Todd Stottlemyre	.05
608	Scott Bradley	.05
609	Mike Hargrove	.05
610	Eric Davis	.05
611	Brian Hunter **RC**	.05
612	Pat Kelly	.05
613	Pedro Munoz	.05
614	Al Osuna	.05
615	Matt Merullo	.05
616	Larry Andersen	.05
617	Junior Ortiz	.05
618	Cesar Hernandez, Steve Hosey, Dan Peltier, Jeff McNeely **RC** Top Prospects-Outfielders	.10
619	Danny Jackson	.05
620	George Brett	.50
621	Dan Gakeler **RC**	.05
622	Steve Buechele	.05
623	Bob Tewksbury	.05
624	Shawn Estes **RC**	.25
625	Kevin McReynolds	.05
626	Chris Haney **RC**	.05
627	Mike Sharperson	.05
628	Mark Williamson	.05
629	Wally Joyner	.05
630	Carlton Fisk	.35
631	Armando Reynoso **RC**	.05
632	Felix Fermin	.05
633	Mitch Williams	.05
634	Manuel Lee	.05
635	Harold Baines	.05
636	Greg Harris	.05
637	Orlando Merced	.05
638	Chris Bosio	.05
639	Wayne Housie **RC**	.05
640	Xavier Hernandez	.05
641	David Howard **RC**	.05
642	Tim Crews	.05
643	Rick Cerone	.05
644	Terry Leach	.05
645	Deion Sanders	.10
646	Craig Wilson	.05
647	Marquis Grissom	.05
648	Scott Fletcher	.05
649	Norm Charlton	.05
650	Jesse Barfield	.05
651	Joe Slusarski **RC**	.05
652	Bobby Rose	.05
653	Dennis Lamp	.05
654	Allen Watson **RC**	.05
655	Brett Butler	.05
656	Rudy Pemberton, Henry Rodriguez, Lee Tinsley, Gerald Williams **RC** Top Prospects-Outfielders	.10
657	Dave Johnson	.05
658	Checklist 5	.05
659	Brian McRae	.05
660	Fred McGriff	.05
661	Bill Landrum	.05
662	Juan Guzman	.05
663	Greg Gagne	.05

664	Ken Hill	.05
665	Dave Haas RC	.05
666	Tom Foley	.05
667	Roberto Hernandez RC	.10
668	Dwayne Henry	.05
669	Jim Fregosi	.05
670	Harold Reynolds	.05
671	Mark Whiten	.05
672	Eric Plunk	.05
673	Todd Hundley	.05
674	Mo Sanford RC	.05
675	Bobby Witt	.05
676	Pat Mahomes, Sam Militello, Roger Salkeld, Turk Wendell RC Top Prospects-Pitchers	.15
677	John Marzano	.05
678	Joe Klink	.05
679	Pete Incaviglia	.05
680	Dale Murphy	.15
681	Rene Gonzales	.05
682	Andy Benes	.05
683	Jim Poole	.05
684	Trever Miller RC	.10
685	Scott Livingstone RC	.05
686	Rich DeLucia	.05
687	Harvey Pulliam RC	.05
688	Tim Belcher	.05
689	Mark Lemke	.05
690	John Franco	.05
691	Walt Weiss	.05
692	Scott Ruskin	.05
693	Jeff King	.05
694	Mike Gardiner	.05
695	Gary Sheffield	.30
696	Joe Boever	.05
697	Mike Felder	.05
698	John Habyan	.05
699	Cito Gaston	.05
700	Ruben Sierra	.05
701	Scott Radinsky	.05
702	Lee Stevens	.05
703	Mark Wohlers RC	.05
704	Curt Young	.05
705	Dwight Evans	.05
706	Rob Murphy	.05
707	Gregg Jefferies	.05
708	Tom Bolton	.05
709	Chris James	.05
710	Kevin Maas	.05
711	Ricky Bones RC	.05
712	Curt Wilkerson	.05
713	Roger McDowell	.05
714	Calvin Reese RC	.10
715	Craig Biggio	.05
716	Kirk Dressendorfer RC	.05
717	Ken Dayley	.05
718	B.J. Surhoff	.05
719	Terry Mulholland	.05
720	Kirk Gibson	.05
721	Mike Pagliarulo	.05
722	Walt Terrell	.05
723	Jose Oquendo	.05
724	Kevin Morton	.05
725	Dwight Gooden	.05
726	Kirt Manwaring	.05
727	Chuck McElroy	.05
728	Dave Burba	.05
729	Art Howe	.05
730	Ramon Martinez	.05
731	Donnie Hill	.05
732	Nelson Santovenia	.05
733	Bob Melvin	.05
734	Scott Hatteberg RC	.10
735	Greg Swindell	.05
736	Lance Johnson	.05
737	Kevin Reimer	.05
738	Dennis Eckersley	.35
739	Rob Ducey	.05
740	Ken Caminiti	.05
741	Mark Gubicza	.05
742	Billy Spiers	.05
743	Darren Lewis	.05
744	Chris Hammond	.05
745	Dave Magadan	.05
746	Bernard Gilkey	.05
747	Willie Banks	.05
748	Matt Nokes	.05
749	Jerald Clark	.05
750	Travis Fryman	.05
751	Steve Wilson	.05
752	Billy Ripken	.05
753	Paul Assenmacher	.05
754	Charlie Hayes	.05
755	Alex Fernandez	.05
756	Gary Pettis	.05
757	Rob Dibble	.05
758	Tim Naehring	.05
759	Jeff Torborg	.05
760	Ozzie Smith	.45
761	Mike Fitzgerald	.05
762	John Burkett	.05
763	Kyle Abbott	.05
764	Tyler Green RC	.05
765	Pete Harnisch	.05
766	Mark Davis	.05
767	Kal Daniels	.05
768	Jim Thome	.35
769	Jack Howell	.05
770	Sid Bream	.05
771	Arthur Rhodes RC	.10
772	Garry Templeton	.05
773	Hal Morris	.05
774	Bud Black	.05
775	Ivan Calderon	.05
776	Doug Henry RC	.05

777	John Olerud	.05
778	Tim Leary	.05
779	Jay Bell	.05
780	Eddie Murray	.35
781	Paul Abbott	.05
782	Phil Plantier	.05
783	Joe Magrane	.05
784	Ken Patterson	.05
785	Albert Belle	.05
786	Royce Clayton	.05
787	Checklist 6	.05
788	Mike Stanton	.05
789	Bobby Valentine	.05
790	Joe Carter	.05
791	Danny Cox	.05
792	Dave Winfield	.35

1992 Topps Gold

MARK LEMKE — Braves

	NM/M
Unopened Fact. Set (793):	75.00
Complete Set (792):	35.00
Common Player:	.20
(Star cards valued at 4X corresponding cards in regular-issue 1992 Topps.)	
86 Steve Finley (Incorrect name, Mark Davidson, on gold strip.)	.20
131 Terry Mathews	.20
264 Rod Beck	1.00
288 Andujar Cedeno (Incorrect team, Yankees, listed on gold strip.)	.60
366 Tony Perezchica	.20
465 Barry Larkin (Incorrect team, Astros, listed on gold strip.)	2.50
527 Terry McDaniel	.20
532 Mike Huff (Incorrect team, Red Sox, listed on gold strip.)	.20
658 John Ramos	.20
787 Brian Williams	.20
793 Brien Taylor (Autographed edition of 12,000; factory sets only.)	7.50

Traded

JEFFREY HAMMONDS — Team USA

	NM/M
Complete Set (132):	50.00
Common Player:	.05
Golds:	2-4X
1	Willie Adams RC (USA)	.05
2	Jeff Alkire (USA)	.05
3	Felipe Alou	.05
4	Moises Alou	.10
5	Ruben Amaro	.05
6	Jack Armstrong	.05
7	Scott Bankhead	.05
8	Tim Belcher	.05
9	George Bell	.05
10	Freddie Benavides	.05
11	Todd Benzinger	.05
12	Joe Boever	.05
13	Ricky Bones	.05
14	Bobby Bonilla	.05
15	Hubie Brooks	.05
16	Jerry Browne	.05
17	Jim Bullinger	.05
18	Dave Burba	.05
19	Kevin Campbell	.05
20	Tom Candiotti	.05
21	Mark Carreon	.05

22	Gary Carter	.75
23	Archi Cianfrocco	.05
24	Phil Clark	.05
25	Chad Curtis RC	.50
26	Eric Davis	.05
27	Tim Davis (USA)	.05
28	Gary DiSarcina	.05
29	Darren Dreifort (USA)	.05
30	Mariano Duncan	.05
31	Mike Fitzgerald	.05
32	John Flaherty	.05
33	Darrin Fletcher	.05
34	Scott Fletcher	.05
35	Ron Fraser (USA)	.05
36	Andres Galarraga	.05
37	Dave Gallagher	.05
38	Mike Gallego	.05
39	Nomar Garciaparra RC (USA)	30.00
40	Jason Giambi (USA)	1.00
41	Danny Gladden	.05
42	Rene Gonzales	.05
43	Jeff Granger (USA)	.05
44	Rick Greene (USA)	.05
45	Jeffrey Hammonds (USA)	.05
46	Charlie Hayes	.05
47	Von Hayes	.05
48	Rick Helling (USA)	.05
49	Butch Henry	.05
50	Carlos Hernandez	.05
51	Ken Hill	.05
52	Butch Hobson	.05
53	Vince Horsman	.05
54	Pete Incaviglia	.05
55	Gregg Jefferies	.05
56	Charles Johnson (USA)	.05
57	Doug Jones	.05
58	Brian Jordan RC	2.00
59	Wally Joyner	.05
60	Daron Kirkreit RC (USA)	.20
61	Bill Krueger	.05
62	Gene Lamont	.05
63	Jim Lefebvre	.05
64	Danny Leon RC	.05
65	Pat Listach	.05
66	Kenny Lofton	.05
67	Dave Martinez	.05
68	Derrick May	.05
69	Kirk McCaskill	.05
70	Chad McConnell RC (USA)	.05
71	Kevin McReynolds	.05
72	Rusty Meacham	.05
73	Keith Miller	.05
74	Kevin Mitchell	.05
75	Jason Moler RC (USA)	.05
76	Mike Morgan	.05
77	Jack Morris	.05
78	Calvin Murray RC (USA)	.05
79	Eddie Murray	.75
80	Randy Myers	.05
81	Denny Neagle	.05
82	Phil Nevin (USA)	.10
83	Dave Nilsson	.05
84	Junior Ortiz	.05
85	Donovan Osborne	.05
86	Bill Pecota	.05
87	Melido Perez	.05
88	Mike Perez	.05
89	Hipolito Pena	.05
90	Willie Randolph	.05
91	Darren Reed	.05
92	Bip Roberts	.05
93	Chris Roberts (USA)	.05
94	Steve Rodriguez (USA)	.05
95	Bruce Ruffin	.05
96	Scott Ruskin	.05
97	Bret Saberhagen	.05
98	Rey Sanchez	.05
99	Steve Sax	.05
100	Curt Schilling	.25
101	Dick Schofield	.05
102	Gary Scott	.05
103	Kevin Seitzer	.05
104	Frank Seminara	.05
105	Gary Sheffield	.35
106	John Smiley	.05
107	Cory Snyder	.05
108	Paul Sorrento	.05
109	Sammy Sosa	1.50
110	Matt Stairs RC	.05
111	Andy Stankiewicz	.05
112	Kurt Stillwell	.05
113	Rick Sutcliffe	.05
114	Bill Swift	.05
115	Jeff Tackett	.05
116	Danny Tartabull	.05
117	Eddie Taubensee	.05
118	Dickie Thon	.05
119	Michael Tucker RC (USA)	.25
120	Scooter Tucker	.05
121	Marc Valdes RC (USA)	.05
122	Julio Valera	.05
123	Jason Varitek RC (USA)	15.00
124	Ron Villone RC (USA)	.05
125	Frank Viola	.05
126	B.J. Wallace RC (USA)	.05
127	Dan Walters	.05
128	Craig Wilson (USA)	.05
129	Chris Wimmer (USA)	.05
130	Dave Winfield	.75
131	Herm Winningham	.05
132	Checklist	

1992 Topps Traded Gold

	NM/M
Complete Unopened Set (132):	75.00

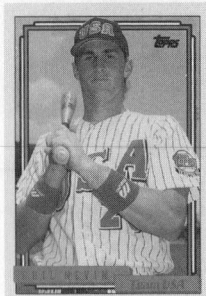

	NM/M
Complete Set (132):	65.00
Common Player:	.25
Stars/Rookies:	4X
(See 1992 Topps Traded for checklist and base card values.)	

1993 Topps

ANDY VAN SLYKE — PIRATES

	NM/M
Unopened Fact. Set (847):	40.00
Complete Set (825):	30.00
Common Player:	.05
Golds:	3X
Series 1 Wax Pack (15):	1.00
Series 1 Wax Box (36):	25.00
Series 2 Wax Pack (15):	.75
Series 2 Wax Box (36):	15.00
Series 1 Jumbo Pack (41):	2.00
Series 1 Jumbo Box (24):	30.00
Series 2 Jumbo Pack (41):	1.50
Series 2 Jumbo Box (24):	20.00
1	Robin Yount	.50
2	Barry Bonds	1.00
3	Ryne Sandberg	.60
4	Roger Clemens	.65
5	Tony Gwynn	.60
6	Jeff Tackett RC	.05
7	Pete Incaviglia	.05
8	Mark Wohlers	.05
9	Kent Hrbek	.05
10	Will Clark	.05
11	Eric Karros	.05
12	Lee Smith	.05
13	Esteban Beltre	.05
14	Greg Briley	.05
15	Marquis Grissom	.05
16	Dan Plesac	.05
17	Dave Hollins	.05
18	Mark Whiten	.05
19	Ed Nunez	.05
20	Tim Salmon	.05
21	Luis Salazar	.05
22	Jim Eisenreich	.05
23	Todd Stottlemyre	.05
24	Tim Naehring	.05
25	John Franco	.05
26	Skeeter Barnes	.05
27	Carlos Garcia RC	.05
28	Joe Orsulak	.05
29	Dwayne Henry	.05
30	Fred McGriff	.05
31	Derek Lilliquist	.05
32	Don Mattingly	.65
33	B.J. Wallace (1992 Draft Pick)	.05
34	Juan Gonzalez	.25
35	John Smoltz	.05
36	Scott Servais	.05
37	Lenny Webster	.05
38	Chris James	.05
39	Roger McDowell	.05
40	Ozzie Smith	.60
41	Alex Fernandez	.05
42	Spike Owen	.05
43	Ruben Amaro	.05
44	Kevin Seitzer	.05
45	Dave Fleming	.05
46	Eric Fox RC	.05
47	Bob Scanlan	.05

48	Bert Blyleven	.05
49	Brian McRae	.05
50	Roberto Alomar	.20
51	Mo Vaughn	.05
52	Bobby Bonilla	.05
53	Frank Tanana	.05
54	Mike LaValliere	.05
55	Mark McLemore	.05
56	Chad Mottola **RC** (1992 Draft Pick)	.10
57	Norm Charlton	.05
58	Jose Melendez	.05
59	Carlos Martinez	.05
60	Roberto Kelly	.05
61	Gene Larkin	.05
62	Rafael Belliard	.05
63	Al Osuna	.05
64	Scott Chiamparino	.05
65	Brett Butler	.05
66	John Burkett	.05
67	Felix Jose	.05
68	Omar Vizquel	.05
69	John Vander Wal	.05
70	Roberto Hernandez	.05
71	Ricky Bones	.05
72	Jeff Grotewold **RC**	.05
73	Mike Moore	.05
74	Steve Buechele	.05
75	Juan Guzman	.05
76	Kevin Appier	.05
77	Junior Felix	.05
78	Greg Harris	.05
79	Dick Schofield	.05
80	Cecil Fielder	.05
81	Lloyd McClendon	.05
82	David Segui	.05
83	Reggie Sanders	.05
84	Kurt Stillwell	.05
85	Sandy Alomar	.05
86	John Habyan	.05
87	Kevin Reimer	.05
88	Mike Stanton	.05
89	Eric Anthony	.05
90	Scott Erickson	.05
91	Craig Colbert	.05
92	Tom Pagnozzi	.05
93	Pedro Astacio **RC**	.10
94	Lance Johnson	.05
95	Larry Walker	.05
96	Russ Swan	.05
97	Scott Fletcher	.05
98	Derek Jeter **RC** (1992 Draft Pick)	10.00
99	Mike Williams **RC**	.05
100	Mark McGwire	.85
101	Jim Bullinger **RC**	.05
102	Brian Hunter	.05
103	Jody Reed	.05
104	Mike Butcher **RC**	.05
105	Gregg Jefferies	.05
106	Howard Johnson	.05
107	John Kiely **RC**	.05
108	Jose Lind	.05
109	Sam Horn	.05
110	Barry Larkin	.05
111	Bruce Hurst	.05
112	Brian Barnes	.05
113	Thomas Howard	.05
114	Mel Hall	.05
115	Robby Thompson	.05
116	Mark Lemke	.05
117	Eddie Taubensee	.05
118	David Hulse	.05
119	Pedro Munoz	.05
120	Ramon Martinez	.05
121	Todd Worrell	.05
122	Joey Cora	.05
123	Moises Alou	.05
124	Franklin Stubbs	.05
125	Pete O'Brien	.05
126	Bob Ayrault **RC**	.05
127	Carney Lansford	.05
128	Kal Daniels	.05
129	Joe Grahe	.05
130	Jeff Montgomery	.05
131	Dave Winfield	.50
132	Preston Wilson **RC** (1992 Draft Pick)	.75
133	Steve Wilson	.05
134	Lee Guetterman	.05
135	Mickey Tettleton	.05
136	Jeff King	.05
137	Alan Mills	.05
138	Joe Oliver	.05
139	Gary Gaetti	.05
140	Gary Sheffield	.30
141	Dennis Cook	.05
142	Charlie Hayes	.05
143	Jeff Huson	.05
144	Kent Mercker	.05
145	Eric Young **RC**	.10
146	Scott Leius	.05
147	Bryan Hickerson	.05
148	Steve Finley	.05
149	Rheal Cormier	.05
150	Frank Thomas	.50
151	Archi Cianfrocco **RC**	.05
152	Rich DeLucia	.05
153	Greg Vaughn	.05
154	Wes Chamberlain	.05
155	Dennis Eckersley	.40
156	Sammy Sosa	.60
157	Gary DiSarcina	.05
158	Kevin Koslofski **RC**	.05
159	Doug Linton **RC**	.05
160	Lou Whitaker	.05
161	Chad McDonnell (1992 Draft Pick)	.05
162	Joe Hesketh	.05
163	Tim Wakefield **RC**	.10
164	Leo Gomez	.05
165	Jose Rijo	.05
166	Tim Scott **RC**	.05
167	Steve Olin	.05
168	Kevin Maas	.05
169	Kenny Rogers	.05
170	Dave Justice	.05
171	Doug Jones	.05
172	Jeff Reboulet **RC**	.05
173	Andres Galarraga	.05
174	Randy Velarde	.05
175	Kirk McCaskill	.05
176	Darren Lewis	.05
177	Lenny Harris	.05
178	Jeff Fassero	.05
179	Ken Griffey Jr.	.75
180	Darren Daulton	.05
181	John Jaha	.05
182	Ron Darling	.05
183	Greg Maddux	.60
184	Damion Easley **RC**	.10
185	Jack Morris	.05
186	Mike Magnante	.05
187	John Dopson	.05
188	Sid Fernandez	.05
189	Tony Phillips	.05
190	Doug Drabek	.05
191	Sean Lowe **RC** (1992 Draft Pick)	.05
192	Bob Milacki	.05
193	Steve Foster **RC**	.05
194	Jerald Clark	.05
195	Pete Harnisch	.05
196	Pat Kelly	.05
197	Jeff Frye	.05
198	Alejandro Pena	.05
199	Junior Ortiz	.05
200	Kirby Puckett	.60
201	Jose Uribe	.05
202	Mike Scioscia	.05
203	Bernard Gilkey	.05
204	Dan Pasqua	.05
205	Gary Carter	.50
206	Henry Cotto	.05
207	Paul Molitor	.50
208	Mike Hartley	.05
209	Jeff Parrett	.05
210	Mark Langston	.05
211	Doug Dascenzo	.05
212	Rick Reed	.05
213	Candy Maldonado	.05
214	Danny Darwin	.05
215	Pat Howell **RC**	.05
216	Mark Leiter	.05
217	Kevin Mitchell	.05
218	Ben McDonald	.05
219	Bip Roberts	.05
220	Benny Santiago	.05
221	Carlos Baerga	.05
222	Bernie Williams	.05
223	Roger Pavlik **RC**	.05
224	Sid Bream	.05
225	Matt Williams	.05
226	Willie Banks	.05
227	Jeff Bagwell	.50
228	Tom Goodwin	.05
229	Mike Perez	.05
230	Carlton Fisk	.50
231	John Wetteland	.05
232	Tino Martinez	.05
233	Rick Greene **RC** (1992 Draft Pick)	.05
234	Tim McIntosh	.05
235	Mitch Williams	.05
236	Kevin Campbell **RC**	.05
237	Jose Vizcaino	.05
238	Chris Donnels	.05
239	Mike Boddicker	.05
240	John Olerud	.05
241	Mike Gardiner	.05
242	Charlie O'Brien	.05
243	Rob Deer	.05
244	Denny Neagle	.05
245	Chris Sabo	.05
246	Gregg Olson	.05
247	Frank Seminara	.05
248	Scott Scudder	.05
249	Tim Burke	.05
250	Chuck Knoblauch	.05
251	Mike Bielecki	.05
252	Xavier Hernandez	.05
253	Jose Guzman	.05
254	Cory Snyder	.05
255	Orel Hershiser	.05
256	Wil Cordero	.05
257	Luis Alicea	.05
258	Mike Schooler	.05
259	Craig Grebeck	.05
260	Duane Ward	.05
261	Bill Wegman	.05
262	Mickey Morandini	.05
263	Vince Horsman **RC**	.05
264	Paul Sorrento	.05
265	Andre Dawson	.25
266	Rene Gonzales	.05
267	Keith Miller	.05
268	Derek Bell	.05
269	Todd Steverson **RC** (1992 Draft Pick)	.05
270	Frank Viola	.05
271	Wally Whitehurst	.05
272	Kurt Knudsen **RC**	.05
273	Dan Walters **RC**	.05
274	Rick Sutcliffe	.05
275	Andy Van Slyke	.05
276	Paul O'Neill	.05
277	Mark Whiten	.05
278	Chris Nabholz	.05
279	Todd Burns	.05
280	Tom Glavine	.25
281	Butch Henry **RC**	.05
282	Shane Mack	.05
283	Mike Jackson	.05
284	Henry Rodriguez	.05
285	Bob Tewksbury	.05
286	Ron Karkovice	.05
287	Mike Gallego	.05
288	Dave Cochrane	.05
289	Jesse Orosco	.05
290	Dave Stewart	.05
291	Tommy Greene	.05
292	Rey Sanchez	.05
293	Rob Ducey	.05
294	Brent Mayne	.05
295	Dave Stieb	.05
296	Luis Rivera	.05
297	Jeff Innis	.05
298	Scott Livingstone	.05
299	Bob Patterson	.05
300	Cal Ripken, Jr.	1.00
301	Cesar Hernandez	.05
302	Randy Myers	.05
303	Brook Jacoby	.05
304	Melido Perez	.05
305	Rafael Palmeiro	.40
306	Damon Berryhill	.05
307	Dan Serafini **RC** (1992 Draft Pick)	.05
308	Darryl Kile	.05
309	J.T. Bruett **RC**	.05
310	Dave Righetti	.05
311	Jay Howell	.05
312	Geronimo Pena	.05
313	Greg Hibbard	.05
314	Mark Gardner	.05
315	Edgar Martinez	.05
316	Dave Nilsson	.05
317	Kyle Abbott	.05
318	Willie Wilson	.05
319	Paul Assenmacher	.05
320	Tim Fortugno **RC**	.05
321	Rusty Meacham	.05
322	Pat Borders	.05
323	Mike Greenwell	.05
324	Willie Randolph	.05
325	Bill Gullickson	.05
326	Gary Varsho	.05
327	Tim Hulett	.05
328	Scott Ruskin	.05
329	Mike Maddux	.05
330	Danny Tartabull	.05
331	Kenny Lofton	.05
332	Geno Petralli	.05
333	Otis Nixon	.05
334	Jason Kendall **RC** (1992 Draft Pick)	.50
335	Mark Portugal	.05
336	Mike Pagliarulo	.05
337	Kirt Manwaring	.05
338	Bob Ojeda	.05
339	Mark Clark **RC**	.05
340	John Kruk	.05
341	Mel Rojas	.05
342	Erik Hanson	.05
343	Doug Henry	.05
344	Jack McDowell	.05
345	Harold Baines	.05
346	Chuck McElroy	.05
347	Luis Sojo	.05
348	Andy Stankiewicz	.05
349	Hipolito Pichardo **RC**	.05
350	Joe Carter	.05
351	Ellis Burks	.05
352	Pete Schourek	.05
353	Buddy Groom **RC**	.05
354	Jay Bell	.05
355	Brady Anderson	.05
356	Freddie Benavides	.05
357	Phil Stephenson	.05
358	Kevin Wickander	.05
359	Mike Stanley	.05
360	Ivan Rodriguez	.40
361	Scott Bankhead	.05
362	Luis Gonzalez	.05
363	John Smiley	.05
364	Trevor Wilson	.05
365	Tom Candiotti	.05
366	Craig Wilson	.05
367	Steve Sax	.05
368	Delino Deshields	.05
369	Jaime Navarro	.05
370	Dave Valle	.05
371	Mariano Duncan	.05
372	Rod Nichols	.05
373	Mike Morgan	.05
374	Julio Valera	.05
375	Wally Joyner	.05
376	Tom Henke	.05
377	Herm Winningham	.05
378	Orlando Merced	.05
379	Mike Munoz	.05
380	Todd Hundley	.05
381	Mike Flanagan	.05
382	Tim Belcher	.05
383	Jerry Browne	.05
384	Mike Benjamin	.05
385	Jim Leyritz	.05
386	Ray Lankford	.05
387	Devon White	.05
388	Jeremy Hernandez	.05
389	Brian Harper	.05
390	Wade Boggs	.60
391	Derrick May	.05
392	Travis Fryman	.05
393	Ron Gant	.05
394	Checklist 1-132	.05
395	Checklist 133-264	.05
396	Checklist 265-396	.05
397	George Brett	.65
398	Bobby Witt	.05
399	Daryl Boston	.05
400	Bo Jackson	.10
401	Fred McGriff, Frank Thomas/AS	.20
402	Ryne Sandberg, Carlos Baerga/AS	.30
403	Gary Sheffield, Edgar Martinez/AS	.05
404	Barry Larkin, Travis Fryman/AS	.05
405	Andy Van Slyke, Ken Griffey Jr./AS	.40
406	Larry Walker, Kirby Puckett/AS	.20
407	Barry Bonds, Joe Carter/AS	.50
408	Darren Daulton, Brian Harper/AS	.05
409	Greg Maddux, Roger Clemens/AS	.25
410	Tom Glavine, Dave Fleming/AS	.05
411	Lee Smith, Dennis Eckersley/AS	.15
412	Jamie McAndrew	.05
413	Pete Smith	.05
414	Juan Guerrero	.05
415	Todd Frohwirth	.05
416	Randy Tomlin	.05
417	B.J. Surhoff	.05
418	Jim Gott	.05
419	Mark Thompson (1992 Draft Pick)	.05
420	Kevin Tapani	.05
421	Curt Schilling	.25
422	J.T. Snow **RC**	.40
423	Ryan Klesko, Ivan Cruz, Bubba Smith, Larry Sutton Top Prospects 1B	.05
424	John Valentin	.05
425	Joe Girardi	.05
426	Nigel Wilson **RC**	.05
427	Bob MacDonald	.05
428	Todd Zeile	.05
429	Milt Cuyler	.05
430	Eddie Murray	.50
431	Rich Amaral	.05
432	Pete Young	.05
433	Roger Bailey, Tom Schmidt Rockies Future Stars	.05
434	Jack Armstrong	.05
435	Willie McGee	.05
436	Greg Harris	.05
437	Chris Hammond	.05
438	Ritchie Moody **RC** (1992 Draft Pick)	.05
439	Bryan Harvey	.05
440	Ruben Sierra	.05
441	Don Lemon, Todd Pridy Marlins Future Stars	.05
442	Kevin McReynolds	.05
443	Terry Leach	.05
444	David Nied	.05
445	Dale Murphy	.15
446	Luis Mercedes	.05
447	Keith Shepherd **RC**	.05
448	Ken Caminiti	.05
449	James Austin	.05
450	Darryl Strawberry	.05
451	Ramon Caraballo, Jon Shave, Brent Gates, Quinton McCracken **RC** Top Prospects 2B	.10
452	Bob Wickman	.05
453	Victor Cole	.05
454	John Johnstone **RC**	.05
455	Chili Davis	.05
456	Scott Taylor	.05
457	Tracy Woodson	.05
458	David Wells	.05
459	Derek Wallace **RC** (1992 Draft Pick)	.05
460	Randy Johnson	.50
461	Steve Reed **RC**	.05
462	Felix Fermin	.05
463	Scott Aldred	.05
464	Greg Colbrunn	.05
465	Tony Fernandez	.05
466	Mike Felder	.05
467	Lee Stevens	.05
468	Matt Whiteside	.05
469	Dave Hansen	.05
470	Rob Dibble	.05
471	Dave Gallagher	.05
472	Chris Gwynn	.05
473	Dave Henderson	.05
474	Ozzie Guillen	.05
475	Jeff Reardon	.05
476	Mark Voisard, Will Scalzitti Rockies Future Stars	.05
477	Jimmy Jones	.05

478 Greg Cadaret .05
479 Todd Pratt .05
480 Pat Listach .05
481 Ryan Luzinski **RC** (1992 Draft Pick) .05
482 Darren Reed .05
483 Brian Griffiths **RC** .05
484 John Wehner .05
485 Glenn Davis .05
486 Eric Wedge **RC** .05
487 Jesse Hollins .05
488 Manuel Lee .05
489 Scott Fredrickson **RC** .05
490 Omar Olivares .05
491 Shawn Hare .05
492 Tom Lampkin .05
493 Jeff Nelson .05
494 Kevin Young, Adell Davenport, Eduardo Perez, Lou Lucca Top Prospects 3B .05
495 Ken Hill .05
496 Reggie Jefferson .05
497 Matt Petersen, Willie Brown Marlins Future Stars .05
498 Bud Black .05
499 Chuck Crim .05
500 Jose Canseco .30
501 Johnny Oates, Bobby Cox Major League Managers .05
502 Butch Hobson, Jim Lefebvre Major League Managers .05
503 Buck Rodgers, Tony Perez Major League Managers .05
504 Gene Lamont, Don Baylor Major League Managers .05
505 Mike Hargrove, Rene Lachemann Major League Managers .05
506 Sparky Anderson, Art Howe Major League Managers .10
507 Hal McRae, Tommy Lasorda Major League Managers .05
508 Phil Garner, Felipe Alou Major League Manager .05
509 Tom Kelly, Jeff Torborg Major League Managers .05
510 Buck Showalter, Jim Fregosi Major League Managers .05
511 Tony LaRussa, Jim Leyland Major League Managers .10
512 Lou Piniella, Joe Torre Major League Managers .10
513 Toby Harrah, Jim Riggleman Major League Managers .05
514 Cito Gaston, Dusty Baker Major League Managers .05
515 Greg Swindell .05
516 Alex Arias .05
517 Bill Pecota .05
518 Benji Grigsby **RC** (1992 Draft Pick) .05
519 David Howard .05
520 Charlie Hough .05
521 Kevin Flora .05
522 Shane Reynolds .05
523 Doug Bochtler **RC** .05
524 Chris Hoiles .05
525 Scott Sanderson .05
526 Mike Sharperson .05
527 Mike Fetters .05
528 Paul Quantrill .05
529 Dave Silvestri, Chipper Jones, Benji Gil, Jeff Patzke Top Propsects SS .25
530 Sterling Hitchcock .05
531 Joe Millette .05
532 Tom Brunansky .05
533 Frank Castillo .05
534 Randy Knorr .05
535 Jose Oquendo .05
536 Dave Haas .05
537 Jason Hutchins, Ryan Turner Rockies Future Stars .05
538 Jimmy Baron (1992 Draft Pick) .05
539 Kerry Woodson .05
540 Ivan Calderon .05
541 Denis Boucher .05
542 Royce Clayton .05
543 Reggie Williams .05
544 Steve Decker .05
545 Dean Palmer .05
546 Hal Morris .05
547 Ryan Thompson **RC** .05
548 Lance Blankenship .05
549 Hensley Meulens .05
550 Scott Radinsky .05
551 Eric Young **RC** .10
552 Jeff Blauser .05
553 Andujar Cedeno .05
554 Arthur Rhodes .05
555 Terry Mulholland .05
556 Darryl Hamilton .05
557 Pedro Martinez .50
558 Ryan Whitman, Mark Skeels Marlins Future Stars .05
559 Jamie Arnold **RC** (1992 Draft Pick) .05
560 Zane Smith .05
561 Matt Nokes .05
562 Bob Zupcic .05
563 Shawn Boskie .05
564 Mike Timlin .05
565 Jerald Clark .05
566 Rod Brewer .05
567 Mark Carreon .05
568 Andy Benes .05
569 Shawn Barton .05
570 Tim Wallach .05
571 Dave Mlicki .05
572 Trevor Hoffman .05
573 John Patterson .05
574 DeShawn Warren (1992 Draft Pick) .05
575 Monty Fariss .05
576 Darrell Sherman, Damon Buford, Cliff Floyd, Michael Moore Top Prospects OF .05
577 Tim Costo .05
578 Dave Magadan .05
579 Neil Garret, Jason Bates Rockies Future Stars .05
580 Walt Weiss .05
581 Chris Haney .05
582 Shawn Abner .05
583 Marvin Freeman .05
584 Casey Candaele .05
585 Ricky Jordan .05
586 Jeff Tabaka .05
587 Manny Alexander .05
588 Mike Trombley .05
589 Carlos Hernandez .05
590 Cal Eldred .05
591 Alex Cole .05
592 Phil Plantier .05
593 Brett Merriman .05
594 Jerry Nielsen .05
595 Shawon Dunston .05
596 Jimmy Key .05
597 Gerald Perry .05
598 Rico Brogna .05
599 Clemente Nunez, Dan Robinson Marlins Future Stars .05
600 Bret Saberhagen .05
601 Craig Shipley .05
602 Henry Mercedes .05
603 Jim Thome .40
604 Rod Beck .05
605 Chuck Finley .05
606 J. Owens .05
607 Dan Smith .05
608 Bill Doran .05
609 Lance Parrish .05
610 Denny Martinez .05
611 Tom Gordon .05
612 Byron Mathews (1992 Draft Pick) .05
613 Joel Adamson .05
614 Brian Williams .05
615 Steve Avery .05
616 Matt Mieske, Tracy Sanders, Midre Cummings, Ryan Freeburg Top Prospects OF .05
617 Craig Lefferts .05
618 Tony Pena .05
619 Billy Spiers .05
620 Todd Benzinger .05
621 Mike Kotarski, Greg Boyd Rockies Future Stars .05
622 Ben Rivera .05
623 Al Martin .05
624 Sam Militello .05
625 Rick Aguilera .05
626 Danny Gladden .05
627 Andres Berumen .05
628 Kelly Gruber .05
629 Cris Carpenter .05
630 Mark Grace .05
631 Jeff Brantley .05
632 Chris Widger (1992 Draft Pick) .05
633 Rodolf Razjigaev, Evgenyi Puchkov, Ilya Bogatyrev Russian Angels .10
634 Mo Sanford .05
635 Albert Belle .05
636 Tim Teufel .05
637 Greg Myers .05
638 Brian Bohanon .05
639 Mike Bordick .05
640 Dwight Gooden .05
641 Pat Leahy, Gavin Baugh Marlins Future Stars .05
642 Milt Hill .05
643 Luis Aquino .05
644 Dante Bichette .05
645 Bobby Thigpen .05
646 Rich Scheid .05
647 Brian Sackinsky (1992 Draft Pick) .05
648 Ryan Hawblitzel .05
649 Tom Marsh .05
650 Terry Pendleton .05
651 Rafael Bournigal **RC** .05
652 Dave West .05
653 Steve Hosey .05
654 Gerald Williams .05
655 Scott Cooper .05
656 Gary Scott .05
657 Mike Harkey .05
658 Jeromy Burnitz, Melvin Nieves, Rich Becker, Shon Walker Top Prospects OF .05
659 Ed Sprague .05
660 Alan Trammell .05
661 Garvin Alston, Mike Case Rockies Future Stars .05
662 Donovan Osborne .05
663 Jeff Gardner .05
664 Calvin Jones .05
665 Darrin Fletcher .05
666 Glenallen Hill .05
667 Jim Rosenbohm (1992 Draft Pick) .05
668 Scott Lewis .05
669 Kip Yaughn .05
670 Julio Franco .05
671 Dave Martinez .05
672 Kevin Bass .05
673 Todd Van Poppel .05
674 Mark Gubicza .05
675 Tim Raines .05
676 Rudy Seanez .05
677 Charlie Leibrandt .05
678 Randy Milligan .05
679 Kim Batiste .05
680 Craig Biggio .05
681 Darren Holmes .05
682 John Candelaria .05
683 Jerry Stafford, Eddie Christian Marlins Future Stars .05
684 Pat Mahomes .05
685 Bob Walk .05
686 Russ Springer .05
687 Tony Sheffield (1992 Draft Picks) .05
688 Dwight Smith .05
689 Eddie Zosky .05
690 Bien Figueroa .05
691 Jim Tatum .05
692 Chad Kreuter .05
693 Rich Rodriguez .05
694 Shane Turner .05
695 Kent Bottenfield .05
696 Jose Mesa .05
697 Darrell Whitmore **RC** .05
698 Ted Wood .05
699 Chad Curtis .05
700 Nolan Ryan 1.00
701 Mike Piazza, Carlos Delgado, Brook Fordyce, Donnie Leshnock Top Prospects C .85
702 Tim Pugh **RC** .05
703 Jeff Kent .05
704 Jon Goodrich, Danny Figueroa Rockies Future Stars .05
705 Bob Welch .05
706 Sherard Clinkscales (1992 Draft Pick) .05
707 Donn Pall .05
708 Greg Olson .05
709 Jeff Juden .05
710 Mike Mussina .30
711 Scott Chiamparino .05
712 Stan Javier .05
713 John Doherty .05
714 Kevin Gross .05
715 Greg Gagne .05
716 Steve Cooke .05
717 Steve Farr .05
718 Jay Buhner .05
719 Butch Henry .05
720 David Cone .05
721 Rick Wilkins .05
722 Chuck Carr .05
723 Kenny Felder **RC** (1992 Draft Pick) .05
724 Guillermo Velasquez .05
725 Billy Hatcher .05
726 Mike Veneziale, Ken Kendrena Marlins Future Stars .05
727 Jonathan Hurst .05
728 Steve Frey .05
729 Mark Leonard .05
730 Charles Nagy .05
731 Donald Harris .05
732 Travis Buckley .05
733 Tom Browning .05
734 Anthony Young .05
735 Steve Shifflett .05
736 Jeff Russell .05
737 Wilson Alvarez .05
738 Lance Painter .05
739 Dave Weathers .05
740 Len Dykstra .05
741 Mike Devereaux .05
742 Rene Arocha, Alan Embree, Tim Crabtree, Brien Taylor Top Prospects/SP .05
743 Dave Landaker (1992 Draft Pick) .05
744 Chris George .05
745 Eric Davis .05
746 Mark Strittmatter, LaMarr Rogers Rockies Future Stars .05
747 Carl Willis .05
748 Stan Belinda .05
749 Scott Kamieniecki .05
750 Rickey Henderson .50
751 Eric Hillman .05
752 Pat Hentgen .05
753 Jim Corsi .05
754 Brian Jordan .05
755 Bill Swift .05
756 Mike Henneman .05
757 Harold Reynolds .05
758 Sean Berry .05
759 Charlie Hayes .05
760 Luis Polonia .05
761 Darrin Jackson .05
762 Mark Lewis .05
763 Rob Maurer .05
764 Willie Greene .05
765 Vince Coleman .05
766 Todd Revenig .05
767 Rich Ireland (1992 Draft Pick) .05
768 Mike MacFarlane .05
769 Francisco Cabrera .05
770 Robin Ventura .05
771 Kevin Ritz .05
772 Chito Martinez .05
773 Cliff Brantley .05
774 Curtis Leskanic .05
775 Chris Bosio .05
776 Jose Offerman .05
777 Mark Guthrie .05
778 Don Slaught .05
779 Rich Monteleone .05
780 Jim Abbott .05
781 Jack Clark .05
782 Rafael Mendoza, Dan Roman Marlins Future Stars .05
783 Heathcliff Slocumb .05
784 Jeff Branson .05
785 Kevin Brown .05
786 Mike Christopher, Ken Ryan, Aaron Taylor, Gus Gandarillas Top Prospects RP .05
787 Mike Matthews (1992 Draft Pick) .05
788 Mackey Sasser .05
789 Jeff Conine .05
790 George Bell .05
791 Pat Rapp .05
792 Joe Boever .05
793 Jim Poole .05
794 Andy Ashby .05
795 Deion Sanders .10
796 Scott Brosius .05
797 Brad Pennington .05
798 Greg Blosser .05
799 Jim Edmonds **RC** 1.00
800 Shawn Jeter .05
801 Jesse Levis .05
802 Phil Clark .05
803 Ed Pierce .05
804 Jose Valentin **RC** .05
805 Terry Jorgensen .05
806 Mark Hutton .05
807 Troy Neel .05
808 Bret Boone .05
809 Chris Colon .05
810 Domingo Martinez **RC** .05
811 Javier Lopez .05
812 Matt Walbeck .05
813 Dan Wilson .05
814 Scooter Tucker .05
815 Billy Ashley **RC** .05
816 Tim Laker **RC** .05
817 Bobby Jones .05
818 Brad Brink .05
819 William Pennyfeather .05
820 Stan Royer .05
821 Doug Brocail .05
822 Kevin Rogers .05
823 Checklist 397-528 .05
824 Checklist 541-691 .05
825 Checklist 692-825 .05

1993 Topps Gold

NM/M

Complete Set (825): 40.00
Common Player: .15
(Star cards valued at 3X corresponding cards in regular 1993 Topps issue.)

394 Bernardo Brito .25
395 Jim McNamara .25
396 Rich Sauveur .25
823 Keith Brown .25
824 Russ McGinnis .25
825 Mike Walker .25

Black Gold

NM/M

Complete Set (44): 7.50
Common Player: .10
Winner A (1-11): 1.00
Winner B (12-22): 1.00
Winner C (23-33): 1.00
Winner D (34-44): 1.00
Winner AB (1-22): 3.00
Winner CD (23-44): 3.00
Winner ABCD (1-44): 5.00
1 Barry Bonds 1.50
2 Will Clark .10

JOE OLIVER

3	Darren Daulton	.10
4	Andre Dawson	.25
5	Delino DeShields	.10
6	Tom Glavine	.20
7	Marquis Grissom	.10
8	Tony Gwynn	.75
9	Eric Karros	.10
10	Ray Lankford	.10
11	Barry Larkin	.10
12	Greg Maddux	.75
13	Fred McGriff	.10
14	Joe Oliver	.10
15	Terry Pendleton	.10
16	Bip Roberts	.10
17	Ryne Sandberg	.75
18	Gary Sheffield	.40
19	Lee Smith	.10
20	Ozzie Smith	.75
21	Andy Van Slyke	.10
22	Larry Walker	.10
23	Roberto Alomar	.20
24	Brady Anderson	.10
25	Carlos Baerga	.10
26	Joe Carter	.10
27	Roger Clemens	.85
28	Mike Devereaux	.10
29	Dennis Eckersley	.60
30	Cecil Fielder	.10
31	Travis Fryman	.10
32	Juan Gonzalez	.35
33	Ken Griffey Jr.	1.00
34	Brian Harper	.10
35	Pat Listach	.10
36	Kenny Lofton	.10
37	Edgar Martinez	.10
38	Jack McDowell	.10
39	Mark McGwire	1.00
40	Kirby Puckett	.75
41	Mickey Tettleton	.10
42	Frank Thomas	.65
43	Robin Ventura	.10
44	Dave Winfield	.65

Traded

GREGG JEFFERIES
CARDINALS

		NM/M
Complete Set (132):		20.00
Common Player:		.05
1	Barry Bonds	2.00
2	Rich Renteria	.05
3	Aaron Sele	.05
4	Carlton Loewer RC (USA)	.10
5	Erik Pappas	.05
6	Greg McMichael RC	.05
7	Freddie Benavides	.05
8	Kirk Gibson	.05
9	Tony Fernandez	.05
10	Jay Gainer RC (USA)	.05
11	Orestes Destrade	.05
12	A.J. Hinch RC (USA)	.40
13	Bobby Munoz	.05
14	Tom Henke	.05
15	Rob Butler	.05
16	Gary Wayne	.05
17	David McCarty	.05
18	Walt Weiss	.05
19	Todd Helton RC (USA)	15.00
20	Mark Whiten	.05

21	Ricky Gutierrez	.05
22	Dustin Hermanson RC (USA)	.40
23	Sherman Obando RC	.05
24	Mike Piazza	2.00
25	Jeff Russell	.05
26	Jason Bere	.05
27	Jack Voight RC	.05
28	Chris Bosio	.05
29	Phil Hiatt	.05
30	Matt Beaumont RC (USA)	.05
31	Andres Galarraga	.05
32	Greg Swindell	.05
33	Vinny Castilla	.05
34	Pat Clougherty RC (USA)	.05
35	Greg Briley	.05
36	Dallas Green, Davey Johnson	.05
37	Tyler Green	.05
38	Craig Paquette	.05
39	Danny Sheaffer	.05
40	Jim Converse	.05
41	Terry Harvey	.05
42	Phil Plantier	.05
43	Doug Saunders RC	.05
44	Benny Santiago	.05
45	Dante Powell RC (USA)	.10
46	Jeff Parrett	.05
47	Wade Boggs	.85
48	Paul Molitor	.75
49	Turk Wendell	.05
50	David Wells	.05
51	Gary Sheffield	.35
52	Kevin Young	.05
53	Nelson Liriano	.05
54	Greg Maddux	.85
55	Derek Bell	.05
56	Matt Turner RC	.05
57	Charlie Nelson RC (USA)	.05
58	Mike Hampton	.05
59	Troy O'Leary RC	.10
60	Benji Gil	.05
61	Mitch Lyden RC	.05
62	J.T. Snow	.05
63	Damon Buford	.05
64	Gene Harris	.05
65	Randy Myers	.05
66	Felix Jose	.05
67	Todd Dunn RC (USA)	.05
68	Jimmy Key	.05
69	Pedro Castellano	.05
70	Mark Merila RC (USA)	.05
71	Rich Rodriguez	.05
72	Matt Mieske	.05
73	Pete Incaviglia	.05
74	Carl Everett	.05
75	Jim Abbott	.05
76	Luis Aquino	.05
77	Rene Arocha RC	.05
78	Jon Shave RC	.05
79	Todd Walker RC (USA)	1.00
80	Jack Armstrong	.05
81	Jeff Richardson	.05
82	Blas Minor	.05
83	Dave Winfield	.75
84	Paul O'Neill	.05
85	Steve Reich RC (USA)	.10
86	Chris Hammond	.05
87	Hilly Hathaway RC	.05
88	Fred McGriff	.05
89	Dave Telgheder RC	.05
90	Richie Lewis RC	.05
91	Brent Gates	.05
92	Andre Dawson	.15
93	Andy Barkett RC (USA)	.05
94	Doug Drabek	.05
95	Joe Klink	.05
96	Willie Blair	.05
97	Danny Graves RC (USA)	.05
98	Pat Meares	.05
99	Mike Lansing	.05
100	Marcos Armas RC	.05
101	Darren Grass RC (USA)	.05
102	Chris Jones	.05
103	Ken Ryan RC	.05
104	Ellis Burks	.05
105	Bobby Kelly	.05
106	Dave Magadan	.05
107	Paul Wilson RC (USA)	.25
108	Rob Natal	.05
109	Paul Wagner	.05
110	Jeromy Burnitz	.05
111	Monty Fariss	.05
112	Kevin Mitchell	.05
113	Scott Pose RC	.05
114	Dave Stewart	.05
115	Russ Johnson RC (USA)	.10
116	Armando Reynoso	.05
117	Geronimo Berroa	.05
118	Woody Williams RC	.15
119	Tim Bogar RC	.05
120	Bob Scafa RC (USA)	.05
121	Henry Cotto	.05
122	Gregg Jefferies	.05
123	Norm Charlton	.05
124	Bret Wagner RC (USA)	.05
125	David Cone	.05
126	Daryl Boston	.05
127	Tim Wallach	.05
128	Mike Martin RC (USA)	.05
129	John Cummings RC	.05
130	Ryan Bowen	.05
131	John Powell RC (USA)	.05
132	Checklist	.05

1994 Topps

Mike Piazza

DODGERS   C

	NM/M
Unopened Retail Set (818):	60.00
Unopened Hobby Set (808):	50.00
Complete Set (792):	35.00
Common Player:	.05
Golds:	2X
Series 1 or 2 Pack (12):	.50
Series 1 or 2 Wax Box (36):	15.00

1	Mike Piazza	.85
2	Bernie Williams	.05
3	Kevin Rogers	.05
4	Paul Carey	.05
5	Ozzie Guillen	.05
6	Derrick May	.05
7	Jose Mesa	.05
8	Todd Hundley	.05
9	Chris Haney	.05
10	John Olerud	.05
11	Andujar Cedeno	.05
12	John Smiley	.05
13	Phil Plantier	.05
14	Willie Banks	.05
15	Jay Bell	.05
16	Doug Henry	.05
17	Lance Blankenship	.05
18	Greg Harris	.05
19	Scott Livingstone	.05
20	Bryan Harvey	.05
21	Wil Cordero	.05
22	Roger Pavlik	.05
23	Mark Lemke	.05
24	Jeff Nelson	.05
25	Todd Zeile	.05
26	Billy Hatcher	.05
27	Joe Magrane	.05
28	Tony Longmire	.05
29	Omar Daal	.05
30	Kirt Manwaring	.05
31	Melido Perez	.05
32	Tim Hulett	.05
33	Jeff Schwarz	.05
34	Nolan Ryan	1.00
35	Jose Guzman	.05
36	Felix Fermin	.05
37	Jeff Innis	.05
38	Brent Mayne	.05
39	Huck Flener RC	.05
40	Jeff Bagwell	.50
41	Kevin Wickander	.05
42	Ricky Gutierrez	.05
43	Pat Mahomes	.05
44	Jeff King	.05
45	Cal Eldred	.05
46	Craig Paquette	.05
47	Richie Lewis	.05
48	Tony Phillips	.05
49	Armando Reynoso	.05
50	Moises Alou	.05
51	Manuel Lee	.05
52	Otis Nixon	.05
53	Billy Ashley	.05
54	Mark Whiten	.05
55	Jeff Russell	.05
56	Chad Curtis	.05
57	Kevin Stocker	.05
58	Mike Jackson	.05
59	Matt Nokes	.05
60	Chris Bosio	.05
61	Damon Buford	.05
62	Tim Belcher	.05
63	Glenallen Hill	.05
64	Bill Wertz	.05
65	Eddie Murray	.50
66	Tom Gordon	.05
67	Alex Gonzalez	.05
68	Eddie Taubensee	.05
69	Jacob Brumfield	.05
70	Andy Benes	.05
71	Rich Becker	.05
72	Steve Cooke	.05
73	Billy Spiers	.05
74	Scott Brosius	.05
75	Alan Trammell	.05
76	Luis Aquino	.05
77	Jerald Clark	.05
78	Mel Rojas	.05
79	Billy Masse, Stanton Cameron, Tim Clark, Craig McClure OF Prospects	.05

80	Jose Canseco	.30
81	Greg McMichael	.05
82	Brian Turang	.05
83	Tom Urban	.05
84	Garret Anderson	.05
85	Tony Pena	.05
86	Ricky Jordan	.05
87	Jim Gott	.05
88	Pat Kelly	.05
89	Bud Black	.05
90	Robin Ventura	.05
91	Rick Sutcliffe	.05
92	Jose Bautista	.05
93	Bob Ojeda	.05
94	Phil Hiatt	.05
95	Tim Pugh	.05
96	Randy Knorr	.05
97	Todd Jones	.05
98	Ryan Thompson	.05
99	Tim Mauser	.05
100	Kirby Puckett	.60
101	Mark Dewey	.05
102	B.J. Surhoff	.05
103	Sterling Hitchcock	.05
104	Alex Arias	.05
105	David Wells	.05
106	Daryl Boston	.05
107	Mike Stanton	.05
108	Gary Redus	.05
109a	Delino DeShields (Red "Expos, 2B.")	2.00
109b	Delino DeShields (Yellow "Expos, 2B.")	.05
110	Lee Smith	.05
111	Greg Litton	.05
112	Frank Rodriguez	.05
113	Russ Springer	.05
114	Mitch Williams	.05
115	Eric Karros	.05
116	Jeff Brantley	.05
117	Jack Voight	.05
118	Jason Bere	.05
119	Kevin Roberson	.05
120	Jimmy Key	.05
121	Reggie Jefferson	.05
122	Jeromy Burnitz	.05
123	Billy Brewer	.05
124	Willie Canate	.05
125	Greg Swindell	.05
126	Hal Morris	.05
127	Brad Ausmus	.05
128	George Tsamis	.05
129	Denny Neagle	.05
130	Pat Listach	.05
131	Steve Karsay	.05
132	Bret Barberie	.05
133	Mark Leiter	.05
134	Greg Colbrunn	.05
135	David Nied	.05
136	Dean Palmer	.05
137	Steve Avery	.05
138	Bill Haselman	.05
139	Tripp Cromer	.05
140	Frank Viola	.05
141	Rene Gonzales	.05
142	Curt Schilling	.25
143	Tim Wallach	.05
144	Bobby Munoz	.05
145	Brady Anderson	.05
146	Rod Beck	.05
147	Mike LaValliere	.05
148	Greg Hibbard	.05
149	Kenny Lofton	.05
150	Dwight Gooden	.05
151	Greg Gagne	.05
152	Ray McDavid	.05
153	Chris Donnels	.05
154	Dan Wilson	.05
155	Todd Stottlemyre	.05
156	David McCarty	.05
157	Paul Wagner	.05
158	Orlando Miller, Brandon Wilson, Derek Jeter, Mike Neal SS Prospects	1.00
159	Mike Fetters	.05
160	Scott Lydy	.05
161	Darrell Whitmore	.05
162	Bob MacDonald	.05
163	Vinny Castilla	.05
164	Denis Boucher	.05
165	Ivan Rodriguez	.40
166	Ron Gant	.05
167	Tim Davis	.05
168	Steve Dixon	.05
169	Scott Fletcher	.05
170	Terry Mulholland	.05
171	Greg Myers	.05
172	Brett Butler	.05
173	Bob Wickman	.05
174	Dave Martinez	.05
175	Fernando Valenzuela	.05
176	Craig Grebeck	.05
177	Shawn Boskie	.05
178	Albie Lopez	.05
179	Butch Huskey	.05
180	George Brett	.65
181	Juan Guzman	.05
182	Eric Anthony	.05
183	Bob Dibble	.05
184	Craig Shipley	.05
185	Kevin Tapani	.05
186	Marcus Moore	.05
187	Graeme Lloyd	.05
188	Mike Bordick	.05
189	Chris Hammond	.05

190 Cecil Fielder .05
191 Curtis Leskanic .05
192 Lou Frazier .05
193 Steve Dreyer .05
194 Javier Lopez .05
195 Edgar Martinez .05
196 Allen Watson .05
197 John Flaherty .05
198 Kurt Stillwell .05
199 Danny Jackson .05
200 Cal Ripken, Jr. 1.00
201 Mike Bell .05
202 Alan Benes **RC** .10
203 Matt Farner .05
204 Jeff Granger **RC** .05
205 Brooks Kieschnick **RC** .05
206 Jeremy Lee .05
207 Charles Peterson **RC** .05
208 Andy Rice .05
209 Billy Wagner **RC** .25
210 Kelly Wunsch .05
211 Tom Candiotti .05
212 Domingo Jean .05
213 John Burkett .05
214 George Bell .05
215 Dan Plesac .05
216 Manny Ramirez .60
217 Mike Maddux .05
218 Kevin McReynolds .05
219 Pat Borders .05
220 Doug Drabek .05
221 Larry Luebbers .05
222 Trevor Hoffman .05
223 Pat Meares .05
224 Danny Miceli .05
225 Greg Vaughn .05
226 Scott Hemond .05
227 Pat Rapp .05
228 Kirk Gibson .05
229 Lance Painter .05
230 Larry Walker .05
231 Benji Gil .05
232 Mark Wohlers .05
233 Rich Amaral .05
234 Erik Pappas .05
235 Scott Cooper .05
236 Mike Butcher .05
237 Curtis Pride, Shawn Green, Mark Sweeney, Eddie Davis OF Prospects .35
238 Kim Batiste .05
239 Paul Assenmacher .05
240 Will Clark .05
241 Jose Offerman .05
242 Todd Frohwirth .05
243 Tim Raines .05
244 Rick Wilkins .05
245 Bret Saberhagen .05
246 Thomas Howard .05
247 Stan Belinda .05
248 Rickey Henderson .50
249 Brian Williams .05
250 Barry Larkin .05
251 Jose Valentin .05
252 Lenny Webster .05
253 Blas Minor .05
254 Tim Teufel .05
255 Bobby Witt .05
256 Walt Weiss .05
257 Chad Kreuter .05
258 Roberto Mejia .05
259 Cliff Floyd .05
260 Julio Franco .05
261 Rafael Belliard .05
262 Marc Newfield .05
263 Gerald Perry .05
264 Ken Ryan .05
265 Chili Davis .05
266 Dave West .05
267 Royce Clayton .05
268 Pedro Martinez .50
269 Mark Hutton .05
270 Frank Thomas .50
271 Brad Pennington .05
272 Mike Harkey .05
273 Sandy Alomar .05
274 Dave Gallagher .05
275 Wally Joyner .05
276 Ricky Trlicek .05
277 Al Osuna .05
278 Calvin Reese .05
279 Kevin Higgins .05
280 Rick Aguilera .05
281 Orlando Merced .05
282 Mike Mohler .05
283 John Jaha .05
284 Robb Nen .05
285 Travis Fryman .05
286 Mark Thompson .05
287 Mike Lansing .05
288 Craig Lefferts .05
289 Damon Berryhill .05
290 Randy Johnson .50
291 Jeff Reed .05
292 Danny Darwin .05
293 J.T. Snow .05
294 Tyler Green .05
295 Chris Hoiles .05
296 Roger McDowell .05
297 Spike Owen .05
298 Salomon Torres .05
299 Wilson Alvarez .05
300 Ryne Sandberg .60
301 Derek Lilliquist .05
302 Howard Johnson .05
303 Greg Cadaret .05
304 Pat Hentgen .05
305 Craig Biggio .05
306 Scott Service .05
307 Melvin Nieves .05
308 Mike Trombley .05
309 Carlos Garcia .05
310 Robin Yount .50
311 Marcos Armas .05
312 Rich Rodriguez .05
313 Justin Thompson .05
314 Danny Sheaffer .05
315 Ken Hill .05
316 Chad Ogea, Duff Brumley, Terrell Wade, Chris Michalak **RC** P Propsects .10
317 Cris Carpenter .05
318 Jeff Blauser .05
319 Ted Power .05
320 Ozzie Smith .60
321 John Dopson .05
322 Chris Turner .05
323 Pete Incaviglia .05
324 Alan Mills .05
325 Jody Reed .05
326 Rich Monteleone .05
327 Mark Carreon .05
328 Donn Pall .05
329 Matt Walbeck .05
330 Charles Nagy .05
331 Jeff McKnight .05
332 Jose Lind .05
333 Mike Timlin .05
334 Doug Jones .05
335 Kevin Mitchell .05
336 Luis Lopez .05
337 Shane Mack .05
338 Randy Tomlin .05
339 Matt Mieske .05
340 Mark McGwire .85
341 Nigel Wilson .05
342 Danny Gladden .05
343 Mo Sanford .05
344 Sean Berry .05
345 Kevin Brown .05
346 Greg Olson .05
347 Dave Magadan .05
348 Rene Arocha .05
349 Carlos Quintana .05
350 Jim Abbott .05
351 Gary DiSarcina .05
352 Ben Rivera .05
353 Carlos Hernandez .05
354 Darren Lewis .05
355 Harold Reynolds .05
356 Scott Ruffcorn .05
357 Mark Gubicza .05
358 Paul Sorrento .05
359 Anthony Young .05
360 Mark Grace .05
361 Rob Butler .05
362 Kevin Bass .05
363 Eric Helfand .05
364 Derek Bell .05
365 Scott Erickson .05
366 Al Martin .05
367 Ricky Bones .05
368 Jeff Branson .05
369 Luis Ortiz, David Bell, Jason Giambi, George Arias **RC** 3B Prospects .30
370a Benny Santiago .05
370b Mark McLemore (Originally checklisted as #379.) .05
371 John Doherty .05
372 Joe Girardi .05
373 Tim Scott .05
374 Marvin Freeman .05
375 Deion Sanders .10
376 Roger Salkeld .05
377 Bernard Gilkey .05
378 Tony Fossas .05
379 (Not issued, see #370)
380 Darren Daulton .05
381 Chuck Finley .05
382 Mitch Webster .05
383 Gerald Williams .05
384 Frank Thomas, Fred McGriff/AS .30
385 Roberto Alomar, Robby Thompson/AS .05
386 Wade Boggs, Matt Williams/AS .35
387 Cal Ripken, Jr., Jeff Blauser/AS .50
388 Ken Griffey Jr., Len Dykstra/AS .40
389 Juan Gonzalez, Dave Justice/AS .10
390 Albert Belle, Barry Bonds/AS .45
391 Mike Stanley, Mike Piazza/AS .45
392 Jack McDowell, Greg Maddux/AS .35
393 Jimmy Key, Tom Glavine/AS .05
394 Jeff Montgomery, Randy Myers/AS .05
395 Checklist 1 .05
396 Checklist 2 .05
397 Tim Salmon (All-Star Rookie) .10
398 Todd Benzinger .05
399 Frank Castillo .05
400 Ken Griffey Jr. .75
401 John Kruk .05
402 Dave Telgheder .05
403 Gary Gaetti .05
404 Jim Edmonds .05
405 Don Slaught .05
406 Jose Oquendo .05
407 Bruce Ruffin .05
408 Phil Clark .05
409 Joe Klink .05
410 Lou Whitaker .05
411 Kevin Seitzer .05
412 Darrin Fletcher .05
413 Kenny Rogers .05
414 Bill Pecota .05
415 Dave Fleming .05
416 Luis Alicea .05
417 Paul Quantrill .05
418 Damion Easley .05
419 Wes Chamberlain .05
420 Harold Baines .05
421 Scott Radinsky .05
422 Rey Sanchez .05
423 Junior Ortiz .05
424 Jeff Kent .05
425 Brian McRae .05
426 Ed Sprague .05
427 Tom Edens .05
428 Willie Greene .05
429 Bryan Hickerson .05
430 Dave Winfield .50
431 Pedro Astacio .05
432 Mike Gallego .05
433 Dave Burba .05
434 Bob Walk .05
435 Darryl Hamilton .05
436 Vince Horsman .05
437 Bob Natal .05
438 Mike Henneman .05
439 Willie Blair .05
440 Denny Martinez .05
441 Dan Peltier .05
442 Tony Tarasco .05
443 John Cummings .05
444 Geronimo Pena .05
445 Aaron Sele .05
446 Stan Javier .05
447 Mike Williams .05
448 Greg Pirkl, Roberto Petagine, D.J. Boston, Shawn Wooten 1B Prospects .05
449 Jim Poole .05
450 Carlos Baerga .05
451 Bob Scanlan .05
452 Lance Johnson .05
453 Eric Hillman .05
454 Keith Miller .05
455 Dave Stewart .05
456 Pete Harnisch .05
457 Roberto Kelly .05
458 Tim Worrell .05
459 Pedro Munoz .05
460 Orel Hershiser .05
461 Randy Velarde .05
462 Trevor Wilson .05
463 Jerry Goff .05
464 Bill Wegman .05
465 Dennis Eckersley .40
466 Jeff Conine .05
467 Joe Boever .05
468 Dante Bichette .05
469 Jeff Shaw .05
470 Rafael Palmeiro .40
471 Phil Leftwich **RC** .05
472 Jay Buhner .05
473 Bob Tewksbury .05
474 Tim Naehring .05
475 Tom Glavine .25
476 Dave Hollins .05
477 Arthur Rhodes .05
478 Joey Cora .05
479 Mike Morgan .05
480 Albert Belle .05
481 John Franco .05
482 Hipolito Pichardo .05
483 Duane Ward .05
484 Luis Gonzalez .05
485 Joe Oliver .05
486 Wally Whitehurst .05
487 Mike Benjamin .05
488 Eric Davis .05
489 Scott Kamieniecki .05
490 Kent Hrbek .05
491 John Hope **RC** .05
492 Jesse Orosco .05
493 Troy Neel .05
494 Ryan Bowen .05
495 Mickey Tettleton .05
496 Chris Jones .05
497 John Wetteland .05
498 David Hulse .05
499 Greg Maddux .60
500 Bo Jackson .10
501 Donovan Osborne .05
502 Mike Greenwell .05
503 Steve Frey .05
504 Jim Eisenreich .05
505 Robby Thompson .05
506 Leo Gomez .05
507 Dave Staton .05
508 Wayne Kirby .05
509 Tim Bogar .05
510 David Cone .05
511 Devon White .05
512 Xavier Hernandez .05
513 Tim Costo .05
514 Gene Harris .05
515 Jack McDowell .05
516 Kevin Gross .05
517 Scott Leius .05
518 Lloyd McClendon .05
519 Alex Diaz **RC** .05
520 Wade Boggs .60
521 Bob Welch .05
522 Henry Cotto .05
523 Mike Moore .05
524 Tim Laker .05
525 Andres Galarraga .05
526 Jamie Moyer .05
527 Norberto Martin, Ruben Santana, Jason Hardtke, Chris Sexton 2B Prospects .05
528 Sid Bream .05
529 Erik Hanson .05
530 Ray Lankford .05
531 Rob Deer .05
532 Rod Correia .05
533 Roger Mason .05
534 Mike Devereaux .05
535 Jeff Montgomery .05
536 Dwight Smith .05
537 Jeremy Hernandez .05
538 Ellis Burks .05
539 Bobby Jones .05
540 Paul Molitor .50
541 Jeff Juden .05
542 Chris Sabo .05
543 Larry Casian .05
544 Jeff Gardner .05
545 Ramon Martinez .05
546 Paul O'Neill .05
547 Steve Hosey .05
548 Dave Nilsson .05
549 Ron Darling .05
550 Matt Williams .05
551 Jack Armstrong .05
552 Bill Krueger .05
553 Freddie Benavides .05
554 Jeff Fassero .05
555 Chuck Knoblauch .05
556 Guillermo Velasquez .05
557 Joel Johnston .05
558 Tom Lampkin .05
559 Todd Van Poppel .05
560 Gary Sheffield .30
561 Skeeter Barnes .05
562 Darren Holmes .05
563 John Vander Wal .05
564 Mike Ignasiak .05
565 Fred McGriff .05
566 Luis Polonia .05
567 Mike Perez .05
568 John Valentin .05
569 Mike Felder .05
570 Tommy Greene .05
571 David Segui .05
572 Roberto Hernandez .05
573 Steve Wilson .05
574 Willie McGee .05
575 Randy Myers .05
576 Darrin Jackson .05
577 Eric Plunk .05
578 Mike MacFarlane .05
579 Doug Brocail .05
580 Steve Finley .05
581 John Roper .05
582 Danny Cox .05
583 Chip Hale .05
584 Scott Bullett .05
585 Kevin Reimer .05
586 Brent Gates .05
587 Matt Turner .05
588 Rich Rowland .05
589 Kent Bottenfield .05
590 Marquis Grissom .05
591 Doug Strange .05
592 Jay Howell .05
593 Omar Vizquel .05
594 Rheal Cormier .05
595 Andre Dawson .25
596 Hilly Hathaway .05
597 Todd Pratt .05
598 Mike Mussina .30
599 Alex Fernandez .05
600 Don Mattingly .65
601 Frank Thomas .25
602 Ryne Sandberg .30
603 Wade Boggs .30
604 Cal Ripken, Jr. .50
605 Barry Bonds .50
606 Ken Griffey Jr. .40
607 Kirby Puckett .35
608 Darren Daulton .05
609 Paul Molitor .25
610 Terry Steinbach .05
611 Todd Worrell .05
612 Jim Thome .40
613 Chuck McElroy .05
614 John Habyan .05
615 Sid Fernandez .05
616 Eddie Zambrano, Glenn Murray, Chad Mottola, Jermaine Allensworth **RC** OF Prospects .05
617 Steve Bedrosian .05
618 Rob Ducey .05
619 Tom Browning .05
620 Tony Gwynn .60
621 Carl Willis .05
622 Kevin Young .05

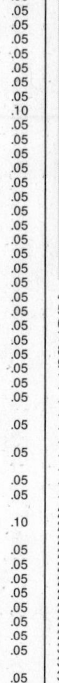

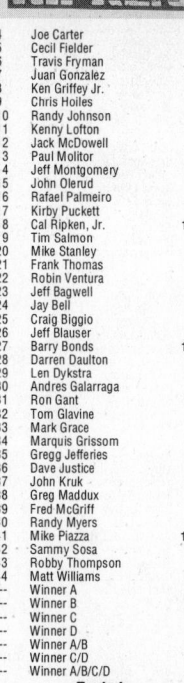

623 Rafael Novoa .05
624 Jerry Browne .05
625 Charlie Hough .05
626 Chris Gomez .05
627 Steve Reed .05
628 Kirk Rueter .05
629 Matt Whiteside .05
630 Dave Justice .05
631 Brad Holman .05
632 Brian Jordan .05
633 Scott Bankhead .05
634 Torey Lovullo .05
635 Len Dykstra .05
636 Ben McDonald .05
637 Steve Howe .05
638 Jose Vizcaino .05
639 Bill Swift .05
640 Darryl Strawberry .05
641 Steve Farr .05
642 Tom Kramer .05
643 Joe Orsulak .05
644 Tom Henke .05
645 Joe Carter .05
646 Ken Caminiti .05
647 Reggie Sanders .05
648 Andy Ashby .05
649 Derek Parks .05
650 Andy Van Slyke .05
651 Juan Bell .05
652 Roger Smithberg .05
653 Chuck Carr .05
654 Bill Gullickson .05
655 Charlie Hayes .05
656 Chris Nabholz .05
657 Karl Rhodes .05
658 Pete Smith .05
659 Bret Boone .05
660 Gregg Jefferies .05
661 Bob Zupcic .05
662 Steve Sax .05
663 Mariano Duncan .05
664 Jeff Tackett .05
665 Mark Langston .05
666 Steve Buechele .05
667 Candy Maldonado .05
668 Woody Williams .05
669 Tim Wakefield .05
670 Danny Tartabull .05
671 Charlie O'Brien .05
672 Felix Jose .05
673 Bobby Ayala .05
674 Scott Servais .05
675 Roberto Alomar .15
676 Pedro Martinez .05
677 Eddie Guardado .05
678 Mark Lewis .05
679 Jaime Navarro .05
680 Ruben Sierra .05
681 Rick Renteria .05
682 Storm Davis .05
683 Cory Snyder .05
684 Ron Karkovice .05
685 Juan Gonzalez .25
686 Chris Howard, Carlos Delgado, Jason Kendall, Paul Bako C Prospects .40
687 John Smoltz .05
688 Brian Dorsett .05
689 Omar Olivares .05
690 Mo Vaughn .05
691 Joe Grahe .05
692 Mickey Morandini .05
693 Tino Martinez .05
694 Brian Barnes .05
695 Mike Stanley .05
696 Mark Clark .05
697 Dave Hansen .05
698 Willie Wilson .05
699 Pete Schourek .05
700 Barry Bonds 1.00
701 Kevin Appier .05
702 Tony Fernandez .05
703 Darryl Kile .05
704 Archi Cianfrocco .05
705 Jose Rijo .05
706 Brian Harper .05
707 Zane Smith .05
708 Dave Henderson .05
709 Angel Miranda .05
710 Orestes Destrade .05
711 Greg Gohr .05
712 Eric Young .05
713 Todd Williams, Ron Watson, Kirk Bullinger, Mike Welch P Prospects .05
714 Tim Spehr .05
715 Hank Aaron (20th Anniversary #715) .50
716 Nate Minchey .05
717 Mike Blowers .05
718 Kent Mercker .05
719 Tom Pagnozzi .05
720 Roger Clemens .65
721 Eduardo Perez .05
722 Milt Thompson .05
723 Gregg Olson .05
724 Kirk McCaskill .05
725 Sammy Sosa .60
726 Alvaro Espinoza .05
727 Henry Rodriguez .05
728 Jim Leyritz .05
729 Steve Scarsone .05
730 Bobby Bonilla .05
731 Chris Gwynn .05
732 Al Leiter .05
733 Bip Roberts .05
734 Mark Portugal .05
735 Terry Pendleton .05
736 Dave Valle .05
737 Paul Kilgus .05
738 Greg Harris .05
739 Jon Ratliff **RC** .05
740 Kirk Presley **RC** .05
741 Josue Estrada **RC** .05
742 Wayne Gomes **RC** .10
743 Pat Watkins **RC** .05
744 Jamey Wright **RC** .05
745 Jay Powell **RC** .05
746 Ryan McGuire **RC** .05
747 Marc Barcelo **RC** .05
748 Sloan Smith **RC** .05
749 John Wasdin **RC** .05
750 Marc Valdes .05
751 Dan Ehler **RC** .05
752 Andre King **RC** .05
753 Greg Keagle **RC** .05
754 Jason Myers **RC** .05
755 Dax Winslett **RC** .05
756 Casey Whitten **RC** .05
757 Tony Fuduric **RC** .05
758 Greg Norton **RC** .05
759 Jeff D'Amico **RC** .05
760 Ryan Hancock **RC** .05
761 David Cooper **RC** .05
762 Kevin Orie **RC** .05
763 John O'Donoghue, Mike Oquist .05
764 Cory Bailey, Scott Hatteberg .05
765 Mark Holzemer, Paul Swingle .05
766 James Baldwin, Rod Bolton .05
767 Jerry DiPoto, Julian Tavarez **RC** .10
768 Danny Bautista, Sean Bergman .05
769 Bob Hamelin, Joe Vitiello .05
770 Mark Kiefer, Troy O'Leary .05
771 Denny Hocking, Oscar Munoz .05
772 Russ Davis, Brien Taylor .05
773 Kurt Abbott, Miguel Jimenez .05
774 Kevin King, Eric Plantenberg .05
775 Jon Shave, Desi Wilson .05
776 Domingo Cedeno, Paul Spoljaric .05
777 Chipper Jones, Ryan Klesko .75
778 Steve Trachsel, Turk Wendell .05
779 Johnny Ruffin, Jerry Spradlin .05
780 Jason Bates, John Burke .05
781 Carl Everett, Dave Weathers .05
782 Gary Mota, James Mouton .05
783 Raul Mondesi, Ben Van Ryn .05
784 Gabe White, Rondell White .05
785 Brook Fordyce, Bill Pulsipher .05
786 Kevin Foster, Gene Schall .05
787 Rich Aude, Midre Cummings .05
788 Brian Barber, Richard Batchelor .05
789 Brian Johnson, Scott Sanders .05
790 Rikkert Faneyte, J.R. Phillips .05
791 Checklist 3 .05
792 Checklist 4 .05

1994 Topps Gold

NM/M

Complete Set (792): 50.00
Common Player: .15
(Star cards valued at 2X corresponding cards in regular Topps issue.)

Black Gold

NM/M

Complete Set (44): 10.00
Complete Series 1 (22): 6.00
Complete Series 2 (22): 4.00
Common Player: .10
1 Roberto Alomar .20
2 Carlos Baerga .10
3 Albert Belle .10

4 Joe Carter .10
5 Cecil Fielder .10
6 Travis Fryman .10
7 Juan Gonzalez .25
8 Ken Griffey Jr. .75
9 Chris Hoiles .10
10 Randy Johnson .45
11 Kenny Lofton .10
12 Jack McDowell .10
13 Paul Molitor .45
14 Jeff Montgomery .10
15 John Olerud .10
16 Rafael Palmeiro .45
17 Kirby Puckett .60
18 Cal Ripken, Jr. 1.50
19 Tim Salmon .10
20 Mike Stanley .10
21 Frank Thomas .50
22 Robin Ventura .10
23 Jeff Bagwell .45
24 Jay Bell .10
25 Craig Biggio .10
26 Jeff Blauser .10
27 Barry Bonds 1.50
28 Darren Daulton .10
29 Len Dykstra .10
30 Andres Galarraga .10
31 Ron Gant .10
32 Tom Glavine .10
33 Mark Grace .10
34 Marquis Grissom .10
35 Gregg Jefferies .10
36 Dave Justice .10
37 John Kruk .10
38 Greg Maddux .60
39 Fred McGriff .10
40 Randy Myers .10
41 Mike Piazza 1.00
42 Sammy Sosa .60
43 Robby Thompson .10
44 Matt Williams .10
--- Winner A .50
--- Winner B .50
--- Winner C .50
--- Winner D .50
--- Winner A/B .60
--- Winner C/D .60
--- Winner A/B/C/D .75

Traded

NM/M

Complete Set (140): 25.00
Common Player: .05
1 Paul Wilson .05
2 Bill Taylor .05
3 Dan Wilson .05
4 Mark Smith .05
5 Toby Borland .05
6 Dave Clark .05
7 Denny Martinez .05
8 Dave Gallagher .05
9 Josias Manzanillo .05
10 Brian Anderson .05
11 Damon Berryhill .05
12 Alex Cole .05
13 Jacob Shumate .05
14 Oddibe McDowell .05
15 Willie Banks .05
16 Jerry Browne .05
17 Donnie Elliott .05
18 Ellis Burks .05
19 Chuck McElroy .05
20 Luis Polonia .05
21 Brian Harper .05
22 Mark Portugal .05
23 Dave Henderson .05
24 Mark Acre .05
25 Julio Franco .05
26 Darren Hall .05
27 Eric Anthony .05
28 Sid Fernandez .05
29 Rusty Greer **RC** .25
30 Riccardo Ingram .05
31 Gabe White .05
32 Tim Belcher .05
33 Terrence Long **RC** .50
34 Mark Dalesandro **RC** .05
35 Mike Kelly .05
36 Jack Morris .05
37 Jeff Brantley .05
38 Larry Barnes **RC** .05
39 Brian Hunter .05
40 Otis Nixon .05
41 Bret Wagner .05
42 Pedro Martinez, Delino DeShields Anatomy of a Trade .25
43 Heathcliff Slocumb .05
44 Ben Grieve **RC** .25
45 John Hudek .05
46 Shawon Dunston .05
47 Greg Colbrunn .05
48 Joey Hamilton .05
49 Marvin Freeman .05
50 Terry Mulholland .05
51 Keith Mitchell .05
52 Dwight Smith .05
53 Shawn Boskie .05
54 Kevin Witt **RC** .05
55 Ron Gant .05
56 Trenidad Hubbard, Jason Schmidt, Larry Sutton, Stephen Larkin 1994 Prospects 3.00
57 Jody Reed .05
58 Rick Helling .05
59 John Powell .05
60 Eddie Murray .60
61 Joe Hall .05
62 Jorge Fabregas .05
63 Mike Mordecai .05
64 Ed Vosberg .05
65 Rickey Henderson .60
66 Tim Grieve .05
67 Jon Lieber .05
68 Chris Howard .05
69 Matt Walbeck .05
70 Chan Ho Park .15
71 Bryan Eversgerd .05
72 John Dettmer .05
73 Erik Hanson .05
74 Mike Thurman .05
75 Bobby Ayala .05
76 Rafael Palmeiro .50
77 Bret Boone .05
78 Paul Shuey .05
79 Kevin Foster .05
80 Dave Magadan .05
81 Bip Roberts .05
82 Howard Johnson .05
83 Xavier Hernandez .05
84 Ross Powell .05
85 Doug Million **RC** .05
86 Geronimo Berroa .05
87 Mark Farris **RC** .05
88 Butch Henry .05
89 Junior Felix .05
90 Bo Jackson .25
91 Hector Carrasco .05
92 Charlie O'Brien .05
93 Omar Vizquel .05
94 David Segui .05
95 Dustin Hermanson .05
96 Gar Finnvold .05
97 Dave Stevens .05
98 Corey Pointer .05
99 Felix Fermin .05
100 Lee Smith .05
101 Reid Ryan .15
102 Bobby Munoz .05
103 Deion Sanders, Roberto Kelly Anatomy of a Trade .05
104 Turner Ward .05
105 William Van Landingham .05
106 Vince Coleman .05
107 Stan Javier .05
108 Darrin Jackson .05
109 C.J. Nitkowski .05
110 Anthony Young .05
111 Kurt Miller .05
112 Paul Konerko **RC** 15.00
113 Walt Weiss .05
114 Daryl Boston .05
115 Will Clark .05
116 Matt Smith **RC** .05
117 Mark Leiter .05
118 Gregg Olson .05
119 Tony Pena .05
120 Jose Vizcaino .05
121 Rick White .05
122 Rich Rowland .05
123 Jeff Reboulet .05
124 Greg Hibbard .05

125 Chris Sabo .05
126 Doug Jones .05
127 Tony Fernandez .05
128 Carlos Reyes .05
129 Kevin Brown .05
130 Ryne Sandberg Commemorative 1.00
131 Ryne Sandberg Commemorative 1.00
132 Checklist 1-132 .05

Traded Finest Inserts

NM/M

Complete Set (8): 6.00
Common Player: .25
1 Greg Maddux 1.50
2 Mike Piazza 2.00
3 Matt Williams .25
4 Raul Mondesi .25
5 Ken Griffey Jr. 2.00
6 Kenny Lofton .25
7 Frank Thomas 1.25
8 Manny Ramirez 1.00

1995 Topps

NM/M

Unopened Hobby Set (677): 100.00
Unopened Retail Set (684): 75.00
Unopened Retail Set (677): 85.00
Complete Set (660): 45.00
Common Player: .05
Series 1 or 2 Pack (15): 1.25
Series 1 or 2 Wax Box (36): 25.00
1 Frank Thomas .75
2 Mickey Morandini .05
3a Babe Ruth (100th Birthday, no gold "Topps" logo) 2.00
3b Babe Ruth (100th Birthday, gold "Topps" logo) 2.00
4 Scott Cooper .05
5 David Cone .05
6 Jacob Shumate .05
7 Trevor Hoffman .05
8 Shane Mack .05
9 Delino DeShields .05
10 Matt Williams .05
11 Sammy Sosa 1.00
12 Gary DiSarcina .05
13 Kenny Rogers .05
14 Jose Vizcaino .05
15 Lou Whitaker .05
16 Ron Darling .05
17 Dave Nilsson .05
18 Chris Hammond .05
19 Sid Bream .05
20 Denny Martinez .05
21 Orlando Merced .05
22 John Wetteland .05
23 Mike Devereaux .05
24 Rene Arocha .05
25 Jay Buhner .05
26 Darren Holmes .05
27 Hal Morris .05
28 Brian Buchanan **RC** .10
29 Keith Miller .05
30 Paul Molitor .75
31 Dave West .05
32 Tony Tarasco .05
33 Scott Sanders .05
34 Eddie Zambrano .05
35 Ricky Bones .05
36 John Valentin .05
37 Kevin Tapani .05
38 Tim Wallach .05
39 Darren Lewis .05
40 Travis Fryman .05
41 Mark Leiter .05
42 Jose Bautista .05
43 Pete Smith .05
44 Bret Barberie .05
45 Dennis Eckersley .65
46 Ken Hill .05
47 Chad Ogea .05
48 Pete Harnisch .05
49 James Baldwin .05
50 Mike Mussina .45
51 Al Martin .05
52 Mark Thompson .05
53 Matt Smith .05
54 Joey Hamilton .05
55 Edgar Martinez .05
56 John Smiley .05
57 Rey Sanchez .05
58 Mike Timlin .05
59 Ricky Bottalico .05
60 Jim Abbott .05
61 Mike Kelly .05
62 Brian Jordan .05
63 Ken Ryan .05
64 Matt Mieske .05
65 Rick Aguilera .05
66 Ismael Valdes .05
67 Royce Clayton .05
68 Junior Felix .05
69 Harold Reynolds .05
70 Juan Gonzalez .35
71 Kelly Stinnett .05
72 Carlos Reyes .05
73 Dave Weathers .05
74 Mel Rojas .05
75 Doug Drabek .05
76 Charles Nagy .05
77 Tim Raines .05
78 Midre Cummings .05
79 Gene Schall, Scott Talanoa, Harold Williams, Ray Brown **RC** 1B Prospects .05
80 Rafael Palmeiro .65
81 Charlie Hayes .05
82 Ray Lankford .05
83 Tim Davis .05
84 C.J. Nitkowski **RC** .05
85 Andy Ashby .05
86 Gerald Williams .05
87 Terry Shumpert .05
88 Heathcliff Slocumb .05
89 Domingo Cedeno .05
90 Mark Grace .05
91 Brad Woodall **RC** .10
92 Gar Finnvold .05
93 Jaime Navarro .05
94 Carlos Hernandez .05
95 Mark Langston .05
96 Chuck Carr .05
97 Mike Gardiner .05
98 David McCarty .05
99 Cris Carpenter .05
100 Barry Bonds 2.00
101 David Segui .05
102 Scott Brosius .05
103 Mariano Duncan .05
104 Kenny Lofton .05
105 Ken Caminiti .05
106 Darrin Jackson .05
107 Jim Poole .05
108 Wil Cordero .05
109 Danny Miceli .05
110 Walt Weiss .05
111 Tom Pagnozzi .05
112 Terrence Long .05
113 Bret Boone .05
114 Daryl Boston .05
115 Wally Joyner .05
116 Rob Butler .05
117 Rafael Belliard .05
118 Luis Lopez .05
119 Tony Fossas .05
120 Len Dykstra .05
121 Mike Morgan .05
122 Denny Hocking .05
123 Kevin Gross .05
124 Todd Benzinger .05
125 John Doherty .05
126 Eduardo Perez .05
127 Dan Smith .05
128 Joe Orsulak .05
129 Brent Gates .05
130 Jeff Conine .05
131 Doug Henry .05
132 Paul Sorrento .05
133 Mike Hampton .05
134 Tim Spehr .05
135 Julio Franco .05
136 Mike Dyer .05
137 Chris Sabo .05
138 Rheal Cormier .05
139 Paul Konerko .25
140 Dante Bichette .05
141 Chuck McElroy .05
142 Mike Stanley .05
143 Bob Hamelin .05
144 Tommy Greene .05
145 John Smoltz .05
146 Ed Sprague .05
147 Ray McDavid .05
148 Otis Nixon .05
149 Turk Wendell .05
150 Chris James .05
151 Derek Parks .05
152 Jose Offerman .05
153 Tony Clark .05
154 Chad Curtis .05
155 Mark Portugal .05
156 Bill Pulsipher .05
157 Troy Neel .05
158 Dave Winfield .75
159 Bill Wegman .05
160 Benny Santiago .05
161 Jose Mesa .05
162 Luis Gonzalez .05
163 Alex Fernandez .05
164 Freddie Benavides .05
165 Ben McDonald .05
166 Blas Minor .05
167 Bret Wagner .05
168 Mac Suzuki .05
169 Roberto Mejia .05
170 Wade Boggs 1.00
171 Calvin Reese .05
172 Hipolito Pichardo .05
173 Kim Batiste .05
174 Darren Hall .05
175 Tom Glavine .25
176 Phil Plantier .05
177 Chris Howard .05
178 Karl Rhodes .05
179 LaTroy Hawkins .05
180 Raul Mondesi .05
181 Jeff Reed .05
182 Milt Cuyler .05
183 Jim Edmonds .05
184 Hector Fajardo .05
185 Jeff Kent .05
186 Wilson Alvarez .05
187 Geronimo Berroa .05
188 Billy Spiers .05
189 Derek Lilliquist .05
190 Craig Biggio .05
191 Roberto Hernandez .05
192 Bob Natal .05
193 Bobby Ayala .05
194 Travis Miller **RC** .10
195 Bob Tewksbury .05
196 Rondell White .05
197 Steve Cooke .05
198 Jeff Branson .05
199 Derek Jeter 2.00
200 Tim Salmon .05
201 Steve Frey .05
202 Kent Mercker .05
203 Randy Johnson .75
204 Todd Worrell .05
205 Mo Vaughn .05
206 Howard Johnson .05
207 John Wasdin .05
208 Eddie Williams .05
209 Tim Belcher .05
210 Jeff Montgomery .05
211 Kirt Manwaring .05
212 Ben Grieve .05
213 Pat Hentgen .05
214 Shawon Dunston .05
215 Mike Greenwell .05
216 Alex Diaz .05
217 Pat Mahomes .05
218 Dave Hanson .05
219 Kevin Rogers .05
220 Cecil Fielder .05
221 Andrew Lorraine .05
222 Jack Armstrong .05
223 Todd Hundley .05
224 Mark Acre .05
225 Darrell Whitmore .05
226 Randy Milligan .05
227 Wayne Kirby .05
228 Darryl Kile .05
229 Bob Zupcic .05
230 Jay Bell .05
231 Dustin Hermanson .05
232 Harold Baines .05
233 Alan Benes .05
234 Felix Fermin .05
235 Ellis Burks .05
236 Jeff Brantley .05
237 Brian Hunter, Jose Malave, Shane Pullen, Karim Garcia **RC** OF Prospects .40
238 Matt Nokes .05
239 Ben Rivera .05
240 Joe Carter .05
241 Jeff Granger .05
242 Terry Pendleton .05
243 Melvin Nieves .05
244 Frank Rodriguez .05
245 Darryl Hamilton .05
246 Brooks Kieschnick .05
247 Todd Hollandsworth .05
248 Joe Rosselli .05
249 Bill Gullickson .05
250 Chuck Knoblauch .05
251 Kurt Miller .05
252 Bobby Jones .05
253 Lance Blankenship .05
254 Matt Whiteside .05
255 Darrin Fletcher .05
256 Eric Plunk .05
257 Shane Reynolds .05
258 Norberto Martin .05
259 Mike Thurman .05
260 Andy Van Slyke .05
261 Dwight Smith .05
262 Allen Watson .05
263 Dan Wilson .05
264 Brent Mayne .05
265 Bip Roberts .05
266 Sterling Hitchcock .05
267 Alex Gonzalez .05
268 Greg Harris .05
269 Ricky Jordan .05
270 Johnny Ruffin .05
271 Mike Stanton .05
272 Rich Rowland .05
273 Steve Trachsel .05
274 Pedro Munoz .05
275 Ramon Martinez .05
276 Dave Henderson .05
277 Chris Gomez .05
278 Joe Grahe .05
279 Rusty Greer .05
280 John Franco .05
281 Mike Bordick .05
282 Jeff D'Amico .05
283 Dave Magadan .05
284 Tony Pena .05
285 Greg Swindell .05
286 Doug Million .05
287 Gabe White .05
288 Trey Beamon .05
289 Arthur Rhodes .05
290 Juan Guzman .05
291 Jose Oquendo .05
292 Willie Blair .05
293 Eddie Taubensee .05
294 Steve Howe .05
295 Greg Maddux 1.00
296 Mike MacFarlane .05
297 Curt Schilling .25
298 Phil Clark .05
299 Woody Williams .05
300 Jose Canseco .40
301 Aaron Sele .05
302 Carl Willis .05
303 Steve Buechele .05
304 Dave Burba .05
305 Orel Hershiser .05
306 Damion Easley .05
307 Mike Henneman .05
308 Josias Manzanillo .05
309 Kevin Seitzer .05
310 Ruben Sierra .05
311 Bryan Harvey .05
312 Jim Thome .45
313 Ramon Castro **RC** .05
314 Lance Johnson .05
315 Marquis Grissom .05
316 Terrell Wade, Juan Acevedo, Matt Arrandale, Eddie Priest **RC** SP Prospects .05
317 Paul Wagner .05
318 Jamie Moyer .05
319 Todd Zeile .05
320 Chris Bosio .05
321 Steve Reed .05
322 Erik Hanson .05
323 Luis Polonia .05
324 Ryan Klesko .05
325 Kevin Appier .05
326 Jim Eisenreich .05
327 Randy Knorr .05
328 Craig Shipley .05
329 Tim Naehring .05
330 Randy Myers .05
331 Alex Cole .05
332 Jim Gott .05
333 Mike Jackson .05
334 John Flaherty .05
335 Chili Davis .05
336 Benji Gil .05
337a Jason Jacome (No Diamond Vision logo on back photo.) .25
337b Jason Jacome (Diamond Vision logo on back photo.) .05
338 Stan Javier .05
339 Mike Fetters .05
340 Rick Renteria .05
341 Kevin Witt .05
342 Scott Servais .05
343 Craig Grebeck .05
344 Kirk Rueter .05
345 Don Slaught .05
346 Armando Benitez **RC** .15
347 Ozzie Smith 1.00
348 Mike Blowers .05
349 Armando Reynoso .05
350 Barry Larkin .05
351 Mike Williams .05
352 Scott Kamieniecki .05
353 Gary Gaetti .05
354 Todd Stottlemyre .05
355 Fred McGriff .05
356 Tim Mauser .05
357 Chris Gwynn .05
358 Frank Castillo .05
359 Jeff Reboulet .05
360 Roger Clemens 1.00
361 Mark Carreon .05
362 Chad Kreuter .05
363 Mark Farris .05
364 Bob Welch .05
365 Dean Palmer .05
366 Jeromy Burnitz .05
367 B.J. Surhoff .05

368 Mike Butcher .05
369 Brad Clontz, Steve Phoenix, Scott Gentile, Bucky Buckles RP Prospects .05
370 Eddie Murray .75
371 Orlando Miller .05
372 Ron Karkovice .05
373 Richie Lewis .05
374 Lenny Webster .05
375 Jeff Tackett .05
376 Tom Urbani .05
377 Tino Martinez .05
378 Mark Dewey .05
379 Charlie O'Brien .05
380 Terry Mulholland .05
381 Thomas Howard .05
382 Chris Haney .05
383 Billy Hatcher .05
384 Jeff Bagwell, Frank Thomas/AS .45
385 Bret Boone, Carlos Baerga/AS .05
386 Matt Williams, Wade Boggs/AS .30
387 Wil Cordero, Cal Ripken Jr./AS 1.00
388 Barry Bonds, Ken Griffey Jr./AS 1.00
389 Tony Gwynn, Albert Belle/AS .50
390 Dante Bichette, Kirby Puckett/AS .50
391 Mike Piazza, Mike Stanley/AS .75
392 Greg Maddux, David Cone/AS .50
393 Danny Jackson, Jimmy Key/AS .05
394 John Franco, Lee Smith/AS .05
395 Checklist 1-198 .05
396 Checklist 199-396 .05
397 Ken Griffey Jr. 1.25
398 Rick Heiserman **RC** .05
399 Don Mattingly 1.00
400 Henry Rodriguez .05
401 Lenny Harris .05
402 Ryan Thompson .05
403 Darren Oliver .05
404 Omar Vizquel .05
405 Jeff Bagwell .75
406 Doug Webb **RC** .05
407 Todd Van Poppel .05
408 Leo Gomez .05
409 Mark Whiten .05
410 Pedro Martinez .05
411 Reggie Sanders .05
412 Kevin Foster .05
413 Danny Tartabull .05
414 Jeff Blauser .05
415 Mike Magnante .05
416 Tom Candiotti .05
417 Rod Beck .05
418 Jody Reed .05
419 Vince Coleman .05
420 Danny Jackson .05
421 Ryan Nye **RC** .05
422 Larry Walker .05
423 Russ Johnson .05
424 Pat Borders .05
425 Lee Smith .05
426 Paul O'Neill .05
427 Devon White .05
428 Jim Bullinger .05
429 Greg Hansell, Brian Sackinsky, Carey Paige, Rob Welch/SP Prospects .05
430 Steve Avery .05
431 Tony Gwynn 1.00
432 Pat Meares .05
433 Bill Swift .05
434 David Wells .05
435 John Briscoe .05
436 Roger Pavlik .05
437 Jayson Peterson **RC** .05
438 Roberto Alomar .15
439 Billy Brewer .05
440 Gary Sheffield .40
441 Lou Frazier .05
442 Terry Steinbach .05
443 Jay Payton **RC** .25
444 Jason Bere .05
445 Denny Neagle .05
446 Andres Galarraga .05
447 Hector Carrasco .05
448 Bill Risley .05
449 Andy Benes .05
450 Jim Leyritz .05
451 Jose Oliva .05
452 Greg Vaughn .05
453 Rich Monteleone .05
454 Tony Eusebio .05
455 Chuck Finley .05
456 Kevin Brown .05
457 Joe Boever .05
458 Bobby Munoz .05
459 Bret Saberhagen .05
460 Kurt Abbott .05
461 Bobby Witt .05
462 Cliff Floyd .05
463 Mark Clark .05
464 Andujar Cedeno .05
465 Marvin Freeman .05
466 Mike Piazza 1.25
467 Willie Greene .05
468 Pat Kelly .05
469 Carlos Delgado .40
470 Willie Banks .05
471 Matt Walbeck .05
472 Mark McGwire 1.50
473 McKay Christensen .05
474 Alan Trammell .05
475 Tom Gordon .05
476 Greg Colbrunn .05
477 Darren Daulton .05
478 Albie Lopez .05
479 Robin Ventura .05
480 Eddie Perez, Jason Kendall, Einar Diaz, Bret Hemphill C Prospects .20
481 Bryan Eversgerd .05
482 Dave Fleming .05
483 Scott Livingstone .05
484 Pete Schourek .05
485 Bernie Williams .05
486 Mark Lemke .05
487 Eric Karros .05
488 Scott Ruffcorn .05
489 Billy Ashley .05
490 Rico Brogna .05
491 John Burkett .05
492 Cade Gaspar **RC** .05
493 Jorge Fabregas .05
494 Greg Gagne .05
495 Doug Jones .05
496 Troy O'Leary .05
497 Pat Rapp .05
498 Butch Henry .05
499 John Olerud .05
500 John Hudek .05
501 Jeff King .05
502 Bobby Bonilla .05
503 Albert Belle .05
504 Rick Wilkins .05
505 John Jaha .05
506 Nigel Wilson .05
507 Sid Fernandez .05
508 Deion Sanders .05
509 Gil Heredia .05
510 Scott Elarton **RC** .10
511 Melido Perez .05
512 Greg McMichael .05
513 Rusty Meacham .05
514 Shawn Green .35
515 Carlos Garcia .05
516 Dave Stevens .05
517 Eric Young .05
518 Omar Daal .05
519 Kirk Gibson .05
520 Spike Owen .05
521 Jacob Cruz **RC** .05
522 Sandy Alomar .05
523 Steve Bedrosian .05
524 Ricky Gutierrez .05
525 Dave Veres .05
526 Gregg Jefferies .05
527 Jose Valentin .05
528 Robb Nen .05
529 Jose Rijo .05
530 Sean Berry .05
531 Mike Gallego .05
532 Roberto Kelly .05
533 Kevin Stocker .05
534 Kirby Puckett 1.00
535 Chipper Jones 1.00
536 Russ Davis .05
537 Jon Lieber .05
538 Trey Moore **RC** .05
539 Joe Girardi .05
540 Quilvio Veras, Arquimedez Pozo, Miguel Cairo, Jason Camilli 2B Prospects .05
541 Tony Phillips .05
542 Brian Anderson .05
543 Ivan Rodriguez .65
544 Jeff Cirillo .05
545 Joey Cora .05
546 Chris Hoiles .05
547 Bernard Gilkey .05
548 Mike Lansing .05
549 Jimmy Key .05
550 Mark Wohlers .05
551 Chris Clemons **RC** .05
552 Vinny Castilla .05
553 Mark Guthrie .05
554 Mike Lieberthal .05
555 Tommy Davis **RC** .05
556 Robby Thompson .05
557 Danny Bautista .05
558 Will Clark .05
559 Rickey Henderson .75
560 Todd Jones .05
561 Jack McDowell .05
562 Carlos Rodriguez .05
563 Mark Eichhorn .05
564 Jeff Nelson .05
565 Eric Anthony .05
566 Randy Velarde .05
567 Javy Lopez .05
568 Kevin Mitchell .05
569 Steve Karsay .05
570 Brian Meadows **RC** .10
571 Rey Ordonez, Mike Metcalfe, Ray Holbert, Kevin Orie SS Prospects .40
572 John Kruk .05
573 Scott Leius .05
574 John Patterson .05
575 Kevin Brown .05
576 Mike Moore .05
577 Manny Ramirez .75
578 Jose Lind .05
579 Derrick May .05
580 Cal Eldred .05
581 David Bell, Joel Chelmis, Lino Diaz, Aaron Boone **RC** 3B Prospects .15
582 J.T. Snow .05
583 Luis Sojo .05
584 Moises Alou .05
585 Dave Clark .05
586 Dave Hollins .05
587 Nomar Garciaparra 2.00
588 Cal Ripken Jr. 2.00
589 Pedro Astacio .05
590 J.R. Phillips .05
591 Jeff Frye .05
592 Bo Jackson .10
593 Steve Ontiveros .05
594 David Nied .05
595 Brad Ausmus .05
596 Carlos Baerga .05
597 James Mouton .05
598 Ozzie Guillen .05
599 Ozzie Timmons, Curtis Goodwin, Johnny Damon, Jeff Abbott **RC** OF Prospects .25
600 Yorkis Perez .05
601 Rich Rodriguez .05
602 Mark McLemore .05
603 Jeff Fassero .05
604 John Roper .05
605 Mark Johnson **RC** .10
606 Wes Chamberlain .05
607 Felix Jose .05
608 Tony Longmire .05
609 Duane Ward .05
610 Brett Butler .05
611 William Van Landingham .05
612 Mickey Tettleton .05
613 Brady Anderson .05
614 Reggie Jefferson .05
615 Mike Kingery .05
616 Derek Bell .05
617 Scott Erickson .05
618 Bob Wickman .05
619 Phil Leftwich .05
620 Dave Justice .05
621 Paul Wilson .05
622 Pedro Martinez .75
623 Terry Mathews .05
624 Brian McRae .05
625 Bruce Ruffin .05
626 Steve Finley .05
627 Ron Gant .05
628 Rafael Bournigal .05
629 Darryl Strawberry .05
630 Luis Alicea .05
631 Mark Smith, Scott Klingenbeck .05
632 Cory Bailey, Scott Hatteberg .05
633 Todd Greene, Troy Percival .05
634 Rod Bolton, Olmedo Saenz .05
635 Herb Perry, Steve Kline .05
636 Sean Bergman, Shannon Penn .05
637 Joe Vitiello, Joe Randa .05
638 Jose Mercedes, Duane Singleton .05
639 Marty Cordova, Marc Barcelo .10
640 Ruben Rivera, Andy Pettitte .10
641 Willie Adams, Scott Spiezio .05
642 Eddie Diaz, Desi Relaford .05
643 Jon Shave, Terrell Lowery .05
644 Paul Spoljaric, Angel Martinez .05
645 Damon Hollins, Tony Graffanino .05
646 Darron Cox, Doug Glanville .05
647 Tim Belk, Pat Watkins .05
648 Rod Pedraza, Phil Schneider .05
649 Marc Valdes, Vic Darensbourg .05
650 Rick Huisman, Roberto Petagine .05
651 Ron Coomer, Roger Cedeno .05
652 Carlos Perez, Shane Andrews .10
653 Jason Isringhausen, Chris Roberts .05
654 Kevin Jordan, Wayne Gomes .05
655 Esteban Loaiza, Steve Pegues .05
656 John Frascatore, Terry Bradshaw .05
657 Bryce Florie, Andres Berumen .05
658 Keith Williams, Dan Carlson .05
659 Checklist .05
660 Checklist .05

Cyberstats

NM/M

Complete Set (396): 25.00
Common Player: .10
1 Frank Thomas .75
2 Mickey Morandini .10
3 Todd Worrell .10
4 David Cone .10

2B/OF — SAN DIEGO PADRES

5 Trevor Hoffman .10
6 Shane Mack .10
7 Delino DeShields .10
8 Matt Williams .10
9 Sammy Sosa 1.00
10 Gary DiSarcina .10
11 Kenny Rogers .10
12 Jose Vizcaino .10
13 Lou Whitaker .10
14 Ron Darling .10
15 Dave Nilsson .10
16 Dennis Martinez .10
17 Orlando Merced .10
18 John Wetteland .10
19 Mike Devereaux .10
20 Rene Arocha .10
21 Jay Buhner .10
22 Hal Morris .10
23 Paul Molitor .75
24 Dave West .10
25 Scott Sanders .10
26 Eddie Zambrano .10
27 Ricky Bones .10
28 John Valentin .10
29 Kevin Tapani .10
30 Tim Wallach .10
31 Darren Lewis .10
32 Travis Fryman .10
33 Bret Barberie .10
34 Dennis Eckersley .65
35 Ken Hill .10
36 Pete Harnisch .10
37 Mike Mussina .50
38 Dave Winfield .75
39 Joey Hamilton .10
40 Edgar Martinez .10
41 John Smiley .10
42 Jim Abbott .10
43 Mike Kelly .10
44 Brian Jordan .10
45 Ken Ryan .10
46 Matt Mieske .10
47 Rick Aguilera .10
48 Ismael Valdes .10
49 Royce Clayton .10
50 Juan Gonzalez .35
51 Mel Rojas .10
52 Doug Drabek .10
53 Charles Nagy .10
54 Tim Raines .10
55 Midre Cummings .10
56 Rafael Palmeiro .65
57 Charlie Hayes .10
58 Ray Lankford .10
59 Tim Davis .10
60 Andy Ashby .10
61 Mark Grace .10
62 Mark Langston .10
63 Chuck Carr .10
64 Barry Bonds 2.00
65 David Segui .10
66 Mariano Duncan .10
67 Kenny Lofton .10
68 Ken Caminiti .10
69 Darrin Jackson .10
70 Wil Cordero .10
71 Walt Weiss .10
72 Tom Pagnozzi .10
73 Bret Boone .10
74 Wally Joyner .10
75 Luis Lopez .10
76 Len Dykstra .10
77 Pedro Munoz .10
78 Kevin Gross .10
79 Eduardo Perez .10
80 Brent Gates .10
81 Jeff Conine .10
82 Paul Sorrento .10
83 Julio Franco .10
84 Chris Sabo .10
85 Dante Bichette .10
86 Mike Stanley .10
87 Bob Hamelin .10
88 Tommy Greene .10
89 Jeff Brantley .10
90 Ed Sprague .10
91 Otis Nixon .10
92 Chad Curtis .10
93 Chuck McElroy .10
94 Troy Neel .10
95 Benito Santiago .10

#	Player	Price	#	Player	Price	#	Player	Price
96	Jose Mesa	.10	211	Reggie Sanders	.10	326	Joey Cora	.10
97	Luis Gonzalez	.10	212	Kevin Foster	.10	327	Chris Hoiles	.10
98	Alex Fernandez	.10	213	Danny Tartabull	.10	328	Bernard Gilkey	.10
99	Ben McDonald	.10	214	Jeff Blauser	.10	329	Mike Lansing	.10
100	Wade Boggs	1.00	215	Mike Magnante	.10	330	Jimmy Key	.10
101	Tom Glavine	.35	216	Tom Candiotti	.10	331	Vinny Castilla	.10
102	Phil Plantier	.10	217	Rod Beck	.10	332	Mark Guthrie	.10
103	Raul Mondesi	.10	218	Jody Reed	.10	333	Mike Lieberthal	.10
104	Jim Edmonds	.10	219	Vince Coleman	.10	334	Will Clark	.10
105	Jeff Kent	.10	220	Danny Jackson	.10	335	Rickey Henderson	.75
106	Wilson Alvarez	.10	221	Larry Walker	.10	336	Todd Jones	.10
107	Geronimo Berroa	.10	222	Pat Borders	.10	337	Jack McDowell	.10
108	Craig Biggio	.10	223	Lee Smith	.10	338	Carlos Rodriguez	.10
109	Roberto Hernandez	.10	224	Paul O'Neill	.10	339	Mark Eichhorn	.10
110	Bobby Ayala	.10	225	Devon White	.10	340	Jeff Nelson	.10
111	Bob Tewksbury	.10	226	Jim Bullinger	.10	341	Eric Anthony	.10
112	Rondell White	.10	227	Steve Avery	.10	342	Randy Velarde	.10
113	Steve Cooke	.10	228	Tony Gwynn	1.00	343	Javier Lopez	.10
114	Tim Salmon	.10	229	Pat Meares	.10	344	Kevin Mitchell	.10
115	Kent Mercker	.10	230	Bill Swift	.10	345	Steve Bedrosian	.10
116	Randy Johnson	.75	231	David Wells	.10	346	John Kruk	.10
117	Mo Vaughn	.10	232	John Briscoe	.10	347	Scott Leius	.10
118	Eddie Williams	.10	233	Roger Pavlik	.10	348	John Patterson	.10
119	Jeff Montgomery	.10	234	Roberto Alomar	.30	349	Kevin Brown	.10
120	Kirt Manwaring	.10	235	Billy Brewer	.10	350	Mike Moore	.10
121	Pat Hentgen	.10	236	Gary Sheffield	.40	351	Manny Ramirez	.75
122	Shawon Dunston	.10	237	Lou Frazier	.10	352	Jose Lind	.10
123	Tim Belcher	.10	238	Terry Steinbach	.10	353	Derrick May	.10
124	Cecil Fielder	.10	239	Omar Daal	.10	354	Cal Eldred	.10
125	Todd Hundley	.10	240	Jason Bere	.10	355	J.T. Snow	.10
126	Mark Acre	.10	241	Denny Neagle	.10	356	Luis Sojo	.10
127	Darrell Whitmore	.10	242	Danny Bautista	.10	357	Moises Alou	.10
128	Darryl Kile	.10	243	Hector Carrasco	.10	358	Dave Clark	.10
129	Jay Bell	.10	244	Bill Risley	.10	359	Dave Hollins	.10
130	Harold Baines	.10	245	Andy Benes	.10	360	Cal Ripken Jr.	2.00
131	Felix Fermin	.10	246	Jim Leyritz	.10	361	Pedro Astacio	.10
132	Ellis Burks	.10	247	Jose Oliva	.10	362	Tony Longmire	.10
133	Joe Carter	.10	248	Greg Vaughn	.10	363	Jeff Frye	.10
134	Terry Pendleton	.10	249	Rich Monteleone	.10	364	Bo Jackson	.20
135	Junior Felix	.10	250	Tony Eusebio	.10	365	Steve Ontiveros	.10
136	Bill Gullickson	.10	251	Chuck Finley	.10	366	David Nied	.10
137	Melvin Nieves	.10	252	Joe Boever	.10	367	Brad Ausmus	.10
138	Chuck Knoblauch	.10	253	Bobby Munoz	.10	368	Carlos Baerga	.10
139	Bobby Jones	.10	254	Bret Saberhagen	.10	369	James Mouton	.10
140	Darrin Fletcher	.10	255	Kurt Abbott	.10	370	Ozzie Guillen	.10
141	Andy Van Slyke	.10	256	Bobby Witt	.10	371	Yorkis Perez	.10
142	Allen Watson	.10	257	Cliff Floyd	.10	372	Rich Rodriguez	.10
143	Dan Wilson	.10	258	Mark Clark	.10	373	Mark McLemore	.10
144	Bip Roberts	.10	259	Andujar Cedeno	.10	374	Jeff Fassero	.10
145	Sterling Hitchcock	.10	260	Marvin Freeman	.10	375	John Roper	.10
146	Johnny Ruffin	.10	261	Mike Piazza	1.25	376	Wes Chamberlain	.10
147	Steve Trachsel	.10	262	Pat Kelly	.10	377	Felix Jose	.10
148	Ramon Martinez	.10	263	Carlos Delgado	.45	378	Brett Butler	.10
149	Dave Henderson	.10	264	Willie Banks	.10	379	William Van Landingham	.10
150	Chris Gomez	.10	265	Matt Walbeck	.10	380	Mickey Tettleton	.10
151	Rusty Greer	.10	266	Mark McGwire	1.50	381	Brady Anderson	.10
152	John Franco	.10	267	Alan Trammell	.10	382	Reggie Jefferson	.10
153	Mike Bordick	.10	268	Tom Gordon	.10	383	Mike Kingery	.10
154	Dave Magadan	.10	269	Greg Colbrunn	.10	384	Derek Bell	.10
155	Greg Swindell	.10	270	Darren Daulton	.10	385	Scott Erickson	.10
156	Arthur Rhodes	.10	271	Albie Lopez	.10	386	Bob Wickman	.10
157	Juan Guzman	.10	272	Robin Ventura	.10	387	Phil Leftwich	.10
158	Greg Maddux	1.00	273	Bryan Eversgerd	.10	388	Dave Justice	.10
159	Mike Macfarlane	.10	274	Dave Fleming	.10	389	Pedro Martinez	.75
160	Curt Schilling	.35	275	Scott Livingstone	.10	390	Terry Mathews	.10
161	Jose Canseco	.40	276	Pete Schourek	.10	391	Brian McRae	.10
162	Aaron Sele	.10	277	Bernie Williams	.10	392	Bruce Ruffin	.10
163	Steve Buechele	.10	278	Mark Lemke	.10	393	Steve Finley	.10
164	Orel Hershiser	.10	279	Eric Karros	.10	394	Rafael Bournigal	.10
165	Mike Henneman	.10	280	Billy Ashley	.10	395	Darryl Strawberry	.10
166	Kevin Seitzer	.10	281	Rico Brogna	.10	396	Luis Alicea	.10
167	Ruben Sierra	.10	282	John Burkett	.10			
168	Alex Cole	.10	283	Jorge Fabregas	.10			
169	Jim Thome	.65	284	Greg Gagne	.10			
170	Lance Johnson	.10	285	Doug Jones	.10			
171	Marquis Grissom	.10	286	Troy O'Leary	.10			
172	Jamie Moyer	.10	287	Pat Rapp	.10			
173	Todd Zeile	.10	288	Butch Henry	.10			
174	Chris Bosio	.10	289	John Olerud	.10			
175	Steve Howe	.10	290	John Hudek	.10			
176	Luis Polonia	.10	291	Jeff King	.10			
177	Ryan Klesko	.10	292	Bobby Bonilla	.10			
178	Kevin Appier	.10	293	Albert Belle	.10			
179	Tim Naehring	.10	294	Rick Wilkins	.10			
180	Randy Myers	.10	295	John Jaha	.10			
181	Mike Jackson	.10	296	Sid Fernandez	.10			
182	Chili Davis	.10	297	Deion Sanders	.10			
183	Jason Jacome	.10	298	Gil Heredia	.10			
184	Stan Javier	.10	299	Melido Perez	.10			
185	Scott Servais	.10	300	Greg McMichael	.10			
186	Kirk Rueter	.10	301	Rusty Meacham	.10			
187	Don Slaught	.10	302	Shawn Green	.35			
188	Ozzie Smith	1.00	303	Carlos Garcia	.10			
189	Barry Larkin	.10	304	Dave Stevens	.10			
190	Gary Gaetti	.10	305	Eric Young	.10			
191	Fred McGriff	.10	306	Kirk Gibson	.10			
192	Roger Clemens	1.00	307	Spike Owen	.10			
193	Dean Palmer	.10	308	Sandy Alomar	.10			
194	Jeromy Burnitz	.10	309	Ricky Gutierrez	.10			
195	Scott Kamieniecki	.10	310	Dave Veres	.10			
196	Eddie Murray	.75	311	Gregg Jefferies	.10			
197	Ron Karkovice	.10	312	Jose Valentin	.10			
198	Tino Martinez	.10	313	Robb Nen	.10			
199	Ken Griffey Jr.	1.25	314	Jose Rijo	.10			
200	Don Mattingly	1.00	315	Sean Berry	.10			
201	Henry Rodriguez	.10	316	Mike Gallego	.10			
202	Lenny Harris	.10	317	Roberto Kelly	.10			
203	Ryan Thompson	.10	318	Kevin Stocker	.10			
204	Darren Oliver	.10	319	Kirby Puckett	1.00			
205	Omar Vizquel	.10	320	Jon Lieber	.10			
206	Jeff Bagwell	.75	321	Joe Girardi	.10			
207	Todd Van Poppel	.10	322	Tony Phillips	.10			
208	Leo Gomez	.10	323	Brian Anderson	.10			
209	Mark Whiten	.10	324	Ivan Rodriguez	.65			
210	Pedro Martinez	.10	325	Jeff Cirillo	.10			

STOLEN BASE LEADER

DEION SANDERS

#	Player	Price
4	Tony Gwynn	1.50
5	Moises Alou	.15
6	Andres Galarraga	.15
7	Matt Williams	.15
8	Barry Bonds	4.00
9	Frank Thomas	.75
10	Jose Canseco	.50
11	Jeff Bagwell	.75
12	Kirby Puckett	1.50
13	Julio Franco	.15
14	Albert Belle	.15
15	Fred McGriff	.15
16	Kenny Lofton	.15
17	Otis Nixon	.15
18	Brady Anderson	.15
19	Deion Sanders	.15
20	Chuck Carr	.15
21	Pat Hentgen	.15
22	Andy Benes	.15
23	Roger Clemens	1.75
24	Greg Maddux	1.50
25	Pedro Martinez	.75
26	Paul O'Neill	.75
27	Jeff Bagwell	.75
28	Frank Thomas	.75
29	Hal Morris	.15
30	Kenny Lofton	.15
31	Ken Griffey Jr.	2.00
32	Jeff Bagwell	.75
33	Albert Belle	.75
34	Fred McGriff	.15
35	Cecil Fielder	.15
36	Matt Williams	.15
37	Joe Carter	.15
38	Dante Bichette	.15
39	Frank Thomas	.75
40	Mike Piazza	2.00
41	Craig Biggio	.15
42	Vince Coleman	.15
43	Marquis Grissom	.15
44	Chuck Knoblauch	.15
45	Darren Lewis	.15
46	Randy Johnson	.75
47	Jose Rijo	.15
48	Chuck Finley	.15
49	Bret Saberhagen	.15
50	Kevin Appier	.15

Cyberstat Season in Review

Juan Gonzalez

		NM/M
Complete Set (7):		10.00
Common Player:		1.00
1	Barry Bonds	6.00
2	Jose Canseco	2.00
3	Juan Gonzalez	1.50
4	Fred McGriff	1.00
5	Carlos Baerga	1.00
6	Ryan Klesko	1.00
7	Kenny Lofton	1.00

League Leaders

		NM/M
Complete Set (50):		20.00
Common Player:		.15
1	Albert Belle	.15
2	Kevin Mitchell	.15
3	Wade Boggs	1.50

1995 Topps Opening Day

Devon White 4 rbi

		NM/M
Complete Set (10):		7.50
Common Player:		.75
1	Kevin Appier	.75
2	Dante Bichette	.75
3	Ken Griffey Jr.	3.50
4	Todd Hundley	.75
5	John Jaha	.75
6	Fred McGriff	.75
7	Raul Mondesi	.75
8	Manny Ramirez	2.50
9	Danny Tartabull	.75
10	Devon White	.75

Total Bases Finest

		NM/M
Complete Set (15):		12.00
Common Player:		.50

1	Jeff Bagwell	1.25
2	Albert Belle	.50
3	Ken Griffey Jr.	2.00
4	Frank Thomas	1.25
5	Matt Williams	.50
6	Dante Bichette	.50
7	Barry Bonds	2.50
8	Moises Alou	.50
9	Andres Galarraga	.50
10	Kenny Lofton	.50
11	Rafael Palmeiro	1.00
12	Tony Gwynn	1.50
13	Kirby Puckett	1.50
14	Jose Canseco	.75
15	Jeff Conine	.50

1995 Topps Embossed

		NM/M
Complete Set (140):		7.50
Common Player:		.10
Embossed Golds:		2X
Wax Pack (6+1):		1.50
Wax Box (24):		22.50
1	Kenny Lofton	.10
2	Gary Sheffield	.35
3	Hal Morris	.10
4	Cliff Floyd	.10
5	Pat Hentgen	.10
6	Tony Gwynn	.75
7	Jose Valentin	.10
8	Jason Bere	.10
9	Jeff Kent	.10
10	John Valentin	.10
11	Brian Anderson	.10
12	Deion Sanders	.10
13	Ryan Thompson	.10
14	Ruben Sierra	.10
15	Jay Bell	.10
16	Chuck Carr	.10
17	Brent Gates	.10
18	Bret Boone	.10
19	Paul Molitor	.60
20	Chili Davis	.10
21	Ryan Klesko	.10
22	Will Clark	.10
23	Greg Vaughn	.10
24	Moises Alou	.10
25	Ray Lankford	.10
26	Jose Rijo	.10
27	Bobby Jones	.10
28	Rick Wilkins	.10
29	Cal Eldred	.10
30	Juan Gonzalez	.30
31	Royce Clayton	.10
32	Bryan Harvey	.10
33	Dave Nilsson	.10
34	Chris Hoiles	.10
35	David Nied	.10
36	Javy Lopez	.10
37	Tim Wallach	.10
38	Bobby Bonilla	.10
39	Danny Tartabull	.10
40	Andy Benes	.10
41	Dean Palmer	.10
42	Chris Gomez	.10
43	Kevin Appier	.10
44	Brady Anderson	.10
45	Alex Fernandez	.10
46	Roberto Kelly	.10
47	Dave Hollins	.10
48	Chuck Finley	.10
49	Wade Boggs	.75
50	Travis Fryman	.10
51	Ken Griffey Jr.	1.00
52	John Olerud	.10
53	Delino DeShields	.10
54	Ivan Rodriguez	.50
55	Tommy Greene	.10
56	Tom Pagnozzi	.10
57	Bip Roberts	.10
58	Luis Gonzalez	.10
59	Rey Sanchez	.10
60	Ken Ryan	.10
61	Darren Daulton	.10
62	Rick Aguilera	.10
63	Wally Joyner	.10
64	Mike Greenwell	.10
65	Jay Buhner	.10
66	Craig Biggio	.10
67	Charles Nagy	.10
68	Devon White	.10
69	Randy Johnson	.60
70	Shawon Dunston	.10
71	Kirby Puckett	.75
72	Paul O'Neill	.10
73	Tino Martinez	.10
74	Carlos Garcia	.10
75	Ozzie Smith	.75
76	Cecil Fielder	.10
77	Mike Stanley	.10
78	Lance Johnson	.10
79	Tony Phillips	.10
80	Bobby Munoz	.10
81	Kevin Tapani	.10
82	William Van Landingham	.10
83	Dante Bichette	.10
84	Tom Candiotti	.10
85	Wil Cordero	.10
86	Jeff Conine	.10
87	Joey Hamilton	.10
88	Mark Whiten	.10
89	Jeff Montgomery	.10
90	Andres Galarraga	.10
91	Roberto Alomar	.20
92	Orlando Merced	.10
93	Mike Mussina	.35
94	Pedro Martinez	.60
95	Carlos Baerga	.10
96	Steve Trachsel	.10
97	Lou Whitaker	.10
98	David Cone	.10
99	Chuck Knoblauch	.10
100	Frank Thomas	.60
101	Dave Justice	.10
102	Raul Mondesi	.10
103	Rickey Henderson	.60
104	Doug Drabek	.10
105	Sandy Alomar	.10
106	Roger Clemens	.85
107	Mark McGwire	1.20
108	Tim Salmon	.10
109	Greg Maddux	.75
110	Mike Piazza	1.00
111	Tom Glavine	.30
112	Walt Weiss	.10
113	Cal Ripken Jr.	1.50
114	Eddie Murray	.60
115	Don Mattingly	.85
116	Ozzie Guillen	.10
117	Bob Hamelin	.10
118	Jeff Bagwell	.60
119	Eric Karros	.10
120	Barry Bonds	1.50
121	Mickey Tettleton	.10
122	Mark Langston	.10
123	Robin Ventura	.10
124	Bret Saberhagen	.10
125	Albert Belle	.10
126	Rafael Palmeiro	.50
127	Fred McGriff	.10
128	Jimmy Key	.10
129	Barry Larkin	.10
130	Tim Raines	.10
131	Len Dykstra	.10
132	Todd Zeile	.10
133	Joe Carter	.10
134	Matt Williams	.10
135	Terry Steinbach	.10
136	Manny Ramirez	.60
137	John Wetteland	.10
138	Rod Beck	.10
139	Mo Vaughn	.10
140	Darren Lewis	.10

Golden Idols

	NM/M
Complete Set (140):	25.00

Common Player:	.25

(Star cards valued at 2X corresponding regular Embossed cards.)

1995 Topps DIII

		NM/M
Complete Set (59):		10.00
Common Player:		.15
Retail Pack (3):		.50
Retail Wax Box (24):		9.00
Hobby Pack (5):		.65
Hobby Wax Box (24):		12.50
1	Dave Justice	.15
2	Cal Ripken Jr.	2.50
3	Ruben Sierra	.15
4	Roberto Alomar	.25
5	Dennis Martinez	.15
6	Todd Zeile	.15
7	Albert Belle	.15
8	Chuck Knoblauch	.15
9	Roger Clemens	1.25
10	Cal Eldred	.15
11	Dennis Eckersley	.75
12	Andy Benes	.15
13	Moises Alou	.15
14	Andres Galarraga	.15
15	Jim Thome	.65
16	Tim Salmon	.15
17	Carlos Garcia	.15
18	Scott Leius	.15
19	Jeff Montgomery	.15
20	Brian Anderson	.15
21	Will Clark	.15
22	Bobby Bonilla	.15
23	Mike Stanley	.15
24	Barry Bonds	2.50
25	Jeff Conine	.15
26	Paul O'Neill	.15
27	Mike Piazza	1.50
28	Tom Glavine	.35
29	Jim Edmonds	.15
30	Lou Whitaker	.15
31	Jeff Frye	.15
32	Ivan Rodriguez	.75
33	Bret Boone	.15
34	Mike Greenwell	.15
35	Mark Grace	.15
36	Darren Lewis	.15
37	Don Mattingly	1.25
38	Jose Rijo	.15
39	Robin Ventura	.15
40	Bob Hamelin	.15
41	Tim Wallach	.15
42	Tony Gwynn	1.00
43	Ken Griffey Jr.	1.50
44	Doug Drabek	.15
45	Rafael Palmeiro	.75
46	Dean Palmer	.15
47	Bip Roberts	.15
48	Barry Larkin	.15
49	Dave Nilsson	.15
50	Wil Cordero	.15
51	Travis Fryman	.15
52	Chuck Carr	.15
53	Rey Sanchez	.15
54	Walt Weiss	.15
55	Joe Carter	.15
56	Len Dykstra	.15
57	Orlando Merced	.15
58	Ozzie Smith	1.00
59	Chris Gomez	.15

Zone

		NM/M
Complete Set (6):		4.00
Common Player:		.50
1	Frank Thomas	1.00
2	Kirby Puckett	1.50
3	Jeff Bagwell	1.00
4	Fred McGriff	.50
5	Raul Mondesi	.50
6	Kenny Lofton	.50

Traded and Rookies

		NM/M
Complete Set (165):		30.00
Common Player:		.05
Pack (11):		2.50
Wax Box (36):		60.00
1	Frank Thomas	1.00
2	Ken Griffey Jr.	.65
3	Barry Bonds	1.00
4	Albert Belle	.05
5	Cal Ripken Jr.	1.00
6	Mike Piazza	.75
7	Tony Gwynn	.60
8	Jeff Bagwell	.45
9	Mo Vaughn	.05
10	Matt Williams	.05
11	Ray Durham	.05
12	Juan LeBron (Photo Carlos Beltran.) RC	5.00
13	Shawn Green (Rookie of the Year Candidate)	.50
14	Kevin Gross	.05
15	Jon Nunnally	.05
16	Brian Maxcy RC	.05
17	Mark Kiefer	.05
18	Carlos Beltran RC (Photo actually Juan Beltran.)	15.00
19	Mike Mimbs RC	.05
20	Larry Walker	.05
21	Chad Curtis	.05
22	Jeff Barry	.05
23	Joe Oliver	.05
24	Tomas Perez RC	.05
25	Michael Barrett RC	1.50
26	Brian McRae	.05
27	Derek Bell	.05
28	Ray Durham (Rookie of the Year Candidate)	.05
29	Todd Williams	.05
30	Ryan Jaroncyk RC	.05
31	Todd Stoverson	.05
32	Mike Devereaux	.05
33	Rheal Cormier	.05
34	Benny Santiago	.05
35	Bobby Higginson RC	.50
36	Jack McDowell	.05
37	Mike Macfarlane	.05
38	Tony McKnight RC	.05
39	Brian Hunter (Rookie of the Year Candidate)	.05
40	Hideo Nomo RC	2.00
41	Brett Butler	.05

42	Donovan Osborne	.05
43	Scott Karl	.05
44	Tony Phillips	.05
45	Marty Cordova (Rookie of the Year Candidate)	.20
46	Dave Mlicki	.05
47	Bronson Arroyo RC	4.00
48	John Burkett	.05
49	J.D. Smart RC	.05
50	Mickey Tettleton	.05
51	Todd Stottlemyre	.05
52	Mike Perez	.05
53	Terry Mulholland	.05
54	Edgardo Alfonzo	.05
55	Zane Smith	.05
56	Jacob Brumfield	.05
57	Andujar Cedeno	.05
58	Jose Parra	.05
59	Manny Alexander	.05
60	Tony Tarasco	.05
61	Orel Hershiser	.05
62	Tim Scott	.05
63	Felix Rodriguez RC	.05
64	Ken Hill	.05
65	Marquis Grissom	.05
66	Lee Smith	.05
67	Jason Bates (Rookie of the Year Candidate)	.05
68	Felipe Lira	.05
69	Alex Hernandez RC	.10
70	Tony Fernandez	.05
71	Scott Radinsky	.05
72	Jose Canseco	.50
73	Mark Grudzielanek RC	.50
74	Ben Davis RC	.25
75	Jim Abbott	.05
76	Roger Bailey	.05
77	Gregg Jefferies	.05
78	Erik Hanson	.05
79	Brad Radke RC	1.50
80	Jaime Navarro	.05
81	John Wetteland	.05
82	Chad Fonville RC	.10
83	John Mabry	.05
84	Glenallen Hill	.05
85	Ken Caminiti	.05
86	Tom Goodwin	.05
87	Darren Bragg	.05
88	Pat Ahearne, Gary Rath, Larry Wimberly, Robbie Bell RC 1995 Prospects/Pitchers	.10
89	Jeff Russell	.05
90	Dave Gallagher	.05
91	Steve Finley	.05
92	Vaughn Eshelman	.05
93	Kevin Jarvis	.05
94	Mark Gubicza	.05
95	Tim Wakefield	.05
96	Bob Tewksbury	.05
97	Sid Roberson RC	.05
98	Tom Henke	.05
99	Michael Tucker	.05
100	Jason Bates	.05
101	Otis Nixon	.05
102	Mark Whiten	.05
103	Dilson Torres	.05
104	Melvin Bunch RC	.05
105	Terry Pendleton	.05
106	Corey Jenkins RC	.05
107	Glenn Dishman, Rob Grable RC On Deck	.05
108	Reggie Taylor RC	.05
109	Curtis Goodwin (Rookie of the Year Candidate)	.05
110	David Cone	.05
111	Antonio Osuna	.05
112	Paul Shuey	.05
113	Doug Jones	.05
114	Mark McLemore	.05
115	Kevin Ritz	.05
116	John Kruk	.05
117	Trevor Wilson	.05
118	Jerald Clark	.05
119	Julian Tavarez	.05
120	Tim Pugh	.05
121	Todd Zeile	.05
122	Mark Sweeney, George Arias, Richie Sexson, Brian Schneider RC 1995 Prospects/Fielders	4.00
123	Bobby Witt	.05
124	Hideo Nomo (Rookie of the Year Candidate)	1.00
125	Joey Cora	.05
126	Jim Scharrer RC	.05
127	Paul Quantrill	.05
128	Chipper Jones (Rookie of the Year Candidate)	.75
129	Kenny James RC	.05
130	Lyle Mouton, Mariano Rivera On Deck	.15
131	Tyler Green (Rookie of the Year Candidate)	.05
132	Brad Clontz	.05
133	Jon Nunnally (Rookie of the Year Candidate)	.05
134	Dave Magadan	.05
135	Al Leiter	.05
136	Bret Barberie	.05
137	Bill Swift	.05
138	Scott Cooper	.05
139	Roberto Kelly	.05
140	Charlie Hayes	.05
141	Pete Harnisch	.05
142	Rich Amaral	.05
143	Rudy Seanez	.05

144	Pat Listach	.05
145	Quilvio Veras (Rookie of the Year Candidate)	.05
146	Jose Olmeda RC	.05
147	Roberto Petagine	.05
148	Kevin Brown	.05
149	Phil Plantier	.05
150	Carlos Perez RC (Rookie of the Year Candidate)	.05
151	Pat Borders	.05
152	Tyler Green	.05
153	Stan Belinda	.05
154	Dave Stewart	.05
155	Andre Dawson	.25
156	Frank Thomas, Fred McGriff/AS	.30
157	Carlos Baerga, Craig Biggio/AS	.05
158	Wade Boggs, Matt Williams/AS	.35
159	Cal Ripken Jr., Ozzie Smith/AS	.75
160	Ken Griffey Jr., Tony Gwynn/AS	.40
161	Albert Belle, Barry Bonds/AS	.75
162	Kirby Puckett, Len Dykstra/AS	.35
163	Ivan Rodriguez, Mike Piazza/AS	.40
164	Randy Johnson, Hideo Nomo/AS	.25
165	Checklist	.05

Traded and Rookies Power Boosters

		NM/M
Complete Set (10):		20.00
Common Player:		.75
1	Frank Thomas	1.50
2	Ken Griffey Jr.	3.00
3	Barry Bonds	5.00
4	Albert Belle	.75
5	Cal Ripken Jr.	5.00
6	Mike Piazza	3.00
7	Tony Gwynn	2.50
8	Jeff Bagwell	1.50
9	Mo Vaughn	.75
10	Matt Williams	.75

1996 Topps

MO VAUGHN

	NM/M
Unopened Hobby Set (449):	40.00
Unopened Retail Set (450):	40.00
Unopened Cereal Box Set (444):	35.00
Complete Set (440):	25.00
Common Player:	.05
Wax Pack (12):	1.50
Wax Box (36):	35.00
Cello Pack (17):	2.50
Cello Box (24):	40.00
Vending Box (500):	12.50
1 Tony Gwynn	.50
2 Mike Piazza	.75
3 Greg Maddux	.50
4 Jeff Bagwell	.40

5	Larry Walker	.05
6	Barry Larkin	.05
7	Mickey Mantle	4.00
8	Tom Glavine	.05
9	Craig Biggio	.05
10	Barry Bonds	1.00
11	Heathcliff Slocumb	.05
12	Matt Williams	.05
13	Todd Helton	.75
14	Mark Redman	.05
15	Michael Barrett	.05
16	Ben Davis	.05
17	Juan LeBron	.05
18	Tony McKnight	.05
19	Ryan Jaroncyk	.05
20	Corey Jenkins	.05
21	Jim Scharrer	.05
22	Mark Bellhorn RC	.10
23	Jarrod Washburn RC	.50
24	Geoff Jenkins RC	1.00
25	Sean Casey RC	3.00
26	Brett Tomko RC	.10
27	Tony Fernandez	.05
28	Rich Becker	.05
29	Andujar Cedeno	.05
30	Paul Molitor	.75
31	Brent Gates	.05
32	Glenallen Hill	.05
33	Mike MacFarlane	.05
34	Manny Alexander	.05
35	Todd Zeile	.05
36	Joe Girardi	.05
37	Tony Tarasco	.05
38	Tim Belcher	.05
39	Tom Goodwin	.05
40	Orel Hershiser	.05
41	Tripp Cromer	.05
42	Sean Bergman	.05
43	Troy Percival	.05
44	Kevin Stocker	.05
45	Albert Belle	.05
46	Tony Eusebio	.05
47	Sid Roberson	.05
48	Todd Hollandsworth	.05
49	Mark Wohlers	.05
50	Kirby Puckett	1.00
51	Darren Holmes	.05
52	Ron Karkovice	.05
53	Al Martin	.05
54	Pat Rapp	.05
55	Mark Grace	.05
56	Greg Gagne	.05
57	Stan Javier	.05
58	Scott Sanders	.05
59	J.T. Snow	.05
60	David Justice	.05
61	Royce Clayton	.05
62	Kevin Foster	.05
63	Tim Naehring	.05
64	Orlando Miller	.05
65	Mike Mussina	.35
66	Jim Eisenreich	.05
67	Felix Fermin	.05
68	Bernie Williams	.05
69	Robb Nen	.05
70	Ron Gant	.05
71	Felipe Lira	.05
72	Jacob Brumfield	.05
73	John Mabry	.05
74	Mark Carreon	.05
75	Carlos Baerga	.05
76	Jim Dougherty	.05
77	Ryan Thompson	.05
78	Scott Leius	.05
79	Roger Pavlik	.05
80	Gary Sheffield	.45
81	Julian Tavarez	.05
82	Andy Ashby	.05
83	Mark Lemke	.05
84	Omar Vizquel	.05
85	Darren Daulton	.05
86	Mike Lansing	.05
87	Rusty Greer	.05
88	Dave Stevens	.05
89	Jose Offerman	.05
90	Tom Henke	.05
91	Troy O'Leary	.05
92	Michael Tucker	.05
93	Marvin Freeman	.05
94	Alex Diaz	.05
95	John Wetteland	.05
96	Cal Ripken Jr.	1.00
97	Mike Mimbs	.05
98	Bobby Higginson	.05
99	Edgardo Alfonzo	.05
100	Frank Thomas	.75
101	Steve Gibralter, Bob Abreu	.05
102	Brian Givens, T.J. Mathews	.05
103	Chris Pritchett, Trenidad Hubbard	.05
104	Eric Owens, Butch Huskey	.05
105	Doug Drabek	.05
106	Tomas Perez	.05
107	Mark Leiter	.05
108	Joe Oliver	.05
109	Tony Castillo	.05
110	Checklist	.05
111	Kevin Seitzer	.05
112	Pete Schourek	.05
113	Sean Berry	.05
114	Todd Stottlemyre	.05
115	Joe Carter	.05
116	Jeff King	.05
117	Dan Wilson	.05
118	Kurt Abbott	.05
119	Lyle Mouton	.05
120	Jose Rijo	.05

121	Curtis Goodwin	.05
122	Jose Valentin RC	.05
123	Ellis Burks	.05
124	David Cone	.05
125	Eddie Murray	.75
126	Brian Jordan	.05
127	Darrin Fletcher	.05
128	Curt Schilling	.05
129	Ozzie Guillen	.05
130	Kenny Rogers	.05
131	Tom Pagnozzi	.05
132	Garret Anderson	.05
133	Bobby Jones	.05
134	Chris Gomez	.05
135	Mike Stanley	.05
136	Hideo Nomo	.35
137	Jon Nunnally	.05
138	Tim Wakefield	.05
139	Steve Finley	.05
140	Ivan Rodriguez	.65
141	Quilvio Veras	.05
142	Mike Fetters	.05
143	Mike Greenwell	.05
144	Bill Pulsipher	.05
145	Mark McGwire	1.50
146	Frank Castillo	.05
147	Greg Vaughn	.05
148	Pat Hentgen	.05
149	Walt Weiss	.05
150	Randy Johnson	.75
151	David Segui	.05
152	Benji Gil	.05
153	Tom Candiotti	.05
154	Geronimo Berroa	.05
155	John Franco	.05
156	Jay Bell	.05
157	Mark Gubicza	.05
158	Hal Morris	.05
159	Wilson Alvarez	.05
160	Derek Bell	.05
161	Ricky Bottalico	.05
162	Bret Boone	.05
163	Brad Radke	.05
164	John Valentin	.05
165	Steve Avery	.05
166	Mark McLemore	.05
167	Danny Jackson	.05
168	Tino Martinez	.05
169	Shane Reynolds	.05
170	Terry Pendleton	.05
171	Jim Edmonds	.05
172	Esteban Loaiza	.05
173	Ray Durham	.05
174	Carlos Perez	.05
175	Raul Mondesi	.05
176	Steve Ontiveros	.05
177	Chipper Jones	1.00
178	Otis Nixon	.05
179	John Burkett	.05
180	Gregg Jefferies	.05
181	Denny Martinez	.05
182	Ken Caminiti	.05
183	Doug Jones	.05
184	Brian McRae	.05
185	Don Mattingly	1.00
186	Mel Rojas	.05
187	Marty Cordova	.05
188	Vinny Castilla	.05
189	John Smoltz	.05
190	Travis Fryman	.05
191	Chris Hoiles	.05
192	Chuck Finley	.05
193	Ryan Klesko	.05
194	Alex Fernandez	.05
195	Dante Bichette	.05
196	Eric Karros	.05
197	Roger Clemens	1.00
198	Randy Myers	.05
199	Tony Phillips	.05
200	Cal Ripken Jr.	2.00
201	Rod Beck	.05
202	Chad Curtis	.05
203	Jack McDowell	.05
204	Gary Gaetti	.05
205	Ken Griffey Jr.	1.25
206	Ramon Martinez	.05
207	Jeff Kent	.05
208	Brad Ausmus	.05
209	Devon White	.05
210	Jason Giambi	.45
211	Nomar Garciaparra	1.00
212	Billy Wagner	.05
213	Todd Greene	.05
214	Paul Wilson	.05
215	Johnny Damon	.25
216	Alan Benes	.05
217	Karim Garcia	.10
218	Dustin Hermanson	.05
219	Derek Jeter	2.00
220	Checklist	.05
221	Kirby Puckett	.50
222	Cal Ripken Jr.	1.00
223	Albert Belle	.50
224	Randy Johnson	.40
225	Wade Boggs	.50
226	Carlos Baerga	.05
227	Ivan Rodriguez	.30
228	Mike Mussina	.25
229	Frank Thomas	.40
230	Ken Griffey Jr.	.75
231	Jose Mesa	.05
232	Matt Morris RC	1.00
233	Craig Wilson RC	.50
234	Alvie Shepherd RC	.05
235	Randy Winn RC	.05
236	David Yocum RC	.05
237	Jason Brester RC	.05

238	Shane Monahan **RC**	.05
239	Brian McNichol **RC**	.05
240	Reggie Taylor	.05
241	Garrett Long	.05
242	Jonathan Johnson **RC**	.05
243	Jeff Liefer **RC**	.05
244	Brian Powell **RC**	.05
245	Brian Buchanan	.05
246	Mike Piazza	1.25
247	Edgar Martinez	.05
248	Chuck Knoblauch	.05
249	Andres Galarraga	.05
250	Tony Gwynn	1.00
251	Lee Smith	.05
252	Sammy Sosa	1.00
253	Jim Thome	.45
254	Frank Rodriguez	.05
255	Charlie Hayes	.05
256	Bernard Gilkey	.05
257	John Smiley	.05
258	Brady Anderson	.05
259	Rico Brogna	.05
260	Kirt Manwaring	.05
261	Len Dykstra	.05
262	Tom Glavine	.25
263	Vince Coleman	.05
264	John Olerud	.05
265	Orlando Merced	.05
266	Kent Mercker	.05
267	Terry Steinbach	.05
268	Brian Hunter	.05
269	Jeff Fassero	.05
270	Jay Buhner	.05
271	Jeff Brantley	.05
272	Tim Raines	.05
273	Jimmy Key	.05
274	Mo Vaughn	.25
275	Andre Dawson	.25
276	Jose Mesa	.05
277	Brett Butler	.05
278	Luis Gonzalez	.05
279	Steve Sparks	.05
280	Chili Davis	.05
281	Carl Everett	.05
282	Jeff Cirillo	.05
283	Thomas Howard	.05
284	Paul O'Neill	.05
285	Pat Meares	.05
286	Mickey Tettleton	.05
287	Bip Roberts	.05
288	Bip Roberts	.05
289	Roberto Alomar	.15
290	Ruben Sierra	.05
291	John Flaherty	.05
292	Bret Saberhagen	.05
293	Barry Larkin	.05
294	Sandy Alomar	.05
295	Ed Sprague	.05
296	Gary DiSarcina	.05
297	Marquis Grissom	.05
298	John Frascatore	.05
299	Will Clark	.05
300	Barry Bonds	2.00
301	Ozzie Smith	1.00
302	Dave Nilsson	.05
303	Pedro Martinez	.75
304	Joey Cora	.05
305	Rick Aguilera	.05
306	Craig Biggio	.05
307	Jose Vizcaino	.05
308	Jeff Montgomery	.05
309	Moises Alou	.05
310	Robin Ventura	.05
311	David Wells	.05
312	Delino DeShields	.05
313	Trevor Hoffman	.05
314	Andy Benes	.05
315	Deion Sanders	.05
316	Jim Bullinger	.05
317	John Jaha	.05
318	Greg Maddux	1.00
319	Tim Salmon	.05
320	Ben McDonald	.05
321	Sandy Martinez **RC**	.05
322	Dan Miceli	.05
323	Wade Boggs	1.00
324	Ismael Valdes	.05
325	Juan Gonzalez	.35
326	Charles Nagy	.05
327	Ray Lankford	.05
328	Mark Portugal	.05
329	Bobby Bonilla	.05
330	Reggie Sanders	.05
331	Jamie Brewington	.05
332	Aaron Sele	.05
333	Pete Harnisch	.05
334	Cliff Floyd	.05
335	Cal Eldred	.05
336	Jason Bates	.05
337	Tony Clark	.05
338	Jose Herrera	.05
339	Alex Ochoa	.05
340	Mark Loretta	.05
341	Donne Wall **RC**	.05
342	Jason Kendall	.05
343	Shannon Stewart	.05
344	Brooks Kieschnick	.05
345	Chris Snopek	.05
346	Ruben Rivera	.05
347	Jeff Suppan	.05
348	Phil Nevin	.05
349	John Wasdin	.05
350	Jay Payton	.05
351	Tim Crabtree	.05
352	Rick Krivda	.05
353	Bob Wolcott	.05
354	Jimmy Haynes	.05

355	Herb Perry	.05
356	Ryne Sandberg	1.00
357	Harold Baines	.05
358	Chad Ogea	.05
359	Lee Tinsley	.05
360	Matt Williams	.05
361	Randy Velarde	.05
362	Jose Canseco	.40
363	Larry Walker	.05
364	Kevin Appier	.05
365	Darryl Hamilton	.05
366	Jose Lima	.05
367	Javy Lopez	.05
368	Dennis Eckersley	.65
369	Jason Isringhausen	.05
370	Mickey Morandini	.05
371	Scott Cooper	.05
372	Jim Abbott	.05
373	Paul Sorrento	.05
374	Chris Hammond	.05
375	Lance Johnson	.05
376	Kevin Brown	.05
377	Luis Alicea	.05
378	Andy Pettitte	.25
379	Dean Palmer	.05
380	Jeff Bagwell	.75
381	Jaime Navarro	.05
382	Rondell White	.05
383	Erik Hanson	.05
384	Pedro Munoz	.05
385	Heathcliff Slocumb	.05
386	Wally Joyner	.05
387	Bob Tewksbury	.05
388	David Bell	.05
389	Fred McGriff	.05
390	Mike Henneman	.05
391	Robby Thompson	.05
392	Norm Charlton	.05
393	Cecil Fielder	.05
394	Benito Santiago	.05
395	Rafael Palmeiro	.65
396	Ricky Bones	.05
397	Rickey Henderson	.75
398	C.J. Nitkowski	.05
399	Shawon Dunston	.05
400	Manny Ramirez	.75
401	Bill Swift	.05
402	Chad Fonville	.05
403	Joey Hamilton	.05
404	Alex Gonzalez	.05
405	Roberto Hernandez	.05
406	Jeff Blauser	.05
407	LaTroy Hawkins	.05
408	Greg Colbrunn	.05
409	Todd Hundley	.05
410	Glenn Dishman	.05
411	Joe Vitiello	.05
412	Todd Worrell	.05
413	Wil Cordero	.05
414	Ken Hill	.05
415	Carlos Garcia	.05
416	Bryan Rekar	.05
417	Shawn Green (Topps Rookie All-Star)	.40
418	Tyler Green	.05
419	Mike Blowers	.05
420	Kenny Lofton	.05
421	Denny Neagle	.05
422	Jeff Conine	.05
423	Mark Langston	.05
424	Steve Cox, Jesse Ibarra, Derrek Lee, Ron Wright **RC** (Prospects)	.10
425	Jim Bonnici, Billy Owens, Richie Sexson, Daryle Ward **RC** (Prospects)	.10
426	Kevin Jordan, Bobby Morris, Desi Relaford, Adam Riggs **RC** (Prospects)	.10
427	Tim Harkrider, Rey Ordonez, Neifi Perez, Enrique Wilson (Prospects)	.05
428	Bartolo Colon, Doug Million, Rafael Orellano, Ray Ricken **RC** (Prospects)	.05
429	Jeff D'Amico, Marty Janzen, Gary Rath, Clint Sodowsky (Prospects)	.05
430	Matt Drews, Rich Hunter, Matt Ruebel, Bret Wagner (Prospects)	.05
431	Jaime Bluma, Dave Coggin, Steve Montgomery, Brandon Reed (Prospects)	.05
432	Mike Figga, Raul Ibanez, Paul Konerko, Julio Mosquera (Prospects)	.25
433	Brian Barber, Marc Kroon, Marc Valdes, Don Wengert (Prospects)	.05
434	George Arias, Chris Haas, Scott Rolen, Scott Spiezio (Prospects)	.50
435	Brian Banks, Vladimir Guerrero, Andruw Jones, Billy McMillon (Prospects)	.50
436	Roger Cedeno, Derrick Gibson, Ben Grieve, Shane Spencer **RC** (Prospects)	.50
437	Anton French, Demond Smith, Daornd Stovall, Keith Williams (Prospects)	.05
438	Michael Coleman, Jacob Cruz, Richard Hidalgo, Charles Peterson (Prospects)	.10

439	Trey Beamon, Yamil Benitez, Jermaine Dye, Angel Echevarria (Prospects)	.05
440	Checklist	.05

Classic Confrontations

		NM/M
Complete Set (15):		3.50
Common Player:		.06
1	Ken Griffey Jr.	.65
2	Cal Ripken Jr.	1.00
3	Edgar Martinez	.05
4	Kirby Puckett	.45
5	Frank Thomas	.35
6	Barry Bonds	1.00
7	Reggie Sanders	.05
8	Andres Galarraga	.05
9	Tony Gwynn	.45
10	Mike Piazza	.65
11	Randy Johnson	.35
12	Mike Mussina	.25
13	Roger Clemens	.50
14	Tom Glavine	.25
15	Greg Maddux	.45

League Leaders Finest Bronze

		NM/M
Complete Set (6):		75.00
Common Player:		10.00
(1)	Mo Vaughn	10.00
(2)	Barry Larkin	10.00
(3)	Randy Johnson	15.00
(4)	Greg Maddux	30.00
(5)	Marty Cordova	10.00
(6)	Hideo Nomo	15.00

Masters of the Game

		NM/M
Complete Set (20):		20.00
Common Player:		.35
1	Dennis Eckersley	.75
2	Denny Martinez	.35
3	Eddie Murray	1.00
4	Paul Molitor	1.00
5	Ozzie Smith	1.50
6	Rickey Henderson	1.00
7	Tim Raines	.35
8	Lee Smith	.35
9	Cal Ripken Jr.	4.00
10	Chili Davis	.35
11	Wade Boggs	1.50
12	Tony Gwynn	1.50
13	Don Mattingly	2.00
14	Bret Saberhagen	.35
15	Kirby Puckett	1.50
16	Joe Carter	.35
17	Roger Clemens	2.00
18	Barry Bonds	4.00
19	Greg Maddux	1.50
20	Frank Thomas	1.00

Mickey Mantle Reprints

	NM/M
Complete Set (19):	90.00
Common Mantle:	5.00
Common SP Mantle (15-19):	8.00

1	1951 Bowman #253		15.00
2	1952 Topps #311		15.00
3	1953 Topps #82		5.00
4	1954 Topps #65		5.00
5	1955 Bowman #202		5.00
6	1956 Topps #135		5.00
7	1957 Topps #95		5.00
8	1958 Topps #150		5.00
9	1959 Topps #10		5.00
10	1960 Topps #350		5.00
11	1961 Topps #300		5.00
12	1962 Topps #200		5.00
13	1963 Topps #200		5.00
14	1964 Topps #50		5.00
15	1965 Topps #350		8.00
16	1966 Topps #50		8.00
17	1967 Topps #150		8.00
18	1968 Topps #280		8.00
19	1969 Topps #500		8.00

Mickey Mantle Finest Reprints

	NM/M
Complete Set (19):	90.00
Common Card (1-14):	6.00
Common Shortprint (15-19):	8.00
Refractors:	3X
Inserted 1:144	

1	1951 Bowman #253	15.00
2	1952 Topps #311	15.00
3	1953 Topps #82	6.00
4	1954 Topps #65	6.00
5	1955 Bowman #202	6.00
6	1956 Topps #135	6.00
7	1957 Topps #95	6.00
8	1958 Topps #150	6.00
9	1959 Topps #10	6.00
10	1960 Topps #350	6.00
11	1961 Topps #300	6.00
12	1962 Topps #200	6.00
13	1963 Topps #200	6.00
14	1964 Topps #50	6.00
15	1965 Topps #350	8.00
16	1966 Topps #50	8.00
17	1967 Topps #150	8.00
18	1968 Topps #280	8.00
19	1969 Topps #500	8.00

Mickey Mantle Commemorative Card Sheet

	NM/M
Framed Sheet:	80.00
Mickey Mantle	

Mickey Mantle Commemorative Last Day

	NM/M
7	Mickey Mantle	5.00

Mickey Mantle Case Inserts

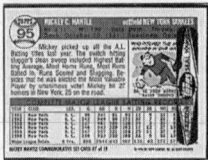

		NM/M
Complete Set (19):		375.00
Common Mantle:		20.00
Common SP Mantle (15-19):		30.00
1	1951 Bowman #253	60.00
2	1952 Topps #311	60.00
3	1953 Topps #82	30.00
4	1954 Bowman #65	20.00
5	1955 Bowman #202	20.00
6	1956 Topps #135	20.00
7	1957 Topps #95	20.00
8	1958 Topps #150	20.00
9	1959 Topps #10	20.00
10	1960 Topps #350	20.00
11	1961 Topps #300	20.00
12	1962 Topps #200	20.00
13	1963 Topps #200	20.00
14	1964 Topps #50	20.00
15	1965 Topps #350	30.00
16	1966 Topps #50	30.00
17	1967 Topps #150	30.00
18	1968 Topps #280	30.00
19	1969 Topps #500	30.00

Mystery Finest

		NM/M
Complete Set (21)		25.00
Common Player:		.50
Refractors:		1.5X
M1	Hideo Nomo	1.00
M2	Greg Maddux	2.00
M3	Randy Johnson	1.50
M4	Chipper Jones	2.00
M5	Marty Cordova	.50
M6	Garret Anderson	.50
M7	Cal Ripken Jr.	4.00
M8	Kirby Puckett	2.00
M9	Tony Gwynn	2.00
M10	Manny Ramirez	1.50
M11	Jim Edmonds	.50
M12	Mike Piazza	2.50
M13	Barry Bonds	4.00
M14	Raul Mondesi	.50
M15	Sammy Sosa	2.00
M16	Ken Griffey Jr.	2.50
M17	Albert Belle	.50
M18	Dante Bichette	.50
M19	Mo Vaughn	.50
M20	Jeff Bagwell	1.50
M21	Frank Thomas	1.50

Power Boosters

		NM/M
Complete Set (26):		30.00
Common Player:		1.00
1	Tony Gwynn	2.00
2	Mike Piazza	3.00
3	Greg Maddux	2.00
4	Jeff Bagwell	1.50
5	Larry Walker	1.00
6	Barry Larkin	1.00
8	Tom Glavine	1.25
9	Craig Biggio	1.00
10	Barry Bonds	4.00
11	Heathcliff Slocumb	1.00
12	Matt Williams	1.00
13	Todd Helton	4.00
14	Mark Redman	1.00
15	Michael Barrett	1.00
16	Ben Davis	1.00
17	Juan LeBron	1.00
18	Tony McKnight	1.00
19	Ryan Jaroncyk	1.00
20	Corey Jenkins	1.00
21	Jim Scharrer	1.00
22	Mark Bellhorn	1.00
23	Jarrod Washburn	1.00
24	Geoff Jenkins	1.00
25	Sean Casey	2.00
26	Brett Tomko	1.00

Profiles-AL

		NM/M
Complete Set (20):		8.00
Common Player:		.25
1	Roberto Alomar	.30
2	Carlos Baerga	.25
3	Albert Belle	.25
4	Cecil Fielder	.25
5	Ken Griffey Jr.	1.00
6	Randy Johnson	.60
7	Paul O'Neill	.25
8	Cal Ripken Jr.	1.50
9	Frank Thomas	.60
10	Mo Vaughn	.25
11	Jay Buhner	.25
12	Marty Cordova	.25
13	Jim Edmonds	.25
14	Juan Gonzalez	.35
15	Kenny Lofton	.25
16	Edgar Martinez	.25
17	Don Mattingly	.75
18	Mark McGwire	1.25
19	Rafael Palmeiro	.50
20	Tim Salmon	.25

Profiles-NL

		NM/M
Complete Set (20):		7.00
Common Player:		.25
1	Jeff Bagwell	.60
2	Derek Bell	.25
3	Barry Bonds	1.50
4	Greg Maddux	.75
5	Fred McGriff	.25
6	Raul Mondesi	.25
7	Mike Piazza	1.00
8	Reggie Sanders	.25
9	Sammy Sosa	.75

		NM/M
10	Larry Walker	.25
11	Dante Bichette	.25
12	Andres Galarraga	.25
13	Ron Gant	.25
14	Tom Glavine	.35
15	Chipper Jones	.75
16	David Justice	.25
17	Barry Larkin	.25
18	Hideo Nomo	.40
19	Gary Sheffield	.40
20	Matt Williams	.25

Road Warriors

		NM/M
Complete Set (20):		9.00
Common Player:		.25
1	Derek Bell	.25
2	Albert Belle	.25
3	Craig Biggio	.25
4	Barry Bonds	2.50
5	Jay Buhner	.25
6	Jim Edmonds	.25
7	Gary Gaetti	.25
8	Ron Gant	.25
9	Edgar Martinez	.25
10	Tino Martinez	.25
11	Mark McGwire	1.50
12	Mike Piazza	1.25
13	Manny Ramirez	1.00
14	Tim Salmon	.25
15	Reggie Sanders	.25
16	Frank Thomas	1.00
17	John Valentin	.25
18	Mo Vaughn	.25
19	Robin Ventura	.25
20	Matt Williams	.25

Wrecking Crew

		NM/M
Complete Set (15):		20.00
Common Player:		.50
1	Jeff Bagwell	1.50
2	Albert Belle	.50
3	Barry Bonds	5.00
4	Jose Canseco	.75
5	Joe Carter	.50
6	Cecil Fielder	.50
7	Ron Gant	.50
8	Juan Gonzalez	.75
9	Ken Griffey Jr.	3.00
10	Fred McGriff	.50
11	Mark McGwire	4.00
12	Mike Piazza	3.00
13	Frank Thomas	1.50
14	Mo Vaughn	.50
15	Matt Williams	.50

5-Star Mystery Finest

		NM/M
Complete Set (5):		12.50
Common Player:		2.00
Refractors:		2X
M22	Hideo Nomo	2.00
M23	Cal Ripken Jr.	5.00

M24	Mike Piazza	3.00
M25	Ken Griffey Jr.	3.00
M26	Frank Thomas	2.50

1996 Topps Chrome

		NM/M
Complete Set (165):		40.00
Common Player:		.10
Refractors:		3X
Pack (4):		2.00
Wax Box (24):		30.00
1	Tony Gwynn	1.00
2	Mike Piazza	1.25
3	Greg Maddux	1.00
4	Jeff Bagwell	.75
5	Larry Walker	.10
6	Barry Larkin	.10
7	Mickey Mantle	9.00
8	Tom Glavine	.10
9	Craig Biggio	.10
10	Barry Bonds	2.00
11	Heathcliff Slocumb	.10
12	Matt Williams	.10
13	Todd Helton	2.00
14	Paul Molitor	1.50
15	Glenallen Hill	.10
16	Troy Percival	.10
17	Albert Belle	.10
18	Mark Wohlers	.10
19	Kirby Puckett	2.00
20	Mark Grace	.10
21	J.T. Snow	.10
22	David Justice	.10
23	Mike Mussina	.75
24	Bernie Williams	.10
25	Ron Gant	.10
26	Carlos Baerga	.10
27	Gary Sheffield	.65
28	Cal Ripken Jr.	2.00
29	Frank Thomas	1.50
30	Kevin Seitzer	.10
31	Joe Carter	.10
32	Jeff King	.10
33	David Cone	.10
34	Eddie Murray	1.50
35	Brian Jordan	.10
36	Garret Anderson	.10
37	Hideo Nomo	.75
38	Steve Finley	.10
39	Ivan Rodriguez	1.25
40	Quilvio Veras	.10
41	Mark McGwire	3.00
42	Greg Vaughn	.10
43	Randy Johnson	1.50
44	David Segui	.10
45	Derek Bell	.10
46	John Valentin	.10
47	Steve Avery	.10
48	Tino Martinez	.10
49	Shane Reynolds	.10
50	Jim Edmonds	.10
51	Raul Mondesi	.10
52	Chipper Jones	2.00
53	Gregg Jefferies	.10
54	Ken Caminiti	.10
55	Brian McRae	.10
56	Don Mattingly	2.25

#	Player	Price
57	Marty Cordova	.10
58	Vinny Castilla	.10
59	John Smoltz	.10
60	Travis Fryman	.10
61	Ryan Klesko	.10
62	Alex Fernandez	.10
63	Dante Bichette	.10
64	Eric Karros	.10
65	Roger Clemens	2.25
66	Randy Myers	.10
67	Cal Ripken Jr.	4.00
68	Rod Beck	.10
69	Jack McDowell	.10
70	Ken Griffey Jr.	2.50
71	Ramon Martinez	.10
72	Jason Giambi	.75
73	Nomar Garciaparra	2.00
74	Billy Wagner	.10
75	Todd Greene	.10
76	Paul Wilson	.10
77	Johnny Damon	.35
78	Alan Benes	.10
79	Karim Garcia	.25
80	Derek Jeter	4.00
81	Kirby Puckett	1.00
82	Cal Ripken Jr.	2.00
83	Albert Belle	.10
84	Randy Johnson	.40
85	Wade Boggs	1.00
86	Carlos Baerga	.10
87	Ivan Rodriguez	.35
88	Mike Mussina	.30
89	Frank Thomas	.75
90	Ken Griffey Jr.	1.25
91	Jose Mesa	.10
92	Matt Morris RC	1.00
93	Mike Piazza	2.50
94	Edgar Martinez	.10
95	Chuck Knoblauch	.10
96	Andres Galarraga	.10
97	Tony Gwynn	2.00
98	Lee Smith	.10
99	Sammy Sosa	2.00
100	Jim Thome	1.25
101	Bernard Gilkey	.10
102	Brady Anderson	.10
103	Rico Brogna	.10
104	Lenny Dykstra	.10
105	Tom Glavine	.35
106	John Olerud	.10
107	Terry Steinbach	.10
108	Brian Hunter	.10
109	Jay Buhner	.10
110	Mo Vaughn	.10
111	Jose Mesa	.10
112	Brett Butler	.10
113	Chili Davis	.10
114	Paul O'Neill	.10
115	Roberto Alomar	.35
116	Barry Larkin	.10
117	Marquis Grissom	.10
118	Will Clark	.10
119	Barry Bonds	4.00
120	Ozzie Smith	2.00
121	Pedro Martinez	1.50
122	Craig Biggio	.10
123	Moises Alou	.10
124	Robin Ventura	.10
125	Greg Maddux	2.00
126	Tim Salmon	.10
127	Wade Boggs	2.00
128	Ismael Valdes	.10
129	Juan Gonzalez	.75
130	Ray Lankford	.10
131	Bobby Bonilla	.10
132	Reggie Sanders	.10
133	Alex Ochoa	.10
134	Mark Loretta	.10
135	Jason Kendall	.10
136	Brooks Kieschnick	.10
137	Chris Snopek	.10
138	Ruben Rivera	.10
139	Jeff Suppan	.10
140	John Wasdin	.10
141	Jay Payton	.10
142	Rick Krivda	.10
143	Jimmy Haynes	.10
144	Ryne Sandberg	2.00
145	Matt Williams	.10
146	Jose Canseco	.65
147	Larry Walker	.10
148	Kevin Appier	.10
149	Javy Lopez	.10
150	Dennis Eckersley	1.25
151	Jason Isringhausen	.10
152	Dean Palmer	.10
153	Jeff Bagwell	1.50
154	Rondell White	.10
155	Wally Joyner	.10
156	Fred McGriff	.10
157	Cecil Fielder	.10
158	Rafael Palmeiro	1.25
159	Rickey Henderson	1.50
160	Shawon Dunston	.10
161	Manny Ramirez	1.50
162	Alex Gonzalez	.10
163	Shawn Green	.45
164	Kenny Lofton	.10
165	Jeff Conine	.10

Wrecking Crew

	NM/M
Complete Set (15):	25.00
Common Player:	1.00
Refractors:	1.5X

#	Player	Price
1	Jeff Bagwell	2.50
2	Albert Belle	1.00
3	Barry Bonds	5.00
4	Jose Canseco	1.50
5	Joe Carter	1.00
6	Cecil Fielder	1.00
7	Ron Gant	1.00
8	Juan Gonzalez	1.25
9	Ken Griffey Jr.	3.50
10	Fred McGriff	1.00
11	Mark McGwire	4.00
12	Mike Piazza	4.00
13	Frank Thomas	2.50
14	Mo Vaughn	1.00
15	Matt Williams	1.00

Masters of the Game

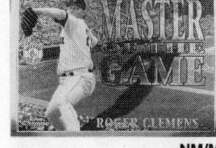

	NM/M
Complete Set (20):	35.00
Common Player:	1.00
Refractors:	1.5X

#	Player	Price
1	Dennis Eckersley	2.00
2	Denny Martinez	1.00
3	Eddie Murray	2.50
4	Paul Molitor	2.50
5	Ozzie Smith	3.50
6	Rickey Henderson	2.50
7	Tim Raines	1.00
8	Lee Smith	1.00
9	Cal Ripken Jr.	6.00
10	Chili Davis	1.00
11	Wade Boggs	3.50
12	Tony Gwynn	3.50
13	Don Mattingly	4.00
14	Bret Saberhagen	1.00
15	Kirby Puckett	3.50
16	Joe Carter	1.00
17	Roger Clemens	4.00
18	Barry Bonds	6.00
19	Greg Maddux	3.50
20	Frank Thomas	2.50

1996 Topps Gallery

MARQUIS GRISSOM

	NM/M
Complete Set (180):	20.00
Common Player:	.10
Private Issue:	8X
Pack (8):	1.50
Wax Box (24):	27.50

#	Player	Price
1	Tom Glavine	.35
2	Carlos Baerga	.10
3	Dante Bichette	.10
4	Mark Langston	.10
5	Ray Lankford	.10
6	Moises Alou	.10
7	Marquis Grissom	.10
8	Ramon Martinez	.10
8p	Ramon Martinez (Unmarked promo, "Pitcher" spelled out under photo on back.)	2.50
9	Steve Finley	.10
10	Todd Hundley	.10
11	Brady Anderson	.10
12	John Valentin	.10
13	Heathcliff Slocumb	.10
14	Ruben Sierra	.10
15	Jeff Conine	.10
16	Jay Buhner	.10
16p	Jay Buhner (Unmarked promo; height, weight and "Bats" on same line.)	2.50
17	Sammy Sosa	1.00
18	Doug Drabek	.10
19	Jose Mesa	.10
20	Jeff King	.10
21	Mickey Tettleton	.10
22	Jeff Montgomery	.10
23	Alex Fernandez	.10
24	Greg Vaughn	.10
25	Chuck Finley	.10
26	Terry Steinbach	.10
27	Rod Beck	.10
28	Jack McDowell	.10
29	Mark Wohlers	.10
30	Lenny Dykstra	.10
31	Bernie Williams	.10
32	Travis Fryman	.10
33	Jose Canseco	.45
34	Ken Caminiti	.10
35	Devon White	.10
36	Bobby Bonilla	.10
37	Paul Sorrento	.10
38	Ryne Sandberg	1.00
39	Derek Bell	.10
40	Bobby Jones	.10
41	J.T. Snow	.10
42	Denny Neagle	.10
43	Tim Wakefield	.10
44	Andres Galarraga	.10
45	David Segui	.10
46	Lee Smith	.10
47	Mel Rojas	.10
48	John Franco	.10
49	Pete Schourek	.10
50	John Wetteland	.10
51	Paul Molitor	.75
52	Ivan Rodriguez	.65
53	Chris Hoiles	.10
54	Mike Greenwell	.10
55	Orel Hershiser	.10
56	Brian McRae	.10
57	Geronimo Berroa	.10
58	Craig Biggio	.10
59	David Justice	.10
59p	David Justice (Unmarked promo; height, weight and "Bats" on same line.)	2.50
60	Lance Johnson	.10
61	Andy Ashby	.10
62	Randy Myers	.10
63	Gregg Jefferies	.10
64	Kevin Appier	.10
65	Rick Aguilera	.10
66	Shane Reynolds	.10
67	John Smoltz	.10
68	Ron Gant	.10
69	Eric Karros	.10
70	Jim Thome	.65
71	Terry Pendleton	.10
72	Kenny Rogers	.10
73	Robin Ventura	.10
74	Dave Nilsson	.10
75	Brian Jordan	.10
76	Glenallen Hill	.10
77	Greg Colbrunn	.10
78	Roberto Alomar	.25
79	Rickey Henderson	.75
80	Carlos Garcia	.10
81	Dean Palmer	.10
82	Mike Stanley	.10
83	Hal Morris	.10
84	Wade Boggs	1.00
85	Chad Curtis	.10
86	Roberto Hernandez	.10
87	John Olerud	.10
88	Frank Castillo	.10
89	Rafael Palmeiro	.65
90	Trevor Hoffman	.10
91	Marty Cordova	.10
92	Hideo Nomo	.35
93	Johnny Damon	.30
94	Bill Pulsipher	.10
95	Garret Anderson	.10
96	Ray Durham	.10
97	Ricky Bottalico	.10
98	Carlos Perez	.10
99	Troy Percival	.10
100	Chipper Jones	1.00
101	Esteban Loaiza	.10
102	John Mabry	.10
103	Jon Nunnally	.10
104	Andy Pettitte	.35
105	Lyle Mouton	.10
106	Jason Isringhausen	.10
107	Brian Hunter	.10
108	Quilvio Veras	.10
109	Jim Edmonds	.10
110	Ryan Klesko	.10
111	Pedro Martinez	.75
112	Joey Hamilton	.10
113	Vinny Castilla	.10
114	Alex Gonzalez	.10
115	Raul Mondesi	.10
116	Rondell White	.10
117	Dan Miceli	.10
118	Tom Goodwin	.10
119	Bret Boone	.10
120	Shawn Green	.35
121	Jeff Cirillo	.10
122	Rico Brogna	.10
123	Chris Gomez	.10
124	Ismael Valdes	.10
125	Javy Lopez	.10
126	Manny Ramirez	.75
127	Paul Wilson	.10
128	Billy Wagner	.10
129	Eric Owens	.10
130	Todd Greene	.10
131	Karim Garcia	.10
132	Jimmy Haynes	.10
133	Michael Tucker	.10
134	John Wasdin	.10
135	Brooks Kieschnick	.10
136	Alex Ochoa	.10
137	Ariel Prieto	.10
138	Tony Clark	.10
139	Mark Loretta	.10
140	Rey Ordonez	.10
141	Chris Snopek	.10
142	Roger Cedeno	.10
143	Derek Jeter	2.00
144	Jeff Suppan	.10
145	Greg Maddux	1.00
146	Ken Griffey Jr.	1.25
147	Tony Gwynn	1.00
148	Darren Daulton	.10
149	Will Clark	.10
150	Mo Vaughn	.10
151	Reggie Sanders	.10
152	Kirby Puckett	1.00
153	Paul O'Neill	.10
154	Tim Salmon	.10
155	Mark McGwire	1.50
156	Barry Bonds	2.00
157	Albert Belle	.10
158	Edgar Martinez	.10
159	Mike Mussina	.35
160	Cecil Fielder	.10
161	Kenny Lofton	.10
162	Randy Johnson	.75
163	Juan Gonzalez	.35
164	Jeff Bagwell	.75
165	Joe Carter	.10
166	Mike Piazza	1.25
167	Eddie Murray	.75
168	Cal Ripken Jr.	2.00
169	Barry Larkin	.10
170	Chuck Knoblauch	.10
171	Chili Davis	.10
172	Fred McGriff	.10
173	Matt Williams	.10
174	Roger Clemens	1.00
175	Frank Thomas	.75
176	Dennis Eckersley	.10
177	Gary Sheffield	.40
178	David Cone	.10
179	Larry Walker	.10
180	Mark Grace	.10

Players Private Issue

ARIEL PRIETO

	NM/M
Complete Set (180):	200.00
Common Player:	1.00
Stars:	8X

(See 1996 Topps Gallery for checklist and base card values.)

Expressionists

	NM/M
Complete Set (20):	20.00
Common Player:	.35

#	Player	Price
1	Mike Piazza	3.00
2	J.T. Snow	.35
3	Ken Griffey Jr.	3.00
4	Kirby Puckett	2.00
5	Carlos Baerga	.35
6	Chipper Jones	2.00
7	Hideo Nomo	.75
8	Mark McGwire	4.00
9	Gary Sheffield	.75
10	Randy Johnson	1.25

11 Ray Lankford .35
12 Sammy Sosa 2.00
13 Denny Martinez .35
14 Jose Canseco .75
15 Tony Gwynn 2.00
16 Edgar Martinez .35
17 Reggie Sanders .35
18 Andres Galarraga .35
19 Albert Belle .35
20 Barry Larkin .35

Masterpiece

NM/M
MP1 Mickey Mantle 6.00

Photo Gallery

NM/M
Complete Set (15): 20.00
Common Player: .75
1 Eddie Murray 2.00
2 Randy Johnson 2.00
3 Cal Ripken Jr. 5.00
4 Bret Boone .75
5 Frank Thomas 2.00
6 Jeff Conine .75
7 Johnny Damon .85
8 Roger Clemens 3.00
9 Albert Belle .75
10 Ken Griffey Jr. 4.00
11 Kirby Puckett 2.50
12 David Justice .75
13 Bobby Bonilla .75
14 Larry Walker, Andres Galarraga, Vinny Castilla, Dante Bichette 1.00
15 Mark Wohlers, Javier Lopez .75

1996 Topps Laser

NM/M
Complete Set (128): 27.50
Common Player: .10
Series 1 or 2 Pack (4): 1.50
Series 1 or 2 Wax Box (24): 22.50
1 Moises Alou .10
2 Derek Bell .10
3 Joe Carter .10
4 Jeff Conine .10
5 Darren Daulton .10
6 Jim Edmonds .10
7 Ron Gant .10
8 Juan Gonzalez .50
9 Brian Jordan .10
10 Ryan Klesko .10
11 Paul Molitor 1.00

12 Tony Phillips .10
13 Manny Ramirez 1.00
14 Sammy Sosa 1.50
15 Devon White .10
16 Bernie Williams .10
17 Garret Anderson .10
18 Jay Bell .10
19 Craig Biggio .10
20 Bobby Bonilla .10
21 Ken Caminiti .10
22 Shawon Dunston .10
23 Mark Grace .10
23p Mark Grace (Unmarked promo, plain, rather than brushed, gold foil.) 2.00
24 Gregg Jefferies .10
25 Jeff King .10
26 Javy Lopez .10
27 Edgar Martinez .10
28 Dean Palmer .10
29 J.T. Snow .10
30 Mike Stanley .10
30p Mike Stanley (Unmarked promo; plain, rather than brushed, gold foil.) 1.00
31 Terry Steinbach .10
32 Robin Ventura .10
33 Roberto Alomar .20
34 Jeff Bagwell 1.00
35 Dante Bichette .10
36 Wade Boggs 1.50
37 Barry Bonds 3.00
38 Jose Canseco .50
39 Vinny Castilla .10
40 Will Clark .10
41 Marty Cordova .10
42 Ken Griffey Jr. 2.00
43 Tony Gwynn 1.50
44 Rickey Henderson 1.00
45 Chipper Jones 1.50
46 Mark McGwire 2.50
47 Brian McRae .10
48 Ryne Sandberg 1.50
49 Andy Ashby .10
50 Alan Benes .10
51 Andy Benes .10
52 Roger Clemens 1.75
53 Doug Drabek .10
54 Dennis Eckersley .75
55 Tom Glavine .35
56 Randy Johnson 1.00
57 Mark Langston .10
58 Denny Martinez .10
59 Jack McDowell .10
60 Hideo Nomo .50
61 Shane Reynolds .10
62 John Smoltz .10
63 Paul Wilson .10
64 Mark Wohlers .10
65 Shawn Green .35
66 Marquis Grissom .10
67 Dave Hollins .10
68 Todd Hundley .10
69 David Justice .10
70 Eric Karros .10
71 Ray Lankford .10
72 Fred McGriff .10
73 Hal Morris .10
74 Eddie Murray 1.00
75 Paul O'Neill .10
76 Rey Ordonez .10
77 Reggie Sanders .10
78 Gary Sheffield .45
79 Jim Thome .75
80 Rondell White .10
81 Travis Fryman .10
82 Derek Jeter 3.00
83 Chuck Knoblauch .10
84 Barry Larkin .10
85 Tino Martinez .10
86 Raul Mondesi .10
87 John Olerud .10
88 Rafael Palmeiro .75
89 Mike Piazza 2.00
90 Cal Ripken Jr. 3.00
91 Ivan Rodriguez .75
92 Frank Thomas 1.00
93 John Valentin .10
94 Mo Vaughn .10
95 Quilvio Veras .10
96 Matt Williams .10
97 Brady Anderson .10
98 Carlos Baerga .10
99 Albert Belle .10
100 Jay Buhner .10
101 Johnny Damon .35
102 Chili Davis .10
103 Ray Durham .10
104 Lenny Dykstra .10
105 Cecil Fielder .10
106 Andres Galarraga .10
107 Brian Hunter .10
108 Kenny Lofton .10
109 Kirby Puckett 1.50
110 Tim Salmon .10
111 Greg Vaughn .10
112 Larry Walker .10
113 Rick Aguilera .10
114 Kevin Appier .10
115 Kevin Brown .10
116 David Cone .10
117 Alex Fernandez .10
118 Chuck Finley .10
119 Joey Hamilton .10
120 Jason Isringhausen .10
121 Greg Maddux 1.50
122 Pedro Martinez 1.00
123 Jose Mesa .10
124 Jeff Montgomery .10
125 Mike Mussina .50
126 Randy Myers .10
127 Kenny Rogers .10
128 Ismael Valdes .10

Series 1 Checklist .05
Series 2 Checklist .05

Bright Spots

NM/M
Complete Set (16): 17.50
Common Player: .50
1 Brian Hunter .50
2 Derek Jeter 4.50
3 Jason Kendall .50
4 Brooks Kieschnick .50
5 Rey Ordonez .50
6 Jason Schmidt .50
7 Chris Snopek .50
8 Bob Wolcott .50
9 Alan Benes .50
10 Marty Cordova .50
11 Jimmy Haynes .50
12 Todd Hollandsworth .50
13 Derek Jeter 4.50
14 Chipper Jones 3.00
15 Hideo Nomo 1.00
16 Paul Wilson .50

Power Cuts

NM/M
Complete Set (16): 20.00
Common Player: .75
1 Albert Belle .75
2 Jay Buhner .75
3 Fred McGriff .75
4 Mike Piazza 3.00
5 Tim Salmon .75
6 Frank Thomas 2.00
7 Mo Vaughn .75
8 Matt Williams .75
9 Jeff Bagwell 2.00
10 Barry Bonds 5.00
11 Jose Canseco 1.00
12 Cecil Fielder .75
13 Juan Gonzalez 1.00
14 Ken Griffey Jr. 3.00
15 Sammy Sosa 2.50
16 Larry Walker .75

Stadium Stars

NM/M
Complete Set (16): 45.00
Common Player: 1.50
1 Carlos Baerga 1.50
2 Barry Bonds 10.00
3 Andres Galarraga 1.50
4 Ken Griffey Jr. 7.50
5 Barry Larkin 1.50
6 Raul Mondesi 1.50
7 Kirby Puckett 5.00
8 Cal Ripken Jr. 10.00
9 Will Clark 1.50
10 Roger Clemens 6.00
11 Tony Gwynn 5.00
12 Randy Johnson 4.00
13 Kenny Lofton 1.50
14 Edgar Martinez 1.50
15 Ryne Sandberg 5.00
16 Frank Thomas 4.00

1997 Topps

NM/M
Unopened Fact. Set (504): 110.00
Unopened Fact. Set (503): 145.00
Complete Set (495): 65.00
Common Player: .05
Ser. 1 or 2 Pack (11): 1.00
Ser. 1 or 2 Wax Box (36): 20.00
Ser. 1 or 2 Vending Box (500): 12.00
1 Barry Bonds 2.00
2 Tom Pagnozzi .05
3 Terrell Wade .05
4 Jose Valentin .05
5 Mark Clark .05
6 Brady Anderson .05
7 Not Issued
8 Wade Boggs 1.00
9 Scott Stahoviak .05
10 Andres Galarraga .05
11 Steve Avery .05
12 Rusty Greer .05
13 Derek Jeter 2.00
14 Ricky Bottalico .05
15 Andy Ashby .05
16 Paul Shuey .05
17 F.P. Santangelo .05
18 Royce Clayton .05
19 Mike Mohler .05
20 Mike Piazza 1.50
21 Jaime Navarro .05
22 Billy Wagner .05
23 Mike Timlin .05
24 Garret Anderson .05
25 Ben McDonald .05
26 Mel Rojas .05
27 John Burkett .05
28 Jeff King .05
29 Reggie Jefferson .05
30 Kevin Appier .05
31 Felipe Lira .05
32 Kevin Tapani .05
33 Mark Portugal .05
34 Carlos Garcia .05
35 Joey Cora .05
36 David Segui .05
37 Mark Grace .05
38 Erik Hanson .05
39 Jeff D'Amico .05
40 Jay Buhner .05

41	B.J. Surhoff	.05
42	Jackie Robinson	1.50
43	Roger Pavlik	.05
44	Hal Morris	.05
45	Mariano Duncan	.05
46	Harold Baines	.05
47	Jorge Fabregas	.05
48	Jose Herrera	.05
49	Jeff Cirillo	.05
50	Tom Glavine	.25
51	Pedro Astacio	.05
52	Mark Gardner	.05
53	Arthur Rhodes	.05
54	Troy O'Leary	.05
55	Bip Roberts	.05
56	Mike Lieberthal	.05
57	Shane Andrews	.05
58	Scott Karl	.05
59	Gary DiSarcina	.05
60	Andy Pettitte	.25
61a	Kevin Elster	.05
61b	Mike Fetters (Should be #84.)	.05
62	Mark McGwire	1.75
63	Dan Wilson	.05
64	Mickey Morandini	.05
65	Chuck Knoblauch	.05
66	Tim Wakefield	.05
67	Raul Mondesi	.05
68	Todd Jones	.05
69	Albert Belle	.05
70	Trevor Hoffman	.05
71	Eric Young	.05
72	Robert Perez	.05
73	Butch Huskey	.05
74	Brian McRae	.05
75	Jim Edmonds	.05
76	Mike Henneman	.05
77	Frank Rodriguez	.05
78	Danny Tartabull	.05
79	Robby Nen	.05
80	Reggie Sanders	.05
81	Ron Karkovice	.05
82	Benny Santiago	.05
83	Mike Lansing	.05
84	Not Issued - See #61b	
85	Craig Biggio	.05
86	Mike Bordick	.05
87	Ray Lankford	.05
88	Charles Nagy	.05
89	Paul Wilson	.05
90	John Wetteland	.05
91	Tom Candiotti	.05
92	Carlos Delgado	.45
93	Derek Bell	.05
94	Mark Lemke	.05
95	Edgar Martinez	.05
96	Rickey Henderson	.75
97	Greg Myers	.05
98	Jim Leyritz	.05
99	Mark Johnson	.05
100	Dwight Gooden	.05
101	Al Leiter	.05
102a	John Mabry (Last line on back ends "... Mabry.")	.05
102b	John Mabry (Last line on back ends "...walked.")	.05
103	Alex Ochoa	.05
104	Mike Piazza	.75
105	Jim Thome	.65
106	Ricky Otero	.05
107	Jamey Wright	.05
108	Frank Thomas	.75
109	Jody Reed	.05
110	Orel Hershiser	.05
111	Terry Steinbach	.05
112	Mark Loretta	.05
113	Turk Wendell	.05
114	Marvin Benard	.05
115	Kevin Brown	.05
116	Robert Person	.05
117	Joey Hamilton	.05
118	Francisco Cordova	.05
119	John Smiley	.05
120	Travis Fryman	.05
121	Jimmy Key	.05
122	Tom Goodwin	.05
123	Mike Greenwell	.05
124	Juan Gonzalez	.35
125	Pete Harnisch	.05
126	Roger Cedeno	.05
127	Ron Gant	.05
128	Mark Langston	.05
129	Tim Crabtree	.05
130	Greg Maddux	1.00
131	William Van Landingham	.05
132	Wally Joyner	.05
133	Randy Myers	.05
134	John Valentin	.05
135	Bret Boone	.05
136	Bruce Ruffin	.05
137	Chris Snopek	.05
138	Paul Molitor	.75
139	Mark McLemore	.05
140	Rafael Palmeiro	.65
141	Herb Perry	.05
142	Luis Gonzalez	.05
143	Doug Drabek	.05
144	Ken Ryan	.05
145	Todd Hundley	.05
146	Ellis Burks	.05
147	Ozzie Guillen	.05
148	Rich Becker	.05
149	Sterling Hitchcock	.05
150	Bernie Williams	.05
151	Mike Stanley	.05
152	Roberto Alomar	.25
153	Jose Mesa	.05
154	Steve Trachsel	.05
155	Alex Gonzalez	.05
156	Troy Percival	.05
157	John Smoltz	.05
158	Pedro Martinez	.75
159	Jeff Conine	.05
160	Bernard Gilkey	.05
161	Jim Eisenreich	.05
162	Mickey Tettleton	.05
163	Justin Thompson	.05
164	Jose Offerman	.05
165	Tony Phillips	.05
166	Ismael Valdes	.05
167	Ryne Sandberg	1.00
168	Matt Mieske	.05
169	Geronimo Berroa	.05
170	Otis Nixon	.05
171	John Mabry	.05
172	Shawon Dunston	.05
173	Omar Vizquel	.05
174	Chris Holles	.05
175	Doc Gooden	.05
176	Wilson Alvarez	.05
177	Todd Hollandsworth	.05
178	Roger Salkeld	.05
179	Rey Sanchez	.05
180	Rey Ordonez	.05
181	Denny Martinez	.05
182	Ramon Martinez	.05
183	Dave Nilsson	.05
184	Marquis Grissom	.05
185	Randy Velarde	.05
186	Ron Coomer	.05
187	Tino Martinez	.05
188	Jeff Brantley	.05
189	Steve Finley	.05
190	Andy Benes	.05
191	Terry Adams	.05
192	Mike Blowers	.05
193	Russ Davis	.05
194	Darryl Hamilton	.05
195	Jason Kendall	.05
196	Johnny Damon	.25
197	Dave Martinez	.05
198	Mike Macfarlane	.05
199	Norm Charlton	.05
200	Doug Million, Damian Moss, Bobby Rodgers	.05
201	Geoff Jenkins, Raul Ibanez, Mike Cameron	.05
202	Sean Casey, Jim Bonnici, Dmitri Young	.15
203	Jed Hansen, Homer Bush, Felipe Crespo	.05
204	Kevin Orie, Gabe Alvarez, Aaron Boone	.05
205	Ben Davis, Kevin Brown, Bobby Estalella	.05
206	Billy McMillon, Bubba Trammell, Dante Powell	.25
207	Jarrod Washburn, Marc Wilkins, Glendon Rusch	.05
208	Brian Hunter	.05
209	Jason Giambi	.45
210	Henry Rodriguez	.05
211	Edgar Renteria	.05
212	Edgardo Alfonzo	.05
213	Fernando Vina	.05
214	Shawn Green	.40
215	Ray Durham	.05
216	Joe Randa	.05
217	Armando Reynoso	.05
218	Eric Davis	.05
219	Bob Tewksbury	.05
220	Jacob Cruz	.05
221	Glenallen Hill	.05
222	Gary Gaetti	.05
223	Donne Wall	.05
224	Brad Clontz	.05
225	Marty Janzen	.05
226	Todd Worrell	.05
227	John Franco	.05
228	David Wells	.05
229	Gregg Jefferies	.05
230	Tim Naehring	.05
231	Thomas Howard	.05
232	Roberto Hernandez	.05
233	Kevin Ritz	.05
234	Julian Tavarez	.05
235	Ken Hill	.05
236	Greg Gagne	.05
237	Bobby Chouinard	.05
238	Joe Carter	.05
239	Jermaine Dye	.05
240	Antonio Osuna	.05
241	Julio Franco	.05
242	Mike Grace	.05
243	Aaron Sele	.05
244	David Justice	.05
245	Sandy Alomar	.05
246	Jose Canseco	.45
247	Paul O'Neill	.05
248	Sean Berry	.05
249	Nick Bierbrodt, Kevin Sweeney **RC**	.05
250	Larry Rodriguez, Vladimir Nunez **RC**	.10
251	Ron Hartman, David Hayman	.05
252	Alex Sanchez, Matt Quatraro	.05
253	Ronni Seberino, Pablo Ortega **RC**	.05
254	Rex Hudler	.05
255	Orlando Miller	.05
256	Mariano Rivera	.10
257	Brad Radke	.05
258	Bobby Higginson	.05
259	Jay Bell	.05
260	Mark Grudzielanek	.05
261	Lance Johnson	.05
262	Ken Caminiti	.05
263	J.T. Snow	.05
264	Gary Sheffield	.45
265	Darrin Fletcher	.05
266	Eric Owens	.05
267	Luis Castillo	.05
268	Scott Rolen	.65
269	Todd Noel, John Oliver	.05
270	Robert Stratton, Corey Lee **RC**	.05
271	Gil Meche, Matt Halloran **RC**	.50
272	Eric Milton, Dermal Brown	.25
273	Josh Garrett, Chris Reitsma **RC**	.10
274	A.J. Zapp, Jason Marquis **RC**	.50
275	Checklist	.05
276a	Checklist	.05
276b	Chipper Jones (Should be #277.)	1.00
277	Not issued	
278	Orlando Merced	.05
279	Ariel Prieto	.05
280	Al Leiter	.05
281	Pat Meares	.05
282	Darryl Strawberry	.05
283	Jamie Moyer	.05
284	Scott Servais	.05
285	Delino DeShields	.05
286	Danny Graves	.05
287	Gerald Williams	.05
288	Todd Greene	.05
289	Rico Brogna	.05
290	Derrick Gibson	.05
291	Joe Girardi	.05
292	Darren Lewis	.05
293	Nomar Garciaparra	1.00
294	Greg Colbrunn	.05
295	Jeff Bagwell	.75
296	Brent Gates	.05
297	Jose Vizcaino	.05
298	Alex Ochoa	.05
299	Sid Fernandez	.05
300	Ken Griffey Jr.	1.50
301	Chris Gomez	.05
302	Wendell Magee	.05
303	Darren Oliver	.05
304	Mel Nieves	.05
305	Sammy Sosa	1.00
306	George Arias	.05
307	Jack McDowell	.05
308	Stan Javier	.05
309	Kimera Bartee	.05
310	James Baldwin	.05
311	Rocky Coppinger	.05
312	Keith Lockhart	.05
313	C.J. Nitkowski	.05
314	Allen Watson	.05
315	Darryl Kile	.05
316	Amaury Telemaco	.05
317	Jason Isringhausen	.05
318	Manny Ramirez	.75
319	Terry Pendleton	.05
320	Tim Salmon	.05
321	Eric Karros	.05
322	Mark Whiten	.05
323	Rick Krivda	.05
324	Brett Butler	.05
325	Randy Johnson	.75
326	Eddie Taubensee	.05
327	Mark Leiter	.05
328	Kevin Gross	.05
329	Ernie Young	.05
330	Pat Hentgen	.05
331	Rondell White	.05
332	Bobby Witt	.05
333	Eddie Murray	.75
334	Tim Raines	.05
335	Jeff Fassero	.05
336	Chuck Finley	.05
337	Willie Adams	.05
338	Chan Ho Park	.05
339	Jay Powell	.05
340	Ivan Rodriguez	.65
341	Jermaine Allensworth	.05
342	Jay Payton	.05
343	T.J. Mathews	.05
344	Tony Batista	.05
345	Ed Sprague	.05
346	Jeff Kent	.05
347	Scott Erickson	.05
348	Jeff Suppan	.05
349	Pete Schourek	.05
350	Kenny Lofton	.05
351	Alan Benes	.05
352	Fred McGriff	.05
353	Charlie O'Brien	.05
354	Darren Bragg	.05
355	Alex Fernandez	.05
356	Al Martin	.05
357	Bob Wells	.05
358	Chad Mottola	.05
359	Devon White	.05
360	David Cone	.05
361	Bobby Jones	.05
362	Scott Sanders	.05
363	Karim Garcia	.15
364	Kirt Manwaring	.05
365	Chili Davis	.05
366	Mike Hampton	.05
367	Chad Ogea	.05
368	Curt Schilling	.25
369	Phil Nevin	.05
370	Roger Clemens	1.25
371	Willie Greene	.05
372	Kenny Rogers	.05
373	Jose Rijo	.05
374	Bobby Bonilla	.05
375	Mike Mussina	.35
376	Curtis Pride	.05
377	Todd Walker	.05
378	Jason Bere	.05
379	Heathcliff Slocumb	.05
380	Dante Bichette	.05
381	Carlos Baerga	.05
382	Livan Hernandez	.05
383	Jason Schmidt	.05
384	Kevin Stocker	.05
385	Matt Williams	.05
386	Bartolo Colon	.05
387	Will Clark	.05
388	Dennis Eckersley	.65
389	Brooks Kieschnick	.05
390	Ryan Klesko	.05
391	Mark Carreon	.05
392	Tim Worrell	.05
393	Dean Palmer	.05
394	Wil Cordero	.05
395	Javy Lopez	.05
396	Rich Aurilia	.05
397	Greg Vaughn	.05
398	Vinny Castilla	.05
399	Jeff Montgomery	.05
400	Cal Ripken Jr.	2.00
401	Walt Weiss	.05
402	Brad Ausmus	.05
403	Ruben Rivera	.05
404	Mark Wohlers	.05
405	Rick Aguilera	.05
406	Tony Clark	.05
407	Lyle Mouton	.05
408	Bill Pulsipher	.05
409	Jose Rosado	.05
410	Tony Gwynn	1.00
411	Cecil Fielder	.05
412	John Flaherty	.05
413	Lenny Dykstra	.05
414	Ugueth Urbina	.05
415	Brian Jordan	.05
416	Bob Abreu	.05
417	Craig Paquette	.05
418	Sandy Martinez	.05
419	Jeff Blauser	.05
420	Barry Larkin	.05
421	Kevin Seitzer	.05
422	Tim Belcher	.05
423	Paul Sorrento	.05
424	Cal Eldred	.05
425	Robin Ventura	.05
426	John Olerud	.05
427	Bob Wolcott	.05
428	Matt Lawton	.05
429	Rod Beck	.05
430	Shane Reynolds	.05
431	Mike James	.05
432	Steve Wojciechowski	.05
433	Vladimir Guerrero	.75
434	Dustin Hermanson	.05
435	Marty Cordova	.05
436	Marc Newfield	.05
437	Todd Stottlemyre	.05
438	Jeffrey Hammonds	.05
439	Dave Stevens	.05
440	Hideo Nomo	.35
441	Mark Thompson	.05
442	Mark Lewis	.05
443	Quinton McCracken	.05
444	Cliff Floyd	.05
445	Denny Neagle	.05
446	John Jaha	.05
447	Mike Sweeney	.05
448	John Wasdin	.05
449	Chad Curtis	.05
450	Mo Vaughn	.05
451	Donovan Osborne	.05
452	Ruben Sierra	.05
453	Michael Tucker	.05
454	Kurt Abbott	.05
455	Andruw Jones	.75
456	Shannon Stewart	.05
457	Scott Brosius	.05
458	Juan Guzman	.05
459	Ron Villone	.05
460	Moises Alou	.05
461	Larry Walker	.05
462	Eddie Murray	.40
463	Paul Molitor	.40
464	Hideo Nomo	.20
465	Barry Bonds	1.00
466	Todd Hundley	.05
467	Rheal Cormier	.05
468	Jason Conti **RC**	.05
469	Rod Barajas **RC**	.05
470	Jared Sandberg, Cedric Bowers **RC**	.05
471	Paul Wilders, Chie Gunner **RC**	.05
472	Mike Decelle, Marcus McCain **RC**	.05
473	Todd Zeile	.05
474	Neifi Perez	.05
475	Jeromy Burnitz	.05
476	Trey Beamon	.05
477	John Patterson, Braden Looper **RC**	.15
478	Danny Peoples, Jake Westbrook **RC**	.25
479	Eric Chavez, Adam Eaton	.75
480	Joe Lawrence, Pete Tucci	.05
481	Kris Benson, Billy Koch **RC**	.25
482	John Nicholson, Andy Prater	.05

483	Mark Kotsay,	
	Mark Johnson	.25
484	Armando Benitez	.05
485	Mike Matheny	.05
486	Jeff Reed	.05
487	Mark Bellhorn, Russ Johnson,	
	Enrique Wilson (Prospects)	.05
488	Ben Grieve, Richard Hidalgo,	
	Scott Morgan **RC**	
	(Prospects)	.05
489	Paul Konerko, Derrek Lee,	
	Ron Wright (Prospects)	.50
490	Wes Helms, Bill Mueller,	
	Brad Seitzer (Prospects)	.50
491	Jeff Abbott, Shane Monahan,	
	Edgard Velazquez (Prospects)	.05
492	Jimmy Anderson, Ron Blazier,	
	Gerald Witasick Jr.	
	(Prospects)	.05
493	Darin Blood, Heath Murray,	
	Carl Pavano (Prospects)	.05
494	Mark Redman, Mike Villano,	
	Nelson Figueroa (Prospects)	.05
495	Checklist	.05
496	Checklist	.05

All-Stars

		NM/M
Complete Set (22):		12.00
Common Player:		.25
1	Ivan Rodriguez	.75
2	Todd Hundley	.25
3	Frank Thomas	1.00
4	Andres Galarraga	.25
5	Chuck Knoblauch	.25
6	Eric Young	.25
7	Jim Thome	.25
8	Chipper Jones	1.50
9	Cal Ripken Jr.	3.00
10	Barry Larkin	.25
11	Albert Belle	.25
12	Barry Bonds	3.00
13	Ken Griffey Jr.	2.00
14	Ellis Burks	.25
15	Juan Gonzalez	.60
16	Gary Sheffield	.50
17	Andy Pettitte	.35
18	Tom Glavine	.35
19	Pat Hentgen	.25
20	John Smoltz	.25
21	Roberto Hernandez	.25
22	Mark Wohlers	.25

Awesome Impact

		NM/M
Complete Set (20):		20.00
Common Player:		.40
1	Jaime Bluma	.40
2	Tony Clark	.40
3	Jermaine Dye	.40
4	Nomar Garciaparra	4.50
5	Vladimir Guerrero	3.00
6	Todd Hollandsworth	.40
7	Derek Jeter	6.00
8	Andruw Jones	3.00
9	Chipper Jones	4.50
10	Jason Kendall	.40

11	Brooks Kieschnick	.40
12	Alex Ochoa	.40
13	Rey Ordonez	.40
14	Neifi Perez	.40
15	Edgar Renteria	.40
16	Mariano Rivera	.50
17	Ruben Rivera	.40
18	Scott Rolen	2.25
19	Billy Wagner	.40
20	Todd Walker	.40

Derek Jeter Autograph

	NM/M
Derek Jeter	130.00

Hobby Masters

		NM/M
Complete Set (20):		30.00
Common Player:		.75
1	Ken Griffey Jr.	3.00
2	Cal Ripken Jr.	4.50
3	Greg Maddux	2.25
4	Albert Belle	.75
5	Tony Gwynn	2.25
6	Jeff Bagwell	1.50
7	Randy Johnson	1.50
8	Raul Mondesi	.75
9	Juan Gonzalez	1.00
10	Kenny Lofton	.75
11	Frank Thomas	1.50
12	Mike Piazza	3.00
13	Chipper Jones	2.25
14	Brady Anderson	.75
15	Ken Caminiti	.75
16	Barry Bonds	4.50
17	Mo Vaughn	.75
18	Derek Jeter	4.50
19	Sammy Sosa	2.25
20	Andres Galarraga	.75

Inter-League Match Ups

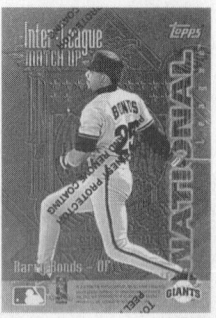

	NM/M
Complete Set (14):	16.00

Common Card:		.50
Refractors:		1.5X
1	Mark McGwire, Barry Bonds	3.00
2	Tim Salmon, Mike Piazza	2.00
3	Ken Griffey Jr.,	
	Dante Bichette	2.00
4	Juan Gonzalez, Tony Gwynn	1.50
5	Frank Thomas, Sammy Sosa	1.50
6	Albert Belle, Barry Larkin	.50
7	Johnny Damon,	
	Brian Jordan	.75
8	Paul Molitor, Jeff King	1.00
9	John Jaha, Jeff Bagwell	1.00
10	Bernie Williams, Todd Hundley	.50
11	Joe Carter, Henry Rodriguez	.50
12	Cal Ripken Jr.,	
	Gregg Jefferies	3.00
13	Mo Vaughn, Chipper Jones	1.50
14	Travis Fryman, Gary Sheffield	.75

Mickey Mantle Reprints

		NM/M
Complete Set (16):		60.00
Common Card:		5.00
Inserted 1:12 Series 1		
21	1953 Bowman #44	5.00
22	1953 Bowman #59	5.00
23	1957 Topps #407	5.00
24	1958 Topps #418	5.00
25	1958 Topps #487	5.00
26	1959 Topps #461	5.00
27	1959 Topps #564	5.00
28	1960 Topps #160	5.00
29	1960 Topps #563	5.00
30	1961 Topps #406	5.00
31	1961 Topps #475	5.00
32	1961 Topps #578	5.00
33	1962 Topps #18	5.00
34	1962 Topps #318	5.00
35	1962 Topps #471	5.00
36	1964 Topps #331	5.00

Mickey Mantle Finest

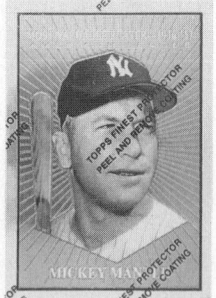

		NM/M
Complete Set (16):		70.00
Common Card:		5.00
Inserted 1:24 Series 2		
Refractor:		4X
Inserted 1:216		
21	1953 Bowman #44	5.00
22	1953 Bowman #59	7.50
23	1957 Topps #407	5.00
24	1958 Topps #418	5.00
25	1958 Topps #487	5.00
26	1959 Topps #461	5.00
27	1959 Topps #564	5.00
28	1960 Topps #160	5.00
29	1960 Topps #563	5.00
30	1961 Topps #406	5.00
31	1961 Topps #475	5.00
32	1961 Topps #578	5.00
33	1962 Topps #18	5.00
34	1962 Topps #318	5.00
35	1962 Topps #471	5.00
36	1964 Topps #331	5.00

Mickey Mantle Case Inserts

		NM/M
Complete Set (16):		160.00
Common Card:		12.50
21	1953 Bowman #44	12.50
22	1953 Bowman #59	18.00
23	1957 Topps #407	12.50
24	1958 Topps #418	12.50
25	1958 Topps #487	12.50
26	1959 Topps #461	12.50
27	1959 Topps #564	12.50
28	1960 Topps #160	12.50
29	1960 Topps #563	12.50
30	1961 Topps #406	12.50
31	1961 Topps #475	12.50
32	1961 Topps #578	12.50
33	1962 Topps #18	12.50
34	1962 Topps #318	12.50
35	1962 Topps #471	12.50
36	1964 Topps #331	12.50

Season's Best

		NM/M
Complete Set (25):		12.00
Common Player:		.25
1	Tony Gwynn	1.50
2	Frank Thomas	1.25
3	Ellis Burks	.25
4	Paul Molitor	1.25
5	Chuck Knoblauch	.25
6	Mark McGwire	3.00
7	Brady Anderson	.25
8	Ken Griffey Jr.	2.00
9	Albert Belle	.25
10	Andres Galarraga	.25
11	Andres Galarraga	.25
12	Albert Belle	.25
13	Juan Gonzalez	.75
14	Mo Vaughn	.25
15	Rafael Palmeiro	1.00
16	John Smoltz	.25
17	Andy Pettitte	.50
18	Pat Hentgen	.50
19	Mike Mussina	.50
20	Andy Benes	.25
21	Kenny Lofton	.25
22	Tom Goodwin	.25
23	Otis Nixon	.25
24	Eric Young	.25
25	Lance Johnson	.25

Sweet Strokes

	NM/M
Complete Set (15):	15.00

Common Player: .35
1 Roberto Alomar .50
2 Jeff Bagwell 1.25
3 Albert Belle .35
4 Barry Bonds 3.00
5 Mark Grace .35
6 Ken Griffey Jr. 2.00
7 Tony Gwynn 1.50
8 Chipper Jones 1.50
9 Edgar Martinez .35
10 Mark McGwire 2.50
11 Rafael Palmeiro 1.00
12 Mike Piazza 2.00
13 Gary Sheffield .75
14 Frank Thomas 1.25
15 Mo Vaughn .35

Team Timber

NM/M
Complete Set (16): 24.00
Common Player: .50
1 Ken Griffey Jr. 3.00
2 Ken Caminiti .50
3 Bernie Williams .50
4 Jeff Bagwell 1.50
5 Frank Thomas 1.50
6 Andres Galarraga .50
7 Barry Bonds 5.00
8 Rafael Palmeiro 1.25
9 Brady Anderson .50
10 Juan Gonzalez .75
11 Mo Vaughn .50
12 Mark McGwire 4.00
13 Gary Sheffield .90
14 Albert Belle .50
15 Chipper Jones 2.50
16 Mike Piazza 3.00

Willie Mays Reprints

NM/M
Complete Set (27): 50.00
Common Card: 3.00
Autographed Card: 120.00
1 1951 Bowman #305 6.00
2 1952 Topps #261 4.00
3 1953 Topps #244 3.00
4 1954 Bowman #89 3.00
5 1954 Topps #90 3.00
6 1955 Bowman #184 3.00
7 1955 Topps #194 3.00
8 1956 Topps #130 3.00
9 1957 Topps #10 3.00
10 1958 Topps #5 3.00
11 1959 Topps #50 3.00
12 1960 Topps #200 3.00
13 1960 Topps #564 3.00
14 1961 Topps #150 3.00
15 1961 Topps #579 3.00
16 1962 Topps #300 3.00
17 1963 Topps #300 3.00
18 1964 Topps #150 3.00
19 1965 Topps #250 3.00
20 1966 Topps #1 3.00
21 1967 Topps #200 3.00
22 1968 Topps #50 3.00
23 1969 Topps #190 3.00
24 1970 Topps #600 3.00
25 1971 Topps #600 3.00
26 1972 Topps #49 3.00
27 1973 Topps #305 3.00

Willie Mays Reprint Autographs

NM/M
Common Card: 120.00
1 1951 Bowman #305 150.00
2 1952 Topps #261 120.00
3 1953 Topps #244 120.00
5 1955 Bowman #184 120.00
7 1955 Topps #194 120.00
9 1957 Topps #10 120.00
10 1958 Topps #5 120.00
12 1960 Topps #200 120.00
13 1960 Topps #564 120.00
14 1961 Topps #150 120.00
15 1961 Topps #579 120.00
17 1963 Topps #300 120.00
18 1964 Topps #150 120.00
19 1965 Topps #250 120.00
20 1966 Topps #1 120.00
23 1969 Topps #190 120.00
24 1970 Topps #600 120.00
26 1972 Topps #49 120.00
27 1973 Topps #305 120.00

Willie Mays Finest

NM/M
Complete Set (27): 60.00
Common Card: 3.00
Refractor: 3X
Inserted 1:180
1 1951 Bowman #305 6.00
2 1952 Topps #261 4.00
3 1953 Topps #244 3.00
4 1954 Bowman #89 3.00
5 1954 Topps #90 3.00
6 1955 Bowman #184 3.00
7 1955 Topps #194 3.00
8 1956 Topps #130 3.00
9 1957 Topps #10 3.00
10 1958 Topps #5 3.00
11 1959 Topps #50 3.00
12 1960 Topps #200 3.00
13 1960 Topps #564 3.00
14 1961 Topps #150 3.00
15 1961 Topps #579 3.00
16 1962 Topps #300 3.00
17 1963 Topps #300 3.00
18 1964 Topps #150 3.00
19 1965 Topps #250 3.00
20 1966 Topps #1 3.00
21 1967 Topps #200 3.00
22 1968 Topps #50 3.00
23 1969 Topps #190 3.00
24 1970 Topps #600 3.00
25 1971 Topps #600 3.00
26 1972 Topps #49 3.00
27 1973 Topps #305 3.00

1997 Topps Chrome

NM/M
Complete Set (165): 35.00
Common Player: .10
Refractors: 2X

Pack (4): 1.50
Wax Box (24): 25.00
1 Barry Bonds 3.00
2 Jose Valentin .10
3 Brady Anderson .10
4 Wade Boggs 1.50
5 Andres Galarraga .10
6 Rusty Greer .10
7 Derek Jeter 3.00
8 Ricky Bottalico .10
9 Mike Piazza 2.00
10 Garret Anderson .10
11 Jeff King .10
12 Kevin Appier .10
13 Mark Grace .10
14 Jeff D'Amico .10
15 Jay Buhner .10
16 Hal Morris .10
17 Harold Baines .10
18 Jeff Cirillo .10
19 Tom Glavine .35
20 Andy Pettitte .35
21 Mark McGwire 2.50
22 Chuck Knoblauch .10
23 Raul Mondesi .10
24 Albert Belle .10
25 Trevor Hoffman .10
26 Eric Young .10
27 Brian McRae .10
28 Jim Edmonds .10
29 Robb Nen .10
30 Reggie Sanders .10
31 Mike Lansing .10
32 Craig Biggio .10
33 Ray Lankford .10
34 Charles Nagy .10
35 Paul Wilson .10
36 John Wetteland .10
37 Derek Bell .10
38 Edgar Martinez .10
39 Rickey Henderson 1.00
40 Jim Thome .75
41 Frank Thomas 1.00
42 Jackie Robinson (Tribute) 2.00
43 Terry Steinbach .10
44 Kevin Brown .10
45 Joey Hamilton .10
46 Travis Fryman .10
47 Juan Gonzalez .50
48 Ron Gant .10
49 Greg Maddux 1.50
50 Wally Joyner .10
51 John Valentin .10
52 Bret Boone .10
53 Paul Molitor 1.00
54 Rafael Palmeiro .75
55 Todd Hundley .10
56 Ellis Burks .10
57 Bernie Williams .10
58 Roberto Alomar .25
59 Jose Mesa .10
60 Troy Percival .10
61 John Smoltz .10
62 Jeff Conine .10
63 Bernard Gilkey .10
64 Mickey Tettleton .10
65 Justin Thompson .10
66 Tony Phillips .10
67 Ryne Sandberg 1.50
68 Geronimo Berroa .10
69 Todd Hollandsworth .10
70 Rey Ordonez .10
71 Marquis Grissom .10
72 Tino Martinez .10
73 Steve Finley .10
74 Andy Benes .10
75 Jason Kendall .10
76 Johnny Damon .35
77 Jason Giambi .50
78 Henry Rodriguez .10
79 Edgar Renteria .10
80 Ray Durham .10
81 Gregg Jefferies .10
82 Roberto Hernandez .10
83 Joe Carter .10
84 Jermaine Dye .10
85 Julio Franco .10
86 David Justice .10
87 Jose Canseco .50
88 Paul O'Neill .10
89 Mariano Rivera .15
90 Bobby Higginson .10
91 Mark Grudzielanek .10
92 Lance Johnson .10
93 Ken Caminiti .10
94 Gary Sheffield .50
95 Luis Castillo .10
96 Scott Rolen .75
97 Chipper Jones 1.50
98 Darryl Strawberry .10
99 Nomar Garciaparra 1.50
100 Jeff Bagwell 1.00
101 Ken Griffey Jr. 2.00
102 Sammy Sosa 1.50
103 Jack McDowell .10
104 James Baldwin .10
105 Rocky Coppinger .10
106 Manny Ramirez 1.00
107 Tim Salmon .10
108 Eric Karros .10
109 Brett Butler .10
110 Randy Johnson 1.00
111 Pat Hentgen .10
112 Rondell White .10
113 Eddie Murray 1.00
114 Ivan Rodriguez .75
115 Jermaine Allensworth .10
116 Ed Sprague .10
117 Kenny Lofton .10
118 Alan Benes .10
119 Fred McGriff .10
120 Alex Fernandez .10
121 Al Martin .10
122 Devon White .10
123 David Cone .10
124 Karim Garcia .25
125 Chili Davis .10
126 Roger Clemens 1.75
127 Bobby Bonilla .10
128 Mike Mussina .50
129 Todd Walker .10
130 Dante Bichette .10
131 Carlos Baerga .10
132 Matt Williams .10
133 Will Clark .10
134 Dennis Eckersley .75
135 Ryan Klesko .10
136 Dean Palmer .10
137 Javy Lopez .10
138 Greg Vaughn .10
139 Vinny Castilla .10
140 Cal Ripken Jr. 3.00
141 Ruben Rivera .10
142 Mark Wohlers .10
143 Tony Clark .10
144 Jose Rosado .10
145 Tony Gwynn 1.50
146 Cecil Fielder .10
147 Brian Jordan .10
148 Bob Abreu .10
149 Barry Larkin .10
150 Robin Ventura .10
151 John Olerud .10
152 Rod Beck .10
153 Vladimir Guerrero 1.00
154 Marty Cordova .10
155 Todd Stottlemyre .10
156 Hideo Nomo .50
157 Denny Neagle .10
158 John Jaha .10
159 Mo Vaughn .10
160 Andruw Jones 1.00
161 Moises Alou .10
162 Larry Walker .10
163 Eddie Murray .75
164 Paul Molitor .75
165 Checklist .10

Jumbos

NM/M
Complete Set (6): 10.00
Common Player: .75
9 Mike Piazza 2.00
94 Gary Sheffield .75
97 Chipper Jones 1.50
101 Ken Griffey Jr. 2.00
102 Sammy Sosa 1.50
140 Cal Ripken Jr. 3.00

All-Stars

NM/M
Complete Set (22): 25.00

Common Player: .75
Refractors: 1.5X
1 Ivan Rodriguez 1.50
2 Todd Hundley .75
3 Frank Thomas 2.00
4 Andres Galarraga .75
5 Chuck Knoblauch .75
6 Eric Young .75
7 Jim Thome 1.50
8 Chipper Jones 3.00
9 Cal Ripken Jr. 6.00
10 Barry Larkin .75
11 Albert Belle .75
12 Barry Bonds 6.00
13 Ken Griffey Jr. 4.00
14 Ellis Burks .75
15 Juan Gonzalez 1.00
16 Gary Sheffield 1.25
17 Andy Pettitte 1.00
18 Tom Glavine 1.00
19 Pat Hentgen .75
20 John Smoltz .75
21 Roberto Hernandez .75
22 Mark Wohlers .75

Diamond Duos

NM/M
Complete Set (10): 17.50
Common Player: .50
Refractors: 1.5X
1 Chipper Jones, Andruw Jones 2.00
2 Derek Jeter, Bernie Williams 4.00
3 Ken Griffey Jr., Jay Buhner 2.50
4 Kenny Lofton, Manny Ramirez 1.50
5 Jeff Bagwell, Craig Biggio 1.50
6 Juan Gonzalez, Ivan Rodriguez 1.25
7 Cal Ripken Jr., Brady Anderson 4.00
8 Mike Piazza, Hideo Nomo 2.50
9 Andres Galarraga, Dante Bichette .50
10 Frank Thomas, Albert Belle 1.50

Season's Best

NM/M
Complete Set (25): 17.50
Common Player: .50
Refractors: 1.5X
1 Tony Gwynn 2.00
2 Frank Thomas 1.50
3 Ellis Burks .50
4 Paul Molitor 1.50
5 Chuck Knoblauch .50
6 Mark McGwire 4.00
7 Brady Anderson .50
8 Ken Griffey Jr. 3.00
9 Albert Belle .50
10 Andres Galarraga .50
11 Andres Galarraga .50
12 Albert Belle .50
13 Juan Gonzalez .75
14 Mo Vaughn .50
15 Rafael Palmeiro 1.25
16 John Smoltz .50
17 Andy Pettitte .75
18 Pat Hentgen .50
19 Mike Mussina .75
20 Andy Benes .50
21 Kenny Lofton .50
22 Tom Goodwin .50
23 Otis Nixon .50
24 Eric Young .50
25 Lance Johnson .50

1997 Topps Gallery

NM/M
Complete Set (180): 20.00
Common Player: .10
Pack (8): 1.50
Wax Box (24): 25.00
1 Paul Molitor .75
2 Devon White .10
3 Andres Galarraga .10
4 Cal Ripken Jr. 3.00
5 Tony Gwynn 1.50
6 Mike Stanley .10
7 Orel Hershiser .10
8 Jose Canseco .50

9 Chili Davis .10
10 Harold Baines .10
11 Rickey Henderson .75
12 Darryl Strawberry .10
13 Todd Worrell .10
14 Cecil Fielder .10
15 Gary Gaetti .10
16 Bobby Bonilla .10
17 Will Clark .10
18 Kevin Brown .10
19 Tom Glavine .35
20 Wade Boggs 1.50
21 Edgar Martinez .10
22 Lance Johnson .10
23 Gregg Jefferies .10
24 Bip Roberts .10
25 Tony Phillips .10
26 Greg Maddux 1.50
27 Mickey Tettleton .10
28 Terry Steinbach .10
29 Ryne Sandberg 1.50
30 Wally Joyner .10
31 Joe Carter .10
32 Ellis Burks .10
33 Fred McGriff .10
34 Barry Larkin .10
35 John Franco .10
36 Rafael Palmeiro .65
37 Mark McGwire 2.50
38 Ken Caminiti .10
39 David Cone .10
40 Julio Franco .10
41 Roger Clemens 1.75
42 Barry Bonds 3.00
43 Dennis Eckersley .65
44 Eddie Murray .75
45 Paul O'Neill .10
46 Craig Biggio .10
47 Roberto Alomar .20
48 Mark Grace .10
49 Matt Williams .10
50 Jay Buhner .10
51 John Smoltz .10
52 Randy Johnson .75
53 Ramon Martinez .10
54 Curt Schilling .35
55 Gary Sheffield .50
56 Jack McDowell .10
57 Brady Anderson .10
58 Dante Bichette .10
59 Ron Gant .10
60 Alex Fernandez .10
61 Moises Alou .10
62 Travis Fryman .10
63 Dean Palmer .10
64 Todd Hundley .10
65 Jeff Brantley .10
66 Bernard Gilkey .10
67 Geronimo Berroa .10
68 John Wetteland .10
69 Robin Ventura .10
70 Ray Lankford .10
71 Kevin Appier .10
72 Larry Walker .10
73 Juan Gonzalez .40
74 Jeff King .10
75 Greg Vaughn .10
76 Steve Finley .10
77 Brian McRae .10
78 Paul Sorrento .10
79 Ken Griffey Jr. 2.00
80 Omar Vizquel .10
81 Jose Mesa .10
82 Albert Belle .10
83 Glenallen Hill .10
84 Sammy Sosa 1.50
85 Andy Benes .10
86 David Justice .10
87 Marquis Grissom .10
88 John Olerud .10
89 Tino Martinez .10
90 Frank Thomas .75
91 Raul Mondesi .10
92 Steve Trachsel .10
93 Jim Edmonds .10
94 Rusty Greer .10
95 Joey Hamilton .10
96 Ismael Valdes .10
97 Dave Nilsson .10
98 John Jaha .10
99 Alex Gonzalez .10

100 Javy Lopez .10
101 Ryan Klesko .10
102 Tim Salmon .10
103 Bernie Williams .10
104 Roberto Hernandez .10
105 Chuck Knoblauch .10
106 Mike Lansing .10
107 Vinny Castilla .10
108 Reggie Sanders .10
109 Mo Vaughn .10
110 Rondell White .10
111 Ivan Rodriguez .65
112 Mike Mussina .40
113 Carlos Baerga .10
114 Jeff Conine .10
115 Jim Thome .65
116 Manny Ramirez .75
117 Kenny Lofton .10
118 Wilson Alvarez .10
119 Eric Karros .10
120 Robb Nen .10
121 Mark Wohlers .10
122 Ed Sprague .10
123 Pat Hentgen .10
124 Juan Guzman .10
125 Derek Bell .10
126 Jeff Bagwell .75
127 Eric Young .10
128 John Valentin .10
129 Al Martin (Photo actually Javy Lopez.) .10
130 Trevor Hoffman .10
131 Henry Rodriguez .10
132 Pedro Martinez .75
133 Mike Piazza 2.00
134 Brian Jordan .10
135 Jose Valentin .10
136 Jeff Cirillo .10
137 Chipper Jones 1.50
138 Ricky Bottalico .10
139 Hideo Nomo .40
140 Troy Percival .10
141 Rey Ordonez .10
142 Edgar Renteria .10
143 Luis Castillo .10
144 Vladimir Guerrero .75
145 Jeff D'Amico .10
146 Andruw Jones .75
147 Darin Erstad .25
148 Bob Abreu .10
149 Carlos Delgado .45
150 Jamey Wright .10
151 Nomar Garciaparra 1.50
152 Jason Kendall .10
153 Jermaine Allensworth .10
154 Scott Rolen .65
155 Rocky Coppinger .10
156 Paul Wilson .10
157 Garret Anderson .10
158 Mariano Rivera .15
159 Ruben Rivera .10
160 Andy Pettitte .35
161 Derek Jeter 3.00
162 Neifi Perez .10
163 Ray Durham .10
164 James Baldwin .10
165 Marty Cordova .10
166 Tony Clark .10
167 Michael Tucker .10
168 Mike Sweeney .10
169 Johnny Damon .25
170 Jermaine Dye .10
171 Alex Ochoa .10
172 Jason Isringhausen .10
173 Mark Grudzielanek .10
174 Jose Rosado .10
175 Todd Hollandsworth .10
176 Alan Benes .10
177 Jason Giambi .45
178 Billy Wagner .10
179 Justin Thompson .10
180 Todd Walker .10

Gallery Players Private Issue

NM/M
Common Player: 1.00
Stars: 5X
(See 1997 Topps/Gallery for checklist and base card values.)

Peter Max

NM/M
Complete Set (10): 60.00
Common Player: 3.00
Peter Max Autographed: 100.00
1 Derek Jeter 10.00
2 Albert Belle 3.00
3 Ken Caminiti 3.00
4 Chipper Jones 6.00
5 Ken Griffey Jr. 7.50
6 Frank Thomas 5.00
7 Cal Ripken Jr. 10.00
8 Mark McGwire 9.00
9 Barry Bonds 10.00
10 Mike Piazza 7.50

Photo Gallery

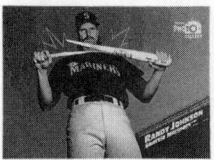

NM/M
Complete Set (16): 15.00
Common Player: .50
1 World Series .50
2 Paul Molitor 1.00
3 Eddie Murray 1.00
4 Ken Griffey Jr. 2.50
5 Chipper Jones 1.50
6 Derek Jeter 3.50
7 Frank Thomas 1.00
8 Mark McGwire 3.00
9 Kenny Lofton .50
10 Gary Sheffield .65
11 Mike Piazza 2.50
12 Vinny Castilla .50
13 Andres Galarraga .50
14 Andy Pettitte .50
15 Robin Ventura .50
16 Barry Larkin .50

of Heroes

NM/M
Complete Set (10): 30.00
Common Player: 1.50
1 Derek Jeter 6.00
2 Chipper Jones 3.00
3 Frank Thomas 2.50
4 Ken Griffey Jr. 4.00
5 Cal Ripken Jr. 6.00
6 Mark McGwire 5.00
7 Mike Piazza 4.00
8 Jeff Bagwell 2.50
9 Tony Gwynn 3.00
10 Mo Vaughn 1.50

1997 Topps Screenplays

		NM/M
Complete Set (20):		25.00
Common Player:		1.00
Pack (1):		2.50
Wax Box (21):		30.00
(1)	Jeff Bagwell	2.00
(2)	Albert Belle	1.00
(3)	Barry Bonds	5.00
(4)	Andres Galarraga	1.00
(5)	Nomar Garciaparra	2.50
(6)	Juan Gonzalez	1.25
(7)	Ken Griffey Jr.	3.00
(8)	Tony Gwynn	2.50
(9)	Derek Jeter	5.00
(10)	Randy Johnson	2.00
(11)	Andruw Jones	2.00
(12)	Chipper Jones	2.50
(13)	Kenny Lofton	1.00
(14)	Mark McGwire	4.00
(15)	Paul Molitor	2.00
(16)	Hideo Nomo	1.25
(17)	Cal Ripken Jr.	5.00
(18)	Sammy Sosa	2.50
(19)	Frank Thomas	2.00
(20)	Jim Thome	1.50

Inserts

		NM/M
Complete Set (6):		35.00
Common Player:		2.00
1	Larry Walker	2.00
2	Cal Ripken Jr.	12.50
3	Chipper Jones	6.00
4	Frank Thomas	5.00
5	Mike Piazza	7.50
6	Ken Griffey Jr.	7.50

1997 Topps Stars

		NM/M
Complete Set (125):		30.00
Common Player:		.10
Always Mint Stars, RC's:		8X
Pack (7):		3.00
Wax Box (24):		65.00
1	Larry Walker	.10
2	Tino Martinez	.10
3	Cal Ripken Jr.	3.00
4	Ken Griffey Jr.	2.00
5	Chipper Jones	1.50
6	David Justice	.10
7	Mike Piazza	2.00
8	Jeff Bagwell	1.00
9	Ron Gant	.10
10	Sammy Sosa	2.00
11	Tony Gwynn	1.50
12	Carlos Baerga	.10
13	Frank Thomas	1.00
14	Moises Alou	.10
15	Barry Larkin	.10
16	Ivan Rodriguez	.75
17	Greg Maddux	1.50
18	Jim Edmonds	.10
19	Jose Canseco	.50
20	Rafael Palmeiro	.75
21	Paul Molitor	1.00
22	Kevin Appier	.10
23	Raul Mondesi	.10
24	Lance Johnson	.10
25	Edgar Martinez	.10
26	Andres Galarraga	.10
27	Mo Vaughn	.10
28	Ken Caminiti	.10
29	Cecil Fielder	.10
30	Harold Baines	.10
31	Roberto Alomar	.25
32	Shawn Estes	.10
33	Tom Glavine	.35
34	Dennis Eckersley	.75
35	Manny Ramirez	1.00
36	John Olerud	.10
37	Juan Gonzalez	.50
38	Chuck Knoblauch	.10
39	Albert Belle	.10
40	Vinny Castilla	.10
41	John Smoltz	.10
42	Barry Bonds	3.00
43	Randy Johnson	1.00
44	Brady Anderson	.10
45	Jeff Blauser	.10
46	Craig Biggio	.10
47	Jeff Conine	.10
48	Marquis Grissom	.10
49	Mark Grace	.10
50	Roger Clemens	1.75
51	Mark McGwire	2.50
52	Fred McGriff	.10
53	Gary Sheffield	.50
54	Bobby Jones	.75
55	Eric Young	.10
56	Robin Ventura	.10
57	Wade Boggs	1.50
58	Joe Carter	.10
59	Ryne Sandberg	1.50
60	Matt Williams	.10
61	Todd Hundley	.10
62	Dante Bichette	.10
63	Chili Davis	.10
64	Kenny Lofton	.10
65	Jay Buhner	.10
66	Will Clark	.10
67	Travis Fryman	.10
68	Pat Hentgen	.10
69	Ellis Burks	.10
70	Mike Mussina	.40
71	Hideo Nomo	.50
72	Sandy Alomar	.10
73	Bobby Bonilla	.10
74	Rickey Henderson	1.00
75	David Cone	.10
76	Terry Steinbach	.10
77	Pedro Martinez	1.00
78	Jim Thome	.75
79	Rod Beck	.10
80	Randy Myers	.10
81	Charles Nagy	.10
82	Mark Wohlers	.10
83	Paul O''Neill	.10
84	Curt Schilling	.35
85	Joey Cora	.10
86	John Franco	.10
87	Kevin Brown	.10
88	Benito Santiago	.10
89	Ray Lankford	.10
90	Bernie Williams	.10
91	Jason Dickson	.10
92	Jeff Cirillo	.10
93	Nomar Garciaparra	2.00
94	Mariano Rivera	.15
95	Javy Lopez	.10
96	Tony Womack RC	.25
97	Jose Rosado	.10
98	Denny Neagle	.10
99	Darryl Kile	.10
100	Justin Thompson	.10
101	Juan Encarnacion	.10
102	Brad Fullmer	.10
103	Kris Benson RC	.75
104	Todd Helton RC	1.00
105	Paul Konerko	.10
106	Travis Lee RC	1.00
107	Todd Greene	.10
108	Mark Kotsay RC	.50
109	Carl Pavano	.10
110	Kerry Wood RC	4.00
111	Jason Romano RC	.10
112	Geoff Goetz RC	.10
113	Scott Hodges RC	.10
114	Aaron Akin RC	.10
115	Vernon Wells RC	6.00
116	Chris Stowe RC	.10
117	Brett Caradonna RC	.10
118	Adam Kennedy RC	1.00
119	Jayson Werth RC	.10
120	Glenn Davis RC	.10
121	Troy Cameron RC	.10
122	J.J. Davis RC	.10
123	Jason Dellaero RC	.10
124	Jason Standridge RC	.10
125	Lance Berkman RC	2.00

Always Mint

		NM/M
Complete Set (125):		250.00
Common Player:		.50

Stars/Rookies:	8X
(See 1997 Topps Stars for checklist and base card values.)	

All-Star Memories

		NM/M
Complete Set (10):		20.00
Common Player:		1.00
1	Cal Ripken Jr.	6.00
2	Jeff Conine	1.00
3	Mike Piazza	4.00
4	Randy Johnson	2.00
5	Ken Griffey Jr.	4.00
6	Fred McGriff	1.00
7	Moises Alou	1.00
8	Hideo Nomo	1.25
9	Larry Walker	1.00
10	Sandy Alomar	1.00

Autographed Rookie Reprints

		NM/M
Common Player:		15.00
(1)	Luis Aparicio	20.00
(3)	Jim Bunning	30.00
(4)	Bob Feller	35.00
(5)	Rollie Fingers	15.00
(6)	Monte Irvin	15.00
(7)	Al Kaline	30.00
(8)	Ralph Kiner	25.00
(9)	Eddie Mathews	75.00
(10)	Hal Newhouser	40.00
(11)	Gaylord Perry	15.00
(12)	Robin Roberts	30.00
(13)	Brooks Robinson	40.00
(14)	Enos Slaughter	30.00
(15)	Earl Weaver	20.00

Future All-Stars

		NM/M
Complete Set (15):		17.50
Common Player:		.75
1	Derek Jeter	4.00
2	Andruw Jones	2.50
3	Vladimir Guerrero	3.00
4	Scott Rolen	2.50
5	Jose Guillen	.75
6	Jose Cruz, Jr.	.75
7	Darin Erstad	2.50
8	Tony Clark	.75
9	Scott Spiezio	.75
10	Kevin Orie	.75
11	Calvin Reese	.75
12	Billy Wagner	.75
13	Matt Morris	.75
14	Jeremi Gonzalez	.75
15	Hideki Irabu	.75

Rookie Reprints

		NM/M
Complete Set (15):		25.00
Common Player:		2.00
(1)	Luis Aparicio	2.00
(2)	Richie Ashburn	2.00
(3)	Jim Bunning	2.00
(4)	Bob Feller	2.00
(5)	Rollie Fingers	2.00
(6)	Monte Irvin	2.00
(7)	Al Kaline	3.00
(8)	Ralph Kiner	2.00
(9)	Eddie Mathews	3.00
(10)	Hal Newhouser	2.00
(11)	Gaylord Perry	2.00
(12)	Robin Roberts	2.00
(13)	Brooks Robinson	3.00
(14)	Enos Slaughter	2.00
(15)	Earl Weaver	2.00

1997 All-Stars

		NM/M
Complete Set (20):		60.00
Common Player:		1.50
1	Greg Maddux	6.00
2	Randy Johnson	4.50
3	Tino Martinez	1.50
4	Jeff Bagwell	4.50
5	Ivan Rodriguez	3.50

6	Mike Piazza	7.50
7	Cal Ripken Jr.	12.00
8	Ken Caminiti	1.50
9	Tony Gwynn	6.00
10	Edgar Martinez	1.50
11	Craig Biggio	1.50
12	Roberto Alomar	2.00
13	Larry Walker	1.50
14	Brady Anderson	1.50
15	Barry Bonds	12.00
16	Ken Griffey Jr.	7.50
17	Ray Lankford	1.50
18	Paul O'Neill	1.50
19	Jeff Blauser	1.50
20	Sandy Alomar	1.50

1998 Topps

	NM/M
Unopened Fact. Set (511):	85.00
Complete Set (503):	40.00
Common Player:	.05
Minted:	6X
Inserted 1:8	
Series 1 or 2 Pack (11):	1.00
Series 1 or 2 Wax Box (36):	25.00

1	Tony Gwynn	1.00
2	Larry Walker	.05
3	Billy Wagner	.05
4	Denny Neagle	.05
5	Vladimir Guerrero	.75
6	Kevin Brown	.05
7	Not Issued	
8	Mariano Rivera	.10
9	Tony Clark	.05
10	Deion Sanders	.05
11	Francisco Cordova	.05
12	Matt Williams	.05
13	Carlos Baerga	.05
14	Mo Vaughn	.05
15	Bobby Witt	.05
16	Matt Stairs	.05
17	Chan Ho Park	.05
18	Mike Bordick	.05
19	Michael Tucker	.05
20	Frank Thomas	.75
21	Roberto Clemente	1.50
22	Dmitri Young	.05
23	Steve Trachsel	.05
24	Jeff Kent	.05
25	Scott Rolen	.50
26	John Thomson	.05
27	Joe Vitiello	.05
28	Eddie Guardado	.05
29	Charlie Hayes	.05
30	Juan Gonzalez	.40
31	Garret Anderson	.05
32	John Jaha	.05
33	Omar Vizquel	.05
34	Brian Hunter	.05
35	Jeff Bagwell	.75
36	Mark Lemke	.05
37	Doug Glanville	.05
38	Dan Wilson	.05
39	Steve Cooke	.05
40	Chili Davis	.05
41	Mike Cameron	.05
42	F.P. Santangelo	.05
43	Brad Ausmus	.05
44	Gary DiSarcina	.05
45	Pat Hentgen	.05
46	Wilton Guerrero	.05
47	Devon White	.05
48	Danny Patterson	.05
49	Pat Meares	.05
50	Rafael Palmeiro	.65
51	Mark Gardner	.05
52	Jeff Blauser	.05
53	Dave Hollins	.05
54	Carlos Garcia	.05
55	Ben McDonald	.05
56	John Mabry	.05
57	Trevor Hoffman	.05
58	Tony Fernandez	.05
59	Rich Loiselle	.05
60	Mark Leiter	.05
61	Pat Kelly	.05
62	John Flaherty	.05
63	Roger Bailey	.05
64	Tom Gordon	.05
65	Ryan Klesko	.05
66	Darryl Hamilton	.05
67	Jim Eisenreich	.05
68	Butch Huskey	.05
69	Mark Grudzielanek	.05
70	Marquis Grissom	.05
71	Mark McLemore	.05
72	Gary Gaetti	.05
73	Greg Gagne	.05
74	Lyle Mouton	.05
75	Jim Edmonds	.05
76	Shawn Green	.25
77	Greg Vaughn	.05
78	Terry Adams	.05
79	Kevin Polcovich **RC**	.05
80	Troy O'Leary	.05
81	Jeff Shaw	.05
82	Rich Becker	.05
83	David Wells	.05
84	Steve Karsay	.05
85	Charles Nagy	.05
86	B.J. Surhoff	.05
87	Jamey Wright	.05
88	James Baldwin	.05
89	Edgardo Alfonzo	.05
90	Jay Buhner	.05
91	Brady Anderson	.05
92	Scott Servais	.05
93	Edgar Renteria	.05
94	Mike Lieberthal	.05
95	Rick Aguilera	.05
96	Walt Weiss	.05
97	Deivi Cruz	.05
98	Kurt Abbott	.05
99	Henry Rodriguez	.05
100	Mike Piazza	1.25
101	Bill Taylor	.05
102	Todd Zeile	.05
103	Rey Ordonez	.05
104	Willie Greene	.05
105	Tony Womack	.05
106	Mike Sweeney	.05
107	Jeffrey Hammonds	.05
108	Kevin Orie	.05
109	Alex Gonzalez	.05
110	Jose Canseco	.50
111	Paul Sorrento	.05
112	Joey Hamilton	.05
113	Brad Radke	.05
114	Steve Avery	.05
115	Esteban Loaiza	.05
116	Stan Javier	.05
117	Chris Gomez	.05
118	Royce Clayton	.05
119	Orlando Merced	.05
120	Kevin Appier	.05
121	Mel Nieves	.05
122	Joe Girardi	.05
123	Rico Brogna	.05
124	Kent Mercker	.05
125	Manny Ramirez	.75
126	Jeromy Burnitz	.05
127	Kevin Foster	.05
128	Matt Morris	.05
129	Jason Dickson	.05
130	Tom Glavine	.25
131	Wally Joyner	.05
132	Rick Reed	.05
133	Todd Jones	.05
134	Dave Martinez	.05
135	Sandy Alomar	.05
136	Mike Lansing	.05
137	Sean Berry	.05
138	Doug Jones	.05
139	Todd Stottlemyre	.05
140	Jay Bell	.05
141	Jaime Navarro	.05
142	Chris Hoiles	.05
143	Joey Cora	.05
144	Scott Spiezio	.05
145	Joe Carter	.05
146	Jose Guillen	.05
147	Damion Easley	.05
148	Lee Stevens	.05
149	Alex Fernandez	.05
150	Randy Johnson	.75
151	J.T. Snow	.05
152	Chuck Finley	.05
153	Bernard Gilkey	.05
154	David Segui	.05
155	Dante Bichette	.05
156	Kevin Stocker	.05
157	Carl Everett	.05
158	Jose Valentin	.05
159	Pokey Reese	.05
160	Derek Jeter	2.00
161	Roger Pavlik	.05
162	Mark Wohlers	.05
163	Ricky Bottalico	.05
164	Ozzie Guillen	.05
165	Mike Mussina	.50
166	Gary Sheffield	.50
167	Hideo Nomo	.40
168	Mark Grace	.05
169	Aaron Sele	.05
170	Darryl Kile	.05
171	Shawn Estes	.05
172	Vinny Castilla	.05
173	Ron Coomer	.05
174	Jose Rosado	.05
175	Kenny Lofton	.05
176	Jason Giambi	.50
177	Hal Morris	.05
178	Darren Bragg	.05
179	Orel Hershiser	.05
180	Ray Lankford	.05
181	Hideki Irabu	.05
182	Kevin Young	.05
183	Javy Lopez	.05
184	Jeff Montgomery	.05
185	Mike Holtz	.05
186	George Williams	.05
187	Cal Eldred	.05
188	Tom Candiotti	.05
189	Glenallen Hill	.05
190	Brian Giles	.05
191	Dave Mlicki	.05
192	Garrett Stephenson	.05
193	Jeff Frye	.05
194	Joe Oliver	.05
195	Bob Hamelin	.05
196	Luis Sojo	.05
197	LaTroy Hawkins	.05
198	Kevin Elster	.05
199	Jeff Reed	.05
200	Dennis Eckersley	.65
201	Bill Mueller	.05
202	Russ Davis	.05
203	Armando Benitez	.05
204	Quilvio Veras	.05
205	Tim Naehring	.05
206	Quinton McCracken	.05
207	Raul Casanova	.05
208	Matt Lawton	.05
209	Luis Alicea	.05
210	Luis Gonzalez	.05
211	Allen Watson	.05
212	Gerald Williams	.05
213	David Bell	.05
214	Todd Hollandsworth	.05
215	Wade Boggs	1.00
216	Jose Mesa	.05
217	Jamie Moyer	.05
218	Darren Daulton	.05
219	Mickey Morandini	.05
220	Rusty Greer	.05
221	Jim Bullinger	.05
222	Jose Offerman	.05
223	Matt Karchner	.05
224	Woody Williams	.05
225	Mark Loretta	.05
226	Mike Hampton	.05
227	Willie Adams	.05
228	Scott Hatteberg	.05
229	Rich Amaral	.05
230	Terry Steinbach	.05
231	Glendon Rusch	.05
232	Bret Boone	.05
233	Robert Person	.05
234	Jose Hernandez	.05
235	Doug Drabek	.05
236	Jason McDonald	.05
237	Chris Widger	.05
238	Tom Martin **RC**	.05
239	Dave Burba	.05
240	Pete Rose II	.05
241	Bobby Ayala	.05
242	Tim Wakefield	.05
243	Dennis Springer	.05
244	Tim Belcher	.05
245	Jon Garland, Geoff Goetz	.05
246	Glenn Davis, Lance Berkman	.05
247	Vernon Wells, Aaron Akin	.10
248	Adam Kennedy, Jason Romano	.10
249	Jason Dellaero, Troy Cameron	.05
250	Alex Sanchez, Jared Sandberg **RC**	.10
251	Pablo Ortega, Jim Manias	.05
252	Jason Conti, Mike Stoner **RC**	.10
253	John Patterson, Larry Rodriguez	.05
254	Adrian Beltre, Ryan Minor, Aaron Boone	.15
255	Ben Grieve, Brian Buchanan, Dermal Brown	.05
256	Carl Pavano, Kerry Wood, Gil Meche	.15
257	David Ortiz, Daryle Ward, Richie Sexson	.50
258	Randy Winn, Juan Encarnacion, Andrew Vessel	.10
259	Kris Benson, Travis Smith, Courtney Duncan	.05
260	Chad Hermansen, Brent Butler, Warren Morris **RC**	.10
261	Ben Davis, Elieser Marrero, Ramon Hernandez	.05
262	Eric Chavez, Russell Branyan, Russ Johnson	.20
263	Todd Dunwoody, John Barnes, Ryan Jackson **RC**	.10
264	Matt Clement, Roy Halladay, Brian Fuentes **RC**	.05
265	Randy Johnson	.15
266	Kevin Brown	.05
267	Ricardo Rincon, Francisco Cordova	.05
268	Nomar Garciaparra	.50
269	Tino Martinez	.05
270	Chuck Knoblauch	.05
271	Pedro Martinez	.40
272	Denny Neagle	.05
273	Juan Gonzalez	.20
274	Andres Galarraga	.05
275	Checklist	.05
276	Checklist	.05
277	Moises Alou	.05
278	Sandy Alomar	.05
279	Gary Sheffield	.05
280	Matt Williams	.05
281	Livan Hernandez	.05
282	Chad Ogea	.05
283	Marlins Win	.05
284	Tino Martinez	.05
285	Roberto Alomar	.20
286	Jeff King	.05
287	Brian Jordan	.05
288	Darin Erstad	.15
289	Ken Caminiti	.05
290	Jim Thome	.60
291	Paul Molitor	.75
292	Ivan Rodriguez	.65
293	Bernie Williams	.05
294	Todd Hundley	.05
295	Andres Galarraga	.05
296	Greg Maddux	1.00
297	Edgar Martinez	.05
298	Ron Gant	.05
299	Derek Bell	.05
300	Roger Clemens	1.00
301	Rondell White	.05
302	Barry Larkin	.05
303	Robin Ventura	.05
304	Jason Kendall	.05
305	Chipper Jones	1.00
306	John Franco	.05
307	Sammy Sosa	1.00
308	Troy Percival	.05
309	Chuck Knoblauch	.05
310	Ellis Burks	.05
311	Al Martin	.05
312	Tim Salmon	.05
313	Moises Alou	.05
314	Lance Johnson	.05
315	Justin Thompson	.05
316	Will Clark	.05
317	Barry Bonds	2.00
318	Craig Biggio	.05
319	John Smoltz	.05
320	Cal Ripken Jr.	2.00
321	Ken Griffey Jr.	1.25
322	Paul O'Neill	.05
323	Todd Helton	.65
324	John Olerud	.05
325	Mark McGwire	1.50
326	Jose Cruz Jr.	.05
327	Jeff Cirillo	.05
328	Dean Palmer	.05
329	John Wetteland	.05
330	Steve Finley	.05
331	Albert Belle	.05
332	Curt Schilling	.25
333	Raul Mondesi	.05
334	Andruw Jones	.75
335	Nomar Garciaparra	1.00
336	David Justice	.05
337	Andy Pettitte	.25
338	Pedro Martinez	.75
339	Travis Miller	.05
340	Chris Stynes	.05
341	Gregg Jefferies	.05
342	Jeff Fassero	.05
343	Craig Counsell	.05
344	Wilson Alvarez	.05
345	Bip Roberts	.05
346	Kelvim Escobar	.05
347	Mark Bellhorn	.05
348	Cory Lidle **RC**	.05
349	Fred McGriff	.05
350	Chuck Carr	.05
351	Bob Abreu	.05
352	Juan Guzman	.05
353	Fernando Vina	.05
354	Andy Benes	.05
355	Dave Nilsson	.05
356	Bobby Bonilla	.05
357	Ismael Valdes	.05
358	Carlos Perez	.05
359	Kirk Rueter	.05
360	Bartolo Colon	.05
361	Mel Rojas	.05
362	Johnny Damon	.25
363	Geronimo Berroa	.05
364	Reggie Sanders	.05
365	Jermaine Allensworth	.05
366	Orlando Cabrera	.05
367	Jorge Fabregas	.05
368	Scott Stahoviak	.05
369	Ken Cloude	.05
370	Donovan Osborne	.05
371	Roger Cedeno	.05
372	Neifi Perez	.05
373	Chris Holt	.05
374	Cecil Fielder	.05
375	Marty Cordova	.05
376	Tom Goodwin	.05
377	Jeff Suppan	.05
378	Jeff Brantley	.05
379	Mark Langston	.05
380	Shane Reynolds	.05
381	Mike Fetters	.05
382	Todd Greene	.05
383	Ray Durham	.05
384	Carlos Delgado	.30
385	Jeff D'Amico	.05
386	Brian McRae	.05
387	Alan Benes	.05
388	Heathcliff Slocumb	.05
389	Eric Young	.05
390	Travis Fryman	.05
391	David Cone	.05

392	Otis Nixon	.05
393	Jeremi Gonzalez	.05
394	Jeff Juden	.05
395	Jose Vizcaino	.05
396	Ugueth Urbina	.05
397	Ramon Martinez	.05
398	Robb Nen	.05
399	Harold Baines	.05
400	Delino DeShields	.05
401	John Burkett	.05
402	Sterling Hitchcock	.05
403	Mark Clark	.05
404	Terrell Wade	.05
405	Scott Brosius	.05
406	Chad Curtis	.05
407	Brian Johnson	.05
408	Roberto Kelly	.05
409	Dave Dellucci **RC**	.15
410	Michael Tucker	.05
411	Mark Kotsay	.05
412	Mark Lewis	.05
413	Ryan McGuire	.05
414	Shawon Dunston	.05
415	Brad Rigby	.05
416	Scott Erickson	.05
417	Bobby Jones	.05
418	Darren Oliver	.05
419	John Smiley	.05
420	T.J. Mathews	.05
421	Dustin Hermanson	.05
422	Mike Timlin	.05
423	Willie Blair	.05
424	Manny Alexander	.05
425	Bob Tewksbury	.05
426	Pete Schourek	.05
427	Reggie Jefferson	.05
428	Ed Sprague	.05
429	Jeff Conine	.05
430	Roberto Hernandez	.05
431	Tom Pagnozzi	.05
432	Jaret Wright	.05
433	Livan Hernandez	.05
434	Andy Ashby	.05
435	Todd Dunn	.05
436	Bobby Higginson	.05
437	Rod Beck	.05
438	Jim Leyritz	.05
439	Matt Williams	.05
440	Brett Tomko	.05
441	Joe Randa	.05
442	Chris Carpenter	.05
443	Dennis Reyes	.05
444	Al Leiter	.05
445	Jason Schmidt	.05
446	Ken Hill	.05
447	Shannon Stewart	.05
448	Enrique Wilson	.05
449	Fernando Tatis	.05
450	Jimmy Key	.05
451	Darrin Fletcher	.05
452	John Valentin	.05
453	Kevin Tapani	.05
454	Eric Karros	.05
455	Jay Bell	.05
456	Walt Weiss	.05
457	Devon White	.05
458	Carl Pavano	.05
459	Mike Lansing	.05
460	John Flaherty	.05
461	Richard Hidalgo	.05
462	Quinton McCracken	.05
463	Karim Garcia	.15
464	Miguel Cairo	.05
465	Edwin Diaz	.05
466	Bobby Smith	.05
467	Yamil Benitez	.05
468	Rich Butler **RC**	.05
469	Ben Ford **RC**	.05
470	Bubba Trammell	.05
471	Brent Brede	.05
472	Brooks Kieschnick	.05
473	Carlos Castillo	.05
474	Brad Radke	.05
475	Roger Clemens	.50
476	Curt Schilling	.05
477	John Olerud	.05
478	Mark McGwire	.75
479	Mike Piazza, Ken Griffey Jr.	.75
480	Jeff Bagwell, Frank Thomas	.50
481	Chipper Jones, Nomar Garciaparra	.75
482	Larry Walker, Juan Gonzalez	.30
483	Gary Sheffield, Tino Martinez	.05
484	Derrick Gibson, Michael Coleman, Norm Hutchins	.05
485	Braden Looper, Cliff Politte, Brian Rose	
486	Eric Milton, Jason Marquis, Corey Lee	.05
487	A.J. Hinch, Mark Osborne, Robert Fick **RC**	.10
488	Aramis Ramirez, Alex Gonzalez, Sean Casey	.15
489	Donnie Bridges, Tim Drew **RC**	.10
490	Ntema Ndungidi, Darnell McDonald **RC**	.10
491	Ryan Anderson, Mark Mangum	.25
492	J.J. Davis, Troy Glaus **RC**	2.00
493	Jayson Werth, Dan Reichert **RC**	.10

494	John Curtice, Mike Cuddyer **RC**	.25
495	Jack Cust, Jason Standridge	1.00
496	Brian Anderson	.05
497	Tony Saunders	.05
498	Vladimir Nunez, Jhensy Sandoval **RC**	.10
499	Brad Penny, Nick Bierbrodt	.05
500	Dustin Carr, Luis Cruz **RC**	.05
501	Marcus McCain, Cedrick Bowers **RC**	.05
502	Checklist	.05
503	Checklist	.05
504	Alex Rodriguez	1.50

Minted in Cooperstown

RANDY JOHNSON SEATTLE MARINERS

	NM/M
Common Card:	.50
Stars/Rookies:	6X

(See 1998 Topps for checklist and base card values.)

Baby Boomers

DEREK JETER

		NM/M
Complete Set (15):		15.00
Common Player:		.75
Inserted 1:36 Retail		
1	Derek Jeter	6.00
2	Scott Rolen	1.00
3	Nomar Garciaparra	3.50
4	Jose Cruz Jr.	.75
5	Darin Erstad	.85
6	Todd Helton	1.50
7	Tony Clark	.75
8	Jose Guillen	.75
9	Andruw Jones	1.00
10	Vladimir Guerrero	1.50
11	Mark Kotsay	.75
12	Todd Greene	.85
13	Andy Pettitte	.85
14	Justin Thompson	.75
15	Alan Benes	.75

Clout 9

Mike Piazza NY

		NM/M
Complete Set (15):		25.00
Common Player:		.75
Inserted 1:36		
1	Juan Gonzalez	.85
2	Nomar Garciaparra	2.50
3	Jose Cruz Jr.	.75
4	Cal Ripken Jr.	5.00

		NM/M
Complete Set (9):		17.50
Common Player:		1.00
Inserted 1:72		
1	Edgar Martinez	1.00
2	Mike Piazza	5.00
3	Frank Thomas	2.00
4	Craig Biggio	1.00
5	Vinny Castilla	1.00
6	Jeff Blauser	1.00
7	Barry Bonds	7.50
8	Ken Griffey Jr.	5.00
9	Larry Walker	1.00

Etch-A-Sketch

		NM/M
Complete Set (9):		20.00
Common Player:		1.00
Inserted 1:36		
1	Albert Belle	1.00
2	Barry Bonds	6.00
3	Ken Griffey Jr.	4.00
4	Greg Maddux	3.00
5	Hideo Nomo	1.50
6	Mike Piazza	4.00
7	Cal Ripken Jr.	6.00
8	Frank Thomas	2.00
9	Mo Vaughn	1.00

Flashback

DEION SANDERS

		NM/M
Complete Set (10):		22.50
Common Player:		1.00
Inserted 1:72		
1	Barry Bonds	7.50
2	Ken Griffey Jr.	5.00
3	Paul Molitor	2.00
4	Randy Johnson	2.00
5	Cal Ripken Jr.	7.50
6	Tony Gwynn	3.00
7	Kenny Lofton	1.00
8	Gary Sheffield	1.50
9	Deion Sanders	1.00
10	Brady Anderson	1.00

Focal Point

FOCAL POINT

		NM/M
Complete Set (15):		25.00
Common Player:		.75
Inserted 1:36		
1	Juan Gonzalez	.85
2	Nomar Garciaparra	2.50
3	Jose Cruz Jr.	.75
4	Cal Ripken Jr.	5.00

5	Ken Griffey Jr.	3.50
6	Ivan Rodriguez	1.00
7	Larry Walker	.75
8	Barry Bonds	5.00
9	Roger Clemens	3.00
10	Frank Thomas	1.50
11	Chuck Knoblauch	.75
12	Mike Piazza	3.50
13	Greg Maddux	2.50
14	Vladimir Guerrero	1.50
15	Andruw Jones	1.50

Hallbound

HALL BOUND KEN GRIFFEY JR

		NM/M
Complete Set (15):		45.00
Common Player:		1.50
1	Paul Molitor	2.50
2	Tony Gwynn	3.50
3	Wade Boggs	3.50
4	Roger Clemens	4.00
5	Dennis Eckersley	2.00
6	Cal Ripken Jr.	7.50
7	Greg Maddux	3.50
8	Rickey Henderson	2.50
9	Ken Griffey Jr.	5.00
10	Frank Thomas	2.50
11	Mark McGwire	6.00
12	Barry Bonds	7.50
13	Mike Piazza	5.00
14	Juan Gonzalez	1.50
15	Randy Johnson	2.50

Inter-League Mystery Finest

		NM/M
Complete Set (20):		35.00
Common Player:		.75
Inserted 1:36		
Refractors:		1.5X
Inserted 1:144		
1	Chipper Jones	3.00
2	Cal Ripken Jr.	6.50
3	Greg Maddux	3.00
4	Rafael Palmeiro	1.50
5	Todd Hundley	.75
6	Derek Jeter	6.50
7	John Olerud	.75
8	Tino Martinez	.75
9	Larry Walker	.75
10	Ken Griffey Jr.	4.00
11	Andres Galarraga	.75
12	Randy Johnson	2.00
13	Mike Piazza	4.00
14	Jim Edmonds	.75
15	Eric Karros	.75
16	Tim Salmon	.75
17	Sammy Sosa	3.00
18	Frank Thomas	2.00
19	Mark Grace	.75
20	Albert Belle	.75

Milestones

MILESTONE

		NM/M
Complete Set (10):		17.50
Common Player:		.75
MS1	Barry Bonds	5.00
MS2	Roger Clemens	2.50
MS3	Dennis Eckersley	1.00
MS4	Juan Gonzalez	.75
MS5	Ken Griffey Jr.	3.00
MS6	Tony Gwynn	2.00
MS7	Greg Maddux	2.00
MS8	Mark McGwire	4.00
MS9	Cal Ripken Jr.	5.00
MS10	Frank Thomas	1.25

Mystery Finest

		NM/M
Complete Set (20):		25.00
Common Player:		.50
Inserted 1:36		
Borderless 1:72:		1.5X
Bordered Refractors 1:108:		1.5X
Borderless Refractors 1:288:		2X
1	Nomar Garciaparra	1.50
2	Chipper Jones	1.50
3	Scott Rolen	.75
4	Albert Belle	.50
5	Mo Vaughn	.50
6	Jose Cruz Jr.	.50
7	Mark McGwire	3.00
8	Derek Jeter	3.50
9	Tony Gwynn	1.50
10	Frank Thomas	1.00
11	Tino Martinez	.50
12	Greg Maddux	1.50
13	Juan Gonzalez	.75
14	Larry Walker	.50
15	Mike Piazza	2.50
16	Cal Ripken Jr.	3.50
17	Jeff Bagwell	1.00
18	Andruw Jones	1.00
19	Barry Bonds	3.50
20	Ken Griffey Jr.	2.50

Roberto Clemente Finest

		NM/M
Complete Set (19):		60.00
Common Card:		4.00
Inserted 1:72		
Refractors:		2X
Inserted 1:288		
1	1955	6.00
2	1956	4.00
3	1957	4.00
4	1958	4.00
5	1959	4.00
6	1960	4.00
7	1961	4.00
8	1962	4.00
9	1963	4.00
10	1964	4.00
11	1965	4.00
12	1966	4.00
13	1967	4.00
14	1968	4.00
15	1969	4.00
16	1970	4.00
17	1971	4.00
18	1972	4.00
19	1973	4.00

Roberto Clemente Reprints

		NM/M
Complete Set (19):		50.00
Common Card:		2.50
Inserted 1:18		
1	1955	4.00
2	1956	2.50
3	1957	2.50
4	1958	2.50
5	1959	2.50

6	1960	2.50
7	1961	2.50
8	1962	2.50
9	1963	2.50
10	1964	2.50
11	1965	2.50
12	1966	2.50
13	1967	2.50
14	1968	2.50
15	1969	2.50
16	1970	2.50
17	1971	2.50
18	1972	2.50
19	1973	2.50

Roberto Clemente Tribute

		NM/M
Complete Set (5):		3.00
Common Clemente:		.75
Inserted 1:12		
1-5	Roberto Clemente	.75

Rookie Class

		NM/M
Complete Set (10):		4.00
Common Player:		.25
Inserted 1:12		
1	Travis Lee	.50
2	Richard Hidalgo	.25
3	Todd Helton	2.00
4	Paul Konerko	.75
5	Mark Kotsay	.25
6	Derrek Lee	1.50
7	Eli Marrero	.25
8	Fernando Tatis	.25
9	Juan Encarnacion	.25
10	Ben Grieve	.25

1998 Topps Chrome

		NM/M
Complete Set (502):		100.00
Common Player:		.10
Refractors:		5X

Inserted 1:12		
Foil Pack (4):		1.50
Foil Box (24):		25.00
1	Tony Gwynn	2.00
2	Larry Walker	.10
3	Billy Wagner	.10
4	Denny Neagle	.10
5	Vladimir Guerrero	1.50
6	Kevin Brown	.10
7	Not Issued	
8	Mariano Rivera	.10
9	Tony Clark	.10
10	Deion Sanders	.10
11	Francisco Cordova	.10
12	Matt Williams	.10
13	Carlos Baerga	.10
14	Mo Vaughn	.10
15	Bobby Witt	.10
16	Matt Stairs	.10
17	Chan Ho Park	.10
18	Mike Bordick	.10
19	Michael Tucker	.10
20	Frank Thomas	1.50
21	Roberto Clemente (Tribute)	2.50
22	Dmitri Young	.10
23	Steve Trachsel	.10
24	Jeff Kent	.10
25	Scott Rolen	.75
26	John Thomson	.10
27	Joe Vitiello	.10
28	Eddie Guardado	.10
29	Charlie Hayes	.10
30	Juan Gonzalez	.75
31	Garret Anderson	.10
32	John Jaha	.10
33	Omar Vizquel	.10
34	Brian Hunter	.10
35	Jeff Bagwell	1.50
36	Mark Lemke	.10
37	Doug Glanville	.10
38	Dan Wilson	.10
39	Steve Cooke	.10
40	Chili Davis	.10
41	Mike Cameron	.10
42	F.P. Santangelo	.10
43	Brad Ausmus	.10
44	Gary DiSarcina	.10
45	Pat Hentgen	.10
46	Wilton Guerrero	.10
47	Devon White	.10
48	Danny Patterson	.10
49	Pat Meares	.10
50	Rafael Palmeiro	1.00
51	Mark Gardner	.10
52	Jeff Blauser	.10
53	Dave Hollins	.10
54	Carlos Garcia	.10
55	Ben McDonald	.10
56	John Mabry	.10
57	Trevor Hoffman	.10
58	Tony Fernandez	.10
59	Rich Loiselle	.10
60	Mark Leiter	.10
61	Pat Kelly	.10
62	John Flaherty	.10
63	Roger Bailey	.10
64	Tom Gordon	.10
65	Ryan Klesko	.10
66	Darryl Hamilton	.10
67	Jim Eisenreich	.10
68	Butch Huskey	.10
69	Mark Grudzielanek	.10
70	Marquis Grissom	.10
71	Mark McLemore	.10
72	Gary Gaetti	.10
73	Greg Gagne	.10
74	Lyle Mouton	.10
75	Jim Edmonds	.10
76	Shawn Green	.35
77	Terry Vaughn	.10
78	Terry Adams	.10
79	Kevin Polcovich RC	.10
80	Troy O'Leary	.10
81	Jeff Shaw	.10
82	Rich Becker	.10
83	David Wells	.10
84	Steve Karsay	.10
85	Charles Nagy	.10
86	B.J. Surhoff	.10
87	Jamey Wright	.10
88	James Baldwin	.10

89	Edgardo Alfonzo	.10
90	Jay Buhner	.10
91	Brady Anderson	.10
92	Scott Servais	.10
93	Edgar Renteria	.10
94	Mike Lieberthal	.10
95	Rick Aguilera	.10
96	Walt Weiss	.10
97	Deivi Cruz	.10
98	Kurt Abbott	.10
99	Henry Rodriguez	.10
100	Mike Piazza	2.25
101	Bill Taylor	.10
102	Todd Zeile	.10
103	Rey Ordonez	.10
104	Willie Greene	.10
105	Tony Womack	.10
106	Mike Sweeney	.10
107	Jeffrey Hammonds	.10
108	Kevin Orie	.10
109	Alex Gonzalez	.10
110	Jose Canseco	.60
111	Paul Sorrento	.10
112	Joey Hamilton	.10
113	Brad Radke	.10
114	Steve Avery	.10
115	Esteban Loaiza	.10
116	Stan Javier	.10
117	Chris Gomez	.10
118	Royce Clayton	.10
119	Orlando Merced	.10
120	Kevin Appier	.10
121	Mel Nieves	.10
122	Joe Girardi	.10
123	Rico Brogna	.10
124	Kent Mercker	.10
125	Manny Ramirez	1.50
126	Jeromy Burnitz	.10
127	Kevin Foster	.10
128	Matt Morris	.10
129	Jason Dickson	.10
130	Tom Glavine	.35
131	Wally Joyner	.10
132	Rick Reed	.10
133	Todd Jones	.10
134	Dave Martinez	.10
135	Sandy Alomar	.10
136	Mike Lansing	.10
137	Sean Berry	.10
138	Doug Jones	.10
139	Todd Stottlemyre	.10
140	Jay Bell	.10
141	Jaime Navarro	.10
142	Chris Holles	.10
143	Joey Cora	.10
144	Scott Spiezio	.10
145	Joe Carter	.10
146	Jose Guillen	.10
147	Damion Easley	.10
148	Lee Stevens	.10
149	Alex Fernandez	.10
150	Randy Johnson	1.50
151	J.T. Snow	.10
152	Chuck Finley	.10
153	Bernard Gilkey	.10
154	David Segui	.10
155	Dante Bichette	.10
156	Kevin Stocker	.10
157	Carl Everett	.10
158	Jose Valentin	.10
159	Pokey Reese	.10
160	Derek Jeter	3.00
161	Roger Pavlik	.10
162	Mark Wohlers	.10
163	Ricky Bottalico	.10
164	Ozzie Guillen	.10
165	Mike Mussina	.60
166	Gary Sheffield	.50
167	Hideo Nomo	.75
168	Mark Grace	.10
169	Aaron Sele	.10
170	Darryl Kile	.10
171	Shawn Estes	.10
172	Vinny Castilla	.10
173	Ron Coomer	.10
174	Jose Rosado	.10
175	Kenny Lofton	.10
176	Jason Giambi	.65
177	Hal Morris	.10
178	Darren Bragg	.10
179	Orel Hershiser	.10
180	Ray Lankford	.10
181	Hideki Irabu	.10
182	Kevin Young	.10
183	Javy Lopez	.10
184	Jeff Montgomery	.10
185	Mike Holtz	.10
186	George Williams	.10
187	Cal Eldred	.10
188	Tom Candiotti	.10
189	Glenallen Hill	.10
190	Brian Giles	.10
191	Dave Mlicki	.10
192	Garrett Stephenson	.10
193	Jeff Frye	.10
194	Joe Oliver	.10
195	Bob Hamelin	.10
196	Luis Sojo	.10
197	LaTroy Hawkins	.10
198	Kevin Elster	.10
199	Jeff Reed	.10
200	Dennis Eckersley	1.00
201	Bill Mueller	.10
202	Russ Davis	.10
203	Armando Benitez	.10

No.	Player	Price
204	Quilvio Veras	.10
205	Tim Naehring	.10
206	Quinton McCracken	.10
207	Raul Casanova	.10
208	Matt Lawton	.10
209	Luis Alicea	.10
210	Luis Gonzalez	.10
211	Allen Watson	.10
212	Gerald Williams	.10
213	David Bell	.10
214	Todd Hollandsworth	.10
215	Wade Boggs	2.00
216	Jose Mesa	.10
217	Jamie Moyer	.10
218	Darren Daulton	.10
219	Mickey Morandini	.10
220	Rusty Greer	.10
221	Jim Bullinger	.10
222	Jose Offerman	.10
223	Matt Karchner	.10
224	Woody Williams	.10
225	Mark Loretta	.10
226	Mike Hampton	.10
227	Willie Adams	.10
228	Scott Hatteberg	.10
229	Rich Amaral	.10
230	Terry Steinbach	.10
231	Glendon Rusch	.10
232	Bret Boone	.10
233	Robert Person	.10
234	Jose Hernandez	.10
235	Doug Drabek	.10
236	Jason McDonald	.10
237	Chris Widger	.10
238	Tom Martin RC	.10
239	Dave Burba	.10
240	Pete Rose	.10
241	Bobby Ayala	.10
242	Tim Wakefield	.10
243	Dennis Springer	.10
244	Tim Belcher	.10
245	Jon Garland, Geoff Goetz	.10
246	Glenn Davis, Lance Berkman	.25
247	Vernon Wells, Aaron Akin	.15
248	Adam Kennedy, Jason Romano	.25
249	Jason Dellaero, Troy Cameron	.10
250	Alex Sanchez, Jared Sandberg RC	.25
251	Pablo Ortega, James Manias RC	.10
252	Jason Conti, Mike Stoner RC	.10
253	John Patterson, Larry Rodriguez	.10
254	Adrian Beltre, Ryan Minor, Aaron Boone	.25
255	Ben Grieve, Brian Buchanan, Dermal Brown	.10
256	Carl Pavano, Kerry Wood, Gil Meche	.75
257	David Ortiz, Daryle Ward, Richie Sexson	.65
258	Randy Winn, Juan Encarnacion, Andrew Vessel	.10
259	Kris Benson, Travis Smith, Courtney Duncan	.15
260	Chad Hermansen, Brent Butler, Warren Morris RC	.15
261	Ben Davis, Elieser Marrero, Ramon Hernandez	.10
262	Eric Chavez, Russell Branyan, Russ Johnson	.25
263	Todd Dunwoody, John Barnes, Ryan Jackson RC	.15
264	Matt Clement, Roy Halladay, Brian Fuentes	.20
265	Randy Johnson	.50
266	Kevin Brown	.10
267	Francisco Cordova, Ricardo Rincon	.10
268	Nomar Garciaparra	.75
269	Tino Martinez	.10
270	Chuck Knoblauch	.10
271	Pedro Martinez	.40
272	Denny Neagle	.10
273	Juan Gonzalez	.20
274	Andres Galarraga	.10
275	Checklist	.10
276	Checklist	.10
277	Moises Alou	.10
278	Sandy Alomar	.10
279	Gary Sheffield	.10
280	Matt Williams	.10
281	Livan Hernandez	.10
282	Chad Ogea	.10
283	Marlins Win	.10
284	Tino Martinez	.10
285	Roberto Alomar	.35
286	Jeff King	.10
287	Brian Jordan	.10
288	Darin Erstad	.30
289	Ken Caminiti	.10
290	Jim Thome	.90
291	Paul Molitor	1.50
292	Ivan Rodriguez	1.00
293	Bernie Williams	.10
294	Todd Hundley	.10
295	Andres Galarraga	.10
296	Greg Maddux	2.00
297	Edgar Martinez	.10
298	Ron Gant	.10
299	Derek Bell	.10
300	Roger Clemens	2.00
301	Rondell White	.10
302	Barry Larkin	.10
303	Robin Ventura	.10
304	Jason Kendall	.10
305	Chipper Jones	2.00
306	John Franco	.10
307	Sammy Sosa	2.00
308	Troy Percival	.10
309	Chuck Knoblauch	.10
310	Ellis Burks	.10
311	Al Martin	.10
312	Tim Salmon	.10
313	Moises Alou	.10
314	Lance Johnson	.10
315	Justin Thompson	.10
316	Will Clark	.10
317	Barry Bonds	3.00
318	Craig Biggio	.10
319	John Smoltz	.10
320	Cal Ripken Jr.	3.00
321	Ken Griffey Jr.	2.25
322	Paul O'Neill	.10
323	Todd Helton	1.50
324	John Olerud	.10
325	Mark McGwire	2.50
326	Jose Cruz Jr.	.10
327	Jeff Cirillo	.10
328	Dean Palmer	.10
329	John Wetteland	.10
330	Steve Finley	.10
331	Albert Belle	.10
332	Curt Schilling	.35
333	Raul Mondesi	.10
334	Andruw Jones	1.50
335	Nomar Garciaparra	2.00
336	David Justice	.10
337	Andy Pettitte	.30
338	Pedro Martinez	1.50
339	Travis Miller	.10
340	Chris Stynes	.10
341	Gregg Jefferies	.10
342	Jeff Fassero	.10
343	Craig Counsell	.10
344	Wilson Alvarez	.10
345	Bip Roberts	.10
346	Kelvim Escobar	.10
347	Mark Bellhorn	.10
348	Cory Lidle	.10
349	Fred McGriff	.10
350	Chuck Carr	.10
351	Bob Abreu	.10
352	Juan Guzman	.10
353	Fernando Vina	.10
354	Andy Benes	.10
355	Dave Nilsson	.10
356	Bobby Bonilla	.10
357	Ismael Valdes	.10
358	Carlos Perez	.10
359	Kirk Rueter	.10
360	Bartolo Colon	.10
361	Mel Rojas	.10
362	Johnny Damon	.35
363	Geronimo Berroa	.10
364	Reggie Sanders	.10
365	Jermaine Allensworth	.10
366	Orlando Cabrera	.10
367	Jorge Fabregas	.10
368	Scott Stahoviak	.10
369	Ken Cloude	.10
370	Donovan Osborne	.10
371	Roger Cedeno	.10
372	Neifi Perez	.10
373	Chris Holt	.10
374	Cecil Fielder	.10
375	Marty Cordova	.10
376	Tom Goodwin	.10
377	Jeff Suppan	.10
378	Jeff Brantley	.10
379	Mark Langston	.10
380	Shane Reynolds	.10
381	Mike Fetters	.10
382	Todd Greene	.10
383	Ray Durham	.10
384	Carlos Delgado	.35
385	Jeff D'Amico	.10
386	Brian McRae	.10
387	Alan Benes	.10
388	Heathcliff Slocumb	.10
389	Eric Young	.10
390	Travis Fryman	.10
391	David Cone	.10
392	Otis Nixon	.10
393	Jeremi Gonzalez	.10
394	Jeff Juden	.10
395	Jose Vizcaino	.10
396	Ugueth Urbina	.10
397	Ramon Martinez	.10
398	Robb Nen	.10
399	Harold Baines	.10
400	Delino DeShields	.10
401	John Burkett	.10
402	Sterling Hitchcock	.10
403	Mark Clark	.10
404	Terrell Wade	.10
405	Scott Brosius	.10
406	Chad Curtis	.10
407	Brian Johnson	.10
408	Roberto Kelly	.10
409	Dave Dellucci RC	.25
410	Michael Tucker	.10
411	Mark Kotsay	.10
412	Mark Lewis	.10
413	Ryan McGuire	.10
414	Shawon Dunston	.10
415	Brad Rigby	.10
416	Scott Erickson	.10
417	Bobby Jones	.10
418	Darren Oliver	.10
419	John Smiley	.10
420	T.J. Mathews	.10
421	Dustin Hermanson	.10
422	Mike Timlin	.10
423	Willie Blair	.10
424	Manny Alexander	.10
425	Bob Tewksbury	.10
426	Pete Schourek	.10
427	Reggie Jefferson	.10
428	Ed Sprague	.10
429	Jeff Conine	.10
430	Roberto Hernandez	.10
431	Tom Pagnozzi	.10
432	Jaret Wright	.10
433	Livan Hernandez	.10
434	Andy Ashby	.10
435	Todd Dunn	.10
436	Bobby Higginson	.10
437	Rod Beck	.10
438	Jim Leyritz	.10
439	Matt Williams	.10
440	Brett Tomko	.10
441	Joe Randa	.10
442	Chris Carpenter	.10
443	Dennis Reyes	.10
444	Al Leiter	.10
445	Jason Schmidt	.10
446	Ken Hill	.10
447	Shannon Stewart	.10
448	Enrique Wilson	.10
449	Fernando Tatis	.10
450	Jimmy Key	.10
451	Darrin Fletcher	.10
452	John Valentin	.10
453	Kevin Tapani	.10
454	Eric Karros	.10
455	Jay Bell	.10
456	Walt Weiss	.10
457	Devon White	.10
458	Carl Pavano	.10
459	Mike Lansing	.10
460	John Flaherty	.10
461	Richard Hidalgo	.10
462	Quinton McCracken	.10
463	Karim Garcia	.20
464	Miguel Cairo	.10
465	Edwin Diaz	.10
466	Bobby Smith	.10
467	Yamil Benitez	.10
468	Rich Butler RC	.10
469	Ben Ford RC	.10
470	Bubba Trammell	.10
471	Brent Brede	.10
472	Brooks Kieschnick	.10
473	Carlos Castillo	.10
474	Brad Radke	.10
475	Roger Clemens	1.00
476	Curt Schilling	.15
477	John Olerud	.10
478	Mark McGwire	1.25
479	Mike Piazza, Ken Griffey Jr.	1.25
480	Jeff Bagwell, Frank Thomas	1.00
481	Chipper Jones, Nomar Garciaparra	1.00
482	Larry Walker,	.20
483	Gary Sheffield, Tino Martinez	.10
484	Derrick Gibson, Michael Coleman, Norm Hutchins	.10
485	Braden Looper, Cliff Politte, Brian Rose	.15
486	Eric Milton, Jason Marquis, Corey Lee	.25
487	A.J. Hinch, Mark Osborne, Robert Fick RC	.25
488	Aramis Ramirez, Alex Gonzalez, Sean Casey	.25
489	Donnie Bridges, Tim Drew RC	.20
490	Ntema Ndungidi, Darnell McDonald RC	.10
491	Ryan Anderson, Mark Mangum	.50
492	J.J. Davis, Troy Glaus RC	3.00
493	Jayson Werth, Dan Reichert	.10
494	John Curtice, Mike Cuddyer RC	.50
495	Jack Cust, Jason Standridge	4.00
496	Brian Anderson	.10
497	Tony Saunders	.10
498	Vladimir Nunez, Jhensy Sandoval RC	.10
499	Brad Penny, Nick Bierbrodt	.10
500	Dustin Carr, Luis Cruz RC	.10
501	Marcus McCain, Cedrick Bowers RC	.10
502	Checklist	.10
503	Checklist	.10
504	Alex Rodriguez	2.50

Refractors

	NM/M
Common Player:	.50
Stars/Rookies:	5X

(See 1998 Topps Chrome for checklist and base card values.)

Baby Boomers

	NM/M
Complete Set (15):	16.00
Common Player:	.75
Inserted 1:24	
Refractors:	1.5X
Inserted 1:72	
1 Derek Jeter	6.00
2 Scott Rolen	.90
3 Nomar Garciaparra	3.50
4 Jose Cruz Jr.	.75
5 Darin Erstad	.90
6 Todd Helton	1.50
7 Tony Clark	.75
8 Jose Guillen	.75
9 Andruw Jones	1.50
10 Vladimir Guerrero	1.50
11 Mark Kotsay	.75
12 Todd Greene	.75
13 Andy Pettitte	.90
14 Justin Thompson	.75
15 Alan Benes	.75

Clout 9

	NM/M
Complete Set (9):	15.00
Common Player:	.75
Inserted 1:24	
Refractors:	1.5X
Inserted 1:72	
1 Edgar Martinez	.75
2 Mike Piazza	3.50
3 Frank Thomas	1.50
4 Craig Biggio	.75
5 Vinny Castilla	.75
6 Jeff Blauser	.75
7 Barry Bonds	6.00
8 Ken Griffey Jr.	3.50
9 Larry Walker	.75

Flashback

	NM/M
Complete Set (10):	16.00
Common Player:	.75
Inserted 1:24	
Refractors:	1.5X
Inserted 1:72	
1 Barry Bonds	6.00
2 Ken Griffey Jr.	3.50
3 Paul Molitor	1.50
4 Randy Johnson	1.50
5 Cal Ripken Jr.	6.00
6 Tony Gwynn	2.50
7 Kenny Lofton	.75
8 Gary Sheffield	.85
9 Deion Sanders	.75
10 Brady Anderson	.75

Hallbound

		NM/M
Complete Set (15):		35.00
Common Player:		1.50
Inserted 1:24		
Refractors:		1.5X
Inserted 1:72		
1	Paul Molitor	2.00
2	Tony Gwynn	2.50
3	Wade Boggs	2.50
4	Roger Clemens	3.00
5	Dennis Eckersley	1.50
6	Cal Ripken Jr.	6.00
7	Greg Maddux	2.50
8	Rickey Henderson	2.00
9	Ken Griffey Jr.	3.50
10	Frank Thomas	2.00
11	Mark McGwire	4.50
12	Barry Bonds	6.00
13	Mike Piazza	3.50
14	Juan Gonzalez	1.50
15	Randy Johnson	2.00

Milestones

		NM/M
Complete Set (10):		25.00
Common Player:		1.00
Inserted 1:24		
Refractors:		1.5X
Inserted 1:72		
1	Barry Bonds	6.00
2	Roger Clemens	3.00
3	Dennis Eckersley	1.00
4	Juan Gonzalez	1.00
5	Ken Griffey Jr.	3.50
6	Tony Gwynn	2.50
7	Greg Maddux	2.50
8	Mark McGwire	4.50
9	Cal Ripken Jr.	6.00
10	Frank Thomas	1.50

Rookie Class

		NM/M
Complete Set (10):		10.00
Common Player:		.75
Inserted 1:12		
Refractors:		1.5X
Inserted 1:24		
1	Travis Lee	1.00
2	Richard Hidalgo	.75
3	Todd Helton	4.50
4	Paul Konerko	1.50
5	Mark Kotsay	.75
6	Derek Lee	3.00
7	Eli Marrero	.75
8	Fernando Tatis	.75
9	Juan Encarnacion	.75
10	Ben Grieve	.75

1998 Topps Gallery

		NM/M
Complete Set (150):		15.00
Common Player:		.10
Pack (6):		1.50
Wax Box (24):		25.00
1	Andruw Jones	1.00
2	Fred McGriff	.10

3	Wade Boggs	1.50
4	Pedro Martinez	1.00
5	Matt Williams	.10
6	Wilson Alvarez	.10
7	Henry Rodriguez	.10
8	Jay Bell	.10
9	Marquis Grissom	.10
10	Darryl Kile	.10
11	Chuck Knoblauch	.10
12	Kenny Lofton	.10
13	Quinton McCracken	.10
14	Andres Galarraga	.10
15	Brian Jordan	.10
16	Mike Lansing	.10
17	Travis Fryman	.10
18	Tony Saunders	.10
19	Moises Alou	.10
20	Travis Lee	.10
21	Garret Anderson	.10
22	Ken Caminiti	.10
23	Pedro Astacio	.10
24	Ellis Burks	.10
25	Albert Belle	.10
26	Alan Benes	.10
27	Jay Buhner	.10
28	Derek Bell	.10
29	Jeromy Burnitz	.10
30	Kevin Appier	.10
31	Jeff Cirillo	.10
32	Bernard Gilkey	.10
33	David Cone	.10
34	Jason Dickson	.10
35	Jose Cruz Jr.	.10
36	Marty Cordova	.10
37	Ray Durham	.10
38	Jaret Wright	.10
39	Billy Wagner	.10
40	Roger Clemens	1.75
41	Juan Gonzalez	.50
42	Jeremi Gonzalez	.10
43	Mark Grudzielanek	.10
44	Tom Glavine	.35
45	Barry Larkin	.10
46	Lance Johnson	.10
47	Bobby Higginson	.10
48	Mike Mussina	.50
49	Al Martin	.10
50	Mark McGwire	2.50
51	Todd Hundley	.10
52	Ray Lankford	.10
53	Jason Kendall	.10
54	Javy Lopez	.10
55	Ben Grieve	.10
56	Randy Johnson	1.00
57	Jeff King	.10
58	Mark Grace	.10
59	Rusty Greer	.10
60	Greg Maddux	1.50
61	Jeff Kent	.10
62	Rey Ordonez	.10
63	Hideo Nomo	.50
64	Charles Nagy	.10
65	Rondell White	.10
66	Todd Helton	.75
67	Jim Thome	.75
68	Denny Neagle	.10
69	Ivan Rodriguez	.75
70	Vladimir Guerrero	1.00
71	Jorge Posada	.10
72	J.T. Snow Jr.	.10
73	Reggie Sanders	.10
74	Scott Rolen	.75
75	Robin Ventura	.10
76	Mariano Rivera	.15
77	Cal Ripken Jr.	3.00
78	Justin Thompson	.10
79	Mike Piazza	2.00
80	Kevin Brown	.10
81	Sandy Alomar	.10
82	Craig Biggio	.10
83	Vinny Castilla	.10
84	Eric Young	.10
85	Bernie Williams	.10
86	Brady Anderson	.10
87	Bobby Bonilla	.10
88	Tony Clark	.10
89	Dan Wilson	.10
90	John Wetteland	.10
91	Barry Bonds	3.00
92	Chan Ho Park	.10
93	Carlos Delgado	.35
94	David Justice	.10
95	Chipper Jones	1.50
96	Shawn Estes	.10
97	Jason Giambi	.60
98	Ron Gant	.10
99	John Olerud	.10
100	Frank Thomas	1.00
101	Jose Guillen	.10
102	Brad Radke	.10
103	Troy Percival	.10
104	John Smoltz	.10
105	Edgardo Alfonzo	.10
106	Dante Bichette	.10
107	Larry Walker	.10
108	John Valentin	.10
109	Roberto Alomar	.30
110	Mike Cameron	.10
111	Eric Davis	.10
112	Johnny Damon	.35
113	Darin Erstad	.30
114	Omar Vizquel	.10
115	Derek Jeter	3.00
116	Tony Womack	.10
117	Edgar Renteria	.10

118	Raul Mondesi	.10
119	Tony Gwynn	1.50
120	Ken Griffey Jr.	2.00
121	Jim Edmonds	.10
122	Brian Hunter	.10
123	Neifi Perez	.10
124	Dean Palmer	.10
125	Alex Rodriguez	2.50
126	Tim Salmon	.10
127	Curt Schilling	.35
128	Kevin Orie	.10
129	Andy Pettitte	.30
130	Gary Sheffield	.50
131	Jose Rosado	.10
132	Manny Ramirez	1.00
133	Rafael Palmeiro	.75
134	Sammy Sosa	1.50
135	Jeff Bagwell	1.00
136	Delino DeShields	.10
137	Ryan Klesko	.10
138	Mo Vaughn	.10
139	Steve Finley	.10
140	Nomar Garciaparra	1.50
141	Paul Molitor	1.00
142	Pat Hentgen	.10
143	Eric Karros	.10
144	Bobby Jones	.10
145	Tino Martinez	.10
146	Matt Morris	.10
147	Livan Hernandez	.10
148	Edgar Martinez	.10
149	Paul O'Neill	.10
150	Checklist	.10

Printing Plates

	NM/M
Common Player, Front:	50.00
Common Player, Back:	35.00
(See 1998 Topps Gallery for checklist and base card values.)	

Player's Private Issue

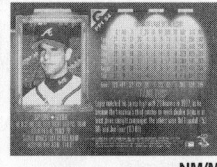

	NM/M
Common Player:	1.00
Stars/Rookies:	4X
Production 250 Sets	
(See 1998 Topps Gallery for checklist and base card values.)	

Player's Private Issue Auction Cards

	NM/M
Complete Set (150):	60.00
Common Player:	.25
Stars/Rookies:	1.5X
(See 1998 Topps Gallery for checklist and base values.)	

Awards Gallery

		NM/M
Complete Set (10):		18.00
Common Player:		1.00
Inserted 1:24		
1	Ken Griffey Jr.	4.00
2	Larry Walker	1.00
3	Roger Clemens	2.50
4	Pedro Martinez	1.50
5	Nomar Garciaparra	2.00
6	Scott Rolen	1.00
7	Frank Thomas	1.50
8	Tony Gwynn	2.00
9	Mark McGwire	5.00
10	Livan Hernandez	1.00

Gallery Proofs

	NM/M
Common Player:	1.50
Stars/Rookies:	4X
Production 125 Sets	
(See 1998 Topps Gallery for checklist and base card values.)	

Gallery of Heroes

		NM/M
Complete Set (15):		80.00
Common Player:		1.25
Inserted 1:24		
Jumbo Version (1:24):		75 Percent
1	Ken Griffey Jr.	8.00
2	Derek Jeter	15.00
3	Barry Bonds	15.00
4	Alex Rodriguez	12.00
5	Frank Thomas	4.00
6	Nomar Garciaparra	6.00
7	Mark McGwire	12.00
8	Mike Piazza	8.00
9	Cal Ripken Jr.	15.00
10	Jose Cruz Jr.	1.25
11	Jeff Bagwell	4.00
12	Chipper Jones	6.00
13	Juan Gonzalez	2.00
14	Hideo Nomo	2.00
15	Greg Maddux	6.00

Photo Gallery

		NM/M
Complete Set (10):		25.00
Common Player:		1.00
Inserted 1:24		
1	Alex Rodriguez	3.00
2	Frank Thomas	2.00
3	Derek Jeter	4.00
4	Cal Ripken Jr.	4.00
5	Ken Griffey Jr.	2.50
6	Mike Piazza	2.50
7	Nomar Garciaparra	2.25
8	Tim Salmon	1.00
9	Jeff Bagwell	2.00
10	Barry Bonds	4.00

1998 Topps Gold Label Class 1
(Fldg, Follow-thru)

	NM/M
Complete Set (100):	12.00
Gold Label Common Player:	.10
Black Label Common Player:	.35
Black Label Stars/RC's:	4X
Red Label Common Player:	1.50
Red Label Stars/RC's:	12X
Pack (5):	2.00
Wax Box (24):	40.00
1 Kevin Brown	.10
2 Greg Maddux	1.25
3 Albert Belle	.10
4 Andres Galarraga	.10
5 Craig Biggio	.10
6 Matt Williams	.10
7 Derek Jeter	3.00
8 Randy Johnson	1.00
9 Jay Bell	.10
10 Jim Thome	.75
11 Roberto Alomar	.30
12 Tom Glavine	.35
13 Reggie Sanders	.10
14 Tony Gwynn	1.25
15 Mark McGwire	2.00
16 Jeromy Burnitz	.10
17 Andruw Jones	1.00
18 Jay Buhner	.10
19 Robin Ventura	.10
20 Jeff Bagwell	1.00
21 Roger Clemens	1.25
22 Masato Yoshii RC	.25
23 Travis Fryman	.10
24 Rafael Palmeiro	.75
25 Alex Rodriguez	2.00
26 Sandy Alomar	.10
27 Chipper Jones	1.25
28 Rusty Greer	.10
29 Cal Ripken Jr.	3.00
30 Tony Clark	.10
31 Derek Bell	.10
32 Fred McGriff	.10
33 Paul O'Neill	.10
34 Moises Alou	.10
35 Henry Rodriguez	.10
36 Steve Finley	.10
37 Marquis Grissom	.10
38 Jason Giambi	.60
39 Javy Lopez	.10
40 Damion Easley	.10
41 Mariano Rivera	.15
42 Mo Vaughn	.10
43 Mike Mussina	.40
44 Jason Kendall	.10
45 Pedro Martinez	1.00
46 Frank Thomas	1.00
47 Jim Edmonds	.10
48 Hideki Irabu	.10
49 Eric Karros	.10
50 Juan Gonzalez	.50
51 Ellis Burks	.10
52 Dean Palmer	.10
53 Scott Rolen	.60
54 Raul Mondesi	.10
55 Quinton McCracken	.10
56 John Olerud	.10
57 Ken Caminiti	.10
58 Brian Jordan	.10
59 Wade Boggs	1.25
60 Mike Piazza	1.50
61 Darin Erstad	.30
62 Curt Schilling	.10
63 David Justice	.10
64 Kenny Lofton	.10
65 Barry Bonds	3.00
66 Ray Lankford	.10
67 Brian Hunter	.10
68 Chuck Knoblauch	.10
69 Vinny Castilla	.10
70 Vladimir Guerrero	1.00
71 Tim Salmon	.10
72 Larry Walker	.10
73 Paul Molitor	1.00
74 Barry Larkin	.10
75 Edgar Martinez	.10
76 Bernie Williams	.10
77 Dante Bichette	.10
78 Nomar Garciaparra	1.25
79 Ben Grieve	.10
80 Ivan Rodriguez	.75
81 Todd Helton	.75
82 Ryan Klesko	.10
83 Sammy Sosa	1.25
84 Travis Lee	.10
85 Jose Cruz	.10
86 Mark Kotsay	.10
87 Richard Hidalgo	.10
88 Rondell White	.10
89 Greg Vaughn	.10
90 Gary Sheffield	.50
91 Paul Konerko	.25
92 Mark Grace	.10
93 Kevin Millwood RC	1.00
94 Manny Ramirez	1.00
95 Tino Martinez	.10
96 Brad Fullmer	.10
97 Todd Walker	.10
98 Carlos Delgado	.45
99 Kerry Wood	.60
100 Ken Griffey Jr.	1.50

Class 2
(Running, Set Position)

	NM/M
Complete Set (100):	50.00
Gold Label Common Player:	.35
Gold Label Stars/RC's:	2X
Black Label Common Player:	1.00
Black Label Stars/RC's:	4X
Red Label Common Player:	4.00
Red Label Stars/RC's:	25X

(See 1998 Topps Gold Label Class 1 for checklist and base card values.)

Class 3
(Hitting, Throwing)

Complete Set (100):	120.00
Common Player:	.75
Gold Label Stars/RC's:	2.5X
Black Label Common Player:	2.00
Black Label Stars/RC's:	6X
Red Label Common Player:	6.00
Red Label Stars/RC's:	35X

(See 1998 Topps Gold Label Class 1 for checklist and base card values.)

Home Run Race

(Due to scarcity and variance in demand, values cannot be quoted.)

Complete Set (4):	7.50
Common Player:	2.00
Black Label:	2X
Red Label:	4X
Pack (6):	1.25
HR1 Roger Maris	3.00
HR2 Mark McGwire	3.00
HR3 Ken Griffey Jr.	2.50
HR4 Sammy Sosa	2.00

1998 Topps Stars

	NM/M
Complete Set, Red or Bronze (150):	24.00
Common Player, Red or Bronze:	.10
Production 9,799 sets each.	
Wax Box (24):	25.00
1 Greg Maddux	1.50
2 Darryl Kile	.10
3 Rod Beck	.10
4 Ellis Burks	.10
5 Gary Sheffield	.40
6 David Ortiz	.10
7 Marquis Grissom	.10
8 Tony Womack	.10
9 Mike Mussina	.60
10 Bernie Williams	.10
11 Andy Benes	.10
12 Rusty Greer	.10
13 Carlos Delgado	.35
14 Jim Edmonds	.10
15 Raul Mondesi	.10
16 Andres Galarraga	.10
17 Wade Boggs	1.50
18 Paul O'Neill	.10
19 Edgar Renteria	.10
20 Tony Clark	.10
21 Vladimir Guerrero	1.00
22 Moises Alou	.10
23 Bernard Gilkey	.10
24 Lance Johnson	.10
25 Ben Grieve	.10
26 Sandy Alomar	.10
27 Ray Durham	.10
28 Shawn Estes	.10
29 David Segui	.10
30 Javy Lopez	.10
31 Steve Finley	.10
32 Rey Ordonez	.10
33 Derek Jeter	3.00
34 Henry Rodriguez	.10
35 Mo Vaughn	.10
36 Richard Hidalgo	.10
37 Omar Vizquel	.10
38 Johnny Damon	.35
39 Brian Hunter	.10
40 Matt Williams	.10
41 Chuck Finley	.10
42 Jeromy Burnitz	.10
43 Livan Hernandez	.10
44 Delino DeShields	.10
45 Charles Nagy	.10
46 Scott Rolen	.75
47 Neifi Perez	.10
48 John Wetteland	.10
49 Eric Milton	.10
50 Mike Piazza	2.00
51 Cal Ripken Jr.	3.00
52 Mariano Rivera	.25
53 Butch Huskey	.10
54 Quinton McCracken	.10
55 Jose Cruz Jr.	.10
56 Brian Jordan	.10
57 Hideo Nomo	.50
58 Masato Yoshii	.10
59 Cliff Floyd	.10
60 Jose Guillen	.10
61 Jeff Shaw	.10
62 Edgar Martinez	.10
63 Rondell White	.10
64 Hal Morris	.10
65 Barry Larkin	.10
66 Eric Young	.10
67 Ray Lankford	.10
68 Derek Bell	.10
69 Charles Johnson	.10
70 Robin Ventura	.10
71 Chuck Knoblauch	.10
72 Kevin Brown	.10
73 Jose Valentin	.10
74 Jay Buhner	.10
75 Tony Gwynn	1.50
76 Andy Pettitte	.30
77 Edgardo Alfonzo	.10
78 Kerry Wood	.40
79 Darin Erstad	.30
80 Paul Konerko	.15
81 Jason Kendall	.10
82 Tino Martinez	.10
83 Brad Radke	.10
84 Jeff King	.10
85 Travis Lee	.10
86 Jeff Kent	.10
87 Trevor Hoffman	.10
88 David Cone	.10
89 Jose Canseco	.40
90 Juan Gonzalez	.50
91 Todd Hundley	.10
92 John Valentin	.10
93 Sammy Sosa	1.50
94 Jason Giambi	.40
95 Chipper Jones	1.50
96 Jeff Blauser	.10
97 Brad Fullmer	.10
98 Derrek Lee	.60
99 Denny Neagle	.10
100 Ken Griffey Jr.	2.00
101 David Justice	.10
102 Tim Salmon	.10
103 J.T. Snow	.10
104 Fred McGriff	.10
105 Brady Anderson	.10
106 Larry Walker	.10
107 Jeff Cirillo	.10
108 Andruw Jones	1.00
109 Manny Ramirez	1.00
110 Justin Thompson	.10
111 Vinny Castilla	.10
112 Chan Ho Park	.10
113 Mark Grudzielanek	.10
114 Mark Grace	.10
115 Ken Caminiti	.10
116 Ryan Klesko	.10
117 Rafael Palmeiro	.75
118 Pat Hentgen	.10
119 Eric Karros	.10
120 Randy Johnson	1.00
121 Roberto Alomar	.25
122 John Olerud	.10
123 Paul Molitor	1.00
124 Dean Palmer	.10
125 Nomar Garciaparra	1.50
126 Curt Schilling	.30
127 Jay Bell	.10
128 Craig Biggio	.10
129 Marty Cordova	.10
130 Ivan Rodriguez	.75
131 Todd Helton	.75
132 Jim Thome	.65
133 Albert Belle	.10
134 Mike Lansing	.10
135 Mark McGwire	2.50
136 Roger Clemens	1.75
137 Tom Glavine	.30
138 Ron Gant	.10
139 Alex Rodriguez	2.50
140 Jeff Bagwell	1.00
141 John Smoltz	.10
142 Kenny Lofton	.10
143 Dante Bichette	.10
144 Pedro Martinez	1.00
145 Barry Bonds	3.00
146 Travis Fryman	.10
147 Bobby Jones	.10
148 Bobby Higginson	.10
149 Reggie Sanders	.10
150 Frank Thomas	1.00
Checklist	.05

Silver

	NM/M
Common Silver:	.50
Silver Stars:	1.5X

Production 4,399 Sets
(See 1998 Topps Stars for checklist and base card values.)

Gold

	NM/M
Common Gold:	1.00
Gold Stars:	2X

Production 2,299 Sets
(See 1998 Topps Stars for checklist and base card values.)

Gold Rainbow

	NM/M
Common Gold Rainbow:	4.00
Gold Rainbow Stars:	8X

Production 99 Sets
(See 1998 Topps Stars for checklist and base card values.)

Galaxy

	NM/M
Complete Set (10):	150.00
Common Player:	7.50
Production 100 Sets	
Silvers:	1.5X
Production 75 Sets	

Golds: 2X
Production 50 Sets
Gold Rainbows: Values Undetermined
Production Five Sets

G1	Barry Bonds	40.00
G2	Jeff Bagwell	15.00
G3	Nomar Garciaparra	20.00
G4	Chipper Jones	20.00
G5	Ken Griffey Jr.	25.00
G6	Sammy Sosa	20.00
G7	Larry Walker	7.50
G8	Alex Rodriguez	35.00
G9	Craig Biggio	7.50
G10	Raul Mondesi	7.50

Luminaries

NM/M
Complete Set (15): 140.00
Common Player: 4.00
Production 100 Sets
Silver (75 Sets): 1.5X
Gold (50 Sets): 1.5X
Gold Rainbow (Five Sets): Values Undetermined

L1	Ken Griffey Jr.	15.00
L2	Mark McGwire	20.00
L3	Juan Gonzalez	5.00
L4	Tony Gwynn	12.50
L5	Frank Thomas	10.00
L6	Mike Piazza	15.00
L7	Chuck Knoblauch	4.00
L8	Kenny Lofton	4.00
L9	Barry Bonds	25.00
L10	Matt Williams	4.00
L11	Raul Mondesi	4.00
L12	Ivan Rodriguez	7.50
L13	Alex Rodriguez	20.00
L14	Nomar Garciaparra	12.50
L15	Ken Caminiti	4.00

Rookie Reprints

NM/M
Complete Set (5): 7.00
Common Player: 1.50
1968 Johnny Bench 1.50
1953 Whitey Ford 1.50
1965 Joe Morgan 1.50
1973 Mike Schmidt 2.50
1960 Carl Yastrzemski 1.50

Rookie Reprints Autographs

NM/M
Complete Set (5): 175.00
Common Player: 25.00
1968 Johnny Bench 75.00

1953 Whitey Ford 50.00
1965 Joe Morgan 25.00
1973 Mike Schmidt 90.00
1960 Carl Yastrzemski 90.00

Supernovas

NM/M
Complete Set (10): 35.00
Common Player: 2.00
Production 100 Sets
Silver: 1.5X
Production 75 Sets
Gold: 1.5X
Production 50 Sets
Gold Rainbow: Values Undetermined
Production Five Sets

S1	Ben Grieve	2.00
S2	Travis Lee	2.00
S3	Todd Helton	10.00
S4	Adrian Beltre	2.50
S5	Derrek Lee	6.00
S6	David Ortiz	6.00
S7	Brad Fullmer	2.00
S8	Mark Kotsay	2.00
S9	Paul Konerko	2.50
S10	Kerry Wood	6.00

1998 Topps Super Chrome

NM/M
Complete Set (36): 20.00
Common Player: .25
Refractors: 1.5X
Inserted 1:12
Pack (3): 2.50
Wax Box (12): 25.00

1	Tony Gwynn	1.00
2	Larry Walker	.25
3	Vladimir Guerrero	.75
4	Mo Vaughn	.25
5	Frank Thomas	.75
6	Barry Larkin	.25
7	Scott Rolen	.65
8	Juan Gonzalez	.75
9	Jeff Bagwell	.75
10	Ryan Klesko	.25
11	Mike Piazza	1.50
12	Randy Johnson	.75
13	Derek Jeter	3.00
14	Gary Sheffield	.50
15	Hideo Nomo	.50
16	Tino Martinez	.25
17	Ivan Rodriguez	.65
18	Bernie Williams	.25
19	Greg Maddux	1.00
20	Roger Clemens	1.25
21	Roberto Clemente	2.00
22	Chipper Jones	1.00
23	Sammy Sosa	1.00
24	Tony Clark	.25
25	Barry Bonds	3.00
26	Craig Biggio	.25
27	Cal Ripken Jr.	3.00
28	Ken Griffey Jr.	1.50
29	Todd Helton	.65
30	Mark McGwire	2.00
31	Jose Cruz	.25
32	Albert Belle	.25
33	Andruw Jones	.75
34	Nomar Garciaparra	1.00
35	Andy Pettitte	.45
36	Alex Rodriguez	2.00

1998 Topps Stars 'N Steel

NM/M
Complete Set (44): 40.00
Common Player: .25
Golds: 2X
Holographics: 7X
Pack (3): 3.50
Wax Box (12): 30.00

1	Roberto Alomar	.50
2	Jeff Bagwell	1.25
3	Albert Belle	.25
4	Dante Bichette	.25
5	Barry Bonds	4.00
6	Jay Buhner	.25
7	Ken Caminiti	.25
8	Vinny Castilla	.25
9	Roger Clemens	2.25
10	Jose Cruz Jr.	.25
11	Andres Galarraga	.25
12	Nomar Garciaparra	2.00
13	Juan Gonzalez	.65
14	Mark Grace	.25
15	Ken Griffey Jr.	2.50
16	Tony Gwynn	2.00
17	Todd Hundley	.25
18	Derek Jeter	4.00
19	Randy Johnson	1.25
20	Andruw Jones	1.25
21	Chipper Jones	2.00
22	David Justice	.25
23	Ray Lankford	.25
24	Barry Larkin	.25
25	Kenny Lofton	.25
26	Greg Maddux	2.00
27	Edgar Martinez	.25
28	Tino Martinez	.25
29	Mark McGwire	3.00
30	Paul Molitor	1.25
31	Rafael Palmeiro	1.00
32	Mike Piazza	2.50
33	Manny Ramirez	.75
34	Cal Ripken Jr.	4.00
35	Ivan Rodriguez	1.00
36	Scott Rolen	.75
37	Tim Salmon	.50
38	Gary Sheffield	.50
39	Sammy Sosa	2.00
40	Frank Thomas	1.25
41	Jim Thome	1.00
42	Mo Vaughn	.25
43	Larry Walker	.25
44	Bernie Williams	.25

1998 Topps TEK

NM/M
Complete Set (90): 75.00
Common Player: .25
Pack (4): 4.00
Wax Box (20): 80.00

1	Ben Grieve	.25
2	Kerry Wood	1.50
3	Barry Bonds	8.00
4	John Olerud	.25
5	Ivan Rodriguez	2.00
6	Frank Thomas	2.50
7	Bernie Williams	.25
8	Dante Bichette	.25
9	Alex Rodriguez	6.00
10	Tom Glavine	.50
11	Eric Karros	.25
12	Craig Biggio	.25
13	Mark McGwire	6.00
14	Derek Jeter	8.00
15	Nomar Garciaparra	4.00
16	Brady Anderson	.25
17	Vladimir Guerrero	2.50
18	David Justice	.25
19	Chipper Jones	4.00
20	Jim Edmonds	.25
21	Roger Clemens	4.50
22	Mark Kotsay	.25
23	Tony Gwynn	4.00
24	Todd Walker	.25
25	Tino Martinez	.25
26	Andruw Jones	2.50
27	Sandy Alomar	.25
28	Sammy Sosa	4.00
29	Gary Sheffield	1.50
30	Ken Griffey Jr.	5.00
31	Aramis Ramirez	.25
32	Curt Schilling	.50
33	Robin Ventura	.25
34	Larry Walker	.25
35	Darin Erstad	1.25
36	Todd Dunwoody	.25
37	Paul O'Neill	.25
38	Vinny Castilla	.25
39	Randy Johnson	2.50
40	Rafael Palmeiro	2.00
41	Pedro Martinez	2.50
42	Derek Bell	.25
43	Carlos Delgado	.50
44	Matt Williams	.25
45	Kenny Lofton	.25
46	Edgar Renteria	.25
47	Albert Belle	.25
48	Jeromy Burnitz	.25
49	Adrian Beltre	.40
50	Greg Maddux	4.00
51	Cal Ripken Jr.	8.00
52	Jason Kendall	.25
53	Ellis Burks	.25
54	Paul Molitor	2.50
55	Moises Alou	.25
56	Raul Mondesi	.25
57	Barry Larkin	.25
58	Tony Clark	.25
59	Travis Lee	.25
60	Juan Gonzalez	1.25
61	Troy Glaus **RC**	3.00
62	Jose Cruz Jr.	.25
63	Paul Konerko	.40
64	Edgar Martinez	.25
65	Javy Lopez	.25
66	Manny Ramirez	2.50
67	Roberto Alomar	.75
68	Ken Caminiti	.25
69	Todd Helton	1.50
70	Chuck Knoblauch	.25
71	Kevin Brown	.25
72	Tim Salmon	.25
73	Orlando Hernandez **RC**	1.00
74	Jeff Bagwell	2.50
75	Brian Jordan	.25
76	Derek Lee	1.50
77	Brad Fullmer	.25
78	Mark Grace	.25
79	Jeff King	.25
80	Mike Mussina	1.50
81	Jay Buhner	.25
82	Quinton McCracken	.25
83	A.J. Hinch	.25
84	Richard Hidalgo	.25
85	Andres Galarraga	.25
86	Mike Piazza	5.00
87	Mo Vaughn	.25
88	Scott Rolen	1.50
89	Jim Thome	2.00
90	Ray Lankford	.25

Diffraction

NM/M
Complete Set (90): 400.00

Common Player: 4.00
Stars/RC's: 4X
(See 1998 Topps TEK for checklist and base card values.)

1999 Topps

		NM/M
Unop. Hobby Set (462):		40.00
Unop. Retail Set (463):		50.00
Complete Set (462):		35.00
Common Player:		.05
MVP Stars/Rookies:		20X
Ser. 1 or 2 Hobby Pack (11):		1.25
Ser. 1 or 2 Hobby Box (36):		40.00
Ser. 1 or 2 Retail Pack (8):		1.00
Ser. 1 or 2 Retail Box (22):		20.00
Ser. 1 or 2 Jumbo Pack (40):		3.50
Ser. 1 or 2 Jumbo Box (12):		30.00
1	Roger Clemens	1.00
2	Andres Galarraga	.05
3	Scott Brosius	.05
4	John Flaherty	.05
5	Jim Leyritz	.05
6	Ray Durham	.05
7	Not Issued	
8	Joe Vizcaino	.05
9	Will Clark	.05
10	David Wells	.05
11	Jose Guillen	.05
12	Scott Hatteberg	.05
13	Edgardo Alfonzo	.05
14	Mike Bordick	.05
15	Manny Ramirez	.75
16	Greg Maddux	1.00
17	David Segui	.05
18	Darryl Strawberry	.05
19	Brad Radke	.05
20	Kerry Wood	.40
21	Matt Anderson	.05
22	Derrek Lee	.60
23	Mickey Morandini	.05
24	Paul Konerko	.15
25	Travis Lee	.15
26	Ken Hill	.05
27	Kenny Rogers	.05
28	Paul Sorrento	.05
29	Quilvio Veras	.05
30	Todd Walker	.05
31	Ryan Jackson	.05
32	John Olerud	.05
33	Doug Glanville	.05
34	Nolan Ryan	2.00
35	Ray Lankford	.05
36	Mark Loretta	.05
37	Jason Dickson	.05
38	Sean Bergman	.05
39	Quinton McCracken	.05
40	Bartolo Colon	.05
41	Brady Anderson	.05
42	Chris Stynes	.05
43	Jorge Posada	.05
44	Justin Thompson	.05
45	Johnny Damon	.30
46	Armando Benitez	.05
47	Brant Brown	.05
48	Charlie Hayes	.05
49	Darren Dreifort	.05
50	Juan Gonzalez	.40
51	Chuck Knoblauch	.05
52	Todd Helton	.75
53	Rick Reed	.05
54	Chris Gomez	.05
55	Gary Sheffield	.45
56	Rod Beck	.05
57	Rey Sanchez	.05
58	Garret Anderson	.05
59	Jimmy Haynes	.05
60	Steve Woodard	.05
61	Rondell White	.05
62	Vladimir Guerrero	.75
63	Eric Karros	.05
64	Russ Davis	.05
65	Mo Vaughn	.05
66	Sammy Sosa	1.00
67	Troy Percival	.05
68	Kenny Lofton	.05
69	Bill Taylor	.05
70	Mark McGwire	1.50
71	Roger Cedeno	.05
72	Javy Lopez	.05
73	Damion Easley	.05
74	Andy Pettitte	.25
75	Tony Gwynn	1.00
76	Ricardo Rincon	.05
77	F.P. Santangelo	.05
78	Jay Bell	.05
79	Scott Servais	.05
80	Jose Canseco	.40
81	Roberto Hernandez	.05
82	Todd Dunwoody	.05
83	John Wetteland	.05
84	Mike Caruso	.05
85	Derek Jeter	2.00
86	Aaron Sele	.05
87	Jose Lima	.05
88	Ryan Christenson	.05
89	Jeff Cirillo	.05
90	Jose Hernandez	.05
91	Mark Kotsay	.05
92	Darren Bragg	.05
93	Albert Belle	.05
94	Matt Lawton	.05
95	Pedro Martinez	.75
96	Greg Vaughn	.05
97	Neifi Perez	.05
98	Gerald Williams	.05
99	Derek Bell	.05
100	Ken Griffey Jr.	1.25
101	David Cone	.05
102	Brian Johnson	.05
103	Dean Palmer	.05
104	Javier Valentin	.05
105	Trevor Hoffman	.05
106	Butch Huskey	.05
107	Dave Martinez	.05
108	Billy Wagner	.05
109	Shawn Green	.30
110	Ben Grieve	.05
111	Tom Goodwin	.05
112	Jaret Wright	.05
113	Aramis Ramirez	.05
114	Dmitri Young	.05
115	Hideki Irabu	.05
116	Roberto Kelly	.05
117	Jeff Fassero	.05
118	Mark Clark	.05
119	Jason McDonald	.05
120	Matt Williams	.05
121	Dave Burba	.05
122	Bret Saberhagen	.05
123	Deivi Cruz	.05
124	Chad Curtis	.05
125	Scott Rolen	.65
126	Lee Stevens	.05
127	J.T. Snow Jr.	.05
128	Rusty Greer	.05
129	Brian Meadows	.05
130	Jim Edmonds	.05
131	Ron Gant	.05
132	A.J. Hinch	.05
133	Shannon Stewart	.05
134	Brad Fullmer	.05
135	Cal Eldred	.05
136	Matt Walbeck	.05
137	Carl Everett	.05
138	Walt Weiss	.05
139	Fred McGriff	.05
140	Darin Erstad	.25
141	Dave Nilsson	.05
142	Eric Young	.05
143	Dan Wilson	.05
144	Jeff Reed	.05
145	Brett Tomko	.05
146	Terry Steinbach	.05
147	Seth Greisinger	.05
148	Pat Meares	.05
149	Livan Hernandez	.05
150	Jeff Bagwell	.75
151	Bob Wickman	.05
152	Omar Vizquel	.05
153	Eric Davis	.05
154	Larry Sutton	.05
155	Magglio Ordonez	.40
156	Eric Milton	.05
157	Darren Lewis	.05
158	Rick Aguilera	.05
159	Mike Lieberthal	.05
160	Robb Nen	.05
161	Brian Giles	.05
162	Jeff Brantley	.05
163	Gary DiSarcina	.05
164	John Valentin	.05
165	David Dellucci	.05
166	Chan Ho Park	.05
167	Masato Yoshii	.05
168	Jason Schmidt	.05
169	LaTroy Hawkins	.05
170	Bret Boone	.05
171	Jerry DiPoto	.05
172	Mariano Rivera	.10
173	Mike Cameron	.05
174	Scott Erickson	.05
175	Charles Johnson	.05
176	Bobby Jones	.05
177	Francisco Cordova	.05
178	Todd Jones	.05
179	Jeff Montgomery	.05
180	Mike Mussina	.40
181	Bob Abreu	.05
182	Ismael Valdes	.05
183	Andy Fox	.05
184	Woody Williams	.05
185	Denny Neagle	.05
186	Jose Valentin	.05
187	Darrin Fletcher	.05
188	Gabe Alvarez	.05
189	Eddie Taubensee	.05
190	Edgar Martinez	.05
191	Jason Kendall	.05
192	Darryl Kile	.05
193	Jeff King	.05
194	Rey Ordonez	.05
195	Andruw Jones	.75
196	Tony Fernandez	.05
197	Jamey Wright	.05
198	B.J. Surhoff	.05
199	Vinny Castilla	.05
200	David Wells	.05
201	Mark McGwire	.75
202	Sammy Sosa	.50
203	Roger Clemens	.50
204	Kerry Wood	.15
205	Lance Berkman, Mike Frank, Gabe Kapler (Prospects)	.15
206	Alex Escobar, Ricky Ledee, Mike Stoner (Prospects)	.25
207	Peter Bergeron, Jeremy Giambi, George Lombard (Prospects)	.30
208	Michael Barrett, Ben Davis, Robert Fick (Prospects)	.05
209	Pat Cline, Ramon Hernandez, Jayson Werth (Prospects)	.05
210	Bruce Chen, Chris Enochs, Ryan Anderson (Prospects)	.05
211	Mike Lincoln, Octavio Dotel, Brad Penny (Prospects)	.05
212	Chuck Abbott, Brent Butler, Danny Klassen (Prospects)	.05
213	Chris Jones, Jeff Urban **RC**	.05
214	Arturo McDowell, Tony Torcato **RC**	.25
215	Josh McKinley, Jason Tyner **RC**	.25
216	Matt Burch, Seth Etherton **RC**	.25
217	Mamon Tucker, Rick Elder **RC**	.10
218	J.M. Gold, Ryan Mills **RC**	.10
219	Adam Brown, Choo Freeman **RC**	.25
220	M. McGwire Home Run Record #1	20.00
220	M. McGwire HR Record #2-60	6.00
220	M. McGwire HR Record #61-62	10.00
220	M. McGwire HR Record #63-69	15.00
220	Mark McGwire HR Record #70	40.00
221	Larry Walker	.05
222	Bernie Williams	.05
223	Mark McGwire	.75
224	Ken Griffey Jr.	.65
225	Sammy Sosa	.50
226	Juan Gonzalez	.20
227	Dante Bichette	.05
228	Alex Rodriguez	.75
229	Sammy Sosa	.50
230	Derek Jeter	1.00
231	Greg Maddux	.50
232	Roger Clemens	.50
233	Ricky Ledee	.05
234	Chuck Knoblauch	.05
235	Bernie Williams	.05
236	Tino Martinez	.05
237	Orlando Hernandez	.05
238	Scott Brosius	.05
239	Andy Pettitte	.05
240	Mariano Rivera	.05
241	Checklist	.05
242	Checklist	.05
243	Tom Glavine	.25
244	Andy Benes	.05
245	Sandy Alomar	.05
246	Wilton Guerrero	.05
247	Alex Gonzalez	.05
248	Roberto Alomar	.30
249	Ruben Rivera	.05
250	Eric Chavez	.15
251	Ellis Burks	.05
252	Richie Sexson	.05
253	Steve Finley	.05
254	Dwight Gooden	.05
255	Dustin Hermanson	.05
256	Kirk Rueter	.05
257	Steve Trachsel	.05
258	Gregg Jefferies	.05
259	Matt Stairs	.05
260	Shane Reynolds	.05
261	Gregg Olson	.05
262	Kevin Tapani	.05
263	Matt Morris	.05
264	Carl Pavano	.05
265	Nomar Garciaparra	1.00
266	Kevin Young	.05
267	Rick Helling	.05
268	Mark Leiter	.05
269	Brian McRae	.05
270	Cal Ripken Jr.	2.00
271	Jeff Abbott	.05
272	Tony Batista	.05
273	Bill Simas	.05
274	Brian Hunter	.05
275	John Franco	.05
276	Devon White	.05
277	Rickey Henderson	.75
278	Chuck Finley	.05
279	Mike Blowers	.05
280	Mark Grace	.05
281	Randy Winn	.05
282	Bobby Bonilla	.05
283	David Justice	.05
284	Shane Monahan	.05
285	Kevin Brown	.05
286	Todd Zeile	.05
287	Al Martin	.05
288	Troy O'Leary	.05
289	Darryl Hamilton	.05
290	Tino Martinez	.05
291	David Ortiz	.45
292	Tony Clark	.05
293	Ryan Minor	.05
294	Reggie Sanders	.05
295	Wally Joyner	.05
296	Cliff Floyd	.05
297	Shawn Estes	.05
298	Pat Hentgen	.05
299	Scott Elarton	.05
300	Alex Rodriguez	1.50
301	Ozzie Guillen	.05
302	Manny Martinez	.05
303	Ryan McGuire	.05
304	Brad Ausmus	.05
305	Alex Gonzalez	.05
306	Brian Jordan	.05
307	John Jaha	.05
308	Mark Grudzielanek	.05
309	Juan Guzman	.05
310	Tony Womack	.05
311	Dennis Reyes	.05
312	Marty Cordova	.05
313	Ramiro Mendoza	.05
314	Robin Ventura	.05
315	Rafael Palmeiro	.60
316	Ramon Martinez	.05
317	John Mabry	.05
318	Dave Hollins	.05
319	Tom Candiotti	.05
320	Al Leiter	.05
321	Rico Brogna	.05
322	Jimmy Key	.05
323	Bernard Gilkey	.05
324	Jason Giambi	.45
325	Craig Biggio	.05
326	Troy Glaus	.65
327	Delino DeShields	.05
328	Fernando Vina	.05
329	John Smoltz	.05
330	Jeff Kent	.05
331	Roy Halladay	.05
332	Andy Ashby	.05
333	Tim Wakefield	.05
334	Tim Belcher	.05
335	Bernie Williams	.05
336	Desi Relaford	.05
337	John Burkett	.05
338	Mike Hampton	.05
339	Royce Clayton	.05
340	Mike Piazza	1.25
341	Jeremi Gonzalez	.05
342	Mike Lansing	.05
343	Jamie Moyer	.05
344	Ron Coomer	.05
345	Barry Larkin	.05
346	Fernando Tatis	.05
347	Chili Davis	.05
348	Bobby Higginson	.05
349	Hal Morris	.05
350	Larry Walker	.05
351	Carlos Guillen	.05
352	Miguel Tejada	.05
353	Travis Fryman	.05
354	Jarrod Washburn	.05
355	Chipper Jones	1.00
356	Todd Stottlemyre	.05
357	Henry Rodriguez	.05
358	Eli Marrero	.05
359	Alan Benes	.05
360	Tim Salmon	.05
361	Luis Gonzalez	.05
362	Scott Spiezio	.05
363	Chris Carpenter	.05
364	Bobby Howry	.05
365	Raul Mondesi	.05
366	Ugueth Urbina	.05
367	Tom Evans	.05
368	Kerry Ligtenberg **RC**	.15
369	Adrian Beltre	.15
370	Ryan Klesko	.05
371	Wilson Alvarez	.05
372	John Thomson	.05
373	Tony Saunders	.05
374	Mike Stanley	.05
375	Ken Caminiti	.05
376	Jay Buhner	.05
377	Bill Mueller	.05
378	Jeff Blauser	.05
379	Edgar Renteria	.05
380	Jim Thome	.60
381	Joey Hamilton	.05
382	Calvin Pickering	.05
383	Marquis Grissom	.05
384	Omar Daal	.05
385	Curt Schilling	.25
386	Jose Cruz Jr.	.05
387	Chris Widger	.05
388	Pete Harnisch	.05
389	Charles Nagy	.05
390	Tom Gordon	.05
391	Bobby Smith	.05
392	Derrick Gibson	.05
393	Jeff Conine	.05
394	Carlos Perez	.05
395	Barry Bonds	2.00
396	Mark McLemore	.05
397	Juan Encarnacion	.05
398	Wade Boggs	1.00
399	Ivan Rodriguez	.65

400	Moises Alou	.05
401	Jeromy Burnitz	.05
402	Sean Casey	.10
403	Jose Offerman	.05
404	Joe Fontenot	.05
405	Kevin Millwood	.05
406	Lance Johnson	.05
407	Richard Hidalgo	.05
408	Mike Jackson	.05
409	Brian Anderson	.05
410	Jeff Shaw	.05
411	Preston Wilson	.05
412	Todd Hundley	.05
413	Jim Parque	.05
414	Justin Baughman	.05
415	Dante Bichette	.05
416	Paul O'Neill	.05
417	Miguel Cairo	.05
418	Randy Johnson	.75
419	Jesus Sanchez	.05
420	Carlos Delgado	.30
421	Ricky Ledee	.05
422	Orlando Hernandez	.05
423	Frank Thomas	.75
424	Pokey Reese	.05
425	Carlos Lee, Mike Lowell, Kit Pellow RC	.25
426	Michael Cuddyer, Mark DeRosa, Jerry Hairston Jr.	.05
427	Marlon Anderson, Ron Belliard, Orlando Cabrera	.10
428	Micah Bowie, Phil Norton, Randy Wolf	.10
429	Jack Cressend, Jason Rakers, John Rocker	.10
430	Ruben Mateo, Scott Morgan, Mike Zywica RC	.10
431	Jason LaRue, Matt LeCroy, Mitch Meluskey	.10
432	Gabe Kapler, Armando Rios, Fernando Seguignol	.05
433	Adam Kennedy, Mickey Lopez, Jackie Rexrode	.10
434	Jose Fernandez, Jeff Liefer, Chris Truby	.10
435	Corey Koskie, Doug Mientkiewicz, Damon Minor	.10
436	Roosevelt Brown, Dernell Stenson, Vernon Wells	.10
437	A.J. Burnett, John Nicholson, Billy Koch	.25
438	Matt Belisle, Matt Roney RC	.10
439	Austin Kearns, Chris George RC	2.50
440	Nate Bump, Nate Cornejo RC	.40
441	Brad Lidge, Mike Nannini RC	.25
442	Matt Holiday, Jeff Winchester RC	.25
443	Adam Everett, Chip Ambres RC	.25
444	Pat Burrell, Eric Valent RC	1.50
445	Roger Clemens	.50
446	Kerry Wood	.15
447	Curt Schilling	.05
448	Randy Johnson	.40
449	Pedro Martinez	.40
450	Jeff Bagwell, Andres Galarraga, Mark McGwire (All-Topps)	.50
451	John Olerud, Jim Thome, Tino Martinez (All-Topps)	.30
452	Alex Rodriguez, Nomar Garciaparra, Derek Jeter (All-Topps)	.60
453	Vinny Castilla, Chipper Jones, Scott Rolen (All-Topps)	.40
454	Sammy Sosa, Ken Griffey Jr., Juan Gonzalez (All-Topps)	.50
455	Barry Bonds, Manny Ramirez, Larry Walker (All-Topps)	.60
456	Frank Thomas, Tim Salmon, David Justice (All-Topps)	.30
457	Travis Lee, Todd Helton, Ben Grieve (All-Topps)	.30
458	Vladimir Guerrero, Greg Vaughn, Bernie Williams (All-Topps)	.25
459	Mike Piazza, Ivan Rodriguez, Jason Kendall (All-Topps)	.50
460	Roger Clemens, Kerry Wood, Greg Maddux (All-Topps)	.45
461	Sammy Sosa Home Run Parade #1	10.00
461	Sammy Sosa HR Parade #2-60	4.00
461	Sammy Sosa HR Parade #61-62	10.00
461	Sammy Sosa HR Parade #63-65	6.00
461	Sammy Sosa HR Parade #66	20.00
462	Checklist	.05
463	Checklist	.05

1999 Topps MVP Promotion

	NM/M
Common Player:	3.00
Stars/Rookies:	20X

(See 1999 Topps for checklist and base card values.)

All-Matrix

	NM/M
Complete Set (30):	45.00
Common Player:	.75

Inserted 1:18

AM1	Mark McGwire	6.00
AM2	Sammy Sosa	3.50
AM3	Ken Griffey Jr.	4.50
AM4	Greg Vaughn	.75
AM5	Albert Belle	.75
AM6	Vinny Castilla	.75
AM7	Jose Canseco	1.25
AM8	Juan Gonzalez	1.25
AM9	Manny Ramirez	2.50
AM10	Andres Galarraga	.75
AM11	Rafael Palmeiro	2.00
AM12	Alex Rodriguez	6.00
AM13	Mo Vaughn	.75
AM14	Eric Chavez	1.25
AM15	Gabe Kapler	.75
AM16	Calvin Pickering	.75
AM17	Ruben Mateo	.75
AM18	Roy Halladay	1.25
AM19	Jeremy Giambi	.75
AM20	Alex Gonzalez	.75
AM21	Ron Belliard	.75
AM22	Marlon Anderson	.75
AM23	Carlos Lee	.75
AM24	Kerry Wood	1.25
AM25	Roger Clemens	3.50
AM26	Curt Schilling	1.25
AM27	Kevin Brown	.75
AM28	Randy Johnson	2.50
AM29	Pedro Martinez	2.50
AM30	Orlando Hernandez	.75

All-Topps Mystery Finest

	NM/M
Complete Set (33):	100.00
Common Player:	1.00

Inserted 1:36

Refractors:	1.5X

Inserted 1:144

M1	Jeff Bagwell	4.25
M2	Andres Galarraga	1.00
M3	Mark McGwire	9.00
M4	John Olerud	1.00
M5	Jim Thome	2.50
M6	Tino Martinez	1.00
M7	Alex Rodriguez	9.00
M8	Nomar Garciaparra	5.00
M9	Derek Jeter	12.50
M10	Vinny Castilla	1.00
M11	Chipper Jones	5.00
M12	Scott Rolen	3.00
M13	Sammy Sosa	5.00
M14	Ken Griffey Jr.	7.50
M15	Juan Gonzalez	2.00
M16	Barry Bonds	12.50
M17	Manny Ramirez	4.50
M18	Larry Walker	1.00
M19	Frank Thomas	4.50
M20	Tim Salmon	1.00
M21	David Justice	1.00
M22	Travis Lee	1.50
M23	Todd Helton	4.50
M24	Ben Grieve	1.00
M25	Vladimir Guerrero	4.50
M26	Greg Vaughn	1.00
M27	Bernie Williams	1.00
M28	Mike Piazza	7.50
M29	Ivan Rodriguez	3.50
M30	Jason Kendall	1.00
M31	Roger Clemens	6.00
M32	Kerry Wood	2.00
M33	Greg Maddux	5.00

Autographs

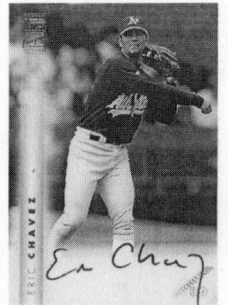

	NM/M
Common Player:	8.00

Series 1 Inserted 1:532 H
Series 2 Inserted 1:501 H

A1	Roger Clemens	100.00
A2	Chipper Jones	50.00
A3	Scott Rolen	25.00
A4	Alex Rodriguez	100.00
A5	Andres Galarraga	8.00
A6	Rondell White	8.00
A7	Ben Grieve	8.00
A8	Troy Glaus	20.00
A9	Moises Alou	15.00
A10	Barry Bonds	180.00
A11	Vladimir Guerrero	35.00
A12	Andruw Jones	20.00
A13	Darin Erstad	12.00
A14	Shawn Green	16.00
A15	Eric Chavez	20.00
A16	Pat Burrell	30.00

Hall of Fame

	NM/M
Complete Set (10):	8.00

	NM/M
Common Player:	.50

Inserted 1:12 H

HOF1	Mike Schmidt	1.50
HOF2	Brooks Robinson	.75
HOF3	Stan Musial	1.50
HOF4	Willie McCovey	.50
HOF5	Eddie Mathews	.75
HOF6	Reggie Jackson	1.50
HOF7	Ernie Banks	1.00
HOF8	Whitey Ford	.75
HOF9	Bob Feller	.50
HOF10	Yogi Berra	1.00

Lords of the Diamond

	NM/M
Complete Set (15):	13.00
Common Player:	.25

Inserted 1:18

LD1	Ken Griffey Jr.	1.25
LD2	Chipper Jones	1.00
LD3	Sammy Sosa	1.00
LD4	Frank Thomas	.75
LD5	Mark McGwire	1.50
LD6	Jeff Bagwell	.75
LD7	Alex Rodriguez	1.50
LD8	Juan Gonzalez	.40
LD9	Barry Bonds	2.00
LD10	Nomar Garciaparra	1.00
LD11	Darin Erstad	.35
LD12	Tony Gwynn	1.00
LD13	Andres Galarraga	.25
LD14	Mike Piazza	1.25
LD15	Greg Maddux	1.00

New Breed

	NM/M
Complete Set (15):	9.00
Common Player:	.25

Inserted 1:18

NB1	Darin Erstad	.50
NB2	Brad Fullmer	.25
NB3	Kerry Wood	.50
NB4	Nomar Garciaparra	1.50

NB5	Travis Lee	.35
NB6	Scott Rolen	.75
NB7	Todd Helton	.75
NB8	Vladimir Guerrero	1.00
NB9	Derek Jeter	3.00
NB10	Alex Rodriguez	2.00
NB11	Ben Grieve	.25
NB12	Andruw Jones	1.00
NB13	Paul Konerko	.40
NB14	Aramis Ramirez	.25
NB15	Adrian Beltre	.35

Nolan Ryan Reprints

		NM/M
Complete Set (27):		40.00
Common Ryan:		3.00
Inserted 1:18		
Nolan Ryan Autograph:		150.00
1	Nolan Ryan/1968	7.50
2	Nolan Ryan/1969	4.50
3	Nolan Ryan/1970	3.00
4	Nolan Ryan/1971	3.00
5	Nolan Ryan/1972	3.00
6	Nolan Ryan/1973	3.00
7	Nolan Ryan/1974	3.00
8	Nolan Ryan/1975	3.00
9	Nolan Ryan/1976	3.00
10	Nolan Ryan/1977	3.00
11	Nolan Ryan/1978	3.00
12	Nolan Ryan/1979	3.00
13	Nolan Ryan/1980	3.00
14	Nolan Ryan/1981	3.00
15	Nolan Ryan/1982	3.00
16	Nolan Ryan/1983	3.00
17	Nolan Ryan/1984	3.00
18	Nolan Ryan/1985	3.00
19	Nolan Ryan/1986	3.00
20	Nolan Ryan/1987	3.00
21	Nolan Ryan/1988	3.00
22	Nolan Ryan/1989	3.00
23	Nolan Ryan/1990	3.00
24	Nolan Ryan/1991	3.00
25	Nolan Ryan/1992	3.00
26	Nolan Ryan/1993	3.00
27	Nolan Ryan/1994	3.00

Nolan Ryan Finest Reprints

		NM/M
Complete Set (27):		125.00
Common Card:		5.00
Refractors:		2X
Inserted 1:288		
1	1968	12.50
2	1969	7.50
3	1970	5.00
4	1971	5.00
5	1972	5.00
6	1973	5.00
7	1974	5.00
8	1975	5.00
9	1976	5.00
10	1977	5.00
11	1978	5.00
12	1979	5.00
13	1980	5.00
14	1981	5.00

15	1982	5.00
16	1983	5.00
17	1984	5.00
18	1985	5.00
19	1986	5.00
20	1987	5.00
21	1988	5.00
22	1989	5.00
23	1990	5.00
24	1991	5.00
25	1992	5.00
26	1992	5.00
27	1992	5.00

Nolan Ryan Reprint Autographs

		NM/M
Common Card:		150.00
1	Nolan Ryan/1968	200.00
2	Nolan Ryan/1969	150.00
3	Nolan Ryan/1970	150.00
4	Nolan Ryan/1971	150.00
5	Nolan Ryan/1972	150.00
6	Nolan Ryan/1973	150.00
7	Nolan Ryan/1974	150.00
8	Nolan Ryan/1975	150.00
9	Nolan Ryan/1976	150.00
10	Nolan Ryan/1977	150.00
11	Nolan Ryan/1978	150.00
12	Nolan Ryan/1979	150.00
13	Nolan Ryan/1980	150.00
14	Nolan Ryan/1981	150.00
15	Nolan Ryan/1982	150.00
16	Nolan Ryan/1983	150.00
17	Nolan Ryan/1984	150.00
18	Nolan Ryan/1985	150.00
19	Nolan Ryan/1986	150.00
20	Nolan Ryan/1987	150.00
21	Nolan Ryan/1988	150.00
22	Nolan Ryan/1989	150.00
23	Nolan Ryan/1990	150.00
24	Nolan Ryan/1991	150.00
25	Nolan Ryan/1992	150.00
26	Nolan Ryan/1993	150.00
27	Nolan Ryan/1994	150.00

Picture Perfect

		NM/M
Complete Set (10):		5.00
Common Player:		.25
Inserted 1:8		
P1	Ken Griffey Jr.	.75
P2	Kerry Wood	.30
P3	Pedro Martinez	.45
P4	Mark McGwire	.90
P5	Greg Maddux	.60
P6	Sammy Sosa	.60
P7	Greg Vaughn	.25
P8	Juan Gonzalez	.30
P9	Jeff Bagwell	.45
P10	Derek Jeter	1.50

Power Brokers

		NM/M
Complete Set (20):		20.00
Common Player:		.25
Inserted 1:36		

Refractors:		1.5X
Inserted 1:144		
PB1	Mark McGwire	3.00
PB2	Andres Galarraga	.25
PB3	Ken Griffey Jr.	2.00
PB4	Sammy Sosa	1.50
PB5	Juan Gonzalez	.50
PB6	Alex Rodriguez	3.00
PB7	Frank Thomas	1.00
PB8	Jeff Bagwell	1.00
PB9	Vinny Castilla	.25
PB10	Mike Piazza	2.00
PB11	Greg Vaughn	.25
PB12	Barry Bonds	4.00
PB13	Mo Vaughn	.25
PB14	Jim Thome	.65
PB15	Larry Walker	.25
PB16	Chipper Jones	1.50
PB17	Nomar Garciaparra	1.50
PB18	Manny Ramirez	1.00
PB19	Roger Clemens	1.75
PB20	Kerry Wood	.65

Record Numbers

		NM/M
Complete Set (10):		8.00
Common Player:		.50
Inserted 1:8		
RN1	Mark McGwire	1.50
RN2	Mike Piazza	1.00
RN3	Curt Schilling	.75
RN4	Ken Griffey Jr.	1.50
RN5	Sammy Sosa	.75
RN6	Nomar Garciaparra	.75
RN7	Kerry Wood	.75
RN8	Roger Clemens	1.50
RN9	Cal Ripken Jr.	2.00
RN10	Mark McGwire	1.50

Record Numbers Gold

		NM/M
Common Player:		8.00
RN1	Mark McGwire/70	40.00
RN2	Mike Piazza/362	15.00
RN3	Curt Schilling/319	8.00
RN4	Ken Griffey Jr./350	20.00
RN5	Sammy Sosa/20	20.00
RN6	Nomar Garciaparra/30	20.00
RN7	Kerry Wood/20	15.00
RN8	Roger Clemens/20	40.00
RN9	Cal Ripken Jr./2,632	15.00
RN10	Mark McGwire/162	20.00

1999 Topps Traded and Rookies

		NM/M
Unopened Set (122):		40.00
Complete Set, No Autograph (121):		15.00
Common Player:		.10
1	Seth Etherton	.10
2	Mark Harriger RC	.10
3	Matt Wise RC	.25
4	Carlos Hernandez RC	.15
5	Julio Lugo RC	.25
6	Mike Nannini	.10
7	Justin Bowles RC	.10
8	Mark Mulder RC	.75
9	Roberto Vaz RC	.10
10	Felipe Lopez RC	.75
11	Matt Belisle	.10
12	Micah Bowie	.10
13	Ruben Quevedo RC	.10
14	Jose Garcia RC	.10
15	David Kelton RC	.25
16	Phillip Norton	.10
17	Corey Patterson RC	.75
18	Ron Walker RC	.10
19	Paul Hoover RC	.10
20	Ryan Rupe RC	.15
21	J.D. Closser RC	.10
22	Rob Ryan RC	.10
23	Steve Colyer RC	.10
24	Bubba Crosby RC	.50
25	Luke Prokopec RC	.10
26	Matt Blank RC	.10
27	Josh McKinley	.10
28	Nate Bump	.10
29	Giuseppe Chiaramonte RC	.10
30	Arturo McDowell	.10
31	Tony Torcato	.10
32	Dave Roberts	.10
33	C.C. Sabathia RC	2.00
34	Sean Spencer RC	.10
35	Chip Ambres	.10
36	A.J. Burnett	.15
37	Mo Bruce RC	.10
38	Jason Tyner	.10
39	Mamon Tucker	.10
40	Sean Burroughs RC	.25
41	Kevin Eberwein RC	.10
42	Junior Herndon RC	.10
43	Bryan Wolff RC	.10
44	Pat Burrell	.50
45	Eric Valent	.10
46	Carlos Pena RC	1.00
47	Mike Zywica	.10
48	Adam Everett	.10
49	Juan Pena RC	.50
50	Adam Dunn RC	3.00
51	Austin Kearns	.75
52	Jacobo Sequea RC	.10
53	Choo Freeman	.10
54	Jeff Winchester	.10
55	Matt Burch	.10
56	Chris George	.10
57	Scott Mullen RC	.10
58	Kit Pellow	.10
59	Mark Quinn RC	.15
60	Nate Cornejo	.10
61	Ryan Mills RC	.25
62	Kevin Beirne RC	.10
63	Kip Wells RC	.50
64	Juan Rivera RC	.25
65	Alfonso Soriano RC	4.00
66	Josh Hamilton RC	8.00
67	Josh Girdley RC	.10
68	Kyle Snyder RC	.15
69	Mike Paradis RC	.10
70	Jason Jennings RC	.25
71	David Walling RC	.10
72	Omar Ortiz RC	.10
73	Jay Gehrke RC	.10
74	Casey Burns RC	.10
75	Carl Crawford RC	2.00
76	Reggie Sanders	.10
77	Will Clark	.10
78	David Wells	.10
79	Paul Konerko	.20
80	Armando Benitez	.10
81	Brant Brown	.10
82	Mo Vaughn	.10
83	Jose Canseco	.10
84	Albert Belle	.10
85	Dean Palmer	.10
86	Greg Vaughn	.10
87	Mark Clark	.10
88	Pat Meares	.10
89	Eric Davis	.10
90	Brian Giles	.10
91	Jeff Brantley	.10
92	Bret Boone	.10
93	Ron Gant	.10
94	Mike Cameron	.10
95	Charles Johnson	.10
96	Denny Neagle	.10
97	Brian Hunter	.10

98	Jose Hernandez	.10
99	Rick Aguilera	.10
100	Tony Batista	.10
101	Roger Cedeno	.10
102	Creighton Gubanich	.10
103	Tim Belcher	.10
104	Bruce Aven	.10
105	Brian Daubach **RC**	.25
106	Ed Sprague	.10
107	Michael Tucker	.10
108	Homer Bush	.10
109	Armando Reynoso	.10
110	Brook Fordyce	.10
111	Matt Mantei	.10
112	Jose Guillen	.10
113	Kenny Rogers	.10
114	Livan Hernandez	.10
115	Butch Huskey	.10
116	David Segui	.10
117	Darryl Hamilton	.10
118	Jim Leyritz	.10
119	Randy Velarde	.10
120	Bill Taylor	.10
121	Kevin Appier	.10

Autographs

		NM/M
Common Player:		3.00
Inserted 1:Set		
1	Seth Etherton	3.00
2	Mark Harriger	3.00
3	Matt Wise	5.00
4	Carlos Hernandez	5.00
5	Julio Lugo	20.00
6	Mike Nannini	3.00
7	Justin Bowles	3.00
8	Mark Mulder	15.00
9	Roberto Vaz	3.00
10	Felipe Lopez	15.00
11	Matt Belisle	3.00
12	Micah Bowie	3.00
13	Ruben Quevedo	5.00
14	Jose Garcia	5.00
15	David Kelton	5.00
16	Phillip Norton	5.00
17	Corey Patterson	15.00
18	Ron Walker	3.00
19	Paul Hoover	3.00
20	Ryan Rupe	4.00
21	J.D. Closser	5.00
22	Rob Ryan	3.00
23	Steve Colyer	5.00
24	Bubba Crosby	10.00
25	Luke Prokopec	3.00
26	Matt Blank	3.00
27	Josh McKinley	5.00
28	Nate Bump	5.00
29	Giuseppe Chiaramonte	3.00
30	Arturo McDowell	3.00
31	Tony Torcato	5.00
32	Dave Roberts	10.00
33	C.C. Sabathia	100.00
34	Sean Spencer	3.00
35	Chip Ambres	3.00
36	A.J. Burnett	25.00
37	Mo Bruce	3.00
38	Jason Tyner	3.00
39	Mamon Tucker	3.00
40	Sean Burroughs	5.00
41	Kevin Eberwein	3.00
42	Junior Herndon	3.00
43	Bryan Wolff	3.00
44	Pat Burrell	35.00
45	Eric Valent	5.00
46	Carlos Pena	30.00
47	Mike Zywica	3.00
48	Adam Everett	10.00
49	Juan Pena	5.00
50	Adam Dunn	80.00
51	Austin Kearns	15.00
52	Jacobo Sequea	3.00
53	Choo Freeman	5.00
54	Jeff Winchester	3.00
55	Matt Burch	3.00
56	Chris George	4.00
57	Scott Mullen	3.00
58	Kit Pellow	3.00
59	Mark Quinn	3.00
60	Nate Cornejo	5.00
61	Ryan Mills	3.00
62	Kevin Beirne	4.00
63	Kip Wells	5.00
64	Juan Rivera	8.00
65	Alfonso Soriano	125.00
66	Josh Hamilton	200.00
67	Josh Girdley	3.00
68	Kyle Snyder	5.00
69	Mike Paradis	3.00
70	Jason Jennings	10.00
71	David Walling	3.00
72	Omar Ortiz	3.00
73	Jay Gehrke	5.00
74	Casey Burns	3.00
75	Carl Crawford	50.00

1999 Topps Chrome

		NM/M
Complete Set (461):		75.00
Common Player:		.15
Refractors:		4X
Inserted 1:12		
Ser. 1 or 2 Pack (4):		1.50
Ser. 1 or 2 Box (24):		30.00
1	Roger Clemens	1.75
2	Andres Galarraga	.15
3	Scott Brosius	.15
4	John Flaherty	.15
5	Jim Leyritz	.15
6	Ray Durham	.15
7	Not Issued	
8	Joe Vizcaino	.15
9	Will Clark	.15
10	David Wells	.15
11	Jose Guillen	.15
12	Scott Hatteberg	.15
13	Edgardo Alfonzo	.15
14	Mike Bordick	.15
15	Manny Ramirez	1.00
16	Greg Maddux	1.50
17	David Segui	.15
18	Darryl Strawberry	.15
19	Brad Radke	.15
20	Kerry Wood	.40
21	Matt Anderson	.15
22	Derrek Lee	.60
23	Mickey Morandini	.15
24	Paul Konerko	.30
25	Travis Lee	.15
26	Ken Hill	.15
27	Kenny Rogers	.15
28	Paul Sorrento	.15
29	Quilvio Veras	.15
30	Todd Walker	.15
31	Ryan Jackson	.15
32	John Olerud	.15
33	Doug Glanville	.15
34	Nolan Ryan	3.00
35	Ray Lankford	.15
36	Mark Loretta	.15
37	Jason Dickson	.15
38	Sean Bergman	.15
39	Quinton McCracken	.15
40	Bartolo Colon	.15
41	Brady Anderson	.15
42	Chris Stynes	.15
43	Jorge Posada	.15
44	Justin Thompson	.15
45	Johnny Damon	.40
46	Armando Benitez	.15
47	Brant Brown	.15
48	Charlie Hayes	.15
49	Darren Dreifort	.15
50	Juan Gonzalez	.50
51	Chuck Knoblauch	.15
52	Todd Helton	1.00
53	Rick Reed	.15
54	Chris Gomez	.15
55	Gary Sheffield	.50
56	Rod Beck	.15
57	Rey Sanchez	.15
58	Garret Anderson	.15
59	Jimmy Haynes	.15
60	Steve Woodard	.15
61	Rondell White	.15
62	Vladimir Guerrero	1.00
63	Eric Karros	.15
64	Russ Davis	.15
65	Mo Vaughn	.15
66	Sammy Sosa	1.50
67	Troy Percival	.15
68	Kenny Lofton	.15
69	Bill Taylor	.15
70	Mark McGwire	2.50
71	Roger Cedeno	.15
72	Javy Lopez	.15
73	Damion Easley	.15
74	Andy Pettitte	.35
75	Tony Gwynn	1.50
76	Ricardo Rincon	.15
77	F.P. Santangelo	.15
78	Jay Bell	.15
79	Scott Servais	.15
80	Jose Canseco	.50
81	Roberto Hernandez	.15
82	Todd Dunwoody	.15
83	John Wetteland	.15
84	Mike Caruso	.15
85	Derek Jeter	3.00
86	Aaron Sele	.15
87	Jose Lima	.15
88	Ryan Christenson	.15
89	Jeff Cirillo	.15
90	Jose Hernandez	.15
91	Mark Kotsay	.15
92	Darren Bragg	.15
93	Albert Belle	.15
94	Matt Lawton	.15
95	Pedro Martinez	1.00
96	Greg Vaughn	.15
97	Neifi Perez	.15
98	Gerald Williams	.15
99	Derek Bell	.15
100	Ken Griffey Jr.	2.00
101	David Cone	.15
102	Brian Johnson	.15
103	Dean Palmer	.15
104	Javier Valentin	.15
105	Trevor Hoffman	.15
106	Butch Huskey	.15
107	Dave Martinez	.15
108	Billy Wagner	.15
109	Shawn Green	.35
110	Ben Grieve	.15
111	Tom Goodwin	.15
112	Jaret Wright	.15
113	Aramis Ramirez	.15
114	Dmitri Young	.15
115	Hideki Irabu	.15
116	Roberto Kelly	.15
117	Jeff Fassero	.15
118	Mark Clark	.15
119	Jason McDonald	.15
120	Matt Williams	.15
121	Dave Burba	.15
122	Bret Saberhagen	.15
123	Deivi Cruz	.15
124	Chad Curtis	.15
125	Scott Rolen	.75
126	Lee Stevens	.15
127	J.T. Snow Jr.	.15
128	Rusty Greer	.15
129	Brian Meadows	.15
130	Jim Edmonds	.15
131	Ron Gant	.15
132	A.J. Hinch	.15
133	Shannon Stewart	.15
134	Brad Fullmer	.15
135	Cal Eldred	.15
136	Matt Walbeck	.15
137	Carl Everett	.15
138	Walt Weiss	.15
139	Fred McGriff	.15
140	Darin Erstad	.40
141	Dave Nilsson	.15
142	Eric Young	.15
143	Dan Wilson	.15
144	Jeff Reed	.15
145	Brett Tomko	.15
146	Terry Steinbach	.15
147	Seth Greisinger	.15
148	Pat Meares	.15
149	Livan Hernandez	.15
150	Jeff Bagwell	1.00
151	Bob Wickman	.15
152	Omar Vizquel	.15
153	Eric Davis	.15
154	Larry Sutton	.15
155	Magglio Ordonez	.45
156	Eric Milton	.15
157	Darren Lewis	.15
158	Rick Aguilera	.15
159	Mike Lieberthal	.15
160	Robb Nen	.15
161	Brian Giles	.15
162	Jeff Brantley	.15
163	Gary DiSarcina	.15
164	John Valentin	.15
165	David Dellucci	.15
166	Chan Ho Park	.15
167	Masato Yoshii	.15
168	Jason Schmidt	.15
169	LaTroy Hawkins	.15
170	Bret Boone	.15
171	Jerry DiPoto	.15
172	Mariano Rivera	.25
173	Mike Cameron	.15
174	Scott Erickson	.15
175	Charles Johnson	.15
176	Bobby Jones	.15
177	Francisco Cordova	.15
178	Todd Jones	.15
179	Jeff Montgomery	.15
180	Mike Mussina	.50
181	Bob Abreu	.15
182	Ismael Valdes	.15
183	Andy Fox	.15
184	Woody Williams	.15
185	Denny Neagle	.15
186	Jose Valentin	.15
187	Darrin Fletcher	.15
188	Gabe Alvarez	.15
189	Eddie Taubensee	.15
190	Edgar Martinez	.15
191	Jason Kendall	.15
192	Darryl Kile	.15
193	Jeff King	.15
194	Rey Ordonez	.15
195	Andruw Jones	1.00
196	Tony Fernandez	.15
197	Jamey Wright	.15
198	B.J. Surhoff	.15
199	Vinny Castilla	.15
200	David Wells	.15
201	Mark McGwire	1.25
202	Sammy Sosa	.75
203	Roger Clemens	.85
204	Kerry Wood	.20
205	Lance Berkman, Mike Frank, Gabe Kapler (Prospects)	.15
206	Alex Escobar, Ricky Ledee, Mike Stoner (Prospects)	.50
207	Peter Bergeron, Jeremy Giambi, George Lombard (Prospects)	.50
208	Michael Barrett, Ben Davis, Robert Fick (Prospects)	.15
209	Pat Cline, Ramon Hernandez, Jayson Werth (Prospects)	.20
210	Bruce Chen, Chris Enochs, Ryan Anderson (Prospects)	.15
211	Mike Lincoln, Octavio Dotel, Brad Penny (Prospects)	.15
212	Chuck Abbott, Brent Butler, Danny Klassen (Prospects)	.15
213	Chris Jones, Jeff Urban **RC**	.15
214	Arturo McDowell, Tony Torcato **RC**	.25
215	Josh McKinley, Jason Tyner **RC**	.30
216	Matt Burch, Seth Etherton **RC**	.15
217	Mamon Tucker, Rick Elder **RC**	.20
218	J.M. Gold, Ryan Mills **RC**	.15
219	Adam Brown, Choo Freeman **RC**	.20
220	Mark McGwire HR #1	15.00
220	Mark McGwire HR #2-60	10.00
220	McGwire HR #61-62	15.00
220	McGwire HR #63-69	12.50
220	McGwire HR #70	40.00
221	Larry Walker	.15
222	Bernie Williams	.15
223	Mark McGwire	1.25
224	Ken Griffey Jr.	1.00
225	Sammy Sosa	.75
226	Juan Gonzalez	.35
227	Dante Bichette	.15
228	Alex Rodriguez	1.25
229	Sammy Sosa	.75
230	Derek Jeter	1.50
231	Greg Maddux	.75
232	Roger Clemens	.75
233	Ricky Ledee	.15
234	Chuck Knoblauch	.15
235	Bernie Williams	.15
236	Tino Martinez	.15
237	Orlando Hernandez	.15
238	Scott Brosius	.15
239	Andy Pettitte	.15
240	Mariano Rivera	.15
241	Checklist	.15
242	Checklist	.15
243	Tom Glavine	.35
244	Andy Benes	.15
245	Sandy Alomar	.15
246	Wilton Guerrero	.15
247	Alex Gonzalez	.15
248	Roberto Alomar	.30
249	Ruben Rivera	.15
250	Eric Chavez	.15
251	Ellis Burks	.15
252	Richie Sexson	.15
253	Steve Finley	.15
254	Dwight Gooden	.15
255	Dustin Hermanson	.15
256	Kirk Rueter	.15
257	Steve Trachsel	.15
258	Gregg Jefferies	.15
259	Matt Stairs	.15
260	Shane Reynolds	.15
261	Gregg Olson	.15
262	Kevin Tapani	.15
263	Matt Morris	.15
264	Carl Pavano	.15
265	Nomar Garciaparra	1.50
266	Kevin Young	.15
267	Rick Helling	.15
268	Matt Franco	.15
269	Brian McRae	.15
270	Cal Ripken Jr.	3.00
271	Jeff Abbott	.15
272	Tony Batista	.15
273	Bill Simas	.15
274	Brian Hunter	.15
275	John Franco	.15
276	Devon White	.15
277	Rickey Henderson	1.00
278	Chuck Finley	.15
279	Mike Blowers	.15
280	Mark Grace	.15

281	Randy Winn	.15
282	Bobby Bonilla	.15
283	David Justice	.15
284	Shane Monahan	.15
285	Kevin Brown	.15
286	Todd Zeile	.15
287	Al Martin	.15
288	Troy O'Leary	.15
289	Darryl Hamilton	.15
290	Tino Martinez	.15
291	David Ortiz	.50
292	Tony Clark	.15
293	Ryan Minor	.15
294	Reggie Sanders	.15
295	Wally Joyner	.15
296	Cliff Floyd	.15
297	Shawn Estes	.15
298	Pat Hentgen	.15
299	Scott Elarton	.15
300	Alex Rodriguez	2.50
301	Ozzie Guillen	.15
302	Hideo Martinez	.15
303	Ryan McGuire	.15
304	Brad Ausmus	.15
305	Alex Gonzalez	.15
306	Brian Jordan	.15
307	Jon Jaha	.15
308	Mark Grudzielanek	.15
309	Juan Guzman	.15
310	Tony Womack	.15
311	Dennis Reyes	.15
312	Marty Cordova	.15
313	Ramiro Mendoza	.15
314	Robin Ventura	.15
315	Rafael Palmeiro	.65
316	Ramon Martinez	.15
317	Pedro Astacio	.15
318	Dave Hollins	.15
319	Tom Candiotti	.15
320	Al Leiter	.15
321	Rico Brogna	.15
322	Reggie Jefferson	.15
323	Bernard Gilkey	.15
324	Jason Giambi	.40
325	Craig Biggio	.15
326	Troy Glaus	.75
327	Delino DeShields	.15
328	Fernando Vina	.15
329	John Smoltz	.15
330	Jeff Kent	.15
331	Roy Halladay	.15
332	Andy Ashby	.15
333	Tim Wakefield	.15
334	Roger Clemens	1.75
335	Bernie Williams	.15
336	Desi Relaford	.15
337	John Burkett	.15
338	Mike Hampton	.15
339	Royce Clayton	.15
340	Mike Piazza	2.00
341	Jeremi Gonzalez	.15
342	Mike Lansing	.15
343	Jamie Moyer	.15
344	Ron Coomer	.15
345	Barry Larkin	.15
346	Fernando Tatis	.15
347	Chili Davis	.15
348	Bobby Higginson	.15
349	Hal Morris	.15
350	Larry Walker	.15
351	Carlos Guillen	.15
352	Miguel Tejada	.30
353	Travis Fryman	.15
354	Jarrod Washburn	.15
355	Chipper Jones	1.50
356	Todd Stottlemyre	.15
357	Henry Rodriguez	.15
358	Eli Marrero	.15
359	Alan Benes	.15
360	Tim Salmon	.15
361	Luis Gonzalez	.15
362	Scott Spiezio	.15
363	Chris Carpenter	.15
364	Bobby Howry	.15
365	Raul Mondesi	.15
366	Ugueth Urbina	.15
367	Tom Evans	.15
368	Kerry Ligtenberg RC	.40
369	Adrian Beltre	.35
370	Ryan Klesko	.15
371	Wilson Alvarez	.15
372	John Thomson	.15
373	Tony Saunders	.15
374	Mike Stanley	.15
375	Ken Caminiti	.15
376	Jay Buhner	.15
377	Bill Mueller	.15
378	Jeff Blauser	.15
379	Edgar Renteria	.15
380	Jim Thome	.60
381	Joey Hamilton	.15
382	Calvin Pickering	.15
383	Marquis Grissom	.15
384	Omar Daal	.15
385	Curt Schilling	.35
386	Jose Cruz Jr.	.15
387	Chris Widger	.15
388	Pete Harnisch	.15
389	Charles Nagy	.15
390	Tom Gordon	.15
391	Bobby Smith	.15
392	Derrick Gibson	.15
393	Jeff Conine	.15
394	Carlos Perez	.15
395	Barry Bonds	3.00

396	Mark McLemore	.15
397	Juan Encarnacion	.15
398	Wade Boggs	1.50
399	Ivan Rodriguez	.75
400	Moises Alou	.15
401	Jeromy Burnitz	.15
402	Sean Casey	.25
403	Jose Offerman	.15
404	Joe Fontenot	.15
405	Kevin Millwood	.15
406	Lance Johnson	.15
407	Richard Hidalgo	.15
408	Mike Jackson	.15
409	Brian Anderson	.15
410	Jeff Shaw	.15
411	Preston Wilson	.15
412	Todd Hundley	.15
413	Jim Parque	.15
414	Justin Baughman	.15
415	Dante Bichette	.15
416	Paul O'Neill	.15
417	Miguel Cairo	.15
418	Randy Johnson	1.00
419	Jesus Sanchez	.15
420	Carlos Delgado	.35
421	Ricky Ledee	.15
422	Orlando Hernandez	.15
423	Frank Thomas	1.00
424	Pokey Reese	.15
425	Carlos Lee, Mike Lowell, Kit Pellow RC	.40
426	Michael Cuddyer, Mark DeRosa, Jerry Hairston Jr. RC	.60
427	Marlon Anderson, Ron Belliard, Orlando Cabrera	.45
428	Micah Bowie, Phil Norton, Randy Wolf	.35
429	Jack Cressend, Jason Rakers, John Rocker	.25
430	Ruben Mateo, Scott Morgan, Mike Zywica RC	.25
431	Jason LaRue, Matt LeCroy, Mitch Meluskey RC	.25
432	Gabe Kapler, Armando Rios, Fernando Seguignol	.25
433	Adam Kennedy, Mickey Lopez, Jackie Rexrode	.25
434	Jose Fernandez, Jeff Liefer, Chris Truby	.25
435	Corey Koskie, Doug Mientkiewicz, Damon Minor	.60
436	Roosevelt Brown, Dernell Stenson, Vernon Wells	.25
437	A.J. Burnett, John Nicholson, Billy Koch	.75
438	Matt Belisle, Matt Roney RC	.30
439	Austin Kearns, Chris George RC	3.00
440	Nate Bump, Nate Cornejo RC	.40
441	Brad Lidge, Mike Nannini RC	.60
442	Matt Holliday, Jeff Winchester RC	8.00
443	Adam Everett, Chip Ambres RC	.30
444	Pat Burrell, Eric Valent RC	3.00
445	Roger Clemens	.85
446	Kerry Wood	.20
447	Curt Schilling	.15
448	Randy Johnson	.50
449	Pedro Martinez	.50
450	Jeff Bagwell, Andres Galarraga, Mark McGwire	1.25
451	John Olerud, Jim Thome, Tino Martinez	.40
452	Alex Rodriguez, Nomar Garciaparra, Derek Jeter	1.50
453	Vinny Castilla, Chipper Jones, Scott Rolen	.75
454	Sammy Sosa, Ken Griffey Jr., Juan Gonzalez	1.50
455	Barry Bonds, Manny Ramirez, Larry Walker	1.50
456	Frank Thomas, Tim Salmon, David Justice	.60
457	Travis Lee, Todd Helton, Ben Grieve	.50
458	Vladimir Guerrero, Greg Vaughn, Bernie Williams	.50
459	Mike Piazza, Ivan Rodriguez, Jason Kendall	1.00
460	Roger Clemens, Kerry Wood, Greg Maddux	1.00
461	Mark McGwire #1 (Home Run Parade)	10.00
461	Sammy Sosa HR #2-60	6.00
461	S. Sosa HR #61-62	10.00
461	S. Sosa HR #63-65	7.50
461	S. Sosa HR #66	20.00
---	Checklist 1-100	.15
---	Checklist - inserts	.15

All-Etch

		NM/M
Complete Set (30):		15.00
Common Player:		.35
Inserted 1:6		
Refractors:		1.5X
Inserted 1:8		
1	Mark McGwire	3.00
2	Sammy Sosa	1.50
3	Ken Griffey Jr.	2.00
4	Greg Vaughn	.25
5	Albert Belle	.25
6	Vinny Castilla	.25
7	Jose Canseco	.50
8	Juan Gonzalez	.50
9	Manny Ramirez	1.00
10	Andres Galarraga	.25
11	Rafael Palmeiro	.75
12	Alex Rodriguez	3.00
13	Mo Vaughn	.25
14	Eric Chavez	.40
15	Gabe Kapler	.25
16	Calvin Pickering	.25
17	Ruben Mateo	.25
18	Roy Halladay	.40
19	Jeremy Giambi	.25
20	Alex Gonzalez	.25
21	Ron Belliard	.25
22	Marlon Anderson	.25
23	Carlos Lee	.25
24	Kerry Wood	.50
25	Roger Clemens	1.50
26	Curt Schilling	.50
27	Kevin Brown	.25
28	Randy Johnson	1.00
29	Pedro Martinez	1.00
30	Orlando Hernandez	.25

Early Road to the Hall

		NM/M
Complete Set (10):		12.00
Common Player:		.50
Inserted 1:12		
Refractors (#d to 100):		6X
ER1	Nomar Garciaparra	1.50
ER2	Derek Jeter	3.00
ER3	Alex Rodriguez	2.50
ER4	Juan Gonzalez	.50
ER5	Ken Griffey Jr.	2.00
ER6	Chipper Jones	1.50
ER7	Vladimir Guerrero	1.00
ER8	Jeff Bagwell	1.00
ER9	Ivan Rodriguez	.75
ER10	Frank Thomas	1.00

Fortune 15

		NM/M
Complete Set (15):		17.50
Common Player:		.50
Inserted 1:12		
Refractors (#'d to 100):		4X
1	Alex Rodriguez	2.25
2	Nomar Garciaparra	1.25
3	Derek Jeter	3.00
4	Troy Glaus	.75
5	Ken Griffey Jr.	1.50
6	Vladimir Guerrero	1.00
7	Kerry Wood	.65
8	Eric Chavez	.65
9	Greg Maddux	1.25
10	Mike Piazza	1.50
11	Sammy Sosa	1.25
12	Mark McGwire	2.25
13	Ben Grieve	.50
14	Chipper Jones	1.25
15	Manny Ramirez	1.00

Lords of the Diamond

		NM/M
Complete Set (15):		20.00
Common Player:		.40
Inserted 1:8		
Refractors:		2X
Inserted 1:24		
LD1	Ken Griffey Jr.	2.00
LD2	Chipper Jones	1.50
LD3	Sammy Sosa	1.50
LD4	Frank Thomas	1.25
LD5	Mark McGwire	2.50
LD6	Jeff Bagwell	1.25
LD7	Alex Rodriguez	2.25
LD8	Juan Gonzalez	.65
LD9	Barry Bonds	3.00
LD10	Nomar Garciaparra	1.50
LD11	Darin Erstad	.50
LD12	Tony Gwynn	1.50
LD13	Andres Galarraga	.40
LD14	Mike Piazza	2.00
LD15	Greg Maddux	1.50

New Breed

		NM/M
Complete Set (15):		30.00
Common Player:		.50
Inserted 1:24		
Refractors:		1.5X
Inserted 1:72		
NB1	Darin Erstad	.75
NB2	Brad Fullmer	.50
NB3	Kerry Wood	.75
NB4	Nomar Garciaparra	5.00
NB5	Travis Lee	.65
NB6	Scott Rolen	2.00
NB7	Todd Helton	3.00
NB8	Vladimir Guerrero	3.00
NB9	Derek Jeter	7.50
NB10	Alex Rodriguez	6.00
NB11	Ben Grieve	.50
NB12	Andruw Jones	3.00
NB13	Paul Konerko	.75
NB14	Aramis Ramirez	.50
NB15	Adrian Beltre	.75

Record Numbers

		NM/M
Complete Set (10):		20.00
Common Player:		.50
Inserted 1:36		
Refractors:		1.5X
Inserted 1:144		
1	Mark McGwire	3.00
2	Craig Biggio	.50
3	Barry Bonds	4.00
4	Ken Griffey Jr.	2.50
5	Sammy Sosa	2.00
6	Alex Rodriguez	3.00
7	Kerry Wood	1.00
8	Roger Clemens	2.00
9	Cal Ripken Jr.	4.00
10	Mark McGwire	3.00

1999 Topps Chrome Traded and Rookies

		NM/M
Complete Set (121):		40.00
Common Player:		.15
1	Seth Etherton	.15
2	Mark Harriger RC	.15
3	Matt Wise RC	.50
4	Carlos Hernandez RC	.50
5	Julio Lugo RC	1.00
6	Mike Nannini	.15
7	Justin Bowles RC	.25
8	Mark Mulder RC	1.00
9	Roberto Vaz RC	.15
10	Felipe Lopez RC	1.50
11	Matt Belisle	.15
12	Micah Bowie	.15
13	Ruben Quevedo RC	.25
14	Jose Garcia RC	.15
15	David Kelton RC	.50
16	Phillip Norton	.15
17	Corey Patterson RC	1.00
18	Ron Walker RC	.15
19	Paul Hoover RC	.15
20	Ryan Rupe RC	.25
21	J.D. Closser RC	.15
22	Rob Ryan RC	.15
23	Steve Colyer RC	.15
24	Bubba Crosby RC	.50
25	Luke Prokopec RC	.15
26	Matt Blank RC	.15
27	Josh McKinley	.15
28	Nate Bump	.15
29	Giuseppe Chiaramonte RC	.15
30	Arturo McDowell	.15
31	Tony Torcato	.15
32	Dave Roberts	.15
33	C.C. Sabathia RC	6.00
34	Sean Spencer RC	.15
35	Chip Ambres	.15
36	A.J. Burnett	.50
37	Mo Bruce RC	.15
38	Jason Tyner	.15
39	Mamon Tucker	.15
40	Sean Burroughs RC	.50
41	Kevin Eberwein RC	.15
42	Junior Herndon RC	.25

43	Bryan Wolff RC	.15
44	Pat Burrell	1.00
45	Eric Valent	.15
46	Carlos Pena RC	3.00
47	Mike Zywica	.15
48	Adam Everett	.15
49	Juan Pena RC	.50
50	Adam Dunn RC	10.00
51	Austin Kearns	1.00
52	Jacobo Sequea RC	.15
53	Choo Freeman	.50
54	Jeff Winchester	.15
55	Matt Burch	.15
56	Chris George	.25
57	Scott Mullen RC	.15
58	Kit Pellow	.15
59	Mark Quinn RC	.50
60	Nate Cornejo	.15
61	Ryan Mills RC	.15
62	Kevin Beirne RC	.15
63	Kip Wells RC	.50
64	Juan Rivera RC	1.00
65	Alfonso Soriano RC	10.00
66	Josh Hamilton RC	18.00
67	Josh Girdley RC	.15
68	Kyle Snyder RC	.25
69	Mike Paradis RC	.25
70	Jason Jennings RC	.25
71	David Walling RC	.25
72	Omar Ortiz RC	.15
73	Jay Gehrke RC	.15
74	Casey Burns RC	.15
75	Carl Crawford RC	8.00
76	Reggie Sanders	.15
77	Will Clark	.15
78	David Wells	.15
79	Paul Konerko	.25
80	Armando Benitez	.15
81	Brant Brown	.15
82	Mo Vaughn	.15
83	Jose Canseco	.50
84	Albert Belle	.25
85	Dean Palmer	.15
86	Greg Vaughn	.15
87	Mark Clark	.15
88	Pat Meares	.15
89	Eric Davis	.15
90	Brian Giles	.15
91	Jeff Brantley	.15
92	Bret Boone	.15
93	Ron Gant	.15
94	Mike Cameron	.15
95	Charles Johnson	.15
96	Denny Neagle	.15
97	Brian Hunter	.15
98	Jose Hernandez	.15
99	Rick Aguilera	.15
100	Tony Batista	.15
101	Roger Cedeno	.15
102	Creighton Gubanich	.15
103	Tim Belcher	.15
104	Bruce Aven	.15
105	Brian Daubach RC	.50
106	Ed Sprague	.15
107	Michael Tucker	.15
108	Homer Bush	.15
109	Armando Reynoso	.15
110	Brook Fordyce	.15
111	Matt Mantei	.15
112	Jose Guillen	.15
113	Kenny Rogers	.15
114	Livan Hernandez	.15
115	Butch Huskey	.15
116	David Segui	.15
117	Darryl Hamilton	.15
118	Jim Leyritz	.15
119	Randy Velarde	.15
120	Bill Taylor	.15
121	Kevin Appier	.15

1999 Topps Gallery

TODD HELTON
1B Colorado Rockies

		NM/M
Complete Set (150):		60.00
Common Player (1-100):		.10
Common Player (101-150):		.25
Player's Private Issue:		5X
PPI SP's:		3X
Production 250 Sets		
Pack (6):		3.00
Wax Box (24):		45.00
1	Mark McGwire	1.50

2	Jim Thome	.35
3	Bernie Williams	.10
4	Larry Walker	.10
5	Juan Gonzalez	.30
6	Ken Griffey Jr.	1.00
7	Raul Mondesi	.10
8	Sammy Sosa	.75
9	Greg Maddux	.75
10	Jeff Bagwell	.60
11	Vladimir Guerrero	.60
12	Scott Rolen	.50
13	Nomar Garciaparra	.75
14	Mike Piazza	1.00
15	Travis Lee	.15
16	Carlos Delgado	.35
17	Darin Erstad	.30
18	David Justice	.10
19	Cal Ripken Jr.	2.00
20	Derek Jeter	2.00
21	Tony Clark	.10
22	Barry Larkin	.10
23	Greg Vaughn	.10
24	Jeff Kent	.10
25	Wade Boggs	.75
26	Andres Galarraga	.10
27	Ken Caminiti	.10
28	Jason Kendall	.10
29	Todd Helton	.60
30	Chuck Knoblauch	.10
31	Roger Clemens	.85
32	Jeromy Burnitz	.10
33	Javy Lopez	.10
34	Roberto Alomar	.25
35	Eric Karros	.10
36	Ben Grieve	.10
37	Eric Davis	.10
38	Rondell White	.10
39	Dmitri Young	.10
40	Ivan Rodriguez	.50
41	Paul O'Neill	.10
42	Jeff Cirillo	.10
43	Kerry Wood	.30
44	Albert Belle	.10
45	Frank Thomas	.60
46	Manny Ramirez	.60
47	Tom Glavine	.25
48	Mo Vaughn	.10
49	Jose Cruz Jr.	.10
50	Sandy Alomar	.10
51	Edgar Martinez	.10
52	John Olerud	.10
53	Todd Walker	.10
54	Tim Salmon	.10
55	Derek Bell	.10
56	Matt Williams	.10
57	Alex Rodriguez	1.50
58	Rusty Greer	.10
59	Vinny Castilla	.10
60	Jason Giambi	.30
61	Mark Grace	.10
62	Jose Canseco	.40
63	Gary Sheffield	.40
64	Brad Fullmer	.10
65	Trevor Hoffman	.10
66	Mark Kotsay	.10
67	Mike Mussina	.25
68	Johnny Damon	.30
69	Tino Martinez	.10
70	Curt Schilling	.25
71	Jay Buhner	.10
72	Kenny Lofton	.10
73	Randy Johnson	.60
74	Kevin Brown	.10
75	Brian Jordan	.10
76	Craig Biggio	.10
77	Barry Bonds	2.00
78	Tony Gwynn	.75
79	Jim Edmonds	.10
80	Shawn Green	.35
81	Todd Hundley	.10
82	Cliff Floyd	.10
83	Jose Guillen	.10
84	Dante Bichette	.10
85	Moises Alou	.10
86	Chipper Jones	.75
87	Ray Lankford	.10
88	Fred McGriff	.10
89	Rod Beck	.10
90	Dean Palmer	.10
91	Pedro Martinez	.60
92	Andruw Jones	.60
93	Robin Ventura	.10
94	Ugueth Urbina	.10
95	Orlando Hernandez	.10
96	Sean Casey	.15
97	Denny Neagle	.10
98	Troy Glaus	.60
99	John Smoltz	.10
100	Al Leiter	.10
101	Ken Griffey Jr.	1.50
102	Frank Thomas	.75
103	Mark McGwire	2.00
104	Sammy Sosa	1.00
105	Chipper Jones	1.00
106	Alex Rodriguez	2.00
107	Nomar Garciaparra	1.00
108	Juan Gonzalez	.40
109	Derek Jeter	3.00
110	Mike Piazza	1.50
111	Barry Bonds	3.00
112	Tony Gwynn	1.00
113	Cal Ripken Jr.	3.00
114	Greg Maddux	1.00
115	Roger Clemens	1.25
116	Brad Fullmer	.25

117	Kerry Wood	.50
118	Ben Grieve	.25
119	Todd Helton	.65
120	Kevin Millwood	.25
121	Sean Casey	.35
122	Vladimir Guerrero	.75
123	Travis Lee	.25
124	Troy Glaus	.65
125	Bartolo Colon	.25
126	Andruw Jones	.75
127	Scott Rolen	.60
128	Alfonso Soriano RC	4.00
129	Nick Johnson RC	1.00
130	Matt Belisle RC	.25
131	Jorge Toca RC	.25
132	Masao Kida RC	.25
133	Carlos Pena RC	1.50
134	Adrian Beltre	.40
135	Eric Chavez	.40
136	Carlos Beltran	.65
137	Alex Gonzalez	.25
138	Ryan Anderson	.25
139	Ruben Mateo	.25
140	Bruce Chen	.25
141	Pat Burrell RC	3.00
142	Michael Barrett	.25
143	Carlos Lee	.25
144	Mark Mulder RC	1.00
145	Choo Freeman RC	.50
146	Gabe Kapler	.25
147	Juan Encarnacion	.25
148	Jeremy Giambi	.25
149	Jason Tyner RC	.35
150	George Lombard	.25
	Checklist Folder 1 (1:3 Packs)	.10
	Checklist Folder 2 (1:3)	.10
	Checklist Folder 3 (1:3)	.10
	Checklist Folder 4 (1:12)	.25
	Checklist Folder 5 (1:240)	1.50
	Checklist Folder 6 (1:640)	3.00

Player's Private Issue

ANDRES GALARRAGA
1B Atlanta Braves

	NM/M
Common Player:	1.00
Stars:	5X
SP's:	3X
Production 250 Sets	
(See 1999 Topps Gallery for checklist and card values.)	

Press Plates

	NM/M
Common Player:	25.00
(See 1999 Topps Gallery for checklist.)	

Autograph Cards

	NM/M
Common Player:	10.00
Inserted 1:209	
GA1	Troy Glaus	15.00

GA2 Adrian Beltre 10.00
GA3 Eric Chavez 10.00

Awards Gallery

	NM/M
Complete Set (10):	12.50
Common Player:	.50
Inserted 1:12	
AG1 Kerry Wood	.75
AG2 Ben Grieve	.50
AG3 Roger Clemens	2.50
AG4 Tom Glavine	.75
AG5 Juan Gonzalez	.75
AG6 Sammy Sosa	3.00
AG7 Ken Griffey Jr.	3.00
AG8 Mark McGwire	4.00
AG9 Bernie Williams	.50
AG10 Larry Walker	.50

Exhibitions

	NM/M
Complete Set (20):	75.00
Common Player:	2.00
Inserted 1:48	
E1 Sammy Sosa	4.50
E2 Mark McGwire	7.50
E3 Greg Maddux	4.50
E4 Roger Clemens	5.00
E5 Ben Grieve	2.00
E6 Kerry Wood	2.25
E7 Ken Griffey Jr.	6.00
E8 Tony Gwynn	4.50
E9 Cal Ripken Jr.	10.00
E10 Frank Thomas	4.00
E11 Jeff Bagwell	4.00
E12 Derek Jeter	10.00
E13 Alex Rodriguez	7.50
E14 Nomar Garciaparra	4.50
E15 Manny Ramirez	4.00
E16 Vladimir Guerrero	4.00
E17 Darin Erstad	2.25
E18 Scott Rolen	3.00
E19 Mike Piazza	6.00
E20 Andres Galarraga	2.00

Gallery of Heroes

	NM/M
Complete Set (10):	30.00
Common Player:	.75
Inserted 1:24	
GH1 Mark McGwire	6.00
GH2 Sammy Sosa	3.50
GH3 Ken Griffey Jr.	4.50
GH4 Mike Piazza	4.50
GH5 Derek Jeter	7.50
GH6 Nomar Garciaparra	4.50
GH7 Kerry Wood	1.50
GH8 Ben Grieve	.75
GH9 Chipper Jones	3.50
GH10 Alex Rodriguez	6.00

Heritage

	NM/M
Complete Set (20):	100.00
Common Player:	2.50
Inserted 1:12	
Heritage Proofs:	1.5X
Inserted 1:48	
TH1 Hank Aaron	10.00
TH2 Ben Grieve	2.50
TH3 Nomar Garciaparra	7.50
TH4 Roger Clemens	8.50
TH5 Travis Lee	2.50
TH6 Tony Gwynn	7.50
TH7 Alex Rodriguez	12.50
TH8 Ken Griffey Jr.	10.00
TH9 Derek Jeter	15.00
TH10 Sammy Sosa	7.50
TH11 Scott Rolen	2.50
TH12 Chipper Jones	7.50
TH13 Cal Ripken Jr.	15.00
TH14 Kerry Wood	3.00
TH15 Barry Bonds	15.00
TH16 Juan Gonzalez	3.00
TH17 Mike Piazza	10.00
TH18 Greg Maddux	7.50
TH19 Frank Thomas	6.00
TH20 Mark McGwire	12.50

1999 Topps Gallery Heritage Lithographs

	NM/M
Complete Set (8):	480.00
Single Player:	60.00
(1) Roger Clemens	60.00
(2) Nomar Garciaparra	60.00
(3) Ken Griffey Jr.	60.00
(4) Derek Jeter	60.00
(5) Mark McGwire	60.00
(6) Mike Piazza	60.00
(7) Cal Ripken Jr.	60.00
(8) Sammy Sosa	60.00

1999 Topps Gallery Heritage Auction Original Art

	NM/M
TH3 Nomar Garciaparra (6/01 Auction)	1,375

TH13 Cal Ripken Jr. (6/01 Auction) ... 3,950

1999 Topps Gold Label Class 1

Pedro Martinez

	NM/M
Complete Set (100):	30.00
Common Gold Label:	.10
Common Black Label:	.50
Black Label Stars:	3X
Common Red Label:	2.00
Red Label Stars:	12X
Pack (5):	3.00
Wax Box (24):	50.00
1 Mike Piazza	2.00
2 Andres Galarraga	.10
3 Mark Grace	.10
4 Tony Clark	.10
5 Jim Thome	.60
6 Tony Gwynn	1.50
7 Kelly Dransfeldt RC	.15
8 Eric Chavez	.25
9 Brian Jordan	.10
10 Todd Hundley	.10
11 Rondell White	.10
12 Dmitri Young	.10
13 Jeff Kent	.10
14 Derek Bell	.10
15 Todd Helton	.75
16 Chipper Jones	1.50
17 Albert Belle	.10
18 Barry Larkin	.10
19 Dante Bichette	.10
20 Gary Sheffield	.50
21 Cliff Floyd	.10
22 Derek Jeter	3.00
23 Jason Giambi	.50
24 Ray Lankford	.10
25 Alex Rodriguez	2.50
26 Ruben Mateo	.10
27 Wade Boggs	1.50
28 Carlos Delgado	.45
29 Tim Salmon	.10
30 Alfonso Soriano RC	5.00
31 Javy Lopez	.10
32 Jason Kendall	.10
33 Nick Johnson RC	1.00
34 A.J. Burnett RC	1.00
35 Troy Glaus	.75
36 Pat Burrell RC	3.00
37 Jeff Cirillo	.10
38 David Justice	.10
39 Ivan Rodriguez	.75
40 Bernie Williams	.10
41 Jay Buhner	.10
42 Mo Vaughn	.10
43 Randy Johnson	1.00
44 Pedro Martinez	1.00
45 Larry Walker	.10
46 Todd Walker	.10
47 Roberto Alomar	.25
48 Kevin Brown	.10
49 Mike Mussina	.40
50 Tom Glavine	.25
51 Curt Schilling	.25
52 Ken Caminiti	.10
53 Brad Fullmer	.10
54 Bobby Seay RC	.10
55 Orlando Hernandez	.10
56 Sean Casey	.10
57 Al Leiter	.10
58 Sandy Alomar	.10
59 Mark Kotsay	.10

60 Matt Williams	.10
61 Raul Mondesi	.10
62 Joe Crede RC	5.00
63 Jim Edmonds	.10
64 Jose Cruz Jr.	.10
65 Juan Gonzalez	.50
66 Sammy Sosa	1.50
67 Cal Ripken Jr.	3.00
68 Vinny Castilla	.10
69 Craig Biggio	.10
70 Mark McGwire	2.50
71 Greg Vaughn	.10
72 Greg Maddux	1.50
73 Paul O'Neill	.10
74 Scott Rolen	.65
75 Ben Grieve	.10
76 Vladimir Guerrero	1.00
77 John Olerud	.10
78 Eric Karros	.10
79 Jeromy Burnitz	.10
80 Jeff Bagwell	1.00
81 Kenny Lofton	.10
82 Manny Ramirez	1.00
83 Andruw Jones	1.00
84 Travis Lee	.15
85 Darin Erstad	.25
86 Nomar Garciaparra	1.50
87 Frank Thomas	1.00
88 Moises Alou	.10
89 Tino Martinez	.10
90 Carlos Pena RC	1.50
91 Shawn Green	.40
92 Rusty Greer	.10
93 Matt Belisle RC	.25
94 Adrian Beltre	.25
95 Roger Clemens	1.75
96 John Smoltz	.10
97 Mark Mulder RC	1.00
98 Kerry Wood	.50
99 Barry Bonds	3.00
100 Ken Griffey Jr.	2.00
Checklist folder	.05

Class 2

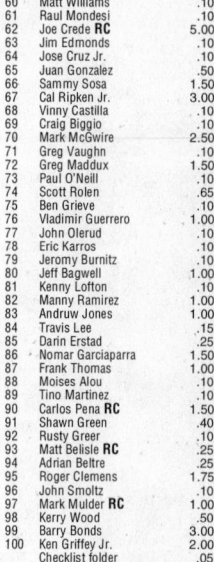

Joe Crede

	NM/M
Complete Set (100):	75.00
Common Gold Label:	.25
Gold Label Stars:	1.5X
Common Black Label:	2.00
Black Label Stars:	4X
Common Red Label:	6.00
Red Label Stars:	15X

(See 1999 Topps Gold Label Class 1 for checklist and base card values.)

Class 3

Complete Set (100):	125.00
Common Gold Label:	.50
Gold Label Stars:	2
Common Black Label:	3.00
Black Label Stars:	6X
Common Red Label:	12.00
Red Label Stars:	35X

(See 1999 Topps Gold Label Class 1 for checklist and base card values.)

One to One

Nomar Garciaparra

	NM/M
Common Player, Base Set:	50.00
Common Player, Race to Aaron:	150.00

(Star/rookie card values cannot be determined due to scarcity.)

Aaron

	NM/M
Complete Set (10):	20.00
Common Player:	1.00
Blacks:	2X
Reds:	12X
1 Mark McGwire	4.50
2 Ken Griffey Jr.	3.00
3 Alex Rodriguez	4.50
4 Vladimir Guerrero	1.50
5 Albert Belle	1.00
6 Nomar Garciaparra	2.50
7 Ken Griffey Jr.	3.00
8 Alex Rodriguez	4.50
9 Juan Gonzalez	1.00
10 Barry Bonds	7.50

1999 Topps Stars

	NM/M
Complete Set (180):	20.00
Common Player:	.05
Pack (6):	1.50
Wax Box (24):	25.00
1 Ken Griffey Jr.	.75
2 Chipper Jones	.50
3 Mike Piazza	.75
4 Nomar Garciaparra	.50
5 Derek Jeter	1.50
6 Frank Thomas	.40
7 Ben Grieve	.05
8 Mark McGwire	1.00
9 Sammy Sosa	.50
10 Alex Rodriguez	1.00
11 Troy Glaus	.05
12 Eric Chavez	.25
13 Kerry Wood	.30
14 Barry Bonds	1.50
15 Vladimir Guerrero	.40
16 Albert Belle	.05
17 Juan Gonzalez	.20
18 Roger Clemens	.60
19 Ruben Mateo	.05
20 Cal Ripken Jr.	1.50
21 Darin Erstad	.25
22 Jeff Bagwell	.40
23 Roy Halladay	.10
24 Todd Helton	.35
25 Michael Barrett	.05
26 Manny Ramirez	.40
27 Fernando Seguignol	.05
28 Pat Burrell RC	2.00
29 Andruw Jones	.40
30 Randy Johnson	.40
31 Jose Canseco	.30
32 Brad Fullmer	.05
33 Alex Escobar RC	.10
34 Alfonso Soriano RC	3.00
35 Larry Walker	.05
36 Matt Clement	.05
37 Mo Vaughn	.05
38 Bruce Chen	.05
39 Travis Lee	.20
40 Adrian Beltre	.10
41 Alex Gonzalez	.05
42 Jason Tyner RC	.10
43 George Lombard	.05
44 Scott Rolen	.25
45 Mark Mulder RC	.50
46 Gabe Kapler	.05
47 Choo Freeman RC	.10
48 Tony Gwynn	.50
49 A.J. Burnett RC	.25
50 Matt Belisle RC	.10
51 Greg Maddux	.50
52 John Smoltz	.05
53 Mark Grace	.05
54 Wade Boggs	.50
55 Bernie Williams	.05
56 Pedro Martinez	.40
57 Barry Larkin	.05
58 Orlando Hernandez	.05
59 Jason Kendall	.05
60 Mark Kotsay	.05
61 Jim Thome	.35
62 Gary Sheffield	.30
63 Preston Wilson	.05
64 Rafael Palmeiro	.35
65 David Wells	.05
66 Shawn Green	.30
67 Tom Glavine	.20
68 Jeromy Burnitz	.05
69 Kevin Brown	.05
70 Rondell White	.05
71 Roberto Alomar	.25
72 Cliff Floyd	.05
73 Craig Biggio	.05
74 Greg Vaughn	.05
75 Ivan Rodriguez	.35
76 Vinny Castilla	.05
77 Todd Walker	.05
78 Paul Konerko	.15
79 Andy Brown RC	.05
80 Todd Hundley	.05
81 Dmitri Young	.05
82 Tony Clark	.05
83 Nick Johnson RC	.50
84 Mike Caruso	.05
85 David Ortiz	.35
86 Matt Williams	.05
87 Raul Mondesi	.05
88 Kenny Lofton	.05
89 Miguel Tejada	.10
90 Dante Bichette	.05
91 Jorge Posada	.05
92 Carlos Beltran	.25
93 Carlos Delgado	.30
94 Javy Lopez	.05
95 Aramis Ramirez	.05
96 Neifi Perez	.05
97 Marlon Anderson	.05
98 David Cone	.05
99 Moises Alou	.05
100 John Olerud	.05
101 Tim Salmon	.05
102 Jason Giambi	.30
103 Sandy Alomar	.05
104 Curt Schilling	.25
105 Andres Galarraga	.05
106 Rusty Greer	.05
107 Bobby Seay RC	.05
108 Eric Young	.05
109 Brian Jordan	.05
110 Eric Davis	.05
111 Will Clark	.05
112 Andy Ashby	.05
113 Edgardo Alfonzo	.05
114 Paul O'Neill	.05
115 Denny Neagle	.05
116 Eric Karros	.05
117 Ken Caminiti	.05
118 Garret Anderson	.05
119 Todd Stottlemyre	.05
120 David Justice	.05
121 Francisco Cordova	.05
122 Robin Ventura	.05
123 Mike Mussina	.25
124 Hideki Irabu	.05
125 Justin Thompson	.05
126 Mariano Rivera	.15
127 Delino DeShields	.05
128 Steve Finley	.05
129 Jose Cruz Jr.	.05
130 Ray Lankford	.05
131 Jim Edmonds	.05
132 Charles Johnson	.05
133 Al Leiter	.05
134 Jose Offerman	.05
135 Eric Milton	.05
136 Dean Palmer	.05
137 Johnny Damon	.25
138 Andy Pettitte	.20
139 Ray Durham	.05
140 Uguieth Urbina	.05
141 Marquis Grissom	.05
142 Ryan Klesko	.05
143 Brady Anderson	.05
144 Bobby Higginson	.05
145 Chuck Knoblauch	.05
146 Rickey Henderson	.40
147 Kevin Millwood	.05
148 Fred McGriff	.05
149 Damion Easley	.05
150 Tino Martinez	.05
151 Greg Maddux	.30
152 Scott Rolen	.20
153 Pat Burrell	.75
154 Roger Clemens	.35
155 Albert Belle	.05
156 Troy Glaus	.25
157 Cal Ripken Jr.	.75
158 Alfonso Soriano	.75
159 Manny Ramirez	.25
160 Eric Chavez	.10
161 Kerry Wood	.20
162 Tony Gwynn	.30
163 Barry Bonds	.75
164 Ruben Mateo	.05
165 Todd Helton	.20
166 Darin Erstad	.05
167 Jeff Bagwell	.25
168 Juan Gonzalez	.15
169 Mo Vaughn	.05
170 Vladimir Guerrero	.25
171 Nomar Garciaparra	.35
172 Derek Jeter	.75
173 Alex Rodriguez	.50
174 Ben Grieve	.05
175 Mike Piazza	.40
176 Chipper Jones	.50
177 Frank Thomas	.25
178 Ken Griffey Jr.	.40
179 Sammy Sosa	.35
180 Mark McGwire	.50
Checklist 1 (1-45)	.05
Checklist 2 (46-136)	.05
Checklist 3 (137-150, inserts)	.05

One-Star

ALEX RODRIGUEZ

	NM/M
Complete Set (100):	25.00
Common Player:	.10
Foils (249 Each):	2X
1 Ken Griffey Jr.	1.25
2 Chipper Jones	1.00
3 Mike Piazza	1.25
4 Nomar Garciaparra	1.00
5 Derek Jeter	2.00
6 Frank Thomas	.75
7 Ben Grieve	.10
8 Mark McGwire	1.50
9 Sammy Sosa	1.00
10 Alex Rodriguez	1.50
11 Troy Glaus	.65
12 Eric Chavez	.25
13 Kerry Wood	.35
14 Barry Bonds	2.00
15 Vladimir Guerrero	.75
16 Albert Belle	.10
17 Juan Gonzalez	.40
18 Roger Clemens	1.00
19 Ruben Mateo	.10
20 Cal Ripken Jr.	2.00
21 Darin Erstad	.30
22 Jeff Bagwell	.75
23 Roy Halladay	.20
24 Todd Helton	.65
25 Michael Barrett	.10
26 Manny Ramirez	.75
27 Fernando Seguignol	.10
28 Pat Burrell	1.00
29 Andruw Jones	.75
30 Randy Johnson	.75
31 Jose Canseco	.40
32 Brad Fullmer	.10
33 Alex Escobar	.10
34 Alfonso Soriano	1.00
35 Larry Walker	.10
36 Matt Clement	.25
37 Mo Vaughn	.10
38 Bruce Chen	.10
39 Travis Lee	.15
40 Adrian Beltre	.20
41 Alex Gonzalez	.10
42 Jason Tyner	.10
43 George Lombard	.10
44 Scott Rolen	.50
45 Mark Mulder	.50
46 Gabe Kapler	.10
47 Choo Freeman	.10
48 Tony Gwynn	1.00
49 A.J. Burnett	.15
50 Matt Belisle	.10
51 Greg Maddux	1.00
52 John Smoltz	.10
53 Mark Grace	.10
54 Wade Boggs	1.00
55 Bernie Williams	.10
56 Pedro Martinez	.75
57 Barry Larkin	.10
58 Orlando Hernandez	.10
59 Jason Kendall	.10
60 Mark Kotsay	.10
61 Jim Thome	.45
62 Gary Sheffield	.40
63 Preston Wilson	.10
64 Rafael Palmeiro	.60
65 David Wells	.10
66 Shawn Green	.30
67 Tom Glavine	.30
68 Jeromy Burnitz	.10
69 Kevin Brown	.10
70 Rondell White	.10
71 Roberto Alomar	.25
72 Cliff Floyd	.10
73 Craig Biggio	.10
74 Greg Vaughn	.10
75 Ivan Rodriguez	.60
76 Vinny Castilla	.10
77 Todd Walker	.10
78 Paul Konerko	.20
79 Andy Brown	.10
80 Todd Hundley	.10
81 Dmitri Young	.10
82 Tony Clark	.10
83 Nick Johnson	.50
84 Mike Caruso	.10
85 David Ortiz	.40
86 Matt Williams	.10
87 Raul Mondesi	.10
88 Kenny Lofton	.10
89 Miguel Tejada	.20
90 Dante Bichette	.10
91 Jorge Posada	.10
92 Carlos Beltran	.20
93 Carlos Delgado	.25
94 Javy Lopez	.10
95 Aramis Ramirez	.10
96 Neifi Perez	.10
97 Marlon Anderson	.10
98 David Cone	.10
99 Moises Alou	.10
100 John Olerud	.10

Two-Star

	NM/M
Complete Set (50):	50.00
Common Player:	.25
Foils:	3X
1 Ken Griffey Jr.	2.00
2 Chipper Jones	1.50
3 Mike Piazza	2.00
4 Nomar Garciaparra	1.50
5 Derek Jeter	3.00
6 Frank Thomas	1.00
7 Ben Grieve	.25
8 Mark McGwire	2.50
9 Sammy Sosa	1.50
10 Alex Rodriguez	2.50
11 Troy Glaus	.75
12 Eric Chavez	.30
13 Kerry Wood	.40
14 Barry Bonds	3.00
15 Vladimir Guerrero	1.00
16 Albert Belle	.25
17 Juan Gonzalez	.50
18 Roger Clemens	1.75
19 Ruben Mateo	.25
20 Cal Ripken Jr.	3.00
21 Darin Erstad	.75
22 Jeff Bagwell	1.00
23 Roy Halladay	.40
24 Todd Helton	.75
25 Michael Barrett	.25
26 Manny Ramirez	1.00
27 Fernando Seguignol	.25
28 Pat Burrell	1.50
29 Andruw Jones	1.00
30 Randy Johnson	1.00
31 Jose Canseco	.25
32 Brad Fullmer	.25
33 Alex Escobar	.25
34 Alfonso Soriano	1.50
35 Larry Walker	.25
36 Matt Clement	.30
37 Mo Vaughn	.25
38 Bruce Chen	.25

39	Travis Lee	.30
40	Adrian Beltre	.30
41	Alex Gonzalez	.25
42	Jason Tyner	.25
43	George Lombard	.25
44	Scott Rolen	.65
45	Mark Mulder	.45
46	Gabe Kapler	.25
47	Choo Freeman	.25
48	Tony Gwynn	1.50
49	A.J. Burnett	.30
50	Matt Belisle	.25

Three-Star

		NM/M
Complete Set (20):		30.00
Common Player:		.50
Foils:		4X
1	Ken Griffey Jr.	2.50
2	Chipper Jones	2.00
3	Mike Piazza	2.50
4	Nomar Garciaparra	2.00
5	Derek Jeter	4.00
6	Frank Thomas	1.50
7	Ben Grieve	.50
8	Mark McGwire	3.00
9	Sammy Sosa	2.00
10	Alex Rodriguez	3.00
11	Troy Glaus	1.25
12	Eric Chavez	.60
13	Kerry Wood	.75
14	Barry Bonds	4.00
15	Vladimir Guerrero	1.50
16	Albert Belle	.50
17	Juan Gonzalez	.75
18	Roger Clemens	2.25
19	Ruben Mateo	.50
20	Cal Ripken Jr.	4.00

Four-Star

		NM/M
Complete Set (10):		30.00
Common Player:		1.00
Foils:		2X
1	Ken Griffey Jr.	4.00
2	Chipper Jones	3.00
3	Mike Piazza	4.00
4	Nomar Garciaparra	3.00
5	Derek Jeter	6.00
6	Frank Thomas	2.50
7	Ben Grieve	1.00
8	Mark McGwire	5.00
9	Sammy Sosa	3.00
10	Alex Rodriguez	5.00

Foil

	NM/M
Complete Base Set (180):	90.00
Common Foil Player:	.15
Foil Stars:	3X

(See 1999 Topps Stars for checklist and base card values.)

Bright Futures

	NM/M
Complete Set (10):	20.00
Common Player:	1.50

Production 1,999 Sets		
Foil (30 Each):		8X
1	Troy Glaus	3.00
2	Eric Chavez	2.00
3	Adrian Beltre	2.00
4	Michael Barrett	1.50
5	Fernando Seguignol	1.50
6	Alex Gonzalez	1.50
7	Matt Clement	1.50
8	Pat Burrell	6.00
9	Ruben Mateo	1.50
10	Alfonso Soriano	6.00

Galaxy

		NM/M
Complete Set (10):		25.00
Common Player:		1.00
Production 1,999 Sets		
Foil (30 Each):		8X
1	Mark McGwire	5.00
2	Roger Clemens	3.00
3	Nomar Garciaparra	4.00
4	Alex Rodriguez	5.00
5	Kerry Wood	1.50
6	Ben Grieve	1.00
7	Derek Jeter	6.00
8	Vladimir Guerrero	2.50
9	Ken Griffey Jr.	4.00
10	Sammy Sosa	3.00

Rookie Reprints

		NM/M
Complete Set (5):		10.00
Common Player:		2.00
Production 2,500 Sets		
1	Frank Robinson	2.00
2	Ernie Banks	3.00
3	Yogi Berra	3.00
4	Bob Gibson	2.00
5	Tom Seaver	3.00

Rookie Reprints Autographs

	NM/M
Complete Set (5):	150.00

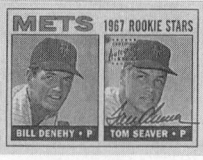

Common Player:		20.00
Inserted 1:406		
Banks Inserted 1:812		
1	Frank Robinson	25.00
2	Ernie Banks	70.00
3	Yogi Berra	35.00
4	Bob Gibson	20.00
5	Tom Seaver	65.00

1999 Topps Stars 'N Steel

		NM/M
Complete Set (44):		65.00
Common Player:		.50
Gold:		4X
Inserted 1:12		
Holographic Dome:		6X
Inserted 1:24		
Pack (3):		4.00
Wax Box (12):		40.00
1	Kerry Wood	1.00
2	Ben Grieve	.50
3	Chipper Jones	3.00
4	Alex Rodriguez	5.00
5	Mo Vaughn	.50
6	Bernie Williams	.50
7	Juan Gonzalez	1.00
8	Vinny Castilla	.50
9	Tony Gwynn	3.00
10	Manny Ramirez	2.00
11	Raul Mondesi	.50
12	Roger Clemens	3.50
13	Darin Erstad	.75
14	Barry Bonds	6.00
15	Cal Ripken Jr.	6.00
16	Barry Larkin	.50
17	Scott Rolen	1.00
18	Albert Belle	.50
19	Craig Biggio	.50
20	Tony Clark	.50
21	Mark McGwire	5.00
22	Andres Galarraga	.50
23	Kenny Lofton	.50
24	Pedro Martinez	2.00
25	Paul O'Neill	.50
26	Ken Griffey Jr.	4.00
27	Travis Lee	75.00
28	Tim Salmon	.50
29	Frank Thomas	2.00
30	Larry Walker	.50
31	Moises Alou	.50
32	Vladimir Guerrero	2.00
33	Ivan Rodriguez	1.50
34	Derek Jeter	6.00
35	Greg Vaughn	.50
36	Gary Sheffield	1.00
37	Carlos Delgado	1.00
38	Greg Maddux	3.00
39	Sammy Sosa	3.00
40	Mike Piazza	4.00
41	Nomar Garciaparra	3.00
42	Dante Bichette	.50
43	Jeff Bagwell	2.00
44	Jim Thome	1.50

1999 Topps TEK

		NM/M
Complete Set (45):		30.00
Common Player:		.25
Common Gold (10 Each Variation):		.25
Gold Stars:		10X
Pack (4):		3.00
Wax Box (20):		45.00
1	Ben Grieve	.25
2	Andres Galarraga	.25
3	Travis Lee	.35
4	Larry Walker	.25
5	Ken Griffey Jr.	2.50
6	Sammy Sosa	2.00
7	Mark McGwire	3.00

8	Roberto Alomar	.40
9	Wade Boggs	2.00
10	Troy Glaus	.75
11	Craig Biggio	.25
12	Kerry Wood	.50
13	Vladimir Guerrero	1.00
14	Albert Belle	.25
15	Mike Piazza	2.50
16	Chipper Jones	2.00
17	Randy Johnson	1.00
18	Adrian Beltre	.45
19	Barry Bonds	4.00
20	Jim Thome	.65
21	Greg Vaughn	.25
22	Scott Rolen	.65
23	Ivan Rodriguez	.75
24	Derek Jeter	4.00
25	Cal Ripken Jr.	4.00
26	Mark Grace	.25
27	Bernie Williams	.25
28	Darin Erstad	.75
29	Eric Chavez	.35
30	Tom Glavine	.50
31	Jeff Bagwell	1.00
32	Manny Ramirez	1.00
33	Tino Martinez	.25
34	Todd Helton	.75
35	Jason Kendall	.25
36	Pat Burrell RC	2.50
37	Tony Gwynn	2.00
38	Nomar Garciaparra	2.00
39	Frank Thomas	1.00
40	Orlando Hernandez	.25
41	Juan Gonzalez	.50
42	Alex Rodriguez	3.00
43	Greg Maddux	2.00
44	Mo Vaughn	.25
45	Roger Clemens	2.25
	Version A Checklist Folder (Orange)	.05
	Version B Checklist Folder (Green)	.05

Gold

	NM/M
Common Gold:	2.00
Gold Stars:	10X

(See 1999 Topps TEK for checklist, base card values.)

Fantastek Phenoms

		NM/M
Complete Set (10):		15.00
Common Player:		.75
Inserted 1:18		
F1	Eric Chavez	1.50
F2	Troy Glaus	4.00
F3	Pat Burrell	4.00
F4	Alex Gonzalez	.75
F5	Carlos Lee	1.00
F6	Ruben Mateo	.75
F7	Carlos Beltran	2.00
F8	Adrian Beltre	1.50

F9	Bruce Chen	.75
F10	Ryan Anderson	.75

Teknicians

		NM/M
Complete Set (10):		24.00
Common Player:		1.00
Inserted 1:18		
T1	Ken Griffey Jr.	3.00
T2	Mark McGwire	4.00
T3	Kerry Wood	1.00
T4	Ben Grieve	1.00
T5	Sammy Sosa	2.50
T6	Derek Jeter	6.00
T7	Alex Rodriguez	4.00
T8	Roger Clemens	2.50
T9	Nomar Garciaparra	2.50
T10	Vladimir Guerrero	1.50

2000 Topps

		NM/M
Complete Set (478):		50.00
Complete Series I Set (239):		25.00
Complete Series II Set (239):		25.00
Common Player:		.10
MVP Stars:		20-40X
Yng Stars & RC's:		10-20X
Production 100 Sets		
5 Versions for 236-240, 475-479		
Pack (11):		1.00
Wax Box (36):		30.00
1	Mark McGwire	1.00
2	Tony Gwynn	.75
3	Wade Boggs	.75
4	Cal Ripken Jr.	1.50
5	Matt Williams	.10
6	Jay Buhner	.10
7	Not Issued	
8	Jeff Conine	.10
9	Todd Greene	.10
10	Mike Lieberthal	.10
11	Steve Avery	.10
12	Bret Saberhagen	.10

13	Magglio Ordonez	.20
14	Brad Radke	.10
15	Derek Jeter	1.50
16	Javy Lopez	.10
17	Russ David	.10
18	Armando Benitez	.10
19	B.J. Surhoff	.10
20	Darryl Kile	.10
21	Mark Lewis	.10
22	Mike Williams	.10
23	Mark McLemore	.10
24	Sterling Hitchcock	.10
25	Darin Erstad	.20
26	Ricky Gutierrez	.10
27	John Jaha	.10
28	Homer Bush	.10
29	Darrin Fletcher	.10
30	Mark Grace	.10
31	Fred McGriff	.10
32	Omar Daal	.10
33	Eric Karros	.10
34	Orlando Cabrera	.15
35	J.T. Snow Jr.	.10
36	Luis Castillo	.10
37	Rey Ordonez	.10
38	Bob Abreu	.20
39	Warren Morris	.10
40	Juan Gonzalez	.20
41	Mike Lansing	.10
42	Chili Davis	.10
43	Dean Palmer	.10
44	Hank Aaron	1.00
45	Jeff Bagwell	.60
46	Jose Valentin	.10
47	Shannon Stewart	.10
48	Kent Bottenfield	.10
49	Jeff Shaw	.10
50	Sammy Sosa	.75
51	Randy Johnson	.60
52	Benny Agbayani	.10
53	Dante Bichette	.10
54	Pete Harnisch	.10
55	Frank Thomas	.60
56	Jorge Posada	.10
57	Todd Walker	.10
58	Juan Encarnacion	.15
59	Mike Sweeney	.10
60	Pedro Martinez	.60
61	Lee Stevens	.10
62	Brian Giles	.10
63	Chad Ogea	.10
64	Ivan Rodriguez	.50
65	Roger Cedeno	.10
66	David Justice	.10
67	Steve Trachsel	.10
68	Eli Marrero	.10
69	Dave Nilsson	.10
70	Ken Caminiti	.10
71	Tim Raines	.10
72	Brian Jordan	.10
73	Jeff Blauser	.10
74	Bernard Gilkey	.10
75	John Flaherty	.10
76	Brent Mayne	.10
77	Jose Vidro	.10
78	Jeff Fassero	.10
79	Bruce Aven	.10
80	John Olerud	.10
81	Pokey Reese	.10
82	Woody Williams	.10
83	Ed Sprague	.10
84	Joe Girardi	.10
85	Barry Larkin	.10
86	Mike Caruso	.10
87	Bobby Higginson	.10
88	Roberto Kelly	.10
89	Edgar Martinez	.10
90	Mark Kotsay	.10
91	Paul Sorrento	.10
92	Eric Young	.10
93	Carlos Delgado	.40
94	Troy Glaus	.50
95	Ben Grieve	.10
96	Jose Lima	.10
97	Garret Anderson	.10
98	Luis Gonzalez	.10
99	Carl Pavano	.10
100	Alex Rodriguez	1.25
101	Preston Wilson	.10
102	Ron Gant	.10
103	Harold Baines	.10
104	Rickey Henderson	.60
105	Gary Sheffield	.40
106	Mickey Morandini	.10
107	Jim Edmonds	.10
108	Kris Benson	.10
109	Adrian Beltre	.20
110	Alex Fernandez	.10
111	Dan Wilson	.10
112	Mark Clark	.10
113	Greg Vaughn	.10
114	Neifi Perez	.10
115	Paul O'Neill	.10
116	Jermaine Dye	.10
117	Todd Jones	.10
118	Terry Steinbach	.10
119	Greg Norton	.10
120	Curt Schilling	.25
121	Todd Zeile	.10
122	Edgardo Alfonzo	.10
123	Ryan McGuire	.10
124	Stan Javier	.10
125	John Smoltz	.10
126	Bob Wickman	.10
127	Richard Hidalgo	.10

128	Chuck Finley	.10
129	Billy Wagner	.10
130	Todd Hundley	.10
131	Dwight Gooden	.10
132	Russ Ortiz	.10
133	Mike Lowell	.10
134	Reggie Sanders	.10
135	John Valentin	.10
136	Brad Ausmus	.10
137	Chad Kreuter	.10
138	David Cone	.10
139	Brook Fordyce	.10
140	Roberto Alomar	.25
141	Charles Nagy	.10
142	Brian Hunter	.10
143	Mike Mussina	.30
144	Robin Ventura	.10
145	Kevin Brown	.10
146	Pat Hentgen	.10
147	Ryan Klesko	.10
148	Derek Bell	.10
149	Andy Sheets	.10
150	Larry Walker	.10
151	Scott Williamson	.10
152	Jose Offerman	.10
153	Doug Mientkiewicz	.10
154	John Snyder **RC**	.10
155	Sandy Alomar	.10
156	Joe Nathan	.10
157	Lance Johnson	.10
158	Odalis Perez	.10
159	Hideo Nomo	.25
160	Steve Finley	.10
161	Dave Martinez	.10
162	Matt Walbeck	.10
163	Bill Spiers	.10
164	Fernando Tatis	.10
165	Kenny Lofton	.10
166	Paul Byrd	.10
167	Aaron Sele	.10
168	Eddie Taubensee	.10
169	Reggie Jefferson	.10
170	Roger Clemens	.85
171	Francisco Cordova	.10
172	Mike Bordick	.10
173	Wally Joyner	.10
174	Marvin Benard	.10
175	Jason Kendall	.10
176	Mike Stanley	.10
177	Chad Allen	.10
178	Carlos Beltran	.25
179	Deivi Cruz	.10
180	Chipper Jones	.75
181	Vladimir Guerrero	.60
182	Dave Burba	.10
183	Tom Goodwin	.10
184	Brian Daubach	.10
185	Jay Bell	.10
186	Roy Halladay	.25
187	Miguel Tejada	.10
188	Armando Rios	.10
189	Fernando Vina	.10
190	Eric Davis	.10
191	Henry Rodriguez	.10
192	Joe McEwing	.10
193	Jeff Kent	.10
194	Mike Jackson	.10
195	Mike Morgan	.10
196	Jeff Montgomery	.10
197	Jeff Zimmerman	.10
198	Tony Fernandez	.10
199	Jason Giambi	.40
200	Jose Canseco	.40
201	Alex Gonzalez	.10
202	Jack Cust, Mike Colangelo, Dee Brown	.10
203	Felipe Lopez, Alfonso Soriano, Pablo Ozuna	.75
204	Erubiel Durazo, Pat Burrell, Nick Johnson	.25
205	John Sneed, Kip Wells, Matt Blank	.10
206	Josh Kalinowski, Michael Tejera, Chris Mears	.10
207	Roosevelt Brown, Corey Patterson, Lance Berkman	.25
208	Kit Pellow, Kevin Barker, Russ Branyan	.10
209	B.J. Garbe, Larry Bigbie **RC**	1.00
210	Eric Munson, Bobby Bradley **RC**	.25
211	Josh Girdley, Kyle Snyder	.10
212	Chance Caple, Jason Jennings	.25
213	Ryan Christiansen, Brett Myers **RC**	1.50
214	Jason Stumm, Rob Purvis **RC**	.25
215	David Walling, Mike Paradis	.10
216	Omar Ortiz, Jay Gehrke	.10
217	David Cone	.10
218	Jose Jimenez	.10
219	Chris Singleton	.10
220	Fernando Tatis	.10
221	Todd Helton	.20
222	Kevin Millwood	.15
223	Todd Pratt	.10
224	Orlando Hernandez	.20
225	Orlando Hernandez (Post-Season Highlights)	.10
226	(Post-Season Highlights)	.10
227	Bernie Williams	.25
228	Mariano Rivera	.20

229	Tony Gwynn	.50
230	Wade Boggs	.25
231	Tim Raines	.10
232	Mark McGwire	2.00
233	Rickey Henderson	.25
234	Rickey Henderson	.25
235	Roger Clemens	1.50
236	Mark McGwire	2.00
237	Hank Aaron	2.00
238	Cal Ripken Jr.	3.00
239	Wade Boggs	.75
240	Tony Gwynn	1.00
	Series 1 checklist (1-201)	.05
	Series 1 checklist (202-240, inserts)	.05
241	Tom Glavine	.25
242	David Wells	.10
243	Kevin Appier	.10
244	Troy Percival	.10
245	Ray Lankford	.10
246	Marquis Grissom	.10
247	Randy Winn	.10
248	Miguel Batista	.10
249	Darren Dreifort	.10
250	Barry Bonds	1.50
251	Harold Baines	.10
252	Cliff Floyd	.10
253	Freddy Garcia	.10
254	Kenny Rogers	.10
255	Ben Davis	.10
256	Charles Johnson	.10
257	John Burkett	.10
258	Desi Relaford	.10
259	Al Martin	.10
260	Andy Pettitte	.20
261	Carlos Lee	.10
262	Matt Lawton	.10
263	Andy Fox	.10
264	Chan Ho Park	.10
265	Billy Koch	.10
266	Dave Roberts	.10
267	Carl Everett	.10
268	Orel Hershiser	.10
269	Trot Nixon	.10
270	Rusty Greer	.10
271	Will Clark	.10
272	Quilvio Veras	.10
273	Rico Brogna	.10
274	Devon White	.10
275	Tim Hudson	.25
276	Mike Hampton	.10
277	Miguel Cairo	.10
278	Darren Oliver	.10
279	Jeff Cirillo	.10
280	Al Leiter	.10
281	Brant Brown	.10
282	Carlos Febles	.10
283	Pedro Astacio	.10
284	Juan Guzman	.10
285	Orlando Hernandez	.20
286	Paul Konerko	.15
287	Tony Clark	.10
288	Aaron Boone	.10
289	Ismael Valdes	.10
290	Moises Alou	.10
291	Kevin Tapani	.10
292	John Franco	.10
293	Todd Zeile	.10
294	Jason Schmidt	.15
295	Johnny Damon	.25
296	Scott Brosius	.10
297	Travis Fryman	.10
298	Jose Vizcaino	.10
299	Eric Chavez	.10
300	Mike Piazza	1.00
301	Matt Clement	.10
302	Cristian Guzman	.10
303	Darryl Strawberry	.10
304	Jeff Abbott	.10
305	Brett Tomko	.10
306	Mike Lansing	.10
307	Eric Owens	.10
308	Livan Hernandez	.10
309	Rondell White	.10
310	Todd Stottlemyre	.10
311	Chris Carpenter	.10
312	Ken Hill	.10
313	Mark Loretta	.10
314	John Rocker	.10
315	Richie Sexson	.25
316	Ruben Mateo	.10
317	Joe Randa	.10
318	Mike Sirotka	.10
319	Jose Rosado	.10
320	Matt Mantei	.10
321	Kevin Millwood	.10
322	Gary DiSarcina	.10
323	Dustin Hermanson	.10
324	Mike Stanton	.10
325	Kirk Rueter	.10
326	Damian Miller	.10
327	Doug Glanville	.10
328	Scott Rolen	.50
329	Ray Durham	.10
330	Butch Huskey	.10
331	Mariano Rivera	.20
332	Darren Lewis	.10
333	Ramiro Mendoza	.10
334	Mark Grudzielanek	.10
335	Mike Cameron	.10
336	Kelvim Escobar	.10
337	Bret Boone	.10
338	Mo Vaughn	.10
339	Craig Biggio	.10
340	Michael Barrett	.10

341	Marlon Anderson	.10
342	Bobby Jones	.10
343	John Halama	.10
344	Todd Ritchie	.10
345	Chuck Knoblauch	.10
346	Rick Reed	.10
347	Kelly Stinnett	.10
348	Tim Salmon	.10
349	A.J. Hinch	.10
350	Jose Cruz Jr.	.10
351	Roberto Hernandez	.10
352	Edgar Renteria	.10
353	Jose Hernandez	.10
354	Brad Fullmer	.10
355	Trevor Hoffman	.10
356	Troy O'Leary	.10
357	Justin Thompson	.10
358	Kevin Young	.10
359	Hideki Irabu	.10
360	Jim Thome	.50
361	Todd Dunwoody	.10
362	Octavio Dotel	.10
363	Omar Vizquel	.10
364	Raul Mondesi	.10
365	Shane Reynolds	.10
366	Bartolo Colon	.10
367	Chris Widger	.10
368	Gabe Kapler	.10
369	Bill Simas	.10
370	Tino Martinez	.10
371	John Thomson	.10
372	Delino DeShields	.10
373	Carlos Perez	.10
374	Eddie Perez	.10
375	Jeromy Burnitz	.10
376	Jimmy Haynes	.10
377	Travis Lee	.10
378	Darryl Hamilton	.10
379	Jamie Moyer	.10
380	Alex Gonzalez	.10
381	John Wetteland	.10
382	Vinny Castilla	.10
383	Jeff Suppan	.10
384	Chad Curtis	.10
385	Robb Nen	.10
386	Wilson Alvarez	.10
387	Andres Galarraga	.10
388	Mike Remlinger	.10
389	Geoff Jenkins	.10
390	Matt Stairs	.10
391	Bill Mueller	.10
392	Mike Lowell	.10
393	Andy Ashby	.10
394	Ruben Rivera	.10
395	Todd Helton	.50
396	Bernie Williams	.10
397	Royce Clayton	.10
398	Manny Ramirez	.60
399	Kerry Wood	.25
400	Ken Griffey Jr.	.75
401	Enrique Wilson	.10
402	Joey Hamilton	.10
403	Shawn Estes	.10
404	Ugueth Urbina	.10
405	Albert Belle	.10
406	Rick Helling	.10
407	Steve Parris	.10
408	Eric Milton	.10
409	Dave Mlicki	.10
410	Shawn Green	.25
411	Jaret Wright	.10
412	Tony Womack	.10
413	Vernon Wells	.15
414	Ron Belliard	.10
415	Ellis Burks	.10
416	Scott Erickson	.10
417	Rafael Palmeiro	.35
418	Damion Easley	.10
419	Jamey Wright	.10
420	Corey Koskie	.10
421	Bobby Howry	.10
422	Ricky Ledee	.10
423	Dmitri Young	.10
424	Sidney Ponson	.10
425	Greg Maddux	.75
426	Jose Guillen	.10
427	Jon Lieber	.10
428	Andy Benes	.10
429	Randy Velarde	.10
430	Sean Casey	.20
431	Torii Hunter	.10
432	Ryan Rupe	.10
433	David Segui	.10
434	Rich Aurilia	.10
435	Nomar Garciaparra	.75
436	Denny Neagle	.10
437	Ron Coomer	.10
438	Chris Singleton	.10
439	Tony Batista	.10
440	Andruw Jones	.60
441	Adam Piatt, Aubrey Huff, Sean Burroughs (Prospects)	.20
442	Rafael Furcal, Jason Dallero, Travis Dawkins (Prospects)	.20
443	Wilton Veras, Joe Crede, Mike Lamb RC (Prospects)	.10
444	Julio Zuleta, Dernell Stenson, Jorge Toca (Prospects)	.20
445	Tim Raines Jr., Gary Mathews Jr., Garry Maddox Jr. RC (Prospects)	.20
446	Matt Riley, Mark Mulder, C.C. Sabathia (Prospects)	.25
447	Scott Downs, Chris George, Matt Belisle (Prospects)	.10

448	Doug Mirabelli, Ben Petrick, Jayson Werth (Prospects)	.10
449	Josh Hamilton, Corey Myers RC	.50
450	Ben Christensen, Brett Myers	.20
451	Barry Zito, Ben Sheets RC	2.00
452	Ty Howington, Kurt Ainsworth RC	.25
453	Rick Asadoorian, Vince Faison RC	.10
454	Keith Reed, Jeff Heaverlo RC	.20
455	Mike MacDougal, Jay Gehrke	.25
456	Mark McGwire	.75
457	Cal Ripken Jr.	1.00
458	Wade Boggs	.25
459	Tony Gwynn	.50
460	Jesse Orosco	.10
461	Nomar Garciaparra, Larry Walker	.50
462	Mark McGwire, Ken Griffey Jr.	.50
463	Mark McGwire, Manny Ramirez	.50
464	Randy Johnson, Pedro Martinez	.25
465	Randy Johnson, Pedro Martinez	.25
466	Luis Gonzalez, Derek Jeter	.50
467	Manny Ramirez, Larry Walker	.25
468	Tony Gwynn	.75
469	Mark McGwire	2.00
470	Frank Thomas	.50
471	Harold Baines	.10
472	Roger Clemens	.75
473	John Franco	.10
474	John Franco	.10
475	Ken Griffey Jr.	1.50
476	Barry Bonds	2.00
477	Sammy Sosa	1.25
478	Derek Jeter	2.50
479	Alex Rodriguez	2.00

2000 Topps Limited Edition

	NM/M
Complete Factory Set (619):	100.00
Common Player:	.50
Stars/Rookies:	1-2X
Inserts:	1X

(See 2000 Topps and inserts for checklists and base card values.)

All-Star Rookie Team

		NM/M
Complete Set (10):		10.00
Common Player:		.25
Inserted 1:36		
"Limited Edition" 4,000 Sets:		1X
1	Mark McGwire	3.00
2	Chuck Knoblauch	.25
3	Chipper Jones	2.00
4	Cal Ripken Jr.	4.00
5	Manny Ramirez	1.00
6	Jose Canseco	.75
7	Ken Griffey Jr.	2.00
8	Mike Piazza	2.00
9	Dwight Gooden	.25
10	Billy Wagner	.25

All-Topps Team

		NM/M
Complete Set (20):		15.00
Common Player:		.25
Inserted 1:12		
"Limited Edition" 4,000 Sets:		1X
1	Greg Maddux	1.50
2	Mike Piazza	1.50
3	Mark McGwire	2.50
4	Craig Biggio	.40
5	Chipper Jones	1.50
6	Barry Larkin	.40
7	Barry Bonds	2.50
8	Andruw Jones	.75
9	Sammy Sosa	1.50
10	Larry Walker	.40
11	Pedro Martinez	1.00
12	Ivan Rodriguez	.50
13	Rafael Palmeiro	.50

		NM/M
14	Roberto Alomar	.50
15	Cal Ripken Jr.	3.00
16	Derek Jeter	3.00
17	Albert Belle	.25
18	Ken Griffey Jr.	1.50
19	Manny Ramirez	.75
20	Jose Canseco	.50

Autographs

		NM/M
Common Player:		8.00
Group A 1:7,589		
Group B 1:4,553		
Group C 1:518		
Group D 1:911		
Group E 1:1,138		
1	Alex Rodriguez/A	100.00
2	Tony Gwynn/A	50.00
3	Vinny Castilla/B	15.00
4	Sean Casey/B	15.00
5	Shawn Green/C	25.00
6	Rey Ordonez/C	8.00
7	Matt Lawton/C	15.00
8	Tony Womack/C	8.00
9	Gabe Kapler/D	10.00
10	Pat Burrell/D	20.00
11	Preston Wilson/D	15.00
12	Troy Glaus/D	30.00
13	Carlos Beltran/D	40.00
14	Josh Girdley/E	8.00
15	B.J. Garbe/E	8.00
16	Derek Jeter/A	125.00
17	Cal Ripken Jr./A	150.00
18	Ivan Rodriguez/B	40.00
19	Rafael Palmeiro/B	40.00
20	Vladimir Guerrero/E	45.00
21	Raul Mondesi/C	15.00
22	Scott Rolen/C	40.00
23	Billy Wagner/C	10.00
24	Fernando Tatis/C	8.00
25	Ruben Mateo/D	8.00
26	Carlos Febles/D	8.00
27	Mike Sweeney/D	10.00
28	Alex Gonzalez/D	10.00
29	Miguel Tejada/D	40.00
30	Josh Hamilton/E	50.00

Century Best

	NM/M
Common Player:	2.00
Ser. 1 1:869 H	
Ser. 2 1:362	
CB1 Tony Gwynn/339	8.00
CB2 Wade Boggs/578	4.00
CB3 Lance Johnson/117	2.00
CB4 Mark McGwire/522	20.00
CB5 Rickey Henderson/1,334	4.00
CB6 Rickey Henderson/2,103	4.00
CB7 Roger Clemens/247	12.00
CB8 Tony Gwynn/3,067	6.00
CB9 Mark McGwire/587	20.00
CB10 Frank Thomas/440	6.00
CB11 Harold Baines/1,583	2.00
CB12 Roger Clemens/3,316	8.00

CB13 John Franco/264	2.00
CB14 John Franco/416	2.00

Combos

		NM/M
Complete Set (10):		15.00
Common Card:		1.00
Inserted 1:18		
"Limited Edition" 4,000 Sets:		1X
1	Roberto Alomar, Manny Ramirez, Kenny Lofton, Jim Thome	1.00
2	Tom Glavine, Greg Maddux, John Smoltz	1.50
3	Derek Jeter, Bernie Williams, Tino Martinez	3.00
4	Ivan Rodriguez, Mike Piazza	1.50
5	Nomar Garciaparra, Alex Rodriguez, Derek Jeter	3.00
6	Sammy Sosa, Mark McGwire	3.00
7	Pedro Martinez, Randy Johnson	1.00
8	Barry Bonds, Ken Griffey Jr.	2.50
9	Chipper Jones, Ivan Rodriguez	1.50
10	Cal Ripken Jr., Tony Gwynn, Wade Boggs	3.00

Hands of Gold

		NM/M
Complete Set (7):		5.00
Common Player:		.25
Inserted 1:18		
"Limited Edition" 4,000 Sets:		1X
1	Barry Bonds	2.50
2	Ivan Rodriguez	.75
3	Ken Griffey Jr.	1.50
4	Roberto Alomar	.75
5	Tony Gwynn	1.00
6	Omar Vizquel	.25
7	Greg Maddux	1.50

Hank Aaron Reprints

		NM/M
Complete Set (23):		60.00
Common Aaron:		3.00
Inserted 1:18		
Autographed:		300.00
"Limited Edition" 4,000 Sets:		1X
1	Hank Aaron/1954	8.00
2	Hank Aaron/1955	3.00
3	Hank Aaron/1956	3.00
4	Hank Aaron/1957	3.00
5	Hank Aaron/1958	3.00
6	Hank Aaron/1959	3.00
7	Hank Aaron/1960	3.00
8	Hank Aaron/1961	3.00
9	Hank Aaron/1962	3.00
10	Hank Aaron/1963	3.00
11	Hank Aaron/1964	3.00
12	Hank Aaron/1965	3.00
13	Hank Aaron/1966	3.00
14	Hank Aaron/1967	3.00
15	Hank Aaron/1968	3.00
16	Hank Aaron/1969	3.00
17	Hank Aaron/1970	3.00
18	Hank Aaron/1971	3.00
19	Hank Aaron/1972	3.00
20	Hank Aaron/1973	3.00
21	Hank Aaron/1974	3.00
22	Hank Aaron/1975	3.00
23	Hank Aaron/1976	3.00

Hank Aaron Chrome Reprints

		NM/M
Complete Set (23):		90.00
Common Aaron:		5.00
Inserted 1:72		
Refractors:		3X
Inserted 1:288		
1	Hank Aaron/1954	10.00
2	Hank Aaron/1955	5.00
3	Hank Aaron/1956	5.00
4	Hank Aaron/1957	5.00
5	Hank Aaron/1958	5.00
6	Hank Aaron/1959	5.00
7	Hank Aaron/1960	5.00
8	Hank Aaron/1961	5.00
9	Hank Aaron/1962	5.00
10	Hank Aaron/1963	5.00
11	Hank Aaron/1964	5.00
12	Hank Aaron/1965	5.00
13	Hank Aaron/1966	5.00
14	Hank Aaron/1967	5.00
15	Hank Aaron/1968	5.00
16	Hank Aaron/1969	5.00
17	Hank Aaron/1970	5.00
18	Hank Aaron/1971	5.00
19	Hank Aaron/1972	5.00
20	Hank Aaron/1973	•5.00
21	Hank Aaron/1974	5.00
22	Hank Aaron/1975	5.00
23	Hank Aaron/1976	5.00

Mark McGwire 1985 Rookie Reprint

		NM/M
Complete Set (1):		6.00
	Mark McGwire	6.00

Own the Game

		NM/M
Complete Set (30):		15.00
Common Player:		.15
Inserted 1:12		
"Limited Edition" 4,000 Sets:		1X
1	Derek Jeter	2.00
2	B.J. Surhoff	.15
3	Luis Gonzalez	.25
4	Manny Ramirez	.50
5	Rafael Palmeiro	.40
6	Mark McGwire	1.50
7	Mark McGwire	1.50
8	Sammy Sosa	1.00
9	Ken Griffey Jr.	1.00
10	Larry Walker	.25
11	Nomar Garciaparra	1.50
12	Derek Jeter	2.00
13	Larry Walker	.25
14	Mark McGwire	1.50
15	Manny Ramirez	.50
16	Pedro Martinez	.75
17	Randy Johnson	.75
18	Kevin Millwood	.25
19	Pedro Martinez	.75
20	Randy Johnson	.75
21	Kevin Brown	.25
22	Chipper Jones	1.00
23	Ivan Rodriguez	.50
24	Mariano Rivera	.25
25	Scott Williamson	.15
26	Carlos Beltran	.25
27	Randy Johnson	.75
28	Pedro Martinez	.75
29	Sammy Sosa	1.00
30	Manny Ramirez	.50

Perennial All-Stars

		NM/M
Complete Set (10):		10.00
Common Player:		.50
Inserted 1:18		
"Limited Edition" 4,000 Sets:		1X
1	Ken Griffey Jr.	1.00
2	Derek Jeter	2.00
3	Sammy Sosa	1.00
4	Cal Ripken Jr.	2.00
5	Mike Piazza	1.00
6	Nomar Garciaparra	1.50
7	Jeff Bagwell	.50
8	Barry Bonds	1.50

9	Alex Rodriguez	1.50
10	Mark McGwire	1.50

Power Players

		NM/M
Complete Set (20):		10.00
Common Player:		.25
Inserted 1:8		
"Limited Edition" 4,000 Sets:		1X
1	Juan Gonzalez	.50
2	Ken Griffey Jr.	1.00
3	Mark McGwire	1.50
4	Nomar Garciaparra	1.50
5	Barry Bonds	1.50
6	Mo Vaughn	.25
7	Larry Walker	.25
8	Alex Rodriguez	1.50
9	Jose Canseco	.25
10	Jeff Bagwell	.50
11	Manny Ramirez	.50
12	Albert Belle	.50
13	Frank Thomas	.50
14	Mike Piazza	1.00
15	Chipper Jones	1.00
16	Sammy Sosa	1.00
17	Vladimir Guerrero	.50
18	Scott Rolen	.50
19	Raul Mondesi	.25
20	Derek Jeter	2.00

Stadium Relics

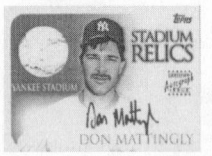

		NM/M
Common Player:		40.00
Inserted 1:165 HTA		
1	Don Mattingly	150.00
2	Carl Yastrzemski	100.00
3	Ernie Banks	75.00
4	Johnny Bench	75.00
5	Willie Mays	150.00
6	Mike Schmidt	100.00
7	Lou Brock	50.00
8	Al Kaline	75.00
9	Paul Molitor	60.00
10	Eddie Matthews	75.00

21st Century Topps

		NM/M
Complete Set (10):		5.00
Common Player:		.25
Inserted 1:18		
"Limited Edition" 4,000 Sets:		1X
1	Ben Grieve	.25
2	Alex Gonzalez	.25
3	Derek Jeter	2.00

4	Sean Casey	.25
5	Nomar Garciaparra	1.50
6	Alex Rodriguez	1.50
7	Scott Rolen	.50
8	Andruw Jones	.50
9	Vladimir Guerrero	.50
10	Todd Helton	.50

2000 Topps Traded and Rookies

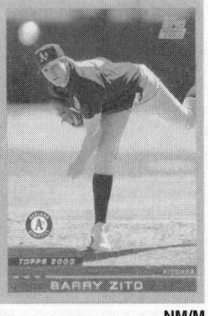

			NM/M
Complete Set (135):			25.00
Common Player:			.10
Unopened Set (136):			50.00
1	Mike MacDougal	**RC**	.20
2	Andy Tracy	**RC**	.20
3	Brandon Phillips	**RC**	1.00
4	Brandon Inge	**RC**	.75
5	Robbie Morrison	**RC**	.25
6	Josh Pressley	**RC**	.20
7	Todd Moser	**RC**	.25
8	Rob Purvis	**RC**	.20
9	Chance Caple	**RC**	.25
10	Ben Sheets		.75
11	Russ Jacobson	**RC**	.10
12	Brian Cole	**RC**	.10
13	Brad Baker	**RC**	.25
14	Alex Cintron	**RC**	.40
15	Lyle Overbay	**RC**	.75
16	Mike Edwards	**RC**	.20
17	Sean McGowan	**RC**	.25
18	Jose Molina	**RC**	.25
19	Marcos Castillo	**RC**	.20
20	Josue Espada	**RC**	.20
21	Alex Gordon	**RC**	.10
22	Rob Pugmire	**RC**	.10
23	Jason Stumm	**RC**	.25
24	Ty Howington	**RC**	.40
25	Brett Myers		.50
26	Maicer Izturis	**RC**	.10
27	John McDonald	**RC**	.10
28	Wilfredo Rodriguez	**RC**	.25
29	Carlos Zambrano	**RC**	3.00
30	Alejandro Diaz	**RC**	.20
31	Geraldo Guzman	**RC**	.20
32	J.R. House	**RC**	.50
33	Elvin Nina	**RC**	.10
34	Juan Pierre	**RC**	.50
35	Ben Johnson	**RC**	.50
36	Jeff Bailey	**RC**	.25
37	Miguel Olivo	**RC**	
38	Francisco Rodriguez	**RC**	2.00
39	Tony Pena Jr.	**RC**	.25
40	Miguel Cabrera	**RC**	10.00
41	Asdrubal Oropeza	**RC**	.10
42	Junior Zamora	**RC**	.10
43	Jovanny Cedeno	**RC**	.25
44	John Sneed	**RC**	.10
45	Josh Kalinowski	**RC**	.10
46	Mike Young	**RC**	3.00
47	Rico Washington	**RC**	.10
48	Chad Durbin	**RC**	.40
49	Junior Brignac	**RC**	.25
50	Carlos Hernandez	**RC**	.40
51	Cesar Izturis	**RC**	.50
52	Oscar Salazar	**RC**	.25
53	Pat Strange	**RC**	.25

#	Player	Value
54	Rick Asadoorian	.15
55	Keith Reed RC	.25
56	Leo Estrella RC	.10
57	Wascar Serrano RC	.10
58	Richard Gomez RC	.25
59	Ramon Santiago RC	.25
60	Jovanny Sosa RC	.25
61	Aaron Rowand RC	.50
62	Junior Guerrero RC	.25
63	Luis Terrero RC	.25
64	Brian Sanches RC	.10
65	Scott Sobkowiak RC	.25
66	Gary Majewski RC	.10
67	Barry Zito	.75
68	Ryan Christianson RC	.40
69	Cristian Guerrero RC	.40
70	Tomas de la Rosa RC	.10
71	Andrew Beinbrink RC	.25
72	Ryan Knox RC	.10
73	Alex Graman RC	.25
74	Juan Guzman RC	.10
75	Ruben Salazar RC	.40
76	Luis Matos RC	.40
77	Tony Mota RC	.10
78	Doug Davis RC	.50
79	Ben Christensen RC	.25
80	Mike Lamb	.10
81	Adrian Gonzalez RC	2.00
82	Mike Stodolka RC	.25
83	Adam Johnson RC	.25
84	Matt Wheatland RC	.25
85	Corey Smith RC	.50
86	Rocco Baldelli RC	1.00
87	Keith Bucktrot RC	.25
88	Adam Wainwright RC	1.50
89	Scott Thorman RC	.50
90	Tripper Johnson RC	.50
91	Jim Edmonds	.25
92	Masato Yoshii	.10
93	Adam Kennedy	.10
94	Darryl Kile	.10
95	Mark McLemore	.10
96	Ricky Gutierrez	.10
97	Juan Gonzalez	.40
98	Melvin Mora	.10
99	Dante Bichette	.10
100	Lee Stevens	.10
101	Roger Cedeno	.10
102	John Olerud	.25
103	Eric Young	.10
104	Mickey Morandini	.10
105	Travis Lee	.10
106	Greg Vaughn	.10
107	Todd Zeile	.10
108	Chuck Finley	.10
109	Ismael Valdes	.10
110	Ron Henika	.10
111	Pat Hentgen	.10
112	Ryan Klesko	.10
113	Derek Bell	.10
114	Hideo Nomo	.40
115	Aaron Sele	.10
116	Fernando Vina	.10
117	Wally Joyner	.10
118	Brian Hunter	.10
119	Joe Girardi	.10
120	Omar Daal	.10
121	Brook Fordyce	.10
122	Jose Valentin	.10
123	Curt Schilling	.40
124	B.J. Surhoff	.10
125	Henry Rodriguez	.10
126	Mike Bordick	.10
127	David Justice	.25
128	Charles Johnson	.10
129	Will Clark	.25
130	Dwight Gooden	.10
131	David Segui	.10
132	Denny Neagle	.10
133	Andy Ashby	.10
134	Bruce Chen	.10
135	Jason Bere	.10

Autographs

ANDREW BEINBRINK

	NM/M
Common Player:	4.00
Inserted 1:Set	
1 Mike MacDougal	4.00
2 Andy Tracy	8.00
3 Brandon Phillips	50.00
4 Brandon Inge	15.00
5 Robbie Morrison	4.00
6 Josh Pressley	4.00
7 Todd Moser	4.00
8 Rob Purvis	4.00
9 Chance Caple	4.00
10 Ben Sheets	40.00
11 Russ Jacobson	4.00
12 Brian Cole	4.00
13 Brad Baker	4.00
14 Alex Cintron	4.00
15 Lyle Overbay	20.00
16 Mike Edwards	4.00
17 Sean McGowan	4.00
18 Jose Molina	4.00
19 Marcos Castillo	4.00
20 Josue Espada	4.00
21 Alex Gordon	4.00
22 Rob Pugmire	4.00
23 Jason Stumm	4.00
24 Ty Howington	4.00
25 Brett Myers	20.00
26 Maicer Izturis	8.00
27 John McDonald	4.00
28 Wilfredo Rodriguez	4.00
29 Carlos Zambrano	150.00
30 Alejandro Diaz	4.00
31 Geraldo Guzman	4.00
32 J.R. House	8.00
33 Elvin Nina	4.00
34 Juan Pierre	25.00
35 Ben Johnson	10.00
36 Jeff Bailey	4.00
37 Miguel Olivo	10.00
38 Francisco Rodriguez	50.00
39 Tony Pena Jr.	4.00
40 Miguel Cabrera	450.00
41 Asdrubal Oropeza	4.00
42 Junior Zamora	4.00
43 Jovanny Cedeno	4.00
44 John Sneed	4.00
45 Josh Kalinowski	8.00
46 Mike Young	100.00
47 Rico Washington	4.00
48 Chad Durbin	4.00
49 Junior Brignac	4.00
50 Carlos Hernandez	8.00
51 Cesar Izturis	10.00
52 Oscar Salazar	4.00
53 Pat Strange	4.00
54 Rick Asadoorian	4.00
55 Keith Reed	4.00
56 Leo Estrella	4.00
57 Wascar Serrano	4.00
58 Richard Gomez	4.00
59 Ramon Santiago	4.00
60 Jovanny Sosa	4.00
61 Aaron Rowand	35.00
62 Junior Guerrero	4.00
63 Luis Terrero	10.00
64 Brian Sanches	4.00
65 Scott Sobkowiak	4.00
66 Gary Majewski	4.00
67 Barry Zito	30.00
68 Ryan Christianson	8.00
69 Cristian Guerrero	4.00
70 Tomas de la Rosa	4.00
71 Andrew Beinbrink	4.00
72 Ryan Knox	4.00
73 Alex Graman	4.00
74 Juan Guzman	4.00
75 Ruben Salazar	4.00
76 Luis Matos	8.00
77 Tony Mota	4.00
78 Doug Davis	10.00
79 Ben Christensen	4.00
80 Mike Lamb	10.00

2000 Topps Chrome

JOSE CANSECO

	NM/M
Complete Set (478):	100.00
Complete Series I Set (239):	50.00
Complete Series II Set (239):	50.00
Common Player:	.25
Pack (4):	1.50
Wax Box (24):	30.00
1 Mark McGwire	3.00
2 Tony Gwynn	1.50
3 Wade Boggs	.75
4 Cal Ripken Jr.	4.00
5 Matt Williams	.40
6 Jay Buhner	.40
7 Not Issued	
8 Jeff Conine	.25
9 Todd Greene	.25
10 Mike Lieberthal	.25
11 Steve Avery	.25
12 Bret Saberhagen	.25
13 Magglio Ordonez	.50
14 Brad Radke	.25
15 Derek Jeter	4.00
16 Javy Lopez	.50
17 Russ David	.25
18 Armando Benitez	.25
19 B.J. Surhoff	.25
20 Darryl Kile	.25
21 Mark Lewis	.25
22 Mike Williams	.25
23 Mark McLemore	.25
24 Sterling Hitchcock	.25
25 Darin Erstad	.50
26 Ricky Gutierrez	.25
27 John Jaha	.25
28 Homer Bush	.25
29 Darrin Fletcher	.25
30 Mark Grace	.75
31 Fred McGriff	.50
32 Omar Daal	.25
33 Eric Karros	.40
34 Orlando Cabrera	.40
35 J.T. Snow Jr.	.25
36 Luis Castillo	.25
37 Rey Ordonez	.25
38 Bob Abreu	.40
39 Warren Morris	.25
40 Juan Gonzalez	1.00
41 Mike Lansing	.25
42 Chili Davis	.25
43 Dean Palmer	.25
44 Hank Aaron	3.00
45 Jeff Bagwell	1.00
46 Jose Valentin	.25
47 Shannon Stewart	.25
48 Kent Bottenfield	.25
49 Jeff Shaw	.25
50 Sammy Sosa	2.00
51 Randy Johnson	1.50
52 Benny Agbayani	.25
53 Dante Bichette	.25
54 Pete Harnisch	.25
55 Frank Thomas	1.00
56 Jorge Posada	.75
57 Todd Walker	.25
58 Juan Encarnacion	.40
59 Mike Sweeney	.25
60 Pedro Martinez	1.50
61 Lee Stevens	.25
62 Brian Giles	.50
63 Chad Ogea	.25
64 Ivan Rodriguez	1.00
65 Roger Cedeno	.25
66 David Justice	.50
67 Steve Trachsel	.25
68 Eli Marrero	.25
69 Dave Nilsson	.25
70 Ken Caminiti	.25
71 Tim Raines	.25
72 Brian Jordan	.25
73 Jeff Blauser	.25
74 Bernard Gilkey	.25
75 John Flaherty	.25
76 Brent Mayne	.25
77 Jose Vidro	.25
78 Jeff Fassero	.25
79 Bruce Aven	.25
80 John Olerud	.50
81 Juan Guzman	.25
82 Woody Williams	.25
83 Ed Sprague	.25
84 Joe Girardi	.25
85 Barry Larkin	.50
86 Mike Caruso	.25
87 Bobby Higginson	.25
88 Roberto Kelly	.25
89 Edgar Martinez	.40
90 Mark Kotsay	.25
91 Paul Sorrento	.25
92 Eric Young	.25
93 Carlos Delgado	1.00
94 Troy Glaus	1.00
95 Ben Grieve	.25
96 Jose Lima	.25
97 Garret Anderson	.50
98 Luis Gonzalez	.50
99 Carl Pavano	.25
100 Alex Rodriguez	3.00
101 Preston Wilson	.40
102 Ron Gant	.40
103 Harold Baines	.25
104 Rickey Henderson	.50
105 Gary Sheffield	.75
106 Mickey Morandini	.25
107 Jim Edmonds	.50
108 Kris Benson	.25
109 Adrian Beltre	.25
110 Alex Fernandez	.25
111 Dan Wilson	.25
112 Mark Clark	.25
113 Greg Vaughn	.25
114 Neifi Perez	.25
115 Paul O'Neill	.50
116 Jermaine Dye	.25
117 Todd Jones	.25
118 Terry Steinbach	.25
119 Greg Norton	.25
120 Curt Schilling	.75
121 Todd Zeile	.25
122 Edgardo Alfonzo	.25
123 Ryan McGuire	.25
124 Stan Javier	.25
125 John Smoltz	.40
126 Bob Wickman	.25
127 Richard Hidalgo	.25
128 Chuck Finley	.25
129 Billy Wagner	.25
130 Todd Hundley	.25
131 Dwight Gooden	.40
132 Russ Ortiz	.25
133 Mike Lowell	.25
134 Reggie Sanders	.25
135 John Valentin	.25
136 Brad Ausmus	.25
137 Chad Kreuter	.25
138 David Cone	.25
139 Brook Fordyce	.25
140 Roberto Alomar	.75
141 Charles Nagy	.25
142 Brian Hunter	.25
143 Mike Mussina	.75
144 Robin Ventura	.40
145 Kevin Brown	.25
146 Pat Hentgen	.25
147 Ryan Klesko	.25
148 Derek Bell	.25
149 Andy Sheets	.25
150 Larry Walker	.50
151 Scott Williamson	.25
152 Jose Offerman	.25
153 Doug Mientkiewicz	.25
154 John Snyder RC	.40
155 Sandy Alomar	.25
156 Joe Nathan	.25
157 Lance Johnson	.25
158 Odalis Perez	.25
159 Hideo Nomo	.75
160 Steve Finley	.25
161 Dave Martinez	.25
162 Matt Walbeck	.25
163 Bill Spiers	.25
164 Fernando Tatis	.25
165 Kenny Lofton	.40
166 Paul Byrd	.25
167 Aaron Sele	.25
168 Eddie Taubensee	.25
169 Reggie Jefferson	.25
170 Roger Clemens	2.50
171 Francisco Cordova	.25
172 Mike Bordick	.25
173 Wally Joyner	.25
174 Marvin Benard	.25
175 Jason Kendall	.40
176 Mike Stanley	.25
177 Chad Allen	.25
178 Carlos Beltran	.50
179 Deivi Cruz	.25
180 Chipper Jones	2.00
181 Vladimir Guerrero	1.50
182 Dave Burba	.25
183 Tom Goodwin	.25
184 Brian Daubach	.25
185 Jay Bell	.25
186 Roy Halladay	.50
187 Miguel Tejada	.50
188 Armando Rios	.25
189 Fernando Vina	.25
190 Eric Davis	.40
191 Henry Rodriguez	.25
192 Joe McEwing	.25
193 Jeff Kent	.50
194 Mike Jackson	.25
195 Mike Morgan	.25
196 Jeff Montgomery	.25
197 Jeff Zimmerman	.25
198 Tony Fernandez	.25
199 Jason Giambi	1.00
200 Jose Canseco	.75
201 Alex Gonzalez	.25
202 Jack Cust, Mike Colangelo, Dee Brown	.50
203 Felipe Lopez, Alfonso Soriano, Pablo Ozuna	3.00
204 Erubiel Durazo, Pat Burrell, Nick Johnson	.75
205 John Sneed, Kip Wells, Matt Blank	.50
206 Josh Kalinowski, Michael Tejera, Chris Mears	.50
207 Roosevelt Brown, Corey Patterson, Lance Berkman	.50
208 Kit Pellow, Kevin Barker, Russ Branyan	.40
209 B.J. Garbe, Larry Bigbie RC	3.00
210 Eric Munson, Bobby Bradley RC	.75
211 Josh Girdley, Kyle Snyder	.50
212 Chance Caple, Jason Jennings	.25
213 Ryan Christianson, Brett Myers RC	6.00
214 Jason Stumm, Rob Purvis RC	.75
215 David Walling, Mike Paradis	.40
216 Omar Ortiz, Jay Gehrke	.40
217 David Cone	.40
218 Jose Jimenez	.25
219 Chris Singleton	.25
220 Fernando Tatis	.25
221 Todd Helton	1.00
222 Kevin Millwood	.50

223	Todd Pratt	.25
224	Orlando Hernandez	.25
225	Post-Season Highlights	.25
226	Post-Season Highlights	.25
227	Bernie Williams	.75
228	Mariano Rivera	.50
229	Tony Gwynn	1.50
230	Wade Boggs	.50
231	Tim Raines	.25
232	Mark McGwire	3.00
233	Rickey Henderson	.75
234	Rickey Henderson	.75
235	Roger Clemens	2.00
236	Mark McGwire	5.00
237	Hank Aaron	5.00
238	Cal Ripken Jr.	6.00
239	Wade Boggs	1.00
240	Tony Gwynn	3.00
	Series 1 checklist (1-201)	.05
	Series 1 checklist (202-240, inserts)	.05
241	Tom Glavine	.50
242	David Wells	.25
243	Kevin Appier	.25
244	Troy Percival	.25
245	Ray Lankford	.25
246	Marquis Grissom	.25
247	Randy Winn	.25
248	Miguel Batista	.25
249	Darren Dreifort	.25
250	Barry Bonds	3.00
251	Harold Baines	.25
252	Cliff Floyd	.25
253	Freddy Garcia	.40
254	Kenny Rogers	.25
255	Ben Davis	.25
256	Charles Johnson	.25
257	John Burkett	.25
258	Desi Relaford	.25
259	Al Martin	.25
260	Andy Pettitte	.50
261	Carlos Lee	.25
262	Matt Lawton	.25
263	Andy Fox	.25
264	Chan Ho Park	.25
265	Billy Koch	.25
266	Dave Roberts	.25
267	Carl Everett	.25
268	Orel Hershiser	.25
269	Trot Nixon	.25
270	Rusty Greer	.25
271	Will Clark	.75
272	Quivio Veras	.25
273	Rico Brogna	.25
274	Devon White	.25
275	Tim Hudson	.50
276	Mike Hampton	.25
277	Miguel Cairo	.25
278	Darren Oliver	.25
279	Jeff Cirillo	.25
280	Al Leiter	.25
281	Brant Brown	.25
282	Carlos Febles	.25
283	Pedro Astacio	.25
284	Juan Guzman	.25
285	Orlando Hernandez	.25
286	Paul Konerko	.25
287	Tony Clark	.25
288	Aaron Boone	.50
289	Ismael Valdes	.25
290	Moises Alou	.50
291	Kevin Tapani	.25
292	John Franco	.25
293	Todd Zeile	.25
294	Jason Schmidt	.25
295	Johnny Damon	.40
296	Scott Brosius	.25
297	Travis Fryman	.40
298	Jose Vizcaino	.25
299	Eric Chavez	.50
300	Mike Piazza	2.00
301	Matt Clement	.25
302	Cristian Guzman	.25
303	Darryl Strawberry	.40
304	Jeff Abbott	.25
305	Brett Tomko	.25
306	Mike Lansing	.25
307	Eric Owens	.25
308	Livan Hernandez	.25
309	Rondell White	.40
310	Todd Stottlemyre	.25
311	Chris Carpenter	.25
312	Ken Hill	.25
313	Mark Loretta	.25
314	John Rocker	.25
315	Richie Sexson	.75
316	Ruben Mateo	.25
317	Ramon Martinez	.25
318	Mike Sirotka	.25
319	Jose Rosado	.25
320	Matt Mantei	.25
321	Kevin Millwood	.50
322	Gary DiSarcina	.25
323	Dustin Hermanson	.25
324	Mike Stanton	.25
325	Kirk Rueter	.25
326	Damian Miller	.25
327	Doug Glanville	.25
328	Scott Rolen	1.00
329	Ray Durham	.25
330	Butch Huskey	.25
331	Mariano Rivera	.50
332	Darren Lewis	.25
333	Ramiro Mendoza	.25
334	Mark Grudzielanek	.25

335	Mike Cameron	.25
336	Kelvim Escobar	.25
337	Bret Boone	.40
338	Mo Vaughn	.40
339	Craig Biggio	.40
340	Michael Barrett	.25
341	Marlon Anderson	.25
342	Bobby Jones	.25
343	John Halama	.25
344	Todd Ritchie	.25
345	Chuck Knoblauch	.25
346	Rick Reed	.25
347	Kelly Stinnett	.25
348	Tim Salmon	.50
349	A.J. Hinch	.25
350	Jose Cruz Jr.	.25
351	Roberto Hernandez	.25
352	Edgar Renteria	.25
353	Jose Hernandez	.25
354	Brad Fullmer	.25
355	Trevor Hoffman	.25
356	Troy O'Leary	.25
357	Justin Thompson	.25
358	Kevin Young	.25
359	Hideki Irabu	.25
360	Jim Thome	1.00
361	Todd Dunwoody	.25
362	Octavio Dotel	.25
363	Omar Vizquel	.40
364	Raul Mondesi	.40
365	Shane Reynolds	.25
366	Bartolo Colon	.25
367	Chris Widger	.25
368	Gabe Kapler	.25
369	Bill Simas	.25
370	Tino Martinez	.50
371	John Thomson	.25
372	Delino DeShields	.25
373	Carlos Perez	.25
374	Eddie Perez	.25
375	Jeromy Burnitz	.25
376	Jimmy Haynes	.25
377	Travis Lee	.25
378	Darryl Hamilton	.25
379	Jamie Moyer	.25
380	Alex Gonzalez	.25
381	John Wetteland	.25
382	Vinny Castilla	.40
383	Jeff Suppan	.25
384	Chad Curtis	.25
385	Robb Nen	.25
386	Wilson Alvarez	.25
387	Andres Galarraga	.50
388	Mike Remlinger	.25
389	Geoff Jenkins	.40
390	Matt Stairs	.25
391	Bill Mueller	.25
392	Mike Lowell	.25
393	Andy Ashby	.25
394	Ruben Rivera	.25
395	Todd Helton	1.00
396	Bernie Williams	.75
397	Royce Clayton	.25
398	Manny Ramirez	1.00
399	Kerry Wood	.75
400	Ken Griffey Jr.	2.00
401	Enrique Wilson	.25
402	Joey Hamilton	.25
403	Shawn Estes	.25
404	Ugueth Urbina	.25
405	Albert Belle	.30
406	Rick Helling	.25
407	Steve Parris	.25
408	Eric Milton	.25
409	Dave Mlicki	.25
410	Shawn Green	.50
411	Jaret Wright	.25
412	Tony Womack	.25
413	Vernon Wells	.50
414	Ron Belliard	.25
415	Ellis Burks	.25
416	Scott Erickson	.25
417	Rafael Palmeiro	.75
418	Damion Easley	.25
419	Jamey Wright	.25
420	Corey Koskie	.25
421	Bobby Howry	.25
422	Ricky Ledee	.25
423	Dmitri Young	.25
424	Sidney Ponson	.25
425	Greg Maddux	2.00
426	Jose Guillen	.25
427	Jon Lieber	.25
428	Andy Benes	.25
429	Randy Velarde	.25
430	Sean Casey	.40
431	Torii Hunter	.50
432	Ryan Rupe	.25
433	David Segui	.25
434	Rich Aurilia	.25
435	Nomar Garciaparra	3.00
436	Denny Neagle	.25
437	Ron Coomer	.25
438	Chris Singleton	.25
439	Tony Batista	.25
440	Andruw Jones	1.00
441	Adam Piatt, Aubrey Huff, Sean Burroughs (Prospects)	.50
442	Rafael Furcal, Jason Dallero, Travis Dawkins (Prospects)	.50
443	Wilton Veras, Joe Crede, Mike Lamb RC (Prospects)	.25
444	Julio Zuleta, Dernell Stenson, Jorge Toca (Prospects)	.25

445	Tim Raines Jr., Gary Mathews Jr., Garry Maddox Jr. RC (Prospects)	.50
446	Matt Riley, Mark Mulder, C.C. Sabathia (Prospects)	.25
447	Scott Downs, Chris George, Matt Belisle (Prospects)	.50
448	Doug Mirabelli, Ben Petrick, Jayson Werth (Prospects)	.25
449	Josh Hamilton, Corey Myers RC	.75
450	Ben Christensen, Brett Myers	.50
451	Barry Zito, Ben Sheets RC	10.00
452	Ty Howington, Kurt Ainsworth RC	2.00
453	Rick Asadoorian, Vince Faison RC	.50
454	Keith Reed, Jeff Heaverlo RC	.50
455	Mike MacDougal, Jay Gehrke	1.50
456	Mark McGwire	3.00
457	Cal Ripken Jr.	4.00
458	Wade Boggs	.75
459	Tony Gwynn	1.50
460	Jesse Orosco	.25
461	Nomar Garciaparra, Larry Walker	1.50
462	Mark McGwire, Ken Griffey Jr.	1.50
463	Mark McGwire, Manny Ramirez	1.50
464	Randy Johnson, Pedro Martinez	1.00
465	Randy Johnson, Pedro Martinez	1.00
466	Luis Gonzalez, Derek Jeter	2.00
467	Manny Ramirez, Larry Walker	.75
468	Tony Gwynn	1.50
469	Mark McGwire	3.00
470	Frank Thomas	.75
471	Harold Baines	.25
472	Roger Clemens	1.50
473	John Franco	.25
474	John Franco	.25
475	Ken Griffey Jr.	3.00
476	Barry Bonds	5.00
477	Sammy Sosa	4.00
478	Derek Jeter	6.00
479	Alex Rodriguez	5.00

Refractors

Stars:	3-5X
Young Stars/RC's:	1-2X
Inserted 1:12	

(See 2000 Topps Chrome for checklist and base card values.)

Allegiance

	NM/M
Complete Set (20):	30.00
Common Player:	.75
Inserted 1:16	
Refractors:	5X
Inserted 1:424	

1	Derek Jeter	6.00
2	Ivan Rodriguez	1.00
3	Alex Rodriguez	5.00
4	Cal Ripken Jr.	6.00
5	Mark Grace	1.00
6	Tony Gwynn	2.00
7	Juan Gonzalez	1.50
8	Frank Thomas	1.50
9	Manny Ramirez	1.50
10	Barry Larkin	.75
11	Bernie Williams	1.50
12	Raul Mondesi	.75
13	Vladimir Guerrero	1.50
14	Craig Biggio	.75
15	Nomar Garciaparra	4.00
16	Andruw Jones	1.00
17	Jim Thome	1.50
18	Scott Rolen	1.50
19	Chipper Jones	3.00
20	Ken Griffey Jr.	3.00

All-Star Rookie Team

	NM/M
Complete Set (10):	10.00
Common Player:	.50
Inserted 1:16	
Refractors:	2-3X
Inserted 1:80	

1	Mark McGwire	3.00
2	Chuck Knoblauch	.50
3	Chipper Jones	2.00
4	Cal Ripken Jr.	4.00
5	Manny Ramirez	1.00
6	Jose Canseco	.75
7	Ken Griffey Jr.	2.00
8	Mike Piazza	2.00
9	Dwight Gooden	.50
10	Billy Wagner	.50

All-Topps Team

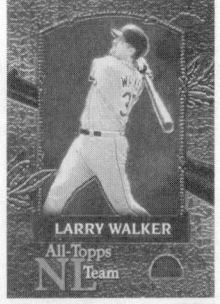

	NM/M
Complete Set (20):	40.00
Complete Series I Set (10):	20.00
Complete Series II Set (10):	20.00
Common Player:	.50
Inserted 1:32	
Refractors:	2-3X
Inserted 1:160	

1	Greg Maddux	3.00
2	Mike Piazza	3.00
3	Mark McGwire	5.00
4	Craig Biggio	1.00
5	Chipper Jones	3.00
6	Barry Larkin	1.00
7	Barry Bonds	5.00
8	Andruw Jones	1.50
9	Sammy Sosa	3.00
10	Larry Walker	1.00
11	Pedro Martinez	2.00
12	Ivan Rodriguez	1.00
13	Rafael Palmeiro	1.00
14	Roberto Alomar	1.00
15	Cal Ripken Jr.	6.00
16	Derek Jeter	6.00
17	Albert Belle	.50
18	Ken Griffey Jr.	3.00
19	Manny Ramirez	1.50
20	Jose Canseco	1.00

Combos

Strikeout Kings
RANDY JOHNSON - PEDRO MARTINEZ

		NM/M
Complete Set (10):		20.00
Common Player:		1.00
Inserted 1:16		
Refractors:		2-3X
Inserted 1:80		
1	Roberto Alomar, Manny Ramirez, Kenny Lofton, Jim Thome	1.00
2	Tom Glavine, Greg Maddux, John Smoltz	2.00
3	Derek Jeter, Bernie Williams, Tino Martinez	4.00
4	Ivan Rodriguez, Mike Piazza	2.00
5	Nomar Garciaparra, Alex Rodriguez, Derek Jeter	4.00
6	Sammy Sosa, Mark McGwire	4.00
7	Pedro Martinez, Randy Johnson	1.50
8	Barry Bonds, Ken Griffey Jr.	3.00
9	Chipper Jones, Ivan Rodriguez	2.00
10	Cal Ripken Jr., Tony Gwynn, Wade Boggs	4.00

Kings

		NM/M
Complete Set (10):		25.00
Common Player:		1.50
Inserted 1:32		
1	Mark McGwire	5.00
2	Sammy Sosa	3.00
3	Ken Griffey Jr.	3.00
4	Mike Piazza	3.00
5	Alex Rodriguez	5.00
6	Manny Ramirez	1.50
7	Barry Bonds	6.00
8	Nomar Garciaparra	4.00
9	Chipper Jones	3.00
10	Vladimir Guerrero	1.50

Mark McGwire 1985 Rookie Reprint

		NM/M
Complete Set (1):		5.00
Inserted 1:32		
Refractor:		50.00
Production 70 cards.		
	Mark McGwire	5.00

Millennium Stars

		NM/M
Complete Set (10):		10.00
Common Player:		.50
Inserted 1:32		
Refractors:		2-3X
Inserted 1:160		
1	Nomar Garciaparra	4.00
2	Vladimir Guerrero	1.50
3	Sean Casey	.75
4	Richie Sexson	1.00
5	Todd Helton	1.50
6	Carlos Beltran	.75
7	Kevin Millwood	.75
8	Ruben Mateo	.50
9	Pat Burrell	1.00
10	Alfonso Soriano	2.00

Own the Game

		NM/M
Complete Set (30):		30.00
Common Player:		.25
Inserted 1:12		
Refractors:		2-3X
Inserted 1:55		
1	Derek Jeter	4.00
2	B.J. Surhoff	.25
3	Luis Gonzalez	.50
4	Manny Ramirez	1.00
5	Rafael Palmeiro	1.00
6	Mark McGwire	3.00
7	Mark McGwire	3.00
8	Sammy Sosa	2.00
9	Ken Griffey Jr.	2.00
10	Larry Walker	.50
11	Nomar Garciaparra	2.00
12	Derek Jeter	4.00
13	Larry Walker	.50
14	Mark McGwire	3.00
15	Manny Ramirez	1.00
16	Pedro Martinez	1.50
17	Randy Johnson	1.50
18	Kevin Millwood	.50
19	Pedro Martinez	1.50
20	Randy Johnson	1.50
21	Kevin Brown	.50
22	Chipper Jones	2.00
23	Ivan Rodriguez	1.00
24	Mariano Rivera	.50
25	Scott Williamson	.25
26	Carlos Beltran	.50
27	Randy Johnson	1.50
28	Pedro Martinez	1.50
29	Sammy Sosa	2.00
30	Manny Ramirez	1.00

Power Players

DEREK JETER

		NM/M
Complete Set (20):		25.00
Common Player:		.25

Inserted 1:8		
Refractors:		2-3X
Inserted 1:40		
1	Juan Gonzalez	1.00
2	Ken Griffey Jr.	2.00
3	Mark McGwire	3.00
4	Nomar Garciaparra	3.00
5	Barry Bonds	3.00
6	Mo Vaughn	.40
7	Larry Walker	.50
8	Alex Rodriguez	3.00
9	Jose Canseco	.75
10	Jeff Bagwell	1.00
11	Manny Ramirez	1.00
12	Albert Belle	.25
13	Frank Thomas	1.00
14	Mike Piazza	2.00
15	Chipper Jones	2.00
16	Sammy Sosa	2.00
17	Vladimir Guerrero	1.00
18	Scott Rolen	1.00
19	Raul Mondesi	.40
20	Derek Jeter	4.00

21st Century Topps

TODD HELTON

		NM/M
Complete Set (10):		10.00
Common Player:		.25
Inserted 1:16		
Refractors:		2-3X
Inserted 1:80		
1	Ben Grieve	.25
2	Alex Gonzalez	.25
3	Derek Jeter	4.00
4	Sean Casey	.50
5	Nomar Garciaparra	3.00
6	Alex Rodriguez	3.00
7	Scott Rolen	1.00
8	Andruw Jones	1.00
9	Vladimir Guerrero	1.00
10	Todd Helton	1.00

2000 Topps Chrome Traded and Rookies

		NM/M
Complete Set (135):		60.00
Common Player:		.25
1	Mike MacDougal RC	.50
2	Andy Tracy RC	.50
3	Brandon Phillips RC	3.00
4	Brandon Inge RC	1.50
5	Robbie Morrison RC	.50
6	Josh Pressley RC	.50
7	Todd Moser RC	.50
8	Rob Purvis RC	.50
9	Chance Caple RC	.50
10	Ben Sheets RC	2.00
11	Russ Jacobson RC	.50
12	Brian Cole RC	.50
13	Brad Baker RC	.50
14	Alex Cintron RC	.50
15	Lyle Overbay RC	1.50
16	Mike Edwards RC	.50
17	Sean McGowan RC	.50
18	Jose Molina RC	.50
19	Marcos Castillo RC	.50
20	Josue Espada RC	.50
21	Alex Gordon RC	.50
22	Rob Pugmire RC	.50
23	Jason Stumm RC	.50
24	Ty Howington RC	.50
25	Brett Myers	.50
26	Maicer Izturis RC	.50
27	John McDonald RC	.50
28	Wilfredo Rodriguez RC	.50
29	Carlos Zambrano RC	6.00
30	Alejandro Diaz RC	.50
31	Geraldo Guzman RC	.50
32	J.R. House RC	.50
33	Elvin Nina RC	.50
34	Juan Pierre RC	2.00
35	Ben Johnson RC	.50
36	Jeff Bailey RC	.50
37	Miguel Olivo RC	.50
38	Francisco Rodriguez RC	4.00
39	Tony Pena Jr. RC	.50
40	Miguel Cabrera RC	30.00
41	Asdrubal Oropeza RC	.50
42	Junior Zamora RC	.50
43	Jovanny Cedeno RC	.50
44	John Sneed RC	.50
45	Josh Kalinowski RC	.50
46	Mike Young RC	6.00
47	Rico Washington RC	.50
48	Chad Durbin RC	.50
49	Junior Brignac RC	.50
50	Carlos Hernandez RC	.50
51	Cesar Izturis RC	.50
52	Oscar Salazar RC	.50
53	Pat Strange RC	.50
54	Rick Asadoorian RC	.50
55	Keith Reed RC	.50
56	Leo Estrella RC	.50
57	Wascar Serrano RC	.50
58	Richard Gomez RC	.50
59	Ramon Santiago RC	.50
60	Jovanny Sosa RC	.50
61	Aaron Rowand RC	3.00
62	Junior Guerrero RC	.50
63	Luis Terrero RC	.50
64	Brian Sanches RC	.50
65	Scott Sobkowiak RC	.50
66	Gary Majewski RC	.50
67	Barry Zito RC	2.00
68	Ryan Christianson RC	.50
69	Cristian Guerrero RC	.50
70	Tomas de la Rosa RC	.50
71	Andrew Beinbrink RC	.50
72	Ryan Knox RC	.50
73	Alex Graman RC	.50
74	Juan Guzman RC	.50
75	Ruben Salazar RC	.50
76	Luis Matos RC	.50
77	Tony Mota RC	.50
78	Doug Davis RC	.50
79	Ben Christensen RC	.50
80	Mike Lamb	.50
81	Adrian Gonzalez RC	5.00
82	Mike Stodolka RC	.50
83	Adam Johnson RC	.50
84	Matt Wheatland RC	.50
85	Corey Smith RC	.50
86	Rocco Baldelli RC	4.00
87	Keith Bucktrot RC	.50
88	Adam Wainwright RC	5.00
89	Scott Thorman RC	1.00
90	Tripper Johnson RC	.50
91	Jim Edmonds	.50
92	Masato Yoshii	.25
93	Adam Kennedy	.25
94	Darryl Kile	.25
95	Mark McLemore	.25
96	Ricky Gutierrez	.25
97	Juan Gonzalez	.50
98	Melvin Mora	.25
99	Dante Bichette	.25
100	Lee Stevens	.25
101	Roger Cedeno	.25
102	John Olerud	.40
103	Eric Young	.25
104	Mickey Morandini	.25
105	Travis Lee	.25
106	Greg Vaughn	.25
107	Todd Zeile	.25
108	Chuck Finley	.25
109	Ismael Valdes	.25
110	Ron Henika	.25
111	Pat Hentgen	.25
112	Ryan Klesko	.40
113	Derek Bell	.25
114	Hideo Nomo	1.00
115	Aaron Sele	.25
116	Fernando Vina	.25
117	Wally Joyner	.25
118	Brian Hunter	.25
119	Joe Girardi	.25
120	Omar Daal	.25
121	Brook Fordyce	.25
122	Jose Valentin	.25
123	Curt Schilling	.50
124	B.J. Surhoff	.25
125	Henry Rodriguez	.25
126	Mike Bordick	.25
127	David Justice	.50
128	Charles Johnson	.25
129	Will Clark	.50
130	Dwight Gooden	.25
131	David Segui	.25
132	Denny Neagle	.25
133	Andy Ashby	.25
134	Bruce Chen	.25
135	Jason Bere	.25

2000 Topps Gallery

		NM/M
Complete Set (150):		40.00
Common Player:		.15
Common (101-150):		.50
Inserted 1:1		
Pack (6):		2.00
Wax Box (24):		40.00
1	Nomar Garciaparra	1.50
2	Kevin Millwood	.25
3	Jay Bell	.15
4	Rusty Greer	.15
5	Bernie Williams	.50
6	Barry Larkin	.25
7	Carlos Beltran	.25
8	Damion Easley	.15
9	Magglio Ordonez	.25
10	Matt Williams	.25
11	Shannon Stewart	.15
12	Ray Lankford	.15
13	Vinny Castilla	.20
14	Miguel Tejada	.25
15	Craig Biggio	.25
16	Chipper Jones	1.00
17	Albert Belle	.20
18	Doug Glanville	.15
19	Brian Giles	.25
20	Shawn Green	.25
21	J.T. Snow Jr.	.15
22	Luis Gonzalez	.25
23	Carlos Delgado	.50
24	J.D. Drew	.25
25	Ivan Rodriguez	.50
26	Tino Martinez	.50
27	Erubiel Durazo	.20
28	Scott Rolen	.50
29	Gary Sheffield	.40
30	Manny Ramirez	.50
31	Luis Castillo	.15
32	Fernando Tatis	.15
33	Darin Erstad	.25
34	Tim Hudson	.25
35	Sammy Sosa	1.00
36	Jason Kendall	.25
37	Todd Walker	.15
38	Orlando Hernandez	.25
39	Pokey Reese	.15
40	Mike Piazza	1.00
41	B.J. Surhoff	.15
42	Tony Gwynn	.75
43	Kevin Brown	.25
44	Preston Wilson	.25
45	Kenny Lofton	.25
46	Rondell White	.20
47	Frank Thomas	.50
48	Neifi Perez	.15
49	Edgardo Alfonzo	.15
50	Ken Griffey Jr.	1.00
51	Barry Bonds	1.50
52	Brian Jordan	.15
53	Raul Mondesi	.25
54	Troy Glaus	.50
55	Curt Schilling	.40
56	Mike Mussina	.50
57	Brian Daubach	.15
58	Roger Clemens	1.00
59	Carlos Febles	.15
60	Todd Helton	.50
61	Mark Grace	.40
62	Randy Johnson	.75
63	Jeff Bagwell	.50
64	Tom Glavine	.25
65	Adrian Beltre	.20
66	Rafael Palmeiro	.25
67	Paul O'Neill	.25
68	Robin Ventura	.15
69	Ray Durham	.15
70	Mark McGwire	1.50
71	Greg Vaughn	.15
72	Javy Lopez	.25
73	Jeromy Burnitz	.15
74	Mike Lieberthal	.15
75	Cal Ripken Jr.	2.00
76	Juan Gonzalez	.50
77	Sean Casey	.25
78	Jermaine Dye	.15
79	John Olerud	.25
80	Jose Canseco	.40
81	Eric Karros	.25
82	Roberto Alomar	.40
83	Ben Grieve	.15
84	Greg Maddux	1.00
85	Pedro Martinez	.75
86	Tony Clark	.15
87	Richie Sexson	.25
88	Cliff Floyd	.15
89	Eric Chavez	.25
90	Andruw Jones	.50
91	Vladimir Guerrero	.50
92	Alex Gonzalez	.15
93	Jim Thome	.50
94	Bob Abreu	.25
95	Derek Jeter	2.00
96	Larry Walker	.25
97	John Smoltz	.25
98	Mo Vaughn	.20
99	Jason Giambi	.50
100	Alex Rodriguez	1.50
101	Mark McGwire	2.50
102	Sammy Sosa	1.50
103	Alex Rodriguez	2.50
104	Derek Jeter	3.00
105	Greg Maddux	1.50
106	Jeff Bagwell	.75
107	Nomar Garciaparra	2.00
108	Mike Piazza	1.50
109	Pedro Martinez	1.00
110	Chipper Jones	1.50
111	Randy Johnson	1.00
112	Barry Bonds	2.50
113	Ken Griffey Jr.	1.50
114	Manny Ramirez	.75
115	Ivan Rodriguez	.75
116	Juan Gonzalez	.75
117	Vladimir Guerrero	.75
118	Tony Gwynn	1.00
119	Larry Walker	.50
120	Cal Ripken Jr.	3.00
121	Josh Hamilton	.50
122	Corey Patterson	.50
123	Pat Burrell	.50
124	Nick Johnson	.50
125	Adam Piatt	.50
126	Rick Ankiel	.50
127	A.J. Burnett	.50
128	Ben Petrick	.50
129	Rafael Furcal	.75
130	Alfonso Soriano	2.00
131	Dee Brown	.50
132	Ruben Mateo	.50
133	Pablo Ozuna	.50
134	Sean Burroughs	.75
135	Mark Mulder	.75
136	Jason Jennings	.50
137	Eric Munson	.50
138	Vernon Wells	.50
139	Brett Myers RC	3.00
140	Ben Christensen RC	.50
141	Bobby Bradley RC	.50
142	Ruben Salazar RC	.50
143	Ryan Christianson RC	.50
144	Corey Myers RC	.50
145	Aaron Rowand RC	1.00
146	Julio Zuleta RC	.50
147	Kurt Ainsworth RC	1.00
148	Scott Downs RC	.50
149	Larry Bigbie RC	1.50
150	Chance Caple RC	.50

Press Plates

	NM/M
Common Player:	50.00

(See 2000 Topps Gallery for checklist.)

Players Private Issue

Stars (1-100):	4-8X
SPs (101-150):	2-4X
Production 250 Sets	

Autographs

		NM/M
Common Player:		5.00
Inserted 1:153		
RA	Rick Ankiel	15.00
RM	Ruben Mateo	5.00
CP	Corey Patterson	15.00

BP	Ben Petrick	5.00
VW	Vernon Wells	20.00

Gallery Exhibits

		NM/M
Complete Set (30):		50.00
Common Player:		.50
Inserted 1:18		
1	Mark McGwire	5.00
2	Jeff Bagwell	1.50
3	Mike Piazza	3.00
4	Alex Rodriguez	5.00
5	Nomar Garciaparra	4.00
6	Ivan Rodriguez	1.50
7	Chipper Jones	3.00
8	Cal Ripken Jr.	6.00
9	Tony Gwynn	2.00
10	Jose Canseco	1.00
11	Albert Belle	.50
12	Greg Maddux	3.00
13	Barry Bonds	5.00
14	Ken Griffey Jr.	3.00
15	Juan Gonzalez	1.50
16	Rickey Henderson	1.00
17	Craig Biggio	.75
18	Vladimir Guerrero	1.50
19	Rey Ordonez	.50
20	Roberto Alomar	1.00
21	Derek Jeter	6.00
22	Manny Ramirez	1.50
23	Shawn Green	1.00
24	Sammy Sosa	3.00
25	Larry Walker	1.00
26	Pedro Martinez	2.00
27	Randy Johnson	2.00
28	Pat Burrell	1.00
29	Josh Hamilton	1.50
30	Corey Patterson	1.00

Lithos

		NM/M
Complete Set (8):		675.00
Common Player:		80.00
Inserted 1:12		
(1)	Shawn Green	80.00
(2)	Ken Griffey Jr.	80.00
(3)	Chipper Jones	80.00
(4)	Pedro Martinez	80.00
(5)	Alex Rodriguez	80.00
(6)	Ivan Rodriguez	80.00
(7)	Nomar Garciaparra, Alex Rodriguez, Derek Jeter Three of a Kind	100.00
(8)	Paul O'Neill, Derek Jeter, Bernie Williams, Tino Martinez Torre's Terrors	100.00

Gallery of Heroes

		NM/M
Complete Set (10):		20.00
Common Player:		1.00
Inserted 1:12		
1	Alex Rodriguez	3.00
2	Chipper Jones	2.00
3	Pedro Martinez	1.50
4	Sammy Sosa	2.00
5	Mark McGwire	3.00
6	Nomar Garciaparra	3.00

7	Vladimir Guerrero	1.00
8	Ken Griffey Jr.	2.00
9	Mike Piazza	2.00
10	Derek Jeter	4.00

Proof Positive

		NM/M
Complete Set (10):		40.00
Common Player:		3.00
Inserted 1:48		
1	Ken Griffey Jr., Ruben Mateo	4.00
2	Derek Jeter, Alfonso Soriano	6.00
3	Mark McGwire, Pat Burrell	6.00
4	Pedro Martinez, A.J. Burnett	3.00
5	Alex Rodriguez, Rafael Furcal	6.00
6	Sammy Sosa, Corey Patterson	4.00
7	Randy Johnson, Rick Ankiel	3.00
8	Chipper Jones, Adam Piatt	4.00
9	Nomar Garciaparra, Pablo Ozuna	6.00
10	Mike Piazza, Eric Munson	6.00

Topps Heritage

		NM/M
Complete Set (20):		100.00
Common Player:		2.00
Inserted 1:12		
Proofs:		1-2X
Inserted 1:27		
1	Mark McGwire	12.00
2	Sammy Sosa	8.00
3	Greg Maddux	8.00
4	Mike Piazza	8.00
5	Ivan Rodriguez	4.00
6	Manny Ramirez	4.00
7	Jeff Bagwell	4.00
8	Sean Casey	2.00
9	Orlando Hernandez	2.00
10	Randy Johnson	5.00
11	Pedro Martinez	5.00
12	Vladimir Guerrero	4.00
13	Shawn Green	2.50
14	Ken Griffey Jr.	8.00
15	Alex Rodriguez	12.00
16	Nomar Garciaparra	10.00
17	Derek Jeter	15.00
18	Tony Gwynn	5.00
19	Chipper Jones	8.00
20	Cal Ripken Jr.	15.00

2000 Topps Gold Label Class 1

Larry Walker

		NM/M
Complete Set (100):		25.00
Common Player:		.25
Gold Parallel:		4-8X
Production 100 Sets		
Pack (3):		2.00
Wax Box (24):		30.00
1	Sammy Sosa	1.50
2	Greg Maddux	1.50
3	Dee Brown	.25
4	Rondell White	.40
5	Fernando Tatis	.25
6	Troy Glaus	.75
7	Nick Johnson	.40
8	Albert Belle	.30
9	Scott Rolen	.75
10	Rafael Palmeiro	.50
11	Tony Gwynn	1.00
12	Kevin Brown	.40
13	Roberto Alomar	.50
14	John Olerud	.40
15	Rick Ankiel	.25
16	Chipper Jones	1.50
17	Craig Biggio	.40
18	Mark Mulder	.40
19	Carlos Delgado	.75
20	Alex Gonzalez	.25
21	Gabe Kapler	.25
22	Derek Jeter	3.00
23	Carlos Beltran	.40
24	Todd Helton	.75
25	Mark McGwire	2.50
26	Ben Grieve	.25
27	Rafael Furcal	.40
28	Vernon Wells	.40
29	Greg Vaughn	.25
30	Vladimir Guerrero	.75
31	Mike Piazza	1.50
32	Roger Clemens	2.00
33	Barry Larkin	.40
34	Pedro Martinez	1.00
35	Matt Williams	.30
36	Mo Vaughn	.30
37	Tim Hudson	.40
38	Andruw Jones	.75
39	Vinny Castilla	.25
40	Frank Thomas	.75
41	Pokey Reese	.25
42	Corey Patterson	.40
43	Jeromy Burnitz	.25
44	Preston Wilson	.40
45	Juan Gonzalez	.75
46	Brian Giles	.40
47	Todd Walker	.25
48	Magglio Ordonez	.40
49	Alfonso Soriano	1.00
50	Ken Griffey Jr.	1.50
51	Michael Barrett	.25
52	Shawn Green	.50
53	Erubiel Durazo	.40
54	Adam Piatt	.25
55	Pat Burrell	.50
56	Mike Mussina	.50
57	Bernie Williams	.75
58	Sean Casey	.40
59	Randy Johnson	1.00
60	Jeff Bagwell	.75
61	Eric Chavez	.50
62	Josh Hamilton	.50
63	A.J. Burnett	.40
64	Jim Thome	.75
65	Raul Mondesi	.40
66	Jason Kendall	.40
67	Mike Lieberthal	.25
68	Robin Ventura	.40
69	Ivan Rodriguez	.50
70	Larry Walker	.40
71	Eric Munson	.25
72	Brian Jordan	.25
73	Edgardo Alfonzo	.25
74	Curt Schilling	.50
75	Nomar Garciaparra	2.00
76	Mark Grace	.50
77	Shannon Stewart	.25
78	J.D. Drew	.40
79	Jack Cust	.25
80	Cal Ripken Jr.	3.00
81	Bob Abreu	.40
82	Ruben Mateo	.25

83	Orlando Hernandez	.25
84	Kris Benson	.25
85	Barry Bonds	2.50
86	Manny Ramirez	.75
87	Jose Canseco	.50
88	Sean Burroughs	.25
89	Kevin Millwood	.40
90	Alex Rodriguez	2.50
91	Brett Myers RC	3.00
92	Rick Asadoorian RC	.40
93	Ben Christensen RC	.40
94	Bobby Bradley RC	.50
95	Corey Myers RC	.50
96	Brad Baisley RC	.50
97	Aaron McNeal RC	.50
98	Aaron Rowand RC	.75
99	Scott Downs RC	.40
100	Michael Tejera RC	.40

Class 2

Kevin Brown

		NM/M
Same prices as Class 1.		
Gold Parallel:		4-8X
Same prices as Class 1.		
Gold Parallel:		4-8X
Production 100 Sets		
Complete Set (10):		125.00
Common Player:		4.00
Inserted 1:53		
1	Jim Thome, Manny Ramirez, Roberto Alomar	6.00
2	Derek Jeter, Orlando Hernandez, Bernie Williams	15.00
3	Chipper Jones, Andruw Jones, Greg Maddux	12.00
4	Alex Rodriguez, Jay Buhner, John Olerud	20.00
5	Nomar Garciaparra, Pedro Martinez, Brian Daubach	15.00
6	Mark McGwire, J.D. Drew, Rick Ankiel	20.00
7	Sammy Sosa, Mark Grace, Kerry Wood	15.00
8	Ken Griffey Jr., Sean Casey, Barry Larkin	20.00
9	Mike Piazza, Edgardo Alfonzo, Robin Ventura	15.00
10	Randy Johnson, Matt Williams, Erubiel Durazo	6.00

End of the Rainbow

Brad Baisley

		NM/M
Complete Set (15):		8.00
Common Player:		.50
Inserted 1:11		
1	Pat Burrell	1.50
2	Corey Patterson	1.00
3	Josh Hamilton	1.50
4	Eric Munson	.75
5	Sean Burroughs	.75
6	Jack Cust	.50
7	Rafael Furcal	.75
8	Ruben Salazar	.50
9	Brett Myers	1.00
10	Wes Anderson	.50
11	Nick Johnson	1.00
12	Scott Downs	.50

13	Choo Freeman	.50
14	Brad Baisley	.50
15	A.J. Burnett	.75

Prospector's Dream

		NM/M
Complete Set (10):		15.00
Common Player:		.50
Inserted 1:26		
1	Mark McGwire	3.00
2	Alex Rodriguez	3.00
3	Nomar Garciaparra	3.00
4	Pat Burrell	.75
5	Todd Helton	1.00
6	Derek Jeter	4.00
7	Adam Piatt	.50
8	Chipper Jones	2.00
9	Shawn Green	.75
10	Josh Hamilton	1.50

The Treasury

Mark Mulder

		NM/M
Complete Set (25):		40.00
Common Player:		.50
Inserted 1:21		
1	Ken Griffey Jr.	3.00
2	Derek Jeter	6.00
3	Chipper Jones	3.00
4	Manny Ramirez	1.50
5	Nomar Garciaparra	4.00
6	Sammy Sosa	3.00
7	Cal Ripken Jr.	6.00
8	Alex Rodriguez	5.00
9	Mike Piazza	3.00
10	Pedro Martinez	2.00
11	Vladimir Guerrero	1.50
12	Jeff Bagwell	1.50
13	Shawn Green	1.00
14	Greg Maddux	3.00
15	Mark McGwire	5.00
16	Josh Hamilton	1.50
17	Corey Patterson	1.00
18	Dee Brown	.50
19	Rafael Furcal	.75
20	Pat Burrell	1.00
21	Alfonso Soriano	3.00
22	Adam Piatt	.75
23	A.J. Burnett	.75
24	Mark Mulder	.75
25	Ruben Mateo	.50

2000 Topps HD

		NM/M
Complete Set (100):		30.00
Common Player:		.25
Platinums:		4-8X
Production 99 Sets		
Pack (4):		1.50
Wax Box (20):		30.00
1	Derek Jeter	3.00
2	Andruw Jones	.75
3	Ben Grieve	.25
4	Carlos Beltran	.40
5	Randy Johnson	1.00
6	Javy Lopez	.40
7	Gary Sheffield	.50
8	John Olerud	.40

TONY GWYNN

9	Vinny Castilla	.25
10	Barry Larkin	.40
11	Tony Clark	.25
12	Roberto Alomar	.50
13	Brian Jordan	.25
14	Wade Boggs	.50
15	Carlos Febles	.25
16	Alfonso Soriano	1.50
17	A.J. Burnett	.25
18	Matt Williams	.25
19	Alex Gonzalez	.25
20	Larry Walker	.40
21	Jeff Bagwell	.75
22	Al Leiter	.25
23	Ken Griffey Jr.	1.50
24	Ruben Mateo	.25
25	Mark Grace	.50
26	Carlos Delgado	.75
27	Vladimir Guerrero	.75
28	Kenny Lofton	.40
29	Rusty Greer	.25
30	Pedro Martinez	1.00
31	Todd Helton	.75
32	Ray Lankford	.25
33	Jose Canseco	.50
34	Raul Mondesi	.40
35	Mo Vaughn	.40
36	Eric Chavez	.40
37	Manny Ramirez	.75
38	Jason Kendall	.40
39	Mike Mussina	.50
40	Dante Bichette	.25
41	Troy Glaus	.75
42	Rickey Henderson	.50
43	Pablo Ozuna	.25
44	Michael Barrett	.25
45	Tony Gwynn	1.00
46	John Smoltz	.40
47	Rafael Palmeiro	.50
48	Curt Schilling	.50
49	Todd Walker	.25
50	Greg Vaughn	.25
51	Orlando Hernandez	.25
52	Jim Thome	.75
53	Pat Burrell	.50
54	Tim Salmon	.40
55	Tom Glavine	.50
56	Travis Lee	.25
57	Gabe Kapler	.25
58	Greg Maddux	1.50
59	Scott Rolen	.75
60	Cal Ripken Jr.	3.00
61	Preston Wilson	.40
62	Ivan Rodriguez	.50
63	Johnny Damon	.40
64	Bernie Williams	.50
65	Barry Bonds	2.50
66	Sammy Sosa	1.50
67	Robin Ventura	.40
68	Tony Fernandez	.25
69	Jay Bell	.25
70	Mark McGwire	2.50
71	Jeromy Burnitz	.25
72	Chipper Jones	1.50
73	Josh Hamilton	.50
74	Darin Erstad	.40
75	Alex Rodriguez	2.50
76	Sean Casey	.40
77	Tino Martinez	.40
78	Juan Gonzalez	.75
79	Cliff Floyd	.25
80	Craig Biggio	.40
81	Shawn Green	.50
82	Adrian Beltre	.25
83	Mike Piazza	1.50
84	Nomar Garciaparra	2.00
85	Kevin Brown	.40
86	Roger Clemens	2.00
87	Frank Thomas	.75
88	Albert Belle	.25
89	Erubiel Durazo	.25
90	David Walling	.25
91	John Sneed RC	.50
92	Larry Bigbie RC	1.50
93	B.J. Garbe RC	.50
94	Bobby Bradley RC	.75
95	Ryan Christiansen RC	.50
96	Jay Gerhke RC	.50
97	Jason Stumm RC	.50
98	Brett Myers RC	4.00
99	Chance Caple RC	.50
100	Corey Myers RC	.75

Autographs

NM/M

Jeter 1:859
Ripken 1:4,386

1	Derek Jeter	150.00
2	Cal Ripken Jr.	250.00

Ballpark Figures

NM/M

Complete Set (10): 15.00
Common Player: .50
Inserted 1:11

1	Mark McGwire	3.00
2	Ken Griffey Jr.	2.00
3	Nomar Garciaparra	3.00
4	Derek Jeter	4.00
5	Sammy Sosa	2.00
6	Mike Piazza	2.00
7	Juan Gonzalez	1.00
8	Larry Walker	.75
9	Ben Grieve	.50
10	Barry Bonds	3.00

Clearly Refined

NM/M

Complete Set (10): 8.00
Common Player: .50
Inserted 1:20

1	Alfonso Soriano	3.00
2	Ruben Mateo	.50
3	Josh Hamilton	1.00
4	Chad Hermansen	.50
5	Ryan Anderson	.50
6	Nick Johnson	1.00
7	Octavio Dotel	.50
8	Peter Bergeron	.50
9	Adam Piatt	.50
10	Pat Burrell	2.00

Image

NM/M

Complete Set (10): 30.00

Common Player: 1.00
Inserted 1:44

1	Sammy Sosa	3.00
2	Mark McGwire	5.00
3	Derek Jeter	6.00
4	Albert Belle	1.00
5	Vladimir Guerrero	1.50
6	Ken Griffey Jr.	3.00
7	Mike Piazza	3.00
8	Alex Rodriguez	5.00
9	Barry Bonds	5.00
10	Nomar Garciaparra	4.00

On The Cutting Edge

NM/M

Complete Set (10): 15.00
Common Player: .50
Inserted 1:22

1	Andruw Jones	1.00
2	Nomar Garciaparra	3.00
3	Barry Bonds	3.00
4	Larry Walker	.50
5	Vladimir Guerrero	1.00
6	Jeff Bagwell	1.00
7	Derek Jeter	4.00
8	Sammy Sosa	2.00
9	Alex Rodriguez	3.00
10	Ken Griffey Jr.	2.00

2000 Topps Opening Day

NM/M

Complete Set (165): 30.00
Common Player: .15
Pack (8): 1.00
Wax Box (36): 25.00

1	Mark McGwire	2.00
2	Tony Gwynn	1.00
3	Wade Boggs	.40
4	Cal Ripken Jr.	2.50
5	Matt Williams	.20
6	Jay Buhner	.15
7	Mike Lieberthal	.15
8	Magglio Ordonez	.25
9	Derek Jeter	2.00
10	Javy Lopez	.25
11	Armando Benitez	.15
12	Darin Erstad	.25
13	Mark Grace	.25
14	Eric Karros	.15
15	J.T. Snow Jr.	.15
16	Luis Castillo	.15
17	Rey Ordonez	.15
18	Bob Abreu	.25
19	Warren Morris	.15
20	Juan Gonzalez	.75
21	Dean Palmer	.15
22	Hank Aaron	2.00
23	Jeff Bagwell	.75
24	Sammy Sosa	1.50
25	Randy Johnson	.75
26	Dante Bichette	.15
27	Frank Thomas	.75
28	Pedro Martinez	.75
29	Brian Giles	.20
30	Ivan Rodriguez	.50
31	Roger Cedeno	.15
32	David Justice	.25

33	Ken Caminiti	.15
34	Brian Jordan	.15
35	John Olerud	.25
36	Pokey Reese	.15
37	Barry Larkin	.25
38	Edgar Martinez	.15
39	Carlos Delgado	.50
40	Troy Glaus	.40
41	Ben Grieve	.15
42	Jose Lima	.15
43	Luis Gonzalez	.15
44	Alex Rodriguez	2.00
45	Preston Wilson	.20
46	Rickey Henderson	.40
47	Gary Sheffield	.25
48	Jim Edmonds	.15
49	Greg Vaughn	.15
50	Neifi Perez	.15
51	Paul O'Neill	.25
52	Jermaine Dye	.15
53	Curt Schilling	.25
54	Edgardo Alfonzo	.15
55	John Smoltz	.20
56	Chuck Finley	.15
57	Billy Wagner	.15
58	David Cone	.25
59	Roberto Alomar	.50
60	Charles Nagy	.15
61	Mike Mussina	.50
62	Robin Ventura	.15
63	Kevin Brown	.15
64	Pat Hentgen	.15
65	Ryan Klesko	.15
66	Derek Bell	.15
67	Larry Walker	.25
68	Scott Williamson	.15
69	Jose Offerman	.15
70	Doug Mientkiewicz	.15
71	John Snyder	.15
72	Sandy Alomar	.15
73	Joe Nathan	.15
74	Steve Finley	.15
75	Dave Martinez	.15
76	Fernando Tatis	.15
77	Kenny Lofton	.20
78	Paul Byrd	.15
79	Aaron Sele	.15
80	Roger Clemens	1.50
81	Francisco Cordova	.15
82	Wally Joyner	.15
83	Jason Kendall	.25
84	Carlos Beltran	.15
85	Chipper Jones	1.50
86	Vladimir Guerrero	.75
87	Tom Goodwin	.15
88	Brian Daubach	.15
89	Jay Bell	.15
90	Roy Halladay	.25
91	Miguel Tejada	.40
92	Eric Davis	.15
93	Henry Rodriguez	.15
94	Joe McEwing	.15
95	Jeff Kent	.25
96	Jeff Zimmerman	.15
97	Tony Fernandez	.15
98	Jason Giambi	.75
99	Jose Canseco	.40
100	Alex Gonzalez	.15
101	Erubiel Durazo, Pat Burrell, Nick Johnson (Prospects)	.40
102	Corey Patterson, Roosevelt Brown, Lance Berkman (Prospects)	.25
103	Eric Munson, Bobby Bradley **RC**	.25
104	Josh Hamilton, Corey Myers **RC**	.25
105	Mark McGwire	2.00
106	Hank Aaron	2.00
107	Cal Ripken Jr.	2.50
108	Wade Boggs	.40
109	Tony Gwynn	1.00
(110)	Hank Aaron (Rookie Reprint)	2.00
111	Tom Glavine	.40
112	Mo Vaughn	.20
113	Tino Martinez	.25
114	Craig Biggio	.25
115	Tim Hudson	.25
116	John Wetteland	.15
117	Ellis Burks	.15
118	David Wells	.15
119	Rico Brogna	.15
120	Greg Maddux	1.50
121	Jeromy Burnitz	.15
122	Raul Mondesi	.25
123	Rondell White	.15
124	Barry Bonds	2.00
125	Orlando Hernandez	.25
126	Bartolo Colon	.15
127	Tim Salmon	.25
128	Kevin Young	.15
129	Troy O'Leary	.15
130	Jim Thome	.50
131	Ray Durham	.15
132	Tony Clark	.15
133	Mariano Rivera	.25
134	Omar Vizquel	.15
135	Ken Griffey Jr.	1.50
136	Shawn Green	.40
137	Cliff Floyd	.15
138	Al Leiter	.15
139	Mike Hampton	.15
140	Mike Piazza	1.50
141	Andy Pettitte	.25

142	Albert Belle	.20
143	Scott Rolen	.75
144	Rusty Greer	.15
145	Kevin Millwood	.25
146	Ivan Rodriguez	.75
147	Nomar Garciaparra	1.50
148	Denny Neagle	.15
149	Manny Ramirez	.75
150	Vinny Castilla	.15
151	Andruw Jones	.50
152	Johnny Damon	.15
153	Eric Milton	.15
154	Todd Helton	.50
155	Rafael Palmeiro	.50
156	Damion Easley	.15
157	Carlos Febles	.15
158	Paul Konerko	.25
159	Bernie Williams	.50
160	Ken Griffey Jr.	1.50
161	Barry Bonds	2.00
162	Sammy Sosa	2.00
163	Derek Jeter	2.00
164	Alex Rodriguez	2.00
165	Checklist	.15

Autographs

NM/M

Common Player: 25.00

1	Edgardo Alfonzo	25.00
2	Wade Boggs	60.00
3	Robin Ventura	25.00
4	Josh Hamilton	50.00
5	Vernon Wells	25.00

2000 Topps Opening Day 2K

NM/M

Complete Set (8): 6.00
Common Player: .50

1	Mark McGwire	2.00
2	Barry Bonds	.75
3	Ivan Rodriguez	.75
4	Sean Casey	.65
5	Derek Jeter	1.00
6	Vladimir Guerrero	1.00
7	Preston Wilson	.65
8	Ben Grieve	.50

2000 Topps Stars

NM/M

Complete Set (200): 35.00
Common Player: .10
Pack (6): 2.00
Box (24): 40.00

1	Vladimir Guerrero	.75
2	Eric Karros	.10
3	Omar Vizquel	.20
4	Ken Griffey Jr.	1.50
5	Preston Wilson	.20
6	Albert Belle	.20
7	Ryan Klesko	.10
8	Bob Abreu	.20
9	Warren Morris	.10
10	Rafael Palmeiro	.40
11	Nomar Garciaparra	2.00
12	Dante Bichette	.10
13	Jeff Cirillo	.10
14	Carlos Beltran	.10

15	Tony Clark	.10
16	Ray Durham	.10
17	Mark McGwire	2.00
18	Jim Thome	.50
19	Todd Walker	.10
20	Richie Sexson	.40
21	Adrian Beltre	.10
22	Jay Bell	.10
23	Craig Biggio	.25
24	Ben Grieve	.15
25	Greg Maddux	1.50
26	Fernando Tatis	.10
27	Jeromy Burnitz	.10
28	Vinny Castilla	.10
29	Mark Grace	.25
30	Derek Jeter	2.00
31	Larry Walker	.25
32	Ivan Rodriguez	.50
33	Curt Schilling	.40
34	Mike Lamb RC	.25
35	Kevin Brown	.20
36	Andruw Jones	.40
37	Chris Mears RC	.10
38	Bartolo Colon	.10
39	Edgardo Alfonzo	.15
40	Brady Anderson	.20
41	Andres Galarraga	.25
42	Scott Rolen	.50
43	Manny Ramirez	.75
44	Carlos Delgado	.50
45	David Cone	.10
46	Carl Everett	.10
47	Chipper Jones	1.50
48	Barry Bonds	2.00
49	Dean Palmer	.10
50	Frank Thomas	.75
51	Paul O'Neill	.25
52	Mo Vaughn	.20
53	Todd Helton	.75
54	Jason Giambi	1.00
55	Brian Jordan	.10
56	Luis Gonzalez	.25
57	Alex Rodriguez	2.00
58	J.D. Drew	.10
59	Javy Lopez	.20
60	Tony Gwynn	1.00
61	Jason Kendall	.20
62	Pedro Martinez	.75
63	Matt Williams	.20
64	Gary Sheffield	.40
65	Roberto Alomar	.50
66	Lyle Overbay RC	1.00
67	Jeff Bagwell	.75
68	Tim Hudson	.40
69	Sammy Sosa	1.50
70	Keith Reed RC	.10
71	Robin Ventura	.20
72	Cal Ripken Jr.	2.50
73	Alex Gonzalez	.10
74	Aaron McNeal RC	.10
75	Mike Lieberthal	.10
76	Brian Giles	.25
77	Kevin Millwood	.10
78	Troy O'Leary	.10
79	Raul Mondesi	.20
80	John Olerud	.20
81	David Justice	.25
82	Erubiel Durazo	.10
83	Shawn Green	.20
84	Tino Martinez	.20
85	Greg Vaughn	.15
86	Tom Glavine	.25
87	Jose Canseco	.40
88	Kenny Lofton	.25
89	Brian Daubach	.10
90	Mike Piazza	1.50
91	Randy Johnson	.75
92	Pokey Reese	.10
93	Troy Glaus	.25
94	Kerry Wood	.25
95	Sean Casey	.20
96	Magglio Ordonez	.40
97	Bernie Williams	.50
98	Juan Gonzalez	.75
99	Barry Larkin	.25
100	Orlando Hernandez	.20
101	Roger Clemens	1.50
102	Bob Gibson	.40
103	Gary Carter	.10
104	Willie Stargell	.40
105	Joe Morgan	.40

106	Brooks Robinson	.50
107	Ozzie Smith	.50
108	Carl Yastrzemski	.25
109	Al Kaline	.40
110	Frank Robinson	.50
111	Lance Berkman	.10
112	Adam Piatt	.25
113	Vernon Wells	.25
114	Rafael Furcal	.25
115	Rick Ankiel	.25
116	Corey Patterson	.25
117	Josh Hamilton	.50
118	Jack Cust	.20
119	Josh Girdley	.10
120	Pablo Ozuna	.10
121	Sean Burroughs	.25
122	Pat Burrell	.25
123	Chad Hermansen	.10
124	Ruben Mateo	.10
125	Ben Petrick	.10
126	Dee Brown	.10
127	Eric Munson	.10
128	Ruben Salazar	.10
129	Kip Wells	.10
130	Alfonso Soriano	1.00
131	Mark Mulder	.25
132	Roosevelt Brown	.10
133	Nick Johnson	.40
134	Kyle Snyder	.10
135	David Walling	.10
136	Geraldo Guzman RC	.25
137	John Sneed RC	.25
138	Ben Christensen RC	.25
139	Corey Myers RC	.25
140	Jose Ortiz RC	3.00
141	Ryan Christianson RC	.25
142	Brett Myers RC	3.00
143	Bobby Bradley RC	.40
144	Rick Asadoorian RC	.40
145	Julio Zuleta RC	.40
146	Ty Howington RC	1.00
147	Josh Kalinowski RC	.40
148	B.J. Garbe RC	.50
149	Scott Downs RC	.25
150	Dan Wright RC	.25
151	Jeff Bagwell	.50
152	Vladimir Guerrero	.50
153	Mike Piazza	1.00
154	Juan Gonzalez	.40
155	Ivan Rodriguez	.25
156	Manny Ramirez	.40
157	Sammy Sosa	1.00
158	Chipper Jones	.75
159	Shawn Green	.20
160	Ken Griffey Jr.	.75
161	Cal Ripken Jr.	1.25
162	Nomar Garciaparra	1.00
163	Derek Jeter	1.00
164	Barry Bonds	1.00
165	Greg Maddux	.75
166	Mark McGwire	1.00
167	Roberto Alomar	.25
168	Alex Rodriguez	1.25
169	Randy Johnson	.40
170	Tony Gwynn	.50
171	Pedro Martinez	.40
172	Bob Gibson	.25
173	Gary Carter	.10
174	Willie Stargell	.25
175	Joe Morgan	.25
176	Brooks Robinson	.25
177	Ozzie Smith	.50
178	Carl Yastrzemski	.20
179	Al Kaline	.25
180	Frank Robinson	.40
181	Adam Piatt (Prospects)	.20
182	Alfonso Soriano (Prospects)	.75
183	Corey Patterson (Prospects)	.25
184	Vernon Wells (Prospects)	.40
185	Pat Burrell (Prospects)	.10
186	Mark Mulder (Prospects)	.10
187	Eric Munson (Prospects)	.10
188	Rafael Furcal (Prospects)	.15
189	Rick Ankiel (Prospects)	.25
190	Ruben Mateo (Prospects)	.10
191	Sean Burroughs (Prospects)	.20
192	Josh Hamilton (Prospects)	.75
193	Brett Myers	1.00
194	Ben Christensen	.20
195	Ty Howington	.20
196	Rick Asadoorian	.20
197	Josh Kalinowski	.20
198	Corey Myers	.25
199	Ryan Christianson	.25
200	John Sneed	.25

Blue

Stars (1-150):		3-5X
Production 299 Sets		
Stars (151-180):		4-8X

Rookies (181-200): 2-4X
Production 99 Sets

All-Star Authority

NM/M

Complete Set (14):		25.00
Common Player:		1.00
Inserted 1:13		
1	Mark McGwire	3.00
2	Sammy Sosa	2.00
3	Ken Griffey Jr.	2.00
4	Cal Ripken Jr.	4.00
5	Tony Gwynn	1.50
6	Barry Bonds	4.00
7	Mike Piazza	2.00
8	Pedro Martinez	1.50
9	Chipper Jones	2.00
10	Manny Ramirez	1.00
11	Alex Rodriguez	3.00
12	Derek Jeter	4.00
13	Nomar Garciaparra	3.00
14	Roberto Alomar	1.00

Autographs

NM/M

Common Player:		10.00
Group A 1:382		
Group B 1:1,636		
RA	Rick Ankiel/A	15.00
GC	Gary Carter/B	60.00
RF	Rafael Furcal/A	15.00
BG	Bob Gibson/A	25.00
DJ	Derek Jeter/A	90.00
AK	Al Kaline/B	50.00
KM	Kevin Millwood/A	15.00
JM	Joe Morgan/A	40.00
BR	Brooks Robinson/B	40.00
FR	Frank Robinson/B	20.00
OS	Ozzie Smith/B	35.00
WS	Willie Stargell/B	50.00
CY	Carl Yastrzemski/B	65.00

Game Gear Jersey

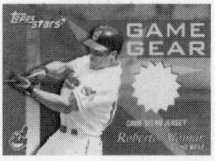

NM/M

Common Player:		10.00
Inserted 1:382		
1	Kevin Millwood	10.00
2	Brad Penny	10.00
3	J.D. Drew	15.00

Game Gear Bats

NM/M

Common Player:		10.00
Group A 1:2,289		

Group B 1:1,153		
Group C 1:409		
1	Rafael Furcal/C	10.00
2	Sean Burroughs/B	10.00
3	Corey Patterson/B	10.00
4	Chipper Jones/B	40.00
5	Vernon Wells/C	15.00
6	Alfonso Soriano/B	25.00
7	Eric Munson/C	10.00
8	Ben Petrick/B	10.00
9	Dee Brown/A	10.00
10	Lance Berkman/C	15.00

Progression

NM/M

Complete Set (9):		15.00
Common Player:		1.00
Inserted 1:13		
1	Bob Gibson, Pedro Martinez, Rick Ankiel	1.50
2	Gary Carter, Mike Piazza, Ben Petrick	2.00
3	Willie Stargell, Mark McGwire, Pat Burrell	3.00
4	Joe Morgan, Roberto Alomar, Ruben Salazar	1.00
5	Brooks Robinson, Chipper Jones, Sean Burroughs	2.00
6	Ozzie Smith, Derek Jeter, Rafael Furcal	3.00
7	Carl Yastrzemski, Barry Bonds, Josh Hamilton	4.00
8	Al Kaline, Ken Griffey Jr., Ruben Mateo	2.00
9	Frank Robinson, Manny Ramirez, Corey Patterson	1.50

Walk of Fame

NM/M

Complete Set (15):		15.00
Common Player:		.75
Inserted 1:8		
1	Cal Ripken Jr.	3.00
2	Ken Griffey Jr.	1.50
3	Mark McGwire	2.00
4	Sammy Sosa	1.50
5	Alex Rodriguez	2.00
6	Derek Jeter	2.50
7	Nomar Garciaparra	2.00
8	Chipper Jones	1.50
9	Manny Ramirez	1.00
10	Mike Piazza	1.50
11	Vladimir Guerrero	1.00
12	Barry Bonds	3.00
13	Tony Gwynn	1.00
14	Roberto Alomar	.75
15	Pedro Martinez	1.00

2000 Topps Subway Series

NM/M

Complete Fact. Set (101):		70.00
Complete Set (100):		20.00
Common Player:		.20
1	Mike Piazza	3.00
2	Jay Payton	.20
3	Edgardo Alfonzo	.40

Rick Reed P
2000 New York City Subway Series

4	Todd Pratt	.20
5	Todd Zeile	.20
6	Mike Bordick	.20
7	Robin Ventura	.40
8	Benny Agbayani	.20
9	Timo Perez	.50
10	Kurt Abbott	.20
11	Matt Franco	.20
12	Bubba Trammell	.20
13	Darryl Hamilton	.20
14	Lenny Harris	.20
15	Joe McEwing	.20
16	Mike Hampton	.40
17	Al Leiter	.40
18	Rick Reed	.20
19	Bobby Jones	.20
20	Glendon Rusch	.20
21	Armando Benitez	.20
22	John Franco	.20
23	Rick White	.20
24	Dennis Cook	.20
25	Turk Wendell	.20
26	Bobby Valentine	.20
27	Derek Jeter	4.00
28	Chuck Knoblauch	.40
29	Tino Martinez	.30
30	Jorge Posada	.40
31	Luis Sojo	.20
32	Scott Brosius	.20
33	Chris Turner	.20
34	Bernie Williams	.75
35	David Justice	.75
36	Paul O'Neill	.40
37	Glenallen Hill	.20
38	Jose Vizcaino	.20
39	Luis Polonia	.20
40	Clay Bellinger	.20
41	Orlando Hernandez	.40
42	Roger Clemens	1.50
43	Andy Pettitte	.50
44	Denny Neagle	.20
45	Dwight Gooden	.30
46	David Cone	.20
47	Mariano Rivera	.50
48	Jeff Nelson	.20
49	Mike Stanton	.20
50	Jason Grimsley	.20
51	Jose Canseco	.75
52	Joe Torre	.50
53	Edgardo Alfonzo	.40
54	Darryl Hamilton	.20
55	John Franco	.20
56	Benny Agbayani	.20
57	Bobby Jones	.20
58	New York Mets	.20
59	Bobby Valentine	.20
60	Mike Piazza	3.00
61	Armando Benitez	.20
62	Mike Piazza	3.00
63	Mike Piazza	3.00
64	Todd Zeile	.20
65	Timo Perez	.50
66	Timo Perez	.50
67	Mike Hampton	.40
68	Andy Pettitte	.50
69	Tino Martinez	.30
70	Joe Torre	.50
71	New York Yankees	.40
72	Orlando Hernandez	.40
73	Bernie Williams	.75
74	Andy Pettitte	.50
75	Mariano Rivera	.50
76	New York Yankees	.40
77	Roger Clemens	1.50
78	Derek Jeter	4.00
79	David Justice	.75
80	Mariano Rivera	.50
81	Tino Martinez	.30
82	New York Yankees	.40
83	Jorge Posada	.40
84	Chuck Knoblauch	.40
85	Jose Vizcaino	.20
86	Roger Clemens	1.50
87	Mike Piazza	3.00
88	Clay Bellinger	.20
89	Robin Ventura	.20
90	Benny Agbayani	.20
91	Orlando Hernandez	.20
92	Derek Jeter	4.00
93	Mike Piazza	3.00
94	Mariano Rivera	.50
95	Derek Jeter	3.00
96	Luis Sojo	.20
97	New York Yankees	.40
98	Mike Hampton	.40
99	David Justice	.75
100	Derek Jeter	4.00

Fan Fare

Mike Piazza
Catcher

		NM/M
Common Player:		25.00
Inserted 1:Set		
1	Timo Perez	35.00
2	Edgardo Alfonzo	40.00
3	Mike Piazza	120.00
4	Robin Ventura	35.00
5	Todd Zeile	25.00
6	Benny Agbayani	25.00
7	Jay Payton	25.00
8	Mike Bordick	25.00
9	Matt Franco	25.00
10	Mike Hampton	40.00
11	Al Leiter	40.00
12	Rick Reed	25.00
13	Bobby Jones	25.00
14	Glendon Rusch	25.00
15	Darryl Hamilton	25.00
16	Turk Wendell	25.00
17	John Franco	25.00
18	Armando Benitez	25.00
19	Chuck Knoblauch	35.00
20	Derek Jeter	200.00
21	David Justice	40.00
22	Bernie Williams	50.00
23	Jorge Posada	40.00
24	Paul O'Neill	50.00
25	Tino Martinez	35.00
26	Luis Sojo	25.00
27	Scott Brosius	25.00
28	Jose Canseco	50.00
29	Orlando Hernandez	35.00
30	Roger Clemens	100.00
31	Andy Pettitte	40.00
32	Denny Neagle	25.00
33	David Cone	25.00
34	Jeff Nelson	25.00
35	Mike Stanton	25.00
36	Mariano Rivera	60.00

2000 Topps TEK

Mike Piazza

		NM/M
Complete Set (45):		25.00
Common Player:		.40
Common Rookie (41-45):		.75
2,000 serial numbered rookies		
Pack (4):		2.00
Box (20):		30.00
1	Mike Piazza	1.50
2	Chipper Jones	1.50
3	Juan Gonzalez	.75
4	Ivan Rodriguez	.50
5	Cal Ripken Jr.	3.00
6	A.J. Burnett	.40
7	Jim Thome	.40
8	Mo Vaughn	.40
9	Andruw Jones	.75
10	Mark McGwire	2.00
11	Jose Canseco	.50
12	Shawn Green	.50
13	Barry Bonds	3.00
14	Bernie Williams	.50
15	Manny Ramirez	.75
16	Greg Maddux	1.50
17	Carlos Beltran	.40
18	Pedro Martinez	1.00
19	Jeff Bagwell	.75
20	Sammy Sosa	2.00
21	J.D. Drew	.40
22	Randy Johnson	1.00
23	Larry Walker	.40
24	Frank Thomas	.75
25	Orlando Hernandez	.40
26	Scott Rolen	.75
27	Tony Gwynn	1.00
28	Rick Ankiel	.50
29	Roberto Alomar	.75
30	Ken Griffey Jr.	1.50
31	Vladimir Guerrero	1.00
32	Derek Jeter	3.00
33	Nomar Garciaparra	2.00
34	Alex Rodriguez	2.50
35	Sean Casey	.40
36	Adam Piatt (Prospects)	.40
37	Corey Patterson (Prospects)	.40
38	Josh Hamilton (Prospects)	.50
39	Pat Burrell (Prospects)	.50
40	Eric Munson (Prospects)	.40
41	Ruben Salazar RC (Rookies)	.75
42	John Sneed RC (Rookies)	.75
43	Josh Girdley RC (Rookies)	.75
44	Brett Myers RC (Rookies)	4.00
45	Rick Asadoorian RC (Rookies)	.75

Color

Ruben Salazar

Patterns 16-20:	1-2X
Inserted 1:10	

Gold

Alex Rodriguez

Stars:	8-15X
Rookies:	4-8X
Production 10 Sets	

ArchiTEKs

		NM/M
Complete Set (18):		20.00
Common Player:		.50
Inserted 1:5		
1	Nomar Garciaparra	2.00
2	Derek Jeter	3.00
3	Chipper Jones	1.50
4	Vladimir Guerrero	1.00

5	Mark McGwire	2.50
7	Ken Griffey Jr.	1.50
8	Mike Piazza	1.50
9	Jeff Bagwell	1.00
10	Larry Walker	.50
11	Manny Ramirez	1.00
12	Alex Rodriguez	2.00
13	Sammy Sosa	2.00
14	Shawn Green	.50
15	Juan Gonzalez	.75
16	Barry Bonds	3.00
17	Pedro Martinez	1.00
18	Cal Ripken Jr.	3.00
19	Ivan Rodriguez	.75

DramaTEK Performers

		NM/M
Complete Set (9):		15.00
Common Player:		1.50
Inserted 1:10		
1	Mark McGwire	3.00
2	Sammy Sosa	2.50
3	Ken Griffey Jr.	2.00
4	Nomar Garciaparra	3.00
5	Chipper Jones	2.00
6	Mike Piazza	2.00
7	Alex Rodriguez	3.00
8	Derek Jeter	3.00
9	Vladimir Guerrero	1.50

TEKtonics

		NM/M
Complete Set (9):		35.00
Common Player:		4.00
Inserted 1:30		
1	Derek Jeter	6.00
2	Mark McGwire	6.00
3	Ken Griffey Jr.	4.00
4	Mike Piazza	4.00
5	Alex Rodriguez	6.00
6	Chipper Jones	4.00
7	Nomar Garciaparra	6.00
8	Sammy Sosa	5.00
9	Cal Ripken Jr.	8.00

2001 Topps

CLARK

		NM/M
Complete Set (790):		70.00
Complete Ser. 1 Set (405):		30.00
Complete Ser. 2 Set (385):		40.00
Common Player:		.10
Complete Factory Set, Blue (795):		75.00
Complete Factory Set, Gold (795):		75.00
Ser. 1 Pack (10):		1.50
Ser. 1 Box (36):		45.00
Ser. 2 Pack (10):		1.50
Ser. 2 Box (36):		45.00
1	Cal Ripken Jr.	1.50
2	Chipper Jones	1.00
3	Roger Cedeno	.10
4	Garret Anderson	.10
5	Robin Ventura	.20
6	Daryle Ward	.10
7	Not Issued	.10
8	Ron Gant	.20
9	Phil Nevin	.10
10	Jermaine Dye	.10
11	Chris Singleton	.10
12	Mike Stanton	.10
13	Brian Hunter	.10
14	Mike Redmond	.10
15	Jim Thome	.25
16	Brian Jordan	.10
17	Joe Girardi	.10
18	Steve Woodard	.10
19	Dustin Hermanson	.10
20	Shawn Green	.30
21	Todd Stottlemyre	.10
22	Dan Wilson	.10
23	Todd Pratt	.10
24	Derek Lowe	.10
25	Juan Gonzalez	.40
26	Clay Bellinger	.10
27	Jeff Fassero	.10
28	Pat Meares	.10
29	Eddie Taubensee	.10
30	Paul O'Neill	.25
31	Jeffrey Hammonds	.10
32	Pokey Reese	.10
33	Mike Mussina	.30
34	Rico Brogna	.10
35	Jay Buhner	.10
36	Steve Cox	.10
37	Quilvio Veras	.10
38	Marquis Grissom	.10
39	Shigetoshi Hasegawa	.10
40	Shane Reynolds	.10
41	Adam Piatt	.10
42	Luis Polonia	.10
43	Brook Fordyce	.10
44	Preston Wilson	.10
45	Ellis Burks	.10
46	Armando Rios	.10
47	Chuck Finley	.10
48	Dan Plesac	.10
49	Shannon Stewart	.10
50	Mark McGwire	1.00
51	Mark Loretta	.10
52	Gerald Williams	.10
53	Eric Young	.10
54	Peter Bergeron	.10
55	Dave Hansen	.10
56	Arthur Rhodes	.10
57	Bobby Jones	.10
58	Matt Clement	.10
59	Mike Benjamin	.10
60	Pedro Martinez	.50
61	Jose Canseco	.40
62	Matt Anderson	.10
63	Torii Hunter	.10
64	Carlos Lee	.10
65	David Cone	.10
66	Ray Sanchez	.10
67	Eric Chavez	.20
68	Rick Helling	.10
69	Manny Alexander	.10
70	John Franco	.10
71	Mike Bordick	.10
72	Andres Galarraga	.25
73	Jose Cruz Jr.	.10
74	Mike Matheny	.10
75	Randy Johnson	.50
76	Richie Sexson	.10
77	Vladimir Nunez	.10
78	Harold Baines	.10
79	Aaron Boone	.10
80	Darin Erstad	.40
81	Alex Gonzalez	.10
82	Gil Heredia	.10
83	Shane Andrews	.10
84	Todd Hundley	.10
85	Bill Mueller	.10
86	Mark McLemore	.10
87	Scott Spiezio	.10
88	Kevin McGlinchy	.10
89	Bubba Trammell	.10
90	Manny Ramirez	.50
91	Mike Lamb	.10
92	Scott Karl	.10
93	Brian Buchanan	.10
94	Chris Turner	.10
95	Mike Sweeney	.10
96	John Wetteland	.10
97	Rob Bell	.10
98	Pat Rapp	.10
99	John Burkett	.10
100	Derek Jeter	1.50
101	J.D. Drew	.25
102	Jose Offerman	.10
103	Rick Reed	.10
104	Will Clark	.30
105	Rickey Henderson	.25
106	Dave Berg	.10
107	Kirk Rueter	.10
108	Lee Stevens	.10
109	Jay Bell	.10
110	Fred McGriff	.20
111	Julio Zuleta	.10
112	Brian Anderson	.10
113	Orlando Cabrera	.10
114	Alex Fernandez	.10
115	Derek Bell	.10
116	Eric Owens	.10
117	Brian Bohannon	.10
118	Dennys Reyes	.10
119	Mike Stanley	.10
120	Jorge Posada	.20
121	Rich Becker	.10
122	Paul Konerko	.10
123	Mike Remlinger	.10
124	Travis Lee	.10
125	Ken Caminiti	.10
126	Kevin Barker	.10
127	Paul Quantrill	.10
128	Ozzie Guillen	.10
129	Kevin Tapani	.10
130	Mark Johnson	.10
131	Randy Wolf	.10
132	Michael Tucker	.10
133	Darren Lewis	.10
134	Joe Randa	.10
135	Jeff Cirillo	.10
136	David Ortiz	.10
137	Herb Perry	.10
138	Jeff Nelson	.10
139	Chris Stynes	.10
140	Johnny Damon	.10
141	Desi Relaford	.10
142	Jason Schmidt	.10
143	Charles Johnson	.10
144	Pat Burrell	.40
145	Gary Sheffield	.25
146	Tom Glavine	.25
147	Jason Isringhausen	.10
148	Chris Carpenter	.10
149	Jeff Suppan	.10
150	Ivan Rodriguez	.50
151	Luis Sojo	.10
152	Ron Villone	.10
153	Mike Sirotka	.10
154	Chuck Knoblauch	.20
155	Jason Kendall	.10
156	Dennis Cook	.10
157	Bobby Estalella	.10
158	Jose Guillen	.10
159	Thomas Howard	.10
160	Carlos Delgado	.50
161	Benji Gil	.10
162	Tim Bogar	.10
163	Kevin Elster	.10
164	Scott Downs	.10
165	Andy Benes	.10
166	Adrian Beltre	.10
167	David Bell	.10
168	Turk Wendell	.10
169	Pete Harnisch	.10
170	Roger Clemens	.75
171	Scott Williamson	.10
172	Kevin Jordan	.10
173	Brad Penny	.10
174	John Flaherty	.10
175	Troy Glaus	.50
176	Kevin Appier	.10
177	Walt Weiss	.10
178	Tyler Houston	.10
179	Michael Barrett	.10
180	Mike Hampton	.10
181	Francisco Cordova	.10
182	Mike Jackson	.10
183	David Segui	.10
184	Carlos Febles	.10
185	Roy Halladay	.10
186	Seth Etherton	.10
187	Charlie Hayes	.10
188	Fernando Tatis	.10
189	Steve Trachsel	.10
190	Livan Hernandez	.10
191	Joe Oliver	.10
192	Stan Javier	.10
193	B.J. Surhoff	.10
194	Rob Ducey	.10
195	Barry Larkin	.25
196	Danny Patterson	.10
197	Bobby Howry	.10
198	Dmitri Young	.10
199	Brian Hunter	.10
200	Alex Rodriguez	1.00
201	Hideo Nomo	.25
202	Luis Alicea	.10
203	Warren Morris	.10
204	Antonio Alfonseca	.10
205	Edgardo Alfonzo	.20
206	Mark Grudzielanek	.10
207	Fernando Vina	.10
208	Willie Greene	.10
209	Homer Bush	.10
210	Jason Giambi	.30
211	Mike Morgan	.10
212	Steve Karsay	.10
213	Matt Lawton	.10
214	Wendell Magee Jr.	.10
215	Rusty Greer	.10
216	Keith Lockhart	.10
217	Billy Koch	.10
218	Todd Hollandsworth	.10
219	Raul Ibanez	.10
220	Tony Gwynn	.75
221	Carl Everett	.20
222	Hector Carrasco	.10
223	Jose Valentin	.10
224	Deivi Cruz	.10
225	Bret Boone	.10
226	Kurt Abbott	.10
227	Melvin Mora	.10
228	Danny Graves	.10
229	Jose Jimenez	.10
230	James Baldwin	.10
231	C.J. Nitkowski	.10
232	Jeff Zimmerman	.10
233	Mike Lowell	.10
234	Hideki Irabu	.10
235	Greg Vaughn	.20
236	Omar Daal	.10
237	Darren Dreifort	.10
238	Gil Meche	.10
239	Damian Jackson	.10
240	Frank Thomas	.75
241	Travis Miller	.10
242	Jeff Frye	.10
243	Dave Magadan	.10
244	Luis Castillo	.10
245	Bartolo Colon	.10
246	Steve Kline	.10
247	Shawon Dunston	.10
248	Rick Aguilera	.10
249	Omar Olivares	.10
250	Craig Biggio	.20
251	Scott Schoeneweis	.10
252	Dave Veres	.10
253	Ramon Martinez	.10
254	Jose Vidro	.10
255	Todd Helton	.50
256	Greg Norton	.10
257	Jacque Jones	.10
258	Jason Grimsley	.10
259	Dan Reichert	.10
260	Robb Nen	.10
261	Mark Clark	.10
262	Scott Hatteberg	.10
263	Doug Brocail	.10
264	Mark Johnson	.10
265	Eric Davis	.20
266	Terry Shumpert	.10
267	Kevin Millar	.10
268	Ismael Valdes	.10
269	Richard Hidalgo	.20
270	Randy Velarde	.10
271	Bengie Molina	.10
272	Tony Womack	.10
273	Enrique Wilson	.10
274	Jeff Brantley	.10
275	Rick Ankiel	.25
276	Terry Mulholland	.10
277	Ron Belliard	.10
278	Terrence Long	.10
279	Alberto Castillo	.10
280	Royce Clayton	.10
281	Joe McEwing	.10
282	Jason McDonald	.10
283	Ricky Bottalico	.10
284	Keith Foulke	.10
285	Brad Radke	.10
286	Gabe Kapler	.10
287	Pedro Astacio	.10
288	Armando Reynoso	.10
289	Darryl Kile	.10
290	Reggie Sanders	.10
291	Esteban Yan	.10
292	Joe Nathan	.10
293	Jay Payton	.10
294	Francisco Cordero	.10
295	Gregg Jefferies	.10
296	LaTroy Hawkins	.10
297	Jeff Tam	.10
298	Jacob Cruz	.10
299	Chris Holt	.10
300	Vladimir Guerrero	.75
301	Marvin Benard	.10
302	Matt Franco	.10
303	Mike Williams	.10
304	Sean Bergman	.10
305	Juan Encarnacion	.10
306	Russ Davis	.10
307	Hanley Frias	.10
308	Ramon Hernandez	.10
309	Matt Walbeck	.10
310	Bill Spiers	.10
311	Bob Wickman	.10
312	Sandy Alomar	.10
313	Eddie Guardado	.10
314	Shane Halter	.10
315	Geoff Jenkins	.20
316	Gerald Witasick	.10
317	Damian Miller	.10
318	Darrin Fletcher	.10
319	Rafael Furcal	.25
320	Mark Grace	.25
321	Mark Mulder	.10
322	Joe Torre	.10
323	Bobby Cox	.10
324	Mike Scioscia	.10
325	Mike Hargrove	.10
326	Jimy Williams	.10
327	Jerry Manuel	.10
328	Buck Showalter	.10
329	Charlie Manuel	.10
330	Don Baylor	.10
331	Phil Garner	.10
332	Jack McKeon	.10
333	Tony Muser	.10
334	Buddy Bell	.10
335	Tom Kelly	.10
336	John Boles	.10
337	Art Howe	.10
338	Larry Dierker	.10
339	Lou Pinella	.10
340	Davey Johnson	.10
341	Larry Rothschild	.10
342	Davey Lopes	.10
343	Johnny Oates	.10
344	Felipe Alou	.10
345	Jim Fregosi	.10
346	Bobby Valentine	.10
347	Terry Francona	.10
348	Gene Lamont	.10
349	Tony LaRussa	.10
350	Bruce Bochy	.10
351	Dusty Baker	.10
352	Adrian Gonzalez, Adam Johnson	.75
353	Matt Wheatland, Brian Digby	.40
354	Tripper Johnson, Scott Thorman	.40
355	Phil Dumatrait, Adam Wainwright	.50
356	Scott Heard, David Parrish **RC**	.40
357	Rocco Baldelli, Mark Folsom **RC**	.40
358	Dominic Rich, Aaron Herr	.40
359	Mike Stodolka, Sean Burnett	.25
360	Derek Thompson, Corey Smith	.40
361	Danny Borrell, Jason Bourgeois **RC**	.40
362	Chin-Feng Chen, Corey Patterson, Josh Hamilton (Prospects)	.25
363	Ryan Anderson, Barry Zito, C.C. Sabathia (Prospects)	.50
364	Scott Sobkowiak, David Walling, Ben Sheets (Prospects)	.50
365	Ty Howington, Josh Kalinowski, Josh Girdley (Prospects)	.10
366	Hee Seop Choi, Aaron McNeal, Jason Hart (Prospects)	1.00
367	Bobby Bradley, Kurt Ainsworth, Chin-Hui Tsao (Prospects)	.40
368	Mike Glendenning, Kenny Kelly, Juan Silvestri **RC** (Prospects)	.25
369	J.R. House, Ramon Castro, Ben Davis (Prospects)	.25
370	Chance Caple, Rafael Soriano, Pasqual Coco (Prospects)	.50
371	Travis Hafner, Eric Munson, Bucky Jacobsen (Prospects)	1.50
372	Jason Conti, Chris Wakeland, Brian Cole (Prospects)	.20
373	Scott Seabol, Aubrey Huff, Joe Crede (Prospects)	.40
374	Adam Everett, Jose Ortiz, Keith Ginter (Prospects)	.25
375	Carlos Hernandez, Geraldo Guzman, Adam Eaton (Prospects)	.25
376	Bobby Kielty, Milton Bradley, Juan Rivera (Prospects)	.25
377	Mark McGwire	.75
378	Don Larsen	.20
379	Bobby Thomson	.10
380	Bill Mazeroski	.20
381	Reggie Jackson	.40
382	Kirk Gibson	.10
383	Roger Maris	.40
384	Cal Ripken Jr.	.75
385	Hank Aaron	.75
386	Joe Carter	.10
387	Cal Ripken Jr.	.75
388	Randy Johnson	.30
389	Ken Griffey Jr.	.50
390	Troy Glaus	.30
391	Kazuhiro Sasaki	.40
392	Sammy Sosa, Troy Glaus	.50
393	Todd Helton, Edgar Martinez	.25
394	Nomar Garciaparra, Todd Helton	.50
395	Barry Bonds, Jason Giambi	.40
396	Todd Helton, Manny Ramirez	.25
397	Todd Helton, Darin Erstad	.25
398	Kevin Brown, Pedro Martinez	.25
399	Randy Johnson, Pedro Martinez	.25
400	Will Clark	.20
401	NY Mets Divisional Highlight	.10
402	NY Yankees Divisional Highlight	.10
403	Seattle Mariners Divisional Highlight	.10
404	Mike Hampton	.10
405	NY Yankees ALCS Highlight	.75
406	World Series Highlight	1.00
407	Jeff Bagwell	.50
408	Brant Brown	.10
409	Brad Fullmer	.10
410	Dean Palmer	.10
411	Gregg Zaun	.10
412	Jose Vizcaino	.10
413	Jeff Abbott	.10
414	Travis Fryman	.15
415	Mike Cameron	.10
416	Matt Mantei	.10
417	Alan Benes	.10
418	Mickey Morandini	.10
419	Troy Percival	.10

420 Eddie Perez	.10	535 Butch Huskey	.10
421 Vernon Wells	.10	536 Orlando Hernandez	.20
422 Ricky Gutierrez	.10	537 Magglio Ordonez	.15
423 Carlos Hernandez	.10	538 Willie Blair	.10
424 Chan Ho Park	.15	539 Kevin Sefcik	.10
425 Armando Benitez	.10	540 Chad Curtis	.10
426 Sidney Ponson	.10	541 John Halama	.10
427 Adrian Brown	.10	542 Andy Fox	.10
428 Ruben Mateo	.20	543 Juan Guzman	.10
429 Alex Ochoa	.10	544 Frank Menechino	.10
430 Jose Rosado	.10	545 Raul Mondesi	.15
431 Masato Yoshii	.10	546 Tim Salmon	.15
432 Corey Koskie	.10	547 Ryan Rupe	.10
433 Andy Pettitte	.20	548 Jeff Reed	.10
434 Brian Daubach	.10	549 Mike Mordecai	.10
435 Sterling Hitchcock	.10	550 Jeff Kent	.15
436 Timo Perez	.10	551 Wiki Gonzalez	.10
437 Shawn Estes	.10	552 Kenny Rogers	.10
438 Tony Armas Jr.	.10	553 Kevin Young	.10
439 Danny Bautista	.10	554 Brian Johnson	.10
440 Randy Winn	.10	555 Tom Goodwin	.10
441 Wilson Alvarez	.10	556 Tony Clark	.10
442 Rondell White	.15	557 Mac Suzuki	.10
443 Jeremy Burnitz	.10	558 Brian Moehler	.10
444 Kelvim Escobar	.10	559 Jim Parque	.10
445 Paul Bako	.10	560 Mariano Rivera	.20
446 Javier Vazquez	.10	561 Trot Nixon	.10
447 Eric Gagne	.10	562 Mike Mussina	.30
448 Kenny Lofton	.20	563 Nelson Figueroa	.10
449 Mark Kotsay	.10	564 Alex Gonzalez	.10
450 Jamie Moyer	.10	565 Benny Agbayani	.10
451 Delino DeShields	.10	566 Ed Sprague	.10
452 Rey Ordonez	.10	567 Scott Erickson	.10
453 Russ Ortiz	.10	568 Abraham Nunez	.10
454 Dave Burba	.10	569 Jerry DiPoto	.10
455 Eric Karros	.15	570 Sean Casey	.10
456 Felix Martinez	.10	571 Wilton Veras	.10
457 Tony Batista	.10	572 Joe Mays	.10
458 Bobby Higginson	.10	573 Bill Simas	.10
459 Jeff D'Amico	.10	574 Doug Glanville	.10
460 Shane Spencer	.10	575 Scott Sauerbeck	.10
461 Brent Mayne	.10	576 Ben Davis	.10
462 Glendon Rusch	.10	577 Jesus Sanchez	.10
463 Chris Gomez	.10	578 Ricardo Rincon	.10
464 Jeff Shaw	.10	579 John Olerud	.15
465 Damon Buford	.10	580 Curt Schilling	.10
466 Mike DiFelice	.10	581 Alex Cora	.10
467 Jimmy Haynes	.10	582 Pat Hentgen	.10
468 Billy Wagner	.10	583 Javy Lopez	.15
469 A.J. Hinch	.10	584 Ben Grieve	.10
470 Gary DiSarcina	.10	585 Frank Castillo	.10
471 Tom Lampkin	.10	586 Kevin Stocker	.10
472 Adam Eaton	.10	587 Mark Sweeney	.10
473 Brian Giles	.15	588 Ray Lankford	.10
474 John Thomson	.10	589 Turner Ward	.10
475 Cal Eldred	.10	590 Felipe Crespo	.10
476 Ramiro Mendoza	.10	591 Omar Vizquel	.15
477 Scott Sullivan	.10	592 Mike Lieberthal	.10
478 Scott Rolen	.25	593 Ken Griffey Jr.	1.00
479 Todd Ritchie	.10	594 Troy O'Leary	.10
480 Pablo Ozuna	.10	595 Dave Mlicki (Front photo actually Brian Moehler.)	.10
481 Carl Pavano	.10	596 Manny Ramirez	.50
482 Matt Morris	.10	597 Mike Lansing	.10
483 Matt Stairs	.10	598 Rich Aurilia	.10
484 Tim Belcher	.10	599 Russ Branyan	.10
485 Lance Berkman	.15	600 Russ Johnson	.10
486 Brian Meadows	.10	601 Gregg Colbrunn	.10
487 Bobby Abreu	.10	602 Andruw Jones	.40
488 John Vander Wal	.10	603 Henry Blanco	.10
489 Donnie Sadler	.10	604 Jarrod Washburn	.10
490 Damion Easley	.10	605 Tony Eusebio	.10
491 David Justice	.25	606 Aaron Sele	.10
492 Ray Durham	.10	607 Charles Nagy	.10
493 Todd Zeile	.10	608 Ryan Klesko	.10
494 Desi Relaford	.10	609 Dante Bichette	.10
495 Cliff Floyd	.10	610 Bill Haselman	.10
496 Scott Downs	.10	611 Jerry Spradlin	.10
497 Barry Bonds	1.00	612 Alex Rodriguez	1.00
498 Jeff D'Amico	.10	613 Jose Silva	.10
499 Octavio Dotel	.10	614 Darren Oliver	.10
500 Kent Mercker	.10	615 Pat Mahomes	.10
501 Craig Grebeck	.10	616 Roberto Alomar	.40
502 Roberto Hernandez	.10	617 Edgar Renteria	.10
503 Matt Williams	.15	618 Jon Lieber	.10
504 Bruce Aven	.10	619 John Rocker	.10
505 Brett Tomko	.10	620 Miguel Tejada	.15
506 Kris Benson	.10	621 Mo Vaughn	.15
507 Neifi Perez	.10	622 Jose Lima	.10
508 Alfonso Soriano	.50	623 Kerry Wood	.15
509 Keith Osik	.10	624 Mike Timlin	.10
510 Matt Franco	.10	625 Wil Cordero	.10
511 Steve Finley	.10	626 Albert Belle	.15
512 Olmedo Saenz	.10	627 Bobby Jones	.10
513 Esteban Loaiza	.10	628 Doug Mirabelli	.10
514 Adam Kennedy	.10	629 Jason Tyner	.10
515 Scott Elarton	.10	630 Andy Ashby	.10
516 Moises Alou	.15	631 Jose Hernandez	.10
517 Bryan Rekar	.10	632 Devon White	.10
518 Darryl Hamilton	.10	633 Ruben Rivera	.10
519 Osvaldo Fernandez	.10	634 Steve Parris	.10
520 Kip Wells	.10	635 David McCarty	.10
521 Bernie Williams	.40	636 Jose Canseco	.25
522 Mike Darr	.10	637 Todd Walker	.10
523 Marlon Anderson	.10	638 Stan Spencer	.10
524 Derrek Lee	.10	639 Wayne Gomes	.10
525 Ugueth Urbina	.10	640 Freddy Garcia	.10
526 Vinny Castilla	.10	641 Jeremy Giambi	.10
527 David Wells	.10	642 Luis Lopez	.10
528 Jason Marquis	.10	643 John Smoltz	.10
529 Orlando Palmeiro	.10	644 Kelly Stinnett	.10
530 Carlos Perez	.10	645 Kevin Brown	.10
531 J.T. Snow Jr.	.10	646 Wilton Guerrero	.10
532 Al Leiter	.15	647 Al Martin	.10
533 Jimmy Anderson	.10	648 Woody Williams	.10
534 Brett Laxton	.10		

649 Brian Rose	.10	746 Mark Dalesandro, Edwin Encarnacion RC	.50
650 Rafael Palmeiro	.30	747 Brian Bass, Odannis Ayala RC	.40
651 Pete Schourek	.10	748 Jason Kaanoi, Michael Mathews RC	.10
652 Kevin Jarvis	.10	749 Stuart McFarland, Adam Sterrett RC	.40
653 Mark Redman	.10	750 David Krynzel, Grady Sizemore	.50
654 Ricky Ledee	.10	751 Keith Bucktrot, Dane Sardinha	.10
655 Larry Walker	.20	752 Anaheim Angels	.10
656 Paul Byrd	.10	753 Arizona Diamondbacks	.10
657 Jason Bere	.10	754 Atlanta Braves	.10
658 Rick White	.10	755 Baltimore Orioles	.10
659 Calvin Murray	.10	756 Boston Red Sox	.10
660 Greg Maddux	1.00	757 Chicago Cubs	.10
661 Ron Gant	.10	758 Chicago White Sox	.10
662 Eli Marrero	.10	759 Cincinnati Reds	.10
663 Graeme Lloyd	.10	760 Cleveland Indians	.10
664 Trevor Hoffman	.10	761 Colorado Rockies	.10
665 Nomar Garciaparra	1.00	762 Detroit Tigers	.10
666 Glenallen Hill	.10	763 Florida Marlins	.10
667 Matt LeCroy	.10	764 Houston Astros	.10
668 Justin Thompson	.10	765 Kansas City Royals	.10
669 Brady Anderson	.10	766 Los Angeles Dodgers	.10
670 Miguel Batista	.10	767 Milwaukee Brewers	.10
671 Erubiel Durazo	.10	768 Minnesota Twins	.10
672 Kevin Millwood	.10	769 Montreal Expos	.10
673 Mitch Meluskey	.10	770 New York Mets	.10
674 Luis Gonzalez	.15	771 New York Yankees	.75
675 Edgar Martinez	.10	772 Oakland Athletics	.10
676 Robert Person	.10	773 Philadelphia Phillies	.10
677 Benito Santiago	.10	774 Pittsburgh Pirates	.10
678 Todd Jones	.10	775 San Diego Padres	.10
679 Tino Martinez	.15	776 San Francisco Giants	.10
680 Carlos Beltran	.10	777 Seattle Mariners	.10
681 Gabe White	.10	778 St. Louis Cardinals	.10
682 Bret Saberhagen	.10	779 Tampa Bay Devil Rays	.10
683 Jeff Conine	.10	780 Texas Rangers	.10
684 Jaret Wright	.10	781 Toronto Blue Jays	.10
685 Bernard Gilkey	.10	782 Bucky Dent	.10
686 Garrett Stephenson	.10	783 Jackie Robinson	1.00
687 Jamey Wright	.10	784 Roberto Clemente	1.00
688 Sammy Sosa	1.00	785 Nolan Ryan)	1.50
689 John Jaha	.10	786 Kerry Wood	.10
690 Ramon Martinez	.10	787 Rickey Henderson	.20
691 Robert Fick	.10	788 Lou Brock	.25
692 Eric Milton	.10	789 David Wells	.10
693 Denny Neagle	.10	790 Andruw Jones	.25
694 Ron Coomer	.10	791 Carlton Fisk	.10
695 John Valentin	.10		
696 Placido Polanco	.10		
697 Tim Hudson	.15		
698 Marty Cordova	.10		
699 Chad Kreuter	.10		
700 Frank Catalanotto	.10		
701 Tim Wakefield	.10		
702 Jim Edmonds	.15		
703 Michael Tucker	.10		
704 Cristian Guzman	.10		
705 Joey Hamilton	.10		
706 Mike Piazza	1.00		
707 Dave Martinez	.10		
708 Mike Hampton	.15		
709 Bobby Bonilla	.10		
710 Juan Pierre	.10		
711 John Parrish	.10		
712 Kory DeHaan	.10		
713 Brian Tollberg	.10		
714 Chris Truby	.10		
715 Emil Brown	.10		
716 Ryan Dempster	.10		
717 Rich Garces	.10		
718 Mike Myers	.10		
719 Luis Ordaz	.10		
720 Kazuhiro Sasaki	.10		
721 Mark Quinn	.10		
722 Ramon Ortiz	.10		
723 Kerry Ligtenberg	.10		
724 Rolando Arrojo	.10		
725 Tsuyoshi Shinjo RC	1.00		
726 Ichiro Suzuki RC	15.00		
727 Roy Oswalt, Pat Strange, Jon Rauch (Prospects)	.25		
728 Phil Wilson, Jake Peavy, Darwin Cubillan RC (Prospects)	.75		
729 Steve Smyth, Mike Bynum, Nathan Haynes (Prospects)	.40		
730 Michael Cuddyer, Joe Lawrence, Choo Freeman (Prospects)	.10		
731 Carlos Pena, Larry Barnes, Dewayne Wise (Prospects)	.10		
732 Gookie Dawkins, Erick Almonte, Felipe Lopez (Prospects)	.40		
733 Alex Escobar, Eric Valent, Brad Wilkerson (Prospects)	.10		
734 Toby Hall, Rod Barajas, Jeff Goldbach RC (Prospects)	.10		
735 Jason Romano, Marcus Giles, Pablo Ozuna (Prospects)	.10		
736 Dee Brown, Jack Cust, Vernon Wells (Prospects)	.10		
737 David Espinosa, Luis Montanez RC	.40		
738 Anthony Pluta, Justin Wayne RC	.50		
739 Josh Axelson, Carmen Cali RC	.50		
740 Shaun Boyd, Chris Morris RC	.50		
741 Tommy Arko, Dan Moylan RC	.10		
742 Luis Cotto, Luis Escobar	.40		
743 Brandon Mims, Blake Williams RC	.40		
744 Chris Russ, Bryan Edwards	.40		
745 Joe Torres, Ben Diggins	.10		

Gold

Stars:	8-15X
Prospects and RC's:	3-6X

Inserted 1:17

Autographs

NM/M

Common Player:	
Group A	1:22,866
Group B	1:3,054
Group C	1:1,431
Group D	1:18,339
Group E	1:13,737
Group F	1:11,015
Group G	1:625

HA	Hank Aaron	275.00
DA	Dick Allen	25.00
RA	Rick Ankiel	30.00
RB	Rocco Baldelli	25.00
EB	Ernie Banks	100.00
YB	Yogi Berra	80.00
LB	Lou Brock	50.00
PB	Pat Burrell	15.00
RC	Rod Carew	50.00
MC	Mike Cuellar	15.00
WF	Whitey Ford	40.00
RF	Rafael Furcal	25.00
BG	Bob Gibson	40.00
AG	Adrian Gonzalez	20.00
SH	Scott Heard	15.00
WH	Willie Hernandez	10.00
AJ	Adam Johnson	10.00
CJ	Chipper Jones	80.00
SK	Sandy Koufax	600.00
ML	Mike Lamb	10.00
VL	Vernon Law	15.00
JM	Jason Marquis	10.00
WM	Willie Mays	250.00
MO	Magglio Ordonez	20.00
AP	Andy Pafko	30.00
BR	Brooks Robinson	80.00
JR	Joe Rudi	15.00
MS	Mike Schmidt	100.00
MS	Mike Stodolka	15.00
RS	Ron Swoboda	30.00
GT	Garry Templeton	20.00
JV	Jose Vidro	20.00
MW	Matt Wheatland	20.00
TZ	Todd Zeile	20.00

Autographs Series 2

Justin Wayne

GOLDEN ANNIVERSARY PROSPECT

NM/M

	Common Player:	10.00
DA	Denny Abreu	10.00
TA	Tony Alvarez	10.00
RB	Rocco Baldelli	25.00
GB	George Bell	10.00
JB	Johnny Bench	75.00
BB	Barry Bonds	180.00
MB	Milton Bradley	15.00
GHB	George Brett	175.00
MAB	Mike Bynum	10.00
EB	Eric Byrnes	15.00
JC	Jorge Cantu	10.00
CC	Chris Clapinski	10.00
WD	Willie Davis	20.00
JDD	J.D. Drew	30.00
TDLR	Tomas de la Rosa	10.00
CD	Chad Durbin	10.00
CE	Carl Erskine	25.00
BE	Brian Esposito	15.00
WF	Whitey Ford	40.00
EF	Eddy Furniss	15.00
BG	Bob Gibson	40.00
MG	Mike Glendenning	15.00
AG	Adrian Gonzalez	20.00
NG	Nick Green	10.00
KG	Kevin Gregg	10.00
DG	Dick Groat	25.00
GG	Geraldo Guzman	10.00
YH	Yamid Haad	10.00
TH	Todd Helton	40.00
AH	Aaron Herr	15.00
KH	Ken Holtzman	15.00
RJ	Reggie Jackson	125.00
NJ	Neil Jenkins	15.00
AJ	Adam Johnson	10.00
TJ	Tripper Johnson	15.00
BK	Bobby Kielty	10.00
JL	John Lackey	20.00
ML	Matt Lawton	15.00
CL	Colby Lewis	16.00
MFL	Mike Lockwood	15.00
GM	Gary Matthews	20.00
LM	Luis Montanez	15.00
EM	Eric Munson	15.00
SM	Stan Musial	180.00
BO	Ben Oglivie	15.00
AO	Augie Ojeda	10.00
ER	Erasmo Ramirez	15.00
CR	Chris Richard	15.00
JR	Juan Rincon	10.00
LR	Luis Rivas	20.00
SR	Scott Rolen	25.00
NR	Nolan Ryan	200.00
JS	Juan Salas	10.00

TS	Tom Seaver	150.00
CS	Carlos Silva	10.00
GS	Grady Sizemore	75.00
CCS	Corey Smith	10.00
MS	Mike Stodolka	10.00
MS	Mike Sweeney	15.00
KT	Kent Tekulve	20.00
DT	Derek Thompson	10.00
ST	Scott Thorman	10.00
BT	Brian Tollberg	15.00
JW	Justin Wayne	20.00
MW	Michael Wenner	15.00
MJW	Matt Wheatland	15.00
WW	Wilbur Wood	20.00
CY	Carl Yastrzemski	80.00

A Look Ahead

DEREK JETER

NM/M

	Complete Set (10):	15.00
	Common Player:	.50
	Inserted 1:25	
1	Vladimir Guerrero	1.50
2	Derek Jeter	4.00
3	Todd Helton	1.00
4	Alex Rodriguez	3.00
5	Ken Griffey Jr.	2.00
6	Nomar Garciaparra	3.00
7	Chipper Jones	2.00
8	Ivan Rodriguez	1.00
9	Pedro Martinez	1.50
10	Rick Ankiel	.50

A Tradition Continued

A TRADITION CONTINUES

NM/M

	Complete Set (30):	50.00
	Common Player:	.50
	Inserted 1:17	
1	Chipper Jones	3.00
2	Cal Ripken Jr.	6.00
3	Mike Piazza	3.00
4	Ken Griffey Jr.	3.00
5	Randy Johnson	1.50
6	Derek Jeter	5.00
7	Scott Rolen	1.50
8	Nomar Garciaparra	4.00
9	Roberto Alomar	1.00
10	Greg Maddux	3.00
11	Ivan Rodriguez	1.50
12	Jeff Bagwell	1.50
13	Ivan Rodriguez	1.50
14	Pedro Martinez	2.00
15	Sammy Sosa	4.00
16	Jim Edmonds	1.00
17	Mo Vaughn	.50
18	Barry Bonds	5.00
19	Larry Walker	.75
20	Mark McGwire	4.00
21	Vladimir Guerrero	2.00
22	Andruw Jones	1.50
23	Todd Helton	1.50
24	Kevin Brown	.75
25	Tony Gwynn	2.00
26	Jim Rincon	1.50
27	Roger Clemens	4.00
28	Frank Thomas	1.50
29	Shawn Green	.75
30	Jim Thome	1.50

Base Hit

BASE HIT

NM/M

	Common Player:	25.00
BH1	Mike Scioscia	35.00
BH2	Larry Dierker	25.00
BH3	Art Howe	25.00
BH4	Jim Fregosi	25.00
BH5	Bobby Cox	35.00
BH6	Davey Lopes	25.00
BH7	Tony LaRussa	30.00
BH8	Don Baylor	35.00
BH9	Larry Rothschild	25.00
BH10	Buck Showalter	30.00
BH11	Davey Johnson	30.00
BH12	Felipe Alou	30.00
BH13	Charlie Manuel	25.00
BH14	Lou Piniella	30.00
BH15	John Boles	25.00
BH16	Bobby Valentine	30.00
BH17	Mike Hargrove	25.00
BH18	Bruce Bochy	25.00
BH19	Terry Francona	25.00
BH20	Gene Lamont	25.00
BH21	Johnny Oates	25.00
BH22	Jimy Williams	25.00
BH23	Jack McKeon	25.00
BH24	Buddy Bell	25.00
BH25	Tony Muser	25.00
BH26	Phil Garner	25.00
BH27	Tom Kelly	25.00
BH28	Jerry Manuel	25.00

Before There Was Topps

Lou Gehrig

NM/M

	Complete Set (10):	20.00
	Common Player:	1.50
	Inserted 1:25	
BT1	Lou Gehrig	4.00
BT2	Babe Ruth	5.00
BT3	Cy Young	2.00
BT4	Walter Johnson	2.00
BT5	Ty Cobb	4.00
BT6	Tris Speaker	1.50
BT7	Honus Wagner	2.00
BT8	Christy Mathewson	1.50
BT9	Grover Alexander	1.50
BT0	Joe DiMaggio	4.00

Combos

LATIN HEAT

VLADIMIR GUERRERO — ROBERTO CLEMENTE

NM/M

	Complete Set (20):	25.00
	Common Player:	1.50
	Inserted 1:12	

1	Yogi Berra, Whitey Ford, Reggie Jackson, Don Mattingly, Derek Jeter		3.00
2	Brooks Robinson, Cal Ripken Jr.		3.00
3	Barry Bonds, Willie Mays		3.00
4	Bob Gibson, Pedro Martinez		1.50
5	Ivan Rodriguez, Johnny Bench		2.00
6	Ernie Banks, Alex Rodriguez		2.50
7	Joe Morgan, Ken Griffey Jr., Barry Larkin, Johnny Bench		2.50
8	Vladimir Guerrero, Roberto Clemente		2.50
9	Ted Williams, Carl Yastrzemski, Nomar Garciaparra		3.00
10	Joe Torre, Casey Stengel		1.50
11	Kevin Brown, Sandy Koufax, Don Drysdale		3.00
12	Mark McGwire, Sammy Sosa, Roger Maris, Babe Ruth		3.00
13	Ted Williams, Carl Yastrzemski, Nomar Garciaparra		3.00
14	Greg Maddux, Roger Clemens, Cy Young		2.00
15	Tony Gwynn, Ted Williams		3.00
16	Cal Ripken Jr., Lou Gehrig		4.00
17	Sandy Koufax, Randy Johnson, Warren Spahn, Steve Carlton		3.00
18	Mike Piazza, Josh Gibson		2.00
19	Barry Bonds, Willie Mays		3.00
20	Jackie Robinson, Larry Doby		2.50

Golden Anniversary

GOLD NUGGETS

CAL RIPKEN

NM/M

	Complete Set (50):	60.00
	Common Player:	.50
	Inserted 1:10	
1	Hank Aaron	3.00
2	Ernie Banks	1.50
3	Mike Schmidt	3.00
4	Willie Mays	4.00
5	Johnny Bench	1.50
6	Tom Seaver	1.00
7	Frank Robinson	1.00
8	Sandy Koufax	3.00
9	Bob Gibson	1.00
10	Ted Williams	4.00
11	Cal Ripken Jr.	5.00
12	Tony Gwynn	1.50
13	Mark McGwire	3.00
14	Ken Griffey Jr.	2.00
15	Greg Maddux	2.00
16	Roger Clemens	3.00
17	Barry Bonds	4.00
18	Rickey Henderson	.75
19	Mike Piazza	2.00
20	Jose Canseco	1.00
21	Derek Jeter	4.00
22	Nomar Garciaparra	3.00
23	Alex Rodriguez	3.00
24	Sammy Sosa	2.50
25	Ivan Rodriguez	1.00
26	Vladimir Guerrero	1.50
27	Chipper Jones	2.00
28	Jeff Bagwell	1.50
29	Pedro Martinez	1.50
30	Randy Johnson	1.50
31	Pat Burrell	1.00
32	Josh Hamilton	.50
33	Nick Johnson	.50
34	Corey Patterson	.50
35	Eric Munson	.50
36	Sean Burroughs	.50
37	Alfonso Soriano	1.50
38	Chin-Feng Chen	.50
39	Barry Zito	.75
40	Adrian Gonzalez	.50
41	Mark McGwire	3.00
42	Nomar Garciaparra	3.00
43	Todd Helton	1.00
44	Matt Williams	.50
45	Troy Glaus	.75
46	Geoff Jenkins	.50
47	Frank Thomas	1.00
48	Mo Vaughn	.50
49	Barry Larkin	.75
50	J.D. Drew	.50

Hit Parade

		NM/M
Complete Set (6):		
Common Player:		25.00
1:2,600 Retail		
HP1	Reggie Jackson	40.00
HP2	Dave Winfield	25.00
HP3	Eddie Murray	25.00
HP4	Rickey Henderson	25.00
HP5	Robin Yount	25.00
HP6	Carl Yastrzemski	65.00

2001 Topps Home Team Advantage

	NM/M
Common Player:	
Star:	+25 Percent

(See 2001 Topps for checklist and base card values.)

King of Kings

		NM/M
Common Card:		25.00
Inserted 1:2,056		
1	Hank Aaron	75.00
2	Nolan Ryan	75.00
3	Rickey Henderson	30.00
5	Bob Gibson	25.00
6	Nolan Ryan	75.00

King of Kings Golden Edition

	NM/M
Production 50 cards.	
KKGE Hank Aaron, Nolan Ryan, Rickey Henderson	250.00

Noteworthy

		NM/M
Complete Set (50):		40.00
Common Player:		.50
Inserted 1:8		
TN1	Mark McGwire	2.00
TN2	Derek Jeter	2.50
TN3	Sammy Sosa	2.00
TN4	Todd Helton	1.00
TN5	Alex Rodriguez	2.00
TN6	Chipper Jones	1.50
TN7	Barry Bonds	3.00
TN8	Ken Griffey Jr.	1.50
TN9	Nomar Garciaparra	2.00
TN10	Frank Thomas	1.00
TN11	Randy Johnson	1.00
TN12	Cal Ripken Jr.	3.00
TN13	Mike Piazza	1.50
TN14	Ivan Rodriguez	1.00
TN15	Jeff Bagwell	1.00
TN16	Vladimir Guerrero	1.00
TN17	Greg Maddux	1.50
TN18	Tony Gwynn	1.00
TN19	Larry Walker	.50
TN20	Juan Gonzalez	.75
TN21	Scott Rolen	1.00
TN22	Jason Giambi	1.00
TN23	Jeff Kent	.50
TN24	Pat Burrell	.75
TN25	Pedro Martinez	1.00
TN26	Willie Mays	2.00
TN27	Whitey Ford	.75
TN28	Jackie Robinson	2.00
TN29	Ted Williams	2.50
TN30	Babe Ruth	3.00
TN31	Warren Spahn	1.00
TN32	Nolan Ryan	3.00
TN33	Yogi Berra	1.00
TN34	Mike Schmidt	2.00
TN35	Steve Carlton	.75
TN36	Brooks Robinson	1.00
TN37	Bob Gibson	1.00
TN38	Reggie Jackson	1.50
TN39	Johnny Bench	1.50
TN40	Ernie Banks	1.00
TN41	Eddie Mathews	.50
TN42	Don Mattingly	2.50
TN43	Duke Snider	.75
TN44	Hank Aaron	2.00
TN45	Roberto Clemente	2.00
TN46	Harmon Killebrew	1.00
TN47	Frank Robinson	1.00
TN48	Stan Musial	2.00
TN49	Lou Brock	.50
TN50	Joe Morgan	.50

Originals

		NM/M
Common Player:		10.00
Series 1 1:1,172		
Series 2 1:1,023		
1	Roberto Clemente/1955	80.00
2	Carl Yastrzemski/1960	30.00
3	Mike Schmidt/1974	30.00
4	Wade Boggs/1983	10.00
5	Chipper Jones/1991	15.00
6	Willie Mays	40.00
7	Lou Brock	15.00
8	Dave Parker	10.00
9	Barry Bonds	40.00
10	Alex Rodriguez	25.00

The Shot Heard Round The World Autograph

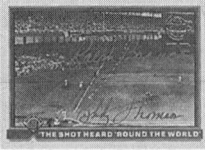

	NM/M
B. Thomson/R. Branca	
Ralph Branca,	
Bobby Thomson	40.00

Through the Years

		NM/M
Complete Set (50):		100.00
Common Player:		1.50
Inserted 1:8		
1	Yogi Berra	2.00
2	Roy Campanella	2.00
3	Willie Mays	5.00
4	Andy Pafko	1.50
5	Jackie Robinson	4.00
6	Stan Musial	4.00
7	Duke Snider	2.00
8	Warren Spahn	2.50
9	Ted Williams	6.00
10	Eddie Matthews	2.00
11	Willie McCovey	1.50
12	Frank Robinson	2.00
13	Ernie Banks	3.00
14	Hank Aaron	5.00
15	Sandy Koufax	4.00
16	Bob Gibson	2.00
17	Harmon Killebrew	2.00
18	Whitey Ford	2.00
19	Roberto Clemente	5.00
20	Juan Marichal	1.50
21	Johnny Bench	3.00
22	Willie Stargell	1.50
23	Joe Morgan	1.50
24	Carl Yastrzemski	2.00
25	Reggie Jackson	2.00
26	Tom Seaver	2.00
27	Steve Carlton	1.50
28	Jim Palmer	1.50
29	Rod Carew	1.50
30	George Brett	5.00
31	Roger Clemens	4.00
32	Don Mattingly	5.00
33	Ryne Sandberg	3.00
34	Mike Schmidt	3.00
35	Cal Ripken Jr.	6.00
36	Tony Gwynn	2.00
37	Ozzie Smith	3.00
38	Wade Boggs	1.50
39	Nolan Ryan	6.00
40	Robin Yount	2.00
41	Mark McGwire	5.00
42	Ken Griffey Jr.	4.00
43	Sammy Sosa	4.00
44	Alex Rodriguez	4.00
45	Barry Bonds	6.00
46	Mike Piazza	3.00
47	Chipper Jones	3.00
48	Greg Maddux	3.00
49	Nomar Garciaparra	4.00
50	Derek Jeter	5.00

Two of a Kind

		NM/M
Inserted 1:30,167		
TK	Bo Jackson, Deion Sanders	75.00

What Could've Been

		NM/M
Complete Set (10):		15.00
Common Player:		1.00
Inserted 1:25		
WCB1	Josh Gibson	3.00
WCB2	Leroy "Satchel" Paige	4.00
WCB3	Walter "Buck" Leonard	2.00

WCB4	James "Cool Papa" Bell	2.00
WCB5	Andrew "Rube" Foster	2.00
WCB6	Martin Dihigo	1.00
WCB7	William "Judy" Johnson	1.50
WCB8	Mule Suttles	1.00
WCB9	Ray Dandridge	1.00
WCB10	John Henry "Pop" Lloyd	2.00

2001 Topps Traded & Rookies

		NM/M
Complete Topps Set (265):		140.00
Common Player:		.10
Chrome Cards:		2-3X
Pack (8 + 2 Chrome):		8.00
Box (24):		175.00
T1	Sandy Alomar Jr.	.10
T2	Kevin Appier	.10
T3	Brad Ausmus	.10
T4	Derek Bell	.10
T5	Bret Boone	.15
T6	Rico Brogna	.10
T7	Ellis Burks	.10
T8	Ken Caminiti	.10
T9	Roger Cedeno	.10
T10	Royce Clayton	.10
T11	Enrique Wilson	.10
T12	Rheal Cormier	.10
T13	Eric Davis	.10
T14	Shawon Duston	.10
T15	Andres Galarraga	.15
T16	Tom Gordon	.10
T17	Mark Grace	.50
T18	Jeffrey Hammonds	.10
T19	Dustin Hermanson	.10
T20	Quinton McCracken	.10
T21	Todd Hundley	.10
T22	Charles Johnson	.10
T23	Marquis Grissom	.10
T24	Jose Mesa	.10
T25	Terry Mulholland	.10
T26	John Rocker	.10
T27	Jeff Frye	.10
T28	Reggie Sanders	.10
T29	David Segui	.10
T30	Mike Sirotka	.10
T31	Fernando Tatis	.10
T32	Steve Trachsel	.10
T33	Ismael Valdes	.10
T34	Randy Velarde	.10
T35	Brian Boehringer	.10
T36	Mike Bordick	.10
T37	Ken Bottenfield	.10
T38	Pat Rapp	.10
T39	Jeff Nelson	.10
T40	Ricky Bottalico	.10
T41	Deion Sanders	.25
T42	Hideo Nomo	.25
T43	Bill Mueller	.10
T44	Roberto Kelly	.10
T45	Chris Holt	.10
T46	Mike Jackson	.10
T47	Devon White	.10
T48	Gerald Williams	.10
T49	Eddie Taubensee	.10
T50	Brian Hunter	.10
T51	Nelson Cruz	.10
T52	Jeff Fassero	.10
T53	Bubba Trammell	.10
T54	Bo Porter	.10
T55	Greg Norton	.10
T56	Benito Santiago	.10
T57	Ruben Rivera	.10
T58	Dee Brown	.10
T59	Jose Canseco	.50
T60	Chris Michalak	.10
T61	Tim Worrell	.10
T62	Matt Clement	.10
T63	Bill Pulsipher	.10
T64	Troy Brohawn	.10
T65	Mark Kotsay	.10
T66	Jose Lima	.10
T67	Shea Hillenbrand	.10
T68	Ted Lilly	.10
T69	Jermaine Dye	.25
T70	Jerry Hairston Jr.	.10
T71	John Mabry	.10
T72	Kurt Abbott	.10
T73	Eric Owens	.10
T74	Jeff Brantley	.10
T75	Vinny Castilla	.10
T76	Ron Villone	.10

T77	Ricky Henderson	.40
T78	Jason Grimsley	.10
T79	Christian Parker RC	.10
T80	Donnie Wall	.10
T81	Alex Arias	.10
T82	Willis Roberts	.10
T83	Ryan Minor	.10
T84	Jason LaRue	.10
T85	Ruben Sierra	.10
T86	Johnny Damon	.75
T87	Juan Gonzalez	.40
T88	Mac Suzuki	.10
T89	Tony Batista	.10
T90	Jay Witasick	.10
T91	Brent Abernathy	.10
T92	Paul LoDuca	.10
T93	Wes Helms	.10
T94	Milton Bradley	.10
T95	Matt LeCroy	.10
T96	A.J. Hinch	.10
T97	Bud Smith RC	.10
T98	Adam Dunn	.50
T99	Albert Pujols, Ichiro Suzuki	15.00
T100	Carlton Fisk	.25
T101	Tim Raines	.25
T102	Juan Marichal	.25
T103	Dave Winfield	.50
T104	Reggie Jackson	1.00
T105	Cal Ripken Jr.	3.00
T106	Ozzie Smith	1.00
T107	Tom Seaver	1.00
T108	Lou Piniella	.25
T109	Dwight Gooden	.25
T110	Bret Saberhagen	.25
T111	Gary Carter	.25
T112	Jack Clark	.25
T113	Rickey Henderson	.75
T114	Barry Bonds	3.00
T115	Bobby Bonilla	.25
T116	Jose Canseco	.50
T117	Will Clark	.50
T118	Andres Galarraga	.25
T119	Bo Jackson	.50
T120	Wally Joyner	.25
T121	Ellis Burks	.25
T122	David Cone	.25
T123	Greg Maddux	1.00
T124	Willie Randolph	.25
T125	Dennis Eckersley	.25
T126	Matt Williams	.40
T127	Joe Morgan	.50
T128	Fred McGriff	.40
T129	Roberto Alomar	.50
T130	Lee Smith	.25
T131	David Wells	.25
T132	Ken Griffey Jr.	2.00
T133	Deion Sanders	.50
T134	Nolan Ryan	2.00
T135	David Justice	.25
T136	Joe Carter	.25
T137	Jack Morris	.25
T138	Mike Piazza	1.50
T139	Barry Bonds	2.00
T140	Terrence Long	.10
T141	Ben Grieve	.10
T142	Richie Sexson	.25
T143	Sean Burroughs	.10
T144	Alfonso Soriano	.50
T145	Bob Boone	.10
T146	Larry Bowa	.10
T147	Bob Brenly	.10
T148	Buck Martinez	.10
T149	Lloyd McClendon	.10
T150	Jim Tracy	.10
T151	Jared Abruzzo RC	.50
T152	Kurt Ainsworth	.10
T153	Willie Bloomquist	.10
T154	Ben Broussard	.10
T155	Bobby Bradley	.10
T156	Mike Bynum	.10
T157	Ken Harvey	.10
T158	Ryan Christianson	.10
T159	Ryan Kohlmeier	.10
T160	Joe Crede	.50
T161	Jack Cust	.10
T162	Ben Diggins	.10
T163	Phil Dumatrait	.10
T164	Alex Escobar	.10
T165	Miguel Olivo	.10
T166	Chris George	.10
T167	Marcus Giles	.10
T168	Keith Ginter	.10
T169	Josh Girdley	.10
T170	Tony Alvarez	.10
T171	Scott Seabol	.10
T172	Josh Hamilton	.50
T173	Jason Hart	.10
T174	Israel Alcantara	.10
T175	Jake Peavy	2.50
T176	Stubby Clapp RC	.40
T177	D'Angelo Jimenez	.10
T178	Nick Johnson	.10
T179	Ben Johnson	.10
T180	Larry Bigbie	.10
T181	Allen Levrault	.10
T182	Felipe Lopez	.10
T183	Sean Burnett	.10
T184	Nick Neugebauer	.10
T185	Austin Kearns	.25
T186	Corey Patterson	.25
T187	Carlos Pena	.25
T188	Ricardo Rodriguez RC	.50
T189	Juan Rivera	.10
T190	Grant Roberts	.10
T191	Adam Pettyjohn RC	.25

T192	Jared Sandberg	.10
T193	Xavier Nady	.25
T194	Dane Sardinha	.10
T195	Shawn Sonnier	.10
T196	Rafael Soriano	.25
T197	Brian Specht RC	.25
T198	Aaron Myette	.10
T199	Juan Uribe RC	.40
T200	Jayson Werth	.10
T201	Brad Wilkerson	.10
T202	Horacio Estrada	.10
T203	Joel Pineiro	.10
T204	Matt LeCroy	.10
T205	Michael Coleman	.10
T206	Ben Sheets	.40
T207	Eric Byrnes	.10
T208	Sean Burroughs	.10
T209	Ken Harvey	.10
T210	Travis Hafner	2.00
T211	Erick Almonte	.10
T212	Jason Belcher RC	.50
T213	Wilson Betemit RC	.75
T214	Hank Blalock RC	2.00
T215	Danny Borrell	.10
T216	John Buck RC	.50
T217	Freddie Bynum RC	.50
T218	Noel Devarez RC	.25
T219	Juan Diaz RC	.25
T220	Felix Diaz RC	.25
T221	Josh Fogg RC	.50
T222	Matt Ford RC	.25
T223	Scott Heard	.10
T224	Ben Hendrickson RC	.25
T225	Cody Ross RC	.50
T226	Adrian Hernandez RC	.40
T227	Alfredo Amezaga RC	.50
T228	Bob Keppel RC	.25
T229	Ryan Madson RC	.75
T230	Octavio Martinez RC	.25
T231	Hee Seop Choi	.40
T232	Thomas Mitchell	.10
T233	Luis Montanez	.10
T234	Andy Morales RC	.40
T235	Justin Morneau RC	5.00
T236	Greg "Toe" Nash RC	.25
T237	Valentino Pasucci RC	.25
T238	Roy Smith RC	.40
T239	Antonio Perez RC	.40
T240	Chad Petty RC	.50
T241	Steve Smyth	.10
T242	Jose Reyes RC	15.00
T243	Eric Reynolds RC	.40
T244	Dominic Rich	.10
T245	Jason Richardson RC	.25
T246	Ed Rogers RC	.40
T247	Albert Pujols RC	40.00
T248	Esix Snead RC	.25
T249	Luis Torres RC	.25
T250	Matt White RC	.40
T251	Blake Williams	.10
T252	Chris Russ	.10
T253	Joe Kennedy RC	.25
T254	Jeff Randazzo RC	.25
T255	Beau Hale RC	.25
256	Brad Hennessey RC	.25
257	Jake Gautreau RC	.25
258	Jeff Mathis RC	.50
259	Aaron Heilman RC	.50
260	Bronson Sardinha RC	.50
261	Irvin Guzman RC	3.00
262	Gabe Gross RC	.50
263	J.D. Martin RC	.40
264	Chris Smith RC	.25
265	Kenny Baugh RC	.40

Autographs

		NM/M
Common Autograph:		15.00
JD	Johnny Damon	30.00
MM	Mike Mussina	25.00

Dual-Traded Relics

		NM/M
Common Player:		4.00
DB	Derek Bell	4.00
MG	Mark Grace	10.00
BG	Ben Grieve	4.00

DH	Dustin Hermanson	4.00
MR	Manny Ramirez	15.00

Farewell Dual Relic

		NM/M
Inserted 1:4,693		
RG	Cal Ripken, Tony Gwynn	80.00

Hall of Fame Relics

		NM/M
Complete Set (1):		
PW	Kirby Puckett,	
	Dave Winfield	40.00

Legends Autographs

		NM/M
Common Player:		
TT51	Ralph Branca	15.00
TTF47	Frank Howard	25.00
TTF50	Mickey Lolich	15.00
TT37	Tug McGraw	15.00
TT48F	Bobby Richardson	20.00
TT36F	Enos Slaughter	25.00
TT13	Warren Spahn	40.00
TT43	Bobby Thomson	20.00

Relics

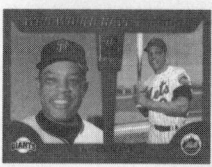

		NM/M
Common Player:		4.00
Inserted 1:29		
SA	Sandy Alomar Jr.	4.00
DB	Derek Bell	4.00
BB	Bobby Bonilla	4.00
BB	Bret Boone	4.00
RB	Rico Brogna	4.00
KC	Ken Caminiti	4.00
JC	Jose Canseco	8.00
ROC	Roger Cedeno	4.00
RSC	Royce Clayton	4.00
JD	Johnny Damon	10.00
ED	Eric Davis	4.00
JD	Jermaine Dye	4.00
AG	Andres Galarraga	4.00
RG	Ron Gant	4.00
JG	Juan Gonzalez	6.00
MG	Mark Grace	8.00
MG	Marquis Grissom	4.00
JH	Jeffrey Hammonds	4.00
MH	Mike Hampton	4.00
DH	Dustin Hermanson	4.00
TH	Todd Hundley	4.00
CJ	Charles Johnson	4.00
FM	Fred McGriff	5.00

BM	Bill Mueller	4.00
DN	Denny Neagle	4.00
HR	Hideo Nomo	25.00
NP	Neifi Perez	4.00
TR	Tim Raines	4.00
RS	Ruben Sierra	4.00
MS	Matt Stairs	4.00
KS	Kelly Stinnett	4.00
FT	Fernando Tatis	4.00
DW	David Wells	4.00
GW	Gerald Williams	4.00
EW	Enrique Wilson	4.00

Rookie Relics

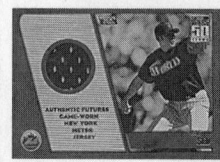

		NM/M
Common Player:		4.00
Inserted 1:91		
AP	Albert Pujols	150.00
TS	Tsuyoshi Shinjo	4.00
AB	Angel Berroa	6.00
BO	Bill Ortega	4.00
HC	Humberto Cota	4.00
JL	Jason Lane	4.00
JS	Jamal Strong	4.00
JV	Jose Valverde	4.00
JY	Jason Young	4.00
NC	Nate Cornejo	4.00
NN	Nick Neugebauer	4.00
PF	Pedro Feliz	4.00
RS	Richard Stahl	4.00
SB	Sean Burroughs	4.00
SS	Jae Weong Seo	4.00
WB	Wilson Betemit	8.00
WR	Wilken Ruan	4.00

Who Would Have Thought

		NM/M
Complete Set (20):		15.00
Common Player:		.75
Inserted 1:8		
WWH1	Nolan Ryan	3.00
WWH2	Ozzie Smith	1.50
WWH3	Tom Seaver	1.50
WWH4	Steve Carlton	.75
WWH5	Reggie Jackson	1.50
WWH6	Frank Robinson	1.00
WWH7	Keith Hernandez	.75
WWH8	Andre Dawson	.75
WWH9	Lou Brock	.75
WWH10	Dennis Eckersley	.75
WWH11	Dave Winfield	1.00
WWH12	Rod Carew	1.00
WWH13	Willie Randolph	.75
WWH14	Doc Gooden	.75
WWH15	Carlton Fisk	1.00
WWH16	Dale Murphy	.75
WWH17	Paul Molitor	.75
WWH18	Gary Carter	.75
WWH19	Wade Boggs	1.00
WWH20	Willie Mays	1.50

2001 Topps American Pie

		NM/M
Complete Set (150):		30.00
Common Player:		.20
Pack (5):		3.00

Box (24):		50.00
1	Al Kaline	.40
2	Al Oliver	.20
3	Andre Dawson	.20
4	Bert Blyleven	.20
5	Bill Buckner	.20
6	Bill Mazeroski	.20
7	Bob Gibson	.50
8	Bill Freeman	.20
9	Bobby Grich	.20
10	Bobby Murcer	.20
11	Bobby Richardson	.20
12	Boog Powell	.20
13	Brooks Robinson	.50
14	Carl Yastrzemski	.75
15	Carlton Fisk	.40
16	Clete Boyer	.20
17	Curt Flood	.20
18	Dale Murphy	.30
19	Tony Conigliaro	.20
20	Dave Parker	.50
21	Dave Winfield	.50
22	Dick Allen	.20
23	Dick Groat	.20
24	Don Drysdale	.50
25	Don Sutton	.20
26	Dwight Evans	.20
27	Eddie Mathews	.75
28	Elston Howard	.20
29	Frank Howard	.50
30	Frank Robinson	.50
31	Fred Lynn	.20
32	Gary Carter	.20
33	Gaylord Perry	.20
34	Norm Cash	.20
35	George Brett	1.50
36	George Foster	.20
37	Goose Gossage	.20
38	Graig Nettles	.20
39	Greg Luzinski	.20
40	Harmon Killebrew	.75
41	Jack Clark	.20
42	Jack Morris	.20
43	Jim Wynn	.20
44	Jim Kaat	.20
45	Jim Palmer	.20
46	Joe Pepitone	.20
47	Joe Rudi	.20
48	Johnny Bench	1.00
49	Juan Marichal	.40
50	Keith Hernandez	.20
51	Bucky Dent	.20
52	Lou Brock	.40
53	Ron Cey	.20
54	Luis Aparicio	.20
55	Luis Tiant	.20
56	Mark Fidrych	.20
57	Maury Wills	.20
58	Mickey Lolich	.20
59	Mickey Rivers	.20
60	Mike Schmidt	1.00
61	Moose Skowron	.20
62	Nolan Ryan	3.00
63	Orlando Cepeda	.20
64	Ozzie Smith	.75
65	Phil Niekro	.20
66	Reggie Jackson	.75
67	Reggie Smith	.20
68	Rico Carty	.20
69	Roberto Clemente	2.00
70	Robin Yount	.75
71	Roger Maris	1.50
72	Rollie Fingers	.20
73	Ron Guidry	.20
74	Ron Santo	.20
75	Ron Swoboda	.20
76	Sal Bando	.20
77	Sam McDowell	.20
78	Steve Carlton	.40
79	Thurman Munson	1.00
80	Tim McCarver	.20
81	Tom Seaver	.75
82	Mike Cuellar	.20
83	Tony Kubek	.20
84	Tommy John	.20
85	Tony Perez	.20
86	Tug McGraw	.20
87	Vida Blue	.20
88	Warren Spahn	.75
89	Whitey Ford	.50
90	Willie Mays	2.00
91	Willie McCovey	.50
92	Willie Stargell	.50
93	Yogi Berra	1.00
94	Stan Musial	1.00
95	Jim Piersall	.20
96	Duke Snider	.50
97	Bruce Sutter	.30
98	Dave Concepcion	.20
99	Darrell Evans	.20
100	Dennis Eckersley	.40
101	Hoyt Wilhelm	.20
102	Minnie Minoso	.20
103	Don Newcombe	.20
104	Richie Ashburn	.20
105	Alan Trammell	.20
106	Jim "Catfish" Hunter	.20
107	Lou Whitaker	.20
108	Johnny Podres	.20
109	Denny Martinez	.20
110	Willie Horton	.20
111	Dean Chance	.20
112	Fergie Jenkins	.20
113	Cecil Cooper	.20
114	Rick Reuschel	.20
115	Space Race	.20
116	Man On The Moon	.50
117		
118	Woodstock	.50
119	Peace Movement/ Flower Power	.20
120	N.Y. Worlds Fair	.20
121	Vietnam War	.20
122	Vietnam Cease Fire	.20
123	Kennedy Elected President	.50
124	Kennedy Assassination	.20
125	Malcom X	.20
126	Nixon Elected President	.20
127	Watergate	.20
128	Nixon Resigns	.20
129	Cuban Missile Crisis	.20
130	Astrodome	.20
131	Secretariat	.20
132	Lyndon Johnson Signs Civil Rights Bill	.20
133	Atomic Bomb Test Ban Treaty	.20
134	Bi Centennial	.20
135	String Bikini	.20
136	Birth Control Pill	.20
137	Studio 54	.20
138	Motown	.20
139	Microsoft Started	.20
140	Internet Developed	.20
141	John F. Kennedy	1.50
142	Marilyn Monroe	1.50
143	Elvis Presley	1.50
144	Jimi Hendrix	1.00
145	Arthur Ashe	.20
146	Richard Nixon	.20
147	James Dean	.20
148	Janis Joplin	.50
149	Frank Sinatra	1.00
150	Malcom X	.50

Autoproofs Baseball Legends

No pricing due to scarcity.
Production 25 Sets

Decade Leaders

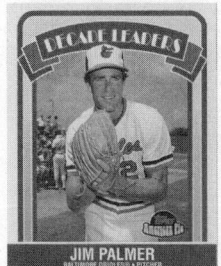

Caption: JIM PALMER — BALTIMORE ORIOLES • PITCHER — 1970s WINS LEADER

		NM/M
Complete Set (10):		15.00
Common Player:		1.00
Inserted 1:12		
DL1	Willie Stargell	1.50
DL2	Harmon Killebrew	1.50
DL3	Johnny Bench	2.00
DL4	Hank Aaron	3.00
DL5	Rod Carew	1.00
DL6	Roberto Clemente	3.00
DL7	Nolan Ryan	4.00
DL8	Bob Gibson	1.50
DL9	Jim Palmer	1.00
DL10	Juan Marichal	1.00

Entertainment Stars

		NM/M
Production 500 Sets		
1	Lou Ferrigno (Incredible Hulk)	50.00
2	Adam West (Batman)	60.00
3	Danny Bonaduce (Partridge Family)	30.00

Legends Autographs

Caption: WILLIE MAYS

	NM/M
Common Player:	10.00

Inserted 1:211		
TT1R	Willie Mays	100.00
TT14R	Johnny Bench	60.00
TT48R	Bobby Richardson	20.00
TT8R	Carl Yastrzemski	50.00
TT13R	Warren Spahn	25.00
TT15R	Reggie Jackson	50.00
TT18R	Bob Gibson	20.00
TT25R	Luis Tiant	10.00
TT29R	Moose Skowron	10.00
TT31R	Clete Boyer	10.00
TT33R	Vida Blue	15.00
TT35R	Joe Pepitone	10.00
TT37R	Tug McGraw	15.00
TT47R	Frank Howard	10.00
TT49R	Tony Kubek	40.00
TT50R	Mickey Lolich	10.00

Piece of American Pie Relics

Caption: AMERICAN PIE — ELVIS PRESLEY — THE KING OF ROCK 'N' ROLL

	NM/M
Common Card:	10.00
Inserted 1:29	
PAPM1 Frank Sinatra	60.00
PAPM2 JFK/Berlin Wall	10.00
PAPM3 Elvis Presley	100.00
PAPM4 Janis Joplin	90.00

Profiles In Courage

Caption: PROFILES IN ... — NEW YORK METS — TOM SEAVER

		NM/M
Complete Set (20):		25.00
Common Player:		1.00
Inserted 1:8		
PIC1	Roger Maris	2.00
PIC2	Lou Brock	1.00
PIC3	Brooks Robinson	1.50
PIC4	Carl Yastrzemski	1.50
PIC5	Mike Schmidt	2.50
PIC6	Hank Aaron	3.00
PIC7	Tom Seaver	1.50
PIC8	Willie Mays	3.00
PIC9	Graig Nettles	1.00
PIC10	Frank Robinson	1.50
PIC11	Rollie Fingers	1.00
PIC12	Tony Perez	1.00
PIC13	George Brett	3.00
PIC14	Robin Yount	1.50
PIC15	Nolan Ryan	4.00
PIC16	Warren Spahn	1.50
PIC17	Johnny Bench	2.00
PIC18	Vida Blue	1.00
PIC19	Roberto Clemente	3.00
PIC20	Thurman Munson	2.00

Rookie Reprint Relics

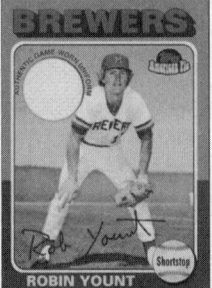

Caption: BREWERS — ROBIN YOUNT — Shortstop

NM/M

Common Player:		10.00
Inserted 1:116		
JB	Johnny Bench	20.00
GB	George Brett	40.00
SC	Steve Carlton	15.00
GC	Gary Carter	10.00
AD	Andre Dawson	10.00
DE	Dennis Eckersley	10.00
MF	Mark Fidrych	10.00
BG	Bobby Grich	10.00
RJ	Reggie Jackson	15.00
JK	Jim Kaat	10.00
TMC	Tim McCarver	10.00
TM	Thurman Munson	35.00
BM	Bobby Murcer	10.00
AO	Al Oliver	10.00
BP	Boog Powell	10.00
OS	Ozzie Smith	20.00
DS	Don Sutton	10.00
DW	Dave Winfield	10.00
RY	Robin Yount	20.00

Timeless Classics Relics

Caption: Dave Winfield

	NM/M
Common Player:	8.00
Inserted 1:80	
Sam McDowell	8.00
Frank Howard	8.00
Dick Groat	8.00
Roger Maris	50.00
Orlando Cepeda	10.00
Willie Mays	40.00
Carl Yastrzemski	30.00
Roberto Clemente	60.00
Harmon Killebrew	20.00
Brooks Robinson	20.00
Tony Conigliaro	15.00
Frank Robinson	15.00
Hank Aaron	40.00
Willie McCovey	15.00
Rico Carty	8.00
Johnny Bench	20.00
Willie Stargell	15.00
Steve Carlton	15.00
Norm Cash	8.00
Reggie Jackson	15.00
Mike Schmidt	30.00
Mickey Rivers	8.00
Tom Seaver	20.00
George Brett	40.00
George Foster	8.00
Graig Nettles	8.00
Nolan Ryan	40.00
Dave Parker	10.00
Dick Allen	8.00
Fred Lynn	8.00
Keith Hernandez	8.00
Dave Winfield	15.00

Woodstock Relics

		NM/M
Common Player:		8.00
Inserted 1:138		
GB	George Brett	40.00
BB	Bill Buckner	8.00
OC	Orlando Cepeda	10.00
DE	Dwight Evans	8.00
CF	Carlton Fisk	15.00
BF	Bill Freehan	8.00
DG	Dick Groat	8.00
RJ	Reggie Jackson	15.00
TK	Ted Kluszewski	8.00
FL	Fred Lynn	8.00
WM	Willie Mays	45.00
SM	Stan Musial	40.00
TP	Tony Perez	8.00
JP	Jimmy Piersall	8.00
BR	Brooks Robinson	15.00
FR	Frank Robinson	15.00
JR	Joe Rudi	8.00
DS	Duke Snider	15.00
WS	Willie Stargell	15.00
MW	Maury Wills	8.00
DW	Dave Winfield	15.00
WS	Woodstock	15.00
JW	Jim Wynn	8.00
CY	Carl Yastrzemski	30.00
RY	Robin Yount	20.00

2001 Topps Archives

		NM/M
Complete Set (450):		150.00
Complete Series 1 (225):		75.00
Complete Series 2 (225):		75.00
Common Player:		.40
Pack (8):		4.50
Box (24):		80.00
1	Johnny Antonelli	.40
2	Yogi Berra	2.50
3	Dom DiMaggio	.40
4	Carl Erskine	.40
5	Joe Garagiola	.50

Roger Maris
OUTFIELD
CLEVELAND INDIANS

6	Monte Irvin	.40
7	Vernon Law	.40
8	Eddie Mathews	2.00
9	Willie Mays	5.00
10	Gil McDougald	.40
11	Andy Pafko	.40
12	Phil Rizzuto	.75
13	Preacher Roe	.40
14	Hank Sauer	.50
15	Bobby Shantz	.40
16	Enos Slaughter	.50
17	Warren Spahn	2.00
18	Mickey Vernon	.40
19	Early Wynn	.40
20	Whitey Ford	1.00
21	Johnny Podres	.40
22	Ernie Banks	2.00
23	Moose Skowron	.40
24	Harmon Killebrew	2.00
25	Ted Williams	6.00
26	Jimmy Piersall	.40
27	Frank Thomas	.40
28	Bill Mazeroski	.50
29	Bobby Richardson	.40
30	Frank Robinson	1.50
31	Stan Musial	3.00
32	Johnny Callison	.40
33	Bob Gibson	2.00
34	Frank Howard	.50
35	Willie McCovey	.40
36	Carl Yastrzemski	2.00
37	Jim Maloney	.40
38	Ron Santo	.40
39	Lou Brock	.75
40	Tim McCarver	.50
41	Joe Pepitone	.40
42	Boog Powell	.50
43	Bill Freehan	.40
44	Dick Allen	.40
45	Willie Horton	.40
46	Mickey Lolich	.40
47	Wilbur Wood	.40
48	Bert Campaneris	.40
49	Rod Carew	1.50
50	Tug McGraw	.40
51	Tony Perez	.75
52	Luis Tiant	.40
53	Bobby Murcer	.40
54	Don Sutton	.75
55	Ken Holtzman	.40
56	Reggie Smith	.40
57	Hal McRae	.40
58	Roy White	.40
59	Reggie Jackson	3.00
60	Graig Nettles	.40
61	Joe Rudi	.40
62	Vida Blue	.50
63	Darrell Evans	.40
64	David Concepcion	.40
65	Bobby Grich	.40
66	Greg Luzinski	.40
67	Cecil Cooper	.40
68	George Hendrick	.40
69	Dwight Evans	.40
70	Gary Matthews	.40
71	Mike Schmidt	3.00
72	Dave Parker	.40
73	Dave Winfield	1.00
74	Gary Carter	.40
75	Dennis Eckersley	.75
76	Kent Tekulve	.40
77	Andre Dawson	.75
78	Denny Martinez	.40
79	Bruce Sutter	.75
80	Jack Morris	.40
81	Ozzie Smith	1.50
82	Lee Smith	.40
83	Don Mattingly	4.00
84	Joe Carter	.40
85	Kirby Puckett	3.00
86	Joe Adcock	.40
87	Gus Bell	.40
88	Roy Campanella	2.00
89	Jackie Jensen	.40
90	Johnny Mize	.75
91	Allie Reynolds	.40
92	Al Rosen	.40
93	Hal Newhouser	.40
94	Harvey Kuenn	.40
95	Nellie Fox	.75
96	Elston Howard	.40
97	Sal Maglie	.40
98	Roger Maris	3.00
99	Norm Cash	.40
100	Thurman Munson	2.50
101	Roy Campanella	1.50
102	Joe Garagiola	.75
103	Dom DiMaggio	.40
104	Johnny Mize	.50
105	Allie Reynolds	.40
106	Preacher Roe	.40
107	Hal Newhouser	.40
108	Monte Irvin	.40
109	Carl Erskine	.40
110	Enos Slaughter	.40
111	Gil McDougald	.40
112	Andy Pafko	.40
113	Sal Maglie	.40
114	Johnny Antonelli	.40
115	Phil Rizzuto	.50
116	Yogi Berra	1.50
117	Early Wynn	.40
118	Mickey Vernon	.40
119	Gus Bell	.40
120	Ted Williams	4.00
121	Frank Thomas	.40
122	Bobby Richardson	.40
123	Whitey Ford	1.00
124	Vernon Law	.40
125	Jimmy Piersall	.40
126	Moose Skowron	.40
127	Joe Adcock	.40
128	Johnny Podres	.40
129	Ernie Banks	1.50
130	Jim Maloney	.40
131	Johnny Callison	.40
132	Eddie Mathews	1.50
133	Joe Pepitone	.40
134	Warren Spahn	1.50
135	Bill Mazeroski	.40
136	Norm Cash	.40
137	Bob Gibson	1.00
138	Harmon Killebrew	1.50
139	Frank Robinson	1.00
140	Ron Santo	.40
141	Hank Sauer	.40
142	Bobby Shantz	.40
143	Nellie Fox	.50
144	Elston Howard	.40
145	Jackie Jensen	.40
146	Al Rosen	.40
147	Dick Allen	.40
148	Bill Freehan	.40
149	Boog Powell	.40
150	Lou Brock	.75
151	Rod Carew	.75
152	Wilbur Wood	.40
153	Thurman Munson	1.50
154	Ken Holtzman	.40
155	Willie Horton	.40
156	Mickey Lolich	.40
157	Tim McCarver	.40
158	Willie McCovey	.40
159	Roy White	.40
160	Bobby Murcer	.40
161	Joe Rudi	.40
162	Reggie Smith	.40
163	Luis Tiant	.40
164	Bert Campaneris	.40
165	Frank Howard	.40
166	Harvey Kuenn	.50
167	Greg Luzinski	.40
168	Tug McGraw	.40
169	Willie Mays	3.00
170	Roger Maris	2.00
171	Vida Blue	.40
172	Bobby Grich	.40
173	Reggie Jackson	2.00
174	Hal McRae	.40
175	Carl Yastrzemski	1.00
176	David Concepcion	.40
177	Cecil Cooper	.40
178	George Hendrick	.40
179	Gary Matthews	.40
180	Stan Musial	2.00
181	Graig Nettles	.40
182	Don Sutton	.50
183	Kent Tekulve	.40
184	Bruce Sutter	.75
185	Darrell Evans	.40
186	Mike Schmidt	2.00
187	Dave Parker	.40
188	Dwight Evans	.40
189	Gary Carter	.40
190	Jack Morris	.40
191	Tony Perez	.50
192	Dave Winfield	.75
193	Andre Dawson	.50
194	Lee Smith	.40
195	Ozzie Smith	1.00
196	Denny Martinez	.40
197	Don Mattingly	2.50
198	Joe Carter	.40
199	Dennis Eckersley	.75
200	Kirby Puckett	2.00
201	Walter Alston	.40
202	Casey Stengel	.75
203	Sparky Anderson	.40
204	Tommy Lasorda	.75
205	Whitey Herzog	.40
206	Harmon Killebrew, Frank Howard, Reggie Jackson	.40
207	Hank Aaron, Early Wynn, Ron Santo, Willie McCovey	2.50
208	Frank Robinson, Harmon Killebrew, Boog Powell	1.50
209	Tony Oliva, Frank Robinson, Frank Howard	.75
210	Hank Aaron, Willie McCovey, Willie Mays, Orlando Cepeda	2.50
211	Hank Aaron, Frank Robinson, Willie Mays, Ernie Banks	2.50
212	Carl Yastrzemski, Harmon Killebrew, Frank Howard	1.50
213	Ernie Banks	1.50
214	Hank Aaron	2.50
215	Willie Mays	2.50
216	Al Kaline	.75
217	Stan Musial	2.00
218	Duke Snider	.75
219	Frank Robinson, Hank Bauer, Frank Robinson	.50
220	Willie Mays, Stan Musial	1.50
221	Whitey Ford	.75
222	Jerry Koosman	.40
223	Bob Gibson	.75
224	Gil Hodges	.40
225	Reggie Jackson	1.50
226	Hank Bauer	.40
227	Ralph Branca	.40
228	Joe Garagiola	.75
229	Bob Feller	2.00
230	Dick Groat	.40
231	George Kell	.40
232	Bob Boone	.40
233	Minnie Minoso	.40
234	Billy Pierce	.40
235	Robin Roberts	.50
236	Johnny Sain	.40
237	Red Schoendienst	.40
238	Curt Simmons	.40
239	Duke Snider	2.00
240	Bobby Thomson	.40
241	Hoyt Wilhelm	.40
242	Elroy Face	.40
243	Ralph Kiner	.75
244	Hank Aaron	4.00
245	Al Kaline	2.00
246	Don Larsen	1.50
247	Tug McGraw	.40
248	Don Newcombe	.75
249	Herb Score	.40
250	Clete Boyer	.40
251	Lindy McDaniel	.40
252	Brooks Robinson	2.50
253	Orlando Cepeda	.60
254	Larry Bowa	.40
255	Mike Cuellar	.40
256	Jim Perry	.40
257	Dave Parker	.40
258	Maury Wills	.40
259	Willie Davis	.40
260	Juan Marichal	.60
261	Jim Bouton	.40
262	Dean Chance	.40
263	Sam McDowell	.40
264	Whitey Ford	3.00
265	Bob Uecker	2.00
266	Willie Stargell	2.00
267	Rico Carty	.40
268	Tommy John	.40
269	Phil Niekro	.60
270	Paul Blair	.40
271	Steve Carlton	3.00
272	Jim Lonborg	.40
273	Tony Perez	.60
274	Ron Swoboda	.40
275	Fergie Jenkins	.75
276	Jim Palmer	1.50
277	Sal Bando	.40
278	Tom Seaver	4.00
279	Johnny Bench	4.00
280	Nolan Ryan	6.00
281	Rollie Fingers	.50
282	Sparky Lyle	.40
283	Al Oliver	.40
284	Bob Watson	.40
285	Bill Buckner	.40
286	Bert Blyleven	.40
287	George Foster	.40
288	Al Hrabosky	.40
289	Cecil Cooper	.40
290	Carlton Fisk	1.00
291	Mickey Rivers	.40
292	Goose Gossage	.40
293	Rick Reuschel	.40
294	Bucky Dent	.40
295	Frank Tanana	.40
296	George Brett	4.00
297	Keith Hernandez	.40
298	Fred Lynn	.40
299	Robin Yount	3.00
300	Ron Guidry	.40
301	Jack Clark	.40
302	Mark Fidrych	.40
303	Dale Murphy	1.50
304	Willie Hernandez	.40
305	Lou Whitaker	.40
306	Kirk Gibson	.75
307	Wade Boggs	3.00
308	Ryne Sandberg	4.00
309	Orel Hershiser	.40
310	Jimmy Key	.40
311	Richie Ashburn	.40
312	Smoky Burgess	.40
313	Gil Hodges	1.50
314	Ted Kluszewski	.40
315	Pee Wee Reese	1.00
316	Jackie Robinson	4.00
317	Harvey Haddix	.40
318	Satchel Paige	3.00
319	Roberto Clemente	5.00
320	Carl Furillo	.40
321	Don Drysdale	2.00
322	Curt Flood	.40
323	Bob Allison	.40
324	Tony Conigliaro	.40
325	Dan Quisenberry	.40
326	Ralph Branca	.40
327	Bob Feller	1.00
328	Satchel Paige	3.00
329	George Kell	.40
330	Pee Wee Reese	1.00
331	Bobby Thomson	.40
332	Carl Furillo	.40
333	Hank Bauer	.40
334	Herb Score	.40
335	Richie Ashburn	.40
336	Billy Pierce	.40
337	Duke Snider	2.00
338	Harvey Haddix	.40
339	Robin Roberts	.40
340	Dick Groat	.40
341	Curt Simmons	.40
342	Bob Uecker	1.00
343	Smoky Burgess	.40
344	Jim Bouton	.40
345	Elroy Face	.40
346	Don Drysdale	1.00
347	Bob Allison	.40
348	Clete Boyer	.40
349	Dean Chance	.40
350	Tony Conigliaro	.40
351	Curt Flood	.40
352	Hoyt Wilhelm	.40
353	Ron Swoboda	.40
354	Roberto Clemente	3.00
355	Tug McGraw	.40
356	Orlando Cepeda	.40
357	Joe Garagiola	.40
358	Juan Marichal	.50
359	Sam McDowell	.40
360	Johnny Sain	.40
361	Ted Kluszewski	.40
362	Al Kaline	2.00
363	Lindy McDaniel	.40
364	Don Newcombe	.40
365	Jim Perry	.40
366	Hank Aaron	4.00
367	Don Larsen	1.00
368	Mike Cuellar	.40
369	Willie Davis	.40
370	Ralph Kiner	.50
371	Minnie Minoso	.40
372	Larry Bowa	.40
373	Brooks Robinson	1.00
374	Bob Boone	.40
375	Jim Lonborg	.40
376	Paul Blair	.40
377	Rico Carty	.40
378	Sal Bando	.40
379	Mark Fidrych	.40
380	Al Hrabosky	.40
381	Willie Stargell	1.00
382	Johnny Bench	2.50
383	Dave Parker	.40
384	Sparky Lyle	.40
385	Fergie Jenkins	.50
386	Jim Palmer	1.00
387	Whitey Ford	2.00
388	Tony Perez	.40
389	Mickey Rivers	.40
390	Bob Watson	.40
391	Rollie Fingers	.40
392	George Foster	.40
393	Al Oliver	.40
394	Tom Seaver	3.00
395	Maury Wills	.40
396	Steve Carlton	1.00
397	Cecil Cooper	.40
398	Bill Buckner	.40
399	Phil Niekro	.40
400	Red Schoendienst	.40
401	Ron Guidry	.40
402	Willie Hernandez	.40
403	Tommy John	.40
404	Gil Hodges	.40
405	Bucky Dent	.40
406	Keith Hernandez	.40
407	Dan Quisenberry	.40
408	Fred Lynn	.40
409	Rick Reuschel	.40
410	Jackie Robinson	3.00
411	Goose Gossage	.40
412	Bert Blyleven	.40
413	Jack Clark	.40
414	Carlton Fisk	.50
415	Dale Murphy	.75
416	Frank Tanana	.40
417	George Brett	3.00
418	Robin Yount	2.50
419	Kirk Gibson	.50
420	Lou Whitaker	.40
421	Ryne Sandberg	2.50
422	Jimmy Key	.40
423	Nolan Ryan	5.00
424	Wade Boggs	.75
425	Orel Hershiser	.40
426	Billy Martin	.40
427	Ralph Houk	.40
428	Chuck Tanner	.40

429	Earl Weaver	.40
430	Leo Durocher	.40
431	Tony Conigliaro, Norm Cash, Willie Horton	.40
432	Ernie Banks, Hank Aaron, Eddie Mathews, Clete Boyer	1.50
433	Norm Cash, Frank Howard, Al Kaline, Jimmy Piersall	.40
434	Goose Gossage, Rollie Fingers	.40
435	Nolan Ryan, Tom Seaver	.40
436	Reggie Jackson, Willie Stargell	.75
437	Johnny Bench, Dick Allen	.75
438	Roger Maris	3.00
439	Carl Yastrzemski	2.00
440	Nolan Ryan	4.00
441	Cincinnati Reds	.75
442	Tony Perez	.40
443	Steve Carlton	.75
444	Wade Boggs	.40
445	Andre Dawson	.40
446	Whitey Ford	1.50
447	Hank Aaron	4.00
448	Bob Gibson	.75
449	Roberto Clemente	4.00
450	Orioles/Jackie Robinson	1.50

Baseball Bucks

NM/M

Valid to 3/02 for Topps merchandise:

TB1	Willie Mays ($1/15,000)	2.00
TB2	Roberto Clemente ($5/1,000)	4.00
TB3	Jackie Robinson ($10/500)	10.00

Autographs

NM/M

Common Player: 10.00
Inserted 1:Box

TAA1	Johnny Antonelli	15.00
TAA2	Hank Bauer	20.00
TAA3	Yogi Berra/50	350.00
TAA4	Ralph Branca	20.00
TAA5	Dom DiMaggio	60.00
TAA6	Joe Garagiola	50.00
TAA7	Carl Erskine	30.00
TAA8	Bob Feller	30.00
TAA10	Dick Groat	50.00
TAA11	Monte Irvin	20.00
TAA12	George Kell	20.00
TAA13	Vernon Law	15.00
TAA14	Bob Boone	10.00
TAA16	Willie Mays/50	500.00
TAA17	Gil McDougald	20.00
TAA18	Minnie Minoso	30.00
TAA19	Andy Pafko	30.00
TAA20	Billy Pierce	10.00
TAA21	Phil Rizzuto/200	120.00
TAA22	Robin Roberts	40.00
TAA23	Preacher Roe	20.00
TAA24	Johnny Sain	25.00
TAA25	Hank Sauer	25.00
TAA26	Red Schoendienst	25.00
TAA27	Bobby Shantz	10.00
TAA28	Curt Simmons	10.00
TAA29	Enos Slaughter	30.00
TAA30	Duke Snider	80.00
TAA31	Warren Spahn	125.00
TAA32	Bobby Thomson	25.00
TAA33	Mickey Vernon	15.00
TAA34	Hoyt Wilhelm	40.00
TAA35	Jim Wynn	10.00
TAA36	Elroy Face	10.00
TAA37	Gaylord Perry	40.00
TAA38	Ralph Kiner	50.00
TAA39	Johnny Podres	20.00
TAA40	Hank Aaron/50	1,400
TAA41	Ernie Banks/50	450.00
TAA42	Al Kaline	150.00
TAA43	Moose Skowron	15.00
TAA44	Don Larsen	200.00
TAA45	Harmon Killebrew	150.00
TAA46	Tug McGraw	35.00
TAA48	Don Newcombe	20.00
TAA49	Jimmy Piersall	20.00
TAA50	Herb Score	20.00
TAA51	Frank Thomas	10.00
TAA52	Clete Boyer	20.00
TAA53	Bill Mazeroski	75.00
TAA54	Lindy McDaniel	15.00
TAA55	Bobby Richardson	15.00
TAA56	Brooks Robinson/SP	200.00
TAA57	Frank Robinson	85.00
TAA58	Orlando Cepeda	80.00
TAA59	Stan Musial/50	300.00
TAA60	Larry Bowa	30.00
TAA61	Johnny Callison	15.00
TAA62	Mike Cuellar	20.00
TAA63	Bob Gibson/SP/50	200.00
TAA64	Jim Perry	15.00
TAA65	Frank Howard	20.00
TAA66	David Palmer	15.00
TAA67	Willie McCovey	100.00
TAA68	Maury Wills	15.00
TAA69	Carl Yastrzemski	220.00
TAA70	Willie Davis	10.00
TAA71	Jim Maloney	10.00
TAA73	Ron Santo	35.00
TAA74	Jim Bouton	30.00
TAA75	Lou Brock/50	200.00
TAA76	Dean Chance	10.00
TAA77	Tim McCarver/200	60.00
TAA78	Sam McDowell	20.00
TAA79	Joe Pepitone	20.00
TAA80	Whitey Ford	140.00
TAA81	Boog Powell	25.00
TAA83	Bill Freehan	10.00
TAA85	Dick Allen	40.00
TAA86	Rico Carty	10.00
TAA87	Willie Horton	10.00
TAA88	Tommy John	15.00
TAA89	Mickey Lolich	10.00
TAA90	Phil Niekro	30.00
TAA91	Wilbur Wood	10.00
TAA92	Paul Blair	10.00
TAA93	Bert Campaneris	10.00
TAA94	Steve Carlton	40.00
TAA96	Jim Lonborg	10.00
TAA97	Luis Aparicio	50.00
TAA98	Tony Perez	40.00
TAA99	Joe Morgan/200	65.00
TAA100	Ron Swoboda	30.00
TAA101	Luis Tiant	15.00
TAA102	Fergie Jenkins	35.00
TAA103	Bobby Murcer	30.00
TAA104	Jim Palmer	80.00
TAA106	Sal Bando	10.00
TAA107	Ken Holtzman	50.00
TAA108	Tom Seaver/50	225.00
TAA110	Johnny Bench	225.00
TAA111	Hal McRae	10.00
TAA112	Nolan Ryan	500.00
TAA113	Roy White	10.00
TAA114	Rollie Fingers	10.00
TAA115	Reggie Jackson/50	225.00
TAA116	Sparky Lyle	15.00
TAA117	Graig Nettles	20.00
TAA118	Al Oliver	10.00
TAA119	Joe Rudi	15.00
TAA120	Bob Watson	10.00
TAA121	Vida Blue	10.00
TAA122	Bill Buckner	10.00
TAA123	Darrell Evans	10.00
TAA124	Bert Blyleven	25.00
TAA125	David Concepcion	20.00
TAA126	George Foster	15.00
TAA127	Bobby Grich	20.00
TAA128	Al Hrabosky	10.00
TAA129	Greg Luzinski	25.00
TAA130	Cecil Cooper	15.00
TAA131	Ron Cey	10.00
TAA132	Carlton Fisk	100.00
TAA133	George Hendrick	10.00
TAA134	Mickey Rivers	10.00
TAA135	Dwight Evans	25.00
TAA136	Goose Gossage	10.00
TAA137	Gary Matthews	10.00
TAA138	Rick Reuschel	10.00
TAA139	Mike Schmidt/SP/50	320.00
TAA140	Bucky Dent	25.00
TAA141	Jim Kaat	25.00
TAA142	Frank Tanana	10.00
TAA143	Dave Winfield/200	100.00
TAA144	George Brett/SP/50	320.00
TAA145	Gary Carter/200	65.00
TAA146	Keith Hernandez	40.00
TAA147	Fred Lynn	40.00
TAA148	Robin Yount/SP/200	150.00
TAA149	Dennis Eckersley/SP/200	120.00
TAA150	Ron Guidry	50.00
TAA151	Kent Tekulve	10.00
TAA152	Jack Clark	10.00
TAA153	Andre Dawson/SP/200	65.00
TAA154	Mark Fidrych	25.00
TAA155	Denny Martinez/SP/200	40.00
TAA156	Dale Murphy	50.00
TAA157	Bruce Sutter	40.00
TAA158	Willie Hernandez	25.00
TAA160	Lou Whitaker	20.00
TAA162	Kirk Gibson	40.00
TAA163	Lee Smith	25.00
TAA164	Wade Boggs	100.00
TAA165	Ryne Sandberg/SP/200	175.00
TAA166	Don Mattingly	150.00
TAA167	Joe Carter/SP/200	50.00
TAA168	Orel Hershiser	50.00
TAA169	Kirby Puckett	160.00
TAA170	Jimmy Key	50.00

Game-Used Bat

NM/M

Common Player:		15.00
1	Johnny Bench	30.00
2	George Brett	50.00
3	Fred Lynn	15.00
4	Reggie Jackson	25.00
5	Mike Schmidt	50.00
6	Willie Stargell	20.00

Game-Used Bat Autograph

NM/M

Common Player: 120.00
Production 25 Sets

1	Johnny Bench	150.00
2	George Brett	200.00
3	Fred Lynn	75.00

Topps Final Autoproof

NM/M

Common Player:	30.00
Carlton Fisk	65.00
Wade Boggs	40.00
Willie Mays	150.00
Willie McCovey	50.00
Jim Palmer	50.00
Robin Roberts	50.00
Duke Snider	50.00
Warren Spahn	60.00
Hoyt Wilhelm	40.00
Carl Yastrzemski	100.00

2001 Topps Archives Reserve

NM/M

Complete Set (100): 90.00

Common Player:		.75
Hobby Pack (5):		8.00
Hobby Box (10 + Auto. Ball):		125.00
1	Joe Adcock	.75
2	Brooks Robinson	3.00
3	Luis Aparicio	.75
4	Richie Ashburn	.75
5	Hank Bauer	.75
6	Johnny Bench	4.00
7	Wade Boggs	2.00
8	Moose Skowron	.75
9	George Brett	5.00
10	Lou Brock	2.00
11	Roy Campanella	4.00
12	Willie Hernandez	.75
13	Steve Carlton	2.00
14	Gary Carter	.75
15	Hoyt Wilhelm	.75
16	Orlando Cepeda	.75
17	Roberto Clemente	8.00
18	Dale Murphy	1.50
19	Dave Concepcion	.75
20	Dom DiMaggio	.75
21	Larry Doby	.75
22	Don Drysdale	4.00
23	Dennis Eckersley	.75
24	Bob Feller	2.00
25	Rollie Fingers	.75
26	Carlton Fisk	2.00
27	Nellie Fox	1.50
28	Mickey Rivers	.75
29	Tommy John	.75
30	Johnny Sain	.75
31	Keith Hernandez	.75
32	Gil Hodges	.75
33	Elston Howard	3.00
34	Frank Howard	.75
35	Bob Gibson	5.00
36	Fergie Jenkins	.75
37	Jackie Jensen	.75
38	Al Kaline	3.00
39	Harmon Killebrew	5.00
40	Ralph Kiner	.75
41	Dick Groat	.75
42	Don Larsen	.75
43	Ralph Branca	.75
44	Mickey Lolich	.75
45	Juan Marichal	3.00
46	Roger Maris	6.00
47	Bobby Thomson	.75
48	Eddie Mathews	4.00
49	Don Mattingly	8.00
50	Willie McCovey	2.00
51	Gil McDougald	.75
52	Tug McGraw	.75
53	Billy Pierce	.75
54	Minnie Minoso	.75
55	Johnny Mize	2.00
56	Elroy Face	.75
57	Joe Morgan	1.50
58	Thurman Munson	5.00
59	Stan Musial	5.00
60	Phil Niekro	.75
61	Paul Blair	.75
62	Andy Pafko	.75
63	Satchel Paige	5.00
64	Tony Perez	.75
65	Sal Bando	.75
66	Jimmy Piersall	.75
67	Kirby Puckett	5.00
68	Phil Rizzuto	3.00
69	Robin Roberts	.75
70	Jackie Robinson	8.00
71	Ryne Sandberg	3.00
72	Mike Schmidt	4.00
73	Red Schoendienst	.75
74	Herb Score	.75
75	Enos Slaughter	.75
76	Ozzie Smith	3.00
77	Warren Spahn	2.00
78	Don Sutton	.75
79	Luis Tiant	.75
80	Ted Kluszewski	.75
81	Whitey Ford	3.00
82	Maury Wills	.75
83	Dave Winfield	2.00
84	Early Wynn	.75
85	Carl Yastrzemski	3.00
86	Robin Yount	4.00
87	Bob Allison	.75
88	Clete Boyer	.75
89	Reggie Jackson	3.00
90	Yogi Berra	5.00
91	Willie Mays	8.00
92	Jim Palmer	.75
93	Pee Wee Reese	2.00
94	Frank Robinson	2.00
95	Boog Powell	.75
96	Willie Stargell	3.00
97	Nolan Ryan	10.00
98	Tom Seaver	4.00
99	Duke Snider	3.00
100	Bill Mazeroski	.75

Autographs

NM/M

Common Autograph: 10.00
Inserted 1:10

1	Willie Mays	175.00
2	Whitey Ford	60.00
3	Nolan Ryan	180.00
4	Carl Yastrzemski	90.00
5	Frank Robinson	40.00
6	Tom Seaver	85.00
7	Warren Spahn	80.00

8	Johnny Bench	100.00
9	Reggie Jackson	85.00
10	Bob Gibson	40.00
11	Bob Feller	20.00
12	Gil McDougald	15.00
13	Luis Tiant	15.00
14	Minnie Minoso	15.00
16	Herb Score	15.00
17	Moose Skowron	20.00
18	Maury Wills	15.00
19	Clete Boyer	20.00
21	Don Larsen	20.00
23	Tug McGraw	30.00
25	Robin Roberts	20.00
26	Frank Howard	20.00
27	Mickey Lolich	15.00
29	Tommy John	15.00
32	Dick Groat	20.00
33	Elroy Face	15.00
34	Paul Blair	10.00

Autographed Baseball

		NM/M
Common Autograph:		20.00
Inserted 1:Box		
1	Johnny Bench/100	80.00
2	Paul Blair/1,000	20.00
3	Clete Boyer/1,000	20.00
4	Ralph Branca/400	30.00
5	Elroy Face/1,000	25.00
6	Bob Feller/1,000	30.00
7	Whitey Ford/100	70.00
8	Bob Gibson/1,000	40.00
9	Dick Groat/1,000	30.00
10	Frank Howard/1,000	25.00
11	Reggie Jackson/100	80.00
12	Don Larsen/100	40.00
13	Mickey Lolich/500	20.00
14	Willie Mays/100	160.00
15	Gil McDougald/500	30.00
16	Tug McGraw/1,000	30.00
17	Minnie Minoso/1,000	30.00
18	Andy Pafko/500	30.00
19	Joe Pepitone/1,000	25.00
20	Robin Roberts/1,000	40.00
21	Frank Robinson/100	50.00
22	Nolan Ryan/100	150.00
23	Herb Score/500	25.00
24	Tom Seaver/100	80.00
25	Moose Skowron/1,000	30.00
26	Warren Spahn/100	80.00
27	Bobby Thomson/400	30.00
28	Luis Tiant/500	25.00
29	Carl Yastrzemski/100	120.00
30	Maury Wills/1,000	25.00

Bat Relics

		NM/M
Common Player:		8.00
Overall Relic Odds 1:10		
21	Al Kaline	20.00
22	Carl Yastrzemski	25.00
23	Carlton Fisk	15.00
24	Dale Murphy	15.00
25	Dave Winfield	15.00
26	Dick Groat	8.00
27	Dom DiMaggio	15.00
28	Don Mattingly	25.00
29	Gary Carter	8.00
30	George Kell	15.00
31	Harmon Killebrew	20.00
32	Jackie Jensen	15.00
33	Jackie Robinson	75.00
34	Jimmy Piersall	10.00
35	Joe Adcock	8.00
36	Joe Carter	8.00
37	Johnny Mize	10.00
38	Kirk Gibson	8.00
39	Mickey Vernon	8.00
40	Mike Schmidt	40.00
41	Ryne Sandberg	40.00
42	Ozzie Smith	25.00
43	Ted Kluszewski	10.00
44	Wade Boggs	15.00
45	Willie Mays	60.00
46	Duke Snider	20.00
47	Harvey Kuenn	8.00
48	Robin Yount	20.00
49	Red Schoendienst	8.00
50	Elston Howard	10.00
51	Bob Allison	8.00

Jersey Relics

		NM/M
Common Player:		8.00
Overall Relic Odds 1:10		
1	Brooks Robinson	15.00
2	Tony Conigliaro	15.00
3	Frank Howard	8.00
4	Don Sutton	10.00
5	Ferguson Jenkins	8.00
6	Frank Robinson	15.00
7	Don Mattingly	40.00
8	Willie Stargell	20.00
9	Moose Skowron	15.00
10	Fred Lynn	8.00
11	George Brett	40.00
12	Nolan Ryan	50.00
13	Orlando Cepeda	10.00
14	Reggie Jackson	20.00
15	Steve Carlton	15.00
16	Tom Seaver	20.00
17	Thurman Munson	25.00
18	Yogi Berra	20.00
19	Willie McCovey	10.00
20	Robin Yount	20.00

2001 Topps Chrome

		NM/M
Complete Set (660):		225.00
Complete Series 1 (330):		100.00
Complete Series 2 (330):		125.00
Common Player:		.25
Series 1 Pack (4):		2.00
Series 1 Box (24):		40.00
Series 2 Pack (4):		6.00
Series 2 Box (24):		120.00
1	Cal Ripken Jr.	3.00
2	Chipper Jones	1.00
3	Roger Cedeno	.25
4	Garret Anderson	.25
5	Robin Ventura	.25
6	Daryle Ward	.25
7	Not Issued (Retired)	
8	Phil Nevin	.25
9	Jermaine Dye	.25
10	Chris Singleton	.25
11	Mike Redmond	.25
12	Jim Thome	1.00
13	Brian Jordan	.25
14	Dustin Hermanson	.25
15	Shawn Green	.25
16	Todd Stottlemyre	.25
17	Dan Wilson	.25
18	Derek Lowe	.25
19	Juan Gonzalez	.50
20	Pat Meares	.25
21	Paul O'Neill	.50
22	Jeffrey Hammonds	.25
23	Pokey Reese	.25
24	Mike Mussina	.75
25	Rico Brogna	.25
26	Jay Buhner	.25
27	Steve Cox	.25
28	Quilvio Veras	.25
29	Marquis Grissom	.25
30	Shigetoshi Hasegawa	.25
31	Shane Reynolds	.25
32	Adam Piatt	.25
33	Preston Wilson	.25
34	Ellis Burks	.25
35	Armando Rios	.25
36	Chuck Finley	.25
37	Shannon Stewart	.25
38	Mark McGwire	2.50
39	Gerald Williams	.25
40	Eric Young	.25
41	Peter Bergeron	.25
42	Arthur Rhodes	.25
43	Bobby Jones	.25
44	Matt Clement	.25
45	Pedro Martinez	1.00
46	Jose Canseco	.50
47	Matt Anderson	.25
48	Torii Hunter	.50
49	Carlos Lee	.50
50	Eric Chavez	.25
51	Rick Helling	.25
52	John Franco	.25
53	Mike Bordick	.25
54	Andres Galarraga	.25
55	Jose Cruz Jr.	.25
56	Mike Matheny	.25
57	Randy Johnson	1.00
58	Richie Sexson	.25
59	Vladimir Nunez	.25
60	Aaron Boone	.25
61	Darin Erstad	.25
62	Alex Gonzalez	.25
63	Gil Heredia	.25
64	Shane Andrews	.25
65	Todd Hundley	.25
66	Bill Mueller	.25
67	Mark McLemore	.25
68	Scott Spiezio	.25
69	Kevin McGlinchy	.25
70	Manny Ramirez	1.00
71	Mike Lamb	.25
72	Brian Buchanan	.25
73	Mike Sweeney	.25
74	John Wetteland	.25
75	Rob Bell	.25
76	John Burkett	.25
77	Derek Jeter	3.00
78	J.D. Drew	.40
79	Jose Offerman	.25
80	Rick Reed	.25
81	Will Clark	.50
82	Rickey Henderson	.75
83	Kirk Rueter	.25
84	Lee Stevens	.25
85	Jay Bell	.25
86	Fred McGriff	.40
87	Julio Zuleta	.25
88	Brian Anderson	.25
89	Orlando Cabrera	.25
90	Alex Fernandez	.25
91	Derek Bell	.25
92	Eric Owens	.25
93	Dennys Reyes	.25
94	Mike Stanley	.25
95	Jorge Posada	.75
96	Paul Konerko	.50
97	Mike Remlinger	.25
98	Travis Lee	.25
99	Ken Caminiti	.25
100	Kevin Barker	.25
101	Ozzie Guillen	.25
102	Randy Wolf	.25
103	Michael Tucker	.25
104	Darren Lewis	.25
105	Joe Randa	.25
106	Jeff Cirillo	.25
107	David Ortiz	1.00
108	Herb Perry	.25
109	Jeff Nelson	.25
110	Chris Stynes	.25
111	Johnny Damon	1.00
112	Jason Schmidt	.25
113	Charles Johnson	.25
114	Pat Burrell	.50
115	Gary Sheffield	.75
116	Tom Glavine	.50
117	Jason Isringhausen	.25
118	Chris Carpenter	.50
119	Jeff Suppan	.25
120	Ivan Rodriguez	.75
121	Luis Sojo	.25
122	Ron Villone	.25
123	Mike Sirotka	.25
124	Chuck Knoblauch	.25
125	Jason Kendall	.25
126	Bobby Estalella	.25
127	Jose Guillen	.25
128	Carlos Delgado	.50
129	Benji Gil	.25
130	Einar Diaz	.25
131	Andy Benes	.25
132	Adrian Beltre	.50
133	Roger Clemens	3.00
134	Scott Williamson	.25
135	Brad Penny	.25
136	Troy Glaus	.40
137	Kevin Appier	.25
138	Walt Weiss	.25
139	Michael Barrett	.25
140	Mike Hampton	.25
141	Francisco Cordova	.25
142	David Segui	.25
143	Carlos Febles	.25
144	Roy Halladay	.50
145	Seth Etherton	.25
146	Fernando Tatis	.25
147	Livan Hernandez	.25
148	B.J. Surhoff	.25
149	Barry Larkin	.50
150	Bobby Howry	.25
151	Dmitri Young	.25
152	Brian Hunter	.25
153	Alex Rodriguez	3.00
154	Hideo Nomo	.50
155	Warren Morris	.25
156	Antonio Alfonseca	.25
157	Edgardo Alfonzo	.25
158	Mark Grudzielanek	.25
159	Fernando Vina	.25
160	Homer Bush	.25
161	Jason Giambi	.75
162	Steve Karsay	.25
163	Matt Lawton	.25
164	Rusty Greer	.25
165	Billy Koch	.25
166	Todd Hollandsworth	.25
167	Raul Ibanez	.25
168	Tony Gwynn	1.00
169	Carl Everett	.25
170	Hector Carrasco	.25
171	Jose Valentin	.25
172	Deivi Cruz	.25
173	Bret Boone	.25
174	Melvin Mora	.25
175	Danny Graves	.25
176	Jose Jimenez	.25
177	James Baldwin	.25
178	C.J. Nitkowski	.25
179	Jeff Zimmerman	.25
180	Mike Lowell	.25
181	Hideki Irabu	.25
182	Greg Vaughn	.25
183	Omar Daal	.25
184	Darren Dreifort	.25
185	Gil Meche	.25
186	Damian Jackson	.25
187	Frank Thomas	1.00
188	Luis Castillo	.25
189	Bartolo Colon	.25
190	Craig Biggio	.50
191	Scott Schoeneweis	.25
192	Dave Veres	.25
193	Ramon Martinez	.25
194	Jose Vidro	.25
195	Todd Helton	.75
196	Greg Norton	.25
197	Jacque Jones	.25
198	Jason Grimsley	.25
199	Dan Reichert	.25
200	Robb Nen	.25
201	Scott Hatteberg	.25
202	Terry Shumpert	.25
203	Kevin Millar	.25
204	Ismael Valdes	.25
205	Richard Hidalgo	.25
206	Randy Velarde	.25
207	Bengie Molina	.25
208	Tony Womack	.25
209	Enrique Wilson	.25
210	Jeff Brantley	.25
211	Rick Ankiel	.50
212	Terry Mulholland	.25
213	Ron Belliard	.25
214	Terrence Long	.25
215	Alberto Castillo	.25
216	Royce Clayton	.25
217	Joe McEwing	.25
218	Jason McDonald	.25
219	Ricky Bottalico	.25
220	Keith Foulke	.25
221	Brad Radke	.25
222	Gabe Kapler	.25
223	Pedro Astacio	.25
224	Armando Reynoso	.25
225	Darryl Kile	.25
226	Reggie Sanders	.25
227	Esteban Yan	.25
228	Joe Nathan	.25
229	Jay Payton	.25
230	Francisco Cordero	.25
231	Gregg Jefferies	.25
232	LaTroy Hawkins	.25
233	Jacob Cruz	.25
234	Chris Holt	.25
235	Vladimir Guerrero	1.00
236	Marvin Benard	.25
237	Alex Ramirez	.25
238	Mike Williams	.25
239	Sean Bergman	.25
240	Juan Encarnacion	.25
241	Russ Davis	.25
242	Ramon Hernandez	.25
243	Sandy Alomar	.25
244	Eddie Guardado	.25
245	Shane Halter	.25
246	Geoff Jenkins	.25
247	Brian Meadows	.25
248	Damian Miller	.25
249	Darrin Fletcher	.25
250	Rafael Furcal	.50
251	Mark Grace	.50
252	Mark Mulder	.25
253	Joe Torre	.75
254	Bobby Cox	.25
255	Mike Scioscia	.25
256	Mike Hargrove	.25
257	Jimy Williams	.25
258	Jerry Manuel	.25
259	Charlie Manuel	.25
260	Don Baylor	.25
261	Phil Garner	.25

262 Tony Muser .25
263 Buddy Bell .25
264 Tom Kelly .25
265 John Boles .25
266 Art Howe .25
267 Larry Dierker .25
268 Lou Pinella .25
269 Larry Rothschild .25
270 Davey Lopes .25
271 Johnny Oates .25
272 Felipe Alou .25
273 Bobby Valentine .25
274 Tony LaRussa .25
275 Bruce Bochy .25
276 Dusty Baker .25
277 Adrian Gonzalez, Adam Johnson 1.00
278 Matt Wheatland, Brian Digby .25
279 Tripper Johnson, Scott Thorman 1.00
280 Phil Dumatrait, Adam Wainwright 1.00
281 Scott Heard, David Parrish **RC** .75
282 Rocco Baldelli, Mark Folsom **RC** 1.00
283 Dominic Rich, Aaron Herr .75
284 Mike Stodolka, Sean Burnett .75
285 Derek Thompson, Corey Smith .75
286 Danny Borrell, Jason Bourgeois **RC** .75
287 Chin-Feng Chen, Corey Patterson, Josh Hamilton .75
288 Ryan Anderson, Barry Zito, C.C. Sabathia .75
289 Scott Sobkowiak, David Walling, Ben Sheets .75
290 Ty Howington, Josh Kalinowski, Josh Girdley .50
291 Hee Seop Choi, Aaron McNeal, Jason Hart 1.00
292 Bobby Bradley, Kurt Ainsworth, Chin-Hui Tsao .75
293 Mike Glendenning, Kenny Kelly, Juan Silvestri .50
294 J.R. House, Ramon Castro, Ben Davis .50
295 Chance Caple, Rafael Soriano, Pascual Coco 1.00
296 Travis Hafner, Eric Munson, Bucky Jacobsen 5.00
297 Jason Conti, Chris Wakeland, Brian Cole .75
298 Scott Seabol, Aubrey Huff, Joe Crede .50
299 Adam Everett, Jose Ortiz, Keith Ginter .50
300 Carlos Hernandez, Geraldo Guzman, Adam Eaton .75
301 Bobby Kielty, Milton Bradley, Juan Rivera .50
302 Mark McGwire 2.00
303 Don Larsen .75
304 Bobby Thomson .25
305 Bill Mazeroski .25
306 Reggie Jackson 1.00
307 Kirk Gibson .25
308 Roger Maris 1.50
309 Cal Ripken Jr. 3.00
310 Hank Aaron 3.00
311 Joe Carter .25
312 Cal Ripken Jr. 3.00
313 Randy Johnson 1.00
314 Ken Griffey Jr. 2.00
315 Troy Glaus .25
316 Kazuhiro Sasaki .25
317 Sammy Sosa, Troy Glaus 1.00
318 Todd Helton, Edgar Martinez .50
319 Todd Helton, Nomar Garciaparra 1.00
320 Barry Bonds, Jason Giambi 1.50
321 Todd Helton, Manny Ramirez .50
322 Todd Helton, Darin Erstad .50
323 Kevin Brown, Pedro Martinez .50
324 Randy Johnson, Pedro Martinez .50
325 Will Clark .40
326 New York Mets .25
327 New York Yankees 1.00
328 Seattle Mariners .25
329 Mike Hampton .25
330 New York Yankees 1.00
331 World Series 1.50
332 Jeff Bagwell 1.00
333 Andy Pettitte .75
334 Tony Armas Jr. .25
335 Jeromy Burnitz .25
336 Javier Vazquez .25
337 Eric Karros .25
338 Brian Giles .25
339 Scott Rolen 1.00
340 David Justice .25
341 Ray Durham .25
342 Todd Zeile .25
343 Cliff Floyd .25
344 Barry Bonds 3.00
345 Matt Williams .40
346 Steve Finley .25
347 Scott Elarton .25
348 Bernie Williams .50
349 David Wells .25
350 J.T. Snow .25
351 Al Leiter .25
352 Maggio Ordonez .50
353 Raul Mondesi .25
354 Tim Salmon .40
355 Jeff Kent .40
356 Mariano Rivera .50
357 John Olerud .25
358 Javy Lopez .25
359 Ben Grieve .25
360 Ray Lankford .25
361 Ken Griffey Jr. 2.00
362 Rich Aurilia .25
363 Andruw Jones .50
364 Ryan Klesko .25
365 Roberto Alomar .50
366 Miguel Tejada .50
367 Mo Vaughn .25
368 Albert Belle .25
369 Jose Canseco .50
370 Kevin Brown .25
371 Rafael Palmeiro .50
372 Mark Redman .25
373 Larry Walker .50
374 Greg Maddux 2.00
375 Nomar Garciaparra .75
376 Kevin Millwood .25
377 Edgar Martinez .25
378 Sammy Sosa .75
379 Tim Hudson .50
380 Jim Edmonds .25
381 Mike Piazza 1.50
382 Brant Brown .25
383 Brad Fullmer .25
384 Alan Benes .25
385 Mickey Morandini .25
386 Troy Percival .25
387 Eddie Perez .25
388 Vernon Wells .50
389 Ricky Gutierrez .25
390 Rondell White .25
391 Kevin Escobar .25
392 Tony Batista .25
393 Jimmy Haynes .25
394 Billy Wagner .25
395 A.J. Hinch .25
396 Matt Morris .25
397 Lance Berkman .75
398 Jeff D'Amico .25
399 Octavio Dotel .25
400 Olmedo Saenz .25
401 Esteban Loaiza .25
402 Adam Kennedy .25
403 Moises Alou .50
404 Orlando Palmeiro .25
405 Kevin Young .25
406 Tom Goodwin .25
407 Mac Suzuki .25
408 Pat Hentgen .25
409 Kevin Stocker .25
410 Mark Sweeney .25
411 Tony Eusebio .25
412 Edgar Renteria .25
413 John Rocker .25
414 Jose Lima .25
415 Kerry Wood .50
416 Mike Timlin .25
417 Jose Hernandez .25
418 Jeremy Giambi .25
419 Luis Lopez .25
420 Mitch Meluskey .25
421 Garrett Stephenson .25
422 Jamey Wright .25
423 John Jaha .25
424 Placido Polanco .25
425 Marty Cordova .25
426 Joey Hamilton .25
427 Travis Fryman .25
428 Mike Cameron .25
429 Matt Mantei .25
430 Chan Ho Park .25
431 Shawn Estes .25
432 Danny Bautista .25
433 Wilson Alvarez .25
434 Kenny Lofton .25
435 Russ Ortiz .25
436 Dave Burba .25
437 Felix Martinez .25
438 Jeff Shaw .25
439 Mike Difelice .25
440 Roberto Hernandez .25
441 Bryan Rekar .25
442 Ugueth Urbina .25
443 Vinny Castilla .25
444 Carlos Perez .25
445 Juan Guzman .25
446 Ryan Rupe .25
447 Mike Mordecai .25
448 Ricardo Rincon .25
449 Curt Schilling .75
450 Alex Cora .25
451 Turner Ward .25
452 Omar Vizquel .25
453 Russ Branyan .25
454 Russ Johnson .25
455 Gregg Colbrunn .25
456 Charles Nagy .25
457 Wil Cordero .25
458 Jason Tyner .25
459 Devon White .25
460 Kelly Stinnett .25
461 Wilton Guerrero .25
462 Jason Bere .25
463 Calvin Murray .25
464 Miguel Batista .25
465 Erubiel Durazo .25
466 Luis Gonzalez .25
467 Jaret Wright .25
468 Chad Kreuter .25
469 Armando Benitez .25
470 Sidney Ponson .25
471 Adrian Brown .25
472 Sterling Hitchcock .25
473 Timoniel Perez .25
474 Jamie Moyer .25
475 Delino DeShields .25
476 Glendon Rusch .25
477 Chris Gomez .25
478 Adam Eaton .25
479 Pablo Ozuna .25
480 Bob Abreu .50
481 Kris Benson .25
482 Keith Osik .25
483 Darryl Hamilton .25
484 Marlon Anderson .25
485 Jimmy Anderson .25
486 John Halama .25
487 Nelson Figueroa .25
488 Alex Gonzalez .25
489 Benny Agbayani .25
490 Ed Sprague .25
491 Scott Erickson .25
492 Doug Glanville .25
493 Jesus Sanchez .25
494 Mike Lieberthal .25
495 Aaron Sele .25
496 Pat Mahomes .25
497 Ruben Rivera .25
498 Wayne Gomes .25
499 Freddy Garcia .25
500 Al Martin .25
501 Woody Williams .25
502 Paul Byrd .25
503 Rick White .25
504 Trevor Hoffman .25
505 Brady Anderson .25
506 Robert Person .25
507 Jeff Conine .25
508 Chris Truby .25
509 Emil Brown .25
510 Ryan Dempster .25
511 Ruben Mateo .25
512 Alex Ochoa .25
513 Jose Rosado .25
514 Masato Yoshii .25
515 Brian Daubach .25
516 Jeff D'Amico .25
517 Brent Mayne .25
518 John Thomson .25
519 Todd Ritchie .25
520 John Vander Wal .25
521 Neifi Perez .25
522 Chad Curtis .25
523 Kenny Rogers .25
524 Trot Nixon .25
525 Sean Casey .25
526 Wilton Veras .25
527 Troy O'Leary .25
528 Dante Bichette .25
529 Jose Silva .25
530 Darren Oliver .25
531 Steve Parris .25
532 David McCarty .25
533 Todd Walker .25
534 Brian Rose .25
535 Pete Schourek .25
536 Ricky Ledee .25
537 Justin Thompson .25
538 Benito Santiago .25
539 Carlos Beltran .75
540 Gabe White .25
541 Bret Saberhagen .25
542 Ramon Martinez .25
543 John Valentin .25
544 Frank Catalanotto .25
545 Tim Wakefield .25
546 Michael Tucker .25
547 Juan Pierre .25
548 Rich Garces .25
549 Luis Ordaz .25
550 Jerry Spradlin .25
551 Corey Koskie .25
552 Cal Eldred .25
553 Alfonso Soriano 1.00
554 Kip Wells .25
555 Orlando Hernandez .25
556 Bill Simas .25
557 Jim Parque .25
558 Joe Mays .25
559 Tim Belcher .25
560 Shane Spencer .25
561 Glenallen Hill .25
562 Matt LeCroy .25
563 Tino Martinez .25
564 Eric Milton .25
565 Ron Coomer .25
566 Cristian Guzman .25
567 Kazuhiro Sasaki .25
568 Mark Quinn .25
569 Eric Gagne .25
570 Kerry Ligtenberg .25
571 Rolando Arrojo .25
572 Jon Lieber .25
573 Jose Vizcaino .25
574 Jeff Abbott .25
575 Carlos Hernandez .25
576 Scott Sullivan .25
577 Matt Stairs .25
578 Tom Lampkin .25
579 Donnie Sadler .25
580 Desi Relaford .25
581 Scott Downs .25
582 Mike Mussina .75
583 Ramon Ortiz .25
584 Mike Myers .25
585 Frank Castillo .25
586 Manny Ramirez 1.00
587 Alex Rodriguez 3.00
588 Andy Ashby .25
589 Felipe Crespo .25
590 Bobby Bonilla .25
591 Denny Neagle .25
592 Dave Martinez .25
593 Mike Hampton .25
594 Gary DiSarcina .25
595 Tsuyoshi Shinjo **RC** .75
596 Albert Pujols **RC** 80.00
597 Roy Oswalt, Pat Strange, Jon Rauch .75
598 Phil Wilson, Jake Peavy, Darwin Cubillan **RC** 10.00
599 Nathan Haynes, Steve Smyth, Mike Bynum .75
600 Joe Lawrence, Choo Freeman, Michael Cuddyer .50
601 Larry Barnes, Dewayne Wise, Carlos Pena .25
602 Felipe Lopez, Gookie Dawkins, Erick Almonte **RC** 1.00
603 Brad Wilkerson, Alex Escobar, Eric Valent .25
604 Jeff Goldbach, Toby Hall, Rod Barajas .25
605 Marcus Giles, Pablo Ozuna, Jason Romano .25
606 Vernon Wells, Jack Cust, Dee Brown .25
607 Luis Montanez, David Espinosa 1.00
608 John Lackey, Justin Wayne **RC** 1.00
609 Josh Axelson, Carmen Cali **RC** 1.00
610 Shaun Boyd, Chris Morris **RC** 1.00
611 Dan Moylan, Tommy Arko **RC** 1.00
612 Luis Cotto, Luis Escobar 1.00
613 Blake Williams, Brandon Mims **RC** 1.00
614 Chris Russ, Bryan Edwards 1.00
615 Joe Torres, Ben Diggins .25
616 Mark Dalesandro, Edwin Encarnacion **RC** 4.00
617 Brian Bass, Odannis Ayala **RC** 1.00
618 Jason Kaanoi, Michael Mathews **RC** .50
619 Stuart McFarland, Adam Sterrett **RC** 1.00
620 David Krynzel, Grady Sizemore 1.00
621 Keith Bucktrot, Dane Sardinha .25
622 Anaheim Angels .25
623 Arizona Diamondbacks .25
624 Atlanta Braves .25
625 Baltimore Orioles .25
626 Boston Red Sox .25
627 Chicago Cubs .25
628 Chicago White Sox .25
629 Cincinnati Reds .25
630 Cleveland Indians .25
631 Colorado Rockies .25
632 Detroit Tigers .25
633 Florida Marlins .25
634 Houston Astros .25
635 Kansas City Royals .25
636 Los Angeles Dodgers .25
637 Milwaukee Brewers .25
638 Minnesota Twins .25
639 Montreal Expos .25
640 New York Mets .25
641 New York Yankees 1.50
642 Oakland Athletics .25
643 Philadelphia Phillies .25
644 Pittsburgh Pirates .25
645 San Diego Padres .25
646 San Francisco Giants .25
647 Seattle Mariners .25
648 St. Louis Cardinals .25
649 Tampa Bay Devil Rays .25
650 Texas Rangers .25
651 Toronto Blue Jays .25
652 Bucky Dent .25
653 Jackie Robinson 1.50
654 Roberto Clemente 1.50
655 Nolan Ryan 2.50
656 Kerry Wood .50
657 Rickey Henderson .75
658 Lou Brock .50
659 David Wells .25
660 Andruw Jones .40
661 Carlton Fisk .25

Retrofractors

Stars: 3-5X
Inserted 1:12

Before There Was Topps

NM/M

Complete Set (10): 40.00
Common Player: 3.00
Inserted 1:20
Refractors: 2-4X

Inserted 1:200		
BT1	Lou Gehrig	8.00
BT2	Babe Ruth	10.00
BT3	Cy Young	5.00
BT4	Walter Johnson	3.00
BT5	Ty Cobb	8.00
BT6	Rogers Hornsby	3.00
BT7	Honus Wagner	4.00
BT8	Christy Mathewson	3.00
BT9	Grover Alexander	3.00
BT10	Joe DiMaggio	8.00

Combos

MOUND MARKSMEN
BOB GIBSON — PEDRO MARTINEZ

		NM/M
Complete Set (20):		80.00
Common Card:		2.00
Inserted 1:12		
Refractors:		2-4X
Inserted 1:120		
1	Derek Jeter, Yogi Berra, Whitey Ford, Don Mattingly, Reggie Jackson	6.00
2	Chipper Jones, Mike Schmidt	6.00
3	Brooks Robinson, Cal Ripken Jr.	8.00
4	Bob Gibson, Pedro Martinez	3.00
5	Ivan Rodriguez, Johnny Bench	4.00
6	Ernie Banks, Alex Rodriguez	6.00
7	Joe Morgan, Ken Griffey Jr., Barry Larkin	5.00
8	Vladimir Guerrero, Roberto Clemente	6.00
9	Ken Griffey Jr., Hank Aaron	6.00
10	Casey Stengel, Joe Torre	2.00
TC11	Kevin Brown, Sandy Koufax, Don Drysdale	5.00
TC12	Mark McGwire, Sammy Sosa, Roger Marris, Babe Ruth	8.00
TC13	Ted Williams, Carl Yastrzemski, Nomar Garciaparra	8.00
TC14	Greg Maddux, Roger Clemens, Cy Young	5.00
TC15	Tony Gwynn, Ted Williams	6.00
TC16	Cal Ripken Jr., Lou Gehrig	10.00
TC17	Sandy Koufax, Randy Johnson, Warren Spahn, Steve Carlton	4.00
TC18	Mike Piazza, Josh Gibson	5.00
TC19	Barry Bonds, Willie Mays	8.00
TC20	Jackie Robinson, Larry Doby	5.00

Golden Anniversary

GOLDEN ANNIVERSARY
HANK AARON

		NM/M
Complete Set (50):		120.00
Common Player:		1.00
Inserted 1:10		
Refractors:		2-4X
Inserted 1:100		
1	Hank Aaron	6.00
2	Ernie Banks	3.00
3	Mike Schmidt	5.00
4	Willie Mays	6.00
5	Johnny Bench	4.00

6	Tom Seaver	3.00
7	Frank Robinson	2.00
8	Sandy Koufax	5.00
9	Bob Gibson	3.00
10	Ted Williams	8.00
11	Cal Ripken Jr.	8.00
12	Tony Gwynn	3.00
13	Mark McGwire	6.00
14	Ken Griffey Jr.	4.00
15	Greg Maddux	4.00
16	Roger Clemens	6.00
17	Barry Bonds	8.00
18	Rickey Henderson	1.50
19	Mike Piazza	4.00
20	Jose Canseco	2.00
21	Derek Jeter	6.00
22	Nomar Garciaparra	5.00
23	Alex Rodriguez	5.00
24	Sammy Sosa	5.00
25	Ivan Rodriguez	2.00
26	Vladimir Guerrero	3.00
27	Chipper Jones	4.00
28	Jeff Bagwell	2.00
29	Pedro Martinez	3.00
30	Randy Johnson	3.00
31	Pat Burrell	1.50
32	Josh Hamilton	1.00
33	Ryan Anderson	1.00
34	Corey Patterson	1.50
35	Eric Munson	1.00
36	Sean Burroughs	1.00
37	C.C. Sabathia	1.00
38	Chin-Feng Chen	1.00
39	Barry Zito	1.50
40	Adrian Gonzalez	1.00
41	Mark McGwire	6.00
42	Nomar Garciaparra	5.00
43	Todd Helton	2.00
44	Matt Williams	1.00
45	Troy Glaus	1.50
46	Geoff Jenkins	1.00
47	Frank Thomas	3.00
48	Mo Vaughn	1.00
49	Barry Larkin	1.50
50	J.D. Drew	1.00

King of Kings

		NM/M
Common Player:		25.00
Inserted 1:5,175 H		
Inserted 1:5,209 R		
KKR1	Hank Aaron	100.00
KKR2	Nolan Ryan	100.00
KKR3	Rickey Henderson	40.00
KKR5	Bob Gibson	25.00
KKR6	Nolan Ryan	100.00

King of Kings Golden Edition

Inserted 1:59,220 H
No Pricing

Past To Present

BARRY BONDS — WILLIE MAYS

		NM/M
Complete Set (10):		20.00
Common Player:		1.50
Inserted 1:18		
Refractors:		1.5-3X
Inserted 1:180		
1	Phil Rizzuto, Derek Jeter	6.00
2	Warren Spahn, Greg Maddux	4.00
3	Yogi Berra, Jorge Posada	4.00
4	Willie Mays, Barry Bonds	6.00
5	Red Schoendienst, Fernando Vina	1.50
6	Duke Snider, Shawn Green	2.00
7	Bob Feller, Bartolo Colon	1.50
8	Johnny Mize, Tino Martinez	1.50
9	Larry Doby, Manny Ramirez	2.00
10	Eddie Mathews, Chipper Jones	3.00

Through The Years

		NM/M
Complete Set (50):		200.00
Common Player:		2.00
Inserted 1:10		

WARREN SPAHN
PITCHER — MILWAUKEE BRAVES

Refractors:		2-4X
Inserted 1:100		
1	Yogi Berra	4.00
2	Roy Campanella	4.00
3	Willie Mays	8.00
4	Andy Pafko	2.00
5	Jackie Robinson	8.00
6	Stan Musial	5.00
7	Duke Snider	4.00
8	Warren Spahn	4.00
9	Ted Williams	10.00
10	Eddie Matthews	4.00
11	Willie McCovey	2.00
12	Frank Robinson	3.00
13	Ernie Banks	5.00
14	Hank Aaron	8.00
15	Sandy Koufax	6.00
16	Bob Gibson	4.00
17	Harmon Killebrew	3.00
18	Whitey Ford	3.00
19	Roberto Clemente	8.00
20	Juan Marichal	2.00
21	Johnny Bench	5.00
22	Willie Stargell	3.00
23	Joe Morgan	2.00
24	Carl Yastrzemski	5.00
25	Reggie Jackson	4.00
26	Tom Seaver	4.00
27	Steve Carlton	3.00
28	Jim Palmer	2.00
29	Rod Carew	3.00
30	George Brett	8.00
31	Roger Clemens	8.00
32	Don Mattingly	3.00
33	Ryne Sandberg	4.00
34	Mike Schmidt	8.00
35	Cal Ripken Jr.	10.00
36	Tony Gwynn	4.00
37	Ozzie Smith	5.00
38	Wade Boggs	3.00
39	Nolan Ryan	10.00
40	Robin Yount	4.00
41	Mark McGwire	8.00
42	Ken Griffey Jr.	5.00
43	Sammy Sosa	6.00
44	Alex Rodriguez	6.00
45	Barry Bonds	8.00
46	Mike Piazza	5.00
47	Chipper Jones	4.00
48	Greg Maddux	5.00
49	Nomar Garciaparra	5.00
50	Derek Jeter	8.00

Topps Originals

ALEX RODRIGUEZ

		NM/M
Common Player:		15.00
Inserted 1:1,783 H		
Inserted 1:1,788 R		
Refractors 10 sets produced.		
1	Roberto Clemente	180.00
2	Carl Yastrzemski	60.00
3	Mike Schmidt	75.00
4	Wade Boggs	20.00
5	Chipper Jones	40.00
6	Lou Brock	20.00
7	Dave Parker	16.00
8	Barry Bonds	80.00
9	Alex Rodriguez	50.00

What Could've Been

LEROY "SATCHEL" PAIGE

		NM/M
Complete Set (10):		25.00
Common Player:		2.00
Inserted 1:30		
Refractors:		2-4X
Inserted 1:300		
WCB1	Josh Gibson	6.00
WCB2	Satchel Paige	6.00
WCB3	Buck Leonard	3.00
WCB4	James "Cool Pap Bell	4.00
WCB5	Andrew "Rube" Foster	3.00
WCB6	Martin Dihigo	2.00
WCB7	William "Judy" Johnson	3.00
WCB8	Mule Suttles	2.00
WCB9	Ray Dandridge	2.00
WCB10	John Henry Lloyd	2.00

2001 Topps Chrome Traded & Rookies

		NM/M
Complete Chrome Set (265):		150.00
Common Player:		.25
T1	Sandy Alomar Jr.	.25
T2	Kevin Appier	.25
T3	Brad Ausmus	.25
T4	Derek Bell	.25
T5	Bret Boone	.40
T6	Rico Brogna	.25
T7	Ellis Burks	.25
T8	Ken Caminiti	.25
T9	Roger Cedeno	.25
T10	Royce Clayton	.25
T11	Enrique Wilson	.25
T12	Rheal Cormier	.25
T13	Eric Davis	.25
T14	Shawon Duston	.25
T15	Andres Galarraga	.40
T16	Tom Gordon	.25
T17	Mark Grace	1.00
T18	Jeffrey Hammonds	.25
T19	Dustin Hermanson	.25
T20	Quinton McCracken	.25
T21	Todd Hundley	.25
T22	Charles Johnson	.25
T23	Marquis Grissom	.25
T24	Jose Mesa	.25
T25	Terry Mulholland	.25
T26	John Rocker	.25
T27	Jeff Frye	.25
T28	Reggie Sanders	.25
T29	David Segui	.25
T30	Mike Sirotka	.25
T31	Fernando Tatis	.25
T32	Steve Trachsel	.25
T33	Ismael Valdes	.25
T34	Randy Velarde	.25
T35	Brian Boehringer	.25
T36	Mike Bordick	.25
T37	Ken Bottenfield	.25
T38	Pat Rapp	.25
T39	Jeff Nelson	.25
T40	Ricky Bottalico	.25
T41	Deion Sanders	.50
T42	Hideo Nomo	1.00
T43	Bill Mueller	.25
T44	Roberto Kelly	.25
T45	Chris Holt	.25
T46	Mike Jackson	.25
T47	Devon White	.25
T48	Gerald Williams	.25
T49	Eddie Taubensee	.25
T50	Brian Hunter	.25
T51	Nelson Cruz	.25
T52	Jeff Fassero	.25
T53	Bubba Trammell	.25
T54	Bo Porter	.25
T55	Greg Norton	.25
T56	Benito Santiago	.25
T57	Ruben Rivera	.25
T58	Dee Brown	.25
T59	Jose Canseco	1.00
T60	Chris Michalak	.25
T61	Tim Worrell	.25
T62	Matt Clement	.25
T63	Bill Pulsipher	.25
T64	Troy Brohawn	.25
T65	Mark Kotsay	.25

T66	Jose Lima	.25
T67	Shea Hillenbrand	.25
T68	Ted Lilly	.25
T69	Jermaine Dye	.25
T70	Jerry Hairston Jr.	.25
T71	John Mabry	.25
T72	Kurt Abbott	.25
T73	Eric Owens	.25
T74	Jeff Brantley	.25
T75	Vinny Castilla	.25
T76	Ron Villone	.25
T77	Ricky Henderson	.75
T78	Jason Grimsley	.25
T79	Christian Parker **RC**	.50
T80	Donnie Wall	.25
T81	Alex Arias	.25
T82	Willis Roberts	.25
T83	Ryan Minor	.25
T84	Jason LaRue	.25
T85	Ruben Sierra	.25
T86	Johnny Damon	1.50
T87	Juan Gonzalez	.75
T88	Mac Suzuki	.25
T89	Tony Batista	.25
T90	Jay Witasick	.25
T91	Brent Abernathy	.25
T92	Paul LoDuca	.25
T93	Wes Helms	.25
T94	Milton Bradley	.25
T95	Matt LeCroy	.25
T96	A.J. Hinch	.25
T97	Bud Smith **RC**	.25
T98	Adam Dunn	1.00
T99	Albert Pujols, Ichiro Suzuki	25.00
T100	Carlton Fisk	.50
T101	Tim Raines	.50
T102	Juan Marichal	.50
T103	Dave Winfield	.75
T104	Reggie Jackson	1.50
T105	Cal Ripken Jr.	4.00
T106	Ozzie Smith	1.50
T107	Tom Seaver	1.50
T108	Lou Piniella	.50
T109	Dwight Gooden	.50
T110	Bret Saberhagen	.25
T111	Gary Carter	.50
T112	Jack Clark	.25
T113	Rickey Henderson	1.00
T114	Barry Bonds	4.00
T115	Bobby Bonilla	.25
T116	Jose Canseco	1.00
T117	Will Clark	1.00
T118	Andres Galarraga	.25
T119	Bo Jackson	1.00
T120	Wally Joyner	.25
T121	Ellis Burks	.25
T122	David Cone	.25
T123	Greg Maddux	2.00
T124	Willie Randolph	.25
T125	Dennis Eckersley	.50
T126	Matt Williams	.75
T127	Joe Morgan	.75
T128	Fred McGriff	.75
T129	Roberto Alomar	.75
T130	Lee Smith	.50
T131	David Wells	.50
T132	Ken Griffey Jr.	3.00
T133	Deion Sanders	1.00
T134	Nolan Ryan	3.00
T135	David Justice	.50
T136	Joe Carter	.50
T137	Jack Morris	.25
T138	Mike Piazza	2.00
T139	Barry Bonds	3.00
T140	Terrence Long	.25
T141	Ben Grieve	.25
T142	Richie Sexson	.50
T143	Sean Burroughs	.25
T144	Alfonso Soriano	1.00
T145	Bob Boone	.25
T146	Larry Bowa	.25
T147	Bob Brenly	.25
T148	Buck Martinez	.25
T149	Lloyd McClendon	.25
T150	Jim Tracy	.25
T151	Jared Abruzzo **RC**	.75
T152	Kurt Ainsworth	.25
T153	Willie Bloomquist	.25
T154	Ben Broussard	.25
T155	Bobby Bradley	.25
T156	Mike Bynum	.25
T157	Ken Harvey	.25
T158	Ryan Christianson	.25
T159	Ryan Kohlmeier	.25
T160	Joe Crede	1.50
T161	Jack Cust	.25
T162	Ben Diggins	.25
T163	Phil Dumatrait	.25
T164	Alex Escobar	.25
T165	Miguel Olivo	.25
T166	Chris George	.25
T167	Marcus Giles	.25
T168	Keith Ginter	.25
T169	Josh Girdley	.25
T170	Tony Alvarez	.25
T171	Scott Seabol	.25
T172	Josh Hamilton	.50
T173	Jason Hart	.25
T174	Israel Alcantara	.25
T175	Jake Peavy	4.00
T176	Stubby Clapp **RC**	.75
T177	D'Angelo Jimenez	.25
T178	Nick Johnson	.25
T179	Ben Johnson	.50
T180	Larry Bigbie	.25
T181	Allen Levrault	.25
T182	Felipe Lopez	.25
T183	Sean Burnett	.25
T184	Nick Neugebauer	.25
T185	Austin Kearns	.50
T186	Corey Patterson	.50
T187	Carlos Pena	.25
T188	Ricardo Rodriguez **RC**	.75
T189	Juan Rivera	.25
T190	Grant Roberts	.25
T191	Adam Pettyjohn **RC**	.50
T192	Jared Sandberg	.25
T193	Xavier Nady	.25
T194	Dane Sardinha	.25
T195	Shawn Sonnier	.25
T196	Rafael Soriano	.25
T197	Brian Specht **RC**	.50
T198	Aaron Myette	.25
T199	Juan Uribe **RC**	.75
T200	Jayson Werth	.25
T201	Brad Wilkerson	.25
T202	Horacio Estrada	.25
T203	Joel Pineiro	.25
T204	Matt LeCroy	.25
T205	Michael Coleman	.25
T206	Ben Sheets	1.00
T207	Eric Byrnes	.25
T208	Sean Burroughs	.25
T209	Ken Harvey	.25
T210	Travis Hafner	5.00
T211	Erick Almonte	.25
T212	Jason Belcher **RC**	1.00
T213	Wilson Betemit **RC**	2.50
T214	Hank Blalock **RC**	4.00
T215	Danny Borrell	.25
T216	John Buck **RC**	.75
T217	Freddie Bynum **RC**	.75
T218	Noel Devarez **RC**	.50
T219	Juan Diaz **RC**	.50
T220	Felix Diaz **RC**	.50
T221	Josh Fogg **RC**	1.00
T222	Matt Ford **RC**	.50
T223	Scott Heard	.25
T224	Ben Hendrickson **RC**	.50
T225	Cody Ross **RC**	1.00
T226	Adrian Hernandez **RC**	.75
T227	Alfredo Amezaga **RC**	.75
T228	Bob Keppel **RC**	.50
T229	Ryan Madson **RC**	1.00
T230	Octavio Martinez **RC**	.50
T231	Hee Seop Choi	.50
T232	Thomas Mitchell	.50
T233	Luis Montanez	.25
T234	Andy Morales **RC**	.75
T235	Justin Morneau **RC**	10.00
T236	Greg "Toe" Nash **RC**	.50
T237	Valentino Pasucci **RC**	.50
T238	Roy Smith **RC**	.75
T239	Antonio Perez **RC**	.75
T240	Chad Petty **RC**	.50
T241	Steve Smyth	.25
T242	Jose Reyes **RC**	30.00
T243	Eric Reynolds **RC**	.75
T244	Dominic Rich	.50
T245	Jason Richardson **RC**	.50
T246	Ed Rogers **RC**	.75
T247	Albert Pujols **RC**	75.00
T248	Esix Snead **RC**	.50
T249	Luis Torres **RC**	.50
T250	Matt White **RC**	.75
T251	Blake Williams	.25
T252	Chris Russ	.25
T253	Joe Kennedy **RC**	.50
T254	Jeff Randazzo **RC**	.50
T255	Beau Hale **RC**	.50
256	Brad Hennessey **RC**	.75
257	Jake Gautreau **RC**	.50
258	Jeff Mathis **RC**	1.00
259	Aaron Heilman **RC**	.75
260	Bronson Sardinha **RC**	.75
261	Irvin Guzman **RC**	6.00
262	Gabe Gross **RC**	1.00
263	J.D. Martin **RC**	.75
264	Chris Smith **RC**	.50
265	Kenny Baugh **RC**	.50
266	Ichiro Suzuki **RC**	25.00

2001 Topps Fusion

		NM/M
Complete Set (250):		100.00
Common Player:		.25
Pack (5):		2.50
Box (24):		50.00
1	Albert Belle	.25
2	Albert Belle	.25
3	Albert Belle	.25
4	Nick Bierbrodt	.25
5	Alex Rodriguez	2.50
6	Alex Rodriguez	2.50
7	Alex Rodriguez	2.50
8	Alex Rodriguez	2.50
9	Eric Munson	.25
10	Barry Bonds	3.00
11	Andruw Jones	.75
12	Antonio Alfonseca	.25
13	Andres Galarraga	.40
14	Joe Crede	.25
15	Barry Larkin	.40
16	Barry Bonds	3.00
17	Barry Bonds	3.00
18	Andruw Jones	.75
19	C.C. Sabathia	.25
20	Bobby Higginson	.25
21	Barry Larkin	.40
22	Ben Grieve	.25
23	Barry Bonds	3.00
24	Corey Patterson	.25
25	Carlos Delgado	.75
26	Bernie Williams	.50
27	Brian Giles	.40
28	Barry Larkin	.40
29	Gookie Dawkins	.25
30	Chipper Jones	1.50
31	Brian Giles	.40
32	Carlos Delgado	.75
33	Ben Grieve	.25
34	Geoff Goetz	.25
35	Cristian Guzman	.25
36	Cal Ripken Jr.	3.00
37	Chipper Jones	1.50
38	Bernie Williams	.50
39	Pablo Ozuna	.25
40	Dante Bichette	.25
41	Carlos Delgado	.75
42	Craig Biggio	.25
43	Cal Ripken Jr.	3.00
44	Tim Redding	.25
45	Darin Erstad	.50
46	Chipper Jones	1.50
47	Darin Erstad	.50
48	Carlos Delgado	.75
49	Josh Hamilton	.50
50	Derek Jeter	3.00
51	Darin Erstad	.50
52	Dean Palmer	.25
53	Chipper Jones	1.50
54	Chin-Feng Chen	.25
55	Edgar Martinez	.25
56	Derek Jeter	3.00
57	Derek Jeter	3.00
58	Craig Biggio	.25
59	Keith Ginter	.25
60	Edgardo Alfonzo	.25
61	Edgar Martinez	.25
62	Edgardo Alfonzo	.25
63	David Justice	.50
64	Roy Oswalt	.25
65	Eric Karros	.25
66	Edgardo Alfonzo	.25
67	Frank Thomas	1.00
68	Dean Palmer	.25
69	Alfonso Soriano	1.00
70	Fernando Vina	.25
71	Frank Thomas	1.00
72	Garret Anderson	.40
73	Derek Jeter	3.00
74	Bobby Bradley	.25
75	Frank Thomas	1.00
76	Gary Sheffield	.50
77	Geoff Jenkins	.25
78	Edgar Martinez	.25
79	Nick Johnson	.25
80	Fred McGriff	.40
81	Geoff Jenkins	.25
82	Greg Maddux	1.50
83	Edgardo Alfonzo	.25
84	Hee Seop Choi **RC**	2.00
85	Garret Anderson	.50
86	Greg Maddux	1.50
87	Ivan Rodriguez	.75
88	Eric Karros	.25
89	Scott Seabol	.25
90	Ivan Rodriguez	.75
91	Ivan Rodriguez	.75
92	J.D. Drew	.25
93	Frank Thomas	1.00
94	Ryan Anderson	.25
95	Jason Giambi	.75
96	Jason Giambi	.75
97	Jason Kendall	.25
98	Gary Sheffield	.50
99	Milton Bradley	.25
100	Jason Kendall	.25
101	Jason Kendall	.25
102	Jeff Bagwell	.75
103	Greg Maddux	1.50
104	Sean Burroughs	.25
105	Jay Bell	.25
106	Jeff Bagwell	.75
107	Jeffrey Hammonds	.25
108	Ivan Rodriguez	.75
109	Ben Petrick	.25
110	Jeff Bagwell	.75
111	Jeff Cirillo	.25
112	Jermaine Dye	.25
113	J.T. Snow Jr.	.25
114	Ben Davis	.25
115	Jeff Cirillo	.25
116	Jeff Kent	.25
117	Jeromy Burnitz	.25
118	Jay Bell	.25
119	Jason Hart	.25
120	Jeff Kent	.25
121	Jermaine Dye	.25
122	John Olerud	.25
123	Jeff Bagwell	.75
124	Jeff Segar **RC**	.50
125	Jeromy Burnitz	.25
126	Jeromy Burnitz	.25
127	Johnny Damon	.25
128	Jim Edmonds	.40
129	Tim Christman **RC**	.50
130	Jim Thome	.75
131	Jim Edmonds	.40
132	Jorge Posada	.50
133	Jim Thome	.75
134	Danny Borrell **RC**	.50
135	Johnny Damon	.25
136	Jim Thome	.75
137	Jose Vidro	.25
138	Ken Griffey Jr.	1.50
139	Sean Burnett	.25
140	Larry Walker	.40
141	Jose Vidro	.25
142	Ken Griffey Jr.	1.50
143	Larry Walker	.40
144	Robert Keppell **RC**	1.00
145	Luis Castillo	.25
146	Ken Griffey Jr.	1.50
147	Kevin Brown	.40
148	Manny Ramirez	.75
149	David Parrish **RC**	.25
150	Manny Ramirez	.75
151	Kevin Brown	.40
152	Luis Castillo	.25
153	Mark Grace	.50
154	Mike Jacobs **RC**	.50
155	Mark Grace	.50
156	Larry Walker	.40
157	Magglio Ordonez	.40
158	Mark McGwire	2.00
159	Adam Johnson	.25
160	Mark McGwire	2.00
161	Magglio Ordonez	.50
162	Mark McGwire	2.00
163	Matt Williams	.40
164	Oscar Ramirez **RC**	.50
165	Mike Piazza	1.50
166	Manny Ramirez	.75
167	Mike Piazza	1.50
168	Mike Mussina	.50
169	Odannis Ayala **RC**	.25
170	Mike Sweeney	.25
171	Mark McGwire	2.00
172	Nomar Garciaparra	2.50
173	Mike Piazza	1.50
174	J.R. House	.25
175	Neifi Perez	.25
176	Mike Piazza	1.50
177	Pedro Martinez	1.00
178	Mo Vaughn	.25
179	Shawn Fagan **RC**	.50
180	Nomar Garciaparra	2.50
181	Mo Vaughn	.25
182	Rafael Palmeiro	.50
183	Nomar Garciaparra	2.50
184	Chris Bass **RC**	.75
185	Raul Mondesi	.25
186	Nomar Garciaparra	2.50
187	Randy Johnson	1.00
188	Omar Vizquel	.25
189	Erick Almonte **RC**	1.00
190	Ray Durham	.25
191	Pedro Martinez	1.00
192	Robb Nen	.25
193	Pedro Martinez	1.00
194	Luis Montanez **RC**	1.00
195	Ray Lankford	.25
196	Rafael Palmeiro	.50
197	Roberto Alomar	.75
198	Rafael Palmeiro	.50
199	Chad Petty **RC**	.50
200	Richard Hidalgo	.25
201	Randy Johnson	1.00
202	Robin Ventura	.25
203	Randy Johnson	1.00
204	Derek Thompson	.25
205	Sammy Sosa	2.00
206	Roberto Alomar	.75
207	Sammy Sosa	2.00
208	Raul Mondesi	.25
209	Scott Heard	.25
210	Scott Rolen	.75
211	Sammy Sosa	2.00
212	Scott Rolen	.75
213	Roberto Alomar	.75
214	Dominic Rich **RC**	.50
215	Sean Casey	.25
216	Scott Rolen	.75
217	Sean Casey	.25
218	Robin Ventura	.25
219	William Smith **RC**	.50
220	Tim Salmon	.40
221	Sean Casey	.25
222	Shannon Stewart	.25
223	Sammy Sosa	2.00
224	Joel Pieniero **RC**	.50
225	Tino Martinez	.25
226	Shawn Green	.40
227	Shawn Green	.40
228	Scott Rolen	.50

229	Greg Morrison RC	.50
230	Tony Gwynn	1.00
231	Todd Helton	.75
232	Steve Finley	.25
233	Scott Williamson	.25
234	Talmadge Nunnari	.25
235	Tony Womack	.25
236	Tony Batista	.25
237	Tim Salmon	.40
238	Shawn Green	.40
239	Carlos Villalobos RC	.50
240	Troy Glaus	.50
241	Troy Glaus	.50
242	Todd Helton	.75
243	Tim Salmon	.40
244	Marco Scutaro RC	.50
245	Troy O'Leary	.25
246	Vladimir Guerrero	1.00
247	Vladimir Guerrero	1.00
248	Vladimir Guerrero	1.00
249	Horacio Estrada	.25
250	Vladimir Guerrero	1.00

Autographs

		NM/M
Common Player:		5.00
Inserted 1:23		
1	Rafael Furcal	15.00
2	Mike Lamb	5.00
3	Jason Marquis	5.00
4	Milton Bradley	8.00
5	Barry Zito	15.00
6	Derrek Lee	20.00
7	Corey Patterson	10.00
8	Josh Hamilton	30.00
9	Sean Burroughs	5.00
10	Jason Hart	5.00
11	Luis Montanez	5.00
12	Robert Keppell	5.00
13	Blake Williams	5.00
14	Phil Wilson	5.00
15	Jake Peavy	250.00
16	Alex Rodriguez	100.00
17	Ivan Rodriguez	20.00
18	Don Larsen	20.00
19	Todd Helton	20.00
20	Carlos Delgado	15.00
21	Geoff Jenkins	5.00
22	Willie Stargell	60.00
23	Frank Robinson	30.00
24	Warren Spahn	40.00
25	Harmon Killebrew	30.00
26	Chipper Jones	40.00
27	Chipper Jones	40.00
28	Chipper Jones	40.00
29	Chipper Jones	40.00
30	Chipper Jones	40.00
31	Rocco Baldelli	10.00
32	Keith Ginter	5.00
33	J.R. House	5.00
34	Alex Cabrera	10.00
35	Tony Alvarez	5.00
36	Pablo Ozuna	5.00
37	Juan Salas	5.00

Double Feature

		NM/M
Common Duo:		10.00
1	Ivan Rodriguez, Rickey Henderson	40.00
2	John Smoltz, Tom Glavine	15.00
3	Willie Stargell, Frank Thomas	20.00
4	Carlos Delgado, Todd Helton	15.00
5	Adrian Gonzalez, Pat Burrell	15.00
6	Jose Vidro, Roberto Alomar	15.00
7	Chipper Jones, Robin Ventura	20.00
8	J.D. Drew, Matt Lawton	10.00
9	Josh Hamilton, Chin-Feng Chen	25.00
10	Rafael Furcal, Miguel Tejada	15.00
11	Josh Beckett, Ryan Anderson	15.00

Feature

		NM/M
Common Player:		4.00
Inserted 1:51		
1	Ivan Rodriguez	8.00
2	Rickey Henderson	15.00
3	John Smoltz	5.00
4	Tom Glavine	8.00
5	Willie Stargell	10.00
6	Frank Thomas	8.00
7	Carlos Delgado	8.00
8	Todd Helton	8.00
9	Adrian Gonzalez	5.00
10	Pat Burrell	8.00
11	Jose Vidro	4.00
12	Roberto Alomar	8.00
13	Chipper Jones	15.00
14	Robin Ventura	5.00
15	J.D. Drew	5.00
16	Matt Lawton	4.00
17	Josh Hamilton	10.00
18	Chin-Feng Chen	25.00
19	Rafael Furcal	8.00
20	Miguel Tejada	8.00
21	Josh Beckett	10.00
22	Ryan Anderson	4.00

2001 Topps Gallery

		NM/M
Complete Set (152):		100.00
Common Player:		.15
Common Rookie:		1.50
Inserted 1:3.5		
Common Prospect:		.50
Inserted 1:2.5		
Common Retired:		1.00
Inserted 1:5		
Pack (6):		5.00
Box (24):		100.00
Set price includes one Suzuki rookie.		
1	Darin Erstad	.40
2	Chipper Jones	1.50
3	Nomar Garciaparra	.75
4	Fernando Vina	.25
5	Bartolo Colon	.25
6	Bobby Higginson	.15
7	Antonio Alfonseca	.15
8	Mike Sweeney	.15
9	Kevin Brown	.25
10	Jose Vidro	.15
11	Derek Jeter	3.00
12	Jason Giambi	.50
13	Pat Burrell	.50
14	Jeff Kent	.25
15	Alex Rodriguez	2.50
16	Rafael Palmeiro	.50
17	Garret Anderson	.40
18	Brad Fullmer	.15
19	Doug Glanville	.15
20	Mark Quinn	.15
21	Mo Vaughn	.25
22	Andruw Jones	.50
23	Pedro Martinez	1.00
24	Ken Griffey Jr.	1.50
25	Roberto Alomar	.50
26	Dean Palmer	.15
27	Jeff Bagwell	.50

28	Jermaine Dye	.15
29	Chan Ho Park	.15
30	Vladimir Guerrero	1.00
31	Bernie Williams	.50
32	Ben Grieve	.15
33	Jason Kendall	.15
34	Barry Bonds	3.00
35	Jim Edmonds	.40
36	Ivan Rodriguez	.50
37	Javy Lopez	.25
38	J.T. Snow	.15
39	Erubiel Durazo	.15
40	Terrence Long	.15
41	Tim Salmon	.25
42	Greg Maddux	1.50
43	Sammy Sosa	1.00
44	Sean Casey	.25
45	Jeff Cirillo	.15
46	Juan Gonzalez	.40
47	Richard Hidalgo	.25
48	Shawn Green	.25
49	Jeromy Burnitz	.15
50	Willie Mays	15.00
51	David Justice	.25
52	Tim Hudson	.40
53	Brian Giles	.25
54	Robb Nen	.15
55	Fernando Tatis	.15
56	Tony Batista	.15
57	Pokey Reese	.15
58	Ray Durham	.15
59	Greg Vaughn	.15
60	Kazuhiro Sasaki	.15
61	Troy Glaus	.40
62	Rafael Furcal	.40
63	Magglio Ordonez	.40
64	Jim Thome	.75
65	Todd Helton	.75
66	Preston Wilson	.15
67	Moises Alou	.25
68	Gary Sheffield	.40
69	Geoff Jenkins	.25
70	Mike Piazza	1.50
71	Jorge Posada	.40
72	Bobby Abreu	.40
73	Phil Nevin	.15
74	John Olerud	.25
75	Mark McGwire	1.50
76	Jose Cruz Jr.	.15
77	David Segui	.15
78	Neifi Perez	.15
79	Omar Vizquel	.25
80	Rick Ankiel	.50
81	Randy Johnson	1.00
82	Albert Belle	.15
83	Frank Thomas	.75
84	Manny Ramirez	.75
85	Larry Walker	.25
86	Luis Castillo	.15
87	Johnny Damon	.50
88	Adrian Beltre	.25
89	Cristian Guzman	.15
90	Jay Payton	.15
91	Miguel Tejada	.40
92	Scott Rolen	.75
93	Ryan Klesko	.40
94	Edgar Martinez	.25
95	Fred McGriff	.25
96	Carlos Delgado	.50
97	Barry Zito	.40
98	Mike Lieberthal	.15
99	Trevor Hoffman	.15
100	Gabe Kapler	.15
101	Edgardo Alfonzo	.15
102	Corey Patterson	.50
103	Alfonso Soriano	1.00
104	Keith Ginter	.50
105	Keith Reed	.50
106	Nick Johnson	.50
107	Carlos Pena	.50
108	Vernon Wells	.50
109	Roy Oswalt	.50
110	Alex Escobar	.50
111	Adam Everett	.50
112	Jimmy Rollins	1.00
113	Marcus Giles	.50
114	Jack Cust	.50
115	Chin-Feng Chen	1.00
116	Pablo Ozuna	.50
117	Ben Sheets	.50
118	Adrian Gonzalez	.50
119	Ben Davis	.50
120	Eric Valent	.50
121	Scott Heard	.50
122	David Parrish RC	1.50
123	Sean Burnett	.50
124	Derek Thompson	.50
125	Tim Christman RC	1.50
126	Mike Jacobs RC	2.00
127	Luis Montanez RC	1.50
128	Chris Bass RC	1.50
129	William Smith RC	1.50
130	Justin Wayne RC	2.00
131	Shawn Fagan RC	1.50
132	Chad Petty RC	1.50
133	J.R. House	.50
134	Joel Pineiro	.50
135	Albert Pujols RC	40.00
136	Carmen Cali RC	1.50
137	Steve Smyth RC	1.50
138	John Lackey	1.50
139	Bob Keppel RC	1.50
140	Dominic Rich RC	1.50
141	Josh Hamilton	1.00
142	Nolan Ryan	5.00

143	Tom Seaver	1.50
144	Reggie Jackson	1.50
145	Johnny Bench	1.50
146	Warren Spahn	1.50
147	Brooks Robinson	1.50
148	Carl Yastrzemski	1.00
149	Al Kaline	1.00
150	Bob Feller	1.00
151a	Ichiro Suzuki/English RC	20.00
151b	Ichiro Suzuki/Japanese RC	20.00

Press Plates

	NM/M
Common Player:	50.00
(See 2001 Topps Gallery for checklist.)	

Autographs

		NM/M
Common Autograph:		15.00
Inserted 1:232		
RA	Rick Ankiel	30.00
BB	Barry Bonds	150.00
PB	Pat Burrell	20.00
AG	Adrian Gonzalez	15.00
AR	Alex Rodriguez	120.00
IR	Ivan Rodriguez	50.00

Heritage

		NM/M
Complete Set (10):		30.00
Common Player:		2.00
Inserted 1:12		
1	Todd Helton	3.00
2	Greg Maddux	4.00
3	Pedro Martinez	3.00
4	Orlando Cepeda	2.00
5	Willie McCovey	2.00
6	Ken Griffey Jr.	4.00
7	Alex Rodriguez	6.00
8	Derek Jeter	8.00
9	Mark McGwire	5.00
10	Vladimir Guerrero	3.00

Heritage Relic

PITCHER
GREG MADDUX

	NM/M
Common Player:	10.00
Inserted 1:133	
Orlando Cepeda	10.00
Greg Maddux	25.00
Pedro Martinez	20.00
Willie McCovey	10.00

Heritage Autographed Relic

	NM/M
Production 25 Sets	
Orlando Cepeda	75.00
Willie McCovey	100.00

Originals Relics

		NM/M
Common Player:		8.00
Inserted 1:133		
RA	Roberto Alomar	10.00
JD	Jermaine Dye	8.00
DE	Darin Erstad	8.00
JG	Jason Giambi	10.00
AG	Adrian Gonzalez	8.00
SG	Shawn Green	10.00
AJ	Andruw Jones	10.00
JK	Jason Kendall	8.00
JFK	Jeff Kent	8.00
RP	Rafael Palmeiro	10.00
PR	Pokey Reese	8.00
SS	Sammy Sosa	20.00
RV	Robin Ventura	8.00
BW	Bernie Williams	10.00
PW	Preston Wilson	8.00

Star Gallery

		NM/M
Complete Set (10):		15.00
Common Player:		1.00
Inserted 1:8		
1	Vladimir Guerrero	1.00
2	Alex Rodriguez	2.50
3	Derek Jeter	3.00
4	Nomar Garciaparra	2.50
5	Ken Griffey Jr.	1.50
6	Mark McGwire	2.00
7	Chipper Jones	1.50
8	Sammy Sosa	2.00
9	Barry Bonds	3.00
10	Mike Piazza	1.50

Team Topps Legends Autographs

SCORE
CHI. WHITE SOX

		NM/M
Common Autograph:		10.00
Inserted 1:286		
23R	Gil McDougald	10.00
27F	Andy Pafko	20.00
10R	Frank Robinson	20.00
28F	Herb Score	10.00
25R	Luis Tiant	10.00

2001 Topps Gold Label

CHIPPER JONES

	NM/M
Complete Set (115):	80.00
Common Player:	.25
Common Rookie:	4.00
Production 999	
Golds:	2-3X
Production 999	
Gold Rookies:	2-3X
Production 99	
Pack (5):	3.00
Box (24):	50.00
1 Adrian Beltre	.40
2 Danny Borrell **RC**	4.00
3 Albert Belle	.25
4 Alex Cabrera	.25
5 Alex Rodriguez	2.50
6 Andruw Jones	.50
7 Antonio Alfonseca	.25
8 Barry Bonds	3.00
9 Barry Larkin	.25
10 Ben Grieve	.25
11 Ben Molina	.25
12 Bernie Williams	.50
13 Bobby Abreu	.40
14 Bobby Higginson	.25
15 Brad Fullmer	.25
16 Brian Giles	.40
17 Cal Ripken Jr.	3.00
18 Carlos Delgado	.50
19 Chad Petty **RC**	4.00
20 Charles Johnson	.25
21 Chipper Jones	1.50
22 Cristian Guzman	.25
23 Darin Erstad	.40
24 David Justice	.40
25 David Segui	.25
26 Derek Jeter	2.50
27 Edgar Martinez	.40
28 Edgardo Alfonzo	.25
29 Fernando Tatis	.25
30 Eric Karros	.25
31 Eric Munson	.25
32 Eric Young	.25
33 Frank Thomas	.75
34 Fernando Vina	.25
35 Garret Anderson	.50
36 Gary Sheffield	.50
37 Geoff Jenkins	.40
38 Greg Maddux	2.00
39 Ivan Rodriguez	.50
40 J.D. Drew	.40
41 J.R. House	.25
42 J.T. Snow Jr.	.25
43 Jason Giambi	.50

44 Jason Kendall	.40
45 Jay Payton	.25
46 Jeff Bagwell	.50
47 Jeff Cirillo	.25
48 Jeff Kent	.40
49 Chan Ho Park	.25
50 Jermaine Dye	.25
51 Jeromy Burnitz	.25
52 Jim Edmonds	.50
53 Jim Thome	.75
54 John Olerud	.50
55 Johnny Damon	.40
56 Jorge Posada	.50
57 Jose Cruz Jr.	.25
58 Jose Vidro	.25
59 Josh Hamilton	.50
60 Juan Gonzalez	.50
61 Steve Smyth **RC**	4.00
62 Justin Wayne **RC**	4.00
63 Kazuhiro Sasaki	.25
64 Ken Griffey Jr.	2.00
65 Kevin Brown	.40
66 Kevin Young	.25
67 Larry Walker	.25
68 Luis Castillo	.25
69 Steve Finley	.25
70 Magglio Ordonez	.50
71 Manny Ramirez	.75
72 Mark McGwire	2.00
73 Mark Quinn	.25
74 Miguel Tejada	.50
75 Mike Piazza	1.50
76 Mike Sweeney	.25
77 Mo Vaughn	.25
78 Moises Alou	.40
79 Nomar Garciaparra	.75
80 Pat Burrell	.50
81 Paul Konerko	.25
82 Pedro Martinez	1.00
83 Phil Nevin	.25
84 Preston Wilson	.25
85 Rafael Furcal	.40
86 Todd Zeile	.25
87 Randy Johnson	1.00
88 Travis Lee	.25
89 Carl Everett	.25
90 Quilvio Veras	.25
91 Rick Ankiel	.50
92 Rick Brosseau **RC**	4.00
93 Robert Keppell **RC**	4.00
94 Roberto Alomar	.50
95 Ryan Klesko	.40
96 Sammy Sosa	1.00
97 Scott Heard	4.00
98 Scott Rolen	.75
99 Sean Casey	.50
100 Shawn Green	.40
101 Terrence Long	.25
102 Tim Salmon	.40
103 Todd Helton	.75
104 Tom Glavine	.50
105 Tony Batista	.25
106 Travis Baptist **RC**	4.00
107 Troy Glaus	.50
108 Victor Hall **RC**	4.00
109 Vladimir Guerrero	1.00
110 Tim Hudson	.40
111 Brian Roberts **RC**	2.00
112 Virgil Chevalier **RC**	4.00
113 Fernando Rodney **RC**	4.00
114 Paul Phillips **RC**	4.00
115 Cesar Bolivar **RC**	4.00

Class 2

	NM/M
Stars:	1-2X
Inserted 1:4	
Rookies:	1-1.5X
Production 699	
Golds:	2-3X
Production 699	
Gold Rookies:	2-3X
Production 69	
(See 2001 Topps Gold Label for	
checklist and base card values.)	

Class 3

	NM/M
Stars:	2-3X
Inserted 1:12	
Rookies:	1-2X
Production 299	
Golds:	3-5X
Production 299	

	NM/M
Gold Rookies:	2-4X
Production 29	
(See 2001 Topps Gold Label for	
checklist and base card values.)	

Masterpiece

	NM/M
Common Player:	50.00
(See 2001 Topps Gold Label for	
checklist.)	

Gold Fixtures

GOLD FIXTURES

	NM/M
Complete Set (10):	150.00
Common Player:	8.00
Inserted 1:374	
1 Alex Rodriguez	20.00
2 Mark McGwire	20.00
3 Derek Jeter	25.00
4 Nomar Garciaparra	20.00
5 Chipper Jones	15.00
6 Sammy Sosa	20.00
7 Ken Griffey Jr.	15.00
8 Carlos Delgado	8.00
9 Frank Thomas	10.00
10 Barry Bonds	25.00

MLB Awards Ceremony

MLB Award Ceremony

	NM/M
Common Player:	4.00

Inserted 1:24

SA	Sandy Alomar/Bat	4.00
JB	Jeff Bagwell/Bat	8.00
AB	Albert Belle/Bat	4.00
CB	Carlos Beltran/Bat	4.00
DB	Dante Bichette	4.00
BB	Barry Bonds/Jsy	25.00
BB	Barry Bonds/Bat	25.00
SB	Scott Brosius/Bat	5.00
JC	Jose Canseco/Jsy	6.00
JC	Jose Canseco/Bat	6.00
WC	Will Clark/Bat	6.00
RC	Roger Clemens/Jsy	20.00
MC	Marty Cordova/Bat	4.00
RF	Rafael Furcal/Bat	6.00
AG	Andres Galarraga/Bat	4.00
NG	Nomar Garciaparra/Jsy	20.00
NG	Nomar Garciaparra/Bat	20.00
JG	Jason Giambi/Bat	8.00
TG	Troy Glaus/Bat	8.00
TG	Tom Glavine/Jsy	6.00
JG	Juan Gonzalez/Jsy	8.00
JG	Juan Gonzalez/Bat	8.00
DG	Dwight Gooden/Jsy	4.00
BG	Ben Grieve/Jsy	4.00
KG	Ken Griffey Jr./Jsy	15.00
KG	Ken Griffey Jr./Bat	15.00
TG	Tony Gwynn/Bat	10.00
TH	Todd Helton/Bat	8.00
RH	Rickey Henderson/Jsy	15.00
TH	Todd Hollandsworth/Bat	4.00
DJ	Derek Jeter/Bat	25.00
RJ	Randy Johnson/Jsy	10.00
CJ	Chipper Jones/Jsy	10.00
DJ	David Justice/Jsy	5.00
JK	Jeff Kent/Bat	4.00
CK	Chuck Knoblauch/Bat	4.00
BL	Barry Larkin/Bat	8.00
GM	Greg Maddux/Jsy	15.00
EM	Edgar Martinez/Bat	6.00
PM	Pedro Martinez/Jsy	10.00
FM	Fred McGriff/Bat	5.00
MM	Mark McGwire/Bat	60.00
MM	Mark McGwire/Jsy	60.00
RM	Raul Mondesi/Bat	4.00
HN	Hideo Nomo/Jsy	25.00
JO	John Olerud/Bat	4.00
PO	Paul O'Neill/Bat	5.00
MP	Mike Piazza/Bat	12.00
CR	Cal Ripken Jr./Jsy	35.00
AR	Alex Rodriguez/Bat	15.00
IR	Ivan Rodriguez/Jsy	8.00
SR	Scott Rolen/Jsy	8.00
TS	Tim Salmon/Jsy	4.00
KS	Kazuhiro Sasaki/Jsy	5.00
GS	Gary Sheffield/Bat	6.00
JS	John Smoltz/Jsy	4.00
SS	Sammy Sosa/Bat	15.00
SS	Sammy Sosa/Jsy	15.00
DS	Darryl Strawberry/Jsy	4.00
DS	Darryl Strawberry/Bat	4.00
FT	Frank Thomas/Bat	8.00
FT	Frank Thomas/Jsy	8.00
MV	Mo Vaughn/Jsy	4.00
MV	Mo Vaughn/Bat	4.00
LW	Larry Walker/Bat	5.00
LW	Larry Walker/Jsy	5.00
JW	John Wetteland/Jsy	4.00
BW	Bernie Williams/Bat	8.00
MW	Matt Williams/Bat	5.00

2001 Topps Heritage

	NM/M
Complete Set (407):	275.00
Complete Master Set (487):	320.00
Common Player:	.50
Common SP (311-407):	2.50
Inserted 1:2	
Pack (8):	13.00
Box (24):	275.00

1	Kris Benson	.50
2	Brian Jordan	.50
3	Fernando Vina	.50
4	Mike Sweeney	.50
5	Rafael Palmeiro	2.00
6	Paul O'Neill	1.00
7	Todd Helton	2.50
8	Ramiro Mendoza	.50
9	Kevin Millwood	1.00
10	Chuck Knoblauch	.75
11	Derek Jeter	10.00
12	Alex Rodriguez	8.00
13	Geoff Jenkins	.75
14	David Justice	1.00
15	David Cone	.50
16	Andres Galarraga	1.00
17	Garret Anderson	1.00
18	Roger Cedeno	.50
19	Randy Velarde	.50
20	Carlos Delgado	2.00
21	Quilvio Veras	.50
22	Jose Vidro	.50
23	Corey Patterson	.75
24	Jorge Posada	1.00
25	Eddie Perez	.50
26	Jack Cust	.50
27	Sean Burroughs	.75
28	Randy Wolf	.50
29	Mike Lamb	.50
30	Rafael Furcal	.75
31	Barry Bonds	8.00
32	Tim Hudson	.75
33	Tom Glavine	1.50
34	Javy Lopez	.75
35	Aubrey Huff	.50
36	Wally Joyner	.50
37	Magglio Ordonez	1.00
38	Matt Lawton	.50
39	Mariano Rivera	1.00
40	Andy Ashby	.50
41	Mark Buehrle	3.00
42	Esteban Loaiza	.50
43	Mark Redman	.50
44	Mark Quinn	.50
45	Tino Martinez	.75
46	Joe Mays	.50
47	Walt Weiss	.50
48	Roger Clemens	6.00
49	Greg Maddux	5.00
50	Richard Hidalgo	.75
51	Orlando Hernandez	.75
52	Chipper Jones	5.00
53	Ben Grieve	.50
54	Jimmy Haynes	.50
55	Ken Caminiti	.50
56	Tim Salmon	1.00
57	Andy Pettitte	1.00
58	Darin Erstad	1.00
59	Marquis Grissom	.50
60	Raul Mondesi	.75
61	Bengie Molina	.50
62	Miguel Tejada	1.00
63	Jose Cruz Jr.	.50
64	Billy Koch	.50
65	Troy Glaus	2.00
66	Cliff Floyd	.50
67	Tony Batista	.50
68	Jeff Bagwell	2.50
69	Billy Wagner	.50
70	Eric Chavez	.75
71	Troy Percival	.50
72	Andruw Jones	2.50
73	Shane Reynolds	.50
74	Barry Zito	2.50
75	Roy Halladay	1.00
76	David Wells	.50
77	Jason Giambi	1.50
78	Scott Elarton	.50
79	Moises Alou	.75
80	Adam Piatt	.75
81	Wilton Veras	.50
82	Darryl Kile	.50
83	Johnny Damon	.50
84	Tony Armas Jr.	.50
85	Ellis Burks	.50
86	Jamey Wright	.50
87	Jose Vizcaino	.50
88	Bartolo Colon	.50
89	Carmen Cali **RC**	.50
90	Kevin Brown	.75
91	Josh Hamilton	.75
92	Jay Buhner	.50
93	Scott Pratt **RC**	.50
94	Alex Cora	.50
95	Luis Montanez **RC**	1.00
96	Dmitri Young	.50
97	J.T. Snow Jr.	.50
98	Damion Easley	.50
99	Greg Norton	.50
100	Matt Wheatland	.50
101	Chin-Feng Chen	.50
102	Tony Womack	.50
103	Adam Kennedy	.50
104	J.D. Drew	.50
105	Carlos Febles	.50
106	Jim Thome	1.00
107	Danny Graves	.50
108	Dave Mlicki	.50
109	Ron Coomer	.50
110	James Baldwin	.50
111	Shaun Boyd **RC**	.75
112	Brian Bohannon	.50
113	Jacque Jones	.50
114	Alfonso Soriano	1.50
115	Tony Clark	.50
116	Terrence Long	.50
117	Todd Hundley	.50
118	Kazuhiro Sasaki	.50
119	Brian Sellier **RC**	.50
120	John Olerud	.75
121	Javier Vazquez	.50
122	Sean Burnett	.50
123	Matt LeCroy	.50
124	Erubiel Durazo	.50
125	Juan Encarnacion	.50
126	Pablo Ozuna	.50
127	Russ Ortiz	.50
128	David Segui	.50
129	Mark McGwire	3.00
130	Mark Grace	1.00
131	Fred McGriff	.75
132	Carl Pavano	.50
133	Derek Thompson	.50
134	Shawn Green	.75
135	B.J. Surhoff	.50
136	Michael Tucker	.50
137	Jason Isringhausen	.50
138	Eric Milton	.50
139	Mike Stodolka	.50
140	Milton Bradley	.50
141	Curt Schilling	.75
142	Sandy Alomar	.50
143	Brent Mayne	.50
144	Todd Jones	.50
145	Charles Johnson	.50
146	Dean Palmer	.50
147	Masato Yoshii	.50
148	Edgar Renteria	.50
149	Joe Randa	.50
150	Adam Johnson	.50
151	Greg Vaughn	.50
152	Adrian Beltre	.75
153	Glenallen Hill	.50
154	David Parrish **RC**	.75
155	Neifi Perez	.50
156	Pete Harnisch	.50
157	Paul Konerko	.50
158	Dennys Reyes	.50
159	Jose Lima	.50
160	Eddie Taubensee	.50
161	Miguel Cairo	.50
162	Jeff Kent	.75
163	Dustin Hermanson	.50
164	Alex Gonzalez	.50
165	Hideo Nomo	.75
166	Sammy Sosa	2.00
167	C.J. Nitkowski	.50
168	Cal Eldred	.50
169	Jeff Abbott	.50
170	Jim Edmonds	.75
171	Mark Mulder	.75
172	Dominic Rich **RC**	.50
173	Ray Lankford	.50
174	Danny Borrell **RC**	.75
175	Rick Aguilera	.50
176	Shannon Stewart	.50
177	Steve Finley	.50
178	Jim Parque	.50
179	Kevin Appier	.50
180	Adrian Gonzalez	.75
181	Tom Goodwin	.50
182	Kevin Tapani	.50
183	Fernando Tatis	.50
184	Mark Grudzielanek	.50
185	Ryan Anderson	.50
186	Jeffrey Hammonds	.50
187	Corey Koskie	.50
188	Brad Fullmer	.50
189	Rey Sanchez	.50
190	Michael Barrett	.50
191	Rickey Henderson	1.00
192	Jermaine Dye	.50
193	Scott Brosius	.50
194	Matt Anderson	.50
195	Brian Buchanan	.50
196	Derrek Lee	.50
197	Larry Walker	.75
198	David Krynzel	.50
199	Vinny Castilla	.50
200	Ken Griffey Jr.	2.00
201	Matt Stairs	.50
202	Ty Howington	.50
203	Andy Benes	.50
204	Luis Gonzalez	.75
205	Brian Moehler	.50
206	Harold Baines	.50
207	Pedro Astacio	.50
208	Cristian Guzman	.50
209	Kip Wells	.50
210	Frank Thomas	1.00
211	Jose Rosado	.50
212	Vernon Wells	.50
213	Bobby Higginson	.50
214	Juan Gonzalez	1.00
215	Omar Vizquel	.75
216	Bernie Williams	1.00
217	Aaron Sele	.50
218	Shawn Estes	.50
219	Roberto Alomar	1.00
220	Rick Ankiel	.50
221	Josh Kalinowski	.50
222	David Bell	.50
223	Keith Foulke	.50
224	Craig Biggio	.75
225	Shawn Fagan **RC**	.50
226	Scott Williamson	.50
227	Ron Belliard	.50
228	Chris Singleton	.50
229	Alex Serrano	.50
230	Deivi Cruz	.50
231	Eric Munson	.50
232	Luis Castillo	.50
233	Edgar Martinez	.75
234	Jeff Shaw	.50
235	Jeromy Burnitz	.50
236	Richie Sexson	.75
237	Will Clark	1.00
238	Ron Villone	.50
239	Kerry Wood	1.00
240	Rich Aurilia	.50
241	Mo Vaughn	.50
242	Travis Fryman	.75
243	Manny Ramirez	1.00
244	Chris Stynes	.50
245	Ray Durham	.50
246	Juan Uribe **RC**	.50
247	Juan Guzman	.50
248	Lee Stevens	.50
249	Devon White	.50
250	Kyle Lohse **RC**	1.50
251	Bryan Wolff	.50
252	Rick Brousseau **RC**	.50
253	Eric Young	.50
254	Freddy Garcia	.50
255	Jay Bell	.50
256	Steve Cox	.50
257	Torii Hunter	.75
258	Jose Canseco	.75
259	Brad Ausmus	.50
260	Jeff Cirillo	.50
261	Brad Penny	.50
262	Antonio Alfonseca	.50
263	Russ Branyan	.50
264	Scott Heard	.50
265	John Lackey	.50
266	Justin Wayne **RC**	1.00
267	Brad Radke	.50
268	Todd Stottlemyre	.50
269	Mark Loretta	.50
270	Matt Williams	.50
271	Kenny Lofton	.50
272	Jeff D'Amico	.50
273	Jamie Moyer	.50
274	Darren Dreifort	.50
275	Denny Neagle	.50
276	Orlando Cabrera	.50
277	Chuck Finley	.50
278	Miguel Batista	.50
279	Carlos Beltran	.50
280	Eric Karros	.50
281	Mark Kotsay	.50
282	Ryan Dempster	.50
283	Barry Larkin	.75
284	Jeff Suppan	.50
285	Gary Sheffield	.75
286	Jose Valentin	.50
287	Robb Nen	.50
288	Chan Ho Park	.50
289	John Halama	.50
290	Steve Smyth **RC**	.50
291	Gerald Williams	.50
292	Preston Wilson	.50
293	Victor Hall **RC**	.75
294	Ben Sheets	.50
295	Eric Davis	.50
296	Kirk Rueter	.50
297	Chad Petty **RC**	.75
298	Kevin Millar	.50
299	Marvin Benard	.50
300	Vladimir Guerrero	1.00
301	Livan Hernandez	.50
302	Travis Baptist **RC**	.75
303	Bill Mueller	.50
304	Mike Cameron	.50
305	Randy Johnson	1.50
306	Alan Mahaffey **RC**	.50
307	Timo Perez (No facsimile autograph.)	.50
308	Pokey Reese	.50
309	Ryan Rupe	.50
310	Carlos Lee	.50
311	Doug Glanville	2.50
312	Jay Payton	2.50
313	Troy O'Leary	2.50
314	Francisco Cordero	2.50
315	Rusty Greer	2.50
316	Cal Ripken Jr.	25.00
317	Ricky Ledee	2.50
318	Brian Daubach	2.50
319	Robin Ventura	2.50
320	Todd Zeile	2.50
321	Francisco Cordova	2.50
322	Henry Rodriguez	2.50
323	Pat Meares	2.50
324	Glendon Rusch	2.50
325	Keith Osik	2.50
326	Robert Keppell **RC**	3.00
327	Bobby Jones	2.50
328	Alex Ramirez	2.50
329	Robert Person	2.50
330	Ruben Mateo	2.50
331	Rob Bell	2.50
332	Carl Everett	2.50
333	Jason Schmidt	2.50
334	Scott Rolen	5.00
335	Jimmy Anderson	2.50
336	Bret Boone	2.50
337	Delino DeShields	2.50
338	Trevor Hoffman	2.50
339	Bob Abreu	3.00
340	Mike Williams	2.50
341	Mike Hampton	2.50
342	John Wetteland	2.50
343	Scott Erickson	2.50
344	Enrique Wilson	2.50
345	Tim Wakefield	2.50
346	Mike Lowell	3.00
347	Todd Pratt	2.50
348	Brook Fordyce	2.50
349	Benny Agbayani	2.50
350	Gabe Kapler	3.00
351	Sean Casey	2.50
352	Darren Oliver	2.50
353	Todd Ritchie	2.50
354	Kenny Rogers	2.50
355	Jason Kendall	2.50
356	John Vander Wal	2.50

357	Ramon Martinez	2.50
358	Edgardo Alfonzo	2.50
359	Phil Nevin	2.50
360	Albert Belle	2.50
361	Ruben Rivera	2.50
362	Pedro Martinez	10.00
363	Derek Lowe	2.50
364	Pat Burrell	5.00
365	Mike Mussina	5.00
366	Brady Anderson	2.50
367	Darren Lewis	2.50
368	Sidney Ponson	2.50
369	Adam Eaton	2.50
370	Eric Owens	2.50
371	Aaron Boone	2.50
372	Matt Clement	2.50
373	Derek Bell	2.50
374	Trot Nixon	2.50
375	Travis Lee	2.50
376	Mike Benjamin	2.50
377	Jeff Zimmerman	2.50
378	Mike Lieberthal	2.50
379	Rick Reed	2.50
380	Nomar Garciaparra	5.00
381	Omar Daal	2.50
382	Ryan Klesko	2.50
383	Rey Ordonez	2.50
384	Kevin Young	2.50
385	Rick Helling	2.50
386	Brian Giles	3.00
387	Tony Gwynn	8.00
388	Ed Sprague	2.50
389	J.R. House	2.50
390	Scott Hatteberg	2.50
391	John Valentin	2.50
392	Melvin Mora	2.50
393	Royce Clayton	2.50
394	Jeff Fassero	2.50
395	Manny Alexander	2.50
396	John Franco	2.50
397	Luis Alicea	2.50
398	Ivan Rodriguez	5.00
399	Kevin Jordan	2.50
400	Jose Offerman	2.50
401	Jeff Conine	2.50
402	Seth Etherton	2.50
403	Mike Bordick	2.50
404	Al Leiter	2.50
405	Mike Piazza	10.00
406	Armando Benitez	2.50
407	Warren Morris	2.50

Chrome

	Common Player:	3.00
	Production 552 Sets	
1	Cal Ripken Jr.	40.00
2	Jim Thome	10.00
3	Derek Jeter	40.00
4	Andres Galarraga	4.00
5	Carlos Delgado	8.00
6	Roberto Alomar	8.00
7	Tom Glavine	10.00
8	Gary Sheffield	8.00
9	Mo Vaughn	3.00
10	Preston Wilson	3.00
11	Mike Mussina	8.00
12	Greg Maddux	30.00
13	Ivan Rodriguez	10.00
14	Al Leiter	3.00
15	Seth Etherton	3.00
16	Edgardo Alfonzo	3.00
17	Richie Sexson	3.00
18	Andruw Jones	10.00
19	Bartolo Colon	3.00
20	Darin Erstad	5.00
21	Kevin Brown	4.00
22	Mike Sweeney	3.00
23	Mike Piazza	30.00
24	Rafael Palmeiro	10.00
25	Terrence Long	3.00
26	Kazuhiro Sasaki	3.00
27	John Olerud	5.00
28	Mark McGwire	30.00
29	Fred McGriff	5.00
30	Todd Helton	10.00
31	Curt Schilling	10.00
32	Alex Rodriguez	30.00
33	Jeff Kent	5.00
34	Pat Burrell	8.00
35	Jim Edmonds	5.00

36	Mark Mulder	3.00
37	Troy Glaus	8.00
38	Jay Payton	3.00
39	Jermaine Dye	5.00
40	Larry Walker	5.00
41	Ken Griffey Jr.	30.00
42	Jeff Bagwell	10.00
43	Rick Ankiel	8.00
44	Mark Redman	3.00
45	Edgar Martinez	5.00
46	Mike Hampton	4.00
47	Manny Ramirez	10.00
48	Ray Durham	3.00
49	Rafael Furcal	5.00
50	Sean Casey	4.00
51	Jose Canseco	8.00
52	Barry Bonds	40.00
53	Tim Hudson	8.00
54	Barry Zito	5.00
55	Chuck Finley	3.00
56	Magglio Ordonez	5.00
57	David Wells	3.00
58	Jason Giambi	8.00
59	Tony Gwynn	15.00
60	Vladimir Guerrero	15.00
61	Randy Johnson	15.00
62	Bernie Williams	8.00
63	Craig Biggio	5.00
64	Jason Kendall	5.00
65	Pedro Martinez	15.00
66	Mark Quinn	3.00
67	Frank Thomas	15.00
68	Nomar Garciaparra	15.00
69	Brian Giles	5.00
70	Shawn Green	5.00
71	Roger Clemens	25.00
72	Sammy Sosa	15.00
73	Juan Gonzalez	8.00
74	Orlando Hernandez	4.00
75	Chipper Jones	20.00
76	Josh Hamilton	10.00
77	Adam Johnson	3.00
78	Shaun Boyd	3.00
79	Alfonso Soriano	15.00
80	Derek Thompson	3.00
81	Adrian Gonzalez	8.00
82	Ryan Anderson	3.00
83	Corey Patterson	5.00
84	J.R. House	3.00
85	Sean Burroughs	3.00
86	Scott Heard	3.00
87	John Lackey	8.00
88	Ben Sheets	3.00
89	Wilson Betemit	3.00
90	Robert Keppell	3.00
91	Luis Montanez	3.00
92	Sean Burnett	3.00
93	Justin Wayne	5.00
94	Eric Munson	3.00
95	Steve Smyth	3.00
96	Rick Brousseau	3.00
97	Carmen Cali	3.00
98	Brian Sellier	3.00
99	David Parrish	3.00
100	Danny Borrell	3.00
101	Chad Petty	3.00
102	Dominic Rich	3.00
103	Shawn Fagan	3.00
104	Alex Serrano	3.00
105	Juan Uribe	3.00
106	Travis Baptist	3.00
107	Alan Mahaffey	3.00
108	Kyle Lohse	5.00
109	Victor Hall	3.00
110	Scott Pratt	3.00

Classic Renditions

Nomar Garciaparra
Boston Red Sox

		NM/M
	Complete Set (10):	15.00
	Common Player:	1.00
	Inserted 1:5	
1	Mark McGwire	2.50
2	Nomar Garciaparra	2.00
3	Barry Bonds	3.00
4	Sammy Sosa	1.50
5	Chipper Jones	1.50
6	Pat Burrell	1.00
7	Frank Thomas	1.50
8	Manny Ramirez	1.00
9	Derek Jeter	3.00
10	Ken Griffey Jr.	2.00

Classic Renditions Autos.

	Production 25 Sets	
BB	Barry Bonds	500.00
CJ	Chipper Jones	350.00
NG	Nomar Garciaparra	150.00

Clubhouse Collection Game-Used

CHIPPER JONES

		NM/M
	Common Player:	25.00
MM	Minnie Monoso	25.00
RS	Red Schoendienst	30.00
DS	Duke Snider	40.00
EM	Eddie Mathews	40.00
CJ	Chipper Jones	40.00
RA	Richie Ashburn	30.00
FT	Frank Thomas	40.00
FV	Fernando Vina	25.00
SG	Shawn Green	30.00
WM	Willie Mays	150.00
BB	Barry Bonds	80.00
SR	Scott Rolen	40.00

Clubhouse Collection Dual Game-Used

		NM/M
	Common Card:	75.00
	Production 52 Sets	
MMFT	Minnie Monoso, Frank Thomas	100.00
RSFV	Red Schoendienst, Fernando Vina	75.00
DSSG	Duke Snider, Shawn Green	150.00
RAPB	Richie Ashburn, Scott Rolen	100.00
EMCJ	Eddie Mathews, Chipper Jones	125.00
WMBB	Willie Mays, Barry Bonds	250.00

Clubhouse Collection Autos.

		NM/M
	Common Player:	
MM	Minnie Monoso/25	120.00
RS	Red Schoendienst/25	150.00

Grandstand Glory

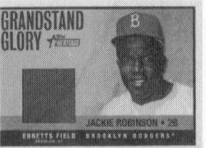

JACKIE ROBINSON • 28

		NM/M
	Common Player:	20.00
	Inserted 1:211	
PR	Phil Rizzuto	30.00
YB	Yogi Berra	30.00
RA	Richie Ashburn	20.00
RR	Robin Roberts	20.00
WM	Willie Mays	60.00
NF	Nellie Fox	20.00
JR	Jackie Robinson	50.00

New Age Performers

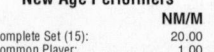

		NM/M
	Complete Set (15):	20.00
	Common Player:	1.00

new age performers

Derek Jeter
NEW YORK YANKEES

	Inserted 1:8	
1	Mike Piazza	1.50
2	Sammy Sosa	2.00
3	Alex Rodriguez	2.50
4	Barry Bonds	3.00
5	Ken Griffey Jr.	1.50
6	Chipper Jones	1.50
7	Randy Johnson	1.00
8	Derek Jeter	3.00
9	Nomar Garciaparra	2.00
10	Mark McGwire	2.50
11	Jeff Bagwell	1.00
12	Pedro Martinez	1.00
13	Todd Helton	1.00
14	Vladimir Guerrero	1.00
15	Greg Maddux	2.00

Real One Autographs

BARRY BONDS

		NM/M
	Common Player:	30.00
	Current MLB Players	
	200 Blue-Inked Produced	
	Red Ink:	1-1.5X
	52 Red-Inked Produced	
	Prices listed for Blue sigs.	
RH	Richard Hidalgo	30.00
TL	Terrence Long	30.00
CD	Carlos Delgado	60.00
CJ	Chipper Jones	160.00
TG	Tom Glavine	100.00
GJ	Geoff Jenkins	40.00
JM	Joe Mays	30.00
FV	Fernando Vina	30.00
CP	Corey Patterson	40.00
JV	Jose Vidro	30.00
BB	Barry Bonds	275.00
AR	Alex Rodriguez	250.00
AH	Aubrey Huff	40.00
SPB	Sean Burroughs	30.00
RW	Randy Wolf	30.00
KB	Kris Benson	30.00
ML	Mike Lamb	30.00
TH	Todd Helton	80.00
MQ	Mark Quinn	30.00
MS	Mike Sweeney	30.00
ML	Matt Lawton	35.00
MO	Magglio Ordonez	40.00
MB	Mark Buehrle	50.00
MR	Mark Redman	30.00
CF	Cliff Floyd	30.00
NG	Nomar Garciaparra	150.00
	1952 MLB Players	
MV	Mickey Vernon	40.00
HB	Hank Bauer	80.00
DD	Dom DiMaggio	100.00
LD	Larry Doby	100.00
JG	Joe Garagiola	80.00
DG	Dick Groat	70.00
MI	Monte Irvin	80.00
VL	Vernon Law	40.00
EM	Eddie Matthews	200.00
WM	Willie Mays	250.00
GM	Gil McDougald	60.00
MM	Minnie Monoso	85.00
AP	Andy Pafko	80.00
PFR	Phil Rizzuto	125.00
PR	Preacher Roe	100.00

JS	Johnny Sain	75.00
HS	Hank Sauer	75.00
RS	Red Schoendienst	80.00
BS	Bobby Shantz	50.00
CS	Curt Simmons	50.00
ES	Enos Slaughter	100.00
DS	Duke Snider	200.00
WS	Warren Spahn	125.00
BT	Bobby Thomson	90.00
HW	Hoyt Wilhelm	90.00
RR	Robin Roberts	80.00

Then and Now

Pee Wee Reese — Brooklyn Dodgers®
Nomar Garciaparra — Boston Red Sox®

		NM/M
Complete Set (10):		15.00
Common Player:		1.50
Inserted 1:8		
1	Yogi Berra, Mike Piazza	1.50
2	Duke Snider,	
	Sammy Sosa	2.00
3	Willie Mays,	
	Ken Griffey Jr.	2.00
4	Phil Rizzuto, Derek Jeter	3.00
5	Pee Wee Reese,	
	Nomar Garciaparra	2.00
6	Jackie Robinson,	
	Alex Rodriguez	2.50
7	Johnny Mize,	
	Mark McGwire	2.50
8	Bob Feller, Pedro Martinez	1.50
9	Robin Roberts,	
	Greg Maddux	2.00
10	Warren Spahn,	
	Randy Johnson	1.50

Time Capsule

		NM/M
Common Player:		20.00
Inserted 1:369		
WM	Willie Mays	75.00
TW	Ted Williams	85.00
DN	Don Newcombe	20.00
WF	Whitey Ford	30.00
WMTW	Ted Williams,	
	Willie Mays/52	200.00

2001 Topps HD

		NM/M
Complete Set (120):		50.00
Common Player:		.25
Common (101-120):		1.00
Inserted 1:6		
Pack (4):		2.50

Box (20):		40.00
1	Derek Jeter	3.00
2	Magglio Ordonez	.50
3	Eric Munson	.25
4	Jermaine Dye	.25
5	Larry Walker	.40
6	Pokey Reese	.25
7	Pedro Martinez	1.00
8	Rafael Palmeiro	.75
9	Jason Kendall	.40
10	Mike Lieberthal	.25
11	Ryan Klesko	.40
12	Cal Ripken Jr.	3.00
13	Mike Piazza	1.50
14	Adam Sterrett RC	.75
15	John Olerud	.40
16	Manny Ramirez	.75
17	Chad Petty RC	.75
18	Vladimir Guerrero	1.00
19	Kevin Brown	.40
20	Luis Cotto RC	.50
21	Josh Hamilton	.75
22	Mark Grace	.50
23	Mark McGwire	2.50
24	Jeromy Burnitz	.25
25	Andruw Jones	.50
26	Raul Mondesi	.40
27	Stuart McFarland RC	.50
28	Craig Biggio	.50
29	Troy Glaus	.50
30	Carlos Delgado	.50
31	Rafael Furcal	.40
32	J.D. Drew	.25
33	Corey Patterson	.40
34	Gary Sheffield	.50
35	Jeff Kent	.40
36	Alex Rodriguez	2.50
37	Edgardo Alfonzo	.25
38	Jeff Segar RC	.25
39	Bobby Abreu	.40
40	Brian Giles	.40
41	Jason Smith RC	.25
42	Mo Vaughn	.25
43	Pat Burrell	.40
44	Barry Larkin	.50
45	Carlos Beltran	.50
46	Eric Mosley RC	.50
47	Alfonso Soriano	1.00
48	Tim Salmon	.40
49	Jason Giambi	.50
50	Greg Maddux	1.50
51	Randy Johnson	1.00
52	Jose Vidro	.25
53	Edgar Martinez	.25
54	Albert Belle	.25
55	Ivan Rodriguez	.75
56	Sean Casey	.25
57	Jorge Posada	.50
58	Preston Wilson	.25
59	Paul Konerko	.25
60	Todd Helton	.75
61	Dominic Rich RC	.50
62	Tony Gwynn	1.00
63	Bernie Williams	.75
64	Anthony Brewer RC	.50
65	Shawn Green	.50
66	Jeff Bagwell	.75
67	Jose Cruz Jr.	.25
68	Darin Erstad	.50
69	Jim Edmonds	.50
70	Frank Thomas	.75
71	Ryan Anderson	.25
72	Scott Rolen	.75
73	Jeff Cirillo	.25
74	Chris Bass RC	.50
75	William Smith RC	.50
76	Trot Nixon	.25
77	Bobby Bradley	.25
78	Odannis Ayala RC	.50
79	Jim Thome	.75
80	Sammy Sosa	1.00
81	Geoff Jenkins	.40
82	Ben Grieve	.25
83	Andres Galarraga	.40
84	Rick Ankiel	.50
85	Barry Bonds	3.00
86	Alex Gonzalez	.25
87	Sean Burroughs	.25
88	Nomar Garciaparra	.75
89	Ken Griffey Jr.	1.50
90	Tim Hudson	.50
91	Chipper Jones	1.50
92	Matt Williams	.40
93	Roberto Alomar	.75
94	Adrian Gonzalez	.40
95	Juan Gonzalez	.50
96	Brian Bass RC	.50
97	Rick Brosseau RC	.50
98	Mariano Rivera	.40
99	James Baldwin	.25
100	Dean Palmer	.25
101	Pedro Martinez	2.00
102	Randy Johnson	2.00
103	Greg Maddux	4.00
104	Sammy Sosa	2.50
105	Mark McGwire	5.00
106	Ivan Rodriguez	1.50
107	Mike Piazza	3.00
108	Chipper Jones	3.00
109	Vladimir Guerrero	2.00
110	Alex Rodriguez	5.00
111	Ken Griffey Jr.	3.00
112	Cal Ripken Jr.	6.00
113	Derek Jeter	6.00
114	Barry Bonds	6.00

115	Nomar Garciaparra	2.00
116	Jeff Bagwell	1.50
117	Todd Helton	1.50
118	Darin Erstad	1.00
119	Shawn Green	1.00
120	Roberto Alomar	1.00

Platinum

Stars (1-100):		4-8X
Stars (101-120):		2-4X
Production 199 Sets		

Autographed Cards

		NM/M
Common Player:		10.00
Inserted 1:431		
1	Todd Helton	25.00
2	Rick Ankiel	20.00
3	Mark Quinn	10.00
4	Adrian Gonzalez	15.00

Game Defined

		NM/M
Complete Set (10):		25.00
Common Player:		1.50
Inserted 1:24		
Platinum:		1.5-2X
Inserted 1:72		
1	Ken Griffey Jr.	3.00
2	Derek Jeter	5.00
3	Sammy Sosa	3.00
4	Mark McGwire	4.00
5	Todd Helton	1.50
6	Mike Piazza	3.00
7	Chipper Jones	2.50
8	Vladimir Guerrero	1.50
9	Alex Rodriguez	4.00
10	Nomar Garciaparra	3.00

Game-Worn Jersey

		NM/M
Common Card:		5.00
Inserted 1:108		
Cards 5-8 are redemptions.		
1	Grant Roberts	5.00
2	Vernon Wells	10.00
3	Travis Dawkins	5.00
4	Ramon Ortiz	5.00
5	Steve Finley	5.00
6	Ramon Hernandez	5.00
7	Jay Payton	8.00
8	Jeromy Burnitz	5.00

Images of Excellence

		NM/M
Complete Set (10):		15.00
Common Player:		1.00
Inserted 1:8		
Platinum:		1.5-2X
Inserted 1:24		
1	Willie Mays	2.50
2	Reggie Jackson	1.00
3	Ernie Banks	1.50
4	Hank Aaron	2.50
5	Ted Williams	2.50
6	Mike Schmidt	2.00
7	Tom Seaver	1.00
8	Johnny Bench	1.50

9	George Brett	2.50
10	Nolan Ryan	3.00

20-20

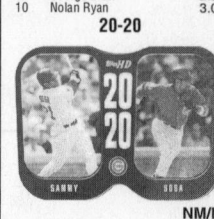

		NM/M
Complete Set (10):		15.00
Common Player:		.50
Inserted 1:12		
Platinum:		1.5-2X
Inserted 1:36		
1	Barry Bonds	4.00
2	Chipper Jones	2.00
3	Ken Griffey Jr.	2.00
4	Alex Rodriguez	3.00
5	Ivan Rodriguez	1.00
6	Sammy Sosa	2.50
7	Roberto Alomar	.75
8	Larry Walker	.50
9	Shawn Green	.75
10	Jeff Bagwell	1.00

2001 Topps Opening Day

		NM/M
Complete Set (165):		35.00
Common Player:		.15
Pack (7):		1.00
Box (24):		20.00
1	Cal Ripken Jr.	2.50
2	Chipper Jones	1.50
3	Garret Anderson	.40
4	Robin Ventura	.20
5	Jermaine Dye	.15
6	Jim Thome	.75
7	Brian Jordan	.15
8	Shawn Green	.40
9	Juan Gonzalez	.75
10	Paul O'Neill	.15
11	Pokey Reese	.15
12	Mike Mussina	.75
13	Jay Buhner	.15
14	Shane Reynolds	.15
15	Adam Piatt	.15
16	Preston Wilson	.15
17	Ellis Burks	.15
18	Chuck Finley	.15
19	Shannon Stewart	.15
20	Mark McGwire	2.00
21	Mark Loretta	.15
22	Bobby Jones	.15
23	Matt Clement	.15
24	Pedro J. Martinez	1.00
25	Carlos Lee	.15
26	John Franco	.15
27	Andres Galarraga	.25
28	Jose Cruz Jr.	.15
29	Randy Johnson	.75
30	Richie Sexson	.40
31	Darin Erstad	.30
32	Manny Ramirez	.75
33	Mike Sweeney	.15
34	John Wetteland	.15
35	Derek Jeter	2.50
36	J.D. Drew	.15
37	Rick Reed	.15
38	Jay Bell	.15
39	Fred McGriff	.25
40	Orlando Cabrera	.15
41	Eric Owens	.15
42	Jorge Posada	.40
43	Jeff Cirillo	.15
44	Johnny Damon	.25
45	Charles Johnson	.15
46	Pat Burrell	.40
47	Gary Sheffield	.40
48	Tom Glavine	.30
49	Ivan Rodriguez	.75
50	Chuck Knoblauch	.15
51	Jason Kendall	.15
52	Carlos Delgado	.60
53	Roger Clemens	1.50

54	Brad Penny	.15
55	Troy Glaus	.75
56	Mike Hampton	.15
57	Carlos Febles	.15
58	Seth Etherton	.15
59	Fernando Tatis	.15
60	Livan Hernandez	.15
61	Barry Larkin	.30
62	Alex Rodriguez	2.00
63	Warren Morris	.15
64	Antonio Alfonseca	.15
65	Edgardo Alfonzo	.15
66	Fernando Vina	.15
67	Jason Giambi	.75
68	Matt Lawton	.15
69	Rusty Greer	.15
70	Tony Gwynn	1.00
71	Carl Everett	.15
72	Bret Boone	.25
73	James Baldwin	.15
74	Greg Vaughn	.15
75	Darren Dreifort	.15
76	Frank Thomas	1.00
77	Luis Castillo	.15
78	Bartolo Colon	.25
79	Craig Biggio	.25
80	Jose Vidro	.15
81	Todd Helton	.75
82	Jacque Jones	.15
83	Robb Nen	.15
84	Richard Hidalgo	.15
85	Tony Womack	.15
86	Rick Ankiel	.15
87	Terrence Long	.15
88	Brad Radke	.15
89	Gabe Kapler	.15
90	Pedro Astacio	.15
91	Darryl Kile	.15
92	Jay Payton	.15
93	Vladimir Guerrero	1.00
94	Juan Encarnacion	.15
95	Ramon Hernandez	.15
96	Sandy Alomar	.15
97	Geoff Jenkins	.25
98	Rafael Furcal	.25
99	Mark Grace	.25
100	Mark Mulder	.25
101	Jim Edmonds	.40
102	Tim Salmon	.25
103	Jeff Bagwell	.75
104	Jose Canseco	.40
105	Ben Grieve	.15
106	Ryan Klesko	.25
107	Javy Lopez	.25
108	Greg Maddux	1.50
109	Andruw Jones	.50
110	Jeromy Burnitz	.15
111	Ray Lankford	.15
112	Sammy Sosa	1.50
113	Raul Mondesi	.25
114	Mike Piazza	1.50
115	Todd Zeile	.15
116	Eric Karros	.15
117	Barry Bonds	2.50
118	J.T. Snow	.15
119	Jeff Kent	.15
120	David Justice	.25
121	Matt Williams	.25
122	Brian Giles	.25
123	Edgar Martinez	.15
124	Ken Griffey Jr.	1.50
125	Al Leiter	.25
126	Kevin Brown	.25
127	John Olerud	.25
128	Roberto Alomar	.40
129	Rafael Palmeiro	.40
130	Steve Finley	.15
131	Tim Hudson	.40
132	Scott Rolen	.75
133	Nomar Garciaparra	1.50
134	Mo Vaughn	.15
135	Larry Walker	.30
136	Albert Belle	.15
137	Ray Durham	.15
138	Andy Pettitte	.40
139	Mariano Rivera	.25
140	Bernie Williams	.50
141	David Wells	.15
142	Magglio Ordonez	.40
143	Kevin Millwood	.15
144	Cliff Floyd	.15
145	Rich Aurilia	.15
146	Eric Chavez	.15
147	Scott Elarton	.15
148	Tony Armas Jr.	.15
149	Mark Redman	.15
150	Javier Vazquez	.15
151	Adrian Gonzalez, Adam Johnson	.50
152	Mike Stodolka, Sean Burnett	
153	David Walling, Ben Sheets	.50
154	Chin-Feng Chen, Corey Patterson, Josh Hamilton	.25
155	Mark McGwire	3.00
156	Bobby Thomson	.15
157	Bill Mazeroski	.15
158	Cal Ripken Jr.	1.00
159	Hank Aaron	1.00
160	Bucky Dent	.15
161	Jackie Robinson	1.00
162	Roberto Clemente	1.00
163	Nolan Ryan	1.00
164	Kerry Wood	.25
165	Checklist	.15

Autographs

		NM/M
	Common Autograph:	20.00
TH	Todd Helton	40.00
CJ	Chipper Jones	100.00
MO	Magglio Ordonez	25.00
CP	Corey Patterson	20.00

Team Logo Stickers

	NM/M
Complete Set (30):	6.00
Sticker:	.25
Each team represented	

2001 Topps Reserve

JASON GIAMBI

		NM/M
	Complete Set (151):	
	Common Player:	.40
	Common SP (101-150):	4.00
	Production 1,500	
	Sealed Hobby Box (10):	125.00
1	Darin Erstad	.40
2	Moises Alou	.50
3	Tony Batista	.40
4	Andruw Jones	.50
5	Edgar Renteria	.40
6	Eric Young	.40
7	Steve Finley	.40
8	Adrian Beltre	.40
9	Vladimir Guerrero	1.00
10	Barry Bonds	3.00
11	Juan Gonzalez	.50
12	Jay Buhner	.40
13	Luis Castillo	.40
14	Cal Ripken Jr.	3.00
15	Bob Abreu	.40
16	Ivan Rodriguez	.75
17	Nomar Garciaparra	.75
18	Todd Helton	.75
19	Bobby Higginson	.40
20	Jorge Posada	.50
21	Tim Salmon	.50
22	Jason Giambi	.75
23	Jose Cruz Jr.	.40
24	Chipper Jones	1.50
25	Jim Edmonds	.50
26	Gerald Williams	.40
27	Randy Johnson	1.00
28	Gary Sheffield	.50
29	Jeff Kent	.40
30	Jim Thome	.75
31	John Olerud	.40
32	Cliff Floyd	.40
33	Mike Lowell	.40
34	Phil Nevin	.40
35	Scott Rolen	.75
36	Alex Rodriguez	2.50
37	Ken Griffey Jr.	2.00
38	Neifi Perez	.40
39	Christian Guzman	.40
40	Mariano Rivera	.50
41	Troy Glaus	.50
42	Johnny Damon	.40
43	Rafael Furcal	.50
44	Jeromy Burnitz	.40
45	Mark McGwire	2.00
46	Fred McGriff	.40
47	Matt Williams	.40
48	Kevin Brown	.40
49	J.T. Snow	.40
50	Kenny Lofton	.40
51	Al Martin	.40
52	Antonio Alfonseca	.40
53	Edgardo Alfonzo	.40
54	Ryan Klesko	.40
55	Pat Burrell	.50
56	Rafael Palmeiro	.50
57	Sean Casey	.40
58	Jeff Cirillo	.40
59	Ray Durham	.40
60	Derek Jeter	3.00
61	Jeff Bagwell	.50
62	Carlos Delgado	.50
63	Tom Glavine	.50
64	Richie Sexson	.40
65	J.D. Drew	.40
66	Ben Grieve	.40
67	Mark Grace	.50
68	Shawn Green	.40
69	Robb Nen	.40
70	Omar Vizquel	.40
71	Edgar Martinez	.40
72	Preston Wilson	.40
73	Mike Piazza	1.50
74	Tony Gwynn	1.00
75	Jason Kendall	.40
76	Manny Ramirez	.75
77	Pokey Reese	.40
78	Mike Sweeney	.40
79	Magglio Ordonez	.50
80	Bernie Williams	.50
81	Richard Hidalgo	.40
82	Brad Fullmer	.40
83	Greg Maddux	2.00
84	Geoff Jenkins	.40
85	Sammy Sosa	1.00
86	Luis Gonzalez	.50
87	Eric Karros	.40
88	Jose Vidro	.40
89	Rich Aurilia	.40
90	Roberto Alomar	.50
91	Mike Cameron	.40
92	Mike Mussina	.50
93	Albert Belle	.40
94	Mike Lieberthal	.40
95	Brian Giles	.40
96	Pedro Martinez	1.00
97	Barry Larkin	.50
98	Jermaine Dye	.40
99	Frank Thomas	.75
100	David Justice	.50
101	Gary Johnson RC	4.00
102	Matt Ford RC	4.00
103	Albert Pujols RC	100.00
104	Brad Cresse RC	4.00
105	Valentino Pascucci RC	4.00
106	Bob Keppel RC	4.00
107	Luis Torres RC	4.00
108	Tony Blanco RC	4.00
109	Ronnie Corona RC	4.00
110	Phil Wilson RC	4.00
111	John Buck RC	6.00
112	Jim Journell RC	4.00
113	Victor Hall RC	4.00
114	Jeff Andra RC	4.00
115	Greg Nash RC	4.00
116	Travis Hafner RC	10.00
117	Casey Fossum RC	4.00
118	Miguel Olivo RC	4.00
119	Elpidio Guzman RC	4.00
120	Jason Belcher RC	4.00
121	Esix Snead RC	4.00
122	Joe Thurston RC	4.00
123	Rafael Soriano RC	6.00
124	Ed Rogers RC	4.00
125	Omar Beltre RC	4.00
126	Brett Gray RC	4.00
127	Deivi Mendez RC	4.00
128	Freddie Bynum RC	4.00
129	David Krynzel RC	4.00
130	Blake Williams RC	4.00
131	Reggie Abercrombie RC	4.00
132	Miguel Vililio RC	4.00
133	Ryan Madson RC	4.00
134	Matt Thompson RC	4.00
135	Mark Burnett RC	4.00
136	Andy Beal RC	4.00
137	Ryan Ludwick RC	15.00
138	Roberto Miniel RC	4.00
139	Steve Smyth RC	4.00
140	Ben Washburn RC	4.00
141	Marvin Seale RC	4.00
142	Reggie Griggs RC	4.00
143	Seung Song RC	4.00
144	Chad Petty RC	4.00
145	Noel Devarez RC	4.00
146	Matt Butler RC	4.00
147	Brett Evert RC	4.00
148	Cesar Izturis RC	4.00
149	Troy Farnsworth RC	4.00
150	Brian Schmitt RC	4.00
151	Ichiro Suzuki RC	30.00

Game-Worn Uniform

AUTHENTIC GAME-WORN UNIFORM

		NM/M
	Common Player:	4.00
	Inserted 1:Box	
RA	Roberto Alomar	8.00
BB	Barry Bonds	25.00
CD	Carlos Delgado	4.00
JE	Jim Edmonds	4.00
NG	Nomar Garciaparra	8.00
JG	Juan Gonzalez	4.00
SG	Shawn Green	4.00
VG	Vladimir Guerrero	8.00
TG	Tony Gwynn	10.00
TH	Todd Helton	8.00
RJ	Randy Johnson	8.00
CJ	Chipper Jones	10.00
DJ	David Justice	4.00
GM	Greg Maddux	15.00
PM	Pedro Martinez	8.00
RP	Rafael Palmeiro	8.00
AR	Alex Rodriguez	15.00
IR	Ivan Rodriguez	8.00
SR	Scott Rolen	8.00
FT	Frank Thomas	8.00

Game-Used Bat

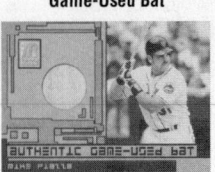

AUTHENTIC GAME-USED BAT

		NM/M
	Common Player:	4.00
	Inserted 1:Box	
JB	Jeff Bagwell	8.00
BB	Barry Bonds	25.00
CD	Carlos Delgado	4.00
JE	Jim Edmonds	4.00
DE	Darin Erstad	4.00
RF	Rafael Furcal	4.00
NG	Nomar Garciaparra	8.00
VG	Vladimir Guerrero	10.00
TG	Tony Gwynn	10.00
CJ	Chipper Jones	10.00
MP	Mike Piazza	15.00
AR	Alex Rodriguez	15.00
IR	Ivan Rodriguez	8.00
BW	Bernie Williams	8.00

Rookie Graded Autograph

VICTOR HALL

	NM/M
Common Rookie:	10.00
Inserted 1:Box	
Prices for PSA 8	
PSA 9s:	1.5X
Reggie Abercrombie	10.00
Jeff Andra	10.00
Andy Beal	10.00
Jason Belcher	10.00
Omar Beltre	10.00
Tony Blanco	10.00
John Buck	10.00
Mark Burnett	10.00
Freddie Bynum	10.00
Ronnie Corona	10.00
Noel Devarez	10.00
Matt Ford	10.00
Brett Gray	10.00
Reggie Griggs	10.00
Elpidio Guzman	10.00
Travis Hafner	40.00
Victor Hall	10.00
Gary Johnson	10.00
Jim Journell	10.00
Bob Keppel	10.00
David Krynzel	10.00
Ryan Ludwick	30.00
Ryan Madson	15.00
Deivi Mendez	10.00
Roberto Miniel	10.00
Greg Nash	10.00
Miguel Olivo	10.00
Valentino Pascucci	10.00
Chad Petty	10.00
Albert Pujols	800.00
Ed Rogers	10.00
Marvin Seale	10.00
Steve Smyth	10.00
Esix Snead	10.00
Seung Song	10.00
Rafael Soriano	15.00
Matt Thompson	15.00
Joe Thurston	15.00
Luis Torres	10.00
Miguel Vililio	10.00
Ben Washburn	10.00
Blake Williams	10.00
Phil Wilson	10.00

Rookie Autographed Baseballs

	NM/M
Common Player:	10.00
Inserted 1:Box w/holder.	
Reggie Abercrombie	10.00
Jeff Andra	10.00
Andy Beal	10.00
Jason Belcher	10.00
Omar Beltre	10.00
Tony Blanco	15.00
John Buck	15.00
Mark Burnett	10.00
Freddie Bynum	10.00
Ronnie Corona	10.00
Noel Devaraz	10.00
Matt Ford	10.00
Casey Fossum	10.00
Brett Gray	10.00
Reggie Griggs	10.00
Elpidio Guzman	10.00
Travis Hafner	40.00
Victor Hall	10.00
Gary Johnson	10.00
Jim Journell	10.00
Bob Keppel	10.00
David Krynzel	10.00
Ryan Ludwick	40.00
Ryan Madson	15.00
Deivi Mendez	10.00
Roberto Miniel	10.00
Greg Nash	10.00
Miguel Olivo	15.00
Valentino Pascucci	10.00
Chad Petty	10.00
Albert Pujols	600.00
Ed Rogers	10.00
Marvin Seale	10.00
Steve Smyth	10.00
Esix Snead	10.00
Seung Song	10.00
Rafael Soriano	10.00
Matt Thompson	10.00
Joe Thurston	10.00
Luis Torres	10.00
Miguel Villilo	10.00
Ben Washbharn	10.00
Blake Williams	10.00
Phil Wilson	10.00

2001 Topps Stars

ALBERT PUJOLS

	NM/M
Complete Set (200):	90.00
Common Player:	.15
Pack (6):	5.00
Box (24):	100.00
1 Darin Erstad	.25
2 Luis Gonzalez	.25
3 Rafael Furcal	.40
4 Dante Bichette	.15
5 Sammy Sosa	.75
6 Ken Griffey Jr.	1.50
7 Jim Thome	.50
8 Bobby Higginson	.15
9 Cliff Floyd	.15
10 Lance Berkman	.50
11 Eric Karros	.15
12 Jeromy Burnitz	.15
13 Jose Vidro	.15
14 Benny Agbayani	.15
15 Jorge Posada	.50
16 Ramon Hernandez	.15
17 Jason Kendall	.25

18 Jeff Kent	.25
19 John Olerud	.40
20 Al Martin	.15
21 Gerald Williams	.15
22 Gabe Kapler	.15
23 Carlos Delgado	.50
24 Mariano Rivera	.50
25 Javy Lopez	.25
26 Paul Konerko	.25
27 Daryle Ward	.15
28 Mike Lieberthal	.15
29 Tom Goodwin	.15
30 Garret Anderson	.40
31 Steve Finley	.15
32 Brian Jordan	.15
33 Nomar Garciaparra	.50
34 Ray Durham	.15
35 Sean Casey	.25
36 Kenny Lofton	.25
37 Dean Palmer	.15
38 Jeff Bagwell	.50
39 Mike Sweeney	.15
40 Adrian Beltre	.15
41 Richie Sexson	.40
42 Vladimir Guerrero	.75
43 Derek Jeter	2.00
44 Miguel Tejada	.40
45 Doug Glanville	.15
46 Brian Giles	.25
47 Marvin Benard	.15
48 Edgar Martinez	.25
49 Edgar Renteria	.15
50 Fred McGriff	.25
51 Ivan Rodriguez	.50
52 Brad Fullmer	.15
53 Antonio Alfonseca	.15
54 Tom Glavine	.50
55 Warren Morris	.15
56 Johnny Damon	.50
57 Dmitri Young	.15
58 Mo Vaughn	.25
59 Randy Johnson	.75
60 Greg Maddux	1.00
61 Carl Everett	.15
62 Magglio Ordonez	.40
63 Pokey Reese	.15
64 Todd Helton	.50
65 Preston Wilson	.15
66 Richard Hidalgo	.15
67 Jermaine Dye	.25
68 Gary Sheffield	.40
69 Geoff Jenkins	.25
70 Edgardo Alfonzo	.15
71 Paul O'Neill	.25
72 Terrence Long	.15
73 Bob Abreu	.40
74 Kevin Young	.15
75 J.T. Snow	.15
76 Alex Rodriguez	1.50
77 Jim Edmonds	.25
78 Mark McGwire	1.50
79 Tony Batista	.15
80 Darrin Fletcher	.15
81 Robb Nen	.15
82 Jose Offerman	.15
83 Travis Fryman	.25
84 Joe Randa	.15
85 Omar Vizquel	.25
86 Tim Salmon	.25
87 Andruw Jones	.40
88 Albert Belle	.15
89 Manny Ramirez	.50
90 Frank Thomas	.50
91 Barry Larkin	.40
92 Neifi Perez	.15
93 Luis Castillo	.15
94 Moises Alou	.25
95 Mark Quinn	.15
96 Kevin Brown	.25
97 Cristian Guzman	.15
98 Mike Piazza	1.00
99 Bernie Williams	.40
100 Jason Giambi	.50
101 Scott Rolen	.75
102 Phil Nevin	.15
103 Rich Aurilia	.15
104 Mike Cameron	.15
105 Fernando Vina	.15
106 Greg Vaughn	.15
107 Jose Cruz	.15
108 Raul Mondesi	.15
109 Ben Molina	.15
110 Pedro Martinez	.75
111 Todd Hollandsworth	.15
112 Jacque Jones	.15
113 Rickey Henderson	.25
114 Troy Glaus	.40
115 Chipper Jones	1.00
116 Delino DeShields	.15
117 Eric Young	.15
118 Jose Valentin	.15
119 Roberto Alomar	.40
120 Jeff Cirillo	.15
121 Mike Lowell	.25
122 Julio Lugo	.15
123 Shawn Green	.25
124 Marquis Grissom	.15
125 Matt Lawton	.15
126 Jay Payton	.15
127 David Justice	.25
128 Eric Chavez	.25
129 Pat Burrell	.50
130 Ryan Klesko	.25
131 Barry Bonds	2.00
132 Jay Buhner	.15

133 J.D. Drew	.25
134 Rafael Palmeiro	.50
135 Shannon Stewart	.15
136 Juan Gonzalez	.40
137 Tony Womack	.15
138 Carlos Lee	.25
139 Derrek Lee	.50
140 Ben Grieve	.15
141 Ron Belliard	.15
142 Stan Musial	1.50
143 Ernie Banks	1.00
144 Jim Palmer	.50
145 Tony Perez	.25
146 Duke Snider	.50
147 Rod Carew	.40
148 Warren Spahn	.75
149 Yogi Berra	.75
150 Juan Marichal	.25
151 Eric Munson	.15
152 Carlos Pena	.15
153 Joe Crede	.15
154 Ryan Anderson	.15
155 Milton Bradley	.15
156 Sean Burroughs	.15
157 Corey Patterson	.25
158 C.C. Sabathia	.40
159 Ben Petrick	.15
160 Aubrey Huff	.15
161 Gookie Dawkins	.15
162 Ben Sheets	.25
163 Pablo Ozuna	.15
164 Eric Valent	.15
165 Rod Barajas	.15
166 Chin-Feng Chen	.40
167 Josh Hamilton	.50
168 Keith Ginter	.15
169 Vernon Wells	.25
170 Dernell Stenson	.75
171 Alfonso Soriano	.75
172 Jason Marquis	.15
173 Nick Johnson	.15
174 Adam Everett	.15
175 Jimmy Rollins	.50
176 Ben Diggins	.15
177 John Lackey	.25
178 Scott Heard	.15
179 Brian Hitchcox RC	.50
180 Odannis Ayala RC	.50
181 Scott Pratt RC	.50
182 Greg Runser RC	.50
183 Chris Russ RC	.50
184 Derek Thompson	.50
185 Jason Jones RC	.50
186 Dominic Rich RC	.50
187 Chad Petty RC	.50
188 Steve Smyth RC	.50
189 Bryan Hebson RC	.50
190 Danny Borrell RC	.50
191 Bob Keppel RC	.50
192 Justin Wayne RC	1.00
193 Reggie Abercrombie RC	1.00
194 Travis Baptist RC	.50
195 Shawn Fagan RC	.50
196 Jose Reyes RC	20.00
197 Chris Bass RC	.50
198 Albert Pujols RC	40.00
199 Luis Cotto RC	.50
200 Jake Peavy RC	4.00

Gold

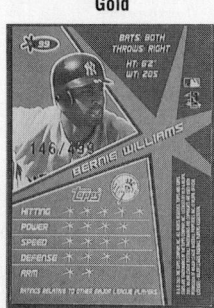

Stars:	2-5X
Production 499 Sets	

Onyx

Stars:	6-12X
Rookies:	4-6X
Production 99 Sets	

Autographs

	NM/M
Common Player:	15.00
Inserted 1:353	
EB Ernie Banks	50.00
YB Yogi Berra	40.00
RC Rod Carew	30.00
CD Carlos Delgado	15.00
TH Todd Helton	30.00
JM Juan Marichal	30.00
EM Eric Munson	10.00
SM Stan Musial	80.00
JP Jim Palmer	25.00
TP Tony Perez	25.00

Eric Munson

IR Ivan Rodriguez	25.00
DS Duke Snider	35.00
WS Warren Spahn	40.00

Elimination

Stars:	5-10X
Production 100 Sets	
Redemp. deadline 10/19/01.	

Game Gear Bats

	NM/M
Common Player:	5.00
Inserted 1:187	
AB Adrian Beltre	5.00
LB Lance Berkman	6.00
SB Sean Burroughs	5.00
MC Michael Cuddyer	5.00
BD Ben Davis	5.00
JDD J.D. Drew	5.00
ED Erubiel Durazo	5.00
JE Juan Encarnacion	5.00
RF Rafael Furcal	8.00
AK Adam Kennedy	5.00
GL George Lombard	5.00
TL Terrence Long	5.00
FL Felipe Lopez	5.00
GM Gary Mathews	5.00
NP Neifi Perez	5.00
AP Adam Piatt	5.00
SR Scott Rolen	15.00
FS Fernando Seguignol	5.00
RS Richie Sexson	10.00

Game Gear Bats Autographs

Inserted 1:12,240
No pricing due to scarcity.

Game Gear Jerseys

BARRY BONDS

	NM/M
Common Player:	4.00
Inserted 1:61	
EA Edgardo Alfonzo	4.00
RA Roberto Alomar	8.00
BB Barry Bonds	25.00
LC Luis Castillo	4.00
TG Tony Gwynn	10.00
TH Todd Helton	8.00
AJ Andruw Jones	8.00
CJ Chipper Jones	10.00
EM Edgar Martinez	8.00
MO Magglio Ordonez	5.00
MP Mike Piazza	15.00
SS Sammy Sosa	25.00

SHS	Shannon Stewart	4.00
FT	Frank Thomas	8.00
JV	Jose Vidro	4.00

Game Gear Jerseys Autographs

Inserted 1:19,288
No pricing due to scarcity.

Player Choice Awards Relics

NM/M
Common Player: 10.00
Inserted 1:1,530

1	Carlos Delgado	15.00
2	Eric Davis	10.00
3	Carlos Delgado	15.00
4	Pedro Martinez	25.00
5	Terrence Long	10.00
6	Frank Thomas	20.00
7	Todd Helton	15.00
8	Randy Johnson	25.00
9	Rafael Furcal	15.00
10	Andres Galarraga	10.00

Players Choice Award Nominees

NM/M
Complete Set (10): 15.00
Common Player: 1.50
Inserted 1:12

1	Barry Bonds, Carlos Delgado, Todd Helton	4.00
2	Gary Sheffield, Eric Davis, Turk Wendell	1.50
3	Alex Rodriguez, Carlos Delgado, Frank Thomas	3.00
4	David Wells, Pedro Martinez, Andy Pettitte	2.00
5	Mark Quinn, Terrence Long, Kazuhiro Sasaki	1.50
6	Jay Buhner, Frank Thomas, Bobby Higginson	1.50
7	Barry Bonds, Todd Helton, Jeff Kent	4.00
8	Tom Glavine, Randy Johnson, Greg Maddux	2.50
9	Rick Ankiel, Rafael Furcal, Jay Payton	1.50
10	Moises Alou, Andres Galarraga, Jeff D'Amico	1.50

Progression

NM/M
Complete Set (9): 10.00
Common Player: 1.00
Inserted 1:8

P1	Ernie Banks, Alex Rodriguez, Felipe Lopez	3.00
P2	Yogi Berra, Ivan Rodriguez, Ramon Hernandez	2.00
P3	Tony Perez, Carlos Delgado, Eric Munson	1.00
P4	Rod Carew, Roberto Alomar, Jose Ortiz	1.00
P5	Stan Musial, Darin Erstad, Alex Escobar	2.00
P6	Jim Palmer, Kevin Brown, Kurt Ainsworth	1.00
P7	Duke Snider, Jim Edmonds, Vernon Wells	1.00
P8	Warren Spahn, Randy Johnson, Ryan Anderson	1.50
P9	Juan Marichal, Bartolo Colon, Bobby Bradley	1.00

2001 Topps Tribute

NM/M
Complete Set (90): 200.00
Common Player: 2.00
Pack (3): 75.00
Box (6): 425.00

1	Pee Wee Reese	2.00
2	Babe Ruth	15.00
3	Ralph Kiner	2.00
4	Brooks Robinson	5.00
5	Don Sutton	2.00
6	Carl Yastrzemski	8.00
7	Roger Maris	10.00
8	Andre Dawson	2.00
9	Luis Aparicio	2.00
10	Wade Boggs	4.00
11	Johnny Bench	8.00
12	Ernie Banks	6.00
13	Thurman Munson	5.00
14	Harmon Killebrew	5.00
15	Ted Kluszewski	2.00
16	Bob Feller	3.00
17	Mike Schmidt	10.00
18	Warren Spahn	4.00
19	Jim Palmer	3.00
20	Don Mattingly	12.00
21	Willie Mays	10.00
22	Gil Hodges	2.00
23	Juan Marichal	2.00
24	Robin Yount	6.00
25	Nolan Ryan	12.00
26	Dave Winfield	3.00
27	Hank Greenberg	2.00
28	Honus Wagner	8.00
29	Nolan Ryan	12.00
30	Phil Niekro	2.00
31	Robin Roberts	2.00
32	Casey Stengel	3.00
33	Willie McCovey	2.00
34	Roy Campanella	4.00
35	Rollie Fingers	2.00
36	Tom Seaver	5.00
37	Jackie Robinson	10.00
38	Hank Aaron	10.00
39	Bob Gibson	4.00
40	Carlton Fisk	4.00
41	Hank Aaron	10.00
42	George Brett	10.00
43	Orlando Cepeda	2.00
44	Red Schoendienst	2.00
45	Don Drysdale	4.00
46	Mel Ott	4.00
47	Casey Stengel	3.00
48	Al Kaline	4.00
49	Reggie Jackson	5.00
50	Tony Perez	2.00
51	Ozzie Smith	6.00
52	Billy Martin	4.00
53	Bill Dickey	2.00
54	Catfish Hunter	4.00
55	Duke Snider	4.00
56	Dale Murphy	2.00
57	Bobby Doerr	2.00
58	Earl Averill	2.00
59	Carlton Fisk	4.00
60	Tom Lasorda	2.00
61	Lou Gehrig	12.00
62	Enos Slaughter	2.00
63	Jim Bunning	2.00
64	Rollie Fingers	2.00
65	Frank Robinson	4.00
66	Earl Weaver	2.00
67	Eddie Mathews	5.00
68	Kirby Puckett	4.00
69	Phil Rizzuto	4.00
70	Lou Brock	4.00
71	Walt Alston	2.00
72	Bill Pierce	2.00
73	Joe Morgan	2.00
74	Roberto Clemente	12.00
75	Whitey Ford	4.00
76	Richie Ashburn	2.00
77	Elston Howard	2.00
78	Gary Carter	2.00
79	Carl Hubbell	2.00
80	Yogi Berra	6.00
81	Ken Boyer	2.00
82	Nolan Ryan	12.00
83	Bill Mazeroski	2.00
84	Dizzy Dean	4.00
85	Nellie Fox	2.00
86	Stan Musial	10.00
87	Steve Carlton	4.00
88	Willie Stargell	4.00
89	Hal Newhouser	2.00
90	Frank Robinson	4.00

Casey Stengel Dual Relic

NM/M
Inserted 1:860

CS	Casey Stengel	100.00

Franchise Figures

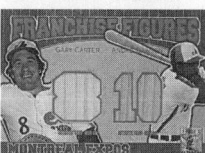

NM/M
Inserted 1:34

AL	Walt Alston, Tommy Lasorda	50.00
AFF	Luis Aparicio, Nellie Fox, Carlton Fisk	125.00
BPKR	Johnny Bench, Tony Perez, Ted Kluszewski, Frank Robinson, Joe Morgan	150.00
CD	Gary Carter, Andre Dawson	40.00
HDB	Bill Dickey, Elston Howard, Yogi Berra	150.00
FY	Carlton Fisk, Carl Yastrzemski	150.00
HSS	Gil Hodges, Casey Stengel, Tom Seaver	150.00
JM	Reggie Jackson, Billy Martin	125.00
KG	Al Kaline, Hank Greenberg	150.00
MMC	Willie Mays, Willie McCovey, Orlando Cepeda	200.00
MCS	Bill Mazeroski, Roberto Clemente, Willie Stargell	185.00
MM	Thurman Munson, Don Mattingly	200.00
MMA	Dale Murphy, Ed Mathews, Hank Aaron	185.00
PK	Kirby Puckett, Harmon Killebrew	100.00
RSC	Pee Wee Reese, Duke Snider, Roy Campanella	160.00
RG	Babe Ruth, Lou Gehrig	500.00
SAC	Mike Schmidt, Richie Ashburn, Steve Carlton	125.00
SBSM	Ozzie Smith, Lou Brock, Red Schoendienst, Stan Musial	125.00

Frank Robinson Dual Relic

NM/M
Inserted 1:860

FR-RO	Frank Robinson	90.00

Game-Used Bat Relics

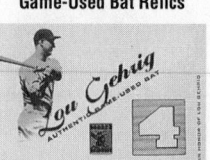

NM/M
Common Player: 20.00
Inserted 1:2

HA	Hank Aaron	50.00
LA	Luis Aparicio	20.00
RA	Richie Ashburn	25.00
KB	Ken Boyer	20.00
GB	George Brett	40.00
LB	Lou Brock	20.00
RC	Roy Campanella	30.00
RCL	Roberto Clemente	80.00
CF	Carlton Fisk	25.00
LG	Lou Gehrig	160.00
HG	Hank Greenberg	50.00
GH	Gil Hodges	25.00
RJ	Reggie Jackson	30.00
AK	Al Kaline	30.00
HK	Harmon Killebrew	30.00
RM	Roger Maris	50.00
BM	Billy Martin	30.00
DM	Don Mattingly	50.00
WM	Willie McCovey	25.00
TM	Thurman Munson	35.00
PWR	Pee Wee Reese	20.00
BRO	Brooks Robinson	30.00
FRR	Frank Robinson	30.00
BR	Babe Ruth	200.00
OS	Ozzie Smith	35.00
CS	Casey Stengel	20.00
HW	Honus Wagner	200.00
CY	Carl Yastrzemski	40.00

Game-Worn Patch And Number Relics

NM/M
Common Player: 60.00
Inserted 1:61

WA	Walt Alston	60.00
JB	Johnny Bench	180.00
YB	Yogi Berra	150.00
WB	Wade Boggs	80.00
LB	Lou Brock	60.00
BD	Bill Dickey	150.00
BDO	Bobby Doerr	100.00
HK	Harmon Killebrew	250.00
TL	Tom Lasorda	80.00
JM	Juan Marichal	75.00
EM	Eddie Mathews	150.00
KB	Kirby Puckett	250.00
NR	Nolan Ryan	300.00
MS	Mike Schmidt	250.00
RS	Red Schoendienst	80.00
DW	Dave Winfield	80.00
CY	Carl Yastrzemski	200.00
RY	Robin Yount	100.00

Nolan Ryan Tri-Relic

NM/M
Randomly inserted.

NR	Nolan Ryan	475.00

Retired Game-Worn Relics

NM/M
Common Player: 20.00
Inserted 1:2

WA	Walt Alston	20.00
EB	Ernie Banks	30.00
EBA	Ernie Banks	30.00
JB	Johnny Bench	30.00
YB	Yogi Berra	30.00
WB	Wade Boggs	20.00

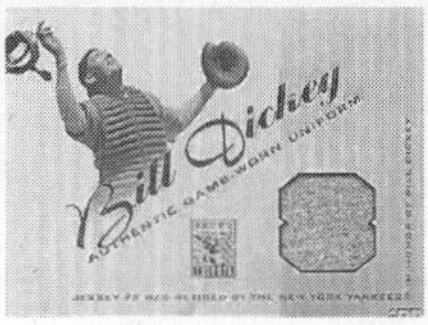

GB	George Brett	50.00
LB	Lou Brock	25.00
SC	Steve Carlton	25.00
DD	Dizzy Dean	40.00
BD	Bill Dickey	20.00
BDO	Bobby Doerr	25.00
NF	Nellie Fox	20.00
HK	Harmon Killebrew	30.00
TL	Tom Lasorda	20.00
JMG	Juan Marichal	30.00
EM	Eddie Mathews	30.00
DM	Don Mattingly	50.00
WMF	Willie Mays	75.00
WMW	Willie Mays	75.00
SM	Stan Musial	75.00
JP	Jim Palmer	20.00
KP	Kirby Puckett	30.00
FR	Frank Robinson	25.00
NRA	Nolan Ryan	80.00
NRH	Nolan Ryan	80.00
NRR	Nolan Ryan	80.00
MSB	Mike Schmidt	50.00
MSW	Mike Schmidt	50.00
RS	Red Schoendienst	20.00
WST	Willie Stargell	20.00
CS	Casey Stengel	20.00
DW	Dave Winfield	20.00
CY	Carl Yastrzemski/White	40.00
CYA	Carl Yastrzemski/Gray	40.00
RY	Robin Yount	30.00

Vintage Buy-Back Cards

No pricing due to scarcity.

2002 Topps

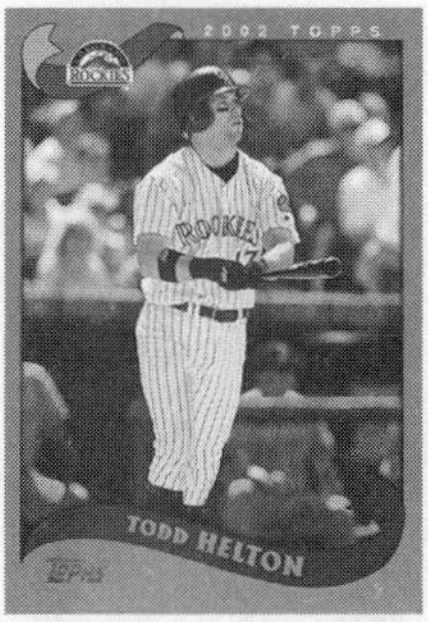

	NM/M
Complete Set (718):	70.00
Complete Factory Set (723):	80.00
Complete Series 1 (365):	35.00
Complete Series 2 (354):	35.00
Common Player:	.10
Pack (10):	1.50
Box (36):	40.00

1	Pedro Martinez	.50
2	Mike Stanton	.10
3	Brad Penny	.10
4	Mike Matheny	.10
5	Johnny Damon	.20
6	Bret Boone	.20
7	Not Issued (Retired)	
8	Chris Truby	.10
9	B.J. Surhoff	.10
10	Mike Hampton	.10
11	Juan Pierre	.10
12	Mark Buehrle	.10
13	Bob Abreu	.20
14	David Cone	.10
15	Aaron Sele	.10
16	Fernando Tatis	.10
17	Bobby Jones	.10
18	Rick Helling	.10
19	Dmitri Young	.10
20	Mike Mussina	.40
21	Mike Sweeney	.10
22	Cristian Guzman	.10
23	Ryan Kohlmeier	.10
24	Adam Kennedy	.10
25	Larry Walker	.25
26	Eric Davis	.10
27	Jason Tyner	.10
28	Eric Young	.10
29	Jason Marquis	.10
30	Luis Gonzalez	.20
31	Kevin Tapani	.10
32	Orlando Cabrera	.10
33	Marty Cordova	.10
34	Brad Ausmus	.10
35	Livan Hernandez	.10
36	Alex Gonzalez	.10
37	Edgar Renteria	.20
38	Bengie Molina	.10
39	Frank Menechino	.10
40	Rafael Palmeiro	.40
41	Brad Fullmer	.10
42	Julio Zuleta	.10
43	Darren Dreifort	.10
44	Trot Nixon	.10
45	Trevor Hoffman	.10
46	Vladimir Nunez	.10
47	Mark Kotsay	.10
48	Kenny Rogers	.10
49	Ben Petrick	.10
50	Jeff Bagwell	.40
51	Juan Encarnacion	.10
52	Ramiro Mendoza	.10
53	Brian Meadows	.10
54	Chad Curtis	.10
55	Aramis Ramirez	.25
56	Mark McLemore	.10
57	Dante Bichette	.10
58	Scott Schoeneweis	.10
59	Jose Cruz Jr.	.10
60	Roger Clemens	1.00
61	Jose Guillen	.10
62	Darren Oliver	.10
63	Chris Reitsma	.10
64	Jeff Abbott	.10
65	Robin Ventura	.10
66	Denny Neagle	.10
67	Al Martin	.10
68	Benito Santiago	.10
69	Roy Oswalt	.20
70	Juan Gonzalez	.40
71	Garret Anderson	.25
72	Bobby Bonilla	.10
73	Danny Bautista	.10
74	J.T. Snow Jr.	.10
75	Derek Jeter	1.50
76	John Olerud	.20
77	Kevin Appier	.10
78	Phil Nevin	.20
79	Sean Casey	.20
80	Troy Glaus	.40
81	Joe Randa	.10
82	Jose Valentin	.10
83	Ricky Bottalico	.10
84	Todd Zeile	.10
85	Barry Larkin	.25
86	Bob Wickman	.10
87	Jeff Shaw	.10
88	Greg Vaughn	.10
89	Fernando Vina	.10
90	Mark Mulder	.25
91	Paul Bako	.10
92	Aaron Boone	.10
93	Esteban Loaiza	.10
94	Richie Sexson	.40
95	Alfonso Soriano	.50
96	Tony Womack	.10
97	Paul Shuey	.10
98	Melvin Mora	.10
99	Tony Gwynn	.50
100	Vladimir Guerrero	.50
101	Keith Osik	.10
102	Randy Velarde	.10
103	Scott Williamson	.10
104	Daryle Ward	.10
105	Doug Mientkiewicz	.10
106	Stan Javier	.10
107	Russ Ortiz	.10
108	Wade Miller	.10
109	Luke Prokopec	.10
110	Andruw Jones	.40
111	Ron Coomer	.10
112	Dan Wilson	.10
113	Luis Castillo	.10
114	Derek Bell	.10
115	Gary Sheffield	.20
116	Ruben Rivera	.10
117	Paul O'Neill	.20
118	Craig Paquette	.10
119	Chris Michalak	.10
120	Brad Radke	.10
121	Jorge Fabregas	.10
122	Randy Winn	.10
123	Tom Goodwin	.10
124	Jaret Wright	.10
125	Manny Ramirez	.40
126	Al Leiter	.20
127	Ben Davis	.10
128	Frank Catalanotto	.10
129	Jose Cabrera	.10
130	Magglio Ordonez	.20
131	Jose Macias	.10
132	Ted Lilly	.10
133	Chris Holt	.10
134	Eric Milton	.10
135	Shannon Stewart	.10
136	Omar Olivares	.10
137	David Segui	.10
138	Jeff Nelson	.10
139	Matt Williams	.25
140	Ellis Burks	.10
141	Jason Bere	.10
142	Jimmy Haynes	.10
143	Ramon Hernandez	.10
144	Craig Counsell (Front photo actually Greg Colbrunn.)	.10
145	John Smoltz	.10
146	Homer Bush	.10
147	Quilvio Veras	.10
148	Esteban Yan	.10
149	Ramon Ortiz	.10
150	Carlos Delgado	.30
151	Lee Stevens	.10
152	Wil Cordero	.10
153	Mike Bordick	.10
154	John Flaherty	.10
155	Omar Daal	.10
156	Todd Ritchie	.10
157	Carl Everett	.10
158	Scott Sullivan	.10
159	Deivi Cruz	.10
160a	Albert Pujols (Back photo is Placido Polanco.) (In cap.)	1.00
160b	Albert Pujols (Back photo corrected) (No cap.)	10.00
161	Royce Clayton	.10
162	Jeff Suppan	.10
163	C.C. Sabathia	.10
164	Jimmy Rollins	.25
165	Rickey Henderson	.25
166	Rey Ordonez	.10
167	Shawn Estes	.10
168	Reggie Sanders	.10
169	Jon Lieber	.10
170	Armando Benitez	.10
171	Mike Remlinger	.10
172	Billy Wagner	.10
173	Troy Percival	.10
174	Devon White	.10
175	Ivan Rodriguez	.40
176	Dustin Hermanson	.10
177	Brian Anderson	.10
178	Graeme Lloyd	.10
179	Russ Branyan	.10
180	Bobby Higginson	.10
181	Alex Gonzalez	.10
182	John Franco	.10
183	Sidney Ponson	.10
184	Jose Mesa	.10
185	Todd Hollandsworth	.10
186	Kevin Young	.10
187	Tim Wakefield	.10
188	Craig Biggio	.20
189	Jason Isringhausen	.10
190	Mark Quinn	.10
191	Glendon Rusch	.10
192	Damian Miller	.10
193	Sandy Alomar	.10
194	Scott Brosius	.10
195	Dave Martinez	.10
196	Danny Graves	.10
197	Shea Hillenbrand	.10
198	Jimmy Anderson	.10
199	Travis Lee	.10
200	Randy Johnson	.50
201	Carlos Beltran	.25
202	Jerry Hairston Jr.	.10
203	Jesus Sanchez	.10
204	Eddie Taubensee	.10
205	David Wells	.10
206	Russ Davis	.10
207	Michael Barrett	.10
208	Marquis Grissom	.10
209	Byung-Hyun Kim	.10
210	Hideo Nomo	.25
211	Ryan Rupe	.10
212	Ricky Gutierrez	.10
213	Darryl Kile	.10
214	Rico Brogna	.10
215	Terrence Long	.10
216	Mike Jackson	.10
217	Jamey Wright	.10
218	Adrian Beltre	.20
219	Benny Agbayani	.10
220	Chuck Knoblauch	.10
221	Randy Wolf	.10
222	Andy Ashby	.10
223	Corey Koskie	.10
224	Roger Cedeno	.10
225	Ichiro Suzuki	1.00
226	Keith Foulke	.10
227	Ryan Minor	.10
228	Shawon Dunston	.10
229	Alex Cora	.10
230	Jeromy Burnitz	.10
231	Mark Grace	.25
232	Aubrey Huff	.10
233	Jeffrey Hammonds	.10
234	Olmedo Saenz	.10
235	Brian Jordan	.10
236	Jeremy Giambi	.10
237	Joe Girardi	.10
238	Eric Gagne	.25
239	Masato Yoshii	.10
240	Greg Maddux	.75
241	Bryan Rekar	.10
242	Ray Durham	.10
243	Torii Hunter	.20
244	Derrek Lee	.20
245	Jim Edmonds	.25
246	Einar Diaz	.10
247	Brian Bohanon	.10
248	Ron Belliard	.10
249	Mike Lowell	.20
250	Sammy Sosa	1.00
251	Richard Hidalgo	.10
252	Bartolo Colon	.10
253	Jorge Posada	.25
254	LaTroy Hawkins	.10
255	Paul LoDuca	.10
256	Carlos Febles	.10
257	Nelson Cruz	.10
258	Edgardo Alfonzo	.10
259	Joey Hamilton	.10
260	Cliff Floyd	.10
261	Wes Helms	.10
262	Jay Bell	.10
263	Mike Cameron	.10
264	Paul Konerko	.10
265	Jeff Kent	.20
266	Robert Fick	.10
267	Allen Levrault	.10
268	Placido Polanco	.10
269	Marlon Anderson	.10
270	Mariano Rivera	.20
271	Chan Ho Park	.10
272	Jose Vizcaino	.10
273	Jeff D'Amico	.10
274	Mark Gardner	.10
275	Travis Fryman	.10
276	Darren Lewis	.10
277	Bruce Bochy	.10
278	Jerry Manuel	.10
279	Bob Brenly	.10
280	Don Baylor	.10
281	Davey Lopes	.10
282	Jerry Narron	.10
283	Tony Muser	.10
284	Hal McRae	.10
285	Bobby Cox	.10
286	Larry Dierker	.10
287	Phil Garner	.10
288	Jimy Williams	.10
289	Bobby Valentine	.10
290	Dusty Baker	.10
291	Lloyd McLendon	.10
292	Mike Scioscia	.10
293	Buck Martinez	.10
294	Larry Bowa	.10
295	Tony LaRussa	.10
296	Jeff Torborg	.10
297	Tom Kelly	.10
298	Mike Hargrove	.10
299	Art Howe	.10
300	Lou Pinella	.10
301	Charlie Manuel	.10
302	Buddy Bell	.10
303	Tony Perez	.10
304	Bob Boone	.10
305	Joe Torre	.25
306	Jim Tracy	.10
307	Jason Lane	.10
308	Chris George	.10
309	Hank Blalock	.25
310	Joe Borchard	.10
311	Marlon Byrd	.10
312	Raymond Cabrera **RC**	.25
313	Freddy Sanchez **RC**	.40
314	Scott Wiggins **RC**	.40
315	Jason Maule **RC**	.30
316	Dionys Cesar **RC**	.40
317	Boof Bonser	.10
318	Juan Tolentino **RC**	.40
319	Earl Snyder **RC**	.25
320	Travis Wade **RC**	.25
321	Napoleon Calzado **RC**	.40
322	Eric Glaser **RC**	.40
323	Craig Kuzmic **RC**	.40
324	Nic Jackson **RC**	.50
325	Mike Rivera	.10
326	Jason Bay **RC**	1.00
327	Chris Smith	.10
328	Jake Gautreau	.10
329	Gabe Gross	.10
330	Kenny Baugh	.10
331	J.D. Martin	.10
332	Barry Bonds	1.00
333	Rickey Henderson	.25
334	Bud Smith	.10
335	Rickey Henderson	.25
336	Barry Bonds	1.00
337	Ichiro Suzuki, Jason Giambi, Roberto Alomar	.50
338	Alex Rodriguez, Ichiro Suzuki, Bret Boone	.50
339	Alex Rodriguez, Jim Thome, Rafael Palmeiro	.40
340	Bret Boone, Juan Gonzalez, Alex Rodriguez	.40
341	Freddy Garcia, Mike Mussina, Joe Mays	.15
342	Hideo Nomo, Mike Mussina, Roger Clemens	.40
343	Larry Walker, Todd Helton, Moises Alou	.25
344	Sammy Sosa, Todd Helton, Barry Bonds	.40
345	Barry Bonds, Sammy Sosa, Luis Gonzalez	.40
346	Sammy Sosa, Todd Helton, Luis Gonzalez	.40
347	Curt Schilling, Randy Johnson, John Burkett	.20
348	Randy Johnson, Curt Schilling, Chan Ho Park	.20
349	Seattle Mariners	.25
350	Oakland A's	.10
351	New York Yankees	.50
352	Cleveland Indians	.10
353	Arizona Diamondbacks	.10
354	Atlanta Braves	.10
355	St. Louis Cardinals	.10
356	Houston Astros	.10
357	D'backs vs. Rockies	.10
358	Mets vs. Pirates	.10
359	Braves vs. Phillies	.10
360	D'backs vs. Phillies	.10
361	Yankees vs. White Sox	.10
362	Cubs vs. Reds	.10
363	Angels vs. Mariners	.10
364	Astros vs. Giants	.10

365	Barry Bonds Race to 70 #1	10.00
365	Barry Bonds HR #2-69	8.00
365	Barry Bonds HR #70	15.00
365	Barry Bonds HR #71	10.00
365	Barry Bonds HR #72	10.00
365	Barry Bonds HR #73	50.00
366	Pat Meares	.10
367	Mike Lieberthal	.10
368	Scott Erickson	.10
369	Ron Gant	.10
370	Moises Alou	.25
371	Chad Kreuter	.10
372	Willis Roberts	.10
373	Toby Hall	.10
374	Miguel Batista	.10
375	John Burkett	.10
376	Cory Lidle	.10
377	Nick Neugebauer	.10
378	Jay Payton	.10
379	Steve Karsay	.10
380	Eric Chavez	.20
381	Kelly Stinnett	.10
382	Jarrod Washburn	.10
383	C.J. Nitkowski	.10
384	Jeff Conine	.10
385	Fred McGriff	.10
386	Marvin Benard	.10
387	Dave Burba	.10
388	Dennis Cook	.10
389	Rick Reed	.10
390	Tom Glavine	.25
391	Rondell White	.15
392	Matt Morris	.20
393	Pat Rapp	.10
394	Robert Person	.10
395	Omar Vizquel	.15
396	Jeff Cirillo	.10
397	Dave Mlicki	.10
398	Jose Ortiz	.10
399	Ryan Dempster	.10
400	Curt Schilling	.25
401	Peter Bergeron	.10
402	Kyle Lohse	.10
403	Craig Wilson	.10
404	David Justice	.20
405	Darin Erstad	.20
406	Jose Mercedes	.10
407	Carl Pavano	.10
408	Albie Lopez	.10
409	Alex Ochoa	.10
410	Chipper Jones	.50
411	Tyler Houston	.10
412	Dean Palmer	.10
413	Damian Jackson	.10
414	Josh Towers	.10
415	Rafael Furcal	.20
416	Ken Caminiti	.10
417	Herb Perry	.10
418	Mike Sirotka	.10
419	Mark Wohlers	.10
420	Nomar Garciaparra	1.00
421	Felipe Lopez	.10
422	Joe McEwing	.10
423	Jacque Jones	.10
424	Julio Franco	.10
425	Frank Thomas	.40
426	So Taguchi **RC**	.50
427	Kazuhisa Ishii **RC**	1.00
428	D'Angelo Jimenez	.10
429	Chris Stynes	.10
430	Kerry Wood	.50
431	Chris Singleton	.10
432	Erubiel Durazo	.10
433	Matt Lawton	.10
434	Bill Mueller	.10
435	Jose Canseco	.25
436	Ben Grieve	.10
437	Terry Mulholland	.10
438	David Bell	.10
439	A.J. Pierzynski	.10
440	Adam Dunn	.40
441	Jon Garland	.10
442	Jeff Fassero	.10
443	Julio Lugo	.10
444	Carlos Guillen	.10
445	Orlando Hernandez	.20
446	Mark Loretta	.10
447	Scott Spiezio	.10
448	Kevin Millwood	.20
449	Jamie Moyer	.10
450	Todd Helton	.40
451	Todd Walker	.10
452	Jose Lima	.10
453	Brook Fordyce	.10
454	Aaron Rowand	.10
455	Barry Zito	.20
456	Eric Owens	.10
457	Charles Nagy	.10
458	Raul Ibanez	.10
459	Joe Mays	.10
460	Jim Thome	.50
461	Adam Eaton	.10
462	Felix Martinez	.10
463	Vernon Wells	.10
464	Donnie Sadler	.10
465	Tony Clark	.10
466	Jose Hernandez	.10
467	Ramon Martinez	.10
468	Rusty Greer	.10
469	Rod Barajas	.10
470	Lance Berkman	.25
471	Brady Anderson	.10
472	Pedro Astacio	.10
473	Shane Halter	.10
474	Bret Prinz	.10
475	Edgar Martinez	.20
476	Steve Trachsel	.10
477	Gary Matthews Jr.	.10
478	Ismael Valdes	.10
479	Juan Uribe	.10
480	Shawn Green	.20
481	Kirk Rueter	.10
482	Damion Easley	.10
483	Chris Carpenter	.10
484	Kris Benson	.10
485	Antonio Alfonseca	.10
486	Kyle Farnsworth	.10
487	Brandon Lyon	.10
488	Hideki Irabu	.10
489	David Ortiz	.25
490	Mike Piazza	1.00
491	Derek Lowe	.10
492	Chris Gomez	.10
493	Mark Johnson	.10
494	John Rocker	.10
495	Eric Karros	.10
496	Bill Haselman	.10
497	Dave Veres	.10
498	Gil Heredia	.10
499	Tomokazu Ohka	.10
500	Barry Bonds	1.50
501	David Dellucci	.10
502	Ed Sprague	.10
503	Tom Gordon	.10
504	Javier Vazquez	.10
505	Ben Sheets	.25
506	Wilton Guerrero	.10
507	John Halama	.10
508	Mark Redman	.10
509	Jack Wilson	.10
510	Bernie Williams	.40
511	Miguel Cairo	.10
512	Denny Hocking	.10
513	Tony Batista	.10
514	Mark Grudzielanek	.10
515	Jose Vidro	.10
516	Sterling Hitchcock	.10
517	Billy Koch	.10
518	Matt Clement	.10
519	Bruce Chen	.10
520	Roberto Alomar	.40
521	Orlando Palmeiro	.10
522	Steve Finley	.10
523	Danny Patterson	.10
524	Terry Adams	.10
525	Tino Martinez	.10
526	Tony Armas Jr.	.10
527	Geoff Jenkins	.20
528	Chris Michalak	.10
529	Corey Patterson	.20
530	Brian Giles	.20
531	Jose Jimenez	.10
532	Joe Kennedy	.10
533	Armando Rios	.10
534	Osvaldo Fernandez	.10
535	Ruben Sierra	.10
536	Octavio Dotel	.10
537	Luis Sojo	.10
538	Brent Butler	.10
539	Pablo Ozuna	.10
540	Freddy Garcia	.10
541	Chad Durbin	.10
542	Orlando Merced	.10
543	Michael Tucker	.10
544	Roberto Hernandez	.10
545	Pat Burrell	.25
546	A.J. Burnett	.10
547	Bubba Trammell	.10
548	Scott Elarton	.10
549	Mike Darr	.10
550	Ken Griffey Jr.	1.00
551	Ugueth Urbina	.10
552	Todd Jones	.10
553	Delino DeShields	.10
554	Adam Piatt	.10
555	Jason Kendall	.10
556	Hector Ortiz	.10
557	Turk Wendell	.10
558	Rob Bell	.10
559	Sun-Woo Kim	.10
560	Raul Mondesi	.10
561	Brent Abernathy	.10
562	Seth Etherton	.10
563	Shawn Wooten	.10
564	Jay Buhner	.10
565	Andres Galarraga	.10
566	Shane Reynolds	.10
567	Rod Beck	.10
568	Dee Brown	.10
569	Pedro Feliz	.10
570	Ryan Klesko	.10
571	John Vander Wal	.10
572	Nick Bierbrodt	.10
573	Joe Nathan	.10
574	James Baldwin	.10
575	J.D. Drew	.20
576	Greg Colbrunn	.10
577	Doug Glanville	.10
578	Rey Sanchez	.10
579	Todd Van Poppel	.10
580	Rich Aurilia	.10
581	Chuck Finley	.10
582	Abraham Nunez	.10
583	Kenny Lofton	.20
584	Brian Daubach	.10
585	Miguel Tejada	.25
586	Nate Cornejo	.10
587	Kazuhiro Sasaki	.10
588	Chris Richard	.10
589	Armando Reynoso	.10
590	Tim Hudson	.20
591	Neifi Perez	.10
592	Steve Cox	.10
593	Henry Blanco	.10
594	Ricky Ledee	.10
595	Tim Salmon	.20
596	Luis Rivas	.10
597	Jeff Zimmerman	.10
598	Matt Stairs	.10
599	Preston Wilson	.10
600	Mark McGwire	1.50
601	Timo Perez	.10
602	Matt Anderson	.10
603	Todd Hundley	.10
604	Rick Ankiel	.25
605	Tsuyoshi Shinjo	.10
606	Woody Williams	.10
607	Jason LaRue	.10
608	Carlos Lee	.10
609	Russ Johnson	.10
610	Scott Rolen	.50
611	Brent Mayne	.10
612	Darrin Fletcher	.10
613	Ray Lankford	.10
614	Troy O'Leary	.10
615	Javier Lopez	.20
616	Randy Velarde	.10
617	Vinny Castilla	.10
618	Milton Bradley	.10
619	Ruben Mateo	.10
620	Jason Giambi	.40
621	Andy Benes	.10
622	Tony Eusebio	.10
623	Andy Pettitte	.20
624	Jose Offerman	.10
625	Mo Vaughn	.20
626	Steve Sparks	.10
627	Mike Matthews	.10
628	Robb Nen	.10
629	Kip Wells	.10
630	Kevin Brown	.20
631	Arthur Rhodes	.10
632	Gabe Kapler	.10
633	Jermaine Dye	.10
634	Josh Beckett	.25
635	Pokey Reese	.10
636	Benji Gil	.10
637	Marcus Giles	.10
638	Julian Tavarez	.10
639	Jason Schmidt	.25
640	Alex Rodriguez	1.25
641	Anaheim Angels	.10
642	Arizona Diamondbacks	.10
643	Atlanta Braves	.10
644	Baltimore Orioles	.10
645	Boston Red Sox	.10
646	Chicago Cubs	.10
647	Chicago White Sox	.10
648	Cincinnati Reds	.10
649	Cleveland Indians	.10
650	Colorado Rockies	.10
651	Detroit Tigers	.10
652	Florida Marlins	.10
653	Houston Astros	.10
654	Kansas City Royals	.10
655	Los Angeles Dodgers	.10
656	Milwaukee Brewers	.10
657	Minnesota Twins	.10
658	Montreal Expos	.10
659	New York Mets	.10
660	New York Yankees	.10
661	Oakland Athletics	.10
662	Philadelphia Phillies	.10
663	Pittsburgh Pirates	.10
664	San Diego Padres	.10
665	San Francisco Giants	.10
666	Seattle Mariners	.10
667	St. Louis Cardinals	.10
668	Tampa Bay Devil Rays	.10
669	Texas Rangers	.10
670	Toronto Blue Jays	.10
671	Juan Cruz	.25
672	Kevin Cash **RC**	.50
673	Jimmy Gobble **RC**	.75
674	Mike Hill **RC**	.40
675	Taylor Buchholz **RC**	.40
676	Bill Hall	.10
677	Brett Roneberg **RC**	.40
678	Royce Huffman **RC**	.40
679	Chris Tritle **RC**	.40
680	Nate Espy **RC**	.40
681	Nick Alvarez **RC**	.50
682	Jason Botts **RC**	.40
683	Ryan Gripp **RC**	.40
684	Dan Phillips **RC**	.50
685	Pablo Arias **RC**	.50
686	John Rodriguez **RC**	.40
687	Rich Harden **RC**	3.00
688	Neal Frendling **RC**	.50
689	Rich Thompson **RC**	.40
690	Greg Montalbano **RC**	.40
691	Leonard Dinardo **RC**	.40
692	Ryan Raburn **RC**	.40
693	Josh Barfield	1.00
694	David Bacani **RC**	.40
695	Dan Johnson **RC**	.50
696	Mike Mussina	.25
697	Ivan Rodriguez	.25
698	Doug Mientkiewicz	.10
699	Roberto Alomar	.25
700	Eric Chavez	.15
701	Omar Vizquel	.10
702	Mike Cameron	.10
703	Torii Hunter	.10
704	Ichiro Suzuki	.50
705	Greg Maddux	.50
706	Brad Ausmus	.10
707	Todd Helton	.25
708	Fernando Vina	.10
709	Scott Rolen	.40
710	Orlando Cabrera	.10
711	Andruw Jones	.15
712	Jim Edmonds	.10
713	Larry Walker	.15
714	Roger Clemens	.50
715	Randy Johnson	.25
716	Ichiro Suzuki	.50
717	Barry Bonds	.75
718	Ichiro Suzuki	.50
719	Albert Pujols	.50

Gold

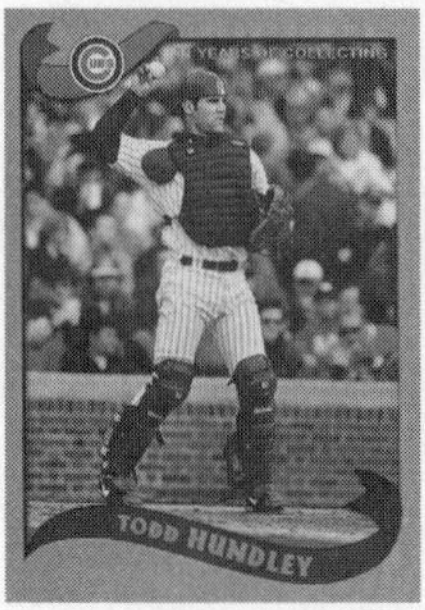

	NM/M
Complete Set (659):	700.00
Stars:	5-10X

Production 2,002 Sets

2002 Topps Limited

	NM/M
Complete Set (790):	165.00

Includes all 73 B. Bonds #365 HR cards.

Aces

		NM/M
Common Player:		10.00
Inserted 1:1,180		
MH	Mike Hampton	10.00
RJ	Randy Johnson	20.00
GM	Greg Maddux	30.00
PM	Pedro Martinez	20.00
MM	Mark Mulder	10.00

All-World Team

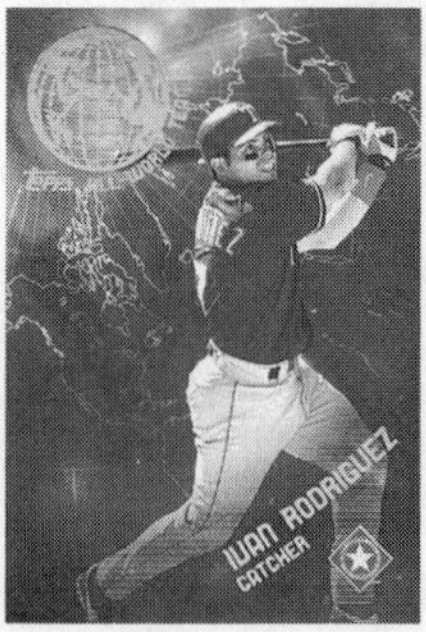

		NM/M
Complete Set (25):		25.00
Common Player:		.50
Inserted 1:12		
AW-1	Ichiro Suzuki	3.00
AW-2	Barry Bonds	4.00
AW-3	Pedro Martinez	1.50
AW-4	Juan Gonzalez	1.00
AW-5	Larry Walker	.50
AW-6	Sammy Sosa	3.00
AW-7	Mariano Rivera	.75
AW-8	Vladimir Guerrero	1.50
AW-9	Alex Rodriguez	3.00
AW-10	Albert Pujols	3.00
AW-11	Luis Gonzalez	.50
AW-12	Ken Griffey Jr.	2.50
AW-13	Kazuhiro Sasaki	.50
AW-14	Bob Abreu	.50
AW-15	Todd Helton	1.00
AW-16	Nomar Garciaparra	2.50
AW-17	Miguel Tejada	.75
AW-18	Roger Clemens	3.00
AW-19	Mike Piazza	2.50
AW-20	Carlos Delgado	1.00
AW-21	Derek Jeter	4.00
AW-22	Hideo Nomo	.75
AW-23	Randy Johnson	1.50
AW-24	Ivan Rodriguez	1.00
AW-25	Chan Ho Park	.50

Autographs

		NM/M
Common Player:		5.00
TA1	Carlos Delgado	40.00
TA2	Ivan Rodriguez	50.00
TA3	Miguel Tejada	30.00
TA4	Geoff Jenkins	10.00
TA5	Johnny Damon	40.00
TA6	Tim Hudson	25.00
TA7	Terrence Long	10.00
TA8	Gabe Kapler	10.00
TA9	Magglio Ordonez	20.00
TA10	Barry Bonds	180.00
TA11	Pat Burrell	20.00
TA12	Mike Mussina	40.00
TA13	Eric Valent	5.00
TA14	Xavier Nady	8.00
TA15	Cristian Guerrero	5.00
TA16	Ben Sheets	15.00
TA17	Corey Patterson	15.00
TA18	Carlos Pena	5.00
TA19	Alex Rodriguez	80.00

Series 2

TA-AB	Adrian Beltre	25.00
TA-JD	Jermaine Dye	15.00
TA-AE	Alex Escobar	
TA-CF	Cliff Floyd	15.00
TA-RF	Rafael Furcal	20.00
TA-BG	Brian Giles	20.00
TA-KG	Keith Ginter	8.00
TA-TG	Troy Glaus	40.00
TA-BGR	Ben Grieve	20.00
TA-CG	Cristian Guzman	15.00
TA-JH	Josh Hamilton	35.00
TA-NJ	Nick Johnson	5.00
TA-RK	Ryan Klesko	20.00
TA-JO	Jose Ortiz	10.00
TA-RO	Roy Oswalt	15.00
TA-RP	Rafael Palmeiro	50.00
TA-AR	Alex Rodriguez	80.00
TA-JR	Jimmy Rollins	25.00
TA-RS	Richie Sexson	25.00
TA-MS	Mike Sweeney	20.00
TA-JW	Justin Wayne	10.00
TA-BW	Brad Wilkerson	10.00

Battery Mates Relic

		NM/M
Inserted 1:4,401		
ML	Greg Maddux,	
	Javy Lopez	30.00
LP	Al Leiter, Mike Piazza	30.00

Coaches Collection Relics

		NM/M
Common Card		8.00
Inserted 1:236 Retail		
AH	Art Howe	8.00
AT	Alan Trammell	15.00
BB	Bruce Bochy	8.00
BM	Buck Martinez	8.00
BV	Bobby Valentine	15.00
BW	Billy Williams	15.00
BBE	Buddy Bell	15.00
BBR	Bob Brenly	15.00
DB	Dusty Baker	20.00
DL	Davey Lopes	15.00
DBA	Don Baylor	15.00
EH	Elrod Hendricks	8.00
EM	Eddie Murray	40.00
FW	Frank White	15.00
HM	Hal McRae	8.00
JT	Joe Torre	15.00
KG	Ken Griffey Sr.	8.00
LB	Larry Bowa	15.00
LP	Lance Parrish	15.00
MH	Mike Hargrove	15.00
MS	Mike Scioscia	15.00
MW	Mookie Wilson	10.00
PG	Phil Garner	10.00
PM	Paul Molitor	40.00
TP	Tony Perez	10.00
WR	Willie Randolph	15.00

Draft Picks

		NM/M
Complete Set (10):		40.00
1-5 in Green Factory Sets		
6-10 in Holiday Factory Sets		
1	Scott Moore	6.00
2	Val Majewski	6.00
3	Brian Slocum	4.00
4	Chris Gruler	6.00
5	Mark Schramek	6.00
6	Joe Saunders	6.00
7	Jeff Francis	8.00
8	Royce Ring	4.00
9	Greg Miller	6.00
10	Brandon Weeden	4.00

Dueces Are Wild

		NM/M
Common Card:		15.00
Inserted 1:1,962		
JG	Randy Johnson,	
	Luis Gonzalez	30.00
BK	Barry Bonds, Jeff Kent	40.00
TA	Jim Thome,	
	Roberto Alomar	30.00
WH	Larry Walker, Todd Helton	25.00
BG	Bret Boone,	
	Freddy Garcia	15.00

Dual Ebbets/ Yankee Seat Relic

No Pricing

Dual Ebbets/Yankee Autographed Seat Relic

No Pricing

East Meets West

		NM/M
Complete Set (8):		6.00
Common Player:		1.00
Inserted 1:24		
EW-HN	Hideo Nomo,	
	Masanori Murakami	2.00
EW-HI	Hideki Irabu,	
	Masanori Murakami	1.00
EW-SH	Shigetoshi Hasegawa,	
	Masanori Murakami	1.00
EW-MY	Masato Yoshii,	
	Masanori Murakami	1.00
EW-TS	Tsuyoshi Shinjo,	
	Masanori Murakami	1.00
EW-KS	Kazuhiro Sasaki,	
	Masanori Murakami	1.00
EW-MS	Mac Suzuki,	
	Masanori Murakami	1.00
EW-TO	Tomo Ohka,	
	Masanori Murakami	1.00

East Meets West Relics

		NM/M
Common Player:		15.00
Inserted 1:3,419		
HN	Hideo Nomo	40.00
KS	Kazuhiro Sasaki	15.00
TS	Tsuyoshi Shinjo	15.00

Ebbets Field Seat Relics

		NM/M
Inserted 1:9,116		
JB	Joe Black	125.00
RC	Roy Campanella	250.00
BC	Billy Cox	125.00
CF	Carl Furillo	125.00
GH	Gil Hodges	250.00
AP	Andy Pafko	125.00
PWR	Pee Wee Reese	250.00
JR	Jackie Robinson	250.00
DS	Duke Snider	200.00

Ebbets Field/Yankee Stadium Seat Dual Relic

No Pricing

Hall of Fame Vintage BuyBacks AutoProofs

		NM/M
Common Autograph:		15.00
BR16	Brooks Robinson	
	82 KM/200	50.00
EW10	Earl Weaver 87/100	15.00
FJ33	Fergie Jenkins 84/100	15.00
GP26	Gaylord Perry 82/100	15.00
GP29	Gaylord Perry 82/100	15.00
GP30	Gaylord Perry 83 SV/200	15.00
OC1	Orlando Cepeda 82 KM/200	15.00
RF15	Rollie Fingers 81/300	15.00
RF16	Rollie Fingers 81 LL/100	15.00
RF18	Rollie Fingers 82/100	15.00
RF19	Rollie Fingers 82 LA/200	15.00
RF21	Rollie Fingers 82 KM/300	15.00
RF22	Rollie Fingers 83/200	15.00
RF24	Rollie Fingers 84/200	15.00
RF27	Rollie Fingers 85/300	15.00
RF28	Rollie Fingers 86/100	15.00
SC5	Steve Carlton 84 LL/100	25.00
SC6	Steve Carlton 85/200	25.00
SC8	Steve Carlton 87/200	25.00

Heart of the Order Relic

		NM/M
Inserted 1:4,247		
KBA	Jeff Kent, Barry Bonds,	
	Rich Aurilia	75.00
TGA	Jim Thome, Juan Gonzalez,	
	Roberto Alomar	50.00
ARB	Bob Abreu, Scott Rolen,	
	Pat Burrell	50.00
OWM	Paul O'Neill, Bernie Williams,	
	Tino Martinez	50.00

Hit and Run Relic

		NM/M
Inserted 1:4,241		
JD	Johnny Damon	10.00
DE	Darin Erstad	10.00
RF	Rafael Furcal	10.00

Hobby Masters

		NM/M
Complete Set (20):		40.00
Common Player:		1.00
Inserted 1:25		
1	Mark McGwire	5.00
2	Derek Jeter	5.00
3	Chipper Jones	2.00
4	Roger Clemens	4.00
5	Vladimir Guerrero	2.00
6	Ichiro Suzuki	3.00

7	Todd Helton	1.50
8	Alex Rodriguez	4.00
9	Albert Pujols	4.00
10	Sammy Sosa	3.00
11	Ken Griffey Jr.	3.00
12	Randy Johnson	2.00
13	Nomar Garciaparra	3.00
14	Ivan Rodriguez	1.50
15	Manny Ramirez	1.50
16	Barry Bonds	5.00
17	Mike Piazza	3.00
18	Pedro Martinez	1.50
19	Jeff Bagwell	1.50
20	Luis Gonzalez	1.00

Jack of All Trades

		NM/M
Inserted 1:1,350		
RO	Roberto Alomar/Bat	20.00
BB	Barry Bonds/Jsy	35.00
AJ	Andruw Jones/Jsy	10.00
IR	Ivan Rodriguez/Jsy	15.00
BW	Bernie Williams/Jsy	15.00

Kings of the Clubhouse

		NM/M
Common Player:		10.00
Inserted 1:1,449 Ser. 2		
TG	Tom Glavine/Jsy	15.00
TH	Todd Helton/Jsy	15.00
RJ	Randy Johnson/Jsy	20.00
EM	Edgar Martinez/Jsy	10.00
PO	Paul O'Neill/Bat	20.00

Like Father Like Son Relic

		NM/M
Common Duo:		
Inserted 1:1,304 Retail		
AL	Roberto Alomar, Sandy Alomar,	
	Sandy Alomar Jr.	40.00
BE	Dale Berra, Yogi Berra	50.00
BON	Bobby Bonds,	
	Barry Bonds	80.00
BOO	Bob Boone, Bret Boone,	
	Aaron Boone	40.00
CR	Jose Cruz, Jose Cruz Jr.	40.00

Own The Game

		NM/M
Complete Set (30):		25.00
Common Player:		.50
Inserted 1:12		
OG1	Moises Alou	.75
OG2	Roberto Alomar	.75
OG3	Luis Gonzalez	.50
OG4	Bret Boone	.75
OG5	Barry Bonds	4.00
OG6	Jim Thome	1.50
OG7	Jimmy Rollins	.75
OG8	Cristian Guzman	.50
OG9	Lance Berkman	.75
OG10	Mike Sweeney	.50
OG11	Rich Aurilia	.50
OG12	Ichiro Suzuki	2.50
OG13	Luis Gonzalez	.50
OG14	Ichiro Suzuki	2.50
OG15	Jimmy Rollins	.75
OG16	Roger Cedeno	.50
OG17	Barry Bonds	4.00
OG18	Jim Thome	1.50
OG19	Curt Schilling	1.00
OG20	Roger Clemens	3.00
OG21	Curt Schilling	1.00
OG22	Brad Radke	.50
OG23	Greg Maddux	2.00
OG24	Mark Mulder	.75
OG25	Jeff Shaw	.50
OG26	Mariano Rivera	.75
OG27	Randy Johnson	1.50
OG28	Pedro Martinez	1.50
OG29	John Burkett	.50
OG30	Tim Hudson	.75

Prime Cuts Pine Tar Series

		NM/M
Common Player:		15.00
Inserted 1:4,420		
BB	Barry Bonds	60.00
LG	Luis Gonzalez	20.00
TG	Tony Gwynn	40.00
TH	Todd Helton	25.00
AP	Albert Pujols	40.00

Series 2

Inserted 1:1,043		
Trademark Series:		1.5-2X
Inserted 1:2,087 Ser. 2		
Prime Cuts Barrel:		2-4X
Inserted 1:7,824 Ser. 2		
WB	Wilson Betemit	15.00
SB	Sean Burroughs	15.00
JC	Joe Crede	20.00
AD	Adam Dunn	30.00
AE	Alex Escobar	15.00
MG	Marcus Giles	15.00
AG	Alexis Gomez	15.00
TH	Toby Hall	15.00
JH	Josh Hamilton	20.00
NJ	Nick Johnson	15.00
XN	Xavier Nady	15.00
CP	Corey Patterson	20.00
CPE	Carlos Pena	15.00
AR	Aaron Rowand	25.00
RS	Ruben Salazar	15.00

Prime Cuts Autograph Series

No Pricing

Ring Masters

		NM/M
Complete Set (10):		15.00
Common Player:		.50
Inserted 1:25		
1	Derek Jeter	4.00
2	Mark McGwire	4.00
3	Mariano Rivera	1.00
4	Gary Sheffield	.75
5	Al Leiter	.50
6	Chipper Jones	1.50
7	Roger Clemens	3.00
8	Greg Maddux	2.00
9	Roberto Alomar	1.00
10	Paul O'Neill	.50

Team Topps Legends Autos.

		NM/M
Common Player:		25.00
TT6R	Whitey Ford	60.00
TT8R	Bob Gibson	40.00
TT47R	Frank Howard	25.00
TT46F	Robin Roberts	25.00
TT13F	Warren Spahn	40.00

Three of a Kind

		NM/M
Common Card:		
Inserted 1:2,039		
SPA	Tsuyoshi Shinjo, Mike Piazza,	
	Edgardo Alfonzo	50.00
LOC	Carlos Lee, Magglio Ordonez,	
	Jose Canseco	50.00
FBJ	Rafael Furcal, Wilson Betemit,	
	Andruw Jones	40.00
PSW	Jorge Posada, Alfonso Soriano,	
	Bernie Williams	50.00
BDB	A.J. Burnett, Ryan Dempster,	
	Josh Beckett	40.00

Trademark Series

No Pricing

Turn Two Relic

		NM/M
Inserted 1:4,401		
TW	Alan Trammell,	
	Lou Whitaker	40.00
VA	Omar Vizquel,	
	Roberto Alomar	40.00

Yankee Stadium Seat Relics

		NM/M
Inserted 1:579		
HB	Hank Bauer	100.00
YB	Yogi Berra	250.00
JC	Joe Collins	100.00
BM	Billy Martin	250.00
GM	Gil McDougald	100.00
JM	Johnny Mize	100.00
AR	Allie Reynolds	100.00
PR	Phil Rizzuto	250.00
GW	Gene Woodling	100.00

1952 Player Autographs

		NM/M
Inserted 1:7,524		
HBA	Hank Bauer	75.00
YBA	Yogi Berra	100.00
PRA	Preacher Roe	70.00

1952 Reprint Autographs

		NM/M
Common Autograph:		25.00
Inserted 1:10,268		
JBA	Joe Black	90.00
CEA	Carl Erskine	50.00
GMA	Gil McDougal	40.00
APA	Andy Pafko	60.00
PRA	Phil Rizzuto	80.00
DSA	Duke Snider	100.00

1952 World Series Tribute

BILLY COX

	NM/M
Complete Set (19):	50.00

Common Player: 3.00
Inserted 1:25
1 Roy Campanella 4.00
2 Duke Snider 4.00
3 Carl Erskine 3.00
4 Andy Pafko 3.00
5 Johnny Mize 3.00
6 Billy Martin 4.00
7 Phil Rizzuto 4.00
8 Gil McDougal 3.00
9 Allie Reynolds 3.00
10 Jackie Robinson 4.00
Series 2
11 Preacher Roe 3.00
12 Gil Hodges 3.00
13 Billy Cox 3.00
14 Yogi Berra 4.00
15 Gene Woodling 3.00
16 Jerry Sain 3.00
17 Ralph Houk 3.00
18 Joe Collins 3.00
19 Hank Bauer 3.00

1952 World Series Highlights

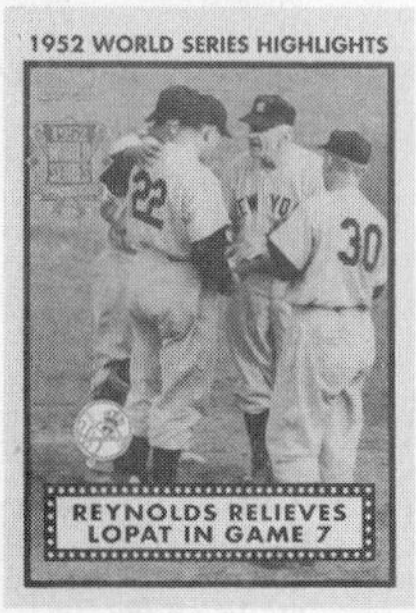
1952 WORLD SERIES HIGHLIGHTS
REYNOLDS RELIEVES LOPAT IN GAME 7

NM/M
Complete Set (7): 10.00
Common Player: 2.00
Inserted 1:25
52WS-1 Dodgers' Game 1 Starting Line Up 3.00
52WS-2 Dodgers Celebrate Game 3 Win! 2.00
52WS-3 Carl Erskine Wins Game 5 2.00
Series 2
52WS-2 Game 2 2.00
52WS-4 Game 4 2.00
52WS-6 Game 6 2.00
52WS-7 Game 7 2.00

2 Bagger Relic

NM/M
Inserted 1:3,733
TG Tony Gwynn 30.00
TH Todd Helton 20.00
SR Scott Rolen 20.00

2002 Topps Traded & Rookies

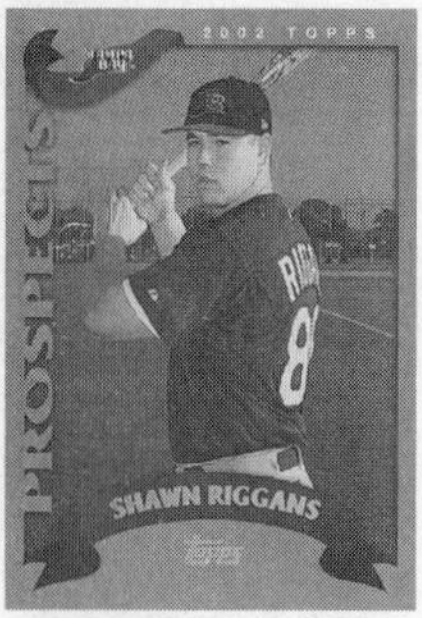
2002 TOPPS
PROSPECTS
SHAWN RIGGANS

NM/M
Complete Set (275): 125.00
Common Player: .15
Common SP (1-110): .50
Chrome Cards: 2-4X
2:Pack
Pack (10): 3.00
Box (24): 60.00
T1 Jeff Weaver .50
T2 Jay Powell .50
T3 Alex Gonzalez .50
T4 Jason Isringhausen .50
T5 Darren Oliver .50
T6 Hector Ortiz .50
T7 Chuck Knoblauch .50
T8 Brian L. Hunter .50
T9 Dustan Mohr .50
T10 Eric Hinske .50
T11 Roger Cedeno .50
T12 Eddie Perez .50
T13 Jeromy Burnitz .50
T14 Bartolo Colon .50
T15 Rick Helling .50
T16 Dan Plesac .50
T17 Scott Strickland .50
T18 Antonio Alfonseca .50
T19 Ricky Gutierrez .50
T20 John Valentin .50
T21 Raul Mondesi .50
T22 Ben Davis .50
T23 Nelson Figueroa .50
T24 Earl Snyder .50
T25 Robin Ventura .50
T26 Jimmy Haynes .50
T27 Kenny Kelly .50
T28 Morgan Ensberg .50
T29 Reggie Sanders .50
T30 Shigetoshi Hasegawa .50
T31 Allen Levrault .50
T32 Russell Branyan .50
T33 Jose Guillen .50
T34 Jose Paniagua .50
T35 Kent Mercker .50
T36 Jesse Orosco .50
T37 Gregg Zaun .50
T38 Reggie Taylor .50
T39 Andres Galarraga .50
T40 Chris Truby .50
T41 Bruce Chen .50
T42 Darren Lewis .50
T43 Ryan Kohlmeier .50
T44 John McDonald .50
T45 Omar Daal .50
T46 Matt Clement .50
T47 Glendon Rusch .50
T48 Chan Ho Park .50
T49 Benny Agbayani .50
T50 Juan Gonzalez 1.50
T51 Carlos Baerga .50
T52 Tim Raines .50
T53 Kevin Appier .50
T54 Marty Cordoua .50
T55 Jeff D'Amico .50
T56 Dmitri Young .50
T57 Roosevelt Brown .50
T58 Dustin Hermanson .50
T59 Jose Rijo .50
T60 Todd Ritchie .50
T61 Lee Stevens .50
T62 Shane Heams .50
T63 Eric Young .50
T64 Chuck Finley .50
T65 Dicky Gonzalez .50
T66 Jose Macias .50
T67 Gabe Kapler .50
T68 Sandy Alomar Jr. .50
T69 Henry Blanco .50
T70 Julian Tavarez .50
T71 Paul Bako .50
T72 Dave Burba .50
T73 Brian Jordan .50
T74 Rickey Henderson 1.00
T75 Kevin Mench .50
T76 Hideo Nomo 1.00
T77 Mark Sweeney .50
T78 Brad Fullmer .50
T79 Carl Everett .50
T80 David Wells .50
T81 Aaron Sele .50
T82 Todd Hollandsworth .50
T83 Vicente Padilla .50
T84 Chris Latham .50
T85 Corky Miller .50
T86 Josh Fogg .50
T87 Calvin Murray .50
T88 Craig Paquette .50
T89 Jay Payton .50
T90 Carlos Pena .50
T91 Juan Encarnacion .50
T92 Rey Sanchez .50
T93 Ryan Dempster .50
T94 Mario Encarnacion .50
T95 Jorge Julio .50
T96 John Mabry .50
T97 Todd Zeile .50
T98 Johnny Damon .50
T99 Deivi Cruz .50
T100 Gary Sheffield 1.00
T101 Ted Lilly .50
T102 Todd Van Poppel .50
T103 Shawn Estes .50
T104 Cesar Izturis .50
T105 Ron Coomer .50
T106 Grady Little .50
T107 Jimy Williams .50
T108 Tony Pena .50
T109 Frank Robinson .50
T110 Ron Gardenhire .50
T111 Dennis Tankersley .15
T112 Alejandro Cadena **RC** .25
T113 Justin Reid **RC** .25
T114 Nate Field **RC** .25
T115 Rene Reyes **RC** .25
T116 Nelson Castro **RC** .25
T117 Miguel Olivo .15
T118 David Espinosa .15
T119 Chris Bootcheck **RC** .40
T120 Rob Henkel **RC** .25
T121 Steve Bechler **RC** .25
T122 Mark Outlaw **RC** .25
T123 Henry Pichardo **RC** .25
T124 Michael Floyd **RC** .25
T125 Richard Lane **RC** .25
T126 Peter Zamora **RC** .25
T127 Javier Colina .15
T128 Greg Sain **RC** .25
T129 Ronnie Merrill .25
T130 Gavin Floyd 1.50
T131 Josh Bonifay **RC** .25
T132 Tommy Marx **RC** .25
T133 Gary Cates Jr. **RC** .25
T134 Neal Cotts .50
T135 Angel Berroa .25
T136 Elio Serrano **RC** .25
T137 J.J. Putz **RC** .25
T138 Ruben Gotay **RC** .25
T139 Eddie Rogers **RC** .25
T140 Wily Mo Pena .25
T141 Tyler Yates **RC** .25
T142 Colin Young **RC** .25
T143 Chance Caple .15
T144 Ben Howard **RC** .25
T145 Ryan Bukvich **RC** .25
T146 Clifford Bartosh **RC** .25
T147 Brandon Claussen .25
T148 Cristian Guerrero .15
T149 Derrick Lewis .15
T150 Eric Miller **RC** .25
T151 Justin Huber **RC** .75
T152 Adrian Gonzalez .15
T153 Brian West **RC** .25
T154 Chris Baker **RC** .25
T155 Drew Henson .15
T156 Scott Hairston .75
T157 Jason Simontacchi **RC** .75
T158 Jason Arnold .40
T159 Brandon Phillips .15
T160 Adam Roller **RC** .25
T161 Scotty Layfield **RC** .25
T162 Freddie Money **RC** .25
T163 Noochie Varner **RC** .50
T164 Terrance Hill **RC** .25
T165 Jeremy Hill **RC** .25
T166 Carlos Cabrera **RC** .25
T167 Jose Morban **RC** .25
T168 Kevin Frederick **RC** .25
T169 Mark Teixeira .40
T170 Brian Rogers .15
T171 Anastacio Martinez **RC** .25
T172 Bobby Jenks **RC** .75
T173 David Gil **RC** .25
T174 Andres Torres .15
T175 James Barrett **RC** .25
T176 Jimmy Journell .15
T177 Brett Kay **RC** .25
T178 Jason Young **RC** .25
T179 Mark Hamilton **RC** .25
T180 Jose Bautista **RC** .50
T181 Blake McGinley **RC** .25
T182 Ryan Mottl **RC** .25
T183 Jeff Austin **RC** .25
T184 Xavier Nady .15
T185 Kyle Kane **RC** .25
T186 Travis Foley .15
T187 Nathan Kaup **RC** .25
T188 Eric Cyr **RC** .25
T189 Josh Cisneros **RC** .25
T190 Brad Nelson **RC** .75
T191 Clint Weibl **RC** .25
T192 Ron Calloway **RC** .25
T193 Jung Bong .15
T194 Rolando Viera **RC** .25
T195 Jason Bulger **RC** .25
T196 Chone Figgins **RC** .75
T197 Jimmy Alvarez **RC** .25
T198 Joel Crump **RC** .25
T199 Ryan Doumit **RC** 1.50
T200 Demetrius Heath **RC** .25
T201 John Ennis **RC** .25
T202 Doug Sessions **RC** .25
T203 Clinton Hosford **RC** .25
T204 Chris Narveson **RC** .25
T205 Ross Peeples **RC** .25
T206 Alexander Requena **RC** .25
T207 Matt Erickson **RC** .25
T208 Brian Forystek **RC** .25
T209 Dewon Brazelton .15
T210 Nathan Haynes .15
T211 Jack Cust .15
T212 Jesse Foppert .75
T213 Jesus Cota **RC** .25
T214 Juan Gonzalez .15
T215 Tim Kalita **RC** .25
T216 Manny Delcarmen **RC** 2.00
T217 Jim Kavourias .15
T218 C.J. Wilson **RC** .25
T219 Edwin Yan **RC** .25
T220 Andy Van Hekken .15
T221 Michael Cuddyer .15
T222 Jeff Verplancke **RC** .25
T223 Mike Wilson **RC** .25
T224 Corwin Malone .15
T225 Chris Snelling **RC** .50
T226 Joe Rogers **RC** .25
T227 Jason Bay .50
T228 Ezequiel Astacio **RC** .25
T229 Joey Hammond **RC** .25
T230 Chris Duffy **RC** .25
T231 Mark Prior 1.00
T232 Hansel Izquierdo **RC** .25
T233 Franklyn German **RC** .25
T234 Alexis Gomez .15
T235 Jorge Padilla **RC** .25
T236 Ryan Snare **RC** .25
T237 Deivis Santos .15
T238 Taggert Bozied **RC** 1.00
T239 Mike Peeples **RC** .25
T240 Ronald Acuna **RC** .25
T241 Koyie Hill .15
T242 Garrett Guzman **RC** .25
T243 Ryan Church **RC** 1.00
T244 Tony Fontana **RC** .25
T245 Keto Anderson **RC** .25
T246 Brad Bouras **RC** .25
T247 Jason Dubois **RC** 1.00
T248 Angel Guzman **RC** 2.00
T249 Joel Hanrahan **RC** .50
T250 Joe Jiannetti **RC** .25
T251 Sean Pierce **RC** .25
T252 Jake Mauer **RC** .25
T253 Marshall McDougall **RC** .50
T254 Edwin Almonte **RC** .25
T255 Shawn Riggans **RC** .25
T256 Steven Shell .15
T257 Kevin Hooper **RC** .40
T258 Michael Frick **RC** .25
T259 Travis Chapman **RC** .40
T260 Tim Hummel **RC** .25
T261 Adam Morrissey **RC** .25
T262 Dontrelle Willis **RC** 5.00
T263 Justin Sherrod **RC** .25
T264 Gerald Smiley **RC** .25
T265 Tony Miller **RC** .25
T266 Nolan Ryan 1.50
T267 Reggie Jackson .50
T268 Steve Garvey .15
T269 Wade Boggs .25
T270 Sammy Sosa 1.00
T271 Curt Schilling .25
T272 Mark Grace .25
T273 Jason Giambi .50
T274 Ken Griffey Jr. .75
T275 Roberto Alomar .40

Gold

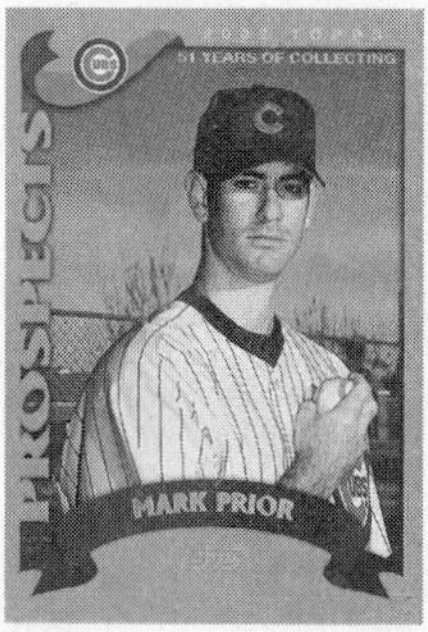
2002 TOPPS
51 YEARS OF COLLECTING
PROSPECTS
MARK PRIOR

Gold Stars: 2-4X
Production 2,002 Sets
Chrome Refractors: 3-5X
Inserted 1:12

Tools of the Trade Relics

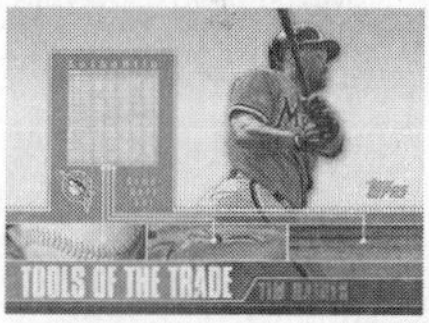
TOOLS OF THE TRADE

NM/M
Common Player: 5.00
Bat Relics 1:34
Jersey Relics 1:426
RAB Roberto Alomar/Bat 8.00
MA Moises Alou/Bat 8.00
DB David Bell/Bat 5.00
JBU Jeromy Burnitz/Bat 5.00
JC Jose Canseco/Bat 10.00
VC Vinny Castilla/Bat 5.00
JCI Jeff Cirillo/Bat 5.00
TC Tony Clark/Bat 5.00
JDB Johnny Damon/Bat 6.00
CE Carl Everett/Bat 5.00
BF Brad Fullmer/Bat 5.00
AG Andres Galarraga/Bat 6.00
JG Juan Gonzalez/Jsy 8.00
RHB Rickey Henderson/Bat 10.00
BJ Brian Jordan/Bat 5.00
DJ David Justice/Bat 5.00
CK Chuck Knoblauch/Bat 5.00
MLB Matt Lawton/Bat 5.00
KL Kenny Lofton/Bat 5.00
TM Tino Martinez/Bat 6.00
CP Carlos Pena/Bat 8.00
JP Josh Phelps/Jsy 6.00
TR Tim Raines/Bat 5.00
RS Reggie Sanders/Bat 5.00
GS Gary Sheffield/Bat 5.00
TS Tsuyoshi Shinjo/Bat 5.00
RSI Ruben Sierra/Bat 5.00
MT Michael Tucker/Bat 5.00
MV Mo Vaughn/Jsy 6.00
MVB Mo Vaughn/Bat 6.00

RV	Robin Ventura/Bat	6.00
RW	Rondell White/Bat	5.00
EY	Eric Young/Bat	5.00

Tools of the Trade Dual Relics

		NM/M
Common Card:		8.00
Inserted 1:539		
MA	Moises Alou	10.00
HN	Hideo Nomo	35.00
CP	Chan Ho Park	8.00

Farewell Relics

		NM/M
Randomly inserted.		
JC	Jose Canseco	10.00

Hall of Fame Relics

		NM/M
Randomly inserted.		
HOF-OS	Ozzie Smith	25.00

Legends Autographs

		NM/M
Common Autograph:		10.00
Inserted 1:1,097		
	Johnny Bench	40.00
	Vida Blue	10.00
	Clete Boyer	12.00
	Whitey Ford	30.00
	Bob Gibson	25.00
	Joe Pepitone	10.00
	Bobby Richardson	10.00
	Bill "Moose" Skowron	10.00
	Enos Slaughter	18.00
	Carl Yastrzemski	60.00

Signature Moves Autos.

		NM/M
Common Autograph:		8.00
Inserted 1:91		
RA	Roberto Alomar	30.00
MA	Moises Alou	15.00
TBL	Tony Blanco	8.00
BB	Boof Bonser	8.00
AC	Antoine Cameron	10.00
BC	Brandon Claussen	15.00
MC	Matt Cooper	8.00
JD	Johnny Damon	30.00
JDA	Jeff DaVanon	8.00
VD	Victor Diaz	12.00
RH	Ryan Hannaman	8.00
KI	Kazuhisa Ishii	40.00
FJ	Forrest Johnson	8.00
TL	Todd Linden	15.00
CM	Corwin Malone	8.00
JM	Jake Mauer	8.00
AM	Andy Morales	8.00
RM	Ramon Moreta	8.00
JMO	Justin Morneau	30.00
JP	Juan Pena	8.00
JS	Juan Silvestre	8.00
CS	Chris Smith	8.00
DT	Dennis Tankersley	8.00
MT	Marcus Thames	8.00
CU	Chase Utley	200.00
JW	Justin Wayne	8.00

2002 Topps American Pie
Spirit of America

AMERICAN TREASURES

JIM THORPE

		NM/M
Complete Set (150):		30.00
Common Player:		.25
Pack (7):		5.00
Box (24):		100.00
1	Warren Spahn	.75
2	Reggie Jackson	.75
3	Bill Mazeroski	.25
4	Carl Yastrzemski	.75
5	Whitey Ford	.75
6	Ralph Houk	.25
7	Rod Carew	.50
8	Kirk Gibson	.25
9	Bobby Thomson	.25
10	Don Newcombe	.25
11	Gaylord Perry	.25
12	Bruce Sutter	.40
13	Bob Gibson	.50
14	Brooks Robinson	1.00
15	Steve Carlton	.50

16	Robin Yount	1.00
17	Ernie Banks	.75
18	Lou Brock	.25
19	Al Kaline	.75
20	Carlton Fisk	.75
21	Frank Robinson	.75
22	Bobby Bonds	.25
23	Andre Dawson	.25
24	Rich "Goose" Gossage	.25
25	Fred Lynn	.25
26	Keith Hernandez	.25
27	Rollie Fingers	.25
28	Juan Marichal	.25
29	Maury Wills	.25
30	Dave Winfield	.50
31	Frank Howard	.25
32	Tony Gwynn	1.00
33	Jim Palmer	.50
34	Mike Schmidt	1.50
35	Bo Jackson	.75
36	Ferguson Jenkins	.25
37	Bobby Richardson	.25
38	Harmon Killebrew	.75
39	Monte Irvin	.25
40	Jim Abbott	.25
41	Wade Boggs	.75
42	Jackie Robinson	2.00
43	Ralph Branca	.25
44	Minnie Minoso	.25
45	Tug McGraw	.25
46	Willie Mays	2.00
47	Nolan Ryan	3.00
48	Duke Snider	1.00
49	Tom Seaver	1.00
50	Casey Stengel	.50
51	D-Day	.75
52	Gulf War	.25
53	Vietnam War	.25
54	Korean War	.25
55	Secret Service	.25
56	Crayons	.25
57	Hoover Dam	.25
58	Penicillin	.25
59	Polio Vaccine	.25
60	Empire State Building	.25
61	Television	.25
62	Free Speech	.25
63	Voyager Mission	.25
64	Space Shuttle	.25
65	Ellis Island	.25
66	Statue of Liberty	.25
67	Battle of the Bulge	.25
68	Battle of Midway	.25
69	Iwo Jima	.25
70	Panama Canal	.25
71	Spirit of St. Louis/	
	Lindbergh	.25
72	Civil Rights/	
	We Shall Overcome	.25
73	Space Race	.25
74	Alaska Pipeline	.25
75	Teddy Bear	.25
76	Sea Biscuit	.25
77	Bazooka Joe	.25
78	Mt. Rushmore	.25
79	Yellowstone Park	.25
80	Niagara Falls	.25
81	Grand Canyon	.25
82	Hoola Hoop	.25
83	George Patton	.25
84	Audie Murphy	.25
85	Amelia Earhart	.25
86	Glen Miller	.25
87	Rick Monday	.25
88	Buzz Aldrin	.25
89	Rosa Parks	.25
90	Edward R. Murrow	.25
91	Susan B. Anthony	.25
92	Bobby Kennedy	.25
93	Gloria Steinem	.25
94	Hank Greenberg	.75
95	Jimmy Doolittle	.25
96	Thurgood Marshall	.25
97	Ernest Hemingway	.75
98	Henry Ford	.25
99	Wright Brothers	.25
100	Thomas Edison	.75
101	Albert Einstein	.75
102	Will Rogers	.25
103	George Gershwin	.25
104	Irving Berlin	.25
105	Frank Lloyd Wright	.25
106	Howard Hughes	.25
107	George M. Cohan	.25
108	Jack Kerouac	.25
109	Harry Houdini	.25
110	Helen Keller	.25
111	John McCain	.25
112	Andrew Carnegie	.25
113	Sandra Day O'Connor	.25
114	Douglas MacArthur	.25
115	Elvis Presley	1.00
116	George Burns	.25
117	Judy Garland	.50
118	Buddy Holly	.25
119	Buddy Holly	.25
120	Don McLean	.25
121	Marilyn Monroe	1.00
122	Humphrey Bogart	.50
123	Gary Cooper	.25
124	The Andrews Sisters	.25
125	Jim Thorpe	1.00
126	Joe Louis	.25
127	Jesse Owens	.50
128	Kate Smith	.25

129	W.C. Fields	.25
130	Bette Davis	.25
131	Jayne Mansfield	.25
132	Teddy Roosevelt	.50
133	Franklin D. Roosevelt	.75
134	Harry Truman	.25
135	Dwight Eisenhower	.50
136	George H.W. Bush	.50
137	George W. Bush	.50
138	John F. Kennedy	1.00
139	Lyndon B. Johnson	.25
140	William Taft	.25
141	Horace Harding	.25
142	Woodrow Wilson	.25
143	Richard Nixon	.25
144	Bill Clinton	.25
145	Jimmy Carter	.25
146	Herbert Hoover	.25
147	Gerald Ford	.25
148	Ronald Reagan	.25
149	Calvin Coolidge	.25
150	William McKinley	.25

Piece of American Pie

JAYNE MANSFIELD

		NM/M
Common Card:		25.00
Inserted 1:119		
HB	Humphrey Bogart	120.00
GB	George Burns	60.00
GC	Gary Cooper	60.00
JD	Judy Garland	80.00
MM	Marilyn Monroe	350.00
EP	Elvis Presley/Shirt	150.00
EP2	Elvis Presley/Coat	150.00
RR	Ronald Reagan/Berlin Wall	25.00
JM	Jayne Mansfield	80.00
BD	Bette Davis	75.00

American Sluggers

AMERICAN SLUGGERS

Kirk Gibson

		NM/M
Complete Set (25):		25.00
Common Player:		.50
Inserted 1:1		
Each card issued in blue, gold, silver		
and red; no value differential.		
AD	Andre Dawson	.50
AK	Al Kaline	1.00
BR	Brooks Robinson	1.00
CC	Cecil Cooper	.50
CF	Carlton Fisk	1.00
CY	Carl Yastrzemski	2.00
DS	Duke Snider	1.00
DW	Dave Winfield	1.00
EM	Eddie Mathews	1.00
FH	Frank Howard	.50
FL	Fred Lynn	.50
FR	Frank Robinson	1.00
GB	George Brett	3.00
GF	George Foster	.50
HK	Harmon Killebrew	1.00
JC	Jack Clark	.50
JCC	Joe Carter	.50
KG	Kirk Gibson	.50
MI	Monte Irvin	.50
MS	Mike Schmidt	3.00
RC	Rod Carew	1.00
RJ	Reggie Jackson	2.50
RS	Ryne Sandberg	2.00
TK	Ted Kluszewski	1.00
WM	Willie Mays	.50

Presidental First Pitch Relics

		NM/M
Common Player:		10.00
Inserted 1:32		
GHWB	George H.W. Bush	10.00

PRESIDENTIAL

FIRST PITCH

GWB	George W. Bush	30.00
BC	Bill Clinton	40.00
CC	Calvin Coolidge	10.00
DE	Dwight Eisenhower	20.00
GF	Gerald Ford	20.00
WH	Warren Harding	10.00
HH	Herbert Hoover	10.00
LBJ	Lyndon B. Johnson	15.00
JFK	John F. Kennedy	35.00
RN	Richard Nixon	30.00
RR	Ronald Reagan	40.00
FDR	Franklin D. Roosevelt	15.00
WT	William Taft	10.00
HT	Harry Truman	20.00
WW	Woodrow Wilson	10.00
Common Player:		8.00
Inserted 1:11		
JA	Jim Abbott	15.00
DA	Dick Allen	8.00
JB	Johnny Bench	20.00
WB	Wade Boggs	10.00
BB	Bill Buckner	8.00
JC	Jack Clark	8.00
AD	Andre Dawson	10.00
KT	Jim Kaat	10.00
EM	Eddie Mathews	15.00
DM	Don Mattingly	40.00
WM	Willie Mays	40.00
MM	Minnie Minoso	15.00
RM	Rick Monday	10.00
JM	Joe Morgan	20.00
TM	Thurman Munson	30.00
AL	Al Oliver	8.00
DP	Dave Parker	10.00
GP	Gaylord Perry	10.00
FR	Frank Robinson	15.00
JR	Joe Rudi	10.00
NR	Nolan Ryan	40.00
TS	Tom Seaver	20.00
WS	Willie Stargell	15.00
DS	Darryl Strawberry	15.00
DW	Dave Winfield	12.00
CY	Carl Yastrzemski	20.00

2002 Topps Archives

		NM/M
Complete Set (200):		70.00
Common Player:		.40
Pack (8):		3.00
Box (20):		50.00
1	Willie Mays	3.00
2	Dale Murphy	.40
3	Dave Winfield	.75
4	Roger Maris	2.00
5	Ron Cey	.40
6	Lee Smith	.40
7	Len Dykstra	.40
8	Ray Fosse	.40
9	Warren Spahn	1.00
10	Herb Score	.40
11	Jim Wynn	.40
12	Sam McDowell	.40
13	Fred Lynn	.40
14	Yogi Berra	1.50
15	Ron Santo	.40
16	Alvin Dark	.40
17	Bill Buckner	.40
18	Rollie Fingers	.60

19	Tony Gwynn	1.50
20	Red Schoendienst	.40
21	Gaylord Perry	.40
22	Jose Cruz	.40
23	Dennis Martinez	.40
24	Dave McNally	.40
25	Norm Cash	.40
26	Ted Kluszewski	.40
27	Rick Reuschel	.40
28	Bruce Sutter	.75
29	Don Larsen	.40
30	Claudell Washington	.40
31	Luis Aparicio	.40
32	Clete Boyer	.40
33	Rich "Goose" Gossage	.40
34	Ray Knight	.40
35	Roy Campanella	1.50
36	Tug McGraw	.40
37	Bob Lemon	.40
38	Willie Stargell	1.00
39	Roberto Clemente	3.00
40	Jim Fregosi	.40
41	Reggie Smith	.40
42	Dave Parker	.40
43	Darrell Evans	.40
44	Ryne Sandberg	2.00
45	Manny Mota	.40
46	Dennis Eckersley	.60
47	Nellie Fox	.40
48	Gil Hodges	.40
49	Reggie Jackson	1.50
50	Bobby Shantz	.40
51	Cecil Cooper	.40
52	Jim Kaat	.40
53	George Hendrick	.40
54	Johnny Podres	.40
55	Bob Gibson	1.00
56	Vern Law	.40
57	Joe Adcock	.40
58	Jack Clark	.40
59	Bill Mazeroski	.40
60	Carl Yastrzemski	1.50
61	Bobby Murcer	.40
62	Davey Johnson	.40
63	Jim Palmer	.75
64	Roy Face	.40
65	Dean Chance	.40
66	Bill "Moose" Skowron	.40
67	Dwight Evans	.40
68	Kirk Gibson	.40
69	Sal Bando	.40
70	Mike Schmidt	2.00
71	Bo Jackson	.75
72	Chris Chambliss	.40
73	Fergie Jenkins	.75
74	Brooks Robinson	1.50
75	Bobby Richardson	.40
76	Duke Snider	1.50
77	Allie Reynolds	.40
78	Harmon Killebrew	1.50
79	Steve Carlton	1.00
80	Bert Blyleven	.40
81	Phil Niekro	.40
82	Lew Burdette	.40
83	Hoyt Wilhelm	.40
84	Curt Flood	.40
85	Guillermo Hernandez	.40
86	Robin Yount	1.50
87	Robin Roberts	.40
88	Whitey Ford	1.00
89	Tony Oliva	.75
90	Don Newcombe	.40
91	Al Oliver	.40
92	Mike Cuellar	.40
93	Mike Scott	.40
94	Dick Allen	.40
95	Jimmy Piersall	.40
96	Bill Freehan	.40
97	Willie Horton	.40
98	Bob Friend	.40
99	Ken Holtzman	.40
100	Rico Carty	.40
101	Gil McDougald	.40
102	Lee May	.40
103	Joe Pepitone	.40
104	Gene Tenace	.40
105	Gary Carter	.40
106	Tim McCarver	.40
107	Ernie Banks	1.50
108	George Foster	.40
109	Lou Brock	1.00
110	Dick Groat	.40
111	Graig Nettles	.40
112	Boog Powell	.40
113	Joe Carter	.40
114	Juan Marichal	.75
115	Larry Doby	.40
116	Fernando Valenzuela	.40
117	Luis Tiant	.40
118	Early Wynn	.40
119	Bill Madlock	.40
120	Eddie Mathews	1.50
121	George Brett	3.00
122	Al Kaline	1.50
123	Frank Howard	.40
124	Mickey Lolich	.40
125	Kirby Puckett	3.00
126	Bob Cerv	.40
127	Will Clark	1.00
128	Vida Blue	.40
129	Kevin Mitchell	.40
130	Bucky Dent	.40
131	Tom Seaver	2.00
132	Jerry Koosman	.40
133	Orlando Cepeda	.40
134	Nolan Ryan	4.00
135	Tony Kubek	.40
136	Don Drysdale	1.00
137	Paul Blair	.40
138	Elston Howard	.40
139	Joe Rudi	.40
140	Tommie Agee	.40
141	Richie Ashburn	.40
142	Jim Bunning	.40
143	Hank Sauer	.40
144	Greg Luzinski	.40
145	Ron Guidry	.40
146	Rod Carew	1.00
147	Andre Dawson	.75
148	Keith Hernandez	.40
149	Carlton Fisk	1.00
150	Cleon Jones	.40
151	Don Mattingly	3.00
152	Vada Pinson	.40
153	Ozzie Smith	1.50
154	Dave Concepcion	.40
155	Al Rosen	.40
156	Tommy John	.40
157	Bob Ojeda	.40
158	Frank Robinson	1.50
159	Darryl Strawberry	.40
160	Bobby Bonds	.40
161	Bert Campaneris	.40
162	Jim "Catfish" Hunter	.40
163	Bud Harrelson	.40
164	Dwight Gooden	.40
165	Wade Boggs	1.00
166	Joe Morgan	1.00
167	Ron Swoboda	.40
168	Hank Aaron	4.00
169	Steve Garvey	.40
170	Mickey Rivers	.40
171	Johnny Bench	3.00
172	Ralph Terry	.40
173	Billy Pierce	.40
174	Thurman Munson	2.50
175	Don Sutton	.40
176	Sparky Anderson	.40
177	Gil Hodges	.40
178	Davey Johnson	.40
179	Frank Robinson	1.50
180	Red Schoendienst	.40
181	Roger Maris	2.00
182	Willie Mays	3.00
183	Luis Aparicio	.40
184	Nellie Fox	.40
185	Ernie Banks	1.50
186	Orlando Cepeda	.75
187	Whitey Ford	1.00
188	Bob Gibson	1.00
189	Bill Mazeroski	.40
190	Hank Aaron	3.00
191	Elston Howard, Harmon Killebrew, Carl Yastrzemski League Leaders	.75
192	Orlando Cepeda, Jackie Robinson, Willie Mays League Leaders	2.00
193	Hank Aaron, Roberto Clemente, Dick Allen League Leaders	2.00
194	Tom Seaver, Phil Niekro, Fergie Jenkins, Juan Marichal League Leaders	1.00
195	Jim Palmer, Jim Hunter, Dennis Eckersley League Leaders	.65
196	Hank Aaron	3.00
197	Brooks Robinson	1.50
198	Tom Seaver	1.50
199	Jim Palmer	.75
200	Lou Brock	1.00

Autographs

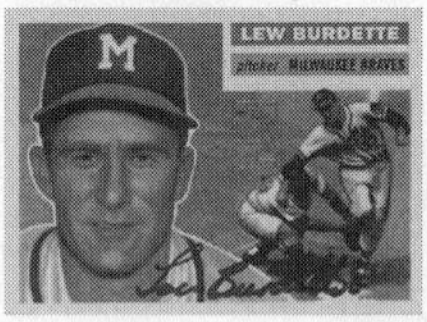

		NM/M
Common Autograph:		10.00
Inserted 1:22		
HA	Hank Aaron	300.00
DA	Dick Allen	25.00
SB	Sal Bando	20.00
EB	Ernie Banks	125.00
BB	Bobby Bonds	25.00
GB	George Brett	250.00
JBU	Jim Bunning	40.00
LB	Lew Burdette	20.00
BC	Bert Campaneris	10.00
GC	Gary Carter	50.00
RCE	Ron Cey	15.00
CC	Chris Chambliss	15.00
JCR	Jose Cruz	15.00
AD	Alvin Dark	25.00
BD	Bucky Dent	20.00
LD	Len Dykstra	20.00
DEV	Darrell Evans	15.00
GF	George Foster	15.00
JF	Jim Fregosi	10.00
SG	Steve Garvey	15.00
DG	Dwight Gooden	25.00
DGR	Dick Groat	15.00
BH	Bud Harrelson	15.00
WH	Willie Hernandez	10.00
KH	Keith Hernandez	40.00
BJ	Bo Jackson	80.00
FJ	Fergie Jenkins	20.00
TJ	Tommy John	15.00
JK	Jim Kaat	20.00
AK	Al Kaline	125.00
HK	Harmon Killebrew	110.00
JKO	Jerry Koosman	65.00
GL	Greg Luzinski	20.00
FL	Fred Lynn	20.00
DM	Dave McNally	20.00
KM	Kevin Mitchell	20.00
DN	Don Newcombe	15.00
TO	Tony Oliva	30.00
JP	Jim Palmer	50.00
DP	Dave Parker	20.00
GP	Gaylord Perry	20.00
BP	Billy Pierce	10.00
JPI	Jimmy Piersall	15.00
JPO	Johnny Podres	15.00
BPO	Boog Powell	25.00
KP	Kirby Puckett	150.00
MR	Mickey Rivers	10.00
BRO	Brooks Robinson	80.00
JR	Joe Rudi	15.00
RS	Ron Santo	30.00
MS	Mike Schmidt	150.00
LS	Lee Smith	20.00
RSM	Reggie Smith	15.00
BS	Bruce Sutter	35.00
RT	Ralph Terry	25.00
HW	Hoyt Wilhelm	20.00
DW	Dave Winfield	85.00
RY	Robin Yount	100.00

AutoProofs

		NM/M
Quantity produced listed		
1	Gary Carter/80	40.00
2	Jose Cruz/95	25.00
4	Bo Jackson/300	50.00
5	Kevin Mitchell/65	25.00
6	Kirby Puckett/65	80.00
7	Mike Schmidt/147	90.00
8	Ozzie Smith/105	75.00
9	Darryl Strawberry/181	40.00
11	Robin Yount/39	100.00

Game-Used Bat

		NM/M
Common Player:		
Group A 1:106		
Group B 1:282		
JB	Johnny Bench	20.00
GB	George Brett	40.00
GC	Gary Carter	10.00
JC	Joe Carter	10.00
NC	Norm Cash	10.00
AD	Andre Dawson	8.00
DE	Dwight Evans	8.00
BF	Bill Freehan	8.00
WH	Willie Horton	10.00
RJ	Reggie Jackson	15.00
DM	Don Mattingly	50.00
RM	Roger Maris	50.00
JM	Joe Morgan	10.00
DP	Dave Parker	10.00
BR	Brooks Robinson	20.00
RS	Ron Santo	20.00
WS	Willie Stargell	15.00
CY	Carl Yastrzemski	40.00
RY	Robin Yount	20.00

Game-Worn Uniform

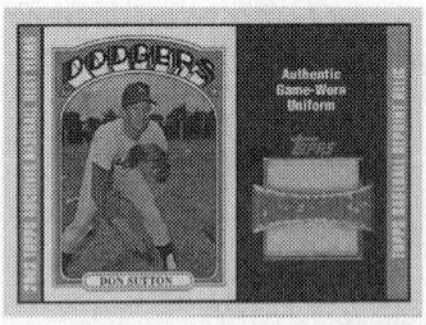

		NM/M
Common Player:		8.00
Inserted 1:28		
SA	Sparky Anderson	10.00
WB	Wade Boggs	15.00
BB	Bobby Bonds	8.00
GB	George Brett	30.00
OC	Orlando Cepeda	10.00
WC	Will Clark	20.00
DC	Dave Concepcion	8.00
DE	Dennis Eckersley	10.00
SG	Steve Garvey	10.00
FL	Fred Lynn	8.00
DM	Dale Murphy	20.00
PN	Phil Niekro	10.00
GP	Gaylord Perry	10.00
KP	Kirby Puckett	20.00
FR	Frank Robinson	15.00
NR	Nolan Ryan	40.00
RS	Ryne Sandberg	30.00
OS	Ozzie Smith	20.00
DS	Don Sutton	10.00
DW	Dave Winfield	10.00

Stadium Seat

		NM/M
Common Player:		8.00
RA	Richie Ashburn	15.00
SA	Sparky Anderson	10.00
EB	Ernie Banks	25.00
YB	Yogi Berra	20.00
JB	Jim Bunning	10.00
RC	Rod Carew	20.00
JC	Joe Carter	10.00
NF	Nellie Fox	15.00
RG	Ron Guidry	10.00
TK	Ted Kluszewski	15.00
BL	Bob Lemon	10.00
ML	Mickey Lolich	10.00
EM	Eddie Mathews	20.00
SM	Sam McDowell	8.00
JP	Jim Palmer	10.00
DP	Dave Parker	10.00
HS	Herb Score	10.00
DS	Duke Snider	20.00
WS	Warren Spahn	15.00

2002 Topps Archives Reserve

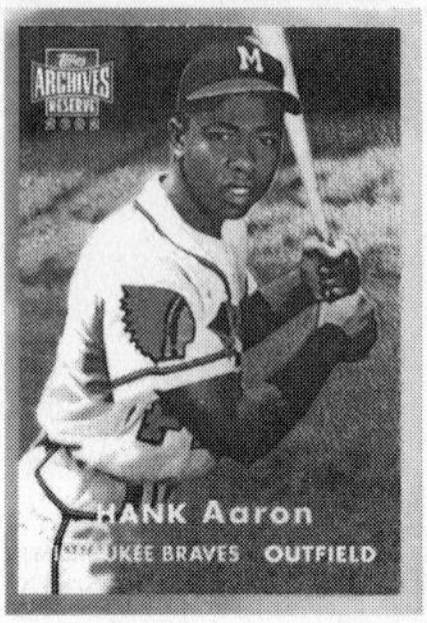

		NM/M
Complete Set (100):		100.00
Common Player:		.75
Box (10 Packs + Auto. Baseball):		125.00
1	Lee Smith	.75
2	Gaylord Perry	.75
3	Al Oliver	.75
4	Rich "Goose" Gossage	.75
5	Bill Madlock	.75
6	Rod Carew	1.50
7	Fred Lynn	.75
8	Frank Robinson	2.00
9	Al Kaline	2.50
10	Len Dykstra	.75
11	Carlton Fisk	1.50
12	Nellie Fox	1.00
13	Reggie Jackson	3.00
14	Bob Gibson	2.00
15	Bill Buckner	.75
16	Harmon Killebrew	2.00
17	Gary Carter	1.50
18	Dave Winfield	1.50
19	Ozzie Smith	2.50
20	Dwight Evans	.75
21	Dave Concepcion	.75
22	Joe Morgan	1.00
23	Clete Boyer	.75
24	Will Clark	1.50
25	Lee May	.75
26	Kevin Mitchell	.75
27	Roger Maris	3.00
28	Mickey Lolich	.75
29	Luis Aparicio	.75
30	George Foster	.75
31	Don Mattingly	6.00
32	Fernando Valenzuela	.75
33	Bobby Bonds	.75
34	Jim Palmer	1.50
35	Dennis Eckersley	1.00
36	Kirby Puckett	3.00
37	Jose Cruz	.75
38	Richie Ashburn	.75
39	Whitey Ford	2.00
40	Robin Roberts	.75
41	Don Newcombe	.75
42	Roy Campanella	2.50
43	Dennis Martinez	.75
44	Larry Doby	1.00
45	Steve Garvey	.75
46	Thurman Munson	3.00
47	Dale Murphy	1.50
48	Bill "Moose" Skowron	.75
49	Tom Seaver	3.00
50	Orlando Cepeda	.75
51	Graig Nettles	.75
52	Willie Stargell	1.50
53	Yogi Berra	2.50
54	Steve Carlton	1.50
55	Don Sutton	.75
56	Brooks Robinson	1.50
57	Vida Blue	.75
58	Rollie Fingers	1.00
59	Jim Bunning	.75
60	Nolan Ryan	8.00
61	Hank Aaron	6.00
62	Fergie Jenkins	.75
63	Andre Dawson	1.00
64	Ernie Banks	2.50
65	Early Wynn	.75

66	Duke Snider	1.50
67	Red Schoendienst	.75
68	Don Drysdale	1.00
69	Jim "Catfish" Hunter	1.00
70	George Brett	6.00
71	Elston Howard	1.00
72	Wade Boggs	1.50
73	Keith Hernandez	.75
74	Billy Pierce	.75
75	Ted Kluszewski	.75
76	Carl Yastrzemski	4.00
77	Bert Blyleven	.75
78	Tony Oliva	.75
79	Joe Carter	.75
80	Johnny Bench	3.00
81	Tony Gwynn	3.00
82	Mike Schmidt	4.00
83	Phil Niekro	.75
84	Juan Marichal	.75
85	Eddie Mathews	2.50
86	Boog Powell	.75
87	Dwight Gooden	.75
88	Darryl Strawberry	.75
89	Roberto Clemente	6.00
90	Ryne Sandberg	5.00
91	Jack Clark	.75
92	Willie Mays	6.00
93	Ron Guidry	.75
94	Kirk Gibson	.75
95	Lou Brock	1.00
96	Robin Yount	2.50
97	Bill Mazeroski	.75
98	Dave Parker	.75
99	Hoyt Wilhelm	.75
100	Warren Spahn	1.50

Autographed Baseballs

	NM/M
Common Auto. Ball:	15.00
Inserted 1:Box	
Luis Aparicio/1,600	25.00
Ernie Banks/50	75.00
Yogi Berra/100	85.00
Lou Brock/400	40.00
Jim Bunning/500	35.00
Gary Carter/500	40.00
Rich Gossage/500	20.00
Fergie Jenkins/1,000	20.00
Al Kaline/250	75.00
Harmon Killebrew/250	60.00
Joe Morgan/250	40.00
Graig Nettles/1,600	15.00
Jim Palmer/400	25.00
Gaylord Perry/500	15.00
Brooks Robinson/500	40.00
Mike Schmidt/250	125.00
Duke Snider/100	65.00
Dave Winfield/1650	30.00
Robin Yount/250	90.00

Best Years Autographs

		NM/M
Common Autograph:		12.00
Inserted 1:15 Hobby		
LA	Luis Aparicio	15.00
EB	Ernie Banks	70.00
YB	Yogi Berra	60.00
LB	Lou Brock	25.00
GC	Gary Carter	20.00
FJ	Fergie Jenkins	12.00
AK	Al Kaline	40.00
HK	Harmon Killebrew	40.00

WM	Willie Mays	120.00
JM	Joe Morgan	25.00
GN	Graig Nettles	12.00
GP	Gaylord Perry	15.00
BR	Brooks Robinson	25.00
MS	Mike Schmidt	125.00
LS	Lee Smith	12.00
DS	Duke Snider	60.00
RY	Robin Yount	80.00

Best Years Game-Worn Uni.

		NM/M
Common Player:		10.00
Inserted 1:7 Hobby		
EB	Ernie Banks	25.00
JBU	Johnny Bench	15.00
WBJ	Wade Boggs	10.00
GCJ	Gary Carter	12.00
WC	Will Clark	15.00
NF	Nellie Fox	15.00
TG	Tony Gwynn	15.00
JM	Juan Marichal	12.00
WM	Willie Mays	35.00
KPJ	Kirby Puckett	18.00
BR	Brooks Robinson	12.00
NR	Nolan Ryan	30.00
RSJ	Red Schoendienst	10.00
WS	Willie Stargell	10.00
RYU	Robin Yount	12.00

Best Years Game-Used Bat

		NM/M
Common Player:		10.00
Inserted 1:22		
HAB	Hank Aaron	40.00
GBB	George Brett	25.00
OC	Orlando Cepeda	10.00
CF	Carlton Fisk	15.00
RM	Roger Maris	70.00
EMB	Eddie Mathews	20.00
DMB	Don Mattingly	30.00
TM	Thurman Munson	30.00
DW	Dave Winfield	10.00
CYB	Carl Yastrzemski	25.00

Team Topps Legends Autos.

	NM/M
Common Player:	
Rich "Goose" Gossage	10.00
Graig Nettles	10.00
Jim Palmer	15.00
Gaylord Perry	15.00

2002 Topps Chrome

	NM/M
Complete Set (685):	200.00
Common Player:	.25
Pack (4):	2.00
Box (24):	40.00
1 Pedro Martinez	1.00
2 Mike Stanton	.25
3 Brad Penny	.25

TODD HELTON

4	Mike Matheny	.25
5	Johnny Damon	.75
6	Bret Boone	.25
7	Retired # not issued	
8	Chris Truby	.25
9	B.J. Surhoff	.25
10	Mike Hampton	.25
11	Juan Pierre	.25
12	Mark Buehrle	.25
13	Bob Abreu	.50
14	David Cone	.25
15	Aaron Sele	.25
16	Fernando Tatis	.25
17	Bobby Jones	.25
18	Rick Helling	.25
19	Dmitri Young	.25
20	Mike Mussina	.50
21	Mike Sweeney	.25
22	Cristian Guzman	.25
23	Ryan Kohlmeier	.25
24	Adam Kennedy	.25
25	Larry Walker	.50
26	Eric Davis	.25
27	Jason Tyner	.25
28	Eric Young	.25
29	Jason Marquis	.25
30	Luis Gonzalez	.25
31	Kevin Tapani	.25
32	Orlando Cabrera	.40
33	Marty Cordova	.25
34	Brad Ausmus	.25
35	Livan Hernandez	.25
36	Alex Gonzalez	.25
37	Edgar Renteria	.50
38	Bengie Molina	.25
39	Frank Menechino	.25
40	Rafael Palmeiro	1.00
41	Brad Fullmer	.25
42	Julio Zuleta	.25
43	Darren Dreifort	.25
44	Trot Nixon	.25
45	Trevor Hoffman	.25
46	Vladimir Nunez	.25
47	Mark Kotsay	.25
48	Kenny Rogers	.25
49	Ben Petrick	.25
50	Jeff Bagwell	.50
51	Juan Encarnacion	.25
52	Ramiro Mendoza	.25
53	Brian Meadows	.25
54	Chad Curtis	.25
55	Aramis Ramirez	.50
56	Mark McLemore	.25
57	Dante Bichette	.25
58	Scott Schoeneweis	.25
59	Jose Cruz	.25
60	Roger Clemens	3.00
61	Jose Guillen	.25
62	Darren Oliver	.25
63	Chris Reitsma	.25
64	Jeff Abbott	.25
65	Robin Ventura	.25
66	Denny Neagle	.25
67	Al Martin	.25
68	Benito Santiago	.25
69	Roy Oswalt	.50
70	Juan Gonzalez	.50
71	Garret Anderson	.40
72	Bobby Bonilla	.25
73	Danny Bautista	.25
74	J.T. Snow	.25
75	Derek Jeter	4.00
76	John Olerud	.40
77	Kevin Appier	.25
78	Phil Nevin	.25
79	Sean Casey	.40
80	Troy Glaus	.50
81	Joe Randa	.25
82	Jose Valentin	.25
83	Ricky Bottalico	.25
84	Todd Zeile	.25
85	Barry Larkin	.50
86	Bob Wickman	.25
87	Jeff Shaw	.25
88	Greg Vaughn	.25
89	Fernando Vina	.25
90	Mark Mulder	.40
91	Paul Bako	.25
92	Aaron Boone	.25
93	Esteban Loaiza	.25
94	Richie Sexson	.40
95	Alfonso Soriano	1.00

96	Tony Womack	.25
97	Paul Shuey	.25
98	Melvin Mora	.25
99	Tony Gwynn	1.50
100	Vladimir Guerrero	1.50
101	Keith Osik	.25
102	Randy Velarde	.25
103	Scott Williamson	.25
104	Daryle Ward	.25
105	Doug Mientkiewicz	.25
106	Stan Javier	.25
107	Russ Ortiz	.25
108	Wade Miller	.25
109	Luke Prokopec	.25
110	Andruw Jones	.50
111	Ron Coomer	.25
112	Dan Wilson	.25
113	Luis Castillo	.25
114	Derek Bell	.25
115	Gary Sheffield	.50
116	Ruben Rivera	.25
117	Paul O'Neill	.50
118	Craig Paquette	.25
119	Kelvim Escobar	.25
120	Brad Radke	.25
121	Jorge Fabregas	.25
122	Randy Winn	.25
123	Tom Goodwin	.25
124	Jaret Wright	.25
125	Bonds-Race to 73	40.00
126	Al Leiter	.25
127	Ben Davis	.25
128	Frank Catalanotto	.25
129	Jose Cabrera	.25
130	Magglio Ordonez	.50
131	Jose Macias	.25
132	Ted Lilly	.25
133	Chris Holt	.25
134	Eric Milton	.25
135	Shannon Stewart	.25
136	Omar Olivares	.25
137	David Segui	.25
138	Jeff Nelson	.25
139	Matt Williams	.25
140	Ellis Burks	.25
141	Jason Bere	.25
142	Jimmy Haynes	.25
143	Ramon Hernandez	.25
144	Craig Counsell	.25
145	John Smoltz	.50
146	Homer Bush	.25
147	Quilvio Veras	.25
148	Esteban Yan	.25
149	Ramon Ortiz	.25
150	Carlos Delgado	.50
151	Lee Stevens	.25
152	Wil Cordero	.25
153	Mike Bordick	.25
154	John Flaherty	.25
155	Omar Daal	.25
156	Todd Ritchie	.25
157	Carl Everett	.25
158	Scott Sullivan	.25
159	Deivi Cruz	.25
160	Albert Pujols	3.00
161	Royce Clayton	.25
162	Jeff Suppan	.25
163	C.C. Sabathia	.50
164	Jimmy Rollins	.75
165	Rickey Henderson	.75
166	Rey Ordonez	.25
167	Shawn Estes	.25
168	Reggie Sanders	.25
169	Jon Lieber	.25
170	Armando Benitez	.25
171	Mike Remlinger	.25
172	Billy Wagner	.25
173	Troy Percival	.25
174	Devon White	.25
175	Ivan Rodriguez	.50
176	Dustin Hermanson	.25
177	Brian Anderson	.25
178	Graeme Lloyd	.25
179	Russell Branyan	.25
180	Bobby Higginson	.25
181	Alex Gonzalez	.25
182	John Franco	.25
183	Sidney Ponson	.25
184	Jose Mesa	.25
185	Todd Hollandsworth	.25
186	Kevin Young	.25
187	Tim Wakefield	.25
188	Craig Biggio	.50
189	Jason Isringhausen	.25
190	Mark Quinn	.25
191	Glendon Rusch	.25
192	Damian Miller	.25
193	Sandy Alomar	.25
194	Scott Brosius	.25
195	Dave Martinez	.25
196	Danny Graves	.25
197	Shea Hillenbrand	.25
198	Jimmy Anderson	.25
199	Travis Lee	.25
200	Randy Johnson	1.50
201	Carlos Beltran	.50
202	Jerry Hairston Jr.	.25
203	Jesus Sanchez	.25
204	Eddie Taubensee	.25
205	David Wells	.25
206	Russ Davis	.25
207	Michael Barrett	.25
208	Marquis Grissom	.25
209	Byung-Hyun Kim	.25
210	Hideo Nomo	.40
211	Ryan Rupe	.25
212	Ricky Gutierrez	.25

213	Darryl Kile	.25
214	Rico Brogna	.25
215	Terrence Long	.25
216	Mike Jackson	.25
217	Jamey Wright	.25
218	Adrian Beltre	.50
219	Benny Agbayani	.25
220	Chuck Knoblauch	.25
221	Randy Wolf	.25
222	Andy Ashby	.25
223	Corey Koskie	.25
224	Roger Cedeno	.25
225	Ichiro Suzuki	3.00
226	Keith Foulke	.25
227	Ryan Minor	.25
228	Shawon Dunston	.25
229	Alex Cora	.25
230	Jeromy Burnitz	.25
231	Mark Grace	.50
232	Aubrey Huff	.25
233	Jeffrey Hammonds	.25
234	Olmedo Saenz	.25
235	Brian Jordan	.25
236	Jeremy Giambi	.25
237	Joe Girardi	.25
238	Eric Gagne	.25
239	Masato Yoshii	.25
240	Greg Maddux	2.00
241	Bryan Rekar	.25
242	Ray Durham	.25
243	Torii Hunter	.50
244	Derrek Lee	.50
245	Jim Edmonds	.40
246	Einar Diaz	.25
247	Brian Bohanon	.25
248	Ron Belliard	.25
249	Mike Lowell	.50
250	Sammy Sosa	.75
251	Richard Hidalgo	.25
252	Bartolo Colon	.25
253	Jorge Posada	.50
254	LaTroy Hawkins	.25
255	Paul LoDuca	.25
256	Carlos Febles	.25
257	Nelson Cruz	.25
258	Edgardo Alfonzo	.25
259	Joey Hamilton	.25
260	Cliff Floyd	.25
261	Wes Helms	.25
262	Jay Bell	.25
263	Mike Cameron	.25
264	Paul Konerko	.40
265	Jeff Kent	.50
266	Robert Fick	.25
267	Allen Levrault	.25
268	Placido Polanco	.25
269	Marlon Anderson	.25
270	Mariano Rivera	.50
271	Chan Ho Park	.25
272	Jose Vizcaino	.25
273	Jeff D'Amico	.25
274	Mark Gardner	.25
275	Travis Fryman	.25
276	Darren Lewis	.25
277	Bruce Bochy	.25
278	Jerry Manuel	.25
279	Bob Brenly	.25
280	Don Baylor	.25
281	Davey Lopes	.25
282	Jerry Narron	.25
283	Tony Muser	.25
284	Hal McRae	.25
285	Bobby Cox	.25
286	Larry Dierker	.25
287	Phil Garner	.25
288	Jimy Williams	.25
289	Bobby Valentine	.25
290	Dusty Baker	.25
291	Lloyd McLendon	.25
292	Mike Scioscia	.25
293	Buck Martinez	.25
294	Larry Bowa	.25
295	Tony LaRussa	.25
296	Jeff Torborg	.25
297	Tom Kelly	.25
298	Mike Hargrove	.25
299	Art Howe	.25
300	Lou Piniella	.25
301	Charlie Manuel	.25
302	Buddy Bell	.25
303	Tony Perez	.25
304	Bob Boone	.25
305	Joe Torre	.25
306	Jim Tracy	.25
307	Jason Lane	.25
308	Chris George	.25
309	Hank Blalock	.50
310	Joe Borchard	.25
311	Marlon Byrd	.50
312	Raymond Cabrera **RC**	.50
313	Freddy Sanchez **RC**	4.00
314	Scott Wiggins **RC**	.50
315	Jason Maule **RC**	.50
316	Dionys Cesar **RC**	.50
317	Boof Bonser	.25
318	Juan Tolentino **RC**	.50
319	Earl Snyder **RC**	.50
320	Travis Wade **RC**	.50
321	Napoleon Calzado **RC**	.50
322	Eric Glaser **RC**	.50
323	Craig Kuzmic **RC**	.50
324	Nic Jackson **RC**	.50
325	Mike Rivera	.25
326	Jason Bay **RC**	8.00
327	Chris Smith	.25
328	Jake Gautreau	.25
329	Gabe Gross	.25
330	Kenny Baugh	.25
331	J.D. Martin	.25
366	Pat Meares	.25
367	Mike Lieberthal	.25
368	Scott Erickson	.25
369	Ron Gant	.25
370	Moises Alou	.50
371	Chad Kreuter	.25
372	Willis Roberts	.25
373	Toby Hall	.25
374	Miguel Batista	.25
375	John Burkett	.25
376	Cory Lidle	.25
377	Nick Neugebauer	.25
378	Jay Payton	.25
379	Steve Karsay	.25
380	Eric Chavez	.50
381	Kelly Stinnett	.25
382	Jarrod Washburn	.25
383	C.J. Nitkowski	.25
384	Jeff Conine	.25
385	Fred McGriff	.50
386	Marvin Benard	.25
387	Dave Burba	.25
388	Dennis Cook	.25
389	Rick Reed	.25
390	Tom Glavine	.75
391	Rondell White	.25
392	Matt Morris	.50
393	Pat Rapp	.25
394	Robert Person	.25
395	Omar Vizquel	.40
396	Jeff Cirillo	.25
397	Dave Mlicki	.25
398	Jose Ortiz	.25
399	Ryan Dempster	.25
400	Curt Schilling	.75
401	Peter Bergeron	.25
402	Kyle Lohse	.25
403	Craig Wilson	.25
404	David Justice	.75
405	Darin Erstad	.50
406	Jose Mercedes	.25
407	Carl Pavano	.25
408	Albie Lopez	.25
409	Alex Ochoa	.25
410	Chipper Jones	1.50
411	Tyler Houston	.25
412	Dean Palmer	.25
413	Damian Jackson	.25
414	Josh Towers	.25
415	Rafael Furcal	.50
416	Mike Morgan	.25
417	Herb Perry	.25
418	Mike Sirotka	.25
419	Mark Wohlers	.25
420	Nomar Garciaparra	.75
421	Felipe Lopez	.25
422	Joe McEwing	.25
423	Jacque Jones	.25
424	Julio Franco	.25
425	Frank Thomas	1.00
426	Kent Bottenfield	.25
427	Mac Suzuki	.25
428	D'Angelo Jimenez	.25
429	Chris Stynes	.25
430	Kerry Wood	.50
431	Chris Singleton	.25
432	Erubiel Durazo	.25
433	Matt Lawton	.25
434	Bill Mueller	.25
435	Jose Canseco	.50
436	Ben Grieve	.25
437	Terry Mulholland	.25
438	David Bell	.25
439	A.J. Pierzynski	.25
440	Adam Dunn	1.00
441	Jon Garland	.25
442	Jeff Fassero	.25
443	Julio Lugo	.25
444	Carlos Guillen	.40
445	Orlando Hernandez	.25
446	Mark Loretta	.25
447	Scott Spiezio	.25
448	Kevin Millwood	.50
449	Jamie Moyer	.25
450	Todd Helton	1.00
451	Todd Walker	.25
452	Jose Lima	.25
453	Brook Fordyce	.25
454	Aaron Rowand	.25
455	Barry Zito	.50
456	Eric Owens	.25
457	Charles Nagy	.25
458	Raul Ibanez	.25
459	Joe Mays	.25
460	Jim Thome	1.00
461	Adam Eaton	.25
462	Felix Martinez	.25
463	Vernon Wells	.25
464	Donnie Sadler	.25
465	Tony Clark	.25
466	Jose Hernandez	.25
467	Ramon Martinez	.25
468	Rusty Greer	.25
469	Rod Barajas	.25
470	Lance Berkman	.75
471	Brady Anderson	.25
472	Pedro Astacio	.25
473	Shane Halter	.25
474	Bret Prinz	.25
475	Edgar Martinez	.50
476	Steve Trachsel	.25
477	Gary Matthews Jr.	.25
478	Ismael Valdes	.25
479	Juan Uribe	.25
480	Shawn Green	.40
481	Kirk Rueter	.25
482	Damion Easley	.25
483	Chris Carpenter	.40
484	Kris Benson	.25
485	Antonio Alfonseca	.25
486	Kyle Farnsworth	.25
487	Brandon Lyon	.25
488	Hideki Irabu	.25
489	David Ortiz	.75
490	Mike Piazza	2.50
491	Derek Lowe	.25
492	Chris Gomez	.25
493	Mark Johnson	.25
494	John Rocker	.25
495	Eric Karros	.25
496	Bill Haselman	.25
497	Dave Veres	.25
498	Gil Heredia	.25
499	Tomokazu Ohka	.25
500	Barry Bonds	4.00
501	David Dellucci	.25
502	Ed Sprague	.25
503	Tom Gordon	.25
504	Javier Vazquez	.25
505	Ben Sheets	.50
506	Wilton Guerrero	.25
507	John Halama	.25
508	Mark Redman	.25
509	Jack Wilson	.25
510	Bernie Williams	.50
511	Miguel Cairo	.25
512	Denny Hocking	.25
513	Tony Batista	.25
514	Mark Grudzielanek	.25
515	Jose Vidro	.25
516	Sterling Hitchcock	.25
517	Billy Koch	.25
518	Matt Clement	.25
519	Bruce Chen	.25
520	Roberto Alomar	1.00
521	Orlando Palmeiro	.25
522	Steve Finley	.25
523	Danny Patterson	.25
524	Terry Adams	.25
525	Tino Martinez	.25
526	Tony Armas Jr.	.25
527	Geoff Jenkins	.25
528	Chris Michalak	.25
529	Corey Patterson	.25
530	Brian Giles	.40
531	Jose Jimenez	.25
532	Joe Kennedy	.25
533	Armando Rios	.25
534	Osvaldo Fernandez	.25
535	Ruben Sierra	.25
536	Octavio Dotel	.25
537	Luis Sojo	.25
538	Brent Butler	.25
539	Pablo Ozuna	.25
540	Freddy Garcia	.25
541	Chad Durbin	.25
542	Orlando Merced	.25
543	Michael Tucker	.25
544	Roberto Hernandez	.25
545	Pat Burrell	.50
546	A.J. Burnett	.25
547	Bubba Trammell	.25
548	Scott Elarton	.25
549	Mike Darr	.25
550	Ken Griffey Jr.	2.50
551	Ugueth Urbina	.25
552	Todd Jones	.25
553	Delino DeShields	.25
554	Adam Piatt	.25
555	Jason Kendall	.25
556	Hector Ortiz	.25
557	Turk Wendell	.25
558	Rob Bell	.25
559	Sun-Woo Kim	.25
560	Raul Mondesi	.50
561	Brent Abernathy	.25
562	Seth Etherton	.25
563	Shawn Wooten	.25
564	Jay Buhner	.25
565	Andres Galarraga	.25
566	Shane Reynolds	.25
567	Rod Beck	.25
568	Dee Brown	.25
569	Pedro Feliz	.25
570	Ryan Klesko	.25
571	John Vander Wal	.25
572	Nick Bierbrodt	.25
573	Joe Nathan	.25
574	James Baldwin	.25
575	J.D. Drew	.40
576	Greg Colbrunn	.25
577	Doug Glanville	.25
578	Rey Sanchez	.25
579	Todd Van Poppel	.25
580	Rich Aurilia	.25
581	Chuck Finley	.25
582	Abraham Nunez	.25
583	Kenny Lofton	.25
584	Brian Daubach	.25
585	Miguel Tejada	.75
586	Nate Cornejo	.25
587	Kazuhiro Sasaki	.25
588	Chris Richard	.25
589	Armando Reynoso	.25
590	Tim Hudson	.75
591	Neifi Perez	.25
592	Steve Cox	.25
593	Henry Blanco	.25
594	Ricky Ledee	.25
595	Tim Salmon	.25
596	Luis Rivas	.25
597	Jeff Zimmerman	.25
598	Matt Stairs	.25
599	Preston Wilson	.25
600	Mark McGwire	4.00
601	Timo Perez	.25
602	Matt Anderson	.25
603	Todd Hundley	.25
604	Rick Ankiel	.50
605	Tsuyoshi Shinjo	.25
606	Woody Williams	.25
607	Jason LaRue	.25
608	Carlos Lee	.50
609	Russ Johnson	.25
610	Scott Rolen	1.00
611	Brent Mayne	.25
612	Darrin Fletcher	.25
613	Ray Lankford	.25
614	Troy O'Leary	.25
615	Javier Lopez	.25
616	Randy Velarde	.25
617	Vinny Castilla	.25
618	Milton Bradley	.25
619	Ruben Mateo	.25
620	Jason Giambi	1.00
621	Andy Benes	.25
622	Joe Mauer **RC**	12.00
623	Andy Pettitte	.75
624	Jose Offerman	.25
625	Mo Vaughn	.40
626	Steve Sparks	.25
627	Mike Matthews	.25
628	Robb Nen	.25
629	Kip Wells	.25
630	Kevin Brown	.25
631	Arthur Rhodes	.25
632	Gabe Kapler	.25
633	Jermaine Dye	.25
634	Josh Beckett	.75
635	Pokey Reese	.25
636	Benji Gil	.25
637	Marcus Giles	.25
638	Julian Tavarez	.25
639	Jason Schmidt	.25
640	Alex Rodriguez	3.00
641	Anaheim Angels	.25
642	Arizona Diamondbacks	.25
643	Atlanta Braves	.25
644	Baltimore Orioles	.25
645	Boston Red Sox	.25
646	Chicago Cubs	.25
647	Chicago White Sox	.25
648	Cincinnati Reds	.25
649	Cleveland Indians	.25
650	Colorado Rockies	.25
651	Detroit Tigers	.25
652	Florida Marlins	.25
653	Houston Astros	.25
654	Kansas City Royals	.25
655	Los Angeles Dodgers	.25
656	Milwaukee Brewers	.25
657	Minnesota Twins	.25
658	Montreal Expos	.25
659	New York Mets	.25
660	New York Yankees	1.00
661	Oakland Athletics	.25
662	Philadelphia Phillies	.25
663	Pittsburgh Pirates	.25
664	San Diego Padres	.25
665	San Francisco Giants	.25
666	Seattle Mariners	.25
667	St. Louis Cardinals	.25
668	Tampa Bay Devil Rays	.25
669	Texas Rangers	.25
670	Toronto Blue Jays	.25
671	Juan Cruz	.25
672	Kevin Cash **RC**	.50
673	Jimmy Gobble **RC**	.50
674	Mike Hill **RC**	.50
675	Taylor Buchholz **RC**	.75
676	Bill Hall	.75
677	Brett Roneberg **RC**	.75
678	Royce Huffman **RC**	.75
679	Chris Tritle **RC**	.50
680	Nate Espy **RC**	.50
681	Nick Alvarez **RC**	.50
682	Jason Botts **RC**	1.00
683	Ryan Gripp **RC**	.75
684	Dan Phillips **RC**	.50
685	Pablo Arias **RC**	.75
686	John Rodriguez **RC**	.75
687	Rich Harden **RC**	10.00
688	Neal Frendling **RC**	1.00
689	Rich Thompson **RC**	.50
690	Greg Montalbano **RC**	1.00
691	Leonard Dinardo **RC**	.75
692	Ryan Raburn **RC**	.50
693	Josh Barfield	.50
694	David Bacani **RC**	.75
695	Dan Johnson **RC**	.50
696	Mike Mussina	.50
697	Ivan Rodriguez	.50
698	Doug Mientkiewicz	.25
699	Roberto Alomar	.50
700	Eric Chavez	.25
701	Omar Vizquel	.25
702	Mike Cameron	.25
703	Torii Hunter	.50
704	Ichiro Suzuki	1.50
705	Greg Maddux	1.00
706	Brad Ausmus	.25
707	Todd Helton	.75
708	Fernando Vina	.25
709	Scott Rolen	.75
710	Orlando Cabrera	.25
711	Andruw Jones	.50
712	Jim Edmonds	.25
713	Larry Walker	.25
714	Roger Clemens	1.50

715	Randy Johnson	.75
716	Ichiro Suzuki	1.50
717	Barry Bonds	2.00
718	Ichiro Suzuki	1.50
719	Albert Pujols	1.50

Black Refractor

Stars: 5-10X
Production 50 Sets

Gold Refractor

Stars: 2-4X
Inserted 1:4

Aces

		NM/M
	Common Player:	10.00
KB	Kevin Brown	10.00
TH	Tim Hudson	10.00
AL	Al Leiter	10.00
CS	Curt Schilling	15.00
BZ	Barry Zito	10.00

Batterymates

		NM/M
	Inserted 1:349	
GL	Tom Glavine, Javy Lopez	20.00
HP	Mike Hampton, Ben Petrick	20.00

Deuces Are Wild

		NM/M
	Common Card:	
	Inserted 1:428	
CA	Andruw Jones, Chipper Jones	40.00
BT	Bernie Williams, Tino Martinez	25.00
RC	Ryan Dempster, Cliff Floyd	10.00

Jack of All Trades

		NM/M
	Common Player:	10.00
CJ	Chipper Jones	20.00
MO	Magglio Ordonez	10.00
AR	Alex Rodriguez	25.00

Kings of the Clubhouse

		NM/M
	Common Player:	15.00
JB	Jeff Bagwell	15.00
TG	Tony Gwynn	20.00
AR	Alex Rodriguez	25.00

Like Father, Like Son Relics

		NM/M
	Inserted 1:790	
WI	Preston Wilson, Mookie Wilson	10.00

Top Of The Order

		NM/M
	Common Player:	8.00
	Inserted 1:106	
BA	Benny Agbayani/Jsy	8.00
PB	Peter Bergeron/Jsy	8.00
CB	Craig Biggio/Jsy	15.00

JD	Johnny Damon/Bat	10.00
RF	Rafael Furcal/Bat	10.00
RH	Rickey Henderson/Bat	20.00
JK	Jason Kendall/Bat	10.00
CK	Chuck Knoblauch/Bat	8.00
PL	Paul LoDuca/Bat	10.00
KL	Kenny Lofton/Jsy	10.00
JP	Juan Pierre/Bat	10.00
SS	Shannon Stewart/Jsy	10.00

Three of a Kind

		NM/M
	Common Card:	
AIR	Alex Rodriguez, Ivan Rodriguez, Rafael Palmeiro	50.00
BEJ	Bret Boone, Edgar Martinez, John Olerud	25.00
JCL	Jeff Bagwell, Craig Biggio, Lance Berkman	40.00

1952 Player Reprints

		NM/M
	Complete Set (19):	50.00
	Common Card:	3.00
	Inserted 1:8	
	Refractors:	2X
	Inserted 1:24	
52R-1	Roy Campanella	4.00
52R-2	Duke Snider	4.00
52R-3	Carl Erskine	3.00
52R-4	Andy Pafko	3.00
52R-5	Johnny Mize	3.00
52R-6	Billy Martin	4.00
52R-7	Phil Rizzuto	4.00
52R-8	Gil McDougald	3.00
52R-9	Allie Reynolds	3.00
52R-10	Jackie Robinson	5.00
52R-11	Preacher Roe	3.00
52R-12	Gil Hodges	3.00
52R-13	Billy Cox	3.00
52R-14	Yogi Berra	4.00
52R-15	Gene Woodling	3.00
52R-16	Johnny Sain	3.00
52R-17	Ralph Houk	3.00
52R-18	Joe Collins	3.00
52R-19	Hank Bauer	3.00

2002 Topps Gallery

		NM/M
	Complete Set (200):	60.00
	Common Player:	.25
	Common (151-200):	.75
	Inserted 1:1	
	Pack (6):	1.50
	Box (24):	30.00
1	Jason Giambi	.50
2	Mark Grace	.40
3	Bret Boone	.40
4	Antonio Alfonseca	.25
5	Kevin Brown	.40
6	Cristian Guzman	.25
7	Magglio Ordonez	.40
8	Luis Gonzalez	.40
9	Jorge Posada	.40
10	Roberto Alomar	.50
11	Mike Sweeney	.25
12	Jeff Kent	.40

13	Matt Morris	.40
14	Alfonso Soriano	.75
15	Adam Dunn	.50
16	Neifi Perez	.25
17	Todd Walker	.25
18	J.D. Drew	.40
19	Eric Chavez	.40
20	Alex Rodriguez	1.50
21	Ray Lankford	.25
22	Roger Cedeno	.25
23	Chipper Jones	.75
24	Jose Canseco	.50
25	Mike Piazza	1.50
26	Freddy Garcia	.25
27	Todd Helton	.50
28	Tino Martinez	.40
29	Kazuhiro Sasaki	.25
30	Curt Schilling	.50
31	Mark Buehrle	.25
32	John Olerud	.40
33	Brad Radke	.25
34	Steve Sparks	.25
35	Jason Tyner	.25
36	Jeff Shaw	.25
37	Mariano Rivera	.40
38	Russ Ortiz	.25
39	Richard Hidalgo	.25
40	Barry Bonds	2.00
41	John Burkett	.25
42	Tim Hudson	.40
43	Mike Hampton	.25
44	Orlando Cabrera	.25
45	Barry Zito	.40
46	C.C. Sabathia	.25
47	Chan Ho Park	.40
48	Tom Glavine	.50
49	Aramis Ramirez	.40
50	Lance Berkman	.40
51	Al Leiter	.25
52	Phil Nevin	.25
53	Javier Vazquez	.25
54	Troy Glaus	.40
55	Tsuyoshi Shinjo	.25
56	Albert Pujols	1.50
57	John Smoltz	.40
58	Derek Jeter	2.00
59	Robb Nen	.25
60	Jason Kendall	.25
61	Eric Gagne	.50
62	Vladimir Guerrero	.75
63	Corey Patterson	.40
64	Rickey Henderson	.50
65	Jack Wilson	.25
66	Jason LaRue	.25
67	Sammy Sosa	1.50
68	Ken Griffey Jr.	1.00
69	Randy Johnson	.75
70	Nomar Garciaparra	1.50
71	Ivan Rodriguez	.75
72	J.T. Snow	.25
73	Darryl Kile	.25
74	Andruw Jones	.50
75	Brian Giles	.40
76	Pedro Martinez	.75
77	Jeff Bagwell	.50
78	Rafael Palmeiro	.50
79	Ryan Dempster	.25
80	Jeff Cirillo	.25
81	Geoff Jenkins	.40
82	Brandon Duckworth	.25
83	Roger Clemens	1.50
84	Fred McGriff	.40
85	Hideo Nomo	.50
86	Larry Walker	.40
87	Sean Casey	.40
88	Trevor Hoffman	.25
89	Robert Fick	.25
90	Armando Benitez	.25
91	Jeromy Burnitz	.25
92	Bernie Williams	.50
93	Carlos Delgado	.50
94	Troy Percival	.25
95	Nate Cornejo	.25
96	Derrek Lee	.40
97	Jose Ortiz	.25
98	Brian Jordan	.25
99	Jose Cruz	.25
100	Ichiro Suzuki	1.50
101	Jose Mesa	.25
102	Tim Salmon	.40
103	Bud Smith	.25
104	Paul LoDuca	.25
105	Juan Pierre	.25
106	Ben Grieve	.25
107	Russell Branyan	.25
108	Bobby Abreu	.40
109	Moises Alou	.25
110	Richie Sexson	.50
111	Jerry Hairston Jr.	.25
112	Marlon Anderson	.25
113	Juan Gonzalez	.50
114	Craig Biggio	.50
115	Carlos Beltran	.50
116	Eric Milton	.25
117	Cliff Floyd	.25
118	Rich Aurilia	.25
119	Adrian Beltre	.40
120	Jason Bere	.25
121	Darin Erstad	.40
122	Ben Sheets	.25
123	Johnny Damon	.40
124	Jimmy Rollins	.50
125	Shawn Green	.40
126	Greg Maddux	1.00
127	Mark Mulder	.40

128	Bartolo Colon	.25
129	Shannon Stewart	.25
130	Ramon Ortiz	.25
131	Kerry Wood	.75
132	Ryan Klesko	.25
133	Preston Wilson	.25
134	Roy Oswalt	.40
135	Rafael Furcal	.25
136	Eric Karros	.25
137	Nick Neugebauer	.25
138	Doug Mientkiewicz	.25
139	Paul Konerko	.40
140	Bobby Higginson	.25
141	Garret Anderson	.40
142	Wes Helms	.25
143	Brent Abernathy	.25
144	Scott Rolen	.75
145	Dmitri Young	.25
146	Jim Thome	.75
147	Raul Mondesi	.25
148	Pat Burrell	.40
149	Gary Sheffield	.40
150	Miguel Tejada	.75
151	Brandon Inge	.75
152	Carlos Pena	.75
153	Jason Lane	.75
154	Nathan Haynes	.75
155	Hank Blalock	1.50
156	Juan Cruz	.75
157	Morgan Ensberg	.75
158	Sean Burroughs	.75
159	Ed Rogers	.75
160	Nick Johnson	.75
161	Orlando Hudson	.75
162	Anastacio Martinez RC	.75
163	Jeremy Affeldt	.75
164	Brandon Claussen	.75
165	Deivis Santos	.75
166	Mike Rivera	.75
167	Carlos Silva	.75
168	Valentino Pascucci	.75
169	Xavier Nady	.75
170	David Espinosa	.75
171	Dan Phillips RC	.75
172	Tony Fontana RC	.75
173	Juan Silvestre	.75
174	Henry Pichardo RC	.75
175	Pablo Arias RC	.75
176	Brett Roneberg RC	.75
177	Chad Qualls RC	.75
178	Greg Sain RC	.75
179	Rene Reyes RC	.75
180	So Taguchi RC	2.00
181	Dan Johnson RC	2.50
182	Justin Backsmeyer RC	.75
183	Juan Gonzalez	.75
184	Jason Ellison RC	.75
185	Kazuhisa Ishii RC	3.00
186	Joe Mauer RC	8.00
187	James Shanks RC	.75
188	Kevin Cash RC	.75
189	J.J. Trujillo RC	.75
190	Jorge Padilla RC	1.00
191	Nolan Ryan	4.00
192	George Brett	3.00
193	Ryne Sandberg	2.00
194	Robin Yount	1.50
195	Tom Seaver	1.00
196	Mike Schmidt	2.00
197	Frank Robinson	1.00
198	Harmon Killebrew	1.00
199	Kirby Puckett	2.00
200	Don Mattingly	4.00

Press Plates

	NM/M
Common Player:	50.00
(See 2002 Topps Gallery for checklist.)	

Autographs

		NM/M
	Common Player:	8.00
	Inserted 1:192	
LB	Lance Berkman	35.00
BBO	Bret Boone	20.00
JD	J.D. Drew	25.00
LG	Luis Gonzalez	20.00
SG	Shawn Green	25.00
JL	Jason Lane	8.00
MO	Magglio Ordonez	20.00

JP	Jorge Posada	40.00
JS	Juan Silvestre	8.00

Heritage

Complete Set (25):		100.00
Common Player:		2.00
Inserted 1:12		
RA	Roberto Alomar	4.00
BBO	Bret Boone	2.00
RC	Roger Clemens	8.00
JG	Jason Giambi	3.00
LG	Luis Gonzalez	2.00
SG	Shawn Green	3.00
KG	Ken Griffey Jr.	6.00
TG	Tony Gwynn	4.00
RJ	Reggie Jackson	4.00
CJ	Chipper Jones	4.00
AK	Al Kaline	4.00
GM	Greg Maddux	4.00
PM	Pedro Martinez	4.00
MM	Mark McGwire	10.00
SM	Stan Musial	5.00
MP	Mike Piazza	6.00
BR	Brooks Robinson	4.00
AR	Alex Rodriguez	8.00
NR	Nolan Ryan	10.00
MS	Mike Schmidt	6.00
TS	Tom Seaver	4.00
TSH	Tsuyoshi Shinjo	2.00
SS	Sammy Sosa	3.00
CY	Carl Yastrzemski	5.00
RY	Robin Yount	5.00

Heritage Autographs

		NM/M
Inserted 1:240		
BBO	Bret Boone	20.00
LG	Luis Gonzalez	25.00
SG	Shawn Green	25.00

Heritage Relics

		NM/M
Common Player:		8.00
Inserted 1:85		
BBO	Bret Boone	8.00
LG	Luis Gonzalez	8.00
TG	Tony Gwynn	15.00
CJ	Chipper Jones	10.00
GM	Greg Maddux	15.00
PM	Pedro Martinez	15.00
MP	Mike Piazza	15.00
AR	Alex Rodriguez	15.00
TS	Tsuyoshi Shinjo	8.00

Originals Relics

		NM/M
Common Player:		8.00
Inserted 1:169		
BBO	Bret Boone	8.00
JC	Jose Canseco	10.00
CD	Carlos Delgado	8.00
JG	Juan Gonzalez	10.00
LG	Luis Gonzalez	8.00
TG	Tony Gwynn	15.00
TH	Todd Helton	12.00
AJ	Andruw Jones	8.00
CJ	Chipper Jones	10.00
TM	Tino Martinez	10.00
MP	Mike Piazza	20.00
AP	Albert Pujols	35.00
AR	Alex Rodriguez	15.00
AS	Alfonso Soriano	10.00
BW	Bernie Williams	10.00

Team Topps Legends Autos.

	NM/M
Inserted 1:1,019	

	Luis Aparicio	15.00
	Jim Bunning	20.00
	Fergie Jenkins	15.00
	Carl Yastrzemski	65.00

2002 Topps Gold Label

		NM/M
Complete Set (200):		60.00
Common Player:		.25
Pack (4):		3.00
Box (18):		40.00
1	Alex Rodriguez	1.50
2	Derek Jeter	2.00
3	Luis Gonzalez	.40
4	Troy Glaus	.40
5	Albert Pujols	1.50
6	Lance Berkman	.40
7	J.D. Drew	.40
8	Chipper Jones	.75
9	Miguel Tejada	.40
10	Randy Johnson	.75
11	Mike Cameron	.25
12	Brian Giles	.40
13	Roger Cedeno	.25
14	Kerry Wood	.75
15	Ken Griffey Jr.	1.00
16	Carlos Lee	.25
17	Todd Helton	.50
18	Gary Sheffield	.40
19	Richie Sexson	.40
20	Vladimir Guerrero	.75
21	Bobby Higginson	.25
22	Roger Clemens	1.50
23	Barry Zito	.40
24	Juan Pierre	.25
25	Pedro Martinez	.75
26	Sean Casey	.40
27	David Segui	.25
28	Jose Garcia	.25
29	Curt Schilling	.50
30	Bernie Williams	.40
31	Ben Grieve	.25
32	Hideo Nomo	.40
33	Aramis Ramirez	.40
34	Cristian Guzman	.25
35	Rich Aurilia	.25
36	Greg Maddux	1.00
37	Eric Chavez	.40
38	Shawn Green	.40
39	Luis Rivas	.25
40	Magglio Ordonez	.40
41	Jose Vidro	.25
42	Mariano Rivera	.40
43	Chris Tritle RC	.50
44	C.C. Sabathia	.40
45	Larry Walker	.40
46	Raul Mondesi	.25
47	Kevin Brown	.40
48	Jeff Bagwell	.50
49	Earl Snyder RC	.50
50	Jason Giambi	.50
51	Ichiro Suzuki	1.50
52	Andruw Jones	.50
53	Ivan Rodriguez	.50
54	Jim Edmonds	.40
55	Preston Wilson	.25
56	Greg Vaughn	.25
57	Jon Lieber	.25
58	Justin Sherrod RC	.50
59	Marcus Giles	.25
60	Roberto Alomar	.40
61	Pat Burrell	.40
62	Doug Mientkiewicz	.25
63	Mark Mulder	.40
64	Mike Hampton	.25
65	Adam Dunn	.50
66	Moises Alou	.25
67	Jose Cruz Jr.	.25
68	Derek Bell	.25
69	Sammy Sosa	1.50
70	Joe Mays	.25
71	Phil Nevin	.25
72	Edgardo Alfonzo	.25
73	Barry Bonds	2.00
74	Edgar Martinez	.40
75	Juan Encarnacion	.25
76	Jason Tyner	.25
77	Edgar Renteria	.40
78	Bret Boone	.40
79	Scott Rolen	.75
80	Nomar Garciaparra	1.50

81	Frank Thomas	.50
82	Roy Oswalt	.40
83	Tsuyoshi Shinjo	.25
84	Ben Sheets	.40
85	Hank Blalock	.40
86	Carlos Delgado	.50
87	Tim Hudson	.40
88	Alfonso Soriano	.75
89	Michael Hill RC	.50
90	Jim Thome	.75
91	Craig Biggio	.40
92	Ryan Klesko	.25
93	Geoff Jenkins	.40
94	Matt Morris	.40
95	Jorge Posada	.40
96	Cliff Floyd	.40
97	Jimmy Rollins	.40
98	Mike Sweeney	.25
99	Frank Catalanotto	.25
100	Mike Piazza	1.25
101	Mark Quinn	.25
102	Torii Hunter	.40
103	Lee Stevens	.25
104	Byung-Hyug Kim	.25
105	Freddy Sanchez RC	.50
106	David Cone	.40
107	Jerry Hairston Jr.	.25
108	Kyle Farnsworth	.25
109	Rafael Furcal	.25
110	Bartolo Colon	.25
111	Juan Rivera	.25
112	Kevin Young	.25
113	Chris Narveson RC	1.00
114	Richard Hidalgo	.25
115	Andy Pettitte	.40
116	Darin Erstad	.40
117	Corey Koskie	.25
118	Rickey Henderson	.50
119	Derrek Lee	.40
120	Sean Burroughs	.25
121	Paul Konerko	.25
122	Ross Peeples RC	.50
123	Terrence Long	.25
124	John Smoltz	.40
125	Brandon Duckworth	.25
126	Luis Maza	.25
127	Morgan Ensberg	.25
128	Eric Valent	.25
129	Shannon Stewart	.25
130	D'Angelo Jimenez	.25
131	Jeff Cirillo	.25
132	Jack Cust	.25
133	Dmitri Young	.25
134	Darryl Kile	.25
135	Reggie Sanders	.25
136	Marlon Byrd	.25
137	Napoleon Calzado RC	.50
138	Javy Lopez	.40
139	Orlando Cabrera	.25
140	Mike Mussina	.40
141	Josh Beckett	.40
142	Kazuhiro Sasaki	.25
143	Jermaine Dye	.25
144	Carlos Beltran	.25
145	Trevor Hoffman	.25
146	Kazuhisa Ishii RC	2.00
147	Alex Gonzalez	.25
148	Marty Cordova	.25
149	Kevin Deaton RC	.50
150	Toby Hall	.25
151	Rafael Palmeiro	.50
152	John Olerud	.40
153	David Eckstein	.25
154	Doug Glanville	.25
155	Johnny Damon	.40
156	Javier Vazquez	.25
157	Jason Bay RC	2.00
158	Robb Nen	.25
159	Rafael Soriano	.25
160	Placido Polanco	.25
161	Garret Anderson	.40
162	Aaron Boone	.25
163	Mike Lieberthal	.25
164	Joe Mauer RC	10.00
165	Matt Lawton	.25
166	Juan Tolentino RC	.50
167	Alex Gonzalez	.25
168	Steve Finley	.25
169	Troy Percival	.25
170	Bud Smith	.25
171	Freddie Garcia	.25
172	Ray Lankford	.25
173	Tim Redding	.25
174	Ryan Dempster	.25
175	Travis Lee	.25
176	Jeff Kent	.40
177	Ramon Hernandez	.25
178	Carl Everett	.25
179	Tom Glavine	.40
180	Juan Gonzalez	.50
181	Nick Johnson	.25
182	Mike Lowell	.40
183	Al Leiter	.25
184	Jason Maule RC	.50
185	Wilson Betemit	.25
186	Tino Martinez	.25
187	Jason Standridge	.25
188	Mike Peeples RC	.50
189	Jason Kendall	.40
190	Fred McGriff	.25
191	John Rodriguez RC	.50
192	Brett Roneberg RC	.50
193	Murphy Tisdale RC	.50
194	J.T. Snow	.25
195	Craig Kuzmic RC	.75

196	Cory Lidle	.25
197	Alex Cintron	.25
198	Fernando Vina	.25
199	Austin Kearns	.50
200	Paul LoDuca	.25

Class One Gold

Stars:	2-4X
Production 500 Sets	

Class Two Platinum

Stars:	4-8X
Production 250 Sets	

Class Three Titanium

Stars:	6-10X
Production 100 Sets	

Platinum Memorabilia

Platinum:	.75-1.5X
Titanium Memorabilia:	1-2X

All-Star MVP Winners

		NM/M
Common Player:		8.00
RA	Roberto Alomar	10.00
SA	Sandy Alomar	8.00
BLB	Bobby Bonds	8.00
DC	Dave Concepcion	8.00
SG2	Steve Garvey	10.00
KG	Ken Griffey Sr.	8.00
BM1	Bill Madlock	10.00
FM	Fred McGriff	8.00
DP3	Dave Parker	8.00
TP	Tony Perez	10.00
MP	Mike Piazza	15.00
KP2	Kirby Puckett	15.00
TR	Tim Raines	8.00

Batting Average

		NM/M
Common Player:		8.00
WB	Wade Boggs	15.00
BB	Bill Buckner	8.00
RC2	Rod Carew	15.00
RAC	Rico Carty	8.00
NC	Norm Cash	15.00
TG1	Tony Gwynn	15.00
TG2	Tony Gwynn	15.00
BM2	Bill Madlock	8.00
DP4	Dave Parker	8.00
KP3	Kirby Puckett	15.00
LW	Larry Walker	8.00
CY2	Carl Yastrzemski	30.00

Cy Young Winners

		NM/M
Common Player:		8.00
RWC	Roger Clemens	15.00
DE	Dennis Eckersley	8.00
RJ	Randy Johnson	12.00
BS	Bret Saberhagen	8.00
JS	John Smoltz	8.00

Home Run Champions

		NM/M
Common Player:		8.00
BB2	Barry Bonds	20.00
GF	George Foster	8.00
TK2	Ted Kluszewski	15.00
KM2	Kevin Mitchell	8.00
DM2	Dale Murphy	40.00
AR	Alex Rodriguez	15.00
DS1	Darryl Strawberry	10.00

League Championship MVP Winners

		NM/M
Common Player:		8.00
GB2	George Brett	40.00
WC	Will Clark	15.00
CC	Craig Counsell	8.00
RH	Rickey Henderson	15.00
JL	Javier Lopez	8.00
AEP	Andy Pettitte	12.00
KP1	Kirby Puckett	15.00
FW	Frank White	8.00
BFW	Bernie Williams	10.00

MLB Moments in Time

		NM/M
Common Player:		8.00
BLB	Barry Bonds	20.00
BB1	Bret Boone	8.00
BB2	Bret Boone	8.00
CD	Carlos Delgado	8.00
TG	Tony Gwynn	15.00
TH	Toby Hall	8.00
CL	Carlos Lee	8.00
JL	Javy Lopez	8.00
MO	Magglio Ordonez	10.00
RP1	Rafael Palmeiro	10.00
RP2	Rafael Palmeiro	10.00
AR	Alex Rodriguez	15.00

MVP Winners

		NM/M
Common Player:		8.00
EB	Ernie Banks	20.00
DB	Don Baylor	8.00
YB	Yogi Berra	15.00
BB1	Barry Bonds	20.00
GB1	George Brett	40.00
SG1	Steve Garvey	8.00
KHG	Kirk Gibson	8.00
KH	Keith Hernandez	10.00
RJ1	Reggie Jackson	15.00
DM	Don Mattingly	40.00
KM1	Kevin Mitchell	8.00
JM	Joe Morgan	8.00
DM1	Dale Murphy	40.00
DP1	Dave Parker	8.00
BR	Brooks Robinson	15.00
FR	Frank Robinson	12.00
RS	Ryne Sandberg	40.00
HS	Hank Sauer	8.00
WS	Willie Stargell	15.00
JT	Joe Torre	10.00
MW	Maury Wills	8.00
CY1	Carl Yastrzemski	30.00
RY	Robin Yount	20.00

Rookie of the Year Winners

		NM/M
Common Player:		8.00
DA	Dick Allen	15.00
AB	Al Bumbry	8.00
RC1	Rod Carew	15.00
CF	Carlton Fisk	8.00
MH	Mike Hargrove	8.00
DJ	Dave Justice	10.00
EM2	Eddie Murray	10.00
LP	Lou Piniella	10.00
AP	Albert Pujols	20.00
DS2	Darryl Strawberry	15.00
FV	Fernando Valenzuela	8.00
BW	Billy Williams	10.00

RBI Leaders

		NM/M
Common Player:		8.00
BRB	Bret Boone	8.00
BRB2	Bret Boone	8.00
GC	Gary Carter	8.00
GL	Greg Luzinski	8.00
EM1	Eddie Murray	12.00
AO	Al Oliver	8.00
DP2	Dave Parker	8.00
DW	Dave Winfield	12.00

World Series MVP Winners

		NM/M
Common Player:		8.00

JB	Johnny Bench	15.00
RCC	Ron Cey	8.00
RJ2	Reggie Jackson	15.00
PM	Paul Molitor	15.00
MR	Mariano Rivera	10.00

2002 Topps Heritage

	NM/M
Complete Set (440):	325.00
Common Player:	.25
Common (364-446):	3.00
Inserted 1:2	
Pack (8):	4.00
Box (24):	90.00
1 Ichiro Suzuki/SP	10.00
2 Darin Erstad	.50
3 Rod Beck	.25
4 Doug Mientkiewicz	.25
5 Mike Sweeney	.25
6 Roger Clemens	2.50
7 Jason Tyner	.25
8 Alex Gonzalez	.25
9 Eric Young	.25
10 Randy Johnson	1.50
10 Randy Johnson/SP	6.00
11 Aaron Sele	.25
12 Tony Clark	.25
13 C.C. Sabathia	.25
14 Melvin Mora	.25
15 Tim Hudson	.50
16 Ben Petrick	.25
17 Tom Glavine	.75
18 Jason Lane	.25
19 Larry Walker	.50
20 Mark Mulder	.50
21 Steve Finley	.25
22 Bengie Molina	.25
23 Rob Bell	.25
24 Nathan Haynes	.25
25 Rafael Furcal	.50
25 Rafael Furcal/SP	3.00
26 Mike Mussina	1.00
27 Paul LoDuca	.25
28 Torii Hunter	.50
29 Carlos Lee	.25
30 Jimmy Rollins	.50
31 Arthur Rhodes	.25
32 Ivan Rodriguez	1.00
33 Wes Helms	.25
34 Cliff Floyd	.25
35 Julian Tavarez	.25
36 Mark McGwire	4.00
37 Chipper Jones/SP	6.00
38 Denny Neagle	.25
39 Odalis Perez	.25
40 Antonio Alfonseca	.25
41 Edgar Renteria	.50
42 Troy Glaus	.75
43 Scott Brosius	.25
44 Abraham Nunez	.25
45 Jamey Wright	.25
46 Bobby Bonilla	.25
47 Ismael Valdes	.25
48 Chris Reitsma	.25
49 Neifi Perez	.25
50 Juan Cruz	.25
51 Kevin Brown	.50
52 Ben Grieve	.25
53 Alex Rodriguez/SP	10.00
54 Charles Nagy	.25
55 Reggie Sanders	.25
56 Nelson Figueroa	.25
57 Felipe Lopez	.25
58 Bill Ortega	.25
59 Mac Suzuki	.25
60 Johnny Estrada	.25
61 Bob Wickman	.25
62 Doug Glanville	.25
63 Jeff Cirillo	.25
63 Jeff Cirillo/SP	3.00
64 Corey Patterson	.50
65 Aaron Myette	.25
66 Magglio Ordonez	.50
67 Ellis Burks	.25
68 Miguel Tejada	.50
69 John Olerud	.50
69 John Olerud/SP	4.00
70 Greg Vaughn	.25
71 Andy Pettitte	.75
72 Mike Matheny	.25
73 Brandon Duckworth	.25

74 Scott Schoeneweis	.25
75 Mike Lowell	.50
76 Einar Diaz	.25
77 Tino Martinez	.50
78 Matt Williams	.50
79 Jason Young RC	1.00
80 Nate Cornejo	.25
81 Andres Galarraga	.40
82 Bernie Williams/SP	6.00
83 Ryan Klesko	.25
84 Dan Wilson	.25
85 Henry Pichardo RC	.50
86 Ray Durham	.25
87 Omar Daal	.25
88 Derrek Lee	.25
89 Al Leiter	.50
90 Darrin Fletcher	.25
91 Josh Beckett	.75
92 Johnny Damon	.50
92 Johnny Damon/SP	5.00
93 Abraham Nunez	.25
94 Ricky Ledee	.25
95 Richie Sexson	.75
96 Adam Kennedy	.25
97 Raul Mondesi	.25
98 John Burkett	.25
99 Ben Sheets	.50
99 Ben Sheets/SP	4.00
100 Preston Wilson	.25
100 Preston Wilson/SP	3.00
101 Boof Bonser	.25
102 Shigetoshi Hasegawa	.25
103 Carlos Febles	.25
104 Jorge Posada/SP	5.00
105 Michael Tucker	.25
106 Roberto Hernandez	.25
107 John Rodriguez RC	.25
108 Danny Graves	.25
109 Rich Aurilia	.25
110 Jon Lieber	.25
111 Tim Hummel RC	.50
112 J.T. Snow	.25
113 Kris Benson	.25
114 Derek Jeter	4.00
115 John Franco	.25
116 Matt Stairs	.25
117 Ben Davis	.25
118 Darryl Kile	.25
119 Mike Peeples RC	.50
120 Kevin Tapani	.25
121 Armando Benitez	.25
122 Damian Miller	.25
123 Jose Jimenez	.25
124 Pedro Astacio	.25
125 Marlyn Tisdale RC	.50
126 Deivi Cruz	.25
127 Paul O'Neill	.75
128 Jermaine Dye	.25
129 Marcus Giles	.25
130 Mark Loretta	.25
131 Garret Anderson	.50
132 Todd Ritchie	.25
133 Joe Crede	.25
134 Kevin Millwood	.50
135 Shane Reynolds	.25
136 Mark Grace	.75
137 Shannon Stewart	.25
138 Nick Neugebauer	.25
139 Nic Jackson RC	.75
140 Robb Nen	.25
141 Dmitri Young	.25
142 Kevin Appier	.25
143 Jack Cust	.25
144 Andres Torres	.25
145 Frank Thomas	1.00
146 Jason Kendall	.25
147 Greg Maddux	2.00
148 David Justice	.50
149 Hideo Nomo	.75
150 Bret Boone	.50
151 Wade Miller	.25
152 Jeff Kent	.50
153 Scott Williamson	.25
154 Julio Lugo	.25
155 Bobby Higginson	.25
156 Geoff Jenkins	.50
157 Darren Dreifort	.25
158 Freddy Sanchez RC	.75
159 Bud Smith	.25
160 Phil Nevin	.25
161 Cesar Izturis	.25
162 Sean Casey	.50
163 Jose Ortiz	.25
164 Brent Abernathy	.25
165 Kevin Young	.25
166 Daryle Ward	.25
167 Trevor Hoffman	.25
168 Rondell White	.25
169 Kip Wells	.25
170 John Vander Wal	.25
171 Jose Lima	.25
172 Wilton Guerrero	.25
173 Aaron Dean	.25
174 Rick Helling	.25
175 Juan Pierre	.25
176 Jay Bell	.25
177 Craig House	.25
178 David Bell	.25
179 Pat Burrell	.50
180 Eric Gagne	.25
181 Adam Pettyjohn	.25
182 Ugueth Urbina	.25
183 Peter Bergeron	.25
184 Adrian Gonzalez	.25
184 Adrian Gonzalez/SP	4.00

185 Damion Easley	.25
186 Gookie Dawkins	.25
187 Matt Lawton	.25
188 Frank Catalanotto	.25
189 David Wells	.25
190 Roger Cedeno	.25
191 Brian Giles	.50
192 Julio Zuleta	.25
193 Timo Perez	.25
194 Billy Wagner	.25
195 Craig Counsell	.25
196 Bart Miadich	.25
197 Gary Sheffield	.75
198 Richard Hidalgo	.50
199 Juan Uribe	.25
200 Curt Schilling	1.00
201 Javy Lopez	.50
202 Jimmy Haynes	.25
203 Jim Edmonds	.75
204 Pokey Reese	.25
204 Pokey Reese/SP	3.00
205 Matt Clement	.25
206 Dean Palmer	.25
207 Nick Johnson	.25
208 Nate Espy RC	.75
209 Pedro Feliz	.25
210 Aaron Rowand	.25
211 Masato Yoshii	.25
212 Jose Cruz	.25
213 Paul Byrd	.25
214 Mark Phillips RC	1.00
215 Benny Agbayani	.25
216 Frank Menechino	.25
217 John Flaherty	.25
218 Brian Boehringer	.25
219 Todd Hollandsworth	.25
220 Sammy Sosa/SP	8.00
221 Steve Sparks	.25
222 Homer Bush	.25
223 Mike Hampton	.50
224 Bobby Abreu	.50
225 Barry Larkin	.75
226 Ryan Rupe	.25
227 Bubba Trammell	.25
228 Todd Zeile	.25
229 Jeff Shaw	.25
230 Alex Ochoa	.25
231 Orlando Cabrera	.25
232 Jeremy Giambi	.25
233 Tomo Ohka	.25
234 Luis Castillo	.25
235 Chris Holt	.25
236 Shawn Green	.50
237 Sidney Ponson	.25
238 Lee Stevens	.25
239 Hank Blalock	.50
240 Randy Winn	.25
241 Pedro Martinez	1.50
242 Vinny Castillo	.25
243 Steve Karsay	.25
244 Barry Bonds/SP	15.00
245 Jason Bere	.25
246 Scott Rolen	1.50
246 Scott Rolen/SP	6.00
247 Ryan Kohlmeier	.25
248 Kerry Wood	1.50
249 Aramis Ramirez	.50
250 Lance Berkman	.75
251 Omar Vizquel	.50
252 Juan Encarnacion	.25
254 David Segui	.25
255 Brian Anderson	.25
256 Jay Payton	.25
257 Mark Grudzielanek	.25
258 Jimmy Anderson	.25
259 Eric Valent	.25
260 Chad Durbin	.25
262 Alex Gonzalez	.25
263 Scott Dunn	.25
264 Scott Elarton	.25
265 Tom Gordon	.25
266 Moises Alou	.50
269 Mark Buehrle	.25
270 Jerry Hairston Jr.	.25
272 Luke Prokopec	.25
273 Graeme Lloyd	.25
274 Bret Prinz	.25
276 Chris Carpenter	.25
277 Ryan Minor	.25
278 Jeff D'Amico	.25
279 Raul Ibanez	.25
280 Joe Mays	.25
281 Livan Hernandez	.25
282 Robin Ventura	.40
283 Gabe Kapler	.40
284 Tony Batista	.25
285 Ramon Hernandez	.25
286 Craig Paquette	.25
287 Mark Kotsay	.25
288 Mike Lieberthal	.25
289 Joe Borchard	.25
290 Cristian Guzman	.25
291 Craig Biggio	.50
292 Joaquin Benoit	.25
293 Ken Caminiti	.25
294 Sean Burroughs	.25
295 Eric Karros	.50
296 Eric Chavez	.50
297 LaTroy Hawkins	.25
298 Alfonso Soriano	1.00
299 John Smoltz	.50
300 Adam Dunn	1.00
301 Ryan Dempster	.25
302 Travis Hafner	.50
303 Russell Branyan	.25

304	Dustin Hermanson	.25
305	Jim Thome	1.50
306	Carlos Beltran	.75
307	Jason Botts RC	.75
308	David Cone	.25
309	Ivanon Coffie	.25
310	Brian Jordan	.25
311	Todd Walker	.25
312	Jeromy Burnitz	.25
313	Tony Armas	.25
314	Jeff Conine	.25
315	Todd Jones	.25
316	Roy Oswalt	.50
317	Aubrey Huff	.25
318	Josh Fogg	.25
319	Jose Vidro	.25
320	Jace Brewer	.25
321	Mike Redmond	.25
322	Noochie Varner RC	1.00
323	Russ Ortiz	.25
324	Edgardo Alfonzo	.25
325	Ruben Sierra	.25
326	Calvin Murray	.25
327	Marlon Anderson	.25
328	Albie Lopez	.25
329	Chris Gomez	.25
330	Fernando Tatis	.25
331	Stubby Clapp	.25
332	Rickey Henderson	.75
333	Brad Radke	.25
334	Brent Mayne	.25
335	Cory Lidle	.25
336	Edgar Martinez	.50
337	Aaron Boone	.25
338	Jay Witasick	.25
339	Benito Santiago	.25
340	Jose Mercedes	.25
341	Fernando Vina	.25
342	A.J. Pierzynski	.25
343	Jeff Bagwell	1.00
344	Brian Bohanon	.25
345	Adrian Beltre	.50
346	Troy Percival	.25
347	Napoleon Calzado RC	.75
348	Ruben Rivera	.25
349	Rafael Soriano	.25
350	Damian Jackson	.25
351	Joe Randa	.25
352	Chan Ho Park	.25
353	Dante Bichette	.25
354	Bartolo Colon	.25
355	Jason Bay RC	5.00
356	Shea Hillenbrand	.25
357	Matt Morris	.50
358	Brad Penny	.25
359	Mark Quinn	.25
360	Marquis Grissom	.25
361	Henry Blanco	.25
362	Billy Koch	.25
363	Mike Cameron	.25
364	Albert Pujols	10.00
365	Paul Konerko	3.00
366	Eric Milton	3.00
367	Nick Bierbrodt	3.00
368	Rafael Palmeiro	5.00
369	Jorge Padilla RC	4.00
370	Jason Giambi	4.00
371	Mike Piazza	10.00
372	Alex Cora	3.00
373	Todd Helton	6.00
374	Juan Gonzalez	6.00
375	Mariano Rivera	4.00
376	Jason LaRue	3.00
377	Tony Gwynn	6.00
378	Wilson Betemit	3.00
379	J.J. Trujillo RC	3.00
380	Brad Ausmus	3.00
381	Chris George	3.00
382	Jose Canseco	5.00
383	Ramon Ortiz	3.00
384	John Rocker	3.00
385	Rey Ordonez	3.00
386	Ken Griffey Jr.	10.00
387	Juan Pena	3.00
388	Michael Barrett	3.00
389	J.D. Drew	4.00
390	Corey Koskie	3.00
391	Vernon Wells	3.00
392	Juan Tolentino RC	3.00
393	Luis Gonzalez	4.00
394	Terrance Long	3.00
395	Travis Lee	3.00
396	Earl Snyder RC	3.00
397	Nomar Garciaparra	10.00
398	Jason Schmidt	4.00
399	David Espinosa	3.00
400	Steve Green	3.00
401	Jack Wilson	3.00
402	Chris Tritle RC	3.00
403	Angel Berroa	3.00
404	Josh Towers	3.00
405	Andruw Jones	4.00
406	Brent Butler	3.00
407	Craig Kuzmic RC	3.00
408	Derek Bell	3.00
409	Eric Glaser RC	3.00
410	Joel Pineiro	3.00
411	Alexis Gomez	3.00
412	Mike Rivera	3.00
413	Shawn Estes	3.00
414	Milton Bradley	3.00
415	Carl Everett	3.00
416	Kazuhiro Sasaki	3.00
417	Tony Fontana RC	3.00
418	Josh Pearce	3.00

419	Gary Matthews Jr.	3.00
420	Raymond Cabrera RC	3.00
421	Joe Kennedy	3.00
422	Jason Maule RC	3.00
423	Casey Fossum	3.00
424	Christian Parker	3.00
425	Laynce Nix RC	5.00
426	Byung-Hyun Kim	3.00
427	Freddy Garcia	3.00
428	Herbert Perry	3.00
429	Jason Marquis	3.00
430	Sandy Alomar Jr.	3.00
431	Roberto Alomar	5.00
432	Tsuyoshi Shinjo	3.00
433	Tim Wakefield	3.00
434	Robert Fick	3.00
435	Vladimir Guerrero	6.00
436	Jose Mesa	3.00
437	Scott Spiezio	3.00
438	Jose Hernandez	3.00
439	Jose Acevedo	3.00
440	Brian West RC	3.00
441	Barry Zito	4.00
442	Luis Maza	3.00
443	Marlon Byrd	4.00
444	A.J. Burnett	3.00
445	Dee Brown	3.00
446	Carlos Delgado	5.00

Chrome

Stars (1-100):		6-10X
RC's:		3-6X
Production 553 Sets		

Classic Renditions

		NM/M
Complete Set (10):		10.00
Common Player:		.50
Inserted 1:12		
CR-1	Kerry Wood	2.00
CR-2	Brian Giles	1.00
CR-3	Roger Cedeno	.50
CR-4	Jason Giambi	1.50
CR-5	Albert Pujols	4.00
CR-6	Mark Buehrle	.50
CR-7	Cristian Guzman	.50
CR-8	Jimmy Rollins	.50
CR-9	Jim Thome	2.00
CR-10	Shawn Green	1.00

Classic Renditions Autos.

Production 25 Sets
No Pricing

Clubhouse Collection

		NM/M
Common Player:		15.00
Jersey 1:332		
Bat 1:498		
RA	Rich Aurilia/Bat	15.00
YB	Yogi Berra/Jsy	40.00
BB	Barry Bonds/Bat	60.00
AD	Alvin Dark/Bat	25.00
NG	Nomar Garciaparra/Bat	50.00
GK	George Kell/Jsy	25.00
GM	Greg Maddux/Jsy	30.00
EM	Eddie Mathews/Jsy	35.00
WM	Willie Mays/Bat	75.00
CP	Corey Patterson/Bat	20.00
JP	Jorge Posada/Bat	25.00
HS	Hank Sauer/Bat	20.00

Clubhouse Collection Dual Relics

		NM/M
Production 53 Sets		
SM	Eddie Mathews, Greg Maddux	150.00
BP	Yogi Berra, Jorge Posada	125.00
SP	Hank Sauer, Corey Patterson	75.00
KR	George Kell, Nomar Garciaparra	100.00
DA	Alvin Dark, Rich Aurilia	100.00
MB	Willie Mays, Barry Bonds	200.00

Clubhouse Collection Autograph Relics

No Pricing
Production 25 Sets

Grandstand Glory Stadium Seat

		NM/M
Common Player:		10.00
Inserted 1:133		
RC	Roy Campanella	25.00
BF	Bob Feller	20.00
WF	Whitey Ford	20.00
TK	Ted Kluszewski	20.00
BM	Billy Martin	25.00
HN	Hal Newhouser	15.00
SP	Satchel Paige	40.00
BP	Billy Pierce	15.00
HS	Hank Sauer	10.00
BS	Bobby Shantz	15.00
WS	Warren Spahn	20.00
EW	Early Wynn	15.00

New Age Performers

		NM/M
Complete Set (15):		30.00
Common Player:		1.00
Inserted 1:15		
NA-1	Luis Gonzalez	1.00
NA-2	Mark McGwire	5.00
NA-3	Barry Bonds	5.00
NA-4	Ken Griffey Jr.	3.00
NA-5	Ichiro Suzuki	3.00
NA-6	Sammy Sosa	3.00
NA-7	Andruw Jones	5.00
NA-8	Derek Jeter	5.00
NA-9	Todd Helton	1.50
NA-10	Alex Rodriguez	4.00
NA-11	Jason Giambi	1.50
NA-12	Bret Boone	1.00
NA-13	Roberto Alomar	1.00
NA-14	Alex Rodriguez	4.00
NA-15	Vladimir Guerrero	1.50

Real One Autographs

		NM/M
Common Autograph:		20.00
Inserted 1:180		
Red Ink:		.75-1.5X
Production 53		
YB	Yogi Berra	100.00
JB	Joe Black	50.00
RB	Ray Boone	60.00
AC	Andy Carey	40.00
RCL	Roger Clemens	125.00
AD	Alvin Dark	60.00
DD	Dom DiMaggio	80.00
JE	Jim Edmonds	50.00
RF	Roy Face	60.00
BF	Bob Feller	60.00
WF	Whitey Ford	80.00
CG	Brian Giles	25.00
CG	Cristian Guzman	20.00
MI	Monte Irvin	60.00
GK	George Kell	60.00
WM	Willie Mays	200.00
GM	Gil McDougald	75.00
OM	Orestes Minoso	60.00
JP	John Podres	60.00
PR	Phil Rizzuto	80.00
ARO	Alex Rodriguez	140.00

PRO	Preacher Roe	60.00
AR	Al Rosen	75.00
ASC	Al Schoendienst	50.00
BS	Bobby Shantz	50.00
ES	Enos Slaughter	80.00
WS	Warren Spahn	100.00
HW	Hoyt Wilhelm	60.00

Team Topps Legends Autos.

		NM/M
Inserted 1:613		
	Vida Blue	20.00
	Frank Howard	30.00
	Mickey Lolich	25.00
	Frank Robinson	40.00
	Bobby Thomson	30.00

Then and Now

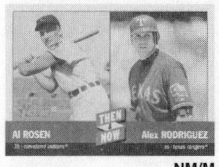

		NM/M
Complete Set (10):		15.00
Common Player:		1.00
Inserted 1:15		
TN-1	Ed Mathews, Barry Bonds	4.00
TN-2	Al Rosen, Alex Rodriguez	4.00
TN-3	Carl Furillo, Larry Walker	1.00
TN-4	Mickey Vernon, Ichiro Suzuki	3.00
TN-5	Roy Campanella, Sammy Sosa	3.00
TN-6	Al Rosen, Bret Boone	1.00
TN-7	Warren Spahn, Randy Johnson	2.00
TN-8	Ed Lopat, Freddy Garcia	1.00
TN-9	Robin Roberts, Randy Johnson	2.00
TN-10	Billy Pierce, Hideo Nomo	1.50

2002 Topps Opening Day

		NM/M
Complete Set (165):		40.00
Common Player:		.10
Pack (7):		1.00
Box (36):		30.00
1	Roy Oswalt	.25
2	Derek Jeter	2.00
3	Dmitri Young	.10
4	Ramon Hernandez	.10
5	Albert Pujols	1.50
6	Sean Casey	.25
7	Joe Randa	.10
8	Craig Counsell	.10
9	John Olerud	.25
10	Troy Glaus	.40
11	Adam Kennedy	.10
12	Carlos Delgado	.40
13	Bobby Abreu	.20
14	J.T. Snow Jr.	.20
15	Ivan Rodriguez	.50
16	Mike Lowell	.10
17	Juan Pierre	.10
18	Magglio Ordonez	.30
19	Greg Maddux	1.00
20	Jorge Posada	.25
21	Johnny Damon	.20
22	Mike Hampton	.10
23	Paul LoDuca	.10
24	Terrence Long	.10
25	Jeff Bagwell	.50
26	Shannon Stewart	.10
27	Brad Radke	.10
28	Brian Jordan	.10
29	Lee Stevens	.10
30	Cliff Floyd	.10
31	Roger Clemens	1.00
32	Mike Matheny	.10
33	Alfonso Soriano	.50

34	Randy Johnson	.75
35	Mike Sweeney	.10
36	Jose Cruz Jr.	.20
37	Fernando Tatis	.10
38	Eric Young	.10
39	Ruben Rivera	.10
40	Mike Mussina	.50
41	Alex Gonzalez	.10
42	Edgardo Alfonzo	.10
43	Torii Hunter	.25
44	Richie Sexson	.25
45	Bret Boone	.20
46	John Smoltz	.20
47	Bengie Molina	.10
48	Trot Nixon	.10
49	Mike Cameron	.10
50	Mariano Rivera	.20
51	Ichiro Suzuki	1.50
52	Cristian Guzman	.10
53	Andruw Jones	.40
54	Jerry Hairston Jr.	.10
55	Brad Fullmer	.10
56	Luis Gonzalez	.25
57	Placido Polanco	.10
58	Jason Tyner	.10
59	Dan Wilson	.10
60	Jim Edmonds	.25
61	Larry Walker	.25
62	Edgar Renteria	.25
63	Orlando Cabrera	.10
64	Sammy Sosa	1.50
65	Derrek Lee	.20
66	C.C. Sabathia	.10
67	Aaron Boone	.10
68	Royce Clayton	.10
69	Darryl Kile	.10
70	Vladimir Guerrero	.75
71	Bud Smith	.10
72	Adrian Beltre	.20
73	Barry Bonds	15.00
74	Ben Petrick	.10
75	Derek Bell	.10
76	Jeff Kent	.20
77	Ricky Gutierrez	.10
78	Rafael Palmeiro	.50
79	Doug Mientkiewicz	.10
80	Fernando Vina	.10
81	Mark Mulder	.20
82	Carlos Beltran	.25
83	Juan Encarnacion	.10
84	Jimmy Rollins	.20
85	Pedro J. Martinez	.50
86	Aramis Ramirez	.25
87	Reggie Sanders	.10
88	Gary Sheffield	.25
89	Bartolo Colon	.10
90	Jose Macias	.10
91	Bobby Higginson	.10
92	Craig Biggio	.20
93	Al Leiter	.20
94	Juan Gonzalez	.50
95	Jose Valentin	.10
96	Jon Lieber	.10
97	Alex Gonzalez	.10
98	Jose Mesa	.10
99	Sandy Alomar	.10
100	Barry Bonds	2.00
101	Todd Walker	.10
102	Kevin Young	.10
103	Ken Griffey Jr.	1.00
104	Mark McGwire	2.00
105	Jason Giambi	.50
106	Todd Helton	.50
107	Mike Piazza	1.00
108	Nomar Garciaparra	1.50
109	Bernie Williams	.40
110	Shawn Wooten	.10
111	Eric Chavez	.20
112	Curt Schilling	.40
113	Roberto Alomar	.50
114	Chipper Jones	.75
115	Edgar Martinez	.20
116	Shawn Green	.20
117	Ben Grieve	.10
118	Jermaine Dye	.10
119	Steve Finley	.10
120	Adam Dunn	.25
121	Preston Wilson	.10
122	Lance Berkman	.20
123	Ben Sheets	.25
124	Ryan Klesko	.10
125	Brian Giles	.25
126	Marcus Giles	.10
127	Craig Wilson	.10
128	Miguel Tejada	.25
129	Andres Galarraga	.20
130	Alex Rodriguez	1.50
131	David Justice	.25
132	Barry Zito	.25
133	Scott Rolen	.75
134	Brent Abernathy	.10
135	Raul Mondesi	.20
136	Josh Towers	.10
137	Rafael Furcal	.10
138	Gabe Kapler	.10
139	Fred McGriff	.25
140	Jeff Conine	.10
141	Mike Lieberthal	.10
142	Frank Thomas	.50
143	Jason Kendall	.10
144	Toby Hall	.10
145	Pat Burrell	.30
146	J.D. Drew	.25
147	Javier Lopez	.25
148	Carlos Lee	.10
149	Doug Glanville	.10
150	Ruben Sierra	.10
151	Julio Franco	.10
152	Tim Hudson	.20
153	Rich Aurilia	.10
154	Geoff Jenkins	.10
155	Tsuyoshi Shinjo	.10
156	Moises Alou	.20
157	Jim Thome	.75
158	Steve Cox	.10
159	Kevin Brown	.20
160	Barry Bonds	.50
161	Rickey Henderson	.20
162	Bud Smith	.10
163	Rickey Henderson	.20
164	Barry Bonds	.50
165	Checklist	.10

Autographs

		NM/M
Common Auto.:		10.00
GJ	Geoff Jenkins	15.00
NJ	Nick Johnson	10.00
BS	Ben Sheets	25.00

2002 Topps Pristine

SAMMY SOSA
CHICAGO CUBS™

		NM/M
Complete Set (210):		
Common Player:		.75
Common Uncommon RC:		3.00
Production 1,999		
Common Rare RC:		5.00
Production 799		
Pack (8):		30.00
Box (5):		125.00
1	Alex Rodriguez	5.00
2	Carlos Delgado	1.50
3	Jimmy Rollins	.75
4	Jason Kendall	.75
5	John Olerud	1.00
6	Albert Pujols	5.00
7	Curt Schilling	2.00
8	Gary Sheffield	1.00
9	Johnny Damon	1.00
10	Ichiro Suzuki	4.00
11	Pat Burrell	1.00
12	Garret Anderson	1.00
13	Andruw Jones	1.50
14	Kerry Wood	2.00
15	Kenny Lofton	1.00
16	Adam Dunn	1.50
17	Juan Pierre	.75
18	Josh Beckett	1.00
19	Roy Oswalt	1.00
20	Derek Jeter	6.00
21	Jose Vidro	.75
22	Richie Sexson	1.50
23	Mike Sweeney	.75
24	Jeff Kent	1.00
25	Jason Giambi	1.50
26	Bret Boone	1.00
27	J.D. Drew	1.00
28	Shannon Stewart	.75
29	Miguel Tejada	1.00
30	Barry Bonds	6.00
31	Randy Johnson	2.00
32	Pedro J. Martinez	2.00
33	Magglio Ordonez	1.00
34	Todd Helton	1.50
35	Craig Biggio	1.00
36	Shawn Green	1.00
37	Vladimir Guerrero	2.00
38	Mo Vaughn	1.00
39	Alfonso Soriano	2.00
40	Barry Zito	1.00
41	Aramis Ramirez	1.00
42	Ryan Klesko	1.00
43	Ruben Sierra	.75
44	Tino Martinez	.75
45	Toby Hall	.75
46	Ivan Rodriguez	1.50
47	Raul Mondesi	.75
48	Carlos Pena	.75
49	Darin Erstad	1.00
50	Sammy Sosa	4.00
51	Bartolo Colon	1.00
52	Robert Fick	.75
53	Cliff Floyd	.75
54	Brian Jordan	.75
55	Torii Hunter	1.00
56	Roberto Alomar	1.00
57	Roger Clemens	4.00
58	Mark Mulder	1.00
59	Brian Giles	1.00
60	Mike Piazza	4.00
61	Rich Aurilia	.75
62	Freddy Garcia	.75
63	Jim Edmonds	1.50
64	Eric Hinske	.75
65	Jeremy Giambi	.75
66	Javier Vazquez	.75
67	Cristian Guzman	.75
68	Paul LoDuca	.75
69	Bobby Abreu	1.00
70	Nomar Garciaparra	4.00
71	Troy Glaus	1.00
72	Chipper Jones	2.00
73	Scott Rolen	2.00
74	Lance Berkman	1.00
75	C.C. Sabathia	.75
76	Bernie Williams	1.00
77	Rafael Palmeiro	1.50
78	Phil Nevin	.75
79	Kazuhiro Sasaki	.75
80	Eric Chavez	1.00
81	Jorge Posada	1.00
82	Edgardo Alfonzo	.75
83	Geoff Jenkins	1.00
84	Preston Wilson	.75
85	Jim Thome	2.00
86	Frank Thomas	1.50
87	Jeff Bagwell	1.50
88	Greg Maddux	3.00
89	Mark Prior	3.00
90	Larry Walker	1.00
91	Luis Gonzalez	1.00
92	Tim Hudson	1.00
93	Tsuyoshi Shinjo	.75
94	Juan Gonzalez	1.50
95	Shea Hillenbrand	.75
96	Paul Konerko	.75
97	Tom Glavine	1.50
98	Marty Cordova	.75
99	Moises Alou	1.00
100	Ken Griffey Jr.	4.00
101	Hank Blalock	1.50
102	Matt Morris	1.00
103	Robb Nen	.75
104	Mike Cameron	.75
105	Mark Buehrle	.75
106	Sean Burroughs	.75
107	Orlando Cabrera	.75
108	Jeromy Burnitz	.75
109	Juan Uribe	.75
110	Eric Milton	.75
111	Carlos Lee	.75
112	Jose Mesa	.75
113	Morgan Ensberg	.75
114	Mike Rivera	.75
115	Juan Cruz	.75
116	Mike Lieberthal	.75
117	Armando Benitez	.75
118	Vinny Castilla	.75
119	Russ Ortiz	.75
120	Mike Lowell	1.00
121	Corey Patterson	1.00
122	Mike Mussina	1.50
123	Rafael Furcal	.75
124	Mark Grace	1.50
125	Ben Sheets	1.00
126	John Smoltz	1.00
127	Fred McGriff	1.00
128	Nick Johnson	.75
129	J.T. Snow	.75
130	Jeff Cirillo	.75
131	Trevor Hoffman	.75
132	Kevin Brown	1.00
133	Mariano Rivera	1.50
134	Marlon Anderson	.75
135	Al Leiter	.75
136	Doug Mientkiewicz	.75
137	Eric Karros	.75
138	Bobby Higginson	.75
139	Sean Casey	1.00
140	Troy Percival	.75
141	Willie Mays	5.00
142	Carl Yastrzemski	3.00
143	Stan Musial	4.00
144	Harmon Killebrew	3.00
145	Mike Schmidt	5.00
146	Duke Snider	2.00
147	Brooks Robinson	3.00
148	Frank Robinson	2.00
149	Nolan Ryan	8.00
150	Reggie Jackson	3.00
151	Joe Mauer/C **RC**	20.00
152	Joe Mauer/U **RC**	25.00
153	Joe Mauer/R **RC**	35.00
154	Colt Griffin/C	3.00
155	Colt Griffin/U	5.00
156	Colt Griffin/R	8.00
157	Jason Simontacchi/C **RC**	2.00
158	Jason Simontacchi/U **RC**	3.00
159	Jason Simontacchi/R **RC**	5.00
160	Casey Kotchman/C	5.00
161	Casey Kotchman/U	8.00
162	Casey Kotchman/R	15.00
163	Greg Sain/C **RC**	1.50
164	Greg Sain/U **RC**	3.00
165	Greg Sain/R **RC**	5.00
166	David Wright/C	40.00
167	David Wright/U	50.00
168	David Wright/R	60.00
169	Scott Hairston/C	4.00
170	Scott Hairston/U	6.00
171	Scott Hairston/R	10.00
172	Rolando Viera/C **RC**	1.50
173	Rolando Viera/U **RC**	3.00
174	Rolando Viera/R **RC**	5.00
175	Tyrell Godwin/C	1.50
176	Tyrell Godwin/U	3.00
177	Tyrell Godwin/R	5.00
178	Jesus Cota/C **RC**	1.50
179	Jesus Cota/U **RC**	3.00
180	Jesus Cota/R **RC**	5.00
181	Dan Johnson/C **RC**	5.00
182	Dan Johnson/U **RC**	10.00
183	Dan Johnson/R **RC**	15.00
184	Mario Ramos/C	1.50
185	Mario Ramos/U	3.00
186	Mario Ramos/R	5.00
187	Jason Dubois/C **RC**	4.00
188	Jason Dubois/U **RC**	6.00
189	Jason Dubois/R **RC**	10.00
190	Jonny Gomes/C **RC**	8.00
191	Jonny Gomes/U **RC**	15.00
192	Jonny Gomes/R **RC**	20.00
193	Chris Snelling/C **RC**	2.00
194	Chris Snelling/U **RC**	4.00
195	Chris Snelling/R **RC**	6.00
196	Hansel Izquierdo/C **RC**	2.00
197	Hansel Izquierdo/U **RC**	4.00
198	Hansel Izquierdo/R **RC**	6.00
199	So Taguchi/C **RC**	3.00
200	So Taguchi/U **RC**	5.00
201	So Taguchi/R **RC**	8.00
202	Kazuhisa Ishii/C **RC**	3.00
203	Kazuhisa Ishii/U **RC**	5.00
204	Kazuhisa Ishii/R **RC**	8.00
205	Jorge Padilla/C **RC**	1.50
206	Jorge Padilla/U **RC**	3.00
207	Jorge Padilla/R **RC**	5.00
208	Earl Snyder/C **RC**	2.00
209	Earl Snyder/U **RC**	4.00
210	Earl Snyder/R **RC**	6.00

Refractors

JAVIER VAZQUEZ
MONTREAL EXPOS™

	NM/M
Stars (1-150):	2-4X
Production 149	
Common Rookies:	.75-1.5X
Production 1,999	
Uncommon Rookies:	1-2X
Production 799	
Rare Rookies:	2-3X
Production 149	
Gold Refractors (1-150):	3-5X
Gold Common RC's:	4-8X
Gold Uncommon RC's:	2-4X
Gold Rare RC's:	1-2X
Production 70 Sets	
All Refractors are uncirculated.	

Fall Memories

FALL
MEMORIES
LUIS
GONZALEZ
ARIZONA DIAMONDBACKS

		NM/M
Common Player:		5.00
Varying quantities produced		
JB	Johnny Bench	15.00
BB	Barry Bonds	30.00
GB	George Brett	25.00
TG	Tom Glavine	8.00
LG	Luis Gonzalez	5.00
MG	Mark Grace	12.00
SG	Shawn Green	6.00
TH	Todd Helton	8.00
RJ	Reggie Jackson	15.00
AJ	Andruw Jones	8.00
CP	Chipper Jones	10.00
TM	Tino Martinez	8.00
WM	Willie Mays	40.00
EM	Eddie Murray	15.00
JP	Jorge Posada	8.00
KP	Kirby Puckett	15.00
CS	Curt Schilling	8.00
GS	Gary Sheffield	5.00

AS	Alfonso Soriano	10.00
BW	Bernie Williams	8.00

In The Gap

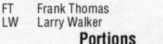

		NM/M
Common Player:		5.00
Varying quantities produced		
RA	Roberto Alomar	10.00
LB	Lance Berkman	8.00
WBE	Wilson Betemit	5.00
WB	Wade Boggs	8.00
BBO	Barry Bonds	25.00
BB	Bret Boone	6.00
EC	Eric Chavez	8.00
CD	Carlos Delgado	6.00
AD	Adam Dunn	10.00
JE	Jim Edmonds	6.00
DE	Darin Erstad	5.00
NG	Nomar Garciaparra	15.00
TG	Tony Gwynn	15.00
TH	Todd Helton	8.00
RH	Rickey Henderson	10.00
AJ	Andruw Jones	10.00
JK	Jeff Kent	5.00
RK	Ryan Klesko	8.00
PL	Paul LoDuca	10.00
RP	Rafael Palmeiro	10.00
MP	Mike Piazza	15.00
AP	Albert Pujols	15.00
ARA	Aramis Ramirez	5.00
AR	Alex Rodriguez	15.00
IR	Ivan Rodriguez	8.00
TS	Tsuyoshi Shinjo	5.00
AS	Alfonso Soriano	10.00
LW	Larry Walker	5.00
BW	Bernie Williams	15.00
PW	Preston Wilson	5.00

Patches

No Pricing
Production 25 Sets

Personal Endorsements

		NM/M
Common Autograph:		8.00
Inserted 1:Box		
RA	Roberto Alomar	30.00
KB	Kenny Baugh	8.00
LB	Lance Berkman	30.00
BB	Barry Bonds	180.00
DB	Dewon Brazelton	15.00
JD	Johnny Damon	30.00
GF	Gavin Floyd	25.00
CG	Cristian Guzman	10.00
IG	Irvin Guzman	10.00
OH	Orlando Hudson	10.00
KI	Kazuhisa Ishii	30.00
CK	Casey Kotchman	20.00
JL	Jason Lane	8.00
CW	Corwin Malone	8.00
NN	Nick Neugebauer	8.00
AP	Albert Pujols	200.00
JR	Jimmy Rollins	25.00
BS	Ben Sheets	20.00
JS	Juan Silvestre	8.00
ST	So Taguchi	15.00
MT	Marcus Thames	8.00

Popular Demand

		NM/M
Common Player:		5.00
Varying quantities produced		
RA	Roberto Alomar	10.00
JB	Jeff Bagwell	10.00
WB	Wade Boggs	8.00
BBO	Barry Bonds	25.00
BB	Bret Boone	5.00
CD	Carlos Delgado	5.00
AD	Adam Dunn	8.00
NG	Nomar Garciaparra	15.00
SG	Shawn Green	5.00
TG	Tony Gwynn	12.00
TH	Todd Helton	8.00
CJ	Chipper Jones	12.00
DM	Don Mattingly	35.00
MP	Mike Piazza	15.00
AP	Albert Pujols	20.00
AR	Alex Rodriguez	15.00
IR	Ivan Rodriguez	8.00
CS	Curt Schilling	8.00

FT	Frank Thomas	10.00
LW	Larry Walker	5.00

Portions

		NM/M
Common Player:		5.00
Varying quantities produced		
RA	Roberto Alomar	10.00
JB	Jeff Bagwell	10.00
LB .	Lance Berkman	10.00
CB	Craig Biggio	8.00
BBO	Barry Bonds	20.00
BB	Bret Boone	5.00
CD	Carlos Delgado	8.00
RD	Ryan Dempster	5.00
AD	Adam Dunn	8.00
CF	Cliff Floyd	5.00
RF	Rafael Furcal	5.00
NG	Nomar Garciaparra	15.00
CG	Cristian Guzman	5.00
TH	Todd Helton	8.00
NJ	Nick Johnson	5.00
LD	Paul LoDuca	5.00
GM	Greg Maddux	10.00
EM	Edgar Martinez	10.00
MM	Mike Mussina	10.00
MO	Magglio Ordonez	8.00
RP	Rafael Palmeiro	8.00
MP	Mike Piazza	15.00
JP	Jorge Posada	8.00
AP	Albert Pujols	15.00
AR	Alex Rodriguez	15.00
IR	Ivan Rodriguez	8.00
NR	Nolan Ryan	30.00
KS	Kazuhiro Sasaki	5.00

2002 Topps Reserve

	NM/M
Complete Set (150):	120.00
Common Player:	.25
Common (136-150):	4.00
Production 999	
Silver parallel (1-135):	4-8X
Silver (136-150):	.75-1.5X
Production 25	
Box:10 Packs &	
1 Auto. Helmet:	100.00

1	Alex Rodriguez	2.50
2	Tsuyoshi Shinjo	.25
3	Craig Biggio	.40
4	Troy Glaus	.50
5	Mike Rivera	.25
6	Curt Schilling	.75
7	Garret Anderson	.50
8	Ben Sheets	.50
9	Todd Helton	.75
10	Paul Konerko	.50
11	Sammy Sosa	2.00
12	Bud Smith	.25
13	Jeff Bagwell	.75
14	Albert Pujols	2.00
15	Jose Vidro	.25
16	Carlos Delgado	.50
17	Torii Hunter	.50
18	Jerry Hairston Jr.	.25
19	Troy Percival	.25
20	Vladimir Guerrero	1.00
21	Geoff Jenkins	.40
22	Carlos Pena	.25
23	Juan Gonzalez	.75
24	Raul Mondesi	.25
25	Jimmy Rollins	.40
26	Mariano Rivera	.50
27	Jorge Posada	.50
28	Magglio Ordonez	.50
29	Roberto Alomar	.50
30	Randy Johnson	1.00
31	Xavier Nady	.25
32	Terrence Long	.25
33	Chipper Jones	1.00
34	Rich Aurilia	.25
35	Aramis Ramirez	.50
36	Jim Thome	1.00
37	Bret Boone	.50
38	Angel Berroa	.25
39	Jeff Conine	.25
40	Cliff Floyd	.25
41	Pedro J. Martinez	1.00
42	J.D. Drew	.50
43	Kazuhiro Sasaki	.25
44	Jon Rauch	.25
45	Orlando Hudson	.25
46	Scott Rolen	1.00
47	Rafael Furcal	.25
48	Brad Penny	.25
49	Miguel Tejada	.50
50	Orlando Cabrera	.25
51	Bobby Abreu	.50
52	Darin Erstad	.25
53	Edgar Martinez	.40
54	Ben Grieve	.25
55	Shawn Green	.50
56	Ivan Rodriguez	.75
57	Josh Beckett	.50
58	Ray Durham	.25
59	Jason Hart	.25
60	Nathan Haynes	.25
61	Jason Giambi	.75
62	Eric Chavez	.50
63	Matt Morris	.40
64	Lance Berkman	.50
65	Jeff Kent	.40
66	Andruw Jones	.50
67	Brian Giles	.50
68	Morgan Ensberg	.25
69	Pat Burrell	.50
70	Ken Griffey Jr.	2.00
71	Carlos Beltran	.50
72	Ichiro Suzuki	2.00
73	Larry Walker	.50
74	J.J. Putz RC	.25
75	Mike Piazza	2.00
76	Rafael Palmeiro	.75
77	Mark Prior	2.00
78	Toby Hall	.25
79	Pokey Reese	.25
80	Mike Mussina	.50
81	Omar Vizquel	.25
82	Shannon Stewart	.25
83	Jeromy Burnitz	.25
84	Bernie Williams	.50
85	C.C. Sabathia	.50
86	Mike Hampton	.25
87	Kevin Brown	.25
88	Juan Cruz	.25
89	Jeff Weaver	.25
90	Jason Lane	.25
91	Adam Dunn	.75
92	Jose Cruz Jr.	.25
93	Marlon Anderson	.25
94	Jeff Cirillo	.25
95	Mark Buehrle	.25
96	Austin Kearns	.50
97	Tim Hudson	.50
98	Brian Jordan	.25
99	Phil Nevin	.25
100	Barry Bonds	3.00
101	Derek Jeter	3.00
102	Javier Vazquez	.25
103	Jason Kendall	.40
104	Jim Edmonds	.50
105	Kenny Kelly	.25
106	Juan Pena	.25
107	Mark Grace	.50
108	Roger Clemens	2.00
109	Barry Zito	.50
110	Greg Vaughn	.25
111	Greg Maddux	1.50
112	Richie Sexson	.25
113	Jermaine Dye	.25
114	Kerry Wood	1.00
115	Matt Lawton	.25
116	Sean Casey	.50
117	Gary Sheffield	.50
118	Preston Wilson	.25
119	Cristian Guzman	.25
120	Mike Sweeney	.25
121	Neifi Perez	.25
122	Paul LoDuca	.25
123	Luis Gonzalez	.50
124	Ryan Klesko	.25
125	Alfonso Soriano	1.00
126	Bobby Higginson	.25
127	Juan Pierre	.25
128	Moises Alou	.50
129	Roy Oswalt	.50
130	Nomar Garciaparra	2.00
131	Fred McGriff	.40
132	Edgardo Alfonzo	.40
133	Johnny Damon	.40
134	Dewon Brazelton	.25
135	Mark Mulder	.50
136	So Taguchi RC	8.00
137	Mario Ramos	4.00
138	Dan Johnson RC	15.00
139	Hansel Izquierdo RC	5.00
140	Kazuhisa Ishii RC	10.00
141	Jon Switzer	4.00
142	Chris Tritle RC	6.00
143	Chris Snelling RC	8.00
144	Chone Figgins RC	8.00
145	Dan Phillips RC	4.00
146	John Rodriguez RC	4.00
147	Colt Griffin	8.00
148	Jonny Gomes RC	15.00
149	Josh Barfield	10.00
150	Joe Mauer RC	30.00

Silver

Stars (1-135):	4-8X
SP's (136-150):	.75-1.5X

Autographed Mini-Helmets

	NM/M
Common Helmet:	20.00
1:Box	
Gold Ink Autographs:	No Pricing
Production 25	

Roberto Alomar	40.00
Moises Alou	25.00
Lance Berkman	40.00
Bret Boone	25.00
Eric Chavez	30.00
Adam Dunn	40.00
Cliff Floyd	20.00
Troy Glaus	40.00
Luis Gonzalez	30.00
Todd Helton	50.00
Magglio Ordonez	25.00
Rafael Palmeiro	40.00
Albert Pujols	220.00
Alex Rodriguez	125.00
Scott Rolen	35.00
Jimmy Rollins	40.00
Alfonso Soriano	50.00
Barry Zito	30.00

Game-Used Baseball

		NM/M
Inserted 1:1,761		
AR	Alex Rodriguez	
I	Ichiro Suzuki	65.00

Game-Used Bat

		NM/M
Common Player:		5.00
Inserted 1:12		
RA	Roberto Alomar	10.00
JB	Jeff Bagwell	10.00
BB	Barry Bonds	20.00
CD	Carlos Delgado	8.00
JG	Juan Gonzalez	8.00
LG	Luis Gonzalez	5.00
TG	Tony Gwynn	12.00
RH	Rickey Henderson	10.00
CJ	Chipper Jones	10.00
AJ	Andruw Jones	8.00
TM	Tino Martinez	8.00
RP	Rafael Palmeiro	8.00
MB	Mike Piazza	15.00
AP	Albert Pujols	15.00
AR	Alex Rodriguez	12.00
IR	Ivan Rodriguez	8.00
TS	Tsuyoshi Shinjo	8.00
AS	Alfonso Soriano	10.00
FT	Frank Thomas	8.00
BW	Bernie Williams	8.00

Game-Worn Patch

No Pricing
Production 25 Sets

Game-Worn Uniform

		NM/M
Common Player:		5.00
Inserted 1:5		
BB	Barry Bonds	20.00
BBO	Bret Boone	5.00
DE	Darin Erstad	5.00

NG	Nomar Garciaparra	15.00
LG	Luis Gonzalez	5.00
TG	Tony Gwynn	10.00
TH	Todd Helton	8.00
RJ	Randy Johnson	10.00
AJ	Andruw Jones	6.00
CJ	Chipper Jones	10.00
GM	Greg Maddux	12.00
PM	Pedro Martinez	10.00
MM	Mark Mulder	5.00
MO	Magglio Ordonez	5.00
RP	Rafael Palmeiro	8.00
MP	Mike Piazza	12.00
AR	Alex Rodriguez	12.00
IR	Ivan Rodriguez	8.00
SR	Scott Rolen	10.00
KS	Kazuhiro Sasaki	5.00
CS	Curt Schilling	8.00
FT	Frank Thomas	8.00
KW	Kerry Wood	10.00

2002 Topps Super Teams

		NM/M
Complete Set:		40.00
Common Player:		.25
Pack (7):		3.50
Box (20):		60.00
1	Leo Durocher	.25
2	Whitey Lockman	.25
3	Alvin Dark	.25
4	Monte Irvin	.50
5	Willie Mays	2.50
6	Wes Westrum	.25
7	Johnny Antonelli	.25
8	Sal Maglie	.25
9	Dusty Rhodes	.25
10	Davey Williams	.25
11	Hoyt Wilhelm	.25
12	Don Mueller	.25
13	Dusty Rhodes	.25
14	Willie Mays, Monte Irvin, Dusty Rhodes	.75
15	Walt Alston	.75
16	Gil Hodges	.75
17	Jim Gilliam	.25
18	Pee Wee Reese	.50
19	Jackie Robinson	2.00
20	Duke Snider	1.00
21	Carl Furillo	.25
22	Roy Campanella	1.00
23	Don Newcombe	.25
24	Don Hoak	.25
25	Johnny Podres	.25
26	Clem Labine	.25
27	Johnny Podres	.25
28	Pee Wee Reese, Jackie Robinson, Duke Snider	1.00
29	Fred Haney	.25
30	Joe Adcock	.25
31	Frank Torre	.25
32	Red Schoendienst	.25
33	Johnny Logan	.25
34	Eddie Mathews	1.00
35	Hank Aaron	3.00
36	Andy Pafko	.25
37	Wes Covington	.25
38	Lew Burdette	.25
39	Warren Spahn	1.00
40	Del Crandall	.25
41	Lew Burdette	.25
42	Warren Spahn, Eddie Mathews, Hank Aaron	1.50
43	Danny Murtaugh	.25
44	Dick Stuart	.25
45	Bill Mazeroski	.25
46	Dick Groat	.25
47	Don Hoak	.25
48	Gino Cimoli	.25
49	Bill Virdon	.25
50	Roberto Clemente	2.50
51	Smoky Burgess	.25
52	Bob Friend	.25
53	Vernon Law	.25
54	Roy Face	.25
55	Bill Mazeroski	.25
56	Roberto Clemente, Bill Mazeroski, Dick Groat	1.00
58	Ralph Houk	.25
59	Bill "Moose" Skowron	.50

60	Bobby Richardson	.25
61	Tony Kubek	.25
62	Clete Boyer	.25
63	Yogi Berra	1.50
64	Bob Cerv	.25
65	Roger Maris	1.50
66	Elston Howard	.25
67	Whitey Ford	1.00
68	Ralph Terry	.25
69	Johnny Blanchard	.25
70	Whitey Ford	1.00
71	Yogi Berra, Roger Maris, Elston Howard, Bill "Moose" Skowron	1.00
72	Red Schoendienst	.25
73	Orlando Cepeda	.40
74	Julian Javier	.25
75	Dal Maxvill	.25
76	Mike Shannon	.25
77	Lou Brock	.75
78	Roger Maris	1.50
79	Curt Flood	.25
80	Tim McCarver	.25
81	Steve Carlton	.75
82	Bob Gibson	1.00
83	Nelson Briles	.25
84	Bobby Tolan	.25
85	Bob Gibson	1.00
86	Bob Gibson, Steve Carlton, Orlando Cepeda, Lou Brock	.50
87	Gil Hodges	.25
88	Ed Kranepool	.25
89	Buddy Harrelson	.25
90	Wayne Garrett	.25
91	Cleon Jones	.25
92	Tommie Agee	.25
93	Ron Swoboda	.25
94	Al Weis	.25
95	Jerry Grote	.25
96	Tom Seaver	1.00
97	Jerry Koosman	.25
98	Tug McGraw	.25
99	Nolan Ryan	3.00
100	Donn Clendenon	.25
101	Tom Seaver, Jerry Koosman, Tug McGraw, Nolan Ryan	1.00
102	Earl Weaver	.25
103	Boog Powell	.25
104	Davey Johnson	.25
105	Mark Belanger	.25
106	Brooks Robinson	1.00
107	Don Buford	.25
108	Paul Blair	.25
109	Frank Robinson	1.00
110	Dick Hall	.25
111	Jim Palmer	.75
112	Mike Cuellar	.25
113	Dave McNally	.25
114	Andy Etchebarren	.25
115	Brooks Robinson	1.00
116	Dick Hall, Jim Palmer, Mike Cuellar, Dave McNally	.40
117	Alvin Dark	.25
118	Gene Tenace	.25
119	Dick Green	.25
120	Bert Campaneris	.25
121	Sal Bando	.25
122	Reggie Jackson	1.00
123	Joe Rudi	.25
124	Claudell Washington	.25
125	Ray Fosse	.25
126	Vida Blue	.40
127	Rollie Fingers	.25
128	Jim "Catfish" Hunter	.50
129	Ken Holtzman	.25
130	Rollie Fingers	.25
131	Jim "Catfish" Hunter, Sal Bando, Reggie Jackson, Rollie Fingers	.50
132	Davey Johnson	.25
133	Keith Hernandez	.25
134	Wally Backman	.25
135	Rafael Santana	.25
136	Ray Knight	.25
137	Len Dykstra	.25
138	Darryl Strawberry	.25
139	Kevin Mitchell	.25
140	Dwight Gooden	.25
141	Bob Ojeda	.25
142	Sid Fernandez	.25
143	Ron Darling	.25
144	Gary Carter	.25
145	Ray Knight	.25
146	Darryl Strawberry, Dwight Gooden, Keith Hernandez	.25

Retrofractor

Cards (1-146):	2-4X

#'d to year team won World Series

Autographs

		NM/M
Common Autograph:		10.00
Inserted 1:19		
YB	Yogi Berra	60.00
VB	Vida Blue	15.00
CB	Clete Boyer	15.00
SC	Steve Carlton	25.00
MI	Monte Irvin	15.00
RJ	Reggie Jackson	50.00
TK	Tony Kubek	30.00
TM	Tug McGraw	15.00
AP	Andy Pafko	20.00
JP	Jim Palmer	25.00
JPO	Johnny Podres	15.00
BR	Bobby Richardson	15.00
BRO	Brooks Robinson	30.00
NR	Nolan Ryan	150.00
TS	Tom Seaver	40.00
MS	Bill "Moose" Skowron	20.00
WS	Warren Spahn	40.00
HW	Hoyt Wilhelm	15.00

A View To A Thrill Autograph Relics

		NM/M
# Produced listed		
WFA	Whitey Ford/61	100.00
BGA	Bob Gibson/67	60.00
WMA	Willie Mays/54	150.00
DSA	Duke Snider/55	80.00
WSA	Warren Spahn/67	60.00

A View To a Thrill Seat Relics

		NM/M
Common Player:		10.00
Inserted 1:30		
HA	Hank Aaron	20.00
YB	Yogi Berra	15.00
LB	Lew Burdette	10.00
RC	Roberto Clemente	50.00
WF	Whitey Ford	15.00
BG	Bob Gibson	15.00
RMB	Roger Maris/Cardinals	20.00
RMY	Roger Maris/Yankees	20.00
EM	Eddie Mathews	15.00
WM	Willie Mays	30.00
BM	Bill Mazeroski	10.00
JP	Jim Palmer	10.00
BP	Boog Powell	10.00
BR	Brooks Robinson	15.00
FR	Frank Robinson	15.00
RS	Red Schoendienst	10.00
DS	Duke Snider	15.00
WS	Warren Spahn	15.00

Classic Combos

		NM/M
Common Card:		40.00
Inserted 1:865		
AJ	Tommie Agee, Cleon Jones	40.00
JR	Reggie Jackson, Joe Rudi	40.00
RR	Brooks Robinson, Frank Robinson	50.00
SK	Tom Seaver, Jerry Koosman	50.00
SRBK	"Moose" Skowron, Bobby Richardson, Clete Boyer, Tony Kubek	80.00

Relics

		NM/M
Common Player:		10.00
TA	Tommie Agee/Bat	20.00
SBB	Sal Bando/Bat	10.00
SBJ	Sal Bando/Jsy	10.00
MB	Mark Belanger/Bat	10.00
PB	Paul Blair/Bat	10.00
CB	Clete Boyer/Bat	10.00
LB	Lew Burdette/Jsy	15.00
SB	Smoky Burgess/Bat	10.00
BC	Bert Campaneris/Jsy	15.00
GC	Gary Carter/Jacket	20.00
CB	Gary Carter/Bat	15.00
GCJ	Gary Carter/Jsy	15.00
OC	Orlando Cepeda/Bat	15.00
BCE	Bob Cerv/Bat	10.00
GCI	Gino Cimoli/Bat	10.00
DC	Del Crandel/Bat	10.00
MC	Mike Cuellar/Jsy	15.00
RD	Ron Darling/Jsy	10.00
LD	Len Dykstra/Bat	15.00
RF	Ray Fosse/Bat	10.00
BF	Bob Friend/Jsy	10.00
WG	Wayne Garrett/Bat	10.00
DG	Dwight Gooden/Jsy	15.00
DH	Don Hoak/Bat	10.00
RH	Ralph Houk/Jsy	15.00
RJ	Reggie Jackson/Bat	35.00
DJ	Davey Johnson/Bat	10.00
CJ	Cleon Jones/Bat	20.00
RK	Ray Knight/Bat	10.00
JK	Jerry Koosman/Jsy	10.00
EK	Ed Kranepool/Jsy	15.00
TK	Tony Kubek/Bat	25.00
TM	Tug McGraw/Jsy	15.00
DM	Dave McNally/Jsy	15.00
KM	Kevin Mitchell/Bat	10.00
AP	Andy Pafko/Bat	10.00
BR	Bobby Richardson/Bat	25.00
BRO	Brooks Robinson/Bat	25.00
FR	Frank Robinson/Bat	20.00
JR	Joe Rudi/Bat	10.00
NR	Nolan Ryan/Bat	75.00
RS	Red Schoendienst/Bat	10.00
TS	Tom Seaver/Bat	20.00
MS	"Moose" Skowron/Bat	20.00
DS	Darryl Strawberry/Bat	20.00
CW	Claudell Washington/Bat	10.00

Super Teammates

		NM/M
Complete Set (5):		10.00
Common Card:		2.00
Inserted 1:10		
BG	Lou Brock, Bob Gibson	2.00
FB	Whitey Ford, Yogi Berra	4.00
MI	Willie Mays, Monte Irvin	4.00
RR	Brooks Robinson, Frank Robinson	3.00
SRBK	Bill "Moose" Skowron, Bobby Richardson, Clete Boyer, Tony Kubek	2.00

Super Teammates Autos.

		NM/M
Production 50 Sets		
BGA	Lou Brock, Bob Gibson	100.00
FBA	Whitey Ford, Yogi Berra	150.00
MIA	Willie Mays, Monte Irvin	180.00
RRA	Brooks Robinson, Frank Robinson	100.00
SRBKA	Bill "Moose" Skowron, Bobby Richardson, Clete Boyer, Tony Kubek	200.00

2002 Topps Ten

		NM/M
Complete Set (200):		40.00
Common Player:		.15
Pack (7):		2.00
Box (24):		40.00
1	Ichiro Suzuki	1.00
2	Rich Aurilia	.15
3	Bret Boone	.25
4	Juan Pierre	.15
5	Shannon Stewart	.15
6	Alex Rodriguez	1.00
7	Luis Gonzalez	.25
8	Todd Helton	.50
9	Garret Anderson	.25
10	Albert Pujols	1.00
11	Lance Berkman	.25
12	Todd Helton	.50
13	Jeff Kent	.15
14	Bob Abreu	.25

15	Jason Giambi	.40
16	Albert Pujols	1.00
17	Mike Sweeney	.15
18	Vladimir Guerrero	.50
19	Cliff Floyd	.15
20	Shannon Stewart	.15
21	Cristian Guzman	.15
22	Roberto Alomar	.40
23	Carlos Beltran	.25
24	Jimmy Rollins	.25
25	Roger Cedeno	.15
26	Juan Pierre	.15
27	Juan Uribe	.15
28	Luis Castillo	.15
29	Ray Durham	.15
30	Mark McLemore	.15
31	Barry Bonds	1.50
32	Sammy Sosa	1.00
33	Luis Gonzalez	.25
34	Alex Rodriguez	1.00
35	Shawn Green	.25
36	Todd Helton	.50
37	Jim Thome	.50
38	Rafael Palmeiro	.40
39	Richie Sexson	.25
40	Phil Nevin	.15
41	Troy Glaus	.40
42	Sammy Sosa	1.00
43	Todd Helton	.50
44	Luis Gonzalez	.25
45	Bret Boone	.25
46	Juan Gonzalez	.40
47	Barry Bonds	1.50
48	Alex Rodriguez	1.00
49	Jeff Bagwell	.50
50	Albert Pujols	1.00
51	Phil Nevin	.15
52	Ichiro Suzuki	1.00
53	Larry Walker	.25
54	Jason Giambi	.40
55	Roberto Alomar	.40
56	Todd Helton	.50
57	Moises Alou	.25
58	Lance Berkman	.25
59	Bret Boone	.25
60	Frank Catalanotto	.15
61	Chipper Jones	.50
62	Barry Bonds	1.50
63	Sammy Sosa	1.00
64	Luis Gonzalez	.25
65	Todd Helton	.50
66	Larry Walker	.25
67	Jason Giambi	.40
68	Jim Thome	.50
69	Alex Rodriguez	1.00
70	Lance Berkman	.25
71	Albert Pujols	1.00
72	Ichiro Suzuki	1.00
73	Roger Cedeno	.15
74	Juan Pierre	.15
75	Jimmy Rollins	.25
76	Alfonso Soriano	.50
77	Mark McLemore	.15
78	Chuck Knoblauch	.15
79	Vladimir Guerrero	.50
80	Bob Abreu	.25
81	Mike Cameron	.15
82	Sammy Sosa	1.00
83	Alex Rodriguez	1.00
84	Todd Helton	.50
85	Barry Bonds	1.50
86	Luis Gonzalez	.25
87	Ichiro Suzuki	1.00
88	Jeff Bagwell	.50
89	Cliff Floyd	.15
90	Shawn Green	.25
91	Craig Biggio	.15
92	Juan Pierre	.15
93	Fernando Vina	.15
94	Paul LoDuca	.15
95	Mark Grace	.25
96	Eric Young	.15
97	Placido Polanco	.15
98	Jason Kendall	.15
99	Ichiro Suzuki	1.00
100	Orlando Cabrera	.15
101	Rey Sanchez	.15
102	Ichiro Suzuki	1.00
103	Edgar Martinez	.25
104	Bret Boone	.25
105	Barry Bonds	1.50
106	Ivan Rodriguez	.40
107	Mike Piazza	1.00
108	Sammy Sosa	1.00
109	John Olerud	.25
110	Roberto Alomar	.40
111	Roberto Alomar	.40
112	Mark McGwire	1.50
113	Barry Larkin	.25
114	Ken Griffey Jr.	1.00
115	Rickey Henderson	.25
116	Barry Bonds	1.50
117	Ivan Rodriguez	.40
118	Mike Piazza	1.00
119	Roger Clemens	1.00
120	Randy Johnson	.50
121	Albert Pujols	1.00
122	Ichiro Suzuki	1.00
123	Roy Oswalt	.25
124	C.C. Sabathia	.15
125	Jimmy Rollins	.25
126	Alfonso Soriano	.50
127	David Eckstein	.15
128	Adam Dunn	.50
129	Bud Smith	.15
130	Tsuyoshi Shinjo	.15
131	Matt Morris	.15
132	Curt Schilling	.25
133	Randy Johnson	.50
134	Mark Mulder	.25
135	Roger Clemens	1.00
136	Jon Lieber	.15
137	Jamie Moyer	.15
138	Freddy Garcia	.15
139	Tim Hudson	.25
140	C.C. Sabathia	.15
141	Randy Johnson	.50
142	Curt Schilling	.25
143	John Burkett	.15
144	Freddy Garcia	.15
145	Greg Maddux	.75
146	Darryl Kile	.15
147	Mike Mussina	.40
148	Joe Mays	.15
149	Matt Morris	.25
150	Russ Ortiz	.15
151	Randy Johnson	.50
152	Curt Schilling	.25
153	Hideo Nomo	.15
154	Chan Ho Park	.15
155	Kerry Wood	.50
156	Mike Mussina	.40
157	Roger Clemens	1.00
158	Javier Vazquez	.15
159	Barry Zito	.25
160	Bartolo Colon	.15
161	Mariano Rivera	.25
162	Robb Nen	.15
163	Kazuhiro Sasaki	.15
164	Armando Benitez	.15
165	Trevor Hoffman	.15
166	Jeff Shaw	.15
167	Keith Foulke	.15
168	Jose Mesa	.15
169	Troy Percival	.15
170	Billy Wagner	.15
171	Pat Burrell	.25
172	Raul Mondesi	.15
173	Gary Sheffield	.25
174	Carlos Beltran	.25
175	Vladimir Guerrero	.50
176	Torii Hunter	.25
177	Jeromy Burnitz	.15
178	Tim Salmon	.15
179	Jim Edmonds	.25
180	Tsuyoshi Shinjo	.15
181	Greg Maddux	.75
182	Roberto Alomar	.40
183	Ken Griffey Jr.	1.00
184	Ivan Rodriguez	.40
185	Omar Vizquel	.15
186	Barry Bonds	1.50
187	Devon White	.15
188	J.T. Snow	.15
189	Larry Walker	.25
190	Robin Ventura	.15
191	Mark Phillips **RC**	3.00
192	Clint Nageotte **RC**	2.00
193	Mauricio Lara **RC**	.75
194	Nic Jackson **RC**	.75
195	Chris Tritle **RC**	.75
196	Ryan Gripp **RC**	.75
197	Greg Montalbano **RC**	.75
198	Noochie Varner **RC**	.75
199	Nick Alvarez **RC**	.75
200	Craig Kuzmic **RC**	.75

Die-Cut

Stars (1-200): 2-4X
Inserted 1:4

Autographs

		NM/M
Common Autograph:		10.00
Inserted 1:67		
BB	Barry Bonds	180.00
BBO	Bret Boone	20.00
RCL	Roger Clemens	100.00
JE	Jim Edmonds	25.00
CF	Cliff Floyd	10.00
LG	Luis Gonzalez	15.00
CG	Cristian Guzman	10.00
RO	Roy Oswalt	15.00
JR	Jimmy Rollins	15.00
BZ	Barry Zito	20.00

Relics

		NM/M
Common Player:		8.00
Bat Relic 1:27		
Jersey Relic 1:26		
BA	Bob Abreu/Bat	12.00
RA	Roberto Alomar/Bat	15.00
MA	Moises Alou/Bat	8.00
GA	Garret Anderson/Bat	10.00
JBA	Jeff Bagwell/Jsy	15.00
CB	Carlos Beltran/Bat	10.00
AB	Armando Benitez/Jsy	8.00
LB	Lance Berkman/Bat	15.00
CBI	Craig Biggio/Jsy	15.00
BB	Barry Bonds/Jsy	25.00
BBO	Bret Boone/Bat	10.00
JBU	John Burkett/Jsy	8.00
JB	Jeromy Burnitz/Jsy	8.00
MC	Mike Cameron/Bat	10.00
LC	Luis Castillo/Bat	8.00
RC	Roger Cedeno/Bat	8.00
BC	Bartolo Colon/Jsy	8.00
RD	Ray Durham/Bat	8.00
JE	Jim Edmonds/Bat	15.00
CF	Cliff Floyd/Bat	8.00
FG	Freddy Garcia/Jsy	8.00
JGO	Juan Gonzalez/Bat	10.00
LG	Luis Gonzalez/Bat	10.00
MG	Mark Grace/Bat	20.00
SG	Shawn Green/Bat	10.00
CG	Cristian Guzman/Bat	10.00
TH	Todd Helton/Bat	15.00
THO	Trevor Hoffman/Jsy	10.00
THU	Torii Hunter/Bat	15.00
RJ	Randy Johnson/Jsy	20.00
CJ	Chipper Jones/Bat	20.00
JK	Jason Kendall/Jsy	10.00
JKE	Jeff Kent/Jsy	10.00
CK	Chuck Knoblauch/Bat	10.00
PL	Paul LoDuca/Bat	10.00
GM	Greg Maddux/Jsy	20.00
EM	Edgar Martinez/Jsy	10.00
MM	Mark McLemore/Bat	8.00
PM	Raul Mondesi/Bat	8.00
PN	Phil Nevin/Bat	8.00
JO	John Olerud/Jsy	10.00
RP	Rafael Palmeiro/Jsy	12.00
CP	Chan Ho Park/Jsy	8.00
MP	Mike Piazza/Jsy	20.00
JP	Juan Pierre/Jsy	10.00
PP	Placido Polanco/Bat	10.00
AP	Albert Pujols/Bat	25.00
AR	Alex Rodriguez/Jsy	15.00
TS	Tim Salmon/Bat	10.00
CS	Curt Schilling/Jsy	15.00
RS	Richie Sexson/Bat	10.00
GS	Gary Sheffield/Jsy	10.00
TSH	Tsuyoshi Shinjo/Bat	10.00
JS	J.T. Snow/Bat	8.00
AS	Alfonso Soriano/Bat	15.00
SS	Shannon Stewart/Bat	8.00
MS	Mike Sweeney/Bat	15.00
JT	Jim Thome/Bat	20.00
RV	Robin Ventura/Bat	8.00
FV	Fernando Vina/Bat	10.00
OV	Omar Vizquel/Bat	10.00
BW	Billy Wagner/Jsy	10.00
LW	Larry Walker/Bat	10.00
DW	Devon White/Bat	8.00
BZ	Barry Zito/Jsy	10.00

Team Topps Legends Autos.

	NM/M
Common Player:	
Carl Yastrzemski	65.00

2002 Topps Total

		NM/M
Complete Set (990):		125.00
Common Player:		.10
Pack (10):		1.00
Box (36):		30.00
1	Joe Mauer **RC**	5.00
2	Derek Jeter	2.00
3	Shawn Green	.25
4	Vladimir Guerrero	.50
5	Mike Piazza	1.50
6	Brandon Duckworth	.10
7	Aramis Ramirez	.10
8	Josh Barfield	1.00
9	Troy Glaus	.40
10	Sammy Sosa	1.00
11	Rod Barajas	.10
12	Tsuyoshi Shinjo	.25
13	Larry Bigbie	.10
14	Tino Martinez	.10
15	Craig Biggio	.25
16	Anastacio Martinez **RC**	.40
17	John McDonald	.10
18	Kyle Kane **RC**	.30
19	Aubrey Huff	.10
20	Juan Cruz	.10
21	Doug Creek	.10
22	Luther Hackman	.10
23	Rafael Furcal	.10
24	Andres Torres	.10
25	Jason Giambi	.50
26	Jose Paniagua	.10
27	Jose Offerman	.10
28	Alex Arias	.10
29	J.M. Gold	.10
30	Jeff Bagwell	.50
31	Brent Cookson **RC**	.20
32	Kelly Wunsch	.10
33	Larry Walker	.25
34	Luis Gonzalez	.25
35	John Franco	.10
36	Roy Oswalt	.25
37	Tom Glavine	.25
38	C.C. Sabathia	.10
39	Jay Gibbons	.10
40	Wilson Betemit	.10
41	Tony Armas	.10
42	Mo Vaughn	.10
43	Gerard Oakes **RC**	.40
44	Dmitri Young	.10
45	Tim Salmon	.10
46	Barry Zito	.10
47	Adrian Gonzalez	.10
48	Joe Davenport	.10
49	Adrian Hernandez	.10
50	Randy Johnson	.50
51	Benito Baez	.10
52	Adam Pettyjohn	.10
53	Alex Escobar	.10
54	Stevenson Agosto **RC**	.25
55	Omar Daal	.10
56	Mike Buddie	.10
57	Dave Williams	.10
58	Marquis Grissom	.10
59	Pat Burrell	.25
60	Mark Prior	2.00
61	Mike Bynum	.10
62	Mike Hill **RC**	.25
63	Brandon Backe **RC**	.25
64	Dan Wilson	.10
65	Nick Johnson	.10
66	Jason Grimsley	.10
67	Russ Johnson	.10
68	Todd Walker	.10
69	Kyle Farnsworth	.10
70	Ben Broussard	.10
71	Garrett Guzman **RC**	.50
72	Terry Mulholland	.10
73	Tyler Houston	.10
74	Jace Brewer	.10
75	Chris Baker **RC**	.25
76	Frank Catalanotto	.10
77	Mike Redmond	.10
78	Matt Wise	.10
79	Fernando Vina	.10
80	Kevin Brown	.10
81	Grant Balfour	.10
82	Clint Nageotte **RC**	.75
83	Jeff Tam	.10
84	Steve Trachsel	.10
85	Tomokazu Ohka	.10
86	Keith McDonald	.10
87	Jose Ortiz	.10
88	Rusty Greer	.10
89	Jeff Suppan	.10
90	Moises Alou	.10
91	Juan Encarnacion	.10
92	Tyler Yates **RC**	.40
93	Scott Strickland	.10
94	Brent Butler	.10
95	Jon Rauch	.10
96	Brian Mallette **RC**	.25
97	Joe Randa	.10
98	Cesar Crespo	.10
99	Felix Rodriguez	.10
100	Chipper Jones	.75
101	Victor Martinez	.10
102	Danny Graves	.10
103	Brandon Berger **RC**	.10
104	Carlos Garcia	.10
105	Alfonso Soriano	.75
106	Allan Simpson **RC**	.25
107	Brad Thomas	.10
108	Devon White	.10
109	Scott Chiasson	.10
110	Cliff Floyd	.10
111	Scott Williamson	.10
112	Julio Zuleta	.10
113	Terry Adams	.10
114	Zach Day	.10
115	Ben Grieve	.10
116	Mark Ellis	.10
117	Bobby Jenks **RC**	.75
118	LaTroy Hawkins	.10
119	Tim Raines Jr.	.10
120	Juan Uribe	.10
121	Bob Scanlan	.10
122	Brad Nelson **RC**	1.50
123	Adam Johnson	.10
124	Raul Casanova	.10
125	Jeff D'Amico	.10
126	Aaron Cook **RC**	.50
127	Alan Benes	.10
128	Mark Little	.10
129	Randy Wolf	.10
130	Phil Nevin	.10
131	Guillermo Mota	.10
132	Nick Neugebauer	.10
133	Pedro Borbon	.10
134	Doug Mientkiewicz	.10

135 Edgardo Alfonzo .10
136 Dustan Mohr .10
137 Dan Reichert .10
138 Dewon Brazelton .10
139 Orlando Cabrera .10
140 Todd Hollandsworth .10
141 Darren Dreifort .10
142 Jose Valentin .10
143 Josh Kalinowski .10
144 Randy Keisler .10
145 Bret Boone .10
146 Roosevelt Brown .10
147 Brent Abernathy .10
148 Jorge Julio .10
149 Alex Gonzalez .10
150 Juan Pierre .10
151 Roger Cedeno .10
152 Javier Vazquez .10
153 Armando Benitez .10
154 Dave Burba .10
155 Brad Penny .10
156 Ryan Jensen .10
157 Jeromy Burnitz .10
158 Matt Childers **RC** .40
159 Wilmy Caceres .10
160 Roger Clemens .10
161 Michael Tejera .10
162 Jason Christiansen .10
163 Pokey Reese .10
164 Ivanon Coffie .10
165 Joaquin Benoit .10
166 Mike Matheny .10
167 Eric Cammack .10
168 Alex Graman .10
169 Brook Fordyce .10
170 Mike Lieberthal .10
171 Giovanni Carrara .10
172 Antonio Perez .10
173 Fernando Tatis .10
174 Jason Bay **RC** 2.00
175 Jason Botts **RC** .50
176 Danys Baez .10
177 Shea Hillenbrand .10
178 Jack Cust .10
179 Clay Bellinger .10
180 Roberto Alomar .10
181 Graeme Lloyd .10
182 Clint Weibl **RC** .40
183 Royce Clayton .10
184 Ben Davis .10
185 Brian Adams .25
186 Jack Wilson .10
187 David Coggin .10
188 Derrick Turnbow .10
189 Vladimir Nunez .10
190 Mariano Rivera .10
191 Wilson Guzman .10
192 Michael Barrett .10
193 Corey Patterson .10
194 Luis Sojo .10
195 Scott Elarton .10
196 Charles Thomas .25
197 Ricky Bottalico .10
198 Wilfredo Rodriguez .10
199 Ricardo Rincon .10
200 John Smoltz .10
201 Travis Miller .10
202 Ben Weber .10
203 T.J. Tucker .10
204 Terry Shumpert .10
205 Bernie Williams .10
206 Russ Ortiz .10
207 Nate Rolison .10
208 Jose Cruz Jr. .10
209 Bill Ortega .10
210 Carl Everett .10
211 Luis Lopez .10
212 Brian Wolfe **RC** .25
213 Doug Davis .10
214 Troy Mattes .10
215 Al Leiter .10
216 Joe Mays .10
217 Bobby Smith .10
218 J.J. Trujillo **RC** .25
219 Hideo Nomo .25
220 Jimmy Rollins .25
221 Bobby Seay .10
222 Mike Thurman .10
223 Bartolo Colon .10
224 Jesus Sanchez .10
225 Ray Durham .10
226 Juan Diaz .10
227 Lee Stevens .10
228 Ben Howard **RC** .75
229 James Moulton .10
230 Paul Quantrill .10
231 Randy Knorr .10
232 Abraham Nunez .10
233 Mike Fetters .10
234 Mario Encarnacion .10
235 Jeremy Fikac .10
236 Travis Lee .10
237 Bob File .10
238 Pete Harnisch .10
239 Randy Galvez **RC** .25
240 Geoff Goetz .10
241 Gary Glover .10
242 Troy Percival .10
243 Lenny Dinardo **RC** .40
244 Jonny Gomes **RC** 2.00
245 Jesus Medrano **RC** .25
246 Rey Ordonez .10
247 Juan Gonzalez .50
248 Jose Guillen .10
249 Franklin German **RC** .25
250 Mike Mussina .40
251 Ugueth Urbina .10
252 Melvin Mora .10
253 Gerald Williams .10
254 Jared Sandberg .10
255 Darrin Fletcher .10
256 A.J. Pierzynski .10
257 Lenny Harris .10
258 Blaine Neal .10
259 Denny Neagle .10
260 Jason Hart .10
261 Henry Mateo .10
262 Rheal Cormier .10
263 Luis Terrero .10
264 Shigetoshi Hasegawa .10
265 Bill Haselman .10
266 Scott Hatteberg .10
267 Adam Hyzdu .10
268 Mike Williams .10
269 Marlon Anderson .10
270 Bruce Chen .10
271 Eli Marrero .10
272 Jimmy Haynes .10
273 Bronson Arroyo .10
274 Kevin Jordan .10
275 Rick Helling .10
276 Mark Loretta .10
277 Dustin Hermanson .10
278 Pablo Ozuna .10
279 Syketo Anderson **RC** .25
280 Jermaine Dye .10
281 Will Smith .10
282 Brian Daubach .10
283 Eric Hinske .10
284 Joe Jiannetti **RC** .40
285 Chan Ho Park .10
286 Curtis Legendre **RC** .25
287 Jeff Reboulet .10
288 Scott Rolen .50
289 Chris Richard .10
290 Eric Chavez .25
291 Scot Shields .10
292 Donnie Sadler .10
293 Dave Veres .10
294 Craig Counsell .10
295 Armando Reynoso .10
296 Kyle Lohse .10
297 Arthur Rhodes .10
298 Sidney Ponson .10
299 Trevor Hoffman .10
300 Kerry Wood .25
301 Danny Bautista .10
302 Scott Sauerbeck .10
303 Johnny Estrada .10
304 Mike Timlin .10
305 Orlando Hernandez .25
306 Tony Clark .10
307 Tomas Perez .10
308 Marcus Giles .10
309 Mike Bordick .10
310 Jorge Posada .25
311 Jason Conti .10
312 Kevin Millar .10
313 Paul Shuey .10
314 Jake Mauer **RC** .75
315 Luke Hudson .10
316 Angel Berroa .10
317 Fred Bastardo **RC** .25
318 Shawn Estes .10
319 Andy Ashby .10
320 Ryan Klesko .10
321 Kevin Appier .10
322 Juan Pena .10
323 Alex Herrera .10
324 Robb Nen .10
325 Orlando Hudson .10
326 Lyle Overbay .10
327 Ben Sheets .25
328 Mike DiFelice .10
329 Pablo Arias **RC** .25
330 Mike Sweeney .10
331 Rick Ankiel .25
332 Tomas De La Rosa .25
333 Kazuhisa Ishii **RC** 1.00
334 Jose Reyes .10
335 Jeremy Giambi .10
336 Jose Mesa .10
337 Ralph Roberts **RC** .25
338 Jose Nunez .10
339 Curt Schilling .40
340 Sean Casey .20
341 Bob Wells .10
342 Carlos Beltran .10
343 Alexis Gomez .10
344 Brandon Claussen .25
345 Buddy Groom .10
346 Mark Phillips **RC** .50
347 Francisco Cordova .10
348 Joe Oliver .10
349 Danny Patterson .10
350 Joel Pineiro .10
351 J.R. House .10
352 Benny Agbayani .10
353 Jose Vidro .10
354 Reed Johnson **RC** .10
355 Mike Lowell .10
356 Scott Schoeneweis .10
357 Brian Jordan .10
358 Steve Finley .10
359 Randy Choate .10
360 Jose Lima .10
361 Miguel Olivo .10
362 Kenny Rogers .10
363 David Justice .20
364 Brandon Knight .10
365 Joe Kennedy .10
366 Eric Valent .10
367 Nelson Cruz .10
368 Brian Giles .25
369 Charles Gibson Jr. .10
370 Juan Pena .10
371 Mark Redman .10
372 Billy Koch .10
373 Ted Lilly .10
374 Craig Paquette .10
375 Kevin Jarvis .10
376 Scott Erickson .10
377 Josh Paul .10
378 Darwin Cubillan .10
379 Nelson Figueroa .10
380 Darin Erstad .20
381 Jeremy Hill **RC** .25
382 Elvin Nina .10
383 David Wells .25
384 Jay Caligiuri **RC** .40
385 Freddy Garcia .10
386 Damian Miller .10
387 Bobby Higginson .10
388 Alejandro Giron **RC** .25
389 Ivan Rodriguez .40
390 Ed Rogers .10
391 Andy Benes .10
392 Matt Blank .10
393 Ryan Vogelsong .10
394 Kelly Ramos **RC** .25
395 Eric Karros .10
396 Bobby Jones .10
397 Omar Vizquel .25
398 Matt Perisho .10
399 Delino DeShields .10
400 Carlos Hernandez .10
401 Derrek Lee .10
402 Kirk Rueter .10
403 David Wright 30.00
404 Paul LoDuca .10
405 Brian Schneider .10
406 Milton Bradley .10
407 Daryle Ward .10
408 Cody Ransom .10
409 Fernando Rodney .10
410 John Suomi **RC** .20
411 Joe Girardi .10
412 Demetrius Heath **RC** .25
413 John Foster **RC** .25
414 Doug Glanville .10
415 Ryan Kohlmeier .10
416 Mike Matthews .10
417 Craig Wilson .10
418 Jay Witasick .10
419 Jay Payton .10
420 Andruw Jones .40
421 Benji Gil .10
422 Jeff Liefer .10
423 Kevin Young .10
424 Richie Sexson .25
425 Cory Lidle .10
426 Shane Halter .10
427 Jesse Foppert .40
428 Jose Molina .10
429 Nick Alvarez **RC** .40
430 Brian L. Hunter .10
431 Clifford Bartosh **RC** .25
432 Junior Spivey .10
433 Eric Good **RC** .25
434 Chin-Feng Chen .10
435 T.J. Mathews .10
436 Rich Rodriguez .10
437 Bobby Abreu .20
438 Joe McEwing .10
439 Michael Tucker .10
440 Preston Wilson .10
441 Mike MacDougal .10
442 Shannon Stewart .10
443 Bob Howry .10
444 Mike Benjamin .10
445 Erik Hiljus .10
446 Ryan Gripp **RC** .25
447 Jose Vizcaino .10
448 Shawn Wooten .10
449 Steve Kent **RC** .25
450 Ramiro Mendoza .10
451 Jake Westbrook .10
452 Joe Lawrence .10
453 Jae Weong Seo .10
454 Ryan Fry **RC** .20
455 Darren Lewis .10
456 Brad Wilkerson .10
457 Gustavo Chacin **RC** .25
458 Adrian Brown .10
459 Mike Cameron .10
460 Bud Smith .10
461 Derrick Lewis .10
462 Derek Lowe .10
463 Matt Williams .10
464 Jason Jennings .10
465 Albie Lopez .10
466 Felipe Lopez .10
467 Luke Allen .10
468 Brian Anderson .10
469 Matt Riley .10
470 Ryan Dempster .10
471 Matt Ginter .10
472 David Ortiz .10
473 Cole Barthel .10
474 Damian Jackson .10
475 Andy Van Hekken .10
476 Doug Brocail .10
477 Denny Hocking .10
478 Sean Douglass .10
479 Eric Owens .10
480 Ryan Ludwick .10
481 Todd Pratt .10
482 Aaron Sele .10
483 Edgar Renteria .10
484 Raymond Cabrera **RC** .25
485 Brandon Lyon .10
486 Chase Utley .75
487 Robert Fick .10
488 Wilfredo Cordero .10
489 Octavio Dotel .10
490 Paul Abbott .10
491 Jason Kendall .10
492 Jarrod Washburn .10
493 Dane Sardinha .10
494 Jung Bong .10
495 J.D. Drew .10
496 Jason Schmidt .10
497 Mike Magnante .10
498 Jorge Padilla **RC** .50
499 Eric Gagne .10
500 Todd Helton .50
501 Jeff Weaver .10
502 Alex Sanchez .10
503 Ken Griffey Jr. .10
504 Abraham Nunez .10
505 Reggie Sanders .10
506 Casey Kotchman 2.00
507 Jim Mann .10
508 Matt LeCroy .10
509 Frank Castillo .10
510 Geoff Jenkins .20
511 Jayson Durocher **RC** .20
512 Ellis Burks .10
513 Aaron Fultz .10
514 Hiram Bocachica .10
515 Nate Espy **RC** .10
516 Placido Polanco .10
517 Kerry Ligtenberg .10
518 Doug Nickle .10
519 Ramon Ortiz .10
520 Greg Swindell .10
521 J.J. Davis .10
522 Sandy Alomar .10
523 Chris Carpenter .10
524 Vance Wilson .10
525 Nomar Garciaparra 1.00
526 Jim Mecir .10
527 Taylor Buchholz **RC** .25
528 Brent Mayne .10
529 John Rodriguez **RC** .25
530 David Segui .10
531 Nate Cornejo .10
532 Gil Heredia .10
533 Esteban Loaiza .10
534 Pat Mahomes .10
535 Matt Morris .20
536 Todd Stottlemyre .10
537 Brian Lesher .10
538 Arturo McDowell .10
539 Felix Diaz .10
540 Mark Mulder .10
541 Kevin Frederick **RC** .25
542 Andy Fox .10
543 Dionys Cesar **RC** .10
544 Justin Miller .10
545 Keith Osik .10
546 Shane Reynolds .10
547 Mike Myers .10
548 Raul Chavez **RC** .25
549 Joe Nathan .10
550 Ryan Anderson .10
551 Jason Marquis .10
552 Marty Cordova .10
553 Kevin Tapani .10
554 Jimmy Anderson .10
555 Pedro Martinez .50
556 Rocky Biddle .10
557 Alex Ochoa .10
558 D'Angelo Jimenez .10
559 Wilkin Ruan .10
560 Terrence Long .10
561 Mark Lukasiewicz .10
562 Jose Santiago .10
563 Brad Fullmer .10
564 Corky Miller .10
565 Matt White .10
566 Mark Grace .30
567 Raul Ibanez .10
568 Josh Towers .10
569 Juan Gonzalez .40
570 Brian Buchanan .10
571 Ken Harvey .10
572 Jeffrey Hammonds .10
573 Wade Miller .10
574 Elpidio Guzman .10
575 Kevin Olsen .10
576 Austin Kearns .40
577 Tim Kalita **RC** .40
578 David Dellucci .10
579 Alex Gonzalez .10
580 Joe Orloski **RC** .20
581 Gary Matthews Jr. .10
582 Ryan Mills .10
583 Erick Almonte .10
584 Jeremy Affeldt .10
585 Chris Tritle **RC** 1.00
586 Michael Cuddyer .10
587 Kris Foster .10
588 Russell Branyan .10
589 Darren Oliver .10
590 Freddie Money **RC** .25
591 Carlos Lee .10
592 Tim Wakefield .10
593 Bubba Trammell .10
594 John Koronka **RC** 3.00

595 Geoff Blum .10
596 Darryl Kile .10
597 Neifi Perez .10
598 Torii Hunter .10
599 Luis Castillo .10
600 Mark Buehrle .10
601 Jeff Zimmerman .10
602 Mike DeJean .10
603 Julio Lugo .10
604 Chad Hermansen .10
605 Keith Foulke .10
606 Lance Davis .10
607 Jeff Austin **RC** .25
608 Brandon Inge .10
609 Orlando Merced .10
610 Johnny Damon .10
611 Doug Henry .10
612 Adam Kennedy .10
613 Wiki Gonzalez .10
614 Brian West **RC** .25
615 Andy Pettitte .25
616 Chone Figgins **RC** .25
617 Matt Lawton .10
618 Paul Rigdon .10
619 Keith Lockhart .10
620 Tim Redding .10
621 John Parrish .10
622 Chad Hutchinson .10
623 Todd Greene .10
624 David Eckstein .10
625 Greg Montalbano **RC** 1.00
626 Joe Beimel .10
627 Adrian Beltre .20
628 Charles Nagy .10
629 Cristian Guzman .10
630 Toby Hall .10
631 Jose Hernandez .10
632 Jose Macias .10
633 Jaret Wright .10
634 Steve Parris .10
635 Gene Kingsdale .10
636 Tim Worrell .10
637 Billy Martin .10
638 Jovanny Cedeno .10
639 Curt Leskanic .10
640 Tim Hudson .20
641 Juan Castro .10
642 Rafael Soriano .10
643 Juan Rincon .10
644 Mark DeRosa .10
645 Carlos Pena .10
646 Robin Ventura .20
647 Odalis Perez .10
648 Damion Easley .10
649 Benito Santiago .10
650 Alex Rodriguez 1.50
651 Aaron Rowand .10
652 Alex Cora .10
653 Bobby Kielty .10
654 Jose Rodriguez .10
655 Herbert Perry .10
656 Jeff Urban .10
657 Paul Bako .10
658 Shane Spencer .10
659 Pat Hentgen .10
660 Jeff Kent .20
661 Mark McLemore .10
662 Chuck Knoblauch .10
663 Blake Stein .10
664 Brett Roneberg **RC** .25
665 Josh Phelps .10
666 Byung-Hyun Kim .10
667 Dave Martinez .10
668 Mike Maroth .10
669 Shawn Chacon .10
670 Billy Wagner .10
671 Luis Alicea .10
672 Sterling Hitchcock .10
673 Adam Piatt .10
674 Ryan Franklin .10
675 Luke Prokopec .10
676 Alfredo Amezega .10
677 Gookie Dawkins .10
678 Eric Byrnes .10
679 Barry Larkin .25
680 Albert Pujols 1.00
681 Edwards Guzman .10
682 Jason Bere .10
683 Adam Everett .10
684 Greg Colbrunn .10
685 Brandon Puffer **RC** .40
686 Mark Kotsay .10
687 Willie Bloomquist .10
688 Hank Blalock .25
689 Travis Hafner .10
690 Lance Berkman .40
691 Joe Crede .10
692 Chuck Finley .10
693 John Grabow .10
694 Randy Winn .10
695 Mike James .10
696 Kris Benson .10
697 Bret Prinz .10
698 Jeff Williams .10
699 Eric Munson .10
700 Mike Hampton .10
701 Ramon E. Martinez .10
702 Hansel Izquierdo **RC** .25
703 Nathan Haynes .10
704 Eddie Taubensee .10
705 Esteban German .10
706 Ross Gload .10
707 Matthew Merricks **RC** .20
708 Chris Piersoll **RC** .25
709 Seth Greisinger .10
710 Ichiro Suzuki 1.00
711 Cesar Izturis .10
712 Brad Cresse .10
713 Carl Pavano .10
714 Steve Sparks .10
715 Dennis Tankersley .10
716 Kelvim Escobar .10
717 Jason LaRue .10
718 Corey Koskie .10
719 Vinny Castilla .10
720 Tim Drew .10
721 Chin-Hui Tsao .10
722 Paul Byrd .10
723 Alex Cintron .10
724 Orlando Palmeiro .10
725 Ramon Hernandez .10
726 Mark Johnson .10
727 B.J. Ryan .10
728 Wendell Magee .10
729 Michael Coleman .10
730 Mario Ramos .50
731 Mike Stanton .10
732 Dee Brown .10
733 Brad Ausmus .10
734 Napoleon Calzado **RC** .25
735 Woody Williams .10
736 Paxton Crawford .10
737 Jason Karnuth .10
738 Michael Restovich .10
739 Ramon Castro .10
740 Magglio Ordonez .25
741 Tom Gordon .10
742 Mark Grudzielanek .10
743 Jamie Moyer .10
744 Marlyn Tisdale **RC** .20
745 Steve Kline .10
746 Adam Eaton .10
747 Eric Glaser **RC** .25
748 Sean DePaula .10
749 Greg Norton .10
750 Steve Reed .10
751 Ricardo Aramboles .10
752 Matt Mantei .10
753 Gene Stechschulte .10
754 Chuck McElroy .10
755 Barry Bonds 1.50
756 Matt Anderson .10
757 Yorvit Torrealba .10
758 Jason Standridge .10
759 Desi Relaford .10
760 Jolbert Cabrera .10
761 Chris George .10
762 Erubiel Durazo .10
763 Paul Konerko .25
764 Tike Redman .10
765 Chad Ricketts **RC** .20
766 Roberto Hernandez .10
767 Mark Lewis .10
768 Livan Hernandez .10
769 Carlos Brackley **RC** .25
770 Kazuhiro Sasaki .10
771 Bill Hall .10
772 Nelson Castro **RC** .25
773 Eric Milton .10
774 Tom Davey .10
775 Todd Ritchie .10
776 Seth Etherton .10
777 Chris Singleton .10
778 Robert Averette **RC** .20
779 Robert Person .10
780 Fred McGriff .25
781 Richard Hidalgo .10
782 Kris Wilson .10
783 John Rocker .10
784 Justin Kaye .10
785 Glendon Rusch .10
786 Greg Vaughn .10
787 Mike Lamb .10
788 Greg Myers .10
789 Nate Field **RC** .25
790 Jim Edmonds .25
791 Olmedo Saenz .10
792 Jason Johnson .10
793 Mike Lincoln .10
794 Todd Coffey .10
795 Jesus Sanchez .10
796 Aaron Myette .10
797 Tony Womack .10
798 Chad Kreuter .10
799 Brady Clark .10
800 Adam Dunn .50
801 Jacque Jones .10
802 Kevin Millwood .10
803 Mike Rivera .10
804 Jim Thome .40
805 Jeff Conine .10
806 Elmer Dessens .10
807 Randy Velarde .10
808 Carlos Delgado .30
809 Steve Karsay .10
810 Casey Fossum .10
811 J.C. Romero .10
812 Chris Truby .10
813 Tony Graffanino .10
814 Wascar Serrano .10
815 Delvin James .10
816 Pedro Feliz .10
817 Damian Rolls .10
818 Scott Linebrink .10
819 Rafael Palmeiro .40
820 Javy Lopez .10
821 Larry Barnes .10
822 Brian Lawrence .10
823 Scotty Layfield **RC** .25
824 Jeff Cirillo .10
825 Willis Roberts .10
826 Rich Harden **RC** 4.00
827 Chris Snelling **RC** 1.00
828 Gary Sheffield .25
829 Jeff Heaverlo .10
830 Matt Clement .10
831 Rich Garces .10
832 Rondell White .10
833 Henry Pichardo **RC** .25
834 Aaron Boone .10
835 Ruben Sierra .10
836 Deivis Santos .10
837 Tony Batista .10
838 Rob Bell .10
839 Frank Thomas .50
840 Jose Silva .10
841 Dan Johnson **RC** .50
842 Steve Cox .10
843 Jose Acevedo .10
844 Jay Bell .10
845 Mike Sirotka .10
846 Garret Anderson .10
847 James Shanks **RC** .25
848 Trot Nixon .10
849 Keith Ginter .10
850 Tim Spooneybarger .10
851 Matt Stairs .10
852 Chris Stynes .10
853 Marvin Bernard .10
854 Raul Mondesi .20
855 Jeremy Owens .10
856 Jon Garland .10
857 Mitch Meluskey .10
858 Chad Durbin .10
859 John Burkett .10
860 Jon Switzer .10
861 Peter Bergeron .10
862 Jesus Colome .10
863 Todd Hundley .10
864 Ben Petrick .10
865 So Taguchi **RC** .75
866 Ryan Drese .10
867 Mike Trombley .10
868 Rick Reed .10
869 Mark Teixeira .20
870 Corey Thurman **RC** .10
871 Brian Roberts .10
872 Mike Timlin .10
873 Chris Reitsma .10
874 Jeff Fassero .10
875 Carlos Valderrama .10
876 John Lackey .10
877 Travis Fryman .10
878 Ismael Valdes .10
879 Rick White .10
880 Edgar Martinez .10
881 Dean Palmer .10
882 Matt Allegra **RC** .20
883 Greg Sain **RC** .25
884 Carlos Silva .10
885 Jose Valverde **RC** .25
886 Dernell Stenson .10
887 Todd Van Poppel .10
888 Wes Anderson .10
889 Bill Mueller .10
890 Morgan Ensberg .10
891 Marcus Thames .10
892 Adam Walker **RC** .10
893 John Halama .10
894 Frank Menechino .10
895 Greg Maddux 1.00
896 Gary Bennett .10
897 Mauricio Lara **RC** .25
898 Mike Young .10
899 Travis Phelps .10
900 Rich Aurilia .10
901 Henry Blanco .10
902 Carlos Febles .10
903 Scott MacRae .10
904 Lou Merloni .10
905 Dicky Gonzalez .10
906 Jeff DaVanon .10
907 A.J. Burnett .10
908 Einar Diaz .10
909 Julio Franco .10
910 John Olerud .25
911 Mark Hamilton **RC** .25
912 David Riske .10
913 Jason Tyner .10
914 Britt Reames .10
915 Vernon Wells .10
916 Eddie Perez .10
917 Edwin Almonte **RC** .25
918 Enrique Wilson .10
919 Chris Gomez .10
920 Jayson Werth .10
921 Jeff Nelson .10
922 Freddy Sanchez **RC** .75
923 John Vander Wal .10
924 Chad Qualls **RC** .25
925 Gabe White .10
926 Chad Harville .10
927 Ricky Gutierrez .10
928 Carlos Guillen .10
929 B.J. Surhoff .10
930 Chris Woodard .10
931 Ricardo Rodriguez .10
932 Jimmy Gobble **RC** 1.00
933 Jon Lieber .10
934 Craig Kuzmic **RC** .25
935 Eric Young .10
936 Gregg Zaun .10
937 Miguel Batista .10
938 Danny Wright .10
939 Todd Zeile .10
940 Chad Zerbe .10
941 Jason Young **RC** .50
942 Ronnie Belliard .10
943 John Ennis **RC** .10
944 John Flaherty .10
945 Jerry Hairston Jr. .10
946 Al Levine .10
947 Antonio Alfonseca .10
948 Brian Moehler .10
949 Calvin Murray .10
950 Nick Bierbrodt .10
951 Sun-Woo Kim .10
952 Noochie Varner **RC** .50
953 Luis Rivas .10
954 Donnie Bridges .10
955 Ramon Vazquez .10
956 Luis Garcia .10
957 Mark Quinn .10
958 Armando Rios .10
959 Chad Fox .10
960 Hee Seop Choi .10
961 Turk Wendell .10
962 Adam Roller **RC** .20
963 Grant Roberts .10
964 Ben Molina .10
965 Juan Rivera .10
966 Matt Kinney .10
967 Rod Beck .10
968 Xavier Nady .10
969 Masato Yoshii .10
970 Miguel Tejada .25
971 Danny Kolb .10
972 Mike Remlinger .10
973 Ray Lankford .10
974 Ryan Minor .10
975 J.T. Snow .10
976 Brad Radke .10
977 Jason Lane .10
978 Jamey Wright .10
979 Tom Goodwin .10
980 Erik Bedard .10
981 Gabe Kapler .10
982 Brian Reith .10
983 Nic Jackson **RC** .50
984 Kurt Ainsworth .10
985 Jason Isringhausen .10
986 Willie Harris .10
987 David Cone .10
988 Bob Wickman .10
989 Wes Helms .10
990 Josh Beckett .25

Award Winners

	NM/M
Complete Set (30):	25.00
Common Player:	.50
Inserted 1:6	
AW1 Ichiro Suzuki	2.00
AW2 Albert Pujols	2.00
AW3 Barry Bonds	3.00
AW4 Ichiro Suzuki	2.00
AW5 Randy Johnson	1.00
AW6 Roger Clemens	2.00
AW7 Jason Giambi	.75
AW8 Bret Boone	.50
AW9 Troy Glaus	.75
AW10 Alex Rodriguez	2.50
AW11 Juan Gonzalez	.75
AW12 Ichiro Suzuki	2.00
AW13 Jorge Posada	.75
AW14 Edgar Martinez	.50
AW15 Todd Helton	.75
AW16 Jeff Kent	.50
AW17 Albert Pujols	2.00
AW18 Rich Aurilia	.50
AW19 Barry Bonds	3.00
AW20 Luis Gonzalez	.50
AW21 Sammy Sosa	2.00
AW22 Mike Piazza	2.00
AW23 Mike Hampton	.50
AW24 Ruben Sierra	.50
AW25 Matt Morris	.50
AW26 Curt Schilling	.75
AW27 Alex Rodriguez	2.50
AW28 Barry Bonds	3.00
AW29 Jim Thome	1.00
AW30 Barry Bonds	3.00

Total Production

	NM/M
Complete Set (10):	15.00

Common Player: .75
Inserted 1:12
TP1	Alex Rodriguez	3.00
TP2	Barry Bonds	3.00
TP3	Ichiro Suzuki	2.00
TP4	Edgar Martinez	.75
TP5	Jason Giambi	1.00
TP6	Todd Helton	1.00
TP7	Nomar Garciaparra	2.50
TP8	Vladimir Guerrero	1.00
TP9	Sammy Sosa	2.00
TP10	Chipper Jones	2.00

Total Topps

MAGGLIO ORDONEZ

NM/M
Complete Set (50): 35.00
Common Player: .50
Inserted 1:3
TT1	Roberto Alomar	.75
TT2	Moises Alou	.50
TT3	Jeff Bagwell	1.00
TT4	Lance Berkman	.75
TT5	Barry Bonds	2.00
TT6	Bret Boone	.50
TT7	Kevin Brown	.50
TT8	Eric Chavez	.50
TT9	Roger Clemens	1.50
TT10	Carlos Delgado	.50
TT11	Cliff Floyd	.50
TT12	Nomar Garciaparra	2.50
TT13	Jason Giambi	1.00
TT14	Brian Giles	.75
TT15	Troy Glaus	.75
TT16	Tom Glavine	.50
TT17	Luis Gonzalez	.50
TT18	Juan Gonzalez	.75
TT19	Shawn Green	.50
TT20	Ken Griffey Jr.	2.50
TT21	Ivan Rodriguez	1.00
TT22	Jorge Posada	.50
TT23	Todd Helton	.50
TT24	Tim Hudson	.50
TT25	Derek Jeter	4.00
TT26	Randy Johnson	1.00
TT27	Andruw Jones	.75
TT28	Chipper Jones	2.00
TT29	Jeff Kent	.50
TT30	Greg Maddux	2.00
TT31	Edgar Martinez	.50
TT32	Pedro Martinez	1.00
TT33	Magglio Ordonez	.50
TT34	Rafael Palmeiro	.50
TT35	Mike Piazza	3.00
TT36	Albert Pujols	2.00
TT37	Aramis Ramirez	.50
TT38	Mariano Rivera	.50
TT39	Alex Rodriguez	3.00
TT40	Ivan Rodriguez	.75
TT41	Curt Schilling	.75
TT42	Gary Sheffield	.50
TT43	Sammy Sosa	2.00
TT44	Ichiro Suzuki	4.00
TT45	Miguel Tejada	.50
TT46	Frank Thomas	1.00
TT47	Jim Thome	.75
TT48	Larry Walker	.50
TT49	Bernie Williams	.50
TT50	Kerry Wood	.50

2002 Topps Tribute

NM/M
Complete Set (90): 120.00
Common Player: 1.50
Pack (5): 35.00
Box (6): 150.00
1	Hank Aaron	6.00
2	Rogers Hornsby	2.50
3	Bobby Thomson	1.50
4	Eddie Collins	1.50
5	Joe Carter	1.50
6	Jim Palmer	1.50
7	Willie Mays	6.00
8	Willie Stargell	2.50
9	Vida Blue	1.50
10	Whitey Ford	3.00
11	Bob Gibson	3.00
12	Nellie Fox	2.00
13	Napoleon Lajoie	2.00
14	Frankie Frisch	1.50
15	Nolan Ryan	10.00
16	Brooks Robinson	2.50
17	Kirby Puckett	5.00

18	Fergie Jenkins	1.50
19	Edd Roush	1.50
20	Honus Wagner	6.00
21	Richie Ashburn	1.50
22	Bob Feller	1.50
23	Joe Morgan	1.50
24	Orlando Cepeda	1.50
25	Steve Garvey	1.50
26	Hank Greenberg	1.50
27	Stan Musial	5.00
28	Sam Crawford	1.50
29	Jim Rice	1.50
30	Hack Wilson	2.50
31	Lou Brock	1.50
32	Mickey Vernon	1.50
33	Chuck Klein	1.50
34	Joe Jackson	6.00
35	Duke Snider	3.00
36	Ryne Sandberg	5.00
37	Johnny Bench	5.00
38	Sam Rice	1.50
39	Lou Gehrig	8.00
40	Robin Yount	3.00
41	Don Sutton	1.50
42	Jim Bottomley	1.50
43	Billy Herman	1.50
44	Zach Wheat	1.50
45	Juan Marichal	1.50
46	Bert Blyleven	1.50
47	Jackie Robinson	6.00
48	Gil Hodges	1.50
49	Mike Schmidt	6.00
50	Dale Murphy	1.50
51	Phil Rizzuto	1.50
52	Ty Cobb	6.00
53	Andre Dawson	1.50
54	Fred Lindstrom	1.50
55	Roy Campanella	3.00
56	Don Larsen	2.00
57	Harry Heilmann	1.50
58	Jim "Catfish" Hunter	1.50
59	Frank Robinson	2.00
60	Bill Mazeroski	1.50
61	Roger Maris	6.00
62	Dave Winfield	2.50
63	Warren Spahn	2.50
64	Babe Ruth	10.00
65	Ernie Banks	4.00
66	Wade Boggs	2.00
67	Carl Yastrzemski	3.00
68	Ron Santo	1.50
69	Dennis Martinez	1.50
70	Yogi Berra	4.00
71	Paul Waner	1.50
72	George Brett	6.00
73	Eddie Mathews	3.00
74	Bill Dickey	1.50
75	Carlton Fisk	2.00
76	Thurman Munson	5.00
77	Reggie Jackson	4.00
78	Phil Niekro	1.50
79	Luis Aparicio	1.50
80	Steve Carlton	1.50
81	Tris Speaker	1.50
82	Johnny Mize	1.50
83	Tom Seaver	4.00
84	Heinie Manush	1.50
85	Tommy John	1.50
86	Joe Cronin	1.50
87	Don Mattingly	8.00
88	Kirk Gibson	1.50
89	Bo Jackson	3.00
90	Mel Ott	1.50

First Impressions

Cards #'d 51-86: 3-5X
Cards #'d 26-50: 4-8X
#'d to last two digits of Rk year
Lasting Impressions
Cards #'d 51-96: 3-5X
Cards #'d 26-50: 4-8X
#'d to last two digits of final season
Production under 25 not priced.

Marks of Excellence

NM/M
Inserted 1:61
LB	Lou Brock	50.00
SC	Steve Carlton	50.00
DL	Don Larsen	50.00
SM	Stan Musial	100.00

MS	Mike Schmidt	85.00
WS	Warren Spahn	65.00

Marks of Excellence Relics

NM/M
Inserted 1:61
FJ	Fergie Jenkins	40.00
DM	Don Mattingly	120.00
JP	Jim Palmer	40.00
BR	Brooks Robinson	75.00
DS	Duke Snider	60.00
RY	Robin Yount	70.00

Matching Marks Dual

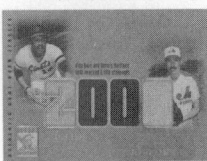

NM/M
Common Card: 10.00
Inserted 1:11
SBA	Ron Santo, Ernie Banks	25.00
YK	Carl Yastrzemski, Chuck Klein	65.00
WY	Dave Winfield, Carl Yastrzemski	25.00
WYO	Dave Winfield, Robin Yount	20.00
SM	Duke Snider, Willie Mays	85.00
RJ	Frank Robinson, Reggie Jackson	50.00
BMA	George Brett, Don Mattingly	90.00
GH	Steve Garvey, Gil Hodges	20.00
AR	Hank Aaron, Babe Ruth	300.00
GA	Hank Greenberg, Richie Ashburn	80.00
PJ	Jim Palmer, Tommy John	20.00
NS	Phil Niekro, Tom Seaver	15.00
SR	Willie Stargell, Jim Rice	15.00
BF	Johnny Bench, Carlton Fisk	50.00
RS	Nolan Ryan, Tom Seaver	125.00
JS	Fergie Jenkins, Tom Seaver	35.00
YP	Robin Yount, Kirby Puckett	60.00
SB	Tris Speaker, George Brett	100.00
BM	Vida Blue, Dennis Martinez	10.00
BB	Wade Boggs, George Brett	40.00
MA	Willie Mays, Hank Aaron	200.00
BS	Bert Blyleven, Don Sutton	15.00

Memorable Materials

NM/M
Common Player: 10.00
Season parallel: 1.5-3X
#'d to last two digits yr event occurred
Jsy Number para.#'d 40-75: 1.5-3X
Under 40 not priced.
Numbered to jersey #.
HA	Hank Aaron	40.00
GB	George Brett	35.00
RC	Roy Campanella	30.00
JC	Joe Carter	10.00
CF	Carlton Fisk	20.00
KG	Kirk Gibson	15.00
BJ	Bo Jackson	25.00
RJ	Reggie Jackson	20.00
CK	Chuck Klein	25.00
RM	Roger Maris	75.00
DM	Don Mattingly	40.00
BM	Bill Mazeroski	15.00
JM	Joe Morgan	15.00
TM	Thurman Munson	50.00
KP	Kirby Puckett	30.00
PR	Phil Rizzuto	25.00
JR	Jackie Robinson	50.00
NR	Nolan Ryan	50.00
BT	Bobby Thomson	15.00
HW	Hack Wilson	40.00
CY	Carl Yastrzemski	30.00

Milestone Materials

NM/M
Common Player: 10.00
Inserted 1:4
Season parallel #'d 51-95: 1.5-3X
#'d to last two digits milestone season
Jersey Number par.#'d 51-95: 1.5-3X
Numbered to Jersey Number.
Under 50 not priced yet.
LA	Luis Aparicio	15.00
EB	Ernie Banks	30.00
JB	Johnny Bench	20.00
YB	Yogi Berra	25.00
WB	Wade Boggs	15.00
JBO	Jim Bottomley	20.00
OC	Orlando Cepeda	15.00
TC	Ty Cobb	150.00
EC	Eddie Collins	30.00
SC	Sam Crawford	25.00
JC	Joe Cronin	20.00
AD	Andre Dawson	15.00
BD	Bill Dickey	15.00
BF	Bob Feller	15.00
WF	Whitey Ford	25.00
NF	Nellie Fox	30.00
FF	Frankie Frisch	25.00
LG	Lou Gehrig	150.00
BG	Bob Gibson	25.00
HH	Harry Heilmann	20.00
BH	Billy Herman	10.00
RH	Rogers Hornsby	50.00
CH	Jim "Catfish" Hunter	12.00
RJ	Reggie Jackson	60.00
NL	Napoleon Lajoie	60.00
FL	Fred Lindstrom	20.00
HM	Heinie Manush	20.00
JMA	Juan Marichal	15.00
EM	Eddie Mathews	20.00
WH	Willie Mays	45.00
JM	Johnny Mize	15.00
DM	Dale Murphy	15.00
MO	Mel Ott	40.00
JP	Jim Palmer	15.00
SR	Sam Rice	20.00
BRO	Brooks Robinson	20.00
FR	Frank Robinson	20.00
ER	Edd Roush	15.00
BR	Babe Ruth	160.00
NR	Nolan Ryan	50.00
RS	Ryne Sandberg	30.00
TS	Tom Seaver	15.00
DS	Duke Snider	20.00
TSP	Tris Speaker	65.00
WS	Willie Stargell	20.00
MV	Mickey Vernon	15.00
HW	Honus Wagner	140.00
PW	Paul Waner	30.00
ZW	Zach Wheat	40.00
RY	Robin Yount	25.00

Pasttime Patches

NM/M
Inserted 1:92
JB	Johnny Bench	125.00
WB	Wade Boggs	90.00
GB	George Brett	200.00
BD	Bill Dickey	100.00
EM	Eddie Mathews	125.00
DM	Don Mattingly	160.00
JP	Jim Palmer	75.00
KP	Kirby Puckett	125.00
NRA	Nolan Ryan	200.00
NRR	Nolan Ryan	200.00
DW	Dave Winfield	100.00
CY	Carl Yastrzemski	180.00
RY	Robin Yount	100.00

"The Catch" Dual

NM/M
Inserted 1:1,023
MW	Willie Mays, Vic Wertz	250.00
MW	Willie Mays, Vic Wertz/54	300.00

Signature Cuts

NM/M
Reported production two each.
Inserted 1:9936

SC-TC Ty Cobb (4/04 Auction) 4,725

2002 Topps206

	NM/M
Complete Set (456):	150.00
Common Player:	.20
Common (141-155, 271-285):	1.00
Inserted 1:2	
Series I Pack (8):	6.00
Series I Box (20):	100.00
Series II Pack (8):	4.00
Series II Box (20):	60.00
Series III Pack (8):	6.00
Series III Box (20):	100.00

1	Vladimir Guerrero	.75
2	Sammy Sosa	1.50
3	Garret Anderson	.40
4	Rafael Palmeiro	.50
5	Juan Gonzalez	.50
6	John Smoltz	.40
7	Mark Mulder	.40
8	Jon Lieber	.20
9	Greg Maddux	1.00
10	Moises Alou	.40
11	Joe Randa	.20
12	Bobby Abreu	.40
13	Ryan Kohlmeier	.20
14	Kerry Wood	.75
15	Craig Biggio	.40
16	Curt Schilling	.50
17	Brian Jordan	.20
18	Edgardo Alfonzo	.20
19	Darren Dreifort	.20
20	Todd Helton	.50
21	Ramon Ortiz	.20
22	Ichiro Suzuki	1.50
23	Jimmy Rollins	.50
24	Darin Erstad	.40
25	Shawn Green	.40
26	Tino Martinez	.30
27	Bret Boone	.40
28	Alfonso Soriano	.75
29	Chan Ho Park	.40
30	Roger Clemens	1.50
31	Cliff Floyd	.20
32	Johnny Damon	.40
33	Frank Thomas	.50
34	Barry Bonds	2.00
35	Luis Gonzalez	.40
36	Carlos Lee	.20
37	Roberto Alomar	.50
38	Carlos Delgado	.50
39	Nomar Garciaparra	1.50
40	Jason Kendall	.40
41	Scott Rolen	.75
42	Tom Glavine	.40
43	Ryan Klesko	.20
44	Brian Giles	.40
45	Bud Smith	.20
46	Charles Nagy	.20
47	Tony Gwynn	.75
48	C.C. Sabathia	.20
49	Manny Ramirez	.75
50	Jerry Hairston Jr.	.20
51	Jeromy Burnitz	.20
52	David Justice	.40
53	Bartolo Colon	.20
54	Andres Galarraga	.30
55	Jeff Weaver	.20
56	Terrance Long	.20
57	Tsuyoshi Shinjo	.20
58	Barry Zito	.40
59	Mariano Rivera	.40
60	John Olerud	.40
61	Randy Johnson	.75
62	Kenny Lofton	.40
63	Jermaine Dye	.20
64	Troy Glaus	.50
65	Larry Walker	.40
66	Hideo Nomo	.40
67	Mike Mussina	.50
68	Paul LoDuca	.20
69	Magglio Ordonez	.40
70	Paul O'Neill	.40
71	Sean Casey	.40
72	Lance Berkman	.40
73	Adam Dunn	.50
74	Aramis Ramirez	.40
75	Rafael Furcal	.40
76	Gary Sheffield	.40
77	Todd Hollandsworth	.20
78	Chipper Jones	1.00
79	Bernie Williams	.50
80	Richard Hidalgo	.25
81	Eric Chavez	.40
82	Mike Piazza	1.50
83	J.D. Drew	.40
84	Ken Griffey Jr.	1.00
85	Joe Kennedy	.20
86	Joel Pineiro	.20
87	Josh Towers	.20
88	Andruw Jones	.50
89	Carlos Beltran	.40
90	Mike Cameron	.20
91	Albert Pujols	1.50
92	Alex Rodriguez	1.50
93	Omar Vizquel	.30
94	Juan Encarnacion	.20
95	Jeff Bagwell	.50
96	Jose Canseco	.40
97	Ben Sheets	.40
98	Mark Grace	.40
99	Mike Sweeney	.20
100	Mark McGwire	2.00
101	Ivan Rodriguez	.75
102	Rich Aurilia	.20
103	Cristian Guzman	.20
104	Roy Oswalt	.40
105	Tim Hudson	.40
106	Brent Abernathy	.20
107	Mike Hampton	.20
108	Miguel Tejada	.40
109	Bobby Higginson	.20
110	Edgar Martinez	.40
111	Jorge Posada	.40
112	Jason Giambi	.50
113	Pedro Astacio	.20
114	Kazuhiro Sasaki	.20
115	Preston Wilson	.20
116	Jason Bere	.20
117	Mark Quinn	.20
118	Pokey Reese	.20
119	Derek Jeter	2.00
120	Shannon Stewart	.20
121	Jeff Kent	.40
122	Jeremy Giambi	.20
123	Pat Burrell	.40
124	Jim Edmonds	.40
125	Mark Buehrle	.20
126	Kevin Brown	.40
127	Raul Mondesi	.20
128	Pedro Martinez	.75
129	Jim Thome	.75
130	Russ Ortiz	.20
131	Brandon Duckworth	.20
132	Ryan Jamison **RC**	.50
133	Brandon Inge	.20
134	Felipe Lopez	.20
135	Jason Lane	.20
136	Forrest Johnson **RC**	.50
137	Greg Nash	.20
138	Covelli Crisp	.20
139	Nick Neugebauer	.20
140	Dustan Mohr	.20
141	Freddy Sanchez **RC**	1.00
142	Justin Backsmeyer **RC**	1.00
143	Jorge Julio	1.00
144	Ryan Mottl **RC**	1.00
145	Chris Tritle **RC**	1.00
146	Noochie Varner **RC**	1.00
147	Brian Rogers	1.00
148	Michael Hill **RC**	1.00
149	Luis Pineda	1.00
150	Rich Thompson **RC**	1.00
151	Bill Hall	1.00
152	Jose Dominguez **RC**	1.50
153	Justin Woodrow **RC**	1.00
154	Nic Jackson **RC**	1.00
155	Laynce Nix **RC**	2.00
156	Hank Aaron	3.00
157	Ernie Banks	1.50
158	Johnny Bench	1.50
159	George Brett	4.00
160	Carlton Fisk	.50
161	Bob Gibson	.75
162	Reggie Jackson	1.00
163	Don Mattingly	4.00
164	Kirby Puckett	1.50
165	Frank Robinson	1.00
166	Nolan Ryan	5.00
167	Tom Seaver	1.00
168	Mike Schmidt	2.00
169	Dave Winfield	.50
170	Carl Yastrzemski	1.00
171	Frank Chance	.75
172	Ty Cobb	3.00
173	Sam Crawford	1.00
174	Johnny Evers	.75
175	John McGraw	1.00
176	Eddie Plank	.50
177	Tris Speaker	1.00
178	Joe Tinker	.50
179	Honus Wagner	5.00
180	Cy Young	2.50
181	Javier Vazquez	.20
182	Mark Mulder	.40
183	Roger Clemens	1.50
184	Kazuhisa Ishii **RC**	1.50
185	Roberto Alomar	.50
186	Lance Berkman	.40
187	Adam Dunn	.50
188	Aramis Ramirez	.40
189	Chuck Knoblauch	.20
190	Nomar Garciaparra	1.50
191	Brad Penny	.20
192	Gary Sheffield	.40
193	Alfonso Soriano	.75
194	Andruw Jones	.50
195	Randy Johnson	.75
196	Corey Patterson	.40
197	Milton Bradley	.20
198	Johnny Damon	.40
199	Paul LoDuca	.20
200	Albert Pujols	1.50
201	Scott Rolen	.75
202	J.D. Drew	.40
203	Vladimir Guerrero	.75
204	Jason Giambi	.50
205	Moises Alou	.40
206	Magglio Ordonez	.40
207	Carlos Febles	.20
208	So Taguchi **RC**	.75
209	Rafael Palmeiro	.50
210	David Wells	.50
211	Orlando Cabrera	.20
212	Sammy Sosa	1.50
213	Armando Benitez	.20
214	Wes Helms	.20
215	Mariano Rivera	.40
216	Jimmy Rollins	.50
217	Matt Lawton	.20
218	Shawn Green	.40
219	Bernie Williams	.50
220	Bret Boone	.40
221	Alex Rodriguez	2.00
222	Roger Cedeno	.20
223	Marty Cordova	.20
224	Fred McGriff	.40
225	Chipper Jones	.75
226	Kerry Wood	.75
227	Larry Walker	.40
228	Robin Ventura	.40
229	Robert Fick	.20
230	Tino Martinez	.40
231	Ben Petrick	.20
232	Neifi Perez	.20
233	Pedro Martinez	.75
234	Brian Jordan	.20
235	Freddy Garcia	.20
236	Derek Jeter	2.00
237	Ben Grieve	.20
238	Barry Bonds	2.00
239	Luis Gonzalez	.40
240	Shane Halter	.20
241	Brian Giles	.40
242	Bud Smith	.20
243	Richie Sexson	.40
244	Barry Zito	.40
245	Eric Milton	.20
246	Ivan Rodriguez	.50
247	Toby Hall	.20
248	Mike Piazza	1.50
249	Ruben Sierra	.20
250	Tsuyoshi Shinjo	.20
251	Jermaine Dye	.20
252	Roy Oswalt	.40
253	Todd Helton	.50
254	Adrian Beltre	.40
255	Doug Mientkiewicz	.20
256	Ichiro Suzuki	1.50
257	C.C. Sabathia	.20
258	Paul Konerko	.20
259	Ken Griffey Jr.	1.00
260	Jeromy Burnitz	.20
261	Hank Blalock	.50
262	Mark Prior	1.50
263	Josh Beckett	.50
264	Carlos Pena	.20
265	Sean Burroughs	.20
266	Austin Kearns	.40
267	Chin-Hui Tsao	.20
268	Dewon Brazelton	.20
269	J.D. Martin	.20
270	Marlon Byrd	.20
271	Joe Mauer **RC**	6.00
272	Jason Botts **RC**	1.00
273	Mauricio Lara **RC**	1.00
274	Jonny Gomes **RC**	3.00
275	Gavin Floyd	1.50
276	Alexander Requena **RC**	1.00
277	Jimmy Gobble **RC**	1.00
278	Chris Duffy **RC**	1.00
279	Colt Griffin	1.00
280	Ryan Church **RC**	1.50
281	Beltran Perez	1.00
282	Clint Nageotte **RC**	1.50
283	Justin Schuda **RC**	1.00
284	Scott Hairston	1.50
285	Mario Ramos	1.00
286	Tom Seaver	2.00
287	Hank Aaron	3.00
288	Mike Schmidt	3.00
289	Robin Yount	1.50
290	Joe Morgan	1.00
291	Frank Robinson	1.00
292	Reggie Jackson	2.00
293	Nolan Ryan	4.00
294	Dave Winfield	1.00
295	Willie Mays	3.00
296	Brooks Robinson	1.50
297	Mark McGwire	3.00
298	Honus Wagner	3.00
299	Sherry Magee	1.00
300	Frank Chance	1.00
301	Larry Doyle	1.00
302	John McGraw	2.00
303	Jimmy Collins	1.00
304	Buck Herzog	1.00
305	Sam Crawford	1.00
306	Cy Young	2.50
307	Honus Wagner	3.00
308	Alex Rodriguez	2.00
308	Alex Rodriguez/SP Blue Jsy	4.00
309	Vernon Wells	.20
310	Barry Bonds	2.00
310	Barry Bonds/SP Cream Jsy	6.00
311	Vicente Padilla	.20
312	Alfonso Soriano	.75
312	A.Soriano/SP No Wristband	1.50
313	Mike Piazza	1.50
314	Jacque Jones	.20
315	Shawn Green/SP	1.50
316	Paul Byrd	.20
317	Lance Berkman	.40
318	Larry Walker	.40
319	Ken Griffey Jr./SP	3.00
320	Shea Hillenbrand	.20
321	Jay Gibbons	.20
322	Andruw Jones	.50
323	Luis Gonzalez/SP	1.50
324	Garret Anderson	.40
325	Roy Halladay	.40
326	Randy Winn	.20
327	Matt Morris	.40
328	Robb Nen	.20
329	Trevor Hoffman	.20
330	Kip Wells	.20
331	Orlando Hernandez	.30
332	Rey Ordonez	.20
333	Torii Hunter	.40
334	Geoff Jenkins	.40
335	Eric Karros	.20
336	Mike Lowell	.40
337	Nick Johnson	.20
338	Randall Simon	.20
339	Ellis Burks	.20
340	Sammy Sosa	1.50
340	Sammy Sosa/SP Blue Jsy	4.00
341	Pedro J. Martinez	.75
342	Junior Spivey	.20
343	Vinny Castilla	.20
344	Randy Johnson/SP	2.00
345	Chipper Jones/SP	1.50
346	Orlando Hudson	.20
347	Albert Pujols/SP	5.00
348	Rondell White	.20
349	Vladimir Guerrero	.75
350	Mark Prior	1.00
350	Mark Prior/SP Red Background	3.00
351	Eric Gagne	.50
352	Todd Zeile	.20
353	Manny Ramirez/SP	2.00
354	Kevin Millwood	.40
355	Troy Percival	.20
356	Jason Giambi	.50
356	Jason Giambi/SP White Jsy	1.50
357	Bartolo Colon	.20
358	Jeremy Giambi	.20
359	Jose Cruz Jr.	.20
360	Ichiro Suzuki	1.50
360	Ichiro/SP Blue Warm-Up	3.00
361	Eddie Guardado	.20
362	Ivan Rodriguez	.50
363	Carl Crawford	.20
364	Jason Simontacchi **RC**	.50
365	Kenny Lofton	.40
366	Raul Mondesi	.20
367	A.J. Pierzynski	.20
368	Ugueth Urbina	.20
369	Rodrigo Lopez	.20
370	Nomar Garciaparra	1.50
370	N. Garciaparra/SP 1 Bat	3.00
371	Craig Counsell	.20
372	Barry Larkin	.40
373	Carlos Pena	.20
374	Luis Castillo	.20
375	Raul Ibanez	.20
376	Kazuhisa Ishii/SP	1.50
377	Derek Lowe	.20
378	Curt Schilling	.50
379	Jim Thome	.75
380	Derek Jeter	2.00
380	D. Jeter/SP Blue background	5.00
381	Pat Burrell	.50
382	Jamie Moyer	.20
383	Eric Hinske	.20
384	Scott Rolen	.75
385	Miguel Tejada/SP	1.50
386	Andy Pettitte	.40
387	Mike Lieberthal	.20
388	Al Leiter	.40
389	Todd Helton/SP	2.00
390	Adam Dunn	.50
390	Adam Dunn/SP with bat	2.00
391	Cliff Floyd	.20
392	Tim Salmon	.40
393	Joe Torre	.50
394	Bobby Cox	.20
395	Tony LaRussa	.20
396	Art Howe	.20
397	Bob Brenly	.20
398	Ron Gardenhire	.20
399	Mike Cuddyer	.20
400	Joe Mauer	2.50
401	Mark Teixeira	.50
402	Hee Seop Choi	.20
403	Angel Berroa	.20
404	Jesse Foppert	.50

405	Bobby Crosby	.50
406	Jose Reyes	.50
407	Casey Kotchman	1.00
408	Aaron Heilman	.20
409	Adrian Gonzalez	.20
410	Delwyn Young RC	.75
411	Brett Myers	.20
412	Justin Huber RC	1.00
413	Drew Henson	.20
414	Taggert Bozied RC	1.00
415	Dontrelle Willis RC	3.00
416	Rocco Baldelli	.50
417	Jason Stokes RC	2.50
418	Brandon Phillips	.20
419	Jake Blalock/SP RC	2.00
420	Micah Schilling/SP RC	1.00
421	Denard Span/SP RC	2.00
422	James Loney/SP RC	4.00
423	Wes Bankston/SP RC	1.50
424	Jeremy Hermida/SP RC	4.00
425	Curtis Granderson/SP RC	3.00
426	Jason Pridie/SP RC	1.00
427	Larry Broadway/SP RC	1.00
428	Khalil Greene/SP RC	5.00
429	Joey Votto/SP RC	2.50
430	B.J. Upton/SP RC	8.00
431	Sergio Santos/SP RC	2.00
432	Brian Dopirak/SP RC	2.00
433	Ozzie Smith/SP	2.00
434	Wade Boggs/SP	1.00
435	Yogi Berra/SP	3.00
436	Al Kaline/SP	2.00
437	Robin Roberts/SP	1.00
438	Roberto Clemente/SP	8.00
439	Gary Carter/SP	1.00
440	Fergie Jenkins/SP	1.00
441	Orlando Cepeda/SP	1.00
442	Rod Carew/SP	1.50
443	Harmon Killebrew/SP	2.50
444	Duke Snider/SP	2.00
445	Stan Musial/SP	5.00
446	Hank Greenberg/SP	1.00
447	Lou Brock/SP	1.00
448	Jim Palmer	.50
449	John McGraw	.75
450	Mordecai Brown	.50
451	Christy Mathewson	1.00
452	Sam Crawford	.50
453	Bill O'Hara	.50
454	Joe Tinker	.50
455	Napoleon Lajoie	.75
456	Honus Wagner	3.00

T206 mini parallel

MONDESI, TORONTO

	NM/M
Polar Bear:	2-3X
Tolstoi Black:	2-5X
Average 4:Box	
Tolstoi Red:	4-8X
Average 2:Box	
Cycle:	6-12X
Average 1:Box	
Series 2	
Polar Bear:	2-3X
Piedmont Black:	3-5X
Piedmont Red:	4-8X
Carolina Brights:	6-12X
Series 3	
Polar Bear:	2-3X
Sweet Caporal Red:	3-5X
Sweet Caporal Blue or Black:	4-6X
Uzit:	6-12X
Bazooka Backs:	No Pricing
Production 30	
Drum Backs:	No Pricing
Production 20	
Lenox Variations:	No Pricing
Production 10	
American Beauty Variation:	No Pricing
Production 5	

Autographs

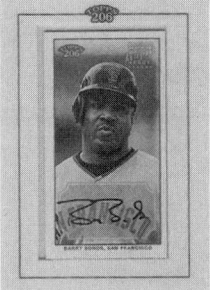

	NM/M
Common Player:	8.00
Inserted 1:41	
BB Barry Bonds	200.00
RC Roger Clemens	120.00
JE Jim Edmonds	30.00
BG Brian Giles	10.00
CG Cristian Guzman	10.00
BI Brandon Inge	10.00
RJ Ryan Jamison	8.00
FJ Forrest Johnson	8.00
JJ Jorge Julio	10.00
FL Felipe Lopez	8.00
GN Greg Nash	8.00
MO Magglio Ordonez	20.00
AR Alex Rodriguez	100.00
JR Jimmy Rollins	25.00
BZ Barry Zito	15.00

Autographs Series 2

	NM/M
Common Player:	8.00
Inserted 1:55	
MA Moises Alou	30.00
LB Lance Berkman	35.00
HB Hank Blalock	20.00
DB Dewon Brazelton	8.00
MB Marlon Byrd	10.00
EC Eric Chavez	15.00
JD Johnny Damon	25.00
GF Gavin Floyd	20.00
LG Luis Gonzalez	15.00
KI Kazuhisa Ishii	15.00
JDM J.D. Martin	8.00
JM Joe Mauer	75.00
MP Mark Prior	20.00
AP Albert Pujols	150.00
SR Scott Rolen	20.00
RS Richie Sexson	15.00
BS Ben Sheets	20.00
BSM Bud Smith	10.00
ST So Taguchi	20.00
CT Chris Tritle	10.00

Autographs Series 3

	NM/M
Common Autograph:	8.00
MB Milton Bradley	10.00
JC Jose Cruz Jr.	15.00
DE David Eckstein	8.00
DH Drew Henson	15.00
ML Mike Lamb	8.00
MT Marcus Thames	8.00
JV Jose Vidro	10.00

Relics

	NM/M
Common Player:	5.00
Overall Relics 1:11	
RA Roberto Alomar/Jsy	10.00
JB Jeff Bagwell/Jsy	10.00
CB Craig Biggio/Jsy	8.00
BB Barry Bonds/Jsy	25.00
BBO Bret Boone/Jsy	8.00
MC Mike Cameron/Jsy	5.00
JC Jose Canseco/Bat	10.00
CD Carlos Delgado/Jsy	8.00
JED Jim Edmonds/Jsy	10.00
CF Cliff Floyd/Jsy	5.00
JGI Jason Giambi/Jsy	8.00
JG Jeremy Giambi/Jsy	5.00
TG Tom Glavine/Jsy	8.00
SG Shawn Green/Jsy	8.00
TGW Tony Gwynn/Jsy	15.00
TH Todd Helton/Jsy	10.00
RJ Randy Johnson/Jsy	15.00
AJ Andruw Jones/Jsy	8.00
CJ Chipper Jones/Jsy	10.00
CL Carlos Lee/Jsy	5.00
KL Kenny Lofton/Jsy	5.00
GM Greg Maddux/Jsy	15.00
EM Edgar Martinez/Jsy	10.00
TM Tino Martinez/Jsy	10.00
JO John Olerud/Jsy	5.00
PO Paul O'Neill/Jsy	8.00
MO Magglio Ordonez/Jsy	6.00
CP Chan Ho Park/Jsy	5.00
MP Mike Piazza/Jsy	15.00
AP Albert Pujols/Bat	25.00
IR Ivan Rodriguez/Jsy	10.00
AS Alfonso Soriano/Jsy	10.00
SS Shannon Stewart/Bat	8.00
FT Frank Thomas/Jsy	10.00
JT Jim Thome/Jsy	20.00
LW Larry Walker/Jsy	5.00
JW Jeff Weaver/Jsy	5.00
BW Bernie Williams/Jsy	5.00
BZ Barry Zito/Jsy	8.00

Relics Series 2

	NM/M
Common Player:	5.00
Jerseys 1:18	
Bats 1:40	
RA Roberto Alomar/Bat	10.00
JB Jeff Bagwell/Jsy	8.00
BB Barry Bonds/Jsy	20.00
BBO Bret Boone/Jsy	6.00
KB Kevin Brown/Jsy	6.00
AB A.J. Burnett/Jsy	5.00
SB Sean Burroughs/Bat	8.00
EC Eric Chavez/Bat	8.00
TC Ty Cobb/Bat	420.00
JC Jimmy Collins/Bat	45.00
SCR Sam Crawford/Bat	50.00
JD Johnny Damon/Bat	12.00
RD Ryan Dempster/Jsy	5.00
BD Brandon Duckworth/Jsy	5.00
AD Adam Dunn/Bat	10.00
DE Darin Erstad/Jsy	5.00
JEV Johnny Evers/Bat	50.00
CF Cliff Floyd/Jsy	5.00
TGL Tom Glavine/Jsy	8.00
JG Juan Gonzalez/Bat	10.00
MG Mark Grace/Bat	9.00
SG Shawn Green/Jsy	6.00
CG Cristian Guzman/Bat	5.00
TG Tony Gwynn/Jsy	15.00
TH Toby Hall/Jsy	5.00
JH Josh Hamilton/Bat	10.00
THE Todd Helton/Jsy	8.00
RH Rickey Henderson/Bat	15.00
BH Buck Herzog/Bat	30.00
JJ Jason Jennings/Jsy	5.00
RJ Randy Johnson/Jsy	10.00
AJ Andruw Jones/Jsy	8.00
CJO Chipper Jones/Jsy	10.00
JK Jeff Kent/Jsy	5.00
BL Barry Larkin/Jsy	5.00
TL Travis Lee/Bat	5.00
GM Greg Maddux/Jsy	12.00
EM Edgar Martinez/Jsy	8.00
TM Tino Martinez/Bat	10.00
JM Joe Mays/Jsy	5.00
JMC John McGraw/Bat	60.00
FM Fred McGriff/Bat	8.00
JO John Olerud/Jsy	5.00
RP Rafael Palmeiro/Jsy	15.00
BP Brad Penny/Jsy	5.00
MP Mike Piazza/Jsy	15.00
AP Albert Pujols/Jsy	15.00
ARA Aramis Ramirez/Bat	10.00
AR Alex Rodriguez/Bat	20.00
IR Ivan Rodriguez/Bat	10.00
CS Curt Schilling/Bat	15.00
GS Gary Sheffield/Bat	8.00
TS Tsuyoshi Shinjo/Bat	5.00
AS Alfonso Soriano/Bat	10.00
MT Miguel Tejada/Bat	8.00
FT Frank Thomas/Bat	8.00
JTH Jim Thome/Bat	15.00
JT Joe Tinker/Bat	40.00
MV Mo Vaughn/Bat	5.00
RV Robin Ventura/Bat	5.00
HWA Honus Wagner/Bat	400.00
LW Larry Walker/Jsy	5.00
BW Bernie Williams/Jsy	8.00
MW Matt Williams/Bat	5.00
PW Preston Wilson/Bat	5.00

Relics Series 3

	NM/M
Common Player:	5.00
RA Roberto Alomar/Bat	8.00
JB Jeff Bagwell/Bat	8.00
WB Wilson Betemit/Bat	5.00
PB Pat Burrell/Bat	10.00
EC Eric Chavez/Bat	8.00
AD Adam Dunn/Bat	10.00
JE Jim Edmonds/Bat	8.00
NG Nomar Garciaparra/Bat	20.00
LG Luis Gonzalez/Jsy	5.00
TG Tony Gwynn/Jsy	10.00
TH Todd Helton/Jsy	8.00
RH Rickey Henderson/Bat	15.00
NJ Nick Johnson/Bat	5.00
RJ Randy Johnson/Jsy	10.00
AJ Andruw Jones/Jsy	8.00
CJ Chipper Jones/Jsy	10.00
PM Pedro Martinez/Jsy	12.00
DM Doug Mientkiewicz/Jsy	6.00
RP Rafael Palmeiro/Jsy	8.00
CP Corey Patterson/Bat	6.00
MP Mike Piazza/Jsy	15.00
AP Albert Pujols/Bat	20.00
AR Alex Rodriguez/Bat	15.00
IR Ivan Rodriguez/Bat	8.00
SR Scott Rolen/Bat	10.00
CS Curt Schilling/Bat	8.00
GS Gary Sheffield/Bat	8.00
TS Tsuyoshi Shinjo/Bat	5.00
AS Alfonso Soriano/Bat	10.00
MTE Miguel Tejada/Jsy	8.00
FT Frank Thomas/Bat	8.00
JT Jim Thome/Jsy	10.00
MV Mo Vaughn/Jsy	5.00
BW Bernie Williams/Jsy	8.00
BZ Barry Zito/Jsy	6.00

Reprint Relics

	NM/M
Common Player:	75.00
SC Sam Crawford	90.00
JE Johnny Evers	90.00
JM John McGraw	75.00
TS Tris Speaker	140.00
HW Honus Wagner	400.00

Team Topps Legends Autographs

	NM/M
Inserted 1:7,093	
Nolan Ryan	400.00

Team Topps Legends Autographs Series 2

	NM/M
Inserted 1:260	
Ralph Branca	25.00
Andy Pafko	20.00
Joe Pepitone	10.00
Tom Seaver	60.00
Warren Spahn	25.00
Luis Tiant	10.00

Team 206

		NM/M
Complete Set (20):		10.00
Common Player:		.25
Inserted 1:Pack		
1	Barry Bonds	2.00
2	Ivan Rodriguez	.50
3	Luis Gonzalez	.25
4	Jason Giambi	.50
5	Pedro Martinez	.75
6	Larry Walker	.25
7	Bobby Abreu	.40
8	Derek Jeter	2.00
9	Bret Boone	.40
10	Mike Piazza	1.00
11	Alex Rodriguez	1.50
12	Roger Clemens	1.50
13	Albert Pujols	1.50
14	Randy Johnson	.75
15	Sammy Sosa	1.50
16	Cristian Guzman	.25
17	Shawn Green	.40
18	Curt Schilling	.50
19	Ichiro Suzuki	1.00
20	Chipper Jones	.75

Team 206 Series 2

RODRIGUEZ, TEXAS

		NM/M
Complete Set (25):		10.00
Common Player:		.25
Inserted 1:1		
1	Alex Rodriguez	1.50
2	Sammy Sosa	1.50
3	Jason Giambi	.50
4	Nomar Garciaparra	1.25

5 Ichiro Suzuki 1.00
6 Chipper Jones .75
7 Derek Jeter 2.00
8 Barry Bonds 2.00
9 Mike Piazza 1.50
10 Randy Johnson .75
11 Shawn Green .25
12 Todd Helton .50
13 Luis Gonzalez .25
14 Albert Pujols 1.50
15 Curt Schilling .50
16 Scott Rolen .75
17 Ivan Rodriguez .50
18 Roberto Alomar .50
19 Cristian Guzman .25
20 Bret Boone .25
21 Barry Zito .40
22 Larry Walker .25
23 Eric Chavez .25
24 Roger Clemens 1.50
25 Pedro Martinez .75

Team 206 Series 3

MATHEWSON, N.Y. NAT'L

NM/M
Complete Set (30): 10.00
Common Player: .25
Inserted 1:1
1 Ichiro Suzuki 1.00
2 Kazuhisa Ishii .25
3 Alex Rodriguez 1.50
4 Mark Prior 1.00
5 Derek Jeter 2.00
6 Sammy Sosa 1.50
7 Nomar Garciaparra 1.25
8 Mike Piazza 1.00
9 Jason Giambi .50
10 Vladimir Guerrero .75
11 Curt Schilling .50
12 Jim Thome .75
13 Adam Dunn .50
14 Albert Pujols 1.50
15 Pat Burrell .50
16 Chipper Jones .75
17 Randy Johnson .75
18 Todd Helton .50
19 Luis Gonzalez .25
20 Alfonso Soriano .75
21 Shawn Green .40
22 Pedro J. Martinez .75
23 Lance Berkman .40
24 Ivan Rodriguez .50
25 Larry Walker .25
26 Andruw Jones .40
27 Ken Griffey Jr. 1.00
28 Eric Hinske .25
29 Mike Sweeney .25
30 Miguel Tejada .50

2003 Topps

NM/M
Complete Set (720): 70.00
Sealed Factory Set (725): 70.00
Complete Series 1 Set (366): 35.00
Complete Series 2 Set (355): 35.00
Common Player: .10
Series 1 & 2 Pack (10): 1.50
Series 1 & 2 Box (36): 35.00

Series 2 Jumbo Box: 45.00
White Topps "throw-back" logo.
Series 1 (1:8852): Value Undetermined
Series 2 (1:4487): Value Undetermined
1a Alex Rodriguez
(Red Topps) 1.00
2 Dan Wilson .10
3 Jimmy Rollins .25
4 Jermaine Dye .10
5 Steve Karsay .10
6 Timoniel Perez .10
7 Not Issued
8 Jose Vidro .10
9 Eddie Guardado .10
10a Mark Prior (Red Topps) .50
11a Curt Schilling (Red Topps) .40
12 Dennis Cook .10
13 Andruw Jones .40
14 David Segui .10
15 Trot Nixon .10
16 Antonio Alfonseca .10
17 Magglio Ordonez .20
18 Jason LaRue .10
19 Danys Baez .10
20a Todd Helton (Red Topps) .40
21 Denny Neagle .10
22 Dave Mlicki .10
23 Roberto Hernandez .10
24 Odalis Perez .10
25 Nick Neugebauer .10
26 David Ortiz .10
27 Andres Galarraga .15
28 Edgardo Alfonzo .10
29 Chad Bradford .10
30a Jason Giambi (Red Topps) .40
31 Brian Giles .25
32 Delvi Cruz .10
33 Robb Nen .10
34 Jeff Nelson .10
35 Edgar Renteria .10
36 Aubrey Huff .10
37 Brandon Duckworth .10
38 Juan Gonzalez .40
39 Sidney Ponson .10
40 Eric Hinske .10
41 Kevin Appier .10
42 Danny Bautista .10
43 Javier Lopez .10
44 Jeff Conine .10
45 Carlos Baerga .10
46 Ugueth Urbina .10
47 Mark Buehrle .10
48 Aaron Boone .10
49 Chuck Finley .10
50a Sammy Sosa
(Red Topps) 1.00
51 Jose Jimenez .10
52 Chris Truby .10
53 Luis Castillo .10
54 Orlando Merced .10
55 Brian Jordan .10
56 Eric Young .10
57 Bobby Kielty .10
58 Luis Rivas .10
59 Brad Wilkerson .10
60 Roberto Alomar .40
61a Roger Clemens
(Red Topps) 1.00
62 Scott Hatteberg .10
63 Andy Ashby .10
64 Mike Williams .10
65 Ron Gant .10
66 Benito Santiago .10
67 Bret Boone .10
68 Matt Morris .10
69 Troy Glaus .40
70 Austin Kearns .25
71 Jim Thome .40
72 Rickey Henderson .40
73a Luis Gonzalez (Red Topps) .20
74 Brad Fullmer .10
75 Benny Agbayani .10
76 Randy Wolf .10
77a Miguel Tejada (Red Topps) .25
78 Jimmy Anderson .10
79 Ramon Martinez .10
80a Ivan Rodriguez
(Red Topps) .40
81 John Flaherty .10
82 Shannon Stewart .10
83 Orlando Palmeiro .10
84 Rafael Furcal .10
85 Kenny Rogers .10
86 Bud Smith .10
87 Mo Vaughn .15
88 Jose Cruz Jr. .10
89 Mike Matheny .10
90a Alfonso Soriano
(Red Topps) .50
91 Orlando Cabrera .10
92 Jeffrey Hammonds .10
93 Hideo Nomo .25
94 Carlos Febles .10
95 Billy Wagner .10
96 Alex Gonzalez .10
97 Todd Zeile .10
98 Omar Vizquel .20
99 Jose Rijo .10
100a Ichiro Suzuki (Red Topps) 1.00
101 Steve Cox .10
102 Hideki Irabu .10
103 Roy Halladay .10
104 David Eckstein .10
105 Greg Maddux .75

106 Chris Richard .10
107 Travis Driskill .10
108 Fred McGriff .15
109 Frank Thomas .50
110 Shawn Green .20
111 Ruben Quevedo .10
112 Jacque Jones .10
113 Tomokazu Ohka .10
114 Joe McEwing .10
115 Ramiro Mendoza .10
116 Mark Mulder .20
117 Mike Lieberthal .10
118 Jack Wilson .10
119 Randall Simon .10
120 Bernie Williams .40
121 Marvin Benard .10
122 Jamie Moyer .10
123 Andy Benes .10
124 Tino Martinez .10
125 Esteban Yan .10
126 Gabe Kapler .10
127 Jason Isringhausen .10
128 Chris Carpenter .10
129 Mike Cameron .10
130a Gary Sheffield (Red Topps) .25
131 Geronimo Gil .10
132 Brian Daubach .10
133 Corey Patterson .10
134 Aaron Rowand .10
135 Chris Reitsma .10
136 Bob Wickman .10
137 Paul Shuey .10
138 Jason Jennings .10
139 Brandon Inge .10
140 Larry Walker .20
141 Ramon Santiago .10
142 Hansel Izquierdo .10
143 Jose Vizcaino .10
144 Mark Quinn .10
145 Michael Tucker .10
146 Darren Dreifort .10
147 Mark Loretta .10
148 Corey Koskie .10
149 Tony Armas Jr. .10
150a Kazuhisa Ishii (Red Topps) .10
151 Al Leiter .10
152 Steve Trachsel .10
153 Mike Stanton .10
154 David Justice .15
155 Marlon Anderson .10
156 Jason Kendall .10
157 Brian Lawrence .10
158 J.T. Snow Jr. .10
159 Edgar Martinez .10
160a Pat Burrell (Red Topps) .25
161 Kerry Robinson .10
162 Greg Vaughn .10
163 Carl Everett .10
164 Vernon Wells .10
165 Jose Mesa .10
166 Troy Percival .10
167 Erubiel Durazo .10
168 Jason Marquis .10
169 Jerry Hairston Jr. .10
170a Vladimir Guerrero
(Red Topps) .50
171 Byung-Hyun Kim .10
172 Marcus Giles .10
173 Johnny Damon .10
174 Jon Lieber .10
175 Ray Durham .10
176 Sean Casey .10
177a Adam Dunn (Red Topps) .40
178 Juan Pierre .10
179 Damion Easley .10
180a Barry Zito (Red Topps) .25
181 Abraham Nunez .10
182 Pokey Reese .10
183 Jeff Kent .20
184 Russ Ortiz .10
185 Ruben Sierra .10
186 Brent Abernathy .10
187 Ismael Valdes .10
188 Darrin Fletcher .10
189 Craig Counsell .10
190 David Wells .10
191 Ramon Hernandez .10
192 Adam Kennedy .10
193 Tony Womack .10
194 Wes Helms .10
195 Tony Batista .10
196 Rolando Arrojo .10
197 Matt Clement .10
198 Sandy Alomar .10
199 Scott Sullivan .10
200a Albert Pujols (Red Topps) 1.00
201 Kirk Rueter .10
202 Phil Nevin .10
203 Kip Wells .10
204 Ron Coomer .10
205 Jeromy Burnitz .10
206 Kyle Lohse .10
207 Paul Bako .10
208 Paul LoDuca .10
209 Carlos Beltran .10
210 Roy Oswalt .25
211 Mike Lowell .10
212 Robert Fick .10
213 Todd Jones .10
214 C.C. Sabathia .10
215 Danny Graves .10
216 Todd Hundley .10
217 Tim Wakefield .10
218 Dustin Hermanson .10
219 Kevin Millwood .10

220 Jorge Posada .25
221 Bobby Jones .10
222 Carlos Guillen .10
223 Fernando Vina .10
224 Ryan Rupe .10
225 Kelvim Escobar .10
226 Ramon Ortiz .10
227 Junior Spivey .10
228 Juan Cruz .10
229 Melvin Mora .10
230a Lance Berkman
(Red Topps) .25
231 Brent Butler .10
232 Matt Anderson .10
233 Derrek Lee .10
234 Matt Lawton .10
235 Chuck Knoblauch .10
236 Eric Gagne .10
237 Alex Sanchez .10
238 Denny Hocking .10
239 Rick Reed .10
240 Rey Ordonez .10
241 Orlando Hernandez .10
242 Robert Person .10
243 Sean Burroughs .10
244 Jeff Cirillo .10
245 Mike Lamb .10
246 Jose Valentin .10
247 Ellis Burks .10
248 Shawn Chacon .10
249 Josh Beckett .10
250a Nomar Garciaparra
(Red Topps) 1.00
251 Craig Biggio .20
252 Joe Randa .10
253 Mark Grudzielanek .10
254 Glendon Rusch .10
255 Michael Barrett .10
256 Tyler Houston .10
257 Ryan Dempster .10
258 Wade Miller .10
259 Adrian Beltre .20
260 Vicente Padilla .10
261 Kazuhiro Sasaki .10
262 Mike Scioscia .10
263 Bobby Cox .10
264 Mike Hargrove .10
265 Grady Little .10
266 Alex Gonzalez .10
267 Jerry Manuel .10
268 Bob Boone .10
269 Joel Skinner .10
270 Clint Hurdle .10
271 Luis Pujols .10
272 Bob Brenly .10
273 Jeff Torborg .10
274 Jimy Williams .10
275 Tony Pena .10
276 Jim Tracy .10
277 Jerry Royster .10
278 Ron Gardenhire .10
279 Frank Robinson .10
280 Bobby Valentine .10
281 Joe Torre .10
282 Art Howe .10
283 Larry Bowa .10
284 Lloyd McClendon .10
285 Bruce Bochy .10
286 Dusty Baker .10
287 Lou Pinella .10
288 Tony LaRussa .10
289 Hal McRae .10
290 Jerry Narron .10
291 Carlos Tosca .10
292 Chris Duncan RC 2.00
293 Franklin Gutierrez RC 1.00
294 Adam LaRoche .25
295 Manuel Ramirez RC .10
296 Il Kim RC .10
297 Wayne Lydon RC .20
298 Daryl Clark RC .25
299 Sean Pierce .10
300a Andy Marte RC
(Red Topps) .50
301 Matt Peterson RC .25
302 Gonzalo Lopez RC .25
303 Bernie Castro RC .10
304 Cliff Lee .10
305 Jason Perry RC .40
306 Jaime Bubela RC .25
307 Alexis Rios .10
308 Brendan Harris RC .40
309 Ramon Martinez .25
310 Terry Tiffee RC .40
311 Kevin Youkilis RC 1.00
312 Ruddy Lugo RC .20
313 C.J. Wilson .10
314 Mike McNutt RC .10
315 Jeff Clark RC .10
316 Mark Malaska RC .10
317 Doug Waechter RC .25
318 Derell McCall RC .10
319 Scott Tyler .10
320 Craig Brazell RC .40
321a Walter Young (Red Topps) .10
322a Marlon Byrd, Jorge Padilla
(Red Topps) .10
323 Chris Snelling,
Shin-Soo Choo .10
324a Hank Blalock, Mark Teixeira
(Red Topps) .10
324b Hank Blalock, Mark Teixeira
(White Topps)

325 Josh Hamilton, Carl Crawford .40
326 Orlando Hudson, Josh Phelps .10
327 Jack Cust, Rene Reyes .10
328 Angel Berroa, Alexis Gomez .10
329 Michael Cuddyer, Michael Restovich .10
330 Juan Rivera, Marcus Thames .10
331 Brandon Puffer, Jung Bong .10
332 Mike Cameron .10
333 Shawn Green .25
334 Team Shot .10
335 Jason Giambi .25
336 Derek Lowe .10
337 Manny Ramirez, Mike Sweeney, Bernie Williams .25
338 Alfonso Soriano, Alex Rodriguez, Derek Jeter .50
339 Alex Rodriguez, Jim Thome, Rafael Palmeiro .40
340 Magglio Ordonez, Alex Rodriguez, Miguel Tejada .40
341 Pedro Martinez, Derek Lowe, Barry Zito .25
342 Pedro Martinez, Roger Clemens, Mike Mussina .25
343 Larry Walker, Vladimir Guerrero, Todd Helton .25
344 Sammy Sosa, Albert Pujols, Shawn Green .40
345 Sammy Sosa, Lance Berkman, Shawn Green .40
346 Lance Berkman, Albert Pujols, Pat Burrell .25
347 Randy Johnson, Greg Maddux, Tom Glavine .25
348 Randy Johnson, Curt Schilling, Kerry Wood .25
349 AL Divison Series .20
350 AL & NL Divison Series .20
351 AL & NL Divison Series .20
352 NL Divison Series .20
353 AL Championship Series .20
354 Postseason Highlight .20
355 NL Championship Series .10
356 Jason Giambi .25
357 Alfonso Soriano .50
358 Alex Rodriguez .75
359 Eric Chavez .10
360 Torii Hunter .10
361 Bernie Williams .20
362 Garret Anderson .10
363 Jorge Posada .20
364 Derek Lowe .10
365 Barry Zito .20
366 Manny Ramirez .25
367 Mike Scioscia .10
368a Francisco Rodriguez (Red Topps) .10
369 Andres Galarraga .10
370a Chipper Jones (Red Topps) .50
371 Chris Singleton .10
372 Cliff Floyd .10
373 Bobby Hill .10
374 Antonio Osuna .10
375 Barry Larkin .25
376 Charles Nagy .10
377 Denny Stark .10
378 Dean Palmer .10
379 Eric Owens .10
380a Randy Johnson (Red Topps) .50
381 Jeff Suppan .10
382 Eric Karros .10
383 Luis Vizcaino .10
384 Johan Santana .10
385 Javier Vazquez .10
386 John Thomson .10
387a Nick Johnson (Red Topps) .10
388 Mark Ellis .10
389 Doug Glanville .10
390a Ken Griffey Jr. (Red Topps) .75
391 Bubba Trammell .10
392 Livan Hernandez .10
393 Desi Relaford .10
394 Eli Marrero .10
395 Jared Sandberg .10
396a Barry Bonds (Red Topps) 1.50
397 Esteban Loaiza .10
398 Aaron Sele .10
399 Geoff Blum .10
400a Derek Jeter (Red Topps) 1.50
401 Eric Byrnes .10
402 Mike Timlin .10
403 Mark Kotsay .10
404 Rich Aurilia .10
405 Joel Pineiro .10
406 Chuck Finley .10
407 Bengie Molina .10
408 Steve Finley .10
409 Julio Franco .10
410 Marty Cordova .10
411 Shea Hillenbrand .10
412 Mark Bellhorn .10
413 Jon Garland .10
414 Reggie Taylor .10
415 Milton Bradley .10
416 Carlos Pena .10
417 Andy Fox .10
418 Brad Ausmus .10
419 Brent Mayne .10
420 Paul Quantrill .10
421a Carlos Delgado (Red Topps) .20
422 Kevin Mench .10
423 Joe Kennedy .10
424 Mike Crudale .10
425 Mark McLemore .10
426 Bill Mueller .10
427 Robert Mackowiak .10
428 Ricky Ledee .10
429 Ted Lilly .10
430 Sterling Hitchcock .10
431 Scott Strickland .10
432 Damion Easley .10
433a Torii Hunter (Red Topps) .25
434 Brad Radke .10
435 Geoff Jenkins .10
436 Paul Byrd .10
437 Morgan Ensberg .10
438 Mike Maroth .10
439 Mike Hampton .10
440 Adam Hyzdu .10
441 Vance Wilson .10
442 Todd Ritchie .10
443 Flash Gordon .10
444 John Burkett .10
445 Rodrigo Lopez .10
446 Tim Spooneybarger .10
447 Quinton McCracken .10
448 Tim Salmon .20
449 Jarrod Washburn .10
450a Pedro Martinez (Red Topps) .50
451 Dustan Mohr .10
452 Julio Lugo .10
453 Scott Stewart .10
454 Armando Benitez .10
455 Raul Mondesi .20
456 Robin Ventura .20
457 Bobby Abreu .20
458 Josh Fogg .10
459 Ryan Klesko .20
460 Tsuyoshi Shinjo .10
461a Jim Edmonds (Red Topps) .25
462 Cliff Politte .10
463 Chan Ho Park .10
464 John Mabry .10
465 Woody Williams .10
466 Jason Michaels .10
467 Scott Schoeneweis .10
468 Brian Anderson .10
469 Brett Tomko .10
470 Scott Erickson .10
471 Tony Clark .10
472 Danny Wright .10
473 Jason Schmidt .10
474 Scott Williamson .10
475 Einar Diaz .10
476 Jay Payton .10
477 Juan Acevedo .10
478 Ben Grieve .10
479 Raul Ibanez .10
480 Richie Sexson .25
481 Rick Reed .10
482 Pedro Astacio .10
483 Adam Piatt .10
484 Bud Smith .10
485 Tomas Perez .10
486 Adam Eaton .10
487 Rafael Palmeiro .25
488 Jason Tyner .10
489a Scott Rolen (Red Topps) .50
490 Randy Winn .10
491 Ryan Jensen .10
492 Trevor Hoffman .10
493 Craig Wilson .10
494 Jeremy Giambi .10
495 Daryle Ward .10
496 Shane Spencer .10
497 Andy Pettitte .25
498 John Franco .10
499 Masato Yoshii .10
500a Mike Piazza (Red Topps) 1.00
501 Cristian Guzman .10
502 Jose Hernandez .10
503 Octavio Dotel .10
504 Brad Penny .10
505 Jose Ortiz .10
506 Ryan Dempster .10
507 Joe Crede .10
508 Chad Hermansen .10
509 Gary Matthews Jr. .10
510 Matt Franco .10
511 Ben Weber .10
512 Dave Berg .10
513 Michael Young .10
514 Frank Catalanotto .10
515a Darin Erstad (Red Topps) .25
516 Matt Williams .10
517 B.J. Surhoff .10
518 Kerry Ligtenberg .10
519 Mike Bordick .10
520 Arthur Rhodes .10
521 Joe Girardi .10
522 D'Angelo Jimenez .10
523 Paul Konerko .10
524 Jose Macias .10
525 Joe Mays .10
526 Marquis Grissom .10
527 Neifi Perez .10
528 Preston Wilson .10
529 Jeff Weaver .10
530a Eric Chavez (Red Topps) .25
531 Placido Polanco .10
532 Ray Lankford .10
533 James Baldwin .10
534 Toby Hall .10
535 Brendan Donnelly .10
536 Benji Gil .10
537 Damian Moss .10
538 Jorge Julio .10
539 Matt Clement .10
540 Brian Moehler .10
541 Lee Stevens .10
542 Jimmy Haynes .10
543 Kevin Millar .10
544 Dave Roberts .10
545 J.C. Romero .10
546 Bartolo Colon .10
547 Roger Cedeno .10
548 Mariano Rivera .20
549 Billy Koch .10
550a Manny Ramirez (Red Topps) .50
551 Travis Lee .10
552 Oliver Perez .10
553 Tim Worrell .10
554 Rafael Soriano .10
555 Damian Miller .10
556 John Smoltz .10
557 Willis Roberts .10
558a Tim Hudson (Red Topps) .25
559 Moises Alou .20
560 Gary Glover .10
561 Corky Miller .10
562 Ben Broussard .10
563 Gabe Kapler .10
564 Chris Woodward .10
565 Paul Wilson .10
566 Todd Hollandsworth .10
567 So Taguchi .10
568 John Olerud .20
569 Reggie Sanders .10
570 Jake Peavy .10
571 Kris Benson .10
572 Todd Pratt .10
573 Ray Durham .10
574 David Wells .10
575 Chris Widger .10
576 Shawn Wooten .10
577 Tom Glavine .25
578 Antonio Alfonseca .10
579 Keith Foulke .10
580 Shawn Estes .10
581 Travis Fryman .10
582 Dmitri Young .10
583 A.J. Burnett .10
584 Richard Hidalgo .10
585a Mike Sweeney (Red Topps) .10
586 Alex Cora .10
587 Matt Stairs .10
588 Doug Mientkiewicz .10
589 Fernando Tatis .10
590 David Weathers .10
591 Cory Lidle .10
592 Dan Plesac .10
593a Jeff Bagwell (Red Topps) .50
594 Steve Sparks .10
595 Sandy Alomar Jr. .10
596 John Lackey .10
597 Rick Helling .10
598 Mark DeRosa .10
599 Carlos Lee .10
600a Garret Anderson (Red Topps) .20
601 Vinny Castilla .10
602 Ryan Drese .10
603 LaTroy Hawkins .10
604 David Bell .10
605 Freddy Garcia .10
606 Miguel Cairo .10
607 Scott Spiezio .10
608 Mike Remlinger .10
609 Tony Graffanino .10
610 Russell Branyan .10
611 Chris Magruder .10
612 Jose Contreras **RC** .75
613 Carl Pavano .10
614 Kevin Brown .10
615 Tyler Houston .10
616 A.J. Pierzynski .10
617 Tony Fiore .10
618 Peter Bergeron .10
619 Rondell White .10
620 Brett Myers .10
621 Kevin Young .10
622 Kenny Lofton .10
623 Ben Davis .10
624 J.D. Drew .10
625 Chris Gomez .10
626 Karim Garcia .10
627 Ricky Gutierrez .10
628 Mark Redman .10
629 Juan Encarnacion .10
630 Anaheim Angels .25
631 Arizona Diamondbacks .10
632 Atlanta Braves .25
633 Baltimore Orioles .10
634 Boston Red Sox .25
635 Chicago Cubs .10
636 Chicago White Sox .10
637 Cincinnati Reds .10
638 Cleveland Indians .10
639 Colorado Rockies .10
640 Detroit Tigers .10
641 Florida Marlins .10
642 Houston Astros .10
643 Kansas City Royals .10
644 Los Angeles Dodgers .10
645 Milwaukee Brewers .10
646 Minnesota Twins .10
647 Montreal Expos .10
648 New York Mets .10
649 New York Yankees .50
650 Oakland Athletics .10
651 Philadelphia Phillies .10
652 Pittsburgh Pirates .10
653 San Diego Padres .10
654 San Francisco Giants .10
655 Seattle Mariners .10
656 St. Louis Cardinals .10
657 Tampa Bay Devil Rays .10
658 Texas Rangers .10
659 Toronto Blue Jays .10
660 Bryan Bullington **RC** .40
661 Jeremy Guthrie .10
662 Joey Gomes .25
663 Evel Bastida-Martinez **RC** .40
664 Brian Wright **RC** .10
665 B.J. Upton .10
666 Jeff Francis .10
667 Drew Meyer .10
668 Jeremy Hermida .10
669 Khalil Greene .75
670 Darrell Rasner .10
671 Cole Hamels .50
672 James Loney .10
673 Sergio Santos .10
674 Jason Pridie .10
675 Brandon Phillips, Victor Martinez .10
676 Hee Seop Choi, Nic Jackson .10
677 Dontrelle Willis, Jason Stokes .10
678 Chad Tracy, Lyle Overbay .10
679 Joe Borchard, Corwin Malone .10
680 Joe Mauer, Justin Morneau .25
681 Drew Henson, Brandon Claussen .10
682 Chase Utley, Gavin Floyd .25
683 Taggert Bozied, Xavier Nady .25
684 Aaron Heilman, Jose Reyes .25
685 Kenny Rogers .10
686 Bengie Molina .10
687 John Olerud .10
688 Bret Boone .10
689 Eric Chavez .15
690 Alex Rodriguez .75
691 Darin Erstad .15
692 Ichiro Suzuki .50
693 Torii Hunter .15
694 Greg Maddux .50
695 Brad Ausmus .10
696 Todd Helton .20
697 Fernando Vina .10
698 Scott Rolen .25
699 Edgar Renteria .10
700 Andruw Jones .20
701 Larry Walker .10
702 Jim Edmonds .10
703 Barry Zito .10
704 Randy Johnson .40
705 Miguel Tejada .15
706 Barry Bonds .75
707 Eric Hinske .10
708 Jason Jennings .10
709 Todd Helton .20
710 Jeff Kent .10
711 Edgar Renteria .10
712 Scott Rolen .25
713 Barry Bonds .75
714 Sammy Sosa .50
715 Vladimir Guerrero .40
716 Mike Piazza .75
717 Curt Schilling .20
718 Randy Johnson .40
719 Bobby Cox .10
720 World Series Card .10
721 World Series Card .10

Gold

Stars: 3-6X
Production 2,003 Sets

Black

Stars: 10-20X
Production 52 Sets

All-Stars

	NM/M
Complete Set (20):	20.00
Common Player:	.50
Inserted 1:15	

Topps All-Stars

TAS1	Alfonso Soriano	1.50
TAS2	Barry Bonds	4.00
TAS3	Ichiro Suzuki	2.00
TAS4	Alex Rodriguez	3.00
TAS5	Miguel Tejada	.75
TAS6	Nomar Garciaparra	2.50
TAS7	Jason Giambi	2.00
TAS8	Manny Ramirez	1.00
TAS9	Derek Jeter	4.00
TAS10	Garret Anderson	.50
TAS11	Barry Zito	.50
TAS12	Sammy Sosa	2.00
TAS13	Adam Dunn	1.00
TAS14	Vladimir Guerrero	1.50
TAS15	Mike Piazza	2.50
TAS16	Shawn Green	.50
TAS17	Luis Gonzalez	.50
TAS18	Todd Helton	.75
TAS19	Torii Hunter	.75
TAS20	Curt Schilling	.75

Autographs

		NM/M
Common Autograph:		8.00
HB	Hank Blalock	20.00
MB	Mark Buehrle	20.00
EC	Eric Chavez	25.00
DE	Darin Erstad	15.00
OH	Orlando Hudson	10.00
AK	Austin Kearns	15.00
JL	Jason Lane	10.00
PL	Paul LoDuca	12.00
JDM	J.D. Martin	8.00
JM	Joe Mauer	40.00
EM	Eric Milton	10.00
NN	Nick Neugebauer	10.00
MP	Mark Prior	40.00
SR	Scott Rolen	50.00
BS	Ben Sheets	15.00
MTE	Mark Teixeira	20.00
MTH	Marcus Thames	8.00

Autographs Series 2

		NM/M
Common Autograph:		8.00
JB	Josh Beckett	30.00
LB	Lance Berkman	40.00
CE	Clint Everts	8.00
CF	Cliff Floyd	20.00
BH	Brad Hawpe	8.00
EH	Eric Hinske	10.00
TH	Torii Hunter	20.00
AK	Austin Kearns	15.00
PK	Paul Konerko	20.00
PL	Paul LoDuca	15.00
MO	Magglio Ordonez	20.00
JPH	Josh Phelps	10.00
AP	Albert Pujols	120.00
MT	Miguel Tejada	30.00
BU	B.J. Upton	25.00
JV	Jose Vidro	10.00
DW	Dontrelle Willis	25.00
BZ	Barry Zito	30.00

Blue Backs

		NM/M
Complete Set (40):		50.00

Common Player: .75
Inserted 1:12

BB1	Albert Pujols	2.00
BB2	Barry Bonds	5.00
BB3	Ichiro Suzuki	3.00
BB4	Sammy Sosa	2.50
BB5	Kazuhisa Ishii	.75
BB6	Alex Rodriguez	4.00
BB7	Derek Jeter	5.00
BB8	Vladimir Guerrero	2.00
BB9	Ken Griffey Jr.	2.50
BB10	Jason Giambi	2.50
BB11	Todd Helton	1.00
BB12	Mike Piazza	3.00
BB13	Nomar Garciaparra	3.00
BB14	Chipper Jones	2.50
BB15	Ivan Rodriguez	1.00
BB16	Luis Gonzalez	.75
BB17	Pat Burrell	1.00
BB18	Mark Prior	1.50
BB19	Adam Dunn	1.50
BB20	Jeff Bagwell	1.50
BB21	Austin Kearns	1.00
BB22	Alfonso Soriano	2.00
BB23	Jim Thome	1.50
BB24	Bernie Williams	1.00
BB25	Pedro J. Martinez	2.00
BB26	Lance Berkman	1.00
BB27	Randy Johnson	2.00
BB28	Rafael Palmeiro	1.00
BB29	Richie Sexson	.75
BB30	Troy Glaus	1.50
BB31	Shawn Green	.75
BB32	Larry Walker	.75
BB33	Eric Hinske	.75
BB34	Andruw Jones	1.50
BB35	Carlos Delgado	1.00
BB36	Curt Schilling	1.50
BB37	Greg Maddux	2.50
BB38	Jimmy Rollins	.75
BB39	Eric Chavez	1.00
BB40	Scott Rolen	1.00

Draft Picks

		NM/M
Complete Set (10):		30.00

1-5 issued in retail sets.
6-10 issued in holiday sets.

1	Brandon Wood	10.00
2	Ryan Wagner	5.00
3	Sean Rodriguez	3.00
4	Chris Lubanski	5.00
5	Chad Billingsley	3.00
6	Javi Herrera	3.00
7	Brian McFall	3.00
8	Nicholas Markakis	5.00
9	Adam Miller	5.00
10	Daric Barton	5.00

Flashback

		NM/M
Complete Set (14):		50.00
Common Player:		2.00

HTA exclusive

GB	George Brett	6.00
LD	Lenny Dykstra	3.00
HK	Harmon Killebrew	6.00
BM	Bill Madlock	2.00
EM	Eddie Mathews	4.00
DM	Dale Murphy	5.00
JP	Jim Palmer	3.00
MP	Mike Piazza	6.00
RR	Robin Roberts	3.00
AR	Al Rosen	4.00
NR	Nolan Ryan	10.00
TS	Tom Seaver	5.00
WS	Warren Spahn	8.00
CY	Carl Yastrzemski	6.00

2003 Topps Futures Game

		NM/M
Complete Set (6):		5.00
Common Player:		.50
1	Alfonso Soriano	2.00
2	Pat Burrell	1.00
3	Adam Dunn	1.00
4	Barry Zito	.75
5	Mark Buehrle	.50
6	Rafael Furcal	.75

Hit Parade

		NM/M
Complete Set (30):		30.00
Common Player:		.50

Inserted 1:15

HP1	Barry Bonds	4.00
HP2	Sammy Sosa	2.50
HP3	Rafael Palmeiro	1.00
HP4	Fred McGriff	.75
HP5	Ken Griffey Jr.	2.50
HP6	Juan Gonzalez	1.00
HP7	Andres Galarraga	.50
HP8	Jeff Bagwell	1.50
HP9	Frank Thomas	1.50
HP10	Matt Williams	.50
HP11	Barry Bonds	4.00
HP12	Rafael Palmeiro	1.00
HP13	Fred McGriff	.75
HP14	Andres Galarraga	.50
HP15	Ken Griffey Jr.	2.50
HP16	Sammy Sosa	2.50
HP17	Jeff Bagwell	1.50
HP18	Juan Gonzalez	1.00
HP19	Frank Thomas	1.50
HP20	Matt Williams	.50
HP21	Rickey Henderson	1.00
HP22	Rafael Palmeiro	1.00
HP23	Roberto Alomar	1.00
HP24	Barry Bonds	4.00
HP25	Mark Grace	1.00
HP26	Fred McGriff	.75
HP27	Julio Franco	.50
HP28	Craig Biggio	.50
HP29	Andres Galarraga	.50
HP30	Barry Larkin	.50

Hobby Masters

		NM/M
Complete Set (20):		40.00
Common Player:		1.00

Inserted 1:18

HM1	Ichiro Suzuki	4.00
HM2	Kazuhisa Ishii	1.00
HM3	Derek Jeter	6.00
HM4	Barry Bonds	5.00
HM5	Sammy Sosa	3.00
HM6	Alex Rodriguez	4.00
HM7	Mike Piazza	4.00
HM8	Chipper Jones	3.00
HM9	Vladimir Guerrero	2.00
HM10	Nomar Garciaparra	4.00
HM11	Todd Helton	1.00
HM12	Jason Giambi	3.00
HM13	Ken Griffey Jr.	3.00
HM14	Albert Pujols	2.00
HM15	Ivan Rodriguez	1.00
HM16	Mark Prior	1.00
HM17	Adam Dunn	1.50
HM18	Randy Johnson	2.00
HM19	Pedro J. Martinez	2.00
HM20	Alfonso Soriano	3.00

Nolan Ryan No-Hitters

		NM/M
Complete Set (7):		45.00

Common Ryan (1-7): 8.00
RB-NR1-RB-NR7 Nolan Ryan 8.00

Nolan Ryan Record Breakers Autographs

		NM/M
Inserted 1:1,894		
HTA Exclusive		
NR	Nolan Ryan	200.00
NRA	Nolan Ryan	200.00
NRR	Nolan Ryan	200.00

Own The Game

		NM/M
Complete Set (30):		30.00
Common Player:		.50

Inserted 1:12

OG1	Ichiro Suzuki	3.00
OG2	Barry Bonds	4.00
OG3	Todd Helton	.75
OG4	Larry Walker	.75
OG5	Mike Sweeney	.50
OG6	Sammy Sosa	2.50
OG7	Lance Berkman	.75
OG8	Alex Rodriguez	4.00
OG9	Jim Thome	1.25
OG10	Shawn Green	.75
OG11	Troy Glaus	1.00
OG12	Richie Sexson	.50
OG13	Paul Konerko	.50
OG14	Jason Giambi	2.50
OG15	Chipper Jones	2.50
OG16	Torii Hunter	.50
OG17	Albert Pujols	1.50
OG18	Jose Vidro	.50
OG19	Alfonso Soriano	2.00
OG20	Luis Castillo	.50
OG21	Mike Lowell	.50
OG22	Garret Anderson	.50
OG23	Jimmy Rollins	.50
OG24	Curt Schilling	1.00
OG25	Kazuhisa Ishii	.50
OG26	Randy Johnson	1.50
OG27	Tom Glavine	.75
OG28	Roger Clemens	2.50
OG29	Pedro J. Martinez	1.50
OG30	Derek Lowe	.50

Prime Cuts Pine Tar Series

		NM/M
Pine Tar Series		
Production 200 Sets		
Trademark Series:		1-1.5X
Production 100 Sets		
Prime Cuts Series:		1.5-2X
Production 50 Sets		
RA	Roberto Alomar	20.00
LB	Lance Berkman	15.00
EC	Eric Chavez	20.00
AD	Adam Dunn	25.00
DE	Darin Erstad	15.00
NG	Nomar Garciaparra	40.00
JG	Juan Gonzalez	15.00
TH	Todd Helton	25.00
AJ	Andruw Jones	20.00
CJ	Chipper Jones	30.00
RP	Rafael Palmeiro	20.00
MP	Mike Piazza	30.00
AP	Albert Pujols	40.00
AR	Alex Rodriguez	25.00
IR	Ivan Rodriguez	25.00
SR	Scott Rolen	25.00
AS	Alfonso Soriano	25.00
MT	Miguel Tejada	15.00
FT	Frank Thomas	30.00
MV	Mo Vaughn	10.00
BW	Bernie Williams	25.00
Pine Tar Series:		
Production 200		
RA	Roberto Alomar	20.00
LB	Lance Berkman	15.00
HB	Hank Blalock	25.00
BBO	Barry Bonds	40.00
EC	Eric Chavez	15.00
CD	Carlos Delgado	10.00
AD	Adam Dunn	25.00
NG	Nomar Garciaparra	30.00
LG	Luis Gonzalez	8.00
TG	Tony Gwynn	20.00
RH	Rickey Henderson	25.00

RJ	Randy Johnson	25.00
EM	Edgar Martinez	20.00
TM	Tino Martinez	15.00
MO	Magglio Ordonez	10.00
RP	Rafael Palmeiro	15.00
JP	Jorge Posada	15.00
AP	Albert Pujols	40.00
MP	Mark Prior	20.00
AR	Alex Rodriguez	25.00
AS	Alfonso Soriano	20.00

Prime Cuts Autograph
NM/M

Production 50 Sets

EC	Eric Chavez	100.00
LB	Lance Berkman	120.00
AJ	Andruw Jones	100.00
CJ	Chipper Jones	150.00
MO	Magglio Ordonez	100.00
MT	Miguel Tejada	120.00

Record Breakers

94 XBHs in 2001
Houston Astros® Extra Base Hits Season Leader
Lance Berkman

NM/M

Complete Set (50): 40.00
Common Player: .50
Inserted 1:6

JB	Jeff Bagwell	1.50
LBE	Lance Berkman	1.00
BB	Barry Bonds	5.00
GB	George Brett	2.50
LB	Lou Brock	.50
RCA	Rod Carew	.50
LC	Luis Castillo	.50
RC	Roger Clemens	2.50
CD	Carlos Delgado	.50
CF	Cliff Floyd	.50
GF	George Foster	.50
AG	Andres Galarraga	.50
JG	Jason Giambi	2.50
BG	Bob Gibson	1.00
TG	Troy Glaus	1.00
JGO	Juan Gonzalez	1.00
LGO	Luis Gonzalez	.50
SG	Shawn Green	.75
HG	Hank Greenberg	.50
KG	Ken Griffey Jr.	3.00
VG	Vladimir Guerrero	1.50
RG	Ron Guidry	.50
TH	Todd Helton	1.00
RH	Rickey Henderson	.75
FJ	Fergie Jenkins	.50
RJ	Randy Johnson	1.50
CJ	Chipper Jones	3.00
HK	Harmon Killebrew	1.00
CK	Chuck Klein	.50
JM	Juan Marichal	.50
PM	Pedro J. Martinez	1.50
EM	Eddie Mathews	1.00
DM	Don Mattingly	4.00
FM	Fred McGriff	.50
JO	John Olerud	.50
RP	Rafael Palmeiro	3.00
MP	Mike Piazza	1.00
FR	Frank Robinson	1.00
AR	Alex Rodriguez	4.00
NR	Nolan Ryan	6.00
MSC	Mike Schmidt	3.00
CS	Curt Schilling	1.00
TS	Tom Seaver	1.00
RS	Richie Sexson	.50
GS	Gary Sheffield	.50
SS	Sammy Sosa	3.00
MS	Mike Sweeney	.50
HW	Hack Wilson	.50
PW	Preston Wilson	.50
RY	Robin Yount	1.00

Record Breakers Autographs
NM/M

Common Autograph:

CF	Cliff Floyd	20.00
LG	Luis Gonzalez	30.00
FJ	Fergie Jenkins	25.00
CJ	Chipper Jones	75.00
HK	Harmon Killebrew	60.00
RP	Rafael Palmeiro	60.00
MS	Mike Schmidt	100.00
RS	Richie Sexson	30.00
MSW	Mike Sweeney	30.00
RY	Robin Yount	75.00

Record Breakers Relics

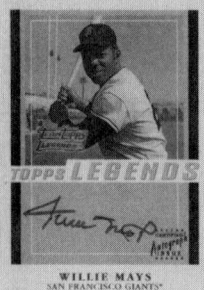

51 2Bs in 1962
Cincinnati Reds® Doubles Season Leader
Frank Robinson

NM/M

Common Player: 6.00

JB	Jeff Bagwell/Jsy	8.00
LB	Lance Berkman/Jsy	10.00
GB	George Brett/Bat	25.00
LC	Luis Castillo/Bat	6.00
CD	Carlos Delgado/Jsy	8.00
LGO	Luis Gonzalez/Jsy	6.00
SG	Shawn Green/Jsy	8.00
HG	Hank Greenberg/Bat	30.00
TH	Todd Helton/Jsy	10.00
RH	Rickey Henderson/Bat	15.00
CJ	Chipper Jones/Jsy	12.00
PM	Pedro Martinez/Jsy	10.00
DM	Don Mattingly/Bat	35.00
MP	Mike Piazza/Bat	15.00
FR	Frank Robinson/Bat	12.00
AR	Alex Rodriguez/Jsy	15.00
NR	Nolan Ryan/Jsy	35.00
MS	Mike Sweeney/Bat	8.00
HW	Hack Wilson/Bat	50.00
RY	Robin Yount/Jsy	15.00

Record Breakers Series 2
NM/M

Complete Set (50): 40.00
Common Player: .50
Inserted 1:6

RA	Roberto Alomar	1.00
GA	Garret Anderson	.75
LA	Luis Aparicio	.50
JB	Jeff Bagwell	1.50
LB	Lance Berkman	1.00
CB	Craig Biggio	.75
WB	Wade Boggs	.75
BB	Barry Bonds	5.00
GB	George Brett	2.50
LBR	Lou Brock	.75
JD	Johnny Damon	.50
CD	Carlos Delgado	.50
LD	Lenny Dykstra	.50
DE	Darin Erstad	.50
BF	Bob Feller	.75
GF	George Foster	.50
NG	Nomar Garciaparra	3.00
LG	Luis Gonzalez	.50
DG	Dwight Gooden	.50
SG	Shawn Green	.75
KG	Ken Griffey Jr.	2.50
VG	Vladimir Guerrero	1.50
TG	Tony Gwynn	1.50
TH	Todd Helton	1.00
RH	Rickey Henderson	1.00
RJ	Randy Johnson	1.50
JK	Jeff Kent	.50
TK	Ted Kluszewski	.50
GM	Greg Maddux	2.50
JM	Juan Marichal	.50
EM	Edgar Martinez	.50
WM	Willie Mays	4.00
JME	Jose Mesa	.50
PM	Paul Molitor	1.00
JP	Jim Palmer	.75
TR	Tim Raines	.50
MR	Manny Ramirez	1.50
JR	Jim Rice	.50
FR	Frank Robinson	1.00
AR	Alex Rodriguez	4.00
TS	Tom Seaver	2.00
RS	Richie Sexson	.75
JS	John Smoltz	.50
SS	Sammy Sosa	2.50
WS	Willie Stargell	1.00
IS	Ichiro Suzuki	2.50
FT	Frank Thomas	1.50
JT	Jim Thome	1.50
LW	Larry Walker	.50
RY	Robin Yount	15.00

Record Breakers Autographs Series 2
NM/M

Common Autograph: 25.00
Inserted 1:2,218

LA	Luis Aparicio	40.00
LB	Lance Berkman	40.00
LBR	Lou Brock	40.00
GF	George Foster	25.00

JM	Juan Marichal	40.00
DM	Don Mattingly	125.00
WM	Willie Mays	150.00

Record Breaker Relics Series 2
NM/M

Common Player: 5.00

WB	Wade Boggs/Bat	10.00
GB	George Brett/Bat	25.00
CD	Carlos Delgado/Jsy	6.00
DE	Darin Erstad/Jsy	8.00
LG	Luis Gonzalez/Jsy	5.00
TH	Todd Helton/Jsy	8.00
RH	Rogers Hornsby/Bat	35.00
TK	Ted Kluszewski/Bat	15.00
EM	Edgar Martinez/Bat	12.00
JR	Jim Rice/Jsy	8.00
FR	Frank Robinson/Bat	12.00
AR	Alex Rodriguez/Jsy	15.00
NRA	Nolan Ryan/Jsy	30.00
RS	Richie Sexson/Jsy	8.00
FT	Frank Thomas/Bat	10.00
RY	Robin Yount	12.00

Red Backs

RAFAEL PALMEIRO

NM/M

Complete Set (40): 50.00
Common Player: .50
Inserted 1:12

TRB1	Nomar Garciaparra	3.00
TRB2	Ichiro Suzuki	2.50
TRB3	Alex Rodriguez	4.00
TRB4	Sammy Sosa	2.50
TRB5	Barry Bonds	5.00
TRB6	Vladimir Guerrero	1.50
TRB7	Derek Jeter	5.00
TRB8	Miguel Tejada	2.00
TRB9	Alfonso Soriano	1.50
TRB10	Manny Ramirez	1.50
TRB11	Adam Dunn	1.50
TRB12	Jason Giambi	2.50
TRB13	Mike Piazza	3.00
TRB14	Scott Rolen	1.50
TRB15	Shawn Green	.75
TRB16	Randy Johnson	1.50
TRB17	Todd Helton	1.00
TRB18	Garret Anderson	1.00
TRB19	Curt Schilling	1.00
TRB20	Albert Pujols	2.00
TRB21	Chipper Jones	2.50
TRB22	Luis Gonzalez	.50
TRB23	Mark Prior	1.50
TRB24	Jim Thome	1.50
TRB25	Ivan Rodriguez	1.00
TRB26	Torii Hunter	1.00
TRB27	Lance Berkman	1.00
TRB28	Troy Glaus	1.50
TRB29	Andruw Jones	1.00
TRB30	Barry Zito	.75
TRB31	Jeff Bagwell	1.50
TRB32	Magglio Ordonez	.75
TRB33	Pat Burrell	.50
TRB34	Mike Sweeney	.50
TRB35	Rafael Palmeiro	1.50
TRB36	Larry Walker	.50
TRB37	Carlos Delgado	.50
TRB38	Brian Giles	1.00
TRB39	Pedro J. Martinez	1.50
TRB40	Greg Maddux	2.50

Stadium Seat Relics
NM/M

Common Player: 15.00
Inserted 1:37 Series 2 HTA

JB	Johnny Bench	30.00
DC	Dave Concepcion	20.00
AD	Adam Dunn	20.00
KG	Ken Griffey Jr.	25.00
AK	Austin Kearns	20.00
BL	Barry Larkin	25.00
JM	Joe Morgan	15.00
PO	Paul O'Neill	15.00
TP	Tony Perez	20.00
TS	Tom Seaver	25.00

Team Topps Legends Autos.

TOPPS LEGENDS

WILLIE MAYS
SAN FRANCISCO GIANTS®

NM/M

Common Player:

Vida Blue	20.00
Bob Feller	25.00
Willie Mays	125.00
Gil McDougald	12.00
Robin Roberts	25.00
Bobby Thomson	20.00
Luis Tiant	8.00
Carl Yastrzemski	50.00

Turn Back The Clock Autos.
NM/M

Common Player:

LD	Lenny Dykstra	15.00
BM	Bill Madlock	10.00
DM	Dale Murphy	40.00
JP	Jim Palmer	20.00

2003 Topps Traded & Rookies

NM/M

Complete Set (275): 50.00
Common Player: .15
Pack (8 + 2 Chrome): 2.00
Box (24): 40.00
Chrome Cards: 2-4X

T1	Juan Pierre	.15
T2	Mark Grudzielanek	.15
T3	Tanyon Sturtze	.15
T4	Greg Vaughn	.15
T5	Greg Myers	.15
T6	Randall Simon	.15
T7	Todd Hundley	.15
T8	Marlon Anderson	.15
T9	Jeff Reboulet	.15
T10	Alex Sanchez	.15
T11	Mike Rivera	.15
T12	Todd Walker	.15
T13	Ray King	.15
T14	Shawn Estes	.15
T15	Gary Mathews Jr.	.15
T16	Jaret Wright	.15
T17	Edgardo Alfonzo	.15
T18	Omar Daal	.15
T19	Ryan Rupe	.15
T20	Tony Clark	.15
T21	Damon Minor	.15
T22	Mike Stanton	.15
T23	Ramon Martinez	.15
T24	Armando Rios	.15
T25	Johnny Estrada	.15
T26	Joe Girardi	.15
T27	Ivan Rodriguez	.75
T28	Robert Fick	.15
T29	Rick White	.15
T30	Robert Person	.15
T31	Alan Benes	.15
T32	Chris Carpenter	.40
T33	Chris Widger	.15
T34	Travis Hafner	.40
T35	Mike Venafro	.15
T36	Jon Lieber	.15
T37	Orlando Hernandez	.15
T38	Aaron Myette	.15
T39	Paul Bako	.15

T40	Erubiel Durazo	.15
T41	Mark Guthrie	.15
T42	Steve Avery	.15
T43	Damian Jackson	.15
T44	Rey Ordonez	.15
T45	John Flaherty	.15
T46	Byung-Hyun Kim	.15
T47	Tom Goodwin	.15
T48	Elmer Dessens	.15
T49	Al Martin	.15
T50	Gene Kingsale	.15
T51	Lenny Harris	.15
T52	David Ortiz	.75
T53	John Rocker	.15
T54	Mike DiFelice	.15
T55	Nick Bierbrodt	.15
T56	Todd Zeile	.15
T57	Roberto Hernandez	.15
T58	Albie Lopez	.15
T59	Roberto Alomar	.50
T60	Russ Ortiz	.15
T61	Brian Daubach	.15
T62	Carl Everett	.15
T63	Jeromy Burnitz	.15
T64	Mark Bellhorn	.15
T65	Ruben Sierra	.15
T66	Mike Fetters	.15
T67	Armando Benitez	.15
T68	Deivi Cruz	.15
T69	Jose Cruz Jr.	.15
T70	Jeremy Fikac	.15
T71	Jeff Kent	.25
T72	Andres Galarraga	.25
T73	Rickey Henderson	.50
T74	Royce Clayton	.15
T75	Troy O'Leary	.15
T76	Ron Coomer	.15
T77	Greg Colbrunn	.15
T78	Wes Helms	.15
T79	Kevin Millwood	.25
T80	Damion Easley	.15
T81	Bobby Kielty	.15
T82	Keith Osik	.15
T83	Ramiro Mendoza	.15
T84	Shea Hillenbrand	.15
T85	Shannon Stewart	.15
T86	Eddie Perez	.15
T87	Ugueth Urbina	.15
T88	Orlando Palmeiro	.15
T89	Graeme Lloyd	.15
T90	John Vander Wal	.15
T91	Gary Bennett	.15
T92	Shane Reynolds	.15
T93	Steve Parris	.15
T94	Julio Lugo	.15
T95	John Halama	.15
T96	Carlos Baerga	.15
T97	Jim Parque	.15
T98	Mike Williams	.15
T99	Fred McGriff	.25
T100	Kenny Rogers	.15
T101	Matt Herges	.15
T102	Jay Bell	.15
T103	Esteban Yan	.15
T104	Eric Owens	.15
T105	Aaron Fultz	.15
T106	Rey Sanchez	.15
T107	Jim Thome	.75
T108	Aaron Boone	.25
T109	Raul Mondesi	.25
T110	Kenny Lofton	.25
T111	Jose Guillen	.15
T112	Aramis Ramirez	.40
T113	Sidney Ponson	.15
T114	Scott Williamson	.15
T115	Robin Ventura	.15
T116	Dusty Baker	.15
T117	Felipe Alou	.15
T118	Buck Showalter	.15
T119	Jack McKeon	.15
T120	Art Howe	.15
T121	Bobby Crosby	.40
T122	Adrian Gonzalez	.25
T123	Kevin Cash	.15
T124	Shin-Soo Choo	.25
T125	Chin-Feng Chen	.25
T126	Miguel Cabrera	.75
T127	Jason Young	.15
T128	Alex Herrera	.15
T129	Jason Dubois	.15
T130	Jeff Mathis	.15
T131	Casey Kotchman	.25
T132	Ed Rogers	.15
T133	Wilson Betemit	.15
T134	Jim Kavourias	.15
T135	Taylor Buchholz	.15
T136	Adam LaRoche	.15
T137	Dallas McPherson	.40
T138	Jesus Cota	.15
T139	Clint Nageotte	.15
T140	Boof Bonser	.15
T141	Walter Young	.15
T142	Joe Crede	.25
T143	Denny Bautista	.15
T144	Victor Diaz	.15
T145	Chris Narveson	.15
T146	Gabe Gross	.15
T147	Jimmy Journell	.15
T148	Rafael Soriano	.15
T149	Jerome Williams	.15
T150	Aaron Cook	.15
T151	Anastacio Martinez	.15
T152	Scott Hairston	.15
T153	John Buck	.15

T154	Ryan Ludwick	.15
T155	Chris Bootcheck	.15
T156	John Rheinecker	.15
T157	Jason Lane	.15
T158	Shelley Duncan	.15
T159	Adam Wainwright	.15
T160	Jason Arnold	.15
T161	Jonny Gomes	.15
T162	James Loney	.50
T163	Mike Fontenot	.15
T164	Khalil Greene	1.00
T165	Sean Burnett	.15
T166	David Martinez	.15
T167	Felix Pie **RC**	2.00
T168	Joe Valentine **RC**	.50
T169	Brandon Webb **RC**	3.00
T170	Matt Diaz **RC**	.25
T171	Lew Ford **RC**	.75
T172	Jeremy Griffiths	.25
T173	Matt Hensley **RC**	.50
T174	Charlie Manning **RC**	.25
T175	Elizardo Ramirez **RC**	.75
T176	Greg Aquino **RC**	.25
T177	Felix Sanchez **RC**	.50
T178	Kelly Shoppach **RC**	.75
T179	Bubba Nelson **RC**	.50
T180	Mike O'Keefe **RC**	.25
T181	Hanley Ramirez **RC**	6.00
T182	Todd Wellemeyer **RC**	.75
T183	Dustin Moseley **RC**	.25
T184	Eric Crozier **RC**	.50
T185	Ryan Shealy **RC**	.75
T186	Jeremy Bonderman	1.50
T187	Thomari Story-Harden **RC**	.40
T188	Dusty Brown **RC**	.50
T189	Rob Hammock **RC**	.40
T190	Jorge Piedra **RC**	.25
T191	Chris De La Cruz **RC**	.25
T192	Eli Whiteside **RC**	.25
T193	Jason Kubel **RC**	.75
T194	Jon Schuerholz **RC**	.25
T195	Stephen Randolph **RC**	.25
T196	Andy Sisco	.75
T197	Sean Smith	.15
T198	Jon-Mark Sprowl **RC**	.75
T199	Matt Kata **RC**	.40
T200	Robinson Cano **RC**	4.00
T201	Nook Logan **RC**	.25
T202	Ben Francisco **RC**	1.00
T203	Arnie Munoz **RC**	.25
T204	Eric Chavez	.15
T205	Eric Riggs **RC**	.25
T206	Beau Kemp **RC**	.25
T207	Travis Wong **RC**	.50
T208	Dustin Yount **RC**	.50
T209	Brian McCann	4.00
T210	Wilton Reynolds **RC**	.25
T211	Matt Bruback **RC**	.25
T212	Andrew Brown **RC**	.50
T213	Edgar Gonzalez **RC**	.25
T214	Eider Torres **RC**	.25
T215	Aquilino Lopez **RC**	.25
T216	Bobby Basham **RC**	.50
T217	Tim Olson **RC**	.50
T218	Nathan Panther **RC**	.50
T219	Bryan Grace **RC**	.25
T220	Dusty Gomon **RC**	.25
T221	Wilfredo Ledezma **RC**	.25
T222	Josh Willingham **RC**	.75
T223	David Cash **RC**	.25
T224	Oscar Villarreal **RC**	.25
T225	Jeff Duncan **RC**	.50
T226	Kade Johnson **RC**	.25
T227	Luke Steidlmayer **RC**	.25
T228	Brandon Watson **RC**	.50
T229	Jose Morales	.25
T230	Mike Gallo **RC**	.25
T231	Tyler Adamczyk **RC**	.50
T232	Adam Stern	.15
T233	Brennan King **RC**	.25
T234	Dan Haren	1.00
T235	Michel Hernandez **RC**	.25
T236	Ben Fritz	.15
T237	Clay Hensley **RC**	.50
T238	Tyler Johnson **RC**	.25
T239	Pete LaForest **RC**	.25
T240	Tyler Martin **RC**	.25
T241	J.D. Durbin **RC**	.50
T242	Shane Victorino **RC**	1.00
T243	Rajai Davis **RC**	1.00
T244	Ismael Castro **RC**	.25
T245	Chien-Ming Wang **RC**	4.00
T246	Travis Ishikawa **RC**	.40
T247	Corey Shafer **RC**	.50
T248	Gary Schneidmiller **RC**	.25
T249	David Pember **RC**	.25
T250	Keith Stamler **RC**	.25
T251	Tyson Graham **RC**	.25
T252	Ryan Cameron **RC**	.25
T253	Eric Eckenstahler **RC**	.25
T254	Matthew Peterson **RC**	.25
T255	Dustin McGowan **RC**	1.00
T256	Prentice Redman **RC**	.40
T257	Haj Turay **RC**	.25
T258	Carlos Guzman **RC**	.40
T259	Matt DeMarco **RC**	.25
T260	Derek Michaelis **RC**	.25
T261	Brian Burgamy **RC**	.25
T262	Jay Sitzman **RC**	.25
T263	Chris Fallon **RC**	.25
T264	Mike Adams **RC**	.25
T265	Clint Barmes **RC**	.75
T266	Eric Reed **RC**	.50
T267	Willie Eyre **RC**	.25

T268	Carlos Duran **RC**	.40
T269	Nick Trzesniak **RC**	.25
T270	Ferdin Tejeda **RC**	.50
T271	Michael Garciaparra	.25
T272	Michael Hinckley **RC**	.75
T273	Branden Florence **RC**	.25
T274	Trent Oeltjen **RC**	.40
T275	Mike Neu **RC**	.25

Gold

Stars:		5-10X
Rookies:		1-2.5X
Production 2003 Sets		

Chrome Refractor

Stars:		4-8X
Rookies:		2-4X
Inserted 1:12		

Future Phenoms

		NM/M
Common Player:		4.00
RB	Rocco Baldelli	6.00
WB	Wilson Betemit	4.00
HB	Hank Blalock	6.00
WPB	Willie Bloomquist	15.00
MB	Marlon Byrd	4.00
CC	Chin-Feng Chen	20.00
CDC	Carl Crawford	6.00
TH	Travis Hafner	6.00
TAH	Trey Hodges	4.00
JM	Justin Morneau	10.00
BP	Brandon Phillips	6.00
MR	Michael Restovich	6.00
CS	Chris Snelling	4.00
MT	Mark Teixeira	8.00
JT	Joe Thurston	4.00

Hall of Fame

		NM/M
Common Player:		8.00
GC	Gary Carter	8.00
EM	Eddie Murray	15.00

Hall of Fame Dual

		NM/M
Complete Set (1):		
CM	Gary Carter,	
	Eddie Murray	25.00

Signature Moves

		NM/M
Common Player:		8.00
EA	Erick Almonte	8.00
DB	David Bell	10.00
JB	Joe Borchard	8.00
BC	Bartolo Colon	12.00
JC	Jose Cruz Jr.	8.00
JJC	Jack Cust	10.00
RF	Robert Fick	8.00
CF	Cliff Floyd	15.00
JF	Jesse Foppert	10.00
JG	Joey Gomes	8.00
KG	Khalil Greene	25.00
JL	James Loney	25.00
VM	Victor Martinez	20.00
FP	Felix Pie	60.00
ER	Elizardo Ramirez	12.00
JR	Jose Reyes	40.00
JS	Jason Stokes	15.00
MT	Mark Teixeira	15.00
BU	B.J. Upton	25.00
WY	Walter Young	10.00

Tools of the Trade

		NM/M
Common Player:		4.00
EA	Edgardo Alfonzo	4.00
DB	David Bell	4.00
JC	Jose Cruz Jr.	4.00
ED	Erubiel Durazo	4.00
RD	Ray Durham	4.00
RF	Robert Fick	4.00
CF	Cliff Floyd	4.00
AG	Andres Galarraga	5.00
JG	Jeremy Giambi	4.00
TG	Tom Glavine	6.00
EK	Eric Karros	5.00
JK	Jeff Kent	5.00
KL	Kenny Lofton	10.00
FL	Felipe Lopez	6.00
FM	Fred McGriff	5.00
KM	Kevin Millar	5.00
RO	Rey Ordonez	4.00
JP	Juan Pierre	5.00
SH	Tsuyoshi Shinjo	4.00
SS	Shane Spencer	4.00
JT	Jim Thome	10.00
BT	Bubba Trammell	4.00
RW	Rondell White	4.00
PW	Preston Wilson	4.00
TZ	Todd Zeile	6.00

Tools of the Trade Dual

		NM/M
Common Player:		10.00
KM	Kevin Millwood	10.00
IR	Ivan Rodriguez	15.00
JT	Jim Thome	15.00

2003 Topps All-Time Fan Favorites

		NM/M
Complete Set (150):		30.00
Common Player:		.25
Pack (6):		4.00
Box (24):		75.00
1	Willie Mays	3.00
2	Whitey Ford	1.00
3	Stan Musial	2.50
4	Paul Blair	.25
5	Harold Reynolds	.25
6	Bob Friend	.25
7	Rod Carew	.75
8	Kirk Gibson	.25
9	Graig Nettles	.25
10	Ozzie Smith	1.00
11	Tony Perez	.25
12	Tim Wallach	.25
13	Bert Campaneris	.25
14	Cory Snyder	.25
15	Dave Parker	.25
16	Darrell Evans	.25

17	Joe Pepitone	.25
18	Don Sutton	.25
19	Dale Murphy	1.00
20	George Brett	2.50
21	Carlton Fisk	.50
22	Bob Watson	.25
23	Wally Joyner	.25
24	Paul Molitor	1.00
25	Keith Hernandez	.25
26	Jerry Koosman	.25
27	George Bell	.25
28	Boog Powell	.25
29	Bruce Sutter	.75
30	Ernie Banks	1.50
31	Steve Lyons	.25
32	Earl Weaver	.25
33	Dave Stieb	.25
34	Alan Trammell	.25
35	Bret Saberhagen	.25
36	J.R. Richard	.25
37	Mickey Rivers	.25
38	Juan Marichal	.75
39	Gaylord Perry	.25
40	Don Mattingly	3.00
41	Bobby Grich	.25
42	Steve Sax	.25
43	Sparky Anderson	.25
44	Luis Aparicio	.25
45	Fergie Jenkins	.50
46	Jim Palmer	.75
47	Howard Johnson	.25
48	Dwight Evans	.25
49	Bill Buckner	.25
50	Cal Ripken Jr.	4.00
51	Jose Cruz	.25
52	Tony Oliva	.25
53	Bobby Richardson	.25
54	Luis Tiant	.25
55	Warren Spahn	1.00
56	Phil Rizzuto	1.00
57	Eric Davis	.25
58	Vida Blue	.25
59	Steve Balboni	.25
60	Mike Schmidt	2.50
61	Ken Griffey Sr.	.25
62	Jim Abbott	.25
63	Whitey Herzog	.25
64	Rich "Goose" Gossage	.25
65	Tony Armas	.25
66	Bill "Moose" Skowron	.25
67	Don Newcombe	.25
68	Bill Madlock	.25
69	Lance Parrish	.25
70	Reggie Jackson	1.50
71	Willie Wilson	.25
72	Terry Pendleton	.25
73	Jimmy Piersall	.25
74	George Foster	.25
75	Bob Horner	.25
76	Chris Sabo	.25
77	Fred Lynn	.25
78	Jim Rice	.25
79	Maury Wills	.25
80	Yogi Berra	1.50
81	Johnny Sain	.25
82	Tom Lasorda	.50
83	Bill Mazeroski	.25
84	John Kruk	.25
85	Bob Feller	.75
86	Frank Robinson	.75
87	Red Schoendienst	.25
88	Gary Carter	.50
89	Andre Dawson	.50
90	Tim McCarver	.25
91	Robin Yount	1.00
92	Phil Niekro	.25
93	Joe Morgan	.25
94	Darren Daulton	.25
95	Bobby Thomson	.25
96	Alvin Davis	.25
97	Robin Roberts	.25
98	Kirby Puckett	1.50
99	Jack Clark	.25
100	Hank Aaron	3.00
101	Orlando Cepeda	.50
102	Vern Law	.25
103	Cecil Cooper	.25
104	Don Larsen	.50
105	Mario Mendoza	.25
106	Tony Gwynn	1.50
107	Ernie Harwell	.25
108a	Monte Irvin (No facsimile autograph.)	.75
108b	Monte Irvin (W/facsimile autograph.)	1.50
109	Tommy John	.25
110	Rollie Fingers	.75
111	Johnny Podres	.25
112	Jeff Reardon	.25
113	Buddy Bell	.25
114	Dwight Gooden	.50
115	Garry Templeton	.25
116	Johnny Bench	2.00
117	Joe Rudi	.25
118	Ron Guidry	.50
119	Vince Coleman	.25
120	Al Kaline	2.00
121	Carl Yastrzemski	1.50
122	Hank Bauer	.25
123	Mark Fidrych	.25
124	Paul O'Neill	.50
125	Ron Cey	.25
126	Willie McGee	.25
127	Harmon Killebrew	1.50
128	Dave Concepcion	.25
129	Harold Baines	.25
130	Lou Brock	.50
131	Lee Smith	.25
132	Willie McCovey	.75
133	Steve Garvey	.25
134	Kent Tekulve	.25
135	Tom Seaver	1.50
136	Bo Jackson	1.00
137	Walt Weiss	.25
138	Brook Jacoby	.25
139	Dennis Eckersley	.50
140	Duke Snider	1.00
141	Lenny Dykstra	.25
142	Greg Luzinski	.25
143	Jim Bunning	.25
144	Jose Canseco	.75
145	Ron Santo	.25
146	Bert Blyleven	.25
147	Wade Boggs	.75
148	Brooks Robinson	1.00
149	Ray Knight	.25
150	Nolan Ryan	4.00

Refractors

Cards (1-150): 3-6X
Production 299 Sets

Autographs

		NM/M
	Common Autograph:	8.00
	SP's Production 50	
HA	Hank Aaron/SP	300.00
JA	Jim Abbott	10.00
SA	Sparky Anderson/SP	30.00
LA	Luis Aparicio	10.00
TA	Tony Armas	10.00
HBA	Harold Baines	15.00
SB	Steve Balboni	8.00
EB	Ernie Banks/SP	120.00
HB	Hank Bauer/SP	35.00
BBE	Buddy Bell	15.00
GB	George Bell	10.00
JBE	Johnny Bench/SP	100.00
YB	Yogi Berra/SP	100.00
BBI	Buddy Biancalana	8.00
PB	Paul Blair	10.00
VB	Vida Blue	15.00
BB	Bert Blyleven	15.00
WB	Wade Boggs/SP	75.00
GBR	George Brett/SP	250.00
LB	Lou Brock/SP	60.00
BBU	Bill Buckner	10.00
JB	Jim Bunning/SP	75.00
BC	Bert Campaneris	10.00
JOS	Jose Canseco/SP	60.00
RCA	Rod Carew/SP	75.00
GC	Gary Carter/SP	40.00
JCA	Joe Carter/SP	35.00
OC	Orlando Cepeda/SP	60.00
RCE	Ron Cey	10.00
JC	Jack Clark	15.00
VC	Vince Coleman	10.00
DC	Dave Concepcion/SP	35.00
CC	Cecil Cooper	10.00
JCR	Jose Cruz	10.00
RDA	Ron Darling	10.00
DD	Darren Daulton	15.00
AD	Alvin Davis	8.00
ED	Eric Davis	15.00
ADA	Andre Dawson/SP	50.00
DDE	Doug DeCinces	15.00
RD	Rob Dibble	15.00
LDU	Leon Durham	10.00
LD	Lenny Dykstra	10.00
DEC	Dennis Eckersley/SP	60.00
DE	Darrell Evans	10.00
DEV	Dwight Evans/SP	40.00
BF	Bob Feller	15.00
MF	Mark Fidrych	10.00
RF	Rollie Fingers/SP	40.00
CF	Carlton Fisk/SP	60.00
WF	Whitey Ford/SP	100.00
GF	George Foster	10.00
BFR	Bob Friend	10.00
SG	Steve Garvey	20.00
KGI	Kirk Gibson/SP	75.00
DG	Dwight Gooden/SP	30.00
RG	Rich "Goose" Gossage/SP	30.00
BGR	Bobby Grich	10.00
KG	Ken Griffey Sr./SP	30.00
RGU	Ron Guidry	15.00
TG	Tony Gwynn/SP	100.00
EH	Ernie Harwell	40.00
KH	Keith Hernandez/SP	60.00
WHE	Willie Hernandez	10.00
TH	Tom Herr	10.00
WH	Whitey Herzog	20.00
BH	Bob Horner	8.00
MI	Monte Irvin/SP	40.00
BJ	Bo Jackson/SP	100.00
RJ	Reggie Jackson/SP	100.00
BJA	Brook Jacoby	8.00
FJ	Fergie Jenkins	15.00
TJ	Tommy John	15.00
HJ	Howard Johnson	10.00
WJ	Wally Joyner	10.00
AK	Al Kaline/SP	75.00
HK	Harmon Killebrew/SP	80.00
RK	Ralph Kiner/SP	65.00
RKI	Ron Kittle	10.00
RY	Ray Knight	10.00
JK	Jerry Koosman	20.00
JKR	John Kruk/SP	60.00
CL	Carney Lansford	15.00
DL	Don Larsen	15.00
TL	Tom Lasorda/SP	40.00
VL	Vern Law	15.00
BL	Bill Lee	10.00
CLE	Chet Lemon	10.00
GL	Greg Luzinski	15.00
FL	Fred Lynn/SP	25.00
SL	Steve Lyons	15.00
BMA	Bill Madlock	10.00
JMA	Juan Marichal/SP	75.00
DON	Don Mattingly/SP	100.00
WM	Willie Mays/SP	150.00
BMZ	Bill Mazeroski/SP	50.00
TM	Tim McCarver/SP	40.00
WMC	Willie McCovey/SP	60.00
MCG	Willie McGee/SP	60.00
TMC	Tug McGraw	20.00
MM	Mario Mendoza	10.00
KM	Kevin Mitchell	10.00
PM	Paul Molitor/SP	60.00
JMO	John Montefusco	10.00
JM	Joe Morgan/SP	30.00
DM	Dale Murphy/SP	60.00
SM	Stan Musial/SP	120.00
GN	Graig Nettles	15.00
DN	Don Newcombe/SP	40.00
PN	Phil Niekro/SP	40.00
AO	Al Oliver	10.00
PO	Paul O'Neill/SP	75.00
MP	Mike Pagliarulo	10.00
JP	Jim Palmer/SP	60.00
DP	Dave Parker/SP	40.00
LP	Lance Parrish	10.00
TP	Terry Pendleton	15.00
JPE	Joe Pepitone	10.00
TPE	Tony Perez/SP	65.00
GP	Gaylord Perry	25.00
BP	Boog Powell	15.00
KP	Kirby Puckett/SP	65.00
JRE	Jeff Reardon	10.00
HR	Harold Reynolds/SP	40.00
JRI	Jim Rice/SP	45.00
JR	J.R. Richard	10.00
CR	Cal Ripken Jr./SP	225.00
MR	Mickey Rivers	10.00
PR	Phil Rizzuto/SP	75.00
RR	Robin Roberts	25.00
BRO	Brooks Robinson/SP	100.00
FR	Frank Robinson/SP	75.00
JRU	Joe Rudi	10.00
NR	Nolan Ryan/SP	200.00
BSA	Bret Saberhagen/SP	40.00
CS	Chris Sabo	8.00
RSA	Ron Santo	25.00
SS	Steve Sax	8.00
MS	Mike Schmidt/SP	150.00
RS	Red Schoendienst	15.00
TSE	Tom Seaver/SP	100.00
KS	Kevin Seitzer	10.00
BS	Bill "Moose" Skowron	15.00
LS	Lee Smith	10.00
OS	Ozzie Smith/SP	100.00
DSN	Duke Snider/SP	60.00
CN	Cory Snyder	15.00
WS	Warren Spahn	40.00
CSP	Chris Speier	10.00
DS	Dave Stieb	15.00
BSU	Bruce Sutter	35.00
DSU	Don Sutton/SP	40.00
KT	Kent Tekulve	10.00
GT	Garry Templeton	10.00
BT	Bobby Thomson/SP	25.00
LT	Luis Tiant/SP	40.00
AT	Alan Trammell	20.00
TW	Tim Wallach	10.00
BW	Bob Watson	10.00
EW	Earl Weaver	10.00
WW	Walt Weiss	8.00
MW	Maury Wills	10.00
WWI	Willie Wilson/SP	25.00
CY	Carl Yastrzemski/SP	150.00
SY	Steve Yeager	10.00
RYO	Robin Yount/SP	100.00

Best Seat Relics

		NM/M
	Common Card:	20.00
BS1	Jim Palmer, Frank Robinson, Brooks Robinson	25.00
BS2	Wally Joyner, Rod Carew, Bobby Grich	20.00
BS3	Phil Garner, Willie Stargell, Dave Parker, Kent Tekulve	20.00
BS4	Rollie Fingers, Robin Yount, Paul Molitor	25.00
BS5	Phil Niekro, Dale Murphy, Bob Horner	20.00

Relics

		NM/M
	Common Player:	8.00
HBA	Harold Baines/Bat	12.00
GBR	George Brett/Jsy	25.00
JOS	Jose Canseco/Bat	12.00
RCA	Rod Carew/Bat	10.00
GC	Gary Carter/Bat	10.00
NC	Norm Cash/Jsy	25.00
VC	Vince Coleman/Bat	8.00
JCR	Jose Cruz/Bat	6.00
RDA	Ron Darling/Jsy	8.00
ADA	Andre Dawson/Bat	8.00
LD	Lenny Dykstra/Bat	8.00
DEC	Dennis Eckersley/Jsy	10.00
CF	Curt Flood/Bat	10.00
GF	George Foster/Bat	8.00
BFR	Bob Friend/Jsy	6.00
SG	Steve Garvey/Bat	6.00
KGI	Kirk Gibson/Bat	8.00
KH	Keith Hernandez/Bat	12.00
WHE	Willie Hernandez/Bat	8.00
BH	Bob Horner/Bat	6.00
BJ	Bo Jackson/Bat	20.00
WJ	Wally Joyner/Bat	8.00
GL	Greg Luzinski/Bat	6.00
FL	Fred Lynn/Bat	10.00
DON	Don Mattingly/Bat	30.00
MCG	Willie McGee/Bat	15.00
TMC	Tug McGraw/Jsy	10.00
KM	Kevin Mitchell/Bat	6.00
JM	Joe Morgan/Bat	10.00
DM	Dale Murphy/Bat	15.00
PO	Paul O'Neill/Bat	8.00
DP	Dave Parker/Bat	6.00
LP	Lance Parrish/Bat	12.00
KP	Kirby Puckett/Bat	15.00
HR	Harold Reynolds/Bat	6.00
JRI	Jim Rice/Bat	8.00
BR	Bobby Richardson/Bat	15.00
JRU	Joe Rudi/Bat	6.00
CS	Chris Sabo/Bat	8.00
MS	Mike Schmidt/Bat	25.00
WS	Willie Stargell/Bat	12.00
AT	Alan Trammell/Bat	15.00
MW	Maury Wills/Bat	6.00

Team Topps Leg. Auto.

	NM/M
Common Autograph:	10.00
Paul Blair	10.00
Lou Brock	30.00
Jim Bunning	15.00
Gary Carter	30.00
Rich "Goose" Gossage	15.00
Al Kaline	50.00
Willie Mays	120.00
Joe Morgan	30.00
Stan Musial	75.00
Graig Nettles	15.00
Johnny Sain	15.00
Mike Schmidt	75.00

2003 Topps Bazooka

	NM/M
Complete Set (280):	40.00
Common Player:	.15
Pack (8):	2.00
Box (24):	40.00

Card #7 has 31 variations.

1	Luis Castillo	.15
2	Randy Winn	.15
3	Orlando Hudson	.15
4	Fernando Vina	.15
5	Pat Burrell	.25
6	Brad Wilkerson	.15
7	Bazooka Joe	.25
8	Javy Lopez	.25
9	Juan Pierre	.15
10	Hideo Nomo	.40
11	Barry Larkin	.25
12	Alfonso Soriano	.75
13	Rodrigo Lopez	.15
14	Mark Ellis	.15
15	Tim Salmon	.25
16	Garret Anderson	.25
17	Aaron Boone	.15
18	Jason Kendall	.15
19	Hee Seop Choi	.15
20	Jorge Posada	.25
21	Sammy Sosa	1.50
22	Mark Prior	.75
23	Mark Teixeira	.50
24	Manny Ramirez	.50
25	Jim Thome	.75
26	A.J. Pierzynski	.15
27	Scott Rolen	.75
28	Austin Kearns	.25
29	Bret Boone	.15
30	Ken Griffey Jr.	1.00
31	Greg Maddux	1.00
32	Derek Lowe	.15
33	David Wells	.15
34	A.J. Burnett	.15
35	Randall Simon	.15
36	Nick Johnson	.15
37	Junior Spivey	.15
38	Eric Gagne	.40
39	Darin Erstad	.25
40	Marty Cordova	.15
41	Brett Myers	.15
42	Mo Vaughn	.15
43	Randy Wolf	.15
44	Vicente Padilla	.15
45	Elmer Dessens	.15
46	Jason Simontacchi	.15
47	John Mabry	.15
48	Torii Hunter	.25
49	Lyle Overbay	.15
50	Kirk Saarloos	.15
51	Bernie Williams	.50
52	Wade Miller	.15
53	Bobby Abreu	.25
54	Wilson Betemit	.15
55	Edwin Almonte	.15
56	Jarrod Washburn	.15
57	Drew Henson	.25
58	Tony Batista	.15
59	Juan Rivera	.15
60	Larry Walker	.25
61	Brandon Phillips	.15
62	Franklyn German	.15
63	Victor Martinez	.25
64	Moises Alou	.25
65	Nomar Garciaparra	1.00
66	Willie Harris	.15
67	Sean Casey	.25
68	Omar Vizquel	.25
69	Robert Fick	.15
70	Curt Schilling	.50
71	Adam Kennedy	.15
72	Scott Hairston	.15
73	Jimmy Journell	.15
74	Rafael Furcal	.25
75	Barry Zito	.25
76	Ed Rogers	.15
77	Cliff Floyd	.15
78	Matt Clement	.15
79	Mike Lowell	.25
80	Randy Johnson	.75
81	Craig Biggio	.25
82	Carlos Beltran	.50
83	Paul LoDuca	.15
84	Jose Vidro	.15
85	Gary Sheffield	.40
86	Jacque Jones	.15
87	Corey Hart	.25
88	Roberto Alomar	.40
89	Robin Ventura	.25
90	Pedro Martinez	.75
91	Scott Hatteberg	.15

92	Marlon Byrd	.15
93	Pokey Reese	.15
94	Sean Burroughs	.15
95	Magglio Ordonez	.25
96	Tsuyoshi Shinjo	.15
97	John Olerud	.15
98	Edgar Renteria	.25
99	Ben Grieve	.15
100	Mariano Rivera	.25
101	Ivan Rodriguez	.50
102	Josh Phelps	.15
103	Nobuaki Yoshida RC	.40
104	Roy Halladay	.15
105	Mark Buehrle	.15
106	Chan Ho Park	.15
107	Joe Kennedy	.15
108	Shin-Soo Choo	.15
109	Ryan Jensen	.15
110	Todd Helton	.50
111	Chris Duncan RC	1.00
112	Taggert Bozied	.15
113	Sean Burnett	.15
114	Mike Lieberthal	.15
115	Josh Beckett	.40
116	Andy Pettitte	.25
117	Jose Reyes	.25
118	Bartolo Colon	.25
119	Justin Morneau	.25
120	Lance Berkman	.40
121	Mike Wodnicki RC	.40
122	Craig Brazell RC	.50
123	Troy Glaus	.40
124	John Smoltz	.25
125	Mike Sweeney	.15
126	Jay Gibbons	.15
127	Kerry Wood	.75
128	Ellis Burks	.15
129	Carlos Pena	.15
130	Shawn Green	.25
131	Jason Stokes	.15
132	Raul Ibanez	.15
133	Francisco Rodriguez	.15
134	Adrian Beltre	.25
135	Richie Sexson	.40
136	Paul Byrd	.15
137	Bobby Kielty	.15
138	Dewon Brazelton	.15
139	Jeremy Griffiths	.15
140	Vladimir Guerrero	.75
141	Jake Peavy	.15
142	Bryan Bullington RC	1.00
143	Orlando Cabrera	.15
144	Scott Erickson	.15
145	Doug Mientkiewicz	.15
146	Derrek Lee	.25
147	Daryl Clark RC	.40
148	Trevor Hoffman	.15
149	Gabe Gross	.15
150	Roger Clemens	1.50
151	Khalil Greene	1.00
152	Cory Doyne RC	.40
153	Brandon Roberson RC	.40
154	Josh Fogg	.15
155	Eric Chavez	.25
156	Kris Benson	.15
157	Billy Koch	.15
158	Jermaine Dye	.15
159	Kip Bouknight RC	.40
160	Brian Giles	.25
161	Justin Huber	.15
162	Mike Restovich	.15
163	Brandon Webb RC	1.00
164	Odalis Perez	.15
165	Phil Nevin	.15
166	Dontrelle Willis	.25
167	Aaron Heilman	.15
168	Dustin Moseley RC	.40
169	Rylan Reed RC	.40
170	Miguel Tejada	.25
171	Nic Jackson	.15
172	Anthony Webster RC	.15
173	Jorge Julio	.15
174	Kevin Millwood	.15
175	Brian Jordan	.15
176	Terry Tiffee RC	.40
177	Dallas McPherson	.15
178	Freddy Garcia	.15
179	Jamie Moyer	.15
180	Rafael Palmeiro	.50
181	Mike O'Keefe RC	.40
182	Kevin Youkilis RC	1.00
183	Kip Wells	.15
184	Joe Mauer	.25
185	Edgar Martinez	.25
186	Jaime Bubela RC	.40
187	Jose Hernandez	.15
188	Josh Hamilton	.40
189	Matt Diaz RC	.40
190	Chipper Jones	1.00
191	Kevin Mench	.15
192	Joey Gomes	.15
193	Shannon Stewart	.15
194	Damian Miller	.15
195	Mike Piazza	1.00
196	Damian Moss	.15
197	Mike Fontenot	.15
198	Shea Hillenbrand	.15
199	Evel Bastida-Martinez RC	.40
200	Jason Giambi	.40
201	Aron Weston RC	.40
202	Frank Thomas	.50
203	Carlos Lee	.15
204	C.C. Sabathia	.15
205	Jim Edmonds	.40
206	Jemel Spearman RC	.40

207	Jason Jennings	.15
208	Jeremy Bonderman	1.00
209	Preston Wilson	.15
210	Eric Hinske	.15
211	Will Smith	.15
212	Matthew Hagen RC	.40
213	Joe Randa	.15
214	James Loney	.15
215	Carlos Delgado	.25
216	Kris Kroski RC	.50
217	Cristian Guzman	.15
218	Tomokazu Ohka	.15
219	Al Leiter	.15
220	Adam Dunn	.50
221	Raul Mondesi	.25
222	Donald Hood RC	.40
223	Mark Mulder	.25
224	Mike Williams	.15
225	Ryan Klesko	.25
226	Rich Aurilia	.15
227	Chris Snelling	.15
228	Gary Schneidmiller RC	.40
229	Ichiro Suzuki	1.50
230	Luis Gonzalez	.25
231	Rocco Baldelli	.15
232	Callix Crabbe RC	.40
233	Adrian Gonzalez	.15
234	Corey Koskie	.15
235	Tom Glavine	.40
236	Kevin Beavers RC	.40
237	Frank Catalanotto	.15
238	Kevin Cash	.15
239	Nick Trzesniak RC	.50
240	Paul Konerko	.25
241	Jose Cruz Jr.	.15
242	Hank Blalock	.50
243	J.D. Drew	.25
244	Kazuhiro Sasaki	.15
245	Jeff Bagwell	.50
246	Jason Schmidt	.25
247	Xavier Nady	.15
248	Aramis Ramirez	.40
249	Jimmy Rollins	.20
250	Alex Rodriguez	1.50
251	Terrence Long	.15
252	Derek Jeter	2.00
253	Edgardo Alfonzo	.15
254	Toby Hall	.15
255	Kazuhisa Ishii	.15
256	Brad Nelson	.15
257	Kevin Brown	.25
258	Roy Oswalt	.25
259	Mike Cameron	.15
260	Juan Gonzalez	.40
261	Dmitri Young	.15
262	Jose Jimenez	.15
263	Wily Mo Pena	.25
264	Joe Borchard	.15
265	Mike Mussina	.50
266	Fred McGriff	.25
267	Johnny Damon	.25
268	Joel Pineiro	.15
269	Andruw Jones	.50
270	Tim Hudson	.25
271	Chad Tracy	.15
272	Brad Fullmer	.15
273	Boof Bonser	.15
274	Clint Nageotte	.15
275	Jeff Kent	.25
276	Tino Martinez	.25
277	Matt Morris	.15
278	Jonny Gomes	.15
279	Benito Santiago	.15
280	Albert Pujols	1.50

Silver

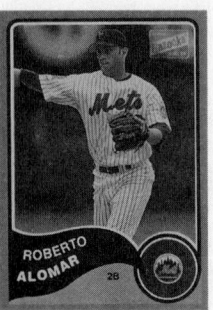

Stars: 1-3X
Inserted 1:1

ROBERTO ALOMAR 2B

Mini

DMITRI YOUNG 1B

Stars: 1-3X
Inserted 1:1

Blasts

		NM/M
Common Player:		4.00
Refractors:		3-4X
Production 25 Sets		
RA	Roberto Alomar	6.00
LB	Lance Berkman	6.00
WB	Wilson Betemit	4.00
JD	Johnny Damon	6.00
CD	Carlos Delgado	5.00
JDD	J.D. Drew	8.00
DE	Darin Erstad	4.00
AG	Andres Galarraga	4.00
LG	Luis Gonzalez	4.00
SG	Shawn Green	6.00
TG	Tony Gwynn	8.00
RH	Rickey Henderson	10.00
DH	Drew Henson	4.00
NJ	Nick Johnson	4.00
CJ	Chipper Jones	10.00
RK	Ryan Klesko	4.00
BL	Barry Larkin	
PL	Paul LoDuca	4.00
EM	Edgar Martinez	8.00
TM	Tino Martinez	4.00
RM	Raul Mondesi	4.00
RP	Rafael Palmeiro	6.00
MP	Mike Piazza	12.00
JP	Jorge Posada	8.00
ANR	Aramis Ramirez	4.00
MR	Manny Ramirez	8.00
AR	Alex Rodriguez	12.00
IR	Ivan Rodriguez	8.00
GS	Gary Sheffield	6.00
TS	Tsuyoshi Shinjo	4.00
AS	Alfonso Soriano	10.00
MS	Mike Sweeney	4.00
RV	Robin Ventura	4.00
BW	Bernie Williams	10.00

Comics

	NM/M
Complete Set (12):	4.00
Common Player:	.30
Inserted 1:4	
Roger Clemens	.40
Nomar Garciaparra	.60
Jason Giambi	.40
Derek Jeter	.75
Randy Johnson	.30
Chipper Jones	.40
Mike Piazza	.50

Albert Pujols	.30
Alex Rodriguez	.60
Alfonso Soriano	.40
Sammy Sosa	.40
Ichiro Suzuki	.50

Piece of Americana

	NM/M
Common Player:	5.00
Refractors:	3-4X
Production 25 Sets	
JB Jeff Bagwell	10.00
CB Craig Biggio	5.00
BB Bret Boone	5.00
DB Dewon Brazelton	5.00
CD Carlos Delgado	5.00
AD Adam Dunn	10.00
JE Jim Edmonds	6.00
RF Rafael Furcal	5.00
NG Nomar Garciaparra	15.00
SG Shawn Green	6.00
CG Cristian Guzman	5.00
TG Tony Gwynn	10.00
THA Toby Hall	5.00
TH Todd Helton	6.00
AH Aubrey Huff	5.00
AJ Andruw Jones	5.00
CJ Chipper Jones	10.00
JK Jeff Kent	5.00
AL Al Leiter	5.00
PL Paul LoDuca	6.00
MM Mike Mussina	8.00
MO Magglio Ordonez	6.00
RP Rafael Palmeiro	6.00
MP Mike Piazza	12.00
PA Albert Pujols	10.00
IR Ivan Rodriguez	5.00
CS Curt Schilling	8.00
FT Frank Thomas	5.00
LW Larry Walker	5.00
PW Preston Wilson	5.00

Stand-Ups

	NM/M
Complete Set (25):	20.00
Common Player:	.40
Inserted 1:8	
1 Albert Pujols	2.50
2 Alfonso Soriano	1.00
3 Ichiro Suzuki	2.00
4 Sammy Sosa	2.00
5 Randy Johnson	1.00
6 Torii Hunter	.50
7 Vladimir Guerrero	1.00
8 Nomar Garciaparra	2.00
9 Alex Rodriguez	3.00
10 Troy Glaus	.50
11 Greg Maddux	1.50
12 Derek Jeter	3.00
13 Lance Berkman	.40
14 Larry Walker	.40
15 Adam Dunn	.50
16 Shawn Green	.50
17 Curt Schilling	.75
18 Todd Helton	.75
19 Pedro Martinez	1.00
20 Pat Burrell	.50
21 Miguel Tejada	.50
22 Manny Ramirez	1.00
23 Mike Piazza	1.50
24 Chipper Jones	1.00
25 Jason Giambi	1.00

4-On-1 Stickers

	NM/M
Complete Set (55):	10.00
Common Sticker:	.20
Inserted 1:4	

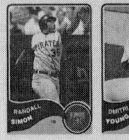

1 Mark Prior, Roy Oswalt, Jarrod Washburn, Barry Zito .30
2 Troy Glaus, Shea Hillenbrand, Eric Chavez, Eric Hinske .30
3 Orlando Hudson, Alfonso Soriano, Roberto Alomar, Jose Vidro .40
4 Nomar Garciaparra, Derek Jeter, Miguel Tejada, Alex Rodriguez .75
5 Jason Giambi, Jim Thome, Todd Helton, Rafael Palmeiro .40
6 Mike Williams, Trevor Hoffman, Billy Koch, John Smoltz .20
7 Jorge Posada, Mike Piazza, A.J. Pierzynski, Ivan Rodriguez .50
8 Vladimir Guerrero, Jim Edmonds, Manny Ramirez, Brad Wilkerson .40
9 Shawn Green, Sammy Sosa, Torii Hunter, Larry Walker .40
10 Bernie Williams, Ken Griffey Jr., Ichiro Suzuki, Adam Dunn .50
11 John Olerud, Mike Lieberthal, Terrence Long, Drew Henson .20
12 Edgar Martinez, Bret Boone, Mo Vaughn, Robert Fisk .20
13 Randy Johnson, Roger Clemens, Pedro Martinez, Greg Maddux .40
14 Curt Schilling, Tim Hudson, Tom Glavine, Kerry Wood .20
15 Paul Konerko, Mike Sweeney, Cristian Guzman, Scott Rolen .20
16 Josh Phelps, Brandon Phillips, Hee Seop Choi, Hank Blalock .20
17 Benito Santiago, Barry Larkin, Gary Sheffield, Carlos Delgado .20
18 Juan Rivera, Jose Reyes, Sean Burroughs, Carlos Pena .20
19 Tony Batista, Tim Salmon, Jeff Bagwell, Raul Ibanez .25
20 Edgardo Alfonzo, Nic Jackson, Luis Castillo, Damian Miller .20
21 David Wells, Ryan Klesko, Phil Nevin, Jeff Kent .20
22 Derek Lowe, Vicente Padilla, Kevin Millwood, Joel Pineiro .20
23 Fernando Vina, Darin Erstad, Jimmy Rollins, Doug Mientkiewicz .20
24 Joe Mauer, Justin Huber, Jason Stokes, Chad Tracy .20
25 Austin Kearns, Junior Spivey, Brett Myers, Victor Martinez .25
26 Kevin Cash, James Loney, .20
27 Albert Pujols, Mark Buehrle, Chipper Jones, Lance Berkman .40
28 Adam Kennedy, Craig Biggio, Johnny Damon, Randy Winn .20
29 Brian Giles, J.D. Drew, Marlon Byrd, Joe Borchard .20
30 Al Leiter, Mike Mussina, Bartolo Colon, Freddy Garcia .20
31 Jason Kendall, Richie Sexson, Mike Lowell, Paul LoDuca .20
32 Pat Burrell, Garret Anderson, Cliff Floyd, Andruw Jones .25
33 Xavier Nady, Bobby Abreu, Taggert Bozied, Adrian Beltre .20
34 Rocco Baldelli, Dontrelle Willis, Chris Snelling, Mark Teixeira .20
35 Willie Harris, Nick Johnson, Jason Jennings, Kazuhisa Ishii .20
36 Mark Mulder, Sean Burnett, Paul Byrd, Josh Beckett .20
37 Corey Koskie, Aramis Ramirez, Tino Martinez, Moises Alou .20
38 Jose Cruz Jr., Roy Halliday, Dewon Brazelton, Jonny Gomes .20
39 Odalis Perez, Kevin Brown, Matt Clement, Randy Wolf .20
40 Eric Gagne, Jose Jimenez, Franklyn German, Edwin Almonte .20
41 Luis Gonzalez, Shannon Stewart, Brian Jordan, Juan Gonzalez .25
42 Toby Hall, Joe Kennedy, Javier Lopez, Damian Moss .20
43 Magglio Ordonez, Carlos Lee, Randall Simon, Dmitri Young .20
44 Sean Casey, Aaron Boone, Jacque Jones, Michael Restovich .20
45 Adrian Gonzalez, Corey Hart, Fred McGriff, Frank Thomas .25
46 C.C. Sabathia, Omar Vizquel, Andy Pettitte, Robin Ventura .20
47 Jason Schmidt, Ellis Burks, Joe Randa, Tsuyoshi Shinjo .20
48 Mike Cameron, Pokey Reese, Jermaine Dye, Preston Wilson .20
49 Chan Ho Park, Kazuhiro Sasaki, Tomokazu Ohka, Hideo Nomo .20
50 Jason Simontacchi, Kip Wells, Matt Morris, Rodrigo Lopez .20
51 Dallas McPherson, Josh Hamilton, Jeremy Bonderman, Aaron Heilman .20
52 Nobuaki Yoshida, Chris Duncan, Craig Brazell, Bryan Bullington .20
53 Daryl Clark, Brandon Webb, Dustin Moseley, Mike O'Keefe .20
54 Kevin Youkilis, Jaime Bubela, Matt Diaz, Joey Gomes .20
55 Kris Kroski, Donald Hood, Gary Schneidmiller, Callix Crabbe .20

2003 Topps Chrome

	NM/M
Complete Set (440):	160.00
Common Player:	.25
Series 1 & 2 Hobby Pack (4):	2.50
Hobby Box (24):	50.00
1 Alex Rodriguez	3.00
2 Eddie Guardado	.25
3 Curt Schilling	1.00
4 Andruw Jones	.50
5 Magglio Ordonez	.75
6 Todd Helton	.75
7 Odalis Perez	.25
8 Edgardo Alfonzo	.25
9 Eric Hinske	.25
10 Danny Bautista	.25
11 Sammy Sosa	1.50
12 Roberto Alomar	.50
13 Roger Clemens	2.00
14 Austin Kearns	.50
15 Luis Gonzalez	.50
16 Mo Vaughn	.50
17 Alfonso Soriano	1.50
18 Orlando Cabrera	.25
19 Hideo Nomo	.75
20 Omar Vizquel	.25
21 Greg Maddux	2.50
22 Fred McGriff	.50
23 Frank Thomas	1.00
24 Shawn Green	.75
25 Jacque Jones	.25
26 Bernie Williams	.75
27 Corey Patterson	.50
28 Cesar Izturis	.25
29 Larry Walker	.25
30 Darren Dreifort	.25
31 Al Leiter	.25
32 Jason Marquis	.25
33 Sean Casey	.25
34 Craig Counsell	.25
35 Albert Pujols	3.00
36 Kyle Lohse	.25
37 Paul LoDuca	.25
38 Roy Oswalt	.50
39 Danny Graves	.25
40 Kevin Millwood	.25
41 Lance Berkman	.75
42 Denny Hocking	.25
43 Jose Valentin	.25
44 Josh Beckett	.75
45 Nomar Garciaparra	.75
46 Craig Biggio	.50
47 Omar Daal	.25
48 Jimmy Rollins	.50
49 Jermaine Dye	.25
50 Edgar Renteria	.25
51 Brandon Duckworth	.25
52 Luis Castillo	.25
53 Andy Ashby	.25
54 Mike Williams	.25
55 Benito Santiago	.25
56 Bret Boone	.25
57 Randy Wolf	.25
58 Ivan Rodriguez	.75
59 Shannon Stewart	.25
60 Jose Cruz Jr.	.25
61 Billy Wagner	.25
62 Alex Gonzalez	.25
63 Ichiro Suzuki	2.50
64 Joe McEwing	.25
65 Mark Mulder	.50
66 Mike Cameron	.25
67 Corey Koskie	.25
68 Marlon Anderson	.25
69 Jason Kendall	.25
70 J.T. Snow Jr.	.25
71 Edgar Martinez	.50
72 Vernon Wells	.25
73 Vladimir Guerrero	1.50
74 Adam Dunn	1.00
75 Barry Zito	.50
76 Jeff Kent	.25
77 Russ Ortiz	.25
78 Phil Nevin	.25
79 Carlos Beltran	1.00
80 Mike Lowell	.50
81 Bob Wickman	.25
82 Junior Spivey	.25
83 Melvin Mora	.25
84 Derrek Lee	.50
85 Chuck Knoblauch	.25
86 Eric Gagne	.75
87 Orlando Hernandez	.25
88 Robert Person	.25
89 Elmer Dessens	.25
90 Wade Miller	.25
91 Adrian Beltre	.50
92 Kazuhiro Sasaki	.25
93 Timoniel Perez	.25
94 Jose Vidro	.25
95 Geronimo Gil	.25
96 Trot Nixon	.25
97 Denny Neagle	.25
98 Roberto Hernandez	.25
99 David Ortiz	1.50
100 Robb Nen	.25
101 Sidney Ponson	.25
102 Kevin Appier	.25
103 Javier Lopez	.50
104 Jeff Conine	.25
105 Mark Buehrle	.25
106 Jason Simontacchi	.25
107 Jose Jimenez	.25
108 Brian Jordan	.25
109 Brad Wilkerson	.25
110 Scott Hatteberg	.25
111 Matt Morris	.50
112 Miguel Tejada	.75
113 Rafael Furcal	.50
114 Steve Cox	.25
115 Roy Halladay	.50
116 David Eckstein	.25
117 Tomokazu Ohka	.25
118 Jack Wilson	.25
119 Randall Simon	.25
120 Jamie Moyer	.25
121 Andy Benes	.25
122 Tino Martinez	.50
123 Esteban Yan	.25
124 Jason Isringhausen	.25
125 Chris Carpenter	.25
126 Aaron Rowand	.25
127 Brandon Inge	.25
128 Jose Vizcaino	.25
129 Jose Mesa	.25
130 Troy Percival	.25
131 Jon Lieber	.25
132 Brian Giles	.50
133 Aaron Boone	.25
134 Bobby Higginson	.25
135 Luis Rivas	.25

No.	Player	Price
136	Troy Glaus	.75
137	Jim Thome	1.00
138	Ramon Martinez	.25
139	Jay Gibbons	.25
140	Mike Lieberthal	.25
141	Juan Uribe	.25
142	Gary Sheffield	.75
143	Ramon Santiago	.25
144	Ben Sheets	.50
145	Tony Armas Jr.	.25
146	Kazuhisa Ishii	.25
147	Erubiel Durazo	.25
148	Jerry Hairston Jr.	.25
149	Byung-Hyun Kim	.25
150	Marcus Giles	.25
151	Johnny Damon	.75
152	Terrence Long	.25
153	Juan Pierre	.25
154	Aramis Ramirez	.75
155	Brent Abernathy	.25
156	Ismael Valdes	.25
157	Mike Mussina	1.00
158	Ramon Hernandez	.25
159	Adam Kennedy	.25
160	Tony Womack	.25
161	Tony Batista	.25
162	Kip Wells	.25
163	Jeromy Burnitz	.25
164	Todd Hundley	.25
165	Tim Wakefield	.25
166	Derek Lowe	.25
167	Jorge Posada	.75
168	Ramon Ortiz	.25
169	Brent Butler	.25
170	Shane Halter	.25
171	Matt Lawton	.25
172	Alex Sanchez	.25
173	Eric Milton	.25
174	Vicente Padilla	.25
175	Steve Karsay	.25
176	Mark Prior	.50
177	Kerry Wood	.50
178	Jason LaRue	.25
179	Danys Baez	.25
180	Nick Neugebauer	.25
181	Andres Galarraga	.25
182	Jason Giambi	.75
183	Aubrey Huff	.25
184	Juan Gonzalez	.50
185	Ugueth Urbina	.25
186	Rickey Henderson	.75
187	Brad Fullmer	.25
188	Todd Zeile	.25
189	Jason Jennings	.25
190	Vladimir Nunez	.25
191	David Justice	.50
192	Brian Lawrence	.25
193	Pat Burrell	.50
194	Pokey Reese	.25
195	Robert Fick	.25
196	C.C. Sabathia	.25
197	Fernando Vina	.25
198	Sean Burroughs	.25
199	Ellis Burks	.25
200	Joe Randa	.25
201	Chris Duncan RC	3.00
202	Franklin Gutierrez RC	1.00
203	Adam LaRoche	.25
204	Manuel Ramirez RC	1.00
205	Il Kim RC	1.00
206	Daryl Clark RC	1.00
207	Sean Pierce	.25
208	Andy Marte RC	1.00
209	Bernie Castro RC	1.00
210	Jason Perry RC	1.00
211	Jaime Bubela RC	1.00
212	Alexis Rios	.25
213	Brendan Harris RC	1.00
214	Ramon A. Martinez RC	.25
215	Terry Tiffee RC	1.00
216	Kevin Youkilis RC	4.00
217	Derell McCall RC	1.00
218	Scott Tyler	1.00
219	Craig Brazell RC	1.00
220	Walter Young	1.00
221	Francisco Rodriguez	.40
222	Chipper Jones	2.00
223	Chris Singleton	.25
224	Cliff Floyd	.25
225	Bobby Hill	.25
226	Antonio Osuna	.25
227	Barry Larkin	.50
228	Dean Palmer	.25
229	Eric Owens	.25
230	Randy Johnson	1.00
231	Jeff Suppan	.25
232	Eric Karros	.25
233	Johan Santana	.25
234	Javier Vazquez	.25
235	John Thomson	.25
236	Nick Johnson	.25
237	Mark Ellis	.25
238	Doug Glanville	.25
239	Ken Griffey Jr.	2.50
240	Bubba Trammell	.25
241	Livan Hernandez	.25
242	Desi Relaford	.25
243	Eli Marrero	.25
244	Jared Sandberg	.25
245	Barry Bonds	3.00
246	Aaron Sele	.25
247	Derek Jeter	3.00
248	Eric Byrnes	.25
249	Rich Aurilia	.25
250	Joel Pineiro	.25
251	Chuck Finley	.25
252	Bengie Molina	.25
253	Steve Finley	.25
254	Marty Cordova	.25
255	Shea Hillenbrand	.25
256	Milton Bradley	.25
257	Carlos Pena	.25
258	Brad Ausmus	.25
259	Carlos Delgado	.75
260	Kevin Mench	.25
261	Joe Kennedy	.25
262	Mark McLemore	.25
263	Bill Mueller	.25
264	Ricky Ledee	.25
265	Ted Lilly	.25
266	Sterling Hitchcock	.25
267	Scott Strickland	.25
268	Damion Easley	.25
269	Torii Hunter	.50
270	Brad Radke	.25
271	Geoff Jenkins	.25
272	Paul Byrd	.25
273	Morgan Ensberg	.25
274	Mike Hampton	.25
275	Flash Gordon	.25
276	John Burkett	.25
277	Rodrigo Lopez	.25
278	Tim Spooneybarger	.25
279	Quinton McCracken	.25
280	Tim Salmon	.50
281	Jarrod Washburn	.25
282	Pedro J. Martinez	1.00
283	Julio Lugo	.25
284	Armando Benitez	.25
285	Raul Mondesi	.50
286	Robin Ventura	.25
287	Bobby Abreu	.50
288	Josh Fogg	.25
289	Ryan Klesko	.50
290	Tsuyoshi Shinjo	.25
291	Jim Edmonds	.75
292	Chan Ho Park	.25
293	John Mabry	.25
294	Woody Williams	.25
295	Scott Schoeneweis	.25
296	Brian Anderson	.25
297	Brett Tomko	.25
298	Scott Erickson	.25
299	Tony Clark	.25
300	Danny Wright	.25
301	Jason Schmidt	.75
302	Scott Williamson	.25
303	Einar Diaz	.25
304	Jay Payton	.25
305	Juan Acevedo	.25
306	Ben Grieve	.25
307	Raul Ibanez	.25
308	Richie Sexson	.75
309	Rick Reed	.25
310	Pedro Astacio	.25
311	Bud Smith	.25
312	Tomas Perez	.25
313	Adam Eaton	.25
314	Rafael Palmeiro	.75
315	Jason Tyner	.25
316	Scott Rolen	1.00
317	Randy Winn	.25
318	Ryan Jensen	.25
319	Trevor Hoffman	.25
320	Craig Wilson	.25
321	Jeremy Giambi	.25
322	Andy Pettitte	.50
323	John Franco	.25
324	Felipe Lopez	.25
325	Mike Piazza	1.50
326	Cristian Guzman	.25
327	Jose Hernandez	.25
328	Octavio Dotel	.25
329	Brad Penny	.25
330	Charles Johnson	.25
331	Ryan Dempster	.25
332	Joe Crede	.25
333	Chad Hermansen	.25
334	Gary Matthews Jr.	.25
335	Frank Catalanotto	.25
336	Darin Erstad	.50
337	Matt Williams	.25
338	B.J. Surhoff	.25
339	Kerry Ligtenberg	.25
340	Mike Bordick	.25
341	Joe Girardi	.25
342	D'Angelo Jimenez	.25
343	Paul Konerko	.25
344	Joe Mays	.25
345	Marquis Grissom	.25
346	Neifi Perez	.25
347	Preston Wilson	.25
348	Jeff Weaver	.25
349	Eric Chavez	.50
350	Placido Polanco	.25
351	Ray Lankford	.25
352	James Baldwin	.25
353	Toby Hall	.25
354	Benji Gil	.25
355	Damian Moss	.25
356	Jorge Julio	.25
357	Matt Clement	.25
358	Lee Stevens	.25
359	Dave Roberts	.25
360	J.C. Romero	.25
361	Bartolo Colon	.25
362	Roger Cedeno	.25
363	Mariano Rivera	.50
364	Billy Koch	.25
365	Manny Ramirez	1.50
366	Travis Lee	.25
367	Oliver Perez	.25
368	Rafael Soriano	.25
369	Damian Miller	.25
370	John Smoltz	.50
371	Willis Roberts	.25
372	Tim Hudson	.50
373	Moises Alou	.50
374	Corky Miller	.25
375	Ben Broussard	.25
376	Gabe Kapler	.25
377	Chris Woodward	.25
378	Todd Hollandsworth	.25
379	So Taguchi	.25
380	John Olerud	.50
381	Reggie Sanders	.25
382	Jake Peavy	.25
383	Kris Benson	.25
384	Ray Durham	.25
385	David Wells	.25
386	Tom Glavine	.75
387	Antonio Alfonseca	.25
388	Keith Foulke	.25
389	Shawn Estes	.25
390	Mark Grace	.50
391	Dmitri Young	.25
392	A.J. Burnett	.25
393	Richard Hidalgo	.25
394	Mike Sweeney	.25
395	Doug Mientkiewicz	.25
396	Cory Lidle	.25
397	Jeff Bagwell	1.00
398	Steve Sparks	.25
399	Sandy Alomar Jr.	.25
400	John Lackey	.25
401	Rick Helling	.25
402	Carlos Lee	.25
403	Garret Anderson	.50
404	Vinny Castilla	.25
405	David Bell	.25
406	Freddy Garcia	.25
407	Scott Spiezio	.25
408	Russell Branyan	.25
409	Jose Contreras RC	3.00
410	Kevin Brown	.50
411	Tyler Houston	.25
412	A.J. Pierzynski	.25
413	Peter Bergeron	.25
414	Brett Myers	.25
415	Kenny Lofton	.25
416	Ben Davis	.25
417	J.D. Drew	.50
418	Ricky Gutierrez	.25
419	Mark Redman	.25
420	Juan Encarnacion	.25
421	Bryan Bullington RC	1.00
422	Jeremy Guthrie	.25
423	Joey Gomes	.50
424	Evel Bastida-Martinez RC	1.00
425	Brian Wright RC	.25
426	B.J. Upton	.25
427	Jeff Francis	.25
428	Jeremy Hermida	.25
429	Khalil Greene	1.00
430	Darrell Rasner	.25
431	Brandon Phillips, Victor Martinez	.75
432	Hee Seop Choi, Nic Jackson	.75
433	Dontrelle Willis, Jason Stokes	1.00
434	Chad Tracy, Lyle Overbay	.25
435	Joe Borchard, Corwin Malone	.25
436	Joe Mauer, Justin Morneau	1.00
437	Drew Henson, Brandon Claussen	.50
438	Chase Utley, Gavin Floyd	.25
439	Taggert Bozied, Xavier Nady	.25
440	Aaron Heilman, Jose Reyes	1.50

Refractors

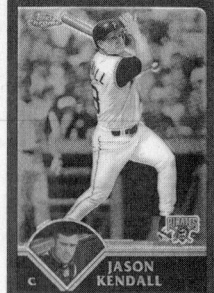

JASON KENDALL

Stars:	1-2X
Production 699 Sets	
Gold Refractors:	1.5-3X
Production 449 Sets	
Black Refractors:	3-5X
Production 199 Sets	

Uncirculated X-Fractors

ADRIAN BELTRE

Stars:	5-10X
Inserted 1:Hobby Box	
Production 50 Sets	

Blue Backs Relics

	NM/M
Common Player:	6.00
Bat Relics Inserted 1:236	
RA	Roberto Alomar/Bat	10.00
JBA	Jeff Bagwell/Jsy	10.00
JB	Josh Beckett/Jsy	8.00
LB	Lance Berkman/Bat	8.00
EC	Eric Chavez/Jsy	6.00
AD	Adam Dunn/Jsy	15.00
NG	Nomar Garciaparra/Jsy	15.00
SG	Shawn Green/Jsy	6.00
NJ	Nick Johnson/Bat	8.00
PK	Paul Konerko/Jsy	8.00
MO	Magglio Ordonez/Jsy	8.00
MP	Mike Piazza/Jsy	15.00
AP	Albert Pujols/Jsy	15.00
AR	Alex Rodriguez/Bat	15.00
JR	Jimmy Rollins/Jsy	8.00
TS	Tsuyoshi Shinjo/Bat	6.00
AS	Alfonso Soriano/Bat	10.00
FT	Frank Thomas/Jsy	8.00
BW	Bernie Williams/Bat	10.00
KW	Kerry Wood/Jsy	8.00

Record Breakers Relics

RECORD BREAKERS

AUTHENTIC GAME-WORN UNIFORM
Slugged .643 in 1996
Texas Season Slugging Pct Leader
Juan Gonzalez

	NM/M
Common Player:	5.00
Bat Relics 1:364	
JB	Jeff Bagwell	10.00

CB	Craig Biggio	5.00
LB	Lou Brock	15.00
CD	Carlos Delgado	5.00
CF	Cliff Floyd	5.00
JG	Juan Gonzalez	8.00
LG	Luis Gonzalez	5.00
TH	Todd Helton	8.00
RH	Rickey Henderson	15.00
RJ	Randy Johnson	10.00
HK	Harmon Killebrew	15.00
JM	Joe Morgan	8.00
SM	Stan Musial	25.00
MP	Mike Piazza	15.00
AR	Alex Rodriguez	15.00
MS	Mike Schmidt	25.00
FT	Frank Thomas	8.00
KS	Kazuhiro Sasaki	5.00
LW	Larry Walker	5.00
RY	Robin Yount	15.00

Record Breakers Relics
Series 2

		NM/M
	Common Player:	5.00
JB	Jeff Bagwell	8.00
BB	Barry Bonds	20.00
BB2	Barry Bonds	20.00
BB3	Barry Bonds	20.00
JC	Jose Canseco	10.00
RC	Rod Carew	8.00
RC2	Rod Carew	8.00
DLE	Dennis Eckersley	8.00
DE	Darin Erstad	5.00
LG	Luis Gonzalez	5.00
RH	Rickey Henderson	15.00
RJ	Randy Johnson	8.00
DM	Don Mattingly	30.00
PM	Paul Molitor	15.00
MR	Manny Ramirez	15.00
HR	Harold Reynolds	5.00
AR	Alex Rodriguez	15.00
TS	Tom Seaver	20.00
JS	John Smoltz	8.00
SS	Sammy Sosa	15.00

Red Backs Relics

		NM/M
	Common Player:	5.00
	Inserted 1:49	
RA	Roberto Alomar	8.00
GA	Garret Anderson	8.00
JB	Jeff Bagwell	8.00
PB	Pat Burrell	5.00
AD	Adam Dunn	8.00
NG	Nomar Garciaparra	12.00
TH	Todd Helton	8.00
TKH	Torii Hunter	8.00
RJ	Randy Johnson	8.00
AJ	Andruw Jones	8.00
CJ	Chipper Jones	10.00
PM	Pedro J. Martinez	10.00
MP	Mike Piazza	10.00
AP	Albert Pujols	15.00
MR	Manny Ramirez	8.00
AR	Alex Rodriguez	10.00
SR	Scott Rolen	10.00
CS	Curt Schilling	8.00
AS	Alfonso Soriano	10.00
MS	Mike Sweeney	5.00

2003 Topps Gallery

JOHNNY DAMON RED SOX

		NM/M
	Complete Set (200):	60.00
	Common Player:	.25
	SP's Inserted 1:20	
	Pack (5):	2.50
	Box (20):	45.00
1	Jason Giambi	.50
1	Jason Giambi/SP/ Drk Blue Jsy	2.00
2	Miguel Tejada	.50
3	Mike Lieberthal	.25
4	Jason Kendall	.40
5	Robb Nen	.25
6	Freddy Garcia	.25
7	Scott Rolen	.75
8	David Wells	.25
9	Rafael Palmeiro	.75
10	Garret Anderson	.50
11	Curt Schilling	.75
12	Greg Maddux	1.00
13	Rodrigo Lopez	.25
14	Nomar Garciaparra	1.50
14	N.Garciaparra/SP/ Navy Elbow Pad	3.00
15	Kerry Wood	.75
16	Frank Thomas	.75
17	Ken Griffey Jr.	1.00
18	Jim Thome	.75
19	Todd Helton	.75
20	Lance Berkman	.50
21	Robert Fick	.25
22	Kevin Brown	.40
23	Richie Sexson	.50
24	Eddie Guardado	.25
25	Vladimir Guerrero	1.00
26	Mike Piazza	1.50
27	Bernie Williams	.50
28	Eric Chavez	.40
29	Jimmy Rollins	.40
30	Ichiro Suzuki	1.50
30	Ichiro Suzuki/SP/ Black Long Shirt	3.00
31	J.D. Drew	.25
32	Nick Johnson	.25
33	Shannon Stewart	.25
34	Tim Salmon	.40
35	Andruw Jones	.75
36	Jay Gibbons	.25
37	Johnny Damon	.50
38	Fred McGriff	.40
39	Carlos Lee	.25
40	Adam Dunn	.75
40	Adam Dunn/SP/ Red Sleeves & Helmet	1.50
41	Jason Jennings	.25
42	Mike Lowell	.40
43	Mike Sweeney	.25
44	Shawn Green	.50
45	Doug Mientkiewicz	.25
46	Bartolo Colon	.40
47	Edgardo Alfonzo	.25
48	Roger Clemens	2.00
49	Randy Wolf	.25
50	Alex Rodriguez	2.00
50	Alex Rodriguez/SP/ Red Undershirt	4.00
51	Vernon Wells	.40
52	Kenny Lofton	.40
53	Mariano Rivera	.40
54	Brian Jordan	.25
55	Roberto Alomar	.50
56	Carlos Pena	.25
57	Moises Alou	.40
58	John Smoltz	.40
59	Adam Kennedy	.25
60	Randy Johnson	1.00
61	Mark Buehrle	.25
62	C.C. Sabathia	.25
63	Craig Biggio	.40
64	Eric Karros	.25
65	Jose Vidro	.25
66	Tim Hudson	.40
67	Trevor Hoffman	.25
68	Bret Boone	.25
69	Carl Crawford	.25
70	Derek Jeter	2.50
71	Troy Percival	.25
72	Gary Sheffield	.50
73	Rickey Henderson	.50
74	Paul Konerko	.25
75	Larry Walker	.40
76	Pat Burrell	.50
77	Brian Giles	.40
78	Jeff Kent	.40
79	Kazuhiro Sasaki	.25
80	Chipper Jones	1.00
81	Darin Erstad	.40
82	Sean Casey	.40
83	Luis Gonzalez	.40
84	Roy Oswalt	.40
85	Dustan Mohr	.25
86	Al Leiter	.25
87	Mike Mussina	.50
88	Vicente Padilla	.25
89	Rich Aurilia	.25
90	Albert Pujols	2.00
91	John Olerud	.40
92	Ivan Rodriguez	.75
93	Eric Hinske	.25
94	Phil Nevin	.25
95	Barry Zito	.50
96	Armando Benitez	.25
97	Torii Hunter	.50
98	Paul LoDuca	.25
99	Preston Wilson	.40
100	Sammy Sosa	1.50
100	Sammy Sosa/SP/ No Shin Guard	4.00
101	Jarrod Washburn	.25
102	Steve Finley	.25
103	Cliff Floyd	.25
104	Mark Prior	1.00
105	Austin Kearns	.50
106	Jeff Bagwell	.75
107	A.J. Pierzynski	.25
108	Pedro J. Martinez	1.00
109	Orlando Cabrera	.25
110	Raul Mondesi	.25
111	Russ Ortiz	.25
112	Ruben Sierra	.25
113	Tino Martinez	.25
114	Manny Ramirez	.75
115	Troy Glaus	.50
116	Magglio Ordonez	.50
117	Omar Vizquel	.40
118	Carlos Beltran	.40
119	Jose Hernandez	.25
120	Javier Vazquez	.25
121	Jorge Posada	.50
122	Aramis Ramirez	.25
123	Jason Schmidt	.40
124	Jamie Moyer	.25
125	Jim Edmonds	.50
126	Aubrey Huff	.25
127	Carlos Delgado	.50
128	Junior Spivey	.25
129	Tom Glavine	.50
130	Marty Cordova	.25
131	Derek Lowe	.25
132	Ellis Burks	.25
133	Barry Bonds	2.50
134	Josh Beckett	.25
135	Raul Ibanez	.25
136	Kazuhisa Ishii	.25
137	Geoff Jenkins	.25
138	Eric Milton	.25
139	Mo Vaughn	.25
140	Mark Mulder	.40
141	Bobby Abreu	.40
142	Ryan Klesko	.40
143	Tsuyoshi Shinjo	.25
144	Jose Mesa	.25
145	Shea Hillenbrand	.25
146	Edgar Renteria	.25
147	Juan Gonzalez	.50
148	Edgar Martinez	.25
149	Matt Morris	.25
150	Alfonso Soriano	1.00
150	Alfonso Soriano/SP/ No Elbow Pad	2.50
151	Bryan Bullington **RC**	1.00
151	Bryan Bullington/SP/ Red Background **RC**	3.00
152	Andy Marte **RC**	3.00
152	Andy Marte/SP/ No Necklace **RC**	3.00
153	Brendan Harris **RC**	1.00
154	Juan Camacho **RC**	1.00
155	Byron Gettis	1.00
156	Daryl Clark **RC**	1.00
157	J.D. Durbin **RC**	1.50
158	Craig Brazell **RC**	1.50
158	Craig Brazell/SP/ Black Jersey **RC**	3.00
159	Jason Kubel **RC**	2.00
160	Brandon Roberson **RC**	1.00
161	Jose Contreras **RC**	2.00
162	Stanley Ramirez **RC**	8.00
163	Jaime Bubela **RC**	1.00
164	Chris Duncan **RC**	2.50
165	Tyler Johnson **RC**	1.00
166	Adam LaRoche	.25
167	Walter Young	.25
168	Ryan Kibler	.25
169	Tommy Whiteman **RC**	.25
170	Trey Hodges	.25
171	Francisco Rodriguez	.25
172	Jason Arnold	.25
173	Brett Myers	.25
174	Rocco Baldelli	.50
175	Adrian Gonzalez	.25
176	Dontrelle Willis	1.00
177	Kris Honel	.25
178	Marlon Byrd	.25
179	Aaron Heilman	.25
180	Casey Kotchman	.25
181	Miguel Cabrera	.25
182	Hee Seop Choi	.50
183	Drew Henson	.25
184	Jose Reyes	.25
185	Michael Cuddyer	.25
186	Brandon Phillips	.25
187	Victor Martinez	.25
188	Joe Mauer	.50
189	Hank Blalock	.75
190	Mark Teixeira	.25
191	Willie Mays	2.00
192	George Brett	2.00
193	Tony Gwynn	1.00
194	Carl Yastrzemski	1.00
195	Nolan Ryan	3.00
196	Reggie Jackson	.75
197	Mike Schmidt	1.50
198	Cal Ripken Jr.	3.00
199	Don Mattingly	2.00
200	Tom Seaver	.75

Rainbow Refractors

Stars (1-200):	2-3X
Inserted 1:1	

Rookies (151-165):	1X
Inserted 1:1	

Currency Collection

		NM/M
	Common Player:	4.00
	Inserted 1:Box	
BA	Bobby Abreu	6.00
HC	Hee Seop Choi	6.00
BC	Bartolo Colon	4.00
LG	Luis Gonzalez	4.00
VG	Vladimir Guerrero	12.00
KI	Kazuhisa Ishii	4.00
AJ	Andruw Jones	8.00
RL	Rodrigo Lopez	4.00
PM	Pedro J. Martinez	10.00
RM	Raul Mondesi	4.00
MO	Magglio Ordonez	8.00
VP	Vicente Padilla	6.00
RP	Rafael Palmeiro	6.00
AP	Albert Pujols	20.00
MR	Manny Ramirez	8.00
ER	Edgar Renteria	6.00
JR	Jose Reyes	8.00
MRI	Mariano Rivera	10.00
FR	Francisco Rodriguez	4.00
KS	Kazuhiro Sasaki	4.00
AS	Alfonso Soriano	8.00
SS	Sammy Sosa	15.00
IS	Ichiro Suzuki	15.00
OV	Omar Vizquel	10.00
LW	Larry Walker	5.00

Heritage

DUKE SNIDER

		NM/M
	Complete Set (25):	75.00
	Common Player:	1.50
	Inserted 1:10	
WB	Wade Boggs	1.50
GB	George Brett	8.00
JC	Jose Canseco	1.50
RC	Roger Clemens	6.00
AD	Adam Dunn	2.00

NG	Nomar Garciaparra	5.00
TG	Tom Glavine	1.50
SG	Shawn Green	1.50
TGW	Tony Gwynn	3.00
RH	Rickey Henderson	2.00
DJ	Derek Jeter	8.00
RJ	Randy Johnson	3.00
HK	Harmon Killebrew	4.00
KR	Jerry Koosman	
	Nolan Ryan	10.00
WM	Willie Mays	8.00
HN	Hideo Nomo	2.00
KP	Kirby Puckett	3.00
IR	Ivan Rodriguez	2.00
DS	Duke Snider	2.00
AS	Alfonso Soriano	3.00
IS	Ichiro Suzuki	5.00
MT	Miguel Tejada	1.50
JT	Jim Thome	2.00
BW	Bernie Williams	2.00
CY	Carl Yastrzemski	3.00

Heritage Autographed Relics
NM/M

Inserted 1:3,260

WB	Wade Boggs	70.00
KP	Kirby Puckett/25	80.00

Heritage Relics

NM/M

Common Player:		5.00
WB	Wade Boggs	5.00
GB	George Brett	20.00
JC	Jose Canseco	8.00
RC	Roger Clemens	15.00
SG	Shawn Green	5.00
TG	Tony Gwynn	10.00
RH	Rickey Henderson	10.00
HK	Harmon Killebrew	25.00
HN	Hideo Nomo	15.00
KP	Kirby Puckett	15.00

Originals Relics

NM/M

Common Player:		5.00
RA	Roberto Alomar	6.00
MA	Moises Alou	5.00
LB	Lance Berkman	5.00
BB	Bret Boone	5.00
AD	Adam Dunn	6.00
NG	Nomar Garciaparra	12.00
LG	Luis Gonzalez	5.00
SG	Shawn Green	5.00
TG	Tony Gwynn	8.00
TH	Todd Helton	8.00
RH	Rickey Henderson	8.00
DH	Drew Henson	5.00
THU	Torii Hunter	8.00
AJ	Andruw Jones	6.00
CJ	Chipper Jones	8.00
JM	Joe Mauer	10.00
MO	Magglio Ordonez	5.00
RP	Rafael Palmeiro	8.00
MP	Mike Piazza	10.00
AP	Albert Pujols	15.00
MR	Manny Ramirez	8.00
AR	Alex Rodriguez	10.00
IR	Ivan Rodriguez	8.00
GS	Gary Sheffield	5.00
AS	Alfonso Soriano	8.00
MT	Miguel Tejada	5.00
FT	Frank Thomas	8.00
JT	Jim Thome	8.00
BW	Bernie Williams	6.00
CY	Carl Yastrzemski	20.00

2003 Topps Gallery HOF Ed.

NM/M

Complete Set (74):		35.00
Common Player:		.40
SP Variations:		2-4X
Inserted 1:1		
Pack (5):		4.00
Box (20):		70.00
1	Willie Mays	2.00
1	Willie Mays/SP/ Gold Background	
2	Al Kaline	1.50
3	Hank Aaron	2.00
4	Carl Yastrzemski	1.00
5	Luis Aparicio	.40
6	Sam Crawford	.40
7	Tom Lasorda	.40
8	John McGraw	.40
9	Edd Roush	.40
10	Reggie Jackson	1.00
11	Jim "Catfish" Hunter	.40
12	Roberto Clemente	2.00
13	Ralph Kiner	.40
14	Frankie Frisch	.40
15	Nolan Ryan	4.00
16	Brooks Robinson	1.00
17	Phil Niekro	.40
18	Joe Cronin	.40
19	Joe Tinker	.40
20	Johnny Bench	1.50
21	Harry Heilmann	.40
22	Ernie Harwell	.40
23	Warren Spahn	1.00
24	George Kelly	.40
25	Phil Rizzuto	1.00
26	Robin Roberts	.40
27	Ozzie Smith	1.00
28	Jim Palmer	.40
29	Duke Snider	1.00
30	Bob Feller	.40
31	Buck Leonard	.40
32	Kirby Puckett	1.00
33	Monte Irvin	.40
34	Chuck Klein	.40
35	Willie Stargell	.75
36	Juan Marichal	.40
37	Lou Brock	.40
38	Bucky Harris	.40
39	Bobby Doerr	.40
40	Lee MacPhail	.40
41	Heinie Manush	.40
42	George Brett	1.50
43	Harmon Killebrew	1.50
44	Whitey Ford	1.00
45	Eddie Mathews	1.50
46	Gaylord Perry	.40
47	Red Schoendienst	.40
48	Earl Weaver	.40
49	Joe Morgan	.40
50	Mike Schmidt	2.00
51	Willie McCovey	.40
52	Stan Musial	2.00
53	Don Sutton	.40
54	Hank Greenberg	.40
55	Robin Yount	1.00
56	Tom Seaver	1.00
57	Tony Perez	.40
58	George Sisler	.40
59	Jim Bottomley	.40
60	Yogi Berra	1.50
61	Fred Lindstrom	.40
62	Napoleon Lajoie	.40
63	Frank Robinson	1.00
64	Carlton Fisk	.40
65	Orlando Cepeda	.40
66	Fergie Jenkins	.40
67	Ernie Banks	1.50
68	Bill Mazeroski	.40
69	Jim Bunning	.40
70	Rollie Fingers	.40
71	Jimmie Foxx	1.50
72	Rod Carew	.40
73	Sparky Anderson	.40
74	George Kell	.40

Refractors

Cards (1-74):		2-4X
Inserted 1:1		
SP Refractors:		4-8X
Inserted 1:Box		

Accent Mark Autograph

NM/M

Common Player:		
Refractors:		1-2X
Production 25 Sets		
YB	Yogi Berra	65.00
BD	Bobby Doerr	40.00
LM	Lee MacPhail	40.00
RR	Robin Roberts	40.00
RS	Red Schoendienst	30.00
WS	Warren Spahn	30.00

ARTifact Relics

NM/M

Common Player:		8.00
Refractors:		1.5-3X
Production 25 Sets		
HA	Hank Aaron/Bat	25.00
SA	Sparky Anderson/Jsy	30.00
LA	Luis Aparicio/Bat	15.00
EB	Ernie Banks/Jsy	30.00
JBE	Johnny Bench/Bat	12.00
JB	Jim Bottomley/Bat	15.00
GB	George Brett/Jsy	25.00
RCA	Rod Carew/Jsy	10.00
OC	Orlando Cepeda/Bat	8.00
TC	Ty Cobb/Bat	80.00
EC	Eddie Collins/Bat	12.00
SC	Sam Crawford/Bat	20.00
BD	Bobby Doerr/Jsy	15.00
CF	Carlton Fisk/Bat	8.00
FF	Frankie Frisch/Bat	15.00
LG	Lou Gehrig/Bat	125.00
HG	Hank Greenberg/Bat	25.00
BH	Bucky Harris/Bat	12.00
HH	Harry Heilmann/Bat	20.00
RJ	Reggie Jackson/Bat	10.00
AK	Al Kaline/Bat	15.00

GK	George Kelly/Bat	20.00
HK	Harmon Killebrew/Jsy	25.00
CK	Chuck Klein/Bat	15.00
TLA	Tom Lasorda/Jsy	15.00
HM	Heinie Manush/Bat	15.00
EM	Eddie Mathews/Jsy	30.00
WM	Willie Mays/Jsy	45.00
WMC	Willie McCovey/Bat	8.00
JM	Joe Morgan/Bat	8.00
SM	Stan Musial/Bat	20.00
PN	Phil Niekro/Jsy	6.00
JP	Jim Palmer/Jsy	20.00
TP	Tony Perez/Bat	8.00
GP	Gaylord Perry/Jsy	8.00
KP	Kirby Puckett/Bat	12.00
BRO	Brooks Robinson/Bat	20.00
FR	Frank Robinson/Bat	10.00
JR	Jackie Robinson/Bat	35.00
ER	Edd Roush/Bat	20.00
BR	Babe Ruth/Bat	140.00
NR	Nolan Ryan/Bat	40.00
MS	Mike Schmidt/Jsy	25.00
TS	Tom Seaver/Bat	25.00
GS	George Sisler/Bat	12.00
OS	Ozzie Smith/Bat	15.00
DS	Duke Snider/Bat	12.00
WS	Willie Stargell/Jsy	10.00
DSU	Don Sutton/Bat	8.00
JT	Joe Tinker/Bat	20.00
HW	Honus Wagner/Bat	140.00
PW	Paul Waner/Bat	20.00
HWI	Hoyt Wilhelm/Jsy	8.00
CY	Carl Yastrzemski/Bat	20.00
RY	Robin Yount/Bat	10.00

ARTifact Auto. Relics
NM/M

Common Player:		30.00
Refractors:		1-1.5X
Production 25 Sets		
OC	Orlando Cepeda	30.00
BD	Bobby Doerr	45.00
AK	Al Kaline	75.00
HK	Harmon Killebrew	75.00
JM	Joe Morgan	40.00
JP	Jim Palmer	50.00
BRO	Brooks Robinson	60.00
MS	Mike Schmidt	225.00
RS	Red Schoendienst	30.00
DS	Duke Snider	50.00
RY	Robin Yount	125.00

Currency Connection

NM/M

Common Player:		12.00
1:Box		
EB	Ernie Banks	20.00
OC	Orlando Cepeda	15.00
TC	Ty Cobb	40.00
BF	Bob Feller	25.00
LG	Lou Gehrig	35.00
HG	Hank Greenberg	20.00
WM	Willie Mays	20.00
WMA	Willie Mays	20.00
WMC	Willie McCovey	12.00
SM	Stan Musial	30.00
JR	Jackie Robinson	25.00
BR	Babe Ruth	60.00

Patch Relics
NM/M

Common Player:		40.00
Production 25 Sets		
GB	George Brett	125.00
CH	Jim "Catfish" Hunter	40.00
FJ	Fergie Jenkins	80.00
HK	Harmon Killebrew	40.00
TL	Tom Lasorda	40.00
EM	Eddie Matthews	80.00
WM	Willie McCovey	40.00
JP	Jim Palmer	40.00
NR	Nolan Ryan	125.00
MS	Mike Schmidt	125.00
OS	Ozzie Smith	75.00
CY	Carl Yastrzemski	80.00
RY	Robin Yount	85.00

Team Topps Legends Autos.
NM/M

Common Player:

	Vern Law	20.00
	Johnny Sain	30.00

2003 Topps Heritage

RANDY JOHNSON
pitcher ARIZ. DIAMONDBACKS™

		NM/M
Complete Set (430):		350.00
Common Player:		.40
Common High # SP (364-430):		4.00
Pack (8):		5.00
Box (24):		100.00
1	Alex Rodriguez	3.00
1	Alex Rodriguez/Black/SP	10.00
2	Jose Cruz Jr.	.40
3	Ichiro Suzuki/SP	10.00
4	Rich Aurilia	.40
5	Trevor Hoffman	.40
6	Brian Giles	.75
6	Brian Giles/Old Logo/SP	5.00
7	Albert Pujols	2.00
7	Albert Pujols/Black/SP	10.00
8	Vicente Padilla	.40
9	Bobby Crosby	.40
10	Derek Jeter	4.00
10	Derek Jeter/Old Logo/SP	15.00
11	Pat Burrell	.50
11	Pat Burrell/Old Logo/SP	5.00
12	Armando Benitez	.40
13	Javier Vazquez	.40
14	Justin Morneau	.75
15	Doug Mientkiewicz	.40
16	Kevin Brown	.40
17	Alexis Gomez	.40
18	Lance Berkman	.75
18	Lance Berkman/Black/SP	5.00
19	Adrian Gonzalez	.50
20	Todd Helton	.75
20	Todd Helton/Black/SP	6.00
21	Carlos Pena	.40
22	Matt Lawton	.40
23	Elmer Dessens	.40
24	Hee Seop Choi	.40
25	Chris Duncan/SP **RC**	6.00
26	Ugueth Urbina	.40
27	Rodrigo Lopez	.40
27	Rodrigo Lopez/Old Logo/SP	4.00
28	Damian Moss	.40
29	Steve Finley	.40
30	Sammy Sosa	1.50
30	Sammy Sosa/Old Logo/SP	6.00
31	Kevin Cash	.40
32	Kenny Rogers	.40
33	Ben Grieve	.40
34	Jason Simontacchi	.40
35	Shin-Soo Choo	.40
36	Freddy Garcia	.40
37	Jesse Foppert	.40
38	Tony LaRussa	.40
39	Mark Kotsay	.40
40	Barry Zito	.75
41	Josh Fogg	.40
42	Marlon Byrd	.40
43	Marcus Thames	.40
44	Al Leiter	.50
45	Michael Barrett	.40
46	Jake Peavy	.75
47	Dustan Mohr	.40
48	Alex Sanchez	.40
49	Chin-Feng Chen	.40
50	Kazuhisa Ishii	.40
50	Kazuhisa Ishii/Black/SP	5.00
51	Carlos Beltran	.75
52	Franklin Gutierrez **RC**	1.50
53	Miguel Cabrera	1.00
54	Roger Clemens	2.50
55	Juan Cruz	.40
56	Jason Young	.40
57	Alex Herrera	.40
58	Aaron Boone	.40
59	Mark Buehrle	.50
60	Larry Walker	.75
61	Morgan Ensberg	.40
62	Barry Larkin	.75
63	Joe Borchard	.40
64	Jason Dubois	.40
65	Juan Acevedo	.40
66	Jay Gibbons	.40
67	Vinny Castilla	.40
68	Jeff Mathis	.40
69	Curt Schilling	1.00
70	Garret Anderson	.50
71	Josh Phelps	.40
72	Chan Ho Park	.40
73	Edgar Renteria	.50
74	Kazuhiro Sasaki	.40
75	Lloyd McClendon	.40
76	Jon Lieber	.40
77	Rolando Viera	.40
78	Jeff Conine	.40
79	Kevin Millwood	.40
80	Randy Johnson	1.50
80	Randy Johnson/Black/SP	8.00
81	Troy Percival	.40
82	Cliff Floyd	.40
83	Tony Graffanino	.40
84	Austin Kearns	.50
85	Manuel Ramirez/SP **RC**	5.00
86	Jim Tracy	.40
87	Rondell White	.40
88	Trot Nixon	.40
89	Carlos Lee	.50
90	Mike Lowell	.50
91	Raul Ibanez	.40
92	Ricardo Rodriguez	.40
93	Ben Sheets	.50
94	Jason Perry/SP **RC**	4.00
95	Mark Teixeira	.75
96	Brad Fullmer	.40
97	Casey Kotchman	.40
98	Craig Counsell	.40
99	Jason Marquis	.40
100	Nomar Garciaparra	2.00
100	Nomar Garciaparra/ Old Logo/SP	5.00
101	Ed Rogers	.40
102	Wilson Betemit	.40
103	Wayne Lydon **RC**	1.00
104	Jack Cust	.40
105	Derrek Lee	.75
106	Jim Kavourias	.40
107	Joe Randa	.40
108	Taylor Buchholz	.40
109	Gabe Kapler	.40
110	Preston Wilson	.40
111	Craig Biggio	.50
112	Paul LoDuca	.40
113	Eddie Guardado	.40
114	Andres Galarraga	.40
115	Edgardo Alfonzo	.40
116	Robin Ventura	.40
117	Jeremy Giambi	.40
118	Ray Durham	.40
119	Mariano Rivera	.50
120	Jimmy Rollins	.50
121	Dennis Tankersley	.40
122	Jason Schmidt	.50
123	Bret Boone	.40
124	Josh Hamilton	.75
125	Scott Rolen	.75
126	Steve Cox	.40
127	Larry Bowa	.40
128	Adam LaRoche/SP	5.00
129	Ryan Klesko	.40
130	Tim Hudson	.50
131	Brandon Claussen	.40
132	Craig Brazell/SP **RC**	4.00
133	Grady Little	.40
134	Jarrod Washburn	.40
135	Lyle Overbay	.40
136	John Burkett	.40
137	Daryl Clark **RC**	.75
138	Kirk Rueter	.40
139	Joe Mauer, Jake Mauer	1.00
139	Joe Mauer, Jake Mauer/Black/SP	6.00
140	Troy Glaus	.75
141	Trey Hodges/SP	4.00
142	Dallas McPherson	.40
143	Art Howe	.40
144	Jesus Cota	.40
145	J.R. House	.40
146	Reggie Sanders	.40
147	Clint Nageotte	.40
148	Jim Edmonds	.50
149	Carl Crawford	.50
150	Mike Piazza	2.00
150	Mike Piazza/Black/SP	10.00
151	Seung Jun Song	.40
152	Roberto Hernandez	.40
153	Marquis Grissom	.40
154	Billy Wagner	.40
155	Josh Beckett	.50
156	Randall Simon	.40
156	Randall Simon/Old Logo/SP	4.00
157	Ben Broussard	.40
158	Russell Branyan	.40
159	Frank Thomas	1.00
160	Alex Escobar	.40
161	Mark Bellhorn	.40
162	Melvin Mora	.40
163	Andruw Jones	.75
164	Danny Bautista	.40
165	Ramon Ortiz	.40
166	Wily Mo Pena	.50
167	Jose Jimenez	.40
168	Mark Redman	.40
169	Angel Berroa	.40
170	Andy Marte/SP **RC**	4.00
171	Juan Gonzalez	.75
172	Fernando Vina	.40
173	Joel Pineiro	.40
174	Boof Bonser	.40
175	Bernie Castro/SP **RC**	4.00
176	Bobby Cox	.40
177	Jeff Kent	.50
178	Oliver Perez	.40
179	Chase Utley	1.00
180	Mark Mulder	.50
181	Bobby Abreu	.50
182	Ramiro Mendoza	.40
183	Aaron Heilman	.40
184	A.J. Pierzynski	.40
185	Eric Gagne	.75
186	Kirk Saarloos	.40
187	Ron Gardenhire	.40
188	Dmitri Young	.40
189	Todd Zeile	.40
190	Jim Thome	1.00
190	Jim Thome/Old Logo/SP	8.00
191	Cliff Lee	.50
192	Matt Morris	.40
193	Robert Fick	.40
194	C.C. Sabathia	.40
195	Alexis Rios	.40
196	D'Angelo Jimenez	.40
197	Edgar Martinez	.50
198	Robb Nen	.40
199	Taggert Bozied	.40
200	Vladimir Guerrero/SP	8.00
201	Walter Young/SP	4.00
202	Brendan Harris **RC**	1.00
203	Mike Hargrove	.40
204	Vernon Wells	.50
205	Hank Blalock	.75
206	Mike Cameron	.40
207	Tony Batista	.40
208	Matt Williams	.40
209	Tony Womack	.40
210	Ramon A. Martinez **RC**	.40
211	Aaron Sele	.40
212	Mark Grace	.75
213	Joe Crede	.75
214	Ryan Dempster	.40
215	Omar Vizquel	.40
216	Juan Pierre	.40
217	Denny Bautista	.40
218	Chuck Knoblauch	.40
219	Eric Karros	.40
220	Victor Diaz	.40
221	Jacque Jones	.40
222	Jose Vidro	.40
223	Joe McEwing	.40
224	Nick Johnson	.40
225	Eric Chavez	.50
226	Jose Mesa	.40
227	Aramis Ramirez	.75
228	John Lackey	.40
229	David Bell	.40
230	John Olerud	.50
231	Tino Martinez	.40
232	Randy Winn	.40
233	Todd Hollandsworth	.40
234	Ruddy Lugo **RC**	.75
235	Carlos Delgado	.75
236	Chris Narveson	.40
237	Tim Salmon	.75
238	Orlando Palmeiro	.40
239	Jeff Clark/SP **RC**	4.00
240	Byung-Hyun Kim	.40
241	Mike Remlinger	.40
242	Johnny Damon	1.00
243	Corey Patterson	.50
244	Paul Konerko	.75
245	Danny Graves	.40
246	Ellis Burks	.40
247	Gavin Floyd	.40
248	Jaime Bubela **RC**	.75
249	Sean Burroughs	.40
250	Alex Rodriguez/SP	10.00
251	Gabe Gross	.40
252	Rafael Palmeiro	.75
253	Dewon Brazelton	.40
254	Jimmy Journell	.40
255	Rafael Soriano	.40
256	Jerome Williams	.40
257	Xavier Nady	.40
258	Mike Williams	.40
259	Randy Wolf	.40
260	Miguel Tejada	.75
260	Miguel Tejada/Black/SP	5.00
261	Juan Rivera	.40
262	Rey Ordonez	.40
263	Bartolo Colon	.40
264	Eric Milton	.40
265	Jeffrey Hammonds	.40
266	Odalis Perez	.40
267	Mike Sweeney	.40
268	Richard Hidalgo	.40
269	Alex Gonzalez	.40
270	Aaron Cook	.40
271	Earl Snyder	.40
272	Todd Walker	.40
273	Aaron Rowand	.40
274	Matt Clement	.40
275	Anastacio Martinez	.40
276	Mike Bordick	.40
277	John Smoltz	.50
278	Scott Hairston	.40
279	David Eckstein	.40
280	Shannon Stewart	.40
281	Carl Everett	.40
282	Aubrey Huff	.40
283	Mike Mussina	.75
284	Ruben Sierra	.40
285	Russ Ortiz	.40
286	Brian Lawrence	.40
287	Kip Wells	.40
288	Placido Polanco	.40
289	Ted Lilly	.40
290	Andy Pettitte	.50
291	John Buck	.40
292	Orlando Cabrera	.40
293	Cristian Guzman	.40
294	Ruben Quevedo	.40
295	Cesar Izturis	.40
296	Ryan Ludwick	.40
297	Roy Oswalt	.75
298	Jason Stokes	.40
299	Mike Hampton	.40
300	Pedro Martinez	1.50
301	Nic Jackson	.40
302	Magglio Ordonez	.50
302	Magglio Ordonez/ Old Logo/SP	5.00
303	Manny Ramirez	1.00
304	Jorge Julio	.40
305	Javy Lopez	.50
306	Roy Halladay	.50
307	Kevin Mench	.40
308	Jason Isringhausen	.40
309	Carlos Guillen	.40
310	Tsuyoshi Shinjo	.40
311	Phil Nevin	.40
312	Pokey Reese	.40
313	Jorge Padilla	.40
314	Jermaine Dye	.40
315	David Wells	.40
316	Mo Vaughn	.40
317	Bernie Williams	.75
318	Michael Restovich	.40
319	Jose Hernandez	.40
320	Richie Sexson	.75
321	Daryle Ward	.40
322	Luis Castillo	.40
323	Rene Reyes	.40
324	Victor Martinez	.40
325	Adam Dunn	.75
325	Adam Dunn/Old Logo/SP	6.00
326	Corwin Malone	.40
327	Kerry Wood	.50
328	Rickey Henderson	.75
329	Marty Cordova	.40
330	Greg Maddux	2.00
331	Miguel Batista	.40
332	Chris Bootcheck	.40
333	Carlos Baerga	.40
334	Antonio Alfonseca	.40
335	Shane Halter	.40
336	Juan Encarnacion	.40
337	Flash Gordon	.40
338	Hideo Nomo	.75
339	Torii Hunter	.75
340	Alfonso Soriano	1.00
340	Alfonso Soriano/Black/SP	6.00
341	Roberto Alomar	.75
342	David Justice	.50
343	Mike Lieberthal	.40
344	Jeff Weaver	.40
345	Timoniel Perez	.40
346	Travis Lee	.40
347	Sean Casey	.40
348	Willie Harris	.40
349	Derek Lowe	.40
350	Tom Glavine	.75
351	Eric Hinske	.40
352	Rocco Baldelli	.40
353	J.D. Drew	.60
354	Jamie Moyer	.40
355	Todd Linden	.40
356	Benito Santiago	.40
357	Brad Baker	.40
358	Alex Gonzalez	.40
359	Brandon Duckworth	.40
360	John Rheinecker	.40
361	Orlando Hernandez	.40
362	Pedro Astacio	.40
363	Brad Wilkerson	.40
364	David Ortiz	8.00
365	Geoff Jenkins	4.00
366	Brian Jordan	4.00
367	Paul Byrd	4.00
368	Jason Lane	4.00
369	Jeff Bagwell	6.00
370	Bobby Higginson	4.00
371	Juan Uribe	4.00
372	Lee Stevens	4.00
373	Jimmy Haynes	4.00
374	Jose Valentin	4.00
375	Ken Griffey Jr.	10.00
376	Shea Hillenbrand	4.00
377	Gary Matthews Jr.	4.00
378	Gary Sheffield	5.00
379	Rick Helling	4.00
380	Junior Spivey	4.00
381	Francisco Rodriguez	4.00
382	Chipper Jones	6.00
383	Orlando Hudson	4.00
384	Ivan Rodriguez	6.00
385	Chris Snelling	4.00
386	Kenny Lofton	4.00
387	Eric Cyr	4.00
388	Jason Kendall	4.00
389	Marlon Anderson	4.00
390	Billy Koch	4.00
391	Shelly Duncan	4.00
392	Jose Reyes	6.00
393	Fernando Tatis	4.00
394	Michael Cuddyer	4.00
395	Mark Prior	6.00
396	Dontrelle Willis	4.00
397	Jay Payton	4.00
398	Brandon Phillips	4.00
399	Dustin Moseley **RC**	4.00
400	Jason Giambi	5.00
401	John Mabry	4.00
402	Ron Gant	4.00
403	J.T. Snow	4.00

404	Jeff Cirillo	4.00
405	Darin Erstad	4.00
406	Luis Gonzalez	4.00
407	Marcus Giles	4.00
408	Brian Daubach	4.00
409	Moises Alou	4.00
410	Raul Mondesi	4.00
411	Adrian Beltre	4.00
412	A.J. Burnett	4.00
413	Jason Jennings	4.00
414	Edwin Almonte	4.00
415	Fred McGriff	4.00
416	Tim Raines Jr.	4.00
417	Rafael Furcal	4.00
418	Erubiel Durazo	4.00
419	Drew Henson	4.00
420	Kevin Appier	4.00
421	Chad Tracy	4.00
422	Adam Wainwright	4.00
423	Choo Freeman	4.00
424	Sandy Alomar Jr.	4.00
425	Corey Koskie	4.00
426	Jeromy Burnitz	4.00
427	Jorge Posada	6.00
428	Jason Arnold	4.00
429	Brett Myers	4.00
430	Shawn Green	5.00

Chrome

		NM/M
Common Player:		1.00
Production 1,954 Sets		
Refractors:		1.5-2X
Production 554 Sets		
THC1	Alex Rodriguez	8.00
THC2	Ichiro Suzuki	8.00
THC3	Brian Giles	1.50
THC4	Albert Pujols	4.00
THC5	Derek Jeter	10.00
THC6	Pat Burrell	3.00
THC7	Lance Berkman	2.00
THC8	Todd Helton	2.00
THC9	Chris Duncan	20.00
THC10	Rodrigo Lopez	1.00
THC11	Sammy Sosa	5.00
THC12	Barry Zito	2.00
THC13	Marlon Byrd	1.00
THC14	Al Leiter	1.00
THC15	Kazuhisa Ishii	1.50
THC16	Franklin Gutierrez	1.00
THC17	Roger Clemens	5.00
THC18	Mark Buehrle	1.00
THC19	Larry Walker	1.00
THC20	Curt Schilling	2.50
THC21	Garret Anderson	1.50
THC22	Randy Johnson	3.00
THC23	Cliff Floyd	1.00
THC24	Austin Kearns	1.00
THC25	Manuel Ramirez	1.00
THC26	Raul Ibanez	1.00
THC27	Jason Perry	1.00
THC28	Mark Teixeira	2.00
THC29	Nomar Garciaparra	6.00
THC30	Wayne Lydon	1.00
THC31	Preston Wilson	1.00
THC32	Paul LoDuca	1.00
THC33	Edgardo Alfonzo	1.00
THC34	Jeremy Giambi	1.00
THC35	Mariano Rivera	1.50
THC36	Jimmy Rollins	2.00
THC37	Bret Boone	1.00
THC38	Scott Rolen	2.00
THC39	Adam LaRoche	1.50
THC40	Tim Hudson	1.50
THC41	Craig Brazell	1.00
THC42	Daryl Clark	1.00
THC43	Joe Mauer, Jake Mauer	3.00
THC44	Troy Glaus	2.50
THC45	Sean Pierce	1.00
THC46	Carl Crawford	1.00
THC47	Mike Piazza	6.00
THC48	Josh Beckett	1.00
THC49	Randall Simon	1.00
THC50	Frank Thomas	2.50
THC51	Andruw Jones	2.00
THC52	Andy Marte	4.00
THC53	Bernie Castro	1.00
THC54	Jim Thome	3.00
THC55	Alexis Rios	1.00
THC56	Vladimir Guerrero	4.00
THC57	Walter Young	1.00

THC58	Hank Blalock	1.50
THC59	Ramon A. Martinez	1.00
THC60	Jacque Jones	1.00
THC61	Nick Johnson	1.00
THC62	Ruddy Lugo	1.00
THC63	Carlos Delgado	1.50
THC64	Jeff Clark	1.00
THC65	Johnny Damon	1.00
THC66	Jaime Bubela	1.00
THC67	Alex Rodriguez	8.00
THC68	Rafael Palmeiro	2.00
THC69	Miguel Tejada	2.00
THC70	Bartolo Colon	1.00
THC71	Mike Sweeney	1.00
THC72	John Smoltz	1.00
THC73	Shannon Stewart	1.00
THC74	Mike Mussina	2.00
THC75	Roy Oswalt	1.50
THC76	Pedro Martinez	4.00
THC77	Magglio Ordonez	2.00
THC78	Manny Ramirez	3.00
THC79	David Wells	1.00
THC80	Richie Sexson	1.50
THC81	Adam Dunn	2.50
THC82	Greg Maddux	5.00
THC83	Alfonso Soriano	5.00
THC84	Roberto Alomar	2.00
THC85	Derek Lowe	1.00
THC86	Tom Glavine	2.00
THC87	Jeff Bagwell	2.50
THC88	Ken Griffey Jr.	6.00
THC89	Shea Hillenbrand	1.00
THC90	Gary Sheffield	1.50
THC91	Chipper Jones	5.00
THC92	Orlando Hudson	1.00
THC93	Jose Cruz Jr.	1.00
THC94	Mark Prior	2.50
THC95	Jason Giambi	5.00
THC96	Luis Gonzalez	1.50
THC97	Drew Henson	1.50
THC98	Cristian Guzman	1.00
THC99	Shawn Green	1.50
THC100	Jose Vidro	1.50

Clubhouse Collection Relics

		NM/M
Common Player:		10.00
EB	Ernie Banks	25.00
AD	Adam Dunn	15.00
JG	Jim Gilliam	12.00
SG	Shawn Green	15.00
CJ	Chipper Jones	15.00
AK	Al Kaline	25.00
EM	Eddie Mathews	20.00
WM	Willie Mays	40.00
AP	Albert Pujols	15.00
AR	Alex Rodriguez	15.00
DS	Duke Snider	25.00
KW	Kerry Wood	10.00

Clubhouse Collection Autograph

No Pricing
Production 25 Sets

Clubhouse Collection Dual Relics

		NM/M
Production 54 Sets		
SG	Duke Snider,	
	Shawn Green	80.00
BW	Ernie Banks,	
	Kerry Wood	80.00
MJ	Eddie Mathews,	
	Chipper Jones	100.00

Flashbacks

RICHIE ASHBURN LEADS THE NATIONAL
LEAGUE IN ON-BASE PERCENTAGE

FLASH BACKS

PHILADELPHIA PHILLIES   RICHIE ASHBURN

		NM/M
Complete Set (10):		12.00
Common Player:		.75
Inserted 1:12		
F1	Willie Mays	3.00
F2	Yogi Berra	2.00
F3	Ted Kluszewski	.75
F4	Stan Musial	3.00
F5	Hank Aaron	3.00
F6	Duke Snider	1.50
F7	Richie Ashburn	.75
F8	Robin Roberts	.75
F9	Mickey Vernon	.75
F10	Don Larsen	.75

Flashbacks Autographs

Production 25
No Pricing

Grandstand Glory

		NM/M
Common Player:		10.00
RA	Richie Ashburn	15.00
EB	Ernie Banks	20.00
YB	Yogi Berra	20.00
DG	Dick Groat	12.00
AK	Al Kaline	15.00
TK	Ted Kluszewski	12.00
EM	Eddie Mathews	12.00
WM	Willie Mays	35.00
AP	Andy Pafko	10.00
PR	Phil Rizzuto	15.00
HS	Hank Sauer	10.00
DS	Duke Snider	15.00
WS	Warren Spahn	15.00

New Age Performers

NEW AGE PERFORMERS

VLADIMIR GUERRERO
montreal expos • outfield

		NM/M
Complete Set (15):		20.00
Common Player:		.75
Inserted 1:15		
NA1	Mike Piazza	3.00
NA2	Ichiro Suzuki	3.00
NA3	Derek Jeter	4.00
NA4	Alex Rodriguez	3.00
NA5	Sammy Sosa	2.00
NA6	Jason Giambi	2.00
NA7	Vladimir Guerrero	1.50
NA8	Albert Pujols	1.50
NA9	Todd Helton	.75
NA10	Nomar Garciaparra	2.50
NA11	Randy Johnson	1.50
NA12	Jim Thome	1.00
NA13	Andruw Jones	1.50
NA14	Miguel Tejada	.75
NA15	Alfonso Soriano	1.50

Real One Autographs

		NM/M
Common Autograph:		15.00
Inserted 1:188		
Special Editions (Red Ink):		1.5-2X
Production 54		
HA	Hank Aaron	300.00
EB	Ernie Banks	150.00
MB	Matt Batts	25.00
HB	Hank Bauer	40.00
LB	Lance Berkman	50.00
YB	Yogi Berra	80.00
MBL	Mike Blyzka	25.00
JC	Jose Cruz Jr.	15.00
RF	Roy Face	40.00
WF	Whitey Ford	60.00
DG	Dick Groat	40.00
GH	Gene Hermanski	25.00
CH	Cal Hogue	25.00
MI	Monte Irvin	50.00
LJ	Larry Jansen	30.00

AK	Al Kaline	80.00
CK	Charlie Kress	25.00
DK	Dick Kryhoski	25.00
TL	Tom Lasorda	70.00
VL	Vern Law	30.00
DL	Don Lenhardt	25.00
DLU	Don Lund	25.00
EM	Eddie Mayo	25.00
WM	Willie Mays	200.00
MM	Mickey Micelotta	25.00
RM	Ray Murray	25.00
AP	Andy Pafko	60.00
PP	Paul Penson	30.00
JPO	Johnny Podres	25.00
JP	Joe Presko	25.00
PR	Phil Rizzuto	50.00
PRO	Preacher Roe	50.00
JR	Jimmy Rollins	25.00
BR	Bob Ross	25.00
JS	Johnny Sain	40.00
MS	Mike Sandlock	25.00
CS	Carl Scheib	25.00
BSH	Bobby Shantz	40.00
BS	Bill "Moose" Skowron	25.00
DS	Duke Snider	80.00
BT	Bob Talbot	25.00
JV	Jose Vidro	15.00
BWE	Bill Werle	25.00
LW	Leroy Wheat	25.00
JW	Jim Willis	25.00

Team Legends Autographs

		NM/M
Common Autograph:		35.00
	Luis Aparicio	35.00
	Jim Bunning	35.00
	Al Kaline	70.00
	Don Larsen	40.00
	Duke Snider	60.00

Then and Now

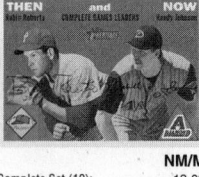

THEN   and   NOW

		NM/M
Complete Set (10):		12.00
Common Card:		.75
Inserted 1:15		
TN1	Ted Kluszewski,	
	Alex Rodriguez	3.00
TN2	Ted Kluszewski,	
	Alex Rodriguez	3.00
TN3	Robin Roberts,	
	Randy Johnson	1.00
TN4	Don Mueller,	
	Alfonso Soriano	1.50
TN5	Stan Musial,	
	Garret Anderson	2.00
TN6	Minnie Minoso,	
	Johnny Damon	.75
TN7	Robin Roberts,	
	Randy Johnson	1.00
TN8	Duke Snider,	
	Alex Rodriguez	3.00
TN9	Robin Roberts,	
	Randy Johnson	1.00
TN10	Johnny Antonelli,	
	Pedro Martinez	1.00

2003 Topps Pristine

JOSE CONTRERAS

NEW YORK YANKEES

		NM/M
Complete Set (190):		
Common Player:		1.00
Common Rookie:		1.00
Common Uncommon RC:		2.50
Production 1,499		
Common Rare RC:		5.00
Production 499		
Pack (8):		30.00
Box (5):		140.00

1	Pedro J. Martinez	2.50
2	Derek Jeter	6.00
3	Alex Rodriguez	6.00
4	Miguel Tejada	1.00
5	Nomar Garciaparra	2.50
6	Austin Kearns	1.50
7	Jose Vidro	1.00
8	Bret Boone	1.00
9	Scott Rolen	2.00
10	Mike Sweeney	1.00
11	Jason Schmidt	1.00
12	Alfonso Soriano	2.50
13	Tim Hudson	1.50
14	A.J. Pierzynski	1.00
15	Lance Berkman	2.00
16	Frank Thomas	2.00
17	Gary Sheffield	1.50
18	Jarrod Washburn	1.00
19	Hideo Nomo	1.50
20	Barry Zito	1.50
21	Kevin Millwood	1.50
22	Matt Morris	1.00
23	Carl Crawford	1.00
24	Carlos Delgado	2.00
25	Mike Piazza	3.00
26	Brad Radke	1.00
27	Richie Sexson	1.50
28	Kevin Brown	1.00
29	Carlos Beltran	2.00
30	Curt Schilling	2.00
31	Chipper Jones	3.00
32	Paul Konerko	1.50
33	Larry Walker	1.50
34	Jeff Bagwell	2.00
35	Jason Giambi	1.50
36	Mark Mulder	1.50
37	Vicente Padilla	1.00
38	Kris Benson	1.00
39	Bernie Williams	1.50
40	Jim Thome	2.00
41	Roger Clemens	5.00
42	Roberto Alomar	1.50
43	Torii Hunter	1.50
44	Bobby Abreu	1.50
45	Jeff Kent	1.00
46	Roy Oswalt	1.50
47	Bartolo Colon	1.00
48	Greg Maddux	4.00
49	Tom Glavine	1.50
50	Sammy Sosa	3.00
51	Ichiro Suzuki	4.00
52	Mark Prior	1.50
53	Manny Ramirez	2.00
54	Andruw Jones	1.50
55	Randy Johnson	3.00
56	Garret Anderson	1.50
57	Roy Halladay	1.00
58	Rafael Palmeiro	2.00
59	Rocco Baldelli	1.50
60	Albert Pujols	6.00
61	Edgar Renteria	1.00
62	John Olerud	1.00
63	Rich Aurilia	1.00
64	Ryan Klesko	1.00
65	Brian Giles	1.50
66	Eric Chavez	1.50
67	Jorge Posada	1.50
68	Cliff Floyd	1.00
69	Vladimir Guerrero	2.00
70	Cristian Guzman	1.00
71	Raul Ibanez	1.00
72	Paul LoDuca	1.00
73	A.J. Burnett	1.00
74	Ken Griffey Jr.	4.00
75	Mark Buehrle	1.50
76	Moises Alou	1.50
77	Adam Dunn	2.00
78	Tony Batista	1.00
79	Troy Glaus	1.50
80	Luis Gonzalez	1.00
81	Shea Hillenbrand	1.00
82	Kerry Wood	1.00
83	Magglio Ordonez	1.00
84	Omar Vizquel	1.00
85	Bobby Higginson	1.00
86	Mike Lowell	1.00
87	Runelvys Hernandez	1.00
88	Shawn Green	1.50
89	Erubiel Durazo	1.00
90	Pat Burrell	1.50
91	Todd Helton	2.00
92	Jim Edmonds	1.50
93	Aubrey Huff	1.00
94	Eric Hinske	1.00
95	Barry Bonds	6.00
96	Willie Mays	5.00
97	Bo Jackson	2.00
98	Carl Yastrzemski	2.00
99	Don Mattingly	5.00
100	Gary Carter	1.50
101	Jose Contreras/C **RC**	2.00
102	Jose Contreras/U **RC**	4.00
103	Jose Contreras/R **RC**	8.00
104	Dan Haren/C	4.00
105	Dan Haren/U	6.00
106	Dan Haren/R	10.00
107	Michel Hernandez/C **RC**	1.00
108	Michel Hernandez/U **RC**	2.50
109	Michel Hernandez/R **RC**	5.00
110	Bobby Basham/C **RC**	1.00
111	Bobby Basham/U **RC**	2.50
112	Bobby Basham/R **RC**	5.00
113	Bryan Bullington/C **RC**	1.50
114	Bryan Bullington/U **RC**	2.50
115	Bryan Bullington/R **RC**	5.00
116	Bernie Castro/C **RC**	1.00
117	Bernie Castro/U **RC**	2.50
118	Bernie Castro/R **RC**	5.00
119	Chien-Ming Wang/C **RC**	25.00
120	Chien-Ming Wang/U **RC**	30.00
121	Chien-Ming Wang/R **RC**	40.00
122	Eric Crozier/C **RC**	1.00
123	Eric Crozier/U **RC**	2.50
124	Eric Crozier/R **RC**	5.00
125	Michael Garciaparra/C	1.00
126	Michael Garciaparra/U	2.50
127	Michael Garciaparra/R	5.00
128	Joey Gomes/C	1.00
129	Joey Gomes/U	2.50
130	Joey Gomes/R	5.00
131	Wilfredo Ledezma/C **RC**	1.00
132	Wilfredo Ledezma/U **RC**	2.50
133	Wilfredo Ledezma/R **RC**	5.00
134	Branden Florence/C **RC**	1.00
135	Branden Florence/U **RC**	2.50
136	Branden Florence/R **RC**	5.00
137	Jeremy Bonderman/C	4.00
138	Jeremy Bonderman/U	6.00
139	Jeremy Bonderman/R	8.00
140	Travis Ishikawa/C **RC**	1.00
141	Travis Ishikawa/U **RC**	2.50
142	Travis Ishikawa/R **RC**	5.00
143	Ben Francisco/C **RC**	2.00
144	Ben Francisco/U **RC**	4.00
145	Ben Francisco/R **RC**	6.00
146	Jason Kubel/C **RC**	3.00
147	Jason Kubel/U **RC**	5.00
148	Jason Kubel/R **RC**	8.00
149	Tyler Martin/C **RC**	1.00
150	Tyler Martin/U **RC**	2.50
151	Tyler Martin/R **RC**	5.00
152	Jason Perry/C	1.50
153	Jason Perry/U	3.00
154	Jason Perry/R	5.00
155	Ryan Shealy/C **RC**	1.50
156	Ryan Shealy/U **RC**	3.00
157	Ryan Shealy/R **RC**	5.00
158	Hanley Ramirez/C **RC**	12.00
159	Hanley Ramirez/U **RC**	15.00
160	Hanley Ramirez/R **RC**	25.00
161	Rajai Davis/C **RC**	2.00
162	Rajai Davis/U **RC**	4.00
163	Rajai Davis/R **RC**	6.00
164	Gary Schneidmiller/C **RC**	1.00
165	Gary Schneidmiller/U **RC**	2.50
166	Gary Schneidmiller/R **RC**	5.00
167	Haj Turay/C **RC**	1.00
168	Haj Turay/U **RC**	2.50
169	Haj Turay/R **RC**	5.00
170	Kevin Youkilis/C **RC**	4.00
171	Kevin Youkilis/U **RC**	8.00
172	Kevin Youkilis/R **RC**	15.00
173	Shane Bazzell/C **RC**	1.00
174	Shane Bazzell/U **RC**	2.50
175	Shane Bazzell/R **RC**	5.00
176	Elizardo Ramirez/C **RC**	1.50
177	Elizardo Ramirez/U **RC**	3.00
178	Elizardo Ramirez/R **RC**	6.00
179	Robinson Cano/C **RC**	15.00
180	Robinson Cano/U **RC**	20.00
181	Robinson Cano/R **RC**	30.00
182	Nook Logan/C **RC**	1.00
183	Nook Logan/U **RC**	2.50
184	Nook Logan/R **RC**	5.00
185	Dustin McGowan/C **RC**	2.00
186	Dustin McGowan/U **RC**	5.00
187	Dustin McGowan/R **RC**	8.00
188	Ryan Howard/C	25.00
189	Ryan Howard/U	25.00
190	Ryan Howard/R	50.00

Refractors

Veterans (1-100):	4-6X
Production 99	
Common RC's:	.75-1.5X
Production 1,599	
Uncommon RC's:	1-2X
Production 499	
Rare RC's:	1.5-3X
Production 99	
Veteran Gold Refrac.(1-100):	4-8X
Rookie Golds (101-190):	2-4X
Production 69 Sets	

Plates

No pricing due to scarcity.
Four plates per player.

Bomb Squad

BOMB SQUAD
ERIC CHAVEZ
oakland athletics

		NM/M
Common Player:		4.00
Refractors:		No Pricing
Production 25 Sets		
MO1	Moises Alou	4.00
MO2	Moises Alou	4.00
GA1	Garret Anderson	5.00
GA2	Garret Anderson	5.00
JRB	Jeff Bagwell	6.00
JB	Johnny Bench	10.00
LB1	Lance Berkman	5.00
LB2	Lance Berkman	5.00
HB	Hank Blalock	5.00
BB	Barry Bonds	15.00
GB1	George Brett	12.00
GB2	George Brett	12.00
GC	Gary Carter	5.00
EC1	Eric Chavez	4.00
EC2	Eric Chavez	4.00
CC	Carl Crawford	4.00
AD	Adam Dunn	6.00
DE1	Darin Erstad	4.00
DE2	Darin Erstad	4.00
CF	Cliff Floyd	4.00
NG1	Nomar Garciaparra	10.00
NG2	Nomar Garciaparra	10.00
JG	Jason Giambi	6.00
TG1	Troy Glaus	5.00
TG2	Troy Glaus	5.00
JAG	Juan Gonzalez	6.00
LG	Luis Gonzalez	4.00
SG	Shawn Green	5.00
VG1	Vladimir Guerrero	8.00
VG2	Vladimir Guerrero	8.00
TH	Todd Helton	6.00
RH	Rickey Henderson	10.00
AJ	Andruw Jones	6.00
CJ	Chipper Jones	8.00
JK	Jeff Kent	4.00
MO	Magglio Ordonez	4.00
RP	Rafael Palmeiro	6.00
MP	Mike Piazza	10.00
AP1	Albert Pujols	15.00
AP2	Albert Pujols	15.00
MR	Manny Ramirez	6.00
AR1	Alex Rodriguez	10.00
AR2	Alex Rodriguez	10.00
TS	Tim Salmon	4.00
MS1	Mike Schmidt	12.00
MS2	Mike Schmidt	12.00
GS	Gary Sheffield	5.00
AS	Alfonso Soriano	8.00
SS1	Sammy Sosa	10.00
SS2	Sammy Sosa	10.00
MT	Miguel Tejada	4.00
FT	Frank Thomas	6.00
JT	Jim Thome	10.00

Borders

PRISTINE BORDERS
TAIWAN
CHIN-FENG CHEN

		NM/M
Common Player:		4.00
Inserted 1:9		
Refractors:		No Pricing
Production 25 Sets		
CC	Chin-Feng Chen	40.00
VG	Vladimir Guerrero	8.00
CG	Cristian Guzman	4.00
KI	Kazuhisa Ishii	4.00
AJ	Andruw Jones	6.00
PM	Pedro J. Martinez	8.00
MO	Maggilo Ordonez	4.00
AP	Albert Pujols	15.00
MR	Manny Ramirez	6.00
IR	Ivan Rodriguez	6.00
TS	Tsuyoshi Shinjo	4.00
AS	Alfonso Soriano	8.00
SS	Sammy Sosa	10.00
MT	Miguel Tejada	4.00
BW	Bernie Williams	6.00

Corners

		NM/M
Common Duo:		6.00
Inserted 1:12		
Refractors:		No Pricing
Production 25 Sets		
CD	Eric Chavez, Erubiel Durazo	6.00
VG	Robin Ventura, Jason Giambi	10.00
WG	Matt Williams, Mark Grace	8.00
RM	Scott Rolen, Tino Martinez	10.00
BM	Adrian Beltre, Fred McGriff	6.00
GS	Troy Glaus, Scott Spiezio	8.00
KM	Corey Koskie, Doug Mientkiewicz	6.00
BT	David Bell, Jim Thome	10.00
BK	Sean Burroughs, Ryan Klesko	6.00
AS	Edgardo Alfonzo, J.T. Snow	6.00
TP	Mark Teixeira, Rafael Palmeiro	10.00

Double Bonds

		NM/M
Common Duo:		25.00
Refractors:		No Pricing
Production 25		
BJ	Barry Bonds, Randy Johnson	50.00
BT	Miguel Tejada, Barry Bonds	25.00
BM	Willie Mays, Barry Bonds	75.00
BR	Alex Rodriguez, Barry Bonds	35.00

Factor

PRISTINE
FACTOR
alex rodriguez | ss

		NM/M
Common Player:		4.00
Inserted 1:9		
Refractors:		No Pricing
Production 25 Sets		
LB	Lance Berkman	4.00
AD	Adam Dunn	6.00
DE	Darin Erstad	4.00
NG	Nomar Garciaparra	10.00
JG	Jason Giambi	6.00
TG	Troy Glaus	5.00
VG	Vladimir Guerrero	8.00
TH	Todd Helton	6.00
TKH	Torii Hunter	5.00
MO	Maggilo Ordonez	4.00
MP	Mike Piazza	10.00
MR	Manny Ramirez	6.00
AR	Alex Rodriguez	10.00
AS	Alfonso Soriano	8.00
SS	Sammy Sosa	10.00

Mini

		NM/M
Common Player:		1.00
RB	Rocco Baldelli	1.50
BWB	Bobby Basham	1.00
JB	Jeremy Bonderman	4.00
BB	Barry Bonds	6.00
BPB	Bryan Bullington	3.00
RJC	Robinson Cano	20.00
BC	Bernie Castro	1.00
EC	Eric Chavez	1.00
RC	Roger Clemens	5.00
JC	Jose Contreras	2.00
ELC	Eric Crozier	1.00
RD	Rajai Davis	1.00
NG	Nomar Garciaparra	5.00
JG	Jason Giambi	2.00
BG	Brian Giles	1.50
VG	Vladimir Guerrero	3.00
DH	Dan Haren	4.00
MH	Michel Hernandez	1.00
RH	Ryan Howard	60.00
DJ	Derek Jeter	6.00
AK	Austin Kearns	2.00
JK	Jeff Kent	1.50
JJK	Jason Kubel	4.00
WL	Wilfredo Ledezma	1.00
NL	Nook Logan	1.00
TM	Tyler Martin	1.00
DM	Dustin McGowan	3.00
MO	Magglio Ordonez	1.00
MJP	Mike Piazza	4.00
MP	Mark Prior	6.00
ER	Elizardo Ramirez	1.00
AR	Alex Rodriguez	6.00
RS	Ryan Shealy	3.00
AS	Alfonso Soriano	3.00
SS	Sammy Sosa	4.00
IS	Ichiro Suzuki	3.00
MT	Miguel Tejada	1.50
JT	Jim Thome	2.00
CW	Chien-Ming Wang	40.00
KY	Kevin Youkilis	6.00

Mini Autograph

		NM/M
Production 100		
RC	Roger Clemens	125.00

Personal Endorsements

	NM/M
Common Autograph:	6.00

Golds: No Pricing
Production 25 Sets

AB	Andrew Brown	6.00
RYC	Ryan Church	10.00
DE	David Eckstein	10.00
LF	Lew Ford	10.00
JG	Jay Gibbons	10.00
RJH	Rich Harden	25.00
KH	Ken Harvey	6.00
PK	Paul Konerko	20.00
ML	Mike Lowell	10.00
VM	Victor Martinez	20.00
BM	Brett Myers	10.00
JP	Josh Phelps	8.00
SR	Scott Rolen	25.00
FS	Felix Sanchez	6.00
KS	Kelly Shoppach	15.00
MS	Mike Sweeney	10.00
FV	Fernando Vina	6.00

Primary Elements
NM/M
Many not priced due to scarcity.
Production 50 Sets
Refractors: No Pricing
Production 10

BRB	Bret Boone	15.00
NG	Nomar Garciaparra	35.00
LG	Luis Gonzalez	10.00
SG	Shawn Green	10.00
TH	Todd Helton	20.00
TKH	Torii Hunter	20.00
KI	Kazuhisa Ishii	10.00
AJ	Andruw Jones	15.00
CJ	Chipper Jones	20.00
PM	Pedro J. Martinez	20.00
MO	Magglio Ordonez	10.00
RP	Rafael Palmeiro	15.00
MP	Mike Piazza	25.00
AR	Alex Rodriguez	50.00
MT	Miguel Tejada	15.00
BZ	Barry Zito	15.00

Solo Bonds
NM/M
Common Bonds: 20.00
Refractors: No Pricing
Production 25

GG	Barry Bonds	20.00
HR	Barry Bonds	20.00
BB	Barry Bonds	20.00
MVP	Barry Bonds	20.00

2003 Topps Retired Signature Edition

NM/M
Complete Set (110): 100.00
Common Player: .50
Pack (5): 30.00
Box (5): 120.00

1	Willie Mays	4.00
2	Tony Perez	1.00
3	Tom Seaver	2.00
4	Johnny Bench	4.00
5	Rod Carew	1.50
6	Red Schoendienst	.50
7	Phil Rizzuto	1.00

8	Ozzie Smith	2.50
9	Maury Wills	.50
10	Hank Aaron	4.00
11	Jim Palmer	1.00
12	Jose Cruz	.50
13	Dave Parker	.50
14	Don Sutton	.75
15	Brooks Robinson	2.00
16	Bo Jackson	1.50
17	Andre Dawson	.75
18	Fergie Jenkins	.75
19	George Foster	.50
20	George Brett	5.00
21	Jerry Koosman	.50
22	John Kruk	.50
23	Kent Tekulve	.50
24	Lee Smith	.50
25	Nolan Ryan	6.00
26	Paul O'Neill	.50
27	Rich "Goose" Gossage	.50
28	Ron Santo	.50
29	Tom Lasorda	.75
30	Tony Gwynn	2.00
31	Vida Blue	.50
32	Whitey Herzog	.50
33	Willie McGee	.50
34	Bill Mazeroski	.50
35	Al Kaline	3.00
36	Bobby Richardson	.50
37	Carlton Fisk	1.00
38	Darrell Evans	.50
39	Dave Concepcion	.50
40	Cal Ripken Jr.	5.00
41	Dwight Evans	.50
42	Earl Weaver	.50
43	Fred Lynn	.50
44	Greg Luzinski	.50
45	Duke Snider	1.50
46	Hank Bauer	.50
47	Jim Rice	.50
48	Johnny Sain	.50
49	Lenny Dykstra	.50
50	Mike Schmidt	4.00
51	Orlando Cepeda	1.00
52	Ralph Kiner	.75
53	Robin Roberts	.50
54	Ron Guidry	.50
55	Steve Garvey	.50
56	Tony Oliva	.75
57	Whitey Ford	1.00
58	Willie McCovey	1.00
59	Phil Niekro	.50
60	Stan Musial	3.00
61	Rollie Fingers	1.00
62	Robin Yount	2.00
63	Alan Trammell	1.00
64	Bill Buckner	.50
65	Bob Feller	1.00
66	Bruce Sutter	.75
67	Dale Murphy	1.00
68	Dennis Eckersley	1.00
69	Don Newcombe	.50
70	Don Mattingly	5.00
71	Dwight Gooden	.50
72	Frank Robinson	1.50
73	Gary Carter	.50
74	Graig Nettles	.50
75	Harmon Killebrew	2.00
76	Jim Bunning	.50
77	Joe Morgan	1.00
78	Joe Rudi	.50
79	Jose Canseco	3.00
80	Ernie Banks	.50
81	Luis Aparicio	.50
82	Luis Tiant	.50
83	Mark Fidrych	.50
84	Kirk Gibson	.50
85	Lou Brock	1.00
86	Juan Marichal	1.00
87	Monte Irvin	1.00
88	Paul Molitor	1.00
89	Tommy John	.50
90	Warren Spahn	1.50
91	Wade Boggs	1.00
92	Reggie Jackson	2.00
93	Kirby Puckett	3.00
94	Boog Powell	.50
95	Carl Yastrzemski	2.00
96	Bobby Thomson	.50
97	Bill "Moose" Skowron	.50
98	Bill Madlock	.50
99	Sparky Anderson	.50
100	Yogi Berra	2.00
101	Bobby Doerr	.50
102	Gaylord Perry	.50
103	George Kell	.50
104	Harold Reynolds	.50
105	Joe Carter	.50
106	Johnny Podres	.50
107	Ron Cey	.50
108	Tim McCarver	.50
109	Tug McGraw	.50
110	Don Larsen	1.00

Black
Cards (1-110): 2-4X
Production 99 Sets

Autographs
NM/M
Common Autograph: 10.00
Inserted 1:1
Refractors: 1-2.5X
Production 25 Sets
HA Hank Aaron/30 300.00

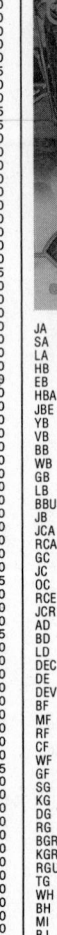
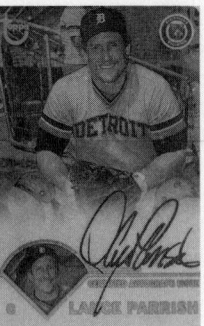

JA	Jim Abbott	20.00
SA	Sparky Anderson	20.00
LA	Luis Aparicio	12.00
HB	Harold Baines	10.00
EB	Ernie Banks/24	175.00
HBA	Hank Bauer	20.00
JBE	Johnny Bench	65.00
YB	Yogi Berra/25	150.00
VB	Vida Blue	15.00
BB	Bert Blyleven	10.00
WB	Wade Boggs/77	125.00
GB	George Brett/25	180.00
LB	Lou Brock/76	120.00
BBU	Bill Buckner	10.00
JB	Jim Bunning/76	100.00
JCA	Jose Canseco	40.00
RCA	Rod Carew	60.00
GC	Gary Carter/77	100.00
JC	Joe Carter	25.00
OC	Orlando Cepeda/75	180.00
RCE	Ron Cey	10.00
JCR	Jose Cruz	10.00
AD	Andre Dawson	20.00
BD	Bobby Doerr	20.00
LD	Lenny Dykstra	20.00
DEC	Dennis Eckersley	65.00
DE	Darrell Evans	10.00
DEV	Dwight Evans/78	80.00
BF	Bob Feller	20.00
MF	Mark Fidrych	25.00
RF	Rollie Fingers	20.00
CF	Carlton Fisk	65.00
WF	Whitey Ford	65.00
GF	George Foster	10.00
SG	Steve Garvey	15.00
KG	Kirk Gibson	40.00
DG	Dwight Gooden	30.00
RG	Rich "Goose" Gossage	15.00
BGR	Bobby Grich	15.00
KGR	Ken Griffey Sr.	15.00
RGU	Ron Guidry	35.00
TG	Tony Gwynn/25	165.00
WH	Whitey Herzog	15.00
BH	Bob Horner	10.00
MI	Monte Irvin	60.00
BJ	Bo Jackson	75.00
RJ	Reggie Jackson	100.00
FJ	Fergie Jenkins	20.00
TJ	Tommy John	25.00
AK	Al Kaline	75.00
GK	George Kell	30.00
HK	Harmon Killebrew/76	150.00
RK	Ralph Kiner	125.00
JK	Jerry Koosman	25.00
JKR	John Kruk	35.00
DL	Don Larsen	15.00
TL	Tom Lasorda/76	100.00
GL	Greg Luzinski	15.00
FL	Fred Lynn	20.00
BM	Bill Madlock	10.00
JMA	Juan Marichal	35.00
DON	Don Mattingly/81	175.00
BMA	Bill Mazeroski	15.00
TM	Tim McCarver	25.00
WMC	Willie McCovey	50.00
WMG	Willie McGee	15.00
TMC	Tug McGraw	50.00
PM	Paul Molitor	75.00
JM	Joe Morgan	35.00
DM	Dale Murphy	40.00
SM	Stan Musial/28	185.00
PN	Phil Niekro	15.00
GN	Graig Nettles	10.00
DN	Don Newcombe	15.00
TO	Tony Oliva	25.00
PO	Paul O'Neill	15.00
JP	Jim Palmer	50.00
DP	Dave Parker	10.00
LP	Lance Parrish	10.00
TP	Terry Pendleton	10.00
TP	Tony Perez	40.00
GP	Gaylord Perry	20.00
JPI	Jimmy Piersall	10.00
JPO	Johnny Podres	10.00
BP	Boog Powell	10.00
HR	Harold Reynolds	10.00
JR	Jim Rice	30.00
BR	Bobby Richardson	15.00
CR	Cal Ripken Jr./25	340.00
PR	Phil Rizzuto/70	140.00
RR	Robin Roberts	25.00
BRO	Brooks Robinson/75	140.00
FR	Frank Robinson	60.00
JRU	Joe Rudi	10.00
NR	Nolan Ryan/77	200.00
BSA	Bret Saberhagen	25.00
RSA	Ron Santo	20.00
MS	Mike Schmidt/83	200.00
RS	Red Schoendienst/83	100.00
TS	Tom Seaver	65.00
BS	Bill "Moose" Skowron	10.00
LS	Lee Smith	15.00
OS	Ozzie Smith	65.00
DSN	Duke Snider/75	100.00
WS	Warren Spahn	50.00
DS	Dave Stieb	15.00
BSU	Bruce Sutter	35.00
DSU	Don Sutton	20.00
KT	Kent Tekulve	20.00
BT	Bobby Thomson	10.00
LT	Luis Tiant	10.00
AT	Alan Trammell	20.00
BW	Bob Watson	10.00
EW	Earl Weaver	12.00
MW	Maury Wills	10.00
CY	Carl Yastrzemski	80.00
RY	Robin Yount/25	150.00

2003 Topps Total

Chien-Ming WANG

NM/M
Complete Set (990): 125.00
Common Player: .10
Pack (10): 1.00
Box (36): 25.00

1	Brent Abernathy	.10
2	Bobby Hill	.10
3	Victor Martinez	.10
4	Chip Ambres	.10
5	Matt Anderson	.10
6	Ricardo Aramboles	.10
7	Carlos Pena	.10
8	Aaron Guiel	.10
9	Luke Allen	.10
10	Francisco Rodriguez	.20
11	Jason Marquis	.10
12	Edwin Almonte	.10
13	Grant Balfour	.10
14	Adam Piatt	.10
15	Andy Phillips	.10
16	Adrian Beltre	.10
17	Brandon Backe	.10
18	Dave Berg	.10
19	Brett Myers	.10
20	Brian Meadows	.10
21	Chin-Feng Chen	.25
22	Blake Williams	.10
23	Josh Bard	.10
24	Josh Beckett	.20
25	Kip Bouknight RC	.20
26	Matt Childers	.10
27	Adam Everett	.10
28	Mike Bordick	.10
29	Antonio Alfonseca	.10
30	Doug Creek	.10
31	J.D. Drew	.20
32	Milton Bradley	.10
33	David Wells	.10
34	Vance Wilson	.10
35	Jeff Fassero	.10
36	Sandy Alomar	.10
37	Ryan Vogelsong	.10
38	Roger Clemens	1.25
39	Juan Gonzalez	.40
40	Dustin Hermanson	.10
41	Andy Ashby	.10
42	Adam Hyzdu	.10
43	Ben Broussard	.10
44	Ryan Klesko	.10
45	Chris Buglovsky	.10
46	Bud Smith	.10
47	Aaron Boone	.10
48	Cliff Floyd	.10
49	Alex Cora	.10
50	Curt Schilling	.40
51	Michael Cuddyer	.10
52	Mike Venafro	.10
53	Carlos Guillen	.10
54	Angel Berroa	.10
55	Eli Marrero	.10
56	A.J. Burnett	.10

57	Oliver Perez	.10
58	Matt Morris	.25
59	Valerio De Los Santos	.10
60	Austin Kearns	.50
61	Darren Dreifort	.10
62	Jason Standridge	.10
63	Carlos Silva	.10
64	Moises Alou	.20
65	Jason Anderson	.10
66	Russell Branyan	.10
67	B.J. Ryan	.10
68	Cory Aldridge	.10
69	Ellis Burks	.10
70	Troy Glaus	.50
71	Kelly Wunsch	.10
72	Brad Wilkerson	.10
73	Jayson Durocher	.10
74	Tony Fiore	.10
75	Brian Giles	.25
76	Billy Wagner	.10
77	Neifi Perez	.10
78	Jose Valverde	.10
79	Brent Butler	.10
80	Mario Ramos	.10
81	Kerry Robinson	.10
82	Brent Mayne	.10
83	Sean Casey	.10
84	Danys Baez	.10
85	Chase Utley	.25
86	Jared Sandberg	.10
87	Terrence Long	.10
88	Kevin Walker	.10
89	Royce Clayton	.10
90	Shea Hillenbrand	.10
91	Brad Lidge	.10
92	Shawn Chacon	.10
93	Kevin Frederick	.10
94	Chris Snelling	.10
95	Omar Vizquel	.20
96	Joe Borchard	.10
97	Matt Belisle	.10
98	Steve Smyth	.10
99	Raul Mondesi	.20
100	Chipper Jones	1.00
101	Victor Alvarez	.10
102	J.M. Gold	.10
103	Willis Roberts	.10
104	Eddie Guardado	.10
105	Brad Voyles	.10
106	Bronson Arroyo	.10
107	Juan Castro	.10
108	Dan Pleasac	.10
109	Ramon Castro	.10
110	Tim Salmon	.25
111	Damion Easley	.10
112	J.D. Closser	.10
113	Mark Buehrle	.10
114	Steve Karsay	.10
115	Cristian Guerrero	.10
116	Brad Ausmus	.10
117	Cristian Guzman	.10
118	Dan Wilson	.10
119	Jake Westbrook	.10
120	Manny Ramirez	.50
121	Jason Giambi	.75
122	Bob Wickman	.10
123	Aaron Cook	.10
124	Alfredo Amezaga	.10
125	Corey Thurman	.10
126	Brandon Puffer	.10
127	Hee Seop Choi	.25
128	Javier Vazquez	.10
129	Carlos Valderrama	.10
130	Jerome Williams	.10
131	Wilson Betemit	.10
132	Bruce Chen	.10
133	Esteban Yan	.10
134	Brandon Berger	.10
135	Bill Hall	.10
136	LaTroy Hawkins	.10
137	Nate Cornejo	.10
138	Jim Mecir	.10
139	Joe Crede	.10
140	Andres Galarraga	.10
141	Dave Williams	.10
142	Joey Eischen	.10
143	Mike Timlin	.10
144	Jose Cruz Jr.	.10
145	Wes Helms	.10
146	Brian Roberts	.10
147	Bret Prinz	.10
148	Brian Hunter	.10
149	Chad Hermansen	.10
150	Andruw Jones	.40
151	Kurt Ainsworth	.10
152	Clifford Bartosh	.10
153	Kyle Lohse	.10
154	Brian Jordan	.10
155	Coco Crisp	.10
156	Tomas Perez	.10
157	Keith Foulke	.10
158	Chris Carpenter	.10
159	Mike Remlinger	.10
160	Dewon Brazelton	.10
161	Brook Fordyce	.10
162	Rusty Greer	.10
163	Scott Downs	.10
164	Jason Dubois	.10
165	David Coggin	.10
166	Jose Hernandez	.10
167	Carlos Hernandez	.10
168	Matt Williams	.10
169	Rheal Cormier	.10
170	Duaner Sanchez	.10
171	Craig Counsell	.10
172	Edgar Martinez	.20
173	Zack Greinke	.10
174	Pedro Feliz	.10
175	Randy Choate	.10
176	Jon Garland	.10
177	Keith Ginter	.10
178	Carlos Febles	.10
179	Gregor Blanco **RC**	.10
180	Jack Cust	.10
181	Koyie Hill	.10
182	Ricky Gutierrez	.10
183	Ben Grieve	.10
184	Livan Hernandez	.10
185	Jason Isringhausen	.10
186	Gookie Dawkins	.10
187	Roberto Alomar	.40
188	Eric Junge	.10
189	Carlos Beltran	.10
190	Denny Hocking	.10
191	Jason Schmidt	.10
192	Cory Lidle	.10
193	Robert Mackowiak	.10
194	Charlton Jimerson **RC**	.10
195	Darin Erstad	.25
196	Jason Davis	.10
197	Luis Castillo	.10
198	Juan Encarnacion	.10
199	Jeffrey Hammonds	.10
200	Nomar Garciaparra	1.50
201	Ryan Christianson	.10
202	Willie Banks	.10
203	Damian Moss	.10
204	Chris Richard	.10
205	Todd Hundley	.10
206	Paul Bako	.10
207	Adam Kennedy	.10
208	Scott Hatteberg	.10
209	Andy Pratt	.10
210	Ken Griffey Jr.	1.00
211	Chris George	.10
212	Lance Niekro	.10
213	Greg Colbrunn	.10
214	Herbert Perry	.10
215	Cody Ransom	.10
216	Craig Biggio	.25
217	Miguel Batista	.10
218	Alex Escobar	.10
219	Willie Harris	.10
220	Scott Strickland	.10
221	Felix Rodriguez	.10
222	Torii Hunter	.25
223	Tyler Houston	.10
224	Darrell May	.10
225	Benito Santiago	.10
226	Ryan Dempster	.10
227	Andy Fox	.10
228	Jung Bong	.10
229	Jose Macias	.10
230	Shannon Stewart	.10
231	Buddy Groom	.10
232	Eric Valent	.10
233	Scott Schoeneweis	.10
234	Corey Hart	.10
235	Brett Tomko	.10
236	Shane Bazzell **RC**	.20
237	Tim Hummel	.10
238	Al Reyes	.10
239	Daryle Ward	.10
240	Ismael Valdes	.10
241	Brian Fuentes	.10
242	Cesar Izturis	.10
243	Mark Bellhorn	.10
244	Geoff Jenkins	.10
245	Derek Jeter	2.00
246	Anderson Machado	.10
247	Dave Roberts	.10
248	Jaime Cerda	.10
249	Woody Williams	.10
250	Vernon Wells	.20
251	Jon Lieber	.10
252	Franklyn German	.10
253	David Segui	.10
254	Freddy Garcia	.10
255	James Baldwin	.10
256	Tony Alvarez	.10
257	Walter Young	.10
258	Alex Herrera	.10
259	Robert Fick	.10
260	Rob Bell	.10
261	Ross Gload	.10
262	Dee Brown	.10
263	Mike Bacsik	.10
264	Corey Patterson	.10
265	Marvin Bernard	.10
266	Eddie Rogers	.10
267	Elio Serrano	.10
268	D'Angelo Jimenez	.10
269	Adam Johnson	.10
270	Gregg Zaun	.10
271	Nick Johnson	.10
272	Geoff Goetz	.10
273	Ryan Drese	.10
274	Eric DuBose	.10
275	Barry Zito	.25
276	Mike Crudale	.10
277	Paul Byrd	.10
278	Eric Gagne	.10
279	Aramis Ramirez	.10
280	Ray Durham	.10
281	Tony Graffanino	.10
282	Jeremy Guthrie	.10
283	Erik Bedard	.10
284	Vince Faison	.10
285	Bobby Kielty	.10
286	Francis Beltran	.10
287	Alexis Gomez	.10
288	Vladimir Guerrero	.75
289	Kevin Appier	.10
290	Gil Meche	.10
291	Marquis Grissom	.10
292	John Burkett	.10
293	Vinny Castilla	.10
294	Tyler Walker	.10
295	Shane Halter	.10
296	Geronimo Gil	.10
297	Eric Hinske	.10
298	Adam Dunn	.50
299	Mike Kinkade	.10
300	Mark Prior	.50
301	Corey Koskie	.10
302	David Dellucci	.10
303	Todd Helton	.40
304	Greg Miller	.10
305	Delvin James	.10
306	Humberto Cota	.10
307	Aaron Harang	.10
308	Jeremy Hill	.10
309	Billy Koch	.10
310	Brandon Claussen	.10
311	Matt Ginter	.10
312	Jason Lane	.10
313	Ben Weber	.10
314	Alan Benes	.10
315	Oscar Herinquez	.10
316	Danny Graves	.10
317	Jason Johnson	.10
318	Jason Grimsley	.10
319	Steve Kline	.10
320	Johnny Damon	.10
321	Jay Gibbons	.10
322	J.J. Putz	.10
323	Stephen Randolph **RC**	.10
324	Bobby Higginson	.10
325	Kazuhisa Ishii	.10
326	Carlos Lee	.10
327	J.R. House	.10
328	Mark Loretta	.10
329	Mike Matheny	.10
330	Ben Diggins	.10
331	Seth Etherton	.10
332	Eli Whiteside **RC**	.20
333	Juan Rivera	.10
334	Jeff Conine	.10
335	John McDonald	.10
336	Erik Hiljus	.10
337	David Eckstein	.10
338	Jeff Bagwell	.50
339	Matt Holliday	.25
340	Jeff Liefer	.10
341	Greg Myers	.10
342	Scott Sauerbeck	.10
343	Omar Infante	.10
344	Ryan Langerhans	.10
345	Abraham Nunez	.10
346	Mike MacDougal	.10
347	Travis Phelps	.10
348	Dan Reichert	.10
349	Alex Rodriguez	1.50
350	Bobby Seay	.10
351	Ichiro Suzuki	1.00
352	Brandon Inge	.10
353	Jack Wilson	.10
354	John Ennis	.10
355	Jamal Strong	.10
356	Jason Jennings	.10
357	Jeff Kent	.20
358	Scott Chiasson	.10
359	Jeremy Griffiths	.10
360	Paul Konerko	.10
361	Jeff Austin	.10
362	Todd Van Poppel	.10
363	Sun-Woo Kim	.10
364	Jerry Hairston	.10
365	Tony Torcato	.10
366	Arthur Rhodes	.10
367	Jose Jimenez	.10
368	Matt LeCroy	.10
369	Curtis Lesanic	.10
370	Ramon Vasquez	.10
371	Joe Randa	.10
372	John Franco	.10
373	Charles Johnson	.10
374	Craig Wilson	.10
375	Michael Young	.10
376	Mark Ellis	.10
377	Joe Mauer	.25
378	Checklist	.10
379	Jason Kendall	.10
380	Checklist	.10
381	Alex Gonzalez	.10
382	Flash Gordon	.10
383	John Buck	.10
384	Shigetoshi Hasegawa	.10
385	Scott Stewart	.10
386	Luke Hudson	.10
387	Todd Jones	.10
388	Fred McGriff	.25
389	Mike Sweeney	.10
390	Marlon Anderson	.10
391	Terry Adams	.10
392	Mark DeRosa	.10
393	Doug Mientkiewicz	.10
394	Miguel Cairo	.10
395	Jamie Moyer	.10
396	Josh Towers	.10
397	Matt Clement	.10
398	Bengie Molina	.10
399	Marcus Thames	.10
400	Nick Bierbrodt	.10
401	Tim Kalita	.10
402	Corwin Malone	.10
403	Jesse Orosco	.10
404	Brandon Phillips	.10
405	Eric Cyr	.10
406	Jason Michaels	.10
407	Julio Lugo	.10
408	Gabe Kapler	.10
409	Mark Mulder	.25
410	Adam Eaton	.10
411	Ken Harvey	.10
412	Jolbert Cabrera	.10
413	Eric Milton	.10
414	Josh Hall **RC**	.20
415	Bob File	.10
416	Brett Evert	.10
417	Ron Chiavacci	.10
418	Jorge De La Rosa	.10
419	Quinton McCracken	.10
420	Luther Hackman	.10
421	Gary Knotts	.10
422	Kevin Brown	.20
423	Jeff Cirillo	.10
424	Damaso Marte	.10
425	Chan Ho Park	.10
426	Nathan Haynes	.10
427	Matt Lawton	.10
428	Mike Stanton	.10
429	Bernie Williams	.40
430	Kevin Jarvis	.10
431	Joe McEwing	.10
432	Mark Kotsay	.10
433	Juan Cruz	.10
434	Russ Ortiz	.10
435	Jeff Nelson	.10
436	Alan Embree	.10
437	Miguel Tejada	.25
438	Kirk Saarloos	.10
439	Cliff Lee	.10
440	Ryan Ludwick	.10
441	Derrek Lee	.10
442	Bobby Abreu	.20
443	Dustan Mohr	.10
444	Nook Logan **RC**	.25
445	Seth McClung	.10
446	Miguel Olivo	.10
447	Henry Blanco	.10
448	Seung Jun Song	.10
449	Kris Wilson	.10
450	Xavier Nady	.10
451	Corky Miller	.10
452	Jim Thome	.50
453	George Lombard	.10
454	Rey Ordonez	.10
455	Deivis Santos	.10
456	Mike Myers	.10
457	Edgar Renteria	.10
458	Braden Looper	.10
459	Guillermo Mota	.10
460	Scott Rolen	.50
461	Lance Berkman	.10
462	Jeff Heaverlo	.10
463	Ramon Hernandez	.10
464	Jason Simontacchi	.10
465	So Taguchi	.10
466	Dave Veres	.10
467	Shane Loux	.10
468	Rodrigo Lopez	.10
469	Bubba Trammell	.10
470	Scott Sullivan	.10
471	Mike Mussina	.40
472	Ramon Ortiz	.10
473	Lyle Overbay	.10
474	Mike Lowell	.10
475	Greg Vaughn	.10
476	Larry Bigbie	.10
477	Rey Sanchez	.10
478	Magglio Ordonez	.25
479	Rondell White	.10
480	Jay Witasick	.10
481	Jimmy Rollins	.25
482	Mike Maroth	.10
483	Mark Quinn	.10
484	Nick Neugebauer	.10
485	Victor Zambrano	.10
486	Travis Lee	.10
487	Bobby Bradley	.10
488	Marcus Giles	.10
489	Steve Trachsel	.10
490	Derek Lowe	.10
491	Hideo Nomo	.25
492	Brad Hawpe	.10
493	Jesus Medrano	.10
494	Rick Ankiel	.25
495	Pasqual Coco	.10
496	Michael Barrett	.10
497	Joe Beimel	.10
498	Marty Cordova	.10
499	Aaron Sele	.10
500	Sammy Sosa	1.00
501	Ivan Rodriguez	.40
502	Keith Osik	.10
503	Hank Blalock	.25
504	Craig Monroe	.10
505	Junior Spivey	.10
506	Edgardo Alfonzo	.10
507	Alex Graman	.10
508	J.J. Davis	.10
509	Roger Cedeno	.10
510	Joe Roa	.10
511	Wily Mo Pena	.10
512	Eric Munson	.10
513	Arnie Munoz **RC**	.10
514	Miguel Asencio	.10
515	Andy Pettitte	.25
516	Jim Edmonds	.25

517	Jeff DaVanon	.10
518	Aaron Myette	.10
519	C.C. Sabathia	.10
520	Gerardo Garcia	.10
521	Brian Schneider	.10
522	Wes Obermueller	.10
523	John Mabry	.10
524	Casey Fossum	.10
525	Toby Hall	.10
526	Denny Neagle	.10
527	Willie Bloomquist	.10
528	A.J. Pierzynski	.10
529	Bartolo Colon	.10
530	Chad Harville	.10
531	Blaine Neal	.10
532	Luis Terrero Jr.	.10
533	Reggie Taylor	.10
534	Melvin Mora	.10
535	Tino Martinez	.10
536	Peter Bergeron	.10
537	Jorge Padilla	.10
538	Oscar Villarreal **RC**	.20
539	David Weathers	.10
540	Mike Lamb	.10
541	Greg Norton	.10
542	Michael Tucker	.10
543	Ben Kozlowski	.10
544	Alex Sanchez	.10
545	Trey Lunsford	.10
546	Abraham Nunez	.10
547	Mike Lincoln	.10
548	Orlando Hernandez	.10
549	Kevin Mench	.10
550	Garret Anderson	.25
551	Kyle Farnsworth	.10
552	Kevin Olsen	.10
553	Joel Pineiro	.10
554	Jorge Julio	.10
555	Jose Mesa	.10
556	Jorge Posada	.40
557	Jose Ortiz	.10
558	Mike Tonis	.10
559	Gabe White	.10
560	Rafael Furcal	.10
561	Matt Franco	.10
562	Trey Hodges	.10
563	Esteban German	.10
564	Josh Fogg	.10
565	Fernando Tatis	.10
566	Alex Cintron	.10
567	Grant Roberts	.10
568	Gene Stechschulte	.10
569	Rafael Palmeiro	.25
570	Mike Hampton	.10
571	Ben Davis	.10
572	Dean Palmer	.10
573	Jerrod Riggan	.10
574	Nate Frese	.10
575	Josh Phelps	.10
576	Freddie Bynum	.10
577	Morgan Ensberg	.10
578	Juan Rincon	.10
579	Kazuhiro Sasaki	.10
580	Yorvit Torrealba	.10
581	Tim Wakefield	.10
582	Sterling Hitchcock	.10
583	Craig Paquette	.10
584	Kevin Millwood	.25
585	Damian Rolls	.10
586	Brad Baisley	.10
587	Kyle Snyder	.10
588	Paul Quantrill	.10
589	Trot Nixon	.10
590	J.T. Snow	.10
591	Kevin Young	.10
592	Tomokazu Ohka	.10
593	Brian Boehringer	.10
594	Danny Patterson	.10
595	Jeff Tam	.10
596	Anastacio Martinez	.10
597	Rod Barajas	.10
598	Octavio Dotel	.10
599	Jason Tyner	.10
600	Gary Sheffield	.40
601	Ruben Quevedo	.10
602	Jay Payton	.10
603	Mo Vaughn	.10
604	Pat Burrell	.40
605	Fernando Vina	.10
606	Wes Anderson	.10
607	Alex Gonzalez	.10
608	Ted Lilly	.10
609	Nick Punto	.10
610	Ryan Madson	.10
611	Odalis Perez	.10
612	Chris Woodward	.10
613	John Olerud	.25
614	Brad Cresse	.10
615	Chad Zerbe	.10
616	Brad Penny	.10
617	Barry Larkin	.40
618	Brandon Duckworth	.10
619	Brad Radke	.10
620	Giovanni Carrara	.10
621	Juan Pierre	.10
622	Rick Reed	.10
623	Omar Daal	.10
624	Jose Hernandez	.10
625	Greg Maddux	1.00
626	Henry Mateo	.10
627	Kip Wells	.10
628	Kevin Cash	.10
629	Mark Redman	.10
630	Luis Gonzalez	.25
631	Jason Conti	.10
632	Ricardo Rincon	.10
633	Mike Bynum	.10
634	Mike Redmond	.10
635	Chance Capel	.10
636	Chris Widger	.10
637	Michael Restovich	.10
638	Mark Grudzielanek	.10
639	Brandon Larson	.10
640	Luis De Los Santos	.10
641	Javy Lopez	.20
642	Rene Reyes	.10
643	Orlando Merced	.10
644	Jason Phillips	.10
645	Luis Ugueto	.10
646	Ron Calloway	.10
647	Josh Paul	.10
648	Todd Greene	.10
649	Joe Giradi	.10
650	Todd Ritchie	.10
651	Lou Merloni	.10
652	Shawn Wooten	.10
653	David Riske	.10
654	Luis Rivas	.10
655	Roy Halladay	.10
656	Travis Driskill	.10
657	Ricky Ledee	.10
658	Tony Perez	.10
659	Fernando Rodney	.10
660	Trevor Hoffman	.10
661	Pat Hentgen	.10
662	Bret Boone	.10
663	Ryan Jensen	.10
664	Ricardo Rodriguez	.10
665	Jeremy Lambert	.10
666	Troy Percival	.10
667	Jon Rauch	.10
668	Mariano Rivera	.25
669	Jason LaRue	.10
670	J.C. Romero	.10
671	Cody Ross	.10
672	Eric Byrnes	.10
673	Paul LoDuca	.10
674	Brad Fullmer	.10
675	Cliff Politte	.10
676	Justin Miller	.10
677	Nic Jackson	.10
678	Kris Benson	.10
679	Carl Sadler	.10
680	Joe Nathan	.10
681	Julio Santana	.10
682	Wade Miller	.10
683	Josh Pearce	.10
684	Tony Armas	.10
685	Al Leiter	.10
686	Raul Ibanez	.10
687	Danny Bautista	.10
688	Travis Hafner	.10
689	Rylan Reed **RC**	.20
690	Pedro J. Martinez	.75
691	Ramon Santiago	.10
692	Felipe Lopez	.10
693	David Ross	.10
694	Chone Figgins	.10
695	Antonio Osuna	.10
696	Jay Powell	.10
697	Roy Smith	.10
698	Alexis Rios	.10
699	Tanyon Sturtze	.10
700	Turk Wendell	.10
701	Richard Hidalgo	.10
702	Joe Mays	.10
703	Jorge Sosa	.10
704	Eric Karros	.10
705	Steve Finley	.10
706	Sean Smith	.10
707	Jeremy Giambi	.10
708	Scott Hodges	.10
709	Vicente Padilla	.10
710	Bert Snow	.10
711	Aaron Rowand	.10
712	Dennis Tankersley	.10
713	Rick Bauer	.10
714	Tim Olson **RC**	.25
715	Jeff Urban	.10
716	Steve Sparks	.10
717	Glendon Rusch	.10
718	Ricky Stone	.10
719	Benji Gil	.10
720	Pete Walker	.10
721	Tim Worrell	.10
722	Michael Tejera	.10
723	David Kelton	.10
724	Britt Reames	.10
725	John Stephens	.10
726	Mark McLemore	.10
727	Jeff Zimmerman	.10
728	Checklist	.10
729	Andres Torres	.10
730	Checklist	.10
731	Johan Santana	.10
732	Dane Sardinha	.10
733	Rodrigo Rosario	.10
734	Frank Thomas	.50
735	Tom Glavine	.25
736	Doug Mirabelli	.10
737	Juan Uribe	.10
738	Ryan Anderson	.10
739	Sean Burroughs	.10
740	Eric Chavez	.25
741	Enrique Wilson	.10
742	Elmer Dessens	.10
743	Marlon Byrd	.10
744	Brendan Donnelly	.10
745	Gary Bennett	.10
746	Roy Oswalt	.25
747	Andy Van Hekken	.10
748	Jesus Colome	.10
749	Erick Almonte	.10
750	Frank Catalanotto	.10
751	Matt Herges	.10
752	Carlos Delgado	.40
753	Ryan Franklin	.10
754	Wilken Ruan	.10
755	Kelvim Escobar	.10
756	Tim Drew	.10
757	Jarrod Washburn	.10
758	Runelvys Hernandez	.10
759	Cory Vance	.10
760	Doug Glanville	.10
761	Ryan Rupe	.10
762	Jermaine Dye	.10
763	Mike Cameron	.10
764	Scott Erickson	.10
765	Richie Sexson	.25
766	Jose Vidro	.10
767	Brian West	.10
768	Shawn Estes	.10
769	Brian Tallet	.10
770	Larry Walker	.25
771	Josh Hamilton	.25
772	Orlando Hudson	.10
773	Justin Morneau	.20
774	Ryan Bukvich	.10
775	Mike Gonzalez	.10
776	Tsuyoshi Shinjo	.10
777	Matt Mantei	.10
778	Jimmy Journell	.10
779	Brian Lawrence	.10
780	Mike Lieberthal	.10
781	Scott Mullen	.10
782	Zach Day	.10
783	John Thomson	.10
784	Ben Sheets	.10
785	Damon Minor	.10
786	Jose Valentin	.10
787	Armando Benitez	.10
788	Jamie Walker	.10
789	Preston Wilson	.10
790	Josh Wilson	.10
791	Phil Nevin	.10
792	Roberto Hernandez	.10
793	Mike Williams	.10
794	Jake Peavy	.10
795	Paul Shuey	.10
796	Chad Bradford	.10
797	Bobby Jenks	.10
798	Sean Douglass	.10
799	Damian Miller	.10
800	Mark Wohlers	.10
801	Ty Wigginton	.10
802	Alfonso Soriano	1.00
803	Randy Johnson	.75
804	Placido Polanco	.10
805	Drew Henson	.10
806	Tony Womack	.10
807	Pokey Reese	.10
808	Albert Pujols	.75
809	Shane Reynolds	.10
810	Mike Rivera	.10
811	John Lackey	.10
812	Brian Wright **RC**	.20
813	Eric Good	.10
814	Dernell Stenson	.10
815	Kirk Rueter	.10
816	Todd Zeile	.10
817	Brad Thomas	.10
818	Shawn Sedlacek	.10
819	Garrett Stephenson	.10
820	Mark Teixeira	.25
821	Tim Hudson	.25
822	Mike Koplove	.10
823	Chris Reitsma	.10
824	Rafael Soriano	.10
825	Ugueth Urbina	.10
826	Matt White	.10
827	Colin Young	.10
828	Pat Strange	.10
829	Juan Pena	.10
830	Joe Thurston	.10
831	Shawn Green	.25
832	Pedro Astacio	.10
833	Danny Wright	.10
834	Weston O'Brien **RC**	.20
835	Luis Lopez	.10
836	Randall Simon	.10
837	Jaret Wright	.10
838	Jayson Werth	.10
839	Endy Chavez	.10
840	Checklist	.10
841	Chad Paronto	.10
842	Randy Winn	.10
843	Sidney Ponson	.10
844	Robin Ventura	.10
845	Rich Aurilia	.10
846	Joaquin Benoit	.10
847	Barry Bonds	2.00
848	Carl Crawford	.10
849	Jeromy Burnitz	.10
850	Orlando Cabrera	.10
851	Luis Vizcaino	.10
852	Randy Wolf	.10
853	Benny Agbayani	.10
854	Jeremy Affeldt	.10
855	Einar Diaz	.10
856	Carl Everett	.10
857	Wiki Gonzalez	.10
858	Steve Belcher	.10
859	Travis Harper	.10
860	Mike Piazza	1.25
861	Will Ohman	.10
862	Eric Young	.10
863	Jason Grabowski	.10
864	Rett Johnson **RC**	.20
865	Aubrey Huff	.10
866	John Smoltz	.10
867	Mickey Callaway	.10
868	Joe Kennedy	.10
869	Tim Redding	.10
870	Colby Lewis	.10
871	Salomon Torres	.10
872	Marco Scutaro	.10
873	Tony Batista	.10
874	Dmitri Young	.10
875	Scott Williamson	.10
876	Scott Spezio	.10
877	John Webb	.10
878	Jose Acevedo	.10
879	Kevin Orie	.10
880	Jacque Jones	.10
881	Ben Francisco **RC**	.75
882	Bobby Basham **RC**	.25
883	Corey Shafer **RC**	.20
884	J.D. Durbin **RC**	.20
885	Chien-Ming Wang **RC**	2.50
886	Adam Stern	.10
887	Wayne Lydon **RC**	.20
888	Derell McCall **RC**	.20
889	Jon Nelson **RC**	.20
890	Willie Eyre **RC**	.20
891	Ramon A. Martinez **RC**	.20
892	Adrian Myers **RC**	.20
893	Jamie Athas **RC**	.20
894	Ismael Castro **RC**	.20
895	David Martinez	.10
896	Terry Tiffee **RC**	.20
897	Nathan Panther **RC**	.25
898	Kyle Roat **RC**	.20
899	Kason Gabbard **RC**	.75
900	Hanley Ramirez **RC**	3.00
901	Bryan Grace **RC**	.15
902	B.J. Barns **RC**	.50
903	Greg Bruso **RC**	.15
904	Mike Neu **RC**	.15
905	Dustin Yount **RC**	.50
906	Shane Victorino **RC**	.20
907	Brian Burgamy **RC**	.20
908	Beau Kemp **RC**	.20
909	Eny Cabreja **RC**	.50
910	Dexter Cooper **RC**	.20
911	Chris Colton **RC**	.20
912	David Cash **RC**	.20
913	Bernie Castro **RC**	.20
914	Luis Hodge **RC**	.20
915	Jeff Clark **RC**	.20
916	Jason Kubel **RC**	1.00
917	T.J. Bohn **RC**	.20
918	Luke Steidlmayer **RC**	.20
919	Matthew Petterson	.10
920	Darrell Rasner	.10
921	Scott Tyler	.10
922	Gary Schneidmiller **RC**	.20
923	Kerry Wood	.40
924	Ryan Cameron **RC**	.20
925	Wilfredo Rodriguez	.10
926	Rajai Davis **RC**	.20
927	Evel Bastida-Martinez **RC**	.20
928	Chris Duncan **RC**	2.00
929	David Pember **RC**	.20
930	Branden Florence **RC**	.20
931	Eric Eckenstahler	.10
932	Hong-Chih Kuo **RC**	1.00
933	Il Kim **RC**	.20
934	Michael Garciaparra	.50
935	Tommy Whiteman **RC**	.10
936	Gary Harris **RC**	.20
937	Derry Hammond	.10
938	Joey Gomes	.10
939	Donald Hood **RC**	.20
940	Clay Hensley **RC**	.50
941	David Pahucki **RC**	.20
942	Wilton Reynolds **RC**	.20
943	Michael Hinckley **RC**	.20
944	Josh Willingham **RC**	.20
945	Pete LaForest **RC**	.20
946	Pete Smart	.10
947	Jay Stizman	.10
948	Mark Malaska **RC**	.20
949	Mike Gallo **RC**	.20
950	Tyler Martin **RC**	.20
951	Shane Victorino	.10
952	Ryan Howard	25.00
953	Daryl Clark **RC**	.20
954	Dayton Buller	.10
955	Carlos Zambrano	.10
956	Chris Booker	.10
957	Brandon Watson **RC**	.20
958	Matt DeMarco **RC**	.20
959	Doug Waechter **RC**	.75
960	Callix Crabbe **RC**	.20
961	Jairo Garcia **RC**	.20
962	Jason Perry **RC**	.20
963	Eric Riggs **RC**	.20
964	Travis Ishikawa **RC**	.40
965	Jorge Piedra **RC**	.20
966	Manuel Ramirez **RC**	.20
967	Tyler Johnson **RC**	.20
968	Jaime Bubela **RC**	.20
969	Haj Turay **RC**	.20
970	Tyson Graham **RC**	.20
971	David DeJesus **RC**	.20
972	Franklin Gutierrez **RC**	.20
973	Craig Brazell **RC**	1.00
974	Keith Stamler **RC**	.20
975	Jemel Spearman **RC**	.20
976	Kade Johnson **RC**	.10

977	Nick Trzesniak RC	.20
978	Bill Simon RC	.20
979	Matthew Hagen RC	.20
980	Kris Kroski RC	.20
981	Prentice Redman RC	.50
982	Kevin Randel RC	.20
983	Thomari Stori-Harden RC	.10
984	Brian Shackelford RC	.20
985	Mike Adams RC	.20
986	Brian McCann	5.00
987	Mike McNutt RC	.20
988	Aron Weston RC	.20
989	Dustin Moseley RC	.20
990	Bryan Bullington RC	1.50

Silver

Jim THOME

Stars (1-990): 1-2X
Inserted 1:1

Award Winners

ALEX RODRIGUEZ

		NM/M
Complete Set (30):		20.00
Common Player:		.50
Inserted 1:12		
AW1	Barry Zito	.75
AW2	Randy Johnson	1.50
AW3	Miguel Tejada	.75
AW4	Barry Bonds	3.00
AW5	Sammy Sosa	2.00
AW6	Barry Bonds	3.00
AW7	Mike Piazza	2.50
AW8	Todd Helton	.75
AW9	Jeff Kent	.50
AW10	Edgar Renteria	.50
AW11	Scott Rolen	.75
AW12	Vladimir Guerrero	1.00
AW13	Mike Hampton	.50
AW14	Jason Giambi	1.50
AW15	Alfonso Soriano	1.50
AW16	Alex Rodriguez	3.00
AW17	Eric Chavez	.50
AW18	Jorge Posada	.50
AW19	Bernie Williams	.75
AW20	Magglio Ordonez	.50
AW21	Garret Anderson	.50
AW22	Manny Ramirez	1.00
AW23	Jason Jennings	.50
AW24	Eric Hinske	.50
AW25	Billy Koch	.50
AW26	John Smoltz	.50
AW27	Alex Rodriguez	3.00
AW28	Barry Bonds	3.00
AW29	Tony LaRussa	.50
AW30	Mike Scioscia	.50

Total Production

		NM/M
Complete Set (10):		10.00
Common Player:		.40
Inserted 1:18		
TP1	Barry Bonds	2.50
TP2	Manny Ramirez	.75
TP3	Albert Pujols	1.00
TP4	Jason Giambi	1.00
TP5	Magglio Ordonez	.40
TP6	Mike Piazza	1.50
TP7	Todd Helton	.75
TP8	Miguel Tejada	.50

TP9	Sammy Sosa	1.50
TP10	Alex Rodriguez	2.50

Total Signatures

		NM/M
Common Autograph:		
Inserted 1:176		
MB	Marlon Byrd	10.00
EM	Eli Marrero	8.00
BP	Brandon Phillips	10.00
MT	Marcus Thames	8.00
TT	Tony Torcato	8.00

Total Topps

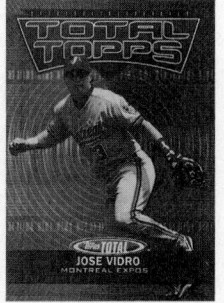

JOSE VIDRO MONTREAL EXPOS

		NM/M
Complete Set (50):		25.00
Common Player:		.25
Inserted 1:7		
TT1	Ichiro Suzuki	1.50
TT2	Alex Rodriguez	2.50
TT3	Barry Bonds	2.50
TT4	Jason Giambi	1.00
TT5	Troy Glaus	.75
TT6	Greg Maddux	1.50
TT7	Albert Pujols	1.00
TT8	Randy Johnson	1.00
TT9	Chipper Jones	1.50
TT10	Magglio Ordonez	.25
TT11	Jim Thome	.75
TT12	Jeff Kent	.40
TT13	Curt Schilling	.50
TT14	Alfonso Soriano	1.00
TT15	Rafael Palmeiro	.50
TT16	Carlos Delgado	.50
TT17	Torii Hunter	.50
TT18	Pat Burrell	.50
TT19	Adam Dunn	.75
TT20	Roberto Alomar	.50
TT21	Eric Chavez	.40
TT22	Derek Jeter	3.00
TT23	Nomar Garciaparra	2.00
TT24	Lance Berkman	.40
TT25	Jim Edmonds	.40
TT26	Todd Helton	.75
TT27	Sammy Sosa	1.50
TT28	Phil Nevin	.25
TT29	Andruw Jones	.40
TT30	Barry Zito	.50
TT31	Richie Sexson	.40
TT32	Ken Griffey Jr.	1.50
TT33	Gary Sheffield	.40
TT34	Shawn Green	.40
TT35	Mike Sweeney	.25
TT36	Mike Lowell	.25
TT37	Larry Walker	.40
TT38	Manny Ramirez	.75
TT39	Miguel Tejada	.40
TT40	Mike Piazza	2.00
TT41	Scott Rolen	.75
TT42	Brian Giles	.40
TT43	Garret Anderson	.40
TT44	Vladimir Guerrero	.75
TT45	Bartolo Colon	.25
TT46	Jorge Posada	.40
TT47	Ivan Rodriguez	.50
TT48	Ryan Klesko	.25
TT49	Jose Vidro	.25
TT50	Pedro J. Martinez	.75

2003 Topps Tribute

GARRET ANDERSON

		NM/M
Complete Set (110):		300.00
Common Player:		1.00
Common Auto. (101-110):		10.00
Pack (5):		35.00
Box (6):		160.00
1	Jim Thome	2.50
2	Edgardo Alfonzo	1.00
3	Edgar Martinez	1.00
4	Scott Rolen	1.50
5	Eric Hinske	1.00
6	Mark Mulder	1.50
7	Jason Giambi	2.50
8	Bernie Williams	2.00
9	Cliff Floyd	1.00
10	Ichiro Suzuki	5.00
11	Pat Burrell	1.50
12	Garret Anderson	1.50
13	Gary Sheffield	1.50
14	Johnny Damon	3.00
15	Kerry Wood	1.50
16	Bartolo Colon	1.00
17	Adam Dunn	2.00
18	Omar Vizquel	1.50
19	Todd Helton	2.00
20	Nomar Garciaparra	4.00
21	A.J. Burnett	1.00
22	Craig Biggio	1.50
23	Carlos Beltran	2.50
24	Kazuhisa Ishii	1.00
25	Vladimir Guerrero	2.50
26	Roberto Alomar	2.00
27	Roger Clemens	6.00
28	Tim Hudson	2.00
29	Brian Giles	1.50
30	Barry Bonds	8.00
31	Jim Edmonds	1.50
32	Rafael Palmeiro	2.00
33	Francisco Rodriguez	1.00
34	Andruw Jones	1.50
35	Shea Hillenbrand	1.00
36	Moises Alou	1.00
37	Luis Gonzalez	1.00
38	Darin Erstad	1.00
39	John Smoltz	1.50
40	Derek Jeter	8.00
41	Aubrey Huff	1.00
42	Eric Chavez	1.00
43	Doug Mientkiewicz	1.00
44	Lance Berkman	2.00
45	Josh Beckett	1.50
46	Austin Kearns	1.50
47	Frank Thomas	2.50
48	Pedro J. Martinez	3.00
49	Tim Salmon	1.50
50	Alex Rodriguez	8.00
51	Ryan Klesko	1.50
52	Tom Glavine	1.50
53	Shawn Green	1.50
54	Jeff Kent	1.50
55	Carlos Pena	1.00
56	Paul Konerko	1.50
57	Troy Glaus	2.00
58	Manny Ramirez	2.50
59	Jason Jennings	1.00
60	Randy Johnson	3.00
61	Ivan Rodriguez	2.00
62	Roy Oswalt	1.50
63	Kevin Brown	1.50
64	Jose Vidro	1.00
65	Jorge Posada	1.50
66	Mike Piazza	5.00
67	Bret Boone	1.50
68	Carlos Delgado	2.00
69	Jimmy Rollins	2.00
70	Alfonso Soriano	3.00
71	Greg Maddux	5.00
72	Mark Prior	2.00
73	Jeff Bagwell	2.50
74	Richie Sexson	2.00
75	Sammy Sosa	4.00
76	Curt Schilling	2.00
77	Mike Sweeney	1.00
78	Torii Hunter	1.50
79	Larry Walker	1.50
80	Miguel Tejada	1.50
81	Rich Aurilia	1.00
82	Bobby Abreu	1.50
83	Phil Nevin	1.00

84	Rodrigo Lopez	1.00
85	Chipper Jones	3.00
86	Ken Griffey Jr.	5.00
87	Mike Lowell	1.00
88	Magglio Ordonez	1.50
89	Barry Zito	1.50
90	Albert Pujols	8.00
91	Corey Shafer RC	2.00
92	Dan Haren	5.00
93	Jeremy Bonderman	6.00
94	Branden Florence RC	2.00
95	Evel Bastida-Martinez RC	2.00
96	Brian Wright RC	2.00
97	Elizardo Ramirez RC	2.00
98	Michael Garciaparra	2.00
99	Clay Hensley RC	3.00
100	Bobby Basham RC	2.00
101	Jose Contreras RC	20.00
102	Bryan Bullington RC	15.00
103	Joey Gomes	10.00
104	Craig Brazell RC	15.00
105	Andy Marte RC	15.00
106	Hanley Ramirez RC	100.00
107	Ryan Shealy RC	15.00
108	Daryl Clark RC	10.00
109	Tyler Johnson RC	15.00
110	Ben Francisco RC	20.00

Red Proof

VLADIMIR GUERRERO

Stars (1-100):	2-4X
Production 225	
Autos. (101-110):	1-2.5X
Production 50	

Gold Proof

Cards (1-100):	No Pricing
Production 25	
Autos. (101-110) are 1 of 1.	

Solo Bonds

		NM/M
Premiere Proof:		1.5X
Production 50		
SB	Barry Bonds	25.00

Double Bonds

		NM/M
Premiere Proof:		1.5X
Production 50		
BT-DB	Barry Bonds	40.00

Triple Bonds

		NM/M
Premiere Proof:		1.5X
Production 50		
TB	Barry Bonds	60.00

Matching Marks Dual Relics

		NM/M
Common Duo:		10.00
Premiere Proofs:		1.5X
Production 50		
PH	Rafael Palmeiro, Rickey Henderson	15.00
GR	Nomar Garciaparra, Alex Rodriguez	25.00

AP	Roberto Alomar,	
	Rafael Palmeiro	15.00
MP	Fred McGriff,	
	Rafael Palmeiro	10.00
HR	Rickey Henderson,	
	Manny Ramirez	15.00
RP	Manny Ramirez,	
	Mike Piazza	20.00
BG	Jeff Bagwell,	
	Juan Gonzalez	10.00
BP	Barry Bonds,	
	Rafael Palmeiro	35.00
SB	Sammy Sosa,	
	Jeff Bagwell	20.00
SG	Alfonso Soriano,	
	Vladimir Guerrero	15.00
PS	Rafael Palmeiro,	
	Sammy Sosa	20.00
MG	Fred McGriff,	
	Juan Gonzalez	10.00
PA	Rafael Palmeiro,	
	Roberto Alomar	15.00

Memorable Materials

		NM/M
Common Player:		8.00
Premiere Proofs:		1.5X
Production 50		
BB	Barry Bonds	30.00
JG	Jason Giambi	8.00
JG2	Jason Giambi	8.00
TG	Troy Glaus	8.00
LG	Luis Gonzalez	8.00
SG	Shawn Green	8.00
VG	Vladimir Guerrero	10.00
RH	Rickey Henderson	10.00
TH	Torii Hunter	8.00
AJ	Andruw Jones	8.00
GM	Greg Maddux	15.00
AP	Albert Pujols	20.00
CR	Cal Ripken Jr.	45.00
AR	Alex Rodriguez	15.00
AS	Alfonso Soriano	10.00
SS	Sammy Sosa	15.00
SS2	Sammy Sosa	15.00
MT	Miguel Tejada	8.00
KW	Kerry Wood	8.00

Milestone Materials

		NM/M
Common Player:		8.00
Premiere Proofs:		1.5X
Production 50		
RA	Roberto Alomar	10.00
JB1	Jeff Bagwell	10.00
JB2	Jeff Bagwell	10.00
BB1	Barry Bonds	25.00
BB2	Barry Bonds	25.00
BB3	Barry Bonds	25.00
BB4	Barry Bonds	25.00
BB5	Barry Bonds	25.00
NG	Nomar Garciaparra	20.00
JG1	Juan Gonzalez	10.00
JG2	Juan Gonzalez	10.00
VG	Vladimir Guerrero	10.00
TH	Todd Helton	10.00
RH1	Rickey Henderson	10.00
RH2	Rickey Henderson	10.00
RH3	Rickey Henderson	10.00
RH4	Rickey Henderson	10.00
RH5	Rickey Henderson	10.00
CJ	Chipper Jones	12.00
FM1	Fred McGriff	8.00
FM2	Fred McGriff	8.00
FM3	Fred McGriff	8.00
RP1	Rafael Palmeiro	10.00
RP2	Rafael Palmeiro	10.00
RP3	Rafael Palmeiro	10.00
RP4	Rafael Palmeiro	10.00
MP1	Mike Piazza	15.00
MP2	Mike Piazza	15.00
MR1	Manny Ramirez	10.00
MR2	Manny Ramirez	10.00
AR	Alex Rodriguez	15.00
SS1	Sammy Sosa	15.00
SS2	Sammy Sosa	15.00
SS3	Sammy Sosa	15.00
FT	Frank Thomas	12.00

Modern Marks Autographs

		NM/M
Common Autograph:		10.00
Premiere Proofs:		1.5X
Production 50		
LB	Lance Berkman	20.00
RC	Roger Clemens	120.00
CF	Cliff Floyd	10.00
EH	Eric Hinske	10.00
TH	Torii Hunter	15.00
PK	Paul Konerko	15.00
PL	Paul LoDuca	15.00
MO	Magglio Ordonez	20.00

Perennial All-Stars Relics

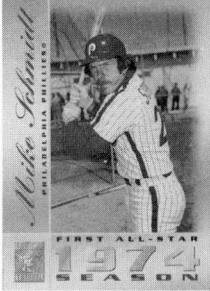

		NM/M
Common Player:		8.00
Premiere Proofs:		1.5X
Production 50		
RA	Roberto Alomar	10.00
CB	Craig Biggio	8.00
BB	Barry Bonds	25.00
RC	Roger Clemens	20.00
RH	Rickey Henderson	15.00
CJ	Chipper Jones	10.00
GM	Greg Maddux	15.00
EM	Edgar Martinez	15.00
EM	Pedro J. Martinez	15.00
MM	Mike Mussina	10.00
MP	Mike Piazza	20.00
MR	Manny Ramirez	10.00
AR	Alex Rodriguez	15.00
IR	Ivan Rodriguez	8.00
BS	Benito Santiago	8.00
CS	Curt Schilling	8.00
GS	Gary Sheffield	8.00
JS	John Smoltz	8.00
SS	Sammy Sosa	20.00
FT	Frank Thomas	10.00
LW	Larry Walker	8.00
BW	Bernie Williams	10.00

Performance Tribute Doubles

		NM/M
Common Duo:		10.00
Premiere Proofs:		1.5X
Production 50		
ZJ	Barry Zito, Randy Johnson	15.00
SA	Alfonso Soriano,	
	Roberto Alomar	15.00
RR	Cal Ripken Jr.,	
	Alex Rodriguez	60.00
RT	Alex Rodriguez,	
	Miguel Tejada	15.00
GG	Luis Gonzalez, Troy Glaus	10.00
PW	Albert Pujols, Kerry Wood	25.00
RG	Alex Rodriguez,	
	Nomar Garciaparra	30.00
BJ	Barry Bonds,	
	Chipper Jones	25.00
SG	Sammy Sosa,	
	Juan Gonzalez	15.00
PS	Mike Piazza,	
	Benito Santiago	15.00
PR	Mike Piazza,	
	Ivan Rodriguez	15.00
MM	Pedro J. Martinez,	
	Greg Maddux	15.00
CM	Roger Clemens,	
	Greg Maddux	35.00
JP	Chipper Jones, Mike Piazza	20.00

Performance Tribute Triples

		NM/M
Common Trio:		20.00
Premiere Proofs:		1.5X
Production 50		

SMP	Sammy Sosa, Rafael Palmeiro,	
	Fred McGriff	25.00
CMJ	Roger Clemens, Greg Maddux,	
	Randy Johnson	30.00
RHP	Manny Ramirez, Mike Piazza,	
	Rickey Henderson	30.00
STB	Sammy Sosa, Frank Thomas,	
	Jeff Bagwell	20.00
BMP	Barry Bonds, Fred McGriff,	
	Rafael Palmeiro	30.00

Team Tribute Doubles

		NM/M
Common Duo:		10.00
Premiere Proofs:		1.5X
Production 50		
MS	Greg Maddux, John Smoltz	35.00
IN	Kazuhisa Ishii,	
	Hideo Nomo	25.00
WH	Larry Walker, Todd Helton	10.00
BB	Craig Biggio, Jeff Bagwell	15.00
RP	Alex Rodriguez,	
	Rafael Palmeiro	15.00
GR	Nomar Garciaparra,	
	Manny Ramirez	20.00

Team Tribute Triples

		NM/M
Common Trio:		15.00
Premiere Proofs:		1.5X
Production 50		
JSJ	Andruw Jones, Gary Sheffield,	
	Chipper Jones	30.00
GRM	Nomar Garciaparra,	
	Manny Ramirez,	
	Pedro J. Martinez	40.00
ASP	Moises Alou, Sammy Sosa,	
	Corey Patterson	30.00
TOK	Frank Thomas, Magglio Ordonez,	
	Paul Konerko	20.00
BBB	Craig Biggio, Lance Berkman,	
	Jeff Bagwell	20.00
MHM	Joe Mauer, Torii Hunter,	
	Doug Mientkiewicz	25.00
SGV	Alfonso Soriano, Jason Giambi,	
	Robin Ventura	25.00
CTM	Eric Chavez, Miguel Tejada,	
	Mark Mulder	15.00
HZM	Tim Hudson, Barry Zito,	
	Mark Mulder	25.00
TBB	Jim Thome, Marlon Byrd,	
	Pat Burrell	25.00
MOB	Edgar Martinez, John Olerud,	
	Bret Boone	20.00
PER	Albert Pujols, Jim Edmonds,	
	Scott Rolen	40.00
RGP	Alex Rodriguez, Juan Gonzalez,	
	Rafael Palmeiro	25.00
RBT	Alex Rodriguez, Hank Blalock,	
	Mark Teixeira	25.00

Tribute to the Stars

		NM/M
Common Player:		10.00
Premiere Proofs:		1.5X
Production 50		
RA	Roberto Alomar	15.00
GA	Garret Anderson	15.00
LB	Lance Berkman	10.00
BB	Barry Bonds	50.00
PB	Pat Burrell	15.00
EC	Eric Chavez	15.00
AD	Adam Dunn	15.00
NG	Nomar Garciaparra	40.00
TG	Troy Glaus	15.00
VG	Vladimir Guerrero	15.00
TH	Todd Helton	15.00
RH	Rickey Henderson	15.00
THU	Torii Hunter	10.00
AJ	Andruw Jones	10.00
CJ	Chipper Jones	15.00
GM	Greg Maddux	20.00
RP	Rafael Palmeiro	10.00
MP	Mike Piazza	20.00
AP	Albert Pujols	40.00
AR	Alex Rodriguez	30.00
AS	Alfonso Soriano	15.00
SS	Sammy Sosa	25.00
FT	Frank Thomas	15.00
JT	Jim Thome	15.00
LW	Larry Walker	15.00

Tribute to the Stars Patchworks

		NM/M
Common Player:		25.00
Production 50 Sets		
JB	Jeff Bagwell	35.00
BB	Barry Bonds	80.00

NG	Nomar Garciaparra	50.00
LG	Luis Gonzalez	25.00
SG	Shawn Green	25.00
TH	Todd Helton	35.00
THU	Torii Hunter	25.00
RJ	Randy Johnson	40.00
CJ	Chipper Jones	35.00
GM	Greg Maddux	50.00
PM	Pedro J. Martinez	40.00
RP	Rafael Palmeiro	30.00
AP	Albert Pujols	80.00
MR	Manny Ramirez	35.00
AR	Alex Rodriguez	50.00
AR2	Alex Rodriguez	50.00
CS	Curt Schilling	25.00
SS	Sammy Sosa	40.00
FT	Frank Thomas	35.00
KW	Kerry Wood	30.00

40/40 Club

		NM/M
Premiere Proof:		1.5X
Production 50		
CBR	Jose Canseco, Barry Bonds,	
	Alex Rodriguez	85.00

600 HR Club Relic

		NM/M
Premiere Proofs:		1.5X
Production 50		
Gold:		No Pricing
Production One Set		
HA-600	Hank Aaron	35.00
BB-600	Barry Bonds	30.00
WM-600	Willie Mays	45.00
BR-600	Babe Ruth	125.00

600 HR Club Double Relic

		NM/M
Premiere Proofs:		1.5X
Production 50		
BA-600	Barry Bonds,	
	Hank Aaron	80.00
BA-600	Barry Bonds,	
	Willie Mays	80.00
BA-600	Barry Bonds,	
	Babe Ruth	200.00

600 HR Club Quad Relic

		NM/M
Premiere Proof:		1X
Production 25		
BA-600	Hank Aaron, Babe Ruth,	
	Willie Mays,	
	Barry Bonds	625.00

2003 Topps Tribute All-Star Edition

		NM/M
Complete Set (50):		50.00
Common Player:		1.00
Pack (5):		40.00
Box (6):		200.00
1	Willie Mays	8.00
2	Don Mattingly	1.00
3	Hoyt Wilhelm	1.00

4	Hank Aaron	8.00
5	Hank Greenberg	1.00
6	Johnny Bench	5.00
7	Duke Snider	3.00
8	Carl Yastrzemski	3.00
9	Jim Palmer	1.00
10	Roberto Clemente	8.00
11	Mike Schmidt	8.00
12	Joe Cronin	1.00
13	Lou Brock	1.00
14	Orlando Cepeda	1.00
15	Bill Mazeroski	1.00
16	Whitey Ford	3.00
17	Rod Carew	1.00
18	Joe Morgan	1.00
19	Luis Aparicio	1.00
20	Nolan Ryan	10.00
21	Bobby Doerr	1.00
22	Dale Murphy	2.00
23	Bob Feller	1.00
24	Paul Molitor	2.00
25	Tom Seaver	3.00
26	Ozzie Smith	3.00
27	Stan Musial	6.00
28	Willie McCovey	1.00
29	Gary Carter	1.00
30	Reggie Jackson	3.00
31	Gaylord Perry	1.00
32	George Brett	8.00
33	Rocky Colavito	1.00
34	Wade Boggs	2.00
35	Cal Ripken Jr.	8.00
36	Carlton Fisk	1.00
37	Al Kaline	3.00
38	Kirby Puckett	4.00
39	Phil Rizzuto	2.00
40	Willie Stargell	1.00
41	Harmon Killebrew	3.00
42	Red Schoendienst	1.00
43	Tony Gwynn	3.00
44	Ralph Kiner	1.00
45	Yogi Berra	4.00
46	Jim "Catfish" Hunter	1.00
47	Frank Robinson	2.00
48	Ernie Banks	4.00
49	Warren Spahn	2.00
50	Brooks Robinson	3.00

Premier Proof

Cards (1-50):		4-8X

Numbered to last two digits of 1st All-Star Year.

1st Class Cuts

		NM/M
Production One Set		
FC-TC	Ty Cobb (3/03 Auction)	7,600
FC-DD	Dizzy Dean	
FC-LG	Lou Gehrig	
FC-JR	Jackie Robinson	
	(3/03 Auction)	3,500
FC-BR	Babe Ruth (6/04 Auction)	7,300
FC-TS	Tris Speaker	
FC-HW	Honus Wagner	

All-Star Signing

		NM/M
Common Autograph:		40.00
Premier Proofs:		1.5-2X
Production 25 Sets		
LB	Lou Brock	50.00
GC	Gary Carter	40.00
OC	Orlando Cepeda	40.00
AD	Andre Dawson	40.00
TG	Tony Gwynn	80.00
AK	Al Kaline	75.00
DMA	Don Mattingly	125.00
DM	Dale Murphy	75.00
JP	Jim Palmer	40.00
MS	Mike Schmidt	100.00
DSN	Duke Snider	45.00

Memorable Match-up Relic

		NM/M
Common Card:		50.00
Production 150 Sets		
Premier Proofs:		1.5-2X
Production 25 Sets		
YB	Carl Yastrzemski, Johnny Bench	70.00
BS	George Brett, Mike Schmidt	120.00
MJ	Willie Mays, Reggie Jackson	65.00
BF	Johnny Bench, Carlton Fisk	50.00
CM	Gary Carter, Don Mattingly	85.00
KA	Harmon Killebrew, Hank Aaron	125.00
BG	Wade Boggs, Tony Gwynn	60.00
PG	Kirby Puckett, Tony Gwynn	60.00
YBR	Carl Yastrzemski, Lou Brock	60.00

Perennial Patch Relics

		NM/M
Common Player:		40.00
Production 30 Sets		
WB	Wade Boggs	75.00
GB	George Brett	220.00
GC	Gary Carter	40.00
TG	Tony Gwynn	125.00
HK	Harmon Killebrew	90.00
WM	Willie McCovey	40.00
JM	Joe Morgan	40.00
DMU	Dale Murphy	120.00
CR	Cal Ripken Jr.	225.00
NR	Nolan Ryan/Rangers	200.00
NRA	Nolan Ryan/Astros	200.00
MS	Mike Schmidt	200.00
OS	Ozzie Smith	120.00
WS	Willie Stargell	75.00
CY	Carl Yastrzemski	190.00

Tribute Relics

		NM/M
Common Player:		10.00
Inserted 1:1		
HA	Hank Aaron	35.00
LA	Luis Aparicio	10.00
EB	Ernie Banks	20.00
JBE	Johnny Bench	20.00
YB	Yogi Berra	40.00
WB	Wade Boggs	15.00
GB	George Brett	40.00
LB	Lou Brock/bat	30.00
LBU	Lou Brock/Jsy	15.00
RCA	Roy Campanella	20.00
ROD	Rod Carew	15.00
GC	Gary Carter	10.00
OC	Orlando Cepeda	12.00
RC	Roberto Clemente	60.00
TC	Ty Cobb	100.00
JCR	Joe Cronin	15.00
AD	Andre Dawson	10.00
DD	Dizzy Dean	40.00
BD	Bobby Doerr	15.00
BF	Bob Feller	15.00
CF	Carlton Fisk	30.00
WF	Whitey Ford	30.00
JF	Jimmie Foxx	40.00
LG	Lou Gehrig	125.00
HG	Hank Greenberg	40.00
TG	Tony Gwynn	20.00
RH	Rogers Hornsby	40.00
CH	Jim "Catfish" Hunter	15.00
RJ	Reggie Jackson	15.00
AK	Al Kaline	25.00
HK	Harmon Killebrew	20.00
NL	Napoleon Lajoie	40.00
EM	Eddie Mathews	15.00
DMA	Don Mattingly	30.00
WM	Willie Mays	40.00
BM	Bill Mazeroski	20.00
WMC	Willie McCovey	18.00
JMI	Johnny Mize	15.00
PM	Paul Molitor	15.00
JMO	Joe Morgan	10.00
TM	Thurman Munson	30.00
DM	Dale Murphy	15.00
SM	Stan Musial	30.00
DN	Don Newcombe	10.00
MO	Mel Ott	30.00
JP	Jim Palmer	10.00
KP	Kirby Puckett	20.00
CRB	Cal Ripken Jr.	40.00
PR	Phil Rizzuto	15.00
BRO	Brooks Robinson	15.00
FR	Frank Robinson	10.00
JR	Jackie Robinson	40.00
BR	Babe Ruth	140.00
NR	Nolan Ryan/Rangers	40.00
NRA	Nolan Ryan/Astros	40.00
MS	Mike Schmidt	40.00
RS	Red Schoendienst	15.00
TSE	Tom Seaver	25.00
OS	Ozzie Smith	20.00
DSN	Duke Snider	20.00
TS	Tris Speaker	75.00
WST	Willie Stargell	20.00
HW	Honus Wagner	125.00
WHI	Hoyt Wilhelm	15.00
CY	Carl Yastrzemski	30.00

2003 Topps Tribute World Series

		NM/M
Complete Set (150):		150.00
Common Player:		1.00
Pack (5):		50.00
Box (6):		260.00
1	Willie Mays	8.00
2	Gary Carter	1.50
3	Yogi Berra	4.00
4	Dennis Eckersley	1.50
5	Willie McCovey	1.50
6	Willie Stargell	1.00
7	Mike Schmidt	8.00
8	Robin Yount	4.00
9	Bucky Harris	1.00
10	Carl Yastrzemski	4.00
11	Lenny Dykstra	1.00
12	Boog Powell	1.00
13	Bill Lee	1.00
14	Lou Brock	1.50
15	Bob Friend	1.00
16	Hank Greenberg	1.50
17	Maury Wills	1.00
18	Tommy Lasorda	1.00
19	Bill "Moose" Skowron	1.00
20	Frank Robinson	2.00
21	Rollie Fingers	1.00
22	Doug DeCinces	1.00
23	Eric Davis	1.00
24	Johnny Podres	1.00
25	Darrell Evans	1.00
26	Ron Cey	1.00
27	Ray Knight	1.00
28	Don Larsen	1.00
29	Harold Baines	1.00
30	Brooks Robinson	4.00
31	Wade Boggs	2.00
32	Joe Morgan	1.00
33	Kirk Gibson	1.00
34	Tommy John	1.00
35	Monte Irvin	2.00
36	Rich "Goose" Gossage	1.00
37	Tug McGraw	1.00
38	Walt Weiss	1.00
39	Bill Madlock	1.00
40	Juan Marichal	2.00
41	Willie McGee	1.00
42	Joe Cronin	1.00
43	Paul Blair	1.00
44	Norm Cash	1.00
45	Ken Griffey Sr.	1.00
46	Bret Saberhagen	1.00
47	Don Sutton	1.00
48	Kirby Puckett	4.00
49	Keith Hernandez	1.00
50	George Brett	8.00
51	Bobby Richardson	1.00
52	Jose Canseco	2.00
53	Greg Luzinski	1.00
54	Bill Mazeroski	1.00
55	Red Schoendienst	1.00
56	Graig Nettles	1.00
57	Jerry Koosman	1.00
58	Tony Perez	1.00
59	Jim Rice	1.00
60	Duke Snider	4.00
61	David Justice	1.00
62	Johnny Sain	1.00
63	Chuck Klein	1.00
64	Sparky Anderson	1.00
65	Alan Trammell	2.00
66	Willie Wilson	1.00
67	Hoyt Wilhelm	1.00
68	Joe Pepitone	1.00
69	Darren Daulton	1.00
70	Tom Seaver	4.00
71	Jim "Catfish" Hunter	1.00
72	Tim McCarver	1.00
73	Dave Parker	1.00
74	Earl Weaver	1.00
75	Ted Kluszewski	1.00
76	John Kruk	1.00
77	Dwight Evans	1.00
78	Ron Darling	1.00
79	Tony Oliva	1.00
80	Johnny Bench	5.00
81	Sam Crawford	1.00
82	Steve Yeager	1.00
83	Paul Molitor	2.00
84	Bert Campaneris	1.00
85	Mickey Rivers	1.00
86	Vince Coleman	1.00
87	Kent Tekulve	1.00
88	Dwight Gooden	1.00
89	Whitey Herzog	1.00
90	Whitey Ford	4.00
91	Warren Spahn	3.00
92	Fred Lynn	1.00
93	Joe Tinker	1.00
94	Bill Buckner	1.00
95	Bob Feller	2.00
96	Hank Bauer	1.00
97	Joe Rudi	1.00
98	Steve Sax	1.00
99	Bruce Sutter	1.50
100	Nolan Ryan	10.00
101	Bobby Thomson	1.00
102	Bob Watson	1.00
103	Vida Blue	1.00
104	Robin Roberts	1.00
105	Orlando Cepeda	2.00
106	Jim Bottomley	1.00
107	Heinie Manush	1.00
108	Jim Gilliam	1.00
109	Dave Concepcion	1.00
110	Al Kaline	5.00
111	Howard Johnson	1.00
112	Phil Rizzuto	2.00
113	Steve Garvey	1.00
114	George Foster	1.00
115	Carlton Fisk	2.00
116	Don Newcombe	1.00
117	Lance Parrish	1.00
118	Reggie Jackson	4.00
119	Luis Aparicio	1.00
120	Jim Palmer	1.50
121	Ron Guidry	1.00
122	Frankie Frisch	1.00
123	Chet Lemon	1.00
124	Cecil Cooper	1.00
125	Harmon Killebrew	4.00
126	Luis Tiant	1.00
127	John McGraw	1.00
128	Paul O'Neill	1.00
129	Jack Clark	1.00
130	Stan Musial	6.00
131	Mike Schmidt	4.00
132	Kirby Puckett	2.00
133	Carlton Fisk	1.50
134	Bill Mazeroski	1.00
135	Johnny Podres	1.00
136	Robin Yount	1.50
137	David Justice	1.00
138	Bobby Thomson	1.00
139	Joe Carter	1.00
140	Reggie Jackson	1.50
141	Kirk Gibson	1.00
142	Whitey Ford	1.50
143	Don Larsen	1.00
144	Duke Snider	1.50
145	Carl Yastrzemski	1.50
146	Johnny Bench	2.00
147	Lou Brock	1.00
148	Ted Kluszewski	1.00
149	Jim Palmer	1.00
150	Willie Mays	5.00

Gold

Golds (1-150):		4-8X
Production 100 Sets		

Autographed Relic

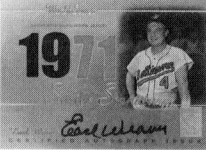

		NM/M
Inserted 1:55		
Golds:		No Pricing
Production 25 Sets		
LB	Lou Brock	40.00

JC	Jose Canseco	40.00
CF	Carlton Fisk	120.00
HK	Harmon Killebrew	75.00
WM	Willie Mays	275.00
BM	Bill Mazeroski	60.00
MS	Mike Schmidt	100.00
BT	Bobby Thomson	40.00

Cut Signature Relic

No pricing due to scarcity.
Production One Set

Fan Fare Relic

		NM/M
Common Player:		10.00
Inserted 1:Box		
HB	Hank Bauer	10.00
YB	Yogi Berra	20.00
WF	Whitey Ford	15.00
DJ	David Justice	10.00
DL	Don Larsen	15.00
BM	Billy Martin	15.00
DN	Don Newcombe	15.00
PO	Paul O'Neill	15.00
JP	Johnny Podres	15.00
PR	Phil Rizzuto	15.00
MS	Bill "Moose" Skowron	10.00
DS	Duke Snider	15.00

Memorab. Match-Up Relic

		NM/M
Common Player:		
Varying quantities produced		
GF	Hank Greenberg, Frankie Frisch/34	90.00
GK	Hank Greenberg, Chuck Klein/35	90.00
PR	Phil Rizzuto, Willie Mays/51	150.00
FS	Whitey Ford, Duke Snider/53	75.00
AS	Luis Aparicio, Duke Snider/59	35.00
MF	Bill Mazeroski, Whitey Ford/60	50.00
KB	Al Kaline, Lou Brock/68	75.00
RS	Frank Robinson, Tom Seaver/69	40.00
RBE	Brooks Robinson, Johnny Bench/70	55.00
AM	Sparky Anderson, Billy Martin/76	25.00
SP	Willie Stargell, Jim Palmer/79	40.00
SB	Mike Schmidt, George Brett/80	80.00
SY	Ozzie Smith, Robin Yount/82	50.00
SRI	Mike Schmidt, Cal Ripken Jr./83	120.00
TG	Alan Trammell, Tony Gwynn/84	50.00
WB	Mookie Wilson, Bill Buckner/86	40.00
EG	Dennis Eckersley, Kirk Gibson/88	35.00

Pastime Patches Relics

No pricing due to scarcity.
Production 15 Sets

Relic

	NM/M
Common Player:	10.00
Production 425 unless noted.	
Golds:	No Pricing
Production 25	

WORLD SERIES TRIBUTE RELIC

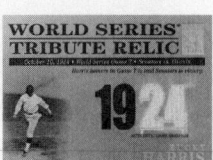

HA	Hank Aaron/50	60.00
HB	Hank Bauer/50	30.00
JBE	Johnny Bench	25.00
YB	Yogi Berra	20.00
WB	Wade Boggs	15.00
JB	Jim Bottomley/50	30.00
GB	George Brett	25.00
LB	Lou Brock	10.00
JC	Jose Canseco	15.00
NC	Norm Cash/50	25.00
OC	Orlando Cepeda/50	30.00
RC	Roberto Clemente/50	120.00
TC	Ty Cobb	120.00
SC	Sam Crawford/50	15.00
CF	Carlton Fisk	40.00
JF	Jimmie Foxx/50	80.00
FF	Frankie Frisch	15.00
LG	Lou Gehrig/50	185.00
HG	Hank Greenberg/50	60.00
TG	Tony Gwynn	20.00
BH	Bucky Harris	10.00
RH	Rogers Hornsby	35.00
CH	Jim "Catfish" Hunter	15.00
RJ	Reggie Jackson	15.00
HK	Harmon Killebrew	25.00
CK	Chuck Klein	10.00
TK	Ted Kluszewski	15.00
HM	Heinie Manush/50	35.00
JM	Juan Marichal	15.00
RM	Roger Maris/50	75.00
BMA	Billy Martin	15.00
WM	Willie Mays	50.00
BM	Bill Mazeroski	15.00
WMC	Willie McCovey	10.00
TM	Thurman Munson	30.00
SM	Stan Musial	30.00
KP	Kirby Puckett	20.00
CR	Cal Ripken Jr.	35.00
FR	Frank Robinson	15.00
JR	Jackie Robinson	40.00
ER	Edd Roush/50	40.00
BR	Babe Ruth	140.00
MS	Mike Schmidt	25.00
RS	Red Schoendienst	15.00
TS	Tom Seaver	15.00
OS	Ozzie Smith	20.00
TSP	Tris Speaker/50	90.00
WS	Willie Stargell/50	15.00
BT	Bobby Thomson	15.00
JT	Joe Tinker	30.00
HW	Honus Wagner/50	150.00
CY	Carl Yastrzemski	30.00
RY	Robin Yount	20.00

World Series Tribute Singles

		NM/M
Common Player:		8.00
Premiere Proofs:		1.5X
Production 50		
TG	Troy Glaus	8.00
MR	Mariano Rivera	10.00

World Series Tribute Doubles

		NM/M
Common Duo:		10.00
Premiere Proofs:		1.5X
Production 50		
PP	Jorge Posada, Andy Pettitte	15.00
WO	Bernie Williams, Paul O'Neill	15.00
LP	John Lackey, Troy Percival	10.00
SJ	Curt Schilling, Randy Johnson	15.00
BG	Barry Bonds, Troy Glaus	35.00
WG	Bernie Williams, Luis Gonzalez	10.00
PC	Mike Piazza, Roger Clemens	35.00

World Series Tribute Triples

		NM/M
Common Trio:		15.00
Premiere Proofs:		1.5X
Production 50		
LGP	John Lackey, Troy Glaus, Troy Percival	15.00
EGS	Darin Erstad, Troy Glaus, Tim Salmon	15.00

Series Signatures

		NM/M
Common Autograph:		25.00
Golds:		No Pricing
Production 25		
SA	Sparky Anderson	25.00
JC	Joe Carter	25.00
WF	Whitey Ford	60.00
SG	Steve Garvey	25.00
KG	Kirk Gibson	30.00
DJ	David Justice	40.00
AK	Al Kaline	50.00
DN	Don Newcombe	40.00
JP	Jim Palmer	30.00
BR	Brooks Robinson	75.00
MS	Bill "Moose" Skowron	25.00
AT	Alan Trammell	25.00
EW	Earl Weaver	25.00
MW	Maury Wills	25.00
MWI	Mookie Wilson	30.00

Team Tribute Relic

		NM/M
Common Card:		15.00
Production 275 unless noted.		
YLK	Carl Yastrzemski, Fred Lynn, Carlton Fisk	50.00
OSD	Paul O'Neill, Chris Sabo, Eric Davis	25.00
FPG	George Foster, Tony Perez, Ken Griffey Jr.	25.00
CPM	Dave Concepcion, Tony Perez, Joe Morgan	50.00
KCA	Al Kaline, Norm Cash	40.00
TA	Alan Trammell, Sparky Anderson	15.00
GT	Kirk Gibson, Alan Trammell	25.00
SB	Bret Saberhagen, George Brett	40.00
CYG	Ron Cey, Steve Yeager, Steve Garvey	
YM	Robin Yount, Paul Molitor	35.00
SRK	Tom Seaver, Nolan Ryan, Jerry Koosman	50.00
HCD	Keith Hernandez, Gary Carter, Lenny Dykstra	30.00
GB	Lou Gehrig, Babe Ruth/25	500.00
EC	Dennis Eckersley, Jose Canseco	25.00
HJ	Jim "Catfish" Hunter, Reggie Jackson	30.00
SPM	Willie Stargell, Dave Parker, Bill Madlock	30.00
CM	Orlando Cepeda, Juan Marichal	30.00
MM	Willie Mays, Willie McCovey	50.00
SMC	Ozzie Smith, Willie McGee, Vince Coleman	40.00

2003 Topps 205

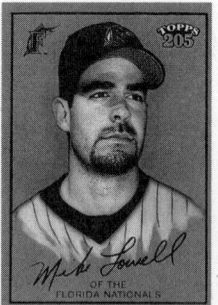

		NM/M
Complete Set (335):		150.00
Common Player:		.20
SP's inserted 1:5		
25 variations in base set and minis		
Mini-Cards(316-335): Exclusive Mini Cards		
Price for minis (316-335) are Polar Bear		
Series 1 or 2 Pack (8):		4.00
Series 1 or 2 Box (20):		65.00
1	Barry Bonds	2.50
1	Barry Bonds/Variation	3.00
2	Bret Boone	.40
3	Albert Pujols	2.00
3	Albert Pujols/Variation	2.00
4	Carl Crawford	.20
5	Bartolo Colon	.20
6	Cliff Floyd	.20
7	John Olerud	.40
8	Jason Giambi	.50
8	Jason Giambi/Variation	.75
9	Edgardo Alfonzo	.20
10	Ivan Rodriguez	.50
11	Jim Edmonds	.50
12	Mike Piazza	1.50
12	Mike Piazza/Variation	2.00

13	Greg Maddux	1.50
14	Jose Vidro	.20
15	Vladimir Guerrero	.75
15	Vladimir Guerrero/Variation	1.00
16	Bernie Williams	.50
17	Roger Clemens	2.00
18	Miguel Tejada	.50
18	Miguel Tejada/Variation	.75
19	Carlos Delgado	.50
20	Alfonso Soriano	.75
20	Alfonso Soriano/Variation	.75
21	Bobby Cox	.20
22	Mike Scioscia	.20
23	John Smoltz	.40
24	Luis Gonzalez	.40
25	Shawn Green	.40
26	Raul Ibanez	.20
27	Andruw Jones	.50
28	Josh Beckett	.40
29	Derek Lowe	.20
30	Todd Helton	.75
31	Barry Larkin	.40
32	Jason Jennings	.20
33	Darin Erstad	.40
34	Magglio Ordonez	.40
35	Mike Sweeney	.20
36	Kazuhisa Ishii	.20
37	Ron Gardenhire	.20
38	Tim Hudson	.40
39	Tim Salmon	.50
40	Pat Burrell	.40
40	Pat Burrell/Variation	.50
41	Manny Ramirez	.75
42	Nick Johnson	.20
43	Tom Glavine	.40
44	Mark Mulder	.40
45	Brian Jordan	.20
46	Rafael Palmeiro	.50
47	Vernon Wells	.40
48	Bob Brenly	.20
49	C.C. Sabathia	.20
50	Alex Rodriguez	2.50
50	Alex Rodriguez/Variation	2.50
51	Sammy Sosa	1.50
51	Sammy Sosa/Variation	2.00
52	Paul Konerko	.20
53	Craig Biggio	.40
54	Moises Alou	.20
55	Johnny Damon	.50
56	Torii Hunter	.40
57	Omar Vizquel	.40
58	Orlando Hernandez	.20
59	Barry Zito	.40
60	Lance Berkman	.50
61	Carlos Beltran	.50
62	Edgar Renteria	.40
63	Ben Sheets	.40
64	Doug Mientkiewicz	.20
65	Troy Glaus	.50
66	Preston Wilson	.20
67	Kerry Wood	.75
68	Frank Thomas	.75
69	Jimmy Rollins	.40
70	Brian Giles	.40
71	Bobby Higginson	.20
72	Larry Walker	.40
73	Randy Johnson	1.00
74	Tony LaRussa	.20
75	Derek Jeter	3.00
75	Derek Jeter/Variation	3.00
76	Bobby Abreu	.40
77	Adam Dunn	.75
77	Adam Dunn/Variation	.75
78	Ryan Klesko	.20
79	Francisco Rodriguez	.20
80	Scott Rolen	.75
81	Roberto Alomar	.50
82	Joe Torre	.50
83	Jim Thome	.75
84	Kevin Millwood	.40
85	J.T. Snow	.20
86	Trevor Hoffman	.20
87	Jay Gibbons	.20
88	Mark Prior	1.00
88	Mark Prior/Variation	1.50
89	Rich Aurilia	.20
90	Chipper Jones	1.00
91	Richie Sexson	.50
92	Gary Sheffield	.50
93	Pedro J. Martinez	1.00
94	Rodrigo Lopez	.20
95	Al Leiter	.20
96	Jorge Posada	.50
97	Luis Castillo	.20
98	Aubrey Huff	.20
99	A.J. Pierzynski	.20
100	Ichiro Suzuki	2.00
100	Ichiro Suzuki/Variation	2.00
101	Eric Chavez	.40
102	Brett Myers	.20
103	Jason Kendall	.20
104	Jeff Kent	.40
105	Eric Hinske	.20
106	Jacque Jones	.20
107	Phil Nevin	.20
108	Roy Oswalt	.40
109	Curt Schilling	.75
110	Nomar Garciaparra	2.00
110	Nomar Garciaparra/Variation	2.00
111	Garret Anderson	.40
112	Eric Gagne	.50
113	Javier Vazquez	.40
114	Jeff Bagwell	.75
115	Mike Lowell	.40
116	Carlos Pena	.20

117	Ken Griffey Jr.	1.50
118	Tony Batista	.20
119	Edgar Martinez	.20
120	Austin Kearns	.50
121	Jason Stokes	.20
122	Jose Reyes	.50
123	Rocco Baldelli	.40
124	Joe Borchard	.20
125	Joe Mauer	.50
126	Gavin Floyd	.20
127	Mark Teixeira	.50
128	Jeremy Guthrie	.20
129	B.J. Upton	.40
130	Khalil Greene	2.00
131	Hanley Ramirez **RC**	3.00
132	Andy Marte **RC**	3.00
133	J.D. Durbin **RC**	1.00
134	Jason Kubel **RC**	2.00
135	Craig Brazell **RC**	.75
136	Bryan Bullington **RC**	1.00
137	Jose Contreras **RC**	1.00
138	Brian Burgamy **RC**	.75
139	Evel Bastida-Martinez **RC**	.50
140	Joey Gomes	1.00
141	Ismael Castro **RC**	.75
142	Travis Wong **RC**	.75
143	Michael Garciaparra	.50
144	Arnaldo Munoz **RC**	.50
145	Louis Sockalexis	2.00
146	Dick Hoblitzell	1.00
147	George "Peaches" Graham	.50
148	Hal Chase	.50
149	John McGraw	1.00
150	Bobby Wallace	.50
151	Dave Shean	.20
152	Dick Hoblitzell SP	3.00
153	Hal Chase	.20
154	George Wiltse	.20
155	George Brett	2.00
156	Willie Mays	3.00
157	Honus Wagner SP	4.00
158	Nolan Ryan	3.00
159	Reggie Jackson	1.00
160	Mike Schmidt	1.50
161	Josh Barfield	.20
162	Grady Sizemore	.40
163	Justin Morneau	.40
164	Laynce Nix	.20
165	Zack Greinke	.20
166	Victor Martinez	.50
167	Jeff Mathis	.20
168	Casey Kotchman	.20
169	Gabe Gross	.20
170	Edwin Jackson **RC**	1.50
171	Delmon Young/SP **RC**	8.00
172	Eric Duncan/SP	2.00
173	Brian Snyder/SP	1.50
174	Chris Lubanski/SP **RC**	3.00
175	Ryan Harvey/SP **RC**	3.00
176	Nicholas Markakis/SP **RC**	8.00
177	Chad Billingsley/ SP **RC**	3.00
178	Elizardo Ramirez	.50
179	Ben Francisco	.50
180	Franklin Gutierrez/SP	4.00
181	Aaron Hill/SP	2.00
182	Kevin Correia	.50
183	Kelly Shoppach **RC**	.75
184	Felix Pie/SP **RC**	4.00
185	Adam Loewen/SP **RC**	4.00
186	Danny Garcia	.50
187	Rickie Weeks/SP **RC**	5.00
188	Robby Hammock/SP	2.00
189	Ryan Wagner/SP **RC**	2.00
190	Matt Kata/SP	1.50
191	Bo Hart/SP **RC**	2.00
192	Brandon Webb/SP **RC**	6.00
193	Bengie Molina	.20
194	Junior Spivey	.20
195	Gary Sheffield	.50
196	Jason Johnson	.20
197	David Ortiz	.75
198	Roberto Alomar	.50
199	Wily Mo Pena	.20
200	Sammy Sosa	2.00
201	Jay Payton	.20
202	Dmitri Young	.20
203	Derek Lee	.40
204	Jeff Bagwell	.75
204	Jeff Bagwell/Variation	.75
205	Runelvys Hernandez	.20
206	Kevin Brown	.40
207	Wes Helms	.20
208	Eddie Guardado	.20
209	Orlando Cabrera	.20
210	Alfonso Soriano	.75
211	Ty Wigginton	.20
212	Rich Harden	.40
212	Rich Harden/Variation	.50
213	Mike Lieberthal	.20
214	Brian Giles	.40
215	Jason Schmidt	.40
216	Jamie Moyer	.20
217	Matt Morris	.20
218	Victor Zambrano	.20
219	Roy Halladay	.50
220	Mike Hampton	.20
221	Kevin Millar	.20
222	Hideo Nomo	.50
223	Milton Bradley	.20
224	Jose Guillen	.20
225	Derek Jeter	3.00
226	Rondell White	.20
227	Hank Blalock	.50
227	Hank Blalock/Variation	.50
228	Shigetoshi Hasegawa	.20
229	Mike Mussina	.50
230	Cristian Guzman	.20
231	Todd Helton	.75
231	Todd Helton/Variation	.75
232	Kenny Lofton	.40
233	Carl Everett	.20
234	Shea Hillenbrand	.20
235	Brad Fullmer	.20
236	Bernie Williams	.50
237	Vicente Padilla	.20
238	Tim Worrell	.20
239	Juan Gonzalez	.40
240	Ichiro Suzuki	2.00
241	Aaron Boone	.20
242	Shannon Stewart	.20
243	Barry Zito	.40
243	Barry Zito/Variation	.40
244	Reggie Sanders	.20
245	Scott Podsednik	.40
246	Miguel Cabrera	.75
247	Angel Berroa	.20
248	Carlos Zambrano	.40
249	Marlon Byrd	.20
250	Mark Prior	1.00
251	Esteban Loaiza	.20
252	David Eckstein	.20
253	Alex Cintron	.20
254	Melvin Mora	.20
255	Russ Ortiz	.20
256	Carlos Lee	.20
257	Tino Martinez	.20
258	Randy Wolf	.20
259	Jason Phillips	.20
260	Vladimir Guerrero	1.00
261	Brad Wilkerson	.20
262	Ivan Rodriguez	.75
263	Matt Lawton	.20
264	Adam Dunn	.50
265	Joe Borowski	.20
266	Jody Gerut	.20
267	Alex Rodriguez	2.50
268	Brendan Donnelly	.20
269	Randy Johnson	1.00
269	Randy Johnson/Variation	1.00
270	Nomar Garciaparra	2.50
271	Javy Lopez	.50
272	Travis Hafner	.20
273	Juan Pierre	.20
274	Morgan Ensberg	.20
275	Albert Pujols	2.00
276	Jason LaRue	.20
277	Paul LoDuca	.20
278	Andy Pettitte	.50
279	Mike Piazza	1.50
280	Jim Thome	1.00
280	Jim Thome/Variation	1.00
281	Marquis Grissom	.20
282	Woody Williams	.20
283	Curt Schilling	.75
283	Curt Schilling/Variation	.75
284	Chipper Jones	1.00
284	Chipper Jones/Variation	1.00
285	Deivi Cruz	.20
286	Johnny Damon	.50
287	Chin-Hui Tsao	.20
288	Alex Gonzalez	.20
289	Billy Wagner	.40
290	Jason Giambi	.50
291	Keith Foulke	.20
292	Jerome Williams	.20
293	Livan Hernandez	.20
294	Aaron Guiel	.20
295	Randall Simon	.20
296	Byung-Hyun Kim	.20
297	Jorge Julio	.20
298	Miguel Batista	.20
299	Rafael Furcal	.40
300	Dontrelle Willis/SP	1.00
300	Dontrelle Willis/Variation	1.00
301	Alex Sanchez	.20
302	Shawn Chacon	.20
303	Matt Clement	.20
304	Luis Matos	.20
305	Steve Finley	.20
306	Marcus Giles	.40
307	David Wells	.20
308	Jeromy Burnitz	.20
309	Mike MacDougal	.20
310	Mariano Rivera	.40
311	Adrian Beltre	.40
312	Mark Loretta	.20
313	Ugueth Urbina	.20
314	Bill Mueller	.40
315	Johan Santana	.50
316	Willie Mays	2.00
317	Delmon Young	4.00
318	Rickie Weeks	4.00
319	Ryan Wagner	.50
320	Brandon Webb	.75
321	Chris Lubanski	1.00
322	Ryan Harvey	3.00
323	Nicholas Markakis	1.00
324	Chad Billingsley	1.00
325	Aaron Hill	.40
326	Brian Snyder	.40
327	Eric Duncan	.40
328	Sammy Sosa	1.50
329	Alfonso Soriano	1.00
330	Ichiro Suzuki	2.00
331	Alex Rodriguez	2.00
332	Nomar Garciaparra	2.00
333	Albert Pujols	2.00
334	Jim Thome	1.00
335	Dontrelle Willis	.50

Mini Parallel

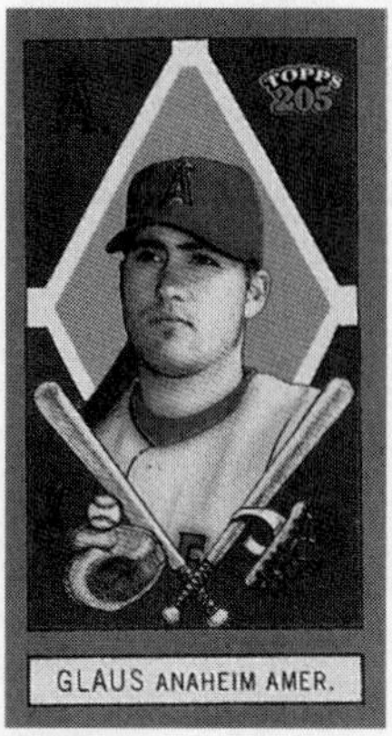

Polar Bear:	1-2X
Sovereign:	1-2X
Sovereign Green:	2-3X
American Beauty:	1-2X
Amer. Beauty Purple:	3-5X
Cycle:	1-2X
Cycle Purple:	3-5X
Drum:	2-4X
Honest:	1-2X
Honest Purple:	3-5X
Piedmont:	1-2X
Piedmont Purple:	3-5X
Sweet Caporal:	1-2X
Sweet Caporal Purple:	3-5X
Bazooka:	No Pricing
Production Five Sets	
Brooklyn:	1.5-4X
Brooklyn:Varies for common, rare & Unc.	

T-205 Relics

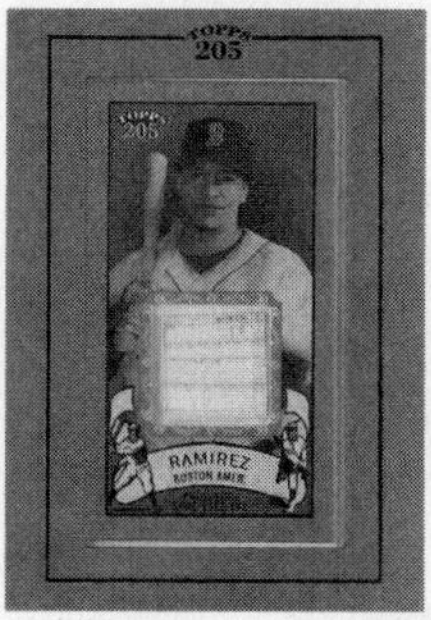

		NM/M
Common Player:		4.00
RA	Roberto Alomar/Bat	6.00
GA	Garret Anderson/Jsy	5.00
JB	Jeff Bagwell/Jsy	6.00
LB	Lance Berkman/Bat	8.00
BB	Barry Bonds	25.00
AB	A.J. Burnett/Jsy	4.00
LC	Luis Castillo/Jsy	4.00
EC	Eric Chavez/Bat	5.00
JD	Johnny Damon/Bat	6.00
AD	Adam Dunn/Bat	8.00
RF	Rafael Furcal/Bat	6.00
EG	Eric Gagne/Jsy	8.00
NG	Nomar Garciaparra/Jsy	15.00
BG	Brian Giles/Bat	5.00
LG	Luis Gonzalez/Jsy	4.00
TH	Todd Helton/Jsy	10.00
KI	Kazuhisa Ishii/Jsy	6.00
JJ	Jason Jennings/Jsy	4.00
NJ	Nick Johnson/Bat	4.00
RJ	Randy Johnson/Jsy	8.00
JK	Jeff Kent/Bat	4.00
AL	Al Leiter/Jsy	4.00
KL	Kenny Lofton/Bat	4.00
DL	Derek Lowe/Jsy	4.00
GM	Greg Maddux/Jsy	15.00
PM	Pedro Martinez/Jsy	10.00
MO	Magglio Ordonez/Jsy	4.00
RO	Roy Oswalt/Jsy	4.00
RP	Rafael Palmeiro/Jsy	6.00
TP	Troy Percival/Jsy	4.00
MP	Mike Piazza/Bat	10.00
AP	Albert Pujols/Jsy	20.00
MR	Manny Ramirez/Bat	8.00
AR	Alex Rodriguez/Jsy	10.00
SR	Scott Rolen/Bat	15.00
CS	Curt Schilling/Jsy	6.00
JS	John Smoltz/Jsy	8.00
AS	Alfonso Soriano/Jsy	10.00
MS	Mike Sweeney/Bat	4.00
JT	Jim Thome/Bat	12.00
MV	Mo Vaughn/Jsy	4.00
BW	Bernie Williams/Bat	10.00
BZ	Barry Zito/Jsy	4.00
Series 2		4.00
RA	Roberto Alomar	6.00
JB	Jeff Bagwell	8.00
RBB	Rocco Baldelli/bat	8.00
RB	Rocco Baldelli/Jsy	8.00
CB	Craig Biggio	4.00
HB	Hank Blalock	6.00
WB	Wade Boggs	15.00
BB	Bret Boone	10.00
GB	George Brett	25.00
KB	Kevin Brown	4.00
SB	Sean Burroughs	4.00
MC	Mike Cameron	4.00
JC	Jose Canseco	8.00
GC	Gary Carter	8.00
RC	Roger Clemens	15.00
CD	Carlos Delgado	6.00
BD	Brandon Duckworth	4.00
JE	Jim Edmonds	6.00
DE	Darin Erstad	4.00
RF	Rafael Furcal	4.00
NG	Nomar Garciaparra	10.00
JG	Jason Giambi	6.00
JGI	Jeremy Giambi	4.00
BG	Brian Giles	4.00
TG	Troy Glaus	6.00
JGO	Juan Gonzalez	6.00
LG	Luis Gonzalez	4.00
MG	Mark Grace	10.00
MGR	Marquis Grissom	4.00
VG	Vladimir Guerrero	8.00
CG	Cristian Guzman	4.00
RH	Rickey Henderson	8.00
RJ	Randy Johnson	8.00
AJ	Andruw Jones	6.00
CJB	Chipper Jones	8.00
KL	Kenny Lofton	4.00
GM	Greg Maddux	10.00
EM	Edgar Martinez	4.00
PM	Pedro J. Martinez	8.00
TM	Tino Martinez	6.00
FM	Fred McGriff	6.00
MM	Mark Mulder	4.00
EMU	Eddie Murray	25.00
JO	John Olerud	4.00
PO	Paul O'Neill	4.00
RP	Rafael Palmeiro	8.00
CP	Corey Patterson	10.00
BP	Brad Penny	4.00
MP	Mike Piazza	10.00
JP	Jorge Posada	15.00
APB	Albert Pujols/bat	20.00
AP	Albert Pujols/jersey	20.00
ARA	Aramis Ramirez	6.00
FR	Frank Robinson	15.00
AR	Alex Rodriguez	10.00
IR	Ivan Rodriguez	8.00
SR	Scott Rolen	8.00
NR	Nolan Ryan	40.00
CS	Curt Schilling	6.00
MS	Mike Schmidt	25.00
GS	Gary Sheffield	6.00
TS	Tsuyoshi Shinjo	4.00
AS	Alfonso Soriano	8.00
SS	Sammy Sosa	15.00
SST	Shannon Stewart	4.00
MT	Mark Teixeira	6.00
MTE	Miguel Tejada	6.00
FT	Frank Thomas	8.00
RV	Robin Ventura	4.00
LW	Larry Walker	4.00
VW	Vernon Wells	8.00
BW	Bernie Williams	6.00
DW	Dontrelle Willis	8.00

T-205 Autographs

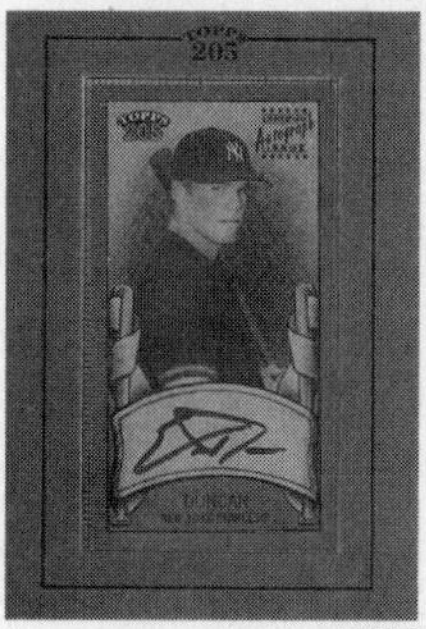

		NM/M
Common Autograph:		12.00
LB	Lance Berkman	25.00
MB	Marlon Byrd	10.00
CF	Cliff Floyd	15.00
TH	Torii Hunter	15.00
PL	Paul LoDuca	15.00
MO	Magglio Ordonez	20.00

JR Jose Reyes 30.00
SR Scott Rolen 40.00
MS Mike Sweeney 20.00
Series 2
HA Hank Aaron/50 280.00
LC Luis Castillo 10.00
ED Eric Duncan 20.00
RH Rich Harden 25.00
FP Felix Pie 40.00
RWA Ryan Wagner 15.00
JW Jerome Williams 20.00
DW Dontrelle Willis 25.00

Team Topps Legends Autos.

NM/M

Common Player:
Stan Musial 65.00
Jim Palmer 20.00
Gaylord Perry 10.00
Robin Yount 75.00

Triple Folder

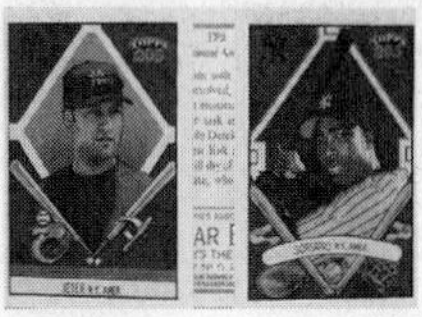

NM/M

Complete Set (100): 60.00
Common Card: .25
Inserted 1:1
Series 1 Brooklyn Variation: 4-8X
Inserted 1:72
Series 2 Brooklyn Variation: 2-4X
Inserted 1:29
TF1 Barry Bonds, Jason LaRue 1.50
TF2 Alfonso Soriano, Derek Jeter 1.50
TF3 Alex Rodriguez, Miguel Tejada 1.50
TF4 Nomar Garciaparra, Derek Jeter 2.00
TF5 Omar Vizquel, Alex Rodriguez 1.50
TF6 Paul Konerko, Omar Vizquel .25
TF7 Paul Konerko, Maggio Ordonez .25
TF8 Doug Mientkiewicz, Darin Erstad .25
TF9 Jason Kendall, Jimmy Rollins .25
TF10 Shawn Green, Roberto Alomar .25
TF11 Derek Jeter, Roberto Alomar 1.50
TF12 Bobby Abreu, Luis Castillo .25
TF13 Randy Johnson, Curt Schilling .75
TF14 Mike Piazza, Kerry Wood 1.00
TF15 Roger Clemens, Jorge Posada 1.00
TF16 Ichiro Suzuki, Ryan Klesko 1.00
TF17 Alfonso Soriano, Chipper Jones 1.00
TF18 Barry Bonds, Nick Johnson 1.50
TF19 Chipper Jones, Andruw Jones .75
TF20 Bobby Abreu, Paul Konerko .25
TF21 Rafael Palmeiro, Alex Rodriguez 1.50
TF22 Eric Hinske, Carlos Delgado .25
TF23 Nomar Garciaparra, Jay Gibbons 1.00
TF24 Mike Piazza, Luis Gonzalez 1.00
TF25 J.T. Snow, Vladimir Guerrero .50
TF26 Jason Giambi, Bernie Williams .75
TF27 Miguel Tejada,Richie Sexson .25
TF28 Doug Mientkiewicz, Jimmy Rollins .25
TF29 Eric Chavez, Derek Jeter 2.00
TF30 Alfonso Soriano, Bret Boone 1.00
TF31 Chipper Jones, Mike Piazza 1.00
TF32 Ichiro Suzuki, Bret Boone 1.00
TF33 Bobby Abreu, Mike Piazza 1.00
TF34 Jimmy Rollins, Pat Burrell .25
TF3 Ichiro Suzuki, Miguel Tejada 1.00
TF36 Jason LaRue, Barry Bonds 1.50
TF37 Derek Jeter, Alfonso Soriano 1.50
TF38 Miguel Tejada, Alex Rodriguez 1.50
TF39 Derek Jeter, Nomar Garciaparra 2.00
TF40 Alex Rodriguez, Omar Vizquel 1.50
TF41 Curt Schilling, Randy Johnson .75
TF42 Jorge Posada, Roger Clemens 1.50
TF43 Ryan Klesko, Ichiro Suzuki 1.00
TF44 Nick Johnson, Barry Bonds 1.50
TF45 Alex Rodriguez, Rafael Palmeiro 1.50
TF46 Vladimir Guerrero, J.T. Snow .50
TF47 Derek Jeter, Eric Chavez 2.00
TF48 Bret Boone, Ichiro Suzuki 1.00
TF49 Mike Piazza, Bobby Abreu 1.00
TF50 Miguel Tejada, Ichiro Suzuki 1.00
TF51 Juan Pierre, Jim Thome .50
TF52 Kevin Millwood, Jim Thome .50
TF53 Hank Blalock, Jorge Posada .40
TF54 Deivi Cruz, Hank Blalock .25
TF55 Rafael Furcal, Ty Wigginton .25
TF56 Jim Thome, Nomar Garciaparra 1.50
TF57 Craig Biggio, Jason Giambi .75
TF58 Aaron Boone, Jason Giambi .75
TF59 Jason Giambi, Bernie Williams .75
TF60 Cristian Guzman, Jody Gerut .25
TF61 Todd Helton, Jose Reyes .50
TF62 Derek Jeter, Hank Blalock 2.00
TF63 Mike Piazza, Jimmy Rollins 1.00
TF64 Bernie Williams, Derek Jeter 2.00
TF65 Andruw Jones, Rafael Furcal .50
TF66 Mike Piazza, Andruw Jones 1.00
TF67 Mike Piazza, Cliff Floyd 1.00
TF68 Jason Kendall, Albert Pujols 1.50
TF69 Nomar Garciaparra, Manny Ramirez 1.50
TF70 Jorge Posada, Alex Rodriguez 1.50
TF71 Derek Jeter, Alex Rodriguez 2.00
TF72 Mike Sweeney, Alex Rodriguez 1.50
TF73 Marquis Grissom, Ivan Rodriguez .50
TF74 Jason Phillips, Gary Sheffield .40
TF75 Chipper Jones, Gary Sheffield 1.00
TF76 Junior Spivey, Gary Sheffield .40
TF77 Al Leiter, Ichiro Suzuki 1.00
TF78 Jose Vidro, Jim Thome .75
TF79 Jimmy Rollins, Paul LoDuca .25
TF80 Alex Rodriguez, Rafael Palmeiro 1.50
TF81 Albert Pujols, Jim Edmonds 1.50
TF82 Eric Chavez, Mike Sweeney .25
TF83 Cristian Guzman, Jimmy Rollins .25
TF84 Alfonso Soriano, Bernie Williams .50
TF85 Ichiro Suzuki, Derek Jeter 2.00
TF86 Jimmy Rollins, Derek Lee .25
TF87 Shawn Green, Paul LoDuca .25
TF88 Carlos Delgado, Jorge Posada .50
TF89 Dmitri Young, C.C. Sabathia .25
TF90 Dontrelle Willis, Shawn Chacon .25
TF91 Edgar Martinez, Alex Rodriguez 1.50
TF92 Edgar Martinez, Carlos Delgado .50
TF93 Edgar Martinez, Esteban Loaiza .25
TF94 Roy Halladay, C.C. Sabathia .25
TF95 Ichiro Suzuki, Albert Pujols 1.50
TF96 Ichiro Suzuki, Shigetoshi Hasegawa 1.00
TF97 Geoff Jenkins, Aaron Boone .25
TF98 Nomar Garciaparra, Alfonso Soriano 1.50
TF99 Jorge Posada, Alfonso Soriano .75
TF100 Vernon Wells, Garret Anderson .25

Triple Folder Autographs

NM/M

Inserted 1:355
RH Rich Harden 40.00
RW Ryan Wagner 40.00
JW Jerome Williams 35.00
DW Dontrelle Willis 40.00

2004 Topps

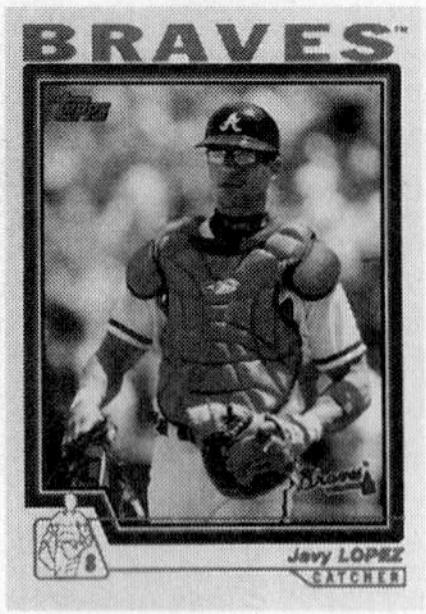

NM/M

Complete Set (732): 60.00
Complete Team Factory Set (737): 75.00
Complete Factory Set (742): 75.00
Common Player: .15
Pack (10): 2.00
Box (36): 55.00
Jumbo Box (12): 65.00
1 Jim Thome .40
2 Aramis Ramirez .25
3 Mark Kotsay .15
4 Edgardo Alfonzo .15
5 Ben Davis .15
6 Mike Matheny .15
8 Marlon Anderson .15
9 Chan Ho Park .15
10 Ichiro Suzuki .75
11 Kevin Millwood .25
12 Bengie Molina .15
13 Tom Glavine .25
14 Junior Spivey .15
15 Marcus Giles .15
16 David Segui .15
17 Kevin Millar .15
18 Corey Patterson .15
19 Aaron Rowand .15
20 Derek Jeter 1.00
21 Jason LaRue .15
22 Chris Hammond .15
23 Jay Payton .15
24 Bobby Higginson .15
25 Lance Berkman .25
26 Juan Pierre .15
27 Brent Mayne .15
28 Fred McGriff .25
29 Richie Sexson .25
30 Tim Hudson .25
31 Mike Piazza .50
32 Brad Radke .15
33 Jeff Weaver .15
34 Ramon Hernandez .15
35 David Bell .15
36 Craig Wilson .15
37 Jake Peavy .15
38 Tim Worrell .15
39 Gil Meche .15
40 Albert Pujols 1.00
41 Michael Young .15
42 Josh Phelps .15
43 Brendan Donnelly .15
44 Steve Finley .15
45 John Smoltz .15
46 Jay Gibbons .15
47 Trot Nixon .15
48 Carl Pavano .15
49 Frank Thomas .40
50 Mark Prior 1.00
51 Danny Graves .15
52 Milton Bradley .15
53 Jose Jimenez .15
54 Shane Halter .15
55 Mike Lowell .15
56 Geoff Blum .15
57 Michael Tucker .15
58 Paul LoDuca .15
59 Vicente Padilla .15
60 Jacque Jones .15
61 Fernando Tatis .15
62 Ty Wigginton .15
63 Pedro Astacio .15
64 Andy Pettitte .25
65 Terrence Long .15
66 Cliff Floyd .15
67 Mariano Rivera .25
68 Mike Williams .15
69 Marlon Byrd .15
70 Mark Mulder .25
71 Damian Moss .15
72 Carlos Guillen .15
73 Fernando Vina .15
74 Lance Carter .15
75 Hank Blalock .25
76 Jimmy Rollins .25
77 Kevin Appier .15
78 Javy Lopez .25
79 Jerry Hairston Jr. .15
80 Andruw Jones .40
81 Rodrigo Lopez .15
82 Johnny Damon .25
83 Hee Seop Choi .15
84 Miguel Olivo .15
85 Scott Sullivan .15
86 Matt Lawton .15
87 Juan Uribe .15
88 Steve Sparks .15
89 Tim Spooneybarger .15
90 Jose Vidro .15
91 Luis Rivas .15
92 Hideo Nomo .25
93 Javier Vazquez .15
94 Al Leiter .15
95 Darren Dreifort .15
96 Mike DeJean .15
97 Zach Day .15
98 Jorge Posada .25
99 John Halama .15
100 Alex Rodriguez 1.00
101 Orlando Palmeiro .15
102 Dave Berg .15
103 Brad Fullmer .15
104 Mike Hampton .15
105 Willis Roberts .15
106 Ramiro Mendoza .15
107 Juan Cruz .15
108 Esteban Loaiza .15
109 Aaron Boone .15
110 Todd Helton .40
111 Braden Looper .15
112 Octavio Dotel .15
113 Mike MacDougal .15
114 Cesar Izturis .15
115 Johan Santana .15
116 Jose Contreras .25
117 Placido Polanco .15
118 Kenny Lofton .25
119 Adam Eaton .15
120 Vernon Wells .25
121 Ben Grieve .15
122 Randy Winn .15
123 Ismael Valdes .15
124 Eric Owens .15
125 Curt Schilling .25
126 Russ Ortiz .15
127 Mark Buehrle .15
128 Danys Baez .15
129 Dmitri Young .15
130 Kazuhisa Ishii .15
131 A.J. Pierzynski .15
132 Michael Barrett .15
133 Joe McEwing .15
134 Robin Ventura .15
135 Tom Wilson .15
136 Carlos Zambrano .15
137 Brett Tomko .15
138 Jeff Nelson .15
139 Jarrod Washburn .15
140 Greg Maddux .75
141 Craig Counsell .15
142 Reggie Taylor .15
143 Omar Vizquel .25
144 Alex Gonzalez .15
145 Billy Wagner .15
146 Brian Jordan .15
147 Wes Helms .15
148 Kyle Lohse .15
149 Timoniel Perez .15
150 Jason Giambi .50
151 Erubiel Durazo .15
152 Mike Lieberthal .15
153 Jason Kendall .15
154 Xavier Nady .15
155 Kirk Rueter .15
156 Mike Cameron .15
157 Miguel Cairo .15
158 Woody Williams .15
159 Toby Hall .15
160 Bernie Williams .40
161 Darin Erstad .25
162 Matt Mantei .15
163 Geronimo Gil .15
164 Bill Mueller .15
165 Damian Miller .15
166 Tony Graffanino .15
167 Sean Casey .15
168 Brandon Phillips .15
169 Mike Remlinger .15
170 Adam Dunn .25
171 Carlos Lee .15
172 Juan Encarnacion .15
173 Angel Berroa .15
174 Desi Relaford .15
175 Paul Quantrill .15
176 Ben Sheets .15
177 Eddie Guardado .15
178 Rocky Biddle .15
179 Mike Stanton .15
180 Eric Chavez .25
181 Jason Michaels .15
182 Terry Adams .15
183 Kip Wells .15
184 Brian Lawrence .15
185 Bret Boone .25
186 Tino Martinez .25
187 Aubrey Huff .15
188 Kevin Mench .15
189 Tim Salmon .25
190 Carlos Delgado .40
191 John Lackey .15
192 Oscar Villarreal .15
193 Sidney Ponson .15
194 Derek Lowe .15
195 Mark Grudzielanek .15
196 Flash Gordon .15
197 Matt Clement .15
198 Scott Williamson .15
199 Brandon Inge .15
200 Nomar Garciaparra 1.00
201 Antonio Osuna .15
202 Jose Mesa .15
203 Randall Simon .15
204 Jack Wilson .15
205 Ray Durham .15
206 Freddy Garcia .15
207 J.D. Drew .15
208 Einar Diaz .15
209 Roy Halladay .25
210 David Eckstein .15
211 Jason Marquis .15
212 Jorge Julio .15
213 Tim Wakefield .15
214 Moises Alou .25
215 Bartolo Colon .25
216 Jimmy Haynes .15
217 Preston Wilson .15
218 Luis Castillo .15
219 Richard Hidalgo .15
220 Manny Ramirez .40
221 Mike Mussina .40
222 Randy Wolf .15
223 Kris Benson .15
224 Ryan Klesko .25
225 Rich Aurilia .15
226 Kelvim Escobar .15
227 Francisco Cordero .15
228 Kazuhiro Sasaki .15
229 Danny Bautista .15
230 Rafael Furcal .15
231 Travis Driskill .15
232 Kyle Farnsworth .15

233	Jose Valentin	.15
234	Felipe Lopez	.15
235	C.C. Sabathia	.15
236	Brad Penny	.15
237	Brad Ausmus	.15
238	Raul Ibanez	.15
239	Adrian Beltre	.15
240	Rocco Baldelli	.25
241	Orlando Hudson	.15
242	Dave Roberts	.15
243	Doug Mientkiewicz	.15
244	Brad Wilkerson	.15
245	Scott Strickland	.15
246	Sterling Hitchcock	.15
247	Chad Bradford	.15
248	Gary Bennett	.15
249	Jose Cruz Jr.	.15
250	Jeff Kent	.25
251	Josh Beckett	.25
252	Ramon Ortiz	.15
253	Miguel Batista	.15
254	Jung Bong	.15
255	Deivi Cruz	.15
256	Alex Gonzalez	.15
257	Shawn Chacon	.15
258	Runelvys Hernandez	.15
259	Joe Mays	.15
260	Eric Gagne	.15
261	Dustan Mohr	.15
262	Tomokazu Ohka	.15
263	Eric Byrnes	.15
264	Frank Catalanotto	.15
265	Cristian Guzman	.15
266	Orlando Cabrera	.15
267	Mike Scioscia	.15
268	Bob Brenly	.15
269	Bobby Cox	.15
270	Mike Hargrove	.15
271	Grady Little	.15
272	Dusty Baker	.15
273	Jerry Manuel	.15
274	Bob Boone	.15
275	Eric Wedge	.15
276	Clint Hurdle	.15
277	Alan Trammell	.15
278	Jack McKeon	.15
279	Jimy Williams	.15
280	Tony Pena	.15
281	Jim Tracy	.15
282	Ned Yost	.15
283	Ron Gardenhire	.15
284	Frank Robinson	.25
285	Art Howe	.15
286	Joe Torre	.25
287	Ken Macha	.15
288	Larry Bowa	.15
289	Lloyd McClendon	.15
290	Bruce Bochy	.15
291	Felipe Alou	.15
292	Bob Melvin	.15
293	Tony LaRussa	.15
294	Lou Piniella	.15
295	Buck Showalter	.15
296	Carlos Tosca	.15
297	Anthony Acevedo **RC**	.25
298	Anthony Lerew **RC**	.75
299	Blake Hawksworth **RC**	.50
300	Brayan Pena **RC**	.50
301	Casey Myers **RC**	.50
302	Craig Ansman **RC**	.50
303	David Murphy	.40
304	David Crouthers	.15
305	Dioner Navarro **RC**	.40
306	Donald Levinski	.15
307	Jesse Roman **RC**	.40
308	Sung Ki Jung **RC**	.25
309	Jon Knott **RC**	.40
310	Josh Labandeira **RC**	.25
311	Kenny Perez **RC**	.25
312	Khalid Ballouli **RC**	.25
313	Kyle Davies **RC**	.40
314	Marcus McBeth **RC**	.40
315	Matt Creighton **RC**	.40
316	Chris O'Riordan **RC**	.50
317	Mike Gosling	.15
318	Nic Ungs **RC**	.40
319	Omar Falcon **RC**	.40
320	Rodney Choy Foo **RC**	.40
321	Tim Frend **RC**	.50
322	Todd Self **RC**	.50
323	Tydus Meadows **RC**	.40
324	Yadier Molina **RC**	.50
325	Zachary Duke **RC**	2.00
326	Zach Miner **RC**	1.00
327	Bernie Castro, Khalil Greene	.15
328	Ryan Madson, Elizardo Ramirez	.15
329	Rich Harden, Bobby Crosby	.15
330	Zack Greinke, Jimmy Gobble	.15
331	Bobby Jenks, Casey Kotchman	.15
332	Sammy Sosa	.50
333	Kevin Millwood	.25
334	Rafael Palmeiro	.25
335	Roger Clemens	.75
336	Eric Gagne	.15
337	Bill Mueller, Manny Ramirez, Derek Jeter	.50
338	Vernon Wells, Ichiro Suzuki, Michael Young	.40
339	Alex Rodriguez, Frank Thomas, Carlos Delgado	.50
340	Carlos Delgado, Alex Rodriguez, Bret Boone	.50
341	Pedro Martinez, Tim Hudson, Esteban Loaiza	.25
342	Esteban Loaiza, Pedro Martinez, Roy Halladay	.25
343	Albert Pujols, Todd Helton, Edgar Renteria	.50
344	Albert Pujols, Todd Helton, Juan Pierre	.50
345	Jim Thome, Richie Sexson, Javy Lopez	.25
346	Preston Wilson, Gary Sheffield, Jim Thome	.25
347	Jason Schmidt, Kevin Brown, Mark Prior	.50
348	Kerry Wood, Mark Prior, Javier Vazquez	.50
349	AL Division Series	.15
350	NL Division Series	.15
351	NL Championship Series	.15
352	AL Championship Series	.25
353	AL & NL Division Series	.15
354	AL Championship Series	.15
355	World Series Highlights	.25
356	Carlos Delgado	.25
357	Bret Boone	.15
358	Alex Rodriguez	.50
359	Bill Mueller	.15
360	Vernon Wells	.15
361	Garret Anderson	.15
362	Magglio Ordonez	.15
363	Jorge Posada	.15
364	Roy Halladay	.15
365	Andy Pettitte	.15
366	Frank Thomas	.25
367	Jody Gerut	.15
368	Sammy Sosa	.75
369	Joe Crede	.15
370	Gary Sheffield	.25
371	Coco Crisp	.15
372	Torii Hunter	.25
373	Derrek Lee	.15
374	Adam Everett	.15
375	Miguel Tejada	.25
376	Jeremy Affeldt	.15
377	Robin Ventura	.15
378	Scott Podsednik	.40
379	Matthew LeCroy	.15
380	Vladimir Guerrero	.40
381	Tony Clark	.15
382	Jeff Nelson	.15
383	Chris Singleton	.15
384	Bobby Abreu	.25
385	Josh Fogg	.15
386	Trevor Hoffman	.15
387	Jesse Foppert	.15
388	Edgar Martinez	.25
389	Edgar Renteria	.25
390	Chipper Jones	.50
391	Eric Munson	.15
392	Dewon Brazelton	.15
393	John Thomson	.15
394	Chris Woodward	.15
395	Aaron Sele	.15
396	Elmer Dessens	.15
397	Johnny Estrada	.15
398	Damian Moss	.15
399	Gabe Kapler	.15
400	Dontrelle Willis	.40
401	Troy Glaus	.25
402	Raul Mondesi	.20
403	Shane Reynolds	.15
404	Kurt Ainsworth	.15
405	Pedro J. Martinez	.50
406	Eric Karros	.15
407	Billy Koch	.15
408	Scott Schoeneweis	.15
409	Paul Wilson	.15
410	Mike Sweeney	.15
411	Jason Bay	.15
412	Mark Redman	.15
413	Jason Jennings	.15
414	Rondell White	.25
415	Todd Hundley	.15
416	Shannon Stewart	.15
417	Jae Weong Seo	.15
418	Livan Hernandez	.15
419	Mark Ellis	.15
420	Pat Burrell	.25
421	Mark Loretta	.15
422	Robb Nen	.15
423	Joel Pineiro	.15
424	Jason Simontacchi	.15
425	Sterling Hitchcock	.15
426	Rey Ordonez	.15
427	Greg Myers	.15
428	Shane Spencer	.15
429	Carlos Baerga	.15
430	Garret Anderson	.25
431	Horacio Ramirez	.15
432	Brian Roberts	.15
433	Damian Jackson	.15
434	Doug Glanville	.15
435	Brian Daubach	.15
436	Alex Escobar	.15
437	Alex Sanchez	.15
438	Jeff Bagwell	.40
439	Darrell May	.15
440	Shawn Green	.25
441	Geoff Jenkins	.25
442	Endy Chavez	.15
443	Nick Johnson	.15
444	Jose Guillen	.15
445	Tomas Perez	.15
446	Phil Nevin	.15
447	Jason Schmidt	.25
448	Julio Mateo	.15
449	So Taguchi	.15
450	Randy Johnson	.40
451	Paul Byrd	.15
452	Chone Figgins	.15
453	Larry Bigbie	.15
454	Scott Williamson	.15
455	Ramon Martinez	.15
456	Roberto Alomar	.25
457	Ryan Dempster	.15
458	Ryan Ludwick	.15
459	Ramon Santiago	.15
460	Jeff Conine	.15
461	Brad Lidge	.15
462	Ken Harvey	.15
463	Guillermo Mota	.15
464	Rick Reed	.15
465	Joey Eischen	.15
466	Wade Miller	.15
467	Steve Karsay	.15
468	Chase Utley	.25
469	Matt Stairs	.15
470	Yorvit Torrealba	.15
471	Joe Kennedy	.15
472	Reed Johnson	.15
473	Victor Zambrano	.15
474	Jeff DaVanon	.15
475	Luis Gonzalez	.25
476	Rod Barajas	.15
477	Ray King	.15
478	Jack Cust	.15
479	Omar Daal	.15
480	Todd Walker	.15
481	Shawn Estes	.15
482	Chris Reitsma	.15
483	Jake Westbrook	.15
484	Jeremy Bonderman	.15
485	A.J. Burnett	.15
486	Roy Oswalt	.25
487	Kevin Brown	.25
488	Eric Milton	.15
489	Claudio Vargas	.15
490	Roger Cedeno	.15
491	David Wells	.15
492	Scott Hatteberg	.15
493	Ricky Ledee	.15
494	Eric Young	.15
495	Armando Benitez	.15
496	Dan Haren	.15
497	Carl Crawford	.15
498	Laynce Nix	.15
499	Eric Hinske	.15
500	Ivan Rodriguez	.40
501	Scot Shields	.15
502	Brandon Webb	.15
503	Mark DeRosa	.15
504	Jhonny Peralta	.15
505	Adam Kennedy	.15
506	Tony Batista	.15
507	Jeff Suppan	.15
508	Kenny Lofton	.25
509	Scott Sullivan	.15
510	Ken Griffey Jr.	.60
511	Billy Traber	.15
512	Larry Walker	.25
513	Mike Maroth	.15
514	Todd Hollandsworth	.15
515	Kirk Saarloos	.15
516	Carlos Beltran	.25
517	Andy Ashby	.15
518	Jose Macias	.15
519	Karim Garcia	.15
520	Jose Reyes	.40
521	Brandon Duckworth	.15
522	Brian Giles	.25
523	J.T. Snow Jr.	.15
524	Jamie Moyer	.15
525	Jason Isringhausen	.15
526	Julio Lugo	.15
527	Mark Teixeira	.25
528	Cory Lidle	.15
529	Lyle Overbay	.15
530	Troy Percival	.15
531	Robby Hammock	.15
532	Robert Fick	.15
533	Jason Johnson	.15
534	Brandon Lyon	.15
535	Antonio Alfonseca	.15
536	Tom Goodwin	.15
537	Paul Konerko	.15
538	D'Angelo Jimenez	.15
539	Ben Broussard	.15
540	Magglio Ordonez	.25
541	Ellis Burks	.15
542	Carlos Pena	.15
543	Chad Fox	.15
544	Jeriome Robertson	.15
545	Travis Hafner	.15
546	Joe Randa	.15
547	Wil Cordero	.15
548	Brady Clark	.15
549	Ruben Sierra	.15
550	Barry Zito	.25
551	Brett Myers	.15
552	Oliver Perez	.15
553	Trey Hodges	.15
554	Benito Santiago	.15
555	David Ross	.15
556	Ramon Vazquez	.15
557	Joe Nathan	.15
558	Dan Wilson	.15
559	Garrett Stephenson	.15
560	Jim Edmonds	.25
561	Shawn Wooten	.15
562	Matt Kata	.15
563	Vinny Castilla	.15
564	Marty Cordova	.15
565	Aramis Ramirez	.15
566	Carl Everett	.15
567	Ryan Freel	.15
568	Jason Davis	.15
569	Mark Bellhorn	.15
570	Craig Monroe	.15
571	Ugueth Urbina	.15
572	Tim Redding	.15
573	Kevin Appier	.15
574	Jeromy Burnitz	.15
575	Miguel Cabrera	.40
576	Orlando Hernandez	.15
577	Casey Blake	.15
578	Aaron Boone	.15
579	Jermaine Dye	.15
580	Jerome Williams	.15
581	John Olerud	.15
582	Scott Rolen	.40
583	Bobby Kielty	.15
584	Travis Lee	.15
585	Jeff Cirillo	.15
586	Scott Spiezio	.15
587	Stephen Randolph	.15
588	Melvin Mora	.15
589	Mike Timlin	.15
590	Kerry Wood	.50
591	Tony Womack	.15
592	Jody Gerut	.15
593	Franklyn German	.15
594	Morgan Ensberg	.15
595	Odalis Perez	.15
596	Michael Cuddyer	.15
597	Jon Lieber	.15
598	Mike Williams	.15
599	Jose Hernandez	.15
600	Alfonso Soriano	.50
601	Marquis Grissom	.15
602	Matt Morris	.25
603	Damian Rolls	.15
604	Juan Gonzalez	.25
605	Aquilino Lopez	.15
606	Jose Valverde	.15
607	Scott Sauerbeck	.15
608	Joe Borowski	.15
609	Josh Bard	.15
610	Austin Kearns	.25
611	Chin-Hui Tsao	.15
612	Wilfredo Ledezma	.15
613	Aaron Guiel	.15
614	LaTroy Hawkins	.15
615	Tony Armas Jr.	.15
616	Steve Trachsel	.15
617	Ted Lilly	.15
618	Todd Pratt	.15
619	Sean Burroughs	.15
620	Rafael Palmeiro	.40
621	Jeremi Gonzalez	.15
622	Quinton McCracken	.15
623	David Ortiz	.25
624	Randall Simon	.15
625	Wily Mo Pena	.15
626	Nate Cornejo	.15
627	Brian Anderson	.15
628	Corey Koskie	.15
629	Keith Foulke	.15
630	Rheal Cormier	.15
631	Sidney Ponson	.15
632	Gary Matthews Jr.	.15
633	Herbert Perry	.15
634	Shea Hillenbrand	.15
635	Craig Biggio	.25
636	Barry Larkin	.25
637	Orlando Merced	.15
638	Anaheim Angels	.15
639	Arizona Diamondbacks	.15
640	Atlanta Braves	.15
641	Baltimore Orioles	.15
642	Boston Red Sox	.25
643	Chicago Cubs	.40
644	Chicago White Sox	.15
645	Cincinnati Reds	.15
646	Cleveland Indians	.15
647	Colorado Rockies	.15
648	Detroit Tigers	.15
649	Florida Marlins	.15
650	Houston Astros	.15
651	Kansas City Royals	.15
652	Los Angeles Dodgers	.15
653	Milwaukee Brewers	.15
654	Minnesota Twins	.15
655	Montreal Expos	.15
656	New York Mets	.15
657	New York Yankees	.50
658	Oakland Athletics	.15
659	Philadelphia Phillies	.15
660	Pittsburgh Pirates	.15
661	San Diego Padres	.15
662	San Francisco Giants	.15
663	Seattle Mariners	.15
664	St. Louis Cardinals	.15
665	Tampa Bay Devil Rays	.15
666	Texas Rangers	.15
667	Toronto Blue Jays	.15
668	Kyle Sleeth	.15
669	Bradley Sullivan	.15
670	Carlos Quentin	.50
671	Conor Jackson	1.00
672	Jeffrey Allison	.15
673	Matthew Moses	.25
674	Tim Stauffer	.15

675	Estee Harris **RC**	.25
676	David Aardsma	.15
677	Omar Quintanilla	.25
678	Aaron Hill	.15
679	Tony Richie	.15
680	Lastings Milledge	3.00
681	Brad Snyder	.15
682	Jason Hirsh	.50
683	Logan Kensing **RC**	.40
684	Chris Lubanski	.15
685	Ryan Harvey	.15
686	Ryan Wagner	.15
687	Rickie Weeks	.50
688	Jeremy Guthrie, Grady Sizemore	.25
689	Edwin Jackson, Greg Miller	.15
690	Neal Cotts, Jeremy Reed	.15
691	Nicholas Markakis, Adam Loewen	.15
692	Delmon Young, B.J. Upton	.75
693	Nomar Garciaparra, Alfonso Soriano	.50
694	Ichiro Suzuki, Albert Pujols	.50
695	Jim Thome, Mike Schmidt	.40
696	Mike Mussina	.25
697	Bengie Molina	.15
698	John Olerud	.15
699	Bret Boone	.25
700	Eric Chavez	.25
701	Alex Rodriguez	.75
702	Mike Cameron	.15
703	Ichiro Suzuki	.75
704	Torii Hunter	.25
705	Mike Hampton	.15
706	Mike Matheny	.15
707	Derrek Lee	.15
708	Luis Castillo	.15
709	Scott Rolen	.40
710	Edgar Renteria	.25
711	Andruw Jones	.25
712	Jose Cruz Jr.	.15
713	Jim Edmonds	.25
714	Roy Halladay	.25
715	Eric Gagne	.25
716	Alex Rodriguez	.75
717	Angel Berroa	.15
718	Dontrelle Willis	.25
719	Todd Helton	.25
720	Marcus Giles	.15
721	Edgar Renteria	.25
722	Scott Rolen	.40
723	Albert Pujols	.75
724	Gary Sheffield	.25
725	Javy Lopez	.25
726	Eric Gagne	.25
727	Randy Wolf	.15
728	Bobby Cox	.15
729	Scott Podsednik	.40
730	World Series Game 4	.15
731	World Series Game 5	.15
732	World Series Game 6	.15
733	World Series MVP	.25

Gold

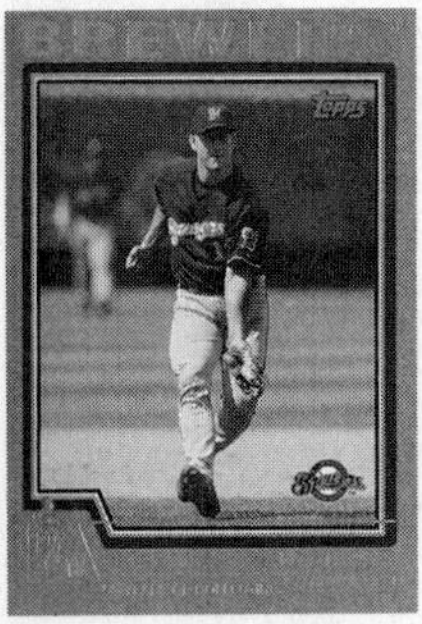

Stars (1-733):	5-10X
Production 2,004 Sets	

Black

Black (1-733):	15-30X
Production 53 Sets	

1st Edition

	NM/M
Stars:	3-5X
HTA Exclusive	
1st Edition Pack (10):	3.00
1st Edition Box (20):	55.00

2004 Topps Team Factory Sets

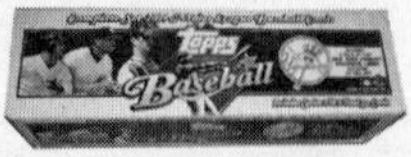

	NM/M
Complete Astros Set (737):	75.00
Complete Cubs Set (737):	75.00
Complete Red Sox Set (737):	75.00
Complete Yankees Set (737):	75.00

Astros Prospects

1	Brooks Conrad	1.00
2	Hector Giminez	1.00
3	Kevin Davidson	1.00
4	Chris Burke	3.00
5	John Buck	1.00

Cubs Prospects

1	Bobby Brownlie	2.00
2	Felix Pie	3.00
3	Jon Connolly	1.00
4	David Kelton	1.00
5	Ricky Nolasco	2.00

Red Sox Prospects

1	David Murphy	1.00
2	Kevin Youkilis	3.00
3	Juan Cedeno	1.00
4	Matt Murton	1.00
5	Kenny Perez	1.00

Yankees Prospects

1	Rudy Guillen	1.00
2	David Parrish	2.00
3	Brad Halsey	1.00
4	Hector Made	1.00
5	Robinson Cano	6.00

All-Stars

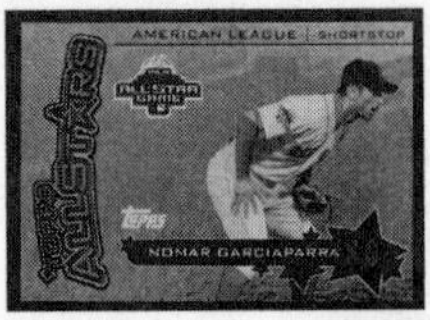

		NM/M
Complete Set (20):		20.00
Common Player:		.50
Inserted 1:16		
TAS1	Jason Giambi	1.50
TAS2	Ichiro Suzuki	2.50
TAS3	Alex Rodriguez	3.00
TAS4	Albert Pujols	3.00
TAS5	Alfonso Soriano	1.50
TAS6	Nomar Garciaparra	2.50
TAS7	Andruw Jones	1.00
TAS8	Carlos Delgado	.75
TAS9	Gary Sheffield	.75
TAS10	Jorge Posada	.75
TAS11	Magglio Ordonez	.75
TAS12	Kerry Wood	1.50
TAS13	Garret Anderson	.75
TAS14	Bret Boone	.50
TAS15	Hank Blalock	.75
TAS16	Mike Lowell	.50
TAS17	Todd Helton	1.00
TAS18	Vernon Wells	.50
TAS19	Roger Clemens	3.00
TAS20	Scott Rolen	1.50

All-Star Stitches

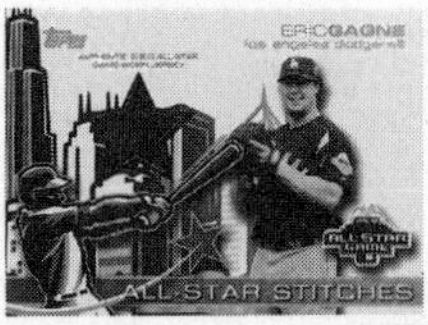

		NM/M
Common Player:		5.00
Inserted 1:137		
GA	Garret Anderson	6.00
HB	Hank Blalock	6.00
AB	Aaron Boone	5.00
BD	Brendan Donnelly	5.00
CE	Carl Everett	5.00
KF	Keith Foulke	5.00
RF	Rafael Furcal	8.00
EGA	Eric Gagne	8.00
NG	Nomar Garciaparra	15.00
TG	Troy Glaus	8.00
EG	Eddie Guardado	5.00
SH	Shigetoshi Hasegawa	5.00
TH	Todd Helton	8.00
RH	Ramon Hernandez	5.00
AJ	Andruw Jones	8.00
EL	Esteban Loaiza	5.00
PL	Paul LoDuca	5.00
JL	Javy Lopez	8.00
ML	Mike Lowell	5.00
EM	Edgar Martinez	8.00
MMO	Melvin Mora	5.00
JM	Jamie Moyer	5.00
MM	Mark Mulder	6.00
RO	Russ Ortiz	6.00
JP	Jorge Posada	8.00
ER	Edgar Renteria	5.00
AR	Alex Rodriguez	15.00
SR	Scott Rolen	10.00
JS	Jason Schmidt	6.00
JV	Jose Vidro	5.00
BW	Billy Wagner	5.00
VW	Vernon Wells	6.00
RWH	Rondell White	5.00
WW	Woody Williams	6.00
PW	Preston Wilson	5.00
RW	Randy Wolf	5.00
KW	Kerry Wood	8.00

All-Star Patch Relics

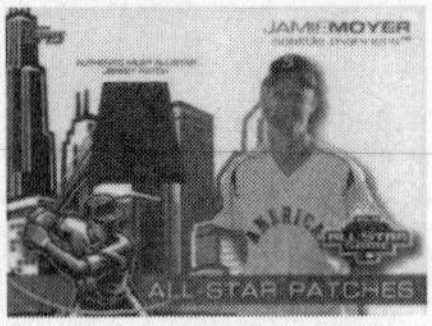

No Pricing
Inserted 1:7,698

American Treasures Cut Signatures

No Pricing
Inserted 1:658,152

American Treasures Dual

No Pricing

American Treasures Presidential Signatures

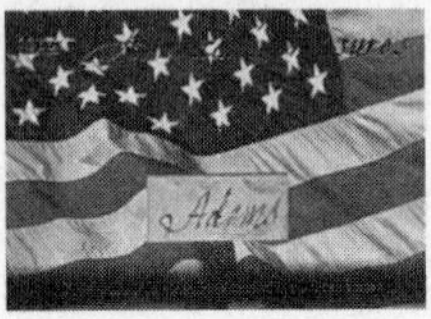

No Pricing
Production One Set

Autographs

		NM/M
Common Player:		
JB	Josh Beckett	50.00
HB	Hank Blalock	20.00
CF	Cliff Floyd	8.00
JG	Jay Gibbons	15.00
KG	Khalil Greene	10.00
EH	Eric Hinske	10.00
TH	Torii Hunter	25.00
AK	Austin Kearns	25.00
PK	Paul Konerko	15.00
PL	Paul LoDuca	10.00
ML	Mike Lowell	8.00
VM	Victor Martinez	20.00
MO	Magglio Ordonez	15.00
JP	Josh Phelps	8.00
MP	Mark Prior	40.00
ER	Elizardo Ramirez	8.00
BS	Benito Santiago	15.00
MS	Mike Sweeney	20.00
MT	Mark Teixeira	25.00
BU	B.J. Upton	20.00
JV	Jose Vidro	8.00
Series 2		
GA	Garret Anderson	35.00
LB	Lance Berkman	35.00
AB	Aaron Boone	35.00
BB	Bobby Brownlie	30.00
MC	Miguel Cabrera	40.00
ZG	Zack Greinke	20.00
AH	Aubrey Huff	20.00
DM	Dustin McGowan	15.00
SP	Scott Podsednik	25.00
JP	Jorge Posada	40.00
IR	Ivan Rodriguez	45.00
SR	Scott Rolen	30.00
DW	Dontrelle Willis	30.00

Derby Digs

		NM/M
Common Player:		8.00
Inserted 1:585		
GA	Garret Anderson	8.00
BB	Bret Boone	8.00
CD	Carlos Delgado	8.00
JE	Jim Edmonds	8.00
JG	Jason Giambi	15.00
AP	Albert Pujols	25.00
RS	Richie Sexson	8.00

Draft Pick Bonus

		NM/M
Complete Set (15):		50.00
Complete Holiday Set (10):		30.00
Complete Retail Set (5):		20.00
1	Josh Johnson	4.00
2	Donny Lucy	4.00
3	Greg Golson	6.00
4	K.C. Herren	4.00
5	Jeff Marquez	4.00
6	Mark Rogers	8.00
7	Eric Hurley	4.00
8	Gio Gonzalez	6.00
9	Thomas Diamond	6.00
10	Matt Bush	8.00
11	Kyle Waldrop	6.00
12	Neil Walker	6.00
13	Mike Ferris	4.00
14	Ray Liotta	6.00
15	Phillip Hughes	15.00

Fall Classic Covers

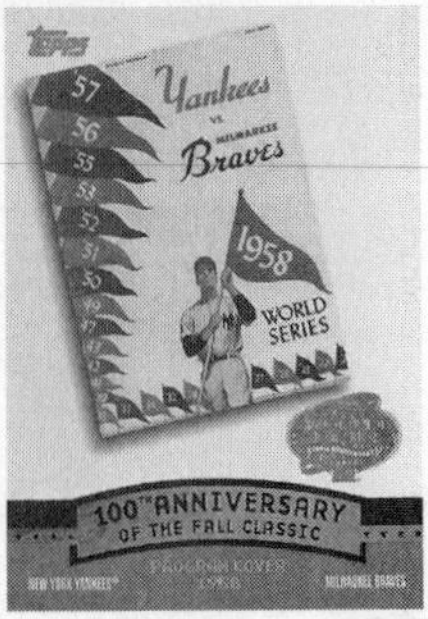

		NM/M
Complete Set (99):		125.00
Common Card:		2.00
Inserted 1:12		
FC1903	1903 World Series	2.00
FC1905	1905 World Series	2.00
FC1906	1906 World Series	2.00
FC1907	1907 World Series	2.00
FC1908	1908 World Series	2.00
FC1909	1909 World Series	2.00
FC1910	1910 World Series	2.00
FC1911	1911 World Series	2.00
FC1912	1912 World Series	2.00
FC1913	1913 World Series	2.00
FC1914	1914 World Series	2.00
FC1915	1915 World Series	2.00
FC1916	1916 World Series	2.00
FC1917	1917 World Series	2.00
FC1918	1918 World Series	2.00
FC1919	1919 World Series	2.00
FC1920	1920 World Series	2.00
FC1921	1921 World Series	2.00
FC1922	1922 World Series	2.00
FC1923	1923 World Series	2.00
FC1924	1924 World Series	2.00
FC1925	1925 World Series	2.00
FC1926	1926 World Series	2.00
FC1927	1927 World Series	2.00
FC1928	1928 World Series	2.00
FC1929	1929 World Series	2.00
FC1930	1930 World Series	2.00
FC1931	1931 World Series	2.00
FC1932	1932 World Series	2.00
FC1933	1933 World Series	2.00
FC1934	1934 World Series	2.00
FC1935	1935 World Series	2.00
FC1936	1936 World Series	2.00
FC1937	1937 World Series	2.00
FC1938	1938 World Series	2.00
FC1939	1939 World Series	2.00
FC1940	1940 World Series	2.00
FC1941	1941 World Series	2.00
FC1942	1942 World Series	2.00
FC1943	1943 World Series	2.00
FC1944	1944 World Series	2.00
FC1945	1945 World Series	2.00
FC1946	1946 World Series	2.00
FC1947	1947 World Series	2.00
FC1948	1948 World Series	2.00
FC1949	1949 World Series	2.00
FC1950	1950 World Series	2.00
FC1951	1951 World Series	2.00
FC1952	1952 World Series	2.00
FC1953	1953 World Series	2.00
FC1954	1954 World Series	2.00
FC1955	1955 World Series	2.00
FC1956	1956 World Series	2.00
FC1957	1957 World Series	2.00
FC1958	1958 World Series	2.00
FC1959	1959 World Series	2.00
FC1960	1960 World Series	2.00
FC1961	1961 World Series	2.00
FC1962	1962 World Series	2.00
FC1963	1963 World Series	2.00
FC1964	1964 World Series	2.00
FC1965	1965 World Series	2.00
FC1966	1966 World Series	2.00
FC1967	1967 World Series	2.00
FC1968	1968 World Series	2.00
FC1969	1969 World Series	2.00
FC1970	1970 World Series	2.00
FC1971	1971 World Series	2.00
FC1972	1972 World Series	2.00
FC1973	1973 World Series	2.00
FC1974	1974 World Series	2.00
FC1975	1975 World Series	2.00
FC1976	1976 World Series	2.00
FC1977	1977 World Series	2.00
FC1978	1978 World Series	2.00
FC1979	1979 World Series	2.00
FC1980	1980 World Series	2.00
FC1981	1981 World Series	2.00
FC1982	1982 World Series	2.00
FC1983	1983 World Series	2.00
FC1984	1984 World Series	2.00
FC1985	1985 World Series	2.00
FC1986	1986 World Series	2.00

FC1987	1987 World Series	2.00
FC1988	1988 World Series	2.00
FC1989	1989 World Series	2.00
FC1990	1990 World Series	2.00
FC1991	1991 World Series	2.00
FC1992	1992 World Series	2.00
FC1993	1993 World Series	2.00
FC1995	1995 World Series	2.00
FC1996	1996 World Series	2.00
FC1997	1997 World Series	2.00
FC1998	1998 World Series	2.00
FC1999	1999 World Series	2.00
FC2000	2000 World Series	2.00
FC2001	2001 World Series	2.00
FC2002	2002 World Series	2.00
FC2003	2003 World Series	2.00

Hit Parade

Rafael Palmeiro

		NM/M
Complete Set (30):		20.00
Common Player:		.50
Inserted 1:7		
HP1	Sammy Sosa	3.00
HP2	Rafael Palmeiro	1.00
HP3	Fred McGriff	.50
HP4	Ken Griffey Jr.	2.00
HP5	Juan Gonzalez	1.00
HP6	Frank Thomas	1.00
HP7	Andres Galarraga	.50
HP8	Jim Thome	1.50
HP9	Jeff Bagwell	1.00
HP10	Mike Piazza	2.00
HP11	Rafael Palmeiro	1.00
HP12	Sammy Sosa	3.00
HP13	Fred McGriff	.50
HP14	Andres Galarraga	.50
HP15	Juan Gonzalez	1.00
HP16	Frank Thomas	1.00
HP17	Jeff Bagwell	1.00
HP18	Ken Griffey Jr.	2.00
HP19	Ruben Sierra	.50
HP20	Ellis Burks	.50
HP21	Rafael Palmeiro	1.00
HP22	Roberto Alomar	.75
HP23	Julio Franco	.50
HP24	Andres Galarraga	.50
HP25	Fred McGriff	.50
HP26	Craig Biggio	.75
HP27	Barry Larkin	.75
HP28	Edgar Martinez	.50
HP29	Ellis Burks	.50
HP30	Sammy Sosa	3.00

Hobby Masters

		NM/M
Complete Set (20):		40.00
Common Player:		.75
Inserted 1:12		
HM1	Albert Pujols	3.00
HM2	Mark Prior	4.00
HM3	Alex Rodriguez	4.00
HM4	Nomar Garciaparra	4.00
HM5	Barry Bonds	3.00
HM6	Sammy Sosa	3.00
HM7	Alfonso Soriano	2.00
HM8	Ichiro Suzuki	2.50
HM9	Derek Jeter	4.00
HM10	Jim Thome	1.50
HM11	Jason Giambi	1.50
HM12	Mike Piazza	2.50
HM13	Barry Zito	1.00
HM14	Randy Johnson	2.00
HM15	Adam Dunn	1.00
HM16	Vladimir Guerrero	2.00
HM17	Gary Sheffield	.75
HM18	Carlos Delgado	1.00
HM19	Chipper Jones	2.50
HM20	Dontrelle Willis	1.00

Own the Game

Garret Anderson

		NM/M
Complete Set (30):		25.00
Common Player:		.50
Inserted 1:18		
OG1	Jim Thome	1.50
OG2	Albert Pujols	3.00
OG3	Alex Rodriguez	3.00
OG4	Barry Bonds	4.00
OG5	Ichiro Suzuki	2.00
OG6	Derek Jeter	3.00
OG7	Nomar Garciaparra	3.00
OG8	Alfonso Soriano	1.50
OG9	Gary Sheffield	.75
OG10	Jason Giambi	1.00
OG11	Todd Helton	1.00
OG12	Garret Anderson	.50
OG13	Carlos Delgado	1.00
OG14	Manny Ramirez	1.00
OG15	Richie Sexson	.75
OG16	Vernon Wells	.50
OG17	Preston Wilson	.50
OG18	Frank Thomas	1.00
OG19	Shawn Green	.75
OG20	Rafael Furcal	.50
OG21	Juan Pierre	.50
OG22	Javy Lopez	.50
OG23	Edgar Renteria	.50
OG24	Mark Prior	3.00
OG25	Pedro J. Martinez	1.50
OG26	Kerry Wood	1.00
OG27	Curt Schilling	.50
OG28	Roy Halladay	.50
OG29	Eric Gagne	.50
OG30	Brandon Webb	.50

Presidential Pastime

		NM/M
Complete Set (42):		100.00
Common President:		3.00
Inserted 1:6		
PP1	George Washington	8.00
PP2	John Adams	4.00
PP3	Thomas Jefferson	4.00
PP4	James Madison	4.00
PP5	James Monroe	4.00
PP6	John Quincy Adams	4.00
PP7	Andrew Jackson	3.00
PP8	Martin Van Buren	3.00
PP9	William H. Harrison	4.00
PP10	John Tyler	4.00
PP11	James K. Polk	3.00
PP12	Zachary Taylor	3.00
PP13	Millard Fillmore	3.00
PP14	Franklin Pierce	3.00
PP15	James Buchanan	3.00
PP16	Abraham Lincoln	6.00
PP17	Andrew Johnson	3.00
PP18	Ulysses S. Grant	5.00
PP19	Rutherford B. Hayes	3.00
PP20	James Garfield	3.00
PP21	Chester A. Arthur	3.00
PP22	Grover Cleveland	3.00
PP23	Benjamin Harrison	3.00
PP24	William McKinley	3.00
PP25	Theodore Roosevelt	4.00
PP26	William H. Taft	4.00
PP27	Woodrow Wilson	4.00
PP28	Warren Harding	4.00
PP29	Calvin Coolidge	4.00
PP30	Herbert Hoover	3.00
PP31	Franklin D. Roosevelt	4.00
PP32	Harry S. Truman	4.00
PP33	Dwight D. Eisenhower	4.00
PP34	John F. Kennedy	6.00
PP35	Lyndon B. Johnson	3.00
PP36	Richard Nixon	4.00
PP37	Gerald Ford	3.00
PP38	Jimmy Carter	3.00
PP39	Ronald Reagan	3.00
PP40	George H.W. Bush	3.00
PP41	Bill Clinton	4.00
PP42	George W. Bush	3.00

Presidential First Pitch Relics

		NM/M
Common Player:		15.00
Inserted 1:592		
GHB	George H.W. Bush	25.00
GB	George W. Bush	25.00
BC	Bill Clinton	40.00
CC	Calvin Coolidge	15.00
DE	Dwight D. Eisenhower	15.00
GF	Gerald Ford	30.00
WH	Warren Harding	30.00
HH	Herbert Hoover	30.00
LJ	Lyndon B. Johnson	20.00
JK	John F. Kennedy	50.00
RN	Richard Nixon	30.00
RR	Ronald Reagan	30.00
FR	Franklin D. Roosevelt	40.00
WT	William H. Taft	25.00
HT	Harry S. Truman	30.00
WW	Woodrow Wilson	25.00

Series Seats Relics

		NM/M
Common Player:		10.00
Inserted 1:316		
LA	Luis Aparicio	15.00
BF	Bob Feller	12.00
RJ	Reggie Jackson	20.00
AK	Al Kaline	20.00
HK	Harmon Killebrew	25.00
WM	Willie Mays	25.00
BM	Bill Mazeroski	20.00
PM	Paul Molitor	15.00
JP	Jim Palmer	15.00
LP	Lou Piniella	10.00
BP	Boog Powell	10.00
BR	Brooks Robinson	15.00
FR	Frank Robinson	15.00
WS	Warren Spahn	15.00
RY	Robin Yount	20.00

Series Stitches Relics

		NM/M
Common Player:		10.00
JBE	Josh Beckett	10.00
JB	Johnny Bench	25.00
GB	George Brett	30.00
JCA	Jose Canseco	15.00
GC	Gary Carter	12.00
JC	Joe Carter	10.00
RC	Roger Clemens	20.00
LD	Lenny Dykstra	15.00
SG	Steve Garvey	15.00
KG	Kirk Gibson	10.00
DG	Dwight Gooden	10.00
RJA	Reggie Jackson	20.00
RJ	Randy Johnson	10.00
CJ	Chipper Jones	15.00
DJ	David Justice	15.00
HK	Harmon Killebrew	30.00
WM	Willie Mays	50.00
PO	Paul O'Neill	20.00
KP	Kirby Puckett	25.00
FR	Frank Robinson	20.00
MS	Mike Schmidt	30.00
TS	Tom Seaver	25.00
AS	Alfonso Soriano	15.00
RY	Robin Yount	20.00

Team Topps Legends Autos.

		NM/M
Inserted 1:766		
SG	Steve Garvey	15.00
BP	Boog Powell	10.00

World Series Highlights

		NM/M
Complete Set (30):		35.00
Common Player:		1.00
Inserted 1:18		
LB	Lou Brock	1.00
CF	Carlton Fisk	1.50
KG	Kirk Gibson	1.00
RJ	Reggie Jackson	2.00

DL	Don Larsen	1.00
MM	Willie Mays	4.00
BM	Bill Mazeroski	1.00
SM	Stan Musial	3.00
JP	Jim Palmer	1.00
KP	Kirby Puckett	2.00
BR	Brooks Robinson	2.00
MS	Mike Schmidt	4.00
TS	Tom Seaver	2.00
CY	Carl Yastrzemski	2.00
RY	Robin Yount	2.00
Series 2		
DB	Dusty Baker	1.00
JB	Johnny Bench	2.50
JCA	Jose Canseco	1.50
JC	Joe Carter	1.00
WF	Whitey Ford	1.00
LG	Luis Gonzalez	1.00
AJ	Andruw Jones	1.50
DJ	David Justice	1.00
AK	Al Kaline	2.00
WM	Willie McCovey	1.00
JP	Johnny Podres	1.00
FR	Frank Robinson	1.50
OS	Ozzie Smith	2.00
DS	Duke Snider	1.50
BT	Bobby Thomson	1.00

World Series Highlights Autographs

		NM/M
Common Player:		
LB	Lou Brock	30.00
CF	Carlton Fisk	50.00
KG	Kirk Gibson	30.00
DL	Don Larsen	25.00
BM	Bill Mazeroski	30.00
JP	Jim Palmer	25.00
BR	Brooks Robinson	40.00
MS	Mike Schmidt	65.00
RY	Robin Yount	50.00
Series 2		
DB	Dusty Baker	20.00
JB	Johnny Bench	50.00
WF	Whitey Ford	35.00
RJ	Reggie Jackson	40.00
DJ	David Justice	30.00
AK	Al Kaline	40.00
SM	Stan Musial	75.00
JP	Johnny Podres	15.00
DS	Duke Snider	35.00
BT	Bobby Thomson	20.00

2004 Topps Traded & Rookies

Alex Rodriguez

		NM/M
Complete Set (220):		50.00
Common Player:		.10
Chrome cards:		2-4X
Pack (10):		4.00
Box (24):		85.00
T1	Pokey Reese	.10
T2	Tony Womack	.10
T3	Michael Barrett	.10
T4	Juan Uribe	.10
T5	J.D. Drew	.25
T6	Marlon Anderson	.10
T7	Carlos Guillen	.10
T8	Royce Clayton	.10
T9	Fernando Vina	.10
T10	Milton Bradley	.10
T11	Eddie Perez	.10
T12	Ben Grieve	.10
T13	Brian Jordan	.10
T14	Tony Graffanino	.10
T15	Billy Wagner	.10
T16	Terrence Long	.10
T17	Casey Fossum	.10
T18	Denny Hocking	.10

T19	Reggie Sanders	.10
T20	Javy Lopez	.25
T21	Jay Payton	.10
T22	Cliff Politte	.10
T23	Eddie Guardado	.10
T24	Andy Pettitte	.50
T25	Richie Sexson	.40
T26	Ronnie Belliard	.10
T27	Michael Tucker	.10
T28	Brad Fullmer	.10
T29	Orlando Palmeiro	.10
T30	Bartolo Colon	.25
T31	Larry Walker	.40
T32	Mark Kotsay	.10
T33	Jason Marquis	.10
T34	Dustan Mohr	.10
T35	Javier Vazquez	.25
T36	Nomar Garciaparra	1.50
T37	Tino Martinez	.25
T38	Hee Seop Choi	.10
T39	Damian Miller	.10
T40	Jose Lima	.10
T41	Todd Zeile	.10
T42	Raul Ibanez	.10
T43	Danys Baez	.10
T44	Tony Clark	.10
T45	Greg Maddux	1.00
T46	Craig Counsell	.10
T47	Orlando Cabrera	.25
T48	Jose Cruz Jr.	.10
T49	Kris Benson	.10
T50	Alex Rodriguez	2.00
T51	Steve Finley	.10
T52	Ramon Hernandez	.10
T53	Esteban Loaiza	.10
T54	Ugueth Urbina	.10
T55	Jeff Weaver	.10
T56	Flash Gordon	.10
T57	Jose Contreras	.10
T58	Paul LoDuca	.10
T59	Junior Spivey	.10
T60	Curt Schilling	1.00
T61	Brad Penny	.10
T62	Braden Looper	.10
T63	Miguel Cairo	.10
T64	Juan Encarnacion	.10
T65	Miguel Batista	.10
T66	Terry Francona	.10
T67	Lee Mazzilli	.10
T68	Al Pedrique	.10
T69	Ozzie Guillen	.10
T70	Phil Garner	.10
T71	Matt Bush **RC**	1.50
T72	Homer Bailey **RC**	4.00
T73	Greg Golson **RC**	2.00
T74	Kyle Waldrop **RC**	1.00
T75	Richie Robnett **RC**	1.00
T76	Jay Rainville **RC**	1.50
T77	Bill Bray **RC**	.50
T78	Phillip Hughes **RC**	8.00
T79	Scott Elbert **RC**	1.00
T80	Josh Fields **RC**	2.00
T81	Justin Orenduff **RC**	.75
T82	Dan Putnam **RC**	.75
T83	Chris Nelson **RC**	2.50
T84	Blake DeWitt **RC**	2.50
T85	J.P. Howell **RC**	1.00
T86	Huston Street **RC**	2.00
T87	Kurt Suzuki **RC**	1.50
T88	Erick San Pedro **RC**	.50
T89	Matt Tuiasosopo **RC**	1.50
T90	Matt Macri **RC**	1.00
T91	Chad Tracy	.20
T92	Scott Hairston	.20
T93	Jonny Gomes	.20
T94	Chin-Feng Chen	.20
T95	Chien-Ming Wang	.50
T96	Dustin McGowan	.20
T97	Chris Burke	.20
T98	Denny Bautista	.20
T99	Preston Larrison	.20
T100	Kevin Youkilis	.40
T101	John Maine	.20
T102	Guillermo Quiroz	.20
T103	David Krynzel	.20
T104	David Kelton	.20
T105	Edwin Encarnacion	.20
T106	Chad Gaudin	.20
T107	Sergio Mitre	.20
T108	Laynce Nix	.20
T109	David Parrish	.20
T110	Brandon Claussen	.20
T111	Frank Francisco **RC**	.25
T112	Brian Dallimore **RC**	.25
T113	Jim Crowell **RC**	.25
T114	Andres Blanco **RC**	.50
T115	Eduardo Villacis **RC**	.50
T116	Kazuhito Tadano **RC**	.50
T117	Aarom Baldiris **RC**	.25
T118	Justin Germano **RC**	.25
T119	Joey Gathright **RC**	1.00
T120	Franklyn Gracesqui **RC**	.25
T121	Chin-Lung Hu **RC**	1.00
T122	Scott Olsen **RC**	1.00
T123	Tyler Davidson	.25
T124	Fausto Carmona **RC**	.50
T125	Tim Hutting **RC**	.25
T126	Ryan Meaux **RC**	.25
T127	Jon Connolly **RC**	.75
T128	Hector Made **RC**	.75
T129	Jamie Brown **RC**	.25
T130	Paul McAnulty **RC**	.50
T131	Chris Saenz **RC**	.25
T132	Marland Williams **RC**	.25
T133	Mike Huggins **RC**	.25
T134	Jesse Crain	.50
T135	Chad Bentz **RC**	.50
T136	Kazuo Matsui **RC**	.75
T137	Paul Maholm **RC**	.75
T138	Brock Jacobsen **RC**	.25
T139	Casey Daigle **RC**	.25
T140	Nyjer Morgan **RC**	.25
T141	Tom Mastny **RC**	.50
T142	Kody Kirkland **RC**	.50
T143	Jose Capellan **RC**	.50
T144	Felix Hernandez **RC**	5.00
T145	Shawn Hill **RC**	.25
T146	Danny Gonzalez **RC**	.25
T147	Scott Dohmann **RC**	.25
T148	Tommy Murphy **RC**	.50
T149	Akinori Otsuka **RC**	.50
T150	Miguel Perez **RC**	.50
T151	Mike Rouse	.25
T152	Ramon Ramirez **RC**	.50
T153	Luke Hughes **RC**	.50
T154	Howard Kendrick **RC**	5.00
T155	Ryan Budde	.25
T156	Charlie Zink **RC**	.25
T157	Warner Madrigal **RC**	.50
T158	Jason Szuminski **RC**	.25
T159	Chad Chop **RC**	.25
T160	Shingo Takatsu **RC**	.50
T161	Matt Lemanczyk **RC**	.25
T162	Wardell Starling **RC**	.50
T163	Nick Gorneault **RC**	.25
T164	Scott Proctor **RC**	.50
T165	Brooks Conrad **RC**	.50
T166	Hector Gimenez **RC**	.50
T167	Kevin Howard **RC**	.50
T168	Vince Perkins **RC**	.50
T169	Brock Peterson **RC**	.25
T170	Chris Shelton **RC**	1.00
T171	Erick Aybar **RC**	1.00
T172	Paul Bacot **RC**	.25
T173	Matt Capps **RC**	.25
T174	Kory Casto	.25
T175	Juan Cedeno **RC**	.25
T176	Vito Chiaravalloti **RC**	.50
T177	Alec Zumwalt **RC**	.25
T178	J.J. Furmaniak **RC**	.50
T179	Lee Gwaltney **RC**	.50
T180	Donald Kelly **RC**	.25
T181	Benji DeQuin **RC**	.25
T182	Brant Colamarino **RC**	.75
T183	Juan Gutierrez **RC**	.50
T184	Carl Loadenthal **RC**	.50
T185	Ricky Nolasco	1.50
T186	Jeff Salazar **RC**	1.00
T187	Rob Tejeda **RC**	.50
T188	Alex Romero **RC**	.25
T189	Yoann Torrealba **RC**	.25
T190	Carlos Sosa **RC**	.25
T191	Tim Bittner **RC**	.50
T192	Chris Aguila **RC**	.25
T193	Jason Frasor **RC**	.25
T194	Reid Gorecki **RC**	.50
T195	Dustin Nippert **RC**	.50
T196	Javier Guzman **RC**	.25
T197	Harvey Garcia **RC**	.50
T198	Ivan Ochoa **RC**	.25
T199	Dave Wallace **RC**	.25
T200	Joel Zumaya **RC**	2.50
T201	Casey Kopitzke **RC**	.25
T202	Lincoln Holdzkom **RC**	.25
T203	Chad Santos **RC**	.25
T204	Brian Pilkington **RC**	.25
T205	Terry Jones **RC**	.25
T206	Jerome Gamble **RC**	.25
T207	Brad Eldred **RC**	.50
T208	David Pauley **RC**	1.00
T209	Kevin Davidson **RC**	.25
T210	Damaso Espino **RC**	.25
T211	Tom Farmer **RC**	.50
T212	Michael Mooney **RC**	.25
T213	James Tomlin **RC**	.25
T214	Greg Thissen **RC**	.25
T215	Calvin Hayes **RC**	.25
T216	Fernando Cortez **RC**	.25
T217	Sergio Silva **RC**	.25
T218	Jon DeVries **RC**	.25
T219	Don Sutton **RC**	1.00
T220	Leo Nunez **RC**	.25
T221	Barry Bonds HTA Redemption	5.00

Gold

Stars:	5-10X
Rookies:	2-3X

Production 2,004 Sets

X-Fractor

No Pricing
Production 20 Sets

Chrome Refractor

Stars:	4-8X
Rookies:	2-4X

Inserted 1:12

Blue Refractor

No Pricing
Production One Set

Printing Plates

No pricing due to scarcity.

Dual Transactions Relic

		NM/M
Common Player:		
Inserted 1:562		
RP	Rafael Palmeiro	15.00
AR	Alex Rodriguez	25.00
CS	Curt Schilling	15.00

Future Phenoms

		NM/M
Common Player:		5.00
KC	Kevin Cash	5.00
BC	Bobby Crosby	10.00
ED	Eric Duncan	5.00
AG	Adrian Gonzalez	8.00
NG	Nick Green	5.00
JH	J.J. Hardy	5.00
EJ	Edwin Jackson	5.00
MM	Mark Malaska	5.00
VM	Victor Martinez	8.00
KM	Kazuo Matsui	10.00
LM	Lastings Milledge	15.00
JM	Justin Morneau	10.00
DN	Dioner Navarro	8.00
RN	Ramon Nivar	5.00
BU	B.J. Upton	12.00
JW	Jayson Werth	10.00
DY	Delmon Young	10.00

Hall of Fame Relic

		NM/M
Common Player:		
DE	Dennis Eckersley	10.00
PM	Paul Molitor	15.00

Hall of Fame Dual Relic

		NM/M
Inserted 1:3,388		
ME	Paul Molitor, Dennis Eckersley	30.00

Signature Moves

		NM/M
Common Autograph:		10.00
MB	Milton Bradley	15.00
MK	Mark Kotsay	10.00
EM	Eli Marrero	10.00
MN	Mike Neu	10.00
AR	Alex Rodriguez	160.00
JV	Javier Vazquez	15.00
FV	Fernando Vina	10.00
AW	Adam Wainwright	35.00

Signature Cuts

No Pricing
Production One Set

Transactions Relics

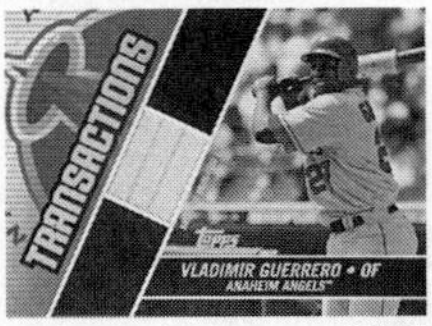
TRANSACTIONS
VLADIMIR GUERRERO • OF
ANAHEIM ANGELS

		NM/M
Common Player:		5.00
Inserted 1:106		
RA	Roberto Alomar	8.00
JB	Jeromy Burnitz	5.00
HC	Hee Seop Choi	5.00
RC	Roger Clemens	15.00
CE	Carl Everett	5.00
JG	Juan Gonzalez	8.00
VG	Vladimir Guerrero	10.00
BJ	Brian Jordan	5.00
KL	Kenny Lofton	5.00
JL	Javy Lopez	5.00
RP	Rafael Palmeiro	8.00
AP	Andy Pettitte	8.00
AR	Alex Rodriguez	25.00
IR	Ivan Rodriguez	10.00
RS	Reggie Sanders	5.00
RLS	Richie Sexson	8.00
GS	Gary Sheffield	10.00
MT	Miguel Tejada	8.00
RW	Rondell White	5.00

2004 Topps All-Time Fan Favorites

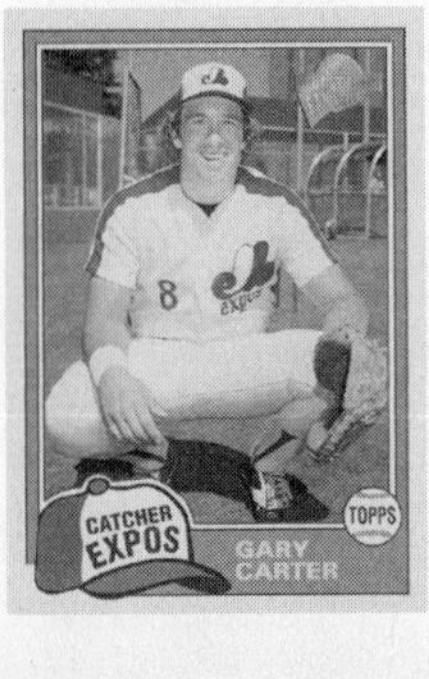
CATCHER
EXPOS
TOPPS
GARY CARTER

		NM/M
Complete Set (150):		35.00
Common Player:		.25
Pack (6):		4.00
Box (24):		80.00
1	Willie Mays	2.50
2	Bob Gibson	.75
3	Dave Steib	.25
4	Tim McCarver	.25
5	Reggie Jackson	.75
6	John Candelaria	.25
7	Lenny Dykstra	.25
8	Tony Oliva	.50
9	Frank Viola	.25
10	Don Mattingly	2.50
11	Garry Maddox	.25
12	Randy Jones	.25
13	Joe Carter	.25
14	Orlando Cepeda	.50
15	Bob Sheppard	.25
16	Bobby Grich	.25
17	George Scott	.25
18	Mickey Rivers	.25
19	Ron Santo	.25
20	Mike Schmidt	2.00
21	Luis Aparicio	.25
22	Cesar Geronimo	.25
23	Jack Morris	.25
24	Jeffrey Loria	.25
25	George Brett	2.00
26	Paul O'Neill	.25
27	Reggie Smith	.25
28	Robin Yount	1.00
29	Andre Dawson	.50
30	Whitey Ford	.75
31	Ralph Kiner	.50
32	Will Clark	.50
33	Keith Hernandez	.25
34	Tony Fernandez	.25
35	Willie McGee	.25
36	Harmon Killebrew	.75
37	Dave Kingman	.25
38	Kirk Gibson	.25
39	Terry Steinbach	.25
40	Frank Robinson	.75
41	Chet Lemon	.25
42	Mike Cuellar	.25
43	Darrell Evans	.25
44	Don Kessinger	.25
45	Dave Concepcion	.25
46	Sparky Anderson	.25
47	Bret Saberhagen	.25
48	Brett Butler	.25
49	Kent Hrbek	.25
50	Hank Aaron	2.50
51	Rudolph Giuliani	.25
52	Clete Boyer	.25
53	Mookie Wilson	.25
54	Dave Stewart	.25
55	Gary Matthews	.25
56	Roy Face	.25
57	Vida Blue	.25
58	Jimmy Key	.25
59	Al Hrabosky	.25
60	Al Kaline	.75
61	Mike Scott	.25
62	Jack McDowell	.25
63	Reggie Jackson	.75
64	Earl Weaver	.25
65	Ernie Harwell	.25
66	David Justice	.25
67	Wilbur Wood	.25
68	Mike Boddicker	.25
69	Don Zimmer	.25
70	Jim Palmer	.50
71	Doug DeCinces	.25
72	Ryne Sandberg	1.00
73	Don Newcombe	.25
74	Denny Martinez	.25
75	Carl Yastrzemski	1.50
76	Bake McBride	.25
77	Andy Van Slyke	.25
78	Bruce Sutter	.50
79	Bobby Valentine	.25
80	Johnny Bench	1.50
81	Orel Hershiser	.25
82	Danny Tartabull	.25
83	Lou Whitaker	.25
84	Alan Trammell	.50
85	Sam McDowell	.25
86	Ray Knight	.25
87	Fernando Valenzuela	.25
88	Ben Oglivie	.25
89	Billy Beane	.25
90	Yogi Berra	1.00
91	Jose Canseco	.50
92	Bobby Bonilla	.25
93	Darren Daulton	.25
94	Harold Reynolds	.25
95	Lou Brock	.50
96	Pete Incaviglia	.25
97	Eric Gregg	.25
98	Devon White	.25
99	Kelly Gruber	.25
100	Nolan Ryan	3.00
101	Carlton Fisk	.50
102	George Foster	.25
103	Dennis Eckersley	.25
104	Rick Sutcliffe	.25
105	Cal Ripken Jr.	3.00
106	Norm Cash	.25
107	Charlie Hough	.25
108	Paul Molitor	.75
109	Maury Wills	.25

#	Player	Price
110	Tom Seaver	1.00
111	Brooks Robinson	1.00
112	Jim Rice	.25
113	Dwight Gooden	.25
114	Harold Baines	.25
115	Tim Raines	.25
116	Roy Smalley	.25
117	Richie Allen	.25
118	Ron Swoboda	.25
119	Ron Guidry	.25
120	Duke Snider	.75
121	Ferguson Jenkins	.50
122	Mark Fidrych	.25
123	Buddy Bell	.25
124	Bo Jackson	.50
125	Stan Musial	1.50
126	Jesse Barfield	.25
127	Tony Gwynn	1.00
128	Phil Garner	.25
129	Dale Murphy	.75
130	Wade Boggs	.50
131	Sid Fernandez	.25
132	Monte Irvin	.25
133	Peter Ueberroth	.25
134	Gary Gaetti	.25
135	Gorman Thomas	.25
136	Davey Lopes	.25
137	Sy Berger	.25
138	Buck O'Neil	.25
139	Herb Score	.25
140	Rod Carew	.75
141	Joe Buck	.25
142	Willie Horton	.25
143	Hal McRae	.25
144	Rollie Fingers	.25
145	Tom Brunansky	.25
146	Fay Vincent	.25
147	Gary Carter	.50
148	Bobby Richardson	.25
149	Steve Garvey	.25
150	Don Larsen	.50

Refractor

Cards (1-150): 3-6X
Production 299 Sets

Autographs

NM/M

Common Autograph:		10.00
SP's Noted		
HA	Hank Aaron/50	350.00
RA	Richie Allen	15.00
SA	Sparky Anderson/100	20.00
LA	Luis Aparicio/100	40.00
HB	Harold Baines/100	20.00
JB	Jesse Barfield	10.00
BB	Billy Beane/100	25.00
BBE	Buddy Bell	20.00
JBE	Johnny Bench/100	150.00
SB	Sy Berger	50.00
YB	Yogi Berra/100	90.00
VB	Vida Blue	15.00
MB	Mike Boddicker	15.00
WB	Wade Boggs/50	100.00
BMB	Bobby Bonilla	20.00
GB	George Brett/50	100.00
LB	Lou Brock/100	60.00
TB	Tom Brunansky	25.00
JB	Joe Buck/100	30.00
JCA	Jose Canseco/100	65.00
RC	Rod Carew/100	60.00
GC	Gary Carter/50	60.00
JC	Joe Carter/100	45.00
OC	Orlando Cepeda/100	65.00
DC	Dave Concepcion/100	40.00
DD	Darren Daulton	15.00
AD	Andre Dawson/100	40.00
LD	Lenny Dykstra/100	20.00
DEC	Dennis Eckersley/100	40.00
DE	Darrell Evans	10.00
SF	Sid Fernandez/100	40.00
TF	Tony Fernandez	15.00
MF	Mark Fidrych/100	40.00
RF	Rollie Fingers/100	40.00
WF	Whitey Ford/100	100.00
GF	George Foster	10.00
SG	Steve Garvey/100	30.00
CG	Cesar Geronimo/100	65.00
BG	Bob Gibson/100	90.00
DG	Dwight Gooden/50	60.00
EG	Eric Gregg	15.00
BGR	Bobby Grich	10.00
RG	Ron Guidry/100	50.00
TG	Tony Gwynn/50	100.00
EH	Ernie Harwell	25.00
KH	Keith Hernandez/50	25.00
OH	Orel Hershiser	30.00
WH	Willie Horton	10.00
CH	Charlie Hough	15.00
AH	Al Hrabosky	15.00
PI	Pete Incaviglia	15.00
MI	Monte Irvin/100	25.00
BJ	Bo Jackson/50	100.00
RJ2	Reggie Jackson	80.00
FJ	Ferguson Jenkins	15.00
RJO	Randy Jones	10.00
DJ	David Justice	25.00
AK	Al Kaline/50	100.00
DKE	Don Kessinger	15.00
JK	Jimmy Key/100	45.00
HK	Harmon Killebrew/100	85.00
RK	Ralph Kiner	40.00
DK	Dave Kingman	40.00
RKN	Ray Knight/100	40.00
DLA	Don Larsen	15.00
CL	Chet Lemon	15.00
DL	Davey Lopes	10.00
GM	Gary Mathews	10.00
DON	Don Mattingly/50	125.00
WM	Willie Mays/50	225.00
TM	Tim McCarver	40.00
JM	Jack McDowell	15.00
SM	Sam McDowell/100	15.00
WMC	Willie McGee/100	50.00
PM	Paul Molitor/50	85.00
JMO	Jack Morris	10.00
DM	Dale Murphy/50	75.00
SM	Stan Musial/100	100.00
BO	Buck O'Neil	30.00
PO	Paul O'Neill/50	60.00
BO	Ben Oglivie	15.00
TO	Tony Oliva	30.00
JP	Jim Palmer/50	100.00
TR	Tim Raines	25.00
HR	Harold Reynolds/100	30.00
JR	Jim Rice/100	40.00
BR	Bobby Richardson	15.00
CR	Cal Ripken Jr./50	200.00
MR	Mickey Rivers	10.00
BRO	Brooks Robinson/50	100.00
FR	Frank Robinson/100	80.00
NR	Nolan Ryan	175.00
BS	Bret Saberhagen/100	45.00
RYN	Ryne Sandberg/100	100.00
RS	Ron Santo	30.00
MS	Mike Schmidt/50	120.00
GS	George Scott	15.00
MSC	Mike Scott	10.00
TSE	Tom Seaver/50	100.00
DSN	Duke Snider/50	75.00
DS	Dave Stewart	10.00
DST	Dave Stieb	25.00
RSU	Rick Sutcliffe/50	40.00
BSU	Bruce Sutter	35.00
RSW	Ron Swoboda	15.00
AT	Alan Trammell/100	60.00
PU	Peter Ueberroth/100	60.00
BV	Bobby Valentine/100	50.00
AV	Andy Van Slyke/100	65.00
FVI	Fay Vincent/100	15.00
EW	Earl Weaver	15.00
MW	Maury Wills	15.00
MWI	Mookie Wilson	10.00
WW	Wilbur Wood	15.00
CY	Carl Yastrzemski/50	100.00
RY	Robin Yount/100	100.00
DZ	Don Zimmer	30.00

Best Seat In The House

BEST SEAT IN THE HOUSE

NM/M

Common Card:		15.00
BS1	Tom Seaver, Johnny Bench, George Foster	15.00
BS2	Frank Robinson, Jim Palmer, Brooks Robinson	15.00
BS3	Dave Parker, Bill Madlock, Bill Mazeroski	15.00
BS4	Kent Hrbek, Rod Carew, Harmon Killebrew	30.00

Relics

FRANK ROBINSON
OUTFIELD • BALTIMORE ORIOLES

NM/M

Common Player:		5.00
WB	Wade Boggs	10.00
GB	George Brett	15.00
LB	Lou Brock	10.00
JC	Jose Canseco/Jsy	8.00
JCB	Jose Canseco/Bat	8.00
GC	Gary Carter	8.00
DE	Dennis Eckersley	5.00
CF	Carlton Fisk	10.00
GF	George Foster	5.00
KG	Kirk Gibson	5.00
KH	Keith Hernandez	5.00
RJ	Reggie Jackson	10.00
DJ	David Justice	5.00
HK	Harmon Killebrew	20.00
WM	Willie Mays	30.00
JM	Joe Morgan	5.00
GN	Graig Nettles	8.00
JP	Jim Palmer	8.00
DP	Dave Parker	5.00
KP	Kirby Puckett	10.00
HR	Harold Reynolds	5.00
JR	Jim Rice	5.00
BR	Brooks Robinson	12.00
FRB	Frank Robinson/Bat	8.00
FR	Frank Robinson/Jsy	8.00
NR	Nolan Ryan	25.00
BS	Bret Saberhagen	5.00
MS	Mike Schmidt	15.00
DS	Darryl Strawberry	8.00
EW	Earl Weaver	8.00
MW	Maury Wills	5.00
CY	Carl Yastrzemski	20.00

2004 Topps Bazooka

ANAHEIM ANGELS
BARTOLO COLON

NM/M

#	Player	Price
Complete Set (300):		40.00
Common Player:		.15
Variations (30):		Same Price
Pack (8):		2.00
Box (24):		40.00
1	Bobby Abreu	.25
2	Jesse Foppert	.15
3	Shea Hillenbrand	.15
4	Jose Lima	.15
5	Manny Ramirez	.50
6	Denny Neagle	.15
7	Frank Thomas	.50
8	A.J. Burnett	.15
9	Carl Everett	.15
10	Scott Podsednik	.25
11	Travis Lee	.15
12	Mike Mussina	.40
13	Runelvys Hernandez	.15
14	Shannon Stewart	.15
15	Miguel Cabrera	.40
16	Edgardo Alfonzo	.15
17	Victor Zambrano	.15
18	Rafael Furcal	.25
19	Eric Hinske	.15
20	Paul LoDuca	.15
21	Phil Nevin	.15
22	Aramis Ramirez	.15
23	Jim Thome	.75
24	Jeromy Burnitz	.15
25	Mark Prior	1.50
26	Ramon Hernandez	.15
27	Cliff Lee	.15
28	Greg Myers	.15
29	Robert Fick	.15
30	Mike Sweeney	.15
31	Carlos Zambrano	.15
32	Roberto Alomar	.40
33	Orlando Cabrera	.25
34	Orlando Hudson	.15
35	Nomar Garciaparra	1.50
36	Esteban Loaiza	.15
37	Laynce Nix	.15
38	Joe Randa	.15
39	Juan Uribe	.15
40	Pat Burrell	.40
41	Steve Finley	.15
42	Livan Hernandez	.15
43	Al Leiter	.15
44	Brett Myers	.15
45	Jody Gerut	.15
46	Mark Teixeira	.40
47	Barry Zito	.40
48	Moises Alou	.25
49	Mike Cameron	.15
50	Albert Pujols	1.50
51	Tim Hudson	.25
52	Kenny Lofton	.25
53	Trot Nixon	.15
54	Tim Redding	.15
55	Marlon Byrd	.15
56	Javier Vazquez	.25
57	Sean Burroughs	.15
58	Cliff Floyd	.15
59	Juan Rivera	.15
60	Mike Lieberthal	.15
61	Xavier Nady	.15
62	Brad Radke	.15
63	Miguel Tejada	.40
64	Ichiro Suzuki	1.00
65	Garret Anderson	.25
66	Sean Casey	.15
67	Jason Giambi	.75
68	Aubrey Huff	.15
69	Javy Lopez	.25
70	Hideo Nomo	.25
71	Mark Redman	.15
72	Jose Vidro	.15
73	Rich Aurilia	.15
74	Luis Castillo	.15
75	Jay Gibbons	.15
76	Torii Hunter	.25
77	Derek Lowe	.15
78	Wes Obermueller	.15
79	Edgar Renteria	.15
80	Jeff Bagwell	.50
81	Fernando Vina	.15
82	Frank Catalanotto	.15
83	Marcus Giles	.15
84	Raul Ibanez	.15
85	Mike Lowell	.25
86	Tomokazu Ohka	.15
87	Jose Reyes	.25
88	Omar Vizquel	.15
89	Shawn Chacon	.15
90	Rocco Baldelli	.25
91	Brian Giles	.25
92	Kazuhisa Ishii	.15
93	Greg Maddux	1.00
94	John Olerud	.25
95	Eric Chavez	.25
96	Doug Waechter	.15
97	Tony Batista	.15
98	Jeriome Robertson	.15
99	Troy Glaus	.25
100	Eric Gagne	.25
101	Pedro J. Martinez	.75
102	Magglio Ordonez	.25
103	Alex Rodriguez	2.00
104	Jason Bay	.15
105	Larry Walker	.25
106	Matt Clement	.15
107	Tom Glavine	.25
108	Geoff Jenkins	.15
109	Victor Martinez	.15
110	David Ortiz	.15
111	Ivan Rodriguez	.40
112	Jarrod Washburn	.15
113	Josh Beckett	.25
114	Bartolo Colon	.15
115	Juan Gonzalez	.40
116	Derek Jeter	2.00
117	Edgar Martinez	.25
118	Ramon Ortiz	.15
119	Scott Rolen	.75
120	Brandon Webb	.25
121	Carlos Beltran	.25
122	Jose Contreras	.25
123	Luis Gonzalez	.25
124	Jason Johnson	.15
125	Luis Matos	.15
126	Russ Ortiz	.15
127	Damian Rolls	.15

128 David Wells .15
129 Adrian Beltre .15
130 Shawn Green .25
131 Nate Cornejo .15
132 Nick Johnson .15
133 Joe Mays .15
134 Roy Oswalt .25
135 C.C. Sabathia .15
136 Vernon Wells .25
137 Kris Benson .15
138 Carl Crawford .15
139 Ken Griffey Jr. 1.00
140 Randy Johnson .75
141 Fred McGriff .25
142 Vicente Padilla .15
143 Tim Salmon .25
144 Kip Wells .15
145 Lance Berkman .25
146 Jose Cruz Jr. .15
147 Marquis Grissom .15
148 Jacque Jones .15
149 Gil Meche .15
150 Vladimir Guerrero .75
151 Reggie Sanders .15
152 Ty Wigginton .15
153 Angel Berroa .15
154 Johnny Damon .25
155 Rafael Palmeiro .50
156 Chipper Jones .75
157 Kevin Millar .15
158 Corey Patterson .25
159 Johan Santana .15
160 Bernie Williams .40
161 Craig Biggio .25
162 Carlos Delgado .50
163 Aaron Guiel .15
164 Wade Miller .15
165 Andruw Jones .50
166 Jay Payton .15
167 Benito Santiago .15
168 Woody Williams .15
169 Casey Blake .15
170 Adam Dunn .40
171 Jose Guillen .15
172 Brian Jordan .15
173 Kevin Millwood .25
174 Carlos Pena .15
175 Curt Schilling .50
176 Jerome Williams .15
177 Hank Blalock .25
178 Erubiel Durazo .15
179 Cristian Guzman .15
180 Austin Kearns .40
181 Raul Mondesi .15
182 Andy Pettitte .25
183 Jason Schmidt .25
184 Jeremy Bonderman .15
185 Dontrelle Willis .25
186 Ray Durham .15
187 Jerry Hairston Jr. .15
188 Jason Kendall .15
189 Melvin Mora .15
190 Jeff Kent .25
191 Jae Weong Seo .15
192 Jack Wilson .15
193 Cesar Izturis .15
194 Jermaine Dye .15
195 Roy Halladay .25
196 Jason Phillips .15
197 Matt Morris .25
198 Mike Piazza 1.00
199 Richie Sexson .40
200 Alfonso Soriano .75
201 Mark Mulder .25
202 David Eckstein .15
203 Mike Hampton .15
204 Ryan Klesko .25
205 Damian Moss .15
206 Juan Pierre .15
207 Ben Sheets .25
208 Randy Winn .15
209 Bret Boone .25
210 Jim Edmonds .25
211 Rich Harden .15
212 Paul Konerko .15
213 Jamie Moyer .15
214 A.J. Pierzynski .15
215 Gary Sheffield .25
216 Randy Wolf .15
217 Kevin Brown .25
218 Morgan Ensberg .15
219 Bo Hart .15
220 Bill Mueller .15
221 Corey Koskie .15
222 Joel Pineiro .15
223 Preston Wilson .15
224 Aaron Boone .15
225 Kerry Wood .50
226 Darin Erstad .25
227 Wes Helms .15
228 Brian Lawrence .15
229 Mark Buehrle .15
230 Sammy Sosa 1.25
231 Sidney Ponson .15
232 Dmitri Young .15
233 Ellis Burks .15
234 Kelvim Escobar .15
235 Todd Helton .50
236 Matt Lawton .15
237 Eric Munson .15
238 Jorge Posada .50
239 Junior Spivey .15
240 Michael Young .15
241 Ramon Nivar .15
242 Edwin Jackson .15
243 Felix Pie .15
244 Ryan Wagner .15
245 Grady Sizemore .25
246 Bobby Jenks .15
247 Chad Billingsley .15
248 Casey Kotchman .15
249 Bobby Crosby .15
250 Khalil Greene .15
251 Danny Garcia .15
252 Nicholas Markakis .15
253 Bernie Castro .15
254 Aaron Hill .15
255 Josh Barfield .15
256 Ryan Wagner .15
257 Ryan Harvey .15
258 Jimmy Gobble .15
259 Ryan Madson .15
260 Zack Greinke .15
261 Rene Reyes .15
262 Eric Duncan .15
263 Chris Lubanski .15
264 Jeff Mathis .15
265 Rickie Weeks .25
266 Justin Morneau .25
267 Brian Snyder .15
268 Neal Cotts .15
269 Joe Borchard .15
270 Larry Bigbie .15
271 Marcus McBeth **RC** .40
272 Tydus Meadows **RC** .40
273 Zach Miner **RC** .50
274 Anthony Lerew **RC** .40
275 Yadier Molina **RC** .40
276 Jon Knott **RC** .40
277 Matthew Moses .40
278 Sung Jung **RC** .40
279 Mike Gosling .15
280 David Murphy .15
281 Tim Frend **RC** .40
282 Casey Myers **RC** .40
283 Brayan Pena **RC** .40
284 Omar Falcon **RC** .40
285 Blake Hawksworth **RC** .40
286 Jesse Roman **RC** .40
287 Kyle Davies **RC** .40
288 Matt Creighton **RC** .40
289 Rodney Choy Foo **RC** .40
290 Kyle Sleeth .15
291 Carlos Quentin .50
292 Khalid Ballouli **RC** .40
293 Tim Stauffer .15
294 Craig Ansman **RC** .40
295 Dioner Navarro **RC** .40
296 Josh Labandeira **RC** .40
297 Jeff Allison .15
298 Anthony Acevedo **RC** .40
299 Brad Sullivan .15
300 Conor Jackson .50

Red

Cards (1-300): 1-2X
Inserted 1:1

Mini

Stars (1-300): 1-2X
Inserted 1:1

Adventures

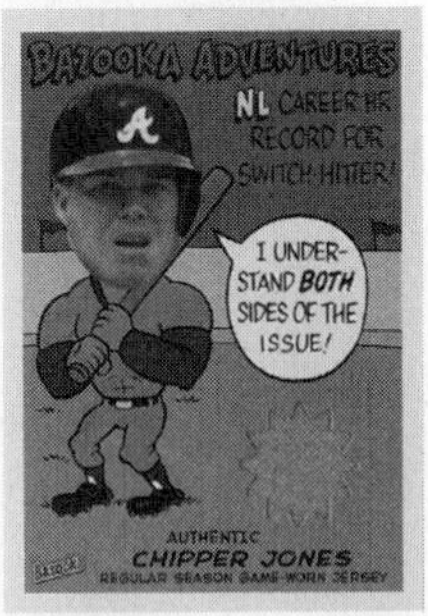

NM/M

Common Player: 4.00
EA Edgardo Alfonzo 4.00
JB Jeff Bagwell 8.00
LB Lance Berkman 6.00
CB Craig Biggio 4.00
KB Kevin Brown 4.00
PB Pat Burrell 6.00
MB Marlon Byrd 4.00
SC Sean Casey 4.00
LC Luis Castillo 4.00
EC Eric Chavez 5.00
AD1 Adam Dunn 6.00
AD2 Adam Dunn 6.00
CE Carl Everett 4.00
CF Cliff Floyd 4.00
NG Nomar Garciaparra 10.00
JG Jason Giambi 8.00
JDG Jeremy Giambi 4.00
TEG Troy Glaus 5.00
TG Tom Glavine 5.00
LG Luis Gonzalez 4.00
SG Shawn Green 5.00
BG Ben Grieve 4.00
VG Vladimir Guerrero 8.00
CG Cristian Guzman 4.00
TH Toby Hall 4.00
TAH1 Tim Hudson 4.00
TAH2 Tim Hudson 4.00
GJ Geoff Jenkins 4.00
RJ Randy Johnson 8.00
AJ Andruw Jones 6.00
CJ Chipper Jones 8.00
JK Jason Kendall 4.00
PK Paul Konerko 4.00
PL Paul LoDuca 4.00
ML Mike Lowell 4.00
GM Greg Maddux 8.00
KM Kevin Millwood 6.00
MM Mark Mulder 5.00
MCM Mike Mussina 6.00
HN Hideo Nomo 8.00
JO John Olerud 4.00
RP1 Rafael Palmeiro 6.00
RP2 Rafael Palmeiro 6.00
BP Brad Penny 4.00
MP1 Mike Piazza 10.00
MP2 Mike Piazza 10.00
AP Albert Pujols 15.00
MR Manny Ramirez 6.00
AR1 Alex Rodriguez 10.00
AR2 Alex Rodriguez 10.00
TJS Tim Salmon 5.00
CS Curt Schilling 8.00
AS Alfonso Soriano 6.00
MT Miguel Tejada 6.00
JT Jim Thome 8.00
LW Larry Walker 4.00
JW Jarrod Washburn 4.00
BW Bernie Williams 6.00
DW Dontrelle Willis 6.00
PW Preston Wilson 4.00
KW Kerry Wood 6.00
BZ Barry Zito 6.00

Blasts

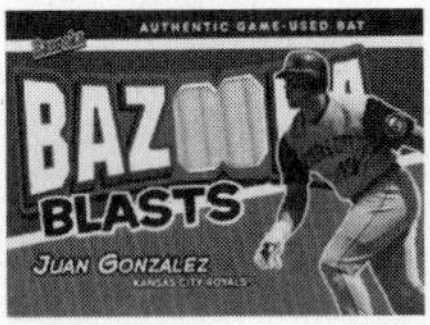

NM/M

Common Player: 4.00
RA Roberto Alomar 6.00
MA Moises Alou 4.00
RSA Rich Aurilia 4.00
JB Jeff Bagwell 8.00
RB Rocco Baldelli 8.00
TB Tony Batista 4.00
CIB Carlos Beltran 4.00
LB Lance Berkman 5.00
CB Craig Biggio 4.00
HB Hank Blalock 6.00
BB Bret Boone 5.00
JNB Jeromy Burnitz 4.00
SB Sean Burroughs 4.00
CC Carl Crawford 4.00
AD Adam Dunn 6.00
CE Carl Everett 4.00
BF Brad Fullmer 4.00
RF Rafael Furcal 5.00
AJG Andres Galarraga 4.00
NG Nomar Garciaparra 12.00
JG Jason Giambi 8.00
TG Troy Glaus 5.00
AG Adrian Gonzalez 4.00
JAG Juan Gonzalez 6.00
LG Luis Gonzalez 4.00
SG Shawn Green 6.00
MG Marquis Grissom 4.00
VG Vladimir Guerrero 8.00
CG Cristian Guzman 4.00
NH Nathan Haynes 4.00
TKH Todd Helton 6.00
AH Aubrey Huff 4.00
TH Torii Hunter 5.00
CJ Chipper Jones 8.00
PK Paul Konerko 4.00
ML Matt Lawton 4.00
CL Carlos Lee 4.00
PL Paul LoDuca 4.00
EM Edgar Martinez 4.00
TM Tino Martinez 6.00
FM Fred McGriff 5.00
DM Doug Mientkiewicz 4.00
JO John Olerud 4.00
MO Magglio Ordonez 4.00
RP Rafael Palmeiro 8.00
CP Corey Patterson 4.00
MP Mike Piazza 10.00
JP Jorge Posada 6.00
AP Albert Pujols 15.00
ANR Aramis Ramirez 4.00
MR Manny Ramirez 6.00
JR Juan Rivera 4.00
AR Alex Rodriguez 10.00
IR Ivan Rodriguez 6.00
SR Scott Rolen 8.00
TJS Tim Salmon 6.00
GS Gary Sheffield 6.00
RS Ruben Sierra 4.00
AS Alfonso Soriano 8.00
SS Shannon Stewart 4.00
ST So Taguchi 5.00
MCT Mark Teixeira 5.00
MT Miguel Tejada 5.00
FT Frank Thomas 8.00
MAT Michael Tucker 4.00
MV Mo Vaughn 4.00
OV Omar Vizquel 4.00
LW Larry Walker 5.00
VW Vernon Wells 5.00
RW Rondell White 4.00
BW Bernie Williams 6.00

Comics

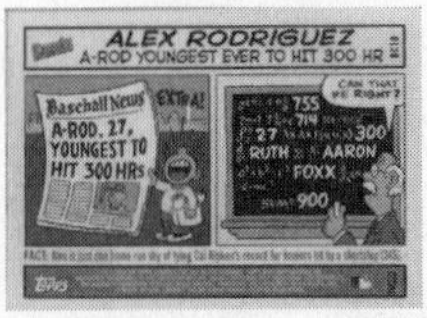

NM/M

Complete Set (24): 6.00
Common Player: .25
Inserted 1:4
BC1 Garret Anderson .25
BC2 Jeff Bagwell .50
BC3 Hank Blalock .25
BC4 Roy Halladay .25
BC5 Dontrelle Willis .25
BC6 Roger Clemens .75
BC7 Carlos Delgado .40
BC8 Rafael Furcal .25
BC9 Eric Gagne .25
BC10 Nomar Garciaparra .75
BC11 Derek Jeter .75
BC12 Esteban Loaiza .25
BC13 Kevin Millwood .25
BC14 Bill Mueller .25
BC15 Rafael Palmeiro .40
BC16 Albert Pujols .75
BC17 Jose Reyes .25
BC18 Alex Rodriguez .75
BC19 Alfonso Soriano .40
BC20 Sammy Sosa .50
BC21 Ichiro Suzuki .50
BC22 Frank Thomas .40
BC23 Brad Wilkerson .25
BC24 Houston Astros .25

One-Liners

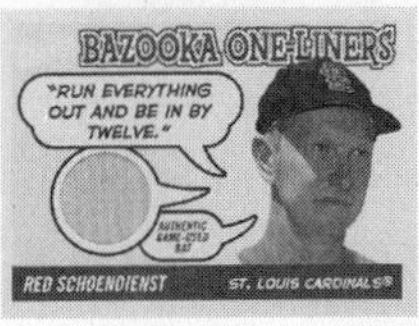

NM/M

Common Player: 5.00
DA Dick Allen 8.00
JB Johnny Bench 10.00
BB Bert Blyleven 5.00
WB1 Wade Boggs 6.00
WB2 Wade Boggs 6.00
GB George Brett 20.00
BC Bert Campaneris 5.00
RC Rod Carew 8.00
GC Gary Carter 5.00
JCA Joe Carter 5.00
OC Orlando Cepeda 5.00
RD Ron Darling 5.00
AD Andre Dawson 8.00
DE Dennis Eckersley 10.00
KG1 Kirk Gibson 5.00
KG2 Kirk Gibson 5.00
DW Dwight Gooden 5.00
KH Keith Hernandez 5.00
RJ Reggie Jackson 10.00
DJ1 David Justice 8.00
DJ2 David Justice 8.00
HK Harmon Killebrew 20.00
JK Jerry Koosman 5.00
BM Bill Madlock 5.00
WM Willie Mays 30.00
WMC Willie McGee 8.00
TM Tug McGraw 8.00
JM Joe Morgan 8.00
DM Dale Murphy 15.00
EM Eddie Murray 10.00
PN Phil Niekro 5.00
DP Dave Parker 5.00
GP Gaylord Perry 5.00
KP1 Kirby Puckett 10.00
KP2 Kirby Puckett 10.00
FR Frank Robinson 10.00
NR Nolan Ryan 15.00
BS Bret Saberhagen 5.00
RSA Ron Santo 10.00
MS Mike Schmidt 15.00
RS Red Schoendienst 5.00
TS Tom Seaver 8.00
WS Willie Stargell 8.00

CY	Carl Yastrzemski	15.00
RY	Robin Yount	10.00

Stand-Ups

VERNON WELLS
TORONTO BLUE JAYS® OUTFIELD

		NM/M
Complete Set (25):		20.00
Common Player:		.50
Inserted 1:8		
1	Jose Reyes	.50
2	Jim Thome	1.00
3	Roy Halladay	.50
4	Jason Giambi	1.00
5	Dontrelle Willis	.50
6	Mike Piazza	1.50
7	Chipper Jones	1.00
8	Mark Prior	2.00
9	Todd Helton	.75
10	Miguel Cabrera	.75
11	Derek Jeter	3.00
12	Nomar Garciaparra	2.00
13	Alex Rodriguez	3.00
14	Miguel Tejada	.50
15	Carlos Delgado	.75
16	Pedro J. Martinez	1.00
17	Sammy Sosa	2.00
18	Ichiro Suzuki	1.50
19	Vladimir Guerrero	1.00
20	Alfonso Soriano	1.00
21	Eric Chavez	.50
22	Albert Pujols	2.50
23	Ivan Rodriguez	.75
24	Vernon Wells	.50
25	Eric Gagne	.50

Tattoos

		NM/M
Complete Set (55):		8.00
Common Player:		.15
Inserted 1:4		
JB	Jeff Bagwell	.25
BAZ	Bazooka Logo	.15
LB	Lance Berkman	.15
CB	Craig Biggio	.15
KB	Kevin Brown	.15
PB	Pat Burrell	.15
MB	Marlon Byrd	.15
SC	Sean Casey	.15
LC	Luis Castillo	.15
EC	Eric Chavez	.15
AD	Adam Dunn	.15
CF	Cliff Floyd	.15
NG	Nomar Garciaparra	.75
JG	Jason Giambi	.40
TFG	Troy Glaus	.25
TG	Tom Glavine	.25
LG	Luis Gonzalez	.15
SG	Shawn Green	.15
VG	Vladimir Guerrero	.40
CG	Cristian Guzman	.15
TH	Toby Hall	.15
TAH	Tim Hudson	.15
GJ	Geoff Jenkins	.15
RJ	Randy Johnson	.40
AJ	Andruw Jones	.25
CJ	Chipper Jones	.40
JK	Jason Kendall	.15
PK	Paul Konerko	.15

PL	Paul LoDuca	.15
ML	Mike Lowell	.15
GM	Greg Maddux	.50
KM	Kevin Millwood	.15
MM	Mark Mulder	.15
MCM	Mike Mussina	.25
HN	Hideo Nomo	.15
JO	John Olerud	.15
RP	Rafael Palmeiro	.25
BP	Brad Penny	.15
MP	Mike Piazza	.25
AP	Albert Pujols	1.00
MR	Manny Ramirez	.25
AR	Alex Rodriguez	1.00
TJS	Tim Salmon	.25
CS	Curt Schilling	.25
AS	Alfonso Soriano	.40
MT	Miguel Tejada	.25
JT	Jim Thome	.40
TOP	Topps Logo	.15
LW	Larry Walker	.15
JW	Jarrod Washburn	.15
BW	Bernie Williams	.15
DW	Dontrelle Willis	.15
PW	Preston Wilson	.15
KW	Kerry Wood	.25
BZ	Barry Zito	.25

4-on-1 Stickers

		NM/M
Complete Set (40):		8.00
Common Player:		.20
Inserted 1:4		
1	Rich Harden, Dontrelle Willis, Jerome Williams, Brandon Webb	.20
2	Eric Duncan, Derek Jeter, Alfonso Soriano, Jason Giambi	.75
3	Grady Sizemore, Rocco Baldelli, Ichiro Suzuki, Vladimir Guerrero	.50
4	Roy Halladay, Pedro J. Martinez, Curt Schilling, Brett Myers	.40
5	Alex Rodriguez, Angel Berroa, Jose Reyes, Khalil Greene	.50
6	Kerry Wood, Adam Dunn, Jeff Kent, Scott Rolen	.40
7	Miguel Cabrera, Scott Podsednik, Bo Hart, Mark Teixeira	.20
8	Rickie Weeks, Josh Barfield, Albert Pujols, Vernon Wells	.50
9	Torii Hunter, Garret Anderson, Bobby Abreu, Ken Griffey Jr.	.40
10	Jay Gibbons, Chipper Jones, Mike Piazza, Mike Sweeney	.50
11	David Ortiz, Nick Johnson, Carlos Delgado, Frank Thomas	.40
12	Todd Helton, Jose Vidro, Mike Lowell, Miguel Tejada	.40
13	Randy Wolf, Mark Mulder, Johan Santana, Randy Johnson	.40
14	Bret Boone, Aubrey Huff, Eric Chavez, Javy Lopez	.20
15	Jason Schmidt, Roy Oswalt, Joel Pineiro, Mark Prior	.50
16	Kevin Millwood, Andy Pettitte, Matt Morris, Tim Hudson	.20
17	Javier Vazquez, Esteban Loaiza, Orlando Cabrera, Roberto Alomar	.20
18	Al Leiter, David Wells, Mike Hampton, Jarrod Washburn	.20
19	Paul LoDuca, Mike Lieberthal, Brian Giles, Andruw Jones	.20
20	Magglio Ordonez, Corey Patterson, Aaron Boone, Jeff Bagwell	.40
21	Troy Glaus, Edgar Martinez, Manny Ramirez, Raul Ibanez	.30
22	Sammy Sosa, Barry Zito, Bartolo Colon, Austin Kearns	.50

23	Jim Edmonds, Gary Sheffield, Preston Wilson, Shawn Green	.20
24	Bernie Williams, Juan Pierre, Josh Beckett, Mike Mussina	.20
25	Ramon Hernandez, Jason Kendall, Jason Phillips, A.J. Pierzynski	.20
26	Pat Burrell, Laynce Nix, Mike Cameron, Cliff Floyd	.20
27	Eric Gagne, Carl Crawford, Jose Guillen, Steve Finley	.20
28	Ellis Burks, Livan Hernandez, Derek Lowe, Kazuhisa Ishii	.20
29	Jorge Posada, Jeff Mathis, Victor Martinez, Ivan Rodriguez	.20
30	Jim Thome, Marcus Giles, Nomar Garciaparra, Hank Blalock	.50
31	Edgar Renteria, Bobby Crosby, Neal Cotts, Russ Ortiz	.20
32	Zack Greinke, Cristian Guzman, Cesar Izturis, Kevin Brown	
33	Bobby Jenks, Ramon Nivar, Richie Sexson, Ryan Klesko	
34	Omar Vizquel, Carlos Pena, Rafael Furcal, Gil Meche	
35	Kenny Lofton, Tim Salmon, Marquis Grissom, Craig Biggio	
36	Kyle Davies, Anthony Lerew, Brayan Pena, Sung Jung	.20
37	Rodney Choy Foo, Craig Ansman, David Murphy, Matthew Moses	.20
38	Carlos Quentin, Dioner Navarro, Marcus McBeth, Josh Labandeira	.20
39	Kyle Sleeth, Conor Jackson, Brad Sullivan, Jeff Allison	.20
40	Yadier Molina, Jon Knott, Blake Hawksworth, Tim Stauffer	.20

2004 Topps Chrome

	NM/M
Complete Set (466):	
Common Player:	.25
Common Rookie Auto.	
(221-246):	10.00
Inserted 1:21	
Series 1 Pack (4):	3.50
Series 1 Box (20):	50.00
Series 2 Pack (4):	3.50
Series 2 Box (20):	50.00

1	Jim Thome	1.00
2	Reggie Sanders	.25
3	Mark Kotsay	.25
4	Edgardo Alfonzo	.25
5	Tim Wakefield	.25
6	Moises Alou	.50
7	Jorge Julio	.25
8	Bartolo Colon	.50
9	Chan Ho Park	.25
10	Ichiro Suzuki	3.00
11	Kevin Millwood	.50
12	Preston Wilson	.40
13	Tom Glavine	.75
14	Junior Spivey	.25
15	Marcus Giles	.40
16	David Segui	.25
17	Kevin Millar	.25
18	Corey Patterson	.40
19	Aaron Rowand	.25
20	Derek Jeter	4.00
21	Luis Castillo	.25
22	Manny Ramirez	1.50
23	Jay Payton	.25
24	Bobby Higginson	.25
25	Lance Berkman	.75
26	Juan Pierre	.25
27	Mike Mussina	1.00
28	Fred McGriff	.50
29	Richie Sexson	.75
30	Tim Hudson	.50
31	Mike Piazza	2.00
32	Brad Radke	.25
33	Jeff Weaver	.25
34	Ramon Hernandez	.25
35	David Bell	.25

36	Randy Wolf	.25
37	Jake Peavy	.50
38	Tim Worrell	.25
39	Gil Meche	.25
40	Albert Pujols	4.00
41	Michael Young	.25
42	Josh Phelps	.25
43	Brendan Donnelly	.25
44	Steve Finley	.50
45	John Smoltz	.50
46	Jay Gibbons	.25
47	Trot Nixon	.25
48	Carl Pavano	.25
49	Frank Thomas	1.00
50	Mark Prior	1.00
51	Danny Graves	.25
52	Milton Bradley	.25
53	Kris Benson	.25
54	Ryan Klesko	.25
55	Mike Lowell	.25
56	Geoff Blum	.25
57	Michael Tucker	.25
58	Paul LoDuca	.25
59	Vicente Padilla	.25
60	Jacque Jones	.25
61	Fernando Tatis	.25
62	Ty Wigginton	.25
63	Rich Aurilia	.25
64	Andy Pettitte	.75
65	Terrence Long	.25
66	Cliff Floyd	.25
67	Mariano Rivera	.50
68	Kelvim Escobar	.25
69	Marlon Byrd	.25
70	Mark Mulder	.50
71	Francisco Cordero	.25
72	Carlos Guillen	.25
73	Fernando Vina	.25
74	Lance Carter	.25
75	Hank Blalock	.75
76	Jimmy Rollins	.50
77	Francisco Rodriguez	.50
78	Javy Lopez	.50
79	Jerry Hairston Jr.	.25
80	Andruw Jones	.75
81	Rodrigo Lopez	.25
82	Johnny Damon	1.00
83	Hee Seop Choi	.25
84	Kazuhiro Sasaki	.25
85	Danny Bautista	.25
86	Matt Lawton	.25
87	Juan Uribe	.25
88	Rafael Furcal	.50
89	Kyle Farnsworth	.25
90	Jose Vidro	.25
91	Luis Rivas	.25
92	Hideo Nomo	.75
93	Javier Vazquez	.50
94	Al Leiter	.40
95	Jose Valentin	.25
96	Alex Cintron	.25
97	Zach Day	.25
98	Jorge Posada	.75
99	C.C. Sabathia	.50
100	Alex Rodriguez	3.00
101	Brad Penny	.25
102	Brad Ausmus	.25
103	Raul Ibanez	.25
104	Mike Hampton	.25
105	Adrian Beltre	.50
106	Ramiro Mendoza	.25
107	Rocco Baldelli	.75
108	Esteban Loaiza	.25
109	Russell Branyan	.25
110	Todd Helton	1.00
111	Braden Looper	.25
112	Octavio Dotel	.25
113	Mike MacDougal	.25
114	Cesar Izturis	.25
115	Johan Santana	1.00
116	Jose Contreras	.50
117	Placido Polanco	.25
118	Jason Phillips	.25
119	Orlando Hudson	.25
120	Vernon Wells	.25
121	Ben Grieve	.25
122	Dave Roberts	.25
123	Ismael Valdes	.25
124	Eric Owens	.25
125	Curt Schilling	1.00
126	Russ Ortiz	.50
127	Mark Buehrle	.50
128	Doug Mientkiewicz	.25
129	Dmitri Young	.25
130	Kazuhisa Ishii	.25
131	A.J. Pierzynski	.25
132	Brad Wilkerson	.25
133	Joe McEwing	.25
134	Alex Cora	.25
135	Jose Cruz Jr.	.25
136	Carlos Zambrano	.50
137	Jeff Kent	.50
138	Shigetoshi Hasegawa	.25
139	Jarrod Washburn	.25
140	Greg Maddux	2.00
141	Josh Beckett	.75
142	Miguel Batista	.25
143	Omar Vizquel	.40
144	Alex Gonzalez	.25
145	Billy Wagner	.25
146	Brian Jordan	.25
147	Wes Helms	.25
148	Deivi Cruz	.25
149	Alex Gonzalez	.25
150	Jason Giambi	1.00

151	Erubiel Durazo	.25
152	Mike Lieberthal	.25
153	Jason Kendall	.25
154	Xavier Nady	.25
155	Kirk Rueter	.25
156	Mike Cameron	.25
157	Miguel Cairo	.25
158	Woody Williams	.25
159	Toby Hall	.25
160	Bernie Williams	.75
161	Darin Erstad	.50
162	Matt Mantei	.25
163	Shawn Chacon	.25
164	Bill Mueller	.25
165	Damian Miller	.25
166	Tony Graffanino	.25
167	Sean Casey	.25
168	Brandon Phillips	.25
169	Runelvys Hernandez	.25
170	Adam Dunn	.75
171	Carlos Lee	.50
172	Juan Encarnacion	.25
173	Angel Berroa	.25
174	Desi Relaford	.25
175	Joe Mays	.25
176	Ben Sheets	.50
177	Eddie Guardado	.25
178	Rocky Biddle	.25
179	Eric Gagne	.50
180	Eric Chavez	.50
181	Jason Michaels	.25
182	Dustan Mohr	.25
183	Kip Wells	.25
184	Brian Lawrence	.25
185	Bret Boone	.25
186	Tino Martinez	.40
187	Aubrey Huff	.25
188	Kevin Mench	.25
189	Tim Salmon	.50
190	Carlos Delgado	1.00
191	John Lackey	.25
192	Eric Byrnes	.25
193	Luis Matos	.25
194	Derek Lowe	.50
195	Mark Grudzielanek	.25
196	Flash Gordon	.25
197	Matt Clement	.25
198	Byung-Hyun Kim	.25
199	Brandon Inge	.25
200	Nomar Garciaparra	1.50
201	Frank Catalanotto	.25
202	Cristian Guzman	.25
203	Bo Hart	.25
204	Jack Wilson	.25
205	Ray Durham	.25
206	Freddy Garcia	.25
207	J.D. Drew	.50
208	Orlando Cabrera	.25
209	Roy Halladay	.50
210	David Eckstein	.25
211	Omar Falcon **RC**	2.00
212	Todd Self **RC**	2.00
213	David Murphy	3.00
214	Dioner Navarro **RC**	4.00
215	Marcus McBeth **RC**	2.00
216	Chris O'Riordan **RC**	2.00
217	Rodney Choy Foo **RC**	2.00
218	Tim Frend **RC**	2.00
219	Yadier Molina **RC**	6.00
220	Zachary Duke **RC**	3.00
221	Anthony Lerew/Auto. **RC**	10.00
222	Blake Hawksworth/ Auto. **RC**	15.00
223	Brayan Pena/Auto. **RC**	10.00
224	Craig Ansman/Auto. **RC**	10.00
225	Jon Knott/Auto. **RC**	10.00
226	Josh Labandeira/Auto. **RC**	10.00
227	Khalid Ballouli/Auto. **RC**	10.00
228	Kyle Davies/Auto. **RC**	15.00
229	Matt Creighton/Auto. **RC**	15.00
230	Mike Gosling/Auto.	15.00
231	Nic Ungs/Auto. **RC**	10.00
232	Zach Miner/Auto. **RC**	10.00
233	Donald Levinski/Auto.	10.00
234	Bradley Sullivan	15.00
235	Carlos Quentin	40.00
236	Conor Jackson	30.00
237	Estee Harris **RC**	15.00
238	Jeffrey Allison	10.00
239	Kyle Sleeth	10.00
240	Matthew Moses	15.00
241	Tim Stauffer	15.00
242	Brad Snyder	10.00
243	Jason Hirsh	15.00
244	Lastings Milledge	40.00
245	Logan Kensing **RC**	15.00
246	Kory Casto	10.00
247	David Aardsma	1.50
248	Omar Quintanilla	2.00
249	Ervin Santana **RC**	2.00
250	Merkin Valdez **RC**	2.00
251	Vito Chiaravalloti **RC**	2.00
252	Travis Blackley **RC**	2.00
253	Chris Shelton **RC**	2.00
254	Rudy Guillen **RC**	3.00
255	Bobby Brownlie **RC**	2.00
256	Paul Maholm **RC**	4.00
257	Roger Clemens	3.00
258	Layne Nix	.25
259	Eric Hinske	.25
260	Ivan Rodriguez	1.00
261	Brandon Webb	.50
262	Jhonny Peralta	.25
263	Adam Kennedy	.25
264	Tony Batista	.25
265	Jeff Suppan	.25
266	Kenny Lofton	.50
267	Scott Sullivan	.25
268	Ken Griffey Jr.	2.00
269	Billy Traber	.25
270	Larry Walker	.50
271	Todd Hollandsworth	.25
272	Carlos Beltran	1.00
273	Carl Crawford	.50
274	Karim Garcia	.25
275	Jose Reyes	.75
276	Brandon Duckworth	.25
277	Brian Giles	.50
278	J.T. Snow Jr.	.25
279	Jamie Moyer	.25
280	Julio Lugo	.25
281	Mark Teixeira	.75
282	Cory Lidle	.25
283	Lyle Overbay	.50
284	Troy Percival	.25
285	Robby Hammock	.25
286	Jason Johnson	.25
287	Brandon Lyon	.25
288	Antonio Alfonseca	.25
289	Tom Goodwin	.25
290	Paul Konerko	.50
291	D'Angelo Jimenez	.25
292	Ben Broussard	.25
293	Magglio Ordonez	.50
294	Carlos Pena	.25
295	Chad Fox	.25
296	Jeriome Robertson	.25
297	Travis Hafner	.50
298	Joe Randa	.25
299	Brady Clark	.25
300	Barry Zito	.75
301	Ruben Sierra	.25
302	Brett Myers	.25
303	Oliver Perez	.25
304	Benito Santiago	.25
305	David Ross	.25
306	Joe Nathan	.25
307	Jim Edmonds	.50
308	Matt Kata	.25
309	Vinny Castilla	.25
310	Marty Cordova	.25
311	Aramis Ramirez	.50
312	Carl Everett	.25
313	Ryan Freel	.25
314	Mark Bellhorn	.25
315	Ugueth Urbina	.25
316	Tim Redding	.25
317	Jeromy Burnitz	.25
318	Miguel Cabrera	1.00
319	Orlando Hernandez	.25
320	Casey Blake	.25
321	Aaron Boone	.25
322	Jermaine Dye	.25
323	Jerome Williams	.25
324	John Olerud	.50
325	Scott Rolen	1.00
326	Bobby Kielty	.25
327	Travis Lee	.25
328	Jeff Cirillo	.25
329	Scott Spiezio	.25
330	Melvin Mora	.25
331	Mike Timlin	.25
332	Kerry Wood	.50
333	Tony Womack	.25
334	Jody Gerut	.25
335	Morgan Ensberg	.25
336	Odalis Perez	.25
337	Michael Cuddyer	.25
338	Jose Hernandez	.25
339	LaTroy Hawkins	.25
340	Marquis Grissom	.25
341	Matt Morris	.50
342	Juan Gonzalez	.75
343	Jose Valverde	.25
344	Joe Borowski	.25
345	Josh Bard	.25
346	Austin Kearns	.50
347	Chin-Hui Tsao	.25
348	Wilfredo Ledezma	.25
349	Aaron Guiel	.25
350	Alfonso Soriano	1.00
351	Ted Lilly	.25
352	Sean Burroughs	.25
353	Rafael Palmeiro	.75
354	Quinton McCracken	.25
355	David Ortiz	1.00
356	Randall Simon	.25
357	Wily Mo Pena	.25
358	Brian Anderson	.25
359	Corey Koskie	.25
360	Keith Foulke	.25
361	Sidney Ponson	.25
362	Gary Matthews Jr.	.25
363	Herbert Perry	.25
364	Shea Hillenbrand	.25
365	Craig Biggio	.50
366	Barry Larkin	.50
367	Orlando Merced	.25
368	Sammy Sosa	1.50
369	Joe Crede	.50
370	Gary Sheffield	.75
371	Coco Crisp	.25
372	Torii Hunter	.50
373	Derrek Lee	.75
374	Adam Everett	.25
375	Miguel Tejada	.75
376	Jeremy Affeldt	.25
377	Robin Ventura	.25
378	Scott Podsednik	.75
379	Matthew LeCroy	.25
380	Vladimir Guerrero	1.50
381	Steve Karsay	.25
382	Jeff Nelson	.25
383	Chase Utley	.75
384	Bobby Abreu	.50
385	Josh Fogg	.25
386	Trevor Hoffman	.25
387	Matt Stairs	.25
388	Edgar Martinez	.50
389	Edgar Renteria	.50
390	Chipper Jones	1.50
391	Eric Munson	.25
392	Dewon Brazelton	.25
393	John Thomson	.25
394	Chris Woodward	.25
395	Joe Kennedy	.25
396	Reed Johnson	.25
397	Johnny Estrada	.25
398	Damian Moss	.25
399	Victor Zambrano	.25
400	Dontrelle Willis	.50
401	Troy Glaus	.75
402	Raul Mondesi	.25
403	Jeff DaVanon	.25
404	Kurt Ainsworth	.25
405	Pedro J. Martinez	1.50
406	Eric Karros	.25
407	Billy Koch	.25
408	Luis Gonzalez	.50
409	Jack Cust	.25
410	Mike Sweeney	.25
411	Jason Bay	.75
412	Mark Redman	.25
413	Jason Jennings	.25
414	Rondell White	.50
415	Todd Hundley	.25
416	Shannon Stewart	.25
417	Jae Weong Seo	.25
418	Livan Hernandez	.25
419	Mark Ellis	.25
420	Pat Burrell	.50
421	Mark Loretta	.25
422	Robb Nen	.25
423	Joel Pineiro	.25
424	Todd Walker	.25
425	Jeremy Bonderman	.50
426	A.J. Burnett	.25
427	Greg Myers	.25
428	Roy Oswalt	.50
429	Carlos Baerga	.25
430	Garret Anderson	.50
431	Horacio Ramirez	.25
432	Brian Roberts	.25
433	Kevin Brown	.50
434	Eric Milton	.25
435	Brian Daubach	.25
436	Alex Escobar	.25
437	Alex Sanchez	.25
438	Jeff Bagwell	1.00
439	Claudio Vargas	.25
440	Shawn Green	.50
441	Geoff Jenkins	.25
442	David Wells	.25
443	Nick Johnson	.25
444	Jose Guillen	.25
445	Scott Hatteberg	.25
446	Phil Nevin	.25
447	Jason Schmidt	.50
448	Ricky Ledee	.25
449	So Taguchi	.25
450	Randy Johnson	.75
451	Eric Young	.25
452	Chone Figgins	.25
453	Larry Bigbie	.25
454	Scott Williamson	.25
455	Ramon Martinez	.25
456	Roberto Alomar	.50
457	Ryan Dempster	.25
458	Ryan Ludwick	.25
459	Ramon Santiago	.25
460	Jeff Conine	.25
461	Brad Lidge	.25
462	Ken Harvey	.25
463	Guillermo Mota	.25
464	Rick Reed	.25
465	Armando Benitez	.25
466	Wade Miller	.25

Refractors

Cards (1-220, 247-466):	1-2X
Inserted 1:4	
Rookie Auto. (221-246):	1.5-2X
Production 100	
Gold Refractor (1-220):	1-2X
Inserted 1:5	
Rookie Gold Refractor (221-246):	2-3X
Production 50	
Black Refractor (1-220):	2-4X
Inserted 1:10	
Rookie Black Refractor:	No Pricing
Production 25	

Fashionably Great

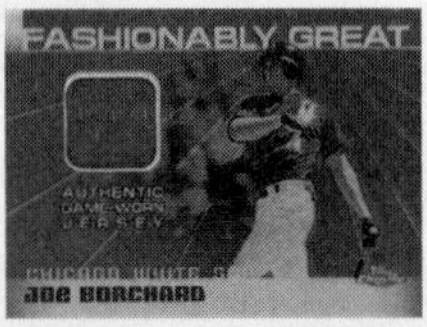

		NM/M
	Common Player:	5.00
	Inserted 1:Box	
JB	Jeff Bagwell	10.00
CB	Craig Biggio	5.00
HB	Hank Blalock	8.00
JBO	Joe Borchard	5.00
KB	Kevin Brown	5.00
EC	Eric Chavez	6.00
CD	Carlos Delgado	6.00
AD	Adam Dunn	6.00
FG	Freddy Garcia	5.00
CF	Cliff Floyd	5.00
NG	Nomar Garciaparra	10.00
TH	Trevor Hoffman	5.00
TH	Tim Hudson	6.00
AJ	Andruw Jones	6.00
CJ	Chipper Jones	8.00
DL	Derek Lowe	6.00
PM	Pedro J. Martinez	8.00
FM	Fred McGriff	8.00
MM	Mark Mulder	6.00
BM	Brett Myers	5.00
JO	John Olerud	6.00
RP	Rafael Palmeiro	8.00
WP	Wily Mo Pena	5.00
MP	Mike Piazza	10.00
AP	Albert Pujols	15.00
MR	Manny Ramirez	8.00
JR	Juan Rivera	5.00
AR	Alex Rodriguez	12.00
IR	Ivan Rodriguez	8.00
CS	Curt Schilling	6.00
JS	John Smoltz	6.00
SS	Sammy Sosa	12.00
MS	Mike Sweeney	5.00
FT	Frank Thomas	10.00
JV	Jose Vidro	5.00
BW	Billy Wagner	6.00
VW	Vernon Wells	5.00

Handle With Care

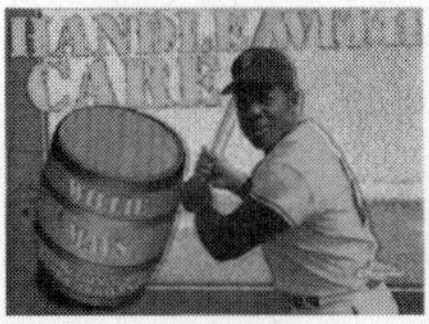

No pricing due to scarcity.
Production Five Sets

Presidential First Pitch Relics

		NM/M
	Common President:	10.00
	Inserted 1:15	
GHB	George H.W. Bush	20.00
GB	George W. Bush	25.00
BC	Bill Clinton	20.00
CC	Calvin Coolidge	20.00
DE	Dwight D. Eisenhower	20.00
GF	Gerald Ford	30.00
WH	Warren Harding	15.00
HH	Herbert Hoover	25.00
LJ	Lyndon B. Johnson	30.00
RN	Richard Nixon	25.00
RR	Ronald Reagan	30.00
FR	Franklin D. Roosevelt	20.00
WT	William H. Taft	25.00
HT	Harry S. Truman	25.00
WW	Woodrow Wilson	10.00

Presidential Pastime

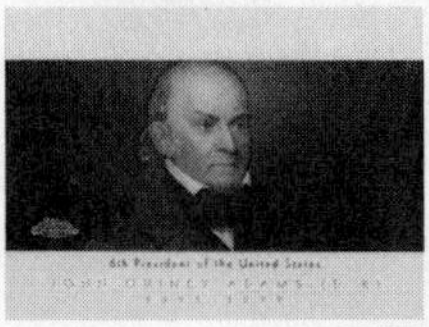

		NM/M
	Common President:	3.00
	X-fractors:	3-5X
	Inserted 1:400	
PP1	George Washington	10.00
PP2	John Adams	3.00
PP3	Thomas Jefferson	6.00
PP4	James Madison	4.00
PP5	James Monroe	4.00
PP6	John Quincy Adams	4.00
PP7	Andrew Jackson	3.00
PP8	Martin Van Buren	3.00
PP9	William H. Harrison	3.00
PP10	John Tyler	3.00
PP11	James K. Polk	3.00
PP12	Zachary Taylor	3.00
PP13	Millard Fillmore	3.00
PP14	Franklin Pierce	3.00
PP15	James Buchanan	3.00
PP16	Abraham Lincoln	8.00
PP17	Andrew Johnson	3.00
PP18	Ulysses S. Grant	5.00
PP19	Rutherford B. Hayes	3.00

PP20	James Garfield	3.00
PP21	Chester A. Arthur	3.00
PP22	Grover Cleveland	3.00
PP23	Benjamin Harrison	3.00
PP24	William McKinley	3.00
PP25	Theodore Roosevelt	3.00
PP26	William H. Taft	3.00
PP27	Woodrow Wilson	3.00
PP28	Warren Harding	3.00
PP29	Calvin Coolidge	3.00
PP30	Herbert Hoover	5.00
PP31	Franklin D. Roosevelt	5.00
PP32	Harry S. Truman	3.00
PP33	Dwight D. Eisenhower	3.00
PP34	John F. Kennedy	8.00
PP35	Lyndon B. Johnson	3.00
PP36	Richard Nixon	4.00
PP37	Gerald Ford	3.00
PP38	Jimmy Carter	3.00
PP39	Ronald Reagan	3.00
PP40	George H.W. Bush	3.00
PP41	Bill Clinton	4.00
PP42	George W. Bush	3.00

Town Heroes

		NM/M
Common Player:		5.00
LB	Lance Berkman	5.00
EC	Eric Chavez	5.00
NG	Nomar Garciaparra	12.00
JG	Jason Giambi	8.00
RH	Rich Harden	5.00
TH	Tim Hudson	8.00
CJ	Chipper Jones	8.00
MM	Mark Mulder	5.00
HN	Hideo Nomo	8.00
RP	Rafael Palmeiro	8.00
MP	Mark Prior	8.00
AP	Albert Pujols	15.00
MR	Manny Ramirez	8.00
JR	Jose Reyes	5.00
AR	Alex Rodriguez	10.00
SS	Sammy Sosa	15.00
SST	Shannon Stewart	5.00
MT	Miguel Tejada	5.00
FT	Frank Thomas	8.00
KW	Kerry Wood	10.00
BZ	Barry Zito	5.00

2004 Topps Clubhouse Collection

		NM/M
Common Player:		4.00
Two Relics Per Pack		
Pack (2):		18.00
Box (10):		140.00
HA	Hank Aaron/113	50.00
BA	Bobby Abreu	6.00
RA	Roberto Alomar	6.00
EA	Edgardo Alfonzo/286	4.00
TA	Tony Armas Jr.	4.00
JB	Jeff Bagwell	8.00
RB	Rocco Baldelli	6.00
TB	Tony Batista	4.00
HB	Hank Bauer	10.00
JPB	Josh Beckett/195	6.00
JBE	Johnny Bench	10.00
AB	Armando Benitez	4.00
LB	Lance Berkman	6.00
YB	Yogi Berra	10.00
HBL	Hank Blalock	6.00
WB	Wade Boggs/250	8.00
BB	Bret Boone	4.00
GB	George Brett	12.00
KB	Kevin Brown	6.00
JBU	Jeromy Burnitz	4.00
PB	Pat Burrell	6.00
MB	Marlon Byrd	4.00
MC	Miguel Cabrera	8.00
GC	Gary Carter/221	8.00
JCA	Joe Carter/259	6.00
RLC	Roger Cedeno	4.00
OC	Orlando Cepeda	8.00
RCE	Ron Cey	4.00
EC	Eric Chavez	6.00
CFC	Chin-Feng Chen	4.00
JC	Jeff Cirillo	4.00
WC	Will Clark	8.00
RC	Roberto Clemente	75.00
DC	Dave Concepcion	8.00

CCR	Carl Crawford	4.00
CD	Carlos Delgado/200	6.00
AD	Adam Dunn	8.00
DE	Dennis Eckersley	10.00
CE	Carl Everett	4.00
SF	Steve Finley	4.00
CFL	Cliff Floyd	4.00
WF	Whitey Ford/296	15.00
BF	Brad Fullmer/200	4.00
JF	Jonathan Fulton	4.00
RF	Rafael Furcal	4.00
EG	Eric Gagne	8.00
NG	Nomar Garciaparra	12.00
JG	Jason Giambi	8.00
TGL	Troy Glaus	8.00
TG	Tom Glavine	8.00
AG	Adrian Gonzalez	4.00
LG	Luis Gonzalez	4.00
JGO	Juan Gonzalez	8.00
MG	Mark Grace	8.00
SG	Shawn Green	6.00
KG	Ken Griffey Jr./200	15.00
MDG	Marquis Grissom	4.00
VG	Vladimir Guerrero	8.00
CG	Cristian Guzman	4.00
TGW	Tony Gwynn	10.00
MH	Mickey Hall	4.00
EH	Estee Harris/206	4.00
THE	Todd Helton	8.00
RHE	Rickey Henderson	10.00
RH	Ramon Hernandez	4.00
OH	Orel Hershiser	8.00
JH	James Houser/182	8.00
OHU	Orlando Hudson	4.00
TH	Tim Hudson	6.00
THU	Torii Hunter	6.00
KI	Kazuhisa Ishii	4.00
RJ	Reggie Jackson	10.00
DJ	Derek Jeter	20.00
AJ	Andruw Jones	6.00
CJ	Chipper Jones	8.00
AK	Al Kaline	15.00
JK	Jason Kendall	
JKE	Jeff Kent/200	8.00
HK	Harmon Killebrew	
PK	Paul Konerko	6.00
BL	Barry Larkin/200	10.00
AL	Al Leiter	4.00
SL	Steve Lerud	4.00
EL	Esteban Loaiza	4.00
PL	Paul LoDuca	4.00
JL	Javy Lopez	6.00
DL	Derek Lowe/200	4.00
CL	Chris Lubanski/209	8.00
GM	Greg Maddux	15.00
EMA	Edgar Martinez/200	6.00
PM	Pedro Martinez/200	10.00
TM	Tino Martinez	6.00
EM	Eddie Mathews/174	25.00
WM	Willie Mays	60.00
FM	Fred McGriff	6.00
KM	Kevin Millwood	4.00
MM	Mark Mulder	6.00
EMU	Eddie Murray	12.00
BM	Brett Myers	4.00
HN	Hideo Nomo/207	8.00
JO	John Olerud	6.00
MO	Magglio Ordonez	4.00
RP	Rafael Palmeiro/200	10.00
CP	Chan Ho Park	4.00
DP	Dave Parker/292	10.00
CPA	Corey Patterson/267	8.00
WP	Wily Mo Pena	8.00
TPE	Troy Percival	4.00
TP	Tony Perez	10.00
MP	Mike Piazza	10.00
JP	Jorge Posada/264	8.00
AP	Albert Pujols	15.00
ARA	Aramis Ramirez	8.00
MR	Manny Ramirez/207	8.00
JRE	Jose Reyes	6.00
CR	Cal Ripken Jr.	20.00
MRI	Mariano Rivera/239	8.00
FR	Frank Robinson	8.00
JR	Jackie Robinson/262	50.00
AR	Alex Rodriguez	10.00
IR	Ivan Rodriguez	8.00
SR	Scott Rolen	10.00
JRO	Jimmy Rollins	8.00
NR	Nolan Ryan	20.00
CS	C.C. Sabathia	4.00
TS	Tim Salmon	6.00
RSA	Ryne Sandberg	8.00
JS	Jay Sborz	6.00
CSC	Curt Schilling	8.00
MS	Mike Schmidt	15.00
RS	Richie Sexson/200	8.00
GS	Gary Sheffield	6.00
RSI	Ruben Sierra	10.00
OS	Ozzie Smith	15.00
JSM	John Smoltz	8.00
DS	Duke Snider	15.00
AS	Alfonso Soriano	8.00
SS	Sammy Sosa	12.00
WS	Willie Stargell/200	10.00
CST	Casey Stengel/217	10.00
MSW	Mike Sweeney	4.00
MTE	Miguel Tejada	6.00
MT	Mark Teixeira	6.00
FT	Frank Thomas	8.00
JT	Jim Thome	8.00
FV	Fernando Valenzuela	4.00
JVI	Jose Vidro	4.00
BWA	Billy Wagner	4.00
LW	Larry Walker	4.00

VW	Vernon Wells/200	4.00
BW	Bernie Williams	6.00
PW	Preston Wilson	4.00
JV	Javier Vazquez	6.00
CY	Carl Yastrzemski	15.00
RY	Robin Yount	12.00
BZ	Barry Zito/230	6.00

Copper

Copper:	.75-1.5X
Production 99 Sets	

Black

Black:	2-3X
Production 25 Sets	

Red

Red:	No Pricing
Production One Set	

All-Star Appeal Ball

No Pricing	
Production 10 Sets	

All-Star Appeal Ball Auto.

		NM/M
Production 30 Sets		
GA	Garret Anderson	30.00
HB	Hank Blalock	35.00
JP	Jorge Posada	50.00

All-Star Appeal Base

		NM/M
Common Player:		5.00
Production 65 Sets		
On Deck Circle:		1X
Production 90 Sets		
GA	Garret Anderson	8.00
HB	Hank Blalock	8.00
BB	Bret Boone	5.00
CD	Carlos Delgado	6.00
JE	Jim Edmonds	6.00
RF	Rafael Furcal	6.00
NG	Nomar Garciaparra	15.00
JG	Jason Giambi	8.00
TG	Troy Glaus	6.00
LG	Luis Gonzalez	6.00
TH	Todd Helton	6.00
AJ	Andruw Jones	6.00
JL	Javy Lopez	6.00
ML	Mike Lowell	6.00
EM	Edgar Martinez	6.00
MO	Magglio Ordonez	6.00
JP	Jorge Posada	6.00
AP	Albert Pujols	25.00
ER	Edgar Renteria	6.00
AR	Alex Rodriguez	15.00
SR	Scott Rolen	10.00
RS	Richie Sexson	6.00
GS	Gary Sheffield	6.00
AS	Alfonso Soriano	10.00
VW	Vernon Wells	6.00
PW	Preston Wilson	5.00

All-Star Appeal Base Auto.

		NM/M
Production 50 Sets		
GA	Garret Anderson	25.00
HB	Hank Blalock	35.00
JP	Jorge Posada	35.00
GS	Gary Sheffield	25.00

All-Star Appeal On Deck Circle

		NM/M
Common Player:		5.00
Production 90 Sets		
GA	Garret Anderson	8.00
HB	Hank Blalock	5.00
AB	Aaron Boone	5.00
BB	Bret Boone	5.00
LC	Luis Castillo	5.00
CD	Carlos Delgado	5.00
JE	Jim Edmonds	8.00
CE	Carl Everett	5.00
RF	Rafael Furcal	6.00
NG	Nomar Garciaparra	15.00
JG	Jason Giambi	8.00
TG	Troy Glaus	5.00
LG	Luis Gonzalez	6.00
TH	Todd Helton	8.00

AJ	Andruw Jones	6.00
PL	Paul LoDuca	5.00
JL	Javy Lopez	8.00
ML	Mike Lowell	6.00
EM	Edgar Martinez	8.00
MM	Melvin Mora	6.00
MO	Magglio Ordonez	6.00
JP	Jorge Posada	8.00
AP	Albert Pujols	20.00
ER	Edgar Renteria	6.00
AR	Alex Rodriguez	15.00
SR	Scott Rolen	10.00
RS	Richie Sexson	6.00
GS	Gary Sheffield	8.00
AS	Alfonso Soriano	10.00
JV	Jose Vidro	5.00
VW	Vernon Wells	6.00
RW	Rondell White	5.00
PW	Preston Wilson	5.00

All-Star Appeal On Deck Autograph

		NM/M
Quantity produced listed		
GA	Garret Anderson/320	15.00
HB	Hank Blalock/920	15.00
JP	Jorge Posada/420	30.00
GS	Gary Sheffield/170	25.00

Legends Relics

		NM/M
Common Player:		
BR1	Babe Ruth/60	175.00
BR2	Babe Ruth/171	150.00
BR3	Babe Ruth/45	200.00
EB1	Ernie Banks/143	15.00
EB3	Ernie Banks/47	20.00
EB6	Ernie Banks/15	15.00
LG1	Lou Gehrig/49	125.00
LG2	Lou Gehrig/184	100.00
LG3	Lou Gehrig/52	125.00
TC3	Ty Cobb/47	120.00
WM1	Willie Mays/52	70.00

Play Relics

		NM/M
Production 75 Sets		
CLE	Omar Vizquel, Brandon Phillips, Travis Hafner	10.00
NYM	Ty Wigginton, Jose Reyes, Mike Piazza	25.00
NYY	Derek Jeter, Alex Rodriguez, Jason Giambi	50.00
PHI	Jimmy Rollins, David Bell, Jim Thome	20.00
SDP	Khalil Greene, Sean Burroughs, Phil Nevin	10.00

Ropes Relics

		NM/M
Common Player:		5.00
Production 50 Sets		
BA	Bobby Abreu	8.00
JB	Jeff Bagwell	10.00
RB	Rocco Baldelli	8.00
JBE	Johnny Bench	20.00
LB	Lance Berkman	5.00
CB	Craig Biggio	6.00
HB	Hank Blalock	10.00
WB	Wade Boggs	8.00
GC	Gary Carter	8.00
EC	Eric Chavez	8.00
ADA	Andre Dawson	8.00
AD	Adam Dunn	10.00
CE	Carl Everett	5.00
RF	Rafael Furcal	5.00
JG	Jason Giambi	8.00
LG	Luis Gonzalez	5.00
SG	Shawn Green	5.00
VG	Vladimir Guerrero	15.00
TH	Todd Helton	10.00
AH	Aubrey Huff	5.00
CJ	Chipper Jones	15.00
PK	Paul Konerko	5.00
EM	Edgar Martinez	5.00
DM	Don Mattingly	40.00
DMU	Dale Murphy	12.00
MO	Magglio Ordonez	5.00
RP	Rafael Palmeiro	10.00
MP	Mike Piazza	15.00

KP Kirby Puckett 15.00
AP Albert Pujols 25.00
MR Manny Ramirez 10.00
JR Jose Reyes 8.00
BR Brooks Robinson 15.00
AR Alex Rodriguez 15.00
IR Ivan Rodriguez 10.00
RS Ryne Sandberg 40.00
MS Mike Schmidt 40.00
GS Gary Sheffield 6.00
OS Ozzie Smith 25.00
DS Duke Snider 15.00
AS Alfonso Soriano 10.00
SS Sammy Sosa 15.00
MT Miguel Tejada 8.00
JT Jim Thome 10.00
BW Bernie Williams 8.00
PW Preston Wilson 5.00
CY Carl Yastrzemski 20.00

Heart of the Line-Up Relics

NM/M

Production 100 unless noted.
ARI Steve Finley, Richie Sexson, Luis Gonzalez 10.00
CHC Sammy Sosa, Moises Alou, Aramis Ramirez 35.00
CHW Magglio Ordonez, Frank Thomas, Carlos Lee/78 20.00
CIN Ken Griffey Jr., Austin Kearns, Adam Dunn 25.00
COL Todd Helton, Larry Walker, Preston Wilson 15.00
NYY Alex Rodriguez, Jason Giambi, Gary Sheffield 35.00
PHI Jim Thome, Pat Burrell, Bobby Abreu 20.00
SEA Edgar Martinez, Bret Boone, John Olerud 10.00
STL Albert Pujols, Jim Edmonds, Scott Rolen 40.00
TEX Alfonso Soriano, Mark Teixeira, Hank Blalock 20.00
TOR Vernon Wells, Carlos Delgado, Eric Hinske 10.00

Place Relics

No Pricing
Production 25 or less.

Pieces Relics

NM/M

Quantity produced listed
CD Carlos Delgado/25 8.00
THU Torii Hunter/48 8.00
AJ Andruw Jones/25 10.00
PM Pedro Martinez/45 10.00
WM Willie Mays/24 85.00
BM Brett Myers/39 5.00
BP Brad Penny/31 5.00
MP Mike Piazza/31 40.00
NR Nolan Ryan/34 50.00
BZ Barry Zito/75 6.00

2004 Topps Cracker Jack

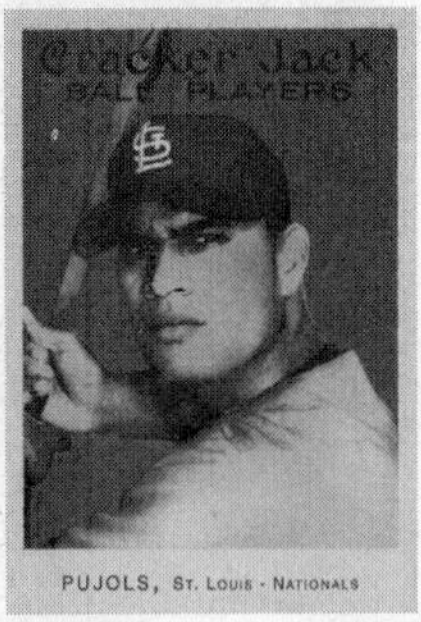

NM/M

Complete Set with SP's (250): 160.00
Common Player: .25
Common SP: 2.00
SP's inserted 1:3
Pack (8): 3.00
Box (24): 60.00
1 Jose Reyes/SP 2.00
2 Edgar Renteria .25
3 Albert Pujols 2.00
3 Albert Pujols/SP/Swinging 6.00
4 Garret Anderson .50
5 Bobby Abreu .40
6 Andruw Jones .75
7 Jeff Kent .40
8 Magglio Ordonez .50
9 Kris Benson .25
10 Luis Gonzalez .40
11 Corey Patterson .50
12 Connie Mack .25
13 Vernon Wells/SP 2.00
14 Jim Edmonds .50
15 Bret Boone .50
16 Travis Lee .25
17 Alex Rodriguez/SP 6.00
No # Alex Rodriguez 2.00
18 Erubiel Durazo .25
19 Brett Myers .25
20 Scott Rolen/SP 3.00
21 Paul LoDuca .25
22 Geoff Jenkins .50
23 Charles Comiskey .25
24 Cliff Floyd .25
25 Jim Thome .75
25 Jim Thome/SP/Fielding 3.00
26 Russ Ortiz .25
27 Bill Mueller .25
28 Kenny Lofton .40
29 Jay Gibbons .40
30 Ken Griffey Jr. 1.50
31 Jeff Bagwell .75
32 Jose Lima .25
33 Brad Radke .25
34 Ramon Hernandez .25
35 Brian Giles/SP 2.00
36 Jeremy Bonderman .25
37 Jerome Williams .25
38 Rafael Palmeiro .50
39 Scott Podsednik .75
40 Rafael Furcal .40
41 Roy Oswalt .40
42 Orlando Hudson .25
43 Todd Helton .75
44 Kerry Wood 1.00
45 Tom Glavine .40
46 David Eckstein .25
47 Trot Nixon .25
48 Preston Wilson .25
50 Eric Gagne/SP 3.00
51 Ichiro Suzuki/SP 5.00
52 Juan Gonzalez .75
53 Torii Hunter .50
54 Bartolo Colon .40
55 Dick Hoblitzell .25
56 Al Leiter .25
57 Johnny Damon .40
58 Larry Walker .40
59 Brian Jordan .25
60 Richie Sexson/SP 3.00
61 Orlando Cabrera .25
62 Jason Phillips .25
63 Phil Nevin .25
64 John Olerud .40
65 Miguel Tejada .50
66 Nap Lajoie .50
67 C.C. Sabathia .25
68 Ty Wigginton .25
69 Troy Glaus .50
70 Mike Piazza 1.50
71 Craig Biggio .40
72 Cristian Guzman .25
73 Dmitri Young .25
74 Roger Clemens 2.00
75 Runelvys Hernandez .25
76 Nomar Garciaparra 2.00
77 Mark Mulder .40
78 Derek Lowe .40
79 Paul Konerko .25
80 Sammy Sosa/SP 5.00
81 Vladimir Guerrero 1.00
82 Xavier Nady .25
83 Joel Pineiro .25
84 Chipper Jones 1.50
85 Manny Ramirez .75
86 Burt Shotton .25
87 Raul Ibanez/SP 2.00
88 Eric Chavez .50
89 Frank Catalanotto .25
90 Dontrelle Willis .50
91 Roy Halladay .50
92 Jermaine Dye .25
93 Jason Kendall .25
94 Jacque Jones .25
95 Gary Sheffield .50
95 Gary Sheffield/SP/Yanks. 3.00
96 Mike Lieberthal .25
97 Adam Dunn .50
98 Carl Crawford .25
99 Reggie Sanders .25
100 Mark Prior/SP 6.00
101 Luis Matos .25
102 Barry Zito .50
103 Randy Johnson 1.00
104 Kevin Brown .50
105 Pat Burrell .50
106 Steve Finley .25
107 Moises Alou .50
108 David Ortiz/SP 3.00
109 Austin Kearns/SP 2.00
110 Carlos Beltran .50
111 Shawn Green .40
112 Javier Vazquez .50
113 Hideo Nomo .50
114 Kazuhisa Ishii .25
115 Corey Koskie .25
116 Kevin Millwood .50
117 Randy Wolf .40
118 Darin Erstad .25
119 Fernando Vina .25
120 Pedro J. Martinez 1.00
121 Melvin Mora .25
122 Carl Everett .25
123 Matt Morris .40
124 Greg Maddux 1.50
125 Jason Schmidt .25
126 Mark Teixeira/SP 3.00
127 Randy Winn .25
128 Rich Aurilia .25
129 Vicente Padilla .25
130 Tim Hudson .50
131 Marlon Byrd .25
132 Jae Weong Seo .25
133 Branch Rickey .25
134 A.J. Pierzynski .25
135 Ryan Klesko .40
136 Eric Hinske .25
137 Mike Cameron .25
138 Roberto Alomar .50
139 Jarrod Washburn .25
140 Curt Schilling .75
140 Curt Schilling/SP/Red Sox 3.00
141 Omar Vizquel .25
142 Mike Sweeney .25
143 Wade Miller .25
144 Jose Vidro .25
145 Rich Harden/SP 2.00
146 Eric Munson .25
147 Lance Berkman .50
148 Mark Buehrle .25
149 Carlos Delgado .75
150 Sean Burroughs .25
151 Kevin Millar .25
152 Frank Thomas .75
153 Adrian Beltre .25
154 Shannon Stewart .25
155 Johan Santana .25
156 Edgardo Alfonzo .25
157 Jose Cruz Jr. .25
158 Sidney Ponson .25
159 Edgar Martinez .50
160 Jamie Moyer .25
161 Tony Batista .25
162 Wes Helms .25
163 Brandon Webb/SP 2.00
164 Gil Meche .25
165 Marcus Giles/SP 2.00
166 Angel Berroa/SP 2.00
167 Rocco Baldelli/SP 3.00
168 Michael Young .25
169 Esteban Loaiza .25
170 Casey Blake .25
171 Jody Gerut .25
172 Bo Hart/SP 2.00
173 Kelvim Escobar .25
174 Aaron Guiel .25
175 Javy Lopez/SP 3.00
176 Aubrey Huff .25
177 Hank Blalock .50
178 Edwin Jackson .25
178 Edwin Jackson/SP/#104 2.00
179 Delmon Young/SP 3.00
180 Bobby Jenks .25
181 Felix Pie .25
181 Felix Pie/SP/#80 2.00
182 Jeremy Reed/SP 2.00
183 Aaron Hill .25
184 Casey Kotchman/SP 2.00
185 Grady Sizemore .50
186 Joe Mauer/SP 3.00
187 Ryan Harvey .25
188 Neal Cotts .25
189 Victor Martinez .25
190 Rene Reyes .25
191 Eric Duncan .25
192 B.J. Upton/SP 3.00
193 Khalil Greene/SP 2.00
194 Bobby Crosby .25
195 Rickie Weeks/SP 3.00
196 Zack Greinke/SP 2.00
197 Laynce Nix .25
198 Vito Chiaravalloti/SP **RC** 2.00
199 Estee Harris **RC** .25
200 Jon Knott/SP **RC** 3.00
201 Dioner Navarro **RC** .75
201 Dioner Navarro/SP/#236 2.00
202 Craig Ansman **RC** .50
203 Travis Blackley **RC** 1.00
204 Yadier Molina **RC** .50
205 Rodney Choy Foo **RC** .50
206 Kyle Sleeth/SP 5.00
207 Jeff Allison 1.00
208 Josh Labandeira **RC** .50
209 Lastings Milledge/SP 10.00
210 Rudy Guillen/SP **RC** 3.00
211 Blake Hawksworth/SP **RC** 3.00
212 David Aardsma .50
213 Shawn Hill **RC** .50
214 Erick Aybar/SP **RC** 3.00
215 Ervin Santana **RC** 1.00
216 Tim Stauffer/SP 3.00
217 Merkin Valdez **RC** 1.00
218 Jack McKeon .25
219 Derrek Lee .50
220 Josh Beckett/SP 3.00
221 Luis Castillo .25
222 Mike Lowell .50
223 Juan Pierre .40
224 Ivan Rodriguez .75
224 Ivan Rodriguez/SP/Tigers 3.00
225 A.J. Burnett .25
226 Miguel Cabrera/SP 4.00
227 Jeffrey Loria .25
228 Joe Torre .50
229 Jason Giambi .75
229 Jason Giambi/SP/Fldg 3.00
230 Aaron Boone .25
231 Jose Contreras .25
232 Derek Jeter/SP 6.00
233 Nick Johnson .25
234 Mike Mussina .75
235 Andy Pettitte .50
236 Jorge Posada/SP 3.00
237 Alfonso Soriano .75
238 Bernie Williams .50

Mini

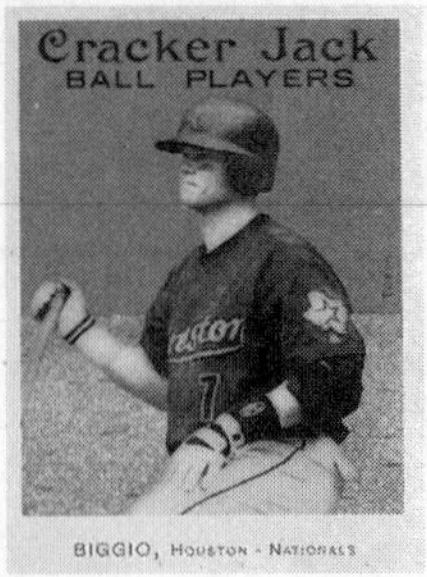

NM/M

Mini: 1-2X
Mini SP: 1X
Inserted 1:Pack
Mini SPs Inserted 1:20
SP's are same as in base set.

Mini Blue

Mini Blue: 3-6X
Mini Blue SP: 1-2X
Inserted 1:10
Mini Blue SP's Inserted 1:60
SP's are same as in base set.

Mini White

No Pricing
Production One Set

Mini Autograph

NM/M

Common Autograph:
Inserted 1:258
95 Gary Sheffield/50 40.00
112 Javier Vazquez 15.00
163 Brandon Webb 15.00
165 Marcus Giles 12.00
221 Luis Castillo 8.00
226 Miguel Cabrera 35.00

Secret Surprise Signatures

NM/M

Common Autograph: 8.00
CF Cliff Floyd 15.00
BG Brian Giles 15.00
AH Aubrey Huff 15.00
ML Mike Lamb 8.00
DM Dustin McGowan 20.00
FP Felix Pie 20.00
SP Scott Podsednik 20.00
SR Scott Rolen 30.00
MV Merkin Valdez 15.00
JW Jerome Williams 20.00
DW Dontrelle Willis 30.00

Sticker

Stickers: 1X
SP Stickers: .5X
Inserted 1:Surprise Pack
SP's Inserted 1:10 Surprise Packs

Take Me Out to/ Ballgame Relics

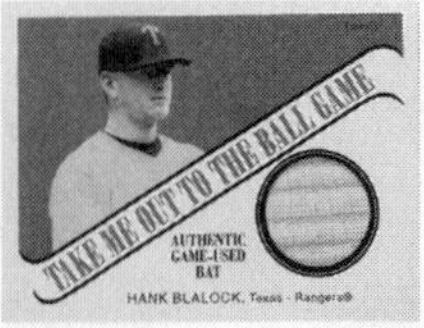

NM/M

Common Player: 5.00
BA Bobby Abreu 5.00
MA Moises Alou 6.00
GA Garret Anderson 8.00
JB Jeff Bagwell 8.00
RB Rocco Baldelli 8.00
LB Lance Berkman 5.00
AB Angel Berroa 5.00
CB Craig Biggio 5.00
HB Hank Blalock 6.00
BB1 Bret Boone/Bat 5.00
BB2 Bret Boone/Jsy 5.00
PB Pat Burrell 6.00
MC Miguel Cabrera 8.00
EC Eric Chavez 5.00
AD Adam Dunn 8.00
JE Jim Edmonds 5.00
RF Rafael Furcal 6.00
NG Nomar Garciaparra/Bat 10.00
NG Nomar Garciaparra/Jsy 10.00
JG Jason Giambi 8.00
MG Marcus Giles 5.00
TG Troy Glaus 8.00
LG Luis Gonzalez 5.00
SG Shawn Green/Bat 6.00

SG Shawn Green/Jsy 6.00
TH Todd Helton 8.00
TKH Torii Hunter 6.00
CJ Chipper Jones 8.00
PL Paul LoDuca 5.00
JL Javy Lopez/Bat 6.00
JL Javy Lopez/Jsy 6.00
MP Mike Piazza 10.00
AP Albert Pujols/Bat 15.00
AP Albert Pujols/Jsy 15.00
MR Manny Ramirez 8.00
JR Jose Reyes 6.00
AR Alex Rodriguez/Bat/Yanks. 15.00
AR Alex Rodriguez/Jsy 10.00
IR Ivan Rodriguez 8.00
JRO Jimmy Rollins 5.00
AS Alfonso Soriano/Bat 8.00
AS Alfonso Soriano/Jsy 8.00
SS Sammy Sosa/Bat 10.00
SS Sammy Sosa/Jsy 10.00
MS Mike Sweeney 5.00
MT Mark Teixeira 6.00
MT Miguel Tejada 6.00
JT Jim Thome 8.00
LW Larry Walker 5.00
VW Vernon Wells 5.00
KW Kerry Wood 8.00
MY Michael Young 5.00

1,2,3 Strikes You're Out Relics

NM/M
Common Player: 4.00
JB Josh Beckett 8.00
KB Kevin Brown 6.00
EG Eric Gagne 8.00
RH Rich Harden 4.00
RJ Randy Johnson 8.00
DL Derek Lowe 6.00
PM Pedro J. Martinez 8.00
KM Kevin Millwood 6.00
MAM Mark Mulder 6.00
MM Mike Mussina 15.00
BM Brett Myers 4.00
HN Hideo Nomo 8.00
CCS C.C. Sabathia 4.00
CS Curt Schilling 15.00
JS John Smoltz 6.00
BW Billy Wagner 4.00
KW Kerry Wood 10.00
BZ Barry Zito 6.00

2004 Topps Heritage

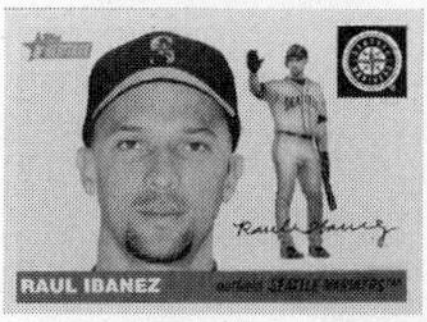

NM/M
Complete Set (475): 400.00
Common Player: .40
Common SP (398-475): 4.00
Variations & SP's Inserted 1:2
Pack (8): 5.00
Box (24): 100.00
1 Jim Thome 1.50
1 Jim Thome/SP/Hitting 8.00
2 Nomar Garciaparra/SP 10.00
3 Aramis Ramirez .50
4 Rafael Palmeiro/SP 6.00
5 Danny Graves .40
6 Casey Blake .40
7 Juan Uribe .40
8 Dmitri Young .40
8 Dmitri Young/SP/Old Logo 4.00
9 Billy Wagner .40
10 Jason Giambi .75
10 Jason Giambi/SP/Batting Stance 6.00
11 Carlos Beltran 1.00
12 Chad Hermansen .40
13 B.J. Upton .75
14 Dustan Mohr .40
15 Endy Chavez .40
16 Cliff Floyd .40
17 Bernie Williams .75
18 Eric Chavez .50
19 Chase Utley .75
20 Randy Johnson 1.50
21 Vernon Wells .50
22 Juan Gonzalez .75
23 Joe Kennedy .40
24 Bengie Molina .40
25 Carlos Lee .40
26 Horacio Ramirez .40
27 Anthony Acevedo **RC** 1.00
28 Sammy Sosa/SP 10.00
29 Jon Garland .40
30 Adam Dunn 1.00
30 Adam Dunn/SP/Hitting 6.00
31 Aaron Rowand .40
32 Jody Gerut .40
33 Chin-Hui Tsao .40
34 Alex Sanchez .40
35 A.J. Burnett .40
36 Brad Ausmus .40
37 Blake Hawksworth **RC** 1.50
38 Francisco Rodriguez .40
39 Alex Cintron .40
40 Chipper Jones 1.50
40 Chipper Jones/SP/Fldg 6.00
41 Deivi Cruz .40
42 Bill Mueller .40
43 Joe Borowski .40
44 Jimmy Haynes .40
45 Mark Loretta .40
46 Jerome Williams .40
47 Gary Sheffield/SP 6.00
48 Richard Hidalgo .40
49 Jason Kendall .40
49 Jason Kendall/SP/Old Logo 4.00
50 Ichiro Suzuki/SP 8.00
51 Jim Edmonds .75
52 Frank Catalanotto .40
53 Jose Contreras .40
54 Mo Vaughn .40
55 Brendan Donnelly .40
56 Luis Gonzalez .50
57 Robert Fick .40
58 Laynce Nix .40
59 Johnny Damon .75
60 Magglio Ordonez .50
60 Magglio Ordonez/SP/Hitting 6.00
61 Matt Clement .40
62 Ryan Ludwick .40
63 Luis Castillo .40
64 David Crouthers .40
65 Dave Berg .40
66 Kyle Davies **RC** 3.00
67 Tim Salmon .50
68 Marcus Giles .40
69 Marty Cordova .40
70 Todd Helton 1.00
70 Todd Helton/SP/Purple Jsy 6.00
71 Jeff Kent .50
72 Michael Tucker .40
73 Cesar Izturis .40
74 Paul Quantrill .40
75 Conor Jackson 3.00
76 Placido Polanco .40
77 Adam Eaton .40
78 Ramon Hernandez .40
79 Edgardo Alfonzo .40
80 Dioner Navarro **RC** 1.00
81 Woody Williams .40
82 Rey Ordonez .40
83 Randy Winn .40
84 Casey Myers **RC** 1.00
85 Rodney Choy Foo **RC** 2.00
85 Rodney Choy Foo/SP/Old Logo 6.00
86 Ray Durham .40
87 Sean Burroughs .40
88 Tim Frend **RC** 3.00
89 Shigetoshi Hasegawa .40
90 Jeff Allison .40
91 Orlando Hudson .40
92 Matt Creighton/SP **RC** 6.00
93 Tim Worrell .40
94 Kris Benson .40
95 Mike Lieberthal .40
96 David Wells .40
97 Jason Phillips .40
98 Bobby Cox .40
99 Johan Santana .75
100 Alex Rodriguez 3.00
100 Alex Rodriguez/SP/Throwing 10.00
101 John Vander Wal .40
102 Orlando Cabrera .50
103 Hideo Nomo .75
104 Todd Walker .40
105 Jason Johnson .40
106 Matt Mantei .40
107 Jarrod Washburn .40
108 Preston Wilson .40
109 Carl Pavano .40
110 Geoff Blum .40
111 Eric Gagne .50
112 Geoff Jenkins .50
113 Joe Torre .50
114 Jon Knott **RC** 1.50
115 Hank Blalock .75
116 John Olerud .50
117 Pat Burrell .75
117 Pat Burrell/Old Logo 5.00
118 Aaron Boone .40
119 Zach Day .40
120 Frank Thomas 1.00
120 Frank Thomas/Old Logo 6.00
121 Kyle Farnsworth .40
122 Derek Lowe .50
123 Zach Miner/SP **RC** 6.00
124 Matt Moses/SP 8.00
125 Jesse Roman **RC** 1.50
126 Josh Phelps .40
127 Nic Ungs **RC** 1.50
128 Dan Haren .40
129 Kirk Rueter .40
130 Jack McKeon .40
131 Keith Foulke .40
132 Garrett Stephenson .40
133 Wes Helms .40
134 Raul Ibanez .50
135 Morgan Ensberg .40
136 Jay Payton .40
137 Billy Koch .40
138 Mark Grudzielanek .40
139 Rodrigo Lopez .40
140 Corey Patterson .40
141 Troy Percival .40
142 Shea Hillenbrand .40
143 Brad Fullmer .40
144 Ricky Nolasco 2.00
145 Mark Teixeira .75
146 Tydus Meadows **RC** 1.50
147 Toby Hall .40
148 Orlando Palmeiro .40
149 Khalid Ballouli **RC** 1.50
150 Grady Little .40
151 David Eckstein .40
152 Kenny Perez **RC** 1.50
153 Ben Grieve .40
154 Ismael Valdes .40
155 Bret Boone .50
156 Jesse Foppert .40
157 Vicente Padilla .40
158 Bobby Abreu .50
159 Scott Hatteberg .40
160 Carlos Quentin 5.00
161 Anthony Lerew **RC** 1.50
162 Lance Carter .40
163 Robb Nen .40
164 Zachary Duke/SP **RC** 10.00
165 Xavier Nady .40
166 Kip Wells .40
167 Kevin Millwood .75
168 Jon Lieber .40
169 Jose Reyes .50
170 Eric Byrnes .40
171 Paul Konerko .40
172 Chris Lubanski .40
173 Jae Weong Seo .40
174 Corey Koskie .40
175 Tim Stauffer .40
176 John Lackey .40
177 Danny Bautista .40
178 Shane Reynolds .40
179 Jorge Julio .40
180 Manny Ramirez 1.00
180 Manny Ramirez/SP/Old Logo 6.00
181 Alex Gonzalez .40
182 Moises Alou .75
182 Moises Alou/SP/Old Logo 6.00
183 Mark Buehrle .40
184 Carlos Guillen .40
185 Nate Cornejo .40
186 Billy Traber .40
187 Jason Jennings .40
188 Eric Munson .40
189 Braden Looper .40
190 Juan Encarnacion .40
191 Dusty Baker .40
192 Travis Lee .40
193 Miguel Cairo .40
194 Rich Aurilia/SP 5.00
195 Flash Gordon .40
196 Freddy Garcia .40
197 Brian Lawrence .40
198 Jorge Posada/SP 8.00
199 Javier Vazquez .40
200 Albert Pujols 3.00
200 Albert Pujols/SP/Old Logo 12.00
201 Victor Zambrano .40
202 Eli Marrero .40
203 Joel Pineiro .40
204 Rondell White .50
205 Craig Ansman **RC** 2.00
206 Michael Young .40
207 Carlos Baerga .40
208 Andruw Jones 1.00
209 Jerry Hairston Jr. .40
210 Shawn Green/SP 6.00
211 Ron Gardenhire .40
212 Darin Erstad .50
213 Brandon Webb .50
213 Brandon Webb/SP/Glove In Air 6.00
214 Greg Maddux 2.00
215 Reed Johnson .40
216 John Thomson .40
217 Tino Martinez .40
218 Mike Cameron .40
219 Edgar Martinez .50
220 Eric Young .40
221 Reggie Sanders .40
222 Randy Wolf .40
223 Erubiel Durazo .40
224 Mike Mussina .75
225 Tom Glavine .75
226 Troy Glaus .75
227 Oscar Villarreal .40
228 David Segui .40
229 Jeff Suppan .40
230 Kenny Lofton .50
231 Esteban Loaiza .40
232 Felipe Lopez .40
233 Matt Lawton .40
234 Mark Bellhorn .40
235 Wilfredo Ledezma .40
236 Todd Hollandsworth .40
237 Octavio Dotel .40
238 Darren Dreifort .40
239 Paul LoDuca .40
240 Richie Sexson .75
241 Doug Mientkiewicz .40
242 Luis Rivas .40
243 Claudio Vargas .40
244 Mark Ellis .40
245 Brett Myers .40
246 Jake Peavy .40
247 Marquis Grissom .40
248 Armando Benitez .40
249 Ryan Franklin .40
250 Alfonso Soriano 1.50
250 Alfonso Soriano/SP/Fldg 6.00
251 Tim Hudson .75
252 Shannon Stewart .40
253 A.J. Pierzynski .40
254 Runelvys Hernandez .40
255 Roy Oswalt .50
256 Shawn Chacon .40
257 Tony Graffanino .40
258 Tim Wakefield .40
259 Damian Miller .40
260 Joe Crede .40
261 Jason LaRue .40
262 Jose Jimenez .40
263 Juan Pierre .40
264 Wade Miller .40
265 Odalis Perez .40
266 Eddie Guardado .40
267 Rocky Biddle .40
268 Jeff Nelson .40
269 Terrence Long .40
270 Ramon Ortiz .40
271 Raul Mondesi .50
272 Ugueth Urbina .40
273 Jeromy Burnitz .40
274 Brad Radke .40
275 Jose Vidro .40
276 Bobby Jenks .40
277 Ty Wigginton .40
278 Jose Guillen .40
279 Delmon Young .75
280 Brian Giles .50
281 Jason Schmidt .50
282 Nicholas Markakis .40
283 Felipe Alou .40
284 Carl Crawford .40
285 Neifi Perez .40
286 Miguel Tejada .75
287 Victor Martinez .40
288 Adam Kennedy .40
289 Kerry Ligtenberg .40
290 Scott Williamson .40
291 Tony Womack .40
292 Travis Hafner .40
293 Bobby Crosby .40
294 Chad Billingsley .40
295 Russ Ortiz .40
296 John Burkett .40
297 Carlos Zambrano .40
298 Randall Simon .40
299 Juan Castro .40
300 Mike Lowell .40
301 Fred McGriff .50
302 Glendon Rusch .40
303 Sung Ki Jung **RC** .40
304 Rocco Baldelli .75
305 Fernando Vina .40
306 Gil Meche .40
307 Jose Cruz Jr. .40
308 Bernie Castro .40
309 Scott Spiezio .40
310 Paul Byrd .40
311 Jay Gibbons .50
311 Jay Gibbons/SP/Old Logo 6.00
312 Trot Nixon .40
313 Chris O'Riordan **RC** 1.50
314 Julio Lugo .40
315 Ben Davis .40
316 Mike Williams .40
317 Trevor Hoffman .40
318 Andy Pettitte .75
319 Orlando Hernandez .40
320 Juan Rivera .40
321 Elizardo Ramirez .40
322 Junior Spivey .40
323 Tony Batista .40
324 Mike Remlinger .40
325 Alex Gonzalez .40
326 Aaron Hill .40
327 Steve Finley .40
328 Vinny Castilla .40
329 Eric Duncan .40
330 Mike Gosling .40
331 Eric Hinske .40
332 Scott Rolen 1.50
333 Benito Santiago .40
334 Jimmy Gobble .40
335 Bobby Higginson .40
336 Kelvim Escobar .40
337 Mike DeJean .40
338 Sidney Ponson .40
339 Todd Self **RC** 1.50
340 Jeff Cirillo .40
341 Jimmy Rollins .50
342 Barry Zito .75
342 Barry Zito/SP/Green Jsy 6.00
343 Felix Pie .40
344 Matt Morris .40
345 Kazuhiro Sasaki .40
346 Jack Wilson .40
347 Nick Johnson .40
348 Wil Cordero .40
349 Ryan Madson .40
350 Torii Hunter .75
351 Andy Ashby .40
352 Aubrey Huff .40
353 Brad Lidge .40
354 Derrek Lee .40
355 Yadier Molina **RC** 2.00
356 Paul Wilson .40
357 Omar Vizquel .50
358 Rene Reyes .40
359 Marlon Anderson .40
360 Bobby Kielty .40
361 Ryan Wagner .40
361 Ryan Wagner/SP/Old Logo 5.00
362 Justin Morneau .50
363 Shane Spencer .40
364 David Bell .40

365	Matt Stairs	.40
366	Joe Borchard	.40
367	Mark Redman	.40
368	Dave Roberts	.40
369	Desi Relaford	.40
370	Rich Harden	.40
371	Fernando Tatis	.40
372	Eric Karros	.40
373	Eric Milton	.40
374	Mike Sweeney	.40
375	Brian Daubach	.40
376	Brian Snyder	.40
377	Chris Reitsma	.40
378	Kyle Lohse	.40
379	Livan Hernandez	.40
380	Robin Ventura	.40
381	Jacque Jones	.40
382	Danny Kolb	.40
383	Casey Kotchman	.40
384	Cristian Guzman	.40
385	Josh Beckett	1.00
386	Khalil Greene	.40
387	Greg Myers	.40
388	Francisco Cordero	.40
389	Donald Levinski	.40
390	Roy Halladay	.75
391	J.D. Drew	.40
392	Jamie Moyer	.40
393	Ken Macha	.40
394	Jeff DaVanon	.40
395	Matt Kata	.40
396	Jack Cust	.40
397	Mike Timlin	.40
398	Zack Greinke	4.00
399	Byung-Hyun Kim	4.00
400	Kazuhisa Ishii	4.00
401	Brayan Pena **RC**	4.00
402	Garret Anderson	6.00
403	Kyle Sleeth	4.00
404	Javy Lopez	4.00
405	Damian Moss	4.00
406	David Ortiz	4.00
407	Pedro J. Martinez	8.00
408	Hee Seop Choi	4.00
409	Carl Everett	4.00
410	Dontrelle Willis	5.00
411	Ryan Harvey	4.00
412	Russell Branyan	4.00
413	Milton Bradley	4.00
414	Marcus McBeth **RC**	4.00
415	Carlos Pena	4.00
416	Ivan Rodriguez	6.00
417	Craig Biggio	5.00
418	Angel Berroa	4.00
419	Brian Jordan	4.00
420	Scott Podsednik	4.00
421	Omar Falcon **RC**	4.00
422	Joe Mays	4.00
423	Brad Wilkerson	4.00
424	Al Leiter	4.00
425	Derek Jeter	15.00
426	Mark Mulder	4.00
427	Marlon Byrd	4.00
428	David Murphy	4.00
429	Phil Nevin	4.00
430	J.T. Snow Jr.	4.00
431	Brad Sullivan	4.00
432	Bo Hart	4.00
433	Josh Labandeira **RC**	4.00
434	Chan Ho Park	4.00
435	Carlos Delgado	6.00
436	Curt Schilling	6.00
437	John Smoltz	5.00
438	Luis Matos	4.00
439	Mark Prior	5.00
440	Roberto Alomar	6.00
441	Coco Crisp	4.00
442	Austin Kearns	4.00
443	Larry Walker	5.00
444	Neal Cotts	4.00
445	Jeff Bagwell	6.00
446	Adrian Beltre	4.00
447	Grady Sizemore	6.00
448	Keith Ginter	4.00
449	Vladimir Guerrero	8.00
450	Lyle Overbay	4.00
451	Rafael Furcal	4.00
452	Melvin Mora	4.00
453	Kerry Wood	4.00
454	Jose Valentin	4.00
455	Ken Griffey Jr.	8.00
456	Brandon Phillips	4.00
457	Miguel Cabrera	8.00
458	Edwin Jackson	4.00
459	Eric Owens	4.00
460	Miguel Batista	4.00
461	Mike Hampton	4.00
462	Kevin Millar	4.00
463	Bartolo Colon	4.00
464	Sean Casey	4.00
465	C.C. Sabathia	5.00
466	Rickie Weeks	4.00
467	Brad Penny	4.00
468	Mike MacDougal	4.00
469	Kevin Brown	4.00
470	Lance Berkman	5.00
471	Ben Sheets	4.00
472	Mariano Rivera	5.00
473	Mike Piazza	8.00
474	Ryan Klesko	4.00
475	Edgar Renteria	4.00

Chrome

	NM/M
Complete Set (110):	
Common Player:	1.00
Production 1,955 Sets	
Refractor:	1.5-2X
Production 555 Sets	
Black Refractor:	2-4X
Production 55 Sets	

THC1	Sammy Sosa	8.00
THC2	Nomar Garciaparra	8.00
THC3	Ichiro Suzuki	6.00
THC4	Rafael Palmeiro	3.00
THC5	Carlos Delgado	2.50
THC6	Troy Glaus	2.00
THC7	Jay Gibbons	1.50
THC8	Frank Thomas	3.00
THC9	Pat Burrell	2.00
THC10	Albert Pujols	8.00
THC11	Brandon Webb	1.50
THC12	Chipper Jones	4.00
THC13	Magglio Ordonez	2.00
THC14	Adam Dunn	3.00
THC15	Todd Helton	2.50
THC16	Jason Giambi	3.00
THC17	Alfonso Soriano	3.00
THC18	Barry Zito	2.00
THC19	Jim Thome	3.00
THC20	Alex Rodriguez	8.00
THC21	Hee Seop Choi	1.00
THC22	Pedro J. Martinez	3.00
THC23	Kerry Wood	2.00
THC24	Bartolo Colon	1.50
THC25	Austin Kearns	2.00
THC26	Ken Griffey Jr.	5.00
THC27	Coco Crisp	1.00
THC28	Larry Walker	1.50
THC29	Ivan Rodriguez	2.50
THC30	Dontrelle Willis	2.00
THC31	Miguel Cabrera	4.00
THC32	Jeff Bagwell	2.50
THC33	Lance Berkman	1.50
THC34	Shawn Green	1.50
THC35	Kevin Brown	1.50
THC36	Vladimir Guerrero	3.00
THC37	Mike Piazza	5.00
THC38	Derek Jeter	10.00
THC39	John Smoltz	1.50
THC40	Mark Prior	8.00
THC41	Gary Sheffield	2.00
THC42	Curt Schilling	2.00
THC43	Randy Johnson	3.00
THC44	Luis Gonzalez	1.50
THC45	Andruw Jones	2.50
THC46	Greg Maddux	5.00
THC47	Tony Batista	1.00
THC48	Esteban Loaiza	1.00
THC49	Chin-Hui Tsao	1.00
THC50	Mike Lowell	1.00
THC51	Jeff Kent	1.50
THC52	Richie Sexson	2.00
THC53	Torii Hunter	2.00
THC54	Jose Vidro	1.00
THC55	Jose Reyes	3.00
THC56	Jimmy Rollins	2.00
THC57	Bret Boone	1.50
THC58	Rocco Baldelli	3.00
THC59	Hank Blalock	2.00
THC60	Rickie Weeks	2.50
THC61	Rodney Choy Foo	1.00
THC62	Zach Miner	3.00
THC63	Brayan Pena	1.00
THC64	David Murphy	1.00
THC65	Matt Creighton	1.00
THC66	Kyle Sleeth	1.00
THC67	Matthew Moses	1.00
THC68	Josh Labandeira	1.00
THC69	Grady Sizemore	2.00
THC70	Edwin Jackson	1.00
THC71	Marcus McBeth	1.00
THC72	Bradley Sullivan	1.00
THC73	Zachary Duke	25.00
THC74	Omar Falcon	1.00
THC75	Conor Jackson	2.00
THC76	Carlos Quentin	4.00
THC77	Craig Ansman	1.00
THC78	Mike Gosling	1.00
THC79	Kyle Davies	1.00
THC80	Anthony Lerew	1.00
THC81	Sung Jung	1.00
THC82	David Crouthers	1.00
THC83	Kenny Perez	1.00
THC84	Jeffrey Allison	1.00
THC85	Nic Ungs	1.00
THC86	Donald Levinski	1.00
THC87	Anthony Acevedo	1.00
THC88	Todd Self	1.00
THC89	Tim Frend	1.00
THC90	Tydus Meadows	1.00
THC91	Khalid Ballouli	1.00
THC92	Dioner Navarro	1.00
THC93	Casey Myers	1.00
THC94	Jon Knott	1.00
THC95	Tim Stauffer	1.00
THC96	Ricky Nolasco	4.00
THC97	Blake Hawksworth	1.00
THC98	Jesse Roman	1.00
THC99	Yadier Molina	1.00
THC100	Chris O'Riordan	1.00
THC101	Cliff Floyd	1.00
THC102	Nick Johnson	1.00
THC103	Edgar Martinez	1.50
THC104	Brett Myers	1.00
THC105	Francisco Rodriguez	1.00
THC106	Scott Rolen	3.00
THC107	Mark Teixeira	2.00
THC108	Miguel Tejada	2.00
THC109	Vernon Wells	1.50
THC110	Jerome Williams	1.00

Clubhouse Collection

	NM/M
Common Player:	5.00
BA	Bobby Abreu	6.00
RB	Rocco Baldelli	12.00
LB	Lance Berkman	6.00
YB	Yogi Berra	35.00
HB	Hank Blalock	8.00
BB	Bret Boone	6.00
KB	Kevin Brown	6.00
EC	Eric Chavez	5.00
RC	Roger Clemens	15.00
JD	Johnny Damon	10.00
AD	Adam Dunn	6.00
RF	Rafael Furcal	6.00
EG	Eric Gagne	8.00
NG	Nomar Garciaparra	15.00
JG	Jason Giambi	8.00
MG	Marcus Giles	8.00
TG	Troy Glaus	6.00
LG	Luis Gonzalez	5.00
SG	Shawn Green	6.00
TH	Tim Hudson	6.00
THU	Torii Hunter	8.00
KI	Kazuhisa Ishii	6.00
RJ	Randy Johnson	10.00
AJ	Andruw Jones	6.00
CJ	Chipper Jones	8.00
AK	Al Kaline	25.00
HK	Harmon Killebrew	30.00
PL	Paul LoDuca	5.00
JL	Javy Lopez	6.00
GM	Greg Maddux	20.00
PM	Pedro J. Martinez	10.00
WM	Willie Mays	100.00
FM	Fred McGriff	6.00
MM	Mark Mulder	5.00
SM	Stan Musial	40.00
BM	Brett Myers	5.00
AP	Albert Pujols	15.00
MR	Manny Ramirez	8.00
JRE	Jose Reyes	8.00
AR	Alex Rodriguez	10.00
IR	Ivan Rodriguez	6.00
SRB	Scott Rolen/bat	8.00
SR	Scott Rolen/jsy	8.00
JR	Jimmy Rollins	6.00
CS	C.C. Sabathia	5.00
GS	Gary Sheffield	8.00
JS	John Smoltz	8.00
DS	Duke Snider	30.00
AS	Alfonso Soriano	10.00
SS	Sammy Sosa	15.00
MS	Mike Sweeney	5.00
MTE	Mark Teixeira	6.00
MT	Miguel Tejada/jsy	6.00
MTB	Miguel Tejada/bat	8.00
JT	Jim Thome	10.00
VW	Vernon Wells	6.00
KW	Kerry Wood	10.00
BZ	Barry Zito	6.00

Clubhouse Collection Auto.

	NM/M
Inserted 15,186	
Production 25 Sets	
WM	Willie Mays	400.00

Clubhouse Collection - Dual

	NM/M
Production 55 Sets	

BC	Yogi Berra, Roger Clemens	160.00
GS	Shawn Green, Duke Snider	150.00

Doubleheader

	NM/M
Complete Set (30):	50.00
Common Player:	.75
Inserted 1:Box	
1	Alex Rodriguez	5.00
2	Nomar Garciaparra	4.00
3	Ichiro Suzuki	4.00
4	Albert Pujols	5.00
5	Sammy Sosa	4.00
6	Derek Jeter	6.00
7	Jim Thome	2.00
8	Adam Dunn	1.00
9	Jason Giambi	2.00
10	Ivan Rodriguez	1.50
11	Todd Helton	1.50
12	Luis Gonzalez	.75
13	Jeff Bagwell	1.50
14	Lance Berkman	1.00
15	Alfonso Soriano	2.00
16	Dontrelle Willis	2.00
17	Mark Prior	4.00
18	Vladimir Guerrero	2.00
19	Mike Piazza	3.00
20	Roger Clemens	4.00
21	Randy Johnson	2.00
22	Curt Schilling	1.50
23	Gary Sheffield	1.00
24	Pedro J. Martinez	2.00
25	Carlos Delgado	1.50
26	Jimmy Rollins	.75
27	Andruw Jones	1.50
28	Chipper Jones	3.00
29	Rocco Baldelli	1.50
30	Hank Blalock	1.00

Flashbacks

	NM/M
Complete Set (10):	8.00
Common Player:	.50
Inserted 1:12	
F1	Duke Snider	1.50
F2	Johnny Podres	.50
F3	Don Newcombe	.50
F4	Al Kaline	1.50
F5	Willie Mays	4.00

F6	Stan Musial	3.00
F7	Harmon Killebrew	2.00
F8	Herb Score	.50
F9	Whitey Ford	1.00
F10	Robin Roberts	.50

Flashbacks Autograph
Inserted 1:30,373
No Pricing

Grandstand Glory

		NM/M
Common Player:		20.00
YB	Yogi Berra	20.00
AK	Al Kaline	30.00
HK	Harmon Killebrew	30.00
SM	Stan Musial	35.00
WS	Warren Spahn	20.00

New Age Performers

JOSH BECKETT
FLORIDA MARLINS · Pitcher
NEW AGE

		NM/M
Complete Set (15):		15.00
Common Player:		.75
Inserted 1:5		
NAP1	Jason Giambi	1.50
NAP2	Ichiro Suzuki	2.50
NAP3	Alex Rodriguez	3.00
NAP4	Alfonso Soriano	1.50
NAP5	Albert Pujols	3.00
NAP6	Nomar Garciaparra	3.00
NAP7	Mark Prior	3.00
NAP8	Derek Jeter	4.00
NAP9	Sammy Sosa	2.50
NAP10	Carlos Delgado	1.00
NAP11	Jim Thome	1.50
NAP12	Todd Helton	1.00
NAP13	Gary Sheffield	.75
NAP14	Vladimir Guerrero	1.50
NAP15	Josh Beckett	1.00

Real One Autograph

		NM/M
Common Autograph:		30.00
Inserted 1:230		
Red Autograph:		1.5-2X
Production 55		
GA	Gair Allie	50.00
EB	Ernie Banks	100.00
YB	Yogi Berra	100.00
BB	Bob Borkowski	40.00
BC	Billy Consolo	55.00
CF	Cliff Floyd	30.00
BG	Bill Glynn	45.00
JG	Johnny Gray	45.00
AH	Aubrey Huff	45.00
AK	Al Kaline	100.00
HK	Harmon Killebrew	90.00
TK	Thornton Kipper	45.00
BK	Bob Kline	45.00
SK	Steve Kraly	60.00
LL	Lou Limmer	45.00
ML	Mike Lowell	40.00
WM	Willie Mays	185.00
BM	Bob Milliken	45.00
SM	Stan Musial	140.00
DN	Don Newcombe	65.00
MO	Magglio Ordonez	35.00
JP	Jim Pearce	45.00
HP	Harry Perkowski	50.00
DP	Duane Pillette	40.00
JPO	Johnny Podres	45.00
SR	Scott Rolen	45.00
FS	Frank Smith	45.00
DS	Duke Snider	85.00
VT	"Jake" Thies	45.00
HV	Harold Valentine	45.00
DW	Dontrelle Willis	50.00
BW	Bill Wilson	40.00
TW	Tom Wright	45.00

Team Topps Legends

	NM/M
Inserted 1:505	
Davey Johnson	12.00
Joe Rudi	15.00

Then And Now

Detroit TIGERS THEN & NOW St. Louis CARDINALS
AL KALINE ALBERT PUJOLS

		NM/M
Complete Set (6):		8.00
Common Player:		1.00
Inserted 1:15		
TN1	Willie Mays, Jim Thome	4.00
TN2	Al Kaline, Albert Pujols	4.00
TN3	Duke Snider, Carlos Delgado	1.50
TN4	Robin Roberts, Roy Halladay	1.00
TN5	Don Newcombe, Johan Santana	1.00
TN6	Herb Score, Kerry Wood	1.50

2004 Topps Opening Day

METS

		NM/M
Complete Set (165):		25.00
Common Player:		.10
Pack (6):		1.00
Box (36):		30.00
1	Jim Thome	.50
2	Edgardo Alfonzo	.10
3	Marlon Anderson	.10
4	Ichiro Suzuki	1.00
5	Frank Thomas	.40
6	Tom Glavine	.25
7	Bo Hart	.10
8	Marcus Giles	.10
9	Kevin Millar	.10
10	Derek Jeter	1.50
11	Corey Patterson	.10
12	Jay Payton	.10
13	Lance Berkman	.20
14	Juan Pierre	.10
15	Mike Piazza	.75
16	Richie Sexson	.40
17	Tim Hudson	.25
18	Fred McGriff	.25
19	Brad Radke	.10
20	John Smoltz	.20
21	Jay Gibbons	.10
22	Michael Young	.10
23	Steve Finley	.10
24	Ramon Hernandez	.10
25	Albert Pujols	1.25
26	Trot Nixon	.10
27	Kevin Millwood	.25
28	Mark Prior	1.00
29	Mike Lowell	.20
30	Paul LoDuca	.10
31	Jacque Jones	.10
32	Ty Wigginton	.10
33	Cliff Floyd	.10
34	Marlon Byrd	.10
35	Mark Mulder	.20
36	Johnny Damon	.20
37	Jimmy Rollins	.25
38	Javy Lopez	.25
39	Andruw Jones	.40
40	Hank Blalock	.25
41	Hee Seop Choi	.10
42	Jose Vidro	.10
43	Hideo Nomo	.25
44	Javier Vazquez	.10
45	Jorge Posada	.25
46	Al Leiter	.10
47	Orlando Cabrera	.10
48	Mike Hampton	.10
49	Esteban Loaiza	.10
50	Todd Helton	.40
51	Jose Contreras	.20
52	Jason L. Phillips	.10
53	Vernon Wells	.20
54	Randy Winn	.10
55	Curt Schilling	.40
56	Mark Buehrle	.10
57	Dmitri Young	.10
58	Kazuhisa Ishii	.10
59	A.J. Pierzynski	.10
60	Greg Maddux	.75
61	Jarrod Washburn	.10
62	Omar Vizquel	.10
63	Alex Gonzalez	.10
64	Sean Casey	.10
65	Eric Chavez	.20
66	Mike Lieberthal	.10
67	Jason Kendall	.10
68	Mike Cameron	.10
69	Woody Williams	.10
70	Nomar Garciaparra	1.00
71	Bernie Williams	.25
72	Darin Erstad	.20
73	Bill Mueller	.10
74	Damian Miller	.10
75	Jason Giambi	.50
76	Adam Dunn	.25
77	Carlos Lee	.10
78	Angel Berroa	.10
79	Erubiel Durazo	.10
80	Bret Boone	.20
81	Aubrey Huff	.20
82	Carlos Delgado	.40
83	Toby Hall	.10
84	Roy Halladay	.25
85	Preston Wilson	.10
86	Bartolo Colon	.20
87	Moises Alou	.20
88	Luis Castillo	.10
89	Manny Ramirez	.40
90	Garret Anderson	.25
91	Ryan Klesko	.20
92	Rich Aurilia	.10
93	Rafael Furcal	.20
94	Rocco Baldelli	.40
95	Eric Gagne	.20
96	Jeff Kent	.20
97	Josh Beckett	.40
98	Alex Gonzalez	.10
99	Jose Cruz Jr.	.10
100	Alex Rodriguez	1.25
101	Troy Glaus	.25
102	Carlos Beltran	.20
103	Luis Gonzalez	.20
104	A.J. Burnett	.10
105	Gary Sheffield	.25
106	Benito Santiago	.10
107	Tony Batista	.10
108	David Ortiz	.20
109	Shannon Stewart	.10
110	Jim Edmonds	.25
111	Kenny Lofton	.20
112	Paul Konerko	.10
113	Rafael Palmeiro	.40
114	Pat Burrell	.25
115	Barry Zito	.25
116	Edgar Martinez	.25
117	Austin Kearns	.25
118	Geoff Jenkins	.20
119	Mike Mussina	.25
120	Alfonso Soriano	.50
121	Shea Hillenbrand	.10
122	Ivan Rodriguez	.40
123	Kerry Wood	.40
124	Scott Rolen	.50
125	Jeff Bagwell	.40
126	Roberto Alomar	.25
127	Carl Crawford	.25
128	Mike Sweeney	.10
129	Melvin Mora	.10
130	Larry Walker	.20
131	Matt Morris	.10
132	Shawn Green	.20
133	Scott Podsednik	.25
134	Phil Nevin	.10
135	Dontrelle Willis	.25
136	Torii Hunter	.25
137	Carl Everett	.10
138	Pedro J. Martinez	.50
139	Roy Oswalt	.25
140	Vladimir Guerrero	.50
141	Chipper Jones	.75
142	Jose Reyes	.25
143	Sammy Sosa	1.00
144	Nick Johnson	.10
145	Miguel Tejada	.25
146	Bobby Abreu	.25
147	Magglio Ordonez	.25
148	Sean Burroughs	.10
149	Jody Gerut	.10
150	Jermaine Dye	.10
151	Craig Biggio	.20
152	Randy Johnson	.50
153	Jeff Conine	.10
154	Edgar Renteria	.25
155	Mark Teixeira	.25
156	Eric Hinske	.10
157	Kevin Brown	.20
158	Ken Griffey Jr.	.75
159	Brandon Webb	.10
160	Brian Giles	.25
161	Jason Schmidt	.20
162	Aramis Ramirez	.10
163	Aaron Boone	.10
164	Miguel Cabrera	.40
165	Checklist	.10

Autograph

		NM/M
Common Autograph:		10.00
Inserted 1:629		
JD	Jeff Duncan	20.00
RH	Rich Harden	20.00
AT	Andres Torres	10.00
RW	Ryan Wagner	25.00
DW	Dontrelle Willis	30.00

2004 Topps Originals Signature Edition

WILLIE MAYS

		NM/M
Common Autograph:		10.00
Pack (4):		45.00
Box (6):		220.00
Second number reflects quantity produced.		
JA1	Jim Abbott 88 TR/339	20.00
SA5	Sparky Anderson 83 MG/67	15.00
SA6	Sparky Anderson 84 MG/97	15.00
SA7	Sparky Anderson 85 MG/73	15.00
LA9	Luis Aparicio 69/49	20.00
LA12	Luis Aparicio 72/15	30.00
HB2	Harold Baines 82/31	25.00
HB3	Harold Baines 83/19	30.00
HB5	Harold Baines 85/97	15.00
HB6	Harold Baines 86/93	15.00
HB7	Harold Baines 87/115	15.00
JB2	Jesse Barfield 83/45	15.00
JB4	Jesse Barfield 85/60	15.00
JB5	Jesse Barfield 86/37	15.00
JB6	Jesse Barfield 87/180	15.00
KB2	Kevin Bass 84/71	10.00
KB3	Kevin Bass 85/30	10.00
KB4	Kevin Bass 86/44	10.00
KB5	Kevin Bass 87/74	10.00
KB6	Kevin Bass 90 TR/35	10.00
BB5	Buddy Bell 79/135	15.00
BB8	Buddy Bell 82/34	15.00
BB9	Buddy Bell 83/83	10.00
BB10	Buddy Bell 84/22	15.00
BB12	Buddy Bell 86/32	15.00
GB2	George Bell 84/67	10.00
GB3	George Bell 85/32	10.00
GB4	George Bell 86/46	15.00
GB5	George Bell 87/204	10.00
JBE2	Johnny Bench 79/14	125.00
JBE5	Johnny Bench 82/16	125.00
YB10	Yogi Berra 85 MG/27	100.00
VB5	Vida Blue 79/21	75.00
VB7	Vida Blue 81/227	15.00
VB8	Vida Blue 82/53	15.00
VB9	Vida Blue 83/45	15.00
BBL4	Bert Blyleven 79/45	25.00
BBL6	Bert Blyleven 81/29	25.00
BBL8	Bert Blyleven 83/41	20.00
BBL10	Bert Blyleven 85/40	20.00
BBL11	Bert Blyleven 86/62	20.00
BBL12	Bert Blyleven 87/54	20.00
MB2	Mike Boddicker 84/56	15.00
MB3	Mike Boddicker 85/139	10.00
MB4	Mike Boddicker 86/66	10.00
MB5	Mike Boddicker 87/88	10.00
WB2	Wade Boggs 84/20	75.00
WB3	Wade Boggs 85/25	75.00
WB5	Wade Boggs 87/45	60.00
LB4	Lou Brock 70/20	50.00
LB13	Lou Brock 79/27	50.00
TB2	Tom Brunansky 83/27	15.00
TB3	Tom Brunansky 84/62	15.00
TB5	Tom Brunansky 86/28	15.00
TB6	Tom Brunansky 87/193	10.00
BU8	Bill Buckner 81/39	20.00
BU9	Bill Buckner 82/38	20.00
BU10	Bill Buckner 83/47	15.00
BU11	Bill Buckner 84/31	20.00
BU12	Bill Buckner 84 TR/24	20.00
BU13	Bill Buckner 85/80	15.00
BU14	Bill Buckner 86/63	15.00
BC5	Bert Campaneris 79/107	10.00
BC7	Bert Campaneris 84/28	15.00
JC2	John Candelaria 79/77	20.00
JC4	John Candelaria 81/19	30.00
JC5	John Candelaria 82/42	25.00
JC6	John Candelaria 83/77	20.00
JC8	John Candelaria 85/36	20.00
JC9	John Candelaria 86/36	20.00
JCA2	Jose Canseco 87/99	60.00
RC4	Rod Carew 79/29	60.00
RC6	Rod Carew 81/21	75.00
RC7	Rod Carew 82/18	75.00
GC3	Gary Carter 79/21	40.00
GC4	Gary Carter 80/24	40.00
GC5	Gary Carter 81/22	40.00
JCR2	Joe Carter 86/24	50.00

JCR3	Joe Carter 87/23	50.00
RCE3	Ron Cey 79/55	15.00
RCE6	Ron Cey 82/34	15.00
RCE7	Ron Cey 83/87	15.00
RCE8	Ron Cey 83 TR/68	15.00
RCE11	Ron Cey 86/43	15.00
VC2	Vince Coleman 87/299	15.00
VC3	Vince Coleman 88/34	20.00
VC4	Vince Coleman 91 TR/23	25.00
DC6	Dave Concepcion 80/21	40.00
DC8	Dave Concepcion 82/43	30.00
DC9	Dave Concepcion 83/34	30.00
DC10	Dave Concepcion 84/24	40.00
DC11	Dave Concepcion 85/41	30.00
DC12	Dave Concepcion 86/69	25.00
JCU8	Jose Cruz Sr. 82/28	15.00
JCU9	Jose Cruz Sr. 83/102	10.00
JCU10	Jose Cruz Sr. 84/67	10.00
JCU11	Jose Cruz Sr. 85/68	10.00
JCU12	Jose Cruz Sr. 86/31	15.00
RD3	Ron Darling 87/224	15.00
DD2	Darren Daulton 87/269	10.00
DD4	Darren Daulton 92/32	15.00
DD5	Darren Daulton 94/17	20.00
DD6	Darren Daulton 96/22	20.00
ED3	Eric Davis 87/336	15.00
AD3	Andre Dawson 80/27	25.00
AD4	Andre Dawson 81/37	25.00
AD5	Andre Dawson 82/55	20.00
AD6	Andre Dawson 83/47	20.00
AD7	Andre Dawson 84/25	25.00
AD8	Andre Dawson 85/22	25.00
AD9	Andre Dawson 86/24	25.00
DDE2	Doug DeCinces 79/38	20.00
DDE3	Doug DeCinces 80/24	20.00
DDE4	Doug DeCinces 81/24	20.00
DDE5	Doug DeCinces 82/42	20.00
DDE6	Doug DeCinces 83/75	15.00
DDE7	Doug DeCinces 84/19	20.00
DDE8	Doug DeCinces 85/54	15.00
DDE9	Doug DeCinces 86/74	15.00
BD6	Bucky Dent 82/49	20.00
BD7	Bucky Dent 83/92	15.00
BD8	Bucky Dent 84/63	15.00
RDI2	Rob Dibble 90/31	25.00
RDI3	Rob Dibble 91/62	20.00
RDI4	Rob Dibble 92/56	20.00
RDI6	Rob Dibble 93/47	15.00
RDI7	Rob Dibble 94/37	15.00
LD2	Leon Durham 82/51	10.00
LD3	Leon Durham 83/52	10.00
LD4	Leon Durham 84/151	10.00
LD7	Leon Durham 87/87	10.00
LDY2	Lenny Dykstra 87/200	15.00
LDY3	Lenny Dykstra 88/30	25.00
LDY4	Lenny Dykstra 89/17	30.00
DE3	Dennis Eckersley 79/44	40.00
DE4	Dennis Eckersley 80/40	40.00
DEV5	Darrell Evans 79/19	20.00
DEV7	Darrell Evans 81/15	20.00
DEV8	Darrell Evans 82/25	20.00
DEV9	Darrell Evans 83/63	15.00
DEV10	Darrell Evans 84/81	10.00
DEV11	Darrell Evans 85/48	15.00
DEV12	Darrell Evans 86/82	10.00
SF2	Sid Fernandez 86/18	30.00
SF3	Sid Fernandez 87/211	15.00
SF4	Sid Fernandez 93/20	25.00
TF2	Tony Fernandez 86/41	15.00
TF3	Tony Fernandez 87/228	10.00
MF3	Mark Fidrych 79/74	25.00
MF4	Mark Fidrych 80/16	40.00
CF2	Cecil Fielder 87/208	30.00
CF3	Cecil Fielder 88/26	50.00
CF4	Cecil Fielder 89/16	50.00
RF3	Rollie Fingers 79/52	20.00
RF4	Rollie Fingers 80/15	40.00
RF5	Rollie Fingers 81/18	40.00
CFI3	Carlton Fisk 79/24	60.00
CFI4	Carlton Fisk 80/32	50.00
CFI6	Carlton Fisk 82/30	50.00
GF6	George Foster 79/20	20.00
GF10	George Foster 83/39	15.00
GF11	George Foster 84/112	10.00
GF12	George Foster 85/76	10.00
GF13	George Foster 86/64	10.00
SG4	Steve Garvey 79/26	30.00
SG7	Steve Garvey 82/122	15.00
SG9	Steve Garvey 84/32	20.00
SG10	Steve Garvey 85/129	15.00
CG3	Cesar Geronimo 79/28	15.00
CG5	Cesar Geronimo 81/21	15.00
CG6	Cesar Geronimo 82/52	10.00
CG7	Cesar Geronimo 83/67	10.00
CG8	Cesar Geronimo 84/70	10.00
KGI2	Kirk Gibson 82/35	20.00
KGI3	Kirk Gibson 83/35	20.00
KGI5	Kirk Gibson 85/44	20.00
KGI6	Kirk Gibson 86/44	20.00
KGI7	Kirk Gibson 87/65	20.00
DG3	Dwight Gooden 87/52	30.00
RG7	Rich "Goose" Gossage 81/21	20.00
RG8	Rich "Goose" Gossage 82/30	20.00
RG9	Rich "Goose" Gossage 83/34	20.00
RG10	Rich "Goose" Gossage 84/90	15.00
RG12	Rich "Goose" Gossage 86/30	15.00
BG1	Bobby Grich 71/1	
BG2	Bobby Grich 79/29	20.00
BG3	Bobby Grich 80/70	15.00
BG4	Bobby Grich 81/14	
BG5	Bobby Grich 82/45	15.00
BG6	Bobby Grich 83/85	10.00
BG7	Bobby Grich 84/57	15.00
BG8	Bobby Grich 85/36	15.00
KG5	Ken Griffey Sr. 80/15	30.00
KG7	Ken Griffey Sr. 82/18	30.00
KG8	Ken Griffey Sr. 83/70	15.00
KG9	Ken Griffey Sr. 84/64	15.00
KG10	Ken Griffey Sr. 85/32	20.00
KG11	Ken Griffey Sr. 86 TR/32	20.00
KGU2	Kelly Gruber 88/77	10.00
KGU3	Kelly Gruber 89/44	10.00
KGU4	Kelly Gruber 90/86	10.00
KGU5	Kelly Gruber 91/52	10.00
KGU6	Kelly Gruber 92/55	10.00
KGU7	Kelly Gruber 93/26	15.00
RGU4	Ron Guidry 80/22	40.00
RGU5	Ron Guidry 81/104	20.00
RGU6	Ron Guidry 82/53	40.00
RGU7	Ron Guidry 83/46	40.00
RGU8	Ron Guidry 84/40	40.00
RGU9	Ron Guidry 85/50	40.00
TG2	Tony Gwynn 84/95	60.00
KH3	Keith Hernandez 80/38	50.00
KH4	Keith Hernandez 81/19	50.00
KH5	Keith Hernandez 82/156	20.00
KH6	Keith Hernandez 83/17	50.00
TH2	Tom Herr 81/22	15.00
TH3	Tom Herr 82/42	15.00
TH4	Tom Herr 83/80	10.00
TH5	Tom Herr 84/30	15.00
TH6	Tom Herr 85/17	15.00
TH7	Tom Herr 86/28	15.00
TH8	Tom Herr 87/134	10.00
OH2	Orel Hershiser 86/23	40.00
OH3	Orel Hershiser 87/218	20.00
WH4	Whitey Herzog 83 MG/63	10.00
WH5	Whitey Herzog 84 MG/85	10.00
WH6	Whitey Herzog 85 MG/75	10.00
WH7	Whitey Herzog 86 MG/66	10.00
WH8	Whitey Herzog 87 MG/29	15.00
WH9	Whitey Herzog 88 MG/35	15.00
BH5	Bob Horner 83/69	15.00
BH6	Bob Horner 84/63	15.00
BH8	Bob Horner 86/118	15.00
BH9	Bob Horner 87/38	15.00
CH2	Charlie Hough 83/19	20.00
CH3	Charlie Hough 84/50	10.00
CH4	Charlie Hough 85/57	10.00
CH5	Charlie Hough 86/66	10.00
CH6	Charlie Hough 87/46	10.00
CH7	Charlie Hough 88/19	20.00
CH8	Charlie Hough 91 TR/70	10.00
CH9	Charlie Hough 92/25	15.00
AH6	Al Hrabosky 78/20	20.00
AH7	Al Hrabosky 79/40	15.00
AH8	Al Hrabosky 80/61	10.00
AH9	Al Hrabosky 81/38	15.00
AH10	Al Hrabosky 82/62	10.00
AH11	Al Hrabosky 89 Sr./20	20.00
BJ2	Bo Jackson 87/100	60.00
RJ8	Reggie Jackson 82/21	75.00
RJ11	Reggie Jackson 85/17	75.00
RJ12	Reggie Jackson 86/17	75.00
BJA2	Brook Jacoby 86/133	10.00
BJA3	Brook Jacoby 87/191	10.00
FJ8	Fergie Jenkins 78/17	40.00
FJ10	Fergie Jenkins 80/37	30.00
FJ11	Fergie Jenkins 81/32	30.00
FJ12	Fergie Jenkins 82/65	20.00
FJ13	Fergie Jenkins 83/22	30.00
FJ14	Fergie Jenkins 84/42	30.00
WJ2	Wally Joyner 87/335	15.00
DJ3	David Justice 93/32	20.00
AK10	Al Kaline 67/18	120.00
AK16	Al Kaline 73/25	140.00
JK2	Jimmy Key 86/21	20.00
JK3	Jimmy Key 87/263	10.00
JK5	Jimmy Key 92/37	20.00
DK4	Dave Kingman 81/25	30.00
DK6	Dave Kingman 83/32	30.00
DK7	Dave Kingman 86/25	30.00
RK2	Ron Kittle 85/86	10.00
RK3	Ron Kittle 86/55	15.00
RK4	Ron Kittle 87/201	10.00
RKN5	Ray Knight 82/25	20.00
RKN6	Ray Knight 83/36	20.00
RKN7	Ray Knight 84/26	20.00
RKN8	Ray Knight 85/68	15.00
RKN9	Ray Knight 86/80	15.00
RKN10	Ray Knight 87 TR/90	15.00
JKR2	John Kruk 87/214	15.00
JKR3	John Kruk 92/22	35.00
CL3	Carney Lansford 81/184	10.00
CL5	Carney Lansford 83/40	15.00
CL6	Carney Lansford 85/35	15.00
CL7	Carney Lansford 86/76	10.00
CLE3	Chet Lemon 79/24	20.00
CLE6	Chet Lemon 82/23	20.00
CLE7	Chet Lemon 83/35	15.00
CLE8	Chet Lemon 84/42	15.00
CLE9	Chet Lemon 85/32	15.00
CLE10	Chet Lemon 86/136	10.00
CLE11	Chet Lemon 87/27	20.00
JL2	Jim Leyritz 91/38	10.00
JL3	Jim Leyritz 93/49	10.00
JL4	Jim Leyritz 94/16	20.00
JL6	Jim Leyritz 97/62	10.00
JL7	Jim Leyritz 98/20	20.00
JL8	Jim Leyritz 99/124	10.00
JL9	Jim Leyritz 00/40	10.00
DL4	Davey Lopes 79/71	10.00
DL5	Davey Lopes 80/19	15.00
DL7	Davey Lopes 82/17	15.00
DL8	Davey Lopes 83/65	10.00
DL10	Davey Lopes 85/24	15.00
DL11	Davey Lopes 86/40	10.00
DL12	Davey Lopes 01 MG/67	10.00
DL13	Davey Lopes 02 MG/19	15.00
GL7	Greg Luzinski 80/21	30.00
GL9	Greg Luzinski 82/34	20.00
GL10	Greg Luzinski 83/75	10.00
GL11	Greg Luzinski 84/85	10.00
GL12	Greg Luzinski 85/92	10.00
BM7	Bill Madlock 82/26	15.00
BM8	Bill Madlock 83/55	15.00
BM9	Bill Madlock 84/69	15.00
BM10	Bill Madlock 85/60	15.00
BM11	Bill Madlock 86/63	15.00
BM12	Bill Madlock 87/42	15.00
GM3	Gary Matthews Sr. 83/20	15.00
GM4	Gary Matthews Sr. 84/43	10.00
GM5	Gary Matthews Sr. 85/39	10.00
GM6	Gary Matthews Sr. 86/38	10.00
GM7	Gary Matthews Sr. 87/82	10.00
GM8	Gary Matthews Sr. 88/30	15.00
DM3	Don Mattingly 87/84	100.00
WM9	Willie Mays 72/25	300.00
TM5	Tim McCarver 79/22	20.00
JM2	Jack McDowell 89/36	20.00
JM3	Jack McDowell 90 TR/61	15.00
JM4	Jack McDowell 91/33	20.00
JM5	Jack McDowell 92/38	20.00
JM6	Jack McDowell 93/27	20.00
JM9	Jack McDowell 96/15	25.00
JM10	Jack McDowell 97/27	20.00
WMC2	Willie McGee 84/66	25.00
WMC3	Willie McGee 85/44	25.00
WMC4	Willie McGee 86/24	40.00
WMC5	Willie McGee 87/117	25.00
PM1	Paul Molitor 79/15	60.00
PM2	Paul Molitor 80/26	50.00
PM4	Paul Molitor 82/32	50.00
JMO9	Joe Morgan 81/32	30.00
JMO10	Joe Morgan 82/18	40.00
JMO11	Joe Morgan 83/49	25.00
JMO13	Joe Morgan 84/73	15.00
JMO14	Joe Morgan 85/40	25.00
DMU2	Dale Murphy 79/38	50.00
DMU6	Dale Murphy 84/29	40.00
DMU8	Dale Murphy 86/25	50.00
DMU9	Dale Murphy 87/91	25.00
SM5	Stan Musial 62/16	150.00
AO6	Al Oliver 79/42	15.00
AO8	Al Oliver 81/54	15.00
AO9	Al Oliver 82/45	15.00
AO10	Al Oliver 83/50	15.00
AO11	Al Oliver 84/51	15.00
AO12	Al Oliver 85/46	15.00
PO2	Paul O'Neill 89/24	50.00
PO3	Paul O'Neill 90/18	50.00
PO4	Paul O'Neill 91/24	50.00
PO5	Paul O'Neill 97/33	40.00
JP3	Jim Palmer 80/33	30.00
JP4	Jim Palmer 81/23	30.00
JP5	Jim Palmer 82/24	30.00
DP6	Dave Parker 82/73	20.00
DP7	Dave Parker 83/30	30.00
DP9	Dave Parker 85/45	25.00
DP10	Dave Parker 86/29	30.00
BP9	Boog Powell 73/17	50.00
BP11	Boog Powell 75/19	40.00
TR2	Tim Raines 82/43	20.00
TR3	Tim Raines 83/26	25.00
TR5	Tim Raines 85/43	20.00
TR6	Tim Raines 86/21	25.00
TR7	Tim Raines 87/211	15.00
HR2	Harold Reynolds 87/255	10.00
JR7	Jim Rice 81/123	20.00
JR8	Jim Rice 82/24	35.00
JR9	Jim Rice 83/71	25.00
CR4	Cal Ripken Jr. 86/74	120.00
MR2	Mickey Rivers 79/35	15.00
MR5	Mickey Rivers 82/49	15.00
MR6	Mickey Rivers 83/79	10.00
MR7	Mickey Rivers 84/91	10.00
MR8	Mickey Rivers 85/34	15.00
BR11	Brooks Robinson 74/20	75.00
BR13	Brooks Robinson 76/17	75.00
JRU9	Joe Rudi 79/24	15.00
JRU10	Joe Rudi 80/45	15.00
JRU11	Joe Rudi 82/26	15.00
JRU12	Joe Rudi 83/75	10.00
NR5	Nolan Ryan 83/23	200.00
NR6	Nolan Ryan 84/20	200.00
NR8	Nolan Ryan 86/20	200.00
BS2	Bret Saberhagen 86/23	25.00
BS3	Bret Saberhagen 87/230	15.00
RS2	Ryne Sandberg 84/37	100.00
RS5	Ryne Sandberg 87/32	100.00
SS2	Steve Sax 83/34	15.00
SS4	Steve Sax 85/33	15.00
SS5	Steve Sax 86/45	15.00
SS6	Steve Sax 87/215	10.00
MS2	Mike Schmidt 80/100	60.00
MSC3	Mike Scott 82/32	15.00
MSC4	Mike Scott 83/55	15.00
MSC5	Mike Scott 84/28	15.00
MSC6	Mike Scott 86/73	10.00
MSC7	Mike Scott 87/36	15.00
MSC8	Mike Scott 88/21	15.00
TS2	Tom Seaver 79/44	85.00
TS4	Tom Seaver 81/16	100.00
TS5	Tom Seaver 82/25	100.00
KS2	Kevin Seitzer 88/88	10.00
KS3	Kevin Seitzer 89/39	10.00
KS4	Kevin Seitzer 90/18	15.00
KS5	Kevin Seitzer 91/39	10.00
KS6	Kevin Seitzer 92/49	10.00
KS9	Kevin Seitzer 93/38	10.00
KS10	Kevin Seitzer 94/22	15.00
KS13	Kevin Seitzer 97/24	15.00
LS5	Lee Smith 86/29	25.00
LS6	Lee Smith 87/237	15.00
LS7	Lee Smith 88/27	25.00
OS2	Ozzie Smith 81/28	60.00
OS3	Ozzie Smith 82/27	60.00
OS5	Ozzie Smith 84/19	75.00
OS6	Ozzie Smith 85/16	75.00
RM8	Reggie Smith 79/15	25.00
RM9	Reggie Smith 80/16	25.00
RM10	Reggie Smith 81/14	25.00
RM11	Reggie Smith 82/32	15.00
RM12	Reggie Smith 83/48	15.00
DS8	Duke Snider 64/18	150.00
CS2	Cory Snyder 87/291	10.00
CS3	Cory Snyder 91/39	15.00
DSW2	Dave Stewart 83/41	15.00
DSW3	Dave Stewart 84/60	15.00
DSW4	Dave Stewart 85/24	15.00
DSW5	Dave Stewart 86/53	15.00
DSW6	Dave Stewart 87/171	10.00
DSE2	Dave Stieb 81/21	35.00
DSE3	Dave Stieb 82/34	30.00
DSE4	Dave Stieb 83/70	25.00
DSE5	Dave Stieb 84/20	35.00
DSE6	Dave Stieb 85/55	25.00
DSE7	Dave Stieb 86/69	25.00
DSE8	Dave Stieb 87/75	25.00
DSR2	Darryl Strawberry 85/32	25.00
DSR3	Darryl Strawberry 86/24	25.00
DSR4	Darryl Strawberry 87/183	20.00
DSR5	Darryl Strawberry 87 AS/110	20.00
RU3	Rick Sutcliffe 82/53	20.00
RU4	Rick Sutcliffe 83/43	20.00
RU5	Rick Sutcliffe 84/33	20.00
RU6	Rick Sutcliffe 85/82	20.00
RU8	Rick Sutcliffe 87/19	25.00
BSU6	Bruce Sutter 82/111	20.00
BSU7	Bruce Sutter 83/45	25.00
BSU8	Bruce Sutter 84/24	30.00
BSU9	Bruce Sutter 85/19	35.00
BSU10	Bruce Sutter 86/78	20.00
BSU11	Bruce Sutter 87/36	25.00
KT5	Kent Tekulve 81/17	20.00
KT6	Kent Tekulve 82/36	15.00
KT7	Kent Tekulve 83/52	15.00
KT8	Kent Tekulve 84/71	15.00
KT9	Kent Tekulve 85/43	15.00
KT10	Kent Tekulve 86/57	15.00
KT11	Kent Tekulve 87/32	15.00
KT12	Kent Tekulve 88/20	20.00
LT2	Luis Tiant 68/16	40.00
LT11	Luis Tiant 79/22	30.00
LT12	Luis Tiant 80/23	30.00
LT13	Luis Tiant 81/20	30.00
LT14	Luis Tiant 82/51	15.00
LT15	Luis Tiant 83/58	15.00
AT2	Alan Trammell 80/17	30.00
AT3	Alan Trammell 81/26	30.00
AT4	Alan Trammell 82/40	30.00
AT5	Alan Trammell 83/21	30.00
AT6	Alan Trammell 84/57	30.00
AT7	Alan Trammell 85/39	30.00
AT8	Alan Trammell 86/23	30.00
AT9	Alan Trammell 87/15	30.00
AV2	Andy Van Slyke 85/35	35.00
AV3	Andy Van Slyke 86/37	35.00
AV4	Andy Van Slyke 87/178	25.00
AV5	Andy Van Slyke 87 TR/130	25.00
FV3	Frank Viola 85/25	25.00
FV4	Frank Viola 86/99	15.00
FV5	Frank Viola 87/209	15.00
TW2	Tim Wallach 83/49	15.00
TW4	Tim Wallach 85/46	15.00
TW5	Tim Wallach 86/44	15.00
TW6	Tim Wallach 87/197	10.00
BW3	Bob Watson 79/77	10.00
BW6	Bob Watson 82/23	20.00
BW7	Bob Watson 83/93	10.00
BW8	Bob Watson 84/64	10.00
BW9	Bob Watson 85/68	10.00
EW4	Earl Weaver 78 MG/52	15.00
EW5	Earl Weaver 83 MG/38	20.00
EW7	Earl Weaver 86 MG/107	15.00
EW8	Earl Weaver 87 MG/175	10.00
WW2	Walt Weiss 89/34	10.00
WW3	Walt Weiss 91/30	10.00
WW4	Walt Weiss 92/71	10.00
WW7	Walt Weiss 97/49	10.00
WW10	Walt Weiss 99/40	10.00
WW11	Walt Weiss 01/51	10.00
MW2	Mookie Wilson 82/20	20.00
MW3	Mookie Wilson 83/41	15.00
MW5	Mookie Wilson 85/51	15.00
MW6	Mookie Wilson 86/47	15.00
MW7	Mookie Wilson 87/67	15.00
CY4	Carl Yastrzemski 80/60	100.00
CY5	Carl Yastrzemski 81/35	120.00
SY5	Steve Yeager 79/23	25.00
SY9	Steve Yeager 83/80	10.00
SY12	Steve Yeager 86/47	15.00
SY13	Steve Yeager 86 TR/100	10.00
RY5	Robin Yount 80/18	100.00
RY6	Robin Yount 81/23	100.00
RY9	Robin Yount 84/15	125.00
RY11	Robin Yount 86/21	100.00

2004 Topps Pristine

NM/M

Complete Set (190):	
Common Player:	1.00
Common Rookie:	1.50

#	Player	Price
Common Uncommon RC:		3.00
Production 999		
Common Rare RC:		6.00
Production 499		
Pack (8):		35.00
Box (5):		140.00
1	Jim Thome	2.00
2	Ryan Klesko	1.00
3	Ichiro Suzuki	4.00
4	Rocco Baldelli	1.00
5	Vernon Wells	1.00
6	Javier Vazquez	1.00
7	Billy Wagner	1.00
8	Jose Reyes	1.00
9	Lance Berkman	1.00
10	Alex Rodriguez	6.00
11	Pat Burrell	1.00
12	Mark Mulder	1.00
13	Mike Piazza	3.00
14	Miguel Cabrera	2.00
15	Larry Walker	1.00
16	Carlos Lee	1.00
17	Mark Prior	2.00
18	Pedro J. Martinez	2.00
19	Melvin Mora	1.00
20	Sammy Sosa	4.00
21	Bartolo Colon	1.00
22	Luis Gonzalez	1.00
23	Marcus Giles	1.00
24	Ken Griffey Jr.	3.00
25	Ivan Rodriguez	1.50
26	Carlos Beltran	1.00
27	Geoff Jenkins	1.00
28	Nick Johnson	1.00
29	Gary Sheffield	1.50
30	Alfonso Soriano	2.00
31	Scott Rolen	2.00
32	Garret Anderson	1.00
33	Richie Sexson	1.00
34	Curt Schilling	1.50
35	Greg Maddux	3.00
36	Adam Dunn	1.50
37	Preston Wilson	1.00
38	Josh Beckett	1.50
39	Roy Oswalt	1.00
40	Derek Jeter	6.00
41	Jason Kendall	1.00
42	Bret Boone	1.00
43	Torii Hunter	1.00
44	Roy Halladay	1.00
45	Edgar Renteria	1.00
46	Troy Glaus	1.00
47	Chipper Jones	2.00
48	Manny Ramirez	1.50
49	C.C. Sabathia	1.00
50	Albert Pujols	5.00
51	Randy Wolf	1.00
52	Eric Chavez	1.00
53	Kevin Brown	1.00
54	Cliff Floyd	1.00
55	Jeff Bagwell	1.50
56	Frank Thomas	1.50
57	David Ortiz	1.50
58	Rafael Palmeiro	1.50
59	Randy Johnson	2.00
60	Vladimir Guerrero	2.00
61	Carlos Delgado	1.00
62	Hank Blalock	1.50
63	Jim Edmonds	1.00
64	Jason Schmidt	1.00
65	Mike Lieberthal	1.00
66	Tim Hudson	1.00
67	Jorge Posada	1.00
68	Jose Vidro	1.00
69	Eric Gagne	1.00
70	Roger Clemens	5.00
71	Mike Lowell	1.00
72	Dontrelle Willis	1.00
73	Austin Kearns	1.00
74	Kerry Wood	2.00
75	Miguel Tejada	1.50
76	Bobby Abreu	1.00
77	Edgar Martinez	1.00
78	Joe Mauer	1.00
79	Mike Sweeney	1.00
80	Jason Giambi	1.00
81	Mark Teixeira	1.00
82	Aubrey Huff	1.00
83	Brian Giles	1.00
84	Barry Zito	1.00
85	Mike Mussina	1.50
86	Brandon Webb	1.00
87	Andruw Jones	1.50
88	Javy Lopez	1.00
89	Bill Mueller	1.00
90	Scott Podsednik	1.00
91	Moises Alou	1.00
92	Esteban Loaiza	1.00
93	Magglio Ordonez	1.00
94	Jeff Kent	1.00
95	Todd Helton	1.50
96	Juan Pierre	1.00
97	Jody Gerut	1.00
98	Angel Berroa	1.00
99	Shawn Green	1.00
100	Nomar Garciaparra	3.00
101	David Aardsma/C	1.50
102	David Aardsma/U	4.00
103	David Aardsma/R	8.00
104	Erick Aybar/C RC	5.00
105	Erick Aybar/U RC	10.00
106	Erick Aybar/R RC	15.00
107	Chad Bentz/C	1.50
108	Chad Bentz/U	3.00
109	Chad Bentz/R	6.00
110	Travis Blackley/C RC	1.50
111	Travis Blackley/U RC	3.00
112	Travis Blackley/R RC	6.00
113	Bobby Brownlie/C RC	4.00
114	Bobby Brownlie/U RC	6.00
115	Bobby Brownlie/R RC	10.00
116	Alberto Callaspo/C RC	1.50
117	Alberto Callaspo/U RC	3.00
118	Alberto Callaspo/R RC	6.00
119	Kazuo Matsui/C RC	5.00
120	Kazuo Matsui/U RC	8.00
121	Kazuo Matsui/R RC	12.00
122	Jesse Crain/C	3.00
123	Jesse Crain/U	5.00
124	Jesse Crain/R	8.00
125	Howard Kendrick/C RC	15.00
126	Howard Kendrick/U RC	20.00
127	Howard Kendrick/R RC	25.00
128	Blake Hawksworth/C RC	1.50
129	Blake Hawksworth/U RC	3.00
130	Blake Hawksworth/R RC	6.00
131	Conor Jackson/C	4.00
132	Conor Jackson/U	8.00
133	Conor Jackson/R	12.00
134	Paul Maholm/C RC	1.50
135	Paul Maholm/U RC	3.00
136	Paul Maholm/R RC	6.00
137	Lastings Milledge/C	8.00
138	Lastings Milledge/U	15.00
139	Lastings Milledge/R	20.00
140	Matt Moses/C	4.00
141	Matt Moses/U	6.00
142	Matt Moses/R	10.00
143	David Murphy/C	1.50
144	David Murphy/R	3.00
145	David Murphy/R	6.00
146	Dioner Navarro/C RC	4.00
147	Dioner Navarro/U RC	6.00
148	Dioner Navarro/R RC	10.00
149	Dustin Nippert/C RC	1.50
150	Dustin Nippert/U RC	3.00
151	Dustin Nippert/R RC	6.00
152	Vito Chiaravalloti/C RC	3.00
153	Vito Chiaravalloti/U RC	5.00
154	Vito Chiaravalloti/R RC	8.00
155	Akinori Otsuka/C RC	3.00
156	Akinori Otsuka/U RC	5.00
157	Akinori Otsuka/R RC	8.00
158	Casey Daigle/C RC	1.50
159	Casey Daigle/U RC	3.00
160	Casey Daigle/R RC	6.00
161	Carlos Quentin/C	5.00
162	Carlos Quentin/U	10.00
163	Carlos Quentin	15.00
164	Omar Quintanilla/C	4.00
165	Omar Quintanilla/U	8.00
166	Omar Quintanilla/U	12.00
167	Chris Saenz/C RC	1.50
168	Chris Saenz/U RC	3.00
169	Chris Saenz/R RC	6.00
170	Ervin Santana/C RC	1.50
171	Ervin Santana/U RC	3.00
172	Ervin Santana/R RC	6.00
173	Chris Shelton/C RC	4.00
174	Chris Shelton/U RC	8.00
175	Chris Shelton/R RC	10.00
176	Kyle Sleeth/C	1.50
177	Kyle Sleeth/U	3.00
178	Kyle Sleeth/R	6.00
179	Brad Snyder/C	4.00
180	Brad Snyder/U	8.00
181	Brad Snyder/R	12.00
182	Tim Stauffer/C	4.00
183	Tim Stauffer/U	8.00
184	Tim Stauffer/R	12.00
185	Shingo Takatsu/C RC	4.00
186	Shingo Takatsu/U RC	8.00
187	Shingo Takatsu/R RC	12.00
188	Merkin Valdez/C RC	1.50
189	Merkin Valdez/U RC	3.00
190	Merkin Valdez/R RC	6.00

Refractors

Veterans (1-100):	4-8X
Production 49	
Common RC's:	.75-1.5X
Production 999	
UnCommon RC's:	1-2X
Production 399	
Rare RC's:	1.5-3X
Production 49	

Gold Refractors

Veterans (1-100):	4-8X
Common RC's:	4-8X
Uncommon RC's:	3-5X
Rare RC's:	1.5-3X
Production 41 Sets	

Fantasy Favorite Relics

		NM/M
Common Player:		4.00
Refractor:		2-4X
Production 25 Sets		
MA	Moises Alou	6.00
JB	Jeff Bagwell	8.00
RB	Rocco Baldelli	6.00
AB	Angel Berroa	6.00
BB	Bret Boone	4.00
JD	Johnny Damon	8.00
CD	Carlos Delgado	5.00
RF	Rafael Furcal	4.00
RFJ	Rafael Furcal	4.00
EG	Eric Gagne	10.00
NG	Nomar Garciaparra	10.00
SG	Shawn Green	4.00
MG	Mark Grudzielanek	4.00
VG	Vladimir Guerrero	8.00
THE	Todd Helton	6.00
TH	Tim Hudson	6.00
DJ	Derek Jeter	20.00
AJ	Andruw Jones	6.00
CJ	Chipper Jones	8.00
CK	Corey Koskie	4.00
KL	Kenny Lofton	4.00
PM	Pedro J. Martinez	6.00
MPI	Mike Piazza	10.00
MP	Mark Prior	8.00
AP	Albert Pujols	15.00
AR	Alex Rodriguez	12.00
JR	Jimmy Rollins	4.00
MT	Mark Teixeira	4.00
FT	Frank Thomas	8.00
JT	Jim Thome	10.00
JV	Jose Vidro	4.00
LW	Larry Walker	4.00
BW	Brandon Webb	4.00
PW	Preston Wilson	4.00
KW	Kerry Wood	8.00

Going, Going, Gone! Relics

		NM/M
Common Player:		4.00
Refractor:		2-4X
Production 25 Sets		
LB	Lance Berkman	4.00
BB	Bret Boone	4.00
AD	Adam Dunn	8.00
JG	Juan Gonzalez	6.00
LG	Luis Gonzalez	4.00
VG	Vladimir Guerrero	8.00
TH	Todd Helton	8.00
CJ	Chipper Jones	8.00
JJ	Jacque Jones	4.00
JK	Jeff Kent	4.00
RK	Ryan Klesko	4.00
MO	Magglio Ordonez	4.00
DO	David Ortiz	10.00
MP	Mike Piazza	10.00
AP	Albert Pujols	15.00
MR	Manny Ramirez	8.00
AR	Alex Rodriguez	12.00
SR	Scott Rolen	8.00
AS	Alfonso Soriano	8.00
SS	Sammy Sosa	10.00
FT	Frank Thomas	8.00
JT	Jim Thome	10.00
VW	Vernon Wells	4.00

Key Acquisitions Relics

		NM/M
Common Player:		4.00
Inserted 1:8		
Refractors:		2-4X
Production 25 Sets		
HC	Hee Seop Choi	4.00
JG	Juan Gonzalez	6.00
VG	Vladimir Guerrero	8.00
JL	Javy Lopez	6.00
AR	Alex Rodriguez	12.00
IR	Ivan Rodriguez	8.00
GS	Gary Sheffield	6.00
AS	Alfonso Soriano	8.00

Mini

		NM/M
Common Player:		2.00
Inserted 1:5		
DA	David Aardsma	5.00
EA	Erick Aybar	4.00
VC	Vito Chiaravalloti	3.00
NG	Nomar Garciaparra	4.00
JG	Jason Giambi	2.00
VG	Vladimir Guerrero	4.00
BH	Blake Hawksworth	4.00
CJA	Conor Jackson	4.00
DJ	Derek Jeter	6.00
CJ	Chipper Jones	3.00
HK	Howard Kendrick	10.00
KM	Kazuo Matsui	4.00
LM	Lastings Milledge	5.00
MM	Matt Moses	6.00
DM	David Murphy	3.00
DN	Dioner Navarro	10.00
AO	Akinori Otsuka	3.00
MPI	Mike Piazza	4.00
MP	Mark Prior	3.00
AP	Albert Pujols	6.00
AR	Alex Rodriguez	6.00
KS	Kyle Sleeth	4.00
SS	Sammy Sosa	4.00
TS	Tim Stauffer	3.00
IS	Ichiro Suzuki	5.00
ST	Shingo Takatsu	4.00
JT	Jim Thome	3.00
MV	Merkin Valdez	3.00
DW	Dontrelle Willis	3.00
KW	Kerry Wood	4.00

Mini Relics

		NM/M
Common Player:		5.00
Inserted 1:51		
JB	Jeff Bagwell	20.00
EG	Eric Gagne	15.00
NG	Nomar Garciaparra	12.00
CJ	Chipper Jones	10.00
PM	Pedro J. Martinez	12.00
MPI	Mike Piazza	12.00
MP	Mark Prior	10.00
AP	Albert Pujols	25.00
PW	Preston Wilson	5.00
KW	Kerry Wood	10.00

Patch Place Relics

		NM/M
Common Player:		5.00
Refractor:		No Pricing
Production 10 Sets		
JB	Jeff Bagwell	20.00
RB	Rocco Baldelli	12.00
JBE	Josh Beckett	15.00
BB	Bret Boone	10.00
LC	Luis Castillo	10.00
CC	Chin-Feng Chen	40.00
CD	Carlos Delgado	10.00
AD	Adam Dunn	15.00

RF	Rafael Furcal	10.00
EG	Eric Gagne	15.00
NG	Nomar Garciaparra	40.00
LG	Luis Gonzalez	10.00
SG	Shawn Green	10.00
THE	Todd Helton	15.00
TH	Tim Hudson	10.00
RJ	Randy Johnson	20.00
AJ	Andruw Jones	10.00
CJ	Chipper Jones	15.00
AK	Austin Kearns	10.00
PL	Paul LoDuca	10.00
ML	Mike Lowell	10.00
PM	Pedro J. Martinez	20.00
MPI	Mike Piazza	35.00
MP	Mark Prior	15.00
AP	Albert Pujols	40.00
JR	Jose Reyes	15.00
JS	John Smoltz	15.00
SS	Sammy Sosa	20.00
FT	Frank Thomas	20.00
DW	Dontrelle Willis	10.00
PW	Preston Wilson	10.00
KW	Kerry Wood	20.00
BZ	Barry Zito	15.00

Personal Endorsements

		NM/M
Common Autograph:		6.00
Golds:		1.5-3X
Production 25 Sets		
DA	David Aardsma	15.00
GA	Garret Anderson	10.00
LB	Lance Berkman	20.00
HB	Hank Blalock	20.00
MC	Miguel Cabrera	30.00
VC	Vito Chiaravalloti	10.00
BC	Bobby Crosby	25.00
JF	Jennie Finch	120.00
MG	Marcus Giles	10.00
VG	Vladimir Guerrero	50.00
EH	Estee Harris	8.00
AH	Aubrey Huff	8.00
CJ	Conor Jackson	20.00
CL	Chris Lubanski	10.00
JM	Joe Mauer	35.00
WM	Willie Mays	200.00
DM	Dustin McGowan	6.00
BM	Brett Myers	10.00
SP	Scott Podsednik	10.00
JP	Jorge Posada	40.00
AR	Alex Rodriguez	150.00
IR	Ivan Rodriguez	40.00
ES	Ervin Santana	10.00
GS	Gary Sheffield	40.00
GS	Grady Sizemore	25.00
JV	Javier Vazquez	15.00
BW	Brandon Webb	6.00
DY	Delmon Young	10.00

Two of a Kind Autograph
Production 13
No Pricing

1, 2, 3 Triple Relics

		NM/M
Inserted 1:171		
Refractor:		1.5-2X
Production 25 Sets		
NYY	Kenny Lofton, Derek Jeter, Alex Rodriguez	50.00
CHC	Mark Grudzielanek, Alex Gonzalez, Sammy Sosa	40.00
BOS	Johnny Damon, Bill Mueller, Nomar Garciaparra	40.00

2004 Topps Retired Signature Edition

		NM/M
Complete Set (110):		125.00
Common Player:		1.00
Pack (5):		35.00
Box (5):		140.00
1	Willie Mays	6.00
2	Tony Gwynn	3.00
3	Dale Murphy	2.00
4	Lenny Dykstra	1.00
5	Johnny Bench	4.00
6	Bill Buckner	1.00
7	Ferguson Jenkins	1.50
8	George Brett	6.00
9	Ralph Kiner	2.00
10	Ernie Banks	4.00
11	Hal McRae	1.00
12	Lou Brock	2.00
13	Keith Hernandez	1.00
14	Jose Canseco	2.00
15	Whitey Ford	2.50
16	Dave Kingman	1.00
17	Tim Raines	1.00
18	Paul O'Neill	1.50
19	Lou Whitaker	1.00
20	Mike Schmidt	5.00
21	Wally Joyner	1.00
22	Kirk Gibson	1.00
23	Ryne Sandberg	5.00
24	Luis Tiant	1.00
25	Al Kaline	4.00
26	Brooks Robinson	3.00
27	Don Zimmer	1.00
28	Nolan Ryan	6.00
29	Maury Wills	1.00
30	Stan Musial	4.00
31	Garry Maddox	1.00
32	Tom Brunansky	1.00
33	Don Mattingly	5.00
34	Earl Weaver	1.00
35	Bobby Grich	1.00
36	Orlando Cepeda	1.50
37	Alan Trammell	1.50
38	Al Hrabosky	1.00
39	Davey Lopes	1.00
40	Rod Carew	2.00
41	Robin Yount	4.00
42	Dwight Gooden	1.50
43	Andre Dawson	1.50
44	Hank Aaron	6.00
45	Norm Cash	1.00
46	Reggie Jackson	2.50
47	Jim Rice	1.00
48	Carlton Fisk	2.00
49	Dave Parker	1.00
50	Cal Ripken Jr.	6.00
51	Roy Face	1.00
52	Bob Gibson	2.50
53	Jimmy Key	1.00
54	Al Oliver	1.00
55	Don Larsen	1.50
56	Tom Seaver	3.00
57	Tony Armas	1.00
58	Dave Stieb	1.00
59	Will Clark	2.00
60	Duke Snider	2.50
61	Cesar Geronimo	1.00
62	Ron Kittle	1.00
63	Ron Santo	2.00
64	Mickey Rivers	1.00
65	Jimmy Piersall	1.00
66	Ron Swoboda	1.00
67	Kent Hrbek	1.00
68	Dennis Eckersley	2.00
69	Greg Luzinski	1.00
70	Harmon Killebrew	3.00
71	Ron Guidry	1.50
72	Steve Garvey	1.00
73	Andy Van Slyke	1.00
74	Rich "Goose" Gossage	1.00
75	Ozzie Smith	3.00
76	Richie Allen	1.00
77	Vida Blue	1.00
78	Tony Oliva	1.00
79	Darryl Strawberry	1.00
80	Frank Robinson	2.00
81	Bruce Sutter	1.50
82	Dave Concepcion	1.00
83	Darrell Evans	1.00
84	Jack Morris	1.00
85	Bo Jackson	2.00
86	Orel Hershiser	1.00
87	Rob Dibble	1.00
88	Wade Boggs	2.00
89	Fernando Valenzuela	1.00
90	Jim Palmer	1.00
91	George Foster	1.00
92	Mike Scott	1.00
93	Paul Molitor	2.50
94	Gary Carter	2.00
95	Bobby Richardson	1.00
96	Rollie Fingers	1.00
97	Tim McCarver	1.00
98	John Candelaria	1.00
99	Dave Winfield	2.00
100	Yogi Berra	3.00
101	Bill Madlock	1.00
102	Jack McDowell	1.00
103	Luis Aparicio	1.00
104	Graig Nettles	1.00
105	Dave Stewart	1.00
106	Darren Daulton	1.00
107	Gary Gaetti	1.00
108	Tony Fernandez	1.00
109	Buddy Bell	1.00
110	Carl Yastrzemski	4.00

Black

Black (1-110):		4-6X
Production 99 Sets		

Chrome Autographs

		NM/M
Common Autograph:		10.00
Inserted 1:1		
Refractor:		2-4X
SP Refractor:		.75-2X
Production 25 Sets		
HA	Hank Aaron/SP/50	320.00
TA	Tony Armas	10.00
EB	Ernie Banks/SP/50	180.00
BBE	Buddy Bell	12.00
JB	Johnny Bench/SP/75	80.00
YB	Yogi Berra/SP/75	80.00
VB	Vida Blue	10.00
WB	Wade Boggs	40.00
TB	Tom Brunansky	10.00
BB	Bill Buckner	12.00
JC	John Candelaria	20.00
JCA	Jose Canseco	35.00
RC	Rod Carew	35.00
GC	Gary Carter	20.00
OC	Orlando Cepeda	15.00
DD	Darren Daulton	10.00
BD	Bucky Dent	10.00
RD	Rob Dibble	12.00
DEC	Dennis Eckersley	30.00
DE	Darrell Evans	10.00
RF	Roy Face	15.00
TF	Tony Fernandez	10.00
WF	Whitey Ford/SP/75	90.00
RF	Rollie Fingers	15.00
CF	Carlton Fisk	40.00
GF	George Foster	12.00
CG	Cesar Geronimo	25.00
BG	Bob Gibson/SP/75	75.00
KG	Kirk Gibson	20.00
DG	Dwight Gooden/SP/75	40.00
GG	Rich "Goose" Gossage	15.00
BGR	Bobby Grich	10.00
TG	Tony Gwynn/SP/75	75.00
OH	Orel Hershiser	25.00
AH	Al Hrabosky	10.00
FJ	Ferguson Jenkins	15.00
WJ	Wally Joyner	10.00
JK	Jimmy Key	10.00
RK	Ralph Kiner	50.00
RKI	Ron Kittle	10.00
DL	Davey Lopes	10.00
GL	Greg Luzinski	15.00
BM	Bill Madlock	10.00
DM	Don Mattingly/SP/75	100.00
JM	Jack McDowell	10.00
PM	Paul Molitor	50.00
DM	Dale Murphy	25.00
SM	Stan Musial/SP/50	160.00
GN	Graig Nettles	10.00
TO	Tony Oliva	20.00
AO	Al Oliver	12.00
PO	Paul O'Neill	40.00
DP	Dave Parker	20.00
JP	Jimmy Piersall	15.00
BR	Bobby Richardson	15.00
CR	Cal Ripken Jr./SP/25	275.00
BRO	Brooks Robinson/SP/75	90.00
FR	Frank Robinson	30.00
NR	Nolan Ryan/SP/25	300.00
RSA	Ryne Sandberg	75.00
RS	Ron Santo	20.00
MS	Mike Schmidt/SP/75	150.00
TS	Tom Seaver/SP/75	75.00
OS	Ozzie Smith/SP/75	100.00
DSN	Duke Snider/SP/50	90.00
DST	Dave Stieb	12.00
DS	Darryl Strawberry	30.00
BS	Bruce Sutter	25.00
RS	Ron Swoboda	10.00
LT	Luis Tiant	10.00
AT	Alan Trammell	20.00
EW	Earl Weaver	10.00
MW	Maury Wills	10.00
CY	Carl Yastrzemski/SP/25	180.00
RY	Robin Yount/SP/25	125.00
DZ	Don Zimmer	20.00

Chrome Co-Signers
No Pricing
Production 25 Sets

2004 Topps Total

		NM/M
Complete Set (880):		100.00
Common Player:		.10
Pack (10):		1.00
Box (36):		30.00
1	Kevin Brown	.25
2	Mike Mordecai	.10
3	Seung Jun Song	.10
4	Mike Maroth	.10
5	Mike Lieberthal	.10
6	Billy Koch	.10
7	Mike Stanton	.10
8	Brad Penny	.10
9	Brooks Kieschnick	.10
10	Carlos Delgado	.40
11	Brady Clark	.10
12	Ramon Martinez	.10
13	Dan Wilson	.10
14	Guillermo Mota	.10

15	Trevor Hoffman	.10
16	Tony Batista	.10
17	Rusty Greer	.10
18	David Weathers	.10
19	Horacio Ramirez	.10
20	Aubrey Huff	.10
21	Casey Blake	.10
22	Ryan Bukvich	.10
23	Garrett Atkins	.10
24	Jose Contreras	.10
25	Chipper Jones	.75
26	Neifi Perez	.10
27	Scott Linebrink	.10
28	Matt Kinney	.10
29	Michael Restovich	.10
30	Scott Rolen	.75
31	John Franco	.10
32	Toby Hall	.10
33	Wily Mo Pena	.10
34	Dennis Tankersley	.10
35	Robb Nen	.10
36	Jose Valverde	.10
37	Chin-Feng Chen	.10
38	Gary Knotts	.10
39	Scott Elarton	.10
40	Bret Boone	.25
41	Josh Phelps	.10
42	Jason Larue	.10
43	Tim Redding	.10
44	Greg Myers	.10
45	Darin Erstad	.25
46	Kip Wells	.10
47	Matt Ford	.10
48	Jerome Williams	.10
49	Brian Meadows	.10
50	Albert Pujols	1.50
51	Kirk Saarloos	.10
52	Scott Eyre	.10
53	John Flaherty	.10
54	Rafael Soriano	.10
55	Shea Hillenbrand	.10
56	Kyle Farnsworth	.10
57	Nate Cornejo	.10
58	Kerry Robinson	.10
59	Yan Vogelsong	.10
60	Ryan Klesko	.20
61	Luke Hudson	.10
62	Justin Morneau	.20
63	Frank Catalanotto	.10
64	Derrick Turnbow	.10
65	Marcus Giles	.10
66	Mark Mulder	.25
67	Matt Anderson	.10
68	Mike Matheny	.10
69	Brian Lawrence	.10
70	Bobby Abreu	.10
71	Damian Moss	.10
72	Richard Hidalgo	.10
73	Mark Kotsay	.10
74	Mike Cameron	.10
75	Troy Glaus	.40
76	Matt Holliday	.25
77	Byung-Hyun Kim	.10
78	Aaron Sele	.10
79	Danny Graves	.10
80	Barry Zito	.40
81	Matt LeCroy	.10
82	Jason Isringhausen	.10
83	Colby Lewis	.10
84	Franklyn German	.10
85	Luis Matos	.10
86	Mike Timlin	.10
87	Miguel Batista	.10
88	John McDonald	.10
89	Joey Eischen	.10
90	Mike Mussina	.50
91	Jack Wilson	.20
92	Aaron Cook	.10
93	John Parrish	.10
94	Jose Valentin	.10
95	Johnny Damon	.20
96	Pat Burrell	.25
97	Brendan Donnelly	.10
98	Lance Carter	.10
99	Omar Daal	.10
100	Ichiro Suzuki	1.00
101	Robin Ventura	.10
102	Brian Shouse	.10
103	Kevin Jarvis	.10
104	Jason Young	.10
105	Moises Alou	.10

106	Wes Obermueller	.10
107	David Segui	.10
108	Mike MacDougal	.10
109	John Buck	.10
110	Gary Sheffield	.25
111	Yorvit Torrealba	.10
112	Matt Kata	.10
113	David Bell	.10
114	Juan Gonzalez	.40
115	Kelvim Escobar	.10
116	Ruben Sierra	.10
117	Todd Wellemeyer	.10
118	Jamie Walker	.10
119	Will Cunnane	.10
120	Cliff Floyd	.10
121	Aramis Ramirez	.40
122	Damaso Marte	.10
123	Juan Castro	.10
124	Chris Woodward	.10
125	Andruw Jones	.50
126	Ben Weber	.10
127	Dee Brown	.10
128	Steve Reed	.10
129	Gabe Kapler	.10
130	Miguel Cabrera	.75
131	Billy McMillon	.10
132	Julio Mateo	.10
133	Preston Wilson	.10
134	Tony Clark	.10
135	Carlos Lee	.20
136	Carlos Baerga	.10
137	Mike Crudale	.10
138	David Ross	.10
139	Josh Fogg	.10
140	Dmitri Young	.10
141	Cliff Lee	.10
142	Mike Lowell	.25
143	Jason Lane	.10
144	Pedro Feliz	.10
145	Ken Griffey Jr.	1.00
146	Dustin Hermanson	.10
147	Scott Hodges	.10
148	Aquilino Lopez	.10
149	Wes Helms	.10
150	Jason Giambi	.50
151	Erasmo Ramirez	.10
152	Sean Burroughs	.10
153	J.T. Snow	.10
154	Eddie Guardado	.10
155	C.C. Sabathia	.10
156	Kyle Lohse	.10
157	Roberto Hernandez	.10
158	Jason Simontacchi	.10
159	Tim Spooneybarger	.10
160	Alfonso Soriano	.50
161	Mike Gonzalez	.10
162	Alex Cora	.10
163	Kevin Gryboski	.10
164	Steve Cox	.10
165	Luis Castillo	.10
166	Odalis Perez	.10
167	Alex Sanchez	.10
168	Robert Mackowiak	.10
169	Francisco Rodriguez	.10
170	Roy Oswalt	.25
171	Omar Infante	.10
172	Ryan Jensen	.10
173	Ben Broussard	.10
174	Mark Hendrickson	.10
175	Manny Ramirez	.50
176	Rob Bell	.10
177	Adam Everett	.10
178	Chris George	.10
179	Ricky Gutierrez	.10
180	Eric Gagne	.40
181	Scott Schoeneweis	.10
182	Kris Benson	.10
183	Amaury Telemaco	.10
184	John Riedling	.10
185	Juan Pierre	.10
186	Ramon Ortiz	.10
187	Luis Rivas	.10
188	Larry Bigbie	.10
189	Robby Hammock	.10
190	Geoff Jenkins	.20
191	Chad Cordero	.10
192	Mark Ellis	.10
193	Mark Loretta	.10
194	Ryan Drese	.10
195	Lance Berkman	.10
196	Kevin Appier	.10
197	Enrique Calero (Kiko)	.10
198	Mickey Callaway	.10
199	Chase Utley	.25
200	Nomar Garciaparra	1.00
201	Kevin Cash	.10
202	Ramiro Mendoza	.10
203	Shane Reynolds	.10
204	Chris Spurling	.10
205	Aaron Guiel	.10
206	Mark Derosa	.10
207	Adam Kennedy	.10
208	Andy Pettitte	.25
209	Rafael Palmeiro	.50
210	Luis Gonzalez	.25
211	Ryan Franklin	.10
212	Bob Wickman	.10
213	Ron Calloway	.10
214	Jae Weong Seo	.10
215	Kazuhisa Ishii	.10
216	Sterling Hitchcock	.10
217	Jimmy Gobble	.10
218	Chad Moeller	.10
219	Jake Peavy	.10
220	John Smoltz	.25
221	Erick Almonte	.10
222	David Wells	.10
223	Brad Lidge	.10
224	Carlos Zambrano	.25
225	Kerry Wood	.75
226	Alex Cintron	.10
227	Javier Lopez	.25
228	Jeremy Griffiths	.10
229	Jon Garland	.10
230	Curt Schilling	.50
231	Alex Gonzalez	.10
232	Jay Gibbons	.10
233	Damian Jackson	.10
234	Jeriome Robertson	.10
235	Johan Santana	.10
236	Jose Guillen	.10
237	Jeff Connie	.10
238	Matt Roney	.10
239	Desi Relaford	.10
240	Frank Thomas	.50
241	Danny Patterson	.10
242	Kevin Mench	.10
243	Mike Redmond	.10
244	Jeff Suppan	.10
245	Carl Everett	.10
246	Jack Cressend	.10
247	Matt Mantei	.10
248	Enrique Wilson	.10
249	Craig Counsell	.10
250	Mark Prior	1.50
251	Jared Sandberg	.10
252	Scott Strickland	.10
253	Lew Ford	.10
254	Hee Seop Choi	.10
255	Jason Phillips	.10
256	Jason Jennings	.10
257	Todd Pratt	.10
258	Matt Herges	.10
259	Kerry Ligtenberg	.10
260	Austin Kearns	.25
261	Jay Witasick	.10
262	Tony Armas Jr.	.10
263	Tom Martin	.10
264	Oliver Perez	.10
265	Jorge Posada	.40
266	Joe Beimel	.10
267	Ben Hendrickson	.10
268	Reggie Sanders	.10
269	Julio Lugo	.10
270	Josh Beckett	.40
271	Kyle Snyder	.10
272	Felipe Lopez	.10
273	Kevin Millar	.10
274	Travis Hafner	.20
275	Magglio Ordonez	.25
276	Marlon Byrd	.10
277	Scott Spiezio	.10
278	Mark Corey	.10
279	Tim Salmon	.25
280	Alex Gonzalez	.10
281	Marquis Grissom	.20
282	Miguel Olivo	.10
283	Orlando Hudson	.10
284	Rondell White	.20
285	Jermaine Dye	.10
286	Paul Shuey	.10
287	Brandon Inge	.10
288	B.J. Surhoff	.10
289	Edgar Gonzalez	.10
290	Angel Berroa	.10
291	Claudio Vargas	.10
292	Cesar Izturis	.10
293	Brandon Phillips	.10
294	Jeff Duncan	.10
295	Randy Wolf	.10
296	Barry Larkin	.25
297	Felix Rodriguez	.10
298	Robb Quinlan	.10
299	Brian Jordan	.10
300	Dontrelle Willis	.25
301	Doug Davis	.10
302	Ricky Stone	.10
303	Travis Harper	.10
304	Jaret Wright	.10
305	Edgardo Alfonzo	.10
306	Quinton McCracken	.10
307	Jason Bay	.10
308	Joe Randa	.10
309	Steve Sparks	.10
310	Roy Halladay	.25
311	Antonio Alfonseca	.10
312	Michael Cuddyer	.10
313	John Patterson	.10
314	Chris Widger	.10
315	Shigetoshi Hasegawa	.10
316	Tim Wakefield	.10
317	Scott Hatteberg	.10
318	Mike Remlinger	.10
319	Jose Vizcaino	.10
320	Rocco Baldelli	.25
321	David Riske	.10
322	Steve Karsay	.10
323	Peter Bergeron	.10
324	Jeff Weaver	.10
325	Larry Walker	.25
326	Jack Cust	.10
327	Bo Hart	.10
328	Rod Beck	.10
329	Jose Acevedo	.10
330	Hank Blalock	.40
331	Flash Gordon	.10
332	Brian Fuentes	.10
333	Tomas Perez	.10
334	Lenny Harris	.10
335	Matt Morris	.25
336	Jeremi Gonzalez	.10
337	David Eckstein	.10
338	Aaron Rowand	.10
339	Rick Bauer	.10
340	Jim Edmonds	.25
341	Joe Borowski	.10
342	Eric Dubose	.10
343	D'Angelo Jimenez	.10
344	Tomokazu Ohka	.10
345	Victor Zambrano	.10
346	Joe McEwing	.10
347	Jorge Sosa	.10
348	Keith Ginter	.10
349	A.J. Pierzynski	.10
350	Mike Sweeney	.10
351	Shawn Chacon	.10
352	Matt Clement	.25
353	Vance Wilson	.10
354	Benito Santiago	.10
355	Eric Hinske	.10
356	Vladimir Guerrero	.75
357	Kenny Rogers	.10
358	Aaron Boone	.10
359	Jay Powell	.10
360	Phil Nevin	.10
361	Willie Harris	.10
362	Ty Wigginton	.10
363	Chad Fox	.10
364	Junior Spivey	.10
365	Brandon Webb	.10
366	Brett Myers	.10
367	Alexis Gomez	.10
368	Dave Roberts	.10
369	LaTroy Hawkins	.10
370	Kevin Millwood	.25
371	Brian Schneider	.10
372	Blaine Neal	.10
373	Jeromy Burnitz	.10
374	Ted Lilly	.10
375	Shawn Green	.25
376	Carlos Pena	.10
377	Gil Meche	.10
378	Jeff Bagwell	.50
379	Alex Escobar	.10
380	Erubiel Durazo	.10
381	Cristian Guzman	.10
382	Rocky Biddle	.10
383	Craig Wilson	.25
384	Rey Sanchez	.10
385	Russ Ortiz	.10
386	Freddy Garcia	.10
387	Luis Vizcaino	.10
388	David Ortiz	.40
389	Jose Molina	.10
390	Edgar Martinez	.25
391	Nate Bump	.10
392	Brent Mayne	.10
393	Ray King	.10
394	Paul Wilson	.10
395	Melvin Mora	.10
396	Morgan Ensberg	.10
397	Ramon Hernandez	.10
398	Juan Rincon	.10
399	Ron Mahay	.10
400	Jeff Kent	.25
401	Cal Eldred	.10
402	Mike Difelice	.10
403	Valerio De Los Santos	.10
404	Steve Finley	.10
405	Trot Nixon	.25
406	Kevin Walker	.10
407	John Vander Wal	.10
408	Ray Durham	.10
409	Aaron Heilman	.10
410	Edgar Renteria	.25
411	Mike Hampton	.10
412	Kirk Rueter	.10
413	Jim Mecir	.10
414	Brian Roberts	.10
415	Paul Konerko	.10
416	Reed Johnson	.10
417	Roger Clemens	1.50
418	Coco Crisp	.10
419	Carlos Hernandez	.10
420	Scott Podsednik	.40
421	Miguel Cairo	.10
422	Abraham Nunez	.10
423	Endy Chavez	.10
424	Eric Munson	.10
425	Torii Hunter	.25
426	Ben Howard	.10
427	Chris Gomez	.10
428	Francisco Cordero	.10
429	Jeffrey Hammonds	.10
430	Shannon Stewart	.10
431	Einar Diaz	.10
432	Eric Byrnes	.10
433	Marty Cordova	.10
434	Matt Ginter	.10
435	Victor Martinez	.10
436	Geronimo Gil	.10
437	Grant Balfour	.10
438	Ramon Vazquez	.10
439	Jose Cruz	.10
440	Orlando Cabrera	.10
441	Joe Kennedy	.10
442	Scott Williamson	.10
443	Troy Percival	.10
444	Derrek Lee	.25
445	Runelvys Hernandez	.10
446	Mark Grudzielanek	.10
447	Trey Hodges	.10
448	Jimmy Haynes	.10
449	Eric Milton	.10
450	Todd Helton	.50
451	Gregg Zaun	.10
452	Woody Williams	.10
453	Todd Walker	.10
454	Gary Matthews	.10
455	Fernando Vina	.10
456	Omar Vizquel	.10
457	Roberto Alomar	.40
458	Bill Hall	.10
459	Juan Rivera	.10
460	Tom Glavine	.40
461	Ramon Castro	.10
462	Cory Vance	.10
463	Dan Miceli	.10
464	Lyle Overbay	.25
465	Craig Biggio	.25
466	Ricky Ledee	.10
467	Michael Barrett	.10
468	Jason Anderson	.10
469	Matt Stairs	.10
470	Jarrod Washburn	.10
471	Todd Hundley	.10
472	Grant Roberts	.10
473	Randy Winn	.10
474	Pat Hentgen	.10
475	Jose Vidro	.10
476	Tony Torcato	.10
477	Jeremy Affeldt	.10
478	Carlos Guillen	.10
479	Paul Quantrill	.10
480	Rafael Furcal	.10
481	Adam Melhuse	.10
482	Jerry Hairston	.10
483	Adam Bernero	.10
484	Terrence Long	.10
485	Paul Lo Duca	.10
486	Corey Koskie	.10
487	John Lackey	.10
488	Chad Zerbe	.10
489	Vinny Castilla	.10
490	Corey Patterson	.20
491	John Olerud	.20
492	Josh Bard	.10
493	Darren Dreifort	.10
494	Jason Standridge	.10
495	Ben Sheets	.25
496	Jose Castillo	.10
497	Jay Payton	.10
498	Rob Bowen	.10
499	Bobby Higginson	.10
500	Alex Rodriguez	1.50
501	Octavio Dotel	.10
502	Rheal Cormier	.10
503	Felix Heredia	.10
504	Dan Wright	.10
505	Michael Young	.10
506	Wilfredo Ledezma	.10
507	Sun-Woo Kim	.10
508	Michael Tejera	.10
509	Herbert Perry	.10
510	Esteban Loaiza	.10
511	Alan Embree	.10
512	Ben Davis	.10
513	Greg Colbrunn	.10
514	Josh Hall	.10
515	Raul Ibanez	.10
516	Jayson Werth	.10
517	Corky Miller	.10
518	Jason Marquis	.10
519	Roger Cedeno	.10
520	Adam Dunn	.50
521	Paul Byrd	.10
522	Sandy Alomar	.10
523	Salomon Torres	.10
524	John Halama	.10
525	Mike Piazza	1.00
526	Buddy Groom	.10
527	Adrian Beltre	.25
528	Chad Harville	.10
529	Javier Vazquez	.20
530	Jody Gerut	.10
531	Elmer Dessens	.10
532	B.J. Ryan	.10
533	Chad Durbin	.10
534	Doug Mirabelli	.10
535	Bernie Williams	.40
536	Jeff Davanon	.10
537	Dave Berg	.10
538	Geoff Blum	.10
539	John Thomson	.10
540	Jeremy Bonderman	.10
541	Jeff Zimmerman	.10
542	Derek Lowe	.10
543	Scot Shields	.10
544	Michael Tucker	.10
545	Tim Hudson	.40
546	Ryan Ludwick	.10
547	Rick Reed	.10
548	Placido Palanco	.10
549	Tony Graffanino	.10
550	Garret Anderson	.40
551	Timoniel Perez	.10
552	Jesus Colome	.10
553	R.A. Dickey	.10
554	Tim Worrell	.10
555	Jason Kendall	.10
556	Tom Goodwin	.10
557	Joaquin Benoit	.10
558	Stephen Randolph	.10
559	Miguel Tejada	.40
560	A.J. Burnett	.10
561	Ben Diggins	.10
562	Juan Cruz	.10
563	Zach Day	.10
564	Antonio Perez	.10
565	Jason Schmidt	.25

No.	Player	Price
566	Armando Benitez	.10
567	Denny Neagle	.10
568	Eric Eckenstahler	.10
569	Chan Ho Park	.10
570	Carlos Beltran	.40
571	Brett Tomko	.10
572	Henry Mateo	.10
573	Ken Harvey	.10
574	Matt Lawton	.10
575	Mariano Rivera	.25
576	Darrell May	.10
577	Jamie Moyer	.10
578	Paul Bako	.10
579	Cory Lidle	.10
580	Jacque Jones	.10
581	Jolbert Cabrera	.10
582	Jason Grimsley	.10
583	Danny Kolb	.10
584	Billy Wagner	.10
585	Rich Aurilia	.10
586	Vicente Padilla	.10
587	Oscar Villarreal	.10
588	Rene Reyes	.10
589	Jon Lieber	.10
590	Nick Johnson	.10
591	Bobby Crosby	.10
592	Steve Trachsel	.10
593	Brian Boehringer	.10
594	Juan Uribe	.10
595	Bartolo Colon	.20
596	Bobby Hill	.10
597	Andy Van Hekken	.10
598	Carl Pavano	.10
599	Kurt Ainsworth	.10
600	Derek Jeter	2.00
601	Doug Mientkiewicz	.10
602	Orlando Palmeiro	.10
603	J.C. Romero	.10
604	Scott Sullivan	.10
605	Brad Radke	.10
606	Fernando Rodney	.10
607	Jim Brower	.10
608	Josh Towers	.10
609	Brad Fullmer	.10
610	Jose Reyes	.25
611	Ryan Wagner	.10
612	Joe Mays	.10
613	Jung Bong	.10
614	Curtis Leskanic	.10
615	Al Leiter	.10
616	Wade Miller	.10
617	Keith Foulke	.10
618	Casey Fossum	.10
619	Craig Monroe	.10
620	Hideo Nomo	.25
621	Bob File	.10
622	Steve Kline	.10
623	Bobby Kielty	.10
624	Dewon Brazelton	.10
625	Eric Chavez	.25
626	Chris Carpenter	.10
627	Trever Miller	.10
628	Jason Davis	.10
629	Jose Jimenez	.10
630	Vernon Wells	.10
631	Kenny Lofton	.25
632	Chad Bradford	.10
633	Brad Wilkerson	.10
634	Pokey Reese	.10
635	Richie Sexson	.40
636	Chin-Hui Tsao	.10
637	Eli Marrero	.10
638	Chris Reitsma	.10
639	Daryle Ward	.10
640	Mark Teixeira	.25
641	Corwin Malone	.10
642	Adam Eaton	.10
643	Jimmy Rollins	.25
644	Brian Anderson	.10
645	Bill Mueller	.10
646	Jake Westbrook	.10
647	Bengie Molina	.10
648	Jorge Julio	.10
649	Billy Traber	.10
650	Randy Johnson	.75
651	Javy Lopez	.25
652	Doug Glanville	.10
653	Jeff Cirillo	.10
654	Tino Martinez	.10
655	Mark Buehrle	.10
656	Jason Michaels	.10
657	Damian Rolls	.10
658	Rosman Garcia	.10
659	Scott Hairston	.10
660	Carl Crawford	.10
661	Livan Hernandez	.10
662	Danny Bautista	.10
663	Brad Ausmus	.10
664	Juan Acevedo	.10
665	Sean Casey	.10
666	Pedro Martinez	.75
667	Milton Bradley	.10
668	Braden Looper	.10
669	Paul Abbott	.10
670	Joel Pineiro	.10
671	Luis Terrero	.10
672	Rodrigo Lopez	.10
673	Joe Crede	.10
674	Mike Koplove	.10
675	Brian Giles	.25
676	Jeff Nelson	.10
677	Russell Branyan	.10
678	Mike DeJean	.10
679	Brian Daubach	.10
680	Ellis Burks	.10
681	Ryan Dempster	.10
682	Cliff Politte	.10
683	Brian Reith	.10
684	Scott Stewart	.10
685	Allan Simpson	.10
686	Shawn Estes	.10
687	Jason Johnson	.10
688	Wil Cordero	.10
689	Kelly Stinnett	.10
690	Jose Lima	.10
691	Gary Bennett	.10
692	T.J. Tucker	.10
693	Shane Spencer	.10
694	Chris Hammond	.10
695	Chris Singleton	.10
696	Xavier Nady	.10
697	Cody Ransom	.10
698	Ron Villone	.10
699	Brook Fordyce	.10
700	Sammy Sosa	1.50
701	Terry Adams	.10
702	Ricardo Rincon	.10
703	Tike Redman	.10
704	Chris Stynes	.10
705	Mark Redman	.10
706	Juan Encarnacion	.10
707	Jhonny Peralta	.10
708	Denny Hocking	.10
709	Ivan Rodriguez	.50
710	Jose Hernandez	.10
711	Brandon Duckworth	.10
712	Dave Burba	.10
713	Joe Nathan	.10
714	Dan Smith	.10
715	Karim Garcia	.10
716	Arthur Rhodes	.10
717	Shawn Wooten	.10
718	Ramon Santiago	.10
719	Luis Ugueto	.10
720	Danys Baez	.10
721	Alfredo Amezaga	.10
722	Sidney Ponson	.10
723	Joe Mauer	.50
724	Jesse Foppert	.10
725	Todd Greene	.10
726	Dan Haren	.10
727	Brandon Larson	.10
728	Bobby Jenks	.10
729	Grady Sizemore	.25
730	Ben Grieve	.10
731	Khalil Greene	.10
732	Chad Gaudin	.10
733	Johnny Estrada	.10
734	Joe Valentine	.10
735	Tim Raines	.10
736	Brandon Claussen	.10
737	Sam Marsonek	.10
738	Delmon Young	.25
739	David Dellucci	.10
740	Sergio Mitre	.10
741	Nick Neugebauer	.10
742	Laynce Nix	.10
743	Joe Thurston	.10
744	Ryan Langerhans	.10
745	Pete LaForest	.10
746	Arnie Munoz	.10
747	Rickie Weeks	.25
748	Neal Cotts	.10
749	Jonny Gomes	.10
750	Jim Thome	.75
751	Jon Rauch	.10
752	Edwin Jackson	.10
753	Ryan Madson	.10
754	Chad Tracy	.10
755	Eddie Perez	.10
756	Joe Borchard	.10
757	Jeremy Guthrie	.10
758	Jose Mesa	.10
759	Doug Waechter	.10
760	J.D. Drew	.25
761	Adam LaRoche	.10
762	Rich Harden	.10
763	Justin Speier	.10
764	Todd Zeile	.10
765	Turk Wendell	.10
766	Mark Bellhorn	.10
767	Mike Jackson	.10
768	Chone Figgins	.10
769	Mike Neu	.10
770	Greg Maddux	.75
771	Frank Brooks	.10
772	Alec Zumwalt RC	.25
773	Glendon Rusch	.10
774	Dustan Mohr	.10
775	Shane Halter	.10
776	Tom Wilson	.10
777	So Taguchi	.10
778	Eric Karros	.10
779	Ramon Nivar	.10
780	Marlon Anderson	.10
781	Brayan Pena RC	.10
782	Chris O'Riordan	.10
783	Dioner Navarro RC	1.50
784	Alberto Callaspo RC	.50
785	Hector Gimenez RC	.25
786	Yadier Molina RC	.40
787	Kevin Richardson	.25
788	Brian Pilkington	.40
789	Adam Greenberg	.50
790	Ervin Santana RC	1.00
791	Brent Colamarino	.75
792	Ben Himes	.10
793	Todd Self RC	.25
794	Brad Vericker	.25
795	Donald Kelly RC	.25
796	Brock Jacobsen	.25
797	Brock Peterson	.25
798	Carlos Sosa	.50
799	Chad Chop	.10
800	Matt Moses	1.00
801	Chris Aguila RC	.25
802	David Murphy	.50
803	Don Sutton RC	1.00
804	Jereme Milons	.10
805	Jon Coutlangus	.10
806	Greg Thissen	.10
807	Jose Capellan RC	1.00
808	Chad Santos RC	.10
809	Wardell Starling RC	.10
810	Kevin Kouzmanoff	2.00
811	Kevin Davidson	.40
812	Michael Mooney	.10
813	Rodney Choy Foo	.10
814	Reid Gorecki	.10
815	Rudy Guillen RC	1.00
816	Harvey Garcia	.10
817	Warner Madrigal RC	.50
818	Kenny Perez	.10
819	Joaquin Arias RC	.10
820	Benji Dequin	.40
821	Lastings Milledge	2.00
822	Blake Hawksworth RC	.50
823	Estee Harris RC	.50
824	Bobby Brownlie	.75
825	Wanell Severino RC	.10
826	Bobby Madritsch	.10
827	Travis Hanson	.40
828	Brandon Medders RC	.10
829	Kevin Howard RC	.50
830	Brian Steffek	.10
831	Terry Jones	.10
832	Anthony Acevedo	.40
833	Kory Casto	.10
834	Brooks Conrad	.10
835	Juan Gutierrez RC	.50
836	Charlie Zink RC	.40
837	David Aardsma	.40
838	Carl Loadenthal	.10
839	Donald Levinski	.10
840	Dustin Nippert RC	.75
841	Calvin Hayes	.10
842	Felix Hernandez RC	4.00
843	Tyler Davidson	.50
844	George Sherrill RC	.10
845	Craig Ansman RC	.10
846	Jeffrey Allison	.50
847	Tommy Murphy RC	.10
848	Jerome Gamble RC	.40
849	Jesse English RC	.10
850	Alex Romero RC	.40
851	Joel Zumaya RC	2.00
852	Carlos Quentin	2.00
853	Jose Valdez	.10
854	J.J. Furmaniak RC	.75
855	Juan Cedeno RC	.25
856	Kyle Sleeth	1.00
857	Josh Labandeira RC	.25
858	Lee Gwaltney	.10
859	Lincoln Holdzkom RC	.25
860	Ivan Ochoa RC	.10
861	Luke Anderson	.10
862	Conor Jackson	1.00
863	Matt Capps RC	.75
864	Merkin Valdez RC	.75
865	Paul Bacot	.50
866	Erick Aybar RC	.50
867	Scott Proctor RC	1.00
868	Tim Stauffer	.50
869	Matt Creighton RC	.50
870	Zach Miner RC	1.00
871	Danny Gonzalez RC	.10
872	Tom Farmer	.10
873	John Santor	.10
874	Logan Kensing RC	.25
875	Vito Chiaravalloti RC	.50
876	Checklist	.10
877	Checklist	.10
878	Checklist	.10
879	Checklist	.10
880	Checklist	.10

Silver

Stars:	2-3X
Inserted 1:1	

Press Plates

No Pricing
Production one for each color.

Autograph

TOTAL SIGNATURES

LARRY BIGBIE

		NM/M
Inserted 1:414		8.00
GB	Grant Balfour	8.00
LB	Larry Bigbie	10.00
BC	Brandon Claussen	8.00
TH	Toby Hall	8.00
JJ	Jimmy Journell	8.00

Total Award Winners

TOTAL AWARD WINNER

Tony Pena

		NM/M
Complete Set (30):		20.00
Common Player:		.50
Inserted 1:12		
AW1	Roy Halladay	.50
AW2	Eric Gagne	.50
AW3	Alex Rodriguez	3.00
AW4	Albert Pujols	3.00
AW5	Alex Rodriguez	3.00
AW6	Jorge Posada	.50
AW7	Javy Lopez	.50
AW8	Carlos Delgado	.50
AW9	Todd Helton	.75
AW10	Bret Boone	.50
AW11	Jose Vidro	.50
AW12	Bill Mueller	.50
AW13	Mike Lowell	.50
AW14	Alex Rodriguez	3.00
AW15	Edgar Renteria	.50
AW16	Garret Anderson	.50
AW17	Albert Pujols	3.00
AW18	Manny Ramirez	1.00
AW19	Vernon Wells	.50
AW20	Gary Sheffield	.50
AW21	Edgar Martinez	.50
AW22	Mike Hampton	.50
AW23	Angel Berroa	.50
AW24	Dontrelle Willis	.50
AW25	Keith Foulke	.50
AW26	Eric Gagne	.50
AW27	Alex Rodriguez	3.00
AW28	Albert Pujols	3.00
AW29	Tony Pena	.50
AW30	Jack McKeon	.50

Total Production

		NM/M
Complete Set (10):		10.00
Common Player:		.50
Inserted 1:18		
TP1	Alex Rodriguez	3.00
TP2	Albert Pujols	3.00
TP3	Sammy Sosa	2.50
TP4	Carlos Delgado	.50
TP5	Gary Sheffield	.50
TP6	Manny Ramirez	1.00
TP7	Jim Thome	1.00
TP8	Todd Helton	.75

TP9	Garret Anderson	.50
TP10	Nomar Garciaparra	2.00

Total Topps

		NM/M
Complete Set (50):		25.00
Common Player:		.50
Inserted 1:7		
TT1	Derek Jeter	3.00
TT2	Jose Reyes	.50
TT3	Miguel Tejada	.50
TT4	Larry Walker	.50
TT5	Frank Thomas	.75
TT6	Carlos Delgado	.50
TT7	Vernon Wells	.50
TT8	Jeff Bagwell	.75
TT9	Jason Giambi	.75
TT10	Mike Lowell	.50
TT11	Shannon Stewart	.50
TT12	Mike Piazza	1.50
TT13	Todd Helton	.75
TT14	Austin Kearns	.50
TT15	Jim Edmonds	.50
TT16	Jose Vidro	.50
TT17	Andruw Jones	.50
TT18	Gary Sheffield	.50
TT19	Eric Chavez	.50
TT20	Magglio Ordonez	.50
TT21	Geoff Jenkins	.50
TT22	Ken Griffey Jr.	1.50
TT23	Jeff Kent	.50
TT24	Jorge Posada	.50
TT25	Albert Pujols	2.00
TT26	Javy Lopez	.50
TT27	Alfonso Soriano	1.00
TT28	Brian Giles	.50
TT29	Mike Sweeney	.50
TT30	Miguel Cabrera	1.00
TT31	Luis Gonzalez	.50
TT32	Scott Rolen	1.00
TT33	Jim Thome	1.00
TT34	Garret Anderson	.75
TT35	Vladimir Guerrero	1.00
TT36	Shawn Green	.50
TT37	Hank Blalock	.75
TT38	Marcus Giles	.50
TT39	Torii Hunter	.50
TT40	Sammy Sosa	2.00
TT41	Nomar Garciaparra	2.00
TT42	Bobby Abreu	.50
TT43	Richie Sexson	.50
TT44	Manny Ramirez	.75
TT45	Troy Glaus	.75
TT46	Preston Wilson	.50
TT47	Ivan Rodriguez	.75
TT48	Ichiro Suzuki	1.50
TT49	Chipper Jones	1.00
TT50	Nomar Garciaparra	3.00

2004 Topps Tribute HOF

		NM/M
Complete Set (80):		120.00
Common Player:		2.00
Pack (5):		50.00
Box (6):		260.00
1	Willie Mays	8.00
2	Richie Ashburn	2.00
3	Babe Ruth	10.00
4	Lou Gehrig	8.00
5	Carl Yastrzemski	5.00
6	Fergie Jenkins	2.00
7	Cool Papa Bell	3.00
8	Johnny Bench	4.00
9	Satchel Paige	4.00
10	Ty Cobb	6.00
11	Robin Roberts	2.00
12	Eddie Mathews	3.00
13	Tom Seaver	3.00
14	Kirby Puckett	3.00
15	Stan Musial	5.00
16	Ralph Kiner	2.00
17	Reggie Jackson	3.00
18	Walter Johnson	4.00
19	Phil Niekro	2.00
20	Mike Schmidt	6.00
21	Brooks Robinson	3.00
22	Jimmie Foxx	4.00
23	Nellie Fox	2.00
24	Joe Morgan	2.00
25	Cy Young	3.00
26	Hank Greenberg	3.00
27	Josh Gibson	3.00
28	Robin Yount	5.00
29	Hoyt Wilhelm	2.00
30	Yogi Berra	3.00
31	Rollie Fingers	2.00
32	Gaylord Perry	2.00
33	Ozzie Smith	4.00
34	Jim Palmer	2.00
35	Harmon Killebrew	4.00
36	Bob Feller	2.00
37	Chuck Klein	2.00
38	Mordecai Brown	2.00
39	Napoleon Lajoie	2.00
40	Al Kaline	3.00
41	Paul Molitor	3.00
42	Jackie Robinson	5.00
43	Mel Ott	3.00
44	Hank Aaron	8.00
45	Rod Carew	2.00
46	Rogers Hornsby	3.00
47	Bob Gibson	2.00
48	Juan Marichal	2.00
49	Bill Mazeroski	2.00
50	Roberto Clemente	8.00
51	Willie McCovey	2.00
52	Red Schoendienst	2.00
53	Nolan Ryan	8.00
54	Dennis Eckersley	2.00
55	Monte Irvin	2.00
56	George Kell	2.00
57	Gary Carter	2.00
58	Tony Perez	2.00
59	Carlton Fisk	3.00
60	Duke Snider	3.00
61	Bobby Doerr	2.00
62	John McGraw	2.00
63	George Sisler	2.00
64	Orlando Cepeda	2.00
65	Earl Weaver	2.00
66	Roy Campanella	3.00
67	Tris Speaker	2.00
68	Sparky Anderson	2.00
69	Willie Stargell	2.00
70	Honus Wagner	3.00
71	Lou Brock	2.00
72	Whitey Ford	3.00
73	George Brett	8.00
74	Luis Aparicio	2.00
75	Ernie Banks	4.00
76	Jim Bunning	2.00
77	Warren Spahn	3.00
78	Jim "Catfish" Hunter	2.00
79	Pee Wee Reese	2.00
80	Frank Robinson	2.00

Gold

Gold Print Run 61-99:	2-3X
Gold p/r 36-60:	2-4X
#'d to last 2 digits of HOF induction yr	

Cooperstown Cut Signatures

		NM/M
No Pricing		
Production One Set		
MO	Mel Ott (8/05 Auction)	2,025

Cooperstown Classmates Dual Cut Signature

No Pricing
Production One Set

Cooperstown Classmates Dual Relic

		NM/M
Common Duo:		20.00
Gold:		.75-1.5X
Production 25		
ME	Paul Molitor, Dennis Eckersley/75	35.00
KK	Chuck Klein, Al Kaline/75	35.00
RB	Nolan Ryan, George Brett/50	60.00
MP	Joe Morgan, Jim Palmer/75	20.00
SK	Duke Snider, Al Kaline/50	60.00
PC	Gaylord Perry, Rod Carew/50	30.00
BY	Johnny Bench, Carl Yastrzemski/75	50.00
CR	Orlando Cepeda, Nolan Ryan/75	60.00
MR	Juan Marichal, Brooks Robinson/50	35.00

Cut Signatures

No Pricing
Production One Set

Dual Cut Signatures

No Pricing
Production One Set

Hall of Fame Patches Relics

		NM/M
Common Player:		20.00
Gold:		.75-1.5X
Production 1-25		
No pricing for production 15 or less.		
GB	George Brett/50	40.00
RC	Rod Carew/100	25.00
DE	Dennis Eckersley/50	25.00
RJ	Reggie Jackson/50	25.00
FR	Frank Robinson/39	35.00
NR	Nolan Ryan/100	50.00
MS	Mike Schmidt/100	40.00
MS2	Mike Schmidt/100	40.00
RY	Robin Yount/35	40.00

Tribute Relics

		NM/M
Common Player:		10.00
Golds:		1-3X
Production 25 Sets		
HA	Hank Aaron/Bat	30.00
JB	Johnny Bench/Jsy/250	15.00
JB2	Johnny Bench/Jsy	15.00
GB	George Brett/Jsy	15.00
GBB	George Brett/Bat	15.00
LBB	Lou Brock/Bat	10.00
GC	Gary Carter/Jsy/200	15.00
GCU	Gary Carter/Jsy	10.00
OC	Orlando Cepeda/Bat/100	20.00
RC	Roberto Clemente/Bat	50.00
TC	Ty Cobb/Jsy/20	275.00
TCB	Ty Cobb/Bat	75.00
CF	Carlton Fisk/Wall/300	20.00
WF	Whitey Ford/Jsy/50	60.00
JF	Jimmie Foxx/Bat/25	100.00
LG	Lou Gehrig/Bat/52	300.00
BG	Bob Gibson/Jsy	15.00
HG	Hank Greenberg/Bat	20.00
RH	Rogers Hornsby/Bat	40.00
RJ	Reggie Jackson/Jsy/110	15.00
RJB	Reggie Jackson/Bat/200	10.00
AK	Al Kaline/Jsy/125	15.00
AKB	Al Kaline/Bat	10.00
HK	Harmon Killebrew/Bat/135	30.00
CK	Chuck Klein/Bat/107	20.00

JMA	Juan Marichal/Jsy/125	10.00
WM1	Willie Mays/Glv/110	150.00
WM2	Willie Mays/Bat	30.00
WM3	Willie Mays/Bat	30.00
WM4	Willie Mays/Jsy	30.00
WM5	Willie Mays/Jsy	30.00
PM	Paul Molitor/Jsy	10.00
PMB	Paul Molitor/Bat	10.00
JM	Joe Morgan/Bat	10.00
SM	Stan Musial/Jsy	20.00
MO	Mel Ott/Bat/25	100.00
JP	Jim Palmer/Jsy	10.00
JP2	Jim Palmer/Jsy	10.00
KP	Kirby Puckett/Jsy/175	15.00
KPB	Kirby Puckett/Bat	10.00
BRO	Brooks Robinson/Bat	10.00
FR	Frank Robinson/Jsy	10.00
FRA	Frank Robinson/Jsy	10.00
FRB	Frank Robinson/Bat	10.00
JR	Jackie Robinson/Bat	25.00
BR	Babe Ruth/Bat/163	150.00
NR	Nolan Ryan/Jsy	25.00
NRA	Nolan Ryan/Jsy/425	25.00
NRJ	Nolan Ryan/Jsy	25.00
MS	Mike Schmidt/Jsy/50	30.00
MSB	Mike Schmidt/Bat	15.00
TS	Tom Seaver/Jsy	15.00
GS	George Sisler/Bat/455	25.00
OS	Ozzie Smith/Bat	15.00
DS	Duke Snider/Bat	10.00
TSP	Tris Speaker/Bat/85	120.00
HW	Honus Wagner/Bat/118	120.00
EW	Earl Weaver/Jsy/25	20.00
CY	Carl Yastrzemski/Wall/300	30.00
CYU	Carl Yastrzemski/Jsy	15.00
RY	Robin Yount/Jsy/50	25.00

Tribute Relic Autographs

		NM/M
Common Player:		40.00
Gold:		No Pricing
Production Five Sets		
AKB	Al Kaline/95	60.00
BRO	Brooks Robinson/95	50.00
NRJ	Nolan Ryan/95	140.00
EW	Earl Weaver/95	40.00
CYU	Carl Yastrzemski/95	85.00

2005 Topps

		NM/M
Complete Set (732):		75.00
Factory Holiday Set (742):		80.00
Factory Hobby Set (737):		80.00
Common Player:		.10
Pack (10):		2.00
Box (36):		60.00
1	Alex Rodriguez	1.50
2	Placido Polanco	.10
3	Torii Hunter	.25
4	Lyle Overbay	.10
5	Johnny Damon	.40
6	Johnny Estrada	.10
7	Francisco Rodriguez	.10
8	Jason LaRue	.10
9	Sammy Sosa	1.00
10	Randy Wolf	.10
11	Jason Bay	.10
12	Tom Glavine	.25
13	Michael Tucker	.10
14	Brian Giles	.20
15	Dan Wilson	.10
16	Jim Edmonds	.40
17	Danys Baez	.10
18	Roy Halladay	.20
19	Hank Blalock	.50
20	Darin Erstad	.10
21	Robby Hammock	.10
22	Mike Hampton	.10
23	Mark Bellhorn	.10
24	Jim Thome	.50
25	Scott Schoeneweis	.10
26	Jody Gerut	.10
27	Vinny Castilla	.10
28	Luis Castillo	.10
29	Matt Morris	.10
30	Ivan Rodriguez	.50
31	Craig Biggio	.20
32	Joe Randa	.10
33	Dave Roberts	.10
34	Scott Podsednik	.10
35	Cliff Floyd	.10
36	Livan Hernandez	.10

37	Eric Byrnes	.10
38	Ricky Ledee	.10
39	Jack Wilson	.10
40	Gary Sheffield	.40
41	Chan Ho Park	.10
42	Carl Crawford	.10
43	Miguel Batista	.10
44	David Bell	.10
45	Jeff DaVanon	.10
46	Brandon Webb	.10
47	Bronson Arroyo	.10
48	Melvin Mora	.10
49	David Ortiz	.50
50	Andruw Jones	.40
51	Chone Figgins	.10
52	Danny Graves	.10
53	Preston Wilson	.10
54	Jeremy Bonderman	.10
55	Chad Fox	.10
56	Dan Miceli	.10
57	Jimmy Gobble	.10
58	Darren Dreifort	.10
59	Matt LeCroy	.10
60	Jose Vidro	.10
61	Al Leiter	.10
62	Javier Vazquez	.10
63	Erubiel Durazo	.10
64	Doug Glanville	.10
65	Scot Shields	.10
66	Edgardo Alfonzo	.10
67	Ryan Franklin	.10
68	Francisco Cordero	.10
69	Brett Myers	.10
70	Curt Schilling	.50
71	Matt Kata	.10
72	Mark DeRosa	.10
73	Rodrigo Lopez	.10
74	Tim Wakefield	.10
75	Frank Thomas	.50
76	Jimmy Rollins	.25
77	Barry Zito	.25
78	Hideo Nomo	.25
79	Brad Wilkerson	.10
80	Adam Dunn	.50
81	Billy Traber	.10
82	Fernando Vina	.10
83	Nate Robertson	.10
84	Brad Ausmus	.10
85	Mike Sweeney	.10
86	Kip Wells	.10
87	Doug Mientkiewicz	.10
88	Zach Day	.10
89	Tony Clark	.10
90	Bret Boone	.10
91	Mark Loretta	.10
92	Jerome Williams	.10
93	Randy Winn	.10
94	Marlon Anderson	.10
95	Aubrey Huff	.10
96	Kevin Mench	.10
97	Frank Catalanotto	.10
98	Flash Gordon	.10
99	Scott Hatteberg	.10
100	Albert Pujols	1.50
101	Jose Molina, Bengie Molina	.10
102	Oscar Villarreal	.10
103	Jay Gibbons	.10
104	Byung-Hyun Kim	.10
105	Joe Borowski	.10
106	Mark Grudzielanek	.10
107	Mark Buehrle	.10
108	Paul Wilson	.10
109	Ronnie Belliard	.10
110	Larry Walker	.40
111	Tim Redding	.10
112	Hee Seop Choi	.10
113	Darrell May	.10
114	Jose Hernandez	.10
115	Ben Sheets	.25
116	Johan Santana	.40
117	Billy Wagner	.20
118	Mariano Rivera	.25
119	Steve Trachsel	.10
120	Akinori Otsuka	.10
121	Bobby Kielty	.10
122	Felix Rodriguez	.10
123	Raul Ibanez	.10
124	Mike Matheny	.10
125	Vernon Wells	.10
126	Jason Isringhausen	.10
127	Jose Guillen	.10
128	Danny Bautista	.10
129	Marcus Giles	.10
130	Javy Lopez	.25
131	Kevin Millar	.10
132	Kyle Farnsworth	.10
133	Carl Pavano	.10
134	D'Angelo Jimenez	.10
135	Casey Blake	.10
136	Matt Holliday	.25
137	Bobby Higginson	.10
138	Ramon Castro	.10
139	Alex Gonzalez	.10
140	Jeff Kent	.20
141	Aaron Guiel	.10
142	Shawn Green	.25
143	Bill Hall	.10
144	Shannon Stewart	.10
145	Juan Rivera	.10
146	Ty Wigginton	.10
147	Mike Mussina	.50
148	Eric Chavez	.25
149	Randall Simon	.10
150	Vladimir Guerrero	.75
151	Alex Cintron	.10
152	Horacio Ramirez	.10
153	Sidney Ponson	.10
154	Trot Nixon	.10
155	Greg Maddux	1.00
156	Esteban Loaiza	.10
157	Ryan Freel	.10
158	Matt Lawton	.10
159	Shawn Chacon	.10
160	Josh Beckett	.25
161	Ken Harvey	.10
162	Juan Cruz	.10
163	Juan Encarnacion	.10
164	Wes Helms	.10
165	Brad Radke	.10
166	Claudio Vargas	.10
167	Mike Cameron	.10
168	Jose Contreras	.10
169	Bobby Crosby	.10
170	Mike Lieberthal	.10
171	Robert Mackowiak	.10
172	Sean Burroughs	.10
173	J.T. Snow Jr.	.10
174	Paul Konerko	.10
175	Luis Gonzalez	.10
176	John Lackey	.10
177	Antonio Alfonseca	.10
178	Brian Roberts	.10
179	Bill Mueller	.10
180	Carlos Lee	.10
181	Corey Patterson	.25
182	Sean Casey	.25
183	Cliff Lee	.10
184	Jason Jennings	.10
185	Dmitri Young	.10
186	Brad Penny	.10
187	Andy Pettitte	.25
188	Juan Gonzalez	.25
189	Paul LoDuca	.10
190	Jason Phillips	.10
191	Rocky Biddle	.10
192	Lew Ford	.10
193	Mark Mulder	.25
194	Bobby Abreu	.25
195	Jason Kendall	.10
196	Terrence Long	.10
197	A.J. Pierzynski	.10
198	Eddie Guardado	.10
199	So Taguchi	.10
200	Jason Giambi	.25
201	Tony Batista	.10
202	Kyle Lohse	.10
203	Trevor Hoffman	.10
204	Tike Redman	.10
205	Neifi Perez	.10
206	Gil Meche	.10
207	Chris Carpenter	.10
208	Josh Phelps	.10
209	Eric Young	.10
210	Doug Waechter	.10
211	Jarrod Washburn	.10
212	Chad Tracy	.10
213	John Smoltz	.25
214	Jorge Julio	.10
215	Alex Gonzalez	.10
216	Shingo Takatsu	.10
217	Jose Acevedo	.10
218	Jason Davis	.10
219	Shawn Estes	.10
220	Lance Berkman	.25
221	Carlos Guillen	.10
222	Jeremy Affeldt	.10
223	Cesar Izturis	.10
224	Scott Sullivan	.10
225	Kazuo Matsui	.25
226	Josh Fogg	.10
227	Jason Schmidt	.25
228	Jason Marquis	.10
229	Scott Spiezio	.10
230	Miguel Tejada	.40
231	Bartolo Colon	.10
232	Jose Valverde	.10
233	Derrek Lee	.25
234	Scott Williamson	.10
235	Joe Crede	.10
236	Cory Lidle	.10
237	Mike MacDougal	.10
238	Eric Gagne	.25
239	Alex Sanchez	.10
240	Miguel Cabrera	.75
241	Luis Rivas	.10
242	Adam Everett	.10
243	Jason Johnson	.10
244	Travis Hafner	.25
245	Jose Valentin	.10
246	Stephen Randolph	.10
247	Rafael Furcal	.25
248	Adam Kennedy	.10
249	Luis Matos	.10
250	Mark Prior	.75
251	Angel Berroa	.10
252	Phil Nevin	.10
253	Oliver Perez	.10
254	Orlando Hudson	.10
255	Victor Zambrano	.10
256	Khalil Greene	.25
257	Tim Worrell	.10
258	Carlos Zambrano	.25
259	Elmer Dessens	.10
260	Gerald Laird	.10
261	Jose Cruz Jr.	.10
262	Michael Barrett	.10
263	Michael Young (Barajas. Uncorrected error - Photo is Rod)	.10
264	Toby Hall	.10
265	Woody Williams	.10
266	Rich Harden	.10
267	Mike Scioscia	.10
268	Al Pedrique	.10
269	Bobby Cox	.10
270	Lee Mazzilli	.10
271	Terry Francona	.10
272	Dusty Baker	.10
273	Ozzie Guillen	.10
274	Dave Miley	.10
275	Eric Wedge	.10
276	Clint Hurdle	.10
277	Alan Trammell	.10
278	Jack McKeon	.10
279	Phil Garner	.10
280	Tony Pena	.10
281	Jim Tracy	.10
282	Ned Yost	.10
283	Ron Gardenhire	.10
284	Frank Robinson	.25
285	Art Howe	.10
286	Joe Torre	.25
287	Ken Macha	.10
288	Larry Bowa	.10
289	Lloyd McClendon	.10
290	Bruce Bochy	.10
291	Felipe Alou	.10
292	Bob Melvin	.10
293	Tony LaRussa	.10
294	Lou Piniella	.10
295	Buck Showalter	.10
296	Carlos Tosca	.10
297	Steven Doetsch **RC**	.10
298	Melky Cabrera **RC**	1.00
299	Luis Ramirez **RC**	.10
300	Chris Seddon **RC**	.10
301	Nate Schierholtz	1.00
302	Ian Kinsler **RC**	2.00
303	Brandon Moss **RC**	1.50
304	Chadd Blasko **RC**	.10
305	Jeremy West **RC**	1.00
306	Sean Marshall **RC**	.75
307	Matt DeSalvo **RC**	.50
308	Ryan Sweeney	1.50
309	Matt Lindstrom **RC**	.10
310	Ryan Goleski **RC**	.50
311	Brett Harper **RC**	.25
312	Chris Roberson **RC**	.10
313	Andre Ethier	1.50
314	Chris Denorfia **RC**	.10
315	Ian Bladergroen **RC**	.75
316	Darren Fenster **RC**	.10
317	Kevin West **RC**	.10
318	Chaz Lytle **RC**	.50
319	James Jurries **RC**	.10
320	Matt Rogelstad **RC**	.10
321	Wade Robinson **RC**	.10
322	Jake Dittler	.10
323	Edgar Huerta **RC**	.10
324	Kole Strayhorn	.10
325	Jose Vaquedano **RC**	.10
326	Elvys Quezada **RC**	.10
327	John Maine, Val Majewski	.10
328	Rickie Weeks, J.J. Hardy	.10
329	Gabe Gross, Guillermo Quiroz	.10
330	David Wright, Craig Brazell	1.50
331	Dallas McPherson, Jeff Mathis	.10
332	Randy Johnson	.10
333	Randy Johnson	.10
334	Ichiro Suzuki	.10
335	Ken Griffey Jr.	.10
336	Greg Maddux	.10
337	Ichiro Suzuki, Melvin Mora, Vladimir Guerrero	.10
338	Ichiro Suzuki, Michael Young, Vladimir Guerrero	.10
339	Manny Ramirez, Paul Konerko, David Ortiz	.10
340	Miguel Tejada, David Ortiz, Manny Ramirez	.10
341	Johan Santana, Curt Schilling, Jake Westbrook	.10
342	Johan Santana, Pedro J. Martinez, Curt Schilling	.10
343	Todd Helton, Mark Loretta, Adrian Beltre	.10
344	Juan Pierre, Mark Loretta, Jack Wilson	.10
345	Adrian Beltre, Adam Dunn, Albert Pujols	.10
346	Vinny Castilla, Scott Rolen, Albert Pujols	.10
347	Jake Peavy, Randy Johnson, Ben Sheets	.10
348	Randy Johnson, Ben Sheets, Jason Schmidt	.10
349	Postseason Highlight	.10
350	Postseason Highlight	.10
351	Postseason Highlight	.10
352	Postseason Highlight	.10
353	Postseason Highlight	.10
354	Postseason Highlight	.10
355	Postseason Highlight	.10
356	Paul Konerko	.10
357	Alfonso Soriano	.10
358	Miguel Tejada	.10
359	Melvin Mora	.10
360	Vladimir Guerrero	.10
361	Ichiro Suzuki	.10
362	Manny Ramirez	.10
363	Ivan Rodriguez	.10
364	Johan Santana	.10
365	Paul Konerko	.10
366	David Ortiz	.10
367	Bobby Crosby	.10
368	Sox Celebration WS4	1.50
369	Garret Anderson	.25
370	Randy Johnson	.75
371	Charles Thomas	.10
372	Rafael Palmeiro	.40
373	Kevin Youkilis	.10
374	Freddy Garcia	.10
375	Magglio Ordonez	.10
376	Aaron Harang	.10
377	Grady Sizemore	.25
378	Chin-Hui Tsao	.10
379	Eric Munson	.10
380	Juan Pierre	.10
381	Brad Lidge	.10
382	Brian Anderson	.10
383	Alex Cora	.10
384	Brady Clark	.10
385	Todd Helton	.40
386	Chad Cordero	.10
387	Kris Benson	.10
388	Brad Halsey	.10
389	Jermaine Dye	.10
390	Manny Ramirez	.50
391	Daryle Ward	.10
392	Adam Eaton	.10
393	Brett Tomko	.10
394	Bucky Jacobsen	.10
395	Dontrelle Willis	.40
396	B.J. Upton	.25
397	Rocco Baldelli	.10
398	Ted Lilly	.10
399	Ryan Drese	.10
400	Ichiro Suzuki	1.25
401	Brendan Donnelly	.10
402	Brandon Lyon	.10
403	Nick Green	.10
404	Jerry Hairston Jr.	.10
405	Mike Lowell	.10
406	Kerry Wood	.50
407	Carl Everett	.10
408	Hideki Matsui	1.25
409	Omar Vizquel	.25
410	Joe Kennedy	.10
411	Carlos Pena	.10
412	Armando Benitez	.10
413	Carlos Beltran	.50
414	Kevin Appier	.10
415	Jeff Weaver	.10
416	Chad Moeller	.10
417	Joe Mays	.10
418	Terrmel Sledge	.10
419	Richard Hidalgo	.10
420	Kenny Lofton	.10
421	Justin Duchscherer	.10
422	Eric Milton	.10
423	Jose Mesa	.10
424	Ramon Hernandez	.10
425	Jose Reyes	.25
426	Joel Pineiro	.10
427	Matt Morris	.10
428	John Halama	.10
429	Gary Matthews Jr.	.10
430	Ryan Madson	.10
431	Mark Kotsay	.10
432	Carlos Delgado	.10
433	Casey Kotchman	.10
434	Greg Aquino	.10
435	Eli Marrero	.10
436	David Newhan	.10
437	Mike Timlin	.10
438	LaTroy Hawkins	.10
439	Jose Contreras	.10
440	Ken Griffey Jr.	1.00
441	C.C. Sabathia	.10
442	Brandon Inge	.10
443	Peter Munro	.10
444	John Buck	.10
445	Hee Seop Choi	.10
446	Chris Capuano	.10
447	Jesse Crain	.10
448	Geoff Jenkins	.10
449	Brian Schneider	.10
450	Mike Piazza	1.00
451	Jorge Posada	.40
452	Nick Swisher	.10
453	Kevin Millwood	.25
454	Mike Gonzalez	.10
455	Jake Peavy	.25
456	Dustin Hermanson	.10
457	Jeremy Reed	.10
458	Julian Tavarez	.10
459	Geoff Blum	.10
460	Alfonso Soriano	.50
461	Alexis Rios	.10
462	David Eckstein	.10
463	Shea Hillenbrand	.10
464	Russ Ortiz	.10
465	Kurt Ainsworth	.10
466	Orlando Cabrera	.10
467	Carlos Silva	.10
468	Ross Gload	.10
469	Josh Phelps	.10
470	Marquis Grissom	.10
471	Mike Maroth	.10
472	Guillermo Mota	.10
473	Chris Burke	.10
474	David DeJesus	.10
475	Jose Lima	.10
476	Cristian Guzman	.10
477	Nick Johnson	.10
478	Victor Zambrano	.10
479	Rod Barajas	.10
480	Damian Miller	.10
481	Chase Utley	.25

482	Todd Pratt	.10
483	Sean Burnett	.10
484	David Wells	.10
485	Dustan Mohr	.10
486	Bobby Madritsch	.10
487	Ray King	.10
488	Reed Johnson	.10
489	R.A. Dickey	.10
490	Scott Kazmir	.25
491	Tony Womack	.10
492	Tomas Perez	.10
493	Esteban Loaiza	.10
494	Tomokazu Ohka	.10
495	Mike Lamb	.10
496	Ramon Ortiz	.10
497	Richie Sexson	.40
498	J.D. Drew	.25
499	David Segui	.10
500	Barry Bonds	2.00
501	Aramis Ramirez	.25
502	Wily Mo Pena	.10
503	Jeromy Burnitz	.10
504	Craig Monroe	.10
505	Nomar Garciaparra	1.00
506	Brandon Backe	.10
507	Marcus Thames	.10
508	Derek Lowe	.10
509	Doug Davis	.10
510	Joe Mauer	.25
511	Endy Chavez	.10
512	Bernie Williams	.25
513	Mark Redman	.10
514	Jason Michaels	.10
515	Craig Wilson	.10
516	Ryan Klesko	.10
517	Ray Durham	.10
518	Jose Lopez	.10
519	Jeff Suppan	.10
520	Julio Lugo	.10
521	Mike Wood	.10
522	David Bush	.10
523	Juan Rincon	.10
524	Paul Quantrill	.10
525	Marlon Byrd	.10
526	Roy Oswalt	.25
527	Rondell White	.10
528	Troy Glaus	.25
529	Scott Hairston	.10
530	Chipper Jones	.75
531	Daniel Cabrera	.10
532	Doug Mientkiewicz	.10
533	Glendon Rusch	.10
534	Jon Garland	.10
535	Austin Kearns	.10
536	Jake Westbrook	.10
537	Aaron Miles	.10
538	Omar Infante	.10
539	Paul LoDuca	.10
540	Morgan Ensberg	.10
541	Tony Graffanino	.10
542	Milton Bradley	.25
543	Keith Ginter	.10
544	Justin Morneau	.40
545	Tony Armas Jr.	.10
546	Mike Stanton	.10
547	Kevin Brown	.10
548	Marco Scutaro	.10
549	Tim Hudson	.10
550	Pat Burrell	.10
551	Ty Wigginton	.10
552	Jeff Cirillo	.10
553	Jim Brower	.10
554	Jamie Moyer	.10
555	Larry Walker	.10
556	Dewon Brazelton	.10
557	Brian Jordan	.10
558	Josh Towers	.10
559	Shigetoshi Hasegawa	.10
560	Octavio Dotel	.10
561	Travis Lee	.10
562	Michael Cuddyer	.10
563	Junior Spivey	.10
564	Zack Greinke	.10
565	Roger Clemens	1.50
566	Chris Shelton	.10
567	Ugueth Urbina	.10
568	Rafael Betancourt	.10
569	Willie Harris	.10
570	Todd Hollandsworth	.10
571	Keith Foulke	.10
572	Larry Bigbie	.10
573	Paul Byrd	.10
574	Troy Percival	.10
575	Pedro Martinez	.75
576	Matt Clement	.10
577	Ryan Wagner	.10
578	Jeff Francis	.10
579	Jeff Conine	.10
580	Wade Miller	.10
581	Matt Stairs	.10
582	Gavin Floyd	.10
583	Kazuhisa Ishii	.10
584	Victor Santos	.10
585	Jacque Jones	.10
586	Sunny Kim	.10
587	Dan Kolb	.10
588	Cory Lidle	.10
589	Jose Castillo	.10
590	Alex Gonzalez	.10
591	Kirk Rueter	.10
592	Jolbert Cabrera	.10
593	Erik Bedard	.10
594	Ben Grieve	.10
595	Ricky Ledee	.10
596	Mark Hendrickson	.10
597	Laynce Nix	.10
598	Jason Frasor	.10
599	Kevin Gregg	.10
600	Derek Jeter	1.50
601	Luis Terrero	.10
602	Jaret Wright	.10
603	Edwin Jackson	.10
604	Dave Roberts	.10
605	Moises Alou	.25
606	Aaron Rowand	.10
607	Kazuhito Tadano	.10
608	Luis Gonzalez	.10
609	A.J. Burnett	.25
610	Jeff Bagwell	.40
611	Brad Penny	.10
612	Craig Counsell	.10
613	Corey Koskie	.10
614	Mark Ellis	.10
615	Felix Rodriguez	.10
616	Jay Payton	.10
617	Hector Luna	.10
618	Miguel Olivo	.10
619	Rob Bell	.10
620	Scott Rolen	.50
621	Ricardo Rodriguez	.10
622	Eric Hinske	.10
623	Tim Salmon	.10
624	Adam LaRoche	.10
625	B.J. Ryan	.10
626	Roberto Alomar	.25
627	Steve Finley	.10
628	Joe Nathan	.10
629	Scott Linebrink	.10
630	Vicente Padilla	.10
631	Raul Mondesi	.10
632	Yadier Molina	.10
633	Tino Martinez	.10
634	Mark Teixeira	.25
635	Kelvim Escobar	.10
636	Pedro Felix	.10
637	Rich Aurilia	.10
638	Los Angeles Angels of Anaheim	.10
639	Arizona Diamondbacks	.10
640	Atlanta Braves	.10
641	Baltimore Orioles	.10
642	Boston Red Sox	.10
643	Chicago Cubs	.10
644	Chicago White Sox	.10
645	Cincinnati Reds	.10
646	Cleveland Indians	.10
647	Colorado Rockies	.10
648	Detroit Tigers	.10
649	Florida Marlins	.10
650	Houston Astros	.10
651	Kansas City Royals	.10
652	Los Angeles Dodgers	.10
653	Milwaukee Brewers	.10
654	Minnesota Twins	.10
655	Montreal Expos	.10
656	New York Mets	.10
657	New York Yankees	.10
658	Oakland Athletics	.10
659	Philadelphia Phillies	.10
660	Pittsburgh Pirates	.10
661	San Diego Padres	.10
662	San Francisco Giants	.10
663	Seattle Mariners	.10
664	St. Louis Cardinals	.10
665	Tampa Bay Devil Rays	.10
666	Texas Rangers	.10
667	Toronto Blue Jays	.10
668	Billy Butler **RC**	1.50
669	Wes Swackhamer **RC**	.25
670	Matt Campbell **RC**	.25
671	Ryan Webb **RC**	.50
672	Glen Perkins **RC**	.25
673	Michael Rogers **RC**	.25
674	Kevin Melillo **RC**	.25
675	Erik Cordier **RC**	.50
676	Landon Powell **RC**	.25
677	Justin Verlander **RC**	1.00
678	Eric Nielsen **RC**	.25
679	Alexander Smit **RC**	.25
680	Ryan Garko **RC**	.50
681	Bobby Livingston **RC**	.25
682	Jeff Niemann **RC**	.50
683	Wladimir Balentien **RC**	.50
684	Chip Cannon **RC**	.50
685	Yorman Bazardo **RC**	.50
686	Michael Bourn	.10
687	Andy LaRoche **RC**	2.00
688	Felix Hernandez, Justin Leone	.50
689	Ryan Howard, Cole Hamels	.75
690	Matt Cain, Merkin Valdez	.25
691	Andy Marte, Jeff Francoeur	.10
692	Chad Billingsley, Joel Guzman	.10
693	Jerry Hairston Jr., Scott Hairston	.10
694	Miguel Tejada, Lance Berkman	.25
695	Kenny Rogers	.10
696	Ivan Rodriguez	.25
697	Darin Erstad	.10
698	Bret Boone	.10
699	Eric Chavez	.10
700	Derek Jeter	1.00
701	Vernon Wells	.10
702	Ichiro Suzuki	.75
703	Torii Hunter	.10
704	Greg Maddux	.50
705	Mike Matheny	.10
706	Todd Helton	.25
707	Luis Castillo	.10
708	Scott Rolen	.40
709	Cesar Izturis	.10
710	Jim Edmonds	.25
711	Andruw Jones	.25
712	Steve Finley	.10
713	Johan Santana	.40
714	Roger Clemens	1.00
715	Vladimir Guerrero	.40
716	Barry Bonds	1.50
717	Bobby Crosby	.10
718	Jason Bay	.10
719	Albert Pujols	1.00
720	Mark Loretta	.10
721	Edgar Renteria	.10
722	Scott Rolen	.40
723	J.D. Drew	.10
724	Jim Edmonds	.25
725	Johnny Estrada	.10
726	Jason Schmidt	.10
727	Chris Carpenter	.10
728	Eric Gagne	.10
729	Jason Bay	.10
730	Bobby Cox	.10
731	Game 1	.50
732	Game 2	.50
733	Game 3	.50
734	Game 4	.50

Black

1st Edition:	20-50X
Production 54 Sets	

Gold

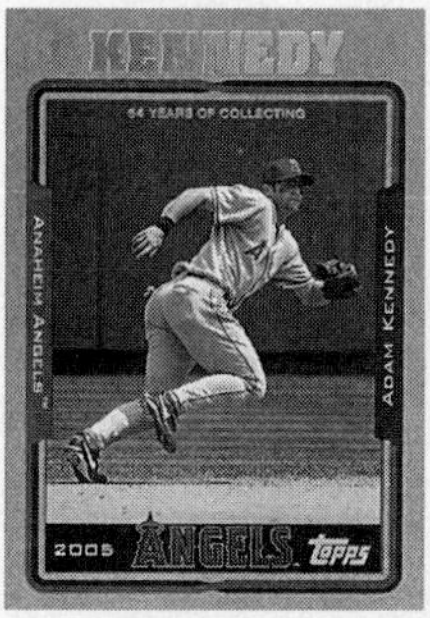

Stars:	5-10X
Production 2,005 Sets	

1st Edition

	NM/M
Stars:	3-5X
HTA Exclusive	
1st Edition Pack (10):	4.00
1st Edition Box (20):	65.00

All-Stars

		NM/M
Complete Set (15):		20.00
Common Player:		
Inserted 1:9		
TAS1	Todd Helton	.75
TAS2	Albert Pujols	3.00
TAS3	Vladimir Guerrero	1.00
TAS4	Ichiro Suzuki	2.00
TAS5	Randy Johnson	1.00
TAS6	Manny Ramirez	1.00
TAS7	Sammy Sosa	2.00
TAS8	Alfonso Soriano	1.00
TAS9	Jim Thome	1.00
TAS10	Barry Bonds	3.00
TAS11	Roger Clemens	3.00
TAS12	Mike Piazza	1.50
TAS13	Derek Jeter	3.00
TAS14	Alex Rodriguez	2.50
TAS15	Carlos Beltran	1.00

All-Star Stitches Relics

		NM/M
Common Player:		5.00
Inserted 1:96		
BA	Bobby Abreu	8.00
MA	Moises Alou	10.00
RB	Ronnie Belliard	5.00
CB	Carlos Beltran	10.00
LB	Lance Berkman	10.00
HB	Hank Blalock	10.00
MC	Miguel Cabrera	10.00
CC	Carl Crawford	5.00
JE	Johnny Estrada	8.00
EG	Eric Gagne	10.00
JG	Jason Giambi	10.00
TG	Tom Glavine	10.00
FG	Flash Gordon	5.00
VG	Vladimir Guerrero	10.00
KH	Ken Harvey	5.00
TH	Todd Helton	10.00
JK	Jeff Kent	8.00
DK	Danny Kolb	8.00
BL	Barry Larkin	10.00
MLA	Matt Lawton	5.00
TL	Ted Lilly	8.00
EL	Esteban Loaiza	5.00
PL	Paul LoDuca	5.00
MLO	Mark Loretta	8.00
ML	Mike Lowell	8.00
VM	Victor Martinez	10.00
MM	Mark Mulder	10.00
JN	Joe Nathan	8.00
DO	David Ortiz	20.00
CP	Carl Pavano	10.00
MP	Mike Piazza	12.00
AP	Albert Pujols	25.00
MR	Manny Ramirez	10.00
ER	Edgar Renteria	8.00
MRI	Mariano Rivera	10.00
FR	Francisco Rodriguez	10.00
IR	Ivan Rodriguez	10.00
SR	Scott Rolen	12.00
CS	C.C. Sabathia	8.00
BS	Ben Sheets	10.00
GS	Gary Sheffield	10.00
AS	Alfonso Soriano	10.00
SS	Sammy Sosa	15.00
MT	Miguel Tejada	10.00
JT	Jim Thome	12.00
JW	Jack Wilson	10.00
MY	Michael Young	15.00
CZ	Carlos Zambrano	10.00

All-Star Patches

No Pricing
Production 25 Sets

Autographs

		NM/M
Common Autograph:		
CB	Carlos Beltran	30.00
MC	Miguel Cabrera	40.00
JC	Jose Capellan	10.00
EC	Eric Chavez	20.00
DD	David DeJesus	10.00
ZG	Zack Greinke	10.00
CK	Casey Kotchman	10.00
JMA	John Maine	25.00
DM	Dallas McPherson	10.00
ARI	Alexis Rios	15.00
AR	Alex Rodriguez	200.00
CT	Chad Tracy	10.00
VW	Vernon Wells	20.00
DW	David Wright	75.00
Series 2		
JB	Jason Bay	25.00
CB	Carlos Beltran	30.00
MB	Milton Bradley	25.00
BB	Billy Butler	25.00
MC	Matt Campbell	10.00
EC	Eric Chavez	20.00
ECO	Erik Cordier	10.00
CC	Carl Crawford	15.00
EG	Eric Gagne	20.00
FH	Felix Hernandez	30.00
SK	Scott Kazmir	25.00
ML	Mark Loretta	15.00
GP	Glen Perkins	15.00
LP	Landon Powell	15.00
AR2	Alex Rodriguez/50	250.00
IR	Ivan Rodriguez	40.00
MR	Michael Rogers	10.00
JS	Johan Santana	40.00
TS	Terrmel Sledge	10.00
CW	Craig Wilson	10.00

Barry Bonds Home Run Highlights

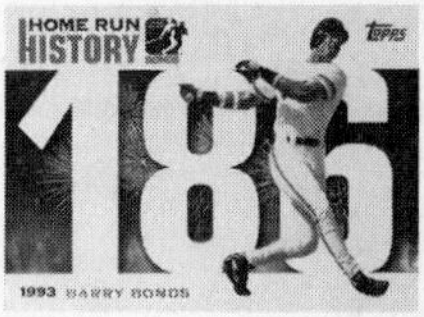

		NM/M
Complete Set (330):		
Common Bonds:		1.50
Inserted 1:4		
BB1-BB330	Barry Bonds	1.50

Bonds MVP

		NM/M
Production 25-500		
BBI2	Barry Bonds/50	40.00
BBI3	Barry Bonds/100	30.00
BBI4	Barry Bonds/200	25.00
BBI5	Barry Bonds/300	20.00
BBI6	Barry Bonds/400	15.00
BBI7	Barry Bonds/500	15.00

Bonds MVP Autographs

No Pricing

Bonds MVP Relics

		NM/M
Production 25-500		
BBR3	Barry Bonds/100	50.00
BBR4	Barry Bonds/200	40.00
BBR5	Barry Bonds/300	40.00
BBR6	Barry Bonds/400	25.00
BBR7	Barry Bonds/500	25.00

Celebrity Threads Relics

		NM/M
Common Player:		8.00
Inserted 1:562		
CC	Cesar Cedeno	8.00
CF	Cecil Fielder	15.00
RF	Rollie Fingers	12.00
GG	Rich "Goose" Gossage	10.00
HR	Harold Reynolds	8.00
MS	Mike Scott	8.00
OS	Ozzie Smith	25.00
DW	Dave Winfield	15.00

Dem Bums

		NM/M
Complete Set (13):		40.00
Common Player:		4.00
Inserted 1:12		
WA	Walter Alston	4.00
BB	Bob Borkowski	4.00
RC	Roy Campanella	6.00
RCR	Roger Craig	4.00
CF	Carl Furillo	4.00
JG	Jim Gilliam	4.00
DH	Don Hoak	4.00
JH	Jim Hughes	4.00
RM	Russ Meyer	4.00
JR	Jackie Robinson	8.00
ER	Ed Roebuck	4.00
GS	George Shuba	4.00
KS	Karl Spooner	4.00

Dem Bums Autographs

		NM/M
Common Autograph:		30.00
CE	Carl Erskine	30.00
CL	Clem Labine	50.00
JP	Johnny Podres	30.00
DS	Duke Snider	50.00
DZ	Don Zimmer	50.00

Dem Bums Cuts

No Pricing
Production One Set

Derby Digs Relics

		NM/M
Common Player:		15.00
Production 100 Sets		
LB	Lance Berkman	15.00
HB	Hank Blalock	20.00
DO	David Ortiz	35.00
SS	Sammy Sosa	40.00
MT	Miguel Tejada	15.00
JT	Jim Thome	25.00

Factory Set Team Bonus

	NM/M
Complete Cubs Set (5):	15.00
Complete Yankees Set (5):	15.00
Complete Red Sox Set (5):	15.00
Complete Giants Set (5):	15.00
Complete Nationals Set (5):	15.00
Complete Tigers Set (5):	15.00
Issued in team themed factory sets.	

Factory Set Draft Picks Bonus

		NM/M
Complete Set (5):		50.00
One set per factory set.		
1	Beau Jones	4.00
2	Cliff Pennington	4.00
3	Chris Volstad	4.00
4	Ricky Romero	4.00
5	Jay Bruce	50.00

Factory Set First Year Draft Bonus

		NM/M
Complete Set (10):		50.00
One set per Green Factory Set		
1	Nick Webber	3.00
2	Aaron Thompson	4.00
3	Matt Garza	8.00
4	Tyler Greene	4.00
5	Ryan Braun	10.00
6	C.J. Henry	4.00
7	Ryan Zimmerman	15.00
8	John Mayberry Jr.	4.00
9	Cesar Carrillo	3.00
10	Mark McCormick	3.00

Factory Set First Year Player Bonus

		NM/M
Complete Set (5):		15.00
Issued in red factory sets		
1	Bill McCarthy	4.00
2	John Hudgins	4.00
3	Kyle Nichols	4.00

4	Thomas Pauly	4.00
5	Philip Humber	4.00

Grudge Match

		NM/M
Complete Set (10):		
Common Duo:		1.00
Inserted 1:24		
GM1	Jorge Posada, Pedro J. Martinez	2.00
GM2	Mike Piazza, Roger Clemens	3.00
GM3	Mariano Rivera, Luis Gonzalez	1.00
GM4	Carlos Zambrano, Jim Edmonds	1.00
GM5	Aaron Boone, Tim Wakefield	1.00
GM6	Manny Ramirez, Roger Clemens	3.00
GM7	Michael Tucker, Eric Gagne	1.00
GM8	Ivan Rodriguez, J.T. Snow	1.00
GM9	Alex Rodriguez, Bronson Arroyo	3.00
GM10	Corky Miller, Sammy Sosa	2.50

Hit Parade

		NM/M
Complete Set (30):		25.00
Common Player:		.50
Inserted 1:12		
HR1	Barry Bonds	4.00
HR2	Sammy Sosa	2.50
HR3	Rafael Palmeiro	1.00
HR4	Ken Griffey Jr.	2.00
HR5	Jeff Bagwell	1.00
HR6	Frank Thomas	1.00
HR7	Juan Gonzalez	.75
HR8	Jim Thome	1.00
HR9	Gary Sheffield	1.00
HR10	Manny Ramirez	1.50
RBI1	Barry Bonds	4.00
RBI2	Rafael Palmeiro	1.00
RBI3	Sammy Sosa	2.50
RBI4	Jeff Bagwell	1.00
RBI5	Ken Griffey Jr.	2.00
RBI6	Frank Thomas	1.00
RBI7	Juan Gonzalez	.75
RBI8	Gary Sheffield	1.00
RBI9	Ruben Sierra	.50
RBI10	Manny Ramirez	1.50
HIT1	Rafael Palmeiro	1.00
HIT2	Barry Bonds	4.00
HIT3	Roberto Alomar	.75
HIT4	Craig Biggio	.50
HIT5	Julio Franco	.50
HIT6	Steve Finley	.50
HIT7	Jeff Bagwell	1.00
HIT8	B.J. Surhoff	.50
HIT9	Marquis Grissom	.50
HIT10	Sammy Sosa	2.50

Hobby Masters

	NM/M
Complete Set (20):	25.00
Common Player:	.75
Inserted 1:18	

HM1	Alex Rodriguez	4.00
HM2	Sammy Sosa	2.50
HM3	Ichiro Suzuki	3.00
HM4	Albert Pujols	4.00
HM5	Derek Jeter	4.00
HM6	Jim Thome	1.50
HM7	Vladimir Guerrero	1.50
HM8	Nomar Garciaparra	2.00
HM9	Mike Piazza	2.00
HM10	Jason Giambi	.75
HM11	Ivan Rodriguez	1.00
HM12	Alfonso Soriano	1.50
HM13	Dontrelle Willis	.75
HM14	Chipper Jones	1.50
HM15	Mark Prior	1.50
HM16	Todd Helton	1.00
HM17	Randy Johnson	1.50
HM18	Hank Blalock	1.00
HM19	Ken Griffey Jr.	2.00
HM20	Roger Clemens	3.00

Midsummer Covers Relics

No Pricing

On-Deck Relics

		NM/M
Inserted 1:1,493		
CB	Carlos Beltran	15.00
HB	Hank Blalock	12.00
TH	Todd Helton	12.00
AP	Albert Pujols	30.00
AR	Alex Rodriguez	25.00
IR	Ivan Rodriguez	15.00
SR	Scott Rolen	15.00
AS	Alfonso Soriano	15.00
SS	Sammy Sosa	25.00
JT	Jim Thome	15.00

Own The Game

		NM/M
Complete Set (30):		15.00
Common Player:		.50
Inserted 1:12		
OG1	Ichiro Suzuki	3.00
OG2	Todd Helton	1.00
OG3	Adrian Beltre	1.00
OG4	Albert Pujols	4.00
OG5	Adam Dunn	1.00
OG6	Jim Thome	1.50
OG7	Miguel Tejada	.75
OG8	David Ortiz	1.50
OG9	Manny Ramirez	1.50
OG10	Scott Rolen	1.50
OG11	Gary Sheffield	.75
OG12	Vladimir Guerrero	1.50
OG13	Jim Edmonds	.50
OG14	Ivan Rodriguez	1.00
OG15	Lance Berkman	.50
OG16	Michael Young	.50
OG17	Juan Pierre	.50
OG18	Craig Biggio	.50
OG19	Johnny Damon	.75
OG20	Jimmy Rollins	.50
OG21	Scott Podsednik	.50
OG22	Bobby Abreu	.50
OG23	Lyle Overbay	.50
OG24	Carl Crawford	.50
OG25	Mark Loretta	.50
OG26	Vinny Castilla	.50
OG27	Curt Schilling	1.00
OG28	Johan Santana	.75
OG29	Randy Johnson	1.50
OG30	Pedro J. Martinez	1.50

Power Brokers Cut Signatures

No Pricing

Spokesman

	NM/M
Complete Set (4):	10.00

Draft Pick

		NM/M
Common Player:		3.00
Inserted 1:24		
ARI1-ARI4	Alex Rodriguez	3.00

Spokesman Autographs

		NM/M
Production 1-200		
ARA3	Alex Rodriguez/100	200.00
ARA4	Alex Rodriguez/200	180.00

Spokesman Relics

		NM/M
Production 1-800		
ARR2	Alex Rodriguez/50	30.00
ARR3	Alex Rodriguez/300	20.00
ARR4	Alex Rodriguez/800	20.00

Spokesman Relic

		NM/M
Inserted 1:5,627		
AR	Alex Rodriguez	50.00

Spokesman Relic Autographs

13 Sets
No Pricing

Touch'em All Relics

No Pricing

World Treasures

No Pricing

World Treasures - Dual

No Pricing
Production One Set

World Champion Red Sox Relics

		NM/M
Common Player:		
OC	Orlando Cabrera	20.00
OC2	Orlando Cabrera	20.00
JD	Johnny Damon	25.00
JD2	Johnny Damon	25.00
DL	Derek Lowe	20.00
PM	Pedro Martinez	20.00
DMI	Doug Mientkiewicz	15.00
KM	Kevin Millar	20.00
BM	Bill Mueller	15.00
BM2	Bill Mueller	15.00
TN	Trot Nixon	20.00
DO	David Ortiz	20.00
DO2	David Ortiz	20.00
MR	Manny Ramirez	25.00
MR2	Manny Ramirez	25.00
MR3	Manny Ramirez	25.00
PR	Pokey Reese	15.00
DR	Dave Roberts	15.00
CS	Curt Schilling	25.00
KY	Kevin Youkilis	15.00

1955 World Series Cut Sigs.

No Pricing

1955 World Series Dual Cut Signatures

No Pricing
Production One Set

2005 Topps Update

		NM/M
Complete Set (330):		35.00
Complete Factory Set (330):		40.00
Common Player:		.10
Pack (10):		2.00
Box (36):		60.00
1	Sammy Sosa	1.00
2	Jeff Francoeur	.25
3	Tony Clark	.10
4	Michael Tucker	.10
5	Mike Matheny	.10
6	Eric Young	.10
7	Jose Valentin	.10
8	Matt Lawton	.10
9	Juan Rivera	.10
10	Shawn Green	.25
11	Aaron Boone	.10
12	Woody Williams	.10
13	Brad Wilkerson	.10
14	Anthony Reyes RC	1.50
15	Russ Adams	.10

16 Gustavo Chacin .10
17 Mike Restovich .10
18 Humberto Quintero .10
19 Matt Ginter .10
20 Scott Podsednik .25
21 Byung-Hyun Kim .10
22 Orlando Hernandez .10
23 Mark Grudzielanek .10
24 Jody Gerut .10
25 Adrian Beltre .25
26 Scott Schoeneweis .10
27 Marlon Anderson .10
28 Jason Vargas .10
29 Claudio Vargas .10
30 Jason Kendall .10
31 Aaron Small .10
32 Juan Cruz .10
33 Placido Polanco .10
34 Jorge Sosa .10
35 John Olerud .10
36 Ryan Langerhans .10
37 Randy Winn .10
38 Zachary Duke .25
39 Garrett Atkins .10
40 Al Leiter .10
41 Shawn Chacon .10
42 Mark DeRosa .10
43 Miguel Ojeda .10
44 A.J. Pierzynski .10
45 Carlos Lee .10
46 LaTroy Hawkins .10
47 Nick Green .10
48 Shawn Estes .10
49 Eli Marrero .10
50 Jeff Kent .10
51 Joe Randa .10
52 Jose Hernandez .10
53 Joe Blanton .10
54 Huston Street .10
55 Marlon Byrd .10
56 Alex Sanchez .10
57 Livan Hernandez .10
58 Chris Young .10
59 Brad Eldred .10
60 Terrence Long .10
61 Phil Nevin .10
62 Kyle Farnsworth .10
63 Jon Lieber .10
64 Antonio Alfonseca .10
65 Tony Graffanino .10
66 Tadahito Iguchi **RC** 1.00
67 Brad Thompson .10
68 Jose Vidro .10
69 Jason Phillips .10
70 Carl Pavano .10
71 Pokey Reese .10
72 Jerome Williams .10
73 Kazuhisa Ishii .10
74 Zach Day .10
75 Edgar Renteria .25
76 Mike Myers .10
77 Jeff Cirillo .10
78 Endy Chavez .10
79 Jose Guillen .10
80 Ugueth Urbina .10
81 Vinny Castilla .10
82 Javier Vazquez .10
83 Willy Taveras .10
84 Mark Mulder .25
85 Mike Hargrove .10
86 Buddy Bell .10
87 Charlie Manuel .10
88 Willie Randolph .10
89 Bob Melvin .10
90 Chris Lambert .10
91 Homer Bailey .20
92 Ervin Santana .10
93 Bill Bray .10
94 Thomas Diamond .10
95 Trevor Plouffe .10
96 James Houser .10
97 Jake Stevens .10
98 Anthony Whittington .10
99 Phillip Hughes .10
100 Greg Golson .10
101 Paul Maholm .10
102 Carlos Quentin .10
103 Dan Johnson .10
104 Mark Rogers .10
105 Neil Walker .10
106 Omar Quintanilla .10
107 Blake DeWitt .10
108 Taylor Tankersley .10
109 David Murphy .10
110 Felix Hernandez .50
111 Craig Biggio .10
112 Greg Maddux .50
113 Bobby Abreu .10
114 Alex Rodriguez .75
115 Trevor Hoffman .10
116 A.J. Pierzynski, Tadahito Iguchi .25
117 Reggie Sanders .10
118 Bengie Molina, Ervin Santana .10
119 Chris Burke, Lance Berkman, Adam LaRoche .10
120 Garret Anderson .25
121 A.J. Pierzynski .10
122 Paul Konerko .25
123 Joe Crede .10
124 Mark Buehrle, Jon Garland .10
125 Freddy Garcia, Jose Contreras .10
126 Reggie Sanders .10
127 Roy Oswalt .10
128 Roger Clemens .75
129 Albert Pujols .75
130 Roy Oswalt .25
131 Joe Crede, Bobby Jenks .10
132 Paul Konerko, Scott Podsednik .25
133 Geoff Blum .10
134 White Sox Sweep .10
135 Alex Rodriguez, David Ortiz, Manny Ramirez .50
136 Michael Young, Alex Rodriguez, Vladimir Guerrero .50
137 David Ortiz, Mark Teixeira, Manny Ramirez .25
138 Bartolo Colon, Jon Garland, Cliff Lee .10
139 Kevin Millwood, Johan Santana, Mark Buehrle .10
140 Johan Santana, Randy Johnson, John Lackey .25
141 Andruw Jones, Derrek Lee, Albert Pujols .50
142 Derek Lee, Albert Pujols, Miguel Cabrera .50
143 Andruw Jones, Albert Pujols, Pat Burrell .50
144 Dontrelle Willis, Chris Carpenter, Roy Oswalt .25
145 Roger Clemens, Andy Pettitte, Dontrelle Willis .50
146 Jake Peavy, Chris Carpenter, Pedro Martinez .25
147 Mark Teixeira .25
148 Brian Roberts .10
149 Michael Young .10
150 Alex Rodriguez 1.00
151 Johnny Damon .25
152 Vladimir Guerrero .25
153 Manny Ramirez .25
154 David Ortiz .25
155 Mariano Rivera .25
156 Joe Nathan .10
157 Albert Pujols 1.00
158 Jeff Kent .10
159 Felipe Lopez .10
160 Morgan Ensberg .10
161 Miguel Cabrera .25
162 Ken Griffey Jr. .50
163 Andruw Jones .25
164 Paul LoDuca .10
165 Chad Cordero .10
166 Ken Griffey Jr. .50
167 Jason Giambi .10
168 Willy Taveras .10
169 Huston Street .10
170 Chris Carpenter .10
171 Bartolo Colon .10
172 Bobby Cox .10
173 Ozzie Guillen .10
174 Andruw Jones .25
175 Johnny Damon .25
176 Alex Rodriguez 1.00
177 David Ortiz .25
178 Manny Ramirez .25
179 Miguel Tejada .25
180 Vladimir Guerrero .25
181 Mark Teixeira .25
182 Ivan Rodriguez .25
183 Brian Roberts .10
184 Mark Buehrle .10
185 Bobby Abreu .25
186 Carlos Beltran .25
187 Albert Pujols 1.00
188 Derrek Lee .25
189 Jim Edmonds .25
190 Aramis Ramirez .10
191 Mike Piazza .50
192 Jeff Kent .10
193 David Eckstein .10
194 Chris Carpenter .10
195 Bobby Abreu .25
196 Ivan Rodriguez .25
197 Carlos Lee .10
198 David Ortiz .25
199 Hee Seop Choi .10
200 Andruw Jones .25
201 Mark Teixeira .25
202 Jason Bay .10
203 Hanley Ramirez .25
204 Shin-Soo Choo .10
205 Justin Huber .10
206 Nelson Cruz **RC** .50
207 Edwin Encarnacion .10
208 Miguel Montero **RC** .50
209 William Bergolla .10
210 Luis Montanez .10
211 Francisco Liriano .50
212 Kevin Thompson .10
213 B.J. Upton .10
214 Conor Jackson .10
215 Delmon Young .25
216 Andy LaRoche .50
217 Ryan Garko .10
218 Josh Barfield .10
219 Chris Young .10
220 Justin Verlander .25
221 Drew Anderson **RC** .25
222 Luis Hernandez **RC** .25
223 Jim Burt **RC** .25
224 Mike Morse **RC** .25
225 Elliot Johnson **RC** .50
226 C.J. Smith **RC** .25
227 Casey McGehee **RC** .25
228 Brian Miller **RC** .15
229 Chris Vines **RC** .40
230 D.J. Houlton **RC** .25
231 Chuck Tiffany **RC** .40
232 Humberto Sanchez **RC** .75
233 Baltazar Lopez **RC** .25
234 Russell Martin **RC** 1.00
235 Dana Eveland **RC** .25
236 Johan Silva **RC** .25
237 Adam Harben **RC** 1.00
238 Brian Bannister **RC** .25
239 Adam Boeve **RC** .25
240 Tom Oldham **RC** .25
241 Cody Haerther **RC** .25
242 Dan Santin **RC** .25
243 Daniel Haigwood **RC** .25
244 Craig Tatum **RC** .25
245 Martin Prado **RC** .40
246 Errol Simonitsch **RC** .40
247 Lorenzo Scott **RC** .25
248 Hayden Penn **RC** .40
249 Heath Totten **RC** .25
250 Nick Masset **RC** .25
251 Pedro Lopez **RC** .25
252 Benjamin Harrison .15
253 Michael Spidale **RC** .25
254 Jeremy Harts **RC** .25
255 Danny Zell **RC** .40
256 Kevin Collins **RC** .15
257 Tony Arnerich **RC** .15
258 Matt Albers **RC** .50
259 Ricky Barrett **RC** .25
260 Hernan Iribarren **RC** .40
261 Sean Tracey **RC** .25
262 Jerry Owens **RC** .40
263 Steve Nelson **RC** .25
264 Brandon McCarthy **RC** 1.00
265 David Shepard **RC** .25
266 Steve Bondurant **RC** .25
267 Billy Sadler .15
268 Ryan Feierabend **RC** .25
269 Stuart Pomeranz **RC** .40
270 Shaun Marcum .25
271 Erik Schindewolf **RC** .25
272 Stefan Bailie **RC** .15
273 Mike Esposito **RC** .25
274 Buck Coats **RC** .40
275 Andy Sides **RC** .25
276 Micah Schnurstein **RC** .40
277 Jesse Gutierrez **RC** .25
278 Jake Postlewait **RC** .25
279 Willy Mota **RC** .50
280 Ryan Speier **RC** .25
281 Frank Mata **RC** .25
282 Jair Jurrjens **RC** 1.50
283 Nick Touchstone **RC** .25
284 Matthew Kemp **RC** 1.50
285 Vinny Rottino **RC** .40
286 J.B. Thurmond **RC** .40
287 Kelvin Pichardo **RC** .25
288 Scott Mitchinson **RC** .25
289 Darwinson Salazar **RC** .25
290 George Kottaras **RC** .50
291 Ken Durost **RC** .40
292 Jonathan Sanchez **RC** 1.00
293 Brandon Moorhead **RC** .25
294 Kennard Bibbs **RC** .25
295 David Gassner **RC** .40
296 Micah Furtado **RC** .25
297 Ismael Ramirez **RC** .25
298 Carlos Gonzalez **RC** 1.50
299 Brandon Sing **RC** .50
300 Jason Motte **RC** .25
301 Chuck James **RC** 1.00
302 Andy Santana **RC** .25
303 Manny Parra **RC** .75
304 Chris Young **RC** 1.00
305 Juan Senreiso **RC** .25
306 Franklin Morales **RC** 1.00
307 Jared Gothreaux **RC** .15
308 Jayce Tingler **RC** .25
309 Matt Brown **RC** .25
310 Frank Diaz **RC** .40
311 Stephen Drew **RC** 2.00
312 Jered Weaver **RC** 4.00
313 Ryan Braun **RC** 4.00
314 John Mayberry Jr. **RC** .75
315 Aaron Thompson **RC** 1.00
316 Cesar Carrillo **RC** .50
317 Jacoby Ellsbury **RC** 6.00
318 Matt Garza **RC** 5.00
319 Cliff Pennington **RC** .75
320 Colby Rasmus **RC** 2.00
321 Chris Volstad **RC** 1.00
322 Ricky Romero **RC** .50
323 Ryan Zimmerman **RC** 2.00
324 C.J. Henry **RC** .75
325 Jay Bruce **RC** 6.00
326 Beau Jones **RC** .50
327 Mark McCormick **RC** .50
328 Eli Iorg **RC** .50
329 Andrew McCutchen **RC** 1.50
330 Mike Costanzo **RC** .50

Blue

No Pricing
Production One Set

Gold

Gold Rookies: 2-4X
Gold Stars: 4-8X
Production 2,005 Sets

Printing Plates

No Pricing
Production one set per color.

All-Star Patches

		NM/M
Common Player:		15.00
BA	Bobby Abreu/65	15.00
MA	Moises Alou/65	20.00
JB	Jason Bay/50	20.00
CB	Carlos Beltran/60	25.00
MB	Mark Buehrle/60	20.00
MC	Miguel Cabrera/70	30.00
CC	Chris Carpenter/70	20.00
MCL	Matt Clement/70	15.00
BC	Bartolo Colon/60	15.00
CCO	Chad Cordero/65	15.00
JD	Johnny Damon/60	25.00
DE	David Eckstein/65	20.00
JE	Jim Edmonds/50	20.00
ME	Morgan Ensberg/60	15.00
JG	Jon Garland/70	20.00
LG	Luis Gonzalez/70	15.00
LH	Livan Hernandez/50	15.00
JI	Jason Isringhausen/65	15.00
AJ	Andruw Jones/70	25.00
JK	Jeff Kent/65	20.00
PK	Paul Konerko/70	20.00
CL	Carlos Lee/65	20.00
DL	Derrek Lee/65	20.00
BL	Brad Lidge/65	15.00
FL	Felipe Lopez/35	20.00
MM	Melvin Mora/30	20.00
JN	Joe Nathan/65	15.00
DO	David Ortiz/70	25.00
RO	Roy Oswalt/60	20.00
JP	Jake Peavy/60	20.00
MP	Mike Piazza/50	30.00
SP	Scott Podsednik/65	20.00
AP	Albert Pujols/35	50.00
ARA	Aramis Ramirez/60	20.00
MR	Manny Ramirez/65	25.00
MRI	Mariano Rivera/65	30.00
AR	Alex Rodriguez/50	30.00
KR	Kenny Rogers/50	15.00
JS	Johan Santana/60	30.00
GS	Gary Sheffield/50	20.00
JSM	John Smoltz/65	30.00
IS	Ichiro Suzuki/50	40.00
MTE	Mark Teixeira/60	20.00
MT	Miguel Tejada/60	20.00
BW	Billy Wagner/50	15.00
DW	Dontrelle Willis/60	20.00
MY	Michael Young/50	20.00

All-Star Stitches

		NM/M
Common Player:		4.00
BA	Bobby Abreu/B	4.00
MA	Moises Alou/C	6.00
JB	Jason Bay/C	4.00
CB	Carlos Beltran/D	6.00
MB	Mark Buehrle/B	4.00
MC	Miguel Cabrera/E	8.00
CC	Chris Carpenter/E	4.00
LC	Luis Castillo/B	4.00
MCL	Matt Clement/B	4.00
BC	Bartolo Colon/D	4.00
CCO	Chad Cordero/D	4.00
JD	Johnny Damon/B	8.00
DE	David Eckstein/B	4.00
JE	Jim Edmonds/A	6.00
ME	Morgan Ensberg/B	4.00
JG	Jon Garland/E	4.00
LG	Luis Gonzalez/C	4.00
LH	Livan Hernandez	4.00
JI	Jason Isringhausen/E	4.00
AJ	Andruw Jones/C	6.00
JK	Jeff Kent/C	4.00
PK	Paul Konerko/A	4.00
CL	Carlos Lee/E	4.00
DL	Derrek Lee/F	6.00
BL	Brad Lidge/D	4.00
FL	Felipe Lopez/B	4.00
MM	Melvin Mora/B	4.00
JN	Joe Nathan/D	4.00
DO	David Ortiz/E	8.00
RO	Roy Oswalt/A	4.00
JP	Jake Peavy/D	4.00
MP	Mike Piazza/E	8.00
SP	Scott Podsednik/A	4.00
AP	Albert Pujols/E	20.00
ARA	Aramis Ramirez/E	4.00
MR	Manny Ramirez/E	8.00
MRI	Mariano Rivera	6.00
BR	Brian Roberts/C	4.00
AR	Alex Rodriguez/D	15.00
IR	Ivan Rodriguez/A	6.00
KR	Kenny Rogers/A	4.00
JS	Johan Santana/C	6.00
GS	Gary Sheffield/D	6.00
JSM	John Smoltz/D	6.00
IS	Ichiro Suzuki/A	20.00
MTE	Mark Teixeira/C	6.00
MT	Miguel Tejada/B	6.00
BW	Billy Wagner/C	4.00
DW	Dontrelle Willis/F	6.00
MY	Michael Young/A	4.00

Derby Digs Jersey

		NM/M
Production 100 Sets		
BA	Bobby Abreu	25.00
JB	Jason Bay	15.00

AJ Andruw Jones 25.00
CL Carlos Lee 10.00
DO David Ortiz 25.00
IR Ivan Rodriguez 25.00
MT Mark Teixeira 25.00

Hall of Fame Bat

NM/M

Complete Set (2):
WB Wade Boggs/A 10.00
RS Ryne Sandberg/B 15.00

Hall of Fame Dual Bat

NM/M

Production 200 Sets
BS Wade Boggs, Ryne Sandberg 25.00

Legendary Sacks

NM/M

Production 300 Sets
JA Jim Abbott 6.00
AD Andre Dawson 6.00
MF Mark Fidrych 4.00
RF Rollie Fingers 4.00
BJ Bo Jackson 8.00
HR Harold Reynolds 4.00
OS Ozzie Smith 8.00
LW Lou Whitaker 4.00
DW Dave Winfield 8.00

Midsummer Covers

NM/M

Production 150 Sets
CB Carlos Beltran 15.00
RC Roger Clemens 25.00
VG Vladimir Guerrero 25.00
DL Derrek Lee 15.00
AP Albert Pujols 40.00
BR Brian Roberts 10.00
AR Alex Rodriguez 30.00
IS Ichiro Suzuki 50.00
MT Miguel Tejada 15.00
DW Dontrelle Willis 10.00

Signature Moves

NM/M

Production 15-475 Sets
Red Foil: No Pricing
Production 25 Sets
MA Matt Albers/475 15.00
TC Travis Chick/475 8.00
TG Troy Glaus/275 20.00
TH Tim Hudson/275 25.00
KI Kazuhisa Ishii/275 15.00
GK George Kottaras/475 15.00
BL Bobby Livingston/475 10.00
MM Mark Mulder/275 25.00
GP Glen Perkins/275 15.00
JP Jake Postlewait/275 10.00
HS Humberto Sanchez 30.00
BS Benito Santiago 20.00
RS Richie Sexson/275 25.00
CJS C.J. Smith/475 10.00
JV Justin Verlander/275 35.00
TW Tony Womack 15.00

Touch Em All Base

NM/M

Production 1,000 Sets
VG Vladimir Guerrero 10.00
DL Derrek Lee 8.00
DO David Ortiz 10.00
AP Albert Pujols 20.00
MR Manny Ramirez 10.00
AR Alex Rodriguez 15.00
IR Ivan Rodriguez 8.00
GS Gary Sheffield 6.00
IS Ichiro Suzuki 20.00
MT Miguel Tejada 10.00

Washington Nationals Inaugural Lineup

NM/M

Inserted 1:10
Ball Relics: No Pricing
Production Five Sets
VC Vinny Castilla .50
JG Jose Guillen 1.00
CG Cristian Guzman .50
LH Livan Hernandez .50
NJ Nick Johnson .50
BS Brian Schneider .50
TS Terrmel Sledge .50
JV Jose Vidro .50
BW Brad Wilkerson .50
TEAM Team Photo 1.00

2005 Topps All-Time Fan Favorites

NM/M

Complete Set (142): 40.00
Common Player: .25
Pack (6): 5.00
Box (24): 110.00
1 Andy Van Slyke .25
2 Bill Freehan .25
3 Bo Jackson .75
4 Mark Grace .50
5 Chuck Knoblauch .25
6 Candy Maldonado .25
7 David Cone .25
8 Don Mattingly 1.50

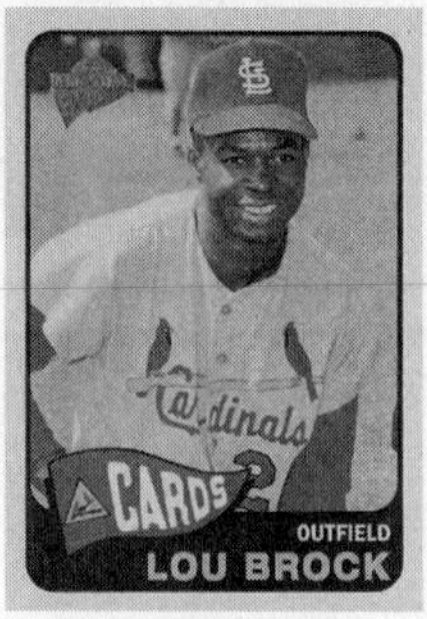

9 Darryl Strawberry .25
10 Dick Williams .25
11 Frank Robinson .75
12 Glenn Hubbard .25
13 Jim Abbott .25
14 Jeff Brantley .25
15 John Elway 2.00
16 Jim Leyland .25
17 Jesse Orosco .25
18 Joe Pepitone .25
19 J.R. Richard .25
20 Jerome Walton .25
21 Kevin Maas .25
22 Lou Brock .50
23 Lou Whitaker .25
24 Carl Erskine .25
25 John Candelaria .25
26 Mike Norris .25
27 Nolan Ryan 2.00
28 Pedro Guerrero .25
29 Roger Craig .25
30 Ron Gant .25
31 Sid Bream .25
32 Sid Fernandez .25
33 Tony LaRussa .25
34 Tom Seaver .75
35 Yogi Berra .75
36 Andre Dawson .25
37 Al Kaline .75
38 Brett Butler .25
39 Bob Gibson .75
40 Bill Mazeroski .25
41 Matty Alou .25
42 Chet Lemon .25
43 Cal Ripken Jr. 2.00
44 Dusty Baker .25
45 Dwight Gooden .25
46 Dave Winfield .50
47 Ernie Banks 1.00
48 Gary Carter .50
49 Howard Johnson .25
50 Mike Schmidt 1.50
51 Matt Williams .25
52 Ozzie Smith 1.00
53 Atlee Hammaker .25
54 Cleon Jones .25
55 Dave Johnson .25
56 Denny McLain .25
57 Don Zimmer .25
58 Gregg Jefferies .25
59 Jay Buhn er .25
60 Johnny Bench .75
61 George Brett 1.50
62 Dale Murphy .50
63 Bob Welch .25
64 Paul O'Neill .25
65 Mark Lemke .25
66 Kevin McReynolds .25
67 Jesus Alou .25
68 Joe Pignatano .25
69 Jim Lonborg .25
70 Jerry Grote .25
71 Joaquin Andujar .25
72 Gary Gaetti .25
73 Edgar Martinez .25
74 Ron Darling .25
75 Duke Snider .75
76 Dave Magadan .25
77 Doug Drabek .25
78 Carl Yastrzemski 1.00
79 Mitch Williams .25
80 Marvin Miller .25
81 Michael Kay .25
82 Lonnie Smith .25
83 John Wetteland .25
84 Johnny Podres .25
85 Joe Morgan .50
86 Juan Marichal .50
87 Jeffrey Leonard .25
88 Bob Feller .50
89 Brooks Robinson .75
90 Clem Labine .25
91 Barry Lyons .25
92 Harmon Killebrew .75
93 Jim Frey .25
94 John Kruk .25
95 Ed Kranepool .25
96 Jose Oquendo .25
97 Johnny Pesky .25
98 John Tudor .25
99 Keith Hernandez .25
100 Monte Irvin .50
101 Marty Barrett .25
102 Oscar Gamble .25
103 Hank Bauer .25
104 Ron Blomberg .25
105 Rod Carew .50
106 Rick Dempsey .25
107 Walt Jocketty .25
108 Tom Kelly .25
109 Steve Carlton .50
110 Rick Monday .25
111 Rob Dibble .25
112 Shawon Dunston .25
113 Tony Gwynn .75
114 Tom Niedenfuer .25
115 Bob Dernier .25
116 Anthony Young .25
117 Reggie Jackson .75
118 Steve Garvey .25
119 Tim Raines .25
120 Whitey Ford .75
121 Rafael Santana .25
122 Scott Brosius .25
123 Stan Musial 1.50
124 Ron Santo .50
125 Wade Boggs .75
126 Jose Canseco .50
127 Brady Anderson .25
128 Vida Blue .25
129 Charlie Hough .25
130 Jim Kaat .25
131 Zane Smith .25
132 Bob Boone .25
133 Travis Fryman .25
134 Harold Baines .25
135 Orlando Cepeda .25
136 Mike Cuellar .25
137 Tito Fuentes .25
138 Daryl Boston .25
139 Jim Leyritz .25
140 Bill "Moose" Skowron .25
141 Theo Epstein .25
142 Barry Bonds 3.00

Refractor

Stars (1-142): 3-5X
Production 299 Sets

Gold Refractor

No Pricing
Production 25 Sets

Printing Plates

No Pricing

Autographs

NM/M

Common Autograph: 15.00
Rainbow: No Pricing
Production 10 Sets
JA Jim Abbott 30.00
JAN Joaquin Andujar 20.00
DB Dusty Baker 25.00
MB Marty Barrett 15.00
JBE Dr. Jim Beckett/SP/90 100.00
JB Johnny Bench/SP/40 125.00
YB Yogi Berra/SP/90 125.00
RB Ron Blomberg 15.00
JBR Jeff Brantley 20.00
SB Sid Bream 20.00
GB George Brett/SP/40 250.00
SBR Scott Brosius/SP/90 85.00
JBU Jay Buhner 20.00
BB Brett Butler 20.00
SC Steve Carlton/SP/90 60.00
GC Gary Carter 25.00
DC David Cone 25.00
RD Rick Dempsey 15.00
DD Doug Drabek 20.00
SD Shawon Dunston 20.00
JE John Elway/SP/40 250.00
BFE Bob Feller 85.00
SF Sid Fernandez 15.00
WF Whitey Ford/SP/90 150.00
BF Bill Freehan 20.00
GG Gary Gaetti 15.00
OG Oscar Gamble 15.00
RG Ron Gant/SP/90 50.00
SG Steve Garvey 50.00
BG Bob Gibson/SP/90 100.00
DG Dwight Gooden 40.00
JG Jerry Grote 30.00
TG Tony Gwynn/SP/90 125.00
AH Atlee Hammaker 15.00
GH Glenn Hubbard 20.00
MI Monte Irvin 50.00
BJ Bo Jackson 70.00
RJ Reggie Jackson/SP/40 100.00
GJ Gregg Jefferies 40.00
WJ Walt Jocketty/SP/90 60.00
DJ Dave Johnson 20.00
HJ Howard Johnson 20.00
CJ Cleon Jones 35.00
AK Al Kaline 60.00
TK Tom Kelly 25.00
HK Harmon Killebrew 85.00
CK Chuck Knoblauch 25.00
JK John Kruk 30.00
CL Clem Labine 40.00
TL Tony LaRussa 30.00
MLE Mark Lemke 15.00
CLE Chet Lemon 15.00
JLE Jim Leyland 20.00
JLO Jim Lonborg 15.00
BL Barry Lyons 15.00
KM Kevin Maas 15.00
DMA Dave Magadan 20.00
CM Candy Maldonado 15.00
JMA Juan Marichal/SP/90 140.00
EM Edgar Martinez 30.00
DM Don Mattingly 140.00
BM Bill Mazeroski 75.00
DMC Denny McLain 30.00
KMC Kevin McReynolds 15.00
MM Marvin Miller/SP/90 80.00
RM Rick Monday 30.00
DMU Dale Murphy 30.00
SM Stan Musial/SP/40 150.00
TN Tom Niedenfuer 15.00
MNO Mike Norris 15.00
PO Paul O'Neill 60.00
JO Jesse Orosco 25.00
JOQ Jose Oquendo 15.00
JPE Joe Pepitone 25.00
JPY Johnny Pesky 65.00
JP Joe Pignatano 30.00
TR Tim Raines 25.00
JR J.R. Richard 15.00
CR Cal Ripken Jr./SP/90 200.00
BR Brooks Robinson/SP/90 125.00
FR Frank Robinson 100.00
NR Nolan Ryan/SP/40 200.00
RS Rafael Santana 20.00
RSA Ron Santo/SP/90 75.00
MS Mike Schmidt/SP/40 160.00
LS Lonnie Smith 15.00
DSN Duke Snider/SP/40 60.00
DS Darryl Strawberry 25.00
JT John Tudor 35.00
AV Andy Van Slyke 25.00
JW Jerome Walton 15.00
BW Bob Welch 30.00
JWE John Wetteland 20.00
LW Lou Whitaker/SP/90 60.00
DWI Dick Williams/SP/90 75.00
MW Matt Williams 25.00
MWI Mitch Williams 25.00
DW Dave Winfield/SP/90 125.00
CY Carl Yastrzemski/SP/90 125.00
AY Anthony Young 15.00
DZ Don Zimmer/SP/40 50.00

Best Seat in House

NM/M

Production 125 unless noted.
Rainbow: No Pricing
Production 25 Sets
MFBJ Don Mattingly, Whitey Ford, Yogi Berra, Reggie Jackson/50 50.00
RRRD Brooks Robinson, Rick Dempsey, Frank Robinson, Cal Ripken Jr. 25.00
RR Brooks Robinson, Cal Ripken Jr. 25.00
CR Cal Ripken Jr., Frank Robinson 25.00
JD Dave Johnson, Rick Dempsey 10.00
KMLW Al Kaline, Lou Whitaker, Chet Lemon, Denny McLain 20.00

Fan Favorite Relics

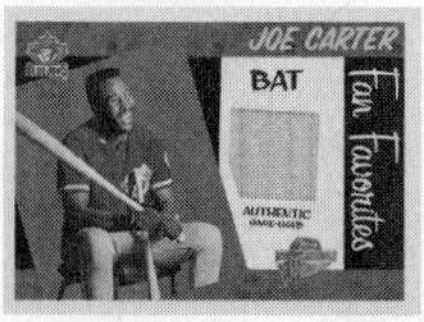

NM/M

Inserted 1:Box
Rainbow: No Pricing
Production 25 Sets
WB Wade Boggs/200 8.00
JCC Jose Canseco/350 8.00
RC Rod Carew/200 8.00
GC Gary Carter/350 5.00
JC Joe Carter/350 5.00
VC Vince Coleman/200 5.00
ED Eric Davis/200 5.00
AD Andre Dawson/350 5.00
BD Bucky Dent/200 5.00
LD Lenny Dykstra/200 5.00
CF Cecil Fielder/200 5.00
TG Tony Gwynn/200 15.00
KH Keith Hernandez/200 5.00
BJ Bo Jackson/200 12.00
RJ Reggie Jackson/350 10.00
WJ Wally Joyner/200 5.00
WM Willie McGee/350 5.00
DM Dale Murphy/200 10.00
SM Stan Musial/50 20.00
PO Paul O'Neill/200 15.00
JR Jim Rice/200 5.00
BR Brooks Robinson/350 10.00
NR Nolan Ryan/135 25.00
DS Darryl Strawberry/350 5.00
BS Bruce Sutter/350 7.50
MW Mookie Wilson/135 5.00
CY Carl Yastrzemski/50 25.00

League Leaders Tr-Signers
Production 50 Sets
No Pricing

Originals Relics
		NM/M
WB	Wade Boggs/Bat	15.00
RC	Rod Carew/Bat	20.00
GC	Gary Carter/Bat	10.00
AD	Andre Dawson/Bat	10.00
TG	Tony Gwynn/Jsy	20.00
BJ	Bo Jackson/Jsy	25.00
RJ	Reggie Jackson/Bat	20.00
DM	Dale Murphy/Bat	15.00
JR	Jim Rice/Bat	15.00
NR	Nolan Ryan/Jsy	35.00

Production 50 Sets
Actual vintage cards used.

Rookie Dual Autograph
		NM/M
Production 50 Sets
SC	Tom Seaver, Rod Carew	160.00

2005 Topps Bazooka

ALEX RODRIGUEZ
NEW YORK YANKEES®

		NM/M
Complete Set (220):		35.00
Common Player:		.15
Common (191-220):		.25
Pack (8):		2.50
Box (24):		50.00
1	Eric Gagne	.40
2	Aramis Ramirez	.40
3	Hank Blalock	.50
4	Jason Kendall	.15
5	Jeromy Burnitz	.15
6	Jose Guillen	.15
7	Tom Glavine	.40
8	Adrian Beltre	.25
9	Jason Bay	.25
10	Mark Teixeira	.40
11	Moises Alou	.25
12	Ronnie Belliard	.15
13	Aaron Guiel	.15
14	Vladimir Guerrero	.75
15	Scott Podsednik	.15
16	Alfonso Soriano	.75
17	Craig Wilson	.15
18	Jose Reyes	.25
19	Mark Prior	.75
20	Preston Wilson	.15
21	Shawn Green	.25
22	Troy Glaus	.25
23	Dmitri Young	.15
24	Garret Anderson	.25
25	Kazuo Matsui	.25
26	Kerry Wood	.25
27	Michael Young	.15
28	Oliver Perez	.15
29	Bartolo Colon	.15
30	Richie Sexson	.40
31	Brad Penny	.15
32	Carlos Guillen	.15
33	Carlos Zambrano	.25
34	David Wright	.50
35	Al Leiter	.25
36	Jack Wilson	.15
37	Ryan Drese	.15
38	Darin Erstad	.15
39	Derrek Lee	.25
40	Ivan Rodriguez	.50
41	Kenny Rogers	.15
42	Mike Piazza	1.00
43	Phil Nevin	.15
44	Geoff Jenkins	.15
45	Jorge Posada	.40
46	Khalil Greene	.40
47	Randy Johnson	.75
48	Rondell White	.15
49	Sammy Sosa	1.25
50	Vernon Wells	.15
51	Ben Sheets	.40
52	Brian Giles	.15
53	Carlos Delgado	.40
54	Derek Jeter	2.00
55	Jeremy Bonderman	.25
56	Maggio Ordonez	.25
57	Chad Tracy	.15
58	Kevin Brown	.15
59	Luis Castillo	.15

60	Lyle Overbay	.15
61	Mark Buehrle	.15
62	Mark Loretta	.15
63	Orlando Hudson	.15
64	Adam Dunn	.50
65	Frank Thomas	.75
66	Jake Peavy	.15
67	Jason Giambi	.40
68	Joe Mauer	.25
69	Marcus Giles	.15
70	Mike Lowell	.25
71	Roy Halladay	.15
72	Aaron Rowand	.15
73	Alex Rodriguez	1.50
74	Brian Lawrence	.15
75	Gabe Gross	.15
76	Johnny Estrada	.25
77	Justin Morneau	.40
78	Miguel Cabrera	.75
79	Alex Rios	.15
80	Gary Sheffield	.40
81	Jason Schmidt	.25
82	Juan Pierre	.15
83	Paul Konerko	.25
84	Jermaine Dye	.15
85	Rafael Furcal	.25
86	Torii Hunter	.25
87	A.J. Pierzynski	.15
88	Carl Pavano	.15
89	Carlos Lee	.25
90	J.D. Drew	.25
91	Javier Vazquez	.25
92	Lew Ford	.15
93	Ted Lilly	.15
94	Austin Kearns	.15
95	Chipper Jones	.75
96	Erubiel Durazo	.15
97	Johan Santana	.50
98	Josh Beckett	.25
99	Mariano Rivera	.25
100	Mark Mulder	.25
101	Andruw Jones	.50
102	Barry Zito	.25
103	Bret Boone	.15
104	Paul LoDuca	.15
105	Shannon Stewart	.15
106	Wily Mo Pena	.25
107	Dontrelle Willis	.25
108	Eric Chavez	.25
109	Jamie Moyer	.15
110	Joe Nathan	.15
111	Sidney Ponson	.15
112	John Smoltz	.25
113	Ichiro Suzuki	1.50
114	Javy Lopez	.25
115	Victor Martinez	.25
116	Ken Griffey Jr.	1.00
117	Lance Berkman	.25
118	Scott Hatteberg	.15
119	Jim Edmonds	.25
120	Kazuhisa Ishii	.15
121	Miguel Tejada	.40
122	Roger Clemens	2.00
123	Ryan Freel	.15
124	Albert Pujols	2.00
125	Hideo Nomo	.25
126	Mark Kotsay	.15
127	Melvin Mora	.15
128	Roy Oswalt	.25
129	Sean Casey	.15
130	Casey Blake	.15
131	Edgar Renteria	.25
132	Jeff Kent	.25
133	Rafael Palmeiro	.50
134	Tim Hudson	.25
135	Tony Batista	.15
136	Andy Pettitte	.25
137	Brian Roberts	.15
138	Jose Vidro	.15
139	Omar Vizquel	.15
140	Rich Harden	.15
141	Scott Rolen	.75
142	Carlos Beltran	.50
143	Chris Carpenter	.15
144	Manny Ramirez	.75
145	Nick Johnson	.15
146	Pat Burrell	.15
147	C.C. Sabathia	.15
148	Johnny Damon	.50
149	Juan Rivera	.15
150	Ken Harvey	.15
151	Kevin Millwood	.15
152	Larry Walker	.50
153	Aubrey Huff	.15
154	Curt Schilling	.75
155	Jake Westbrook	.15
156	Randy Wolf	.15
157	Zach Day	.15
158	Zack Greinke	.25
159	Brad Wilkerson	.15
160	Carl Crawford	.25
161	Jim Thome	.75
162	Mike Sweeney	.25
163	Pedro J. Martinez	.15
164	Travis Hafner	.15
165	Bobby Abreu	.25
166	Cliff Floyd	.15
167	David DeJesus	.15
168	David Ortiz	.75
169	Rocco Baldelli	.25
170	Todd Helton	.50
171	Dallas McPherson	.25
172	Kevin Youkilis	.25
173	Val Majewski	.15
174	Grady Sizemore	.25

175	Joey Gathright	.15
176	Rickie Weeks	.25
177	Jason Kubel	.25
178	Robinson Cano	.25
179	Nick Swisher	.25
180	Ryan Howard	.50
181	Tim Stauffer	.15
182	Merkin Valdez	.15
183	B.J. Upton	.40
184	Scott Kazmir	.40
185	Chris Burke	.25
186	Felix Hernandez	.50
187	Freddy Guzman	.15
188	Josh Labandeira	.15
189	Willy Taveras	.15
190	Casey Kotchman	.25
191	Steven Doetsch RC	.25
192	Melky Cabrera RC	.75
193	Luis Ramirez RC	.25
194	Chris Seddon RC	.40
195	Chad Orvella RC	.50
196	Ian Kinsler RC	1.50
197	Brandon Moss RC	1.00
198	Chadd Blasko RC	.50
199	Jeremy West RC	.75
200	Sean Marshall RC	.50
201	Matt DeSalvo RC	.50
202	Ryan Sweeney RC	1.50
203	Matt Lindstrom RC	.50
204	Ryan Goleski RC	.40
205	Brett Harper RC	.25
206	Chris Roberson RC	.25
207	Andre Ethier RC	1.00
208	Chris Denorfia RC	.25
209	Darren Fenster RC	.25
210	Elvys Quezada RC	.25
211	Kevin West RC	.50
212	Chaz Lytle RC	.50
213	James Jurries RC	.25
214	Matt Rogelstad RC	.25
215	Wade Robinson RC	.25
216	Ian Bladergroen RC	.75
217	Jake Dittler RC	.25
218	Nate McLouth RC	.50
219	Kole Strayhorn RC	.25
220	Jose Vaquedano RC	.25

Gold Chunks

ARAMIS RAMIREZ
CHICAGO CUBS™

Golds:	1-2X
Inserted 1:1	

Minis
Mini:	1-2x
Inserted 1:1	

Blasts

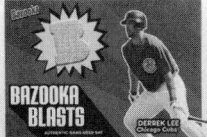

BAZOOKA BLASTS
AUTHENTIC GAME-WORN BAT
DERREK LEE
Chicago Cubs

		NM/M
Common Bat:		4.00
RA	Roberto Alomar	6.00
RB	Ron Belliard	4.00
AB	Angel Berroa	4.00
CB	Craig Biggio	8.00
HB	Hank Blalock	8.00
JB	Jeromy Burnitz	4.00
SB	Sean Burroughs	4.00
MC	Miguel Cabrera	10.00
VC	Vinny Castilla	4.00
TC	Tony Clark	4.00
JC	Jeff Conine	4.00
JCJ	Jose Cruz Jr.	4.00
AD	Adam Dunn	6.00
ME	Morgan Ensberg	4.00
DE	Darin Erstad	4.00
CE	Carl Everett	4.00
CF	Chone Figgins	4.00
JF	Julio Franco	4.00
NG	Nomar Garciaparra	8.00
AGO	Adrian Gonzalez	4.00
AG	Alex Gonzalez	4.00

LG	Luis Gonzalez	4.00
VG	Vladimir Guerrero	8.00
CGU	Carlos Guillen	4.00
CG	Cristian Guzman	4.00
TH	Todd Helton	6.00
LH	Livan Hernandez	4.00
RH	Richard Hidalgo	4.00
JK	Jeff Kent	4.00
PK	Paul Konerko	4.00
DL	Derrek Lee	4.00
ML	Mike Lowell	6.00
PM	Pedro Martinez	6.00
TM	Tino Martinez	6.00
VM	Victor Martinez	4.00
KM	Kazuo Matsui	8.00
MO	Maggio Ordonez	4.00
DO	David Ortiz	10.00
ARA	Aramis Ramirez	6.00
MR	Manny Ramirez	6.00
AR	Alex Rodriguez	20.00
CS	Curt Schilling	6.00
GS	Gary Sheffield	4.00
RS	Ruben Sierra	4.00
MT	Miguel Tejada	6.00
BU	B.J. Upton	10.00
JV	Jose Valentin	4.00
JVI	Jose Vidro	4.00
LW	Larry Walker	6.00
JW	Jayson Werth	4.00
PW	Preston Wilson	4.00
DW	David Wright	10.00
MY	Michael Young	4.00

Comics
		NM/M
Complete Set (24):		8.00
Common Player:		.25
Inserted 1:4		
1	Randy Johnson	.50
2	Gary Sheffield	.25
3	Ken Griffey Jr.	.75
4	Alex Rodriguez	.75
5	Vladimir Guerrero	.50
6	David Bell	.25
7	Carlos Pena	.25
8	Eric Gagne	.25
9	Jim Thome	.50
10	Cleveland Indians	.25
11	Greg Maddux	.50
12	Miguel Tejada	.25
13	Ichiro Suzuki	.75
14	Mariano Rivera	.25
15	Juan Pierre	.25
16	Carl Crawford	.25
17	Mike Mussina	.25
18	Vladimir Guerrero	.50
19	Oliver Perez	.25
20	Ichiro Suzuki	.75
21	Johan Santana	.25
22	Kevin Brown	.25
23	Mike Piazza	.50
24	Randy Johnson	.50

Fun Facts Relics

BAZOOKA FUN FACT
DARREN DAULTON

		NM/M
Common Relic:		4.00
HB	Harold Baines	4.00
WB	Wade Boggs	6.00
GB	George Brett	12.00
JC	Jose Canseco	8.00
RC	Rod Carew	12.00
GC	Gary Carter	4.00
DD	Darren Daulton	4.00
DE	Darrell Evans	4.00
CF	Cecil Fielder	8.00
KG	Ken Griffey Sr.	4.00
WH	Willie Horton	4.00
WJ	Wally Joyner	4.00
DJ	David Justice	4.00
DJ2	David Justice	4.00
RK	Ron Kittle	4.00
JL	Jim Leyritz	4.00
DP	Dave Parker	4.00
HR	Harold Reynolds	4.00
MR	Mickey Rivers	4.00
MS	Mike Schmidt	10.00
OS	Ozzie Smith	20.00
CS	Cory Snyder	4.00
DS	Darryl Strawberry	4.00
WW	Walt Weiss	4.00

Moments Relics
		NM/M
Common Relic:		6.00
MB	Matt Bush	8.00
RH	Ramon Hernandez	6.00
TL	Terrence Long	6.00
MM	Mark Mulder	6.00
MP	Mike Piazza	12.00
JP	Jorge Posada	8.00
AP	Albert Pujols	25.00
AR	Alex Rodriguez	12.00

IR	Ivan Rodriguez	8.00
KR	Kenny Rogers	6.00
AS	Alfonso Soriano	6.00
MT	Mark Teixeira	6.00
FT	Frank Thomas	6.00

Tatoos

NM/M

Common Player: .25
Inserted 1:4

1	Alex Rodriguez	.50
2	Randy Johnson	.50
3	Jim Thome	.25
4	Pedro Martinez	.50
5	Roger Clemens	.50
6	Troy Glaus	.25
7	Todd Helton	.25
8	Albert Pujols	.50
9	Sammy Sosa	.50
10	David Wright	.50
11	Mike Piazza	.50
12	Gary Sheffield	.25
13	David Ortiz	.50
14	Hank Blalock	.25
15	Miguel Tejada	.25
16	Dontrelle Willis	.25
17	Ivan Rodriguez	.25
18	Nomar Garciaparra	.50
19	Alfonso Soriano	.25
20	Adrian Beltre	.25
21	Torii Hunter	.25
22	Brian Giles	.25
23	Chipper Jones	.25
24	Carlos Beltran	.25
25	Manny Ramirez	.50

4-on-1 Stickers

NM/M

Common Sticker: .50
Inserted 1:3 Hobby

1	Alex Rodriguez, Hank Blalock, Scott Rolen, Mike Lowell	1.50
2	Jorge Posada, Ivan Rodriguez, Joe Mauer, Johnny Estrada	.75
3	Ichiro Suzuki, Carlos Beltran, Jim Edmonds, Brian Giles	1.50
4	Jim Thome, Mark Teixeira, Paul Konerko, Lyle Overbay	1.00
5	Jose Reyes, Mark Loretta, Jose Vidro, Luis Castillo	.50
6	Miguel Tejada, Derek Jeter, Michael Young, Edgar Renteria	2.00
7	Roy Oswalt, Rich Harden, Johan Santana, Mark Prior	1.00
8	Mariano Rivera, Eric Gagne, Joe Nathan, John Smoltz	.50
9	Larry Walker, Carl Crawford, Preston Wilson, Garret Anderson	.50
10	Wily Mo Pena, Mark Kotsay, Alex Rios, Geoff Jenkins	.50
11	Victor Martinez, David Wright, Justin Morneau, Jason Bay	.75
12	Carlos Lee, Andruw Jones, Ronnie Belliard, Eric Chavez	.25
13	Vladimir Guerrero, Vernon Wells, Miguel Cabrera, Adrian Beltre	1.00
14	David Ortiz, Marcus Giles, Jeff Kent, Bobby Abreu	1.00
15	Juan Pierre, Torii Hunter, J.D. Drew, Austin Kearns	.50
16	Bartolo Colon, Manny Ramirez, Ken Griffey Jr., Dontrelle Willis	1.50
17	Andy Pettitte, Tim Hudson, Curt Schilling, Randy Johnson	1.00
18	Jamie Moyer, Zach Day, Al Leiter, Oliver Perez	.50
19	Kazuo Matsui, Roger Clemens, Khalil Greene, Javier Vazquez	1.00
20	Pedro Martinez, Rocco Baldelli, Mike Piazza, Melvin Mora	1.50
21	Hideo Nomo, Kazuhisa Ishii, Ken Harvey, Mike Sweeney	.50
22	Casey Blake, Ryan Freel, Bret Boone, Javy Lopez	.50
23	Craig Wilson, Shawn Green, Aramis Ramirez, Darin Erstad	.50
24	Troy Glaus, Lance Berkman, Scott Podsednik, Adam Dunn	.50
25	Albert Pujols, Gary Sheffield, Chipper Jones, Magglio Ordonez	2.00
26	Johnny Damon, Carlos Zambrano, Jason Schmidt, Ted Lilly	1.00
27	Sidney Ponson, Chris Carpenter, C.C. Sabathia, Kevin Millwood	.50
28	Carl Pavano, Mark Mulder, Rafael Furcal, Jack Wilson	.50
29	Jeremy Bonderman, Jake Westbrook, Zack Greinke, Tom Glavine	.50
30	Omar Vizquel, Carlos Guillen, Roy Halladay, Ben Sheets	.50
31	Kerry Wood, Kevin Brown, Moises Alou, Travis Hafner	.75
32	Nick Johnson, Erubiel Durazo, Alfonso Soriano, Jason Giambi	.75
33	Chad Tracy, Richie Sexson, Aubrey Huff, Brian Roberts	.50
34	Todd Helton, Dmitri Young, Jeromy Burnitz, Jose Guillen	.75
35	Juan Rivera, Shannon Stewart, Sammy Sosa, Cliff Floyd	1.00
36	Pat Burrell, Gabe Gross, Aaron Guiel, Paul LoDuca	.50
37	A.J. Pierzynski, Orlando Hudson, David DeJesus, Brian Lawrence	.50
38	Josh Beckett, Barry Zito, Mark Buehrle, Randy Wolf	.50
39	Brad Penny, Jake Peavy, Rondell White, Brad Wilkerson	.50
40	Ryan Drese, Kenny Rogers, Jermaine Dye, Lew Ford	.50
41	Aaron Rowand, Jason Kendall, Tony Batista, Derrek Lee	.50
42	Phil Nevin, Sean Casey, Rafael Palmeiro, Frank Thomas	.75
43	Scott Hatteberg, Josh Labandeira, Jason Kubel, Nick Swisher	.50
44	Freddy Guzman, Tim Stauffer, Merkin Valdez, Felix Hernandez	.50
45	Willy Taveras, Grady Sizemore, Joey Gathright, Carlos Delgado	.50
46	Scott Kazmir, Rickie Weeks, Dallas McPherson, Kevin Youkilis	1.00
47	Val Majewski, Casey Kotchman, Ryan Howard, Chris Burke	.50
48	Robinson Cano, B.J. Upton, Jake Dittler, Ian Bladergroen	1.00
49	Brett Harper, James Jurries, Jeremy West, Matt Rogelstad	1.00
50	Darren Fenster, Nate Schierholtz, Brandon Moss, Ryan Sweeney	2.00
51	Chris Roberson, Steven Doetsch, Andre Ethier, Kevin West	.50
52	Melky Cabrera, Ryan Goleski, Chris Denorfia, Chaz Lytle	.50
53	Luis Ramirez, Matt DeSalvo, Sean Marshall, Jose Vaquedano	.50
54	Chris Seddon, Chadd Blasko, Elvys Quezada, Wade Robinson	.50
55	Nate McLouth, Matt Lindstrom, Kole Strayhorn, Ian Kinsler	2.50

2005 Topps Chrome

NM/M

Complete Set (472):

	Common Player:	.25
	Common Rookie Auto. (221-252):	10.00
	Inserted 1:20	
	Series 1 Hobby Pack (4):	3.00
	Series 1 Hobby Box (20):	50.00
	Series 2 Hobby Pack (4):	5.00
	Series 2 Hobby Box (20):	90.00
1	Alex Rodriguez	2.50
2	Placido Polanco	.25
3	Torii Hunter	.25
4	Lyle Overbay	.25
5	Johnny Damon	.75
6	Johnny Estrada	.25
7	Rich Harden	.25
8	Francisco Rodriguez	.25
9	Jarrod Washburn	.25
10	Sammy Sosa	1.00
11	Randy Wolf	.25
12	Jason Bay	.50
13	Tom Glavine	.50
14	Michael Tucker	.25
15	Brian Giles	.25
16	Chad Tracy	.25
17	Jim Edmonds	.50
18	John Smoltz	.50
19	Roy Halladay	.50
20	Hank Blalock	.25
21	Darin Erstad	.50
22	Todd Walker	.25
23	Mike Hampton	.25
24	Mark Bellhorn	.25
25	Jim Thome	1.00
26	Shingo Takatsu	.25
27	Jody Gerut	.25
28	Vinny Castilla	.25
29	Luis Castillo	.25
30	Ivan Rodriguez	.75
31	Craig Biggio	.50
32	Joe Randa	.25
33	Adrian Beltre	.50
34	Scott Podsednik	.25
35	Cliff Floyd	.25
36	Livan Hernandez	.25
37	Eric Byrnes	.25
38	Jose Acevedo	.25
39	Jack Wilson	.25
40	Gary Sheffield	.75
41	Chan Ho Park	.25
42	Carl Crawford	.25
43	Shawn Estes	.25
44	David Bell	.25
45	Jeff DaVanon	.25
46	Brandon Webb	.25
47	Lance Berkman	.50
48	Melvin Mora	.25
49	David Ortiz	1.00
50	Andruw Jones	.50
51	Chone Figgins	.25
52	Danny Graves	.25
53	Preston Wilson	.25
54	Jeremy Bonderman	.25
55	Carlos Guillen	.25
56	Cesar Izturis	.25
57	Kazuo Matsui	.25
58	Jason Schmidt	.50
59	Jason Marquis	.25
60	Jose Vidro	.25
61	Al Leiter	.40
62	Javier Vazquez	.25
63	Erubiel Durazo	.25
64	Scott Spiezio	.25
65	Scot Shields	.25
66	Edgardo Alfonzo	.25
67	Miguel Tejada	.50
68	Francisco Cordero	.25
69	Brett Myers	.25
70	Curt Schilling	1.00
71	Matt Kata	.25
72	Bartolo Colon	.25
73	Rodrigo Lopez	.25
74	Tim Wakefield	.25
75	Frank Thomas	.50
76	Jimmy Rollins	.50
77	Barry Zito	.50
78	Hideo Nomo	.50
79	Brad Wilkerson	.25
80	Adam Dunn	.75
81	Derrek Lee	.25
82	Joe Crede	.25
83	Nate Robertson	.25
84	John Thomson	.25
85	Mike Sweeney	.25
86	Kip Wells	.25
87	Eric Gagne	.50
88	David Wells	.25
89	Alex Sanchez	.25
90	Bret Boone	.25
91	Mark Loretta	.25
92	Miguel Cabrera	1.00
93	Randy Winn	.25
94	Adam Everett	.25
95	Aubrey Huff	.25
96	Kevin Mench	.25
97	Frank Catalanotto	.25
98	Flash Gordon	.25
99	Scott Hatteberg	.25
100	Albert Pujols	3.00
101	Jose Molina, Bengie Molina	.25
102	Jason Johnson	.25
103	Jay Gibbons	.25
104	Byung-Hyun Kim	.25
105	Joe Borowski	.25
106	Mark Grudzielanek	.25
107	Mark Buehrle	.25
108	Paul Wilson	.25
109	Ronnie Belliard	.25
110	Reggie Sanders	.25
111	Tim Redding	.25
112	Brian Lawrence	.25
113	Travis Hafner	.40
114	Jose Hernandez	.25
115	Ben Sheets	.50
116	Johan Santana	.75
117	Billy Wagner	.40
118	Mariano Rivera	.50
119	Steve Trachsel	.25
120	Akinori Otsuka	.25
121	Jose Valentin	.25
122	Orlando Hernandez	.25
123	Raul Ibanez	.25
124	Mike Matheny	.25
125	Vernon Wells	.50
126	Jason Isringhausen	.25
127	Jose Guillen	.25
128	Danny Bautista	.25
129	Marcus Giles	.25
130	Javy Lopez	.40
131	Kevin Millar	.25
132	Kyle Farnsworth	.25
133	Carl Pavano	.25
134	Rafael Furcal	.25
135	Casey Blake	.25
136	Matt Holliday	.50
137	Bobby Higginson	.25
138	Adam Kennedy	.25
139	Alex Gonzalez	.25
140	Jeff Kent	.40
141	Aaron Guiel	.25
142	Shawn Green	.40
143	Bill Hall	.25
144	Shannon Stewart	.25
145	Juan Rivera	.25
146	Coco Crisp	.25
147	Mike Mussina	.50
148	Eric Chavez	.50
149	Jon Lieber	.25
150	Vladimir Guerrero	1.00
151	Alex Cintron	.25
152	Luis Matos	.25
153	Sidney Ponson	.25
154	Trot Nixon	.25
155	Greg Maddux	2.00
156	Edgar Renteria	.50
157	Ryan Freel	.25
158	Matt Lawton	.25
159	Mark Prior	1.00
160	Josh Beckett	.50
161	Ken Harvey	.25
162	Angel Berroa	.25
163	Juan Encarnacion	.25
164	Wes Helms	.25
165	Brad Radke	.25
166	Phil Nevin	.25
167	Mike Cameron	.25
168	Billy Koch	.25
169	Bobby Crosby	.50
170	Mike Lieberthal	.25
171	Robert Mackowiak	.25
172	Sean Burroughs	.25
173	J.T. Snow Jr.	.25
174	Paul Konerko	.40
175	Luis Gonzalez	.50
176	John Lackey	.25
177	Oliver Perez	.25
178	Brian Roberts	.25
179	Bill Mueller	.25
180	Carlos Lee	.25
181	Corey Patterson	.50
182	Sean Casey	.40
183	Cliff Lee	.40
184	Jason Jennings	.25
185	Dmitri Young	.25
186	Juan Uribe	.25
187	Andy Pettitte	.50
188	Juan Gonzalez	.50
189	Orlando Hudson	.25
190	Jason Phillips	.25
191	Braden Looper	.25
192	Lew Ford	.25
193	Mark Mulder	.40
194	Bobby Abreu	.40
195	Jason Kendall	.25
196	Khalil Greene	.50
197	A.J. Pierzynski	.25
198	Tim Worrell	.25
199	So Taguchi	.25
200	Jason Giambi	.50
201	Tony Batista	.25
202	Carlos Zambrano	.50
203	Trevor Hoffman	.25
204	Odalis Perez	.25
205	Jose Cruz Jr.	.25
206	Michael Barrett	.25
207	Chris Carpenter	.25
208	Michael Young	.25
209	Toby Hall	.25
210	Woody Williams	.25
211	Chris Denorfia RC	1.00
212	Darren Fenster RC	1.00
213	Elvys Quezada RC	2.00
214	Ian Kinsler RC	5.00
215	Matt Lindstrom RC	2.00
216	Ryan Goleski RC	2.00
217	Ryan Sweeney RC	3.00
218	Sean Marshall RC	1.00
219	Steven Doetsch RC	2.00
220	Wade Robinson RC	3.00
221	Andre Ethier	30.00
222	Brandon Moss RC	20.00
223	Chadd Blasko RC	10.00
224	Chris Roberson RC	10.00
225	Chris Seddon RC	10.00
226	Ian Bladergroen RC	10.00
227	Jake Dittler	10.00

#	Player	Price
228	Jose Vaquedano RC	10.00
229	Jeremy West RC	10.00
230	Kole Strayhorn	10.00
231	Kevin West RC	10.00
232	Luis Ramirez RC	10.00
233	Melky Cabrera RC	30.00
234	Nate Schierholtz	15.00
235	Billy Butler RC	40.00
236	Brandon Szymanski RC	10.00
237	Chad Orvella RC	10.00
238	Chip Cannon RC	10.00
239	Eric Nielsen RC	10.00
240	Erik Cordier RC	10.00
241	Glen Perkins RC	15.00
242	Justin Verlander RC	50.00
243	Kevin Melillo RC	10.00
244	Landon Powell RC	10.00
245	Matt Campbell RC	10.00
246	Michael Rogers RC	15.00
247	Nate McLouth RC	20.00
248	Scott Mathieson RC	10.00
249	Shane Costa	10.00
250	Tony Giarratano RC	10.00
251	Tyler Pelland RC	10.00
252	Wes Swackhamer RC	10.00
253	Garret Anderson	.50
254	Randy Johnson	1.00
255	Charles Thomas	.25
256	Rafael Palmeiro	.75
257	Kevin Youkilis	.25
258	Freddy Garcia	.25
259	Magglio Ordonez	.25
260	Aaron Harang	.25
261	Grady Sizemore	.50
262	Chin-Hui Tsao	.25
263	Eric Munson	.25
264	Juan Pierre	.25
265	Brad Lidge	.25
266	Brian Anderson	.25
267	Todd Helton	.75
268	Chad Cordero	.25
269	Kris Benson	.25
270	Brad Halsey	.25
271	Jermaine Dye	.25
272	Manny Ramirez	1.00
273	Adam Eaton	.25
274	Brett Tomko	.25
275	Bucky Jacobsen	.25
276	Dontrelle Willis	.50
277	B.J. Upton	.25
278	Rocco Baldelli	.25
279	Ryan Drese	.25
280	Ichiro Suzuki	2.50
281	Brandon Lyon	.25
282	Nick Green	.25
283	Jerry Hairston	.25
284	Mike Lowell	.25
285	Kerry Wood	1.00
286	Omar Vizquel	.25
287	Carlos Beltran	.50
288	Carlos Pena	.25
289	Jeff Weaver	.25
290	Chad Moeller	.25
291	Joe Mays	.25
292	Terrmel Sledge	.25
293	Richard Hidalgo	.25
294	Justin Duchscherer	.25
295	Eric Milton	.25
296	Ramon Hernandez	.25
297	Jose Reyes	.50
298	Joel Pineiro	.25
299	Matt Morris	.25
300	John Halama	.25
301	Gary Matthews	.25
302	Ryan Madson	.25
303	Mark Kotsay	.25
304	Carlos Delgado	.50
305	Casey Kotchman	.25
306	Greg Aquino	.25
307	LaTroy Hawkins	.25
308	Jose Contreras	.25
309	Ken Griffey Jr.	2.00
310	C.C. Sabathia	.25
311	Brandon Inge	.25
312	John Buck	.25
313	Hee Seop Choi	.25
314	Chris Capuano	.25
315	Jesse Crain	.25
316	Geoff Jenkins	.25
317	Mike Piazza	2.00
318	Jorge Posada	.50
319	Nick Swisher	.25
320	Kevin Millwood	.25
321	Mike Gonzalez	.25
322	Jake Peavy	.25
323	Dustin Hermanson	.25
324	Jeremy Reed	.25
325	Alfonso Soriano	1.00
326	Alexis Rios	.25
327	David Eckstein	.25
328	Shea Hillenbrand	.25
329	Russ Ortiz	.25
330	Kurt Ainsworth	.25
331	Orlando Cabrera	.25
332	Carlos Silva	.25
333	Ross Gload	.25
334	Josh Phelps	.25
335	Mike Maroth	.25
336	Guillermo Mota	.25
337	Chris Burke	.25
338	David DeJesus	.25
339	Jose Lima	.25
340	Cristian Guzman	.25
341	Nick Johnson	.25
342	Victor Zambrano	.25
343	Rod Barajas	.25
344	Damian Miller	.25
345	Chase Utley	.50
346	Sean Burnett	.25
347	David Wells	.25
348	Dustan Mohr	.25
349	Bobby Madritsch	.25
350	Reed Johnson	.25
351	R.A. Dickey	.25
352	Scott Kazmir	.25
353	Tony Womack	.25
354	Thomas Perez	.25
355	Esteban Loaiza	.25
356	Tomokazu Ohka	.25
357	Ramon Ortiz	.25
358	Richie Sexson	.50
359	J.D. Drew	.40
360	Barry Bonds	4.00
361	Aramis Ramirez	.50
362	Wily Mo Pena	.25
363	Jeromy Burnitz	.25
364	Nomar Garciaparra	2.00
365	Brandon Backe	.25
366	Derek Lowe	.25
367	Doug Davis	.25
368	Joe Mauer	.75
369	Endy Chavez	.25
370	Bernie Williams	.50
371	Jason Michaels	.25
372	Craig Wilson	.25
373	Ryan Klesko	.25
374	Ray Durham	.25
375	Jose Lopez	.25
376	Jeff Suppan	.25
377	David Bush	.25
378	Marlon Byrd	.25
379	Roy Oswalt	.40
380	Rondell White	.25
381	Troy Glaus	.50
382	Scott Hairston	.25
383	Chipper Jones	1.00
384	Daniel Cabrera	.25
385	Jon Garland	.25
386	Austin Kearns	.25
387	Jake Westbrook	.25
388	Aaron Miles	.25
389	Omar Infante	.25
390	Paul LoDuca	.25
391	Morgan Ensberg	.25
392	Tony Graffanino	.25
393	Milton Bradley	.25
394	Keith Ginter	.25
395	Justin Morneau	.75
396	Tony Armas Jr.	.25
397	Kevin Brown	.25
398	Marco Scutaro	.25
399	Tim Hudson	.50
400	Pat Burrell	.40
401	Jeff Cirillo	.25
402	Larry Walker	.50
403	Dewon Brazelton	.25
404	Shigetoshi Hasegawa	.25
405	Octavio Dotel	.25
406	Michael Cuddyer	.25
407	Junior Spivey	.25
408	Zack Greinke	.25
409	Roger Clemens	3.00
410	Chris Shelton	.25
411	Ugueth Urbina	.25
412	Rafael Betancourt	.25
413	Willie Harris	.25
414	Keith Foulke	.25
415	Larry Bigbie	.25
416	Paul Byrd	.25
417	Troy Percival	.25
418	Pedro J. Martinez	1.00
419	Matt Clement	.25
420	Ryan Wagner	.25
421	Jeff Francis	.25
422	Jeff Conine	.25
423	Wade Miller	.25
424	Gavin Floyd	.25
425	Kazuhisa Ishii	.25
426	Victor Santos	.25
427	Jacque Jones	.25
428	Hideki Matsui	2.00
429	Cory Lidle	.25
430	Jose Castillo	.25
431	Alex Gonzalez	.25
432	Kirk Rueter	.25
433	Jolbert Cabrera	.25
434	Erik Bedard	.25
435	Ricky Ledee	.25
436	Mark Hendrickson	.25
437	Laynce Nix	.25
438	Jason Frasor	.25
439	Kevin Gregg	.25
440	Derek Jeter	3.00
441	Jaret Wright	.25
442	Edwin Jackson	.25
443	Moises Alou	.50
444	Aaron Rowand	.25
445	Kazuhito Tadano	.25
446	Luis Gonzalez	.25
447	A.J. Burnett	.40
448	Jeff Bagwell	.50
449	Brad Penny	.25
450	Corey Koskie	.25
451	Mark Ellis	.25
452	Hector Luna	.25
453	Miguel Olivo	.25
454	Scott Rolen	1.00
455	Ricardo Rodriguez	.25
456	Eric Hinske	.25
457	Tim Salmon	.25
458	Adam LaRoche	.25
459	B.J. Ryan	.25
460	Steve Finley	.25
461	Joe Nathan	.25
462	Vicente Padilla	.25
463	Yadier Molina	.25
464	Tino Martinez	.25
465	Mark Teixeira	.50
466	Kelvim Escobar	.25
467	Pedro Feliz	.25
468	Ryan Garko RC	4.00
469	Bobby Livingston RC	2.00
470	Yorman Bazardo RC	3.00
471	Michael Bourn	2.00
472	Andy LaRoche RC	10.00

Refractor

Refractor:	2-3X
Inserted 1:6	
Rookie Auto. (221-252):	1-1.5X
Production 500	

Black Refractor

Black Refractor:	3-5X
Production 225	
Rookie Auto. (221-252):	1.5-3X
Production 200	

X-Fractor

Cards (1-220):	5-10X
Rookie Auto. (221-234):	No Pricing
Production 25 Sets	

Gold Refractor

No Pricing
Production One Set

Printing Plates

No Pricing
Production one set per color.

A-Rod Throwbacks

	NM/M
Common A-Rod:	3.00
ARI1-ARI4 Alex Rodriguez	3.00

Chrome The Game Relics

	NM/M
Common Player:	5.00
Inserted 1:Box	

		NM/M
JB	Jeff Bagwell	8.00
WB	Wade Boggs	6.00
TH	Torii Hunter	5.00
MPI	Mike Piazza	8.00
JP	Jorge Posada	6.00
MP	Mark Prior	8.00
AR	Alex Rodriguez	15.00
JS	John Smoltz	8.00
AS	Alfonso Soriano	8.00
SS	Sammy Sosa	8.00
MY	Michael Young	5.00

Chrome The Game Patch Relics

		NM/M
Common Player:		10.00
JB	Jeff Bagwell	15.00
JBE	Josh Beckett	10.00
LB	Lance Berkman	10.00
BB	Bret Boone	10.00
AD1	Adam Dunn	15.00
AD2	Adam Dunn	15.00
TG	Troy Glaus	10.00
TH	Todd Helton	15.00
KI	Kazuhisa Ishii	10.00
CJ	Chipper Jones	20.00
PL	Paul LoDuca	10.00
ML	Mike Lowell	10.00
PM	Pedro Martinez	20.00
HN	Hideo Nomo	20.00
MO	Magglio Ordonez	10.00
MPI	Mike Piazza	10.00
AP	Albert Pujols	25.00
AR	Alex Rodriguez	25.00
CS	C.C. Sabathia	10.00
SS	Sammy Sosa	20.00
MT	Mark Teixeira	15.00
FT	Frank Thomas	15.00
DW	Dontrelle Willis	10.00
KW	Kerry Wood	20.00

Dem Bums Autographs

		NM/M
Inserted 1:1,816		
CE	Carl Erskine	50.00
DS	Duke Snider	85.00

2005 Topps Chrome Update

		NM/M
Complete Set (237):		
Common Player:		.25
Common Rookie (106-215):		.50
Common Rk Auto. (221-237):		10.00
Pack (4):		4.00
Box (20):		70.00
UH1	Sammy Sosa	1.00
UH2	Jeff Francoeur	.50
UH3	Tony Clark	.25
UH4	Michael Tucker	.25
UH5	Mike Matheny	.25
UH6	Eric Young	.25
UH7	Jose Valentin	.25
UH8	Matt Lawton	.25
UH9	Juan Rivera	.25
UH10	Shawn Green	.50
UH11	Aaron Boone	.25
UH12	Woody Williams	.25
UH13	Brad Wilkerson	.25
UH14	Anthony Reyes RC	3.00
UH15	Gustavo Chacin	.25
UH16	Mike Restovich	.25
UH17	Humberto Quintero	.25
UH18	Matt Ginter	.25
UH19	Scott Podsednik	.50
UH20	Byung-Hyun Kim	.25
UH21	Orlando Hernandez	.25
UH22	Mark Grudzielanek	.25
UH23	Jody Gerut	.25
UH24	Adrian Beltre	.50
UH25	Scott Schoeneweis	.25
UH26	Marlon Anderson	.25
UH27	Jason Vargas	.25
UH28	Claudio Vargas	.25
UH29	Jason Kendall	.25
UH30	Aaron Small	.25
UH31	Juan Cruz	.25
UH32	Placido Polanco	.25
UH33	Jorge Sosa	.25
UH34	John Olerud	.25
UH35	Ryan Langerhans	.25
UH36	Randy Winn	.25
UH37	Zachary Duke	.50
UH38	Garrett Atkins	.25
UH39	Al Leiter	.25
UH40	Shawn Chacon	.25
UH41	Mark DeRosa	.25
UH42	Miguel Ojeda	.25
UH43	A.J. Pierzynski	.25
UH44	Carlos Lee	.25
UH45	LaTroy Hawkins	.25
UH46	Nick Green	.25

UH47	Shawn Estes	.25
UH48	Eli Marrero	.25
UH49	Jeff Kent	.25
UH50	Joe Randa	.25
UH51	Jose Hernandez	.25
UH52	Joe Blanton	.25
UH53	Huston Street	.25
UH54	Marlon Byrd	.25
UH55	Alex Sanchez	.25
UH56	Livan Hernandez	.25
UH57	Chris Young	.25
UH58	Brad Eldred	.25
UH59	Terrence Long	.25
UH60	Phil Nevin	.25
UH61	Kyle Farnsworth	.25
UH62	Jon Lieber	.25
UH63	Antonio Alfonseca	.25
UH64	Tony Graffanino	.25
UH65	Tadahito Iguchi	1.00
UH66	Brad Thompson	.25
UH67	Jose Vidro	.25
UH68	Jason Phillips	.25
UH69	Carl Pavano	.25
UH70	Pokey Reese	.25
UH71	Jerome Williams	.25
UH72	Kazuhisa Ishii	.25
UH73	Felix Hernandez	.50
UH74	Edgar Renteria	.50
UH75	Mike Myers	.25
UH76	Jeff Cirillo	.25
UH77	Endy Chavez	.25
UH78	Jose Guillen	.25
UH79	Ugueth Urbina	.25
UH80	Zach Day	.25
UH81	Javier Vazquez	.25
UH82	Willy Taveras	.25
UH83	Mark Mulder	.50
UH84	Vinny Castilla	.25
UH85	Russ Adams	.25
UH86	Homer Bailey	.25
UH87	Ervin Santana	.25
UH88	Bill Bray	.25
UH89	Thomas Diamond	.25
UH90	Trevor Plouffe	.25
UH91	James Houser	.25
UH92	Jake Stevens	.25
UH93	Anthony Whittington	.25
UH94	Phillip Hughes	.25
UH95	Greg Golson	.25
UH96	Paul Maholm	.25
UH97	Carlos Quentin	.25
UH98	Dan Johnson	.25
UH99	Mark Rogers	.25
UH100	Neil Walker	.25
UH101	Omar Quintanilla	.25
UH102	Blake DeWitt	.25
UH103	Taylor Tankersley	.25
UH104	David Murphy	.25
UH105	Chris Lambert	.25
UH106	Drew Anderson **RC**	.50
UH107	Luis Hernandez **RC**	.50
UH108	Jim Burt **RC**	.50
UH109	Mike Morse **RC**	.50
UH110	Elliot Johnson **RC**	2.00
UH111	C.J. Smith **RC**	.50
UH112	Casey McGehee **RC**	.50
UH113	Brian Miller **RC**	.50
UH114	Chris Vines **RC**	.50
UH115	D.J. Houlton **RC**	.50
UH116	Chuck Tiffany **RC**	2.00
UH117	Humberto Sanchez **RC**	3.00
UH118	Baltazar Lopez **RC**	.50
UH119	Russell Martin **RC**	4.00
UH120	Dana Eveland **RC**	1.00
UH121	Johan Silva **RC**	.50
UH122	Adam Harben **RC**	1.00
UH123	Brian Bannister **RC**	1.50
UH124	Adam Boeve **RC**	.75
UH125	Tom Oldham **RC**	.75
UH126	Cody Haerther **RC**	1.50
UH127	Dan Santin **RC**	.75
UH128	Daniel Haigwood **RC**	1.00
UH129	Craig Tatum **RC**	.50
UH130	Martin Prado **RC**	.75
UH131	Errol Simonitsch **RC**	.50
UH132	Lorenzo Scott **RC**	.75
UH133	Hayden Penn **RC**	1.00
UH134	Heath Totten **RC**	.50
UH135	Nick Masset **RC**	.50
UH136	Pedro Lopez **RC**	.75
UH137	Benjamin Harrison **RC**	.50
UH138	Michael Spidale **RC**	.50
UH139	Jeremy Harts **RC**	.50
UH140	Danny Zell **RC**	.50
UH141	Kevin Collins **RC**	.50
UH142	Tony Arnerich **RC**	.50
UH143	Matt Albers **RC**	2.50
UH144	Ricky Barrett **RC**	.50
UH145	Hernan Iribarren **RC**	.75
UH146	Sean Tracey **RC**	.50
UH147	Jerry Owens **RC**	1.00
UH148	Steve Nelson **RC**	.50
UH149	Brandon McCarthy **RC**	2.00
UH150	David Shepard **RC**	.75
UH151	Steve Bondurant **RC**	.75
UH152	Billy Sadler	.75
UH153	Ryan Feierabend **RC**	.75
UH154	Stuart Pomeranz **RC**	.75
UH155	Shawn Marcum **RC**	1.00
UH156	Erik Schindewolf **RC**	.50
UH157	Stefan Bailie **RC**	.50
UH158	Mike Esposito **RC**	.50
UH159	Buck Coats **RC**	.75
UH160	Andy Sides **RC**	.50
UH161	Micah Schnurstein **RC**	.75
UH162	Jesse Gutierrez **RC**	.50
UH163	Jake Postlewait **RC**	.50
UH164	Willy Mota **RC**	.50
UH165	Ryan Speier **RC**	.50
UH166	Frank Mata **RC**	.50
UH167	Jair Jurrjens **RC**	4.00
UH168	Nick Touchstone **RC**	.50
UH169	Matthew Kemp **RC**	6.00
UH170	Vinny Rottino **RC**	.50
UH171	J.B. Thurmond **RC**	.50
UH172	Kelvin Pichardo **RC**	.50
UH173	Scott Mitchinson **RC**	.50
UH174	Darwinson Salazar **RC**	.50
UH175	George Kottaras **RC**	1.50
UH176	Ken Durost **RC**	.75
UH177	Jonathan Sanchez **RC**	3.00
UH178	Brandon Moorhead **RC**	.75
UH179	Kennard Bibbs **RC**	.75
UH180	David Gassner **RC**	.50
UH181	Micah Furtado **RC**	.50
UH182	Ismael Ramirez **RC**	.50
UH183	Carlos Gonzalez **RC**	5.00
UH184	Brandon Sing **RC**	.75
UH185	Jason Motte **RC**	.50
UH186	Chuck James **RC**	3.00
UH187	Andy Santana **RC**	.50
UH188	Manny Parra **RC**	3.00
UH189	Chris Young **RC**	5.00
UH190	Juan Senreiso **RC**	.50
UH191	Franklin Morales **RC**	3.00
UH192	Jared Gothreaux **RC**	.50
UH193	Jayce Tingler **RC**	.50
UH194	Matt Brown **RC**	.50
UH195	Frank Diaz **RC**	1.50
UH196	Stephen Drew **RC**	8.00
UH197	Jered Weaver **RC**	10.00
UH198	Ryan Braun **RC**	25.00
UH199	John Mayberry Jr. **RC**	2.50
UH200	Aaron Thompson **RC**	2.00
UH201	Ben Copeland **RC**	4.00
UH202	Jacoby Ellsbury **RC**	25.00
UH203	Garrett Olson **RC**	3.00
UH204	Cliff Pennington **RC**	2.50
UH205	Colby Rasmus **RC**	10.00
UH206	Chris Volstad **RC**	3.00
UH207	Ricky Romero **RC**	2.00
UH208	Ryan Zimmerman **RC**	8.00
UH209	C.J. Henry **RC**	2.00
UH210	Nelson Cruz **RC**	1.00
UH211	Josh Wall **RC**	1.50
UH212	Nick Webber **RC**	.50
UH213	Paul Kelly **RC**	1.00
UH214	Kyle Winters **RC**	1.50
UH215	Mitch Boggs **RC**	.75
UH216	Craig Biggio	.50
UH217	Greg Maddux	1.00
UH218	Bobby Abreu	.25
UH219	Alex Rodriguez	2.00
UH220	Trevor Hoffman	.25
UH221	Trevor Bell **RC**	20.00
UH222	Jay Bruce **RC**	100.00
UH223	Travis Buck **RC**	20.00
UH224	Cesar Carrillo **RC**	15.00
UH225	Mike Costanzo **RC**	20.00
UH226	Brent Cox **RC**	10.00
UH227	Matt Garza **RC**	30.00
UH228	Josh Geer **RC**	10.00
UH229	Tyler Greene **RC**	10.00
UH230	Eli Iorg **RC**	10.00
UH231	Craig Italiano **RC**	20.00
UH232	Beau Jones **RC**	15.00
UH233	Mark McCormick **RC**	10.00
UH234	Andrew McCutchen **RC**	50.00
UH235	Micah Owings **RC**	25.00
UH236	Cesar Ramos **RC**	10.00
UH237	Chaz Roe **RC**	10.00

Refractor

Stars (1-105):	2-3X
Rookies (106-215):	1-2X
Inserted 1:5	
Refractor Auto. (221-237):	1-1.5X
Production 500	

Black Refractor

Black (1-105):	2-4X
Black (106-215):	2-3X
Production 250	
Black Auto. (221-237):	1-2.5X
Production 200	

Gold SuperFractor

No Pricing
Production One Set

Red X-Fractor

Red (1-105):	4-8X
Red (106-215):	6-12X
Production 65	
Red Auto. (221-237):	No Pricing
Production 25	

Printing Plates

No Pricing
Production one set per color.

Barry Bonds Home Run History

	NM/M
Complete Set (15):	40.00
Common Bonds:	3.00
Inserted 1:12	
Refractor:	1-2X
Inserted 1:71	
Black Refractor:	2-3X
Production 200 Sets	
Red X-Fractor:	4-6X

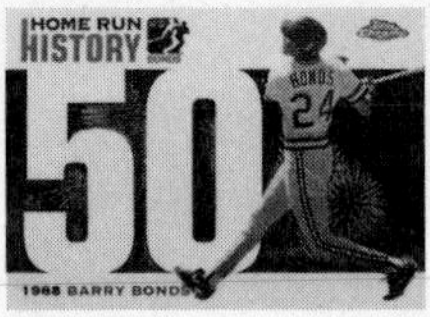

Production 25 Sets		
Gold Super:		No Pricing
Production One Set		
BB1	Barry Bonds	3.00
BB25	Barry Bonds	3.00
BB50	Barry Bonds	3.00
BB75	Barry Bonds	3.00
BB100	Barry Bonds	3.00
BB125	Barry Bonds	3.00
BB150	Barry Bonds	3.00
BB175	Barry Bonds	3.00
BB200	Barry Bonds	3.00
BB225	Barry Bonds	3.00
BB250	Barry Bonds	3.00
BB275	Barry Bonds	3.00
BB300	Barry Bonds	3.00
BB325	Barry Bonds	3.00
BB350	Barry Bonds	3.00

2005 Topps Cracker Jack

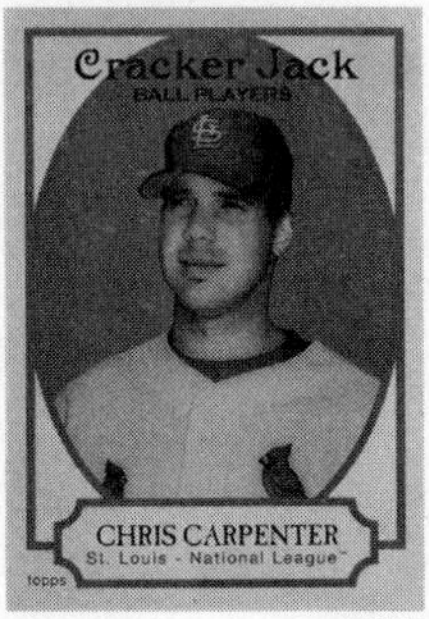

		NM/M
Complete Set (240):		
Common Player:		.25
Common SP:		3.00
Inserted 1:3		
Pack (8):		4.00
Box (20):		70.00
1	David Wright/SP	8.00
2	Rafael Furcal	.25
3	Alex Rodriguez	1.50
3	Alex Rodriguez/SP/Fldg	5.00
4	Victor Martinez/SP	3.00
5	Ken Griffey Jr.	1.50
6	Bobby Crosby/SP	3.00
7	Ivan Rodriguez	.50
8	Darin Erstad	.25
9	Javy Lopez	.25
10	Brian Giles	.25
11	Aaron Rowand/SP	3.00
12	Joe Torre	.25
13	Zack Greinke/SP	3.00
14	Shannon Stewart	.25
15	Jack Wilson	.25
16	Jose Vidro	.25
17	Josh Beckett	.40
---	Josh Beckett (No number.)	4.00
18	Barry Zito	.40
19	Bret Boone	.25
20	Greg Maddux	1.00
21	Carl Crawford/SP	3.00
22	Mark Teixeira	.50
23	Jason Schmidt	.40
24	Kazuhisa Ishii	.25
25	Mike Piazza	1.00
26	Daniel Cabrera/SP	3.00
27	Mike Lieberthal	.25
28	Gil Meche	.25
29	Phil Nevin	.25
30	Adrian Beltre/SP	3.00
31	Chipper Jones/SP	4.00
32	Zach Day	.25
33	Ben Sheets	.40
34	Carlos Zambrano	.40
35	Melvin Mora	.25
36	Joe Mauer	.75
37	Ken Harvey	.25
38	Bernie Williams	.40
39	Mike Maroth	.25
40	Eric Chavez	.40
41	Matt Lawton/SP	3.00
42	Ray Durham	.25
43	Vernon Wells	.25
44	Mike Lowell	.25
45	Jim Thome	.50
46	Joel Pineiro	.25
47	Lance Berkman	.40
48	Ryan Klesko	.25
49	Adam Dunn	.50
50	Vladimir Guerrero	.75
51	Eric Gagne/SP	4.00
52	Richie Sexson	.40
53	Javier Vazquez	.25
54	Roy Oswalt	.40
55	Carlos Delgado	.50
56	John Buck/SP	3.00
57	Kenny Rogers	.25
58	Sidney Ponson	.25
59	Vicente Padilla	.25
60	Mark Prior/SP	.75
60	Mark Prior/SP/Portrait	4.00
61	A.J. Pierzynski	.25
62	Aubrey Huff	.25
63	Shea Hillenbrand	.25
64	Carlos Guillen	.25
65	Lyle Overbay	.25
66	Al Leiter	.25
67	Eric Hinske	.25
68	Laynce Nix	.25
69	Scott Hairston	.25
70	Roger Clemens	2.00
71	Cesar Izturis/SP	3.00
72	Shawn Green	.25
73	Marcus Giles	.25
74	Rafael Palmeiro	.50
75	Melky Cabrera/SP	3.00
75	Gary Sheffield/SP	4.00
76	Juan Pierre	.25
77	Pat Burrell	.40
78	Sean Burroughs	.25
79	Frank Thomas	.50
80	Andruw Jones	.40
81	C.C. Sabathia	.25
82	Jeff Bagwell	.50
83	Tom Glavine	.40
84	Craig Wilson/SP	3.00
85	Johan Santana	.75
85	Johan Santana/SP/Portrait	4.00
86	Raul Ibanez	.25
87	Sean Casey	.25
88	Bucky Jacobsen	.25
89	B.J. Upton	.40
90	Bobby Abreu	.40
91	Geoff Jenkins	.25
92	Troy Glaus	.40
93	Dontrelle Willis	.40
94	Jose Lima	.25
95	Rocco Baldelli	.25
96	Aramis Ramirez	.40
97	Paul LoDuca	.25
98	Torii Hunter	.40
99	Jay Payton	.25
100	Carlos Beltran	.50
101	Jaret Wright	.25
102	Jason Bay	.40
103	Cliff Floyd	.25
104	Mike Sweeney	.25
105	Sammy Sosa	1.50
106	Khalil Greene/SP	4.00
107	David DeJesus	.25
108	Jermaine Dye	.25
109	Miguel Cabrera	.75
110	Miguel Tejada/SP	5.00
111	Johnny Estrada/SP	3.00
112	Ronnie Belliard/SP	3.00
113	Austin Kearns	.25
114	Erubiel Durazo	.25
115	Preston Wilson	.25
116	Hideo Nomo	.40
117	Dmitri Young	.25
118	Jon Lieber	.25
119	Derrek Lee	.40
120	Todd Helton	.50
121	Omar Vizquel	.25
122	Wily Mo Pena	.40
123	J.D. Drew	.40
124	Matt Holliday	.25
125	Ichiro Suzuki	1.50
126	Mark Buehrle/SP	3.00
127	Eric Munson	.25
128	Jeff Kent	.25
129	Kerry Wood	.75
130	Mariano Rivera	.50
131	Nick Johnson	.25
132	Randy Winn	.25
133	Phil Garner	.25
134	Jose Reyes	.50
135	Michael Young/SP	3.00
135	Ian Kinsler/SP	6.00
136	Jose Contreras	.25
137	Oliver Perez	.25
138	Roy Halladay	.40
139	Kevin Millwood	.25
140	Jorge Posada	.40
141	Mike Cameron	.25
142	Edgardo Alfonzo	.25
143	Chris Shelton	.25
144	Luis Castillo	.25
145	Alfonso Soriano	.75
146	Ryan Drese/SP	3.00
147	Mark Mulder	.40
148	Jason Giambi	.25
149	Travis Hafner	.25
150	Randy Johnson	.75
151	Paul Konerko/SP	3.00
152	Mike Mussina	.50
153	Brad Wilkerson	.25
154	Tim Hudson	.40
155	Garret Anderson	.40
156	Chase Utley/SP	3.00
157	Jamie Moyer	.25
158	Scott Kazmir	.40
159	Brett Myers	.25
160	Kazuo Matsui	.25
161	Orlando Hudson	.25

162	Luis Gonzalez	.25
163	Kevin Youkilis	.25
164	Jason Kendall/SP	.25
164	Landon Powell/SP	3.00
165	Hank Blalock	.50
166	Mark Loretta/SP	3.00
167	Miguel Cairo	.25
168	Corey Patterson	.40
169	Carlos Zambrano	.25
170	Magglio Ordonez	.25
171	J.T. Snow	.25
172	Randy Wolf	.25
173	Rich Harden	.40
174	Bartolo Colon	.25
175	Derek Jeter	2.00
176	Casey Kotchman/SP	3.00
177	Val Majewski	.25
178	Grady Sizemore	.50
179	Rickie Weeks	.25
180	Robinson Cano	.75
181	Nick Swisher/SP	3.00
182	Ryan Howard	1.50
183	John Van Benschoten	.25
184	Delmon Young	.50
185	Aaron Hill	.25
186	Chris Burke/SP	3.00
187	Merkin Valdez	.25
188	Jeremy Reed	.25
189	Conor Jackson	.25
190	Melky Cabrera	.25
191	Joey Gathright/SP	3.00
192	Gavin Floyd	.25
193	Joe Blanton	.25
194	Jason Kubel	.25
195	Jeff Francis	.25
196	Angel Guzman/SP	3.00
197	Dallas McPherson	.25
198	Melky Cabrera **RC**	1.50
199	Jake Dittler	.25
200	Elvys Quezada **RC**	.50
201	Ian Kinsler/SP **RC**	6.00
202	Nate McLouth **RC**	1.00
203	Chris Seddon **RC**	.75
204	Chad Orvella **RC**	.50
205	Ian Bladergroen **RC**	1.00
206	James Jurries/SP **RC**	4.00
207	Landon Powell **RC**	.75
208	Eric Nielsen **RC**	.50
209	Chris Roberson **RC**	.50
210	Andre Ethier	2.00
211	Chris Denorfia/SP **RC**	4.00
212	Darren Fenster **RC**	.50
213	Jeremy West **RC**	1.00
214	Sean Marshall **RC**	.50
215	Ryan Sweeney	1.50
216	Steven Doetsch/SP **RC**	3.00
217	Kevin Melillo **RC**	.50
218	Chip Cannon **RC**	1.00
219	Tony LaRussa	.25
220	Chris Carpenter	.25
221	Edgar Renteria/SP/Red Sox	3.00
221	Edgar Renteria/SP/Cardinals	3.00
222	Albert Pujols	2.00
223	Jim Edmonds	.40
224	Jason Marquis	.25
225	Scott Rolen/SP	4.00
226	Larry Walker/SP	4.00
227	Matt Morris	.25
228	Mike Matheny	3.00
228	Mike Matheny/SP/Cardinals	3.00
229	Jeromy Burnitz	.25
230	Terry Francona	.25
231	Johnny Damon/SP	4.00
232	Keith Foulke	.25
233	Trot Nixon	.25
234	Manny Ramirez	.75
235	David Ortiz/SP	4.00
236	Pedro Martinez/SP/Mets	4.00
236	Pedro J. Martinez/ SP/Red Sox	4.00
237	Curt Schilling	.75
238	Kevin Millar	.25
239	Bill Mueller	.25
240	Mark Bellhorn	.25
	Josh Beckett/SP	3.00

Mini Blue

Stars: 8-15X
SP's: 4-6X
Production 50 Sets

Mini Grey

No Pricing
Production 25 Sets

Mini Red

Stars: 1-2X
Inserted 1:1
SP's: .75-1.5X
Inserted 1:20

Mini White

No Pricing
Production One Set

Autographs

NM/M

Production 50 Sets
Bonds Production 25

GA	Garret Anderson/50	30.00
CB	Carlos Beltran/50	80.00
EC	Eric Chavez/50	30.00
CC	Carl Crawford/50	40.00
EG	Eric Gagne	40.00
AR	Alex Rodriguez	250.00
CS	C.C. Sabathia/50	50.00
JS	Johan Santana	60.00
CW	Craig Wilson/50	25.00
DW	David Wright/50	150.00

Mini Stickers

Stars: 1-2X
Inserted 1:1
SP's: .75-1.5X
Inserted 1:20

Secret Surprise Autographs

NM/M

	Common Auto.:	8.00
GA	Garret Anderson	15.00
EC	Eric Chavez	15.00
CC	Carl Crawford	10.00
EG	Eric Gagne	20.00
AG	Angel Guzman	8.00
SK	Scott Kazmir	25.00
MK	Mark Kotsay/100	15.00
ML	Mark Loretta/100	15.00
DM	Dallas McPherson/100	15.00
KM	Kevin Millar	15.00
MM	Melvin Mora	15.00
CN	Chris Nelson	10.00
RR	Richie Robnett	10.00
AR	Alex Rodriguez/100	250.00
CS	C.C. Sabathia	20.00
JS	Johan Santana	50.00
CT	Curtis Thigpen	15.00
CW	Craig Wilson	10.00
DW	David Wright	50.00

Take Me Out To/ Ballgame Relics

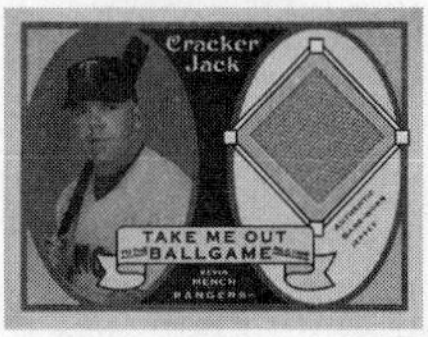

NM/M

Inserted 1:16

JB	Jeff Bagwell	6.00
RB	Ronnie Belliard	4.00
CB	Carlos Beltran	8.00
AB	Adrian Beltre	6.00
LB1	Lance Berkman	6.00
LB2	Lance Berkman	6.00
AB1	Angel Berroa	4.00
AB2	Angel Berroa	4.00
CBI	Craig Biggio	6.00
HB1	Hank Blalock	8.00
HB2	Hank Blalock	8.00
HB3	Hank Blalock	8.00
SB	Sean Burroughs	4.00
MC	Miguel Cabrera	8.00
VC	Vinny Castilla	4.00
EC1	Eric Chavez	6.00
EC2	Eric Chavez	6.00
BC	Bobby Cox	6.00
CC	Coco Crisp	4.00
BCR	Bobby Crosby	6.00
AD	Adam Dunn	8.00
JE1	Jim Edmonds	6.00
JE2	Jim Edmonds	6.00
DE	Darin Erstad	4.00
JE	Johnny Estrada	4.00
RF	Rafael Furcal	6.00
JG	Jody Gerut	4.00
JGI	Jay Gibbons	4.00
MG	Marcus Giles	4.00
TG	Troy Glaus	6.00
LG	Luis Gonzalez	4.00
NG	Nick Green	4.00
SG	Shawn Green	4.00
VG	Vladimir Guerrero	10.00
JGU	Jose Guillen	6.00
CG	Cristian Guzman	4.00
TH	Todd Helton	8.00
THU	Torii Hunter	6.00
JJ	Jacque Jones	4.00
JK	Jason Kendall	4.00
BK	Bobby Kielty	4.00
RK	Ryan Klesko	4.00
PK	Paul Konerko	4.00
MK	Mark Kotsay	4.00
AL	Adam LaRoche	6.00
VM	Victor Martinez	6.00
KME	Kevin Mench	4.00
DM	Doug Mientkiewicz	4.00
KM	Kevin Millar	10.00
MM	Melvin Mora	6.00
PN	Phil Nevin	4.00
LN	Laynce Nix	4.00
MO	Magglio Ordonez	4.00
DO	David Ortiz	10.00
RP	Rafael Palmeiro	8.00
CP	Corey Patterson	6.00
MP	Mike Piazza	12.00
JP1	Jorge Posada	8.00
JP2	Jorge Posada	8.00
AP	Albert Pujols	20.00
MR	Manny Ramirez	10.00
JR	Jeremy Reed	8.00
MRE	Mike Restovich	4.00
AR	Alex Rodriguez	15.00
ARA	Aramis Ramirez	6.00
IR1	Ivan Rodriguez	8.00
IR2	Ivan Rodriguez	8.00
RS	Reggie Sanders	4.00
BS	Benito Santiago	4.00
GS	Gary Sheffield	8.00
AS	Alfonso Soriano	8.00
MT1	Mark Teixeira	8.00
MT2	Mark Teixeira	8.00
MT3	Mark Teixeira	8.00
MTE1	Miguel Tejada	8.00
MTE2	Miguel Tejada	8.00
CT	Charles Thomas	4.00
JT	Jim Thome	8.00
JTO	Joe Torre	10.00
OV	Omar Vizquel	6.00
BW	Bernie Williams	6.00
DW	Dontrelle Willis	8.00
MY	Michael Young	6.00

1,2,3 Strikes You're Out Relics

NM/M

Inserted 1:204

JB	Josh Beckett	8.00
RD	Ryan Drese	5.00
RO	Russ Ortiz	5.00
BR	Brad Radke	8.00
CS	Curt Schilling	15.00
JW	Jaret Wright	8.00

2005 Topps Gallery

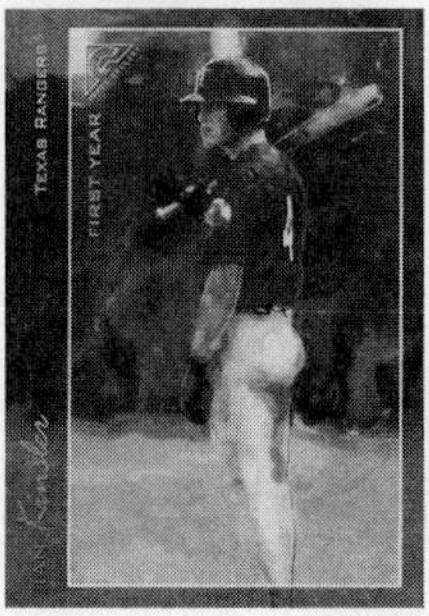

NM/M

	Complete Set (195):	175.00
	Common Player:	.25
	Common SP (151-195):	1.00
	Inserted 1:1	
	Variations 1:40	
	Pack (5):	6.00
	Box (20):	100.00
1	Alex Rodriguez	2.50
1	Alex Rodriguez/ SP/Black Bat Glove	8.00
2	Eric Chavez	.50
3	Mike Piazza	1.50
4	Bret Boone	.25
5	Albert Pujols	3.00
6	Vernon Wells	.25
7	Andruw Jones	.50
8	Miguel Tejada	.50
9	Johnny Damon	.75
10	Nomar Garciaparra	2.00
11	Pat Burrell	.40
12	Bartolo Colon	.25
13	Johnny Estrada	.25
14	Luis Gonzalez	.40
15	Jay Gibbons	.25
16	Curt Schilling	1.00
17	Aramis Ramirez	.50
18	Frank Thomas	.75
19	Adam Dunn	.75
20	Sammy Sosa	2.00
21	Matt Lawton	.25
22	Preston Wilson	.25
23	Carlos Pena	.25
24	Josh Beckett	.50
25	Carlos Beltran	.75
26	Juan Gonzalez	.50
27	Adrian Beltre	.50
28	Lyle Overbay	.25
29	Justin Morneau	.50
30	Derek Jeter	3.00
31	Barry Zito	.50
32	Bobby Abreu	.40
33	Jason Bay	.25
34	Jose Reyes	.50
35	Nick Johnson	.25
36	Lew Ford	.25
37	Scott Podsednik	.25
38	Rocco Baldelli	.40
39	Eric Hinske	.25
40	Ichiro Suzuki	2.50
40	Ichiro Suzuki/SP/ Writing On Wall	8.00
41	Larry Walker	.50
42	Mark Teixeira	.50
43	Khalil Greene	.50
44	Edgardo Alfonzo	.25
45	Javier Vazquez	.25
46	Cliff Floyd	.25
47	Geoff Jenkins	.25
48	Ken Griffey Jr.	2.00
49	Vinny Castilla	.25
50	Mark Prior	1.00
51	Jose Guillen	.25
52	J.D. Drew	.50
53	Rafael Palmeiro	.75
54	Kevin Youkilis	.25
55	Derrek Lee	.50
56	Freddy Garcia	.25
57	Wily Mo Pena	.25
58	C.C. Sabathia	.25
59	Craig Biggio	.40
60	Ivan Rodriguez	.75
61	Angel Berroa	.25
62	Ben Sheets	.50
63	Johan Santana	.75
64	Al Leiter	.40
65	Bernie Williams	.50
66	Bobby Crosby	.50
67	Jack Wilson	.25
68	A.J. Pierzynski	.25
69	Jimmy Rollins	.50
70	Jason Giambi	.50
71	Tom Glavine	.50
72	Kevin Brown	.25
73	B.J. Upton	.50
74	Edgar Renteria	.50
75	Alfonso Soriano	1.00
76	Mike Lieberthal	.25
77	Kazuo Matsui	.25
78	Phil Nevin	.25
79	Shawn Green	.40
80	Miguel Cabrera	1.00
81	Todd Helton	.75
82	Magglio Ordonez	.40
83	Manny Ramirez	1.00
84	Bill Mueller	.25
85	Troy Glaus	.50
86	Richie Sexson	.50
87	Javy Lopez	.40
88	David Ortiz	1.00
89	Greg Maddux	1.50
90	Vladimir Guerrero	1.00
91	Jeromy Burnitz	.25
92	Jeff Kent	.40
93	Travis Hafner	.40
94	Mark Buehrle	.25
95	Paul LoDuca	.25
96	Roy Oswalt	.40
97	Torii Hunter	.40
98	Gary Sheffield	.75
99	Erubiel Durazo	.25
100	Jim Thome	1.00
100	Jim Thome/SP/ Kid's Shirt Is Red	6.00
101	Ken Harvey	.25
102	Shannon Stewart	.25
103	Dmitri Young	.25
104	Kevin Millar	.50
105	Kerry Wood	1.00
106	Paul Konerko	.40
107	Ronnie Belliard	.25
108	Mike Lowell	.40
109	Hee Seop Choi	.25
110	Joe Mauer	.50
111	David Wright	.50
112	Jorge Posada	.50
113	Tim Hudson	.50
114	Brian Giles	.25
115	Jason Schmidt	.50
116	Aubrey Huff	.25
117	Hank Blalock	.75
118	Jim Edmonds	.50
119	Raul Ibanez	.25
120	Carlos Delgado	.50
121	Craig Wilson	.40
122	Ryan Klesko	.25
123	Mark Mulder	.50
124	Jose Vidro	.25
125	Mike Sweeney	.25
126	Lance Berkman	.50
127	Juan Pierre	.25
128	Austin Kearns	.25
129	Moises Alou	.50
130	Garret Anderson	.50
131	Pedro J. Martinez	1.00
132	Melvin Mora	.25
133	Marcus Giles	.25
134	Corey Patterson	.50
135	Carlos Lee	.25
136	Sean Casey	.40
137	Jody Gerut	.25
138	Jose Valentin	.25
139	Aaron Miles	.25
140	Randy Johnson	1.00
141	Carlos Guillen	.25
142	Dontrelle Willis	.50
143	Jeff Bagwell	.75
144	Jason Kendall	.25
145	Mark Loretta	.25
146	Scott Rolen	1.00
147	Carl Crawford	.25
148	Michael Young	.25
149	Jermaine Dye	.25
150	Chipper Jones	1.00
151	Melky Cabrera **RC**	4.00
152	Chris Seddon **RC**	4.00
153	Nate Schierholtz	4.00
154	Ian Kinsler **RC**	8.00
154	Ian Kinsler/SP/ Gold Background	20.00
155	Brandon Moss **RC**	4.00
155	Brandon Moss/SP/Red Hat	10.00
156	Chadd Blasko **RC**	2.00
157	Jeremy West **RC**	2.00

157	Jeremy West/SP/	
	Navy Blue Jersey	6.00
158	Sean Marshall RC	2.00
159	Ryan Sweeney	4.00
160	Matt Lindstrom RC	2.00
161	Ryan Goleski RC	4.00
162	Brett Harper RC	2.00
163	Chris Roberson RC	3.00
164	Andre Ethier	8.00
165	Ian Bladergroen RC	2.00
165	Ian Bladergroen/	
	SP/Swinging	6.00
166	James Jurries RC	2.00
167	Billy Butler RC	5.00
167	Billy Butler/SP/Black Jsy	10.00
168	Michael Rogers RC	3.00
168	Michael Rogers/SP/	
	Baseball In Hand	8.00
169	Tyler Clippard RC	10.00
170	Luis Ramirez RC	3.00
171	Casey Kotchman	2.00
172	Chris Burke	2.00
173	Dallas McPherson	2.00
174	Edwin Jackson	1.00
175	Felix Hernandez	4.00
176	Gavin Floyd	1.00
177	Guillermo Quiroz	1.00
178	Jason Kubel	1.00
179	Jeff Mathis	1.00
180	Rickie Weeks	1.00
181	Ryan Howard	3.00
182	Franklin Gutierrez	1.00
183	Jeremy Reed	5.00
184	Carlos Quentin	5.00
185	Jeff Francis	5.00
186	Nolan Ryan	6.00
187	Hank Aaron	6.00
187	Hank Aaron/SP/Red 755	15.00
188	Duke Snider	4.00
189	Mike Schmidt	5.00
190	Ernie Banks	4.00
191	Frank Robinson	3.00
192	Harmon Killebrew	4.00
193	Al Kaline	3.00
194	Rod Carew	3.00
195	Johnny Bench	4.00

Artist's Proof

Stars (1-150): 2-4X
SP's (151-195): 1-2X
Inserted 1:1

Printing Plates

No Pricing
Production one for each color.

Cut Signatures

No Pricing

Gallo's Gallery Sketches

HANK BLALOCK • TEXAS RANGERS®

		NM/M
Complete Set (20):		50.00
Common Player:		1.50
Inserted 1:15		
HA	Hank Aaron	6.00
HB	Hank Blalock	1.50
NG	Nomar Garciaparra	4.00
VG	Vladimir Guerrero	2.00

TH	Todd Helton	1.50
DJ	Derek Jeter	6.00
RJ	Randy Johnson	2.00
CJ	Chipper Jones	2.00
MPI	Mike Piazza	4.00
MP	Mark Prior	2.00
AP	Albert Pujols	6.00
AR	Alex Rodriguez	5.00
IR	Ivan Rodriguez	1.50
NR	Nolan Ryan	6.00
MS	Mike Schmidt	5.00
AS	Alfonso Soriano	2.00
SS	Sammy Sosa	4.00
IS	Ichiro Suzuki	4.00
MT	Miguel Tejada	1.50
JT	Jim Thome	4.00

Heritage Insert

JOHNNY BENCH Catcher
REDS

		NM/M
Complete Set (25):		65.00
Common Player:		2.00
Inserted 1:15		
EB	Ernie Banks	4.00
CB	Carlos Beltran	3.00
JB	Johnny Bench	4.00
HB	Hank Blalock	2.00
GB	George Brett	6.00
JC	Jose Canseco	2.00
BG	Bob Gibson	3.00
AK	Al Kaline	6.00
DM	Don Mattingly	3.00
RP	Rafael Palmeiro	3.00
JP	Jim Palmer	2.00
AP	Albert Pujols	8.00
BR	Brooks Robinson	3.00
FR	Frank Robinson	2.00
RR	Frank Robinson,	
	Brooks Robinson	3.00
RJ	Alex Rodriguez,	
	Derek Jeter	8.00
IR	Ivan Rodriguez	3.00
NR	Nolan Ryan	8.00
CS	Curt Schilling	3.00
MS	Mike Schmidt	5.00
TS	Jim Thome, Mike Schmidt	5.00
OS	Ozzie Smith	3.00
DSN	Duke Snider	3.00
DS	Darryl Strawberry	2.00
DW	Dontrelle Willis	2.00

Heritage Relics

		NM/M
Common Player:		5.00
Inserted 1:40		
GB	George Brett	12.00
JC	Jose Canseco	8.00
DM	Don Mattingly	15.00
AP	Albert Pujols	15.00
AR	Alex Rodriguez	15.00
IR	Ivan Rodriguez	8.00
NR	Nolan Ryan	20.00
OS	Ozzie Smith	8.00
DS	Darryl Strawberry	5.00
DW	Dontrelle Willis	5.00

Heritage Relic Autographs

		NM/M
Production 25 Sets		
DM	Don Mattingly	75.00
AR	Alex Rodriguez	300.00
IR	Ivan Rodriguez	
NR	Nolan Ryan	150.00

Murray Olderman Sketches

No Pricing
Production One Set

Originals Relics

FRANK THOMAS CHICAGO WHITE SOX

		NM/M
Common Player:		4.00
Inserted 1:10		
JB	Jeff Bagwell	8.00
RB	Rocco Baldelli	4.00
JBE	Josh Beckett	4.00
LB	Lance Berkman	4.00
AB	Angel Berroa	4.00
HB	Hank Blalock	4.00
HBB	Hank Blalock	8.00
MC	Miguel Cabrera	8.00
JD	Johnny Damon	8.00
RD	Ryan Drese	4.00
JG	Jason Giambi	6.00
MG	Marcus Giles	4.00
VG	Vladimir Guerrero	8.00
RH	Rich Harden	4.00
TH	Todd Helton	8.00
CJ	Chipper Jones	8.00
JL	Javy Lopez	4.00
ML	Mike Lowell	4.00
PM	Pedro J. Martinez	8.00
KM	Kazuo Matsui	6.00
LN	Laynce Nix	4.00
DO	David Ortiz	8.00
MP	Mike Piazza	8.00
MPB	Mike Piazza	8.00
MPR	Mark Prior	8.00
AP	Albert Pujols	15.00
MR	Manny Ramirez	8.00
JR	Jose Reyes	6.00
AR	Alex Rodriguez	12.00
IR	Ivan Rodriguez	8.00
AS	Alfonso Soriano	8.00
SS	Sammy Sosa	10.00
MT	Mark Teixeira	4.00
MTE	Miguel Tejada	6.00
FT	Frank Thomas	8.00
BU	B.J. Upton	4.00
BW	Bernie Williams	6.00
DW	Dontrelle Willis	4.00
KW	Kerry Wood	8.00
MY	Michael Young	4.00

Penmanship Autographs

		NM/M
Common Autograph:		10.00
JB	Jason Bartlett	10.00
TB	Taylor Buchholz	10.00
EC	Eric Chavez	15.00
FH	Felix Hernandez	30.00
AH	Aubrey Huff	15.00
JJ	Justin Jones	15.00
DM	Dallas McPherson	25.00
AR	Alex Rodriguez	250.00
VW	Vernon Wells	10.00

2005 Topps Heritage

DALLAS McPHERSON

		NM/M
Complete Set (475):		400.00
Common Player:		.40
Common SP (398-475):		4.00
SP's & Variations Inserted 1:2		
Pack (8):		5.00
Box (24):		100.00
1	Will Harridge	.40
2	Warren Giles	.40
3	Alfonso Soriano	1.00
3	Alfonso Soriano/	
	SP/Running	5.00
4	Mark Mulder	.75
5	Todd Helton/SP	5.00
6	Jason Bay	.40
6	Jason Bay/SP/	
	1956 Pirates Uniform	5.00

7	Ichiro Suzuki	2.50
7	Ichiro Suzuki/SP/	
	Squatting On-Deck	8.00
8	Jim Tracy	.40
9	Gavin Floyd	.40
10	John Smoltz	.75
11	Chicago Cubs	.50
12	Darin Erstad	.40
13	Chad Tracy	.40
14	Charles Thomas	.40
15	Miguel Tejada	.75
16	Andre Ethier	6.00
17	Jeff Francis	.40
18	Derrek Lee	.50
19	Juan Uribe	.40
20	Jim Edmonds/SP	5.00
21	Kenny Lofton	.40
22	Brad Ausmus	.40
23	Jon Garland	.40
24	Edwin Jackson	.40
25	Joe Mauer	.75
26	Wes Helms	.40
27	Brian Schneider	.40
28	Kazuo Matsui	.40
29	Tom Gordon	.40
30	Hideo Nomo/SP	4.00
31	Albert Pujols/SP	15.00
31	Albert Pujols/SP/	
	1956 Cards Uniform	15.00
32	Carl Crawford	.40
33	Vladimir Guerrero/SP	6.00
34	Nick Green	.40
35	Jay Gibbons	.40
36	Kevin Youkilis	.40
37	Billy Wagner	.40
38	Terrence Long	.40
39	Kevin Mench	.40
40	Garret Anderson	.50
41	Reed Johnson	.40
42	Reggie Sanders	.40
43	Kirk Rueter	.40
44	Jay Payton	.40
45	Tike Redman	.40
46	Mike Lieberthal	.40
47	Damian Miller	.40
48	Zach Day	.40
49	Juan Rincon	.40
50	Jim Thome	1.00
50	Jim Thome/SP/Fldg	6.00
51	Jose Guillen	.40
52	Richie Sexson	.75
53	Juan Cruz	.40
54	Byung-Hyun Kim	.40
55	Carlos Zambrano	.50
56	Carlos Lee	.40
57	Adam Dunn	.75
58	David Riske	.40
59	Carlos Guillen	.40
60	Larry Bowa	.40
61	Barry Bonds	4.00
62	Chris Woodward	.40
63	Matt DeSalvo RC	2.50
64	Brian Stavisky RC	1.00
65	Scot Shields	.40
66	J.D. Drew	.50
67	Erik Bedard	.40
68	Scott Williamson	.40
69	Mark Prior	1.00
69	Mark Prior/SP/	
	1956 Cubs Uniform	6.00
70	Ken Griffey Jr.	2.00
71	Kazuhito Tadano	.40
72	Philadelphia Phillies	.40
73	Jeremy Reed	.40
74	Ricardo Rodriguez	.40
75	Carlos Delgado	.50
76	Eric Milton	.40
77	Miguel Olivo	.40
78	Edgardo Alfonzo	.40
78	Edgardo Alfonzo/SP/	
	1956 Giants Uniform	4.00
79	Kazuhisa Ishii/SP	4.00
80	Jason Giambi	.75
81	Cliff Floyd	.40
82	Torii Hunter	.50
82	Torii Hunter/SP/	
	1956 Senators Uniform	4.00
83	Odalis Perez	.40
84	Scott Podsednik	.40
85	Cleveland Indians	.40
86	Jeff Suppan	.40
87	Ray Durham	.40
88	Tyler Clippard RC	10.00
89	Ryan Howard	2.00
90	Cincinnati Reds	.40
91	Bengie Molina	.40
92	Danny Bautista	.40
93	Eli Marrero	.40
94	Larry Bigbie	.40
95	Atlanta Braves	.40
96	Merkin Valdez	.40
97	Rocco Baldelli	.40
98	Woody Williams	.40
99	Jason Frasor	.40
100	Baltimore Orioles	.40
101	Ivan Rodriguez/SP	6.00
102	Joe Kennedy	.40
103	Mike Lowell	.50
104	Armando Benitez	.40
105	Craig Biggio	.50
106	David DeJesus	.40
107	Adrian Beltre	.75
108	Phil Nevin	.40
109	Cristian Guzman	.40

110 Jorge Posada/SP 6.00
111 Boston Red Sox .75
112 Jeff Mathis .40
113 Bartolo Colon .40
114 Alex Cintron .40
115 Russ Ortiz .40
116 Doug Mientkiewicz .40
117 Placido Polanco .40
118 Magglio Ordonez .40
118 Magglio Ordonez/SP/ 1956 White Sox Uni. 4.00
119 Chris Seddon **RC** 1.00
120 Bobby Abreu .50
121 Pittsburgh Pirates .40
122 Dallas McPherson .75
123 Rodrigo Lopez .40
124 Mark Bellhorn .40
125 Nomar Garciaparra 2.00
125 Nomar Garciaparra/SP/ 1956 Cubs Uniform 8.00
126 Sean Casey .40
127 Ronnie Belliard .40
128 Tom Goodwin .40
129 Preston Wilson .40
130 Andruw Jones/SP 5.00
131 Roberto Alomar .75
132 John Buck .40
133 Jason LaRue .40
134 St. Louis Cardinals .75
135 Alex Rodriguez/SP 10.00
135 Alex Rodriguez/SP/Fldg 10.00
136 Nate Robertson .40
137 Juan Pierre .40
138 Morgan Ensberg .40
139 Vinny Castilla .40
140 Jake Dittler 1.00
141 Chan Ho Park .40
142 Felix Hernandez 2.50
143 Jason Isringhausen .40
144 Dustan Mohr .40
145 Khalil Greene .75
146 Minnesota Twins .40
147 Vicente Padilla .40
148 Oliver Perez .40
149 Brian Giles .40
150 Shawn Green .40
151 Matt Lawton .40
152 Casey Blake .40
153 Frank Thomas .75
154 Orlando Hernandez .40
155 Eric Chavez .50
155 Eric Chavez/SP/ 1956 Kansas City Uni. 4.00
156 Chase Utley .75
157 John Olerud .40
158 Adam Eaton .40
159 Josh Fogg .40
160 Michael Tucker .40
161 Kevin Brown .40
162 Bobby Crosby .50
163 Jason Schmidt .50
164 Shannon Stewart .40
165 Tony Womack .40
166 Los Angeles Dodgers .40
167 Franklin Gutierrez .40
168 Ted Lilly .40
169 Mark Teixeira .50
170 Matt Morris .40
171 Bucky Jacobsen .40
172 Steven Doetsch **RC** 1.00
173 Jeff Weaver .40
174 Tony Graffanino .40
175 Jeff Bagwell .75
176 Carl Pavano .50
177 Junior Spivey .40
178 Carlos Silva .40
179 Tim Redding .40
180 Brett Myers .40
181 Mike Mussina .75
182 Richard Hidalgo .40
183 Nick Johnson .40
184 Lew Ford .40
185 Barry Zito .50
186 Jimmy Rollins .50
187 Jack Wilson .40
188 Chicago White Sox .40
189 Guillermo Quiroz .40
190 Mark Hendrickson .40
191 Jeremy Bonderman .40
192 Jason Jennings .40
193 Paul LoDuca .40
194 A.J. Burnett .40
195 Ken Harvey .40
196 Geoff Jenkins .40
197 Joe Mays .40
198 Jose Vidro .40
199 David Wright .75
200 Randy Johnson 1.00
201 Jeff DeVanon .40
202 Paul Byrd .40
203 David Ortiz 1.00
204 Kyle Farnsworth .40
205 Keith Foulke .40
206 Joe Crede .40
207 Austin Kearns .40
208 Jody Gerut .40
209 Shawn Chacon .40
210 Carlos Pena .40
211 Luis Castillo .40
212 Chris Denorfia **RC** 1.00
213 Detroit Tigers .40
214 Aubrey Huff .40
215 Brad Fullmer .40
216 Frank Catalanotto .40
217 Raul Ibanez .40
218 Ryan Klesko .40
219 Octavio Dotel .40
220 Robert Mackowiak .40
221 Scott Hatteberg .40
222 Pat Burrell .40
223 Bernie Williams .50
224 Kris Benson .40
225 Eric Gagne .50
226 San Francisco Giants .40
227 Roy Oswalt .40
228 Josh Beckett .50
229 Lee Mazzilli .40
230 Rickie Weeks .40
231 Troy Glaus .50
232 Chone Figgins .40
233 John Thomson .40
234 Trot Nixon .40
235 Brad Penny .40
236 Oakland Athletics .40
237 Miguel Batista .40
238 Ryan Drese .40
239 Aaron Miles .40
240 Randy Wolf .40
241 Brian Lawrence .40
242 A.J. Pierzynski .40
243 Jamie Moyer .40
244 Chris Carpenter .40
245 So Taguchi .40
246 Rob Bell .40
247 Francisco Cordero .40
248 Tom Glavine .50
249 Jermaine Dye .40
250 Cliff Lee .50
251 New York Yankees .75
252 Vernon Wells .40
253 R.A. Dickey .40
254 Larry Walker .50
255 Randy Winn .40
256 Pedro Feliz .40
257 Mark Loretta .40
258 Tim Worrell .40
259 Kip Wells .40
260 Cesar Izturis/SP 4.00
261 Carlos Beltran .75
261 Carlos Beltran/SP/Btg 6.00
262 Juan Encarnacion .40
263 Luis Gonzalez .40
264 Grady Sizemore .75
265 Paul Wilson .40
266 Mark Buehrle .40
267 Todd Hollandsworth .40
268 Orlando Cabrera .50
269 Sidney Ponson .40
270 Mike Hampton .40
271 Luis Gonzalez .50
272 Brendan Donnelly .40
273 Chipper Jones 1.00
273 Chipper Jones/SP/ Blue Background 6.00
274 Brandon Webb .40
275 Marty Cordova .40
276 Greg Maddux 2.00
277 Jose Contreras .40
278 Aaron Harang .40
279 Coco Crisp .40
280 Bobby Higginson .40
281 Guillermo Mota .40
282 Andy Pettitte .50
283 Jeremy West **RC** 3.00
284 Craig Brazell .40
285 Eric Hinske .40
286 Hank Blalock .75
286 Hank Blalock/SP/Fldg 6.00
287 B.J. Upton .75
288 Jason Marquis .40
289 Matt Herges .40
290 Ramon Hernandez .40
291 Marlon Byrd .40
292 Ryan Sweeney/SP 8.00
293 Esteban Loaiza .40
294 Al Leiter .50
295 Alex Gonzalez .40
296 Johan Santana .75
296 Johan Santana/SP/ 1956 Senators Uniform 6.00
297 Milton Bradley .40
298 Mike Sweeney .40
299 Wade Miller .40
300 Sammy Sosa 2.00
300 Sammy Sosa/SP/Blue Jsy 8.00
301 Wily Mo Pena .40
302 Tim Wakefield .40
303 Rafael Palmeiro .75
304 Rafael Furcal .40
305 David Eckstein .40
306 David Segui .40
307 Kevin Millar .40
308 Matt Clement .40
309 Wade Robinson **RC** 1.00
310 Brad Radke .40
311 Steve Finley .40
312 Lance Berkman .50
312 Lance Berkman/SP/Fldg 5.00
313 Joe Randa .40
314 Miguel Cabrera 1.00
315 Billy Koch .40
316 Alex Sanchez .40
317 Chin-Hui Tsao .40
318 Omar Vizquel .40
319 Ryan Freel .40
320 LaTroy Hawkins .40
321 Aaron Rowand .40
322 Paul Konerko .40
323 Joe Borowski .40
324 Jarrod Washburn .40
325 Jaret Wright .40
326 Johnny Damon .75
327 Corey Patterson .50
328 Travis Hafner .40
329 Shingo Takatsu .40
330 Dmitri Young .40
331 Matt Holliday .50
332 Jeff Kent .50
333 Desi Relaford .40
334 Jose Hernandez .40
335 Lyle Overbay .40
336 Jacque Jones .40
337 Termel Sledge .40
338 Victor Zambrano .40
339 Gary Sheffield .75
340 Brad Wilkerson .40
341 Ian Kinsler **RC** 5.00
342 Jesse Crain .40
343 Orlando Hudson .40
344 Laynce Nix .40
345 Jose Cruz Jr. .40
346 Edgar Renteria .50
347 Eddie Guardado .40
348 Jerome Williams .40
349 Trevor Hoffman .40
350 Mike Piazza 1.50
351 Jason Kendall .40
352 Kevin Millwood .40
353 Tim Hudson .50
353 Tim Hudson/SP/ 1956 Braves Uniform 5.00
354 Paul Quantrill .40
355 Jon Lieber .40
356 Braden Looper .40
357 Chad Cordero .40
358 Joe Nathan .40
359 Doug Davis .40
360 Ian Bladergroen **RC** 1.00
361 Val Majewski .40
362 Francisco Rodriguez .40
363 Kelvim Escobar .40
364 Marcus Giles .40
365 Darren Fenster **RC** 1.00
366 David Bell .40
367 Shea Hillenbrand .40
368 Manny Ramirez 1.00
369 Ben Broussard .40
370 Luis Ramirez **RC** 1.00
371 Dustin Hermanson .40
372 Akinori Otsuka .40
373 Chadd Blasko **RC** 1.00
374 Delmon Young .75
375 Michael Young .40
376 Bret Boone .40
377 Jake Peavy .40
378 Matt Lindstrom **RC** 1.00
379 Sean Burroughs .40
380 Rich Harden .40
381 Chris Roberson **RC** 1.00
382 John Lackey .40
383 Johnny Estrada .40
384 Matt Rogelstad **RC** 1.00
385 Toby Hall .40
386 Adam LaRoche .40
387 Bill Hall .40
388 Tim Salmon .50
389 Curt Schilling 1.00
389 Curt Schilling/SP/ Looking In 6.00
390 Michael Barrett .40
391 Jose Acevedo .40
392 Nate Schierholtz 1.00
393 J.T. Snow Jr. .40
394 Mark Redman .40
395 Ryan Madson .40
396 Kevin West **RC** 1.00
397 Ramon Ortiz .40
398 Derek Lowe 4.00
399 Kerry Wood 6.00
400 Derek Jeter 15.00
401 Livan Hernandez 4.00
402 Casey Kotchman 6.00
403 Chaz Lytle **RC** 6.00
404 Alexis Rios 5.00
405 Scott Spiezio 4.00
406 Craig Wilson 4.00
407 Felix Rodriguez 4.00
408 D'Angelo Jimenez 4.00
409 Rondell White 4.00
410 Shawn Estes 4.00
411 Troy Percival 4.00
412 Melvin Mora 4.00
413 Aramis Ramirez 6.00
414 Carl Everett 4.00
415 Elvys Quezada **RC** 6.00
416 Ben Sheets 5.00
417 Matt Stairs 4.00
418 Adam Everett 4.00
419 Jason Johnson 4.00
420 Billy Butler **RC** 10.00
421 Justin Morneau 6.00
422 Jose Reyes 6.00
423 Mariano Rivera 5.00
424 Jose Vaquedano **RC** 6.00
425 Gabe Gross 5.00
426 Scott Rolen 6.00
427 Ty Wigginton 4.00
428 James Jurries **RC** 6.00
429 Pedro J. Martinez 6.00
430 Mark Grudzielanek 4.00
431 Josh Phelps 4.00
432 Ryan Goleski **RC** 5.00
433 Mike Matheny 4.00
434 Bobby Kielty 4.00
435 Tony Batista 4.00
436 Corey Koskie 4.00
437 Brad Lidge 4.00
438 Dontrelle Willis 4.00
439 Angel Berroa 4.00
440 Jason Kubel 4.00
441 Roy Halladay 4.00
442 Brian Roberts 4.00
443 Bill Mueller 4.00
444 Adam Kennedy 4.00
445 Brandon Moss **RC** 5.00
446 Sean Burnett 4.00
447 Eric Byrnes 4.00
448 Matt Campbell **RC** 6.00
449 Ryan Webb **RC** 6.00
450 Jose Valentin 4.00
451 Jake Westbrook 4.00
452 Glen Perkins **RC** 6.00
453 Alex Gonzalez 4.00
454 Jeromy Burnitz 4.00
455 Zack Greinke 4.00
456 Sean Marshall **RC** 6.00
457 Erubiel Durazo 4.00
458 Michael Cuddyer 4.00
459 Hee Seop Choi 4.00
460 Melky Cabrera **RC** 10.00
461 Jerry Hairston Jr. 4.00
462 Moises Alou 5.00
463 Michael Rogers **RC** 6.00
464 Javy Lopez 4.00
465 Freddy Garcia 4.00
466 Brett Harper **RC** 5.00
467 Juan Gonzalez 5.00
468 Kevin Melillo **RC** 5.00
469 Todd Walker 5.00
470 C.C. Sabathia 4.00
471 Kole Strayhorn 5.00
472 Mark Kotsay 4.00
473 Javier Vazquez 4.00
474 Mike Cameron 4.00
475 Wes Swackhamer **RC** 6.00

Chrome Parallel

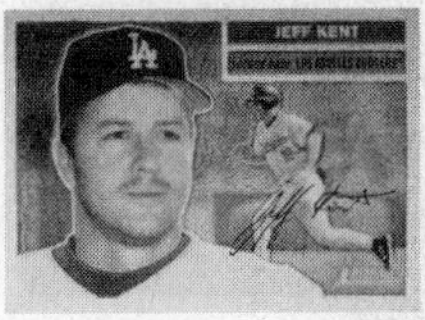

NM/M

Complete Set (110):
Common Player: 1.00
Production 1,956 Sets
Refractors: 1.5-2X
Production 556 Sets
Black Refractor: 3-5X
Production 56 Sets
THC1 Will Harridge 2.00
THC2 Warren Giles 2.00
THC3 Alex Rodriguez 10.00
THC4 Alfonso Soriano 5.00
THC5 Barry Bonds 12.00
THC6 Todd Helton 3.00
THC7 Kazuo Matsui 2.00
THC8 Garret Anderson 1.50
THC9 Mark Prior 5.00
THC10 Jim Thome 4.00
THC11 Jason Giambi 2.00
THC12 Ivan Rodriguez 4.00
THC13 Mike Lowell 1.00
THC14 Vladimir Guerrero 5.00
THC15 Adrian Beltre 2.00
THC16 Andruw Jones 2.00
THC17 Jose Vidro 1.00
THC18 Josh Beckett 1.50
THC19 Mike Sweeney 1.00
THC20 Sammy Sosa 6.00
THC21 Scott Rolen 5.00
THC22 Javy Lopez 1.50
THC23 Albert Pujols 12.00
THC24 Adam Dunn 3.00
THC25 Ken Griffey Jr. 6.00
THC26 Torii Hunter 1.50
THC27 Jorge Posada 2.00
THC28 Magglio Ordonez 1.00
THC29 Shawn Green 1.50
THC30 Frank Thomas 3.00
THC31 Barry Zito 1.50
THC32 David Ortiz 5.00
THC33 Pat Burrell 1.50
THC34 Luis Gonzalez 1.50
THC35 Chipper Jones 5.00
THC36 Hank Blalock 3.00
THC37 Rafael Palmeiro 3.00
THC38 Lance Berkman 2.00
THC39 Miguel Cabrera 5.00
THC40 Paul Konerko 1.00
THC41 Jeff Kent 1.50
THC42 Gary Sheffield 3.00
THC43 Mike Piazza 6.00
THC44 Bret Boone 1.00
THC45 Kerry Wood 5.00
THC46 Derek Jeter 12.00
THC47 Pedro J. Martinez 5.00
THC48 Jason Bay 2.00
THC49 Ichiro Suzuki 8.00
THC50 Miguel Tejada 3.00
THC51 Richie Sexson 2.00

THC52	Jeff Bagwell	3.00
THC53	Lew Ford	1.00
THC54	Randy Johnson	5.00
THC55	Carlos Beltran	3.00
THC56	Greg Maddux	6.00
THC57	Lyle Overbay	1.00
THC58	Michael Young	1.00
THC59	Curt Schilling	5.00
THC60	Jose Reyes	3.00
THC61	Dontrelle Willis	1.50
THC62	Nomar Garciaparra	6.00
THC63	Paul LoDuca	1.00
THC64	Larry Walker	2.00
THC65	Andre Ethier	8.00
THC66	Matt DeSalvo	5.00
THC67	Brian Stavisky	2.00
THC68	Tyler Clippard	20.00
THC69	Chris Seddon	3.00
THC70	Steven Doetsch	3.00
THC71	Chris Denorfia	3.00
THC72	Jeremy West	3.00
THC73	Ryan Sweeney	5.00
THC74	Ian Kinsler	10.00
THC75	Ian Bladergroen	4.00
THC76	Darren Fenster	4.00
THC77	Luis Ramirez	4.00
THC78	Chadd Blasko	2.00
THC79	Matt Lindstrom	2.00
THC80	Chris Roberson	3.00
THC81	Matt Rogelstad	4.00
THC82	Nate Schierholtz	4.00
THC83	Kevin West	4.00
THC84	Chaz Lytle	4.00
THC85	Elvys Quezada	4.00
THC86	Billy Butler	10.00
THC87	Jose Vaquedano	4.00
THC88	James Jurries	4.00
THC89	Ryan Goleski	4.00
THC90	Brandon Moss	4.00
THC91	Matt Campbell	4.00
THC92	Ryan Webb	5.00
THC93	Glen Perkins	5.00
THC94	Sean Marshall	4.00
THC95	Melky Cabrera	8.00
THC96	Michael Rogers	4.00
THC97	Brett Harper	4.00
THC98	Kevin Melillo	4.00
THC99	Kole Strayhorn	4.00
THC100	Wes Swackhamer	4.00
THC101	Rickie Weeks	2.00
THC102	Delmon Young	4.00
THC103	Kazuhito Tadano	1.00
THC104	Kazuhisa Ishii	1.00
THC105	David Wright	4.00
THC106	Eric Gagne	3.00
THC107	So Taguchi	1.00
THC108	B.J. Upton	4.00
THC109	Shingo Takatsu	1.00
THC110	Akinori Otsuka	1.00

Clubhouse Collection Relic Auto.

Production 25 Sets

LA	Luis Aparicio	165.00
EB	Ernie Banks	200.00
AK	Al Kaline	200.00
HK	Harmon Killebrew	200.00
RS	Red Schoendienst	165.00

Clubhouse Collection Relics

		NM/M
Common Player:		5.00
LA	Luis Aparicio	8.00
EB	Ernie Banks	15.00
LB	Lance Berkman	5.00
MC	Miguel Cabrera	8.00
AK	Al Kaline	15.00
HK	Harmon Killebrew	15.00
AP	Albert Pujols	20.00
MR	Manny Ramirez	8.00
AR	Alex Rodriguez	15.00
RS	Red Schoendienst	8.00
GS	Gary Sheffield	8.00
AS	Alfonso Soriano	8.00
MT	Miguel Tejada	8.00
BW	Bernie Williams	5.00
DW	Dontrelle Willis	5.00

Clubhouse Collection Dual Relics

		NM/M
Production 56 Sets		
MP	Stan Musial, Albert Pujols	85.00
KR	Al Kaline, Ivan Rodriguez	65.00
BG	Ernie Banks, Nomar Garciaparra	85.00

Flashbacks

		NM/M
Complete Set (10):		8.00
Common Player:		.50
Inserted 1:12		
HA	Hank Aaron	4.00
LA	Luis Aparicio	.50
EB	Ernie Banks	2.00
BF	Bob Feller	.50
AK	Al Kaline	1.50
DL	Don Larsen	.50
SM	Stan Musial	2.00
FR	Frank Robinson	1.00
HS	Herb Score	.50
DS	Duke Snider	1.00

Flashbacks Autographs

		NM/M
Common Player:		
Production 25 Sets		
LA	Luis Aparicio	125.00
EB	Ernie Banks	200.00
BF	Bob Feller	165.00
AK	Al Kaline	165.00
DL	Don Larsen	175.00
SM	Stan Musial	200.00
FR	Frank Robinson	200.00
HS	Herb Score	150.00

Flashbacks Relic Autos.

		NM/M
Production 25 Sets		
LA	Luis Aparicio	150.00
EB	Ernie Banks	200.00
BF	Bob Feller	175.00
AK	Al Kaline	175.00
DL	Don Larsen	175.00
SM	Stan Musial	200.00
FR	Frank Robinson	200.00
HS	Herb Score	150.00

Flashbacks Relics

		NM/M
Common Player:		8.00
Inserted 1:96		
HA	Hank Aaron	15.00
LA	Luis Aparicio	8.00
EB	Ernie Banks	15.00
BF	Bob Feller	10.00
AK	Al Kaline	15.00
DL	Don Larsen	8.00
SM	Stan Musial	15.00
FR	Frank Robinson	10.00

HS	Herb Score	8.00
DS	Duke Snider	10.00

New Age Performers

Complete Set (15):		15.00
Common Player:		1.00
Inserted 1:15		
NAP1	Alfonso Soriano	1.50
NAP2	Alex Rodriguez	3.00
NAP3	Ichiro Suzuki	3.00
NAP4	Albert Pujols	4.00
NAP5	Vladimir Guerrero	1.50
NAP6	Jim Thome	1.50
NAP7	Derek Jeter	4.00
NAP8	Sammy Sosa	2.50
NAP9	Ivan Rodriguez	1.00
NAP10	Manny Ramirez	1.50
NAP11	Todd Helton	1.00
NAP12	David Ortiz	1.50
NAP13	Gary Sheffield	1.00
NAP14	Nomar Garciaparra	2.00
NAP15	Randy Johnson	1.50

Real One Autographs

		NM/M
Production 200 Sets		
Red Ink:		1.5-2X
Production 56 Sets		
HA	Hank Aaron	275.00
JA	Joe Astroth	50.00
EB	Ernie Banks	125.00
YB	Yogi Berra	100.00
JB	Jim Brady	50.00
CD	Chuck Diering	50.00
BF	Bob Feller	70.00
JG	Jim Greengrass	50.00
MI	Monte Irvin	60.00
SJ	Spook Jacobs	50.00
FM	Fred Marsh	50.00
JM	Jake Martin	50.00
RM	Rudy Minarcin	50.00
PM	Paul Minner	50.00
BN	Bob Nelson	50.00
LP	Laurin Pepper	40.00
LPO	Leroy Powell	60.00
JSA	Jose Santiago	50.00
JS	Johnny Schmitz	50.00
DS	Duke Snider	85.00
AS	Art Swanson	50.00
BT	Bill Tremel	50.00
WW	Wally Westlake	50.00

Then and Now

		NM/M
Complete Set (10):		8.00
Common Duo:		.50
Inserted 1:15		
TN1	Hank Aaron, Ichiro Suzuki	4.00
TN2	Don Newcombe, Curt Schilling	1.50
TN3	Robin Roberts, Livan Hernandez	.50
TN4	Bob Friend, Livan Hernandez	.50
TN5	Herb Score, Randy Johnson	1.50
TN6	Whitey Ford, Jake Peavy	1.00
TN7	Jimmy Piersall, Lyle Overbay	.50
TN8	Clem Labine, Mariano Rivera	.75
TN9	Bill Bruton, Carl Crawford	.50
TN10	Eddie Yost, Bobby Abreu	.50

1956 Cuts - Cut Signatures

No Pricing
Production One Set

2005 Topps Opening Day

		NM/M
Complete Set (165):		30.00
Common Player:		.15
Pack (6):		1.00
Box (36):		30.00
1	Alex Rodriguez	1.50
2	Placido Polanco	.15
3	Torii Hunter	.25
4	Lyle Overbay	.15
5	Johnny Damon	.50
6	Mike Cameron	.15
7	Ichiro Suzuki	1.50
8	Francisco Rodriguez	.15
9	Bobby Crosby	.15
10	Sammy Sosa	1.25
11	Randy Wolf	.15
12	Jason Bay	.25
13	Mike Lieberthal	.15
14	Paul Konerko	.25
15	Brian Giles	.15
16	Luis Gonzalez	.25
17	Jim Edmonds	.40
18	Carlos Lee	.25
19	Corey Patterson	.40
20	Hank Blalock	.25
21	Sean Casey	.25
22	Dmitri Young	.25
23	Mark Mulder	.25
24	Bobby Abreu	.25
25	Jim Thome	.25
26	Jason Kendall	.15
27	Jason Giambi	.15
28	Vinny Castilla	.15
29	Tony Batista	.15
30	Ivan Rodriguez	.50
31	Craig Biggio	.25
32	Chris Carpenter	.15
33	Adrian Beltre	.40
34	Scott Podsednik	.15
35	Cliff Floyd	.15
36	Chad Tracy	.15
37	John Smoltz	.25
38	Shingo Takatsu	.15
39	Jack Wilson	.15
40	Gary Sheffield	.50
41	Lance Berkman	.25
42	Carl Crawford	.25
43	Carlos Guillen	.15
44	David Bell	.15
45	Kazuo Matsui	.15
46	Jason Schmidt	.15
47	Jason Marquis	.15
48	Melvin Mora	.15
49	David Ortiz	.50
50	Andruw Jones	.40
51	Miguel Tejada	.50
52	Bartolo Colon	.15
53	Derrek Lee	.25
54	Eric Gagne	.25
55	Miguel Cabrera	.75
56	Travis Hafner	.15
57	Jose Valentin	.15
58	Mark Prior	.75
59	Phil Nevin	.15
60	Jose Vidro	.25
61	Khalil Greene	.25
62	Carlos Zambrano	.40
63	Erubiel Durazo	.15
64	Michael Young	.15
65	Woody Williams	.15
66	Edgardo Alfonzo	.15
67	Troy Glaus	.40
68	Garret Anderson	.25
69	Richie Sexson	.40
70	Curt Schilling	.75
71	Randy Johnson	.75
72	Chipper Jones	.75
73	J.D. Drew	.25
74	Russ Ortiz	.15
75	Frank Thomas	.50
76	Jimmy Rollins	.25
77	Barry Zito	.25
78	Rafael Palmeiro	.50
79	Brad Wilkerson	.15
80	Adam Dunn	.50
81	Doug Mientkiewicz	.15
82	Manny Ramirez	.75
83	Pedro J. Martinez	.75
84	Moises Alou	.25
85	Mike Sweeney	.15
86	Boston Red Sox WC	1.00
87	Matt Clement	.15

88	Nomar Garciaparra	1.00
89	Magglio Ordonez	.15
90	Bret Boone	.15
91	Mark Loretta	.15
92	Jose Contreras	.15
93	Randy Winn	.15
94	Austin Kearns	.15
95	Ken Griffey Jr.	1.25
96	Jake Westbrook	.15
97	Kazuhito Tadano	.15
98	C.C. Sabathia	.15
99	Todd Helton	.50
100	Albert Pujols	2.00
101	Jose Molina	.15
102	Aaron Miles	.15
103	Mike Lowell	.25
104	Paul LoDuca	.15
105	Juan Pierre	.15
106	Dontrelle Willis	.40
107	Jeff Bagwell	.40
108	Carlos Beltran	.50
109	Ronnie Belliard	.15
110	Roy Oswalt	.25
111	Zack Greinke	.15
112	Steve Finley	.15
113	Kazuhisa Ishii	.15
114	Justin Morneau	.40
115	Ben Sheets	.25
116	Johan Santana	.50
117	Billy Wagner	.15
118	Mariano Rivera	.25
119	Corey Koskie	.15
120	Akinori Otsuka	.15
121	Joe Mauer	.40
122	Jacque Jones	.15
123	Joe Nathan	.15
124	Nick Johnson	.15
125	Vernon Wells	.15
126	Mike Piazza	1.00
127	Jose Guillen	.15
128	Jose Reyes	.25
129	Marcus Giles	.15
130	Javy Lopez	.15
131	Kevin Millar	.15
132	Jorge Posada	.40
133	Carl Pavano	.25
134	Bernie Williams	.40
135	Kerry Wood	.75
136	Matt Holliday	.15
137	Kevin Brown	.15
138	Derek Jeter	2.00
139	Barry Bonds	2.00
140	Jeff Kent	.25
141	Mark Kotsay	.15
142	Shawn Green	.25
143	Tim Hudson	.25
144	Shannon Stewart	.15
145	Pat Burrell	.25
146	Gavin Floyd	.15
147	Mike Mussina	.50
148	Eric Chavez	.25
149	Jon Lieber	.15
150	Vladimir Guerrero	.75
151	Vicente Padilla	.15
152	Ryan Klesko	.15
153	Jake Peavy	.25
154	Scott Rolen	.75
155	Greg Maddux	1.00
156	Edgar Renteria	.25
157	Larry Walker	.25
158	Scott Kazmir	.25
159	B.J. Upton	.25
160	Mark Teixeira	.50
161	Ken Harvey	.15
162	Alfonso Soriano	.75
163	Carlos Delgado	.40
164	Alexis Rios	.15
165	Checklist	.15

Autographs

		NM/M
	Complete Set (6):	
	Common Player:	
CC	Chad Cordero	10.00
FH	Felix Hernandez	25.00
AH	Aaron Hill	8.00
PM	Paul Maholm	8.00
OQ	Omar Quintanilla	15.00
AW	Anthony Whittington	8.00

MLB Game Worn Jersey Collection

		NM/M
	Target Retail Exclusive	
37	Vladimir Guerrero	8.00
38	Albert Pujols	15.00
39	Torii Hunter	4.00
40	Alfonso Soriano	6.00
41	Bobby Abreu	4.00
42	Moises Alou	6.00
43	Sean Burroughs	4.00
44	Shannon Stewart	4.00
45	Troy Glaus	6.00
46	Fernando Vina	4.00
47	Dan Wilson	4.00
48	Paul Konerko	4.00
49	Jimmy Rollins	6.00
50	Livan Hernandez	4.00
51	Sean Casey	4.00
52	Paul LoDuca	4.00
53	Richie Sexson	6.00
54	Aubrey Huff	4.00

2005 Topps Pack Wars

		NM/M
	Complete Set (175):	40.00
	Common Player:	.25
	Pack (7):	20.00
	Box (7):	120.00
1	Alex Rodriguez	3.00
2	Eric Chavez	.40
3	Jimmy Rollins	.40
4	Jason Bay	.50
5	Nomar Carciaparra	2.00
6	Melvin Mora	.25
7	Bobby Abreu	.50
8	Bartolo Colon	.25
9	Orlando Cabrera	1.00
10	Albert Pujols	3.00
11	Barry Zito	.40
12	Vernon Wells	.25
13	J.D. Drew	.25
14	Darin Erstad	.25
15	Manny Ramirez	1.00
16	Derrek Lee	.40
17	Juan Uribe	.25
18	Wily Mo Pena	.25
19	Jeromy Burnitz	.25
20	Dontrelle Willis	.25
21	Craig Biggio	.40
22	Cesar Izturis	.25
23	Geoff Jenkins	.25
24	Joe Mauer	.50
25	Derek Jeter	3.00
26	David Wright	1.00
27	Jose Vidro	.25
28	Bobby Crosby	.25
29	Khalil Greene	.50
30	Ichiro Suzuki	2.00
31	Reggie Sanders	.25
32	A.J. Pierzynski	.25
33	Corey Patterson	.40
34	Frank Thomas	.75
35	Craig Wilson	.25
36	Carl Crawford	.25
37	Michael Young	.25
38	Mark Kotsay	.25
39	Javier Vazquez	.25
40	Kazuo Matsui	.25
41	Lew Ford	.25
42	Corey Koskie	.25
43	Larry Walker	.50
44	Mike Lowell	.40
45	Todd Helton	.75
46	Travis Hafner	.25
47	Sean Casey	.25
48	Ken Griffey Jr.	1.50
49	Milton Bradley	.25
50	Ivan Rodriguez	.75
51	Carlos Lee	.25
52	Aramis Ramirez	.50
53	Curt Schilling	1.00
54	Russ Ortiz	.25
55	Randy Johnson	1.00
56	Preston Wilson	.25
57	Jay Gibbons	.25
58	Mike Liebenthal	.25
59	Johnny Damon	.50
60	Mark Prior	1.00
61	Freddy Garcia	.25
62	Casey Blake	.25
63	Chipper Jones	1.00
64	Carlos Guillen	.25
65	Juan Pierre	.25
66	Tom Glavine	.50
67	Alex Sanchez	.25
68	Tony Batista	.25
69	Paul LoDuca	.25
70	Hank Blalock	.75
71	Pedro Feliz	.25
72	Jim Edmonds	.50
73	Phil Nevin	.25
74	Rocco Baldelli	.25
75	Alfonso Soriano	1.00
76	David Bell	.25
77	Eric Hinske	.25
78	Jose Guillen	.25
79	Marcus Giles	.25
80	Rafael Palmeiro	.75
81	Jeff Bagwell	.75
82	Kerry Wood	1.00
83	Johan Santana	.50
84	Troy Glaus	.40

85	Andruw Jones	.50
86	Barry Bonds	3.00
87	Jermaine Dye	.25
88	Carlos Zambrano	.50
89	Aaron Rowand	.25
90	Garret Anderson	.40
91	Ryan Klesko	.25
92	Paul Konerko	.25
93	Jeff Kent	.40
94	Richie Sexson	.50
95	Lyle Overbay	.25
96	Torii Hunter	.40
97	Mike Cameron	.25
98	Eric Byrnes	.25
99	Jason Kendall	.25
100	Vladimir Guerrero	1.00
101	Johnny Estrada	.25
102	Mark Bellhorn	.25
103	Moises Alou	.40
104	Ronnie Belliard	.25
105	Adam Dunn	.75
106	Dmitri Young	.25
107	Luis Castillo	.25
108	Carlos Beltran	.75
109	Steve Finley	.25
110	Shannon Stewart	.25
111	Al Leiter	.25
112	Bernie Williams	.50
113	Roy Oswalt	.40
114	Sean Burroughs	.25
115	Randy Winn	.25
116	Tony Womack	.25
117	Jim Thome	1.00
118	Aubrey Huff	.25
119	Bret Boone	.25
120	Carlos Delgado	.40
121	Jason Schmidt	.50
122	Rafael Furcal	.25
123	Miguel Tejada	.75
124	Bill Mueller	.25
125	Pedro Martinez	1.00
126	Michael Barrett	.25
127	Jody Gerut	.25
128	Vinny Castilla	.25
129	Rondell White	.25
130	Magglio Ordonez	.25
131	Lance Berkman	.25
132	Alex Gonzalez	.25
133	Mike Sweeney	.25
134	Ben Sheets	.50
135	Jacque Jones	.25
136	Brad Wilkerson	.25
137	Cliff Floyd	.25
138	Kevin Brown	.25
139	Scott Hatteberg	.25
140	Gary Sheffield	.50
141	Justin Morneau	.50
142	Scott Podsednik	.25
143	Shawn Green	.40
144	David Ortiz	1.00
145	Josh Beckett	.50
146	Tim Hudson	.50
147	Matt Lawton	.25
148	Mark Buehrle	.25
149	Todd Walker	.25
150	Jason Giambi	.50
151	Brian Giles	.25
152	Erubiel Durazo	.25
153	Jack Wilson	.25
154	Jose Reyes	.25
155	Scott Rolen	1.00
156	Raul Ibanez	.25
157	Mark Teixeira	.50
158	Luis Gonzalez	.25
159	Javy Lopez	.25
160	Greg Maddux	1.50
161	Kevin Millar	.25
162	Jose Valentin	.25
163	C.C. Sabathia	.25
164	Carlos Pena	.25
165	Miguel Cabrera	1.00
166	Adrian Beltre	.50
167	Sammy Sosa	2.00
168	Nick Johnson	.25
169	Jorge Posada	.50
170	Mike Piazza	1.50
171	Mark Mulder	.50
172	Mark Loretta	.25
173	Edgardo Alfonzo	.25
174	Edgar Renteria	.50
175	Pat Burrell	.25

Autographs

		NM/M
	Common Autograph:	15.00
CB	Carlos Beltran	30.00
HB	Hank Blalock	20.00
AB	Aaron Boone	20.00
MC	Miguel Cabrera	25.00
EC	Eric Chavez	15.00
JE	Johnny Estrada	10.00
ZG	Zack Greinke	15.00

VM	Victor Martinez	15.00
CS	C.C. Sabathia	15.00
VW	Vernon Wells	10.00
MY	Michael Young	15.00

Collector Chips

		NM/M
	Common Player:	8.00
	Inserted 1:Box	
	Blue:	No Pricing
	Production 25 Sets	
	Red:	No Pricing
	Production 10 Sets	
2	Ichiro Suzuki	30.00
3	Jim Thome	20.00
4	Albert Pujols	30.00
5	Vladimir Guerrero	15.00
6	Derek Jeter	30.00
7	Sammy Sosa	20.00
9	Ivan Rodriguez	10.00
11	Nomar Garciaparra	20.00
12	Ken Griffey Jr.	20.00
13	Mark Prior	10.00
14	Todd Helton	10.00
15	Mike Piazza	20.00
16	Jorge Posada	10.00
17	Chipper Jones	10.00
18	Randy Johnson	15.00
19	Gary Sheffield	8.00
20	Mike Schmidt	25.00
21	Ernie Banks	20.00
22	Frank Robinson	20.00
23	Reggie Jackson	10.00
24	George Brett	25.00
25	Nolan Ryan	30.00

Cut Signatures

No Pricing

Relics

		NM/M
	Common Player:	8.00
RC	Roger Clemens	12.00
NG	Nomar Garciaparra	15.00
VG	Vladimir Guerrero	10.00
TH	Todd Helton	8.00
THB	Todd Helton	8.00
CJ	Chipper Jones	8.00
CJB	Chipper Jones	8.00
GM	Greg Maddux	10.00
PM	Pedro Martinez	8.00
RP	Rafael Palmeiro	8.00
MP	Mike Piazza	10.00
AP.	Albert Pujols	15.00
MR	Manny Ramirez	10.00
MRB	Manny Ramirez	10.00
AR	Alex Rodriguez	15.00
IR	Ivan Rodriguez	8.00
SR	Scott Rolen	10.00
GS	Gary Sheffield	8.00
AS	Alfonso Soriano	8.00
SS	Sammy Sosa	10.00
FT	Frank Thomas	8.00
JT	Jim Thome	8.00

Relic Autographs

		NM/M
	Common Autograph:	15.00
	Production 200 Sets	
CB	Carlos Beltran	40.00
HB	Hank Blalock	25.00
MC	Miguel Cabrera	30.00
EC	Eric Chavez	20.00
JE	Johnny Estrada	15.00
VM	Victor Martinez	15.00
MY	Michael Young	20.00

2005 Topps Pristine

		NM/M
	Common 1-100	.75
	Common Rookie (101-130):	1.00
	Common (131-180):	3.00
	Production 500	
	Common (181-205):	10.00
	Production 100	
	Common (206-210):	
	Production 49	
	Pack (8):	30.00
	Box (5):	125.00
1	Alex Rodriguez	3.00
2	Jake Peavy	.75

3	Bobby Crosby	.75
4	J.D. Drew	.75
5	Scott Rolen	1.50
6	Bobby Abreu	.75
7	Ken Griffey Jr.	2.50
8	Jeremy Bonderman	.75
9	Mike Sweeney	.75
10	Mark Prior	1.50
11	Tim Hudson	.75
12	Clint Barmes	.75
13	Jeff Bagwell	1.00
14	Andruw Jones	1.50
15	Carlos Delgado	.75
16	Rocco Baldelli	.75
17	Adam Dunn	1.50
18	Greg Maddux	2.00
19	Torii Hunter	.75
20	Miguel Tejada	1.50
21	Lyle Overbay	.75
22	Craig Wilson	.75
23	Scott Kazmir	.75
24	Alex Rios	.75
25	Ichiro Suzuki	3.00
26	Jorge Posada	1.00
27	Jose Reyes	.75
28	Hank Blalock	.75
29	Troy Glaus	1.00
30	Todd Helton	1.50
31	Javy Lopez	.75
32	Barry Zito	1.00
33	Jimmy Rollins	1.00
34	Mark Loretta	.75
35	Richie Sexson	1.00
36	Nick Johnson	.75
37	Ivan Rodriguez	1.00
38	Jeff Kent	.75
39	Jake Westbrook	.75
40	Carlos Beltran	1.00
41	Rich Harden	.75
42	Joe Mauer	1.00
43	Luis Gonzalez	.75
44	Frank Thomas	1.00
45	Michael Young	.75
46	Jason Schmidt	.75
47	Eric Chavez	.75
48	Vinny Castilla	.75
49	John Smoltz	1.00
50	Barry Bonds	4.00
51	Jim Edmonds	1.00
52	Edgar Renteria	.75
53	Jose Vidro	.75
54	Chipper Jones	1.50
55	Curt Schilling	1.50
56	Victor Martinez	.75
57	Josh Beckett	.75
58	Derrek Lee	1.50
59	Shawn Green	.75
60	Roger Clemens	4.00
61	Orlando Cabrera	.75
62	Mike Piazza	2.00
63	Gary Sheffield	1.00
64	Carl Crawford	.75
65	Johan Santana	1.50
66	Oliver Perez	.75
67	Manny Ramirez	1.50
68	Paul Konerko	1.00
69	Preston Wilson	.75
70	Sammy Sosa	2.00
71	Eric Gagne	.75
72	Geoff Jenkins	.75
73	Magglio Ordonez	.75
74	Kerry Wood	1.00
75	Albert Pujols	4.00
76	Roy Halladay	1.00
77	Aubrey Huff	.75
78	Nomar Garciaparra	1.50
79	Brian Roberts	.75
80	Randy Johnson	1.50
81	Pat Burrell	.75
82	Brian Giles	.75
83	Mike Mussina	1.00
84	Mark Teixeira	1.00
85	Pedro Martinez	1.50
86	Jason Bay	.75
87	Mark Buehrle	.75
88	Rafael Furcal	.75
89	Juan Pierre	.75
90	Jim Thome	1.00
91	Ben Sheets	1.00
92	Alfonso Soriano	1.50
93	Adrian Beltre	.75
94	Miguel Cabrera	1.50
95	Derek Jeter	4.00
96	Vernon Wells	.75
97	Lance Berkman	1.00
98	Hideki Matsui	2.50
99	David Ortiz	1.50
100	Vladimir Guerrero	1.50
101	Justin Verlander **RC**	3.00
102	Billy Butler **RC**	6.00
103	Wladimir Balentien **RC**	1.50
104	Jeremy West **RC**	2.00
105	Philip Humber **RC**	3.00
106	Tyler Pelland **RC**	1.00
107	Andy LaRoche **RC**	5.00
108	Hernan Iribarren **RC**	1.00
109	Luke Scott **RC**	1.00
110	Landon Powell **RC**	1.00
111	Alexander Smit **RC**	1.00
112	Ryan Garko **RC**	1.00
113	Bear Bay **RC**	1.00
114	Ian Bladergroen **RC**	1.00
115	Manny Parra **RC**	3.00
116	Andy Sides **RC**	1.00
117	Travis Chick **RC**	1.00
118	Stefan Bailie **RC**	1.00
119	Chuck Tiffany **RC**	2.00
120	Buck Coats **RC**	1.00
121	Jeff Niemann **RC**	2.00
122	Jake Postlewait **RC**	1.00
123	Matt Campbell **RC**	1.00
124	Kevin Melillo **RC**	2.00
125	Mike Morse **RC**	3.00
126	Anthony Reyes **RC**	6.00
127	Casey McGehee **RC**	1.00
128	Cody Haerther **RC**	1.00
129	Brandon McCarthy **RC**	4.00
130	Glen Perkins **RC**	2.00
131	Moises Alou	3.00
132	Nomar Garciaparra	6.00
133	Scott Rolen	6.00
134	Miguel Tejada	4.00
135	Alex Rodriguez	10.00
136	Michael Young	3.00
137	Tim Hudson	5.00
138	Troy Glaus	3.00
139	Eric Chavez	3.00
140	David Ortiz	10.00
141	Andruw Jones	5.00
142	Richie Sexson	5.00
143	Jim Thome	5.00
144	Javy Lopez	3.00
145	Lance Berkman	3.00
146	Gary Sheffield	5.00
147	Dontrelle Willis	4.00
148	Curt Schilling	5.00
149	Jorge Posada	5.00
150	Vladimir Guerrero	8.00
151	Adam Dunn	5.00
152	Ryan Drese	3.00
153	Hank Blalock	3.00
154	Kerry Wood	4.00
155	Alfonso Soriano	5.00
156	Aramis Ramirez	4.00
157	Mark Mulder	4.00
158	Paul Konerko	4.00
159	Jim Edmonds	6.00
160	Roger Clemens	10.00
161	Mariano Rivera	6.00
162	Rafael Palmeiro	6.00
163	Mark Teixeira	6.00
164	Eric Gagne	3.00
165	Sammy Sosa	8.00
166	Brett Myers	3.00
167	Kazuhisa Ishii	3.00
168	Ken Harvey	3.00
169	Johnny Estrada	3.00
170	Todd Helton	5.00
171	Rich Harden	3.00
172	Johnny Damon	6.00
173	Manny Ramirez	6.00
174	Benito Santiago	3.00
175	Albert Pujols	15.00
176	Chipper Jones	.75
177	Miguel Cabrera	8.00
178	Jeff Bagwell	5.00
179	Ivan Rodriguez	5.00
180	Mike Piazza	8.00
181	Chip Cannon **RC**	15.00
182	Erik Cordier **RC**	15.00
183	Billy Butler **RC**	30.00
184	C.J. Smith **RC**	10.00
185	Alfonso Soriano	25.00
186	Bobby Livingston **RC**	15.00
187	Wladimir Balentien **RC**	15.00
188	Mike Morse **RC**	15.00
189	Wes Swackhamer **RC**	15.00
190	Justin Verlander **RC**	50.00
191	Jake Postlewait **RC**	15.00
192	Michael Rogers **RC**	20.00
193	Matt Campbell **RC**	20.00
194	Eric Nielsen **RC**	15.00
195	Gary Sheffield	30.00
196	Glen Perkins **RC**	25.00
197	Kevin Melillo **RC**	20.00
198	Chad Orvella **RC**	10.00
199	Jeff Niemann **RC**	25.00
200	Alex Rodriguez	180.00
201	Brian Stavisky **RC**	15.00
202	Brian Miller **RC**	15.00
203	Landon Powell **RC**	20.00
204	Philip Humber **RC**	20.00
205	Mariano Rivera	100.00
206	Curt Schilling	50.00
207	Nolan Ryan	150.00

Red

Red (1-130):	2-4X
Production 66	
Red (131-210):	No Pricing
Production Three Sets	

Printing Plates

No Pricing
Production one set for each color.

Uncirculated Bronze

Bronze (1-130):	1.5-3X
Production 375	
Bronze (131-180):	1-1.5X
Production 100	
Bronze (181-205):	No Pricing
Production 18	
Bronze (206-210):	No Pricing
Production 10	

Doubles Act Autographs

No Pricing
Production Five Sets

Fielder's Choice

No Pricing
Production Nine Sets

In The Name Patch

No Pricing
One card for each letter.

Personal Endorsements

		NM/M
Common		
Production 497 Sets		
Uncirculated:		No Pricing
Production Three Sets		
MB	Milton Bradley	10.00
BB	Billy Butler	20.00
LC	Lance Cormier	5.00
SE	Scott Elbert	8.00
JF	Josh Fields	5.00
LH	Livan Hernandez	12.00
JPH	J.P. Howell	8.00
PH	Philip Humber	10.00
ZJ	Zach Jackson	8.00
BJ	Blake Johnson	5.00
BL	Bobby Livingston	8.00
CO	Chad Orvella	5.00
GP	Glen Perkins	15.00
LP	Landon Powell	8.00
MR	Mike Rodriguez	5.00
MRO	Mark Rogers	8.00
TS	Terrmel Sledge	5.00
CJS	C.J. Smith	5.00
JS	Jeremy Sowers	10.00
JV	Justin Verlander	20.00
Uncommon		
Production 247 Sets		
JB	Jason Bay	25.00
AB	Aaron Boone	10.00
MB	Matt Bush	15.00
BB	Billy Butler	20.00
CC	Chip Cannon	8.00
CE	Carl Erskine	10.00
HK	Harmon Killebrew	25.00
BL	Bobby Livingston	8.00
ML	Mark Loretta	8.00
DO	David Ortiz	40.00
CW	Craig Wilson	10.00
DW	David Wright	60.00
DZ	Don Zimmer	15.00
Rare		
Production 97 Sets		
GA	Garret Anderson	15.00
EB	Ernie Banks	50.00
SM	Stan Musial	50.00
MR	Mariano Rivera	100.00
TS	Tom Seaver	30.00
AS	Alfonso Soriano	25.00

Personal Pieces

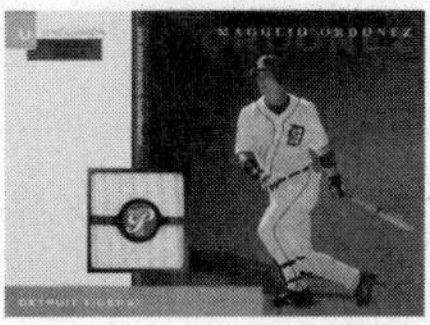

		NM/M
Common		
Production 425		
Uncirculated:		No Pricing
Production Three Sets		
JB	Jeff Bagwell	5.00
RB	Ronnie Belliard	3.00
AB	Adrian Beltre	3.00
LB	Lance Berkman	5.00
HB	Hank Blalock	5.00
EC	Eric Chavez	3.00
RC	Roger Clemens	12.00
BC	Bobby Crosby	5.00
JDD	J.D. Drew	3.00
AD	Adam Dunn	5.00
JE	Jim Edmonds	5.00
JES	Johnny Estrada	3.00
JG	Jason Giambi	5.00
JGI	Jay Gibbons	3.00
SG	Shawn Green	3.00
VG	Vladimir Guerrero	8.00
CG	Cristian Guzman	3.00
THA	Travis Hafner	3.00
TH	Todd Helton	5.00
THU	Tim Hudson	5.00
AJ	Andruw Jones	5.00
CJ	Chipper Jones	8.00
JL	Javy Lopez	3.00
ML	Mark Loretta	3.00
MLO	Mike Lowell	3.00
PM	Pedro Martinez	8.00
VM	Victor Martinez	3.00
KM	Kevin Millar	3.00
MM	Mark Mulder	5.00
BM	Brett Myers	3.00
LN	Laynce Nix	3.00
MP	Mike Piazza	8.00
MPR	Mark Prior	5.00
AP	Albert Pujols	15.00
BR	Brad Radke	3.00
MR	Manny Ramirez	8.00
ER	Edgar Renteria	3.00
MRI	Mariano Rivera	6.00
SR	Scott Rolen	5.00
CS	Curt Schilling	6.00
GS	Gary Sheffield	5.00
AS	Alfonso Soriano	5.00
MTE	Mark Teixeira	5.00
MT	Miguel Tejada	5.00
FT	Frank Thomas	8.00
JT	Jim Thome	5.00
BJU	B.J. Upton	3.00
BW	Bernie Williams	5.00
KW	Kerry Wood	5.00
BZ	Barry Zito	3.00
Uncommon		
Production 200		
CB	Carlos Beltran	5.00
AB	Adrian Beltre	3.00
MC	Miguel Cabrera	8.00
RC	Roger Clemens	12.00
JE	Jim Edmonds	5.00
EG	Eric Gagne	3.00
TG	Troy Glaus	3.00
TH	Torii Hunter	3.00
AJ	Andruw Jones	5.00
CJ	Chipper Jones	8.00
MM	Mark Mulder	5.00
MO	Magglio Ordonez	3.00
DO	David Ortiz	8.00
MP	Mike Piazza	8.00
JP	Jorge Posada	5.00
AP	Albert Pujols	15.00
MR	Manny Ramirez	8.00
MRI	Mariano Rivera	6.00
AR	Alex Rodriguez	15.00
IR	Ivan Rodriguez	5.00
SR	Scott Rolen	5.00
CS	Curt Schilling	6.00
AS	Alfonso Soriano	5.00
SS	Sammy Sosa	8.00
JT	Jim Thome	5.00
Rare		
CB	Carlos Beltran	10.00
BB	Barry Bonds	40.00
RC	Roger Clemens	20.00
JD	Johnny Damon	12.00
EG	Eric Gagne	8.00
VG	Vladimir Guerrero	10.00
TH	Todd Helton	10.00
PM	Pedro Martinez	10.00
AP	Albert Pujols	25.00
AR	Alex Rodriguez	25.00

Power Core

No Pricing	
Production 3-10	
Power Stick:	No Pricing
Production One Set	

Selective Swatch

No Pricing
Production One Set

2005 Topps Pristine Legends

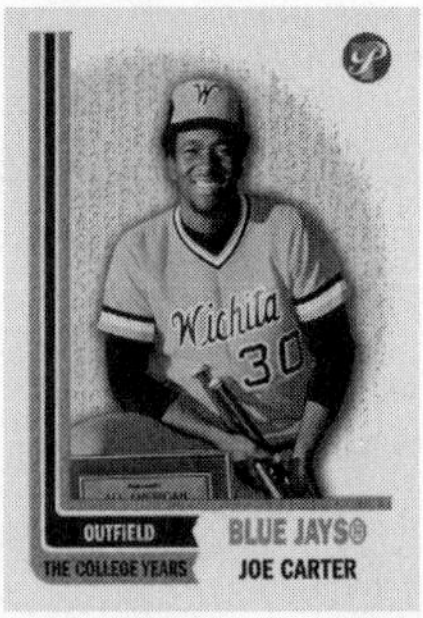

		NM/M
Complete Set (140):		
Common Player:		1.00
Common SP (101-125):		2.00
Production 1,999		
Common SP (126-135):		3.00
Production 999		
Common SP (136-140):		4.00
Production 499		
Pack (8):		30.00
Box (5):		120.00
1	Vida Blue	1.00
2	Bert Blyleven	1.00
3	Joe Carter	1.00
4	Bill Buckner	1.00
5	Luis Aparicio	1.00
6	Ernie Banks	2.50
7	Wade Boggs	2.00
8	George Brett	4.00
9	Lou Brock	2.00
10	Rod Carew	2.00
11	Gary Carter	1.00
12	Andre Dawson	1.00
13	Dennis Eckersley	1.00
14	Rollie Fingers	1.00
15	Steve Garvey	1.00
16	Dwight Gooden	1.00
17	Rich "Goose" Gossage	1.00
18	Ron Guidry	1.00
19	Keith Hernandez	1.00

20	Charlie Hough	1.00
21	Bo Jackson	2.50
22	Monte Irvin	2.00
23	Reggie Jackson	2.00
24	Ferguson Jenkins	1.00
25	Ralph Kiner	1.00
26	Juan Marichal	1.00
27	Stan Musial	4.00
28	Tony Oliva	1.00
29	Jim Palmer	1.50
30	Dave Parker	1.00
31	Gaylord Perry	1.00
32	Jimmy Piersall	1.00
33	Johnny Podres	1.00
34	Brooks Robinson	2.00
35	Frank Robinson	2.00
36	Nolan Ryan	5.00
37	Tom Seaver	2.00
38	Ozzie Smith	3.00
39	Duke Snider	2.00
40	Bobby Thomson	1.00
41	Carl Yastrzemski	3.00
42	Maury Wills	1.00
43	Robin Yount	3.00
44	Matt Williams	1.00
45	Orel Hershiser	1.00
46	Tim McCarver	1.00
47	Don Newcombe	1.00
48	Paul O'Neill	1.00
49	Al Kaline	2.00
50	Harmon Killebrew	2.00
51	Dave Kingman	1.00
52	Ken Griffey	1.00
53	George Foster	1.00
54	Mark Fidrych	1.00
55	Orlando Cepeda	1.00
56	Don Larsen	1.00
57	Bill Madlock	1.00
58	Dale Murphy	1.50
59	Graig Nettles	1.00
60	Phil Niekro	1.00
61	Al Oliver	1.00
62	Harold Reynolds	1.00
63	Bobby Richardson	1.00
64	Mike Scott	1.00
65	Dave Stewart	1.00
66	Rick Sutcliffe	1.00
67	Bruce Sutter	1.50
68	Luis Tiant	1.00
69	Bob Watson	1.00
70	Walt Weiss	1.00
71	Don Zimmer	1.00
72	Tommy John	1.00
73	Ray Knight	1.00
74	Jack Morris	1.00
75	Mickey Rivers	1.00
76	Lee Smith	1.00
77	Darryl Strawberry	1.00
78	David Justice	1.00
79	Wally Joyner	1.00
80	Jimmy Key	1.00
81	John Kruk	1.00
82	Greg Luzinski	1.00
83	Mookie Wilson	1.00
84	Wilbur Wood	1.00
85	Tim Raines	1.00
86	Jim Rice	1.00
87	Tony Armas	1.00
88	Harold Baines	1.00
89	Bucky Dent	1.00
90	Darrell Evans	1.00
91	Cecil Fielder	1.00
92	Jose Cruz	1.00
93	Dave Concepcion	1.00
94	Ron Cey	1.00
95	Davey Lopes	1.00
96	Boog Powell	1.00
97	Buddy Bell	1.00
98	George Bell	1.00
99	Bert Campaneris	1.00
100	Chet Lemon	1.00
101	Bo Jackson	4.00
102	Will Clark	2.00
103	Cecil Fielder	2.00
104	Ron Cey	2.00
105	Tony Gwynn	5.00
106	Orel Hershiser	2.00
107	Jimmy Key	2.00
108	Paul Molitor	3.00
109	Pete Incaviglia	2.00
110	Wally Joyner	2.00
111	Dave Kingman	2.00
112	Ron Guidry	2.00
113	Ron Darling	2.00
114	Mookie Wilson	2.00
115	Reggie Jackson	3.00
116	Walt Weiss	2.00
117	Joe Carter	2.00
118	Cory Snyder	2.00
119	Dave Winfield	3.00
120	Terry Steinbach	2.00
121	Matt Williams	2.00
122	Ozzie Smith	5.00
123	Jack McDowell	2.00
124	Bob Horner	2.00
125	Don Kessinger	2.00
126	Minnie Minoso	3.00
127	Cecil Kaiser	3.00
128	Buck O'Neil	3.00
129	Monte Irvin	4.00
130	Jim Gilliam	3.00
131	Josh Gibson	4.00
132	Ernie Banks	6.00
133	Don Newcombe	3.00
134	Red Moore	3.00
135	Willie Pope	3.00
136	Gary Carter	4.00
137	Bo Jackson	6.00
138	George Brett	8.00
139	Joe Carter	4.00
140	Nolan Ryan	8.00

Refractor

Refractor (1-100):	1-1.5X
Production 549	
Refractor (101-125):	1.5-2X
Production 199	
Refractor (126-135):	1.5-2.5X
Production 99	
Refractor (136-140):	No Pricing
Production 25	

Refractors Gold Die-Cut

Gold (1-100):	3-4X
Gold (101-135):	1-2.5X
Gold (136-140):	1-1.5X
Production 65 Sets	

Printing Plates

No Pricing
One set produced per color.

SuperFractor

No Pricing
Production One Set

Celebrity Threads

NM/M

Inserted 1:18
Refractor: No Pricing
Production 25 Sets

MM	Marilyn Monroe	75.00
EP	Elvis Presley	65.00

Leading Indicators

TOTAL BASES LEADER – 1978
JIM RICE RED SOX

NM/M

Common Player:	4.00
Refractor:	No Pricing
Production one or 25.	

WB	Wade Boggs	10.00
LB	Lou Brock	
RC	Rod Carew	8.00
AD	Andre Dawson	8.00
BF	Bob Feller	10.00
CF	Cecil Fielder	8.00
GF	George Foster	4.00
TG	Tony Gwynn	10.00
AK	Al Kaline	12.00
DK	Dave Kingman	6.00
RM	Roger Maris	35.00
DM	Don Mattingly	15.00
DBM	Dale Murphy	10.00
TO	Tony Oliva	6.00
PO	Paul O'Neill	10.00
DP	Dave Parker	4.00
GP	Gaylord Perry	4.00
TR	Tim Raines	8.00
TR2	Jim Rice	6.00
JR	Jim Rice	6.00
NR	Nolan Ryan	20.00
MS	Mike Scott	10.00
TS	Tom Seaver	10.00
DS	Darryl Strawberry	6.00
MW	Maury Wills	10.00
CY	Carl Yastrzemski	15.00

Personal Endorsements

NM/M

Common Autograph:	10.00
Gold:	No Pricing
Production 25 Sets	

JA	Jim Abbott	15.00
LA	Luis Aparicio	15.00
BB	Bert Blyleven	15.00

GB	George Brett	50.00
GC	Gary Carter	15.00
RD	Ron Darling	15.00
AD	Andre Dawson	15.00
DE	Dennis Eckersley	15.00
DWE	Darrell Evans	15.00
CF	Carlton Fisk	25.00
GF	George Foster	10.00
GG	Rich "Goose" Gossage	10.00
BG	Bobby Grich	10.00
KH	Keith Hernandez	12.00
BJ	Bo Jackson	60.00
RJ	Reggie Jackson	50.00
AK	Al Kaline	40.00
DL	Don Larsen	15.00
JM	Jack McDowell	10.00
SM	Stan Musial	50.00
GN	Graig Nettles	15.00
JO	Jesse Orosco	10.00
JP	Jim Palmer	15.00
JAP	Jimmy Piersall	15.00
CR	Cal Ripken Jr.	125.00
BR	Brooks Robinson	30.00
NR	Nolan Ryan	90.00
DS	Duke Snider	40.00
EW	Earl Weaver	15.00
CY	Carl Yastrzemski	50.00
RY	Robin Yount	50.00

Signature Marks

NM/M

No Pricing
Production One Set

RR	Sugar Ray Robinson (12/05 Auction)	1,000

Title Threads

NM/M

Common Player:	4.00
Refractors:	No Pricing
Production 25 Sets	

WB	Wade Boggs	10.00
GC	Gary Carter	6.00
JC	Joe Carter	6.00
OC	Orlando Cepeda	8.00
BD	Bucky Dent	6.00
LD	Lenny Dykstra	6.00
RF	Rollie Fingers	8.00
GF	George Foster	4.00
CS	Cesar Geronimo	6.00
GG	Rich "Goose" Gossage	6.00
KG	Ken Griffey Sr.	6.00
OH	Orel Hershiser	8.00
WH	Willie Horton	10.00
MI	Monte Irvin	12.00
DJ	David Justice	6.00
JK	Jimmy Key	6.00
EK	Ed Kranepool	6.00
TM	Tim McCarver	6.00
PO	Paul O'Neill	10.00
JP	Jim Palmer	8.00
DS	Darryl Strawberry	6.00
MW	Mookie Wilson	4.00

Valuable Performances

KEITH HERNANDEZ MVP 1979 CARDINALS

NM/M

Common Player:	4.00
Refractor:	No Pricing
Production one of 25.	

YB	Yogi Berra	15.00
JC	Jose Canseco	10.00
AD	Andre Dawson	6.00
DE	Dennis Eckersley	8.00
CF	Cecil Fielder	8.00
SG	Steve Garvey	6.00
KH	Keith Hernandez	4.00
RJ	Reggie Jackson	10.00
HK	Harmon Killebrew	12.00
DBM	Don Mattingly	15.00
JM	Joe Morgan	6.00
DM	Dale Murphy	15.00
SM	Stan Musial	15.00
DP	Dave Parker	4.00
JR	Jim Rice	8.00
CR	Cal Ripken Jr.	25.00
FR	Frank Robinson	8.00
MS	Mike Schmidt	15.00
CY	Carl Yastrzemski	15.00
RY	Robin Yount	8.00

2005 Topps Retired Signature Edition

GIBSON — St. Louis Cardinals

NM/M

Complete Set (110):	150.00
Common Player:	1.00
Pack (5):	30.00
Box (5):	125.00

1	Josh Gibson	1.00
2	Andre Dawson	1.00
3	Al Kaline	2.00
4	Andy Van Slyke	1.00
5	Brett Butler	1.00
6	Bob Gibson	1.50
7	Bo Jackson	2.00
8	Carlton Fisk	1.00
9	Chuck Knoblauch	1.00
10	Cal Ripken Jr.	6.00
11	Carl Yastrzemski	3.00
12	Tom Niedenfuer	1.00
13	Dennis Eckersley	1.00
14	Darryl Strawberry	1.00
15	Dwight Gooden	1.00
16	Davey Johnson	1.00
17	Don Mattingly	3.00
18	Dave Winfield	1.50
19	Don Zimmer	1.00
20	Ernie Banks	2.00
21	George Brett	3.00
22	Gary Carter	1.00
23	Gregg Jefferies	1.00
24	Harold Baines	1.00
25	Ryne Sandberg	2.00
26	Howard Johnson	1.00
27	Jim Abbott	1.00
28	Johnny Bench	2.00
29	Jay Buhner	1.00
30	Johnny Podres	1.00
31	Jose Canseco	1.50
32	Keith Hernandez	1.00
33	Lou Brock	1.00
34	Lou Whitaker	1.00
35	Mark Fidrych	1.00
36	Orlando Cepeda	1.00
37	Ozzie Smith	2.00
38	Paul O'Neill	1.00
39	Reggie Jackson	1.50
40	Sid Fernandez	1.00
41	Tony Gwynn	2.00
42	Tim Raines	1.00
43	Tom Seaver	1.50
44	Vida Blue	1.00
45	Brady Anderson	1.00
46	Bob Brenly	1.00
47	Bob Feller	1.50
48	Bill Mazeroski	1.00
49	Brooks Robinson	1.50
50	Harmon Killebrew	1.50
51	Bob Welch	1.00
52	Carl Erskine	1.00
53	Dale Murphy	1.50
54	Denny McClain	1.00
55	Dave Magadan	1.00
56	Duke Snider	1.50
57	Ed Kranepool	1.00
58	Frank Robinson	1.50

No.	Player	Price
59	Jesus Alou	1.00
60	Joe Girardi	1.00
61	John Kruk	1.00
62	Jim Leyland	1.00
63	Juan Marichal	1.00
64	Johnny Pesky	1.00
65	Ken Singleton	1.00
66	Jesse Orosco	1.00
67	Matty Alou	1.00
68	Monte Irvin	1.00
69	Matt Williams	1.00
70	Pedro Guerrero	1.00
71	Ron Blomberg	1.00
72	Rod Carew	1.50
73	Rafael Santana	1.00
74	Ralph Kiner	1.00
75	Wade Boggs	1.00
76	Roger Craig	1.00
77	Robin Yount	2.00
78	Steve Carlton	1.00
79	Shawon Dunston	1.00
80	Steve Garvey	1.00
81	Stan Musial	3.00
82	Travis Fryman	1.00
83	Tito Fuentes	1.00
84	Mike Cuellar	1.00
85	Roberto Clemente	4.00
86	Whitey Ford	1.50
87	Yogi Berra	2.00
88	Atlee Hammaker	1.00
89	Bill Freehan	1.00
90	Brian Cashman	1.00
91	Bobby Richardson	1.00
92	Bob Boone	1.00
93	Charlie Hough	1.00
94	Glenn Hubbard	1.00
95	Grady Little	1.00
96	Jimmy Piersall	1.00
97	Jim Frey	1.00
98	Jerry Grote	1.00
99	Jim Leyritz	1.00
100	Nolan Ryan	5.00
101	Jim Kaat	1.00
102	Joe Pepitone	1.00
103	J.R. Richard	1.00
104	John Candelaria	1.00
105	Bill "Moose" Skowron	1.00
106	Rick Cerone	1.00
107	Ron Santo	1.00
108	Rick Dempsey	1.00
109	Roy White	1.00
110	Tippy Martinez	1.00

Black

Black (1-110): 4-6X
Production 54 Sets

Gold

Gold (1-110): 2-4X
Production 500 Sets

Holographic

No Pricing
Production One Set

Autographs

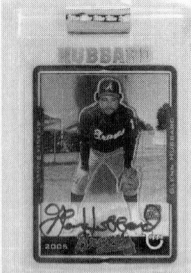

NM/M
Common Autograph: 10.00

JAA	Jim Abbott	20.00
JA	Jesus Alou	15.00
MA	Matty Alou	15.00
BA	Brady Anderson	15.00
HB	Harold Baines	15.00
EB	Ernie Banks	150.00
JB	Johnny Bench	200.00
YB	Yogi Berra	200.00
RB	Ron Blomberg	15.00
VB	Vida Blue	25.00
WB	Wade Boggs	50.00
BRB	Bob Boone	20.00
DLB	Daryl Boston	10.00
BEB	Bob Brenly	10.00
GB	George Brett	150.00
LB	Lou Brock	25.00
JCB	Jay Buhner	25.00
BB	Brett Butler	20.00
JRC	John Candelaria	15.00
JC	Jose Canseco	50.00
RCC	Rod Carew	30.00
SC	Steve Carlton	35.00
GC	Gary Carter	20.00
BC	Brian Cashman	85.00
OC	Orlando Cepeda	15.00
RC	Rick Cerone	15.00
RLC	Roger Craig	15.00
MC	Mike Cuellar	15.00
RD	Ron Darling	15.00
AD	Andre Dawson	25.00
RRD	Rick Dempsey	15.00
BD	Bob Dernier	20.00
SD	Shawon Dunston	35.00
CE	Carl Erskine	30.00
BF	Bob Feller	30.00
SF	Sid Fernandez	20.00
CF	Carlton Fisk	30.00
BAF	Bill Freehan	10.00
JF	Jim Frey	15.00
TDF	Travis Fryman	15.00
TF	Tito Fuentes	15.00
REG	Ron Gant	25.00
SG	Steve Garvey	20.00
BG	Bob Gibson	150.00
DG	Dwight Gooden	20.00
JG	Jerry Grote	20.00
PG	Pedro Guerrero	15.00
TG	Tony Gwynn	100.00
AH	Atlee Hammaker	10.00
TH	Toby Harrah	10.00
KH	Keith Hernandez	20.00
CH	Charlie Hough	10.00
GH	Glenn Hubbard	10.00
MI	Monte Irvin	50.00
BJ	Bo Jackson	100.00
RJ	Reggie Jackson	150.00
GJ	Gregg Jefferies	20.00
HJ	Howard Johnson	25.00
JLK	Jim Kaat	15.00
AK	Al Kaline	40.00
HK	Harmon Killebrew	100.00
RK	Ralph Kiner	35.00
EK	Ed Kranepool	15.00
JK	John Kruk	20.00
TL	Tony LaRussa	20.00
JL	Jim Leyland	15.00
JJL	Jim Leyritz	15.00
GL	Grady Little	15.00
JRL	Jim Lonborg	15.00
DJM	Dave Magadan	15.00
JM	Juan Marichal	25.00
TM	Tippy Martinez	10.00
DM	Don Mattingly	140.00
BM	Bill Mazeroski	45.00
DDM	Denny McLain	20.00
DBM	Dale Murphy	30.00
TN	Tom Niedenfuer	10.00
PO	Paul O'Neill	40.00
JO	Jesse Orosco	10.00
JP	Joe Pepitone	20.00
JMP	Johnny Pesky	20.00
JAP	Jimmy Piersall	20.00
JJP	Johnny Podres	50.00
TR	Tim Raines	25.00
JR	J.R. Richard	20.00
BCR	Bobby Richardson	20.00
CR	Cal Ripken Jr.	180.00
BR	Brooks Robinson	80.00
FR	Frank Robinson	60.00
NR	Nolan Ryan	250.00
RS	Ryne Sandberg	90.00
RFS	Rafael Santana	10.00
RES	Ron Santo	30.00
TS	Tom Seaver	100.00
MS	Bill "Moose" Skowron	15.00
OS	Ozzie Smith	125.00
ZS	Zane Smith	15.00
DS	Duke Snider	60.00
DES	Darryl Strawberry	50.00
BW	Bob Welch	15.00
LW	Lou Whitaker	35.00
RW	Roy White	10.00
MW	Matt Williams	30.00
DW	Dave Winfield	50.00
CY	Carl Yastrzemski	120.00
AY	Anthony Young	10.00
RY	Robin Yount	125.00
DZ	Don Zimmer	30.00

Co-Signers

NM/M
Some not priced.

Code	Players	Price
BS	Wade Boggs, Ryne Sandberg/49	140.00
BF	Johnny Bench, Carlton Fisk/49	125.00
GF	Bob Gibson, Whitey Ford/49	100.00

2005 Topps Total

Barry Bonds

NM/M

Complete Set (770):		120.00
Common Player:		.15
Pack (10):		1.00
Box (36):		35.00

No.	Player	Price
1	Rafael Furcal	.15
2	Tony Clark	.15
3	Hideki Matsui	1.25
4	Zach Day	.15
5	Garret Anderson	.40
6	B.J. Surhoff	.15
7	Trevor Hoffman	.15
8	Kenny Lofton	.15
9	Ross Gload	.15
10	Jorge Cantu	.15
11	Joel Pineiro	.15
12	Alex Cintron	.15
13	Mike Matheny	.15
14	Rod Barajas	.15
15	Ray Durham	.15
16	Danys Baez	.15
17	Brian Schneider	.15
18	Tike Redman	.15
19	Ricardo Rodriguez	.15
20	Mike Sweeney	.15
21	Greg Myers	.15
22	Chone Figgins	.15
23	Brian Lawrence	.15
24	Joe Nathan	.15
25	Placido Polanco	.15
26	Yadier Molina	.15
27	Gary Bennett	.15
28	Yorvit Torrealba	.15
29	Javier Valentin	.15
30	Jason Giambi	.25
31	Brandon Claussen	.15
32	Miguel Olivo	.15
33	Josh Bard	.15
34	Ramon Hernandez	.15
35	Geoff Jenkins	.15
36	Bobby Kielty	.15
37	Luis A. Gonzalez	.15
38	Benito Santiago	.15
39	Brandon Inge	.15
40	Mark Prior	.50
41	Mike Lieberthal	.15
42	Toby Hall	.15
43	Brad Ausmus	.15
44	Damian Miller	.15
45	Mark Kotsay	.15
46	John Buck	.15
47	Oliver Perez	.25
48	Matt Morris	.25
49	Raul Chavez	.15
50	Randy Johnson	.50
51	David Bush	.15
52	Jose Macias	.15
53	Paul Wilson	.15
54	Wilfredo Ledezma	.15
55	J.D. Drew	.25
56	Pedro Martinez	.50
57	Josh Towers	.15
58	Jamie Moyer	.15
59	Scott Elarton	.15
60	Ken Griffey Jr.	1.00
61	Steve Trachsel	.15
62	Bubba Crosby	.15
63	Michael Barrett	.15
64	Odalis Perez	.15
65	B.J. Upton	.25
66	Eric Bruntlett	.15
67	Carlos Zambrano	.15
68	Brandon League	.15
69	Carlos Silva	.15
70	Lyle Overbay	.25
71	Runelvys Hernandez	.15
72	Brad Penny	.15
73	Ty Wigginton	.15
74	Orlando Hudson	.15
75	Roy Oswalt	.25
76	Jason LaRue	.15
77	Ismael Valdez	.15
78	Calvin Pickering	.15
79	Bill Hall	.15
80	Carl Crawford	.15
81	Tomas Perez	.15
82	Joe Kennedy	.15
83	Chris Woodward	.15
84	Jason Lane	.15
85	Steve Finley	.15
86	Jeff Francis	.15
87	Felipe Lopez	.15
88	Chan Ho Park	.15
89	Joe Crede	.15
90	Jose Vidro	.15
91	Casey Kotchman	.25
92	Brandon Backe	.15
93	Mike Hampton	.15
94	Ryan Dempster	.15
95	Wily Mo Pena	.25
96	Matt Holliday	.15
97	A.J. Pierzynski	.15
98	Jason Jennings	.15
99	Eli Marrero	.15
100	Carlos Beltran	.40
101	Scott Kazmir	.25
102	Kenny Rogers	.15
103	Roy Halladay	.25
104	Alex Cora	.15
105	Richie Sexson	.25
106	Ben Sheets	.25
107	Bartolo Colon	.25
108	Eddie Perez	.15
109	Vicente Padilla	.15
110	Sammy Sosa	1.00
111	Mark Ellis	.15
112	Woody Williams	.15
113	Todd Greene	.15
114	Nook Logan	.15
115	Francisco Rodriguez	.15
116	Miguel Batista	.15
117	Livan Hernandez	.15
118	Chris Aguila	.15
119	Coco Crisp	.15
120	Jose Reyes	.25
121	Ricky Ledee	.15
122	Brad Radke	.15
123	Carlos Guillen	.15
124	Paul Bako	.15
125	Tom Glavine	.25
126	Chad Moeller	.15
127	Mark Buehrle	.15
128	Casey Blake	.15
129	Juan Rivera	.15
130	Preston Wilson	.15
131	Nate Robertson	.15
132	Julio Franco	.15
133	Derek Lowe	.15
134	Rob Bell	.15
135	Javy Lopez	.25
136	Javier Vazquez	.25
137	Desi Relaford	.15
138	Danny Graves	.15
139	Josh Fogg	.15
140	Bobby Crosby	.25
141	Ramon Castro	.15
142	Jerry Hairston Jr.	.15
143	Morgan Ensberg	.15
144	Brandon Webb	.25
145	Jack Wilson	.15
146	Bill Mueller	.15
147	Troy Glaus	.25
148	Armando Benitez	.15
149	Adam LaRoche	.15
150	Hank Blalock	.40
151	Ryan Franklin	.15
152	Kevin Millwood	.15
153	Jason Marquis	.15
154	Dewon Brazelton	.15
155	Al Leiter	.15
156	Garrett Atkins	.15
157	Todd Walker	.15
158	Kris Benson	.15
159	Eric Milton	.15
160	Bret Boone	.15
161	Matthew LeCroy	.15
162	Chris Widger	.15
163	Ruben Gotay	.15
164	Craig Monroe	.15
165	Travis Hafner	.25
166	Vance Wilson	.15
167	Jason Grabowski	.15
168	Tim Salmon	.25
169	Henry Blanco	.15
170	Josh Beckett	.25
171	Jake Westbrook	.15
172	Paul LoDuca	.15
173	Julio Lugo	.15
174	Juan Cruz	.15
175	Mark Mulder	.25
176	Juan Castro	.15
177	Damion Easley	.15
178	LaTroy Hawkins	.15
179	Jon Lieber	.25
180	Vernon Wells	.25
181	Jeff DaVanon	.15
182	Dustan Mohr	.15
183	Ryan Freel	.15
184	Doug Davis	.15
185	Sean Casey	.25
186	Robb Quinlan	.15
187	J.D. Closser	.15
188	Tim Wakefield	.15
189	Brian Jordan	.15
190	Adam Dunn	.40
191	Antonio Perez	.15
192	Brett Tomko	.15
193	John Flaherty	.15
194	Michael Cuddyer	.15

195	Ronnie Belliard	.15
196	Tony Womack	.15
197	Jason Johnson	.15
198	Victor Santos	.15
199	Dan Haren	.15
200	Derek Jeter	1.50
201	Brian Anderson	.15
202	Carlos Pena	.15
203	Jaret Wright	.15
204	Paul Byrd	.15
205	Shannon Stewart	.15
206	Chris Carpenter	.15
207	Matt Stairs	.15
208	Brad Hawpe	.15
209	Bobby Higginson	.15
210	Torii Hunter	.25
211	Shawn Green	.25
212	Todd Hollandsworth	.15
213	Scott Erickson	.15
214	C.C. Sabathia	.15
215	Mike Mussina	.40
216	Jason Kendall	.15
217	Todd Pratt	.15
218	Danny Kolb	.15
219	Tony Armas	.15
220	Edgar Renteria	.25
221	Dave Roberts	.15
222	Luis Rivas	.15
223	Adam Everett	.15
224	Jeff Cirillo	.15
225	Orlando Hernandez	.15
226	Ken Harvey	.15
227	Corey Patterson	.25
228	Humberto Cota	.15
229	A.J. Burnett	.25
230	Roger Clemens	1.50
231	Joe Randa	.15
232	David Dellucci	.15
233	Troy Percival	.15
234	Dustin Hermanson	.15
235	Eric Gagne	.25
236	Terry Tiffee	.15
237	Tony Graffanino	.15
238	Jayson Werth	.15
239	Michael Sweeney	.15
240	Chipper Jones	.75
241	Aramis Ramirez	.40
242	Frank Catalanotto	.15
243	Mike Maroth	.15
244	Kelvim Escobar	.15
245	Bobby Abreu	.25
246	Kyle Lohse	.15
247	Jason Isringhausen	.15
248	Jose Lima	.15
249	Adrian Gonzalez	.15
250	Alex Rodriguez	1.50
251	Ramon Ortiz	.15
252	Frank Menechino	.15
253	Keith Ginter	.15
254	Kip Wells	.15
255	Dmitri Young	.15
256	Craig Biggio	.25
257	Ramon E. Martinez	.15
258	Jason Bartlett	.15
259	Brad Lidge	.15
260	Brian Giles	.25
261	Luis Terrero	.15
262	Miguel Ojeda	.15
263	Rich Harden	.25
264	Jacque Jones	.15
265	Marcus Giles	.25
266	Carlos Zambrano	.25
267	Michael Tucker	.15
268	Wes Obermueller	.15
269	Peter Orr	.50
270	Jim Thome	.50
271	Omar Vizquel	.25
272	Jose Valentin	.15
273	Juan Uribe	.15
274	Doug Mirabelli	.15
275	Jeff Kent	.25
276	Brad Wilkerson	.15
277	Chris Burke	.25
278	Endy Chavez	.15
279	Richard Hidalgo	.15
280	John Smoltz	.25
281	Jarrod Washburn	.15
282	Larry Bigbie	.15
283	Edgardo Alfonzo	.15
284	Cliff Lee	.15
285	Carlos Lee	.25
286	Olmedo Saenz	.15
287	Tomokazu Ohka	.15
288	Ruben Sierra	.15
289	Nick Swisher	.15
290	Frank Thomas	.40
291	Aaron Cook	.15
292	Cody McKay	.15
293	Hee Seop Choi	.15
294	Carl Pavano	.25
295	Scott Rolen	.50
296	Matt Kata	.15
297	Terrence Long	.15
298	Jimmy Gobble	.15
299	Jason Repko	.15
300	Manny Ramirez	.50
301	Dan Wilson	.15
302	Jhonny Peralta	.15
303	John Mabry	.15
304	Adam Melhuse	.15
305	Kerry Wood	.50
306	Ryan Langerhans	.15
307	Antonio Alfonseca	.15
308	Marco Scutaro	.15
309	Jamey Carroll	.15
310	Lance Berkman	.25
311	Willie Harris	.15
312	Phil Nevin	.25
313	Gregg Zaun	.15
314	Michael Ryan	.15
315	Zack Greinke	.15
316	Ted Lilly	.15
317	David Eckstein	.15
318	Tony Torcato	.15
319	Robert Mackowiak	.15
320	Mark Teixeira	.40
321	Jason Phillips	.15
322	Jeremy Reed	.15
323	Bengie Molina	.15
324	Termel Sledge	.15
325	Justin Morneau	.40
326	Sandy Alomar Jr.	.15
327	Jon Garland	.25
328	Jay Payton	.15
329	Tino Martinez	.25
330	Jason Bay	.25
331	Jeff Conine	.15
332	Shawn Chacon	.15
333	Angel Berroa	.15
334	Reggie Sanders	.15
335	Kevin Brown	.15
336	Brady Clark	.15
337	Casey Fossum	.15
338	Raul Ibanez	.15
339	Derrek Lee	.40
340	Victor Martinez	.25
341	Kazuhisa Ishii	.15
342	Royce Clayton	.15
343	Trot Nixon	.25
344	Eric Young	.15
345	Aubrey Huff	.15
346	Brett Myers	.25
347	Joey Gathright	.15
348	Mark Grudzielanek	.15
349	Scott Spiezio	.15
350	Eric Chavez	.25
351	Einar Diaz	.15
352	Dallas McPherson	.25
353	John Thomson	.15
354	Neifi Perez	.15
355	Larry Walker	.25
356	Billy Wagner	.25
357	Mike Cameron	.15
358	Jimmy Rollins	.25
359	Kevin Mench	.15
360	Joe Mauer	.25
361	Jose Molina	.15
362	Joe Borchard	.15
363	Kevin Cash	.15
364	Jay Gibbons	.15
365	Khalil Greene	.25
366	Justin Leone	.15
367	Eddie Guardado	.15
368	Mike Lamb	.15
369	Matt Riley	.15
370	Luis Gonzalez	.25
371	Alfredo Amezaga	.15
372	J.J. Hardy	.15
373	Hector Luna	.15
374	Greg Aquino	.15
375	Jim Edmonds	.25
376	Joe Blanton	.15
377	Russell Branyan	.15
378	J.T. Snow	.15
379	Magglio Ordonez	.25
380	Rafael Palmeiro	.40
381	Andruw Jones	.25
382	David DeJesus	.15
383	Marquis Grissom	.15
384	Bobby Hill	.15
385	Kazuo Matsui	.15
386	Mark Loretta	.15
387	Chris Shelton	.15
388	Johnny Estrada	.15
389	Adam Hyzdu	.15
390	Nomar Garciaparra	1.00
391	Mark Teahen	.15
392	Chris Capuano	.15
393	Ben Broussard	.15
394	Daniel Cabrera	.15
395	Jeremy Bonderman	.25
396	Darin Erstad	.25
397	Alex S. Gonzalez	.15
398	Kevin Millar	.15
399	Freddy Garcia	.15
400	Alfonso Soriano	.50
401	Koyie Hill	.15
402	Omar Infante	.15
403	Alex Gonzalez	.15
404	Pat Burrell	.25
405	Wes Helms	.15
406	Junior Spivey	.15
407	Joe Mays	.15
408	Jason Stanford	.15
409	Gil Meche	.15
410	Tim Hudson	.25
411	Chase Utley	.25
412	Matt Clement	.25
413	Nick Green	.15
414	Jose Vizcaino	.15
415	Ryan Klesko	.15
416	Vinny Castilla	.15
417	Brian Roberts	.40
418	Geronimo Gil	.15
419	Gary Matthews	.15
420	Jeff Weaver	.15
421	Jerome Williams	.15
422	Andy Pettitte	.40
423	Randy Wolf	.15
424	D'Angelo Jimenez	.15
425	Moises Alou	.25
426	Eric Byrnes	.15
427	Mark Redman	.15
428	Jermaine Dye	.15
429	Cory Lidle	.15
430	Jason Schmidt	.25
431	Jason W. Smith	.15
432	Jose Castillo	.15
433	Pokey Reese	.15
434	Matt Lawton	.15
435	Jose Guillen	.25
436	Craig Counsell	.15
437	Jose Hernandez	.15
438	Braden Looper	.15
439	Scott Hatteberg	.15
440	Gary Sheffield	.40
441	Gabe Gross	.15
442	Chris Gomez	.15
443	Dontrelle Willis	.40
444	Jamey Wright	.15
445	Rocco Baldelli	.15
446	Bernie Williams	.25
447	Sean Burroughs	.15
448	Willie Bloomquist	.15
449	Luis Castillo	.15
450	Mike Piazza	1.00
451	Ryan Drese	.15
452	Pedro Feliz	.15
453	Horacio Ramirez	.15
454	Luis Matos	.15
455	Craig Wilson	.15
456	Russ Ortiz	.15
457	Xavier Nady	.15
458	Hideo Nomo	.25
459	Miguel Cairo	.15
460	Mike Lowell	.25
461	Corky Miller	.15
462	Bobby Madritsch	.15
463	Jose Contreras	.15
464	Johnny Damon	.75
465	Miguel Cabrera	.50
466	Eric Hinske	.15
467	Marlon Byrd	.15
468	Aaron Miles	.15
469	Ramon Vazquez	.15
470	Michael Young	.15
471	Alex Sanchez	.15
472	Shea Hillenbrand	.15
473	Jeff Bagwell	.40
474	Erik Bedard	.15
475	Jake Peavy	.40
476	Jody Gerut	.15
477	Randy Winn	.15
478	Kevin Youkilis	.15
479	Eric Dubose	.15
480	David Wright	.75
481	Wilson Valdez	.15
482	Cliff Floyd	.15
483	Jose Mesa	.25
484	Doug Mientkiewicz	.15
485	Jorge Posada	.40
486	Sidney Ponson	.15
487	David Krynzel	.15
488	Octavio Dotel	.15
489	Matt Treanor	.15
490	Johan Santana	.40
491	John Patterson	.15
492	So Taguchi	.15
493	Carl Everett	.15
494	Jason Dubois	.15
495	Albert Pujols	1.50
496	Kirk Rueter	.15
497	Geoff Blum	.15
498	Juan Encarnacion	.15
499	Mark Hendrickson	.15
500	Barry Bonds	2.00
501	Cesar Izturis	.15
502	David Wells	.15
503	Jorge Julio	.15
504	Cristian Guzman	.15
505	Juan Pierre	.15
506	Adam Eaton	.15
507	Nick Johnson	.25
508	Mike Redmond	.15
509	Daryle Ward	.15
510	Adrian Beltre	.25
511	Laynce Nix	.15
512	Reed Johnson	.15
513	Jeremy Affeldt	.15
514	R.A. Dickey	.15
515	Alex Rios	.15
516	Orlando Palmeiro	.15
517	Mark Belhorn	.15
518	Adam Kennedy	.15
519	Curtis Granderson	.15
520	Todd Helton	.40
521	Aaron Boone	.15
522	Milton Bradley	.25
523	Timoniel Perez	.15
524	Jeff Suppan	.15
525	Austin Kearns	.15
526	Charles Thomas	.15
527	Bronson Arroyo	.15
528	Roger Cedeno	.15
529	Russ Adams	.15
530	Barry Zito	.25
531	Bob Wickman	.15
532	Deivi Cruz	.15
533	Mariano Rivera	.40
534	J.J. Davis	.15
535	Greg Maddux	1.00
536	Ryan Vogelsong	.15
537	Josh Phelps	.15
538	Scott Hairston	.15
539	Vladimir Guerrero	.75
540	Ivan Rodriguez	.50
541	David Newhan	.15
542	David Bell	.15
543	Lew Ford	.15
544	Grady Sizemore	.25
545	David Ortiz	.75
546	Jose Cruz Jr.	.15
547	Aaron Rowand	.15
548	Marcus Thames	.15
549	Scott Podsednik	.25
550	Ichiro Suzuki	1.25
551	Eduardo Perez	.15
552	Chris Snyder	.15
553	Corey Koskie	.15
554	Miguel Tejada	.50
555	Orlando Cabrera	.25
556	Rondell White	.15
557	Wade Miller	.15
558	Rodrigo Lopez	.15
559	Chad Tracy	.15
560	Paul Konerko	.25
561	Wil Cordero	.15
562	John McDonald	.15
563	Jason Ellison	.15
564	Jason Michaels	.15
565	Melvin Mora	.25
566	Ryan Church	.15
567	Ryan Ludwick	.15
568	Erubiel Durazo	.15
569	Noah Lowry	.15
570	Curt Schilling	.50
571	Esteban Loaiza	.15
572	Freddy Sanchez	.15
573	Rich Aurilia	.15
574	Travis Lee	.15
575	Dennis Tankersley, Chris George	.15
576	Jason Christiansen, Kevin Correia	.15
577	Ryan Bukvich, Randy Williams	.15
578	Terry Agams, Gavin Floyd	.15
579	Seth Etherton, Dan Meyer	.15
580	Justin Lehr, Derrick Turnbow	.15
581	Mike Gosling, Brad Halsey	.15
582	Jim Mecir, Logan Kensing	.15
583	Brad Hennessey, Jeff Fassero	.15
584	Jason Grilli, John Adkins	.15
585	Jesse Crain, Juan Rincon	.15
586	Jaime Cerda, Nate Field	.15
587	Bartolome Fortunato, Jae Weong Seo	.15
588	Frank Brooks, Yhency Brazoban	.15
589	Jamie Walker, Ugueth Urbina	.15
590	Bret Prinz, Scott Proctor	.15
591	Bob Howry, Jason Davis	.15
592	Amaury Telemaco, Tim Worrell	.15
593	Jose Acevedo, Kent Mercker	.15
594	Chris Hammond, Scott Linebrink	.15
595	Fernando Nieve, John Franco	.15
596	Mike Lincoln, Randy Flores	.15
597	Joe Borowski, Kyle Farnsworth	.15
598	Jesus Colome, Lance Carter	.15
599	Abe Alvarez, Lenny DiNardo	.15
600	Chad Bradford, Kiko Calero	.15
601	David Aardsma, Jim Brower	.15
602	Geoff Geary, Ryan Madson	.15
603	Ben Howard, Nate Bump	.15
604	Chin-Hui Tsao, Jason Young	.15
605	Aaron Harang, Ryan Wagner	.15
606	Rick Bauer, Steve Kline	.15
607	Lance Cormier, Randy Choate	.15
608	Jon Leicester, Todd Wellemeyer	.15
609	Jason Frasor, Vinnie Chulk	.15
610	Brian Fuentes, Scott Dohmann	.15
611	Matt Ginter, Tyler Yates	.15
612	Cory Stewart, Salomon Torres	.15
613	Cal Eldred, Mike Myers	.15
614	Carlos Almanzar, Doug Brocail	.15
615	George Sherrill, J.J. Putz	.15
616	Bruce Chen, Matt Riley	.15
617	Ben Weber, David Weathers	.15
618	Dennys Reyes, Rudy Seanez	.15
619	Ricardo Rincon, Tim Harikkala	.15
620	D.J. Carrasco, Shawn Camp	.15
621	Allan Simpson, Javier Lopez	.15
622	Glendon Rusch, Mike Remlinger	.15

623	Kevin Gryboski, Roman Colon	.15
624	Chris Reitsma, Tom Martin	.15
625	Chad Qualls, Dan Wheeler	.15
626	Brooks Kieschnick, Matt Wise	.15
627	Justin Speier, Kerry Ligtenberg	.15
628	Francisco Cordero, Frank Francisco	.15
629	Matt Thornton, Rafael Soriano	.15
630	Mike Stanton, Steve Karsay	.15
631	Mike MacDougal, Scott Sullivan	.15
632	Brian Bruney, Oscar Villarreal	.15
633	Jeff Bennett, Mike Adams	.15
634	Dave Borkowski, Eddy Rodriguez	.15
635	David Riske, Rafael Betancourt	.15
636	Gary Glover, Jorge De La Rosa	.15
637	Justin Wayne, Matt Perisho	.15
638	Jeff Bajenaru, Luis Vizcaino	.15
639	Erasmo Ramirez, Ron Mahay	.15
640	John Grabow, Mike Gonzalez	.15
641	J.C. Romero, Matt Guerrier	.15
642	Brandon Duckworth, Tim Redding	.15
643	Franklin Nunez, Travis Harper	.15
644	Matt Herges, Tyler Walker	.15
645	Elmer Dessens, Wilson Alvarez	.15
646	Anastacio Martinez, Mark Malaska	.15
647	Gary Knotts, Roberto Novoa	.15
648	Jairo Garcia, Justin Duchscherer	.15
649	Aaron Rakers, Todd Williams	.15
650	Paul Quantrill, Tom Gordon	.15
651	Brandon Lyon, Shawn Estes	.15
652	Gustavo Chacin, Justin Miller	.15
653	John Lackey, Scot Shields	.15
654	Bobby Seay, Jorge Sosa	.15
655	Chad Cordero, Luis Ayala	.15
656	Julio Mateo, Ron Villone	.15
657	Byung-Hyun Kim, Matt Mantei	.15
658	Cliff Politte, Damaso Marte	.15
659	Joe Valentine, Luke Hudson	.15
660	John Riedling, Todd Jones	.15
661	Aaron Heilman, Heath Bell	.15
662	Akinori Otsuka, Blaine Neal	.15
663	Joe Horgan, Joey Eischen	.15
664	Grant Balfour, J.D. Durbin	.15
665	Alan Embree, Mike Timlin	.15
666	Keith Foulke	.15
667	Aaron Fultz, Rheal Cormier	.15
668	Kevin Gregg, Scott Dunn	.15
669	Franklyn German, Steve Coyler	.15
670	Scott Eyre, Wayne Franklin	.15
671	Brian Meadows, Mike Johnston	.15
672	Guillermo Mota, Tim Spooneybarger	.15
673	B.J. Ryan, Jason Grimsley	.15
674	Neal Cotts, Shingo Takatsu	.15
675	Felix Heredia, Mike DeJean	.15
676	Brian Shackelford, Josh Hancock	.15
677	Jon Rauch, T.J. Tucker	.15
678	Brian Shouse, Nick Regilio	.15
679	Julian Tavarez, Ray King	.15
680	Mike Wuertz, Stephen Randolph	.15
681	Gabe White, Jorge Vasquez	.15
682	Jose Valverde, Mike Koplove	.15
683	Arthur Rhodes, Scott Sauerbeck	.15
684	Felix Rodriguez, Tanyon Sturtze	.15
685	Duaner Sanchez, Giovanni Carrara	.15
686	Chad Harville, Mike Gallo	.15
687	Dave Williams, Sean Burnett	.15
688	Scott Atchison, Shigetoshi Hasegawa	.15
689	Claudio Vargas, Francis Beltran	.15
690	Brendan Donnelly, Esteban Yan	.15
691	Ervin Santana, Jeff Mathis	.15
692	Bill Bray, Clint Everts	.15
693	Jason Kubel, Trevor Plouffe	.15
694	Andy Marte, Jake Stevens	.15
695	Aaron Hill, Chad Gaudin	.15
696	Carlos Quentin, Jesus Cota	.15
697	Chris Young, Thomas Diamond	.15
698	Dan Johnson, Omar Quintanilla	.15
699	John Maine, Val Majewski	.15
700	James Houser, Jonny Gomes	.15
701	David Murphy, Hanley Ramirez	.25
702	Chris Lambert, Rick Ankiel	.25
703	Angel Guzman, Felix Pie	.15
704	Merkin Valdez, Nate Schierholtz	.15

705	Arnie Munoz, Gio Gonzalez	.15
706	Felix Hernandez, Travis Blackley	.15
707	Edwin Encarnacion, Tony Blanco	.15
708	Justin Germano, Tim Stauffer	.15
709	Jeremy Guthrie, Jeremy Sowers	
710	Jorge Cortes, Tom Gorzelanny	
711	Logan Kensing, Taylor Tankersley	
712	Neil Walker, Paul Maholm	.15
713	Carlos Hernandez, Willy Taveras	.50
714	Greg Golson, Ryan Howard	1.00
715	Blake DeWitt, Edwin Jackson	.15
716	Dan Putnam, Huston Street	.15
717	Mark Rogers, Rickie Weeks	.25
718	Phillip Hughes, Robinson Cano	.40
719	Jay Rainville, Kyle Waldrop	.15
720	Craig Brazell, Yusmeiro Petit	
721	Baltazar Lopez, Matt Brown **RC**	.25
722	Brett Price, Jerry Owens **RC**	.50
723	Dan Uggla, Kyle Nichols **RC**	10.00
724	Francisco Rosario, Jayce Tingler	.25
725	Eulogio de la Cruz, Tony Giarratano **RC**	.25
726	Matt Campbell, Shane Costa **RC**	.25
727	Bill McCarthy, Martin Prado **RC**	.25
728	Edinson Volquez, Ian Kinsler **RC**	4.00
729	Lorenzo Scott, Luis Ramirez **RC**	.25
730	Chris Seddon, Elliot Johnson **RC**	.75
731	Chris Dickerson, Thomas Pauly **RC**	.15
732	Jason Motte, Stuart Pomeranz **RC**	.25
733	Jose Vaquedano, Stefan Bailie **RC**	.25
734	D.J. Houlton, Wade Robinson **RC**	.25
735	Matt DeSalvo, Melky Cabrera **RC**	1.00
736	Brian Stavisky, Landon Powell **RC**	.25
737	Scott Mathieson, Scott Mitchinson **RC**	.50
738	Bear Bay, Sean Marshall **RC**	.50
739	Brandon McCarthy, Pedro Lopez **RC**	1.50
740	Alexander Smit, Jair Jurrjens **RC**	2.00
741	Matt Rogelstad, Ryan Feierabend **RC**	.25
742	Adam Boeve, Nate McLouth **RC**	1.00
743	Kevin Melillo, Michael Rogers **RC**	.25
744	Heath Totten, Matthew Kemp **RC**	2.00
745	Trevor Hutchinson, Yorman Bazardo **RC**	.15
746	Jesse Gutierrez, Tyler Pelland **RC**	.25
747	Jeremy West, Willy Mota **RC**	.25
748	Ryan Barbo, Ryan Goleski **RC**	.50
749	Bryan Triplett, Jared Gothreaux **RC**	.25
750	Glen Perkins, Kevin West **RC**	.25
751	Michael Esposito, Zachary Parker **RC**	.25
752	Brian Miller, Ryan Sweeney	.25
753	Buck Coats, Casey McGehee **RC**	.25
754	Nate Cabrera, Zachary Cline **RC**	.15
755	Bobby Livingston, Mike Morse **RC**	.25
756	Brendan Ryan, Wes Swackhamer **RC**	.25
757	John Hudgins, Nick Masset **RC**	.25
758	George Kottaras, Peeter Ramos **RC**	.25
759	Elvys Quezada, T.J. Beam **RC**	.25
760	Dana Eveland, Travis Hinton **RC**	.25
761	Chris Vines, James Jurries **RC**	.25
762	Humberto Sanchez, Justin Verlander **RC**	2.00
763	Ian Bladergroen, Shawn Bowman **RC**	.50
764	J.B. Thurmond, Pat Misch **RC**	.25

765	Christian Colonel, Neil Wilson **RC**	.25
766	Checklist 1	.15
767	Checklist 2	.15
768	Checklist 3	.15
769	Checklist 4	.15
770	Checklist 5	.15

Press Plates

	NM/M
Common Card Front P. Plate:	25.00
Common Card Back P. Plate:	15.00
Stars not priced.	
Production one set per color (4)	

Silver

Stars:	1-3X
Inserted 1:1	

Award Winners

DAVID ORTIZ

TOTAL AWARD WINNER

	NM/M
Complete Set (30):	15.00
Common Player:	.25
Inserted 1:10	
AW1	Barry Bonds	2.00
AW2	Vladimir Guerrero	.75
AW3	Roger Clemens	2.00
AW4	Johan Santana	.75
AW5	Jason Bay	.25
AW6	Bobby Crosby	.25
AW7	Eric Gagne	.40
AW8	Mariano Rivera	.50
AW9	Albert Pujols	.50
AW10	Mark Teixeira	.50
AW11	Mark Loretta	.25
AW12	Alfonso Soriano	.75
AW13	Jack Wilson	.25
AW14	Miguel Tejada	.50
AW15	Adrian Beltre	.40
AW16	Melvin Mora	.25
AW17	Barry Bonds	2.00
AW18	Jim Edmonds	.50
AW19	Bobby Abreu	.40
AW20	Manny Ramirez	.75
AW21	Gary Sheffield	.50
AW22	Vladimir Guerrero	.75
AW23	Johnny Estrada	.25
AW24	Victor Martinez	.25
AW25	Ivan Rodriguez	.50
AW26	Livan Hernandez	.25
AW27	David Ortiz	.75
AW28	Bobby Cox	.25
AW29	Buck Showalter	.25
AW30	Barry Bonds	2.00

Domination

	NM/M
Complete Set (30):	15.00
Common Player:	.25
Inserted 1:10	
40	Mark Prior	.75
50	Randy Johnson	.75
56	Pedro Martinez	.75
60	Ken Griffey Jr.	1.00
100	Carlos Beltran	.50
110	Sammy Sosa	1.50
147	Troy Glaus	.50
150	Hank Blalock	.50
180	Vernon Wells	.25
190	Adam Dunn	.50
200	Derek Jeter	2.00
230	Roger Clemens	2.00
250	Alex Rodriguez	1.50
260	Brian Giles	.25
270	Jim Thome	.75
280	Frank Thomas	.50
290	Manny Ramirez	.75
300	Manny Ramirez	.75
345	Aubrey Huff	.25
350	Eric Chavez	.25
400	Alfonso Soriano	.75
465	Miguel Cabrera	.50
490	Johan Santana	.50
495	Albert Pujols	2.00
500	Barry Bonds	2.00
510	Adrian Beltre	.40
520	Todd Helton	.50
575	Vladimir Guerrero	.50
540	Ivan Rodriguez	.50
545	David Ortiz	.75
554	Miguel Tejada	.50

Domination Autograph

Production 10
No Pricing

Production

Total Production

GIANTS

Barry Bonds

	NM/M
Complete Set (10):	8.00
Common Player:	.40
Inserted 1:15	
AB	Adrian Beltre	.40
BB	Barry Bonds	2.00
VG	Vladimir Guerrero	.75
TH	Todd Helton	.50
AP	Albert Pujols	2.00
MR	Manny Ramirez	.75
AR	Alex Rodriguez	1.50
AS	Alfonso Soriano	.75
MT	Miguel Tejada	.50
JT	Jim Thome	.75

Signatures

	NM/M
Common Autograph:	8.00
BB	Brian Bruney	8.00
RC	Robinson Cano	35.00
JG	Joey Gathright	10.00
ZG	Zack Greinke	12.00
BM	Brett Myers	12.00
TT	Terry Tiffee	15.00
DW	David Wright	50.00

Team Checklists

Topps Total TEAM SET GIANTS

	NM/M
Complete Set (30):	8.00
Common Player:	.15
3	Miguel Tejada	.50
6	Frank Thomas	.50
8	Victor Martinez	.25
9	Todd Helton	.50
10	Ivan Rodriguez	.50
11	Miguel Cabrera	.50
12	Roger Clemens	1.00
13	Zack Greinke	.15
14	Vladimir Guerrero	.50
16	Ben Sheets	.25
17	Johan Santana	.50
18	Carlos Beltran	.25
19	Alex Rodriguez	1.00
20	Eric Chavez	.25
21	Jim Thome	.50
22	Jason Bay	.25
23	Brian Giles	.25
24	Barry Bonds	1.50
25	Ichiro Suzuki	1.00
26	Albert Pujols	1.00
27	Carl Crawford	.50
28	Alfonso Soriano	.50
29	Roy Halladay	.25
30	Jose Vidro	.15
7	Adam Dunn	.50
5	Kerry Wood	.50
1	Luis Gonzalez	.25
2	John Smoltz	.25
4	David Ortiz	.50
15	Eric Gagne	.25

Total Topps

	NM/M
Complete Set (20):	12.00
Common Player:	.25

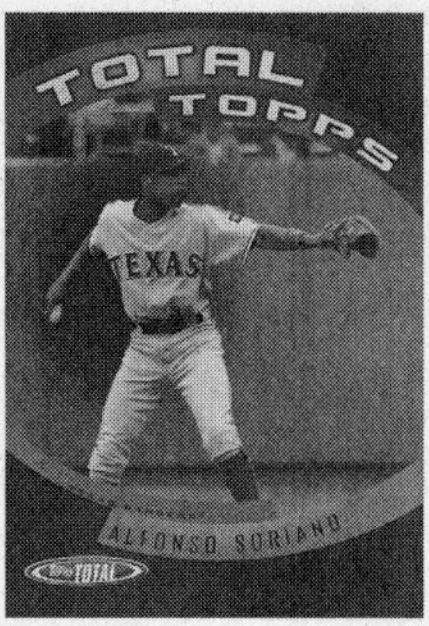

Inserted 1:15

CB	Carlos Beltran	.50
AB	Adrian Beltre	.40
BB	Barry Bonds	2.00
EC	Eric Chavez	.25
RC	Roger Clemens	2.00
VG	Vladimir Guerrero	.75
TH	Todd Helton	.50
DJ	Derek Jeter	2.00
RJ	Randy Johnson	.75
GM	Greg Maddux	1.00
MP	Mike Piazza	1.00
AP	Albert Pujols	2.00
MR	Manny Ramirez	.75
AR	Alex Rodriguez	1.50
IR	Ivan Rodriguez	.50
JS	Johan Santana	.50
AS	Alfonso Soriano	.75
SS	Sammy Sosa	1.50
MT	Miguel Tejada	.50
JT	Jim Thome	.50

2005 Topps Rookie Cup

NM/M

Complete Set (160):	35.00
Common Player (1-150):	.15
Common Rookie Auto. (151-160):	8.00
Inserted 1:62	
Pack (7):	4.00
Box (24):	75.00

1	Pat Corrales	.15
2	Ron Santo	.25
3	Joe Torre	.40
4	Boog Powell	.15
5	Tom Tresh	.15
6	Jonny Gomes	.15
7	Rico Carty	.15
8	Bert Campaneris	.15
9	Tony Oliva	.25
10	Ron Swoboda	.15
11	Tony Perez	.40
12	Joe Morgan	.40
13	Davey Johnson	.15
14	Cleon Jones	.15
15	Tom Seaver	.75
16	Rod Carew	.50
17	Rick Monday	.15
18	Johnny Bench	.75
19	Bobby Cox	.15
20	Jerry Koosman	.15
21	Al Oliver	.25
22	Lou Piniella	.25
23	Larry Bowa	.25
24	Chris Chambliss	.15
25	Bill Buckner	.15
26	Don Baylor	.15
27	Buddy Bell	.15
28	Carlton Fisk	.50
29	Gary Mathews	.15
30	Davey Lopes	.15
31	Bob Boone	.15
32	Bill Madlock	.15
33	Claudell Washington	.15
34	Jim Rice	.25
35	Gary Carter	.15
36	Willie Randolph	.15
37	Chet Lemon	.15
38	Andre Dawson	.25
39	Eddie Murray	.50
40	Paul Molitor	.50
41	Ozzie Smith	1.00
42	Jeffrey Leonard	.15
43	Lonnie Smith	.15
44	Mookie Wilson	.15
45	Tim Wallach	.15
46	Tim Raines	.25
47	Fernando Valenzuela	.15
48	Cal Ripken Jr.	2.00
49	Ryne Sandberg	1.00
50	Willie McGee	.15
51	Darryl Strawberry	.15
52	Julio Franco	.15
53	Brook Jacoby	.15
54	Dwight Gooden	.15
55	Roger McDowell	.15
56	Ozzie Guillen	.15
57	Vince Coleman	.15
58	Pete Incaviglia	.15
59	Wally Joyner	.15
60	Jose Canseco	.50
61	Cory Snyder	.15
62	Devon White	.15
63	Walt Weiss	.15
64	Mark Grace	.40
65	Ron Gant	.15
66	Chris Sabo	.15
67	Jay Buhner	.15
68	Gary Sheffield	.40
69	Gregg Jefferies	.15
70	Ken Griffey Jr.	1.50
71	Tom Gordon	.15
72	Jim Abbott	.15
73	David Justice	.25
74	Larry Walker	.25
75	Sandy Alomar	.15
76	Chuck Knoblauch	.15
77	Jeff Bagwell	.50
78	Luis Gonzalez	.25
79	Ivan Rodriguez	.50
80	Eric Karros	.15
81	Jeff Kent	.15
82	Kenny Lofton	.15
83	Moises Alou	.25
84	Reggie Sanders	.15
85	Jeff Conine	.15
86	J.T. Snow	.15
87	Tim Salmon	.25
88	Mike Piazza	1.00
89	Manny Ramirez	.75
90	Ryan Klesko	.15
91	Javy Lopez	.15
92	Chipper Jones	.75
93	Ray Durham	.15
94	Garret Anderson	.25
95	Shawn Green	.15
96	Hideo Nomo	.25
97	Jermaine Dye	.15
98	Tony Clark	.15
99	Joe Randa	.15
100	Derek Jeter	2.00
101	Jason Kendall	.15
102	Billy Wagner	.15
103	Andruw Jones	.50
104	Dmitri Young	.15
105	Scott Rolen	.50
106	Nomar Garciaparra	.75
107	Jose Cruz Jr.	.15
108	Scott Hatteberg	.15
109	Mark Kotsay	.15
110	Todd Helton	.50
111	Miguel Cairo	.15
112	Magglio Ordonez	.25
113	Kerry Wood	.25
114	Preston Wilson	.15
115	Alex Gonzalez	.15
116	Carlos Beltran	.50
117	Rafael Furcal	.25
118	Pat Burrell	.15
119	Adam Kennedy	.15
120	Terrence Long	.15
121	Jay Payton	.15
122	Bengie Molina	.15
123	Albert Pujols	2.00
124	Craig Wilson	.15
125	Alfonso Soriano	.50
126	Jimmy Rollins	.25
127	Adam Dunn	.50
128	Ichiro Suzuki	1.50
129	Roy Oswalt	.25
130	C.C. Sabathia	.15
131	Brad Wilkerson	.15
132	Nick Johnson	.15
133	Eric Hinske	.15
134	Austin Kearns	.25
135	Dontrelle Willis	.40
136	Mark Teixeira	.50
137	Rocco Baldelli	.15
138	Scott Podsednik	.25
139	Brandon Webb	.15
140	Jason Bay	.25
141	Adam LaRoche	.15
142	Khalil Greene	.25
143	Joe Mauer	.50
144	Matt Holliday	.25
145	Chad Tracy	.15
146	Garrett Atkins	.15
147	Tadahito Iguchi	1.00
148	Russ Adams	.15
149	Huston Street	.15
150	Dan Johnson	.15
151	J. Brent Cox **RC**	15.00
152	John Drennen **RC**	20.00
153	Ryan Tucker **RC**	10.00
154	Yunel Escobar **RC**	40.00
155	Jacob Marceaux **RC**	10.00
156	Mark Pawelek **RC**	25.00
157	Brandon Snyder **RC**	25.00
158	Wade Townsend **RC**	15.00
159	Troy Tulowitzki **RC**	50.00
160	Kevin Whelan **RC**	12.00

Printing Plates

No Pricing
Production one set per color.

Blue

Blue (1-150):	3-6X
Blue (151-160):	1-2X
Production 50 Sets	

Gold

No Pricing
Production One Set

Green

Green (1-150):	2-4X
Production 199	
Green (151-160):	1-2X
Production 99	

Orange

Orange (1-150):	1.5-3X
Production 399	
Orange (151-160):	1X
Production 299	

Red

Red (1-150):	1-2X
Production 499	
Red (151-160):	1X
Production 399	

Silver

No Pricing
Production One Set

Yellow

Yellow (1-150):	2-3X
Production 299	
Yellow (151-160):	1X
Production 199	

Autographs

NM/M

Common Autograph:		
Silver:		No Pricing
Production Five Sets		
Gold:		No Pricing
Production One Set		
JBA	Jason Bay	20.00
JB	Johnny Bench	65.00
AD	Andre Dawson	15.00
JD	Jermaine Dye	8.00
RF	Rafael Furcal	12.00
MG	Mark Grace	25.00
DRJ	Dan Johnson	15.00
DJ	Davey Johnson	8.00
AJ	Andruw Jones	40.00
CJ	Chipper Jones	40.00
DJ	David Justice	20.00
EK	Eric Karros	8.00
MK	Mark Kotsay	8.00
CK	Chuck Knoblauch	20.00
RM	Roger McDowell	10.00
PM	Paul Molitor	50.00
BP	Boog Powell	15.00
MR	Manny Ramirez	50.00
JR	Jim Rice	30.00
RSA	Ron Santo	25.00
TS	Tom Seaver	50.00
GS	Gary Sheffield	25.00
DS	Darryl Strawberry	15.00
RS	Ron Swoboda	10.00
JT	Joe Torre	25.00
BW	Brad Wilkerson	8.00
DW	Dontrelle Willis	20.00

Dual Autographs

NM/M

Inserted 1:118

GS	Mark Grace, Ron Santo	80.00
BW	Jason Bay, Dontrelle Willis	50.00
WD	Brad Wilkerson, Andre Dawson	50.00
CS	J. Brent Cox, Tom Seaver	40.00
RTW	Ryan Tucker, Dontrelle Willis	20.00
EF	Yunel Escobar, Rafael Furcal	25.00
MM	Jacob Marceaux, Roger McDowell	20.00
SP	Brandon Snyder, Boog Powell	25.00
TS	Wade Townsend, Tom Seaver	50.00
TW	Troy Tulowitzki, Walt Weiss	30.00
WM	Kevin Whelan, Roger McDowell	15.00

Original Relics

No Pricing
Production 1-10

Reprints

NM/M

Complete Set (150):	60.00
Common Player:	.25
Reprints:	1-2X Base Card
2 Per Hobby Pack	
1 Per Retail Pack	
Chrome:	No Pricing
Production 25 Sets	
Refractor:	No Pricing
15 Sets	
Chrome Gold:	No Pricing
Production One Set	

1	Pat Corrales/66	.25
2	Ron Santo/61	.50
3	Joe Torre/62	.75
4	Boog Powell/63	.25
5	Tom Tresh/63	.25
6	Jonny Gomes/06	.25
7	Rico Carty/65	.25
8	Bert Campaneris/65	.25
9	Tony Oliva/65	.50
10	Ron Swoboda/66	.25
11	Tony Perez/66	.75
12	Joe Morgan/66	.75
13	Davey Johnson/67	.25
14	Cleon Jones/67	.25
15	Tom Seaver/68	1.00
16	Rod Carew/68	.75
17	Rick Monday/68	.25
18	Johnny Bench/69	1.50
19	Bobby Cox/69	.25
20	Jerry Koosman/69	.25
21	Al Oliver/70	.50
22	Lou Piniella/70	.40
23	Larry Bowa/71	.40
24	Chris Chambliss/72	.25
25	Bill Buckner/72	.25
26	Don Baylor/73	.25
27	Buddy Bell/73	.25
28	Carlton Fisk/73	.75
29	Gary Mathews/74	.25
30	Davey Lopes/74	.25
31	Bob Boone/74	.25
32	Bill Madlock/75	.25
33	Claudell Washington/75	.25
34	Jim Rice/76	.40
35	Gary Carter/76	.25
36	Willie Randolph/77	.25
37	Chet Lemon/77	.25
38	Andre Dawson/78	.40
39	Eddie Murray/78	.75
40	Paul Molitor/79	.75
41	Ozzie Smith/79	1.50
42	Jeffrey Leonard/80	.25
43	Lonnie Smith/81	.25
44	Mookie Wilson/82	.25
45	Tim Wallach/82	.25
46	Tim Raines/82	.40
47	Fernando Valenzuela/82	.25
48	Cal Ripken Jr./83	3.00
49	Ryne Sandberg/84	1.50
50	Willie McGee/83	.25
51	Darryl Strawberry/84	.25
52	Julio Franco/84	.25
53	Brook Jacoby/85	.25
54	Dwight Gooden/85	.25
55	Roger McDowell/86	.25
56	Ozzie Guillen/86	.25
57	Vince Coleman/86	.25
58	Pete Incaviglia/87	.25
59	Wally Joyner/87	.25
60	Jose Canseco/87	.75
61	Cory Snyder/87	.25
62	Devon White/88	.25
63	Walt Weiss/89	.25
64	Mark Grace/89	.50
65	Ron Gant/89	.25
66	Chris Sabo/89	.25
67	Jay Buhner/89	.25
68	Gary Sheffield/90	.50
69	Gregg Jefferies/90	.25
70	Ken Griffey Jr./90	2.00
71	Tom Gordon/90	.25
72	Jim Abbott/90	.25
73	David Justice/91	.40
74	Larry Walker/91	.40
75	Sandy Alomar Jr./91	.25
76	Chuck Knoblauch/92	.25
77	Jeff Bagwell/92	.50
78	Luis Gonzalez/92	.25
79	Ivan Rodriguez/92	.50
80	Eric Karros/93	.25
81	Jeff Kent/93	.25
82	Kenny Lofton/93	.25
83	Moises Alou/93	.25
84	Reggie Sanders/93	.25
85	Jeff Conine/94	.25
86	J.T. Snow/94	.25
87	Tim Salmon/94	.25
88	Mike Piazza/94	1.50
89	Manny Ramirez/95	.75
90	Ryan Klesko/95	.25
91	Javy Lopez/95	.25
92	Chipper Jones/96	1.00
93	Ray Durham/96	.25
94	Garret Anderson/96	.25
95	Shawn Green/96	.25
96	Hideo Nomo/96	.40
97	Jermaine Dye/97	.25
98	Tony Clark/97	.25
99	Joe Randa/97	.25
100	Derek Jeter/97	3.00
101	Jason Kendall/97	.25
102	Billy Wagner/97	.25
103	Andruw Jones/98	.75
104	Dmitri Young/98	.25
105	Scott Rolen/98	.75
106	Nomar Garciaparra/98	.75
107	Jose Cruz Jr./98	.25
108	Scott Hatteberg/98	.25
109	Mark Kotsay/99	.25
110	Todd Helton/99	.50
111	Miguel Cairo/99	.25
112	Maggio Ordonez/99	.25
113	Kerry Wood/99	.40
114	Preston Wilson/00	.25
115	Alex Gonzalez/00	.25
116	Carlos Beltran/00	.50
117	Rafael Furcal/01	.25
118	Pat Burrell/01	.25
119	Adam Kennedy/01	.25
120	Terrence Long/01	.25
121	Jay Payton/01	.25
122	Bengie Molina/01	.25
123	Albert Pujols/02	3.00
124	Craig Wilson/02	.25
125	Alfonso Soriano/02	.50
126	Jimmy Rollins/02	.50
127	Adam Dunn/02	.75
128	Ichiro Suzuki/02	2.00
129	Roy Oswalt/02	.40

130	C.C. Sabathia/02	.25
131	Brad Wilkerson/03	.25
132	Nick Johnson/03	.25
133	Eric Hinske/03	.25
134	Austin Kearns/03	.25
135	Dontrelle Willis/04	.75
136	Mark Teixeira/04	.75
137	Rocco Baldelli/04	.25
138	Scott Podsednik/04	.25
139	Brandon Webb/04	.25
140	Jason Bay/05	.25
141	Adam LaRoche/05	.25
142	Khalil Greene/05	.25
143	Joe Mauer/05	.50
144	Matt Holliday/05	.25
145	Chad Tracy/05	.25
146	Garrett Atkins/06	.25
147	Tadahito Iguchi/06	1.50
148	Russ Adams/06	.25
149	Huston Street/06	.25
150	Dan Johnson/06	.25

2005 Topps Turkey Red

NM/M

Complete Set (315):		
Common Player:		.25
Common SP:		4.00
Inserted 1:4		
Pack (8):		5.00
Box (24):		100.00
1	Barry Bonds/Gray Uni./SP	15.00
1	Barry Bonds	4.00
2	Michael Young	.25
3	Jim Edmonds	.50
4	Cliff Floyd	.25
5	Roger Clemens/Blue Sky SP	12.00
5	Roger Clemens/Yellow Sky SP	12.00
6	Hal Chase	.25
7	Shannon Stewart	.25
8	Fred Clarke	.25
9	Travis Hafner	.50
10	Sammy Sosa/w/Name/SP	6.00
10	Sammy Sosa/ w/o Name/SP	6.00
11	Jermaine Dye	.25
12	Lyle Overbay	.25
13	Oliver Perez	.25
14	Red Dooin	.25
15	Kid Elberfeld	.25
16	Mike Piazza/Blue Uni. SP	6.00
16	Mike Piazza/Pinstripe	1.50
17	Bret Boone	.25
18	Hughie Jennings	.25
19	Jeff Francis	.25
20	Manny Ramirez/SP	6.00
21	Russ Ortiz	.25
22	Carlos Zambrano	.50
23	Luis Castillo	.25
24	David DeJesus	.25
25	Carlos Beltran/SP	5.00
26	Doug Davis	.25
27	Bobby Abreu	.50
28	Rich Harden/SP	4.00
29	Brian Giles	.25
30	Richie Sexson/SP	4.00
31	Nick Johnson	.25
32	Roy Halladay	.50
33	Andy Pettitte	.50
34	Miguel Cabrera	1.00
35	Jeff Kent	.25
36	Chone Figgins	.25
37	Carlos Lee	.25
38	Greg Maddux	2.00
39	Preston Wilson	.25
40	Chipper Jones	1.00
41	Coco Crisp	.25
42	Adam Dunn	.75
43	Miguel Tejada CL	.50
44	Gary Sheffield CL	.50
45	Javy Lopez CL	.25
46	Scott Rolen CL	.50
47	Todd Helton CL	.50
48	Roger Clemens CL	1.00
49	Jimmy Rollins CL	.40
50	Ichiro Suzuki CL	1.00
51	Cliff Floyd CL	.25
52	Johan Santana CL	.50
53	Mark Teixeira	.75
54	Chris Carpenter	.25
55	Roy Oswalt/SP	4.00

56	Casey Kotchman	.25
57	Torii Hunter	.25
58	Jose Reyes	.50
59	Wily Mo Pena/SP	4.00
60	Magglio Ordonez/SP	4.00
61	Aaron Miles	.25
62	Dallas McPherson	.25
63	Javy Lopez	.25
64	Luis Gonzalez	.25
65	David Ortiz	1.00
66	Jorge Posada	.50
67	Xavier Nady	.25
68	Larry Walker	.50
69	Mark Loretta	.25
70	Jim Thome/SP	5.00
71	Livan Hernandez	.25
72	Garrett Atkins	.25
73	Milton Bradley	.25
74	B.J. Upton	.25
75	Ichiro Suzuki/w/Name/SP	8.00
75	Ichiro Suzuki/w/o Name/SP	8.00
76	Aramis Ramirez	.25
77	Eric Milton	.25
78	Troy Glaus SP	4.00
79	David Newhan	.25
80	Delmon Young	.50
81	Justin Morneau	.40
82	Ramon Ortiz	.25
83	Eric Chavez/Blue Sky	.25
83	Eric Chavez/Purple Sky/SP	4.00
84	Sean Burroughs	.25
85	Scott Rolen/SP	6.00
86	Rocco Baldelli	.25
87	Joe Mauer SP	5.00
88	Tony Womack	.25
89	Ken Griffey Jr.	2.00
90	Alfonso Soriano/SP	6.00
91	Paul Konerko	.25
92	Guillermo Mota	.25
93	Lance Berkman	.50
94	Mark Buehrle	.25
95	Matt Clement	.25
96	Melvin Mora	.25
97	Khalil Greene	.50
98	David Wright	1.50
99	Jack Wilson	.25
100	Alex Rodriguez/w/Bat/SP	10.00
100	Alex Rodriguez/w/Glove/SP	10.00
101	Joe Nathan	.25
102	Adrian Beltre/Gray Uni. SP	4.00
102	Adrian Beltre/White Uni.	.25
103	Mike Sweeney	.25
104	Brad Lidge	.25
105	Shawn Green	.25
106	Miguel Tejada/SP	5.00
107	Derrek Lee	.75
108	Eric Hinske	.25
109	Eric Byrnes	.25
110	Hideki Matsui/SP	8.00
111	Tom Glavine	.50
112	Jimmy Rollins	.40
113	Ryan Drese	.25
114	Josh Beckett	.25
115	Curt Schilling/SP	6.00
116	Jeremy Bonderman	.25
117	Hideki Matsui	.25
118	Chase Utley	.50
119	Troy Percival	.25
120	Vladimir Guerrero/w/Bat/SP	6.00
120	Vladimir Guerrero/w/Glove/SP	6.00
121	Gary Sheffield	.50
122	Jeromy Burnitz	.25
123	Javier Vazquez	.25
124	Kevin Millar	.25
125	Randy Johnson/Blue Sky	1.00
125	Randy Johnson/Purple Sky/SP	5.00
126	Pat Burrell	.25
127	Jason Schmidt	.25
128	Jose Vidro	.25
129	Kip Wells	.25
130	Ivan Rodriguez/w/Cap	.75
130	Ivan Rodriguez/ w/Helmet/SP	6.00
131	C.C. Sabathia	.25
132	Carlos Delgado/SP	4.00
133	Bartolo Colon	.25
134	Andruw Jones	.50
135	Kerry Wood	.50
136	Sidney Ponson	.25
137	Eric Gagne	.25
138	Rickie Weeks	.25
139	Mariano Rivera	.50
140	Bobby Crosby	.25
141	Jamie Moyer	.25
142	Corey Koskie	.25
143	John Smoltz	.50
144	Frank Thomas	.75
145	Cristian Guzman	.25
146	Paul LoDuca	.25
147	Geoff Jenkins	.25
148	Nick Swisher	.25
149	Jason Bay/SP	4.00
150	Albert Pujols/SP	10.00
151	Edwin Jackson	.25
152	Carl Crawford	.25
153	Mark Mulder	.50
154	Rafael Palmeiro	.75
155	Pedro Martinez/SP	6.00
156	Jake Westbrook	.25
157	Sean Casey	.25
158	Aaron Rowand	.25

159	J.D. Drew	.25
160	Johan Santana/Glove on Knee/SP	5.00
160	Johan Santana/Throwing/SP	5.00
161	Gavin Floyd	.25
162	Vernon Wells	.25
163	Aubrey Huff	.25
164	Jeff Bagwell	.50
165	David Wells	.25
166	Brad Penny	.25
167	Austin Kearns	.25
168	Mike Mussina	.50
169	Randy Wolf	.25
170	Tim Hudson/SP	4.00
171	Casey Blake	.25
172	Edgar Renteria	.50
173	Ben Sheets	.50
174	Kevin Brown	.25
175	Nomar Garciaparra/SP	8.00
176	Armando Benitez	.25
177	Jody Gerut	.25
178	Craig Biggio	.50
179	Omar Vizquel	.25
180	Jake Peavy	.25
181	Gustavo Chacin/SP	4.00
182	Johnny Damon	.75
183	Mike Lieberthal	.25
184	Felix Hernandez/SP	10.00
185	Zach Day/SP	4.00
186	Matt Cain	.25
187	Erubiel Durazo	.25
188	Zack Greinke	.25
189	Matt Morris	.25
190	Billy Wagner	.25
191	Al Leiter	.25
192	Miguel Olivo	.25
193	Jose Capellan/SP	4.00
194	Adam Eaton	.25
195	Steven White/SP	4.00
196	Joe Randa	.25
197	Richard Hidalgo	.25
198	Orlando Cabrera	.25
199	Joel Guzman/SP	6.00
200	Garret Anderson	.50
201	Endy Chavez	.25
202	Andy Marte	.25
203	Jose Guillen	.25
204	Victor Martinez	.25
205	Johnny Estrada	.25
206	Damian Miller	.25
207	Ken Harvey	.25
208	Ronnie Belliard	.25
209	Chan Ho Park	.25
210	Laynce Nix	.25
211	Lew Ford	.25
212	Moises Alou	.50
213	Kris Benson	.25
214	Mike Gonzalez/SP	4.00
215	Chris Burke	.25
216	Juan Pierre	.25
217	Phil Nevin	.25
218	Jerry Hairston Jr.	.25
219	Jeremy Reed	.25
220	Scott Kazmir/SP	4.00
221	Mike Maroth	.25
222	Alex Rios	.25
223	Esteban Loaiza	.25
224	Terrmel Sledge	.25
225	Mark Prior/Blue Sky/SP	5.00
225	Mark Prior/Yellow Sky/SP	5.00
226	Hank Blalock	.50
227	Craig Wilson	.25
228	Cesar Izturis	.25
229	Dmitri Young	.25
230	Derek Jeter/Blue Sky SP	15.00
230	Derek Jeter/Purple Sky/SP	15.00
231	Mark Kotsay	.25
232	Darin Erstad	.25
233	Brandon Backe/SP	4.00
234	Mike Lowell	.25
235	Scott Podsednik	.25
236	Michael Barrett	.25
237	Chad Tracy	.25
238	David Dellucci	.25
239	Brady Clark	.25
240	Jorge Cantu	.25
241	Wilfredo Ledezma	.25
242	Morgan Ensberg	.25
243	Omar Infante	.25
244	Corey Patterson	.25
245	Matt Holliday	.25
246	Vinny Castilla	.25
247	Jason Bartlett	.25
248	Noah Lowry	.25
249	Huston Street	.25
250	Russell Branyan	.25
251	Juan Uribe	.25
252	Larry Bigbie	.25
253	Grady Sizemore	.50
254	Pedro Feliz	.25
255	Brad Wilkerson	.25
256	Brandon Inge	.25
257	Dewon Brazelton	.25
258	Rodrigo Lopez	.25
259	Jacque Jones	.25
260	Jason Giambi	.50
261	Clint Barmes	.25
262	Willy Taveras	.25
263	Marcus Giles	.25
264	Joe Blanton	.25
265	John Thomson	.25
266	Steve Finley/SP	4.00
267	Kevin Millwood	.25
268	David Eckstein	.25

269	Barry Zito	.50
270	Todd Helton/Purple Sky/SP	5.00
270	Todd Helton/Yellow Sky/SP	5.00
271	Landon Powell RC	1.00
272	Justin Verlander RC	3.00
273	Wes Swackhamer RC	1.00
274	Wladimir Balentien RC	1.00
275	Philip Humber RC	1.00
276	Kevin Melillo RC	2.00
277	Billy Butler RC	4.00
278	Michael Rogers RC	1.00
279	Bobby Livingston RC	1.00
280	Glen Perkins RC	1.00
281	Michael Bourn RC	1.00
282	Tyler Pelland RC	1.00
283	Jeremy West RC	2.00
284	Brandon McCarthy RC	4.00
285	Ian Kinsler RC	3.00
286	Chris Roberson RC	1.00
287	Melky Cabrera RC	2.00
288	Ryan Sweeney RC	1.00
289	Chip Cannon RC	1.50
290	Andy LaRoche RC	5.00
291	Chuck Tiffany RC	1.00
292	Ian Bladergroen RC	1.00
293	Bear Bay RC	1.00
294	Hernan Iribarren RC	1.00
295	Stuart Pomeranz RC	1.00
296	Luke Scott RC	1.00
297	Chuck James RC	2.00
298	Kennard Bibbs RC	1.50
299	Steve Bondurant RC	1.50
300	Tom Oldham RC	1.00
301	Nolan Ryan	3.00
302	Reggie Jackson	1.50
303	Tom Seaver	1.00
304	Al Kaline	1.50
305	Cal Ripken Jr.	4.00
306	Josh Gibson	1.50
307	Frank Robinson	1.00
308	Duke Snider	1.00
309	Wade Boggs	1.50
310	Tony Gwynn	2.00
311	Carl Yastrzemski	2.00
312	Ryne Sandberg	2.00
313	Gary Carter	1.00
314	Brooks Robinson	1.50
315	Ernie Banks	1.50

Black
Stars (1-315):	3-5X
SP's:	1.5-2X
Inserted 1:20	

Gold
Stars (1-315):	5-10X
SP's:	3-5X
Production 50 Sets	

Red

Stars (1-315):	1-2X
SP's:	.5-1X

Suede
No Pricing
Production One Set

White

Stars (1-315):	2-3X

SP's:		1-1.5X
Inserted 1:4		

Autographs

		NM/M
Common Auto.:		10.00
Cards are not serial numbered.		
MB	Matt Bush/17	20.00
CC	Carl Crawford/17	30.00
SE	Scott Elbert	20.00
JF	Josh Fields	15.00
EG	Eric Gagne/142	20.00
JG	Jody Gerut	10.00
JPH	J.P. Howell	15.00
ZJ	Zach Jackson	12.00
JJ	Jason Jaramillo	12.00
BJ	Blake Johnson	15.00
BM	Brett Myers/67	20.00
CN	Chris Nelson	10.00
DO	David Ortiz	50.00
ZP	Zachary Parker	12.00
DP	Dustin Pedroia	40.00
MR	Mariano Rivera/192	90.00
MRO	Mike Rodriguez	10.00
GS	Gary Sheffield	40.00
AS	Alfonso Soriano/142	40.00
JS	Jeremy Sowers	20.00

B-18 Blanket Boxloaders

	NM/M
Common Blanket	8.00
Barry Bonds	20.00
Roger Clemens	20.00
Todd Helton	8.00
Derek Jeter	20.00
Alex Rodriguez	15.00
Curt Schilling	12.00
Alfonso Soriano	8.00
Ichiro Suzuki	15.00

Cabinet Boxloaders

		NM/M
Inserted 1:Box		
BB	Barry Bonds	25.00
GB	George W. Bush	10.00
RJ	Randy Johnson	12.00
MP	Mike Piazza	12.00
AP	Albert Pujols	20.00
MR	Manny Ramirez	12.00
AR	Alex Rodriguez	20.00
SR	Scott Rolen	10.00
JS	Johan Santana	12.00
SS	Sammy Sosa	15.00
WT	William H. Taft	15.00
MT	Miguel Tejada	10.00
JT	Jim Thome	10.00
GW	George Washington	25.00

Cabinet Auto Relics

		NM/M
Production 5-450		
MB	Matt Bush/450	25.00
CC	Carl Crawford/450	25.00
JG	Jody Gerut/450	20.00
MK	Mark Kotsay/450	30.00
BM	Brett Myers/150	40.00
DO	David Ortiz/75	100.00
MR	Mariano Rivera/25	90.00
AR	Alex Rodriguez/25	400.00
GS	Gary Sheffield/25	100.00
AS	Alfonso Soriano/75	75.00

Cut Signatures

Production One Set
No Pricing

Relics

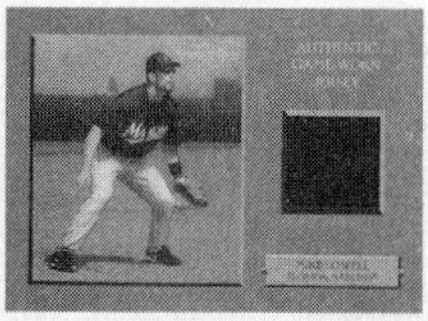

		NM/M
Common Player:		4.00
JB	Jeff Bagwell	6.00
CB	Carlos Beltran	6.00
AB	Adrian Beltre	6.00
HB	Hank Blalock	6.00
BB	Barry Bonds	20.00
MC	Miguel Cabrera	8.00
RC	Roger Clemens	15.00
RC2	Roger Clemens	15.00
JD	Johnny Damon	10.00
JD2	Johnny Damon	10.00
VG	Vladimir Guerrero	8.00
TH	Todd Helton	6.00
CJ	Chipper Jones	8.00
ML	Mike Lowell	4.00
MM	Mark Mulder	4.00
MO	Magglio Ordonez	4.00
DO	David Ortiz	8.00
RP	Rafael Palmeiro	6.00
MP	Mike Piazza	8.00
MPR	Mark Prior	6.00
AP	Albert Pujols	15.00
MR	Manny Ramirez	8.00
AR	Alex Rodriguez	12.00
AR2	Alex Rodriguez	12.00
CS	Curt Schilling	8.00
GS	Gary Sheffield	6.00
AS	Alfonso Soriano	8.00
SS	Sammy Sosa	10.00
MTE	Mark Teixeira	6.00
MT	Miguel Tejada	8.00
JT	Jim Thome	6.00
LW	Larry Walker	4.00

2006 Topps

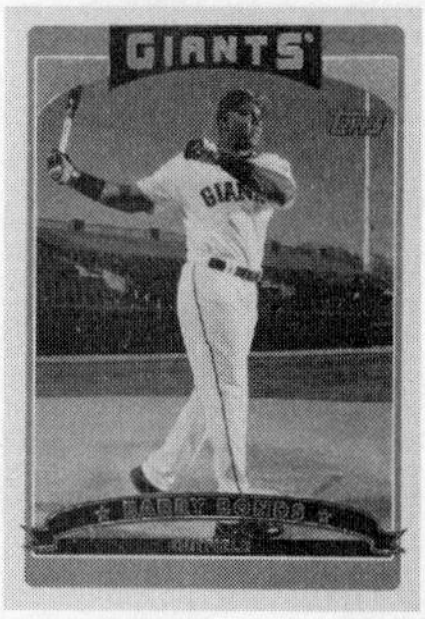

	NM/M
Complete Set (659):	60.00
Complete Hobby Set (664):	75.00
Complete Holiday Set (659):	75.00
Complete Cardinals Set (664):	75.00
Complete Cubs Set (664):	75.00
Complete Pirates Set (664):	75.00
Complete Red Sox Set (664):	75.00
Complete Yankees Set (664):	75.00
Common Player:	.10
Series 1 & 2 hobby pack (10):	1.50
Series 1 & 2 hobby box (36):	40.00
Jumbo Pack (35):	4.00
Jumbo Box (12):	40.00

1	Alex Rodriguez	1.50
2	Jose Valentin	.10
3	Garrett Atkins	.25
4	Scott Hatteberg	.10
5	Carl Crawford	.25
6	Armando Benitez	.10
7	Mickey Mantle	5.00
8	Mike Morse	.10
9	Damian Miller	.10
10	Clint Barmes	.10
11	Michael Barrett	.10
12	Coco Crisp	.10
13	Tadahito Iguchi	.25
14	Chris Snyder	.10
15	Brian Roberts	.25
16	David Wright	1.00
17	Victor Santos	.10
18	Trevor Hoffman	.20
19	Jeremy Reed	.10
20	Bobby Abreu	.25
21	Lance Berkman	.25
22	Zach Day	.10
23	Jonny Gomes	.10
24	Jason Marquis	.10
25	Chipper Jones	.50
26	Scott Hairston	.10
27	Ryan Dempster	.10
28	Brandon Inge	.10
29	Aaron Harang	.20
30	Jon Garland	.10
31	Pokey Reese	.10
32	Mike MacDougal	.10
33	Mike Lieberthal	.10
34	Cesar Izturis	.10
35	Brad Wilkerson	.10
36	Jeff Suppan	.10
37	Adam Everett	.10
38	Bengie Molina	.10
39	Rickie Weeks	.25
40	Jorge Posada	.25
41	Rheal Cormier	.10
42	Reed Johnson	.10
43	Layne Nix	.10
44	Carl Everett	.10
45	Greg Maddux	1.00
46	Jeff Francis	.10
47	Felipe Lopez	.10
48	Dan Johnson	.10
49	Humberto Cota	.10
50	Manny Ramirez	.50
51	Juan Uribe	.10
52	Jaret Wright	.10
53	Tomokazu Ohka	.10
54	Mike Matheny	.10
55	Joe Mauer	.25
56	Jarrod Washburn	.10
57	Randy Winn	.10
58	Pedro Feliz	.10
59	Kenny Rogers	.10
60	Rocco Baldelli	.10
61	Eric Hinske	.10
62	Damaso Marte	.10
63	Desi Relaford	.10
64	Juan Encarnacion	.10
65	Nomar Garciaparra	.50
66	Shawn Estes	.10
67	Brian Jordan	.10
68	Steve Kline	.10
69	Braden Looper	.10
70	Carlos Lee	.10
71	Tom Glavine	.25
72	Craig Biggio	.25
73	Steve Finley	.10
74	David Newhan	.10
75	Eric Gagne	.20
76	Tony Graffanino	.10
77	Dallas McPherson	.10
78	Nick Punto	.10
79	Mark Kotsay	.10
80	Kerry Wood	.25
81	Kyle Farnsworth	.10
82	Huston Street	.20
83	Endy Chavez	.10
84	So Taguchi	.10
85	Hank Blalock	.25
86	Brad Radke	.10
87	Chien-Ming Wang	.50
88	B.J. Surhoff	.10
89	Glendon Rusch	.10
90	Mark Buehrle	.25
91	Rafael Betancourt	.10
92	Lance Cormier	.10
93	Alex Gonzalez	.10
94	Matt Stairs	.10
95	Andy Pettitte	.25
96	Jesse Crain	.10
97	Kenny Lofton	.10
98	Geoff Blum	.10
99	Mark Redman	.10
100	Barry Bonds	1.50
101	Chad Orvella	.10
102	Xavier Nady	.10
103	Junior Spivey	.10
104	Bernie Williams	.25
105	Victor Martinez	.25
106	Nook Logan	.10
107	Mark Teahen	.10
108	Mike Lamb	.10
109	Jayson Werth	.10
110	Mariano Rivera	.25
111	Erubiel Durazo	.10
112	Ryan Vogelsong	.10
113	Bobby Madritsch	.10
114	Travis Lee	.10
115	Adam Dunn	.40
116	David Riske	.10
117	Troy Percival	.10
118	Chad Tracy	.20
119	Andy Marte	.10
120	Edgar Renteria	.20
121	Jason Giambi	.25
122	Justin Morneau	.40
123	J.T. Snow	.10
124	Danys Baez	.10
125	Carlos Delgado	.25
126	John Buck	.10
127	Shannon Stewart	.10
128	Mike Cameron	.10
129	Joe McEwing	.10
130	Richie Sexson	.25
131	Rod Barajas	.10
132	Russ Adams	.10
133	J.D. Closser	.10
134	Ramon Ortiz	.10
135	Josh Beckett	.50
136	Ryan Freel	.10
137	Victor Zambrano	.10
138	Ronnie Belliard	.10
139	Jason Michaels	.10
140	Brian Giles	.20
141	Randy Wolf	.10
142	Robinson Cano	.50
143	Joe Blanton	.10
144	Esteban Loaiza	.10
145	Troy Glaus	.25
146	Matt Clement	.10
147	Geoff Jenkins	.10
148	John Thomson	.10
149	A.J. Pierzynski	.10
150	Pedro Martinez	.50
151	Roger Clemens	1.50
152	Jack Wilson	.10
153	Ray King	.10
154	Ryan Church	.10
155	Paul LoDuca	.10
156	Dan Wheeler	.10
157	Carlos Zambrano	.25
158	Mike Timlin	.10
159	Brandon Claussen	.10
160	Travis Hafner	.25
161	Chris Shelton	.10
162	Rafael Furcal	.25
163	Flash Gordon	.10
164	Noah Lowry	.10
165	Larry Walker	.25
166	Dave Roberts	.10
167	Scott Schoeneweis	.10
168	Julian Tavarez	.10
169	Jhonny Peralta	.25
170	Vernon Wells	.25
171	Jorge Cantu	.10
172	Todd Greene	.10
173	Willy Taveras	.10
174	Corey Patterson	.10
175	Ivan Rodriguez	.40
176	Bobby Kielty	.10
177	Jose Reyes	.50
178	Barry Zito	.25
179	Deivi Cruz	.10
180	Mark Teixeira	.50
181	Chone Figgins	.25
182	Aaron Rowand	.10
183	Tim Wakefield	.10
184	Mike Maroth	.10
185	Johnny Damon	.50
186	Vicente Padilla	.10
187	Ryan Klesko	.10
188	Gary Matthews	.10
189	Jose Mesa	.10
190	Nick Johnson	.10
191	Freddy 1arcia	.10
192	Larry Bigbie	.10
193	Chris Ray	.10
194	Torii Hunter	.25
195	Mike Sweeney	.10
196	Brad Penny	.10
197	Jason Frasor	.10
198	Kevin Mench	.10
199	Adam Kennedy	.10
200	Albert Pujols	1.50
201	Jody Gerut	.10
202	Luis Gonzalez	.10
203	Zack Greinke	.25
204	Miguel Cairo	.10
205	Jimmy Rollins	.50
206	Edgardo Alfonzo	.10
207	Billy Wagner	.10
208	B.J. Ryan	.10
209	Orlando Hudson	.10
210	Preston Wilson	.10
211	Melvin Mora	.10
212	Bill Mueller	.10
213	Javy Lopez	.10
214	Wilson Betemit	.10
215	Garret Anderson	.10
216	Russell Branyan	.10
217	Jeff Weaver	.10
218	Doug Mientkiewicz	.10
219	Mark Ellis	.10
220	Jason Bay	.25
221	Adam LaRoche	.10
222	C.C. Sabathia	.25
223	Humberto Quintero	.10
224	Bartolo Colon	.20
225	Ichiro Suzuki	1.00
226	Brett Tomko	.10
227	Corey Koskie	.10
228	David Eckstein	.10
229	Cristian Guzman	.10
230	Jeff Kent	.25
231	Chris Capuano	.10
232	Rodrigo Lopez	.10
233	Jason Phillips	.10
234	Luis Rivas	.10
235	Cliff Floyd	.10
236	Gil Meche	.10
237	Adam Eaton	.10
238	Matt Morris	.10
239	Kyle Davies	.10
240	David Wells	.10
241	John Smoltz	.25
242	Felix Hernandez	.50
243	Kenny Rogers	.10
244	Mark Teixeira	.25
245	Orlando Hudson	.10
246	Derek Jeter	1.00
247	Eric Chavez	.20
248	Torii Hunter	.20
249	Vernon Wells	.20
250	Ichiro Suzuki	.50
251	Greg Maddux	.50
252	Mike Matheny	.10
253	Derrek Lee	.25
254	Luis Castillo	.10
255	Omar Vizquel	.10
256	Mike Lowell	.25
257	Andruw Jones	.25
258	Jim Edmonds	.20
259	Bobby Abreu	.25
260	Bartolo Colon	.10
261	Chris Carpenter	.25
262	Alex Rodriguez	1.00
263	Albert Pujols	1.00
264	Huston Street	.10
265	Ryan Howard	.50
266	Bob Melvin	.10
267	Bobby Cox	.10
268	Baltimore Orioles	.10
269	Boston Red Sox	.25
270	Chicago White Sox	.25
271	Dusty Baker	.10
272	Jerry Narron	.10
273	Cleveland Indians	.10
274	Clint Hurdle	.10
275	Detroit Tigers	.10
276	Jack McKeon	.10
277	Phil Garner	.10
278	Kansas City Royals	.10
279	Jim Tracy	.10
280	Angels	.10
281	Milwaukee Brewers	.10
282	Minnesota Twins	.10
283	Willie Randolph	.10
284	New York Yankees	.50
285	Oakland Athletics	.10
286	Charlie Manuel	.10
287	Pete Mackanin	.10
288	Bruce Bochy	.10
289	Felipe Alou	.10
290	Seattle Mariners	.10
291	Tony LaRussa	.10
292	Tampa Bay Devil Rays	.10
293	Texas Rangers	.10
294	Toronto Blue Jays	.10
295	Frank Robinson	.25
296	Anderson Hernandez **(RC)**	.10

297a Alex Gordon (Complete card. Not officially issued.) 800.00
297b Alex Gordon (Cut-out card.) 80.00
297c Alex Gordon Blank Gold 80.00
298 Jason Botts **(RC)** .10
299 Jeff Mathis **(RC)** .10
300 Ryan Garko **(RC)** .25
301 Charlton Jimerson **(RC)** .25
302 Chris Denorfia **(RC)** .25
303 Anthony Reyes **(RC)** .25
304 Bryan Bullington **(RC)** .25
305 Chuck James **(RC)** .25
306 Danny Sandoval **RC** .25
307 Walter Young **(RC)** .25
308 Fausto Carmona **(RC)** .25
309 Francisco Liriano **(RC)** 1.00
310 Hong-Chih Kuo **(RC)** .75
311 Joe Saunders **(RC)** .25
312 John Koronka **(RC)** .25
313 Robert Andino **RC** .25
314 Shaun Marcum **(RC)** .25
315 Tom Gorzelanny **(RC)** .25
316 Craig Breslow **RC** .25
317 Chris Demaria **RC** .50
318 Brayan Pena **(RC)** .25
319 Rich Hill **(RC)** .50
320 Rick Short **RC** .25
321 C.J. Wilson **(RC)** .25
322 Marshall McDougall **(RC)** .25
323 Darrell Rasner **(RC)** .25
324 Brandon Watson **(RC)** .25
325 Paul McAnulty **(RC)** .25
326 Derek Jeter, Alex Rodriguez .50
327 Miguel Tejada, Melvin Mora .25
328 Marcus Giles, Chipper Jones .25
329 Manny Ramirez, David Ortiz .25
330 Michael Barrett, Greg Maddux .25
331 Matt Holliday .50
332 Orlando Cabrera .25
333 Ryan Langerhans .10
334 Lew Ford .10
335 Mark Prior .25
336 Ted Lilly .10
337 Michael Young .25
338 Livan Hernandez .10
339 Yadier Molina .10
340 Eric Chavez .10
341 Miguel Batista .10
342 Bruce Chen .10
343 Sean Casey .10
344 Doug Davis .10
345 Andruw Jones .25
346 Hideki Matsui 1.00
347 Joe Randa .10
348 Reggie Sanders .10
349 Jason Jennings .10
350 Joe Nathan .10
351 Jose Lopez .10
352 John Lackey .10
353 Claudio Vargas .10
354 Grady Sizemore .50
355 Jonathan Papelbon **(RC)** 2.00
356 Luis Matos .10
357 Orlando Hernandez .10
358 Jamie Moyer .10
359 Chase Utley .50
360 Moises Alou .25
361 Chad Cordero .10
362 Brian McCann .25
363 Jermaine Dye .10
364 Ryan Madson .10
365 Aramis Ramirez .25
366 Matt Treanor .10
367 Ray Durham .10
368 Khalil Greene .10
369 Mike Hampton .10
370 Mike Mussina .25
371 Brad Hawpe .10
372 Marlon Byrd .10
373 Woody Williams .10
374 Victor Diaz .10
375 Brady Clark .10
376 Luis Gonzalez .10
377 Raul Ibanez .10
378 Tony Clark .10
379 Shawn Chacon .10
380 Marcus Giles .10
381 Odalis Perez .10
382 Steve Trachsel .10
383 Russ Ortiz .10
384 Toby Hall .10
385 Bill Hall .10
386 Luke Hudson .10
387 Ken Griffey Jr. 1.00
388 Tim Hudson .25
389 Brian Moehler .10
390 Jake Peavy .25
391 Casey Blake .10
392 Sidney Ponson .10
393 Brian Schneider .10
394 J.J. Hardy .10
395 Austin Kearns .25
396 Pat Burrell .25
397 Jason Vargas .10
398 Ryan Howard .75
399 Joe Crede .10
400 Vladimir Guerrero .50
401 Roy Halladay .25
402 David Dellucci .10
403 Brandon Webb .25
404 Marlon Anderson .10
405 Miguel Tejada .25
406 Ryan Doumit .10
407 Kevin Youkilis .25
408 Jon Lieber .10
409 Edwin Encarnacion .10
410 Miguel Cabrera .50
411 A.J. Burnett .25
412 David Bell .10
413 Gregg Zaun .10
414 Lance Niekro .10
415 Shawn Green .10
416 Roberto Hernandez .10
417 Jay Gibbons .10
418 Johnny Estrada .10
419 Omar Vizquel .10
420 Gary Sheffield .25
421 Brad Halsey .10
422 Aaron Cook .10
423 David Ortiz .50
424 Tony Womack .10
425 Joe Kennedy .10
426 Dustin McGowan .10
427 Carl Pavano .10
428 Nick Green .10
429 Francisco Cordero .10
430 Octavio Dotel .10
431 Julio Franco .10
432 Brett Myers .10
433 Casey Kotchman .10
434 Frank Catalanotto .10
435 Paul Konerko .25
436 Keith Foulke .10
437 Juan Rivera .10
438 Todd Pratt .10
439 Ben Broussard .10
440 Scott Kazmir .25
441 Rich Aurilia .10
442 Craig Monroe .10
443 Danny Kolb .10
444 Curtis Granderson .25
445 Jeff Francoeur .25
446 Dustin Hermanson .10
447 Jacque Jones .10
448 Bobby Crosby .10
449 Jason LaRue .10
450 Derrek Lee .40
451 Curt Schilling .50
452 Jake Westbrook .10
453 Daniel Cabrera .10
454 Bobby Jenks .10
455 Dontrelle Willis .25
456 Brad Lidge .10
457 Shea Hillenbrand .10
458 Luis Castillo .10
459 Mark Hendrickson .10
460 Randy Johnson .50
461 Placido Polanco .10
462 Aaron Boone .10
463 Todd Walker .10
464 Nick Swisher .25
465 Joel Pineiro .10
466 Jay Payton .10
467 Cliff Lee .10
468 Johan Santana .50
469 Josh Willingham **(RC)** .10
470 Jeremy Bonderman .10
471 Runelvys Hernandez .10
472 Duaner Sanchez .10
473 Jason Lane .10
474 Trot Nixon .10
475 Ramon Hernandez .10
476 Mike Lowell .25
477 Chan Ho Park .10
478 Doug Waechter .10
479 Carlos Silva .10
480 Jose Contreras .10
481 Vinny Castilla .10
482 Chris Reitsma .10
483 Jose Guillen .10
484 Aaron Hill .10
485 Kevin Millwood .10
486 Wily Mo Pena .10
487 Rich Harden .10
488 Chris Carpenter .25
489 Jason Bartlett .10
490 Magglio Ordonez .25
491 John Rodriguez .10
492 Bob Wickman .10
493 Eddie Guardado .10
494 Kip Wells .10
495 Adrian Beltre .25
496 Jose Capellan **(RC)** .10
497 Scott Podsednik .10
498 Brad Thompson .10
499 Aaron Heilman .10
500 Derek Jeter 1.50
501 Emil Brown .10
502 Morgan Ensberg .20
503 Nate Bump .10
504 Phil Nevin .10
505 Jason Schmidt .10
506 Michael Cuddyer .10
507 John Patterson .10
508 Dan Haren .25
509 Freddy Sanchez .10
510 J.D. Drew .25
511 Dmitri Young .10
512 Eric Milton .10
513 Ervin Santana .10
514 Mark Loretta .10
515 Mark Grudzielanek .10
516 Derrick Turnbow .10
517 Danny Bautista .10
518 Lyle Overbay .10
519 Julio Lugo .10
520 Carlos Beltran .40
521 Jose Cruz Jr. .10
522 Jason Isringhausen .10
523 Bronson Arroyo .10
524 Ben Sheets .25
525 Zachary Duke .10
526 Ryan Wagner .10
527 Jose Vidro .10
528 Doug Mirabelli .10
529 Kris Benson .10
530 Carlos Guillen .25
531 Juan Pierre .25
532 Scot Shields .10
533 Scott Hatteberg .10
534 Tim Stauffer .10
535 Jim Edmonds .25
536 Scott Eyre .10
537 Ben Johnson **(RC)** .10
538 Mark Mulder .25
539 Juan Rincon .10
540 Gustavo Chacin .10
541 Oliver Perez .10
542 Chris Young .25
543 Edinson Volquez .50
544 Mark Bellhorn .10
545 Kelvim Escobar .10
546 Andrew Sisco .10
547 Derek Lowe .25
548 Sean Burroughs .10
549 Erik Bedard .25
550 Alfonso Soriano .40
551 Matt Murton .10
552 Eric Byrnes .10
553 Chris Duffy .10
554 Kazuo Matsui .10
555 Scott Rolen .40
556 Robert Mackowiak .10
557 Chris Burke .10
558 Jeromy Burnitz .10
559 Jerry Hairston Jr. .10
560 Jim Thome .40
561 Miguel Olivo .10
562 Jose Castillo .10
563 Brad Ausmus .10
564 Yorvit Torrealba .10
565 David DeJesus .10
566 Paul Byrd .10
567 Brandon Backe .10
568 Aubrey Huff .10
569 Mike Jacobs **(RC)** .25
570 Todd Helton .40
571 Angel Berroa .10
572 Todd Jones .10
573 Jeff Bagwell .25
574 Darin Erstad .10
575 Roy Oswalt .25
576 Rondell White .10
577 Alex Rios .25
578 Wes Helms .10
579 Javier Vazquez .10
580 Frank Thomas .40
581 Brian Fuentes .10
582 Francisco Rodriguez .10
583 Craig Counsell .10
584 Jorge Sosa .10
585 Mike Piazza .50
586 Mike Scioscia .10
587 Joe Torre .25
588 Ken Macha .10
589 John Gibbons .10
590 Joe Maddon .10
591 Eric Wedge .10
592 Mike Hargrove .10
593 Sam Perlozzo .10
594 Buck Showalter .10
595 Terry Francona .10
596 Buddy Bell .10
597 Jim Leyland .10
598 Ron Gardenhire .10
599 Ozzie Guillen .10
600 Ned Yost .10
601 Atlanta Braves .10
602 Philadelphia Phillies .10
603 New York Mets .10
604 Washington Nationals .10
605 Florida Marlins .10
606 Houston Astros .10
607 Chicago Cubs .25
608 St. Louis Cardinals .25
609 Pittsburgh Pirates .10
610 Cincinnati Reds .10
611 Colorado Rockies .10
612 Los Angeles Dodgers .25
613 San Francisco Giants .10
614 San Diego Padres .10
615 Arizona Diamondbacks .10
616 Kenji Johjima **RC** 2.00
617 Ryan Zimmerman **(RC)** 2.00
618 Craig Hansen **RC** 1.00
619 Joey Devine **RC** .50
620 Hanley Ramirez **(RC)** .50
621 Scott Olsen **(RC)** .25
622 Jason Bergmann **RC** .25
623 Geovany Soto **(RC)** .50
624 J.J. Furmaniak **(RC)** .25
625 Jeremy Accardo **RC** .25
626 Mark Woodyard **(RC)** .25
627 Matt Capps **(RC)** .25
628 Tim Corcoran **RC** .25
629 Ryan Jorgensen **RC** .25
630 Ronny Paulino **(RC)** .25
631 Dan Uggla **(RC)** 1.00
632 Ian Kinsler **(RC)** .50
633 Josh Barfield **(RC)** .25
634 Reggie Abercrombie **(RC)** .25
635 Joel Zumaya **(RC)** .50
636 Matt Cain **(RC)** .50
637 Conor Jackson **(RC)** .25
638 Bryan Anderson **(RC)** .25
639 Prince Fielder **(RC)** 1.00
640 Jeremy Hermida **(RC)** .25
641 Justin Verlander **(RC)** 1.00
642 Brian Bannister **(RC)** .25
643 Willie Eyre **(RC)** .25
644 Ricky Nolasco **(RC)** .25
645 Paul Maholm **(RC)** .25
646 Johnny Damon, Jason Giambi .25
647 Rondell White, Lew Ford .10
648 Orlando Hernandez, Orlando Hudson .10
649 Adam Dunn, Ken Griffey Jr. .25
650 Pat Burrell, Mike Lieberthal .10
651 Jose Reyes, Kazuo Matsui .10
652 Hank Blalock, Michael Young .10
653 Prince Fielder, Rickie Weeks .50
654 Travis Lee, Rocco Baldelli .10
655 Derrick Lee, Aramis Ramirez .25
656 Grady Sizemore, Aaron Boone .25
657 Luis Gonzalez, Shawn Green, Koyie Hill .10
658 Ivan Rodriguez, Carlos Guillen .10
659 Alex Rodriguez, Gary Sheffield .25
660 Ervin Santana, Francisco Rodriguez .10

Black

Stars: 15-25X
Production 55 Sets
HTA Exclusive

Gold

Stars: 5-10X
Production 2,006 Sets

Platinum

No Pricing
Production One Set

Factory Set Rookie Bonus

NM/M

1-5 issued in retail factory sets
6-10 issued in hobby factory sets
11-20 issued in holiday factory sets
1 Nicholas Markakis 5.00
2 Kelly Shoppach 3.00
3 Jordan Tata 3.00
4 Ruddy Lugo 3.00
5 Josh Wilson 3.00
6 Fernando Nieve 3.00
7 Sendy Rleal 3.00
8 Jason Kubel 3.00
9 James Loney 5.00
10 Fabio Castro 3.00
11 Jonathan Broxton 3.00
12 Eliezer Alfonzo 3.00
13 Jason Hirsh 3.00
14 Rajai Davis 3.00
15 Henry Owens 5.00
16 Kevin Frandsen 3.00
17 Matt Garza 5.00
18 Chris Duncan 3.00
19 Chris Coste 3.00
20 Jeff Karstens 5.00

Factory Set Team Bonus

NM/M

Issued in specified factory team sets.
BRS1 Jonathan Papelbon 10.00
BRS2 Manny Ramirez 5.00
BRS3 David Ortiz 5.00
BRS4 Josh Beckett 3.00
BRS5 Curt Schilling 4.00
CC1 Sean Marshall 3.00
CC2 Freddie Bynum 3.00
CC3 Derrek Lee 4.00
CC4 Juan Pierre 3.00
CC5 Carlos Zambrano 3.00
NYY1 Wilbert Nieves 3.00
NYY2 Alex Rodriguez 6.00
NYY3 Derek Jeter 8.00
NYY4 Mariano Rivera 5.00
NYY5 Randy Johnson 5.00
PP1 Matt Capps 3.00
PP2 Paul Maholm 3.00
PP3 Nate McLouth 3.00
PP4 John Van Benschoten 3.00
PP5 Jason Bay 3.00
SLC1 Adam Wainwright 4.00
SLC2 Skip Schumaker 3.00
SLC3 Albert Pujols 10.00
SLC4 Jim Edmonds 3.00
SLC5 Scott Rolen 5.00

Autographs

NM/M

Common Player:
WB Wade Boggs/250 50.00
BB Barry Bonds/10
JB Jason Botts 10.00
MB Milton Bradley 20.00
CB Craig Breslow 10.00
FC Fausto Carmona 15.00
BC Brian Cashman/100 175.00

EC	Eric Chavez/200	60.00
LC	Lance Cormier	15.00
NC	Nelson Cruz	8.00
DD	Doug DeVore	8.00
TE	Theo Epstein/100	120.00
RG	Ryan Garko	20.00
AG	Alex Gordon	100.00
CG	Carlos Guillen	20.00
LH	Livan Hernandez	10.00
RH	Rich Hill	20.00
CJ	Chuck James	25.00
JJ	Josh Johnson	15.00
AL	Anthony Lerew	10.00
FL	Francisco Liriano	30.00
JM	Jeff Mathis	15.00
GN	Graig Nettles	25.00
SO	Scott Olsen	15.00
TO	Tim Olson	8.00
DO	David Ortiz/100	100.00
HR	Horacio Ramirez	10.00
DR	Darrell Rasner	10.00
ARE	Anthony Reyes	25.00
CR	Cal Ripken Jr./100	200.00
AR	Alex Rodriguez/100	450.00
RS	Ryne Sandberg/100	140.00
GS	Gary Sheffield/200	60.00
TS	Terrmel Sledge	15.00
BW	Brad Wilkerson	15.00
DW	Dave Winfield/100	150.00
MY	Michael Young	25.00

Series 2

GA	Garrett Atkins	20.00
CB	Clint Barmes	15.00
JB	Jose Bautista	15.00
BB	Barry Bonds/120	400.00
RC	Robinson Cano	50.00
GC	Gary Carter/250	40.00
BC	Brandon Claussen	10.00
DD	Doug Drabek/250	20.00
JF	Jeff Francis	20.00
DJ	Dan Johnson	15.00
AJ	Andruw Jones/50	50.00
SK	Scott Kazmir	25.00
DL	Derrek Lee/250	50.00
BM	Brandon McCarthy	15.00
CO	Chad Orvella	10.00
JP	Jonathan Papelbon	60.00
WP	Wily Mo Pena/250	30.00
BR	Brian Roberts/250	40.00
DSN	Duke Snider/250	60.00
DS	Darryl Strawberry/250	25.00
CV	Claudio Vargas	15.00
RZ	Ryan Zimmerman	40.00

Hit Parade

	NM/M
Common Player:	.50
RB11 Barry Bonds	3.00
RB12 Ken Griffey Jr.	2.00
RB13 Jeff Bagwell	.75
RB14 Gary Sheffield	.75
RB15 Frank Thomas	.75
RB16 Manny Ramirez	1.00
RB17 Ruben Sierra	.50
RB18 Jeff Kent	.50
RB19 Luis Gonzalez	.50
RB110 Alex Rodriguez	3.00
HR1 Barry Bonds	3.00
HR2 Ken Griffey Jr.	2.00
HR3 Jeff Bagwell	.75
HR4 Gary Sheffield	.75
HR5 Frank Thomas	.75
HR6 Manny Ramirez	1.00
HR7 Jim Thome	1.00
HR8 Alex Rodriguez	3.00
HR9 Mike Piazza	1.00
HR10 Carlos Delgado	.75
HT1 Craig Biggio	.50
HT2 Barry Bonds	3.00
HT3 Julio Franco	.50
HT4 Steve Finley	.50
HT5 Gary Sheffield	.75
HT6 Jeff Bagwell	.75
HT7 Ken Griffey Jr.	2.00
HT8 Omar Vizquel	.50
HT9 Marquis Grissom	.50
HT10 Bernie Williams	.50

Hobby Masters

	NM/M
Complete Set (20):	20.00
Common Player:	.75
Inserted 1:18	
HM1 Derrek Lee	1.00
HM2 Albert Pujols	4.00
HM3 Nomar Garciaparra	1.00
HM4 Alfonso Soriano	.75
HM5 Derek Jeter	4.00
HM6 Miguel Tejada	1.00
HM7 Alex Rodriguez	4.00
HM8 Jim Edmonds	.75
HM9 Mark Prior	1.00
HM10 Roger Clemens	4.00
HM11 Randy Johnson	1.50
HM12 Manny Ramirez	1.50
HM13 Curt Schilling	1.50
HM14 Vladimir Guerrero	1.50
HM15 Barry Bonds	4.00
HM16 Ichiro Suzuki	2.50
HM17 Pedro Martinez	1.50
HM18 Carlos Beltran	1.00
HM19 David Ortiz	1.50
HM20 Andruw Jones	1.50

King of England Cut Sig

Production One
No Pricing

Mantle Homerun History

	NM/M
Inserted 1:4	
MHR1 Mickey Mantle	2.00
Common Mantle:	2.00
MHR2-101 Mickey Mantle	2.00

Mantle Homerun History Relic

Inserted 1:4,540
Production Seven Sets
No Pricing

Mantle Homerun History Cut Signature

Production One
No Pricing

Opening Day

	NM/M
Common Team:	.50
WI Chicago White Sox	.50
MN New York Mets	2.00
RR Texas Rangers	1.00
BP Milwaukee Brewers	.50
RC Cincinnati Reds	1.00
PC Philadelphia Phillies	1.00
OD Baltimore Orioles	1.00
RD Colorado Rockies	.50
DB Los Angeles Dodgers	2.00
RT Kansas City Royals	.50
MA Seattle Mariners	1.00
AM Houston Astros	1.00
PG San Diego Padres	1.00
AY Oakland Athletics	2.00
JT Toronto Blue Jays	1.00

Own the Game

	NM/M
Complete Set (30):	20.00
Common Player:	.50
Inserted 1:12	
OG1 Derrek Lee	1.00
OG2 Michael Young	.75
OG3 Albert Pujols	3.00
OG4 Roger Clemens	3.00
OG5 Andy Pettitte	.75
OG6 Dontrelle Willis	.75
OG7 Michael Young	.75
OG8 Ichiro Suzuki	2.00
OG9 Derek Jeter	3.00
OG10 Andruw Jones	.75
OG11 Alex Rodriguez	3.00
OG12 David Ortiz	1.00
OG13 David Ortiz	1.00
OG14 Manny Ramirez	1.00
OG15 Mark Teixeira	1.00
OG16 Albert Pujols	3.00
OG17 Alex Rodriguez	3.00
OG18 Derek Jeter	3.00
OG19 Chad Cordero	.50
OG20 Francisco Rodriguez	.50
OG21 Mariano Rivera	.75
OG22 Chone Figgins	.50
OG23 Jose Reyes	.75
OG24 Scott Podsednik	.50
OG25 Jake Peavy	.75
OG26 Johan Santana	1.00
OG27 Pedro Martinez	1.00
OG28 Dontrelle Willis	.75
OG29 Chris Carpenter	.50
OG30 Bartolo Colon	.50

Signers of the Declaration of Independence

	NM/M
Complete Set (56):	80.00
Common Signer:	1.50
Inserted 1:4	
JA John Adams	3.00
SA Samuel Adams	3.00
JB Josiah Bartlett	1.50
CB Carter Braxton	1.50
CC Charles Carroll	1.50
SC Samuel Chase	1.50
AC Abraham Clark	1.50
GC George Clymer	1.50
WE William Ellery	1.50
WF William Floyd	1.50
BF Benjamin Franklin	4.00
EG Elbridge Gerry	1.50
BG Button Gwinnett	1.50
LH Lyman Hall	1.50
JH John Hancock	3.00
BH Benjamin Harrison	1.50
JHA John Hart	1.50
JHE Joseph Hewes	1.50
TH Thomas Heyward Jr.	1.50
WH William Hooper	1.50
SH Stephen Hopkins	1.50
FH Francis Hopkinson	1.50
SHU Samuel Huntington	1.50
TJ Thomas Jefferson	4.00
FLL Francis Lightfoot Lee	1.50
RHL Richard Henry Lee	1.50
FL Francis Lewis	1.50
PL Philip Livingston	1.50
TL Thomas Lynch Jr.	1.50
TM Thomas McKean	1.50
AM Arthur Middleton	1.50
LM Lewis Morris	1.50
RM Robert Morris	1.50
JM John Morton	1.50
TN Thomas Nelson Jr.	1.50
WP William Paca	1.50
RTP Robert Treat Paine	1.50
JP John Penn	1.50
GRE George Read	1.50
CR Caesar Rodney	1.50
GR George Ross	1.50
BR Benjamin Rush	1.50
ER Edward Rutledge	1.50
RS Roger Sherman	1.50
JS James Smith	1.50
RST Richard Stockton	1.50
TS Thomas Stone	1.50
GT George Taylor	1.50
MT Matthew Thornton	1.50
GW George Walton	1.50
WW William Whipple	1.50
WWI William Williams	1.50
JW James Wilson	1.50
JWI John Witherspoon	1.50
OW Oliver Wolcott	1.50
GWY George Wythe	1.50

Declaration of Independence Cuts

No Pricing
Production One Set

Signers of the Constitution

	NM/M
Common Signer:	1.50
Inserted 1:8	
AB Abraham Baldwin	1.50
RB Richard Bassett	1.50
GB Gunning Bedford Jr.	1.50
JB John Blair	1.50
WB William Blount	1.50
DB David Brearly	1.50
JBR Jacob Broom	1.50
PB Pierce Butler	1.50
DC Daniel Carroll	1.50
GC George Clymer	1.50
JD Jonathan Dayton	1.50
JDI John Dickinson	1.50
WF William Few	1.50
TF Thomas Fitzsimons	1.50
BF Benjamin Franklin	4.00
NG Nicholas Gilman	1.50
NGO Nathaniel Gorham	1.50
AH Alexander Hamilton	3.00
JI Jared Ingersoll	1.50
DJ Daniel of St. Thomas Jenifer	1.50
WJ William Samuel Johnson	1.50
RK Rufus King	1.50
JL John Langdon	1.50
WL William Livingston	1.50
JM James Madison	2.00
JMC James McHenry	1.50
TM Thomas Mifflin	1.50
GM Gouverneur Morris	1.50
RM Robert Morris	1.50
WP William Paterson	1.50
CCP Charles Cotesworth Pinckney	1.50
CP Charles Pinckney	1.50
GR George Read	1.50
JR John Rutledge	1.50
RS Roger Sherman	1.50
RDS Richard Dobbs Spaight	1.50
GW George Washington	4.00
HW Hugh Williamson	1.50
JW James Wilson	1.50

Signers of the Constitution Cut Signatures

No Pricing

Stars

	NM/M
Common Player:	.75
BB Barry Bonds	3.00
MC Miguel Cabrera	1.00
RC Roger Clemens	3.00
VG Vladimir Guerrero	1.00
TH Todd Helton	.75
DJ Derek Jeter	3.00
PM Pedro Martinez	1.00
HM Hideki Matsui	2.00
DO David Ortiz	1.00
AP Albert Pujols	3.00
MR Manny Ramirez	1.00
AR Alex Rodriguez	3.00
AS Alfonso Soriano	.75
IS Ichiro Suzuki	2.00
MT Miguel Tejada	.75

Trading Places

	NM/M
Common Player:	.50
MB Milton Bradley	.50
CC Coco Crisp	.50
JD Johnny Damon	1.00
CD Carlos Delgado	.75
JDN Juan Encarnacion	.50
RF Rafael Furcal	.50
NG Nomar Garciaparra	1.00
TG Troy Glaus	.50
RH Ramon Hernandez	.50
KL Kenny Lofton	.50
BM Bill Mueller	.50
CP Corey Patterson	.50
MJP Mike Piazza	1.00
JP Juan Pierre	.50
ER Edgar Renteria	.50
AS Alfonso Soriano	.75
FT Frank Thomas	.75
JT Jim Thome	1.00
BW Brad Wilkerson	.50
PW Preston Wilson	.50

Trading Places Autographs

	NM/M
Autographed Relics:	No Pricing
Production 25 Sets	
JE Johnny Estrada	10.00
KJ Kenji Johjima	140.00
PL Paul LoDuca	20.00
ML Mike Lowell	25.00
BR B.J. Ryan	30.00
TS Terrmel Sledge	10.00
BW Billy Wagner	30.00

Trading Places Autographed Relics

No Pricing
Production 25 Sets

Trading Places Relics

NM/M

Common Player: 4.00
MB Milton Bradley 4.00
CC Coco Crisp 6.00
JD Johnny Damon 15.00
JE Johnny Estrada 6.00
NG Nomar Garciaparra 10.00
RH Ramon Hernandez 4.00
KJ Kenji Johjima 15.00
PL Paul LoDuca 6.00
KL Kenny Lofton 6.00
ML Mike Lowell 10.00
BM Bill Mueller 4.00
CP Corey Patterson 8.00
JP Juan Pierre 6.00
ER Edgar Renteria 6.00
BR B.J. Ryan 4.00
TS Termel Sledge 4.00
AS Alfonso Soriano 8.00
FT Frank Thomas 8.00
JT Jim Thome 10.00
BW Billy Wagner 6.00
BW Brad Wilkerson 4.00
PW Preston Wilson 4.00

The Mantle Collection

NM/M

Complete Set (10): 65.00
Common Mantle: 8.00
Inserted 1:36
Black: No Pricing
Production Seven Sets
MM2005 Mickey Mantle 8.00
MM2004 Mickey Mantle 8.00
MM2003 Mickey Mantle 8.00
MM2002 Mickey Mantle 8.00
MM2001 Mickey Mantle 8.00
MM2000 Mickey Mantle 8.00
MM1999 Mickey Mantle 8.00
MM1998 Mickey Mantle 8.00
MM1997 Mickey Mantle 8.00
MM1996 Mickey Mantle 8.00

The Mantle Collection Gold

NM/M

Varying quantities produced
MM2005 Mickey Mantle/977 30.00
MM2004 Mickey Mantle/877 30.00
MM2003 Mickey Mantle/777 40.00
MM2002 Mickey Mantle/677 40.00
MM2001 Mickey Mantle/577 50.00
MM2000 Mickey Mantle/477 50.00
MM1999 Mickey Mantle/377 50.00
MM1998 Mickey Mantle/277 60.00
MM1997 Mickey Mantle/177 100.00
MM1996 Mickey Mantle/77 150.00

The Mantle Collection Relics

NM/M

Production 77-167
Gold:
Black: No Pricing
Production Seven Sets
MM2005 Mickey Mantle/167 160.00
MM2004 Mickey Mantle/157 160.00
MM2003 Mickey Mantle/147 160.00
MM2002 Mickey Mantle/137 160.00
MM2001 Mickey Mantle/127 200.00
MM2000 Mickey Mantle/117 200.00
MM1999 Mickey Mantle/107 200.00
MM1998 Mickey Mantle/97 200.00
MM1997 Mickey Mantle/87 200.00
MM1996 Mickey Mantle/77 200.00

Rookie of the Week

NM/M

Issued one per week via HTA shops.
1 Mickey Mantle 10.00
2 Barry Bonds 3.00
3 Roger Clemens 3.00
4 Ernie Banks 2.00
5 Nolan Ryan 5.00
6 Albert Pujols 4.00
7 Roberto Clemente 5.00
8 Frank Robinson 1.50
9 Brooks Robinson 1.50
10 Harmon Killebrew 1.50
11 Reggie Jackson 1.50
12 George Brett 3.00
13 Ichiro Suzuki 3.00
14 Cal Ripken Jr. 6.00
15 Tom Seaver 1.50
16 Johnny Bench 1.50
17 Mike Schmidt 2.00
18 Derek Jeter 5.00
19 Bob Gibson 1.50
20 Ozzie Smith 2.00
21 Rickey Henderson 1.50
22 Tony Gwynn 1.50
23 Wade Boggs 1.50
24 Ryne Sandberg 3.00
25 Mickey Mantle 10.00

Walmart Cards

NM/M

Complete Set (18): 25.00
Common Player: .50
WM1 Stan Musial 2.00
WM2 Ted Williams 3.00
WM3 Yogi Berra 2.00
WM5 Mickey Mantle 10.00
WM6 Mickey Mantle 10.00
WM7 Alex Rodriguez 3.00
WM9 Gary Carter .50
WM10 Roy Oswalt .50
WM13 Carlos Lee .50
WM14 Johan Santana 1.00
WM15 Roberto Clemente 3.00
WM16 Carl Yastrzemski 1.50
WM21 Chipper Jones 1.00
WM22 Ichiro Suzuki 2.00
WM23 Bobby Abreu .50
WM24 Tom Seaver 1.00
WM25 Alfonso Soriano .75
WM26 Andruw Jones 1.00
WM28 Adam Dunn .75
WM30 Mark Teixeira 1.00
WM31 Albert Pujols 3.00
WM32 Cal Ripken Jr. 4.00
WM33 Ryne Sandberg 2.00
WM34 Don Mattingly 2.00
WM35 Roger Clemens 3.00
WM36 Jose Reyes .50
WM38 Derrek Lee 1.00
WM39 Miguel Cabrera 1.00
WM41 Barry Bonds 3.00
WM42 Barry Bonds 3.00
WM44 Livan Hernandez .50
WM45 Derek Jeter 3.00
WM46 David Ortiz 1.00
WM48 Ivan Rodriguez .75
WM52 Alex Rodriguez 3.00
WM53 Vladimir Guerrero 1.00

World Series Relics

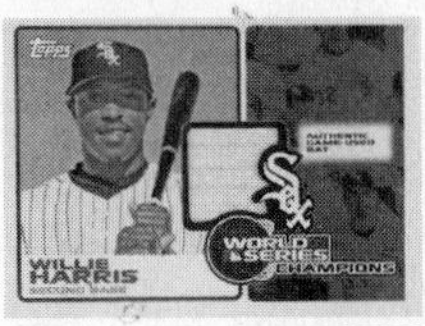

NM/M

Common Player:
MB Mark Buehrle/Glv/100 200.00
JC Joe Crede 35.00
JD Jermaine Dye 20.00
CEB Carl Everett 15.00
CEU Carl Everett/Uni./100 90.00
JG Jon Garland 20.00
WH Willie Harris 10.00
TI Tadahito Iguchi 25.00
BJ Bobby Jenks/Glv/100 275.00
PKB Paul Konerko 15.00
PKU Paul Konerko 15.00
TP Timoniel Perez 15.00
AP A.J. Pierzynski 20.00
SP Scott Podsednik 25.00
AR Aaron Rowand 25.00
FT Frank Thomas 25.00
JU Juan Uribe 20.00

2006 Topps Updates & Highlights

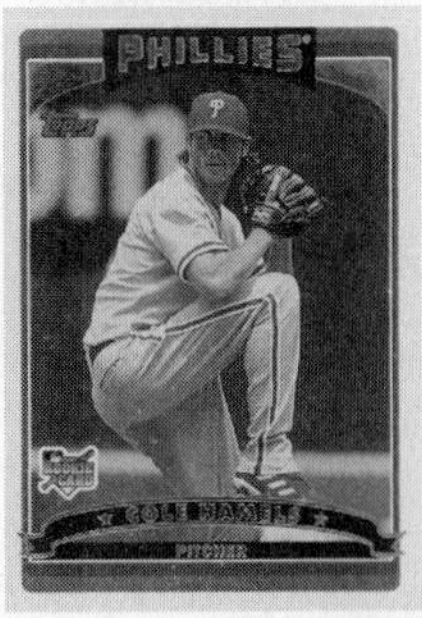

NM/M

Complete Factory Set (333): 40.00
Complete Set (330): 30.00
Common Player: .10
UH1 Austin Kearns .25
UH2 Adam Eaton .10
UH3 Juan Encarnacion .10
UH4 Jarrod Washburn .10
UH5 Alex Gonzalez .10
UH6 Toby Hall .10
UH7 Preston Wilson .10
UH8 Ramon Ortiz .10
UH9 Jason Michaels .10
UH10 Jeff Weaver .10
UH11 Russell Branyan .10
UH12 Brett Tomko .10
UH13 Doug Mientkiewicz .10
UH14 David Wells .10
UH15 Corey Koskie .10
UH16 Russ Ortiz .10
UH17 Carlos Pena .25
UH18 Mark Hendrickson .10
UH19 Julian Tavarez .10
UH20 Jeff Conine .10
UH21 Dioner Navarro .10
UH22 Bob Wickman .10
UH23 Felipe Lopez .10
UH24 Eddie Guardado .10
UH25 David Dellucci .10
UH26 Ryan Wagner .10
UH27 Nick Green .10
UH28 Gary Majewski .10
UH29 Shea Hillenbrand .10
UH30 Jae Weong Seo .10
UH31 Royce Clayton .10
UH32 David Riske .10
UH33 Joey Gathright .10
UH34 Robinson Tejeda .10
UH35 Edwin Jackson .10
UH36 Aubrey Huff .10
UH37 Akinori Otsuka .10
UH38 Juan Castro .10
UH39 Zach Day .10
UH40 Jeremy Accardo .10
UH41 Shawn Green .10
UH42 Kazuo Matsui .10
UH43 J.J. Putz .10
UH44 David Ross .10
UH45 Scott Williamson .10
UH46 Joe Borchard .10
UH47 Elmer Dessens .10
UH48 Odalis Perez .10
UH49 Kelly Shoppach .10
UH50 Brandon Phillips .25
UH51 Guillermo Mota .10
UH52 Alex Cintron .10
UH53 Denny Bautista .10
UH54 Josh Bard .10
UH55 Julio Lugo .10
UH56 Doug Mirabelli .10
UH57 Kip Wells .10
UH58 Adrian Gonzalez .25
UH59 Shawn Chacon .10
UH60 Marcus Thames .10
UH61 Craig Wilson .10
UH62 Cory Sullivan .10
UH63 Ben Broussard .10
UH64 Todd Walker .10
UH65 Greg Maddux 1.00
UH66 Xavier Nady .20
UH67 Oliver Perez .10
UH68 Sean Casey .10
UH69 Kyle Lohse .10
UH70 Carlos Lee .25
UH71 Rheal Cormier .10
UH72 Ronnie Belliard .10
UH73 Cory Lidle .10
UH74 David Bell .10
UH75 Wilson Betemit .10
UH76 Danys Baez .10
UH77 Mike Stanton .10
UH78 Kevin Mench .10
UH79 Sandy Alomar .10
UH80 Cesar Izturis .10
UH81 Jeremy Affeldt .10
UH82 Matt Stairs .10
UH83 Hector Luna .10
UH84 Tony Graffanino .10
UH85 J.P. Howell .10
UH86 Bengie Molina .10
UH87 Maicer Izturis .10
UH88 Marco Scutaro .10
UH89 Daryle Ward .10
UH90 Sal Fasano .10
UH91 Oscar Villarreal .10
UH92 Gabe Gross .10
UH93 Phil Nevin .10
UH94 Damon Hollins .10
UH95 Juan Cruz .10
UH96 Marlon Anderson .10
UH97 Jason Davis .10
UH98 Ryan Shealy .10
UH99 Francisco Cordero .10
UH100 Bobby Abreu .25
UH101 Roberto Hernandez .10
UH102 Gary Bennett .10
UH103 Aaron Sele .10
UH104 Nook Logan .10
UH105 Alfredo Amezaga .10
UH106 Chris Woodward .10
UH107 Kevin Jarvis .10
UH108 B.J. Upton .25
UH109 Alan Embree .10
UH110 Milton Bradley .20
UH111 Peter Orr .10
UH112 Jeff Cirillo .10
UH113 Corey Patterson .10
UH114 Josh Paul .10
UH115 Fernando Rodney .10
UH116 Jerry Hairston .10
UH117 Scott Proctor .10
UH118 Ambiorix Burgos .10
UH119 Jose Bautista .10
UH120 Livan Hernandez .10
UH121 John McDonald .10
UH122 Ronny Cedeno .10
UH123 Nate Robertson .10
UH124 Jamey Carroll .10
UH125 Alex Escobar .10
UH126 Endy Chavez .10
UH127 Jorge Julio .10
UH128 Kenny Lofton .10
UH129 Matt Diaz .10
UH130 David Bush .10
UH131 Jose Molina .10
UH132 Mike MacDougal .10
UH133 Benjamin Zobrist **(RC)** .50
UH134 Shane Komine **RC** .25
UH135 Casey Janssen **RC** .50
UH136 Kevin Frandsen **(RC)** .25
UH137 John Rheinecker **(RC)** .25
UH138 Matthew Kemp **(RC)** .75
UH139 Scott Mathieson **(RC)** .25
UH140 Jered Weaver **(RC)** .75
UH141 Joel Guzman **(RC)** .25
UH142 Anibal Sanchez **(RC)** .25
UH143 Melky Cabrera **(RC)** .50
UH144 Howie Kendrick **(RC)** .50
UH145 Cole Hamels **(RC)** 1.00
UH146 Willy Aybar **(RC)** .25
UH147 James Shields **RC** .50
UH148 Kevin Thompson **(RC)** .25
UH149 Jon Lester **(RC)** 1.00
UH150 Stephen Drew **(RC)** .75
UH151 Andre Ethier **(RC)** .50
UH152 Jordan Tata **RC** .50
UH153 Michael Napoli **RC** 1.00
UH154 Kason Gabbard **(RC)** .25
UH155 Lastings Milledge **(RC)** .50
UH156 Erick Aybar **(RC)** .50
UH157 Fausto Carmona **(RC)** .50
UH158 Russell Martin **(RC)** .75
UH159 David Pauley **(RC)** .25
UH160 Andy Marte **(RC)** .25
UH161 Carlos Quentin **(RC)** .50
UH162 Franklin Gutierrez **(RC)** .25
UH163 Taylor Buchholz **(RC)** .25
UH164 Josh Johnson **(RC)** .25
UH165 Chad Billingsley **(RC)** .50
UH166 Kendry Morales **(RC)** .25
UH167 Adam Loewen **(RC)** .25
UH168 Yusmeiro Petit **(RC)** .25
UH169 Matt Albers **(RC)** .25
UH170 John Maine **(RC)** .50
UH171 Alex Rodriguez 1.00
UH172 Mike Piazza .50
UH173 Cory Sullivan .10
UH174 Anibal Sanchez .10
UH175 Trevor Hoffman .10
UH176 Barry Bonds .75
UH177 Derek Jeter 1.00
UH178 Jose Reyes .50
UH179 Manny Ramirez .25
UH180 Vladimir Guerrero .25
UH181 Mariano Rivera .25
UH182 Postseason Highlights .25
UH183 Postseason Highlights .25
UH184 Postseason Highlights .25
UH185 Postseason Highlights .25
UH186 Postseason Highlights .25
UH187 Postseason Highlights .25
UH188 Postseason Highlights .25
UH189 Postseason Highlights .25
UH190 Postseason Highlights .25
UH191 Postseason Highlights .25
UH192 Postseason Highlights .25
UH193 Postseason Highlights .25
UH194 Postseason Highlights .25
UH195 Postseason Highlights .25
UH196 Postseason Highlights .25
UH197 Postseason Highlights .25
UH198 Postseason Highlights .25
UH199 Postseason Highlights .25
UH200 Postseason Highlights .25
UH201 Postseason Highlights .25
UH202 David Ortiz, Jermaine Dye, Travis Hafner .25
UH203 Joe Mauer, Derek Jeter, Robinson Cano .50
UH204 David Ortiz, Justin Morneau, Raul Ibanez .25
UH205 Carl Crawford, Chone Figgins, Ichiro Suzuki .50
UH206 Johan Santana, Chien-Ming Wang, Jon Garland .50
UH207 Johan Santana, Roy Halladay, C.C. Sabathia .25
UH208 Johan Santana, Jeremy Bonderman, John Lackey .25
UH209 Francisco Rodriguez, Bobby Jenks, B.J. Ryan .10
UH210 Ryan Howard, Albert Pujols, Alfonso Soriano 1.00
UH211 Freddy Sanchez, Miguel Cabrera, Albert Pujols .50
UH212 Ryan Howard, Albert Pujols, Lance Berkman 1.00
UH213 Jose Reyes, Juan Pierre, Hanley Ramirez .50
UH214 Derek Lowe, Brandon Webb, Carlos Zambrano .25
UH215 Roy Oswalt, Chris Carpenter, Brandon Webb .25
UH216 Aaron Harang, Jake Peavy, John Smoltz .10
UH217 Trevor Hoffman, Billy Wagner, Joe Borowski .10
UH218 Ichiro Suzuki .50
UH219 Derek Jeter .75
UH220 Alex Rodriguez .75
UH221 David Ortiz .50
UH222 Vladimir Guerrero .25
UH223 Ivan Rodriguez .25
UH224 Vernon Wells .25
UH225 Mark Loretta .10

UH226	Kenny Rogers	.10
UH227	Alfonso Soriano	.50
UH228	Carlos Beltran	.25
UH229	Albert Pujols	.75
UH230	Jason Bay	.25
UH231	Edgar Renteria	.25
UH232	David Wright	.50
UH233	Chase Utley	.50
UH234	Paul LoDuca	.10
UH235	Brad Penny	.10
UH236	Derrick Turnbow	.10
UH237	Mark Redman	.10
UH238	Francisco Liriano	.25
UH239	A.J. Pierzynski	.10
UH240	Grady Sizemore	.25
UH241	Jose Contreras	.10
UH242	Jermaine Dye	.25
UH243	Jason Schmidt	.10
UH244	Nomar Garciaparra	.25
UH245	Scott Kazmir	.25
UH246	Johan Santana	.25
UH247	Chris Capuano	.10
UH248	Magglio Ordonez	.25
UH249	Gary Matthews	.10
UH250	Carlos Lee	.25
UH251	David Eckstein	.10
UH252	Michael Young	.25
UH253	Matt Holliday	.25
UH254	Lance Berkman	.25
UH255	Scott Rolen	.25
UH256	Bronson Arroyo	.10
UH257	Barry Zito	.10
UH258	Brian McCann	.25
UH259	Jose Lopez	.10
UH260	Chris Carpenter	.25
UH261	Roy Halladay	.25
UH262	Jim Thome	.25
UH263	Dan Uggla	.25
UH264	Mariano Rivera	.25
UH265	Roy Oswalt	.10
UH266	Tom Gordon	.10
UH267	Troy Glaus	.25
UH268	Bobby Jenks	.10
UH269	Freddy Sanchez	.10
UH270	Paul Konerko	.25
UH271	Joe Mauer	.25
UH272	B.J. Ryan	.10
UH273	Ryan Howard	.75
UH274	Brian Fuentes	.10
UH275	Miguel Cabrera	.25
UH276	Brandon Webb	.25
UH277	Mark Buehrle	.10
UH278	Trevor Hoffman	.10
UH279	Jonathan Papelbon	.25
UH280	Andruw Jones	.25
UH281	Miguel Tejada	.25
UH282	Carlos Zambrano	.25
UH283	Ryan Howard	.75
UH284	David Wright	.50
UH285	Miguel Cabrera	.25
UH286	David Ortiz	.25
UH287	Jermaine Dye	.10
UH288	Miguel Tejada	.25
UH289	Lance Berkman	.25
UH290	Troy Glaus	.25
UH291	David Wright, Tom Glavine	.25
UH292	Ryan Howard, Tom Gordon	.50
UH293	Miguel Cabrera, Dontrelle Willis	.25
UH294	Andruw Jones, John Smoltz	.25
UH295	Alfonso Soriano	.25
UH296	Albert Pujols, Chris Carpenter	.50
UH297	Adam Dunn, Bronson Arroyo	.10
UH298	Lance Berkman, Roy Oswalt	.25
UH299	Chris Capuano, Prince Fielder	.50
UH300	Freddy Sanchez, Jason Bay	.10
UH301	Carlos Zambrano, Juan Pierre	.10
UH302	Adrian Gonzalez, Trevor Hoffman	.10
UH303	Derek Lowe, Rafael Furcal	.10
UH304	Omar Vizquel, Jason Schmidt	.10
UH305	Brandon Webb, Chad Tracy	.10
UH306	Matt Holliday, Garrett Atkins	.25
UH307	Alex Rodriguez, Chien-Ming Wang	.50
UH308	Curt Schilling, David Ortiz	.25
UH309	Roy Halladay, Vernon Wells	.10
UH310	Miguel Tejada, Erik Bedard	.10
UH311	Carl Crawford, Scott Kazmir	.10
UH312	Jeremy Bonderman, Magglio Ordonez	.10
UH313	Justin Morneau, Johan Santana	.25
UH314	Jon Garland, Jermaine Dye	.10
UH315	Travis Hafner, C.C. Sabathia	.10
UH316	Emil Brown, Mark Grudzielanek	.10
UH317	Frank Thomas, Barry Zito	.25
UH318	Jered Weaver, Vladimir Guerrero	.25
UH319	Michael Young, Gary Matthews	.10
UH320	Ichiro Suzuki, J.J. Putz	.50

UH321	Derek Jeter, Robinson Cano	.50
UH232	Mark Mulder, Chris Carpenter	.25
UH323	Trevor Schmidt, Jason Schmidt	.10
UH324	David Wright, Paul LoDuca	.25
UH325	Lance Berkman, Roy Oswalt	.25
UH326	Derek Jeter, Jose Reyes	.50
UH327	David Wright, Cliff Floyd	.25
UH328	Johan Santana, Francisco Liriano	.25
UH329	Stephen Drew, J.D. Drew	.25
UH330	Jeff Weaver	.25

Black

Black: 15-25X
Production 55 Sets

First Edition

1st Edition: 4-6X
Inserted 1:Hobby Box

Gold

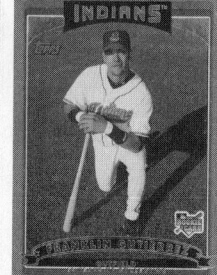

Gold: 5-10X
Production 2,006 Sets

Platinum

Production One Set

All-Star Autographs

No Pricing
Production 25 Sets

All-Star Stitches

NM/M
Common Player: 4.00
Inserted 1:43
Patch: No Pricing
Production 10 Sets

BA	Bronson Arroyo	8.00
JB	Jason Bay	15.00
CB	Carlos Beltran	10.00
LB	Lance Berkman	10.00
MB	Mark Buehrle	8.00
MC	Miguel Cabrera	10.00
RC	Robinson Cano	10.00
CFC	Chris Capuano	4.00
CC	Chris Carpenter	10.00
JC	Jose Contreras	8.00
JD	Jermaine Dye	6.00
DE	David Eckstein	15.00
BF	Brian Fuentes	4.00
TEG	Troy Glaus	6.00
TMG	Tom Glavine	8.00
TG	Tom Gordon	4.00
VG	Vladimir Guerrero	8.00
RH	Roy Halladay	6.00
TH	Trevor Hoffman	6.00
MH	Matt Holliday	6.00
RJH	Ryan Howard	25.00
BJ	Bobby Jenks	4.00
AJ	Andruw Jones	8.00
SK	Scott Kazmir	6.00
PK	Paul Konerko	8.00
CL	Carlos Lee	8.00

PL	Paul LoDuca	6.00
JL	Jose Lopez	4.00
ML	Mark Loretta	4.00
GM	Gary Matthews	6.00
JM	Joe Mauer	10.00
BM	Brian McCann	15.00
MO	Magglio Ordonez	8.00
DO	David Ortiz	15.00
RO	Roy Oswalt	6.00
JP	Jonathan Papelbon	20.00
BP	Brad Penny	4.00
AJP	A.J. Pierzynski	4.00
AP	Albert Pujols	25.00
MAR	Mark Redman	4.00
ER	Edgar Renteria	6.00
JR	Jose Reyes	15.00
MR	Mariano Rivera	10.00
AR	Alex Rodriguez	15.00
IR	Ivan Rodriguez	6.00
KR	Kenny Rogers	6.00
SR	Scott Rolen	8.00
BR	B.J. Ryan	4.00
FS	Freddy Sanchez	6.00
JS	Johan Santana	10.00
JDS	Jason Schmidt	8.00
GS	Grady Sizemore	10.00
AS	Alfonso Soriano	8.00
MT	Miguel Tejada	8.00
JT	Jim Thome	10.00
DT	Derrick Turnbow	4.00
DU	Dan Uggla	10.00
CU	Chase Utley	10.00
BW	Brandon Webb	10.00
VW	Vernon Wells	8.00
DW	David Wright	20.00
MY	Michael Young	6.00
CZ	Carlos Zambrano	8.00

All-Star Patches

No Pricing
Production 10 Sets

Barry Bonds HR History

NM/M
Common Bonds HR History: 1.00
Inserted 1:6
Autographs: No Pricing
Production Five Sets
BB709-734 Barry Bonds 1.00

Barry Bonds 715

NM/M
Inserted 1:36
715-BB Barry Bonds 3.00

Barry Bonds 715 Relic

NM/M
Production 715
Barry Bonds 35.00

Chrome RC Box Topper

NM/M
Production 599
Inserted one per box.
Refractors: 2-4X
Production 25 Sets

1	Aaron Zobrist	3.00
2	Shane Komine	3.00
3	Casey Janssen	3.00
4	Kevin Frandsen	3.00
5	John Rheinecker	3.00
6	Matthew Kemp	8.00
7	Scott Mathieson	3.00
8	Jered Weaver	8.00
9	Joel Guzman	3.00
10	Anibal Sanchez	3.00
11	Melky Cabrera	6.00
12	Howie Kendrick	6.00
13	Cole Hamels	8.00
14	Willy Aybar	3.00
15	James Shields	5.00
16	Kevin Thompson	3.00
17	Jon Lester	20.00
18	Stephen Drew	6.00
19	Andre Ethier	5.00
20	Jordan Tata	3.00
21	Michael Napoli	6.00
22	Kason Gabbard	3.00
23	Lastings Milledge	5.00
24	Erick Aybar	3.00

25	Fausto Carmona	5.00
26	Russell Martin	6.00
27	David Pauley	3.00
28	Andy Marte	3.00
29	Carlos Quentin	5.00
30	Franklin Gutierrez	4.00
31	Taylor Buchholz	3.00
32	Josh Johnson	3.00
33	Chad Billingsley	6.00
34	Kendry Morales	3.00
35	Adam Loewen	3.00
36	Yusmeiro Petit	3.00
37	Matt Albers	3.00
38	John Maine	6.00
39	Josh Willingham	5.00
40	Taylor Tankersley	3.00
41	Pat Neshek	30.00
42	Francisco Rosario	3.00
43	Matt Smith	3.00
44	Jonathan Sanchez	5.00
45	Chris Demaria	3.00
46	Manuel Corpas	3.00
47	Kevin Reese	3.00
48	Brent Clevlen	3.00
49	Anderson Hernandez	3.00
50	Chris Roberson	3.00

Derby Digs Relics

NM/M
Inserted 1:4,200
JD Jermaine Dye 25.00
TG Troy Glaus 25.00

Mickey Mantle HR History Relics

NM/M
Common Mantle: 140.00
Production Seven Sets

Mickey Mantle HR History

NM/M
Common Mantle (102-201): 2.00
Inserted 1:4

Midsummer Covers

No Pricing
Production 10 Sets

Rookie Debut

NM/M
Common Player: 1.00
Inserted 1:4

RD1	Joel Zumaya	2.00
RD2	Ian Kinsler	2.00
RD3	Kenji Johjima	3.00
RD4	Josh Barfield	1.00
RD5	Nicholas Markakis	2.00
RD6	Dan Uggla	2.00
RD7	Eric Reed	1.00
RD8	Carlos Martinez	1.00
RD9	Angel Pagan	1.50
RD10	Jason Childers	1.00
RD11	Ruddy Lugo	1.00
RD12	James Loney	2.50
RD13	Fernando Nieve	1.00
RD14	Reggie Abercrombie	1.00
RD15	Boone Logan	1.00
RD16	Brian Bannister	1.50
RD17	Ricky Nolasco	1.50
RD18	Willie Eyre	1.00
RD19	Fabio Castro	1.00
RD20	Jordan Tata	1.00
RD21	Taylor Buchholz	1.50
RD22	Sean Marshall	1.00
RD23	John Rheinecker	1.00
RD24	Casey Janssen	1.00
RD25	Russell Martin	1.50
RD26	Yusmeiro Petit	1.00
RD27	Kendry Morales	1.50

RD28	Alay Soler	1.00
RD29	Jered Weaver	3.00
RD30	Matthew Kemp	2.00
RD31	Enrique Gonzalez	1.00
RD32	Lastings Milledge	2.00
RD33	James Shields	1.00
RD34	David Pauley	1.00
RD35	Zach Jackson	1.00
RD36	Zach Miner	1.00
RD37	Jon Lester	3.00
RD38	Chad Billingsley	2.00
RD39	Scott Thorman	1.00
RD40	Anibal Sanchez	2.00
RD41	Mike Thompson	1.00
RD42	T.J. Beam	1.00
RD43	Stephen Drew	3.00
RD44	Joe Saunders	1.00
RD45	Carlos Quentin	1.50

Rookie Debut Autographs

		NM/M
Common Autograph:		15.00
RA	Reggie Abercrombie	10.00
MA	Matt Albers	20.00
FC	Fausto Carmona	15.00
FF	Emiliano Fruto	15.00
IK	Ian Kinsler	20.00
JL	Jon Lester	40.00
BL	Bobby Livingston	15.00
AL	Adam Loewen	40.00
MN	Michael Napoli	30.00
RN	Ricky Nolasco	15.00
YP	Yusmeiro Petit	15.00
MP	Martin Prado	15.00
JS	Jeremy Sowers	15.00
ST	Scott Thorman	15.00

Signature Moves

		NM/M
Common Autograph:		
AH	Aubrey Huff	15.00
JL	Julio Lugo	15.00
BP	Brandon Phillips	20.00
BW	Brad Wilkerson	10.00
CW	Craig Wilson	10.00

Touch 'Em All Relics

		NM/M
Inserted 1:610		
CB	Carlos Beltran	20.00
RH	Ryan Howard	30.00
JM	Joe Mauer	15.00
DO	David Ortiz	20.00
AP	Albert Pujols	30.00
AR	Alex Rodriguez	25.00
IS	Ichiro Suzuki	25.00
MT	Miguel Tejada	10.00
DW	David Wright	25.00
MY	Michael Young	8.00

2006 Topps AFLAC

		NM/M
Common Player:		15.00
BB	Blake Beavan	50.00
BK	Brett Krill	40.00
CC	Christian Colon	40.00
CR	Cameron Rupp	25.00
DB	Drake Britton	15.00
DD	Derek Dietrich	25.00
DM	D.J. LeMahieu	25.00
DR	Danny Rams	25.00
ED	Evan Danieli	30.00
EG	Erik Goeddel	30.00
FF	Freddie Freeman	25.00
GP	Greg Peavey	30.00
HM	Hunter Morris	40.00
JG	Jon Gilmore	25.00
JH	Jason Heyward	65.00
JL	Joe Leftridge	20.00
JS	Josh Smoker	40.00
JT	John Tolisano	25.00
JV	Josh Vitters	125.00
KB	Kyle Blair	15.00
KK	Kevin Keyes	15.00
MB	Madison Bumgarner	75.00
MH	Matt Harvey	60.00
MM	Michael Main	40.00
NN	Nick Noonan	15.00
NR	Neil Ramirez	25.00
PD	Paul Demny	15.00
RP	Rick Porcello	75.00
RS	Robert Stock	50.00
SB	Steven Brooks	25.00
SS	Sequoyah Stonecipher	75.00
TA	Tim Alderson	25.00
YG	Yasmani Grandal	25.00

2006 Topps Allen & Ginter

		NM/M
Complete Set (350):		
Common Player:		.25
Common SP:		.50
SP's Inserted 1:2		
Pack (7):		8.00
Box (24):		160.00
1	Albert Pujols	3.00
2	Aubrey Huff	.25
3	Mark Teixeira	.75
4	Vernon Wells	.50
5	Ken Griffey Jr./SP	4.00
6	Nick Swisher	.25
7	Jose Reyes	.75
8	David Wright	2.00
9	Vladimir Guerrero	1.00

10	Andruw Jones	.50
11	Ramon Hernandez	.25
12	Miguel Tejada	.75
13	Juan Pierre	.25
14	Jim Thome	.75
15	Austin Kearns/SP	.50
16	Jhonny Peralta	.25
17	Clint Barmes	.25
18	Angel Berroa	.25
19	Nomar Garciaparra	.75
20	Joe Nathan	.25
21	Brandon Webb	.75
22	Chad Tracy	.25
23	Derek Jeter	3.00
24	Conor Jackson **(RC)**	.50
25	Jason Giambi/SP	1.00
26	Johnny Estrada	.25
27	Luis Gonzalez	.40
28	Javier Vazquez	.25
29	Orlando Hudson	.25
30	Shawn Green	.40
31	Mark Buehrle	.40
32	Wily Mo Pena	.25
33	C.C. Sabathia	.50
34	Ronnie Belliard	.25
35	Travis Hafner/SP	1.00
36	Mike Jacobs **(RC)**	.50
37	Roy Oswalt	.50
38	Zack Greinke	.50
39	J.D. Drew	.40
40	Jeff Kent	.40
41	Ben Sheets	.40
42	Luis Castillo	.25
43	Carlos Delgado	.75
44	Cliff Floyd	.25
45	Danny Haren/SP	.50
46	Bobby Abreu	.50
47	Jeromy Burnitz	.25
48	Khalil Greene	.25
49	Moises Alou	.50
50	Alex Rodriguez/SP	5.00
51	Ervin Santana/SP	.50
52	Bartolo Colon/SP	.50
53	John Smoltz/SP	1.00
54	David Ortiz/SP	2.00
55	Hideki Matsui/SP	3.00
56	Jermaine Dye/SP	.50
57	Victor Martinez/SP	.50
58	Willy Taveras/SP	.50
59	Brady Clark/SP	.50
60	Justin Morneau	.50
61	Xavier Nady	.25
62	Rich Harden	.25
63	Jack Wilson	.25
64	Brian Giles	.25
65	Jon Lieber/SP	.50
66	Dan Johnson	.25
67	Billy Wagner	.25
68	Rickie Weeks	.40
69	Chris Ray **(RC)**	.50
70	Chris Shelton	.25
71	Dmitri Young	.25
72	Ivan Rodriguez	.75
73	Jeremy Bonderman	.50
74	Justin Verlander **(RC)**	1.00
75	Randy Johnson	1.00
76	Magglio Ordonez	.50
77	Brandon Inge	.25
78	Placido Polanco	.25
79	Ryan Howard	1.00
80	Jason Bay	.50
81	Sean Casey	.25
82	Jeremy Hermida **(RC)**	.50
83	Mike Cameron	.25
84	Trevor Hoffman	.25
85	Mike Matheny/SP	.50
86	Steve Finley	.25
87	Adam Everett	.25
88	Jason Isringhausen	.25
89	Jonny Gomes	.25
90	Barry Zito	.50
91	Bobby Crosby	.25
92	Eric Chavez	.25
93	Frank Thomas	.75
94	Huston Street	.25
95	Jorge Posada	.50
96	Casey Kotchman	.25
97	Darin Erstad	.25
98	Chipper Jones	1.00
99	Jeff Francoeur	.50
100	Barry Bonds	3.00
101	Alfonso Soriano	1.00
102	Brandon Claussen	.25
103	Aaron Boone	.25
104	Roger Clemens	3.00
105	Andy Pettitte/SP	.75
106	Nick Johnson	.25
107	Tom Gordon	.25
108	Orlando Hernandez	.25
109	Francisco Rodriguez	.25
110	Orlando Cabrera	.25
111	Edgar Renteria	.50
112	Tim Hudson	.50
113	Coco Crisp	.25
114	Matt Clement	.25
115	Greg Maddux/SP	3.00
116	Paul Konerko	.50
117	Felipe Lopez	.25
118	Garrett Atkins	.50
119	Akinori Otsuka	.25
120	Craig Biggio	.50
121	Danys Baez	.25
122	Brad Penny	.25
123	Eric Gagne	.25
124	Lew Ford	.25
125	Mariano Rivera/SP	1.00
126	Carlos Beltran	.75
127	Pedro Martinez	1.00
128	Todd Helton	.75
129	Aaron Rowand	.25
130	Mike Lieberthal	.25
131	Oliver Perez	.25
132	Ryan Klesko	.25
133	Randy Winn	.25
134	Yuniesky Betancourt	.25
135	David Eckstein/SP	.50
136	Chad Orvella	.25
137	Toby Hall	.25
138	Hank Blalock	.50
139	B.J. Ryan	.25
140	Roy Halladay	.50
141	Livan Hernandez	.25
142	John Patterson	.25
143	Bengie Molina	.25
144	Brad Wilkerson	.25
145	Jorge Cantu/SP	.50
146	Mark Mulder	.50
147	Felix Hernandez	.50
148	Paul LoDuca	.25
149	Prince Fielder **(RC)**	4.00
150	Johnny Damon/SP	2.00
151	Ryan Langerhans/SP	.50
152	Kris Benson/SP	.50
153	Curt Schilling/SP	2.00
154	Manny Ramirez/SP	2.00
155	Robinson Cano/SP	1.50
156	Derrek Lee/SP	1.50
157	A.J. Pierzynski/SP	.50
158	Adam Dunn/SP	1.00
159	Cliff Lee/SP	.50
160	Grady Sizemore	.50
161	Jeff Francis	.25
162	Dontrelle Willis	.50
163	Brad Ausmus	.25
164	Preston Wilson	.25
165	Derek Lowe/SP	.50
166	Chris Capuano	.25
167	Joe Mauer	.50
168	Torii Hunter	.40
169	Chase Utley	.75
170	Zachary Duke	.25
171	Jason Schmidt	.40
172	Adrian Beltre	.25
173	Eddie Guardado	.25
174	Richie Sexson	.50
175	Miguel Cabrera/SP	2.00
176	Julio Lugo	.25
177	Francisco Cordero	.25
178	Kevin Millwood	.25
179	A.J. Burnett	.25
180	Jose Guillen	.25
181	Larry Bigbie	.25
182	Raul Ibanez	.25
183	Jake Peavy	.50
184	Pat Burrell	.50
185	Tom Glavine/SP	.75
186	J.J. Hardy	.25
187	Emil Brown	.25
188	Lance Berkman	.50
189	Marcus Giles	.25
190	Scott Podsednik	.25
191	Chone Figgins	.50
192	Melvin Mora	.25
193	Mark Loretta	.25
194	Carlos Zambrano	.50
195	Chien-Ming Wang	.75
196	Mark Prior	.50
197	Bobby Jenks	.25
198	Brian Fuentes	.25
199	Garret Anderson	.25
200	Ichiro Suzuki	2.00
201	Brian Roberts	.50
202	Jason Kendall	.25
203	Milton Bradley	.25
204	Jimmy Rollins	.75
205	Brett Myers/SP	.50
206	Joe Randa	.25
207	Mike Piazza	1.00
208	Matt Morris	.25
209	Omar Vizquel	.25
210	Jeremy Reed	.25
211	Chris Carpenter	.50
212	Jim Edmonds	.50
213	Scott Kazmir	.50
214	Travis Lee	.25
215	Michael Young/SP	.75
216	Rod Barajas	.25
217	Gustavo Chacin	.25
218	Lyle Overbay	.25
219	Troy Glaus	.50
220	Chad Cordero	.25
221	Jose Vidro	.25
222	Scott Rolen	.75
223	Carl Crawford	.50
224	Rocco Baldelli	.25
225	Mike Mussina	.50
226	Kelvim Escobar	.25
227	Corey Patterson	.25
228	Javy Lopez	.25
229	Jonathan Papelbon/SP **(RC)**	5.00
230	Aramis Ramirez	.50
231	Tadahito Iguchi	.50
232	Morgan Ensberg	.25
233	Mark Grudzielanek	.25
234	Mike Sweeney	.25
235	Shawn Chacon/SP	.50
236	Nick Punto	.25
237	Geoff Jenkins	.25
238	Carlos Lee	.50
239	David DeJesus	.25
240	Brad Lidge	.25
241	Bob Wickman	.25
242	Jon Garland	.25
243	Kerry Wood	.50
244	Bronson Arroyo	.25
245	Matt Holliday/SP	.75
246	Josh Beckett	.75
247	Johan Santana	.75
248	Rafael Furcal	.50
249	Shannon Stewart	.25
250	Gary Sheffield	.50
251	Josh Barfield **(RC)**	.50
252	Kenji Johjima **RC**	2.00
253	Ian Kinsler **(RC)**	.50
254	Brian Anderson **(RC)**	.50
255	Matt Cain **(RC)**	1.00
256	Josh Willingham/SP **(RC)**	.50
257	John Koronka **(RC)**	.50
258	Chris Duffy **(RC)**	.50
259	Brian McCann **(RC)**	.50
260	Hanley Ramirez **(RC)**	1.00
261	Hong-Chih Kuo **(RC)**	.75
262	Francisco Liriano **(RC)**	2.00
263	Anderson Hernandez **(RC)**	.50
264	Ryan Zimmerman **(RC)**	4.00
265	Brian Bannister/SP **(RC)**	.50
266	Nolan Ryan	2.00
267	Frank Robinson	1.00
268	Roberto Clemente	3.00
269	Hank Greenberg	.50
270	Napoleon Lajoie	.50
271	Lloyd Waner	.25
272	Paul Waner	.25
273	Frankie Frisch	.25
274	Bill "Moose" Skowron	.25
275	Mickey Mantle	6.00
276	Brooks Robinson	1.00
277	Carl Yastrzemski	1.00
278	Johnny Pesky	.25
279	Stan Musial	1.50
280	Bill Mazeroski	.50
281	Harmon Killebrew	.75
282	Monte Irvin	.50
283	Bob Gibson	1.00
284	Ted Williams	2.00
285	Yogi Berra/SP	2.00
286	Ernie Banks	1.00
287	Bobby Doerr	.25
288	Josh Gibson	.50
289	Bob Feller	.25
290	Cal Ripken Jr.	3.00
291	Bobby Cox	.25
292	Terry Francona	.25
293	Dusty Baker	.25
294	Ozzie Guillen	.25
295	Jim Leyland	.50
296	Willie Randolph	.25
297	Joe Torre	.50
298	Felipe Alou	.25
299	Tony LaRussa	.25
300	Frank Robinson	.50
301	Mike Tyson	2.00
302	Duke Paoa Kahanamoku	.25
303	Jennie Finch	2.00
304	Brandi Chastain	.25
305	Danica Patrick/SP	10.00
306	Wendy Guey	.25
307	Hulk Hogan	.25
308	Carl Lewis	.25
309	John Wooden	.25
310	Randy Couture	.25
311	Andy Irons	.25
312	Takeru Kobayashi	.25
313	Leon Spinks	.25
314	Jim Thorpe	1.00
315	Jerry Bailey/SP	.50
316	Adrian C. Anson	.25
317	John M. Ward	.25
318	Mike Kelly	.25
319	Cpt. Jack Glasscock	.25
320	Aaron Hill	.25
321	Derrick Turnbow	.25
322	Nicholas Markakis	.25
323	Brad Hawpe	.25
324	Kevin Mench	.25
325	John Lackey/SP	.50
326	Chester A. Arthur	.25
327	Ulysses S. Grant	.50
328	Abraham Lincoln	1.00
329	Grover Cleveland	.25
330	Benjamin Harrison	.25

331	Theodore Roosevelt	.50
332	Rutherford B. Hayes	.25
333	Chancellor Otto Von Bismarck	.25
334	Kaiser Wilhelm II	.25
335	Queen Victoria/SP	.50
336	Pope Leo XIII	.25
337	Thomas Edison	.50
338	Orville Wright	.50
339	Wilbur Wright	.50
340	Nathaniel Hawthorne	.25
341	Herman Melville	.25
342	Stonewall Jackson	.50
343	Robert E. Lee	.50
344	Andrew Carnegie	.50
345	John Rockefeller/SP	.50
346	Bob Fitzsimmons	.25
347	Billy the Kid	.25
348	Buffalo Bill	.25
349	Jesse James	.25
350	Statue of Liberty	.25

Mini

BRONSON ARROYO.
ALLEN & GINTER'S
BROOKLYN   NEW YORK

Mini:	2-4X
SP's:	1-2X
Mini SP's Inserted 1:13	
Mini (351-375):	No Pricing
#'s 351-375 Inserted In Rip Cards	
Allen & Ginter Back:	3-6X
Inserted 1:5	
A & G Back SP's:	2-3X
Inserted 1:65	
Bazooka Mini:	No Pricing
Production 25 Sets	
Black Mini:	5-10X
Inserted 1:10	
Black SP:	3-5X
Inserted 1:130	
Wood:	No Pricing
Production One Set	

Printing Plates
No Pricing
Production one set per color.

Autographs
NM/M

Cards are not serial numbered.

JB	Jerry Bailey/200	80.00
JBA	Josh Barfield	15.00
CB	Clint Barmes	15.00
BB	Barry Bonds/25	500.00
MC	Miguel Cabrera/100	150.00
RC	Robinson Cano	60.00
BC	Brandi Chastain/200	75.00
EC	Eric Chavez	15.00
RA	Randy Couture	150.00
BF	Bob Feller	75.00
PF	Prince Fielder	100.00
JF	Jennie Finch/200	150.00
LF	Lew Ford	10.00
JG	Jonny Gomes	15.00
VG	Vladimir Guerrero/50	225.00
WG	Wendy Guey	30.00
TG	Tony Gwynn/50	250.00
TH	Travis Hafner	25.00
HH	Hulk Hogan/200	250.00
RH	Ryan Howard	150.00
AI	Andy Irons/200	40.00
KJ	Kenji Johjima/50	275.00
SK	Sal Kazmir	30.00
TK	Takeru Kobayashi/200	75.00
DL	Derrek Lee	40.00
CL	Carl Lewis/200	120.00
FL	Francisco Liriano	40.00
VM	Victor Martinez	30.00
SM	Stan Musial/50	400.00
DP	Danica Patrick/100	500.00
WMP	Wily Mo Pena	20.00
CR	Cal Ripken Jr./50	300.00
AR	Alex Rodriguez/50	400.00
BJR	B.J. Ryan	15.00
NR	Nolan Ryan/50	375.00
ES	Ervin Santana	15.00
JS	Johan Santana/100	125.00

GS	Gary Sheffield/50	140.00
OS	Ozzie Smith/75	200.00
LS	Leon Spinks/200	75.00
HS	Huston Street	40.00
MT	Mike Tyson/200	275.00
CU	Chase Utley	80.00
BW	Billy Wagner	25.00
CMW	Chien-Ming Wang/100	400.00
DWI	Dontrelle Willis/100	40.00
JW	John Wooden/200	200.00
DW	David Wright	140.00
CY	Carl Yastrzemski/50	325.00
MY	Michael Young	35.00
RZ	Ryan Zimmerman	40.00

Allen & Ginter N43
NM/M

Inserted 1:2 Hobby Boxes

1	Alex Rodriguez	4.00
2	Barry Bonds	4.00
3	Albert Pujols	4.00
4	Josh Gibson	2.00
5	Nolan Ryan	4.00
6	Ichiro Suzuki	3.00
7	Mickey Mantle	10.00
8	Ted Williams	4.00
9	David Wright	3.00
10	Ken Griffey Jr.	3.00
11	Mark Teixeira	1.50
12	Adrian C. Anson	2.00
13	Mike Tyson	3.00
14	Kenji Johjima	2.00
15	Ryan Zimmerman	2.00

Allen & Ginter N43 Autos
Production 10 Sets
No Pricing

Allen & Ginter N43 Relics
NM/M
Production 50 Sets

AP	Albert Pujols	100.00
JG	Josh Gibson	250.00

Dick Perez Sketches

NM/M

Common Player		.25
Inserted 1:1		
Originals:		No Pricing
Production One Set		
ARI	Shawn Green	.25
ATL	Andruw Jones	.50
BAL	Miguel Tejada	.50
BOS	David Ortiz	1.00
CHC	Derrek Lee	.50
CHW	Paul Konerko	.50
CIN	Ken Griffey Jr.	1.00
CLE	Travis Hafner	.50
COL	Todd Helton	.50
DET	Ivan Rodriguez	.50
FLA	Miguel Cabrera	.75
HOU	Lance Berkman	.25
KC	Mike Sweeney	.25
LAA	Vladimir Guerrero	.75
LAD	Rafael Furcal	.25
MIL	Carlos Lee	.25
MIN	Johan Santana	.50
NYM	David Wright	1.00
NYY	Alex Rodriguez	2.00
OAK	Huston Street	.25
PHI	Bobby Abreu	.50
PIT	Jason Bay	.50
SDP	Jake Peavy	.50
SEA	Ichiro Suzuki	1.50
SFG	Barry Bonds	2.00
STL	Albert Pujols	2.00
TAM	Aubrey Huff	.25
TEX	Mark Teixeira	.50
TOR	Vernon Wells	.50
WAS	Alfonso Soriano	.75

Personalized Postcards
One Set Produced
No Pricing

Postcards
NM/M
Inserted 1:2 Hobby Boxes

BB	Barry Bonds	4.00
JG	Josh Gibson	2.00
KG	Ken Griffey Jr.	3.00

VG	Vladimir Guerrero	2.00
DJ	Derek Jeter	4.00
MM	Mickey Mantle	10.00
DO	David Ortiz	2.00
AP	Albert Pujols	4.00
MR	Manny Ramirez	2.00
CR	Cal Ripken Jr.	6.00
AR	Alex Rodriguez	4.00
I	Ichiro Suzuki	3.00
MT	Miguel Tejada	1.50
TW	Ted Williams	4.00
DW	David Wright	3.00

Relics

NM/M

Common Player:		4.00
CBA	Clint Barmes	4.00
CB	Carlos Beltran	10.00
BB	Barry Bonds	20.00
MB	Mark Buehrle	8.00
GWB	George W. Bush	300.00
MC	Miguel Cabrera	10.00
RC	Robinson Cano	20.00
JC	Jorge Cantu	6.00
EC	Eric Chavez	6.00
BC	Bobby Crosby	6.00
JD	Johnny Damon	12.00
CD	Carlos Delgado	8.00
ZD	Zachary Duke	8.00
JDY	Jermaine Dye	8.00
JF	Jeff Francoeur	15.00
JG	Jonny Gomes	6.00
VG	Vladimir Guerrero	10.00
TH	Travis Hafner	10.00
FH	Felix Hernandez	8.00
MH	Matt Holliday	8.00
RH	Ryan Howard	30.00
JFK	John F. Kennedy	375.00
PK	Paul Konerko	6.00
HCK	Hong-Chih Kuo	20.00
RL	Ryan Langerhans	8.00
MM	Mickey Mantle	125.00
PM	Pedro Martinez	10.00
VM	Victor Martinez	8.00
HM	Hideki Matsui	15.00
BM	Brandon McCarthy	4.00
DO	David Ortiz	15.00
RO	Roy Oswalt	6.00
JP	Jake Peavy	6.00
APE	Andy Pettitte	6.00
MPZ	Mike Piazza	10.00
MP	Mark Prior	8.00
AP	Albert Pujols	20.00
MR	Manny Ramirez	10.00
AR	Alex Rodriguez	20.00
JS	Johan Santana	10.00
CS	Curt Schilling	10.00
GS	Gary Sheffield	8.00
HS	Huston Street	6.00
NS	Nick Swisher	8.00
WT	Willy Taveras	6.00
MT	Miguel Tejada	10.00
FT	Frank Thomas	8.00
JT	Jim Thome	10.00
CU	Chase Utley	15.00
CMW	Chien-Ming Wang	50.00
DWI	Dontrelle Willis	8.00
DW	David Wright	15.00

Rip Card
NM/M

All prices for unripped cards.

1-4:	Production 10 Sets
5-9:	Production 15 Sets
10-19:	Production 25 Sets
20-50:	Production 99 Sets

RIP20	Kenji Johjima	100.00
RIP21	Cap Anson	100.00
RIP22	Ryan Zimmerman	100.00
RIP23	Andruw Jones	100.00
RIP24	Barry Bonds	150.00
RIP25	Cal Ripken Jr.	150.00
RIP26	David Ortiz	100.00
RIP27	Hideki Matsui	150.00
RIP28	Ken Griffey Jr.	100.00
RIP29	Manny Ramirez	100.00
RIP30	Mickey Mantle	200.00
RIP31	Alex Rodriguez	150.00
RIP32	Miguel Cabrera	100.00
RIP33	Miguel Tejada	100.00
RIP34	Pedro Martinez	100.00
RIP35	Albert Pujols	150.00
RIP36	Alex Rodriguez	150.00
RIP37	Alex Rodriguez, Derek Jeter	150.00
RIP38	Barry Bonds	150.00
RIP39	Derek Jeter	180.00
RIP40	Ichiro Suzuki	150.00
RIP41	Ichiro Suzuki, Hideki Matsui	150.00
RIP42	Josh Gibson	150.00
RIP43	Mickey Mantle	200.00
RIP44	Jonathan Papelbon	100.00
RIP45	Mickey Mantle, Ted Williams	200.00
RIP46	Albert Pujols	150.00
RIP47	Roberto Clemente	150.00
RIP48	Roger Clemens	150.00
RIP49	Ted Williams	150.00
RIP50	Vladimir Guerrero	100.00

2006 Topps Bazooka

NM/M

Complete Set (220):		30.00
Common Player:		.10
Pack (8):		2.50
Box (24):		50.00
1	Josh Gibson	.25
2	Scott Podsednik	.10
3	Sammy Sosa	.75
4	Ivan Rodriguez	.40
5	Derek Jeter	1.50
6	Manny Ramirez	.50
7	Nook Logan	.10
8	Adam Dunn	.40
9	Travis Hafner	.25
10	Felix Hernandez	.40
11	Larry Bigbie	.10
12	Magglio Ordonez	.25
13	Josh Beckett	.25
14	Mike Sweeney	.10
15	Mickey Mantle	2.00
16	Grady Sizemore	.25
17	Brian Fuentes	.10
18	Wily Mo Pena	.10
19	Morgan Ensberg	.10
20	Tim Hudson	.25
21	Justin Verlander (RC)	.25
22	Jermaine Dye	.10
23	Miguel Cabrera	.25
24	Greg Maddux	1.00
25	Jason Giambi	.25
26	Ben Sheets	.25
27	Brad Radke	.10
28	Torii Hunter	.25
29	Mike Piazza	.75
30	Jason Kendall	.10
31	Pat Burrell	.25
32	Khalil Greene	.10
33	Brian Roberts	.10
34	C.C. Sabathia	.10
35	Mike Mussina	.40
36	Bob Wickman	.10
37	Dmitri Young	.10
38	Dontrelle Willis	.25
39	David DeJesus	.10
40	J.D. Drew	.25
41	Chad Tracy	.10
42	Joe Mauer	.25

43	Melvin Mora	.10
44	Carlos Zambrano	.25
45	Mariano Rivera	.25
46	Coco Crisp	.10
47	Derrek Lee	.50
48	Cliff Floyd	.10
49	Willy Taveras	.10
50	Albert Pujols	1.50
51	Aaron Boone	.10
52	Mark Mulder	.10
53	Brad Wilkerson	.10
54	Hank Blalock	.25
55	Hideki Matsui	1.00
56	Victor Martinez	.10
57	Jeremy Bonderman	.10
58	Felipe Lopez	.10
59	Paul LoDuca	.10
60	Derek Lowe	.10
61	Luis Gonzalez	.10
62	Paul Konerko	.25
63	Miguel Tejada	.40
64	Jeromy Burnitz	.10
65	Orlando Hernandez	.10
66	Curt Schilling	.50
67	Joe Nathan	.10
68	Jose Reyes	.25
69	David Wright	.75
70	Eric Chavez	.25
71	Rich Harden	.25
72	A.J. Pierzynski	.10
73	Trevor Hoffman	.10
74	Adrian Beltre	.25
75	Alex Rodriguez	1.50
76	Larry Walker	.25
77	Jorge Cantu	.10
78	Mark Teixeira	.40
79	Jeff Bagwell	.40
80	Jeff Francoeur	.25
81	Ichiro Suzuki	1.00
82	Jhonny Peralta	.10
83	Todd Helton	.40
84	Brad Penny	.10
85	Shawn Chacon	.10
86	Billy Wagner	.10
87	Jason Schmidt	.25
88	Austin Kearns	.10
89	Chris Carpenter	.10
90	Chipper Jones	.50
91	Shawn Green	.25
92	A.J. Burnett	.25
93	Joe Crede	.10
94	Mark Prior	.40
95	Andy Pettitte	.25
96	Edgar Renteria	.25
97	Roy Halladay	.25
98	Eric Milton	.10
99	Craig Biggio	.25
100	Barry Bonds	1.50
101	Troy Glaus	.10
102	Aaron Rowand	.10
103	Aramis Ramirez	.25
104	Nomar Garciaparra	.50
105	Randy Johnson	.50
106	David Ortiz	.50
107	Vinny Castilla	.10
108	Carl Crawford	.25
109	Zachary Duke	.10
110	Barry Zito	.25
111	Darin Erstad	.10
112	Chris Capuano	.10
113	Javy Lopez	.10
114	Lew Ford	.10
115	Robinson Cano	.25
116	Ronnie Belliard	.10
117	Placido Polanco	.10
118	Rickie Weeks	.25
119	Brad Lidge	.10
120	Andruw Jones	.40
121	Nick Swisher	.10
122	Bartolo Colon	.10
123	Juan Pierre	.10
124	Johan Santana	.50
125	Jorge Posada	.25
126	Jeff Francis	.10
127	Matt Holliday	.25
128	Carlos Delgado	.25
129	Zack Greinke	.10
130	Lyle Overbay	.10
131	Conor Jackson (RC)	.10
132	Mark Buehrle	.25
133	Chone Figgins	.10
134	Pedro Martinez	.50
135	Roger Clemens	1.50
136	Raul Ibanez	.10
137	Jim Edmonds	.25
138	Michael Young	.10
139	Preston Wilson	.10
140	Rafael Furcal	.10
141	Bobby Abreu	.25
142	Tadahito Iguchi	.25
143	B.J. Ryan	.10
144	Francisco Rodriguez	.25
145	J.T. Snow	.10
146	Aubrey Huff	.10
147	Mike Morse	.10
148	Jason Bay	.25
149	Roy Oswalt	.25
150	Carlos Beltran	.40
151	Carlos Lee	.25
152	Emil Brown	.10
153	Craig Monroe	.10
154	Kris Benson	.10
155	Gary Sheffield	.40
156	Jake Peavy	.25
157	David Eckstein	.10

158	Tom Glavine	.25
159	Jeff Kent	.25
160	Livan Hernandez	.10
161	Orlando Hudson	.10
162	Randy Winn	.10
163	Jimmy Rollins	.20
164	Luis Castillo	.10
165	Nick Johnson	.10
166	Johnny Damon	.50
167	Eric Gagne	.25
168	Geoff Jenkins	.10
169	Mike Cameron	.10
170	Marcus Giles	.10
171	Huston Street	.25
172	Moises Alou	.25
173	Scott Rolen	.50
174	Jose Vidro	.10
175	Alfonso Soriano	.40
176	Toby Hall	.10
177	Orlando Cabrera	.10
178	Brian Giles	.10
179	Erubiel Durazo	.10
180	Matt Morris	.10
181	Jack Wilson	.10
182	Brady Clark	.10
183	Shannon Stewart	.10
184	Kerry Wood	.25
185	Carl Pavano	.10
186	Chase Utley	.25
187	Omar Vizquel	.10
188	Vladimir Guerrero	.50
189	Richie Sexson	.25
190	John Smoltz	.25
191	Garret Anderson	.10
192	Jon Garland	.10
193	Julio Lugo	.10
194	Rocco Baldelli	.10
195	Jaret Wright	.10
196	Matt Clement	.10
197	Vernon Wells	.10
198	Sean Casey	.10
199	Lance Berkman	.25
200	Justin Morneau	.20
201	Shaun Marcum (RC)	.20
202	Chuck James (RC)	.20
203	Hong-Chih Kuo (RC)	.20
204	Darrell Rasner (RC)	.20
205	Anthony Reyes (RC)	.25
206	Francisco Liriano (RC)	.50
207	Joe Saunders (RC)	.20
208	Fausto Carmona (RC)	.20
209	Charlton Jimerson (RC)	.20
210	Bryan Bullington (RC)	.20
211	Tom Gorzelanny (RC)	.20
212	Anderson Hernandez (RC)	.20
213	Ryan Garko (RC)	.20
214	John Koronka (RC)	.20
215	Chris Denorfia (RC)	.20
216	Jeff Mathis (RC)	.20
217	Jose Bautista (RC)	.20
218	Danny Sandoval (RC)	.20
219	Robert Andino RC	.20
220	Justin Huber (RC)	.20

Gold

Stars:	1-2X
Inserted 1:1	

Autographs

		NM/M
BM	Brandon McCarthy	12.00
KM	Kevin Millar	20.00
MM	Mike Morse	15.00
VZ	Victor Zambrano	15.00

Bazooka Blasts

		NM/M
BA	Bobby Abreu	4.00
MA	Moises Alou	4.00
JB	Jason Bay	8.00
CB	Carlos Beltran	6.00
HB	Hank Blalock	4.00
BB	Barry Bonds	20.00
CC	Coco Crisp	4.00
JD	Johnny Damon	8.00
JD	J.D. Drew	4.00
AD	Adam Dunn	6.00
CF	Cliff Floyd	4.00
TG	Troy Glaus	4.00
VG	Vladimir Guerrero	6.00
GJ	Geoff Jenkins	4.00
AJ	Andruw Jones	6.00
CJ	Chipper Jones	8.00
PK	Paul Konerko	6.00
DL	Derrek Lee	6.00
PL	Paul LoDuca	4.00
ML	Mark Loretta	4.00
MM	Mickey Mantle/100	175.00
VM	Victor Martinez	4.00
TN	Trot Nixon	4.00
DO	David Ortiz	8.00
CP	Corey Patterson	4.00

MP	Mike Piazza	8.00
AR	Aramis Ramirez	6.00
AR	Alex Rodriguez	15.00
GS	Gary Sheffield	6.00
SS	Sammy Sosa	8.00
MT	Miguel Tejada	8.00
JT	Jim Thome	6.00
PW	Preston Wilson	4.00
DW	David Wright	10.00

Bazooka Basics

		NM/M
BA	Bobby Abreu	4.00
LB	Lance Berkman	6.00
CB	Craig Biggio	4.00
HB	Hank Blalock	4.00
SB	Sean Burroughs	4.00
MC	Miguel Cabrera	8.00
JD	Johnny Damon	8.00
CD	Carlos Delgado	4.00
EG	Eric Gagne	6.00
MG	Marcus Giles	4.00
MH	Matt Holliday	4.00
TH	Tim Hudson	6.00
AJ	Andruw Jones	6.00
CJ	Chipper Jones	8.00
ML	Mike Lowell	4.00
PM	Pedro Martinez	10.00
MM	Mark Mulder	4.00
MMU	Mike Mussina	6.00
AP	Albert Pujols	15.00
MR	Manny Ramirez	4.00
JR	Jose Reyes	4.00
BR	Brian Roberts	4.00
CS	Curt Schilling	8.00
MT	Mark Teixeira	6.00
BW	Bernie Williams	6.00
DW	Dontrelle Willis	6.00

Bazooka Rewind

		NM/M
CB	Clint Barmes	4.00
WB	William Bergolla	4.00
LB	Lance Berkman	6.00
CBI	Craig Biggio	6.00
JB	Jason Botts	4.00
PB	Pat Burrell	4.00
RC	Robinson Cano	15.00
SC	Shin-Soo Choo	6.00
CC	Carl Crawford	6.00
NC	Nelson Cruz	6.00
JDA	Johnny Damon	8.00
JD	Jermaine Dye	4.00
CE	Carl Everett	4.00
RG	Ryan Garko	4.00
JG	Jon Garland	4.00
MG	Mark Grudzielanek	4.00
JG	Jose Guillen	4.00
CG	Cristian Guzman	4.00
JH	Justin Huber	4.00
MJ	Mike Jacobs	8.00
NJ	Nick Johnson	4.00
AJ	Andruw Jones	6.00
AK	Adam Kennedy	4.00
PK	Paul Konerko	6.00
AML	Adam LaRoche	4.00
CL	Carlos Lee	4.00
FL	Francisco Liriano	8.00
LM	Luis Montanez	4.00
MM	Miguel Montero	4.00
AP	A.J. Pierzynski	6.00
SP	Scott Podsednik	6.00
HR	Hanley Ramirez	8.00
MR	Manny Ramirez	8.00
ER	Edgar Renteria	4.00
BR	Brian Roberts	4.00
AR	Alex Rodriguez	15.00
JR	Jimmy Rollins	4.00
AR	Aaron Rowand	4.00
TS	Terrmel Sledge	4.00
WT	Willy Taveras	4.00
FT	Frank Thomas	6.00
KT	Ken Thompson	4.00
CU	Chase Utley	8.00
JV	Justin Verlander	8.00
RW	Rickie Weeks	4.00
DW	Dontrelle Willis	6.00
CY	Chris Young	4.00

Comics

	NM/M
Complete Set (24):	10.00
Common Player:	.25

Inserted 1:4

1	Greg Maddux	1.00
2	Alex Rodriguez	1.00
3	Trevor Hoffman	.25
4	Rafael Palmeiro	.50
5	Roy Oswalt	.25
6	Bobby Abreu	.25
7	Miguel Tejada	.50
8	Vladimir Guerrero	.50
9	Mark Teixeira	.25
10	Zachary Duke	.25
11	Xavier Nady	.25
12	Alex Rodriguez	1.00
13	Jeremy Hermida	.25
14	Craig Biggio	.50
15	Manny Ramirez	.50
16	Texas Rangers	.25
17	Oakland A's	.25
18	Alex Rodriguez	1.00
19	Jason Giambi	.50
20	Aaron Small	.25
21	Jimmy Rollins	.25
22	Roger Clemens	1.00
23	White Sox/Mariners	.50
24	Andruw Jones	.50

Fortune

Stars:	1-2X
Inserted 1:1	

Mickey Mantle Oversized Reprint

		NM/M
1952	Mickey Mantle	40.00
1953	Mickey Mantle	30.00
1956	Mickey Mantle	25.00
1957	Mickey Mantle	25.00
1958	Mickey Mantle	25.00
1959	Mickey Mantle	25.00
1960	Mickey Mantle	25.00
1961	Mickey Mantle	25.00
1962	Mickey Mantle	25.00
1963	Mickey Mantle	20.00
1964	Mickey Mantle	25.00
1965	Mickey Mantle	25.00
1966	Mickey Mantle	25.00
1967	Mickey Mantle	25.00
1968	Mickey Mantle	25.00
1969	Mickey Mantle	25.00

Stamps

	NM/M
Complete Set (30):	15.00
Common Player:	.50

Inserted 1:3 Hobby

1	Bobby Abreu	.50
2	Lance Berkman	.50
3	Hank Blalock	.50
4	Barry Bonds	2.00
5	Mark Buehrle	.50
6	Miguel Cabrera	1.00
7	Jim Edmonds	.50
8	Morgan Ensberg	.50
9	Jeff Francoeur	.50
10	Roy Halladay	.50
11	Tim Hudson	.50
12	Derek Jeter	2.00
13	Andruw Jones	.75
14	Chipper Jones	1.00
15	Derrek Lee	.75
16	Mickey Mantle	3.00
17	Victor Martinez	.50

18 Justin Morneau .50
19 Manny Ramirez 1.00
20 Brian Roberts .50
21 Alex Rodriguez 2.00
22 Ivan Rodriguez .50
23 Johan Santana .50
24 Alfonso Soriano .50
25 Huston Street .50
26 Ichiro Suzuki 1.00
27 Mark Teixeira .50
28 Miguel Tejada .50
29 Rickie Weeks .50
30 Dontrelle Willis .50

4-on-1 Stickers
NM/M

1 Josh Gibson, Mickey Mantle,
Alex Rodriguez,
Barry Bonds 2.00
2 Jason Giambi, David Ortiz,
Carlos Delgado, Jeff Bagwell .75
3 Vernon Wells, Shannon Stewart,
Carl Crawford, Torii Hunter .50
4 Jason Kendall, Javy Lopez,
Joe Mauer, Jorge Posada .50
5 Roger Clemens, Andy Pettitte,
Mike Mussina,
Orlando Hernandez 1.00
6 Ivan Rodriguez, Rafael Palmeiro,
Alfonso Soriano,
Hank Blalock .50
7 Pedro Martinez, Curt Schilling,
Matt Clement, Derek Lowe .75
8 J.D. Drew, Andruw Jones,
Gary Sheffield,
Vladimir Guerrero .50
9 Tim Hudson, Greg Maddux,
Tom Glavine, John Smoltz .75
10 Justin Morneau, Albert Pujols,
Mark Teixeira, Derrek Lee 1.00
11 B.J. Ryan, Bob Wickman,
Mariano Rivera,
Trevor Hoffman .50
12 Mike Morse, Mike Cameron,
Mike Piazza, Mike Sweeney .75
13 Michael Young, Jimmy Rollins,
David Eckstein,
Orlando Cabrera .50
14 A.J. Burnett, A.J. Pierzynski,
C.C. Sabathia, J.T. Snow .50
15 Hideki Matsui, Ichiro Suzuki,
Tadahito Iguchi,
Chase Utley 1.00
16 Barry Zito, Zachary Duke,
Zack Greinke, Jeff Francis .50
17 Mark Buehrle, Mark Mulder,
Mark Prior, Marcus Giles .75
18 Sammy Sosa, Manny Ramirez,
Bobby Abreu, Wily Mo Pena .75
19 Scott Podsednik, Preston Wilson,
Juan Pierre, Carlos Beltran .50
20 Francisco Rodriguez,
Billy Wagner, Huston Street,
Joe Nathan .50
21 Melvin Mora, Morgan Ensberg,
Scott Rolen, Eric Chavez .50
22 Garret Anderson, Jim Edmonds,
Johnny Damon, Moises Alou .50
23 Derek Jeter, Edgar Renteria,
Miguel Tejada, Julio Lugo 1.00
24 Felix Hernandez, Dontrelle Willis,
Rich Harden, Brian Fuentes .50
25 Bartolo Colon, Jason Schmidt,
Jeremy Bonderman,
Carlos Zambrano .50
26 Randy Johnson, Johan Santana,
Roy Halladay, Chris Carpenter .75
27 Roy Oswalt, Shawn Chacon,
Kris Benson, Josh Beckett .50
28 Jose Reyes, Felipe Lopez,
Rafael Furcal, Jhonny Peralta .50
29 Justin Verlander, Kerry Wood,
Livan Hernandez, Matt Morris .50
30 Khalil Greene, Nomar Garciaparra,
Omar Vizquel, Jack Wilson .50
31 Pat Burrell, Rocco Baldelli,
Shawn Green, Jason Bay .50
32 Brad Lidge, Brad Penny,
Brad Radke, Brian Roberts .50
33 Jeff Francoeur, Willy Taveras,
Rickie Weeks, Robinson Cano .50
34 Geoff Jenkins, Lance Berkman,
Larry Bigbie, Matt Holliday .50
35 Paul LoDuca, Toby Hall,
Victor Martinez, Carlos Lee .50
36 Aramis Ramirez, Chipper Jones,
David Wright, Troy Glaus .75
37 Randy Winn, Brad Wilkerson,
Craig Monroe, Aaron Rowand .50
38 Aaron Boone, Adrian Beltre,
Vinny Castilla,
Chone Figgins .50
39 Larry Walker, Cliff Floyd,
Luis Gonzalez, Adam Dunn .50
40 Ronnie Belliard, Jeff Kent,
Jorge Cantu, Placido Polanco .50
41 Craig Biggio, Jose Vidro,
Luis Castillo, Orlando Hudson .50

42 Grady Sizemore, Lew Ford,
Nick Swisher, Brian Giles .50
43 David DeJesus, Emil Brown,
Coco Crisp, Jeromy Burnitz .50
44 Eric Gagne, Eric Milton,
Jake Peavy, Jaret Wright .50
45 Aubrey Huff, Austin Kearns,
Brady Clark, Nook Logan .50
46 Ben Sheets, Carl Pavano,
Chris Capuano, Jon Garland .50
47 Darin Erstad, Dmitri Young,
Erubiel Durazo, Travis Hafner .50
48 Magglio Ordonez, Miguel Cabrera,
Jermaine Dye, Conor Jackson .50
49 Richie Sexson, Sean Casey,
Chad Tracy, Lyle Overbay .50
50 Nick Johnson, Paul Konerko,
Raul Ibanez, Todd Helton .50
51 Shaun Marcum, Chuck James,
Hong-Chih Kuo,
Darrell Rasner .50
52 Anthony Reyes, Francisco Liriano,
Joe Saunders,
Fausto Carmona .50
53 Charlton Jimerson,
Bryan Bullington,
Tom Gorzelanny,
Anderson Hernandez .50
54 Ryan Garko, John Koronka,
Chris Denorfia, Jeff Mathis .50
55 Jose Bautista, Danny Sandoval,
Robert Andino, Alex Gordon .50

2006 Topps Chrome

NM/M

Complete Set (354):
Common Player: .25
Common Auto. (331-354): 10.00
Pack (4): 3.00
Box (24): 60.00
1 Alex Rodriguez 3.00
2 Garrett Atkins .25
3 Carl Crawford .50
4 Clint Barmes .25
5 Tadahito Iguchi .50
6 Brian Roberts .50
7 Mickey Mantle 8.00
8 David Wright 2.00
9 Jeremy Reed .25
10 Bobby Abreu .50
11 Lance Berkman .50
12 Jonny Gomes .25
13 Jason Marquis .25
14 Chipper Jones 1.00
15 Jon Garland .25
16 Brad Wilkerson .25
17 Rickie Weeks .50
18 Jorge Posada .50
19 Greg Maddux 2.00
20 Jeff Francis .25
21 Felipe Lopez .25
22 Dan Johnson .25
23 Manny Ramirez 1.00
24 Joe Mauer .75
25 Randy Winn .25
26 Pedro Feliz .25
27 Kenny Rogers .25
28 Rocco Baldelli .25
29 Nomar Garciaparra .50
30 Carlos Lee .50
31 Tom Glavine .50
32 Craig Biggio .50
33 Steve Finley .25
34 Eric Gagne .40
35 Dallas McPherson .25
36 Mark Kotsay .25
37 Kerry Wood .50
38 Huston Street .25
39 Hank Blalock .50
40 Brad Radke .25
41 Chien-Ming Wang .75
42 Mark Buehrle .40
43 Andy Pettitte .50
44 Bernie Williams .50
45 Victor Martinez .50
46 Darin Erstad .40
47 Gustavo Chacin .25
48 Carlos Guillen .50
49 Lyle Overbay .25

50 Barry Bonds 3.00
51 Nook Logan .25
52 Mark Teahen .25
53 Mike Lamb .25
54 Jayson Werth .25
55 Mariano Rivera .50
56 Julio Lugo .25
57 Adam Dunn .75
58 Troy Percival .25
59 Chad Tracy .25
60 Edgar Renteria .50
61 Jason Giambi .75
62 Justin Morneau .75
63 Carlos Delgado .50
64 John Buck .25
65 Shannon Stewart .25
66 Mike Cameron .25
67 Richie Sexson .50
68 Russ Adams .25
69 Josh Beckett .75
70 Ryan Freel .25
71 Victor Zambrano .25
72 Ronnie Belliard .25
73 Brian Giles .40
74 Randy Wolf .25
75 Robinson Cano .75
76 Joe Blanton .25
77 Esteban Loaiza .25
78 Troy Glaus .50
79 Matt Clement .25
80 Geoff Jenkins .25
81 Roy Oswalt .50
82 A.J. Pierzynski .25
83 Pedro Martinez 1.00
84 Roger Clemens 3.00
85 Jack Wilson .25
86 Mike Piazza 1.00
87 Paul LoDuca .25
88 Jeff Bagwell .50
89 Carlos Zambrano .50
90 Brandon Claussen .25
91 Travis Hafner .50
92 Chris Shelton .25
93 Rafael Furcal .50
94 Frank Thomas .75
95 Noah Lowry .25
96 Jhonny Peralta .25
97 Vernon Wells .50
98 Jorge Cantu .25
99 Willy Taveras .25
100 Ivan Rodriguez .50
101 Jose Reyes .75
102 Barry Zito .50
103 Mark Teixeira .75
104 Chone Figgins .50
105 Todd Helton .75
106 Tim Wakefield .25
107 Mike Maroth .25
108 Johnny Damon .75
109 David DeJesus .25
110 Ryan Klesko .25
111 Nick Johnson .25
112 Freddy Garcia .25
113 Torii Hunter .50
114 Mike Sweeney .25
115 Scott Rolen .50
116 Jim Thome .75
117 Adam Kennedy .25
118 Albert Pujols 3.00
119 Kazuo Matsui .25
120 Zack Greinke .25
121 Jimmy Rollins .75
122 Edgar Alfonzo .25
123 Billy Wagner .25
124 B.J. Ryan .25
125 Orlando Hudson .25
126 Preston Wilson .25
127 Melvin Mora .25
128 Alfonso Soriano .75
129 Javy Lopez .25
130 Wilson Betemit .25
131 Garret Anderson .25
132 Jason Bay .50
133 Adam LaRoche .25
134 C.C. Sabathia .50
135 Bartolo Colon .25
136 Ichiro Suzuki 2.00
137 Jim Edmonds .50
138 David Eckstein .25
139 Cristian Guzman .25
140 Jeff Kent .40
141 Chris Capuano .25
142 Cliff Floyd .25
143 Zachary Duke .25
144 Matt Morris .25
145 Jose Vidro .25
146 David Wells .25
147 John Smoltz .50
148 Felix Hernandez .50
149 Orlando Cabrera .25
150 Mark Prior .50
151 Ted Lilly .25
152 Michael Young .50
153 Livan Hernandez .25
154 Yadier Molina .25
155 Eric Chavez .50
156 Miguel Batista .25
157 Ben Sheets .50
158 Oliver Perez .25
159 Doug Davis .25
160 Andruw Jones .50
161 Hideki Matsui 1.50
162 Reggie Sanders .25
163 Joe Nathan .25
164 John Lackey .50

165 Matt Murton .25
166 Grady Sizemore .75
167 Brad Thompson .25
168 Kevin Millwood .25
169 Orlando Hernandez .25
170 Mark Mulder .25
171 Chase Utley .75
172 Moises Alou .50
173 Wily Mo Pena .25
174 Brian McCann .50
175 Jermaine Dye .40
176 Ryan Madson .25
177 Aramis Ramirez .50
178 Khalil Greene .25
179 Mike Hampton .25
180 Mike Mussina .50
181 Rich Harden .25
182 Woody Williams .25
183 Chris Carpenter .50
184 Brady Clark .25
185 Luis Gonzalez .25
186 Raul Ibanez .25
187 Magglio Ordonez .50
188 Adrian Beltre .25
189 Marcus Giles .25
190 Odalis Perez .25
191 Derek Jeter 3.00
192 Jason Schmidt .25
193 Toby Hall .25
194 Danny Haren .50
195 Tim Hudson .50
196 Jake Peavy .50
197 Casey Blake .25
198 J.D. Drew .25
199 Ervin Santana .40
200 J.J. Hardy .25
201 Austin Kearns .25
202 Pat Burrell .40
203 Jason Vargas .25
204 Ryan Howard 1.50
205 Joe Crede .25
206 Vladimir Guerrero 1.00
207 Roy Halladay .50
208 David Dellucci .25
209 Brandon Webb .50
210 Ryan Church .25
211 Miguel Tejada .50
212 Mark Loretta .25
213 Kevin Youkilis .50
214 Jon Lieber .25
215 Miguel Cabrera 1.00
216 A.J. Burnett .50
217 David Bell .25
218 Eric Byrnes .25
219 Lance Niekro .25
220 Shawn Green .25
221 Ken Griffey Jr. 2.00
222 Johnny Estrada .25
223 Omar Vizquel .25
224 Gary Sheffield .50
225 Brad Halsey .25
226 Aaron Cook .25
227 David Ortiz 1.00
228 Scott Kazmir .50
229 Dustin McGowan .25
230 Gregg Zaun .25
231 Carlos Beltran .75
232 Bob Wickman .25
233 Brett Myers .25
234 Casey Kotchman .25
235 Jeff Francoeur .50
236 Paul Konerko .50
237 Juan Rivera .25
238 Bobby Crosby .25
239 Derrek Lee .75
240 Curt Schilling 1.00
241 Jake Westbrook .25
242 Dontrelle Willis .25
243 Brad Lidge .25
244 Randy Johnson 1.00
245 Nick Swisher .50
246 Johan Santana .75
247 Jeremy Bonderman .25
248 Ramon Hernandez .25
249 Mike Lowell .50
250 Javier Vazquez .25
251 Jose Contreras .25
252 Aubrey Huff .25
253 Kenny Rogers .50
254 Mark Teixeira .25
255 Orlando Hudson .25
256 Derek Jeter 2.00
257 Eric Chavez .25
258 Torii Hunter .50
259 Vernon Wells .50
260 Ichiro Suzuki 1.00
261 Greg Maddux 1.00
262 Mike Matheny .25
263 Derrek Lee .50
264 Luis Castillo .25
265 Omar Vizquel .25
266 Mike Lowell .25
267 Andruw Jones .25
268 Jim Edmonds .25
269 Bobby Abreu .25
270 Bartolo Colon .25
271 Chris Carpenter .25
272 Alex Rodriguez 2.00
273 Albert Pujols 2.00
274 Huston Street .25
275 Ryan Howard .75
276 Chris Denorfia (RC) .25
277 John Van Benschoten (RC) .25
278 Russell Martin (RC) 1.00
279 Fausto Carmona (RC) .50

280	Freddie Bynum **(RC)**	.50
281	Kelly Shoppach **(RC)**	.50
282	Chris Demaria **RC**	.50
283	Jordan Tata **RC**	.50
284	Ryan Zimmerman **(RC)**	4.00
285	Kenji Johjima **RC**	3.00
285	Kenji Johjima Auto **RC**	50.00
286	Ruddy Lugo **(RC)**	.50
287	Tommy Murphy **(RC)**	.50
288	Bobby Livingston **RC**	.50
289	Anderson Hernandez **RC**	.50
290	Brian Slocum **(RC)**	.50
291	Sendy Rleal **RC**	.50
292	Ryan Spilborghs **(RC)**	.50
293	Brandon Fahey **RC**	1.00
294	Jason Kubel **(RC)**	.50
295	James Loney **(RC)**	1.00
296	Jeremy Accardo **RC**	.50
297	Fabio Castro **RC**	.50
298	Matt Capps **(RC)**	.75
299	Casey Janssen **RC**	1.00
300	Martin Prado **(RC)**	1.00
301	Ronny Paulino **(RC)**	.75
302	Josh Barfield **(RC)**	.50
303	Joel Zumaya **(RC)**	1.00
304	Matt Cain **(RC)**	1.00
305	Conor Jackson **(RC)**	1.00
306	Brian Anderson **(RC)**	.50
307	Prince Fielder **(RC)**	4.00
308	Jeremy Hermida **(RC)**	.75
309	Justin Verlander **(RC)**	4.00
310	Brian Bannister **(RC)**	.50
311	Josh Willingham **(RC)**	.50
312	John Rheinecker **(RC)**	.50
313	Nicholas Markakis **(RC)**	1.00
314	Jonathan Papelbon **(RC)**	6.00
315	Mike Jacobs **(RC)**	1.50
316	Jose Capellan **(RC)**	.50
317	Michael Napoli **RC**	4.00
318	Ricky Nolasco **(RC)**	.50
319	Ben Johnson **(RC)**	.50
320	Paul Maholm **(RC)**	.50
321	Drew Meyer **(RC)**	.50
322	Jeff Mathis **(RC)**	.50
323	Fernando Nieve **(RC)**	.50
324	John Koronka **(RC)**	.50
325	Wilbert Nieves **(RC)**	.50
326	Nate McLouth **(RC)**	1.00
327	Howard Kendrick **(RC)**	2.00
328	Sean Marshall **(RC)**	.75
329	Brandon Watson **(RC)**	.50
330	Skip Schumaker **(RC)**	.50
331	Ryan Garko/Auto. **(RC)**	15.00
332	Jason Bergmann/Auto. **RC**	15.00
333	Chuck James/Auto. **(RC)**	15.00
334	Adam Wainwright/ Auto. **(RC)**	20.00
335	Daniel Ortmeier/Auto. **(RC)**	10.00
336	Francisco Liriano/ Auto. **(RC)**	25.00
337	Craig Breslow/Auto. **RC**	10.00
338	Darrell Rasner/Auto. **(RC)**	15.00
339	Jason Botts/Auto. **(RC)**	10.00
340	Ian Kinsler/Auto. **(RC)**	25.00
341	Joey Devine/Auto. **RC**	10.00
342	Miguel Perez/Auto. **(RC)**	10.00
343	Scott Olsen/Auto. **(RC)**	15.00
344	Tyler Johnson/Auto. **(RC)**	10.00
345	Anthony Lerew/Auto. **(RC)**	10.00
346	Nelson Cruz/Auto. **(RC)**	10.00
347	Willie Eyre/Auto. **(RC)**	10.00
348	Josh Johnson/Auto. **(RC)**	10.00
349	Shawn Marcum Auto **(RC)**	15.00
350	Dustin Nippert/Auto. **(RC)**	10.00
351	Josh Wilson/Auto. **(RC)**	10.00
352	Hanley Ramirez/ Auto. **(RC)**	30.00
353	Reggie Abercrombie/ Auto. **(RC)**	10.00
354	Dan Uggla/Auto. **(RC)**	30.00

Refractors

Cards (1-330): 2-3X
Inserted 1:4
Rookie Auto. (331-354): 1-1.5X
Production 500

Black Refractors

Cards (1-330): 3-5X
Production 549
Rookie Auto. (331-354): 1.5-2X
Production 200

Blue Refractors

Cards (1-330): 2-4X
Inserted 1:8

Gold Super-Fractor

No Pricing
Production One Set

Red Refractors

Cards (1-330): 4-8X
Production 90
Rookie Auto. (331-354): No Pricing
Production 25

X-Fractor

Cards (1-330): 2-4X
Inserted 1:6 Retail

Printing Plates

No Pricing
Production one set per color.

Bonds Home Run History

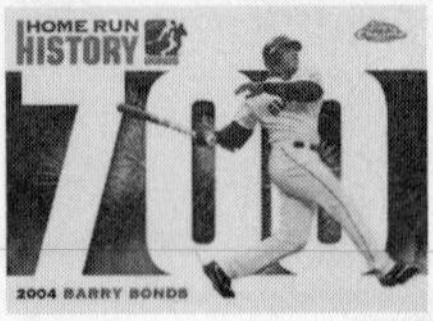

NM/M

Common Bonds: 2.00
Inserted 1:6
Refractors: 2-4X
Production 500 Sets
Black Refractor: 3-5X
Production 200 Sets
Red Refractor: 10-20X
Production 25 Sets

BBC375	Barry Bonds	2.00
BBC400	Barry Bonds	2.00
BBC425	Barry Bonds	2.00
BBC450	Barry Bonds	2.00
BBC475	Barry Bonds	2.00
BBC500	Barry Bonds	2.00
BBC525	Barry Bonds	2.00
BBC550	Barry Bonds	2.00
BBC575	Barry Bonds	2.00
BBC600	Barry Bonds	2.00
BBC625	Barry Bonds	2.00
BBC650	Barry Bonds	2.00
BBC675	Barry Bonds	2.00
BBC700	Barry Bonds	2.00

Mantle Home Run History

NM/M

Common Mantle: 3.00
Inserted 1:6
Refractor: 2-4X
Production 500 Sets
Black Refractor: 3-5X
Production 200 Sets
Red Refractor: 15-20X
Production 25 Sets

MHRC1	Mickey Mantle	3.00
MHRC7	Mickey Mantle	3.00
MHRC10	Mickey Mantle	3.00
MHRC20	Mickey Mantle	3.00
MHRC30	Mickey Mantle	3.00
MHRC40	Mickey Mantle	3.00
MHRC40	Mickey Mantle	3.00
MHRC50	Mickey Mantle	3.00
MHRC60	Mickey Mantle	3.00
MHRC70	Mickey Mantle	3.00
MHRC80	Mickey Mantle	3.00
MHRC90	Mickey Mantle	3.00
MHRC100	Mickey Mantle	3.00
MHRC110	Mickey Mantle	3.00

Signers of the Constitution

NM/M

Common Signer: 1.50
Inserted 1:7
Refractors: 1-2X
Inserted 1:11

AB	Abraham Baldwin	1.50
RB	Richard Bassett	1.50
GB	Gunning Bedford Jr.	1.50
JB	John Blair	1.50
WB	William Blount	1.50
DB	David Brearly	1.50
JBR	Jacob Broom	1.50
PB	Pierce Butler	1.50
DC	Daniel Carroll	1.50
GC	George Clymer	1.50
JD	Jonathan Dayton	1.50
JDI	John Dickinson	1.50
WF	William Few	1.50
TF	Thomas Fitzsimons	1.50
BF	Benjamin Franklin	4.00
NG	Nicholas Gilman	1.50
NGO	Nathaniel Gorham	1.50
AH	Alexander Hamilton	3.00
JI	Jared Ingersoll	1.50
DJ	Daniel of St. Thomas Jenifer	1.50
WJ	William Samuel Johnson	1.50
RK	Rufus King	1.50
JL	John Langdon	1.50
WL	William Livingston	1.50
JM	James Madison	2.00
JMC	James McHenry	1.50
TM	Thomas Mifflin	1.50
GM	Gouverneur Morris	1.50
RM	Robert Morris	1.50
WP	William Paterson	1.50
CCP	Charles Cotesworth Pinckney	1.50
CP	Charles Pinckney	1.50
GR	George Read	1.50
JR	John Rutledge	1.50
RS	Roger Sherman	1.50
RDS	Richard Dobbs Spaight	1.50
GW	George Washington	4.00
HW	Hugh Williamson	1.50
JW	James Wilson	1.50

Signers of Declaration/Independence

NM/M

Common Signer: 1.50
Inserted 1:5
Refractors: 1-2X
Inserted 1:9

JA	John Adams	2.00
SA	Samuel Adams	1.50
JB	Josiah Bartlett	1.50
CB	Carter Braxton	1.50
CC	Charles Carroll	1.50
SC	Samuel Chase	1.50
AC	Abraham Clark	1.50
GC	George Clymer	1.50
WE	William Ellery	1.50
WF	William Floyd	1.50
BF	Benjamin Franklin	4.00
EG	Elbridge Gerry	1.50
BG	Button Gwinnett	1.50
LH	Lyman Hall	1.50
JH	John Hancock	3.00
BH	Benjamin Harrison	1.50
JHA	John Hart	1.50
JHE	Joseph Hewes	1.50
TH	Thomas Heyward Jr.	1.50
WH	William Hooper	1.50
SH	Stephen Hopkins	1.50
FH	Francis Hopkinson	1.50
SHU	Samuel Huntington	1.50
TJ	Thomas Jefferson	4.00
FL	Francis Lewis	1.50
FLL	Francis Lightfoot Lee	1.50
RHL	Richard Henry Lee	1.50
PL	Philip Livingston	1.50
TL	Thomas Lynch Jr.	1.50
TM	Thomas McKean	1.50
AM	Arthur Middleton	1.50
LM	Lewis Morris	1.50
RM	Robert Morris	1.50
JM	John Morton	1.50
TN	Thomas Nelson Jr.	1.50
WP	William Paca	1.50
RTP	Robert Treat Paine	1.50
JP	John Penn	1.50
GRE	George Read	1.50
CR	Caesar Rodney	1.50
GR	George Ross	1.50
BR	Benjamin Rush	1.50
ER	Edward Rutledge	1.50
RS	Roger Sherman	1.50
JS	James Smith	1.50
RST	Richard Stockton	1.50
TS	Thomas Stone	1.50
GT	George Taylor	1.50
MT	Matthew Thornton	1.50
GW	George Walton	1.50
WW	William Whipple	1.50
WWI	William Williams	1.50
JW	James Wilson	1.50
JWI	John Witherspoon	1.50
OW	Oliver Wolcott	1.50
GWY	George Wythe	1.50

2006 Topps Co-Signers

NM/M

Complete Set (120):
Common Player (1-100): .25
Common Auto. (101-120): 10.00
Pack (6): 12.00
Box (12): 120.00
Note: Each parallel has three versions.

1	Albert Pujols	3.00
2	Roger Clemens	3.00
3	Paul Konerko	.50
4	Jeff Francoeur	.50
5	Miguel Tejada	.75
6	Curt Schilling	1.00
7	Mickey Mantle	4.00
8	Miguel Cabrera	1.00
9	Derrek Lee	1.00
10	Jeff Kent	.50
11	Gary Sheffield	.50
12	Rich Harden	.25
13	Scott Rolen	.75
14	David Wright	1.50
15	Troy Glaus	.50
16	Torii Hunter	.50
17	Nolan Ryan	2.00
18	Alfonso Soriano	.75
19	Hank Blalock	.50
20	Chase Utley	1.00
21	Ryan Howard	1.00
22	Robinson Cano	1.00
23	Derek Jeter	3.00
24	Huston Street	.25
25	Jason Giambi	.50
26	Rafael Furcal	.50
27	Rickie Weeks	.25
28	Ivan Rodriguez	.50
29	Travis Hafner	.50
30	Greg Maddux	2.00
31	Andruw Jones	.50
32	Andy Pettitte	.50
33	Scott Podsednik	.25
34	Francisco Rodriguez	.25
35	Josh Beckett	.75
36	Lance Berkman	.50
37	Roy Oswalt	.50
38	Pedro Martinez	1.00
39	Jimmy Rollins	.75
40	Johan Santana	.75
41	Randy Johnson	1.00
42	Mariano Rivera	.50
43	Nick Johnson	.25
44	Josh Gibson	.75
45	Shawn Green	.25
46	Adrian Beltre	.50
47	Johnny Damon	1.00
48	Joe Mauer	.50
49	Todd Helton	.50
50	Alex Rodriguez	2.50
51	Jake Peavy	.50
52	David Ortiz	1.00
53	Mark Buehrle	.50
54	Eric Gagne	.25
55	Hideki Matsui	1.50
56	Bobby Abreu	.50
57	Victor Martinez	.50
58	Brian Roberts	.50
59	Chipper Jones	1.00
60	Carlos Beltran	.75
61	Tim Hudson	.50
62	Carlos Lee	.50
63	Barry Zito	.50
64	Moises Alou	.50
65	Mark Teixeira	.75
66	Lyle Overbay	.25
67	Kerry Wood	.50
68	B.J. Ryan	.25
69	Jim Edmonds	.50
70	Carlos Delgado	.50
71	Maggilo Ordonez	.50
72	Juan Pierre	.25
73	Manny Ramirez	1.00
74	Dontrelle Willis	.50
75	Ichiro Suzuki	2.00
76	Nomar Garciaparra	.50
77	Zachary Duke	.25
78	Chris Carpenter	.50
79	A.J. Burnett	.50
80	Scott Kazmir	.50
81	Carl Crawford	.50
82	Mark Prior	.50
83	Adam Dunn	.75
84	Justin Morneau	.50
85	Morgan Ensberg	.25
86	Pat Burrell	.50
87	Paul LoDuca	.25
88	Jason Bay	.50
89	Aubrey Huff	.25
90	Kevin Millwood	.25
91	Vernon Wells	.50
92	Javy Lopez	.25
93	Michael Young	.50
94	Felix Hernandez	.50
95	Ken Griffey Jr.	2.00
96	Bartolo Colon	.25
97	Billy Wagner	.25
98	Vladimir Guerrero	1.00
99	Jose Reyes	1.00
100	Barry Bonds	3.00
101	Anthony LeRew/Auto. **(RC)**	10.00
102	Ryan Zimmerman/ 440/Auto. **(RC)**	30.00
103	Craig Hansen/250/ Auto. **RC**	25.00
104	Francisco Liriano/ Auto. **(RC)**	25.00
105	Jason Botts/Auto. **(RC)**	10.00
106	Josh Johnson/Auto. **(RC)**	10.00
107	Hanley Ramirez/Auto. **(RC)**	30.00
108	Adam Wainwright/ Auto. **(RC)**	20.00
109	Kenji Johjima/200/Auto. **RC**	75.00

110 Daniel Ortmeier/Auto. **(RC)** 10.00
111 Darrell Rasner/Auto. **(RC)** 15.00
112 Chuck James/Auto. **(RC)** 15.00
113 Nelson Cruz/Auto. **(RC)** 10.00
114 Hong-Chih Kuo/
Auto. **(RC)** 25.00
115 Ryan Garko/Auto. **(RC)** 15.00
116 R. Abercrombie/Auto. **(RC)** 10.00
117 Ian Kinsler/Auto. **(RC)** 25.00
118 Joel Zumaya/Auto. **(RC)** 15.00
119 Willie Eyre/Auto. **(RC)** 10.00
120 Dan Uggla/Auto. **(RC)** 25.00

Bronze
Bronze (1-100): 2-3X
Production 150 Sets

Blue
Blue (1-100): 2-3X
Production 125 Sets

Gold
Gold (1-100): 2-3X
Production 115 Sets

Hyper Silver - Bronze
Hyper Silver/Bronze (1-100): 2-3X
Production 75 Sets

Hyper Silver - Blue
Hyper Silver/Blue: No Pricing
Production 10 Sets

Hyper Silver - Gold
Hyper Silver/Gold: No Pricing
Production Five Sets

Hyper Silver - Red
Hyper Silver/Red: No Pricing
Production 25 Sets

Silver - Bronze
Silver/Bronze (1-100): 2-3X
Production 125 Sets

Silver - Blue
Silver/Blue (1-100): 2-3X
Production 75 Sets

Silver - Gold
Silver/Gold (1-100): 3-4X
Production 50 Sets

Silver - Red
Silver/Red (1-100): 2-3X
Production 100 Sets

Dual Autographs
NM/M
Cards are not serial #'d.
CS2 David Wright,
Alex Rodriguez/25 275.00
CS3 Victor Martinez,
Kenji Johjima/25 75.00
CS4 Kenji Johjima,
Felix Hernandez/18 200.00
CS5 David Ortiz,
Manny Ramirez/25 150.00
CS6 Nolan Ryan,
Roger Clemens/25 350.00
CS7 David Ortiz,
Albert Pujols/25 350.00
CS8 Chipper Jones,
Dale Murphy/25 100.00
CS11 Stan Musial,
Albert Pujols/20 500.00
CS15 Prince Fielder,
Ryan Zimmerman 50.00
CS16 Cal Ripken Jr.,
Ozzie Smith/25 275.00
CS18 Don Larsen,
Yogi Berra/25 200.00
CS19 Mike Schmidt,
Brooks Robinson/25 125.00
CS20 Ryan Zimmerman,
Wade Boggs/25 50.00
CS22 Ryan Howard,
Derrek Lee/75 80.00
CS23 Jeff Mathis, Chris Snyder 15.00
CS25 Ray Knight, Keith
Hernandez/100 25.00
CS26 Mike Schmidt,
Chase Utley/25 100.00
CS27 Billy Wagner,
Paul LoDuca/50 70.00
CS28 Tony Gwynn,
Wade Boggs/25 140.00
CS30 Dwight Gooden,
Darryl Strawberry/50 40.00
CS31 Ryan Howard,
Huston Street 40.00
CS32 Mariano Rivera,
Huston Street/25 140.00
CS33 Prince Fielder,
Ryan Howard/50 60.00
CS34 Robinson Cano,
Chase Utley/75 60.00
CS36 David Justice,
Chipper Jones/25 80.00
CS37 Jose Reyes,
David Wright/50 200.00
CS38 Jeff Mathis, Ryan Garko 15.00
CS39 Brandon McCarthy,
Pedro Lopez 15.00
CS40 David Justice,
Dale Murphy/100 50.00
CS42 Joe Mauer,
Francisco Liriano 40.00
CS44 Ryan Zimmerman,
David Wright/100 100.00
CS45 Rick Rhoden,
Dave Parker/100 40.00
CS46 Jonathan Papelbon,
Craig Breslow 40.00
CS48 Dan Johnson,
Prince Fielder/100 30.00
CS49 Victor Martinez,
Ryan Garko 20.00
CS50 Ben Hendrickson,
Anthony Reyes 15.00
CS51 Nelson Cruz,
Prince Fielder/100 30.00
CS52 Jonathan Papelbon,
Anthony Reyes 30.00
CS53 Ben Hendrickson, Rich Hill 20.00
CS54 Shin-Soo Choo,
Kenji Johjima/25 85.00
CS55 Francisco Liriano,
Johan Santana/100 100.00
CS56 Brandon McCarthy,
Zachary Duke 15.00
CS57 Josh Johnson, Scott Olsen 15.00
CS58 Tommy John, Bob Welch 15.00
CS59 Roy White, Joe Pepitone 25.00
CS60 Cecil Fielder, Prince Fielder 60.00
CS62 Conor Jackson,
Ryan Howard 50.00
CS63 Dontrelle Willis,
Zachary Duke/50 25.00
CS64 Mariano Rivera,
Billy Wagner/25 150.00
CS65 Hong-Chih Kuo,
Shin-Soo Choo 30.00
CS66 Jim Leyritz, Cecil Fielder 50.00
CS67 Scott Kazmir,
Francisco Liriano 40.00
CS68 Scott Kazmir,
Roy Oswalt/50 50.00
CS69 Chuck James,
Anthony LeRew 15.00
CS70 Cecil Fielder,
Ryan Howard 60.00
CS71 Chien-Ming Wang,
Hong-Chih Kuo/25 200.00
CS72 Shin-Soo Choo,
Chien-Ming Wang/50 160.00
CS73 Nelson Cruz,
Jason Botts 15.00
CS74 Francisco Liriano,
Ervin Santana 30.00
CS75 Adam Wainwright,
Anthony Reyes 30.00
CS76 Ervin Santana,
Scott Kazmir 30.00
CS77 Robinson Cano,
Gary Sheffield 50.00
CS78 David Wright,
Miguel Cabrera/50 120.00
CS79 Dan Johnson,
Conor Jackson 15.00
CS80 Frank Tanana,
Mickey Tettleton 15.00
CS81 Andruw Jones,
Chipper Jones 75.00
CS82 Morgan Ensberg,
Roy Oswalt 25.00
CS83 Michael Young,
Ozzie Smith 50.00
CS84 Grady Sizemore,
Nick Swisher 40.00
CS85 Garrett Atkins,
Clint Barmes 20.00

Dual Cut Signatures
No Pricing

Solo Sigs
NM/M
Cards are not serial #'d.
CB Clint Barmes 10.00
CBR Craig Breslow 10.00
RC Robinson Cano 50.00
GC Gustavo Chacin 10.00
SSC Shin-Soo Choo 15.00
JC Jack Clark 10.00
AD Andre Dawson 10.00
ZD Zachary Duke 10.00
CF Cecil Fielder 20.00
PF Prince Fielder/250 40.00
RHI Rich Hill 20.00
RH Ryan Howard/100 60.00
DJ Dan Johnson/250 10.00
CJ Chipper Jones/25 80.00
AK Al Kaline/100 50.00
SK Scott Kazmir 20.00
DL Don Larsen 20.00
DLE Derrek Lee/50 40.00
VM Victor Martinez/50 25.00
JM Jeff Mathis 10.00
DM Don Mattingly/50 120.00
JMA Joe Mauer/75 30.00
CM Craig Monroe 10.00
SO Scott Olsen 15.00
DO David Ortiz/25 60.00
JP Jonathan Papelbon 60.00
ARE Anthony Reyes 10.00
RR Rick Rhoden 10.00
CR Cal Ripken Jr./20 200.00
AR Alex Rodriguez/20 200.00
NR Nolan Ryan/20 125.00
ES Ervin Santana/250 10.00
JS Johan Santana/50 40.00
CS Chris Snyder 8.00
DS Darryl Strawberry 15.00
HS Huston Street/250 20.00
DWI Dontrelle Willis 15.00
DW David Wright/75 80.00

2006 Topps Heritage

NM/M
Complete Set (485):
Common Player: .40
Common SP: 4.00
Pack (8): 4.00
Box (24): 75.00
1 David Ortiz/SP 8.00
2 Mike Piazza/SP 8.00
3 Daryle Ward .40
4 Rafael Furcal .75
5 Derek Lowe .40
6 Eric Chavez .50
7 Juan Uribe .40
8 C.C. Sabathia .75
9 Sean Casey .40
10 Barry Bonds/SP 15.00
11 Gary Sheffield .75
12 Ted Lilly .50
13 Lew Ford .40
14 Tom Gordon .40
15 Curt Schilling 1.00
16 Jason Kendall .40
17 Frank Catalanotto .40
18 Pedro Martinez/SP 8.00
19 David Dellucci .40
20 Andruw Jones .75
20 Andruw Jones/w/Seats/SP 6.00
21 Brad Halsey .40
22 Vernon Wells .75
23 Derek Jeter 4.00
23 Derek Jeter/Blue Letter/SP 15.00
24 Todd Helton 1.00
25 Randy Johnson/SP 8.00
26 Jay Gibbons .40
27 Joe Mays .40
28 Paul Konerko .75
29 Lyle Overbay .40
30 Jorge Posada .75
31 Brandon Webb .75
32 Marcus Giles .40
33 J.T. Snow .40
34 Todd Walker .40
35 Wily Mo Pena/SP 5.00
36 Carlos Delgado .75
37 David Wright 2.00
38 Shea Hillenbrand .40
39 Daniel Cabrera .40
40 Trevor Hoffman .40
41 Matt Morris .40
42 Mariano Rivera .75
43 Jeff Bagwell 1.00
44 J.D. Drew .50
45 Carl Pavano .40
46 Placido Polanco .40
47 Adrian Beltre .75
48 J.D. Closser .40
49 Paul LoDuca .40
50 Scott Rolen .75
51 Bernie Williams .75
52 Jose Guillen .40
53 Aubrey Huff .40
54 Greg Maddux 2.50
55 Derrek Lee/SP 8.00
56 Hideki Matsui 2.50
57 Jose Bautista .40
58 Kyle Farnsworth .40
59 Nate Robertson .40
60 Sammy Sosa 1.00
61 Javier Vazquez .40
62 Jeff Mathis **(RC)** .40
63 Mark Buehrle .75
64 Orlando Hernandez .40
65 Brandon Claussen .40
66 Miguel Batista .40
67 Eddie Guardado .40
68 Alex Gonzalez .40
69 Kris Benson .40
70 Bobby Abreu/SP 6.00
71 Vinny Castilla .40
72 Ben Broussard .40
73 Travis Hafner .75
74 Dmitri Young .40
75 Alex S. Gonzalez .40
76 Jason Bay/SP 6.00
77 Charlton Jimerson .40
78 Ryan Garko **(RC)** .50
79 Lance Berkman .75
80 Tim Hudson .75
80 Tim Hudson/Blue Letter/SP 5.00
81 Guillermo Mota .40
82 Chris Young .75
83 Brad Lidge .40
84 A.J. Pierzynski .40
85 Maicer Izturis .40
86 Vladimir Guerrero 1.50
87 J.J. Hardy .40
88 Cesar Izturis .40
89 Mark Ellis .40
90 Chipper Jones 1.50
91 Chris Snelling/SP 4.00
92 Jose Reyes 1.00
93 Mike Lieberthal .40
94 Octavio Dotel .40
95 Alex Rodriguez/Fldg/SP 10.00
95 Alex Rodriguez/w/Bat/SP 10.00
96 Brett Myers .40
97 New York Yankees 1.00
98 Ryan Klesko .40
99 Brian Jordan/SP 4.00
100 William Harridge,
Warren Giles .40
101 Adam Eaton .40
102 Aaron Boone .40
103 Alex Rios .75
104 Andy Pettitte .75
105 Barry Zito .50
106 Bengie Molina/SP 4.00
107 Austin Kearns .50
108 Adam Everett .40
109 A.J. Burnett .75
110 Mark Prior .75
111 Russ Ortiz .40
112 Adam Dunn 1.00
113 Byung-Hyun Kim .40
114 Atlanta Braves .50
115 Carlos Silva .40
116 Chad Cordero .40
117 Chone Figgins .75
118 Chris Reitsma .40
119 Coco Crisp .40
120 David DeJesus .40
121 Chris Snyder .40
122 Brad Eldred .40
123 Humberto Cota/SP 5.00
124 Erubiel Durazo .40
125 Josh Beckett 1.00
126 Kenny Lofton .40
127 Joe Nathan/SP 5.00
128 Bryan Bullington .40
129 Jim Thome 1.00
130 Shawn Green .75
131 LaTroy Hawkins .40
132 Mark Kotsay .40
133 Matt Lawton .40
134 Luis Castillo .40
135 Michael Barrett .40
136 Preston Wilson .40
137 Orlando Cabrera .40
138 Chuck James **(RC)** .40
139 Raul Ibanez .40
140 Frank Thomas 1.00
141 Orlando Hudson .40
142 Scott Kazmir .75
143 Steve Finley .40
144 Danny Sandoval **RC** 1.00
145 Javy Lopez .40
146 Tony Giarratano .40
147 Terrence Long .40
148 Victor Martinez .75
149 Toby Hall .40
150 Fausto Carmona **(RC)** .75
151 Tim Wakefield .40
152 Troy Percival .40
153 Chris Denorfia **(RC)** .40
154 Junior Spivey .40
155 Desi Relaford .40
156 Francisco Liriano **(RC)** .75
157 Corey Koskie .40
158 Chris Carpenter .75
159 Robert Andino **RC** 1.00
160 Cliff Floyd .40
161 Pittsburgh Pirates .40
162 Anderson Hernandez **(RC)** .40
163 Mike Maroth .40
164 Aaron Rowand .75
165 Albert Pujols 4.00
165 Albert Pujols/Red Shirt/SP 15.00
166 David Bell .40
167 Angel Berroa .40
168 B.J. Ryan .40
169 Bartolo Colon .40
170 Hong-Chih Kuo .75
171 Cincinnati Reds .40
172 Bill Mueller .40
173 John Koronka **(RC)** .40
174 Billy Wagner .40
175 Zack Greinke .75
176 Rick Short **RC** 1.00
177 Yadier Molina .40
178 Willy Taveras .40
179 Wes Helms .40
180 Wade Miller .40

181 Luis Gonzalez .40
182 Carlos Zambrano .75
183 Chicago Cubs .50
184 Victor Santos .40
185 Tyler Walker .40
186 Bobby Crosby .40
187 Trot Nixon .40
188 Nick Johnson .40
189 Nick Swisher .75
190 Brian Roberts .75
191 Nomar Garciaparra 1.00
192 Oliver Perez .40
193 Ramon Hernandez .40
194 Randy Winn .40
195 Ryan Church .40
196 Ryan Wagner .40
197 Todd Hollandsworth .40
198 Detroit Tigers .40
199 Tino Martinez .75
200 Roger Clemens 3.00
200 Roger Clemens/Red Shirt/SP 12.00
201 Shawn Estes .40
202 Justin Morneau .75
203 Jeff Francis .40
204 Oakland Athletics .40
205 Jeff Francoeur .75
206 C.J. Wilson .40
207 Francisco Rodriguez .40
208 Edgardo Alfonzo .40
209 David Eckstein .40
210 Cory Lidle .40
211 Chase Utley 1.50
212 Rocco Baldelli .40
212 Rocco Baldelli/Blue Letter/SP 5.00
213 So Taguchi .40
214 Philadelphia Phillies .40
215 Brad Hawpe .40
216 Walter Young .40
217 Tom Gorzelanny **(RC)** .75
218 Shaun Marcum **(RC)** .40
219 Ryan Howard 2.00
220 Damian Jackson .40
221 Craig Counsell .40
222 Damian Miller .40
223 Derrick Turnbow .40
224 Hank Blalock .75
225 Brayan Pena .40
226 Grady Sizemore 1.00
227 Ivan Rodriguez 1.00
228 Jason Isringhausen .40
229 Brian Fuentes .40
230 Jason Phillips .40
231 Jason Schmidt .50
232 Javier Valentin .40
233 Jeff Kent .75
234 John Buck .40
235 Mike Matheny .40
236 Jorge Cantu .40
237 Jose Castillo .40
238 Kenny Rogers .40
239 Kerry Wood .75
240 Kevin Mench .40
241 Tim Stauffer .40
242 Eric Milton .40
243 St. Louis Cardinals .75
244 Shawn Chacon .40
245 Mike Jacobs **(RC)** 1.00
246 Ryan Dempster .40
247 Todd Jones .40
248 Tom Glavine .75
249 Tony Graffanino .40
250 Ichiro Suzuki 2.50
251 Baltimore Orioles .50
252 Brad Radke .40
253 Brad Wilkerson .40
254 Carlos Lee .75
255 Alex Gordon/Cut-Out 150.00
256 Gustavo Chacin .40
257 Jermaine Dye .75
258 Jose Mesa .40
259 Julio Lugo .40
260 Mark Redman .40
261 Brandon Watson **(RC)** .40
262 Pedro Feliz .40
263 Esteban Loaiza .40
264 Anthony Reyes .40
265 Jose Contreras/SP 4.00
266 Tadahito Iguchi/SP 6.00
267 Mark Loretta/SP 4.00
268 Ray Durham/SP 4.00
269 Neifi Perez/SP 4.00
270 Washington Nationals .40
271 Troy Glaus/SP 6.00
272 Matt Holliday/SP 8.00
273 Kevin Millwood/SP 4.00
274 Jon Lieber/SP 4.00
275 Cleveland Indians .40
276 Jeremy Reed/SP 4.00
277 Garrett Atkins/SP 6.00
278 Geoff Jenkins/SP 4.00
279 Joey Gathright/SP 4.00
280 Ben Sheets/SP 6.00
281 Melvin Mora/SP 4.00
282 Jonathan Papelbon/SP **(RC)** 10.00
283 John Smoltz/SP 6.00
284 Jake Peavy/SP 6.00
285 Felix Hernandez/SP 6.00
286 Alfonso Soriano/SP 6.00
287 Bronson Arroyo/SP 4.00
288 Adam LaRoche/SP 5.00
289 Aramis Ramirez/SP 6.00
290 Brad Hennessey/SP 4.00
291 Conor Jackson/SP **(RC)** 5.00
292 Rod Barajas/SP 4.00
293 Chris Young/SP 5.00
294 Jeremy Bonderman/SP 4.00
295 Jack Wilson/SP 4.00
296 Jay Payton/SP 4.00
297 Danys Baez/SP 4.00
298 Jose Lima/SP 4.00
299 Luis A. Gonzalez/SP 4.00
300 Mike Sweeney/SP 4.00
301 Nelson Cruz/SP **(RC)** 4.00
302 Eric Gagne/SP 4.00
303 Juan Castro/SP 4.00
304 Joe Mauer/SP 5.00
305 Richie Sexson/SP 5.00
306 Roy Oswalt/SP 5.00
307 Rickie Weeks/SP 5.00
308 Pat Borders/SP 4.00
309 Mike Morse/SP 4.00
310 Matt Stairs/SP 4.00
311 Chad Tracy/SP 4.00
312 Matt Cain/SP **(RC)** 6.00
313 Mark Mulder/SP 4.00
314 Mark Grudzielanek/SP 4.00
315 Johnny Damon/SP 8.00
316 Casey Kotchman/SP 4.00
317 San Francisco Giants .40
318 Chris Burke/SP 4.00
319 Carl Crawford/SP 5.00
320 Edgar Renteria/SP 5.00
321 Chan Ho Park/SP 4.00
322 Boston Red Sox 5.00
323 Robinson Cano/SP 8.00
324 Los Angeles Dodgers .40
325 Miguel Tejada/w/Bat/SP 6.00
325 Miguel Tejada/Hand Up/SP 6.00
326 Jimmy Rollins/SP 6.00
327 Juan Pierre/SP 4.00
328 Dan Johnson/SP 4.00
329 Chicago White Sox .40
330 Pat Burrell/SP 5.00
331 Ramon Ortiz/SP 4.00
332 Rondell White/SP 4.00
333 David Wells/SP 4.00
334 Michael Young/SP 5.00
335 Mike Mussina/SP 5.00
336 Moises Alou/SP 5.00
337 Scott Podsednik/SP 4.00
338 Rich Harden/SP 5.00
339 Mark Teahen/SP 4.00
340 Jacque Jones/SP 4.00
341 Jason Giambi/SP 5.00
342 Bill Hall/SP 4.00
343 Jon Garland/SP 4.00
344 Dontrelle Willis/SP 4.00
345 Danny Haren/SP 5.00
346 Brian Giles/SP 4.00
347 Brad Penny/SP 4.00
348 Brandon McCarthy/SP 4.00
349 Chien-Ming Wang/SP 8.00
350 Torii Hunter/Blue Letter/SP 5.00
350 Torii Hunter/Red/Blue Letter/SP 5.00
351 Yhency Brazoban/SP 4.00
352 Rodrigo Lopez/SP 4.00
353 Paul McAnulty .40
354 Francisco Cordero .40
355 Brandon Inge .40
356 Jason Lane .40
357 Brian Schneider .40
358 Dustin Hermanson .40
359 Eric Hinske .40
360 Jarrod Washburn .40
361 Jayson Werth .40
362 Craig Breslow **RC** 1.00
363 Jeff Weaver .40
364 Jeromy Burnitz .40
365 Jhonny Peralta .75
366 Joe Crede .40
367 Johan Santana 1.50
368 Jose Valentin .40
369 Keith Foulke .40
370 Larry Bigbie .40
371 Manny Ramirez 1.50
372 Jim Edmonds .75
373 Horacio Ramirez .40
374 Garret Anderson .75
375 Felipe Lopez .75
376 Eric Byrnes .40
377 Darin Erstad .50
378 Carlos Zambrano .75
379 Craig Biggio .75
380 Darrell Rasner **(RC)** .40
381 Dave Roberts .40
382 Hanley Ramirez **(RC)** 1.50
383 Geoff Blum .40
384 Joel Pineiro .40
385 Kip Wells .40
386 Kelvim Escobar .40
387 John Patterson .40
388 Jody Gerut .40
389 Marshall McDougall .40
390 Mike MacDougal .40
391 Orlando Palmeiro .40
392 Rich Aurilia .40
393 Ronnie Belliard .40
394 Rich Hill .50
395 Scott Hatteberg .40
396 Ryan Langerhans .40
397 Richard Hidalgo .40
398 Omar Vizquel .40
399 Mike Lowell .75
400 Astros' Aces/SP 8.00
401 Mike Cameron .40
402 Matt Clement .40
403 Miguel Cabrera 1.50
404 Milton Bradley .40
405 Laynce Nix .40
406 Robert Mackowiak .40
407 White Sox Power Hitters/SP 10.00
408 Mark Teixeira 1.00
409 Brady Clark .40
410 Johnny Estrada .40
411 Juan Encarnacion .40
412 Morgan Ensberg .40
413 Nook Logan .40
414 Phil Nevin .40
415 Reggie Sanders .40
416 Roy Halladay .75
417 Livan Hernandez .40
418 Jose Vidro .40
419 Shannon Stewart .40
420 Brian Bruney .40
421 Royce Clayton .40
422 Chris Demaria **RC** .75
423 Eduardo Perez .40
424 Jeff Suppan .40
425 Jaret Wright .40
426 Joe Randa .40
427 Bobby Kielty .40
428 Jason Ellison .40
429 Gregg Zaun .40
430 Runelvys Hernandez .40
431 Joe McEwing .40
432 Jason LaRue .40
433 Aaron Miles .40
434 Adam Kennedy .40
435 Ambiorix Burgos .40
436 Armando Benitez .40
437 Brad Ausmus .40
438 Brandon Backe .40
439 Brian Anderson **(RC)** .40
440 Bruce Chen .40
441 Carlos Guillen .75
442 Casey Blake .40
443 Chris Capuano .40
444 Chris Duffy .40
445 Chris Ray .40
446 Clint Barmes .40
447 Andrew Sisco .40
448 Dallas McPherson .40
449 Tanyon Sturtze .40
450 Carlos Beltran 1.50
451 Jason Vargas .40
452 Ervin Santana .50
453 Jason Marquis .40
454 Juan Rivera .40
455 Jake Westbrook .40
456 Jason Johnson .40
457 Joe Blanton .40
458 Kevin Millar .40
459 John Thomson .40
460 J.P. Howell .40
461 Justin Verlander **(RC)** 1.00
462 Kelly Johnson .40
463 Kyle Davies .40
464 Lance Niekro .40
465 Magglio Ordonez .75
466 Melky Cabrera .75
467 Nick Punto .40
468 Paul Byrd .40
469 Randy Wolf .40
470 Ruben Gotay .40
471 Ryan Madson .40
472 Victor Diaz .40
473 Xavier Nady .40
474 Zachary Duke .40
475 Huston Street .75
475 Huston Street/Blue Letter/SP 6.00
476 Brad Thompson .40
477 Jonny Gomes .40
478 B.J. Upton .75
479 Jamey Carroll .40
480 Mike Hampton .40
481 Tony Clark .40
482 Antonio Alfonseca .40
483 Justin Duchscherer .40
484 Mike Timlin .40
485 Joe Saunders .40

Chrome

Heritage
Helton
COLORADO ROCKIES

NM/M

Common Player: 2.00
Production 1,957 Sets
Refractor: 1.5-2X
Production 557 Sets
Black Refractor: 3-6X
Production 57 Sets

1 Rafael Furcal 3.00
2 C.C. Sabathia 3.00
3 Sean Casey 2.00
4 Gary Sheffield 3.00
5 William Harridge, Warren Giles 2.00
6 Curt Schilling 3.00
7 Jay Gibbons 2.00
8 Paul Konerko 3.00
9 Lyle Overbay 2.00
10 Jorge Posada 3.00
11 Todd Walker 2.00
12 Carlos Delgado 3.00
13 David Wright 6.00
14 Matt Morris 2.00
15 Mariano Rivera 3.00
16 Jeff Bagwell 3.00
17 Carl Pavano 2.00
18 Adrian Beltre 3.00
19 Scott Rolen 3.00
20 Aubrey Huff 2.00
21 Hideki Matsui 6.00
22 Andruw Jones 3.00
23 Sammy Sosa 4.00
24 Mark Buehrle 3.00
25 Orlando Hernandez 2.00
26 Travis Hafner 3.00
27 Vladimir Guerrero 4.00
28 Chipper Jones 4.00
29 Jose Reyes 4.00
30 Roger Clemens 6.00
31 Aaron Boone 2.00
32 Andy Pettitte 3.00
33 David DeJesus 2.00
34 Shawn Green 2.00
35 Luis Castillo 2.00
36 Frank Thomas 3.00
37 Javy Lopez 2.00
38 Victor Martinez 3.00
39 Tim Wakefield 2.00
40 Cliff Floyd 2.00
41 Bartolo Colon 2.00
42 Billy Wagner 2.00
43 Dmitri Young 2.00
44 Mark Prior 2.00
45 Nick Johnson 2.00
46 Brian Roberts 3.00
47 Nomar Garciaparra 3.00
48 Jorge Cantu 2.00
49 Jeff Francoeur 3.00
50 Barry Bonds 8.00
51 Francisco Rodriguez 2.00
52 Rocco Baldelli 2.00
53 Ryan Howard 5.00
54 Hank Blalock 3.00
55 Ivan Rodriguez 3.00
56 Jason Schmidt 2.00
57 Jeff Kent 3.00
58 Jose Castillo 2.00
59 Kerry Wood 3.00
60 Chase Utley 4.00
61 Shawn Chacon 2.00
62 Tom Glavine 4.00
63 Ichiro Suzuki 6.00
64 Carlos Lee 3.00
65 Jeff Weaver 2.00
66 Jeromy Burnitz 2.00
67 Jhonny Peralta 2.00
68 Johan Santana 4.00
69 Keith Foulke 2.00
70 Manny Ramirez 4.00
71 Jim Edmonds 2.00
72 Garret Anderson 3.00
73 Felipe Lopez 2.00
74 Craig Biggio 3.00
75 Ryan Langerhans 2.00
76 Mike Cameron 2.00
77 Matt Clement 2.00
78 Miguel Cabrera 4.00
79 Mark Teixeira 3.00
80 Johnny Estrada 2.00
81 Nook Logan 2.00
82 Livan Hernandez 2.00
83 Roy Halladay 3.00
84 Jose Vidro 2.00
85 Shannon Stewart 2.00
86 Brian Bruney 2.00
87 Jaret Wright 2.00
88 Gregg Zaun 2.00
89 Jason LaRue 2.00
90 Adam Kennedy 2.00
91 Armando Benitez 2.00
92 Chris Ray 2.00
93 Clint Barmes 2.00
94 Ervin Santana 2.00
95 Justin Verlander 3.00
96 Magglio Ordonez 3.00
97 Todd Helton 3.00
98 Zachary Duke 2.00
99 Huston Street 2.00
100 Alex Rodriguez 8.00
101 Mike Hampton 2.00
102 Tony Clark 2.00
104 Barry Zito 2.00
105 Anderson Hernandez 2.00
106 B.J. Upton 3.00
107 Albert Pujols 10.00
108 Tim Hudson 3.00
109 Derek Jeter 10.00
110 Greg Maddux 6.00

Clubhouse Collection Relics

		NM/M
Common Player:		4.00
CB	Clint Barmes	4.00
BB	Barry Bonds	20.00
MC	Miguel Cabrera	8.00
RC	Robinson Cano	15.00
EC	Eric Chavez	4.00
SC	Shin-Soo Choo	4.00
CC	Carl Crawford	6.00
JD	Johnny Damon	6.00
JD2	Johnny Damon	6.00
AD	Adam Dunn	6.00
JE	Jim Edmonds	4.00
ME	Morgan Ensberg	4.00
JF	Jeff Francis	4.00
EG	Eric Gagne	4.00
KG	Khalil Greene	4.00
VG	Vladimir Guerrero	8.00
MH	Matt Holliday	8.00
TI	Tadahito Iguchi	4.00
CJ	Conor Jackson	4.00
AJ	Andruw Jones	6.00
AK	Al Kaline	20.00
DL	Derrek Lee	8.00
MM	Mickey Mantle	200.00
PM	Pedro Martinez	8.00
BM	Bill Mazeroski	30.00
MMU	Mark Mulder	4.00
SM	Stan Musial	35.00
DO	David Ortiz	10.00
JP	Jake Peavy	6.00
MP	Mike Piazza	8.00
AP	Albert Pujols	20.00
MR	Manny Ramirez	8.00
MR2	Manny Ramirez	8.00
BR	Brian Roberts	4.00
BR2	Brian Roberts	4.00
BRO	Brooks Robinson	30.00
FR	Frank Robinson	20.00
AR	Alex Rodriguez	20.00
AR2	Alex Rodriguez	20.00
JS	Johan Santana	6.00
CS	Curt Schilling	8.00
GS	Gary Sheffield	6.00
AS	Alfonso Soriano	6.00
MTE	Mark Teixeira	6.00
MT	Miguel Tejada	6.00
RW	Rickie Weeks	6.00
DWI	Dontrelle Willis	4.00
DW	David Wright	10.00

Clubhouse Collection Relic Autograph

		NM/M
Production 25 Sets		
CCA-3	Brooks Robinson	125.00
CCA-4	Al Kaline	200.00
CCA-5	Stan Musial	250.00

Clubhouse Collection Dual Relics

		NM/M
Production 57 Sets		
BR	Brooks Robinson, Bobby Roberts	75.00
MR	Mickey Mantle, Alex Rodriguez	250.00
MP	Stan Musial, Albert Pujols	150.00

Clubhouse Collection Cut Signature Relic

Production One Set
No Pricing

Flashbacks

		NM/M
Complete Set (10):		10.00
Common Player:		.50
Inserted 1:12		
EB	Ernie Banks	1.50
YB	Yogi Berra	1.50
WF	Whitey Ford	1.00
AK	Al Kaline	1.50
MM	Mickey Mantle	5.00
BM	Bill Mazeroski	.50
SM	Stan Musial	1.50
BRI	Bobby Richardson	.50
BR	Brooks Robinson	1.00
FR	Frank Robinson	1.00

Flashbacks Autographs

No Pricing
Production 25 Sets

Flashbacks Relics

		NM/M
EB	Ernie Banks	15.00
YB	Yogi Berra	20.00
WF	Whitey Ford	20.00
AK	Al Kaline	15.00
MM	Mickey Mantle	40.00
BM	Bill Mazeroski	10.00
SM	Stan Musial	50.00
BRI	Bobby Richardson	15.00
BR	Brooks Robinson	10.00
FR	Frank Robinson	10.00

Flashbacks Relic Autographs

No Pricing
Production 25 Sets

New Age Performers

		NM/M
Complete Set (15):		20.00
Common Player:		1.00
Inserted 1:15		
BB	Barry Bonds	4.00
MC	Miguel Cabrera	1.50
RC	Roger Clemens	4.00
CL	Carlos Lee	1.00
DL	Derrek Lee	1.50
PM	Pedro Martinez	1.50
DO	David Ortiz	1.50
GM	Mark Prior	1.00
AP	Albert Pujols	4.00
MR	Manny Ramirez	1.50
AR	Alex Rodriguez	4.00
GS	Gary Sheffield	1.00
I	Ichiro Suzuki	2.50
MT	Mark Teixeira	1.50

Real One Autographs

		NM/M
Production 200 Sets		
Red Ink:		1.5-2X
Production 57 Sets		
EB	Ernie Banks	120.00
YB	Yogi Berra	100.00
TB	Tommy Byrne	60.00
BC	Bob Chakales	50.00
JAC	Jack Collum	40.00
JCR	Jack Crimian	50.00
JD	Jack Dittmer	60.00
WF	Whitey Ford	100.00
DK	Don Kaiser	40.00
NK	Nellie King	50.00
LK	Lou Kretlow	50.00
PL	Paul LaPalme	50.00
JM	Joe Margoneri	60.00
WM	Windy McCall	40.00
JRM	John (Red) Murff	50.00
SM	Stan Musial	150.00
RN	Ron Negray	40.00
EOB	Eddie O'Brien	50.00
KO	Karl Olson	50.00
EO	Ernie Oravetz	50.00
MP	Mel Parnell	60.00
JP	Jim Pyburn	50.00
DR	Dusty Rhodes	50.00
FR	Frank Robinson	100.00
JSM	Jim Small	50.00
DS	Duke Snider	120.00
JSN	Jerry Snyder	60.00
CT	Charles Thompson	50.00
BW	Bob Wiesler	60.00

Real One Cut Signatures

Production One Set
No Pricing

Then and Now

		NM/M
Complete Set (10):		20.00
Common Duo:		1.00
Inserted 1:15		
TN1	Mickey Mantle, Alex Rodriguez	6.00
TN2	Ted Williams, Michael Young	3.00
TN3	Mickey Mantle, Jason Giambi	6.00
TN4	Luis Aparicio, Chone Figgins	1.00
TN5	Ted Williams, Alex Rodriguez	4.00
TN6	Stan Musial, Derrek Lee	2.00
TN7	Stan Musial, Derrek Lee	2.00
TN8	Red Schoendienst, Derrek Lee	1.50
TN9	Johnny Podres, Roger Clemens	4.00
TN10	Clem Labine, Chad Cordero	1.00

2006 Topps Opening Day

		NM/M
Complete Set (165):		25.00
Common Player:		.10
Pack (6):		1.00
Box (36):		30.00
1	Alex Rodriguez	1.50
2	Jhonny Peralta	.20
3	Garrett Atkins	.10
4	Vernon Wells	.25
5	Carl Crawford	.25
6	Josh Beckett	.25
7	Mickey Mantle	3.00
8	Willy Taveras	.10
9	Ivan Rodriguez	.40
10	Clint Barmes	.10
11	Jose Reyes	.25
12	Travis Hafner	.40
13	Tadahito Iguchi	.25
14	Barry Zito	.25
15	Brian Roberts	.25
16	David Wright	1.00
17	Mark Teixeira	.50
18	Roy Halladay	.25
19	Scott Rolen	.40
20	Bobby Abreu	.25
21	Lance Berkman	.25
22	Moises Alou	.20
23	Chone Figgins	.10
24	Aaron Rowand	.10
25	Chipper Jones	.50
26	Johnny Damon	.50
27	Matt Clement	.10
28	Nick Johnson	.10
29	Freddy Garcia	.10
30	Jon Garland	.10
31	Torii Hunter	.20
32	Mike Sweeney	.10
33	Mike Lieberthal	.10
34	Rafael Furcal	.20
35	Brad Wilkerson	.10
36	Brad Penny	.10
37	Jorge Cantu	.10
38	Paul Konerko	.25
39	Rickie Weeks	.25
40	Jorge Posada	.25
41	Albert Pujols	1.50
42	Zack Greinke	.10
43	Jimmy Rollins	.25
44	Mark Prior	.40
45	Greg Maddux	1.00
46	Jeff Francis	.10
47	Felipe Lopez	.10
48	Dan Johnson	.10
49	B.J. Ryan	.10
50	Manny Ramirez	.50
51	Melvin Mora	.20
52	Javy Lopez	.10
53	Garret Anderson	.20
54	Jason Bay	.25
55	Joe Mauer	.20
56	C.C. Sabathia	.10
57	Bartolo Colon	.20
58	Ichiro Suzuki	1.00
59	Andruw Jones	.50
60	Rocco Baldelli	.10
61	Jeff Kent	.20
62	Cliff Floyd	.10
63	John Smoltz	.25
64	Shawn Green	.20
65	Nomar Garciaparra	.50
66	Miguel Cabrera	.50
67	Vladimir Guerrero	.50
68	Gary Sheffield	.25
69	Jake Peavy	.25
70	Carlos Lee	.20
71	Tom Glavine	.25
72	Craig Biggio	.25
73	Steve Finley	.10
74	Adrian Beltre	.10
75	Eric Gagne	.25
76	Aubrey Huff	.10
77	Livan Hernandez	.10
78	Scott Podsednik	.10
79	Todd Helton	.40
80	Kerry Wood	.25
81	Randy Johnson	.50
82	Huston Street	.20
83	Pedro Martinez	.50
84	Roger Clemens	1.50
85	Hank Blalock	.20
86	Carlos Beltran	.40
87	Chien-Ming Wang	.25
88	Rich Harden	.25
89	Mike Mussina	.25
90	Mark Buehrle	.25
91	Michael Young	.20
92	Mark Mulder	.20
93	Khalil Greene	.10
94	Johan Santana	.50
95	Andy Pettitte	.25
96	Derek Jeter	1.50
97	Jack Wilson	.10
98	Ben Sheets	.25
99	Miguel Tejada	.40
100	Barry Bonds	1.50
101	Dontrelle Willis	.20
102	Curt Schilling	.50
103	Jose Contreras	.10
104	Jeremy Bonderman	.20
105	David Ortiz	.50
106	Lyle Overbay	.10
107	Robinson Cano	.25
108	Tim Hudson	.10
109	Paul LoDuca	.10
110	Mariano Rivera	.25
111	Derrek Lee	.50
112	Morgan Ensberg	.20
113	Wily Mo Pena	.10
114	Roy Oswalt	.25
115	Adam Dunn	.40
116	Hideki Matsui	1.00
117	Pat Burrell	.25
118	Jason Schmidt	.20
119	Alfonso Soriano	.40
120	Aramis Ramirez	.25
121	Jason Giambi	.25
122	Orlando Hernandez	.25
123	Magglio Ordonez	.10
124	Troy Glaus	.25
125	Carlos Delgado	.25
126	Kevin Millwood	.10
127	Shannon Stewart	.10
128	Luis Castillo	.10
129	Jim Edmonds	.25
130	Richie Sexson	.10
131	Dmitri Young	.10
132	Russ Adams	.10
133	Nick Swisher	.25
134	Jermaine Dye	.10
135	Anderson Hernandez (RC)	.10
136	Justin Huber (RC)	.10
137	Jason Botts (RC)	.10
138	Jeff Mathis (RC)	.10
139	Ryan Garko (RC)	.10
140	Charlton Jimerson (RC)	.10
141	Chris Denorfia (RC)	.10
142	Anthony Reyes (RC)	.10
143	Bryan Bullington (RC)	.10
144	Chuck James (RC)	.10
145	Danny Sandoval RC	.25
146	Walter Young (RC)	.10
147	Fausto Carmona (RC)	.10
148	Francisco Liriano (RC)	.25
149	Hong-Chih Kuo (RC)	.10
150	Joe Saunders (RC)	.10
151	John Koronka (RC)	.10
152	Robert Andino RC	.10
153	Shaun Marcum (RC)	.10
154	Tom Gorzelanny (RC)	.10
155	Craig Breslow RC	.25
156	Chris Demaria RC	.50
157	Brayan Pena (RC)	.10
158	Rich Hill (RC)	.25
159	Rick Short RC	.25
160	Darrell Rasner (RC)	.10
161	C.J. Wilson (RC)	.10
162	Brandon Watson (RC)	.10
163	Paul McAnulty (RC)	.10
164	Marshall McDougall (RC)	.10
165	Checklist	.10

Red Foil

Red:	2-3X
Production 2,006 Sets	

Printing Plates

No Pricing
Production one set per color.

Autographs

		NM/M
BE	Brad Eldred	10.00
JE	Johnny Estrada	10.00
TH	Toby Hall	10.00
MK	Mark Kotsay	10.00
EM	Eli Marrero	10.00
VZ	Victor Zambrano	10.00

Opening Day Relics

		NM/M
Common Team:		25.00
WI	Chicago White Sox	40.00
MN	New York Mets	40.00
RR	Texas Rangers	30.00
BP	Milwaukee Brewers	25.00
RC	Cincinnati Reds	30.00
PC	Philadelphia Phillies	40.00
OD	Baltimore Orioles	25.00
RD	Colorado Rockies	25.00

DB	Los Angeles Dodgers	40.00
RT	Kansas City Royals	25.00
MA	Seattle Mariners	30.00
AM	Houston Astros	30.00
PG	San Diego Padres	40.00
AY	Oakland Athletics	40.00
JT	Toronto Blue Jays	30.00

SI For Kids

		NM/M
1	Vladimir Guerrero	.50
2	Marcus Giles	.15
3	Michael Young	.15
4	Derek Jeter	1.50
5	Barry Bonds	1.50
6	Ivan Rodriguez	.40
7	Miguel Cabrera	.50
8	Jim Edmonds	.25
9	Jack Wilson	.15
10	Khalil Greene	.15
11	Miguel Tejada	.40
12	Eric Chavez	.25
13	Shannon Stewart	.15
14	Julio Lugo	.15
15	Andruw Jones	.50
16	Nick Johnson, Randy Johnson	.50
17	Tadahito Iguchi, Ivan Rodriguez	.25
18	Roy Oswalt, Jose Reyes	.25
19	Manny Ramirez, Ronnie Belliard	.50
20	Todd Helton, Khalil Greene	.25
21	David Ortiz, Dontrelle Willis	.50
22	Ichiro Suzuki, Johnny Damon	.75
23	Craig Biggio, Jack Wilson	.15
24	Brian Roberts, Richie Sexson	.25
25	Chipper Jones, Marcus Giles	.50

2006 Topps Sterling

		NM/M
Common Player:		10.00
Production 250 Sets		
Box (Five Cards):		300.00
1-19	Barry Bonds	10.00
20-39	Mickey Mantle	25.00
40-43	Josh Gibson	30.00
44-53	Rickey Henderson	10.00
54-62	Ted Williams	15.00
63-67	Roberto Clemente	25.00
68-77	Nolan Ryan	20.00
78-96	Cal Ripken Jr.	20.00
97-101	Stan Musial	15.00
102-106	Reggie Jackson	15.00
107-111	Johnny Bench	15.00
112-121	George Brett	15.00
122-131	Don Mattingly	15.00
132-136	Roger Maris	20.00
137-146	Rod Carew	10.00
147-151	Yogi Berra	15.00
152-156	Mike Schmidt	15.00
157-175	Carl Yastrzemski	15.00
176-185	Tony Gwynn	15.00
186-190	Ryne Sandberg	15.00
191-200	Ozzie Smith	15.00

Framed Burgundy

Burgundy (1-200): 3-5X
Production 10 Sets

Framed Silver

No Pricing
Production One Set

Framed White

White (1-200): 1-1.5X
Production 50 Sets

Baseball Cut Signatures

		NM/M
SA	Sparky Anderson	40.00
LA	Luis Aparicio	40.00
LB	Lou Brock	50.00
RC	Rod Carew	50.00
SC	Steve Carlton	50.00
GC	Gary Carter	50.00
OC	Orlando Cepeda	35.00
DE	Dennis Eckersley	40.00
BF	Bob Feller	40.00
RF	Rollie Fingers	40.00
CF	Carlton Fisk	60.00
BG	Bob Gibson	50.00
MI	Monte Irvin	40.00
AK	Al Kaline	60.00
GK	George Kell	40.00
HK	Harmon Killebrew	70.00
RK	Ralph Kiner	50.00
JM	Juan Marichal	40.00
JMO	Joe Morgan	50.00
PN	Phil Niekro	40.00
JP	Jim Palmer	40.00
TP	Tony Perez	40.00
GP	Gaylord Perry	40.00
RR	Robin Roberts	40.00
BR	Brooks Robinson	60.00
FR	Frank Robinson	60.00
RS	Ryne Sandberg	80.00
MS	Mike Schmidt	75.00
RSH	Red Schoendienst	60.00
DS	Duke Snider	75.00
EW	Earl Weaver	30.00
RY	Robin Yount	70.00

Career Stats Relics

No Pricing
Production 10 Sets
Prime: No Pricing
Production One Set
Sterling Silver: No Pricing
Production One Set

Career Stats Relics Autos.

Production 10 Sets
Prime: No Pricing
Production One Set
Sterling Silver: No Pricing
Production One Set

Cut from the Same Cloth Signatures

Production 1-5
No Pricing

Cut Signatures

		NM/M
46	Elmer Valo	80.00
53	Carl Furillo	100.00
61	Hal Newhouser	60.00
64	Dick Sisler	65.00
65	Frank Shea	75.00
66	Monty Stratton	80.00
67	Lloyd Waner	150.00
68	Sal Maglie	70.00
69	Waite Hoyt	80.00
70	Warren Spahn	100.00
72	A.B. Chandler	60.00
73	Al Barlick	75.00
74	Bill Dickey	100.00
75	Bill Terry	80.00
76	Billy Herman	75.00
77	Bob Lemon	60.00
78	Buck Leonard	80.00
79	Charles Gehringer	100.00
81	Earl Averill	60.00
82	Hoyt Wilhelm	80.00
83	Jim "Catfish" Hunter	100.00
84	Joe Sewell	80.00
85	Judy Johnson	80.00
86	Carl Hubbell	85.00
87	Lou Boudreau	65.00
88	Luke Appling	80.00
89	Ray Dandridge	75.00
90	Rick Ferrell	60.00
91	Stan Coveleski	75.00
92	Willie Stargell	120.00

Five Relics

Production 10 Sets
Prime: No Pricing
Production 10 Sets
Sterling Silver: No Pricing
Production One Set

Five Relics Autographs

Production 10 Sets
Prime: No Pricing
Production 10 Sets
Sterling Silver: No Pricing
Production One Set

Josh Gibson Bat Barrel

Production One
No Pricing

Jumbo Jersey

Production 10 Sets
Prime: No Pricing
Production One Set
Patch: No Pricing
Production 10 Sets
Sterling Silver: No Pricing
Production One Set

Moments Relics

		NM/M
Production 10 Sets		
Prime:		No Pricing
Production One Set		
BB	Barry Bonds HR 1	75.00
BB	Barry Bonds HR 2	75.00
BB	Barry Bonds HR 3	75.00
BB	Barry Bonds HR 4	75.00
BB	Barry Bonds HR 5	75.00
BB	Barry Bonds HR 6	75.00
BB	Barry Bonds HR 7	75.00
BB	Barry Bonds HR 8	75.00
BB	Barry Bonds HR 9	75.00
BB	Barry Bonds HR 1	75.00
BB	Barry Bonds HR 2	75.00
BB	Barry Bonds HR 3	75.00
BB	Barry Bonds HR 4	75.00
BB	Barry Bonds HR 5	75.00
BB	Barry Bonds HR 6	75.00
BB	Barry Bonds HR 7	75.00
BB	Barry Bonds HR 8	75.00
BB	Barry Bonds HR 1	75.00
BB	Barry Bonds HR 2	75.00
BB	Barry Bonds HR 3	75.00
BB	Barry Bonds HR 4	75.00
BB	Barry Bonds HR 5	75.00
BB	Barry Bonds HR 6	75.00
BB	Barry Bonds HR 7	75.00
BB	Barry Bonds HR 8	75.00
BB	Barry Bonds	75.00
BB	Barry Bonds 1993	75.00
BB	Barry Bonds 1994	75.00
BB	Barry Bonds 1995	75.00
BB	Barry Bonds 1996	75.00
BB	Barry Bonds 1997	75.00
BB	Barry Bonds 1998	75.00
BB	Barry Bonds 1999	75.00
BB	Barry Bonds 1993	75.00
BB	Barry Bonds 2001	75.00
BB	Barry Bonds 2002	75.00
BB	Barry Bonds 2003	75.00
BB	Barry Bonds 2004	75.00
BB	Barry Bonds 1993	75.00
BB	Barry Bonds 1994	75.00
BB	Barry Bonds 1995	75.00
BB	Barry Bonds 1996	75.00
BB	Barry Bonds 1997	75.00
BB	Barry Bonds 1998	75.00
BB	Barry Bonds 2000	75.00
BB	Barry Bonds 2001	75.00
BB	Barry Bonds 2002	75.00
BB	Barry Bonds 2003	75.00
BB	Barry Bonds 2004	75.00
BB	Barry Bonds 2002	75.00
BB	Barry Bonds 2004	75.00
BB	Barry Bonds 1993	75.00
BB	Barry Bonds 1994	75.00
BB	Barry Bonds 1996	75.00
BB	Barry Bonds 1997	75.00
BB	Barry Bonds 2000	75.00
BB	Barry Bonds 2001	75.00
BB	Barry Bonds 2002	75.00
BB	Barry Bonds 2003	75.00
BB	Barry Bonds 2004	75.00
BB	Barry Bonds 1993	75.00
BB	Barry Bonds 2001	75.00
BB	Barry Bonds 2002	75.00
BB	Barry Bonds 2003	75.00
BB	Barry Bonds 2004	75.00
MM	Mickey Mantle WS HR 1	350.00
MM	Mickey Mantle WS HR 2	350.00
MM	Mickey Mantle WS HR 3	350.00
MM	Mickey Mantle WS HR 4	350.00
MM	Mickey Mantle WS HR 5	350.00
MM	Mickey Mantle WS HR 6	350.00
MM	Mickey Mantle WS HR 7	350.00
MM	Mickey Mantle WS HR 8	350.00
MM	Mickey Mantle WS HR 9	350.00
MM	Mickey Mantle WS HR 10	350.00
MM	Mickey Mantle WS HR 11	350.00
MM	Mickey Mantle WS HR 12	350.00
MM	Mickey Mantle WS HR 13	350.00
MM	Mickey Mantle WS HR 14	350.00
MM	Mickey Mantle WS HR 15	350.00
MM	Mickey Mantle WS HR 16	350.00
MM	Mickey Mantle WS HR 17	350.00
MM	Mickey Mantle WS HR 18	350.00
MM	Mickey Mantle 1952	350.00
MM	Mickey Mantle 1956	350.00
MM	Mickey Mantle 1957	350.00
MM	Mickey Mantle 1962	350.00
MM	Mickey Mantle 1953	350.00
MM	Mickey Mantle 1954	350.00
MM	Mickey Mantle 1955	350.00
MM	Mickey Mantle 1958	350.00
MM	Mickey Mantle 1959	350.00
MM	Mickey Mantle 1960	350.00
MM	Mickey Mantle 1961	350.00
MM	Mickey Mantle 1963	350.00
MM	Mickey Mantle 1964	350.00
MM	Mickey Mantle 1965	350.00
MM	Mickey Mantle 1967	350.00
MM	Mickey Mantle 1968	350.00
MM	Mickey Mantle HR 1	350.00
MM	Mickey Mantle HR 7	350.00
MM	Mickey Mantle HR 10	350.00
MM	Mickey Mantle HR 2	350.00
MM	Mickey Mantle HR 3	350.00
MM	Mickey Mantle HR 4	350.00
MM	Mickey Mantle HR 5	350.00
MM	Mickey Mantle HR 6	350.00
MM	Mickey Mantle HR 8	350.00
MM	Mickey Mantle HR 9	350.00
MM	Mickey Mantle HR 11	350.00
MM	Mickey Mantle HR 12	350.00
MM	Mickey Mantle HR 13	350.00
MM	Mickey Mantle HR 14	350.00
MM	Mickey Mantle HR 15	350.00
MM	Mickey Mantle HR 16	350.00
MM	Mickey Mantle HR 17	350.00
MM	Mickey Mantle HR 18	350.00
MM	Mickey Mantle HR 19	350.00
MM	Mickey Mantle HR 20	350.00
MM	Mickey Mantle HR 25	350.00
MM	Mickey Mantle HR 21	350.00
MM	Mickey Mantle HR 22	350.00
MM	Mickey Mantle HR 23	350.00
MM	Mickey Mantle HR 24	350.00
MM	Mickey Mantle HR 26	350.00
MM	Mickey Mantle HR 27	350.00
MM	Mickey Mantle HR 28	350.00
MM	Mickey Mantle HR 29	350.00
MM	Mickey Mantle HR 30	350.00
MM	Mickey Mantle HR 31	350.00
MM	Mickey Mantle HR 32	350.00
MM	Mickey Mantle HR 33	350.00
MM	Mickey Mantle HR 34	350.00
MM	Mickey Mantle HR 35	350.00
MM	Mickey Mantle HR 36	350.00
MM	Mickey Mantle HR 37	350.00
MM	Mickey Mantle HR 38	350.00
MM	Mickey Mantle HR 39	350.00
MM	Mickey Mantle HR 40	350.00
MM	Mickey Mantle HR 50	350.00
MM	Mickey Mantle HR 60	350.00
MM	Mickey Mantle HR 41	350.00
MM	Mickey Mantle HR 42	350.00
MM	Mickey Mantle HR 43	350.00
MM	Mickey Mantle HR 44	350.00
MM	Mickey Mantle HR 45	350.00
MM	Mickey Mantle HR 46	350.00
MM	Mickey Mantle HR 47	350.00
MM	Mickey Mantle HR 48	350.00
MM	Mickey Mantle HR 49	350.00
MM	Mickey Mantle HR 51	350.00
MM	Mickey Mantle HR 52	350.00
MM	Mickey Mantle HR 53	350.00
MM	Mickey Mantle HR 54	350.00
MM	Mickey Mantle HR 55	350.00
MM	Mickey Mantle HR 56	350.00
MM	Mickey Mantle HR 57	350.00
MM	Mickey Mantle HR 58	350.00
MM	Mickey Mantle HR 59	350.00
MM	Mickey Mantle HR 75	350.00
MM	Mickey Mantle HR 61	350.00
MM	Mickey Mantle HR 62	350.00
MM	Mickey Mantle HR 63	350.00
MM	Mickey Mantle HR 64	350.00
MM	Mickey Mantle HR 65	350.00
MM	Mickey Mantle HR 66	350.00
MM	Mickey Mantle HR 67	350.00
MM	Mickey Mantle HR 68	350.00
MM	Mickey Mantle HR 69	350.00
MM	Mickey Mantle HR 70	350.00
MM	Mickey Mantle HR 71	350.00
MM	Mickey Mantle HR 72	350.00
MM	Mickey Mantle HR 73	350.00
MM	Mickey Mantle HR 74	350.00
MM	Mickey Mantle HR 76	350.00
MM	Mickey Mantle HR 77	350.00
MM	Mickey Mantle HR 78	350.00
MM	Mickey Mantle HR 79	350.00
MM	Mickey Mantle HR 80	350.00
MM	Mickey Mantle HR 90	350.00
MM	Mickey Mantle HR 81	350.00
MM	Mickey Mantle HR 82	350.00
MM	Mickey Mantle HR 83	350.00
MM	Mickey Mantle HR 84	350.00
MM	Mickey Mantle HR 85	350.00
MM	Mickey Mantle HR 86	350.00
MM	Mickey Mantle HR 87	350.00
MM	Mickey Mantle HR 88	350.00
MM	Mickey Mantle HR 89	350.00
MM	Mickey Mantle HR 91	350.00
MM	Mickey Mantle HR 92	350.00
MM	Mickey Mantle HR 93	350.00
MM	Mickey Mantle HR 94	350.00
MM	Mickey Mantle HR 95	350.00
MM	Mickey Mantle HR 96	350.00
MM	Mickey Mantle HR 97	350.00
MM	Mickey Mantle HR 98	350.00
MM	Mickey Mantle HR 99	350.00
MM	Mickey Mantle HR 100	350.00
JG	Josh Gibson	500.00
JG	Josh Gibson	500.00
JG	Josh Gibson	500.00
JG	Josh Gibson	500.00
JG	Josh Gibson	500.00
JG	Josh Gibson	500.00
JG	Josh Gibson	500.00
JG	Josh Gibson	500.00
RH	Rickey Henderson 1980	60.00
RH	Rickey Henderson 1981	60.00
RH	Rickey Henderson 1982	60.00
RH	Rickey Henderson 1983	60.00
RH	Rickey Henderson 1984	60.00
RH	Rickey Henderson 1990	60.00
RH	Rickey Henderson 1998	60.00
RH	Rickey Henderson 1989	60.00
RH	Rickey Henderson 1991	60.00
RH	Rickey Henderson 1985	60.00
RH	Rickey Henderson 1986	60.00
RH	Rickey Henderson 1987	60.00
RH	Rickey Henderson 1980	60.00
RH	Rickey Henderson 1983	60.00
RH	Rickey Henderson 1990	60.00
RH	Rickey Henderson 1982	60.00
RH	Rickey Henderson 1984	60.00
RH	Rickey Henderson 1991	60.00
RH	Rickey Henderson 1985	60.00
RH	Rickey Henderson 1987	60.00
RH	Rickey Henderson 1986	60.00
RH	Rickey Henderson 1988	60.00
RH	Rickey Henderson 1981	60.00
RH	Rickey Henderson 1990	60.00
RH	Rickey Henderson 1989	60.00
RH	Rickey Henderson 1986	60.00
RH	Rickey Henderson 1985	60.00
RH	Rickey Henderson 1983	60.00
RH	Rickey Henderson 1998	60.00

RH	Rickey Henderson 1982	60.00
RH	Rickey Henderson 1989	60.00
RH	Rickey Henderson 1990	60.00
RH	Rickey Henderson 1981	60.00
RH	Rickey Henderson 1985	60.00
TW	Ted Williams 0.406	150.00
TW	Ted Williams 0.5	150.00
TW	Ted Williams 0.308	150.00
TW	Ted Williams 0.341	150.00
TW	Ted Williams 0.421	150.00
TW	Ted Williams 0.436	150.00
TW	Ted Williams 0.42	150.00
TW	Ted Williams 0.405	150.00
TW	Ted Williams 0.397	150.00
TW	Ted Williams 0.4	150.00
TW	Ted Williams 0.414	150.00
TW	Ted Williams 0.409	150.00
TW	Ted Williams 0.411	150.00
TW	Ted Williams 0.399	150.00
TW	Ted Williams 0.404	150.00
TW	Ted Williams HR 1	150.00
TW	Ted Williams HR 10	150.00
TW	Ted Williams HR 20	150.00
TW	Ted Williams HR 30	150.00
TW	Ted Williams HR 36	150.00
TW	Ted Williams HR 1	150.00
TW	Ted Williams HR 10	150.00
TW	Ted Williams HR 20	150.00
TW	Ted Williams HR 30	150.00
TW	Ted Williams HR 32	150.00
RC	Roberto Clemente HIT 1	200.00
RC	Roberto Clemente HIT 2	200.00
RC	Roberto Clemente HIT 3	200.00
RC	Roberto Clemente HIT 4	200.00
RC	Roberto Clemente HIT 5	200.00
RC	Roberto Clemente HIT 6	200.00
RC	Roberto ClementeHIT 7	200.00
RC	Roberto Clemente HIT 8	200.00
RC	Roberto Clemente HIT 9	200.00
RC	Roberto Clemente HIT 10	200.00
RC	Roberto Clemente HIT 11	200.00
RC	Roberto Clemente HIT 12	200.00
RC	Roberto Clemente HIT 21	200.00
RC	Roberto Clemente HIT 13	200.00
RC	Roberto Clemente HIT 14	200.00
RC	Roberto Clemente HIT 15	200.00
RC	Roberto Clemente HIT 16	200.00
RC	Roberto Clemente HIT 17	200.00
RC	Roberto Clemente HIT 18	200.00
RC	Roberto Clemente HIT 19	200.00
RC	Roberto Clemente HIT 20	200.00
RC	Roberto Clemente 1966	200.00
RC	Roberto Clemente 1971	200.00
RC	Roberto Clemente 1972	200.00
RC	Roberto Clemente 1961	200.00
RC	Roberto Clemente 1962	200.00
RC	Roberto Clemente1963	200.00
RC	Roberto Clemente 1964	200.00
RC	Roberto Clemente 1965	200.00
RC	Roberto Clemente 1967	200.00
RC	Roberto Clemente 1968	200.00
RC	Roberto Clemente 1969	200.00
RC	Roberto Clemente 1970	200.00
NR	Nolan Ryan SO 1	100.00
NR	Nolan Ryan SO 50	100.00
NR	Nolan Ryan SO 100	100.00
NR	Nolan Ryan SO 200	100.00
NR	Nolan Ryan SO 10	100.00
NR	Nolan Ryan SO 20	100.00
NR	Nolan Ryan SO 30	100.00
NR	Nolan Ryan SO 40	100.00
NR	Nolan Ryan SO 60	100.00
NR	Nolan Ryan SO 70	100.00
NR	Nolan Ryan SO 80	100.00
NR	Nolan Ryan SO 90	100.00
NR	Nolan Ryan SO 125	100.00
NR	Nolan Ryan SO 150	100.00
NR	Nolan Ryan SO 175	100.00
NR	Nolan Ryan SO 225	100.00
NR	Nolan Ryan SO 300	100.00
NR	Nolan Ryan SO 350	100.00
NR	Nolan Ryan SO 380	100.00
NR	Nolan Ryan SO 382	100.00
NR	Nolan Ryan SO 383	100.00
NR	Nolan Ryan SO 250	100.00
NR	Nolan Ryan SO 275	100.00
NR	Nolan Ryan SO 310	100.00
NR	Nolan Ryan SO 320	100.00
NR	Nolan Ryan SO 330	100.00
NR	Nolan Ryan SO 340	100.00
NR	Nolan Ryan SO 360	100.00
NR	Nolan Ryan SO 370	100.00
NR	Nolan Ryan SO 375	100.00
NR	Nolan Ryan NO HIT 1	100.00
NR	Nolan Ryan NO HIT 2	100.00
NR	Nolan Ryan NO HIT 3	100.00
NR	Nolan Ryan NO HIT 4	100.00
NR	Nolan Ryan NO HIT 5	100.00
NR	Nolan Ryan NO HIT 6	100.00
NR	Nolan Ryan NO HIT 7	100.00
CR	Cal Ripken Jr. 1983	100.00
CR	Cal Ripken Jr. 1985	100.00
CR	Cal Ripken Jr. 1987	100.00
CR	Cal Ripken Jr. 1989	100.00
CR	Cal Ripken Jr. 1991	100.00
CR	Cal Ripken Jr. 1993	100.00
CR	Cal Ripken Jr. 1995	100.00
CR	Cal Ripken Jr. 1997	100.00
CR	Cal Ripken Jr. 1999	100.00
CR	Cal Ripken Jr. 2001	100.00
CR	Cal Ripken Jr. 1984	100.00
CR	Cal Ripken Jr. 1986	100.00
CR	Cal Ripken Jr. 1988	100.00
CR	Cal Ripken Jr. 1990	100.00
CR	Cal Ripken Jr. 1992	100.00
CR	Cal Ripken Jr. 1994	100.00
CR	Cal Ripken Jr. 1996	100.00
CR	Cal Ripken Jr. 1998	100.00
CR	Cal Ripken Jr. 2000	100.00
CR	Cal Ripken Jr. 1984	100.00
CR	Cal Ripken Jr. 1986	100.00
CR	Cal Ripken Jr. 1991	100.00
CR	Cal Ripken Jr. 1994	100.00
CR	Cal Ripken Jr. 1983	100.00
CR	Cal Ripken Jr. 1985	100.00
CR	Cal Ripken Jr. 1989	100.00
CR	Cal Ripken Jr. 1993	100.00
CR	Cal Ripken Jr. HIT 1	100.00
CR	Cal Ripken Jr. 1000	100.00
CR	Cal Ripken Jr. 1500	100.00
CR	Cal Ripken Jr. 2000	100.00
CR	Cal Ripken Jr. 2500	100.00
CR	Cal Ripken Jr. 2900	100.00
CR	Cal Ripken Jr. 3000	100.00
CR	Cal Ripken Jr. 3184	100.00
CR	Cal Ripken Jr. 100	100.00
CR	Cal Ripken Jr. 200	100.00
CR	Cal Ripken Jr. 300	100.00
CR	Cal Ripken Jr. 400	100.00
CR	Cal Ripken Jr. 500	100.00
CR	Cal Ripken Jr. 2100	100.00
CR	Cal Ripken Jr. 2200	100.00
CR	Cal Ripken Jr. 2300	100.00
CR	Cal Ripken Jr. 2400	100.00
CR	Cal Ripken Jr. 2600	100.00
CR	Cal Ripken Jr. 2700	100.00
CR	Cal Ripken Jr. 2800	100.00
CR	Cal Ripken Jr. HR 1	100.00
CR	Cal Ripken Jr. HR 100	100.00
CR	Cal Ripken Jr. HR 200	100.00
CR	Cal Ripken Jr. HR 300	100.00
CR	Cal Ripken Jr. HR 400	100.00
CR	Cal Ripken Jr. HR 431	100.00
CR	Cal Ripken Jr. HR 10	100.00
CR	Cal Ripken Jr. HR 25	100.00
CR	Cal Ripken Jr. HR 50	100.00
CR	Cal Ripken Jr. HR 75	100.00
CR	Cal Ripken Jr. HR 125	100.00
CR	Cal Ripken Jr. HR 150	100.00
CR	Cal Ripken Jr. HR 175	100.00
CR	Cal Ripken Jr. HR 225	100.00
CR	Cal Ripken Jr. HR 250	100.00
CR	Cal Ripken Jr. HR 275	100.00
CR	Cal Ripken Jr. HR 325	100.00
CR	Cal Ripken Jr. HR 350	100.00
CR	Cal Ripken Jr. HR 375	100.00
CR	Cal Ripken Jr. HR 425	100.00
CR	Cal Ripken Jr. GM 1	100.00
CR	Cal Ripken Jr. 500	100.00
CR	Cal Ripken Jr. 1000	100.00
CR	Cal Ripken Jr. 2000	100.00
CR	Cal Ripken Jr. 2130	100.00
CR	Cal Ripken Jr. 2131	100.00
CR	Cal Ripken Jr. 2632	100.00
CR	Cal Ripken Jr. 100	100.00
CR	Cal Ripken Jr. 200	100.00
CR	Cal Ripken Jr. 300	100.00
CR	Cal Ripken Jr. 400	100.00
CR	Cal Ripken Jr. 600	100.00
CR	Cal Ripken Jr. 700	100.00
CR	Cal Ripken Jr. 800	100.00
CR	Cal Ripken Jr. 900	100.00
CR	Cal Ripken Jr. 1250	100.00
CR	Cal Ripken Jr. 1500	100.00
CR	Cal Ripken Jr. 1750	100.00
CR	Cal Ripken Jr. 2500	100.00
CR	Cal Ripken Jr. 2600	100.00
SM	Stan Musial 1943	75.00
SM	Stan Musial 1946	75.00
SM	Stan Musial 1948	75.00
SM	Stan Musial 1950	75.00
SM	Stan Musial 1952	75.00
SM	Stan Musial 1942	75.00
SM	Stan Musial 1944	75.00
SM	Stan Musial 1947	75.00
SM	Stan Musial 1949	75.00
SM	Stan Musial 1951	75.00
SM	Stan Musial 1954	75.00
SM	Stan Musial 1956	75.00
SM	Stan Musial 1958	75.00
SM	Stan Musial 1960	75.00
SM	Stan Musial 1962	75.00
SM	Stan Musial 1953	75.00
SM	Stan Musial 1955	75.00
SM	Stan Musial 1957	75.00
SM	Stan Musial 1959	75.00
SM	Stan Musial 1961	75.00
RJ	Reggie Jackson HR 1	60.00
RJ	Reggie Jackson HR 100	60.00
RJ	Reggie Jackson HR 200	60.00
RJ	Reggie Jackson HR 250	60.00
RJ	Reggie Jackson HR 300	60.00
RJ	Reggie Jackson HR 350	60.00
RJ	Reggie Jackson HR 400	60.00
RJ	Reggie Jackson HR 450	60.00
RJ	Reggie Jackson HR 550	60.00
RJ	Reggie Jackson HR 25	60.00
RJ	Reggie Jackson HR 50	60.00
RJ	Reggie Jackson HR 75	60.00
RJ	Reggie Jackson HR 150	60.00
JB	Johnny Bench 1968	65.00
JB	Johnny Bench 1969	65.00
JB	Johnny Bench 1971	65.00
JB	Johnny Bench 1973	65.00
JB	Johnny Bench 1975	65.00
JB	Johnny Bench 1976	65.00
GB	George Brett HIT 1	60.00
GB	George Brett HIT 3	60.00
GB	George Brett HIT 5	60.00
GB	George Brett HIT 7	60.00
GB	George Brett HIT 10	60.00
GB	George Brett HIT 12	60.00
GB	George Brett HIT 15	60.00
GB	George Brett HIT 16	60.00
GB	George Brett HIT 17	60.00
GB	George Brett HIT 18	60.00
GB	George Brett HIT 2	60.00
GB	George Brett HIT 4	60.00
GB	George Brett HIT 6	60.00
GB	George Brett HIT 8	60.00
GB	George Brett HIT 9	60.00
GB	George Brett HIT 11	60.00
GB	George Brett HIT 13	60.00
GB	George Brett HIT 14	60.00
GB	George Brett 1976	60.00
GB	George Brett 1980	60.00
GB	George Brett 1990	60.00
GB	George Brett 1976	60.00
GB	George Brett 1977	60.00
GB	George Brett 1979	60.00
GB	George Brett 1981	60.00
GB	George Brett 1983	60.00
GB	George Brett 1985	60.00
GB	George Brett 1988	60.00
GB	George Brett 1978	60.00
GB	George Brett 1980	60.00
GB	George Brett 1982	60.00
GB	George Brett 1984	60.00
GB	George Brett 1986	60.00
GB	George Brett 1980	60.00
GB	George Brett 1985	60.00
GB	George Brett 1988	60.00
RM	Roger Maris HR 1	125.00
RM	Roger Maris HR 2	125.00
RM	Roger Maris HR 5	125.00
RM	Roger Maris HR 9	125.00
RM	Roger Maris HR 10	125.00
RM	Roger Maris HR 15	125.00
RM	Roger Maris HR 3	125.00
RM	Roger Maris HR 4	125.00
RM	Roger Maris HR 6	125.00
RM	Roger Maris HR 7	125.00
RM	Roger Maris HR 8	125.00
RM	Roger Maris HR 11	125.00
RM	Roger Maris HR 12	125.00
RM	Roger Maris HR 13	125.00
RM	Roger Maris HR 14	125.00
RM	Roger Maris HR 20	125.00
RM	Roger Maris HR 25	125.00
RM	Roger Maris HR 30	125.00
RM	Roger Maris HR 16	125.00
RM	Roger Maris HR 17	125.00
RM	Roger Maris HR 18	125.00
RM	Roger Maris HR 19	125.00
RM	Roger Maris HR 21	125.00
RM	Roger Maris HR 22	125.00
RM	Roger Maris HR 23	125.00
RM	Roger Maris HR 24	125.00
RM	Roger Maris HR 26	125.00
RM	Roger Maris HR 27	125.00
RM	Roger Maris HR 28	125.00
RM	Roger Maris HR 29	125.00
YB	Yogi Berra 1951	75.00
YB	Yogi Berra 1951	75.00
YB	Yogi Berra 1954	75.00
YB	Yogi Berra 1955	75.00
MS	Mike Schmidt HR 1	50.00
MS	Mike Schmidt HR 2	50.00
MS	Mike Schmidt HR 3	50.00
MS	Mike Schmidt HR 4	50.00
CY	Carl Yastrzemski HR 1	60.00
CY	Carl Yastrzemski HR 5	60.00
CY	Carl Yastrzemski HR 10	60.00
CY	Carl Yastrzemski HR 15	60.00
CY	Carl Yastrzemski HR 2	60.00
CY	Carl Yastrzemski HR 3	60.00
CY	Carl Yastrzemski HR 4	60.00
CY	Carl Yastrzemski HR 6	60.00
CY	Carl Yastrzemski HR 7	60.00
CY	Carl Yastrzemski HR 8	60.00
CY	Carl Yastrzemski HR 9	60.00
CY	Carl Yastrzemski HR 11	60.00
CY	Carl Yastrzemski HR 12	60.00
CY	Carl Yastrzemski HR 13	60.00
CY	Carl Yastrzemski HR 14	60.00
CY	Carl Yastrzemski HR 20	60.00
CY	Carl Yastrzemski HR 25	60.00
CY	Carl Yastrzemski HR 30	60.00
CY	Carl Yastrzemski HR 16	60.00
CY	Carl Yastrzemski HR 17	60.00
CY	Carl Yastrzemski HR 18	60.00
CY	Carl Yastrzemski HR 19	60.00
CY	Carl Yastrzemski HR 21	60.00
CY	Carl Yastrzemski HR 22	60.00
CY	Carl Yastrzemski HR 23	60.00
CY	Carl Yastrzemski HR 24	60.00
CY	Carl Yastrzemski HR 26	60.00
CY	Carl Yastrzemski HR 27	60.00
CY	Carl Yastrzemski HR 28	60.00
CY	Carl Yastrzemski HR 29	60.00
CY	Carl Yastrzemski HR 35	60.00
CY	Carl Yastrzemski HR 40	60.00
CY	Carl Yastrzemski HR 44	60.00
CY	Carl Yastrzemski HR 31	60.00
CY	Carl Yastrzemski HR 32	60.00
CY	Carl Yastrzemski HR 33	60.00
CY	Carl Yastrzemski HR 34	60.00
CY	Carl Yastrzemski HR 36	60.00
CY	Carl Yastrzemski HR 37	60.00
CY	Carl Yastrzemski HR 38	60.00
CY	Carl Yastrzemski HR 39	60.00
CY	Carl Yastrzemski HR 41	60.00
CY	Carl Yastrzemski HR 42	60.00
CY	Carl Yastrzemski HR 43	60.00
CY	Carl Yastrzemski 1961	60.00
CY	Carl Yastrzemski 1964	60.00
CY	Carl Yastrzemski 1966	60.00
CY	Carl Yastrzemski 1967	60.00
CY	Carl Yastrzemski 1970	60.00
CY	Carl Yastrzemski 1972	60.00
CY	Carl Yastrzemski 1962	60.00
CY	Carl Yastrzemski 1963	60.00
CY	Carl Yastrzemski 1965	60.00
CY	Carl Yastrzemski 1968	60.00
CY	Carl Yastrzemski 1969	60.00
CY	Carl Yastrzemski 1971	60.00
CY	Carl Yastrzemski 1973	60.00
CY	Carl Yastrzemski 1975	60.00
CY	Carl Yastrzemski 1977	60.00
CY	Carl Yastrzemski 1980	60.00
CY	Carl Yastrzemski 1983	60.00
CY	Carl Yastrzemski 1974	60.00
CY	Carl Yastrzemski 1976	60.00
CY	Carl Yastrzemski 1978	60.00
CY	Carl Yastrzemski 1979	60.00
CY	Carl Yastrzemski 1981	60.00
CY	Carl Yastrzemski 1982	60.00
CY	Carl Yastrzemski 1963	60.00
CY	Carl Yastrzemski 1965	60.00
CY	Carl Yastrzemski 1966	60.00
CY	Carl Yastrzemski 1967	60.00
CY	Carl Yastrzemski 1968	60.00
CY	Carl Yastrzemski 1969	60.00
CY	Carl Yastrzemski 1970	60.00
CY	Carl Yastrzemski 1971	60.00
CY	Carl Yastrzemski 1972	60.00
CY	Carl Yastrzemski 1973	60.00
CY	Carl Yastrzemski 1974	60.00
CY	Carl Yastrzemski 1975	60.00
CY	Carl Yastrzemski 1976	60.00
CY	Carl Yastrzemski 1977	60.00
CY	Carl Yastrzemski 1978	60.00
CY	Carl Yastrzemski 1979	60.00
CY	Carl Yastrzemski 1982	60.00
CY	Carl Yastrzemski 1983	60.00
TG	Tony Gwynn 1984	60.00
TG	Tony Gwynn 1987	60.00
TG	Tony Gwynn 1988	60.00
TG	Tony Gwynn 1989	60.00
TG	Tony Gwynn 1994	60.00
TG	Tony Gwynn 1995	60.00
TG	Tony Gwynn 1996	60.00
TG	Tony Gwynn 1997	60.00
RS	Ryne Sandberg 1984	70.00
RS	Ryne Sandberg 1988	70.00
RS	Ryne Sandberg 1990	70.00
RS	Ryne Sandberg 1992	70.00
RS	Ryne Sandberg 1983	70.00
RS	Ryne Sandberg 1985	70.00
RS	Ryne Sandberg 1987	70.00
RS	Ryne Sandberg 1989	70.00

Moments Relics Autographs

NM/M

Production 10 Sets

Prime: No Pricing

Production One Set

BB	Barry Bonds	
RH	Rickey Henderson 1980	125.00
RH	Rickey Henderson 1981	125.00
RH	Rickey Henderson 1982	125.00
RH	Rickey Henderson 1983	125.00
RH	Rickey Henderson 1984	125.00
RH	Rickey Henderson 1990	125.00
RH	Rickey Henderson 1998	125.00
RH	Rickey Henderson 1985	125.00
RH	Rickey Henderson 1986	125.00
RH	Rickey Henderson 1987	125.00
RH	Rickey Henderson 1980	125.00
RH	Rickey Henderson 1983	125.00
RH	Rickey Henderson 1990	125.00
RH	Rickey Henderson 1985	125.00
RH	Rickey Henderson 1987	125.00
RH	Rickey Henderson 1981	125.00
RH	Rickey Henderson 1990	125.00
RH	Rickey Henderson 1986	125.00
RH	Rickey Henderson 1983	125.00
RH	Rickey Henderson 1998	125.00
RH	Rickey Henderson 1990	125.00
NR	Nolan Ryan SO 1	300.00
NR	Nolan Ryan SO 50	300.00
NR	Nolan Ryan SO 100	300.00
NR	Nolan Ryan SO 200	300.00
NR	Nolan Ryan SO 300	300.00
NR	Nolan Ryan SO 350	300.00
NR	Nolan Ryan SO 380	300.00
NR	Nolan Ryan SO 382	300.00
NR	Nolan Ryan SO 383	300.00
NR	Nolan Ryan NO HIT 1	300.00
NR	Nolan Ryan NO HIT 2	300.00
NR	Nolan Ryan NO HIT 3	300.00
NR	Nolan Ryan NO HIT 4	300.00
NR	Nolan Ryan NO HIT 5	300.00
NR	Nolan Ryan NO HIT 6	300.00
NR	Nolan Ryan NO HIT 7	300.00
CR	Cal Ripken Jr. 1983	300.00
CR	Cal Ripken Jr. 1985	300.00
CR	Cal Ripken Jr. 1987	300.00
CR	Cal Ripken Jr. 1989	300.00
CR	Cal Ripken Jr. 1991	300.00
CR	Cal Ripken Jr. 1993	300.00
CR	Cal Ripken Jr. 1995	300.00
CR	Cal Ripken Jr. 1997	300.00
CR	Cal Ripken Jr. 1999	300.00
CR	Cal Ripken Jr. 2001	300.00
CR	Cal Ripken Jr. 1984	300.00
CR	Cal Ripken Jr. 1986	300.00
CR	Cal Ripken Jr. 1991	300.00
CR	Cal Ripken Jr. 1994	300.00
CR	Cal Ripken Jr. HIT 1	300.00

CR	Cal Ripken Jr. 1000	300.00
CR	Cal Ripken Jr. 1500	300.00
CR	Cal Ripken Jr. 2000	300.00
CR	Cal Ripken Jr. 2500	300.00
CR	Cal Ripken Jr. 2900	300.00
CR	Cal Ripken Jr. 3000	300.00
CR	Cal Ripken Jr. 3184	300.00
CR	Cal Ripken Jr. HR 1	300.00
CR	Cal Ripken Jr. HR 100	300.00
CR	Cal Ripken Jr. HR 200	300.00
CR	Cal Ripken Jr. HR 300	300.00
CR	Cal Ripken Jr. HR 400	300.00
CR	Cal Ripken Jr. HR 431	300.00
CR	Cal Ripken Jr. GM 1	300.00
CR	Cal Ripken Jr. 500	300.00
CR	Cal Ripken Jr. 1000	300.00
CR	Cal Ripken Jr. 2000	300.00
CR	Cal Ripken Jr. 2130	300.00
CR	Cal Ripken Jr. 2131	300.00
CR	Cal Ripken Jr. 2632	300.00
SM	Stan Musial 1941	150.00
SM	Stan Musial 1943	150.00
SM	Stan Musial 1946	150.00
SM	Stan Musial 1948	150.00
SM	Stan Musial 1950	150.00
SM	Stan Musial 1952	150.00
SM	Stan Musial 1954	150.00
SM	Stan Musial 1956	150.00
SM	Stan Musial 1958	150.00
SM	Stan Musial 1960	150.00
SM	Stan Musial 1962	150.00
SM	Stan Musial 1963	150.00
RJ	Reggie Jackson HR 1	150.00
RJ	Reggie Jackson HR 100	150.00
RJ	Reggie Jackson HR 200	150.00
RJ	Reggie Jackson HR 250	150.00
RJ	Reggie Jackson HR 300	150.00
RJ	Reggie Jackson HR 350	150.00
RJ	Reggie Jackson HR 400	150.00
RJ	Reggie Jackson HR 450	150.00
RJ	Reggie Jackson HR 500	150.00
RJ	Reggie Jackson HR 550	150.00
RJ	Reggie Jackson HR 563	150.00
RJ	Reggie Jackson WS HR 1	150.00
RJ	Reggie Jackson WS HR 2	150.00
RJ	Reggie Jackson WS HR 3	150.00
RJ	Reggie Jackson 500 HR	150.00
JB	Johnny Bench 1968	150.00
JB	Johnny Bench 1969	150.00
JB	Johnny Bench 1970	150.00
JB	Johnny Bench 1971	150.00
JB	Johnny Bench 1972	150.00
JB	Johnny Bench 1973	150.00
JB	Johnny Bench 1974	150.00
JB	Johnny Bench 1975	150.00
JB	Johnny Bench 1976	150.00
JB	Johnny Bench 1977	150.00
JB	Johnny Bench 1975	150.00
JB	Johnny Bench 1976	150.00
GB	George Brett HIT 1	150.00
GB	George Brett HIT 3	150.00
GB	George Brett HIT 5	150.00
GB	George Brett HIT 7	150.00
GB	George Brett HIT 10	150.00
GB	George Brett HIT 12	150.00
GB	George Brett HIT 15	150.00
GB	George Brett HIT 16	150.00
GB	George Brett HIT 17	150.00
GB	George Brett HIT 18	150.00
GB	George Brett 1976	150.00
GB	George Brett 1980	150.00
GB	George Brett 1990	150.00
GB	George Brett 1976	150.00
GB	George Brett 1977	150.00
GB	George Brett 1979	150.00
GB	George Brett 1981	150.00
GB	George Brett 1983	150.00
GB	George Brett 1985	150.00
GB	George Brett 1988	150.00
DM	Don Mattingly GS 1	140.00
DM	Don Mattingly GS 2	140.00
DM	Don Mattingly GS 3	140.00
DM	Don Mattingly GS 4	140.00
DM	Don Mattingly GS 5	140.00
DM	Don Mattingly GS 6	140.00
DM	Don Mattingly HR 1	140.00
DM	Don Mattingly HR 2	140.00
DM	Don Mattingly HR 3	140.00
DM	Don Mattingly HR 4	140.00
DM	Don Mattingly HR 5	140.00
DM	Don Mattingly HR 6	140.00
DM	Don Mattingly HR 7	140.00
DM	Don Mattingly HR 8	140.00
DM	Don Mattingly HR 9	140.00
DM	Don Mattingly 1985	140.00
DM	Don Mattingly 1986	140.00
DM	Don Mattingly 1987	140.00
DM	Don Mattingly 1988	140.00
DM	Don Mattingly 1989	140.00
DM	Don Mattingly 1991	140.00
DM	Don Mattingly 1992	140.00
DM	Don Mattingly 1993	140.00
DM	Don Mattingly 1994	140.00
DM	Don Mattingly 1984	140.00
DM	Don Mattingly 1985	140.00
DM	Don Mattingly 1986	140.00
DM	Don Mattingly 1987	140.00
DM	Don Mattingly 1988	140.00
DM	Don Mattingly 1989	140.00
DM	Don Mattingly HR 1	140.00
DM	Don Mattingly HR 2	140.00
DM	Don Mattingly HR 3	140.00
DM	Don Mattingly HR 4	140.00
DM	Don Mattingly HR 5	140.00
DM	Don Mattingly HR 6	140.00
DM	Don Mattingly HR 7	140.00
DM	Don Mattingly HR 8	140.00
DM	Don Mattingly HR 9	140.00
RC	Rod Carew 1967	80.00
RC	Rod Carew 1968	80.00
RC	Rod Carew 1969	80.00
RC	Rod Carew 1970	80.00
RC	Rod Carew 1971	80.00
RC	Rod Carew 1972	80.00
RC	Rod Carew 1973	80.00
RC	Rod Carew 1974	80.00
RC	Rod Carew 1975	80.00
RC	Rod Carew 1976	80.00
RC	Rod Carew 1977	80.00
RC	Rod Carew 1978	80.00
RC	Rod Carew 1979	80.00
RC	Rod Carew 1980	80.00
RC	Rod Carew 1981	80.00
RC	Rod Carew 1982	80.00
RC	Rod Carew 1983	80.00
RC	Rod Carew 1984	80.00
RC	Rod Carew SH 1	80.00
RC	Rod Carew SH 2	80.00
RC	Rod Carew SH 3	80.00
RC	Rod Carew SH 4	80.00
RC	Rod Carew SH 5	80.00
RC	Rod Carew SH 6	80.00
RC	Rod Carew SH 7	80.00
RC	Rod Carew 100	80.00
RC	Rod Carew 200	80.00
RC	Rod Carew 300	80.00
RC	Rod Carew 400	80.00
RC	Rod Carew 500	80.00
RC	Rod Carew 600	80.00
RC	Rod Carew 700	80.00
RC	Rod Carew 800	80.00
RC	Rod Carew 900	80.00
RC	Rod Carew 1969	80.00
RC	Rod Carew 1972	80.00
RC	Rod Carew 1973	80.00
RC	Rod Carew 1974	80.00
RC	Rod Carew 1975	80.00
RC	Rod Carew 1977	80.00
RC	Rod Carew 1978	80.00
YB	Yogi Berra 1947	160.00
YB	Yogi Berra 1949	160.00
YB	Yogi Berra 1950	160.00
YB	Yogi Berra 1951	160.00
YB	Yogi Berra 1952	160.00
YB	Yogi Berra 1953	160.00
YB	Yogi Berra 1956	160.00
YB	Yogi Berra 1958	160.00
YB	Yogi Berra 1961	160.00
YB	Yogi Berra 1962	160.00
YB	Yogi Berra 1948	160.00
YB	Yogi Berra 1949	160.00
YB	Yogi Berra 1950	160.00
YB	Yogi Berra 1951	160.00
YB	Yogi Berra 1952	160.00
YB	Yogi Berra 1953	160.00
YB	Yogi Berra 1954	160.00
YB	Yogi Berra 1955	160.00
YB	Yogi Berra 1956	160.00
YB	Yogi Berra 1957	160.00
YB	Yogi Berra 1958	160.00
YB	Yogi Berra 1959	160.00
YB	Yogi Berra 1960	160.00
YB	Yogi Berra 1961	160.00
YB	Yogi Berra 1962	160.00
MS	Mike Schmidt HR 1	140.00
MS	Mike Schmidt HR 2	140.00
MS	Mike Schmidt HR 3	140.00
MS	Mike Schmidt HR 4	140.00
MS	Mike Schmidt HIT 1	140.00
MS	Mike Schmidt HIT 2	140.00
MS	Mike Schmidt HIT 3	140.00
MS	Mike Schmidt HIT 4	140.00
MS	Mike Schmidt HIT 5	140.00
MS	Mike Schmidt HIT 6	140.00
MS	Mike Schmidt HIT 7	140.00
MS	Mike Schmidt HIT 8	140.00
MS	Mike Schmidt RUN 1	140.00
MS	Mike Schmidt RUN 2	140.00
MS	Mike Schmidt RUN 3	140.00
MS	Mike Schmidt RUN 4	140.00
MS	Mike Schmidt RUN 5	140.00
MS	Mike Schmidt RUN 6	140.00
CY	Carl Yastrzemski HR 1	125.00
CY	Carl Yastrzemski HR 5	125.00
CY	Carl Yastrzemski HR 10	125.00
CY	Carl Yastrzemski HR 15	125.00
CY	Carl Yastrzemski HR 20	125.00
CY	Carl Yastrzemski HR 25	125.00
CY	Carl Yastrzemski HR 30	125.00
CY	Carl Yastrzemski HR 35	125.00
CY	Carl Yastrzemski HR 40	125.00
CY	Carl Yastrzemski HR 44	125.00
CY	Carl Yastrzemski 1961	125.00
CY	Carl Yastrzemski 1964	125.00
CY	Carl Yastrzemski 1966	125.00
CY	Carl Yastrzemski 1967	125.00
CY	Carl Yastrzemski 1970	125.00
CY	Carl Yastrzemski 1972	125.00
CY	Carl Yastrzemski 1973	125.00
CY	Carl Yastrzemski 1975	125.00
CY	Carl Yastrzemski 1977	125.00
CY	Carl Yastrzemski 1980	125.00
CY	Carl Yastrzemski 1983	125.00
CY	Carl Yastrzemski 1963	125.00
CY	Carl Yastrzemski 1965	125.00
CY	Carl Yastrzemski 1966	125.00
CY	Carl Yastrzemski 1967	125.00
CY	Carl Yastrzemski 1968	125.00
CY	Carl Yastrzemski 1969	125.00
CY	Carl Yastrzemski 1970	125.00
CY	Carl Yastrzemski 1971	125.00
CY	Carl Yastrzemski 1972	125.00
CY	Carl Yastrzemski 1973	125.00
CY	Carl Yastrzemski 1974	125.00
CY	Carl Yastrzemski 1975	125.00
CY	Carl Yastrzemski 1976	125.00
CY	Carl Yastrzemski 1977	125.00
CY	Carl Yastrzemski 1978	125.00
CY	Carl Yastrzemski 1979	125.00
CY	Carl Yastrzemski 1982	125.00
CY	Carl Yastrzemski 1983	125.00
TG	Tony Gwynn 1983	120.00
TG	Tony Gwynn 1984	120.00
TG	Tony Gwynn 1985	120.00
TG	Tony Gwynn 1986	120.00
TG	Tony Gwynn 1987	120.00
TG	Tony Gwynn 1988	120.00
TG	Tony Gwynn 1989	120.00
TG	Tony Gwynn 1990	120.00
TG	Tony Gwynn 1991	120.00
TG	Tony Gwynn 1992	120.00
TG	Tony Gwynn 1993	120.00
TG	Tony Gwynn 1994	120.00
TG	Tony Gwynn 1994	120.00
TG	Tony Gwynn 1995	120.00
TG	Tony Gwynn 1996	120.00
TG	Tony Gwynn 1997	120.00
TG	Tony Gwynn 1998	120.00
TG	Tony Gwynn 1999	120.00
TG	Tony Gwynn 2000	120.00
TG	Tony Gwynn 2001	120.00
TG	Tony Gwynn 1984	120.00
TG	Tony Gwynn 1987	120.00
TG	Tony Gwynn 1988	120.00
\G	Tony Gwynn 1989	120.00
TG	Tony Gwynn 1994	120.00
TG	Tony Gwynn 1995	120.00
TG	Tony Gwynn 1996	120.00
TG	Tony Gwynn 1997	120.00
TG	Tony Gwynn 1984	120.00
TG	Tony Gwynn 1985	120.00
TG	Tony Gwynn 1986	120.00
TG	Tony Gwynn 1987	120.00
TG	Tony Gwynn 1989	120.00
TG	Tony Gwynn 1990	120.00
TG	Tony Gwynn 1991	120.00
TG	Tony Gwynn 1992	120.00
TG	Tony Gwynn 1993	120.00
TG	Tony Gwynn 1994	120.00
TG	Tony Gwynn 1995	120.00
TG	Tony Gwynn 1996	120.00
TG	Tony Gwynn 1997	120.00
TG	Tony Gwynn 1998	120.00
TG	Tony Gwynn 1999	120.00
TG	Tony Gwynn 1984	120.00
TG	Tony Gwynn 1986	120.00
TG	Tony Gwynn 1987	120.00
TG	Tony Gwynn 1989	120.00
TG	Tony Gwynn 1994	120.00
TG	Tony Gwynn 1995	120.00
TG	Tony Gwynn 1997	120.00
RS	Ryne Sandberg 1984	150.00
RS	Ryne Sandberg 1985	150.00
RS	Ryne Sandberg 1988	150.00
RS	Ryne Sandberg 1989	150.00
RS	Ryne Sandberg 1990	150.00
RS	Ryne Sandberg 1991	150.00
RS	Ryne Sandberg 1992	150.00
RS	Ryne Sandberg 1983	150.00
RS	Ryne Sandberg 1984	150.00
RS	Ryne Sandberg 1985	150.00
RS	Ryne Sandberg 1986	150.00
RS	Ryne Sandberg 1987	150.00
RS	Ryne Sandberg 1988	150.00
RS	Ryne Sandberg 1989	150.00
RS	Ryne Sandberg 1990	150.00
RS	Ryne Sandberg 1991	150.00
OS	Ozzie Smith 1980	100.00
OS	Ozzie Smith 1981	100.00
OS	Ozzie Smith 1982	100.00
OS	Ozzie Smith 1983	100.00
OS	Ozzie Smith 1984	100.00
OS	Ozzie Smith 1985	100.00
OS	Ozzie Smith 1986	100.00
OS	Ozzie Smith 1987	100.00
OS	Ozzie Smith 1988	100.00
OS	Ozzie Smith 1989	100.00
OS	Ozzie Smith 1990	100.00
OS	Ozzie Smith 1991	100.00
OS	Ozzie Smith 1992	100.00
OS	Ozzie Smith 2B 1	100.00
OS	Ozzie Smith 2B 2	100.00
OS	Ozzie Smith 2B 3	100.00
OS	Ozzie Smith 2B 4	100.00
OS	Ozzie Smith 2B 5	100.00
OS	Ozzie Smith 2B 6	100.00
OS	Ozzie Smith 2B 7	100.00
OS	Ozzie Smith 2B 8	100.00
OS	Ozzie Smith 2B 9	100.00
OS	Ozzie Smith 2B 10	100.00
OS	Ozzie Smith 2B 11	100.00
OS	Ozzie Smith 2B 12	100.00
OS	Ozzie Smith 2B 13	100.00
OS	Ozzie Smith 2B 14	100.00
OS	Ozzie Smith 2B 15	100.00
OS	Ozzie Smith 2B 16	100.00
OS	Ozzie Smith 2B 17	100.00
OS	Ozzie Smith 2B 18	100.00
OS	Ozzie Smith 2B 19	100.00
OS	Ozzie Smith 2B 20	100.00
OS	Ozzie Smith 2B 21	100.00
OS	Ozzie Smith 2B 22	100.00
OS	Ozzie Smith 2B 23	100.00
OS	Ozzie Smith 2B 24	100.00
OS	Ozzie Smith 2B 25	100.00
OS	Ozzie Smith 2B 26	100.00
OS	Ozzie Smith 2B 27	100.00
OS	Ozzie Smith 2B 28	100.00
OS	Ozzie Smith 2B 29	100.00
OS	Ozzie Smith 2B 30	100.00
OS	Ozzie Smith 2B 31	100.00
OS	Ozzie Smith 2B 32	100.00
OS	Ozzie Smith 2B 33	100.00
OS	Ozzie Smith 2B 34	100.00
OS	Ozzie Smith 2B 35	100.00
OS	Ozzie Smith 2B 36	100.00
OS	Ozzie Smith 2B 37	100.00
OS	Ozzie Smith 2B 38	100.00
OS	Ozzie Smith 2B 39	100.00
OS	Ozzie Smith 2B 40	100.00

Moments Relics Cut Signatures

Production 10 Sets
Prime: No Pricing
Production One Set

Quad Relics

Production 10 Sets
Prime: No Pricing
Production 10 Sets
Sterling Silver: No Pricing
Production One Set

Quad Relics Autographs

Production 10 Sets
Prime: No Pricing
Production 10 Sets
Sterling Silver: No Pricing
Production One Set

Season Stats Relics

Production 10 Sets
Prime: No Pricing
Production One Set
Sterling Silver: No Pricing
Production One Set

Season Stats Relics Autos.

Production 10 Sets
Prime: No Pricing
Production One Set
Sterling Silver: No Pricing
Production One Set

Six Relics

Production 10 Sets
Prime: No Pricing
Production 10 Sets
Sterling Silver: No Pricing
Production One Set

Six Relics Autographs

Production 10 Sets
Prime: No Pricing
Production 10 Sets
Sterling Silver: No Pricing
Production One Set

Triple Relics Autographs

Production 10 Sets
Prime: No Pricing
Production 10 Sets
Sterling Silver: No Pricing
Production One Set

2006 Topps Triple Threads

		NM/M
Complete Set (120):		
Common (1-100):		.50
Common (101-120):		10.00
Production 225		
Pack (6):		140.00
Box (2):		250.00
1	Hideki Matsui	3.00
2	Josh Gibson	2.00
3	Roger Clemens	4.00
4	Paul Konerko	1.00
5	Brooks Robinson	1.00
6	Stan Musial	2.00
7	Dontrelle Willis	.50
8	Yogi Berra	1.50
9	John Smoltz	.75
10	Brian Roberts	.75
11	Gary Sheffield	.75
12	Wade Boggs	1.00
13	Alex Rodriguez	4.00
14	Ernie Banks	2.00
15	Ichiro Suzuki	3.00
16	Whitey Ford	1.00
17	Vladimir Guerrero	1.50
18	Tadahito Iguchi	.50
19	Robin Yount	1.50
20	Jason Schmidt	.50
21	Roberto Clemente	3.00
22	Andruw Jones	1.00
23	Don Mattingly	2.00
24	Joe Mauer	.50
25	Barry Bonds	4.00
26	Johnny Damon	1.50
27	Chris Carpenter	.75
28	Garret Anderson	.50
29	Scott Rolen	1.50
30	Tim Hudson	.75
31	Dave Winfield	.75
32	Steve Carlton	.75
33	Miguel Tejada	1.00
34	Nolan Ryan	3.00
35	Mark Buehrle	.75
36	Travis Hafner	.75
37	Rickie Weeks	.75
38	Sammy Sosa	1.50

39	Carlos Beltran	1.00
40	Todd Helton	1.00
41	Tom Seaver	1.00
42	Ted Williams	3.00
43	Alfonso Soriano	1.00
44	Reggie Jackson	1.00
45	Pedro Martinez	1.50
46	Randy Johnson	1.50
47	Ted Williams	3.00
48	Torii Hunter	.50
49	Manny Ramirez	1.50
50	George Brett	3.00
51	Chipper Jones	1.50
52	Nomar Garciaparra	1.00
53	Richie Sexson	.75
54	David Ortiz	1.50
55	Derek Jeter	4.00
56	Mickey Mantle	8.00
57	Michael Young	.75
58	Aramis Ramirez	.75
59	Bartolo Colon	.50
60	Troy Glaus	.75
61	Carlos Delgado	.75
62	Mike Sweeney	.50
63	Jorge Cantu	.50
64	Mike Mussina	.75
65	Hank Blalock	.75
66	Frank Robinson	1.50
67	Carl Yastrzemski	2.00
68	Adam Dunn	1.00
69	Eric Chavez	.50
70	Curt Schilling	1.50
71	Jeff Francoeur	.75
72	C.C. Sabathia	.75
73	Roy Oswalt	.75
74	Carlos Lee	.75
75	Barry Zito	.75
76	Derrek Lee	1.00
77	Greg Maddux	3.00
78	Ivan Rodriguez	.75
79	Jeff Kent	.75
80	Gary Carter	.75
81	Jose Reyes	1.00
82	Johan Santana	1.50
83	Magglio Ordonez	.75
84	Mark Prior	.75
85	Johnny Bench	2.00
86	Vernon Wells	.75
87	Mark Mulder	.50
88	Cal Ripken Jr.	6.00
89	Mark Teixeira	1.00
90	Miguel Cabrera	1.50
91	Duke Snider	1.00
92	Jason Giambi	.75
93	Albert Pujols	4.00
94	Carl Crawford	.75
95	Jim Edmonds	.50
96	Jose Contreras	.50
97	Victor Martinez	.75
98	Jeremy Bonderman	.50
99	Lance Berkman	.75
100	Rocco Baldelli	.50
101	Zach Duke/Auto. Jsy	15.00
102	Felix Hernandez/Auto. Jsy	40.00
103	Dan Johnson/Auto. Jsy	10.00
104	Brandon McCarthy/ Auto. Jsy	10.00
105	Huston Street/Auto. Jsy	15.00
106	Robinson Cano/Auto. Jsy	50.00
107	Jason Bay/Auto. Jsy	20.00
108	Ryan Howard/Auto. Jsy	80.00
109	Ervin Santana/Auto. Jsy	15.00
110	Rich Harden/Auto. Jsy	15.00
111	Aaron Hill/Auto. Jsy	15.00
112	David Wright/Auto. Jsy	75.00
113	Rich Hill/Auto. Jsy **(RC)**	20.00
114	Nelson Cruz/ Auto. Jsy **(RC)**	15.00
115	Francisco Liriano/ Auto. Jsy **(RC)**	40.00
116	Hong-Chih Kuo/ Auto. Jsy **(RC)**	75.00
117	Ryan Garko/ Auto. Jsy **(RC)**	20.00
118	Craig Hansen/ Auto. Jsy **RC**	30.00
119	Shin-Soo Choo/ Auto. Jsy **(RC)**	20.00
120	Darrell Rasner/ Auto. Jsy **(RC)**	20.00

Sepia Tone

Sepia (1-100): 3-4X
Production 150
Sepia (101-120): 1X
Production 125

Emerald

Emerald (1-100): 4-6X
Production 99
Emerald (101-120): 1X
Production 75

Gold

Gold (1-100): 5-10X
Gold (101-120): 1-1.5X
Production 50 Sets

Sapphire

Sapphire (1-100): 8-15X
Sapphire (101-120): 1-2X
Production 25 Sets

Platinum

Platinum: No Pricing
Production One Set

Printing Plates

No Pricing
Production one set per color.

Heroes

NM/M

Inserted 1:Pack
Die-Cut: 2-3X
Production 50 Sets
Autograph: No Pricing
Production Three Sets

MM1	Mickey Mantle	8.00
MM2	Mickey Mantle	8.00
MM3	Mickey Mantle	8.00
MM4	Mickey Mantle	8.00
MM5	Mickey Mantle	8.00
MM6	Mickey Mantle	8.00
MM7	Mickey Mantle	8.00
MM8	Mickey Mantle	8.00
MM9	Mickey Mantle	8.00
MM10	Mickey Mantle	8.00
TW1	Ted Williams	5.00
TW2	Ted Williams	5.00
TW3	Ted Williams	5.00
TW4	Ted Williams	5.00
TW5	Ted Williams	5.00
TW1	Ted Williams	5.00
TW2	Ted Williams	5.00
TW3	Ted Williams	5.00
TW4	Ted Williams	5.00
TW5	Ted Williams	5.00
FR1	Frank Robinson	4.00
FR2	Frank Robinson	4.00
FR3	Frank Robinson	4.00
FR4	Frank Robinson	4.00
FR5	Frank Robinson	4.00
FR6	Frank Robinson	4.00
FR7	Frank Robinson	4.00
FR8	Frank Robinson	4.00
FR9	Frank Robinson	4.00
FR10	Frank Robinson	4.00
CY1	Carl Yastrzemski	4.00
CY2	Carl Yastrzemski	4.00
CY3	Carl Yastrzemski	4.00
CY4	Carl Yastrzemski	4.00
CY5	Carl Yastrzemski	4.00
CY6	Carl Yastrzemski	4.00
CY7	Carl Yastrzemski	4.00
CY8	Carl Yastrzemski	4.00
CY9	Carl Yastrzemski	4.00
CY10	Carl Yastrzemski	4.00

Heroes Co-Signer Autos.

No Pricing
Production Three Sets

Heroes Quad Signers

Production One Card
No Pricing

Heroes Cut Signatures

Production One Set
No Pricing

Triple Signed Hides

Production One Set
No Pricing

Triple Relic

NM/M

Production 18 Sets
Gold: No Pricing
Production Nine Sets
Platinum: No Pricing
Production Three Sets

1	Adam Dunn	30.00
2	Adam Dunn	30.00
3	Adrian Beltre	20.00
4	Adrian Beltre	20.00
5	Al Kaline	35.00
6	Al Kaline	35.00
7	Al Kaline	35.00
8	Albert Pujols	75.00
9	Albert Pujols	75.00
10	Albert Pujols	75.00
11	Albert Pujols	75.00
12	Alex Rodriguez	100.00
13	Alex Rodriguez	100.00
14	Alex Rodriguez	100.00
15	Alex Rodriguez	100.00
16	Alex Rodriguez	100.00
17	Alex Rodriguez	100.00
18	Alex Rodriguez	100.00
19	Alex Rodriguez	100.00
20	Alex Rodriguez	100.00
21	Alfonso Soriano	25.00
22	Alfonso Soriano	25.00
23	Andruw Jones	25.00
24	Andruw Jones	25.00
25	Andy Pettitte	30.00
26	Andy Pettitte	30.00
27	Aramis Ramirez	25.00
28	B.J. Upton	25.00
29	Barry Bonds	75.00
30	Barry Bonds	75.00
31	Barry Bonds	75.00
32	Barry Bonds	75.00
33	Barry Bonds	75.00
34	Barry Bonds	75.00
35	Barry Bonds	75.00
36	Barry Bonds	75.00
37	Barry Zito	20.00
38	Barry Zito	20.00
39	Ben Sheets	25.00
40	Bill Mazeroski	40.00
41	Bob Feller	30.00
42	Bobby Abreu	25.00
43	Bobby Cox	25.00
44	Bobby Doerr	20.00
45	Brad Lidge	20.00
46	Brian Giles	20.00
47	Brian Roberts	25.00
48	Cal Ripken Jr.	75.00
49	Cal Ripken Jr.	75.00
50	Cal Ripken Jr.	75.00
51	Carl Yastrzemski	50.00
52	Carl Yastrzemski	50.00
53	Carl Yastrzemski	50.00
54	Carlos Beltran	30.00
55	Carlos Beltran	30.00
56	Carlos Delgado	30.00
57	Carlton Fisk	40.00
58	Carlton Fisk	40.00
59	Carlton Fisk	40.00
60	Chipper Jones	50.00
61	Chipper Jones	50.00
62	Chipper Jones	50.00
63	Chris Carpenter	25.00
64	Craig Biggio	30.00
65	Craig Biggio	30.00
66	Curt Schilling	30.00
67	Curt Schilling	30.00
68	Curt Schilling	30.00
69	Curt Schilling	35.00
70	Dale Murphy	40.00
71	Darryl Strawberry	25.00
72	Darryl Strawberry	25.00
73	Dave Winfield	25.00
74	Dave Winfield	25.00
75	Dave Winfield	25.00
76	David Ortiz	35.00
77	David Ortiz	35.00
78	David Ortiz	35.00
79	Derrek Lee	35.00
80	Don Mattingly	40.00
81	Don Mattingly	40.00
82	Don Mattingly	40.00
83	Dontrelle Willis	20.00
84	Dontrelle Willis	20.00
85	Duke Snider	35.00
86	Dwight Gooden	25.00
87	Dwight Gooden	25.00
88	Eric Chavez	20.00
89	Ernie Banks	40.00
90	Ernie Banks	40.00
91	Ernie Banks	40.00
92	Frank Robinson	35.00
93	Frank Robinson	35.00
94	Frankie Frisch	30.00
95	Gary Carter	25.00
96	Gary Sheffield	25.00
97	Gary Sheffield	25.00
98	George Brett	50.00
99	George Brett	50.00
100	Greg Maddux	50.00
101	Hank Blalock	25.00
102	Hank Greenberg	75.00
103	Hank Greenberg	75.00
104	Hideki Matsui	80.00
105	Hideki Matsui	80.00
106	Hideki Matsui	80.00
107	Ichiro Suzuki	100.00
108	Ichiro Suzuki	100.00
109	Ichiro Suzuki	125.00
110	Ivan Rodriguez	25.00
111	Ivan Rodriguez	25.00
112	Ivan Rodriguez	25.00
113	Ivan Rodriguez	25.00
114	Jake Peavy	25.00
115	Javy Lopez	20.00
116	Jeff Bagwell	35.00
117	Jim Edmonds	20.00
118	Jim Thome	30.00
119	Joe Mauer	20.00
120	Joe Torre	25.00
121	Johan Santana	30.00
122	Johan Santana	30.00
123	Johnny Bench	40.00
124	Johnny Bench	40.00
125	Johnny Damon	30.00
126	Jon Garland	20.00
127	Jon Garland	20.00
128	Jorge Posada	30.00
129	Jorge Posada	30.00
130	Jose Canseco	25.00
131	Jose Reyes	25.00
132	Juan Marichal	25.00
133	Kerry Wood	25.00
134	Kerry Wood	25.00
135	Lance Berkman	30.00
136	Lance Berkman	30.00
137	Lloyd Waner	75.00
138	Lloyd Waner	75.00
139	Lou Brock	25.00
140	Manny Ramirez	30.00
141	Manny Ramirez	30.00
142	Mariano Rivera	40.00
143	Mariano Rivera	40.00
144	Mark Buehrle	20.00
145	Mark Mulder	20.00
146	Mark Mulder	20.00
147	Mark Prior	25.00
148	Mark Teixeira	30.00
149	Michael Young	25.00
150	Michael Young	25.00
151	Mickey Mantle	200.00
152	Mickey Mantle	200.00
153	Mickey Mantle	200.00
154	Mickey Mantle	200.00
155	Mickey Mantle	200.00
156	Miguel Cabrera	30.00
157	Miguel Tejada	25.00
158	Miguel Tejada	25.00
159	Miguel Tejada	25.00
160	Miguel Tejada	25.00
161	Mike Mussina	25.00
162	Mike Mussina	25.00
163	Mike Piazza	60.00
164	Mike Piazza	50.00
165	Mike Piazza	60.00
166	Mike Schmidt	40.00
167	Mike Schmidt	40.00
168	Mike Schmidt	40.00
169	Monte Irvin	30.00
170	Morgan Ensberg	20.00
171	Nolan Ryan	65.00
172	Nolan Ryan	65.00
173	Nolan Ryan	65.00
174	Nolan Ryan	65.00
175	Wade Boggs	40.00
176	Ozzie Smith	40.00
177	Ozzie Smith	40.00
178	Pat Burrell	25.00
179	Paul Konerko	20.00
180	Paul Konerko	20.00
181	Paul Konerko	20.00
182	Paul Molitor	30.00
183	Pedro Martinez	35.00
184	Pedro Martinez	35.00
185	Pedro Martinez	35.00
186	Randy Johnson	35.00
187	Randy Johnson	35.00
188	Reggie Jackson	40.00
189	Reggie Jackson	40.00
190	Rickey Henderson	40.00
191	Rickey Henderson	40.00
192	Rickey Henderson	40.00
193	Rickey Henderson	40.00
194	Rickie Weeks	20.00
195	Rickie Weeks	20.00
196	Roberto Clemente	125.00
197	Roberto Clemente	125.00
198	Robin Yount	40.00
199	Rod Carew	30.00
200	Roger Clemens	50.00
201	Roger Clemens	50.00
202	Roger Clemens	50.00
203	Roger Clemens	50.00
204	Roger Clemens	50.00
205	Roger Clemens	50.00
206	Roy Halladay	25.00
207	Roy Oswalt	25.00
208	Roy Oswalt	25.00
209	Ryne Sandberg	60.00
210	Ryne Sandberg	60.00
211	Sammy Sosa	50.00
212	Sammy Sosa	50.00
213	Sammy Sosa	50.00
214	Sammy Sosa	50.00
215	Sammy Sosa	50.00
216	Scott Rolen	25.00
217	Scott Rolen	25.00
218	Sean Burroughs	20.00
219	Stan Musial	50.00
220	Steve Carlton	25.00
221	Steve Carlton	25.00
222	Steve Carlton	25.00
223	Steve Garvey	20.00
224	Tadahito Iguchi	25.00
225	Ted Williams	120.00
226	Ted Williams	120.00
227	Tim Hudson	20.00
228	Tim Hudson	20.00
229	Todd Helton	25.00
230	Todd Helton	25.00
231	Todd Helton	25.00
232	Tom Seaver	40.00
233	Tony Gwynn	40.00
234	Tony Gwynn	40.00
235	Tony Gwynn	40.00
236	Torii Hunter	20.00
237	Torii Hunter	20.00
238	Travis Hafner	25.00
239	Vladimir Guerrero	40.00
240	Vladimir Guerrero	40.00
241	Wade Boggs	30.00
242	Willie Stargell	40.00
243	Willie Stargell	40.00
244	Willie Stargell	40.00
245	Willy Taveras	25.00

Triple Relic Combo

NM/M

Production 18 Sets
Gold: No Pricing
Production Nine Sets
Platinum: No Pricing
Production Three Sets

1	Albert Pujols, Alex Rodriguez, Barry Bonds	100.00
2	Alex Rodriguez, Barry Bonds, Albert Pujols	100.00
3	Albert Pujols, Alex Rodriguez, Manny Ramirez	100.00
4	Albert Pujols, Barry Bonds, Ted Williams	125.00
5	Alex Rodriguez, Barry Bonds, Chipper Jones	75.00
6	Alex Rodriguez, Roberto Clemente, Barry Bonds	125.00
7	Alex Rodriguez, Vladimir Guerrero, Ichiro Suzuki	80.00

8 Alex Rodriguez, Stan Musial, Ted Williams 120.00
9 Andruw Jones, Alfonso Soriano, Vladimir Guerrero 40.00
10 Barry Bonds, Ichiro Suzuki, Roberto Clemente 150.00
11 Barry Bonds, Lloyd Waner, Roberto Clemente 160.00
12 Barry Bonds, Manny Ramirez, Andruw Jones 60.00
13 Barry Bonds, Manny Ramirez, Ted Williams 100.00
14 Barry Bonds, Roberto Clemente, Willie Stargell 125.00
15 Carl Yastrzemski, Paul Molitor, Manny Ramirez 40.00
16 Don Mattingly, Paul Molitor, Manny Ramirez 40.00
17 Don Mattingly, Rod Carew, Tony Gwynn 70.00
18 Gary Sheffield, Vladimir Guerrero, Ivan Rodriguez 30.00
19 Hank Greenberg, Stan Musial, Ted Williams 125.00
20 Ichiro Suzuki, Chipper Jones, Barry Bonds 80.00
21 Ichiro Suzuki, Ted Williams, Roberto Clemente 150.00
22 Joe Morgan, Paul Molitor, Gary Carter 35.00
23 Manny Ramirez, Vladimir Guerrero, Roberto Clemente 90.00
24 Mike Piazza, Paul Molitor, Rickey Henderson 40.00
25 Napoleon Lajoie, Stan Musial, Ted Williams
26 Paul Molitor, Andruw Jones, Robin Yount 40.00
27 Paul Molitor, Andruw Jones, Alfonso Soriano 35.00
28 Reggie Jackson, Vladimir Guerrero, Andruw Jones 35.00
29 Rickey Henderson, Wade Boggs, Tony Gwynn 60.00
30 Roberto Clemente, Ted Williams, Tony Gwynn
31 Stan Musial, Ted Williams, Tony Gwynn 70.00
32 Ted Williams, Ichiro Suzuki, Wade Boggs 140.00
33 Albert Pujols, Ted Williams, Mickey Mantle 250.00
34 Andruw Jones, George Brett, Chipper Jones 60.00
35 Greg Maddux, Nolan Ryan, Steve Carlton 60.00
36 Greg Maddux, Steve Carlton, Tom Seaver 50.00
37 Nolan Ryan, Steve Carlton, Tom Seaver 50.00
38 Nolan Ryan, Tom Seaver, Roger Clemens 60.00
39 Roger Clemens, Nolan Ryan, Tom Seaver 60.00
40 Barry Bonds, Rickey Henderson, Tony Gwynn 60.00
41 Cal Ripken Jr., Carl Yastrzemski, Paul Molitor 60.00
42 Cal Ripken Jr., George Brett, Roberto Clemente 100.00
43 Cal Ripken Jr., George Brett, Tony Gwynn 85.00
44 Cal Ripken Jr., Paul Molitor, Rickey Henderson 85.00
45 Cal Ripken Jr., Paul Molitor, Tony Gwynn 85.00
46 George Brett, Cal Ripken Jr., Rod Carew 80.00
47 George Brett, Cal Ripken Jr., Rod Carew 80.00
48 George Brett, Robin Yount, Rod Carew 50.00
49 George Brett, Tony Gwynn, Wade Boggs 60.00
50 George Brett, Tony Gwynn, Wade Boggs 60.00
51 Paul Molitor, Robin Yount, Wade Boggs 40.00
52 Paul Waner, Rickey Henderson, Stan Musial 60.00
53 Paul Waner, Rickey Henderson, Wade Boggs 50.00
54 Paul Waner, Rod Carew, Wade Boggs 50.00
55 Rickey Henderson, Stan Musial, Wade Boggs 60.00
56 Roberto Clemente, Robin Yount, Rod Carew 80.00
57 Roberto Clemente, Robin Yount, Rod Carew 90.00
58 Roberto Clemente, Robin Yount, Tony Gwynn 90.00
59 Rod Carew, Stan Musial, Tony Gwynn 50.00
60 Stan Musial, Tony Gwynn, Wade Boggs 50.00
61 Wade Boggs 30.00

62 Barry Bonds, Mickey Mantle, Frank Robinson 140.00
63 Barry Bonds, Ted Williams, Mickey Mantle 160.00
64 Barry Bonds, Frank Robinson, Reggie Jackson 70.00
65 Barry Bonds, Frank Robinson, Harmon Killebrew 60.00
66 Frank Robinson, Barry Bonds, Mike Schmidt 60.00
67 Frank Robinson, Harmon Killebrew, Mickey Mantle 150.00
68 Josh Gibson, Barry Bonds, Mickey Mantle 200.00
69 Josh Gibson, Barry Bonds, Ted Williams 150.00
70 Mike Schmidt, Harmon Killebrew, Reggie Jackson 75.00
71 Dave Winfield, Vladimir Guerrero, Reggie Jackson 50.00
72 Rod Carew, Reggie Jackson, Vladimir Guerrero 30.00
73 Andruw Jones, Chipper Jones, Jeff Francoeur 30.00
74 Bobby Cox, Andruw Jones, Chipper Jones 50.00
75 Chipper Jones, Greg Maddux, Andruw Jones 50.00
76 Brian Roberts, Sammy Sosa, Miguel Tejada 40.00
77 Brooks Robinson, Cal Ripken Jr., Jim Palmer 65.00
78 Brooks Robinson, Jim Palmer, Frank Robinson 40.00
79 Cal Ripken Jr., Brooks Robinson, Miguel Tejada 50.00
80 Cal Ripken Jr., Frank Robinson, Sammy Sosa 80.00
81 Frank Robinson, Reggie Jackson, Brooks Robinson 75.00
82 Jim Palmer, Frank Robinson, Reggie Jackson 60.00
83 Jim Palmer, Reggie Jackson, Sammy Sosa 50.00
84 Jim Palmer, Sammy Sosa, Miguel Tejada 40.00
85 Miguel Tejada, Brian Roberts, Cal Ripken Jr. 80.00
86 Reggie Jackson, Frank Robinson, Sammy Sosa 50.00
87 Bobby Doerr, Carl Yastrzemski, Ted Williams 80.00
88 Carl Yastrzemski, David Ortiz, Manny Ramirez 60.00
89 Carl Yastrzemski, Ted Williams, David Ortiz 80.00
90 Carl Yastrzemski, Ted Williams, Manny Ramirez 80.00
91 Curt Schilling, David Ortiz, Johnny Damon 40.00
92 Curt Schilling, David Ortiz, Manny Ramirez 40.00
93 Curt Schilling, Manny Ramirez, Johnny Damon 40.00
94 David Ortiz, Johnny Damon, Manny Ramirez 50.00
95 Johnny Damon, Manny Ramirez, Ted Williams 60.00
96 Manny Ramirez, David Ortiz, Pedro Martinez 40.00
97 Manny Ramirez, Ted Williams, David Ortiz 60.00
98 Pedro Martinez, Roger Clemens, Manny Ramirez 50.00
99 Greg Maddux, Randy Johnson, Roger Clemens 50.00
100 Johan Santana, Pedro Martinez, Roger Clemens 50.00
101 Roger Clemens 50.00
102 Roger Clemens 50.00
103 Randy Johnson, Curt Schilling, Roger Clemens 75.00
104 Derrek Lee, Aramis Ramirez, Mark Prior 35.00
105 Derrek Lee, Ryne Sandberg, Sammy Sosa 65.00
106 Ernie Banks, Ryne Sandberg, Derrek Lee 60.00
107 Ernie Banks, Ryne Sandberg, Sammy Sosa 60.00
108 Greg Maddux, Ryne Sandberg, Ernie Banks 75.00
109 Mark Prior, Kerry Wood, Greg Maddux 60.00
110 Sammy Sosa, Ernie Banks, Derrek Lee 60.00
111 Frank Robinson, Joe Morgan, Johnny Bench 40.00
112 Johnny Bench, Frank Robinson, Tom Seaver 50.00
113 Johnny Bench, Tom Seaver, Joe Morgan 50.00
114 Jermaine Dye, Scott Podsednik, Tadahito Iguchi 40.00
115 Jim Thome, Paul Konerko, Tadahito Iguchi 60.00
116 Jon Garland, Scott Podsednik, Mark Buehrle 25.00

117 Jon Garland, Tadahito Iguchi, Mark Buehrle 30.00
118 Paul Konerko, Sammy Sosa, Carlton Fisk 40.00
119 Paul Konerko, Tadahito Iguchi, Jermaine Dye 40.00
120 Al Kaline, Ivan Rodriguez, Hank Greenberg 60.00
121 Greg Maddux, Johan Santana, Roger Clemens 60.00
122 Juan Marichal, Nolan Ryan, Roger Clemens 80.00
123 Nolan Ryan, Randy Johnson, Whitey Ford 60.00
124 Cal Ripken Jr., Ozzie Smith, Mike Schmidt 60.00
125 Mike Schmidt, Cal Ripken Jr., Ozzie Smith 60.00
126 Al Kaline, Frank Robinson, Paul Waner 60.00
127 Al Kaline, Harmon Killebrew, Frank Robinson 75.00
128 Al Kaline, Mickey Mantle, Reggie Jackson 125.00
129 Al Kaline, Reggie Jackson, Stan Musial 60.00
130 Al Kaline, Robin Yount, Paul Waner 40.00
131 Barry Bonds, Chipper Jones, Manny Ramirez 65.00
132 Bob Feller, Juan Marichal, Nolan Ryan 60.00
133 Bob Feller, Whitey Ford, Steve Carlton 40.00
134 Bobby Doerr, Ted Williams, Wade Boggs 80.00
135 Brooks Robinson, Ozzie Smith, Ryne Sandberg 50.00
136 Carl Yastrzemski, George Brett, Paul Molitor 50.00
137 Carlton Fisk, Carl Yastrzemski, Wade Boggs 75.00
138 Joe Morgan, George Brett, Mike Schmidt 50.00
139 Yogi Berra, Carlton Fisk, Gary Carter 50.00
140 Andy Pettitte, Nolan Ryan, Brad Lidge 50.00
141 Andy Pettitte, Nolan Ryan, Randy Johnson 50.00
142 Andy Pettitte, Nolan Ryan, Roger Clemens 60.00
143 Andy Pettitte, Randy Johnson, Brad Lidge 30.00
144 Andy Pettitte, Roy Oswalt, Roger Clemens 50.00
145 Brad Lidge, Roy Oswalt, Andy Pettitte 35.00
146 Craig Biggio, Jeff Bagwell, Lance Berkman 40.00
147 Nolan Ryan, Roger Clemens, Randy Johnson 80.00
148 Roger Clemens, Brad Lidge, Andy Pettitte 50.00
149 Roger Clemens, Randy Johnson, Andy Pettitte 50.00
150 Ichiro Suzuki, Hideki Matsui 160.00
151 Ichiro Suzuki, Hideki Matsui, Kazuo Matsui 140.00
152 Ichiro Suzuki, Tadahito Iguchi, Hideki Matsui 150.00
153 Eric Gagne, Mike Piazza, Duke Snider 100.00
154 Gary Sheffield, Rickie Weeks, Paul Molitor 30.00
155 Paul Molitor, Gary Sheffield, Robin Yount 35.00
156 Robin Yount, Paul Molitor, Rickie Weeks 30.00
157 Harmon Killebrew, Rod Carew, Johan Santana 40.00
158 Harmon Killebrew, Torii Hunter, Rod Carew 40.00
159 Johan Santana, Joe Mauer, Torii Hunter 35.00
160 Paul Molitor, Rod Carew, Harmon Killebrew 40.00
161 Albert Pujols, Ichiro Suzuki, Barry Bonds 180.00
162 Alex Rodriguez, Barry Bonds, George Brett 60.00
163 Alex Rodriguez, Barry Bonds, Mickey Mantle 150.00
164 Alex Rodriguez, Ichiro Suzuki, Mickey Mantle 180.00
165 Alex Rodriguez, Reggie Jackson, Yogi Berra 50.00
166 Alex Rodriguez, Ted Williams, Mickey Mantle 200.00
167 Alex Rodriguez, Yogi Berra, Don Mattingly 60.00
168 Alex Rodriguez, Barry Bonds, Don Mattingly 70.00
169 Alex Rodriguez, Cal Ripken Jr., Miguel Tejada 60.00
170 Barry Bonds, Harmon Killebrew, Reggie Jackson 70.00

171 Barry Bonds, Roberto Clemente, Willie Stargell 120.00
172 Barry Bonds, Alex Rodriguez, Albert Pujols 100.00
173 Barry Bonds, Cal Ripken Jr., Mickey Mantle 200.00
174 Barry Bonds, Josh Gibson, Albert Pujols 120.00
175 Barry Bonds, Vladimir Guerrero, Ichiro Suzuki 75.00
176 Brooks Robinson, George Brett, Mike Schmidt 60.00
177 Cal Ripken Jr., Barry Bonds, Ichiro Suzuki 120.00
178 Cal Ripken Jr., Don Mattingly, George Brett 90.00
179 Cal Ripken Jr., George Brett, Don Mattingly 90.00
180 Cal Ripken Jr., Mike Schmidt, Don Mattingly 100.00
181 Cal Ripken Jr., Roger Clemens, Don Mattingly 125.00
182 Chipper Jones, Dale Murphy, Don Mattingly 75.00
183 Don Mattingly, Mickey Mantle, Reggie Jackson 150.00
184 George Brett, Johnny Bench, Mike Schmidt 60.00
185 George Brett, Johnny Bench, Mike Schmidt 60.00
186 Ichiro Suzuki, Barry Bonds, Mickey Mantle 180.00
187 Ivan Rodriguez, Vladimir Guerrero, Miguel Tejada 35.00
188 Ivan Rodriguez, Yogi Berra, Johnny Bench 50.00
189 Ivan Rodriguez, Yogi Berra, Johnny Bench 50.00
190 Johnny Bench, Mike Piazza, Yogi Berra 50.00
191 Mickey Mantle, Barry Bonds, Ted Williams 200.00
192 Mickey Mantle, Ichiro Suzuki, Roberto Clemente 200.00
193 Mickey Mantle, Roberto Clemente, Stan Musial 200.00
194 Mickey Mantle, Ted Williams, Roberto Clemente 220.00
195 Mickey Mantle, Vladimir Guerrero, Roberto Clemente 200.00
196 Miguel Tejada, Reggie Jackson, Rickey Henderson 40.00
197 Reggie Jackson, Alex Rodriguez, Yogi Berra 50.00
198 Roberto Clemente, Mickey Mantle, Barry Bonds 180.00
199 Buck O'Neil, Josh Gibson, Monte Irvin 100.00
200 Carlos Beltran, Carlos Delgado, David Wright 60.00
201 Carlos Beltran, Carlos Delgado, Jose Reyes 50.00
202 Carlos Beltran, David Wright, Pedro Martinez 60.00
203 Darryl Strawberry, Dwight Gooden, Gary Carter 30.00
204 David Wright, Carlos Beltran, Mike Piazza 60.00
205 David Wright, Mike Piazza, Jose Reyes 75.00
206 Jose Reyes, Kazuo Matsui, David Wright 40.00
207 Alex Rodriguez, Don Mattingly, Mickey Mantle 180.00
208 Alex Rodriguez, Hideki Matsui, Joe Torre 80.00
209 Alex Rodriguez, Hideki Matsui, Mickey Mantle 200.00
210 Don Mattingly, Mickey Mantle, Roger Clemens 200.00
211 Hideki Matsui, Gary Sheffield, Alex Rodriguez 50.00
212 Hideki Matsui, Gary Sheffield, Jorge Posada 50.00
213 Jorge Posada, Roger Clemens, Mike Mussina 75.00
214 Mickey Mantle, Whitey Ford, Yogi Berra 200.00
215 Mike Mussina, Whitey Ford, Roger Clemens 65.00
216 Roger Clemens, Mickey Mantle, Alex Rodriguez 200.00
217 Wade Boggs, Joe Torre, Alfonso Soriano 30.00
218 Barry Zito, Mark Mulder, Tim Hudson 25.00
219 Jose Canseco, Reggie Jackson, Rickey Henderson 40.00
220 Mark Mulder, Miguel Tejada, Tim Hudson 40.00
221 Bobby Abreu, Pat Burrell, Jim Thome 40.00
222 Curt Schilling, Mike Schmidt, Steve Carlton 50.00
223 Mike Schmidt, Pat Burrell, Scott Rolen 50.00

224 Barry Bonds, Roberto Clemente, Josh Gibson 150.00
225 Paul Waner, Roberto Clemente, Lloyd Waner 150.00
226 Willie Stargell, Bill Mazeroski, Roberto Clemente 140.00
227 Albert Pujols, Carlos Beltran, Dontrelle Willis 60.00
228 Albert Pujols, Dontrelle Willis, Ichiro Suzuki 90.00
229 Cal Ripken Jr., Albert Pujols, Orlando Cepeda 90.00
230 Cal Ripken Jr., Carlton Fisk, Tom Seaver 80.00
231 Cal Ripken Jr., Rod Carew, Carlton Fisk 75.00
232 Cal Ripken Jr., Rod Carew, Carlton Fisk 75.00
233 Jeff Bagwell, Albert Pujols, Mike Piazza 100.00
234 Mike Piazza, Jeff Bagwell, Scott Rolen 80.00
235 Rickey Henderson, Steve Garvey, Tony Gwynn 50.00
236 Adrian Beltre, Ichiro Suzuki, Alex Rodriguez 80.00
237 Ichiro Suzuki, Alex Rodriguez, Randy Johnson 100.00
238 Barry Bonds, Juan Marichal, Orlando Cepeda 75.00
239 Juan Marichal, Monte Irvin, Orlando Cepeda 40.00
240 Orlando Cepeda, Monte Irvin, Barry Bonds 60.00
241 Albert Pujols, Frankie Frisch, Stan Musial 120.00
242 Albert Pujols, Mark Mulder, Scott Rolen 65.00
243 Scott Rolen, Jim Edmonds, Albert Pujols 75.00
244 Stan Musial, Ozzie Smith, Albert Pujols 120.00
245 Alex Rodriguez, Ivan Rodriguez, Alfonso Soriano 50.00
246 Alex Rodriguez, Mark Teixeira, Alfonso Soriano 50.00
247 Alex Rodriguez, Nolan Ryan, Alfonso Soriano 60.00
248 Alfonso Soriano, Hank Blalock, Mark Teixeira 30.00
249 Alfonso Soriano, Hank Blalock, Michael Young 25.00
250 Mark Teixeira, Alfonso Soriano, Michael Young 30.00

Triple Relic Autograph

NM/M

Production 18 Sets
Gold: No Pricing
Production Nine Sets
Platinum: No Pricing
Production Three Sets

1-3 Albert Pujols 475.00
4-6 Alex Rodriguez 275.00
7 Derrek Lee 60.00
8 Barry Bonds 400.00
9-10 Ben Sheets 35.00
11-12 Brad Lidge 35.00
13-15 Cal Ripken Jr. 220.00
16-18 Carl Yastrzemski 100.00
19-20 Chase Utley 70.00
21-24 Chien-Ming Wang 800.00
25-26 Chris Carpenter 100.00
27-28 Clint Barmes 25.00
29-30 Conor Jackson 40.00
31 David Ortiz 125.00
32-34 Don Mattingly 120.00
35-36 Duke Snider 75.00
37 Ernie Banks 120.00
38-40 Frank Robinson 65.00
41-42 Garrett Atkins 35.00
43-45 Derrek Lee 60.00
46-47 J.J. Hardy 40.00
48-49 Jake Peavy 50.00
50-51 Jeff Francis 30.00
52-53 Joe Mauer 40.00
54-55 Joey Devine 25.00
56-59 Johan Santana 75.00
60-62 Johnny Bench 80.00
63 Johnny Damon 80.00
64-65 Jonny Gomes 40.00
66-67 Jose Reyes 50.00
68-69 Justin Morneau 40.00
70-73 Lou Brock 60.00
74 Manny Ramirez 100.00
75 Mariano Rivera 150.00
76 Mark Prior 50.00
77-80 Miguel Cabrera 70.00
81-83 Mike Schmidt 100.00
84-85 Morgan Ensberg 35.00
86-87 Nick Swisher 40.00
88-90 Nolan Ryan 150.00
91-92 Zach Duke 30.00
93-95 Ozzie Smith 80.00
96 Pedro Martinez 125.00
97-99 Robin Yount 75.00
100-103 Rod Carew 50.00
104-105 Roger Clemens 180.00
106-107 Ryan Langerhans 40.00
108-110 Ryne Sandberg 100.00
111-112 Scott Kazmir 40.00
113-115 Stan Musial 100.00
116-118 Steve Carlton 40.00
119-120 Steve Garvey 40.00
121-123 Tony Gwynn 100.00
124-125 Travis Hafner 40.00
126-127 Victor Martinez 40.00
128-130 Wade Boggs 60.00

Triple Relic Combos Auto.

NM/M

Production 18 Sets
Gold: No Pricing
Production Nine Sets
Platinum: No Pricing
Production Three Sets

1 Albert Pujols, Barry Bonds, Alex Rodriguez 1,000
2 Felix Hernandez, Alex Rodriguez, Shin-Soo Choo 150.00
3 Nolan Ryan, Roger Clemens, Felix Hernandez 300.00
4 Johnny Damon, Alex Rodriguez, Robinson Cano 300.00
5 Manny Ramirez, Carl Yastrzemski, David Ortiz 250.00
6 Michael Young, Cal Ripken Jr., Ozzie Smith 300.00
7 Brian Roberts, Cal Ripken Jr., Frank Robinson 250.00
8 Stan Musial, Ozzie Smith, Lou Brock 180.00
9 Ozzie Smith, Stan Musial, Lou Brock 180.00
10 Tony Gwynn, Stan Musial, Rod Carew 180.00
11 Brooks Robinson, Cal Ripken Jr., Brian Roberts 200.00
12 Rod Carew, Robin Yount, Paul Molitor 120.00
13 Derrek Lee, Ryne Sandberg, Mark Prior 180.00
14 Chien-Ming Wang, Steve Carlton, Dontrelle Willis 275.00
15 Brad Lidge, Mariano Rivera, Huston Street 180.00
16 Morgan Ensberg, Wade Boggs, David Wright 120.00
17 Ben Sheets, Steve Carlton, Felix Hernandez 80.00
18 Victor Martinez, Johnny Bench, Joe Mauer 125.00
19 David Wright, Mike Schmidt, Aaron Hill 160.00
20 Chase Utley, Mike Schmidt, Ryan Howard 200.00
21 Felix Hernandez, Steve Carlton, Brandon McCarthy 75.00
22 David Wright, Miguel Cabrera, Jason Bay 140.00
23 Robinson Cano, Don Mattingly, Chien-Ming Wang 350.00
24 Justin Morneau, Don Mattingly, Travis Hafner 100.00
25 Steve Garvey, Don Mattingly, Dan Johnson 100.00
26 Travis Hafner, Miguel Cabrera, Jason Bay 100.00
27 Ben Sheets, Johan Santana, Jake Peavy 75.00
28 Ervin Santana, Johan Santana, Ben Sheets 70.00
29 Chris Carpenter, Johan Santana, Rich Harden 120.00
30 Zach Duke, Johan Santana, Brandon McCarthy 75.00

2006 Topps Turkey Red

NM/M

Complete Set (316-630):
Common Player: .25
Common SP: 4.00
Inserted 1:4
Pack (8): 4.00
Box (24): 75.00

316 Alex Rodriguez 3.00
316 Alex Rodriguez/Rangers/SP 8.00
316 Alex Rodriguez/M's/SP 8.00
317 Jeff Francoeur/SP 4.00
318 Shawn Green .25
319 Daniel Cabrera .25
320 Craig Biggio .50
321 Jeremy Bonderman .40
322 Mark Kotsay .25
323 Cliff Floyd .25
324 Jimmy Rollins 1.00
325 Magglio Ordonez .50
325 Magglio Ordonez/W. Sox/SP 4.00
326 C.C. Sabathia .75
327 Oliver Perez .25
328 Orlando Hudson .25
329 Chris Ray .25
330 Manny Ramirez 1.00
331 Paul Konerko .50
332 Joe Mauer/SP 4.00
333 Jorge Posada .50
334 Mark Ellis .25
335 A.J. Burnett .50
336 Mike Sweeney .25
337 Shannon Stewart .25
338 Jake Peavy/SP 4.00
339 Carlos Delgado/Mets/SP 5.00
339 Carlos Delgado/B. Jays/SP 5.00
340 Brian Roberts .50
341 Dontrelle Willis .50
342 Aaron Rowand .50
343 Richie Sexson .50
343 Richie Sexson/Brewers/SP 4.00
344 Chris Carpenter .75
345 Carlos Zambrano .50
346 Nomar Garciaparra .75
347 Carlos Lee .50
348 Preston Wilson .25
348 Preston Wilson/Marlins/SP 4.00
349 Mariano Rivera .50
350 Ichiro Suzuki/SP 8.00
351 Mike Piazza 1.00
351 Mike Piazza/Mets/SP 4.00
352 Jason Schmidt .25
353 Jeff Weaver .25
354 Rocco Baldelli .25
355 Adam Dunn .75
356 Jeromy Burnitz .25
357 Chris Shelton/SP 4.00
358 Chone Figgins/SP 4.00
359 Javier Vazquez .25
360 Chipper Jones 1.00
361 Frank Thomas 1.00
362 Mark Loretta .25
363 Hideki Matsui 2.00
364 J.J. Hardy/SP 4.00
365 Todd Helton .75
366 Reggie Sanders .25
367 Jay Gibbons .25
368 Johnny Estrada .25
369 Grady Sizemore 1.00
370 Jim Thome 1.00
371 Ivan Rodriguez .75
372 Jason Bay .75
373 Carl Crawford .50
374 Adrian Beltre .50
375 Derrek Lee/SP 6.00
376 Miguel Olivo .25
377 Roy Oswalt .50
378 Coco Crisp .25
379 Moises Alou .50
380 Kevin Millwood .25
381 Mark Grudzielanek .25
382 Justin Morneau .75
383 Austin Kearns .40
384 Brad Penny .25
385 Troy Glaus .50
386 Cliff Lee .25
387 Armando Benitez .25
388 Clint Barmes .25
389 Orlando Cabrera .50
390 Jim Edmonds SP 4.00
391 Jermaine Dye .50
392 Morgan Ensberg/SP 4.00
393 Paul LoDuca .25
394 Eric Chavez .25
395 Greg Maddux/SP 8.00
396 Jack Wilson .25
397 Omar Vizquel .25
398 Joe Nathan .25
399 Bobby Abreu .50
400 Barry Bonds/SP 8.00
401 Gary Sheffield .50
402 John Patterson .25
403 J.D. Drew .50
404 Bruce Chen .25
405 Johnny Damon 1.00
406 Aubrey Huff .25
407 Mark Mulder .25
408 Jamie Moyer .25
409 Carlos Guillen .50
410 Andruw Jones/SP 5.00
411 Jhonny Peralta/SP 4.00
412 Doug Davis .25
413 Aaron Miles .25
414 Jon Lieber .25
415 Aaron Hill .25
416 Josh Beckett/SP 5.00
417 Bobby Crosby .25
418 Noah Lowry/SP 4.00
419 Sidney Ponson .25
420 Luis Castillo .25
421 Brad Wilkerson .25
422 Felix Hernandez/SP 4.00
423 Vinny Castilla .25
424 Tom Glavine .50
425 Vladimir Guerrero 1.00
426 Javy Lopez .25
427 Ronnie Belliard .25
428 Dmitri Young .25
429 Johan Santana 1.00
430 David Ortiz/Red Sox/SP 5.00
430 David Ortiz/Twins/SP 5.00
431 Ben Sheets .50
432 Matt Holliday .75
433 Brian McCann .50
434 Joe Blanton .25
435 Sean Casey .25
436 Brad Lidge .25
437 Chad Tracy .25
438 Brett Myers .25
439 Matt Morris .25
440 Brian Giles .25
441 Zach Duke .25
442 Jose Lopez .25
443 Kris Benson .25
444 Jose Reyes SP 5.00
445 Travis Hafner .75
446 Orlando Hernandez .25
447 Edgar Renteria .40
448 Scott Podsednik .25
449 Nick Swisher SP 4.00
450 Derek Jeter SP 10.00
451 Scott Kazmir SP 4.00
452 Hank Blalock .50
453 Jake Westbrook .25
454 Miguel Cabrera 1.00
455 Ken Griffey Jr. 2.00
455 Ken Griffey Jr./M's SP 8.00
456 Rafael Furcal .50
457 Lance Berkman .50
458 Aramis Ramirez .50
459 Xavier Nady .25
459 Xavier Nady/Padres SP 4.00
460 Randy Johnson 1.00
460 Randy Johnson/Astros SP 6.00
461 Khalil Greene .25
462 Bartolo Colon .25
463 Mike Lowell .50
464 David DeJesus .25
465 Ryan Howard SP 8.00
466 Tim Salmon SP 4.00
467 Mark Buehrle SP 4.00
468 Curtis Granderson .75
469 Kerry Wood .50
470 Miguel Tejada .75
471 Geoff Jenkins .25
472 Jeremy Reed .25
473 David Eckstein .25
474 Lyle Overbay .25
475 Michael Young .50
476 Nick Johnson/Nats SP 4.00
476 Nick Johnson/Yanks SP 4.00
477 Carlos Beltran 1.00
478 Huston Street .25
479 Brandon Webb .75
480 Phil Nevin .25
481 Ryan Madson SP 4.00
482 Jason Giambi .75
483 Angel Berroa .25
484 Casey Blake .25
485 Pat Burrell .50
486 B.J. Ryan .25
487 Torii Hunter .50
488 Garret Anderson .25
489 Chase Utley SP 6.00
490 Matt Murton .25
491 Rich Harden .25
492 Garrett Atkins .50
493 Tadahito Iguchi/SP 4.00
494 Jarrod Washburn .25
495 Carl Everett .25
496 Kameron Loe .25
497 Jorge Cantu/SP 4.00
498 Chris Young .50
499 Marcus Giles .25
500 Albert Pujols 3.00
501 Alfonso Soriano/Nats/SP 5.00
501 Alfonso Soriano/Yanks/SP 5.00
502 Randy Winn .25
503 Roy Halladay .50
504 Victor Martinez .50
505 Pedro Martinez 1.00
506 Rickie Weeks .50
507 Dan Johnson .25
508 Tim Hudson .50
508 Tim Hudson/A's/SP 4.00
509 Mark Prior .50
510 Melvin Mora .25
511 Matt Clement .25
512 Brandon Inge .25
513 Mike Mussina .75
514 Mike Cameron .25
515 Barry Zito .50
516 Luis Gonzalez .25
517 Jose Castillo .25
518 Andy Pettitte .50
519 Wily Mo Pena .25
520 Billy Wagner .25
521 Ervin Santana/SP 4.00
522 Juan Pierre .25
523 Dan Haren .50
524 Adrian Gonzalez/SP 4.00
525 Robinson Cano .75
526 Jeff Kent .50
527 Cory Sullivan .25
528 Joe Crede SP 4.00
529 John Smoltz .50
530 David Wright 2.00
531 Chad Cordero .25
532 Scott Rolen SP 5.00
533 Edwin Jackson .25
534 Doug Mientkiewicz .25
535 Mark Teixeira SP 5.00

536	Kelvim Escobar	.25
537	Alex Rios	.50
538	Jose Vidro	.25
539	Alex Gonzalez	.25
540	Yadier Molina	.25
541	Ronny Cedeno SP	4.00
542	Mark Hendrickson	.25
543	Russ Adams	.25
544	Chris Capuano	.25
545	Raul Ibanez	.25
546	Vicente Padilla	.25
547	Chris Duffy	.25
548	Bengie Molina	.25
549	Chien-Ming Wang	1.00
550	Curt Schilling	.50
551	Craig Wilson	.25
552	Mike Lieberthal	.25
553	Kazuo Matsui	.25
554	Jeff Francis	.25
555	Brady Clark	.25
556	Willy Taveras	.25
557	Mike Maroth	.25
558	Bernie Williams	.50
559	Edwin Encarnacion	.25
560	Vernon Wells	.25
561	Livan Hernandez/Nats	.25
561	Livan Hernandez/Giants SP	4.00
562	Kenny Rogers	.25
563	Steve Finley	.25
564	Trot Nixon	.25
565	Jonny Gomes SP	4.00
566	Brandon Phillips	.50
567	Shawn Chacon	.25
568	David Bush	.25
569	Jose Guillen	.25
570	Gustavo Chacin	.25
571	A. Rod Safe at the Plate CL	1.00
572	Pujols At Bat CL	1.00
573	Bonds On Deck CL	1.00
574	Breaking Up Two CL	.25
575	Conference On The Mound CL	.25
576	Touch Em All CL	.50
577	Avoiding The Runner CL	.25
578	Bunting The Runner Over CL	.25
579	In The Hole CL	.50
580	Jeter Steals Third CL	1.00
581	Nolan Ryan	2.00
582	Cal Ripken Jr.	3.00
583	Carl Yastrzemski	1.00
584	Duke Snider	1.00
585	Tom Seaver	1.00
586	Mickey Mantle	5.00
587	Jim Palmer	.50
588	Gary Carter	.25
589	Stan Musial	1.50
590	Luis Aparicio	.25
591	Prince Fielder **(RC)**	4.00
592	Conor Jackson **(RC)**	.50
593	Jeremy Hermida **(RC)**	1.00
594	Jeff Mathis **(RC)**	.50
595	Alay Soler **RC**	1.00
596	Ryan Spilborghs **(RC)**	.50
597	Chuck James **(RC)**	1.00
598	Josh Barfield **(RC)**	.50
599	Ian Kinsler **(RC)**	1.00
600	Val Majewski **(RC)**	.50
601	Brian Slocum **(RC)**	.50
602	Matthew Kemp **(RC)**	2.00
603	Nate McLouth **(RC)**	1.00
604	Sean Marshall **(RC)**	.50
605	Brian Bannister **(RC)**	.50
606	Ryan Zimmerman **(RC)**	4.00
607	Kendry Morales **(RC)**	1.00
608	Jonathan Papelbon **(RC)**	4.00
609	Matt Cain **(RC)**	1.00
610	Anderson Hernandez **(RC)**	.50
611	Jose Capellan **(RC)**	.50
612	Lastings Milledge **(RC)**	1.50
613	Francisco Liriano **(RC)**	2.00
614	Hanley Ramirez **(RC)**	3.00
615	Bryan Anderson **(RC)**	.50
616	Reggie Abercrombie **(RC)**	.50
617	Erick Aybar **(RC)**	1.00
618	James Loney **(RC)**	1.00
619	Joel Zumaya **(RC)**	1.00
620	Travis Ishikawa **(RC)**	.50
621	Jason Kubel **(RC)**	.50
622	Drew Meyer **(RC)**	.50
623	Kenji Johjima **RC**	3.00
624	Fausto Carmona **(RC)**	1.00
625	Nicholas Markakis **(RC)**	1.00
626	John Rheinecker **(RC)**	.50
627	Melky Cabrera **(RC)**	1.00
628	Mike Pelfrey **RC**	4.00
629	Dan Uggla **(RC)**	1.50
630	Justin Verlander **(RC)**	4.00

Black

Stars (316-630): 3-5X
SP's: 1.5-2X
Inserted 1:20

Gold

Stars (316-630): 5-10X
SP's: 3-5X
Inserted 1:60

Red

Stars (316-630): 1-2X
SP's: .5-1X

Suede

No Pricing
Production One Set

White

Stars (316-630): 2-3X
SP's: 1X
Inserted 1:4

Autographs

NM/M

Common Auto.: 8.00
Suede: No Pricing
Production One Set

GA	Garrett Atkins	15.00
JB	Josh Barfield	8.00
CB	Clint Barmes	10.00
MC	Miguel Cabrera	40.00
RC	Robinson Cano	60.00
JG	Jonny Gomes	25.00
RH	Ryan Howard	100.00
CJA	Conor Jackson	15.00
KJ	Kenji Johjima	90.00
DJ	Dan Johnson	15.00
CJ	Chipper Jones	60.00
DL	Derrek Lee	40.00
PL	Paul LoDuca	25.00
BM	Brian McCann	30.00
BMC	Brandon McCarthy/Exch.	10.00
MM	Mike Morse	10.00
RO	Roy Oswalt	25.00
AR	Alex Rodriguez	250.00
JS	Johan Santana/Exch.	65.00
HS	Huston Street/Exch.	25.00
NS	Nick Swisher/Exch.	20.00
CV	Claudio Vargas/Exch.	8.00
DW	David Wright	85.00

Autographs Black

NM/M

Production 15 or 99

GA	Garrett Atkins/99	20.00
JB	Josh Barfield/99	15.00
CB	Clint Barmes/99	15.00
CJA	Conor Jackson/99	20.00
DJ	Dan Johnson/99	15.00
BM	Brian McCann/99	40.00
BMC	Brandon McCarthy/ 99 Exch.	15.00
MM	Mike Morse/99	15.00
NS	Nick Swisher/99 Exch.	20.00
CV	Claudio Vargas/99 Exch.	15.00

Autographs Gold

NM/M

Production 5 or 25

JB	Josh Barfield/25	25.00
BM	Brian McCann/25	75.00
MM	Mike Morse/25	25.00
NS	Nick Swisher/25 Exch.	30.00

Autographs Red

NM/M

Production 50 or 475

GA	Garrett Atkins/475	20.00
JB	Josh Barfield/475	15.00
CB	Clint Barmes/475	15.00
MC	Miguel Cabrera/50	60.00
RC	Robinson Cano/50	100.00
JG	Jonny Gomes/50	25.00
RH	Ryan Howard/50	125.00
CJA	Conor Jackson/475	20.00
KJ	Kenji Johjima/50	100.00
DJ	Dan Johnson/475	15.00
CJ	Chipper Jones/50	100.00
DL	Derrek Lee/50	40.00
PL	Paul LoDuca/50	30.00
BM	Brian McCann/475	30.00
BMC	Brandon McCarthy/ 475 Exch.	15.00
MM	Mike Morse/475	10.00
RO	Roy Oswalt/50	30.00
AR	Alex Rodriguez/50	250.00
JS	Johan Santana/50 Exch.	75.00
HS	Huston Street/50 Exch.	30.00
NS	Nick Swisher/475 Exch.	20.00
CV	Claudio Vargas/475 Exch.	8.00
DW	David Wright/50	100.00

Autographs White

NM/M

Production 25 or 100

GA	Garrett Atkins/200	20.00
JB	Josh Barfield/200	15.00
CB	Clint Barmes/200	15.00
CJA	Conor Jackson/200	20.00
DJ	Dan Johnson/200	15.00
BM	Brandon McCarthy/ 200 Exch.	15.00
BMC	Brandon McCarthy/ 200 Exch.	15.00
MM	Mike Morse/200	10.00
NS	Nick Swisher/200 Exch.	20.00
CV	Claudio Vargas/200 Exch.	10.00

B-18 Blankets

NM/M

Inserted 1:2 Boxes
Original B-18 Blanket: No Pricing
Inserted 1:159 Boxes

BB1	Barry Bonds/White	15.00
BB2	Barry Bonds/Red	15.00
VG1	Vladimir Guerrero/White	10.00
VG2	Vladimir Guerrero/Green	10.00
KJ1	Kenji Johjima/White	10.00
KJ2	Kenji Johjima/Green	10.00
DL1	Derrek Lee/White	10.00
DL2	Derrek Lee/Red	10.00
MM1	Mickey Mantle/White	25.00
MM2	Mickey Mantle/Blue	25.00
HM1	Hideki Matsui/White	10.00
HM2	Hideki Matsui/Blue	10.00
DO1	David Ortiz/White	10.00
DO2	David Ortiz/Orange	10.00
MR1	Manny Ramirez/White	10.00
MR2	Manny Ramirez/Orange	10.00
AR1	Alex Rodriguez/White	15.00
AR2	Alex Rodriguez/Blue	15.00
IS1	Ichiro Suzuki/White	10.00
IS2	Ichiro Suzuki/Green	10.00

Cabinet

NM/M

Common Player:
Inserted 1:2 Boxes
Cabinet Original: No Pricing
Inserted 1:4,340 Boxes
Suede: No Pricing
Inserted 1:634 Boxes

JB	Josh Barfield	10.00
JBE	Josh Beckett	10.00
BB	Barry Bonds	25.00
JC	Jorge Cantu	10.00
CCA	Chris Carpenter	10.00
GC	Gary Carter	10.00
CC	Carl Crawford	10.00
JD	Johnny Damon	20.00
CD	Carlos Delgado	10.00
PF	Prince Fielder	20.00
JF	Jeff Francoeur	15.00
NG	Nomar Garciaparra	15.00
TG	Troy Glaus	10.00
JG	Jonny Gomes	10.00
KG	Ken Griffey Jr.	20.00
RH	Ryan Howard	20.00
DJ	Derek Jeter	30.00
NJ	Nick Johnson	10.00
RJ	Randy Johnson	20.00
AJ	Andruw Jones	15.00
DL	Derrek Lee	10.00
FL	Francisco Liriano	10.00
MM	Mickey Mantle	50.00
NM	Nicholas Markakis	10.00
PM	Pedro Martinez	15.00
HM	Hideki Matsui	15.00
DO	David Ortiz	20.00
JPA	Jonathan Papelbon	25.00
JP	Jake Peavy	10.00
MP	Mike Piazza	15.00
AP	Albert Pujols	30.00
AR	Alex Rodriguez	25.00
IR	Ivan Rodriguez	10.00
JR	Jimmy Rollins	15.00
NR	Nolan Ryan	25.00
JS	Johan Santana	15.00
DS	Duke Snider	20.00
AS	Alfonso Soriano	20.00
IS	Ichiro Suzuki	20.00
JT	Jim Thome	15.00
DW	David Wright	15.00
CY	Carl Yastrzemski	25.00

Cabinet Auto Relics

No Pricing
Inserted 1:86 Boxes
Suede: No Pricing
Production One Set

Cabinet Auto Relics Dual

No Pricing
Inserted 1:1,368 Boxes
Suede: No Pricing
Production One Set

Relics

NM/M

Common Player: 4.00
Red: 1-1.5X
Production 150 Sets
White: 1.5-2X
Production 99 Sets
Black: 2-3X
Production 50 Sets
Gold: 2-4X
Production 25 Sets
Suede: No Pricing
Production One Set

CBA	Clint Barmes	4.00
CB	Carlos Beltran	8.00
LB	Lance Berkman	6.00
HB	Hank Blalock	4.00
MC	Miguel Cabrera	8.00
RC	Robinson Cano	15.00
CC	Chris Carpenter	8.00
EC	Eric Chavez	4.00
JC	Jose Contreras	6.00
JD	Johnny Damon	15.00
CD	Carlos Delgado	6.00
JE	Jim Edmonds	4.00
ME	Morgan Ensberg	4.00
JF	Jeff Francoeur	8.00
JG	Jon Garland	4.00
VG	Vladimir Guerrero	8.00
RHA	Roy Halladay	6.00
RIH	Rich Harden	4.00
JH	Jeremy Hermida	4.00
RH	Ryan Howard	25.00
TH	Torii Hunter	6.00
CJ	Andruw Jones	6.00
CJ	Chipper Jones	10.00
PK	Paul Konerko	8.00
DL	Derrek Lee	8.00
BL	Brad Lidge	6.00
PL	Paul LoDuca	4.00
PM	Pedro Martinez	10.00
HM	Hideki Matsui	15.00
JM	Joe Mauer	10.00
MM	Mike Mussina	10.00
DO	David Ortiz	15.00
RO	Roy Oswalt	6.00
APE	Andy Pettitte	6.00
MP	Mike Piazza	10.00
AP	Albert Pujols	20.00
MR	Manny Ramirez	10.00
JR	Jose Reyes	8.00
MRI	Mariano Rivera	15.00
BR	Brian Roberts	6.00
AR	Alex Rodriguez	15.00
JS	Johan Santana	10.00
IS	Ichiro Suzuki	25.00
MT	Mark Teixeira	8.00
BW	Bernie Williams	8.00
DWI	Dontrelle Willis	4.00
DW	David Wright	15.00
MY	Michael Young	

2006 Topps 1952 Edition

NM/M

Complete Set (312):
Common Player: .25
Common SP (276-312): 5.00
Common 52 Logo Variation: 4.00
Inserted 1:5
Pack (8): 4.50
Box (20): 80.00

1	Howie Kendrick **(RC)**	1.50
2	Enrique Gonzalez **(RC)**	.25
3	Chuck James **(RC)**	.75
4	Chris Britton **RC**	.50
5	David Pauley **(RC)**	.50
6	Angel Pagan **(RC)**	.25
7	Pat Neshek **RC**	4.00
8	Walter Young **(RC)**	.25
9	Chris Denorfia **(RC)**	.25
10	Rafael Perez **RC**	.50
11	Ryan Spilborghs **(RC)**	.25
12	Jon Huber **RC**	.50
13	Jordan Tata **RC**	.50
14	Eric Reed **(RC)**	.25
15	Norris Hopper **RC**	.75
16	Scott Olsen **(RC)**	.25
17	Fernando Nieve **(RC)**	.25
18	Chris Booker **(RC)**	.25
19	Chad Billingsley **(RC)**	.75
20	Carlos Villanueva **RC**	.50
21	Craig Hansen **RC**	1.50
22	David Gassner **(RC)**	.25
23	Mike Pelfrey **RC**	4.00
24	Matt Smith **(RC)**	1.00
25	Chris Roberson **(RC)**	.50
26	John Van Benschoten **(RC)**	.25
27	Kevin Frandsen **(RC)**	.25
28	Les Walrond **(RC)**	.50
29	James Shields **RC**	.50
30	Russell Martin **(RC)**	1.00
31	Benjamin Zobrist **(RC)**	.25
32	John Rheinecker **(RC)**	.25
33	Francisco Rosario **(RC)**	.25
34	Santiago Ramirez **(RC)**	.25
35	Michael Napoli **RC**	1.50
36	Tony Pena **(RC)**	.25
37	Jeff Karstens **RC**	1.00
37	Jeff Karstens/ 52 Logo SP **RC**	5.00
38	Phil Stockman **(RC)**	.25
39	Kurt Birkins **RC**	1.00
40	Dustin Pedroia **(RC)**	.50
41	Buck Coats **(RC)**	.25
42	Jim Johnson **RC**	1.00
43	Angel Guzman **(RC)**	.25
44	Kelly Shoppach **(RC)**	.25
45	Josh Wilson **(RC)**	.25
46	Jack Hannahan **RC**	.75
47	Ricky Nolasco **(RC)**	.25
48	T.J. Bohn **(RC)**	.25
49	Joel Zumaya **(RC)**	1.00
50	Philip Barzilla **RC**	.75
51	Justin Huber **(RC)**	.25
52	Willy Aybar **(RC)**	.25
52	Willy Aybar/ 52 Logo SP **(RC)**	4.00
53	Tony Gwynn Jr. **(RC)**	.50
54	Chris Barnwell **RC**	.50

55	Henry Owens **RC**	.75
56	Jeff Bajenaru **(RC)**	.25
57	Jonah Bayliss **RC**	.50
58	Joshua Sharpless **RC**	.50
59	Eliezer Alfonzo **RC**	.50
60	Bobby Livingston **(RC)**	.25
61	John Gall **(RC)**	.25
62	Ruddy Lugo **(RC)**	.25
63	Fabio Castro **RC**	.50
64	Casey Janssen **RC**	.75
65	Mike O'Connor **RC**	.50
66	Kendry Morales **(RC)**	.50
67	James Hoey **RC**	.75
68	Dustin Moseley **(RC)**	.25
69	Peter Moylan **RC**	.50
70	Manny Delcarmen **(RC)**	.50
71	Rich Hill **(RC)**	.50
72	Boone Logan **RC**	.50
73	Cody Ross **(RC)**	.25
74	Fausto Carmona **(RC)**	.50
75	Ramon Ramirez **(RC)**	.25
76	Zach Miner **(RC)**	.25
77	Hanley Ramirez **(RC)**	.50
78	Josh Johnson **(RC)**	.25
79	Taylor Buchholz **(RC)**	.25
80	Joe Nelson **(RC)**	.25
81	Hong-Chih Kuo **(RC)**	.50
82	Chris Mabeus **(RC)**	.25
83	Willie Eyre **(RC)**	.25
84	John Maine **(RC)**	.50
85	Yurendell DeCaster **(RC)**	.25
86	Mike Thompson **RC**	.50
87	Brian Wilson **RC**	.50
88	Matt Cain **(RC)**	.50
88	Matt Cain/52 Logo SP **(RC)**	8.00
89	Josh Rupe **RC**	.25
90	Tyler Johnson **(RC)**	.25
91	Jason Childers **RC**	.50
92	Wes Littleton **(RC)**	.25
93	Ty Taubenheim **RC**	.50
94	Saul Rivera **(RC)**	.25
95	Reggie Willits **(RC)**	1.00
96	Carlos Quentin **(RC)**	.50
97	Macay McBride **(RC)**	.25
98	Brandon Fahey **RC**	.50
99	Sean Marshall **(RC)**	.25
100	Sean Tracey **(RC)**	.25
101	Brian Slocum **(RC)**	.25
102	Choo Freeman **(RC)**	.25
103	Brent Clevlen **(RC)**	.25
104	Josh Willingham **(RC)**	.25
105	Chris Resop **(RC)**	.25
106	Chris Sampson **RC**	1.00
107	James Loney **(RC)**	.50
107	James Loney/ 52 Logo SP **(RC)**	8.00
108	Matthew Kemp **(RC)**	.50
109	Jason Kubel **(RC)**	.25
110	Brian Bannister **(RC)**	1.50
111	Kevin Thompson **(RC)**	.25
112	Jeremy Brown **(RC)**	.25
113	Brian Sanches **(RC)**	.25
114	Nate McLouth **(RC)**	.50
115	Ben Johnson **(RC)**	.25
116	Jonathan Sanchez **(RC)**	.50
117	Mark Lowe **(RC)**	.25
118	Skip Schumaker **(RC)**	.50
119	Jason Hammel **(RC)**	.25
120	Drew Meyer **(RC)**	.25
121	Melvin Dorta **RC**	.50
122	Jeff Mathis **(RC)**	.25
123	Davis Romero **(RC)**	.25
124	Joey Devine **RC**	.50
125	Sendy Rleal **RC**	.50
126	Freddie Bynum **(RC)**	.25
127	Bryan Anderson **(RC)**	.25
128	Jeremy Sowers **(RC)**	.25
129	Ryan Shealy **(RC)**	.25
130	Reggie Abercrombie **(RC)**	.25
131	Matt Albers **(RC)**	.25
132	Lastings Milledge **(RC)**	.50
133	Robert Andino **RC**	.25
134	Chris Demaria **RC**	.50
135	Boof Bonser **(RC)**	.25
136	Alay Soler **RC**	.50
137	Wilbert Nieves **(RC)**	.25
138	Mike Rouse **(RC)**	.25
139	Carlos Ruiz **(RC)**	.25
140	Matt Capps **(RC)**	.25
141	Travis Ishikawa **(RC)**	.25
142	Josh Kinney **RC**	1.00
143	Josh Rupe **(RC)**	.25
144	Shaun Marcum **(RC)**	.25
145	Jason Bergmann **(RC)**	.25
146	Tommy Murphy **(RC)**	.25
147	Martin Prado **(RC)**	.25
148	Val Majewski **(RC)**	.25
149	Ian Kinsler **(RC)**	.50
150	Joe Winkelsas **(RC)**	.25
151	Agustin Montero **(RC)**	.25
152	Joe Inglett **RC**	1.00
153	Manuel Corpas **RC**	.50
154	Yusmeiro Petit **(RC)**	.25
155	Mark Woodyard **(RC)**	.25
156	Jeff Fulchino **RC**	.50
157	Stephen Andrade **(RC)**	.25
158	Tim Hamulack **(RC)**	.25
159	Colter Bean **(RC)**	.25
160	Anderson Hernandez **(RC)**	.25
161	Kevin Reese **(RC)**	.25
162	Jason Windsor **(RC)**	.25
163	Paul Maholm **(RC)**	.25
163	Paul Maholm/ 52 Logo SP **(RC)**	4.00
164	Jeremy Accardo **RC**	.50
165	Joel Guzman **(RC)**	.25
166	Erick Aybar **(RC)**	.50
167	Scott Thorman **(RC)**	.25
168	Adam Loewen **(RC)**	.25
169	Carlos Marmol **RC**	.50
170	Bill Bray **(RC)**	.25
171	Edward Mujica **RC**	.50
172	Jeremy Hermida **(RC)**	.50
173	Taylor Tankersley **(RC)**	.25
174	Bobby Keppel **(RC)**	.25
175	Chris Young **(RC)**	.50
176	Josh Rabe **RC**	1.00
177	T.J. Beam **(RC)**	.25
178	Shane Komine **RC**	1.00
178	Shane Komine/52 Logo SP	6.00
179	Scott Mathieson **(RC)**	.25
180	Josh Barfield **(RC)**	.25
181	Justin Knoedler **(RC)**	.25
182	Emiliano Fruto **RC**	.50
183	Adam Wainwright **(RC)**	.50
184	Nick Masset **(RC)**	.25
185	Ryan Roberts **RC**	.50
186	Brandon Watson **(RC)**	.25
187	Chris Bootcheck **(RC)**	.25
188	Daniel Ortmeier **(RC)**	.25
189	Kevin Barry **(RC)**	.25
190	Cory Morris **RC**	.50
191	Kason Gabbard **(RC)**	.25
192	Tom Mastny **(RC)**	.25
193	David Aardsma **(RC)**	.25
194	Anthony Reyes **(RC)**	.25
195	Mike Jacobs **(RC)**	.50
196	Conor Jackson **(RC)**	.25
197	Kenji Johjima **RC**	2.50
198	Jack Taschner **(RC)**	.25
199	Renyel Pinto **(RC)**	.25
200	Chad Santos **(RC)**	.25
201	Aaron Rakers **(RC)**	.25
202	Franklin Gutierrez **(RC)**	.25
203	Chris Coste **RC**	1.50
204	Chris Iannetta **RC**	.50
205	Michael Vento **(RC)**	.25
206	Ryan O'Malley **RC**	1.00
207	Jason Botts **(RC)**	.25
208	John Hattig Jr. **(RC)**	.25
209	Brandon Harper **RC**	.50
210	Ryan Theriot **(RC)**	1.00
211	Travis Hughes **(RC)**	.25
212	Paul Hoover **(RC)**	.25
213	Brayan Pena **(RC)**	.25
214	Craig Breslow **RC**	.75
215	Eude Brito **(RC)**	.25
216	Melky Cabrera **(RC)**	.50
216	Melky Cabrera/ 52 Logo SP	8.00
217	Jonathan Broxton **(RC)**	.50
217	Jonathan Broxton/ 52 Logo SP **(RC)**	5.00
218	Bryan Corey **(RC)**	.25
219	Ron Flores **RC**	.50
220	Andrew Brown **(RC)**	.25
221	Jaime Bubela **(RC)**	.25
222	Jason Bulger **(RC)**	.25
223	Alberto Callaspo **(RC)**	.25
224	Jose Capellan **(RC)**	.25
225	Cole Hamels **(RC)**	.50
225	Cole Hamels/ 52 Logo SP **(RC)**	6.00
226	Bernie Castro **(RC)**	.25
227	Shin-Soo Choo **(RC)**	.25
228	Doug Clark **(RC)**	.25
229	Roy Corcoran **RC**	.50
230	Tim Corcoran **RC**	.75
231	Nelson Cruz **(RC)**	.25
232	Rajai Davis **(RC)**	.25
233	Chris Duncan **(RC)**	.25
233	Chris Duncan/ 52 Logo SP **(RC)**	5.00
234	Scott Dunn **(RC)**	.25
235	Mike Esposito **(RC)**	.25
236	Scott Feldman **RC**	.50
237	Luis Figueroa **RC**	.50
238	Bartolome Fortunato **(RC)**	.25
239	Alejandro Freire **RC**	.50
240	J.J. Furmaniak **(RC)**	.25
241	Nicholas Markakis **(RC)**	.50
242	Matt Garza **(RC)**	1.00
243	Justin Germano **(RC)**	.25
244	Alexis Gomez **(RC)**	.25
245	Tom Gorzelanny **(RC)**	.25
246	Dan Uggla **(RC)**	.75
247	Jeremy Guthrie **(RC)**	.25
248	Stephen Drew **(RC)**	1.00
249	Brendan Harris **(RC)**	.25
250	Jeff Harris **RC**	.50
251	Corey Hart **(RC)**	.50
252	Chris Heintz **(RC)**	.25
253	Prince Fielder **(RC)**	1.00
254	Francisco Liriano **(RC)**	.50
255	Jason Hirsh **(RC)**	.25
256	J.R. House **(RC)**	.25
257	Zach Jackson **(RC)**	.25
258	Charlton Jimerson **(RC)**	.25
259	Greg Jones **(RC)**	.25
260	Mitch Jones **(RC)**	.25
261	Ryan Jorgensen **RC**	.50
262	Logan Kensing **(RC)**	.25
263	John Koronka **(RC)**	.25
264	Anthony Lerew **(RC)**	.25
265	Anibal Sanchez **(RC)**	.25
266	Juan Mateo **RC**	.50
267	Paul McAnulty **(RC)**	.25
268	Dustin McGowan **(RC)**	.50
269	Marty McLeary **(RC)**	.25
270	Ryan Zimmerman **(RC)**	2.00
271	Dustin Nippert **(RC)**	.25
272	Eric O'Flaherty **RC**	.50
273	Ronny Paulino **(RC)**	.25
274	Tony Pena **(RC)**	.25
275	Hayden Penn **(RC)**	.25
276	Miguel Perez **(RC)**	5.00
277	Paul Phillips **(RC)**	5.00
278	Omar Quintanilla **(RC)**	5.00
279	Guillermo Quiroz **(RC)**	5.00
280	Darrell Rasner **(RC)**	5.00
281	Kenny Ray **(RC)**	5.00
282	Royce Ring **(RC)**	5.00
283	Brian Rogers **(RC)**	5.00
284	Ed Rogers **(RC)**	5.00
285	Danny Sandoval **RC**	5.00
286	Joe Saunders **(RC)**	5.00
287	Chris Schroder **RC**	5.00
288	Mike Smith **(RC)**	5.00
289	Travis Smith **(RC)**	5.00
290	Geovany Soto **(RC)**	8.00
291	Brian Sweeney **(RC)**	5.00
292	Jon Switzer **(RC)**	5.00
293	Joe Thurston **(RC)**	5.00
294	Jermaine Van Buren **(RC)**	5.00
295	Ryan Garko **(RC)**	5.00
296	Cla Meredith **(RC)**	5.00
297	Luke Scott **(RC)**	5.00
298	Andy Marte **(RC)**	5.00
299	Jered Weaver **(RC)**	10.00
300	Freddy Guzman **(RC)**	5.00
301	Jonathan Papelbon **(RC)**	10.00
302	John-Ford Griffin **(RC)**	5.00
303	Jon Lester **(RC)**	10.00
304	Shawn Hill **(RC)**	5.00
305	Brian Myrow **RC**	5.00
306	Anderson Garcia **RC**	5.00
307	Andre Ethier **(RC)**	6.00
308	Ben Hendrickson **(RC)**	5.00
309	Alejandro Machado **(RC)**	5.00
310	Justin Verlander **(RC)**	8.00
311	Mickey Mantle/Blue	40.00
311	Mickey Mantle/Black	15.00
311	Mickey Mantle/Green	15.00
311	Mickey Mantle/Orange	15.00
311	Mickey Mantle/Red	15.00
311	Mickey Mantle/Yellow	15.00
312	Steve Stemle **RC**	5.00

Chrome

		NM/M
Common Player:		1.50
Production 1,952 Sets		
Refractor:		2-3X
Production 552 Sets		
Gold Refractor:		4-6X
Production 52 Sets		
1	Howie Kendrick	2.00
2	David Pauley	1.50
3	Chris Denorfia	1.50
4	Jordan Tata	2.00
5	Fernando Nieve	1.50
6	Craig Hansen	2.00
7	Mickey Mantle	25.00
8	James Shields	3.00
9	Francisco Rosario	1.50
10	Jeff Karstens	3.00
11	Buck Coats	1.50
12	Josh Wilson	1.50
13	Joel Zumaya	2.00
14	Tony Gwynn Jr.	2.00
15	Jonah Bayliss	1.50
16	John Gall	1.50
17	Mike O'Connor	1.50
18	Peter Moylan	1.50
19	Cody Ross	1.50
20	Hanley Ramirez	4.00
21	Hong-Chih Kuo	3.00
22	Yurendell DeCaster	1.50
23	Sean Green	1.50
24	Ty Taubenheim	1.50
25	Macay McBride	1.50
26	Brian Slocum	1.50
27	Chris Resop	1.50
28	Jason Kubel	1.50
29	Brian Sanches	1.50
30	Mark Lowe	1.50
31	Melvin Dorta	1.50
32	Sendy Rleal	1.50
33	Ryan Shealy	1.50
34	Robert Andino	1.50
35	Wilbert Nieves	1.50
36	Travis Ishikawa	1.50
37	Jason Bergmann	1.50
38	Ian Kinsler	3.00
39	Manuel Corpas	1.50
40	Stephen Andrade	1.50
41	Kevin Reese	1.50
42	Joel Guzman	1.50
43	Carlos Marmol	3.00
44	Taylor Tankersley	1.50
45	T.J. Beam	1.50
46	Justin Knoedler	1.50
47	Ryan Roberts	1.50
48	Kevin Barry	1.50
49	David Aardsma	1.50
50	Kenji Johjima	3.00
51	Aaron Rakers	1.50
52	Michael Vento	1.50
53	Brandon Harper	1.50
54	Brayan Pena	1.50
55	Jonathan Broxton	2.00
56	Jaime Bubela	1.50
57	Cole Hamels	5.00
58	Roy Corcoran	1.50
59	Chris Duncan	4.00
60	Luis Figueroa	1.50
61	Kendry Morales	1.50
62	Tom Gorzelanny	1.50
63	Brendan Harris	1.50
64	Anibal Sanchez	1.50
65	Zach Jackson	1.50
66	Ryan Jorgensen	1.50
67	Josh Johnson	1.50
68	Marty McLeary	2.00
69	Ronny Paulino	1.50
70	Tyler Johnson	1.50
2	Reggie Abercrombie	1.50
72	Nick Markakis	5.00
73	J.J. Furmaniak	2.00
74	Prince Fielder	5.00
75	Enrique Gonzalez	1.50
76	Angel Pagan	1.50
77	Rafael Perez	2.00
78	Eric Reed	1.50
79	Chris Booker	1.50
80	David Gassner	1.50
81	John Van Benschoten	1.50
82	Russell Martin	3.00
83	Santiago Ramirez	1.50
84	Phil Stockman	1.50
85	Jim Johnson	1.50
86	Jack Hannahan	1.50
87	Philip Barzilla	1.50
88	Chris Barnwell	1.50
89	Joshua Sharpless	1.50
90	Chris Roberson	1.50

Autograph

		NM/M
Common Auto.:		8.00
Red Ink:		2-3X
Production 52 Sets		
RA	Reggie Abercrombie	8.00
MA	Matt Albers	8.00
BA	Brian Anderson	8.00
EA	Erick Aybar	10.00
BPB	Brian Bannister	10.00
TJB	T.J. Bohn	8.00
BB	Boof Bonser	20.00
WB	Bill Bray	8.00
MC	Melky Cabrera	30.00
MTC	Matt Cain	25.00
FC	Fabio Castro	8.00
BC	Buck Coats	8.00
YD	Yurendell DeCaster	8.00
SD	Stephen Drew	25.00
KF	Kevin Frandsen	8.00
EF	Emiliano Fruto	8.00
MG	Matt Garza	20.00
EG	Enrique Gonzalez	8.00
FG	Franklin Gutierrez	10.00
AG	Angel Guzman	8.00
JG	Joel Guzman	8.00
CI	Chris Iannetta	10.00
CHJ	Chuck James	10.00
JWK	Jeff Karstens	20.00
MK	Matthew Kemp	25.00
HK	Howie Kendrick	30.00
JK	Josh Kinney	8.00
HCK	Hong-Chih Kuo	40.00
AL	Anthony Lerew	8.00

CM	Chris Mabeus	8.00
TM	Tom Mastny	15.00
SM	Scott Mathieson	8.00
JM	Jeff Mathis	8.00
KM	Kendry Morales	8.00
EM	Edward Mujica	8.00
MN	Michael Napoli	15.00
RO	Ryan O'Malley	8.00
AP	Angel Pagan	8.00
JP	Jonathan Papelbon	40.00
YP	Yusmeiro Petit	10.00
AS	Anibal Sanchez	8.00
JFS	Joe Saunders	15.00
JS	Joshua Sharpless	8.00
BS	Brian Slocum	8.00
DU	Dan Uggla	25.00
JVB	John Van Benschoten	10.00
JV	Justin Verlander	50.00
JW	Jered Weaver	40.00
RZ	Ryan Zimmerman	40.00
BZ	Benjamin Zobrist	8.00
JZ	Joel Zumaya	20.00

Debut Flashbacks

	NM/M
Common Player:	2.00
Chrome:	1.5-2X
Production 1,952 Sets	
Refractor:	2-3X
Production 552 Sets	
Gold Refractor:	4-6X
Production 52 Sets	
1 Dontrelle Willis	2.00
2 Carlos Beltran	3.00
3 Albert Pujols	8.00
4 Ichiro Suzuki	5.00
5 Mike Piazza	4.00
6 Nomar Garciaparra	3.00
7 Scott Rolen	3.00
8 Mariano Rivera	3.00
9 David Ortiz	4.00
10 Johnny Damon	4.00
11 Tom Glavine	3.00
12 David Wright	5.00
13 Greg Maddux	5.00
14 Manny Ramirez	4.00
15 Alex Rodriguez	6.00
16 Roger Clemens	6.00
17 Alfonso Soriano	3.00
18 Frank Thomas	3.00
19 Chipper Jones	4.00
20 Ivan Rodriguez	3.00

Dynamic Duos

DYNAMIC DUOS
ANDRE ETHIER   RUSSELL MARTIN

	NM/M
Common Duo:	1.00
Inserted 1:4	
1 Stephen Drew, Carlos Quentin	2.00
2 Jonathan Papelbon, Jon Lester	3.00
3 Joel Zumaya, Justin Verlander	4.00
4 Dan Uggla, Hanley Ramirez	1.50
5 Jonathan Broxton, Chad Billingsley	1.00
6 Francisco Liriano, Matt Garza	1.50
7 Lastings Milledge, John Maine	1.50
8 Chris Coste, Cole Hamels	1.50
9 Michael Napoli, Howie Kendrick	1.50
10 Joe Inglett, Andy Marte	1.00
11 Jeremy Hermida, Josh Willingham	1.00
12 Matthew Kemp, James Loney	1.50
13 Andre Ethier, Russell Martin	1.50
14 Melky Cabrera, Jeff Karstens	1.50
15 Ricky Nolasco, Scott Olsen, Josh Johnson, Anibal Sanchez	1.50

Ticket to Stardom Relics

No Pricing
Production 10 Sets

2007 Topps

	NM/M
Complete Set (661):	75.00
Common Player:	.10
Series 1 Hobby Pack (10):	3.00
Series 1 Hobby Box (36):	100.00
Series 1 Jumbo Pack (50):	15.00
Series 1 Jumbo Box (10):	140.00
Series 1 Rack Pack (22):	5.00
Series 1 Rack Box (24):	100.00
Series 2 Hobby Pack (10):	2.00
Series 2 Hobby Box (36):	60.00
Series 2 Jumbo Pack (50):	10.00
Series 2 Jumbo Box (10):	90.00
Series 2 Rack Pack (22):	4.00
Series 2 Rack Box (24):	85.00
Series 1 Variations:	No Pricing
Inserted 1:3700 Wal-Mart	
1 John Lackey	.10
2 Nick Swisher	.25
3 Brad Lidge	.10
4 Bengie Molina	.10
5 Bobby Abreu	.25
6 Edgar Renteria	.25
7 Mickey Mantle	5.00
8 Preston Wilson	.10
9 Ryan Dempster	.10
10 C.C. Sabathia	.10
11 Julio Lugo	.10
12 J.D. Drew	.25
13 Miguel Batista	.10
14 Eliezer Alfonzo	.10
15 Andrew Miller RC	3.00
15 Andrew Miller/Posed RC	.10
16 Yuniesky Betancourt	.10
17 Saul Rivera	.10
18 Orlando Hernandez	.10
19 Alfredo Amezaga	.10
20 Delmon Young/Face Right (RC)	.50
20 Delmon Young/Face Left (RC)	.10
21 Javy Lopez	.10
22 Corey Patterson	.10
23 Josh Bard	.10
24 Tom Gordon	.10
25 Gary Matthews	.10
26 Jason Jennings	.10
27 Joey Gathright	.10
28 Brandon Inge	.10
29 Pat Neshek	.10
30 Bronson Arroyo	.10
31 Jay Payton	.10
32 Andy Pettitte	.25
33 Ervin Santana	.10
34 Paul Konerko	.25
35 Joel Zumaya	.25
36 Gregg Zaun	.10
37 Tony Gwynn	.50
38 Adam LaRoche	.10
39 Jim Edmonds	.25
40 Derek Jeter	15.00
41 Rich Hill	.25
42 Livan Hernandez	.10
43 Aubrey Huff	.10
44 Todd Greene	.10
45 Andre Ethier	.25
46 Jeremy Sowers	.10
47 Ben Broussard	.10
48 Darren Oliver	.10
49 Nook Logan	.10
50 Miguel Cabrera	.50
51 Carlos Lee	.25
52 Jose Castillo	.10
53 Mike Piazza	.75
54 Daniel Cabrera	.10
55 Cole Hamels	.40
56 Mark Loretta	.10
57 Brian Fuentes	.10
58 Todd Coffey	.10
59 Brent Clevlen	.10
60 John Smoltz	.25
61 Ross Gload	.10
62 Dan Wheeler	.10
63 Scott Proctor	.10
64 Bobby Kielty	.10
65 Dan Uggla	.25
66 Lyle Overbay	.10
67 Geoff Jenkins	.10
68 Michael Barrett	.10
69 Casey Fossum	.10
70 Ivan Rodriguez	.40
71 Jose Lopez	.10
72 Jake Westbrook	.10
73 Moises Alou	.25
74 Jose Valverde	.10
75 Jered Weaver	.25
76 Lastings Milledge	.25
77 Austin Kearns	.10
78 Adam Loewen	.10
79 Josh Barfield	.10
80 Johan Santana	.40
81 Ian Kinsler	.10
82 Ian Snell	.10
83 Mike Lowell	.10
84 Elizardo Ramirez	.10
85 Scott Rolen	.40
86 Shannon Stewart	.10
87 Alexis Gomez	.10
88 Jimmy Gobble	.10
89 Jamey Carroll	.10
90 Chipper Jones	.50
91 Carlos Silva	.10
92 Joe Crede	.25
93 Michael Napoli	.10
94 Willy Travis	.10
95 Rafael Furcal	.25
96 Phil Nevin	.10
97 David Bush	.10
98 Marcus Giles	.10
99 Joe Blanton	.10
100 Dontrelle Willis	.25
101 Scott Kazmir	.25
102 Jeff Kent	.25
103 Pedro Feliz	.10
104 Johnny Estrada	.10
105 Travis Hafner	.25
106 Ryan Garko	.10
107 Rafael Soriano	.10
108 Wes Helms	.10
109 Billy Wagner	.10
110 Aaron Rowand	.10
111 Felipe Lopez	.10
112 Jeff Conine	.10
113 Nicholas Markakis	.25
114 John Koronka	.10
115 B.J. Ryan	.10
116 Tim Wakefield	.10
117 David Ross	.10
118 Emil Brown	.10
119 Michael Cuddyer	.10
120 Jason Giambi	.40
121 Alex Cintron	.10
122 Luke Scott	.10
123 Chone Figgins	.10
124 Huston Street	.10
125 Carlos Delgado	.40
126 Daryle Ward	.10
127 Chris Duncan	.10
128 Damian Miller	.10
129 Aramis Ramirez	.25
130 Albert Pujols	1.50
131 Chris Snyder	.10
132 Ray Durham	.10
133 Franklin Gutierrez	.10
134 Mike Jacobs	.10
135 Troy Tulowitzki (RC)	.50
135 Troy Tulowitzki/Throw (RC)	.50
136 Jon Rauch	.10
137 Jay Gibbons	.10
138 Adrian Gonzalez	.10
139 Randy Wolf	.10
140 Freddy Sanchez	.10
141 Rich Aurilia	.10
142 Trot Nixon	.10
143 Vicente Padilla	.10
144 Jack Wilson	.10
145 Jake Peavy	.25
146 Luke Hudson	.10
147 Javier Vazquez	.10
148 Scott Podsednik	.10
149 Ivan Rodriguez, Magglio Ordonez	.25
150 Todd Helton	.40
151 Kendry Morales	.10
152 Adam Everett	.10
153 Bob Wickman	.10
154 Bill Hall	.25
155 Jeremy Bonderman	.25
156 Ryan Theriot	.10
157 Rocco Baldelli	.10
158 Noah Lowry	.10
159 Jason Michaels	.10
160 Justin Verlander	.50
161 Eduardo Perez	.10
162 Chris Ray	.10
163 Dave Roberts	.10
164 Zachary Duke	.10
165 Mark Buehrle	.10
166 Hank Blalock	.25
167 Royce Clayton	.10
168 Mark Teahen	.10
169 Todd Jones	.10
170 Chien-Ming Wang	.50
171 Nick Punto	.10
172 Morgan Ensberg	.10
173 Robert Mackowiak	.10
174 Frank Catalanotto	.10
175 Matt Murton	.10
176 Alfonso Soriano, Carlos Beltran	.40
177 Francisco Cordero	.10
178 Jason Marquis	.10
179 Joe Nathan	.10
180 Roy Halladay	.25
181 Melvin Mora	.10
182 Ramon Ortiz	.10
183 Jose Valentin	.10
184 Gil Meche	.10
185 B.J. Upton	.25
186 Grady Sizemore	.40
187 Matt Cain	.25
188 Eric Byrnes	.10
189 Carl Crawford	.25
190 J.J. Putz	.10
191 Cla Meredith	.10
192 Matt Capps	.10
193 Rod Barajas	.10
194 Edwin Encarnacion	.10
195 James Loney	.10
196 Johnny Damon	.50
197 Freddy Garcia	.10
198 Mike Redmond	.10
199 Ryan Shealy	.10
200 Carlos Beltran	.40
201 Chuck James	.10
202 Mark Ellis	.10
203 Brad Ausmus	.10
204 Juan Rivera	.10
205 Cory Sullivan	.10
206 Ben Sheets	.25
207 Mark Mulder	.10
208 Carlos Quentin	.10
209 Jonathan Broxton	.10
210 Kazuo Matsui	.10
211 Armando Benitez	.10
212 Richie Sexson	.40
213 Josh Johnson	.10
214 Brian Schneider	.10
215 Craig Monroe	.10
216 Chris Duffy	.10
217 Chris Coste	.10
218 Clay Hensley	.10
219 Chris Gomez	.10
220 Hideki Matsui	.75
221 Robinson Tejeda	.10
222 Scott Hatteberg	.10
223 Jeff Francis	.10
224 Matt Thornton	.10
225 Robinson Cano	.40
226 New York Yankees	1.00
227 Oakland A's	.25
228 St. Louis Cardinals	.50
229 Minnesota Twins	.25
230 Barry Zito	.25
231 Baltimore Orioles	.25
232 Seattle Mariners	.25
233 Houston Astros	.25
234 Florida Marlins	.25
235 Reed Johnson	.10
236 Toronto Blue Jays	.25
237 Cincinnati Reds	.25
238 Philadelphia Phillies	.25
239 Anaheim Angels	.25
240 Chris Carpenter	.25
241 Atlanta Braves	.25
242 Washington Nationals	.25
243 Joe Torre	.25
244 Tampa Bay Devil Rays	.25
245 Chad Tracey	.10
246 Mike Hargrove	.10
247 Mike Scioscia	.10
248 Ron Gardenhire	.10
249 Tony LaRussa	.10
250 Anibal Sanchez	.10
251 Charlie Manuel	.10
252 John Gibbons	.10
253 Ken Macha	.10
254 Jerry Narron	.10
255 Brad Penny	.10
256 Bobby Cox	.10
257 Bob Melvin	.10
258 Mike Hargrove	.10
259 Phil Garner	.10
260 David Wright	1.00
261 Vinny Rottino (RC)	.25
262 Ryan Braun (RC)	2.00
263 Kevin Kouzmanoff (RC)	.50
264 David Murphy (RC)	.25
265 Jimmy Rollins	.25
266 Joe Maddon	.10
267 Grady Little	.10
268 Ryan Sweeney (RC)	.25
269 Fred Lewis (RC)	.25
270 Alfonso Soriano	.50
271 Delwyn Young (RC)	.25
271 Delwyn Young/Swing (RC)	.25
272 Jeff Salazar (RC)	.25
273 Miguel Montero (RC)	.25
274 Shawn Riggans (RC)	.25
275 Greg Maddux	1.00
276 Brian Stokes (RC)	.25
277 Philip Humber (RC)	.25
278 Scott Moore (RC)	.25
279 Adam Lind (RC)	.25
280 Curt Schilling	.50
281 Chris Narveson (RC)	.25
282 Oswaldo Navarro RC	.50
283 Drew Anderson (RC)	.25
284 Jerry Owens (RC)	.25
285 Randy Johnson	.50
286 Joaquin Arias (RC)	.25
287 Jose Garcia (RC)	.25
288 Shane Youman RC	.50
289 Brian Burres (RC)	.25
290 Matt Holliday	.25
291 Ryan Feierabend (RC)	.25
292 Josh Fields (RC)	.25
292 Josh Fields/Running (RC)	.10
293 Glen Perkins (RC)	.25
294 Mike Rabelo RC	.50
295 Jorge Posada	.25

296 Ubaldo Jimenez **(RC)** .25
297 Brad Ausmus .10
298 Eric Chavez .25
299 Orlando Hudson .10
300 Vladimir Guerrero .50
301 Derek Jeter 1.00
302 Scott Rolen .25
303 Mark Grudzielanek .10
304 Kenny Rogers .10
305 Frank Thomas .25
306 Mike Cameron .10
307 Torii Hunter .10
308 Albert Pujols 1.00
309 Mark Teixeira .25
310 Jonathan Papelbon .50
311 Greg Maddux .50
312 Carlos Beltran .25
313 Ichiro Suzuki .75
314 Andruw Jones .25
315 Manny Ramirez .50
316 Vernon Wells .25
317 Omar Vizquel .10
318 Ivan Rodriguez .25
319 Brandon Webb .25
320 Magglio Ordonez .25
321 Johan Santana .25
322 Ryan Howard 1.00
323 Justin Morneau .25
324 Hanley Ramirez .40
325 Joe Mauer .25
326 Justin Verlander .25
327 Derek Jeter, Bobby Abreu .50
328 Carlos Delgado, David Wright .50
329 Yadier Molina, Albert Pujols .50
330 Ryan Howard .50
331 Kelly Johnson .10
332 Chris Young .25
333 Mark Kotsay .10
334 A.J. Burnett .10
335 Brian McCann .10
336 Woody Williams .10
337 Jason Isringhausen .10
338 Juan Pierre .10
339 Jonny Gomes .10
340 Roger Clemens 1.50
341 Akinori Iwamura **RC** 1.50
342 Bengie Molina .10
343 Shin-Soo Choo .10
344 Kenji Johjima .25
345 Joe Borowski .10
346 Shawn Green .25
347 Chicago Cubs .10
348 Rodrigo Lopez .10
349 Brian Giles .25
350 Chase Utley .50
351 Mark DeRosa .10
352 Carl Pavano .10
353 Kyle Lohse .10
354 Chris Iannetta .10
355 Oliver Perez .10
356 Curtis Granderson .10
357 Sean Casey .10
358 Jason Tyner .10
359 Jon Garland .10
360 David Ortiz .75
361 Adam Kennedy .10
362 Chris Burke .10
363 Bobby Crosby .10
364 Conor Jackson .10
365 Tim Hudson .25
366 Rickie Weeks .25
367 Cristian Guzman .10
368 Mark Prior .25
369 Benjamin Zobrist .10
370 Troy Glaus .25
371 Kenny Lofton .25
372 Shane Victorino .25
373 Cliff Lee .10
374 Adrian Beltre .25
375 Miguel Olivo .10
376 Endy Chavez .10
377 Zack Segovia **(RC)** .25
378 Ramon Hernandez .10
379 Chris Young .25
380 Jason Schmidt .25
381 Ronny Paulino .10
382 Kevin Millwood .10
383 Jon Lester .25
384 Alex Gonzalez .10
385 Brad Hawpe .10
386 Placido Polanco .10
387 Nate Robertson .10
388 Torii Hunter .25
389 Gavin Floyd .10
390 Roy Oswalt .40
391 Kelvim Escobar .10
392 Craig Wilson .10
393 Milton Bradley .10
394 Aaron Hill .10
395 Matt Diaz .10
396 Chris Capuano .10
397 Juan Encarnacion .10
398 Jacque Jones .10
399 James Shields .10
400 Ichiro Suzuki .75
401 Matthew Kemp .10
402 Matt Morris .10
403 Casey Blake .10
404 Corey Hart .10
405 Josh Willingham .10
406 Ryan Madson .10
407 Nick Johnson .10
408 Kevin Millar .10
409 Khalil Greene .10
410 Tom Glavine .25
411 Jason Bay .25
412 Gerald Laird .10
413 Coco Crisp .10
414 Brandon Phillips .10
415 Aaron Cook .10
416 Mark Redman .10
417 Mike Maroth .10
418 Boof Bonser .10
419 Jorge Cantu .10
420 Jeff Weaver .10
421 Melky Cabrera .25
422 Francisco Rodriguez .10
423 Mike Lamb .10
424 Danny Haren .25
425 Tomokazu Ohka .10
426 Jeff Francoeur .25
427 Randy Wolf .10
428 So Taguchi .10
429 Carlos Zambrano .25
430 Justin Morneau .50
431 Luis Gonzalez .25
432 Takashi Saito .25
433 Brandon Morrow **RC** .75
434 Victor Martinez .25
435 Felix Hernandez .25
436 Ricky Nolasco .10
437 Paul LoDuca .10
438 Chad Cordero .10
439 Miguel Tejada .40
440 Mark Teixeira .40
441 Pat Burrell .25
442 Paul Maholm .10
443 Mike Cameron .25
444 Josh Beckett .25
445 Pablo Ozuna .10
446 Jaret Wright .10
447 Angel Berroa .10
448 Fernando Rodney .10
449 Francisco Liriano .25
450 Ken Griffey Jr. 1.00
451 Bobby Jenks .10
452 Mike Mussina .40
453 Howie Kendrick .25
454 Milwaukee Brewers .10
455 Dan Johnson .10
456 Ted Lilly .10
457 Mike Hampton .10
458 J.J. Hardy .25
459 Jeff Suppan .10
460 Jose Reyes 1.00
461 Jae Weong Seo .10
462 Edgar Gonzalez .10
463 Russell Martin .25
464 Omar Vizquel .10
465 Jhonny Peralta .25
466 Raul Ibanez .10
467 Hanley Ramirez .50
468 Kerry Wood .25
469 Ryan Church .10
470 Gary Sheffield .40
471 David Wells .10
472 David Dellucci .10
473 Xavier Nady .10
474 Michael Young .25
475 Kevin Youkilis .40
476 Aaron Harang .10
477 Brian Lawrence .10
478 Octavio Dotel .10
479 Chris Shelton .10
480 Matt Garza .25
481 Jim Thome .40
482 Jose Contreras .10
483 Kris Benson .10
484 John Maine .25
485 Tadahito Iguchi .10
486 Wandy Rodriguez .10
487 Eric Chavez .25
488 Vernon Wells .25
489 Doug Davis .10
490 Andruw Jones .40
491 David Eckstein .10
492 Michael Barrett .10
493 Greg Norton .10
494 Orlando Hudson .10
495 Wilson Betemit .10
496 Ryan Klesko .10
497 Fausto Carmona .10
498 Jarrod Washburn .10
499 Aaron Boone .10
500 Pedro Martinez .50
501 Mike O'Connor .10
502 Brian Roberts .25
503 Jeff Cirillo .10
504 Brett Myers .25
505 Jose Bautista .10
506 Akinori Otsuka .10
507 Shea Hillenbrand .10
508 Ryan Langerhans .10
509 Josh Fogg .10
510 Alex Rodriguez 1.50
511 Kenny Rogers .10
512 Jason Kubel .10
513 Jermaine Dye .25
514 Mark Grudzielanek .10
515 Josh Phelps .10
516 Bartolo Colon .25
517 Craig Biggio .25
518 Esteban Loaiza .10
519 Alex Rios .25
520 Adam Dunn .40
521 Derrick Turnbow .10
522 Anthony Reyes .10
523 Derrek Lee .40
524 Ty Wigginton .10
525 Jeremy Hermida .10
526 Derek Lowe .25
527 Randy Winn .10
528 Paul Byrd .10
529 Chris Snelling .10
530 Brandon Webb .25
531 Julio Franco .10
532 Jose Vidro .10
533 Erik Bedard .25
534 Termel Sledge .10
535 Jon Lieber .10
536 Tom Gorzelanny .10
537 Kip Wells .10
538 Wily Mo Pena .10
539 Eric Milton .10
540 Chad Billingsley .10
541 David DeJesus .10
542 Omar Infante .10
543 Rondell White .10
544 Juan Uribe .10
545 Miguel Cairo .10
546 Orlando Cabrera .25
547 Byung-Hyun Kim .10
548 Jason Kendall .10
549 Horacio Ramirez .10
550 Trevor Hoffman .25
551 Ronnie Belliard .10
552 Chris Woodward .10
553 Ramon Martinez .10
554 Elizardo Ramirez .10
555 Andy Marte .10
556 John Patterson .10
557 Scott Olsen .10
558 Steve Trachsel .10
559 Doug Mientkiewicz .10
560 Randy Johnson .50
561 Chan Ho Park .10
562 Jamie Moyer .10
563 Mike Gonzalez .10
564 Nelson Cruz .10
565 Alex Cora .10
566 Ryan Freel .10
567 Chris Stewart **RC** .50
568 Carlos Guillen .10
569 Jason Bartlett .10
570 Mariano Rivera .40
571 Norris Hopper .10
572 Alex Escobar .10
573 Gustavo Chacin .10
574 Brandon McCarthy .10
575 Seth McClung .10
576 Yuniesky Betancourt .10
577 Jason LaRue .10
578 Dustin Pedroia .25
579 Taylor Tankersley .10
580 Garret Anderson .10
581 Mike Sweeney .10
582 Scott Thorman .10
583 Joe Inglett .10
584 Clint Barmes .10
585 Willie Bloomquist .10
586 Willy Aybar .10
587 Brian Bannister .10
588 Jose Guillen .10
589 Brad Wilkerson .10
590 Lance Berkman .25
591 Toronto Blue Jays .10
592 Florida Marlins .10
593 Washington Nationals .10
594 Los Angeles Angels .10
595 Cleveland Indians .10
596 Texas Rangers .10
597 Detroit Tigers .10
598 Arizona Diamondbacks .10
599 Kansas City Royals .10
600 Ryan Zimmerman .40
601 Colorado Rockies .10
602 Minnesota Twins .10
603 Los Angeles Dodgers .10
604 San Diego Padres .10
605 Bruce Bochy .10
606 Ron Washington .10
607 Manny Acta .10
608 Sam Perlozzo .10
609 Terry Francona .10
610 Jim Leyland .10
611 Eric Wedge .10
612 Ozzie Guillen .10
613 Buddy Bell .10
614 Bob Geren .10
615 Lou Piniella .10
616 Fredi Gonzalez .10
617 Ned Yost .10
618 Willie Randolph .10
619 Bud Black .10
620 Garrett Atkins .10
621 Alexi Casilla **RC** .25
622 Matt Chico **(RC)** .25
623 Alejandro De Aza **RC** .75
624 Jeremy Brown .10
625 Josh Hamilton **(RC)** .50
626 Doug Slaten **RC** .50
627 Andy Cannizaro **RC** .50
628 Juan Salas **(RC)** .25
629 Levale Speigner **RC** .50
630 Daisuke Matsuzaka **RC** 6.00
631 Elijah Dukes **RC** 1.00
632 Kevin Cameron **RC** .50
633 Juan Perez **RC** .50
634 Alex Gordon **RC** 4.00
635 Juan Lara **RC** .50
636 Mike Rabelo **RC** .50
637 Justin Hampson **(RC)** .25
638 Cesar Jimenez **RC** .50
639 Joe Smith **RC** .50
640 Kei Igawa **RC** 1.00
641 Hideki Okajima **RC** 2.00
642 Sean Henn **(RC)** .25
643 Jay Marshall **RC** .50
644 Jared Burton **RC** .50
645 Angel Sanchez **RC** .50
646 Devern Hansack **RC** 1.00
647 Juan Morillo **(RC)** .25
648 Hector Gimenez **(RC)** .25
649 Brian Barden **RC** .50
650 Alex Rodriguez, Jason Giambi 1.00
651 Jason Michaels, Travis Hafner .25
652 J. Johnson, Miguel Olivo .10
653 Sean Casey, Placido Polanco .10
654 Ivan Rodriguez, Fernando Rodney .25
655 Dan Uggla, H. Ramirez .25
656 Carlos Beltran, Jose Reyes .50
657 Alex Rodriguez, Derek Jeter 1.00
658 Aaron Rowand, Jimmy Rollins .25
659 Angel Berroa, Andres Blanco .10
660 Yadier Molina .10
661 Barry Bonds 2.00

Copper

Copper: 25-50X
Production 56 Sets

Gold

Gold: 8-15X
Production 2,007 Sets

Platinum

No Pricing
Production One Set

1st Edition

1st Edition: 5-10X
Hobby Exclusive 1:36

Red Back

Red Back (1-330): 1-2.5X
Inserted 2:Hobby, 10:HTA

Printing Plates

Production one set per color.

All-Stars

		NM/M
Complete Set (12):		15.00
Common Player:		1.00
Inserted 1:Rack Pack		
1	Alfonso Soriano	2.00
2	Paul Konerko	1.50
3	Carlos Beltran	2.00
4	Troy Glaus	1.00
5	Jason Bay	1.50
6	Vladimir Guerrero	2.50
7	Chase Utley	3.00
8	Michael Young	1.00
9	David Wright	3.00
10	Gary Matthews	1.00
11	Brad Penny	1.00
12	Roy Halladay	1.00

All-Star Rookies

		NM/M
Complete Set (10):		12.00
Common Player:		1.50
Inserted 1:Rack Pack		
1	Prince Fielder	2.00
2	Dan Uggla	1.50
3	Ryan Zimmerman	2.00
4	Hanley Ramirez	2.00
5	Melky Cabrera	1.50
6	Andre Ethier	1.50
7	Nicholas Markakis	1.50
8	Justin Verlander	2.00
9	Francisco Liriano	2.00
10	Russell Martin	1.50

A-Rod Road to 500

NM/M

Series 1 A-Rod (1-25): 3.00
Series 2 A-Rod (201-225): 3.00

A-Rod Road to 500 Autographs

Production One Set

Distinguished Service

NM/M

Complete Set (20): 25.00
Common Player: 2.00
Inserted 1:12 Hobby, 1:12 HTA

1	Duke Snider	3.00
2	Yogi Berra	3.00
3	Bob Feller	2.00
4	Bobby Doerr	2.00
5	Monte Irvin	2.00
6	Dwight D. Eisenhower	2.00
7	George Marshall	2.00
8	Franklin D. Roosevelt	2.00
9	Harry S. Truman	2.00
10	Douglas MacArthur	2.00
11	Ralph Kiner	2.00
12	Hank Sauer	2.00
13	Elmer Valo	2.00
14	Bob Lemon	2.00
15	Hoyt Wilhelm	2.00
16	James Doolittle	2.00
17	Curtis Lemay	2.00
18	Omar Bradley	2.00
19	Chester Nimitz	2.00
20	Mark Clark	2.00
21	Joe DiMaggio	4.00
22	Warren Spahn	3.00
23	Stan Musial	3.00
24	Red Schoendienst	2.00
25	Ted Williams	4.00
26	Winston Churchill	3.00
27	Charles de Gaulle	2.00
28	George Bush	2.00
29	John F. Kennedy	2.00
30	Richard Bong	2.00

Distinguished Service Autograph

NM/M

Inserted 1:20,000 Hobby

BD	Bobby Doerr	50.00
BF	Bob Feller	60.00
DS	Duke Snider	75.00
MI	Monte Irvin	50.00
RK	Ralph Kiner	75.00

Distinguished Service Cut Signatures

Production One Set
No Pricing

Generation Now

NM/M

All Ryan Howard's:	2.00
All Chase Utley's:	1.00
All C. Ming Wang's:	3.00

All Mike Napoli's:	.50
All Justin Morneau's:	1.00
All David Wright's:	2.00
All Jered Weaver's:	1.00
All Andre Ethier's:	1.00
All Ryan Zimmerman's:	1.00
All Delmon Young's:	1.00
All Russell Martin's:	.75
All Justin Verlander's:	1.00
All Hanley Ramirez's:	1.00
All Nick Markakis's:	1.00
All Nick Swisher's:	.75

Generation Now Autographs

NM/M

Production One Set

Highlights Autographs

NM/M

Short prints are not serial #'d

JH	John Hattig Jr.	8.00
AM	Andrew Miller	8.00
AS	Anibal Sanchez	10.00
MN	Michael Napoli	10.00
JL	James Loney	20.00
MH	Matt Holliday	25.00
TT	Troy Tulowitzki	25.00
HR	Hanley Ramirez	20.00
JF	Josh Fields	15.00
CQ	Carlos Quentin	15.00
MG	Matt Garza	10.00
JM	John Maine	25.00
MP	Mike Piazza/50	120.00
TH	Travis Hafner	20.00
KM	Kevin Mench	10.00
CU	Chase Utley	50.00
DW	David Wright	60.00
JM	Justin Morneau	25.00
JS	Johan Santana/250	60.00
MC	Miguel Cabrera/250	30.00
DY	Delmon Young	20.00
DWW	Dontrelle Willis	20.00
CW	Chien-Ming Wang/100	250.00
JS	John Smoltz/250	50.00
AS	Alfonso Soriano/100	80.00
DO	David Ortiz/100	80.00
RH	Ryan Howard/100	100.00
GS	Gary Sheffield/25	
JD	Johnny Damon/25	
VG	Vladimir Guerrero/25	
AR	Alex Rodriguez/25	250.00
CMS	Curt Schilling/25	
AP	Albert Pujols/25	
EF	Emiliano Fruto	10.00
RZ	Ryan Zimmerman	25.00

Series 2

AB	Aaron Boone	10.00
AJ	Andruw Jones	35.00
AP	Albert Pujols	250.00
AR	Anthony Reyes	15.00
CG	Curtis Granderson	30.00
CW	Craig Wilson	15.00
DO	David Ortiz	80.00
DT	Derrick Turnbow	15.00
DU	Dan Uggla	20.00
DW	David Wright	50.00
DWW	Dontrelle Willis	20.00
EC	Endy Chavez	40.00
ES	Ervin Santana	15.00
JT	Jim Thome	40.00
JD	Johnny Damon	100.00
JG	Jon Garland	15.00
JV	Justin Verlander	50.00
JZ	Joel Zumaya	20.00
KE	Kelvim Escobar	20.00
KM	Kendry Morales	10.00
LM	Lastings Milledge	20.00
MC	Melky Cabrera	25.00
MTC	Matt Cain	20.00
PL	Paul LoDuca	40.00
RC	Robinson Cano	30.00
RH	Ryan Howard	100.00
RM	Russell Martin	20.00
RZ	Ryan Zimmerman	25.00
SC	Shawn Chacon	10.00
SP	Scott Podsednik	15.00
SR	Shawn Riggans	10.00
SSC	Shin-Soo Choo	20.00
ST	Steve Trachsel	25.00
TG	Tom Glavine	75.00
VG	Vladimir Guerrero	150.00

Highlights Relics

NM/M

Common Player: 5.00

AP	Albert Pujols	25.00
AR	Alex Rodriguez	20.00
AS	Alfonso Soriano	15.00
BM	Brian McCann	15.00
CB	Carlos Beltran	10.00
CD	Carlos Delgado	8.00
CQ	Carlos Quentin	10.00
CB	Craig Biggio	10.00
CS	Curt Schilling	10.00
DO	David Ortiz	10.00
DW	Dontrelle Willis	8.00
ER	Edgar Renteria	5.00
FT	Frank Thomas	10.00
GS	Gary Sheffield	8.00
IS	Ichiro Suzuki	25.00
IR	Ivan Rodriguez	10.00
JB	Jason Bay	10.00
JPM	Joe Mauer	15.00
JAS	Johan Santana	20.00

2006 HIGHLIGHTS

AUTHENTIC GAME WORN PANTS
ALEX RODRIGUEZ

JS	John Smoltz	10.00
JR	Jose Reyes	15.00
JM	Justin Morneau	15.00
MO	Magglio Ordonez	5.00
MAR	Manny Ramirez	10.00
MR	Mariano Rivera	15.00
MT	Miguel Tejada	8.00
PK	Paul Konerko	10.00
RC	Robinson Cano	15.00
RO	Roy Oswalt	8.00
RH	Ryan Howard	20.00
SK	Scott Kazmir	8.00
SR	Scott Rolen	10.00
TG	Tom Glavine	8.00
TG	Troy Glaus	5.00
VW	Vernon Wells	8.00

Series 2

AB	Adrian Beltre	5.00
AER	Alex Rodriguez	20.00
AJ	Andruw Jones	8.00
ALR	Anthony Reyes	5.00
AP	Albert Pujols	25.00
AR	Aramis Ramirez	8.00
AS	Alfonso Soriano	10.00
BB	Barry Bonds	
CJ	Chipper Jones	10.00
DE	David Eckstein	20.00
DO	David Ortiz	15.00
DW	David Wright	15.00
DWW	Dontrelle Willis	8.00
GA	Garrett Atkins	5.00
GS	Grady Sizemore	10.00
JD	Jermaine Dye	5.00
JDD	Johnny Damon	15.00
JT	Jim Thome	10.00
JV	Justin Verlander	20.00
LB	Lance Berkman	8.00
MC	Matt Cain	8.00
MCT	Mark Teixeira	8.00
MEC	Melky Cabrera	8.00
MR	Manny Ramirez	10.00
MT	Miguel Tejada	8.00
NS	Nick Swisher	8.00
PK	Paul Konerko	8.00
PM	Pedro Martinez	8.00
RC	Robinson Cano	15.00
RH	Roy Halladay	10.00
RJH	Ryan Howard	20.00
SK	Scott Kazmir	8.00
TG	Tom Glavine	10.00
VG	Vladimir Guerrero	8.00
VW	Vernon Wells	8.00

Hit Parade

HIT PARADE
LUIS GONZALEZ
HITS

NM/M

Inserted 1:9

1	Barry Bonds	2.00
2	Ken Griffey Jr.	1.50
3	Frank Thomas	1.00
4	Jim Thome	.75
5	Manny Ramirez	1.00
6	Alex Rodriguez	2.00
7	Gary Sheffield	.75
8	Mike Piazza	1.00
9	Carlos Delgado	.75
10	Chipper Jones	1.00
11	Barry Bonds	2.00
12	Ken Griffey Jr.	1.50

13	Frank Thomas	1.00
14	Manny Ramirez	1.00
15	Gary Sheffield	.75
16	Jeff Kent	.50
17	Alex Rodriguez	2.00
18	Luis Gonzalez	.50
19	Jim Thome	.75
20	Mike Piazza	1.00
21	Craig Biggio	.50
22	Barry Bonds	2.00
23	Julio Franco	.50
24	Steve Finley	.50
25	Omar Vizquel	.50
26	Ken Griffey Jr.	1.50
27	Gary Sheffield	.75
28	Luis Gonzalez	.50
29	Ivan Rodriguez	.75
30	Bernie Williams	.50

Hobby Masters

ALBERT PUJOLS ST. LOUIS CARDINALS®

NM/M

Common Player: .50
Inserted 1:6

1	David Wright	3.00
2	Albert Pujols	4.00
3	David Ortiz	1.50
4	Ryan Howard	3.00
5	Alfonso Soriano	1.50
6	Delmon Young	1.50
7	Jered Weaver	1.50
8	Derek Jeter	4.00
9	Freddy Sanchez	.50
10	Alex Rodriguez	3.00
11	Johan Santana	1.50
12	Ichiro Suzuki	2.50
13	Andruw Jones	1.50
14	Vladimir Guerrero	1.50
15	Miguel Cabrera	1.50
16	Todd Helton	1.00
17	Manny Ramirez	1.50
18	Carlos Beltran	1.00
19	Justin Morneau	1.00
20	Francisco Liriano	1.00

Home Run Derby

NM/M

Production 999 Sets

DO	David Ortiz	4.00
RH	Ryan Howard	8.00
JD	Jermaine Dye	2.00
AP	Albert Pujols	10.00
TH	Travis Hafner	2.00
AS	Alfonso Soriano	4.00
JT	Jim Thome	3.00
LB	Lance Berkman	2.00
FT	Frank Thomas	4.00
CB	Carlos Beltran	2.00
TG	Troy Glaus	2.00
AJ	Andruw Jones	4.00
JG	Jason Giambi	3.00
AD	Adam Dunn	2.00
PK	Paul Konerko	2.00
CD	Carlos Delgado	3.00
MR	Manny Ramirez	4.00
AR	Aramis Ramirez	3.00
AER	Alex Rodriguez	10.00
JB	Jason Bay	2.00
NS	Nick Swisher	2.00
BH	Bill Hall	2.00
JM	Justin Morneau	4.00
MH	Matt Holliday	2.00
RS	Richie Sexson	2.00
AL	Adam LaRoche	2.00
VG	Vladimir Guerrero	4.00
CU	Chase Utley	4.00
RI	Raul Ibanez	2.00
GA	Garrett Atkins	2.00
MT	Mark Teixeira	4.00
PB	Pat Burrell	2.00
VW	Vernon Wells	2.00
PF	Prince Fielder	10.00
TKH	Torii Hunter	3.00
CL	Carlos Lee	2.00
CM	Craig Monroe	2.00
KG	Ken Griffey Jr.	10.00
JC	Joe Crede	2.00
DU	Dan Uggla	2.00
GS	Grady Sizemore	4.00
MC	Miguel Cabrera	4.00
MOT	Miguel Tejada	3.00
DW	David Wright	8.00

DY	Delmon Young	4.00
MMT	Marcus Thames	2.00
JDD	Johnny Damon	4.00
JF	Jeff Francoeur	3.00
AB	Adrian Beltre	2.00
MP	Mike Piazza	4.00

In The Name
Production One Set

Josh Gibson HR History

NM/M
Common Gibson: 1.00
Inserted 1:9

Mickey Mantle Home Run History

NM/M
Common Mantle HR History: 2.00
Inserted 1:9 Hobby

Mickey Mantle Home Run History Relics
NM/M
Common Mantle: 150.00
Production Seven Sets

Opening Day

NM/M
Inserted 1:12

1	New York Mets, St. Louis Cardinals	2.00
2	Atlanta Braves, Philadelphia Phillies	1.00
3	Florida Marlins, Washington Nationals	1.00
4	Tampa Bay Devil Rays, New York Yankees	2.00
5	Toronto Blue Jays, Detroit Tigers	1.00
6	Cleveland Indians, Chicago White Sox	1.00
7	Los Angeles Dodgers, Milwaukee Brewers	1.00
8	Chicago Cubs, Cincinnati Reds	1.00
9	Arizona Diamondbacks, Colorado Rockies	1.00
10	Boston Red Sox, Kansas City Royals	2.00
11	Oakland Athletics, Seattle Mariners	1.00
12	Baltimore Orioles, Minnesota Twins	1.00
13	Pittsburgh Pirates, Houston Astros	1.00
14	Texas Rangers, Anaheim Angels	1.00
15	San Diego Padres, San Francisco Giants	1.00

Own The Game
NM/M
Common Player: .50

Inserted 1:6

1	Ryan Howard	2.50
2	David Ortiz	1.00
3	Alfonso Soriano	1.00
4	Albert Pujols	3.00
5	Lance Berkman	.75
6	Jermaine Dye	.50
7	Travis Hafner	.75
8	Jim Thome	1.00
9	Carlos Beltran	1.00
10	Adam Dunn	.75
11	Ryan Howard	2.50
12	David Ortiz	1.00
13	Albert Pujols	3.00
14	Lance Berkman	.75
15	Justin Morneau	.75
16	Andruw Jones	1.00
17	Jermaine Dye	.50
18	Travis Hafner	.75
19	Alex Rodriguez	3.00
20	David Wright	2.00
21	Johan Santana	1.00
22	Chris Carpenter	.75
23	Brandon Webb	.50
24	Roy Oswalt	.75
25	Josh Johnson	.50

Ted Williams 406
NM/M
Complete Set (18): 30.00
Common Williams: 2.50
Inserted 1:4 Target

The Mickey Mantle Story

NM/M
Complete Set (30): 40.00
Common Mantle: 3.00

The Streak

NM/M
Common Joe DiMaggio (1-56): 1.50
Inserted 1:9

The Streak Before The Streak
NM/M
Common Joe DiMaggio (1-61): 1.50
Inserted 1:9

Topps Stars
NM/M
Inserted 1:9

1	Ryan Howard	1.50
2	Alfonso Soriano	1.00
3	Todd Helton	.75
4	Johan Santana	.75

5	David Wright	1.50
6	Albert Pujols	2.00
7	Daisuke Matsuzaka	3.00
8	Miguel Cabrera	1.00
9	David Ortiz	1.00
10	Alex Rodriguez	2.00
11	Vladimir Guerrero	1.00
12	Ichiro Suzuki	1.50
13	Derek Jeter	2.00
14	Lance Berkman	.50
15	Ryan Zimmerman	.50

Trading Places

NM/M
Inserted 1:9

1	Jeff Weaver	.50
2	Frank Thomas	1.00
3	Mike Piazza	1.00
4	Alfonso Soriano	1.00
5	Freddy Garcia	.50
6	Jason Marquis	.50
7	Ted Lilly	.50
8	Mark Loretta	.50
9	Marcus Giles	.50
10	Barry Zito	.50
11	Andy Pettitte	.75
12	J.D. Drew	.50
13	Gary Matthews	.50
14	Jay Payton	.50
15	Aubrey Huff	.50
16	Brian Bannister	.50
17	Jeff Conine	.50
18	Gary Sheffield	.75
19	Shea Hillenbrand	.50
20	Wes Helms	.50
21	Frank Catalanotto	.50
22	Adam LaRoche	.50
23	Mike Gonzalez	.50
24	Greg Maddux	1.50
25	Jason Schmidt	.50

Trading Places Autographs
NM/M
Common Auto: 10.00

AL	Adam LaRoche	10.00
BB	Brian Bannister	15.00
FC	Frank Catalanotto	10.00
FG	Freddy Garcia	10.00
GS	Gary Sheffield	40.00
JS	Jason Schmidt	15.00
MG	Mike Gonzalez	10.00
SH	Shea Hillenbrand	10.00
WH	Wes Helms	10.00

Trading Places Relics
NM/M

AP	Andy Pettitte	10.00
AS	Alfonso Soriano	10.00
BZ	Barry Zito	8.00
FT	Frank Thomas	10.00
GM	Greg Maddux	20.00
GS	Gary Sheffield	15.00
JW	Jeff Weaver	8.00
MG	Marcus Giles	5.00
ML	Mark Loretta	8.00
MP	Mike Piazza	20.00

Unlock the Mick

NM/M
Complete Set (5):
Common Mantle: 2.00
Inserted 1:18
1-5 Mickey Mantle 2.00

Wal-Mart
NM/M
Complete Set (18): 40.00
Common Player: 1.50
Three per $9.99 Wal-Mart box.

1	Frank Thomas	3.00
2	Mike Piazza	3.00
3	Ivan Rodriguez	2.00
4	David Ortiz	3.00
5	David Wright	4.00
6	Greg Maddux	4.00
7	Mickey Mantle	8.00
8	Jose Reyes	4.00
9	John Smoltz	1.50
10	Jim Edmonds	1.50
11	Ryan Howard	4.00
12	Miguel Cabrera	3.00
13	Carlos Delgado	2.00
14	Miguel Tejada	2.00
15	Ichiro Suzuki	4.00
16	Albert Pujols	5.00
17	Derek Jeter	5.00
18	Vladimir Guerrero	3.00

World Champion Relics
NM/M
Production 100 Sets
Cards are not serial #'d.

1	Jeff Weaver	60.00
2	Chris Duncan	60.00
3	Chris Carpenter	75.00
4	Yadier Molina	40.00
5	Albert Pujols	160.00
6	Jim Edmonds	65.00
7	Ronnie Belliard	50.00
8	So Taguchi	80.00
9	Juan Encarnacion	50.00
10	Scott Rolen	75.00
11	Anthony Reyes	60.00
12	Preston Wilson	50.00
13	Jeff Suppan	60.00
14	Adam Wainwright	120.00
15	David Eckstein	100.00

1952 Mickey Mantle Reprint Relic
Production 52
52MM Mickey Mantle

1953 Mickey Mantle Reprint Relic
Production 53
53MM Mickey Mantle

2007 Topps Update

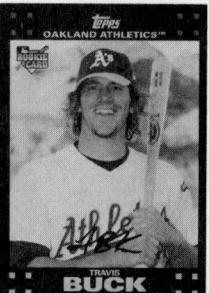

NM/M
Complete Set (330): 40.00
Common Player: .10
Pack (10): 2.00

Box (36):		65.00
1	Tony Armas Jr.	.10
2	Shannon Stewart	.10
3	Jason Marquis	.10
4	Josh Wilson	.10
5	Steve Trachsel	.10
6	J.D. Drew	.25
7	Ronnie Belliard	.10
8	Trot Nixon	.10
9	Adam LaRoche	.25
10	Mark Loretta	.10
11	Matt Morris	.10
12	Marlon Anderson	.10
13	Jorge Julio	.10
14	Brady Clark	.10
15	David Wells	.10
16	Francisco Rosario	.10
17	Jason Ellison	.10
18	Adam Jones	.10
19	Russell Branyan	.10
20	Rob Bowen	.10
21	J.D. Durbin	.10
22	Jeff Salazar	.10
23	Tadahito Iguchi	.10
24	Brad Hennessey	.10
25	Mark Hendrickson	.10
26	Kameron Loe	.10
27	Yusmeiro Petit	.10
28	Olmedo Saenz	.10
29	Carlos Silva	.10
30	Kevin Frandsen	.10
31	Tony Pena	.10
32	Russ Ortiz	.10
33	Hong-Chih Kuo	.10
34	Paul McAnulty	.10
35	Hiram Bocachica	.10
36	Justin Germano	.10
37	Jason Simontacchi	.10
38	Jose Cruz	.10
39	Wilfredo Ledezma	.10
40	Chris Denorfia	.10
41	Ryan Langerhans	.10
42	Chris Snelling	.10
43	Ubaldo Jimenez	.10
44	Scott Spiezio	.10
45	Byung-Hyun Kim	.10
46	Brandon Lyon	.10
47	Scott Hairston	.10
48	Chad Durbin	.10
49	Sammy Sosa	.50
50	Jason Smith	.10
51	Zack Greinke	.10
52	Armando Benitez	.10
53	Randy Messenger	.10
54	Mark Teixeira	.50
55	Mike Maroth	.10
56	Jamie Burke	.10
57	Carlos Marmol	.10
58	David Weathers	.10
59	Ryan Doumit	.10
60	Michael Barrett	.10
61	Shawn Chacon	.10
62	Mike Fontenot	.10
63	Cesar Izturis	.10
64	Cliff Floyd	.10
65	Angel Pagan	.10
66	Aaron Miles	.10
67	Tony Graffanino	.10
68	Kevin Mench	.10
69	Claudio Vargas	.10
70	Jose Capellan	.10
71	A.J. Pierzynski	.10
72	Darin Erstad	.10
73	Boone Logan	.10
74	Luis Castillo	.10
75	Marcus Thames	.10
76	Neifi Perez	.10
77	Esteban German	.10
78	Tony Pena	.10
79	Adam Wainwright	.25
80	Reggie Sanders	.10
81	Kelly Shoppach	.10
82	Rafael Betancourt	.10
83	Tom Mastny	.10
84	Kyle Farnsworth	.10
85	Rick Ankiel	.25
86	Kevin Thompson	.10
87	Jeff Karstens	.10
88	Eric Hinske	.10
89	Doug Mirabelli	.10
90	Julian Tavarez	.10
91	Carlos Pena	.25
92	Brendan Harris	.10
93	Chris Sampson	.10
94	Al Reyes	.10
95	Dmitri Young	.10
96	Jason Bergmann	.10
97	Shawn Hill	.10
98	Greg Dobbs	.10
99	Carlos Ruiz	.10
100	Abraham Nunez	.10
100b	Jacoby Ellsbury **(RC)**	100.00
101	Jayson Werth	.10
102	Adam Eaton	.10
103	Antonio Alfonseca	.10
104	Jorge Sosa	.10
105	Ramon Castro	.10
106	Ruben Gotay	.10
107	Damion Easley	.10
108	David Newhan	.10
109	Jason Wood	.10
110	Reggie Abercrombie	.10
111	Kevin Gregg	.10
112	Henry Owens	.10
113	Willie Harris	.10
114	Peter Orr	.10
115	Casey Janssen	.10
116	Jason Frasor	.10
117	Jeremy Accardo	.10
118	John McDonald	.10
119	Matt Stairs	.10
120	Jason Phillips	.10
121	Justin Duchscherer	.10
122	Rich Harden	.10
123	Jack Cust	.10
124	Lenny DiNardo	.10
125	Joe Kennedy	.10
126	Chad Gaudin	.10
127	Marco Scutaro	.10
128	Brad Thompson	.10
129	Dustin Moseley	.10
130	Eric Gagne	.10
131	Marlon Byrd	.10
132	Scot Shields	.10
133	Victor Diaz	.10
134	Reggie Willits	.25
135	Jose Molina	.10
136	Ramon Vazquez	.10
137	Erick Aybar	.10
138	Sean Marshall	.25
139	Casey Kotchman	.25
140	Ryan Spilborghs	.10
141	Cameron Maybin **RC**	2.50
142	Jeremy Guthrie	.10
143	Jeff Baker	.10
144	Edwin Jackson	.10
145	Macay McBride	.10
146	Freddie Bynum	.10
147	Eric Patterson	.10
148	Dustin McGowan	.10
149	Homer Bailey **(RC)**	1.00
150	Ryan Braun **(RC)**	2.50
151	Tony Abreu **RC**	.50
152	Tyler Clippard **(RC)**	.50
153	Mark Reynolds **RC**	1.00
154	Jesse Litsch **RC**	.50
155	Carlos Gomez **RC**	2.00
156	Matt DeSalvo **(RC)**	.50
157	Andy LaRoche **(RC)**	1.00
158	Tim Lincecum **RC**	5.00
159	Jarrod Saltalamacchia **(RC)**	.50
160	Hunter Pence **(RC)**	2.00
161	Brandon Wood **(RC)**	.50
162	Phil Hughes **(RC)**	2.00
163	Rocky Cherry **RC**	.50
164	Chase Wright **RC**	.50
165	Dallas Braden **RC**	.50
166	Felix Pie **(RC)**	.50
167	Zach McClellan **RC**	.50
168	Rick Vanden Hurk **RC**	.50
169	Micah Owings **(RC)**	.50
170	Jon Coutlangus **(RC)**	.25
171	Andrew Sonnanstine **RC**	.50
172	Yunel Escobar **(RC)**	.25
173	Kevin Slowey **(RC)**	.50
174	Curtis Thigpen **(RC)**	.25
175	Masumi Kuwata **RC**	2.00
176	Kurt Suzuki **(RC)**	.50
177	Travis Buck **(RC)**	.25
178	Matt Lindstrom **(RC)**	.25
179	Jesus Flores **RC**	.50
180	Joakim Soria **RC**	.50
181	Nathan Haynes **RC**	.25
182	Matthew Brown **RC**	.50
183	Travis Metcalf **RC**	.50
184	Yovani Gallardo **(RC)**	1.00
185	Nate Schierholtz **(RC)**	.25
186	Kyle Kendrick **RC**	1.00
187	Kevin Melillo **(RC)**	.25
188	Ryan Rowland-Smith	.25
189	Lee Gronkiewicz **RC**	.50
190	Eulogio De La Cruz **(RC)**	.25
191	Brett Carroll **RC**	.50
192	Terry Evans **RC**	.50
193	Chase Headley **(RC)**	.50
194	Guillermo Rodriguez **RC**	.50
195	Marcus McBeth **(RC)**	.25
196	Brian Wolfe **(RC)**	.25
197	Troy Cate **RC**	.50
198	Mike Zagurski **RC**	.50
199	Yoel Hernandez	.25
200	Brad Salmon **RC**	.50
201	Alberto Arias **RC**	.50
202	Danny Putnam **(RC)**	.25
203	Jamie Vermilyea **RC**	.50
204	Kyle Lohse	.10
205	Sammy Sosa	.25
206	Tom Glavine	.25
207	Prince Fielder	.50
208	Mark Buehrle	.10
209	Troy Tulowitzki	1.00
210	Daisuke Matsuzaka **RC**	5.00
211	Randy Johnson	.50
212	Justin Verlander	.25
213	Trevor Hoffman	.10
214	Alex Rodriguez	1.00
215	Ivan Rodriguez	.25
216	David Ortiz	.50
217	Placido Polanco	.10
218	Derek Jeter	1.00
219	Alex Rodriguez	1.00
220	Vladimir Guerrero	.50
221	Magglio Ordonez	.25
222	Ichiro Suzuki	.75
223	Russell Martin	.25
224	Prince Fielder	.50
225	Chase Utley	.50
226	Jose Reyes	.50
227	David Wright	.50
228	Carlos Beltran	.25
229	Barry Bonds	1.00
230	Ken Griffey Jr.	.75
231	Torii Hunter	.25
232	Jonathan Papelbon	.25
233	J.J. Putz	.10
234	Francisco Rodriguez	.10
235	C.C. Sabathia	.25
236	Johan Santana	.50
237	Justin Verlander	.25
238	Francisco Cordero	.10
239	Mike Lowell	.25
240	Cole Hamels	.25
241	Trevor Hoffman	.10
242	Manny Ramirez	.50
243	Jake Peavy	.25
244	Brad Penny	.10
245	Takashi Saito	.10
246	Ben Sheets	.25
247	Hideki Okajima	.25
248	Roy Oswalt	.25
249	Billy Wagner	.10
250	Carl Crawford	.25
251	Chris Young	.10
252	Brian McCann	.10
253	Derrek Lee	.25
254	Albert Pujols	1.00
255	Dmitri Young	.10
256	Orlando Hudson	.10
257	J.J. Hardy	.25
258	Miguel Cabrera	.50
259	Freddy Sanchez	.10
260	Matt Holliday	.25
261	Carlos Lee	.25
262	Aaron Rowand	.10
263	Alfonso Soriano	.50
264	Victor Martinez	.25
265	Jorge Posada	.25
266	Justin Morneau	.25
267	Brian Roberts	.25
268	Carlos Guillen	.10
269	Grady Sizemore	.50
270	Josh Beckett	.25
271	Danny Haren	.10
272	Bobby Jenks	.10
273	John Lackey	.10
274	Gil Meche	.10
275	Mike Fontenot, Khalil Greene	.10
276	Alex Rodriguez, Russell Martin	.50
277	Troy Tulowitzki, Jose Reyes	.50
278	Jorge Posada, Derek Jeter, Alex Rodriguez	1.00
279	Chase Utley, Ichiro Suzuki	.50
280	Carl Crawford, Carlos Guillen	.10
281	Cole Hamels, Russell Martin	.25
282	Jonathan Papelbon, Jorge Posada	.25
283	Carl Crawford, Victor Martinez	.25
284	Alfonso Soriano, J.J. Hardy	.25
285	Justin Morneau	.25
286	Prince Fielder	.50
287	Alex Rios	.25
288	Vladimir Guerrero	.50
289	Albert Pujols	1.00
290	Ryan Howard	.75
291	Magglio Ordonez	.25
292	Matt Holliday	.25
293	Wilson Betemit	.10
294	Todd Wellemeyer	.10
295	Scott Baker	.10
296	Edgar Gonzalez	.10
297	J.P. Howell	.10
298	Shaun Marcum	.10
299	Edinson Volquez	.50
300	Kason Gabbard	.10
301	Bob Howry	.10
302	J.A. Happ	.10
303	Scott Feldman	.10
304	D'Angelo Jimenez	.10
305	Orlando Palmeiro	.10
306	Paul Bako	.10
307	Kyle Davies	.10
308	Gabe Gross	.10
309	John Wasdin	.10
310	Jon Knott	.10
311	Josh Phelps	.10
312	Joba Chamberlain **RC**	8.00
312	Joba Chamberlain/ Reverse Negative	150.00
313	Octavio Dotel	.10
314	Craig Monroe	.10
315	Edward Mujica	.10
316	Brandon Watson	.10
317	Chris Schroder	.10
318	Scott Proctor	.10
319	Ty Wigginton	.10
320	Troy Percival	.10
321	Scott Linebrink	.10
322	David Murphy	.10
323	Jorge Cantu	.10
324	Dan Wheeler	.10
325	Jason Kendall	.10
326	Milton Bradley	.10
327	Justin Upton **RC**	3.00
328	Kenny Lofton	.10
329	Roger Clemens	1.00
330	Brian Burres	.10
SQ1	Poley Walnuts	40.00

1st Edition

1st Edition: 5-10X
Hobby Exclusive 1:36

Copper

Copper: 25-50X
Production 56 Sets

Gold

Gold: 8-15X
Production 2,007 Sets

Platinum

No Pricing
Production One Set

Red Back

Red Back (1-330): 1-2.5X
Inserted 2:Hobby, 10:HTA

Printing Plates

Production one set per color.

All-Star Stitches

		NM/M
Common Player:		8.00
Inserted 1:45		
Patch:		No Pricing
Production 10 Sets		
AIR	Alex Rios	10.00
AP	Albert Pujols	25.00
AR	Alex Rodriguez	25.00
ARR	Aaron Rowand	10.00
BF	Brian Fuentes	8.00
BJ	Bobby Jenks	10.00
BM	Brian McCann	15.00
BR	Brian Roberts	8.00
BS	Ben Sheets	10.00
BW	Brandon Webb	10.00
CB	Carlos Beltran	10.00
CC	Carl Crawford	10.00
CH	Cole Hamels	15.00
CL	Carlos Lee	10.00
CS	C.C. Sabathia	15.00
CU	Chase Utley	15.00
CY	Chris Young	8.00
DO	David Ortiz	15.00
DW	David Wright	15.00
DY	Dmitri Young	8.00
FR	Francisco Rodriguez	8.00
FC	Francisco Cordero	8.00
FS	Freddy Sanchez	10.00
GM	Gil Meche	8.00
GS	Grady Sizemore	15.00
HO	Hideki Okajima	20.00
IR	Ivan Rodriguez	10.00
IS	Ichiro Suzuki	30.00
JB	Josh Beckett	20.00
JEP	Jake Peavy	10.00
JH	J.J. Hardy	10.00
JL	John Lackey	10.00
JM	Justin Morneau	10.00
JP	J.J. Putz	8.00
JR	Jose Reyes	20.00
JRP	Jorge Posada	10.00
JRV	Jose Valverde	8.00
JS	Johan Santana	10.00
JV	Justin Verlander	10.00
MH	Matt Holliday	10.00
ML	Mike Lowell	10.00
MR	Manny Ramirez	15.00
OH	Orlando Hudson	8.00
PF	Prince Fielder	15.00
RH	Ryan Howard	20.00
RM	Russell Martin	15.00
RO	Roy Oswalt	10.00
TH	Torii Hunter	10.00
TS	Takashi Saito	15.00
TWH	Trevor Hoffman	8.00
VM	Victor Martinez	10.00

All-Star Dual Stitches

Production 25 Sets
No Pricing

All-Star Triple Stitches

Production 25 Sets
No Pricing

A-Rod Road to 500

NM/M
A-Rod (376-400): 3.00

A-Rod Road to 500 Autographs
Production One Set

Barry Bonds Home Run History

NM/M
Common Bonds (735-756): 3.00
Inserted 1:12

Barry Bonds Home Run King

NM/M
Inserted 1:36
HRK Barry Bonds 5.00

Barry Bonds Home Run King Relic
NM/M
Production 756
HRK Barry Bonds 50.00

Barry Bonds Home Run King Relic Auto.
Production 20

Chrome
		NM/M
Common Player:		5.00
Production 415 Sets		
1	Homer Bailey	10.00
2	Ryan Braun	25.00
3	Tony Abreu	5.00
4	Tyler Clippard	8.00
5	Mark Reynolds	10.00
6	Jesse Litsch	5.00
7	Carlos Gomez	15.00
8	Matt DeSalvo	5.00
9	Andy LaRoche	10.00
10	Tim Lincecum	20.00
11	Jarrod Saltalamacchia	15.00
12	Hunter Pence	20.00
13	Brandon Wood	8.00
14	Phil Hughes	10.00
15	Rocky Cherry	5.00
16	Chase Wright	5.00
17	Dallas Braden	5.00
18	Felix Pie	5.00
19	Zach McClellan	5.00
20	Rick Vanden Hurk	8.00
21	Micah Owings	5.00
22	Jon Coutlangus	5.00
23	Andrew Sonnanstine	5.00
24	Yunel Escobar	5.00
25	Kevin Slowey	10.00
26	Curtis Thigpen	5.00
27	Masumi Kuwata	15.00
28	Kurt Suzuki	5.00
29	Travis Buck	5.00
30	Matt Lindstrom	5.00
31	Jesus Flores	5.00
32	Joakim Soria	5.00
33	Nathan Haynes	5.00
34	Matthew Brown	5.00
35	Travis Metcalf	5.00
36	Yovani Gallardo	8.00
37	Nate Schierholtz	5.00
38	Kyle Kendrick	10.00
39	Kevin Melillo	5.00
40	Cameron Maybin	25.00
41	Lee Gronkiewicz	5.00
42	Eulogio De La Cruz	5.00
43	Brett Carroll	5.00
44	Terry Evans	5.00
45	Chase Headley	5.00
46	Guillermo Rodriguez	5.00
47	Marcus McBeth	5.00
48	Brian Wolfe	5.00
49	Troy Cate	5.00
50	Justin Upton	30.00
51	Joba Chamberlain	60.00
52	Brad Salmon	5.00
53	Alberto Arias	5.00
54	Danny Putnam	5.00
55	Jamie Vermilyea	5.00

Generation Now

NM/M
All Ryan Zimmerman's: 1.00
All Justin Verlander's: 1.00
All Prince Fielder's: 2.00
All Ian Kinsler's: 1.00
All Kenji Johjima's: 1.00
All Jonathan Papelbon's: 1.00
All Jose Reyes': 2.00
All Curtis Granderson's: 1.00
All Josh Barfield's: .50

Generation Now Autographs
Production One Set

Highlights Autographs
NM/M
Some not priced due to scarcity
DW	David Wright	60.00
RH	Ryan Howard	60.00
AR	Alex Rodriguez	200.00
JT	Jim Thome	40.00
AP	Albert Pujols	200.00
AJ	Andruw Jones	25.00
AG	Alex Gordon	35.00
GS	Gary Sheffield	30.00
JS	Jarrod Saltalamacchia	20.00
CJ	Conor Jackson	15.00
RC	Robinson Cano	30.00
PF	Prince Fielder	40.00
AE	Andre Ethier	15.00
JR	Jimmy Rollins	40.00
AL	Anthony Lerew	10.00
FC	Francisco Cordero	15.00
BB	Brian Bruney	10.00
AH	Aaron Heilman	10.00
CS	C.C. Sabathia	20.00
TT	Troy Tulowitzki	25.00
RB	Rod Barajas	10.00
RW	Ron Washington	10.00
AC	Asdrubal Cabrera	15.00
DE	Damion Easley	10.00
MC	Miguel Cairo	10.00

Mickey Mantle Home Run History

NM/M
Common Mantle HR History: 2.00
Inserted 1:9 Hobby

Mickey Mantle Home Run History Relics
NM/M
Common Mantle: 125.00
Production Seven Sets

Mickey Mantle Story

NM/M
Complete Set (15): 30.00
Common Mantle: 3.00
Inserted 1:18

Target
Common Mantle
Target Exclusive
No Pricing

World Series Watch

NM/M
Inserted 1:36
1	New York Mets	1.00
2	Detroit Tigers	1.00
3	Boston Red Sox	5.00
4	Milwaukee Brewers	1.00
5	Cleveland Indians	1.00
6	Angels	1.00
7	San Diego Padres	1.00
8	Los Angeles Dodgers	1.00
9	Philadelphia Phillies	1.00
10	Chicago Cubs	1.00
11	St. Louis Cardinals	1.00
12	Arizona Diamondbacks	1.00
13	New York Yankees	1.00
14	Seattle Mariners	1.00
15	Atlanta Braves	1.00

1954 Mickey Mantle Reprint Relic
Production 54
No Pricing

2007 Topps Allen & Ginter

NM/M
Complete Set (390):
Common Player: .25
Mini Exclusives (351-390): No Pricing
Inserted in Rip Cards
Common SP: 2.00
Inserted 1:2
Pack (8): 5.00
Box (24): 110.00
1	Ryan Howard	3.00
2	Mike Gonzalez	.25
3	Austin Kearns	.25
4	Josh Hamilton (RC)	.50
5	Stephen Drew/SP	2.00
6	Matt Murton	.25
7	Mickey Mantle	5.00
8	Howie Kendrick	.25
9	Alexander Graham Bell	.25
10	Jason Bay	.50
11	Hank Blalock	.50
12	Johan Santana	.75
13	Eleanor Roosevelt	.25
14	Kei Igawa RC	1.00
15	Jeff Francoeur	.50
16	Carl Crawford	.50
17	Jhonny Peralta	.25
18	Mariano Rivera	.50
19	Mario Andretti	.25
20	Vladimir Guerrero	.75
21	Adam Wainwright	.50
22	Huston Street	.25
23	Cael Sanderson	.25
24	Susan B. Anthony	.25
25	Jay Payton	.25
26	P.T. Barnum	.25
27	Scott Podsednik	.25
28	Willie Randolph	.25
29	Sean Casey	.25
30	Eiffel Tower	.25
31	Kenji Johjima	.25
32	Felix Hernandez	.50
33	Elijah Dukes RC	1.00
34	Mark Grudzielanek	.25
35	J.D. Drew	.25
36	Kevin Kouzmanoff (RC)	.50
37	Jonathan Papelbon	.50
38	Bobby Crosby	.25
39	Brooklyn Bridge	.25
40	Adam Dunn	.50
41	Lyle Overbay	.25
42	Brian Fuentes	.25
43	Scott Rolen/SP	3.00
44	Matt Lindstrom (RC)	.50
45	Carlos Zambrano	.50
46	Cole Hamels	.50
47	Matthew Kemp	.25
48	Gary Matthews/SP	2.00
49	J.J. Putz	.25
50	Albert Pujols	2.00
51	Danny Haren	.25
52	Aaron Harang	.25
53	Ferris Wheel	.25
54	Juan Rivera	.25
55	Ken Griffey Jr.	1.50
56	Chien-Ming Wang	1.00
57	Sean Henn (RC)	.50
58	Mike Mussina/SP	3.00
59	Ian Snell	.25
60	Josh Barfield	.25
61	Justin Morneau	.75
62	Dwight D. Eisenhower	.25
63	Bengie Molina/SP	2.00
64	Brett Myers	.25
65	Andy Marte	.25
66	Bill Hall	.25
67	Ryan Shealy	.25
68	Joe Scott	.25
69	Mike Rabelo RC	.50
70	Jermaine Dye	.25
71	Andre Ethier	.25
72	Bruce Lee	1.00
73	Nick Punto	.25
74	Ervin Santana	.25
75	Troy Tulowitzki (RC)	1.00
76	Garret Anderson	.25
77	Ryan Freel	.25
78	Carlos Guillen	.50
79	John Smoltz	.50
80	Chase Utley	.75
81	Mike Sweeney	.25
82	Joe Frazier	1.00
83	Brad Lidge	.25
84	Casey Blake	.25
85	Ivan Rodriguez	.50
86	Roy Oswalt	.25
87	Akinori Iwamura RC	2.00
88	Francisco Rodriguez	.25
89	John Lackey	.25
90	Miguel Cabrera	.75
91	Kevin Mench	.25
92	Victor Martinez	.50
93	Chad Tracy	.25
94	Charlie Manuel	.25
95	Hanley Ramirez	.75
96	Dontrelle Willis	.50
97	Doug Slaten RC	.25
98	Noah Lowry	.25
99	Shawn Green	.25
100	David Ortiz	1.00
101	Mark Reynolds RC	2.00
102	Preston Wilson	.25
103	Mohandas Gandhi	.25
104	Jeff Kent	.50
105	Lance Berkman	.50
106	C.C. Sabathia	.50
107	Jason Varitek/SP	3.00
108	Mark Twain	.25
109	Melvin Mora	.25
110	Michael Young/SP	2.00
111	Scott Hatteberg	.25
112	Erik Bedard	.50
113	Sitting Bull	.25
114	Homer Bailey (RC)	1.00
115	Mark Teahen	.25
116	Ryan Braun (RC)	3.00
117	John Miles	.25
118	Coco Crisp	.25
119	Hunter Pence/SP (RC)	4.00
120	Delmon Young (RC)	1.00
121	Aramis Ramirez	.50
122	Magglio Ordonez	.50
123	Tadahito Iguchi	.25
124	Mark Selby	.25

125	Gil Meche	.25
126	Curt Schilling	.75
127	Brandon Phillips	.25
128	Milton Bradley	.25
129	Craig Monroe	.25
130	Jason Schmidt/SP	2.00
131	Nick Markakis	.50
132	Paul Konerko	.25
133	Carlos Gomez RC	1.50
134	Garrett Atkins	.25
135	Jered Weaver	.50
136	Edgar Renteria	.50
137	Jason Isringhausen/SP	2.00
138	Ray Durham	.25
139	Bob Baffert	.25
140	Nick Swisher	.50
141	Brian McCann	.50
142	Orlando Hudson	.25
143	Brian Bannister	.25
144	Manny Acta	.25
145	Jose Vidro	.25
146	Carlos Quentin	.25
147	Billy Butler (RC)	1.00
148	Kenny Rogers	.25
149	Tom Gordon	.25
150	Derek Jeter	2.00
151	Bob Wickman	.25
152	Carlos Lee/SP	2.00
153	Willy Taveras	.25
154	Paul LoDuca	.25
155	Ben Sheets	.50
156	Brian Roberts	.50
157	Freddy Adu	.25
158	Jason Kendall	.25
159	Michael Barrett/SP	2.00
160	Frank Thomas	.75
161	Manny Ramirez	.75
162	Stanley Glenn	.25
163	Robinson Cano	.50
164	Phil Hughes (RC)	1.50
165	Joe Mauer	.50
166	Derrek Lee	.75
167	Jeff Weaver	.25
168	Joe Smith RC	.50
169	Louis Pasteur	.50
170	Gary Sheffield	.50
171	Luis Castillo	.25
172	Joe Torre	.50
173	Andy LaRoche (RC)	.50
174	Jamie Fischer	.50
175	Carlos Beltran	.50
176	Bronson Arroyo	.25
177	Rafael Furcal	.50
178	Juan Pierre/SP	2.00
179	Matt Cain	.50
180	Alfonso Soriano	.75
181	Joe Borowski	.25
182	Conor Jackson	.25
183	Groundhog Day	.25
184	Pat Burrell	.25
185	Troy Glaus	.50
186	Joel Zumaya	.25
187	Russell Martin	.50
188	Josh Willingham	.25
189	Jarrod Saltalamacchia (RC)	.50
190	Scott Kazmir	.50
191	Jeremy Hermida	.25
192	Tower Bridge	.50
193	Rich Hill/SP	2.00
194	Francisco Cordero/SP	2.00
195	Mike Piazza	1.00
196	Brad Ausmus	.25
197	Greg Louganis	.25
198	Frank Catalanotto	.25
199	Alejandro De Aza RC	1.00
200	David Wright	1.00
201	Freddy Sanchez	.25
202	Shea Hillenbrand	.25
203	Justin Verlander/SP	3.00
204	Alex Gordon RC	4.00
205	Jimmy Rollins	.50
206	Mike Napoli	.25
207	Chris Burke	.25
208	Chipper Jones	.75
209	Randy Johnson	.75
210	Daisuke Matsuzaka RC	5.00
211	Orlando Cabrera	.25
212	B.J. Upton	.50
213	Lou Piniella	.25
214	Mike Cameron	.25
215	Luis Gonzalez	.25
216	Rickie Weeks	.25
217	Hideki Okajima RC	1.00
218	Johnny Estrada	.25
219	Dan Uggla/SP	2.00
220	Ryan Zimmerman	.25
221	Tony Gwynn Jr.	.25
222	Rocco Baldelli/SP	2.00
223	Xavier Nady	.25
224	Josh Bard/SP	2.00
225	Raul Ibanez	.25
226	Chris Carpenter	.25
227	Matt DeSalvo (RC)	.50
228	Jack the Ripper	.25
229	Eric Chavez	.25
230	Jose Reyes	1.00
231	Glen Perkins (RC)	.50
232	Gregg Zaun	.25
233	Jim Thome	.25
234	Joe Crede	.25
235	Barry Zito	.50
236	Yoel Hernandez RC	1.00
237	Kelly Johnson	.25
238	Chris Young	.25
239	Fyodor Dostoevsky	.25
240	Miguel Tejada	.50
241	Doug Mientkiewicz	.25
242	Bobby Jenks	.25
243	Brad Hawpe/SP	2.00
244	Jay Marshall RC	.50
245	Brad Penny	.25
246	Johnny Damon	.75
247	Dave Roberts	.25
248	Ron Washington	.25
249	Mike Aponte	.25
250	Brandon Webb	.50
251	Andy Pettitte	.50
252	Bud Black	.25
253	Mike Cuddyer	.25
254	Chris Stewart RC	.50
255	Mark Teixeira	.75
256	Hideki Matsui	1.50
257	Curtis Granderson	.25
258	A.J. Pierzynski	.25
259	Tony LaRussa	.25
260	Andruw Jones	.75
261	Torii Hunter	.50
262	Mark Loretta	.25
263	Jim Edmonds/SP	2.00
264	Aaron Rowand	.25
265	Roy Halladay	.50
266	Freddy Garcia	.25
267	Reggie Sanders	.25
268	Washington Monument	.25
269	Franklin D. Roosevelt	.50
270	Alex Rodriguez	2.00
271	Wes Helms	.25
272	Mia Hamm	.50
273	Jorge Posada	.50
274	Tim Lincecum RC	5.00
275	Bobby Abreu	.50
276	Zachary Duke	.25
277	Carlos Delgado	.50
278	Julio Juarez	.25
279	Brandon Inge	.25
280	Todd Helton	.50
281	Marcus Giles	.25
282	Josh Johnson	.25
283	Chris Capuano	.25
284	B.J. Ryan	.25
285	Nick Johnson	.25
286	Khalil Greene	.25
287	Travis Hafner	.50
288	Ted Lilly	.25
289	Jim Leyland	.25
290	Prince Fielder	1.00
291	Trevor Hoffman	.25
292	Brian Giles	.25
293	Omar Vizquel	.25
294	Julio Lugo	.25
295	Jake Peavy	.50
296	Adrian Beltre	.25
297	Josh Beckett	.50
298	Harry S. Truman	.50
299	Mark Buehrle	.25
300	Ichiro Suzuki	1.50
301	Chris Duncan/SP	2.00
302	Augie Garrido/SP	2.00
303	Tyler Clippard/SP (RC)	2.00
304	Ramon Hernandez	.25
305	Jeremy Bonderman	.50
306	Morgan Ensberg/SP	2.00
307	J.J. Hardy/SP	2.00
308	Mark Zupan/SP	2.00
309	Laila Ali/SP	4.00
310	Greg Maddux/SP	4.00
311	David Ross	.25
312	Chris Duffy	.25
313	Moises Alou	.50
314	Yadier Molina	.25
315	Corey Patterson	.25
316	Dan O'Brien/SP	2.00
317	Michael Bourn/SP (RC)	2.00
318	Jonny Gomes/SP	2.00
319	Ken Jennings/SP	2.00
320	Barry Bonds/SP	5.00
321	Gary Hall Jr./SP	2.00
322	Kerri Walsh/SP	2.00
323	Craig Biggio	.50
324	Ian Kinsler	.25
325	Grady Sizemore/SP	3.00
326	Alex Rios/SP	3.00
327	Ted Toles/SP	2.00
328	Jason Jennings	.25
329	Vernon Wells	.50
330	Bob Geren/SP	2.00
331	Dennis Rodman/SP	2.00
332	Tom Glavine	.50
333	Pedro Martinez	.75
334	Gustavo Molina/SP RC	3.00
335	Bartolo Colon/SP	2.00
336	Misty May-Treanor/SP	2.00
337	Randy Winn	.25
338	Eric Byrnes	.50
339	Jason McElwain/SP	2.00
340	Placido Polanco/SP	2.00
341	Adrian Gonzalez	.50
342	Chad Coredo	.25
343	Jeff Francis	.25
344	Lastings Milledge	.25
345	Sammy Sosa/SP	3.00
346	Jacque Jones	.25
347	Anibal Sanchez	.25
348	Roger Clemens/SP	4.00
349	Jesse Litsch/SP RC	2.00
350	Adam LaRoche/SP	2.00

Mini

Mini:	2-3X
Mini (351-390):	No Pricing
#'s 351-390 Inserted in Rip Cards	
Allen & Ginter Back:	3-4X
Inserted 1:5	
Black Border:	4-6X
Inserted 1:10	
No Number:	10-20X
Production 50 Sets	
Bazooka Mini:	No Pricing
Production 25 Sets	
Wood:	No Pricing
Production One Set	

Printing Plates

Production one set per color.

Autographs

		NM/M
Short-prints are noted.		
Red Ink:		No Pricing
Production 10 Sets		
CS	Cael Sanderson/200	100.00
MS	Mark Selby/200	50.00
SJF	Joe Frazier/120	250.00
DR	Dennis Rodman/200	125.00
MZ	Mark Zupan/200	50.00
FA	Freddy Adu/200	125.00
BB	Bob Baffert/200	120.00
TT	Ted Toles/200	100.00
KJ	Ken Jennings/200	120.00
GH	Gary Hall Jr./200	80.00
DO	Dan O'Brien/200	75.00
JF	Jamie Fischer/200	40.00
GL	Greg Louganis/200	50.00
MA	Mike Aponte/200	40.00
JJ	Julio Juarez/200	40.00
KW	Kerri Walsh/200	100.00
LA	Laila Ali/200	120.00
TS	Tommie Smith/200	120.00
MGA	Mario Andretti/200	150.00
AG	Augie Garrido/200	100.00
JMC	Jason McElwain/200	60.00
SG	Stanley Glenn/200	125.00
JMM	John Miles/200	125.00
JBS	Joe Scott/200	120.00
MH	Mia Hamm/200	220.00
MMT	Misty May-Treanor/200	100.00
BC	Brian Cashman/200	200.00
CMW	Chien-Ming Wang/200	250.00
AI	Akinori Iwamura	40.00
RH	Ryan Howard/100	125.00
HR	Hanley Ramirez	50.00
HK	Howie Kendrick	25.00
AR	Alex Rodriguez/225	300.00
DW	David Wright/200	120.00
RM	Russell Martin	40.00
AE	Andre Ethier	25.00
JT	Jim Thome/100	100.00
JM	Justin Morneau	40.00
ES	Ervin Santana	25.00
BH	Bill Hall	30.00
CH	Cole Hamels	75.00
MEI	Maicer Izturis	20.00
CG	Curtis Granderson	50.00
AG2	Adrian Gonzalez	25.00
TT	Troy Tulowitzki	30.00
VW	Vernon Wells	25.00
JS	Johan Santana/100	150.00
JP	Jonathan Papelbon	50.00
MC	Miguel Cabrera/100	60.00
BPB	Brian Bannister	25.00
TH	Torii Hunter	30.00
RZ	Ryan Zimmerman	40.00
NM	Nicholas Markakis	40.00
JH	Jeremy Hermida	20.00
MN	Mike Napoli	25.00
NL	Nook Logan	20.00

Cut Signatures

Production One Set
No Pricing

Dick Perez Sketch Cards

		NM/M
Complete Set (30):		15.00
Common Player:		.50
Inserted 1:1		
Dick Perez Originals:		No Pricing
Production One Set		
1	Brandon Webb	.50
2	Chipper Jones	1.00
3	Nick Markakis	.50
4	Daisuke Matsuzaka	2.00
5	Alfonso Soriano	1.00
6	Jermaine Dye	.50
7	Adam Dunn	.50
8	Grady Sizemore	1.00
9	Troy Tulowitzki	.50
10	Gary Sheffield	.75
11	Hanley Ramirez	.75
12	Carlos Lee	.50
13	Mark Teahen	.50
14	Gary Matthews	.50
15	Andre Ethier	.50
16	Prince Fielder	1.50
17	Joe Mauer	.75
18	Jose Reyes	1.00
19	Derek Jeter	2.00
20	Nick Swisher	.50
21	Ryan Howard	1.50
22	Freddy Sanchez	.50
23	Greg Maddux	1.50
24	Raul Ibanez	.50
25	Barry Zito	.50
26	Jim Edmonds	.50
27	Delmon Young	.50
28	Michael Young	.50
29	Roy Halladay	.50
30	Ryan Zimmerman	.75

Mini Flags

	NM/M
Common Card:	2.00
1 Angola	2.00
2 Argentina	2.00
3 Australia	2.00
4 Austria	2.00
5 Belgium	2.00
6 Brazil	2.00
7 Bulgaria	2.00
8 Canada	2.00
9 Chile	2.00
10 China	2.00
11 Colombia	2.00
12 Costa Rica	2.00
13 Denmark	2.00
14 Dominican Republic	2.00
15 Ecuador	2.00
16 Egypt	2.00
17 France	2.00
18 Germany	2.00
19 Greece	2.00
20 Greenland	2.00
21 Honduras	2.00
22 Iceland	2.00
23 India	2.00
24 Indonesia	2.00
25 Ireland	2.00
26 Israel	2.00
27 Italy	2.00
28 Ivory Coast	2.00
29 Jamaica	2.00
30 Japan	2.00
31 Kenya	2.00
32 Mexico	2.00
33 Morocco	2.00
34 Netherlands	2.00
35 Nigeria	2.00
36 Norway	2.00
37 Panama	2.00
38 Peru	2.00
39 Phillipines	2.00
40 Portugal	2.00
41 Puerto Rico	2.00
42 Russian Federation	2.00
43 Spain	2.00
44 Switzerland	2.00
45 Taiwan	2.00
46 Thailand	2.00
47 Turkey	2.00
48 United Arab Emirates	2.00
49 United Kingdom	2.00
50 United States	2.00

Mini Snakes

	NM/M
Common Mini Snake:	25.00
1 Arizona Coral Snake	25.00
2 Copperhead	25.00
3 Black Mamba	25.00
4 King Cobra	25.00
5 Cottonmouth	25.00
	25.00

Mini Emperors

	NM/M
Common Emperor:	5.00
1 Julius Caesar	5.00
2 Caesar Augustus	5.00
3 Tiberius	5.00
4 Caligula	5.00
5 Claudius	5.00
6 Nero	5.00
7 Titus	5.00
8 Hadrian	5.00
9 Marcus Aurelius	5.00
10 Septimus Severus	5.00

National Pride Box Loaders

	NM/M
Common Card:	5.00
Inserted 1:Box	
1 Kei Igawa, Daisuke Matsuzaka, Hideki Matsui, Ichiro Suzuki	8.00
2 Hideki Okajima, Akinori Iwamura, Kenji Johjima, Tadahito Iguchi	6.00
3 Bobby Abreu, Miguel Cabrera, Felix Hernandez, Johan Santana	5.00
4 Shin-Soo Choo, Chan Ho Park, Byung-Hyun Kim, Jae-Kuk Ryu	5.00
5 Jason Bay, Russell Martin, Justin Morneau, Rich Harden	6.00
6 Hanley Ramirez, Manny Ramirez, Aramis Ramirez, Vladimir Guerrero	8.00
7 Jose Reyes, Pedro Martinez, David Ortiz, Albert Pujols	8.00
8 Carlos Beltran, Carlos Delgado, Ivan Rodriguez, Jorge Posada	6.00
9 Prince Fielder, Alex Rodriguez, Ryan Howard, David Wright	8.00
10 Brandon Webb, Justin Verlander, Greg Maddux, John Smoltz	5.00

N43 Box Loader

	NM/M
Common Player:	4.00
Inserted 1:Box	
AR Alex Rodriguez	8.00
RH Ryan Howard	6.00
DW David Wright	6.00
IS Ichiro Suzuki	8.00
AP Albert Pujols	8.00
DM Daisuke Matsuzaka	10.00
VG Vladimir Guerrero	4.00
BB Barry Bonds	8.00
PF Prince Fielder	6.00
RZ Ryan Zimmerman	4.00
DJ Ch Felicity's Diamond Jim	15.00
BL Bruce Lee	10.00
MA Mario Andretti	4.00
GL Greg Louganis	4.00
JF Joe Frazier	6.00

N43 Box Loader Autographs

Production 10 Sets
No Pricing

N43 Box Loader Relics

Production 25 Sets
No Pricing

Relics

	NM/M
Common Relic:	5.00
KJ Ken Jennings/250	40.00
JF Jamie Fischer/250	30.00
TS Tommie Smith/250	50.00
KW Kerri Walsh/250	60.00
LA Laila Ali/250	50.00
JJ Julio Juarez/250	25.00
MH Mia Hamm/250	70.00
BL Bruce Lee/250	300.00
DO Dan O'Brien/250	20.00
SJF Joe Frazier/250	80.00
GH Gary Hall Jr./250	50.00
AL Adam LaRoche	8.00
AP Albert Pujols	30.00
AR Aramis Ramirez	8.00
CB Carlos Beltran	8.00
CC Carl Crawford	8.00
CK Casey Kotchman	5.00
EC Eric Chavez	5.00
EG Eric Gagne	8.00
HB Hank Blalock	5.00
HR Hanley Ramirez	8.00
JB Jason Bay	5.00
JG Jason Giambi	8.00
MC1 Miguel Cabrera	10.00
MC2 Miguel Cabrera	10.00
MG Marcus Giles	5.00
MMU Mark Mulder	5.00
MCM Mike Mussina	8.00
MP Mike Piazza	15.00
MR Manny Ramirez	10.00
MT Miguel Tejada	8.00
NS Nick Swisher	5.00
PF Prince Fielder	20.00
PK Paul Konerko	8.00
RC Robinson Cano	20.00
RH Rich Harden	5.00
RW Randy Winn	5.00
SD Stephen Drew	8.00
SP Scott Podsednik	8.00
SR1 Scott Rolen	8.00
SR2 Scott Rolen	8.00
TG Troy Glaus	5.00
VG Vladimir Guerrero	10.00
DAO David Ortiz/250	20.00
AER Alex Rodriguez/250	30.00
BB Barry Bonds/250	35.00
MM Mickey Mantle/250	150.00
BR Brian Roberts	8.00
BZ Barry Zito	5.00
CMS Curt Schilling	10.00
DW Dontrelle Willis	5.00
IR Ivan Rodriguez	8.00
PL Paul LoDuca	5.00
CLC Coco Crisp	8.00
CP Corey Patterson	5.00
CT Chad Tracy	5.00
DL Derrek Lee	8.00
RA Rich Aurilia	5.00
SS Sammy Sosa	10.00
TN Trot Nixon	5.00
BC Brian Cashman/250	35.00
AS Arthur Shorin/50	150.00
KO Keith Olbermann/100	150.00

Rip Cards

	NM/M
Production 10-99	75.00
Prices are for unripped cards	
Ripped cards 10-15 percen.	
1 Grady Sizemore/90	125.00
2 Miguel Cabrera/75	125.00
3 Adam Dunn/95	100.00
4 Jose Reyes/99	150.00
5 Alfonso Soriano/99	125.00
6 Chase Utley/99	125.00
7 Frank Thomas/95	150.00
8 Andruw Jones/95	125.00
9 Nick Markakis/75	100.00
10 Felix Hernandez/99	125.00
11 Jered Weaver/99	125.00
12 Ivan Rodriguez/99	125.00
13 Joe Mauer/99	150.00
14 Derek Jeter/99	180.00
17 Miguel Tejada/95	100.00
18 Vladimir Guerrero/75	125.00
19 Greg Maddux/99	150.00
20 Michael Young/99	100.00
21 Barry Zito/99	100.00
22 Russell Martin/95	150.00
23 Daisuke Matsuzaka/99	180.00
24 Stephen Drew/95	100.00
25 Alex Rodriguez/99	150.00
26 J.D. Drew/99	100.00
27 Paul Konerko/99	100.00
28 Josh Hamilton/99	100.00
29 Mike Piazza/99	125.00
31 Carl Crawford/99	100.00
32 Adam LaRoche/99	100.00
33 Bill Hall/95	100.00
34 Scott Kazmir/95	100.00
35 Gary Matthews/99	100.00
36 Gary Sheffield/99	125.00
37 Francisco Rodriguez/95	100.00
38 Todd Helton/99	100.00
40 David Wright/99	150.00
42 Barry Bonds/99	180.00
43 Johan Santana/75	125.00
44 Albert Pujols/90	200.00
45 Carlos Lee/99	75.00
46 Cole Hamels/95	125.00
47 Prince Fielder/99	125.00
48 Hanley Ramirez/99	125.00
49 Ryan Zimmerman/90	125.00
50 Kei Igawa/99	100.00

2007 Topps Chrome

	NM/M
Complete Set (363):	
Common Player:	.25
Common RC Auto. (331-363):	10.00
Pack (4):	3.00
Box (24):	60.00
1 Nick Swisher	.50
2 Bobby Abreu	.50
3 Edgar Renteria	.50
4 Mickey Mantle	5.00
5 Preston Wilson	.25
6 C.C. Sabathia	.50
7 Julio Lugo	.25
8 J.D. Drew	.50
9 Jason Varitek	.50
10 Orlando Hernandez	.25
11 Corey Patterson	.25
12 Josh Bard	.25
13 Gary Matthews	.25
14 Jason Jennings	.25
15 Bronson Arroyo	.25
16 Andy Pettitte	.50
17 Ervin Santana	.25
18 Paul Konerko	.50
19 Adam LaRoche	.25
20 Jim Edmonds	.50
21 Derek Jeter	3.00
22 Aubrey Huff	.25
23 Andre Ethier	.25
24 Jeremy Sowers	.25
25 Miguel Cabrera	1.00
26 Carlos Lee	.50
27 Mike Piazza	1.00
28 Cole Hamels	.75
29 Mark Loretta	.25
30 John Smoltz	.50
31 Dan Uggla	.25
32 Lyle Overbay	.25
33 Michael Barrett	.25
34 Ivan Rodriguez	.75
35 Jake Westbrook	.25
36 Moises Alou	.50
37 Jered Weaver	.50
38 Lastings Milledge	.50
39 Austin Kearns	.25
40 Adam Loewen	.25
41 Josh Barfield	.25
42 Johan Santana	1.00
43 Ian Kinsler	.50
44 Mike Lowell	.50
45 Scott Rolen	.75
46 Chipper Jones	1.00
47 Joe Crede	.25
48 Rafael Furcal	.50
49 David Bush	.25
50 Marcus Giles	.25
51 Joe Blanton	.25
52 Dontrelle Willis	.50
53 Scott Kazmir	.50
54 Jeff Kent	.50
55 Travis Hafner	.50
56 Ryan Garko	.25
57 Nicholas Markakis	.50
58 Michael Cuddyer	.25
59 Jason Giambi	.50
60 Chone Figgins	.50
61 Carlos Delgado	.50
62 Aramis Ramirez	.50
63 Albert Pujols	3.00
64 Gary Sheffield	.75
65 Adrian Gonzalez	.50
66 Prince Fielder	1.50
67 Freddy Sanchez	.25
68 Jack Wilson	.25
69 Jake Peavy	.50
70 Javier Vazquez	.25
71 Todd Helton	.75
72 Bill Hall	.25
73 Jeremy Bonderman	.25
74 Rocco Baldelli	.25
75 Noah Lowry	.25
76 Justin Verlander	.75
77 Mark Buehrle	.50
78 Hank Blalock	.25
79 Mark Teahen	.25
80 Chien-Ming Wang	1.00
81 Roy Halladay	.50
82 Melvin Mora	.25
83 Grady Sizemore	.75
84 Matt Cain	.50
85 Carl Crawford	.50
86 Johnny Damon	.75
87 Freddy Garcia	.25
88 Ryan Shealy	.25
89 Carlos Beltran	.75
90 Chuck James	.25
91 Ben Sheets	.50
92 Mark Mulder	.25
93 Carlos Quentin	.25
94 Richie Sexson	.50
95 Brian Schneider	.25
96 Hideki Matsui	2.00
97 Robinson Tejada	.25
98 Scott Hatteberg	.25
99 Jeff Francis	.25
100 Robinson Cano	.50
101 Barry Zito	.50
102 Reed Johnson	.25
103 Chris Carpenter	.50
104 Chad Tracy	.25
105 Anibal Sanchez	.25
106 Brad Penny	.25
107 David Wright	2.00
108 Jimmy Rollins	.75
109 Alfonso Soriano	1.00
110 Greg Maddux	2.00
111 Curt Schilling	.75
112 Stephen Drew	.25
113 Matt Holliday	.50
114 Jorge Posada	.50
115 Vladimir Guerrero	1.00
116 Frank Thomas	.75
117 Jonathan Papelbon	.50
118 Manny Ramirez	1.00
119 Magglio Ordonez	.50
120 Joe Mauer	.50
121 Ryan Howard	2.00
122 Chris Young	.50
123 A.J. Burnett	.25
124 Brian McCann	.50
125 Juan Pierre	.25

#	Player	Price
126	Jonny Gomes	.25
127	Roger Clemens	2.50
128	Chad Billingsley	.50
129	Kenji Johjima	.25
130	Brian Giles	.25
131	Chase Utley	1.00
132	Carl Pavano	.25
133	Curtis Granderson	.50
134	Sean Casey	.25
135	Jon Garland	.25
136	David Ortiz	1.00
137	Bobby Crosby	.25
138	Conor Jackson	.25
139	Tim Hudson	.50
140	Rickie Weeks	.25
141	Mark Prior	.25
142	Benjamin Zobrist	.25
143	Troy Glaus	.25
144	Cliff Lee	.50
145	Adrian Beltre	.50
146	Endy Chavez	.25
147	Ramon Hernandez	.25
148	Chris Young	.25
149	Jason Schmidt	.25
150	Kevin Millwood	.25
151	Placido Polanco	.25
152	Torii Hunter	.50
153	Roy Oswalt	.50
154	Kelvim Escobar	.25
155	Milton Bradley	.25
156	Chris Capuano	.25
157	Juan Encarnacion	.25
158	Ichiro Suzuki	2.00
159	Matthew Kemp	.50
160	Matt Morris	.25
161	Casey Blake	.25
162	Josh Willingham	.25
163	Nick Johnson	.25
164	Khalil Greene	.25
165	Tom Glavine	.75
166	Jason Bay	.50
167	Brandon Phillips	.50
168	Jorge Cantu	.25
169	Jeff Weaver	.25
170	Melky Cabrera	.50
171	Danny Haren	.50
172	Jeff Francoeur	.50
173	Randy Wolf	.25
174	Carlos Zambrano	.50
175	Justin Morneau	.75
176	Takashi Saito	.50
177	Victor Martinez	.50
178	Felix Hernandez	.50
179	Paul LoDuca	.25
180	Miguel Tejada	.75
181	Mark Teixeira	.75
182	Pat Burrell	.50
183	Mike Cameron	.25
184	Josh Beckett	.50
185	Francisco Liriano	.50
186	Ken Griffey Jr.	2.00
187	Mike Mussina	.50
188	Howie Kendrick	.25
189	Ted Lilly	.25
190	Mike Hampton	.25
191	Jeff Suppan	.25
192	Jose Reyes	2.00
193	Russell Martin	.50
194	Jhonny Peralta	.50
195	Raul Ibanez	.25
196	Hanley Ramirez	1.00
197	Kerry Wood	.25
198	Gary Sheffield	.50
199	David Dellucci	.25
200	Xavier Nady	.25
201	Michael Young	.50
202	Kevin Youkilis	.50
203	Aaron Harang	.25
204	Mario Garza	.25
205	Jim Thome	.50
206	Jose Contreras	.25
207	Tadahito Iguchi	.25
208	Eric Chavez	.50
209	Vernon Wells	.50
210	Doug Davis	.25
211	Andruw Jones	.75
212	David Eckstein	.25
213	J.J. Hardy	.25
214	Orlando Hudson	.25
215	Pedro Martinez	.50
216	Brian Roberts	.50
217	Brett Myers	.25
218	Alex Rodriguez	3.00
219	Kenny Rogers	.25
220	Jason Kubel	.25
221	Jermaine Dye	.50
222	Bartolo Colon	.25
223	Craig Biggio	.50
224	Alex Rios	.50
225	Adam Dunn	.75
226	Anthony Reyes	.25
227	Derrek Lee	.50
228	Jeremy Hermida	.25
229	Derek Lowe	.25
230	Randy Winn	.25
231	Brandon Webb	.50
232	Jose Vidro	.25
233	Erik Bedard	.25
234	Jon Lieber	.25
235	Wily Mo Pena	.25
236	Kelly Johnson	.25
237	David DeJesus	.25
238	Andy Marte	.25
239	Scott Olsen	.25
240	Randy Johnson	1.00
241	Nelson Cruz	.25
242	Carlos Guillen	.50
243	Brandon McCarthy	.25
244	Garret Anderson	.25
245	Mike Sweeney	.25
246	Brian Bannister	.25
247	Jose Guillen	.25
248	Brad Wilkerson	.25
249	Lance Berkman	.50
250	Ryan Zimmerman	.50
251	Garrett Atkins	.50
252	Johan Santana	1.00
253	Brandon Webb	.50
254	Justin Verlander	.75
255	Hanley Ramirez	1.00
256	Justin Morneau	.75
257	Ryan Howard	2.00
258	Eric Chavez	.25
259	Scott Rolen	.75
260	Derek Jeter	3.00
261	Omar Vizquel	.25
262	Mark Grudzielanek	.25
263	Orlando Hudson	.25
264	Mark Teixeira	.50
265	Albert Pujols	3.00
266	Ivan Rodriguez	.75
267	Brad Ausmus	.25
268	Torii Hunter	.50
269	Mike Cameron	.25
270	Ichiro Suzuki	2.00
271	Carlos Beltran	.75
272	Vernon Wells	.50
273	Andruw Jones	.50
274	Kenny Rogers	.25
275	Greg Maddux	2.00
276	Danny Putnam (RC)	1.00
277	Chase Wright (RC)	2.00
278	Zach McClellan RC	1.00
279	Jamie Vermilyea RC	1.00
280	Felix Pie (RC)	2.00
281	Phil Hughes (RC)	5.00
282	Jon Knott (RC)	1.00
283	Micah Owings (RC)	1.50
284	Devern Hansack RC	2.00
285	Andy Cannizaro (RC)	1.00
286	Lee Gardner (RC)	1.00
287	Josh Hamilton (RC)	2.00
288	Angel Sanchez/Auto. RC	10.00
289	J.D. Durbin (RC)	1.00
290	Jamie Burke (RC)	1.00
291	Joseph Bisenius RC	1.00
292	Rick Vanden Hurk RC	2.00
293	Brian Barden (RC)	1.00
294	Levale Speigner RC	1.00
295	Kevin Cameron (RC)	1.00
296	Donald Kelly (RC)	1.00
297	Hideki Okajima RC	2.50
298	Andrew Miller RC	4.00
299	Delmon Young (RC)	1.00
300	Vinny Rottino (RC)	1.00
301	Philip Humber (RC)	1.00
302	Drew Anderson (RC)	1.00
303	Jerry Owens (RC)	1.00
304	Jose Garcia RC	1.00
305	Shane Youman RC	1.00
306	Ryan Feierabend (RC)	1.00
307	Mike Rabelo RC	1.00
308	Josh Fields (RC)	1.00
309	Jon Coutlangus (RC)	1.00
310	Travis Buck (RC)	1.00
311	Doug Slaten (RC)	1.00
312	Ryan Braun RC	3.00
313	Juan Salas (RC)	1.00
314	Matt Lindstrom (RC)	1.00
315	Cesar Jimenez RC	1.00
316	Jay Marshall RC	1.00
317	Jared Burton RC	1.00
318	Juan Perez RC	1.00
319	Elijah Dukes RC	1.00
320	Jura Lara RC	1.00
321	Justin Hampson (RC)	1.00
322	Kei Igawa RC	1.50
323	Zack Segovia (RC)	1.00
324	Alejandro De Aza RC	1.00
325	Brandon Morrow RC	2.00
326	Gustavo Molina RC	1.00
327	Joe Smith RC	1.00
328	Jesus Flores RC	2.00
329	Jeff Baker (RC)	1.00
330	Daisuke Matsuzaka RC	6.00
331	Troy Tulowitzki/Auto. (RC)	25.00
332	John Danks/Auto. (RC)	20.00
333	Kevin Kouzmanoff/ Auto. (RC)	15.00
334	David Murphy/Auto. (RC)	15.00
335	Ryan Sweeney/Auto. (RC)	15.00
336	Fred Lewis/Auto. (RC)	15.00
337	Delwyn Young/Auto. (RC)	15.00
338	Matt Chico/Auto. (RC)	10.00
339	Miguel Montero/Auto. (RC)	10.00
340	Shawn Riggans/Auto. (RC)	10.00
341	Brian Stokes/Auto. (RC)	10.00
342	Scott Moore/Auto. (RC)	10.00
343	Adam Lind/Auto. (RC)	10.00
344	Chris Narveson/Auto. (RC)	10.00
345	Alex Gordon/Auto. RC	40.00
346	Joaquin Arias/Auto. (RC)	10.00
347	Brian Burres/Auto. (RC)	10.00
348	Glen Perkins/Auto. (RC)	10.00
349	Ubaldo Jimenez/Auto. (RC)	15.00
350	Chris Stewart/Auto. (RC)	10.00
351	Beltran Perez/Auto. (RC)	10.00
352	Dennis Sarfate/Auto. (RC)	10.00
353	Carlos Maldonado/ Auto. (RC)	10.00
354	Mitch Maier/Auto. RC	10.00
355	Kory Casto/Auto. (RC)	10.00
356	Juan Morillo/Auto. (RC)	10.00
357	Hector Gimenez/Auto. (RC)	10.00
358	Alexi Casilla/Auto. RC	15.00
359	Michael Bourn/Auto. (RC)	15.00
360	Sean Henn/Auto. (RC)	10.00
361	Tim Gradoville/Auto. RC	10.00
362	Akinori Iwamura/Auto. RC	25.00
363	Oswaldo Navarro/Auto. RC	10.00

Refractor

Refractor (1-330):	2-3X
Ref. RC Auto. (288, 331-363):	1-1.5X
Auto Production 500	

Red Refractor

Red Ref. (1-330):	4-8X
Production 99	
Red Auto. (288, 331-363):	3-4X
Auto. Production 25	

White Refractor

White Ref. (1-330):	3-4X
Production 660	
White Auto. (288, 331-363):	1-1.5X
Auto. Production 200	

Printing Plates

Production one set per color.

A-Rod Road to 500

	NM/M
Complete Set (226-250):	40.00
Common A-Rod:	2.00

A-Rod Road to 500 Autographs

	NM/M
Production One Set	40.00

Generation Now

	NM/M
Common Player:	.50
Refractor:	2-3X
Production 500 Sets	
White Refractor:	3-4X
Production 200 Sets	
Red Refractor:	3-5X
Production 99 Sets	
GN201 Ryan Howard	2.00
GN203 Ryan Howard	2.00
GN204 Ryan Howard	2.00
GN205 Ryan Howard	2.00
GN208 Ryan Howard	2.00
GN209 Chase Utley	2.00
GN210 Chien-Ming Wang	3.00
GN211 Mike Napoli	.50
GN213 Justin Morneau	2.00
GN214 Justin Morneau	2.00
GN215 Justin Morneau	2.00
GN216 Justin Morneau	2.00
GN217 Jered Weaver	1.00
GN218 Andre Ethier	1.00
GN219 Ryan Zimmerman	1.00
GN238 Ryan Zimmerman	1.00
GN264 Ryan Zimmerman	1.00
GN265 Delmon Young	1.00
GN269 Delmon Young	1.00
GN274 Delmon Young	1.00
GN278 Delmon Young	1.00
GN279 Russell Martin	1.00
GN280 Russell Martin	1.00
GN281 Russell Martin	1.00
GN282 Russell Martin	1.00
GN283 Justin Verlander	1.50
GN292 Justin Verlander	1.50
GN297 Justin Verlander	1.50
GN298 Justin Verlander	1.50
GN299 Hanley Ramirez	1.50
GN308 Hanley Ramirez	1.50
GN318 Hanley Ramirez	1.50
GN328 Hanley Ramirez	1.50
GN338 Hanley Ramirez	1.50
GN349 Hanley Ramirez	1.00
GN350 Nicholas Markakis	1.00
GN359 Nicholas Markakis	1.00
GN360 Nick Swisher	.50
GN364 Nick Swisher	.50
GN379 Nick Swisher	.50
GN394 Nick Swisher	.50

Mickey Mantle Home Run History

	NM/M
Common Mantle:	2.00
Refractor:	2-3X
Production 500 Sets	
White Refractor:	3-5X
Production 200 Sets	
Red Refractor:	4-8X
Production 99 Sets	

The Mickey Mantle Story

	NM/M
Complete Set (30):	50.00
Common Mantle:	2.00
Refractor:	2-3X
Production 500 Sets	
White Refractor:	3-4X
Production 200 Sets	
Red Refractor:	3-6X
Production 99 Sets	
1-30 Mickey Mantle	2.00

2007 Topps Co-Signers

	NM/M
Complete Set (122):	
Common Player:	.25
Common RC Auto.:	10.00
Pack (6):	10.00
Box (12):	100.00
1 Ryan Howard	2.00
2 Jered Weaver	.50
3 Brian McCann	.25
4 Garrett Atkins	.25
5 Travis Hafner	.50
6 Jason Schmidt	.25
7 Curtis Granderson	.50
8 Ben Sheets	.50
9 Chien-Ming Wang	1.50
10 Francisco Liriano	.50
11 Freddy Sanchez	.50
12 Roy Oswalt	.75
13 Jim Edmonds	.50
14 Matt Cain	.50
15 Jake Peavy	.75
16 Ryan Zimmerman	.75
17 Troy Glaus	.50
18 Kenji Johjima	.50
19 Curt Schilling	1.00
20 Alfonso Soriano	1.00
21 Adam Dunn	.75
22 Hanley Ramirez	.75
23 Mark Teahen	.25
24 Todd Helton	.75

#	Player	Price
25	Alex Rodriguez	3.00
26	Mike Mussina	.75
27	Jason Bay	.50
28	Carl Crawford	.50
29	Vernon Wells	.50
30	Rich Harden	.25
31	Justin Morneau	1.00
32	Andre Ethier	.25
33	Ramon Hernandez	.25
34	Erik Bedard	.50
35	Vladimir Guerrero	1.00
36	Stephen Drew	.50
37	Felix Hernandez	.50
38	C.C. Sabathia	.50
39	Adrian Gonzalez	.50
40	Prince Fielder	1.00
41	Carlos Delgado	.75
42	Jimmy Rollins	.75
43	Raul Ibanez	.25
44	Jorge Cantu	.25
45	Michael Young	.25
46	Austin Kearns	.25
47	Ivan Rodriguez	.75
48	Chad Billingsley	.25
49	David Ortiz	1.00
50	David Wright	1.50
51	Justin Verlander	.75
52	Nicholas Markakis	.50
53	Miguel Cabrera	1.00
54	Lance Berkman	.50
55	Robinson Cano	.75
56	Jon Lieber	.25
57	Andruw Jones	.75
58	Danny Haren	.50
59	Grady Sizemore	.75
60	Gary Sheffield	.75
61	Paul LoDuca	.25
62	Cole Hamels	1.00
63	Richie Sexson	.50
64	David Eckstein	.25
65	Carlos Zambrano	.50
66	Scott Kazmir	.25
67	Anthony Reyes	.25
68	Mark Kotsay	.25
69	Miguel Tejada	.25
70	Pedro Martinez	1.00
71	Jack Wilson	.25
72	Joe Mauer	.75
73	Brian Giles	.25
74	Jonathan Papelbon	1.00
75	Albert Pujols	3.00
76	Nick Swisher	.50
77	Bill Hall	.50
78	Jose Contreras	.25
79	David DeJesus	.25
80	Bobby Abreu	.50
81	John Smoltz	.50
82	Chipper Jones	1.00
83	Mark Buehrle	.25
84	Josh Barfield	.25
85	Derrek Lee	.75
86	Jim Thome	.75
87	Kenny Rogers	.25
88	Jeremy Sowers	.25
89	Brandon Webb	.50
90	Roy Halladay	.50
91	Tadahito Iguchi	.25
92	Jeff Kent	.50
93	Johnny Damon	1.00
94	Daisuke Matsuzaka RC	5.00
95	Mark Teixeira	.75
96a	Delmon Young RC	2.00
96b	Delmon Young/Auto.	20.00
97a	Jeff Baker RC	1.00
97b	Jeff Baker/Auto.	10.00
98a	Michael Bourn (RC)	1.00
98b	Michael Bourn/Auto.	10.00
99a	Ubaldo Jimenez RC	1.00
99b	Ubaldo Jimenez/Auto.	10.00
100a	Andrew Miller (RC)	5.00
100b	Andrew Miller/Auto.	25.00
101	Angel Sanchez/Auto. (RC)	10.00
102	Troy Tulowitzki/Auto. (RC)	25.00
103	Joaquin Arias/Auto. RC	10.00
104	Beltran Perez/Auto. RC	10.00
105	Josh Fields/Auto. RC	10.00
106	Hector Gimenez/Auto. RC	10.00
107	Kevin Kouzmanoff/Auto. RC	15.00
108	Miguel Montero/Auto. RC	10.00
109	Philip Humber/Auto. RC	15.00
110	Jerry Owens/Auto. RC	10.00
111	Shawn Riggans/Auto. RC	10.00
112	Brian Stokes/Auto. RC	10.00
113	Scott Moore/Auto. RC	10.00
114	David Murphy/Auto. (RC)	10.00
115	Mitch Maier/Auto. RC	10.00
116	Adam Lind/Auto. RC	10.00
117	Adam Lind/Auto. RC	10.00
118	Dennis Sarfate/Auto. RC	10.00
119	Elijah Dukes/Auto. (RC)	10.00
120	Josh Hamilton/Auto. (RC)	30.00
121	Alex Gordon/Auto. RC	40.00
122	Barry Bonds	3.00

Bronze

Bronze Non-Auto.:	2-3X
Bronze RC Auto.:	1X
Production 250 Sets	

Blue

Blue Non-Auto.:	2-3X
Blue RC Auto.:	1X
Production 225 Sets	

Gold

Gold Non-Auto.:	2-3X
Gold RC Auto.:	1X
Production 200 Sets	

Red

Red Non-Auto.:	2-3X
Production 299 Sets	
Red RC Auto.:	1X
Production 275 Sets	

Silver-Red

Silver Red Non-Auto.:	2-3X
Silver Red RC Auto.:	1X
Production 175 Sets	

Silver-Bronze

Silver Bronze Non-Auto.:	2-4X
Silver Bronze RC Auto.:	1-1.5X
Production 150 Sets	

Silver-Blue

Silver Blue Non-Auto.:	2-4X
Silver Blue RC Auto.:	1-1.5X
Production 125 Sets	

Silver-Gold

Silver Gold Non-Auto.:	2-4X
Silver Gold RC Auto.:	1-1.5X
Production 100 Sets	

Hyper Silver-Red

Hyper Silver Red Non-Auto.:	2-4X
Hyper Silver Red RC Auto.:	1-1.5X
Production 75 Sets	

Hyper Silver-Bronze

Hyper Silver Bronze Non-Auto.:	3-4X
Hyper Silver Bronze Auto.:	1-2X
Production 50 Sets	

Hyper Silver Blue

No Pricing
Production 25 Sets

Hyper Silver Gold

No Pricing
Production Five Sets

Hyper Plaid Silver

No Pricing
Production One Set

Printing Plates

No Pricing
Production one set per color.

A-Rod Road to 500

NM/M

Common A-Rod:	3.00
2:Box	
Autograph:	No Pricing
Production One Set	

Cut Signatures Dual

Production One Set
No Pricing

Dual Autograph

NM/M

Common Dual Auto.:		10.00
AH	Garrett Atkins, Matt Holliday	30.00
AI	Matt Albers, Chris Iannetta	10.00
AS	Matt Albers, Brian Slocum	10.00
BB	Brian Bannister, Floyd Bannister	20.00
BDE	Erik Bedard, Zachary Duke	20.00
BG	Jeremy Bonderman, Curtis Granderson	10.00
BS	Jeff Baker, Jeff Salazar	10.00
BV	Jeremy Bonderman, Justin Verlander	50.00
CC	Melky Cabrera, Robinson Cano	60.00
CJ	Chris Granderson, Tyler Johnson	40.00
CK	Robinson Cano, Chuck Knoblauch	40.00
CM	Fabio Castro, Scott Mathieson	15.00
CW	Miguel Cabrera, Dontrelle Willis	30.00
CY	Alberto Callaspo, Chris Young	20.00
CZ	Alberto Callaspo, Benjamin Zobrist	15.00
GB	Garrett Atkins, Clint Barmes	15.00
GC	Curtis Granderson, Melky Cabrera	25.00
GM	Hector Gimenez, Miguel Montero	15.00
GS	Dwight Gooden, Darryl Strawberry	40.00
HH	Bill Hall, J.J. Hardy	30.00
HO	Ryan Howard, David Ortiz	100.00
IK	Chris Iannetta, Matthew Kemp	15.00
IM	Chris Iannetta, Miguel Montero	15.00
JJ	Andruw Jones, David Justice	50.00
JS	Ubaldo Jimenez, Dennis Sarfate	10.00
JY	Conor Jackson, Chris Young	25.00

KA	Howie Kendrick, Erick Aybar	25.00
KF	Kevin Kouzmanoff, Josh Fields	20.00
KG	Matthew Kemp, Franklin Gutierrez	15.00
KM	Josh Kinney, Tom Mastny	15.00
KMA	Jeff Karstens, Scott Mathieson	15.00
KZ	Austin Kearns, Ryan Zimmerman	25.00
LG	Adam LaRoche, Tom Gorzelanny	20.00
LK	Francisco Liriano, Jim Kaat	20.00
LL	Tony Larussa, Jim Leyland	50.00
LP	Francisco Liriano, Jonathan Papelbon	35.00
LV	Francisco Liriano, Justin Verlander	40.00
LY	Adam Lind, Delmon Young	20.00
MB	Nicholas Markakis, Brian Roberts	30.00
MC	Omar Minaya, Brian Cashman	60.00
MCA	Nicholas Markakis, Melky Cabrera	30.00
MG	Craig Monroe, Curtis Granderson	30.00
MH	John Maine, Philip Humber	30.00
MM	Lastings Milledge, John Maine	25.00
MMA	David Murphy, Mitch Maier	15.00
MP	Andrew Miller, Glen Perkins	30.00
MQ	Nicholas Markakis, Carlos Quentin	20.00
MS	Justin Morneau, Nick Swisher	30.00
MSL	Tom Mastny, Brian Slocum	10.00
MW	Lastings Milledge, David Wright	50.00
OB	Jerry Owens, Michael Bourn	15.00
PC	Angel Pagan, Buck Coats	15.00
PS	Yusmeiro Petit, Anibal Sanchez	15.00
PV	Jonathan Papelbon, Justin Verlander	50.00
SH	Jonathan Sanchez, Brad Hennessey	15.00
SM	Freddy Sanchez, Joe Mauer	30.00
SMA	Chris Stewart, Carlos Maldonado	15.00
SR	Brian Stokes, Shawn Riggans	15.00
VF	Justin Verlander, Mark Fidrych	50.00
VM	John Van Benschoten, Scott Mathieson	15.00
VP	Jason Varitek, Jorge Posada	80.00
WC	David Wright, Robinson Cano	80.00
WS	Dontrelle Willis, Anibal Sanchez	20.00
YL	Chris Young, Nook Logan	15.00
YU	Delmon Young, B.J. Upton	35.00
ZG	Benjamin Zobrist, Joel Guzman	15.00

Moon Shots Autographs

NM/M

Common Auto.:		80.00
BA	Buzz Aldrin	200.00
WC	Walt Cunningham	80.00
WS	Wally Schirra	180.00
RC	Robert Crippen	80.00
CD	Charles Duke	80.00
AW	Alfred Worden	90.00
EM	Edgar Mitchell	90.00
FH	Fred Haise	100.00
RG	Richard Gordon	100.00
SC	Scott Carpenter	100.00

Moon Shots Autographs Dual

NM/M

Common Dual Auto.:		100.00
AC	Garrett Atkins, Scott Carpenter	100.00
AD	Andre Dawson, Alfred Worden	140.00
DG	Jermaine Dye, Richard Gordon	100.00
HC	Ryan Howard, W. Cunningham	140.00
OS	David Ortiz, Wally Schirra	150.00
RA	Alex Rodriguez, Buzz Aldrin	375.00
SC	Alfonso Soriano, Robert Crippen	150.00
SH	Duke Snider, Fred Haise	160.00
WD	David Wright, Charles Duke	180.00
WM	Dave Winfield, Edgar Mitchell	125.00

Solo Sigs

NM/M

Common Autograph:		10.00
AH	Aaron Hill	10.00
AL	Anthony Lerew	10.00
AS	Anibal Sanchez	10.00

BB	Boof Bonser	10.00
CB	Clint Barmes	10.00
CH	Cole Hamels	25.00
CJ	Chuck James	10.00
CQ	Carlos Quentin	15.00
DH	Dave Henderson	10.00
DU	Dan Uggla	15.00
ES	Ervin Santana	15.00
FL	Francisco Liriano	20.00
FS	Freddy Sanchez	10.00
GA	Garrett Atkins	10.00
HK	Howie Kendrick	15.00
HM	Hideki Matsui	250.00
HR	Hanley Ramirez	25.00
JM	Justin Morneau	25.00
JS	Jeremy Sowers	10.00
MC	Matt Cain	20.00
MH	Matt Holliday	30.00
NM	Nicholas Markakis	25.00
RC	Robinson Cano	30.00
RCE	Ronny Cedeno	10.00
RG	Ryan Garko	10.00
RH	Ryan Howard	60.00
RR	Rick Rhoden	10.00
VG	Vladimir Guerrero	50.00

Tri-Signers

NM/M

Inserted 1:288

ANS	Joaquin Arias, Oswaldo Navarro, Angel Sanchez	20.00
CPC	Melky Cabrera, Wily Mo Pena, Miguel Cabrera	40.00
HLC	Brad Hennessey, J. Sanchez, Matt Cain	40.00
JGK	Conor Jackson, Ryan Garko, Howie Kendrick	40.00
JHS	Chuck James, Cole Hamels, Jeremy Sowers	50.00
LNB	Francisco Liriano, Joe Nathan, Boof Bonser	50.00
MAR	Justin Morneau, Garrett Atkins, Brian Roberts	40.00
MLM	Justin Morneau, Francisco Liriano, Matt Garza	60.00
MLP	Justin Morneau, Francisco Liriano, Glen Perkins	50.00
MSG	Justin Morneau, Nick Swisher, Adrian Gonzalez	50.00
MYT	Andrew Miller, Delmon Young, Troy Tulowitzki	60.00
OPV	David Ortiz, Jonathan Papelbon, Jason Varitek	150.00
OWH	David Ortiz, David Wright, Ryan Howard	150.00
QJY	Carlos Quentin, Conor Jackson, Chris Young	40.00
RCC	Alex Rodriguez, Melky Cabrera, Robinson Cano	250.00
RWH	Alex Rodriguez, David Wright, Ryan Howard	250.00
SHH	Huston Street, Rich Harden, Danny Haren	50.00
TPW	Taylor Tankersley, Yusmeiro Petit, Dontrelle Willis	35.00
URW	Dan Uggla, Hanley Ramirez, Dontrelle Willis	

Yankees Cut Signatures

Production One Set
No Pricing

2007 Topps Heritage

Adrian Gonzalez — 1st Base — SAN DIEGO PADRES

NM/M

Complete Set (495):	325.00
Common Player:	.40
Common SP:	5.00
Inserted 1:2	
Common Variation:	5.00
Inserted 1:6	
Pack (8):	3.00
Box (24):	65.00
1 David Ortiz	1.50
2 Roger Clemens	3.00

2 Roger Clemens/ Yellow Team Name SP 15.00
3 David Wells .40
4 Ronny Paulino/SP 5.00
5 Derek Jeter/SP 15.00
6 Felix Hernandez 2.00
7 Todd Helton 1.00
8 David Eckstein .40
8 David Eckstein/ Yellow Name SP 5.00
9 Craig Wilson .40
10 John Smoltz .75
11 Robert Mackowiak .40
11 Robert Mackowiak/ Yellow Team Name/SP 5.00
12 Scott Hatteberg .40
13 Wilfredo Ledezma/SP 5.00
13 Wilfredo Ledezma/ Yellow Team Name/SP 5.00
14 Bobby Abreu/SP 8.00
15 Austin Kearns .40
16 Wilson Betemit .40
17 Darren Oliver .40
18 Josh Beckett .40
19 San Francisco Giants .40
20 Robinson Cano 1.00
20 Robinson Cano/ Yellow Team Name/SP 8.00
21 Matt Cain 1.00
22 Jason Kendall/SP 5.00
23 Mark Kotsay/SP 5.00
23 Mark Kotsay/ Yellow Name/SP 5.00
24 Yadier Molina .40
24 Yadier Molina/ Yellow Name/SP 5.00
25 Brad Penny .40
26 Adrian Gonzalez .50
27 Danny Haren .40
28 Brian Giles .50
29 Jose Lopez .40
30 Ichiro Suzuki 2.50
30 Ichiro Suzuki/ Yellow Name/SP 10.00
31 Beltran Perez/SP **(RC)** 5.00
32 Brad Hawpe/SP 5.00
33 Jim Thome 1.50
33 Jim Thome/ Yellow Team Name/SP 8.00
34 Mark DeRosa .40
35 Woody Williams .40
35 Woody Williams/ Yellow Team Name/SP 5.00
36 Luis Gonzalez .40
37 Billy Sadler **(RC)** 1.00
38 Dave Roberts .40
39 Mitch Maier **(RC)** 1.00
40 Francisco Cordero SP 5.00
41 Anthony Reyes SP 8.00
42 Russell Martin .40
43 Scott Proctor .40
44 Washington Nationals .40
45 Shane Victorino .40
46 Joel Zumaya 1.00
46 Joel Zumaya/ Yellow Name SP 5.00
47 Delmon Young **(RC)** 1.00
48 Alex Rios .40
49 Willy Taveras SP 5.00
50 Mark Buehrle SP 5.00
50 Mark Buehrle/ Yellow Team Name/SP 5.00
51 Livan Hernandez .40
52 Jason Bay 1.00
52 Jason Bay/ Yellow Team Name/SP 5.00
53 Jose Valentin .40
53 Jose Valentin/ Yellow Name/SP 5.00
54 Kevin Reese .40
55 Felipe Lopez .40
56 Ryan Sweeney **(RC)** 1.00
57 Kelvim Escobar .40
57 Kelvim Escobar/ Yellow Name/SP 5.00
58 Nick Swisher/SP 5.00
58 Nick Swisher/ Yellow Team Name/SP 8.00
59 Kevin Millwood/SP 5.00
60 Preston Wilson .40
60 Preston Wilson/ Yellow Name/SP 5.00
61 Mariano Rivera .75
61 Mariano Rivera/ Yellow Name/SP 8.00
62 Josh Barfield .40
63 Ryan Freel .40
64 Tim Hudson .75
65 Chris Narveson **(RC)** 1.00
65 Chris Narveson/ Yellow Name/SP 5.00
66 Matt Murton .40
67 Melvin Mora/SP 5.00
68 Jason Jennings/SP 5.00
69 Emil Brown .40
70 Magglio Ordonez .40
70 Magglio Ordonez/ Yellow Name/SP 5.00
71 Los Angeles Dodgers .40
72 Huston Street .40
73 David Ross .40
74 Juan Uribe .40
75 Scott Podsednik .40
76 Cole Hamels/SP 8.00
76 Cole Hamels/ Yellow Team Name/SP 8.00
77 Rafael Furcal/SP 5.00
77 Rafael Furcal/ Yellow Team Name/SP 5.00
78 Ryan Theriot .40
78 Ryan Theriot/ Yellow Name/SP 5.00
79 Corey Patterson .40
79 Corey Patterson/ Yellow Team Name/SP 5.00
80 Jered Weaver .40
81 Stephen Drew .75
81 Stephen Drew/ Yellow Team Name/SP 8.00
82 Adam Kennedy .40
83 Tony Gwynn Jr. .40
84 Erik Bedard .40
85 Omar Vizquel/SP 5.00
85 Omar Vizquel/ Yellow Team Name/SP 5.00
86 Fred Lewis/SP **(RC)** 5.00
87 Brad Radke .40
87 Shawn Chacon/ Yellow Name/SP 5.00
88 Frank Catalanotto .40
89 Orlando Hudson .40
90 Pat Burrell .40
91 David DeJesus .40
92 David Wright 2.50
92 David Wright/ Yellow Name/SP 10.00
93 Conor Jackson .40
94 Xavier Nady/SP 5.00
95 Bill Hall SP 8.00
96 Andre Ethier .75
97 Jeff Suppan .40
97 Jeff Suppan/ Yellow Name/SP 5.00
98 Ryan Zimmerman .75
98 Ryan Zimmerman/ Yellow Name/SP 8.00
99 Yuniesky Betancourt .40
100 Jose Contreras .40
100 Jose Contreras/ Yellow Team Name/SP 5.00
101 Miguel Cairo .40
101 Miguel Cairo/ Yellow Name/SP 5.00
102 Brian Roberts .40
103 Carl Crawford/SP 8.00
104 Mike Lamb/SP 5.00
105 Mark Ellis .40
106 Scott Rolen 1.50
107 Garrett Atkins .40
108 Hanley Ramirez .75
108 Hanley Ramirez/ Yellow Team Name/SP 8.00
109 Trot Nixon .40
110 Edgar Renteria .40
111 Jeff Francis .40
112 Marcus Thames/SP 5.00
113 Brian Burres/SP **(RC)** 5.00
114 Brian Schneider .40
115 Jeremy Bonderman .75
116 Ryan Madson .40
117 Gerald Laird .40
118 Roy Halladay .75
119 Victor Martinez .40
120 Greg Maddux 2.50
121 Jay Payton/SP 5.00
122 Jacque Jones/SP 5.00
123 Juan Lara **RC** 1.00
124 Derrick Turnbow .40
125 Adam Everett .40
126 Michael Cuddyer .40
127 Gil Meche .40
128 Willy Aybar .40
129 Jerry Owens **RC** 1.00
130 Manny Ramirez/SP 10.00
131 Howie Kendrick/SP 8.00
132 Byung-Hyun Kim .40
133 Kevin Kouzmanoff **(RC)** 1.00
134 Philadelphia Phillies .40
135 Joe Blanton .40
136 Ray Durham .40
137 Luke Hudson .40
138 Eric Byrnes .40
139 Ryan Braun/SP **(RC)** 8.00
140 Johnny Damon/SP 10.00
141 Ambiorix Burgos .40
142 Hideki Matsui .40
143 Josh Johnson .40
144 Miguel Cabrera .40
146 Delwyn Young **(RC)** 1.00
147 Chuck James .40
148 Morgan Ensberg .40
149 Jose Vidro/SP 5.00
150 Alex Rodriguez/SP 15.00
151 Carlos Maldonado **(RC)** 1.00
152 Jason Schmidt .40
153 Alex Escobar .40
154 Chris Gomez .40
155 Endy Chavez .40
156 Kris Benson .40
157 Bronson Arroyo .40
158 Cleveland Indians/SP 8.00
159 Chris Ray/SP 5.00
160 Richie Sexson .40
161 Huston Street .40
162 Kevin Youkilis .40
163 Armando Benitez .40
164 Vinny Rottino **(RC)** 1.00
165 Garret Anderson .40
166 Todd Greene .40
167 Brian Stokes/SP **(RC)** 5.00
168 Albert Pujols/SP 15.00
169 Todd Coffey .40
170 Jason Michaels .40
171 David Dellucci .40
172 Eric Milton .40
173 Austin Kearns .40
174 Kansas City Royals .40
175 Andy Cannizaro **RC** 2.00
176 David Weathers/SP 5.00
177 Jermaine Dye/SP 5.00
178 Wily Mo Pena .40
179 Chris Burke .40
180 Jeff Weaver .40
181 Juan Encarnacion .40
182 Jeremy Hermida .40
183 Tim Wakefield .40
184 Rich Hill .50
185 Aaron Hill/SP 5.00
186 Scot Shields/SP 5.00
187 Randy Johnson .40
188 Dan Johnson .40
189 Sean Marshall .40
190 Marcus Giles .40
191 Jonathan Broxton .40
192 Mike Piazza .40
193 Carlos Quentin .40
194 Derek Lowe/SP 5.00
195 Russell Branyan/SP 5.00
196 Jason Marquis .40
197 Khalil Greene .40
198 Ryan Dempster .40
199 Ronnie Belliard .40
200 Josh Fogg .40
201 Carlos Lee .40
202 Chris Denorfia .40
203 Kendry Morales/SP 5.00
204 Rafael Soriano/SP 5.00
205 Brandon Phillips .40
206 Andrew Miller **RC** 5.00
207 John Koronka .40
208 Luis Castillo .40
209 Angel Guzman .40
210 Jim Edmonds .40
211 Patrick Misch **(RC)** 1.00
212 Ty Wigginton/SP 5.00
213 Brandon Inge/SP 5.00
214 Royce Clayton .40
215 Ben Broussard .40
216 St. Louis Cardinals .40
217 Mark Mulder .40
218 Kenji Johjima .40
219 Joe Crede .40
220 Danny Haren .40
221 Josh Fields/SP **(RC)** 8.00
222 Pat Neshek/SP 10.00
223 Reed Johnson .40
224 Mike Mussina .40
225 Randy Winn .40
226 Brian Rogers **(RC)** .40
227 Juan Rivera .40
228 Shawn Green .40
229 Mike Napoli .40
230 Chase Utley/SP 10.00
231 John Nelson/SP **(RC)** 10.00
232 Casey Blake .40
233 Lyle Overbay .40
234 Adam LaRoche .40
235 Jeff Weaver .40
236 Johnny Estrada .40
237 James Shields .40
238 Jose Castillo .40
239 Doug Davis/SP 5.00
240 Jason Giambi/SP 8.00
241 Mike Gonzalez .40
242 Scott Downs .40
243 Joe Inglett .40
244 Matthew Kemp .40
245 Ted Lilly .40
246 New York Yankees .40
247 Jamey Carroll .40
248 Adam Wainwright/SP 8.00
249 Matt Thornton/SP 5.00
250 Alfonso Soriano .40
251 Tom Gordon .40
252 Dennis Sarfate **(RC)** .40
253 Zachary Duke .40
254 Hank Blalock .40
255 Johan Santana .40
256 Chicago White Sox .40
257 Aaron Cook/SP 5.00
258 Cliff Lee/SP 5.00
259 Miguel Tejada .40
260 Mike Lowell .40
261 Ian Snell .40
262 Jason Tyner .40
263 Troy Tulowitzki **(RC)** .75
264 Ervin Santana .40
265 Jon Lester .40
266 Andy Pettitte/SP 8.00
267 A.J. Pierzynski/SP 5.00
268 Rich Aurilia .40
269 Phil Nevin .40
270 Tom Glavine .40
271 Chris Coste .40
272 Moises Alou .40
273 J.D. Drew .40
274 Abraham Nunez .40
275 Jorge Posada/SP 8.00
276 Jeff Conine/SP 5.00
277 Chad Cordero .40
278 Nick Johnson .40
279 Kevin Millar .40
280 Mark Grudzielanek .40
281 Chris Stewart **RC** 1.00
282 Nate Robertson .40
283 Drew Anderson **(RC)** 1.00
284 Doug Mientkiewicz/SP 5.00
285 Ken Griffey Jr./SP 10.00
286 Cory Sullivan .40
287 Chris Carpenter .40
288 Gary Matthews .40
289 Justin Verlander, Jeff Weaver .40
290 Vicente Padilla .40
291 Chris Roberson .40
292 Chris Young .40
293 Ryan Garko/SP 5.00
294 Miguel Batista/SP 5.00
295 B.J. Upton .40
296 Justin Verlander .40
297 Benjamin Zobrist .40
298 Ben Sheets .40
299 Eric Chavez .40
300 William Harridge, Warren Giles .40
301 Placido Polanco .40
302 Angel Sanchez/SP **RC** 5.00
303 Freddy Sanchez/SP 5.00
304 Magglio Ordonez, Carlos Guillen .40
305 A.J. Burnett .40
306 Juan Perez **RC** 1.00
307 Chris Britton .40
308 Jon Garland .40
309 Pedro Feliz .40
310 Ryan Howard .40
311 Aaron Harang/SP 5.00
312 Boston Red Sox/SP 8.00
313 Chad Billingsley .40
314 Bobby Cox, Chipper Jones .40
315 Johan Santana .40
316 Juan Pierre .40
317 Luke Scott .40
318 Javier Valentin .40
319 Mark Loretta .40
320 Kenny Lofton/SP 5.00
321 Vladimir Guerrero/SP, Ivan Rodriguez/SP 8.00
322 Josh Willingham .40
323 Lance Berkman .40
324 Anibal Sanchez .40
325 Maicer Izturis .40
326 Brett Myers .40
327 Chicago Cubs .40
328 Francisco Liriano .40
329 Craig Monroe/SP 5.00
330 Paul LoDuca/SP 5.00
331 Steve Trachsel .40
332 Bernie Williams .40
333 Carlos Guillen .40
334 Johan Santana, Francisco Liriano .40
335 David Bush .40
336 Carlos Beltran .40
337 Jason Isringhausen .40
338 Todd Walker/SP 5.00
339 Jarrod Washburn/SP 5.00
340 Brandon Webb .40
341 Pittsburgh Pirates .40
342 Derrick Turnbow .40
343 Chad Santos .40
344 Brad Lidge .40
345 Brad Ausmus .40
346 Carlos Delgado .40
347 Boone Logan/SP 5.00
348 Jimmy Rollins/SP 8.00
349 Orlando Hernandez .40
350 Gary Sheffield .40
351 Albert Pujols, Yadier Molina, Jim Edmonds, Chris Duncan .40
352 Jake Peavy .40
353 Jason Varitek .40
354 Freddy Garcia .40
355 Matt Diaz .40
356 Bernie Castro/SP 5.00
357 Eric Stults/SP **RC** 5.00
358 John Lackey .40
359 Bobby Jenks .40
360 Mark Teixeira .40
361 Jonathan Papelbon .40
362 Paul Konerko .40
363 Erik Bedard .40
364 Eliezer Alfonzo .40
365 Fernando Rodney/SP 5.00
366 Chris Duncan/SP 8.00
367 Jose Diaz **RC** 1.00
368 Travis Hafner .40
369 Matt Capps .40
370 Ivan Rodriguez .40
371 David Murphy **(RC)** 1.00
372 Carlos Zambrano .40
373 Chris Iannetta .40
374 Jose Mesa/SP 5.00
375 Michael Young/SP 8.00
376 Bill Bray .40
377 Milwaukee Brewers .40
378 Robert Mackowiak .40
379 Barry Zito .40
380 Clay Hensley .40
381 J.J. Putz .40
382 C.C. Sabathia .40
383 Eduardo Perez/SP 5.00
384 Scott Moore/SP **(RC)** 8.00
385 Scott Olsen .40
386 Ryan Howard, Chase Utley .50
387 Aaron Rowand .40

#	Player	Price
388	Mike Rouse	.40
389	Alexis Gomez	.40
390	Brian McCann	.40
391	Ryan Shealy	.40
392	Shane Youman/SP RC	8.00
393	Melky Cabrera/SP	8.00
394	Jeremy Sowers	.40
395	Casey Janssen	.40
396	Miguel Perez	.40
397	Detroit Tigers	.40
398	Reggie Abercrombie	.40
399	Ricky Nolasco	.40
400	Tadahito Iguchi	.40
401	Jose Reyes	10.00
402	Juan Encarnacion/SP	5.00
403	Brandon Harper	.40
404	Torii Hunter	.40
405	Dan Uggla	.40
406	Orlando Cabrera	.40
407	Jose Capellan	.40
408	Baltimore Orioles	.40
409	Frank Thomas	.40
410	Francisco Rodriguez/SP	5.00
411	Ian Kinsler/SP	5.00
412	Billy Wagner	.40
413	Andy Marte	.40
414	Mike Jacobs	.40
415	Raul Ibanez	.40
416	Jhonny Peralta	.40
417	Chris Young	.40
418	Albert Pujols, Craig Monroe	.40
419	Scott Kazmir/SP	8.00
420	Norris Hopper/SP	5.00
421	Chris Capuano	.40
422	Troy Glaus	.40
423	Roy Oswalt	.40
424	Grady Sizemore	.40
425	Chone Figgins	.40
426	Chad Tracy	.40
427	Brian Fuentes	.40
428	Cincinnati Reds/SP	8.00
429	Ramon Hernandez/SP	5.00
430	Mike Cameron	.40
431	Dontrelle Willis	.40
432	Joshua Sharpless	.40
433	Adrian Beltre	.40
434	Curtis Granderson	.40
435	B.J. Ryan	.40
436	Ryan Howard, David Wright	.40
437	Vernon Wells/SP	8.00
438	Vladimir Guerrero/SP	8.00
439	Jake Westbrook	.40
440	Chipper Jones	.40
441	James Loney	.40
442	St. Louis Cardinals	.40
443	Oswaldo Navarro	.40
444	Joe Mauer	.40
445	Miguel Montero	.40
446	Franklin Gutierrez/SP	5.00
447	Mark Redman/SP	5.00
448	Mike Rabelo RC	1.00
449	Philip Humber	.40
450	Justin Morneau	.40
451	Hector Gimenez	.40
452	Matt Holliday	.50
453	Akinori Otsuka	.40
454	Prince Fielder	.50
455	Chien-Ming Wang/SP	10.00
456	Shawn Riggans/SP	8.00
457	John Maine	.40
458	Adam Lind (RC)	1.00
459	Ubaldo Jimenez	.40
460	Drew Anderson	.40
461	Cla Meredith	.40
462	Joaquin Arias	.40
463	Kenny Rogers	.40
464	Jose Garcia/SP	5.00
465	Pedro Martinez/SP	8.00
466	Jeff Salazar	.40
467	Glen Perkins (RC)	.40
468	Travis Ishikawa	.40
469	Joe Borowski	.40
470	Jeremy Brown	.40
471	Andre Ethier	.40
472	Taylor Tankersley	.40
473	Lastings Milledge/SP	8.00
474	Brian Sanchez/SP	8.00
475	Ozzie Guillen, Phil Garner	.40
476	Albert Pujols	.40
477	David Ortiz	.40
478	Chase Utley	.50
479	Mark Loretta	.40
480	David Wright	.40
481	Alex Rodriguez	.40
482	Edgar Renteria/SP	5.00
483	Derek Jeter/SP	15.00
484	Alfonso Soriano	.40
485	Vladimir Guerrero	.40
486	Carlos Beltran	.40
487	Vernon Wells	.40
488	Jason Bay	.40
489	Ichiro Suzuki	.40
490	Paul LoDuca	.40
491	Ivan Rodriguez/SP	8.00
492	Brad Penny/SP	5.00
493	Roy Halladay	.40
494	Brian Fuentes	.40
495	Kenny Rogers	.40

Chrome

		NM/M
Common Player:		2.00

Production 1,958 Sets
Refractors: 1.5-2X
Production 558 Sets

Freddy Garcia — PITCHER — PHILA. PHILS.®

Black Refractors: 3-6X
Production 58 Sets

#	Player	Price
1	David Ortiz	6.00
2	John Smoltz	3.00
4	Brian Giles	2.00
5	Billy Sadler	4.00
6	Joel Zumaya	2.00
7	Felipe Lopez	3.00
8	Tim Hudson	3.00
9	David Ross	2.00
10	Adam Kennedy	2.00
11	David DeJesus	2.00
12	Jose Contreras	2.00
13	Trot Nixon	2.00
14	Roy Halladay	2.00
15	Gil Meche	2.00
16	Ray Durham	2.00
17	Delwyn Young	2.00
18	Endy Chavez	2.00
19	Vinny Rottino	3.00
20	Austin Kearns	3.00
21	Jeremy Hermida	3.00
22	Jonathan Broxton	4.00
23	Josh Fogg	2.00
24	Angel Guzman	4.00
25	Kenji Johjima	4.00
26	Juan Rivera	2.00
27	Johnny Estrada	2.00
28	Ted Lilly	2.00
29	Hank Blalock	3.00
30	Troy Tulowitzki	5.00
31	Moises Alou	3.00
32	Chris Stewart	2.00
33	Vicente Padilla	2.00
34	Eric Chavez	3.00
35	Jon Garland	2.00
36	Luke Scott	3.00
37	Brett Myers	5.00
38	David Bush	2.00
39	Brad Lidge	2.00
40	Jason Varitek	5.00
41	Paul Konerko	4.00
42	David Murphy	2.00
43	Clay Hensley	2.00
44	Alexis Gomez	2.00
45	Reggie Abercrombie	2.00
46	Jose Capellan	2.00
47	Jhonny Peralta	3.00
48	Chone Figgins	2.00
49	Curtis Granderson	4.00
50	Oswaldo Navarro	3.00
51	Matt Holliday	4.00
52	Cla Meredith	2.00
53	Jeremy Brown	3.00
54	Mark Loretta	2.00
55	Jason Bay	4.00
56	Roger Clemens	8.00
57	Robert Mackowiak	2.00
58	Robinson Cano	6.00
59	Jose Lopez	3.00
60	Dave Roberts	2.00
61	Delmon Young	6.00
62	Ryan Sweeney	3.00
63	Chris Narveson	3.00
64	Juan Uribe	2.00
65	Tony Gwynn Jr.	2.00
66	David Wright	8.00
67	Miguel Cairo	2.00
68	Edgar Renteria	2.00
69	Victor Martinez	3.00
70	Willy Aybar	2.00
71	Luke Hudson	2.00
72	Chuck James	2.00
73	Kris Benson	2.00
74	Garret Anderson	2.00
75	Tim Wakefield	2.00
77	Mike Piazza	6.00
78	Carlos Lee	4.00
79	Jim Edmonds	4.00
80	Joe Crede	2.00
81	Shawn Green	3.00
82	James Shields	8.00
84	Julian Santana	8.00
85	Ervin Santana	2.00
86	J.D. Drew	4.00
87	Nate Robertson	2.00
88	Chris Roberson	3.00
90	Pedro Feliz	2.00
91	Javier Valentin	2.00
93	Carlos Beltran	5.00
94	Brad Ausmus	2.00
95	Freddy Garcia	2.00
96	Erik Bedard	4.00
97	Carlos Zambrano	4.00
98	J.J. Putz	2.00
99	Brian McCann	4.00
100	Ricky Nolasco	2.00
102	Chris Young	4.00
103	Chad Tracy	2.00
104	B.J. Ryan	2.00
105	Joe Mauer	5.00
106	Akinori Otsuka	2.00
107	Joaquin Arias	2.00
108	Andre Ethier	4.00
109	David Wright	10.00
110	Ichiro Suzuki	8.00

A-Rod Road to 500

	NM/M
Common A-Rod:	3.00

Inserted 1:24
Autograph: No Pricing
Production 1 Set
51-75 Alex Rodriguez 3.00

Clubhouse Collection

		NM/M
	Common Player:	8.00
SM	Stan Musial	30.00
DS	Duke Snider	20.00
FR	Frank Robinson	20.00
BR	Brooks Robinson	15.00
YB	Yogi Berra	25.00
AK	Al Kaline	20.00
AW	Adam Wainwright	15.00
AJP	Albert Pujols	20.00
AR	Alex Rodriguez	20.00
ALR	Anthony Reyes	10.00
BU	B.J. Upton	8.00
BZ	Barry Zito	8.00
BS	Ben Sheets	10.00
BW	Billy Wagner	8.00
BR	Brian Roberts	10.00
CU	Chase Utley	15.00
CC	Chris Carpenter	15.00
CD	Chris Duncan	10.00
CJ	Conor Jackson	10.00
DE	David Eckstein	20.00
DO	David Ortiz	15.00
DW	David Wright	30.00
DY	Delmon Young	10.00
DWW	Dontrelle Willis	8.00
DM	Doug Mientkiewicz	8.00
ER	Edgar Renteria	8.00
EC	Eric Chavez	8.00
ES	Ervin Santana	8.00
FL	Francisco Liriano	10.00
GS	Gary Sheffield	10.00
HB	Hank Blalock	8.00
IR	Ivan Rodriguez	10.00
JS	Jeff Suppan	10.00
JW	Jeff Weaver	8.00
JR	Jimmy Rollins	10.00
JD	Johnny Damon	15.00
JRP	Jorge Posada	10.00
JBR	Jose Reyes	20.00
JV	Jose Vidro	8.00
JP	Juan Pierre	8.00
JM	Justin Morneau	15.00
LB	Lance Berkman	10.00
LG	Luis Gonzalez	8.00
MO	Magglio Ordonez	8.00
MR	Manny Ramirez	10.00
MK	Mark Kotsay	8.00
MT	Mark Teixeira	10.00
MM	Melvin Mora	8.00
MC	Miguel Cabrera	10.00
MOT	Miguel Tejada	8.00
MP	Mike Piazza	15.00
MA	Moises Alou	8.00
NS	Nick Swisher	10.00
OV	Omar Vizquel	8.00
PB	Pat Burrell	10.00
PP	Placido Polanco	8.00
RF	Rafael Furcal	8.00
RS	Richie Sexson	8.00
RB	Ronnie Belliard	8.00
RH	Ryan Howard	30.00
TH	Todd Helton	10.00
TKH	Torii Hunter	10.00
VM	Victor Martinez	8.00
YM	Yadier Molina	15.00

Clubhouse Collection Dual Relic

		NM/M

Production 58 Sets

MP	Stan Musial, Albert Pujols	180.00
KR	Al Kaline, Ivan Rodriguez	80.00

Clubhouse Coll. Relic Autograph

Production 25 Sets
No Pricing

Felt Team Emblem

	NM/M

Inserted 1:Box

Los Angeles Dodgers	3.00
Washington Senators	3.00
San Francisco Giants	3.00
Boston Red Sox	5.00
Cincinnati Redlegs	3.00
Pittsburgh Pirates	3.00
Milwaukee Braves	3.00
Chicago Cubs	5.00
Baltimore Orioles	3.00
New York Yankees	5.00
Cleveland Indians	3.00
St. Louis Cardinals	5.00
Kansas City Athletics	3.00
Detroit Tigers	3.00
Chicago White Sox	3.00
Philadelphia Phillies	3.00

Flashbacks

BALTIMORE WELCOMES BROOKS — BROOKS ROBINSON — APRIL 15, 1955

		NM/M
	Common Player:	1.00

Inserted 1:12

SM	Stan Musial	2.00
AK	Al Kaline	2.00
BR	Brooks Robinson	2.00
RS	Red Schoendienst	1.00
LA	Luis Aparicio	1.00
WS	Warren Spahn	2.00
HS	Hank Sauer	1.00
LB	Lew Burdette	1.00
EY	Eddie Yost	1.00
JB	Jim Bunning	1.00

Flashback Autograph

No Pricing
Production 25 Sets

Flashbacks Relics

		NM/M
	Common Player:	20.00
SM	Stan Musial	30.00
AK	Al Kaline	25.00
BR	Brooks Robinson	25.00
RS	Red Schoendienst	20.00
WS	Warren Spahn	25.00
LB	Lew Burdette	25.00
EY	Eddie Yost	20.00
JB	Jim Bunning	20.00

Flashbacks Relic Autograph

Production 25 Sets
No Pricing

Dual Flashbacks

Production 10 Sets
No Pricing

New Age Performers

		NM/M
	Common Player:	1.00

Inserted 1:15

RH	Ryan Howard	3.00
AR	Alex Rodriguez	3.00
AS	Alfonso Soriano	2.00
DO	David Ortiz	2.00
TH	Trevor Hoffman	3.00
DJ	Derek Jeter	4.00
AAS	Anibal Sanchez	3.00
RC	Roger Clemens	3.00
JS	Johan Santana	4.00
AP	Albert Pujols	4.00

CJ Chipper Jones 2.00
FT Frank Thomas 2.00
IR Ivan Rodriguez 1.50
IS Ichiro Suzuki 3.00
CB Craig Biggio 1.00

Real One Autographs

NM/M

Common Autograph:
Red Ink: 1.5-2X
Production 58 Sets
AK Al Kaline 150.00
BH Bob Henrich 60.00
BM Bobby Morgan 60.00
BP Buddy Pritchard 65.00
BR Brooks Robinson 100.00
BT Bill Taylor 50.00
BW Bill Wight 50.00
CH Chuck Harmon 50.00
CJD Jim Derrington 40.00
CR Charley Rabe 60.00
DM Dave Melton 60.00
DS Duke Snider 100.00
DW David Wright 120.00
DWW Dontrelle Willis 40.00
DY Delmon Young 60.00
DZ Don Zimmer 50.00
EM Ed Mayer 40.00
GK George Kell 75.00
HP Harding Peterson 60.00
JC Joe Caffie 60.00
JD Joe Durham 70.00
JL Joe Lonnett 50.00
JM Justin Morneau 60.00
JP Johnny Podres 60.00
LA Luis Aparicio 60.00
LM Lloyd Merritt 50.00
LS Lou Sleater 50.00
MB Milt Bolling 50.00
MEB Mack Burk 60.00
OH Orlando Hudson 40.00
PS Paul Smith 60.00
RC Ray Crone 50.00
RH Ryan Howard 250.00
RS Red Schoendienst 85.00
SP Stan Palys 60.00
TT Tim Thompson 50.00

Then and Now

NM/M

Common Player: 1.00
Inserted 1:15
RH Ryan Howard 3.00
DO David Ortiz 2.00
JM Joe Mauer 1.50
JR Jose Reyes 2.00
JS Johan Santana 2.00
AH Aaron Harang 1.00
IS Ichiro Suzuki 3.00
TH Travis Hafner 1.50
FR Francisco Rodriguez 1.00
CW Chien-Ming Wang 2.00

1958 A.L. Home Run Champion

NM/M

Common Mantle: 3.00
Inserted 1:6
1-42 Mickey Mantle 3.00

1958 Cut Signatures

Production One Set
No Pricing

2007 Topps Moments & Milestones

NM/M

Complete Set (193):
Common Player: .50
Common RC (170-193): 5.00
Production 150 Sets
Pack (6): 7.00
Box (18): 100.00
1 Albert Pujols (37/5550) 4.00
2 Albert Pujols (130/19500) 4.00
3 Albert Pujols (194/29100) 4.00
4 Albert Pujols (112/16800) 4.00
5 Albert Pujols (47/7050) 4.00
6 Ichiro Suzuki (242/36300) 2.50
7 Ichiro Suzuki (34/5100) 2.50
8 Ichiro Suzuki (8/1200) 5.00
9 Ichiro Suzuki (56/8400) 2.50
10 Ichiro Suzuki (69/10350) 2.50
11 Ichiro Suzuki (8/1200) 5.00
12 Greg Maddux (20/3000) 3.00
13 Greg Maddux (199/29850) 3.00
14 Greg Maddux (20/3000) 3.00
15 Greg Maddux (197/29550) 3.00
16 Roger Clemens (24/3600) 3.00
17 Roger Clemens (10/1500) 5.00
18 Roger Clemens (238/35700) 3.00
19 Roger Clemens (20/3000) 3.00
20 Roger Clemens (256/38400) 3.00
21 Chipper Jones (45/6750) 1.50
22 Chipper Jones (110/16500) 1.50
23 Chipper Jones (181/27150) 1.50
24 Chipper Jones (116/17400) 1.50
25 Chipper Jones (41/6150) 1.50
26 Chipper Jones (25/3750) 1.50
27 Alex Rodriguez (47/7050) 4.00
28 Alex Rodriguez (118/17700) 4.00
29 Alex Rodriguez (181/27150) 4.00
30 Alex Rodriguez (124/18600) 4.00
31 Alex Rodriguez (30/4500) 4.00
32 Alex Rodriguez (17/2550) 8.00
33 Alex Rodriguez (48/7200) 4.00
34 Alex Rodriguez (130/19500) 4.00
35 Alex Rodriguez (194/29100) 4.00
36 Alex Rodriguez (124/18600) 4.00
37 Alex Rodriguez (29/4350) 6.00
38 Alex Rodriguez (21/3150) 6.00
39 Vladimir Guerrero (39/5850) 1.50
40 Vladimir Guerrero (126/18900) 1.50
41 Vladimir Guerrero (206/30900) 1.50
42 Vladimir Guerrero (124/18600) 1.50
43 Vladimir Guerrero (39/5850) 1.50
44 Vladimir Guerrero (13/1950) 1.50
45 Ken Griffey Jr. (56/8400) 3.00
46 Ken Griffey Jr. (147/22050) 3.00
47 Ken Griffey Jr. (185/27750) 3.00
48 Barry Zito (23/3450) .75
49 Barry Zito (182/27300) .75
50 Randy Johnson (18/2700) 1.50
51 Randy Johnson (294/44100) 1.50
52 Randy Johnson (6/900) 5.00
53 Randy Johnson (3/450) 20.00
54 Randy Johnson (17/2550) 1.50
55 Randy Johnson (364/54600) 1.50
56 Randy Johnson (12/1800) 1.50
57 Randy Johnson (2/300) 20.00
58 Prince Fielder (35/5250) 2.00
59 Prince Fielder (81/12150) 2.00
60 Dan Uggla (26/3900) .50
61 Dan Uggla (27/4050) .50
62 Dan Uggla (172/25800) .50
63 Justin Verlander (17/2550) 3.00
64 Justin Verlander (124/18600) 1.50
65 Francisco Liriano (12/1800) 1.50
66 Francisco Liriano (144/21600) 1.50
67 Ryan Zimmerman (176/26400) 1.00
68 Ryan Zimmerman (110/16500) 1.00
69 Ryan Zimmerman (84/12600) 1.00
70 Hanley Ramirez (51/7650) 1.50
71 Hanley Ramirez (119/17850) 1.50
72 Hanley Ramirez (185/27750) 1.50
73 Russ Martin (65/9750) 1.00
74 Russ Martin (26/3900) 1.00
75 Mickey Mantle (173/25950) 5.00
76 Mickey Mantle (121/18150) 5.00
77 Mickey Mantle (146/21900) 5.00
78 Mickey Mantle (94/14100) 5.00
79 Mike Piazza (35/5250) 1.50
80 Mike Piazza (112/16800) 1.50
81 Derek Jeter (10/1500) 4.00
82 Derek Jeter (78/1700) 4.00
83 Derek Jeter (183/27450) 4.00
84 Dontrelle Willis (14/2100) .75
85 Dontrelle Willis (142/21300) .75
86 Dontrelle Willis (2/300) 2.50
87 Bobby Crosby (22/3300) .50
88 Bobby Crosby (64/9600) .50
89 Ryan Howard (22/3300) 3.00
90 Ryan Howard (63/9450) 3.00
91 Curt Schilling (21/3150) 1.50
92 Curt Schilling (203/30450) 1.50
93 Andruw Jones (52/7800) 1.50
94 Andruw Jones (128/19200) 1.50
95 Andruw Jones (11/1650) 1.50
96 Hideki Matsui (23/3450) 2.50
97 Hideki Matsui (116/17400) 2.50
98 Hideki Matsui (192/28800) 2.50
99 David Wright (27/4050) 2.50
100 David Wright (102/15300) 2.50
101 David Wright (42/6300) 2.50
102 David Wright (17/2550) 2.50
103 David Ortiz (75/11250) 2.00
104 David Wright (47/7050) 2.00
105 David Ortiz (11/1650) 2.00
106 Frank Thomas (38/5700) 1.50
107 Frank Thomas (101/15150) 1.50
108 Craig Biggio (40/6000) 1.00
109 Miguel Cabrera (33/4950) 2.00
110 Miguel Cabrera (116/17400) 2.00
111 Vernon Wells (12/1800) 1.00
112 Michael Young (24/3600) 1.00
113 Michael Young (40/6000) 1.00
114 Joe Mauer (144/21600) 1.50
115 Gary Sheffield (34/5100) 1.00
116 Jim Edmonds (42/6300) 1.00
117 Jorge Posada (19/2850) 1.00
118 Jorge Posada (23/3450) 1.00
119 Pat Burrell (32/4800) .75
120 Adam Dunn (40/6000) 1.00
121 Johnny Damon (35/5250) 2.00
122 Scott Rolen (34/5100) 1.50
123 Paul Konerko (6/900) 3.00
124 Roy Halladay (22/3300) 1.00
125 Grady Sizemore (22/3300) 1.50
126 Grady Sizemore (37/5550) 1.50
127 John Smoltz (24/3600) 1.00
128 Jeff Kent (29/4350) .75
129 Billy Wagner (38/5700) .50
130 Mark Prior (18/2700) .75
131 Eric Chavez (32/4800) .75
132 Jimmy Rollins (41/6150) 1.50
133 Manny Ramirez (7/1050) 1.50
134 Manny Ramirez (45/6750) 1.50
135 Manny Ramirez (144/21600) 1.50
136 Derrek Lee (46/6900) 1.50
137 Derrek Lee (107/16050) 1.50
138 Tom Glavine (14/2100) 1.00
139 Tom Glavine (20/3000) 1.00
140 Jose Reyes (17/2550) 2.00
141 Pedro Martinez (15/2250) 1.50
142 Pedro Martinez (208/31200) 1.50
143 Mark Teixeira (43/6450) 1.00
144 Jake Peavy (13/1950) 1.00
145 Carlos Lee (32/4800) .75
146 Josh Beckett (16/2400) .75
147 Johan Santana (20/3000) 2.00
148 Todd Helton (33/4950) 1.50
149 Mariano Rivera (43/6450) 1.50
150 Travis Hafner (33/4950) 1.50
151 Jason Bay (24/3600) 1.00
152 Bobby Abreu (30/4500) 1.00
153 Mike Mussina (13/1950) 1.00
154 Miguel Tejada (34/5100) 1.00
155 Miguel Tejada (150/22500) 1.00
156 Robinson Cano (14/2100) 1.50
157 Robinson Cano (34/5100) 1.50
158 Ryan Zimmerman (23/3450) 1.00
159 Carlos Beltran (16/2400) 1.50
160 Carlos Beltran (17/2550) 1.50
161 Roger Clemens (18/2700) 3.00
162 Roger Clemens (218/32700) 3.00
163 Mickey Mantle (52/7800) 5.00
164 Mickey Mantle (130/19500) 5.00
165 Mickey Mantle (188/28200) 5.00
166 Mickey Mantle (132/19800) 5.00
167 Mickey Mantle (42/6300) 5.00
168 Mickey Mantle (97/14550) 5.00
169 Mickey Mantle (127/19050) 5.00
170 Daisuke Matsuzaka **RC** 80.00
171 Daisuke Matsuzaka **RC** 80.00
172 Daisuke Matsuzaka **RC** 80.00
173 Delmon Young **(RC)** 5.00
174 Delmon Young **(RC)** 5.00
175 Delmon Young **(RC)** 5.00
176 Andrew Miller **RC** 20.00
177 Andrew Miller **RC** 20.00
178 Andrew Miller **RC** 20.00
179 Troy Tulowitzki **(RC)** 8.00
180 Troy Tulowitzki **(RC)** 8.00
181 Troy Tulowitzki **(RC)** 8.00
182 Josh Fields **(RC)** 5.00
183 Josh Fields **(RC)** 5.00
184 Josh Fields **(RC)** 5.00
185 Jeff Baker **(RC)** 5.00
186 Jeff Baker **(RC)** 5.00
187 Jeff Baker **(RC)** 5.00
188 Philip Humber **(RC)** 5.00
189 Philip Humber **(RC)** 5.00
190 Philip Humber **(RC)** 5.00
191 Kevin Kouzmanoff **(RC)** 5.00
192 Kevin Kouzmanoff **(RC)** 5.00
193 Kevin Kouzmanoff **(RC)** 5.00

Black

Stars: 2-3X
Production 29 Sets

Red

No Pricing
Production One Set

Printing Plates

No Pricing
Production one set per color.

A-Rod Road to 500

NM/M

Common A-Rod (101-125): 3.00
Inserted 2:Box

A-Rod Road to 500 Auto

NM/M

Production One Set 3.00

Milestone Autographs

NM/M

Common Auto.: 10.00
Black: 1-1.5X
Production 40 Sets
Red: No Pricing
Production One Set
AJ Andruw Jones/100 50.00
AR Alex Rodriguez/100 180.00
BP Brandon Phillips 15.00
BR Brian Roberts 15.00
CJ Conor Jackson 15.00
DO David Ortiz 60.00
DW David Wright 60.00
GA Garrett Atkins 15.00
GS Gary Sheffield/100 35.00
HS Huston Street/200 20.00
JF Jeff Francoeur 40.00
JG Jason Giambi/100 50.00
JJG Jonny Gomes 10.00
JL Julio Lugo 15.00
JP Jonathan Papelbon 40.00
JR Jose Reyes/200 40.00
JS Jeremy Sowers 10.00
KJ Kenji Johjima 35.00
KM Kendry Morales 10.00
LM Lastings Milledge 15.00
MK Matthew Kemp 15.00
MN Mike Napoli 15.00
MP Martin Prado 15.00
NS Nick Swisher 15.00
RH Ryan Howard/200 75.00
RP Ronny Paulino 10.00
TH Travis Hafner 15.00
VG Vladimir Guerrero/100 50.00
WP Wily Mo Pena/100 20.00

Rookie Autographs

NM/M

Common Auto.: 10.00
Black: 2-3X
Production 40 Sets
Red: No Pricing
Production One Set

AL	Adam Lind	10.00
AM	Andrew Miller	25.00
DM	David Murphy	10.00
HG	Hector Gimenez	10.00
JA	Joaquin Arias	10.00
KK	Kevin Kouzmanoff	15.00
MB	Michael Bourn	15.00
MM	Miguel Montero	10.00
SR	Shawn Riggans	10.00
TT	Troy Tulowitzki	20.00

2007 Topps Opening Day

		NM/M
Complete Set (220):		35.00
Common Player:		.15
Pack (6):		1.25
Box (36):		40.00
1	Bobby Abreu	.25
2	Mike Piazza	.75
3	Jake Westbrook	.15
4	Zachary Duke	.15
5	David Wright	1.00
6	Adrian Gonzalez	.25
7	Mickey Mantle	3.00
8	Bill Hall	.15
9	Robinson Cano	.25
10	Dontrelle Willis	.25
11	J.D. Drew	.25
12	Paul Konerko	.25
13	Austin Kearns	.15
14	Mike Lowell	.15
15	Magglio Ordonez	.15
16	Rafael Furcal	.25
17	Matt Cain	.25
18	Craig Monroe	.15
19	Matt Holliday	.25
20	Edgar Renteria	.25
21	Mark Buehrle	.15
22	Carlos Quentin	.15
23	C.C. Sabathia	.25
24	Nicholas Markakis	.25
25	Chipper Jones	.50
26	Jason Giambi	.40
27	Barry Zito	.25
28	Jake Peavy	.25
29	Hank Blalock	.25
30	Johnny Damon	.25
31	Chad Tracy	.15
32	Nick Swisher	.25
33	Willy Taveras	.15
34	Chuck James	.15
35	Carlos Delgado	.40
36	Livan Hernandez	.15
37	Freddy Garcia	.15
38	Bronson Arroyo	.15
39	Jack Wilson	.15
40	Dan Uggla	.15
41	Chris Carpenter	.50
42	Jorge Posada	.25
43	Joe Mauer	.40
44	Corey Patterson	.15
45	Chien-Ming Wang	.50
46	Derek Jeter	1.50
47	Carlos Beltran	.50
48	Jim Edmonds	.25
49	Jeremy Sowers	.15
50	Randy Johnson	.50
51	Jered Weaver	.25
52	Josh Barfield	.15
53	Scott Rolen	.40
54	Ryan Shealy	.15
55	Freddy Sanchez	.15
56	Javier Vazquez	.15
57	Jeremy Bonderman	.25
58	Miguel Cabrera	.50
59	Kazuo Matsui	.15
60	Curt Schilling	.50
61	Alfonso Soriano	.50
62	Orlando Hernandez	.15
63	Joe Blanton	.15
64	Aramis Ramirez	.25
65	Ben Sheets	.25
66	Jimmy Rollins	.25
67	Mark Loretta	.15
68	Cole Hamels	.25
69	Albert Pujols	1.50
70	Moises Alou	.25
71	Mark Teahen	.15
72	Roy Halladay	.25
73	Cory Sullivan	.15
74	Frank Thomas	.50
75	Ryan Howard	1.50
76	Rocco Baldelli	.25
77	Manny Ramirez	.50
78	Ray Durham	.15
79	Gary Sheffield	.40
80	Jay Gibbons	.15
81	Todd Helton	.40
82	Gary Matthews	.15
83	Brandon Inge	.15
84	Jonathan Papelbon	.40
85	John Smoltz	.25
86	Chone Figgins	.15
87	Hideki Matsui	.75

88	Carlos Lee	.25
89	Jose Reyes	.75
90	Lyle Overbay	.25
91	Johan Santana	.50
92	Ian Kinsler	.15
93	Scott Kazmir	.25
94	Hanley Ramirez	.40
95	Greg Maddux	1.00
96	Johnny Estrada	.15
97	B.J. Upton	.25
98	Francisco Liriano	.25
99	Chase Utley	.50
100	Preston Wilson	.15
101	Marcus Giles	.15
102	Jeff Kent	.25
103	Grady Sizemore	.50
104	Ken Griffey Jr.	1.00
105	Garret Anderson	.15
106	Brian McCann	.25
107	Jon Garland	.15
108	Troy Glaus	.25
109	Brandon Webb	.25
110	Jason Schmidt	.25
111	Ramon Hernandez	.15
112	Justin Morneau	.50
113	Mike Cameron	.15
114	Andruw Jones	.40
115	Russell Martin	.25
116	Vernon Wells	.25
117	Orlando Hudson	.15
118	Derek Lowe	.15
119	Alex Rodriguez	1.50
120	Chad Billingsley	.15
121	Kenji Johjima	.15
122	Nick Johnson	.15
123	Danny Haren	.25
124	Mark Teixeira	.40
125	Jeff Francoeur	.25
126	Ted Lilly	.15
127	Jhonny Peralta	.15
128	Aaron Harang	.15
129	Ryan Zimmerman	.25
130	Jermaine Dye	.25
131	Orlando Cabrera	.15
132	Juan Pierre	.25
133	Brian Giles	.25
134	Jason Bay	.25
135	David Ortiz	.50
136	Chris Capuano	.15
137	Carlos Zambrano	.25
138	Luis Gonzalez	.25
139	Jeff Weaver	.15
140	Lance Berkman	.25
141	Raul Ibanez	.15
142	Jim Thome	.40
143	Jose Contreras	.15
144	David Eckstein	.15
145	Adam Dunn	.40
146	Alex Rios	.15
147	Garrett Atkins	.25
148	A.J. Burnett	.25
149	Jeremy Hermida	.15
150	Conor Jackson	.15
151	Adrian Beltre	.25
152	Torii Hunter	.25
153	Andrew Miller **RC**	2.00
154	Ichiro Suzuki	1.00
155	Mark Redman	.15
156	Paul LoDuca	.25
157	Xavier Nady	.15
158	Stephen Drew	.25
159	Eric Chavez	.25
160	Pedro Martinez	.50
161	Derrek Lee	.40
162	David DeJesus	.15
163	Troy Tulowitzki **(RC)**	.50
164	Vinny Rottino **(RC)**	.25
165	Philip Humber **(RC)**	.25
166	Jerry Owens **(RC)**	.25
167	Ubaldo Jimenez **(RC)**	.25
168	Michael Young	.25
169	Ryan Braun **(RC)**	.25
170	Kevin Kouzmanoff **(RC)**	.25
171	Oswaldo Navarro **RC**	.25
172	Miguel Montero **(RC)**	.25
173	Roy Oswalt	.25
174	Shane Youman **RC**	.25
175	Josh Fields **(RC)**	.25
176	Adam Lind **(RC)**	.25
177	Miguel Tejada	.40
178	Delwyn Young **(RC)**	.25
179	Scott Moore **(RC)**	.25
180	Fred Lewis **(RC)**	.25
181	Glen Perkins **(RC)**	.25
182	Vladimir Guerrero	.50
183	Drew Anderson **(RC)**	.25
184	Jeff Salazar **(RC)**	.25
185	Tom Gordon	.15
186	The Bird	.15
187	Justin Verlander	.40
188	Delmon Young **(RC)**	.50
189	Homer	.15
190	Wally the Green Monster	.15
191	Southpaw	.15
192	Dinger	.15
193	Carl Crawford	.15
194	Slider	.15
195	Gapper	.15
196	Paws	.15
197	Billy the Marlin	.15
198	Ivan Rodriguez	.25
199	Slugger	.15
200	Junction Jack	.15
201	Bernie the Brewer	.15
202	Travis Hafner	.40
203	Stomper	.15
204	Mr. Met	.15

205	The Moose	.15
206	Phillie Phanatic	.15
207	Prince Fielder	.50
208	Julio Lugo	.15
209	Pirate Parrot	.15
210	Joel Zumaya	.25
211	Swinging Friar	.15
212	Jay Payton	.15
213	Lou Seal	.15
214	Fredbird	.15
215	Screech	.15
216	TC Bear	.15
217	Andre Ethier	.15
218	Ervin Santana	.15
219	Melvin Mora	.15
220	Checklist	.15

Autographs

		NM/M
Common Auto.:		10.00
EF	Emiliano Fruto	10.00
HK	Howie Kendrick	25.00
JT	Jordan Tata	25.00
JM	Juan Morillo	10.00
MC	Matt Cain	20.00
MK	Matthew Kemp	25.00
MN	Mike Napoli	15.00
OH	Orlando Hudson	15.00
RM	Robert Mackowiak	10.00
SS	Shannon Stewart	10.00

A-Rod Road to 500

		NM/M
Common A-Rod (76-100):		3.00

A-Rod Road to 500 Autograph

Production One Set

Diamond Stars

		NM/M
Common Player:		.25
1	Ryan Howard	1.50
2	Alfonso Soriano	.75
3	Alex Rodriguez	1.50
4	David Ortiz	.75
5	Raul Ibanez	.25
6	Matt Holliday	.50
7	Delmon Young	.50
8	Derrick Turnbow	.25
9	Freddy Sanchez	.25
10	Troy Glaus	.25
11	A.J. Pierzynski	.25
12	Dontrelle Willis	.50
13	Justin Morneau	.75
14	Jose Reyes	1.00
15	Derek Jeter	1.50
16	Ivan Rodriguez	.50
17	Jay Payton	.25
18	Adrian Gonzalez	.25
19	David Eckstein	.25
20	Chipper Jones	.75
21	Aramis Ramirez	.50
22	David Wright	1.00
23	Mark Teixeira	.50
24	Stephen Drew	.50
25	Ichiro Suzuki	1.00

Movie Gallery

		NM/M
Alex Rodriguez		1.00

Puzzle

		NM/M
Complete Puzzle:		10.00
Common Player:		.25
1	Adam Dunn	.25
2	Adam Dunn	.25
3	Miguel Tejada	.25
4	Miguel Tejada	.25
5	Hanley Ramirez	.25
6	Hanley Ramirez	.25
7	Johan Santana	.50
8	Johan Santana	.50
9	Brandon Webb	.25
10	Brandon Webb	.25
11	David Wright	.75
12	David Wright	.75
13	Alex Rodriguez	.75
14	Alex Rodriguez	.75
15	Ryan Howard	.75
16	Ryan Howard	.75
17	Albert Pujols	1.00
18	Albert Pujols	1.00
19	Andruw Jones	.50
20	Andruw Jones	.50
21	Alfonso Soriano	.50
22	Alfonso Soriano	.50
23	Vladimir Guerrero	.50
24	Vladimir Guerrero	.50
25	David Ortiz	.50
26	David Ortiz	.50
27	Ichiro Suzuki	.75
28	Ichiro Suzuki	.75

2007 Topps Triple Threads

		NM/M
Complete Set (189):		
Common Player (1-125):		1.00
Production 1,350		
Common Auto. (126-189):		10.00
Production 99		
Pack (6):		100.00
Box (2):		200.00
1	Alex Rodriguez	4.00
2	Barry Zito	1.00
3	Corey Patterson	1.00
4	Roberto Clemente	5.00
5	David Wright	3.00
6	Dontrelle Willis	1.00
7	Mickey Mantle	8.00
8	Adam Dunn	1.50
9	Richie Ashburn	2.00
10	Ryan Howard	3.00
11	Miguel Tejada	1.50
12	Ernie Banks	4.00
13	Ken Griffey Jr.	3.00
14	Johnny Bench	3.00
15	Ichiro Suzuki	3.00
16	Gil Meche	1.00
17	Kazuo Matsui	1.00
18	Matt Holliday	1.50
19	Juan Pierre	1.00
20	Yogi Berra	3.00
21	Bill Hall	1.00
22	Wade Boggs	2.00
23	Jason Bay	1.50

24 Troy Glaus 1.50
25 Paul Konerko 1.50
26 Rod Carew 2.00
27 Jay Gibbons 1.00
28 Frank Thomas 2.00
29 Joe Mauer 1.50
30 Carlos Beltran 2.00
31 Frank Robinson 3.00
32 Bobby Abreu 1.50
33 Roy Oswalt 1.50
34 Edgar Renteria 1.50
35 Magglio Ordonez 1.50
36 Mike Piazza 2.00
37 Trevor Hoffman 1.50
38 Eddie Mathews 3.00
39 Albert Pujols 4.00
40 Dennis Eckersley 1.00
41 Andruw Jones 2.00
42 Alfonso Soriano 2.00
43 Bob Feller 2.00
44 J.D. Drew 1.00
45 Jason Schmidt 1.00
46 Vladimir Guerrero 2.00
47 Reggie Jackson 3.00
48 Lance Berkman 1.50
49 Michael Young 1.00
50 Carlton Fisk 2.00
51 Brandon Webb 1.50
52 Adrian Beltre 1.00
53 Hideki Matsui 2.50
54 Bronson Arroyo 1.00
55 Tony Gwynn 3.00
56 Ray Durham 1.00
57 Garrett Atkins 1.50
58 Nolan Ryan 4.00
59 Daisuke Matsuzaka **RC** 15.00
60 Todd Helton 1.50
61 Carl Crawford 1.50
62 Jake Peavy 2.00
63 Rafael Furcal 1.50
64 Joe Morgan 2.00
65 Greg Maddux 3.00
66 Luis Aparicio 1.00
67 Derrek Lee 1.50
68 Johnny Damon 1.50
69 Mike Lowell 1.50
70 Roger Maris 4.00
71 Vernon Wells 1.50
72 Monte Irvin 2.00
73 Jermaine Dye 1.50
74 Miguel Cabrera 2.50
75 Barry Bonds 4.00
76 Stan Musial 3.00
77 Derek Lowe 1.00
78 Don Mattingly 4.00
79 Lyle Overbay 1.00
80 Chien-Ming Wang 3.00
81 Carlos Zambrano 1.50
82 Kei Igawa **RC** 2.00
83 Cole Hamels 2.00
84 Gary Sheffield 1.50
85 Nick Johnson 1.00
86 Brooks Robinson 3.00
87 Curt Schilling 2.00
88 Ryne Sandberg 3.00
89 Mike Cameron 1.00
90 Mike Schmidt 3.00
91 Chris Carpenter 1.50
92 Scott Rolen 1.50
93 Rocco Baldelli 1.00
94 C.C. Sabathia 1.50
95 Jeff Francis 1.00
96 Ozzie Smith 3.00
97 Aramis Ramirez 1.50
98 Aaron Harang 1.00
99 Duke Snider 3.00
100 David Ortiz 2.00
101 Raul Ibanez 1.00
102 Bruce Sutter 1.00
103 Gary Matthews 1.00
104 Chipper Jones 3.00
105 Craig Biggio 1.50
106 Roy Halladay 1.50
107 Hoyt Wilhelm 1.00
108 Manny Ramirez 2.00
109 Randy Johnson 2.00
110 Carl Yastrzemski 3.00
111 Mark Teixeira 2.00
112 Derek Jeter 4.00
113 Stephen Drew 1.00
114 Darryl Strawberry 1.00
115 Travis Hafner 1.50
116 Torii Hunter 1.50
117 Jim Edmonds 1.00
118 John Smoltz 1.50
119 Bo Jackson 3.00
120 Roger Clemens 3.00
121 Pedro Martinez 2.00
122 Rickey Henderson 2.00
123 Ivan Rodriguez 1.50
124 Robin Yount 3.00
125 Johan Santana 2.00
126a Robinson Cano/Auto. 40.00
126b Robinson Cano/Auto. 40.00
127a Jose Reyes/Auto. 60.00
127b Jose Reyes/Auto. 60.00
128a Justin Morneau/Auto. 25.00
128b Justin Morneau/Auto. 25.00
129a Curtis Granderson/Auto. 30.00
129b Curtis Granderson/Auto. 30.00
130a Justin Verlander/Auto. 40.00
130b Justin Verlander/Auto. 40.00
131 Prince Fielder/Auto. 50.00
132a Ryan Zimmerman/Auto. 30.00
132b Ryan Zimmerman/Auto. 30.00
133 Mike Napoli/Auto. 15.00
134 Melky Cabrera/Auto. 30.00
135 Jonathan Papelbon/Auto. 40.00
136a Nicholas Markakis/Auto. 30.00
136b Nicholas Markakis/Auto. 30.00
137 B.J. Upton/Auto. 25.00
138a Joel Zumaya/Auto. 20.00
138b Joel Zumaya/Auto. 20.00
140 Nick Swisher/Auto. 25.00
141 Andre Ethier/Auto. 20.00
142a Jered Weaver/Auto. 25.00
142b Jered Weaver/Auto. 25.00
143 Matt Cain/Auto. 25.00
144 Lastings Milledge/Auto. 25.00
145 Brian McCann/Auto. 35.00
146 Shin-Soo Choo/Auto. 20.00
147a Dan Uggla/Auto. 25.00
147b Dan Uggla/Auto. 25.00
148 Hanley Ramirez/Auto. 40.00
149 Russell Martin/Auto. 40.00
150 Francisco Liriano/Auto. 25.00
151 Anthony Reyes/Auto. 10.00
152 Josh Barfield/Auto. 10.00
153 Anibal Sanchez/Auto. 10.00
154 Jeremy Hermida/Auto. 15.00
155 Kendry Morales/Auto. 10.00
156 Matthew Kemp/Auto. 30.00
157 Freddy Sanchez/Auto. 15.00
158 Howie Kendrick/Auto. 20.00
159 Scott Thorman/Auto. 10.00
160 Franklin Gutierrez/Auto. 15.00
161 Jason Bartlett/Auto. 10.00
162 Chris Duncan/Auto. 40.00
163 Maicer Izturis/Auto. 10.00
164 Jason Botts/Auto. 10.00
165 Tony Gwynn Jr./Auto. 30.00
166 Jorge Cantu/Auto. 10.00
167 Adam Jones/Auto. 30.00
168 Edinson Volquez/Auto. 40.00
169 Joey Gathright/Auto. 10.00
170 Carlos Marmol/Auto. 30.00
171 Benjamin Zobrist/Auto. 10.00
172 Josh Willingham/Auto. 10.00
173 Brad Thompson/Auto. 15.00
174a Chris Ray/Auto. 15.00
174b Ervin Santana/Auto. 25.00
175 Ronny Paulino/Auto. 10.00
176 Tyler Johnson/Auto. 15.00
177 J.J. Hardy/Auto. 25.00
178 Adrian Gonzalez/Auto. 20.00
179 Scott Kazmir/Auto. 25.00
180 Juan Morillo/Auto. **(RC)** 10.00
181a Shawn Riggans/Auto. **(RC)** 15.00
181b Shawn Riggans/Auto. **(RC)** 10.00
182 Brian Stokes/Auto. **(RC)** 10.00
183 Delmon Young/Auto. **(RC)** 25.00
184a Troy Tulowitzki/Auto. **(RC)** 50.00
184b Troy Tulowitzki/Auto. **(RC)** 50.00
185 Adam Lind/Auto. **(RC)** 15.00
186 David Murphy/Auto. **(RC)** 20.00
187a Philip Humber/Auto. **(RC)** 15.00
187b Philip Humber/Auto. **(RC)** 15.00
188a Andrew Miller/Auto. **RC** 30.00
188b Andrew Miller/Auto. **RC** 30.00
189a Glen Perkins/Auto. **(RC)** 10.00
189b Glen Perkins/Auto. **(RC)** 10.00

Sepia

Sepia (1-125): 1-2X
Production 559 Sets
Autos. (126-189): 1X
Production 75 Sets

Emerald

Emerald (1-125): 2-3X
Production 239 Sets
Autos. (126-189): 1-1.5X
Production 50 Sets

Gold

Gold (1-125): 3-4X
Production 99 Sets
Autos. (126-189): 1-2X
Production 25 Sets

Sapphire

Sapphire (1-125): 4-8X
Production 25 Sets
Autos. (126-189): No Pricing
Production 10 Sets

Platinum

Production One Set

Printing Plates

Production one set per color.

All-Star Triple Patches

No Pricing
Production Nine Sets
Platinum: No Pricing
Production One Set

Bat-Barrels

No Pricing

Logo Man

No Pricing
Production One Set

Relics

NM/M

Common Player: 20.00
Production 36 Sets
Sepia: 1X
Production 27 Sets
Emerald: 1-1.5X
Production 18 Sets
Gold: No Pricing
Production Nine Sets
Sapphire: No Pricing
Production Three Sets
Platinum: No Pricing
Production One Set
1-3 Carl Yastrzemski 30.00
4-9 Roberto Clemente 100.00
10-15 Alex Rodriguez 50.00
16-18 Ryan Howard 40.00
19-21 David Wright 40.00
22-24 Chien-Ming Wang 100.00
25-27 Ichiro Suzuki 80.00
28-30 Hideki Matsui 60.00
31-33 Luis Aparicio 20.00
34-36 Joe DiMaggio 100.00
37-39 Ted Williams 100.00
40-45 Mickey Mantle 150.00
45 Mickey Mantle 150.00
46-48 Mickey Mantle 120.00
49-51 David Ortiz 30.00
52-54 Albert Pujols 50.00
55-57 Justin Morneau 25.00
58-63 Nolan Ryan 50.00
64-66 Manny Ramirez 20.00
67-69 Roger Maris 80.00
70-72 Daisuke Matsuzaka 100.00
73-75 Brian Cashman 25.00
76-78 Ernie Banks 40.00
79-81 Stan Musial 50.00
82-84 Duke Snider 30.00
85-87 Yogi Berra 50.00
88-90 Harmon Killebrew 40.00
91-93 Joe Mauer 25.00
94-96 Alfonso Soriano 25.00
97-102 Reggie Jackson 35.00
103-105 Vladimir Guerrero 20.00
106-108 Pedro Martinez 30.00
109-111 Roger Clemens 40.00
112-114 Randy Johnson 25.00
115-117 Don Mattingly 50.00
118-120 Bill Dickey 50.00
121a Barry Bonds 100.00
121b Bruce Sutter 20.00
122a Barry Bonds 100.00
122b Bruce Sutter 20.00
123a Barry Bonds 100.00
123b Bruce Sutter 20.00
124-126 John F. Kennedy 200.00
127-129 Johnny Bench 35.00
130-132 Mark Teixeira 20.00
133-135 Johan Santana 30.00
136-138 Alex Rodriguez 50.00
139-141 Brooks Robinson 30.00
142-144 Rickey Henderson 30.00
145-147 Ozzie Smith 50.00
148-150 Chipper Jones 30.00

Relics Autographs

NM/M

Production 18 Sets
Gold: No Pricing
Production Nine Sets
Sapphire: No Pricing
Production Three Sets
Platinum: No Pricing
Production One Set
1-3 Alex Rodriguez 275.00
4-6 Chien-Ming Wang 200.00
7-9 David Ortiz 100.00
10-12 Manny Ramirez 75.00
13-15 Johnny Damon 75.00
16-18 Miguel Tejada 50.00
19-21 Carl Crawford 40.00
22-24 Johan Santana 60.00
25-27 Francisco Liriano 30.00
28-30 Bob Feller 60.00
31-33 Vladimir Guerrero 75.00
34-36 Ernie Banks 150.00
37-39 Yogi Berra 100.00
40-42 Nolan Ryan 150.00
43-45 Ozzie Smith 100.00
46-48 David Wright 100.00
49-51 Albert Pujols 350.00
52-54 Ryan Howard 120.00
55-57 Don Mattingly 100.00
58-60 Brooks Robinson 60.00
61-63 Robin Yount 75.00
64-66 Mike Schmidt 100.00
67-69 Carl Yastrzemski 100.00
70-72 Wade Boggs 65.00
73-75 Andre Dawson 50.00
76-78 Reggie Jackson 75.00
79-81 Miguel Cabrera 60.00
82-84 Tom Seaver 75.00
85-87 Ralph Kiner 65.00
88-90 Chipper Jones 100.00
91-93 Andruw Jones 40.00
94-96 Dontrelle Willis 30.00
97-99 Bob Gibson 80.00
100-102 Johnny Bench 85.00
103-105 Joe Morgan 50.00
106-108 Ryne Sandberg 120.00
109-111 Dwight Gooden 40.00
112-114 Johnny Podres 60.00
115-117 Monte Irvin 50.00
118-120 Orlando Cepeda 50.00
121-123 Bo Jackson 140.00
124-126 Gary Sheffield 60.00
127-129 Tom Glavine 100.00
130-132 Tony LaRussa 40.00
133-135 Jim Leyland 50.00
136-138 Joe Torre 60.00
139-141 Gary Carter 75.00
142-144 Roy Oswalt 50.00
145-147 Carlos Delgado 50.00
148-150 Jason Varitek 75.00
151-153 Bobby Abreu 50.00
154-156 Juan Marichal 60.00
157-159 Frank Robinson 65.00
160-162 Jorge Posada 80.00
163-165 Luis Aparicio 50.00
166-168 Carlton Fisk 50.00
169-171 Dale Murphy 80.00
172-174 Mark Teixeira 60.00
175-177 Darryl Strawberry 50.00
178-180 Justin Morneau 50.00

Relics Combos Autographs

NM/M

Production 36 Sets
Sepia: 1X
Production 27 Sets
Emerald: 1-1.5X
Production 18 Sets
Gold: No Pricing
Production Nine Sets
Sapphire: No Pricing
Production Three Sets
Platinum: No Pricing
Production One Set
1 Brooks Robinson, Robin Yount, Johnny Bench 125.00
2 Reggie Jackson, Joe Morgan, Ryne Sandberg 125.00
3 Tom Seaver, Bob Gibson, Nolan Ryan 180.00
4 Albert Pujols, Alex Rodriguez, Vladimir Guerrero 375.00
5 Tom Seaver, Roger Clemens, Dwight Gooden 160.00
6 Johan Santana, Tom Glavine, Roger Clemens 200.00
7 Alex Rodriguez, Chien-Ming Wang, Don Mattingly 300.00
8 Ryan Howard, Mike Schmidt, Bobby Abreu 150.00
9 Ryan Howard, David Ortiz, Albert Pujols 350.00
10 Alex Rodriguez, David Wright, Jose Reyes 300.00
11 Miguel Cabrera, Manny Ramirez, David Ortiz 125.00
12 Justin Verlander, Jered Weaver, Chien-Ming Wang 250.00
13 Ralph Kiner, Duke Snider, Yogi Berra 125.00
14 Ryan Howard, Alex Rodriguez, Andruw Jones 260.00
15 Adam Lind, Brian Stokes, David Murphy 30.00
16 Andrew Miller, Brian Stokes, Glen Perkins 50.00
17 Shawn Riggans, Troy Tulowitzki, Andrew Miller 80.00
18 Glen Perkins, Lastings Milledge, Troy Tulowitzki 50.00

Relics Combos

NM/M

Production 36 Sets
Sepia: 1X
Production 27 Sets
Emerald: 1-1.5X
Production 18 Sets
Gold: No Pricing
Production Nine Sets
Sapphire: No Pricing
Production Three Sets
Platinum: No Pricing
Production One Set
1 Albert Pujols, Manny Ramirez, David Ortiz 40.00
2 Albert Pujols, Pedro Martinez, Vladimir Guerrero 40.00
3 Ivan Rodriguez, Carlos Delgado, Roberto Clemente 60.00
4 Roberto Clemente, Bernie Williams, Carlos Beltran 65.00
5 Jose Reyes, Alfonso Soriano, Miguel Tejada 30.00
6 Carl Crawford, Jose Reyes, Juan Pierre 25.00
7 Hideki Matsui, Ichiro Suzuki, So Taguchi 60.00
8 Miguel Cabrera, Johan Santana, Bobby Abreu 25.00
9 Alex Rodriguez, Mariano Rivera, Hideki Matsui 60.00
10 Reggie Jackson, Alex Rodriguez, Don Mattingly 50.00
11 Yogi Berra, Don Mattingly, Reggie Jackson 75.00
12 David Ortiz, Wade Boggs, Manny Ramirez 25.00
13 David Ortiz, Manny Ramirez, Pedro Martinez 30.00
14 Miguel Tejada, Eddie Murray, Brooks Robinson 30.00
15 Joe Mauer, Justin Morneau, Johan Santana 30.00
16 Harmon Killebrew, Joe Mauer, Justin Morneau 40.00

No.	Players	Price
17	Justin Verlander, Ivan Rodriguez, Joel Zumaya	25.00
18	Barry Zito, Dennis Eckersley, Huston Street	20.00
19	Reggie Jackson, Rod Carew, Vladimir Guerrero	30.00
20	Vladimir Guerrero, Pedro Martinez, Moises Alou	30.00
21	Michael Young, Mark Teixeira, Alex Rodriguez	40.00
22	Edgar Martinez, Ichiro Suzuki, Alex Rodriguez	70.00
23	David Wright, Carlos Delgado, Jose Reyes	40.00
24	Jose Reyes, Pedro Martinez, David Wright	50.00
25	Jose Reyes, Carlos Beltran, David Wright	40.00
26	Ryan Howard, Chase Utley, Jimmy Rollins	50.00
27	Jeff Francoeur, Chipper Jones, Brian McCann	30.00
28	John Smoltz, Tom Glavine, Greg Maddux	40.00
29	Chipper Jones, Jeff Francoeur, Andruw Jones	40.00
30	Nolan Ryan, Pedro Martinez, Tom Seaver	50.00
31	Mike Schmidt, Jim Thome, Ryan Howard	40.00
32	Stan Musial, Albert Pujols, Ozzie Smith	60.00
33	Albert Pujols, David Eckstein, Jim Edmonds	50.00
34	Lance Berkman, Roy Oswalt, Craig Biggio	25.00
35	Roger Clemens, Roy Oswalt, Nolan Ryan	40.00
36	Frank Robinson, Joe Morgan, Johnny Bench	40.00
37	Paul Molitor, Prince Fielder, Robin Yount	40.00
38	Ernie Banks, Alfonso Soriano, Ryne Sandberg	50.00
39	Andre Ethier, Matthew Kemp, Jered Weaver	25.00
40	Chien-Ming Wang, Alex Rodriguez, Mariano Rivera	100.00
41	Albert Pujols, Ichiro Suzuki, Vladimir Guerrero	50.00
42	Albert Pujols, Alex Rodriguez, Ichiro Suzuki	75.00
43	Ryan Howard, Justin Morneau, Albert Pujols	50.00
44	Albert Pujols, Roberto Clemente, Ichiro Suzuki	100.00
45	Albert Pujols, Roberto Clemente, Mickey Mantle	150.00
46	Joe DiMaggio, Mickey Mantle, Alex Rodriguez	150.00
47	Ted Williams, Joe DiMaggio, Mickey Mantle	200.00
48	Roberto Clemente, Mickey Mantle, Reggie Jackson	125.00
49	Stan Musial, Roberto Clemente, Frank Robinson	100.00
50	Albert Pujols, Johnny Bench, Mickey Mantle	100.00
51	Carl Yastrzemski, Ted Williams, Mickey Mantle	140.00
52	Brandon Webb, Tom Seaver, Johan Santana	30.00
53	Roger Clemens, Dwight Gooden, Pedro Martinez	40.00
54	Johan Santana, Greg Maddux, Roger Clemens	35.00
55	Johan Santana, Pedro Martinez, Roger Clemens	30.00
56	Randy Johnson, Roger Clemens, Tom Glavine	30.00
57	Justin Verlander, Ryan Howard, Ichiro Suzuki	50.00
58	Dontrelle Willis, Carlos Beltran, Jason Bay	20.00
59	Albert Pujols, Scott Rolen, Ryan Howard	40.00
60	Roberto Clemente, Joe DiMaggio, Mickey Mantle	200.00
61	Stan Musial, Ernie Banks, Mickey Mantle	140.00
62	Mike Schmidt, Joe Morgan, Johnny Bench	35.00
63	George Brett, Robin Yount, Ozzie Smith	60.00
64	Albert Pujols, Ichiro Suzuki, Rod Carew	50.00
65	Alfonso Soriano, Mickey Mantle, Alex Rodriguez	100.00
66	Don Mattingly, Wade Boggs, Tony Gwynn	50.00
67	Rod Carew, Vladimir Guerrero, Garret Anderson	25.00
68	Tony Gwynn, Wade Boggs, George Brett	50.00
69	Vladimir Guerrero, Alfonso Soriano, Bobby Abreu	30.00
70	Darryl Strawberry, Carlos Beltran, Howard Johnson	30.00
71	Jim Thome, Manny Ramirez, Frank Thomas	30.00
72	Mickey Mantle, Mike Piazza, Mike Schmidt	120.00
73	Carl Yastrzemski, Alex Rodriguez, Dave Winfield	50.00
74	Johan Santana, Pedro Martinez, Roger Clemens	30.00
75	Greg Maddux, Nolan Ryan, Tom Seaver	60.00
76	Bob Gibson, Dwight Gooden, Greg Maddux	50.00
77	Roberto Clemente, Reggie Jackson, Manny Ramirez	75.00
78	Johnny Podres, Don Larsen, Lew Burdette	30.00
79	Ichiro Suzuki, Kenji Johjima, Tadahito Iguchi	70.00
80	Paul Molitor, Jimmy Rollins, Chase Utley	35.00
81	Gary Carter, Paul LoDuca, Mike Piazza	60.00
82	George Brett, Alex Rodriguez, David Wright	50.00
83	Hoyt Wilhelm, Phil Niekro, Tim Wakefield	35.00
84	Franklin D. Roosevelt, Harry S. Truman, Dwight D. Eisenhower	80.00
85	Ichiro Suzuki, Eric Chavez, Torii Hunter	50.00
86	Richard Nixon, Ronald Reagan, George W. Bush	100.00
87	John Smoltz, Carlos Delgado, Edgar Martinez	30.00
88	Manny Ramirez, Vladimir Guerrero, David Ortiz	30.00
89	Livan Hernandez, Orel Hershiser, Willie Stargell	20.00
90	David Ortiz, Ryan Howard, Albert Pujols	50.00
91	Chien-Ming Wang, Johan Santana, Jon Garland	80.00
92	Deion Sanders, Bo Jackson, Brian Jordan	60.00
93	Franklin D. Roosevelt, John F. Kennedy, Bill Clinton	125.00
94	Vladimir Guerrero, Ichiro Suzuki, Vernon Wells	50.00
95	Jim Thome, Jermaine Dye, Paul Konerko	25.00
96	A.J. Pierzynski, Kelvim Escobar, Josh Paul	20.00
97	Joe Carter, Rickey Henderson, Paul Molitor	50.00
98	Kirk Gibson, Dennis Eckersley	25.00
99	Luis Castillo, Moises Alou, Mark Prior	20.00
100	Mookie Wilson, Ray Knight, Bill Buckner	20.00

Relics Combos Double

	NM/M
Production 36 Sets	
Sepia:	No Pricing
Production 27 Sets	
Emerald:	1-1.5X
Production 18 Sets	
Gold:	No Pricing
Production Nine Sets	
Sapphire:	No Pricing
Production Three Sets	
Platinum:	No Pricing
Production One Set	

No.	Players	Price
1	Mickey Mantle, Joe DiMaggio	250.00
2	Alex Rodriguez, Chien-Ming Wang, Johnny Damon, Manny Ramirez, David Ortiz, Jason Varitek	100.00
3	David Wright, Carlos Beltran, Tom Glavine, Chipper Jones, Andruw Jones, John Smoltz	50.00
4	David Wright	50.00
5	Albert Pujols	70.00
6	Chien-Ming Wang	100.00
7	David Wright, Ryan Howard	60.00
8	Alex Rodriguez	70.00
9	Ryan Howard	60.00
10	Ichiro Suzuki	100.00
11	Albert Pujols, Pedro Martinez, David Ortiz, Vladimir Guerrero, Manny Ramirez, Alfonso Soriano	70.00
12	Ichiro Suzuki, So Taguchi, Hideki Matsui, Kazuo Matsui, Tadahito Iguchi, Kenji Johjima	140.00
13	Roberto Clemente, Ivan Rodriguez, Carlos Beltran, Bernie Williams, Carlos Delgado, Javy Lopez	125.00
14	Johan Santana, Miguel Cabrera, Bobby Abreu, Omar Vizquel, Ozzie Guillen, Luis Aparicio	50.00
15	Mickey Mantle, Joe DiMaggio, Ted Williams, Ernie Banks, Yogi Berra, Stan Musial	200.00
16	Mickey Mantle, Albert Pujols, Vladimir Guerrero, Ted Williams, Roberto Clemente, Joe DiMaggio	200.00
17	Mickey Mantle, Alex Rodriguez, Don Mattingly, Yogi Berra, Chien-Ming Wang, Reggie Jackson	200.00
18	Carl Yastrzemski, Manny Ramirez, David Ortiz, Pedro Martinez, Johnny Damon, Carlton Fisk	60.00
19	Justin Morneau, Torii Hunter, Joe Mauer, Johan Santana, Francisco Liriano, Harmon Killebrew	60.00
20	Justin Verlander, Joel Zumaya, Curtis Granderson, Magglio Ordonez, Ivan Rodriguez, Kenny Rogers	50.00
21	Nick Swisher, Huston Street, Reggie Jackson, Barry Zito, Jose Canseco, Dennis Eckersley	40.00
22	Vladimir Guerrero, Rod Carew, Jered Weaver, Reggie Jackson, Garret Anderson, Francisco Rodriguez	50.00
23	Vladimir Guerrero, Pedro Martinez, Moises Alou, Gary Carter, Andre Dawson, Randy Johnson	50.00
24	Nolan Ryan, Mark Teixeira, Michael Young, Alex Rodriguez, Ivan Rodriguez, Hank Blalock	65.00
25	Kenji Johjima, Ichiro Suzuki, Alex Rodriguez, Randy Johnson, Edgar Martinez, Richie Sexson	90.00
26	David Wright, Jose Reyes, Carlos Beltran, Pedro Martinez, Tom Glavine, Carlos Delgado	75.00
27	David Eckstein, Albert Pujols, Chris Carpenter, Stan Musial, Ozzie Smith, Jim Edmonds	75.00
28	Nolan Ryan, Andy Pettitte, Roger Clemens, Roy Oswalt, Lance Berkman, Craig Biggio	75.00
29	Ryan Howard, Chase Utley, Mike Schmidt, Jimmy Rollins, Richie Ashburn, Steve Carlton	100.00
30	Jeff Francoeur, Brian McCann, Chipper Jones, Andruw Jones, John Smoltz, Tim Hudson	70.00
31	Alfonso Soriano, Ernie Banks, Ryne Sandberg, Kerry Wood, Mark Prior, Andre Dawson	60.00
32	David Wright, Justin Morneau, Ryan Howard, Chien-Ming Wang, Chase Utley, Jose Reyes	75.00
33	David Ortiz	35.00
34	Roger Maris, Stan Musial, Roberto Clemente, Ernie Banks, Johnny Bench, Carl Yastrzemski	150.00
35	Albert Pujols, Jim Edmonds, Scott Rolen, Ivan Rodriguez, Kenny Rogers, Magglio Ordonez	50.00
36	Derrek Lee, Juan Pierre, Greg Maddux, Paul Konerko, Jermaine Dye, Jim Thome	60.00
37	David Wright, Paul LoDuca, Jose Reyes, Alex Rodriguez, Jason Giambi, Johnny Damon	75.00
38	Joe Mauer, Freddy Sanchez, Robinson Cano, Miguel Cabrera, Albert Pujols, Miguel Cabrera	75.00
39	Ryan Howard, David Ortiz, Albert Pujols, Alfonso Soriano, Lance Berkman, Jermaine Dye	75.00
40	David Wright, Albert Pujols, David Ortiz, Lance Berkman, Justin Morneau, Andruw Jones	75.00
41	Johan Santana, Roy Oswalt, Chris Carpenter, Brandon Webb, Roy Halladay, C.C. Sabathia	50.00
42	Chien-Ming Wang, Johan Santana, Jon Garland, Randy Johnson, Kenny Rogers, Freddy Garcia	85.00
43	Johan Santana, Aaron Harang, Jake Peavy, John Smoltz, Carlos Zambrano, Jeremy Bonderman	50.00
44	Jeff Suppan, Roy Oswalt, Albert Pujols, Placido Polanco, Paul Konerko, David Ortiz	50.00
45	Orlando Cepeda, Monte Irvin, Bobby Thomson, Duke Snider, Johnny Podres, Don Zimmerman	75.00
46	Ryne Sandberg, Wade Boggs, Dennis Eckersley, Paul Molitor, Gary Carter, Eddie Murray	70.00
47	Jermaine Dye, Paul Konerko, A.J. Pierzynski, Craig Biggio, Lance Berkman, Morgan Ensberg	50.00
48	Roger Clemens, Randy Johnson, Greg Maddux, Curt Schilling, Pedro Martinez, John Smoltz	85.00
49	David Wright, Brooks Robinson, George Brett, Mike Schmidt, Alex Rodriguez, Eddie Murray	80.00
50	Alfonso Soriano, Bobby Abreu, Carlos Beltran, Vladimir Guerrero, Alex Rodriguez, Preston Wilson	70.00

Triple Signed Hide

Production One Set
No Pricing

2007 Topps Turkey Red

	NM/M
Complete Set (186):	
Common Player:	.25
Common SP:	4.00
Inserted 1:4	
Pack (8):	4.00
Box (24):	80.00
1 Ryan Howard	2.00
1 Ryan Howard/SP Ad Back	8.00
2 Dontrelle Willis	.25
3 Matt Cain	.50
4 John Maine	.50
5 Cole Hamels	.75
6 Corey Patterson	.25
7 Mickey Mantle/SP	25.00
8 Johan Santana/CL	.75
9 Josh Beckett	.75
10 Jimmy Rollins	1.00
11 Kenji Johjima	.50
12 Orlando Hernandez	.25
13 Jorge Posada/CL	.50
14 Ivan Rodriguez	.75
15 Ichiro Suzuki	2.00
15 Ichiro Suzuki/SP Ad Back	6.00
16 Ken Griffey Jr./CL	1.00
17 Stephen Drew	.25
18 B.J. Upton	.50
19 Mickey Mantle	3.00
20 Alex Rodriguez	3.00
20 Alex Rodriguez/SP Ad Back	8.00
21 Adam Dunn	.75
22 Adam Lind/SP (RC)	6.00
23 Adrian Gonzalez	.50
24 Akinori Iwamura RC	2.00
25 Albert Pujols	6.00
25 Albert Pujols/SP Ad Back	8.00
26 Frank Thomas	1.00
27 Roy Halladay	.50
28 Alejandro De Aza RC	.50
29 Alex Gordon RC	4.00
30 Barry Bonds	3.00
31 Andrew Miller RC	4.00
32 Andruw Jones	.75
33 Kurt Suzuki/SP (RC)	5.00
34 Mickey Mantle	3.00
35 Andy Pettitte	.50
36 Tadahito Iguchi	.25
37 Edgar Renteria	.50
38 Tim Hudson	.50
39 Micah Owings (RC)	.50
40 Chipper Jones	1.00
40 Chipper Jones/SP Ad Back	6.00
41 Barry Zito	.50

42	Daisuke Matsuzaka/CL	2.00
43	Jarrod Saltalamacchia/SP **(RC)**	6.00
44	Bill Hall	.25
45	Billy Butler **(RC)**	1.00
46	Billy Wagner	.25
47	Rich Harden/SP	4.00
48	Albert Pujols/CL	1.00
49	Brandon Inge	.25
50	Jason Giambi	.50
51	Brandon Webb	.75
52	Brandon Wood **(RC)**	1.00
53	Carl Crawford/CL	.50
54	Brian Giles	.25
55	Josh Hamilton **(RC)**	1.00
56	Chase Utley	1.50
56	Chase Utley/SP Ad Back	6.00
57	Miguel Montero **(RC)**	.50
58	Carl Crawford	.50
59	Carlos Beltran	1.00
60	Mariano Rivera	.50
61	Carlos Delgado	.75
62	Carlos Lee/SP	5.00
63	Carlos Zambrano/SP	5.00
64	Miguel Tejada	.50
65	Mike Cameron	.25
66	Chase Utley SP	8.00
67	Chase Wright **RC**	1.00
68	Chien-Ming Wang	1.00
69	Nick Swisher	.50
70	David Wright	1.50
71	Mike Piazza/SP	5.00
72	Chris Carpenter	1.00
73	Mark Buehrle/SP	4.00
74	Torii Hunter/SP	5.00
75	Tyler Clippard **(RC)**	.50
76	Nicholas Markakis	.50
77	Mickey Mantle	3.00
78	Curt Schilling	1.00
79	Curtis Granderson	.75
80	Craig Biggio	.50
81	Juan Pierre	.50
82	Dallas Braden/SP **RC**	4.00
83	Dan Haren/SP	6.00
84	Dan Uggla	.50
85	Danny Putnam **(RC)**	.50
86	David DeJesus	.25
87	David Eckstein	.25
88	Tim Lincecum **RC**	6.00
89	Johnny Damon/SP	6.00
90	Justin Morneau	1.00
91	Delmon Young **(RC)**	1.00
92	Homer Bailey **(RC)**	1.00
93	Carlos Gomez **RC**	1.00
94	Josh Fields/SP **(RC)**	4.00
95	Derek Jeter	3.00
95	Derek Jeter/SP Ad Back	8.00
96	Derrek Lee	.75
97	Donald Kelly **(RC)**	.50
98	Doug Slaten **RC**	.50
99	Dustin Moseley	.25
100	Gary Sheffield	.75
101	Orlando Hudson/SP	4.00
102	Elijah Dukes **RC**	1.00
103	Eric Byrnes/SP	4.00
104	Eric Chavez	.50
105	Phil Hughes **(RC)**	1.00
105	Phil Hughes/SP Ad Back	5.00
106	Felix Hernandez/SP	4.00
106	Felix Hernandez/SP Ad Back	6.00
107	Mickey Mantle	3.00
108	Felix Pie **(RC)**	1.00
109	Derek Jeter/CL	1.00
110	Daisuke Matsuzaka **RC**	5.00
110	Daisuke Matsuzaka/SP Ad Back **RC**	10.00
111	Francisco Rodriguez	.50
112	Ramon Hernandez	.25
113	Randy Johnson	1.00
114	Gary Matthews	.25
115	Prince Fielder	1.00
116	Vladimir Guerrero CL	.50
117	Mickey Mantle	3.00
118	Hideki Matsui	2.00
119	Hideki Okajima **RC**	1.00
120	Manny Ramirez	1.00
121	Hunter Pence/SP **(RC)**	10.00
122	Roy Oswalt	.50
123	Josh Willingham/SP	4.00
124	Tom Gordon/SP	4.00
125	Michael Young	.50
126	J.D. Drew	.25
127	Ryan Zimmerman	.50
128	James Shields/SP	4.00
129	Jack Wilson	.25
130	David Ortiz	1.00
130	David Ortiz/SP Ad Back	6.00
131	Jose Reyes/CL	.50
132	Jamie Vermilyea **RC**	.50
133	Jason Bay	.50
134	Scott Kazmir/SP	4.00
135	Jason Isringhausen/SP	4.00
136	Jason Marquis/SP	4.00
137	Jason Schmidt	.50
138	Shawn Green	.25
139	Jeff Francoeur/SP	5.00
140	Alfonso Soriano	1.00
141	Kevin Kouzmanoff **(RC)**	.50
142	Jered Weaver	.50
143	Todd Helton/SP	5.00
144	Jermaine Dye	.50
145	Jim Thome	.75
146	Tom Glavine/SP	5.00
147	Joe Mauer	.75
148	Joe Nathan	.50
149	Joe Smith **RC**	.50
150	Ken Griffey Jr.	2.00
150	Ken Griffey Jr./SP Ad Back	6.00
151	Grady Sizemore	1.00
152	Sammy Sosa/SP	5.00
153	Andy LaRoche **(RC)**	1.00
154	Travis Buck **(RC)**	.50
155	Alex Rios	.50
156	Travis Hafner	.50
157	Jake Peavy	.50
158	Jeff Kent	.50
159	Johan Santana	1.00
159	Johan Santana/SP Ad Back	5.00
160	Ivan Rodriguez	.75
161	Trevor Hoffman	.50
162	Troy Glaus	.50
163	Troy Tulowitzki **(RC)**	1.00
164	Jorge Posada	.50
165	Kei Igawa/SP **RC**	5.00
166	Jose Reyes	1.00
167	Mickey Mantle	3.00
168	Chase Utley/CL	.50
169	Justin Verlander	.50
170	Hanley Ramirez	1.00
171	Kelly Johnson/SP	4.00
172	Kelvin Jimenez **RC**	.50
173	Roger Clemens	2.00
174	Khalil Greene/SP	5.00
175	Lance Berkman	.50
176	Hanley Ramirez/CL	.50
177	Kyle Kendrick **RC**	2.00
178	Magglio Ordonez	.50
179	Marcus Giles/SP	4.00
180	Miguel Cabrera	1.00
180	Miguel Cabrera/SP Ad Back	5.00
181	Mark Teahen	.25
182	Mark Teixeira/SP	5.00
183	Matt Chico/SP **(RC)**	4.00
184	Matt Holliday	.75
185	Vladimir Guerrero	1.00
185	Vladimir Guerrero/SP Ad Back	5.00
186	Yovani Gallardo **(RC)**	1.00

Chrome

Chrome:	2-3X
Chrome SP's:	1X
Production 1,999 Sets	

Chrome Refractors

Refractors:	3-4X
Refractor SP's:	1-2X
Production 999 Sets	

Chrome Black Refractors

Refractors:	5-10X
Refractor SP's:	2-4X
Production 99 Sets	

A-Rod Road to 500

Common A-Rod (301-325)
Inserted 2:Box

A-Rod Road to 500 Autographs

Production One Set

Cabinet

		NM/M
Common Player:		3.00
Inserted 1:Box		
JB	Jason Bay	5.00
LB	Lance Berkman	6.00
MC	Miguel Cabrera	6.00
CC	Chris Carpenter	8.00
SD	Stephen Drew	4.00
ED	Elijah Dukes	4.00
JD	Jermaine Dye	4.00
AD	Adam Dunn	4.00
PF	Prince Fielder	15.00
JF	Jeff Francoeur	10.00
AG	Alex Gordon	15.00
KG	Ken Griffey Jr.	15.00
VG	Vladimir Guerrero	8.00
FH	Felix Hernandez	5.00
RH	Ryan Howard	15.00
KI	Kei Igawa	4.00
AI	Akinori Iwamura	3.00
DJ	Derek Jeter	20.00
AJ	Andruw Jones	5.00
CL	Carlos Lee	4.00
MM	Mickey Mantle	25.00
NM	Nicholas Markakis	8.00
DM	Daisuke Matsuzaka	15.00
JM	Joe Mauer	5.00
JEM	Justin Morneau	5.00
HO	Hideki Okajima	8.00
DO	David Ortiz	15.00
MP	Mike Piazza	10.00
AP	Albert Pujols	20.00
HR	Hanley Ramirez	10.00
MR	Manny Ramirez	10.00
JR	Jose Reyes	15.00
AR	Alex Rodriguez	20.00
FR	Francisco Rodriguez	4.00
IR	Ivan Rodriguez	5.00
JS	Johan Santana	8.00
JDS	Jason Schmidt	3.00
GS	Grady Sizemore	10.00
AS	Alfonso Soriano	8.00
IS	Ichiro Suzuki	15.00
MT	Miguel Tejada	5.00
TT	Troy Tulowitzki	8.00
CU	Chase Utley	10.00
JV	Justin Verlander	5.00
CW	Chien-Ming Wang	8.00
BW	Brandon Webb	4.00
DW	David Wright	15.00
DY	Delmon Young	5.00
MY	Michael Young	5.00
RZ	Ryan Zimmerman	10.00
BZ	Barry Zito	3.00

Cabinet Dick Perez Autographs

		NM/M
Production 25 Sets		
JB	Jason Bay	30.00
LB	Lance Berkman	30.00
MC	Miguel Cabrera	30.00
CC	Chris Carpenter	30.00
SD	Stephen Drew	25.00
ED	Elijah Dukes	20.00
AD	Adam Dunn	25.00
JD	Jermaine Dye	30.00
PF	Prince Fielder	40.00
JF	Jeff Francoeur	30.00
AG	Alex Gordon	35.00
KG	Ken Griffey Jr.	50.00
VG	Vladimir Guerrero	30.00
FH	Felix Hernandez	30.00
RH	Ryan Howard	40.00
KI	Kei Igawa	25.00
AI	Akinori Iwamura	30.00
AJ	Andruw Jones	30.00
CL	Carlos Lee	30.00
MM	Mickey Mantle	100.00
NM	Nicholas Markakis	30.00
JM	Joe Mauer	30.00
JEM	Justin Morneau	30.00
HO	Hideki Okajima	30.00
DO	David Ortiz	50.00
MP	Mike Piazza	40.00
AP	Albert Pujols	80.00
HR	Hanley Ramirez	40.00
MR	Manny Ramirez	30.00
JR	Jose Reyes	40.00
AR	Alex Rodriguez	80.00
FR	Francisco Rodriguez	25.00
IR	Ivan Rodriguez	30.00
JS	Johan Santana	30.00
JDS	Jason Schmidt	25.00
GS	Grady Sizemore	40.00
AS	Alfonso Soriano	50.00
IS	Ichiro Suzuki	80.00
MT	Miguel Tejada	30.00
TT	Troy Tulowitzki	30.00
CU	Chase Utley	50.00
JV	Justin Verlander	30.00
CW	Chien-Ming Wang	50.00
BW	Brandon Webb	30.00
DW	David Wright	50.00
DY	Delmon Young	30.00
MY	Michael Young	30.00
RZ	Ryan Zimmerman	25.00
BZ	Barry Zito	30.00

Chromographs

		NM/M
Common Autograph:		10.00
AG	Alex Gordon	40.00
AK	Austin Kearns	10.00
AR	Alex Rodriguez	250.00
BJ	Bobby Jenks	25.00
BW	Brad Wilkerson	10.00
CAH	Clay Hensley	10.00
CG	Curtis Granderson	75.00
CH	Cole Hamels	30.00
CJ	Chuck James	15.00
DE	Darin Erstad	10.00
DU	Dan Uggla	15.00
EC	Eric Chavez	10.00
FP	Felix Pie	20.00
GS	Gary Sheffield	40.00
HCK	Hong-Chih Kuo	20.00
HR	Hanley Ramirez	30.00
JB	Jason Bay	40.00
JD	Johnny Damon	40.00
JM	John Maine	20.00
JZ	Joel Zumaya	15.00
KE	Kelvim Escobar	10.00
LM	Lastings Milledge	20.00
MC	Melky Cabrera	30.00
MG	Mike Gonzalez	10.00
NM	Nicholas Markakis	25.00
NR	Nate Robertson	15.00
PL	Paul LoDuca	15.00
RC	Robinson Cano	40.00
RH	Ryan Howard	80.00
RJH	Rich Hill	15.00
RM	Robert Mackowiak	10.00
RNM	Russell Martin	25.00
SC	Sean Casey	25.00
SP	Scott Podsednik	10.00
SV	Shane Victorino	15.00
TG	Tony Gwynn Jr.	15.00
WN	Wilbert Nieves	10.00

Presidents

		NM/M
Common President:		1.00
Inserted 1:12		
1	George Washington	4.00
2	John Adams	2.00
3	Thomas Jefferson	3.00
4	James Madison	2.00
5	James Monroe	2.00
6	John Quincy Adams	2.00
7	Andrew Jackson	2.00
8	Martin Van Buren	1.00
9	William H. Harrison	1.00
10	John Tyler	1.00
11	James K. Polk	1.00
12	Zachary Taylor	1.00
13	Millard Fillmore	1.00
14	Franklin Pierce	1.00
15	James Buchanan	1.00
16	Abraham Lincoln	4.00
17	Andrew Johnson	1.00
18	Ulysses S. Grant	2.00
19	Rutherford B. Hayes	1.00
20	James Garfield	1.00
21	Chester A. Arthur	1.00
22	Grover Cleveland	1.00
23	Benjamin Harrison	1.00
24	Grover Cleveland	1.00
25	William McKinley	1.00
26	Theodore Roosevelt	3.00
27	William H. Taft	1.00
28	Woodrow Wilson	1.00
29	Warren G. Harding	1.00
30	Calvin Coolidge	1.00
31	Herbert Hoover	1.00
32	Franklin D. Roosevelt	3.00
33	Harry S. Truman	2.00
34	Dwight D. Eisenhower	3.00
35	John F. Kennedy	4.00
36	Lyndon B. Johnson	1.00
37	Richard Nixon	2.00
38	Gerald Ford	1.00
39	Jimmy Carter	2.00
40	Ronald Reagan	2.00
41	George H.W. Bush	2.00
42	Bill Clinton	2.00
43	George W. Bush	2.00

Relics

		NM/M
Common Relic:		4.00
AB	Adrian Beltre	4.00
AD	Adam Dunn	6.00
AH	Aaron Harang	4.00
AJ1	Andruw Jones	6.00
AJ2	Andruw Jones	6.00

AM	Andrew Miller	8.00
ANB	Angel Berroa	4.00
AS	Alfonso Soriano	10.00
BB	Barry Bonds	30.00
BC	Bobby Crosby	4.00
BJR	B.J. Ryan	4.00
BR	Brian Roberts	6.00
BS	Brian Stokes	4.00
BT	Brad Thompson	4.00
BW	Brandon Webb	6.00
BZ	Benjamin Zobrist	6.00
CB1	Carlos Beltran	8.00
CB2	Carlos Beltran	8.00
CC	Coco Crisp	6.00
CD	Carlos Delgado	8.00
CH	Cole Hamels	10.00
CJ	Chipper Jones	10.00
CJC	Chris Carpenter	8.00
CL	Carlos Lee	6.00
CR	Chris Ray	4.00
CS	C.C. Sabathia	6.00
DN	Dioner Navarro	4.00
DO	David Ortiz	10.00
DR	Darrell Rasner	4.00
DU	Dan Uggla	6.00
DW	David Wright	15.00
DWA	Daryle Ward	4.00
DWW	Dontrelle Willis	6.00
DY	Delmon Young	6.00
ES	Ervin Santana	4.00
GP	Glen Perkins	4.00
HB	Hank Blalock	8.00
HR	Hanley Ramirez	10.00
IR	Ivan Rodriguez	8.00
IS	Ichiro Suzuki	20.00
JB	Josh Beckett	6.00
JC	Jorge Cantu	4.00
JD	Jermaine Dye	6.00
JE	Jim Edmonds	6.00
JF	Jeff Francoeur	15.00
JG	Jon Garland	4.00
JH	Josh Hamilton	10.00
JK	Jeff Kent	4.00
JM	Justin Morneau	8.00
JP	Josh Paul	4.00
JPM	Joe Mauer	6.00
JR	Jose Reyes	10.00
JRB	Jason Bay	6.00
JS	John Smoltz	8.00
JV2	Jason Varitek	10.00
JW	Jered Weaver	8.00
JZ	Joel Zumaya	8.00
KM	Kazuo Matsui	6.00
LB	Lance Berkman	6.00
LC	Luis Castillo	4.00
MC	Melky Cabrera	8.00
ME	Morgan Ensberg	4.00
MG	Marcus Giles	4.00
MJC	Miguel Cairo	4.00
MM	Mickey Mantle	125.00
MP	Mike Piazza	10.00
MR	Manny Ramirez	8.00
MT	Miguel Tejada	6.00
MY	Michael Young	6.00
NM	Nicholas Markakis	20.00
NP	Neifi Perez	4.00
NS	Nick Swisher	6.00
PM	Pedro Martinez	8.00
PP	Placido Polanco	6.00
RB1	Rocco Baldelli	4.00
RB2	Rocco Baldelli	4.00
RH	Ryan Howard	15.00
RJH	Rich Hill	6.00
RK	Ryan Klesko	4.00
RS	Reggie Sanders	4.00
RZ	Ryan Zimmerman	10.00
SR	Scott Rolen	8.00
SS	Sammy Sosa	8.00
ST	So Taguchi	4.00
TB	Travis Buck	4.00
TH	Travis Hafner	8.00
TI	Tadahito Iguchi	6.00
TJ	Tyler Johnson	8.00
VG	Vladimir Guerrero	8.00
VW	Vernon Wells	6.00

Silks

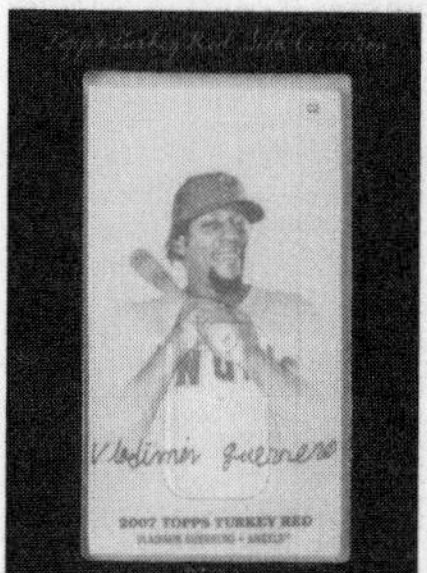

		NM/M
Common Player:		15.00
Production 99 Sets		
AD	Adam Dunn	15.00
AI	Akinori Iwamura	15.00
AIR	Alex Rios	15.00
AP	Albert Pujols	50.00
AR	Alex Rodriguez	50.00
AS	Alfonso Soriano	20.00
BB	Billy Butler	20.00
BLB	Barry Bonds	40.00
CH	Cole Hamels	25.00
CJ	Chipper Jones	25.00
CS	C.C. Sabathia	15.00
CY	Adrian Gonzalez	15.00
DH	Danny Haren	15.00
DJ	Derek Jeter	50.00
DM	Daisuke Matsuzaka	80.00
DO	David Ortiz	30.00
DU	Dan Uggla	15.00
DW	David Wright	30.00
DWW	Dontrelle Willis	20.00
EB	Erik Bedard	20.00
GS	Grady Sizemore	25.00
HP	Hunter Pence	30.00
HR	Hanley Ramirez	20.00
IS	Ichiro Suzuki	50.00
JAS	John Smoltz	20.00
JB	Josh Beckett	20.00
JBR	Jose Reyes	25.00
JD	Jermaine Dye	15.00
JH	J.J. Hardy	15.00
JL	John Lackey	15.00
JM	Justin Morneau	20.00
JP	Jake Peavy	20.00
JR	Jimmy Rollins	25.00
JRB	Jason Bay	15.00
JS	Johan Santana	25.00
JV	Justin Verlander	25.00
KG	Ken Griffey Jr.	40.00
MAR	Manny Ramirez	25.00
MH	Matt Holliday	25.00
MM	Mickey Mantle	80.00
MO	Magglio Ordonez	25.00
MR	Mark Reynolds	15.00
MT	Mark Teixeira	20.00
NS	Nick Swisher	20.00
PF	Prince Fielder	30.00
RH	Ryan Howard	40.00
RM	Russell Martin	20.00
RZ	Ryan Zimmerman	20.00
TH	Torii Hunter	15.00
VG	Vladimir Guerrero	15.00

2007 Topps 1952 Edition

		NM/M
Complete Set (221):		
Common RC:		.25
Common Action Variation:		
Inserted 1:6 Hobby		
Common SP (208-221):		4.00
Inserted 1:6 Hobby		
Hobby Pack (8):		5.00
Hobby Box (20):		90.00
1	Akinori Iwamura **RC**	1.00
2	Angel Sanchez **RC**	.50
3	Luis Hernandez **(RC)**	.25
4	Joaquin Arias **(RC)**	.25
5	Troy Tulowitzki **(RC)**	2.00
5	Troy Tulowitzki/Action/SP	5.00
6	Jesus Flores **RC**	.50
7	Mickey Mantle	3.00
8	Kory Casto **(RC)**	.25
9	Tony Abreu **RC**	.50
10	Kevin Kouzmanoff **(RC)**	.50
11	Travis Buck **(RC)**	.25
12	Kurt Suzuki **(RC)**	.25
13	Matt DeSalvo **(RC)**	.25
14	Jerry Owens **(RC)**	.25
15	Alex Gordon **RC**	3.00
16	Jeff Baker **(RC)**	.25
17	Ben Francisco **(RC)**	.25
18	Nate Schierholtz **(RC)**	.25
19	Nathan Haynes **(RC)**	.25
20	Ryan Braun **(RC)**	3.00
20	Ryan Braun/Action/SP	8.00
21	Brian Barden **RC**	.50
22	Sean Barker **RC**	.50
23	Alejandro De Aza **RC**	.50
24	Jamie Burke **(RC)**	.25
25	Michael Bourn **(RC)**	.25
26	Jeff Salazar **(RC)**	.25
27	Chase Headley **(RC)**	.50
28	Chris Basak **RC**	.50
29	Mike Fontenot **(RC)**	.25
30	Hunter Pence **(RC)**	3.00
30	Hunter Pence/Action/SP	8.00
31	Masumi Kuwata **RC**	1.00
32	Ryan Rowland-Smith **RC**	.50
33	Tyler Clippard **(RC)**	.25
34	Matt Lindstrom **(RC)**	.25
35	Fred Lewis **(RC)**	.25
36	Brett Carroll **RC**	.50
37	Alexi Casilla **RC**	.50
38	Nick Gorneault **(RC)**	.25
39	Dennis Sarfate **(RC)**	.25
40	Felix Pie **(RC)**	.25
41	Miguel Montero **(RC)**	.25
42	Danny Putnam **(RC)**	.25
43	Shane Youman **(RC)**	.25
44	Andy LaRoche **(RC)**	1.00
45	Jarrod Saltalamacchia **(RC)**	.50
46	Kei Igawa **RC**	1.00
47	Don Kelly **(RC)**	.25
48	Fernando Cortez **(RC)**	.25
49	Travis Metcalf **RC**	.50
50	Daisuke Matsuzaka **RC**	4.00
50	Daisuke Matsuzaka/ Action/SP	8.00
51	Edwar Ramirez **RC**	.50
52	Ryan Sweeney **(RC)**	.25
53	Shawn Riggans **(RC)**	.25
54	Billy Sadler **(RC)**	.25
55	Billy Butler **(RC)**	.50
56	Andy Cavazos **RC**	.50
57	Sean Henn **(RC)**	.25
58	Brian Esposito **(RC)**	.25
59	Brandon Morrow **RC**	.50
60	Adam Lind **(RC)**	.25
61	Joe Smith **RC**	.50
62	Chris Stewart **RC**	.50
63	Eulogio De La Cruz **(RC)**	.25
64	Sean Gallagher **(RC)**	.25
65	Carlos Gomez **RC**	1.00
66	Jailen Peguero **RC**	.50
67	Juan Perez **RC**	.50
68	Levale Speigner **RC**	.50
69	Jamie Vermilyea **RC**	.50
70	Delmon Young **(RC)**	.50
70	Delmon Young/Action/SP	3.00
71	Jo Jo Reyes **(RC)**	.25
72	Zack Segovia **(RC)**	.25
73	Andrew Sonnanstine **RC**	.50
74	Chase Wright **RC**	1.00
75	Josh Fields **(RC)**	.25
76	Jon Knott **(RC)**	.25
77	Guillermo Rodriguez **RC**	.50
78	Jon Coutlangus **(RC)**	.25
79	Kevin Cameron **RC**	.50
80	Mark Reynolds **RC**	.50
81	Brian Stokes **(RC)**	.25
82	Alberto Arias **RC**	.50
83	Yoel Hernandez **RC**	.50
84	David Murphy **(RC)**	.25
85	Josh Hamilton **(RC)**	.50
86	Justin Hampson **(RC)**	.25
87	Doug Slaten **RC**	.50
88	Joseph Bisenius **RC**	.50
89	Troy Cate **RC**	.50
90	Homer Bailey **(RC)**	1.00
91	Jacoby Ellsbury **(RC)**	5.00
92	Devern Hansack **RC**	.50
93	Zach McClellan **RC**	.50
94	Vinny Rottino **(RC)**	.25
95	Elijah Dukes **RC**	.50
96	Ryan Braun **RC**	.50
97	Lee Gardner **(RC)**	.25
98	Joakim Soria **RC**	.50
99	Jason Miller **(RC)**	.50
100	Hideki Okajima **RC**	1.00
100	Hideki Okajima/Action/SP	4.00
101	John Danks **(RC)**	.50
102	Garrett Jones **(RC)**	.25
103	Jensen Lewis **RC**	.50
104	Clay Rapada **RC**	.50
105	Kyle Kendrick **RC**	.50
106	Eric Stults **RC**	.50
107	Jared Burton **RC**	.50
108	Julio DePaula **RC**	.50
109	Jesse Litsch **RC**	.50
110	Micah Owings **(RC)**	.25
111	Cory Doyne **(RC)**	.25
112	Jay Marshall **RC**	.50
113	Mike Schultz **RC**	.50
114	Juan Salas **(RC)**	.25
115	Matt Chico **(RC)**	.25
116	Brad Salmon **RC**	.50
117	Jeff Bailey **(RC)**	.25
118	Gustavo Molina **RC**	.50
119	Brian Burres **(RC)**	.25
120	Yovani Gallardo **(RC)**	2.00
121	Hector Gimenez **(RC)**	.25
122	Kelvin Jimenez **RC**	.50
123	Rick Vanden Hurk **RC**	.50
124	Billy Petrick **(RC)**	.25
125	Andrew Miller **RC**	3.00
126	Rocky Cherry **RC**	.50
127	Jordan DeJong **RC**	.50
128	Eric Hull **RC**	.50
129	Kevin Mahar **RC**	.50
130	Tim Lincecum **RC**	3.00
130	Tim Lincecum/Action/SP	8.00
131	Garrett Olson **(RC)**	.25
132	Neal Musser **RC**	.50
133	Mike Rabelo **RC**	.50
134	Dennis Dove **(RC)**	.25
135	J.D. Durbin **(RC)**	.25
136	Jose Garcia **RC**	.50
137	Marcus McBeth **(RC)**	.25
138	Curtis Thigpen **(RC)**	.25
139	Mike Zagurski **RC**	.50
140	Kevin Slowey **(RC)**	.25
141	Dewon Day **RC**	.50
142	Glen Perkins **(RC)**	.25
143	Brian Wolfe **(RC)**	.25
144	Dallas Braden **RC**	.50
145	J.A. Happ **(RC)**	.25
146	Lee Gronkiewicz **RC**	.50
147	Cesar Jimenez **RC**	.50
148	Mark McLemore **(RC)**	.25
149	Connor Robertson **RC**	.50
150	Phil Hughes **(RC)**	2.00
150	Phil Hughes/Action/SP	5.00
151	Matthew Brown **RC**	.50
152	Ryan Feierabend **(RC)**	.25
153	Brendan Ryan **(RC)**	.25
154	Terry Evans **RC**	.50
155	Eric Patterson **(RC)**	.25
156	Patrick Misch **(RC)**	.25
157	Darren Clarke **RC**	.50
158	Kevin Melillo **(RC)**	.25
159	Edwin Bellorin **RC**	.50
160	Ubaldo Jimenez **(RC)**	.25
161	Ryan Budde **(RC)**	.25
162	Brian Buscher **RC**	.50
163	Juan Gutierrez **RC**	.50
164	Franklin Morales **(RC)**	.25
165	Carmen Pignatiello **(RC)**	.25
166	Jair Jurrjens **(RC)**	.50
167	Manny Acosta **(RC)**	.25
168	Ian Stewart **(RC)**	.25
169	Daniel Barone **(RC)**	.25
170	Justin Upton **RC**	3.00
170	Justin Upton/Action/SP	8.00
171	Tommy Watkins **RC**	.50
172	Ross Wolf **RC**	.50
173	Jack Cassel **RC**	.50
174	Asdrubal Cabrera **RC**	1.00
175	Mauro Zarate **RC**	.50
176	Aaron Laffey **RC**	.50
177	Marcus Gwyn **RC**	.50
178	Danny Richar **RC**	.50
179	Joel Hanrahan **(RC)**	.25
180	Cameron Maybin **RC**	2.00
181	John Lannan **RC**	.50
182	Shelley Duncan **(RC)**	.25
183	Brandon Wood **(RC)**	.50
184	Delwyn Young **(RC)**	.25
185	Manny Parra **(RC)**	.25
186	Ehren Wassermann **RC**	.50
187	Jose Reyes **RC**	.50
188	Jose Ascanio **RC**	.50
190	Alvin Colina **RC**	.50
190	Joba Chamberlain/ Action/SP	15.00
191	Yunel Escobar **(RC)**	.25
192	Carlos Maldonado **(RC)**	.25
193	Dan Meyer **(RC)**	.25
194	Scott Moore **(RC)**	.25
195	Romulo Sanchez **RC**	.50
196	Tom Shearn **(RC)**	.25
197	Craig Stansberry **(RC)**	.25
201	Joba Chamberlain **RC**	6.00
202	John Nelson SP **(RC)**	5.00
203	Phil Dumatrait **(RC)**	.25
204	Brandon Moss **(RC)**	.25
205	Beltran Perez **(RC)**	.25
206	Drew Anderson **RC**	.50
207	Brett Campbell **RC**	.50
208	Andy Cannizaro/SP **RC**	8.00
209	Travis Chick/SP **(RC)**	5.00
210	Francisco Cruceta/SP **(RC)**	4.00
211	Jose Diaz/SP **(RC)**	4.00
212	Jeff Fiorentino/SP **(RC)**	5.00
213	Tim Gradoville/SP **RC**	4.00
214	Kevin Hooper/SP **(RC)**	4.00
215	Philip Humber/SP **(RC)**	5.00
216	Juan Lara/SP **RC**	5.00
217	Mitch Maier/SP **RC**	4.00
218	Juan Morillo/SP **(RC)**	4.00
219	A.J. Murray/SP **RC**	5.00
220	Chris Narveson/SP **(RC)**	5.00
221	Oswaldo Navarro/SP **RC**	6.00

Black Back

Black Backs:	2-4X
Inserted 1:6 Hobby	

A-Rod Road to 500

	NM/M
A-Rod (476-500):	3.00

A-Rod Road to 500 Autograph

	NM/M
Production One Set	3.00

Chrome

		NM/M
Common player:		1.50
Production 1,952 Sets		
Refractor:		2-3X
Production 552 Sets		
Gold Refractor:		4-6X
Production 52 Sets		
1	Akinori Iwamura	2.00
2	Angel Sanchez	1.50
3	Luis Hernandez	1.50
4	Troy Tulowitzki	5.00
5	Joaquin Arias	1.50
6	Jesus Flores	1.50
7	Brandon Wood	2.00
8	Kory Casto	1.50
9	Kevin Kouzmanoff	2.00
10	Tony Abreu	1.50
11	Travis Buck	1.50
12	Kurt Suzuki	1.50
13	Alejandro De Aza	1.50
14	Alex Gordon	6.00
15	Jerry Owens	1.50
16	Ryan Braun	8.00
17	Michael Bourn	1.50
18	Hunter Pence	6.00
19	Jeff Baker	1.50
20	Ben Francisco	1.50
21	Nate Schierholtz	1.50
22	Nathan Haynes	1.50
23	Andrew Miller	4.00
24	Sean Barker	1.50
25	Matt DeSalvo	1.50
26	Fred Lewis	1.50
27	Jamie Burke	1.50
28	Jeff Salazar	1.50
29	Chase Headley	2.00
30	Chris Basak	1.50
31	Mike Fontenot	1.50
32	Felix Pie	2.00
33	Masumi Kuwata	1.50
34	Daisuke Matsuzaka	8.00
35	Tim Lincecum	6.00

36 Jarrod Saltalamacchia 3.00
37 Tyler Clippard 2.00
38 Billy Butler 4.00
39 Matt Lindstrom 1.50
40 Brett Carroll 1.50
41 Alexi Casilla 1.50
42 Nick Gorneault 1.50
43 Matt Chico 1.50
44 Adam Lind 1.50
45 Miguel Montero 1.50
46 Danny Putnam 1.50
47 Delmon Young 2.00
48 Josh Fields 1.50
49 Carlos Gomez 3.00
50 Mark Reynolds 3.00
51 Shane Youman 2.00
52 Andy LaRoche 3.00
53 Kei Igawa 1.50
54 Don Kelly 1.50
55 Cameron Maybin 5.00
56 Travis Metcalf 1.50
57 Ubaldo Jimenez 1.50
58 Ryan Sweeney 1.50
59 Shawn Riggans 1.50
60 Jacoby Ellsbury 15.00
61 Andy Cavazos 1.50
62 Josh Hamilton 5.00
63 Homer Bailey 3.00
64 Sean Henn 1.50
65 Elijah Dukes 1.50
66 Brian Esposito 1.50
67 Brandon Morrow 1.50
68 Joe Smith 1.50
69 Chris Stewart 1.50
70 Eulogio De La Cruz 1.50
71 Sean Gallagher 1.50
72 Jailen Peguero 1.50
73 Juan Perez 1.50
74 Levale Speigner 1.50
75 Jamie Vermilyea 1.50
76 Hideki Okajima 2.00
77 Eric Patterson 1.50
78 Zack Segovia 1.50
79 Kyle Kendrick 1.50
80 Andrew Sonnanstine 1.50
81 Chase Wright 1.50
82 Jon Knott 1.50
83 Guillermo Rodriguez 1.50
84 Jon Coutlangus 1.50
85 Kevin Cameron 1.50
86 Brian Stokes 1.50
87 Alberto Arias 1.50
88 Delwyn Young 1.50
89 David Murphy 1.50
90 Micah Owings 1.50
91 Yovani Gallardo 4.00
92 Justin Hampson 1.50
93 Doug Slaten 1.50
94 Justin Upton 5.00
95 Joba Chamberlain 20.00

Dynamic Duos

NM/M

Common Duo: 1.00
Inserted 1:4
1 Tim Lincecum, Nate Schierholtz 2.00
2 Joba Chamberlain, Phil Hughes 6.00
3 Ryan Braun, Yovani Gallardo 3.00
4 Kyle Kendrick, Michael Bourn 1.00
5 Delmon Young, Elijah Dukes 1.00
6 Hideki Okajima, Daisuke Matsuzaka 5.00
7 Justin Upton, Mark Reynolds 2.00
8 Eric Patterson, Felix Pie 1.00
9 Josh Hamilton, Homer Bailey 1.50
10 Ubaldo Jimenez, Troy Tulowitzki 2.00
11 Alex Gordon, Billy Butler 3.00
12 Delwyn Young, Andy LaRoche 2.00
13 Andrew Miller, Cameron Maybin 2.00
14 Joe Smith, Carlos Gomez 1.00
15 David Murphy, Jarrod Saltalamacchia 1.00

Debut Flashbacks

NM/M

Complete Set (15): 10.00
Common Player: .50
Inserted 1:6
Chrome: 2X
Production 1,952 Sets
Refractor: 3-4X
Production 552 Sets
Gold Refractor: 4-8X
Production 52 Sets
1 Vladimir Guerrero 1.50
2 Ken Griffey Jr. 3.00
3 Pedro Martinez 1.50
4 Carlos Delgado .75
5 Gary Sheffield 1.00
6 Curt Schilling 1.00
7 Jorge Posada .75
8 Miguel Tejada .75
9 Trevor Hoffman .50
10 Francisco Cordero .50
11 Travis Hafner .75
12 Paul LoDuca .50
13 Jimmy Rollins 1.50
14 Magglio Ordonez .75
15 Jim Edmonds .50

Diamond Debut Tix Relics

Production 20 Sets
No Pricing

Signatures

NM/M

Common Auto.: 5.00
Red Ink: 1.5-2X
Production 52 Sets
AA Alberto Arias 5.00
AC Alexi Casilla 8.00
AG Alex Gordon 30.00
AI Akinori Iwamura 20.00
AL Andy LaRoche 25.00
AM Andrew Miller 30.00
AS Angel Sanchez 5.00
ASL Aaron Laffey 15.00
BB Brian Barden 8.00
BC Brett Carroll 8.00
BE Brian Esposito 8.00
BF Ben Francisco 8.00
BP Ben Petrick 10.00
BPB Brian Buscher 10.00
BS Brian Stokes 8.00
BW Brian Wolfe 8.00
CD Cory Doyne 8.00
CM Cameron Maybin 40.00
CS Chris Stewart 8.00
CW Chase Wright 20.00
DC Darren Clarke 8.00
ER Edwar Ramirez 15.00
FC Francisco Cordero/SP 60.00
FL Fred Lewis 15.00
FP Felix Pie 25.00
GS Gary Sheffield/SP 60.00
HO Hideki Okajima 60.00
HP Hunter Pence 50.00
JA Joaquin Arias 10.00
JB Jared Burton 20.00
JC Jon Coutlangus 10.00
JCH Joba Chamberlain 150.00
JH Joel Hanrahan 20.00
JJR Jo Jo Reyes 20.00
JL Jensen Lewis 10.00
JM Jason Miller 10.00
JRB Joseph Bisenius 8.00
JSS Jarrod Saltalamacchia 25.00
JU Justin Upton 60.00
KK Kevin Kouzmanoff 15.00
KS Kurt Suzuki 15.00
LS Levale Speigner 8.00
MB Michael Bourn 20.00
MBB Matthew Brown 8.00
ML Matt Lindstrom 10.00
MM Mark McLemore 8.00
NG Nick Gorneault 15.00
NH Nathan Haynes 8.00
PD Phil Dumatrait 10.00
PH Phil Hughes 50.00
PL Paul LoDuca 20.00
RB Ryan Braun 75.00
RC Rocky Cherry 10.00
RDB Ryan Budde 10.00
RZB Ryan Braun 10.00
TB Travis Buck 15.00
TC Tyler Clippard 25.00
TL Tim Lincecum 75.00
TM Travis Metcalf 25.00
TPC Troy Cate 8.00
YG Yovani Gallardo 30.00
ZS Zack Segovia 10.00

Signatures Combos

NM/M

Production 25 Sets
LO Tim Lincecum, Hideki Okajima 125.00
ML Andrew Miller, Matt Lindstrom 60.00
OI Hideki Okajima, Akinori Iwamura 125.00
LB Matt Lindstrom, Michael Bourn 40.00

2008 Topps

NM/M

Complete Set (660): 50.00
Common Player: .10
Hobby Pack (10): 2.00
Hobby Box (36): 60.00
1 Alex Rodriguez 1.50
2 Barry Zito .10
3 Jeff Suppan .10
4 Rick Ankiel .25
5 Scott Kazmir .25
6 Felix Pie .10
7 Mickey Mantle 4.00
8 Stephen Drew .25
9 Randy Wolf .10
10 Miguel Cabrera .50
11 Yorvit Torrealba .10
12 Jason Bartlett .10
13 Kendry Morales .10
14 Lenny DiNardo .10
15 Magglio Ordonez, Ichiro Suzuki, Placido Polanco .50
16 Kevin Gregg .10
17 Cristian Guzman .10
18 J.D. Durbin .10
19 Robinson Tejeda .10
20 Daisuke Matsuzaka 1.00
21 Edwin Encarnacion .10
22 Ron Washington .10
23 Chin-Lung Hu **(RC)** .25
24 Alex Rodriguez, Magglio Ordonez, Vladimir Guerrero .50
25 Kazuo Matsui .10
26 Manny Ramirez .50
27 Bob Melvin .10
28 Kyle Kendrick .10
29 Anibal Sanchez .10
30 Jimmy Rollins .50
31 Ronny Paulino .10
32 Howie Kendrick .10
33 Joe Mauer .25
34 Aaron Cook .10
35 Cole Hamels .25
36 Brendan Harris .10
37 Jason Marquis .10
38 Preston Wilson .10
39 Yovani Gallardo .25
40 Miguel Tejada .25
41 Rich Aurilia .10
42 Corey Hart .25
43 Ryan Dempster .10
44 Jonathan Broxton .10
45 Dontrelle Willis .10
46 Zack Greinke .10
47 Orlando Cabrera .25
48 Zachary Duke .10
49 Orlando Hernandez .10
50 Jake Peavy .25
51 Erik Bedard .25
52 Trevor Hoffman .10
53 Hank Blalock .10
54 Victor Martinez .25
55 Chris Young .10
56 Seth Smith **(RC)** .25
57 Wladimir Balentien **(RC)** .25
58 Matt Holliday, Ryan Howard, Miguel Cabrera .50
59 Grady Sizemore .50
60 Jose Reyes .50
61 Alex Rodriguez, Carlos Pena, David Ortiz .50
62 Rich Thompson **(RC)** .25
63 Jason Michaels .10
64 Mike Lowell .10
65 Billy Wagner .10
66 Brad Wilkerson .10
67 Wes Helms .10
68 Kevin Millar .10
69 Bobby Cox .10
70 Dan Uggla .10
71 Jarrod Washburn .10
72 Mike Piazza .40
73 Mike Napoli .10
74 Garrett Atkins .25
75 Felix Hernandez .25
76 Ivan Rodriguez .25
77 Angel Guzman .10
78 Radhames Liz **RC** .50
79 Omar Vizquel .10
80 Alex Rios .25
81 Ray Durham .10
82 So Taguchi .10
83 Mark Reynolds .10
84 Brian Fuentes .10
85 Jason Bay .25
86 Scott Podsednik .10
87 Maicer Izturis .10
88 Jack Cust .10
89 Josh Willingham .10
90 Vladimir Guerrero .50
91 Marcus Giles .10
92 Ross Detwiler **RC** 1.00
93 Kenny Lofton .10
94 Bud Black .10
95 John Lackey .10
96 Sam Fuld **RC** .50
97 Clint Sammons **(RC)** .25
98 Ryan Howard, Chase Utley .50
99 David Ortiz, Manny Ramirez .25
100 Ryan Howard .75
101 Ryan Braun .50
102 Ross Ohlendorf **RC** .50
103 Jonathan Albaladejo **RC** 1.00
104 Kevin Youkilis .25
105 Roger Clemens 1.00
106 Josh Bard .10
107 Shawn Green .10
108 B.J. Ryan .10
109 Joe Nathan .10
110 Justin Morneau .40
111 Ubaldo Jimenez .10
112 Jacque Jones .10
113 Kevin Frandsen .10
114 Mike Fontenot .10
115 Johan Santana .50
116 Chuck James .10
117 Boof Bonser .10
118 Marco Scutaro .10
119 Jeremy Hermida .10
120 Andruw Jones .25
121 Mike Cameron .10
122 Jason Varitek .25
123 Terry Francona .10
124 Bob Geren .10
125 Tim Hudson .25
126 Brandon Jones **RC** .50
127 Steve Pearce **RC** 1.00
128 Kenny Lofton .10
129 Kevin Hart **(RC)** .25
130 Justin Upton .50
131 Norris Hopper .10
132 Ramon Vazquez .10
133 Mike Bacsik .10
134 Matt Stairs .10
135 Brad Penny .10
136 Robinson Cano .40
137 Jamey Carroll .10
138 Dan Wheeler .10
139 Johnny Estrada .10
140 Brandon Webb .25
141 Ryan Klesko .10
142 Chris Duncan .10
143 Willie Harris .10
144 Jerry Owens .10
145 Magglio Ordonez .25
146 Aaron Hill .10
147 Marlon Anderson .10
148 Gerald Laird .10
149 Luke Hochevar **RC** 1.00
150 Alfonso Soriano .40
151 Adam Loewen .10
152 Bronson Arroyo .10
153 Luis Mendoza **(RC)** .50
154 David Ross .10
155 Carlos Zambrano .25
156 Brandon McCarthy .10
157 Tim Redding .10
158 Jose Bautista .10
159 Luke Scott .10
160 Ben Sheets .25
161 Matt Garza .10
162 Andy LaRoche .25
163 Doug Davis .10
164 Nate Schierholtz .10
165 Tim Lincecum .25
166 Andrew Sonnanstine .10
167 Jason Hirsh .10
168 Phil Hughes .25
169 Adam Lind .10
170 Scott Rolen .25
171 John Maine .10
172 Chris Ray .10
173 Jamie Moyer .10
174 Julian Tavarez .10
175 Delmon Young .25
176 Troy Patton **(RC)** .25
177 Josh Anderson **(RC)** .50
178 Dustin Pedroia .25
179 Chris Young .25
180 Jose Valverde .10
181 Joe Borowski, Bobby Jenks, J.J. Putz .10
182 Billy Buckner **(RC)** .25
183 Paul Byrd .10
184 Tadahito Iguchi .10
185 Yunel Escobar .10
186 Lastings Milledge .10
187 Dustin McGowan .10
188 Kei Igawa .10
189 Esteban German .10
190 Russell Martin .25
191 Orlando Hudson .10
192 Jim Edmonds .10
193 J.J. Hardy .10
194 Chad Billingsley .10
195 Todd Helton .25
196 Ross Gload .10
197 Melky Cabrera .25
198 Shannon Stewart .10
199 Adrian Beltre .10
200 Manny Ramirez .40
201 Matt Capps .10
202 Mike Lamb .10
203 Jason Tyner .10
204 Rafael Furcal .10
205 Gil Meche .10
206 Geoff Jenkins .10
207 Jeff Kent .10
208 David DeJesus .10
209 Andy Phillips .10
210 Mark Teahen .10
211 Lyle Overbay .10
212 Moises Alou .10
213 Michael Barrett .10
214 C.J. Wilson .10
215 Bobby Jenks .10
216 Ryan Garko .10
217 Josh Beckett .40
218 Clint Hurdle .10
219 Kevin Kouzmanoff .25
220 Roy Oswalt .25
221 Ian Snell .10
222 Mark Grudzielanek .10
223 Odalis Perez .10
224 Mark Buehrle .10

225 Hunter Pence .25
226 Kurt Suzuki .10
227 Alfredo Amezaga .10
228 Geoff Blum .10
229 Dustin Pedroia .25
230 Roy Halladay .25
231 Casey Blake .10
232 Clay Buchholz **(RC)** .50
233 Jimmy Rollins .50
234 Boston Red Sox .25
234 Boston Red Sox with Giuliani 15.00
235 Rich Harden .10
236 Joe Koshansky **(RC)** .25
237 Eric Wedge .10
238 Shane Victorino .10
239 Richie Sexson .25
240 Jim Thome .25
241 Ervin Santana .10
242 Manny Acta .10
243 Akinori Iwamura .10
244 Adam Wainwright .10
245 Danny Haren .10
246 Jason Isringhausen .10
247 Edgar Gonzalez .10
248 Jose Contreras .10
249 Chris Sampson .10
250 Jonathan Papelbon .25
251 Dan Johnson .10
252 Dmitri Young .10
253 Bronson Sardinha **(RC)** .25
254 David Murphy .10
255 Brandon Phillips .10
256 Alex Rodriguez 1.00
257 Austin Kearns, Dmitri Young .10
258 Manny Ramirez, Kevin Youkilis .25
259 Emilio Bonifacio **RC** .50
260 Chad Cordero .10
261 Josh Barfield .10
262 Brett Myers .10
263 Nook Logan .10
264 Byung-Hyun Kim .10
265 Fredi Gonzalez .10
266 Ryan Doumit .10
267 Chris Burke .10
268 Daric Barton **(RC)** .25
269 James Loney .25
270 C.C. Sabathia .25
271 Chad Tracy .10
272 Anthony Reyes .10
273 Rafael Soriano .10
274 Jermaine Dye .10
275 C.C. Sabathia .25
276 Brad Ausmus .10
277 Aubrey Huff .10
278 Xavier Nady .10
279 Damion Easley .10
280 Willie Randolph .10
281 Carlos Ruiz .10
282 Jon Lester .10
283 Jorge Sosa .10
284 Lance Broadway **RC** .25
285 Tony LaRussa .10
286 Jeff Clement **(RC)** .25
287 Justin Morneau, Johan Santana, Joe Mauer .25
288 Ivan Rodriguez, Justin Verlander .25
289 Justin Ruggiano **RC** .50
290 Edgar Renteria .10
291 Eugenio Velez **RC** .50
292 Mark Loretta .10
293 Gavin Floyd .10
294 Brian McCann .25
295 Tim Wakefield .10
296 Paul Konerko .25
297 Jorge Posada .25
298 Prince Fielder, Ryan Howard, Adam Dunn .50
299 Cesar Izturis .10
300 Chien-Ming Wang .50
301 Chris Duffy .10
302 Horacio Ramirez .10
303 Jose Lopez .10
304 Jose Vidro .10
305 Carlos Delgado .25
306 Scott Olsen .10
307 Shawn Hill .10
308 Felipe Lopez .10
309 Ryan Church .10
310 Kelvim Escobar .10
311 Jeremy Guthrie .10
312 Ramon Hernandez .10
313 Kameron Loe .10
314 Ian Kinsler .10
315 David Weathers .10
316 Scott Hatteberg .10
317 Cliff Lee .10
318 Ned Yost .10
319 Joey Votto **(RC)** .50
320 Ichiro Suzuki 1.00
321 J.R. Towles **RC** 1.00
322 Scott Kazmir, Johan Santana, Erik Bedard .25
323 Jose Valverde, Francisco Cordero, Trevor Hoffman .10
324 Jake Peavy .25
325 Jim Leyland .10
326 Matt Holliday, Chipper Jones, Hanley Ramirez .25
327 Jake Peavy, Aaron Harang, John Smoltz .25
328 Nyjer Morgan **(RC)** .50
329 Lou Piniella .10
330 Curtis Granderson .25
331 Dave Roberts .10
332 Grady Sizemore, Jhonny Peralta .25
333 Jayson Nix **(RC)** .25
334 Oliver Perez .10
335 Eric Byrnes .25
336 Jhonny Peralta .25
337 Livan Hernandez .10
338 Matt Diaz .10
339 Troy Percival .10
340 David Wright .75
341 Daniel Cabrera .10
342 Matt Belisle .10
343 Kason Gabbard .10
344 Mike Rabelo .10
345 Carl Crawford .25
346 Adam Everett .10
347 Chris Capuano .10
348 Craig Monroe .10
349 Mike Mussina .25
350 Mark Teixeira .40
351 Bobby Crosby .10
352 Miguel Batista .10
353 Brendan Ryan .10
354 Edwin Jackson .10
355 Brian Roberts .25
356 Manny Corpas .10
357 Jeremy Accardo .10
358 John Patterson .10
359 Evan Meek **RC** .50
360 David Ortiz .50
361 Wesley Wright **RC** .50
362 Fernando Hernandez **RC** .50
363 Brian Barton **RC** .50
364 Al Reyes .10
365 Derrek Lee .40
366 Jeff Weaver .10
367 Khalil Greene .10
368 Michael Bourn .10
369 Luis Castillo .10
370 Adam Dunn .40
371 Rickie Weeks .25
372 Matt Kemp .25
373 Casey Kotchman .10
374 Jason Jennings .10
375 Fausto Carmona .25
376 Willy Taveras .25
377 Jake Westbrook .10
378 Ozzie Guillen .10
379 Hideki Okajima .25
380 Grady Sizemore .50
381 Jeff Francoeur .40
382 Micah Owings .10
383 Jered Weaver .25
384 Carlos Quentin .25
385 Troy Tulowitzki .25
386 Julio Lugo .10
387 Sean Marshall .10
388 Jorge Cantu .10
389 Callix Crabbe **(RC)** .25
390 Troy Glaus .25
391 Nick Markakis .40
392 Joey Gathright .10
393 Michael Cuddyer .10
394 Mark Ellis .10
395 Lance Berkman .40
396 Randy Johnson .40
397 Brian Wilson .10
398 Kenji Johjima .10
399 Jarrod Saltalamacchia .10
400 Matt Holliday .40
401 Scott Hairston .10
402 Taylor Buchholz .10
403 Nate Robertson .10
404 Cecil Cooper .10
405 Travis Hafner .25
406 Takashi Saito .10
407 Johnny Damon .40
408 Edinson Volquez .25
409 Jason Giambi .25
410 Alex Gordon .25
411 Jason Kubel .10
412 Joel Zumaya .10
413 Wandy Rodriguez .10
414 Andrew Miller .25
415 Derek Lowe .10
416 Elijah Dukes .10
417 Brian Bass .25
418 Dioner Navarro .10
419 Bengie Molina .10
420 Nick Swisher .25
421 Brandon Backe .10
422 Erick Aybar .10
423 Mike Scioscia .10
424 Aaron Harang .10
425 Hanley Ramirez .50
426 Franklin Gutierrez .10
427 Carlos Guillen .25
428 Jair Jurrjens .10
429 Billy Butler .10
430 Ryan Braun .50
431 Delwyn Young .10
432 Jason Kendall .10
433 Carlos Silva .10
434 Ron Gardenhire .10
435 Torii Hunter .25
436 Joe Blanton .10
437 Brandon Wood .10
438 Jay Payton .10
439 Josh Hamilton .40
440 Pedro Martinez .50
441 Miguel Olivo .10
442 Luis Gonzalez .10
443 Greg Dobbs .10
444 Jack Wilson .10
445 Hideki Matsui .75
446 Randor Bierd **RC** .50
447 Chipper Jones, Mark Teixeira .40
448 Cameron Maybin .10
449 Braden Looper .10
450 Prince Fielder .40
451 Brian Giles .10
452 Kevin Slowey .10
453 Josh Fogg .10
454 Mike Hampton .10
455 Derek Jeter 1.50
456 Chone Figgins .25
457 Josh Fields .10
458 Brad Hawpe .10
459 Mike Sweeney .10
460 Chase Utley .50
461 Jacoby Ellsbury .50
462 Freddy Sanchez .10
463 John McLaren .10
464 Rocco Baldelli .10
465 Huston Street .10
466 Miguel Cabrera, Ivan Rodriguez .25
467 Nick Blackburn **RC** 1.00
468 Gregor Blanco **(RC)** .25
469 Brian Bocock **RC** .50
470 Tom Gorzelanny .10
471 Brian Schneider .10
472 Shaun Marcum .10
473 Joe Maddon .10
474 Yuniesky Betancourt .10
475 Adrian Gonzalez .25
476 Johnny Cueto **RC** 1.00
477 Ben Broussard .10
478 Geovany Soto .25
479 Bobby Abreu .25
480 Matt Cain .25
481 Manny Parra .10
482 Kazuo Fukumori **RC** .50
483 Mike Jacobs .10
484 Todd Jones .10
485 J.J. Putz .10
486 Javier Vazquez .10
487 Corey Patterson .10
488 Mike Gonzalez .10
489 Joakim Soria .10
490 Albert Pujols 1.50
491 Cliff Floyd .10
492 Harvey Garcia **(RC)** .25
493 Steve Holm **RC** .50
494 Paul Maholm .10
495 James Shields .25
496 Brad Lidge .10
497 Cla Meredith .10
498 Matt Chico .10
499 Milton Bradley .10
500 Chipper Jones .50
501 Elliot Johnson **(RC)** .25
502 Alex Cora .10
503 Jeremy Bonderman .10
504 Conor Jackson .25
505 B.J. Upton .25
506 Jay Gibbons .10
507 Mark DeRosa .10
508 John Danks .10
509 Alex Gonzalez .10
510 Justin Verlander .25
511 Jeff Francis .10
512 Placido Polanco .10
513 Rick Vanden Hurk .10
514 Tony Pena .10
515 A.J. Burnett .10
516 Jason Schmidt .10
517 Bill Hall .10
518 Ian Stewart .10
519 Travis Buck .10
520 Vernon Wells .10
521 Jayson Werth .10
522 Nate McLouth .10
523 Noah Lowry .10
524 Raul Ibanez .10
525 Gary Matthews .10
526 Juan Encarnacion .10
527 Marlon Byrd .10
528 Paul LoDuca .50
529 Masahide Kobayashi **RC** .10
530 Ryan Zimmerman .25
531 Hiroki Kuroda **RC** 1.00
532 Tim Lahey **RC** .50
533 Kyle McClellan **RC** .50
534 Matt Tupman **RC** .50
535 Francisco Rodriguez .10
536 Albert Pujols, Prince Fielder .50
537 Scott Moore .10
538 Alex Romero **(RC)** .25
539 Clete Thomas **RC** .50
540 John Smoltz .40
541 Adam Jones .10
542 Adam Kennedy .10
543 Carlos Lee .25
544 Chad Gaudin .10
545 Chris Young .25
546 Francisco Liriano .25
547 Fred Lewis .10
548 Garrett Olson .10
549 Gregg Zaun .10
550 Curt Schilling .40
551 Erick Threets **(RC)** .25
552 J.D. Drew .25
553 Jo Jo Reyes .10
554 Joe Borowski .10
555 Josh Beckett .40
556 John Gibbons .10
557 John McDonald .10
558 John Russell .10
559 Jonny Gomes .10
560 Aramis Ramirez .40
561 Matt Tolbert **RC** .50
562 Ronnie Belliard .10
563 Ramon Troncoso **RC** .50
564 Frank Catalanotto .10
565 A.J. Pierzynski .10
566 Kevin Millwood .10
567 David Eckstein .10
568 Jose Guillen .10
569 Brad Hennessey .10
570 Homer Bailey .10
571 Eric Gagne .10
572 Adam Eaton .10
573 Tom Gordon .10
574 Scott Baker .10
575 Ty Wigginton .10
576 David Bush .10
577 John Buck .10
578 Ricky Nolasco .10
579 Jesse Litsch .10
580 Ken Griffey Jr. 1.00
581 Kazuo Matsui .10
582 Dusty Baker .10
583 Nick Punto .10
584 Ryan Theriot .10
585 Brian Bannister .10
586 Coco Crisp .10
587 Chris Snyder .10
588 Tony Gwynn .10
589 Dave Trembley .10
590 Mariano Rivera .25
591 Rico Washington **(RC)** .25
592 Matt Morris .10
593 Randy Wells **RC** .50
594 Mike Morse .10
595 Francisco Cordero .10
596 Joba Chamberlain 1.00
597 Kyle Davies .10
598 Bruce Bochy .10
599 Austin Kearns .10
600 Tom Glavine .25
601 Felipe Paulino **RC** .50
602 Lyle Overbay, Vernon Wells .10
603 Blake DeWitt **(RC)** .25
604 Wily Mo Pena .10
605 Andre Ethier .10
606 Jason Bergmann .10
607 Ryan Spilborghs .10
608 Brian Burres .10
609 Ted Lilly .10
610 Carlos Beltran .40
611 Garret Anderson .10
612 Kelly Johnson .10
613 Melvin Mora .10
614 Rich Hill .10
615 Pat Burrell .10
616 Jon Garland .10
617 Asdrubal Cabrera .10
618 Pat Neshek .10
619 Sergio Mitre .10
620 Gary Sheffield .40
621 Denard Span .10
622 Jorge De La Rosa .10
623 Trey Hillman .10
624 Joe Torre .10
625 Greg Maddux 1.00
626 Mike Redmond .10
627 Mike Pelfrey .10
628 Andy Pettitte .25
629 Eric Chavez .10
630 Chris Carpenter .25
631 Joe Girardi .10
632 Charlie Manuel .10
633 Adam LaRoche .10
634 Kenny Rogers .10
635 Michael Young .25
636 Rafael Betancourt .10
637 Jose Castillo .10
638 Juan Pierre .10
639 Juan Uribe .10
640 Carlos Pena .25
641 Marcus Thames .10
642 Mark Kotsay .10
643 Matt Murton .10
644 Reggie Willits .10
645 Andy Marte .10
646 Rajai Davis .10
647 Randy Winn .10
648 Ryan Freel .10
649 Joe Crede .10
650 Frank Thomas .40
651 Martin Prado .10
652 Rod Barajas .10
653 Endy Chavez .10
654 Willy Aybar .10
655 Aaron Rowand .10
656 Darin Erstad .10
657 Jeff Keppinger .10
658 Kerry Wood .10
659 Vicente Padilla .10
660 Yadier Molina .10

Gold

Gold:	5-10X
Production 2,008 Sets	

Gold Foil

Gold Foil:	1-2X

Black

Black:	20-30X
Production 57 Sets	

Platinum

No Pricing
Production One Set

Printing Plates

No Pricing
Production one set per color.

Campaign 2008

	NM/M
Common Candidate:	1.00
Inserted 1:9	
JB	Joseph Biden	1.00
HC	Hillary Clinton	3.00
JE	John Edwards	2.00
RG	Rudy Giuliani	2.00
MH	Mike Huckabee	1.00
DK	Dennis Kucininch	1.00
JM	John McCain	3.00
BO	Barack Obama	6.00
RP	Ron Paul	1.00
BR	Bill Richardson	1.00
MR	Mitt Romney	1.00
FT	Fred Thompson	2.00

Campaign '08 Letter Patches

		NM/M
Inserted 1:2,642		
HC	Hillary Clinton	50.00
BO	Barack Obama	150.00
JM	John McCain	60.00

Commemorative Patch Relics

		NM/M
Production 499-539		
AIR	Alex Rios	15.00
AP	Albert Pujols	20.00
AR	Alex Rodriguez	25.00
BW	Brandon Webb	10.00
CC	Carl Crawford	8.00
CH	Cole Hamels	20.00
CMS	Curt Schilling	15.00
CS	C.C. Sabathia	15.00
CU	Chase Utley	20.00
DAO	David Ortiz	30.00
DO	David Ortiz	15.00
DP	Dustin Pedroia	25.00
DW	David Wright	20.00
GS	Grady Sizemore	15.00
HO	Hideki Okajima	10.00
IS	Ichiro Suzuki	30.00
JAV	Jason Varitek	20.00
JB	Josh Beckett	25.00
JCL	Julio Lugo	15.00
JDD	J.D. Drew	20.00
JE	Jacoby Ellsbury	40.00
JL	Jon Lester	25.00
JM	Justin Morneau	20.00
JP	Jake Peavy	15.00
JR	Jose Reyes	25.00
JRP	Jonathan Papelbon	25.00
JV	Justin Verlander	15.00
KY	Kevin Youkilis	20.00
MH	Matt Holliday	15.00
ML	Mike Lowell	25.00
MR	Manny Ramirez	20.00
MT	Mike Timlin	15.00
PF	Prince Fielder	20.00
RH	Ryan Howard	25.00
RM	Russell Martin	15.00

Historical Campaign Match-Ups

		NM/M
Inserted 1:6		
1792	George Washington, John Adams	2.00
1796	John Adams, Thomas Jefferson	1.00

1800	Thomas Jefferson, Aaron Burr	1.00
1804	Thomas Jefferson, Charles Pinckney	1.00
1808	James Madison, Charles Pinckney	.50
1812	James Madison, DeWitt Clinton	.50
1816	James Monroe, Rufus King	.50
1820	James Monroe, John Quincy Adams	.50
1824	John Quincy Adams, Andrew Jackson	.50
1828	Andrew Jackson, John Quincy Adams	.50
1832	Andrew Jackson, Henry Clay	.50
1836	Martin Van Buren, William Henry Harrison	.50
1840	William Henry Harrison, Martin Van Buren	.50
1844	James K. Polk, Henry Clay	.50
1848	Zachary Taylor, Lewis Cass	.50
1852	Franklin Pierce, Winfield Scott	.50
1856	James Buchanan, John C. Fremont	.50
1860	Abraham Lincoln, John C. Breckinridge	2.00
1864	Abraham Lincoln, George B. McClellan	2.00
1868	Ulysses S. Grant, Horatio Seymour	1.00
1872	Ulysses S. Grant, Horace Greeley	1.00
1876	Rutherford B. Hayes, Samuel J. Tilden	.50
1880	James Garfield, Winfield Scott Hancock	.50
1884	Grover Cleveland, James G. Blaine	.50
1888	Benjamin Harrison, Grover Cleveland	.50
1892	Grover Cleveland, Benjamin Harrison	.50
1896	William McKinley, William Jennings Bryan	.50
1900	William McKinley, William Jennings Bryan	.50
1904	Theodore Roosevelt, Alton B. Parker	.50
1908	William H. Taft, William Jennings Bryan	.50
1912	Woodrow Wilson, Theodore Roosevelt	.50
1916	Woodrow Wilson, Charles Evans Hughes	.50
1920	Warren G. Harding, James M. Cox	.50
1924	Calvin Coolidge, John W. Davis	.50
1928	Herbert Hoover, Al Smith	.50
1932	Franklin D. Roosevelt, Herbert Hoover	1.00
1936	Franklin D. Roosevelt, Alf Landon	1.00
1940	Franklin D. Roosevelt, Wendell Willkie	1.00
1944	Franklin D. Roosevelt, Thomas E. Dewey	1.00
1948	Harry S. Truman, Thomas E. Dewey	.50
1952	Dwight D. Eisenhower, Adlai Stevenson	.50
1956	Dwight D. Eisenhower, Adlai Stevenson	.50
1960	John F. Kennedy, Richard Nixon	2.00
1964	Lyndon B. Johnson, Barry Goldwater	.50
1968	Richard Nixon, Hubert H. Humphrey	.50
1972	Richard Nixon, George McGovern	.50
1976	Jimmy Carter, Gerald Ford	.50
1980	Ronald Reagan, Jimmy Carter	1.00
1984	Ronald Reagan, Walter Mondale	1.00
1988	George H.W. Bush, Michael Dukakis	.50
1992	Bill Clinton, George H.W. Bush	1.00
1996	Bill Clinton, Bob Dole	1.00
2000	George W. Bush, Al Gore	1.00
2004	George W. Bush, John Kerry	1.00
2008D	Hillary Clinton, Barack Obama	2.00

Historical Campaign Match-Ups Cut Signatures

Production One Set
No Pricing

Home Run Derby

		NM/M
Common Player:		3.00
Production 999 Sets		
1	Alex Rodriguez	15.00
2	Ryan Braun	8.00
3	Carlos Beltran	5.00
4	Alfonso Soriano	5.00
5	Prince Fielder	4.00
6	Carlos Lee	15.00
7	Albert Pujols	4.00
8	Chris Young	4.00
9	Justin Morneau	4.00
10	Ryan Howard	8.00
11	Dan Uggla	3.00
12	Pat Burrell	4.00
13	Adrian Gonzalez	4.00
14	Ken Griffey Jr.	10.00
15	Carlos Pena	4.00
16	Brandon Phillips	4.00
17	Jimmy Rollins	5.00
18	David Wright	8.00
19	Jim Thome	4.00
20	Adam Dunn	4.00
21	Chipper Jones	8.00
22	Hanley Ramirez	5.00
23	Brad Hawpe	3.00
24	Jermaine Dye	3.00
25	Matt Holliday	5.00
26	Magglio Ordonez	4.00
27	Aaron Rowand	3.00
28	Andruw Jones	3.00
29	Khalil Greene	3.00
30	David Ortiz	6.00
31	Frank Thomas	4.00
32	Victor Martinez	4.00
33	Russell Martin	4.00
34	Gary Sheffield	4.00
35	Vladimir Guerrero	5.00
36	Carlos Delgado	4.00
37	Travis Hafner	3.00
38	Alex Rios	3.00
39	Grady Sizemore	4.00
40	Miguel Cabrera	4.00
41	Ryan Zimmerman	4.00
42	Nick Markakis	4.00
43	Jason Bay	3.00
44	Delmon Young	3.00
45	Lance Berkman	4.00
46	Manny Ramirez	5.00
47	Jorge Posada	4.00
48	Derrek Lee	4.00
49	B.J. Upton	4.00
50	Chase Utley	5.00

In The Name Relics

No Pricing

Mickey Mantle Home Run History

		NM/M
Common Mantle (502-536):		2.00
Inserted 1:9		

Mickey Mantle 1956 Reprint Relic

	NM/M
Production 56	
56MM Mickey Mantle	100.00

New York Commemorative Patch Relics

		NM/M
Common Patch:		20.00
Production 100 Sets		
AR	Alex Rodriguez	75.00
JP	Jorge Posada	30.00
DJ	Derek Jeter	75.00
RC	Robinson Cano	30.00
JD	Johnny Damon	30.00
BA	Bobby Abreu	30.00
CMW	Chien-Ming Wang	50.00
MR	Mariano Rivera	40.00
PH	Phil Hughes	35.00
JC	Joba Chamberlain	50.00
MC	Melky Cabrera	25.00
JG	Jason Giambi	25.00
AP	Andy Pettitte	35.00
HM	Hideki Matsui	40.00
MM	Mike Mussina	40.00
DW	David Wright	40.00
JR	Jose Reyes	35.00
CD	Carlos Delgado	20.00
CB	Carlos Beltran	25.00
PM	Pedro Martinez	25.00

JM	John Maine	20.00
BW	Billy Wagner	20.00
MA	Moises Alou	20.00
RMC	Ryan Church	20.00
OP	Oliver Perez	20.00
BS	Brian Schneider	20.00
LC	Luis Castillo	20.00
EC	Endy Chavez	20.00
OH	Orlando Hernandez	20.00
MP	Mike Pelfrey	20.00

Own the Game

		NM/M
Complete Set (25):		10.00
Common Player:		.50
Inserted 1:6		
1	Alex Rodriguez	2.00
2	Prince Fielder	1.00
3	Ryan Howard	1.00
4	Carlos Pena	.50
5	Adam Dunn	.50
6	Matt Holliday	.75
7	David Ortiz	1.00
8	Jim Thome	.50
9	Lance Berkman	.50
10	Miguel Cabrera	.75
11	Alex Rodriguez	2.00
12	Magglio Ordonez	.50
13	Matt Holliday	.75
14	Ryan Howard	1.00
15	Vladimir Guerrero	.75
16	Carlos Pena	.50
17	Mike Lowell	.50
18	Miguel Cabrera	.75
19	Prince Fielder	1.00
20	Carlos Lee	.50
21	Jake Peavy	.50
22	John Lackey	.50
23	Brandon Webb	.50
24	Brad Penny	.50
25	Fausto Carmona	.50

Red Hot Rookie Redemptions

		NM/M
Will be announced throughout season.		
1	Jay Bruce/Auto.	50.00
2	Justin Masterson	15.00
3	John Bowker	10.00
4	Kosuke Fukudome	30.00
5	Mike Aviles	15.00
6	Chris Davis	25.00
7	Chris Volstad	15.00
8	Jeff Samardzija	25.00
9	Brad Ziegler	15.00
10	Gio Gonzalez	8.00
11	Clayton Kershaw	12.00
12	Daniel Murphy	20.00
13	Chris Dickerson	15.00
14	Pablo Sandoval	15.00
15	Nick Evans	15.00
16	Clayton Richard	10.00

Silk

		NM/M
Common Player:		10.00
Production 50 Sets		
1	Alex Rodriguez	75.00
2	Scott Kazmir	10.00
3	Ivan Rodriguez	15.00
4	Joe Mauer	15.00
5	Ken Griffey Jr.	50.00
6	Nick Markakis	25.00
7	Mickey Mantle	100.00
8	Erik Bedard	15.00
9	Derrek Lee	20.00
10	Miguel Cabrera	20.00
11	Yovani Gallardo	15.00
12	Victor Martinez	15.00
13	Curtis Granderson	20.00
14	Chris Young	15.00
15	Jimmy Rollins	15.00
16	Dan Uggla	10.00
17	Felix Hernandez	20.00
18	Alex Rios	15.00
19	Jason Bay	15.00
20	Jose Reyes	25.00
21	Mike Lowell	15.00
22	Carl Crawford	15.00
23	Chipper Jones	40.00
24	Troy Glaus	10.00
25	Cole Hamels	20.00

26	Chris Young	15.00
27	Torii Hunter	15.00
28	Hideki Matsui	25.00
29	Freddy Sanchez	10.00
30	Josh Beckett	25.00
31	Mark Buehrle	10.00
32	Brian Bannister	10.00
33	Carlos Beltran	20.00
34	Dontrelle Willis	10.00
35	Vladimir Guerrero	25.00
36	Matt Holliday	20.00
37	Adam Dunn	20.00
38	Gary Matthews Jr.	10.00
39	Travis Hafner	15.00
40	Chase Utley	30.00
41	Vernon Wells	10.00
42	Lance Berkman	20.00
43	Jeff Francis	10.00
44	Curt Schilling	20.00
45	Alfonso Soriano	20.00
46	Jarrod Saltalamacchia	15.00
47	Hideki Okajima	20.00
48	Pedro Martinez	25.00
49	Jorge Posada	20.00
50	Justin Upton	20.00
51	Tom Gorzelanny	10.00
52	Carlos Delgado	15.00
53	Edgar Renteria	10.00
54	Chien-Ming Wang	30.00
55	C.C. Sabathia	20.00
56	B.J. Upton	20.00
57	Delmon Young	15.00
58	Tim Lincecum	25.00
59	Carlos Zambrano	20.00
60	Magglio Ordonez	15.00
61	Brandon Webb	15.00
62	Ben Sheets	15.00
63	Brad Penny	10.00
64	John Lackey	10.00
65	Hanley Ramirez	25.00
66	Gary Sheffield	20.00
67	Ubaldo Jimenez	10.00
68	Barry Zito	10.00
69	Daisuke Matsuzaka	60.00
70	Justin Morneau	20.00
71	Jacoby Ellsbury	75.00
72	John Smoltz	20.00
73	Chris Carpenter	15.00
74	Ryan Braun	35.00
75	Prince Fielder	25.00
76	Carlos Lee	20.00
77	Ryan Zimmerman	20.00
78	Troy Tulowitzki	20.00
79	Michael Young	15.00
80	Johan Santana	25.00
81	Hunter Pence	30.00
82	Adrian Gonzalez	15.00
83	Jake Peavy	20.00
84	Derek Jeter	75.00
85	Ichiro Suzuki	35.00
86	Miguel Tejada	20.00
87	Trevor Hoffman	10.00
88	Kevin Youkilis	20.00
89	David Wright	35.00
90	Albert Pujols	75.00
91	Todd Helton	20.00
92	Rich Harden	10.00
93	Fausto Carmona	10.00
94	Mark Teixeira	20.00
95	Justin Verlander	25.00
96	Tim Hudson	15.00
97	Jeff Francoeur	20.00
98	Manny Ramirez	25.00
99	David Ortiz	30.00
100	Ryan Howard	40.00

Stars

		NM/M
Complete Set (25):		15.00
Common Player:		.50
Inserted 1:6		
1	Alex Rodriguez	2.00
2	Magglio Ordonez	.50
3	Justin Morneau	.50
4	Josh Beckett	.75
5	David Wright	1.00
6	Jimmy Rollins	.75
7	Ichiro Suzuki	1.00
8	Chipper Jones	1.00
9	Brandon Webb	.75
10	Ryan Howard	1.00

11	Derek Jeter	2.00
12	Vladimir Guerrero	.75
13	Manny Ramirez	.75
14	Jake Peavy	.50
15	David Ortiz	.75
16	Jose Reyes	.75
17	Miguel Cabrera	.75
18	Victor Martinez	.50
19	C.C. Sabathia	.50
20	Prince Fielder	.75
21	Alfonso Soriano	.75
22	Grady Sizemore	.75
23	Albert Pujols	2.00
24	Pedro Martinez	.75
25	Matt Holliday	.75

The Mickey Mantle Story

	NM/M
Complete Set (20):	40.00
Complete Series 1 Set (10):	20.00
Complete Series 2 Set (10):	20.00
Common Mantle:	3.00
Inserted 1:18	

The Presidential Stamp Collection

		NM/M
Production 90 Sets		
GW1	George Washington	50.00
GW2	George Washington	50.00
GW3	George Washington	50.00
GW4	George Washington	50.00
GW5	George Washington	50.00
GW6	George Washington	50.00
TJ1	Thomas Jefferson	60.00
TJ2	Thomas Jefferson	60.00
TJ3	Thomas Jefferson	60.00
TJ4	Thomas Jefferson	60.00
JM1	James Monroe	60.00
JQA1	John Quincy Adams	60.00
AJ1	Andrew Jackson	60.00
WHH1	William Henry Harrison	40.00
JT1	John Tyler	60.00
ZT1	Zachary Taylor	50.00
JB1	James Buchanan	60.00
AL1	Abraham Lincoln	60.00
AL2	Abraham Lincoln	60.00
AL3	Abraham Lincoln	60.00
JG1	James Garfield	50.00
BH1	Benjamin Harrison	50.00
TR1	Teddy Roosevelt	60.00
WW1	Woodrow Wilson	60.00
WGH1	Warren G. Harding	50.00
HH1	Herbert Hoover	50.00
FDR1	Franklin Delano Roosevelt	50.00
DDE1	Dwight D. Eisenhower	60.00
JFK1	John F. Kennedy	100.00
JFK2	John F. Kennedy	100.00
Series 2		
GW7	George Washington	60.00
GW8	George Washington	60.00
GW9	George Washington	60.00
GW10	George Washington	60.00
GW11	George Washington	60.00
GW12	George Washington	60.00
GW13	George Washington	60.00
JM2	James Monroe	60.00
AL4	Abraham Lincoln	100.00
JG2	James Garfield	50.00
TR2	Theodore Roosevelt	60.00
TR3	Theodore Roosevelt	60.00
WW2	Woodrow Wilson	50.00
WGH2	Warren Harding	60.00
RBH1	Rutherford B. Hayes	60.00
RBH2	Rutherford B. Hayes	60.00
WM1	William McKinley	50.00
LBJ1	Lyndon B. Johnson	60.00
USG1	Ulysses S. Grant	60.00
USG2	Ulysses S. Grant	60.00
WHT1	William Taft	50.00
RN1	Richard Nixon	60.00
CAA1	Chester A. Arthur	50.00
AJO1	Andrew Johnson	50.00
HST1	Harry S. Truman	60.00
JMA1	James Madison	60.00
JKP1	James K. Polk	60.00
GC1	Grover Cleveland	60.00
MF1	Millard Fillmore	60.00
MVB1	Martin Van Buren	60.00
FP1	Franklin Pierce	60.00

Trading Card History

	NM/M
Common Player:	.50
Inserted 1:2	
#26-50 HTA Exclusive	
#51-75 Series 2	

1	Jacoby Ellsbury	2.00
2	Joba Chamberlain	4.00
3	Daisuke Matsuzaka	3.00
4	Prince Fielder	1.00

JUSTIN MORNEAU

5	Clay Buchholz	2.00
6	Alex Rodriguez	3.00
7	Mickey Mantle	4.00
8	Ryan Braun	2.00
9	Albert Pujols	3.00
10	Joe Mauer	.50
11	Jose Reyes	1.50
12	Joey Votto	.50
13	Johan Santana	1.00
14	Hunter Pence	1.00
15	Hideki Okajima	.50
16	Cameron Maybin	.50
17	Roger Clemens	1.50
18	Tim Lincecum	1.00
19	Mark Teixeira, Jeff Francoeur	.50
20	Justin Upton	1.00
21	Alfonso Soriano	1.00
22	Pedro Martinez	1.00
23	Chien-Ming Wang	1.50
24	Ichiro Suzuki	2.00
25	Grady Sizemore	1.00
26	Ryan Howard	2.00
27	David Wright	2.00
28	Chin-Lung Hu	.50
29	Justin Morneau	1.00
30	Ken Griffey Jr.	3.00
31	Chipper Jones	2.50
32	Justin Verlander	1.00
33	Manny Ramirez	1.50
34	Chase Utley	1.50
35	Ivan Rodriguez	.75
36	Josh Beckett	1.00
37	Tom Glavine	1.00
38	Vladimir Guerrero	1.50
39	Lance Berkman	1.00
40	Gary Sheffield	1.00
41	Luke Hochevar	.50
42	David Ortiz	1.50
43	Miguel Cabrera	1.50
44	Andruw Jones	.75
45	Hideki Matsui	2.50
46	C.C. Sabathia	1.00
47	Magglio Ordonez	1.00
48	Pedro Martinez	1.50
49	Curtis Granderson	1.00
50	Derek Jeter	4.00
51	Victor Martinez	.75
52	Hanley Ramirez	1.00
53	Jake Peavy	.75
54	Brandon Webb	.75
55	Matt Holliday	.75
56	Hiroki Kuroda	.50
57	Mike Lowell	.75
58	Carlos Lee	.75
59	Nick Markakis	.75
60	Carlos Beltran	.75
61	Francisco Rodriguez	.50
62	Troy Tulowitzki	.75
63	Russell Martin	.75
64	Justin Morneau	.75
65	Phil Hughes	.75
66	Torii Hunter	.75
67	Adam Dunn	.75
68	Raul Ibanez	.50
69	Robinson Cano	.75
70	Brad Hawpe	.50
71	Michael Young	.50
72	Jim Thome	.75
73	Chris Young	.75
74	Carlos Zambrano	.75
75	Felix Hernandez	1.00

World Champion Relics

		NM/M
Production 100 Sets		
1	Josh Beckett	60.00
2	Hideki Okajima	50.00
3	Curt Schilling	60.00
4	Jason Varitek	60.00
5	Mike Lowell	60.00
6	Jacoby Ellsbury	80.00
7	Dustin Pedroia	70.00
8	Jonathan Papelbon	60.00
9	Julio Lugo	50.00
10	Manny Ramirez	60.00
11	David Ortiz	60.00
12	Eric Gagne	40.00
13	Jon Lester	50.00
14	J.D. Drew	50.00
15	Kevin Youkilis	50.00

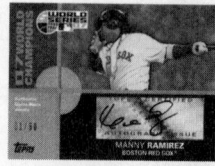

World Champion Autograph Relics

		NM/M
Production 50 Sets		
1	Josh Beckett	
2	Hideki Okajima	150.00
3	Curt Schilling	150.00
4	Jason Varitek	150.00
5	Mike Lowell	150.00
6	Jacoby Ellsbury	300.00
7	Dustin Pedroia	200.00
8	Julio Lugo	100.00
10	Manny Ramirez	225.00

Year In Review

BYRNES ENDS GAME WITH WALK-OFF

ERIC BYRNES ARIZONA DIAMONDBACKS

		NM/M
Complete Set (120):		60.00
Common Player:		.50
#'s 61-120 in Series 2		
Inserted 1:6		
1	Paul LoDuca	.50
2	Felix Hernandez	.75
3	Ian Snell	.50
4	Carlos Beltran	.50
5	Daisuke Matsuzaka	1.50
6	Jose Reyes	1.00
7	Alex Rodriguez	2.00
8	Scott Kazmir	.75
9	Adam Everett	.50
10	Josh Beckett, Josh Hamilton	.75
11	Craig Monroe	.50
12	Justin Morneau	.75
13	Roy Halladay	.75
14	Jeff Suppan	.50
15	Marco Scutaro	.50
16	Ivan Rodriguez	.50
17	Dmitri Young	.50
18	Mark Buehrle	.50
19	Alex Rodriguez	2.00
20	Joe Saunders	.50
21	Russell Martin	.75
22	Manny Ramirez	.75
23	Chase Utley	1.00
24	Travis Hafner	.50
25	Jake Peavy	.75
26	Shawn Hill	.50
27	Daisuke Matsuzaka	1.50
28	Matt Belisle	.50
29	Troy Tulowitzki	.75
30	Andruw Jones	.75
31	Phil Hughes	.75
32	Derek Lee	.75
33	Ichiro Suzuki	1.50
34	Julio Franco	.50
35	Chien-Ming Wang	1.00
36	Hideki Matsui	1.00
37	Brad Penny	.50
38	Jack Wilson	.50
39	Francisco Cordero	.50
40	Omar Vizquel	.50
41	Tim Lincecum	.75
42	Bartolo Colon	.50
43	Fred Lewis	.50
44	Jeff Kent	.50
45	Randy Johnson	1.00
46	Rafael Furcal	.75
47	Delmon Young	.75
48	Andrew Miller	.75
49	David Ortiz, Mike Lowell	1.00
50	Justin Verlander	.75
51	C.C. Sabathia	.75
52	Felipe Lopez	.50
53	Oliver Perez	.50
54	John Smoltz	.75
55	Mark Reynolds	.50
56	Jeremy Accardo	.50
57	Todd Helton	.75

58 Adrian Beltre .50
59 Carlos Delgado .50
60 Chris Young .75
61 Roy Halladay .75
62 Kevin Youkilis .75
63 Joe Blanton .50
64 Chad Gaudin .50
65 Derek Lowe .50
66 C.C. Sabathia .75
67 Luis Castillo .50
68 Curt Schilling .75
69 Pedro Feliz .50
70 James Shields .50
71 Masumi Kuwata .50
72 Raul Ibanez .50
73 Justin Verlander .75
74 Tim Lincecum .75
75 Hideki Matsui 1.00
76 Julio Franco .50
77 Russell Branyan .50
78 Chipper Jones 1.00
79 Chone Figgins .75
80 Chris Young .75
81 Sammy Sosa .75
82 Miguel Tejada .75
83 Wilfredo Ledezma .50
84 Victor Martinez .75
85 Dustin McGowan .50
86 Mike Fontenot .50
87 Mark Ellis .50
88 Ryan Howard 1.50
89 Frank Thomas .75
90 Aubrey Huff .50
91 Jake Peavy .75
92 Dan Haren .50
93 Damian Miller .50
94 Billy Butler .50
95 Dmitri Young .50
96 Chipper Jones 1.00
97 Justin Morneau .75
98 Erik Bedard .75
99 Scott Hatteberg .50
100 Vladimir Guerrero 1.00
101 Ichiro Suzuki 1.50
102 Jose Reyes 1.00
103 Ryan Garko .50
104 Jeff Francoeur .75
105 Joe Mauer .50
106 Manny Ramirez .75
107 Chase Utley 1.00
108 Magglio Ordonez .50
109 Chris Young .75
110 B.J. Upton .75
111 Willie Harris .50
112 Shelley Duncan .50
113 Jon Lester .75
114 Travis Buck .50
115 Ryan Raburn .50
116 Eric Byrnes .50
117 Kenny Lofton .50
118 Jason Isringhausen .50
119 Todd Helton .75
120 Carl Crawford .50

50th Anniversary All-Rookie Team

NM/M
Complete Set (110): 75.00
Common Player: .50
#'s 56-110 in Series 2
Inserted 1:5
1 Darryl Strawberry .50
2 Gary Sheffield .75
3 Dwight Gooden .50
4 Melky Cabrera .75
5 Gary Carter .50
6 Lou Piniella .50
7 David Justice .50
8 Andre Dawson .75
9 Mark Ellis .50
10 Dave Johnson .50
11 Jermaine Dye .50
12 Dan Johnson .50
13 Alfonso Soriano .75
14 Prince Fielder 1.50
15 Hanley Ramirez 1.00
16 Matt Holliday .75
17 Justin Verlander 1.00
18 Mark Teixeira .75
19 Julio Franco .50
20 Ivan Rodriguez .75
21 Jason Bay .75
22 Brandon Webb .75
23 Dontrelle Willis .50
24 Brad Wilkerson .50
25 Dan Uggla .50
26 Ozzie Smith 1.00
27 Andruw Jones .75
28 Garret Anderson .50
29 Jimmy Rollins 1.00
30 Brian McCann .50
31 Scott Podsednik .50
32 Garrett Atkins .50
33 Billy Wagner .50
34 Chipper Jones 1.00
35 Roger McDowell .50
36 Austin Kearns .50
37 Boog Powell .50
38 Ron Swoboda .50
39 Roy Oswalt .75
40 Mike Piazza 1.00
41 Albert Pujols 3.00
42 Ichiro Suzuki 2.00
43 C.C. Sabathia .75
44 Todd Helton .75
45 Scott Rolen .75
46 Derek Jeter 3.00
47 Shawn Green .50
48 Manny Ramirez 1.00
49 Tom Seaver 1.00
50 Kenny Lofton .50
51 Francisco Liriano .75
52 Ryan Zimmerman .75
53 Jeff Francoeur .75
54 Joe Mauer .75
55 Magglio Ordonez .75
56 Carlos Beltran 1.00
57 Andre Ethier .50
58 Brian Bannister .50
59 Chris Young .75
60 Troy Tulowitzki .75
61 Hideki Okajima .75
62 Delmon Young .50
63 Craig Wilson .50
64 Hunter Pence 1.00
65 Tadahito Iguchi .50
66 Mark Kotsay .50
67 Nick Markakis 1.00
68 Russ Adams .50
69 Russell Martin 1.00
70 James Loney .75
71 Ryan Braun 1.50
72 Jonny Gomes .50
73 Carlos Ruiz .50
74 Willy Taveras .50
75 Joe Torre .50
76 Jeff Kent .50
77 Huston Street .50
78 Dustin Pedroia 1.00
79 Gustavo Chacin .50
80 Adam Dunn 1.00
81 Pat Burrell .75
82 Rocco Baldelli .50
83 Chad Tracy .50
84 Adam LaRoche .50
85 Aaron Miles .50
86 Khalil Greene .50
87 Daniel Cabrera .50
88 Mike Gonzalez .50
89 Ty Wigginton .50
90 Angel Berroa .50
91 Moises Alou .50
92 Miguel Olivo .50
93 Nick Johnson .50
94 Eric Hinske .50
95 Ramon Santiago .50
96 Jason Jennings .50
97 Adam Kennedy .50
98 Mike Lamb .50
99 Rafael Furcal .50
100 Jay Payton .50
101 Bengie Molina .50
102 Mark Redman .50
103 Alex Gonzalez .50
104 Ray Durham .50
105 Miguel Cairo .50
106 Kerry Wood .75
107 Dmitri Young .50
108 Jose Cruz .50
109 Jose Guillen .50
110 Scott Hatteberg .50

50th Anniv. All-Rookie Team Relics

NM/M
Production 50 Sets
DS Darryl Strawberry 20.00
AD Andre Dawson 40.00
DW Dontrelle Willis 10.00
MP Mike Piazza 40.00
TS Tom Seaver 40.00
OS Ozzie Smith 40.00
IR Ivan Rodriguez 25.00
DG Dwight Gooden 15.00
GC Gary Carter 20.00
AS Alfonso Soriano 30.00
IS Ichiro Suzuki 40.00
MH Matt Holliday 25.00
JR Jimmy Rollins 30.00
PF Prince Fielder 40.00
DJ David Justice 20.00
JV Justin Verlander 40.00
AJ Andruw Jones 20.00
CJ Chipper Jones 30.00
RO Roy Oswalt 20.00
BW Brandon Webb 25.00
Series 2
BM Brian McCann 15.00
HR Hanley Ramirez 30.00
DU Dan Uggla 10.00
GA Garret Anderson 10.00
JB Jason Bay 10.00
MT Mark Teixeira 20.00
SP Scott Podsednik 10.00
JM Joe Mauer 10.00
AP Albert Pujols 40.00
AD Adam Dunn 15.00
CS C.C. Sabathia 15.00
NJ Nick Johnson 10.00
PB Pat Burrell 15.00
TH Todd Helton 15.00
MO Magglio Ordonez 10.00
GS Gary Sheffield 15.00
RB Rocco Baldelli 10.00
AE Andre Ethier 10.00
NM Nick Markakis 20.00
FL Francisco Liriano 15.00

50th Anniversary All-Rookie Team Autos.

Production 25 Sets
No Pricing

2007 Highlight Relics

NM/M
Common Relic: 5.00
CB Carlos Beltran 10.00
DO David Ortiz 15.00
DW David Wright 10.00
IR Ivan Rodriguez 8.00
LB Lance Berkman 8.00
MT Miguel Tejada 5.00
TH Todd Helton 8.00
JV Justin Verlander 15.00
MH Matt Holliday 8.00
AP Albert Pujols 20.00
VG Vladimir Guerrero 8.00
JR Jose Reyes 10.00
PF Prince Fielder 15.00
CC Carl Crawford 5.00
MR Manny Ramirez 8.00
IS Ichiro Suzuki 20.00
EC Eric Chavez 5.00
CM Cameron Maybin 10.00
CS Curt Schilling 8.00
DWW Dontrelle Willis 5.00
Series 2
JT Jim Thome 8.00
JB Jeremy Bonderman 5.00
BP Brandon Phillips 8.00
AG Alex Gordon 10.00
RH Ryan Howard 10.00
CU Chase Utley 15.00
RZ Ryan Zimmerman 8.00
DU Dan Uggla 5.00
HR Hanley Ramirez 8.00
BU B.J. Upton 8.00
DY Delmon Young 5.00
VG Vladimir Guerrero 8.00
RO Roy Oswalt 5.00
PF Prince Fielder 10.00
RB Ryan Braun 15.00
AP Albert Pujols 15.00
JR Jose Reyes 10.00
DW David Wright 10.00
IS Ichiro Suzuki 15.00
AR Aramis Ramirez 8.00
DL Derrek Lee 8.00
BW Brandon Webb 8.00
RF Rafael Furcal 5.00
JL James Loney 8.00
CMW Chien-Ming Wang 20.00
ST Scott Thorman 5.00
DO David Ortiz 10.00
JP Jake Peavy 8.00
CM Cameron Maybin 8.00
CC Carl Crawford 5.00

2007 Highlight Relic Autograph

Production 25 Sets
No Pricing

2007 Highlight Autographs

NM/M
Common Auto.: 10.00
AP Albert Pujols
AS Alfonso Soriano 50.00
CMW Chien-Ming Wang 125.00
GS Gary Sheffield 40.00
JD Johnny Damon 50.00
JP Jake Peavy 30.00
JV Jason Varitek 50.00
MR Manny Ramirez 80.00
RJC Robinson Cano 40.00
VG Vladimir Guerrero 50.00
BP Brad Penny 25.00
DH Danny Haren 25.00
DW David Wright 60.00
HR Hanley Ramirez 40.00
JBR Jose Reyes 60.00
JR Jimmy Rollins 50.00
JTD Jermaine Dye 20.00
MY Michael Young 20.00
PF Prince Fielder 50.00
CB Clay Buchholz 80.00
CP Carlos Pena 20.00
ED Eulogio de la Cruz 15.00
ES Ervin Santana 10.00
FC Fausto Carmona 20.00
FS Freddy Sanchez 15.00
JF Josh Fields 15.00
JL John Lackey 15.00
LC Luis Castillo 15.00
MG Matt Garza 15.00
NM Nicholas Markakis 20.00
RM Russell Martin 20.00
WN Wilbert Nieves 15.00
YG Yovani Gallardo 20.00
HK Howie Kendrick 15.00
JB John Buck 10.00
JM Jose Molina 10.00
RC Ramon Castro 10.00
RH Rich Hill 20.00
CV Carlos Villanueva 10.00
DM Dustin Moseley 10.00
MB Mike Bacsik 10.00
ME Mark Ellis 10.00
RJM Randy Messenger 10.00
SM Scott Moore 10.00
TG Tom Gorzelanny 15.00
UJ Ubaldo Jimenez 10.00
AL Adam Lind 10.00
JA Josh Anderson 15.00
DB Daric Barton 15.00
LB Lance Broadway 10.00
SF Sam Fuld 20.00
NJM Nyjer Morgan 20.00
SS Seth Smith 15.00
Series 2
DW David Wright 120.00
JM Justin Morneau 25.00
JR Jimmy Rollins 50.00
MT Mark Teixeira 40.00
CMW Chien-Ming Wang 75.00
DO David Ortiz 75.00
CD Carlos Delgado 20.00
VG Vladimir Guerrero 75.00
JD Johnny Damon 40.00
CF Chone Figgins 15.00
KM Kendry Morales 8.00
RN Ricky Nolasco 8.00
TT Taylor Tankersley 10.00
JW Josh Willingham 15.00
JC Joba Chamberlain 90.00
JKM John Maine 20.00
MG Matt Garza 15.00
BC Bobby Crosby 10.00
SV Shane Victorino 20.00
NM Nick Markakis 20.00
FL Francisco Liriano 15.00
RM Russell Martin 20.00
MC Melky Cabrera 20.00
RB Ryan Braun 35.00
DE Darin Erstad 10.00
JB Jeremy Bonderman 15.00
JTD Jermaine Dye 15.00
AH Aaron Heilman 10.00
CC Carl Crawford 15.00
JZ Joel Zumaya 10.00
MMT Marcus Thames 10.00
PJF Pedro Feliciano 15.00
CM Craig Monroe 10.00
NR Nate Robertson 10.00
EC Eric Chavez 10.00
PF Prince Fielder 30.00
RC Robinson Cano 20.00
JAR Jo Jo Reyes 15.00
DB Dallas Braden 15.00
AK Austin Kearns 8.00
CV Claudio Vargas 8.00
HCK Hong-Chih Kuo 20.00
JLC Jorge Cantu 10.00
CW Chase Wright 8.00
DY Delwyn Young 8.00
RP Ronny Paulino 8.00
ZG Zack Greinke 10.00
JAB Jason Bartlett 10.00
PH Philip Humber 8.00
RR Ryan Roberts 8.00
TG Tom Gorzelanny 8.00
ES Ervin Santana 10.00
FC Fausto Carmona 10.00

2007 Highlight Dual Relics

NM/M
Production 25 Sets
No Pricing

2008 Topps Allen & Ginter

NM/M
Common Player (1-300): .25
Common SP (301-350): 2.00
Inserted 1:2
Mini Exclusives (351-400): No Pricing
Rip Card Exclusive
Pack (8): 5.00
Box (24): 110.00
1 Alex Rodriguez 2.00
2 Juan Pierre .25
3 Benjamin Franklin .50
4 Roy Halladay .50
5 C.C. Sabathia .50
6 Brian Barton **RC** 2.00
7 Mickey Mantle 5.00
8 Brian Bass **(RC)** 1.50
9 Ian Kinsler .50
10 Manny Ramirez .75
11 Michael Cuddyer .25
12 Ian Snell .25
13 Mike Lowell .50
14 Adrian Gonzalez .50
15 B.J. Upton .50
16 Hiroki Kuroda **RC** 2.50
17 Kenji Johjima .25
18 James Loney .25
19 Albert Einstein .25
20 Vladimir Guerrero .50
21 Miguel Tejada .40
22 Chin-Lung Hu **(RC)** 2.00
23 A.J. Burnett .25
24 Bobby Jenks .25
25 Aramis Ramirez .50
26 Corey Hart .40
27 Brad Hawpe .25

28	Adam LaRoche	.25
29	Empire State Building	.25
30	Miguel Cabrera	.75
31	Ryan Zimmerman	.40
32	Mark Ellis	.25
33	Nick Swisher	.25
34	Bill Hall	.25
35	Eric Byrnes	.25
36	Michael Young	.40
37	Pedro Martinez	.50
38	Andruw Jones	.25
39	J.R. Towles **RC**	2.00
40	Justin Upton	.40
41	Paul Konerko	.40
42	Luke Scott	.25
43	Rickie Weeks	.25
44	Adam Wainwright	.25
45	Justin Morneau	.50
46	Chris Young	.40
47	Chad Billingsley	.40
48	Kazuo Matsui	.25
49	Shane Victorino	.40
50	Albert Pujols	2.00
51	Brian McCann	.50
52	Carlos Delgado	.40
53	Chien-Ming Wang	.50
54	Takashi Saito	.25
55	Josh Beckett	.50
56	Nick Johnson	.25
57	Ben Sheets	.40
58	Johnny Damon	.50
59	Nicky Hayden	.25
60	Prince Fielder	.50
61	Adam Dunn	.40
62	Dustin Pedroia	.50
63	Jacoby Ellsbury	.50
64	Brad Penny	.25
65	Victor Martinez	.40
66	Joe Mauer	.40
67	Kevin Kouzmanoff	.25
68	Frank Thomas	.50
69	Stevie Williams	.25
70	Matt Holliday	.50
71	Fausto Carmona	.25
72	Clayton Kershaw **RC**	4.00
73	Tadahito Iguchi	.25
74	Khalil Greene	.25
75	Travis Hafner	.40
76	Jim Thome	.50
77	Joba Chamberlain	.75
78	Ivan Rodriguez	.40
79	Jose Guillen	.25
80	Hanley Ramirez	.75
81	Vernon Wells	.40
82	Jayson Nix **(RC)**	1.00
83	Masahide Kobayashi **RC**	2.00
84	Bonnie Blair	.25
85	Curtis Granderson	.50
86	Kelvim Escobar	.25
87	Aaron Rowand	.25
88	Troy Glaus	.40
89	Billy Wagner	.25
90	Jose Reyes	.50
91	Scott Rolen	.40
92	Dan Jansen	.25
93	David Eckstein	.25
94	Tom Gorzelanny	.25
95	Garrett Atkins	.40
96	Carlos Zambrano	.50
97	Jeff Francis	.25
98	Kazuo Fukumori **RC**	2.00
99	John Bowker **(RC)**	1.00
100	David Wright	.75
101	Adrian Beltre	.40
102	Ray Durham	.25
103	Kerri Strug	.25
104	Orlando Hudson	.25
105	Jonathan Papelbon	.50
106	Brian Schneider	.25
107	Matt Biondi	.25
108	Alex Romero **(RC)**	1.00
109	Joey Chestnut	.25
110	Chase Utley	.75
111	Dan Uggla	.40
112	Akinori Iwamura	.25
113	Curt Schilling	.50
114	Trevor Hoffman	.25
115	Alex Rios	.40
116	Mariano Rivera	.50
117	Jeff Niemann **(RC)**	1.00
118	Geovany Soto	.50
119	Billy Mitchell	.25
120	Derek Jeter	2.00
121	Yovani Gallardo	.40
122	The Gateway Arch	.25
123	Josh Willingham	.25
124	Greg Maddux	1.50
125	John Lackey	.40
126	Chris Young	.40
127	Billy Butler	.25
128	Golden Gate Bridge	.25
129	Joey Votto **(RC)**	2.00
130	Tim Wakefield	.25
131	Todd Helton	.50
132	Gary Matthews Jr.	.25
133	Wild Bill Hickok	.25
134	Jason Varitek	.40
135	Robinson Cano	.50
136	Javier Vazquez	.25
137	Annie Oakley	.25
138	Andy Pettitte	.50
139	Greg Reynolds **RC**	1.50
140	Jimmy Rollins	.50
141	Jermaine Dye	.40
142	Eugenio Velez **RC**	1.50
143	J.J. Hardy	.25
144	Grand Canyon	.25
145	Bobby Abreu	.40
146	Scott Kazmir	.40
147	James Fennimore Cooper	.25
148	Mark Buehrle	.25
149	Freddy Sanchez	.25
150	Johan Santana	.50
151	Orlando Cabrera	.25
152	Lyle Overbay	.25
153	Clay Buchholz **(RC)**	3.00
154	Jesse Carlson **RC**	1.50
155	Troy Tulowitzki	.40
156	Delmon Young	.40
157	Ross Ohlendorf **RC**	2.00
158	Mary Shelley	.25
159	James Shields	.40
160	Alfonso Soriano	.50
161	Randy Winn	.25
162	Austin Kearns	.25
163	Jeremy Hermida	.25
164	Jorge Posada	.50
165	Justin Verlander	.50
166	Bram Stoker	.25
167	Marie Curie	.25
168	Melky Cabrera	.25
169	Howie Kendrick	.25
170	Jake Peavy	.50
171	J.D. Drew	.25
172	Pablo Picasso	.25
173	Rick Ankiel	.50
174	Jose Valverde	.25
175	Chipper Jones	.75
176	Claude Monet	.25
177	Evan Longoria **RC**	5.00
178	Jose Vidro	.25
179	Hideki Matsui	.75
180	Ryan Braun	.75
181	Moises Alou	.40
182	Nate McLouth	.25
183	Harriet Tubman	.25
184	Felix Hernandez	.50
185	Carlos Pena	.25
186	Jarrod Saltalamacchia	.25
187	Les Miles	.25
188	Kelly Johnson	.25
189	"Rampage" Jackson	1.00
190	Grady Sizemore	.50
191	Francisco Cordero	.25
192	Yunel Escobar	.25
193	Edwin Encarnacion	.25
194	Melvin Mora	.25
195	Russell Martin	.40
196	Edgar Renteria	.25
197	Bigfoot	.25
198	Steve Holm **RC**	1.00
199	Daric Barton **(RC)**	2.00
200	David Ortiz	.75
201	Tim Lincecum	.50
202	Jeff King	.25
203	Jhonny Peralta	.25
204	Julio Lugo	.25
205	J.J. Putz	.25
206	Jeff Francoeur	.25
207	Yuniesky Betancourt	.25
208	Bruce Jenner	.25
209	Clete Thomas **RC**	2.00
210	Carlos Lee	.50
211	Josh Hamilton	.75
212	Pyotr Ilyich Tchaikovsky	.25
213	Brendan Harris	.25
214	Dustin McGowan	.25
215	Aaron Harang	.25
216	Brett Myers	.25
217	Friedrich Nietzsche	.25
218	John Maine	.25
219	Charles Dickens	.25
220	Erik Bedard	.25
221	Tim Hudson	.25
222	Jeremy Bonderman	.25
223	Nyjer Morgan **(RC)**	1.00
224	Johnny Cueto **RC**	2.00
225	Roy Oswalt	.40
226	Rich Hill	.25
227	Frederick Douglass	.25
228	Derek Lowe	.25
229	Joe Blanton	.25
230	Carlos Beltran	.50
231	Huston Street	.25
232	Davy Crockett	.25
233	Pluto	.25
234	Jered Weaver	.25
235	Dan Haren	.40
236	Alex Gordon	.40
237	Zack Greinke	.25
238	Todd Clever	.25
239	Brian Bannister	.25
240	Magglio Ordonez	.40
241	Ryan Garko	.25
242	Takudzwa Ngwenya	.25
243	Gil Meche	.25
244	Mark Teahen	.25
245	Carlos Guillen	.25
246	Jeff Kent	.25
247	Lisa Leslie	.25
248	Lastings Milledge	.25
249	Serena Williams	.25
250	Ichiro Suzuki	1.00
251	Matt Cain	.25
252	Callix Crabbe **(RC)**	1.00
253	Nick Blackburn **RC**	2.00
254	Hunter Pence	.40
255	Cole Hamels	.50
256	Garret Anderson	.25
257	Luis Gonzalez	.25
258	Eric Chavez	.25
259	Francisco Rodriguez	.25
260	Mark Teixeira	.50
261	Bob Motley	.25
262	Mark Spitz	.25
263	Yadier Molina	.25
264	Adam Jones	.25
265	Brian Roberts	.25
266	Matt Kemp	.25
267	Andrew Miller	.25
268	Dean Karnazes	.25
269	Gary Sheffield	.40
270	Lance Berkman	.50
271	Paul LoDuca	.25
272	Matt Tolbert **RC**	1.00
273	Jay Bruce **(RC)**	5.00
274	John Smoltz	.50
275	Nick Markakis	.50
276	Oscar Wilde	.25
277	Dontrelle Willis	.25
278	Kevin Van Dam	.25
279	Jim Edmonds	.25
280	Brandon Webb	.50
281	Joe Nathan	.25
282	Jeanette Lee	.25
283	Andrew "William Ocean" Litz	.25
284	Daisuke Matsuzaka	1.00
285	Brandon Phillips	.50
286	Pat Burrell	.50
287	Chris Carpenter	.40
288	Pete Weber	.25
289	Derrek Lee	.50
290	Ken Griffey Jr.	1.50
291	Rich Thompson **(RC)**	1.00
292	Elijah Dukes	.25
293	Pedro Feliz	.25
294	Torii Hunter	.50
295	Chone Figgins	.25
296	Hideki Okajima	.25
297	Max Scherzer **RC**	2.00
298	Greg Smith **RC**	1.00
299	Rafael Furcal	.40
300	Ryan Howard	.75
301	Felix Pie	2.00
302	Brad Lidge	2.00
303	Jason Bay	2.50
304	Victor Hugo	2.00
305	Randy Johnson	3.00
306	Carlos Gomez	2.00
307	Pat Neshek	2.00
308	Jed Lowrie **(RC)**	4.00
309	Ryan Church	2.00
310	Michael Bourn	2.00
311	B.J. Ryan	2.00
312	Brandon Wood	2.00
313	Harriet Beecher Stowe	2.00
314	Mike Cameron	2.00
315	Tom Glavine	3.00
316	Ervin Santana	3.00
317	Geoff Jenkins	2.00
318	Andre Ethier	2.00
319	Jason Giambi	3.00
320	Dmitri Young	2.00
321	Wily Mo Pena	2.00
322	Hank Blalock	2.00
323	James Bowie	2.00
324	Casey Kotchman	2.00
325	Stephen Drew	2.00
326	Adam Kennedy	2.00
327	A.J. Pierzynski	2.00
328	Richie Sexson	2.00
329	Jeff Clement **(RC)**	3.00
330	Luke Hochevar **RC**	4.00
331	Luis Castillo	2.00
332	Dave Roberts	2.00
333	Coco Crisp	2.00
334	Jo Jo Reyes	2.00
335	Phil Hughes	3.00
336	Allen Fisher	2.00
337	Jason Schmidt	2.00
338	Placido Polanco	2.00
339	Jack Cust	2.00
340	Carl Crawford	3.00
341	Ty Wigginton	2.00
342	Aubrey Huff	2.00
343	Bengie Molina	2.00
344	Matt Diaz	2.00
345	Francisco Liriano	3.00
346	Brandon Boggs **(RC)**	3.00
347	David DeJesus	2.00
348	Justin Masterson **RC**	4.00
349	Frank Morris	2.00
350	Kevin Youkilis	3.00

Mini

Mini:	2-3X
Mini (351-390):	No Pricing
#'s 351-390 Inserted in Rip Cards	
Allen & Ginter Back:	3-4X
Inserted 1:5	
Black Border:	4-6X
Inserted 1:10	
No Number:	10-20X
Production 50 Sets	
Bazooka Back:	No Pricing
Production 25 Sets	
Framed Cloth:	No Pricing
Production 10 sets	
Wood:	No Pricing
Production One Set	

Ancient Icons

		NM/M
Common Icon:		5.00
1	Gilgamesh	5.00
2	Marduk	5.00
3	Beowulf	5.00
4	Poseidon	5.00
5	The Sphinx	5.00
6	Tutankhamen	5.00
7	Alexander the Great	5.00
8	Cleopatra	5.00
9	Sun Tzu	5.00
10	Quetzalcoatl	5.00
11	Isis	5.00
12	Hercules	5.00
13	King Arthur	5.00
14	Miyamoto Musashi	5.00
15	Genghis Khan	5.00
16	Zeus	5.00
17	Achilles	5.00
18	Confucius	5.00
19	Attila the Hun	5.00
20	Romulus & Remus	5.00

Autographs

		NM/M
Common Auto.:		15.00
SP Autos are noted		
RH	Ryan Howard/90	100.00
DO	David Ortiz/90	100.00
MR	Manny Ramirez/90	100.00
MH	Matt Holliday/90	70.00
PF	Prince Fielder/90	80.00
JR	Jose Reyes/90	100.00
HP	Hunter Pence/90	75.00
DW	David Wright/240	140.00
BP	Brad Penny/240	35.00
HR	Hanley Ramirez/240	50.00
TLH	Travis Hafner/240	25.00
CC	Carl Crawford/240	30.00
TH	Torii Hunter/240	25.00
JC	Joba Chamberlain	120.00
NM	Nick Markakis	35.00
CG	Curtis Granderson	25.00
GJ	Geoff Jenkins	20.00
ALR	Alex Rios	20.00
MK	Matt Kemp	20.00
CB	Clay Buchholz	30.00
OH	Orlando Hudson	15.00
JF	Jeff Francis	15.00
FCC	Fausto Carmona	15.00
ES	Ervin Santana	15.00
FC	Francisco Cordero	15.00
JS	Jarrod Saltalamacchia	15.00
BPB	Brian Bannister	15.00
AE	Andre Ethier	15.00
IK	Ian Kinsler	20.00
JBF	Jeff Francoeur	25.00
MH	Marcus Henderson/ Guitar Pick/100	200.00
BJ	Bruce Jenner/190	100.00
AF	Andrea Farina/190	40.00
AFI	Allen Fisher/190	35.00
AL	Andrew "William Ocean" Litz/190	40.00
BB	Bonnie Blair/190	75.00
BM	Bob Motley/190	60.00
BPM	Billy Mitchell/190	85.00
DJ	Dan Jansen/190	70.00
DK	Dean Karnazes/190	50.00
FM	Frank Morris/190	40.00
JJC	Joey Chestnut/190	75.00
JK	Jeff King/190	20.00
JL	Jeanette Lee/190	150.00
KS	Kerri Strug/190	75.00
KVD	Kevin Van Dam/190	60.00
LL	Lisa Leslie/190	75.00
LM	Les Miles/190	60.00
MB	Matt Biondi/190	50.00
MS	Mark Spitz/190	85.00
NH	Nicky Hayden/240	70.00
PW	Pete Weber/190	65.00
RJ	"Rampage" Jackson/190	140.00
SW	Serena Williams/190	140.00
TC	Todd Clever/190	50.00
SW	Stevie Williams/240	60.00
TN	Takudzwa Ngwenya/190	50.00
AM	Adriano Moraes/190	40.00
DB	Deep Blue/190	65.00

Baseball Icons

		NM/M
Inserted 1:48		
1	Cy Young	8.00

2	Walter Johnson	8.00
3	Jackie Robinson	8.00
4	Thurman Munson	8.00
5	Mel Ott	6.00
6	Honus Wagner	8.00
7	Pee Wee Reese	8.00
8	Tris Speaker	8.00
9	Christy Mathewson	6.00
10	Ty Cobb	8.00
11	Johnny Mize	6.00
12	Jimmie Foxx	8.00
13	Lou Gehrig	10.00
14	Roy Campanella	8.00
15	George Sisler	6.00
16	Rogers Hornsby	8.00
17	Babe Ruth	15.00

Cabinet Boxloader Autograph

NM/M

Production 200

BF	Bigfoot	80.00

Cabinet Boxloaders

NM/M

Common Card: 4.00
Inserted 1:Box

BH1	Matt Holliday, Jamey Carroll, Michael Barrett, Brian Giles	4.00
BH2	Mike Lowell, Manny Ramirez, Jonathan Papelbon, Josh Beckett	6.00
BH3	Ryan Howard, Jimmy Rollins, Chase Utley, Cole Hamels	6.00
BH4	Alex Rodriguez, Frank Thomas, Jim Thome	6.00
BH5	Justin Verlander, Mark Buehrle, Clay Buchholz	4.00
HB1	General George Washington, General Nathanael Greene	4.00
HB2	General Horatio Gates, General John Burgoyne	4.00
HB3	General George Meade, General Robert E. Lee	4.00
HB4	Lt. Col. William B. Travis, Colonel James Bowie, Colonel Davy Crockett, General Antonio Lopez, de Santa Ana	4.00
HB5	General Dwight D. Eisenhower, Field Marshall Bernard Montgomery	4.00

Cut Signatures

Production One Set
No Pricing

Dick Perez Originals

Production One Set
No Pricing

N43 Boxloaders

NM/M

Inserted 1:Box

RH	Ryan Howard	6.00
DO	David Ortiz	6.00
MR	Manny Ramirez	4.00
DW	David Wright	6.00
PF	Prince Fielder	5.00
JC	Joba Chamberlain	6.00
JR	Jose Reyes	4.00
HR	Hanley Ramirez	5.00
MH	Matt Holliday	4.00
CG	Curtis Granderson	4.00
CU	Chase Utley	5.00
RZ	Ryan Zimmerman	4.00
VG	Vladimir Guerrero	5.00
IS	Ichiro Suzuki	6.00
RB	Ryan Braun	6.00

N43 Boxloader Autographs

Production 15 Sets
No Pricing

N43 Boxloader Relics

No Pricing
Production 25 Sets

Relics

NM/M

Common Relic: 4.00

ER	Edgar Renteria	4.00
JD	J.D. Drew	5.00
PF	Prince Fielder	8.00
JV1	Jason Varitek	6.00
JG	Jay Gibbons	4.00
JDD	Johnny Damon	6.00
BR2	Brian Roberts	4.00
CC2	Carl Crawford	5.00
AD2	Adam Dunn	6.00
DY	Dmitri Young	4.00
RF	Rafael Furcal	5.00
BA	Bobby Abreu	6.00
IR2	Ivan Rodriguez	5.00
ALR	Alex Rios	5.00
VG	Vladimir Guerrero	8.00
WMP	Wily Mo Pena	4.00
JK	Jeff Kent	4.00
PL	Paul LoDuca	4.00
AK	Austin Kearns	4.00
DO1	David Ortiz	8.00
DW	David Wright	10.00
JTD	Jermaine Dye	5.00
IS	Ichiro Suzuki	15.00
BR1	Brian Roberts	5.00
HB	Hank Blalock	5.00
CK	Casey Kotchman	4.00
CS	Curt Schilling	6.00
AR	Aramis Ramirez	6.00
IR1	Ivan Rodriguez	5.00
SD	Stephen Drew	5.00
DO2	David Ortiz	8.00
AER	Alex Rodriguez	20.00
AP2	Albert Pujols	20.00
EC	Eric Chavez	4.00
CJ	Chipper Jones	10.00
JF	Jeff Francoeur	6.00
TG	Tom Glavine	6.00
AP1	Albert Pujols	20.00
VM	Victor Martinez	5.00
TH	Tim Hudson	5.00
ATK	Adam Kennedy	4.00
PK	Paul Konerko	5.00
AJP	A.J. Pierzynski	4.00
TLH	Todd Helton	6.00
AD1	Adam Dunn	6.00
CC1	Carl Crawford	5.00
MR	Manny Ramirez	8.00
JT	Jim Thome	6.00
RS	Richie Sexson	4.00
GA	Garret Anderson	4.00
JB	Jason Bay	5.00
RH	Ryan Howard	10.00
TPH	Travis Hafner	5.00
DM	Daisuke Matsuzaka	25.00
JV2	Jason Varitek	6.00
MH	Mike Hampton	4.00
MC	Melky Cabrera	6.00
DRY	Delwyn Young	4.00
MK	Matt Kemp	6.00
CZ	Carlos Zambrano	6.00
MT	Mark Teixeira	6.00
TSG	Tom Gorzelanny	4.00
MDC	Matt Capps	4.00
CAM	Carlos Marmol	6.00
JS	John Smoltz	6.00
BH	Brad Hawpe	5.00
BMM	Brian McCann	8.00
CG	Curtis Granderson	8.00
TT	Troy Tulowitzki	6.00
CU	Chase Utley	8.00
LB	Lance Berkman	6.00
RO	Roy Oswalt	6.00
MY	Michael Young	5.00
JJH	J.J. Hardy	5.00
JM	Joe Mauer	6.00
BC	Bobby Crosby	4.00
APB	Aaron Pryor/100	25.00
AW	Andre Ward/100	30.00
DG	Danny Green/100	30.00
EM	Edison Miranda/100	40.00
JFB	Jeff Fenech/100	25.00
JCJ	Joel Casamayor/100	25.00
KP	Kelly Pavlik/100	100.00
RM	Ray Mancini/75	75.00
SP	Samuel Peter/100	35.00
AM	Archie Moore/100	50.00
NH	Nicky Hayden/250	30.00
SW	Stevie Williams/250	20.00
BB	Bonnie Blair/250	25.00
DJ	Dan Jansen/250	20.00
KS	Kerri Strug/250	30.00
MB	Matt Biondi/250	20.00
TC	Todd Clever/250	25.00
TN	Takudzwa Ngwenya/250	15.00
LL	Lisa Leslie/250	30.00
SJW	Serena Williams/250	25.00
JC	Joey Chestnut/250	25.00
BM	Billy Mitchell/250	30.00
MS	Mark Spitz/250	30.00
FM	Frank Morris/250	20.00
AF	Andrea Farina/250	20.00
DK	Dean Karnazes/250	20.00
KVD	Kevin Van Dam/250	20.00
JL	Jeanette Lee/250	30.00
AL	Andrew "William Ocean" Litz/250	30.00
PW	Pete Weber/250	40.00
AFI	Allen Fisher/250	25.00
LM	Les Miles/250	20.00
RJ	"Rampage" Jackson/250	40.00
JKI	Jeff King/250	25.00
BJ	Bruce Jenner/250	20.00
BF	Bigfoot/250	60.00
ASM	Adriano Moraes/250	20.00

Rip Cards

NM/M

Prices for unripped cards.
Ripped cards 10 percent.

1	Erik Bedard/99	100.00
2	Jacoby Ellsbury/75	150.00
3	Chris Carpenter/99	100.00
4	Brandon Phillips/99	100.00
5	Daric Barton/99	100.00
6	Brian McCann/99	125.00
8	Dan Uggla/75	90.00
9	James Loney/99	100.00
10	James Shields/99	80.00
11	Curtis Granderson/75	100.00
12	Jason Bay/99	80.00
13	Alex Gordon/75	100.00
14	Travis Hafner/99	80.00
15	Derek Jeter/28	250.00
16	Pedro Feliz/99	80.00
17	Thurman Munson/50	150.00
18	Grady Sizemore/75	120.00
19	Alex Rios/99	100.00
20	David Ortiz/50	150.00
21	Walter Johnson/28	200.00
22	Scott Rolen/99	100.00
23	John Smoltz/99	100.00
24	Mel Ott/28	200.00
25	Ryan Howard/50	180.00
26	Hiroki Kuroda/99	100.00
27	Johnny Damon/99	125.00
28	Jose Reyes/75	125.00
29	Felix Hernandez/99	100.00
30	John Lackey/99	100.00
32	Mark Teixeira/99	100.00
33	Jim Edmonds/99	100.00
34	Prince Fielder/50	150.00
35	Brian Bannister/99	90.00
36	Chipper Jones/50	150.00
37	Edgar Renteria/99	90.00
38	Roy Campanella/50	180.00
39	Troy Tulowitzki/99	100.00
40	Adam LaRoche/99	90.00
41	Phil Hughes/99	100.00
42	Pee Wee Reese/50	160.00
43	Adam Jones/99	100.00
44	Huston Street/99	90.00
45	Cliff Lee/99	100.00
46	Delmon Young/99	100.00
47	Joe Mauer/99	100.00
48	Johan Santana/28	150.00
49	Dmitri Young/99	80.00
50	Todd Helton/99	100.00
51	Carlos Beltran/75	140.00
52	J.J. Putz/99	100.00
53	Carlos Lee/99	100.00
54	Billy Butler/99	100.00
55	Miguel Cabrera/99	125.00
56	Derrek Lee/99	100.00
57	Alfonso Soriano/75	100.00
58	Cole Hamels/99	100.00
59	Hanley Ramirez/75	120.00
60	Adrian Gonzalez/99	100.00
61	B.J. Upton/99	100.00
62	Tim Lincecum/75	150.00
63	Gary Matthews Jr./99	90.00
64	Justin Upton/75	140.00
65	Zack Greinke/99	100.00
66	Roy Oswalt/75	100.00
67	Jimmy Rollins/28	150.00
68	Miguel Tejada/99	100.00
69	Clay Buchholz/99	100.00
70	Andruw Jones/99	80.00
71	Chase Utley/75	100.00
72	Aaron Rowand/99	90.00
73	Johnny Mize/50	150.00
74	Jonathan Papelbon/75	125.00
75	Jarrod Saltalamacchia/99	90.00
76	Lance Berkman/50	100.00
77	Vernon Wells/99	90.00
78	Dontrelle Willis/99	90.00
79	Jim Thome/99	100.00
80	Torii Hunter/99	100.00
81	Russell Martin/75	100.00
82	Jake Peavy/99	100.00
83	Carlos Zambrano/99	100.00
84	Troy Glaus/99	90.00
85	Ryan Zimmerman/75	100.00
86	Evan Longoria/75	100.00
87	Yovani Gallardo/99	100.00
89	Josh Hamilton/75	125.00
90	Matt Holliday/50	125.00
91	Matt Cain/99	100.00
92	Francisco Cordero/99	80.00
93	Derek Lowe/99	100.00
94	Brandon Webb/75	100.00
95	Carlos Pena/99	100.00
97	Khalil Greene/99	90.00
99	C.C. Sabathia/75	100.00
100	Victor Martinez/99	100.00

U.S. State Cards

NM/M

Common Card: .25
Inserted 1:1

1	Alex Rios	.50
2	Curt Schilling	.50
3	Brian Bannister	.25
4	Torii Hunter	.50
5	Chase Utley	.75
6	Roy Halladay	.50
7	Brad Ausmus	.25
8	Ian Snell	.25
9	Lastings Milledge	.25
10	Nick Markakis	.50
11	Shane Victorino	.50
12	Jason Schmidt	.25
13	Curtis Granderson	.50
14	Scott Rolen	.50
15	Casey Blake	.25
16	Nate Robertson	.25
17	Brandon Webb	.50
18	Jonathan Papelbon	.50
19	Tim Stauffer	.25
20	Mark Teixeira	.50
21	Chris Capuano	.25
22	Jason Varitek	.50
23	Joe Mauer	.50
24	Dmitri Young	.25
25	Ryan Howard	.75
26	Taylor Tankersley	.25
27	Alex Gordon	.50
28	Barry Zito	.25
29	Chris Carpenter	.50
30	Derek Jeter	2.00
31	Cody Ross	.25
32	Alex Rodriguez	2.00
33	Ryan Zimmerman	.50
34	Travis Hafner	.50
35	Nick Swisher	.25
36	Matt Holliday	.50
37	Jacoby Ellsbury	.50
38	Ken Griffey Jr.	1.50
39	Paul Konerko	.50
40	Orlando Hudson	.25
41	Mark Ellis	.25
42	Todd Helton	.50
43	Adam Dunn	.50
44	Brandon Lyon	.25
45	Daric Barton	.25
46	David Wright	.75
47	Grady Sizemore	.50
48	Seth McClung	.25
49	Pat Neshek	.25
50	John Buck	.25

World's Greatest Victories

NM/M

Complete Set (20): 40.00
Common Card: 3.00

1	Kerri Strug	3.00
2	Mark Spitz	3.00
3	Jonas Salk	3.00
4	Man Walks on the Moon	3.00
5	Jon Lester	3.00
6	The Fall of the Berlin Wall	3.00
7	David and Goliath	3.00
8	Gary Carter and the '86 Mets	3.00
9	The Battle of Gettysburg	3.00
10	Deep Blue	3.00
11	The Allied Forces	3.00
12	Don Larsen	3.00
13	Truman Defeats Dewey	3.00
14	The American Revolution	3.00
15	2004 ALCS	3.00
16	The Battle of Thermopylae	3.00
17	Brown v. Board of Education	3.00
18	Team Orange	3.00
19	Bill Mazeroski	3.00
20	Cinderella	3.00

World Leaders

NM/M

Common World Leader: 2.50

1	Cristina Fernandez de Kirchner	2.50
2	Kevin Rudd	2.50
3	Guy Verhofstadt	2.50
4	Luiz Inacio Lula da Silva	2.50
5	Stephen Harper	2.50
6	Michelle Bachelet Jeria	2.50
7	Oscar Arias Sanchez	2.50
8	Mirek Topolanek	2.50
9	Anders Fogh Rasmussen	2.50
10	Leonel Fernandez Reyna	2.50
11	Mohamed Hosni Mubarak	2.50
12	Tarja Halonen	2.50
13	Nicolas Sarkozy	2.50
14	Yahya A.J.J. Jammeh	2.50
15	Angela Merkel	2.50
16	Konstandinos Karamanlis	2.50
17	Benedict XVI	2.50
18	Geir H. Haarde	2.50
19	Manmohan Singh	2.50
20	Susilo Bambang Yudhoyono	2.50
21	Bertie Ahern	2.50
22	Ehud Olmert	2.50
23	Bruce Golding	2.50
24	Yasuo Fukuda	2.50
25	Mwai Kibaki	2.50
26	Felipe de Jesus Calderon Hinojosa	2.50
27	Sanjaa Bayar	2.50
28	Armando Guebuza	2.50
29	Girija Prasad Koirala	2.50
30	Jan Peter Balkenende	2.50
31	Helen Clark	2.50
32	Jens Stoltenberg	2.50
33	Qaboos bin Said al-Said	2.50
34	Alan Garcia Perez	2.50
35	Gloria Macapagal-Arroyo	2.50
36	Donald Tusk	2.50
37	Vladimir Vladimirovich Putin	2.50
38	Robert Fico	2.50
39	Thabo Mbeki	2.50
40	Lee Myung-bak	2.50
41	Jose Luis Rodriguez Zapatero	2.50
42	Fredrik Reinfeldt	2.50
43	Pascal Couchepin	2.50
44	Jakaya Kikwete	2.50
45	Samak Sundavavej	2.50
46	Tenzin Gyatso	2.50
47	Patrick Manning	2.50
48	Gordon Brown	2.50
49	George W. Bush	2.50
50	Nguyen Tan Dung	2.50

1 of 1 Relic Cards

Production One Set
No Pricing

2008 Topps Chrome

NM/M

Complete Set (239):
Common Player (1-220): .25
Common RC Auto. (221-239): 10.00
Hobby Pack (4): 3.00
Hobby Box (24): 65.00

1	Alex Rodriguez	3.00
2	Barry Zito	.25
3	Scott Kazmir	.50
4	Stephen Drew	.50
5	Miguel Cabrera	1.00

6	Daisuke Matsuzaka	1.00
7	Mickey Mantle	4.00
8	Jimmy Rollins	.75
9	Joe Mauer	.40
10	Cole Hamels	.50
11	Yovani Gallardo	.40
12	Miguel Tejada	.50
13	Dontrelle Willis	.25
14	Orlando Cabrera	.25
15	Jake Peavy	.50
16	Erik Bedard	.50
17	Victor Martinez	.50
18	Chris Young	.50
19	Jose Reyes	1.00
20	Mike Lowell	.40
21	Dan Uggla	.50
22	Garrett Atkins	.40
23	Felix Hernandez	.50
24	Ivan Rodriguez	.50
25	Alex Rios	.50
26	Jason Bay	.50
27	Vladimir Guerrero	1.00
28	John Lackey	.25
29	Ryan Howard	1.00
30	Kevin Youkilis	.50
31	Justin Morneau	.50
32	Johan Santana	.75
33	Jeremy Hermida	.25
34	Andruw Jones	.40
35	Mike Cameron	.25
36	Jason Varitek	.50
37	Tim Hudson	.40
38	Justin Upton	.50
39	Brad Penny	.50
40	Robinson Cano	.50
41	Brandon Webb	.50
42	Magglio Ordonez	.40
43	Aaron Hill	.25
44	Alfonso Soriano	.75
45	Carlos Zambrano	.50
46	Ben Sheets	.50
47	Tim Lincecum	.50
48	Phil Hughes	.50
49	Scott Rolen	.50
50	John Maine	.50
51	Delmon Young	.40
52	Tadahito Iguchi	.25
53	Yunel Escobar	.25
54	Russell Martin	.50
55	Orlando Hudson	.25
56	Jim Edmonds	.50
57	Todd Helton	.50
58	Melky Cabrera	.25
59	Adrian Beltre	.50
60	Manny Ramirez	1.00
61	Gil Meche	.25
62	David DeJesus	.25
63	Roy Oswalt	.50
64	Mark Buehrle	.25
65	Hunter Pence	.50
66	Dustin Pedroia	.40
67	Roy Halladay	.50
68	Rich Harden	.40
69	Jim Thome	.50
70	Akinori Iwamura	.25
71	Dan Haren	.50
72	Brandon Phillips	.50
73	Brett Myers	.25
74	James Loney	.40
75	C.C. Sabathia	.50
76	Jermaine Dye	.40
77	Carlos Ruiz	.25
78	Brian McCann	.50
79	Paul Konerko	.50
80	Jorge Posada	.50
81	Chien-Ming Wang	.75
82	Carlos Delgado	.50
83	Ichiro Suzuki	2.00
84	Elijah Dukes	.25
85	David Wright	1.00
86	Carl Crawford	.50
87	Mark Teixeira	.50
88	Bobby Crosby	.25
89	Brian Roberts	.25
90	David Ortiz	1.00
91	Derrek Lee	.75
92	Adam Dunn	.50
93	Fausto Carmona	.25
94	Grady Sizemore	.75
95	Jeff Francoeur	.50
96	Jered Weaver	.25

97	Troy Tulowitzki	.50
98	Troy Glaus	.40
99	Nick Markakis	.50
100	Lance Berkman	.75
101	Randy Johnson	.75
102	Kenji Johjima	.25
103	Jarrod Saltalamacchia	.25
104	Matt Holliday	.75
105	Travis Hafner	.40
106	Johnny Damon	.50
107	Alex Gordon	.50
108	Derek Lowe	.50
109	Nick Swisher	.40
110	Aaron Harang	.25
111	Hanley Ramirez	1.00
112	Carlos Guillen	.50
113	Ryan Braun	1.00
114	Torii Hunter	.50
115	Joe Blanton	.25
116	Josh Hamilton	.50
117	Pedro Martinez	.75
118	Hideki Matsui	1.00
119	Cameron Maybin	.50
120	Prince Fielder	.75
121	Derek Jeter	3.00
122	Chone Figgins	.50
123	Chase Utley	1.00
124	Jacoby Ellsbury	.75
125	Freddy Sanchez	.25
126	Rocco Baldelli	.25
127	Tom Gorzelanny	.25
128	Adrian Gonzalez	.50
129	Geovany Soto	.50
130	Bobby Abreu	.50
131	Albert Pujols	3.00
132	Chipper Jones	1.00
133	Jeremy Bonderman	.25
134	B.J. Upton	.50
135	Justin Verlander	.50
136	Jeff Francis	.25
137	A.J. Burnett	.25
138	Travis Buck	.25
139	Vernon Wells	.50
140	Raul Ibanez	.25
141	Ryan Zimmerman	.50
142	John Smoltz	.50
143	Carlos Lee	.50
144	Chris Young	.50
145	Francisco Liriano	.50
146	Curt Schilling	.50
147	Josh Beckett	.75
148	Aramis Ramirez	.25
149	Ronnie Belliard	.25
150	Homer Bailey	.25
151	Curtis Granderson	.50
152	Ken Griffey Jr.	2.00
153	Kazuo Matsui	.25
154	Brian Bannister	.25
155	Joba Chamberlain	1.50
156	Tom Glavine	.50
157	Carlos Beltran	.75
158	Kelly Johnson	.25
159	Rich Hill	.25
160	Pat Burrell	.50
161	Asdrubal Cabrera	.25
162	Gary Sheffield	.50
163	Greg Maddux	1.00
164	Eric Chavez	.50
165	Chris Carpenter	.50
166	Michael Young	.50
167	Carlos Pena	.50
168	Frank Thomas	.75
169	Aaron Rowand	.40
170	Yadier Molina	.25
171	Luis Castillo	.25
172	Ryan Theriot	.25
173	Andre Ethier	.25
174	Casey Kotchman	.25
175	Rickie Weeks	.40
176	Milton Bradley	.25
177	Daniel Cabrera	.25
178	Jo Jo Reyes	.25
179	Livan Hernandez	.25
180	Hideki Okajima	.25
181	Matt Kemp	.50
182	Jonny Gomes	.25
183	Billy Butler	.25
184	Adam LaRoche	.25
185	Brad Hawpe	.25
186	Paul Maholm	.25
187	Placido Polanco	.25
188	Noah Lowry	.25
189	Gregg Zaun	.25
190	Nate McLouth	.25
191	Edinson Volquez	.25
192	Jeff Niemann (RC)	1.00
193	Evan Longoria (RC)	8.00
194	Adam Jones	.50
195	Eugenio Velez RC	1.00
196	Joey Votto (RC)	2.00
197	Nick Blackburn RC	2.00
198	Harvey Garcia (RC)	1.00
199	Hiroki Kuroda RC	2.00
200	Elliot Johnson (RC)	1.00
201	Luis Mendoza (RC)	1.00
202	Alex Romero (RC)	1.00
203	Gregor Blanco (RC)	1.00
204	Rico Washington (RC)	1.00
205	Brian Bocock RC	1.00
206	Evan Meek RC	1.00
207	Steve Holm RC	1.00
208	Matt Tupman RC	1.00
209	Fernando Hernandez RC	1.00
210	Randor Bierd RC	1.00
211	Blake DeWitt (RC)	2.00

212	Randy Wells RC	1.00
213	Wesley Wright RC	1.00
214	Clete Thomas RC	1.00
215	Kyle McClellan RC	1.00
216	Brian Bixler (RC)	1.00
217	Kazuo Fukumori RC	1.50
218	Burke Badenhop RC	1.00
219	Denard Span (RC)	1.00
220	Brian Bass (RC)	1.00
221	J.R. Towles/Auto. RC	15.00
222	Felipe Paulino/Auto. RC	10.00
223	Sam Fuld/Auto. RC	15.00
224	Kevin Hart/Auto. (RC)	10.00
225	Nyjer Morgan/Auto. (RC)	10.00
226	Daric Barton/Auto. (RC)	10.00
227	Armando Galarraga/Auto. RC	25.00
228	Chin-Lung Hu/Auto. (RC)	20.00
229	Clay Buchholz/Auto. (RC)	20.00
230	Rich Thompson/Auto. (RC)	10.00
231	Brian Barton/Auto. RC	15.00
232	Ross Ohlendorf/Auto. RC	15.00
233	Masahide Kobayashi/Auto. RC	20.00
234	Callix Crabbe/Auto. (RC)	10.00
235	Matt Tolbert/Auto. RC	15.00
236	Jayson Nix/Auto. (RC)	10.00
237	Johnny Cueto/Auto. RC	25.00
238	Evan Meek/Auto. RC	10.00
239	Randy Wells/Auto. RC	10.00

Refractor

Refractor (1-220):	2-3X
Inserted 1:3	
Refractor Auto. (221-239):	1-1.25X
Autos Production 500	

Blue Refractor

Blue Autos. (221-239):	1-1.5X
Production 200 Sets	

Copper Refractor

Copper Ref. (1-220):	3-4X
Production 599	
Copper Autos. (221-239):	1.5-2X
Autos Production 50	

Red Refractor

Red Ref. (1-220):	10-20X
Red Autos. (221-239):	3-4X
Production 25 Sets	

Superfractor

Production One Set

Printing Plates

Production one set per color.

All-Rookie Team

		NM/M
Complete Set (23):		15.00
Common Player:		.50
Inserted 1:9		
1	Gary Sheffield	.75
2	Ivan Rodriguez	.50
3	Mike Piazza	1.00
4	Manny Ramirez	1.00
5	Chipper Jones	1.50
6	Derek Jeter	3.00
7	Andruw Jones	.50
8	Alfonso Soriano	1.00
9	Jimmy Rollins	1.00
10	Albert Pujols	3.00
11	Ichiro Suzuki	2.00
12	Mark Teixeira	.75
13	Matt Holliday	.75
14	Joe Mauer	.50
15	Prince Fielder	1.00
16	Hideki Okajima	.50
17	Roy Oswalt	.50

18	Hunter Pence	.75
19	Nick Markakis	.75
20	Ryan Zimmerman	.50
21	Ryan Braun	1.50
22	C.C. Sabathia	.75
23	Dustin Pedroia	.50

Mickey Mantle HR History

	NM/M
Common Mantle:	2.00
Inserted 1:12	
Refractor:	2-3X
Production 400 Sets	
Copper Refractor:	3-5X
Production 100 Sets	
Red Refractor:	No Pricing
Production 25 Sets	

Target Continuity

Complete Set (30):	
Common Player:	
Target Exclusive	
No Pricing	

The Mickey Mantle Story

	NM/M
Complete Set (10):	20.00
Common Mantle (46-55):	3.00
Inserted 1:20	
Refractor:	2-3X
Production 400 Sets	
Copper Refractor:	3-4X
Production 100 Sets	
Red Refractor:	No Pricing
Production 25 Sets	

Topps Heritage Chrome

	NM/M
Common Player (101-200):	3.00
Production 1,959 Sets	
Refractor:	1-1.5X
Production 559 Sets	
Black Refractor:	4-8X
Production 59 Sets	
C101	Phil Hughes	4.00
C102	Hideki Okajima	3.00
C103	Chone Figgins	4.00
C104	Jose Vidro	3.00
C105	Johan Santana	8.00
C106	Paul Konerko	5.00
C107	Alfonso Soriano	8.00
C108	Kei Igawa	3.00
C109	Lastings Milledge	3.00
C110	Asdrubal Cabrera	3.00
C111	Brandon Jones	3.00
C112	Tom Gorzelanny	3.00
C113	Delmon Young	4.00
C114	Daric Barton	3.00
C115	David DeJesus	3.00
C116	Ryan Howard	8.00
C117	Tom Glavine	5.00
C118	Frank Thomas	5.00
C119	J.R. Towles	4.00
C120	Jeremy Bonderman	3.00
C121	Adrian Beltre	4.00
C122	Dan Haren	4.00

C123 Kazuo Matsui 3.00
C124 Joe Blanton 3.00
C125 Dan Uggla 4.00
C126 Stephen Drew 4.00
C127 Daniel Cabrera 3.00
C128 Jeff Clement 5.00
C129 Pedro Martinez 5.00
C130 Josh Anderson 3.00
C131 Orlando Hudson 3.00
C132 Jason Bay 4.00
C133 Eric Chavez 3.00
C134 Johnny Damon 5.00
C135 Lance Broadway 3.00
C136 Jake Peavy 5.00
C137 Carl Crawford 4.00
C138 Kenji Johjima 3.00
C139 Melky Cabrera 3.00
C140 Aaron Hill 3.00
C141 Carlos Lee 4.00
C142 Mark Buehrle 3.00
C143 Carlos Beltran 5.00
C144 Chin-Lung Hu 4.00
C145 C.C. Sabathia 5.00
C146 Dustin Pedroia 4.00
C147 Freddy Sanchez 3.00
C148 Kevin Youkilis 5.00
C149 Radhames Liz 4.00
C150 Jim Thome 5.00
C151 Greg Maddux 8.00
C152 Rich Hill 3.00
C153 Andy LaRoche 4.00
C154 Gil Meche 4.00
C155 Victor Martinez 4.00
C156 Mariano Rivera 5.00
C157 Kyle Kendrick 3.00
C158 Jarrod Saltalamacchia 3.00
C159 Tadahito Iguchi 3.00
C160 Eric Gagne 3.00
C161 Garrett Atkins 4.00
C162 Pat Burrell 4.00
C163 Akinori Iwamura 3.00
C164 Melvin Mora 5.00
C165 Joey Votto 5.00
C166 Brian Roberts 4.00
C167 Brett Myers 3.00
C168 Michael Young 3.00
C169 Adam Jones 3.00
C170 Carlos Zambrano 5.00
C171 Jeff Francoeur 5.00
C172 Brad Hawpe 4.00
C173 Andy Pettitte 5.00
C174 Ryan Garko 3.00
C175 Adrian Gonzalez 4.00
C176 Ted Lilly 3.00
C177 J.J. Hardy 4.00
C178 Jon Lester 3.00
C179 Carlos Pena 4.00
C180 Ross Detwiler 5.00
C181 Andruw Jones 3.00
C182 Gary Sheffield 4.00
C183 Dmitri Young 3.00
C184 Carlos Guillen 3.00
C185 Yovani Gallardo 3.00
C186 Alex Gordon 4.00
C187 Aaron Harang 4.00
C188 Travis Hafner 4.00
C189 Orlando Cabrera 4.00
C190 Bobby Abreu 5.00
C191 Randy Johnson 5.00
C192 Scott Kazmir 4.00
C193 Jason Varitek 3.00
C194 Mike Lowell 4.00
C195 A.J. Burnett 3.00
C196 Garret Anderson 3.00
C197 Chris Carpenter 4.00
C198 Jermaine Dye 4.00
C199 Luke Hochevar 5.00
C200 Steve Pearce 5.00

Trading Card History

NM/M
Common Player (1-50): .50
Inserted in 1:4
1 Jacoby Ellsbury 1.00
2 Joba Chamberlain 2.00
3 Daisuke Matsuzaka 1.50
4 Prince Fielder 1.00
5 Alex Rodriguez 3.00
6 Mickey Mantle 4.00
7 Ryan Braun 1.50
8 Albert Pujols 2.00

9 Joe Mauer .50
10 Jose Reyes 1.50
11 Johan Santana 1.00
12 Hunter Pence .75
13 Hideki Okajima .50
14 Cameron Maybin .50
15 Tim Lincecum 1.00
16 Mark Teixeira, Jeff Francoeur .75
17 Justin Upton .75
18 Alfonso Soriano .75
19 Ichiro Suzuki 2.00
20 Grady Sizemore .75
21 Ryan Howard 1.00
22 David Wright 1.00
23 Jimmy Rollins 1.00
24 Ken Griffey Jr. 2.00
25 Chipper Jones 1.00
26 Justin Verlander .75
27 Manny Ramirez 1.00
28 Chase Utley 1.00
29 Ivan Rodriguez .75
30 Josh Beckett .75
31 Vladimir Guerrero 1.00
32 Lance Berkman .75
33 Gary Sheffield .75
34 David Ortiz 1.00
35 Andruw Jones .50
36 Hideki Matsui 1.50
37 C.C. Sabathia .75
38 Magglio Ordonez .50
39 Pedro Martinez 1.00
40 Derek Jeter 3.00
41 Hanley Ramirez .50
42 Jake Peavy .50
43 Brandon Webb .50
44 Matt Holliday .50
45 Carlos Beltran .75
46 Troy Tulowitzki .75
47 Justin Morneau .75
48 Phil Hughes .75
49 Torii Hunter .75
50 Brad Hawpe .50

Wal-Mart Continuity

Complete Set (20):
Common Player:
Wal-Mart Exclusive
No Pricing

2008 Topps Co-Signers

NM/M
Common Player (1-100): .25
Common RC Auto. (99-112): 10.00
Pack (6): 10.00
Box (12): 100.00
1 Jacoby Ellsbury 1.00
2 Michael Young .50
3 Cameron Maybin .25
4 Dmitri Young .25
5 Grady Sizemore .75
6 Brandon Webb .75
7 Derrek Lee .25
8 Jeff Francis .25
9 Aaron Harang .25
10 John Smoltz .50
11 Nicholas Markakis .50
12 Tom Gorzelanny .25
13 Miguel Cabrera 1.00
14 Josh Beckett 1.00
15 Magglio Ordonez .50
16 Joe Mauer .50
17 Carl Crawford .50
18 Barry Zito .25
19 Brad Penny .25
20 C.C. Sabathia .50
21 Mark Buehrle .25
22 Carlos Lee .50
23 Chipper Jones 1.00
24 Chase Utley 1.00
25 David Ortiz 1.00
26 Justin Morneau .50
27 Erik Bedard .50
28 Greg Maddux 2.00
29 Joba Chamberlain 3.00
30 Vernon Wells .50
31 Orlando Hudson .25
32 Kevin Youkilis .50
33 Curtis Granderson .75
34 Chone Figgins .25
35 Jorge Posada .75
36 Ken Griffey Jr. 2.00

37 Tim Hudson .50
38 Nick Swisher .50
39 Carlos Beltran .75
40 Alex Gordon .50
41 Andre Ethier .25
42 Todd Helton .75
43 Miguel Tejada .50
44 Yadier Molina .25
45 Hanley Ramirez 1.00
46 Justin Verlander .50
47 Adam Dunn .75
48 Raul Ibanez .25
49 Scott Rolen .50
50 Alex Rodriguez 3.00
51 Garret Anderson .25
52 Andruw Jones .25
53 Matt Cain .50
54 Daisuke Matsuzaka 1.50
55 Ichiro Suzuki 2.00
56 Scott Kazmir .50
57 Jeff Kent .50
58 Aubrey Huff .25
59 Justin Upton .75
60 Prince Fielder 1.00
61 Alex Rios .50
62 Alfonso Soriano .75
63 Paul Konerko .50
64 Matt Holliday .75
65 Felix Hernandez .50
66 Ivan Rodriguez .50
67 John Maine .50
68 Roy Oswalt .50
69 Brian McCann .50
70 Albert Pujols 3.00
71 John Lackey .25
72 Travis Hafner .50
73 Gil Meche .25
74 Ben Sheets .50
75 Ryan Howard 1.00
76 Hideki Matsui 1.50
77 Mike Lowell .50
78 Danny Haren .50
79 Adrian Gonzalez .50
80 David Wright 1.50
81 Jason Bay .50
82 Carlos Zambrano .50
83 Johan Santana 1.00
84 David DeJesus .25
85 Ryan Zimmerman .50
86 Bobby Abreu .50
87 Richie Sexson .25
88 Eric Chavez .25
89 Derek Lowe .25
90 Jake Peavy .50
91 Joe Blanton .25
92 Jermaine Dye .25
93 Pedro Martinez .75
94 B.J. Upton .50
95 Vladimir Guerrero 1.00
96 Ross Ohlendorf RC 1.00
97 J.R. Towles RC 3.00
98 Jonathan Meloan RC 1.00
99 Chin-Lung Hu (RC) 2.00
99 Chin-Lung Hu/Auto. (RC) 25.00
100 Clay Buchholz (RC) 3.00
100 Clay Buchholz/Auto. (RC) 35.00
101 Willie Collazo/Auto. RC 15.00
102 David Davidson/Auto. RC 10.00
103 Joe Koshansky/Auto. (RC) 10.00
104 Sam Fuld/Auto. RC 10.00
105 Nyjer Morgan/Auto. RC 10.00
106 Clint Sammons/Auto. (RC) 10.00
107 Josh Anderson/Auto. (RC) 10.00
108 Bronson Sardinha/ Auto. (RC) 10.00
109 Wladimir Balentien/ Auto. (RC) 15.00
110 Kevin Hart/Auto. RC 10.00
111 Felipe Paulino/Auto. RC 10.00
112 Rob Johnson/Auto. (RC) 10.00

Gold

Gold (1-100): 2-3X
Autos. (99-112): 1-1.5X
Production 150 Sets

Green

Green (1-100): 2-3X
Autos. (99-112): 1X
Production 200 Sets

Blue

Blue (1-100): 2-3X
Non-Auto. Production 250
Autos (99-112): 1X
Auto Production 300

Tri-Signers

NM/M
Common Trio:
Some not priced.
PBG Manny Parra, Ryan Braun, Yovani Gallardo 75.00

Bronze

Bronze (1-100): 2-3X
Non-Auto. Production 300
Autos (99-112): 1X
Auto. Production 400

Quad-Signers

No Pricing

Red

Red (1-100): 2-3X
Non-Auto. Production 400

Autos. (99-112): 1X
Auto. Production 500

Hyper Plaid Silver

Production One Set

Hyper Plaid Gold

No Pricing
Production 10 Sets

Hyper Plaid Green

Hyper-P Green (1-100): 5-10X
Autos. (99-112): No Pricing
Production 25 Sets

Hyper Plaid Blue

Hyper-P Blue (1-100): 3-5X
Autos. (99-112): 1.5X
Production 50 Sets

Hyper Plaid Bronze

Hyper-P Bronze (1-100): 3-4X
Autos. (99-112): 1-1.5X
Production 75 Sets

Hyper Plaid Red

Hyper-P Red (1-100): 2-3X
Autos. (99-112): 1-1.5X
Production 100 Sets

Cut Signatures

No Pricing

Cowhide Dual Sigs

Production One Set
No Pricing

Dual Autos.

NM/M
Common Dual Auto.: 15.00
CE Jack Cust, Mark Ellis 20.00
CC Robinson Cano, Asdrubal Cabrera 30.00
HC Felix Hernandez, Joba Chamberlain 100.00
SP Geovany Soto, Felix Pie 35.00
MM Andrew Miller, Cameron Maybin 20.00
GS Tom Gorzelanny, Freddy Sanchez 15.00
SG Andrew Sonnanstine, Matt Garza 15.00
PS Steve Pearce, Freddy Sanchez 15.00
BZ Jason Bartlett, Benjamin Zobrist 15.00
BB Daric Barton, Clay Buchholz 25.00
RO Edwar Ramirez, Ross Ohlendorf 20.00
JA Brandon Jones, Josh Anderson 15.00
OB Garrett Olson, Brian Burres 15.00
DR Chris Duncan, Brendan Ryan 30.00
FH Jeff Francis, Jason Hirsh 15.00
MS Carlos Marmol, Geovany Soto 50.00
PKS Glen Perkins, Kevin Slowey 15.00
BA Josh Banks, Jeremy Accardo 15.00
SC Brian Schneider, Ramon Castro 20.00
FP Sam Fuld, Felix Pie 25.00
RM Alex Rios, Nicholas Markakis 30.00
FJ Jeff Francis, Ubaldo Jimenez 15.00
BJ Erik Bedard, Adam Jones 40.00
VC Joey Votto, Daric Barton 25.00
LH Andy LaRoche, Chin-Lung Hu 25.00
MD Lastings Milledge, Elijah Dukes 20.00
CV Francisco Cordero, Edinson Volquez
SZ Alex Smith, Ryan Zimmerman 20.00
MP Joe Mason, Jonathan Papelbon 20.00
KC Tim Kelly, Joba Chamberlain 60.00
HCA Josue Herrera, Fausto Carmona
BM Bill Buck, Cameron Maybin 20.00
JM Dave Jennings, Nicholas Markakis 25.00
CG Jerome Cochran, Curtis Granderson 20.00
OBA Dan Ontiveros, Daric Barton 15.00
EH Bob Engle, Felix Hernandez 20.00
LG Don Lyle, Ryan Garko 15.00
DD Juan Diaz, Julio Diaz 15.00

CB Steve Cunningham, Shannon Briggs 25.00
CCC Martin Castillo, Julio Cesar Chavez Jr. 30.00
PP Samuel Peter, Aaron Pryor 35.00
MMJ Juan Manuel Marquez, Chris John 15.00
PG Daniel Ponce de Leon, Joan Guzman 15.00
MV Rafael Marquez, Israel Vasquez 20.00
DB Chad Dawson, Andre Berto 20.00
DG Vic Darchinyan, Danny Green 15.00
CLC Joel Casamayor, Jose Luis Castillo 20.00
KA Roman Karmazin, Arthur Abraham 15.00
MB Edison Miranda, O'Neil Bell 15.00
AC Jorge Arce, Ivan Calderon 20.00
FC Chone Figgins, Carl Crawford 25.00
PO Jonathan Papelbon, Hideki Okajima 60.00
RR Jimmy Rollins, Jose Reyes 50.00
FHO Prince Fielder, Ryan Howard 50.00
WF Dontrelle Willis, Mark Fidrych 20.00
RW Jose Reyes, David Wright 100.00
SE Arthur Shorin, Michael Eisner 70.00

Quad Cut Signatures
Production One Set
No Pricing

Solo Sigs Boxers

NM/M
Common Boxer Auto.: 10.00
KP Kelly Pavlik 60.00
EM Edison Miranda 15.00
SB Shannon Briggs 25.00
SP Samuel Peter 20.00
JD Juan Diaz 20.00
JUD Julio Diaz 15.00
JC Joel Casamayor 20.00
CJ Chris John 15.00
SC Steve Cunningham 15.00
OB O'Neil Bell 10.00
DP Daniel Ponce de Leon 15.00
JM Juan Manuel Marquez 15.00
RM Rafael Marquez 20.00
VD Vic Darchinyan 10.00
JA Jorge Arce 20.00
AA Arthur Abraham 15.00
JG Joan Guzman 15.00
JLC Jose Luis Castillo 20.00
JCC Julio Cesar Chavez Jr. 15.00
AB Andre Berto 15.00
CD Chad Dawson 15.00
AW Andre Ward 15.00
AP Aaron Pryor 30.00
RBBM Ray Boom Boom Mancini 50.00
JF Jeff Fenech 20.00
IC Ivan Calderon 15.00
RK Roman Karmazin 15.00
TA Teddy Atlas 20.00
BS Bert Sugar 20.00
FM Fernando Montiel 20.00
IV Israel Vasquez 25.00
MC Martin Castillo 10.00
DAG Danny Green 20.00

2008 Topps Heritage
NM/M
Complete Set (500): 275.00
Common Player: .40
Common SP: 5.00
Inserted 1:3
Common Black Back: 3.00
Pack (8): 3.50
Box (24): 75.00
1 Vladimir Guerrero 1.00
2 Placido Polanco .40
2 Placido Polanco/Black Back 3.00
3 Eric Byrnes .50
3 Eric Byrnes/Black Back 4.00
4 Mark Teixeira .75
5 Javier Vazquez .40

5 Javier Vazquez/Black Back 3.00
6 Jacoby Ellsbury 2.00
7 Joey Gathright .40
7 Joey Gathright/Black Back 3.00
8 Philadelphia Phillies .75
8 Philadelphia Phillies/ Black Back 4.00
9 Andre Ethier .40
9 Andre Ethier/Black Back 3.00
10 Alex Rodriguez 4.00
11 Luke Scott SP 5.00
12 Curt Schilling 1.00
12 Curt Schilling/Black Back 4.00
13 Billy Wagner .40
13 Billy Wagner/Black Back 3.00
14 Gary Matthews Jr. .40
14 Gary Matthews Jr./ Black Back .50
15 Sean Marshall .50
16 Ichiro Suzuki 2.00
16 Ichiro Suzuki/Black Back 5.00
17 Jason Bay, Freddy Sanchez, Jack Wilson .40
18 Dontrelle Willis .40
18 Dontrelle Willis/Black Back 3.00
19 Josh Willingham .40
20 Jeff Kent .50
21 Troy Tulowitzki .75
21 Troy Tulowitzki/Black Back 4.00
22 Brian Fuentes .40
22 Brian Fuentes/Black Back 3.00
23 Robinson Cano .75
23 Robinson Cano/Black Back 4.00
24 Felix Hernandez .40
24 Felix Hernandez/Black Back 4.00
25 Edwin Encarnacion .40
26 Fausto Carmona .40
27 Greg Maddux 1.50
28 Ivan Rodriguez .75
28 Ivan Rodriguez/Black Back 4.00
29 Joe Nathan .40
30 Paul Konerko .40
31 Nook Logan .40
32 Derek Lowe .40
33 Jose Lopez .40
34 Magglio Ordonez, Curtis Granderson .50
34 Ordonez, Granderson/ Black Back 3.00
35 Adam LaRoche .40
35 Adam LaRoche/Black Back 3.00
36 Kenny Lofton .40
37 Matt Capps .40
38 Mark Reynolds .40
39 Joe Mauer .50
40 Tim Hudson .40
40 Tim Hudson/Black Back 3.00
41 Kelvim Escobar .40
41 Kelvim Escobar/Black Back 3.00
42 Jason Jennings .40
42 Jason Jennings/Black Back 3.00
43 Victor Martinez .75
44 Jason Kendall .40
45 Chris Ray .40
45 Chris Ray/Black Back 3.00
46 Jason Bergmann .40
47 Jason Marquis .40
48 Baltimore Orioles .50
49 Bill Hall .40
49 Bill Hall/Black Back 3.00
50 Ken Griffey Jr. 2.00
51 Chad Cordero .40
52 Omar Vizquel .40
52 Omar Vizquel/Black Back 3.00
53 Jim Edmonds .50
54 Justin Upton 1.00
54 Justin Upton/Black Back 4.00
55 Josh Beckett 1.00
56 Jeff Francis .40
57 Brad Lidge .40
57 Brad Lidge/Black Back 3.00
58 Paul LoDuca .40
58 Paul LoDuca/Black Back 3.00
59 John Patterson .40
60 Andy Pettitte .75
60 Andy Pettitte/Black Back 3.00
61 Brendan Harris .40
61 Brendan Harris/Black Back 3.00
62 Chris Young .50
62 Chris Young/Black Back 3.00

63 Eric Chavez .40
64 Francisco Rodriguez .50
65 Jason Giambi .75
65 Jason Giambi/Black Back 3.00
66 B.J. Ryan .40
67 Rich Hill .50
67 Rich Hill/Black Back 3.00
68 Derek Jeter 3.00
69 San Francisco Giants .50
69 San Francisco Giants/ Black Back 3.00
70 Carlos Guillen .50
71 Trevor Hoffman .40
71 Trevor Hoffman/Black Back .40
72 Zachary Duke .40
73 Dustin Pedroia .50
74 Ryan Zimmerman, Dmitri Young .50
76 Cole Hamels .75
76 Carlos Delgado .50
77 Jonathan Broxton .40
78 Josh Hamilton .50
78 Josh Hamilton/Black Back 5.00
79 Mark Loretta .40
79 Mark Loretta/Black Back 3.00
80 Grady Sizemore 1.00
81 Torii Hunter .75
81 Torii Hunter/Black Back 3.00
82 Carlos Beltran 1.00
82 Carlos Beltran/Black Back 4.00
83 Jason Isringhausen .40
83 Jason Isringhausen/ Black Back 3.00
84 Brad Penny .40
84 Brad Penny/Black Back 3.00
85 Jayson Werth .40
86 Alex Gordon .75
87 David DeJesus .40
88 Clay Buchholz (RC) .75
89 Conor Jackson .40
90 Hideki Matsui 1.50
90 Hideki Matsui/Black Back 5.00
91 Matt Garza .40
91 Matt Garza/Black Back 3.00
92 Phil Hughes 1.00
92 Phil Hughes/Black Back 5.00
93 Mike Piazza .75
94 Chicago White Sox .40
94 Chicago White Sox/ Black Back 3.00
95 Buddy Carlyle .40
96 Mark DeRosa .40
97 Brandon Webb .75
98 Jon Garland .40
98 Jon Garland/Black Back 3.00
99 Mariano Rivera .75
100 Jack Cust .40
101 Carlos Ruiz .40
102 Moises Alou .50
102 Moises Alou/Black Back 3.00
103 Bengie Molina .40
104 Adam Jones .40
105 Alfonso Soriano 1.00
106 Troy Glaus .75
107 John Maine .50
108 Pat Burrell .50
109 David Eckstein .40
110 Homer Bailey .50
111 Cincinnati Reds .50
112 Corey Hart .50
113 Orlando Hernandez .40
114 Orlando Cabrera .50
115 Ryan Garko .40
116 Wladimir Balentien .40
116 Wladimir Balentien/ Black Back 3.00
117 Daric Barton .40
117 Daric Barton/Black Back 3.00
118 Emilio Bonifacio RC .40
119 Lance Broadway RC .75
120 Jeff Clement .40
121 David Davidson RC .40
122 Ross Detwiler RC 1.00
122 Ross Detwiler/Black Back 3.00
123 Sam Fuld RC 1.00
124 Armando Galarraga RC 2.00
125 Harvey Garcia .40
126 Daniel Giese .40
126 Daniel Giese/Black Back 3.00
127 Alberto Gonzalez (RC) .50
127 Alberto Gonzalez/Black Back 3.00
128 Kevin Hart .40
129 Luke Hochevar RC 1.00
129 Luke Hochevar/Black Back 4.00
130 Chin-Lung Hu (RC) .40
130 Chin-Lung Hu/Black Back 3.00
131 Brandon Jones RC .75
132 Joe Koshansky .40
133 Radhames Liz RC .50
134 Donny Lucy .40
135 Mitch Stetter RC .50
135 Mitch Stetter/Black Back 3.00
136 Nyjer Morgan .40
137 Ross Ohlendorf RC .40
138 Steve Pearce RC 1.00
139 Jeff Ridgway RC .75
140 Bronson Sardinha .40
141 Seth Smith .40
142 Rich Thompson .40
143 Erick Threets .40
144 J.R. Towles RC 1.50
145 Eugenio Velez RC .50
146 Joey Votto .75

147 Alfonso Soriano, Aramis Ramirez, Derrek Lee .50
148 Hunter Pence .75
149 Barry Zito .40
150 Albert Pujols 3.00
150 Albert Pujols/Black Back 6.00
151 Sammy Sosa .40
152 Brian Bannister .40
153 Reggie Willits .40
154 Bobby Abreu .75
155 Johnny Damon .50
155 Johnny Damon/Black Back 4.00
156 Brandon Webb, Jake Peavy .50
157 Aramis Ramirez .75
158 Mark Buehrle .40
159 David Weathers .40
160 Jack Wilson .40
161 Josh Fogg .40
162 Garrett Atkins .40
163 Brad Ausmus .40
164 Gil Meche .40
165 Jeff Francoeur .50
166 Grady Sizemore, Travis Hafner, Victor Martinez .50
167 Juan Pierre .40
168 Rafael Furcal .40
169 J.J. Hardy .40
170 Nicholas Markakis .50
171 Delmon Young .40
172 Oakland A's .40
173 Ronny Paulino .40
173 Ronny Paulino/Black Back 3.00
174 Mike Cameron .40
174 Mike Cameron/Black Back 3.00
175 Jeff Weaver .40
175 Jeff Weaver/Black Back 3.00
176 Preston Wilson .40
176 Preston Wilson/Black Back 3.00
177 Robinson Tejeda .40
177 Robinson Tejeda/Black Back 3.00
178 Adam Lind .40
178 Adam Lind/Black Back 3.00
179 Austin Kearns .40
179 Austin Kearns/Black Back 3.00
180 Jorge Posada .75
180 Jorge Posada/Black Back 4.00
181 Tadahito Iguchi .40
182 Matt Cain .50
183 Yuniesky Betancourt .40
184 Bronson Arroyo .40
185 Brad Hawpe .40
185 Brad Hawpe/Black Back 3.00
186 Rickie Weeks .50
186 Rickie Weeks/Black Back 3.00
187 Carlos Silva .40
187 Carlos Silva/Black Back 3.00
188 Adrian Gonzalez .50
189 Kenji Johjima .40
190 Chris Duncan .40
191 James Shields .50
192 Akinori Iwamura .40
193 David Murphy .40
194 Alex Rios .75
195 Carlos Quentin .40
195 Carlos Quentin/Black Back 3.00
196 Jose Valverde .40
196 Jose Valverde/Black Back 3.00
197 Derrek Lee .75
197 Derrek Lee/Black Back 4.00
198 Jerry Owens .40
198 Jerry Owens/Black Back 3.00
199 Russell Martin .75
200 Yovani Gallardo .75
201 Johan Santana 1.00
202 Nick Swisher .50
203 So Taguchi .40
204 Justin Morneau .75
205 Milton Bradley .40
206 Jake Westbrook .40
207 Dave Roberts .40
208 Billy Butler .40
209 Lance Berkman .75
210 J.J. Putz .40
210 J.J. Putz/Black Back 3.00
211 Mike Sweeney .40
211 Mike Sweeney/Black Back 3.00
212 Andruw Jones, Chipper Jones .50
213 Ricky Nolasco .40
214 Andy LaRoche .40
215 Ray Durham .40
216 Francisco Cordero .40
217 Jered Weaver .50
218 Rafael Soriano .40
219 Orlando Hudson .40
220 Mike Lowell .40
221 Chris Snyder .40
222 Cesar Izturis .40
223 St. Louis Cardinals .50
224 David Wright 1.50
224 David Wright/Black Back 5.00
225 Pedro Martinez 1.00
225 Pedro Martinez/Black Back 4.00
226 Rich Harden .40
226 Rich Harden/Black Back 3.00
227 Shane Victorino .50
227 Shane Victorino/Black Back 3.00
228 Andrew Miller .40
228 Andrew Miller/Black Back 3.00
229 Chris Young .50
230 Andruw Jones .50
231 Kevin Gregg SP 5.00
232 C.C. Sabathia .40
233 Hanley Ramirez 1.00
234 Wandy Rodriguez .40
235 Roy Oswalt .75

236 Mark Grudzielanek .40
237 Derek Jeter, Chien-Ming Wang, Robinson Cano 1.00
238 Todd Helton .75
239 Zack Greinke .40
240 Carlos Gomez .40
241 Lastings Milledge .40
242 Huston Street .40
243 Danny Haren .40
244 Carlos Pena .75
245 Brad Wilkerson .40
246 Roy Halladay .40
247 Dmitri Young .40
248 Boston Red Sox 1.00
249 Jonathan Papelbon .75
250 Felix Pie .40
251 Alex Gonzalez .40
252 Bobby Crosby .40
253 Justin Ruggiano **RC** .75
254 Freddy Garcia .40
255 Khalil Greene .50
256 Rich Aurilia .40
257 Jarrod Washburn .40
258 B.J. Upton .50
259 Michael Young .40
260 Carlos Zambrano .75
261 Livan Hernandez .40
262 Derek Lowe, Brad Penny, Chad Billingsley .40
262 Lowe, Penny, Billingsley/ Black Back 3.00
263 Melky Cabrera .50
263 Melky Cabrera/Black Back 3.00
264 Shannon Stewart .40
264 Shannon Stewart/Black Back 3.00
265 Aaron Rowand .50
265 Aaron Rowand/Black Back 3.00
266 Matt Morris .40
266 Matt Morris/Black Back 3.00
267 Xavier Nady .50
267 Xavier Nady/Black Back 3.00
268 Jim Thome .75
269 Horacio Ramirez .40
270 Prince Fielder 1.00
271 Andy Phillips .40
272 Aaron Harang .40
273 Josh Barfield .40
274 Ubaldo Jimenez .40
275 Anibal Sanchez .40
276 Carlos Lee .50
277 Mark Teahen .40
278 Delwyn Young .40
279 Kurt Suzuki .40
280 Nate Schierholtz .40
281 Raul Ibanez .40
282 Jose Vidro .40
283 Miguel Cabrera 1.00
283 Miguel Cabrera/Black Back 4.00
284 Luis Gonzalez .40
284 Luis Gonzalez/Black Back 3.00
285 Chad Billingsley .40
285 Chad Billingsley/Black Back 3.00
286 Tony Gwynn Jr. .40
286 Tony Gwynn Jr./Black Back 3.00
287 Matthew Kemp .75
288 James Loney .50
289 Brett Myers .40
290 Nate McLouth .40
291 Matt Chico, Jason Bergmann .40
291 Matt Chico, Jason Bergmann/Black Back 3.00
292 Chad Tracy .40
293 Edgar Renteria .40
294 Jay Payton .40
295 Josh Johnson .40
296 Josh Banks .40
297 Bill Murphy .40
298 Ben Sheets .50
299 Jose Reyes 1.00
300 Chase Utley 1.00
301 Ronnie Belliard .40
301 Ronnie Belliard/Black Back 3.00
302 Wily Mo Pena .40
303 Tim Lincecum .75
304 Chicago Cubs .75
305 John Lackey .40
306 Stephen Drew .75
307 Kelly Johnson .40
308 Daisuke Matsuzaka 2.00
309 Craig Monroe .40
310 Jerry Owens .40
311 Jeff Suppan .40
312 Tom Glavine .75
313 Kei Igawa .40
314 Mark Kotsay .40
315 Jacque Jones SP 5.00
316 Melvin Mora .40
317 Matt Holliday, Hanley Ramirez .75
318 Jarrod Saltalamacchia .50
319 A.J. Burnett .40
320 Casey Kotchman .40
321 Randy Winn .40
321 Randy Winn/Black Back 3.00
322 Richie Sexson .50
322 Richie Sexson/Black Back 3.00
323 Juan Encarnacion .40
323 Juan Encarnacion/Black Back 3.00
324 Rick Ankiel .50
324 Rick Ankiel/Black Back 3.00
325 Dan Wheeler .40
325 Dan Wheeler/Black Back 3.00
326 Brian Roberts .50
327 David Ortiz 1.00
328 Garret Anderson .40
329 Detroit Tigers .50
330 Ty Wigginton .40
330 Ty Wigginton/Black Back 3.00
331 Travis Hafner .50
332 Howie Kendrick .50
332 Howie Kendrick/Black Back 3.00
333 Kevin Kouzmanoff .50
333 Kevin Kouzmanoff/ Black Back 3.00
334 Matt Holliday .75
334 Matt Holliday/Black Back 4.00
335 Brandon Phillips .50
335 Brandon Phillips/Black Back 3.00
336 Ian Kinsler .50
336 Ian Kinsler/Black Back 3.00
337 Lyle Overbay .50
337 Lyle Overbay/Black Back 3.00
338 Justin Verlander .75
338 Justin Verlander/Black Back 4.00
339 Ian Snell .50
340 Hank Blalock .50
341 Vernon Wells .50
342 Matt Chico .40
343 Tim Wakefield .40
344 Michael Bourn .40
345 Chris Carpenter .50
346 Josh Beckett, Daisuke Matsuzaka 1.00
347 Chuck James .40
347 Chuck James/Black Back 3.00
348 Joba Chamberlain 3.00
349 Erik Bedard .75
350 Jimmy Rollins .75
350 Jimmy Rollins/Black Back 4.00
351 Anthony Reyes .40
352 Carl Crawford .50
353 Jeremy Hermida .40
354 Ervin Santana .40
355 Edgar Gonzalez .40
356 Yunel Escobar .40
357 Yorvit Torrealba .40
358 Hideki Okajima .50
359 Paul Byrd .40
360 Magglio Ordonez .50
360 Magglio Ordonez/Black Back 3.00
361 Joe Borowski .40
362 Clint Sammons .40
363 Chris Duffy .40
364 Fred Lewis .40
365 Adrian Beltre .50
366 Alex Rodriguez 3.00
367 Troy Tulowitzki .75
368 Prince Fielder 1.00
369 Clay Buchholz .75
370 Justin Verlander .75
370 Justin Verlander/Black Back 4.00
371 Pedro Martinez 1.00
371 Pedro Martinez/Black Back 4.00
372 Ryan Howard 1.00
372 Ryan Howard/Black Back 5.00
373 Ichiro Suzuki 2.00
374 Kenny Lofton .40
375 Manny Ramirez .75
376 Randy Johnson 1.00
377 Chris Capuano .40
378 Johnny Estrada .40
379 Franklin Morales .40
380 Ryan Howard 1.00
381 Casey Blake SP 5.00
382 Coco Crisp .40
383 John Maine, Willie Randolph .40
384 Jeremy Guthrie .40
385 Geoff Jenkins .40
386 Marlon Byrd .40
387 Jeremy Bonderman .50
388 Ryan Howard 1.00
389 Joe Girardi .40
390 Ryan Braun 1.00
391 Ryan Zimmerman .75
392 Dustin Pedroia, Kevin Youkilis, Mike Lowell .50
393 Pittsburgh Pirates .40
394 Ryan Spilborghs .40
395 Eric Gagne .40
396 Joe Blanton .40
397 Washington Nationals .40
398 Ryan Church .40
399 Ted Lilly .40
400 Manny Ramirez .75
401 Chad Gaudin .40
402 Dustin McGowan .40
403 Scott Baker .40
404 Franklin Gutierrez .40
405 David Bush .40
406 Aubrey Huff .40
407 Jermaine Dye .40
408 Chase Utley, Jimmy Rollins .75
409 Jon Lester SP 5.00
410 Aaron Cook .40
411 Sergio Mitre .40
412 Jason Bartlett .40
413 Edwin Jackson .40
414 J.D. Drew .40
415 Freddy Sanchez .40
415 Freddy Sanchez/Black Back 3.00
416 Asdrubal Cabrera .40
417 Nate Robertson .40
418 Shaun Marcum .40
419 Noah Lowry .40
420 Atlanta Braves .50
421 Jamie Moyer .40
422 Michael Cuddyer .40
423 Randy Wolf .40
424 Juan Uribe .40
425 Brian McCann .50
426 Kyle Lohse/SP 5.00
427 Doug Davis/SP 5.00
428 Ian Snell, Tom Gorzelanny, Matt Capps/SP 5.00
429 Miguel Batista/SP 5.00
430 Chien-Ming Wang/SP 10.00
431 Jeff Salazar/SP 5.00
432 Yadier Molina/SP 5.00
433 Adam Wainwright/SP 5.00
434 Scott Kazmir/SP 5.00
435 Adam Dunn/SP 6.00
436 Ryan Freel/SP 5.00
437 Jhonny Peralta/SP 5.00
438 Kazuo Matsui/SP 5.00
439 Daniel Cabrera .40
440 John Smoltz .75
441 Emil Brown/SP 5.00
442 Gary Sheffield/SP 5.00
443 Jake Peavy/SP 8.00
444 Scott Rolen/SP 5.00
445 Kason Gabbard/SP 5.00
446 Aaron Hill/SP 5.00
447 Felipe Lopez/SP 5.00
448 Dan Uggla/SP 5.00
449 Willy Taveras/SP 5.00
450 Chipper Jones/SP 6.00
451 Josh Anderson/SP 5.00
452 Eric Byrnes, Chris Young, Justin Upton/SP 5.00
453 Braden Looper/SP 5.00
454 Brandon Inge/SP 5.00
455 Brian Giles/SP 5.00
456 Corey Patterson/SP 5.00
457 Los Angeles Dodgers/SP 5.00
458 Sean Casey/SP 5.00
459 Pedro Feliz/SP 5.00
460 Tom Gorzelanny .40
461 Chone Figgins/SP 5.00
462 Kyle Kendrick/SP 5.00
463 Tony Pena/SP 5.00
464 Marcus Giles/SP 5.00
465 Augie Ojeda/SP 5.00
466 Micah Owings/SP 5.00
467 Ryan Theriot/SP 5.00
468 Shawn Green/SP 5.00
469 Frank Thomas/SP 6.00
470 Lenny DiNardo/SP 5.00
471 Jose Bautista/SP 5.00
472 Manny Corpas/SP 5.00
473 Kevin Millwood/SP 5.00
474 Kevin Youkilis/SP 5.00
475 Jose Contreras/SP 5.00
476 Cleveland Indians .50
477 Julio Lugo/SP 5.00
478 Jason Bay .75
479 Tony LaRussa/SP 5.00
480 Jim Leyland/SP 5.00
481 Derrek Lee/SP 6.00
482 Justin Morneau/SP 6.00
483 Orlando Hudson/SP 5.00
484 Brian Roberts/SP 5.00
485 Miguel Cabrera/SP 6.00
486 Mike Lowell/SP 5.00
487 J.J. Hardy/SP 5.00
488 Carlos Guillen/SP 5.00
489 Ken Griffey Jr./SP 8.00
490 Vladimir Guerrero/SP 6.00
491 Alfonso Soriano/SP 6.00
492 Ichiro Suzuki/SP 8.00
493 Matt Holliday/SP 6.00
494 Magglio Ordonez/SP 5.00
495 Brian McCann/SP 5.00
496 Victor Martinez/SP 5.00
497 Brad Penny/SP 5.00
498 Josh Beckett/SP 6.00
499 Cole Hamels/SP 6.00
500 Justin Verlander/SP 6.00

Chrome

billy wagner
NEW YORK METS
PITCHER

NM/M

Complete Set (100): 200.00
Common Player: 2.00
Production 1,959 Sets
Refractor: 2X
Production 559 Sets
Black Refractor: 4-6X
Production 59 Sets
1 Hunter Pence 4.00
2 Andre Ethier 2.00
3 Curt Schilling 4.00
4 Gary Matthews Jr. 2.00
5 Dontrelle Willis 2.00
6 Troy Tulowitzki 5.00
7 Robinson Cano 4.00
8 Felix Hernandez 4.00
9 Josh Hamilton 5.00
10 Justin Upton 4.00
11 Brad Penny 2.00
12 Hideki Matsui 6.00
13 J.J. Putz 2.00
14 Jorge Posada 3.00
15 Albert Pujols 8.00
16 Aaron Rowand 2.00
17 Ronnie Belliard 2.00
18 Rick Ankiel 3.00
19 Ian Kinsler 3.00
20 Justin Verlander 4.00
21 Lyle Overbay 2.00
22 Tim Hudson 3.00
23 Ryan Zimmerman 3.00
24 Ryan Braun 5.00
25 Jimmy Rollins 5.00
26 Kelvim Escobar 2.00
27 Adam LaRoche 2.00
28 Ivan Rodriguez 3.00
29 Billy Wagner 2.00
30 Ichiro Suzuki 8.00
31 Chris Young 3.00
32 Trevor Hoffman 2.00
33 Torii Hunter 3.00
34 Jason Isringhausen 2.00
35 Jose Valverde 2.00
36 Derrek Lee 4.00
37 Rich Harden 2.00
38 Andrew Miller 2.00
39 Miguel Cabrera 4.00
40 David Wright 8.00
41 Brandon Phillips 2.00
42 Magglio Ordonez 2.00
43 Eric Byrnes 2.00
44 John Smoltz 3.00
45 Brandon Webb 3.00
46 Barry Zito 2.00
47 Sammy Sosa 3.00
48 James Shields 3.00
49 Alex Rios 3.00
50 Matt Holliday 4.00
51 Chris Young 4.00
52 Roy Oswalt 3.00
53 Matthew Kemp 3.00
54 Tim Lincecum 4.00
55 Hanley Ramirez 4.00
56 Vladimir Guerrero 4.00
57 Mark Teixeira 3.00
58 Fausto Carmona 2.00
59 B.J. Ryan 2.00
60 Manny Ramirez 4.00
61 Carlos Delgado 3.00
62 Matt Cain 2.00
63 Brian Bannister 2.00
64 Russell Martin 3.00
65 Todd Helton 3.00
66 Roy Halladay 2.00
67 Lance Berkman 3.00
68 John Lackey 2.00
69 Daisuke Matsuzaka 5.00
70 Joe Mauer 3.00
71 Francisco Rodriguez 2.00
72 Derek Jeter 10.00
73 Homer Bailey 2.00
74 Jonathan Papelbon 3.00
75 Billy Butler 2.00
76 B.J. Upton 2.00
77 Ubaldo Jimenez 2.00
78 Erik Bedard 2.00
79 Jeff Kent 2.00
80 Ken Griffey Jr. 8.00
81 Josh Beckett 3.00
82 Jeff Francis 2.00
83 Grady Sizemore 4.00
84 John Maine 2.00
85 Cole Hamels 3.00
86 Nicholas Markakis 3.00
87 Ben Sheets 2.00
88 Jose Reyes 5.00
89 Vernon Wells 2.00
90 Justin Morneau 2.00
91 Brian McCann 2.00
92 Jacoby Ellsbury 5.00
93 Clay Buchholz 3.00
94 Prince Fielder 4.00
95 David Ortiz 4.00
96 Joba Chamberlain 5.00
97 Chien-Ming Wang 6.00
98 Chipper Jones 4.00
99 Chase Utley 4.00
100 Alex Rodriguez 10.00

Advertising Panels

NM/M

Common Panel: 3.00

Autographs

NM/M

Inserted 1:247
Red Ink: 1.5X
Production 59 Sets
MB Mike Baxes 50.00
BB Bob Blaylock 60.00
JB Jim Bolger 60.00
TC Tom Carroll 50.00
PC Phil Clark 50.00
CE Carl Erskine 60.00
RH Russ Heman 50.00
RJ Randy Jackson 60.00

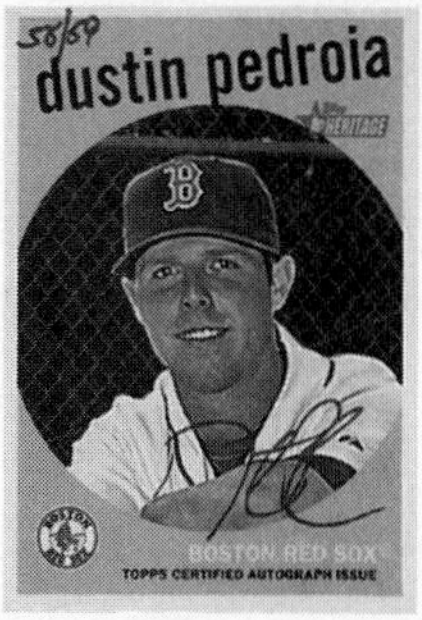
dustin pedroia
BOSTON RED SOX
TOPPS CERTIFIED AUTOGRAPH ISSUE

TK Ted Kazanski 50.00
CK Chick King 50.00
KL Ken Lehman 50.00
MM Morrie Martin 60.00
BM Bob Martyn 50.00
LM Les Moss 60.00
JO Johnny O'Brien 50.00
HP Herb Plews 50.00
JP J.W. Porter 60.00
TQ Tom Qualters 50.00
BR Bill Renna 50.00
BS Bob Smith 50.00
BSP Bob Speake 60.00
LT Lee Tate 50.00
VV Vito Valentinetti 40.00
GEZ Gus Zernial 60.00
GZ George Zuverink 60.00
MIM Minnie Minoso 65.00
YB Yogi Berra 120.00
LA Luis Aparicio 80.00
WM Bill Mazeroski 85.00
JC Joba Chamberlain 150.00
FS Freddy Sanchez 40.00
AR Aramis Ramirez 40.00
SP Scott Podsednik 40.00

Clubhouse Collection

NM/M

Common Player: 5.00
MIM Minnie Minoso 25.00
YB Yogi Berra 25.00
LA Luis Aparicio 15.00
BG Bob Gibson 20.00
WM Bill Mazeroski 20.00
AD Adam Dunn 8.00
AJ Andruw Jones 8.00
AR Aramis Ramirez 10.00
BA Bobby Abreu 8.00
CC Carl Crawford 8.00
CB Carlos Beltran 8.00
CD Carlos Delgado 8.00
CL Carlos Lee 5.00
CAB Craig Biggio 8.00
DL Derrek Lee 8.00
DO David Ortiz 15.00
DY Dmitri Young 5.00
EC Eric Chavez 5.00
FT Frank Thomas 10.00
GA Garret Anderson 5.00
HB Hank Blalock 5.00
IR Ivan Rodriguez 8.00
JE Jim Edmonds 5.00
JS John Smoltz 8.00
JD Johnny Damon 10.00
JP Jorge Posada 5.00
JV Justin Verlander 10.00
LB Lance Berkman 8.00
MC Miguel Cabrera 10.00
MT Miguel Tejada 5.00
MM Mike Mussina 8.00
PM Pedro Martinez 8.00
RS Richie Sexson 5.00
RO Roy Oswalt 8.00
RH Ryan Howard 15.00
RZ Ryan Zimmerman 8.00
SG Shawn Green 5.00
TH Todd Helton 8.00
TKH Torii Hunter 8.00
TLH Travis Hafner 8.00

Clubhouse Collection Dual Relics

NM/M

Production 59 Sets
MB Bill Mazeroski, Jason Bay 125.00
BL Ernie Banks, Derrek Lee 150.00
GE Bob Gibson, Jim Edmonds 125.00
MH Minnie Minoso, Travis Hafner 125.00
AK Luis Aparicio, Paul Konerko 80.00

Clubhouse Collection Relic Auto.

NM/M

Production 25 Sets
BG Bob Gibson 250.00
JC Joba Chamberlain 280.00

Dual Autographs

Production 25 Sets
No Pricing

Flashbacks

NM/M

Complete Set (10): 10.00
Common Player: .50
Inserted 1:12
1 Minnie Minoso .50
2 Luis Aparicio .50
3 Ernie Banks 1.50
4 Bill Mazeroski .50
5 Bob Gibson 1.50
6 Frank Robinson 1.50
7 Brooks Robinson 1.50
8 Mickey Mantle 3.00
9 Orlando Cepeda .50
10 Eddie Mathews 1.50

Flashbacks Autographs

NM/M

Production 25 Sets 10.00

Flashbacks Relics

NM/M

Common Player:
MIM Minnie Minoso 20.00
LA Luis Aparicio 15.00
EB Ernie Banks 25.00
WM Bill Mazeroski 20.00
BG Bob Gibson 20.00
FR Frank Robinson 20.00
BR Brooks Robinson 20.00
MM Mickey Mantle 50.00
OC Orlando Cepeda 20.00
EM Eddie Mathews 20.00

Flashbacks Dual Relics

No Pricing
Production 10 Sets

Flashbacks Stadium Relics

NM/M

Common Player:
MM Minnie Minoso 20.00
LA Luis Aparicio 15.00
EB Ernie Banks 25.00
WM Bill Mazeroski 20.00
BG Bob Gibson 20.00

New Age Performers

NM/M

Complete Set (15): 12.00
Common Player: .50
Inserted 1:15
1 Maggilo Ordonez 1.00
2 Ichiro Suzuki 2.00
3 Matt Holliday 1.00
4 Prince Fielder 1.00
5 David Wright 2.00
6 Jake Peavy .75
7 Alex Rodriguez 3.00
8 John Lackey .50
9 Vladimir Guerrero 1.00
10 Ryan Howard 1.00
11 Brandon Webb .50
12 Manny Ramirez 1.00
13 Josh Beckett 1.00
14 Jimmy Rollins 1.00
15 David Ortiz 1.00

News Flashbacks

NM/M

Complete Set (10): 10.00
Common Card: 1.00
Inserted 1:12
1 Alaska becomes 49th State 1.00
2 The Day the Music Died 1.00
3 Castro becomes Prime Minister of Cuba 1.00
4 Dalai Lama flees to India 1.00
5 NASA 1st 7 Astronauts 1.00
6 Nixon and Khrushchev 1.00
7 Hawaii becomes 50th State 1.00
8 USSR's Luna 2 1.00
9 In Cold Blood murders committed 1.00
10 Antarctic Treaty 1.00

Then & Now

ichiro
Then & Now
minnie minoso
CLEVELAND INDIANS

NM/M

Complete Set (10): 12.00
Common Duo: 1.00
Inserted 1:15
1 Alex Rodriguez, Eddie Mathews 3.00
2 Alex Rodriguez, Ernie Banks 3.00
3 Maggilo Ordonez, Orlando Cepeda 1.00
4 Jose Reyes, Luis Aparicio 1.50
5 David Ortiz, Mickey Mantle 3.00
6 Erik Bedard, Johnny Podres 1.00
7 Josh Beckett, Early Wynn 1.00
8 Ichiro Suzuki, Minnie Minoso 2.00
9 David Ortiz, Frank Robinson 1.50
10 Jake Peavy, Don Drysdale 1.00

1959 Cut Signatures

Production One Set
No Pricing

1959 Topps Originals

See 1959 Topps pricing.

2008 Topps Moments & Milestones

NM/M

Common Player: .50
Production 150 Sets
Pack (6): 5.00
Box (18): 80.00
1-2 Alex Rodriguez 3.00
3 Frank Thomas 1.00
4-7 Mickey Mantle 4.00
8 Greg Maddux 2.00
9 Troy Tulowitzki 1.00
10-11 Hunter Pence 1.00
12-15 Albert Pujols 3.00
16-17 David Ortiz 1.50
18-19 David Wright 2.00
20 Aaron Hill .50
21 Eric Byrnes .50
22 Dmitri Young .50
23 Garret Anderson .50
24-25 Jimmy Rollins 1.50
26 Joba Chamberlain 5.00
27 Magglio Ordonez 1.00
28-31 Ryan Howard 2.00
32 Trevor Hoffman .50
33 Ken Griffey Jr. 2.00
34 Travis Hafner .50
35 Joe Mauer .75
36-37 Daisuke Matsuzaka 2.00
38-41 Curtis Granderson 1.50
42 Alex Gordon 1.00
43 Aramis Ramirez 1.00
44 Jonathan Papelbon 1.50
45 B.J. Upton 1.00
46 C.C. Sabathia 1.00
47 Carl Crawford .75
48 Jason Bay .75
49 Carlos Beltran 1.00
50 Carlos Guillen .75
51 C.C. Sabathia 1.00
52 Gary Sheffield 1.00
53 Chris Young .75
54 Dontrelle Willis .50
55 Dustin Pedroia 1.00
56 Alfonso Soriano 1.50
57 Derek Jeter 3.00
58-61 Chase Utley 1.50
62-63 Ichiro Suzuki 2.50
64-65 Jorge Posada 1.00
66 Jose Reyes 2.00
67-68 Miguel Tejada .75
69 Nick Swisher .75
70 Robinson Cano 1.00
71 Roy Halladay .75
72 Ryan Zimmerman 1.00
73 Scott Rolen .75
74 Tim Lincecum 1.00
75 Vernon Wells .75
76-82 Roger Clemens 2.00
83 Michael Young .75
84 John Smoltz 1.00
85 Jim Thome 1.00
86-87 Johan Santana 1.50
88-89 Jack Cust .50
90 Jake Peavy 1.00
91-92 Hanley Ramirez 1.50
93 Hideki Okajima .50
94 Grady Sizemore 1.00
95 Erik Bedard .50
96-97 Derrek Lee 1.00
98-99 Delmon Young .50
100 Cole Hamels 1.00
101 Brad Hawpe .50
102 Mike Lowell 1.00
103 Placido Polanco .50
104 Nick Swisher .50
105 Adrian Gonzalez .75
106 Adrian Gonzalez .75
107 Scott Kazmir .50
108 Freddy Sanchez .50
109 Jeremy Guthrie .50
110 Chipper Jones 1.50
111 Chris Carpenter .75
112 Andy Pettitte 1.00
113 Andruw Jones .75
114 Bobby Abreu .75
115 Eric Chavez .50
116 Eric Chavez .50
117 Josh Hamilton 1.00
118-119 Manny Ramirez 1.00
120 Mariano Rivera 1.00
121 Kelly Johnson .50
122 Jeff Kent .75
123 Mark Teixeira 1.00
124 Matt Holliday 1.00
125 Matt Holliday 1.00
126 Huston Street .50
127 Carlos Lee .75
128 Brian Bannister .50
129 Carlos Pena .75
130 Brian McCann 1.00
131 Prince Fielder 1.50
132 Randy Johnson 1.50
133 Russell Martin 1.00
134 Ryan Braun 1.50
135-136 Vladimir Guerrero 1.50
137 Tom Glavine 1.00
138-140 Miguel Cabrera 1.00
141-142 Pedro Martinez 1.00
143 Yovani Gallardo .75
144 Brian Roberts .50
150-153 Clay Buchholz **(RC)** 2.00
154-156 Billy Buckner 1.00
157-159 Jeff Clement 1.00
160-162 Radhames Liz .50
163-165 Bronson Sardinha .50
166-168 Seth Smith .50
172-174 Wladimir Balentien 1.00
175-177 Josh Banks .50
178-180 Ross Detwiler .50
181-183 Felipe Paulino .50
184-186 Troy Patton .50
187-189 Brandon Jones 1.00

Black

Black: 2-4X
Production 25 Sets

Blue

Blue: 3-5X
Production 10 Sets

Red

No Pricing
Production One Set

Printing Plates

No Pricing
Production one set per color.

Autographs

NM/M

Common Auto: 5.00
Black: 1-1.5X
Production 25 Sets
Blue: No Pricing
Production 10 Sets
Red: No Pricing
Production One Set
CB Clay Buchholz 30.00
JK Joe Koshansky 8.00
NM Nyjer Morgan 8.00
CH Chin-Lung Hu 20.00
RT Rich Thompson 8.00
SF Sam Fuld 10.00
DB Daric Barton 8.00
JA Josh Anderson 8.00
JM Jonathan Meloan 8.00
JT J.R. Towles 15.00
SP Steve Pearce 10.00
RO Ross Ohlendorf 15.00
JR Justin Ruggiano 8.00
LB Lance Broadway 8.00
WB Wladimir Balentien 10.00
AG Armando Galarraga 20.00
FP Felipe Paulino 8.00
JM Jose Morales 8.00
RJ Rob Johnson 10.00
BJ Brandon Jones 8.00
BP Brandon Phillips 20.00
MC Melky Cabrera 15.00
MCA Matt Cain 15.00
CR Carlos Ruiz 8.00
BR B.J. Ryan 10.00
TG Tom Gorzelanny 8.00
AL Adam Lind 10.00
RB Ryan Braun 30.00
TJ Todd Jones 8.00
BC Bobby Crosby 8.00
FC Fausto Carmona 15.00
FS Freddy Sanchez 10.00
CP Carlos Pena 15.00
JD Jermaine Dye 10.00
CM Cameron Maybin 15.00
JC Jack Cust 10.00
RM Russell Martin 10.00
AC Asdrubal Cabrera 10.00
LM Lastings Milledge 10.00
BH Brad Hawpe 15.00
RC Robinson Cano 20.00
RH Rich Harden 8.00
CC Carl Crawford 10.00
TH Tim Hudson 15.00
DW David Wright 50.00
AS Alfonso Soriano 20.00
HR Hanley Ramirez 20.00
JR Jose Reyes 30.00
MH Matt Holliday 20.00
JP Jorge Posada 40.00
MIC Miguel Cabrera 25.00
JH Josh Hamilton 15.00

2008 Topps Opening Day

NM/M

Complete Set (220): 30.00
Common Player: .15
Pack (6): 1.00
Box (36): 30.00
1 Alex Rodriguez 1.50
2 Barry Zito .25
3 Jeff Suppan .15
4 Placido Polanco .15
5 Scott Kazmir .25
6 Ivan Rodriguez .40
7 Mickey Mantle 2.00
8 Stephen Drew .25
9 Ken Griffey Jr. 1.00

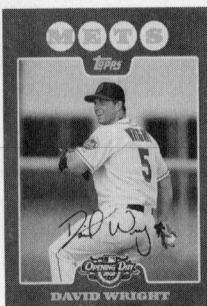

DAVID WRIGHT

#	Player	Value
10	Miguel Cabrera	.50
11	Yorvit Torrealba	.15
12	Daisuke Matsuzaka	.75
13	Kyle Kendrick	.15
14	Jimmy Rollins	.50
15	Joe Mauer	.25
16	Cole Hamels	.25
17	Yovani Gallardo	.25
18	Miguel Tejada	.25
19	Corey Hart	.25
20	Nicholas Markakis	.25
21	Zack Greinke	.15
22	Orlando Cabrera	.25
23	Jake Peavy	.25
24	Erik Bedard	.25
25	Trevor Hoffman	.15
26	Derrek Lee	.40
27	Hank Blalock	.25
28	Victor Martinez	.25
29	Chris Young	.25
30	Jose Reyes	.50
31	Mike Lowell	.25
32	Curtis Granderson	.25
33	Dan Uggla	.25
34	Mike Piazza	.50
35	Garrett Atkins	.25
36	Felix Hernandez	.40
37	Alex Rios	.25
38	Mark Reynolds	.15
39	Jason Bay	.25
40	Josh Beckett	.25
41	Jack Cust	.15
42	Vladimir Guerrero	.50
43	Marcus Giles	.15
44	Kenny Lofton	.15
45	John Lackey	.15
46	Ryan Howard	1.00
47	Kevin Youkilis	.25
48	Gary Sheffield	.25
49	Justin Morneau	.25
50	Albert Pujols	1.00
51	Ubaldo Jimenez	.15
52	Johan Santana	.50
53	Chuck James	.15
54	Jeremy Hermida	.15
55	Andruw Jones	.25
56	Jason Varitek	.25
57	Tim Hudson	.25
58	Justin Upton	.50
59	Brad Penny	.15
60	Robinson Cano	.40
61	Johnny Estrada	.15
62	Brandon Webb	.25
63	Chris Duncan	.15
64	Aaron Hill	.15
65	Alfonso Soriano	.50
66	Carlos Zambrano	.25
67	Ben Sheets	.25
68	Andy LaRoche	.15
69	Tim Lincecum	.25
70	Phil Hughes	.25
71	Magglio Ordonez	.25
72	Scott Rolen	.25
73	John Maine	.15
74	Delmon Young	.25
75	Chase Utley	.50
76	Jose Valverde	.15
77	Tadahito Iguchi	.15
78	Checklist	.15
79	Russell Martin	.25
80	B.J. Upton	.25
81	Orlando Hudson	.15
82	Jim Edmonds	.15
83	J.J. Hardy	.15
84	Todd Helton	.40
85	Melky Cabrera	.15
86	Adrian Beltre	.25
87	Manny Ramirez	.50
88	Rafael Furcal	.25
89	Gil Meche	.15
90	Grady Sizemore	.50
91	Jeff Kent	.25
92	David DeJesus	.15
93	Lyle Overbay	.15
94	Moises Alou	.25
95	Frank Thomas	.50
96	Ryan Garko	.15
97	Kevin Kouzmanoff	.15
98	Roy Oswalt	.25
99	Mark Buehrle	.25
100	David Ortiz	.50

#	Player	Value
101	Hunter Pence	.25
102	David Wright	.75
103	Dustin Pedroia	.15
104	Roy Halladay	.25
105	Derek Jeter	1.50
106	Casey Blake	.15
107	Rich Harden	.15
108	Shane Victorino	.15
109	Richie Sexson	.25
110	Jim Thome	.40
111	Akinori Iwamura	.15
112	Danny Haren	.15
113	Jose Contreras	.15
114	Jonathan Papelbon	.25
115	Prince Fielder	.50
116	Dan Johnson	.15
117	Dmitri Young	.15
118	Brandon Phillips	.25
119	Brett Myers	.15
120	James Loney	.15
121	C.C. Sabathia	.25
122	Jermaine Dye	.15
123	Aubrey Huff	.15
124	Carlos Ruiz	.15
125	Hanley Ramirez	.50
126	Edgar Renteria	.15
127	Mark Loretta	.15
128	Brian McCann	.25
129	Paul Konerko	.25
130	Jorge Posada	.25
131	Chien-Ming Wang	.75
132	Jose Vidro	.15
133	Carlos Delgado	.25
134	Kelvim Escobar	.15
135	Pedro Martinez	.40
136	Jeremy Guthrie	.15
137	Ramon Hernandez	.15
138	Ian Kinsler	.25
139	Ichiro Suzuki	1.00
140	Garret Anderson	.15
141	Tom Gorzelanny	.15
142	Bobby Crosby	.15
143	Jeff Francoeur	.25
144	Josh Hamilton	.25
145	Mark Teixeira	.50
146	Fausto Carmona	.25
147	Alex Gordon	.40
148	Nick Swisher	.25
149	Justin Verlander	.40
150	Pat Burrell	.25
151	Chris Carpenter	.25
152	Matt Holliday	.50
153	Adam Dunn	.40
154	Curt Schilling	.40
155	Kelly Johnson	.15
156	Aaron Rowand	.15
157	Brian Roberts	.25
158	Bobby Abreu	.25
159	Carlos Beltran	.40
160	Lance Berkman	.25
161	Gary Matthews	.15
162	Jeff Francis	.15
163	Vernon Wells	.25
164	Dontrelle Willis	.25
165	Travis Hafner	.25
166	Brian Bannister	.15
167	Carlos Pena	.25
168	Raul Ibanez	.15
169	Aramis Ramirez	.25
170	Eric Byrnes	.25
171	Greg Maddux	1.00
172	John Smoltz	.25
173	Jarrod Saltalamacchia	.25
174	Hideki Okajima	.25
175	Javier Vazquez	.25
176	Aaron Harang	.25
177	Jhonny Peralta	.25
178	Carlos Lee	.25
179	Ryan Braun	1.00
180	Torii Hunter	.25
181	Hideki Matsui	1.00
182	Eric Chavez	.15
183	Freddy Sanchez	.25
184	Adrian Gonzalez	.25
185	Bengie Molina	.15
186	Kenji Johjima	.15
187	Carl Crawford	.25
188	Chipper Jones	.50
189	Chris Young	.25
190	Michael Young	.15
191	Troy Glaus	.25
192	Ryan Zimmerman	.25
193	Brian Giles	.15
194	Troy Tulowitzki	.40
195	Chin-Lung Hu **(RC)**	.50
196	Seth Smith **(RC)**	.25
197	Wladimir Balentien **(RC)**	.25
198	Rich Thompson **(RC)**	.25
199	Radhames Liz **RC**	.25
200	Ross Detwiler **RC**	.25
201	Sam Fuld **RC**	.25
202	Clint Sammons **(RC)**	.25
203	Ross Ohlendorf **RC**	.25
204	Jonathan Albaladejo **RC**	.25
205	Brandon Jones **RC**	.50
206	Steve Pearce **RC**	.75
207	Kevin Hart **(RC)**	.25
208	Luke Hochevar **RC**	.75
209	Troy Patton **(RC)**	.25
210	Josh Anderson **(RC)**	.25
211	Clay Buchholz **RC**	.50
212	Joe Koshansky **(RC)**	.25
213	Bronson Sardinha **RC**	.25
214	Emilio Bonifacio **RC**	.25
215	Daric Barton **(RC)**	.25

#	Player	Value
216	Lance Broadway **RC**	.25
217	Jeff Clement **(RC)**	.25
218	Joey Votto **(RC)**	.50
219	J.R. Towles **RC**	.50
220	Nyjer Morgan **(RC)**	.25

Gold

Gold: 2-3X

Autographs

		NM/M
Common Auto.:		
JB	Jeff Baker	15.00
KG	Kevin Gregg	15.00
AL	Anthony Lerew	15.00
NS	Nate Schierholtz	20.00
JCB	Jason Botts	15.00

Flapper Cards

		NM/M
Common Player:		.50
AR	Alex Rodriguez	1.00
RH	Ryan Howard	.75
DW	David Wright	.75
DO	David Ortiz	.75
PF	Prince Fielder	.75
AP	Albert Pujols	1.00
IS	Ichiro Suzuki	.75
VG	Vladimir Guerrero	.50
DJ	Derek Jeter	1.00
JR	Jose Reyes	.75
KG	Ken Griffey Jr.	.75
GM	Greg Maddux	.75
MM	Mickey Mantle	.75
MR	Manny Ramirez	.75
JB	Josh Beckett	.50
CJ	Chipper Jones	.50
RC	Roger Clemens	.75
DM	Daisuke Matsuzaka	.75

Puzzle

	NM/M
Common Puzzle Card:	.50
Matt Holliday	.50
Vladimir Guerrero	.50
Jose Reyes	.50
Josh Beckett	.50
Albert Pujols	.50
Alex Rodriguez	.50
Jake Peavy	.50
David Ortiz	.50
Ryan Howard	.50
Ichiro	.50
Hanley Ramirez	.50
Grady Sizemore	.50
David Wright	.50
Alex Rios	.50

Tattoos

		NM/M
Common Tattoo:		.25
PP	Phillie Phanatic	.25
WM	Wally the Green Monster	.25
MM	Mr. Met	.25
TM	The Moose	.25
LS	Lou Seal	.25
ST	Stomper	.25

BM	Billy the Marlin	.25
SL	Slider	.25
SF	Swinging Friar	.25
JJ	Junction Jack	.25
PIP	Pirate Parrot	.25
BB	Bernie Brewer	.25
FB	Fredbird	.25
TB	TC Bear	.25
PW	Paws	.25
NYY	New York Yankees	.25
NYM	N.Y. Mets	.25
BRS	Boston Red Sox	.25
SFG	San Francisco Giants	.25
CC	Chicago Cubs	.25
CL	Cleveland Indians	.25
CWS	Chicago White Sox	.25
LAA	L.A. Angels	.25
CR	Cincinnati Reds	.25
FM	Florida Marlins	.25
TBJ	Toronto Blue Jays	.25
AB	Atlanta Braves	.25
AD	Arizona Diamondbacks	.25
TDR	Tampa Bay Rays	.25
TR	Texas Rangers	.25

2008 Topps Triple Threads

	NM/M
Common (1-145, 221-251):	1.00
Production 1,350	
Common Jsy Auto. RC (146-170):	10.00
Production 99	
Team Initial Die-Cut variation:	1X
Box (2):	160.00

#	Player	Value
1	David Wright	3.00
2	Nolan Ryan	5.00
3	Johnny Damon	1.50
4	Joe Mauer	1.50
5	Francisco Rodriguez	1.00
6	Carlos Beltran	1.50
7	Mickey Mantle	8.00
8	Brian Roberts	1.00
9	Lou Gehrig	5.00
10	Babe Ruth	6.00
11	Ryne Sandberg	3.00
12	Bob Gibson	2.00
13	Matt Kemp	1.00
14	Jered Weaver	1.00
15	Johnny Bench	2.00
16	Magglio Ordonez	1.00
17	Carl Yastrzemski	2.50
18	Derek Jeter	5.00
19	Gil Meche	1.00
20	Hanley Ramirez	2.00
21	Edgar Martinez	1.00
22	Steve Carlton	1.00
23	C.C. Sabathia	2.00
24	Chase Utley	2.00
25	Francisco Cordero	1.00
26	Mark Ellis	1.00
27	Jeff Kent	1.00
28	Brian Fuentes	1.00
29	Johan Santana	2.00
30	Ichiro Suzuki	3.00
31	Ken Griffey Jr.	4.00
32	Steve Garvey	1.00
33	Rafael Furcal	1.00
34	Chipper Jones	3.00
35	Roberto Clemente	5.00
36	Rich Harden	1.00
37	Cy Young	2.00
38	Albert Pujols	5.00
39	Dontrelle Willis	1.00
40	Mark Teixeira	1.50
41	Daisuke Matsuzaka	3.00
42	Harmon Killebrew	2.50
43	Darryl Strawberry	1.00
44	Eric Chavez	1.00
45	Don Larsen	1.50
46	Huston Street	1.00
47	Albert Belle	1.00
48	Prince Fielder	2.00
49	Garret Anderson	1.00
50	Matt Holliday	1.50
51	Travis Buck	1.00
52	Ben Sheets	1.00
53	George Brett	3.00
54	Dmitri Young	1.00
55	Phil Rizzuto	2.00
56	Jimmy Rollins	2.00
57	Manny Ramirez	2.00
58	Ozzie Smith	3.00
59	Dale Murphy	1.50
60	Bobby Crosby	1.00
61	Trevor Hoffman	1.00
62	Chien-Ming Wang	2.50
63	Jose Reyes	2.00
64	Vladimir Guerrero	2.00
65	Vida Blue	1.00
66	Rod Carew	1.50
67	Aaron Rowand	1.00
68	Hong-Chih Kuo	1.00
69	Mike Schmidt	3.00
70	Rogers Hornsby	1.50
71	Alex Rodriguez	5.00
72	Roger Maris	2.50
73	Travis Hafner	1.00
74	Tom Glavine	1.50
75	Pat Burrell	1.50
76	Pedro Martinez	2.00
77	Joba Chamberlain	3.00
78	Jason Varitek	1.50
79	Hideo Nomo	1.00
80	Frank Thomas	2.00
81	Rollie Fingers	1.00
82	Carl Crawford	1.50

83 Bobby Jenks 1.00
84 Victor Martinez 1.00
85 Ernie Banks 2.50
86 Josh Beckett 1.50
87 Jose Valverde 1.00
88 Reggie Jackson 1.50
89 Duke Snider 1.50
90 Mike Lowell 1.00
91 Dom DiMaggio 1.00
92 Torii Hunter 1.00
93 Alfonso Soriano 2.00
94 Justin Morneau 1.50
95 Carlos Delgado 1.00
96 Ty Cobb 4.00
97 Andruw Jones 1.00
98 Yogi Berra 2.00
99 Joe DiMaggio 4.00
100 Willie Randolph 1.00
101 Miguel Cabrera 2.00
102 Grady Sizemore 2.00
103 Michael Young 1.00
104 Wade Boggs 1.50
105 Rich "Goose" Gossage 1.00
106 Robin Roberts 1.00
107 Brooks Robinson 1.50
108 Jim Palmer 1.50
109 Jorge Posada 1.50
110 Keith Hernandez 1.00
111 Ivan Rodriguez 1.50
112 Carlos Lee 1.50
113 John Lackey 1.50
114 Alex Rios 1.50
115 Carlton Fisk 1.50
116 Gary Matthews 1.00
117 Bill Martin 1.00
118 Paul Molitor 2.00
119 Hideki Matsui 2.00
120 Al Kaline 2.00
121 Takashi Saito 1.00
122 Stan Musial 3.00
123 Ryan Howard 3.00
124 Whitey Ford 2.00
125 John Smoltz 1.50
126 Roy Oswalt 1.50
127 Jim Thome 1.50
128 Tony Gwynn 2.50
129 Dennis Eckersley 1.00
130 Ted Williams 5.00
131 Justin Verlander 1.50
132 David Ortiz 3.00
133 Tom Gordon 1.00
134 Tom Seaver 1.50
135 Red Schoendienst 1.00
136 Johnny Podres 1.00
137 Paul Konerko 1.50
138 Robin Yount 2.50
139 Todd Helton 1.50
140 Frank Robinson 2.00
141 J.J. Putz 1.00
142 Jackie Robinson 3.00
143 Brandon Webb 1.50
144 Eddie Murray 2.00
145 Freddy Sanchez 1.00
146 Josh Anderson **(RC)** 20.00
147 Daric Barton **(RC)** 15.00
148 Steve Pearce **RC** 15.00
149 Chin-Lung Hu **(RC)** 35.00
150 Clay Buchholz **(RC)** 30.00
151 J.R. Towles **RC** 20.00
152 Brandon Jones **RC** 15.00
153 Lance Broadway **RC** 15.00
154 Nyjer Morgan **(RC)** 15.00
155 Ross Ohlendorf **RC** 15.00
156 Chris Seddon **(RC)** 10.00
157 Jonathan Albaladejo **RC** 15.00
158 Seth Smith **(RC)** 10.00
159 Kevin Hart **(RC)** 20.00
160 Bill White **RC** 15.00
161 Wladimir Balentien **(RC)** 15.00
162 Justin Ruggiano **RC** 15.00
163 Clint Sammons **(RC)** 15.00
164 Rich Thompson **(RC)** 15.00
165 David Davidson **RC** 10.00
166 Troy Patton **(RC)** 20.00
167 Joe Koshansky **(RC)** 15.00
168 Colt Morton **RC** 15.00
169 Armando Galarraga **RC** 30.00
170 Sam Fuld **RC** 15.00
171 Dustin Moseley 15.00
172 Tim Lincecum 60.00
173 Ryan Braun 60.00
174 Phil Hughes 25.00
175 Joba Chamberlain 75.00
176 Hunter Pence 25.00
177 Fausto Carmona 15.00
178 Ubaldo Jimenez 15.00
179 Cameron Maybin 20.00
180 Adam Jones 20.00
181 Brian Bannister 15.00
182 Jarrod Saltalamacchia 15.00
183 Alex Gordon 25.00
184 Russell Martin 20.00
185 John Maine 15.00
186 Hideki Okajima 25.00
187 Curtis Granderson 30.00
188 Delmon Young 15.00
189 Jo Jo Reyes 10.00
190 Yovani Gallardo 20.00
191 Ryan Zimmerman 20.00
192 Jeremy Guthrie 15.00
193 Dan Uggla 20.00
194 Andre Ethier 20.00
195 Chris Young 20.00
196 Elijah Dukes 15.00
197 Nick Markakis 25.00
198 Melky Cabrera 20.00
199 Cole Hamels 30.00
200 James Loney 15.00
201 Kevin Slowey 15.00
202 Carlos Marmol 25.00
203 Akinori Iwamura 20.00
204 Adrian Gonzalez 15.00
205 Brandon Phillips 20.00
206 J.J. Hardy 20.00
207 Tom Gorzelanny 10.00
208 Matt Cain 20.00
209 Matt Capps 10.00
210 Jeff Francis 15.00
211 Brian McCann 20.00
212 Matt Garza 20.00
213 Robinson Cano 25.00
214 Felix Hernandez 30.00
215 Yunel Escobar 15.00
216 Francisco Liriano 20.00
217 Rich Hill 10.00
218 Taylor Buchholz 10.00
219 Asdrubal Cabrera 15.00
220 Lastings Milledge 15.00
221 Honus Wagner 2.50
222 Walter Johnson 2.50
223 Thurman Munson 2.50
224 Roy Campanella 2.50
225 George Sisler 1.50
226 Pee Wee Reese 1.50
227 Johnny Mize 1.50
228 Jimmie Foxx 2.50
229 Tris Speaker 1.50
230 Christy Mathewson 2.50
231 Mel Ott 2.00
232 Ralph Kiner 1.00
233 Joey Votto **RC** 1.50
234 Hiroki Kuroda **RC** 1.50
235 John Bowker **(RC)** 1.00
236 Lance Berkman 1.50
237 Aaron Harang 1.00
238 B.J. Upton 1.50
239 Zack Greinke 1.00
240 Cal Ripken Jr. 6.00
241 Justin Upton 1.00
242 Roy Halladay 1.50
243 Orlando Hudson 1.00
244 Scott Kazmir 1.00
245 Matt Kemp 1.50
246 Mark Buehrle 1.00
247 Adam Dunn 1.50
248 Erik Bedard 1.00
249 Carlos Zambrano 1.50
250 Jeff Francoeur 1.00
251 Brad Penny 1.00

Emerald

Emerald (1-145, 221-251): 1-1.5X
Production 240
Emerald Auto. (146-220): 1X
Auto Production 50

Gold

Gold (1-145, 221-251): 2-3X
Production 99
Gold Auto. (146-220): 1-1.5X
Auto Production 25

Sapphire

Sapphire: (1-145, 221-251): 4-8X
Production 25
Sapphire Auto. (146-220): No Pricing
Auto Production 10

Sepia

Sepia (1-145, 221-251): .75-1X
Production 525
Sepia Auto. (146-220): 1X
Auto Production 75

Printing Plates

Production one set per color.

Auto. RC Relic Pairs

NM/M

Common Duo: 20.00
Production 50 Sets
Gold: 1-1.25X
Production 25 Sets
Sapphire: No Pricing
Production 10 Sets
Platinum: No Pricing
Production One Set
1 Steve Pearce, Nyjer Morgan 30.00
2 Cameron Maybin, Curtis Granderson 40.00
3 Melky Cabrera, Robinson Cano 40.00
4 Lastings Milledge, Elijah Dukes 20.00
5 Rich Hill, Sam Fuld 25.00
6 J.R. Towles, Jarrod Saltalamacchia 20.00
7 Clay Buchholz, Fausto Carmona 30.00
8 Ryan Braun, Ryan Zimmerman 50.00
9 Phil Hughes, Joba Chamberlain 80.00
10 Brandon Phillips, Homer Bailey 25.00

Triple Th. Auto. Relic Pairs

NM/M

Production 18 Sets
Gold: No Pricing
Production 9 Sets
Sapphire: No Pricing
Production 3 Sets
Platinum: No Pricing
Production One Set
1 Ryan Howard, David Wright 100.00
2 Manny Ramirez, David Ortiz 100.00
3 Frank Thomas, Jim Thome 80.00
4 Eddie Murray, Mike Schmidt 80.00
5 Paul Molitor, Prince Fielder 80.00
6 Jimmy Rollins, Ryan Howard 100.00
7 C.C. Sabathia, Johan Santana 80.00
8 Travis Hafner, Fausto Carmona 40.00
9 Robin Yount, Ozzie Smith 100.00
10 Whitey Ford, Yogi Berra 150.00

T.T. Auto Relic Double Combos

Production 3 Sets
No Pricing

Presidential Cut Above

1 Set
No Pricing

T.T. "Cut Above" Relics

Production One Set
No Pricing

Triple Threads Auto Relics

NM/M

Production 18 Sets
Gold: No Pricing
Production 9 Sets
Sapphire: No Pricing
Production 3 Sets
Platinum: No Pricing
Production One Set
1-3 Prince Fielder 60.00
4-6 Vladimir Guerrero 75.00
7-9 Bob Gibson 50.00
10-12 Chien-Ming Wang 180.00
13-15 Johnny Podres 50.00
16-18 Frank Robinson 50.00
19-21 Robin Yount 60.00
22-24 David Ortiz 75.00
25-27 Chipper Jones 80.00
28-30 Cal Ripken Jr. 200.00
31-33 Carlton Fisk 50.00
34-36 Jason Varitek 50.00
37-39 Ernie Banks 80.00
40-42 Harmon Killebrew 75.00
43-45 Travis Hafner 40.00
46-48 Manny Ramirez 75.00
49-51 Tony Gwynn 75.00
52-54 Alfonso Soriano 50.00
55-57 Carl Yastrzemski 100.00
58-60 Jim Palmer 50.00
61-63 Jimmy Rollins 60.00
64-66 Frank Thomas 75.00
67-69 Brooks Robinson 75.00
70-72 Dom DiMaggio 50.00
73-75 George Kell 40.00
76-78 Wade Boggs 60.00
79-81 Johan Santana 60.00
82-84 Jose Reyes 80.00
85-87 Hanley Ramirez 50.00
88-90 Johnny Bench 75.00
91-93 Mike Lowell 50.00
94-96 Tom Seaver 60.00
97-99 John Smoltz 70.00
100-102 Ozzie Smith 75.00
103-105 Duke Snider 60.00
106-108 Steve Carlton 40.00
109-111 Jorge Posada 50.00
112-114 Andruw Jones 30.00
115-117 Reggie Jackson 75.00
118-120 C.C. Sabathia 50.00
121-123 Jim Thome 50.00
124-126 Mike Schmidt 75.00
127-129 Yogi Berra 100.00
130-132 Dontrelle Willis 35.00
133-135 Nolan Ryan 120.00
136-138 Rich "Goose" Gossage 40.00
139-141 Al Kaline 75.00
142-144 David Wright 100.00
145-147 Miguel Cabrera 50.00
148-150 Ryne Sandberg 100.00
151-153 Tom Glavine 70.00
154-156 Paul Molitor 50.00
157-159 Eddie Murray 60.00
160-162 Justin Verlander 40.00
163-165 Dale Murphy 60.00
166-168 Whitey Ford 75.00
169-171 Matt Holliday 40.00
172-174 Albert Pujols 250.00
175-177 Stan Musial 100.00
178-180 Ryan Howard 80.00
181-183 Johnny Cueto 30.00
184-186 Evan Longoria 180.00

T.T. Auto Relic Combos

NM/M

Production 36 Sets
Emerald: No Pricing
Production 18 Sets
Gold: No Pricing
Production 9 Sets
Sepia: 1X
Production 27 Sets
Sapphire: No Pricing
Production 3 Sets
Platinum: No Pricing
Production One Set
1 Jose Reyes, Ozzie Smith, Hanley Ramirez 80.00
2 Albert Pujols, Manny Ramirez, Vladimir Guerrero 200.00
3 Keith Hernandez, Mike Schmidt, Dale Murphy 100.00
4 Frank Robinson, Carl Yastrzemski, Harmon Killebrew 180.00
5 Bob Gibson, Tom Seaver, Steve Carlton 90.00
6 Harmon Killebrew, Rod Carew, Brooks Robinson 150.00
7 David Wright, Ryan Howard, Albert Pujols 200.00
8 Prince Fielder, Eddie Murray, Ryan Howard 100.00
9 Nolan Ryan, George Brett, Robin Yount 180.00
10 Johnny Bench, Ivan Rodriguez, Carlton Fisk 80.00
11 Yogi Berra, Whitey Ford, Jorge Posada 150.00
12 Tony Gwynn, Dale Murphy, Darryl Strawberry 90.00
13 Mike Lowell, Manny Ramirez, David Ortiz 120.00
14 Joba Chamberlain, Jorge Posada, Chien-Ming Wang 160.00
15 Jeff Francis, Taylor Buchholz, Ubaldo Jimenez 25.00
16 Melky Cabrera, Ross Ohlendorf, Robinson Cano 40.00
17 Dan Uggla, Chris Seddon, Hanley Ramirez 30.00
18 Alex Gordon, Evan Longoria, Ryan Zimmerman 60.00
19 Chris Young, Lastings Milledge, Melky Cabrera 25.00
20 Rich Hill, Johnny Cueto, Tom Gorzelanny 25.00
21 Dustin Moseley, Francisco Liriano, Felix Hernandez 35.00
22 Hanley Ramirez, James Loney, J.J. Hardy 40.00
23 Armando Galarraga, Fausto Carmona, Troy Patton 30.00

Triple Threads XXIV Relics

No Pricing
Production 18 Sets
Gold: No Pricing
Production 9 Sets
Sapphire: No Pricing
Production 3 Sets
Platinum: No Pricing
Production One Set

Triple Threads Jumbo Plus Relics

Production 3 Sets
Platinum: No Pricing
Production One Set
No Pricing

Triple Threads Letter Plus Relics

Production 3 Sets
Platinum: No Pricing
Production One Set
No Pricing

Tr. Threads All-Star Patches

Production 9 Sets
No Pricing

T.T. All-Star Logo Man

1 of 1
No Pricing

Triple Threads Bat Barrels

Production One Set
No Pricing

Triple Threads Relics

NM/M

Production 36 Sets
Emerald: 1-1.2X
Production 18 Sets
Gold: No Pricing
Production 9 Sets
Sapphire: No Pricing
Production 3 Sets
Sepia: 1X
Production 27 Sets
Platinum: No Pricing
Production One Set
1-3 David Wright 30.00
4-6 Alex Rodriguez 40.00
7-9 Mickey Mantle 140.00
10-12 Duke Snider 25.00
13-15 Carlton Fisk 25.00
16-18 Ichiro Suzuki 50.00
19-21 Wade Boggs 25.00
22-24 Chien-Ming Wang 30.00
25-27 Alfonso Soriano 20.00
28-30 Ernie Banks 30.00

31-33	Jimmy Rollins	20.00
34-36	Bob Gibson	30.00
37-39	Brooks Robinson	30.00
40-42	Joe DiMaggio	80.00
43-45	Hideo Nomo	40.00
46-48	Ted Williams	75.00
49-51	David Ortiz	25.00
52-54	Frank Robinson	20.00
55-57	Tony Gwynn	25.00
58-60	Jose Reyes	25.00
61-63	Roger Maris	75.00
64-66	Mike Schmidt	30.00
67-69	Eddie Murray	20.00
70-72	Johnny Bench	25.00
73-75	Roberto Clemente	80.00
76-78	Steve Carlton	15.00
79-81	Grady Sizemore	25.00
82-84	Robin Yount	25.00
85-87	Hanley Ramirez	20.00
88-90	Al Kaline	25.00
91-93	Vladimir Guerrero	25.00
94-96	George Kell	25.00
97-99	Reggie Jackson	25.00
100-102	Tom Seaver	25.00
103-105	Johan Santana	20.00
106-108	Jason Varitek	20.00
109-111	Ryan Howard	25.00
112-114	Manny Ramirez	20.00
115-117	Miguel Cabrera	20.00
118-120	Jorge Posada	20.00
121-123	Nolan Ryan	40.00
124-126	Paul Molitor	15.00
127-129	Chipper Jones	25.00
130-132	Carl Yastrzemski	30.00
133-135	Whitey Ford	30.00
136-138	Yogi Berra	50.00
139-141	Albert Pujols	40.00
142-144	Jim Palmer	15.00
145-147	Harmon Killebrew	40.00
148-150	Ozzie Smith	25.00
151-153	Stan Musial	35.00
154-156	Ryne Sandberg	30.00
157-159	Matt Holliday	20.00
160-162	Carlos Beltran	15.00
163-165	Prince Fielder	20.00
166-168	Ivan Rodriguez	15.00
169-171	Victor Martinez	15.00
172-174	Justin Verlander	20.00
175-177	Reggie Jackson	25.00
178-180	Alfonso Soriano	20.00
181-183	Prince Fielder	20.00
184-186	Ichiro Suzuki	50.00
187-189	David Wright	30.00
190-192	Eddie Murray	20.00
193-195	Manny Ramirez	20.00
196-198	Mike Schmidt	30.00
199-201	Johnny Bench	25.00
202-204	Matt Holliday	20.00
205-207	Alex Rodriguez	40.00
208-210	Jose Reyes	25.00
211-213	Jimmy Rollins	20.00
214-216	David Ortiz	25.00
217-219	Robin Yount	25.00
220-222	Nolan Ryan	40.00
223-225	Ryan Howard	25.00
226	John F. Kennedy	200.00
227	Ty Cobb	150.00
228	Jimmie Foxx	75.00
229	Rogers Hornsby	75.00
230	George Sisler	75.00
231	Mel Ott	80.00
232	Jackie Robinson	120.00
233	Tris Speaker	80.00
234	Honus Wagner	250.00
235	Lou Gehrig	125.00
236	Pee Wee Reese	30.00
237	Roy Campanella	60.00
238	Johnny Mize	30.00
239	Thurman Munson	60.00
240	Babe Ruth	350.00

Triple Threads Relics Combos

NM/M

Production 36 Sets
Emerald: 1-1.25X
Production 18 Sets
Gold: No Pricing
Production 9 Sets
Sepia: 1-1.2X
Production 27 Sets
Sapphire: No Pricing
Production 3 Sets
Platinum: No Pricing
Production One Set

1 Alex Rodriguez, David Wright, Ryan Howard 50.00
2 Mickey Mantle, Ted Williams, Joe DiMaggio 180.00
3 Ted Williams, Carl Yastrzemski, Manny Ramirez 50.00
4 Magglio Ordonez, Ichiro Suzuki, Placido Polanco 35.00
5 Alex Rodriguez, Prince Fielder, Ryan Howard 40.00
6 Alex Rodriguez, Matt Holliday, Magglio Ordonez 30.00
7 Jose Reyes, Juan Pierre, Hanley Ramirez 30.00
8 Chien-Ming Wang, Alex Rodriguez, Mariano Rivera 40.00
9 Jake Peavy, Scott Kazmir, Johan Santana 25.00
10 Joe DiMaggio, Roberto Clemente, Mickey Mantle 180.00
11 Mark Buehrle, Justin Verlander, Clay Buchholz 20.00
12 Magglio Ordonez, Al Kaline, Curtis Granderson 35.00
13 Russell Martin, Andruw Jones, Rafael Furcal 20.00
14 Jason Varitek, Jorge Posada, Ivan Rodriguez 20.00
15 Yogi Berra, Mickey Mantle, Roger Maris 125.00
16 Gary Matthews, Vladimir Guerrero, Torii Hunter 15.00
17 Troy Tulowitzki, Matt Holliday, Todd Helton 25.00
18 Roberto Clemente, Carl Yastrzemski, Reggie Jackson 75.00
19 Ernie Banks, Alfonso Soriano, Ryne Sandberg 50.00
20 Mickey Mantle, Albert Pujols, Roberto Clemente 150.00
21 Lance Berkman, Carlos Lee, Hunter Pence 20.00
22 Alex Gordon, Ryan Braun, Ryan Zimmerman 25.00
23 Mickey Mantle, Alex Rodriguez, Ted Williams 150.00
24 Justin Morneau, Harmon Killebrew, Joe Mauer 40.00
25 Trevor Hoffman, Dennis Eckersley, Mariano Rivera 30.00
26 Jose Reyes, David Wright, John Maine 35.00
27 Daisuke Matsuzaka, Ichiro Suzuki, Hideki Matsui 85.00
28 Stan Musial, Albert Pujols, Rogers Hornsby 85.00
29 Vince DiMaggio, Joe DiMaggio, Dom DiMaggio 90.00
30 Mike Schmidt, George Brett, Steve Carlton 35.00
31 Nick Markakis, Brooks Robinson, Brian Roberts 35.00
32 Prince Fielder, Paul Molitor, Ryan Braun 30.00
33 Tim Lincecum, Joba Chamberlain, Brian Bannister 35.00
34 Prince Fielder, Ryan Howard, Andruw Jones 25.00
35 Alex Rodriguez, David Ortiz, Manny Ramirez 40.00
36 Jim Palmer, Pedro Martinez, Tom Seaver 35.00
37 Ichiro Suzuki, Todd Helton, Albert Pujols 40.00
38 Pedro Martinez, Roy Oswalt, Greg Maddux 35.00
39 Yogi Berra, Joe DiMaggio, Phil Rizzuto 125.00
40 Ernie Banks, Roberto Clemente, Carl Yastrzemski 60.00
41 Justin Morneau, Ryan Howard, Prince Fielder 30.00
42 Alex Gordon, George Brett, Brian Bannister 25.00
43 Ryan Howard, Albert Pujols, Manny Ramirez 40.00
44 Alex Rodriguez, Vladimir Guerrero, Prince Fielder 35.00
45 Randy Johnson, Nolan Ryan, Hideo Nomo 40.00
46 Rollie Fingers, Reggie Jackson, Vida Blue 25.00
47 Roberto Clemente, Ichiro Suzuki, Mickey Mantle 150.00
48 Brooks Robinson, Jim Palmer, Frank Robinson 30.00
49 Reggie Jackson, Steve Garvey, Willie Randolph 50.00
50 David Ortiz, Ted Williams, Manny Ramirez 50.00
51 Mickey Mantle, Alex Rodriguez, Joe DiMaggio 175.00
52 Duke Snider, Russell Martin, Steve Garvey 50.00
53 Ichiro Suzuki, Alfonso Soriano, Carlos Beltran 35.00
54 Chase Utley, Dan Uggla, Dustin Pedroia 35.00
55 Jose Reyes, Jimmy Rollins, Hanley Ramirez 30.00
56 Jimmy Rollins, Joe DiMaggio, Chase Utley 80.00
57 Johnny Bench, Ivan Rodriguez, Carlton Fisk 35.00
58 Pedro Martinez, Nolan Ryan, Johan Santana 40.00
59 Jose Reyes, Ozzie Smith, Jimmy Rollins 30.00
60 Jimmy Rollins, Jake Peavy, Ryan Braun 35.00
61 Alex Rodriguez, C.C. Sabathia, Dustin Pedroia 40.00
62 Delmon Young, Alex Rodriguez, Justin Upton 40.00
63 Alex Rodriguez, Frank Thomas, Jim Thome 40.00
64 Roger Maris, Mickey Mantle, Harmon Killebrew 125.00
65 Carlos Beltran, Chipper Jones, Jose Reyes 30.00
66 Jimmy Rollins, Matt Holliday, Prince Fielder 25.00
67 Alex Rodriguez, Magglio Ordonez, Vladimir Guerrero 30.00
68 Jake Peavy, Brandon Webb, Brad Penny 20.00
69 C.C. Sabathia, Josh Beckett, John Lackey 25.00
70 Ryan Braun, Troy Tulowitzki, Hunter Pence 25.00
71 Dustin Pedroia, Delmon Young, Brian Bannister 20.00
72 Victor Martinez, Grady Sizemore, Travis Hafner 25.00
73 Magglio Ordonez, Ichiro Suzuki, Vladimir Guerrero 35.00
74 Dan Uggla, Hanley Ramirez, Cameron Maybin 20.00
75 Ichiro Suzuki, Daisuke Matsuzaka, Akinori Iwamura 50.00
76 Jason Varitek, Alex Rodriguez, Chase Utley 25.00
77 Tris Speaker, Manny Ramirez, Travis Hafner 20.00
78 Eddie Mathews, Chipper Jones, Dale Murphy 50.00
79 Mike Schmidt, Ryan Howard, Richie Ashburn 50.00
80 Jimmy Rollins, Ryan Howard, Chase Utley 35.00
81 Matt Holliday, Carlos Beltran, Carlos Lee 20.00
82 Vladimir Guerrero, Magglio Ordonez, Ichiro Suzuki 30.00
83 Andruw Jones, Jeff Francoeur, Aaron Rowand, Carlos Beltran
84 Grady Sizemore, Ichiro Suzuki, Torii Hunter 35.00
85 Stan Musial, Carl Yastrzemski, Ted Williams 75.00
86 Alex Rodriguez 30.00
87 Chipper Jones, Brian McCann, Jeff Francoeur 35.00
88 Nolan Ryan 40.00
89 David Ortiz, Paul Molitor, Edgar Martinez 20.00
90 Alex Rodriguez, Albert Pujols, Manny Ramirez 40.00
91 Randy Johnson, Luis Gonzalez, Mariano Rivera 40.00
92 Rich "Goose" Gossage, George Brett, Billy Martin 40.00
93 Fausto Carmona, Joba Chamberlain, Grady Sizemore 30.00
94 Brian Giles, Matt Holliday, Michael Barrett 15.00
95 Franklin D. Roosevelt, Harry S. Truman, John F. Kennedy 75.00
96 George H.W. Bush, George W. Bush, Ronald Reagan 60.00
97 William Taft, Woodrow Wilson, Warren G. Harding 50.00
98 Johnny Damon, Chipper Jones, Matt Holliday 25.00
99 David Ortiz, Jose Reyes, Alfonso Soriano 25.00
100 Adrian Beltre, Albert Pujols, Placido Polanco 25.00
101 Joe DiMaggio, Mickey Mantle, Lou Gehrig 180.00
102 Ty Cobb, Babe Ruth, Honus Wagner 300.00
103 Roy Campanella, Thurman Munson, Johnny Bench 50.00
104 Pee Wee Reese, Jackie Robinson, Roy Campanella 120.00
105 Roberto Clemente, Ralph Kiner, Honus Wagner 175.00
106 Johnny Mize, Mel Ott, Rogers Hornsby 75.00
107 Reggie Jackson, Thurman Munson, Billy Martin 50.00
108 Jimmie Foxx, Lou Gehrig, Mel Ott 150.00
109 Roger Maris, Babe Ruth, Mickey Mantle 275.00
110 Honus Wagner, Ty Cobb, Tris Speaker 250.00
111 Jimmie Foxx, Ted Williams, Manny Ramirez 75.00

Triple Threads Relic Double Combos

NM/M

Production 36 Sets
Sepia: 1X
Production 27 Sets
Emerald: No Pricing
Production 18 Sets
Gold: No Pricing
Production 9 Sets
Sapphire: No Pricing
Production 3 Sets
Platinum: No Pricing
Production One Set

1 Joe DiMaggio, Mickey Mantle, Roger Maris, Roberto Clemente, Ted Williams, Tris Speaker 200.00
2 Ty Cobb, Rogers Hornsby, Joe DiMaggio, Ted Williams, Tony Gwynn, Ichiro Suzuki 200.00
3 Troy Tulowitzki, Chipper Jones, Kelly Johnson, Edgar Renteria 50.00
4 Albert Pujols, Bob Gibson, Rogers Hornsby, Stan Musial, Ozzie Smith, Red Schoendienst 100.00
5 Ryan Howard, Albert Pujols, Prince Fielder, Vladimir Guerrero, Alex Rodriguez, David Ortiz 65.00
6 Tom Seaver, Nolan Ryan, Steve Carlton, Dennis Eckersley, Jim Palmer, Whitey Ford 80.00
7 Jose Reyes, Hanley Ramirez, Jimmy Rollins, Carl Crawford, Brian Roberts, Ichiro Suzuki 50.00
8 Russell Martin, Brian McCann, Jorge Posada, Mike Piazza, Carlton Fisk, Yogi Berra 40.00
9 Joe DiMaggio, Mickey Mantle 180.00
10 Joe DiMaggio, Mickey Mantle, Roger Maris, Billy Martin, Phil Rizzuto, Whitey Ford 180.00
11 Frank Robinson, Carl Yastrzemski, Roberto Clemente, Mickey Mantle, Ted Williams, Harmon Killebrew 160.00
12 Roy Oswalt, Peter Munro, Kirk Saarloos, Brad Lidge, Octavio Dotel, Billy Wagner 30.00
13 Mickey Mantle, Joe DiMaggio, Ted Williams, David Wright, Ryan Howard, Alex Rodriguez 160.00
14 Alex Rodriguez, Hideki Matsui, Jorge Posada, Johnny Damon, Chien-Ming Wang, Joba Chamberlain 75.00
15 Akinori Iwamura, Hideki Matsui, Hideki Okajima, Kazuo Matsui, Ichiro Suzuki, Kenji Johjima 80.00
16 Russell Martin, Jason Bay, Erik Bedard, Rich Harden, Justin Morneau, Shawn Hill 40.00
17 Carlos Beltran, David Wright, Carlos Delgado, Jose Reyes, Pedro Martinez, John Maine 50.00
18 Travis Hafner, Victor Martinez, Grady Sizemore, C.C. Sabathia, Fausto Carmona, Bob Feller 40.00
19 Brooks Robinson, Jim Palmer, Eddie Murray, Brian Roberts, Nick Markakis, Melvin Mora 40.00
20 David Ortiz, Jason Varitek, Josh Beckett, Manny Ramirez, Mike Lowell, Hideki Okajima 75.00
21 Jose Vidro, Alex Rodriguez, Ichiro Suzuki, J.J. Putz, Edgar Martinez, Kenji Johjima 60.00
22 Alex Rodriguez, C.C. Sabathia, Dustin Pedroia, Jimmy Rollins, Jake Peavy, Ryan Braun 50.00
23 Mickey Mantle 200.00
24 Joe DiMaggio 100.00
25 Roberto Clemente 100.00
26 Carlos Lee, Roy Oswalt, Lance Berkman, Hunter Pence, Nolan Ryan, Kazuo Matsui 40.00
27 Jimmy Rollins, Mike Schmidt, Chase Utley, Cole Hamels, Robin Roberts, Ryan Howard 50.00
28 Johnny Podres, Whitey Ford, Brooks Robinson, Ernie Banks, Duke Snider, Bob Gibson 40.00
29 Ted Williams 80.00
30 Justin Morneau, Rod Carew, Francisco Liriano, Joe Mauer, Delmon Young, Harmon Killebrew 75.00
31 Justin Morneau, Ryan Howard, Albert Pujols, Prince Fielder, Carlos Delgado, Mark Teixeira 50.00

32	Magglio Ordonez, Al Kaline, Ivan Rodriguez, Curtis Granderson, Ty Cobb, Gary Sheffield	90.00
33	Carlton Fisk, Jim Thome, Jermaine Dye, Mark Buehrle, Paul Konerko, Luis Aparicio	40.00
34	Keith Hernandez, Dwight Gooden, Darryl Strawberry, David Wright, Pedro Martinez, Jose Reyes	40.00
35	Chipper Jones, John Smoltz, Brian McCann, Jeff Francoeur, Mark Teixeira, Tom Glavine	40.00
36	David Ortiz, Manny Ramirez, Jason Varitek, Alex Rodriguez, Jorge Posada, Johnny Damon	75.00
37	Roger Maris, Mickey Mantle	220.00
38	Ichiro Suzuki	60.00
39	Albert Pujols	50.00
40	Robin Yount, Paul Molitor, Rollie Fingers, Prince Fielder, Ryan Braun, Ben Sheets	50.00
41	Nolan Ryan, Alex Rodriguez, Ivan Rodriguez, Ian Kinsler, Michael Young, Hank Blalock	50.00
42	Vladimir Guerrero, John Lackey, Jered Weaver, Garret Anderson, Torii Hunter, Gary Matthews	35.00
43	Tim Lincecum, Rich Aurilia, Barry Zito, Eric Chavez, Mark Ellis, Bobby Crosby	35.00
44	Russell Martin, Rafael Furcal, Andruw Jones, Matt Kemp, Jeff Kent, Hong-Chih Kuo	40.00
45	David Wright, Carlos Beltran, Jose Reyes, Ryan Howard, Jimmy Rollins, Chase Utley	50.00
46	Chien-Ming Wang	60.00
47	Ichiro Suzuki, Alex Rodriguez, David Ortiz, Magglio Ordonez, Ivan Rodriguez, Vladimir Guerrero	50.00
48	Manny Ramirez, David Ortiz, Mike Lowell, Travis Hafner, Victor Martinez, Grady Sizemore	50.00
49	Matt Holliday, Todd Helton, Troy Tulowitzki, Orlando Hudson, Stephen Drew, Chris Young	35.00
50	Manny Ramirez, David Ortiz, Mike Lowell, Matt Holliday, Todd Helton, Troy Tulowitzki	50.00
51	Alex Rodriguez, Mickey Mantle	75.00
52	Albert Pujols, Vladimir Guerrero, Manny Ramirez, David Ortiz, Pedro Martinez, Alfonso Soriano	50.00
53	Joe DiMaggio, Ty Cobb, Babe Ruth, Lou Gehrig, Ted Williams, Mickey Mantle	500.00
54	George Sisler, Johnny Mize, Rogers Hornsby, Jimmie Foxx, Mel Ott, Pee Wee Reese	160.00
55	Jackie Robinson, Duke Snider, Roy Campanella, Phil Rizzuto, Mickey Mantle, Yogi Berra	160.00

2008 Topps Update

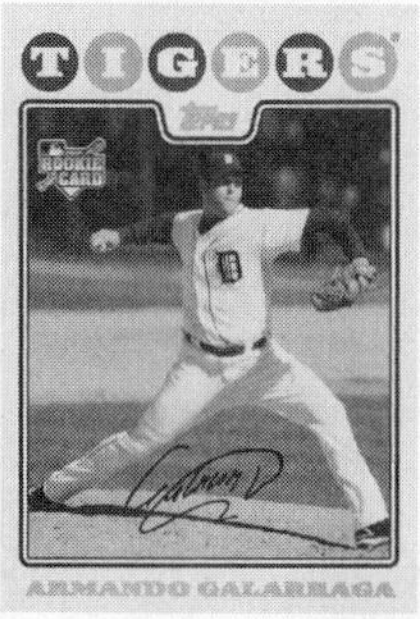

	NM/M
Complete Set (330):	40.00
Common player:	.15
Hobby Pack (10):	2.00
Hobby Box (36):	60.00

1	Kosuke Fukudome **RC**	3.00
1	Kosuke Fukudome Upside down image	40.00
2	Sean Casey	.15
3	Freddie Bynum	.15
4	Brent Lillibridge **(RC)**	.25
5	Chipper Jones	.75
6	Yamid Haad	.15
7	Josh Anderson	.15
8	Jeff Mathis	.15
9	Shawn Riggans	.15
10	Evan Longoria **RC**	5.00
10	Evan Longoria upside down image	75.00
11	Matt Holliday	.40
12	Trot Nixon	.15
13	Geoff Blum	.15
14	Bartolo Colon	.15
15	Kevin Cash	.15
16	Paul Janish **(RC)**	.25
17	Russell Martin	.25
18	Andy Phillips	.15
19	Johnny Estrada	.15
20	Justin Masterson **RC**	2.50
21	Darrell Rasner	.15
22	Brian Moehler	.15
23	Cristian Guzman	.15
24	Tony Armas Jr.	.15
25	Lance Berkman	.40
26	Chris Iannetta	.15
27	Reid Brignac	.25
28	Miguel Tejada	.25
29	Ryan Ludwick	.25
30	Brendan Harris	.15
31	Marco Scutaro	.15
32	Cody Ross	.15
33	Carlos Marmol	.15
34	Nate McLouth	.25
35	Hanley Ramirez	.75
36	Xavier Nady	.15
37	Connor Robertson	.15
38	Carlos Villanueva	.15
39	Jose Molina	.15
40	Jon Rauch	.15
41	Joe Mauer	.40
42	Chip Ambres	.15
43	Jason Bartlett	.15
44	Ryan Sweeney	.15
45	Eric Hurley **(RC)**	.50
46	Kevin Youkilis	.25
47	Dustin Pedroia	.50
48	Grant Balfour	.15
49	Ryan Ludwick	.25
50	Matt Garza	.15
51	Fernando Tatis	.15
52	Derek Jeter	1.50
53	Justin Duchscherer	.15
54	Matt Ginter	.15
55	Cesar Izturis	.15
56	Roy Halladay	.25
57	Ramon Castro	.15
58	Scott Kazmir	.25
59	Cliff Lee	.25
60	Jim Edmonds	.25
61	Randy Wolf	.15
62	Matt Albers	.15
63	Eric Bruntlett	.15
64	Joe Nathan	.15
65	Alex Rodriguez	1.00
66	Robinson Cancel	.15
67	Jamey Carroll	.15
68	Jonathan Papelbon	.40
69	Chad Moeller	.15
70	George Sherrill	.15
71	Mariano Rivera	.40
72	Peter Orr	.15
73	Jonathan Albaladejo	.15
74	Corey Patterson	.15
75	Matt Treanor	.15
76	Francisco Rodriguez	.15
77	Ervin Santana	.15
78	Dallas Braden	.15
79	Willie Harris	.15
80	Erik Bedard	.15
81	J.C. Romero	.15
82	Joe Saunders	.15
83	George Sherrill	.15
84	Julian Tavarez	.15
85	Chad Gaudin	.15
86	David Aardsma	.15
87	Ryan Langerhans	.15
88	Dan Haren, Russ Martin	.25
89	Joakim Soria	.15
90	Dan Haren	.25
91	Billy Buckner	.15
92	Eric Hinske	.15
93	Chris Coste	.15
94	Edinson Volquez, Russ Martin	.25
95	Ichiro Suzuki	1.00
96	Vladimir Nunez	.15
97	Sean Gallagher	.15
98	Denny Bautista	.15
99	Hanley Ramirez, David Ortiz	.50
100	Jay Bruce **(RC)**	3.00
100	Jay Bruce upside down image	50.00
101	Dioner Navarro	.15
102	Matt Murton	.15
103	Chris Burke	.15
104	Omar Infante	.15
105	Daniel Giese **(RC)**	.25
106	Carlos Guillen, Josh Hamilton	.25
107	Jason Varitek	.25
108	Shin-Soo Choo	.15
109	Alberto Callaspo	.15
110	Jose Valverde	.15
111	Brandon Boggs **(RC)**	.25
112	Josh Hamilton, J.D. Drew	.25
113	Justin Morneau	.25
114	Billy Traber	.15
115	Mike Lamb	.15
116	Odalis Perez	.15
117	Jed Lowrie **(RC)**	1.00
118	Justin Morneau, David Ortiz	.50
119	Ken Griffey Jr.	1.00
120	Angel Berroa	.15
121	Jacque Jones	.15
122	Dewayne Wise	.15
123	Matt Joyce **RC**	.75
124	Alex Rodriguez, Evan Longoria	1.50
125	John Smoltz	.40
126	Morgan Ensberg	.15
127	Michael Young, Derek Jeter	1.00
128	LaTroy Hawkins	.15
129	Nick Adenhart **(RC)**	.75
130	Mike Cameron	.15
131	Manny Ramirez	.75
132	Jorge De La Rosa	.15
133	Tadahito Iguchi	.15
134	Joey Devine	.15
135	Jose Arredondo **RC**	.50
136	Hanley Ramirez, Albert Pujols	1.00
137	Evan Longoria	3.00
138	T.J. Beam	.15
139	Jon Lieber	.15
140	Dana Eveland	.15
141	Michael Aubrey **RC**	.75
142	Adrian Gonzalez, Matt Holliday	.25
143	Chipper Jones	.50
144	Robinson Tejeda	.15
145	Kip Wells	.15
146	Carlos Gonzalez **(RC)**	.50
147	Josh Banks **(RC)**	.25
148	David Wright	.75
149	Paul Hoover	.15
150	Jon Lester	.50
151	Darin Erstad	.15
152	Steve Trachsel	.15
153	Armando Galarraga **RC**	1.00
154	Grady Sizemore	.50
155	Jay Bruce	1.00
156	Juan Rincon	.15
157	Mark Hendrickson	.15
158	Chad Durbin	.15
159	Mike Aviles **RC**	1.00
160	Orlando Cabrera	.25
161	Asdrubal Cabrera	.15
162	Eric Stults	.15
163	Miguel Cairo	.15
164	Jason LaRue	.15
165	Burke Badenhop **RC**	.25
166	Ryan Braun	.50
167	Justin Morneau	.25
168	Benjamin Zobrist	.15
169	Eulogio de la Cruz	.15
170	Greg Smith **(RC)**	.25
171	Brian Bixler **(RC)**	.25
172	Evan Longoria	2.00
173	Randy Johnson	.50
174	D.J. Carrasco	.15
175	Luis Vizcaino	.15
176	Brad Wilkerson	.15
177	Emmanuel Burriss **RC**	.25
178	Lance Berkman	.25
179	Johnny Damon	.25
180	Scott Rolen	.25
181	Runelvys Hernandez	.15
182	Sidney Ponson	.15
183	Greg Reynolds **RC**	.25
184	Chase Utley	.50
185	Joey Votto	.50
186	Wes Littleton	.15
187	Rod Barajas	.15
188	Ray Durham	.15
189	Micah Hoffpauir **RC**	1.00
190	Manny Ramirez	.50
191	Ian Kinsler	.25
192	Craig Hansen	.15
193	Jeremy Affeldt	.15
194	Gary Bennett	.15
195	Chris Carter **(RC)**	.25
196	Dan Uggla	.25
197	Michael Young	.25
198	Andy LaRoche	.15
199	Lance Cormier	.15
200	Luke Scott	.15
201	Travis Denker **RC**	.50
202	Josh Hamilton	.75
203	Joe Crede	.15
204	Franquelis Osoria	.15
205	Octavio Dotel	.15
206	Russell Branyan	.15
207	Alberto Gonzalez **RC**	.50
208	Kerry Wood	.15
209	Carlos Guillen	.15
210	Joe Saunders	.15
211	Brett Tomko	.15
212	Guillermo Mota	.15
213	German Duran **RC**	.25
214	Carlos Zambrano	.25
215	Josh Hamilton	.50
216	Jason Bay	.25
217	Willy Aybar	.15
218	Salomon Torres	.15
219	Damaso Marte	.15
220	Geoff Jenkins	.15
221	J.D. Drew	.25
222	Dave Borkowski	.15
223	Jeff Ridgway	.15
224	Angel Pagan	.15
225	Ryan Tucker **(RC)**	.25
226	Brian McCann	.25
227	Carlos Quentin	.25
228	Joe Blanton	.15
229	Adrian Gonzalez	.25
230	Jason Jennings	.15
231	Chris Davis **RC**	1.00
232	Geovany Soto	.50
233	Grady Sizemore	.50
234	Carl Pavano	.15
235	Eddie Guardado	.15
236	Chris Snelling	.15
237	Manny Ramirez	.50
238	Dan Uggla	.25
239	Milton Bradley	.15
240	Clayton Kershaw **RC**	1.00
241	Chase Utley	.50
242	Raul Chavez	.15
243	Joe Mather	.15
244	Brandon Webb	.25
245	Ryan Braun	.75
246	Kelvin Jimenez	.15
247	Scott Podsednik	.15
248	Doug Mientkiewicz	.15
249	Chris Volstad **(RC)**	.50
250	Pedro Feliz	.15
251	Mark Redman	.15
252	Tony Clark	.15
253	Josh Johnson	.15
254	Jose Castillo	.15
255	Brian Horwitz **RC**	.25
256	Aramis Ramirez	.25
257	Casey Blake	.15
258	Arthur Rhodes	.15
259	Aaron Boone	.15
260	Emil Brown	.15
261	Matt Macri **(RC)**	.25
262	Brian Wilson	.15
263	Eric Patterson	.15
264	David Ortiz	.75
265	Tony Abreu	.15
266	Robert Mackowiak	.15
267	Gregorio Petit **RC**	.50
268	Alfonso Soriano	.50
269	Robert Andino	.15
270	Justin Duchscherer	.15
271	Brad Thompson	.15
272	Guillermo Quiroz	.15
273	Chris Perez **RC**	.50
274	Albert Pujols	1.00
275	Rich Harden	.15
276	Corey Hart	.25
277	John Rheinecker	.15
278	So Taguchi	.15
279	Alex Hinshaw **RC**	.50
280	Max Scherzer **RC**	1.00
281	Chris Aguila	.15
282	Carlos Marmol	.15
283	Alex Cintron	.15
284	Curtis Thigpen	.15
285	Kosuke Fukudome	1.50
286	Aaron Cook	.15
287	Chase Headley	.25
288	Evan Longoria	2.00
289	Chris Gomez	.15
290	Carlos Gomez	.15
291	Jonathan Herrera **RC**	.50
292	Ryan Dempster	.15
293	Adam Dunn	.40
294	Mark Teixeira	.40
295	Aaron Miles	.15
296	Gabe Gross	.15
297	Cory Wade **(RC)**	.25
298	Dan Haren	.25
299	Jolbert Cabrera	.15
300	C.C. Sabathia	.50
301	Tony Pena	.15
302	Brandon Moss	.15
303	Taylor Teagarden **RC**	.75
304	Brad Lidge	.15
305	Ben Francisco	.15
306	Casey Kotchman	.15
307	Greg Norton	.15
308	Shelley Duncan	.15
309	John Bowker **(RC)**	.50
310	Kyle Lohse	.15
311	Oscar Salazar	.15
312	Ivan Rodriguez	.25
313	Tim Lincecum	.50
314	Wilson Betemit	.15
315	Sean Rodriguez **(RC)**	.25
316	Ben Sheets	.25
317	Brian Buscher	.15
318	Kyle Farnsworth	.15
319	Ruben Gotay	.15
320	Heath Bell	.15
321	Jeff Niemann **(RC)**	.25
322	Edinson Volquez	.50
323	Jorge Velandia	.15
324	Ken Griffey Jr.	1.00
325	Clay Hensley	.15
326	Kevin Mench	.15
327	Hernan Iribarren **(RC)**	.50
328	Billy Wagner	.15
329	Jeremy Sowers	.15
330	Johan Santana	.50

Black

Black:	20-30X
Production 57 Sets	

Gold

ALL-STARS

57 YEARS OF COLLECTING

JONATHAN PAPELBON

Gold:	5-10X
Production 2,008 Sets	

Gold Foil

Gold Foil:	1-2X

Platinum

Production One Set

All-Star Stitches

	NM/M
Common player:	4.00
Inserted 1:44	
Gold:	1-2X
Production 50 Sets	
Platinum:	No Pricing
Production One Set	
AC	Aaron Cook	4.00
AG	Adrian Gonzalez	8.00
AP	Albert Pujols	15.00
AR	Aramis Ramirez	8.00
AER	Alex Rodriguez	15.00
AS	Alfonso Soriano	8.00
BL	Brad Lidge	8.00
BM	Brian McCann	8.00
BS	Ben Sheets	6.00
WW	Billy Wagner	4.00
BTW	Brandon Webb	8.00
CG	Cristian Guzman	4.00
CAG	Carlos Guillen	4.00
CH	Corey Hart	6.00
CJ	Chipper Jones	10.00
CL	Cliff Lee	8.00
CM	Carlos Marmol	6.00
CQ	Carlos Quentin	8.00
CU	Chase Utley	10.00
CZ	Carlos Zambrano	8.00
DH	Dan Haren	6.00
DN	Dioner Navarro	4.00
DO	David Ortiz	10.00
DP	Dustin Pedroia	10.00
DU	Dan Uggla	8.00
DW	David Wright	10.00
EL	Evan Longoria	25.00
ES	Ervin Santana	8.00
EV	Edinson Volquez	8.00
FR	Francisco Rodriguez	8.00
GPS	Geovany Soto	15.00
GFS	George Sherrill	4.00
GS	Grady Sizemore	10.00
HR	Hanley Ramirez	8.00
IK	Ian Kinsler	10.00
IS	Ichiro Suzuki	25.00
JC	Joe Crede	6.00
JCD	Justin Duchscherer	6.00
JD	J.D. Drew	6.00
JH	Josh Hamilton	20.00
JM	Joe Mauer	6.00
JN	Joe Nathan	6.00
JP	Jonathan Papelbon	8.00
JES	Joe Saunders	4.00
JS	Joakim Soria	4.00
JV	Jason Varitek	10.00
KF	Kosuke Fukudome	20.00
KW	Kerry Wood	8.00
KY	Kevin Youkilis	10.00
LB	Lance Berkman	6.00
MB	Milton Bradley	8.00
MH	Matt Holliday	8.00
MR	Manny Ramirez	8.00
MSR	Mariano Rivera	10.00
MT	Miguel Tejada	6.00
MY	Michael Young	6.00
NM	Nate McLouth	4.00
RB	Ryan Braun	10.00
RD	Ryan Dempster	6.00
RH	Roy Halladay	8.00

RL	Ryan Ludwick	10.00
RM	Russ Martin	8.00
SK	Scott Kazmir	8.00
TL	Tim Lincecum	15.00

All-Star Stitches Auto.

		NM/M
Production 25 Sets		
CJ	Chipper Jones	160.00
DU	Dan Uggla	40.00
TL	Tim Lincecum	160.00
JH	Josh Hamilton	150.00
DP	Dustin Pedroia	125.00
JV	Jason Varitek	90.00
RB	Ryan Braun	75.00
EV	Edinson Volquez	60.00
HR	Hanley Ramirez	60.00
RM	Russ Martin	100.00

All-Star Stitches Dual

		NM/M
Production 25 Sets		
HM	Josh Hamilton, Ryan Braun	40.00
RR	Alex Rodriguez, Manny Ramirez	50.00
FS	Kosuke Fukudome, Ichiro Suzuki	75.00
UU	Chase Utley, Dan Uggla	40.00
HW	Dan Haren, Brandon Webb	
LV	Tim Lincecum, Edinson Volquez	25.00
LS	Cliff Lee, Ben Sheets	20.00
BP	Lance Berkman, Albert Pujols	50.00
RT	Hanley Ramirez, Miguel Tejada	25.00
RR	Mariano Rivera, Francisco Rodriguez	50.00

All-Star Stitches Triple

		NM/M
Production 25 Sets		
RSS	Francisco Rodriguez, Ervin Santana, Joe Saunders	40.00
HRI	Josh Hamilton, Manny Ramirez, Ichiro Suzuki	50.00
RWJ	Alex Rodriguez, David Wright, Chipper Jones	75.00
HFB	Matt Holliday, Kosuke Fukudome, Ryan Braun	50.00
PDO	Dustin Pedroia, J.D. Drew, David Ortiz	50.00
ZRD	Carlos Zambrano, Aramis Ramirez, Ryan Dempster	75.00
PGB	Albert Pujols, Adrian Gonzalez, Lance Berkman	50.00
WLW	Kerry Wood, Brad Lidge, Billy Wagner	40.00
MNM	Russ Martin, Dioner Navarro, Brian McCann	
KBY	Ian Kinsler, Milton Bradley, Michael Young	15.00

All-Star Jumbo Patches

No Pricing
Production 6 Sets

All-Star Jumbo Patches Auto.

Production 6 Sets
No Pricing

First Couples

MARTHA THOMAS
JEFFERSON
FIRST COUPLE 1801-1809

	NM/M
Common Couple:	.75
Inserted 1:6	
1	George Washington, Martha Washington	2.50
2	John Adams, Abigail Adams	1.50
3	Thomas Jefferson, Martha Jefferson	1.50
4	James Madison, Dolly Madison	1.00
5	James Monroe, Elizabeth Kotright Monroe	.75
6	John Quincy Adams, Louisa Catherine Adams	1.00
7	Andrew Jackson, Rachel Jackson	1.00
8	Martin Van Buren, Hannah Van Buren	.75
9	William Henry Harrison, Anna Harrison	.75
10	John Tyler, Julia Tyler	.75
11	James K. Polk, Sarah Polk	.75
12	Zachary Taylor, Margaret Taylor	.75

13	Millard Fillmore, Abigail Fillmore	.75
14	Franklin Pierce, Jane M. Pierce	.75
15	Abraham Lincoln, Mary Lincoln	2.50
16	Andrew Johnson, Eliza Johnson	1.50
17	Ulysses S. Grant, Julia Grant	1.50
18	Rutherford B. Hayes, Lucy Hayes	.75
19	James A. Garfield, Lucretia Garfield	.75
20	Chester A. Arthur, Elien Arthur	.75
21	Grover Cleveland, Frances Cleveland	.75
22	Benjamin Harrison, Caroline Harrison	.75
23	William McKinley, Ida McKinley	.75
24	Theodore Roosevelt, Edith Roosevelt	1.50
25	William H. Taft, Helen Taft	.75
26	Woodrow Wilson, Edith Wilson	.75
27	Warren G. Harding, Florence Harding	.75
28	Calvin Coolidge, Grace Coolidge	.75
29	Herbert Hoover, Lou Hoover	.75
30	Franklin D. Roosevelt, Eleanor Roosevelt	1.50
31	Harry S. Truman, Bess Truman	1.50
32	Dwight D. Eisenhower, Mamie Eisenhower	1.50
33	John F. Kennedy, Jacqueline Kennedy	3.00
34	Lyndon B. Johnson, Lady Bird Johnson	1.00
35	Richard M. Nixon, Pat Nixon	.75
36	Gerald R. Ford, Betty Ford	.75
37	Jimmy Carter, Rosalynn Carter	1.00
38	Ronald Reagan, Nancy Reagan	2.00
39	George H.W. Bush, Barbara Bush	2.00
40	Bill Clinton, Hillary Rodham Clinton	2.00
41	George W. Bush, Laura Bush	2.00

First Lady Cut Signatures

Production One Set
No Pricing

Presidential Stamp Collection

		NM/M
Inserted 1:867		
AL4	Abraham Lincoln	50.00
AL5	Abraham Lincoln	50.00
AL6	Abraham Lincoln	50.00
AJWS1	Andrew Jackson, Winfield Scott	30.00
FDR1	Franklin D. Roosevelt	40.00
FDR2	Franklin D. Roosevelt	40.00
FDR3	Franklin D. Roosevelt	40.00
FDR4	Franklin D. Roosevelt	40.00
FDR5	Franklin D. Roosevelt	40.00
GW18	George Washington	40.00
GW19	George Washington	40.00
GW20	George Washington	40.00
GW21	George Washington	40.00
GW22	George Washington	40.00
GW23	George Washington	40.00
GW24	George Washington	40.00
GW25	George Washington	40.00
GW26	George Washington (Inauguration)	50.00
JG3	James Garfield	25.00
JA1	John Adams	30.00
WW3	Woodrow Wilson	25.00

Rookie Box Loaders

		NM/M
Inserted 1:Box		3.00
All cards are refractors.		
1	Jay Bruce	10.00
2	Daniel Giese	5.00
3	Brandon Boggs	3.00
4	Jed Lowrie	8.00
5	Matt Joyce	6.00
6	Nick Adenhart	4.00
7	Jose Arredondo	3.00
8	Michael Aubrey	3.00
9	Josh Banks	3.00
10	Armando Galarraga	4.00
11	Mike Aviles	6.00
12	Burke Badenhop	3.00
13	Reid Brignac	5.00
14	Emmanuel Burriss	3.00
15	Greg Reynolds	3.00
16	Chris Volstad	4.00
17	Brian Bixler	3.00
18	Chris Carter	3.00
19	Travis Denker	3.00
20	Alberto Gonzalez	5.00
21	Robinzon Diaz	3.00
22	Brett Gardner	5.00
23	Mick Hoffpauir	5.00
24	Hernan Iribarren	3.00
25	Greg Smith	3.00
26	German Duran	3.00
27	Kosuke Fukudome	10.00

28	Ryan Tucker	3.00
29	Paul Janish	3.00
30	Clayton Kershaw	8.00
31	Chris Davis	8.00
32	Joe Mather	5.00
33	Nick Hundley	5.00
34	Brian Horwitz	3.00
35	Carlos Gonzalez	6.00
36	Matt Macri	3.00
37	Gregorio Petit	3.00
38	Chris Perez	5.00
39	Alex Hinshaw	3.00
40	Max Scherzer	8.00
41	Jonathan Van Every	3.00
42	Jonathan Herrera	3.00
43	Cory Wade	4.00
44	Max Ramirez	5.00
45	John Bowker	3.00
46	Sean Rodriguez	3.00
47	Jeff Niemann	3.00
48	Taylor Teagarden	5.00
49	Mark Worrell	4.00
50	Evan Longoria	20.00
51	Chris Smith	4.00
52	Brent Lillibridge	3.00
53	Colt Morton	3.00
54	Eric Hurley	3.00
55	Justin Masterson	10.00

Silk

		NM/M
Production 50 sets		
101	Johan Santana	25.00
102	Cristian Guzman	8.00
103	Brendan Harris	8.00
104	Randy Wolf	10.00
105	Cliff Lee	20.00
106	Roy Halladay	20.00
107	Dustin Pedroia	25.00
108	Chris Iannetta	10.00
109	Kerly Wood	10.00
110	Jim Edmonds	15.00
111	Jon Rauch	8.00
112	Ryan Sweeney	10.00
113	Ryan Ludwick	20.00
114	George Sherrill	10.00
115	Matt Garza	15.00
116	Nate McLouth	20.00
117	Eric Hinske	10.00
118	Adrian Gonzalez	15.00
119	Carlos Marmol	15.00
120	Jose Valverde	10.00
121	Shane Victorino	20.00
122	Brad Wilkerson	10.00
123	Dana Eveland	10.00
124	Luke Scott	10.00
125	Mike Cameron	10.00
126	Ervin Santana	20.00
127	Ryan Dempster	15.00
128	Geoff Jenkins	10.00
129	Billy Wagner	10.00
130	Pedro Feliz	10.00
131	Stephen Drew	15.00
132	Mark Hendrickson	8.00
133	Orlando Hudson	10.00
134	Pat Burrell	20.00
135	Russell Martin	30.00
136	James Loney	15.00
137	Justin Masterson	50.00
138	Matt Kemp	20.00
139	Hiroki Kuroda	20.00
140	Joe Crede	10.00
141	Joakim Soria	10.00
142	Armando Galarraga	20.00
143	Jason Varitek	15.00
144	Aaron Cook	15.00
145	Orlando Cabrera	10.00
146	Ian Kinsler	20.00
147	Carlos Gomez	20.00
148	Mike Aviles	25.00
149	Carlos Guillen	15.00
150	Erik Bedard	15.00
151	J.D. Drew	15.00
152	Marco Scutaro	10.00
153	James Shields	15.00
154	Cesar Izturis	10.00
155	Akinori Iwamura	15.00
156	Aramis Ramirez	20.00
157	Joe Mauer	25.00
158	Brad Lidge	15.00
159	Milton Bradley	15.00
160	Jay Bruce	30.00
161	Andrew Miller	15.00
162	Mark Reynolds	15.00
163	Johnny Damon	20.00
164	Michael Bourn	10.00
165	Andre Ethier	15.00
166	Carlos Pena	20.00
167	Joe Nathan	20.00
168	Cody Ross	8.00
169	Joba Chamberlain	35.00
170	Clayton Kershaw	25.00
171	Francisco Rodriguez	15.00
172	Mark DeRosa	15.00
173	Ben Sheets	15.00
174	Brian Wilson	10.00
175	Emil Brown	10.00
176	Geovany Soto	25.00
177	Jason Giambi	15.00
178	Shaun Marcum	10.00
179	Edinson Volquez	15.00
180	Max Scherzer	20.00
181	Kelly Johnson	10.00
182	Mariano Rivera	25.00
183	Chris Perez	20.00

184	Jose Guillen	10.00
185	Kyle Lohse	10.00
186	Kosuke Fukudome	25.00
187	Takashi Saito	15.00
188	Mike Mussina	20.00
189	J.J. Putz	10.00
190	Evan Longoria	50.00
191	Jered Weaver	15.00
192	Grady Sizemore	30.00
193	Carlos Gonzalez	15.00
194	Brian McCann	15.00
195	Jonathan Papelbon	20.00
196	Dioner Navarro	10.00
197	Bobby Abreu	15.00
198	Carlos Quentin	15.00
199	Josh Hamilton	50.00
200	Dan Haren	15.00

Sketch Cards

NM/M

Inserted 1:214

1	Adam Dunn	30.00
2	Adrian Gonzalez	30.00
3	Albert Pujols	100.00
4	Alex Gordon	40.00
5	Alex Rios	40.00
6	Alex Rodriguez	100.00
7	Alfonso Soriano	40.00
8	Aramis Ramirez	25.00
9	B.J. Upton	40.00
10	Ben Sheets	30.00
11	Bobby Jenks	20.00
12	Brandon Webb	30.00
13	Brian McCann	25.00
14	C.C. Sabathia	30.00
15	Carl Crawford	40.00
16	Carlos Beltran	40.00
17	Carlos Gomez	30.00
18	Carlos Lee	25.00
19	Carlos Quentin	40.00
20	Carlos Zambrano	35.00
21	Chase Utley	50.00
22	Chipper Jones	50.00
23	Chien-Ming Wang	60.00
24	Chris Young	30.00
25	Clayton Kershaw	25.00
26	Cliff Lee	30.00
27	Cole Hamels	40.00
28	Daisuke Matsuzaka	40.00
29	Dan Haren	30.00
30	Dan Uggla	25.00
31	David Ortiz	60.00
32	David Wright	75.00
33	Derek Jeter	100.00
34	Derrek Lee	30.00
35	Dustin Pedroia	40.00
36	Edinson Volquez	30.00
37	Ervin Santana	35.00
39	Felix Hernandez	50.00
40	Francisco Rodriguez	30.00
41	Geovany Soto	40.00
42	Grady Sizemore	60.00
43	Hanley Ramirez	50.00
45	Hunter Pence	20.00
46	Ichiro Suzuki	100.00
47	Jacoby Ellsbury	50.00
48	Jake Peavy	25.00
49	Jason Bay	25.00
50	Jay Bruce	50.00
51	Jeff Francoeur	25.00
52	Ryan Zimmerman	30.00
53	Jimmy Rollins	40.00
54	Joba Chamberlain	50.00
57	Johan Santana	40.00
58	John Smoltz	50.00
59	Johnny Cueto	40.00
60	Jonathan Papelbon	40.00
62	Jose Reyes	40.00
63	Jose Valverde	15.00
64	Josh Beckett	40.00
64	Josh Hamilton	75.00
65	Justin Morneau	30.00
67	Justin Verlander	40.00
68	Lance Berkman	35.00
69	Magglio Ordonez	25.00
70	Manny Ramirez	50.00
72	Mark Teixeira	40.00
73	Matt Garza	20.00
75	Matt Kemp	25.00
78	Miguel Cabrera	40.00
80	Nick Markakis	40.00
81	Pat Burrell	30.00
82	Pedro Martinez	25.00
83	Prince Fielder	50.00
85	Rick Ankiel	40.00
87	Roy Halladay	25.00
90	Ryan Braun	60.00
91	Ryan Howard	50.00
92	Scott Kazmir	25.00
93	Tim Hudson	30.00
94	Tim Lincecum	80.00
95	Torii Hunter	40.00
96	Troy Tulowitzki	25.00
97	Vernon Wells	40.00
99	Vladimir Guerrero	40.00

Take Me Out to the Ballgame

NM/M

Inserted 1:72

1	100th Anniversary	2.00

The Mickey Mantle Story

NM/M

Common Mantle: 2.00

Inserted 1:18
66-75 Mickey Mantle   2.00

Year in Review

FIELDER BECOMES YOUNGEST TO 50 HRs

PRINCE FIELDER
MILWAUKEE BREWERS

NM/M

Common player: .50
Inserted 1:6

121	Mark Teixeira	.75
122	Alex Gordon	.75
123	Jermaine Dye	.50
124	Vladimir Guerrero	.75
125	Alex Rodriguez	2.00
126	Tom Glavine	.75
127	Scott Rolen	.50
128	Billy Wagner	.50
129	Rick Ankiel	.75
130	Jack Cust	.50
131	Mike Mussina	.75
132	Magglio Ordonez	.75
133	Placido Polanco	.50
134	Russell Branyan	.50
135	David Price	3.00
136	Mike Cameron	.50
137	Brandon Webb	.75
138	Cameron Maybin	.75
139	Johan Santana	.75
140	Bobby Jenks	.50
141	Garret Anderson	.50
142	Jarrod Saltalamacchia	.50
143	Adrian Gonzalez	.75
144	Carlos Guillen	.50
145	Tom Shearn	.50
146	John Lackey	.50
147	Jayson Werth	.50
148	Aaron Harang	.50
149	Chien-Ming Wang	1.00
150	Scott Baker	.50
151	Clay Buchholz	.50
152	Tom Glavine	.75
153	Pedro Martinez	.75
154	Doug Davis	.50
155	Brandon Phillips	.75
156	Jason Varitek	1.00
157	Jim Thome	.75
158	Alex Rodriguez	2.00
159	Curtis Granderson	1.00
160	Scott Kazmir	.75
161	Marlon Byrd	.50
162	David Ortiz	1.00
163	David Wells	.50
164	Johnny Damon	.75
165	Carlos Lee	.50
166	Jim Thome	.75
167	Frank Thomas	.75
168	Greg Maddux	1.50
169	Matt Holliday	.75
170	J.R. Towles	.50
171	Lance Berkman	.75
172	Melky Cabrera	.75
173	Vladimir Guerrero	.75
174	Nick Markakis	.75
175	Prince Fielder	1.00
176	Moises Alou	.50
177	Micah Owings	.50
178	Carlos Zambrano	.75

World Series Ring of Honor

1965 WORLD SERIES CHAMPION

RING OF HONOR

DAVID JUSTICE

NM/M

Common player: 1.50
Inserted 1:18
Gold: No Pricing
Production 25 Sets

RK	Ray Knight	1.50
BS	Bruce Sutter	1.50
JP	Johnny Podres	2.00
LA	Luis Aparicio	1.50
MI	Monte Irvin	2.00
DC	David Cone	1.50
DJ	David Justice	1.50
ML	Mike Lowell	1.50
WF	Whitey Ford	3.00
DS	Duke Snider	3.00
OC	Orlando Cepeda	1.50

World Series Ring of Honor Autos.

NM/M

Inserted 1:2,569

BS	Bruce Sutter	50.00
JP	Johnny Podres	35.00
LA	Luis Aparicio	35.00
MI	Monte Irvin	40.00
DC	David Cone	50.00
DJ	David Justice	40.00
ML	Mike Lowell	30.00
WF	Whitey Ford	60.00
DS	Duke Snider	60.00
OC	Orlando Cepeda	40.00

1957 Mickey Mantle Reprint Relic

NM/M

Production 57 Cards

57	Mickey Mantle/Bat	125.00

1986 N.Y. Mets Ring of Honor Autos.

NM/M

Inserted 1:2,849

HJ	Howard Johnson	30.00
RD	Ron Darling	30.00
JO	Jesse Orosco	40.00
DJ	Davey Johnson	25.00
KM	Kevin Mitchell	30.00
DS	D.J. Strawberry	30.00
DG	Dwight Gooden	30.00
GC	Gary Carter	40.00
RK	Ray Knight	30.00
KH	Keith Hernandez	40.00

1986 N.Y. Mets Ring of Honor

NM/M

Common player: 1.50
Inserted 1:18
Gold: No Pricing
Production 25 Sets

HJ	Howard Johnson	1.50
RD	Ron Darling	1.50
JO	Jesse Orosco	1.50
DJ	Davey Johnson	1.50
KM	Kevin Mitchell	1.50
DS	Darryl Strawberry	1.50
DG	Dwight Gooden	1.50
GC	Gary Carter	1.50
RK	Ray Knight	1.50
KH	Keith Hernandez	1.50

2008 Presidential Picks

NM/M

Production 100 sets

JM	John McCain	50.00
BO	Barack Obama	250.00

2008 Highlight Autographs

NM/M

Common Auto.:   8.00
Some not priced due to scarcity.

RB	Ryan Braun	100.00
CK	Clayton Kershaw	75.00
BP	Brandon Phillips	15.00
NM	Nick Markakis	25.00
JH	Josh Hamilton	80.00
MS	Max Scherzer	25.00
AC	Asdrubal Cabrera	15.00
BD	Blake DeWitt	30.00
MK	Masahide Kobayashi	15.00
DM	Dustin McGowan	15.00
CG	Carlos Gomez	10.00
ZG	Zack Greinke	25.00
BB	Billy Butler	20.00
JV	Joey Votto	40.00
EV	Edinson Volquez	20.00
AG	Armando Galarraga	20.00
BR	B.J. Ryan	10.00
JR	Jo Jo Reyes	8.00
BDB	Brian Barton	8.00
SH	Steve Holm	8.00
CR	Carlos Ruiz	10.00
SS	Seth Smith	8.00
JS	Jeff Salazar	8.00
MW	Mark Worrell	8.00

2009 World Baseball Classic

NM/M

Complete Set (25):   20.00
Common Player: .50
Inserted 1:9

1	Daisuke Matsuzaka	2.00
2	Alexei Ramirez	4.00

CUBA

3	Derrek Lee	1.00
4	Akinori Iwamura	.50
5	Chase Utley	1.50
6	Jose Reyes	1.50
7	Jake Peavy	1.00
8	Justin Huber	.50
9	Justin Morneau	1.00
10	Ichiro Suzuki	3.00
11	Adrian Gonzalez	1.00
12	Carlos Zambrano	1.00
13	Miguel Cabrera	1.00
14	Carlos Beltran	1.00
15	Albert Pujols	3.00
16	Paul Bell	.50
17	Frank Catalanotto	.50
18	Jason Varitek	.75
19	Andruw Jones	.50
20	Johan Santana	1.00
21	Carlos Lee	.50
22	David Ortiz	1.50
23	Francisco Rodriguez	.50
24	Chin-Lung Hu	.50
25	Kosuke Fukudome	2.00

U

1991 Ultra

FLEER '91
ULTRA

GEORGE BELL
CUBS
OUTFIELD

NM/M

Complete Set (400):   12.00
Common Player: .05
Wax Pack (14):   .50
Wax Box (36):   9.00

1	Steve Avery	.05
2	Jeff Blauser	.05
3	Francisco Cabrera	.05
4	Ron Gant	.05
5	Tom Glavine	.25
6	Tommy Gregg	.05
7	Dave Justice	.05
8	Oddibe McDowell	.05
9	Greg Olson	.05
10	Terry Pendleton	.05
11	Lonnie Smith	.05
12	John Smoltz	.15
13	Jeff Treadway	.05
14	Glenn Davis	.05
15	Mike Devereaux	.05
16	Leo Gomez	.05
17	Chris Hoiles	.05
18	Dave Johnson	.05
19	Ben McDonald	.05
20	Randy Milligan	.05
21	Gregg Olson	.05
22	Joe Orsulak	.05
23	Bill Ripken	.05
24	Cal Ripken, Jr.	1.50
25	David Segui	.05
26	Craig Worthington	.05
27	Wade Boggs	.60
28	Tom Bolton	.05
29	Tom Brunansky	.05
30	Ellis Burks	.05
31	Roger Clemens	.65
32	Mike Greenwell	.05
33	Greg Harris	.05
34	Daryl Irvine	.05
35	Mike Marshall	.05
36	Tim Naehring	.05
37	Tony Pena	.05
38	Phil Plantier **RC**	.05
39	Carlos Quintana	.05
40	Jeff Reardon	.05
41	Jody Reed	.05
42	Luis Rivera	.05
43	Jim Abbott	.05
44	Chuck Finley	.05

#	Player	Price
45	Bryan Harvey	.05
46	Donnie Hill	.05
47	Jack Howell	.05
48	Wally Joyner	.05
49	Mark Langston	.05
50	Kirk McCaskill	.05
51	Lance Parrish	.05
52	Dick Schofield	.05
53	Lee Stevens	.05
54	Dave Winfield	.50
55	George Bell	.05
56	Damon Berryhill	.05
57	Mike Bielecki	.05
58	Andre Dawson	.25
59	Shawon Dunston	.05
60	Joe Girardi	.05
61	Mark Grace	.05
62	Mike Harkey	.05
63	Les Lancaster	.05
64	Greg Maddux	.60
65	Derrick May	.05
66	Ryne Sandberg	.60
67	Luis Salazar	.05
68	Dwight Smith	.05
69	Hector Villanueva	.05
70	Jerome Walton	.05
71	Mitch Williams	.05
72	Carlton Fisk	.50
73	Scott Fletcher	.05
74	Ozzie Guillen	.05
75	Greg Hibbard	.05
76	Lance Johnson	.05
77	Steve Lyons	.05
78	Jack McDowell	.05
79	Dan Pasqua	.05
80	Melido Perez	.05
81	Tim Raines	.05
82	Sammy Sosa	.60
83	Cory Snyder	.05
84	Bobby Thigpen	.05
85	Frank Thomas	.50
86	Robin Ventura	.05
87	Todd Benzinger	.05
88	Glenn Braggs	.05
89	Tom Browning	.05
90	Norm Charlton	.05
91	Eric Davis	.05
92	Rob Dibble	.05
93	Bill Doran	.05
94	Mariano Duncan	.05
95	Billy Hatcher	.05
96	Barry Larkin	.05
97	Randy Myers	.05
98	Hal Morris	.05
99	Joe Oliver	.05
100	Paul O'Neill	.05
101a	Jeff Reed	.05
101b	Beau Allred (Should be #104.)	.05
102	Jose Rijo	.05
103a	Chris Sabo	.05
103b	Carlos Baerga (Should be #106.)	
104	Not Issued (See #101b.)	
105	Sandy Alomar,Jr.	.05
106	Not Issued (See #103b.)	
107	Albert Belle	.05
108	Jerry Browne	.05
109	Tom Candiotti	.05
110	Alex Cole	.05
111a	John Farrell	.05
111b	Chris James (Should be #114.)	.05
112	Felix Fermin	.05
113	Brook Jacoby	.05
114	Not Issued (See #111b.)	
115	Doug Jones	.05
116a	Steve Olin	.05
116b	Mitch Webster (Should be #119.)	.05
117	Greg Swindell	.05
118	Turner Ward	.05
119	Not Issued (See #116b.)	
120	Dave Bergman	.05
121	Cecil Fielder	.05
122	Travis Fryman	.05
123	Mike Henneman	.05
124	Lloyd Moseby	.05
125	Dan Petry	.05
126	Tony Phillips	.05
127	Mark Salas	.05
128	Frank Tanana	.05
129	Alan Trammell	.05
130	Lou Whitaker	.05
131	Eric Anthony	.05
132	Craig Biggio	.05
133	Ken Caminiti	.05
134	Casey Candaele	.05
135	Andujar Cedeno	.05
136	Mark Davidson	.05
137	Jim Deshaies	.05
138	Mark Portugal	.05
139	Rafael Ramirez	.05
140	Mike Scott	.05
141	Eric Yelding	.05
142	Gerald Young	.05
143	Kevin Appier	.05
144	George Brett	.65
145	Jeff Conine RC	.40
146	Jim Eisenreich	.05
147	Tom Gordon	.05
148	Mark Gubicza	.05
149	Bo Jackson	.10
150	Brent Mayne	.05
151	Mike Macfarlane	.05
152	Brian McRae RC	.10
153	Jeff Montgomery	.05
154	Bret Saberhagen	.05
155	Kevin Seitzer	.05
156	Terry Shumpert	.05
157	Kurt Stillwell	.05
158	Danny Tartabull	.05
159	Tim Belcher	.05
160	Kal Daniels	.05
161	Alfredo Griffin	.05
162	Lenny Harris	.05
163	Jay Howell	.05
164	Ramon Martinez	.05
165	Mike Morgan	.05
166	Eddie Murray	.50
167	Jose Offerman	.05
168	Juan Samuel	.05
169	Mike Scioscia	.05
170	Mike Sharperson	.05
171	Darryl Strawberry	.05
172	Greg Brock	.05
173	Chuck Crim	.05
174	Jim Gantner	.05
175	Ted Higuera	.05
176	Mark Knudson	.05
177	Tim McIntosh	.05
178	Paul Molitor	.50
179	Dan Plesac	.05
180	Gary Sheffield	.35
181	Bill Spiers	.05
182	B.J. Surhoff	.05
183	Greg Vaughn	.05
184	Robin Yount	.50
185	Rick Aguilera	.05
186	Greg Gagne	.05
187	Dan Gladden	.05
188	Brian Harper	.05
189	Kent Hrbek	.05
190	Gene Larkin	.05
191	Shane Mack	.05
192	Pedro Munoz	.05
193	Al Newman	.05
194	Junior Ortiz	.05
195	Kirby Puckett	.60
196	Kevin Tapani	.05
197	Dennis Boyd	.05
198	Tim Burke	.05
199	Ivan Calderon	.05
200	Delino DeShields	.05
201	Mike Fitzgerald	.05
202	Steve Frey	.05
203	Andres Galarraga	.05
204	Marquis Grissom	.05
205	Dave Martinez	.05
206	Dennis Martinez	.05
207	Junior Noboa	.05
208	Spike Owen	.05
209	Scott Ruskin	.05
210	Tim Wallach	.05
211	Daryl Boston	.05
212	Vince Coleman	.05
213	David Cone	.05
214	Ron Darling	.05
215	Kevin Elster	.05
216	Sid Fernandez	.05
217	John Franco	.05
218	Dwight Gooden	.05
219	Tom Herr	.05
220	Todd Hundley	.05
221	Gregg Jefferies	.05
222	Howard Johnson	.05
223	Dave Magadan	.05
224	Kevin McReynolds	.05
225	Keith Miller	.05
226	Mackey Sasser	.05
227	Frank Viola	.05
228	Jesse Barfield	.05
229	Greg Cadaret	.05
230	Alvaro Espinoza	.05
231	Bob Geren	.05
232	Lee Guetterman	.05
233	Mel Hall	.05
234	Andy Hawkins	.05
235	Roberto Kelly	.05
236	Tim Leary	.05
237	Jim Leyritz	.05
238	Kevin Maas	.05
239	Don Mattingly	.65
240	Hensley Meulens	.05
241	Eric Plunk	.05
242	Steve Sax	.05
243	Todd Burns	.05
244	Jose Canseco	.35
245	Dennis Eckersley	.40
246	Mike Gallego	.05
247	Dave Henderson	.05
248	Rickey Henderson	.50
249	Rick Honeycutt	.05
250	Carney Lansford	.05
251	Mark McGwire	1.00
252	Mike Moore	.05
253	Terry Steinbach	.05
254	Dave Stewart	.05
255	Walt Weiss	.05
256	Bob Welch	.05
257	Curt Young	.05
258	Wes Chamberlain	.05
259	Pat Combs	.05
260	Darren Daulton	.05
261	Jose DeJesus	.05
262	Len Dykstra	.05
263	Charlie Hayes	.05
264	Von Hayes	.05
265	Ken Howell	.05
266	John Kruk	.05
267	Roger McDowell	.05
268	Mickey Morandini	.05
269	Terry Mulholland	.05
270	Dale Murphy	.15
271	Randy Ready	.05
272	Dickie Thon	.05
273	Stan Belinda	.05
274	Jay Bell	.05
275	Barry Bonds	1.50
276	Bobby Bonilla	.05
277	Doug Drabek	.05
278	Carlos Garcia RC	.05
279	Neal Heaton	.05
280	Jeff King	.05
281	Bill Landrum	.05
282	Mike LaValliere	.05
283	Jose Lind	.05
284	Orlando Merced RC	.10
285	Gary Redus	.05
286	Don Slaught	.05
287	Andy Van Slyke	.05
288	Jose DeLeon	.05
289	Pedro Guerrero	.05
290	Ray Lankford	.05
291	Joe Magrane	.05
292	Jose Oquendo	.05
293	Tom Pagnozzi	.05
294	Bryn Smith	.05
295	Lee Smith	.05
296	Ozzie Smith	.60
297	Milt Thompson	.05
298	Craig Wilson RC	.05
299	Todd Zeile	.05
300	Shawn Abner	.05
301	Andy Benes	.05
302	Paul Faries	.05
303	Tony Gwynn	.60
304	Greg Harris	.05
305	Thomas Howard	.05
306	Bruce Hurst	.05
307	Craig Lefferts	.05
308	Fred McGriff	.05
309	Dennis Rasmussen	.05
310	Bip Roberts	.05
311	Benito Santiago	.05
312	Garry Templeton	.05
313	Ed Whitson	.05
314	Dave Anderson	.05
315	Kevin Bass	.05
316	Jeff Brantley	.05
317	John Burkett	.05
318	Will Clark	.05
319	Steve Decker	.05
320	Scott Garrelts	.05
321	Terry Kennedy	.05
322	Mark Leonard	.05
323	Darren Lewis	.05
324	Greg Litton	.05
325	Willie McGee	.05
326	Kevin Mitchell	.05
327	Don Robinson	.05
328	Andres Santana	.05
329	Robby Thompson	.05
330	Jose Uribe	.05
331	Matt Williams	.05
332	Scott Bradley	.05
333	Henry Cotto	.05
334	Alvin Davis	.05
335	Ken Griffey Sr.	.05
336	Ken Griffey Jr.	.75
337	Erik Hanson	.05
338	Brian Holman	.05
339	Randy Johnson	.50
340	Edgar Martinez	.05
341	Tino Martinez	.05
342	Pete O'Brien	.05
343	Harold Reynolds	.05
344	David Valle	.05
345	Omar Vizquel	.05
346	Brad Arnsberg	.05
347	Kevin Brown	.05
348	Julio Franco	.05
349	Jeff Huson	.05
350	Rafael Palmeiro	.40
351	Geno Petralli	.05
352	Gary Pettis	.05
353	Kenny Rogers	.05
354	Jeff Russell	.05
355	Nolan Ryan	1.50
356	Ruben Sierra	.15
357	Bobby Witt	.05
358	Roberto Alomar	.15
359	Pat Borders	.05
360	Joe Carter	.05
361	Kelly Gruber	.05
362	Tom Henke	.05
363	Glenallen Hill	.05
364	Jimmy Key	.05
365	Manny Lee	.05
366	Rance Mulliniks	.05
367	John Olerud	.05
368	Dave Stieb	.05
369	Duane Ward	.05
370	David Wells	.05
371	Mark Whiten	.05
372	Mookie Wilson	.05
373	Willie Banks	.05
374	Steve Carter	.05
375	Scott Chiamparino	.05
376	Steve Chitren	.05
377	Darrin Fletcher	.05
378	Rich Garces	.05
379	Reggie Jefferson	.05
380	Eric Karros RC	.50
381	Pat Kelly	.05
382	Chuck Knoblauch	.05
383	Denny Neagle	.05
384	Dan Opperman	.05
385	John Ramos	.05
386	Henry Rodriguez RC	.05
387	Mo Vaughn	.05
388	Gerald Williams	.05
389	Mike York	.05
390	Eddie Zosky	.05
391	Barry Bonds	.75
392	Cecil Fielder	.05
393	Rickey Henderson	.25
394	Dave Justice	.05
395	Nolan Ryan	.75
396	Bobby Thigpen	.05
397	Checklist	.05
398	Checklist	.05
399	Checklist	.05
400	Checklist	.05

Gold

BO JACKSON
KANSAS CITY ROYALS • OUTFIELD

		NM/M
Complete Set (10):		5.00
Common Player:		.15
1	Barry Bonds	2.50
2	Will Clark	.15
3	Doug Drabek	.15
4	Ken Griffey Jr.	1.50
5	Rickey Henderson	.75
6	Bo Jackson	.25
7	Ramon Martinez	.15
8	Kirby Puckett	1.00
9	Chris Sabo	.15
10	Ryne Sandberg	1.00

Update

RICK WILKINS   CUBS CATCHER

		NM/M
Complete Set (120):		15.00
Common Player:		.05
1	Dwight Evans	.05
2	Chito Martinez	.05
3	Bob Melvin	.05
4	Mike Mussina RC	3.00
5	Jack Clark	.05
6	Dana Kiecker	.05
7	Steve Lyons	.05
8	Gary Gaetti	.05
9	Dave Gallagher	.05
10	Dave Parker	.05
11	Luis Polonia	.05
12	Luis Sojo	.05
13	Wilson Alvarez	.05
14	Alex Fernandez	.05
15	Craig Grebeck	.05
16	Ron Karkovice	.05
17	Warren Newson	.05
18	Scott Radinsky	.05
19	Glenallen Hill	.05
20	Charles Nagy	.05
21	Mark Whiten	.05
22	Milt Cuyler	.05
23	Paul Gibson	.05
24	Mickey Tettleton	.05
25	Todd Benzinger	.05
26	Storm Davis	.05
27	Kirk Gibson	.05
28	Bill Pecota	.05

29 Gary Thurman .05
30 Darryl Hamilton .05
31 Jaime Navarro .05
32 Willie Randolph .05
33 Bill Wegman .05
34 Randy Bush .05
35 Chili Davis .05
36 Scott Erickson .05
37 Chuck Knoblauch .05
38 Scott Leius .05
39 Jack Morris .05
40 John Habyan .05
41 Pat Kelly .05
42 Matt Nokes .05
43 Scott Sanderson .05
44 Bernie Williams .05
45 Harold Baines .05
46 Brook Jacoby .05
47 Ernest Riles .05
48 Willie Wilson .05
49 Jay Buhner .05
50 Rich DeLucia .05
51 Mike Jackson .05
52 Bill Krueger .05
53 Bill Swift .05
54 Brian Downing .05
55 Juan Gonzalez .75
56 Dean Palmer .05
57 Kevin Reimer .05
58 Ivan Rodriguez **RC** 6.00
59 Tom Candiotti .05
60 Juan Guzman .05
61 Bob MacDonald .05
62 Greg Myers .05
63 Ed Sprague .05
64 Devon White .05
65 Rafael Belliard .05
66 Juan Berenguer .05
67 Brian Hunter .05
68 Kent Mercker .05
69 Otis Nixon .05
70 Danny Jackson .05
71 Chuck McElroy .05
72 Gary Scott .05
73 Heathcliff Slocumb .05
74 Chico Walker .05
75 Rick Wilkins .05
76 Chris Hammond .05
77 Luis Quinones .05
78 Herm Winningham .05
79 Jeff Bagwell **RC** 6.00
80 Jim Corsi .05
81 Steve Finley .05
82 Luis Gonzalez **RC** 1.00
83 Pete Harnisch .05
84 Darryl Kile .05
85 Brett Butler .05
86 Gary Carter 1.00
87 Tim Crews .05
88 Orel Hershiser .05
89 Bob Ojeda .05
90 Bret Barberie .05
91 Barry Jones .05
92 Gilberto Reyes .05
93 Larry Walker .05
94 Hubie Brooks .05
95 Tim Burke .05
96 Rick Cerone .05
97 Jeff Innis .05
98 Wally Backman .05
99 Tommy Greene .05
100 Ricky Jordan .05
101 Mitch Williams .05
102 John Smiley .05
103 Randy Tomlin .05
104 Gary Varsho .05
105 Cris Carpenter .05
106 Ken Hill .05
107 Felix Jose .05
108 Omar Oliveras **RC** .05
109 Gerald Perry .05
110 Jerald Clark .05
111 Tony Fernandez .05
112 Darrin Jackson .05
113 Mike Maddux .05
114 Tim Teufel .05
115 Bud Black .05
116 Kelly Downs .05
117 Mike Felder .05
118 Willie McGee .05
119 Trevor Wilson .05
120 Checklist .05

1992 Ultra

NM/M

Complete Set (600): 12.00
Common Player: .05
Ser. 1 or 2 Pack (14): .60
Ser. 1 or 2 Box (36): 12.50
Tony Gwynn Auto. 60.00
1 Glenn Davis .05
2 Mike Devereaux .05
3 Dwight Evans .05
4 Leo Gomez .05
5 Chris Hoiles .05
6 Sam Horn .05
7 Chito Martinez .05
8 Randy Milligan .05
9 Mike Mussina .30
10 Billy Ripken .05
11 Cal Ripken, Jr. 1.00
12 Tom Brunansky .05
13 Ellis Burks .05
14 Jack Clark .05
15 Roger Clemens .60

JOE CARTER
TORONTO BLUE JAYS • OUTFIELD

16 Mike Greenwell .05
17 Joe Hesketh .05
18 Tony Pena .05
19 Carlos Quintana .05
20 Jeff Reardon .05
21 Jody Reed .05
22 Luis Rivera .05
23 Mo Vaughn .05
24 Gary DiSarcina .05
25 Chuck Finley .05
26 Gary Gaetti .05
27 Bryan Harvey .05
28 Lance Parrish .05
29 Luis Polonia .05
30 Dick Schofield .05
31 Luis Sojo .05
32 Wilson Alvarez .05
33 Carlton Fisk .40
34 Craig Grebeck .05
35 Ozzie Guillen .05
36 Greg Hibbard .05
37 Charlie Hough .05
38 Lance Johnson .05
39 Ron Karkovice .05
40 Jack McDowell .05
41 Donn Pall .05
42 Melido Perez .05
43 Tim Raines .05
44 Frank Thomas .40
45 Sandy Alomar, Jr. .05
46 Carlos Baerga .05
47 Albert Belle .05
48 Jerry Browne .05
49 Felix Fermin .05
50 Reggie Jefferson .05
51 Mark Lewis .05
52 Carlos Martinez .05
53 Steve Olin .05
54 Jim Thome .35
55 Mark Whiten .05
56 Dave Bergman .05
57 Milt Cuyler .05
58 Rob Deer .05
59 Cecil Fielder .05
60 Travis Fryman .05
61 Scott Livingstone .05
62 Tony Phillips .05
63 Mickey Tettleton .05
64 Alan Trammell .05
65 Lou Whitaker .05
66 Kevin Appier .05
67 Mike Boddicker .05
68 George Brett .60
69 Jim Eisenreich .05
70 Mark Gubicza .05
71 David Howard .05
72 Joel Johnston .05
73 Mike Macfarlane .05
74 Brent Mayne .05
75 Brian McRae .05
76 Jeff Montgomery .05
77 Terry Shumpert .05
78 Don August .05
79 Dante Bichette .05
80 Ted Higuera .05
81 Paul Molitor .40
82 Jamie Navarro .05
83 Gary Sheffield .30
84 Bill Spiers .05
85 B.J. Surhoff .05
86 Greg Vaughn .05
87 Robin Yount .40
88 Rick Aguilera .05
89 Chili Davis .05
90 Scott Erickson .05
91 Brian Harper .05
92 Kent Hrbek .05
93 Chuck Knoblauch .05
94 Scott Leius .05
95 Shane Mack .05
96 Mike Pagliarulo .05
97 Kirby Puckett .50
98 Kevin Tapani .05
99 Jesse Barfield .05
100 Alvaro Espinoza .05
101 Mel Hall .05
102 Pat Kelly .05
103 Roberto Kelly .05
104 Kevin Maas .05
105 Don Mattingly .60
106 Hensley Meulens .05
107 Matt Nokes .05
108 Steve Sax .05
109 Harold Baines .05
110 Jose Canseco .30
111 Ron Darling .05
112 Mike Gallego .05
113 Dave Henderson .05
114 Rickey Henderson .40
115 Mark McGwire .75
116 Terry Steinbach .05
117 Dave Stewart .05
118 Todd Van Poppel .05
119 Bob Welch .05
120 Greg Briley .05
121 Jay Buhner .05
122 Rich DeLucia .05
123 Ken Griffey Jr. .65
124 Erik Hanson .05
125 Randy Johnson .40
126 Edgar Martinez .05
127 Tino Martinez .05
128 Pete O'Brien .05
129 Harold Reynolds .05
130 Dave Valle .05
131 Julio Franco .05
132 Juan Gonzalez .20
133 Jeff Huson .05
134 Mike Jeffcoat .05
135 Terry Mathews .05
136 Rafael Palmeiro .35
137 Dean Palmer .05
138 Geno Petralli .05
139 Ivan Rodriguez .35
140 Jeff Russell .05
141 Nolan Ryan 1.00
142 Ruben Sierra .05
143 Roberto Alomar .15
144 Pat Borders .05
145 Joe Carter .05
146 Kelly Gruber .05
147 Jimmy Key .05
148 Manny Lee .05
149 Rance Mulliniks .05
150 Greg Myers .05
151 John Olerud .05
152 Dave Stieb .05
153 Todd Stottlemyre .05
154 Duane Ward .05
155 Devon White .05
156 Eddie Zosky .05
157 Steve Avery .05
158 Rafael Belliard .05
159 Jeff Blauser .05
160 Sid Bream .05
161 Ron Gant .05
162 Tom Glavine .25
163 Brian Hunter .05
164 Dave Justice .05
165 Mark Lemke .05
166 Greg Olson .05
167 Terry Pendleton .05
168 Lonnie Smith .05
169 John Smoltz .05
170 Mike Stanton .05
171 Jeff Treadway .05
172 Paul Assenmacher .05
173 George Bell .05
174 Shawon Dunston .05
175 Mark Grace .05
176 Danny Jackson .05
177 Les Lancaster .05
178 Greg Maddux .50
179 Luis Salazar .05
180 Rey Sanchez .05
181 Ryne Sandberg .50
182 Jose Vizcaino .05
183 Chico Walker .05
184 Jerome Walton .05
185 Glenn Braggs .05
186 Tom Browning .05
187 Rob Dibble .05
188 Bill Doran .05
189 Chris Hammond .05
190 Billy Hatcher .05
191 Barry Larkin .05
192 Hal Morris .05
193 Joe Oliver .05
194 Paul O'Neill .05
195 Jeff Reed .05
196 Jose Rijo .05
197 Chris Sabo .05
198 Jeff Bagwell .40
199 Craig Biggio .05
200 Ken Caminiti .05
201 Andujar Cedeno .05
202 Steve Finley .05
203 Luis Gonzalez .05
204 Pete Harnisch .05
205 Xavier Hernandez .05
206 Darryl Kile .05
207 Al Osuna .05
208 Curt Schilling .25
209 Brett Butler .05
210 Kal Daniels .05
211 Lenny Harris .05
212 Stan Javier .05
213 Ramon Martinez .05
214 Roger McDowell .05
215 Jose Offerman .05
216 Juan Samuel .05
217 Mike Scioscia .05
218 Mike Sharperson .05
219 Darryl Strawberry .05
220 Delino DeShields .05
221 Tom Foley .05
222 Steve Frey .05
223 Dennis Martinez .05
224 Spike Owen .05
225 Gilberto Reyes .05
226 Tim Wallach .05
227 Daryl Boston .05
228 Tim Burke .05
229 Vince Coleman .05
230 David Cone .05
231 Kevin Elster .05
232 Dwight Gooden .05
233 Todd Hundley .05
234 Jeff Innis .05
235 Howard Johnson .05
236 Dave Magadan .05
237 Mackey Sasser .05
238 Anthony Young .05
239 Wes Chamberlain .05
240 Darren Daulton .05
241 Len Dykstra .05
242 Tommy Greene .05
243 Charlie Hayes .05
244 Dave Hollins .05
245 Ricky Jordan .05
246 John Kruk .05
247 Mickey Morandini .05
248 Terry Mulholland .05
249 Dale Murphy .25
250 Jay Bell .05
251 Barry Bonds 1.00
252 Steve Buechele .05
253 Doug Drabek .05
254 Mike LaValliere .05
255 Jose Lind .05
256 Lloyd McClendon .05
257 Orlando Merced .05
258 Don Slaught .05
259 John Smiley .05
260 Zane Smith .05
261 Randy Tomlin .05
262 Andy Van Slyke .05
263 Pedro Guerrero .05
264 Felix Jose .05
265 Ray Lankford .05
266 Omar Olivares .05
267 Jose Oquendo .05
268 Tom Pagnozzi .05
269 Bryn Smith .05
270 Lee Smith .05
271 Ozzie Smith .50
272 Milt Thompson .05
273 Todd Zeile .05
274 Andy Benes .05
275 Jerald Clark .05
276 Tony Fernandez .05
277 Tony Gwynn .50
278 Greg Harris .05
279 Thomas Howard .05
280 Bruce Hurst .05
281 Mike Maddux .05
282 Fred McGriff .05
283 Benito Santiago .05
284 Kevin Bass .05
285 Jeff Brantley .05
286 John Burkett .05
287 Will Clark .05
288 Royce Clayton .05
289 Steve Decker .05
290 Kelly Downs .05
291 Mike Felder .05
292 Darren Lewis .05
293 Kirt Manwaring .05
294 Willie McGee .05
295 Robby Thompson .05
296 Matt Williams .05
297 Trevor Wilson .05
298 Sandy Alomar, Jr. Checklist 1-108 .05
299 Rey Sanchez Checklist 109-208 .05
300 Nolan Ryan Checklist 209-300 .25
301 Brady Anderson .05
302 Todd Frohwirth .05
303 Ben McDonald .05
304 Mark McLemore .05
305 Jose Mesa .05
306 Bob Milacki .05
307 Gregg Olson .05
308 David Segui .05
309 Rick Sutcliffe .05
310 Jeff Tackett .05
311 Wade Boggs .50
312 Scott Cooper .05
313 John Flaherty .05
314 Wayne Housie .05
315 Peter Hoy .05
316 John Marzano .05
317 Tim Naehring .05
318 Phil Plantier .05
319 Frank Viola .05
320 Matt Young .05
321 Jim Abbott .05
322 Hubie Brooks .05
323 Chad Curtis **RC** .25
324 Alvin Davis .05
325 Junior Felix .05
326 Von Hayes .05
327 Mark Langston .05
328 Scott Lewis .05
329 Don Robinson .05
330 Bobby Rose .05
331 Lee Stevens .05
332 George Bell .05
333 Esteban Beltre .05
334 Joey Cora .05

335	Alex Fernandez	.05
336	Roberto Hernandez	.05
337	Mike Huff	.05
338	Kirk McCaskill	.05
339	Dan Pasqua	.05
340	Scott Radinsky	.05
341	Steve Sax	.05
342	Bobby Thigpen	.05
343	Robin Ventura	.05
344	Jack Armstrong	.05
345	Alex Cole	.05
346	Dennis Cook	.05
347	Glenallen Hill	.05
348	Thomas Howard	.05
349	Brook Jacoby	.05
350	Kenny Lofton	.05
351	Charles Nagy	.05
352	Rod Nichols	.05
353	Junior Ortiz	.05
354	Dave Otto	.05
355	Tony Perezchica	.05
356	Scott Scudder	.05
357	Paul Sorrento	.05
358	Skeeter Barnes	.05
359	Mark Carreon	.05
360	John Doherty	.05
361	Dan Gladden	.05
362	Bill Gullickson	.05
363	Shawn Hare	.05
364	Mike Henneman	.05
365	Chad Kreuter	.05
366	Mark Leiter	.05
367	Mike Munoz	.05
368	Kevin Ritz	.05
369	Mark Davis	.05
370	Tom Gordon	.05
371	Chris Gwynn	.05
372	Gregg Jefferies	.05
373	Wally Joyner	.05
374	Kevin McReynolds	.05
375	Keith Miller	.05
376	Rico Rossy	.05
377	Curtis Wilkerson	.05
378	Ricky Bones	.05
379	Chris Bosio	.05
380	Cal Eldred	.05
381	Scott Fletcher	.05
382	Jim Gantner	.05
383	Darryl Hamilton	.05
384	Doug Henry	.05
385	Pat Listach RC	.05
386	Tim McIntosh	.05
387	Edwin Nunez	.05
388	Dan Plesac	.05
389	Kevin Seitzer	.05
390	Franklin Stubbs	.05
391	William Suero	.05
392	Bill Wegman	.05
393	Willie Banks	.05
394	Jarvis Brown	.05
395	Greg Gagne	.05
396	Mark Guthrie	.05
397	Bill Krueger	.05
398	Pat Mahomes RC	.05
399	Pedro Munoz	.05
400	John Smiley	.05
401	Gary Wayne	.05
402	Lenny Webster	.05
403	Carl Willis	.05
404	Greg Cadaret	.05
405	Steve Farr	.05
406	Mike Gallego	.05
407	Charlie Hayes	.05
408	Steve Howe	.05
409	Dion James	.05
410	Jeff Johnson	.05
411	Tim Leary	.05
412	Jim Leyritz	.05
413	Melido Perez	.05
414	Scott Sanderson	.05
415	Andy Stankiewicz	.05
416	Mike Stanley	.05
417	Danny Tartabull	.05
418	Lance Blankenship	.05
419	Mike Bordick	.05
420	Scott Brosius RC	.05
421	Dennis Eckersley	.35
422	Scott Hemond	.05
423	Carney Lansford	.05
424	Henry Mercedes	.05
425	Mike Moore	.05
426	Gene Nelson	.05
427	Randy Ready	.05
428	Bruce Walton	.05
429	Willie Wilson	.05
430	Rich Amaral	.05
431	Dave Cochrane	.05
432	Henry Cotto	.05
433	Calvin Jones	.05
434	Kevin Mitchell	.05
435	Clay Parker	.05
436	Omar Vizquel	.05
437	Floyd Bannister	.05
438	Kevin Brown	.05
439	John Cangelosi	.05
440	Brian Downing	.05
441	Monty Fariss	.05
442	Jose Guzman	.05
443	Donald Harris	.05
444	Kevin Reimer	.05
445	Kenny Rogers	.05
446	Wayne Rosenthal	.05
447	Dickie Thon	.05
448	Derek Bell	.05
449	Juan Guzman	.05

450	Tom Henke	.05
451	Candy Maldonado	.05
452	Jack Morris	.05
453	David Wells	.05
454	Dave Winfield	.40
455	Juan Berenguer	.05
456	Damon Berryhill	.05
457	Mike Bielecki	.05
458	Marvin Freeman	.05
459	Charlie Leibrandt	.05
460	Kent Mercker	.05
461	Otis Nixon	.05
462	Alejandro Pena	.05
463	Ben Rivera	.05
464	Deion Sanders	.10
465	Mark Wohlers	.05
466	Shawn Boskie	.05
467	Frank Castillo	.05
468	Andre Dawson	.25
469	Joe Girardi	.05
470	Chuck McElroy	.05
471	Mike Morgan	.05
472	Ken Patterson	.05
473	Bob Scanlan	.05
474	Gary Scott	.05
475	Dave Smith	.05
476	Sammy Sosa	.50
477	Hector Villanueva	.05
478	Scott Bankhead	.05
479	Tim Belcher	.05
480	Freddie Benavides	.05
481	Jacob Brumfield	.05
482	Norm Charlton	.05
483	Dwayne Henry	.05
484	Dave Martinez	.05
485	Bip Roberts	.05
486	Reggie Sanders	.05
487	Greg Swindell	.05
488	Ryan Bowen	.05
489	Casey Candaele	.05
490	Juan Guerrero	.05
491	Pete Incaviglia	.05
492	Jeff Juden	.05
493	Rob Murphy	.05
494	Mark Portugal	.05
495	Rafael Ramirez	.05
496	Scott Servais	.05
497	Ed Taubensee	.05
498	Brian Williams	.05
499	Todd Benzinger	.05
500	John Candelaria	.05
501	Tom Candiotti	.05
502	Tim Crews	.05
503	Eric Davis	.05
504	Jim Gott	.05
505	Dave Hansen	.05
506	Carlos Hernandez	.05
507	Orel Hershiser	.05
508	Eric Karros	.05
509	Bob Ojeda	.05
510	Steve Wilson	.05
511	Moises Alou	.05
512	Bret Barberie	.05
513	Ivan Calderon	.05
514	Gary Carter	.40
515	Archi Cianfrocco	.05
516	Jeff Fassero	.05
517	Darrin Fletcher	.05
518	Marquis Grissom	.05
519	Chris Haney	.05
520	Ken Hill	.05
521	Chris Nabholz	.05
522	Bill Sampen	.05
523	John VanderWal	.05
524	David Wainhouse	.05
525	Larry Walker	.05
526	John Wetteland	.05
527	Bobby Bonilla	.05
528	Sid Fernandez	.05
529	John Franco	.05
530	Dave Gallagher	.05
531	Paul Gibson	.05
532	Eddie Murray	.40
533	Junior Noboa	.05
534	Charlie O'Brien	.05
535	Bill Pecota	.05
536	Willie Randolph	.05
537	Bret Saberhagen	.05
538	Dick Schofield	.05
539	Pete Schourek	.05
540	Ruben Amaro	.05
541	Andy Ashby	.05
542	Kim Batiste	.05
543	Cliff Brantley	.05
544	Mariano Duncan	.05
545	Jeff Grotewold	.05
546	Barry Jones	.05
547	Julio Peguero	.05
548	Curt Schilling	.25
549	Mitch Williams	.05
550	Stan Belinda	.05
551	Scott Bullett	.05
552	Cecil Espy	.05
553	Jeff King	.05
554	Roger Mason	.05
555	Paul Miller	.05
556	Denny Neagle	.05
557	Vocente Palacios	.05
558	Bob Patterson	.05
559	Tom Prince	.05
560	Gary Redus	.05
561	Gary Varsho	.05
562	Juan Agosto	.05
563	Cris Carpenter	.05
564	Mark Clark RC	.05

565	Jose DeLeon	.05
566	Rich Gedman	.05
567	Bernard Gilkey	.05
568	Rex Hudler	.05
569	Tim Jones	.05
570	Donovan Osborne	.05
571	Mike Perez	.05
572	Gerald Perry	.05
573	Bob Tewksbury	.05
574	Todd Worrell	.05
575	Dave Eiland	.05
576	Jeremy Hernandez	.05
577	Craig Lefferts	.05
578	Jose Melendez	.05
579	Randy Myers	.05
580	Gary Pettis	.05
581	Rich Rodriguez	.05
582	Gary Sheffield	.30
583	Craig Shipley	.05
584	Kurt Stillwell	.05
585	Tim Teufel	.05
586	Rod Beck RC	.05
587	Dave Burba	.05
588	Craig Colbert	.05
589	Bryan Hickerson	.05
590	Mike Jackson	.05
591	Mark Leonard	.05
592	Jim McNamara	.05
593	John Patterson	.05
594	Dave Righetti	.05
595	Cory Snyder	.05
596	Bill Swift	.05
597	Ted Wood	.05
598	Scott Sanderson	
	Checklist 301-403	.05
599	Junior Ortiz Checklist 404-498	.05
600	Mike Morgan	
	Checklist 499-600	.05

All-Rookies

NM/M

Complete Set (10):		2.00
Common Player:		.25
1	Eric Karros	.35
2	Andy Stankiewicz	.25
3	Gary DiSarcina	.25
4	Archi Cianfrocco	.25
5	Jim McNamara	.25
6	Chad Curtis	.25
7	Kenny Lofton	.35
8	Reggie Sanders	.25
9	Pat Mahomes	.25
10	Donovan Osborne	.25

All-Stars

NM/M

Complete Set (20):		7.50
Common Player:		.15
1	Mark McGwire	1.25
2	Roberto Alomar	.30
3	Cal Ripken, Jr.	1.50
4	Wade Boggs	.75
5	Mickey Tettleton	.15
6	Ken Griffey Jr.	1.00
7	Roberto Kelly	.15
8	Kirby Puckett	.75
9	Frank Thomas	.65

10	Jack McDowell	.15
11	Will Clark	.15
12	Ryne Sandberg	.75
13	Barry Larkin	.15
14	Gary Sheffield	.35
15	Tom Pagnozzi	.15
16	Barry Bonds	1.50
17	Deion Sanders	.15
18	Darryl Strawberry	.15
19	David Cone	.15
20	Tom Glavine	.30

Award Winners

CAL RIPKEN, JR.

NM/M

Complete Set (26):		10.00
Common Player:		.20
1	Jack Morris	.20
2	Chuck Knoblauch	.20
3	Jeff Bagwell	.75
4	Terry Pendleton	.20
5	Cal Ripken, Jr.	2.00
6	Roger Clemens	1.25
7	Tom Glavine	.35
8	Tom Pagnozzi	.20
9	Ozzie Smith	1.00
10	Andy Van Slyke	.20
11	Barry Bonds	2.00
12	Tony Gwynn	1.00
13	Matt Williams	.20
14	Will Clark	.20
15	Robin Ventura	.20
16	Mark Langston	.20
18	Devon White	.20
19	Don Mattingly	1.25
20	Roberto Alomar	.40
21a	Cal Ripken, Jr. (Reversed negative.)	2.00
21b	Cal Ripken, Jr. (Correct)	2.00
22	Ken Griffey Jr.	1.50
23	Kirby Puckett	1.00
24	Greg Maddux	1.00
25	Ryne Sandberg	1.00

Tony Gwynn

TONY GWYNN
COMMEMORATIVE SERIES

NM/M

Complete Set (12):		9.00
Common Card:		.75
Certified Autograph Card:		60.00
INSERT CARDS		
1	Tony Gwynn/Fldg	.75
2	Tony Gwynn/Btg	.75
3	Tony Gwynn/Fldg	.75
4	Tony Gwynn/Btg	.75
5	Tony Gwynn/Base-running	.75
6	Tony Gwynn/Awards	.75
7	Tony Gwynn/Bunting	.75
8	Tony Gwynn/Btg	.75
9	Tony Gwynn/Running	.75
10	Tony Gwynn/Btg	.75
SEND-AWAY CARDS		
1	Tony Gwynn/Btg	2.00
2	Tony Gwynn/Fldg	2.00
SPECIAL CARDS		
---	Tony Gwynn, Paul Mullan	3.00
---	Tony Gwynn/ Casa de Amparo	7.50

1993 Ultra

		NM/M
Complete Set (650):		15.00
Common Player:		.05
Series 1 or 2 Pack (14):		.75
Series 1 or 2 Wax Box (36):		15.00
1	Steve Avery	.05
2	Rafael Belliard	.05
3	Damon Berryhill	.05
4	Sid Bream	.05
5	Ron Gant	.05
6	Tom Glavine	.20
7	Ryan Klesko	.05
8	Mark Lemke	.05
9	Javier Lopez	.05
10	Greg Olson	.05
11	Terry Pendleton	.05
12	Deion Sanders	.05
13	Mike Stanton	.05
14	Paul Assenmacher	.05
15	Steve Buechele	.05
16	Frank Castillo	.05
17	Shawon Dunston	.05
18	Mark Grace	.05
19	Derrick May	.05
20	Chuck McElroy	.05
21	Mike Morgan	.05
22	Bob Scanlan	.05
23	Dwight Smith	.05
24	Sammy Sosa	.60
25	Rick Wilkins	.05
26	Tim Belcher	.05
27	Jeff Branson	.05
28	Bill Doran	.05
29	Chris Hammond	.05
30	Barry Larkin	.05
31	Hal Morris	.05
32	Joe Oliver	.05
33	Jose Rijo	.05
34	Bip Roberts	.05
35	Chris Sabo	.05
36	Reggie Sanders	.05
37	Craig Biggio	.05
38	Ken Caminiti	.05
39	Steve Finley	.05
40	Luis Gonzalez	.05
41	Juan Guerrero	.05
42	Pete Harnisch	.05
43	Xavier Hernandez	.05
44	Doug Jones	.05
45	Al Osuna	.05
46	Eddie Taubensee	.05
47	Scooter Tucker	.05
48	Brian Williams	.05
49	Pedro Astacio	.05
50	Rafael Bournigal	.05
51	Brett Butler	.05
52	Tom Candiotti	.05
53	Eric Davis	.05
54	Lenny Harris	.05
55	Orel Hershiser	.05
56	Eric Karros	.05
57	Pedro Martinez	.50
58	Roger McDowell	.05
59	Jose Offerman	.05
60	Mike Piazza	.75
61	Moises Alou	.05
62	Kent Bottenfield	.05
63	Archi Cianfrocco	.05
64	Greg Colbrunn	.05
65	Wil Cordero	.05
66	Delino DeShields	.05
67	Darrin Fletcher	.05
68	Ken Hill	.05
69	Chris Nabholz	.05
70	Mel Rojas	.05
71	Larry Walker	.05
72	Sid Fernandez	.05
73	John Franco	.05
74	Dave Gallagher	.05
75	Todd Hundley	.05
76	Howard Johnson	.05
77	Jeff Kent	.05
78	Eddie Murray	.50
79	Bret Saberhagen	.05
80	Chico Walker	.05
81	Anthony Young	.05
82	Kyle Abbott	.05
83	Ruben Amaro Jr.	.05
84	Juan Bell	.05
85	Wes Chamberlain	.05
86	Darren Daulton	.05
87	Mariano Duncan	.05
88	Dave Hollins	.05
89	Ricky Jordan	.05
90	John Kruk	.05
91	Mickey Morandini	.05
92	Terry Mulholland	.05
93	Ben Rivera	.05
94	Mike Williams	.05
95	Stan Belinda	.05
96	Jay Bell	.05
97	Jeff King	.05
98	Mike LaValliere	.05
99	Lloyd McClendon	.05
100	Orlando Merced	.05
101	Zane Smith	.05
102	Randy Tomlin	.05
103	Andy Van Slyke	.05
104	Tim Wakefield	.05
105	John Wehner	.05
106	Bernard Gilkey	.05
107	Brian Jordan	.05
108	Ray Lankford	.05
109	Donovan Osborne	.05
110	Tom Pagnozzi	.05
111	Mike Perez	.05
112	Lee Smith	.05
113	Ozzie Smith	.60
114	Bob Tewksbury	.05
115	Todd Zeile	.05
116	Andy Benes	.05
117	Greg Harris	.05
118	Darrin Jackson	.05
119	Fred McGriff	.05
120	Rich Rodriguez	.05
121	Frank Seminara	.05
122	Gary Sheffield	.35
123	Craig Shipley	.05
124	Kurt Stillwell	.05
125	Dan Walters	.05
126	Rod Beck	.05
127	Mike Benjamin	.05
128	Jeff Brantley	.05
129	John Burkett	.05
130	Will Clark	.05
131	Royce Clayton	.05
132	Steve Hosey	.05
133	Mike Jackson	.05
134	Darren Lewis	.05
135	Kirt Manwaring	.05
136	Bill Swift	.05
137	Robby Thompson	.05
138	Brady Anderson	.05
139	Glenn Davis	.05
140	Leo Gomez	.05
141	Chito Martinez	.05
142	Ben McDonald	.05
143	Alan Mills	.05
144	Mike Mussina	.30
145	Gregg Olson	.05
146	David Segui	.05
147	Jeff Tackett	.05
148	Jack Clark	.05
149	Scott Cooper	.05
150	Danny Darwin	.05
151	John Dopson	.05
152	Mike Greenwell	.05
153	Tim Naehring	.05
154	Tony Pena	.05
155	Paul Quantrill	.05
156	Mo Vaughn	.05
157	Frank Viola	.05
158	Bob Zupcic	.05
159	Chad Curtis	.05
160	Gary DiScarcina	.05
161	Damion Easley	.05
162	Chuck Finley	.05
163	Tim Fortugno	.05
164	Rene Gonzales	.05
165	Joe Grahe	.05
166	Mark Langston	.05
167	John Orton	.05
168	Luis Polonia	.05
169	Julio Valera	.05
170	Wilson Alvarez	.05
171	George Bell	.05
172	Joey Cora	.05
173	Alex Fernandez	.05
174	Lance Johnson	.05
175	Ron Karkovice	.05
176	Jack McDowell	.05
177	Scott Radinsky	.05
178	Tim Raines	.05
179	Steve Sax	.05
180	Bobby Thigpen	.05
181	Frank Thomas	.50
182	Sandy Alomar Jr.	.05
183	Carlos Baerga	.05
184	Felix Fermin	.05
185	Thomas Howard	.05
186	Mark Lewis	.05
187	Derek Lilliquist	.05
188	Carlos Martinez	.05
189	Charles Nagy	.05
190	Scott Scudder	.05
191	Paul Sorrento	.05
192	Jim Thome	.40
193	Mark Whiten	.05
194	Milt Cuyler	.05
195	Rob Deer	.05
196	John Doherty	.05
197	Travis Fryman	.05
198	Dan Gladden	.05
199	Mike Henneman	.05
200	John Kiely	.05
201	Chad Kreuter	.05
202	Scott Livingstone	.05
203	Tony Phillips	.05
204	Alan Trammell	.05
205	Mike Boddicker	.05
206	George Brett	.65
207	Tom Gordon	.05
208	Mark Gubicza	.05
209	Gregg Jefferies	.05
210	Wally Joyner	.05
211	Kevin Koslofski	.05
212	Brent Mayne	.05
213	Brian McRae	.05
214	Kevin McReynolds	.05
215	Rusty Meacham	.05
216	Steve Shifflett	.05
217	James Austin	.05
218	Cal Eldred	.05
219	Darryl Hamilton	.05
220	Doug Henry	.05
221	John Jaha	.05
222	Dave Nilsson	.05
223	Jesse Orosco	.05
224	B.J. Surhoff	.05
225	Greg Vaughn	.05
226	Bill Wegman	.05
227	Robin Yount	.50
228	Rick Aguilera	.05
229	J.T. Bruett	.05
230	Scott Erickson	.05
231	Kent Hrbek	.05
232	Terry Jorgensen	.05
233	Scott Leius	.05
234	Pat Mahomes	.05
235	Pedro Munoz	.05
236	Kirby Puckett	.60
237	Kevin Tapani	.05
238	Lenny Webster	.05
239	Carl Willis	.05
240	Mike Gallego	.05
241	John Habyan	.05
242	Pat Kelly	.05
243	Kevin Maas	.05
244	Don Mattingly	.65
245	Hensley Meulens	.05
246	Sam Militello	.05
247	Matt Nokes	.05
248	Melido Perez	.05
249	Andy Stankiewicz	.05
250	Randy Velarde	.05
251	Bob Wickman	.05
252	Bernie Williams	.05
253	Lance Blankenship	.05
254	Mike Bordick	.05
255	Jerry Browne	.05
256	Ron Darling	.05
257a	Dennis Eckersley	.40
257b	Dennis Eckersley (Wt. 195; no "MLBPA" on back - unmarked sample card.)	1.50
257c	Dennis Eckersley (Wt, 195; no "Printed in USA" on back - unmarked sample card.)	1.50
258	Rickey Henderson	.50
259	Vince Horsman	.05
260	Troy Neel	.05
261	Jeff Parrett	.05
262	Terry Steinbach	.05
263	Bob Welch	.05
264	Bobby Witt	.05
265	Rich Amaral	.05
266	Bret Boone	.05
267	Jay Buhner	.05
268	Dave Fleming	.05
269	Randy Johnson	.50
270	Edgar Martinez	.05
271	Mike Schooler	.05
272	Russ Swan	.05
273	Dave Valle	.05
274	Omar Vizquel	.05
275	Kerry Woodson	.05
276	Kevin Brown	.05
277	Julio Franco	.05
278	Jeff Frye	.05
279	Juan Gonzalez	.25
280	Jeff Huson	.05
281	Rafael Palmeiro	.40
282	Dean Palmer	.05
283	Roger Pavlik	.05
284	Ivan Rodriguez	.40
285	Kenny Rogers	.05
286	Derek Bell	.05
287	Pat Borders	.05
288	Joe Carter	.05
289	Bob MacDonald	.05
290	Jack Morris	.05
291	John Olerud	.05
292	Ed Sprague	.05
293	Todd Stottlemyre	.05
294	Mike Timlin	.05
295	Duane Ward	.05
296	David Wells	.05
297	Devon White	.05
298	Ray Lankford Checklist	.05
299	Bobby Witt Checklist	.05
300	Mike Piazza Checklist	.40
301	Steve Bedrosian	.05
302	Jeff Blauser	.05
303	Francisco Cabrera	.05
304	Marvin Freeman	.05
305	Brian Hunter	.05
306	Dave Justice	.05
307	Greg Maddux	.60
308	Greg McMichael **RC**	.05
309	Kent Mercker	.05
310	Otis Nixon	.05
311	Pete Smith	.05
312	John Smoltz	.05
313	Jose Guzman	.05
314	Mike Harkey	.05
315	Greg Hibbard	.05
316	Candy Maldonado	.05
317	Randy Myers	.05
318	Dan Plesac	.05
319	Rey Sanchez	.05
320	Ryne Sandberg	.60
321	Tommy Shields **RC**	.05
322	Jose Vizcaino	.05
323	Matt Walbeck **RC**	.05
324	Willie Wilson	.05
325	Tom Browning	.05
326	Tim Costo	.05
327	Rob Dibble	.05
328	Steve Foster	.05
329	Roberto Kelly	.05
330	Randy Milligan	.05
331	Kevin Mitchell	.05
332	Tim Pugh **RC**	.05
333	Jeff Reardon	.05
334	John Roper **RC**	.05
335	Juan Samuel	.05
336	John Smiley	.05
337	San Wilson	.05
338	Scott Aldred	.05
339	Andy Ashby	.05
340	Freddie Benavides	.05
341	Dante Bichette	.05
342	Willie Blair	.05
343	Daryl Boston	.05
344	Vinny Castilla	.05
345	Jerald Clark	.05
346	Alex Cole	.05
347	Andres Galarraga	.05
348	Joe Girardi	.05
349	Ryan Hawblitzel **RC**	.05
350	Charlie Hayes	.05
351	Butch Henry	.05
352	Darren Holmes	.05
353	Dale Murphy	.20
354	David Nied	.05
355	Jeff Parrett	.05
356	Steve Reed **RC**	.05
357	Bruce Ruffin	.05
358	Danny Sheaffer **RC**	.05
359	Bryn Smith	.05
360	Jim Tatum **RC**	.05
361	Eric Young	.05
362	Gerald Young	.05
363	Luis Aquino	.05
364	Alex Arias **RC**	.05
365	Jack Armstrong	.05
366	Bret Barberie	.05
367	Ryan Bowen	.05
368	Greg Briley	.05
369	Cris Carpenter	.05
370	Chuck Carr	.05
371	Jeff Conine **RC**	.25
372	Steve Decker	.05
373	Orestes Destrade	.05
374	Monty Fariss	.05
375	Junior Felix	.05
376	Chris Hammond	.05
377	Bryan Harvey	.05
378	Trevor Hoffman **RC**	.25
379	Charlie Hough	.05
380	Joe Klink	.05
381	Richie Lewis **RC**	.05
382	Dave Magadan	.05
383	Bob McClure	.05
384	Scott Pose **RC**	.05
385	Rich Renteria **RC**	.05
386	Benito Santiago	.05
387	Walt Weiss	.05
388	Nigel Wilson	.05
389	Eric Anthony	.05
390	Jeff Bagwell	.50
391	Andujar Cedeno	.05
392	Doug Drabek	.05
393	Darryl Kile	.05
394	Mark Portugal	.05
395	Karl Rhodes	.05
396	Scott Servais	.05
397	Greg Swindell	.05
398	Tom Goodwin	.05
399	Kevin Gross	.05
400	Carlos Hernandez	.05
401	Ramon Martinez	.05
402	Raul Mondesi	.05
403	Jody Reed	.05
404	Mike Sharperson	.05
405	Cory Snyder	.05
406	Darryl Strawberry	.05
407	Rick Trlicek **RC**	.05
408	Tim Wallach	.05
409	Todd Worrell	.05
410	Tavo Alvarez	.05
411	Sean Berry **RC**	.05
412	Frank Bolick **RC**	.05
413	Cliff Floyd	.05
414	Mike Gardiner	.05
415	Marquis Grissom	.05
416	Tim Laker **RC**	.05
417	Mike Lansing **RC**	.10
418	Dennis Martinez	.05
419	John Vander Wal	.05
420	John Wetteland	.05
421	Rondell White	.05
422	Bobby Bonilla	.05

423	Jeromy Burnitz	.05
424	Vince Burnitz RC	.05
425	Mike Draper RC	.05
426	Tony Fernandez	.05
427	Dwight Gooden	.05
428	Jeff Innis	.05
429	Bobby Jones	.05
430	Mike Maddux	.05
431	Charlie O'Brien	.05
432	Joe Orsulak	.05
433	Pete Schourek	.05
434	Frank Tanana	.05
435	Ryan Thompson RC	.05
436	Kim Batiste	.05
437	Mark Davis	.05
438	Jose DeLeon	.05
439	Len Dykstra	.05
440	Jim Eisenreich	.05
441	Tommy Greene	.05
442	Pete Incaviglia	.05
443	Danny Jackson	.05
444	Todd Pratt RC	.05
445	Curt Schilling	.20
446	Milt Thompson	.05
447	David West	.05
448	Mitch Williams	.05
449	Steve Cooke	.05
450	Carlos Garcia	.05
451	Al Martin	.05
452	Blas Minor RC	.05
453	Dennis Moeller	.05
454	Denny Neagle	.05
455	Don Slaught	.05
456	Lonnie Smith	.05
457	Paul Wagner	.05
458	Bob Walk	.05
459	Kevin Young	.05
460	Rene Arocha RC	.05
461	Brian Barber	.05
462	Rheal Cormier	.05
463	Gregg Jefferies	.05
464	Joe Magrane	.05
465	Omar Olivares	.05
466	Geronimo Pena	.05
467	Allen Watson	.05
468	Mark Whiten	.05
469	Derek Bell	.05
470	Phil Clark	.05
471	Pat Gomez RC	.05
472	Tony Gwynn	.60
473	Jeremy Hernandez	.05
474	Bruce Hurst	.05
475	Phil Plantier	.05
476	Scott Sanders RC	.05
477	Tim Scott RC	.05
478	Darrell Sherman RC	.05
479	Guillermo Velasquez	.05
480	Tim Worrell RC	.05
481	Todd Benzinger	.05
482	Bud Black	.05
483	Barry Bonds	1.50
484	Dave Burba	.05
485	Bryan Hickerson	.05
486	Dave Martinez	.05
487	Willie McGee	.05
488	Jeff Reed	.05
489	Kevin Rogers	.05
490	Matt Williams	.05
491	Trevor Wilson	.05
492	Harold Baines	.05
493	Mike Devereaux	.05
494	Todd Frohwirth	.05
495	Chris Hoiles	.05
496	Luis Mercedes	.05
497	Sherman Obando RC	.05
498	Brad Pennington RC	.05
499	Harold Reynolds	.05
500	Arthur Rhodes	.05
501	Cal Ripken, Jr.	1.50
502	Rick Sutcliffe	.05
503	Fernando Valenzuela	.05
504	Mark Williamson	.05
505	Scott Bankhead	.05
506	Greg Blosser	.05
507	Ivan Calderon	.05
508	Roger Clemens	.65
509	Andre Clemens	.05
510	Scott Fletcher	.05
511	Greg Harris	.05
512	Billy Hatcher	.05
513	Bob Melvin	.05
514	Carlos Quintana	.05
515	Luis Rivera	.05
516	Jeff Russell	.05
517	Ken Ryan RC	.05
518	Chili Davis	.05
519	Jim Edmonds RC	1.50
520	Gary Gaetti	.05
521	Torey Lovullo	.05
522	Tony Percival RC	.05
523	Tim Salmon	.05
524	Scott Sanderson	.05
525	J.T. Snow RC	.75
526	Jerome Walton	.05
527	Jason Bere	.05
528	Rod Bolton RC	.05
529	Ellis Burks	.05
530	Carlton Fisk	.05
531	Craig Grebeck	.05
532	Ozzie Guillen	.05
533	Roberto Hernandez	.05
534	Bo Jackson	.10
535	Kirk McCaskill	.05
536	Dave Stieb	.05
537	Robin Ventura	.05

538	Albert Belle	.05
539	Mike Bielecki	.05
540	Glenallen Hill	.05
541	Reggie Jefferson	.05
542	Kenny Lofton	.05
543	Jeff Mutis RC	.05
544	Junior Ortiz	.05
545	Manny Ramirez	.50
546	Jeff Treadway	.05
547	Kevin Wickander	.05
548	Cecil Fielder	.05
549	Kirk Gibson	.05
550	Greg Gohr RC	.05
551	David Haas	.05
552	Bill Krueger	.05
553	Mike Moore	.05
554	Mickey Tettleton	.05
555	Lou Whitaker	.05
556	Kevin Appier	.05
557	Billy Brewer RC	.05
558	David Cone	.05
559	Greg Gagne	.05
560	Mark Gardner	.05
561	Phil Hiatt	.05
562	Felix Jose	.05
563	Jose Lind	.05
564	Mike Macfarlane	.05
565	Keith Miller	.05
566	Jeff Montgomery	.05
567	Hipolito Pechardo	.05
568	Ricky Bones	.05
569	Tom Brunansky	.05
570	Joe Kmak RC	.05
571	Pat Listach	.05
572	Graeme Lloyd RC	.05
573	Carlos Maldonado RC	.05
574	Josias Manzanillo	.05
575	Matt Mieske	.05
576	Kevin Reimer	.05
577	Bill Spiers	.05
578	Dickie Thon	.05
579	Willie Banks	.05
580	Jim Deshaies	.05
581	Mark Guthrie	.05
582	Brian Harper	.05
583	Chuck Knoblauch	.05
584	Gene Larkin	.05
585	Shane Mack	.05
586	David McCarty	.05
587	Mike Pagliarulo	.05
588	Mike Trombley	.05
589	Dave Winfield	.50
590	Jim Abbott	.05
591	Wade Boggs	.60
592	Russ Davis RC	.05
593	Steve Farr	.05
594	Steve Howe	.05
595	Mike Humphreys RC	.05
596	Jimmy Key	.05
597	Jim Leyritz	.05
598	Bobby Munoz RC	.05
599	Paul O'Neill	.05
600	Spike Owen	.05
601	Mike Stanley	.05
602	Danny Tartabull	.05
603	Scott Brosius	.05
604	Storm Davis	.05
605	Eric Fox	.05
606	Goose Gossage	.05
607	Scott Hammond	.05
608	Dave Henderson	.05
609	Mark McGwire	1.00
610	Mike Mohler RC	.05
611	Edwin Nunez	.05
612	Kevin Seitzer	.05
613	Ruben Sierra	.05
614	Chris Bosio	.05
615	Norm Charlton	.05
616	Jim Converse RC	.05
617	John Cummings RC	.05
618	Mike Felder	.05
619	Ken Griffey Jr.	.75
620	Mike Hampton	.05
621	Erik Hanson	.05
622	Bill Haselman	.05
623	Tino Martinez	.05
624	Lee Tinsley	.05
625	Fernando Vina RC	.05
626	David Wainhouse RC	.05
627	Jose Canseco	.30
628	Benji Gil	.05
629	Tom Henke	.05
630	David Hulse RC	.05
631	Manuel Lee	.05
632	Craig Lefferts	.05
633	Robb Nen RC	.05
634	Gary Redus	.05
635	Bill Ripken	.05
636	Nolan Ryan	1.50
637	Dan Smith	.05
638	Matt Whiteside RC	.05
639	Roberto Alomar	.25
640	Juan Guzman	.05
641	Pat Hentgen	.05
642	Darrin Jackson	.05
643	Randy Knorr	.05
644	Domingo Martinez RC	.05
645	Paul Molitor	.50
646	Dick Schofield	.05
647	Dave Stewart	.05
648	Rey Sanchez Checklist	.05
649	Jeremy Hernandez Checklist	.05
650	Junior Ortiz Checklist	.05

All-Rookies

MIKE PIAZZA

NM/M

Complete Set (10):		4.00
Common Player:		.25
1	Rene Arocha	.25
2	Jeff Conine	.25
3	Phil Hiatt	.25
4	Mike Lansing	.25
5	Al Martin	.25
6	David Nied	.25
7	Mike Piazza	3.00
8	Tim Salmon	.50
9	J.T. Snow	.45
10	Kevin Young	.25

All-Stars

NM/M

Complete Set (20):		17.50
Common Player:		.25
1	Darren Daulton	.25
2	Will Clark	.35
3	Ryne Sandberg	1.50
4	Barry Larkin	.25
5	Gary Sheffield	.40
6	Barry Bonds	3.00
7	Ray Lankford	.25
8	Larry Walker	.25
9	Greg Maddux	1.50
10	Lee Smith	.25
11	Ivan Rodriguez	.75
12	Mark McGwire	2.50
13	Carlos Baerga	.25
14	Cal Ripken, Jr.	3.00
15	Edgar Martinez	.25
16	Juan Gonzalez	1.00
17	Ken Griffey Jr.	2.00
18	Kirby Puckett	1.50
19	Frank Thomas	1.25
20	Mike Mussina	.65

Award Winners

NM/M

Complete Set (25):		12.00
Common Player:		.25
1	Greg Maddux	.75
2	Tom Pagnozzi	.25
3	Mark Grace	.25
4	Jose Lind	.25
5	Terry Pendleton	.25
6	Ozzie Smith	.75
7	Barry Bonds	2.00
8	Andy Van Slyke	.25
9	Larry Walker	.25
10	Mark Langston	.25

11	Ivan Rodriguez	.60
12	Don Mattingly	.75
13	Roberto Alomar	.35
14	Robin Ventura	.25
15	Cal Ripken, Jr.	2.00
16	Ken Griffey Jr.	1.00
17	Kirby Puckett	.75
18	Devon White	.25
19	Pat Listach	.25
20	Eric Karros	.25
21	Pat Borders	.25
22	Greg Maddux	.75
23	Dennis Eckersley	.60
24	Barry Bonds	2.00
25	Gary Sheffield	.45

1993 Ultra Commemorative

NM/M

Dennis Eckersley, Paul Mullan	5.00

Dennis Eckersley Career Highlights

NM/M

Complete Set (12):		6.00
Common Card:		.50
Autographed Card:		35.00
1	"Perfection" (A's 1987-92)	.50
2	"The Kid" (Indians 1975-77)	.50
3	"The Warrior" (Indians 1975-77)	.50
4	"Beantown Blazer" (Red Sox 1978-84)	.50
5	"Eckspeak" (Red Sox 1978-84)	.50
6	"Down to Earth" (Red Sox 1978-84)	.50
7	"Wrigley Bound" (Cubs 1984-86)	.50
8	"No Relief" (A's 1987-92)	.50
9	"In Control" (A's 1987-92)	.50
10	"Simply the Best" (A's 1987-92)	.50
11	"Reign of Perfection" (A's 1987-92)	.50
12	"Leaving His Mark" (A's 1987-92)	.50

Home Run Kings

NM/M

Complete Set (10):		8.00
Common Player:		.50
1	Juan Gonzalez	.65
2	Mark McGwire	2.50
3	Cecil Fielder	.50
4	Fred McGriff	.50
5	Albert Belle	.50
6	Barry Bonds	2.50
7	Joe Carter	.50
8	Gary Sheffield	.65

Joe Carter
TORONTO BLUE JAYS

		NM/M
9	Darren Daulton	.50
10	Dave Hollins	.50

Performers

ULTRA PERFORMERS
J.T. SNOW

		NM/M
Complete Set (10):		5.00
Common Player:		.25
1	Barry Bonds	2.50
2	Juan Gonzalez	.30
3	Ken Griffey Jr.	1.00
4	Eric Karros	.25
5	Pat Listach	.25
6	Greg Maddux	.75
7	David Nied	.25
8	Gary Sheffield	.40
9	J.T. Snow	.25
10	Frank Thomas	.65

Strikeout Kings

RANDY JOHNSON

		NM/M
Complete Set (5):		7.50
Common Player:		.25
1	Roger Clemens	2.50
2	Juan Guzman	.25
3	Randy Johnson	1.25
4	Nolan Ryan	5.00
5	John Smoltz	.50

1994 Ultra

		NM/M
Complete Set (600):		15.00
Common Player:		.05
Series 1 or 2 Pack (14):		.50
Series 1 or 2 Wax Box (36):		15.00
1	Jeffrey Hammonds	.05
2	Chris Hoiles	.05
3	Ben McDonald	.05
4	Mark McLemore	.05
5	Alan Mills	.05
6	Jamie Moyer	.05
7	Brad Pennington	.05
8	Jim Poole	.05
9	Cal Ripken, Jr.	1.50
10	Jack Voigt	.05

11	Roger Clemens	.65
12	Danny Darwin	.05
13	Andre Dawson	.25
14	Scott Fletcher	.05
15	Greg Harris	.05
16	Billy Hatcher	.05
17	Jeff Russell	.05
18	Aaron Sele	.05
19	Mo Vaughn	.05
20	Mike Butcher	.05
21	Rod Correia	.05
22	Steve Frey	.05
23	Phil Leftwich **RC**	.05
24	Torey Lovullo	.05
25	Ken Patterson	.05
26	Eduardo Perez	.05
27	Tim Salmon	.05
28	J.T. Snow	.05
29	Chris Turner	.05
30	Wilson Alvarez	.05
31	Jason Bere	.05
32	Joey Cora	.05
33	Alex Fernandez	.05
34	Roberto Hernandez	.05
35	Lance Johnson	.05
36	Ron Karkovice	.05
37	Kirk McCaskill	.05
38	Jeff Schwarz	.05
39	Frank Thomas	.50
40	Sandy Alomar Jr.	.05
41	Albert Belle	.05
42	Felix Fermin	.05
43	Wayne Kirby	.05
44	Tom Kramer	.05
45	Kenny Lofton	.05
46	Jose Mesa	.05
47	Eric Plunk	.05
48	Paul Sorrento	.05
49	Jim Thome	.35
50	Bill Wertz	.05
51	John Doherty	.05
52	Cecil Fielder	.05
53	Travis Fryman	.05
54	Chris Gomez	.05
55	Mike Henneman	.05
56	Chad Kreuter	.05
57	Bob MacDonald	.05
58	Mike Moore	.05
59	Tony Phillips	.05
60	Lou Whitaker	.05
61	Kevin Appier	.05
62	Greg Gagne	.05
63	Chris Gwynn	.05
64	Bob Hamelin	.05
65	Chris Haney	.05
66	Phil Hiatt	.05
67	Felix Jose	.05
68	Jose Lind	.05
69	Mike Macfarlane	.05
70	Jeff Montgomery	.05
71	Hipolito Pichardo	.05
72	Juan Bell	.05
73	Cal Eldred	.05
74	Darryl Hamilton	.05
75	Doug Henry	.05
76	Mike Ignasiak	.05
77	John Jaha	.05
78	Graeme Lloyd	.05
79	Angel Miranda	.05
80	Dave Nilsson	.05
81	Troy O'Leary	.05
82	Kevin Reimer	.05
83	Willie Banks	.05
84	Larry Casian	.05
85	Scott Erickson	.05
86	Eddie Guardado	.05
87	Kent Hrbek	.05
88	Terry Jorgensen	.05
89	Chuck Knoblauch	.05
90	Pat Meares	.05
91	Mike Trombley	.05
92	Dave Winfield	.05
93	Wade Boggs	.60
94	Scott Kamieniecki	.05
95	Pat Kelly	.05
96	Jimmy Key	.05
97	Jim Leyritz	.05
98	Bobby Munoz	.05
99	Paul O'Neill	.05
100	Melido Perez	.05
101	Mike Stanley	.05
102	Danny Tartabull	.05

103	Bernie Williams	.05
104	Kurt Abbott **RC**	.05
105	Mike Bordick	.05
106	Ron Darling	.05
107	Brent Gates	.05
108	Miguel Jimenez	.05
109	Steve Karsay	.05
110	Scott Lydy	.05
111	Mark McGwire	1.00
112	Troy Neel	.05
113	Craig Paquette	.05
114	Bob Welch	.05
115	Bobby Witt	.05
116	Rich Amaral	.05
117	Mike Blowers	.05
118	Jay Buhner	.05
119	Dave Fleming	.05
120	Ken Griffey Jr.	.75
121	Tino Martinez	.05
122	Marc Newfield	.05
123	Ted Power	.05
124	Mackey Sasser	.05
125	Omar Vizquel	.05
126	Kevin Brown	.05
127	Juan Gonzalez	.25
128	Tom Henke	.05
129	David Hulse	.05
130	Dean Palmer	.05
131	Roger Pavlik	.05
132	Ivan Rodriguez	.40
133	Kenny Rogers	.05
134	Doug Strange	.05
135	Pat Borders	.05
136	Joe Carter	.05
137	Darnell Coles	.05
138	Pat Hentgen	.05
139	Al Leiter	.05
140	Paul Molitor	.50
141	John Olerud	.05
142	Ed Sprague	.05
143	Dave Stewart	.05
144	Mike Timlin	.05
145	Duane Ward	.05
146	Devon White	.05
147	Steve Avery	.05
148	Steve Bedrosian	.05
149	Damon Berryhill	.05
150	Jeff Blauser	.05
151	Tom Glavine	.20
152	Chipper Jones	.75
153	Mark Lemke	.05
154	Fred McGriff	.05
155	Greg McMichael	.05
156	Deion Sanders	.05
157	John Smoltz	.05
158	Mark Wohlers	.05
159	Jose Bautista	.05
160	Steve Buechele	.05
161	Mike Harkey	.05
162	Greg Hibbard	.05
163	Chuck McElroy	.05
164	Mike Morgan	.05
165	Kevin Roberson	.05
166	Ryne Sandberg	.60
167	Jose Vizcaino	.05
168	Rick Wilkins	.05
169	Willie Wilson	.05
170	Willie Greene	.05
171	Roberto Kelly	.05
172	Larry Luebbers	.05
173	Kevin Mitchell	.05
174	Joe Oliver	.05
175	John Roper	.05
176	Johnny Ruffin	.05
177	Reggie Sanders	.05
178	John Smiley	.05
179	Jerry Spradlin	.05
180	Freddie Benavides	.05
181	Dante Bichette	.05
182	Willie Blair	.05
183	Kent Bottenfield	.05
184	Jerald Clark	.05
185	Joe Girardi	.05
186	Roberto Mejia	.05
187	Steve Reed	.05
188	Armando Reynoso	.05
189	Bruce Ruffin	.05
190	Eric Young	.05
191	Luis Aquino	.05
192	Bret Barberie	.05
193	Ryan Bowen	.05
194	Chuck Carr	.05
195	Orestes Destrade	.05
196	Richie Lewis	.05
197	Dave Magadan	.05
198	Bob Natal	.05
199	Gary Sheffield	.30
200	Matt Turner	.05
201	Darrell Whitmore	.05
202	Eric Anthony	.05
203	Jeff Bagwell	.50
204	Andujar Cedeno	.05
205	Luis Gonzalez	.05
206	Xavier Hernandez	.05
207	Doug Jones	.05
208	Darryl Kile	.05
209	Scott Servais	.05
210	Greg Swindell	.05
211	Brian Williams	.05
212	Pedro Astacio	.05
213	Brett Butler	.05
214	Omar Daal	.05
215	Jim Gott	.05
216	Raul Mondesi	.05
217	Jose Offerman	.05

218	Mike Piazza	.75
219	Cory Snyder	.05
220	Tim Wallach	.05
221	Todd Worrell	.05
222	Moises Alou	.05
223	Sean Berry	.05
224	Wil Cordero	.05
225	Jeff Fassero	.05
226	Darrin Fletcher	.05
227	Cliff Floyd	.05
228	Marquis Grissom	.05
229	Ken Hill	.05
230	Mike Lansing	.05
231	Kirk Rueter	.05
232	John Wetteland	.05
233	Rondell White	.05
234	Tim Bogar	.05
235	Jeromy Burnitz	.05
236	Dwight Gooden	.05
237	Todd Hundley	.05
238	Jeff Kent	.05
239	Josias Manzanillo	.05
240	Joe Orsulak	.05
241	Ryan Thompson	.05
242	Kim Batiste	.05
243	Darren Daulton	.05
243a	Darren Daulton (Promotional Sample)	1.00
244	Tommy Greene	.05
245	Dave Hollins	.05
246	Pete Incaviglia	.05
247	Danny Jackson	.05
248	Ricky Jordan	.05
249	John Kruk	.05
249a	John Kruk (Promotional Sample)	1.00
250	Mickey Morandini	.05
251	Terry Mulholland	.05
252	Ben Rivera	.05
253	Kevin Stocker	.05
254	Jay Bell	.05
255	Steve Cooke	.05
256	Jeff King	.05
257	Al Martin	.05
258	Danny Micelli	.05
259	Blas Minor	.05
260	Don Slaught	.05
261	Paul Wagner	.05
262	Tim Wakefield	.05
263	Kevin Young	.05
264	Rene Arocha	.05
265	Richard Batchelor **RC**	.05
266	Gregg Jefferies	.05
267	Brian Jordan	.05
268	Jose Oquendo	.05
269	Donovan Osborne	.05
270	Erik Pappas	.05
271	Mike Perez	.05
272	Bob Tewksbury	.05
273	Mark Whiten	.05
274	Todd Zeile	.05
275	Andy Ashby	.05
276	Brad Ausmus	.05
277	Phil Clark	.05
278	Jeff Gardner	.05
279	Ricky Gutierrez	.05
280	Tony Gwynn	.60
281	Tim Mauser	.05
282	Scott Sanders	.05
283	Frank Seminara	.05
284	Wally Whitehurst	.05
285	Rod Beck	.05
286	Barry Bonds	1.50
287	Dave Burba	.05
288	Mark Carreon	.05
289	Royce Clayton	.05
290	Mike Jackson	.05
291	Darren Lewis	.05
292	Kirt Manwaring	.05
293	Dave Martinez	.05
294	Billy Swift	.05
295	Salomon Torres	.05
296	Matt Williams	.05
297	Checklist 1-103 (Joe Orsulak)	.05
298	Checklist 104-201 (Pete Incaviglia)	.05
299	Checklist 202-300 (Todd Hundley)	.05
300	Checklist - Inserts (John Doherty)	.05
301	Brady Anderson	.05
302	Harold Baines	.05
303	Damon Buford	.05
304	Mike Devereaux	.05
305	Sid Fernandez	.05
306	Rick Krivda	.05
307	Mike Mussina	.30
308	Rafael Palmeiro	.40
309	Arthur Rhodes	.05
310	Chris Sabo	.05
311	Lee Smith	.05
312	Gregg Zaun **RC**	.05
313	Scott Cooper	.05
314	Mike Greenwell	.05
315	Tim Naehring	.05
316	Otis Nixon	.05
317	Paul Quantrill	.05
318	John Valentin	.05
319	Dave Valle	.05
320	Frank Viola	.05
321	Brian Anderson **RC**	.10
322	Garret Anderson	.05
323	Chad Curtis	.05
324	Chili Davis	.05

325	Gary DiSarcina	.05
326	Damion Easley	.05
327	Jim Edmonds	.05
328	Chuck Finley	.05
329	Joe Grahe	.05
330	Bo Jackson	.10
331	Mark Langston	.05
332	Harold Reynolds	.05
333	James Baldwin	.05
334	Ray Durham RC	.50
335	Julio Franco	.05
336	Craig Grebeck	.05
337	Ozzie Guillen	.05
338	Joe Hall	.05
339	Darrin Jackson	.05
340	Jack McDowell	.05
341	Tim Raines	.05
342	Robin Ventura	.05
343	Carlos Baerga	.05
344	Derek Lilliquist	.05
345	Dennis Martinez	.05
346	Jack Morris	.05
347	Eddie Murray	.50
348	Chris Nabholz	.05
349	Charles Nagy	.05
350	Chad Ogea	.05
351	Manny Ramirez	.50
352	Omar Vizquel	.05
353	Tim Belcher	.05
354	Eric Davis	.05
355	Kirk Gibson	.05
356	Rick Greene	.05
357	Mickey Tettleton	.05
358	Alan Trammell	.05
359	David Wells	.05
360	Stan Belinda	.05
361	Vince Coleman	.05
362	David Cone	.05
363	Gary Gaetti	.05
364	Tom Gordon	.05
365	Dave Henderson	.05
366	Wally Joyner	.05
367	Brent Mayne	.05
368	Brian McRae	.05
369	Michael Tucker	.05
370	Ricky Bones	.05
371	Brian Harper	.05
372	Tyrone Hill	.05
373	Mark Kiefer	.05
374	Pat Listach	.05
375	Mike Matheny RC	.10
376	Jose Mercedes RC	.05
377	Jody Reed	.05
378	Kevin Seitzer	.05
379	B.J. Surhoff	.05
380	Greg Vaughn	.05
381	Turner Ward	.05
382	Wes Weger RC	.05
383	Bill Wegman	.05
384	Rick Aguilera	.05
385	Rich Becker	.05
386	Alex Cole	.05
387	Steve Dunn	.05
388	Keith Garagozzo RC	.05
389	LaTroy Hawkins RC	.05
390	Shane Mack	.05
391	David McCarty	.05
392	Pedro Munoz	.05
393	Derek Parks RC	.05
394	Kirby Puckett	.60
395	Kevin Tapani	.05
396	Matt Walbeck	.05
397	Jim Abbott	.05
398	Mike Gallego	.05
399	Xavier Hernandez	.05
400	Don Mattingly	.65
401	Terry Mulholland	.05
402	Matt Nokes	.05
403	Luis Polonia	.05
404	Bob Wickman	.05
405	Mark Acre	.05
406	Fausto Cruz RC	.05
407	Dennis Eckersley	.45
408	Rickey Henderson	.50
409	Stan Javier	.05
410	Carlos Reyes RC	.05
411	Ruben Sierra	.05
412	Terry Steinbach	.05
413	Bill Taylor	.05
414	Todd Van Poppel	.05
415	Eric Anthony	.05
416	Bobby Ayala	.05
417	Chris Bosio	.05
418	Tim Davis	.05
419	Randy Johnson	.50
420	Kevin King	.05
421	Anthony Manahan RC	.05
422	Edgar Martinez	.05
423	Keith Mitchell	.05
424	Roger Salkeld	.05
425	Mac Suzuki RC	.05
426	Dan Wilson	.05
427	Duff Brumley RC	.05
428	Jose Canseco	.30
429	Will Clark	.05
430	Steve Dreyer	.05
431	Rick Helling	.05
432	Chris James	.05
433	Matt Whiteside	.05
434	Roberto Alomar	.20
435	Scott Brow	.05
436	Domingo Cedeno RC	.05
437	Carlos Delgado	.35
438	Juan Guzman	.05
439	Paul Spoljaric	.05
440	Todd Stottlemyre	.05
441	Woody Williams	.05
442	Dave Justice	.05
443	Mike Kelly	.05
444	Ryan Klesko	.05
445	Javier Lopez	.05
446	Greg Maddux	.60
447	Kent Mercker	.05
448	Charlie O'Brien	.05
449	Terry Pendleton	.05
450	Mike Stanton	.05
451	Tony Tarasco	.05
452	Terrell Wade RC	.05
453	Willie Banks	.05
454	Shawon Dunston	.05
455	Mark Grace	.05
456	Jose Guzman	.05
457	Jose Hernandez	.05
458	Glenallen Hill	.05
459	Blaise Ilsley	.05
460	Brooks Kieschnick RC	.05
461	Derrick May	.05
462	Randy Myers	.05
463	Karl Rhodes	.05
464	Sammy Sosa	.05
465	Steve Trachsel RC	.10
466	Anthony Young	.05
467	Eddie Zambrano RC	.05
468	Bret Boone	.05
469	Tom Browning	.05
470	Hector Carrasco RC	.05
471	Rob Dibble	.05
472	Erik Hanson	.05
473	Thomas Howard	.05
474	Barry Larkin	.05
475	Hal Morris	.05
476	Jose Rijo	.05
477	John Burke	.05
478	Ellis Burks	.05
479	Marvin Freeman	.05
480	Andres Galarraga	.05
481	Greg Harris	.05
482	Charlie Hayes	.05
483	Darren Holmes	.05
484	Howard Johnson	.05
485	Marcus Moore RC	.05
486	David Nied	.05
487	Mark Thompson	.05
488	Walt Weiss	.05
489	Kurt Abbott	.05
490	Matias Carrillo	.05
491	Jeff Conine	.05
492	Chris Hammond	.05
493	Bryan Harvey	.05
494	Charlie Hough	.05
495	Yorkis Perez RC	.05
496	Pat Rapp	.05
497	Benito Santiago	.05
498	David Weathers	.05
499	Craig Biggio	.05
500	Ken Caminiti	.05
501	Doug Drabek	.05
502	Tony Eusebio RC	.10
503	Steve Finley	.05
504	Pete Harnisch	.05
505	Brian Hunter	.05
506	Domingo Jean	.05
507	Todd Jones	.05
508	Orlando Miller	.05
509	James Mouton	.05
510	Roberto Petagine	.05
511	Shane Reynolds	.05
512	Mitch Williams	.05
513	Billy Ashley	.05
514	Tom Candiotti	.05
515	Delino DeShields	.05
516	Kevin Gross	.05
517	Orel Hershiser	.05
518	Eric Karros	.05
519	Ramon Martinez	.05
520	Chan Ho Park RC	.75
521	Henry Rodriguez	.05
522	Joey Eischen	.05
523	Rod Henderson	.05
524	Pedro Martinez	.50
525	Mel Rojas	.05
526	Larry Walker	.05
527	Gabe White RC	.10
528	Bobby Bonilla	.05
529	Jonathan Hurst	.05
530	Bobby Jones	.05
531	Kevin McReynolds	.05
532	Bill Pulsipher	.05
533	Bret Saberhagen	.05
534	David Segui	.05
535	Pete Smith	.05
536	Kelly Stinnett RC	.05
537	Dave Telgheder	.05
538	Quilvio Veras RC	.05
539	Jose Vizcaino	.05
540	Pete Walker	.05
541	Ricky Bottalico	.05
542	Wes Chamberlain	.05
543	Mariano Duncan	.05
544	Len Dykstra	.05
545	Jim Eisenreich	.05
546	Phil Geisler RC	.05
547	Wayne Gomes RC	.10
548	Doug Jones	.05
549	Jeff Juden	.05
550	Mike Lieberthal	.05
551	Tony Longmire RC	.05
552	Tom Marsh	.05
553	Bobby Munoz	.05
554	Curt Schilling	.15
555	Carlos Garcia	.05
556	Ravelo Manzanillo RC	.05
557	Orlando Merced	.05
558	Will Pennyfeather RC	.05
559	Zane Smith	.05
560	Andy Van Slyke	.05
561	Rick White	.05
562	Luis Alicea	.05
563	Brian Barber RC	.05
564	Clint Davis RC	.05
565	Bernard Gilkey	.05
566	Ray Lankford	.05
567	Tom Pagnozzi	.05
568	Ozzie Smith	.60
569	Rick Sutcliffe	.05
570	Allen Watson	.05
571	Dmitri Young	.05
572	Derek Bell	.05
573	Andy Benes	.05
574	Archi Cianfrocco	.05
575	Joey Hamilton	.05
576	Gene Harris	.05
577	Trevor Hoffman	.05
578	Tim Hyers RC	.05
579	Brian Johnson RC	.05
580	Keith Lockhart RC	.05
581	Pedro Martinez	.05
582	Ray McDavid	.05
583	Phil Plantier	.05
584	Bip Roberts	.05
585	Dave Staton	.05
586	Todd Benzinger	.05
587	John Burkett	.05
588	Bryan Hickerson	.05
589	Willie McGee	.05
590	John Patterson	.05
591	Mark Portugal	.05
592	Kevin Rogers	.05
593	Joe Rosselli RC	.05
594	Steve Soderstrom RC	.05
595	Robby Thompson	.05
596	125th Anniversary card	.05
597	Checklist	.05
598	Checklist	.05
599	Checklist	.05
600	Checklist	.05

All-Rookie Team

		NM/M
Complete Set (10):		4.00
Common Player:		.35
1	Kurt Abbott	.35
2	Carlos Delgado	3.00
3	Cliff Floyd	.35
4	Jeffrey Hammonds	.35
5	Ryan Klesko	.35
6	Javier Lopez	.35
7	Raul Mondesi	.35
8	James Mouton	.35
9	Chan Ho Park	.50
10	Dave Staton	.35

All-Stars

		NM/M
Complete Set (20):		5.00
Common Player:		.15
1	Chris Hoiles	.15

2	Frank Thomas	.35
3	Roberto Alomar	.20
4	Cal Ripken, Jr.	1.00
5	Robin Ventura	.15
6	Albert Belle	.15
7	Juan Gonzalez	.20
8	Ken Griffey Jr.	.50
9	John Olerud	.15
10	Jack McDowell	.15
11	Mike Piazza	.50
12	Fred McGriff	.15
13	Ryne Sandberg	.40
14	Jay Bell	.15
15	Matt Williams	.15
16	Barry Bonds	1.00
17	Len Dykstra	.15
18	Dave Justice	.15
19	Tom Glavine	.20
20	Greg Maddux	.40

Award Winners

		NM/M
Complete Set (25):		5.00
Common Player:		.10
1	Ivan Rodriguez	.25
2	Don Mattingly	.45
3	Roberto Alomar	.20
4	Robin Ventura	.10
5	Omar Vizquel	.10
6	Ken Griffey Jr.	.50
7	Kenny Lofton	.10
8	Devon White	.10
9	Mark Langston	.10
10	Kirt Manwaring	.10
11	Mark Grace	.10
12	Robby Thompson	.10
13	Matt Williams	.10
14	Jay Bell	.10
15	Barry Bonds	.60
16	Marquis Grissom	.10
17	Larry Walker	.10
18	Greg Maddux	.40
19	Frank Thomas	.35
20	Barry Bonds	.60
21	Paul Molitor	.35
22	Jack McDowell	.10
23	Greg Maddux	.40
24	Tim Salmon	.10
25	Mike Piazza	.50

Career Achievement Awards

		NM/M
Complete Set (5):		4.00
Common Player:		.50
1	Joe Carter	.50
2	Paul Molitor	.75
3	Cal Ripken, Jr.	2.00
4	Ryne Sandberg	1.00
5	Dave Winfield	.75

Firemen

RANDY MYERS

		NM/M
Complete Set (10):		2.00
Common Player:		.25
1	Jeff Montgomery	.25
2	Duane Ward	.25

3	Tom Henke	.25
4	Roberto Hernandez	.25
5	Dennis Eckersley	1.25
6	Randy Myers	.25
7	Rod Beck	.25
8	Bryan Harvey	.25
9	John Wetteland	.25
10	Mitch Williams	.25

Hitting Machines

		NM/M
Complete Set (10):		4.00
Common Player:		.15
1	Roberto Alomar	.25
2	Carlos Baerga	.15
3	Barry Bonds	2.00
4	Andres Galarraga	.15
5	Juan Gonzalez	.25
6	Tony Gwynn	.50
7	Paul Molitor	.40
8	John Olerud	.15
9	Mike Piazza	.75
10	Frank Thomas	.40

Home Run Kings

		NM/M
Complete Set (12):		15.00
Common Player:		.75
1	Juan Gonzalez	1.00
2	Ken Griffey Jr.	2.50
3	Frank Thomas	2.00
4	Albert Belle	.75
5	Rafael Palmeiro	1.50
6	Joe Carter	.75
7	Barry Bonds	4.00
8	Dave Justice	.75
9	Matt Williams	.75
10	Fred McGriff	.75
11	Ron Gant	.75
12	Mike Piazza	2.50

League Leaders

Andres Galarraga
League Leader
N.L. Batting Average

		NM/M
Complete Set (10):		3.00
Common Player:		.25
1	John Olerud	.25
2	Rafael Palmeiro	1.00
3	Kenny Lofton	.25
4	Jack McDowell	.25
5	Randy Johnson	1.50
6	Andres Galarraga	.25
7	Len Dykstra	.25
8	Chuck Carr	.25
9	Tom Glavine	.35
10	Jose Rijo	.25

On-Base Leaders

		NM/M
Complete Set (12):		25.00
Common Player:		1.50
1	Roberto Alomar	2.00
2	Barry Bonds	6.50
3	Len Dykstra	1.50
4	Andres Galarraga	1.50
5	Mark Grace	1.50
6	Ken Griffey Jr.	5.00
7	Gregg Jefferies	1.50
8	Orlando Merced	1.50
9	Paul Molitor	3.50
10	John Olerud	1.50
11	Tony Phillips	1.50
12	Frank Thomas	3.50

Phillies Finest

		NM/M
Complete Set (24):		4.00
Common Player:		.25
Autographed Daulton:		45.00
Autographed Kruk:		30.00
1-5	Darren Daulton	.25
6-10	John Kruk	.25
11-15	Darren Daulton	.25
16-20	John Kruk	.25
9a	John Kruk (PROMOTIONAL SAMPLE)	1.50
	MAIL-IN CARDS	
1M, 3M	Darren Daulton	.75
2M, 4M	John Kruk	.75

Rising Stars

		NM/M
Complete Set (12):		15.00
Common Player:		1.00
1	Carlos Baerga	1.00
2	Jeff Bagwell	5.00
3	Albert Belle	1.00
4	Cliff Floyd	1.00
5	Travis Fryman	1.00
6	Marquis Grissom	1.00

7	Kenny Lofton	1.00
8	John Olerud	1.00
9	Mike Piazza	7.50
10	Kirk Rueter	1.00
11	Tim Salmon	1.00
12	Aaron Sele	1.00

RBI Kings

		NM/M
Complete Set (12):		16.00
Common Player:		1.00
1	Albert Belle	1.00
2	Frank Thomas	2.50
3	Joe Carter	1.00
4	Juan Gonzalez	1.25
5	Cecil Fielder	1.00
6	Carlos Baerga	1.00
7	Barry Bonds	5.00
8	David Justice	1.00
9	Ron Gant	1.00
10	Mike Piazza	3.50
11	Matt Williams	1.00
12	Darren Daulton	1.00

Second Year Standouts

		NM/M
Complete Set (10):		5.00
Common Player:		.25
1	Jason Bere	.25
2	Brent Gates	.25
3	Jeffrey Hammonds	.25
4	Tim Salmon	.50
5	Aaron Sele	.25
6	Chuck Carr	.25
7	Jeff Conine	.25
8	Greg McMichael	.25
9	Mike Piazza	4.00
10	Kevin Stocker	.25

Strikeout Kings

GREG MADDUX

		NM/M
Complete Set (5):		2.00
Common Player:		.25
1	Randy Johnson	.75
2	Mark Langston	.25
3	Greg Maddux	1.00
4	Jose Rijo	.25
5	John Smoltz	.25

1995 Ultra

	NM/M
Complete Set (450):	10.00
Common Player:	.05
Gold Medallion:	2X
Series 1 or 2 Pack (12):	.50

Series 1 or 2 Wax Box (36):		12.50
1	Brady Anderson	.05
2	Sid Fernandez	.05
3	Jeffrey Hammonds	.05
4	Chris Hoiles	.05
5	Ben McDonald	.35
6	Mike Mussina	.05
7	Rafael Palmeiro	.65
8	Jack Voigt	.05
9	Wes Chamberlain	.05
10	Roger Clemens	1.00
11	Chris Howard	.05
12	Tim Naehring	.05
13	Otis Nixon	.05
14	Rich Rowland	.05
15	Ken Ryan	.05
16	John Valentin	.05
17	Mo Vaughn	.05
18	Brian Anderson	.05
19	Chili Davis	.05
20	Damion Easley	.05
21	Jim Edmonds	.05
22	Mark Langston	.05
23	Tim Salmon	.05
24	J.T. Snow	.05
25	Chris Turner	.05
26	Wilson Alvarez	.05
27	Joey Cora	.05
28	Alex Fernandez	.05
29	Roberto Hernandez	.05
30	Lance Johnson	.05
31	Ron Karkovice	.05
32	Kirk McCaskill	.05
33	Tim Raines	.05
34	Frank Thomas	.75
35	Sandy Alomar	.05
36	Albert Belle	.05
37	Mark Clark	.05
38	Kenny Lofton	.05
39	Eddie Murray	.75
40	Eric Plunk	.05
41	Manny Ramirez	.75
42	Jim Thome	.60
43	Omar Vizquel	.05
44	Danny Bautista	.05
45	Junior Felix	.05
46	Cecil Fielder	.05
47	Chris Gomez	.05
48	Chad Kreuter	.05
49	Mike Moore	.05
50	Tony Phillips	.05
51	Alan Trammell	.05
52	David Wells	.05
53	Kevin Appier	.05
54	Billy Brewer	.05
55	David Cone	.05
56	Greg Gagne	.05
57	Bob Hamelin	.05
58	Jose Lind	.05
59	Brent Mayne	.05
60	Brian McRae	.05
61	Terry Shumpert	.05
62	Ricky Bones	.05
63	Mike Fetters	.05
64	Darryl Hamilton	.05
65	John Jaha	.05
66	Graeme Lloyd	.05
67	Matt Mieske	.05
68	Kevin Seitzer	.05
69	Jose Valentin	.05
70	Turner Ward	.05
71	Rick Aguilera	.05
72	Rich Becker	.05
73	Alex Cole	.05
74	Scott Leius	.05
75	Pat Meares	.05
76	Kirby Puckett	1.00
77	Dave Stevens	.05
78	Kevin Tapani	.05
79	Matt Walbeck	.05
80	Wade Boggs	1.00
81	Scott Kamieniecki	.05
82	Pat Kelly	.05
83	Jimmy Key	.05
84	Paul O'Neill	.05
85	Luis Polonia	.05
86	Mike Stanley	.05
87	Danny Tartabull	.05
88	Bob Wickman	.05
89	Mark Acre	.05
90	Geronimo Berroa	.05

#	Player	Price
91	Mike Bordick	.05
92	Ron Darling	.05
93	Stan Javier	.05
94	Mark McGwire	1.50
95	Troy Neel	.05
96	Ruben Sierra	.05
97	Terry Steinbach	.05
98	Eric Anthony	.05
99	Chris Bosio	.05
100	Dave Fleming	.05
101	Ken Griffey Jr.	1.25
102	Reggie Jefferson	.05
103	Randy Johnson	.75
104	Edgar Martinez	.05
105	Bill Risley	.05
106	Dan Wilson	.05
107	Cris Carpenter	.05
108	Will Clark	.05
109	Juan Gonzalez	.40
110	Rusty Greer	.05
111	David Hulse	.05
112	Roger Pavlik	.05
113	Ivan Rodriguez	.75
114	Doug Strange	.05
115	Matt Whiteside	.05
116	Roberto Alomar	.20
117	Brad Cornett	.05
118	Carlos Delgado	.45
119	Alex Gonzalez	.05
120	Darren Hall	.05
121	Pat Hentgen	.05
122	Paul Molitor	.75
123	Ed Sprague	.05
124	Devon White	.05
125	Tom Glavine	.25
126	Dave Justice	.05
127	Roberto Kelly	.05
128	Mark Lemke	.05
129	Greg Maddux	1.00
130	Charles Johnson	.05
131	Kent Mercker	.05
132	Charlie O'Brien	.05
133	John Smoltz	.05
134	Willie Banks	.05
135	Steve Buechele	.05
136	Kevin Foster	.05
137	Glenallen Hill	.05
138	Ray Sanchez	.05
139	Sammy Sosa	1.00
140	Steve Trachsel	.05
141	Rick Wilkins	.05
142	Jeff Brantley	.05
143	Hector Carrasco	.05
144	Kevin Jarvis	.05
145	Barry Larkin	.05
146	Chuck McElroy	.05
147	Jose Rijo	.05
148	Johnny Ruffin	.05
149	Deion Sanders	.05
150	Eddie Taubensee	.05
151	Dante Bichette	.05
152	Ellis Burks	.05
153	Joe Girardi	.05
154	Charlie Hayes	.05
155	Mike Kingery	.05
156	Steve Reed	.05
157	Kevin Ritz	.05
158	Bruce Ruffin	.05
159	Eric Young	.05
160	Kurt Abbott	.05
161	Chuck Carr	.05
162	Chris Hammond	.05
163	Bryan Harvey	.05
164	Terry Mathews	.05
165	Yorkis Perez	.05
166	Pat Rapp	.05
167	Gary Sheffield	.40
168	Dave Weathers	.05
169	Jeff Bagwell	.75
170	Ken Caminiti	.05
171	Doug Drabek	.05
172	Steve Finley	.05
173	John Hudek	.05
174	Todd Jones	.05
175	James Mouton	.05
176	Shane Reynolds	.05
177	Scott Servais	.05
178	Tom Candiotti	.05
179	Omar Daal	.05
180	Darren Dreifort	.05
181	Eric Karros	.05
182	Ramon Martinez	.05
183	Raul Mondesi	.05
184	Henry Rodriguez	.05
185	Todd Worrell	.05
186	Moises Alou	.05
187	Sean Berry	.05
188	Wil Cordero	.05
189	Jeff Fassero	.05
190	Darrin Fletcher	.05
191	Butch Henry	.05
192	Ken Hill	.05
193	Mel Rojas	.05
194	John Wetteland	.05
195	Bobby Bonilla	.05
196	Rico Brogna	.05
197	Bobby Jones	.05
198	Jeff Kent	.05
199	Josias Manzanillo	.05
200	Kelly Stinnett	.05
201	Ryan Thompson	.05
202	Jose Vizcaino	.05
203	Lenny Dykstra	.05
204	Jim Eisenreich	.05
205	Dave Hollins	.05
206	Mike Lieberthal	.05
207	Mickey Morandini	.05
208	Bobby Munoz	.05
209	Curt Schilling	.20
210	Heathcliff Slocumb	.05
211	David West	.05
212	Dave Clark	.05
213	Steve Cooke	.05
214	Midre Cummings	.05
215	Carlos Garcia	.05
216	Jeff King	.05
217	Jon Lieber	.05
218	Orlando Merced	.05
219	Don Slaught	.05
220	Rick White	.05
221	Rene Arocha	.05
222	Bernard Gilkey	.05
223	Brian Jordan	.05
224	Tom Pagnozzi	.05
225	Vicente Palacios	.05
226	Geronimo Pena	.05
227	Ozzie Smith	1.00
228	Allen Watson	.05
229	Mark Whiten	.05
230	Brad Ausmus	.05
231	Derek Bell	.05
232	Andy Benes	.05
233	Tony Gwynn	1.00
234	Joey Hamilton	.05
235	Luis Lopez	.05
236	Pedro A. Martinez	.05
237	Scott Sanders	.05
238	Eddie Williams	.05
239	Rod Beck	.05
240	Dave Burba	.05
241	Darren Lewis	.05
242	Kirt Manwaring	.05
243	Mark Portugal	.05
244	Darryl Strawberry	.05
245	Robby Thompson	.05
246	William Van Landingham	.05
247	Matt Williams	.05
248	Checklist	.05
249	Checklist	.05
250	Checklist	.05
251	Harold Baines	.05
252	Bret Barberie	.05
253	Armando Benitez	.05
254	Mike Devereaux	.05
255	Leo Gomez	.05
256	Jamie Moyer	.05
257	Arthur Rhodes	.05
258	Cal Ripken Jr.	2.00
259	Luis Alicea	.05
260	Jose Canseco	.45
261	Scott Cooper	.05
262	Andre Dawson	.25
263	Mike Greenwell	.05
264	Aaron Sele	.05
265	Garret Anderson	.05
266	Chad Curtis	.05
267	Gary DiSarcina	.05
268	Chuck Finley	.05
269	Rex Hudler	.05
270	Andrew Lorraine	.05
271	Spike Owen	.05
272	Lee Smith	.05
273	Jason Bere	.05
274	Ozzie Guillen	.05
275	Norberto Martin	.05
276	Scott Ruffcorn	.05
277	Robin Ventura	.05
278	Carlos Baerga	.05
279	Jason Grimsley	.05
280	Dennis Martinez	.05
281	Charles Nagy	.05
282	Paul Sorrento	.05
283	Dave Winfield	.75
284	John Doherty	.05
285	Travis Fryman	.05
286	Kirk Gibson	.05
287	Lou Whitaker	.05
288	Gary Gaetti	.05
289	Tom Gordon	.05
290	Mark Gubicza	.05
291	Wally Joyner	.05
292	Mike Macfarlane	.05
293	Jeff Montgomery	.05
294	Jeff Cirillo	.05
295	Cal Eldred	.05
296	Pat Listach	.05
297	Jose Mercedes	.05
298	Dave Nilsson	.05
299	Duane Singleton	.05
300	Greg Vaughn	.05
301	Scott Erickson	.05
302	Denny Hocking	.05
303	Chuck Knoblauch	.05
304	Pat Mahomes	.05
305	Pedro Munoz	.05
306	Erik Schullstrom	.05
307	Jim Abbott	.05
308	Tony Fernandez	.05
309	Sterling Hitchcock	.05
310	Jim Leyritz	.05
311	Don Mattingly	1.00
312	Jack McDowell	.05
313	Melido Perez	.05
314	Bernie Williams	.05
315	Scott Brosius	.05
316	Dennis Eckersley	.65
317	Brent Gates	.05
318	Rickey Henderson	.75
319	Steve Karsay	.05
320	Steve Ontiveros	.05
321	Bill Taylor	.05
322	Todd Van Poppel	.05
323	Bob Welch	.05
324	Bobby Ayala	.05
325	Mike Blowers	.05
326	Jay Buhner	.05
327	Felix Fermin	.05
328	Tino Martinez	.05
329	Marc Newfield	.05
330	Greg Pirkl	.05
331	Alex Rodriguez	1.50
332	Kevin Brown	.05
333	John Burkett	.05
334	Jeff Frye	.05
335	Kevin Gross	.05
336	Dean Palmer	.05
337	Joe Carter	.05
338	Shawn Green	.35
339	Juan Guzman	.05
340	Mike Huff	.05
341	Al Leiter	.05
342	John Olerud	.05
343	Dave Stewart	.05
344	Todd Stottlemyre	.05
345	Steve Avery	.05
346	Jeff Blauser	.05
347	Chipper Jones	1.00
348	Mike Kelly	.05
349	Ryan Klesko	.05
350	Javier Lopez	.05
351	Fred McGriff	.05
352	Jose Oliva	.05
353	Terry Pendleton	.05
354	Mike Stanton	.05
355	Tony Tarasco	.05
356	Mark Wohlers	.05
357	Jim Bullinger	.05
358	Shawon Dunston	.05
359	Mark Grace	.05
360	Derrick May	.05
361	Randy Myers	.05
362	Karl Rhodes	.05
363	Bret Boone	.05
364	Brian Dorsett	.05
365	Ron Gant	.05
366	Brian R. Hunter	.05
367	Hal Morris	.05
368	Jack Morris	.05
369	John Roper	.05
370	Reggie Sanders	.05
371	Pete Schourek	.05
372	John Smiley	.05
373	Marvin Freeman	.05
374	Andres Galarraga	.05
375	Mike Munoz	.05
376	David Nied	.05
377	Walt Weiss	.05
378	Greg Colbrunn	.05
379	Jeff Conine	.05
380	Charles Johnson	.05
381	Kurt Miller	.05
382	Robb Nen	.05
383	Benito Santiago	.05
384	Craig Biggio	.05
385	Tony Eusebio	.05
386	Luis Gonzalez	.05
387	Brian L. Hunter	.05
388	Darryl Kile	.05
389	Orlando Miller	.05
390	Phil Plantier	.05
391	Greg Swindell	.05
392	Billy Ashley	.05
393	Pedro Astacio	.05
394	Brett Butler	.05
395	Delino DeShields	.05
396	Orel Hershiser	.05
397	Garey Ingram	.05
398	Chan Ho Park	.05
399	Mike Piazza	1.25
400	Ismael Valdes	.05
401	Tim Wallach	.05
402	Cliff Floyd	.05
403	Marquis Grissom	.05
404	Mike Lansing	.05
405	Pedro Martinez	.75
406	Kirk Rueter	.05
407	Tim Scott	.05
408	Jeff Shaw	.05
409	Larry Walker	.05
410	Rondell White	.05
411	John Franco	.05
412	Todd Hundley	.05
413	Jason Jacome	.05
414	Joe Orsulak	.05
415	Bret Saberhagen	.05
416	David Segui	.05
417	Darren Daulton	.05
418	Mariano Duncan	.05
419	Tommy Greene	.05
420	Gregg Jefferies	.05
421	John Kruk	.05
422	Kevin Stocker	.05
423	Jay Bell	.05
424	Al Martin	.05
425	Denny Neagle	.05
426	Zane Smith	.05
427	Andy Van Slyke	.05
428	Paul Wagner	.05
429	Tom Henke	.05
430	Danny Jackson	.05
431	Ray Lankford	.05
432	John Mabry	.05
433	Bob Tewksbury	.05
434	Todd Zeile	.05
435	Andy Ashby	.05
436	Andujar Cedeno	.05
437	Donnie Elliott	.05
438	Bryce Florie	.05
439	Trevor Hoffman	.05
440	Melvin Nieves	.05
441	Bip Roberts	.05
442	Barry Bonds	2.00
443	Royce Clayton	.05
444	Mike Jackson	.05
445	John Patterson	.05
446	J.R. Phillips	.05
447	Bill Swift	.05
448	Checklist	.05
449	Checklist	.05
450	Checklist	.05

1995 Ultra Gold Medallion

	NM/M
Complete Set (450):	60.00
Common Player:	.25
Stars/Rookies:	2X

(See 1995 Ultra for checklist and base card values.)

All-Rookies

		NM/M
Complete Set (10):		2.25
Common Player:		.15
Gold Medallion:		2X
1	Cliff Floyd	.15
2	Chris Gomez	.15
3	Rusty Greer	.15
4	Bob Hamelin	.15
5	Joey Hamilton	.15
6	John Hudek	.15
7	Ryan Klesko	.15
8	Raul Mondesi	.15
9	Manny Ramirez	2.00
10	Steve Trachsel	.15

All-Stars

		NM/M
Complete Set (20):		7.50
Common Player:		.15
Gold Medallion:		2X
1	Moises Alou	.15
2	Albert Belle	.15
3	Craig Biggio	.15
4	Wade Boggs	.60
5	Barry Bonds	1.50
6	David Cone	.15
7	Ken Griffey Jr.	.75
8	Tony Gwynn	.60
9	Chuck Knoblauch	.15
10	Barry Larkin	.15
11	Kenny Lofton	.15
12	Greg Maddux	.60
13	Fred McGriff	.15
14	Paul O'Neill	.15
15	Mike Piazza	.75
16	Kirby Puckett	.60
17	Cal Ripken Jr.	1.50
18	Ivan Rodriguez	.45
19	Frank Thomas	.50
20	Matt Williams	.15

Award Winners

ALL-STAR GAME M.V.P.

		NM/M
Complete Set (25):		6.00
Common Player:		.10
Gold Medallion:		2X
1	Ivan Rodriguez	.30
2	Don Mattingly	.65
3	Roberto Alomar	.20
4	Wade Boggs	.60
5	Omar Vizquel	.10
6	Ken Griffey Jr.	.75
7	Kenny Lofton	.10
8	Devon White	.10
9	Mark Langston	.10
10	Tom Pagnozzi	.10
11	Jeff Bagwell	.45
12	Craig Biggio	.10
13	Matt Williams	.10
14	Barry Larkin	.10
15	Barry Bonds	1.00
16	Marquis Grissom	.10
17	Darren Lewis	.10
18	Greg Maddux	.60
19	Frank Thomas	.45
20	Jeff Bagwell	.45
21	David Cone	.10
22	Greg Maddux	.60
23	Bob Hamelin	.10
24	Raul Mondesi	.10
25	Moises Alou	.10

Golden Prospects

GOLDEN PROSPECT MICHAEL TUCKER

		NM/M
Complete Set (10):		5.00
Common Player:		.10
Gold Medallion:		2X
1	James Baldwin	.10
2	Alan Benes	.10
3	Armando Benitez	.10
4	Ray Durham	.10
5	LaTroy Hawkins	.10
6	Brian Hunter	.10
7	Derek Jeter	3.00
8	Charles Johnson	.10
9	Alex Rodriguez	2.00
10	Michael Tucker	.10

Hitting Machines

		NM/M
Complete Set (10):		6.00
Common Player:		.40
Gold Medallion:		2X
1	Jeff Bagwell	.65
2	Albert Belle	.25
3	Dante Bichette	.25
4	Barry Bonds	2.50
5	Jose Canseco	.50
6	Ken Griffey Jr.	1.00
7	Tony Gwynn	.75
8	Fred McGriff	.25
9	Mike Piazza	1.00
10	Frank Thomas	.65

Home Run Kings

		NM/M
Complete Set (10):		7.50
Common Player:		.25
Gold Medallion:		2X
1	Ken Griffey Jr.	2.00
2	Frank Thomas	.75
3	Albert Belle	.25
4	Jose Canseco	.50
5	Cecil Fielder	.25
6	Matt Williams	.25
7	Jeff Bagwell	.75

8	Barry Bonds	3.00
9	Fred McGriff	.25
10	Andres Galarraga	.25

League Leaders

TONY GWYNN

		NM/M
Complete Set (10):		2.50
Common Player:		.15
Gold Medallion:		2X
1	Paul O'Neill	.15
2	Kenny Lofton	.15
3	Jimmy Key	.15
4	Randy Johnson	.50
5	Lee Smith	.15
6	Tony Gwynn	.75
7	Craig Biggio	.15
8	Greg Maddux	.75
9	Andy Benes	.15
10	John Franco	.15

On-Base Leaders

		NM/M
Complete Set (10):		15.00
Common Player:		1.00
Gold Medallion:		2X
1	Jeff Bagwell	2.00
2	Albert Belle	1.00
3	Craig Biggio	1.00
4	Wade Boggs	2.50
5	Barry Bonds	6.00
6	Will Clark	1.00
7	Tony Gwynn	2.50
8	Dave Justice	1.00
9	Paul O'Neill	1.00
10	Frank Thomas	2.00

Power Plus

		NM/M
Complete Set (6):		7.50
Common Player:		.50
Gold Medallion:		2X
1	Albert Belle	.50
2	Ken Griffey Jr.	2.00
3	Frank Thomas	1.00
4	Jeff Bagwell	1.00

5	Barry Bonds	4.00
6	Matt Williams	.50

Rising Stars

		NM/M
Complete Set (9):		7.00
Common Player:		.50
Gold Medallion:		2X
1	Moises Alou	.50
2	Jeff Bagwell	1.50
3	Albert Belle	.65
4	Juan Gonzalez	1.50
5	Chuck Knoblauch	.50
6	Kenny Lofton	.50
7	Raul Mondesi	.50
8	Mike Piazza	2.50
9	Frank Thomas	1.50

RBI Kings

JULIO FRANCO RBI KING CHICAGO WHITE SOX

		NM/M
Complete Set (10):		12.00
Common Player:		.50
Gold Medallion:		2X
1	Kirby Puckett	3.00
2	Joe Carter	.50
3	Albert Belle	.50
4	Frank Thomas	2.00
5	Julio Franco	.50
6	Jeff Bagwell	2.00
7	Matt Williams	.50
8	Dante Bichette	.50
9	Fred McGriff	.50
10	Mike Piazza	4.00

Second Year Standouts

2ND YEAR STANDOUTS

		NM/M
Complete Set (15):		3.50
Common Player:		.15
Gold Medallion:		2X
1	Cliff Floyd	.15
2	Chris Gomez	.15
3	Rusty Greer	.15
4	Darren Hall	.15
5	Bob Hamelin	.15
6	Joey Hamilton	.15
7	Jeffrey Hammonds	.15
8	John Hudek	.15
9	Ryan Klesko	.15
10	Raul Mondesi	.15
11	Manny Ramirez	3.00
12	Bill Risley	.15
13	Steve Trachsel	.15
14	William Van Landingham	.15
15	Rondell White	.15

Strikeout Kings

STRIKEOUT KING

		NM/M
Complete Set (6):		3.00
Common Player:		.10
Gold Medallion:		2X
1	Andy Benes	.10
2	Roger Clemens	1.50
3	Randy Johnson	.75
4	Greg Maddux	1.00
5	Pedro Martinez	.75
6	Jose Rijo	.10

1996 Ultra

		NM/M
Complete Set (600):		22.50
Common Player:		.05
Gold Medallions:		2X
Series 1 or 2 Pack (12):		1.25
Series 1 or 2 Wax Box (24):		20.00
1	Manny Alexander	.05
2	Brady Anderson	.05
3	Bobby Bonilla	.05
4	Scott Erickson	.05
5	Curtis Goodwin	.05
6	Chris Hoiles	.05
7	Doug Jones	.05
8	Jeff Manto	.05
9	Mike Mussina	.35
10	Rafael Palmeiro	.50
11	Cal Ripken Jr.	1.50
12	Rick Aguilera	.05
13	Luis Alicea	.05
14	Stan Belinda	.05
15	Jose Canseco	.40
16	Roger Clemens	.85
17	Mike Greenwell	.05
18	Mike Macfarlane	.05
19	Tim Naehring	.05
20	Troy O'Leary	.05
21	John Valentin	.05
22	Mo Vaughn	.05
23	Tim Wakefield	.05
24	Brian Anderson	.05
25	Garret Anderson	.05
26	Chili Davis	.05
27	Gary DiSarcina	.05
28	Jim Edmonds	.05
29	Jorge Fabregas	.05
30	Chuck Finley	.05
31	Mark Langston	.05
32	Troy Percival	.05
33	Tim Salmon	.05
34	Lee Smith	.05
35	Wilson Alvarez	.05
36	Ray Durham	.05

37	Alex Fernandez	.05
38	Ozzie Guillen	.05
39	Roberto Hernandez	.05
40	Lance Johnson	.05
41	Ron Karkovice	.05
42	Lyle Mouton	.05
43	Tim Raines	.05
44	Frank Thomas	.60
45	Carlos Baerga	.05
46	Albert Belle	.05
47	Orel Hershiser	.05
48	Kenny Lofton	.05
49	Dennis Martinez	.05
50	Jose Mesa	.05
51	Eddie Murray	.60
52	Chad Ogea	.05
53	Manny Ramirez	.60
54	Jim Thome	.50
55	Omar Vizquel	.05
56	Dave Winfield	.60
57	Chad Curtis	.05
58	Cecil Fielder	.05
59	John Flaherty	.05
60	Travis Fryman	.05
61	Chris Gomez	.05
62	Bob Higginson	.05
63	Felipe Lira	.05
64	Brian Maxcy	.05
65	Alan Trammell	.05
66	Lou Whitaker	.05
67	Kevin Appier	.05
68	Gary Gaetti	.05
69	Tom Goodwin	.05
70	Tom Gordon	.05
71	Jason Jacome	.05
72	Wally Joyner	.05
73	Brent Mayne	.05
74	Jeff Montgomery	.05
75	Jon Nunnally	.05
76	Joe Vitiello	.05
77	Ricky Bones	.05
78	Jeff Cirillo	.05
79	Mike Fetters	.05
80	Darryl Hamilton	.05
81	David Hulse	.05
82	Dave Nilsson	.05
83	Kevin Seitzer	.05
84	Steve Sparks	.05
85	B.J. Surhoff	.05
86	Jose Valentin	.05
87	Greg Vaughn	.05
88	Marty Cordova	.05
89	Chuck Knoblauch	.05
90	Pat Meares	.05
91	Pedro Munoz	.05
92	Kirby Puckett	.75
93	Brad Radke	.05
94	Scott Stahoviak	.05
95	Dave Stevens	.05
96	Mike Trombley	.05
97	Matt Walbeck	.05
98	Wade Boggs	.75
99	Russ Davis	.05
100	Jim Leyritz	.05
101	Don Mattingly	.85
102	Jack McDowell	.05
103	Paul O'Neill	.05
104	Andy Pettitte	.30
105	Mariano Rivera	.15
106	Ruben Sierra	.05
107	Darryl Strawberry	.05
108	John Wetteland	.05
109	Bernie Williams	.05
110	Geronimo Berroa	.05
111	Scott Brosius	.05
112	Dennis Eckersley	.50
113	Brent Gates	.05
114	Rickey Henderson	.60
115	Mark McGwire	1.25
116	Ariel Prieto	.05
117	Terry Steinbach	.05
118	Todd Stottlemyre	.05
119	Todd Van Poppel	.05
120	Steve Wojciechowski	.05
121	Rich Amaral	.05
122	Bobby Ayala	.05
123	Mike Blowers	.05
124	Chris Bosio	.05
125	Joey Cora	.05
126	Ken Griffey Jr.	1.00
127	Randy Johnson	.60
128	Edgar Martinez	.05
129	Tino Martinez	.05
130	Alex Rodriguez	1.25
131	Dan Wilson	.05
132	Will Clark	.05
133	Jeff Frye	.05
134	Benji Gil	.05
135	Juan Gonzalez	.30
136	Rusty Greer	.05
137	Mark McLemore	.05
138	Roger Pavlik	.05
139	Ivan Rodriguez	.50
140	Kenny Rogers	.05
141	Mickey Tettleton	.05
142	Roberto Alomar	.20
143	Joe Carter	.05
144	Tony Castillo	.05
145	Alex Gonzalez	.05
146	Shawn Green	.35
147	Pat Hentgen	.05
148	Sandy Martinez **RC**	.05
149	Paul Molitor	.60
150	John Olerud	.05
151	Ed Sprague	.05
152	Jeff Blauser	.05
153	Brad Clontz	.05
154	Tom Glavine	.30
155	Marquis Grissom	.05
156	Chipper Jones	.75
157	David Justice	.05
158	Ryan Klesko	.05
159	Javier Lopez	.05
160	Greg Maddux	.75
161	John Smoltz	.05
162	Mark Wohlers	.05
163	Jim Bullinger	.05
164	Frank Castillo	.05
165	Shawon Dunston	.05
166	Kevin Foster	.05
167	Luis Gonzalez	.05
168	Mark Grace	.05
169	Rey Sanchez	.05
170	Scott Servais	.05
171	Sammy Sosa	.75
172	Ozzie Timmons	.05
173	Steve Trachsel	.05
174	Bret Boone	.05
175	Jeff Branson	.05
176	Jeff Brantley	.05
177	Dave Burba	.05
178	Ron Gant	.05
179	Barry Larkin	.05
180	Darren Lewis	.05
181	Mark Portugal	.05
182	Reggie Sanders	.05
183	Pete Schourek	.05
184	John Smiley	.05
185	Jason Bates	.05
186	Dante Bichette	.05
187	Ellis Burks	.05
188	Vinny Castilla	.05
189	Andres Galarraga	.05
190	Darren Holmes	.05
191	Armando Reynoso	.05
192	Kevin Ritz	.05
193	Bill Swift	.05
194	Larry Walker	.05
195	Kurt Abbott	.05
196	John Burkett	.05
197	Greg Colbrunn	.05
198	Jeff Conine	.05
199	Andre Dawson	.25
200	Chris Hammond	.05
201	Charles Johnson	.05
202	Robb Nen	.05
203	Terry Pendleton	.05
204	Quilvio Veras	.05
205	Jeff Bagwell	.60
206	Derek Bell	.05
207	Doug Drabek	.05
208	Tony Eusebio	.05
209	Mike Hampton	.05
210	Brian Hunter	.05
211	Todd Jones	.05
212	Orlando Miller	.05
213	James Mouton	.05
214	Shane Reynolds	.05
215	Dave Veres	.05
216	Billy Ashley	.05
217	Brett Butler	.05
218	Chad Fonville	.05
219	Todd Hollandsworth	.05
220	Eric Karros	.05
221	Ramon Martinez	.05
222	Raul Mondesi	.05
223	Hideo Nomo	.30
224	Mike Piazza	1.00
225	Kevin Tapani	.05
226	Ismael Valdes	.05
227	Todd Worrell	.05
228	Moises Alou	.05
229	Wil Cordero	.05
230	Jeff Fassero	.05
231	Darrin Fletcher	.05
232	Mike Lansing	.05
233	Pedro Martinez	.60
234	Carlos Perez	.05
235	Mel Rojas	.05
236	David Segui	.05
237	Tony Tarasco	.05
238	Rondell White	.05
239	Edgardo Alfonzo	.05
240	Rico Brogna	.05
241	Carl Everett	.05
242	Todd Hundley	.05
243	Butch Huskey	.05
244	Jason Isringhausen	.05
245	Bobby Jones	.05
246	Jeff Kent	.05
247	Bill Pulsipher	.05
248	Jose Vizcaino	.05
249	Ricky Bottalico	.05
250	Darren Daulton	.05
251	Jim Eisenreich	.05
252	Tyler Green	.05
253	Charlie Hayes	.05
254	Gregg Jefferies	.05
255	Tony Longmire	.05
256	Michael Mimbs	.05
257	Mickey Morandini	.05
258	Paul Quantrill	.05
259	Heathcliff Slocumb	.05
260	Jay Bell	.05
261	Jacob Brumfield	.05
262	Angelo Encarnacion **RC**	.05
263	John Ericks	.05
264	Mark Johnson	.05
265	Esteban Loaiza	.05
266	Al Martin	.05
267	Orlando Merced	.05
268	Dan Miceli	.05
269	Denny Neagle	.05
270	Brian Barber	.05
271	Scott Cooper	.05
272	Tripp Cromer	.05
273	Bernard Gilkey	.05
274	Tom Henke	.05
275	Brian Jordan	.05
276	John Mabry	.05
277	Tom Pagnozzi	.05
278	Mark Petkovsek **RC**	.05
279	Ozzie Smith	.75
280	Andy Ashby	.05
281	Brad Ausmus	.05
282	Ken Caminiti	.05
283	Glenn Dishman	.05
284	Tony Gwynn	.75
285	Joey Hamilton	.05
286	Trevor Hoffman	.05
287	Phil Plantier	.05
288	Jody Reed	.05
289	Eddie Williams	.05
290	Barry Bonds	1.50
291	Jamie Brewington	.05
292	Mark Carreon	.05
293	Royce Clayton	.05
294	Glenallen Hill	.05
295	Mark Leiter	.05
296	Kirt Manwaring	.05
297	J.R. Phillips	.05
298	Deion Sanders	.05
299	William Van Landingham	.05
300	Matt Williams	.05
301	Roberto Alomar	.20
302	Armando Benitez	.05
303	Mike Devereaux	.05
304	Jeffrey Hammonds	.05
305	Jimmy Haynes	.05
306	Scott McClain **RC**	.05
307	Kent Mercker	.05
308	Randy Myers	.05
309	B.J. Surhoff	.05
310	Tony Tarasco	.05
311	David Wells	.05
312	Wil Cordero	.05
313	Alex Delgado	.05
314	Tom Gordon	.05
315	Dwayne Hosey	.05
316	Jose Malave	.05
317	Kevin Mitchell	.05
318	Jamie Moyer	.05
319	Aaron Sele	.05
320	Heathcliff Slocumb	.05
321	Mike Stanley	.05
322	Jeff Suppan	.05
323	Jim Abbott	.05
324	George Arias	.05
325	Todd Greene	.05
326	Bryan Harvey	.05
327	J.T. Snow	.05
328	Randy Velarde	.05
329	Tim Wallach	.05
330	Harold Baines	.05
331	Jason Bere	.05
332	Darren Lewis	.05
333	Norberto Martin	.05
334	Tony Phillips	.05
335	Bill Simas	.05
336	Chris Snopek	.05
337	Kevin Tapani	.05
338	Danny Tartabull	.05
339	Robin Ventura	.05
340	Sandy Alomar	.05
341	Julio Franco	.05
342	Jack McDowell	.05
343	Charles Nagy	.05
344	Julian Tavarez	.05
345	Kimera Bartee	.05
346	Greg Keagle	.05
347	Mark Lewis	.05
348	Jose Lima	.05
349	Melvin Nieves	.05
350	Mark Parent	.05
351	Eddie Williams	.05
352	Johnny Damon	.30
353	Sal Fasano	.05
354	Mark Gubicza	.05
355	Bob Hamelin	.05
356	Chris Haney	.05
357	Keith Lockhart	.05
358	Mike Macfarlane	.05
359	Jose Offerman	.05
360	Bip Roberts	.05
361	Michael Tucker	.05
362	Chuck Carr	.05
363	Bobby Hughes	.05
364	John Jaha	.05
365	Mark Loretta	.05
366	Mike Matheny	.05
367	Ben McDonald	.05
368	Matt Mieske	.05
369	Angel Miranda	.05
370	Fernando Vina	.05
371	Rick Aguilera	.05
372	Rich Becker	.05
373	LaTroy Hawkins	.05
374	Dave Hollins	.05
375	Roberto Kelly	.05
376	Matt Lawton **RC**	.25
377	Paul Molitor	.60
378	Dan Naulty **RC**	.05
379	Rich Robertson	.05
380	Frank Rodriguez	.05
381	David Cone	.05
382	Mariano Duncan	.05
383	Andy Fox **RC**	.05
384	Joe Girardi	.05
385	Dwight Gooden	.05
386	Derek Jeter	1.50
387	Pat Kelly	.05
388	Jimmy Key	.05
389	Matt Luke **RC**	.05
390	Tino Martinez	.05
391	Jeff Nelson	.05
392	Melido Perez	.05
393	Tim Raines	.05
394	Ruben Rivera	.05
395	Kenny Rogers	.05
396	Tony Batista **RC**	.25
397	Allen Battle	.05
398	Mike Bordick	.05
399	Steve Cox	.05
400	Jason Giambi	.40
401	Doug Johns	.05
402	Pedro Munoz	.05
403	Phil Plantier	.05
404	Scott Spiezio	.05
405	George Williams	.05
406	Ernie Young	.05
407	Darren Bragg	.05
408	Jay Buhner	.05
409	Norm Charlton	.05
410	Russ Davis	.05
411	Sterling Hitchcock	.05
412	Edwin Hurtado	.05
413	Raul Ibanez **RC**	.05
414	Mike Jackson	.05
415	Luis Sojo	.05
416	Paul Sorrento	.05
417	Bob Wolcott	.05
418	Damon Buford	.05
419	Kevin Gross	.05
420	Darryl Hamilton	.05
421	Mike Henneman	.05
422	Ken Hill	.05
423	Dean Palmer	.05
424	Bobby Witt	.05
425	Tilson Brito	.05
426	Giovanni Carrara	.05
427	Domingo Cedeno	.05
428	Felipe Crespo	.05
429	Carlos Delgado	.40
430	Juan Guzman	.05
431	Erik Hanson	.05
432	Marty Janzen **RC**	.05
433	Otis Nixon	.05
434	Robert Perez	.05
435	Paul Quantrill	.05
436	Bill Risley	.05
437	Steve Avery	.05
438	Jermaine Dye	.05
439	Mark Lemke	.05
440	Marty Malloy **RC**	.05
441	Fred McGriff	.05
442	Greg McMichael	.05
443	Wonderful Monds	.05
444	Eddie Perez	.05
445	Jason Schmidt	.05
446	Terrell Wade	.05
447	Terry Adams	.05
448	Scott Bullett	.05
449	Robin Jennings **RC**	.05
450	Doug Jones	.05
451	Brooks Kieschnick	.05
452	Dave Magadan	.05
453	Jason Maxwell **RC**	.05
454	Brian McRae	.05
455	Rodney Myers	.05
456	Jaime Navarro	.05
457	Ryne Sandberg	.75
458	Vince Coleman	.05
459	Eric Davis	.05
460	Steve Gibralter	.05
461	Thomas Howard	.05
462	Mike Kelly	.05
463	Hal Morris	.05
464	Eric Owens	.05
465	Jose Rijo	.05
466	Chris Sabo	.05
467	Eddie Taubensee	.05
468	Trenidad Hubbard	.05
469	Curt Leskanic	.05
470	Quinton McCracken	.05
471	Jayhawk Owens	.05
472	Steve Reed	.05
473	Bryan Rekar	.05
474	Bruce Ruffin	.05
475	Bret Saberhagen	.05
476	Walt Weiss	.05
477	Eric Young	.05
478	Kevin Brown	.05
479	Al Leiter	.05
480	Pat Rapp	.05
481	Gary Sheffield	.35
482	Devon White	.05
483	Bob Abreu	.05
484	Sean Berry	.05
485	Craig Biggio	.05
486	Jim Dougherty	.05
487	Richard Hidalgo	.05
488	Darryl Kile	.05
489	Derrick May	.05
490	Greg Swindell	.05
491	Rick Wilkins	.05
492	Mike Blowers	.05
493	Tom Candiotti	.05
494	Roger Cedeno	.05
495	Delino DeShields	.05
496	Greg Gagne	.05

497	Karim Garcia	.10
498	Wilton Guerrero **RC**	.05
499	Chan Ho Park	.05
500	Israel Alcantara	.05
501	Shane Andrews	.05
502	Yamil Benitez	.05
503	Cliff Floyd	.05
504	Mark Grudzielanek	.05
505	Ryan McGuire	.05
506	Sherman Obando	.05
507	Jose Paniagua	.05
508	Henry Rodriguez	.05
509	Kirk Rueter	.05
510	Juan Acevedo	.05
511	John Franco	.05
512	Bernard Gilkey	.05
513	Lance Johnson	.05
514	Rey Ordonez	.05
515	Robert Person	.05
516	Paul Wilson	.05
517	Toby Borland	.05
518	David Doster **RC**	.05
519	Lenny Dykstra	.05
520	Sid Fernandez	.05
521	Mike Grace **RC**	.05
522	Rich Hunter **RC**	.05
523	Benito Santiago	.05
524	Gene Schall	.05
525	Curt Schilling	.15
526	Kevin Sefcik **RC**	.05
527	Lee Tinsley	.05
528	David West	.05
529	Mark Whiten	.05
530	Todd Zeile	.05
531	Carlos Garcia	.05
532	Charlie Hayes	.05
533	Jason Kendall	.05
534	Jeff King	.05
535	Mike Kingery	.05
536	Nelson Liriano	.05
537	Dan Plesac	.05
538	Paul Wagner	.05
539	Luis Alicea	.05
540	David Bell	.05
541	Alan Benes	.05
542	Andy Benes	.05
543	Mike Busby **RC**	.05
544	Royce Clayton	.05
545	Dennis Eckersley	.50
546	Gary Gaetti	.05
547	Ron Gant	.05
548	Aaron Holbert	.05
549	Ray Lankford	.05
550	T.J. Mathews	.05
551	Willie McGee	.05
552	Miguel Mejia **RC**	.05
553	Todd Stottlemyre	.05
554	Sean Bergman	.05
555	Willie Blair	.05
556	Andujar Cedeno	.05
557	Steve Finley	.05
558	Rickey Henderson	.60
559	Wally Joyner	.05
560	Scott Livingstone	.05
561	Marc Newfield	.05
562	Bob Tewksbury	.05
563	Fernando Valenzuela	.05
564	Rod Beck	.05
565	Doug Creek	.05
566	Shawon Dunston	.05
567	Osvaldo Fernandez **RC**	.20
568	Stan Javier	.05
569	Marcus Jensen	.05
570	Steve Scarsone	.05
571	Robby Thompson	.05
572	Allen Watson	.05
573	Roberto Alomar (Ultra Stars)	.10
574	Jeff Bagwell (Ultra Stars)	.30
575	Albert Belle (Ultra Stars)	.05
576	Wade Boggs (Ultra Stars)	.40
577	Barry Bonds (Ultra Stars)	.75
578	Juan Gonzalez (Ultra Stars)	.15
579	Ken Griffey Jr. (Ultra Stars)	.50
580	Tony Gwynn (Ultra Stars)	.40
581	Randy Johnson (Ultra Stars)	.30
582	Chipper Jones (Ultra Stars)	.40
583	Barry Larkin (Ultra Stars)	.05
584	Kenny Lofton (Ultra Stars)	.05
585	Greg Maddux (Ultra Stars)	.40
586	Raul Mondesi (Ultra Stars)	.05
587	Mike Piazza (Ultra Stars)	.50
588	Cal Ripken Jr. (Ultra Stars)	.75
589	Tim Salmon (Ultra Stars)	.05
590	Frank Thomas (Ultra Stars)	.35
591	Mo Vaughn (Ultra Stars)	.05
592	Matt Williams (Ultra Stars)	.05
593	Marty Cordova (Raw Power)	.05
594	Jim Edmonds (Raw Power)	.05
595	Cliff Floyd (Raw Power)	.05
596	Chipper Jones (Raw Power)	.40
597	Ryan Klesko (Raw Power)	.05
598	Raul Mondesi (Raw Power)	.05
599	Manny Ramirez (Raw Power)	.30
600	Ruben Rivera (Raw Power)	.05

1996 Ultra Gold Medallion

	NM/M
Complete Set (600):	75.00
Common Player:	.25

(Star cards valued at 2X regular edition Fleer Ultra.)

Call to the Hall

		NM/M
Complete Set (10):		10.00
Common Player:		1.00
Gold Medallion Edition:		2X
1	Barry Bonds	3.00
2	Ken Griffey Jr.	2.00
3	Tony Gwynn	1.25
4	Rickey Henderson	1.00
5	Greg Maddux	1.25
6	Eddie Murray	1.00
7	Cal Ripken Jr.	3.00
8	Ryne Sandberg	1.25
9	Ozzie Smith	1.25
10	Frank Thomas	1.00

Diamond Producers

		NM/M
Complete Set (12):		15.00
Common Player:		.50
Gold Medallions:		2X
1	Albert Belle	.50
2	Barry Bonds	3.00
3	Ken Griffey Jr.	2.00
4	Tony Gwynn	1.50
5	Greg Maddux	1.50
6	Hideo Nomo	.75
7	Mike Piazza	2.00
8	Kirby Puckett	1.50
9	Cal Ripken Jr.	3.00
10	Frank Thomas	1.25
11	Mo Vaughn	.75
12	Matt Williams	.50

Fresh Foundations

		NM/M
Complete Set (10):		2.00
Common Player:		.25
Gold Medallions:		2X
1	Garret Anderson	.15
2	Marty Cordova	.15
3	Jim Edmonds	.15
4	Brian Hunter	.15
5	Chipper Jones	.50
6	Ryan Klesko	.15
7	Raul Mondesi	.15
8	Hideo Nomo	.25

9	Manny Ramirez	.40
10	Rondell White	.15

Golden Prospects, Series 1

		NM/M
Complete Set (10):		7.00
Common Player:		.25
Gold Medallions:		2X
1	Yamil Benitez	.25
2	Alberto Castillo	.25
3	Roger Cedeno	.25
4	Johnny Damon	1.00
5	Micah Franklin	.25
6	Jason Giambi	1.00
7	Jose Herrera	.25
8	Derek Jeter	5.00
9	Kevin Jordan	.25
10	Ruben Rivera	.25

Golden Prospects, Series 2

		NM/M
Complete Set (15):		10.00
Common Player:		1.00
Gold Medallions:		2X
1	Bob Abreu	1.50
2	Israel Alcantara	1.00
3	Tony Batista	1.00
4	Mike Cameron	1.00
5	Steve Cox	1.00
6	Jermaine Dye	1.00
7	Wilton Guerrero	1.00
8	Richard Hidalgo	1.00
9	Raul Ibanez	1.00
10	Marty Janzen	1.00
11	Robin Jennings	1.00
12	Jason Maxwell	1.00
13	Scott McClain	1.00
14	Wonderful Monds	1.00
15	Chris Singleton	1.00

Hitting Machines

	NM/M
Complete Set (10):	35.00
Common Player:	2.00
Gold Medallion:	2X
1	Albert Belle	2.00
2	Barry Bonds	12.00
3	Juan Gonzalez	2.50
4	Ken Griffey Jr.	6.00
5	Edgar Martinez	2.00
6	Rafael Palmeiro	3.00
7	Mike Piazza	6.00
8	Tim Salmon	2.00
9	Frank Thomas	4.00
10	Matt Williams	2.00

Home Run Kings

		NM/M
Complete Set (12):		50.00
Common Player:		2.50
Gold Medallions:		2X
1	Albert Belle	2.50
2	Dante Bichette	2.50
3	Barry Bonds	12.50
4	Jose Canseco	5.00
5	Juan Gonzalez	3.00
6	Ken Griffey Jr.	9.00
7	Mark McGwire	10.00
8	Manny Ramirez	6.50
9	Tim Salmon	2.50
10	Frank Thomas	6.50
11	Mo Vaughn	2.50
12	Matt Williams	2.50

On-Base Leaders

		NM/M
Complete Set (10):		4.50
Common Player:		.25
Gold Medallion:		2X
1	Wade Boggs	.75
2	Barry Bonds	2.00
3	Tony Gwynn	.75
4	Rickey Henderson	.60
5	Chuck Knoblauch	.25
6	Edgar Martinez	.25
7	Mike Piazza	1.00
8	Tim Salmon	.25
9	Frank Thomas	.60
10	Jim Thome	.50

Power Plus

	NM/M
Complete Set (12):	10.00
Common Player:	.40
Gold Medallions:	2X

1	Jeff Bagwell	1.25
2	Barry Bonds	3.00
3	Ken Griffey Jr.	2.00
4	Raul Mondesi	.40
5	Rafael Palmeiro	1.00
6	Mike Piazza	2.00
7	Manny Ramirez	1.25
8	Tim Salmon	.40
9	Reggie Sanders	.40
10	Frank Thomas	1.25
11	Larry Walker	.40
12	Matt Williams	.40

Prime Leather

		NM/M
Complete Set (18):		17.50
Common Player:		.50
Gold Medallions:		2X
1	Ivan Rodriguez	1.50
2	Will Clark	.50
3	Roberto Alomar	.65
4	Cal Ripken Jr.	4.00
5	Wade Boggs	2.00
6	Ken Griffey Jr.	2.50
7	Kenny Lofton	.50
8	Kirby Puckett	2.00
9	Tim Salmon	.65
10	Mike Piazza	2.50
11	Mark Grace	.50
12	Craig Biggio	.50
13	Barry Larkin	.50
14	Matt Williams	.50
15	Barry Bonds	4.00
16	Tony Gwynn	2.00
17	Brian McRae	.50
18	Raul Mondesi	.50

R-E-S-P-E-C-T

		NM/M
Complete Set (10):		20.00
Common Player:		.50
Gold Medallion:		2X
1	Joe Carter	.50
2	Ken Griffey Jr.	3.00
3	Tony Gwynn	2.50
4	Greg Maddux	2.50
5	Eddie Murray	2.00
6	Kirby Puckett	2.50
7	Cal Ripken Jr.	5.00
8	Ryne Sandberg	2.50
9	Frank Thomas	2.00
10	Mo Vaughn	.50

Rawhide

		NM/M
Complete Set (10):		10.00
Common Player:		.45
Gold Medallion:		2X
1	Roberto Alomar	.65
2	Barry Bonds	3.00
3	Mark Grace	.45
4	Ken Griffey Jr.	1.50
5	Kenny Lofton	.45
6	Greg Maddux	1.00
7	Raul Mondesi	.45
8	Mike Piazza	1.50
9	Cal Ripken Jr.	3.00
10	Matt Williams	.45

Rising Stars

		NM/M
Complete Set (10):		4.00
Common Player:		.20
Gold Medallion:		2X
1	Garret Anderson	.20
2	Marty Cordova	.20
3	Jim Edmonds	.35
4	Cliff Floyd	.20
5	Brian Hunter	.20
6	Chipper Jones	2.00
7	Ryan Klesko	.20
8	Hideo Nomo	.65
9	Manny Ramirez	1.25
10	Rondell White	.20

RBI Kings

		NM/M
Complete Set (10):		4.00
Common Player:		.10
Gold Medallions:		2X
1	Derek Bell	.10
2	Albert Belle	.10
3	Dante Bichette	.10
4	Barry Bonds	2.00
5	Jim Edmonds	.15
6	Manny Ramirez	1.00
7	Reggie Sanders	.10
8	Sammy Sosa	1.50
9	Frank Thomas	1.00
10	Mo Vaughn	.10

Season Crowns

		NM/M
Complete Set (10):		12.50
Common Player:		.75
Gold Medallions:		2X
1	Barry Bonds	4.00
2	Tony Gwynn	2.00
3	Randy Johnson	1.25
4	Kenny Lofton	.75
5	Greg Maddux	2.00
6	Edgar Martinez	.75
7	Hideo Nomo	1.00
8	Cal Ripken Jr.	4.00

9	Frank Thomas	1.25
10	Tim Wakefield	.75

Thunderclap

		NM/M
Complete Set (20):		45.00
Common Player:		1.00
Gold Medallion:		2X
1	Albert Belle	1.00
2	Barry Bonds	7.50
3	Bobby Bonilla	1.00
4	Jose Canseco	1.50
5	Joe Carter	1.00
6	Will Clark	1.00
7	Andre Dawson	1.50
8	Cecil Fielder	1.00
9	Andres Galarraga	1.00
10	Juan Gonzalez	1.50
11	Ken Griffey Jr.	5.00
12	Fred McGriff	1.00
13	Mark McGwire	6.00
14	Eddie Murray	2.50
15	Rafael Palmeiro	2.00
16	Kirby Puckett	4.00
17	Cal Ripken Jr.	7.50
18	Ryne Sandberg	4.00
19	Frank Thomas	2.50
20	Matt Williams	1.00

1996 Ultra Diamond Dust

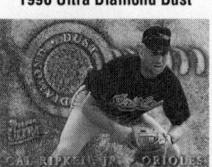

	NM/M
Cal Ripken Jr. (Numbered)	40.00
Cal Ripken Jr. (Unnumbered)	20.00

1997 Ultra

		NM/M
Complete Set (553):		80.00
Common Player:		.05
Gold Medallion:		3X
Platinum Medallion:		25X
Series 1 Wax Pack (10):		1.25
Series 1 Wax Box (24):		20.00
Series 2 Wax Pack (10):		5.00
Series 2 Wax Box (24):		90.00
1	Roberto Alomar	.25
2	Brady Anderson	.05
3	Rocky Coppinger	.05
4	Jeffrey Hammonds	.05
5	Chris Hoiles	.05
6	Eddie Murray	.75
7	Mike Mussina	.45
8	Jimmy Myers	.05
9	Randy Myers	.05
10	Arthur Rhodes	.05

11	Cal Ripken Jr.	2.50
12	Jose Canseco	.50
13	Roger Clemens	1.25
14	Tom Gordon	.05
15	Jose Malave	.05
16	Tim Naehring	.05
17	Troy O'Leary	.05
18	Bill Selby	.05
19	Heathcliff Slocumb	.05
20	Mike Stanley	.05
21	Mo Vaughn	.05
22	Garret Anderson	.05
23	George Arias	.05
24	Chili Davis	.05
25	Jim Edmonds	.05
26	Darin Erstad	.25
27	Chuck Finley	.05
28	Todd Greene	.05
29	Troy Percival	.05
30	Tim Salmon	.05
31	Jeff Schmidt	.05
32	Randy Velarde	.05
33	Shad Williams	.05
34	Wilson Alvarez	.05
35	Harold Baines	.05
36	James Baldwin	.05
37	Mike Cameron	.05
38	Ray Durham	.05
39	Ozzie Guillen	.05
40	Roberto Hernandez	.05
41	Darren Lewis	.05
42	Jose Munoz	.05
43	Tony Phillips	.05
44	Frank Thomas	.75
45	Sandy Alomar Jr.	.05
46	Albert Belle	.05
47	Mark Carreon	.05
48	Julio Franco	.05
49	Orel Hershiser	.05
50	Kenny Lofton	.05
51	Jack McDowell	.05
52	Jose Mesa	.05
53	Charles Nagy	.05
54	Manny Ramirez	.75
55	Julian Tavarez	.05
56	Omar Vizquel	.05
57	Raul Casanova	.05
58	Tony Clark	.05
59	Travis Fryman	.05
60	Bob Higginson	.05
61	Melvin Nieves	.05
62	Curtis Pride	.05
63	Justin Thompson	.05
64	Alan Trammell	.05
65	Kevin Appier	.05
66	Johnny Damon	.35
67	Keith Lockhart	.05
68	Jeff Montgomery	.05
69	Jose Offerman	.05
70	Bip Roberts	.05
71	Jose Rosado	.05
72	Chris Stynes	.05
73	Mike Sweeney	.05
74	Jeff Cirillo	.05
75	Jeff D'Amico	.05
76	John Jaha	.05
77	Scott Karl	.05
78	Mike Matheny	.05
79	Ben McDonald	.05
80	Matt Mieske	.05
81	Marc Newfield	.05
82	Dave Nilsson	.05
83	Jose Valentin	.05
84	Fernando Vina	.05
85	Rick Aguilera	.05
86	Marty Cordova	.05
87	Chuck Knoblauch	.05
88	Matt Lawton	.05
89	Pat Meares	.05
90	Paul Molitor	.75
91	Greg Myers	.05
92	Dan Naulty	.05
93	Kirby Puckett	1.00
94	Frank Rodriguez	.05
95	Wade Boggs	1.00
96	Cecil Fielder	.05
97	Joe Girardi	.05
98	Dwight Gooden	.05
99	Derek Jeter	2.50
100	Tino Martinez	.05
101	Ramiro Mendoza RC	.05

102 Andy Pettitte .20
103 Mariano Rivera .15
104 Ruben Rivera .05
105 Kenny Rogers .05
106 Darryl Strawberry .05
107 Bernie Williams .05
108 Tony Batista .05
109 Geronimo Berroa .05
110 Bobby Chouinard .05
111 Brent Gates .05
112 Jason Giambi .60
113 Damon Mashore **RC** .05
114 Mark McGwire 2.00
115 Scott Spiezio .05
116 John Wasdin .05
117 Steve Wojciechowski .05
118 Ernie Young .05
119 Norm Charlton .05
120 Joey Cora .05
121 Ken Griffey Jr. 1.50
122 Sterling Hitchcock .05
123 Raul Ibanez .05
124 Randy Johnson .75
125 Edgar Martinez .05
126 Alex Rodriguez 2.00
127 Matt Wagner .05
128 Bob Wells .05
129 Dan Wilson .05
130 Will Clark .05
131 Kevin Elster .05
132 Juan Gonzalez .40
133 Rusty Greer .05
134 Darryl Hamilton .05
135 Mike Henneman .05
136 Ken Hill .05
137 Mark McLemore .05
138 Dean Palmer .05
139 Roger Pavlik .05
140 Ivan Rodriguez .65
141 Joe Carter .05
142 Carlos Delgado .50
143 Alex Gonzalez .05
144 Juan Guzman .05
145 Pat Hentgen .05
146 Marty Janzen .05
147 Otis Nixon .05
148 Charlie O'Brien .05
149 John Olerud .05
150 Robert Perez .05
151 Jermaine Dye .05
152 Tom Glavine .30
153 Andruw Jones .75
154 Chipper Jones 1.00
155 Ryan Klesko .05
156 Javier Lopez .05
157 Greg Maddux 1.00
158 Fred McGriff .05
159 Wonderful Monds .05
160 John Smoltz .05
161 Terrell Wade .05
162 Mark Wohlers .05
163 Brant Brown .05
164 Mark Grace .05
165 Tyler Houston .05
166 Robin Jennings .05
167 Jason Maxwell .05
168 Ryne Sandberg 1.00
169 Sammy Sosa 1.00
170 Amaury Telemaco .05
171 Steve Trachsel .05
172 Pedro Valdes **RC** .05
173 Tim Belk .05
174 Bret Boone .05
175 Jeff Brantley .05
176 Eric Davis .05
177 Barry Larkin .05
178 Chad Mottola .05
179 Mark Portugal .05
180 Reggie Sanders .05
181 John Smiley .05
182 Eddie Taubensee .05
183 Dante Bichette .05
184 Ellis Burks .05
185 Andres Galarraga .05
186 Curt Leskanic .05
187 Quinton McCracken .05
188 Jeff Reed .05
189 Kevin Ritz .05
190 Walt Weiss .05
191 Jamey Wright .05
192 Eric Young .05
193 Kevin Brown .05
194 Luis Castillo .05
195 Jeff Conine .05
196 Andre Dawson .25
197 Charles Johnson .05
198 Al Leiter .05
199 Ralph Milliard .05
200 Robb Nen .05
201 Edgar Renteria .05
202 Gary Sheffield .40
203 Bob Abreu .10
204 Jeff Bagwell .75
205 Derek Bell .05
206 Sean Berry .05
207 Richard Hidalgo .05
208 Todd Jones .05
209 Darryl Kile .05
210 Orlando Miller .05
211 Shane Reynolds .05
212 Billy Wagner .05
213 Donne Wall .05
214 Roger Cedeno .05
215 Greg Gagne .05
216 Karim Garcia .10
217 Wilton Guerrero .05
218 Todd Hollandsworth .05
219 Ramon Martinez .05
220 Raul Mondesi .05
221 Hideo Nomo .40
222 Chan Ho Park .05
223 Mike Piazza 1.50
224 Ismael Valdes .05
225 Moises Alou .05
226 Derek Aucoin .05
227 Yamil Benitez .05
228 Jeff Fassero .05
229 Darrin Fletcher .05
230 Mark Grudzielanek .05
231 Barry Manuel .05
232 Pedro Martinez .75
233 Henry Rodriguez .05
234 Ugueth Urbina .05
235 Rondell White .05
236 Carlos Baerga .05
237 John Franco .05
238 Bernard Gilkey .05
239 Todd Hundley .05
240 Butch Huskey .05
241 Jason Isringhausen .05
242 Lance Johnson .05
243 Bobby Jones .05
244 Alex Ochoa .05
245 Rey Ordonez .05
246 Paul Wilson .05
247 Ron Blazier .05
248 David Doster .05
249 Jim Eisenreich .05
250 Mike Grace .05
251 Mike Lieberthal .05
252 Wendell Magee .05
253 Mickey Morandini .05
254 Ricky Otero .05
255 Scott Rolen .60
256 Curt Schilling .20
257 Todd Zeile .05
258 Jermaine Allensworth .05
259 Trey Beamon .05
260 Carlos Garcia .05
261 Mark Johnson .05
262 Jason Kendall .05
263 Jeff King .05
264 Al Martin .05
265 Denny Neagle .05
266 Matt Ruebel .05
267 Marc Wilkins **RC** .05
268 Alan Benes .05
269 Dennis Eckersley .65
270 Ron Gant .05
271 Aaron Holbert .05
272 Brian Jordan .05
273 Ray Lankford .05
274 John Mabry .05
275 T.J. Mathews .05
276 Ozzie Smith 1.00
277 Todd Stottlemyre .05
278 Mark Sweeney .05
279 Andy Ashby .05
280 Steve Finley .05
281 John Flaherty .05
282 Chris Gomez .05
283 Tony Gwynn 1.00
284 Joey Hamilton .05
285 Rickey Henderson .75
286 Trevor Hoffman .05
287 Jason Thompson .05
288 Fernando Valenzuela .05
289 Greg Vaughn .05
290 Barry Bonds 2.50
291 Jay Canizaro .05
292 Jacob Cruz .05
293 Shawon Dunston .05
294 Shawn Estes .05
295 Mark Gardner .05
296 Marcus Jensen .05
297 Bill Mueller **RC** .35
298 Chris Singleton .05
299 Allen Watson .05
300 Matt Williams .05
301 Rod Beck .05
302 Jay Bell .05
303 Shawon Dunston .05
304 Reggie Jefferson .05
305 Darren Oliver .05
306 Benito Santiago .05
307 Gerald Williams .05
308 Damon Buford .05
309 Jeromy Burnitz .05
310 Sterling Hitchcock .05
311 Dave Hollins .05
312 Mel Rojas .05
313 Robin Ventura .05
314 David Wells .05
315 Cal Eldred .05
316 Gary Gaetti .05
317 John Hudek .05
318 Brian Johnson .05
319 Denny Neagle .05
320 Larry Walker .05
321 Russ Davis .05
322 Delino DeShields .05
323 Charlie Hayes .05
324 Jermaine Dye .05
325 John Ericks .05
326 Jeff Fassero .05
327 Nomar Garciaparra 1.00
328 Willie Greene .05
329 Greg McMichael .05
330 Damion Easley .05
331 Ricky Bones .05
332 John Burkett .05
333 Royce Clayton .05
334 Greg Colbrunn .05
335 Tony Eusebio .05
336 Gregg Jefferies .05
337 Wally Joyner .05
338 Jim Leyritz .05
339 Paul O'Neill .05
340 Bruce Ruffin .05
341 Michael Tucker .05
342 Andy Benes .05
343 Craig Biggio .05
344 Rex Hudler .05
345 Brad Radke .05
346 Deion Sanders .05
347 Moises Alou .05
348 Brad Ausmus .05
349 Armando Benitez .05
350 Mark Gubicza .05
351 Terry Steinbach .05
352 Mark Whiten .05
353 Ricky Bottalico .05
354 Brian Giles **RC** .75
355 Eric Karros .05
356 Jimmy Key .05
357 Carlos Perez .05
358 Alex Fernandez .05
359 J.T. Snow .05
360 Bobby Bonilla .05
361 Scott Brosius .05
362 Greg Swindell .05
363 Jose Vizcaino .05
364 Matt Williams .05
365 Darren Daulton .05
366 Shane Andrews .05
367 Jim Eisenreich .05
368 Ariel Prieto .05
369 Bob Tewksbury .05
370 Mike Bordick .05
371 Rheal Cormier .05
372 Cliff Floyd .05
373 David Justice .05
374 John Wetteland .05
375 Mike Blowers .05
376 Jose Canseco .50
377 Roger Clemens 1.25
378 Kevin Mitchell .05
379 Todd Zeile .05
380 Jim Thome .60
381 Turk Wendell .05
382 Rico Brogna .05
383 Eric Davis .05
384 Mike Lansing .05
385 Devon White .05
386 Marquis Grissom .05
387 Todd Worrell .05
388 Jeff Kent .05
389 Mickey Tettleton .05
390 Steve Avery .05
391 David Cone .05
392 Scott Cooper .05
393 Lee Stevens .05
394 Kevin Elster .05
395 Tom Goodwin .05
396 Shawn Green .25
397 Pete Harnisch .05
398 Eddie Murray .75
399 Joe Randa .05
400 Scott Sanders .05
401 John Valentin .05
402 Todd Jones .05
403 Terry Adams .05
404 Brian Hunter .05
405 Pat Listach .05
406 Kenny Lofton .05
407 Hal Morris .05
408 Ed Sprague .05
409 Rich Becker .05
410 Edgardo Alfonzo .05
411 Albert Belle .05
412 Jeff King .05
413 Kirt Manwaring .05
414 Jason Schmidt .05
415 Allen Watson .05
416 Lee Tinsley .05
417 Brett Butler .05
418 Carlos Garcia .05
419 Mark Lemke .05
420 Jaime Navarro .05
421 David Segui .05
422 Ruben Sierra .05
423 B.J. Surhoff .05
424 Julian Tavarez .05
425 Billy Taylor .05
426 Ken Caminiti .05
427 Chuck Carr .05
428 Benji Gil .05
429 Terry Mulholland .05
430 Mike Stanton .05
431 Wil Cordero .05
432 Chili Davis .05
433 Mariano Duncan .05
434 Orlando Merced .05
435 Kent Mercker .05
436 John Olerud .05
437 Quilvio Veras .05
438 Mike Fetters .05
439 Glenallen Hill .05
440 Bill Swift .05
441 Tim Wakefield .05
442 Pedro Astacio .05
443 Vinny Castilla .05
444 Doug Drabek .05
445 Alan Embree .05
446 Lee Smith .05
447 Darryl Hamilton .05
448 Brian McRae .05
449 Mike Timlin .05
450 Bob Wickman .05
451 Jason Dickson .05
452 Chad Curtis .05
453 Mark Leiter .05
454 Damon Berryhill .05
455 Kevin Orie .05
456 Dave Burba .05
457 Chris Holt .05
458 Ricky Ledee **RC** .10
459 Mike Devereaux .05
460 Pokey Reese .05
461 Tim Raines .05
462 Ryan Jones .05
463 Shane Mack .05
464 Darren Dreifort .05
465 Mark Parent .05
466 Mark Portugal .05
467 Dante Powell .05
468 Craig Grebeck .05
469 Ron Villone .05
470 Dmitri Young .05
471 Shannon Stewart .05
472 Rick Helling .05
473 Bill Haselman .05
474 Albie Lopez .05
475 Glendon Rusch .05
476 Derrick May .05
477 Chad Ogea .05
478 Kirk Reuter .05
479 Chris Hammond .05
480 Russ Johnson .05
481 James Mouton .05
482 Mike Macfarlane .05
483 Scott Ruffcorn .05
484 Jeff Frye .05
485 Richie Sexson .05
486 Emil Brown **RC** .05
487 Desi Wilson .05
488 Brent Gates .05
489 Tony Graffanino .05
490 Dan Miceli .05
491 Orlando Cabrera **RC** .65
492 Tony Womack **RC** .20
493 Jerome Walton .05
494 Mark Thompson .05
495 Jose Guillen .05
496 Willie Blair .05
497 T.J. Staton **RC** .05
498 Scott Kamieniecki .05
499 Vince Coleman .05
500 Jeff Abbott .05
501 Chris Widger .05
502 Kevin Tapani .05
503 Carlos Castillo **RC** .05
504 Luis Gonzalez .05
505 Tim Belcher .05
506 Armando Reynoso .05
507 Jamie Moyer .05
508 Randall Simon **RC** .05
509 Vladimir Guerrero .75
510 Wady Almonte **RC** .05
511 Dustin Hermanson .05
512 Deivi Cruz **RC** .25
513 Luis Alicea .05
514 Felix Heredia **RC** .15
515 Don Slaught .05
516 Shigetosi Hasegawa .05
517 Matt Walbeck .05
518 David Arias **RC**
(Last name actually Ortiz.) 40.00
519 Brady Raggio **RC** .05
520 Rudy Pemberton .05
521 Wayne Kirby .05
522 Calvin Maduro .05
523 Mark Lewis .05
524 Mike Jackson .05
525 Sid Fernandez .05
526 Mike Bielecki .05
527 Bubba Trammell **RC** .05
528 Brent Brede **RC** .05
529 Matt Morris .05
530 Joe Borowski .05
531 Orlando Miller .05
532 Jim Bullinger .05
533 Robert Person .05
534 Doug Glanville .05
535 Terry Pendleton .05
536 Jorge Posada .05
537 Marc Sagmoen **RC** .05
538 Fernando Tatis **RC** .20
539 Aaron Sele .05
540 Brian Banks .05
541 Derrek Lee .50
542 John Wasdin .05
543 Justin Towle **RC** .05
544 Pat Cline .05
545 Dave Magadan .05
546 Jeff Blauser .05
547 Phil Nevin .05
548 Todd Walker .05
549 Elieser Marrero .05
550 Bartolo Colon .05
551 Jose Cruz Jr. **RC** .50
552 Todd Dunwoody .05
553 Hideki Irabu **RC** .25

1997 Ultra Gold Medallion Edition

	NM/M
Complete Set (553):	100.00
Common Player:	.25
Stars/Rookies:	3X

(See 1997 Ultra for checklist and base card values.)

1997 Ultra Platinum Medallion Edition

	NM/M
Common Player:	2.00
Stars/Rookies:	25X

(See 1997 Ultra for checklist and base card values.)

Baseball Rules!

		NM/M
Complete Set (10):		45.00
Common Player:		.50
1	Barry Bonds	10.00
2	Ken Griffey Jr.	6.00
3	Derek Jeter	10.00
4	Chipper Jones	5.00
5	Greg Maddux	5.00
6	Mark McGwire	7.50
7	Troy Percival	.50
8	Mike Piazza	6.00
9	Cal Ripken Jr.	10.00
10	Frank Thomas	4.00

Diamond Producers

		NM/M
Complete Set (12):		110.00
Common Player:		2.50
1	Jeff Bagwell	7.00
2	Barry Bonds	20.00
3	Ken Griffey Jr.	12.50
4	Chipper Jones	10.00
5	Kenny Lofton	2.50
6	Greg Maddux	10.00

		NM/M
7	Mark McGwire	15.00
8	Mike Piazza	12.50
9	Cal Ripken Jr.	20.00
10	Alex Rodriguez	15.00
11	Frank Thomas	7.50
12	Matt Williams	2.50

Double Trouble

		NM/M
Complete Set (20):		10.00
Common Player:		.15
1	Roberto Alomar, Cal Ripken Jr.	1.50
2	Mo Vaughn, Jose Canseco	.40
3	Jim Edmonds, Tim Salmon	.15
4	Harold Baines, Frank Thomas	.50
5	Albert Belle, Kenny Lofton	.15
6	Chuck Knoblauch, Marty Cordova	.15
7	Andy Pettitte, Derek Jeter	1.50
8	Jason Giambi, Mark McGwire	1.00
9	Ken Griffey Jr., Alex Rodriguez	1.00
10	Juan Gonzalez, Will Clark	.30
11	Greg Maddux, Chipper Jones	.75
12	Mark Grace, Sammy Sosa	.60
13	Dante Bichette, Andres Galarraga	.15
14	Jeff Bagwell, Derek Bell	.50
15	Hideo Nomo, Mike Piazza	.75
16	Henry Rodriguez, Moises Alou	.15
17	Rey Ordonez, Alex Ochoa	.15
18	Ray Lankford, Ron Gant	.15
19	Tony Gwynn, Rickey Henderson	.60
20	Barry Bonds, Matt Williams	1.50

Fame Game

		NM/M
Complete Set (18):		20.00
Common Player:		.35
1	Ken Griffey Jr.	1.75
2	Frank Thomas	1.00
3	Alex Rodriguez	2.00
4	Cal Ripken Jr.	3.00
5	Mike Piazza	1.75
6	Greg Maddux	1.25
7	Derek Jeter	3.00
8	Jeff Bagwell	1.00
9	Juan Gonzalez	.50
10	Albert Belle	.35
11	Tony Gwynn	1.25
12	Mark McGwire	2.00

		NM/M
13	Andy Pettitte	.45
14	Kenny Lofton	.35
15	Roberto Alomar	.40
16	Ryne Sandberg	1.25
17	Barry Bonds	3.00
18	Eddie Murray	1.00

Fielder's Choice

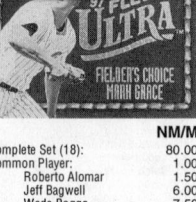

		NM/M
Complete Set (18):		80.00
Common Player:		1.00
1	Roberto Alomar	1.50
2	Jeff Bagwell	6.00
3	Wade Boggs	7.50
4	Barry Bonds	15.00
5	Mark Grace	1.00
6	Ken Griffey Jr.	10.00
7	Marquis Grissom	1.00
8	Charles Johnson	1.00
9	Chuck Knoblauch	1.00
10	Barry Larkin	1.00
11	Kenny Lofton	1.00
12	Greg Maddux	7.50
13	Raul Mondesi	1.00
14	Rey Ordonez	1.00
15	Cal Ripken Jr.	15.00
16	Alex Rodriguez	12.50
17	Ivan Rodriguez	5.00
18	Matt Williams	1.00

Golden Prospects

		NM/M
Complete Set (10):		3.00
Common Player:		.25
1	Andruw Jones	1.50
2	Vladimir Guerrero	1.50
3	Todd Walker	.25
4	Karim Garcia	.25
5	Kevin Orie	.25
6	Brian Giles	.25
7	Jason Dickson	.25
8	Jose Guillen	.25
9	Ruben Rivera	.25
10	Derrek Lee	1.00

Hitting Machines

		NM/M
Complete Set (18):		60.00
Common Player:		1.00
1	Andruw Jones	3.00
2	Ken Griffey Jr.	5.00
3	Frank Thomas	3.00
4	Alex Rodriguez	6.50
5	Cal Ripken Jr.	9.00
6	Mike Piazza	5.00

		NM/M
7	Derek Jeter	9.00
8	Albert Belle	1.00
9	Tony Gwynn	4.00
10	Jeff Bagwell	3.00
11	Mark McGwire	6.50
12	Kenny Lofton	1.00
13	Manny Ramirez	3.00
14	Roberto Alomar	1.25
15	Ryne Sandberg	4.00
16	Eddie Murray	3.00
17	Sammy Sosa	4.00
18	Ken Caminiti	1.00

HR Kings

		NM/M
Complete Set (12):		30.00
Common Player:		1.00
1	Albert Belle	1.00
2	Barry Bonds	7.50
3	Juan Gonzalez	1.50
4	Ken Griffey Jr.	4.50
5	Todd Hundley	1.00
6	Ryan Klesko	1.00
7	Mark McGwire	6.00
8	Mike Piazza	4.50
9	Sammy Sosa	3.50
10	Frank Thomas	2.50
11	Mo Vaughn	1.00
12	Matt Williams	1.00

Leather Shop

		NM/M
Complete Set (12):		9.00
Common Player:		.25
1	Ken Griffey Jr.	1.25
2	Alex Rodriguez	1.50
3	Cal Ripken Jr.	2.00
4	Derek Jeter	2.00
5	Juan Gonzalez	.45
6	Tony Gwynn	1.00
7	Jeff Bagwell	.75
8	Roberto Alomar	.40
9	Ryne Sandberg	1.00
10	Ken Caminiti	.25
11	Kenny Lofton	.25
12	John Smoltz	.25

Power Plus Series 2

		NM/M
Complete Set (12):		6.50
Common Player:		.25
1	Ken Griffey Jr.	.75
2	Frank Thomas	.50
3	Alex Rodriguez	1.00
4	Cal Ripken Jr.	1.50
5	Mike Piazza	.75
6	Chipper Jones	.75
7	Albert Belle	.25
8	Juan Gonzalez	.35
9	Jeff Bagwell	.50
10	Mark McGwire	.75

11	Mo Vaughn	.25
12	Barry Bonds	1.50

Power Plus Series 1

		NM/M
Complete Set (12):		15.00
Common Player:		.50
1	Jeff Bagwell	.75
2	Barry Bonds	3.00
3	Juan Gonzalez	.60
4	Ken Griffey Jr.	1.50
5	Chipper Jones	1.00
6	Mark McGwire	2.00
7	Mike Piazza	1.50
8	Cal Ripken Jr.	3.00
9	Alex Rodriguez	2.00
10	Sammy Sosa	1.00
11	Frank Thomas	.75
12	Matt Williams	.50

Rookie Reflections

		NM/M
Complete Set (10):		3.50
Common Player:		.25
1	James Baldwin	.25
2	Jermaine Dye	.25
3	Darin Erstad	.40
4	Todd Hollandsworth	.25
5	Derek Jeter	3.00
6	Jason Kendall	.25
7	Alex Ochoa	.25
8	Rey Ordonez	.25
9	Edgar Renteria	.25
10	Scott Rolen	.50

RBI Kings

		NM/M
Complete Set (10):		12.50
Common Player:		.75
1	Jeff Bagwell	1.50
2	Albert Belle	.75
3	Dante Bichette	.75
4	Barry Bonds	4.00

5	Jay Buhner	.75
6	Juan Gonzalez	1.00
7	Ken Griffey Jr.	2.50
8	Sammy Sosa	2.00
9	Frank Thomas	1.50
10	Mo Vaughn	.75

Season Crowns

		NM/M
Complete Set (12):		10.00
Common Player:		.50
1	Albert Belle	.50
2	Dante Bichette	.50
3	Barry Bonds	3.00
4	Kenny Lofton	.50
5	Edgar Martinez	.50
6	Mark McGwire	2.00
7	Andy Pettitte	.50
8	Mike Piazza	1.50
9	Alex Rodriguez	2.00
10	John Smoltz	.50
11	Sammy Sosa	1.25
12	Frank Thomas	1.00

Starring Role

		NM/M
Complete Set (12):		175.00
Common Player:		7.50
1	Andruw Jones	12.00
2	Ken Griffey Jr.	20.00
3	Frank Thomas	12.00
4	Alex Rodriguez	25.00
5	Cal Ripken Jr.	30.00
6	Mike Piazza	20.00
7	Greg Maddux	15.00
8	Chipper Jones	15.00
9	Derek Jeter	30.00
10	Juan Gonzalez	9.00
11	Albert Belle	7.50
12	Tony Gwynn	15.00

Thunderclap

		NM/M
Complete Set (10):		20.00

Common Player:		.75
1	Barry Bonds	5.00
2	Mo Vaughn	.75
3	Mark McGwire	4.00
4	Jeff Bagwell	1.50
5	Juan Gonzalez	1.00
6	Alex Rodriguez	4.00
7	Chipper Jones	2.50
8	Ken Griffey Jr.	3.00
9	Mike Piazza	3.00
10	Frank Thomas	2.00

Top 30

		NM/M
Complete Set (30):		12.00
Common Player:		.20
Gold Medallions:		6X
1	Andruw Jones	.75
2	Ken Griffey Jr.	1.25
3	Frank Thomas	.75
4	Alex Rodriguez	1.50
5	Cal Ripken Jr.	2.00
6	Mike Piazza	1.25
7	Greg Maddux	1.00
8	Chipper Jones	1.00
9	Derek Jeter	2.00
10	Juan Gonzalez	.40
11	Albert Belle	.20
12	Tony Gwynn	1.00
13	Jeff Bagwell	.75
14	Mark McGwire	1.50
15	Andy Pettitte	.30
16	Mo Vaughn	.20
17	Kenny Lofton	.20
18	Manny Ramirez	.75
19	Roberto Alomar	.40
20	Ryne Sandberg	1.00
21	Hideo Nomo	.40
22	Barry Bonds	2.00
23	Eddie Murray	.75
24	Ken Caminiti	.20
25	John Smoltz	.20
26	Pat Hentgen	.20
27	Todd Hollandsworth	.20
28	Matt Williams	.20
29	Bernie Williams	.20
30	Brady Anderson	.20

1998 Ultra

		NM/M
Complete Set (501):		75.00
Common Player:		.05
Alex Rodriguez Autograph (750):		50.00
Pack (10):		1.25
Wax Box (24):		20.00
1	Ken Griffey Jr.	1.25
2	Matt Morris	.05
3	Roger Clemens	1.00
4	Matt Williams	.05
5	Roberto Hernandez	.05
6	Rondell White	.05
7	Tim Salmon	.05
8	Brad Radke	.05
9	Brett Butler	.05
10	Carl Everett	.05
11	Chili Davis	.05
12	Chuck Finley	.05
13	Darryl Kile	.05

14	Deivi Cruz	.05
15	Gary Gaetti	.05
16	Matt Stairs	.05
17	Pat Meares	.05
18	Will Cunnane	.05
19	Steve Woodard **RC**	.15
20	Andy Ashby	.05
21	Bobby Higginson	.05
22	Brian Jordan	.05
23	Craig Biggio	.05
24	Jim Edmonds	.05
25	Ryan McGuire	.05
26	Scott Hatteberg	.05
27	Willie Greene	.05
28	Albert Belle	.05
29	Ellis Burks	.05
30	Hideo Nomo	.40
31	Jeff Bagwell	.75
32	Kevin Brown	.05
33	Nomar Garciaparra	1.00
34	Pedro Martinez	.75
35	Raul Mondesi	.05
36	Ricky Bottalico	.05
37	Shawn Estes	.05
38	Shawon Dunston	.05
39	Terry Steinbach	.05
40	Tom Glavine	.25
41	Todd Dunwoody	.05
42	Deion Sanders	.05
43	Gary Sheffield	.45
44	Mike Lansing	.05
45	Mike Lieberthal	.05
46	Paul Sorrento	.05
47	Paul O'Neill	.05
48	Tom Goodwin	.05
49	Andruw Jones	.75
50	Barry Bonds	2.00
51	Bernie Williams	.05
52	Jeremi Gonzalez	.05
53	Mike Piazza	1.25
54	Russ Davis	.05
55	Vinny Castilla	.05
56	Rod Beck	.05
57	Andres Galarraga	.05
58	Ben McDonald	.05
59	Billy Wagner	.05
60	Charles Johnson	.05
61	Fred McGriff	.05
62	Dean Palmer	.05
63	Frank Thomas	.75
64	Ismael Valdes	.05
65	Mark Bellhorn	.05
66	Jeff King	.05
67	John Wetteland	.05
68	Mark Grace	.05
69	Mark Kotsay	.05
70	Scott Rolen	.60
71	Todd Hundley	.05
72	Todd Worrell	.05
73	Wilson Alvarez	.05
74	Bobby Jones	.05
75	Jose Canseco	.50
76	Kevin Appier	.05
77	Neifi Perez	.05
78	Paul Molitor	.75
79	Quilvio Veras	.05
80	Randy Johnson	.75
81	Glendon Rusch	.05
82	Curt Schilling	.15
83	Alex Rodriguez	1.50
84	Rey Ordonez	.05
85	Jeff Juden	.05
86	Mike Cameron	.05
87	Ryan Klesko	.05
88	Trevor Hoffman	.05
89	Chuck Knoblauch	.05
90	Larry Walker	.05
91	Mark McLemore	.05
92	B.J. Surhoff	.05
93	Darren Daulton	.05
94	Ray Durham	.05
95	Sammy Sosa	1.00
96	Eric Young	.05
97	Gerald Williams	.05
98	Javy Lopez	.05
99	John Smiley	.05
100	Juan Gonzalez	.40
101	Shawn Green	.30
102	Charles Nagy	.05
103	David Justice	.05
104	Joey Hamilton	.05

105	Pat Hentgen	.05
106	Raul Casanova	.05
107	Tony Phillips	.05
108	Tony Gwynn	1.00
109	Will Clark	.05
110	Jason Giambi	.50
111	Jay Bell	.05
112	Johnny Damon	.30
113	Alan Benes	.05
114	Jeff Suppan	.05
115	Kevin Polcovich **RC**	.05
116	Shigetosi Hasegawa	.05
117	Steve Finley	.05
118	Tony Clark	.05
119	David Cone	.05
120	Jose Guillen	.05
121	Kevin Millwood **RC**	1.00
122	Greg Maddux	1.00
123	Dave Nilsson	.05
124	Hideki Irabu	.05
125	Jason Kendall	.05
126	Jim Thome	.60
127	Delino DeShields	.05
128	Edgar Renteria	.05
129	Edgardo Alfonzo	.05
130	J.T. Snow	.05
131	Jeff Abbott	.05
132	Jeffrey Hammonds	.05
133	Rich Loiselle	.05
134	Vladimir Guerrero	.75
135	Jay Buhner	.05
136	Jeff Cirillo	.05
137	Jeromy Burnitz	.05
138	Mickey Morandini	.05
139	Tino Martinez	.05
140	Jeff Shaw	.05
141	Rafael Palmeiro	.65
142	Bobby Bonilla	.05
143	Cal Ripken Jr.	2.00
144	Chad Fox **RC**	.05
145	Dante Bichette	.05
146	Dennis Eckersley	.65
147	Mariano Rivera	.15
148	Mo Vaughn	.05
149	Reggie Sanders	.05
150	Derek Jeter	2.00
151	Rusty Greer	.05
152	Brady Anderson	.05
153	Brett Tomko	.05
154	Jaime Navarro	.05
155	Kevin Orie	.05
156	Roberto Alomar	.20
157	Edgar Martinez	.05
158	John Olerud	.05
159	John Smoltz	.05
160	Ryne Sandberg	1.00
161	Billy Taylor	.05
162	Chris Holt	.05
163	Damion Easley	.05
164	Darin Erstad	.25
165	Joe Carter	.05
166	Kelvim Escobar	.05
167	Ken Caminiti	.05
168	Pokey Reese	.05
169	Ray Lankford	.05
170	Livan Hernandez	.05
171	Steve Kline	.05
172	Tom Gordon	.05
173	Travis Fryman	.05
174	Al Martin	.05
175	Andy Pettitte	.25
176	Jeff Kent	.05
177	Jimmy Key	.05
178	Mark Grudzielanek	.05
179	Tony Saunders	.05
180	Barry Larkin	.05
181	Bubba Trammell	.05
182	Carlos Delgado	.50
183	Carlos Baerga	.05
184	Derek Bell	.05
185	Henry Rodriguez	.05
186	Jason Dickson	.05
187	Ron Gant	.05
188	Tony Womack	.05
189	Justin Thompson	.05
190	Fernando Tatis	.05
191	Mark Wohlers	.05
192	Takashi Kashiwada	.05
193	Garret Anderson	.05
194	Jose Cruz, Jr.	.05
195	Ricardo Rincon	.05
196	Tim Naehring	.05
197	Moises Alou	.05
198	Eric Karros	.05
199	John Jaha	.05
200	Marty Cordova	.05
201	Travis Lee	.10
202	Mark Davis	.05
203	Vladimir Nunez	.05
204	Stanton Cameron	.05
205	Mike Stoner **RC**	.05
206	Rolando Arrojo **RC**	.40
207	Rick White	.05
208	Luis Polonia	.05
209	Greg Blosser	.05
210	Cesar Devarez	.05
211	Jeff Bagwell	1.00
212	Barry Bonds	3.00
213	Roger Clemens	1.75
214	Nomar Garciaparra	1.50
215	Ken Griffey Jr.	2.00
216	Tony Gwynn	1.50
217	Randy Johnson	1.00
218	Mark McGwire	3.00
219	Scott Rolen	.75

220	Frank Thomas	1.25
221	Matt Perisho	.25
222	Wes Helms	.25
223	David Dellucci **RC**	.25
224	Todd Helton	1.00
225	Brian Rose	.25
226	Aaron Boone	.25
227	Keith Foulke	.25
228	Homer Bush	.25
229	Shannon Stewart	.25
230	Richard Hidalgo	.25
231	Russ Johnson	.25
232	Henry Blanco **RC**	.25
233	Paul Konerko	.35
234	Antone Williamson	.25
235	Shane Bowers **RC**	.25
236	Jose Vidro	.25
237	Derek Wallace	.25
238	Ricky Ledee	.25
239	Ben Grieve	.25
240	Lou Collier	.25
241	Derrek Lee	.65
242	Ruben Rivera	.25
243	Jorge Velandia	.25
244	Andrew Vessel	.25
245	Chris Carpenter	.25
246	Ken Griffey Jr. Checklist	.65
247	Andruw Jones Checklist	.50
248	Alex Rodriguez Checklist	.75
249	Frank Thomas Checklist	.60
250	Cal Ripken Jr. Checklist	1.00
251	Carlos Perez	.05
252	Larry Sutton	.05
253	Brad Rigby	.05
254	Wally Joyner	.05
255	Todd Stottlemyre	.05
256	Nerio Rodriguez	.05
257	Jeff Frye	.05
258	Pedro Astacio	.05
259	Cal Eldred	.05
260	Chili Davis	.05
261	Freddy Garcia	.05
262	Bobby Witt	.05
263	Michael Coleman	.05
264	Mike Caruso	.05
265	Mike Lansing	.05
266	Dennis Reyes	.05
267	F.P. Santangelo	.05
268	Darryl Hamilton	.05
269	Mike Fetters	.05
270	Charlie Hayes	.05
271	Royce Clayton	.05
272	Doug Drabek	.05
273	James Baldwin	.05
274	Brian Hunter	.05
275	Chan Ho Park	.05
276	John Franco	.05
277	David Wells	.05
278	Eli Marrero	.05
279	Kerry Wood	.40
280	Donnie Sadler	.05
281	Scott Winchester **RC**	.05
282	Hal Morris	.05
283	Brad Fullmer	.05
284	Bernard Gilkey	.05
285	Ramiro Mendoza	.05
286	Kevin Brown	.05
287	David Segui	.05
288	Willie McGee	.05
289	Darren Oliver	.05
290	Antonio Alfonseca	.05
291	Eric Davis	.05
292	Mickey Morandini	.05
293	Frank Catalanotto **RC**	.20
294	Derrek Lee	.50
295	Todd Zeile	.05
296	Chuck Knoblauch	.05
297	Wilson Delgado	.05
298	Raul Ibanez	.05
299	Orel Hershiser	.05
300	Ozzie Guillen	.05
301	Aaron Sele	.05
302	Joe Carter	.05
303	Darryl Kile	.05
304	Shane Reynolds	.05
305	Todd Dunn	.05
306	Bob Abreu	.10
307	Doug Strange	.05
308	Jose Canseco	.50
309	Lance Johnson	.05
310	Harold Baines	.05
311	Todd Pratt	.05
312	Greg Colbrunn	.05
313	Masato Yoshii **RC**	.25
314	Felix Heredia	.05
315	Dennis Martinez	.05
316	Geronimo Berroa	.05
317	Darren Lewis	.05
318	Billy Ripken	.05
319	Enrique Wilson	.05
320	Alex Ochoa	.05
321	Doug Glanville	.05
322	Mike Stanley	.05
323	Gerald Williams	.05
324	Pedro Martinez	.75
325	Jaret Wright	.05
326	Terry Pendleton	.05
327	LaTroy Hawkins	.05
328	Emil Brown	.05
329	Walt Weiss	.05
330	Omar Vizquel	.05
331	Carl Everett	.05
332	Fernando Vina	.05
333	Mike Blowers	.05
334	Dwight Gooden	.05

335	Mark Lewis	.05
336	Jim Leyritz	.05
337	Kenny Lofton	.05
338	John Halama **RC**	.05
339	Jose Valentin	.05
340	Desi Relaford	.05
341	Dante Powell	.05
342	Ed Sprague	.05
343	Reggie Jefferson	.05
344	Mike Hampton	.05
345	Marquis Grissom	.05
346	Heathcliff Slocumb	.05
347	Francisco Cordova	.05
348	Ken Cloude	.05
349	Benito Santiago	.05
350	Denny Neagle	.05
351	Sean Casey	.15
352	Robb Nen	.05
353	Orlando Merced	.05
354	Adrian Brown	.05
355	Gregg Jefferies	.05
356	Otis Nixon	.05
357	Michael Tucker	.05
358	Eric Milton	.05
359	Travis Fryman	.05
360	Gary DiSarcina	.05
361	Mario Valdez	.05
362	Craig Counsell	.05
363	Jose Offerman	.05
364	Tony Fernandez	.05
365	Jason McDonald	.05
366	Sterling Hitchcock	.05
367	Donovan Osborne	.05
368	Troy Percival	.05
369	Henry Rodriguez	.05
370	Dmitri Young	.05
371	Jay Powell	.05
372	Jeff Conine	.05
373	Orlando Cabrera	.10
374	Butch Huskey	.05
375	Mike Lowell **RC**	1.00
376	Kevin Young	.05
377	Jamie Moyer	.05
378	Jeff D'Amico	.05
379	Scott Erickson	.05
380	Magglio Ordonez **RC**	2.50
381	Melvin Nieves	.05
382	Ramon Martinez	.05
383	A.J. Hinch	.05
384	Jeff Brantley	.05
385	Kevin Elster	.05
386	Allen Watson	.05
387	Moises Alou	.05
388	Jeff Blauser	.05
389	Pete Harnisch	.05
390	Shane Andrews	.05
391	Rico Brogna	.05
392	Stan Javier	.05
393	David Howard	.05
394	Darryl Strawberry	.05
395	Kent Mercker	.05
396	Juan Encarnacion	.05
397	Sandy Alomar	.05
398	Al Leiter	.05
399	Tony Graffanino	.05
400	Terry Adams	.05
401	Bruce Aven	.05
402	Derrick Gibson	.05
403	Jose Cabrera	.05
404	Rich Becker	.05
405	David Ortiz	.50
406	Brian McRae	.05
407	Bobby Estalella	.05
408	Bill Mueller	.05
409	Dennis Eckersley	.65
410	Sandy Martinez	.05
411	Jose Vizcaino	.05
412	Jermaine Allensworth	.05
413	Miguel Tejada	.20
414	Turner Ward	.05
415	Glenallen Hill	.05
416	Lee Stevens	.05
417	Cecil Fielder	.05
418	Ruben Sierra	.05
419	Jon Nunnally	.05
420	Rod Myers	.05
421	Dustin Hermanson	.05
422	James Mouton	.05
423	Dan Wilson	.05
424	Roberto Kelly	.05
425	Antonio Osuna	.05
426	Jacob Cruz	.05
427	Brent Mayne	.05
428	Matt Karchner	.05
429	Damian Jackson	.05
430	Roger Cedeno	.05
431	Rickey Henderson	.75
432	Joe Randa	.05
433	Greg Vaughn	.05
434	Andres Galarraga	.05
435	Rod Beck	.05
436	Curtis Goodwin	.05
437	Brad Ausmus	.05
438	Bob Hamelin	.05
439	Todd Walker	.05
440	Scott Brosius	.05
441	Lenny Dykstra	.05
442	Abraham Nunez	.05
443	Brian Johnson	.05
444	Randy Myers	.05
445	Bret Boone	.15
446	Oscar Henriquez	.05
447	Mike Sweeney	.05
448	Kenny Rogers	.05
449	Mark Langston	.05

450	Luis Gonzalez	.05
451	John Burkett	.05
452	Bip Roberts	.05
453	Travis Lee	.15
454	Felix Rodriguez	.05
455	Andy Benes	.05
456	Willie Blair	.05
457	Brian Anderson	.05
458	Jay Bell	.05
459	Matt Williams	.05
460	Devon White	.05
461	Karim Garcia	.10
462	Jorge Fabregas	.05
463	Wilson Alvarez	.05
464	Roberto Hernandez	.05
465	Tony Saunders	.05
466	Rolando Arrojo **RC**	.35
467	Wade Boggs	1.00
468	Fred McGriff	.05
469	Paul Sorrento	.05
470	Kevin Stocker	.05
471	Bubba Trammell	.05
472	Quinton McCracken	.05
473	Ken Griffey Jr. Checklist	.65
474	Cal Ripken Jr. Checklist	1.00
475	Frank Thomas Checklist	.60
476	Ken Griffey Jr. (Pizzazz)	1.75
477	Cal Ripken Jr. (Pizzazz)	3.00
478	Frank Thomas (Pizzazz)	1.25
479	Alex Rodriguez (Pizzazz)	2.00
480	Nomar Garciaparra (Pizzazz)	1.50
481	Derek Jeter (Pizzazz)	3.00
482	Andruw Jones (Pizzazz)	1.00
483	Chipper Jones (Pizzazz)	1.50
484	Greg Maddux (Pizzazz)	1.50
485	Mike Piazza (Pizzazz)	1.75
486	Juan Gonzalez (Pizzazz)	.60
487	Jose Cruz (Pizzazz)	.50
488	Jaret Wright (Pizzazz)	.50
489	Hideo Nomo (Pizzazz)	.60
490	Scott Rolen (Pizzazz)	.65
491	Tony Gwynn (Pizzazz)	1.50
492	Roger Clemens (Pizzazz)	1.60
493	Darin Erstad (Pizzazz)	.50
494	Mark McGwire (Pizzazz)	2.00
495	Jeff Bagwell (Pizzazz)	1.00
496	Mo Vaughn (Pizzazz)	.50
497	Albert Belle (Pizzazz)	.50
498	Kenny Lofton (Pizzazz)	.50
499	Ben Grieve (Pizzazz)	.50
500	Barry Bonds (Pizzazz)	2.50
501	Mike Piazza (Mets)	1.50

1998 Ultra Gold Medallion

	NM/M
Common Player:	.25
Stars/RC's:	2X
Checklists:	2X
Season Crowns:	1X
Prospects:	1X
Pizzazz:	1X

(See 1998 Ultra for checklist and base card values.)

1998 Ultra Platinum Medallion

	NM/M
Common Player:	5.00
Stars/RC's:	25X
Checklists:	25X

Season Crowns: 8X
Prospects: 8X
Pizzazz: 8X
(See 1998 Ultra for checklist and base card values.)

Masterpiece

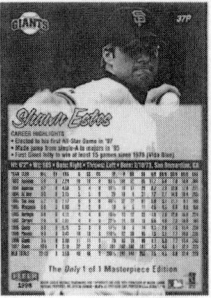

NM/M
Common Player: 50.00
(Individual players cannot be priced due to scarcity and fluctuating demand.)

Artistic Talents

		NM/M
Complete Set (18):		12.00
Common Player:		.40
Inserted 1:8		
1	Ken Griffey Jr.	1.00
2	Andruw Jones	.60
3	Alex Rodriguez	1.25
4	Frank Thomas	.60
5	Cal Ripken Jr.	1.50
6	Derek Jeter	1.50
7	Chipper Jones	.75
8	Greg Maddux	.75
9	Mike Piazza	1.00
10	Albert Belle	.40
11	Darin Erstad	.50
12	Juan Gonzalez	.50
13	Jeff Bagwell	.60
14	Tony Gwynn	.75
15	Mark McGwire	1.25
16	Scott Rolen	.50
17	Barry Bonds	1.50
18	Kenny Lofton	.40

Back to the Future

		NM/M
Complete Set (15):		4.00
Common Player:		.10
Inserted 1:6		
1	Andruw Jones	.50
2	Alex Rodriguez	1.00
3	Derek Jeter	1.50
4	Darin Erstad	.25
5	Mike Cameron	.10
6	Scott Rolen	.35
7	Nomar Garciaparra	.75
8	Hideki Irabu	.10
9	Jose Cruz, Jr.	.10
10	Vladimir Guerrero	.50
11	Mark Kotsay	.10
12	Tony Womack	.10
13	Jason Dickson	.10
14	Jose Guillen	.10
15	Tony Clark	.10

Big Shots

		NM/M
Complete Set (15):		4.00
Common Player:		.10
Inserted 1:4		
1	Ken Griffey Jr.	.75
2	Frank Thomas	.35
3	Chipper Jones	.50
4	Albert Belle	.10
5	Juan Gonzalez	.25
6	Jeff Bagwell	.35
7	Mark McGwire	1.00
8	Barry Bonds	1.50
9	Manny Ramirez	.35
10	Mo Vaughn	.10
11	Matt Williams	.10
12	Jim Thome	.30
13	Tino Martinez	.10
14	Mike Piazza	.75
15	Tony Clark	.10

Diamond Producers

		NM/M
Complete Set (15):		180.00
Common Player:		7.50
Inserted 1:288		
1	Ken Griffey Jr.	30.00
2	Andruw Jones	12.50
3	Alex Rodriguez	40.00
4	Frank Thomas	12.50
5	Cal Ripken Jr.	50.00
6	Derek Jeter	50.00
7	Chipper Jones	20.00
8	Greg Maddux	20.00
9	Mike Piazza	30.00
10	Juan Gonzalez	9.00
11	Jeff Bagwell	12.50
12	Tony Gwynn	20.00
13	Mark McGwire	40.00
14	Barry Bonds	50.00
15	Jose Cruz, Jr.	7.50

Diamond Immortals

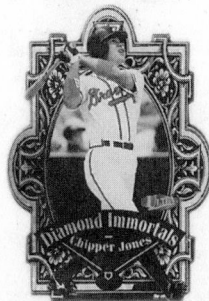

		NM/M
Complete Set (15):		330.00
Common Player:		7.50
Inserted 1:288		
1	Ken Griffey Jr.	30.00
2	Frank Thomas	12.50
3	Alex Rodriguez	40.00
4	Cal Ripken Jr.	50.00
5	Mike Piazza	30.00
6	Mark McGwire	40.00
7	Greg Maddux	20.00
8	Andruw Jones	12.50
9	Chipper Jones	20.00
10	Derek Jeter	50.00
11	Tony Gwynn	20.00
12	Juan Gonzalez	9.00
13	Jose Cruz	7.50
14	Roger Clemens	25.00
15	Barry Bonds	50.00

Double Trouble

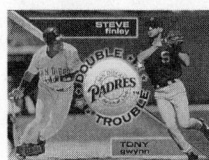

		NM/M
Complete Set (20):		12.00
Common Player:		.15
Inserted 1:4		
1	Ken Griffey Jr., Alex Rodriguez	1.25
2	Vladimir Guerrero, Pedro Martinez	.60
3	Andruw Jones, Kenny Lofton	.60
4	Chipper Jones, Greg Maddux	.75
5	Derek Jeter, Tino Martinez	1.50
6	Frank Thomas, Albert Belle	.60
7	Cal Ripken Jr., Roberto Alomar	1.50
8	Mike Piazza, Hideo Nomo	1.00
9	Darin Erstad, Jason Dickson	.15
10	Juan Gonzalez, Ivan Rodriguez	.25
11	Jeff Bagwell, Darryl Kile	.60
12	Tony Gwynn, Steve Finley	.65
13	Mark McGwire, Ray Lankford	1.00
14	Barry Bonds, Jeff Kent	1.50
15	Andy Pettitte, Bernie Williams	.25
16	Mo Vaughn, Nomar Garciaparra	.65
17	Matt Williams, Jim Thome	.15
18	Hideki Irabu, Mariano Rivera	.25
19	Roger Clemens, Jose Cruz, Jr.	.75
20	Manny Ramirez, David Justice	.60

Fall Classics

		NM/M
Complete Set (15):		35.00
Common Player:		1.00
Inserted 1:18		
1	Ken Griffey Jr.	3.00
2	Andruw Jones	1.50
3	Alex Rodriguez	4.00
4	Frank Thomas	1.50
5	Cal Ripken Jr.	5.00
6	Derek Jeter	5.00
7	Chipper Jones	2.00
8	Greg Maddux	2.00
9	Mike Piazza	4.00
10	Albert Belle	1.00
11	Juan Gonzalez	1.00
12	Jeff Bagwell	1.50
13	Tony Gwynn	2.00
14	Mark McGwire	3.00
15	Barry Bonds	5.00

Kid Gloves

		NM/M
Complete Set (12):		9.00
Common Player:		.25
Inserted 1:8		
1	Andruw Jones	.75
2	Alex Rodriguez	2.00
3	Derek Jeter	3.00
4	Chipper Jones	1.00
5	Darin Erstad	.35
6	Todd Walker	.25
7	Scott Rolen	.65
8	Nomar Garciaparra	1.00
9	Jose Cruz, Jr.	.25
10	Charles Johnson	.25
11	Rey Ordonez	.25
12	Vladimir Guerrero	.75

Millennium Men

		NM/M
Complete Set (15):		30.00
Common Player:		.75
Inserted 1:35		
1	Jose Cruz	.75
2	Ken Griffey Jr.	3.50
3	Cal Ripken Jr.	6.00
4	Derek Jeter	6.00
5	Andruw Jones	2.00
6	Alex Rodriguez	4.50
7	Chipper Jones	2.50
8	Scott Rolen	1.00
9	Nomar Garciaparra	2.50
10	Frank Thomas	2.00
11	Mike Piazza	3.50
12	Greg Maddux	2.50
13	Juan Gonzalez	1.00
14	Ben Grieve	.75
15	Jaret Wright	.75

Power Plus

		NM/M
Complete Set (10):		16.00
Common Player:		1.00

Inserted 1:36
1	Ken Griffey Jr.	4.00
2	Andruw Jones	2.00
3	Alex Rodriguez	3.00
4	Frank Thomas	2.00
5	Mike Piazza	3.00
6	Albert Belle	1.00
7	Juan Gonzalez	1.25
8	Jeff Bagwell	2.00
9	Barry Bonds	5.00
10	Jose Cruz, Jr.	1.00

Prime Leather

		NM/M
Complete Set (18):		135.00
Common Player:		2.00
Inserted 1:144		
1	Ken Griffey Jr.	12.50
2	Andruw Jones	7.50
3	Alex Rodriguez	15.00
4	Frank Thomas	7.50
5	Cal Ripken Jr.	20.00
6	Derek Jeter	20.00
7	Chipper Jones	10.00
8	Greg Maddux	10.00
9	Mike Piazza	12.50
10	Albert Belle	2.00
11	Darin Erstad	3.00
12	Juan Gonzalez	3.00
13	Jeff Bagwell	7.50
14	Tony Gwynn	10.00
15	Roberto Alomar	2.50
16	Barry Bonds	20.00
17	Kenny Lofton	2.00
18	Jose Cruz, Jr.	2.00

Notables

		NM/M
Complete Set (20):		13.50
Common Player:		.20
Inserted 1:4		
1	Frank Thomas	.50
2	Ken Griffey Jr.	1.25
3	Edgar Renteria	.20
4	Albert Belle	.20
5	Juan Gonzalez	.30
6	Jeff Bagwell	.50
7	Mark McGwire	1.50
8	Barry Bonds	2.25
9	Scott Rolen	.40
10	Mo Vaughn	.20
11	Andruw Jones	.50
12	Chipper Jones	.75
13	Tino Martinez	.20
14	Mike Piazza	1.25
15	Tony Clark	.20
16	Jose Cruz	.20
17	Nomar Garciaparra	.75
18	Cal Ripken Jr.	2.25
19	Alex Rodriguez	1.50
20	Derek Jeter	2.25

Rocket to Stardom

		NM/M
Complete Set (15):		15.00
Common Player:		.75
Inserted 1:20		

1	Ben Grieve	.75
2	Magglio Ordonez	4.00
3	Travis Lee	1.00
4	Carl Pavano	.75
5	Brian Rose	.75
6	Brad Fullmer	.75
7	Michael Coleman	.75
8	Juan Encarnacion	.75
9	Karim Garcia	1.00
10	Todd Helton	7.50
11	Richard Hildalgo	.75
12	Paul Konerko	1.50
13	Rod Myers	.75
14	Jaret Wright	.75
15	Miguel Tejada	1.50

Win Now

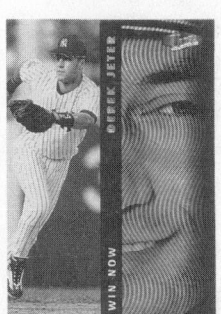

		NM/M
Complete Set (20):		100.00
Common Player:		2.50
Inserted 1:72		
1	Alex Rodriguez	10.00
2	Andruw Jones	4.00
3	Cal Ripken Jr.	12.50
4	Chipper Jones	5.00
5	Darin Erstad	3.00
6	Derek Jeter	12.50
7	Frank Thomas	4.00
8	Greg Maddux	5.00
9	Hideo Nomo	3.00
10	Jeff Bagwell	4.00
11	Jose Cruz	2.50
12	Juan Gonzalez	3.00
13	Ken Griffey Jr.	7.50
14	Mark McGwire	10.00
15	Mike Piazza	7.50
16	Mo Vaughn	2.50
17	Nomar Garciaparra	5.00
18	Roger Clemens	6.00
19	Scott Rolen	3.00
20	Tony Gwynn	5.00

Ticket Studs

		NM/M
Complete Set (15):		150.00
Common Player:		2.50
Inserted 1:144		
1	Travis Lee	3.00
2	Tony Gwynn	12.00
3	Scott Rolen	6.00
4	Nomar Garciaparra	12.00
5	Mike Piazza	15.00
6	Mark McGwire	17.50
7	Ken Griffey Jr.	15.00
8	Juan Gonzalez	5.00
9	Jose Cruz	2.50
10	Frank Thomas	9.00
11	Derek Jeter	20.00
12	Chipper Jones	12.00
13	Cal Ripken Jr.	20.00

14	Andruw Jones	9.00
15	Alex Rodriguez	17.50

Top 30

		NM/M
Complete Set (30):		20.00
Common Player:		.15
Inserted 1:1 R		
1	Barry Bonds	2.00
2	Ivan Rodriguez	.65
3	Kenny Lofton	.15
4	Albert Belle	.15
5	Mo Vaughn	.15
6	Jeff Bagwell	.75
7	Mark McGwire	1.50
8	Darin Erstad	.35
9	Roger Clemens	1.00
10	Tony Gwynn	1.00
11	Scott Rolen	.45
12	Hideo Nomo	.35
13	Juan Gonzalez	.35
14	Mike Piazza	1.25
15	Greg Maddux	1.00
16	Chipper Jones	1.00
17	Andruw Jones	.75
18	Derek Jeter	2.00
19	Nomar Garciaparra	1.00
20	Alex Rodriguez	1.50
21	Frank Thomas	.75
22	Cal Ripken Jr.	2.00
23	Ken Griffey Jr.	1.25
24	Jose Cruz Jr.	.15
25	Jaret Wright	.15
26	Travis Lee	.30
27	Wade Boggs	1.00
28	Chuck Knoblauch	.15
29	Joe Carter	.15
30	Ben Grieve	.15

1999 Ultra

	NM/M
Complete Set (250):	35.00
Common Player:	.05
Common Season Crown:	.25
Inserted 1:8	
Common Prospect:	.25
Inserted 1:4	
Gold Medallion (1-215):	2X
Inserted 1:1	
Gold Medall. Prospect:	4X
Inserted 1:40	
Gold Medall. Season Crown:	3X
Inserted 1:80	
Platinums (1-215):	25X
Production 99 Sets	
Platinum Prospects:	6X
Production 65 Sets	
Platinum Season Crowns:	20X
Production 50 Sets	
Pack (10):	1.50

Wax Box (24):		25.00
1	Greg Maddux	1.00
2	Greg Vaughn	.05
3	John Wetteland	.05
4	Tino Martinez	.05
5	Todd Walker	.05
6	Troy O'Leary	.05
7	Barry Larkin	.05
8	Mike Lansing	.05
9	Delino DeShields	.05
10	Brett Tomko	.05
11	Carlos Perez	.05
12	Mark Langston	.05
13	Jamie Moyer	.05
14	Jose Guillen	.05
15	Bartolo Colon	.05
16	Brady Anderson	.05
17	Walt Weiss	.05
18	Shane Reynolds	.05
19	David Segui	.05
20	Vladimir Guerrero	.75
21	Freddy Garcia	.05
22	Carl Everett	.05
23	Jose Cruz Jr.	.05
24	David Ortiz	.40
25	Andruw Jones	.75
26	Darren Lewis	.05
27	Ray Lankford	.05
28	Wally Joyner	.05
29	Charles Johnson	.05
30	Derek Jeter	2.00
31	Sean Casey	.10
32	Bobby Bonilla	.05
33	Todd Zeile	.05
34	Todd Helton	.65
35	David Wells	.05
36	Darin Erstad	.30
37	Ivan Rodriguez	.65
38	Antonio Osuna	.05
39	Mickey Morandini	.05
40	Rusty Greer	.05
41	Rod Beck	.05
42	Larry Sutton	.05
43	Edgar Renteria	.05
44	Otis Nixon	.05
45	Eli Marrero	.05
46	Reggie Jefferson	.05
47	Trevor Hoffman	.05
48	Andres Galarraga	.05
49	Scott Brosius	.05
50	Vinny Castilla	.05
51	Bret Boone	.05
52	Masato Yoshii	.05
53	Matt Williams	.05
54	Robin Ventura	.05
55	Jay Powell	.05
56	Dean Palmer	.05
57	Eric Milton	.05
58	Willie McGee	.05
59	Tony Gwynn	1.00
60	Tom Gordon	.05
61	Dante Bichette	.05
62	Jaret Wright	.05
63	Devon White	.05
64	Frank Thomas	.75
65	Mike Piazza	1.25
66	Jose Offerman	.05
67	Pat Meares	.05
68	Brian Meadows	.05
69	Nomar Garciaparra	1.00
70	Mark McGwire	1.50
71	Tony Graffanino	.05
72	Ken Griffey Jr.	1.25
73	Ken Caminiti	.05
74	Todd Jones	.05
75	A.J. Hinch	.05
76	Marquis Grissom	.05
77	Jay Buhner	.05
78	Albert Belle	.05
79	Brian Anderson	.05
80	Quinton McCracken	.05
81	Omar Vizquel	.05
82	Todd Stottlemyre	.05
83	Cal Ripken Jr.	2.00
84	Magglio Ordonez	.30
85	John Olerud	.05
86	Hal Morris	.05
87	Derrek Lee	.40
88	Doug Glanville	.05
89	Marty Cordova	.05
90	Kevin Brown	.05

91	Kevin Young	.05
92	Rico Brogna	.05
93	Wilson Alvarez	.05
94	Bob Wickman	.05
95	Jim Thome	.50
96	Mike Mussina	.35
97	Al Leiter	.05
98	Travis Lee	.10
99	Jeff King	.05
100	Kerry Wood	.40
101	Cliff Floyd	.05
102	Jose Valentin	.05
103	Manny Ramirez	.75
104	Butch Huskey	.05
105	Scott Erickson	.05
106	Ray Durham	.05
107	Johnny Damon	.30
108	Craig Counsell	.05
109	Rolando Arrojo	.05
110	Bob Abreu	.05
111	Tony Womack	.05
112	Mike Stanley	.05
113	Kenny Lofton	.05
114	Eric Davis	.05
115	Jeff Conine	.05
116	Carlos Baerga	.05
117	Rondell White	.05
118	Billy Wagner	.05
119	Ed Sprague	.05
120	Jason Schmidt	.05
121	Edgar Martinez	.05
122	Travis Fryman	.05
123	Armando Benitez	.05
124	Matt Stairs	.05
125	Roberto Hernandez	.05
126	Jay Bell	.05
127	Justin Thompson	.05
128	John Jaha	.05
129	Mike Caruso	.05
130	Miguel Tejada	.20
131	Geoff Jenkins	.05
132	Wade Boggs	1.00
133	Andy Benes	.05
134	Aaron Sele	.05
135	Bret Saberhagen	.05
136	Mariano Rivera	.15
137	Neifi Perez	.05
138	Paul Konerko	.15
139	Barry Bonds	2.00
140	Garret Anderson	.05
141	Bernie Williams	.05
142	Gary Sheffield	.40
143	Rafael Palmeiro	.65
144	Orel Hershiser	.05
145	Craig Biggio	.05
146	Dmitri Young	.05
147	Damion Easley	.05
148	Henry Rodriguez	.05
149	Brad Radke	.05
150	Pedro Martinez	.75
151	Mike Lieberthal	.05
152	Jim Leyritz	.05
153	Chuck Knoblauch	.05
154	Darryl Kile	.05
155	Brian Jordan	.05
156	Chipper Jones	1.00
157	Pete Harnisch	.05
158	Moises Alou	.05
159	Ismael Valdes	.05
160	Stan Javier	.05
161	Mark Grace	.05
162	Jason Giambi	.40
163	Chuck Finley	.05
164	Juan Encarnacion	.05
165	Chan Ho Park	.05
166	Randy Johnson	.75
167	J.T. Snow	.05
168	Tim Salmon	.05
169	Brian Hunter	.05
170	Rickey Henderson	.75
171	Cal Eldred	.05
172	Curt Schilling	.05
173	Alex Rodriguez	1.50
174	Dustin Hermanson	.05
175	Mike Hampton	.05
176	Shawn Green	.30
177	Roberto Alomar	.20
178	Sandy Alomar Jr.	.05
179	Larry Walker	.05
180	Mo Vaughn	.05
181	Raul Mondesi	.05
182	Hideki Irabu	.05
183	Jim Edmonds	.05
184	Shawn Estes	.05
185	Tony Clark	.05
186	Dan Wilson	.05
187	Michael Tucker	.05
188	Jeff Shaw	.05
189	Mark Grudzielanek	.05
190	Roger Clemens	1.00
191	Juan Gonzalez	.40
192	Sammy Sosa	1.00
193	Troy Percival	.05
194	Robb Nen	.05
195	Bill Mueller	.05
196	Ben Grieve	.05
197	Luis Gonzalez	.05
198	Will Clark	.05
199	Jeff Cirillo	.05
200	Scott Rolen	.50
201	Reggie Sanders	.05
202	Fred McGriff	.05
203	Denny Neagle	.05
204	Brad Fullmer	.05
205	Royce Clayton	.05
206	Jose Canseco	.50
207	Jeff Bagwell	.75
208	Hideo Nomo	.40
209	Karim Garcia	.15
210	Kenny Rogers	.05
211	Kerry Wood Checklist	.25
212	Alex Rodriguez Checklist	.75
213	Cal Ripken Jr. Checklist	1.00
214	Frank Thomas Checklist	.50
215	Ken Griffey Jr. Checklist	.65
216	Alex Rodriguez	1.00
217	Greg Maddux	.50
218	Juan Gonzalez	.20
219	Ken Griffey Jr.	.75
220	Kerry Wood	.25
221	Mark McGwire	1.00
222	Mike Piazza	.75
223	Rickey Henderson	.40
224	Sammy Sosa	.50
225	Travis Lee	.25
226	Gabe Alvarez	.25
227	Matt Anderson	.25
228	Adrian Beltre	.35
229	Orlando Cabrera	.35
230	Orlando Hernandez	.25
231	Aramis Ramirez	.25
232	Troy Glaus	1.00
233	Gabe Kapler	.25
234	Jeremy Giambi	.25
235	Derrick Gibson	.25
236	Carlton Loewer	.25
237	Mike Frank	.25
238	Carlos Guillen	.25
239	Alex Gonzalez	.25
240	Enrique Wilson	.25
241	J.D. Drew	.75
242	Bruce Chen	.25
243	Ryan Minor	.25
244	Preston Wilson	.35
245	Josh Booty	.25
246	Luis Ordaz	.25
247	George Lombard	.25
248	Matt Clement	.25
249	Eric Chavez	.75
250	Corey Koskie	.30

Gold Medallion

	NM/M
Common Player (1-215):	.25
Stars/RC's:	2X
Season Crowns (216-225):	4X
Prospects (226-250):	3X

(See 1999 Ultra for checklist and base card values.)

Platinum Medallion

	NM/M
Common Player (1-215):	5.00
Stars/RC's:	25X
Season Crowns (216-225):	20X
Prospects (226-250):	6X

(See 1999 Ultra for checklist and base card values.)

Masterpiece

	NM/M
Common Player:	50.00

(Individual player cards cannot be valued due to scarcity and fluctuating demand.)

Book On

		NM/M
Complete Set (20):		13.50
Common Player:		.25
Inserted 1:6		
1	Kerry Wood	.35
2	Ken Griffey Jr.	1.00
3	Frank Thomas	.65
4	Albert Belle	.25
5	Juan Gonzalez	.35
6	Jeff Bagwell	.65
7	Mark McGwire	1.25
8	Barry Bonds	1.50
9	Andruw Jones	.65
10	Mo Vaughn	.25
11	Scott Rolen	.40
12	Travis Lee	.25
13	Tony Gwynn	.75
14	Greg Maddux	.75
15	Mike Piazza	1.00
16	Chipper Jones	.75
17	Nomar Garciaparra	.75
18	Cal Ripken Jr.	1.50
19	Derek Jeter	1.50
20	Alex Rodriguez	1.25

Damage Inc.

		NM/M
Complete Set (15):		50.00
Common Player:		1.00
Inserted 1:72		
1	Alex Rodriguez	5.00
2	Greg Maddux	3.50
3	Cal Ripken Jr.	7.50
4	Chipper Jones	4.00
5	Derek Jeter	7.50
6	Frank Thomas	2.50
7	Juan Gonzalez	1.50
8	Ken Griffey Jr.	4.00
9	Kerry Wood	1.25
10	Mark McGwire	5.00
11	Mike Piazza	4.00
12	Nomar Garciaparra	3.50
13	Scott Rolen	1.50
14	Tony Gwynn	3.50
15	Travis Lee	1.00

Diamond Producers

		NM/M
Complete Set (10):		140.00
Common Player:		6.00
Inserted 1:288		
1	Ken Griffey Jr.	17.50
2	Frank Thomas	12.00
3	Alex Rodriguez	20.00
4	Cal Ripken Jr.	25.00
5	Mike Piazza	17.50
6	Mark McGwire	20.00
7	Greg Maddux	15.00
8	Kerry Wood	6.00
9	Chipper Jones	15.00
10	Derek Jeter	25.00

RBI Kings

		NM/M
Complete Set (30):		12.00
Common Player:		.15
Inserted 1:1 R		
1	Rafael Palmeiro	.40
2	Mo Vaughn	.15
3	Ivan Rodriguez	.40
4	Barry Bonds	1.25
5	Albert Belle	.15
6	Jeff Bagwell	.45
7	Mark McGwire	1.00
8	Darin Erstad	.25
9	Manny Ramirez	.45
10	Chipper Jones	.75
11	Jim Thome	.40
12	Scott Rolen	.35
13	Tony Gwynn	.60
14	Juan Gonzalez	.25
15	Mike Piazza	.75
16	Sammy Sosa	.60
17	Andruw Jones	.45
18	Derek Jeter	1.25
19	Nomar Garciaparra	.60
20	Alex Rodriguez	1.00
21	Frank Thomas	.45
22	Cal Ripken Jr.	1.25
23	Ken Griffey Jr.	.75
24	Travis Lee	.25
25	Paul O'Neill	.15
26	Greg Vaughn	.15
27	Andres Galarraga	.15
28	Tino Martinez	.15
29	Jose Canseco	.30
30	Ben Grieve	.15

Thunderclap

		NM/M
Complete Set (15):		35.00
Common Player:		.75
Inserted 1:36		
1	Alex Rodriguez	4.00
2	Andruw Jones	1.50
3	Cal Ripken Jr.	6.00
4	Chipper Jones	2.50
5	Darin Erstad	.75
6	Derek Jeter	6.00
7	Frank Thomas	1.50
8	Jeff Bagwell	1.50
9	Juan Gonzalez	.75
10	Ken Griffey Jr.	3.00
11	Mark McGwire	4.00
12	Mike Piazza	3.00
13	Travis Lee	.75
14	Nomar Garciaparra	2.50
15	Scott Rolen	1.00

World Premiere

		NM/M
Complete Set (15):		8.00
Common Player:		.50
Inserted 1:18		
1	Gabe Alvarez	.50
2	Kerry Wood	1.50
3	Orlando Hernandez	.60
4	Mike Caruso	.50
5	Matt Anderson	.50
6	Randall Simon	.50
7	Adrian Beltre	.65
8	Scott Elarton	.50
9	Karim Garcia	.60
10	Mike Frank	.50
11	Richard Hidalgo	.50
12	Paul Konerko	.60
13	Travis Lee	.65
14	J.D. Drew	1.50
15	Miguel Tejada	.75

2000 Ultra

		NM/M
Complete Set (300):		35.00
Common Player:		.10
Common Player (251-300):		.50
Inserted 1:4		
Pack (10):		2.00
Wax Box (24):		35.00
1	Alex Rodriguez	1.50
2	Shawn Green	.25
3	Magglio Ordonez	.25
4	Tony Gwynn	.75
5	Joe McEwing	.10
6	Jose Rosado	.10
7	Sammy Sosa	1.00
8	Gary Sheffield	.25
9	Mickey Morandini	.10
10	Mo Vaughn	.15
11	Todd Hollandsworth	.10
12	Tom Gordon	.10
13	Charles Johnson	.10
14	Derek Bell	.10
15	Kevin Young	.10
16	Jay Buhner	.15
17	J.T. Snow	.10
18	Jay Bell	.10
19	John Rocker	.10
20	Ivan Rodriguez	.40
21	Pokey Reese	.10
22	Paul O'Neill	.20
23	Ronnie Belliard	.10
24	Ryan Rupe	.10
25	Travis Fryman	.20
26	Trot Nixon	.10
27	Wally Joyner	.10
28	Andy Pettitte	.25
29	Dan Wilson	.10
30	Orlando Hernandez	.20
31	Dmitri Young	.10
32	Edgar Renteria	.10
33	Eric Karros	.20
34	Fernando Seguignol	.10
35	Jason Kendall	.20
36	Jeff Shaw	.10
37	Matt Lawton	.10

38	Robin Ventura	.20
39	Scott Williamson	.10
40	Ben Grieve	.10
41	Billy Wagner	.10
42	Javy Lopez	.20
43	Joe Randa	.10
44	Neifi Perez	.10
45	David Justice	.20
46	Ray Durham	.10
47	Dustin Hermanson	.10
48	Andres Galarraga	.20
49	Brad Fullmer	.10
50	Nomar Garciaparra	1.50
51	David Cone	.15
52	David Nilsson	.10
53	David Wells	.10
54	Miguel Tejada	.25
55	Ismael Valdes	.10
56	Jose Lima	.10
57	Juan Encarnacion	.10
58	Fred McGriff	.20
59	Kenny Rogers	.10
60	Vladimir Guerrero	.75
61	Benito Santiago	.10
62	Chris Singleton	.10
63	Carlos Lee	.10
64	Sean Casey	.20
65	Tom Goodwin	.10
66	Todd Hundley	.10
67	Ellis Burks	.10
68	Tim Hudson	.25
69	Matt Stairs	.10
70	Chipper Jones	1.00
71	Craig Biggio	.20
72	Brian Rose	.10
73	Carlos Delgado	.40
74	Eddie Taubensee	.10
75	John Smoltz	.20
76	Ken Caminiti	.15
77	Rafael Palmeiro	.40
78	Sidney Ponson	.10
79	Todd Helton	.50
80	Juan Gonzalez	.50
81	Bruce Aven	.10
82	Desi Relaford	.10
83	Johnny Damon	.20
84	Albert Belle	.15
85	Mark McGwire	1.50
86	Rico Brogna	.10
87	Tom Glavine	.25
88	Harold Baines	.10
89	Chad Allen	.10
90	Barry Bonds	2.00
91	Mark Grace	.25
92	Paul Byrd	.10
93	Roberto Alomar	.40
94	Roberto Hernandez	.10
95	Steve Finley	.10
96	Bret Boone	.20
97	Charles Nagy	.10
98	Eric Chavez	.20
99	Jamie Moyer	.10
100	Ken Griffey Jr.	1.00
101	J.D. Drew	.20
102	Todd Stottlemyre	.10
103	Tony Fernandez	.10
104	Jeromy Burnitz	.10
105	Jeremy Giambi	.10
106	Livan Hernandez	.10
107	Marlon Anderson	.10
108	Troy Glaus	.50
109	Troy O'Leary	.10
110	Scott Rolen	.50
111	Bernard Gilkey	.10
112	Brady Anderson	.15
113	Chuck Knoblauch	.15
114	Jeff Weaver	.10
115	B.J. Surhoff	.10
116	Alex Gonzalez	.10
117	Vinny Castilla	.10
118	Tim Salmon	.20
119	Brian Jordan	.10
120	Corey Koskie	.10
121	Dean Palmer	.10
122	Gabe Kapler	.15
123	Jim Edmonds	.25
124	John Jaha	.10
125	Mark Grudzielanek	.10
126	Mike Bordick	.10
127	Mike Lieberthal	.10
128	Pete Harnisch	.10
129	Russ Ortiz	.10
130	Kevin Brown	.20
131	Troy Percival	.10
132	Alex Gonzalez	.10
133	Bartolo Colon	.10
134	John Valentin	.10
135	Jose Hernandez	.10
136	Marquis Grissom	.10
137	Wade Boggs	.25
138	Dante Bichette	.10
139	Bobby Higginson	.10
140	Frank Thomas	.50
141	Geoff Jenkins	.20
142	Jason Giambi	.50
143	Jeff Cirillo	.10
144	Sandy Alomar Jr.	.10
145	Luis Gonzalez	.20
146	Preston Wilson	.20
147	Carlos Beltran	.20
148	Greg Vaughn	.10
149	Carlos Febles	.10
150	Jose Canseco	.40
151	Kris Benson	.10
152	Chuck Finley	.10

153	Michael Barrett	.10
154	Rey Ordonez	.10
155	Adrian Beltre	.20
156	Andruw Jones	.50
157	Barry Larkin	.20
158	Brian Giles	.20
159	Carl Everett	.10
160	Manny Ramirez	.50
161	Darryl Kile	.10
162	Edgar Martinez	.20
163	Jeff Kent	.20
164	Matt Williams	.20
165	Mike Piazza	1.00
166	Pedro J. Martinez	.75
167	Ray Lankford	.10
168	Roger Cedeno	.10
169	Ron Coomer	.10
170	Cal Ripken Jr.	2.00
171	Jose Offerman	.10
172	Kenny Lofton	.20
173	Kent Bottenfield	.10
174	Kevin Millwood	.20
175	Omar Daal	.10
176	Orlando Cabrera	.10
177	Pat Hentgen	.10
178	Tino Martinez	.20
179	Tony Clark	.10
180	Roger Clemens	1.25
181	Brad Radke	.10
182	Darin Erstad	.20
183	Jose Jimenez	.10
184	Jim Thome	.50
185	John Wetteland	.10
186	Justin Thompson	.10
187	John Hamala	.10
188	Lee Stevens	.10
189	Miguel Cairo	.10
190	Mike Mussina	.40
191	Raul Mondesi	.15
192	Armando Rios	.10
193	Trevor Hoffman	.10
194	Tony Batista	.10
195	Will Clark	.40
196	Brad Ausmus	.10
197	Chili Davis	.10
198	Cliff Floyd	.10
199	Curt Schilling	.25
200	Derek Jeter	2.00
201	Henry Rodriguez	.10
202	Jose Cruz Jr.	.10
203	Omar Vizquel	.20
204	Randy Johnson	.75
205	Reggie Sanders	.10
206	Al Leiter	.10
207	Damion Easley	.10
208	David Bell	.10
209	Fernando Tatis	.10
210	Kerry Wood	.25
211	Kevin Appier	.10
212	Mariano Rivera	.20
213	Mike Caruso	.10
214	Moises Alou	.20
215	Randy Winn	.10
216	Roy Halladay	.20
217	Shannon Stewart	.10
218	Todd Walker	.10
219	Jim Parque	.10
220	Travis Lee	.10
221	Andy Ashby	.10
222	Ed Sprague	.10
223	Larry Walker	.20
224	Rick Helling	.10
225	Rusty Greer	.10
226	Todd Zeile	.10
227	Freddy Garcia	.15
228	Hideo Nomo	.40
229	Marty Cordova	.10
230	Greg Maddux	1.00
231	Rondell White	.20
232	Paul Konerko	.15
233	Warren Morris	.10
234	Bernie Williams	.40
235	Bobby Abreu	.20
236	John Olerud	.25
237	Doug Glanville	.10
238	Eric Young	.10
239	Robb Nen	.10
240	Jeff Bagwell	.50
241	Sterling Hitchcock	.10
242	Todd Greene	.10
243	Bill Mueller	.10
244	Rickey Henderson	.25
245	Chan Ho Park	.10
246	Jason Schmidt	.10
247	Jeff Zimmerman	.10
248	Jermaine Dye	.10
249	Randall Simon	.10
250	Richie Sexson	.10
251	Micah Bowie	.50
252	Joe Nathan	.50
253	Chris Woodward	.50
254	Lance Berkman	.75
255	Ruben Mateo	.50
256	Russell Branyan	.50
257	Randy Wolf	.75
258	A.J. Burnett	.50
259	Mark Quinn	.50
260	Buddy Carlyle	.50
261	Ben Davis	.50
262	Yamid Haad	.50
263	Mike Colangelo	.50
264	Rick Ankiel	.75
265	Jacque Jones	.75
266	Kelly Dransfeldt	.50
267	Matt Riley	.50

268	Adam Kennedy	.50
269	Octavio Dotel	.50
270	Francisco Cordero	.50
271	Wilton Veras	.50
272	Calvin Pickering	.50
273	Alex Sanchez	.50
274	Tony Armas Jr.	.50
275	Pat Burrell	1.00
276	Chad Meyers	.50
277	Ben Petrick	.50
278	Ramon Hernandez	.50
279	Ed Yarnall	.50
280	Erubiel Durazo	.50
281	Vernon Wells	1.00
282	Gary Matthews	.50
283	Kip Wells	.50
284	Peter Bergeron	.50
285	Travis Dawkins	.50
286	Jorge Toca	.50
287	Cole Liniak	.50
288	Chad Hermansen	.50
289	Eric Gagne	.50
290	Chad Hutchinson	.50
291	Eric Munson	.50
292	Wiki Gonzalez	.50
293	Alfonso Soriano	1.50
294	Trent Durrington	.50
295	Ben Molina	.50
296	Aaron Myette	.50
297	Willi Mo Pena	.75
298	Kevin Barker	.50
299	Geoff Blum	.50
300	Josh Beckett	.75

Gold Medallion

Stars:	2X
Inserted 1:1	
Prospects (251-300):	2-4X
Inserted 1:24	

(See 2000 Ultra for checklist and base card values.)

Platinum Medallion

Stars:	15-30X
Production 50 Sets	
Prospects (251-300):	4-8X
Production 25 Sets	

(See 2000 Ultra for checklist and base card values.)

Masterpiece Edition

(Star card values undetermined because of unique status.)

Diamond Mine

		NM/M
Complete Set (15):		20.00
Common Player:		1.00
Inserted 1:6		
1	Greg Maddux	1.50
2	Mark McGwire	2.00
3	Ken Griffey Jr.	1.50
4	Cal Ripken Jr.	3.00
5	Nomar Garciaparra	2.50
6	Mike Piazza	2.00
7	Alex Rodriguez	2.50
8	Frank Thomas	1.00
9	Juan Gonzalez	1.00

GREG MADDUX

10	Derek Jeter	2.50
11	Tony Gwynn	1.00
12	Chipper Jones	1.50
13	Sammy Sosa	2.00
14	Roger Clemens	1.50
15	Vladimir Guerrero	1.00

Club 3000

	NM/M
Common Player:	3.00
Inserted 1:24	
Wade Boggs	2.00
Tony Gwynn	3.00
Carl Yastrzemski	3.00

Club 3000 Memorabilia

	NM/M
Wade Boggs/Bat/250	20.00
Wade Boggs/Hat/100	40.00
Wade Boggs/Jsy/440	20.00
Wade Boggs/Bat, Jsy/100	40.00
Wade Boggs/ Bat, Hat, Jsy/25	150.00
Tony Gwynn/Bat/260	40.00
Tony Gwynn/Hat/115	60.00
Tony Gwynn/Jsy/450	25.00
Tony Gwynn/Bat, Jsy/100	65.00
Tony Gwynn/ Bat, Hat, Jsy/25	375.00
Carl Yastrzemski/Bat/250	40.00
Carl Yastrzemski/Hat/100	60.00
Carl Yastrzemski/Jsy/440	25.00
Carl Yastrzemski/ Bat, Jsy/100	75.00
Carl Yastrzemski/ Bat, Hat, Jsy/25	300.00

Crunch Time

		NM/M
Complete Set (15):		50.00
Common Player:		2.00
Inserted 1:72		
1	Nomar Garciaparra	8.00
2	Ken Griffey Jr.	5.00
3	Mark McGwire	8.00
4	Alex Rodriguez	8.00
5	Derek Jeter	8.00
6	Sammy Sosa	6.00
7	Mike Piazza	5.00
8	Cal Ripken Jr.	10.00
9	Frank Thomas	3.00
10	Juan Gonzalez	3.00

11	J.D. Drew	2.00
12	Greg Maddux	5.00
13	Tony Gwynn	3.00
14	Vladimir Guerrero	3.00
15	Ben Grieve	2.00

Feel the Game

	NM/M
Common Player:	5.00
Roberto Alomar	10.00
J.D. Drew	5.00
Tony Gwynn/SP	40.00
Randy Johnson	20.00
Greg Maddux	20.00
Edgar Martinez	10.00
Pedro Martinez	20.00
Kevin Millwood	10.00
Cal Ripken Jr.	40.00
Alex Rodriguez	25.00
Scott Rolen	10.00
Curt Schilling	10.00
Chipper Jones	20.00
Frank Thomas/SP	40.00
Robin Ventura	5.00

Fresh Ink

		NM/M
Common Player:		5.00
1	Bobby Abreu/400	10.00
2	Chad Allen/1,000	5.00
3	Marlon Anderson/1,000	5.00
4	Glen Barker/1,000	5.00
5	Michael Barrett/1,000	5.00
6	Carlos Beltran/1,000	15.00
7	Adrian Beltre/1,000	8.00
8	Wade Boggs/250	40.00
9	Barry Bonds/250	150.00
10	Peter Bergeron/1,000	5.00
11	Pat Burrell/500	20.00
12	Roger Cedeno/500	5.00
13	Eric Chavez/750	10.00
14	Bruce Chen/600	5.00
15	Johnny Damon/750	8.00
16	Ben Davis/1,000	5.00
17	Carlos Delgado/300	10.00
18	Einar Diaz/1,000	5.00
19	Octavio Dotel/1,000	6.00
20	J.D. Drew/600	8.00
21	Scott Elarton/1,000	5.00
22	Freddy Garcia/500	8.00
23	Jeremy Giambi/1,000	5.00
24	Troy Glaus/500	20.00
25	Shawn Green/350	30.00
26	Tony Gwynn/250	50.00
27	Richard Hidalgo/500	8.00
28	Bobby Higginson/1,000	6.00
29	Tim Hudson/1,000	10.00
30	Norm Hutchins/1,000	5.00
31	Derek Jeter/95	200.00
32	Randy Johnson/150	50.00
33	Gabe Kapler/750	8.00
34	Jason Kendall/400	8.00
35	Paul Konerko/500	8.00
36	Matt Lawton/1,000	6.00
37	Carlos Lee/1,000	8.00
38	Jose Macias/1,000	5.00
39	Greg Maddux/250	65.00
40	Ruben Mateo/250	8.00
41	Kevin Millwood/500	10.00
42	Warren Morris/1,000	5.00
43	Eric Munson/1,000	6.00
44	Heath Murray/1,000	5.00
45	Joe Nathan/1,000	5.00
46	Magglio Ordonez/350	10.00
47	Angel Pena/1,000	5.00
48	Cal Ripken Jr./350	125.00
49	Alex Rodriguez/350	80.00
50	Scott Rolen/250	35.00

51	Ryan Rupe/1,000	5.00
52	Curt Schilling/375	25.00
53	Randall Simon/1,000	5.00
54	Alfonso Soriano/1,000	60.00
55	Shannon Stewart/300	5.00
56	Miguel Tejada/1,000	25.00
57	Frank Thomas/150	60.00
58	Jeff Weaver/1,000	6.00
59	Randy Wolf/1,000	8.00
60	Ed Yarnall/1,000	5.00
61	Kevin Young/1,000	5.00
62	Tony Gwynn, Wade Boggs, Nolan Ryan/100	450.00
63	Rick Ankiel/500	10.00

Swing King

		NM/M
Complete Set (10):		20.00
Common Player:		1.00
Inserted 1:24		
1	Cal Ripken Jr.	4.00
2	Nomar Garciaparra	3.00
3	Frank Thomas	1.00
4	Tony Gwynn	1.50
5	Ken Griffey Jr.	2.00
6	Chipper Jones	2.00
7	Mark McGwire	3.00
8	Sammy Sosa	2.50
9	Derek Jeter	3.00
10	Alex Rodriguez	3.00

Ultra Talented

		NM/M
Common Player:		5.00
Production 100 Sets		
1	Sammy Sosa	15.00
2	Derek Jeter	20.00
3	Alex Rodriguez	15.00
4	Mike Piazza	15.00
5	Ken Griffey Jr.	15.00
6	Nomar Garciaparra	20.00
7	Mark McGwire	20.00
8	Cal Ripken Jr.	25.00
9	Frank Thomas	8.00
10	J.D. Drew	5.00

World Premiere

		NM/M
Complete Set (10):		5.00
Common Player:		.50
Inserted 1:12		
1	Ruben Mateo	.50
2	Lance Berkman	1.00
3	Octavio Dotel	.50
4	Ben Davis	.50
5	Warren Morris	.50
6	Carlos Beltran	.75
7	Rick Ankiel	.50
8	Adam Kennedy	.50

9	Tim Hudson	1.00
10	Jorge Toca	.50

2001 Ultra

BRIAN JORDAN

		NM/M
Complete Set (275):		65.00
Common Player:		.15
Common Prospect (251-275):		1.00
Inserted 1:4		
Pack (10):		3.00
Box (24):		55.00
1	Pedro Martinez	.75
2	Derek Jeter	2.00
3	Cal Ripken Jr.	2.00
4	Alex Rodriguez	1.50
5	Vladimir Guerrero	.75
6	Troy Glaus	.40
7	Sammy Sosa	1.25
8	Mike Piazza	1.00
9	Tony Gwynn	.75
10	Tim Hudson	.25
11	John Flaherty	.15
12	Jeff Cirillo	.15
13	Ellis Burks	.15
14	Carlos Lee	.15
15	Carlos Beltran	.25
16	Ruben Rivera	.15
17	Richard Hidalgo	.15
18	Omar Vizquel	.25
19	Michael Barrett	.15
20	Jose Canseco	.40
21	Jason Giambi	.50
22	Greg Maddux	1.00
23	Charles Johnson	.15
24	Sandy Alomar	.15
25	Rick Ankiel	.25
26	Richie Sexson	.40
27	Matt Williams	.25
28	Joe Girardi	.15
29	Jason Kendall	.25
30	Brad Fullmer	.15
31	Alex Gonzalez	.15
32	Rick Helling	.15
33	Mike Mussina	.50
34	Joe Randa	.15
35	J.T. Snow	.15
36	Edgardo Alfonzo	.15
37	Dante Bichette	.15
38	Brad Ausmus	.15
39	Bobby Abreu	.25
40	Warren Morris	.15
41	Tony Womack	.15
42	Russell Branyan	.15
43	Mike Lowell	.15
44	Mark Grace	.40
45	Jeromy Burnitz	.15
46	J.D. Drew	.25
47	David Justice	.25
48	Alex Gonzalez	.15
49	Tino Martinez	.25
50	Raul Mondesi	.25
51	Rafael Furcal	.25
52	Marquis Grissom	.15
53	Kevin Young	.15
54	Jon Lieber	.15
55	Henry Rodriguez	.15
56	Dave Burba	.15

57	Shannon Stewart	.15	172	Juan Gonzalez	.50
58	Preston Wilson	.15	173	Ivan Rodriguez	.50
59	Paul O'Neill	.25	174	Al Leiter	.25
60	Jimmy Haynes	.15	175	Vinny Castilla	.15
61	Darryl Kile	.15	176	Peter Bergeron	.15
62	Bret Boone	.25	177	Pedro Astacio	.15
63	Bartolo Colon	.25	178	Paul Konerko	.15
64	Andres Galarraga	.25	179	Mitch Meluskey	.15
65	Trot Nixon	.15	180	Kevin Millwood	.25
66	Steve Finley	.15	181	Ben Grieve	.15
67	Shawn Green	.30	182	Barry Bonds	2.00
68	Robert Person	.15	183	Rusty Greer	.15
69	Kenny Rogers	.15	184	Miguel Tejada	.40
70	Bobby Higginson	.15	185	Mark Quinn	.15
71	Barry Larkin	.30	186	Larry Walker	.25
72	Al Martin	.15	187	Jose Valentin	.15
73	Tom Glavine	.40	188	Jose Vidro	.15
74	Rondell White	.15	189	Delino DeShields	.15
75	Ray Lankford	.15	190	Darin Erstad	.25
76	Moises Alou	.25	191	Bill Mueller	.15
77	Matt Clement	.15	192	Ray Durham	.15
78	Geoff Jenkins	.25	193	Ken Caminiti	.15
79	David Wells	.15	194	Jim Thome	.75
80	Chuck Finley	.15	195	Javy Lopez	.25
81	Andy Pettitte	.25	196	Fernando Vina	.15
82	Travis Fryman	.25	197	Eric Chavez	.25
83	Ron Coomer	.15	198	Eric Owens	.15
84	Mark McGwire	1.50	199	Brad Radke	.15
85	Kerry Wood	.50	200	Travis Lee	.15
86	Jorge Posada	.40	201	Tim Salmon	.25
87	Jeff Bagwell	.50	202	Rafael Palmeiro	.50
88	Andruw Jones	.50	203	Nomar Garciaparra	1.50
89	Ryan Klesko	.25	204	Mike Hampton	.15
90	Mariano Rivera	.25	205	Kevin Brown	.25
91	Lance Berkman	.25	206	Juan Encarnacion	.15
92	Kenny Lofton	.25	207	Danny Graves	.15
93	Jacque Jones	.15	208	Carlos Guillen	.15
94	Eric Young	.15	209	Phil Nevin	.15
95	Edgar Renteria	.15	210	Matt Lawton	.15
96	Chipper Jones	1.00	211	Manny Ramirez	.50
97	Todd Helton	.50	212	James Baldwin	.15
98	Shawn Estes	.15	213	Fernando Tatis	.15
99	Mark Mulder	.25	214	Craig Biggio	.25
100	Lee Stevens	.15	215	Brian Jordan	.15
101	Jermaine Dye	.15	216	Bernie Williams	.40
102	Greg Vaughn	.15	217	Ryan Dempster	.15
103	Chris Singleton	.15	218	Roger Clemens	1.50
104	Brady Anderson	.15	219	Jose Cruz Jr.	.15
105	Terrence Long	.15	220	John Valentin	.15
106	Quilvio Veras	.15	221	Dmitri Young	.15
107	Magglio Ordonez	.40	222	Curt Schilling	.40
108	Johnny Damon	.25	223	Jim Edmonds	.30
109	Jeffrey Hammonds	.15	224	Chan Ho Park	.25
110	Fred McGriff	.25	225	Brian Giles	.25
111	Carl Pavano	.15	226	Jimmy Anderson	.15
112	Bobby Estalella	.15	227	Adam Piatt	.15
113	Todd Hundley	.15	228	Kenny Kelly	.15
114	Scott Rolen	.75	229	Randy Choate	.15
115	Robin Ventura	.25	230	Eric Cammack	.15
116	Pokey Reese	.15	231	Yovanny Lara	.15
117	Luis Gonzalez	.25	232	Wayne Franklin	.15
118	Jose Offerman	.15	233	Cameron Cairncross	.15
119	Edgar Martinez	.25	234	J.C. Romero	.15
120	Dean Palmer	.15	235	Geraldo Guzman	.15
121	David Segui	.15	236	Morgan Burkhart	.15
122	Troy O'Leary	.15	237	Pascual Coco	.15
123	Tony Batista	.15	238	John Parrish	.15
124	Todd Zeile	.15	239	Keith McDonald	.15
125	Randy Johnson	.75	240	Carlos Casimiro	.15
126	Luis Castillo	.15	241	Daniel Garibay	.15
127	Kris Benson	.15	242	Sang-Hoon Lee	.15
128	John Olerud	.25	243	Hector Ortiz	.15
129	Eric Karros	.25	244	Jeff Sparks	.15
130	Eddie Taubensee	.15	245	Jason Boyd	.15
131	Neifi Perez	.15	246	Mark Buehrle	.15
132	Matt Stairs	.15	247	Adam Melhuse	.15
133	Luis Alicea	.15	248	Kane Davis	.15
134	Jeff Kent	.25	249	Mike Darr	.15
135	Javier Vazquez	.15	250	Vicente Padilla	.15
136	Garret Anderson	.25	251	Barry Zito	4.00
137	Frank Thomas	.50	252	Tim Drew	1.00
138	Carlos Febles	.15	253	Luis Matos	2.00
139	Albert Belle	.15	254	Alex Cabrera	1.00
140	Tony Clark	.15	255	Jon Garland	1.00
141	Pat Burrell	.50	256	Milton Bradley	1.50
142	Mike Sweeney	.15	257	Juan Pierre	2.00
143	Jay Buhner	.15	258	Ismael Villegas	1.00
144	Gabe Kapler	.15	259	Eric Munson	1.00
145	Derek Bell	.15	260	Tomas De La Rosa	1.00
146	B.J. Surhoff	.15	261	Chris Richard	1.00
147	Adam Kennedy	.15	262	Jason Tyner	1.00
148	Aaron Boone	.15	263	B.J. Waszgis	1.00
149	Todd Stottlemyre	.15	264	Jason Marquis	1.00
150	Roberto Alomar	.40	265	Dusty Allen	1.00
151	Orlando Hernandez	.25	266	Corey Patterson	2.00
152	Jason Varitek	.15	267	Eric Byrnes	2.00
153	Gary Sheffield	.40	268	Xavier Nady	2.00
154	Cliff Floyd	.15	269	George Lombard	1.00
155	Chad Hermansen	.15	270	Timoniel Perez	1.00
156	Carlos Delgado	.50	271	Gary Matthews Jr.	1.00
157	Aaron Sele	.15	272	Chad Durbin	1.00
158	Sean Casey	.15	273	Tony Armas Jr.	2.00
159	Ruben Mateo	.15	274	Francisco Cordero	1.00
160	Mike Bordick	.15	275	Alfonso Soriano	5.00
161	Mike Cameron	.15			
162	Doug Glanville	.15			
163	Damion Easley	.15			
164	Carl Everett	.15			
165	Bengie Molina	.15			
166	Adrian Beltre	.25			
167	Tom Goodwin	.15			
168	Rickey Henderson	.40			
169	Mo Vaughn	.25			
170	Mike Lieberthal	.15			
171	Ken Griffey Jr.	1.00			

Gold Medallion

Stars (1-250):	1-2X
Inserted 1:1	

Prospects (251-275):	1-2X
Inserted 1:24	

Platinum Medallion

Stars (1-250):	15-25X
Production 50 Sets	
Prospects (251-275):	5-10X
Production 25 Sets	

Autographics

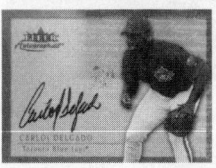

	NM/M
Common Player:	5.00
Inserted 1:48	
Silvers:	1-1.5X
Production 250 Sets	
1 Roberto Alomar	25.00
2 Jimmy Anderson	5.00
3 Lance Berkman	15.00
4 Barry Bonds	150.00
5 Roosevelt Brown	5.00
6 Jeromy Burnitz	5.00
7 Pat Burrell	10.00
8 Alex Cabrera	5.00
9 Eric Chavez	10.00
10 Joe Crede	5.00
11 Johnny Damon	30.00
12 Carlos Delgado	20.00
13 Adam Dunn	20.00
14 Jim Edmonds	15.00
15 Chad Green	5.00
16 Dustin Hermanson	5.00
17 Randy Johnson	50.00
18 Corey Lee	5.00
19 Derrek Lee	25.00
20 Terrence Long	5.00
21 Julio Lugo	5.00
22 Edgar Martinez	20.00
23 Justin Miller	5.00
24 Russ Ortiz	5.00
25 Pablo Ozuna	5.00
26 Adam Piatt	5.00
27 Mark Redman	5.00
28 Richie Sexson	15.00
29 Gary Sheffield	25.00
30 Alfonso Soriano	25.00
31 Jose Vidro	8.00
32 Vernon Wells	10.00
33 Preston Wilson	10.00
34 Jamey Wright	5.00
35 Julio Zuleta	5.00

Decade of Dominance

	NM/M
Complete Set (15):	15.00
Common Player:	.50

Inserted 1:8	
1 Barry Bonds	3.00
2 Mark McGwire	2.00
3 Sammy Sosa	2.00
4 Ken Griffey Jr.	1.50
5 Cal Ripken Jr.	3.00
6 Tony Gwynn	1.00
7 Albert Belle	.50
8 Frank Thomas	1.00
9 Randy Johnson	1.00
10 Juan Gonzalez	.75
11 Greg Maddux	1.50
12 Craig Biggio	.50
13 Edgar Martinez	.50
14 Roger Clemens	2.00
15 Andres Galarraga	.50

Fall Classics

	NM/M
Complete Set (37):	150.00
Common Player:	2.00
Inserted 1:20	
1 Jackie Robinson	8.00
2 Enos Slaughter	2.00
3 Mariano Rivera	2.00
4 Hank Bauer	2.00
5 Cal Ripken Jr.	12.00
6 Babe Ruth	15.00
7 Thurman Munson	5.00
8 Tom Glavine	3.00
9 Fred Lynn	2.00
10 Johnny Bench	6.00
11 Tony Lazzeri	2.00
12 Al Kaline	5.00
13 Reggie Jackson	5.00
14 Derek Jeter	10.00
15 Willie Stargell	3.00
16 Roy Campanella	4.00
17 Phil Rizzuto	4.00
18 Roberto Clemente	12.00
19 Carlton Fisk	4.00
20 Duke Snider	4.00
21 Ted Williams	12.00
22 Bill Skowron	2.00
23 Bucky Dent	2.00
24 Mike Schmidt	8.00
25 Lou Brock	3.00
26 Whitey Ford	5.00
27 Brooks Robinson	4.00
28 Roberto Alomar	4.00
29 Yogi Berra	5.00
30 Joe Carter	2.00
31 Bill Mazeroski	2.00
32 Bob Gibson	5.00
33 Hank Greenberg	4.00
34 Andruw Jones	4.00
35 Bernie Williams	3.00
36 Don Larsen	3.00
37 Billy Martin	3.00

Fall Classics Memorabilia

	NM/M
Common Player:	10.00
Inserted 1:288	
1 Jackie Robinson/Pants	80.00
2 Enos Slaughter/Bat	15.00

3	Mariano Rivera/Jsy	15.00
4	Hank Bauer/Bat	10.00
5	Cal Ripken Jr./Jsy	40.00
6	Thurman Munson/Bat	25.00
7	Tom Glavine/Jsy	15.00
8	Fred Lynn/Bat	10.00
9	Babe Ruth/Bat	200.00
10	Tony Lazzeri/Bat	10.00
11	Al Kaline/Jersey	20.00
12	Reggie Jackson/Jsy	20.00
13	Derek Jeter/Jsy	40.00
14	Willie Stargell/Bat	15.00
15	Roy Campanella/Bat	50.00
16	Phil Rizzuto/Bat	20.00
17	Roberto Clemente/Bat	120.00
18	Carlton Fisk/Jsy	20.00
19	Duke Snider/Bat	25.00
20	Ted Williams/Bat	120.00
21	Bill Skowron/Bat	10.00
22	Bucky Dent/Bat	10.00
23	Mike Schmidt/Jsy	40.00
24	Lou Brock/Jsy	15.00
25	Brooks Robinson/Bat	20.00
26	Johnny Bench/	25.00

Fall Classics Memorabilia Autographs

No pricing due to scarcity.

Feel the Game

		NM/M
Common Player:		5.00
Inserted 1:48		
Golds:		2X
Production 50 Sets		
1	Moises Alou	5.00
2	Brady Anderson	5.00
3	Adrian Beltre	5.00
4	Carlos Delgado	8.00
5	J.D. Drew	5.00
6	Jermaine Dye	5.00
7	Jason Giambi	8.00
8	Richard Hidalgo	5.00
9	Chipper Jones	10.00
10	Eric Karros	5.00
11	Raul Mondesi	5.00
12	Chan Ho Park	5.00
13	Ivan Rodriguez	8.00
14	Matt Stairs	5.00
15	Frank Thomas	8.00
16	Jose Vidro	5.00
17	Matt Williams	5.00
18	Preston Wilson	5.00

Power Plus

		NM/M
Complete Set (10):		15.00
Common Player:		1.00
Inserted 1:24		
1	Vladimir Guerrero	1.50
2	Mark McGwire	3.00
3	Mike Piazza	2.00
4	Derek Jeter	4.00
5	Chipper Jones	2.00
6	Carlos Delgado	1.00
7	Sammy Sosa	2.00

8	Ken Griffey Jr.	2.00
9	Nomar Garciaparra	2.50
10	Alex Rodriguez	3.00

Season Pass

No Pricing

The Greatest Hits of ...

		NM/M
Complete Set (10):		10.00
Common Player:		.50
Inserted 1:12		
1	Mark McGwire	2.00
2	Alex Rodriguez	2.00
3	Ken Griffey Jr.	1.50
4	Ivan Rodriguez	.75
5	Cal Ripken Jr.	3.00
6	Todd Helton	.75
7	Derek Jeter	3.00
8	Pedro Martinez	1.00
9	Tony Gwynn	1.00
10	Jim Edmonds	.50

Tomorrow's Legends

		NM/M
Complete Set (15):		10.00
Common Player:		.25
Inserted 1:4		
1	Rick Ankiel	.25
2	J.D. Drew	.40
3	Carlos Delgado	.75
4	Todd Helton	.75
5	Andruw Jones	.75
6	Troy Glaus	.75
7	Jermaine Dye	.25
8	Vladimir Guerrero	1.00
9	Brian Giles	.25
10	Scott Rolen	.75
11	Darin Erstad	.40
12	Derek Jeter	3.00
13	Alex Rodriguez	3.00
14	Pat Burrell	.50
15	Nomar Garciaparra	2.00

2002 Ultra

		NM/M
Complete Set (285):		100.00
Common Player:		.15
Common SP (201-285):		.50
Inserted 1:4		
Pack (10):		2.00
Box (24):		40.00
1	Jeff Bagwell	.50
2	Derek Jeter	2.00
3	Alex Rodriguez	1.50

4	Eric Chavez	.40
5	Tsuyoshi Shinjo	.15
6	Chris Stynes	.15
7	Ivan Rodriguez	.50
8	Cal Ripken Jr.	2.00
9	Freddy Garcia	.15
10	Chipper Jones	.75
11	Hideo Nomo	.40
12	Rafael Furcal	.25
13	Preston Wilson	.15
14	Jimmy Rollins	.25
15	Cristian Guzman	.15
16	Garret Anderson	.40
17	Todd Helton	.50
18	Moises Alou	.25
19	Tony Gwynn	.75
20	Jorge Posada	.40
21	Sean Casey	.25
22	Kazuhiro Sasaki	.15
23	Ray Lankford	.15
24	Manny Ramirez	.50
25	Barry Bonds	2.00
26	Fred McGriff	.25
27	Vladimir Guerrero	.75
28	Jermaine Dye	.15
29	Adrian Beltre	.25
30	Ken Griffey Jr.	1.00
31	Ramon Hernandez	.15
32	Kerry Wood	.75
33	Greg Maddux	1.00
34	Rondell White	.15
35	Mike Mussina	.50
36	Jim Edmonds	.40
37	Scott Rolen	.75
38	Mike Lowell	.25
39	Al Leiter	.25
40	Tony Clark	.15
41	Joe Mays	.15
42	Mo Vaughn	.25
43	Geoff Jenkins	.25
44	Curt Schilling	.50
45	Pedro Martinez	.75
46	Andy Pettitte	.40
47	Tim Salmon	.25
48	Carl Everett	.15
49	Lance Berkman	.25
50	Troy Glaus	.40
51	Ichiro Suzuki	1.00
52	Alfonso Soriano	.75
53	Tomo Ohka	.15
54	Dean Palmer	.15
55	Kevin Brown	.15
56	Albert Pujols	1.50
57	Homer Bush	.15
58	Tim Hudson	.40
59	Frank Thomas	.50
60	Joe Randa	.15
61	Chan Ho Park	.15
62	Bobby Higginson	.15
63	Bartolo Colon	.15
64	Aramis Ramirez	.40
65	Jeff Cirillo	.15
66	Roberto Alomar	.50
67	Mark Kotsay	.15
68	Mike Cameron	.15
69	Mike Hampton	.15
70	Trot Nixon	.15
71	Juan Gonzalez	.50
72	Damian Rolls	.15
73	Brad Fullmer	.15
74	David Ortiz	.25
75	Brandon Inge	.15
76	Orlando Hernandez	.15
77	Matt Stairs	.15
78	Jay Gibbons	.15
79	Greg Vaughn	.15
80	Brady Anderson	.15
81	Jim Thome	.75
82	Ben Sheets	.40
83	Rafael Palmeiro	.50
84	Edgar Renteria	.25
85	Doug Mientkiewicz	.15
86	Raul Mondesi	.15
87	Shane Reynolds	.15
88	Steve Finley	.15
89	Jose Cruz Jr.	.15
90	Edgardo Alfonzo	.15
91	Jose Valentin	.15
92	Mark McGwire	2.00
93	Mark Grace	.40
94	Mike Lieberthal	.15
95	Barry Larkin	.25
96	Chuck Knoblauch	.15
97	Deivi Cruz	.15
98	Jeromy Burnitz	.15
99	Shannon Stewart	.15
100	David Wells	.15
101	Brook Fordyce	.15
102	Rusty Greer	.15
103	Andruw Jones	.50
104	Jason Kendall	.15
105	Nomar Garciaparra	1.25
106	Shawn Green	.25
107	Craig Biggio	.25
108	Masato Yoshii	.15
109	Ben Petrick	.15
110	Gary Sheffield	.40
111	Travis Lee	.15
112	Matt Williams	.25
113	Billy Wagner	.15
114	Robin Ventura	.15
115	Jerry Hairston Jr.	.15
116	Paul LoDuca	.15
117	Darin Erstad	.25
118	Ruben Sierra	.15

119	Ricky Gutierrez	.15
120	Bret Boone	.25
121	John Rocker	.15
122	Roger Clemens	1.50
123	Eric Karros	.15
124	J.D. Drew	.25
125	Carlos Delgado	.40
126	Jeffrey Hammonds	.15
127	Jeff Kent	.25
128	David Justice	.25
129	Cliff Floyd	.15
130	Omar Vizquel	.25
131	Matt Morris	.25
132	Rich Aurilia	.15
133	Larry Walker	.25
134	Miguel Tejada	.25
135	Eric Young	.15
136	Aaron Sele	.15
137	Eric Milton	.15
138	Travis Fryman	.15
139	Magglio Ordonez	.25
140	Sammy Sosa	1.50
141	Pokey Reese	.15
142	Adam Eaton	.15
143	Adam Kennedy	.15
144	Mike Piazza	1.00
145	Larry Barnes	.15
146	Darryl Kile	.15
147	Tom Glavine	.25
148	Ryan Klesko	.15
149	Jose Vidro	.15
150	Joe Kennedy	.15
151	Bernie Williams	.40
152	C.C. Sabathia	.15
153	Alex Ochoa	.15
154	A.J. Pierzynski	.15
155	Johnny Damon	.15
156	Omar Daal	.15
157	A.J. Burnett	.15
158	Eric Munson	.15
159	Fernando Vina	.15
160	Chris Singleton	.15
161	Juan Pierre	.15
162	John Olerud	.25
163	Randy Johnson	.75
164	Paul Konerko	.25
165	Tino Martinez	.25
166	Richard Hidalgo	.15
167	Luis Gonzalez	.25
168	Ben Grieve	.15
169	Matt Lawton	.15
170	Gabe Kapler	.15
171	Mariano Rivera	.25
172	Kenny Lofton	.25
173	Brad Radke	.15
174	Brian Giles	.25
175	Mark Quinn	.15
176	Neifi Perez	.15
177	Ellis Burks	.15
178	Bobby Abreu	.40
179	Jeff Weaver	.15
180	Andres Galarraga	.25
181	Javy Lopez	.25
182	Todd Walker	.15
183	Fernando Tatis	.15
184	Charles Johnson	.15
185	Pat Burrell	.40
186	Jay Bell	.15
187	Aaron Boone	.15
188	Jason Giambi	.50
189	Jay Payton	.15
190	Carlos Lee	.15
191	Phil Nevin	.15
192	Mike Sweeney	.15
193	J.T. Snow	.15
194	Dmitri Young	.15
195	Richie Sexson	.40
196	Derrek Lee	.25
197	Corey Koskie	.15
198	Edgar Martinez	.25
199	Wade Miller	.15
200	Tony Batista	.15
201	John Olerud	.50
202	Bret Boone	.50
203	Cal Ripken Jr.	3.00
204	Alex Rodriguez	2.50
205	Ichiro Suzuki	2.00
206	Manny Ramirez	.75
207	Juan Gonzalez	.75
208	Ivan Rodriguez	.75
209	Roger Clemens	2.00
210	Edgar Martinez	.50
211	Todd Helton	.75
212	Jeff Kent	.50
213	Chipper Jones	1.00
214	Rich Aurilia	.15
215	Barry Bonds	3.00
216	Sammy Sosa	2.00
217	Luis Gonzalez	.50
218	Mike Piazza	2.00
219	Randy Johnson	1.00
220	Larry Walker	.50
221	Todd Helton, Juan Uribe	.50
222	Pat Burrell, Eric Valent	.50
223	Edgar Martinez, Ichiro Suzuki	2.00
224	Ben Grieve, Jason Tyner	.50
225	Mark Quinn, Dee Brown	.50
226	Cal Ripken Jr., Brian Roberts	3.00
227	Cliff Floyd, Abraham Nunez	.50
228	Jeff Bagwell, Adam Everett	.75
229	Mark McGwire, Albert Pujols	3.00
230	Doug Mientkiewicz, Luis Rivas	.50
231	Juan Gonzalez, Danny Peoples	.75
232	Kevin Brown, Luke Prokopec	.50
233	Richie Sexson, Ben Sheets	.50

234	Jason Giambi, Jason Hart	.75
235	Barry Bonds,	
	Carlos Valderrama	3.00
236	Tony Gwynn, Cesar Crespo	1.00
237	Ken Griffey Jr., Adam Dunn	1.50
238	Frank Thomas, Joe Crede	.75
239	Derek Jeter, Drew Henson	3.00
240	Chipper Jones,	
	Wilson Betemit	1.00
241	Luis Gonzalez, Junior Spivey	.50
242	Bobby Higginson,	
	Andres Torres	.50
243	Carlos Delgado, Vernon Wells	.50
244	Sammy Sosa,	
	Corey Patterson	2.00
245	Nomar Garciaparra,	
	Shea Hillenbrand	2.00
246	Alex Rodriguez,	
	Jason Romano	2.50
247	Troy Glaus, David Eckstein	.75
248	Mike Piazza, Alex Escobar	2.00
249	Brian Giles, Jack Wilson	.50
250	Vladimir Guerrero,	
	Scott Hodges	1.00
251	Bud Smith	1.00
252	Juan Diaz	1.00
253	Wilkin Ruan	1.00
254	Chris Spurling RC	1.00
255	Toby Hall	1.00
256	Jason Jennings	1.00
257	George Perez	1.00
258	D'Angelo Jimenez	1.00
259	Jose Acevedo	1.00
260	Josue Perez	1.00
261	Brian Rogers	1.00
262	Carlos Maldonado	1.00
263	Travis Phelps	1.00
264	Rob Mackowiak	1.50
265	Ryan Drese	1.00
266	Carlos Garcia	1.00
267	Alexis Gomez	1.00
268	Jeremy Affeldt	1.00
269	Scott Podsednik	3.00
270	Adam Johnson	1.00
271	Pedro Santana	1.00
272	Les Walrond	1.00
273	Jackson Melian	1.00
274	Carlos Hernandez	1.00
275	Mark Nussbeck RC	1.00
276	Cory Aldridge	1.00
277	Troy Mattes	1.00
278	Brent Abernathy	1.00
279	J.J. Davis	1.00
280	Brandon Duckworth	1.00
281	Kyle Lohse	1.00
282	Justin Kaye	1.00
283	Cody Ransom	1.00
284	Dave Williams	1.00
285	Luis Lopez	1.00

Gold Medallion

Stars (1-200):	2-3X
Inserted 1:1	
Stars (201-250):	2-4X
Inserted 1:24	
Prospects (251-285):	4-8X
Production 100	

Fall Classic

	NM/M
Complete Set (39):	180.00
Common Player:	2.50
Inserted 1:20	
1FC Ty Cobb	10.00
2FC Lou Gehrig	10.00
3FC Babe Ruth	15.00
4FC Stan Musial	8.00
5FC Ted Williams	12.00

6FC Dizzy Dean	6.00
7FC Mickey Cochrane	2.50
8FC Jimmie Foxx	8.00
9FC Mel Ott	5.00
10FC Rogers Hornsby	6.00
11FC Hank Aaron	10.00
12FC Clete Boyer	2.50
13FC George Brett	10.00
14FC Bob Gibson	5.00
15FC Carlton Fisk	4.00
16FC Johnny Bench	8.00
17FC Rusty Staub	2.50
18FC Willie McCovey	2.50
19FC Paul Molitor	5.00
20FC Jim Palmer	4.00
21FC Frank Robinson	5.00
22FC Derek Jeter	10.00
23FC Earl Weaver	2.50
24FC Lefty Grove	2.50
25FC Tony Perez	2.50
26FC Reggie Jackson	5.00
27FC Sparky Anderson	2.50
28FC Casey Stengel	2.50
29FC Roy Campanella	6.00
30FC Roberto Clemente	10.00
31FC Don Drysdale	6.00
32FC Joe Morgan	4.00
33FC Eddie Murray	5.00
34FC Nolan Ryan	15.00
35FC Tom Seaver	8.00
36FC Bill Mazeroski	2.50
37FC Jackie Robinson	8.00
38FC Kirk Gibson	2.50
39FC Robin Yount	8.00

Fall Classic Game Used

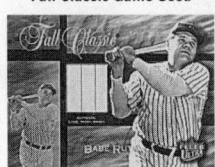

	NM/M
Inserted 1:113	
Sparky Anderson/Pants	5.00
Johnny Bench/Jsy	15.00
Johnny Bench/Pants	10.00
George Brett/Bat	5.00
George Brett/Blue/Jsy/65	45.00
George Brett/White/Jsy	15.00
Roy Campanella/Bat/21	225.00
Carlton Fisk/Bat/42	35.00
Carlton Fisk/Jersey	8.00
Jimmie Foxx/Bat	35.00
Bob Gibson/Jsy	10.00
Kirk Gibson/Bat	5.00
Reggie Jackson/Bat	10.00
Reggie Jackson/Jsy/73	20.00
Derek Jeter/Pants	30.00
Willie McCovey/Jsy	5.00
Paul Molitor/Bat	10.00
Paul Molitor/Jsy	10.00
Joe Morgan/Bat	8.00
Joe Morgan/Jsy	8.00
Eddie Murray/Bat	10.00
Eddie Murray/Jsy/91	35.00
Jim Palmer/Gray Jsy/85	20.00
Jim Palmer/White Jsy	5.00
Tony Perez/Bat	8.00
Frank Robinson/Bat/40	25.00
Jackie Robinson/Jsy	50.00
Babe Ruth/Bat/44	200.00
Nolan Ryan/Pants	30.00
Tom Seaver/Jsy	10.00
Earl Weaver/Jsy	5.00
Ted Williams/Bat/30	200.00
Ted Williams/Jsy	75.00
Robin Yount/Bat	10.00
Robin Yount/Gray Jsy	10.00
Robin Yount/White Jsy/30	30.00

Fall Classic Autographs

	NM/M
Common Autograph:	10.00
Inserted 1:240	
1 Sparky Anderson	15.00
2 Johnny Bench/SP	40.00
3 George Brett/SP	80.00
4 Carlton Fisk	25.00
5 Bob Gibson	25.00
6 Kirk Gibson	15.00
7 Reggie Jackson/SP	40.00
9 Bill Mazeroski	20.00
10 Willie McCovey/SP	30.00
11 Joe Morgan	15.00
12 Eddie Murray/SP	40.00
14 Jim Palmer	15.00
15 Tony Perez	15.00
16 Frank Robinson	20.00
17 Nolan Ryan/SP	175.00
18 Tom Seaver/SP	30.00
19 Earl Weaver	10.00
20 Robin Yount/SP	50.00

Glove Works

	NM/M
Complete Set (15):	25.00
Common Player:	1.00

Inserted 1:20	
1GW Andruw Jones	1.50
2GW Derek Jeter	6.00
3GW Cal Ripken Jr.	8.00
4GW Larry Walker	1.00
5GW Chipper Jones	2.00
6GW Barry Bonds	6.00
7GW Scott Rolen	2.00
8GW Jim Edmonds	1.00
9GW Robin Ventura	1.00
10GW Darin Erstad	1.00
11GW Barry Larkin	1.00
12GW Raul Mondesi	1.00
13GW Mark Grace	1.50
14GW Bernie Williams	1.00
15GW Ivan Rodriguez	1.50

Glove Works Game Worn

	NM/M
Common Player:	10.00
Production 450 Sets	
Platinum (25 Sets) randomly inserted.	
Derek Jeter	35.00
Cal Ripken Jr.	50.00
Barry Bonds	40.00
Robin Ventura	10.00
Barry Larkin/SP	15.00
Raul Mondesi	10.00
Ivan Rodriguez	15.00

Hitting Machine

	NM/M
Complete Set (25):	60.00
Common Player:	1.00
Inserted 1:20	
1HM Frank Thomas	2.00
2HM Derek Jeter	8.00
3HM Vladimir Guerrero	3.00
4HM Jim Edmonds	1.50
5HM Mike Piazza	5.00
6HM Ivan Rodriguez	2.00
7HM Chipper Jones	3.00
8HM Tony Gwynn	3.00
9HM Manny Ramirez	2.00
10HM Andruw Jones	2.00
11HM Carlos Delgado	1.50
12HM Bernie Williams	1.50
13HM Larry Walker	1.00
14HM Juan Gonzalez	2.00
15HM Ichiro Suzuki	5.00
16HM Albert Pujols	6.00
17HM Barry Bonds	8.00
18HM Cal Ripken Jr.	8.00
19HM Edgar Martinez	1.50
20HM Luis Gonzalez	1.00
21HM Moises Alou	1.50
22HM Roberto Alomar	2.00
23HM Todd Helton	1.50
24HM Rafael Palmeiro	2.00
25HM Bobby Abreu	1.50

Hitting Machine Game Worn

	NM/M
Common Player:	8.00
Inserted 1:81	
Platinum (25 Sets) randomly inserted.	
Frank Thomas	15.00
Derek Jeter	25.00
Jim Edmonds	10.00
Mike Piazza	15.00
Ivan Rodriguez	15.00
Chipper Jones	15.00
Tony Gwynn	15.00
Manny Ramirez	10.00
Andruw Jones	10.00
Carlos Delgado	10.00
Bernie Williams	10.00
Larry Walker	8.00

Juan Gonzalez	10.00
Albert Pujols	30.00
Barry Bonds	25.00
Cal Ripken Jr.	40.00
Edgar Martinez	10.00
Luis Gonzalez	8.00
Moises Alou	10.00
Roberto Alomar	15.00
Todd Helton	15.00
Rafael Palmeiro	10.00
Bobby Abreu	10.00

On the Road Game Used

	NM/M
Common Player:	10.00
Inserted 1:93	
Platinum (25 Sets) randomly inserted.	
Derek Jeter	30.00
Ivan Rodriguez	10.00
Carlos Delgado	8.00
Larry Walker	8.00
Roberto Alomar	15.00
Tony Gwynn	15.00
Barry Bonds	30.00
Todd Helton	15.00
Kazuhiro Sasaki	10.00
Jeff Bagwell	15.00
Omar Vizquel	8.00
Chan Ho Park	10.00
Tom Glavine	10.00

Rising Stars

	NM/M
Complete Set (15):	15.00
Common Player:	.50
Inserted 1:12	
1RS Ichiro Suzuki	2.50
2RS Derek Jeter	4.00
3RS Albert Pujols	3.00
4RS Jimmy Rollins	1.00
5RS Adam Dunn	1.00
6RS Sean Casey	1.00
7RS Kerry Wood	2.00
8RS Tsuyoshi Shinjo	.50
9RS Shea Hillenbrand	.50
10RS Pat Burrell	1.00
11RS Ben Sheets	1.00
12RS Alfonso Soriano	1.50
13RS J.D. Drew	1.00
14RS Kazuhiro Sasaki	.50
15RS Corey Patterson	.75

Rising Stars Game Worn

	NM/M
Common Player:	20.00
Production 100 Sets	
Platinum (25 Sets) randomly seeded.	
Derek Jeter	75.00
Albert Pujols	50.00
Tsuyoshi Shinjo	25.00
Alfonso Soriano	25.00
J.D. Drew	25.00
Kazuhiro Sasaki	20.00

2003 Ultra

	NM/M
Complete Set (250):	75.00
Common Player:	.15
Common SP (201-250):	.50
Inserted 1:4	
Hobby Pack (10):	2.00
Hobby Box (24):	35.00
1 Barry Bonds	2.00
2 Derek Jeter	2.50
3 Ichiro Suzuki	1.50
4 Mike Lowell	.15
5 Hideo Nomo	.50
6 Javier Vazquez	.15
7 Jeremy Giambi	.15
8 Jamie Moyer	.15
9 Rafael Palmeiro	.40
10 Magglio Ordonez	.25
11 Trot Nixon	.15
12 Luis Castillo	.15
13 Paul Byrd	.15
14 Adam Kennedy	.15
15 Trevor Hoffman	.15
16 Matt Morris	.15
17 Nomar Garciaparra	1.50
18 Matt Lawton	.15
19 Carlos Beltran	.15
20 Jason Giambi	1.25
21 Brian Giles	.25
22 Jim Edmonds	.25
23 Garret Anderson	.25
24 Tony Batista	.15
25 Aaron Boone	.15
26 Mike Hampton	.15
27 Billy Wagner	.15
28 Kazuhisa Ishii	.15
29 Al Leiter	.25
30 Pat Burrell	.40
31 Jeff Kent	.25
32 Randy Johnson	.75
33 Ray Durham	.15
34 Josh Beckett	.15
35 Cristian Guzman	.15
36 Roger Clemens	1.25
37 Freddy Garcia	.15
38 Roy Halladay	.15
39 David Eckstein	.15
40 Jerry Hairston Jr.	.15
41 Barry Larkin	.25
42 Larry Walker	.25
43 Craig Biggio	.25
44 Edgardo Alfonzo	.15
45 Marlon Byrd	.15
46 J.T. Snow	.15
47 Juan Gonzalez	.50
48 Ramon Ortiz	.15
49 Jay Gibbons	.15
50 Adam Dunn	.60
51 Juan Pierre	.15
52 Jeff Bagwell	.60
53 Kevin Brown	.15
54 Pedro Astacio	.15
55 Mike Lieberthal	.15
56 Johnny Damon	.25
57 Tim Salmon	.25
58 Mike Bordick	.15
59 Ken Griffey Jr.	1.50
60 Jason Jennings	.15
61 Lance Berkman	.50
62 Jeromy Burnitz	.15
63 Jimmy Rollins	.25
64 Tsuyoshi Shinjo	.15
65 Alex Rodriguez	2.00
66 Greg Maddux	1.25
67 Mark Prior	.40
68 Mike Maroth	.15
69 Geoff Jenkins	.15
70 Tony Armas Jr.	.15
71 Jermaine Dye	.15
72 Albert Pujols	.75
73 Shannon Stewart	.15
74 Troy Glaus	.60
75 Brook Fordyce	.15
76 Juan Encarnacion	.15
77 Todd Hollandsworth	.15
78 Roy Oswalt	.25
79 Paul LoDuca	.15
80 Mike Piazza	1.50
81 Bobby Abreu	.15
82 Sean Burroughs	.15
83 Randy Winn	.15
84 Curt Schilling	.50
85 Chris Singleton	.15
86 Sean Casey	.25
87 Todd Zeile	.15
88 Richard Hidalgo	.15
89 Roberto Alomar	.50
90 Tim Hudson	.25
91 Ryan Klesko	.15
92 Greg Vaughn	.15
93 Tony Womack	.15
94 Fred McGriff	.25
95 Tom Glavine	.40
96 Todd Walker	.15
97 Travis Fryman	.15
98 Shane Reynolds	.15
99 Shawn Green	.25
100 Mo Vaughn	.25
101 Adam Piatt	.15
102 Deivi Cruz	.15
103 Steve Cox	.15
104 Luis Gonzalez	.25
105 Russell Branyan	.15
106 Daryle Ward	.15
107 Mariano Rivera	.25
108 Phil Nevin	.15
109 Ben Grieve	.15
110 Moises Alou	.15
111 Omar Vizquel	.25
112 Joe Randa	.15
113 Jorge Posada	.40
114 Mark Kotsay	.15
115 Ryan Rupe	.15
116 Javy Lopez	.15
117 Corey Patterson	.15
118 Bobby Higginson	.15
119 Jose Vidro	.15
120 Barry Zito	.25
121 Matt Morris	.15
122 Gary Sheffield	.25
123 Kerry Wood	.15
124 Brandon Inge	.15
125 Jose Hernandez	.15
126 Michael Barrett	.15
127 Miguel Tejada	.40
128 Edgar Renteria	.15
129 Junior Spivey	.15
130 Jose Valentin	.15
131 Derrek Lee	.15
132 A.J. Pierzynski	.15
133 Mike Mussina	.50
134 Bret Boone	.15
135 Chan Ho Park	.15
136 Steve Finley	.15
137 Mark Buehrle	.15
138 A.J. Burnett	.15
139 Ben Sheets	.15
140 David Ortiz	.15
141 Nick Johnson	.15
142 Randall Simon	.15
143 Carlos Delgado	.40
144 Darin Erstad	.25
145 Shea Hillenbrand	.15
146 Todd Helton	.40
147 Preston Wilson	.15
148 Eric Gagne	.15
149 Vladimir Guerrero	.75
150 Brandon Duckworth	.15
151 Rich Aurilia	.15
152 Ivan Rodriguez	.50
153 Andruw Jones	.50
154 Carlos Lee	.15
155 Robert Fick	.15
156 Jacque Jones	.15
157 Bernie Williams	.50
158 John Olerud	.25
159 Eric Hinske	.15
160 Matt Clement	.15
161 Dmitri Young	.15
162 Torii Hunter	.15
163 Carlos Pena	.15
164 Mike Cameron	.15
165 Raul Mondesi	.15
166 Pedro J. Martinez	.75
167 Bob Wickman	.15
168 Mike Sweeney	.15
169 David Wells	.15
170 Jason Kendall	.15
171 Tino Martinez	.15
172 Matt Williams	.15
173 Frank Thomas	.60
174 Cliff Floyd	.15
175 Corey Koskie	.15
176 Orlando Hernandez	.15
177 Edgar Martinez	.15
178 Richie Sexson	.25
179 Manny Ramirez	.60
180 Jim Thome	.50
181 Andy Pettitte	.40
182 Aramis Ramirez	.15
183 J.D. Drew	.25
184 Brian Jordan	.15
185 Sammy Sosa	1.25
186 Jeff Weaver	.15
187 Jeffrey Hammonds	.15
188 Eric Milton	.15
189 Eric Chavez	.25
190 Kazuhiro Sasaki	.15
191 Jose Cruz Jr.	.15
192 Derek Lowe	.15
193 C.C. Sabathia	.15
194 Adrian Beltre	.15
195 Alfonso Soriano	1.00
196 Jack Wilson	.15
197 Fernando Vina	.15
198 Chipper Jones	1.25
199 Paul Konerko	.15
200 Rusty Greer	.15
201 Jason Giambi	2.00
202 Alfonso Soriano	2.00
203 Shea Hillenbrand	.50
204 Alex Rodriguez	3.00
205 Jorge Posada	.60
206 Ichiro Suzuki	3.00
207 Manny Ramirez	1.00
208 Torii Hunter	.50
209 Todd Helton	.75
210 Roberto Alomar	.75
211 Scott Rolen	.75
212 Jimmy Rollins	.50
213 Mike Piazza	3.00
214 Barry Bonds	3.00
215 Sammy Sosa	2.00
216 Vladimir Guerrero	1.50
217 Lance Berkman	.75
218 Derek Jeter	4.00
219 Nomar Garciaparra	3.00
220 Luis Gonzalez	.75
221 Kazuhisa Ishii	1.00
222 Satoru Komiyama	.50
223 So Taguchi	.50
224 Jorge Padilla	.50
225 Ben Howard	.50
226 Jason Simontacchi	.50
227 Barry Wesson	.50
228 Howie Clark	.50
229 Aaron Guiel	.50
230 Oliver Perez	.75
231 David Ross	.50
232 Julius Matos	.50
233 Chris Snelling	.50
234 Rodrigo Lopez	.50
235 Wilbert Nieves	.50
236 Brendan Donnelly	.50
237 Aaron Cook	.50
238 Anderson Machado	.50
239 Corey Thurman	.50
240 Tyler Yates	.50
241 Coco Crisp	4.00
242 Andy Van Hekken	1.50
243 Jim Rushford	2.00
244 Jerome Robertson	1.00
245 Shane Nance	1.00
246 Kevin Cash	.50
247 Kirk Saarloos	1.50
248 Josh Bard	2.00
249 David Pember RC	1.00
250 Freddy Sanchez	1.50

Gold Medallion

Stars (1-200):	2-3X
Inserted 1:1	
Stars (201-220):	3-4X
Inserted 1:24	
Rookies (221-250):	1-3X
Inserted 1:24	

Back 2 Back

	NM/M
Complete Set (17):	60.00
Common Player:	2.00
Production 1,000 Sets	
1B2B Derek Jeter	10.00
2B2B Barry Bonds	8.00
3B2B Mike Piazza	6.00
4B2B Alex Rodriguez	8.00
5B2B Todd Helton	2.00
6B2B Edgar Martinez	2.00
7B2B Chipper Jones	5.00
8B2B Shawn Green	4.00
9B2B Chan Ho Park	2.00
10B2B Preston Wilson	4.00
11B2B Manny Ramirez	3.00
12B2B Aramis Ramirez	2.00
13B2B Pedro J. Martinez	4.00
14B2B Ivan Rodriguez	2.00
15B2B Ichiro Suzuki	6.00
16B2B Sammy Sosa	5.00
17B2B Jason Giambi	5.00

Back 2 Back Memorabilia

	NM/M
Common Player:	5.00
Production 500 Sets	
Golds:	1.5-3X
Production 50 Sets	
Derek Jeter	25.00
Barry Bonds/Bat	20.00
Mike Piazza/Jsy	12.00
Alex Rodriguez/Jsy	12.00
Todd Helton/Jsy	8.00
Edgar Martinez/Jsy	6.00
Chipper Jones/Jsy	15.00
Shawn Green/Jsy	6.00
Chan Ho Park/Bat	6.00
Preston Wilson/Jsy	5.00
Manny Ramirez/Jsy	8.00
Aramis Ramirez/Jsy	5.00
Pedro Martinez/Jsy	10.00
Ivan Rodriguez/Jsy	8.00
Ichiro Suzuki/Base	15.00
Sammy Sosa/Base	10.00
Jason Giambi/Base	8.00

Double Up

	NM/M
Complete Set (16):	30.00
Common Card:	1.00
Inserted 1:8	
1DU Derek Jeter, Mike Piazza	4.00

2DU	Alex Rodriguez, Rafael Palmeiro	3.00
3DU	Chipper Jones, Andruw Jones	2.00
4DU	Derek Jeter, Alex Rodriguez	4.00
5DU	Nomar Garciaparra, Derek Jeter	4.00
6DU	Barry Bonds, Jason Giambi	3.00
7DU	Ichiro Suzuki, Hideo Nomo	3.00
8DU	Randy Johnson, Curt Schilling	1.00
9DU	Pedro J. Martinez, Nomar Garciaparra	2.50
10DU	Roger Clemens, Kevin Brown	2.00
11DU	Nomar Garciaparra, Manny Ramirez	2.50
12DU	Kazuhiro Sasaki, Hideo Nomo	1.00
13DU	Mike Piazza, Ivan Rodriguez	3.00
14DU	Ichiro Suzuki, Ken Griffey Jr.	3.00
15DU	Barry Bonds, Sammy Sosa	3.00
16DU	Alfonso Soriano, Roberto Alomar	2.00

Double Up Memorabilia

	NM/M
Common Card:	15.00
Production 100 Sets	
Derek Jeter, Mike Piazza	50.00
Alex Rodriguez, Rafael Palmeiro	25.00
Chipper Jones, Andruw Jones	15.00
Derek Jeter, Alex Rodriguez	50.00
Nomar Garciaparra, Derek Jeter	50.00
Barry Bonds, Jason Giambi	30.00
Ichiro Suzuki, Hideo Nomo	80.00
Randy Johnson, Curt Schilling	20.00
Pedro J. Martinez, Nomar Garciaparra	30.00
Roger Clemens, Kevin Brown	25.00
Nomar Garciaparra, Manny Ramirez	25.00
Kazuhiro Sasaki, Hideo Nomo	50.00
Mike Piazza, Ivan Rodriguez	25.00
Ichiro Suzuki, Ken Griffey Jr.	50.00
Barry Bonds, Sammy Sosa	40.00
Alfonso Soriano, Roberto Alomar	25.00

Moonshots

	NM/M
Complete Set (20):	30.00
Common Player:	.75
Inserted 1:12	
1M Mike Piazza	4.00
2M Alex Rodriguez	4.00
3M Manny Ramirez	1.50
4M Ivan Rodriguez	1.00
5M Luis Gonzalez	.75

6M	Shawn Green	.75
7M	Barry Bonds	5.00
8M	Jason Giambi	3.00
9M	Nomar Garciaparra	4.00
10M	Edgar Martinez	.75
11M	Mo Vaughn	.75
12M	Chipper Jones	3.00
13M	Todd Helton	1.00
14M	Raul Mondesi	.75
15M	Preston Wilson	.75
16M	Rafael Palmeiro	1.00
17M	Jim Edmonds	.75
18M	Bernie Williams	1.00
19M	Vladimir Guerrero	2.00
20M	Alfonso Soriano	2.00

Moonshots Memorabilia

NM/M

Common Player:		4.00
Inserted 1:20		
	Mike Piazza/Jsy	12.00
	Alex Rodriguez/Jsy	12.00
	Manny Ramirez/Jsy	5.00
	Ivan Rodriguez/Jsy	5.00
	Luis Gonzalez/Jsy	4.00
	Shawn Green/Jsy	4.00
	Barry Bonds/Jsy	12.00
	Jason Giambi/Base	8.00
	Nomar Garciaparra/Jsy	12.00
	Edgar Martinez/Jsy	5.00
	Mo Vaughn/Jsy	4.00
	Chipper Jones/Jsy	8.00
	Todd Helton/Jsy	6.00
	Raul Mondesi/Jsy	5.00
	Preston Wilson/Jsy	4.00
	Rafael Palmeiro/Jsy	5.00
	Jim Edmonds/Jsy	5.00
	Bernie Williams/Jsy	6.00
	Vladimir Guerrero/Base	8.00
	Alfonso Soriano/Jsy	5.00

Photo Effex

Vladimir Guerrero
Montreal Expos™

Photo Effex

NM/M

Complete Set (20):		45.00
Common Player:		1.00
Inserted 1:12		
Golds:		6-12X
Production 25 Sets		
1PE	Derek Jeter	6.00
2PE	Barry Bonds	5.00
3PE	Sammy Sosa	3.00
4PE	Troy Glaus	1.50
5PE	Albert Pujols	2.00
6PE	Alex Rodriguez	5.00
7PE	Ichiro Suzuki	4.00
8PE	Greg Maddux	3.00
9PE	Nomar Garciaparra	4.00
10PE	Jeff Bagwell	1.50
11PE	Chipper Jones	3.00
12PE	Mike Piazza	3.00
13PE	Randy Johnson	2.00
14PE	Vladimir Guerrero	3.00
15PE	Alfonso Soriano	3.00
16PE	Lance Berkman	1.00
17PE	Todd Helton	1.00
18PE	Mike Lowell	1.00
19PE	Carlos Delgado	1.00
20PE	Jason Giambi	3.00

When it was a Game

NM/M

Complete Set (40):		125.00
Common Player:		2.00
Inserted 1:20		
1WG	Derek Jeter	10.00
2WG	Barry Bonds	8.00
3WG	Luis Aparicio	2.00
4WG	Richie Ashburn	2.00
5WG	Ernie Banks	5.00
6WG	Enos Slaughter	3.00
7WG	Yogi Berra	5.00
8WG	Lou Boudreau	2.00
9WG	Lou Brock	4.00
10WG	Jim Bunning	2.00
11WG	Rod Carew	4.00
12WG	Orlando Cepeda	2.00
13WG	Larry Doby	4.00
14WG	Bobby Doerr	2.00
15WG	Bob Feller	3.00
16WG	Brooks Robinson	5.00
17WG	Rollie Fingers	2.00
18WG	Whitey Ford	3.00
19WG	Bob Gibson	4.00
20WG	Jim "Catfish" Hunter	3.00
21WG	Nolan Ryan	15.00
22WG	Reggie Jackson	5.00
23WG	Fergie Jenkins	3.00
24WG	Al Kaline	6.00
25WG	Mike Schmidt	8.00
26WG	Harmon Killebrew	8.00
27WG	Ralph Kiner	4.00
28WG	Willie Stargell	4.00
29WG	Billy Williams	2.00
30WG	Tom Seaver	5.00
31WG	Juan Marichal	3.00
32WG	Eddie Mathews	6.00
33WG	Willie McCovey	4.00
34WG	Joe Morgan	4.00
35WG	Stan Musial	8.00
36WG	Robin Roberts	4.00
37WG	Robin Yount	8.00
38WG	Jim Palmer	3.00
39WG	Phil Rizzuto	4.00
40WG	Pee Wee Reese	4.00

When it was a Game Memorabilia

NM/M

Common Player:		
Varying quantities produced		
	Derek Jeter/Jsy/200	35.00
	Barry Bonds/Bat/200	25.00
	Yogi Berra/100	35.00
	Larry Doby/Bat/150	20.00
	Catfish Hunter/Jsy	8.00
	Reggie Jackson/Bat	12.00
	Tom Seaver/Jsy	15.00
	Juan Marichal/Jsy	8.00
	Eddie Mathews/Bat	25.00
	Willie McCovey/Jsy/150	15.00
	Joe Morgan/Jsy/200	10.00
	Jim Palmer/Jsy/300	10.00

When it was a Game Autograph

No Pricing

2004 Ultra

Richie Weeks
Brewers

NM/M

Complete Set (220):		45.00
Common Player:		.15
Common All-Rookie (201-220):		.50
Common Player (221-295):		.25
Minor Stars (221-295):		.40
Unlisted Stars (221-295):		.60
Common Player (296-382):		2.00
Inserted 2:1		

Common Player (383-395):		15.00
Production 500 Sets		
Pack (8):		3.00
Box (24):		60.00
1	Magglio Ordonez	.40
2	Bobby Abreu	.25
3	Eric Munson	.15
4	Eric Byrnes	.15
5	Bartolo Colon	.25
6	Juan Encarnacion	.15
7	Jody Gerut	.15
8	Eddie Guardado	.15
9	Shea Hillenbrand	.15
10	Andruw Jones	.50
11	Carlos Lee	.15
12	Pedro J. Martinez	.75
13	Barry Larkin	.25
14	Angel Berroa	.15
15	Edgar Martinez	.25
16	Sidney Ponson	.15
17	Mariano Rivera	.25
18	Richie Sexson	.40
19	Frank Thomas	.50
20	Jerome Williams	.15
21	Barry Zito	.40
22	Roberto Alomar	.50
23	Rocky Biddle	.15
24	Orlando Cabrera	.25
25	Placido Polanco	.15
26	Morgan Ensberg	.15
27	Jason Giambi	.75
28	Jim Thome	.75
29	Vladimir Guerrero	.75
30	Tim Hudson	.40
31	Jacque Jones	.15
32	Derrek Lee	.25
33	Rafael Palmeiro	.40
34	Mike Mussina	.40
35	Corey Patterson	.15
36	Mike Cameron	.15
37	Ivan Rodriguez	.50
38	Ben Sheets	.15
39	Woody Williams	.15
40	Ichiro Suzuki	1.00
41	Moises Alou	.25
42	Craig Biggio	.25
43	Jorge Posada	.40
44	Craig Monroe	.15
45	Darin Erstad	.25
46	Jay Gibbons	.25
47	Aaron Guiel	.15
48	Travis Lee	.15
49	Jorge Julio	.15
50	Torii Hunter	.25
51	Luis Matos	.15
52	Brett Myers	.15
53	Sean Casey	.25
54	Mark Prior	1.50
55	Alex Rodriguez	1.50
56	Gary Sheffield	.40
57	Jason Varitek	.15
58	Dontrelle Willis	.40
59	Garret Anderson	.25
60	Casey Blake	.15
61	Jay Payton	.15
62	Carl Crawford	.25
63	Carl Everett	.15
64	Marcus Giles	.15
65	Jose Guillen	.15
66	Eric Karros	.15
67	Mike Lieberthal	.15
68	Hideki Matsui	3.00
69	Xavier Nady	.15
70	Hank Blalock	.40
71	Albert Pujols	1.50
72	Jose Cruz Jr.	.15
73	Randall Simon	.15
74	Javier Vazquez	.15
75	Preston Wilson	.15
76	Danys Baez	.15
77	Alex Cintron	.15
78	Jake Peavy	.15
79	Scott Rolen	.50
80	Robert Fick	.15
81	Brian Giles	.25
82	Roy Halladay	.25
83	Kazuhisa Ishii	.15
84	Austin Kearns	.40
85	Paul LoDuca	.15
86	Darrell May	.15
87	Phil Nevin	.15
88	Carlos Pena	.15
89	Manny Ramirez	.50
90	C.C. Sabathia	.15
91	John Smoltz	.25
92	Jose Vidro	.15
93	Randy Wolf	.15
94	Jeff Bagwell	.50
95	Barry Bonds	2.00
96	Frank Catalanotto	.15
97	Zach Day	.15
98	David Ortiz	.15
99	Troy Glaus	.40
100	Bo Hart	.15
101	Geoff Jenkins	.25
102	Jason Kendall	.15
103	Esteban Loiaza	.15
104	Doug Mientkiewicz	.15
105	Trot Nixon	.15
106	Troy Percival	.15
107	Aramis Ramirez	.15
108	Alex Sanchez	.15
109	Alfonso Soriano	.75
110	Omar Vizquel	.25
111	Kerry Wood	.50
112	Rocco Baldelli	.15
113	Bret Boone	.25
114	Shawn Chacon	.15
115	Carlos Delgado	.50
116	Shawn Green	.40
117	Tim Worrell	.15
118	Tom Glavine	.25
119	Shigetoshi Hasegawa	.15
120	Derek Jeter	2.00
121	Jeff Kent	.25
122	Braden Looper	.15
123	Kevin Millwood	.25
124	Hideo Nomo	.40
125	Jason Phillips	.15
126	Tim Redding	.15
127	Reggie Sanders	.15
128	Sammy Sosa	1.25
129	Billy Wagner	.25
130	Miguel Batista	.15
131	Milton Bradley	.15
132	Eric Chavez	.25
133	J.D. Drew	.15
134	Keith Foulke	.15
135	Luis Gonzalez	.25
136	LaTroy Hawkins	.15
137	Randy Johnson	.75
138	Byung-Hyun Kim	.15
139	Javy Lopez	.25
140	Melvin Mora	.15
141	Aubrey Huff	.15
142	Mike Piazza	1.00
143	Mark Redman	.15
144	Kazuhiro Sasaki	.15
145	Shannon Stewart	.15
146	Larry Walker	.25
147	Dmitri Young	.15
148	Josh Beckett	.50
149	Jae Weong Seo	.15
150	Hee Seop Choi	.15
151	Adam Dunn	.40
152	Rafael Furcal	.25
153	Juan Gonzalez	.50
154	Todd Helton	.50
155	Carlos Zambrano	.15
156	Ryan Klesko	.25
157	Mike Lowell	.15
158	Jamie Moyer	.15
159	Russ Ortiz	.15
160	Juan Pierre	.15
161	Edgar Renteria	.15
162	Curt Schilling	.40
163	Mike Sweeney	.15
164	Brandon Webb	.15
165	Michael Young	.15
166	Carlos Beltran	.25
167	Sean Burroughs	.15
168	Luis Castillo	.15
169	David Eckstein	.15
170	Eric Gagne	.25
171	Chipper Jones	1.00
172	Livan Hernandez	.15
173	Nick Johnson	.15
174	Corey Koskie	.15
175	Jason Schmidt	.15
176	Bill Mueller	.15
177	Steve Finley	.15
178	A.J. Pierzynski	.15
179	Rene Reyes	.15
180	Jason Johnson	.15
181	Mark Teixeira	.15
182	Kip Wells	.15
183	Mike MacDougal	.15
184	Lance Berkman	.25
185	Victor Zambrano	.15
186	Roger Clemens	1.50
187	Jim Edmonds	.25
188	Nomar Garciaparra	1.50
189	Ken Griffey Jr.	1.00
190	Richard Hidalgo	.15
191	Cliff Floyd	.15
192	Greg Maddux	1.00
193	Mark Mulder	.25
194	Roy Oswalt	.25
195	Marlon Byrd	.15
196	Jose Reyes	.25
197	Kevin Brown	.25
198	Miguel Tejada	.25
199	Vernon Wells	.25
200	Joel Pineiro	.15
201	Rickie Weeks	5.00
202	Chad Gaudin	1.50
203	Ryan Wagner	1.50
204	Chris Bootcheck	.50
205	Koyie Hill	.50
206	Jeff Duncan	1.00
207	Rich Harden	1.00
208	Edwin Jackson	.50
209	Robby Hammock	.50
210	Khalil Greene	.50
211	Chien-Ming Wang	.50
212	Prentice Redman	.50
213	Todd Wellemeyer	.50
214	Clint Barmes	.50
215	Matt Kata	.50
216	Jon Leicester	.50
217	Jeremy Guthrie	.50
218	Chin-Hui Tsao	1.50
219	Dan Haren	1.00
220	Delmon Young	5.00
221	Vladimir Guerrero	1.00
222	Andy Pettitte	.60
223	Gary Sheffield	.60
224	Javier Vazquez	.25
225	Alex Rodriguez	2.50
226	Billy Wagner	.25

#	Player	Price
227	Miguel Tejada	.60
228	Greg Maddux	1.50
229	Ivan Rodriguez	.60
230	Roger Clemens	2.50
231	Alfonso Soriano	1.00
232	Miguel Cabrera	.75
233	Javy Lopez	.40
234	David Wells	.25
235	Eric Milton	.25
236	Armando Benitez	.25
237	Mike Cameron	.25
238	J.D. Drew	.40
239	Carlos Beltran	.60
240	Bartolo Colon	.40
241	Jose Guillen	.25
242	Kevin Brown	.40
243	Carlos Guillen	.25
244	Kenny Lofton	.25
245	Pokey Reese	.25
246	Rafael Palmeiro	.75
247	Nomar Garciaparra	2.50
248	Hee Seop Choi	.25
249	Juan Uribe	.25
250	Nick Johnson	.25
251	Scott Podsednik	.25
252	Richie Sexson	.60
253	Keith Foulke	.25
254	Jaret Wright	.25
255	Johnny Estrada	.25
256	Michael Barrett	.25
257	Bernie Williams	.60
258	Octavio Dotel	.25
259	Jeromy Burnitz	.25
260	Kevin Youkilis	.25
261	Derrek Lee	.40
262	Jack Wilson	.25
263	Craig Wilson	.25
264	Richard Hidalgo	.25
265	Royce Clayton	.25
266	Curt Schilling	.60
267	Joe Mauer	.75
268	Bobby Crosby	.25
269	Zack Greinke	.25
270	Victor Martinez	.25
271	Pedro Feliz	.25
272	Tony Batista	.25
273	Casey Kotchman	.25
274	Freddy Garcia	.25
275	Adam Everett	.25
276	Alexis Rios	.25
277	Lew Ford	.25
278	Adam LaRoche	.25
279	Lyle Overbay	.25
280	Juan Gonzalez	.40
281	A.J. Pierzynski	.25
282	Scott Hairston	.25
283	Danny Bautista	.25
284	Brad Penny	.25
285	Paul Konerko	.25
286	Matt Lawton	.25
287	Carl Pavano	.25
288	Pat Burrell	.40
289	Kenny Rogers	.25
290	Laynce Nix	.25
291	Johnny Damon	.40
292	Paul Wilson	.25
293	Vinny Castilla	.25
294	Aaron Miles	.25
295	Ken Harvey	.25
296	Onil Joseph RC	2.00
297	Kazuhito Tadano RC	3.00
298	Jeff Bennett RC	2.00
299	Chad Bentz RC	2.00
300	Akinori Otsuka RC	3.00
301	Jon Knott RC	2.00
302	Ian Snell RC	2.00
303	Fernando Nieve RC	2.00
304	Mike Rouse	2.00
305	Dennis Sarfate RC	2.00
306	Josh Labandeira RC	3.00
307	Chris Oxspring RC	2.00
308	Alfredo Simon RC	2.00
309	Rusty Tucker RC	2.00
310	Lincoln Holdzkom RC	2.00
311	Justin Leone RC	2.00
312	Jorge Sequea RC	2.00
313	Brian Dallimore RC	2.00
314	Tim Bittner RC	2.00
315	Ronny Cedeno RC	2.00
316	Justin Hampson RC	2.00
317	Ryan Wing RC	2.00
318	Mariano Gomez RC	2.00
319	Carlos Vasquez RC	2.00
320	Casey Daigle RC	2.00
321	Renyel Pinto RC	2.00
322	Chris Shelton RC	4.00
323	Mike Gosling RC	2.00
324	Aaron Baldiris RC	2.00
325	Ramon Ramirez RC	2.00
326	Roberto Novoa RC	2.00
327	Sean Henn RC	2.00
328	Nick Regilio RC	2.00
329	David Crouthers RC	2.00
330	Greg Dobbs RC	2.00
331	Angel Chavez RC	2.00
332	Luis A. Gonzalez RC	2.00
333	Justin Knoedler RC	2.00
334	Jason Frasor RC	2.00
335	Jerry Gil RC	2.00
336	Carlos Hines RC	2.00
337	Ivan Ochoa RC	3.00
338	Jose Capellan RC	3.00
339	Hector Gimenez RC	3.00
340	Shawn Hill RC	3.00
341	Freddy Guzman RC	2.00
342	Scott Proctor RC	2.00
343	Frank Francisco RC	2.00
344	Brandon Medders RC	2.00
345	Andy Green RC	2.00
346	Eddy Rodriguez RC	2.00
347	Tim Hamulack RC	2.00
348	Mike Wuertz RC	2.00
349	Arnie Munoz RC	2.00
350	Enemencio Pacheco RC	2.00
351	Dusty Bergman RC	2.00
352	Charles Thomas RC	5.00
353	William Bergolla RC	2.00
354	Ramon Castro RC	2.00
355	Justin Lehr RC	2.00
356	Lino Urdaneta RC	2.00
357	Donnie Kelly RC	2.00
358	Kevin Cave RC	2.00
359	Franklyn Gracesqui RC	2.00
360	Chris Aguila RC	2.00
361	Jorge Vasquez RC	2.00
362	Andres Blanco RC	2.00
363	Orlando Rodriguez RC	2.00
364	Colby Miller RC	2.00
365	Shawn Camp RC	2.00
366	Jake Woods RC	2.00
367	George Sherrill RC	2.00
368	Justin Huisman RC	2.00
369	Jimmy Serrano RC	3.00
370	Mike Johnston RC	3.00
371	Ryan Meaux RC	3.00
372	Scott Dohmann RC	3.00
373	Brad Halsey RC	5.00
374	Joey Gathright RC	3.00
375	Yadier Molina RC	3.00
376	Travis Blackley RC	2.00
377	Steve Andrade RC	2.00
378	Phil Stockman RC	2.00
379	Roman Colon RC	2.00
380	Jesse Crain RC	2.00
381	Edwardo Sierra RC	2.00
382	Justin Germano RC	2.00
383	Kazuo Matsui RC	30.00
384	Shingo Takatsu RC	20.00
385	John Gall RC	15.00
386	Chris Saenz RC	15.00
387	Merkin Valdez RC	20.00
388	Jamie Brown RC	15.00
389	Jason Bartlett RC	20.00
390	David Aardsma RC	20.00
391	Scott Kazmir	30.00
392	David Wright	40.00
393	Dioner Navarro RC	30.00
394	B.J. Upton	25.00
395	Gavin Floyd	30.00

Gold Medallion

Cards (1-200):	2-3X
Inserted 1:1	
All-Rookies (201-220):	3-4X
Inserted 1:8	
Cards (221-295):	.75-1.5X
Inserted 1:1	
Cards (296-382):	.75-1.25X
Cards (383-395):	.25-.75X
Inserted 1:4	

Platinum Medallion

Cards (1-200):	8-15X
All-Rookies (201-220):	5-10X
Production 66 Sets	
Cards (221-295):	4-8X
Cards (296-382):	2-4X
Production 100 Sets	
Cards (383-395):	No Pricing
Production 13 Sets	

Diamond Producers

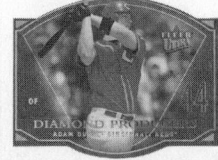

	NM/M
Complete Set (10):	60.00
Common Player:	4.00
Inserted 1:144	
1DP Greg Maddux	8.00
2DP Dontrelle Willis	4.00
3DP Jim Thome	5.00
4DP Alfonso Soriano	6.00
5DP Alex Rodriguez	10.00
6DP Sammy Sosa	10.00
7DP Nomar Garciaparra	10.00
8DP Derek Jeter	15.00
9DP Adam Dunn	4.00
10DP Mark Prior	8.00

Diamond Producers Memorabilia

	NM/M
Production 1,000 Sets	
Dontrelle Willis	15.00
Alfonso Soriano	10.00
Alex Rodriguez	10.00
Sammy Sosa	10.00
Nomar Garciaparra	10.00
Derek Jeter	15.00
Mark Prior	10.00

Diamond Producers UltraSwatch

	NM/M
Numbered to Jersey #.	
Dontrelle Willis/35	25.00

Hitting Machines

	NM/M
Common Player:	3.00
Inserted 1:12	
Die-Cut:	1-2X
1HM Albert Pujols	6.00
2HM Ken Griffey Jr.	4.00
3HM Vladimir Guerrero	3.50
4HM Mike Piazza	4.00
5HM Ichiro Suzuki	5.00
6HM Miguel Cabrera	3.00
7HM Hideki Matsui	6.00
8HM Nomar Garciaparra	6.00
9HM Derek Jeter	8.00
10HM Chipper Jones	4.00

HR Kings

	NM/M
Complete Set (10):	35.00
Inserted 1:96	
Golds:	2-3X
Production 50 Sets	
1HK Barry Bonds	8.00
2HK Albert Pujols	6.00
3HK Jason Giambi	3.00
4HK Jeff Bagwell	2.00
5HK Ken Griffey Jr.	4.00
6HK Alex Rodriguez	6.00
7HK Sammy Sosa	5.00
8HK Alfonso Soriano	3.00
9HK Chipper Jones	4.00
10HK Mike Piazza	4.00

Legendary 13 Memorabilia

	NM/M
Numbered to 13 each.	

Each player's jersey swatch on each card
Masterpiece 1/1 auto. by named player.
Inserted 1:192 Series 2 Hobby players on each card.

Legendary 13 Memorabilia Autographs

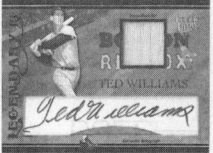

	NM/M
Numbered to five each.	
Masterpiece:	1/1

Numbered with "L13A-" prefix
Limited pricing due to scarcity.

TW Ted Williams	900.00

Legendary 13 Dual Memorabilia Autographs

Numbered to three each.
Masterpiece 1/1
No pricing due to scarcity.

Performers

	NM/M
Complete Set (15):	12.00
Common Player:	.50
Inserted 1:6	
1UP Ichiro Suzuki	1.50
2UP Albert Pujols	2.00
3UP Barry Bonds	3.00
4UP Hideki Matsui	2.00
5UP Randy Johnson	1.00
6UP Jason Giambi	1.00
7UP Pedro J. Martinez	1.00
8UP Hank Blalock	.50
9UP Chipper Jones	1.50
10UP Mike Piazza	1.50
11UP Derek Jeter	3.00
12UP Vladimir Guerrero	1.00
13UP Barry Zito	.75
14UP Rocco Baldelli	.50
15UP Hideo Nomo	.75

Performers Memorabilia

	NM/M
Common Player:	6.00
Production 500 Sets	
Albert Pujols	15.00
Barry Bonds/Base	15.00
Randy Johnson	8.00
Jason Giambi	8.00
Pedro J. Martinez	10.00
Hank Blalock	6.00
Chipper Jones	10.00
Mike Piazza	15.00
Derek Jeter	15.00
Vladimir Guerrero	8.00
Rocco Baldelli	10.00
Hideo Nomo	15.00

Performers UltraSwatch

	NM/M
Numbered to Jersey #.	
Randy Johnson/51	15.00
Pedro Martinez/45	20.00
Mike Piazza/31	25.00
Vladimir Guerrero/27	20.00

RBI Kings

	NM/M
Complete Set (10):	15.00

Inserted 1:32
Golds: 3-4X
Production 50 Sets

1RK	Hideki Matsui	4.00
2RK	Albert Pujols	4.00
3RK	Todd Helton	1.50
4RK	Jim Thome	1.50
5RK	Carlos Delgado	1.50
6RK	Alex Rodriguez	4.00
7RK	Barry Bonds	5.00
8RK	Manny Ramirez	1.50
9RK	Vladimir Guerrero	1.50
10RK	Nomar Garciaparra	4.00

Season Crowns Memorabilia

AUTHENTIC GAME-WORN JERSEY

NM/M
Common Player: 4.00
Production 399 Sets
Golds: 1-2X
Production 99 Sets
Platinums: No Pricing
Production 25 Sets

Adam Dunn	6.00
Carlos Pena	4.00
Torii Hunter	8.00
Gary Sheffield	8.00
Sean Casey	4.00
Lance Berkman	4.00
Tom Glavine	6.00
Sean Burroughs	4.00
Shawn Green	6.00
Jason Kendall	4.00
Vladimir Guerrero	10.00
Todd Helton	8.00
Tim Hudson	8.00
Troy Glaus	6.00
Larry Walker	4.00
Carlos Beltran	6.00
Hideo Nomo	10.00
Kazuhiro Sasaki	4.00
Mike Piazza	10.00
Scott Rolen	8.00
Carlos Delgado	6.00
Andruw Jones	8.00
Alfonso Soriano	10.00
Angel Berroa	4.00
Brandon Webb	6.00
Jason Giambi	8.00
Pedro J. Martinez	10.00
Manny Ramirez	8.00
Alex Rodriguez	10.00
Derek Jeter	15.00
Mark Mulder	6.00
Greg Maddux	10.00
Sammy Sosa	15.00
Jim Thome	10.00
Hank Blalock	6.00
Roberto Alomar	8.00
Omar Vizquel	5.00
Austin Kearns	8.00
Jeff Bagwell	8.00
Frank Thomas	8.00
Randy Johnson	8.00
Rocco Baldelli	12.00
Albert Pujols	15.00
Jose Reyes	8.00
Dontrelle Willis	12.00
Hideki Matsui/Base	20.00
Barry Bonds/Base	15.00
Ichiro Suzuki/Base	15.00
Chipper Jones	10.00
Roger Clemens	15.00

Season Crowns Autograph

NM/M
Common Player: 15.00
Production 150 Sets
Golds: No Pricing
Production 25 Sets

Rocco Baldelli	35.00
Hank Blalock	15.00
Bo Hart	30.00
Aubrey Huff	15.00
Chipper Jones	60.00
Austin Kearns	15.00
Mike Lowell	15.00
Corey Patterson	20.00
Carlos Pena	15.00
Jose Reyes	30.00
Scott Rolen	20.00
Miguel Tejada	25.00

Brandon Webb	15.00
Rickie Weeks	30.00
Dontrelle Willis	35.00

Strikeout Kings

NM/M
Complete Set (10): 10.00
Common Player: .75
Inserted 1:24
Golds: 3-5X
Production 50 Sets

1KK	Randy Johnson	1.50
2KK	Pedro J. Martinez	1.50
3KK	Curt Schilling	1.00
4KK	Roger Clemens	3.00
5KK	Mike Mussina	1.00
6KK	Roy Halladay	.75
7KK	Kerry Wood	1.00
8KK	Dontrelle Willis	1.00
9KK	Greg Maddux	2.00
10KK	Mark Prior	2.00

Turn Back the Clock

NM/M
Common Player: 1.50
Inserted 1:6

1	Roger Clemens	5.00
2	Alex Rodriguez	5.00
3	Randy Johnson	2.00
4	Pedro Martinez	2.00
5	Alfonso Soriano	2.00
6	Curt Schilling	1.50
7	Miguel Tejada	1.50
8	Scott Rolen	1.50
9	Jim Thome	2.00
10	Manny Ramirez	1.50
11	Vladimir Guerrero	2.00
12	Tom Glavine	1.50
13	Andy Pettitte	1.50
14	Ivan Rodriguez	1.50
15	Jason Giambi	2.00
16	Rafael Palmeiro	2.00
17	Greg Maddux	3.00
18	Hideo Nomo	1.50
19	Mike Mussina	1.50
20	Sammy Sosa	4.00

Turn Back the Clock Game-Used Copper

NM/M
Common Player: 8.00
Production 399 Sets
Silver: .75-1.5X
Production 199 Sets
Gold: 1-2X
Production 99 Sets
Platinum Patch: 2-5X
Production 29 Sets

RC	Roger Clemens	12.00
JG	Jason Giambi	10.00
TG	Tom Glavine	8.00
VG	Vladimir Guerrero	10.00
RJ	Randy Johnson	10.00
GM	Greg Maddux	12.00
PR	Pedro Martinez	10.00
MM	Mike Mussina	8.00
HM	Hideo Nomo	8.00
RP	Rafael Palmeiro	10.00
AP	Andy Pettitte	8.00
MR	Manny Ramirez	10.00
IR	Ivan Rodriguez	8.00
SR	Scott Rolen	10.00
CS	Curt Schilling	8.00
AS	Alfonso Soriano	8.00
SS	Sammy Sosa	12.00
MT	Miguel Tejada	8.00
JT	Jim Thome	10.00

3 Kings

NM/M
Production 33 Sets

Mike Piazza, Roger Clemens, Alex Rodriguez	70.00
Albert Pujols, Mark Prior, Todd Helton	50.00
Alfonso Soriano, Dontrelle Willis, Albert Pujols	60.00
P. Martinez, Sammy Sosa, Albert Pujols	70.00
Randy Johnson, Albert Pujols, Todd Helton	50.00
Dontrelle Willis, Chipper Jones, Albert Pujols	60.00
Dontrelle Willis, Jeff Bagwell, Jim Thome	40.00
Greg Maddux, Jason Giambi, Manny Ramirez	50.00

2005 Ultra

NM/M
Common Player (1-200): .15
Minor Stars (1-200): .25
Unlisted Stars (1-200): .50
Common Player (201-220): 2.00
Minor Stars (201-220): 3.00
Inserted 1:4
Pack (8): 3.50
Box (24): 75.00

1	Andy Pettitte	.40
2	Jose Cruz	.15
3	Cliff Floyd	.25
4	Paul Konerko	.15
5	Joe Mauer	.75
6	Scott Spiezio	.15
7	Ben Sheets	.25
8	Kerry Wood	.50
9	Carl Pavano	.15
10	Matt Morris	.15
11	Kazuo Matsui	.75
12	Ivan Rodriguez	.40
13	Victor Martinez	.15
14	Justin Morneau	.25
15	Adam Everett	.15
16	Carl Crawford	.25
17	David Ortiz	.25
18	Jason Giambi	.75
19	Derrek Lee	.25
20	Magglio Ordonez	.25
21	Bobby Abreu	.25
22	Milton Bradley	.15
23	Jeff Bagwell	.25
24	Jim Edmonds	.25
25	Garret Anderson	.25
26	Jacque Jones	.15
27	Ted Lilly	.15
28	Greg Maddux	1.00
29	Jermaine Dye	.15
30	Bill Mueller	.15
31	Roy Oswalt	.15
32	Tony Womack	.15
33	Andruw Jones	.50
34	Tom Glavine	.25
35	Mariano Rivera	.50
36	Sean Casey	.15
37	Edgardo Alfonzo	.15
38	Brad Penny	.15
39	Johan Santana	.25
40	Mark Teixeira	.25
41	Manny Ramirez	.50
42	Gary Sheffield	.40
43	Matt Lawton	.15
44	Troy Percival	.15
45	Rocco Baldelli	.40
46	Doug Mientkiewicz	.15
47	Corey Patterson	.15
48	Austin Kearns	.15
49	Edgar Martinez	.25
50	Brad Radke	.15
51	Barry Larkin	.25
52	Chone Figgins	.15
53	Alexis Rios	.15
54	Alex Rodriguez	1.50
55	Vinny Castilla	.15
56	Javier Vazquez	.15
57	Javy Lopez	.25
58	Mike Cameron	.15
59	Brian Giles	.25
60	Dontrelle Willis	.25
61	Rafael Furcal	.15
62	Trot Nixon	.15
63	Mark Mulder	.25
64	Josh Beckett	.50
65	J.D. Drew	.25
66	Brandon Webb	.15
67	Wade Miller	.15
68	Lyle Overbay	.15
69	Pedro J. Martinez	.75
70	Rich Harden	.15
71	Al Leiter	.15
72	Adam Eaton	.15
73	Mike Sweeney	.15
74	Steve Finley	.15
75	Kris Benson	.15
76	Jim Thome	.75
77	Juan Pierre	.15
78	Bartolo Colon	.25
79	Carlos Delgado	.50
80	Jack Wilson	.15
81	Ken Harvey	.15
82	Nomar Garciaparra	1.50
83	Paul LoDuca	.15
84	Cesar Izturis	.15
85	Adrian Beltre	.25
86	Brian Roberts	.15
87	David Eckstein	.15
88	Jimmy Rollins	.15
89	Roger Clemens	1.00
90	Randy Johnson	.75
91	Orlando Hudson	.15
92	Tim Hudson	.25
93	Dmitri Young	.15
94	Chipper Jones	1.00
95	John Smoltz	.25
96	Billy Wagner	.15
97	Hideo Nomo	.15
98	Sammy Sosa	1.25
99	Darin Erstad	.25
100	Todd Helton	.50
101	Aubrey Huff	.15
102	Alfonso Soriano	.75
103	Jose Vidro	.15
104	Carlos Lee	.15
105	Corey Koskie	.15
106	Bret Boone	.25
107	Torii Hunter	.40
108	Aramis Ramirez	.15
109	Chase Utley	.15
110	Reggie Sanders	.15
111	Livan Hernandez	.15
112	Jeromy Burnitz	.15
113	Carlos Zambrano	.15
114	Hank Blalock	.40
115	Sidney Ponson	.15
116	Zack Greinke	.15
117	Trevor Hoffman	.15
118	Jeff Kent	.25
119	Richie Sexson	.40
120	Melvin Mora	.15
121	Eric Chavez	.25
122	Miguel Cabrera	.50
123	Ryan Freel	.15
124	Russ Ortiz	.15
125	Craig Wilson	.15
126	Craig Biggio	.25
127	Curt Schilling	.40
128	Kazuhisa Ishii	.15
129	Marquis Grissom	.15
130	Bernie Williams	.40
131	Travis Hafner	.15
132	Hee Seop Choi	.15
133	Scott Rolen	.15
134	Tony Batista	.15
135	Frank Thomas	.75
136	Jason Varitek	.50
137	Ichiro Suzuki	1.25
138	Junior Spivey	.15
139	Adam Dunn	.40
140	Jorge Posada	.40
141	Edgar Renteria	.15
142	Hideki Matsui	1.50
143	Carlos Guillen	.15
144	Jody Gerut	.15
145	Wily Mo Pena	.15
146	Derek Jeter	2.00
147	C.C. Sabathia	.15
148	Geoff Jenkins	.25
149	Albert Pujols	1.50
150	Eric Munson	.15
151	Moises Alou	.25
152	Jerry Hairston	.15
153	Ray Durham	.15
154	Mike Piazza	1.00
155	Omar Vizquel	.25
156	A.J. Pierzynski	.15
157	Michael Young	.15
158	Jason Bay	.25
159	Mark Loretta	.15
160	Shawn Green	.25
161	Luis Gonzalez	.25
162	Johnny Damon	.25
163	Eric Milton	.15
164	Mike Lowell	.15
165	Jose Guillen	.15
166	Eric Hinske	.15
167	Jason Kendall	.25
168	Carlos Beltran	.40
169	Johnny Estrada	.15
170	Scott Hatteberg	.15
171	Laynce Nix	.15
172	Eric Gagne	.25
173	Richard Hidalgo	.15
174	Bobby Crosby	.15

175	Woody Williams	.15
176	Justin Leone	.15
177	Orlando Cabrera	.15
178	Mark Prior	1.50
179	Jorge Julio	.15
180	Jamie Moyer	.15
181	Jose Reyes	.40
182	Ken Griffey Jr.	1.00
183	Mike Lieberthal	.15
184	Kenny Rogers	.15
185	Mike Mussina	.40
186	Preston Wilson	.15
187	Khalil Greene	.50
188	Angel Berroa	.15
189	Miguel Tejada	.40
190	Freddy Garcia	.15
191	Pat Burrell	.25
192	Luis Castillo	.15
193	Vladimir Guerrero	.75
194	Roy Halladay	.25
195	Barry Zito	.40
196	Lance Berkman	.25
197	Rafael Palmeiro	.50
198	Nate Robertson	.15
199	Jason Schmidt	.25
200	Scott Podsednik	.15
201	Casey Kotchman	3.00
202	Scott Kazmir	4.00
203	Bucky Jacobsen	4.00
204	Jeff Keppinger	2.00
205	David Bush	2.00
206	Gavin Floyd	5.00
207	David Wright	3.00
208	B.J. Upton	3.00
209	David Aardsma	2.00
210	Jason Bartlett	3.00
211	Dioner Navarro	2.00
212	Jason Kubel	3.00
213	Ryan Howard	2.00
214	Charles Thomas RC	2.00
215	Freddy Guzman	3.00
216	Brad Halsey	3.00
217	Joey Gathright	2.00
218	Jeff Francis	2.00
219	Terry Tiffee	2.00
220	Nick Swisher	5.00

Gold

Cards 1-200: 1-3X
Inserted 1:1
Cards 201-220: .5-1X
Inserted 1:8

Platinum
Cards 1-200: 5-8X
Cards 201-220: 3-5X
Production 50 Sets

Follow the Leader

	NM/M
Common Player:	1.50
Inserted 1:6	
Copper Game-Used:	3-5X
Inserted 1:72 (Hobby Only)	
Red Game-Used:	2-4X
Inserted 1:48 (Retail Only)	
Gold Game-Used:	4-6X
Production 250 Sets	
Platinum Game-Used:	5-8X
Production 99 Sets	
Ultra Game-Used:	
Numbered 26-51:	5-10X
Numbered 25 or less:	No Pricing
Production to player's jersey number.	
1 Roger Clemens	3.00
2 Albert Pujols	3.00
3 Sammy Sosa	2.50
4 Manny Ramirez	1.50
5 Vladimir Guerrero	2.00

6	Ivan Rodriguez	1.50
7	Mike Piazza	2.00
8	Scott Rolen	2.00
9	Ichiro Suzuki	2.50
10	Randy Johnson	2.00
11	Mark Prior	2.00
12	Jim Thome	2.00
13	Greg Maddux	2.00
14	Pedro J. Martinez	2.00
15	Miguel Cabrera	1.50

HR Kings

	NM/M
Common Player:	2.50
Inserted 1:96	
Ultra Kings Gold:	1-3X
Production 50 Sets	
1 Jim Thome	4.00
2 David Ortiz	3.00
3 Adam Dunn	3.00
4 Albert Pujols	8.00
5 Manny Ramirez	3.50
6 Vladimir Guerrero	4.00
7 Miguel Tejada	3.00
8 Rafael Palmeiro	3.50
9 Mark Teixeira	2.50
10 Sammy Sosa	6.00
11 Frank Thomas	3.50
12 Pat Burrell	2.50
13 Adrian Beltre	2.50
14 Miguel Cabrera	3.50
15 Gary Sheffield	3.00

RBI Kings

	NM/M
Common Player:	2.50
Inserted 1:32	
Ultra Kings Gold:	2-4X
Production 50 Sets	
1 Sean Casey	2.50
2 Ivan Rodriguez	2.50
3 Mike Piazza	4.00
4 Todd Helton	3.00
5 Scott Rolen	3.50
6 Hideki Matsui	6.00
7 Gary Sheffield	2.50
8 Alfonso Soriano	3.50
9 Bobby Abreu	2.50
10 Lance Berkman	2.50
11 Miguel Tejada	2.50
12 Travis Hafner	2.50
13 Hank Blalock	2.50
14 Jeff Bagwell	3.00
15 Chipper Jones	4.00

**Season Crowns Copper
Game-Used**

	NM/M
Common Player:	5.00
Production 399 Sets	
Gold:	.75-1.5X
Production 99 Sets	
Platinum:	No Pricing
Production 25 Sets	
1 Andy Pettitte/Jsy	8.00
3 Cliff Floyd/Jsy	5.00
7 Ben Sheets/Jsy	5.00
8 Kerry Wood/Jsy	8.00
11 Kazuo Matsui/Bat	15.00
13 Victor Martinez/Jsy	5.00
17 David Carr/Jsy	8.00
20 Magglio Ordonez/Bat	5.00
21 Bobby Abreu/Bat	5.00
24 Jim Edmonds/Jsy	5.00
31 Roy Oswalt/Jsy	5.00
33 Andruw Jones/Jsy	8.00
34 Tom Glavine/Bat	5.00
36 Sean Casey/Jsy	5.00
37 Edgardo Alfonzo/Bat	5.00
41 Manny Ramirez/Bat	8.00
42 Gary Sheffield/Bat	8.00
45 Rocco Baldelli/Jsy	5.00
48 Austin Kearns/Jsy	5.00
49 Edgar Martinez/Jsy	5.00
60 Dontrelle Willis/Jsy	5.00
65 J.D. Drew/Jsy	5.00
70 Rich Harden/Jsy	5.00
71 Al Leiter/Jsy	5.00
80 Jack Wilson/Bat	5.00

93	Dmitri Young/Bat	5.00
94	Chipper Jones/Bat	10.00
97	Hideo Nomo/Jsy	8.00
98	Sammy Sosa/Bat	12.00
100	Todd Helton/Bat	8.00
102	Alfonso Soriano/Bat	8.00
107	Torii Hunter/Jsy	8.00
114	Hank Blalock/Bat	8.00
119	Richie Sexson/Jsy	8.00
121	Eric Chavez/Jsy	5.00
130	Bernie Williams/Bat	8.00
135	Frank Thomas/Bat	8.00
139	Adam Dunn/Bat	8.00
142	Hideki Matsui/Bat	15.00
144	Jody Gerut/Bat	8.00
154	Mike Piazza/Bat	10.00
158	Jason Bay/Bat	8.00
162	Johnny Damon/Jsy	10.00
168	Carlos Beltran/Bat	8.00
173	Richard Hidalgo/Jsy	5.00
181	Jose Reyes/Bat	8.00
187	Khalil Greene/Jsy	15.00
191	Pat Burrell/Bat	8.00
193	Vladimir Guerrero/Bat	8.00
197	Rafael Palmeiro/Jsy	8.00

**Season Crown Autographs
Copper**

	NM/M
Common Player:	20.00
Stated Production 199 Sets	
All 199 cards not released for some players.	
31 Roy Oswalt/50	25.00
80 Jack Wilson/199	20.00
125 Craig Wilson/130	20.00
157 Michael Young/150	20.00

**Season Crown Autographs
Gold**

	NM/M
Common Player:	20.00
Stated Production 99 Sets	
All 99 cards not released for some players.	
21 Roy Oswalt/99	20.00
50 Brad Radke/89	20.00
51 Barry Larkin/99	20.00
62 Trot Nixon/37	25.00
70 Rich Harden/41	25.00
80 Jack Wilson/99	20.00
88 Jimmy Rollins/45	25.00
121 Eric Chavez/69	20.00
125 Craig Wilson/99	20.00
157 Michael Young/99	20.00
200 Scott Podsednik/99	20.00

**Season Crown Autographs
Platinum**

	NM/M
Common Player:	25.00
Stated Production 50 Sets	
All 50 cards not released	
for some players.	
Masterpiece:	No Pricing
Production One Set	
20 Magglio Ordonez/50	25.00
25 Garret Anderson/50	25.00
31 Roy Oswalt/50	25.00
40 Mark Teixeira/50	30.00
50 Brad Radke/50	25.00
51 Barry Larkin/50	30.00
62 Trot Nixon/50	25.00
70 Rich Harden/50	25.00
87 David Eckstein/45	25.00
88 Jimmy Rollins/50	25.00
96 Billy Wagner/50	30.00
116 Zack Greinke/49	25.00
121 Eric Chavez/50	25.00
125 Craig Wilson/50	25.00
157 Michael Young/50	25.00
161 Luis Gonzalez/50	25.00
185 Mike Mussina/50	30.00
195 Barry Zito/50	25.00
199 Jason Schmidt/50	25.00
200 Scott Podsednik/50	25.00
201 Casey Kotchman/50	25.00

Strikeout Kings

	NM/M
Common Player:	2.50
Inserted 1:24	
Ultra Kings Gold:	2-4X
Production 50 Sets	
1 Pedro J. Martinez	3.50
2 Randy Johnson	3.50
3 Mark Mulder	2.50
4 Barry Zito	2.50
5 Roger Clemens	6.00
6 Mark Prior	5.00
7 Ben Sheets	2.50

8	Curt Schilling	2.50
9	Billy Wagner	2.50
10	Eric Gagne	2.50
11	Josh Beckett	3.00
12	Kerry Wood	3.00
13	Jason Schmidt	2.50
14	Roy Halladay	2.50
15	Greg Maddux	4.00

Ultra Kings Game-Used Gold

	NM/M
Common Player:	8.00
Production 150 Sets	
Ultra Swatch	
Numbered 51-75:	.75-1.5X
Numbered 26-50:	1-2X
Numbered 25 or less:	No Pricing
Production to player's jersey number.	
Platinum:	No Pricing
Production 25 Sets	
1 Pedro J. Martinez	12.00
2 Randy Johnson	12.00
3 Mark Mulder	8.00
4 Barry Zito	8.00
5 Roger Clemens	25.00
6 Mark Prior	20.00
7 Ben Sheets	8.00
8 Curt Schilling	8.00
9 Billy Wagner	8.00
10 Eric Gagne	8.00
11 Josh Beckett	10.00
12 Kerry Wood	10.00
13 Jason Schmidt	8.00
14 Roy Halladay	8.00
15 Greg Maddux	15.00
16 Sean Casey	8.00
17 Ivan Rodriguez	8.00
18 Mike Piazza	15.00
19 Todd Helton	10.00
20 Scott Rolen	12.00
21 Hideki Matsui	30.00
22 Gary Sheffield	8.00
23 Alfonso Soriano	12.00
24 Bobby Abreu	8.00
25 Lance Berkman	8.00
26 Miguel Tejada	8.00
27 Travis Hafner	8.00
28 Hank Blalock	8.00
29 Jeff Bagwell	10.00
30 Chipper Jones	15.00
31 Jim Thome	12.00
32 David Ortiz	8.00
33 Adam Dunn	8.00
34 Albert Pujols	25.00
35 Manny Ramirez	10.00
36 Vladimir Guerrero	12.00
37 Miguel Tejada	8.00
38 Rafael Palmeiro	10.00
39 Mark Teixeira	8.00
40 Sammy Sosa	20.00
41 Frank Thomas	10.00
42 Pat Burrell	8.00
43 Adrian Beltre	8.00
44 Miguel Cabrera	10.00
45 Gary Sheffield	8.00

Ultra 3 Kings Triple Swatch

	NM/M
Common Card:	40.00
Production 33 Sets	
1 Greg Maddux, Mark Prior, Kerry Wood	75.00
2 Mark Teixeira, Hank Blalock, Alfonso Soriano	40.00
3 Jeff Bagwell, Roger Clemens, Lance Berkman	60.00
4 Jim Thome, Pat Burrell, Billy Wagner	40.00
5 Gary Sheffield, Hideki Matsui, Mike Piazza	75.00
6 Scott Rolen, Chipper Jones, Adrian Beltre	40.00
7 Albert Pujols, Adam Dunn, Miguel Cabrera	50.00
8 Curt Schilling, Pedro J. Martinez, Manny Ramirez	60.00
9 Randy Johnson, Greg Maddux, Pedro J. Martinez	50.00
10 Josh Beckett, Miguel Cabrera, Ivan Rodriguez	40.00

2006 Ultra

	NM/M
Complete Set (251):	60.00
Common Player:	.15
Common SP (201-250):	.50
Inserted 1:4	
Production 5,000 for #251	
Pack (8):	2.50
Box (24):	50.00
1 Vladimir Guerrero	.75

No.	Player	Price
2	Bartolo Colon	.15
3	Francisco Rodriguez	.15
4	Darin Erstad	.15
5	Chone Figgins	.25
6	Bengie Molina	.15
7	Roger Clemens	2.00
8	Lance Berkman	.50
9	Morgan Ensberg	.15
10	Roy Oswalt	.25
11	Andy Pettitte	.25
12	Craig Biggio	.25
13	Eric Chavez	.25
14	Barry Zito	.25
15	Huston Street	.15
16	Bobby Crosby	.15
17	Nick Swisher	.25
18	Rich Harden	.15
19	Vernon Wells	.25
20	Roy Halladay	.25
21	Alex Rios	.25
22	Orlando Hudson	.15
23	Shea Hillenbrand	.15
24	Gustavo Chacin	.15
25	Chipper Jones	.75
26	Andruw Jones	.50
27	Jeff Francoeur	.50
28	John Smoltz	.25
29	Tim Hudson	.25
30	Marcus Giles	.15
31	Carlos Lee	.25
32	Ben Sheets	.25
33	Rickie Weeks	.25
34	Chris Capuano	.15
35	Geoff Jenkins	.15
36	Brady Clark	.15
37	Albert Pujols	2.00
38	Jim Edmonds	.25
39	Chris Carpenter	.25
40	Mark Mulder	.25
41	Yadier Molina	.15
42	Scott Rolen	.75
43	Derrek Lee	.50
44	Mark Prior	.25
45	Aramis Ramirez	.40
46	Carlos Zambrano	.25
47	Greg Maddux	1.50
48	Nomar Garciaparra	.50
49	Jonny Gomes	.25
50	Carl Crawford	.25
51	Scott Kazmir	.25
52	Jorge Cantu	.15
53	Julio Lugo	.15
54	Aubrey Huff	.15
55	Luis Gonzalez	.15
56	Brandon Webb	.50
57	Troy Glaus	.25
58	Shawn Green	.25
59	Craig Counsell	.15
60	Conor Jackson (RC)	.25
61	Jeff Kent	.25
62	Eric Gagne	.15
63	J.D. Drew	.25
64	Milton Bradley	.15
65	Jeff Weaver	.15
66	Cesar Izturis	.15
67	Jason Schmidt	.25
68	Moises Alou	.15
69	Pedro Feliz	.15
70	Randy Winn	.15
71	Omar Vizquel	.15
72	Noah Lowry	.15
73	Travis Hafner	.40
74	Victor Martinez	.25
75	C.C. Sabathia	.40
76	Grady Sizemore	.40
77	Coco Crisp	.15
78	Cliff Lee	.25
79	Raul Ibanez	.15
80	Ichiro Suzuki	1.00
81	Richie Sexson	.25
82	Felix Hernandez	.25
83	Adrian Beltre	.25
84	Jamie Moyer	.15
85	Miguel Cabrera	.75
86	A.J. Burnett	.25
87	Juan Pierre	.15
88	Carlos Delgado	.50
89	Dontrelle Willis	.25
90	Juan Encarnacion	.15
91	Carlos Beltran	.50
92	Jose Reyes	.75
93	David Wright	.75
94	Tom Glavine	.25
95	Mike Piazza	.75
96	Pedro Martinez	.75
97	Ryan Zimmerman (RC)	2.00
98	Nick Johnson	.15
99	Jose Vidro	.15
100	Jose Guillen	.15
101	Livan Hernandez	.15
102	John Patterson	.15
103	Miguel Tejada	.25
104	Melvin Mora	.15
105	Brian Roberts	.25
106	Erik Bedard	.25
107	Javy Lopez	.15
108	Rodrigo Lopez	.15
109	Jake Peavy	.50
110	Mike Cameron	.15
111	Mark Loretta	.15
112	Brian Giles	.25
113	Trevor Hoffman	.15
114	Ramon Hernandez	.15
115	Bobby Abreu	.25
116	Chase Utley	.75
117	Pat Burrell	.25
118	Jimmy Rollins	.25
119	Ryan Howard	.75
120	Billy Wagner	.15
121	Jason Bay	.40
122	Oliver Perez	.15
123	Jack Wilson	.15
124	Zach Duke	.15
125	Robert Mackowiak	.15
126	Freddy Sanchez	.15
127	Mark Teixeira	.50
128	Michael Young	.25
129	Alfonso Soriano	.50
130	Hank Blalock	.25
131	Kenny Rogers	.15
132	Kevin Mench	.15
133	Manny Ramirez	.75
134	Josh Beckett	.50
135	David Ortiz	.75
136	Johnny Damon	.75
137	Edgar Renteria	.25
138	Curt Schilling	.25
139	Ken Griffey Jr.	1.50
140	Adam Dunn	.25
141	Felipe Lopez	.15
142	Wily Mo Pena	.15
143	Aaron Harang	.15
144	Sean Casey	.15
145	Todd Helton	.50
146	Garrett Atkins	.25
147	Matt Holliday	.40
148	Jeff Francis	.15
149	Clint Barmes	.15
150	Luis Gonzalez	.15
151	Mike Sweeney	.15
152	Zack Greinke	.25
153	Angel Berroa	.15
154	Emil Brown	.15
155	David DeJesus	.15
156	Ivan Rodriguez	.50
157	Jeremy Bonderman	.15
158	Brandon Inge	.15
159	Craig Monroe	.15
160	Chris Shelton	.15
161	Dmitri Young	.15
162	Johan Santana	.75
163	Joe Mauer	.25
164	Torii Hunter	.25
165	Shannon Stewart	.15
166	Scott Baker	.15
167	Brad Radke	.15
168	Jon Garland	.15
169	Tadahito Iguchi	.15
170	Paul Konerko	.25
171	Scott Podsednik	.15
172	Mark Buehrle	.15
173	Joe Crede	.15
174	Derek Jeter	2.00
175	Alex Rodriguez	1.50
176	Hideki Matsui	1.00
177	Randy Johnson	.75
178	Gary Sheffield	.40
179	Mariano Rivera	.40
180	Jason Giambi	.25
181	Joey Devine RC	.50
182	Alejandro Freire RC	.75
183	Craig Hansen RC	2.00
184	Robert Andino RC	.50
185	Ryan Jorgensen RC	.50
186	Chris Demaria RC	.50
187	Jonah Bayliss RC	.50
188	Ryan Theriot (RC)	.75
189	Steve Stemle RC	.50
190	Brian Myrow RC	.50
191	Chris Heintz RC	.50
192	Ron Flores RC	.50
193	Danny Sandoval RC	.50
194	Craig Breslow RC	1.00
195	Jeremy Accardo RC	.50
196	Jeff Harris RC	.50
197	Tim Corcoran RC	.50
198	Scott Feldman RC	1.00
199	Robinson Cano	.50
200	Jason Bergmann RC	2.00
201	Ken Griffey Jr.	4.00
202	Frank Thomas	1.00
203	Chipper Jones	2.00
204	Tony Clark	.50
205	Mike Lieberthal	.50
206	Manny Ramirez	2.00
207	Phil Nevin	.50
208	Derek Jeter	6.00
209	Preston Wilson	.50
210	Billy Wagner	.50
211	Alex Rodriguez	6.00
212	Trot Nixon	.50
213	Jaret Wright	.50
214	Nomar Garciaparra	1.50
215	Paul Konerko	1.00
216	Paul Wilson	.50
217	Dustin Hermanson	.50
218	Todd Walker	.50
219	Matt Morris	.50
220	Darin Erstad	.50
221	Todd Helton	1.50
222	Geoff Jenkins	.50
223	Eric Chavez	.50
224	Kris Benson	.50
225	Jon Garland	.50
226	Troy Glaus	1.00
227	Vernon Wells	1.00
228	Michael Cuddyer	.50
229	Justin Verlander (RC)	2.00
230	Pat Burrell	2.00
231	Mark Mulder	1.00
232	Corey Patterson	1.00
233	J.D. Drew	1.00
234	Austin Kearns	1.00
235	Felipe Lopez	.50
236	Sean Burroughs	.50
237	Ben Sheets	1.00
238	Brett Myers	.50
239	Josh Beckett	1.50
240	Barry Zito	.75
241	Adrian Gonzalez	1.00
242	Rocco Baldelli	.50
243	Chris Burke	.50
244	Joe Mauer	1.50
245	Mark Prior	1.00
246	Mark Teixeira	2.00
247	Khalil Greene	.50
248	Zack Greinke	.50
249	Prince Fielder (RC)	6.00
250	Rickie Weeks	1.00
251	Kenji Johjima RC	10.00

Gold

Gold (1-200):	2-3X
Inserted 1:1	
Gold (201-251):	2-3X
Inserted 1:13	

AUTOGRAPHics

Inserted 1:576 Hobby
No Pricing

Diamond Producers

		NM/M
Complete Set (25):		15.00
Common Player:		.50
DP1	Derek Jeter	3.00
DP2	Chipper Jones	1.00
DP3	Jim Edmonds	.75
DP4	Ken Griffey Jr.	2.00
DP5	David Ortiz	1.00
DP6	Manny Ramirez	1.00
DP7	Mark Teixeira	.75
DP8	Alex Rodriguez	3.00
DP9	Jeff Kent	.50
DP10	Albert Pujols	3.00
DP11	Todd Helton	.75
DP12	Miguel Cabrera	1.00
DP13	Hideki Matsui	2.00
DP14	Derek Lee	.75
DP15	Vladimir Guerrero	1.00
DP16	Miguel Tejada	.75
DP17	Jorge Cantu	.50
DP18	Travis Hafner	.75
DP19	Pat Burrell	.50
DP20	Bobby Abreu	.50
DP21	David Wright	2.00
DP22	Jason Bay	.50
DP23	Adam Dunn	.75
DP24	Eric Chavez	.50
DP25	Paul Konerko	.50

Feel the Game

		NM/M
Common Player:		4.00
BA	Bobby Abreu	4.00
JB	Josh Beckett	6.00
CB	Carlos Beltran	8.00
AB	Adrian Beltre	4.00
EC	Eric Chavez	4.00
MC	Matt Clement/SP	6.00
CD	Carlos Delgado	4.00
BG	Brian Giles	4.00
TG	Troy Glaus	6.00
SG	Shawn Green	4.00
KG	Ken Griffey Jr.	20.00
VG	Vladimir Guerrero	8.00
FH	Felix Hernandez	6.00
DJ	Derek Jeter	20.00
RJ	Randy Johnson/SP	10.00

Feel the Game
TROY GLAUS

AJ	Andruw Jones	8.00
CJ	Chipper Jones	8.00
GM	Greg Maddux	10.00
MO	Magglio Ordonez	4.00
MP	Mike Piazza	10.00
AP	Albert Pujols	20.00
MR	Manny Ramirez	10.00
JR	Jose Reyes/SP	8.00
IR	Ivan Rodriguez	6.00
RS	Richie Sexson	4.00
AS	Alfonso Soriano	8.00
MT	Miguel Tejada	8.00
FT	Frank Thomas/SP	8.00
PW	Preston Wilson	4.00
DW	David Wright	15.00

Fine Fabrics

		NM/M
BA	Bobby Abreu	6.00
JB	Josh Beckett	6.00
CB	Carlos Beltran	8.00
AB	Adrian Beltre	6.00
HB	Hank Blalock	6.00
SB	Sean Burroughs	4.00
EC	Eric Chavez	4.00
RC	Roger Clemens SP	15.00
MC	Matt Clement	4.00
BC	Bobby Crosby	4.00
CD	Carlos Delgado	6.00
JD	J.D. Drew	4.00
AD	Adam Dunn	8.00
SF	Steve Finley	4.00
JG	Jason Giambi	10.00
BG	Brian Giles	4.00
TG	Troy Glaus	6.00
SG	Shawn Green	4.00
KH	Khalil Greene SP	8.00
KG	Ken Griffey Jr.	20.00
VG	Vladimir Guerrero	8.00
TH	Travis Hafner	8.00
FH	Felix Hernandez	8.00
RH	Ramon Hernandez	4.00
RY	Ryan Howard	15.00
DJ	Derek Jeter	20.00
RJ	Randy Johnson SP	10.00
AJ	Andruw Jones	8.00
CJ	Chipper Jones	8.00
JK	Jeff Kent	4.00
RK	Ryan Klesko	4.00
DL	Derrek Lee	8.00
GM	Greg Maddux	10.00
MO	Magglio Ordonez	4.00
DO	David Ortiz	8.00
CP	Corey Patterson	4.00
MP	Mike Piazza	10.00
JP	Jorge Posada	4.00
AP	Albert Pujols	20.00
MR	Manny Ramirez	8.00
JR	Jose Reyes	6.00
BR	Brian Roberts	6.00
IR	Ivan Rodriguez	6.00
SR	Scott Rolen	10.00
RS	Richie Sexson	6.00
JS	John Smoltz	8.00
AS	Alfonso Soriano	8.00
SS	Sammy Sosa	10.00
HS	Huston Street	4.00
TX	Mark Teixeira	8.00
MT	Miguel Tejada	8.00
FT	Frank Thomas	8.00
CU	Chase Utley	15.00
VW	Vernon Wells	6.00
BW	Bernie Williams	6.00
WI	Dontrelle Willis	6.00
PW	Preston Wilson	4.00
KW	Kerry Wood	6.00
DW	David Wright	15.00
BZ	Barry Zito	6.00

Home Run Kings

	NM/M
Complete Set (15):	10.00
Common Player:	.50
HRK1 Albert Pujols	3.00
HRK2 Ken Griffey Jr.	2.00
HRK3 Andruw Jones	1.00
HRK4 Alex Rodriguez	3.00
HRK5 David Ortiz	1.00
HRK6 Manny Ramirez	1.00
HRK7 Derrek Lee	.75
HRK8 Mark Teixeira	.75
HRK9 Adam Dunn	.75
HRK10 Paul Konerko	.50
HRK11 Richie Sexson	.50
HRK12 Alfonso Soriano	.75
HRK13 Vladimir Guerrero	.75
HRK14 Gary Sheffield	.75
HRK15 Mike Piazza	1.00

Midsummer Classic Kings

	NM/M
Complete Set (10):	10.00
Common Player:	.50
MCK1 Ken Griffey Jr.	2.00
MCK2 Mike Piazza	1.00
MCK3 Derek Jeter	3.00
MCK4 Roger Clemens	3.00
MCK5 Randy Johnson	1.00
MCK6 Miguel Tejada	.75
MCK7 Alfonso Soriano	.75
MCK8 Garret Anderson	.50
MCK9 Pedro Martinez	1.00
MCK10 Ivan Rodriguez	.75

Rising Stars

	NM/M
Complete Set (10):	10.00
Common Player:	.50
URS1 Ryan Howard	3.00
URS2 Huston Street	.50
URS3 Jeff Francoeur	.75
URS4 Felix Hernandez	1.50
URS5 Chase Utley	2.00
URS6 Robinson Cano	1.00
URS7 Zachary Duke	.50
URS8 Scott Kazmir	1.00
URS9 Willy Taveras	.50
URS10 Tadahito Iguchi	1.00

RBI Kings

	NM/M
Complete Set (20):	15.00
Common Player:	.50
RBI1 Ken Griffey Jr.	2.00
RBI2 David Ortiz	1.00
RBI3 Manny Ramirez	1.00
RBI4 Mark Teixeira	.75
RBI5 Alex Rodriguez	3.00
RBI6 Andruw Jones	1.00
RBI7 Jeff Bagwell	.75
RBI8 Gary Sheffield	.75
RBI9 Richie Sexson	.50
RBI10 Jeff Kent	.50
RBI11 Albert Pujols	3.00
RBI12 Todd Helton	.75
RBI13 Miguel Cabrera	1.00
RBI14 Hideki Matsui	2.00
RBI15 Carlos Delgado	.75
RBI16 Carlos Lee	.50
RBI17 Derrek Lee	.75
RBI18 Vladimir Guerrero	1.00
RBI19 Luis Gonzalez	.50
RBI20 Mike Piazza	1.00

Strikeout Kings

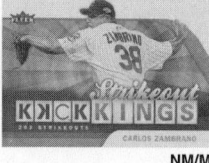

	NM/M
Complete Set (10):	8.00
Common Player:	.50
SOK1 Roger Clemens	3.00
SOK2 Johan Santana	1.00
SOK3 Jake Peavy	.50
SOK4 Randy Johnson	1.00
SOK5 Curt Schilling	1.00
SOK6 Chris Carpenter	.75
SOK7 Pedro Martinez	1.00
SOK8 Mark Prior	.75
SOK9 Carlos Zambrano	.50
SOK10 John Smoltz	.50

2007 Ultra

	NM/M
Complete Set (250):	
Common player (1-200):	.15
Common RC (201-250):	.25
Hobby SE Pack (15):	12.00
Hobby SE Box (5):	55.00
1 Brandon Webb	.25
2 Randy Johnson	.75
3 Conor Jackson	.15
4 Stephen Drew	.25
5 Eric Byrnes	.25
6 Carlos Quentin	.25
7 Andruw Jones	.50
8 Chipper Jones	.75
9 Jeff Francoeur	.50
10 Tim Hudson	.25
11 John Smoltz	.50
12 Ed Renteria	.25
13 Erik Bedard	.25
14 Kris Benson	.15
15 Miguel Tejada	.50
16 Nicholas Markakis	.25
17 Brian Roberts	.25
18 Melvin Mora	.15
19 Aubrey Huff	.15
20 Curt Schilling	.75
21 Jonathan Papelbon	1.00
22 Josh Beckett	.50
23 Jason Varitek	.25
24 David Ortiz	1.00
25 Manny Ramirez	.75
26 J.D. Drew	.15
27 Carlos Zambrano	.25
28 Derrek Lee	.50
29 Aramis Ramirez	.25
30 Alfonso Soriano	.75
31 Rich Hill	.15
32 Jacque Jones	.15
33 A.J. Pierzynski	.15
34 Jermaine Dye	.25
35 Paul Konerko	.25
36 Bobby Jenks	.15
37 Jon Garland	.15
38 Mark Buehrle	.25
39 Tadahito Iguchi	.15
40 Adam Dunn	.50
41 Ken Griffey Jr.	1.50
42 Aaron Harang	.15
43 Bronson Arroyo	.15
44 Ryan Freel	.15
45 Brandon Phillips	.25
46 Grady Sizemore	1.00
47 Travis Hafner	.25
48 Victor Martinez	.25
49 Jhonny Peralta	.25
50 C.C. Sabathia	.25
51 Jeremy Sowers	.15
52 Ryan Garko	.15
53 Garrett Atkins	.25
54 Willy Taveras	.15
55 Todd Helton	.50
56 Jeff Francis	.15
57 Brad Hawpe	.15
58 Matt Holliday	.50
59 Justin Verlander	.75
60 Jeremy Bonderman	.25
61 Maggilo Ordonez	.50
62 Ivan Rodriguez	.50
63 Gary Sheffield	.25
64 Kenny Rogers	.15
65 Brandon Inge	.15
66 Anibal Sanchez	.15
67 Scott Olsen	.15
68 Dontrelle Willis	.25
69 Dan Uggla	.15
70 Hanley Ramirez	1.00
71 Miguel Cabrera	1.00
72 Jeremy Hermida	.15
73 Roy Oswalt	.50
74 Brad Lidge	.15
75 Lance Berkman	.50
76 Carlos Lee	.50
77 Morgan Ensberg	.15
78 Craig Biggio	.50
79 Reggie Sanders	.15
80 Mike Sweeney	.15
81 Mark Teahen	.15
82 John Buck	.15
83 Mark Grudzielanek	.15
84 Gary Matthews	.25
85 Vladimir Guerrero	1.00
86 Garret Anderson	.25
87 Howie Kendrick	.25
88 Jered Weaver	.50
89 Chone Figgins	.25
90 Bartolo Colon	.15
91 Francisco Rodriguez	.25
92 Nomar Garciaparra	.75
93 Andre Ethier	.15
94 Rafael Furcal	.25
95 Jeff Kent	.50
96 Derek Lowe	.25
97 Jason Schmidt	.15
98 Takashi Saito	.15
99 Ben Sheets	.25
100 Prince Fielder	1.00
101 Bill Hall	.25
102 Rickie Weeks	.25
103 Francisco Cordero	.15
104 J.J. Hardy	.25
105 Johan Santana	.75
106 Justin Morneau	.50
107 Joe Mauer	.25
108 Joe Nathan	.15
109 Torii Hunter	.25
110 Michael Cuddyer	.15
111 Boof Bonser	.15
112 Tom Glavine	.50
113 Pedro Martinez	.75
114 Billy Wagner	.15
115 Jose Reyes	1.00
116 David Wright	1.00
117 Carlos Delgado	.50
118 Carlos Beltran	.50
119 Alex Rodriguez	2.00
120 Chien-Ming Wang	1.00
121 Mariano Rivera	.50
122 Bobby Abreu	.50
123 Hideki Matsui	1.50
124 Johnny Damon	.75
125 Robinson Cano	.75
126 Derek Jeter	2.00
127 Nick Swisher	.25
128 Eric Chavez	.25
129 Jason Kendall	.15
130 Bobby Crosby	.15
131 Huston Street	.15
132 Danny Haren	.15
133 Rich Harden	.15
134 Mike Piazza	.75
135 Chase Utley	1.00
136 Jimmy Rollins	.75
137 Aaron Rowand	.25
138 Jamie Moyer	.15
139 Cole Hamels	.50
140 Pat Burrell	.25
141 Ryan Howard	1.50
142 Freddy Sanchez	.15
143 Zachary Duke	.15
144 Ian Snell	.15
145 Jack Wilson	.15
146 Jason Bay	.25
147 Albert Pujols	2.00
148 Scott Rolen	.50
149 Jim Edmonds	.25
150 Chris Carpenter	.50
151 Yadier Molina	.15
152 Adam Wainwright	.25
153 David Eckstein	.15
154 Trevor Hoffman	.15
155 Brian Giles	.15
156 Adrian Gonzalez	.25
157 Jake Peavy	.50
158 Khalil Greene	.25
159 Chris Young	.25
160 Greg Maddux	1.00
161 Mike Cameron	.15
162 Matt Cain	.15
163 Matt Morris	.15
164 Pedro Feliz	.15
165 Omar Vizquel	.15
166 Randy Winn	.15
167 Barry Zito	.25
168 Adrian Beltre	.15
169 Yuniesky Betancourt	.15
170 Richie Sexson	.25
171 Raul Ibanez	.15
172 Kenji Johjima	.15
173 Ichiro Suzuki	1.50
174 Felix Hernandez	.50
175 Scott Kazmir	.25
176 Carl Crawford	.25
177 B.J. Upton	.25
178 James Shields	.15
179 Rocco Baldelli	.15
180 Jorge Cantu	.15
181 Ty Wigginton	.15
182 Mark Teixeira	.50
183 Hank Blalock	.25
184 Ian Kinsler	.25
185 Michael Young	.25
186 Vicente Padilla	.15
187 Akinori Otsuka	.15
188 Kenny Lofton	.15
189 A.J. Burnett	.15
190 Roy Halladay	.25
191 B.J. Ryan	.15
192 Vernon Wells	.25
193 Alex Rios	.50
194 Troy Glaus	.25
195 Frank Thomas	.75
196 Ryan Zimmerman	.50
197 Michael O'Connor	.15
198 Chad Cordero	.15
199 Nick Johnson	.15
200 Felipe Lopez	.15
201 Miguel Montero	1.00
202 Doug Slaten RC	1.00
203 Joseph Bisenius RC	1.00
204 Jared Burton RC	1.00
205 Kevin Cameron RC	1.00
206 Matt Chico (RC)	1.00
207 Chris Stewart RC	1.00
208 Joe Smith RC	2.00
209 Zack Segovia (RC)	1.00
210 John Danks (RC)	2.00
211 Lee Gardner (RC)	1.00
212 Jeff Baker (RC)	2.00
213 Jamie Burke (RC)	1.00
214 Phil Hughes (RC)	3.00
215 Mike Rabelo RC	1.00
216 Jose Garcia RC	1.00
217 Hector Gimenez (RC)	1.00
218 Jesus Flores RC	1.00
219 Brandon Morrow RC	3.00
220 Hideki Okajima RC	3.00
221 Jay Marshall RC	1.00
222 Matt Lindstrom (RC)	1.00
223 Juan Salas (RC)	1.00
224 Juan Perez RC	1.00
225 Sean Henn (RC)	1.00
226 Travis Buck (RC)	1.00
227 Gustavo Molina RC	1.00
228 Hunter Pence (RC)	6.00
229 Michael Bourn (RC)	1.00
230 Brian Barden RC	1.00
231 Donald Kelly (RC)	1.00
232 Joakim Soria RC	3.00
233 Cesar Jimenez RC	1.00
234 Levale Speigner RC	2.00
235 Micah Owings (RC)	1.00
236 Brian Stokes (RC)	1.00
237 Joaquin Arias (RC)	1.00
238 Josh Hamilton (RC)	4.00
239 Daisuke Matsuzaka RC	5.00
240 Alejandro De Aza RC	1.00
241 Kory Casto (RC)	1.00
242 Troy Tulowitzki RC	4.00
243 Akinori Iwamura RC	2.00
244 Angel Sanchez RC	1.00
245 Ryan Braun (RC)	8.00
246 Alex Gordon RC	5.00
247 Elijah Dukes RC	1.00
248 Kei Igawa RC	1.00
249 Kevin Kouzmanoff (RC)	1.00
250 Delmon Young (RC)	1.00

Gold

Gold (1-200):	2-3X
Gold RC (201-250):	1X
Inserted 1:10 Hobby	

Retail

Retail (1-200):	.5X
Retail RC (201-250):	.5X

Printing Plates

Production one set per color.

Autographics

	NM/M
Common Auto:	

AG	Alex Gordon/499	30.00
AH	Aaron Harang/499	15.00
CH	Clay Hensley/499	10.00
JA	Jason Bay/499	15.00
JB	Joe Blanton/499	10.00
JE	Johnny Estrada/132	10.00
JS	Johan Santana/173	30.00
KG	Khalil Greene/499	15.00
KI	Kei Igawa/199	25.00

Dual Materials
NM/M

Common Player: 5.00
Production 160 unless noted.
Gold: 1-1.5x
Production 20-75
Patch: No Pricing
Production 25 Sets

AB	A.J. Burnett	5.00
AE	Andre Ethier	5.00
AJ	Andruw Jones	8.00
AK	Austin Kearns	5.00
AL	Adam LaRoche	5.00
AN	Garret Anderson	5.00
AP	Albert Pujols	20.00
AS	Anibal Sanchez	5.00
BA	Bobby Abreu	5.00
BC	Bobby Crosby	5.00
BE	Adrian Beltre	5.00
BG	Brian Giles	5.00
BI	Craig Biggio	8.00
BJ	Bobby Jenks	5.00
BL	Brad Lidge	5.00
BM	Brandon McCarthy	5.00
BR	Brian Roberts	8.00
BS	Ben Sheets	5.00
BW	Brandon Webb	5.00
CA	Carlos Beltran	10.00
CB	Chris Burke	5.00
CC	Carl Crawford	5.00
CF	Chone Figgins	5.00
CH	Chris Carpenter	8.00
CJ	Conor Jackson	5.00
CK	Casey Kotchman	5.00
CL	Carlos Lee	8.00
CP	Corey Patterson	5.00
CR	Coco Crisp	5.00
CS	C.C. Sabathia	8.00
CU	Curt Schilling	10.00
DJ	Derek Jeter	20.00
DL	Derek Lowe	5.00
DO	David Ortiz	10.00
DR	J.D. Drew	5.00
DU	Dan Uggla	5.00
DW	David Wells	5.00
ED	Jim Edmonds	5.00
ES	Ervin Santana	5.00
FG	Freddy Garcia	5.00
FH	Felix Hernandez	5.00
GA	Garrett Atkins	5.00
GJ	Geoff Jenkins	5.00
GM	Greg Maddux	15.00
GS	Gary Sheffield	10.00
HE	Todd Helton	10.00
HO	Trevor Hoffman	8.00
HR	Hanley Ramirez	10.00
HU	Torii Hunter	8.00
IS	Ian Snell	5.00
JB	Jeremy Bonderman	8.00
JC	Chipper Jones	10.00
JD	Jermaine Dye	8.00
JG	Jonny Gomes	5.00
JH	J.J. Hardy	8.00
JJ	Josh Johnson	5.00
JK	Jeff Kent	8.00
JM	Justin Morneau	10.00
JN	Joe Nathan	5.00
JO	Josh Beckett	15.00
JP	Jorge Posada	10.00
JS	James Shields	8.00
JV	Jason Varitek	10.00
JW	Josh Willingham	5.00
KG	Khalil Greene	8.00
KW	Kerry Wood	5.00
LB	Lance Berkman	8.00
LE	Derrek Lee	10.00
LG	Luis Gonzalez	5.00
LM	Lastings Milledge	8.00
LS	Luke Scott	5.00
MC	Matt Cain	8.00
ME	Melky Cabrera	10.00
MH	Matt Holliday	8.00
MI	Mike Mussina	10.00
MM	Melvin Mora	5.00
MO	Magglio Ordonez	8.00
MR	Manny Ramirez	10.00
MS	Mike Sweeney	5.00
MT	Miguel Tejada	8.00
MU	Mark Mulder	5.00
PE	Andy Pettitte	8.00
PF	Prince Fielder	15.00
PJ	Jhonny Peralta	5.00
RH	Rich Harden	5.00
SC	Jason Schmidt	5.00
SI	Grady Sizemore	20.00
SO	Scott Olsen	5.00
TE	Mark Teixeira	10.00
TH	Travis Hafner	8.00
TW	Tim Wakefield	5.00
VG	Vladimir Guerrero	10.00
VM	Victor Martinez	8.00
VW	Vernon Wells	5.00
WI	Dontrelle Willis	5.00
ZD	Zachary Duke	5.00

Faces of the Game

TOM GLAVINE
NEW YORK METS

		NM/M
	Common Player:	.50
AB	Adrian Beltre	.50
AJ	Andruw Jones	.75
BS	Ben Sheets	.50
CJ	Chipper Jones	1.00
CS	C.C. Sabathia	.75
CU	Chase Utley	1.00
DJ	Derek Jeter	3.00
FR	Francisco Rodriguez	.50
GM	Greg Maddux	2.00
HO	Trevor Hoffman	.50
JB	Jason Bay	.75
JG	Jason Giambi	.75
KG	Ken Griffey Jr.	2.00
LG	Luis Gonzalez	.50
MC	Miguel Cabrera	1.00
MP	Mike Piazza	1.00
MR	Mariano Rivera	.75
OV	Omar Vizquel	.50
TG	Tom Glavine	.75
TH	Torii Hunter	.50

Faces of the Game Materials
NM/M

	Common Jersey:	5.00
AB	Adrian Beltre	5.00
AJ	Andruw Jones	8.00
BS	Ben Sheets	8.00
CJ	Chipper Jones	8.00
CS	C.C. Sabathia	5.00
CU	Chase Utley	10.00
DJ	Derek Jeter	20.00
FR	Francisco Rodriguez	5.00
GM	Greg Maddux	10.00
HU	Torii Hunter	5.00
JB	Jason Bay	5.00
JG	Jason Giambi	5.00
KG	Ken Griffey Jr.	15.00
LG	Luis Gonzalez	5.00
MC	Miguel Cabrera	8.00
MP	Mike Piazza	8.00
MR	Mariano Rivera	8.00
OV	Omar Vizquel	5.00
TG	Tom Glavine	8.00
TH	Trevor Hoffman	5.00

Feel the Game
NM/M

	Common Player:	.50
AP	Albert Pujols	3.00
BA	Bobby Abreu	.50
BR	Brian Roberts	.50
BW	Brandon Webb	.50
CC	Chris Carpenter	.75
CJ	Chipper Jones	1.00
CR	Carl Crawford	.50
CS	Curt Schilling	1.00
CZ	Carlos Zambrano	.50
DJ	Derek Jeter	3.00
DW	Dontrelle Willis	.50
EC	Eric Chavez	.50
GS	Grady Sizemore	1.00
HR	Hanley Ramirez	1.00
IR	Ivan Rodriguez	.75
JM	Justin Morneau	.75
JP	Jonathan Papelbon	.75
JR	Jose Reyes	2.00
JS	John Smoltz	.75
KG	Ken Griffey Jr.	2.00
KJ	Kenji Johjima	.50
LB	Lance Berkman	.50
LG	Luis Gonzalez	.50
MC	Miguel Cabrera	1.00
RC	Robinson Cano	1.00
RJ	Randy Johnson	1.00
SA	Johan Santana	1.00
SC	Jason Schmidt	.50
VG	Vladimir Guerrero	1.00

Feel the Game Materials
NM/M

	Common Jersey:	5.00
AP	Albert Pujols	20.00
BA	Bobby Abreu	5.00
BR	Brian Roberts	5.00
BW	Brandon Webb	5.00
CC	Chris Carpenter	5.00
CJ	Chipper Jones	8.00

Bobby Abreu Outfield

FEEL THE GAME

YANKEES

CR	Carl Crawford	5.00
CS	Curt Schilling	8.00
CU	Chase Utley	10.00
CZ	Carlos Zambrano	8.00
DJ	Derek Jeter	20.00
DW	Dontrelle Willis	5.00
EC	Eric Chavez	5.00
GS	Grady Sizemore	10.00
HR	Hanley Ramirez	8.00
IR	Ivan Rodriguez	8.00
JM	Justin Morneau	8.00
JP	Jonathan Papelbon	10.00
JR	Jose Reyes	10.00
JS	John Smoltz	8.00
KJ	Ken Griffey Jr.	15.00
KJ	Kenji Johjima	8.00
LB	Lance Berkman	5.00
LG	Luis Gonzalez	5.00
MC	Miguel Cabrera	8.00
RC	Robinson Cano	10.00
RJ	Randy Johnson	8.00
SA	Johan Santana	8.00
SC	Jason Schmidt	5.00
VG	Vladimir Guerrero	8.00

Hitting Machines
NM/M

	Common Player:	.50
AR	Aramis Ramirez	.75
AS	Alfonso Soriano	1.00
BI	Craig Biggio	.50
CB	Carlos Beltran	1.00
DO	David Ortiz	1.00
FS	Freddy Sanchez	.50
FT	Frank Thomas	1.00
JK	Jeff Kent	.50
JM	Joe Mauer	.75
JT	Jim Thome	.75
MT	Mark Teixeira	1.00
NS	Nick Swisher	.50
TE	Miguel Tejada	.75
TG	Troy Glaus	.75
TH	Todd Helton	.75

Hitting Machines Materials
NM/M

	Common Jersey:	5.00
AR	Aramis Ramirez	5.00
AS	Alfonso Soriano	8.00
BI	Craig Biggio	8.00
CB	Carlos Beltran	8.00
DO	David Ortiz	8.00
FS	Freddy Sanchez	5.00
FT	Frank Thomas	10.00
JK	Jeff Kent	5.00
JM	Joe Mauer	8.00
JT	Jim Thome	8.00
MT	Mark Teixeira	8.00
NS	Nick Swisher	5.00
TE	Miguel Tejada	5.00
TG	Troy Glaus	5.00
TH	Todd Helton	8.00

Iron Man

Cal Ripken Jr. - Orioles

NM/M
Common Ripken (1-50): 3.00
Autograph: No Pricing
Production 10 Sets

Lucky 13 Rookies Auto.
NM/M

Quantity produced listed 10.00
Parallel: 1-1.5x
Production 99 or 199

238	Josh Hamilton/499	35.00
241	Kory Casto/499	10.00
242	Troy Tulowitzki/499	30.00
245	Ryan Braun/499	100.00
246	Alex Gordon/499	30.00
248	Kei Igawa/299	40.00
249	Kevin Kouzmanoff/499	15.00

Lucky 13 Rookies Auto.-Retail
NM/M

	Common Autograph:	10.00
238	Josh Hamilton	35.00
241	Kory Casto	10.00
242	Troy Tulowitzki	30.00
246	Alex Gordon/SP	30.00
248	Kei Igawa/SP	40.00
249	Kevin Kouzmanoff	15.00

Rookies Auto.
NM/M

Production 299 unless noted.
Parallel: 1x
Production 99-349

201	Miguel Montero	10.00
202	Doug Slaten	10.00
203	Joseph Bisenius	10.00
204	Jared Burton	10.00
205	Kevin Cameron	10.00
206	Matt Chico	10.00
207	Chris Stewart	10.00
209	Zack Segovia	15.00
210	John Danks	15.00
213	Jamie Burke	15.00
215	Mike Rabelo	15.00
217	Hector Gimenez	10.00
219	Brandon Morrow	25.00
221	Jay Marshall	10.00
225	Sean Henn	10.00
226	Travis Buck	10.00
227	Gustavo Molina	10.00
229	Michael Bourn	15.00
232	Joakim Soria	25.00
234	Levale Speigner	10.00
236	Brian Stokes	10.00
237	Joaquin Arias	10.00

Rookies Auto-Retail
NM/M

	Common Autograph:	10.00
201	Miguel Montero	10.00
202	Doug Slaten	10.00
204	Jared Burton/SP	10.00
205	Kevin Cameron/SP	10.00
206	Matt Chico	10.00
207	Chris Stewart	10.00
209	Zack Segovia	10.00
215	Mike Rabelo	15.00
217	Hector Gimenez	10.00
225	Sean Henn	10.00
229	Michael Bourn/SP	15.00
234	Levale Speigner	10.00
236	Brian Stokes	10.00
237	Joaquin Arias	10.00

Stike Zone
NM/M

	Common Player:	.50
BZ	Barry Zito	.50
CC	C.C. Sabathia	.75
CZ	Carlos Zambrano	.75
DW	Dontrelle Willis	.50
JS	Johan Santana	1.00
JV	Justin Verlander	1.00
MM	Mike Mussina	.75
PM	Pedro Martinez	1.00
RH	Roy Halladay	.75
RO	Roy Oswalt	.75

Strike Zone Materials
NM/M

	Common Player:	5.00
BZ	Barry Zito	5.00
CC	C.C. Sabathia	5.00
CZ	Carlos Zambrano	5.00
DW	Dontrelle Willis	5.00
JS	Johan Santana	8.00
JV	Justin Verlander	8.00
MM	Mike Mussina	8.00
PM	Pedro Martinez	8.00
RH	Roy Halladay	8.00
RO	Roy Oswalt	8.00

Swing Kings
NM/M

	Common Player:	.50
AD	Adam Dunn	.75
AJ	Andruw Jones	1.00
AP	Albert Pujols	3.00
AR	Aramis Ramirez	.75
AS	Alfonso Soriano	1.00
CB	Carlos Beltran	.75
CL	Carlos Lee	.75
DJ	Derek Jeter	3.00
DO	David Ortiz	1.00
FT	Frank Thomas	1.00
GS	Gary Sheffield	.75
HE	Todd Helton	.75
JM	Joe Mauer	.75

JR	Jose Reyes	2.00
JT	Jim Thome	.75
KG	Ken Griffey Jr.	2.00
MC	Miguel Cabrera	1.00
MR	Manny Ramirez	1.00
MT	Miguel Tejada	.75
NG	Nomar Garciaparra	1.00
PB	Pat Burrell	.75
TE	Mark Teixeira	.75
TH	Travis Hafner	.75
VG	Vladimir Guerrero	1.00
VW	Vernon Wells	.50

Swing Kings Materials

	Common Player:	NM/M
		5.00
AD	Adam Dunn	8.00
AJ	Andruw Jones	8.00
AP	Albert Pujols	20.00
AR	Aramis Ramirez	8.00
AS	Alfonso Soriano	8.00
CB	Carlos Beltran	8.00
CL	Carlos Lee	5.00
DJ	Derek Jeter	20.00
DO	David Ortiz	8.00
FT	Frank Thomas	10.00
GS	Gary Sheffield	8.00
HE	Todd Helton	8.00
JM	Joe Mauer	8.00
JR	Jose Reyes	10.00
JT	Jim Thome	8.00
KG	Ken Griffey Jr.	15.00
MC	Miguel Cabrera	8.00
MR	Manny Ramirez	8.00
MT	Miguel Tejada	5.00
NG	Nomar Garciaparra	8.00
PB	Pat Burrell	5.00
TE	Mark Teixeira	8.00
TH	Travis Hafner	5.00
VG	Vladimir Guerrero	8.00
VW	Vernon Wells	5.00

Ultragraphs

	Common Auto.:	NM/M
		8.00
AK	Austin Kearns/499	10.00
AL	Adam LaRoche/499	8.00
AN	Garret Anderson/499	10.00
BB	Boof Bonser/499	10.00
GA	Garrett Atkins/499	10.00
JJ	Jorge Julio/499	8.00
JN	Joe Nathan/299	10.00
JW	Jered Weaver/499	10.00
MM	Mark Mulder/319	8.00
RW	Rickie Weeks/499	10.00
TH	Travis Hafner/499	10.00
ZG	Zack Greinke/199	8.00

1989 Upper Deck

Dale Murphy

	NM/M
Unopened Fact. Set (800):	80.00
Complete Set (800):	45.00
Complete Low Set (700):	40.00
Complete High Set (100):	5.00
Common Player:	.05
Low Foil Pack (15):	4.00
Low Foil Box (36):	100.00

High Foil Pack (15):	2.00
High Foil Box (36):	60.00
1 Ken Griffey Jr. **RC**	40.00
2 Luis Medina **RC**	.05
3 Tony Chance **RC**	.05
4 Dave Otto **RC**	.05
5 Sandy Alomar, Jr. **RC**	1.00
6 Rolando Roomes **RC**	.05
7 David West **RC**	.05
8 Cris Carpenter **RC**	.05
9 Gregg Jefferies	.25
10 Doug Dascenzo **RC**	.05
11 Ron Jones **RC**	.05
12 Luis de los Santos **RC**	.05
13a Gary Sheffield **RC** ("SS" upside-down)	8.00
13b Gary Sheffield **RC** ("SS" correct)	8.00
14 Mike Harkey **RC**	.05
15 Lance Blankenship **RC**	.05
16 William Brennan **RC**	.05
17 John Smoltz	.25
18 Ramon Martinez **RC**	.25
19 Mark Lemke **RC**	.05
20 Juan Bell **RC**	.05
21 Rey Palacios **RC**	.05
22 Felix Jose **RC**	.05
23 Van Snider **RC**	.05
24 Dante Bichette **RC**	.75
25 Randy Johnson **RC**	10.00
26 Carlos Quintana **RC**	.05
27 Star Rookie Checklist 1-26	.05
28 Mike Schooler **RC**	.05
29 Randy St. Claire	.05
30 Jerald Clark **RC**	.05
31 Kevin Gross	.05
32 Dan Firova **RC**	.05
33 Jeff Calhoun	.05
34 Tommy Hinzo	.05
35 Ricky Jordan **RC**	.05
36 Larry Parrish	.05
37 Bret Saberhagen	.05
38 Mike Smithson	.05
39 Dave Dravecky	.05
40 Ed Romero	.05
41 Jeff Musselman	.05
42 Ed Hearn	.05
43 Rance Mulliniks	.05
44 Jim Eisenreich	.05
45 Sil Campusano **RC**	.05
46 Mike Krukow	.05
47 Paul Gibson **RC**	.05
48 Mike LaCoss	.05
49 Larry Herndon	.05
50 Scott Garrelts	.05
51 Dwayne Henry	.05
52 Jim Acker	.05
53 Steve Sax	.05
54 Pete O'Brien	.05
55 Paul Runge	.05
56 Rick Rhoden	.05
57 John Dopson **RC**	.05
58 Casey Candaele	.05
59 Dave Righetti	.05
60 Joe Hesketh	.05
61 Frank DiPino	.05
62 Tim Laudner	.05
63 Jamie Moyer	.05
64 Fred Toliver	.05
65 Mitch Webster	.05
66 John Tudor	.05
67 John Cangelosi	.05
68 Mike Devereaux	.05
69 Brian Fisher	.05
70 Mike Marshall	.05
71 Zane Smith	.05
72a Brian Holton (Ball not visible on card front, photo a ctually Shawn Hillegas.)	.75
72b Brian Holton (Ball visible, correct photo.)	.05
73 Jose Guzman	.05
74 Rick Mahler	.05
75 John Shelby	.05
76 Jim Deshaies	.05
77 Bobby Meacham	.05
78 Bryn Smith	.05
79 Joaquin Andujar	.05
80 Richard Dotson	.05
81 Charlie Lea	.05
82 Calvin Schiraldi	.05
83 Les Straker	.05
84 Les Lancaster	.05
85 Allan Anderson	.05
86 Junior Ortiz	.05
87 Jesse Orosco	.05
88 Felix Fermin	.05
89 Dave Anderson	.05
90 Rafael Belliard	.05
91 Franklin Stubbs	.05
92 Cecil Espy	.05
93 Albert Hall	.05
94 Tim Leary	.05
95 Mitch Williams	.05
96 Tracy Jones	.05
97 Danny Darwin	.05
98 Gary Ward	.05
99 Neal Heaton	.05
100 Jim Pankovits	.05
101 Bill Buckner	.05
102 Tim Wallach	.05
103 Joe Magrane	.05
104 Ozzie Virgil	.05
105 Alvin Davis	.05

106 Tom Brookens	.05
107 Shawon Dunston	.05
108 Tracy Woodson	.05
109 Nelson Liriano	.05
110 Devon White	.05
111 Steve Balboni	.05
112 Buddy Bell	.05
113 German Jimenez **RC**	.05
114 Ken Dayley	.05
115 Andres Galarraga	.05
116 Mike Scioscia	.05
117 Gary Pettis	.05
118 Ernie Whitt	.05
119 Bob Boone	.05
120 Ryne Sandberg	1.50
121 Bruce Benedict	.05
122 Hubie Brooks	.05
123 Mike Moore	.05
124 Wallace Johnson	.05
125 Bob Horner	.05
126 Chili Davis	.05
127 Manny Trillo	.05
128 Chet Lemon	.05
129 John Cerutti	.05
130 Orel Hershiser	.05
131 Terry Pendleton	.05
132 Jeff Blauser	.05
133 Mike Fitzgerald	.05
134 Henry Cotto	.05
135 Gerald Young	.05
136 Luis Salazar	.05
137 Alejandro Pena	.05
138 Jack Howell	.05
139 Tony Fernandez	.05
140 Mark Grace	.05
141 Ken Caminiti	.05
142 Mike Jackson	.05
143 Larry McWilliams	.05
144 Andres Thomas	.05
145 Nolan Ryan	2.00
146 Mike Davis	.05
147 DeWayne Buice	.05
148 Jody Davis	.05
149 Jesse Barfield	.05
150 Matt Nokes	.05
151 Jerry Reuss	.05
152 Rick Cerone	.05
153 Storm Davis	.05
154 Marvell Wynne	.05
155 Will Clark	.05
156 Luis Aguayo	.05
157 Willie Upshaw	.05
158 Randy Bush	.05
159 Ron Darling	.05
160 Kal Daniels	.05
161 Spike Owen	.05
162 Luis Polonia	.05
163 Kevin Mitchell	.05
164 Dave Gallagher **RC**	.05
165 Benito Santiago	.05
166 Greg Gagne	.05
167 Ken Phelps	.05
168 Sid Fernandez	.05
169 Bo Diaz	.05
170 Cory Snyder	.05
171 Eric Show	.05
172 Robby Thompson	.05
173 Marty Barrett	.05
174 Dave Henderson	.05
175 Ozzie Guillen	.05
176 Barry Lyons	.05
177 Kelvin Torve **RC**	.05
178 Don Slaught	.05
179 Steve Lombardozzi	.05
180 Chris Sabo **RC**	.05
181 Jose Uribe	.05
182 Shane Mack	.05
183 Ron Karkovice	.05
184 Todd Benzinger	.05
185 Dave Stewart	.05
186 Julio Franco	.05
187 Ron Robinson	.05
188 Wally Backman	.05
189 Randy Velarde	.05
190 Joe Carter	.05
191 Bob Welch	.05
192 Kelly Paris	.05
193 Chris Brown	.05
194 Rick Reuschel	.05
195 Roger Clemens	1.60
196 Dave Concepcion	.05
197 Al Newman	.05
198 Brook Jacoby	.05
199 Mookie Wilson	.05
200 Don Mattingly	1.60
201 Dick Schofield	.05
202 Mark Gubicza	.05
203 Gary Gaetti	.05
204 Dan Pasqua	.05
205 Andre Dawson	.35
206 Chris Speier	.05
207 Kent Tekulve	.05
208 Rod Scurry	.05
209 Scott Bailes	.05
210 Rickey Henderson	1.00
211 Harold Baines	.05
212 Tony Armas	.05
213 Kent Hrbek	.05
214 Darrin Jackson	.05
215 George Brett	1.60
216 Rafael Santana	.05
217 Andy Allanson	.05
218 Brett Butler	.05
219 Steve Jeltz	.05
220 Jay Buhner	.05

221 Bo Jackson	.15
222 Angel Salazar	.05
223 Kirk McCaskill	.05
224 Steve Lyons	.05
225 Bert Blyleven	.05
226 Scott Bradley	.05
227 Bob Melvin	.05
228 Ron Kittle	.05
229 Phil Bradley	.05
230 Tommy John	.05
231 Greg Walker	.05
232 Juan Berenguer	.05
233 Pat Tabler	.05
234 Terry Clark **RC**	.05
235 Rafael Palmeiro	.75
236 Paul Zuvella	.05
237 Willie Randolph	.05
238 Bruce Fields	.05
239 Mike Aldrete	.05
240 Lance Parrish	.05
241 Greg Maddux	1.50
242 John Moses	.05
243 Melido Perez	.05
244 Willie Wilson	.05
245 Mark McLemore	.05
246 Von Hayes	.05
247 Matt Williams	.05
248 John Candelaria	.05
249 Harold Reynolds	.05
250 Greg Swindell	.05
251 Juan Agosto	.05
252 Mike Felder	.05
253 Vince Coleman	.05
254 Larry Sheets	.05
255 George Bell	.05
256 Terry Steinbach	.05
257 Jack Armstrong **RC**	.05
258 Dickie Thon	.05
259 Ray Knight	.05
260 Darryl Strawberry	.05
261 Doug Sisk	.05
262 Alex Trevino	.05
263 Jeff Leonard	.05
264 Tom Henke	.05
265 Ozzie Smith	1.50
266 Dave Bergman	.05
267 Tony Phillips	.05
268 Mark Davis	.05
269 Kevin Elster	.05
270 Barry Larkin	.05
271 Manny Lee	.05
272 Tom Brunansky	.05
273 Craig Biggio	.05
274 Jim Gantner	.05
275 Eddie Murray	1.00
276 Jeff Reed	.05
277 Tim Teufel	.05
278 Rick Honeycutt	.05
279 Guillermo Hernandez	.05
280 John Kruk	.05
281 Luis Alicea **RC**	.15
282 Jim Clancy	.05
283 Billy Ripken	.05
284 Craig Reynolds	.05
285 Robin Yount	1.00
286 Jimmy Jones	.05
287 Ron Oester	.05
288 Terry Leach	.05
289 Dennis Eckersley	.75
290 Alan Trammell	.05
291 Jimmy Key	.05
292 Chris Bosio	.05
293 Jose DeLeon	.05
294 Jim Traber	.05
295 Mike Scott	.05
296 Roger McDowell	.05
297 Garry Templeton	.05
298 Doyle Alexander	.05
299 Nick Esasky	.05
300 Mark McGwire	1.75
301 Darryl Hamilton **RC**	.05
302 Dave Smith	.05
303 Rick Sutcliffe	.05
304 Dave Stapleton	.05
305 Alan Ashby	.05
306 Pedro Guerrero	.05
307 Ron Guidry	.05
308 Steve Farr	.05
309 Curt Ford	.05
310 Claudell Washington	.05
311 Tom Prince	.05
312 Chad Kreuter **RC**	.15
313 Ken Oberkfell	.05
314 Jerry Browne	.05
315 R.J. Reynolds	.05
316 Scott Bankhead	.05
317 Milt Thompson	.05
318 Mario Diaz	.05
319 Bruce Ruffin	.05
320 Dave Valle	.05
321a Gary Varsho **RC** (Batting righty on card back, photo actually Mike Bielecki.)	1.00
321b Gary Varsho **RC** (Batting lefty on card back, correct photo.)	.05
322 Paul Mirabella	.05
323 Chuck Jackson	.05
324 Drew Hall	.05
325 Don August	.05
326 Israel Sanchez **RC**	.05
327 Denny Walling	.05
328 Joel Skinner	.05
329 Danny Tartabull	.05
330 Tony Pena	.05

331	Jim Sundberg	.05
332	Jeff Robinson	.05
333	Odibbe McDowell	.05
334	Jose Lind	.05
335	Paul Kilgus	.05
336	Juan Samuel	.05
337	Mike Campbell	.05
338	Mike Maddux	.05
339	Darnell Coles	.05
340	Bob Dernier	.05
341	Rafael Ramirez	.05
342	Scott Sanderson	.05
343	B.J. Surhoff	.05
344	Billy Hatcher	.05
345	Pat Perry	.05
346	Jack Clark	.05
347	Gary Thurman	.05
348	Timmy Jones **RC**	.05
349	Dave Winfield	1.00
350	Frank White	.05
351	Dave Collins	.05
352	Jack Morris	.05
353	Eric Plunk	.05
354	Leon Durham	.05
355	Ivan DeJesus	.05
356	Brian Holman **RC**	.05
357a	Dale Murphy (Reversed negative.)	20.00
357b	Dale Murphy (Corrected)	.25
358	Mark Portugal	.05
359	Andy McGaffigan	.05
360	Tom Glavine	.25
361	Keith Moreland	.05
362	Todd Stottlemyre	.05
363	Dave Leiper	.05
364	Cecil Fielder	.05
365	Carmelo Martinez	.05
366	Dwight Evans	.05
367	Kevin McReynolds	.05
368	Rich Gedman	.05
369	Len Dykstra	.05
370	Jody Reed	.05
371	Jose Canseco	.60
372	Rob Murphy	.05
373	Mike Henneman	.05
374	Walt Weiss	.05
375	Rob Dibble **RC**	.05
376	Kirby Puckett	1.50
377	Denny Martinez	.05
378	Ron Gant	.05
379	Brian Harper	.05
380	Nelson Santovenia **RC**	.05
381	Lloyd Moseby	.05
382	Lance McCullers	.05
383	Dave Stieb	.05
384	Tony Gwynn	1.50
385	Mike Flanagan	.05
386	Bob Ojeda	.05
387	Bruce Hurst	.05
388	Dave Magadan	.05
389	Wade Boggs	1.50
390	Gary Carter	1.00
391	Frank Tanana	.05
392	Curt Young	.05
393	Jeff Treadway	.05
394	Darrell Evans	.05
395	Glenn Hubbard	.05
396	Chuck Cary	.05
397	Frank Viola	.05
398	Jeff Parrett	.05
399	Terry Blocker **RC**	.05
400	Dan Gladden	.05
401	Louie Meadows **RC**	.05
402	Tim Raines	.05
403	Joey Meyer	.05
404	Larry Andersen	.05
405	Rex Hudler	.05
406	Mike Schmidt	1.60
407	John Franco	.05
408	Brady Anderson	.05
409	Don Carman	.05
410	Eric Davis	.05
411	Bob Stanley	.05
412	Pete Smith	.05
413	Jim Rice	.25
414	Bruce Sutter	.75
415	Oil Can Boyd	.05
416	Ruben Sierra	.05
417	Mike LaValliere	.05
418	Steve Buechele	.05
419	Gary Redus	.05
420	Scott Fletcher	.05
421	Dale Sveum	.05
422	Bob Knepper	.05
423	Luis Rivera	.05
424	Ted Higuera	.05
425	Kevin Bass	.05
426	Ken Gerhart	.05
427	Shane Rawley	.05
428	Paul O'Neill	.05
429	Joe Orsulak	.05
430	Jackie Gutierrez	.05
431	Gerald Perry	.05
432	Mike Greenwell	.05
433	Jerry Royster	.05
434	Ellis Burks	.05
435	Ed Olwine	.05
436	Dave Rucker	.05
437	Charlie Hough	.05
438	Bob Walk	.05
439	Bob Brower	.05
440	Barry Bonds	2.00
441	Tom Foley	.05
442	Rob Deer	.05
443	Glenn Davis	.05
444	Dave Martinez	.05
445	Bill Wegman	.05
446	Lloyd McClendon	.05
447	Dave Schmidt	.05
448	Darren Daulton	.05
449	Frank Williams	.05
450	Don Aase	.05
451	Lou Whitaker	.05
452	Goose Gossage	.05
453	Ed Whitson	.05
454	Jim Walewander	.05
455	Damon Berryhill	.05
456	Tim Burke	.05
457	Barry Jones	.05
458	Joel Youngblood	.05
459	Floyd Youmans	.05
460	Mark Salas	.05
461	Jeff Russell	.05
462	Darrell Miller	.05
463	Jeff Kunkel	.05
464	Sherman Corbett **RC**	.05
465	Curtis Wilkerson	.05
466	Bud Black	.05
467	Cal Ripken, Jr.	2.00
468	John Farrell	.05
469	Terry Kennedy	.05
470	Tom Candiotti	.05
471	Roberto Alomar	.20
472	Jeff Robinson	.05
473	Vance Law	.05
474	Randy Ready	.05
475	Walt Terrell	.05
476	Kelly Downs	.05
477	Johnny Paredes **RC**	.05
478	Shawn Hillegas	.05
479	Bob Brenly	.05
480	Otis Nixon	.05
481	Johnny Ray	.05
482	Geno Petralli	.05
483	Stu Cliburn	.05
484	Pete Incaviglia	.05
485	Brian Downing	.05
486	Jeff Stone	.05
487	Carmen Castillo	.05
488	Tom Niedenfuer	.05
489	Jay Bell	.05
490	Rick Schu	.05
491	Jeff Pico **RC**	.05
492	Mark Parent **RC**	.05
493	Eric King	.05
494	Al Nipper	.05
495	Andy Hawkins	.05
496	Daryl Boston	.05
497	Ernie Riles	.05
498	Pascual Perez	.05
499	Bill Long	.05
500	Kirt Manwaring	.05
501	Chuck Crim	.05
502	Candy Maldonado	.05
503	Dennis Lamp	.05
504	Glenn Braggs	.05
505	Joe Price	.05
506	Ken Williams	.05
507	Bill Pecota	.05
508	Rey Quinones	.05
509	Jeff Bittiger **RC**	.05
510	Kevin Seitzer	.05
511	Steve Bedrosian	.05
512	Todd Worrell	.05
513	Chris James	.05
514	Jose Oquendo	.05
515	David Palmer	.05
516	John Smiley	.05
517	Dave Clark	.05
518	Mike Dunne	.05
519	Ron Washington	.05
520	Bob Kipper	.05
521	Lee Smith	.05
522	Juan Castillo	.05
523	Don Robinson	.05
524	Kevin Romine	.05
525	Paul Molitor	1.00
526	Mark Langston	.05
527	Donnie Hill	.05
528	Larry Owen	.05
529	Jerry Reed	.05
530	Jack McDowell	.05
531	Greg Mathews	.05
532	John Russell	.05
533	Dan Quisenberry	.05
534	Greg Gross	.05
535	Danny Cox	.05
536	Terry Francona	.05
537	Andy Van Slyke	.05
538	Mel Hall	.05
539	Jim Gott	.05
540	Doug Jones	.05
541	Criag Lefferts	.05
542	Mike Boddicker	.05
543	Greg Brock	.05
544	Atlee Hammaker	.05
545	Tom Bolton	.05
546	Mike Macfarlane **RC**	.25
547	Rich Renteria **RC**	.05
548	John Davis	.05
549	Floyd Bannister	.05
550	Mickey Brantley	.05
551	Duane Ward	.05
552	Dan Petry	.05
553	Mickey Tettleton	.05
554	Rick Leach	.05
555	Mike Witt	.05
556	Sid Bream	.05
557	Bobby Witt	.05
558	Tommy Herr	.05
559	Randy Milligan	.05
560	Jose Cecena **RC**	.05
561	Mackey Sasser	.05
562	Carney Lansford	.05
563	Rick Aguilera	.05
564	Ron Hassey	.05
565	Dwight Gooden	.05
566	Paul Assenmacher	.05
567	Neil Allen	.05
568	Jim Morrison	.05
569	Mike Pagliarulo	.05
570	Ted Simmons	.05
571	Mark Thurmond	.05
572	Fred McGriff	.05
573	Wally Joyner	.05
574	Jose Bautista **RC**	.05
575	Kelly Gruber	.05
576	Cecilio Guante	.05
577	Mark Davidson	.05
578	Bobby Bonilla	.05
579	Mike Stanley	.05
580	Gene Larkin	.05
581	Stan Javier	.05
582	Howard Johnson	.05
583a	Mike Gallego (Photo on card back reversed.)	.75
583b	Mike Gallego (Correct photo.)	.05
584	David Cone	.05
585	Doug Jennings **RC**	.05
586	Charlie Hudson	.05
587	Dion James	.05
588	Al Leiter	.05
589	Charlie Puleo	.05
590	Roberto Kelly	.05
591	Thad Bosley	.05
592	Pete Stanicek	.05
593	Pat Borders **RC**	.25
594	Bryan Harvey **RC**	.05
595	Jeff Ballard	.05
596	Jeff Reardon	.05
597	Doug Drabek	.05
598	Edwin Correa	.05
599	Keith Atherton	.05
600	Dave LaPoint	.05
601	Don Baylor	.05
602	Tom Pagnozzi	.05
603	Tim Flannery	.05
604	Gene Walter	.05
605	Dave Parker	.05
606	Mike Diaz	.05
607	Chris Gwynn	.05
608	Odell Jones	.05
609	Carlton Fisk	1.00
610	Jay Howell	.05
611	Tim Crews	.05
612	Keith Hernandez	.05
613	Willie Fraser	.05
614	Jim Eppard	.05
615	Jeff Hamilton	.05
616	Kurt Stillwell	.05
617	Tom Browning	.05
618	Jeff Montgomery	.05
619	Jose Rijo	.05
620	Jamie Quirk	.05
621	Willie McGee	.05
622	Mark Grant	.05
623	Bill Swift	.05
624	Orlando Mercado	.05
625	John Costello **RC**	.05
626	Jose Gonzalez	.05
627a	Bill Schroeder (Putting on shin guards on card back, photo actually Ronn Reynolds.)	.75
627b	Bill Schroeder (Arms crossed on card back, correct photo.)	.05
628a	Fred Manrique (Throwing on card back, photo actually Ozzie Guillen.)	.75
628b	Fred Manrique (Batting on card back, correct photo.)	.05
629	Ricky Horton	.05
630	Dan Plesac	.05
631	Alfredo Griffin	.05
632	Chuck Finley	.05
633	Kirk Gibson	.05
634	Randy Myers	.05
635	Greg Minton	.05
636	Herm Winningham	.05
637	Charlie Leibrandt	.05
638	Tim Birtsas	.05
639	Bill Buckner	.05
640	Danny Jackson	.05
641	Greg Booker	.05
642	Jim Presley	.05
643	Gene Nelson	.05
644	Rod Booker	.05
645	Dennis Rasmussen	.05
646	Juan Nieves	.05
647	Bobby Thigpen	.05
648	Tim Belcher	.05
649	Mike Young	.05
650	Ivan Calderon	.05
651	Oswaldo Peraza **RC**	.05
652a	Pat Sheridan (No position on front.)	8.00
652b	Pat Sheridan (Position on front.)	.05
653	Mike Morgan	.05
654	Mike Heath	.05
655	Jay Tibbs	.05
656	Fernando Valenzuela	.05
657	Lee Mazzilli	.05
658	Frank Viola	.05
659	Jose Canseco	.60
660	Walt Weiss	.05
661	Orel Hershiser	.05
662	Kirk Gibson	.05
663	Chris Sabo	.05
664	Dennis Eckersley	.75
665	Orel Hershiser	.05
666	Kirk Gibson	.05
667	Orel Hershiser	.05
668	Wally Joyner (TC)	.05
669	Nolan Ryan (TC)	1.00
670	Jose Canseco (TC)	.30
671	Fred McGriff (TC)	.05
672	Dale Murphy (TC)	.20
673	Paul Molitor (TC)	.50
674	Ozzie Smith (TC)	.75
675	Ryne Sandberg (TC)	.40
676	Kirk Gibson (TC)	.05
677	Andres Galarraga (TC)	.05
678	Will Clark (TC)	.05
679	Cory Snyder (TC)	.05
680	Alvin Davis (TC)	.05
681	Darryl Strawberry (TC)	.05
682	Cal Ripken, Jr. (TC)	1.00
683	Tony Gwynn (TC)	.40
684	Mike Schmidt (TC)	.85
685	Andy Van Slyke (TC)	.05
686	Ruben Sierra (TC)	.05
687	Wade Boggs (TC)	.40
688	Eric Davis (TC)	.05
689	George Brett (TC)	.85
690	Alan Trammell (TC)	.05
691	Frank Viola (TC)	.05
692	Harold Baines (TC)	.05
693	Don Mattingly (TC)	.85
694	Checklist 1-100	.05
695	Checklist 101-200	.05
696	Checklist 201-300	.05
697	Checklist 301-400	.05
698	Checklist 401-500	.05
699	Checklist 501-600	.05
700	Checklist 601-700	.05
701	Checklist 701-800	.05
702	Jessie Barfield	.05
703	Walt Terrell	.05
704	Dickie Thon	.05
705	Al Leiter	.05
706	Dave LaPoint	.05
707	Charlie Hayes **RC**	.05
708	Andy Hawkins	.05
709	Mickey Hatcher	.05
710	Lance McCullers	.05
711	Ron Kittle	.05
712	Bert Blyleven	.05
713	Rick Dempsey	.05
714	Ken Williams	.05
715	Steve Rosenberg **(RC)**	.05
716	Joe Skalski **(RC)**	.05
717	Spike Owen	.05
718	Todd Burns	.05
719	Kevin Gross	.05
720	Tommy Herr	.05
721	Rob Ducey	.05
722	Gary Green **(RC)**	.05
723	Gregg Olson **RC**	.10
724	Greg Harris **(RC)**	.05
725	Craig Worthington **(RC)**	.05
726	Tom Howard **(RC)**	.05
727	Dale Mohorcic	.05
728	Rich Yett	.05
729	Mel Hall	.05
730	Floyd Youmans	.05
731	Lonnie Smith	.05
732	Wally Backman	.05
733	Trevor Wilson	.05
734	Jose Alvarez	.05
735	Bob Milacki **(RC)**	.05
736	Tom Gordon **RC**	.50
737	Wally Whitehurst **(RC)**	.05
738	Mike Aldrete	.05
739	Keith Miller	.05
740	Randy Milligan	.05
741	Jeff Parrett	.05
742	Steve Finley **RC**	.75
743	Junior Felix **RC**	.05
744	Pete Harnisch **RC**	.25
745	Bill Spiers **(RC)**	.05
746	Hensley Meulens **(RC)**	.05
747	Juan Bell	.05
748	Steve Sax	.05
749	Phil Bradley	.05
750	Rey Quinones	.05
751	Tommy Gregg **(RC)**	.05
752	Kevin Brown **(RC)**	.25
753	Derek Lilliquist **(RC)**	.05
754	Todd Zeile **RC**	.75
755	Jim Abbott	.05
756	Ozzie Canseco **RC**	.05
757	Nick Esasky	.05
758	Mike Moore	.05
759	Rob Murphy	.05
760	Rick Mahler	.05
761	Fred Lynn	.05
762	Kevin Blankenship **RC**	.05
763	Eddie Murray	1.00
764	Steve Searcy **RC**	.05
765	Jerome Walton **RC**	.05
766	Erik Hanson **RC**	.05
767	Bob Boone	.05
768	Edgar Martinez **(RC)**	.05
769	Jose DeJesus **RC**	.05
770	Greg Briley **RC**	.05
771	Steve Peters **RC**	.05
772	Rafael Palmeiro	.75
773	Jack Clark	.05
774	Nolan Ryan	2.00

775 Lance Parrish .05
776 Joe Girardi **RC** .30
777 Willie Randolph .05
778 Mitch Williams .05
779 Dennis Cook **RC** .05
780 Dwight Smith **RC** .05
781 Lenny Harris **RC** .10
782 Torey Lovullo **RC** .05
783 Norm Charlton **RC** .15
784 Chris Brown .05
785 Todd Benzinger .05
786 Shane Rawley .05
787 Omar Vizquel **RC** 2.00
788 LaVel Freeman **RC** .05
789 Jeffrey Leonard .05
790 Eddie Williams **RC** .05
791 Jamie Moyer .05
792 Bruce Hurst .05
793 Julio Franco .05
794 Claudell Washington .05
795 Jody Davis .05
796 Oddibe McDowell .05
797 Paul Kilgus .05
798 Tracy Jones .05
799 Steve Wilson **(RC)** .05
800 Pete O'Brien .05

1990 Upper Deck

Tom Gordon

	NM/M
Unopened Factory Set (800):	20.00
Complete Set (800):	15.00
Complete Low Set (700):	12.00
Complete High Set (100):	5.00
Common Player:	.05
Low or High Foil Pack (15):	.50
Low or High Foil Box (36):	12.00

1 Star Rookie Checklist .05
2 Randy Nosek **(RC) RC** .05
3 Tom Drees **(RC) RC** .05
4 Curt Young .05
5 Devon White Angels checklist .05
6 Luis Salazar .05
7 Von Hayes Phillies checklist .05
8 Jose Bautista .05
9 Marquis Grissom **RC** .50
10 Orel Hershiser Dodgers checklist .05
11 Rick Aguilera .05
12 Benito Santiago Padres checklist .05
13 Deion Sanders .10
14 Marvell Wynne .05
15 David West .05
16 Bobby Bonilla Pirates checklist .05
17 Sammy Sosa **RC** 5.00
18 Steve Sax Yankees checklist .05
19 Jack Howell .05
20 Mike Schmidt Mike Schmidt Retires .75
21 Robin Ventura .05
22 Brian Meyer **(RC)** .05
23 Blaine Beatty **(RC) RC** .05
24 Ken Griffey Jr. Mariners checklist .50
25 Greg Vaughn .05
26 Xavier Hernandez **RC** .05
27 Jason Grimsley **RC** .05
28 Eric Anthony **RC** .05
29 Tim Raines Expos checklist .05
30 David Wells .05
31 Hal Morris **(RC)** .05
32 Bo Jackson Royals checklist .10
33 Kelly Mann **(RC) RC** .05
34 Nolan Ryan Nolan Ryan 5000 Strikeouts 1.00
35 Scott Service **(RC) RC** .05
36 Mark McGwire Athletics checklist .50
37 Tino Martinez .05
38 Chili Davis .05
39 Scott Sanderson .05
40 Kevin Mitchell Giants checklist .05
41 Lou Whitaker Tigers checklist .05
42 Scott Coolbaugh **(RC) RC** .05
43 Jose Cano **(RC) RC** .05
44 Jose Vizcaino **RC** .10
45 Bob Hamelin **RC** .05
46 Jose Offerman **RC** .15
47 Kevin Blankenship .05
48 Kirby Puckett Twins checklist .40
49 Tommy Greene **RC** .05
50 Will Clark N.L. Top Vote Getter .05
51 Rob Nelson **(RC)** .05
52 Chris Hammond **RC** .15
53 Joe Carter Indians checklist .05
54a Ben McDonald **RC** (Orioles Logo) 1.00
54b Ben McDonald **RC** (Star Rookie logo) .25
55 Andy Benes .05
56 John Olerud **RC** 1.00
57 Roger Clemens Red Sox checklist .45
58 Tony Armas .05
59 George Canale **(RC) RC** .05
60a Mickey Tettleton Orioles checklist (#683 Jamie Weston) 1.00
60b Mickey Tettleton Orioles checklist (#683 Mickey Weston) .05
61 Mike Stanton **(RC) RC** .05
62 Dwight Gooden Mets checklist .05
63 Kent Mercker **RC** .10
64 Francisco Cabrera **RC** .05
65 Steve Avery .05
66 Jose Canseco .35
67 Matt Merullo **(RC) RC** .05
68 Vince Coleman Cardinals checklist .05
69 Ron Karkovice .05
70 Kevin Maas **RC** .05
71 Dennis Cook .05
72 Juan Gonzalez **RC** 2.00
73 Andre Dawson Cubs checklist .10
74 Dean Palmer **RC** .25
75 Bo Jackson A.L. Top Vote Getter .10
76 Rob Richie **(RC) RC** .05
77 Bobby Rose **(RC) RC** .05
78 Brian DuBois **(RC) RC** .05
79 Ozzie Guillen White Sox checklist .05
80 Gene Nelson .05
81 Bob McClure .05
82 Julio Franco Rangers checklist .05
83 Greg Minton .05
84 John Smoltz Braves checklist .05
85 Willie Fraser .05
86 Neal Heaton .05
87 Kevin Tapani **RC** .05
88 Mike Scott Astros checklist .05
89a Jim Gott (Incorrect photo.) 1.00
89b Jim Gott (Correct photo.) .05
90 Lance Johnson .05
91 Robin Yount Brewers checklist .35
92 Jeff Parrett .05
93 Julio Machado **(RC) RC** .05
94 Ron Jones .05
95 George Bell Blue Jays checklist .05
96 Jerry Reuss .05
97 Brian Fisher .05
98 Kevin Ritz **(RC) RC** .05
99 Barry Larkin Reds checklist .05
100 Checklist 1-100 .05
101 Gerald Perry .05
102 Kevin Appier .05
103 Julio Franco .05
104 Craig Biggio .05
105 Bo Jackson .10
106 Junior Felix **RC** .05
107 Mike Harkey **(RC)** .05
108 Fred McGriff .05
109 Rick Sutcliffe .05
110 Pete O'Brien .05
111 Kelly Gruber .05
112 Pat Borders .05
113 Dwight Evans .05
114 Dwight Gooden .05
115 Kevin Batiste **RC** .05
116 Eric Davis .05
117 Kevin Mitchell .05
118 Ron Oester .05
119 Brett Butler .05
120 Danny Jackson .05
121 Tommy Gregg .05
122 Ken Caminiti .05
123 Kevin Brown .05
124 George Brett .85
125 Mike Scott .05
126 Cory Snyder .05
127 George Bell .05
128 Mark Grace .05
129 Devon White .05
130 Tony Fernandez .05
131 Don Aase .05
132 Rance Mulliniks .05
133 Marty Barrett .05
134 Nelson Liriano .05
135 Mark Carreon **(RC)** .05
136 Candy Maldonado .05
137 Tim Birtsas .05
138 Tom Brookens .05
139 John Franco .05
140 Mike LaCoss .05
141 Jeff Treadway .05
142 Pat Tabler .05
143 Darrell Evans .05
144 Rafael Ramirez .05
145 Oddibe McDowell .05
146 Brian Downing .05
147 Curtis Wilkerson .05
148 Ernie Whitt .05
149 Bill Schroeder .05
150 Domingo Ramos .05
151 Rick Honeycutt .05
152 Don Slaught .05
153 Mitch Webster .05
154 Tony Phillips .05
155 Paul Kilgus .05
156 Ken Griffey Jr. 1.50
157 Gary Sheffield .35
158 Wally Backman .05
159 B.J. Surhoff .05
160 Louie Meadows .05
161 Paul O'Neill .05
162 Jeff McKnight **(RC) RC** .05
163 Alvaro Espinoza **(RC)** .05
164 Scott Scudder **(RC) RC** .05
165 Jeff Reed .05
166 Gregg Jefferies .05
167 Barry Larkin .05
168 Gary Carter .60
169 Robby Thompson .05
170 Rolando Roomes .05
171 Mark McGwire 1.50
172 Steve Sax .05
173 Mark Williamson .05
174 Mitch Williams .05
175 Brian Holton .05
176 Rob Deer .05
177 Tim Raines .05
178 Mike Felder .05
179 Harold Reynolds .05
180 Terry Francona .05
181 Chris Sabo .05
182 Darryl Strawberry .05
183 Willie Randolph .05
184 Billy Ripken .05
185 Mackey Sasser .05
186 Todd Benzinger .05
187 Kevin Elster .05
188 Jose Uribe .05
189 Tom Browning .05
190 Keith Miller .05
191 Don Mattingly .85
192 Dave Parker .05
193 Roberto Kelly .05
194 Phil Bradley .05
195 Ron Hassey .05
196 Gerald Young .05
197 Hubie Brooks .05
198 Bill Doran .05
199 Al Newman .05
200 Checklist 101-200 .05
201 Terry Puhl .05
202 Frank DiPino .05
203 Jim Clancy .05
204 Bob Ojeda .05
205 Alex Trevino .05
206 Dave Henderson .05
207 Henry Cotto .05
208 Rafael Belliard .05
209 Stan Javier .05
210 Jerry Reed .05
211 Doug Dascenzo .05
212 Andres Thomas .05
213 Greg Maddux .75
214 Mike Schooler .05
215 Lonnie Smith .05
216 Jose Rijo .05
217 Greg Gagne .05
218 Jim Gantner .05
219 Allan Anderson .05
220 Rick Mahler .05
221 Jim Deshaies .05
222 Keith Hernandez .05
223 Vince Coleman .05
224 David Cone .05
225 Ozzie Smith .75
226 Matt Nokes .05
227 Barry Bonds 2.00
228 Felix Jose .05
229 Dennis Powell .05
230 Mike Gallego .05
231 Shawon Dunston .05
232 Ron Gant .05
233 Omar Vizquel .05
234 Derek Lilliquist .05
235 Erik Hanson .05
236 Kirby Puckett .75
237 Bill Spiers .05
238 Dan Gladden .05
239 Bryan Clutterbuck **(RC)** .05
240 John Moses .05
241 Ron Darling .05
242 Joe Magrane .05
243 Dave Magadan .05
244 Pedro Guerrero .05
245 Glenn Davis .05
246 Terry Steinbach .05
247 Fred Lynn .05
248 Gary Redus .05
249 Kenny Williams .05
250 Sid Bream .05
251 Bob Welch .05
252 Bill Buckner .05
253 Carney Lansford .05
254 Paul Molitor .60
255 Jose DeJesus .05
256 Orel Hershiser .05
257 Tom Brunansky .05
258 Mike Davis .05
259 Jeff Ballard .05
260 Scott Terry .05
261 Sid Fernandez .05
262 Mike Marshall .05
263 Howard Johnson .05
264 Kirk Gibson .05
265 Kevin McReynolds .05
266 Cal Ripken, Jr. 2.00
267 Ozzie Guillen .05
268 Jim Traber .05
269 Bobby Thigpen .05
270 Joe Orsulak .05
271 Bob Boone .05
272 Dave Stewart .05
273 Tim Wallach .05
274 Luis Aquino .05
275 Mike Moore .05
276 Tony Pena .05
277 Eddie Murray .60
278 Milt Thompson .05
279 Alejandro Pena .05
280 Ken Dayley .05
281 Carmen Castillo .05
282 Tom Henke .05
283 Mickey Hatcher .05
284 Roy Smith **(RC)** .05
285 Manny Lee .05
286 Dan Pasqua .05
287 Larry Sheets .05
288 Garry Templeton .05
289 Eddie Williams .05
290 Brady Anderson .05
291 Spike Owen .05
292 Storm Davis .05
293 Chris Bosio .05
294 Jim Eisenreich .05
295 Don August .05
296 Jeff Hamilton .05
297 Mickey Tettleton .05
298 Mike Scioscia .05
299 Kevin Hickey **(RC)** .05
300 Checklist 201-300 .05
301 Shawn Abner .05
302 Kevin Bass .05
303 Bip Roberts **(RC)** .05
304 Joe Girardi .05
305 Danny Darwin .05
306 Mike Heath .05
307 Mike Macfarlane .05
308 Ed Whitson .05
309 Tracy Jones .05
310 Scott Fletcher .05
311 Darnell Coles .05
312 Mike Brumley .05
313 Bill Swift .05
314 Charlie Hough .05
315 Jim Presley .05
316 Luis Polonia .05
317 Mike Morgan .05
318 Lee Guetterman .05
319 Jose Oquendo .05
320 Wayne Tollenson .05
321 Jody Reed .05
322 Damon Berryhill .05
323 Roger Clemens .85
324 Ryne Sandberg .75
325 Benito Santiago .05
326 Bret Saberhagen .05
327 Lou Whitaker .05
328 Dave Gallagher .05
329 Mike Pagliarulo .05
330 Doyle Alexander .05
331 Jeffrey Leonard .05
332 Torey Lovullo .05
333 Pete Incaviglia .05
334 Rickey Henderson .60
335 Rafael Palmeiro .50
336 Ken Hill **(RC)** .05
337 Dave Winfield .60
338 Alfredo Griffin .05
339 Andy Hawkins .05
340 Ted Power .05
341 Steve Wilson .05
342 Jack Clark .05
343 Ellis Burks .05
344 Tony Gwynn .75
345 Jerome Walton .05
346 Roberto Alomar .20
347 Carlos Martinez **(RC) RC** .05
348 Chet Lemon .05
349 Willie Wilson .05
350 Greg Walker .05
351 Tom Bolton .05
352 German Gonzalez **(RC)** .05
353 Harold Baines .05
354 Mike Greenwell .05
355 Ruben Sierra .05
356 Andres Galarraga .05
357 Andre Dawson .25
358 Jeff Brantley **(RC) RC** .05
359 Mike Bielecki .05
360 Ken Oberkfell .05
361 Kurt Stillwell .05
362 Brian Holman .05
363 Kevin Seitzer .05
364 Alvin Davis .05
365 Tom Gordon .05
366 Bobby Bonilla .05
367 Carlton Fisk .60
368 Steve Carter **(RC) RC** .05
369 Joel Skinner .05
370 John Cangelosi .05
371 Cecil Espy .05
372 Gary Wayne **(RC) RC** .05
373 Jim Rice .20
374 Mike Dyer **(RC) RC** .05
375 Joe Carter .05
376 Dwight Smith .05
377 John Wetteland **RC** .15
378 Ernie Riles .05
379 Otis Nixon .05
380 Vance Law .05

381	Dave Bergman	.05
382	Frank White	.05
383	Scott Bradley	.05
384	Israel Sanchez	.05
385	Gary Pettis	.05
386	Donn Pall **(RC)**	.05
387	John Smiley	.05
388	Tom Candiotti	.05
389	Junior Ortiz	.05
390	Steve Lyons	.05
391	Brian Harper	.05
392	Fred Manrique	.05
393	Lee Smith	.05
394	Jeff Kunkel	.05
395	Claudell Washington	.05
396	John Tudor	.05
397	Terry Kennedy	.05
398	Lloyd McClendon	.05
399	Craig Lefferts	.05
400	Checklist 301-400	.05
401	Keith Moreland	.05
402	Rich Gedman	.05
403	Jeff Robinson	.05
404	Randy Ready	.05
405	Rick Cerone	.05
406	Jeff Blauser	.05
407	Larry Andersen	.05
408	Joe Boever	.05
409	Felix Fermin	.05
410	Glenn Wilson	.05
411	Rex Hudler	.05
412	Mark Grant	.05
413	Dennis Martinez	.05
414	Darrin Jackson	.05
415	Mike Aldrete	.05
416	Roger McDowell	.05
417	Jeff Reardon	.05
418	Darren Daulton	.05
419	Tim Laudner	.05
420	Don Carman	.05
421	Lloyd Moseby	.05
422	Doug Drabek	.05
423	Lenny Harris	.05
424	Jose Lind	.05
425	Dave Johnson **RC**	.05
426	Jerry Browne	.05
427	Eric Yelding **(RC) RC**	.05
428	Brad Komminsk **(RC)**	.05
429	Jody Davis	.05
430	Mariano Duncan **(RC)**	.05
431	Mark Davis	.05
432	Nelson Santovenia	.05
433	Bruce Hurst	.05
434	Jeff Huson **(RC) RC**	.05
435	Chris James	.05
436	Mark Guthrie **(RC) RC**	.05
437	Charlie Hayes **(RC)**	.05
438	Shane Rawley	.05
439	Dickie Thon	.05
440	Juan Berenguer	.05
441	Kevin Romine	.05
442	Bill Landrum	.05
443	Todd Frohwirth	.05
444	Craig Worthington	.05
445	Fernando Valenzuela	.05
446	Albert Belle	.05
447	Ed Whited **(RC) RC**	.05
448	Dave Smith	.05
449	Dave Clark	.05
450	Juan Agosto	.05
451	Dave Valle	.05
452	Kent Hrbek	.05
453	Von Hayes	.05
454	Gary Gaetti	.05
455	Greg Briley	.05
456	Glenn Braggs	.05
457	Kirt Manwaring	.05
458	Mel Hall	.05
459	Brook Jacoby	.05
460	Pat Sheridan	.05
461	Rob Murphy	.05
462	Jimmy Key	.05
463	Nick Esasky	.05
464	Rob Ducey	.05
465	Carlos Quintana	.05
466	Larry Walker **RC**	1.00
467	Todd Worrell	.05
468	Kevin Gross	.05
469	Terry Pendleton	.05
470	Dave Martinez	.05
471	Gene Larkin	.05
472	Len Dykstra	.05
473	Barry Lyons	.05
474	Terry Mulholland **(RC)**	.05
475	Chip Hale **(RC) RC**	.05
476	Jesse Barfield	.05
477	Dan Plesac	.05
478a	Scott Garrelts (Photo actually Bill Bathe.)	1.00
478b	Scott Garrelts (Correct photo.)	.05
479	Dave Righetti	.05
480	Gus Polidor **(RC)**	.05
481	Mookie Wilson	.05
482	Luis Rivera	.05
483	Mike Flanagan	.05
484	Dennis "Oil Can" Boyd	.05
485	John Cerutti	.05
486	John Costello	.05
487	Pascual Perez	.05
488	Tommy Herr	.05
489	Tom Foley	.05
490	Curt Ford	.05
491	Steve Lake	.05
492	Tim Teufel	.05
493	Randy Bush	.05
494	Mike Jackson	.05
495	Steve Jeltz	.05
496	Paul Gibson	.05
497	Steve Balboni	.05
498	Bud Black	.05
499	Dale Sveum	.05
500	Checklist 401-500	.05
501	Timmy Jones	.05
502	Mark Portugal	.05
503	Ivan Calderon	.05
504	Rick Rhoden	.05
505	Willie McGee	.05
506	Kirk McCaskill	.05
507	Dave LaPoint	.05
508	Jay Howell	.05
509	Johnny Ray	.05
510	Dave Anderson	.05
511	Chuck Crim	.05
512	Joe Hesketh	.05
513	Dennis Eckersley	.40
514	Greg Brock	.05
515	Tim Burke **(RC)**	.05
516	Frank Tanana	.05
517	Jay Bell	.05
518	Guillermo Hernandez	.05
519	Randy Kramer **(RC)**	.05
520	Charles Hudson	.05
521	Jim Corsi **(RC)**	.05
522	Steve Rosenberg	.05
523	Cris Carpenter	.05
524	Matt Winters **(RC) RC**	.05
525	Melido Perez	.05
526	Chris Gwynn **(RC)**	.05
527	Bert Blyleven	.05
528	Chuck Cary **(RC)**	.05
529	Daryl Boston	.05
530	Dale Mohorcic	.05
531	Geronimo Berroa **(RC)**	.05
532	Edgar Martinez	.05
533	Dale Murphy	.20
534	Jay Buhner	.05
535	John Smoltz	.05
536	Andy Van Slyke	.05
537	Mike Henneman **(RC)**	.05
538	Miguel Garcia **(RC)**	.05
539	Frank Williams **(RC)**	.05
540	R.J. Reynolds	.05
541	Shawn Hillegas **(RC)**	.05
542	Walt Weiss	.05
543	Greg Hibbard **(RC) RC**	.05
544	Nolan Ryan	2.00
545	Todd Zeile	.05
546	Hensley Meulens	.05
547	Tim Belcher **(RC)**	.05
548	Mike Witt	.05
549	Greg Cadaret **(RC)**	.05
550	Franklin Stubbs	.05
551	Tony Castillo **(RC) RC**	.05
552	Jeff Robinson	.05
553	Steve Olin **(RC) RC**	.05
554	Alan Trammell	.05
555	Wade Boggs	.75
556	Will Clark	.05
557	Jeff King	.05
558	Mike Fitzgerald	.05
559	Ken Howell **(RC)**	.05
560	Bob Kipper	.05
561	Scott Bankhead **(RC)**	.05
562a	Jeff Innis **(RC) RC** (Photo actually David West.)	1.00
562b	Jeff Innis **(RC) RC** (Correct photo.)	.05
563	Randy Johnson	.60
564	Wally Whitehurst **(RC) RC**	.05
565	Gene Harris **(RC) RC**	.05
566	Norm Charlton **(RC)**	.05
567	Robin Yount	.60
568	Joe Oliver **RC**	.05
569	Mark Parent	.05
570	John Farrell **(RC)**	.05
571	Tom Glavine	.20
572	Rod Nichols **(RC)**	.05
573	Jack Morris	.05
574	Greg Swindell **(RC)**	.05
575	Steve Searcy **(RC)**	.05
576	Ricky Jordan **(RC)**	.05
577	Matt Williams	.05
578	Mike LaValliere **(RC)**	.05
579	Bryn Smith	.05
580	Bruce Ruffin **(RC)**	.05
581	Randy Myers	.05
582	Rick Wrona **(RC) RC**	.05
583	Juan Samuel	.05
584	Les Lancaster **(RC)**	.05
585	Jeff Musselman	.05
586	Rob Dibble **(RC)**	.05
587	Eric Show	.05
588	Jesse Orosco	.05
589	Herm Winningham	.05
590	Andy Allanson	.05
591	Dion James	.05
592	Carmelo Martinez **(RC)**	.05
593	Luis Quinones **(RC)**	.05
594	Dennis Rasmussen **(RC)**	.05
595	Rich Yett	.05
596	Bob Walk **(RC)**	.05
597a	Andy McGaffigan (Thompson. Player #48, photo actually Rich)	.75
597b	Andy McGaffigan (Player #27, correct photo.)	.05
598	Billy Hatcher **(RC)**	.05
599	Bob Knepper	.05
600	Checklist 501-600	.05
601	Joey Cora **(RC)**	.05
602	Steve Finley **RC**	.20
603	Kal Daniels	.05
604	Gregg Olson	.05
605	Dave Steib	.05
606	Kenny Rogers **(RC) RC**	.05
607	Zane Smith	.05
608	Bob Geren **(RC) RC**	.05
609	Chad Kreuter	.05
610	Mike Smithson **(RC)**	.05
611	Jeff Wetherby **(RC) RC**	.05
612	Gary Mielke **(RC) RC**	.05
613	Pete Smith	.05
614	Jack Daugherty **(RC) RC**	.05
615	Lance McCullers	.05
616	Don Robinson **(RC)**	.05
617	Jose Guzman	.05
618	Steve Bedrosian **(RC)**	.05
619	Jamie Moyer	.05
620	Atlee Hammaker **(RC)**	.05
621	Rick Luecken **(RC) RC**	.05
622	Greg W. Harris **(RC)**	.05
623	Pete Harnisch	.05
624	Jerald Clark **(RC)**	.05
625	Jack McDowell	.05
626	Frank Viola	.05
627	Ted Higuera	.05
628	Marty Pevey **(RC) RC**	.05
629	Bill Wegman	.05
630	Eric Plunk **(RC)**	.05
631	Drew Hall	.05
632	Doug Jones **(RC)**	.05
633	Geno Petralli	.05
634	Jose Alvarez **(RC)**	.05
635	Bob Milacki	.05
636	Bobby Witt **(RC)**	.05
637	Trevor Wilson	.05
638	Jeff Russell **(RC)**	.05
639	Mike Krukow	.05
640	Rick Leach **(RC)**	.05
641	Dave Schmidt	.05
642	Terry Leach **(RC)**	.05
643	Calvin Schiraldi	.05
644	Bob Melvin **(RC)**	.05
645	Jim Abbott	.05
646	Jaime Navarro **RC**	.05
647	Mark Langston	.05
648	Juan Nieves **(RC)**	.05
649	Damaso Garcia	.05
650	Charlie O'Brien **(RC)**	.05
651	Eric King	.05
652	Mike Boddicker	.05
653	Duane Ward	.05
654	Bob Stanley	.05
655	Sandy Alomar, Jr.	.05
656	Danny Tartabull	.05
657	Randy McCament	.05
658	Charlie Leibrandt	.05
659	Dan Quisenberry	.05
660	Paul Assenmacher **(RC)**	.05
661	Walt Terrell	.05
662	Tim Leary	.05
663	Randy Milligan	.05
664	Bo Diaz **(RC)**	.05
665	Mark Lemke	.05
666	Jose Gonzalez **(RC)**	.05
667	Chuck Finley	.05
668	John Kruk	.05
669	Dick Schofield	.05
670	Tim Crews	.05
671	John Dopson	.05
672	John Orton **RC**	.05
673	Eric Hetzel **(RC)**	.05
674	Lance Parrish	.05
675	Ramon Martinez	.05
676	Mark Gubicza	.05
677	Greg Litton	.05
678	Greg Mathews	.05
679	Dave Dravecky	.05
680	Steve Farr **(RC)**	.05
681	Mike Devereaux	.05
682	Ken Griffey Sr.	.05
683a	Jamie Weston **(RC) RC** (First name incorrect.)	1.00
683b	Mickey Weston **(RC) RC** (Corrected)	.05
684	Jack Armstrong	.05
685	Steve Buechele	.05
686	Bryan Harvey	.05
687	Lance Blankenship	.05
688	Dante Bichette	.05
689	Todd Burns **(RC)**	.05
690	Dan Petry	.05
691	Kent Anderson **RC**	.05
692	Todd Stottlemyre	.05
693	Wally Joyner	.05
694	Mike Rochford **(RC)**	.05
695	Floyd Bannister	.05
696	Rick Reuschel	.05
697	Jose DeLeon **(RC)**	.05
698	Jeff Montgomery	.05
699	Kelly Downs	.05
700a	Checklist 601-700 (#683 Jamie Weston)	.05
700b	Checklist 601-700 (# 683 Mickey Weston)	.05
701	Jim Gott	.05
702	Delino DeShields, Larry Walker, Marquis Grissom "Rookie Threats"	.25
703	Alejandro Pena	.05
704	Willie Randolph	.05
705	Tim Leary	.05
706	Chuck McElroy **(RC)**	.05
707	Gerald Perry **(RC)**	.05
708	Tom Brunansky	.05
709	John Franco	.05
710	Mark Davis	.05
711	Dave Justice **RC**	1.50
712	Storm Davis	.05
713	Scott Ruskin **(RC)**	.05
714	Glenn Braggs	.05
715	Kevin Bearse **(RC)**	.05
716	Jose Nunez **(RC)**	.05
717	Tim Layana **(RC)**	.05
718	Greg Myers **(RC)**	.05
719	Pete O'Brien	.05
720	John Candelaria	.05
721	Craig Grebeck	.05
722	Shawn Boskie **(RC)**	.05
723	Jim Leyritz **(RC)**	.10
724	Bill Sampen **(RC)**	.05
725	Scott Radinsky **(RC)**	.05
726	Todd Hundley **RC**	.25
727	Scott Hemond **(RC)**	.05
728	Lenny Webster **(RC)**	.05
729	Jeff Reardon	.05
730	Mitch Webster	.05
731	Brian Bohanon **(RC)**	.05
732	Rick Parker **(RC)**	.05
733	Terry Shumpert **(RC)**	.05
734a	Nolan Ryan (300-win stripe on front)	1.50
734b	Nolan Ryan (No stripe.)	4.00
735	John Burkett	.05
736	Derrick May **RC**	.05
737	Carlos Baerga **RC**	.05
738	Greg Smith **(RC)**	.05
739	Joe Kraemer **(RC)**	.05
740	Scott Sanderson **(RC)**	.05
741	Hector Villanueva **(RC)**	.05
742	Mike Fetters **(RC)**	.05
743	Mark Gardner **(RC)**	.05
744	Matt Nokes **(RC)**	.05
745	Dave Winfield	.60
746	Delino DeShields **RC**	.15
747	Dann Howitt **(RC)**	.05
748	Tony Pena	.05
749	Oil Can Boyd	.05
750	Mike Benjamin **(RC)**	.05
751	Alex Cole **(RC)**	.05
752	Eric Gunderson **(RC)**	.05
753	Howard Farmer **(RC)**	.05
754	Joe Carter	.05
755	Ray Lankford **RC**	.25
756	Sandy Alomar,Jr.	.05
757	Alex Sanchez **(RC)**	.05
758	Nick Esasky	.05
759	Stan Belinda **(RC)**	.05
760	Jim Presley **(RC)**	.05
761	Gary DiSarcina **(RC)**	.05
762	Wayne Edwards **(RC)**	.05
763	Pat Combs **(RC)**	.05
764	Mickey Pina **(RC)**	.05
765	Wilson Alvarez **RC**	.25
766	Dave Parker	.05
767	Mike Blowers **(RC)**	.05
768	Tony Phillips	.05
769	Pascual Perez	.05
770	Gary Pettis	.05
771	Fred Lynn	.05
772	Mel Rojas **RC**	.10
773	David Segui **(RC)**	.25
774	Gary Carter	.60
775	Rafael Valdez **(RC)**	.05
776	Glenallen Hill **(RC)**	.05
777	Keith Hernandez	.05
778	Billy Hatcher	.05
779	Marty Clary **(RC)**	.05
780	Candy Maldonado **(RC)**	.05
781	Mike Marshall	.05
782	Billy Jo Robidoux **(RC)**	.05
783	Mark Langston	.05
784	Paul Sorrento **RC**	.05
785	Dave Hollins **RC**	.05
786	Cecil Fielder	.05
787	Matt Young	.05
788	Jeff Huson	.05
789	Lloyd Moseby	.05
790	Ron Kittle	.05
791	Hubie Brooks	.05
792	Craig Lefferts	.05
793	Kevin Bass	.05
794	Bryn Smith **(RC)**	.05
795	Juan Samuel	.05
796	Sam Horn	.05
797	Randy Myers	.05
798	Chris James **(RC)**	.05
799	Bill Gullickson	.05
800	Checklist 701-800	.05

Baseball Heroes Reggie Jackson

	NM/M
Complete Set (10):	5.00
Common Player:	.50
Autographed Card:	100.00
1 Reggie Jackson 1969 Emerging Superstar	.50
2 Reggie Jackson 1973 An MVP Year	.50
3 Reggie Jackson 1977 "Mr. October"	.50
4 Reggie Jackson 1978 Jackson vs. Welch	.50
5 Reggie Jackson 1982 Under the Halo	.50
6 Reggie Jackson 1984 500!	.50
7 Reggie Jackson 1986 Moving Up the List	.50
8 Reggie Jackson 1987 A Great Career Ends	.50
9 Reggie Jackson Heroes Checklist 1-9	.50
---- Header Card	.50

1991 Upper Deck

	NM/M
Unopened Factory Set (800):	20.00
Complete Set (800):	10.00
Complete Low Series (700):	9.00
Complete High Series (100):	1.00
Common Player:	.05
Low or High Wax Pack (15):	.60
Low or High Wax Box (36):	13.50

1 Star Rookie Checklist .05
2 Phil Plantier **RC** .05
3 D.J. Dozier **(RC) RC** .05
4 Dave Hansen **(RC)** .05
5 Mo Vaughn **(RC)** .10
6 Leo Gomez **RC** .05
7 Scott Aldred **(RC) RC** .05
8 Scott Chiamparino **RC** .05
9 Lance Dickson **RC** .05
10 Sean Berry **RC** .05
11 Bernie Williams **(RC)** .25
12 Brian Barnes **RC** .05
13 Narciso Elvira **RC** .05
14 Mike Gardiner **RC** .05
15 Greg Colbrunn **RC** .05
16 Bernard Gilkey **RC** .05
17 Mark Lewis **(RC)** .05
18 Mickey Morandini **RC** .05
19 Charles Nagy **(RC)** .05
20 Geronimo Pena **RC** .05
21 Henry Rodriguez **RC** .05
22 Scott Cooper **(RC)** .05
23 Andujar Cedeno **RC** .05
24 Eric Karros **RC** .25
25 Steve Decker **RC** .05
26 Kevin Belcher **RC** .05
27 Jeff Conine **RC** .25
28 Dave Stewart Oakland Athletics checklist .05
29 Carlton Fisk Chicago White Sox checklist .20
30 Rafael Palmeiro Texas Rangers checklist .20
31 Chuck Finley California Angels checklist .05
32 Harold Reynolds Seattle Mariners checklist .05
33 Bret Saberhagen Kansas City Royals checklist .05
34 Gary Gaetti Minnesota Twins checklist .05
35 Scott Leius .05
36 Neal Heaton .05
37 Terry Lee **RC** .05
38 Gary Redus .05
39 Barry Jones .05
40 Chuck Knoblauch .05
41 Larry Andersen .05
42 Darryl Hamilton .05
43 Mike Greenwell Boston Red Sox checklist .05
44 Kelly Gruber Toronto Blue Jays checklist .05
45 Jack Morris Detroit Tigers checklist .05
46 Sandy Alomar Jr. Cleveland Indians checklist .05
47 Gregg Olson Baltimore Orioles checklist .05
48 Dave Parker Milwaukee Brewers checklist .05
49 Roberto Kelly New York Yankees checklist .05
50 Top Prospect '91 checklist .05
51 Kyle Abbott **RC** .10
52 Jeff Juden **(RC)** .05
53 Todd Van Poppel **RC** .10
54 Steve Karsay **RC** .10
55 Chipper Jones **RC** 6.00
56 Chris Johnson **RC** .05
57 John Ericks **RC** .05
58 Gary Scott **RC** .05
59 Kiki Jones **(RC)** .05
60 Wil Cordero **RC** .05
61 Royce Clayton **RC** .05
62 Tim Costo **RC** .05
63 Roger Salkeld **(RC)** .05
64 Brook Fordyce **RC** .05
65 Mike Mussina **RC** 1.00
66 Dave Staton **RC** .05
67 Mike Lieberthal **RC** .50
68 Kurt Miller **RC** .05
69 Dan Peltier **RC** .05
70 Greg Blosser **(RC)** .05
71 Reggie Sanders **RC** .25
72 Brent Mayne **(RC)** .05
73 Rico Brogna **RC** .05
74 Willie Banks **RC** .05
75 Len Brutcher **RC** .05
76 Pat Kelly **RC** .05
77 Chris Sabo Cincinnati Reds checklist .05
78 Ramon Martinez Los Angeles Dodgers checklist .05
79 Matt Williams San Francisco Giants checklist .05
80 Roberto Alomar San Diego Padres checklist .05
81 Glenn Davis Houston Astros checklist .05
82 Ron Gant Atlanta Braves checklist .05
83 Cecil Fielder "Fielder's Feat" .05
84 Orlando Merced **RC** .10
85 Domingo Ramos .05
86 Tom Bolton .05
87 Andres Santana **(RC) RC** .05
88 John Dopson **(RC)** .05
89 Kenny Williams .05
90 Marty Barrett .05
91 Tom Pagnozzi .05
92 Carmelo Martinez .05
93 Bobby Thigpen "Save Master" .05
94 Barry Bonds Pittsburgh Pirates checklist .50
95 Gregg Jefferies New York Mets checklist .05
96 Tim Wallach Montreal Expos checklist .05
97 Lenny Dykstra Philadelphia Phillies checklist .05
98 Pedro Guerrero St. Louis Cardinals checklist .05
99 Mark Grace Chicago Cubs checklist .05
100 Checklist 1-100 .05
101 Kevin Elster .05
102 Tom Brookens .05
103 Mackey Sasser .05
104 Felix Fermin **(RC)** .05
105 Kevin McReynolds .05
106 Dave Steib .05
107 Jeffrey Leonard .05
108 Dave Henderson .05
109 Sid Bream .05
110 Henry Cotto .05
111 Shawon Dunston .05
112 Mariano Duncan **(RC)** .05
113 Joe Girardi .05
114 Billy Hatcher .05
115 Greg Maddux .50
116 Jerry Browne **(RC)** .05
117 Juan Samuel .05
118 Steve Olin .05
119 Alfredo Griffin .05
120 Mitch Webster **(RC)** .05
121 Joel Skinner .05
122 Frank Viola .05
123 Cory Snyder .05
124 Howard Johnson .05
125 Carlos Baerga .05
126 Tony Fernandez .05
127 Dave Stewart .05
128 Jay Buhner .05
129 Mike LaValliere .05
130 Scott Bradley .05
131 Tony Phillips .05
132 Ryne Sandberg .50
133 Paul O'Neill .05
134 Mark Grace .05
135 Chris Sabo .05
136 Ramon Martinez .05
137 Brook Jacoby .05
138 Candy Maldonado .05
139 Mike Scioscia .05
140 Chris James **(RC)** .05
141 Craig Worthington .05
142 Manny Lee .05
143 Tim Raines .05
144 Sandy Alomar, Jr. .05
145 John Olerud .05
146 Ozzie Canseco **RC** .05
147 Pat Borders .05
148 Harold Reynolds .05
149 Tom Henke .05
150 R.J. Reynolds .05
151 Mike Gallego .05
152 Bobby Bonilla .05
153 Terry Steinbach .05
154 Barry Bonds 1.00
155 Jose Canseco .30
156 Gregg Jefferies .05
157 Matt Williams .05
158 Craig Biggio .05
159 Daryl Boston .05
160 Ricky Jordan .05
161 Stan Belinda .05
162 Ozzie Smith .50
163 Tom Brunansky .05
164 Todd Zeile .05
165 Mike Greenwell .05
166 Kal Daniels .05
167 Kent Hrbek .05
168 Franklin Stubbs .05
169 Dick Schofield .05
170 Junior Ortiz .05
171 Hector Villanueva **RC** .05
172 Dennis Eckersley .35
173 Mitch Williams .05
174 Mark McGwire .75
175 Fernando Valenzuela .05
176 Gary Carter .40
177 Dave Magadan .05
178 Robby Thompson .05
179 Bob Ojeda .05
180 Ken Caminiti .05
181 Don Slaught .05
182 Luis Rivera .05
183 Jay Bell .05
184 Jody Reed .05
185 Wally Backman .05
186 Dave Martinez .05
187 Luis Polonia .05
188 Shane Mack .05
189 Spike Owen .05
190 Scott Bailes .05
191 John Russell .05
192 Walt Weiss .05
193 Jose Oquendo .05
194 Carney Lansford .05
195 Jeff Huson .05
196 Keith Miller .05
197 Eric Yelding .05
198 Ron Darling .05
199 John Kruk .05
200 Checklist 101-200 .05
201 John Shelby .05
202 Bob Geren .05
203 Lance McCullers .05
204 Alvaro Espinoza .05
205 Mark Salas .05
206 Mike Pagliarulo .05
207 Jose Uribe .05
208 Jim Deshaies **(RC)** .05
209 Ron Karkovice .05
210 Rafael Ramirez .05
211 Donnie Hill .05
212 Brian Harper **(RC)** .05
213 Jack Howell .05
214 Wes Gardner .05
215 Tim Burke .05
216 Doug Jones **(RC)** .05
217 Hubie Brooks .05
218 Tom Candiotti .05
219 Gerald Perry .05
220 Jose DeLeon **(RC)** .05
221 Wally Whitehurst .05
222 Alan Mills **RC** .05
223 Alan Trammell .05
224 Dwight Gooden .05
225 Travis Fryman .05
226 Joe Carter .05
227 Julio Franco .05
228 Craig Lefferts .05
229 Gary Pettis .05
230 Dennis Rasmussen .05
231a Brian Downing (No position on front.) 2.00
231b Brian Downing (DH on front) .05
232 Carlos Quintana **(RC)** .05
233 Gary Gaetti .05
234 Mark Langston .05
235 Tim Wallach .05
236 Greg Swindell .05
237 Eddie Murray .40
238 Jeff Manto **(RC)** .05
239 Lenny Harris .05
240 Jesse Orosco .05
241 Scott Lusader .05
242 Sid Fernandez .05
243 Jim Leyritz .05
244 Cecil Fielder .05
245 Darryl Strawberry .05
246 Frank Thomas **(RC)** .50
247 Kevin Mitchell .05
248 Lance Johnson **(RC)** .05
249 Rick Rueschel .05
250 Mark Portugal .05
251 Derek Lilliquist .05
252 Brian Holman **(RC)** .05
253 Rafael Valdez .05
254 B.J. Surhoff .05
255 Tony Gwynn .50
256 Andy Van Slyke .05
257 Todd Stottlemyre .05
258 Jose Lind .05
259 Greg Myers .05
260 Jeff Ballard **(RC)** .05
261 Bobby Thigpen .05
262 Jimmy Kremers **(RC) RC** .05
263 Robin Ventura .05
264 John Smoltz .05
265 Sammy Sosa .50
266 Gary Sheffield .30
267 Len Dykstra .05
268 Bill Spiers .05
269 Charlie Hayes .05
270 Brett Butler .05
271 Bip Roberts .05
272 Rob Deer .05
273 Fred Lynn .05
274 Dave Parker .05
275 Andy Benes .05
276 Glenallen Hill **(RC)** .05
277 Steve Howard **(RC) RC** .05
278 Doug Drabek .05
279 Joe Oliver .05
280 Todd Benzinger .05
281 Eric King .05
282 Jim Presley .05
283 Ken Patterson **(RC)** .05
284 Jack Daugherty **(RC)** .05
285 Ivan Calderon .05
286 Edgar Diaz **(RC) RC** .05
287 Kevin Bass .05
288 Don Carman **(RC)** .05
289 Greg Brock .05
290 John Franco .05
291 Joey Cora .05
292 Bill Wegman .05
293 Eric Show .05
294 Scott Bankhead .05
295 Garry Templeton .05
296 Mickey Tettleton .05
297 Luis Sojo .05
298 Jose Rijo .05
299 Dave Johnson .05
300 Checklist 201-300 .05
301 Mark Grant .05
302 Pete Harnisch .05
303 Greg Olson .05
304 Anthony Telford **(RC) RC** .05
305 Lonnie Smith .05
306 Chris Hoiles .05
307 Bryn Smith .05
308 Mike Devereaux .05
309a Milt Thompson ("86" in stats obscured by "bull's eye") .50
309b Milt Thompson ("86" visible) .05
310 Bob Melvin .05
311a Luis Salazar (Circled dot over "i" in Luis on back.) 2.00
311b Luis Salazar (Corrected) .05
312 Ed Whitson **(RC)** .05
313 Charlie Hough .05
314 Dave Clark .05
315 Eric Gunderson **RC** .05
316 Dan Petry .05
317 Dante Bichette .05
318 Mike Heath .05
319 Damon Berryhill .05
320 Walt Terrell .05
321 Scott Fletcher .05
322 Dan Plesac .05
323 Jack McDowell .05
324 Paul Molitor .40
325 Ozzie Guillen .05
326 Gregg Olson .05
327 Pedro Guerrero .05
328 Bob Milacki **(RC)** .05
329 John Tudor .05
330 Steve Finley .05
331 Jack Clark .05
332 Jerome Walton .05
333 Andy Hawkins .05
334 Derrick May .05
335 Roberto Alomar .20
336 Jack Morris .05
337 Dave Winfield .40
338 Steve Searcy .05
339 Chili Davis .05
340 Larry Sheets .05
341 Ted Higuera .05

342 David Segui **RC** .10
343 Greg Cadaret .05
344 Robin Yount .40
345 Nolan Ryan 1.00
346 Ray Lankford .05
347 Cal Ripken, Jr. 1.00
348 Lee Smith .05
349 Brady Anderson .05
350 Frank DiPino .05
351 Hal Morris .05
352 Deion Sanders .10
353 Barry Larkin .05
354 Don Mattingly .60
355 Eric Davis .05
356 Jose Offerman .05
357 Mel Rojas .05
358 Rudy Seanez **(RC)** .05
359 Oil Can Boyd .05
360 Nelson Liriano .05
361 Ron Gant .05
362 Howard Farmer **RC** .05
363 Dave Justice .05
364 Delino DeShields .05
365 Steve Avery .05
366 David Cone .05
367 Lou Whitaker .05
368 Von Hayes .05
369 Frank Tanana .05
370 Tim Teufel .05
371 Randy Myers .05
372 Roberto Kelly .05
373 Jack Armstrong .05
374 Kelly Gruber .05
375 Kevin Maas .05
376 Randy Johnson .40
377 David West .05
378 Brent Knackert **RC** .05
379 Rick Honeycutt .05
380 Kevin Gross .05
381 Tom Foley .05
382 Jeff Blauser .05
383 Scott Ruskin **RC** .05
384 Andres Thomas **(RC)** .05
385 Dennis Martinez .05
386 Mike Henneman .05
387 Felix Jose .05
388 Alejandro Pena .05
389 Chet Lemon .05
390 Craig Wilson **RC** .05
391 Chuck Crim .05
392 Mel Hall .05
393 Mark Knudson .05
394 Norm Charlton .05
395 Mike Felder .05
396 Tim Layana **RC** .05
397 Steve Frey **(RC)** .05
398 Bill Doran .05
399 Dion James .05
400 Checklist 301-400 .05
401 Ron Hassey .05
402 Don Robinson .05
403 Gene Nelson .05
404 Terry Kennedy .05
405 Todd Burns .05
406 Roger McDowell .05
407 Bob Kipper .05
408 Darren Daulton .05
409 Chuck Cary .05
410 Bruce Ruffin .05
411 Juan Berenguer .05
412 Gary Ward .05
413 Al Newman .05
414 Danny Jackson .05
415 Greg Gagne .05
416 Tom Herr .05
417 Jeff Parrett .05
418 Jeff Reardon .05
419 Mark Lemke .05
420 Charlie O'Brien **(RC)** .05
421 Willie Randolph .05
422 Steve Bedrosian .05
423 Mike Moore .05
424 Jeff Brantley **(RC)** .05
425 Bob Welch .05
426 Terry Mulholland .05
427 Willie Blair **(RC) RC** .05
428 Darrin Fletcher **(RC)** .05
429 Mike Witt .05
430 Joe Boever .05
431 Tom Gordon .05
432 Pedro Munoz **RC** .05
433 Kevin Seitzer .05
434 Kevin Tapani .05
435 Bret Saberhagen .05
436 Ellis Burks .05
437 Chuck Finley .05
438 Mike Boddicker .05
439 Francisco Cabrera .05
440 Todd Hundley .05
441 Kelly Downs .05
442 Dann Howitt **(RC) RC** .05
443 Scott Garrelts .05
444 Rickey Henderson .40
445 Will Clark .05
446 Ben McDonald .05
447 Dale Murphy .20
448 Dave Righetti .05
449 Dickie Thon .05
450 Ted Power .05
451 Scott Coolbaugh .05
452 Dwight Smith .05
453 Pete Incaviglia .05
454 Andre Dawson .25
455 Ruben Sierra .05
456 Andres Galarraga .05
457 Alvin Davis .05
458 Tony Castillo .05
459 Pete O'Brien .05
460 Charlie Leibrandt .05
461 Vince Coleman .05
462 Steve Sax .05
463 Omar Oliveras **(RC) RC** .05
464 Oscar Azocar **(RC) RC** .05
465 Joe Magrane **(RC)** .05
466 Karl Rhodes **RC** .05
467 Benito Santiago .05
468 Joe Klink **(RC) RC** .05
469 Sil Campusano **(RC)** .05
470 Mark Parent .05
471 Shawn Boskie **RC** .05
472 Kevin Brown .05
473 Rick Sutcliffe .05
474 Rafael Palmeiro .35
475 Mike Harkey .05
476 Jaime Navarro .05
477 Marquis Grissom .05
478 Marty Clary .05
479 Greg Briley **(RC)** .05
480 Tom Glavine .25
481 Lee Guetterman .05
482 Rex Hudler .05
483 Dave LaPoint **(RC)** .05
484 Terry Pendleton .05
485 Jesse Barfield .05
486 Jose DeJesus .05
487 Paul Abbott **(RC) RC** .05
488 Ken Howell .05
489 Greg W. Harris .05
490 Roy Smith .05
491 Paul Assenmacher .05
492 Geno Petralli .05
493 Steve Wilson .05
494 Kevin Reimer **(RC)** .05
495 Bill Long .05
496 Mike Jackson **(RC)** .05
497 Oddibe McDowell .05
498 Bill Swift .05
499 Jeff Treadway .05
500 Checklist 401-500 .05
501 Gene Larkin .05
502 Bob Boone .05
503 Allan Anderson .05
504 Luis Aquino **(RC)** .05
505 Mark Guthrie .05
506 Joe Orsulak .05
507 Dana Kiecker **(RC) RC** .05
508 Dave Gallagher **(RC)** .05
509 Greg A. Harris .05
510 Mark Williamson .05
511 Casey Candaele .05
512 Mookie Wilson .05
513 Dave Smith .05
514 Chuck Carr **RC** .05
515 Glenn Wilson .05
516 Mike Fitzgerald **(RC)** .05
517 Devon White .05
518 Dave Hollins .05
519 Mark Eichhorn .05
520 Otis Nixon .05
521 Terry Shumpert **RC** .05
522 Scott Erickson **RC** .15
523 Danny Tartabull .05
524 Orel Hershiser .05
525 George Brett .60
526 Greg Vaughn .05
527 Tim Naehring **(RC)** .05
528 Curt Schilling **(RC)** .25
529 Chris Bosio .05
530 Sam Horn .05
531 Mike Scott .05
532 George Bell .05
533 Eric Anthony .05
534 Julio Valera **RC** .05
535 Glenn Davis .05
536 Larry Walker .05
537 Pat Combs .05
538 Chris Nabholz **RC** .05
539 Kirk McCaskill .05
540 Randy Ready .05
541 Mark Gubicza .05
542 Rick Aguilera .05
543 Brian McRae **RC** .05
544 Kirby Puckett .50
545 Bo Jackson .10
546 Wade Boggs .50
547 Tim McIntosh **(RC)** .05
548 Randy Milligan **(RC)** .05
549 Dwight Evans .05
550 Billy Ripken .05
551 Erik Hanson .05
552 Lance Parrish .05
553 Tino Martinez .05
554 Jim Abbott .05
555 Ken Griffey Jr. .65
556 Milt Cuyler **(RC)** .05
557 Mark Leonard **(RC) RC** .05
558 Jay Howell .05
559 Lloyd Moseby .05
560 Chris Gwynn .05
561 Mark Whiten **(RC) RC** .05
562 Harold Baines .05
563 Junior Felix .05
564 Darren Lewis .05
565 Fred McGriff .05
566 Kevin Appier .05
567 Luis Gonzalez **RC** 1.00
568 Frank White .05
569 Juan Agosto .05
570 Mike Macfarlane .05
571 Bert Blyleven .05
572 Ken Griffey Sr. .05
573 Lee Stevens **(RC)** .05
574 Edgar Martinez .05
575 Wally Joyner .05
576 Tim Belcher .05
577 John Burkett .05
578 Mike Morgan .05
579 Paul Gibson .05
580 Jose Vizcaino **(RC)** .05
581 Duane Ward .05
582 Scott Sanderson .05
583 David Wells .05
584 Willie McGee .05
585 John Cerutti .05
586 Danny Darwin .05
587 Kurt Stillwell .05
588 Rich Gedman .05
589 Mark Davis .05
590 Bill Gullickson .05
591 Matt Young .05
592 Bryan Harvey **(RC)** .05
593 Omar Vizquel .05
594 Scott Lewis **RC** .05
595 Dave Valle .05
596 Tim Crews **(RC)** .05
597 Mike Bielecki .05
598 Mike Sharperson .05
599 Dave Bergman .05
600 Checklist 501-600 .05
601 Steve Lyons .05
602 Bruce Hurst .05
603 Donn Pall .05
604 Jim Vatcher **(RC) RC** .05
605 Dan Pasqua .05
606 Kenny Rogers .05
607 Jeff Schulz **(RC) RC** .05
608 Brad Arnsberg **(RC)** .05
609 Willie Wilson .05
610 Jamie Moyer .05
611 Ron Oester .05
612 Dennis Cook **(RC)** .05
613 Rick Mahler .05
614 Bill Landrum .05
615 Scott Scudder .05
616 Tom Edens **(RC) RC** .05
617 "1917 Revisited"(Chicago White Sox team photo.) .05
618 Jim Gantner .05
619 Darrel Akerfelds **(RC)** .05
620 Ron Robinson .05
621 Scott Radinsky .05
622 Pete Smith .05
623 Melido Perez .05
624 Jerald Clark **(RC)** .05
625 Carlos Martinez .05
626 Wes Chamberlain **RC** .05
627 Bobby Witt .05
628 Ken Dayley **(RC)** .05
629 John Barfield **(RC) RC** .05
630 Bob Tewksbury .05
631 Glenn Braggs .05
632 Jim Neidlinger **(RC) RC** .05
633 Tom Browning .05
634 Kirk Gibson .05
635 Rob Dibble .05
636 Lou Brock, Rickey Henderson "Stolen Base Leaders" .15
637 Jeff Montgomery .05
638 Mike Schooler .05
639 Storm Davis .05
640 Rich Rodriguez **(RC) RC** .05
641 Phil Bradley .05
642 Kent Mercker .05
643 Carlton Fisk .40
644 Mike Bell .05
645 Alex Fernandez **RC** .05
646 Juan Gonzalez .30
647 Ken Hill .05
648 Jeff Russell .05
649 Chuck Malone **(RC) RC** .05
650 Steve Buechele .05
651 Mike Benjamin .05
652 Tony Pena .05
653 Trevor Wilson .05
654 Alex Cole .05
655 Roger Clemens .60
656 Mark McGwire "The Bashing Years" .50
657 Joe Grahe **(RC) RC** .05
658 Jim Eisenreich .05
659 Dan Gladden .05
660 Steve Farr **(RC)** .05
661 Bill Sampen **RC** .05
662 Dave Rohde **(RC) RC** .05
663 Mark Gardner .05
664 Mike Simms **RC** .05
665 Moises Alou .05
666 Mickey Hatcher .05
667 Jimmy Key .05
668 John Wetteland .05
669 John Smiley .05
670 Jim Acker .05
671 Pascual Perez .05
672 Reggie Harris **RC** .05
673 Matt Nokes .05
674 Rafael Novoa **RC** .05
675 Hensley Meulens .05
676 Jeff M. Robinson **(RC)** .05
677 "Ground Breaking" (New Comiskey Park) .15
678 Johnny Ray .05
679 Greg Hibbard .05
680 Paul Sorrento .05
681 Mike Marshall .05
682 Jim Clancy .05
683 Rob Murphy .05
684 Dave Schmidt **(RC)** .05
685 Jeff Gray **(RC) RC** .05
686 Mike Hartley **(RC)** .05
687 Jeff King .05
688 Stan Javier **(RC)** .05
689 Bob Walk .05
690 Jim Gott .05
691 Mike LaCoss .05
692 John Farrell .05
693 Tim Leary .05
694 Mike Walker **RC** .05
695 Eric Plunk .05
696 Mike Fetters .05
697 Wayne Edwards .05
698 Tim Drummond **(RC)** .05
699 Willie Fraser .05
700 Checklist 601-700 .05
701 Mike Heath .05
702 Luis Gonzalez, Karl Rhodes, Jeff Bagwell "Rookie Threats" .45
703 Jose Mesa .05
704 Dave Smith **(RC)** .05
705 Danny Darwin .05
706 Rafael Belliard .05
707 Rob Murphy .05
708 Terry Pendleton .05
709 Mike Pagliarulo .05
710 Sid Bream .05
711 Junior Felix .05
712 Dante Bichette .05
713 Kevin Gross .05
714 Luis Sojo .05
715 Bob Ojeda .05
716 Julio Machado **(RC)** .05
717 Steve Farr .05
718 Franklin Stubbs .05
719 Mike Boddicker .05
720 Willie Randolph .05
721 Willie McGee .05
722 Chili Davis .05
723 Danny Jackson .05
724 Cory Snyder .05
725 Andre Dawson, George Bell, Ryne Sandberg "MVP Lineup" .20
726 Rob Deer .05
727 Rich DeLucia **(RC)** .05
728 Mike Perez **(RC)** .05
729 Mickey Tettleton .05
730 Mike Blowers .05
731 Gary Gaetti .05
732 Brett Butler .05
733 Dave Parker .05
734 Eddie Zosky **(RC)** .05
735 Jack Clark .05
736 Jack Morris .05
737 Kirk Gibson .05
738 Steve Bedrosian .05
739 Candy Maldonado .05
740 Matt Young .05
741 Rich Garces **(RC)** .05
742 George Bell .05
743 Deion Sanders .10
744 Bo Jackson .10
745 Luis Mercedes **(RC)** .05
746 Reggie Jefferson **(RC)** .05
747 Pete Incaviglia .05
748 Chris Hammond .05
749 Mike Stanton .05
750 Scott Sanderson .05
751 Paul Faries **(RC)** .05
752 Al Osuna **(RC)** .05
753 Steve Chitren **(RC)** .05
754 Tony Fernandez .05
755 Jeff Bagwell **RC** 1.50
756 Kirk Dressendorfer **(RC)** .05
757 Glenn Davis .05
758 Gary Carter .40
759 Zane Smith .05
760 Vance Law .05
761 Denis Boucher **(RC)** .05
762 Turner Ward **(RC)** .05
763 Roberto Alomar .20
764 Albert Belle .05
765 Joe Carter .05
766 Pete Schourek **(RC)** .05
767 Heathcliff Slocumb **(RC)** .05
768 Vince Coleman .05
769 Mitch Williams .05
770 Brian Downing .05
771 Dana Allison **(RC)** .05
772 Pete Harnisch .05
773 Tim Raines .05
774 Darryl Kile **(RC)** .05
775 Fred McGriff .05
776 Dwight Evans .05
777 Joe Slusarski .05
778 Dave Righetti .05
779 Jeff Hamilton .05
780 Ernest Riles .05
781 Ken Dayley .05
782 Eric King .05
783 Devon White .05
784 Beau Allred **(RC)** .05
785 Mike Timlin **(RC)** .05
786 Ivan Calderon .05
787 Hubie Brooks .05
788 Juan Agosto **(RC)** .05
789 Barry Jones .05
790 Wally Backman .05
791 Jim Presley .05
792 Charlie Hough .05
793 Larry Andersen .05
794 Steve Finley .05

795 Shawn Abner .05
796 Jeff M. Robinson .05
797 Joe Bitker (RC) .05
798 Eric Show .05
799 Bud Black .05
800 Checklist 701-800 .05
SP1 Michael Jordan 3.00
SP2 Rickey Henderson, Nolan Ryan "A Day to Remember" 1.00
HH1 Hank Aaron (Hologram) 1.00

Final Edition

Oil Can Boyd

NM/M
Complete Set (100): 9.00
Common Player: .05
1 Ryan Klesko, Reggie Sanders (Minor League Diamond Skills Checklist) .10
2 Pedro Martinez (RC) RC 5.00
3 Lance Dickson (RC) .05
4 Royce Clayton .05
5 Scott Bryant (RC) .05
6 Dan Wilson (RC) .05
7 Dmitri Young (RC) .50
8 Ryan Klesko (RC) RC .50
9 Tom Goodwin (RC) .05
10 Rondell White (RC) RC .25
11 Reggie Sanders .05
12 Todd Van Poppel .05
13 Arthur Rhodes (RC) .05
14 Eddie Zosky .05
15 Gerald Williams (RC) .05
16 Robert Eenhoorn (RC) .05
17 Jim Thome (RC) RC 3.00
18 Marc Newfield (RC) .05
19 Kerwin Moore (RC) .05
20 Jeff McNeely (RC) .05
21 Frankie Rodriguez .05
22 Andy Mota (RC) .05
23 Chris Haney (RC) .05
24 Kenny Lofton RC .25
25 Dave Nilsson (RC) .05
26 Derek Bell .05
27 Frank Castillo (RC) .05
28 Candy Maldonado .05
29 Chuck McElroy .05
30 Chito Martinez (RC) .05
31 Steve Howe (RC) .05
32 Freddie Benavides (RC) .05
33 Scott Kamieniecki .05
34 Denny Neagle (RC) .05
35 Mike Humphreys (RC) .05
36 Mike Remlinger (RC) .05
37 Scott Coolbaugh .05
38 Darren Lewis .05
39 Thomas Howard (RC) .05
40 John Candelaria .05
41 Todd Benzinger .05
42 Wilson Alvarez .05
43 Patrick Lennon (RC) .05
44 Rusty Meacham (RC) .05
45 Ryan Bowen RC .05
46 Rick Wilkins RC .10
47 Ed Sprague RC .05
48 Bob Scanlan RC .05
49 Tom Candiotti .05
50 Dennis Martinez (Perfecto) .05
51 Oil Can Boyd .05
52 Glenallen Hill .05
53 Scott Livingstone RC .05
54 Brian Hunter RC .05
55 Ivan Rodriguez RC 1.50
56 Keith Mitchell RC .05
57 Roger McDowell .05
58 Otis Nixon .05
59 Juan Bell RC .05
60 Bill Krueger .05
61 Chris Donnels RC .05
62 Tommy Greene .05
63 Doug Simons (RC) .05
64 Andy Ashby RC .15
65 Anthony Young RC .05
66 Kevin Morton RC .05
67 Bret Barberie RC .05
68 Scott Servais RC .05
69 Ron Darling .05
70 Vicente Palacios .05
71 Tim Burke RC .05
72 Gerald Alexander RC .05
73 Reggie Jefferson .05
74 Dean Palmer .05

75 Mark Whiten .05
76 Randy Tomlin (RC) .05
77 Mark Wohlers RC .05
78 Brook Jacoby .05
79 Ken Griffey Jr., Ryne Sandberg (All-Star Checklist) .25
80 Jack Morris/AS .05
81 Sandy Alomar, Jr./AS .05
82 Cecil Fielder/AS .05
83 Roberto Alomar/AS .10
84 Wade Boggs/AS .25
85 Cal Ripken, Jr./AS .60
86 Rickey Henderson/AS .15
87 Ken Griffey Jr./AS .60
88 Dave Henderson/AS .05
89 Danny Tartabull/AS .05
90 Tom Glavine/AS .10
91 Benito Santiago/AS .05
92 Will Clark/AS .05
93 Ryne Sandberg/AS .50
94 Chris Sabo/AS .05
95 Ozzie Smith/AS .50
96 Ivan Calderon/AS .05
97 Tony Gwynn/AS .25
98 Andre Dawson/AS .05
99 Bobby Bonilla/AS .05
100 Checklist .05

Baseball Heroes Hank Aaron

NM/M
Complete Set (10): 4.00
Common Aaron: .50
Autographed Card: 180.00
Aaron Header: 1.00
19 1954 Rookie Year .50
20 1957 MVP .50
21 1966 Move to Atlanta .50
22 1970 3,000 .50
23 1974 715 .50
24 1975 Return to Milwaukee .50
25 1976 755 .50
26 1982 Hall of Fame .50
27 Checklist - Heroes 19-27 .50

Baseball Heroes Nolan Ryan

NM/M
Complete Set (10): 3.00
Common Player: .50
Ryan Header Card: 1.00
Autographed Card: 200.00
"Strike Out King" Auto.: 575.00
10 1968 Victory #1 .50
11 1973 A Career Year .50
12 1975 Double Milestone .50
13 1979 Back Home .50
14 1981 All-Time Leader .50
15 1989 5,000 .50
16 1990 The Sixth .50
17 1990 ... and Still Counting .50
18 Checklist - Heroes 10-18 .50

1991 Upper Deck Heroes of Baseball

NM/M
Complete Set (4): 7.00
Common Card: 2.00

1 Harmon Killebrew 2.00
1a Harmon Killebrew/Auto. 10.00
2 Gaylord Perry 2.00
2a Gaylord Perry/Auto. 10.00
3 Ferguson Jenkins 2.00
3a Ferguson Jenkins/Auto. 10.00
4 Gaylord Perry, Ferguson Jenkins, Harmon Killebrew 2.00

Silver Sluggers

Alan Trammell

NM/M
Complete Set (18): 5.00
Common Player: .15
1 Julio Franco .15
2 Alan Trammell .15
3 Rickey Henderson .75
4 Jose Canseco .50
5 Barry Bonds 2.00
6 Eddie Murray .75
7 Kelly Gruber .15
8 Ryne Sandberg 1.00
9 Darryl Strawberry .15
10 Ellis Burks .15
11 Lance Parrish .15
12 Cecil Fielder .15
13 Matt Williams .15
14 Dave Parker .15
15 Bobby Bonilla .15
16 Don Robinson .15
17 Benito Santiago .15
18 Barry Larkin .15

1992 Upper Deck

NM/M
Unopened Fact. Set (800): 20.00
Complete Set (800): 15.00
Common Player: .05
Low or High Pack (15): .50
Low or High Box (36): 12.50
Jumbo Pack (27): 1.00
Jumbo Box (20): 16.00
Bench/Morgan Auto. 75.00
Ted Williams Auto. 425.00
1 Ryan Klesko, Jim Thome Star Rookie Checklist .25
2 Royce Clayton .05
3 Brian Jordan RC .30
4 Dave Fleming RC .40
5 Jim Thome .40
6 Jeff Juden .05
7 Roberto Hernandez RC .15
8 Kyle Abbott (RC) .05
9 Chris George RC .05
10 Rob Maurer RC .05

11 Donald Harris (RC) RC .05
12 Ted Wood RC .05
13 Patrick Lennon RC .05
14 Willie Banks .05
15 Roger Salkeld (RC) .05
16 Wil Cordero .05
17 Arthur Rhodes RC .05
18 Pedro Martinez .40
19 Andy Ashby RC .10
20 Tom Goodwin .05
21 Braulio Castillo RC .05
22 Todd Van Poppel .05
23 Brian Williams RC .05
24 Ryan Klesko .05
25 Kenny Lofton .05
26 Derek Bell .05
27 Reggie Sanders .05
28 Dave Winfield (Winfield's 400th) .25
29 Dave Justice Atlanta Braves Checklist .05
30 Rob Dibble Cincinnati Reds Checklist .05
31 Craig Biggio (RC) Houston Astros Checklist .05
32 Eddie Murray Los Angeles Dodgers Checklist .20
33 Fred McGriff San Diego Padres Checklist .05
34 Willie McGee San Francisco Giants Checklist .05
35 Shawon Dunston Chicago Cubs Checklist .05
36 Delino DeShields Montreal Expos Checklist .05
37 Howard Johnson New York Mets Checklist .05
38 John Kruk Philadelphia Phillies Checklist .05
39 Doug Drabek Pittsburgh Pirates Checklist .05
40 Todd Zeile St. Louis Cardinals Checklist .05
41 Steve Avery (Playoff Perfection) .05
42 Jeremy Hernandez RC .05
43 Doug Henry RC .05
44 Chris Donnels RC .05
45 Mo Sanford RC .05
46 Scott Kamieniecki RC .10
47 Mark Lemke .05
48 Steve Farr .05
49 Francisco Oliveras .05
50 Ced Landrum RC .05
51 Rondell White, Marc Newfield Top Prospect Checklist .05
52 Eduardo Perez RC .10
53 Tom Nevers RC .05
54 David Zancanaro RC .05
55 Shawn Green RC 1.50
56 Mark Wohlers RC .05
57 Dave Nilsson .05
58 Dmitri Young .05
59 Ryan Hawblitzel (RC) RC .05
60 Raul Mondesi .05
61 Rondell White .05
62 Steve Hosey .05
63 Manny Ramirez RC 2.00
64 Marc Newfield .05
65 Jeromy Burnitz .05
66 Mark Smith RC .05
67 Joey Hamilton RC .10
68 Tyler Green RC .05
69 John Farrell RC .05
70 Kurt Miller RC .05
71 Jeff Plympton RC .05
72 Dan Wilson .05
73 Joe Vitiello RC .05
74 Rico Brogna .05
75 David McCarty RC .05
76 Bob Wickman RC .05
77 Carlos Rodriguez RC .05
78 Jim Abbott (Stay in School) .05
79 Pedro Martinez, Ramon Martinez Bloodlines .25
80 Kevin Mitchell, Keith Mitchell Bloodlines .05
81 Sandy Jr. & Roberto Alomar, Sandy Jr. & Roberto Alomar Bloodlines .10
82 Cal Jr. & Billy Ripken, Cal Jr. & Billy Ripken Bloodlines .40
83 Tony & Chris Gwynn, Tony & Chris Gwynn Bloodlines .20
84 Dwight Gooden, Gary Sheffield Bloodlines .15
85 Ken, Sr.; Ken, Jr.; & Craig Griffey, Ken, Sr.; Ken, Jr.; & Craig Griffey, Ken, Sr.; Ken, Jr.; & Craig Griffey Bloodlines .30
86 Jim Abbott California Angels Checklist .05
87 Frank Thomas Chicago White Sox Checklist .25
88 Danny Tartabull Kansas City Royals Checklist .05
89 Scott Erickson Minnesota Twins Checklist .05
90 Rickey Henderson Oakland Athletics Checklist .25

91	Edgar Martinez Seattle Mariners Checklist	.05
92	Nolan Ryan Texas Rangers Checklist	.50
93	Ben McDonald Baltimore Orioles Checklist	.05
94	Ellis Burks Boston Red Sox Checklist	.05
95	Greg Swindell Cleveland Indians Checklist	.05
96	Cecil Fielder Detroit Tigers Checklist	.05
97	Greg Vaughn Milwaukee Brewers Checklist	.05
98	Kevin Maas New York Yankees Checklist	.05
99	Dave Steib Toronto Blue Jays Checklist	.05
100	Checklist 1-100	.05
101	Joe Oliver	.05
102	Hector Villanueva	.05
103	Ed Whitson	.05
104	Danny Jackson	.05
105	Chris Hammond	.05
106	Ricky Jordan	.05
107	Kevin Bass	.05
108	Darrin Fletcher	.05
109	Junior Ortiz	.05
110	Tom Bolton	.05
111	Jeff King	.05
112	Dave Magadan	.05
113	Mike LaValliere	.05
114	Hubie Brooks	.05
115	Jay Bell	.05
116	David Wells	.05
117	Jim Leyritz	.05
118	Manuel Lee	.05
119	Alvaro Espinoza	.05
120	B.J. Surhoff	.05
121	Hal Morris	.05
122	Shawon Dunston	.05
123	Chris Sabo	.05
124	Andre Dawson	.25
125	Eric Davis	.05
126	Chili Davis	.05
127	Dale Murphy	.15
128	Kirk McCaskill	.05
129	Terry Mulholland	.05
130	Rick Aguilera	.05
131	Vince Coleman	.05
132	Andy Van Slyke	.05
133	Gregg Jefferies	.05
134	Barry Bonds	1.00
135	Dwight Gooden	.05
136	Dave Stieb	.05
137	Albert Belle	.05
138	Teddy Higuera	.05
139	Jesse Barfield	.05
140	Pat Borders	.05
141	Bip Roberts	.05
142	Rob Dibble	.05
143	Mark Grace	.05
144	Barry Larkin	.05
145	Ryne Sandberg	.50
146	Scott Erickson	.05
147	Luis Polonia	.05
148	John Burkett	.05
149	Luis Sojo	.05
150	Dickie Thon	.05
151	Walt Weiss	.05
152	Mike Scioscia	.05
153	Mark McGwire	.75
154	Matt Williams	.05
155	Rickey Henderson	.40
156	Sandy Alomar, Jr.	.05
157	Brian McRae	.05
158	Harold Baines	.05
159	Kevin Appier	.05
160	Felix Fermin	.05
161	Leo Gomez	.05
162	Craig Biggio	.05
163	Ben McDonald	.05
164	Randy Johnson	.40
165	Cal Ripken, Jr.	1.00
166	Frank Thomas	.40
167	Delino DeShields	.05
168	Greg Gagne	.05
169	Ron Karkovice	.05
170	Charlie Leibrandt	.05
171	Dave Righetti	.05
172	Dave Henderson	.05
173	Steve Decker	.05
174	Darryl Strawberry	.05
175	Will Clark	.05
176	Ruben Sierra	.05
177	Ozzie Smith	.50
178	Charles Nagy	.05
179	Gary Pettis	.05
180	Kirk Gibson	.05
181	Randy Milligan	.05
182	Dave Valle	.05
183	Chris Hoiles	.05
184	Tony Phillips	.05
185	Brady Anderson	.05
186	Scott Fletcher	.05
187	Gene Larkin	.05
188	Lance Johnson	.05
189	Greg Olson	.05
190	Melido Perez	.05
191	Lenny Harris	.05
192	Terry Kennedy	.05
193	Mike Gallego	.05
194	Willie McGee	.05
195	Juan Samuel	.05
196	Jeff Huson	.05
197	Alex Cole	.05
198	Ron Robinson	.05
199	Joel Skinner	.05
200	Checklist 101-200	.05
201	Kevin Reimer	.05
202	Stan Belinda	.05
203	Pat Tabler	.05
204	Jose Guzman	.05
205	Jose Lind	.05
206	Spike Owen	.05
207	Joe Orsulak	.05
208	Charlie Hayes	.05
209	Mike Devereaux	.05
210	Mike Fitzgerald	.05
211	Willie Randolph	.05
212	Rod Nichols	.05
213	Mike Boddicker	.05
214	Bill Spiers	.05
215	Steve Olin	.05
216	David Howard **(RC) RC**	.05
217	Gary Varsho	.05
218	Mike Harkey	.05
219	Luis Aquino	.05
220	Chuck McElroy **(RC)**	.05
221	Doug Drabek	.05
222	Dave Winfield	.40
223	Rafael Palmeiro	.35
224	Joe Carter	.05
225	Bobby Bonilla	.05
226	Ivan Calderon	.05
227	Gregg Olson	.05
228	Tim Wallach	.05
229	Terry Pendleton	.05
230	Gilberto Reyes **(RC)**	.05
231	Carlos Baerga	.05
232	Greg Vaughn	.05
233	Bret Saberhagen	.05
234	Gary Sheffield	.30
235	Mark Lewis	.05
236	George Bell	.05
237	Danny Tartabull	.05
238	Willie Wilson	.05
239	Doug Dascenzo	.05
240	Bill Pecota	.05
241	Julio Franco	.05
242	Ed Sprague	.05
243	Juan Gonzalez	.20
244	Chuck Finley	.05
245	Ivan Rodriguez	.35
246	Len Dykstra	.05
247	Deion Sanders	.10
248	Dwight Evans	.05
249	Larry Walker	.05
250	Billy Ripken	.05
251	Mickey Tettleton	.05
252	Tony Pena	.05
253	Benito Santiago	.05
254	Kirby Puckett	.50
255	Cecil Fielder	.05
256	Howard Johnson	.05
257	Andujar Cedeno	.05
258	Jose Rijo	.05
259	Al Osuna	.05
260	Todd Hundley	.05
261	Orel Hershiser	.05
262	Ray Lankford	.05
263	Robin Ventura	.05
264	Felix Jose	.05
265	Eddie Murray	.40
266	Kevin Mitchell	.05
267	Gary Carter	.40
268	Mike Benjamin	.05
269	Dick Schofield	.05
270	Jose Uribe	.05
271	Pete Incaviglia	.05
272	Tony Fernandez	.05
273	Alan Trammell	.05
274	Tony Gwynn	.50
275	Mike Greenwell	.05
276	Jeff Bagwell	.40
277	Frank Viola	.05
278	Randy Myers	.05
279	Ken Caminiti	.05
280	Bill Doran	.05
281	Dan Pasqua	.05
282	Alfredo Griffin	.05
283	Jose Oquendo	.05
284	Kal Daniels	.05
285	Bobby Thigpen	.05
286	Robby Thompson	.05
287	Mark Eichhorn	.05
288	Mike Felder	.05
289	Dave Gallagher	.05
290	Dave Anderson	.05
291	Mel Hall	.05
292	Jerald Clark	.05
293	Al Newman	.05
294	Rob Deer	.05
295	Matt Nokes	.05
296	Jack Armstrong	.05
297	Jim Deshaies	.05
298	Jeff Innis	.05
299	Jeff Reed	.05
300	Checklist 201-300	.05
301	Lonnie Smith	.05
302	Jimmy Key	.05
303	Junior Felix	.05
304	Mike Heath	.05
305	Mark Langston	.05
306	Greg W. Harris	.05
307	Brett Butler	.05
308	Luis Rivera **(RC)**	.05
309	Bruce Ruffin	.05
310	Paul Faries	.05
311	Terry Leach	.05
312	Scott Brosius **RC**	.10
313	Scott Leius	.05
314	Harold Reynolds	.05
315	Jack Morris	.05
316	David Segui	.05
317	Bill Gullickson	.05
318	Todd Frohwirth	.05
319	Mark Leiter **(RC) RC**	.05
320	Jeff M. Robinson	.05
321	Gary Gaetti	.05
322	John Smoltz	.05
323	Andy Benes	.05
324	Kelly Gruber	.05
325	Jim Abbott	.05
326	John Kruk	.05
327	Kevin Seitzer	.05
328	Darrin Jackson	.05
329	Kurt Stillwell **(RC)**	.05
330	Mike Maddux	.05
331	Dennis Eckersley	.35
332	Dan Gladden	.05
333	Jose Canseco	.30
334	Kent Hrbek	.05
335	Ken Griffey Sr.	.05
336	Greg Swindell	.05
337	Trevor Wilson **(RC)**	.05
338	Sam Horn	.05
339	Mike Henneman	.05
340	Jerry Browne	.05
341	Glenn Braggs	.05
342	Tom Glavine	.20
343	Wally Joyner	.05
344	Fred McGriff	.05
345	Ron Gant	.05
346	Ramon Martinez	.05
347	Wes Chamberlain	.05
348	Terry Shumpert	.05
349	Tim Teufel	.05
350	Wally Backman	.05
351	Joe Girardi	.05
352	Devon White	.05
353	Greg Maddux	.50
354	Ryan Bowen **RC**	.05
355	Roberto Alomar	.20
356	Don Mattingly	.60
357	Pedro Guerrero	.05
358	Steve Sax	.05
359	Joey Cora	.05
360	Jim Gantner	.05
361	Brian Barnes **(RC)**	.05
362	Kevin McReynolds	.05
363	Bret Barberie **RC**	.05
364	David Cone	.05
365	Dennis Martinez	.05
366	Brian Hunter **RC**	.05
367	Edgar Martinez	.05
368	Steve Finley	.05
369	Greg Briley	.05
370	Jeff Blauser	.05
371	Todd Stottlemyre	.05
372	Luis Gonzalez	.05
373	Rick Wilkins	.05
374	Darryl Kile **RC**	.05
375	John Olerud	.05
376	Lee Smith	.05
377	Kevin Maas	.05
378	Dante Bichette	.05
379	Tom Pagnozzi	.05
380	Mike Flanagan	.05
381	Charlie O'Brien	.05
382	Dave Martinez	.05
383	Keith Miller	.05
384	Scott Ruskin	.05
385	Kevin Elster	.05
386	Alvin Davis	.05
387	Casey Candaele	.05
388	Pete O'Brien	.05
389	Jeff Treadway **(RC)**	.05
390	Scott Bradley	.05
391	Mookie Wilson	.05
392	Jimmy Jones	.05
393	Candy Maldonado	.05
394	Eric Yelding	.05
395	Tom Henke	.05
396	Franklin Stubbs	.05
397	Milt Thompson	.05
398	Mark Carreon	.05
399	Randy Velarde	.05
400	Checklist 301-400	.05
401	Omar Vizquel	.05
402	Joe Boever	.05
403	Bill Krueger	.05
404	Jody Reed	.05
405	Mike Schooler **(RC)**	.05
406	Jason Grimsley	.05
407	Greg Myers	.05
408	Randy Ready	.05
409	Mike Timlin **RC**	.15
410	Mitch Williams	.05
411	Garry Templeton	.05
412	Greg Cadaret	.05
413	Donnie Hill	.05
414	Wally Whitehurst	.05
415	Scott Sanderson	.05
416	Thomas Howard	.05
417	Neal Heaton	.05
418	Charlie Hough	.05
419	Jack Howell	.05
420	Greg Hibbard	.05
421	Carlos Quintana	.05
422	Kim Batiste **RC**	.05
423	Paul Molitor	.40
424	Ken Griffey Jr.	.65
425	Phil Plantier	.05
426	Denny Neagle	.05
427	Von Hayes	.05
428	Shane Mack	.05
429	Darren Daulton	.05
430	Dwayne Henry	.05
431	Lance Parrish	.05
432	Mike Humphreys **RC**	.05
433	Tim Burke	.05
434	Bryan Harvey	.05
435	Pat Kelly	.05
436	Ozzie Guillen	.05
437	Bruce Hurst	.05
438	Sammy Sosa	.50
439	Dennis Rasmussen	.05
440	Ken Patterson	.05
441	Jay Buhner	.05
442	Pat Combs	.05
443	Wade Boggs	.50
444	George Brett	.60
445	Mo Vaughn	.05
446	Chuck Knoblauch	.05
447	Tom Candiotti	.05
448	Mark Portugal	.05
449	Mickey Morandini	.05
450	Duane Ward	.05
451	Otis Nixon	.05
452	Bob Welch	.05
453	Rusty Meacham	.05
454	Keith Mitchell	.05
455	Marquis Grissom	.05
456	Robin Yount	.40
457	Harvey Pulliam **RC**	.05
458	Jose DeLeon **(RC)**	.05
459	Mark Gubicza	.05
460	Darryl Hamilton	.05
461	Tom Browning	.05
462	Monty Fariss	.05
463	Jerome Walton	.05
464	Paul O'Neill	.05
465	Dean Palmer	.05
466	Travis Fryman	.05
467	John Smiley	.05
468	Lloyd Moseby	.05
469	John Wehner **RC**	.05
470	Skeeter Barnes **(RC)**	.05
471	Steve Chitren	.05
472	Kent Mercker	.05
473	Terry Steinbach	.05
474	Andres Galarraga	.05
475	Steve Avery	.05
476	Tom Gordon	.05
477	Cal Eldred	.05
478	Omar Olivares **(RC)**	.05
479	Julio Machado	.05
480	Bob Milacki	.05
481	Les Lancaster	.05
482	John Candelaria	.05
483	Brian Downing	.05
484	Roger McDowell	.05
485	Scott Scudder	.05
486	Zane Smith	.05
487	John Cerutti	.05
488	Steve Buechele	.05
489	Paul Gibson	.05
490	Curtis Wilkerson	.05
491	Marvin Freeman	.05
492	Tom Foley	.05
493	Juan Berenguer	.05
494	Ernest Riles	.05
495	Sid Bream	.05
496	Chuck Crim	.05
497	Mike Macfarlane	.05
498	Dale Sveum	.05
499	Storm Davis	.05
500	Checklist 401-500	.05
501	Jeff Reardon	.05
502	Shawn Abner	.05
503	Tony Fossas	.05
504	Cory Snyder	.05
505	Matt Young	.05
506	Allan Anderson **(RC)**	.05
507	Mark Lee	.05
508	Gene Nelson	.05
509	Mike Pagliarulo	.05
510	Rafael Belliard	.05
511	Jay Howell	.05
512	Bob Tewksbury	.05
513	Mike Morgan	.05
514	John Franco	.05
515	Kevin Gross	.05
516	Lou Whitaker	.05
517	Orlando Merced	.05
518	Todd Benzinger	.05
519	Gary Redus	.05
520	Walt Terrell	.05
521	Jack Clark	.05
522	Dave Parker	.05
523	Tim Naehring	.05
524	Mark Whiten	.05
525	Ellis Burks	.05
526	Frank Castillo **(RC) RC**	.05
527	Brian Harper	.05
528	Brook Jacoby	.05
529	Rick Sutcliffe	.05
530	Joe Klink	.05
531	Terry Bross	.05
532	Jose Offerman	.05
533	Todd Zeile	.05
534	Eric Karros	.05
535	Anthony Young **RC**	.05
536	Milt Cuyler	.05
537	Randy Tomlin	.05
538	Scott Livingstone **(RC) RC**	.05
539	Jim Eisenreich	.05
540	Don Slaught	.05

541	Scott Cooper	.05
542	Joe Grahe (RC)	.05
543	Tom Brunansky	.05
544	Eddie Zosky	.05
545	Roger Clemens	.60
546	Dave Justice	.05
547	Dave Stewart	.05
548	David West	.05
549	Dave Smith	.05
550	Dan Plesac	.05
551	Alex Fernandez	.05
552	Bernard Gilkey	.05
553	Jack McDowell	.05
554	Tino Martinez	.05
555	Bo Jackson	.10
556	Bernie Williams	.05
557	Mark Gardner	.05
558	Glenallen Hill	.05
559	Oil Can Boyd	.05
560	Chris James	.05
561	Scott Servais RC	.05
562	Rey Sanchez RC	.05
563	Paul McClellan (RC) RC	.05
564	Andy Mota RC	.05
565	Darren Lewis	.05
566	Jose Melendez (RC) RC	.05
567	Tommy Greene	.05
568	Rich Rodriguez	.05
569	Heathcliff Slocumb RC	.05
570	Joe Hesketh (RC)	.05
571	Carlton Fisk	.40
572	Erik Hanson	.05
573	Wilson Alvarez	.05
574	Rheal Cormier RC	.05
575	Tim Raines	.05
576	Bobby Witt	.05
577	Roberto Kelly	.05
578	Kevin Brown	.05
579	Chris Nabholz	.05
580	Jesse Orosco	.05
581	Jeff Brantley	.05
582	Rafael Ramirez	.05
583	Kelly Downs	.05
584	Mike Simms	.05
585	Mike Remlinger RC	.05
586	Dave Hollins	.05
587	Larry Andersen	.05
588	Mike Gardiner	.05
589	Craig Lefferts	.05
590	Paul Assenmacher (RC)	.05
591	Bryn Smith	.05
592	Donn Pall	.05
593	Mike Jackson	.05
594	Scott Radinsky	.05
595	Brian Holman	.05
596	Geronimo Pena	.05
597	Mike Jeffcoat	.05
598	Carlos Martinez (RC)	.05
599	Geno Petralli	.05
600	Checklist 501-600	.05
601	Jerry Don Gleaton	.05
602	Adam Peterson (RC)	.05
603	Craig Grebeck	.05
604	Mark Guthrie	.05
605	Frank Tanana	.05
606	Hensley Meulens (RC)	.05
607	Mark Davis	.05
608	Eric Plunk	.05
609	Mark Williamson	.05
610	Lee Guetterman (RC)	.05
611	Bobby Rose	.05
612	Bill Wegman	.05
613	Mike Hartley	.05
614	Chris Beasley (RC) RC	.05
615	Chris Bosio	.05
616	Henry Cotto	.05
617	Chico Walker (RC) RC	.05
618	Russ Swan (RC)	.05
619	Bob Walk	.05
620	Billy Swift	.05
621	Warren Newson RC	.05
622	Steve Bedrosian (RC)	.05
623	Ricky Bones (RC) RC	.05
624	Kevin Tapani	.05
625	Juan Guzman RC	.05
626	Jeff Johnson (RC) RC	.05
627	Jeff Montgomery	.05
628	Ken Hill	.05
629	Gary Thurman	.05
630	Steve Howe (RC)	.05
631	Jose DeJesus	.05
632	Bert Blyleven	.05
633	Jaime Navarro	.05
634	Lee Stevens (RC)	.05
635	Pete Harnisch	.05
636	Bill Landrum	.05
637	Rich DeLucia	.05
638	Luis Salazar (RC)	.05
639	Rob Murphy	.05
640	Rickey Henderson, Jose Canseco	
	A.L. Diamond Skills Checklist	.05
641	Roger Clemens	.40
642	Jim Abbott	.05
643	Travis Fryman	.05
644	Jesse Barfield	.05
645	Cal Ripken, Jr.	.50
646	Wade Boggs	.35
647	Cecil Fielder	.05
648	Rickey Henderson	.20
649	Jose Canseco	.15
650	Ken Griffey Jr.	.45
651	Kenny Rogers	.05
652	Luis Mercedes (RC) RC	.05
653	Mike Stanton	.05
654	Glenn Davis	.05

655	Nolan Ryan	1.00
656	Reggie Jefferson	.05
657	Javier Ortiz (RC) RC	.05
658	Greg A. Harris	.05
659	Mariano Duncan	.05
660	Jeff Shaw	.05
661	Mike Moore	.05
662	Chris Haney (RC) RC	.05
663	Joe Slusarski RC	.05
664	Wayne Housie RC	.05
665	Carlos Garcia	.05
666	Bob Ojeda	.05
667	Bryan Hickerson RC	.05
668	Tim Belcher	.05
669	Ron Darling	.05
670	Rex Hudler (RC)	.05
671	Sid Fernandez	.05
672	Chito Martinez RC	.05
673	Pete Schourek RC	.05
674	Armando Reonso RC	.05
675	Mike Mussina	.30
676	Kevin Morton (RC)	.05
677	Norm Charlton	.05
678	Danny Darwin	.05
679	Eric King	.05
680	Ted Power	.05
681	Barry Jones	.05
682	Carney Lansford	.05
683	Mel Rojas	.05
684	Rick Honeycutt	.05
685	Jeff Fassero (RC) RC	.05
686	Cris Carpenter (RC)	.05
687	Tim Crews	.05
688	Scott Terry	.05
689	Chris Gwynn	.05
690	Gerald Perry	.05
691	John Barfield	.05
692	Bob Melvin	.05
693	Juan Agosto	.05
694	Alejandro Pena (RC)	.05
695	Jeff Russell	.05
696	Carmelo Martinez	.05
697	Bud Black	.05
698	Dave Otto (RC)	.05
699	Billy Hatcher	.05
700	Checklist 601-700	.05
701	Clemente Nunez (RC)	.05
702	Donovan Osborne, Brian Jordan,	
	Mark Clark "Rookie Threats"	.05
703	Mike Morgan	.05
704	Keith Miller	.05
705	Kurt Stillwell	.05
706	Damon Berryhill	.05
707	Von Hayes	.05
708	Rick Sutcliffe	.05
709	Hubie Brooks	.05
710	Ryan Turner (RC)	.05
711	Barry Bonds, Andy Van Slyke	
	N.L. Diamond Skills Checklist	.30
712	Jose Rijo	.05
713	Tom Glavine	.05
714	Shawon Dunston	.05
715	Andy Van Slyke	.05
716	Ozzie Smith	.35
717	Tony Gwynn	.35
718	Will Clark	.05
719	Marquis Grissom	.05
720	Howard Johnson	.05
721	Barry Bonds	.50
722	Kirk McCaskill	.05
723	Sammy Sosa	.50
724	George Bell	.05
725	Gregg Jefferies	.05
726	Gary DiSarcina (RC)	.05
727	Mike Bordick	.05
728	Eddie Murray	.05
	(400 Home Run Club)	.20
729	Rene Gonzales	.05
730	Mike Bielecki	.05
731	Calvin Jones (RC)	.05
732	Jack Morris	.05
733	Frank Viola	.05
734	Dave Winfield	.40
735	Kevin Mitchell	.05
736	Billy Swift	.05
737	Dan Gladden	.05
738	Mike Jackson	.05
739	Mark Carreon	.05
740	Kirt Manwaring	.05
741	Randy Myers	.05
742	Kevin McReynolds	.05
743	Steve Sax	.05
744	Wally Joyner	.05
745	Gary Sheffield	.25
746	Danny Tartabull	.05
747	Julio Valera	.05
748	Denny Neagle	.05
749	Lance Blankenship	.05
750	Mike Gallego	.05
751	Bret Saberhagen	.05
752	Ruben Amaro (RC)	.05
753	Eddie Murray	.40
754	Kyle Abbott (RC)	.05
755	Bobby Bonilla	.05
756	Eric Davis	.05
757	Eddie Taubensee (RC)	.05
758	Andres Galarraga	.05
759	Pete Incaviglia	.05
760	Tom Candiotti	.05
761	Tim Belcher	.05
762	Ricky Bones	.05
763	Bip Roberts	.05
764	Pedro Munoz	.05
765	Greg Swindell	.05

766	Kenny Lofton	.05
767	Gary Carter	.40
768	Charlie Hayes	.05
769	Dickie Thon	.05
770	Donovan Osborne Diamond	
	Debuts Checklist	.05
771	Bret Boone	.10
772	Archi Cianfrocco RC	.05
773	Mark Clark RC	.05
774	Chad Curtis RC	.20
775	Pat Listach RC	.05
776	Pat Mahomes RC	.05
777	Donovan Osborne RC	.05
778	John Patterson RC	.05
779	Andy Stankiewicz RC	.05
780	Turk Wendell RC	.10
781	Bill Krueger	.05
782	Rickey Henderson	
	(Grand Theft)	.20
783	Kevin Seitzer	.05
784	Dave Martinez	.05
785	John Smiley	.05
786	Matt Stairs	.05
787	Scott Scudder	.05
788	John Wetteland	.05
789	Jack Armstrong	.05
790	Ken Hill	.05
791	Dick Schofield	.05
792	Mariano Duncan	.05
793	Bill Pecota	.05
794	Mike Kelly RC	.05
795	Willie Randolph	.05
796	Butch Henry RC	.05
797	Carlos Hernandez RC	.05
798	Doug Jones	.05
799	Melido Perez	.05
800	Checklist	.05
SP3	Deion Sanders "Prime Time's	
	Two"	.25
SP4	Tom Selleck, Frank Thomas "Mr.	
	Baseball"	2.00
HH2	Ted Williams (Hologram)	2.00

Baseball Heroes Bench/Morgan

		NM/M
Complete Set (10):		4.00
Common Player:		.50
Autographed Card:		65.00
---	Header Card	.75
37	Johnny Bench	
	1968 Rookie of the Year	.75
38	Johnny Bench 1968-77 Ten	
	Straight Gold Gloves	.75
39	Johnny Bench	
	1970 & 1972 MVP	.75
40	Joe Morgan 1965 Rookie Year	.50
41	Joe Morgan	
	1975-76 Back-to-Back MVP	.50
42	Joe Morgan	
	1980-83 The Golden Years	.50
43	Johnny Bench, Joe Morgan	
	1972-79 Big Red Machine	.60
44	Johnny Bench, Joe Morgan	
	1989 & 1990 Hall of Fame	.60
45	Johnny Bench, Joe Morgan	
	Checklist - Heroes 37-45	.60

Baseball Heroes Ted Williams

		NM/M
Complete Set (10):		3.00
Common Player:		.50
Autographed Card:		425.00
---	Header Card	.75
28	Ted Williams	
	1939 Rookie Year	.50

29	Ted Williams 1941 .406!	.50
30	Ted Williams	
	1942 Triple Crown Year	.50
31	Ted Williams	
	1946 & 1949 MVP	.50
32	Ted Williams	
	1947 Second Triple Crown	.50
33	Ted Williams	
	1950s Player of the Decade	.50
34	Ted Williams	
	1960 500 Home Run Club	.50
35	Ted Williams	
	1966 Hall of Fame	.50
36	Ted Williams Checklist -	
	Heroes 28-36	.50

1992 Upper Deck Hall of Fame Heroes

ROLLIE FINGERS

	NM/M
Complete Set (4):	2.50
Common Player:	.50
5 Vida Blue	.50
5a Vida Blue/Auto.	20.00
6 Lou Brock	1.00
6a Lou Brock/Auto.	35.00
7 Rollie Fingers	.50
7a Rollie Fingers/Auto.	30.00
8 Vida Blue, Lou Brock,	
Rollie Fingers	1.00

1992 Upper Deck Heroes Highlights

BROOKS ROBINSON

	NM/M
Complete Set (10):	4.00
Common Player:	.45
1 Bobby Bonds	.45
2 Lou Brock	.45
3 Rollie Fingers	.45
4 Bob Gibson	.45
5 Reggie Jackson	.75
6 Gaylord Perry	.45
7 Robin Roberts	.45
8 Brooks Robinson	.45
9 Billy Williams	.45
10 Ted Williams	2.00

Home Run Heroes

	NM/M
Complete Set (26):	5.00
Common Player:	.15
1 Jose Canseco	.45
2 Cecil Fielder	.15
3 Howard Johnson	.15
4 Cal Ripken, Jr.	1.50
5 Matt Williams	.15
6 Joe Carter	.15
7 Ron Gant	.15
8 Frank Thomas	.75
9 Andre Dawson	.40
10 Fred McGriff	.15
11 Danny Tartabull	.15
12 Chili Davis	.15
13 Albert Belle	.15
14 Jack Clark	.15
15 Paul O'Neill	.15

CECIL FIELDER

		NM/M
Complete Set (20):		3.00
Common Player:		.12
1	Wade Boggs	.50
2	Barry Bonds	1.00
3	Jose Canseco	.25
4	Will Clark	.10
5	Cecil Fielder	.10
6	Tony Gwynn	.50
7	Rickey Henderson	.40
8	Fred McGriff	.10
9	Kirby Puckett	.50
10	Ruben Sierra	.10
11	Roberto Alomar	.20
12	Jeff Bagwell	.40
13	Albert Belle	.10
14	Juan Gonzalez	.20
15	Ken Griffey Jr.	.75
16	Chris Hoiles	.10
17	Dave Justice	.10
18	Phil Plantier	.10
19	Frank Thomas	.40
20	Robin Ventura	.10

16	Darryl Strawberry	.15
17	Dave Winfield	.75
18	Jay Buhner	.15
19	Juan Gonzalez	.25
20	Greg Vaughn	.15
21	Barry Bonds	1.50
22	Matt Nokes	.15
23	John Kruk	.15
24	Ivan Calderon	.15
25	Jeff Bagwell	.75
26	Todd Zeile	.15

Scouting Report

SCOUTING REPORT

MARK WOHLERS

		NM/M
Complete Set (25):		2.00
Common Player:		.25
1	Andy Ashby	.25
2	Willie Banks	.25
3	Kim Batiste	.25
4	Derek Bell	.25
5	Archi Cianfrocco	.25
6	Royce Clayton	.25
7	Gary DiSarcina	.25
8	Dave Fleming	.25
9	Butch Henry	.25
10	Todd Hundley	.25
11	Brian Jordan	.25
12	Eric Karros	.25
13	Pat Listach	.25
14	Scott Livingstone	.25
15	Kenny Lofton	.25
16	Pat Mahomes	.25
17	Denny Neagle	.25
18	Dave Nilsson	.25
19	Donovan Osborne	.25
20	Reggie Sanders	.25
21	Andy Stankiewicz	.25
22	Jim Thome	1.50
23	Julio Valera	.25
24	Mark Wohlers	.25
25	Anthony Young	.25

Ted Williams' Best Hitters/Future

Ted Williams
BEST HITTERS OF THE FUTURE
ROBERTO ALOMAR

1993 Upper Deck

		NM/M
Unopened Fact. Set (840):		30.00
Complete Set (840):		25.00
Common Player:		.05
Gold Hologram:		4X
Series 1 or 2 Pack (15):		.75
Series 1 or 2 Wax Box (36):		17.50
Jumbo Pack, USA (27):		1.50
Jumbo Box, USA (20):		17.50
Jumbo Pack, Canada (23):		2.00
Jumbo Box, Canada (20):		20.00
1	Tim Salmon (Checklist)	.05
2	Mike Piazza	1.25
3	Rene Arocha RC	.05
4	Willie Greene RC	.05
5	Manny Alexander RC	.05
6	Dan Wilson	.05
7	Dan Smith RC	.05
8	Kevin Rogers RC	.05
9	Nigel Wilson RC	.05
10	Joe Vitko RC	.05
11	Tim Costo (RC)	.05
12	Alan Embree	.05
13	Jim Tatum RC	.05
14	Cris Colon RC	.05
15	Steve Hosey (RC)	.05
16	Sterling Hitchcock RC	.15
17	Dave Mlicki RC	.05
18	Jessie Hollins RC	.05
19	Bobby J. Jones RC	.05
20	Kurt Miller RC	.05
21	Melvin Nieves RC	.05
22	Billy Ashley RC	.05
23	J.T. Snow RC	.05
24	Chipper Jones	1.00
25	Tim Salmon	.25
26	Tim Pugh RC	.05
27	David Nied	.05
28	Mike Trombley RC	.05
29	Javier Lopez	.05
30	Jim Abbott Community Heroes Checklist	.05
31	Jim Abbott	.05
32	Dale Murphy	.10
33	Tony Pena	.05
34	Kirby Puckett	.40
35	Harold Reynolds	.05
36	Cal Ripken, Jr.	.65
37	Nolan Ryan	.65
38	Ryne Sandberg	.35
39	Dave Stewart	.05
40	Dave Winfield	.25
41	Joe Carter, Mark McGwire Teammates Checklist	.50
42	Joe Carter, Roberto Alomar Blockbuster Trade	.05
43	Pat Listach, Robin Yount, Paul Molitor Brew Crew	.15
44	Brady Anderson, Cal Ripken, Jr. Iron and Steal	.45
45	Albert Belle, Sandy Alomar Jr., Jim Thome, Carlos Baerga, Kenny Lofton Youthful Tribe	.25
46	Cecil Fielder, Mickey Tettleton Motown Mashers	.05
47	Roberto Kelly, Don Mattingly Yankee Pride	.45
48	Frank Viola, Roger Clemens Boston Cy Sox	.30
49	Ruben Sierra, Mark McGwire Bash Brothers	.50
50	Kent Hrbek, Kirby Puckett Twin Titles	.35
51	Robin Ventura, Frank Thomas Southside Sluggers	.35
52	Jose Canseco, Ivan Rodriguez, Rafael Palmeiro, Juan Gonzalez Latin Stars	.35
53	Mark Langston, Jim Abbott, Chuck Finley Lethal Lefties	.05
54	Gregg Jefferies, George Brett, Wally Joyner Royal Family	.35
55	Kevin Mitchell, Jay Buhner, Ken Griffey Jr. Pacific Sox Exchange	.40
56	George Brett	.85
57	Scott Cooper	.05
58	Mike Maddux	.05
59	Rusty Meacham RC	.05
60	Wil Cordero	.05
61	Tim Teufel	.05
62	Jeff Montgomery	.05
63	Scott Livingstone (RC)	.05
64	Doug Dascenzo	.05
65	Bret Boone	.05
66	Tim Wakefield RC	.10
67	Curt Schilling	.20
68	Frank Tanana	.05
69	Len Dykstra	.05
70	Derek Lilliquist	.05
71	Anthony Young (RC)	.05
72	Hipolito Pichardo RC	.05
73	Rod Beck (RC)	.05
74	Kent Hrbek	.05
75	Tom Glavine	.20
76	Kevin Brown	.05
77	Chuck Finley	.05
78	Bob Walk	.05
79	Rheal Cormier	.05
80	Rick Sutcliffe	.05
81	Harold Baines	.05
82	Lee Smith	.05
83	Geno Petralli	.05
84	Jose Oquendo	.05
85	Mark Gubicza	.05
86	Mickey Tettleton	.05
87	Bobby Witt	.05
88	Mark Lewis	.05
89	Kevin Appier	.05
90	Mike Stanton	.05
91	Rafael Belliard	.05
92	Kenny Rogers	.05
93	Randy Velarde	.05
94	Luis Sojo	.05
95	Mark Leiter	.05
96	Jody Reed	.05
97	Pete Harnisch	.05
98	Tom Candiotti	.05
99	Mark Portugal	.05
100	Dave Valle	.05
101	Shawon Dunston	.05
102	B.J. Surhoff	.05
103	Jay Bell	.05
104	Sid Bream	.05
105	Frank Thomas Checklist 1-105	.35
106	Mike Morgan	.05
107	Bill Doran	.05
108	Lance Blankenship	.05
109	Mark Lemke	.05
110	Brian Harper	.05
111	Brady Anderson	.05
112	Bip Roberts	.05
113	Mitch Williams	.05
114	Craig Biggio	.05
115	Eddie Murray	.65
116	Matt Nokes	.05
117	Lance Parrish	.05
118	Bill Swift	.05
119	Jeff Innis	.05
120	Mike LaValliere	.05
121	Hal Morris	.05
122	Walt Weiss	.05
123	Ivan Rodriguez	.60
124	Andy Van Slyke	.05
125	Roberto Alomar	.20
126	Robby Thompson	.05
127	Sammy Sosa	.75
128	Mark Langston	.05
129	Jerry Browne	.05
130	Chuck McElroy	.05
131	Frank Viola	.05
132	Leo Gomez	.05
133	Ramon Martinez	.05
134	Don Mattingly	.85
135	Roger Clemens	.85
136	Rickey Henderson	.65
137	Darren Daulton	.05
138	Ken Hill	.05
139	Ozzie Guillen	.05
140	Jerald Clark	.05
141	Dave Fleming	.05
142	Delino DeShields	.05
143	Matt Williams	.05
144	Larry Walker	.05
145	Ruben Sierra	.05
146	Ozzie Smith	.75
147	Chris Sabo	.05
148	Carlos Hernandez RC	.05
149	Pat Borders	.05
150	Orlando Merced	.05
151	Royce Clayton	.05
152	Kurt Stillwell	.05
153	Dave Hollins	.05
154	Mike Greenwell	.05
155	Nolan Ryan	1.50
156	Felix Jose	.05
157	Junior Felix	.05
158	Derek Bell	.05
159	Steve Buechele	.05
160	John Burkett	.05
161	Pat Howell RC	.05
162	Milt Cuyler	.05
163	Terry Pendleton	.05
164	Jack Morris	.05
165	Tony Gwynn	.75
166	Deion Sanders	.10
167	Mike Devereaux	.05
168	Ron Darling	.05
169	Orel Hershiser	.05
170	Mike Jackson	.05
171	Doug Jones	.05
172	Dan Walters (RC) RC	.05
173	Darren Lewis	.05
174	Carlos Baerga	.05
175	Ryne Sandberg	.75
176	Gregg Jefferies	.05
177	John Jaha	.05
178	Luis Polonia	.05
179	Kirt Manwaring	.05
180	Mike Magnante	.05
181	Billy Ripken	.05
182	Mike Moore	.05
183	Eric Anthony	.05
184	Lenny Harris	.05
185	Tony Pena	.05
186	Mike Felder	.05
187	Greg Olson	.05
188	Rene Gonzales	.05
189	Mike Bordick	.05
190	Mel Rojas	.05
191	Todd Frohwirth	.05
192	Darryl Hamilton	.05
193	Mike Fetters	.05
194	Omar Olivares (RC)	.05
195	Tony Phillips	.05
196	Paul Sorrento	.05
197	Trevor Wilson	.05
198	Kevin Gross	.05
199	Ron Karkovice	.05
200	Brook Jacoby	.05
201	Mariano Duncan	.05
202	Dennis Cook	.05
203	Daryl Boston	.05
204	Mike Perez	.05
205	Manuel Lee	.05
206	Steve Olin	.05
207	Charlie Hough	.05
208	Scott Scudder	.05
209	Charlie O'Brien	.05
210	Barry Bonds	
	Checklist 106-210	.60
211	Jose Vizcaino	.05
212	Scott Leius	.05
213	Kevin Mitchell	.05
214	Brian Barnes	.05
215	Pat Kelly	.05
216	Chris Hammond	.05
217	Rob Deer	.05
218	Cory Snyder	.05
219	Gary Carter	.65
220	Danny Darwin	.05
221	Tom Gordon	.05
222	Gary Sheffield	.40
223	Joe Carter	.05
224	Jay Buhner	.05
225	Jose Offerman	.05
226	Jose Rijo	.05
227	Mark Whiten	.05
228	Randy Milligan	.05
229	Bud Black	.05
230	Gary DiSarcina	.05
231	Steve Finley	.05
232	Dennis Martinez	.05
233	Mike Mussina	.30
234	Joe Oliver	.05
235	Chad Curtis	.05
236	Shane Mack	.05
237	Jaime Navarro	.05
238	Brian McRae	.05
239	Chili Davis	.05
240	Jeff King	.05
241	Dean Palmer	.05
242	Danny Tartabull	.05
243	Charles Nagy	.05
244	Ray Lankford	.05
245	Barry Larkin	.05
246	Steve Avery	.05
247	John Kruk	.05
248	Derrick May	.05
249	Stan Javier	.05
250	Roger McDowell	.05
251	Dan Gladden	.05
252	Wally Joyner	.05
253	Pat Listach	.05
254	Chuck Knoblauch	.05
255	Sandy Alomar Jr.	.05
256	Jeff Bagwell	.65
257	Andy Stankiewicz	.05
258	Darrin Jackson	.05
259	Brett Butler	.05
260	Joe Orsulak	.05
261	Andy Benes	.05
262	Kenny Lofton	.05
263	Robin Ventura	.05

264 Ron Gant .05
265 Ellis Burks .05
266 Juan Guzman .05
267 Wes Chamberlain .05
268 John Smiley .05
269 Franklin Stubbs .05
270 Tom Browning .05
271 Dennis Eckersley .60
272 Carlton Fisk .65
273 Lou Whitaker .05
274 Phil Plantier .05
275 Bobby Bonilla .05
276 Ben McDonald .05
277 Bob Zupcic .05
278 Terry Steinbach .05
279 Terry Mulholland .05
280 Lance Johnson .05
281 Willie McGee .05
282 Bret Saberhagen .05
283 Randy Myers .05
284 Randy Tomlin .05
285 Mickey Morandini .05
286 Brian Williams .05
287 Tino Martinez .05
288 Jose Melendez .05
289 Jeff Huson .05
290 Joe Grahe .05
291 Mel Hall .05
292 Otis Nixon .05
293 Todd Hundley .05
294 Casey Candaele .05
295 Kevin Seitzer .05
296 Eddie Taubensee .05
297 Moises Alou .05
298 Scott Radinsky .05
299 Thomas Howard .05
300 Kyle Abbott .05
301 Omar Vizquel .05
302 Keith Miller .05
303 Rick Aguilera .05
304 Bruce Hurst .05
305 Ken Caminiti .05
306 Mike Pagiarulo .05
307 Frank Seminara .05
308 Andre Dawson .30
309 Jose Lind .05
310 Joe Boever .05
311 Jeff Parrett **(RC)** .05
312 Alan Mills .05
313 Kevin Tapani .05
314 Darryl Kile .05
315 Will Clark Checklist 211-315 .05
316 Mike Sharperson .05
317 John Orton .05
318 Bob Tewksbury .05
319 Xavier Hernandez .05
320 Paul Assenmacher .05
321 John Franco .05
322 Mike Timlin .05
323 Jose Guzman .05
324 Pedro Martinez .65
325 Bill Spiers .05
326 Melido Perez .05
327 Mike Macfarlane .05
328 Ricky Bones .05
329 Scott Bankhead .05
330 Rich Rodriguez .05
331 Geronimo Pena .05
332 Bernie Williams .05
333 Paul Molitor .65
334 Roger Mason .05
335 David Cone .05
336 Randy Johnson .65
337 Pat Mahomes .05
338 Erik Hanson .05
339 Duane Ward .05
340 Al Martin .05
341 Pedro Munoz .05
342 Greg Colbrunn .05
343 Julio Valera .05
344 John Olerud .05
345 George Bell .05
346 Devon White .05
347 Donovan Osborne .05
348 Mark Gardner .05
349 Zane Smith .05
350 Wilson Alvarez .05
351 Kevin Koslofski **RC** .05
352 Roberto Hernandez .05
353 Glenn Davis .05
354 Reggie Sanders .05
355 Ken Griffey Jr. 1.00
355a Ken Griffey Jr. (Promo, 1992-dated hologram on back.) 3.00
355b Ken Griffey Jr. (8-1/2" x 11" limited edition of 1,000) 15.00
356 Marquis Grissom .05
357 Jack McDowell .05
358 Jimmy Key .05
359 Stan Belinda .05
360 Gerald Williams .05
361 Sid Fernandez .05
362 Alex Fernandez .05
363 John Smoltz .05
364 Travis Fryman .05
365 Jose Canseco .50
366 Dave Justice .05
367 Pedro Astacio **RC** .10
368 Tim Belcher .05
369 Steve Sax .05
370 Gary Gaetti .05
371 Jeff Frye .05
372 Bob Wickman .05
373 Ryan Thompson **RC** .05
374 David Hulse **RC** .05
375 Cal Eldred .05
376 Ryan Klesko .05
377 Damion Easley **RC** .10
378 John Kiely **RC** .05
379 Jim Bullinger **(RC) RC** .05
380 Brian Bohanon .05
381 Rod Brewer .05
382 Fernando Ramsey **RC** .05
383 Sam Militello .05
384 Arthur Rhodes .05
385 Eric Karros .05
386 Rico Brogna .05
387 John Valentin **RC** .10
388 Kerry Woodson **RC** .05
389 Ben Rivera **RC** .05
390 Matt Whiteside **RC** .05
391 Henry Rodriguez .05
392 John Wetteland .05
393 Kent Mercker .05
394 Bernard Gilkey .05
395 Doug Henry .05
396 Mo Vaughn .05
397 Scott Erickson .05
398 Bill Gullickson .05
399 Mark Guthrie .05
400 Dave Martinez .05
401 Jeff Kent **RC** .50
402 Chris Hoiles .05
403 Mike Henneman .05
404 Chris Nabholz .05
405 Tom Pagnozzi .05
406 Kelly Gruber .05
407 Bob Welch .05
408 Frank Castillo .05
409 John Dopson .05
410 Steve Farr .05
411 Henry Cotto .05
412 Bob Patterson .05
413 Todd Stottlemyre .05
414 Greg A. Harris .05
415 Denny Neagle .05
416 Bill Wegman .05
417 Willie Wilson .05
418 Terry Leach .05
419 Willie Randolph .05
420 Mark McGwire Checklist 316-420 .65
421 Calvin Murray (Top Prospects Checklist) .05
422 Pete Janicki **RC** (Top Prospect) .05
423 Todd Jones **(RC)** (Top Prospect) .05
424 Mike Neill (Top Prospect) .05
425 Carlos Delgado (Top Prospect) .40
426 Jose Oliva (Top Prospect) .05
427 Tyrone Hill (Top Prospect) .05
428 Dmitri Young (Top Prospect) .05
429 Derek Wallace **RC** (Top Prospect) .05
430 Michael Moore **RC** (Top Prospect) .05
431 Cliff Floyd (Top Prospect) .05
432 Calvin Murray (Top Prospect) .05
433 Manny Ramirez (Top Prospect) .75
434 Marc Newfield (Top Prospect) .05
435 Charles Johnson (Top Prospect) .05
436 Butch Huskey (Top Prospect) .05
437 Brad Pennington (Top Prospect) .05
438 Ray McDavid **RC** (Top Prospect) .05
439 Chad McConnell (Top Prospect) .05
440 Midre Cummings **RC** (Top Prospect) .05
441 Benji Gil (Top Prospect) .05
442 Frank Rodriguez (Top Prospect) .05
443 Chad Mottola **RC** (Top Prospect) .05
444 John Burke **RC** (Top Prospect) .05
445 Michael Tucker (Top Prospect) .05
446 Rick Greene (Top Prospect) .05
447 Rich Becker (Top Prospect) .05
448 Mike Robertson (Top Prospect) .05
449 Derek Jeter **RC** (Top Prospect) 10.00
450 David McCarty, Ivan Rodriguez Checklist 451-470 Inside the Numbers .05
451 Jim Abbott (Inside the Numbers) .05
452 Jeff Bagwell (Inside the Numbers) .40
453 Jason Bere (Inside the Numbers) .05
454 Delino DeShields (Inside the Numbers) .05
455 Travis Fryman (Inside the Numbers) .05
456 Alex Gonzalez (Inside the Numbers) .05
457 Phil Hiatt (Inside the Numbers) .05
458 Dave Hollins (Inside the Numbers) .05
459 Chipper Jones (Inside the Numbers) .75
460 Dave Justice (Inside the Numbers) .05
461 Ray Lankford (Inside the Numbers) .05
462 David McCarty (Inside the Numbers) .05
463 Mike Mussina (Inside the Numbers) .15
464 Jose Offerman (Inside the Numbers) .05
465 Dean Palmer (Inside the Numbers) .05
466 Geronimo Pena (Inside the Numbers) .05
467 Eduardo Perez (Inside the Numbers) .05
468 Ivan Rodriguez (Inside the Numbers) .25
469 Reggie Sanders (Inside the Numbers) .05
470 Bernie Williams (Inside the Numbers) .05
471 Barry Bonds, Matt Williams, Will Clark Checklist 472-485 Team Stars .45
472 John Smoltz, Steve Avery, Greg Maddux, Tom Glavine Strike Force .10
473 Jose Rijo, Rob Dibble, Roberto Kelly, Reggie Sanders, Barry Larkin Red October .10
474 Gary Sheffield, Phil Plantier, Tony Gwynn, Fred McGriff Four Corners .20
475 Doug Drabek, Craig Biggio, Jeff Bagwell Shooting Stars .15
476 Will Clark, Barry Bonds, Matt Williams Giant Sticks .40
477 Darryl Strawberry, Eric Davis Boyhood Friends .05
478 Dante Bichette, David Nied, Andres Galarraga Rock Solid .05
479 Dave Magadan, Orestes Destrade, Bret Barbarie, Jeff Conine Inaugural Catch .05
480 Tim Wakefield, Andy Van Slyke, Jay Bell Steel City Champions .05
481 Marquis Grissom, Delino DeShields, Dennis Martinez, Larry Walker "Les Grandes Etoiles" .05
482 Geronimo Pena, Ray Lankford, Ozzie Smith, Bernard Gilkey Runnin' Redbirds .10
483 Ryne Sandberg, Mark Grace, Randy Myers Ivy Leaguers .15
484 Eddie Murray, Bobby Bonilla, Howard Johnson Big Apple Power Switch .10
485 John Kruk, Dave Hollins, Darren Daulton, Len Dykstra Hammers & Nails .05
486 Barry Bonds (Award Winners) .60
487 Dennis Eckersley (Award Winners) .30
488 Greg Maddux (Award Winners) .40
489 Dennis Eckersley (Award Winners) .30
490 Eric Karros (Award Winners) .05
491 Pat Listach (Award Winners) .05
492 Gary Sheffield (Award Winners) .10
493 Mark McGwire (Award Winners) .75
494 Gary Sheffield (Award Winners) .10
495 Edgar Martinez (Award Winners) .05
496 Fred McGriff (Award Winners) .05
497 Juan Gonzalez (Award Winners) .20
498 Darren Daulton (Award Winners) .05
499 Cecil Fielder (Award Winners) .05
500 Brent Gates Checklist 501-510 Diamond Debuts .05
501 Tavo Alvarez (Diamond Debuts) .05
502 Rod Bolton (Diamond Debuts) .05
503 John Cummings **RC** (Diamond Debuts) .05
504 Brent Gates (Diamond Debuts) .05
505 Tyler Green (Diamond Debuts) .05
506 Jose Martinez **RC** (Diamond Debuts) .05
507 Troy Percival (Diamond Debuts) .05
508 Kevin Stocker (Diamond Debuts) .05
509 Matt Walbeck **RC** (Diamond Debuts) .10
510 Rondell White (Diamond Debuts) .05
511 Billy Ripken .05
512 Mike Moore .05
513 Jose Lind .05
514 Chito Martinez .05
515 Jose Guzman .05
516 Kim Batiste .05
517 Jeff Tackett .05
518 Charlie Hough .05
519 Marvin Freeman .05
520 Carlos Martinez .05
521 Eric Young .05
522 Pete Incaviglia .05
523 Scott Fletcher .05
524 Orestes Destrade .05
525 Ken Griffey Jr. Checklist 421-525 .40
526 Ellis Burks .05
527 Juan Samuel .05
528 Dave Magadan .05
529 Jeff Parrett .05
530 Bill Krueger .05
531 Frank Bolick .05
532 Alan Trammell .05
533 Walt Weiss .05
534 David Cone .05
535 Greg Maddux .75
536 Kevin Young .05
537 Dave Hansen .05
538 Alex Cole .05
539 Greg Hibbard .05
540 Gene Larkin .05
541 Jeff Reardon .05
542 Felix Jose .05
543 Jimmy Key .05
544 Reggie Jefferson .05
545 Gregg Jefferies .05
546 Dave Stewart .05
547 Tim Wallach .05
548 Spike Owen .05
549 Tommy Greene .05
550 Fernando Valenzuela .05
551 Rich Amaral .05
552 Bret Barberie .05
553 Edgar Martinez .05
554 Jim Abbott .05
555 Frank Thomas .65
556 Wade Boggs .75
557 Tom Henke .05
558 Milt Thompson .05
559 Lloyd McClendon .05
560 Vinny Castilla .05
561 Ricky Jordan .05
562 Andujar Cedeno .05
563 Greg Vaughn .05
564 Cecil Fielder .05
565 Kirby Puckett .75
566 Mark McGwire 1.25
567 Barry Bonds 1.50
568 Jody Reed .05
569 Todd Zeile .05
570 Mark Carreon .05
571 Joe Girardi .05
572 Luis Gonzalez .05
573 Mark Grace .05
574 Rafael Palmeiro .60
575 Darryl Strawberry .05
576 Will Clark .05
577 Fred McGriff .05
578 Kevin Reimer .05
579 Dave Righetti .05
580 Juan Bell .05
581 Jeff Brantley .05
582 Brian Hunter .05
583 Tim Naehring .05
584 Glenallen Hill .05
585 Cal Ripken, Jr. 1.50
586 Albert Belle .05
587 Robin Yount .65
588 Chris Bosio .05
589 Pete Smith .05
590 Chuck Carr .05
591 Jeff Blauser .05
592 Kevin McReynolds .05
593 Andres Galarraga .05
594 Kevin Maas .05
595 Eric Davis .05
596 Brian Jordan .05
597 Tim Raines .05
598 Rick Wilkins .05
599 Steve Cooke .05
600 Mike Gallego .05
601 Mike Munoz .05
602 Luis Rivera .05
603 Junior Ortiz .05
604 Brent Mayne .05
605 Luis Alicea .05
606 Damon Berryhill .05
607 Dave Henderson .05
608 Kirk McCaskill .05
609 Jeff Fassero .05
610 Mike Harkey .05
611 Francisco Cabrera .05
612 Rey Sanchez .05
613 Scott Servais .05
614 Darrin Fletcher .05
615 Felix Fermin .05
616 Kevin Seitzer .05
617 Bob Scanlan .05
618 Billy Hatcher .05
619 John Vander Wal .05
620 Joe Hesketh .05
621 Hector Villanueva .05
622 Randy Milligan .05
623 Tony Tarasco **RC** .05
624 Russ Swan .05
625 Willie Wilson .05

626 Frank Tanana .05
627 Pete O'Brien .05
628 Lenny Webster .05
629 Mark Clark .05
630 Roger Clemens
Checklist 526-630 .40
631 Alex Arias .05
632 Chris Gwynn .05
633 Tom Bolton .05
634 Greg Briley .05
635 Kent Bottenfield .05
636 Kelly Downs .05
637 Manuel Lee .05
638 Al Leiter .05
639 Jeff Gardner .05
640 Mike Gardiner .05
641 Mark Gardner .05
642 Jeff Branson .05
643 Paul Wagner .05
644 Sean Berry .05
645 Phil Hiatt .05
646 Kevin Mitchell .05
647 Charlie Hayes .05
648 Jim Deshaies .05
649 Dan Pasqua .05
650 Mike Maddux .05
651 Domingo Martinez **RC** .05
652 Greg McMichael **RC** .05
653 Eric Wedge **RC** .05
654 Mark Whiten .05
655 Bobby Kelly .05
656 Julio Franco .05
657 Gene Harris .05
658 Pete Schourek .05
659 Mike Bielecki .05
660 Ricky Gutierrez .05
661 Chris Hammond .05
662 Tim Scott .05
663 Norm Charlton .05
664 Doug Drabek .05
665 Dwight Gooden .05
666 Jim Gott .05
667 Randy Myers .05
668 Darren Holmes .05
669 Tim Spehr .05
670 Bruce Ruffin .05
671 Bobby Thigpen .05
672 Tony Fernandez .05
673 Darrin Jackson .05
674 Gregg Olson .05
675 Rob Dibble .05
676 Howard Johnson .05
677 Mike Lansing **RC** .15
678 Charlie Leibrandt .05
679 Kevin Bass .05
680 Hubie Brooks .05
681 Scott Brosius .05
682 Randy Knorr .05
683 Dante Bichette .05
684 Bryan Harvey .05
685 Greg Gohr .05
686 Willie Banks .05
687 Robb Nen .05
688 Mike Scioscia .05
689 John Farrell .05
690 John Candelaria .05
691 Damon Buford .05
692 Todd Worrell .05
693 Pat Hentgen .05
694 John Smiley .05
695 Greg Swindell .05
696 Derek Bell .05
697 Terry Jorgensen .05
698 Jimmy Jones .05
699 David Wells .05
700 Dave Martinez .05
701 Steve Bedrosian .05
702 Jeff Russell .05
703 Joe Magrane .05
704 Matt Mieske .05
705 Paul Molitor .65
706 Dale Murphy .15
707 Steve Howe .05
708 Greg Gagne .05
709 Dave Eiland .05
710 David West .05
711 Luis Aquino .05
712 Joe Orsulak .05
713 Eric Plunk .05
714 Mike Felder .05
715 Joe Klink .05
716 Lonnie Smith .05
717 Monty Fariss .05
718 Craig Lefferts .05
719 John Habyan .05
720 Willie Blair .05
721 Darnell Coles .05
722 Mark Williamson .05
723 Bryn Smith .05
724 Greg W. Harris .05
725 Graeme Lloyd **RC** .05
726 Cris Carpenter .05
727 Chico Walker .05
728 Tracy Woodson .05
729 Jose Uribe .05
730 Stan Javier .05
731 Jay Howell .05
732 Freddie Benavides .05
733 Jeff Reboulet .05
734 Scott Sanderson .05
735 Ryne Sandberg
Checklist 631-735 .20
736 Archi Cianfrocco .05
737 Daryl Boston .05
738 Craig Grebeck .05
739 Doug Dascenzo .05
740 Gerald Young .05
741 Candy Maldonado .05
742 Joey Cora .05
743 Don Slaught .05
744 Steve Decker .05
745 Blas Minor .05
746 Storm Davis .05
747 Carlos Quintana .05
748 Vince Coleman .05
749 Todd Burns .05
750 Steve Frey .05
751 Ivan Calderon .05
752 Steve Reed **RC** .05
753 Danny Jackson .05
754 Jeff Conine .05
755 Juan Gonzalez .35
756 Mike Kelly .05
757 John Doherty .05
758 Jack Armstrong .05
759 John Wehner .05
760 Scott Bankhead .05
761 Jim Tatum .05
762 Scott Pose **RC** .05
763 Andy Ashby .05
764 Ed Sprague .05
765 Harold Baines .05
766 Kirk Gibson .05
767 Troy Neel .05
768 Dick Schofield .05
769 Dickie Thon .05
770 Butch Henry .05
771 Junior Felix .05
772 Ken Ryan **RC** .05
773 Trevor Hoffman .05
774 Phil Plantier .05
775 Bo Jackson .10
776 Benito Santiago .05
777 Andre Dawson .25
778 Bryan Hickerson .05
779 Dennis Moeller .05
780 Ryan Bowen .05
781 Eric Fox .05
782 Joe Kmak .05
783 Mike Hampton .05
784 Darrell Sherman **RC** .05
785 J.T. Snow .05
786 Dave Winfield .65
787 Jim Austin .05
788 Craig Shipley .05
789 Greg Myers .05
790 Todd Benzinger .05
791 Cory Snyder .05
792 David Segui .05
793 Armando Reynoso .05
794 Chili Davis .05
795 Dave Nilsson .05
796 Paul O'Neill .05
797 Jerald Clark .05
798 Jose Mesa .05
799 Brian Holman .05
800 Jim Eisenreich .05
801 Mark McLemore .05
802 Luis Sojo .05
803 Harold Reynolds .05
804 Dan Plesac .05
805 Dave Stieb .05
806 Tom Brunansky .05
807 Kelly Gruber .05
808 Bob Ojeda .05
809 Dave Burba .05
810 Joe Boever .05
811 Jeremy Hernandez .05
812 Tim Salmon Angels Checklist .05
813 Jeff Bagwell Astros Checklist .35
814 Mark McGwire
Athletics Checklist .75
815 Roberto Alomar
Blue Jays Checklist .10
816 Steve Avery Braves Checklist .05
817 Pat Listach Brewers Checklist .05
818 Gregg Jefferies
Cardinals Checklist .05
819 Sammy Sosa Cubs Checklist .40
820 Darryl Strawberry
Dodgers Checklist .05
821 Dennis Martinez
Expos Checklist .05
822 Robby Thompson
Giants Checklist .05
823 Albert Belle Indians Checklist .05
824 Randy Johnson
Mariners Checklist .30
825 Nigel Wilson Marlins Checklist .05
826 Bobby Bonilla Mets Checklist .05
827 Glenn Davis Orioles Checklist .05
828 Gary Sheffield
Padres Checklist .10
829 Darren Daulton
Phillies Checklist .05
830 Jay Bell Pirates Checklist .05
831 Juan Gonzalez
Rangers Checklist .20
832 Andre Dawson
Red Sox Checklist .10
833 Hal Morris Reds Checklist .05
834 David Nied Rockies Checklist .05
835 Felix Jose Royals Checklist .05
836 Travis Fryman Tigers Checklist .05
837 Shane Mack Twins Checklist .05
838 Robin Ventura
White Sox Checklist .05
839 Danny Tartabull
Yankees Checklist .05
840 Roberto Alomar
Checklist 736-840 .10
SP5 Robin Yount, George Brett
3,000 Hits .50
SP6 Nolan Ryan 1.50

1993 Upper Deck All-Time Heroes

NM/M

Complete Set (165): 35.00
Common Player: .10
Wax Pack (12): 2.00
Wax Box (24): 30.00
1 Hank Aaron 2.00
2 Tommie Agee .10
3 Bob Allison .10
4 Matty Alou .10
5 Sal Bando .10
6 Hank Bauer .15
7 Don Baylor .10
8 Glenn Beckert .10
9 Yogi Berra .50
10 Buddy Biancalana .10
11 Jack Billingham .10
12 Joe Black .10
13 Paul Blair .10
14 Steve Blass .10
15 Ray Boone .10
16 Lou Boudreau .10
17 Ken Brett .10
18 Nellie Briles .10
19 Bobby Brown .10
20 Bill Buckner .10
21 Don Buford .10
22 Al Bumbry .10
23 Lew Burdette .10
24 Jeff Burroughs .10
25 Johnny Callison .10
26 Bert Campaneris .10
27 Rico Carty .10
28 Dave Cash .10
29 Cesar Cedeno .10
30 Frank Chance .25
31 Joe Charboneau .15
32 Ty Cobb 2.00
33 Jerry Coleman .10
34 Cecil Cooper .10
35 Frankie Crossetti .10
36 Alvin Dark .10
37 Tommy Davis .10
38 Dizzy Dean .25
39 Doug DeCinces .10
40 Bucky Dent .10
41 Larry Dierker .10
42 Larry Doby .20
43 Moe Drabowsky .10
44 Dave Dravecky .10
45 Del Ennis .10
46 Carl Erskine .10
47 Johnny Evers .25
48 Elroy Face .10
49 Rick Ferrell .10
50 Mark Fidrych .15
51 Curt Flood .10
52 Whitey Ford .50
53 George Foster .10
54 Jimmie Foxx .25
55 Jim Fregosi .10
56 Phil Garner .10
57 Ralph Garr .10
58 Lou Gehrig 2.00
59 Bobby Grich .10
60 Jerry Grote .10
61 Harvey Haddix .10
62 Toby Harrah .10
63 Bud Harrelson .10
64 Jim Hegan .10
65 Gil Hodges .25
66 Ken Holtzman .10
67 Bob Horner .10
68 Rogers Hornsby .25
69 Carl Hubbell .25
70 Ron Hunt .10
71 Monte Irvin .10
72a Reggie Jackson (Regular issue, black printing on back.) .50
72b Reggie Jackson (Dealer promo, red printing on back.) 6.00
73 Larry Jansen .10
74 Ferguson Jenkins .10
75 Tommy John .10
76 Cliff Johnson .10
77 Davey Johnson .10
78 Walter Johnson .45
79 George Kell .10
80 Don Kessinger .10
81 Vern Law .10
82 Dennis Leonard .10
83 Johnny Logan .10
84 Mickey Lolich .10
85 Jim Lonborg .10
86 Bill Madlock .10
87 Mickey Mantle 4.00
88 Billy Martin .25
89 Christy Mathewson .45
90 Lee May .10
91 Willie Mays 2.00
92 Bill Mazeroski .25
93 Gil McDougald .15
94 Sam McDowell .10
95 Minnie Minoso .15
96 Johnny Mize .25
97 Rick Monday .10
98 Wally Moon .10
99 Manny Mota .10
100 Bobby Murcer .10
101 Ron Necciai .10
102 Al Oliver .10
103 Mel Ott .15
104 Mel Parnell .10
105 Jimmy Piersall .10
106 Johnny Podres .15
107 Bobby Richardson .15
108 Robin Roberts .15
109 Al Rosen .10
110 Babe Ruth 3.00
111 Joe Sambito .10
112 Manny Sanguillen .10
113 Ron Santo .10
114 Bill Skowron .15
115 Enos Slaughter .15
116 Warren Spahn .20
117 Tris Speaker .20
118 Frank Thomas .10
119 Bobby Thomson .10
120 Andre Thornton .10
121 Marv Throneberry .10
122 Luis Tiant .10
123 Joe Tinker .25
124 Honus Wagner .50
125 Bill White .10
126 Ted Williams 1.00
127 Earl Wilson .10
128 Joe Wood .10
129 Cy Young .40
130 Richie Zisk .10
131 Babe Ruth, Lou Gehrig 2.00
132 Ted Williams,
Rogers Hornsby 1.00
133 Lou Gehrig, Babe Ruth 2.00
134 Babe Ruth, Mickey Mantle 3.00
135 Mickey Mantle,
Reggie Jackson 1.00
136 Mel Ott, Carl Hubbell .15
137 Mickey Mantle, Willie Mays 2.00
138 Cy Young, Walter Johnson .25
139 Honus Wagner,
Rogers Hornsby .25
140 Mickey Mantle, Whitey Ford 2.00
141 Mickey Mantle, Billy Martin 2.00
142 Cy Young, Walter Johnson .25
143 Christy Mathewson,
Walter Johnson .25
144 Warren Spahn,
Christy Mathewson .15
145 Honus Wagner, Ty Cobb .50
146 Babe Ruth, Ty Cobb 1.00
147 Joe Tinker, Johnny Evers .15
148 Johnny Evers, Frank Chance .15
149 Hank Aaron, Babe Ruth 1.00
150 Willie Mays, Hank Aaron 1.00
151 Babe Ruth, Willie Mays 1.00
152 Babe Ruth, Whitey Ford 1.00
153 Larry Doby, Minnie Minoso .25
154 Joe Black, Monte Irvin .10
155 Joe Wood, Christy Mathewson .15
156 Christy Mathewson, Cy Young .25
157 Cy Young, Joe Wood .15
158 Cy Young, Whitey Ford .20
159 Cy Young, Ferguson Jenkins .15
160 Ty Cobb, Rogers Hornsby .45
161 Tris Speaker, Ted Williams 1.00
162 Rogers Hornsby,
Ted Williams 1.00
163 Willie Mays, Monte Irvin .50
164 Willie Mays, Bobby Thomson .50
165 Reggie Jackson,
Mickey Mantle 2.00

1993 Upper Deck Baseball Heroes Reggie Jackson Supers

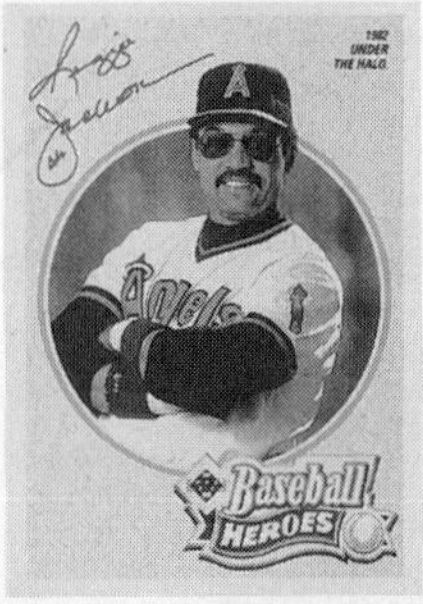

NM/M

Complete Set (10): 25.00

Common Card:	3.00
1 Reggie Jackson	
1969 Emerging Superstar	3.00
2 Reggie Jackson	
1973 An MVP Year	3.00
3 Reggie Jackson	
1977 "Mr. October"	3.00
4 Reggie Jackson	
1978 Jackson vs. Welch	3.00
5 Reggie Jackson	
1982 Under the Halo	3.00
6 Reggie Jackson 1984 500!	3.00
7 Reggie Jackson	
1986 Moving Up the List	3.00
8 Reggie Jackson	
1987 A Great Career Ends	3.00
9 Reggie Jackson	
Heroes Checklist	3.00
--- Header Card	3.00

Baseball Heroes Willie Mays

	NM/M
Complete Set (10):	4.00
Common Card:	.50
Header Card:	1.00
46 1951 Rookie-of-the-Year	.50
47 1954 The Catch	.50
48 1956-57 30-30 Club	.50
49 1961 Four-Homer Game	.50
50 1965 Most Valuable Player	.50
51 1969 600-Home Run Club	.50
52 1972 New York Homecoming	.50
53 1979 Hall of Fame	.50
54 Checklist - Heroes 46-54	.50

Clutch Performers

	NM/M
Complete Set (20):	8.00
Common Player:	.25
1 Roberto Alomar	.30
2 Wade Boggs	1.00
3 Barry Bonds	2.50
4 Jose Canseco	.40
5 Joe Carter	.25
6 Will Clark	.25
7 Roger Clemens	1.25
8 Dennis Eckersley	.60
9 Cecil Fielder	.25
10 Juan Gonzalez	.60
11 Ken Griffey Jr.	2.00
12 Rickey Henderson	.75
13 Barry Larkin	.25
14 Don Mattingly	1.25
15 Fred McGriff	.25
16 Terry Pendleton	.25
17 Kirby Puckett	1.00
18 Ryne Sandberg	1.00
19 John Smoltz	.25
20 Frank Thomas	.75

1993 Upper Deck Diamond Gallery

	NM/M
Complete Set (36):	6.00

Common Player:	.10
1 Tim Salmon	.10
2 Jeff Bagwell	.30
3 Mark McGwire	.75
4 Roberto Alomar	.25
5 Terry Pendleton	.10
6 Robin Yount	.30
7 Ray Lankford	.10
8 Ryne Sandberg	.40
9 Darryl Strawberry	.10
10 Marquis Grissom	.10
11 Barry Bonds	1.00
12 Carlos Baerga	.10
13 Ken Griffey Jr.	.65
14 Benito Santiago	.10
15 Dwight Gooden	.10
16 Cal Ripken, Jr.	1.00
17 Tony Gwynn	.40
18 Dave Hollins	.10
19 Andy Van Slyke	.10
20 Juan Gonzalez	.25
21 Roger Clemens	.50
22 Barry Larkin	.10
23 Dave Nied	.10
24 George Brett	.50
25 Travis Fryman	.10
26 Kirby Puckett	.40
27 Frank Thomas	.30
28 Don Mattingly	.50
29 Rickey Henderson	.30
30 Nolan Ryan	1.00
31 Ozzie Smith	.40
32 Wil Cordero	.10
33 Phil Hiatt	.10
34 Mike Piazza	.65
35 J.T. Snow	.10
36 Kevin Young	.10

Future Heroes

	NM/M
Complete Set (10):	5.00
Common Player:	.50
Header Card:	.25
55 Roberto Alomar	.50
56 Barry Bonds	2.50
57 Roger Clemens	1.00
58 Juan Gonzalez	.50
59 Ken Griffey Jr.	1.50
60 Mark McGwire	2.00
61 Kirby Puckett	.85
62 Frank Thomas	.75
63 Checklist	.05

Highlights

	NM/M
Complete Set (20):	20.00
Common Player:	.25
1 Roberto Alomar	.50
2 Steve Avery	.25
3 Harold Baines	.25
4 Damon Berryhill	.25
5 Barry Bonds	7.50
6 Bret Boone	.25
7 George Brett	4.00
8 Francisco Cabrera	.25
9 Ken Griffey Jr.	5.00
10 Rickey Henderson	2.00

11 Kenny Lofton	.25
12 Mickey Morandini	.25
13 Eddie Murray	2.00
14 David Nied	.25
15 Jeff Reardon	.25
16 Bip Roberts	.25
17 Nolan Ryan	7.50
18 Ed Sprague	.25
19 Dave Winfield	2.00
20 Robin Yount	2.00

Home Run Heroes

Albert Belle Upper Deck

	NM/M
Complete Set (28):	7.50
Common Player:	.15
1 Juan Gonzalez	.50
2 Mark McGwire	2.25
3 Cecil Fielder	.15
4 Fred McGriff	.15
5 Albert Belle	.15
6 Barry Bonds	2.50
7 Joe Carter	.15
8 Darren Daulton	.15
9 Ken Griffey Jr.	2.00
10 Dave Hollins	.15
11 Ryne Sandberg	1.00
12 George Bell	.15
13 Danny Tartabull	.15
14 Mike Devereaux	.15
15 Greg Vaughn	.15
16 Larry Walker	.15
17 Dave Justice	.15
18 Terry Pendleton	.15
19 Eric Karros	.15
20 Ray Lankford	.15
21 Matt Williams	.15
22 Eric Anthony	.15
23 Bobby Bonilla	.15
24 Kirby Puckett	1.00
25 Mike Macfarlane	.15
26 Tom Brunansky	.15
27 Paul O'Neill	.15
28 Gary Gaetti	.15

Iooss Collection

The Upper Deck Iooss Collection

	NM/M
Complete Set (27):	10.00
Common Player:	.25
Header Card:	.25
1 Tim Salmon	.25
2 Jeff Bagwell	.75
3 Mark McGwire	1.50
4 Roberto Alomar	.35
5 Steve Avery	.25
6 Paul Molitor	.75
7 Ozzie Smith	1.00
8 Mark Grace	.25
9 Eric Karros	.25
10 Delino DeShields	.25
11 Will Clark	.25
12 Albert Belle	.35
13 Ken Griffey Jr.	1.50
14 Howard Johnson	.25
15 Cal Ripken, Jr.	2.00
16 Fred McGriff	.25
17 Darren Daulton	.25
18 Andy Van Slyke	.25

19 Nolan Ryan	2.00
20 Wade Boggs	1.00
21 Barry Larkin	.25
22 George Brett	1.25
23 Cecil Fielder	.25
24 Kirby Puckett	1.00
25 Frank Thomas	.75
26 Don Mattingly	1.25

Next Generation

	NM/M
Complete Set (18):	100.00
Common Player:	1.50
Electic Diamond	
Complete Set (18):	
Electic Diamond Singles (1.5X)	
1 Roberto Alomar	2.50
2 Carlos Delgado	4.00
3 Cliff Floyd	1.50
4 Alex Gonzalez	1.50
5 Juan Gonzalez	3.00
6 Ken Griffey Jr.	10.00
7 Jeffrey Hammonds	1.50
8 Michael Jordan	30.00
9 Dave Justice	1.50
10 Ryan Klesko	1.50
11 Javier Lopez	1.50
12 Raul Mondesi	1.50
13 Mike Piazza	10.00
14 Kirby Puckett	7.50
15 Manny Ramirez	6.50
16 Alex Rodriguez	30.00
17 Tim Salmon	1.50
18 Gary Sheffield	4.00
ED Trade Card (Ken Griffey Jr.)	30.00

On Deck

	NM/M
Complete Set (25):	10.00
Common Player:	.15
1 Jim Abbott	.15
2 Roberto Alomar	.25
3 Carlos Baerga	.15
4 Albert Belle	.15
5 Wade Boggs	1.00
6 George Brett	1.25
7 Jose Canseco	.45
8 Will Clark	.15
9 Roger Clemens	1.25
10 Dennis Eckersley	.65
11 Cecil Fielder	.15
12 Juan Gonzalez	.40
13 Ken Griffey Jr.	1.50
14 Tony Gwynn	1.00
15 Bo Jackson	.20
16 Chipper Jones	1.00
17 Eric Karros	.15
18 Mark McGwire	2.00
19 Kirby Puckett	1.00
20 Nolan Ryan	2.50
21 Tim Salmon	.15
22 Ryne Sandberg	1.00
23 Darryl Strawberry	.15
24 Frank Thomas	.75
25 Andy Van Slyke	.15

Then And Now

		NM/M
Complete Set (18):		30.00
Common Player:		.75
1	Wade Boggs	2.00
2	George Brett	2.50
3	Rickey Henderson	1.25
4	Cal Ripken, Jr.	4.00
5	Nolan Ryan	4.00
6	Ryne Sandberg	2.00
7	Ozzie Smith	2.00
8	Darryl Strawberry	.75
9	Dave Winfield	1.25
10	Dennis Eckersley	1.00
11	Tony Gwynn	2.00
12	Howard Johnson	.75
13	Don Mattingly	2.50
14	Eddie Murray	1.25
15	Robin Yount	1.25
16	Reggie Jackson	2.00
17	Mickey Mantle	6.00
17a	Mickey Mantle (5" x 7")	13.50
18	Willie Mays	3.00

Triple Crown Contenders

		NM/M
Complete Set (10):		6.00
Common Player:		.25
1	Barry Bonds	1.50
2	Jose Canseco	.45
3	Will Clark	.25
4	Ken Griffey Jr.	1.25
5	Fred McGriff	.25
6	Kirby Puckett	.75
7	Cal Ripken, Jr.	1.50
8	Gary Sheffield	.35
9	Frank Thomas	.60
10	Larry Walker	.25

5th Anniversary

		NM/M
Complete Set (15):		7.00
Common Player:		.25
1	Ken Griffey Jr.	1.50
2	Gary Sheffield	.35
3	Roberto Alomar	.35
4	Jim Abbott	.25
5	Nolan Ryan	2.00
6	Juan Gonzalez	.35
7	Dave Justice	.25
8	Carlos Baerga	.25
9	Reggie Jackson	1.00
10	Eric Karros	.25
11	Chipper Jones	1.00
12	Ivan Rodriguez	.50
13	Pat Listach	.25
14	Frank Thomas	.90
15	Tim Salmon	.25

SP Insert

		NM/M
Complete Set (15):		60.00
Common Player:		.50
EASTERN REGION		
1	Roberto Alomar	1.00
2	Cliff Floyd	.50
3	Javier Lopez	.50
4	Don Mattingly	6.00
5	Cal Ripken, Jr.	10.00
CENTRAL REGION		
1	Jeff Bagwell	3.00
2	Michael Jordan	10.00
3	Kirby Puckett	6.00
4	Manny Ramirez	3.00
5	Frank Thomas	4.00
WESTERN REGION		
1	Barry Bonds	10.00
2	Juan Gonzalez	1.50
3	Ken Griffey Jr.	5.00
4	Mike Piazza	5.00
5	Tim Salmon	.50

1994 Upper Deck

		NM/M
Complete Set (550):		30.00
Complete Series 1 (280):		25.00
Complete Series 2 (270):		5.00
Common Player:		.05
Series 1 Hobby Pack (12):		2.50
Series 1 Hobby Box (36):		65.00
Series 1 Retail Pack (12):		2.00
Series 1 Retail Box (36):		40.00
Series 2 Hobby Pack (12):		.75
Series 2 Hobby Box (36):		20.00
Series 2 Retail Pack (12):		1.25
Series 2 Retail Box (36):		25.00
1	Brian Anderson RC (Star Rookie)	.15
2	Shane Andrews (Star Rookie)	.05
3	James Baldwin (Star Rookie)	.05
4	Rich Becker (Star Rookie)	.05
5	Greg Blosser (Star Rookie)	.05
6	Ricky Bottalico RC (Star Rookie)	.05
7	Midre Cummings	.05
8	Carlos Delgado (Star Rookie)	.50
9	Steve Dreyer RC (Star Rookie)	.05
10	Joey Eischen RC (Star Rookie)	.05
11	Carl Everett (Star Rookie)	.05
12	Cliff Floyd (Star Rookie)	.05
13	Alex Gonzalez (Star Rookie)	.05
14	Jeff Granger (Star Rookie)	.05
15	Shawn Green (Star Rookie)	.35
16	Brian Hunter (Star Rookie)	.05
17	Butch Huskey (Star Rookie)	.05
18	Mark Hutton (Star Rookie)	.05
19	Michael Jordan RC (Star Rookie)	5.00
20	Steve Karsay (Star Rookie)	.05
21	Jeff McNeely (Star Rookie)	.05
22	Marc Newfield (Star Rookie)	.05
23	Manny Ramirez (Star Rookie)	.60
24	Alex Rodriguez RC (Star Rookie)	20.00
25	Scott Ruffcorn (Star Rookie)	.05
26	Paul Spoljaric (Star Rookie)	.05
27	Salomon Torres RC (Star Rookie)	.05
28	Steve Trachsel (Star Rookie)	.05
29	Chris Turner RC (Star Rookie)	.05
30	Gabe White (Star Rookie)	.05
31	Randy Johnson (Fantasy Team)	.40
32	John Wetteland (Fantasy Team)	.05
33	Mike Piazza (Fantasy Team)	.65
34	Rafael Palmeiro (Fantasy Team)	.35
35	Roberto Alomar (Fantasy Team)	.10
36	Matt Williams (Fantasy Team)	.05
37	Travis Fryman (Fantasy Team)	.05
38	Barry Bonds (Fantasy Team)	1.00
39	Marquis Grissom (Fantasy Team)	.05
40	Albert Belle (Fantasy Team)	.05
41	Steve Avery (Future/Now)	.05
42	Jason Bere (Future/Now)	.05
43	Alex Fernandez (Future/Now)	.05
44	Mike Mussina (Future/Now)	.15
45	Aaron Sele (Future/Now)	.05
46	Rod Beck (Future/Now)	.05
47	Mike Piazza (Future/Now)	.65
48	John Olerud (Future/Now)	.05
49	Carlos Baerga (Future/Now)	.05
50	Gary Sheffield (Future/Now)	.20
51	Travis Fryman (Future/Now)	.05
52	Juan Gonzalez (Future/Now)	.20
53	Ken Griffey Jr. (Future/Now)	.65
54	Tim Salmon (Future/Now)	.05
55	Frank Thomas (Future/Now)	.45
56	Tony Phillips	.05
57	Julio Franco	.05
58	Kevin Mitchell	.05
59	Raul Mondesi	.05
60	Rickey Henderson	.75
61	Jay Buhner	.05
62	Bill Swift	.05
63	Brady Anderson	.05
64	Ryan Klesko	.05
65	Darren Daulton	.05
66	Damion Easley	.05
67	Mark McGwire	1.50
68	John Roper	.05
69	Dave Telgheder	.05
70	Dave Nied	.05
71	Mo Vaughn	.05
72	Tyler Green	.05
73	Dave Magadan	.05
74	Chili Davis	.05
75	Archi Cianfrocco	.05
76	Joe Girardi	.05
77	Chris Hoiles	.05
78	Ryan Bowen	.05
79	Greg Gagne	.05
80	Aaron Sele	.05
81	Dave Winfield	.75
82	Chad Curtis	.05
83	Andy Van Slyke	.05
84	Kevin Stocker	.05
85	Deion Sanders	.05
86	Bernie Williams	.05
87	John Smoltz	.05
88	Ruben Santana RC	.05
89	Dave Stewart	.05
90	Don Mattingly	1.00
91	Joe Carter	.05
92	Ryne Sandberg	.90
93	Chris Gomez	.05
94	Tino Martinez	.05
95	Terry Pendleton	.05
96	Andre Dawson	.25
97	Wil Cordero	.05
98	Kent Hrbek	.05
99	John Olerud	.05
100	Kirt Manwaring	.05
101	Tim Bogar	.05
102	Mike Mussina	.30
103	Nigel Wilson	.05
104	Ricky Gutierrez	.05
105	Roberto Mejia	.05
106	Tom Pagnozzi	.05
107	Mike Macfarlane	.05
108	Jose Bautista	.05
109	Luis Ortiz	.05
110	Brent Gates	.05
111	Tim Salmon	.05
112	Wade Boggs	.90
113	Tripp Cromer RC	.05
114	Denny Hocking	.05
115	Carlos Baerga	.05
116	J.R. Phillips RC	.05
117	Bo Jackson	.10
118	Lance Johnson	.05
119	Bobby Jones	.05
120	Bobby Witt	.05
121	Ron Karkovice	.05
122	Jose Vizcaino	.05
123	Danny Darwin	.05
124	Eduardo Perez	.05
125	Brian Looney	.05
126	Pat Hentgen	.05
127	Frank Viola	.05
128	Darren Holmes	.05
129	Wally Whitehurst	.05
130	Matt Walbeck	.05
131	Albert Belle	.05
132	Steve Cooke	.05
133	Kevin Appier	.05
134	Joe Oliver	.05
135	Benji Gil	.05
136	Steve Buechele	.05
137	Devon White	.05
138	Sterling Hitchcock	.05
139	Phil Leftwich RC	.05
140	Jose Canseco	.45
141	Rick Aguilera	.05
142	Rod Beck	.05
143	Jose Rijo	.05
144	Tom Glavine	.25
145	Phil Plantier	.05
146	Jason Bere	.05
147	Jamie Moyer	.05
148	Wes Chamberlain	.05
149	Glenallen Hill	.05
150	Mark Whiten	.05
151	Bret Barberie	.05
152	Chuck Knoblauch	.05
153	Trevor Hoffman	.05
154	Rick Wilkins	.05
155	Juan Gonzalez	.40
156	Ozzie Guillen	.05
157	Jim Eisenreich	.05
158	Pedro Astacio	.05
159	Joe Magrane	.05
160	Ryan Thompson	.05
161	Jose Lind	.05
162	Jeff Conine	.05
163	Todd Benzinger	.05
164	Roger Salkeld	.05
165	Gary DiSarcina	.05
166	Kevin Gross	.05
167	Charlie Hayes	.05
168	Tim Costo	.05
169	Wally Joyner	.05
170	Johnny Ruffin	.05
171	Kirk Rueter RC	.10
172	Len Dykstra	.05
173	Ken Hill	.05
174	Mike Bordick	.05
175	Billy Hall	.05
176	Rob Butler	.05
177	Jay Bell	.05
178	Jeff Kent	.05
179	David Wells	.05
180	Dean Palmer	.05
181	Mariano Duncan	.05
182	Orlando Merced	.05
183	Brett Butler	.05
184	Milt Thompson	.05
185	Chipper Jones	1.00
186	Paul O'Neill	.05
187	Mike Greenwell	.05
188	Harold Baines	.05
189	Todd Stottlemyre	.05
190	Jeromy Burnitz	.05
191	Rene Arocha	.05
192	Jeff Fassero	.05
193	Robby Thompson	.05
194	Greg W. Harris	.05
195	Todd Van Poppel	.05
196	Jose Guzman	.05
197	Shane Mack	.05
198	Carlos Garcia	.05
199	Kevin Roberson	.05
200	David McCarty	.05
201	Alan Trammell	.05
202	Chuck Carr	.05
203	Tommy Greene	.05
204	Wilson Alvarez	.05
205	Dwight Gooden	.05
206	Tony Tarasco	.05
207	Darren Lewis	.05
208	Eric Karros	.05
209	Chris Hammond	.05
210	Jeffrey Hammonds	.05
211	Rich Amaral	.05
212	Danny Tartabull	.05
213	Jeff Russell	.05
214	Dave Staton	.05
215	Kenny Lofton	.05
216	Manuel Lee	.05
217	Brian Koelling	.05
218	Scott Lydy	.05
219	Tony Gwynn	.90
220	Cecil Fielder	.05
221	Royce Clayton	.05
222	Reggie Sanders	.05
223	Brian Jordan	.05
224	Ken Griffey Jr.	1.25
224a	Ken Griffey Jr. (Promo Card)	3.00
225	Fred McGriff	.05
226	Felix Jose	.05
227	Brad Pennington	.05
228	Chris Bosio	.05
229	Mike Stanley	.05
230	Willie Greene	.05
231	Alex Fernandez	.05
232	Brad Ausmus	.05
233	Darrell Whitmore	.05
234	Marcus Moore	.05
235	Allen Watson	.05
236	Jose Offerman	.05
237	Rondell White	.05
238	Jeff King	.05
239	Luis Alicea	.05
240	Dan Wilson	.05
241	Ed Sprague	.05

#	Player	Price
242	Todd Hundley	.05
243	Al Martin	.05
244	Mike Lansing	.05
245	Ivan Rodriguez	.65
246	Dave Fleming	.05
247	John Doherty	.05
248	Mark McLemore	.05
249	Bob Hamelin	.05
250	Curtis Pride RC	.05
251	Zane Smith	.05
252	Eric Young	.05
253	Brian McRae	.05
254	Tim Raines	.05
255	Javier Lopez	.05
256	Melvin Nieves	.05
257	Randy Myers	.05
258	Willie McGee	.05
259	Jimmy Key	.05
260	Tom Candiotti	.05
261	Eric Davis	.05
262	Craig Paquette	.05
263	Robin Ventura	.05
264	Pat Kelly	.05
265	Gregg Jefferies	.05
266	Cory Snyder	.05
267	Dave Justice (Home Field Advantage)	.05
268	Sammy Sosa (Home Field Advantage)	.45
269	Barry Larkin (Home Field Advantage)	.05
270	Andres Galarraga (Home Field Advantage)	.05
271	Gary Sheffield (Home Field Advantage)	.20
272	Jeff Bagwell (Home Field Advantage)	.40
273	Mike Piazza (Home Field Advantage)	.65
274	Larry Walker (Home Field Advantage)	.05
275	Bobby Bonilla (Home Field Advantage)	.05
276	John Kruk (Home Field Advantage)	.05
277	Jay Bell (Home Field Advantage)	.05
278	Ozzie Smith (Home Field Advantage)	.45
279	Tony Gwynn (Home Field Advantage)	.45
280	Barry Bonds (Home Field Advantage)	1.00
281	Cal Ripken, Jr. (Home Field Advantage)	1.00
282	Mo Vaughn (Home Field Advantage)	.05
283	Tim Salmon (Home Field Advantage)	.05
284	Frank Thomas (Home Field Advantage)	.40
285	Albert Belle (Home Field Advantage)	.05
286	Cecil Fielder (Home Field Advantage)	.05
287	Wally Joyner (Home Field Advantage)	.05
288	Greg Vaughn (Home Field Advantage)	.05
289	Kirby Puckett (Home Field Advantage)	.45
290	Don Mattingly (Home Field Advantage)	.50
291	Terry Steinbach (Home Field Advantage)	.05
292	Ken Griffey Jr. (Home Field Advantage)	.90
293	Juan Gonzalez (Home Field Advantage)	.20
294	Paul Molitor (Home Field Advantage)	.40
295	Tavo Alvarez (Classic Alumni)	.05
296	Matt Brunson (Classic Alumni)	.05
297	Shawn Green (Classic Alumni)	.20
298	Alex Rodriguez (Classic Alumni)	2.00
299	Shannon Stewart (Classic Alumni)	.05
300	Frank Thomas	.75
301	Mickey Tettleton	.05
302	Pedro Munoz	.05
303	Jose Valentin	.05
304	Orestes Destrade	.05
305	Pat Listach	.05
306	Scott Brosius	.05
307	Kurt Miller RC	.05
308	Rob Dibble	.05
309	Mike Blowers	.05
310	Jim Abbott	.05
311	Mike Jackson	.05
312	Craig Biggio	.05
313	Kurt Abbott RC	.05
314	Chuck Finley	.05
315	Andres Galarraga	.05
316	Mike Moore	.05
317	Doug Strange	.05
318	Pedro J. Martinez	.75
319	Kevin McReynolds	.05
320	Greg Maddux	.90
321	Mike Henneman	.05
322	Scott Leius	.05
323	John Franco	.05
324	Jeff Blauser	.05
325	Kirby Puckett	.90
326	Darryl Hamilton	.05
327	John Smiley	.05
328	Derrick May	.05
329	Jose Vizcaino	.05
330	Randy Johnson	.75
331	Jack Morris	.05
332	Graeme Lloyd	.05
333	Dave Valle	.05
334	Greg Myers	.05
335	John Wetteland	.05
336	Jim Gott	.05
337	Tim Naehring	.05
338	Mike Kelly	.05
339	Jeff Montgomery	.05
340	Rafael Palmeiro	.65
341	Eddie Murray	.75
342	Xavier Hernandez	.05
343	Bobby Munoz	.05
344	Bobby Bonilla	.05
345	Travis Fryman	.05
346	Steve Finley	.05
347	Chris Sabo	.05
348	Armando Reynoso	.05
349	Ramon Martinez	.05
350	Will Clark	.05
351	Moises Alou	.05
352	Jim Thome	.50
353	Bob Tewksbury	.05
354	Andujar Cedeno	.05
355	Orel Hershiser	.05
356	Mike Devereaux	.05
357	Mike Perez	.05
358	Dennis Martinez	.05
359	Dave Nilsson	.05
360	Ozzie Smith	.90
361	Eric Anthony	.05
362	Scott Sanders	.05
363	Paul Sorrento	.05
364	Tim Belcher	.05
365	Dennis Eckersley	.60
366	Mel Rojas	.05
367	Tom Henke	.05
368	Randy Tomlin	.05
369	B.J. Surhoff	.05
370	Larry Walker	.05
371	Joey Cora	.05
372	Mike Harkey	.05
373	John Valentin	.05
374	Doug Jones	.05
375	Dave Justice	.05
376	Vince Coleman	.05
377	David Hulse	.05
378	Kevin Seitzer	.05
379	Pete Harnisch	.05
380	Ruben Sierra	.05
381	Mark Lewis	.05
382	Bip Roberts	.05
383	Paul Wagner	.05
384	Stan Javier	.05
385	Barry Larkin	.05
386	Mark Portugal	.05
387	Roberto Kelly	.05
388	Andy Benes	.05
389	Felix Fermin	.05
390	Marquis Grissom	.05
391	Troy Neel	.05
392	Chad Kreuter	.05
393	Gregg Olson	.05
394	Charles Nagy	.05
395	Jack McDowell	.05
396	Luis Gonzalez	.05
397	Benito Santiago	.05
398	Chris James	.05
399	Terry Mulholland	.05
400	Barry Bonds	2.00
401	Joe Grahe	.05
402	Duane Ward	.05
403	John Burkett	.05
404	Scott Servais	.05
405	Bryan Harvey	.05
406	Bernard Gilkey	.05
407	Greg McMichael	.05
408	Tim Wallach	.05
409	Ken Caminiti	.05
410	John Kruk	.05
411	Darrin Jackson	.05
412	Mike Gallego	.05
413	David Cone	.05
414	Lou Whitaker	.05
415	Sandy Alomar Jr.	.05
416	Bill Wegman	.05
417	Pat Borders	.05
418	Roger Pavlik	.05
419	Pete Smith	.05
420	Steve Avery	.05
421	David Segui	.05
422	Rheal Cormier	.05
423	Harold Reynolds	.05
424	Edgar Martinez	.05
425	Cal Ripken, Jr.	2.00
426	Jaime Navarro	.05
427	Sean Berry	.05
428	Bret Saberhagen	.05
429	Bob Welch	.05
430	Juan Guzman	.05
431	Cal Eldred	.05
432	Dave Hollins	.05
433	Sid Fernandez	.05
434	Willie Banks	.05
435	Darryl Kile	.05
436	Henry Rodriguez	.05
437	Tony Fernandez	.05
438	Walt Weiss	.05
439	Kevin Tapani	.05
440	Mark Grace	.05
441	Brian Harper	.05
442	Kent Mercker	.05
443	Anthony Young	.05
444	Todd Zeile	.05
445	Greg Vaughn	.05
446	Ray Lankford	.05
447	David Weathers	.05
448	Bret Boone	.05
449	Charlie Hough	.05
450	Roger Clemens	1.00
451	Mike Morgan	.05
452	Doug Drabek	.05
453	Danny Jackson	.05
454	Dante Bichette	.05
455	Roberto Alomar	.20
456	Ben McDonald	.05
457	Kenny Rogers	.05
458	Bill Gullickson	.05
459	Darrin Fletcher	.05
460	Curt Schilling	.20
461	Billy Hatcher	.05
462	Howard Johnson	.05
463	Mickey Morandini	.05
464	Frank Castillo	.05
465	Delino DeShields	.05
466	Gary Gaetti	.05
467	Steve Farr	.05
468	Roberto Hernandez	.05
469	Jack Armstrong	.05
470	Paul Molitor	.75
471	Melido Perez	.05
472	Greg Hibbard	.05
473	Jody Reed	.05
474	Tom Gordon	.05
475	Gary Sheffield	.35
476	John Jaha	.05
477	Shawon Dunston	.05
478	Reggie Jefferson	.05
479	Don Slaught	.05
480	Jeff Bagwell	.75
481	Tim Pugh	.05
482	Kevin Young	.05
483	Ellis Burks	.05
484	Greg Swindell	.05
485	Mark Langston	.05
486	Omar Vizquel	.05
487	Kevin Brown	.05
488	Terry Steinbach	.05
489	Mark Lemke	.05
490	Matt Williams	.05
491	Pete Incaviglia	.05
492	Karl Rhodes	.05
493	Shawn Green	.30
494	Hal Morris	.05
495	Derek Bell	.05
496	Luis Polonia	.05
497	Otis Nixon	.05
498	Ron Darling	.05
499	Mitch Williams	.05
500	Mike Piazza	1.25
501	Pat Meares	.05
502	Scott Cooper	.05
503	Scott Erickson	.05
504	Jeff Juden	.05
505	Lee Smith	.05
506	Bobby Ayala	.05
507	Dave Henderson	.05
508	Erik Hanson	.05
509	Bob Wickman	.05
510	Sammy Sosa	.90
511	Hector Carrasco (Diamond Debuts)	.05
512	Tim Davis (Diamond Debuts)	.05
513	Joey Hamilton (Diamond Debuts)	.05
514	Robert Eenhoorn (Diamond Debuts)	.05
515	Jorge Fabregas (Diamond Debuts)	.05
516	Tim Hyers (Diamond Debuts)	.05
517	John Hudek (Diamond Debuts)	.05
518	James Mouton RC (Diamond Debuts)	.05
519	Herbert Perry (Diamond Debuts)	.05
520	Chan Ho Park RC (Diamond Debuts)	.75
521	Bill VanLandingham (Diamond Debuts)	.05
522	Paul Shuey (Diamond Debuts)	.05
523	Ryan Hancock RC (Top Prospects)	.05
524	Billy Wagner RC (Top Prospects)	.25
525	Jason Giambi (Top Prospects)	.50
526	Jose Silva RC (Top Prospects)	.05
527	Terrell Wade RC (Top Prospects)	.05
528	Todd Dunn (Top Prospects)	.05
529	Alan Benes RC (Top Prospects)	.05
530	Brooks Kieschnick RC (Top Prospects)	.05
531	Todd Hollandsworth (Top Prospects)	.05
532	Brad Fullmer RC (Top Prospects)	.15
533	Steve Soderstrom RC (Top Prospects)	.05
534	Daron Kirkreit (Top Prospects)	.05
535	Arquimedez Pozo RC (Top Prospects)	.05
536	Charles Johnson (Top Prospects)	.05
537	Preston Wilson (Top Prospects)	.10
538	Alex Ochoa (Top Prospects)	.05
539	Derrek Lee RC (Top Prospects)	3.00
540	Wayne Gomes RC (Top Prospects)	.05
541	Jermaine Allensworth RC (Top Prospects)	.05
542	Mike Bell RC (Top Prospects)	.05
543	Trot Nixon RC (Top Prospects)	1.25
544	Pokey Reese (Top Prospects)	.05
545	Neifi Perez RC (Top Prospects)	.05
546	Johnny Damon (Top Prospects)	.30
547	Matt Brunson (Top Prospects)	.05
548	LaTroy Hawkins RC (Top Prospects)	.05
549	Eddie Pearson RC (Top Prospects)	.05
550	Derek Jeter (Top Prospects)	2.00

1994 Upper Deck Electric Diamond

NM/M
Complete Set (550): 75.00
Common Player: .25
Stars: 1.5X
(See 1994 Upper Deck for checklist and base card values.)

Alex Rodriguez Autograph

NM/M
A298 Alex Rodriguez (Classic Alumni, Autographed) 500.00

1994 Upper Deck All-Stars

NM/M
Complete Set (48): 9.00
Common Player: .15
Gold: 4X

#	Player	Price
1	Ken Griffey Jr.	1.00
2	Ruben Sierra, Todd Van Poppel	.15
3	Bryan Harvey, Gary Sheffield	.35
4	Gregg Jefferies, Brian Jordan	.15
5	Ryne Sandberg	.75
6	Matt Williams, John Burkett	.15

7	Darren Daulton, John Kruk	.15
8	Don Mattingly, Wade Boggs	.75
9	Pat Listach, Greg Vaughn	.15
10	Tim Salmon, Eduardo Perez	.25
11	Fred McGriff, Tom Glavine	.25
12	Mo Vaughn, Andre Dawson	.35
13	Brian McRae, Kevin Appier	.15
14	Kirby Puckett, Kent Hrbek	.75
15	Cal Ripken, Jr.	2.00
16	Roberto Alomar, Paul Molitor	.65
17	Tony Gwynn, Phil Plantier	.75
18	Greg Maddux, Steve Avery	.75
19	Mike Mussina, Chris Hoiles	.75
20	Randy Johnson	.65
21	Roger Clemens, Aaron Sele	.75
22	Will Clark, Dean Palmer	.25
23	Cecil Fielder, Travis Fryman	.15
24	John Olerud, Joe Carter	.15
25	Juan Gonzalez	.65
26	Jose Rijo, Barry Larkin	.15
27	Andy Van Slyke, Jeff King	.15
28	Larry Walker, Marquis Grissom	.15
29	Kenny Lofton, Albert Belle	.25
30	Mark Grace, Sammy Sosa	1.00
31	Mike Piazza	1.00
32	Ramon Martinez, Orel Hershiser	.15
33	Dave Justice, Terry Pendleton	.15
34	Ivan Rodriguez, Jose Canseco	.15
35	Barry Bonds	2.00
36	Jeff Bagwell, Craig Biggio	.65
37	Jay Bell, Orlando Merced	.15
38	Jeff Kent, Dwight Gooden	.15
39	Andres Galarraga, Charlie Hayes	.15
40	Frank Thomas	.70
41	Bobby Bonilla	.15
42	Jack McDowell, Tim Raines	.15
43	1869 Red Stockings	.15
44	Ty Cobb	.50
45	Babe Ruth	1.50
46	Mickey Mantle	2.50
47	Reggie Jackson	.50
48	Ken Griffey Jr.	1.00
48a	Ken Griffey Jr. (Promo Card)	1.00

Baseball Heroes Mickey Mantle

		NM/M
Complete Set (10):		25.00
Common Card:		3.00
64	Mickey Mantle 1951 - The Early Years	3.00
65	Mickey Mantle 1953 - Tape Measure Home Runs	3.00
66	Mickey Mantle 1956 - Triple Crown Season	3.00
67	Mickey Mantle 1957 - 2nd Consecutive MVP	3.00
68	Mickey Mantle 1961 - Chases The Babe	3.00
69	Mickey Mantle 1964 - Series Home Run Record	3.00
70	Mickey Mantle 1967 - 500th Home Run	3.00
71	Mickey Mantle 1974: Hall of Fame	3.00
72	Mickey Mantle (Portrait)	3.00
----	Mickey Mantle Header Card	5.00

Diamond Collection

		NM/M
Complete Set (30):		40.00
Common Player:		.50
Complete Central (10):		20.00
1	Michael Jordan	10.00

2	Jeff Bagwell	2.00
3	Barry Larkin	1.00
4	Kirby Puckett	4.00
5	Manny Ramirez	3.00
6	Ryne Sandberg	3.00
7	Ozzie Smith	3.00
8	Frank Thomas	3.00
9	Andy Van Slyke	.50
10	Robin Yount	3.00
Complete East (10):		12.00
1	Roberto Alomar	1.00
2	Roger Clemens	4.00
3	Len Dykstra	.50
4	Cecil Fielder	.50
5	Cliff Floyd	.50
6	Dwight Gooden	.50
7	Dave Justice	.50
8	Don Mattingly	3.00
9	Cal Ripken, Jr.	6.00
10	Gary Sheffield	1.00
Complete West (10):		15.00
1	Barry Bonds	5.00
2	Andres Galarraga	.50
3	Juan Gonzalez	1.00
4	Ken Griffey Jr.	4.00
5	Tony Gwynn	2.50
6	Rickey Henderson	1.50
7	Bo Jackson	1.00
8	Mark McGwire	3.00
9	Mike Piazza	3.00
10	Tim Salmon	.50

1994 Upper Deck Ken Griffey Jr. 5th Anniversary Jumbo

	NM/M
Ken Griffey Jr.	20.00

Mantle-Griffey Autographed Inserts

		NM/M
KG1	Ken Griffey Jr., Mickey Mantle (Griffey Autograph)	250.00
MM1	Ken Griffey Jr., Mickey Mantle (Mantle Autograph)	650.00
GM1	Ken Griffey Jr., Mickey Mantle (Both Autographs)	1,150

Mickey Mantle's Long Shots

		NM/M
Complete Set (21):		20.00
Common Player:		.50
Electric Diamonds:		1X
(1)	Mickey Mantle Trade Card (Silver): (Redeemable for 21-card Mantle Long Shots set.)	
(2)	Mickey Mantle Trade Card (Blue): (Redeemable for Electric Diamond version Mantle Long Shots set.)	4.00
1	Jeff Bagwell	1.50
2	Albert Belle	.50
3	Barry Bonds	4.00
4	Jose Canseco	.75
5	Joe Carter	.50
6	Carlos Delgado	.75
7	Cecil Fielder	.50
8	Cliff Floyd	.50
9	Juan Gonzalez	.75
10	Ken Griffey Jr.	2.50
11	David Justice	.50
12	Fred McGriff	.50
13	Mark McGwire	3.00
14	Dean Palmer	.50
15	Mike Piazza	2.50
16	Manny Ramirez	1.50
17	Tim Salmon	.50
18	Frank Thomas	1.50
19	Mo Vaughn	.50
20	Matt Williams	.50
21	Mickey Mantle Header	4.00

1995 Upper Deck

	NM/M
Complete Set (450):	20.00
Common Player:	.05
Electric Diamond:	2X
Electric Diamond Golds:	8X

Chicago White Sox - OF

Series 1 or 2 Pack (12):		.85
Series 1 or 2 Wax Box (36):		20.00
1	Ruben Rivera (Top Prospect)	.05
2	Bill Pulsipher (Top Prospect)	.05
3	Ben Grieve (Top Prospect)	.05
4	Curtis Goodwin (Top Prospect)	.05
5	Damon Hollins (Top Prospect)	.05
6	Todd Greene (Top Prospect)	.05
7	Glenn Williams (Top Prospect)	.05
8	Bret Wagner (Top Prospect)	.05
9	Karim Garcia RC (Top Prospect)	.50
10	Nomar Garciaparra (Top Prospect)	1.00
11	Raul Casanova RC (Top Prospect)	.10
12	Matt Smith (Top Prospect)	.05
13	Paul Wilson (Top Prospect)	.05
14	Jason Isringhausen (Top Prospect)	.05
15	Reid Ryan (Top Prospect)	.05
16	Lee Smith	.05
17	Chili Davis	.05
18	Brian Anderson	.05
19	Gary DiSarcina	.05
20	Bo Jackson	.10
21	Chuck Finley	.05
22	Darryl Kile	.05
23	Shane Reynolds	.05
24	Tony Eusebio	.05
25	Craig Biggio	.05
26	Doug Drabek	.05
27	Brian L. Hunter	.05
28	James Mouton	.05
29	Geronimo Berroa	.05
30	Rickey Henderson	.75
31	Steve Karsay	.05
32	Steve Ontiveros	.05
33	Ernie Young	.05
34	Dennis Eckersley	.05
35	Mark McGwire	1.50
36	Dave Stewart	.05
37	Pat Hentgen	.05
38	Carlos Delgado	.45
39	Joe Carter	.05
40	Roberto Alomar	.20
41	John Olerud	.05
42	Devon White	.05
43	Roberto Kelly	.05
44	Jeff Blauser	.05
45	Fred McGriff	.05
46	Tom Glavine	.25
47	Mike Kelly	.05
48	Javy Lopez	.05
49	Greg Maddux	1.00
50	Matt Mieske	.05
51	Troy O'Leary	.05
52	Jeff Cirillo	.05
53	Cal Eldred	.05
54	Pat Listach	.05
55	Jose Valentin	.05
56	John Mabry	.05
57	Bob Tewksbury	.05
58	Brian Jordan	.05
59	Gregg Jefferies	.05
60	Ozzie Smith	1.00
61	Geronimo Pena	.05
62	Mark Whiten	.05
63	Rey Sanchez	.05
64	Willie Banks	.05
65	Mark Grace	.05
66	Randy Myers	.05
67	Steve Trachsel	.05
68	Derrick May	.05
69	Brett Butler	.05
70	Eric Karros	.05
71	Tim Wallach	.05
72	Delino DeShields	.05
73	Darren Dreifort	.05
74	Orel Hershiser	.05
75	Billy Ashley	.05
76	Sean Berry	.05
77	Ken Hill	.05
78	John Wetteland	.05
79	Moises Alou	.05
80	Cliff Floyd	.05
81	Marquis Grissom	.05
82	Larry Walker	.05
83	Rondell White	.05
84	William VanLandingham	.05

85	Matt Williams	.05
86	Rod Beck	.05
87	Darren Lewis	.05
88	Robby Thompson	.05
89	Darryl Strawberry	.05
90	Kenny Lofton	.05
91	Charles Nagy	.05
92	Sandy Alomar Jr.	.05
93	Mark Clark	.05
94	Dennis Martinez	.05
95	Dave Winfield	.75
96	Jim Thome	.60
97	Manny Ramirez	.75
98	Goose Gossage	.05
99	Tino Martinez	.05
100	Ken Griffey Jr.	1.25
100a	Ken Griffey Jr./OPS	2.00
101	Greg Maddux (Analysis: '90s Midpoint)	.50
102	Randy Johnson (Analysis: '90s Midpoint)	.40
103	Barry Bonds (Analysis: '90s Midpoint)	1.00
104	Juan Gonzalez (Analysis: '90s Midpoint)	.20
105	Frank Thomas (Analysis: '90s Midpoint)	.40
106	Matt Williams (Analysis: '90s Midpoint)	.05
107	Paul Molitor (Analysis: '90s Midpoint)	.40
108	Fred McGriff (Analysis: '90s Midpoint)	.05
109	Carlos Baerga (Analysis: '90s Midpoint)	.05
110	Ken Griffey Jr. (Analysis: '90s Midpoint)	.65
111	Reggie Jefferson	.05
112	Randy Johnson	.75
113	Marc Newfield	.05
114	Robb Nen	.05
115	Jeff Conine	.05
116	Kurt Abbott	.05
117	Charlie Hough	.05
118	Dave Weathers	.05
119	Juan Castillo	.05
120	Bret Saberhagen	.05
121	Rico Brogna	.05
122	John Franco	.05
123	Todd Hundley	.05
124	Jason Jacome	.05
125	Bobby Jones	.05
126	Bret Barberie	.05
127	Ben McDonald	.05
128	Harold Baines	.05
129	Jeffrey Hammonds	.05
130	Mike Mussina	.30
131	Chris Hoiles	.05
132	Brady Anderson	.05
133	Eddie Williams	.05
134	Andy Benes	.05
135	Tony Gwynn	1.00
136	Bip Roberts	.05
137	Joey Hamilton	.05
138	Luis Lopez	.05
139	Ray McDavid	.05
140	Lenny Dykstra	.05
141	Mariano Duncan	.05
142	Fernando Valenzuela	.05
143	Bobby Munoz	.05
144	Kevin Stocker	.05
145	John Kruk	.05
146	Jon Lieber	.05
147	Zane Smith	.05
148	Steve Cooke	.05
149	Andy Van Slyke	.05
150	Jay Bell	.05
151	Carlos Garcia	.05
152	John Dettmer	.05
153	Darren Oliver	.05
154	Dean Palmer	.05
155	Otis Nixon	.05
156	Rusty Greer	.05
157	Rick Helling	.05
158	Jose Canseco	.40
159	Roger Clemens	1.00
160	Andre Dawson	.25
161	Mo Vaughn	.05
162	Aaron Sele	.05
163	John Valentin	.05
164	Brian Hunter	.05
165	Bret Boone	.05
166	Hector Carrasco	.05
167	Pete Schourek	.05
168	Willie Greene	.05
169	Kevin Mitchell	.05
170	Deion Sanders	.05
171	John Roper	.05
172	Charlie Hayes	.05
173	David Nied	.05
174	Ellis Burks	.05
175	Dante Bichette	.05
176	Marvin Freeman	.05
177	Eric Young	.05
178	David Cone	.05
179	Greg Gagne	.05
180	Bob Hamelin	.05
181	Wally Joyner	.05
182	Jeff Montgomery	.05
183	Jose Lind	.05
184	Chris Gomez	.05
185	Travis Fryman	.05
186	Kirk Gibson	.05
187	Mike Moore	.05

188	Lou Whitaker	.05
189	Sean Bergman	.05
190	Shane Mack	.05
191	Rick Aguilera	.05
192	Denny Hocking	.05
193	Chuck Knoblauch	.05
194	Kevin Tapani	.05
195	Kent Hrbek	.05
196	Ozzie Guillen	.05
197	Wilson Alvarez	.05
198	Tim Raines	.05
199	Scott Ruffcorn	.05
200	Michael Jordan	2.00
201	Robin Ventura	.05
202	Jason Bere	.05
203	Darrin Jackson	.05
204	Russ Davis	.05
205	Jimmy Key	.05
206	Jack McDowell	.05
207	Jim Abbott	.05
208	Paul O'Neill	.05
209	Bernie Williams	.05
210	Don Mattingly	1.00
211	Orlando Miller (Star Rookie)	.05
212	Alex Gonzalez (Star Rookie)	.05
213	Terrell Wade (Star Rookie)	.05
214	Jose Oliva (Star Rookie)	.05
215	Alex Rodriguez (Star Rookie)	1.50
216	Garret Anderson (Star Rookie)	.05
217	Alan Benes (Star Rookie)	.05
218	Armando Benitez (Star Rookie)	.05
219	Dustin Hermanson (Star Rookie)	.05
220	Charles Johnson (Star Rookie)	.05
221	Julian Tavarez (Star Rookie)	.05
222	Jason Giambi (Star Rookie)	.50
223	LaTroy Hawkins (Star Rookie)	.05
224	Todd Hollandsworth (Star Rookie)	.05
225	Derek Jeter (Star Rookie)	2.00
226	Hideo Nomo **RC** (Star Rookie)	2.00
227	Tony Clark (Star Rookie)	.05
228	Roger Cedeno (Star Rookie)	.05
229	Scott Stahoviak (Star Rookie)	.05
230	Michael Tucker (Star Rookie)	.05
231	Joe Rosselli (Star Rookie)	.05
232	Antonio Osuna (Star Rookie)	.05
233	Bobby Higginson (Star Rookie)	.25
234	Mark Grudzielanek **RC** (Star Rookie)	.25
235	Ray Durham (Star Rookie)	.05
236	Frank Rodriguez (Star Rookie)	.05
237	Quilvio Veras (Star Rookie)	.05
238	Darren Bragg (Star Rookie)	.05
239	Ugueth Urbina (Star Rookie)	.05
240	Jason Bates (Star Rookie)	.05
241	David Bell (Diamond Debuts)	.05
242	Ron Villone (Diamond Debuts)	.05
243	Joe Randa (Diamond Debuts)	.05
244	Carlos Perez **RC** (Diamond Debuts)	.05
245	Brad Clontz (Diamond Debuts)	.05
246	Steve Rodriguez (Diamond Debuts)	.05
247	Joe Vitiello (Diamond Debuts)	.05
248	Ozzie Timmons (Diamond Debuts)	.05
249	Rudy Pemberton (Diamond Debuts)	.05
250	Marty Cordova (Diamond Debuts)	.05
251	Tony Graffanino (Top Prospect)	.05
252	Mark Johnson **RC** (Top Prospect)	.05
253	Tomas Perez **RC** (Top Prospect)	.05
254	Jimmy Hurst (Top Prospect)	.05
255	Edgardo Alfonzo (Top Prospect)	.05
256	Jose Malave (Top Prospect)	.05
257	Brad Radke **RC** (Top Prospect)	.30
258	Jon Nunnally (Top Prospect)	.05
259	Dilson Torres (Top Prospect)	.05
260	Esteban Loaiza (Top Prospect)	.05
261	Freddy Garcia **RC** (Top Prospect)	.05
262	Don Wengert (Top Prospect)	.05
263	Robert Person **RC** (Top Prospect)	.05
264	Tim Unroe **RC** (Top Prospect)	.05
265	Juan Acevedo (Top Prospect)	.05
266	Eduardo Perez	.05
267	Tony Phillips	.05
268	Jim Edmonds	.05
269	Jorge Fabregas	.05
270	Tim Salmon	.05
271	Mark Langston	.05
272	J.T. Snow	.05
273	Phil Plantier	.05
274	Derek Bell	.05
275	Jeff Bagwell	.75
276	Luis Gonzalez	.05
277	John Hudek	.05
278	Todd Stottlemyre	.05
279	Mark Acre	.05
280	Ruben Sierra	.05
281	Mike Bordick	.05
282	Ron Darling	.05

283	Brent Gates	.05
284	Todd Van Poppel	.05
285	Paul Molitor	.75
286	Ed Sprague	.05
287	Juan Guzman	.05
288	David Cone	.05
289	Shawn Green	.30
290	Marquis Grissom	.05
291	Kent Mercker	.05
292	Steve Avery	.05
293	Chipper Jones	1.00
294	John Smoltz	.05
295	Dave Justice	.05
296	Ryan Klesko	.05
297	Joe Oliver	.05
298	Ricky Bones	.05
299	John Jaha	.05
300	Greg Vaughn	.05
301	Dave Nilsson	.05
302	Kevin Seitzer	.05
303	Bernard Gilkey	.05
304	Allen Battle	.05
305	Ray Lankford	.05
306	Tom Pagnozzi	.05
307	Allen Watson	.05
308	Danny Jackson	.05
309	Ken Hill	.05
310	Todd Zeile	.05
311	Kevin Roberson	.05
312	Steve Buechele	.05
313	Rick Wilkins	.05
314	Kevin Foster	.05
315	Sammy Sosa	1.00
316	Howard Johnson	.05
317	Greg Hansell	.05
318	Pedro Astacio	.05
319	Rafael Bournigal	.05
320	Mike Piazza	1.25
321	Ramon Martinez	.05
322	Raul Mondesi	.05
323	Ismael Valdes	.05
324	Wil Cordero	.05
325	Tony Tarasco	.05
326	Roberto Kelly	.05
327	Jeff Fassero	.05
328	Mike Lansing	.05
329	Pedro J. Martinez	.75
330	Kirk Rueter	.05
331	Glenallen Hill	.05
332	Kirt Manwaring	.05
333	Royce Clayton	.05
334	J.R. Phillips	.05
335	Barry Bonds	2.00
336	Mark Portugal	.05
337	Terry Mulholland	.05
338	Omar Vizquel	.05
339	Carlos Baerga	.05
340	Albert Belle	.05
341	Eddie Murray	.75
342	Wayne Kirby	.05
343	Chad Ogea	.05
344	Tim Davis	.05
345	Jay Buhner	.05
346	Bobby Ayala	.05
347	Mike Blowers	.05
348	Dave Fleming	.05
349	Edgar Martinez	.05
350	Andre Dawson	.30
351	Darrell Whitmore	.05
352	Chuck Carr	.05
353	John Burkett	.05
354	Chris Hammond	.05
355	Gary Sheffield	.40
356	Pat Rapp	.05
357	Greg Colbrunn	.05
358	David Segui	.05
359	Jeff Kent	.05
360	Bobby Bonilla	.05
361	Pete Harnisch	.05
362	Ryan Thompson	.05
363	Jose Vizcaino	.05
364	Brett Butler	.05
365	Cal Ripken Jr.	2.00
366	Rafael Palmeiro	.65
367	Leo Gomez	.05
368	Andy Van Slyke	.05
369	Arthur Rhodes	.05
370	Ken Caminiti	.05
371	Steve Finley	.05
372	Melvin Nieves	.05
373	Andujar Cedeno	.05
374	Trevor Hoffman	.05
375	Fernando Valenzuela	.05
376	Ricky Bottalico	.05
377	Dave Hollins	.05
378	Charlie Hayes	.05
379	Tommy Greene	.05
380	Darren Daulton	.05
381	Curt Schilling	.25
382	Midre Cummings	.05
383	Al Martin	.05
384	Jeff King	.05
385	Orlando Merced	.05
386	Denny Neagle	.05
387	Don Slaught	.05
388	Dave Clark	.05
389	Kevin Gross	.05
390	Will Clark	.05
391	Ivan Rodriguez	.65
392	Benji Gil	.05
393	Jeff Frye	.05
394	Kenny Rogers	.05
395	Juan Gonzalez	.40
396	Mike Macfarlane	.05
397	Lee Tinsley	.05

398	Tim Naehring	.05
399	Tim Vanegmond	.05
400	Mike Greenwell	.05
401	Ken Ryan	.05
402	John Smiley	.05
403	Tim Pugh	.05
404	Reggie Sanders	.05
405	Barry Larkin	.05
406	Hal Morris	.05
407	Jose Rijo	.05
408	Lance Painter	.05
409	Joe Girardi	.05
410	Andres Galarraga	.05
411	Mike Kingery	.05
412	Roberto Mejia	.05
413	Walt Weiss	.05
414	Bill Swift	.05
415	Larry Walker	.05
416	Billy Brewer	.05
417	Pat Borders	.05
418	Tom Gordon	.05
419	Kevin Appier	.05
420	Gary Gaetti	.05
421	Greg Gohr	.05
422	Felipe Lira	.05
423	John Doherty	.05
424	Chad Curtis	.05
425	Cecil Fielder	.05
426	Alan Trammell	.05
427	David McCarty	.05
428	Scott Erickson	.05
429	Pat Mahomes	.05
430	Kirby Puckett	1.00
431	Dave Stevens	.05
432	Pedro Munoz	.05
433	Chris Sabo	.05
434	Alex Fernandez	.05
435	Frank Thomas	.75
436	Roberto Hernandez	.05
437	Lance Johnson	.05
438	Jim Abbott	.05
439	John Wetteland	.05
440	Melido Perez	.05
441	Tony Fernandez	.05
442	Pat Kelly	.05
443	Mike Stanley	.05
444	Danny Tartabull	.05
445	Wade Boggs	1.00
446	Robin Yount (Final Tribute)	.75
447	Ryne Sandberg (Final Tribute)	1.00
448	Nolan Ryan (Final Tribute)	2.00
449	George Brett (Final Tribute)	1.00
450	Mike Schmidt (Final Tribute)	1.00

Electric Diamond

	NM/M
Complete Set (1-450):	60.00
Common Player:	.25
Stars/Rookies:	2X

(See 1995 Upper Deck for checklist and base card values.)

Autographed Jumbos

		NM/M
Complete Set (2):		100.00
(1)	Roger Clemens	50.00
(2)	Alex Rodriguez	75.00

Autograph Redemption Cards

	NM/M
Complete Set (5):	220.00
Common Player:	15.00
AC1	Reggie Jackson	20.00
AC2	Willie Mays	100.00
AC3	Frank Robinson	30.00
AC4	Roger Clemens	125.00
AC5	Raul Mondesi	10.00

Baseball Heroes Babe Ruth

	NM/M
Complete Set (10):	45.00
Common Card:	6.00
73	Babe Ruth 1914-18 Pitching Career	6.00
74	Babe Ruth 1919 - Move to Outfield	6.00
75	Babe Ruth 1920 - Renaissance Man	6.00
76	Babe Ruth 1923 - House That Ruth Built	6.00
77	Babe Ruth 1927 - 60-Homer Season	6.00
78	Babe Ruth 1928 - Three-homer Game	6.00
79	Babe Ruth 1932 - The Called Shot	6.00
80	Babe Ruth 1930-35 - Milestones	6.00
81	Babe Ruth 1935 - The Last Hurrah	6.00
---	Header Card	7.50

1995 Upper Deck Cal Ripken Commemorative Jumbo

	NM/M
Cal Ripken Jr. (Silver edition of 5,000.)	10.00
Cal Ripken Jr. (Gold edition of 2,131.)	13.50

Special Edition

	NM/M
Complete Set (270):	60.00
Common Player:	.10
Gold:	3X
1	Cliff Floyd	.10
2	Wil Cordero	.10
3	Pedro Martinez	1.50
4	Larry Walker	.10
5	Derek Jeter	4.00
6	Mike Stanley	.10
7	Melido Perez	.10
8	Jim Leyritz	.10
9	Danny Tartabull	.10
10	Wade Boggs	2.00
11	Ryan Klesko	.10
12	Steve Avery	.10
13	Damon Hollins	.10

#	Player	Price
14	Chipper Jones	2.00
15	Dave Justice	.10
16	Glenn Williams	.10
17	Jose Oliva	.10
18	Terrell Wade	.10
19	Alex Fernandez	.10
20	Frank Thomas	1.50
21	Ozzie Guillen	.10
22	Roberto Hernandez	.10
23	Albie Lopez	.10
24	Eddie Murray	1.50
25	Albert Belle	.10
26	Omar Vizquel	.10
27	Carlos Baerga	.10
28	Jose Rijo	.10
29	Hal Morris	.10
30	Reggie Sanders	.10
31	Jack Morris	.10
32	Raul Mondesi	.10
33	Karim Garcia	.15
34	Todd Hollandsworth	.10
35	Mike Piazza	2.50
36	Chan Ho Park	.10
37	Ramon Martinez	.10
38	Kenny Rogers	.10
39	Will Clark	.75
40	Juan Gonzalez	.75
41	Ivan Rodriguez	1.25
42	Orlando Miller	.10
43	John Hudek	.10
44	Luis Gonzalez	.10
45	Jeff Bagwell	1.50
46	Cal Ripken Jr.	4.00
47	Mike Oquist	.10
48	Armando Benitez	.10
49	Ben McDonald	.10
50	Rafael Palmeiro	1.25
51	Curtis Goodwin	.10
52	Vince Coleman	.10
53	Tom Gordon	.10
54	Mike Macfarlane	.10
55	Brian McRae	.10
56	Matt Smith	.10
57	David Segui	.10
58	Paul Wilson	.10
59	Bill Pulsipher	.10
60	Bobby Bonilla	.10
61	Jeff Kent	.10
62	Ryan Thompson	.10
63	Jason Isringhausen	.10
64	Ed Sprague	.10
65	Paul Molitor	1.50
66	Juan Guzman	.10
67	Alex Gonzalez	.10
68	Shawn Green	.50
69	Mark Portugal	.10
70	Barry Bonds	4.00
71	Robby Thompson	.10
72	Royce Clayton	.10
73	Ricky Bottalico	.10
74	Doug Jones	.10
75	Darren Daulton	.10
76	Gregg Jefferies	.10
77	Scott Cooper	.10
78	Nomar Garciaparra	2.00
79	Ken Ryan	.10
80	Mike Greenwell	.10
81	LaTroy Hawkins	.10
82	Rich Becker	.10
83	Scott Erickson	.10
84	Pedro Munoz	.10
85	Kirby Puckett	2.00
86	Orlando Merced	.10
87	Jeff King	.10
88	Midre Cummings	.10
89	Bernard Gilkey	.10
90	Ray Lankford	.10
91	Todd Zeile	.10
92	Alan Benes	.10
93	Bret Wagner	.10
94	Rene Arocha	.10
95	Cecil Fielder	.10
96	Alan Trammell	.10
97	Tony Phillips	.10
98	Junior Felix	.10
99	Brian Harper	.10
100	Greg Vaughn	.10
101	Ricky Bones	.10
102	Walt Weiss	.10
103	Lance Painter	.10
104	Roberto Mejia	.10
105	Andres Galarraga	.10
106	Todd Van Poppel	.10
107	Ben Grieve	.10
108	Brent Gates	.10
109	Jason Giambi	1.00
110	Ruben Sierra	.10
111	Terry Steinbach	.10
112	Chris Hammond	.10
113	Charles Johnson	.10
114	Jesus Tavarez	.10
115	Gary Sheffield	.40
116	Chuck Carr	.10
117	Bobby Ayala	.10
118	Randy Johnson	1.50
119	Edgar Martinez	.10
120	Alex Rodriguez	3.00
121	Kevin Foster	.10
122	Kevin Roberson	.10
123	Sammy Sosa	2.00
124	Steve Trachsel	.10
125	Eduardo Perez	.10
126	Tim Salmon	.10
127	Todd Greene	.10
128	Jorge Fabregas	.10
129	Mark Langston	.10
130	Mitch Williams	.10
131	Raul Casanova	.10
132	Mel Nieves	.10
133	Andy Benes	.10
134	Dustin Hermanson	.10
135	Trevor Hoffman	.10
136	Mark Grudzielanek	.10
137	Ugueth Urbina	.10
138	Moises Alou	.10
139	Roberto Kelly	.10
140	Rondell White	.10
141	Paul O'Neill	.10
142	Jimmy Key	.10
143	Jack McDowell	.10
144	Ruben Rivera	.10
145	Don Mattingly	2.25
146	John Wetteland	.10
147	Tom Glavine	.25
148	Marquis Grissom	.10
149	Javy Lopez	.10
150	Fred McGriff	.10
151	Greg Maddux	2.00
152	Chris Sabo	.10
153	Jay Durham	.10
154	Robin Ventura	.10
155	Jim Abbott	.10
156	Jimmy Hurst	.10
157	Tim Raines	.10
158	Dennis Martinez	.10
159	Kenny Lofton	.10
160	Dave Winfield	1.50
161	Manny Ramirez	1.50
162	Jim Thome	1.00
163	Barry Larkin	.10
164	Bret Boone	.10
165	Deion Sanders	.10
166	Ron Gant	.10
167	Benito Santiago	.10
168	Hideo Nomo	.75
169	Billy Ashley	.10
170	Roger Cedeno	.10
171	Ismael Valdes	.10
172	Eric Karros	.10
173	Rusty Greer	.10
174	Rick Helling	.10
175	Nolan Ryan	4.00
176	Dean Palmer	.10
177	Phil Plantier	.10
178	Darryl Kile	.10
179	Derek Bell	.10
180	Doug Drabek	.10
181	Craig Biggio	.10
182	Kevin Brown	.10
183	Harold Baines	.10
184	Jeffrey Hammonds	.10
185	Chris Hoiles	.10
186	Mike Mussina	.50
187	Bob Hamelin	.10
188	Jeff Montgomery	.10
189	Michael Tucker	.10
190	George Brett	2.25
191	Edgardo Alfonzo	.10
192	Brett Butler	.10
193	Bobby Jones	.10
194	Todd Hundley	.10
195	Bret Saberhagen	.10
196	Pat Hentgen	.10
197	Roberto Alomar	.30
198	David Cone	.10
199	Carlos Delgado	1.00
200	Joe Carter	.10
201	William Van Landingham	.10
202	Rod Beck	.10
203	J.R. Phillips	.10
204	Darren Lewis	.10
205	Matt Williams	.10
206	Lenny Dykstra	.10
207	Dave Hollins	.10
208	Mike Schmidt	2.25
209	Charlie Hayes	.10
210	Mo Vaughn	.10
211	Jose Malave	.10
212	Roger Clemens	2.25
213	Jose Canseco	.75
214	Mark Whiten	.10
215	Marty Cordova	.10
216	Rick Aguilera	.10
217	Kevin Tapani	.10
218	Chuck Knoblauch	.10
219	Al Martin	.10
220	Jay Bell	.10
221	Carlos Garcia	.10
222	Freddy Garcia	.10
223	Jon Lieber	.10
224	Danny Jackson	.10
225	Ozzie Smith	2.00
226	Brian Jordan	.10
227	Ken Hill	.10
228	Scott Cooper	.10
229	Chad Curtis	.10
230	Lou Whitaker	.10
231	Kirk Gibson	.10
232	Travis Fryman	.10
233	Jose Valentin	.10
234	Dave Nilsson	.10
235	Cal Eldred	.10
236	Matt Mieske	.10
237	Bill Swift	.10
238	Marvin Freeman	.10
239	Jason Bates	.10
240	Larry Walker	.10
241	David Nied	.10
242	Dante Bichette	.10
243	Dennis Eckersley	1.25
244	Todd Stottlemyre	.10
245	Rickey Henderson	1.50
246	Geronimo Berroa	.10
247	Mark McGwire	3.00
248	Quilvio Veras	.10
249	Terry Pendleton	.10
250	Andre Dawson	.30
251	Jeff Conine	.10
252	Kurt Abbott	.10
253	Jay Buhner	.10
254	Darren Bragg	.10
255	Ken Griffey Jr.	2.50
256	Tino Martinez	.10
257	Mark Grace	.10
258	Ryne Sandberg	2.00
259	Randy Myers	.10
260	Howard Johnson	.10
261	Lee Smith	.10
262	J.T. Snow	.10
263	Chili Davis	.10
264	Chuck Finley	.10
265	Eddie Williams	.10
266	Joey Hamilton	.10
267	Ken Caminiti	.10
268	Andujar Cedeno	.10
269	Steve Finley	.10
270	Tony Gwynn	2.00

Steal of a Deal

		NM/M
Complete Set (15):		25.00
Common Player:		1.00
1	Mike Piazza	6.00
2	Fred McGriff	1.00
3	Kenny Lofton	1.00
4	Jose Oliva	1.00
5	Jeff Bagwell	3.00
6	Roberto Alomar, Joe Carter	1.00
7	Steve Karsay	1.00
8	Ozzie Smith	4.00
9	Dennis Eckersley	2.00
10	Jose Canseco	1.50
11	Carlos Baerga	1.00
12	Cecil Fielder	1.00
13	Don Mattingly	5.00
14	Bret Boone	1.00
15	Michael Jordan	10.00

Update

		NM/M
Complete Set (45):		7.50
Common Player:		.25
451	Jim Abbott	.25
452	Danny Tartabull	.25
453	Ariel Prieto	.25
454	Scott Cooper	.25
455	Tom Henke	.25
456	Todd Zeile	.25
457	Brian McRae	.25
458	Luis Gonzalez	.25
459	Jaime Navarro	.25
460	Todd Worrell	.25
461	Roberto Kelly	.25
462	Chad Fonville	.25
463	Shane Andrews	.25
464	David Segui	.25
465	Deion Sanders	.50
466	Orel Hershiser	.25
467	Ken Hill	.25
468	Andy Benes	.25
469	Terry Pendleton	.25
470	Bobby Bonilla	.25
471	Scott Erickson	.25
472	Kevin Brown	.25
473	Glenn Dishman	.25
474	Phil Plantier	.75
475	Gregg Jefferies	.25
476	Tyler Green	.25
477	Heathcliff Slocumb	.25
478	Mark Whiten	.25
479	Mickey Tettleton	.25
480	Tim Wakefield	.25
481	Vaughn Eshelman	.25
482	Rick Aguilera	.25
483	Erik Hanson	.25
484	Willie McGee	.25
485	Troy O'Leary	.25
486	Benito Santiago	.25
487	Darren Lewis	.25
488	Dave Burba	.25
489	Ron Gant	.25
490	Bret Saberhagen	.25
491	Vinny Castilla	.25
492	Frank Rodriguez	.25
493	Andy Pettitte	5.00
494	Ruben Sierra	.25
495	David Cone	.25

1996 Upper Deck

		NM/M
Unopened Wood Box Set (510):		40.00
Unopened Fact. Set (510):		35.00
Complete Set (480):		20.00
Common Player:		.05
Wax Pack (10):		.75
Wax Box (32):		17.50
1	Cal Ripken Jr. (Milestones)	1.00
2	Eddie Murray (Milestones)	.40
3	Mark Wohlers	.05
4	Dave Justice	.05
5	Chipper Jones	1.00
6	Javier Lopez	.05
7	Mark Lemke	.05
8	Marquis Grissom	.05
9	Tom Glavine	.25
10	Greg Maddux	1.00
11	Manny Alexander	.05
12	Curtis Goodwin	.05
13	Scott Erickson	.05
14	Chris Hoiles	.05
15	Rafael Palmeiro	.65
16	Rick Krivda	.05
17	Jeff Manto	.05
18	Mo Vaughn	.05
19	Tim Wakefield	.05
20	Roger Clemens	1.00
21	Tim Naehring	.05
22	Troy O'Leary	.05
23	Mike Greenwell	.05
24	Stan Belinda	.05
25	John Valentin	.05
26	J.T. Snow	.05
27	Gary DiSarcina	.05
28	Mark Langston	.05
29	Brian Anderson	.05
30	Jim Edmonds	.05
31	Garret Anderson	.05
32	Orlando Palmeiro	.05
33	Brian McRae	.05
34	Kevin Foster	.05
35	Sammy Sosa	1.00
36	Todd Zeile	.05
37	Jim Bullinger	.05
38	Luis Gonzalez	.05
39	Lyle Mouton	.05
40	Ray Durham	.05

41	Ozzie Guillen	.05
42	Alex Fernandez	.05
43	Brian Keyser	.05
44	Robin Ventura	.05
45	Reggie Sanders	.05
46	Pete Schourek	.05
47	John Smiley	.05
48	Jeff Brantley	.05
49	Thomas Howard	.05
50	Bret Boone	.05
51	Kevin Jarvis	.05
52	Jeff Branson	.05
53	Carlos Baerga	.05
54	Jim Thome	.50
55	Manny Ramirez	.75
56	Omar Vizquel	.05
57	Jose Mesa	.05
58	Julian Tavarez	.05
59	Orel Hershiser	.05
60	Larry Walker	.05
61	Bret Saberhagen	.05
62	Vinny Castilla	.05
63	Eric Young	.05
64	Bryan Rekar	.05
65	Andres Galarraga	.05
66	Steve Reed	.05
67	Chad Curtis	.05
68	Bobby Higginson	.05
69	Phil Nevin	.05
70	Cecil Fielder	.05
71	Felipe Lira	.05
72	Chris Gomez	.05
73	Charles Johnson	.05
74	Quilvio Veras	.05
75	Jeff Conine	.05
76	John Burkett	.05
77	Greg Colbrunn	.05
78	Terry Pendleton	.05
79	Shane Reynolds	.05
80	Jeff Bagwell	.75
81	Orlando Miller	.05
82	Mike Hampton	.05
83	James Mouton	.05
84	Brian L. Hunter	.05
85	Derek Bell	.05
86	Kevin Appier	.05
87	Joe Vitiello	.05
88	Wally Joyner	.05
89	Michael Tucker	.05
90	Johnny Damon	.20
91	Jon Nunnally	.05
92	Jason Jacome	.05
93	Chad Fonville	.05
94	Chan Ho Park	.05
95	Hideo Nomo	.40
96	Ismael Valdes	.05
97	Greg Gagne	.05
98	Diamondbacks-Devil Rays (Expansion Card)	.10
99	Raul Mondesi	.05
100	Dave Winfield (Young at Heart)	.75
101	Dennis Eckersley (Young at Heart)	.35
102	Andre Dawson (Young at Heart)	.15
103	Dennis Martinez (Young at Heart)	.05
104	Lance Parrish (Young at Heart)	.05
105	Eddie Murray (Young at Heart)	.40
106	Alan Trammell (Young at Heart)	.05
107	Lou Whitaker (Young at Heart)	.05
108	Ozzie Smith (Young at Heart)	.50
109	Paul Molitor (Young at Heart)	.40
110	Rickey Henderson (Young at Heart)	.40
111	Tim Raines (Young at Heart)	.05
112	Harold Baines (Young at Heart)	.05
113	Lee Smith (Young at Heart)	.05
114	Fernando Valenzuela (Young at Heart)	.05
115	Cal Ripken Jr. (Young at Heart)	1.00
116	Tony Gwynn (Young at Heart)	.50
117	Wade Boggs (Young at Heart)	.50
118	Todd Hollandsworth	.05
119	Dave Nilsson	.05
120	Jose Valentin **RC**	.05
121	Steve Sparks	.05
122	Chuck Carr	.05
123	John Jaha	.05
124	Scott Karl	.05
125	Chuck Knoblauch	.05
126	Brad Radke	.05
127	Pat Meares	.05
128	Ron Coomer	.05
129	Pedro Munoz	.05
130	Kirby Puckett	1.00
131	David Segui	.05
132	Mark Grudzielanek	.05
133	Mike Lansing	.05
134	Sean Berry	.05
135	Rondell White	.05
136	Pedro Martinez	.75
137	Carl Everett	.05
138	Dave Mlicki	.05
139	Bill Pulsipher	.05
140	Jason Isringhausen	.05
141	Rico Brogna	.05
142	Edgardo Alfonzo	.05
143	Jeff Kent	.05
144	Andy Pettitte	.25
145	Mike Piazza (Beat the Odds)	.65
146	Cliff Floyd (Beat the Odds)	.05
147	Jason Isringhausen (Beat the Odds)	.05
148	Tim Wakefield (Beat the Odds)	.05
149	Chipper Jones (Beat the Odds)	.50
150	Hideo Nomo (Beat the Odds)	.20
151	Mark McGwire (Beat the Odds)	.75
152	Ron Gant (Beat the Odds)	.05
153	Gary Gaetti (Beat the Odds)	.05
154	Don Mattingly	1.00
155	Paul O'Neill	.05
156	Derek Jeter	2.00
157	Joe Girardi	.05
158	Ruben Sierra	.05
159	Jorge Posada	.05
160	Geronimo Berroa	.05
161	Steve Ontiveros	.05
162	George Williams	.05
163	Doug Johns	.05
164	Ariel Prieto	.05
165	Scott Brosius	.05
166	Mike Bordick	.05
167	Tyler Green	.05
168	Mickey Morandini	.05
169	Darren Daulton	.05
170	Gregg Jefferies	.05
171	Jim Eisenreich	.05
172	Heathcliff Slocumb	.05
173	Kevin Stocker	.05
174	Esteban Loaiza	.05
175	Jeff King	.05
176	Mark Johnson	.05
177	Denny Neagle	.05
178	Orlando Merced	.05
179	Carlos Garcia	.05
180	Brian Jordan	.05
181	Mike Morgan	.05
182	Mark Petkovsek	.05
183	Bernard Gilkey	.05
184	John Mabry	.05
185	Tom Henke	.05
186	Glenn Dishman	.05
187	Andy Ashby	.05
188	Bip Roberts	.05
189	Melvin Nieves	.05
190	Ken Caminiti	.05
191	Brad Ausmus	.05
192	Deion Sanders	.05
193	Jamie Brewington	.05
194	Glenallen Hill	.05
195	Barry Bonds	2.00
196	William Van Landingham	.05
197	Mark Carreon	.05
198	Royce Clayton	.05
199	Joey Cora	.05
200	Ken Griffey Jr.	1.25
201	Jay Buhner	.05
202	Alex Rodriguez	1.50
203	Norm Charlton	.05
204	Andy Benes	.05
205	Edgar Martinez	.05
206	Juan Gonzalez	.40
207	Will Clark	.05
208	Kevin Gross	.05
209	Roger Pavlik	.05
210	Ivan Rodriguez	.65
211	Rusty Greer	.05
212	Angel Martinez	.05
213	Tomas Perez	.05
214	Alex Gonzalez	.05
215	Joe Carter	.05
216	Shawn Green	.30
217	Edwin Hurtado	.05
218	Edgar Martinez, Tony Pena (Post Season Checklist)	.05
219	Chipper Jones, Barry Larkin (Post Season Checklist)	.25
220	Orel Hershiser (Post Season Checklist)	.05
221	Mike Devereaux (Post Season Checklist)	.05
222	Tom Glavine (Post Season Checklist)	.05
223	Karim Garcia (Star Rookies)	.10
224	Arquimedez Pozo (Star Rookies)	.05
225	Billy Wagner (Star Rookies)	.05
226	John Wasdin (Star Rookies)	.05
227	Jeff Suppan (Star Rookies)	.05
228	Steve Gibralter (Star Rookies)	.05
229	Jimmy Haynes (Star Rookies)	.05
230	Ruben Rivera (Star Rookies)	.05
231	Chris Snopek (Star Rookies)	.05
232	Alex Ochoa (Star Rookies)	.05
233	Shannon Stewart (Star Rookies)	.05
234	Quinton McCracken (Star Rookies)	.05
235	Trey Beamon (Star Rookies)	.05
236	Billy McMillon (Star Rookies)	.05
237	Steve Cox (Star Rookies)	.05
238	George Arias (Star Rookies)	.05
239	Yamil Benitez (Star Rookies)	.05
240	Todd Greene (Star Rookies)	.05
241	Jason Kendall (Star Rookie)	.05
242	Brooks Kieschnick (Star Rookie)	.05
243	Osvaldo Fernandez **RC** (Star Rookie)	.15
244	Livan Hernandez **RC** (Star Rookie)	.35
245	Rey Ordonez (Star Rookie)	.05
246	Mike Grace **RC** (Star Rookie)	.05
247	Jay Canizaro (Star Rookie)	.05
248	Bob Wolcott (Star Rookie)	.05
249	Jermaine Dye (Star Rookie)	.05
250	Jason Schmidt (Star Rookie)	.05
251	Mike Sweeney **RC** (Star Rookie)	1.00
252	Marcus Jensen (Star Rookie)	.05
253	Mendy Lopez (Star Rookie)	.05
254	Wilton Guerrero **RC** (Star Rookie)	.10
255	Paul Wilson (Star Rookie)	.05
256	Edgar Renteria (Star Rookie)	.05
257	Richard Hidalgo (Star Rookie)	.05
258	Bob Abreu (Star Rookie)	.10
259	Robert Smith **RC** (Diamond Debuts)	.05
260	Sal Fasano (Diamond Debuts)	.05
261	Enrique Wilson (Diamond Debuts)	.05
262	Rich Hunter **RC** (Diamond Debuts)	.05
263	Sergio Nunez (Diamond Debuts)	.05
264	Dan Serafini (Diamond Debuts)	.05
265	David Doster **RC** (Diamond Debuts)	.05
266	Ryan McGuire (Diamond Debuts)	.05
267	Scott Spiezio (Diamond Debuts)	.05
268	Rafael Orellano (Diamond Debuts)	.05
269	Steve Avery	.05
270	Fred McGriff	.05
271	John Smoltz	.05
272	Ryan Klesko	.05
273	Jeff Blauser	.05
274	Brad Clontz	.05
275	Roberto Alomar	.20
276	B.J. Surhoff	.05
277	Jeffrey Hammonds	.05
278	Brady Anderson	.05
279	Bobby Bonilla	.05
280	Cal Ripken Jr.	2.00
281	Mike Mussina	.30
282	Wil Cordero	.05
283	Mike Stanley	.05
284	Aaron Sele	.05
285	Jose Canseco	.40
286	Tom Gordon	.05
287	Heathcliff Slocumb	.05
288	Lee Smith	.05
289	Troy Percival	.05
290	Tim Salmon	.05
291	Chuck Finley	.05
292	Jim Abbott	.05
293	Chili Davis	.05
294	Steve Trachsel	.05
295	Mark Grace	.05
296	Rey Sanchez	.05
297	Scott Servais	.05
298	Jaime Navarro	.05
299	Frank Castillo	.05
300	Frank Thomas	.75
301	Jason Bere	.05
302	Danny Tartabull	.05
303	Darren Lewis	.05
304	Roberto Hernandez	.05
305	Tony Phillips	.05
306	Wilson Alvarez	.05
307	Jose Rijo	.05
308	Hal Morris	.05
309	Mark Portugal	.05
310	Barry Larkin	.05
311	Dave Burba	.05
312	Eddie Taubensee	.05
313	Sandy Alomar Jr.	.05
314	Dennis Martinez	.05
315	Albert Belle	.15
316	Eddie Murray	.75
317	Charles Nagy	.05
318	Chad Ogea	.05
319	Kenny Lofton	.05
320	Dante Bichette	.05
321	Armando Reynoso	.05
322	Walt Weiss	.05
323	Ellis Burks	.05
324	Kevin Ritz	.05
325	Bill Swift	.05
326	Jason Bates	.05
327	Tony Clark	.05
328	Travis Fryman	.05
329	Mark Parent	.05
330	Alan Trammell	.05
331	C.J. Nitkowski	.05
332	Jose Lima	.05
333	Phil Plantier	.05
334	Kurt Abbott	.05
335	Andre Dawson	.25
336	Chris Hammond	.05
337	Robb Nen	.05
338	Pat Rapp	.05
339	Al Leiter	.05
340	Gary Sheffield	.35
341	Todd Jones	.05
342	Doug Drabek	.05
343	Greg Swindell	.05
344	Tony Eusebio	.05
345	Craig Biggio	.05
346	Darryl Kile	.05
347	Mike Macfarlane	.05
348	Jeff Montgomery	.05
349	Chris Haney	.05
350	Bip Roberts	.05
351	Tom Goodwin	.05
352	Mark Gubicza	.05
353	Joe Randa	.05
354	Ramon Martinez	.05
355	Eric Karros	.05
356	Delino DeShields	.05
357	Brett Butler	.05
358	Todd Worrell	.05
359	Mike Blowers	.05
360	Mike Piazza	1.25
361	Ben McDonald	.05
362	Ricky Bones	.05
363	Greg Vaughn	.05
364	Matt Mieske	.05
365	Kevin Seitzer	.05
366	Jeff Cirillo	.05
367	LaTroy Hawkins	.05
368	Frank Rodriguez	.05
369	Rick Aguilera	.05
370	Roberto Alomar (Best of a Generation)	.15
371	Albert Belle (Best of a Generation)	.05
372	Wade Boggs (Best of a Generation)	.50
373	Barry Bonds (Best of a Generation)	1.00
374	Roger Clemens (Best of a Generation)	.65
375	Dennis Eckersley (Best of a Generation)	.35
376	Ken Griffey Jr. (Best of a Generation)	.65
377	Tony Gwynn (Best of a Generation)	.50
378	Rickey Henderson (Best of a Generation)	.40
379	Greg Maddux (Best of a Generation)	.50
380	Fred McGriff (Best of a Generation)	.05
381	Paul Molitor (Best of a Generation)	.40
382	Eddie Murray (Best of a Generation)	.40
383	Mike Piazza (Best of a Generation)	.65
384	Kirby Puckett (Best of a Generation)	.50
385	Cal Ripken Jr. (Best of a Generation)	1.00
386	Ozzie Smith (Best of a Generation)	.50
387	Frank Thomas (Best of a Generation)	.45
388	Matt Walbeck	.05
389	Dave Stevens	.05
390	Marty Cordova	.05
391	Darrin Fletcher	.05
392	Cliff Floyd	.05
393	Mel Rojas	.05
394	Shane Andrews	.05
395	Moises Alou	.05
396	Carlos Perez	.05
397	Jeff Fassero	.05
398	Bobby Jones	.05
399	Todd Hundley	.05
400	John Franco	.05
401	Jose Vizcaino	.05
402	Bernard Gilkey	.05
403	Pete Harnisch	.05
404	Pat Kelly	.05
405	David Cone	.05
406	Bernie Williams	.05
407	John Wetteland	.05
408	Scott Kamieniecki	.05
409	Tim Raines	.05
410	Wade Boggs	1.00
411	Terry Steinbach	.05
412	Jason Giambi	.40
413	Todd Van Poppel	.05
414	Pedro Munoz	.05
415	Eddie Murray-1990 (Strange But True)	.40
416	Dennis Eckersley-1990 (Strange But True)	.35
417	Bip Roberts-1992 (Strange But True)	.05
418	Glenallen Hill-1992 (Strange But True)	.05
419	John Hudek-1994 (Strange But True)	.05
420	Derek Bell-1995 (Strange But True)	.05
421	Larry Walker-1995 (Strange But True)	.05
422	Greg Maddux-1995 (Strange But True)	.50
423	Ken Caminiti-1995 (Strange But True)	.05
424	Brent Gates	.05
425	Mark McGwire	1.50
426	Mark Whiten	.05
427	Sid Fernandez	.05
428	Ricky Bottalico	.05
429	Mike Mimbs	.05
430	Lenny Dykstra	.05

431	Todd Zeile	.05
432	Benito Santiago	.05
433	Danny Miceli	.05
434	Al Martin	.05
435	Jay Bell	.05
436	Charlie Hayes	.05
437	Mike Kingery	.05
438	Paul Wagner	.05
439	Tom Pagnozzi	.05
440	Ozzie Smith	1.00
441	Ray Lankford	.05
442	Dennis Eckersley	.65
443	Ron Gant	.05
444	Alan Benes	.05
445	Rickey Henderson	.75
446	Jody Reed	.05
447	Trevor Hoffman	.05
448	Andujar Cedeno	.05
449	Steve Finley	.05
450	Tony Gwynn	1.00
451	Joey Hamilton	.05
452	Mark Leiter	.05
453	Rod Beck	.05
454	Kirt Manwaring	.05
455	Matt Williams	.05
456	Robby Thompson	.05
457	Shawon Dunston	.05
458	Russ Davis	.05
459	Paul Sorrento	.05
460	Randy Johnson	.75
461	Chris Bosio	.05
462	Luis Sojo	.05
463	Sterling Hitchcock	.05
464	Benji Gil	.05
465	Mickey Tettleton	.05
466	Mark McLemore	.05
467	Darryl Hamilton	.05
468	Ken Hill	.05
469	Dean Palmer	.05
470	Carlos Delgado	.40
471	Ed Sprague	.05
472	Otis Nixon	.05
473	Pat Hentgen	.05
474	Juan Guzman	.05
475	John Olerud	.05
476	Buck Showalter Checklist	.05
477	Bobby Cox Checklist	.05
478	Tommy Lasorda Checklist	.05
479	Jim Leyland Checklist	.05
480	Sparky Anderson Checklist	.05

1996 Upper Deck A Cut Above

(See 1996 Collector's Choice A Cut Above.)

Blue Chip Prospects

		NM/M
Complete Set (20):		50.00
Common Player:		1.00
1	Hideo Nomo	4.00
2	Johnny Damon	3.50
3	Jason Isringhausen	1.00
4	Bill Pulsipher	1.00
5	Marty Cordova	1.00
6	Michael Tucker	1.00
7	John Wasdin	1.00
8	Karim Garcia	1.50
9	Ruben Rivera	1.00
10	Chipper Jones	10.00
11	Billy Wagner	1.00
12	Brooks Kieschnick	1.00
13	Alex Ochoa	1.00
14	Roger Cedeno	1.00
15	Alex Rodriguez	15.00
16	Jason Schmidt	1.00
17	Derek Jeter	20.00
18	Brian L. Hunter	1.00
19	Garret Anderson	1.00
20	Manny Ramirez	7.50

Cal Ripken Collection

		NM/M
Complete Set (8):		12.50
Common Card:		2.00
Header:		2.00
5-17	Cal Ripken Jr.	2.00

1996 Upper Deck Diamond Destiny

		NM/M
Complete Set (Bronze):		35.00
Common Player (Bronze):		.30
Silver:		6X
Gold:		12X
1	Chipper Jones	1.50
2	Fred McGriff	.30
3	Ryan Klesko	.30
4	John Smoltz	.30
5	Greg Maddux	1.50
6	Cal Ripken Jr.	3.00
7	Roberto Alomar	.45
8	Eddie Murray	1.25
9	Brady Anderson	.30
10	Mo Vaughn	.30
11	Roger Clemens	1.75
12	Darin Erstad	.60
13	Sammy Sosa	1.50
14	Frank Thomas	1.25
15	Barry Larkin	.30
16	Albert Belle	.30
17	Manny Ramirez	1.25
18	Kenny Lofton	.30
19	Dante Bichette	.30
20	Gary Sheffield	.75
21	Jeff Bagwell	1.25
22	Hideo Nomo	.65
23	Mike Piazza	2.00
24	Kirby Puckett	1.50
25	Paul Molitor	1.25
26	Chuck Knoblauch	.30
27	Wade Boggs	1.50
28	Derek Jeter	3.00
29	Rey Ordonez	.30
30	Mark McGwire	2.50
31	Ozzie Smith	1.50
32	Tony Gwynn	1.50
33	Barry Bonds	3.00
34	Matt Williams	.30
35	Ken Griffey Jr.	2.00
36	Jay Buhner	.30
37	Randy Johnson	1.25
38	Alex Rodriguez	2.00
39	Juan Gonzalez	.65
40	Joe Carter	.30

Gameface

		NM/M
Complete Set (10):		6.00
Common Player:		.15
1	Ken Griffey Jr.	1.00
2	Frank Thomas	.65
3	Barry Bonds	1.50
4	Albert Belle	.15
5	Cal Ripken Jr.	1.50
6	Mike Piazza	1.00
7	Chipper Jones	.75
8	Matt Williams	.15
9	Hideo Nomo	.40
10	Greg Maddux	.75

Future Stock

		NM/M
Complete Set (20):		4.00
Common Player:		.25
1	George Arias	.25
2	Brian Barnes	.25
3	Trey Beamon	.25
4	Yamil Benitez	.25
5	Jamie Brewington	.25
6	Tony Clark	.25
7	Steve Cox	.25
8	Carlos Delgado	.75
9	Chad Fonville	.25
10	Steve Gibralter	.25
11	Curtis Goodwin	.25
12	Todd Greene	.25
13	Jimmy Haynes	.25
14	Quinton McCracken	.25
15	Billy McMillon	.25
16	Chan Ho Park	.25
17	Arquimedez Pozo	.25
18	Chris Snopek	.25
19	Shannon Stewart	.25
20	Jeff Suppan	.25

1996 Upper Deck Hideo Nomo R.O.Y.

	NM/M
Hideo Nomo	15.00

Hot Commodities

		NM/M
Complete Set (20):		30.00
Common Player:		.75
1	Ken Griffey Jr.	3.00
2	Hideo Nomo	1.50
3	Roberto Alomar	1.50
4	Paul Wilson	.75
5	Albert Belle	.75
6	Manny Ramirez	2.25
7	Kirby Puckett	2.50
8	Johnny Damon	2.00
9	Randy Johnson	2.25
10	Greg Maddux	2.50
11	Chipper Jones	2.50
12	Barry Bonds	5.00
13	Mo Vaughn	.75
14	Mike Piazza	3.00
15	Cal Ripken Jr.	5.00
16	Tim Salmon	.75
17	Sammy Sosa	2.50
18	Kenny Lofton	.75
19	Tony Gwynn	2.50
20	Frank Thomas	2.25

Lovero Collection

		NM/M
Complete Set (20):		17.50
Common Player:		.25
1	Rod Carew	1.00
2	Hideo Nomo	.50
3	Derek Jeter	3.00
4	Barry Bonds	3.00
5	Greg Maddux	1.50
6	Mark McGwire (W/Will Clark.)	2.50
7	Jose Canseco	.50
8	Ken Caminiti	.25
9	Raul Mondesi	.25
10	Ken Griffey Jr.	2.50
11	Jay Buhner	.25
12	Randy Johnson	1.00
13	Roger Clemens	2.00
14	Brady Anderson	.25
15	Frank Thomas	1.00
16	Angels Outfielders	.25
17	Mike Piazza	2.50
18	Dante Bichette	.25
19	Tony Gwynn	1.50
20	Jim Abbott	.25

1996 Upper Deck National Heroes

	NM/M
Complete Set (2):	20.00
Complete Set, Autographed (2):	190.00
(1) Ken Griffey Jr.	7.50
(1a) Ken Griffey Jr./Auto.	90.00
(2) Cal Ripken Jr.	10.00
(2a) Cal Ripken Jr./Auto.	100.00

Nomo Highlights

	NM/M
Complete Set (5):	3.00
Common Card:	.75
1-5 Hideo Nomo	.75

Power Driven

	NM/M
Complete Set (20):	24.00
Common Player:	.30
1 Albert Belle	.30
2 Barry Bonds	5.00
3 Jay Buhner	.30
4 Jose Canseco	.75
5 Cecil Fielder	.30
6 Juan Gonzalez	.75
7 Ken Griffey Jr.	3.00
8 Eric Karros	.30
9 Fred McGriff	.30
10 Mark McGwire	4.00
11 Rafael Palmeiro	1.25
12 Mike Piazza	3.00
13 Manny Ramirez	1.50
14 Tim Salmon	.30
15 Reggie Sanders	.30
16 Sammy Sosa	2.50
17 Frank Thomas	1.50
18 Mo Vaughn	.30
19 Larry Walker	.30
20 Matt Williams	.30

Run Producers

	NM/M
Complete Set (20):	50.00
Common Player:	1.00

1	Albert Belle	1.00
2	Dante Bichette	1.00
3	Barry Bonds	10.00
4	Jay Buhner	1.00
5	Jose Canseco	2.00
6	Juan Gonzalez	1.50
7	Ken Griffey Jr.	6.00
8	Tony Gwynn	5.00
9	Kenny Lofton	1.00
10	Edgar Martinez	1.00
11	Fred McGriff	1.00
12	Mark McGwire	7.50
13	Rafael Palmeiro	2.50
14	Mike Piazza	6.00
15	Manny Ramirez	3.00
16	Tim Salmon	1.00
17	Sammy Sosa	5.00
18	Frank Thomas	3.00
19	Mo Vaughn	1.00
20	Matt Williams	1.00

1996 Upper Deck Update

	NM/M
Complete Set (30):	8.00
Common Player:	.25
481 Randy Myers	.25
482 Kent Mercker	.25
483 David Wells	.35
484 Kevin Mitchell	.25
485 Randy Velarde	.25
486 Ryne Sandberg	4.00
487 Doug Jones	.25
488 Terry Adams	.25
489 Kevin Tapani	.25
490 Harold Baines	.25
491 Eric Davis	.25
492 Julio Franco	.25
493 Jack McDowell	.25
494 Devon White	.25
495 Kevin Brown	.35
496 Rick Wilkins	.25
497 Sean Berry	.25
498 Keith Lockhart	.25
499 Mark Loretta	.25
500 Paul Molitor	2.50
501 Roberto Kelly	.25
502 Lance Johnson	.25
503 Tino Martinez	.25
504 Kenny Rogers	.25
505 Todd Stottlemyre	.25
506 Gary Gaetti	.25
507 Royce Clayton	.25
508 Andy Benes	.25
509 Wally Joyner	.25
510 Erik Hanson	.25

1997 Upper Deck

	NM/M
Complete Set (550):	75.00
Complete 1 Set (240):	35.00
Complete Update Set (241-270):	5.00
Complete Series 2 Set (271-520):	35.00
Complete Update Set (521-550):	7.50
Common Player:	.05
Series 1 or 2 Pack (12):	1.50
Series 1 or 2 Wax Box (28):	25.00
1 Jackie Robinson	.50
2 Jackie Robinson	.50
3 Jackie Robinson	.50
4 Jackie Robinson	.50
5 Jackie Robinson	.50
6 Jackie Robinson	.50
7 Jackie Robinson	.50
8 Jackie Robinson	.50
9 Jackie Robinson	.50
10 Chipper Jones	1.00
11 Marquis Grissom	.05
12 Jermaine Dye	.05
13 Mark Lemke	.05
14 Terrell Wade	.05
15 Fred McGriff	.20
16 Tom Glavine	.20
17 Mark Wohlers	.05
18 Randy Myers	.05
19 Roberto Alomar	.25
20 Cal Ripken Jr.	2.00
21 Rafael Palmeiro	.65
22 Mike Mussina	.30
23 Brady Anderson	.05
24 Jose Canseco	.50
25 Mo Vaughn	.05

26	Roger Clemens	1.00
27	Tim Naehring	.05
28	Jeff Suppan	.05
29	Troy Percival	.05
30	Sammy Sosa	1.00
31	Amaury Telemaco	.05
32	Rey Sanchez	.05
33	Scott Servais	.05
34	Steve Trachsel	.05
35	Mark Grace	.05
36	Wilson Alvarez	.05
37	Harold Baines	.05
38	Tony Phillips	.05
39	James Baldwin	.05
40	Frank Thomas (Wrong (Ken Griffey Jr.'s) vital data.)	.85
41	Lyle Mouton	.05
42	Chris Snopek	.05
43	Hal Morris	.05
44	Eric Davis	.05
45	Barry Larkin	.05
46	Reggie Sanders	.05
47	Pete Schourek	.05
48	Lee Smith	.05
49	Charles Nagy	.05
50	Albert Belle	.05
51	Julio Franco	.05
52	Kenny Lofton	.15
53	Orel Hershiser	.05
54	Omar Vizquel	.05
55	Eric Young	.05
56	Curtis Leskanic	.05
57	Quinton McCracken	.05
58	Kevin Ritz	.05
59	Walt Weiss	.05
60	Dante Bichette	.05
61	Marc Lewis	.05
62	Tony Clark	.05
63	Travis Fryman	.05
64	John Smoltz (Strike Force)	.05
65	Greg Maddux (Strike Force)	.50
66	Tom Glavine (Strike Force)	.10
67	Mike Mussina (Strike Force)	.15
68	Andy Pettitte (Strike Force)	.15
69	Mariano Rivera (Strike Force)	.10
70	Hideo Nomo (Strike Force)	.20
71	Kevin Brown (Strike Force)	.05
72	Randy Johnson (Strike Force)	.40
73	Felipe Lira	.05
74	Kimera Bartee	.05
75	Alan Trammell	.05
76	Kevin Brown	.05
77	Edgar Renteria	.05
78	Al Leiter	.05
79	Charles Johnson	.05
80	Andre Dawson	.25
81	Billy Wagner	.05
82	Donne Wall	.05
83	Jeff Bagwell	.75
84	Keith Lockhart	.05
85	Jeff Montgomery	.05
86	Tom Goodwin	.05
87	Tim Belcher	.05
88	Mike Macfarlane	.05
89	Joe Randa	.05
90	Brett Butler	.05
91	Todd Worrell	.05
92	Todd Hollandsworth	.05
93	Ismael Valdes	.05
94	Hideo Nomo	.40
95	Mike Piazza	1.25
96	Jeff Cirillo	.05
97	Ricky Bones	.05
98	Fernando Vina	.05
99	Ben McDonald	.05
100	John Jaha	.05
101	Mark Loretta	.05
102	Paul Molitor	.75
103	Rick Aguilera	.05
104	Marty Cordova	.05
105	Kirby Puckett	1.00
106	Dan Naulty	.05
107	Frank Rodriguez	.05
108	Shane Andrews	.05
109	Henry Rodriguez	.05
110	Mark Grudzielanek	.05
111	Pedro Martinez	.75
112	Ugueth Urbina	.05
113	David Segui	.05
114	Rey Ordonez	.05
115	Bernard Gilkey	.05
116	Butch Huskey	.05
117	Paul Wilson	.05
118	Alex Ochoa	.05
119	John Franco	.05
120	Dwight Gooden	.05
121	Ruben Rivera	.05
122	Andy Pettitte	.20
123	Tino Martinez	.05
124	Bernie Williams	.05
125	Wade Boggs	1.00
126	Paul O'Neill	.05
127	Scott Brosius	.05
128	Ernie Young	.05
129	Doug Johns	.05
130	Geronimo Berroa	.05
131	Jason Giambi	.50
132	John Wasdin	.05
133	Jim Eisenreich	.05
134	Ricky Otero	.05
135	Ricky Bottalico	.05
136	Mark Langston (Defensive Gems)	.05

137	Greg Maddux (Defensive Gems)	.50
138	Ivan Rodriguez (Defensive Gems)	.35
139	Charles Johnson (Defensive Gems)	.05
140	J.T. Snow (Defensive Gems)	.05
141	Mark Grace (Defensive Gems)	.05
142	Roberto Alomar (Defensive Gems)	.15
143	Craig Biggio (Defensive Gems)	.05
144	Ken Caminiti (Defensive Gems)	.05
145	Matt Williams (Defensive Gems)	.05
146	Omar Vizquel (Defensive Gems)	.05
147	Cal Ripken Jr. (Defensive Gems)	1.00
148	Ozzie Smith (Defensive Gems)	.40
149	Rey Ordonez (Defensive Gems)	.05
150	Ken Griffey Jr. (Defensive Gems)	.65
151	Devon White (Defensive Gems)	.05
152	Barry Bonds (Defensive Gems)	1.00
153	Kenny Lofton (Defensive Gems)	.05
154	Mickey Morandini	.05
155	Gregg Jefferies	.05
156	Curt Schilling	.20
157	Jason Kendall	.05
158	Francisco Cordova	.05
159	Dennis Eckersley	.65
160	Ron Gant	.05
161	Ozzie Smith	1.00
162	Brian Jordan	.05
163	John Mabry	.05
164	Andy Ashby	.05
165	Steve Finley	.05
166	Fernando Valenzuela	.05
167	Archi Cianfrocco	.05
168	Wally Joyner	.05
169	Greg Vaughn	.05
170	Barry Bonds	2.00
171	William Van Landingham	.05
172	Marvin Benard	.05
173	Rich Aurilia	.05
174	Jay Canizaro	.05
175	Ken Griffey Jr.	1.25
176	Bob Wells	.05
177	Jay Buhner	.05
178	Sterling Hitchcock	.05
179	Edgar Martinez	.05
180	Rusty Greer	.05
181	Dave Nilsson (Global Impact)	.05
182	Larry Walker (Global Impact)	.05
183	Edgar Renteria (Global Impact)	.05
184	Rey Ordonez (Global Impact)	.05
185	Rafael Palmeiro (Global Impact)	.35
186	Osvaldo Fernandez (Global Impact)	.05
187	Raul Mondesi (Global Impact)	.05
188	Manny Ramirez (Global Impact)	.40
189	Sammy Sosa (Global Impact)	.50
190	Robert Eenhoorn (Global Impact)	.05
191	Devon White (Global Impact)	.05
192	Hideo Nomo (Global Impact)	.20
193	Mac Suzuki (Global Impact)	.05
194	Chan Ho Park (Global Impact)	.05
195	Fernando Valenzuela (Global Impact)	.05
196	Andruw Jones (Global Impact)	.40
197	Vinny Castilla (Global Impact)	.05
198	Dennis Martinez (Global Impact)	.05
199	Ruben Rivera (Global Impact)	.05
200	Juan Gonzalez (Global Impact)	.20
201	Roberto Alomar (Global Impact)	.30
202	Edgar Martinez (Global Impact)	.05
203	Ivan Rodriguez (Global Impact)	.35
204	Carlos Delgado (Global Impact)	.20
205	Andres Galarraga (Global Impact)	.05
206	Ozzie Guillen (Global Impact)	.05
207	Midre Cummings (Global Impact)	.05
208	Roger Pavlik	.05
209	Darren Oliver	.05
210	Dean Palmer	.05
211	Ivan Rodriguez	.65
212	Otis Nixon	.05
213	Pat Hentgen	.05
214	Ozzie Smith, Andre Dawson, Kirby Puckett CL (Season Highlights)	.10
215	Barry Bonds, Gary Sheffield, Brady Anderson (Checklist/Season Highlights)	.25

216 Ken Caminiti (Checklist/Season Highlights) .05
217 John Smoltz (Checklist/Season Highlights) .05
218 Eric Young (Checklist/Season Highlights) .05
219 Juan Gonzalez (Checklist/Season Highlights) .10
220 Eddie Murray (Checklist/Season Highlights) .15
221 Tommy Lasorda (Checklist/Season Highlights) .05
222 Paul Molitor (Checklist/Season Highlights) .15
223 Luis Castillo .05
224 Justin Thompson .05
225 Rocky Coppinger .05
226 Jermaine Allensworth .05
227 Jeff D'Amico .05
228 Jamey Wright .05
229 Scott Rolen .60
230 Darin Erstad .25
231 Marty Janzen .05
232 Jacob Cruz .05
233 Raul Ibanez .05
234 Nomar Garciaparra 1.00
235 Todd Walker .05
236 Brian Giles **RC** .75
237 Matt Beech .05
238 Mike Cameron .05
239 Jose Paniagua .05
240 Andruw Jones .75
241 Brant Brown (Star Rookies) .25
242 Robin Jennings (Star Rookies) .25
243 Willie Adams (Star Rookies) .25
244 Ken Caminiti (Division Series) .25
245 Brian Jordan (Division Series) .25
246 Chipper Jones (Division Series) 2.50
247 Juan Gonzalez (Division Series) 1.00
248 Bernie Williams (Division Series) .25
249 Roberto Alomar (Division Series) .30
250 Bernie Williams (Post-Season) .25
251 David Wells (Post-Season) .25
252 Cecil Fielder (Post-Season) .25
253 Darryl Strawberry (Post-Season) .25
254 Andy Pettitte (Post-Season) .40
255 Javier Lopez (Post-Season) .25
256 Gary Gaetti (Post-Season) .25
257 Ron Gant (Post-Season) .25
258 Brian Jordan (Post-Season) .25
259 John Smoltz (Post-Season) .25
260 Greg Maddux (Post-Season) 2.50
261 Tom Glavine (Post-Season) .45
262 Chipper Jones (World Series) 2.50
263 Greg Maddux (World Series) 2.50
264 David Cone (World Series) .25
265 Jim Leyritz (World Series) .25
266 Andy Pettitte (World Series) .40
267 John Wetteland (World Series) .25
268 Dario Veras **RC** (Star Rookie) .25
269 Neifi Perez (Star Rookie) .25
270 Bill Mueller (Star Rookie) .25
271 Vladimir Guerrero (Star Rookie) .75
272 Dmitri Young (Star Rookie) .05
273 Nerio Rodriguez **RC** (Star Rookie) .05
274 Kevin Orie (Star Rookie) .05
275 Felipe Crespo (Star Rookie) .05
276 Danny Graves (Star Rookie) .05
277 Roderick Myers (Star Rookie) .05
278 Felix Heredia **RC** (Star Rookie) .25
279 Ralph Milliard (Star Rookie) .05
280 Greg Norton (Star Rookie) .05
281 Derek Wallace (Star Rookie) .05
282 Trot Nixon (Star Rookie) .10
283 Bobby Chouinard (Star Rookie) .05
284 Jay Witasick (Star Rookie) .05
285 Travis Miller (Star Rookie) .05
286 Brian Bevil (Star Rookie) .05
287 Bobby Estalella (Star Rookie) .05
288 Steve Soderstrom (Star Rookie) .05
289 Mark Langston .05
290 Tim Salmon .05
291 Jim Edmonds .05
292 Garret Anderson .05
293 George Arias .05
294 Gary DiSarcina .05
295 Chuck Finley .05
296 Todd Greene .05
297 Randy Velarde .05
298 David Justice .05
299 Ryan Klesko .05
300 John Smoltz .05
301 Javier Lopez .05
302 Greg Maddux 1.00
303 Denny Neagle .05
304 B.J. Surhoff .05
305 Chris Hoiles .05
306 Eric Davis .05
307 Scott Erickson .05
308 Mike Bordick .05
309 John Valentin .05
310 Heathcliff Slocumb .05
311 Tom Gordon .05
312 Mike Stanley .05
313 Reggie Jefferson .05
314 Darren Bragg .05
315 Troy O'Leary .05
316 John Mabry (Season Highlight) .05
317 Mark Whiten (Season Highlight) .05
318 Edgar Martinez (Season Highlight) .05
319 Alex Rodriguez (Season Highlight) .75
320 Mark McGwire (Season Highlight) .75
321 Hideo Nomo (Season Highlight) .20
322 Todd Hundley (Season Highlight) .05
323 Barry Bonds (Season Highlight) 1.00
324 Andruw Jones (Season Highlight) .40
325 Ryne Sandberg 1.00
326 Brian McRae .05
327 Frank Castillo .05
328 Shawon Dunston .05
329 Ray Durham .05
330 Robin Ventura .05
331 Ozzie Guillen .05
332 Roberto Hernandez .05
333 Albert Belle .25
334 Dave Martinez .05
335 Willie Greene .05
336 Jeff Brantley .05
337 Kevin Jarvis .05
338 John Smiley .05
339 Eddie Taubensee .05
340 Bret Boone .05
341 Kevin Seitzer .05
342 Jack McDowell .05
343 Sandy Alomar Jr. .05
344 Chad Curtis .05
345 Manny Ramirez .75
346 Chad Ogea .05
347 Jim Thome .05
348 Mark Thompson .05
349 Ellis Burks .05
350 Andres Galarraga .05
351 Vinny Castilla .05
352 Kirt Manwaring .05
353 Larry Walker .05
354 Omar Olivares .05
355 Bobby Higginson .05
356 Melvin Nieves .05
357 Brian Johnson .05
358 Devon White .05
359 Jeff Conine .05
360 Gary Sheffield .35
361 Robb Nen .05
362 Mike Hampton .05
363 Bob Abreu .10
364 Luis Gonzalez .05
365 Derek Bell .05
366 Sean Berry .05
367 Craig Biggio .05
368 Darryl Kile .05
369 Shane Reynolds .05
370 Jeff Bagwell (Capture the Flag) .40
371 Ron Gant (Capture the Flag) .05
372 Andy Benes (Capture the Flag) .05
373 Gary Gaetti (Capture the Flag) .05
374a Ramon Martinez (Capture the Flag)(Gold back.)) .05
374b Ramon Martinez (Capture the Flag)(White back.)) .05
375 Raul Mondesi (Capture the Flag) .05
376a Steve Finley (Capture the Flag)(Gold back.)) .05
376b Steve Finley (Capture the Flag)(White back.)) .05
377 Ken Caminiti (Capture the Flag) .05
378 Tony Gwynn (Capture the Flag) .40
379 Dario Veras (Capture the Flag) .05
380 Andy Pettitte (Capture the Flag) .10
381 Ruben Rivera (Capture the Flag) .05
382 David Cone (Capture the Flag) .05
383 Roberto Alomar (Capture the Flag) .20
384 Edgar Martinez (Capture the Flag) .05
385 Ken Griffey Jr. (Capture the Flag) .65
386 Mark McGwire (Capture the Flag) .75
387 Rusty Greer (Capture the Flag) .05
388 Jose Rosado .05
389 Kevin Appier .05
390 Johnny Damon .25
391 Jose Offerman .05
392 Michael Tucker .05
393 Craig Paquette .05
394 Bip Roberts .05
395 Ramon Martinez .05
396 Greg Gagne .05
397 Chan Ho Park .05
398 Karim Garcia .10
399 Wilton Guerrero .05
400 Eric Karros .05
401 Raul Mondesi .05
402 Matt Mieske .05
403 Mike Fetters .05
404 Dave Nilsson .05
405 Jose Valentin .05
406 Scott Karl .05
407 Marc Newfield .05
408 Cal Eldred .05
409 Rich Becker .05
410 Terry Steinbach .05
411 Chuck Knoblauch .05
412 Pat Meares .05
413 Brad Radke .05
414 Not Issued
415a Kirby Puckett (should be #414) 1.00
415b Andruw Jones (Griffey Hot List) 1.50
416 Chipper Jones (Griffey Hot List) 2.00
417 Mo Vaughn (Griffey Hot List) .50
418 Frank Thomas (Griffey Hot List) 1.50
419 Albert Belle (Griffey Hot List) .50
420 Mark McGwire (Griffey Hot List) 3.00
421 Derek Jeter (Griffey Hot List) 4.50
422 Alex Rodriguez (Griffey Hot List) 3.00
423 Juan Gonzalez (Griffey Hot List) .75
424 Ken Griffey Jr. (Griffey Hot List) 2.50
425 Rondell White .05
426 Darrin Fletcher .05
427 Cliff Floyd .05
428 Mike Lansing .05
429 F.P. Santangelo .05
430 Todd Hundley .05
431 Mark Clark .05
432 Pete Harnisch .05
433 Jason Isringhausen .05
434 Bobby Jones .05
435 Lance Johnson .05
436 Carlos Baerga .05
437 Mariano Duncan .05
438 David Cone .05
439 Mariano Rivera .15
440 Derek Jeter 2.00
441 Joe Girardi .05
442 Charlie Hayes .05
443 Tim Raines .05
444 Darryl Strawberry .05
445 Cecil Fielder .05
446 Ariel Prieto .05
447 Tony Batista .05
448 Brent Gates .05
449 Scott Spiezio .05
450 Mark McGwire 1.50
451 Don Wengert .05
452 Mike Lieberthal .05
453 Lenny Dykstra .05
454 Rex Hudler .05
455 Darren Daulton .05
456 Kevin Stocker .05
457 Trey Beamon .05
458 Midre Cummings .05
459 Mark Johnson .05
460 Al Martin .05
461 Kevin Elster .05
462 Jon Lieber .05
463 Jason Schmidt .05
464 Paul Wagner .05
465 Andy Benes .05
466 Alan Benes .05
467 Royce Clayton .05
468 Gary Gaetti .05
469 Curt Lyons (Diamond Debuts) .05
470 Eugene Kingsale (Diamond Debuts) .05
471 Damian Jackson (Diamond Debuts) .05
472 Wendell Magee (Diamond Dubuts) .05
473 Kevin L. Brown (Diamond Debuts) .05
474 Raul Casanova (Diamond Debuts) .05
475 Ramiro Mendoza **RC** (Diamond Debuts) .25
476 Todd Dunn (Diamond Debuts) .05
477 Chad Mottola (Diamond Debuts) .05
478 Andy Larkin (Diamond Debuts) .05
479 Jaime Bluma (Diamond Debuts) .05
480 Mac Suzuki (Diamond Debuts) .05
481 Brian Banks (Diamond Debuts) .05
482 Desi Wilson (Diamond Debuts) .05
483 Einar Diaz (Diamond Debuts) .05
484 Tom Pagnozzi .05
485 Ray Lankford .05
486 Todd Stottlemyre .05
487 Donovan Osborne .05
488 Trevor Hoffman .05
489 Chris Gomez .05
490 Ken Caminiti .05
491 John Flaherty .05
492 Tony Gwynn 1.00
493 Joey Hamilton .05
494 Rickey Henderson .75
495 Glenallen Hill .05
496 Rod Beck .05
497 Osvaldo Fernandez .05
498 Rick Wilkins .05
499 Joey Cora .05
500 Alex Rodriguez 1.50
501 Randy Johnson .75
502 Paul Sorrento .05
503 Dan Wilson .05
504 Jamie Moyer .05
505 Will Clark .05
506 Mickey Tettleton .05
507 John Burkett .05
508 Ken Hill .05
509 Mark McLemore .05
510 Juan Gonzalez .40
511 Bobby Witt .05
512 Carlos Delgado .40
513 Alex Gonzalez .05
514 Shawn Green .25
515 Joe Carter .05
516 Juan Guzman .05
517 Charlie O'Brien .05
518 Ed Sprague .05
519 Mike Timlin .05
520 Roger Clemens 1.00
521 Eddie Murray 2.00
522 Jason Dickson .25
523 Jim Leyritz .25
524 Michael Tucker .25
525 Kenny Lofton .25
526 Jimmy Key .25
527 Mel Rojas .25
528 Deion Sanders .25
529 Bartolo Colon .25
530 Matt Williams .25
531 Marquis Grissom .25
532 David Justice .25
533 Bubba Trammell **RC** .35
534 Moises Alou .25
535 Bobby Bonilla .25
536 Alex Fernandez .25
537 Jay Bell .25
538 Chili Davis .25
539 Jeff King .25
540 Todd Zeile .25
541 John Olerud .25
542 Jose Guillen .25
543 Derrek Lee 1.00
544 Dante Powell .25
545 J.T. Snow .25
546 Jeff Kent .25
547 Jose Cruz Jr. **RC** .75
548 John Wetteland .25
549 Orlando Merced .25
550 Hideki Irabu **RC** .50

Amazing Greats

	NM/M
Complete Set (20):	140.00
Common Player:	2.50
1 Ken Griffey Jr.	12.50
2 Roberto Alomar	3.00
3 Alex Rodriguez	15.00
4 Paul Molitor	7.50
5 Chipper Jones	10.00
6 Tony Gwynn	10.00
7 Kenny Lofton	2.50
8 Albert Belle	2.50
9 Matt Williams	2.50
10 Frank Thomas	7.50
11 Greg Maddux	10.00
12 Sammy Sosa	10.00
13 Kirby Puckett	10.00
14 Jeff Bagwell	7.50
15 Cal Ripken Jr.	20.00
16 Manny Ramirez	7.50
17 Barry Bonds	20.00
18 Mo Vaughn	2.50
19 Eddie Murray	7.50
20 Mike Piazza	12.50

Blue Chip Prospects

	NM/M
Common Player:	6.00
Production 500 Sets	
1 Andruw Jones	25.00
2 Derek Jeter	60.00
3 Scott Rolen	15.00

4	Manny Ramirez	25.00
5	Todd Walker	6.00
6	Rocky Coppinger	6.00
7	Nomar Garciaparra	30.00
8	Darin Erstad	7.50
9	Jermaine Dye	6.00
10	Vladimir Guerrero	25.00
11	Edgar Renteria	6.00
12	Bob Abreu	7.50
13	Karim Garcia	6.00
14	Jeff D'Amico	6.00
15	Chipper Jones	30.00
16	Todd Hollandsworth	6.00
17	Andy Pettitte	9.00
18	Ruben Rivera	6.00
19	Jason Kendall	6.00
20	Alex Rodriguez	40.00

Game Jersey

		NM/M
Complete Set (3):		160.00
Common Player:		15.00
GJ1	Ken Griffey Jr.	150.00
GJ2	Tony Gwynn	25.00
GJ3	Rey Ordonez	15.00

1997 Upper Deck Home Team Heroes

		NM/M
Complete Set (12):		10.00
Common Player:		.50
1	Alex Rodriguez, Ken Griffey Jr.	2.00
2	Bernie Williams, Derek Jeter	2.50
3	Bernard Gilkey, Randy Hundley	.50
4	Hideo Nomo, Mike Piazza	1.50
5	Andruw Jones, Chipper Jones	.50
6	John Smoltz, Greg Maddux	1.00
7	Mike Mussina, Cal Ripken Jr.	2.50
8	Andres Galarraga, Dante Bichette	.50
9	Juan Gonzalez, Ivan Rodriguez	.65
10	Albert Belle, Frank Thomas	.75
11	Jim Thome, Manny Ramirez	.75
12	Ken Caminiti, Tony Gwynn	1.00

Hot Commodities

		NM/M
Complete Set (20):		20.00
Common Player:		.30
1	Alex Rodriguez	2.00
2	Andruw Jones	1.00

3	Derek Jeter	2.50
4	Frank Thomas	1.00
5	Ken Griffey Jr.	1.50
6	Chipper Jones	1.25
7	Juan Gonzalez	.50
8	Cal Ripken Jr.	2.50
9	John Smoltz	.30
10	Mark McGwire	2.00
11	Barry Bonds	2.50
12	Albert Belle	.30
13	Mike Piazza	1.50
14	Manny Ramirez	1.00
15	Mo Vaughn	.30
16	Tony Gwynn	1.25
17	Vladimir Guerrero	1.00
18	Hideo Nomo	.50
19	Greg Maddux	1.25
20	Kirby Puckett	1.25

1997 Upper Deck Jackie Robinson Tribute

APRIL 15, 1947

	NM/M
Jackie Robinson	3.50

Long Distance Connection

		NM/M
Complete Set (20):		32.50
Common Player:		.60
1	Mark McGwire	4.00
2	Brady Anderson	.60
3	Ken Griffey Jr.	3.00
4	Albert Belle	.60
5	Juan Gonzalez	1.25
6	Andres Galarraga	.60
7	Jay Buhner	.60
8	Mo Vaughn	.60
9	Barry Bonds	5.00
10	Gary Sheffield	1.25
11	Todd Hundley	.60
12	Frank Thomas	2.00
13	Sammy Sosa	2.50
14	Rafael Palmeiro	1.75
15	Alex Rodriguez	4.00
16	Mike Piazza	3.00
17	Ken Caminiti	.60
18	Chipper Jones	2.50
19	Manny Ramirez	2.00
20	Andruw Jones	2.00

1997 Upper Deck Memorable Moments

	NM/M
Complete Set (20):	20.00

Common Player:		.50
SERIES 1		
1	Andruw Jones	.75
2	Chipper Jones	1.00
3	Cal Ripken Jr.	2.50
4	Frank Thomas	.75
5	Manny Ramirez	.75
6	Mike Piazza	1.50
7	Mark McGwire	2.00
8	Barry Bonds	2.50
9	Ken Griffey Jr.	1.50
10	Alex Rodriguez	2.00
SERIES 2		
1	Ken Griffey Jr.	1.50
2	Albert Belle	.50
3	Derek Jeter	2.50
4	Greg Maddux	1.00
5	Tony Gwynn	1.00
6	Ryne Sandberg	1.00
7	Juan Gonzalez	.60
8	Roger Clemens	1.25
9	Jose Cruz Jr.	.50
10	Mo Vaughn	.50

Power Package

		NM/M
Complete Set (20):		30.00
Common Player:		1.00
1	Ken Griffey Jr.	3.50
2	Joe Carter	1.00
3	Rafael Palmeiro	1.75
4	Jay Buhner	1.00
5	Sammy Sosa	3.00
6	Fred McGriff	1.00
7	Jeff Bagwell	2.00
8	Albert Belle	1.00
9	Matt Williams	1.00
10	Mark McGwire	4.00
11	Gary Sheffield	1.25
12	Tim Salmon	1.00
13	Ryan Klesko	1.00
14	Manny Ramirez	2.00
15	Mike Piazza	3.50
16	Barry Bonds	5.00
17	Mo Vaughn	1.00
18	Jose Canseco	1.25
19	Juan Gonzalez	1.25
20	Frank Thomas	3.00

Rock Solid Foundation

JASON KENDALL

		NM/M
Complete Set (20):		7.50
Common Player:		.15
1	Alex Rodriguez	1.50
2	Rey Ordonez	.15
3	Derek Jeter	2.00
4	Darin Erstad	.35
5	Chipper Jones	1.25
6	Johnny Damon	.35
7	Ryan Klesko	.15
8	Charles Johnson	.15
9	Andy Pettitte	.30
10	Manny Ramirez	.75
11	Ivan Rodriguez	.65
12	Jason Kendall	.15
13	Rondell White	.15
14	Alex Ochoa	.15
15	Javy Lopez	.15

16	Pedro Martinez	.75
17	Carlos Delgado	.50
18	Paul Wilson	.15
19	Alan Benes	.15
20	Raul Mondesi	.15

Run Producers

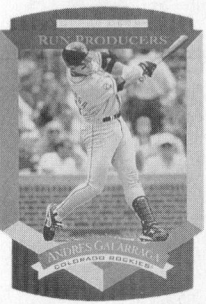

		NM/M
Complete Set (24):		45.00
Common Player:		.50
1	Ken Griffey Jr.	5.00
2	Barry Bonds	7.50
3	Albert Belle	.50
4	Mark McGwire	6.00
5	Frank Thomas	3.00
6	Juan Gonzalez	1.50
7	Brady Anderson	.50
8	Andres Galarraga	.50
9	Rafael Palmeiro	2.50
10	Alex Rodriguez	6.00
11	Jay Buhner	.50
12	Gary Sheffield	1.50
13	Sammy Sosa	4.00
14	Dante Bichette	.50
15	Mike Piazza	5.00
16	Manny Ramirez	3.00
17	Kenny Lofton	.50
18	Mo Vaughn	.50
19	Tim Salmon	.50
20	Chipper Jones	4.00
21	Jim Thome	2.00
22	Ken Caminiti	.50
23	Jeff Bagwell	3.00
24	Paul Molitor	3.00

1997 Upper Deck Star Attractions

		NM/M
Complete Set (20):		30.00
Common Player:		.30
Gold:		1.5X
1	Ken Griffey Jr.	3.00
2	Barry Bonds	5.00
3	Jeff Bagwell	2.00
4	Nomar Garciaparra	2.50
5	Tony Gwynn	2.50
6	Roger Clemens	2.75
7	Chipper Jones	2.50
8	Tino Martinez	.30
9	Albert Belle	.30
10	Kenny Lofton	.30
11	Alex Rodriguez	4.00
12	Mark McGwire	4.00
13	Cal Ripken Jr.	5.00
14	Larry Walker	.30
15	Mike Piazza	3.00
16	Frank Thomas	2.00
17	Juan Gonzalez	.65
18	Greg Maddux	2.50
19	Jose Cruz Jr.	.30
20	Mo Vaughn	.30

Ticket to Stardom

		NM/M
Complete Set (20):		35.00
Common Player:		.75
1	Chipper Jones	5.00
2	Jermaine Dye	.75

3	Rey Ordonez	.75
4	Alex Ochoa	.75
5	Derek Jeter	7.50
6	Ruben Rivera	.75
7	Billy Wagner	.75
8	Jason Kendall	.75
9	Darin Erstad	1.00
10	Alex Rodriguez	6.00
11	Bob Abreu	.75
12	Richard Hidalgo	.75
13	Karim Garcia	1.00
14	Andruw Jones	4.00
15	Carlos Delgado	1.50
16	Rocky Coppinger	.75
17	Jeff D'Amico	.75
18	Johnny Damon	2.00
19	John Wasdin	.75
20	Manny Ramirez	4.00

1997 Upper Deck Tony Gwynn Commemorative

NM/M

	Tony Gwynn	7.50

1997 Upper Deck UD3

NM/M

Complete Set (60):		30.00
Common Player:		.15
Pack (3):		1.50
Wax Box (24):		30.00
1	Mark McGwire	2.50
2	Brady Anderson	.15
3	Ken Griffey Jr.	2.00
4	Albert Belle	.15
5	Andres Galarraga	.15
6	Juan Gonzalez	.40
7	Jay Buhner	.15
8	Mo Vaughn	.15
9	Barry Bonds	3.00
10	Gary Sheffield	.40
11	Todd Hundley	.15
12	Ellis Burks	.15
13	Ken Caminiti	.15
14	Vinny Castilla	.15
15	Sammy Sosa	1.50
16	Frank Thomas	.75
17	Rafael Palmeiro	.65
18	Mike Piazza	2.00
19	Matt Williams	.15
20	Eddie Murray	.75
21	Roger Clemens	1.75
22	Tim Salmon	.15
23	Robin Ventura	.15
24	Ron Gant	.15
25	Cal Ripken Jr.	3.00
26	Bernie Williams	.15
27	Hideo Nomo	.40
28	Ivan Rodriguez	.65
29	John Smoltz	.15
30	Paul Molitor	.75
31	Greg Maddux	1.50
32	Raul Mondesi	.40
33	Roberto Alomar	.25
34	Barry Larkin	.15
35	Tony Gwynn	1.50

36	Jim Thome	.60
37	Kenny Lofton	.15
38	Jeff Bagwell	.75
39	Ozzie Smith	1.50
40	Kirby Puckett	1.50
41	Andruw Jones	.75
42	Vladimir Guerrero	.75
43	Edgar Renteria	.15
44	Luis Castillo	.15
45	Darin Erstad	.30
46	Nomar Garciaparra	1.50
47	Todd Greene	.15
48	Jason Kendall	.15
49	Rey Ordonez	.15
50	Alex Rodriguez	2.50
51	Manny Ramirez	.75
52	Todd Walker	.15
53	Ruben Rivera	.15
54	Andy Pettitte	.30
55	Derek Jeter	3.00
56	Todd Hollandsworth	.15
57	Rocky Coppinger	.15
58	Scott Rolen	.60
59	Jermaine Dye	.15
60	Chipper Jones	1.50

Generation Next

NM/M

Complete Set (20):		35.00
Common Player:		1.00
1	Alex Rodriguez	5.00
2	Vladimir Guerrero	2.50
3	Luis Castillo	1.00
4	Rey Ordonez	1.00
5	Andruw Jones	2.50
6	Darin Erstad	1.25
7	Edgar Renteria	1.00
8	Jason Kendall	1.00
9	Jermaine Dye	1.00
10	Chipper Jones	3.00
11	Rocky Coppinger	1.00
12	Andy Pettitte	1.25
13	Todd Greene	1.00
14	Todd Hollandsworth	1.00
15	Derek Jeter	6.00
16	Ruben Rivera	1.00
17	Todd Walker	1.00
18	Nomar Garciaparra	3.00
19	Scott Rolen	2.00
20	Manny Ramirez	2.50

Marquee Attraction

NM/M

Complete Set (10):		40.00
Common Player:		1.25
1	Ken Griffey Jr.	6.00
2	Mark McGwire	7.50
3	Juan Gonzalez	1.75
4	Barry Bonds	9.00
5	Frank Thomas	2.50
6	Albert Belle	1.25
7	Mike Piazza	6.00
8	Cal Ripken Jr.	9.00
9	Mo Vaughn	1.25
10	Alex Rodriguez	7.50

Superb Signatures

NM/M

Complete Set (4):		450.00
Common Autograph:		15.00
1	Ken Caminiti	45.00
2	Ken Griffey Jr.	150.00
3	Vladimir Guerrero	50.00
4	Derek Jeter	225.00

1998 Upper Deck

NM/M

Complete Set (750):		100.00
Complete Series 1 Set (270):		25.00
Complete Series 2 Set (270):		25.00
Complete Series 3 Set (210):		75.00
Common Emminent Prestige		
(601-630):		.25
Common Player:		.05
Series 1 or 2 Pack (12):		1.50
Series 3 Pack (10):		1.50
Series 1 or 2 Wax Box (24):		35.00
Series 3 Wax Box (24):		35.00
1	Tino Martinez	
	(History in the Making)	.05
2	Jimmy Key	
	(History in the Making)	.05
3	Jay Buhner	
	(History in the Making)	.05
4	Mark Gardner	
	(History in the Making)	.05
5	Greg Maddux	
	(History in the Making)	.25
6	Pedro Martinez	
	(History in the Making)	.20
7	Hideo Nomo, Shigetosi Hasegawa	
	(History in the Making)	.25
8	Sammy Sosa	
	(History in the Making)	.35
9	Mark McGwire	
	(Griffey Hot List)	.50
10	Ken Griffey Jr.	
	(Griffey Hot List)	.45
11	Larry Walker (Griffey Hot List)	.05
12	Tino Martinez	
	(Griffey Hot List)	.05
13	Mike Piazza (Griffey Hot List)	.40
14	Jose Cruz, Jr.	
	(Griffey Hot List)	.05
15	Tony Gwynn (Griffey Hot List)	.05
16	Greg Maddux	
	(Griffey Hot List)	.25
17	Roger Clemens	
	(Griffey Hot List)	.35
18	Alex Rodriguez	
	(Griffey Hot List)	.50
19	Shigetosi Hasegawa	.05
20	Eddie Murray	.50
21	Jason Dickson	.05
22	Darin Erstad	.25
23	Chuck Finley	.05
24	Dave Hollins	.05
25	Garret Anderson	.05
26	Michael Tucker	.05
27	Kenny Lofton	.25
28	Javier Lopez	.05
29	Fred McGriff	.05
30	Greg Maddux	.65
31	Jeff Blauser	.05
32	John Smoltz	.05
33	Mark Wohlers	.05
34	Scott Erickson	.05
35	Jimmy Key	.05
36	Harold Baines	.05
37	Randy Myers	.05
38	B.J. Surhoff	.05
39	Eric Davis	.05
40	Rafael Palmeiro	.35
41	Jeffrey Hammonds	.05
42	Mo Vaughn	.25
43	Tom Gordon	.05
44	Tim Naehring	.05
45	Darren Bragg	.05
46	Aaron Sele	.05
47	Troy O'Leary	.05
48	John Valentin	.05
49	Doug Glanville	.05
50	Ryne Sandberg	.65
51	Steve Trachsel	.05
52	Mark Grace	.05
53	Kevin Foster	.05
54	Kevin Tapani	.05
55	Kevin Orie	.05
56	Lyle Mouton	.05
57	Ray Durham	.05
58	Jaime Navarro	.05
59	Mike Cameron	.05
60	Albert Belle	.05

61	Doug Drabek	.05
62	Chris Snopek	.05
63	Eddie Taubensee	.05
64	Terry Pendleton	.05
65	Barry Larkin	.05
66	Willie Greene	.05
67	Deion Sanders	.05
68	Pokey Reese	.05
69	Jeff Shaw	.05
70	Jim Thome	.35
71	Orel Hershiser	.05
72	Omar Vizquel	.05
73	Brian Giles	.05
74	David Justice	.05
75	Bartolo Colon	.05
76	Sandy Alomar Jr.	.05
77	Neifi Perez	.05
78	Eric Young	.05
79	Vinny Castilla	.05
80	Dante Bichette	.05
81	Quinton McCracken	.05
82	Jamey Wright	.05
83	John Thomson	.05
84	Damion Easley	.05
85	Justin Thompson	.05
86	Willie Blair	.05
87	Raul Casanova	.05
88	Bobby Higginson	.05
89	Bubba Trammell	.05
90	Tony Clark	.05
91	Livan Hernandez	.05
92	Charles Johnson	.05
93	Edgar Renteria	.05
94	Alex Fernandez	.05
95	Gary Sheffield	.30
96	Moises Alou	.05
97	Tony Saunders	.05
98	Robb Nen	.05
99	Darryl Kile	.05
100	Craig Biggio	.05
101	Chris Holt	.05
102	Bob Abreu	.10
103	Luis Gonzalez	.05
104	Billy Wagner	.05
105	Brad Ausmus	.05
106	Chili Davis	.05
107	Tim Belcher	.05
108	Dean Palmer	.05
109	Jeff King	.05
110	Jose Rosado	.05
111	Mike Macfarlane	.05
112	Jay Bell	.05
113	Todd Worrell	.05
114	Chan Ho Park	.05
115	Raul Mondesi	.05
116	Brett Butler	.05
117	Greg Gagne	.05
118	Hideo Nomo	.25
119	Todd Zeile	.05
120	Eric Karros	.05
121	Cal Eldred	.05
122	Jeff D'Amico	.05
123	Antone Williamson	.05
124	Doug Jones	.05
125	Dave Nilsson	.05
126	Gerald Williams	.05
127	Fernando Vina	.05
128	Ron Coomer	.05
129	Matt Lawton	.05
130	Paul Molitor	.50
131	Todd Walker	.05
132	Rick Aguilera	.05
133	Brad Radke	.05
134	Bob Tewksbury	.05
135	Vladimir Guerrero	.50
136	Tony Gwynn	
	(Define The Game)	.25
137	Roger Clemens	
	(Define The Game)	.35
138	Dennis Eckersley	
	(Define The Game)	.15
139	Brady Anderson	
	(Define The Game)	.05
140	Ken Griffey Jr.	
	(Define The Game)	.40
141	Derek Jeter	
	(Define The Game)	.75
142	Ken Caminiti	
	(Define The Game)	.05
143	Frank Thomas	
	(Define The Game)	.20
144	Barry Bonds	
	(Define The Game)	.75
145	Cal Ripken Jr.	
	(Define The Game)	.75
146	Alex Rodriguez	
	(Define The Game)	.50
147	Greg Maddux	
	(Define The Game)	.25
148	Kenny Lofton	
	(Define The Game)	.05
149	Mike Piazza	
	(Define The Game)	.40
150	Mark McGwire	
	(Define The Game)	.50
151	Andruw Jones	
	(Define The Game)	.20
152	Rusty Greer	
	(Define The Game)	.05
153	F.P. Santangelo	
	(Define The Game)	.05
154	Mike Lansing	.05
155	Lee Smith	.05

156 Carlos Perez .05
157 Pedro Martinez .50
158 Ryan McGuire .05
159 F.P. Santangelo .05
160 Rondell White .05
161 Takashi Kashiwada **RC** .05
162 Butch Huskey .05
163 Edgardo Alfonzo .05
164 John Franco .05
165 Todd Hundley .05
166 Rey Ordonez .05
167 Armando Reynoso .05
168 John Olerud .05
169 Bernie Williams .05
170 Andy Pettitte .15
171 Wade Boggs .65
172 Paul O'Neill .05
173 Cecil Fielder .05
174 Charlie Hayes .05
175 David Cone .05
176 Hideki Irabu .05
177 Mark Bellhorn .05
178 Steve Karsay .05
179 Damon Mashore .05
180 Jason McDonald .05
181 Scott Spiezio .05
182 Ariel Prieto .05
183 Jason Giambi .30
184 Wendell Magee .05
185 Rico Brogna .05
186 Garrett Stephenson .05
187 Wayne Gomes .05
188 Ricky Bottalico .05
189 Mickey Morandini .05
190 Mike Lieberthal .05
191 Kevin Polcovich **RC** .05
192 Francisco Cordova .05
193 Kevin Young .05
194 Jon Lieber .05
195 Kevin Elster .05
196 Tony Womack .05
197 Lou Collier .05
198 Mike Defelice **RC** .05
199 Gary Gaetti .05
200 Dennis Eckersley .40
201 Alan Benes .05
202 Willie McGee .05
203 Ron Gant .05
204 Fernando Valenzuela .05
205 Mark McGwire 1.00
206 Archi Cianfrocco .05
207 Andy Ashby .05
208 Steve Finley .05
209 Quilvio Veras .05
210 Ken Caminiti .05
211 Rickey Henderson .50
212 Joey Hamilton .05
213 Derrek Lee .30
214 Bill Mueller .05
215 Shawn Estes .05
216 J.T. Snow .05
217 Mark Gardner .05
218 Terry Mulholland .05
219 Dante Powell .05
220 Jeff Kent .05
221 Jamie Moyer .05
222 Joey Cora .05
223 Jeff Fassero .05
224 Dennis Martinez .05
225 Ken Griffey Jr. .75
226 Edgar Martinez .05
227 Russ Davis .05
228 Dan Wilson .05
229 Will Clark .05
230 Ivan Rodriguez .40
231 Benji Gil .05
232 Lee Stevens .05
233 Mickey Tettleton .05
234 Julio Santana .05
235 Rusty Greer .05
236 Bobby Witt .05
237 Ed Sprague .05
238 Pat Hentgen .05
239 Kevin Escobar .05
240 Joe Carter .05
241 Carlos Delgado .25
242 Shannon Stewart .05
243 Benito Santiago .05
244 Tino Martinez (Season Highlights) .05
245 Ken Griffey Jr. (Season Highlights) .40
246 Kevin Brown (Season Highlights) .05
247 Ryne Sandberg (Season Highlights) .35
248 Mo Vaughn (Season Highlights) .05
249 Darryl Hamilton (Season Highlights) .05
250 Randy Johnson (Season Highlights) .20
251 Steve Finley (Season Highlights) .05
252 Bobby Higginson (Season Highlights) .05
253 Brett Tomko (Star Rookie) .05
254 Mark Kotsay (Star Rookie) .05
255 Jose Guillen (Star Rookie) .05
256 Elieser Marrero (Star Rookie) .05
257 Dennis Reyes (Star Rookie) .05
258 Richie Sexson (Star Rookie) .05
259 Pat Cline (Star Rookie) .05
260 Todd Helton (Star Rookie) .50
261 Juan Melo (Star Rookie) .05
262 Matt Morris (Star Rookie) .05
263 Jeremi Gonzalez (Star Rookie) .05
264 Jeff Abbott (Star Rookie) .05
265 Aaron Boone (Star Rookie) .05
266 Todd Dunwoody (Star Rookie) .05
267 Jaret Wright (Star Rookie) .05
268 Derrick Gibson (Star Rookie) .05
269 Mario Valdez (Star Rookie) .05
270 Fernando Tatis (Star Rookie) .05
271 Craig Counsell (Star Rookie) .05
272 Brad Rigby (Star Rookie) .05
273 Danny Clyburn (Star Rookie) .05
274 Brian Rose (Star Rookie) .05
275 Miguel Tejada (Star Rookie) .15
276 Jason Varitek (Star Rookie) .05
277 David Dellucci **RC** (Star Rookie) .15
278 Michael Coleman (Star Rookie) .05
279 Adam Riggs (Star Rookie) .05
280 Ben Grieve (Star Rookie) .05
281 Brad Fullmer (Star Rookie) .05
282 Ken Cloude (Star Rookie) .05
283 Tom Evans (Star Rookie) .05
284 Kevin Millwood **RC** (Star Rookie) .75
285 Paul Konerko (Star Rookie) .15
286 Juan Encarnacion (Star Rookie) .05
287 Chris Carpenter (Star Rookie) .05
288 Tom Fordham (Star Rookie) .05
289 Gary DiSarcina .05
290 Tim Salmon .05
291 Troy Percival .05
292 Todd Greene .05
293 Ken Hill .05
294 Dennis Springer .05
295 Jim Edmonds .05
296 Allen Watson .05
297 Brian Anderson .05
298 Keith Lockhart .05
299 Tom Glavine .20
300 Chipper Jones .75
301 Randall Simon .05
302 Mark Lemke .05
303 Ryan Klesko .05
304 Denny Neagle .05
305 Andruw Jones .50
306 Mike Mussina .30
307 Brady Anderson .05
308 Chris Hoiles .05
309 Mike Bordick .05
310 Cal Ripken Jr. 1.50
311 Geronimo Berroa .05
312 Armando Benitez .05
313 Roberto Alomar .25
314 Tim Wakefield .05
315 Reggie Jefferson .05
316 Jeff Frye .05
317 Scott Hatteberg .05
318 Steve Avery .05
319 Robinson Checo .05
320 Nomar Garciaparra .65
321 Lance Johnson .05
322 Tyler Houston .05
323 Mark Clark .05
324 Terry Adams .05
325 Sammy Sosa .65
326 Scott Servais .05
327 Manny Alexander .05
328 Norberto Martin .05
329 Scott Eyre **RC** .05
330 Frank Thomas .50
331 Robin Ventura .05
332 Matt Karchner .05
333 Keith Foulke .05
334 James Baldwin .05
335 Chris Stynes .05
336 Bret Boone .05
337 Jon Nunnally .05
338 Dave Burba .05
339 Eduardo Perez .05
340 Reggie Sanders .05
341 Mike Remlinger .05
342 Pat Watkins .05
343 Chad Ogea .05
344 John Smiley .05
345 Kenny Lofton .05
346 Jose Mesa .05
347 Charles Nagy .05
348 Bruce Aven .05
349 Enrique Wilson .05
350 Manny Ramirez .50
351 Jerry DiPoto .05
352 Ellis Burks .05
353 Kirt Manwaring .05
354 Vinny Castilla .05
355 Larry Walker .05
356 Kevin Ritz .05
357 Pedro Astacio .05
358 Scott Sanders .05
359 Deivi Cruz .05
360 Brian L. Hunter .05
361 Pedro Martinez (History in the Making) .20
362 Tom Glavine (History in the Making) .05
363 Willie McGee (History in the Making) .05
364 J.T. Snow (History in the Making) .05
365 Rusty Greer (History in the Making) .05
366 Mike Grace (History in the Making) .05
367 Tony Clark (History in the Making) .05
368 Ben Grieve (History in the Making) .05
369 Gary Sheffield (History in the Making) .10
370 Joe Oliver .05
371 Todd Jones .05
372 Frank Catalanotto **RC** .10
373 Brian Moehler .05
374 Cliff Floyd .05
375 Bobby Bonilla .05
376 Al Leiter .05
377 Josh Booty .05
378 Darren Daulton .05
379 Jay Powell .05
380 Felix Heredia .05
381 Jim Eisenreich .05
382 Richard Hidalgo .05
383 Mike Hampton .05
384 Shane Reynolds .05
385 Jeff Bagwell .50
386 Derek Bell .05
387 Ricky Gutierrez .05
388 Bill Spiers .05
389 Jose Offerman .05
390 Johnny Damon .25
391 Jermaine Dye .05
392 Jeff Montgomery .05
393 Glendon Rusch .05
394 Mike Sweeney .05
395 Kevin Appier .05
396 Joe Vitiello .05
397 Ramon Martinez .05
398 Darren Dreifort .05
399 Wilton Guerrero .05
400 Mike Piazza .75
401 Eddie Murray .50
402 Ismael Valdes .05
403 Todd Hollandsworth .05
404 Mark Loretta .05
405 Jeromy Burnitz .05
406 Jeff Cirillo .05
407 Scott Karl .05
408 Mike Matheny .05
409 Jose Valentin .05
410 John Jaha .05
411 Terry Steinbach .05
412 Torii Hunter .05
413 Pat Meares .05
414 Marty Cordova .05
415 Jaret Wright (Postseason Headliners) .05
416 Mike Mussina (Postseason Headliners) .10
417 John Smoltz (Postseason Headliners) .05
418 Devon White (Postseason Headliners) .05
419 Denny Neagle (Postseason Headliners) .05
420 Livan Hernandez (Postseason Headliners) .05
421 Kevin Brown (Postseason Headliners) .05
422 Marquis Grissom (Postseason Headliners) .05
423 Mike Mussina (Postseason Headliners) .10
424 Eric Davis (Postseason Headliners) .05
425 Tony Fernandez (Postseason Headliners) .05
426 Moises Alou (Postseason Headliners) .05
427 Sandy Alomar Jr. (Postseason Headliners) .05
428 Gary Sheffield (Postseason Headliners) .10
429 Jaret Wright (Postseason Headliners) .05
430 Livan Hernandez (Postseason Headliners) .05
431 Chad Ogea (Postseason Headliners) .05
432 Edgar Renteria (Postseason Headliners) .05
433 LaTroy Hawkins .05
434 Rich Robertson .05
435 Chuck Knoblauch .05
436 Jose Vidro .05
437 Dustin Hermanson .05
438 Jim Bullinger .05
439 Orlando Cabrera (Star Rookie) .10
440 Vladimir Guerrero .50
441 Ugueth Urbina .05
442 Brian McRae .05
443 Matt Franco .05
444 Bobby Jones .05
445 Bernard Gilkey .05
446 Dave Mlicki .05
447 Brian Bohanon .05
448 Mel Rojas .05
449 Tim Raines .05
450 Derek Jeter 1.50
451 Roger Clemens (Upper Echelon) .35
452 Nomar Garciaparra (Upper Echelon) .35
453 Mike Piazza (Upper Echelon) .40
454 Mark McGwire (Upper Echelon) .50
455 Ken Griffey Jr. (Upper Echelon) .40
456 Larry Walker (Upper Echelon) .05
457 Alex Rodriguez (Upper Echelon) .50
458 Tony Gwynn (Upper Echelon) .25
459 Frank Thomas (Upper Echelon) .20
460 Tino Martinez .05
461 Chad Curtis .05
462 Ramiro Mendoza .05
463 Joe Girardi .05
464 David Wells .05
465 Mariano Rivera .15
466 Willie Adams .05
467 George Williams .05
468 Dave Telgheder .05
469 Dave Magadan .05
470 Matt Stairs .05
471 Billy Taylor .05
472 Jimmy Haynes .05
473 Gregg Jefferies .05
474 Midre Cummings .05
475 Curt Schilling .15
476 Mike Grace .05
477 Mark Leiter .05
478 Matt Beech .05
479 Scott Rolen .35
480 Jason Kendall .05
481 Esteban Loaiza .05
482 Jermaine Allensworth .05
483 Mark Smith .05
484 Jason Schmidt .05
485 Jose Guillen .05
486 Al Martin .05
487 Delino DeShields .05
488 Todd Stottlemyre .05
489 Brian Jordan .05
490 Ray Lankford .05
491 Matt Morris .05
492 Royce Clayton .05
493 John Mabry .05
494 Wally Joyner .05
495 Trevor Hoffman .05
496 Chris Gomez .05
497 Sterling Hitchcock .05
498 Pete Smith .05
499 Greg Vaughn .05
500 Tony Gwynn .65
501 Will Cunnane .05
502 Darryl Hamilton .05
503 Brian Johnson .05
504 Kirk Rueter .05
505 Barry Bonds 1.50
506 Osvaldo Fernandez .05
507 Stan Javier .05
508 Julian Tavarez .05
509 Rich Aurilia .05
510 Alex Rodriguez 1.00
511 David Segui .05
512 Rich Amaral .05
513 Raul Ibanez .05
514 Jay Buhner .05
515 Randy Johnson .50
516 Heathcliff Slocumb .05
517 Tony Saunders .05
518 Kevin Elster .05
519 John Burkett .05
520 Juan Gonzalez .25
521 John Wetteland .05
522 Domingo Cedeno .05
523 Darren Oliver .05
524 Roger Pavlik .05
525 Jose Cruz Jr. .05
526 Woody Williams .05
527 Alex Gonzalez .05
528 Robert Person .05
529 Juan Guzman .05
530 Roger Clemens .70
531 Shawn Green .20
532 Cordova, Ricon, Smith (Season Highlights) .05
533 Nomar Garciaparra (Season Highlights) .35
534 Roger Clemens (Season Highlights) .35
535 Mark McGwire (Season Highlights) .50
536 Larry Walker (Season Highlights) .05
537 Mike Piazza (Season Highlights) .40
538 Curt Schilling (Season Highlights) .05
539 Tony Gwynn (Season Highlights) .25
540 Ken Griffey Jr. (Season Highlights) .40
541 Carl Pavano (Star Rookies) .05
542 Shane Monahan (Star Rookies) .05
543 Gabe Kapler **RC** (Star Rookies) .25
544 Eric Milton (Star Rookies) .05
545 Gary Matthews Jr. **RC** (Star Rookies) .05
546 Mike Kinkade **RC** (Star Rookies) .25
547 Ryan Christenson **RC** (Star Rookies) .10

548 Corey Koskie **RC** (Star Rookies) .25
549 Norm Hutchins (Star Rookies) .05
550 Russell Branyan (Star Rookies) .05
551 Masato Yoshii **RC** (Star Rookies) .25
552 Jesus Sanchez **RC** (Star Rookies) .05
553 Anthony Sanders (Star Rookies) .05
554 Edwin Diaz (Star Rookies) .05
555 Gabe Alvarez (Star Rookies) .05
556 Carlos Lee **RC** (Star Rookies) .25
557 Mike Darr (Star Rookies) .05
558 Kerry Wood (Star Rookies) .20
559 Carlos Guillen (Star Rookies) .05
560 Sean Casey (Star Rookies) .15
561 Manny Aybar **RC** (Star Rookies) .05
562 Octavio Dotel (Star Rookies) .05
563 Jarrod Washburn (Star Rookies) .05
564 Mark L. Johnson (Star Rookies) .05
565 Ramon Hernandez (Star Rookies) .05
566 Rich Butler **RC** (Star Rookies) .05
567 Mike Caruso (Star Rookies) .05
568 Cliff Politte (Star Rookies) .05
569 Scott Elarton (Star Rookies) .05
570 Magglio Ordonez **RC** (Star Rookies) 1.50
571 Adam Butler **RC** (Star Rookies) .05
572 Marlon Anderson (Star Rookies) .05
573 Julio Ramirez **RC** (Star Rookies) .05
574 Darron Ingram **RC** (Star Rookies) .05
575 Bruce Chen (Star Rookies) .05
576 Steve Woodard **RC** (Star Rookies) .05
577 Hiram Bocachica (Star Rookies) .05
578 Kevin Witt (Star Rookies) .05
579 Javier Vazquez (Star Rookies) .10
580 Alex Gonzalez (Star Rookies) .05
581 Brian Powell (Star Rookies) .05
582 Wes Helms (Star Rookies) .05
583 Ron Wright (Star Rookies) .05
584 Rafael Medina (Star Rookies) .05
585 Daryle Ward (Star Rookies) .05
586 Geoff Jenkins (Star Rookies) .05
587 Preston Wilson (Star Rookies) .10
588 Jim Chamblee **RC** (Star Rookies) .05
589 Mike Lowell **RC** (Star Rookies) 2.00
590 A.J. Hinch (Star Rookies) .05
591 Francisco Cordero **RC** (Star Rookies) .10
592 Rolando Arrojo **RC** (Star Rookies) .25
593 Braden Looper (Star Rookies) .05
594 Sidney Ponson (Star Rookies) .05
595 Matt Clement (Star Rookies) .05
596 Carlton Loewer (Star Rookies) .05
597 Brian Meadows (Star Rookies) .05
598 Danny Klassen (Star Rookies) .05
599 Larry Sutton (Star Rookies) .05
600 Travis Lee (Star Rookies) .15
601 Randy Johnson (Eminent Prestige) 1.50
602 Greg Maddux (Eminent Prestige) 2.00
603 Roger Clemens (Eminent Prestige) 2.25
604 Jaret Wright (Eminent Prestige) .25
605 Mike Piazza (Eminent Prestige) 2.50
606 Tino Martinez (Eminent Prestige) .25
607 Frank Thomas (Eminent Prestige) 1.50
608 Mo Vaughn (Eminent Prestige) .25
609 Todd Helton (Eminent Prestige) 1.00
610 Mark McGwire (Eminent Prestige) 3.00
611 Jeff Bagwell (Eminent Prestige) 1.50
612 Travis Lee (Eminent Prestige) .40
613 Scott Rolen (Eminent Prestige) 1.00
614 Cal Ripken Jr. (Eminent Prestige) 4.00
615 Chipper Jones (Eminent Prestige) 2.00
616 Nomar Garciaparra (Eminent Prestige) 2.00
617 Alex Rodriguez (Eminent Prestige) 3.00
618 Derek Jeter (Eminent Prestige) 4.00
619 Tony Gwynn (Eminent Prestige) 2.00
620 Ken Griffey Jr. (Eminent Prestige) 2.50
621 Kenny Lofton (Eminent Prestige) .25
622 Juan Gonzalez (Eminent Prestige) .75
623 Jose Cruz Jr. (Eminent Prestige) .25
624 Larry Walker (Eminent Prestige) .25
625 Barry Bonds (Eminent Prestige) 4.00
626 Ben Grieve (Eminent Prestige) .25
627 Andruw Jones (Eminent Prestige) 1.50
628 Vladimir Guerrero (Eminent Prestige) 1.50
629 Paul Konerko (Eminent Prestige) .50
630 Paul Molitor (Eminent Prestige) 1.50
631 Cecil Fielder .05
632 Jack McDowell .05
633 Mike James .05
634 Brian Anderson .05
635 Jay Bell .05
636 Devon White .05
637 Andy Stankiewicz .05
638 Tony Batista .05
639 Omar Daal .05
640 Matt Williams .05
641 Brent Brede .05
642 Jorge Fabregas .05
643 Karim Garcia .10
644 Felix Rodriguez .05
645 Andy Benes .05
646 Willie Blair .05
647 Jeff Suppan .05
648 Yamil Benitez .05
649 Walt Weiss .05
650 Andres Galarraga .05
651 Doug Drabek .05
652 Ozzie Guillen .05
653 Joe Carter .05
654 Dennis Eckersley .40
655 Pedro Martinez .50
656 Jim Leyritz .05
657 Henry Rodriguez .05
658 Rod Beck .05
659 Mickey Morandini .05
660 Jeff Blauser .05
661 Ruben Sierra .05
662 Mike Sirotka .05
663 Pete Harnisch .05
664 Damian Jackson .05
665 Dmitri Young .05
666 Steve Cooke .05
667 Geronimo Berroa .05
668 Shawon Dunston .05
669 Mike Jackson .05
670 Travis Fryman .05
671 Dwight Gooden .05
672 Paul Assenmacher .05
673 Eric Plunk .05
674 Mike Lansing .05
675 Darryl Kile .05
676 Luis Gonzalez .05
677 Frank Castillo .05
678 Joe Randa .05
679 Bip Roberts .05
680 Derrek Lee .30
681a Mike Piazza (Marlins) 2.00
681b Mike Piazza (Mets) 1.00
682 Sean Berry .05
683 Ramon Garcia .05
684 Carl Everett .05
685 Moises Alou .05
686 Hal Morris .05
687 Jeff Conine .05
688 Gary Sheffield .25
689 Jose Vizcaino .05
690 Charles Johnson .05
691 Bobby Bonilla .05
692 Marquis Grissom .05
693 Alex Ochoa .05
694 Mike Morgan .05
695 Orlando Merced .05
696 David Ortiz .30
697 Brent Gates .05
698 Otis Nixon .05
699 Trey Moore .05
700 Derrick May .05
701 Rich Becker .05
702 Al Leiter .05
703 Chili Davis .05
704 Scott Brosius .05
705 Chuck Knoblauch .05
706 Kenny Rogers .05
707 Mike Blowers .05
708 Mike Fetters .05
709 Tom Candiotti .05
710 Rickey Henderson .50
711 Bob Abreu .05
712 Mark Lewis .05
713 Doug Glanville .05
714 Desi Relaford .05
715 Kent Mercker .05
716 J. Kevin Brown .05
717 James Mouton .05
718 Mark Langston .05
719 Greg Myers .05
720 Orel Hershiser .05
721 Charlie Hayes .05
722 Robb Nen .05
723 Glenallen Hill .05
724 Tony Saunders .05
725 Wade Boggs .65
726 Kevin Stocker .05
727 Wilson Alvarez .05
728 Albie Lopez .05
729 Dave Martinez .05
730 Fred McGriff .05
731 Quinton McCracken .05
732 Bryan Rekar .05
733 Paul Sorrento .05
734 Roberto Hernandez .05
735 Bubba Trammell .05
736 Miguel Cairo .05
737 John Flaherty .05
738 Terrell Wade .05
739 Roberto Kelly .05
740 Mark Mclemore (McLemore) .05
741 Danny Patterson .05
742 Aaron Sele .05
743 Tony Fernandez .05
744 Randy Myers .05
745 Jose Canseco .30
746 Darrin Fletcher .05
747 Mike Stanley .05
748 Marquis Grissom (Season Highlights) .05
749 Fred McGriff (Season Highlights) .05
750 Travis Lee (Season Highlights) .05

Amazing Greats

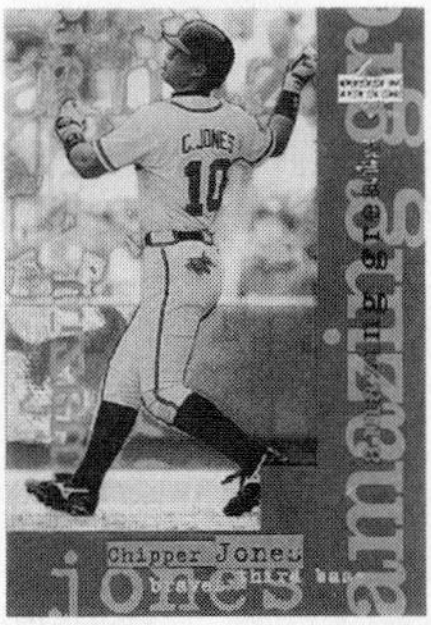

NM/M

Complete Set (30): 75.00
Common Player: .60
Die-Cuts (250): 8X

1 Ken Griffey Jr. 5.00
2 Derek Jeter 7.50
3 Alex Rodriguez 6.00
4 Paul Molitor 3.00
5 Jeff Bagwell 3.00
6 Larry Walker .60
7 Kenny Lofton .60
8 Cal Ripken Jr. 7.50
9 Juan Gonzalez 1.50
10 Chipper Jones 4.00
11 Greg Maddux 4.00
12 Roberto Alomar 1.25
13 Mike Piazza 5.00
14 Andres Galarraga .60
15 Barry Bonds 7.50
16 Andy Pettitte 1.25
17 Nomar Garciaparra 4.00
18 Hideki Irabu .60
19 Tony Gwynn 4.00
20 Frank Thomas 3.00
21 Roger Clemens 4.50
22 Sammy Sosa 5.00
23 Jose Cruz, Jr. .60
24 Manny Ramirez 3.00
25 Mark McGwire 6.00
26 Randy Johnson 3.00
27 Mo Vaughn .60
28 Gary Sheffield 1.50
29 Andruw Jones 3.00
30 Albert Belle .60

A Piece of the Action

NM/M

Complete Set (14): 250.00
Common Player: 5.00
Inserted 1:2,500

SERIES 1

(1) Jay Buhner/Bat 20.00
(2) Tony Gwynn/Bat 25.00
(3) Tony Gwynn/Jsy 25.00
(4) Todd Hollandsworth/Bat 5.00
(5) Todd Hollandsworth/Jsy 5.00
(6) Greg Maddux/Jsy 40.00
(7) Alex Rodriguez/Bat 40.00
(8) Alex Rodriguez/Jsy 40.00
(9) Gary Sheffield/Bat 15.00
(10) Gary Sheffield/Jsy 15.00

SERIES 2

RA Roberto Alomar 35.00
JB Jay Buhner 10.00

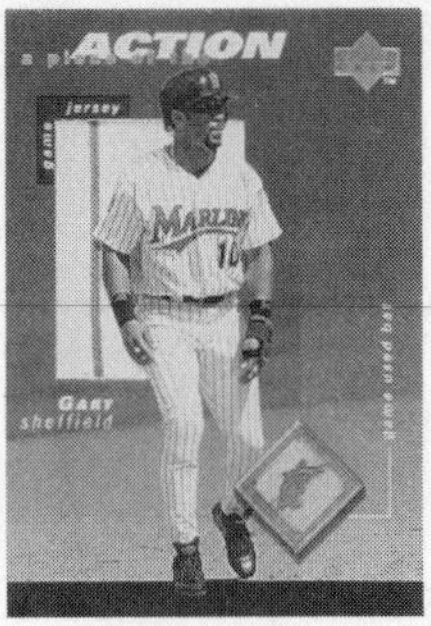

AJ Andruw Jones 20.00
GS Gary Sheffield 15.00

Blue Chip Prospects

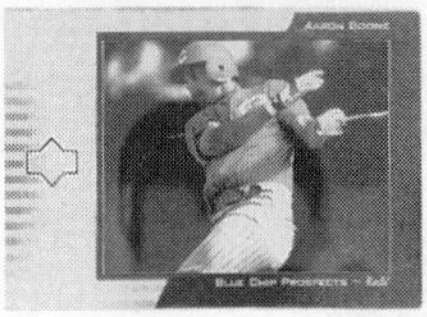

NM/M

Complete Set (30): 75.00
Common Player: 2.00

1 Nomar Garciaparra 8.00
2 Scott Rolen 5.00
3 Jason Dickson 2.00
4 Darin Erstad 3.00
5 Brad Fullmer 2.00
6 Jaret Wright 2.00
7 Justin Thompson 2.00
8 Matt Morris 2.00
9 Fernando Tatis 2.00
10 Alex Rodriguez 12.00
11 Todd Helton 6.50
12 Andy Pettitte 2.50
13 Jose Cruz Jr. 2.00
14 Mark Kotsay 2.00
15 Derek Jeter 15.00
16 Paul Konerko 3.00
17 Todd Dunwoody 2.00
18 Vladimir Guerrero 6.00
19 Miguel Tejada 5.00
20 Chipper Jones 8.00
21 Kevin Orie 2.00
22 Juan Encarnacion 2.00
23 Brian Rose 2.00
24 Andruw Jones 6.00
25 Livan Hernandez 2.00
26 Brian Giles 2.00
27 Brett Tomko 2.00
28 Jose Guillen 2.00
29 Aaron Boone 2.00
30 Ben Grieve 2.00

Clearly Dominant

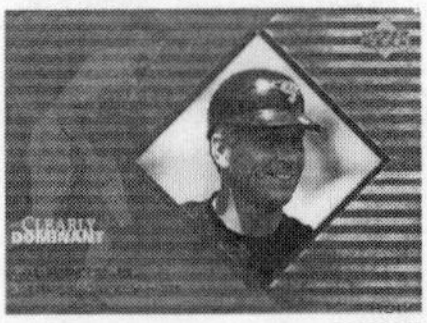

NM/M

Complete Set (30): 300.00
Common Player: 3.00
Production 250 Sets

1 Mark McGwire 25.00
2 Derek Jeter 30.00
3 Alex Rodriguez 25.00
4 Paul Molitor 12.00
5 Jeff Bagwell 12.00
6 Ivan Rodriguez 10.00
7 Kenny Lofton 3.00
8 Cal Ripken Jr. 30.00
9 Albert Belle 3.00
10 Chipper Jones 15.00
11 Gary Sheffield 5.00
12 Roberto Alomar 4.00
13 Mo Vaughn 3.00
14 Andres Galarraga 3.00
15 Nomar Garciaparra 15.00
16 Randy Johnson 12.00
17 Mike Mussina 6.00
18 Greg Maddux 15.00
19 Tony Gwynn 15.00
20 Frank Thomas 12.00
21 Roger Clemens 17.50
22 Dennis Eckersley 10.00
23 Juan Gonzalez 6.00

24	Tino Martinez	3.00
25	Andruw Jones	12.00
26	Larry Walker	3.00
27	Ken Caminiti	3.00
28	Mike Piazza	20.00
29	Barry Bonds	30.00
30	Ken Griffey Jr.	20.00

Ken Griffey Jr.'s HR Chronicles

	NM/M
Complete Set (56):	45.00
Common Card:	1.00
Inserted 1:9	
1-56	Ken Griffey Jr.

1998 Upper Deck Mark McGwire's Chase for 62

	NM/M
Complete Boxed Set:	7.50
Common Card:	.50
1-30	Mark McGwire	.50
---	Mark McGwire (3-1/2" x 5" HR #61/62)	3.00

National Pride

	NM/M
Complete Set (42):	65.00
Common Player:	.75
1	Dave Nilsson	.75
2	Larry Walker	.75
3	Edgar Renteria	.75
4	Jose Canseco	1.25
5	Rey Ordonez	.75
6	Rafael Palmeiro	2.50
7	Livan Hernandez	.75
8	Andruw Jones	3.00
9	Manny Ramirez	3.00
10	Sammy Sosa	4.00
11	Raul Mondesi	.75
12	Moises Alou	.75
13	Pedro Martinez	3.00
14	Vladimir Guerrero	3.00
15	Chili Davis	.75
16	Hideo Nomo	1.50
17	Hideki Irabu	.75
18	Shigetosi Hasegawa	.75
19	Takashi Kashiwada	.75
20	Chan Ho Park	.75
21	Fernando Valenzuela	.75
22	Vinny Castilla	.75
23	Armando Reynoso	.75
24	Karim Garcia	1.00
25	Marvin Benard	.75
26	Mariano Rivera	1.00

27	Juan Gonzalez	1.50
28	Roberto Alomar	1.00
29	Ivan Rodriguez	2.50
30	Carlos Delgado	1.00
31	Bernie Williams	.75
32	Edgar Martinez	.75
33	Frank Thomas	3.00
34	Barry Bonds	7.50
35	Mike Piazza	5.00
36	Chipper Jones	4.00
37	Cal Ripken Jr.	7.50
38	Alex Rodriguez	6.00
39	Ken Griffey Jr.	5.00
40	Andres Galarraga	.75
41	Omar Vizquel	.75
42	Ozzie Guillen	.75

Prime Nine

	NM/M
Complete Set (60):	50.00
Common Griffey:	1.00
Common Piazza:	1.25
Common Thomas:	.60
Common McGwire:	1.25
Common Ripken:	1.75
Common Gonzalez:	.50
Common Gwynn:	.70
Common Bonds:	1.75
Common Maddux:	.70
Inserted 1:5	
PN1	Ken Griffey Jr./1989-1992	1.00
PN2	Ken Griffey Jr./1993	1.00
PN3	Ken Griffey Jr./1994	1.00
PN4	Ken Griffey Jr./1995	1.00
PN5	Ken Griffey Jr./1996	1.00
PN6	Ken Griffey Jr./1997	1.00
PN7	Ken Griffey Jr./1997	1.00
PN8	Mike Piazza/1991	1.00
PN9	Mike Piazza/1992	1.00
PN10	Mike Piazza/1993	1.00
PN11	Mike Piazza/1994	1.00
PN12	Mike Piazza/1995	1.00
PN13	Mike Piazza/1996	1.00
PN14	Mike Piazza/1997	1.00
PN15	Frank Thomas/1991	.60
PN16	Frank Thomas/1992	.60
PN17	Frank Thomas/1993	.60
PN18	Frank Thomas/1994	.60
PN19	Frank Thomas/1995	.60
PN20	Frank Thomas/1996	.60
PN21	Frank Thomas/1997	.60
PN22	Mark McGwire/1987	1.25
PN23	Mark McGwire/1988-1990	1.25
PN24	Mark McGwire/1992	1.25
PN25	Mark McGwire/1995-1996	1.25
PN26	Mark McGwire/1997	1.25
PN27	Mark McGwire/1997	1.25
PN28	Mark McGwire/1997	1.25
PN29	Cal Ripken Jr./1982	1.75
PN30	Cal Ripken Jr./1983	1.75
PN31	Cal Ripken Jr./1989	1.75
PN32	Cal Ripken Jr./1991	1.75
PN33	Cal Ripken Jr./1995	1.75
PN34	Cal Ripken Jr./1996	1.75
PN35	Cal Ripken Jr./1997	1.75
PN36	Juan Gonzalez/1992	.50
PN37	Juan Gonzalez/1993	.50
PN38	Juan Gonzalez/1994	.50
PN39	Juan Gonzalez/1995	.50
PN40	Juan Gonzalez/1996	.50
PN41	Juan Gonzalez/1996	.50
PN42	Juan Gonzalez/1997	.50
PN43	Tony Gwynn/1984	.75
PN44	Tony Gwynn/1987-1989	.75
PN45	Tony Gwynn/1990-1993	.75
PN46	Tony Gwynn/1994	.75
PN47	Tony Gwynn/1996	.75
PN48	Tony Gwynn/1997	.75
PN49	Tony Gwynn/1997	.75
PN50	Barry Bonds/1986-1992	1.75
PN51	Barry Bonds/1990-1993	1.75
PN52	Barry Bonds/1993	1.75
PN53	Barry Bonds/1994	1.75
PN54	Barry Bonds/1996	1.75
PN55	Barry Bonds/1997	1.75
PN56	Greg Maddux/1992	.75
PN57	Greg Maddux/1993-1994	.75
PN58	Greg Maddux/1995	.75
PN59	Greg Maddux/1996	.75
PN60	Greg Maddux/1997	.75

Rookie Edition Preview

	NM/M
Complete Set (10):	5.00
Common Player:	.50
1	Nomar Garciaparra	2.00
2	Scott Rolen	1.00
3	Mark Kotsay	.50
4	Todd Helton	1.50
5	Paul Konerko	.60
6	Juan Encarnacion	.50
7	Brad Fullmer	.50
8	Miguel Tejada	.65
9	Richard Hidalgo	.50
10	Ben Grieve	.50

Superstar Xcitement

	NM/M
Complete Set (10):	275.00
Common Player:	10.00
Production 250 Sets	
PZ1	Jose Cruz Jr.	10.00
PZ2	Frank Thomas	25.00
PZ3	Juan Gonzalez	10.00
PZ4	Mike Piazza	40.00
PZ5	Mark McGwire	45.00
PZ6	Barry Bonds	50.00
PZ7	Greg Maddux	35.00
PZ8	Alex Rodriguez	45.00
PZ9	Nomar Garciaparra	35.00
PZ10	Ken Griffey Jr.	40.00

Tape Measure Titans

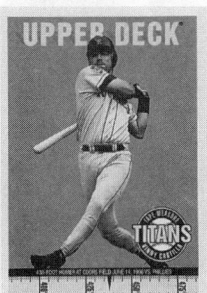

	NM/M
Complete Set (30):	45.00
Common Player:	.40
Inserted 1:23	
Gold:	1.5X
1	Mark McGwire	
2	Andres Galarraga	.40
3	Jeff Bagwell	2.00
4	Larry Walker	.40
5	Frank Thomas	2.50
6	Rafael Palmeiro	1.50

7	Nomar Garciaparra	4.00
8	Mo Vaughn	.40
9	Albert Belle	.60
10	Ken Griffey Jr.	4.00
11	Manny Ramirez	2.00
12	Jim Thome	.40
13	Tony Clark	.40
14	Juan Gonzalez	2.00
15	Mike Piazza	4.00
16	Jose Canseco	1.00
17	Jay Buhner	.40
18	Alex Rodriguez	5.00
19	Jose Cruz Jr.	.40
20	Tino Martinez	.40
21	Carlos Delgado	.75
22	Andruw Jones	2.00
23	Chipper Jones	3.00
24	Fred McGriff	.40
25	Matt Williams	.40
26	Sammy Sosa	4.00
27	Vinny Castilla	.40
28	Tim Salmon	.60
29	Ken Caminiti	.40
30	Barry Bonds	6.00

10th Anniversary Preview

	NM/M
Complete Set (60):	45.00
Common Player:	.30
1	Greg Maddux	2.00
2	Mike Mussina	.50
3	Roger Clemens	2.25
4	Hideo Nomo	.75
5	David Cone	.30
6	Tom Glavine	.45
7	Andy Pettitte	.60
8	Jimmy Key	.30
9	Randy Johnson	1.50
10	Dennis Eckersley	1.00
11	Lee Smith	.30
12	John Franco	.30
13	Randy Myers	.30
14	Mike Piazza	2.50
15	Ivan Rodriguez	1.25
16	Todd Hundley	.30
17	Sandy Alomar Jr.	.30
18	Frank Thomas	1.50
19	Rafael Palmeiro	1.25
20	Mark McGwire	3.00
21	Mo Vaughn	.30
22	Fred McGriff	.30
23	Andres Galarraga	.30
24	Mark Grace	.30
25	Jeff Bagwell	1.50
26	Roberto Alomar	.45
27	Chuck Knoblauch	.30
28	Ryne Sandberg	2.00
29	Eric Young	.30
30	Craig Biggio	.30
31	Carlos Baerga	.30
32	Robin Ventura	.30
33	Matt Williams	.30
34	Wade Boggs	2.00
35	Dean Palmer	.30
36	Chipper Jones	2.00
37	Vinny Castilla	.30
38	Ken Caminiti	.30
39	Omar Vizquel	.30
40	Cal Ripken Jr.	3.50
41	Derek Jeter	3.50
42	Alex Rodriguez	3.00
43	Barry Larkin	.30
44	Mark Grudzielanek	.30
45	Albert Belle	.30
46	Manny Ramirez	1.50
47	Jose Canseco	.75
48	Ken Griffey Jr.	2.50
49	Juan Gonzalez	.75
50	Kenny Lofton	.30
51	Sammy Sosa	2.00
52	Larry Walker	.30
53	Gary Sheffield	.60
54	Rickey Henderson	1.50
55	Tony Gwynn	2.00
56	Barry Bonds	3.50
57	Paul Molitor	1.50
58	Edgar Martinez	.30
59	Chili Davis	.30
60	Eddie Murray	1.50

Rookie Edition A Piece of the Action

	NM/M
Common Card:	15.00
KG	Ken Griffey Jr./300	100.00
KGS	Ken Griffey Jr./Auto./24	300.00
BG	Ben Grieve/200	15.00
JC	Jose Cruz Jr./200	15.00
TL	Travis Lee/200	15.00

Rookie Edition All-Star Credentials

		NM/M
Complete Set (30):		25.00
Common Player:		.25
Inserted 1:9		
AS1	Ken Griffey Jr.	1.50
AS2	Travis Lee	.40
AS3	Ben Grieve	.25
AS4	Jose Cruz Jr.	.25
AS5	Andruw Jones	.75
AS6	Craig Biggio	.25
AS7	Hideo Nomo	.40
AS8	Cal Ripken Jr.	2.50
AS9	Jaret Wright	.25
AS10	Mark McGwire	2.00
AS11	Derek Jeter	2.50
AS12	Scott Rolen	.60
AS13	Jeff Bagwell	.75
AS14	Manny Ramirez	.75
AS15	Alex Rodriguez	2.00
AS16	Chipper Jones	1.00
AS17	Larry Walker	.25
AS18	Barry Bonds	2.50
AS19	Tony Gwynn	1.00
AS20	Mike Piazza	1.50
AS21	Roger Clemens	1.25
AS22	Greg Maddux	1.00
AS23	Jim Thome	.60
AS24	Tino Martinez	.25
AS25	Nomar Garciaparra	1.00
AS26	Juan Gonzalez	.40
AS27	Kenny Lofton	.25
AS28	Randy Johnson	.75
AS29	Todd Helton	.65
AS30	Frank Thomas	.75

Rookie Edition Destination Stardom

	NM/M
Complete Set (60):	40.00
Common Player:	.50

1	Travis Lee	.75
2	Nomar Garciaparra	3.50
3	Alex Gonzalez	.50
4	Richard Hidalgo	.50
5	Jaret Wright	.50
6	Mike Kinkade	.50
7	Matt Morris	.50
8	Gary Mathews Jr.	.50
9	Brett Tomko	.50
10	Todd Helton	2.00
11	Scott Elarton	.50
12	Scott Rolen	1.50
13	Jose Cruz Jr.	.50
14	Jarrod Washburn	.50
15	Sean Casey	.50
16	Magglio Ordonez	2.00
17	Gabe Alvarez	.50
18	Todd Dunwoody	.50
19	Kevin Witt	.50
20	Ben Grieve	.50
21	Daryle Ward	.50
22	Matt Clement	.50
23	Carlton Loewer	.50
24	Javier Vazquez	.50
25	Paul Konerko	.75
26	Preston Wilson	.60
27	Wes Helms	.50
28	Derek Jeter	5.00
29	Corey Koskie	.50
30	Russell Branyan	.50
31	Vladimir Guerrero	2.50
32	Ryan Christenson	.50
33	Carlos Lee	.60
34	David Dellucci	.50
35	Bruce Chen	.50
36	Ricky Ledee	.50
37	Ron Wright	.50
38	Derrek Lee	1.50
39	Miguel Tejada	.75
40	Brad Fullmer	.50
41	Rich Butler	.50
42	Chris Carpenter	.50
43	Alex Rodriguez	4.00
44	Darron Ingram	.50
45	Kerry Wood	1.50
46	Jason Varitek	.50
47	Ramon Hernandez	.50
48	Aaron Boone	.50
49	Juan Encarnacion	.50
50	A.J. Hinch	.50
51	Mike Lowell	1.00
52	Fernando Tatis	.50
53	Jose Guillen	.50
54	Mike Caruso	.50
55	Carl Pavano	.50
56	Chris Clemons	.50
57	Mark L. Johnson	.50
58	Ken Cloude	.50
59	Rolando Arrojo	.50
60	Mark Kotsay	.50

1998 Upper Deck Rookie Edition Eminent Prestige 5x7

		NM/M
Complete Set (10):		25.00
Common Player:		2.00
605	Mike Piazza	3.50
607	Frank Thomas	2.50
610	Mark McGwire	4.00
611	Jeff Bagwell	2.50
612	Travis Lee	2.00
614	Cal Ripken Jr.	5.00
616	Nomar Garciaparra	3.00
617	Alex Rodriguez	4.00
619	Tony Gwynn	3.00
620	Ken Griffey Jr.	3.50

Rookie Edition Retrospectives

		NM/M
Complete Set (30):		55.00
Common Player:		.50
Inserted 1:24		
1	Dennis Eckersley	2.50
2	Rickey Henderson	3.00
3	Harold Baines	.50
4	Cal Ripken Jr.	7.50
5	Tony Gwynn	4.00
6	Wade Boggs	4.00
7	Orel Hershiser	.50
8	Joe Carter	.50
9	Roger Clemens	4.50
10	Barry Bonds	7.50
11	Mark McGwire	6.00
12	Greg Maddux	4.00
13	Fred McGriff	.50
14	Rafael Palmeiro	3.00
15	Craig Biggio	.50
16	Brady Anderson	.50
17	Randy Johnson	3.00
18	Gary Sheffield	1.00
19	Albert Belle	.50
20	Ken Griffey Jr.	5.00
21	Juan Gonzalez	1.50
22	Larry Walker	.50
23	Tino Martinez	.50
24	Frank Thomas	3.00
25	Jeff Bagwell	3.00
26	Kenny Lofton	.50
27	Mo Vaughn	.50
28	Mike Piazza	5.00
29	Alex Rodriguez	5.00
30	Chipper Jones	4.00

Rookie Edition Unparalleled

		NM/M
Complete Set (20):		75.00
Common Player:		1.00
Inserted 1:72		
1	Ken Griffey Jr.	6.00
2	Travis Lee	1.50
3	Ben Grieve	1.00
4	Jose Cruz Jr.	1.00
5	Nomar Garciaparra	1.75
6	Hideo Nomo	1.75
7	Kenny Lofton	1.00
8	Cal Ripken Jr.	10.00
9	Roger Clemens	5.50
10	Mike Piazza	6.00
11	Jeff Bagwell	3.50
12	Chipper Jones	5.00
13	Greg Maddux	5.00
14	Randy Johnson	3.50
15	Alex Rodriguez	7.50
16	Barry Bonds	10.00
17	Frank Thomas	3.50
18	Juan Gonzalez	1.75
19	Tony Gwynn	5.00
20	Mark McGwire	7.50

1998 Upper Deck Special F/X

		NM/M
Complete Set (150):		30.00
Common Player:		.05
1	Ken Griffey Jr.	
	(Griffey Hot List)	1.00
2	Mark McGwire	
	(Griffey Hot List)	1.25
3	Alex Rodriguez	
	(Griffey Hot List)	2.50
4	Larry Walker (Griffey Hot List)	.05
5	Tino Martinez	
	(Griffey Hot List)	.05
6	Mike Piazza (Griffey Hot List)	2.50
7	Jose Cruz Jr. (Griffey Hot List)	.05
8	Greg Maddux	
	(Griffey Hot List)	.75
9	Tony Gwynn (Griffey Hot List)	.75
10	Roger Clemens	
	(Griffey Hot List)	1.75
11	Jason Dickson	.05
12	Darin Erstad	.25
13	Chuck Finley	.05
14	Dave Hollins	.05
15	Garret Anderson	.05
16	Michael Tucker	.05
17	Javier Lopez	.05
18	John Smoltz	.05
19	Mark Wohlers	.05
20	Greg Maddux	1.50
21	Scott Erickson	.05
22	Jimmy Key	.05
23	B.J. Surhoff	.05
24	Eric Davis	.05
25	Rafael Palmeiro	.75
26	Tim Naehring	.05
27	Darren Bragg	.05
28	Troy O'Leary	.05
29	John Valentin	.05
30	Mo Vaughn	.05
31	Mark Grace	.05
32	Kevin Foster	.05
33	Kevin Tapani	.05
34	Kevin Orie	.05
35	Albert Belle	.05
36	Ray Durham	.05
37	Jaime Navarro	.05
38	Mike Cameron	.05
39	Eddie Taubensee	.05
40	Barry Larkin	.05
41	Willie Greene	.05
42	Jeff Shaw	.05
43	Omar Vizquel	.05
44	Brian Giles	.05
45	Jim Thome	.60
46	David Justice	.05
47	Sandy Alomar Jr.	.05
48	Neifi Perez	.05
49	Dante Bichette	.05
50	Vinny Castilla	.05
51	John Thomson	.05
52	Damion Easley	.05
53	Justin Thompson	.05
54	Bobby Higginson	.05
55	Tony Clark	.05
56	Charles Johnson	.05
57	Edgar Renteria	.05
58	Alex Fernandez	.05
59	Gary Sheffield	.50
60	Livan Hernandez	.05
61	Craig Biggio	.05
62	Chris Holt	.05
63	Billy Wagner	.05
64	Brad Ausmus	.05
65	Dean Palmer	.05
66	Tim Belcher	.05
67	Jeff King	.05
68	Jose Rosado	.05
69	Chan Ho Park	.05
70	Raul Mondesi	.05
71	Hideo Nomo	.50
72	Todd Zeile	.05
73	Eric Karros	.05
74	Cal Eldred	.05
75	Jeff D'Amico	.05
76	Doug Jones	.05
77	Dave Nilsson	.05
78	Todd Walker	.05
79	Rick Aguilera	.05
80	Paul Molitor	1.00
81	Brad Radke	.05
82	Vladimir Guerrero	1.00
83	Carlos Perez	.05
84	F.P. Santangelo	.05
85	Rondell White	.05
86	Butch Huskey	.05
87	Edgardo Alfonzo	.05
88	John Franco	.05
89	John Olerud	.05
90	Todd Hundley	.05
91	Bernie Williams	.05
92	Andy Pettitte	.30
93	Paul O'Neill	.05
94	David Cone	.05
95	Jason Giambi	.50
96	Damon Mashore	.05
97	Scott Spiezio	.05
98	Ariel Prieto	.05
99	Rico Brogna	.05
100	Mike Lieberthal	.05
101	Garrett Stephenson	.05
102	Ricky Bottalico	.05
103	Kevin Polcovich	.05
104	Jon Lieber	.05
105	Kevin Young	.05
106	Tony Womack	.05
107	Gary Gaetti	.05
108	Alan Benes	.05
109	Willie McGee	.05
110	Mark McGwire	2.50
111	Ron Gant	.05
112	Andy Ashby	.05
113	Steve Finley	.05
114	Quilvio Veras	.05
115	Ken Caminiti	.05
116	Joey Hamilton	.05
117	Bill Mueller	.05
118	Mark Gardner	.05
119	Shawn Estes	.05
120	J.T. Snow	.05

121	Dante Powell	.05
122	Jeff Kent	.05
123	Jamie Moyer	.05
124	Joey Cora	.05
125	Ken Griffey Jr.	2.00
126	Jeff Fassero	.05
127	Edgar Martinez	.05
128	Will Clark	.05
129	Lee Stevens	.05
130	Ivan Rodriguez	.75
131	Rusty Greer	.05
132	Ed Sprague	.05
133	Pat Hentgen	.05
134	Shannon Stewart	.05
135	Carlos Delgado	.40
136	Brett Tomko (Star Rookie)	.05
137	Jose Guillen (Star Rookie)	.05
138	Elieser Marrero (Star Rookie)	.05
139	Dennis Reyes (Star Rookie)	.05
140	Mark Kotsay (Star Rookie)	.05
141	Richie Sexson (Star Rookie)	.05
142	Todd Helton (Star Rookie)	.75
143	Jeremi Gonzalez (Star Rookie)	.05
144	Jeff Abbott (Star Rookie)	.05
145	Matt Morris (Star Rookie)	.05
146	Aaron Boone (Star Rookie)	.05
147	Todd Dunwoody (Star Rookie)	.05
148	Mario Valdez (Star Rookie)	.05
149	Fernando Tatis (Star Rookie)	.05
150	Jaret Wright (Star Rookie)	.05

OctoberBest

Complete Set (15):		40.00
Common Player:		1.00
Inserted 1:34		
PZ1	Frank Thomas	3.00
PZ2	Juan Gonzalez	1.50
PZ3	Mike Piazza	5.00
PZ4	Mark McGwire	6.00
PZ5	Jeff Bagwell	3.00
PZ6	Barry Bonds	7.50
PZ7	Ken Griffey Jr.	5.00
PZ8	John Smoltz	1.00
PZ9	Andruw Jones	3.00
PZ10	Greg Maddux	3.00
PZ11	Sandy Alomar Jr.	1.00
PZ12	Roberto Alomar	1.25
PZ13	Chipper Jones	4.00
PZ14	Kenny Lofton	1.00
PZ15	Tom Glavine	1.25

Power Driven

		NM/M
Complete Set (10):		40.00
Common Player:		1.50
Inserted 1:69		
PZ1	Frank Thomas	4.50
PZ2	Juan Gonzalez	2.50
PZ3	Mike Piazza	6.00
PZ4	Larry Walker	1.50
PZ5	Mark McGwire	7.50
PZ6	Jeff Bagwell	4.50
PZ7	Mo Vaughn	1.50
PZ8	Barry Bonds	10.00
PZ9	Tino Martinez	1.50
PZ10	Ken Griffey Jr.	6.00

Power Zone

		NM/M
Complete Set (20):		40.00
Common Player:		.50
Inserted 1:7		
PZ1	Jose Cruz Jr.	.50
PZ2	Frank Thomas	2.50
PZ3	Juan Gonzalez	1.25
PZ4	Mike Piazza	4.50
PZ5	Mark McGwire	4.50
PZ6	Barry Bonds	6.00
PZ7	Greg Maddux	3.00
PZ8	Alex Rodriguez	4.50
PZ9	Nomar Garciaparra	3.00
PZ10	Ken Griffey Jr.	3.50
PZ11	John Smoltz	.50
PZ12	Andruw Jones	2.50
PZ13	Sandy Alomar Jr.	.50
PZ14	Roberto Alomar	1.00
PZ15	Chipper Jones	3.00
PZ16	Kenny Lofton	.50
PZ17	Larry Walker	.50
PZ18	Jeff Bagwell	2.50
PZ19	Mo Vaughn	.50
PZ20	Tom Glavine	1.00

1998 Upper Deck UD 3

	NM/M
Complete Set (270):	200.00
Common Future Impact (1-30):	.50
Inserted 1:12	
Die-Cuts (2,000 Sets):	1X
Common Power Corps (31-60):	.25
Inserted 1:1	
Die-Cuts (2,000 Sets):	3X
Common Establishment (61-90):	.25
Inserted 1:6	
Die-Cuts (2,000 Sets):	2X
Common Future Impact Embossed (91-120):	.25
Inserted 1:6	
Die-Cuts (1,000 Sets):	3X
Common Power Corps Embossed (121-150):	.25
Inserted 1:4	
Die-Cuts (1,000 Sets):	6X
Common Establishment Embossed (151-180):	.25
Inserted 1:1	
Die-Cuts (1,000 Sets):	12X
Common Future Impact Rainbow (181-210):	.25
Inserted 1:1	
Die-Cuts (100 Sets):	15X
Common Power Corps Rainbow (211-240):	.50
Inserted 1:1	
Die-Cuts (100 Sets):	8X
Common Establishment Rainbow (241-270):	.75
Inserted 1:24	
Die-Cuts (100 Sets):	5X
Pack (3):	1.00
Wax Box (24):	20.00

LIGHT FX FUTURE IMPACT (1:12)

1	Travis Lee	.50
2	A.J. Hinch	.50
3	Mike Caruso	.50
4	Miguel Tejada	.75
5	Brad Fullmer	.50
6	Eric Milton	.50
7	Mark Kotsay	.50
8	Darin Erstad	.75
9	Magglio Ordonez	1.00
10	Ben Grieve	.50
11	Brett Tomko	.50
12	Mike Kinkade RC	.75
13	Rolando Arrojo	.50
14	Todd Helton	1.00
15	Scott Rolen	1.00
16	Bruce Chen	.50
17	Daryle Ward	.50
18	Jaret Wright	.50
19	Sean Casey	.65
20	Paul Konerko	.65
21	Kerry Wood	1.00
22	Russell Branyan	.50
23	Gabe Alvarez	.50
24	Juan Encarnacion	.50
25	Andruw Jones	1.50
26	Vladimir Guerrero	1.50
27	Eli Marrero	.50
28	Matt Clement	.50
29	Gary Matthews Jr.	.50
30	Derrek Lee	1.50

LIGHT FX POWER CORPS (1:1)

31	Ken Caminiti	.25
32	Gary Sheffield	.50
33	Jay Buhner	.25
34	Ryan Klesko	.25
35	Nomar Garciaparra	.75
36	Vinny Castilla	.25
37	Tony Clark	.25
38	Sammy Sosa	.75
39	Tino Martinez	.25
40	Mike Piazza	1.00
41	Manny Ramirez	.65
42	Larry Walker	.25
43	Jose Cruz Jr.	.25
44	Matt Williams	.25
45	Frank Thomas	.65
46	Jim Edmonds	.25
47	Raul Mondesi	.25
48	Alex Rodriguez	1.50
49	Albert Belle	.25
50	Mark McGwire	1.50
51	Tim Salmon	.25
52	Andres Galarraga	.25
53	Jeff Bagwell	.65
54	Jim Thome	.50
55	Barry Bonds	2.50
56	Carlos Delgado	.40
57	Mo Vaughn	.25
58	Chipper Jones	.75
59	Juan Gonzalez	.40
60	Ken Griffey Jr.	1.00

LIGHT FX THE ESTABLISHMENT (1:6)

61	David Cone	.25
62	Hideo Nomo	.75
63	Edgar Martinez	.25
64	Fred McGriff	.25
65	Cal Ripken Jr.	4.00
66	Todd Hundley	.25
67	Barry Larkin	.25
68	Dennis Eckersley	1.00
69	Randy Johnson	1.50
70	Paul Molitor	1.50
71	Eric Karros	.25
72	Rafael Palmeiro	1.00
73	Chuck Knoblauch	.25
74	Ivan Rodriguez	1.25
75	Greg Maddux	2.00
76	Dante Bichette	.25
77	Brady Anderson	.25
78	Craig Biggio	.25
79	Derek Jeter	4.00
80	Roger Clemens	2.25
81	Roberto Alomar	.40
82	Wade Boggs	2.00
83	Charles Johnson	.25
84	Mark Grace	.25
85	Kenny Lofton	.25
86	Mike Mussina	1.00
87	Pedro Martinez	1.50
88	Curt Schilling	.50
89	Bernie Williams	.25
90	Tony Gwynn	2.00

EMBOSSED FUTURE IMPACT (1:6)

91	Travis Lee	.40
92	A.J. Hinch	.25
93	Mike Caruso	.25
94	Miguel Tejada	.40
95	Brad Fullmer	.25
96	Eric Milton	.25
97	Mark Kotsay	.25
98	Darin Erstad	1.00
99	Magglio Ordonez	1.00
100	Ben Grieve	.25
101	Brett Tomko	.25
102	Mike Kinkade RC	.40
103	Rolando Arrojo	.25
104	Todd Helton	1.00
105	Scott Rolen	1.00
106	Bruce Chen	.25
107	Daryle Ward	.25
108	Jaret Wright	.25
109	Sean Casey	.40
110	Paul Konerko	.40
111	Kerry Wood	1.00
112	Russell Branyan	.25
113	Gabe Alvarez	.25
114	Juan Encarnacion	.25
115	Andruw Jones	1.50
116	Vladimir Guerrero	1.50
117	Eli Marrero	.25
118	Matt Clement	.25
119	Gary Matthews Jr.	.25
120	Derrek Lee	.25

EMBOSSED POWER CORPS (1:4)

121	Ken Caminiti	.25
122	Gary Sheffield	.50
123	Jay Buhner	.25
124	Ryan Klesko	.25
125	Nomar Garciaparra	1.50
126	Vinny Castilla	.25
127	Tony Clark	.25
128	Sammy Sosa	1.50
129	Tino Martinez	.25
130	Mike Piazza	2.00
131	Manny Ramirez	1.00
132	Larry Walker	.25
133	Jose Cruz Jr.	.25
134	Matt Williams	.25
135	Frank Thomas	1.00
136	Jim Edmonds	.25
137	Raul Mondesi	.25
138	Alex Rodriguez	3.00
139	Albert Belle	.25
140	Mark McGwire	3.00
141	Tim Salmon	.25
142	Andres Galarraga	.25
143	Jeff Bagwell	1.00
144	Jim Thome	.75
145	Barry Bonds	5.00
146	Carlos Delgado	.50
147	Mo Vaughn	.25
148	Chipper Jones	1.50
149	Juan Gonzalez	.50
150	Ken Griffey Jr.	2.00

EMBOSSED THE ESTABLISHMENT (1:1)

151	David Cone	.25
152	Hideo Nomo	.40
153	Edgar Martinez	.25
154	Fred McGriff	.25
155	Cal Ripken Jr.	2.00
156	Todd Hundley	.25
157	Barry Larkin	.25
158	Dennis Eckersley	.65
159	Randy Johnson	.75
160	Paul Molitor	.75
161	Eric Karros	.25
162	Rafael Palmeiro	.65
163	Chuck Knoblauch	.25
164	Ivan Rodriguez	.65
165	Greg Maddux	1.00
166	Dante Bichette	.25
167	Brady Anderson	.25
168	Craig Biggio	.25
169	Derek Jeter	2.00
170	Roger Clemens	1.25
171	Roberto Alomar	.30
172	Wade Boggs	1.00
173	Charles Johnson	.25
174	Mark Grace	.25
175	Kenny Lofton	.25
176	Mike Mussina	.40
177	Pedro Martinez	.75
178	Curt Schilling	.25
179	Bernie Williams	.25
180	Tony Gwynn	1.00

RAINBOW FUTURE IMPACT (1:1)

181	Travis Lee	.40
182	A.J. Hinch	.25
183	Mike Caruso	.25
184	Miguel Tejada	.40
185	Brad Fullmer	.25
186	Eric Milton	.25
187	Mark Kotsay	.25
188	Darin Erstad	.50
189	Magglio Ordonez	1.25
190	Ben Grieve	.25
191	Brett Tomko	.25
192	Mike Kinkade RC	.40
193	Rolando Arrojo	.25
194	Todd Helton	.65
195	Scott Rolen	.60
196	Bruce Chen	.25
197	Daryle Ward	.25
198	Jaret Wright	.25
199	Sean Casey	.40
200	Paul Konerko	.40
201	Kerry Wood	.60
202	Russell Branyan	.25
203	Gabe Alvarez	.25
204	Juan Encarnacion	.25
205	Andruw Jones	1.50
206	Vladimir Guerrero	1.50
207	Eli Marrero	.25
208	Matt Clement	.25
209	Gary Matthews Jr.	.25
210	Derrek Lee	1.00

RAINBOW POWER CORPS (1:12)

211	Ken Caminiti	1.00
212	Gary Sheffield	1.00
213	Jay Buhner	.50
214	Ryan Klesko	.50
215	Nomar Garciaparra	3.00
216	Vinny Castilla	.50
217	Tony Clark	.50
218	Sammy Sosa	3.00
219	Tino Martinez	.50
220	Mike Piazza	4.00
221	Manny Ramirez	2.00
222	Larry Walker	.50
223	Jose Cruz Jr.	.50
224	Matt Williams	.50
225	Frank Thomas	2.00
226	Jim Edmonds	.50
227	Raul Mondesi	.50
228	Alex Rodriguez	6.00
229	Albert Belle	.50
230	Mark McGwire	6.00
231	Tim Salmon	.50
232	Andres Galarraga	.50

233	Jeff Bagwell	2.00
234	Jim Thome	1.50
235	Barry Bonds	9.00
236	Carlos Delgado	.75
267	Mo Vaughn	.50
238	Chipper Jones	3.00
239	Juan Gonzalez	1.00
240	Ken Griffey Jr.	4.00

RAINBOW THE ESTABLISHMENT (1:24)

241	David Cone	.75
242	Hideo Nomo	1.50
243	Edgar Martinez	.75
244	Fred McGriff	.75
245	Cal Ripken Jr.	12.00
246	Todd Hundley	.75
247	Barry Larkin	.75
248	Dennis Eckersley	3.00
249	Randy Johnson	4.50
250	Paul Molitor	4.50
251	Eric Karros	.75
252	Rafael Palmeiro	3.50
253	Chuck Knoblauch	.75
254	Ivan Rodriguez	4.00
255	Greg Maddux	6.00
256	Dante Bichette	.75
257	Brady Anderson	.75
258	Craig Biggio	.75
259	Derek Jeter	12.00
260	Roger Clemens	6.50
261	Roberto Alomar	1.25
262	Wade Boggs	6.00
263	Charles Johnson	.75
264	Mark Grace	.75
265	Kenny Lofton	.75
266	Mike Mussina	1.25
267	Pedro Martinez	4.50
268	Curt Schilling	1.50
269	Bernie Williams	.75
270	Tony Gwynn	6.00

1998 Upper Deck UD 3 Die-Cut

NM/M

Light FX Die-Cuts (2,000 Each)
Future Impact (1-30): .75X
Power Corps (31-60): 3X
Establishment (61-90): 2X
Embossed Die-Cuts (1,000 Each)
Future Impact (91-120): 1X
Power Corps (121-150): 3X
Establishment (151-180): 6X
Rainbow Die-Cuts (100 Each)
Future Impact (181-210): 20X
Power Corps (211-240): 4X
Establishment (241-270): 12X
(See 1998 UD 3 for checklist and base card values.)

1998 UD Retro

NM/M

Complete Set (129): 15.00
Common Player: .05
Pack (6): 2.25
Lunchbox (24): 40.00

1	Jim Edmonds	.05
2	Darin Erstad	.25
3	Tim Salmon	.05
4	Jay Bell	.05
5	Matt Williams	.05
6	Andres Galarraga	.05
7	Andruw Jones	.60
8	Chipper Jones	.75
9	Greg Maddux	.75
10	Rafael Palmeiro	.50
11	Cal Ripken Jr.	2.00
12	Brooks Robinson	.15
13	Nomar Garciaparra	.75
14	Pedro Martinez	.60
15	Mo Vaughn	.05
16	Ernie Banks	.50
17	Mark Grace	.05
18	Gary Matthews	.05
19	Sammy Sosa	.75
20	Albert Belle	.05
21	Carlton Fisk	.15
22	Frank Thomas	.60
23	Ken Griffey Sr.	.05
24	Paul Konerko	.15
25	Barry Larkin	.05
26	Sean Casey	.10
27	Tony Perez	.05
28	Bob Feller	.15
29	Kenny Lofton	.05
30	Manny Ramirez	.60
31	Jim Thome	.45
32	Omar Vizquel	.05
33	Dante Bichette	.05
34	Larry Walker	.05
35	Tony Clark	.05
36	Damion Easley	.05
37	Cliff Floyd	.05
38	Livan Hernandez	.05
39	Jeff Bagwell	.60
40	Craig Biggio	.05
41	Al Kaline	.15
42	Johnny Damon	.20
43	Dean Palmer	.05
44	Charles Johnson	.05
45	Eric Karros	.05
46	Gaylord Perry	.05
47	Raul Mondesi	.05
48	Gary Sheffield	.30
49	Eddie Mathews	.15
50	Warren Spahn	.15
51	Jeromy Burnitz	.05
52	Jeff Cirillo	.05
53	Marquis Grissom	.05
54	Paul Molitor	.60
55	Kirby Puckett	.75
56	Brad Radke	.05
57	Todd Walker	.05
58	Vladimir Guerrero	.60
59	Brad Fullmer	.05
60	Rondell White	.05
61	Bobby Jones	.05
62	Hideo Nomo	.30
63	Mike Piazza	1.00
64	Tom Seaver	.15
65	Frank J. Thomas	.05
66	Yogi Berra	.50
67	Derek Jeter	2.00
68	Tino Martinez	.05
69	Paul O'Neill	.05
70	Andy Pettitte	.20
71	Rollie Fingers	.05
72	Rickey Henderson	.05
73	Matt Stairs	.05
74	Scott Rolen	.50
75	Curt Schilling	.25
76	Jose Guillen	.05
77	Jason Kendall	.05
78	Lou Brock	.10
79	Bob Gibson	.05
80	Ray Lankford	.05
81	Mark McGwire	1.50
82	NOT ISSUED	
83	Kevin Brown	.05
84	Ken Caminiti	.05
85	Tony Gwynn	.75
86	Greg Vaughn	.05
87	Barry Bonds	2.00
88	Willie Stargell	.10
89	Willie McCovey	.10
90	Ken Griffey Jr.	1.00
91	Randy Johnson	.60
92	Alex Rodriguez	1.50
93	Quinton McCracken	.05
94	Fred McGriff	.05
95	Juan Gonzalez	.30
96	Ivan Rodriguez	.05
97	Nolan Ryan	1.50
98	Jose Canseco	.45
99	Roger Clemens	.90
100	Jose Cruz Jr.	.05
101	Justin Baughman RC	.05
102	David Dellucci RC (Futurama)	.15
103	Travis Lee (Futurama)	.15
104	Troy Glaus RC (Futurama)	1.00
105	Kerry Wood (Futurama)	.40
106	Mike Caruso (Futurama)	.05
107	Jim Parque RC (Futurama)	.10
108	Brett Tomko (Futurama)	.05
109	Russell Branyan (Futurama)	.05
110	Jaret Wright (Futurama)	.05
111	Todd Helton (Futurama)	.60
112	Gabe Alvarez (Futurama)	.05
113	Matt Anderson RC (Futurama)	.10
114	Alex Gonzalez (Futurama)	.05
115	Mark Kotsay (Futurama)	.10
116	Derrek Lee (Futurama)	.50
117	Richard Hidalgo (Futurama)	.05
118	Adrian Beltre (Futurama)	.10
119	Geoff Jenkins (Futurama)	.05
120	Eric Milton (Futurama)	.05
121	Brad Fullmer (Futurama)	.05
122	Vladimir Guerrero (Futurama)	.60
123	Carl Pavano (Futurama)	.05
124	Orlando Hernandez RC (Futurama)	.25
125	Ben Grieve (Futurama)	.05
126	A.J. Hinch (Futurama)	.05
127	Matt Clement (Futurama)	.05
128	Gary Matthews Jr. RC (Futurama)	.05
129	Aramis Ramirez (Futurama)	.05
130	Rolando Arrojo (Futurama)	.05

Big Boppers

NM/M

Complete Set (30): 80.00
Common Player: 1.00
Production 500 Sets

B1	Darin Erstad	1.50
B2	Rafael Palmeiro	3.00
B3	Cal Ripken Jr.	10.00
B4	Nomar Garciaparra	5.00
B5	Mo Vaughn	1.00
B6	Frank Thomas	4.00
B7	Albert Belle	1.00
B8	Jim Thome	2.50
B9	Manny Ramirez	4.00
B10	Tony Clark	1.00
B11	Tino Martinez	1.00
B12	Ben Grieve	1.00
B13	Ken Griffey Jr.	6.00
B14	Alex Rodriguez	7.50
B15	Jay Buhner	1.00
B16	Juan Gonzalez	2.00
B17	Jose Cruz Jr.	1.00
B18	Jose Canseco	2.50
B19	Travis Lee	1.50
B20	Chipper Jones	5.00
B21	Andres Galarraga	1.00
B22	Andruw Jones	4.00
B23	Sammy Sosa	5.00
B24	Vinny Castilla	1.00
B25	Larry Walker	1.00
B26	Jeff Bagwell	1.00
B27	Gary Sheffield	2.00
B28	Mike Piazza	6.00
B29	Mark McGwire	7.50
B30	Barry Bonds	10.00

Groovy Kind of Glove

NM/M

Complete Set (30): 50.00
Common Player: .60
Inserted 1:7

G1	Roberto Alomar	1.00
G2	Cal Ripken Jr.	7.50
G3	Nomar Garciaparra	3.50
G4	Frank Thomas	2.25
G5	Robin Ventura	.60
G6	Omar Vizquel	.60
G7	Kenny Lofton	.60
G8	Ben Grieve	.60
G9	Alex Rodriguez	6.00
G10	Ken Griffey Jr.	5.00
G11	Ivan Rodriguez	1.50
G12	Travis Lee	.75
G13	Matt Williams	.60
G14	Greg Maddux	3.50
G15	Andres Galarraga	.60
G16	Andruw Jones	2.25
G17	Kerry Wood	1.25
G18	Mark Grace	.60
G19	Craig Biggio	.60
G20	Charles Johnson	.60
G21	Raul Mondesi	.60
G22	Mike Piazza	5.00
G23	Rey Ordonez	.60
G24	Derek Jeter	7.50
G25	Scott Rolen	1.25
G26	Mark McGwire	6.00
G27	Ken Caminiti	.60
G28	Tony Gwynn	3.50
G29	J.T. Snow	.60
G30	Barry Bonds	7.50

Legendary Cut

NM/M

LC	Babe Ruth (Three issued; 1/04 auction.)	9,500

Lunchbox

NM/M

Complete Set (6): 40.00
Common Lunchbox: 4.00

Nomar Garciaparra	6.00
Ken Griffey Jr.	7.50
Chipper Jones	6.00
Travis Lee	4.00
Mark McGwire	10.00
Cal Ripken Jr.	12.00

New Frontier

NM/M

Complete Set (30): 45.00
Common Player: 1.00
Production 1,000 Sets

NF1	Justin Baughman	1.00
NF2	David Dellucci	1.00
NF3	Travis Lee	1.50
NF4	Troy Glaus	6.00
NF5	Mike Caruso	1.00
NF6	Jim Parque	1.00
NF7	Kerry Wood	2.00
NF8	Brett Tomko	1.00
NF9	Russell Branyan	1.00
NF10	Jaret Wright	1.00
NF11	Todd Helton	5.00
NF12	Gabe Alvarez	1.00
NF13	Matt Anderson	1.00
NF14	Alex Gonzalez	1.00
NF15	Mark Kotsay	1.00
NF16	Derrek Lee	3.00
NF17	Richard Hidalgo	1.00
NF18	Adrian Beltre	2.00
NF19	Geoff Jenkins	1.00
NF20	Eric Milton	1.00
NF21	Brad Fullmer	1.00
NF22	Vladimir Guerrero	6.00
NF23	Carl Pavano	1.00
NF24	Orlando Hernandez	1.25
NF25	Ben Grieve	1.00
NF26	A.J. Hinch	1.00
NF27	Matt Clement	1.00
NF28	Gary Matthews	1.00
NF29	Aramis Ramirez	1.00
NF30	Rolando Arrojo	1.00

Quantum Leap

NM/M

Common Player: 15.00
Production 50 Sets

Q1	Darin Erstad	20.00
Q2	Cal Ripken Jr.	100.00
Q3	Nomar Garciaparra	50.00
Q4	Frank Thomas	40.00
Q5	Kenny Lofton	15.00
Q6	Ben Grieve	15.00
Q7	Ken Griffey Jr.	60.00

Q8	Alex Rodriguez	75.00
Q9	Juan Gonzalez	20.00
Q10	Jose Cruz Jr.	15.00
Q11	Roger Clemens	55.00
Q12	Travis Lee	15.00
Q13	Chipper Jones	50.00
Q14	Greg Maddux	50.00
Q15	Kerry Wood	20.00
Q16	Jeff Bagwell	40.00
Q17	Mike Piazza	60.00
Q18	Scott Rolen	30.00
Q19	Mark McGwire	75.00
Q20	Tony Gwynn	50.00
Q21	Larry Walker	15.00
Q22	Derek Jeter	100.00
Q23	Sammy Sosa	50.00
Q24	Barry Bonds	100.00
Q25	Mo Vaughn	15.00
Q26	Roberto Alomar	20.00
Q27	Todd Helton	30.00
Q28	Ivan Rodriguez	30.00
Q29	Vladimir Guerrero	40.00
Q30	Albert Belle	15.00

Sign of the Times

		NM/M
Common Autograph:		7.50
Inserted 1:36		
EB	Ernie Banks/300	40.00
YB	Yogi Berra/150	60.00
RB	Russell Branyan/750	8.00
LB	Lou Brock/300	25.00
JC	Jose Cruz Jr./300	8.00
RF	Rollie Fingers/600	10.00
BF	Bob Feller/600	20.00
CF	Carlton Fisk/600	30.00
BGi	Bob Gibson/300	30.00
BGr	Ben Grieve/300	5.00
KGj	Ken Griffey Jr./100	185.00
KGs	Ken Griffey Sr./600	10.00
TG	Tony Gwynn/200	35.00
AK	Al Kaline/600	30.00
PK	Paul Konerko/750	15.00
TLe	Travis Lee/300	8.00
EM	Eddie Mathews/600	60.00
GMj	Gary Matthews Jr./750	8.00
GMs	Gary Matthews/600	8.00
WM	Willie McCovey/600	30.00
TP	Tony Perez/600	20.00
GP	Gaylord Perry/1,000	10.00
KP	Kirby Puckett/450	80.00
BR	Brooks Robinson/300	30.00
SR	Scott Rolen/300	20.00
NR	Nolan Ryan/500	100.00
TS	Tom Seaver/300	30.00
WS	Warren Spahn/600	40.00
WiS	Willie Stargell/600	50.00
FT	Frank Thomas/600	15.00
KW	Kerry Wood/200	25.00

Time Capsule

		NM/M
Complete Set (50):		35.00
Common Player:		.25
Inserted 1:2		
TC1	Mike Mussina	.50
TC2	Rafael Palmeiro	.65
TC3	Cal Ripken Jr.	3.00
TC4	Nomar Garciaparra	1.50
TC5	Pedro Martinez	1.00
TC6	Mo Vaughn	.25
TC7	Albert Belle	.25
TC8	Frank Thomas	1.00
TC9	David Justice	.25
TC10	Kenny Lofton	.25
TC11	Manny Ramirez	1.00
TC12	Jim Thome	.60
TC13	Derek Jeter	3.00
TC14	Tino Martinez	.25
TC15	Ben Grieve	.25
TC16	Rickey Henderson	1.00
TC17	Ken Griffey Jr.	2.00
TC18	Randy Johnson	1.00
TC19	Alex Rodriguez	2.50
TC20	Wade Boggs	1.50
TC21	Fred McGriff	.25
TC22	Juan Gonzalez	.50
TC23	Ivan Rodriguez	.75
TC24	Nolan Ryan	2.50
TC25	Jose Canseco	.50
TC26	Roger Clemens	1.75
TC27	Jose Cruz Jr.	.25
TC28	Travis Lee	.40
TC29	Matt Williams	.25
TC30	Andres Galarraga	.25
TC31	Andruw Jones	1.00
TC32	Chipper Jones	1.50
TC33	Greg Maddux	1.50
TC34	Kerry Wood	.50
TC35	Barry Larkin	.25
TC36	Dante Bichette	.25
TC37	Larry Walker	.25
TC38	Livan Hernandez	.25
TC39	Jeff Bagwell	1.00
TC40	Craig Biggio	.25
TC41	Charles Johnson	.25
TC42	Gary Sheffield	.50
TC43	Marquis Grissom	.25
TC44	Mike Piazza	2.00
TC45	Scott Rolen	.65
TC46	Curt Schilling	.40
TC47	Mark McGwire	2.50
TC48	Ken Caminiti	.25
TC49	Tony Gwynn	1.50
TC50	Barry Bonds	3.00

1999 Upper Deck

		NM/M
Complete Set (525):		45.00
Complete Series 1 (255):		25.00
Complete Series 2 (270):		20.00
Common Player:		.05
Exclusive Stars/RC's:		15X
Production 100 each		
Pack (10):		1.50
Wax Box (24):		35.00
1	Troy Glaus (Star Rookies)	.60
2	Adrian Beltre (Star Rookies)	.25
3	Matt Anderson (Star Rookies)	.05
4	Eric Chavez (Star Rookies)	.15
5	Jin Cho (Star Rookies)	.05
6	Robert Smith **RC** (Star Rookies)	.05
7	George Lombard (Star Rookies)	.05
8	Mike Kinkade (Star Rookies)	.05
9	Seth Greisinger (Star Rookies)	.05
10	J.D. Drew (Star Rookies)	.50
11	Aramis Ramirez (Star Rookies)	.05
12	Carlos Guillen (Star Rookies)	.05
13	Justin Baughman (Star Rookies)	.05
14	Jim Parque (Star Rookies)	.05
15	Ryan Jackson (Star Rookies)	.05
16	Ramon Martinez (Star Rookies)	.05
17	Orlando Hernandez (Star Rookies)	.05
18	Jeremy Giambi (Star Rookies)	.05
19	Gary DiSarcina	.05
20	Darin Erstad	.25
21	Troy Glaus	.50
22	Chuck Finley	.05
23	Dave Hollins	.05
24	Troy Percival	.05
25	Tim Salmon	.05
26	Brian Anderson	.05
27	Jay Bell	.05
28	Andy Benes	.05
29	Brent Brede	.05
30	David Dellucci	.05
31	Karim Garcia	.10
32	Travis Lee	.20
33	Andres Galarraga	.05
34	Ryan Klesko	.05
35	Keith Lockhart	.05
36	Kevin Millwood	.05
37	Denny Neagle	.05
38	John Smoltz	.05
39	Michael Tucker	.05
40	Walt Weiss	.05
41	Dennis Martinez	.05
42	Javy Lopez	.05
43	Brady Anderson	.05
44	Harold Baines	.05
45	Mike Bordick	.05
46	Roberto Alomar	.20
47	Scott Erickson	.05
48	Mike Mussina	.30
49	Cal Ripken Jr.	2.00
50	Darren Bragg	.05
51	Dennis Eckersley	.50
52	Nomar Garciaparra	.75
53	Scott Hatteberg	.05
54	Troy O'Leary	.05
55	Bret Saberhagen	.05
56	John Valentin	.05
57	Rod Beck	.05
58	Jeff Blauser	.05
59	Brant Brown	.05
60	Mark Clark	.05
61	Mark Grace	.05
62	Kevin Tapani	.05
63	Henry Rodriguez	.05
64	Mike Cameron	.05
65	Mike Caruso	.05
66	Ray Durham	.05
67	Jaime Navarro	.05
68	Magglio Ordonez	.30
69	Mike Sirotka	.05
70	Sean Casey	.15
71	Barry Larkin	.05
72	Jon Nunnally	.05
73	Paul Konerko	.15
74	Chris Stynes	.05
75	Brett Tomko	.05
76	Dmitri Young	.05
77	Sandy Alomar	.05
78	Bartolo Colon	.05
79	Travis Fryman	.05
80	Brian Giles	.05
81	David Justice	.05
82	Omar Vizquel	.05
83	Jaret Wright	.05
84	Jim Thome	.40
85	Charles Nagy	.05
86	Pedro Astacio	.05
87	Todd Helton	.50
88	Darryl Kile	.05
89	Mike Lansing	.05
90	Neifi Perez	.05
91	John Thomson	.05
92	Larry Walker	.05
93	Tony Clark	.05
94	Deivi Cruz	.05
95	Damion Easley	.05
96	Brian L. Hunter	.05
97	Todd Jones	.05
98	Brian Moehler	.05
99	Gabe Alvarez	.05
100	Craig Counsell	.05
101	Cliff Floyd	.05
102	Livan Hernandez	.05
103	Andy Larkin	.05
104	Derrek Lee	.35
105	Brian Meadows	.05
106	Moises Alou	.05
107	Sean Berry	.05
108	Craig Biggio	.05
109	Ricky Gutierrez	.05
110	Mike Hampton	.05
111	Jose Lima	.05
112	Billy Wagner	.05
113	Hal Morris	.05
114	Johnny Damon	.30
115	Jeff King	.05
116	Jeff Montgomery	.05
117	Glendon Rusch	.05
118	Larry Sutton	.05
119	Bobby Bonilla	.05
120	Jim Eisenreich	.05
121	Eric Karros	.05
122	Matt Luke	.05
123	Ramon Martinez	.05
124	Gary Sheffield	.40
125	Eric Young	.05
126	Charles Johnson	.05
127	Jeff Cirillo	.05
128	Marquis Grissom	.05
129	Jeromy Burnitz	.05
130	Bob Wickman	.05
131	Scott Karl	.05
132	Mark Loretta	.05
133	Fernando Vina	.05
134	Matt Lawton	.05
135	Pat Meares	.05
136	Eric Milton	.05
137	Paul Molitor	.60
138	David Ortiz	.35
139	Todd Walker	.05
140	Shane Andrews	.05
141	Brad Fullmer	.05
142	Vladimir Guerrero	.60
143	Dustin Hermanson	.05
144	Ryan McGuire	.05
145	Ugueth Urbina	.05
146	John Franco	.05
147	Butch Huskey	.05
148	Bobby Jones	.05
149	John Olerud	.05
150	Rey Ordonez	.05
151	Mike Piazza	1.25
152	Hideo Nomo	.30
153	Masato Yoshii	.05
154	Derek Jeter	2.00
155	Chuck Knoblauch	.05
156	Paul O'Neill	.05
157	Andy Pettitte	.20
158	Mariano Rivera	.15
159	Darryl Strawberry	.05
160	David Wells	.05
161	Jorge Posada	.05
162	Ramiro Mendoza	.05
163	Miguel Tejada	.15
164	Ryan Christenson	.05
165	Rickey Henderson	.60
166	A.J. Hinch	.05
167	Ben Grieve	.05
168	Kenny Rogers	.05
169	Matt Stairs	.05
170	Bob Abreu	.05
171	Rico Brogna	.05
172	Doug Glanville	.05
173	Mike Grace	.05
174	Desi Relaford	.05
175	Scott Rolen	.40
176	Jose Guillen	.05
177	Francisco Cordova	.05
178	Al Martin	.05
179	Jason Schmidt	.05
180	Turner Ward	.05
181	Kevin Young	.05
182	Mark McGwire	1.50
183	Delino DeShields	.05
184	Eli Marrero	.05
185	Tom Lampkin	.05
186	Ray Lankford	.05
187	Willie McGee	.05
188	Matt Morris	.05
189	Andy Ashby	.05
190	Kevin Brown	.05
191	Ken Caminiti	.05
192	Trevor Hoffman	.05
193	Wally Joyner	.05
194	Greg Vaughn	.05
195	Danny Darwin	.05
196	Shawn Estes	.05
197	Orel Hershiser	.05
198	Jeff Kent	.05
199	Bill Mueller	.05
200	Robb Nen	.05
201	J.T. Snow	.05
202	Ken Cloude	.05
203	Russ Davis	.05
204	Jeff Fassero	.05
205	Ken Griffey Jr.	1.00
206	Shane Monahan	.05
207	David Segui	.05
208	Dan Wilson	.05
209	Wilson Alvarez	.05
210	Wade Boggs	.75
211	Miguel Cairo	.05
212	Bubba Trammell	.05
213	Quinton McCracken	.05
214	Paul Sorrento	.05
215	Kevin Stocker	.05
216	Will Clark	.05
217	Rusty Greer	.05
218	Rick Helling	.05
219	Mike McLemore	.05
220	Ivan Rodriguez	.50
221	John Wetteland	.05
222	Jose Canseco	.40
223	Roger Clemens	.85
224	Carlos Delgado	.25
225	Darrin Fletcher	.05
226	Alex Gonzalez	.05
227	Jose Cruz Jr.	.05
228	Shannon Stewart	.05
229	Rolando Arrojo (Foreign Focus)	.05
230	Livan Hernandez (Foreign Focus)	.05
231	Orlando Hernandez (Foreign Focus)	.05
232	Raul Mondesi (Foreign Focus)	.05
233	Moises Alou (Foreign Focus)	.05
234	Pedro Martinez (Foreign Focus)	.30
235	Sammy Sosa (Foreign Focus)	.50
236	Vladimir Guerrero (Foreign Focus)	.40
237	Bartolo Colon (Foreign Focus)	.05
238	Miguel Tejada (Foreign Focus)	.05
239	Ismael Valdes (Foreign Focus)	.05
240	Mariano Rivera (Foreign Focus)	.05
241	Jose Cruz Jr. (Foreign Focus)	.05
242	Juan Gonzalez (Foreign Focus)	.20
243	Ivan Rodriguez (Foreign Focus)	.15
244	Sandy Alomar (Foreign Focus)	.05
245	Roberto Alomar (Foreign Focus)	.10
246	Magglio Ordonez (Foreign Focus)	.05
247	Kerry Wood (Highlights Checklist)	.10
248	Mark McGwire (Highlights Checklist)	.75
249	David Wells (Highlights Checklist)	.05
250	Rolando Arrojo (Highlights Checklist)	.05

#	Player	Price
251	Ken Griffey Jr. (Highlights Checklist)	.65
252	Trevor Hoffman (Highlights Checklist)	.05
253	Travis Lee (Highlights Checklist)	.05
254	Roberto Alomar (Highlights Checklist)	.10
255	Sammy Sosa (Highlights Checklist)	.50
266	Pat Burrell RC (Star Rookie)	2.00
267	Shea Hillenbrand RC (Star Rookie)	.65
268	Robert Fick (Star Rookie)	.05
269	Roy Halladay (Star Rookie)	.05
270	Ruben Mateo (Star Rookie)	.05
271	Bruce Chen (Star Rookie)	.05
272	Angel Pena (Star Rookie)	.05
273	Michael Barrett (Star Rookie)	.05
274	Kevin Witt (Star Rookie)	.05
275	Damon Minor (Star Rookie)	.05
276	Ryan Minor (Star Rookie)	.05
277	A.J. Pierzynski (Star Rookie)	.05
278	A.J. Burnett RC (Star Rookie)	.50
279	Dermal Brown (Star Rookie)	.05
280	Joe Lawrence (Star Rookie)	.05
281	Derrick Gibson (Star Rookie)	.05
282	Carlos Febles (Star Rookie)	.05
283	Chris Haas (Star Rookie)	.05
284	Cesar King (Star Rookie)	.05
285	Calvin Pickering (Star Rookie)	.05
286	Mitch Meluskey (Star Rookie)	.05
287	Carlos Beltran (Star Rookie)	.50
288	Ron Belliard (Star Rookie)	.05
289	Jerry Hairston Jr. (Star Rookie)	.05
290	Fernando Seguignol (Star Rookie)	.05
291	Kris Benson (Star Rookie)	.05
292	Chad Hutchinson RC (Star Rookie)	.05
293	Jarrod Washburn	.05
294	Jason Dickson	.05
295	Mo Vaughn	.05
296	Garrett Anderson	.05
297	Jim Edmonds	.05
298	Ken Hill	.05
299	Shigetosi Hasegawa	.05
300	Todd Stottlemyre	.05
301	Randy Johnson	.60
302	Omar Daal	.05
303	Steve Finley	.05
304	Matt Williams	.05
305	Danny Klassen	.05
306	Tony Batista	.05
307	Brian Jordan	.05
308	Greg Maddux	.75
309	Chipper Jones	.75
310	Bret Boone	.05
311	Ozzie Guillen	.05
312	John Rocker	.05
313	Tom Glavine	.25
314	Andruw Jones	.60
315	Albert Belle	.05
316	Charles Johnson	.05
317	Will Clark	.05
318	B.J. Surhoff	.05
319	Delino DeShields	.05
320	Heathcliff Slocumb	.05
321	Sidney Ponson	.05
322	Juan Guzman	.05
323	Reggie Jefferson	.05
324	Mark Portugal	.05
325	Tim Wakefield	.05
326	Jason Varitek	.05
327	Jose Offerman	.05
328	Pedro Martinez	.60
329	Trot Nixon	.05
330	Kerry Wood	.30
331	Sammy Sosa	.75
332	Glenallen Hill	.05
333	Gary Gaetti	.05
334	Mickey Morandini	.05
335	Benito Santiago	.05
336	Jeff Blauser	.05
337	Frank Thomas	.65
338	Paul Konerko	.15
339	Jaime Navarro	.05
340	Carlos Lee	.05
341	Brian Simmons	.05
342	Mark Johnson	.05
343	Jeff Abbot	.05
344	Steve Avery	.05
345	Mike Cameron	.05
346	Michael Tucker	.05
347	Greg Vaughn	.05
348	Hal Morris	.05
349	Pete Harnisch	.05
350	Denny Neagle	.05
351	Manny Ramirez	.60
352	Roberto Alomar	.20
353	Dwight Gooden	.05
354	Kenny Lofton	.05
355	Mike Jackson	.05
356	Charles Nagy	.05
357	Enrique Wilson	.05
358	Russ Branyan	.05
359	Richie Sexson	.05
360	Vinny Castilla	.05
361	Dante Bichette	.05
362	Kirt Manwaring	.05
363	Darryl Hamilton	.05
364	Jamey Wright	.05
365	Curt Leskanic	.05
366	Jeff Reed	.05
367	Bobby Higginson	.05
368	Justin Thompson	.05
369	Brad Ausmus	.05
370	Dean Palmer	.05
371	Gabe Kapler	.05
372	Juan Encarnacion	.05
373	Karim Garcia	.10
374	Alex Gonzalez	.05
375	Braden Looper	.05
376	Preston Wilson	.05
377	Todd Dunwoody	.05
378	Alex Fernandez	.05
379	Mark Kotsay	.05
380	Mark Mantei	.05
381	Ken Caminiti	.05
382	Scott Elarton	.05
383	Jeff Bagwell	.60
384	Derek Bell	.05
385	Ricky Gutierrez	.05
386	Richard Hidalgo	.05
387	Shane Reynolds	.05
388	Carl Everett	.05
389	Scott Service	.05
390	Jeff Suppan	.05
391	Joe Randa	.05
392	Kevin Appier	.05
393	Shane Halter	.05
394	Chad Kreuter	.05
395	Mike Sweeney	.05
396	Kevin Brown	.05
397	Devon White	.05
398	Todd Hollandsworth	.05
399	Todd Hundley	.05
400	Chan Ho Park	.05
401	Mark Grudzielanek	.05
402	Raul Mondesi	.05
403	Ismael Valdes	.05
404	Rafael Roque	.05
405	Sean Berry	.05
406	Kevin Barker	.05
407	Dave Nilsson	.05
408	Geoff Jenkins	.05
409	Jim Abbott	.05
410	Bobby Hughes	.05
411	Corey Koskie	.05
412	Rick Aguilera	.05
413	LaTroy Hawkins	.05
414	Ron Coomer	.05
415	Denny Hocking	.05
416	Marty Cordova	.05
417	Terry Steinbach	.05
418	Rondell White	.05
419	Wilton Guerrero	.05
420	Shane Andrews	.05
421	Orlando Cabrera	.05
422	Carl Pavano	.05
423	Jeff Vasquez	.05
424	Chris Widger	.05
425	Robin Ventura	.05
426	Rickey Henderson	.60
427	Al Leiter	.05
428	Bobby Jones	.05
429	Brian McRae	.05
430	Roger Cedeno	.05
431	Bobby Bonilla	.05
432	Edgardo Alfonzo	.05
433	Bernie Williams	.05
434	Ricky Ledee	.05
435	Chili Davis	.05
436	Tino Martinez	.05
437	Scott Brosius	.05
438	David Cone	.05
439	Joe Girardi	.05
440	Roger Clemens	.85
441	Chad Curtis	.05
442	Hideki Irabu	.05
443	Jason Giambi	.40
444	Scott Spezio	.05
445	Tony Phillips	.05
446	Ramon Hernandez	.05
447	Mike Macfarlane	.05
448	Tom Candiotti	.05
449	Billy Taylor	.05
450	Bobby Estella	.05
451	Curt Schilling	.25
452	Carlton Loewer	.05
453	Marlon Anderson	.05
454	Kevin Jordan	.05
455	Ron Gant	.05
456	Chad Ogea	.05
457	Abraham Nunez	.05
458	Jason Kendall	.05
459	Pat Meares	.05
460	Brant Brown	.05
461	Brian Giles	.05
462	Chad Hermansen	.05
463	Freddy Garcia	.05
464	Edgar Renteria	.05
465	Fernando Tatis	.05
466	Eric Davis	.05
467	Darren Bragg	.05
468	Donovan Osborne	.05
469	Manny Aybar	.05
470	Jose Jimenez	.05
471	Kent Mercker	.05
472	Reggie Sanders	.05
473	Ruben Rivera	.05
474	Tony Gwynn	.75
475	Jim Leyritz	.05
476	Chris Gomez	.05
477	Matt Clement	.05
478	Carlos Hernandez	.05
479	Sterling Hitchcock	.05
480	Ellis Burks	.05
481	Barry Bonds	2.00
482	Marvin Bernard	.05
483	Kirk Rueter	.05
484	F.P. Santangelo	.05
485	Stan Javier	.05
486	Jeff Kent	.05
487	Alex Rodriguez	1.50
488	Tom Lampkin	.05
489	Jose Mesa	.05
490	Jay Buhner	.05
491	Edgar Martinez	.05
492	Butch Huskey	.05
493	John Mabry	.05
494	Jamie Moyer	.05
495	Roberto Hernandez	.05
496	Tony Saunders	.05
497	Fred McGriff	.05
498	Dave Martinez	.05
499	Jose Canseco	.40
500	Rolando Arrojo	.05
501	Esteban Yan	.05
502	Juan Gonzalez	.30
503	Rafael Palmeiro	.05
504	Aaron Sele	.05
505	Royce Clayton	.05
506	Todd Zeile	.05
507	Tom Goodwin	.05
508	Lee Stevens	.05
509	Esteban Loaiza	.05
510	Joey Hamilton	.05
511	Homer Bush	.05
512	Willie Greene	.05
513	Shawn Green	.25
514	David Wells	.05
515	Kelvim Escobar	.05
516	Tony Fernandez	.05
517	Pat Hentgen	.05
518	Mark McGwire (Arms Race)	.75
519	Ken Griffey Jr. (Arms Race)	.65
520	Sammy Sosa (Arms Race)	.65
521	Juan Gonzalez (Arms Race)	.20
522	J.D. Drew (Arms Race)	.10
523	Chipper Jones (Arms Race)	.05
524	Alex Rodriguez (Arms Race)	.75
525	Mike Piazza (Arms Race)	.65
526	Nomar Garciaparra (Arms Race)	.50
527	Mark McGwire Season Highlights Checklist	.50
528	Sammy Sosa Season Highlights Checklist	.50
529	Scott Brosius Season Highlights Checklist	.05
530	Cal Ripken Jr. Season Highlights Checklist	1.00
531	Barry Bonds Season Highlights Checklist	1.00
532	Roger Clemens Season Highlights Checklist	.40
533	Ken Griffey Jr. Season Highlights Checklist	.65
534	Alex Rodriguez Season Highlights Checklist	.75
535	Curt Schilling Season Highlights Checklist	.05

Exclusives

	NM/M
Common Player:	3.00
Stars/Rookies:	15X
Greens (1-255):	Values Undetermined
Greens (266-535):	100X

(See 1999 Upper Deck for checklist and base card values.)

Babe Ruth Piece of History Bat

		NM/M
PH	Babe Ruth/Bat	900.00
PHLC	Babe Ruth/Legendary Cut Auto.	25,000

Crowning Glory

	NM/M
Complete Set (3):	22.50
Common Player:	6.00
Inserted 1:23	
Doubles (1,000 Sets):	2X
Triples (25 Sets):	8X
Home Runs (1 Set):Values Undetermined	
CG1 Roger Clemens, Kerry Wood	6.00
CG2 Mark McGwire, Barry Bonds	12.00
CG3 Ken Griffey Jr., Mark McGwire	7.50

Forte

	NM/M
Complete Set (30):	50.00
Common Player:	.50
Inserted 1:23	
Doubles (2,000 Sets):	3X
Triples (10):	15X
Quadruples (10):	40X
1 Darin Erstad	1.50
2 Troy Glaus	1.50
3 Mo Vaughn	.50
4 Greg Maddux	2.50
5 Andres Galarraga	.50
6 Chipper Jones	2.50
7 Cal Ripken Jr.	5.00
8 Albert Belle	.50
9 Nomar Garciaparra	2.50
10 Sammy Sosa	2.50
11 Kerry Wood	1.00
12 Frank Thomas	2.00
13 Jim Thome	1.50
14 Jeff Bagwell	2.00
15 Vladimir Guerrero	2.00
16 Mike Piazza	3.00
17 Derek Jeter	5.00
18 Ben Grieve	.50
19 Eric Chavez	.50
20 Scott Rolen	1.50
21 Mark McGwire	4.00
22 J.D. Drew	1.00
23 Tony Gwynn	2.50
24 Barry Bonds	5.00
25 Alex Rodriguez	4.00
26 Ken Griffey Jr.	3.00
27 Ivan Rodriguez	1.50
28 Juan Gonzalez	1.00
29 Roger Clemens	2.75
30 Andruw Jones	2.00

Game Jersey

		NM/M
	Common Player:	6.00
AB	Adrian Beltre H1	10.00
EC	Eric Chavez H2	6.00
JD	J.D. Drew H2	10.00
JDs	J.D. Drew/Auto./8 H2	150.00
DE	Darin Erstad H1	10.00
BF	Brad Fullmer H2	4.50
JG	Juan Gonzalez HR1	15.00
BG	Ben Grieve H1	6.00
KG	Ken Griffey Jr. H1	20.00
KGs	Ken Griffey Jr./Auto./24 H1	150.00
JR	Ken Griffey Jr. HR2	20.00
JRs	Ken Griffey Jr./Auto./24 HR2	150.00
TGw	Tony Gwynn H2	15.00
TH	Todd Helton H1	15.00
CJ	Charles Johnson HR1	6.00
CJ	Chipper Jones H2	15.00
TL	Travis Lee H1	6.00
GM	Greg Maddux H2	15.00
MP	Mike Piazza HR1	20.00
MR	Manny Ramirez H2	10.00
AR	Alex Rodriguez HR1	25.00
IR	Ivan Rodriguez H1	7.50
NRa	Nolan Ryan/Astros H2	15.00
NRas	Nolan Ryan H2 Auto./34	450.00
NRb	Nolan Ryan/Rangers HR2	15.00
SS	Sammy Sosa H2	20.00
BT	Bubba Trammell H2	15.00
FT	Frank Thomas HR2	15.00
KW	Kerry Wood HR1	15.00
KWs	Kerry Wood/Auto./34 HR1	150.00

1999 Upper Deck Hitter.Net Ted Williams

		NM/M
9	Ted Williams	7.50

1999 Upper Deck Homerun Heroes

		NM/M
	Complete Set (10):	10.00
	Common Player:	.50
	Complete Set Cans (6):	10.00
	Common Player Can:	2.00
H1	Ken Griffey Jr.	1.25
H2	Mark McGwire	2.00
H3	Sammy Sosa	1.00
H4	Troy Glaus	.75
H5	Mike Piazza	2.00
H6	Chipper Jones	1.00
H7	Vladimir Guerrero	.75
H8	Frank Thomas	.75
H9	Juan Gonzalez	.50
H10	Alex Rodriguez	2.00
	SEALED CANS	
1	Ken Griffey Jr.	2.50
2	Mark McGwire	2.50
3	Sammy Sosa	2.00
4	Troy Glaus	1.50
5	Mike Piazza	2.50
6	Chipper Jones	2.00

Immaculate Perception

		NM/M
	Complete Set (27):	45.00
	Common Player:	.25
	Inserted 1:23	
	Doubles (1,000 Sets):	1.5X
	Triples (25):	8X
	Home Runs (1):	Values Undetermined
I1	Jeff Bagwell	2.00
I2	Craig Biggio	.25
I3	Barry Bonds	5.00
I4	Roger Clemens	2.75
I5	Jose Cruz Jr.	.25
I6	Nomar Garciaparra	2.50
I7	Tony Clark	.25
I8	Ben Grieve	.25
I9	Ken Griffey Jr.	3.00
I10	Tony Gwynn	2.50
I11	Randy Johnson	2.00
I12	Chipper Jones	2.50
I13	Travis Lee	.40
I14	Kenny Lofton	.25
I15	Greg Maddux	2.50
I16	Mark McGwire	4.00
I17	Hideo Nomo	1.00
I18	Mike Piazza	3.00
I19	Manny Ramirez	2.00
I20	Cal Ripken Jr.	5.00
I21	Alex Rodriguez	4.00
I22	Scott Rolen	1.50
I23	Frank Thomas	2.00
I24	Kerry Wood	1.00
I25	Larry Walker	.25
I26	Vinny Castilla	.25
I27	Derek Jeter	5.00

Ken Griffey Jr. 1989 Buyback Autograph

		NM/M
	Ken Griffey Jr./100	1,250

Piece of History 500 Club Babe Ruth

		NM/M
BR	Babe Ruth/50	4,000

Textbook Excellence

		NM/M
	Complete Set (30):	12.50
	Common Player:	.25
	Inserted 1:4	
	Doubles (2,000 Sets):	1.5X
	Triples (100):	5X
	Quadruples (10):	40X
T1	Mo Vaughn	.25
T2	Greg Maddux	.75
T3	Chipper Jones	.75
T4	Andruw Jones	.60
T5	Cal Ripken Jr.	2.00
T6	Albert Belle	.25
T7	Roberto Alomar	.30
T8	Nomar Garciaparra	.75
T9	Kerry Wood	.30
T10	Sammy Sosa	.75
T11	Greg Vaughn	.25
T12	Jeff Bagwell	.60
T13	Kevin Brown	.25
T14	Vladimir Guerrero	.60
T15	Mike Piazza	1.00
T16	Bernie Williams	.25
T17	Derek Jeter	2.00
T18	Ben Grieve	.25
T19	Eric Chavez	.25
T29	Scott Rolen	.50
T21	Mark McGwire	1.50
T22	David Wells	.25
T23	J.D. Drew	.50
T24	Tony Gwynn	.75
T25	Barry Bonds	2.00
T26	Alex Rodriguez	1.50
T27	Ken Griffey Jr.	.50
T28	Juan Gonzalez	.30
T29	Ivan Rodriguez	.50
T30	Roger Clemens	.85

View to a Thrill

		NM/M
	Complete Set (30):	25.00
	Common Player:	.35
	Inserted 1:7	
	Doubles (2,000 Sets):	1.5X
	Triples (100):	4X
	Quadruples (10):	30X
V1	Mo Vaughn	.35
V2	Darin Erstad	.40
V3	Travis Lee	.40
V4	Chipper Jones	1.50
V5	Greg Maddux	1.50
V6	Gabe Kapler	.35
V7	Cal Ripken Jr.	3.00
V8	Nomar Garciaparra	1.50
V9	Kerry Wood	.40
V10	Frank Thomas	1.00
V11	Manny Ramirez	1.00
V12	Larry Walker	.35
V13	Tony Clark	.35
V14	Jeff Bagwell	1.00
V15	Craig Biggio	.35
V16	Vladimir Guerrero	1.00
V17	Mike Piazza	2.00
V18	Bernie Williams	.35
V19	Derek Jeter	3.00
V20	Ben Grieve	.35
V21	Eric Chavez	.35
V22	Scott Rolen	.65
V23	Mark McGwire	2.50
V24	Tony Gwynn	1.50
V25	Barry Bonds	3.00
V26	Ken Griffey Jr.	2.00
V27	Alex Rodriguez	2.50
V28	J.D. Drew	.65
V29	Juan Gonzalez	.50
V30	Roger Clemens	1.75

Wonder Years

		NM/M
	Complete Set (30):	30.00
	Common Player:	.50
	Inserted 1:7	
	Doubles (2,000):	2.5X
	Triples (50):	10X
	Home Runs (1):	Values Undetermined
WY1	Kerry Wood	.75
WY2	Travis Lee	.65
WY3	Jeff Bagwell	1.50
WY4	Barry Bonds	4.00
WY5	Roger Clemens	2.25
WY6	Jose Cruz Jr.	.50
WY7	Andres Galarraga	.50
WY8	Nomar Garciaparra	2.00
WY9	Juan Gonzalez	.75
WY10	Ken Griffey Jr.	2.50
WY11	Tony Gwynn	2.00

WY12	Derek Jeter	4.00
WY13	Randy Johnson	1.50
WY14	Andruw Jones	1.50
WY15	Chipper Jones	2.00
WY16	Kenny Lofton	.50
WY17	Greg Maddux	2.00
WY18	Tino Martinez	.50
WY19	Mark McGwire	3.00
WY20	Paul Molitor	1.50
WY21	Mike Piazza	2.50
WY22	Manny Ramirez	1.50
WY23	Cal Ripken Jr.	4.00
WY24	Alex Rodriguez	3.00
WY25	Sammy Sosa	2.00
WY26	Frank Thomas	1.50
WY27	Mo Vaughn	.50
WY28	Larry Walker	.50
WY29	Scott Rolen	1.00
WY30	Ben Grieve	.50

10th Anniversary Team

		NM/M
	Complete Set (30):	20.00
	Common Player:	.15
	Inserted 1:4	
	Doubles (4,000 Sets):	2X
	Triples (100):	6X
	Home Runs (1):	Values Undetermined
X1	Mike Piazza	1.50
X2	Mark McGwire	2.00
X3	Roberto Alomar	.30
X4	Chipper Jones	1.00
X5	Cal Ripken Jr.	3.00
X6	Ken Griffey Jr.	1.50
X7	Barry Bonds	3.00
X8	Tony Gwynn	1.00
X9	Nolan Ryan	3.00
X10	Randy Johnson	.75
X11	Dennis Eckersley	.65
X12	Ivan Rodriguez	.65
X13	Frank Thomas	.75
X14	Craig Biggio	.15
X15	Wade Boggs	1.00
X16	Alex Rodriguez	2.00
X17	Albert Belle	.15
X18	Juan Gonzalez	.40
X19	Rickey Henderson	.75
X20	Greg Maddux	1.00
X21	Tom Glavine	.35
X22	Randy Myers	.15
X23	Sandy Alomar	.15
X24	Jeff Bagwell	.75
X25	Derek Jeter	3.00
X26	Matt Williams	.15
X27	Kenny Lofton	.15
X28	Sammy Sosa	1.00
X29	Larry Walker	.15
X30	Roger Clemens	1.25

1999 Upper Deck Black Diamond

	NM/M
Complete Set (120):	30.00
Common Player:	.10
Common Diamond Debut (91-120):	.25
Inserted 1:4	

Double Diamonds (3,000 Each):		3X
Double Diamond Debuts (2,500):		2X
Triple Diamonds (1,500):		6X
Triple Diamond Debuts (1,000):		3X
Pack (6):		2.00
Wax Box (30):		40.00
1	Darin Erstad	.25
2	Tim Salmon	.10
3	Jim Edmonds	.10
4	Matt Williams	.10
5	David Dellucci	.10
6	Jay Bell	.10
7	Andres Galarraga	.10
8	Chipper Jones	1.00
9	Greg Maddux	1.00
10	Andruw Jones	.75
11	Cal Ripken Jr.	2.50
12	Rafael Palmeiro	.65
13	Brady Anderson	.10
14	Mike Mussina	.40
15	Nomar Garciaparra	1.00
16	Mo Vaughn	.10
17	Pedro Martinez	.75
18	Sammy Sosa	1.00
19	Henry Rodriguez	.10
20	Frank Thomas	.75
21	Magglio Ordonez	.40
22	Albert Belle	.10
23	Paul Konerko	.20
24	Sean Casey	.10
25	Jim Thome	.60
26	Kenny Lofton	.10
27	Sandy Alomar Jr.	.10
28	Jaret Wright	.10
29	Larry Walker	.10
30	Todd Helton	.65
31	Vinny Castilla	.10
32	Tony Clark	.10
33	Damion Easley	.10
34	Mark Kotsay	.10
35	Derrek Lee	.50
36	Moises Alou	.10
37	Jeff Bagwell	.75
38	Craig Biggio	.10
39	Randy Johnson	.75
40	Dean Palmer	.10
41	Johnny Damon	.35
42	Chan Ho Park	.10
43	Raul Mondesi	.10
44	Gary Sheffield	.40
45	Jeromy Burnitz	.10
46	Marquis Grissom	.10
47	Jeff Cirillo	.10
48	Paul Molitor	.75
49	Todd Walker	.10
50	Vladimir Guerrero	.75
51	Brad Fullmer	.10
52	Mike Piazza	1.50
53	Hideo Nomo	.40
54	Carlos Baerga	.10
55	John Olerud	.10
56	Derek Jeter	2.50
57	Hideki Irabu	.10
58	Tino Martinez	.10
59	Bernie Williams	.10
60	Miguel Tejada	.25
61	Ben Grieve	.10
62	Jason Giambi	.55
63	Scott Rolen	.60
64	Doug Glanville	.10
65	Desi Relaford	.10
66	Tony Womack	.10
67	Jason Kendall	.10
68	Jose Guillen	.10
69	Tony Gwynn	1.00
70	Ken Caminiti	.10
71	Greg Vaughn	.10
72	Kevin Brown	.10
73	Barry Bonds	2.50
74	J.T. Snow	.10
75	Jeff Kent	.10
76	Ken Griffey Jr.	1.50
77	Alex Rodriguez	2.00
78	Edgar Martinez	.10
79	Jay Buhner	.10
80	Mark McGwire	2.00
81	Delino DeShields	.10
82	Brian Jordan	.10
83	Quinton McCracken	.10
84	Fred McGriff	.10
85	Juan Gonzalez	.40
86	Ivan Rodriguez	.65
87	Will Clark	.10
88	Roger Clemens	1.25
89	Jose Cruz Jr.	.10
90	Babe Ruth	2.00
91	Troy Glaus (Diamond Debut)	1.00
92	Jarrod Washburn (Diamond Debut)	.25
93	Travis Lee (Diamond Debut)	.75
94	Bruce Chen (Diamond Debut)	.25
95	Mike Caruso (Diamond Debut)	.25
96	Jim Parque (Diamond Debut)	.25
97	Kerry Wood (Diamond Debut)	.50
98	Jeremy Giambi (Diamond Debut)	.25
99	Matt Anderson (Diamond Debut)	.25
100	Seth Greisinger (Diamond Debut)	.25
101	Gabe Alvarez (Diamond Debut)	.25
102	Rafael Medina (Diamond Debut)	.25
103	Daryle Ward (Diamond Debut)	.25
104	Alex Cora (Diamond Debut)	.25
105	Adrian Beltre (Diamond Debut)	.50
106	Geoff Jenkins (Diamond Debut)	.25
107	Eric Milton (Diamond Debut)	.25
108	Carl Pavano (Diamond Debut)	.25
109	Eric Chavez (Diamond Debut)	.50
110	Orlando Hernandez (Diamond Debut)	.25
111	A.J. Hinch (Diamond Debut)	.25
112	Carlton Loewer (Diamond Debut)	.25
113	Aramis Ramirez (Diamond Debut)	.25
114	Cliff Politte (Diamond Debut)	.25
115	Matt Clement (Diamond Debut)	.25
116	Alex Gonzalez (Diamond Debut)	.25
117	J.D. Drew (Diamond Debut)	.75
118	Shane Monahan (Diamond Debut)	.25
119	Rolando Arrojo (Diamond Debut)	.25
120	George Lombard (Diamond Debut)	.25

Double Diamond

NM/M

Complete Set (120):		200.00
Common Player (1-90):		.25
Common Diamond Debut (91-120):		1.00
Stars (1-90):		3X
Diamond Debuts (91-120):		2X

(See 1999 Upper Deck Black Diamond for checklist and base card values.)

Triple Diamond

NM/M

Common Player (1-90):		1.00
Common Diamond Debut (91-120):		1.50
Stars (1-90):		6X
Diamond Debuts (91-120):		3X

(See 1999 Upper Deck Black Diamond for checklist and base card values.)

Quadruple Diamond

NM/M

Common Player (1-90):		4.00
Production 150 each.		
Common Diamond Debut (91-120):		6.00
Production 100 each.		
Stars (1-90):		25X
Diamond Debuts (91-120):		8X
18	Sammy Sosa/66	50.00
76	Ken Griffey Jr. /56	60.00
80	Mark McGwire/70	75.00

(See 1999 Upper Deck Black Diamond for checklist and base card values.)

A Piece of History

NM/M

Common Player:		5.00
JG	Juan Gonzalez	7.50
TG	Tony Gwynn	10.00
BW	Bernie Williams	5.00
MM	Mark McGwire	200.00
MV	Mo Vaughn	5.00
SS	Sammy Sosa	25.00

Diamond Dominance

NM/M

Complete Set (30):		65.00
Common Player:		.50
Production 1,500 Sets		
D01	Kerry Wood	1.00
D02	Derek Jeter	6.00
D03	Alex Rodriguez	5.00
D04	Frank Thomas	2.00
D05	Jeff Bagwell	2.00
D06	Mo Vaughn	.50
D07	Ivan Rodriguez	1.00
D08	Cal Ripken Jr.	6.00
D09	Rolando Arrojo	.50
D10	Chipper Jones	3.00
D11	Kenny Lofton	.50
D12	Paul Konerko	.75
D13	Mike Piazza	4.00
D14	Ben Grieve	.50
D15	Nomar Garciaparra	3.00
D16	Travis Lee	.65
D17	Scott Rolen	1.00
D18	Juan Gonzalez	1.00
D19	Tony Gwynn	3.00
D20	Tony Clark	.50
D21	Roger Clemens	3.50
D22	Sammy Sosa	3.00
D23	Larry Walker	.50
D24	Ken Griffey Jr.	4.00
D25	Mark McGwire	5.00
D26	Barry Bonds	6.00
D27	Vladimir Guerrero	2.00
D28	Tino Martinez	.50
D29	Greg Maddux	3.00
D30	Babe Ruth	5.00

Mystery Numbers

NM/M

Complete Set (30):		100.00
Common Player:		.75
M1	Babe Ruth/100	25.00
M2	Ken Griffey Jr./200	12.50
M3	Kerry Wood/300	4.00
M4	Mark McGwire/400	12.50
M5	Alex Rodriguez/500	12.50
M6	Chipper Jones/600	6.00
M7	Nomar Garciaparra/700	6.00
M8	Derek Jeter/800	10.00
M9	Mike Piazza/900	6.00
M10	Roger Clemens/1,000	4.50
M11	Greg Maddux/1,100	4.00
M12	Scott Rolen/1,200	1.25
M13	Cal Ripken Jr./1,300	7.50
M14	Ben Grieve/1,400	.75
M15	Troy Glaus/1,500	3.00
M16	Sammy Sosa/1,600	4.50
M17	Darin Erstad/1,700	1.25
M18	Juan Gonzalez/1,800	1.25
M19	Pedro Martinez/1,900	1.50
M20	Larry Walker/2,000	.75
M21	Vladimir Guerrero/2,100	1.50
M22	Jeff Bagwell/2,200	1.50
M23	Jaret Wright/2,300	.75
M24	Travis Lee/2,400	.75
M25	Barry Bonds/2,500	6.00
M26	Orlando Hernandez/2,600	.75
M27	Frank Thomas/2,700	1.50
M28	Tony Gwynn/2,800	2.00
M29	Andres Galarraga/2,900	.75
M30	Craig Biggio/3,000	.75

Piece of History 500 Club

NM/M

Reggie Jackson	165.00
Reggie Jackson/Auto.	500.00

1999 Upper Deck Century Legends

NM/M

Complete Set (131):		20.00
Common Player:		.10
Century Collection:		20X
Production 100 Sets		
Pack (5):		3.00
Wax Box (24):		60.00
1	Babe Ruth (Top 50)	2.00
1	Babe Ruth (SAMPLE overprint on back.)	2.00
2	Willie Mays (Top 50)	1.00
3	Ty Cobb (Top 50)	1.00
4	Walter Johnson (Top 50)	.40

5	Hank Aaron (Top 50)	1.00
6	Lou Gehrig (Top 50)	1.50
7	Christy Mathewson (Top 50)	.40
8	Ted Williams (Top 50)	1.25
9	Rogers Hornsby (Top 50)	.25
10	Stan Musial (Top 50)	.65
12	Grover Alexander (Top 50)	.25
13	Honus Wagner (Top 50)	.40
14	Cy Young (Top 50)	.40
15	Jimmie Foxx (Top 50)	.25
16	Johnny Bench (Top 50)	.50
17	Mickey Mantle (Top 50)	2.00
18	Josh Gibson (Top 50)	.25
19	Satchel Paige (Top 50)	.50
20	Roberto Clemente (Top 50)	1.50
21	Warren Spahn (Top 50)	.20
22	Frank Robinson (Top 50)	.20
23	Lefty Grove (Top 50)	.20
24	Eddie Collins (Top 50)	.10
27	Tris Speaker (Top 50)	.25
28	Mike Schmidt (Top 50)	.50
29	Napoleon LaJoie (Top 50)	.20
30	Steve Carlton (Top 50)	.25
31	Bob Gibson (Top 50)	.25
32	Tom Seaver (Top 50)	.25
33	George Sisler (Top 50)	.10
34	Barry Bonds (Top 50)	1.50
35	Joe Jackson (Top 50)	1.25
36	Bob Feller (Top 50)	.25
37	Hank Greenberg (Top 50)	.25
38	Ernie Banks (Top 50)	.40
39	Greg Maddux (Top 50)	.75
40	Yogi Berra (Top 50)	.40
41	Nolan Ryan (Top 50)	2.00
42	Mel Ott (Top 50)	.25
43	Al Simmons (Top 50)	.10
44	Jackie Robinson (Top 50)	1.25
45	Carl Hubbell (Top 50)	.25
46	Charley Gehringer (Top 50)	.10
47	Buck Leonard (Top 50)	.10
48	Reggie Jackson (Top 50)	.40
49	Tony Gwynn (Top 50)	.75
50	Roy Campanella (Top 50)	.40
51	Ken Griffey Jr. (Contemporaries)	1.00
52	Barry Bonds (Contemporaries)	1.50
53	Roger Clemens (Contemporaries)	.85
54	Tony Gwynn (Contemporaries)	.75
55	Cal Ripken Jr. (Contemporaries)	1.50
56	Greg Maddux (Contemporaries)	.75
57	Frank Thomas (Contemporaries)	.65
58	Mark McGwire (Contemporaries)	1.25
59	Mike Piazza (Contemporaries)	1.00
60	Wade Boggs (Contemporaries)	.75
61	Alex Rodriguez (Contemporaries)	1.25
62	Juan Gonzalez (Contemporaries)	.30
63	Mo Vaughn (Contemporaries)	.10
64	Albert Belle (Contemporaries)	.10
65	Sammy Sosa (Contemporaries)	.75
66	Nomar Garciaparra (Contemporaries)	.75
67	Derek Jeter (Contemporaries)	1.50
68	Kevin Brown (Contemporaries)	.10
69	Jose Canseco (Contemporaries)	.35
70	Randy Johnson (Contemporaries)	.60
71	Tom Glavine (Contemporaries)	.25
72	Barry Larkin (Contemporaries)	.10
73	Curt Schilling (Contemporaries)	.25
74	Moises Alou (Contemporaries)	.10
75	Fred McGriff (Contemporaries)	.10

76	Pedro Martinez (Contemporaries)	.65
77	Andres Galarraga (Contemporaries)	.10
78	Will Clark (Contemporaries)	.10
79	Larry Walker (Contemporaries)	.10
80	Ivan Rodriguez (Contemporaries)	.50
81	Chipper Jones (Contemporaries)	.75
82	Jeff Bagwell (Contemporaries)	.60
83	Craig Biggio (Contemporaries)	.10
84	Kerry Wood (Contemporaries)	.35
85	Roberto Alomar (Contemporaries)	.20
86	Vinny Castilla (Contemporaries)	.10
87	Kenny Lofton (Contemporaries)	.10
88	Rafael Palmeiro (Contemporaries)	.10
89	Manny Ramirez (Contemporaries)	.60
90	David Wells (Contemporaries)	.10
91	Mark Grace (Contemporaries)	.10
92	Bernie Williams (Contemporaries)	.10
93	David Cone (Contemporaries)	.10
94	John Olerud (Contemporaries)	.10
95	John Smoltz (Contemporaries)	.10
96	Tino Martinez (Contemporaries)	.10
97	Raul Mondesi (Contemporaries)	.10
98	Gary Sheffield (Contemporaries)	.35
99	Orel Hershiser (Contemporaries)	.10
100	Rickey Henderson (Contemporaries)	.65
101	J.D. Drew (21st Century Phenoms)	.50
102	Troy Glaus (21st Century Phenoms)	.50
103	Nomar Garciaparra (21st Century Phenoms)	.75
104	Scott Rolen (21st Century Phenoms)	.45
105	Ryan Minor (21st Century Phenoms)	.10
106	Travis Lee (21st Century Phenoms)	.20
107	Roy Halladay (21st Century Phenoms)	.10
108	Carlos Beltran (21st Century Phenoms)	.50
109	Alex Rodriguez (21st Century Phenoms)	1.25
110	Eric Chavez (21st Century Phenoms)	.20
111	Vladimir Guerrero (21st Century Phenoms)	.60
112	Ben Grieve (21st Century Phenoms)	.15
113	Kerry Wood (21st Century Phenoms)	.30
114	Alex Gonzalez (21st Century Phenoms)	.10
115	Darin Erstad (21st Century Phenoms)	.30
116	Derek Jeter (21st Century Phenoms)	1.50
117	Jaret Wright (21st Century Phenoms)	.10
118	Jose Cruz Jr. (21st Century Phenoms)	.25
119	Chipper Jones (21st Century Phenoms)	.75
120	Gabe Kapler (21st Century Phenoms)	.10
121	Satchel Paige (Century Memories)	.50
122	Willie Mays (Century Memories)	1.00
123	Roberto Clemente (Century Memories)	1.50
124	Lou Gehrig (Century Memories)	1.50
125	Mark McGwire (Century Memories)	1.25
127	Bob Gibson (Century Memories)	.25
128	Johnny Vander Meer (Century Memories)	.10
129	Walter Johnson (Century Memories)	.25
130	Ty Cobb (Century Memories)	.75
131	Don Larsen (Century Memories)	.20
132	Jackie Robinson (Century Memories)	1.00
133	Tom Seaver (Century Memories)	.25
134	Johnny Bench (Century Memories)	.35
135	Frank Robinson (Century Memories)	.25

Century Collection

NM/M	
Common Player:	2.00
Stars:	30X

(See 1999 Upper Deck Century Legends for checklist and base card values.)

All-Century Team

NM/M

Complete Set (10):		30.00
Common Player:		2.50
Inserted 1:23		
1	Babe Ruth	7.50
2	Ty Cobb	3.50
3	Willie Mays	3.50
4	Lou Gehrig	6.00
5	Jackie Robinson	5.00
6	Mike Schmidt	2.50
7	Ernie Banks	2.50
8	Johnny Bench	2.50
9	Cy Young	2.50
10	Lineup Sheet	.25

Century Artifacts

No Pricing

Century Epic Signatures

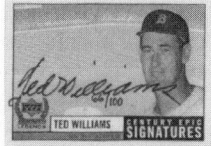

NM/M

Common Player:	20.00
Production 100 Sets	
EB Ernie Banks	85.00
JB Johnny Bench	90.00
YB Yogi Berra	75.00
BB Barry Bonds	240.00
SC Steve Carlton	50.00
BD Bucky Dent	20.00
BF Bob Feller	50.00
CF Carlton Fisk	40.00
BG Bob Gibson	60.00
JG Juan Gonzalez	60.00
Jr. Ken Griffey Jr.	165.00
Sr. Ken Griffey Sr.	20.00
VG Vladimir Guerrero	70.00
TG Tony Gwynn	90.00
RJ Reggie Jackson	60.00
HK Harmon Killebrew	75.00
DL Don Larsen	30.00
GM Greg Maddux	150.00
EMa Eddie Mathews	90.00
WM Willie Mays	300.00
BM Bill Mazeroski	25.00
WMc Willie McCovey	50.00
SM Stan Musial	100.00
FR Frank Robinson	50.00

AR	Alex Rodriguez	200.00
NR	Nolan Ryan	200.00
MS	Mike Schmidt	125.00
TS	Tom Seaver	75.00
WS	Warren Spahn	80.00
FT	Frank Thomas	80.00
BT	Bobby Thomson	20.00
TW	Ted Williams	750.00

Century MVPs

One Set Produced
Values Undetermined
No Pricing

Epic Milestones

NM/M

Complete Set (9):		5.00
Common Player:		.25
Inserted 1:12		
2	Jackie Robinson	.75
3	Nolan Ryan	1.00
4	Mark McGwire	.75
5	Roger Clemens	.60
6	Sammy Sosa	.50
7	Cal Ripken Jr.	1.00
8	Rickey Henderson	.25
9	Hank Aaron	.75
10	Barry Bonds	1.00

Epic Signatures

NM/M

Common Player:	10.00
Inserted 1:24	
EB Ernie Banks	65.00
JB Johnny Bench	40.00
YB Yogi Berra	50.00
BB Barry Bonds	180.00
SC Steve Carlton	20.00
BD Bucky Dent	10.00
BF Bob Feller	15.00
CF Carlton Fisk	25.00
BG Bob Gibson	25.00
JG Juan Gonzalez	20.00
Jr. Ken Griffey Jr.	100.00
Sr. Ken Griffey Sr.	10.00
VG Vladimir Guerrero	30.00
TG Tony Gwynn	40.00
RJ Reggie Jackson	40.00
HK Harmon Killebrew	30.00
DL Don Larsen	15.00
GM Greg Maddux	100.00
EMa Eddie Mathews	80.00
BM Bill Mazeroski	30.00
WMc Willie McCovey	20.00
SM Stan Musial	80.00
FR Frank Robinson	30.00
AR Alex Rodriguez	150.00
NR Nolan Ryan	150.00
MS Mike Schmidt	50.00
TS Tom Seaver	40.00
WS Warren Spahn	60.00
FT Frank Thomas	60.00
BT Bobby Thomson	10.00

1999 Upper Deck Century Legends Hank Aaron Blowup

NM/M

5	Hank Aaron	125.00

Jerseys of the Century

NM/M

Common Player:	12.50
Inserted 1:418	
GB George Brett	25.00
RC Roger Clemens	25.00
TG Tony Gwynn	20.00
GM Greg Maddux	20.00
EM Eddie Murray	15.00

NR	Nolan Ryan	90.00
MS	Mike Schmidt	25.00
OZ	Ozzie Smith	20.00
DW	Dave Winfield	15.00

Legendary Cuts

NM/M

Values Undetermined

CY	Cy Young (11/00 Auction)	1,850

Memorable Shots

NM/M

Complete Set (10):		15.00
Common Player:		.50
Inserted 1:12		
1	Babe Ruth	5.00
2	Bobby Thomson	1.00
3	Kirk Gibson	.50
4	Carlton Fisk	.50
5	Bill Mazeroski	1.00
6	Bucky Dent	.50
7	Mark McGwire	2.00
8	Mickey Mantle	5.00
9	Joe Carter	.50
10	Mark McGwire	2.00

500 Club Piece History

NM/M

JF	Jimmie Foxx	125.00

1999 Upper Deck Challengers for 70

NM/M

Complete Set (90):		15.00
Common Player:		.05
Challenger's Edition (600 Sets):		5X
Pack (5):		2.00
Wax Box (20):		25.00
1	Mark McGwire (Power Elite)	1.50
2	Sammy Sosa (Power Elite)	1.00
3	Ken Griffey Jr. (Power Elite)	1.25
4	Alex Rodriguez (Power Elite)	1.50
5	Albert Belle (Power Elite)	.05
6	Mo Vaughn (Power Elite)	.05
7	Mike Piazza (Power Elite)	1.25
8	Frank Thomas (Power Elite)	.75
9	Juan Gonzalez (Power Elite)	.35
10	Barry Bonds (Power Elite)	2.00
11	Rafael Palmeiro (Power Corps)	.60
12	Jose Canseco (Power Corps)	.50
13	Nomar Garciaparra (Power Corps)	1.00
14	Carlos Delgado (Power Corps)	.20
15	Brian Jordan (Power Corps)	.05
16	Vladimir Guerrero (Power Corps)	.65
17	Vinny Castilla (Power Corps)	.05
18	Chipper Jones (Power Corps)	1.00
19	Jeff Bagwell (Power Corps)	.65
20	Moises Alou (Power Corps)	.05
21	Tony Clark (Power Corps)	.05
22	Jim Thome (Power Corps)	.05
23	Tino Martinez (Power Corps)	.05
24	Greg Vaughn (Power Corps)	.05
25	Javy Lopez (Power Corps)	.05
26	Jeromy Burnitz (Power Corps)	.05
27	Cal Ripken Jr. (Power Corps)	2.00
28	Manny Ramirez (Power Corps)	.65
29	Darin Erstad (Power Corps)	.25
30	Ken Caminiti (Power Corps)	.05
31	Edgar Martinez (Power Corps)	.05
32	Ivan Rodriguez (Power Corps)	.60
33	Larry Walker (Power Corps)	.05
34	Todd Helton (Power Corps)	.60
35	Andruw Jones (Power Corps)	.65
36	Ray Lankford (Power Corps)	.05
37	Travis Lee (Power Corps)	.10
38	Raul Mondesi (Power Corps)	.05
39	Scott Rolen (Power Corps)	.50
40	Ben Grieve (Power Corps)	.05
41	J.D. Drew (Rookie Power)	.50
42	Troy Glaus (Rookie Power)	.60
43	Eric Chavez (Rookie Power)	.10
44	Gabe Kapler (Rookie Power)	.05
45	Michael Barrett (Rookie Power)	.05
46	Mark McGwire (HR Highlights)	.75
47	Jose Canseco (HR Highlights)	.25
48	Greg Vaughn (HR Highlights)	.05
49	Albert Belle (HR Highlights)	.05
50	Mark McGwire (HR Highlights)	.75
51	Vinny Castilla (HR Highlights)	.05
52	Vladimir Guerrero (HR Highlights)	.35
53	Andres Galarraga (HR Highlights)	.05
54	Rafael Palmeiro (HR Highlights)	.30
55	Juan Gonzalez (HR Highlights)	.20
56	Ken Griffey Jr. (HR Highlights)	.60
57	Barry Bonds (HR Highlights)	1.00
58	Mo Vaughn (HR Highlights)	.05
59	Nomar Garciaparra (HR Highlights)	.50
60	Tino Martinez (HR Highlights)	.05
61	Mark McGwire (HR Highlights)	.75
62	Mark McGwire (HR Highlights)	.75
63	Mark McGwire (HR Highlights)	.75
64	Mark McGwire (HR Highlights)	.75
65	Mark McGwire (HR Highlights)	.75
66	Sammy Sosa (HR Highlights)	.50
67	Mark McGwire (HR Highlights)	.75
68	Mark McGwire (HR Highlights)	.75
69	Mark McGwire (HR Highlights)	.75
70	Mark McGwire (HR Highlights)	.75
71	Mark McGwire (HR Highlights)	.75
72	Scott Brosius (HR Highlights)	.05
73	Tony Gwynn (HR Highlights)	.40
74	Chipper Jones (HR Highlights)	.50
75	Jeff Bagwell (HR Highlights)	.35
76	Moises Alou (HR Highlights)	.05
77	Manny Ramirez (HR Highlights)	.35
78	Carlos Delgado (HR Highlights)	.05
79	Kerry Wood (HR Highlights)	.20
80	Ken Griffey Jr. (HR Highlights)	.60
81	Cal Ripken Jr. (HR Highlights)	1.00
82	Alex Rodriguez (HR Highlights)	.75
83	Barry Bonds (HR Highlights)	1.00
84	Ken Griffey Jr. (HR Highlights)	.60
85	Travis Lee (HR Highlights)	.15
86	George Lombard (HR Highlights)	.05
87	Michael Barrett (HR Highlights)	.05
88	Jeremy Giambi (HR Highlights)	.05
89	Troy Glaus (HR Highlights)	.30
90	J.D. Drew (HR Highlights)	.25

Autographed Swinging

NM/M

Complete Set (6):		200.00
Common Player:		5.00
JR	Ken Griffey Jr.	95.00
VG	Vladimir Guerrero	25.00
TH	Todd Helton	15.00
GK	Gabe Kapler	5.00

TL	Travis Lee	7.50
AR	Alex Rodriguez	90.00

Challengers Insert

NM/M

Complete Set (30):		9.00
Common Player:		.15
Parallel Edition (70 Sets):		15X
1	Mark McGwire	1.00
2	Sammy Sosa	.65
3	Ken Griffey Jr.	.75
4	Alex Rodriguez	1.00
5	Albert Belle	.15
6	Mo Vaughn	.15
7	Mike Piazza	.75
8	Frank Thomas	.50
9	Juan Gonzalez	.25
10	Barry Bonds	1.50
11	Rafael Palmeiro	.35
12	Nomar Garciaparra	.65
13	Vladimir Guerrero	.45
14	Vinny Castilla	.15
15	Chipper Jones	.75
16	Jeff Bagwell	.45
17	Moises Alou	.15
18	Tony Clark	.15
19	Jim Thome	.35
20	Tino Martinez	.15
21	Greg Vaughn	.15
22	Manny Ramirez	.45
23	Darin Erstad	.25
24	Ken Caminiti	.15
25	Ivan Rodriguez	.35
26	Andruw Jones	.45
27	Travis Lee	.25
28	Scott Rolen	.35
29	Ben Grieve	.15
30	J.D. Drew	.35

Longball Legends

NM/M

Complete Set (30):		20.00
Common Player:		.50
1	Ken Griffey Jr.	1.50
2	Mark McGwire	2.00
3	Sammy Sosa	1.00
4	Cal Ripken Jr.	2.50
5	Barry Bonds	2.50
6	Larry Walker	.50
7	Fred McGriff	.50
8	Alex Rodriguez	2.00
9	Frank Thomas	.75
10	Juan Gonzalez	.60
11	Jeff Bagwell	.75
12	Mo Vaughn	.50
13	Albert Belle	.50
14	Mike Piazza	1.50
15	Vladimir Guerrero	.75
16	Chipper Jones	1.00
17	Ken Caminiti	.50
18	Rafael Palmeiro	.65
19	Nomar Garciaparra	1.00
20	Jim Thome	.60
21	Edgar Martinez	.50
22	Ivan Rodriguez	.65
23	Andres Galarraga	.50
24	Scott Rolen	.60
25	Darin Erstad	.65
26	Moises Alou	.50
27	J.D. Drew	.65
28	Andruw Jones	.75
29	Manny Ramirez	.75
30	Tino Martinez	.50

Mark on History

NM/M

Complete Set (25):		25.00
Common McGwire:		1.50
Parallel:		8X
01-25 Mark McGwire		1.50

Piece of History 500

NM/M

Harmon Killebrew		120.00
Harmon Killebrew/Auto.		450.00

Swinging/Fences

NM/M

Complete Set (15):		15.00
Common Player:		.50
1	Ken Griffey Jr.	1.50
2	Mark McGwire	2.00
3	Sammy Sosa	1.25
4	Alex Rodriguez	2.00
5	Nomar Garciaparra	1.25
6	J.D. Drew	.75
7	Vladimir Guerrero	1.00
8	Ben Grieve	.50
9	Chipper Jones	1.25

10	Gabe Kapler	.50
11	Travis Lee	.60
12	Todd Helton	.75
13	Juan Gonzalez	.60
14	Mike Piazza	1.50
15	Mo Vaughn	.50

1999 Upper Deck Encore

		NM/M
Complete Set (180):		75.00
Common Player (1-90):		.05
Common Player (91-135):		.25
Inserted 1:4		
Common Player (136-165):		.35
Inserted 1:6		
Common Player (166-180):		.50
Inserted 1:8		
Gold (1-90):		10X
Gold (91-135):		1.5X
Gold (136-165):		3X
Gold (166-180):		4X
Production 125 Sets		
Pack (6):		1.50
Wax Box (24):		25.00
1	Darin Erstad	.25
2	Mo Vaughn	.05
3	Travis Lee	.15
4	Randy Johnson	.60
5	Matt Williams	.05
6	John Smoltz	.05
7	Greg Maddux	.75
8	Chipper Jones	.75
9	Tom Glavine	.25
10	Andruw Jones	.60
11	Cal Ripken Jr.	1.50
12	Mike Mussina	.30
13	Albert Belle	.05
14	Nomar Garciaparra	.75
15	Jose Offerman	.05
16	Pedro Martinez	.60
17	Trot Nixon	.10
18	Kerry Wood	.40
19	Sammy Sosa	.75
20	Frank Thomas	.60
21	Paul Konerko	.15
22	Sean Casey	.15
23	Barry Larkin	.15
24	Greg Vaughn	.05
25	Travis Fryman	.05
26	Jaret Wright	.05
27	Jim Thome	.45
28	Manny Ramirez	.60
29	Roberto Alomar	.20
30	Kenny Lofton	.05
31	Todd Helton	.60
32	Larry Walker	.05
33	Vinny Castilla	.05
34	Dante Bichette	.05
35	Tony Clark	.05
36	Dean Palmer	.05
37	Gabe Kapler	.05
38	Juan Encarnacion	.05
39	Alex Gonzalez	.05
40	Preston Wilson	.05
41	Mark Kotsay	.05
42	Moises Alou	.05
43	Craig Biggio	.05
44	Ken Caminiti	.05
45	Jeff Bagwell	.60
46	Johnny Damon	.30
47	Gary Sheffield	.25
48	Kevin Brown	.05
49	Raul Mondesi	.05
50	Jeff Cirillo	.05
51	Jeromy Burnitz	.05
52	Todd Walker	.05
53	Corey Koskie	.05
54	Brad Fullmer	.05
55	Vladimir Guerrero	.60
56	Mike Piazza	1.25
57	Robin Ventura	.05
58	Rickey Henderson	.60
59	Derek Jeter	1.50
60	Paul O'Neill	.05
61	Bernie Williams	.05
62	Tino Martinez	.05
63	Roger Clemens	.85
64	Ben Grieve	.05
65	Jason Giambi	.35
66	Bob Abreu	.10
67	Scott Rolen	.40

68	Curt Schilling	.25
69	Marlon Anderson	.05
70	Kevin Young	.05
71	Jason Kendall	.05
72	Brian Giles	.05
73	Mark McGwire	1.25
74	Fernando Tatis	.05
75	Eric Davis	.05
76	Trevor Hoffman	.05
77	Tony Gwynn	.75
78	Matt Clement	.05
79	Robb Nen	.05
80	Barry Bonds	1.50
81	Ken Griffey Jr.	1.00
82	Alex Rodriguez	1.25
83	Wade Boggs	.75
84	Fred McGriff	.05
85	Jose Canseco	.30
86	Ivan Rodriguez	.50
87	Juan Gonzalez	.30
88	Rafael Palmeiro	.50
89	Carlos Delgado	.25
90	David Wells	.05
91	Troy Glaus (Star Rookies)	1.00
92	Adrian Beltre (Star Rookies)	.50
93	Matt Anderson (Star Rookies)	.50
94	Eric Chavez (Star Rookies)	.40
95	Jeff Weaver RC (Star Rookies)	.50
96	Warren Morris (Star Rookies)	.25
97	George Lombard (Star Rookies)	.25
98	Mike Kinkade (Star Rookies)	.25
99	Kyle Farnsworth RC (Star Rookies)	.25
100	J.D. Drew (Star Rookies)	.50
101	Joe McEwing RC (Star Rookies)	.50
102	Carlos Guillen (Star Rookies)	.25
103	Kelly Dransfeldt RC (Star Rookies)	.25
104	Eric Munson RC (Star Rookies)	.50
105	Armando Rios (Star Rookies)	.25
106	Ramon Martinez (Star Rookies)	.25
107	Orlando Hernandez (Star Rookies)	.45
108	Jeremy Giambi (Star Rookies)	.25
109	Pat Burrell RC (Star Rookies)	2.50
110	Shea Hillenbrand RC (Star Rookies)	1.00
111	Billy Koch (Star Rookies)	.25
112	Roy Halladay (Star Rookies)	.35
113	Ruben Mateo (Star Rookies)	.25
114	Bruce Chen (Star Rookies)	.25
115	Angel Pena (Star Rookies)	.25
116	Michael Barrett (Star Rookies)	.25
117	Kevin Witt (Star Rookies)	.25
118	Damon Minor (Star Rookies)	.25
119	Ryan Minor (Star Rookies)	.25
120	A.J. Pierzynski (Star Rookies)	.25
121	A.J. Burnett RC (Star Rookies)	.50
122	Christian Guzman (Star Rookies)	.25
123	Joe Lawrence (Star Rookies)	.25
124	Derrick Gibson (Star Rookies)	.25
125	Carlos Febles (Star Rookies)	.25
126	Chris Haas (Star Rookies)	.25
127	Cesar King (Star Rookies)	.25
128	Calvin Pickering (Star Rookies)	.25
129	Mitch Meluskey (Star Rookies)	.25
130	Carlos Beltran (Star Rookies)	1.00
131	Ron Belliard (Star Rookies)	.25
132	Jerry Hairston Jr. (Star Rookies)	.25
133	Fernando Seguignol (Star Rookies)	.25
134	Kris Benson (Star Rookies)	.25
135	Chad Hutchinson RC (Star Rookies)	.25
136	Ken Griffey Jr. (Homer Odyssey)	1.50
137	Mark McGwire (Homer Odyssey)	2.00
138	Sammy Sosa (Homer Odyssey)	1.25
139	Albert Belle (Homer Odyssey)	.35
140	Mo Vaughn (Homer Odyssey)	.35
141	Alex Rodriguez (Homer Odyssey)	2.00
142	Manny Ramirez (Homer Odyssey)	.75
143	J.D. Drew (Homer Odyssey)	.50
144	Juan Gonzalez (Homer Odyssey)	.45
145	Vladimir Guerrero (Homer Odyssey)	.75
146	Fernando Tatis (Homer Odyssey)	.35
147	Mike Piazza (Homer Odyssey)	2.00
148	Barry Bonds (Homer Odyssey)	2.50
149	Ivan Rodriguez (Homer Odyssey)	.60
150	Jeff Bagwell (Homer Odyssey)	.75
151	Raul Mondesi (Homer Odyssey)	.35

152	Nomar Garciaparra (Homer Odyssey)	1.25
153	Jose Canseco (Homer Odyssey)	.50
154	Greg Vaughn (Homer Odyssey)	.35
155	Scott Rolen (Homer Odyssey)	.50
156	Vinny Castilla (Homer Odyssey)	.35
157	Troy Glaus (Homer Odyssey)	.65
158	Craig Biggio (Homer Odyssey)	.35
159	Tino Martinez (Homer Odyssey)	.35
160	Jim Thome (Homer Odyssey)	.60
161	Frank Thomas (Homer Odyssey)	1.00
162	Tony Clark (Homer Odyssey)	.35
163	Ben Grieve (Homer Odyssey)	.35
164	Matt Williams (Homer Odyssey)	.35
165	Derek Jeter (Homer Odyssey)	2.50
166	Ken Griffey Jr. (Strokes of Genius)	2.00
167	Tony Gwynn (Strokes of Genius)	1.50
168	Mike Piazza (Strokes of Genius)	2.00
169	Mark McGwire (Strokes of Genius)	2.50
170	Sammy Sosa (Strokes of Genius)	1.50
171	Juan Gonzalez (Strokes of Genius)	.60
172	Mo Vaughn (Strokes of Genius)	.50
173	Derek Jeter (Strokes of Genius)	3.00
174	Bernie Williams (Strokes of Genius)	.50
175	Ivan Rodriguez (Strokes of Genius)	.75
176	Barry Bonds (Strokes of Genius)	3.00
177	Scott Rolen (Strokes of Genius)	.75
178	Larry Walker (Strokes of Genius)	.50
179	Chipper Jones (Strokes of Genius)	1.50
180	Alex Rodriguez (Strokes of Genius)	2.50

FX Gold

	NM/M
Common Player:	1.00
Gold (1-90):	10X
Gold (91-135):	1.5X
Gold (136-165):	3X
Gold (166-180):	4X
(See 1999 Upper Deck Encore for checklist and base card values.)	

Batting Practice Caps

		NM/M
Complete Set (15):		85.00
Common Player:		4.00
Inserted 1:750		
CB	Carlos Beltran	8.00
BB	Barry Bonds	30.00
VC	Vinny Castilla	4.00
EC	Eric Chavez	6.00
TC	Tony Clark	4.00
JD	J.D. Drew	6.00
VG	Vladimir Guerrero	8.00
TG	Tony Gwynn	15.00

TH	Todd Helton	8.00
GK	Gabe Kapler	4.00
JK	Jason Kendall	4.00
DP	Dean Palmer	4.00
BH	Frank Thomas	8.00
GV	Greg Vaughn	4.00
TW	Todd Walker	4.00

Driving Forces

		NM/M
Complete Set (15):		30.00
Common Player:		1.00
Inserted 1:23		
Gold (10 Sets):		30X
D1	Ken Griffey Jr.	3.00
D2	Mark McGwire	4.00
D3	Sammy Sosa	2.50
D4	Albert Belle	1.00
D5	Alex Rodriguez	4.00
D6	Mo Vaughn	1.00
D7	Juan Gonzalez	1.00
D8	Jeff Bagwell	2.00
D9	Mike Piazza	3.00
D10	Frank Thomas	2.00
D11	Barry Bonds	5.00
D12	Vladimir Guerrero	2.00
D13	Chipper Jones	2.50
D14	Tony Gwynn	2.50
D15	J.D. Drew	1.50

McGwired!

		NM/M
Complete Set (10):		12.50
Common Card:		1.50
Inserted 1:23		
Parallel:		2X
Production 500 Sets		
1	Mark McGwire, Carl Pavano	1.50
2	Mark McGwire, Michael Morgan	1.50
3	Mark McGwire, Steve Trachsel	1.50
4	Mark McGwire	2.50
5	Mark McGwire	2.50
6	Mark McGwire, Scott Elarton	1.50
7	Mark McGwire, Jim Parque	1.50
8	Mark McGwire	2.50
9	Mark McGwire, Rafael Roque	1.50
10	Mark McGwire, Jaret Wright	1.50

Pure Excitement

		NM/M
Complete Set (30):		35.00
Common Player:		.50
Inserted 1:7		
1	Mo Vaughn	.50
2	Darin Erstad	.75
3	Travis Lee	.65
4	Chipper Jones	1.50
5	Greg Maddux	1.50
6	Gabe Kapler	.50
7	Cal Ripken Jr.	4.00
8	Nomar Garciaparra	1.50
9	Kerry Wood	.75
10	Frank Thomas	1.00
11	Manny Ramirez	1.00
12	Larry Walker	.50

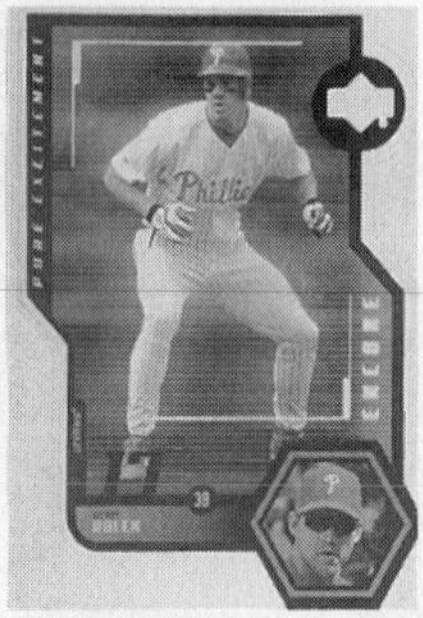

13	Tony Clark	.50
14	Jeff Bagwell	1.00
15	Craig Biggio	.50
16	Vladimir Guerrero	1.00
17	Mike Piazza	2.00
18	Bernie Williams	.60
19	Derek Jeter	4.00
20	Ben Grieve	.60
21	Eric Chavez	.60
22	Scott Rolen	.75
23	Mark McGwire	3.00
24	Tony Gwynn	1.50
25	Barry Bonds	4.00
26	Ken Griffey Jr.	2.00
27	Alex Rodriguez	3.00
28	J.D. Drew	.75
29	Juan Gonzalez	.60
30	Roger Clemens	1.75

Rookie Encore

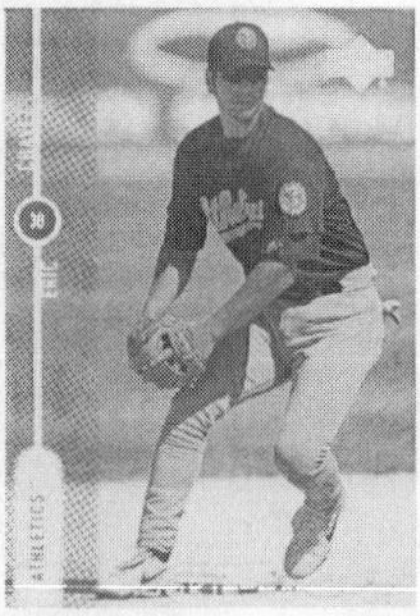

		NM/M
Complete Set (10):		17.50
Common Player:		1.00
Inserted 1:23		
FX Gold:		2X
Production 500 Sets		
1	J.D. Drew	2.00
2	Eric Chavez	1.00
3	Gabe Kapler	1.00
4	Bruce Chen	1.00
5	Carlos Beltran	3.00
6	Troy Glaus	5.00
7	Roy Halladay	1.00
8	Adrian Beltre	2.00
9	Michael Barrett	1.00
10	Pat Burrell	5.00

Upper Realm

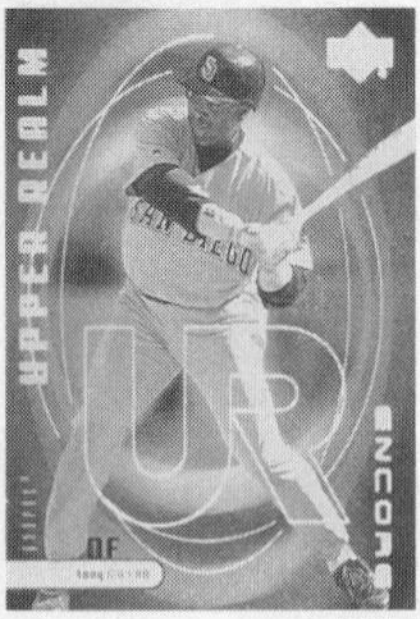

		NM/M
Complete Set (15):		13.00
Common Player:		.30
Inserted 1:11		
1	Ken Griffey Jr.	1.25
2	Mark McGwire	1.50
3	Sammy Sosa	.75
4	Tony Gwynn	.75
5	Alex Rodriguez	1.50
6	Juan Gonzalez	.40
7	J.D. Drew	.50
8	Roger Clemens	.85
9	Greg Maddux	.75
10	Randy Johnson	.60
11	Mo Vaughn	.30
12	Derek Jeter	2.00
13	Vladimir Guerrero	.60
14	Cal Ripken Jr.	2.00
15	Nomar Garciaparra	.75

UD Authentics

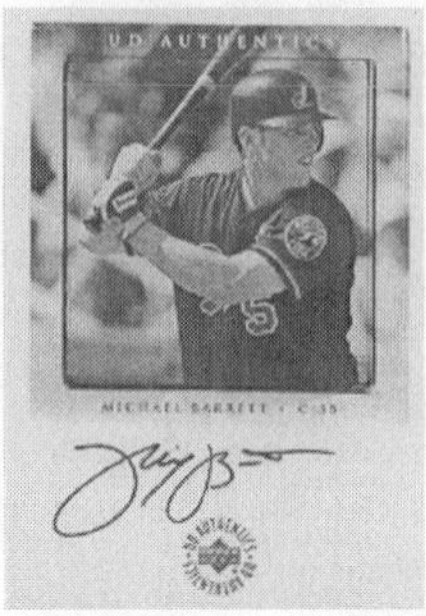

		NM/M
Complete Set (6):		130.00
Common Player:		5.00
Inserted 1:288		
MB	Michael Barrett	4.00
PB	Pat Burrell	10.00
JD	J.D. Drew	12.00
NG	Nomar Garciaparra	70.00
TG	Troy Glaus	12.00
JR	Ken Griffey Jr.	90.00

2K Countdown

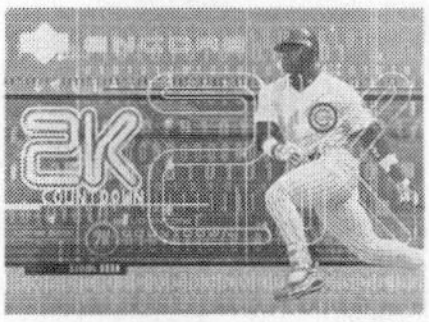

		NM/M
Complete Set (10):		16.00
Common Player:		.75
Inserted 1:11		
1	Ken Griffey Jr.	2.00
2	Derek Jeter	3.00
3	Mike Piazza	2.00
4	J.D. Drew	.75
5	Vladimir Guerrero	1.00
6	Chipper Jones	1.50
7	Alex Rodriguez	2.50
8	Nomar Garciaparra	1.50
9	Mark McGwire	2.50
10	Sammy Sosa	1.50

1999 Upper Deck HoloGrFX

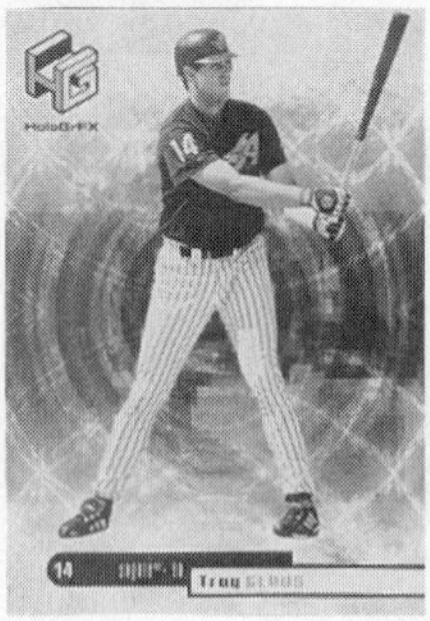

		NM/M
Complete Set (60):		12.00
Common Player:		.10
AUsome:		1.5X
Inserted 1:8		
Pack (3):		1.00
Wax Box (36):		20.00
1	Mo Vaughn	.10
2	Troy Glaus	.60
3	Tim Salmon	.10
4	Randy Johnson	.65
5	Travis Lee	.25
6	Chipper Jones	.75
7	Greg Maddux	.75
8	Andruw Jones	.65
9	Tom Glavine	.25
10	Cal Ripken Jr.	1.50
11	Albert Belle	.10
12	Nomar Garciaparra	.75
13	Pedro J. Martinez	.65
14	Sammy Sosa	.75
15	Frank Thomas	.65
16	Greg Vaughn	.10
17	Kenny Lofton	.10
18	Jim Thome	.50
19	Manny Ramirez	.65
20	Todd Helton	.60
21	Larry Walker	.10
22	Tony Clark	.10
23	Juan Encarnacion	.10
24	Mark Kotsay	.10
25	Jeff Bagwell	.65
26	Craig Biggio	.10
27	Ken Caminiti	.10
28	Carlos Beltran	.50
29	Jeremy Giambi	.10
30	Raul Mondesi	.10
31	Kevin Brown	.10
32	Jeromy Burnitz	.10
33	Corey Koskie	.10
34	Todd Walker	.10
35	Vladimir Guerrero	.65
36	Mike Piazza	1.00
37	Robin Ventura	.10
38	Derek Jeter	1.50
39	Roger Clemens	.85
40	Bernie Williams	.10
41	Orlando Hernandez	.10
42	Ben Grieve	.10
43	Eric Chavez	.15
44	Scott Rolen	.45
45	Pat Burrell **RC**	1.50
46	Warren Morris	.10
47	Jason Kendall	.10
48	Mark McGwire	1.25
49	J.D. Drew	.50
50	Tony Gwynn	.75
51	Trevor Hoffman	.10
52	Barry Bonds	1.50
53	Ken Griffey Jr.	1.00
54	Alex Rodriguez	1.25
55	Jose Canseco	.35
56	Juan Gonzalez	.30
57	Ivan Rodriguez	.60
58	Rafael Palmeiro	.60
59	David Wells	.10
60	Carlos Delgado	.25

Future Fame

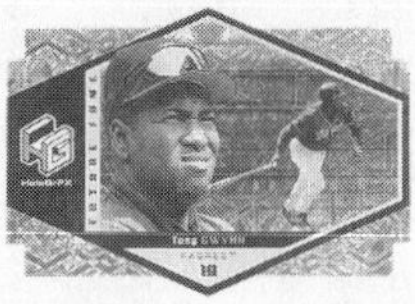

		NM/M
Complete Set (6):		15.00
Common Player:		2.50
Inserted 1:34		
Gold:		2X
Inserted 1:210		
1	Tony Gwynn	2.50
2	Cal Ripken Jr.	5.00
3	Mark McGwire	4.00
4	Ken Griffey Jr.	3.50
5	Greg Maddux	2.50
6	Roger Clemens	3.00

Launchers

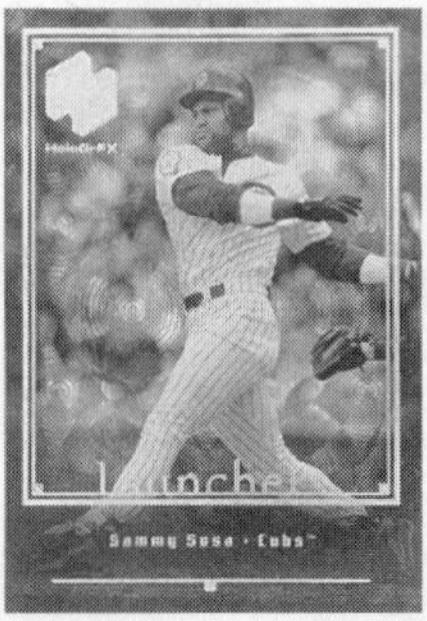

		NM/M
Complete Set (15):		20.00
Common Player:		.50
Inserted 1:3		
Gold:		2X
Inserted 1:105		
1	Mark McGwire	3.00
2	Ken Griffey Jr.	2.50
3	Sammy Sosa	2.00
4	J.D. Drew	.75
5	Mo Vaughn	.50
6	Juan Gonzalez	.50
7	Mike Piazza	2.50
8	Alex Rodriguez	3.00
9	Chipper Jones	2.00
10	Nomar Garciaparra	2.00
11	Vladimir Guerrero	1.00
12	Albert Belle	.50
13	Barry Bonds	4.00
14	Frank Thomas	1.00
15	Jeff Bagwell	1.00

StarView

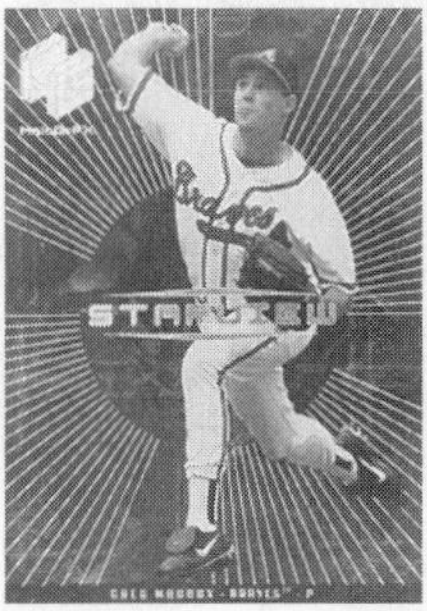

		NM/M
Complete Set (9):		25.00
Common Player:		2.50
Inserted 1:17		
Gold:		2X
Inserted 1:210		
1	Mark McGwire	5.00
2	Ken Griffey Jr.	4.00
3	Sammy Sosa	2.50
4	Nomar Garciaparra	2.50
5	Roger Clemens	3.00
6	Greg Maddux	2.50
7	Mike Piazza	4.00
8	Alex Rodriguez	5.00
9	Chipper Jones	2.50

UD Authentics

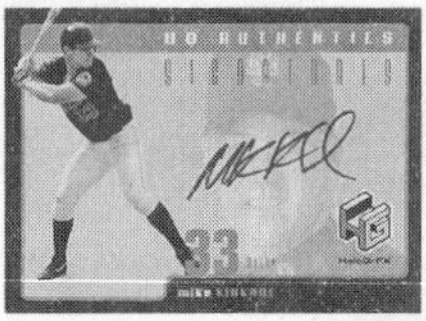

		NM/M
Common Player:		4.00
Inserted 1:431		
CB	Carlos Beltran	25.00
BC	Bruce Chen	4.00
JD	J.D. Drew	12.00
AG	Alex Gonzalez	4.00
JR	Ken Griffey Jr.	80.00
CJ	Chipper Jones	50.00
GK	Gabe Kapler	6.00
MK	Mike Kinkade	4.00
CK	Corey Koskie	7.50
GL	George Lombard	4.00
RM	Ryan Minor	4.00
SM	Shane Monahan	4.00

500 Club Piece of History

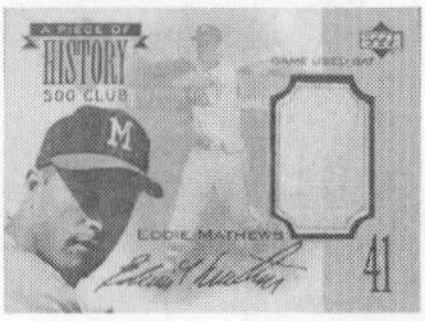

	NM/M
Eddie Mathews/350	150.00
Eddie Mathews/Auto./41	550.00
Willie McCovey/350	120.00
Willie McCovey/Auto./44	650.00

1999 Upper Deck MVP

	NM/M
Complete Set (220):	10.00
Common Player:	.05
Silver Script:	1X
Inserted 1:2	
Gold Script:	10X
Production 100 Sets	
Super Script:	30X
Production 25 Sets	
Pack (10):	1.00

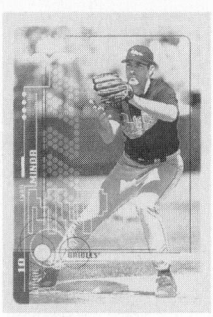

Wax Box (36):		20.00
1	Mo Vaughn	.05
2	Tim Belcher	.05
3	Jack McDowell	.05
4	Troy Glaus	.60
5	Darin Erstad	.40
6	Tim Salmon	.15
7	Jim Edmonds	.05
8	Randy Johnson	.60
9	Steve Finley	.05
10	Travis Lee	.15
11	Matt Williams	.05
12	Todd Stottlemyre	.05
13	Jay Bell	.05
14	David Dellucci	.05
15	Chipper Jones	.75
16	Andruw Jones	.60
17	Greg Maddux	.75
18	Tom Glavine	.25
19	Javy Lopez	.05
20	Brian Jordan	.05
21	George Lombard	.05
22	John Smoltz	.05
23	Cal Ripken Jr.	1.50
24	Charles Johnson	.05
25	Albert Belle	.15
26	Brady Anderson	.05
27	Mike Mussina	.35
28	Calvin Pickering	.05
29	Ryan Minor	.05
30	Jerry Hairston Jr.	.05
31	Nomar Garciaparra	1.00
32	Pedro Martinez	.60
33	Jason Varitek	.05
34	Troy O'Leary	.05
35	Donnie Sadler	.05
36	Mark Portugal	.05
37	John Valentin	.05
38	Kerry Wood	.35
39	Sammy Sosa	1.00
40	Mark Grace	.10
41	Henry Rodriguez	.05
42	Rod Beck	.05
43	Benito Santiago	.05
44	Kevin Tapani	.05
45	Frank Thomas	.60
46	Mike Caruso	.05
47	Magglio Ordonez	.40
48	Paul Konerko	.05
49	Ray Durham	.05
50	Jim Parque	.05
51	Carlos Lee	.05
52	Denny Neagle	.05
53	Pete Harnisch	.05
54	Michael Tucker	.05
55	Sean Casey	.15
56	Eddie Taubensee	.05
57	Barry Larkin	.05
58	Pokey Reese	.05
59	Sandy Alomar	.05
60	Roberto Alomar	.25
61	Bartolo Colon	.05
62	Kenny Lofton	.05
63	Omar Vizquel	.05
64	Travis Fryman	.05
65	Jim Thome	.05
66	Manny Ramirez	.60
67	Jaret Wright	.05
68	Darryl Kile	.05
69	Kirt Manwaring	.05
70	Vinny Castilla	.05
71	Todd Helton	.60
72	Dante Bichette	.05
73	Larry Walker	.05
74	Derrick Gibson	.05
75	Gabe Kapler	.05
76	Dean Palmer	.05
77	Matt Anderson	.05
78	Bobby Higginson	.05
79	Damion Easley	.05
80	Tony Clark	.05
81	Juan Encarnacion	.05
82	Livan Hernandez	.05
83	Alex Gonzalez	.05
84	Preston Wilson	.05
85	Derrek Lee	.05
86	Mark Kotsay	.05
87	Todd Dunwoody	.05
88	Cliff Floyd	.05
89	Ken Caminiti	.05
90	Jeff Bagwell	.60

91	Moises Alou	.05
92	Craig Biggio	.05
93	Billy Wagner	.05
94	Richard Hidalgo	.05
95	Derek Bell	.05
96	Hipolito Pichardo	.05
97	Jeff King	.05
98	Carlos Beltran	.40
99	Jeremy Giambi	.05
100	Larry Sutton	.05
101	Johnny Damon	.20
102	Dee Brown	.05
103	Kevin Brown	.10
104	Chan Ho Park	.05
105	Raul Mondesi	.05
106	Eric Karros	.05
107	Adrian Beltre	.15
108	Devon White	.05
109	Gary Sheffield	.35
110	Sean Berry	.05
111	Alex Ochoa	.05
112	Marquis Grissom	.05
113	Fernando Vina	.05
114	Jeff Cirillo	.05
115	Geoff Jenkins	.05
116	Jeromy Burnitz	.05
117	Brad Radke	.05
118	Eric Milton	.05
119	A.J. Pierzynski	.05
120	Todd Walker	.05
121	David Ortiz	.05
122	Corey Koskie	.05
123	Vladimir Guerrero	.60
124	Rondell White	.05
125	Brad Fullmer	.05
126	Ugueth Urbina	.05
127	Dustin Hermanson	.05
128	Michael Barrett	.05
129	Fernando Seguignol	.05
130	Mike Piazza	1.00
131	Rickey Henderson	.60
132	Rey Ordonez	.05
133	John Olerud	.05
134	Robin Ventura	.05
135	Hideo Nomo	.60
136	Mike Kinkade	.05
137	Al Leiter	.05
138	Brian McRae	.05
139	Derek Jeter	1.50
140	Bernie Williams	.15
141	Paul O'Neill	.05
142	Scott Brosius	.05
143	Tino Martinez	.05
144	Roger Clemens	.85
145	Orlando Hernandez	.10
146	Mariano Rivera	.10
147	Ricky Ledee	.05
148	A.J. Hinch	.05
149	Ben Grieve	.10
150	Eric Chavez	.15
151	Miguel Tejada	.15
152	Matt Stairs	.05
153	Ryan Christenson	.05
154	Jason Giambi	.35
155	Curt Schilling	.25
156	Scott Rolen	.45
157	Pat Burrell **RC**	1.50
158	Doug Glanville	.05
159	Bobby Abreu	.05
160	Rico Brogna	.05
161	Ron Gant	.05
162	Jason Kendall	.05
163	Aramis Ramirez	.05
164	Jose Guillen	.05
165	Emil Brown	.05
166	Pat Meares	.05
167	Kevin Young	.05
168	Brian Giles	.05
169	Mark McGwire	1.25
170	J.D. Drew	.40
171	Edgar Renteria	.05
172	Fernando Tatis	.05
173	Matt Morris	.05
174	Eli Marrero	.05
175	Ray Lankford	.05
176	Tony Gwynn	.75
177	Sterling Hitchcock	.05
178	Ruben Rivera	.05
179	Wally Joyner	.05
180	Trevor Hoffman	.05
181	Jim Leyritz	.05
182	Carlos Hernandez	.05
183	Barry Bonds	1.50
184	Ellis Burks	.05
185	F.P. Santangelo	.05
186	J.T. Snow	.05
187	Ramon Martinez	.05
188	Jeff Kent	.05
189	Robb Nen	.05
190	Ken Griffey Jr.	1.00
191	Alex Rodriguez	1.25
192	Shane Monahan	.05
193	Carlos Guillen	.05
194	Edgar Martinez	.05
195	David Segui	.05
196	Jose Mesa	.05
197	Jose Canseco	.35
198	Rolando Arrojo	.05
199	Wade Boggs	.75
200	Fred McGriff	.05
201	Quinton McCracken	.05
202	Bobby Smith	.05
203	Bubba Trammell	.05
204	Juan Gonzalez	.60
205	Ivan Rodriguez	.45

206	Rafael Palmeiro	.45
207	Royce Clayton	.05
208	Rick Helling	.05
209	Todd Zeile	.05
210	Rusty Greer	.05
211	David Wells	.05
212	Roy Halladay	.05
213	Carlos Delgado	.25
214	Darrin Fletcher	.05
215	Shawn Green	.15
216	Kevin Witt	.05
217	Jose Cruz Jr.	.05
218	Ken Griffey Jr. Checklist	.45
219	Sammy Sosa Checklist	.45
220	Mark McGwire Checklist	.50

Scripts/Super Scripts

Silver Script:	1X
Gold Script:	10X
Super Script:	30X

(See 1999 UD MVP for checklist and base card values.)

1999 Upper Deck MVP All-Star Game

		NM/M
Complete Set (30):		12.50
Common Player:		.25
1	Mo Vaughn	.25
2	Randy Johnson	.60
3	Chipper Jones	.75
4	Greg Maddux	.75
5	Cal Ripken Jr.	2.00
6	Albert Belle	.35
7	Nomar Garciaparra	1.00
8	Pedro Martinez	.60
9	Sammy Sosa	1.00
10	Frank Thomas	.60
11	Sean Casey	.35
12	Roberto Alomar	.30
13	Manny Ramirez	.60
14	Larry Walker	.25
15	Jeff Bagwell	.60
16	Craig Biggio	.25
17	Raul Mondesi	.25
18	Vladimir Guerrero	.60
19	Mike Piazza	1.00
20	Derek Jeter	2.00
21	Roger Clemens	.85
22	Scott Rolen	.40
23	Mark McGwire	1.50
24	Tony Gwynn	.75
25	Barry Bonds	2.00
26	Ken Griffey Jr.	1.00
27	Alex Rodriguez	1.50
28	Jose Canseco	.40
29	Juan Gonzalez	.60
30	Ivan Rodriguez	.50

Dynamics

		NM/M
Complete Set (15):		17.50
Common Player:		.60
Inserted 1:28		
1	Ken Griffey Jr.	2.00
2	Alex Rodriguez	2.50
3	Nomar Garciaparra	2.00
4	Mike Piazza	2.00
5	Mark McGwire	2.25
6	Sammy Sosa	2.00
7	Chipper Jones	1.50
8	Mo Vaughn	.60
9	Tony Gwynn	1.50
10	Vladimir Guerrero	1.25
11	Derek Jeter	3.00
12	Jeff Bagwell	1.25
13	Cal Ripken Jr.	3.00
14	Juan Gonzalez	1.25
15	J.D. Drew	.90

Game Used Souvenirs

		NM/M
Complete Set (9):		75.00
Common Player:		5.00
Inserted 1:144		
JB	Jeff Bagwell	8.00
BB	Barry Bonds	20.00
JD	J.D. Drew	8.00
KGj	Ken Griffey Jr.	15.00
CJ	Chipper Jones	10.00
MP	Mike Piazza	15.00
CR	Cal Ripken Jr.	20.00
SR	Scott Rolen	8.00
MV	Mo Vaughn	5.00

Power Surge

		NM/M
Complete Set (15):		12.50
Common Player:		.50
Inserted 1:9		
1	Mark McGwire	1.50
2	Sammy Sosa	1.25
3	Ken Griffey Jr.	1.25
4	Alex Rodriguez	1.50
5	Juan Gonzalez	.75
6	Nomar Garciaparra	1.25
7	Vladimir Guerrero	.75
8	Chipper Jones	1.00
9	Albert Belle	.50
10	Frank Thomas	.75
11	Mike Piazza	1.25
12	Jeff Bagwell	.75
13	Manny Ramirez	.75
14	Mo Vaughn	.50
15	Barry Bonds	2.00

ProSign

		NM/M
Common Autograph:		5.00
Inserted 1:216 R		
MA	Matt Anderson	5.00
CB	Carlos Beltran	15.00
RB	Russ Branyan	5.00
EC	Eric Chavez	10.00
BC	Bruce Chen	5.00
BF	Brad Fuller	5.00
NG	Nomar Garciaparra	80.00
JG	Jeremy Giambi	5.00
DG	Derrick Gibson	5.00
CG	Chris Gomez	5.00
AG	Alex Gonzalez	5.00
BG	Ben Grieve	5.00

JR.	Ken Griffey Jr.	80.00
RH	Richard Hidalgo	5.00
SH	Shea Hillenbrand	10.00
CJ	Chipper Jones/SP	50.00
GK	Gabe Kapler	6.00
SK	Scott Karl	5.00
CK	Corey Koskie	7.50
RL	Ricky Ledee	5.00
ML	Mike Lincoln	5.00
GL	George Lombard	5.00
MLo	Mike Lowell	7.50
RM	Ryan Minor	5.00
SM	Shane Monahan	5.00
AN	Abraham Nunez	5.00
JP	Jim Parque	5.00
CP	Calvin Pickering	5.00
JRa	Jason Rakers	5.00
RR	Ruben Rivera	5.00
IR	Ivan Rodriguez/SP	50.00
KW	Kevin Witt	5.00

Scout's Choice

		NM/M
Complete Set (15):		5.00
Common Player:		.25
Inserted 1:9		
1	J.D. Drew	.65
2	Ben Grieve	.35
3	Troy Glaus	1.50
4	Gabe Kapler	.25
5	Carlos Beltran	.45
6	Aramis Ramirez	.25
7	Pat Burrell	1.00
8	Kerry Wood	.65
9	Ryan Minor	.25
10	Todd Helton	1.00
11	Eric Chavez	.35
12	Russ Branyon	.25
13	Travis Lee	.35
14	Ruben Mateo	.25
15	Roy Halladay	.35

Signed Game Used Souvenirs

		NM/M
KGj	Ken Griffey Jr.	300.00
CJ	Chipper Jones	200.00

Super Tools

		NM/M
Complete Set (15):		25.00
Common Player:		.50
Inserted 1:14		
1	Ken Griffey Jr.	2.50
2	Alex Rodriguez	3.00
3	Sammy Sosa	2.00
4	Derek Jeter	4.00
5	Vladimir Guerrero	1.50
6	Ben Grieve	.50
7	Mike Piazza	2.50
8	Kenny Lofton	.50
9	Barry Bonds	4.00
10	Darin Erstad	1.00
11	Nomar Garciaparra	2.00
12	Cal Ripken Jr.	4.00

13	J.D. Drew	1.00
14	Larry Walker	.50
15	Chipper Jones	2.00

Swing Time

		NM/M
Complete Set (12):		5.00
Common Player:		.35
Inserted 1:6		
1	Ken Griffey Jr.	.75
2	Mark McGwire	1.00
3	Sammy Sosa	.60
4	Tony Gwynn	.60
5	Alex Rodriguez	1.00
6	Nomar Garciaparra	.60
7	Barry Bonds	1.50
8	Frank Thomas	.45
9	Chipper Jones	.60
10	Ivan Rodriguez	.35
11	Mike Piazza	.75
12	Derek Jeter	1.50

500 Club Piece of History

	NM/M
Mike Schmidt/350	160.00
Mike Schmidt/Auto./20	1,250

1999 Upper Deck Ovation

		NM/M
Complete Set (90):		20.00
Common Player:		.05

Common World Premiere:		.15
Inserted 1:3.5		
Common Superstar Spotlight:		.60
Inserted 1:6		
Pack (5):		2.00
Box (20):		30.00
1	Ken Griffey Jr.	1.50
2	Rondell White	.05
3	Tony Clark	.05
4	Barry Bonds	2.50
5	Larry Walker	.05
6	Greg Vaughn	.05
7	Mark Grace	.05
8	John Olerud	.05
9	Matt Williams	.05
10	Craig Biggio	.05
11	Quinton McCracken	.05
12	Kerry Wood	.35
13	Derek Jeter	2.50
14	Frank Thomas	.75
15	Tino Martinez	.05
16	Albert Belle	.05
17	Ben Grieve	.05
18	Cal Ripken Jr.	2.50
19	Johnny Damon	.30
20	Jose Cruz Jr.	.05
21	Barry Larkin	.05
22	Jason Giambi	.45
23	Sean Casey	.10
24	Scott Rolen	.60
25	Jim Thome	.45
26	Curt Schilling	.25
27	Moises Alou	.05
28	Alex Rodriguez	2.00
29	Mark Kotsay	.05
30	Darin Erstad	.25
31	Mike Mussina	.30
32	Todd Walker	.05
33	Nomar Garciaparra	1.00
34	Vladimir Guerrero	.75
35	Jeff Bagwell	.75
36	Mark McGwire	2.00
37	Travis Lee	.15
38	Dean Palmer	.05
39	Fred McGriff	.05
40	Sammy Sosa	1.00
41	Mike Piazza	1.50
42	Andres Galarraga	.05
43	Pedro Martinez	.75
44	Juan Gonzalez	.40
45	Greg Maddux	1.00
46	Jeromy Burnitz	.05
47	Roger Clemens	1.25
48	Vinny Castilla	.05
49	Kevin Brown	.05
50	Mo Vaughn	.05
51	Raul Mondesi	.05
52	Randy Johnson	.75
53	Ray Lankford	.05
54	Jaret Wright	.05
55	Tony Gwynn	1.00
56	Chipper Jones	1.00
57	Gary Sheffield	.40
58	Ivan Rodriguez	.65
59	Kenny Lofton	.05
60	Jason Kendall	.05
61	J.D. Drew (World Premiere)	.75
62	Gabe Kapler (World Premiere)	.15
63	Adrian Beltre (World Premiere)	.40
64	Carlos Beltran (World Premiere)	.50
65	Eric Chavez (World Premiere)	.35
66	Mike Lowell (World Premiere)	.25
67	Troy Glaus (World Premiere)	1.00
68	George Lombard (World Premiere)	.15
69	Alex Gonzalez (World Premiere)	.15
70	Mike Kinkade (World Premiere)	.15
71	Jeremy Giambi (World Premiere)	.15
72	Bruce Chen (World Premiere)	.15
73	Preston Wilson (World Premiere)	.25
74	Kevin Witt (World Premiere)	.15
75	Carlos Guillen (World Premiere)	.15
76	Ryan Minor (World Premiere)	.15
77	Corey Koskie (World Premiere)	.15
78	Robert Fick (World Premiere)	.15
79	Michael Barrett (World Premiere)	.15
80	Calvin Pickering (World Premiere)	.15
81	Ken Griffey Jr. (Superstar Spotlight)	1.00
82	Mark McGwire (Superstar Spotlight)	1.50
83	Cal Ripken Jr. (Superstar Spotlight)	2.00
84	Derek Jeter (Superstar Spotlight)	2.00
85	Chipper Jones (Superstar Spotlight)	.75
86	Nomar Garciaparra (Garciaparra) (Superstar Spotlight)	.75
87	Sammy Sosa (Superstar Spotlight)	.75
88	Juan Gonzalez (Superstar Spotlight)	.30

89	Mike Piazza (Superstar Spotlight)	1.00
90	Alex Rodriguez (Superstar Spotlight)	1.50

Standing Ovation

	NM/M
Stars (1-60):	3X
World Premiere (61-80):	1.5X
Superstar Spotlight (81-90):	2X
Production 500 Sets	
(See 1999 Upper Deck Ovation for checklist and base card values.)	

Curtain Calls

		NM/M
Complete Set (20):		20.00
Common Player:		.25
Inserted 1:8		
R1	Mark McGwire	2.00
R2	Sammy Sosa	1.00
R3	Ken Griffey Jr.	1.50
R4	Alex Rodriguez	2.00
R5	Roger Clemens	1.25
R6	Cal Ripken Jr.	2.50
R7	Barry Bonds	2.50
R8	Kerry Wood	.40
R9	Nomar Garciaparra	1.00
R10	Derek Jeter	2.50
R11	Juan Gonzalez	.50
R12	Greg Maddux	1.00
R13	Pedro Martinez	1.00
R14	David Wells	.25
R15	Moises Alou	.25
R16	Tony Gwynn	1.00
R17	Albert Belle	.25
R18	Mike Piazza	1.50
R19	Ivan Rodriguez	.65
R20	Randy Johnson	.75

Major Production

	NM/M
Complete Set (20):	45.00

Common Player:		.75
Inserted 1:45		
S1	Mike Piazza	4.00
S2	Mark McGwire	5.00
S3	Chipper Jones	3.00
S4	Cal Ripken Jr.	6.00
S5	Ken Griffey Jr.	4.00
S6	Barry Bonds	6.00
S7	Tony Gwynn	3.00
S8	Randy Johnson	2.50
S9	Ivan Rodriguez	2.00
S10	Frank Thomas	2.50
S11	Alex Rodriguez	5.00
S12	Albert Belle	.75
S13	Juan Gonzalez	1.25
S14	Greg Maddux	3.00
S15	Jeff Bagwell	2.50
S16	Derek Jeter	6.00
S17	Matt Williams	.75
S18	Kenny Lofton	.75
S19	Sammy Sosa	3.00
S20	Roger Clemens	3.50

Piece of History

		NM/M
Common Player:		5.00
Inserted 1:247		
BB	Barry Bonds	25.00
CJ	Chipper Jones	15.00
BW	Bernie Williams	5.00
KGj	Ken Griffey Jr.	20.00
NG	Nomar Garciaparra	15.00
JG	Juan Gonzalez	5.00
DJ	Derek Jeter	25.00
SS	Sammy Sosa	15.00
TG	Tony Gwynn	15.00
AR	Alex Rodriguez	20.00
CR	Cal Ripken Jr.	25.00
BG	Ben Grieve	5.00
VG	Vladimir Guerrero	10.00
MP	Mike Piazza	20.00
BGAU	Ben Grieve/Auto./25)	30.00
KWAU	Kerry Wood/Auto./25)	50.00

ReMarkable

		NM/M
Complete Set (15):		20.00
Common #1-5:		1.50
Inserted 1:9		
Common #6-10:		2.25
Inserted 1:25		
Common # 11-15		3.00
Inserted 1:99		
MM1-5	Mark McGwire	1.50
MM6-10	Mark McGwire	3.00
MM11-15	Mark McGwire	5.00

500 Club Piece of History

		NM/M
MIC-P	Mickey Mantle/350	600.00
	Mickey Mantle/Bat Auto	8,000

1999 Upper Deck PowerDeck

		NM/M
Complete Set (25):		20.00
Common Player:		.50
Pack (3):		1.50
Wax Box (24):		20.00
1	Ken Griffey Jr.	2.00
2	Mark McGwire	2.50
3	Cal Ripken Jr.	3.00
4	Sammy Sosa	1.50
5	Derek Jeter	3.00
6	Mike Piazza	2.00
7	Nomar Garciaparra	1.50
8	Greg Maddux	1.50
9	Tony Gwynn	1.50
10	Roger Clemens	1.75
11	Scott Rolen	1.00
12	Alex Rodriguez	2.50
13	Manny Ramirez	1.25
14	Chipper Jones	1.50
15	Juan Gonzalez	.65
16	Ivan Rodriguez	1.00
17	Frank Thomas	1.25
18	Mo Vaughn	.50
19	Barry Bonds	3.00
20	Vladimir Guerrero	1.25
21	Jose Canseco	.65
22	Jeff Bagwell	1.25
23	Pedro Martinez	1.25
24	Gabe Kapler	.50
25	J.D. Drew	.75
---	Checklist	.10

Auxiliary Power

		NM/M
Complete Set (25):		6.00
Common Player:		.10
1	Ken Griffey Jr.	.50
2	Mark McGwire	.60
3	Cal Ripken Jr.	.75
4	Sammy Sosa	.40
5	Derek Jeter	.75
6	Mike Piazza	.50
7	Nomar Garciaparra	.40
8	Greg Maddux	.40
9	Tony Gwynn	.40
10	Roger Clemens	.45
11	Scott Rolen	.25
12	Alex Rodriguez	.60
13	Manny Ramirez	.30
14	Chipper Jones	.40
15	Juan Gonzalez	.15
16	Ivan Rodriguez	.25
17	Frank Thomas	.30
18	Mo Vaughn	.10
19	Barry Bonds	.75
20	Vladimir Guerrero	.30
21	Jose Canseco	.20
22	Jeff Bagwell	.30
23	Pedro Martinez	.30
24	Gabe Kapler	.10
25	J.D. Drew	.25

1999 Upper Deck PowerDeck A Season to Remember

	NM/M
Mark McGwire	3.00

Most Valuable Performances

		NM/M
Complete Set (7):		75.00
Common Player:		6.00
Inserted 1:287		
1	Sammy Sosa	10.00
2	Barry Bonds	20.00
3	Cal Ripken Jr.	20.00
4	Juan Gonzalez	6.00

5	Ken Griffey Jr.	12.50
6	Roger Clemens	10.00
7	Mark McGwire,	
	Sammy Sosa	12.50

MVP Auxiliary

		NM/M
Complete Set (7):		60.00
Common Player:		4.00
Inserted 1:287		
1	Sammy Sosa	7.50
2	Barry Bonds	15.00
3	Cal Ripken Jr.	15.00
4	Juan Gonzalez	4.00
5	Ken Griffey Jr.	10.00
6	Roger Clemens	7.50
7	Mark McGwire,	
	Sammy Sosa	12.50

Powerful Moments

		NM/M
Complete Set (6):		10.00
Common Player:		1.00
Inserted 1:7		
1	Mark McGwire	2.00
2	Sammy Sosa	1.00
3	Cal Ripken Jr.	3.00
4	Ken Griffey Jr.	1.50
5	Derek Jeter	3.00
6	Alex Rodriguez	2.00

Powerful Moments Auxiliary

		NM/M
Complete Set (6):		10.00
Common Player:		1.00
Inserted 1:7		
Gold (One each.):		Value Undetermined
1	Mark McGwire	2.00
2	Sammy Sosa	1.00
3	Cal Ripken Jr.	3.00
4	Ken Griffey Jr.	1.50
5	Derek Jeter	3.00
6	Alex Rodriguez	2.00

Time Capsule

		NM/M
Complete Set (6):		12.50
Common Player:		1.00
Inserted 1:23		
1	Ken Griffey Jr.	2.50
2	Mike Piazza	2.50
3	Mark McGwire	3.00
4	Derek Jeter	4.00
5	Jose Canseco	1.00
6	Nomar Garciaparra	2.00

Time Capsule-Auxiliary Power

		NM/M
Complete Set (6):		15.00
Common Player:		1.00
Inserted 1:23		
Gold (One of each.): Values Undetermined		
1	Ken Griffey Jr.	2.50
2	Mike Piazza	2.50

3	Mark McGwire	3.00
4	Derek Jeter	4.00
5	Jose Canseco	1.00
6	Nomar Garciaparra	2.00

1999 Upper Deck Ultimate Victory

		NM/M
Complete Set (180):		125.00
Common Player:		.10
Common 99 Rookie (121-150):		.50
Common McGwire Magic (151-180):		1.00
Victory (1-120):		3.5X
Victory SP (121-180):		2X
Inserted 1:12		
Ultimate (1-120):		12X
Ultimate SP (121-180):		5X
Production 100 Sets		
Pack (5):		4.50
Wax Box (24):		75.00
1	Troy Glaus	.65
2	Tim Salmon	.10
3	Mo Vaughn	.10
4	Garret Anderson	.10
5	Darin Erstad	.30
6	Randy Johnson	.75
7	Matt Williams	.10
8	Travis Lee	.25
9	Jay Bell	.10
10	Steve Finley	.10
11	Luis Gonzalez	.10
12	Greg Maddux	1.00
13	Chipper Jones	1.00
14	Javy Lopez	.10
15	Tom Glavine	.35
16	John Smoltz	.10
17	Cal Ripken Jr.	3.00
18	Charles Johnson	.10
19	Albert Belle	.10
20	Mike Mussina	.40
21	Pedro Martinez	.75
22	Nomar Garciaparra	1.00
23	Jose Offerman	.10
24	Sammy Sosa	1.00
25	Mark Grace	.10
26	Kerry Wood	.35
27	Frank Thomas	.75
28	Ray Durham	.10
29	Paul Konerko	.20
30	Pete Harnisch	.10
31	Greg Vaughn	.10
32	Sean Casey	.20
33	Manny Ramirez	.75
34	Jim Thome	.65
35	Sandy Alomar	.10
36	Roberto Alomar	.30
37	Travis Fryman	.10
38	Kenny Lofton	.10
39	Omar Vizquel	.10
40	Larry Walker	.10
41	Todd Helton	.65
42	Vinny Castilla	.10
43	Tony Clark	.10
44	Juan Encarnacion	.10
45	Dean Palmer	.10
46	Damion Easley	.10
47	Mark Kotsay	.10
48	Cliff Floyd	.10
49	Jeff Bagwell	.75
50	Ken Caminiti	.10
51	Craig Biggio	.10
52	Moises Alou	.10
53	Johnny Damon	.35
54	Larry Sutton	.10
55	Kevin Brown	.10
56	Adrian Beltre	.25
57	Raul Mondesi	.10
58	Gary Sheffield	.50
59	Jeromy Burnitz	.10
60	Sean Berry	.10
61	Jeff Cirillo	.10
62	Brad Radke	.10
63	Todd Walker	.10
64	Matt Lawton	.10
65	Vladimir Guerrero	.75
66	Rondell White	.10
67	Dustin Hermanson	.10
68	Mike Piazza	2.00
69	Rickey Henderson	.75

70	Robin Ventura	.10
71	John Olerud	.10
72	Derek Jeter	3.00
73	Roger Clemens	1.25
74	Orlando Hernandez	.10
75	Paul O'Neill	.10
76	Bernie Williams	.10
77	Chuck Knoblauch	.10
78	Tino Martinez	.10
79	Jason Giambi	.50
80	Ben Grieve	.10
81	Matt Stairs	.10
82	Scott Rolen	.60
83	Ron Gant	.10
84	Bobby Abreu	.10
85	Curt Schilling	.35
86	Brian Giles	.10
87	Jason Kendall	.10
88	Kevin Young	.10
89	Mark McGwire	2.00
90	Fernando Tatis	.10
91	Ray Lankford	.10
92	Eric Davis	.10
93	Tony Gwynn	1.00
94	Reggie Sanders	.10
95	Wally Joyner	.10
96	Trevor Hoffman	.10
97	Robb Nen	.10
98	Barry Bonds	3.00
99	Jeff Kent	.10
100	J.T. Snow	.10
101	Ellis Burks	.10
102	Ken Griffey Jr.	1.50
103	Alex Rodriguez	2.00
104	Jay Buhner	.10
105	Edgar Martinez	.10
106	David Bell	.10
107	Bobby Smith	.10
108	Wade Boggs	1.00
109	Fred McGriff	.10
110	Rolando Arrojo	.10
111	Jose Canseco	.50
112	Ivan Rodriguez	.65
113	Juan Gonzalez	.40
114	Rafael Palmeiro	.65
115	Rusty Greer	.10
116	Todd Zeile	.10
117	Jose Cruz Jr.	.10
118	Carlos Delgado	.35
119	Shawn Green	.30
120	David Wells	.10
121	Eric Munson RC (99 Rookie)	2.50
122	Lance Berkman (99 Rookie)	2.00
123	Ed Yarnall (99 Rookie)	.50
124	Jacque Jones (99 Rookie)	1.00
125	Kyle Farnsworth (99 Rookie)	1.00
126	Ryan Rupe (99 Rookie)	1.00
127	Jeff Weaver RC (99 Rookie)	2.00
128	Gabe Kapler (99 Rookie)	.50
129	Alex Gonzalez (99 Rookie)	.50
130	Randy Wolf (99 Rookie)	1.00
131	Ben Davis (99 Rookie)	.50
132	Carlos Beltran (99 Rookie)	2.00
133	Jim Morris (99 Rookie)	2.00
134	Jeff Zimmerman (99 Rookie)	2.00
135	Bruce Aven (99 Rookie)	.50
136	Alfonso Soriano RC (99 Rookie)	50.00
137	Tim Hudson RC (99 Rookie)	10.00
138	Josh Beckett RC (99 Rookie)	50.00
139	Michael Barrett (99 Rookie)	.50
140	Eric Chavez (99 Rookie)	1.00
141	Pat Burrell RC (99 Rookie)	10.00
142	Kris Benson (99 Rookie)	1.00
143	J.D. Drew (99 Rookie)	2.00
144	Matt Clement (99 Rookie)	1.00
145	Rick Ankiel RC (99 Rookie)	25.00
146	Vernon Wells (99 Rookie)	1.00
147	Ruben Mateo (99 Rookie)	.50
148	Roy Halladay (99 Rookie)	1.00
149	Joe McEwing (99 Rookie)	.50
150	Freddy Garcia RC (99 Rookie)	8.00
151-180	Mark McGwire (McGwire Magic)	

Ultimate Collection

	NM/M
Common Player (1-120, 151-180):	2.00
Common Player (121-150):	12.00
Stars (1-120):	12X

RAY LANKFORD
Cardinals / Outfield

Stars (121-150):   5X
(See 1999 Upper Deck Ultimate Victory for checklist and base card values.)

Victory Collection

STEVE FINLEY
Diamondbacks / Outfield

	NM/M
Common Player (1-120, 151-180):	1.00
Common Player (121-150):	5.00
Stars (1-120):	3.5X
Stars (121-150):	2X

(See 1999 Ultimate Victory for checklist and base card values.)

Bleacher Reachers

		NM/M
Complete Set (11):		20.00
Common Player:		.75
Inserted 1:23		
1	Ken Griffey Jr.	2.50
2	Mark McGwire	3.00
3	Sammy Sosa	2.00
4	Barry Bonds	4.00
5	Nomar Garciaparra	2.00
6	Juan Gonzalez	.75
7	Jose Canseco	.75
8	Manny Ramirez	1.50
9	Mike Piazza	2.50
10	Jeff Bagwell	1.50
11	Alex Rodriguez	3.00

Fame-Used Combo

	NM/M
Edition of 99:	
HOF Nolan Ryan, George Brett, Robin Yount, Orlando Cepeda	250.00

Fame-Used Memorabilia

ORLANDO CEPEDA
GIANTS
FAME-USED

	NM/M
Complete Set (4):	50.00
Common Player:	7.50

Production 350 Cards

GB	George Brett	20.00
OC	Orlando Cepeda	7.50
NR	Nolan Ryan	25.00
RY	Robin Yount	10.00

Frozen Ropes

		NM/M
Complete Set (10):		15.00
Common Player:		.50
Inserted 1:23		
1	Ken Griffey Jr.	2.00
2	Mark McGwire	2.50
3	Sammy Sosa	1.50
4	Derek Jeter	3.00
5	Tony Gwynn	1.50
6	Nomar Garciaparra	1.50
7	Alex Rodriguez	2.50
8	Mike Piazza	2.00
9	Mo Vaughn	.50
10	Craig Biggio	.50

STATure

STAT [URE]
34 HR
CHIPPER JONES · BRAVES

		NM/M
Complete Set (15):		9.00
Common Player:		.30
Inserted 1:6		
1	Ken Griffey Jr.	.75
2	Mark McGwire	1.00
3	Sammy Sosa	.65
4	Nomar Garciaparra	.65
5	Roger Clemens	.65
6	Greg Maddux	.65
7	Alex Rodriguez	1.00
8	Derek Jeter	1.50
9	Juan Gonzalez	.30
10	Manny Ramirez	.50
11	Mike Piazza	.75
12	Tony Gwynn	.65
13	Chipper Jones	.75
14	Pedro Martinez	.50
15	Frank Thomas	.50

Tribute 1999

		NM/M
Complete Set (4):		5.00
Common Player:		1.00
Inserted 1:11		
1	Nolan Ryan	2.00
2	Robin Yount	1.50
3	George Brett	1.50
4	Orlando Cepeda	1.00

Ultimate Competitors

		NM/M
Complete Set (12):		20.00
Common Player:		.60
Inserted 1:23		
1	Ken Griffey Jr.	3.00
2	Roger Clemens	2.50
3	Scott Rolen	1.00
4	Greg Maddux	2.00
5	Mark McGwire	4.00
6	Derek Jeter	5.00
7	Randy Johnson	1.50
8	Cal Ripken Jr.	5.00

Ultimate COMPETITORS
Ken Griffey Jr.

9	Craig Biggio	.50
10	Kevin Brown	.50
11	Chipper Jones	2.00
12	Vladimir Guerrero	1.50

Ultimate Hit Men

ULTIMATE HIT MEN
alex rodriguez • Mariners • ss

		NM/M
Complete Set (8):		15.00
Common Player:		1.00
Inserted 1:23		
1	Tony Gwynn	2.00
2	Cal Ripken Jr.	4.00
3	Wade Boggs	2.00
4	Larry Walker	1.00
5	Alex Rodriguez	3.00
6	Derek Jeter	4.00
7	Ivan Rodriguez	1.25
8	Ken Griffey Jr.	2.50

1999 Upper Deck Victory

CARLOS DELGADO
Blue Jays / First Base

	NM/M
Complete Set (470):	30.00
Common Player:	.05
Pack (12):	.75
Wax Box (36):	20.00

1	Anaheim Angels (Team Checklist)	.05
2	Mark Harriger RC (99 Rookie)	.10
3	Mo Vaughn (Power Trip)	.05
4	Darin Erstad (Big Play Makers)	.10
5	Troy Glaus	.45
6	Tim Salmon	.05
7	Mo Vaughn	.05
8	Darin Erstad	.25
9	Garret Anderson	.05
10	Todd Greene	.05
11	Troy Percival	.05
12	Chuck Finley	.05
13	Jason Dickson	.05
14	Jim Edmonds	.05

15	Arizona Diamondbacks (Team Checklist)	.05
16	Randy Johnson	.50
17	Matt Williams	.05
18	Travis Lee	.15
19	Jay Bell	.05
20	Tony Womack	.05
21	Steve Finley	.05
22	Bernard Gilkey	.05
23	Tony Batista	.05
24	Todd Stottlemyre	.05
25	Omar Daal	.05
26	Atlanta Braves (Team Checklist)	.05
27	Bruce Chen (99 Rookie)	.05
28	George Lombard (99 Rookie)	.05
29	Chipper Jones (Power Trip)	.40
30	Chipper Jones (Big Play Makers)	.40
31	Greg Maddux	.65
32	Chipper Jones	.75
33	Javy Lopez	.05
34	Tom Glavine	.25
35	John Smoltz	.05
36	Andruw Jones	.50
37	Brian Jordan	.05
38	Walt Weiss	.05
39	Bret Boone	.05
40	Andres Galarraga	.05
41	Baltimore Orioles (Team Checklist)	.05
42	Ryan Minor (99 Rookie)	.05
43	Jerry Hairston Jr. (99 Rookie)	.05
44	Calvin Pickering (99 Rookie)	.05
45	Cal Ripken Jr. (History in the Making)	.75
46	Cal Ripken Jr.	1.50
47	Charles Johnson	.05
48	Albert Belle	.05
49	Delino DeShields	.05
50	Mike Mussina	.30
51	Scott Erickson	.05
52	Brady Anderson	.05
53	B.J. Surhoff	.05
54	Harold Baines	.05
55	Will Clark	.05
56	Boston Red Sox (Team Checklist)	.05
57	Shea Hillenbrand **RC** (99 Rookie)	.50
58	Trot Nixon (99 Rookie)	.10
59	Jin Ho Cho (99 Rookie)	.05
60	Nomar Garciaparra (Power Trip)	.35
61	Nomar Garciaparra (Big Play Makers)	.35
62	Pedro Martinez	.50
63	Nomar Garciaparra	.65
64	Jose Offerman	.05
65	Jason Varitek	.05
66	Darren Lewis	.05
67	Troy O'Leary	.05
68	Donnie Sadler	.05
69	John Valentin	.05
70	Tim Wakefield	.05
71	Bret Saberhagen	.05
72	Chicago Cubs (Team Checklist)	.05
73	Kyle Farnsworth **RC** (99 Rookie)	.10
74	Sammy Sosa (Power Trip)	.35
75	Sammy Sosa (Big Play Makers)	.35
76	Sammy Sosa (History in the Making)	.35
77	Kerry Wood (History in the Making)	.10
78	Sammy Sosa	.65
79	Mark Grace	.05
80	Kerry Wood	.25
81	Kevin Tapani	.05
82	Benito Santiago	.05
83	Gary Gaetti	.05
84	Mickey Morandini	.05
85	Glenallen Hill	.05
86	Henry Rodriguez	.05
87	Rod Beck	.05
88	Chicago White Sox (Team Checklist)	.05
89	Carlos Lee (99 Rookie)	.10
90	Mark Johnson (99 Rookie)	.05
91	Frank Thomas (Power Trip)	.30
92	Frank Thomas	.50
93	Jim Parque	.05
94	Mike Sirotka	.05
95	Mike Caruso	.05
96	Ray Durham	.05
97	Magglio Ordonez	.25
98	Paul Konerko	.15
99	Bob Howry	.05
100	Brian Simmons	.05
101	Jaime Navarro	.05
102	Cincinnati Reds (Team Checklist)	.05
103	Denny Neagle	.05
104	Pete Harnisch	.05
105	Greg Vaughn	.05
106	Brett Tomko	.05
107	Mike Cameron	.05
108	Sean Casey	.10
109	Aaron Boone	.05
110	Michael Tucker	.05
111	Dmitri Young	.05
112	Barry Larkin	.05
113	Cleveland Indians (Team Checklist)	.05
114	Russ Branyan (99 Rookie)	.05
115	Jim Thome (Power Trip)	.20
116	Manny Ramirez (Power Trip)	.25
117	Manny Ramirez	.50
118	Jim Thome	.40
119	David Justice	.05
120	Sandy Alomar	.05
121	Roberto Alomar	.20
122	Jaret Wright	.05
123	Bartolo Colon	.05
124	Travis Fryman	.05
125	Kenny Lofton	.05
126	Omar Vizquel	.05
127	Colorado Rockies (Team Checklist)	.05
128	Derrick Gibson (99 Rookie)	.05
129	Larry Walker (Big Play Makers)	.05
130	Larry Walker	.05
131	Dante Bichette	.05
132	Todd Helton	.45
133	Neifi Perez	.05
134	Vinny Castilla	.05
135	Darryl Kile	.05
136	Pedro Astacio	.05
137	Darryl Hamilton	.05
138	Mike Lansing	.05
139	Kirt Manwaring	.05
140	Detroit Tigers (Team Checklist)	.05
141	Jeff Weaver **RC** (99 Rookie)	.50
142	Gabe Kapler (99 Rookie)	.05
143	Tony Clark (Power Trip)	.05
144	Tony Clark	.05
145	Juan Encarnacion	.05
146	Dean Palmer	.05
147	Damion Easley	.05
148	Bobby Higginson	.05
149	Karim Garcia	.05
150	Justin Thompson	.05
151	Matt Anderson	.05
152	Willie Blair	.05
153	Brian Hunter	.05
154	Florida Marlins (Team Checklist)	.05
155	Alex Gonzalez (99 Rookie)	.05
156	Mark Kotsay	.05
157	Livan Hernandez	.05
158	Cliff Floyd	.05
159	Todd Dunwoody	.05
160	Alex Fernandez	.05
161	Mark Mantei	.05
162	Derrek Lee	.40
163	Kevin Orie	.05
164	Craig Counsell	.05
165	Rafael Medina	.05
166	Houston Astros (Team Checklist)	.05
167	Daryle Ward (99 Rookie)	.05
168	Mitch Meluskey (99 Rookie)	.05
169	Jeff Bagwell (Power Trip)	.25
170	Jeff Bagwell	.50
171	Ken Caminiti	.05
172	Craig Biggio	.05
173	Derek Bell	.05
174	Moises Alou	.05
175	Billy Wagner	.05
176	Shane Reynolds	.05
177	Carl Everett	.05
178	Scott Elarton	.05
179	Richard Hidalgo	.05
180	Kansas City Royals (Team Checklist)	.05
181	Carlos Beltran (99 Rookie)	.60
182	Carlos Febles (99 Rookie)	.05
183	Jeremy Giambi (99 Rookie)	.05
184	Johnny Damon	.30
185	Joe Randa	.05
186	Jeff King	.05
187	Hipolito Pichardo	.05
188	Kevin Appier	.05
189	Chad Kreuter	.05
190	Rey Sanchez	.05
191	Larry Sutton	.05
192	Jeff Montgomery	.05
193	Jermaine Dye	.05
194	Los Angeles Dodgers (Team Checklist)	.05
195	Adam Riggs (99 Rookie)	.05
196	Angel Pena (99 Rookie)	.05
197	Todd Hundley	.05
198	Kevin Brown	.05
199	Ismael Valdes	.05
200	Chan Ho Park	.05
201	Adrian Beltre	.15
202	Mark Grudzielanek	.05
203	Raul Mondesi	.05
204	Gary Sheffield	.35
205	Eric Karros	.05
206	Devon White	.05
207	Milwaukee Brewers (Team Checklist)	.05
208	Ron Belliard (99 Rookie)	.05
209	Rafael Roque (99 Rookie)	.05
210	Jeromy Burnitz	.05
211	Fernando Vina	.05
212	Scott Karl	.05
213	Jim Abbott	.05
214	Sean Berry	.05
215	Marquis Grissom	.05
216	Geoff Jenkins	.05
217	Jeff Cirillo	.05
218	Dave Nilsson	.05
219	Jose Valentin	.05
220	Minnesota Twins (Team Checklist)	.05
221	Corey Koskie (99 Rookie)	.05
222	Christian Guzman (99 Rookie)	.05
223	A.J. Pierzynski (99 Rookie)	.05
224	David Ortiz	.05
225	Brad Radke	.05
226	Todd Walker	.05
227	Matt Lawton	.05
228	Rick Aguilera	.05
229	Eric Milton	.05
230	Marty Cordova	.05
231	Torii Hunter	.05
232	Ron Coomer	.05
233	LaTroy Hawkins	.05
234	Montreal Expos (Team Checklist)	.05
235	Fernando Seguignol (99 Rookie)	.05
236	Michael Barrett (99 Rookie)	.05
237	Vladimir Guerrero (Big Play Makers)	.25
238	Vladimir Guerrero	.50
239	Brad Fullmer	.05
240	Rondell White	.05
241	Ugueth Urbina	.05
242	Dustin Hermanson	.05
243	Orlando Cabrerra	.05
244	Wilton Guerrero	.05
245	Carl Pavano	.05
246	Javier Vasquez	.05
247	Chris Widger	.05
248	New York Mets (Team Checklist)	.05
249	Mike Kinkade (99 Rookie)	.05
250	Octavio Dotel (99 Rookie)	.05
251	Mike Piazza (Power Trip)	.40
252	Mike Piazza	.75
253	Rickey Henderson	.50
254	Edgardo Alfonzo	.05
255	Robin Ventura	.05
256	Al Leiter	.05
257	Brian McRae	.05
258	Rey Ordonez	.05
259	Bobby Bonilla	.05
260	Orel Hershiser	.05
261	John Olerud	.05
262	New York Yankees (Team Checklist)	.05
263	Ricky Ledee (99 Rookie)	.05
264	Bernie Williams (Big Play Makers)	.05
265	Derek Jeter (Big Play Makers)	.75
266	Scott Brosius (History in the Making)	.05
267	Derek Jeter	1.50
268	Roger Clemens	.65
269	Orlando Hernandez	.05
270	Scott Brosius	.05
271	Paul O'Neill	.05
272	Bernie Williams	.05
273	Chuck Knoblauch	.05
274	Tino Martinez	.05
275	Mariano Rivera	.10
276	Jorge Posada	.05
277	Oakland Athletics (Team Checklist)	.05
278	Eric Chavez (99 Rookie)	.15
279	Ben Grieve (History in the Making)	.05
280	Jason Giambi	.30
281	John Jaha	.05
282	Miguel Tejada	.15
283	Ben Grieve	.05
284	Matt Stairs	.05
285	Ryan Christenson	.05
286	A.J. Hinch	.05
287	Kenny Rogers	.05
288	Tom Candiotti	.05
289	Scott Spezio	.05
290	Philadelphia Phillies (Team Checklist)	.05
291	Pat Burrell **RC** (99 Rookie)	1.50
292	Marlon Anderson (99 Rookie)	.05
293	Scott Rolen (Big Play Makers)	.20
294	Scott Rolen	.40
295	Doug Glanville	.05
296	Rico Brogna	.05
297	Ron Gant	.05
298	Bobby Abreu	.05
299	Desi Relaford	.05
300	Curt Schilling	.25
301	Chad Ogea	.05
302	Kevin Jordan	.05
303	Carlton Loewer	.05
304	Pittsburgh Pirates (Team Checklist)	.05
305	Kris Benson (99 Rookie)	.05
306	Brian Giles	.05
307	Jason Kendall	.05
308	Jose Guillen	.05
309	Pat Meares	.05
310	Brant Brown	.05
311	Kevin Young	.05
312	Ed Sprague	.05
313	Francisco Cordova	.05
314	Aramis Ramirez	.05
315	Freddy Garcia	.05
316	Saint Louis Cardinals (Team Checklist)	.05
317	J.D. Drew (99 Rookie)	.40
318	Chad Hutchinson **RC** (99 Rookie)	.05
319	Mark McGwire (Power Trip)	.50
320	J.D. Drew (Power Trip)	.20
321	Mark McGwire (Big Play Makers)	.50
322	Mark McGwire (History in the Making)	.50
323	Mark McGwire	1.00
324	Fernando Tatis	.05
325	Edgar Renteria	.05
326	Ray Lankford	.05
327	Willie McGee	.05
328	Ricky Bottalico	.05
329	Eli Marrero	.05
330	Matt Morris	.05
331	Eric Davis	.05
332	Darren Bragg	.05
333	Padres (Team Checklist)	.05
334	Matt Clement (99 Rookie)	.05
335	Ben Davis (99 Rookie)	.05
336	Gary Matthews Jr. (99 Rookie)	.05
337	Tony Gwynn (Big Play Makers)	.35
338	Tony Gwynn (History in the Making)	.35
339	Tony Gwynn	.65
340	Reggie Sanders	.05
341	Ruben Rivera	.05
342	Wally Joyner	.05
343	Sterling Hitchcock	.05
344	Carlos Hernandez	.05
345	Andy Ashby	.05
346	Trevor Hoffman	.05
347	Chris Gomez	.05
348	Jim Leyritz	.05
349	San Francisco Giants (Team Checklist)	.05
350	Armando Rios (99 Rookie)	.05
351	Barry Bonds (Power Trip)	.75
352	Barry Bonds (Big Play Makers)	.75
353	Barry Bonds (History in the Making)	.75
354	Robb Nen	.05
355	Bill Mueller	.05
356	Barry Bonds	1.50
357	Jeff Kent	.05
358	J.T. Snow	.05
359	Ellis Burks	.05
360	F.P. Santangelo	.05
361	Marvin Benard	.05
362	Stan Javier	.05
363	Shawn Estes	.05
364	Seattle Mariners (Team Checklist)	.05
365	Carlos Guillen (99 Rookie)	.05
366	Ken Griffey Jr. (Power Trip)	.40
367	Alex Rodriguez (Power Trip)	.50
368	Ken Griffey Jr. (Big Play Makers)	.40
369	Alex Rodriguez (Big Play Makers)	.50
370	Ken Griffey Jr. (History in the Making)	.40
371	Alex Rodriguez (History in the Making)	.50
372	Ken Griffey Jr.	.75
373	Alex Rodriguez	1.00
374	Jay Buhner	.05
375	Edgar Martinez	.05
376	Jeff Fassero	.05
377	David Bell	.05
378	David Segui	.05
379	Russ Davis	.05
380	Dan Wilson	.05
381	Jamie Moyer	.05
382	Tampa Bay Devil Rays (Team Checklist)	.05
383	Roberto Hernandez	.05
384	Bobby Smith	.05
385	Wade Boggs	.65
386	Fred McGriff	.05
387	Rolando Arrojo	.05
388	Jose Canseco	.35
389	Wilson Alvarez	.05
390	Kevin Stocker	.05
391	Miguel Cairo	.05
392	Quinton McCracken	.05
393	Texas Rangers (Team Checklist)	.05
394	Ruben Mateo (99 Rookie)	.05
395	Cesar King (99 Rookie)	.05
396	Juan Gonzalez (Power Trip)	.15
397	Juan Gonzalez (Big Play Makers)	.15

398	Ivan Rodriguez	.40
399	Juan Gonzalez	.25
400	Rafael Palmeiro	.40
401	Rick Helling	.05
402	Aaron Sele	.05
403	John Wetteland	.05
404	Rusty Greer	.05
405	Todd Zeile	.05
406	Royce Clayton	.05
407	Tom Goodwin	.05
408	Toronto Blue Jays (Team Checklist)	.05
409	Kevin Witt (99 Rookie)	.05
410	Roy Halladay (99 Rookie)	.05
411	Jose Cruz Jr.	.05
412	Carlos Delgado	.30
413	Willie Greene	.05
414	Shawn Green	.25
415	Homer Bush	.05
416	Shannon Stewart	.05
417	David Wells	.05
418	Kelvim Escobar	.05
419	Joey Hamilton	.05
420	Alex Gonzalez	.05
421-450	Mark McGwire (McGwire Magic)	.20
451	Chipper Jones '93 (Rookie Flashback)	.40
452	Cal Ripken Jr. '81 (Rookie Flashback)	.75
453	Roger Clemens '84 (Rookie Flashback)	.40
454	Wade Boggs '82 (Rookie Flashback)	.35
455	Greg Maddux '86 (Rookie Flashback)	.35
456	Frank Thomas '90 (Rookie Flashback)	.30
457	Jeff Bagwell '91 (Rookie Flashback)	.25
458	Mike Piazza '92 (Rookie Flashback)	.45
459	Randy Johnson '88 (Rookie Flashback)	.25
460	Mo Vaughn '91 (Rookie Flashback)	.05
461	Mark McGwire '86 (Rookie Flashback)	.50
462	Rickey Henderson '79 (Rookie Flashback)	.25
463	Barry Bonds '86 (Rookie Flashback)	.75
464	Tony Gwynn '82 (Rookie Flashback)	.35
465	Ken Griffey Jr. '89 (Rookie Flashback)	.45
466	Alex Rodriguez '94 (Rookie Flashback)	.50
467	Sammy Sosa '89 (Rookie Flashback)	.35
468	Juan Gonzalez '89 (Rookie Flashback)	.15
469	Kevin Brown '86 (Rookie Flashback)	.05
470	Fred McGriff '86 (Rookie Flashback)	.05

1999 Upper Deck UD Choice

		NM/M
Complete Set (155):		7.50
Common Player:		.03
Prime Choice Reserve Stars:		10X
Production 100 Sets		
Pack (12):		.50
Wax Box (36):		10.00
1	Gabe Kapler (Rookie Class)	.05
2	Jin Ho Cho (Rookie Class)	.05
3	Matt Anderson (Rookie Class)	.05
4	Ricky Ledee (Rookie Class)	.05
5	Bruce Chen (Rookie Class)	.05
6	Alex Gonzalez (Rookie Class)	.05
7	Ryan Minor (Rookie Class)	.05
8	Michael Barrett (Rookie Class)	.05
9	Carlos Beltran (Rookie Class)	.05
10	Ramon Martinez (Rookie Class)	.05
11	Dermal Brown (Rookie Class)	.05
12	Robert Fick (Rookie Class)	.05

13	Preston Wilson (Rookie Class)	.05
14	Orlando Hernandez (Rookie Class)	.05
15	Troy Glaus (Rookie Class)	.65
16	Calvin Pickering (Rookie Class)	.05
17	Corey Koskie (Rookie Class)	.05
18	Fernando Seguignol (Rookie Class)	.05
19	Carlos Guillen (Rookie Class)	.05
20	Kevin Witt (Rookie Class)	.05
21	Mike Kinkade (Rookie Class)	.05
22	Eric Chavez (Rookie Class)	.15
23	Mike Lowell (Rookie Class)	.10
24	Adrian Beltre (Rookie Class)	.10
25	George Lombard (Rookie Class)	.05
26	Jeremy Giambi (Rookie Class)	.05
27	J.D. Drew (Rookie Class)	.40
28	Mark McGwire (Cover Glory)	.60
29	Kerry Wood (Cover Glory)	.15
30	David Wells (Cover Glory)	.05
31	Juan Gonzalez (Cover Glory)	.15
32	Randy Johnson (Cover Glory)	.35
33	Derek Jeter (Cover Glory)	.75
34	Tony Gwynn (Cover Glory)	.45
35	Greg Maddux (Cover Glory)	.45
36	Cal Ripken Jr. (Cover Glory)	.75
37	Ken Griffey Jr. (Cover Glory)	.50
38	Bartolo Colon (Cover Glory)	.05
39	Troy Glaus (Cover Glory)	.30
40	Ben Grieve (Cover Glory)	.05
41	Roger Clemens (Cover Glory)	.50
42	Chipper Jones (Cover Glory)	.50
43	Scott Rolen (Cover Glory)	.25
44	Nomar Garciaparra (Cover Glory)	.45
45	Sammy Sosa (Cover Glory)	.45
46	Tim Salmon	.05
47	Darin Erstad	.05
48	Chuck Finley	.05
49	Garrett Anderson	.05
50	Matt Williams	.05
51	Jay Bell	.05
52	Travis Lee	.10
53	Andruw Jones	.65
54	Andres Galarraga	.05
55	Chipper Jones	.75
56	Greg Maddux	.75
57	Javy Lopez	.05
58	Cal Ripken Jr.	1.50
59	Brady Anderson	.05
60	Rafael Palmeiro	.50
61	B.J. Surhoff	.05
62	Nomar Garciaparra	.75
63	Troy O'Leary	.05
64	Pedro Martinez	.65
65	Jason Varitek	.35
66	Kerry Wood	.35
67	Sammy Sosa	.75
68	Mark Grace	.05
69	Mickey Morandini	.05
70	Albert Belle	.05
71	Mike Caruso	.05
72	Frank Thomas	.65
73	Sean Casey	.10
74	Pete Harnisch	.05
75	Dmitri Young	.05
76	Manny Ramirez	.65
77	Omar Vizquel	.05
78	Travis Fryman	.05
79	Jim Thome	.40
80	Kenny Lofton	.05
81	Todd Helton	.50
82	Larry Walker	.05
83	Vinny Castilla	.05
84	Gabe Alvarez	.05
85	Tony Clark	.05
86	Damion Easley	.05
87	Livan Hernandez	.05
88	Mark Kotsay	.05
89	Cliff Floyd	.05
90	Jeff Bagwell	.65
91	Moises Alou	.05
92	Randy Johnson	.65
93	Craig Biggio	.05
94	Larry Sutton	.05
95	Dean Palmer	.05
96	Johnny Damon	.20
97	Charles Johnson	.05
98	Gary Sheffield	.25
99	Raul Mondesi	.05
100	Mark Grudzielanek	.05
101	Jeromy Burnitz	.05
102	Jeff Cirillo	.05
103	Jose Valentin	.05
104	Mark Loretta	.05
105	Todd Walker	.05
106	David Ortiz	.35
107	Brad Radke	.05
108	Brad Fullmer	.05
109	Rondell White	.05
110	Vladimir Guerrero	.65
111	Mike Piazza	1.00
112	Brian McRae	.05
113	John Olerud	.05
114	Rey Ordonez	.05
115	Derek Jeter	1.50
116	Bernie Williams	.05
117	David Wells	.05
118	Paul O'Neill	.05
119	Tino Martinez	.05
120	A.J. Hinch	.05

121	Jason Giambi	.30
122	Miguel Tejada	.10
123	Ben Grieve	.05
124	Scott Rolen	.50
125	Desi Relaford	.05
126	Bobby Abreu	.10
127	Jose Guillen	.05
128	Jason Kendall	.05
129	Aramis Ramirez	.05
130	Mark McGwire	1.25
131	Ray Lankford	.05
132	Eli Marrero	.05
133	Wally Joyner	.05
134	Greg Vaughn	.05
135	Trevor Hoffman	.05
136	Kevin Brown	.05
137	Tony Gwynn	.75
138	Bill Mueller	.05
139	Ellis Burks	.05
140	Barry Bonds	1.50
141	Robb Nen	.05
142	Ken Griffey Jr.	1.00
143	Alex Rodriguez	1.25
144	Jay Buhner	.05
145	Edgar Martinez	.05
146	Rolando Arrojo	.05
147	Robert Smith	.05
148	Quinton McCracken	.05
149	Ivan Rodriguez	.50
150	Will Clark	.05
151	Mark McLemore	.05
152	Juan Gonzalez	.35
153	Jose Cruz Jr.	.15
154	Carlos Delgado	.25
155	Roger Clemens	.85

Prime Choice Reserve

	NM/M
Common Player:	2.50
Stars:	10X

(See 1999 UD Choice for checklist and base card values.)

1999 Upper Deck UD Choice All-Star Game '99

		NM/M
Complete Set (21):		12.50
Common Player:		.35
1	Kenny Lofton	.35
2	Pedro Martinez	.75
3	Nomar Garciaparra	1.00
4	Ken Griffey Jr.	1.25
5	Derek Jeter	2.00
6	Manny Ramirez	.75
7	Ivan Rodriguez	.65
8	Bernie Williams	.35
9	Cal Ripken Jr.	2.00
10	Jim Thome	.60
11	Mike Piazza	1.25
12	Jeff Bagwell	.75
13	Craig Biggio	.35
14	Mark McGwire	1.50
15	Matt Williams	.35
16	Chipper Jones	.75
17	Tony Gwynn	1.00
18	Sammy Sosa	1.00

19	Raul Mondesi	.35
20	Larry Walker	.35
---	Header Card	.05

Mini Bobbing Head

	NM/M
Complete Set (30):	15.00
Common Player:	.25

Inserted 1:5

B1	Randy Johnson	.50
B2	Troy Glaus	.50
B3	Chipper Jones	.75
B4	Cal Ripken Jr.	1.50
B5	Nomar Garciaparra	.65
B6	Pedro Martinez	.50
B7	Kerry Wood	.35
B8	Sammy Sosa	.65
B9	Frank Thomas	.50
B10	Paul Konerko	.35
B11	Omar Vizquel	.25
B12	Kenny Lofton	.25
B13	Gabe Kapler	.25
B14	Adrian Beltre	.35
B15	Orlando Hernandez	.25
B16	Derek Jeter	1.50
B17	Mike Piazza	.75
B18	Tino Martinez	.25
B19	Ben Grieve	.25
B20	Rickey Henderson	.50
B21	Scott Rolen	.40
B22	Aramis Ramirez	.25
B23	Greg Vaughn	.25
B24	Tony Gwynn	.65
B25	Barry Bonds	1.50
B26	Alex Rodriguez	1.00
B27	Ken Griffey Jr.	.75
B28	Mark McGwire	1.00
B29	J.D. Drew	.45
B30	Juan Gonzalez	.30

Piece of History 500 Club

		NM/M
EM	Eddie Murray/350	150.00

StarQuest

	NM/M
Complete Set (30):	7.50
Common Player:	.10

Inserted 1:1

Green (1:8):		1.5X
Red (1:23):		3X
Gold (100 Sets):		50X
SQ1	Ken Griffey Jr.	.60
SQ2	Sammy Sosa	.50
SQ3	Alex Rodriguez	.75
SQ4	Derek Jeter	1.00
SQ5	Troy Glaus	.50
SQ6	Mike Piazza	.60
SQ7	Barry Bonds	1.00
SQ8	Tony Gwynn	.50
SQ9	Juan Gonzalez	.20
SQ10	Chipper Jones	.50
SQ11	Greg Maddux	.50
SQ12	Randy Johnson	.40
SQ13	Roger Clemens	.55
SQ14	Ben Grieve	.25

SQ15	Nomar Garciaparra	.50
SQ16	Travis Lee	.15
SQ17	Frank Thomas	.40
SQ18	Vladimir Guerrero	.40
SQ19	Scott Rolen	.30
SQ20	Ivan Rodriguez	.35
SQ21	Cal Ripken Jr.	1.00
SQ22	Mark McGwire	.75
SQ23	Jeff Bagwell	.40
SQ24	Tony Clark	.10
SQ25	Kerry Wood	.25
SQ26	Kenny Lofton	.25
SQ27	Adrian Beltre	.15
SQ28	Larry Walker	.10
SQ29	Curt Schilling	.25
SQ30	Jim Thome	.40

Yard Work

NM/M

Complete Set (30): 20.00
Common Player: .35
Inserted 1:13

Y1	Andres Galarraga	.35
Y2	Chipper Jones	1.50
Y3	Rafael Palmeiro	.75
Y4	Nomar Garciaparra	1.50
Y5	Sammy Sosa	1.50
Y6	Frank Thomas	1.00
Y7	J.D. Drew	.75
Y8	Albert Belle	.35
Y9	Jim Thome	.60
Y10	Manny Ramirez	1.00
Y11	Larry Walker	.35
Y12	Vinny Castilla	.35
Y13	Tony Clark	.35
Y14	Jeff Bagwell	1.00
Y15	Moises Alou	.35
Y16	Dean Palmer	.35
Y17	Gary Sheffield	.35
Y18	Vladimir Guerrero	1.00
Y19	Mike Piazza	1.75
Y20	Tino Martinez	.35
Y21	Ben Grieve	.35
Y22	Greg Vaughn	.35
Y23	Ken Caminiti	.35
Y24	Barry Bonds	3.00
Y25	Ken Griffey Jr.	1.75
Y26	Alex Rodriguez	2.25
Y27	Mark McGwire	2.25
Y28	Juan Gonzalez	.50
Y29	Jose Canseco	.50
Y30	Jose Cruz Jr.	.35

1999 UD Ionix

NM/M

Complete Set (90): 45.00
Common Player (1-60): .25
Common Techno (61-90): .50
Inserted 1:4
Reciprocals (1-60): 3X
Production 750 Sets
Techno Reciprocals (61-90): 1.5X
Production 100 Sets
Pack (4): 2.00
Wax Box (20): 25.00

1	Troy Glaus	.60
2	Darin Erstad	.50
3	Travis Lee	.35
4	Matt Williams	.25
5	Chipper Jones	.75
6	Greg Maddux	.75
7	Andruw Jones	.65
8	Andres Galarraga	.25
9	Tom Glavine	.35
10	Cal Ripken Jr.	2.00
11	Ryan Minor	.25
12	Nomar Garciaparra	1.00
13	Mo Vaughn	.25
14	Pedro Martinez	.65
15	Sammy Sosa	.75
16	Kerry Wood	.50
17	Albert Belle	.25
18	Frank Thomas	.65
19	Sean Casey	.25
20	Kenny Lofton	.25
21	Manny Ramirez	.65
22	Jim Thome	.60
23	Bartolo Colon	.25
24	Jaret Wright	.25
25	Larry Walker	.25
26	Tony Clark	.25
27	Gabe Kapler	.25
28	Edgar Renteria	.25
29	Randy Johnson	.65
30	Craig Biggio	.65
31	Jeff Bagwell	.65
32	Moises Alou	.25
33	Johnny Damon	.50
34	Adrian Beltre	.35
35	Jeromy Burnitz	.25
36	Todd Walker	.25
37	Corey Koskie	.25
38	Vladimir Guerrero	.65
39	Mike Piazza	1.00
40	Hideo Nomo	.35
41	Derek Jeter	2.00
42	Tino Martinez	.25
43	Orlando Hernandez	.25
44	Ben Grieve	.25
45	Rickey Henderson	.65
46	Scott Rolen	.60
47	Curt Schilling	.35
48	Aramis Ramirez	.25
49	Tony Gwynn	.75
50	Kevin Brown	.25
51	Barry Bonds	2.00
52	Ken Griffey Jr.	1.00
53	Alex Rodriguez	1.50
54	Mark McGwire	1.50
55	J.D. Drew	.60
56	Rolando Arrojo	.25
57	Ivan Rodriguez	.60
58	Juan Gonzalez	.35
59	Roger Clemens	.85
60	Jose Cruz Jr.	.65
61	Travis Lee (Techno)	.65
62	Andres Galarraga (Techno)	.50
63	Andruw Jones (Techno)	1.50
64	Chipper Jones (Techno)	2.00
65	Greg Maddux (Techno)	2.00
66	Cal Ripken Jr. (Techno)	4.00
67	Nomar Garciaparra (Techno)	2.00
68	Mo Vaughn (Techno)	.50
69	Sammy Sosa (Techno)	2.00
70	Frank Thomas (Techno)	1.50
71	Kerry Wood (Techno)	.75
72	Kenny Lofton (Techno)	.50
73	Manny Ramirez (Techno)	1.50
74	Larry Walker (Techno)	.50
75	Jeff Bagwell (Techno)	1.50
76	Randy Johnson (Techno)	1.50
77	Paul Molitor (Techno)	1.50
78	Derek Jeter (Techno)	4.00
79	Tino Martinez (Techno)	.50
80	Mike Piazza (Techno)	2.50
81	Ben Grieve (Techno)	.50
82	Scott Rolen (Techno)	.75
83	Mark McGwire (Techno)	3.00
84	Tony Gwynn (Techno)	2.00
85	Barry Bonds (Techno)	4.00
86	Ken Griffey Jr. (Techno)	2.50
87	Alex Rodriguez (Techno)	3.00
88	Juan Gonzalez (Techno)	.75
89	Roger Clemens (Techno)	2.25
90	J.D. Drew (Techno)	1.00
100	Ken Griffey Jr. (SAMPLE)	2.50

Reciprocal

NM/M

Stars (1-60): 3X
Stars (61-90): 1.5X
(See 1999 UD Ionix for checklist and base card values.)

Cyber

NM/M

Complete Set (25): 125.00
Common Player: 2.00

C01	Ken Griffey Jr.	8.00
C02	Cal Ripken Jr.	12.50
C03	Frank Thomas	5.00
C04	Greg Maddux	6.50
C05	Mike Piazza	8.00
C06	Alex Rodriguez	10.00
C07	Chipper Jones	8.00
C08	Derek Jeter	12.50
C09	Mark McGwire	10.00
C10	Juan Gonzalez	2.50
C11	Kerry Wood	2.50
C12	Tony Gwynn	6.50
C13	Scott Rolen	4.00
C14	Nomar Garciaparra	6.50
C15	Roger Clemens	7.00
C16	Sammy Sosa	6.50
C17	Travis Lee	2.00
C18	Ben Grieve	2.00
C19	Jeff Bagwell	5.00
C20	Ivan Rodriguez	4.00
C21	Barry Bonds	12.50
C22	J.D. Drew	4.00
C23	Kenny Lofton	2.00
C24	Andruw Jones	5.00
C25	Vladimir Guerrero	5.00

HoloGrFX

NM/M

Complete Set (10): 800.00
Common Player: 50.00
Inserted 1:1,500

HG01	Ken Griffey Jr.	100.00
HG02	Cal Ripken Jr.	150.00
HG03	Frank Thomas	75.00
HG04	Greg Maddux	90.00
HG05	Mike Piazza	100.00
HG06	Alex Rodriguez	125.00
HG07	Chipper Jones	90.00
HG08	Derek Jeter	150.00
HG09	Mark McGwire	125.00
HG10	Juan Gonzalez	50.00

Hyper

NM/M

Complete Set (20): 37.00
Common Player: .75
Inserted 1:9

H01	Ken Griffey Jr.	3.00
H02	Cal Ripken Jr.	4.50
H03	Frank Thomas	1.50
H04	Greg Maddux	2.25
H05	Mike Piazza	3.00
H06	Alex Rodriguez	3.75
H07	Chipper Jones	2.50
H08	Derek Jeter	4.50
H09	Mark McGwire	3.75
H10	Juan Gonzalez	.75

H11	Kerry Wood	1.00
H12	Tony Gwynn	2.25
H13	Scott Rolen	1.00
H14	Nomar Garciaparra	2.25
H15	Roger Clemens	2.75
H16	Sammy Sosa	2.25
H17	Travis Lee	1.00
H18	Ben Grieve	.75
H19	Jeff Bagwell	1.50
H20	J.D. Drew	1.00

Nitro

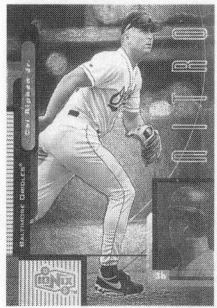

NM/M

Complete Set (10): 18.00
Common Player: 1.00
Inserted 1:18

N01	Ken Griffey Jr.	2.50
N02	Cal Ripken Jr.	4.00
N03	Frank Thomas	1.50
N04	Greg Maddux	2.00
N05	Mike Piazza	2.50
N06	Alex Rodriguez	3.00
N07	Chipper Jones	2.00
N08	Derek Jeter	4.00
N09	Mark McGwire	3.00
N10	J.D. Drew	1.00

Warp Zone

NM/M

Complete Set (15): 195.00
Common Player: 6.00
Inserted 1:216

WZ1	Ken Griffey Jr.	20.00
WZ2	Cal Ripken Jr.	30.00
WZ3	Frank Thomas	10.00
WZ4	Greg Maddux	15.00
WZ5	Mike Piazza	20.00
WZ6	Alex Rodriguez	25.00
WZ7	Chipper Jones	15.00
WZ8	Derek Jeter	30.00
WZ9	Mark McGwire	25.00
WZ10	Juan Gonzalez	6.00
WZ11	Kerry Wood	6.00

WZ12	Tony Gwynn	15.00
WZ13	Scott Rolen	6.00
WZ14	Nomar Garciaparra	15.00
WZ15	J.D. Drew	6.00

500 Club Piece of History

		NM/M
FR	Frank Robinson/350	165.00
FRA	Frank Robinson/Auto. 20	650.00

1999 UD Retro

	NM/M
Complete Set (110):	15.00
Common Player:	.05
Gold:	12X
Production 250 Sets	
Platinum 1/1:	Values Undetermined
Wax Pack (6):	2.50
Lunchbox (24):	45.00

1	Mo Vaughn	.05
2	Troy Glaus	.65
3	Tim Salmon	.05
4	Randy Johnson	.75
5	Travis Lee	.15
6	Matt Williams	.05
7	Greg Maddux	.85
8	Chipper Jones	1.00
9	Andruw Jones	.75
10	Tom Glavine	.25
11	Javy Lopez	.05
12	Albert Belle	.05
13	Cal Ripken Jr.	2.00
14	Brady Anderson	.05
15	Nomar Garciaparra	.75
16	Pedro J. Martinez	.75
17	Sammy Sosa	.85
18	Mark Grace	.05
19	Frank Thomas	.75
20	Ray Durham	.05
21	Sean Casey	.10
22	Greg Vaughn	.05
23	Barry Larkin	.05
24	Manny Ramirez	.75
25	Jim Thome	.50
26	Jaret Wright	.05
27	Kenny Lofton	.05
28	Larry Walker	.05
29	Todd Helton	.65
30	Vinny Castilla	.05
31	Tony Clark	.05
32	Juan Encarnacion	.05
33	Dean Palmer	.05
34	Mark Kotsay	.05
35	Alex Gonzalez	.05
36	Shane Reynolds	.05
37	Ken Caminiti	.05
38	Jeff Bagwell	.75
39	Craig Biggio	.05
40	Carlos Febles	.05
41	Carlos Beltran	.35
42	Jeremy Giambi	.05
43	Raul Mondesi	.05
44	Adrian Beltre	.10
45	Kevin Brown	.05
46	Jeromy Burnitz	.05
47	Jeff Cirillo	.05
48	Corey Koskie	.05
49	Todd Walker	.05
50	Vladimir Guerrero	.75
51	Michael Barrett	.05
52	Mike Piazza	1.00
53	Robin Ventura	.05
54	Edgardo Alfonzo	.05
55	Derek Jeter	2.00
56	Roger Clemens	.90
57	Tino Martinez	.05
58	Orlando Hernandez	.05
59	Chuck Knoblauch	.05
60	Bernie Williams	.05
61	Eric Chavez	.10
62	Ben Grieve	.05
63	Jason Giambi	.40
64	Scott Rolen	.60
65	Curt Schilling	.25
66	Bobby Abreu	.10
67	Jason Kendall	.05
68	Kevin Young	.05
69	Mark McGwire	1.50
70	J.D. Drew	.60
71	Eric Davis	.05
72	Tony Gwynn	.85
73	Trevor Hoffman	.05
74	Barry Bonds	2.00
75	Robb Nen	.05
76	Ken Griffey Jr.	1.00
77	Alex Rodriguez	1.50
78	Jay Buhner	.05
79	Carlos Guillen	.05
80	Jose Canseco	.40
81	Bobby Smith	.05
82	Juan Gonzalez	.40
83	Ivan Rodriguez	.65
84	Rafael Palmeiro	.65
85	Rick Helling	.05
86	Jose Cruz Jr.	.05
87	David Wells	.05
88	Carlos Delgado	.20
89	Nolan Ryan	1.50
90	George Brett	.90
91	Robin Yount	.50
92	Paul Molitor	.50
93	Dave Winfield	.50
94	Steve Garvey	.25
95	Ozzie Smith	.85
96	Ted Williams	1.50
97	Don Mattingly	.90
98	Mickey Mantle	2.50
99	Harmon Killebrew	.25
100	Rollie Fingers	.10
101	Kirk Gibson	.05
102	Bucky Dent	.05
103	Willie Mays	1.00
104	Babe Ruth	1.50
105	Gary Carter	.50
106	Reggie Jackson	.85
107	Frank Robinson	.25
108	Ernie Banks	.50
109	Eddie Murray	.50
110	Mike Schmidt	.90

Gold/Platinum

	NM/M
Common Gold:	1.00
Gold Stars:	15X
Platinum 1/1:	Values Undetermined

(See 1999 UD Retro for checklist and base card values.)

Distant Replay

	NM/M
Complete Set (15):	30.00
Common Player:	1.00
Inserted 1:8	
Level 2:	6X
Production 100 Sets	

1	Ken Griffey Jr.	2.50
2	Mark McGwire	3.00
3	Cal Ripken Jr.	4.00
4	Greg Maddux	2.00
5	Nomar Garciaparra	2.00
6	Roger Clemens	2.25
7	Alex Rodriguez	3.00
8	Frank Thomas	1.50
9	Mike Piazza	2.50
10	Chipper Jones	2.00
11	Juan Gonzalez	1.00
12	Tony Gwynn	2.00
13	Barry Bonds	4.00
14	Ivan Rodriguez	1.00
15	Derek Jeter	4.00

INKredible

	NM/M
Common Player:	4.00
Inserted 1:23	

CBe	Carlos Beltran	30.00
GB	George Brett/SP	80.00
PB	Pat Burrell	10.00
SC	Sean Casey	10.00
TC	Tony Clark	4.00
BD	Bucky Dent	8.00
DE	Darin Erstad	15.00
RF	Rollie Fingers	8.00
SG	Steve Garvey	10.00
KG	Kirk Gibson	10.00
RG	Rusty Greer	4.00
JR	Ken Griffey Jr.	80.00
TG	Tony Gwynn	30.00
CJ	Chipper Jones	40.00
GK	Gabe Kapler	5.00
HK	Harmon Killebrew	30.00
FL	Fred Lynn	10.00
DM	Don Mattingly	50.00
PM	Paul Molitor	20.00
EM	Eddie Murray/SP	50.00
PO	Paul O'Neill	15.00
AP	Angel Pena	4.00
MR	Manny Ramirez	30.00
IR	Ivan Rodriguez	25.00
NR	Nolan Ryan	150.00
OZ	Ozzie Smith	30.00
DWe	David Wells	15.00
BW	Bernie Williams	40.00
DW	Dave Winfield	20.00
RY	Robin Yount	35.00

INKredible Level 2

	NM/M
Common Player:	10.00
Limited to player's jersey #.	

CBe	Carlos Beltran/36	60.00
PB	Pat Burrell/76	50.00
SC	Sean Casey/21	40.00
TC	Tony Clark/17	20.00
BD	Bucky Dent/20	25.00
DE	Darin Erstad/17	50.00
RF	Rollie Fingers/34	25.00
KG	Kirk Gibson/23	30.00
RG	Rusty Greer/29	30.00
JR	Ken Griffey Jr./24	200.00
TG	Tony Gwynn/19	150.00
GK	Gabe Kapler/23	40.00
FL	Fred Lynn/19	30.00
DM	Don Mattingly/23	200.00
EM	Eddie Murray/33	80.00
PO	Paul O'Neill/21	50.00
AP	Angel Pena/36	10.00
MR	Manny Ramirez/24	80.00
NR	Nolan Ryan/34	400.00
DWe	David Wells/33	60.00
BW	Bernie Williams/51	60.00
DW	Dave Winfield/31	90.00
RY	Robin Yount/19	90.00

Lunchbox

	NM/M
Complete Set (17):	140.00
Common Lunchbox	7.50
One dual-player per case.	
Roger Clemens	7.50
Ken Griffey Jr.	7.50
Mickey Mantle	10.00

Mark McGwire	10.00
Mike Piazza	7.50
Alex Rodriguez	7.50
Babe Ruth	10.00
Sammy Sosa	7.50
Ted Williams	10.00
Ken Griffey Jr., Mark McGwire	12.50
Ken Griffey Jr., Babe Ruth	12.50
Ken Griffey Jr., Ted Williams	12.50
Mickey Mantle, Babe Ruth	15.00
Mark McGwire, Mickey Mantle	15.00
Mark McGwire, Babe Ruth	15.00
Mark McGwire, Ted Williams	15.00

Old/New School

	NM/M
Complete Set (30):	35.00
Common Player:	.40
Production 1,000 Sets	
Level 2:	5X
Production 50 Sets	

1	Ken Griffey Jr.	2.50
2	Alex Rodriguez	3.00
3	Frank Thomas	1.50
4	Cal Ripken Jr.	4.00
5	Chipper Jones	2.00
6	Craig Biggio	.40
7	Greg Maddux	2.00
8	Jeff Bagwell	1.50
9	Juan Gonzalez	.75
10	Mark McGwire	3.00
11	Mike Piazza	2.50
12	Mo Vaughn	.40
13	Roger Clemens	2.25
14	Sammy Sosa	2.00
15	Tony Gwynn	2.00
16	Gabe Kapler	.40
17	J.D. Drew	1.00
18	Pat Burrell	1.00
19	Roy Halladay	.40
20	Jeff Weaver	.40
21	Troy Glaus	1.00
22	Vladimir Guerrero	1.50
23	Michael Barrett	.40
24	Carlos Beltran	.40
25	Scott Rolen	1.00
26	Nomar Garciaparra	2.00
27	Warren Morris	.40
28	Alex Gonzalez	.40
29	Kyle Farnsworth	.40
30	Derek Jeter	4.00

Piece of History 500 Club

		NM/M
TW	Ted Williams/350	250.00

Throwback Attack

	NM/M
Complete Set (15):	20.00

Common Player:	.50
Inserted 1:5	
Level 2:	3X
Production 500 Sets	

1	Ken Griffey Jr.	2.00
2	Mark McGwire	2.50
3	Sammy Sosa	1.25
4	Roger Clemens	1.50
5	J.D. Drew	.75
6	Alex Rodriguez	2.50
7	Greg Maddux	1.25
8	Mike Piazza	2.00
9	Juan Gonzalez	.50
10	Mo Vaughn	.50
11	Cal Ripken Jr.	3.00
12	Frank Thomas	1.00
13	Nomar Garciaparra	1.25
14	Vladimir Guerrero	1.00
15	Tony Gwynn	1.25

2000 Upper Deck

	NM/M
Complete Set (540):	40.00
Complete Series I (270):	20.00
Complete Series II (270):	20.00
Common Player:	.15
Silver Stars:	5-10X
Rookies:	2-4X
Hobby Pack (10):	3.00
Hobby Box (24):	55.00

1	Rick Ankiel (Star Rookie)	.25
2	Vernon Wells (Star Rookie)	.50
3	Ryan Anderson (Star Rookie)	.15
4	Ed Yarnall (Star Rookie)	.15
5	Brian McNichol (Star Rookie)	.15
6	Ben Petrick (Star Rookie)	.15
7	Kip Wells (Star Rookie)	.15
8	Eric Munson (Star Rookie)	.20
9	Matt Riley (Star Rookie)	.15
10	Peter Bergeron (Star Rookie)	.15
11	Eric Gagne (Star Rookie)	.25
12	Ramon Ortiz (Star Rookie)	.25
13	Josh Beckett (Star Rookie)	.50
14	Alfonso Soriano (Star Rookie)	1.50
15	Jorge Toca (Star Rookie)	.15
16	Buddy Carlyle (Star Rookie)	.15
17	Chad Hermansen (Star Rookie)	.15
18	Matt Perisho (Star Rookie)	.15
19	Tomokazu Ohka **RC** (Star Rookie)	.75
20	Jacque Jones (Star Rookie)	.15
21	Josh Paul (Star Rookie)	.15
22	Dermal Brown (Star Rookie)	.15
23	Adam Kennedy (Star Rookie)	.15
24	Chad Harville (Star Rookie)	.15
25	Calvin Murray (Star Rookie)	.15
26	Chad Meyers (Star Rookie)	.15
27	Brian Cooper (Star Rookie)	.15
28	Troy Glaus	.50
29	Ben Molina	.15
30	Troy Percival	.15
31	Ken Hill	.15
32	Chuck Finley	.15
33	Todd Greene	.15
34	Tim Salmon	.25
35	Gary DiSarcina	.15
36	Luis Gonzalez	.25
37	Tony Womack	.15
38	Omar Daal	.15
39	Randy Johnson	.50
40	Erubiel Durazo	.20
41	Jay Bell	.15
42	Steve Finley	.15
43	Travis Lee	.15
44	Greg Maddux	1.00
45	Bret Boone	.25
46	Brian Jordan	.15
47	Kevin Millwood	.25
48	Odalis Perez	.15
49	Javy Lopez	.25
50	John Smoltz	.25
51	Bruce Chen	.15
52	Albert Belle	.15
53	Jerry Hairston Jr.	.15
54	Will Clark	.40
55	Sidney Ponson	.15
56	Charles Johnson	.15
57	Cal Ripken Jr.	2.00
58	Ryan Minor	.15
59	Mike Mussina	.40
60	Tom Gordon	.15
61	Jose Offerman	.15
62	Trot Nixon	.15
63	Pedro Martinez	.75
64	John Valentin	.15
65	Jason Varitek	.15
66	Juan Pena	.15
67	Troy O'Leary	.15
68	Sammy Sosa	1.25
69	Henry Rodriguez	.15
70	Kyle Farnsworth	.15
71	Glenallen Hill	.15
72	Lance Johnson	.15
73	Mickey Morandini	.15
74	Jon Lieber	.15
75	Kevin Tapani	.15
76	Carlos Lee	.15
77	Ray Durham	.15
78	Jim Parque	.15
79	Bob Howry	.15
80	Magglio Ordonez	.25
81	Paul Konerko	.20
82	Mike Caruso	.15
83	Chris Singleton	.15
84	Sean Casey	.20
85	Barry Larkin	.25
86	Pokey Reese	.15
87	Eddie Taubensee	.15
88	Scott Williamson	.15
89	Jason LaRue	.15
90	Aaron Boone	.20
91	Jeffrey Hammonds	.15
92	Omar Vizquel	.20
93	Manny Ramirez	.50
94	Kenny Lofton	.20
95	Jaret Wright	.15
96	Einar Diaz	.15
97	Charles Nagy	.15
98	David Justice	.25
99	Richie Sexson	.25
100	Steve Karsay	.15
101	Todd Helton	.50
102	Dante Bichette	.15
103	Larry Walker	.25
104	Pedro Astacio	.15
105	Neifi Perez	.15
106	Brian Bohanon	.15
107	Edgard Clemente	.15
108	Dave Veres	.15
109	Gabe Kapler	.15
110	Juan Encarnacion	.15
111	Jeff Weaver	.15
112	Damion Easley	.15
113	Justin Thompson	.15
114	Brad Ausmus	.15
115	Frank Catalanotto	.15
116	Todd Jones	.15
117	Preston Wilson	.25
118	Cliff Floyd	.15
119	Mike Lowell	.15
120	Jorge Fabregas	.15
121	Alex Gonzalez	.15
122	Braden Looper	.15
123	Bruce Aven	.15
124	Richard Hidalgo	.15
125	Mitch Meluskey	.15
126	Jeff Bagwell	.50
127	Jose Lima	.15
128	Derek Bell	.15
129	Billy Wagner	.15
130	Shane Reynolds	.15
131	Moises Alou	.25
132	Carlos Beltran	.25
133	Carlos Febles	.15
134	Jermaine Dye	.15
135	Jeremy Giambi	.15
136	Joe Randa	.15
137	Jose Rosado	.15
138	Chad Kreuter	.15
139	Jose Vizcaino	.15
140	Adrian Beltre	.25
141	Kevin Brown	.25
142	Ismael Valdes	.15
143	Angel Pena	.15
144	Chan Ho Park	.15
145	Mark Grudzielanek	.15
146	Jeff Shaw	.15
147	Geoff Jenkins	.20
148	Jeromy Burnitz	.15
149	Hideo Nomo	.25
150	Ron Belliard	.15
151	Sean Berry	.15
152	Mark Loretta	.15
153	Steve Woodard	.15
154	Joe Mays	.15
155	Eric Milton	.15
156	Corey Koskie	.15
157	Ron Coomer	.15
158	Brad Radke	.15
159	Terry Steinbach	.15
160	Christian Guzman	.15
161	Vladimir Guerrero	.50
162	Wilton Guerrero	.15
163	Michael Barrett	.15
164	Chris Widger	.15
165	Fernando Seguignol	.15
166	Ugueth Urbina	.15
167	Dustin Hermanson	.15
168	Kenny Rogers	.15
169	Edgardo Alfonzo	.15
170	Orel Hershiser	.15
171	Robin Ventura	.20
172	Octavio Dotel	.15
173	Rickey Henderson	.25
174	Roger Cedeno	.15
175	John Olerud	.25
176	Derek Jeter	2.00
177	Tino Martinez	.25
178	Orlando Hernandez	.20
179	Chuck Knoblauch	.15
180	Bernie Williams	.40
181	Chili Davis	.15
182	David Cone	.20
183	Ricky Ledee	.15
184	Paul O'Neill	.25
185	Jason Giambi	.50
186	Eric Chavez	.25
187	Matt Stairs	.15
188	Miguel Tejada	.25
189	Olmedo Saenz	.15
190	Tim Hudson	.40
191	John Jaha	.15
192	Randy Velarde	.15
193	Rico Brogna	.15
194	Mike Lieberthal	.20
195	Marlon Anderson	.15
196	Bobby Abreu	.25
197	Ron Gant	.15
198	Randy Wolf	.15
199	Desi Relaford	.15
200	Doug Glanville	.15
201	Warren Morris	.15
202	Kris Benson	.15
203	Kevin Young	.15
204	Brian Giles	.25
205	Jason Schmidt	.15
206	Ed Sprague	.15
207	Francisco Cordova	.15
208	Mark McGwire	2.00
209	Jose Jimenez	.15
210	Fernando Tatis	.15
211	Kent Bottenfield	.15
212	Eli Marrero	.15
213	Edgar Renteria	.15
214	Joe McEwing	.15
215	J.D. Drew	.20
216	Tony Gwynn	.75
217	Gary Matthews Jr.	.15
218	Eric Owens	.15
219	Damian Jackson	.15
220	Reggie Sanders	.15
221	Trevor Hoffman	.15
222	Ben Davis	.15
223	Shawn Estes	.15
224	F.P. Santangelo	.15
225	Livan Hernandez	.15
226	Ellis Burks	.15
227	J.T. Snow	.15
228	Jeff Kent	.25
229	Robb Nen	.15
230	Marvin Benard	.15
231	Ken Griffey Jr.	1.00
232	John Halama	.15
233	Gil Meche	.15
234	David Bell	.15
235	Brian L. Hunter	.15
236	Jay Buhner	.25
237	Edgar Martinez	.25
238	Jose Mesa	.15
239	Wilson Alvarez	.15
240	Wade Boggs	.40
241	Fred McGriff	.25
242	Jose Canseco	.40
243	Kevin Stocker	.15
244	Roberto Hernandez	.15
245	Bubba Trammell	.15
246	John Flaherty	.15
247	Ivan Rodriguez	.40
248	Rusty Greer	.15
249	Rafael Palmeiro	.40
250	Jeff Zimmerman	.15
251	Royce Clayton	.15
252	Todd Zeile	.15
253	John Wetteland	.15
254	Ruben Mateo	.15
255	Kelvim Escobar	.15
256	David Wells	.15
257	Shawn Green	.40
258	Homer Bush	.15
259	Shannon Stewart	.15
260	Carlos Delgado	.50
261	Roy Halladay	.25
262	Fernando Tatis CL	.15
263	Jose Jimenez CL	.15
264	Tony Gwynn CL	.40
265	Wade Boggs CL	.25
266	Cal Ripken Jr. CL	1.00
267	David Cone CL	.15
268	Mark McGwire CL	.75
269	Pedro Martinez CL	.40
270	Nomar Garciaparra CL	.75
271	Nick Johnson (Star Rookie)	.40
272	Mark Quinn (Star Rookie)	.15
273	Roosevelt Brown (Star Rookie)	.15
274	Adam Everett (Star Rookie)	.15
275	Jason Marquis (Star Rookie)	.15
276	Kazuhiro Sasaki **RC** (Star Rookie)	1.50
277	Aaron Myette (Star Rookie)	.15
278	Danys Baez **RC** (Star Rookie)	.50
279	Travis Dawkins (Star Rookie)	.15
280	Mark Mulder (Star Rookie)	.25
281	Chris Haas (Star Rookie)	.15
282	Milton Bradley (Star Rookie)	.15
283	Brad Penny (Star Rookie)	.15
284	Rafael Furcal (Star Rookie)	.25
285	Luis Matos **RC** (Star Rookie)	1.00
286	Victor Santos (Star Rookie)	.15
287	Rico Washington **RC** (Star Rookie)	.15
288	Rob Bell (Star Rookie)	.15
289	Joe Crede (Star Rookie)	.15
290	Pablo Ozuna (Star Rookie)	.15
291	Wascar Serrano **RC** (Star Rookie)	.15
292	Sang-Hoon Lee **RC** (Star Rookie)	.25
293	Chris Wakeland (Star Rookie)	.15
294	Luis Rivera (Star Rookie)	.15
295	Mike Lamb **RC** (Star Rookie)	.20
296	Wily Pena (Star Rookie)	.20
297	Mike Meyers **RC** (Star Rookie)	.15
298	Mo Vaughn	.20
299	Darin Erstad	.25
300	Garret Anderson	.25
301	Tim Belcher	.15
302	Scott Spiezio	.15
303	Kent Bottenfield	.15
304	Orlando Palmeiro	.15
305	Jason Dickson	.15
306	Matt Williams	.20
307	Brian Anderson	.15
308	Hanley Frias	.15
309	Todd Stottlemyre	.15
310	Matt Mantei	.15
311	David Dellucci	.15
312	Armando Reynoso	.15
313	Bernard Gilkey	.15
314	Chipper Jones	1.00
315	Tom Glavine	.25
316	Quilvio Veras	.15
317	Andruw Jones	.50
318	Bobby Bonilla	.15
319	Reggie Sanders	.15
320	Andres Galarraga	.20
321	George Lombard	.15
322	John Rocker	.15
322	Wally Joyner	.15
324	B.J. Surhoff	.15
325	Scott Erickson	.15
326	Delino DeShields	.15
327	Jeff Conine	.15
328	Mike Timlin	.15
329	Brady Anderson	.15
330	Mike Bordick	.15
331	Harold Baines	.15
332	Nomar Garciaparra	1.50
333	Bret Saberhagen	.15
334	Ramon Martinez	.15
335	Donnie Sadler	.15
336	Wilton Veras	.15
337	Mike Stanley	.15
338	Brian Rose	.15
339	Carl Everett	.15
340	Tim Wakefield	.15
341	Mark Grace	.25
342	Kerry Wood	.30
343	Eric Young	.15
344	Jose Nieves	.15
345	Ismael Valdes	.15
346	Joe Girardi	.15
347	Damon Buford	.15
348	Ricky Gutierrez	.15
349	Frank Thomas	.50
350	Brian Simmons	.15
351	James Baldwin	.15
352	Brook Fordyce	.15
353	Jose Valentin	.15
354	Mike Sirotka	.15
355	Greg Norton	.15
356	Dante Bichette	.15
357	Deion Sanders	.25
358	Ken Griffey Jr.	1.00
359	Denny Neagle	.15
360	Dmitri Young	.15
361	Pete Harnisch	.15
362	Michael Tucker	.15
363	Roberto Alomar	.40
364	Dave Roberts	.15
365	Jim Thome	.50
366	Bartolo Colon	.15
367	Travis Fryman	.20
368	Chuck Finley	.15
369	Russell Branyan	.15
370	Alex Ramirez	.15
371	Jeff Cirillo	.15
372	Jeffrey Hammonds	.15
373	Scott Karl	.15

374	Brent Mayne	.15
375	Tom Goodwin	.15
376	Jose Jimenez	.15
377	Rolando Arrojo	.15
378	Terry Shumpert	.15
379	Juan Gonzalez	.50
380	Bobby Higginson	.15
381	Tony Clark	.15
382	Dave Mlicki	.15
383	Deivi Cruz	.15
384	Brian Moehler	.15
385	Dean Palmer	.15
386	Luis Castillo	.15
387	Mike Redmond	.15
388	Alex Fernandez	.15
389	Brant Brown	.15
390	Dave Berg	.15
391	A.J. Burnett	.15
392	Mark Kotsay	.15
393	Craig Biggio	.20
394	Daryle Ward	.15
395	Lance Berkman	.25
396	Roger Cedeno	.15
397	Scott Elarton	.15
398	Octavio Dotel	.15
399	Ken Caminiti	.25
400	Johnny Damon	.25
401	Mike Sweeney	.15
402	Jeff Suppan	.15
403	Rey Sanchez	.15
404	Blake Stein	.15
405	Ricky Bottalico	.15
406	Jay Witasick	.15
407	Shawn Green	.40
408	Orel Hershiser	.15
409	Gary Sheffield	.40
410	Todd Hollandsworth	.15
411	Terry Adams	.15
412	Todd Hundley	.15
413	Eric Karros	.15
414	F.P. Santangelo	.15
415	Alex Cora	.15
416	Marquis Grissom	.15
417	Henry Blanco	.15
418	Jose Hernandez	.15
419	Kyle Peterson	.15
420	John Snyder RC	.15
421	Bob Wickman	.15
422	Jamey Wright	.15
423	Chad Allen	.15
424	Todd Walker	.15
425	J.C. Romero RC	.15
426	Butch Huskey	.15
427	Jacque Jones	.15
428	Matt Lawton	.15
429	Rondell White	.25
430	Jose Vidro	.15
431	Hideki Irabu	.15
432	Javier Vazquez	.15
433	Lee Stevens	.15
434	Mike Thurman	.15
435	Geoff Blum	.15
436	Mike Hampton	.15
437	Mike Piazza	1.00
438	Al Leiter	.15
439	Derek Bell	.15
440	Armando Benitez	.15
441	Rey Ordonez	.15
442	Todd Zeile	.15
443	Roger Clemens	1.25
444	Ramiro Mendoza	.15
445	Andy Pettitte	.25
446	Scott Brosius	.15
447	Mariano Rivera	.25
448	Jim Leyritz	.15
449	Jorge Posada	.25
450	Omar Olivares	.15
451	Ben Grieve	.15
452	A.J. Hinch	.15
453	Gil Heredia	.15
454	Kevin Appier	.15
455	Ryan Christenson	.15
456	Ramon Hernandez	.15
457	Scott Rolen	.50
458	Alex Arias	.15
459	Andy Ashby	.15
460	(Not issued, see #474.)	
460		.15
461	Robert Person	.15
462	Paul Byrd	.15
463	Curt Schilling	.25
464	Mike Jackson	.15
465	Jason Kendall	.25
466	Pat Meares	.15
467	Bruce Aven	.15
468	Todd Ritchie	.15
469	Wil Cordero	.15
470	Aramis Ramirez	.15
471	Andy Benes	.15
472	Ray Lankford	.15
473	Fernando Vina	.15
474a	Jim Edmonds	.25
474b	Kevin Jordan	
	(should be #460)	.15
475	Craig Paquette	.15
476	Pat Hentgen	.15
477	Darryl Kile	.15
478	Sterling Hitchcock	.15
479	Ruben Rivera	.15
480	Ryan Klesko	.15
481	Phil Nevin	.15
482	Woody Williams	.15
483	Carlos Hernandez	.15
484	Brian Meadows	.15
485	Bret Boone	.25

486	Barry Bonds	1.50
487	Russ Ortiz	.15
488	Bobby Estalella	.15
489	Rich Aurilia	.15
490	Bill Mueller	.15
491	Joe Nathan	.15
492	Russ Davis	.15
493	John Olerud	.25
494	Alex Rodriguez	1.50
495	Fred Garcia	.15
496	Carlos Guillen	.15
497	Aaron Sele	.15
498	Brett Tomko	.15
499	Jamie Moyer	.15
500	Mike Cameron	.15
501	Vinny Castilla	.15
502	Gerald Williams	.15
503	Mike DiFelice	.15
504	Ryan Rupe	.15
505	Greg Vaughn	.15
506	Miguel Cairo	.15
507	Juan Guzman RC	.15
508	Jose Guillen	.15
509	Gabe Kapler	.15
510	Rick Helling	.15
511	David Segui	.15
512	Doug Davis	.15
513	Justin Thompson	.15
514	Chad Curtis	.15
515	Tony Batista	.15
516	Billy Koch	.15
517	Raul Mondesi	.20
518	Joey Hamilton	.15
519	Darrin Fletcher	.15
520	Brad Fullmer	.15
521	Jose Cruz Jr.	.15
522	Kevin Witt	.15
523	Mark McGwire (All-UD Team)	1.00
524	Roberto Alomar (All-UD Team)	.25
525	Chipper Jones (All-UD Team)	.50
526	Derek Jeter (All-UD Team)	1.00
527	Ken Griffey Jr. (All-UD Team)	.50
528	Sammy Sosa (All-UD Team)	.75
529	Manny Ramirez (All-UD Team)	.40
530	Ivan Rodriguez (All-UD Team)	.25
531	Pedro J. Martinez (All-UD Team)	.40
532	Mariano Rivera (Season Highlights Checklist)	.15
533	Sammy Sosa (Season Highlights Checklist)	.75
534	Cal Ripken Jr. (Season Highlights Checklist)	1.00
535	Vladimir Guerrero (Season Highlights Checklist)	.40
536	Tony Gwynn (Season Highlights Checklist)	.25
537	Mark McGwire (Season Highlights Checklist)	1.00
538	Bernie Williams (Season Highlights Checklist)	.25
539	Pedro J. Martinez (Season Highlights Checklist)	.40
540	Ken Griffey Jr. (Season Highlights Checklist)	.50

Exclusives

	NM/M
Common Silver Exclusive:	1.00
Silver Stars/Rookies:	8X

(See 2000 Upper Deck for checklist and base card values.)

Cooperstown Calling

	NM/M
Complete Set (15):	25.00

Common Player:		.75
Inserted 1:23		
1	Roger Clemens	3.00
2	Cal Ripken Jr.	5.00
3	Ken Griffey Jr.	3.00
4	Mike Piazza	3.00
5	Tony Gwynn	2.00
6	Sammy Sosa	2.50
7	Jose Canseco	1.00
8	Larry Walker	.75
9	Barry Bonds	4.00
10	Greg Maddux	2.50
11	Derek Jeter	5.00
12	Mark McGwire	4.00
13	Randy Johnson	2.00
14	Frank Thomas	1.50
15	Jeff Bagwell	1.50

e-Card

		NM/M
Complete Set (6):		10.00
Common Player:		1.00
Inserted 1:12		
1	Ken Griffey Jr.	2.00
2	Alex Rodriguez	3.00
3	Cal Ripken Jr.	3.00
4	Jeff Bagwell	1.00
5	Barry Bonds	3.00
6	Manny Ramirez	1.00

eVolve Jersey

		NM/M
Common Player:		15.00
Production 300 Sets		
1	Ken Griffey Jr.	30.00
2	Alex Rodriguez	40.00
3	Cal Ripken Jr.	50.00
4	Jeff Bagwell	15.00
5	Barry Bonds	40.00
6	Manny Ramirez	20.00

eVolve Signature

		NM/M
Common Player:		40.00
Production 200 Sets		
1	Ken Griffey Jr.	85.00
2	Alex Rodriguez	85.00
3	Cal Ripken Jr.	150.00
4	Jeff Bagwell	40.00
5	Barry Bonds	120.00
6	Manny Ramirez	40.00

eVolve Signed Jersey

		NM/M
Common Player:		80.00
Production 50 Sets		
1	Ken Griffey Jr.	150.00
2	Alex Rodriguez	150.00
3	Cal Ripken Jr.	200.00
4	Jeff Bagwell	60.00
5	Barry Bonds	150.00
6	Manny Ramirez	60.00

Faces of the Game

		NM/M
Complete Set (20):		30.00
Common Player:		.75
Inserted 1:11		
Silver:		4-8X
Production 100 Sets		
1	Ken Griffey Jr.	2.50
2	Mark McGwire	3.00
3	Sammy Sosa	2.00
4	Alex Rodriguez	3.00
5	Manny Ramirez	1.00
6	Derek Jeter	4.00
7	Jeff Bagwell	1.00
8	Roger Clemens	2.00
9	Scott Rolen	.75
10	Tony Gwynn	1.50
11	Nomar Garciaparra	2.50
12	Randy Johnson	1.50
13	Greg Maddux	2.00
14	Mike Piazza	2.50
15	Frank Thomas	1.00
16	Cal Ripken Jr.	4.00
17	Ivan Rodriguez	.75
18	Mo Vaughn	.75
19	Chipper Jones	2.00
20	Sean Casey	.75

Five-Tool Talents

		NM/M
Complete Set (15):		15.00
Common Player:		.50
Inserted 3:11		
1	Vladimir Guerrero	1.50
2	Barry Bonds	3.00
3	Jason Kendall	.50
4	Derek Jeter	4.00
5	Ken Griffey Jr.	2.50
6	Andruw Jones	.75
7	Bernie Williams	.75
8	Jose Canseco	.75
9	Scott Rolen	.75
10	Shawn Green	.50
11	Nomar Garciaparra	2.50
12	Jeff Bagwell	1.00
13	Larry Walker	.75
14	Chipper Jones	2.00
15	Alex Rodriguez	3.00

Game Balls

		NM/M
Common Player:		10.00
JB	Jeff Bagwell	10.00
RC	Roger Clemens	30.00
KG	Ken Griffey Jr.	25.00
VG	Vladimir Guerrero	15.00
TG	Tony Gwynn	25.00

DJ	Derek Jeter	40.00
CJ	Chipper Jones	20.00
GM	Greg Maddux	20.00
MM	Mark McGwire	50.00
AR	Alex Rodriguez	30.00
BW	Bernie Williams	10.00

Game Jersey

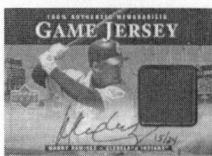

		NM/M
Common Player:		10.00
Inserted 1:2,500		
JC	Jose Canseco	15.00
JG	Juan Gonzalez	15.00
VG	Vladimir Guerrero	20.00
TH	Todd Helton	15.00
CJ	Chipper Jones	25.00
GK	Gabe Kapler	10.00
GM	Greg Maddux	35.00
MR	Manny Ramirez	20.00
CR	Cal Ripken Jr.	60.00
GV	Greg Vaughn	10.00

Game Jersey Hobby

		NM/M
Common Player:		10.00
Inserted 1:288		
JB	Jeff Bagwell	15.00
TG	Troy Glaus	15.00
CY	Tom Glavine	10.00
Jr.	Ken Griffey Jr.	25.00
DJ	Derek Jeter	40.00
PM	Pedro J. Martinez	20.00
MP	Mike Piazza	30.00
AR	Alex Rodriguez	30.00
FT	Frank Thomas	15.00
LW	Larry Walker	10.00

Game Jersey Series 2

		NM/M
Common Player:		10.00
AR	Alex Rodriguez	30.00
TG	Tony Gwynn	20.00
FT	Frank Thomas	15.00
MW	Matt Williams	10.00
JT	Jim Thome	15.00
MV	Mo Vaughn	15.00
TGl	Tom Glavine	15.00
BG	Ben Grieve	10.00
TrG	Troy Glaus	15.00
RJ	Randy Johnson	20.00
KM	Kevin Millwood	10.00
KG	Ken Griffey Jr.	25.00
AB	Albert Belle	10.00
DC	David Cone	10.00
MH	Mike Hampton	10.00
EC	Eric Chavez	10.00
EM	Edgar Martinez	15.00
PW	Preston Wilson	10.00
RV	Robin Ventura	10.00

Game Jersey Patch

		NM/M
Common Player:		40.00
Inserted 1:10,000		
JB	Jeff Bagwell	60.00
JC	Jose Canseco	60.00
TG	Troy Glaus	50.00
CY	Tom Glavine	60.00
Jr.	Ken Griffey Jr.	100.00
VG	Vladimir Guerrero	100.00
TH	Todd Helton	60.00
DJ	Derek Jeter	150.00
CJ	Chipper Jones	75.00
GK	Gabe Kapler	40.00
GM	Greg Maddux	100.00
PM	Pedro J. Martinez	100.00
MP	Mike Piazza	100.00
MR	Manny Ramirez	80.00
CR	Cal Ripken Jr.	200.00
AR	Alex Rodriguez	125.00
FT	Frank Thomas	80.00
GV	Greg Vaughn	40.00
LW	Larry Walker	50.00

Game Jersey Patch Series 2

		NM/M
Common Player:		50.00
JB	Jeff Bagwell	75.00
BB	Barry Bonds	200.00
JC	Jose Canseco	75.00
TGl	Troy Glaus	75.00
KG	Ken Griffey Jr.	125.00
VG	Vladimir Guerrero	100.00
TG	Tony Gwynn	100.00
DJ	Derek Jeter	150.00
RJ	Randy Johnson	100.00
AJ	Andruw Jones	80.00
CJ	Chipper Jones	100.00
GM	Greg Maddux	100.00
PM	Pedro Martinez	100.00
MR	Manny Ramirez	100.00
CR	Cal Ripken Jr.	200.00
SR	Scott Rolen	75.00
AR	Alex Rodriguez	150.00
IR	Ivan Rodriguez	90.00
FT	Frank Thomas	100.00
MV	Mo Vaughn	50.00
MW	Matt Williams	50.00

Game Jersey Auto. Hobby Series 2

		NM/M
Common Player:		30.00
H-KG	Ken Griffey Jr.	100.00
H-CR	Cal Ripken Jr.	150.00
H-DJ	Derek Jeter	150.00
H-IR	Ivan Rodriguez	40.00
H-AR	Alex Rodriguez	100.00
H-MR	Manny Ramirez	100.00
H-JC	Jose Canseco	30.00
H-BB	Barry Bonds	180.00
H-SR	Scott Rolen	40.00
H-PO	Paul O'Neill	40.00
H-JK	Jason Kendall	30.00
H-VG	Vladimir Guerrero	50.00
H-JB	Jeff Bagwell	40.00

Hit Brigade

		NM/M
Complete Set (15):		15.00
Common Player:		.50
Inserted 1:8		
Silver:		5-10X
Production 100 Sets		
1	Ken Griffey Jr.	2.00

2	Tony Gwynn	1.00
3	Alex Rodriguez	2.50
4	Derek Jeter	3.00
5	Mike Piazza	2.00
6	Sammy Sosa	1.50
7	Juan Gonzalez	.75
8	Scott Rolen	.50
9	Nomar Garciaparra	2.00
10	Barry Bonds	2.50
11	Craig Biggio	.50
12	Chipper Jones	1.50
13	Frank Thomas	.75
14	Larry Walker	.50
15	Mark McGwire	2.50

Hot Properties

		NM/M
Complete Set (15):		10.00
Common Player:		.50
Inserted 1:11		
1	Carlos Beltran	1.00
2	Rick Ankiel	.50
3	Sean Casey	1.00
4	Preston Wilson	1.00
5	Vernon Wells	1.00
6	Pat Burrell	1.50
7	Eric Chavez	1.00
8	J.D. Drew	1.00
9	Alfonso Soriano	2.00
10	Gabe Kapler	.50
11	Rafael Furcal	1.00
12	Ruben Mateo	.50
13	Corey Koskie	.75
14	Kip Wells	.50
15	Ramon Ortiz	.75

Pennant Driven

		NM/M
Complete Set (10):		8.00
Common Player:		.50
Inserted 1:4		
1	Derek Jeter	2.00
2	Roberto Alomar	.50
3	Chipper Jones	1.50
4	Jeff Bagwell	.75
5	Roger Clemens	1.00
6	Nomar Garciaparra	1.50
7	Manny Ramirez	.75
8	Mike Piazza	1.50
9	Ivan Rodriguez	.75
10	Randy Johnson	.75

Piece of History-500 Club

		NM/M
755HR	Hank Aaron	300.00
HAAU	Hank Aaron/Auto./44	1,200

Power Deck

		NM/M
Complete Set (11):		60.00
Common Player:		2.50
Inserted 1:23		
1	Ken Griffey Jr.	5.00
2	Cal Ripken Jr.	7.50
3	Mark McGwire	6.00
4	Tony Gwynn	3.50
5	Roger Clemens	3.50
6	Alex Rodriguez	6.00
7	Sammy Sosa	3.50
8	Derek Jeter	7.50
9	Ken Griffey Jr.	25.00
10	Mark McGwire	30.00
11	Reggie Jackson	15.00

Power MARK

		NM/M
Complete Set (10):		25.00
Common McGwire:		3.00
Inserted 1:23		
Silver:		5-10X
Production 100 Sets		
1-10	Mark McGwire	3.00

Power Rally

		NM/M
Complete Set (15):		20.00
Common Player:		.75
Inserted 1:11		
Silver:		4-8X
Production 100 Sets		
1	Ken Griffey Jr.	2.50
2	Mark McGwire	3.00
3	Sammy Sosa	2.00
4	Jose Canseco	.75
5	Juan Gonzalez	1.00
6	Bernie Williams	.75

7	Jeff Bagwell	1.00
8	Chipper Jones	2.00
9	Vladimir Guerrero	1.50
10	Mo Vaughn	.75
11	Derek Jeter	4.00
12	Mike Piazza	2.50
13	Barry Bonds	3.00
14	Alex Rodriguez	3.00
15	Nomar Garciaparra	2.50

Prime Performers

		NM/M
Complete Set (10):		10.00
Common Player:		.50
Inserted 1:8		
1	Manny Ramirez	.75
2	Pedro Martinez	1.00
3	Carlos Delgado	.50
4	Ken Griffey Jr.	2.00
5	Derek Jeter	3.00
6	Chipper Jones	1.50
7	Sean Casey	.50
8	Shawn Green	.50
9	Sammy Sosa	1.50
10	Alex Rodriguez	2.50

STATitude

		NM/M
Complete Set (30):		25.00
Common Player:		.40
Inserted 1:4		
Silver:		5-10X
Production 100 Sets		
1	Mo Vaughn	.40
2	Matt Williams	.40
3	Travis Lee	.40
4	Chipper Jones	1.50
5	Greg Maddux	1.50
6	Gabe Kapler	.40
7	Cal Ripken Jr.	3.00
8	Nomar Garciaparra	2.00
9	Sammy Sosa	1.50
10	Frank Thomas	.75
11	Manny Ramirez	.75
12	Larry Walker	.50
13	Ivan Rodriguez	.50
14	Jeff Bagwell	.75
15	Craig Biggio	.50
16	Vladimir Guerrero	1.00
17	Mike Piazza	2.00
18	Bernie Williams	.50
19	Derek Jeter	3.00
20	Jose Canseco	.50
21	Eric Chavez	.50
22	Scott Rolen	.50
23	Mark McGwire	2.50
24	Tony Gwynn	1.00
25	Barry Bonds	2.50
26	Ken Griffey Jr.	2.00
27	Alex Rodriguez	2.50
28	J.D. Drew	.50
29	Juan Gonzalez	.50
30	Roger Clemens	1.50

The People's Choice

		NM/M
Complete Set (15):		20.00
Common Player:		.75
Inserted 1:23		
1	Mark McGwire	3.00
2	Nomar Garciaparra	3.00
3	Derek Jeter	3.00
4	Shawn Green	.75
5	Manny Ramirez	1.00
6	Pedro Martinez	1.50
7	Ivan Rodriguez	.75
8	Alex Rodriguez	3.00
9	Juan Gonzalez	1.00
10	Ken Griffey Jr.	2.00
11	Sammy Sosa	2.50
12	Jeff Bagwell	1.00
13	Chipper Jones	2.00
14	Cal Ripken Jr.	4.00
15	Mike Piazza	2.00

2K Plus

		NM/M
Complete Set (12):		15.00
Common Player:		.50
Inserted 1:23		
Silver:		5-10X
Production 100 Sets		
1	Ken Griffey Jr.	2.00
2	J.D. Drew	.50
3	Derek Jeter	3.00
4	Nomar Garciaparra	3.00
5	Pat Burrell	.75
6	Ruben Mateo	.50
7	Carlos Beltran	.50
8	Vladimir Guerrero	1.00
9	Scott Rolen	1.00
10	Chipper Jones	2.00
11	Alex Rodriguez	3.00
12	Magglio Ordonez	.75

3,000 Hit Club Series 2

		NM/M
HA-B	Hank Aaron/Bat/350	75.00
HA-JB	Hank Aaron/Bat/Jsy/100	150.00
HA-J	Hank Aaron/Jsy/350	75.00
HA-JBS	Hank Aaron/ Auto. Bat/Jsy/44	1,000

3,000 Hit Club Series 1

		NM/M
CR-B	Cal Ripken Jr./Bat/350	25.00
CR-J	Cal Ripken Jr./Jsy/350	25.00
CR-JB	Cal Ripken Jr./ Jsy/Bat/100	150.00
EM-B	Eddie Murray/Bat/350	10.00
EM-J	Eddie Murray/Jsy/350	8.00
EM-JB	Eddie Murray/Jsy/Bat/100	60.00

2000 Upper Deck Black Diamond

		NM/M
Complete Set (120):		25.00
Common Player:		.15
Common Diamond Debut:		.50
Pack (6):		1.50
Wax Box (24):		30.00
1	Darin Erstad	.25
2	Tim Salmon	.25
3	Mo Vaughn	.20
4	Matt Williams	.25
5	Travis Lee	.15
6	Randy Johnson	.75
7	Tom Glavine	.40
8	Chipper Jones	1.50
9	Greg Maddux	1.50
10	Andruw Jones	.50

11	Brian Jordan	.15
12	Cal Ripken Jr.	2.50
13	Albert Belle	.20
14	Mike Mussina	.50
15	Nomar Garciaparra	2.00
16	Troy O'Leary	.15
17	Pedro J. Martinez	1.00
18	Sammy Sosa	1.50
19	Henry Rodriguez	.15
20	Frank Thomas	.75
21	Magglio Ordonez	.40
22	Greg Vaughn	.15
23	Barry Larkin	.25
24	Sean Casey	.25
25	Jim Thome	.75
26	Kenny Lofton	.25
27	Roberto Alomar	.50
28	Manny Ramirez	.75
29	Larry Walker	.25
30	Todd Helton	.75
31	Gabe Kapler	.15
32	Tony Clark	.15
33	Dean Palmer	.15
34	Cliff Floyd	.15
35	Alex Gonzalez	.15
36	Moises Alou	.25
37	Jeff Bagwell	.75
38	Craig Biggio	.25
39	Richard Hidalgo	.15
40	Carlos Beltran	.25
41	Johnny Damon	.25
42	Adrian Beltre	.25
43	Gary Sheffield	.40
44	Kevin Brown	.25
45	Jeromy Burnitz	.15
46	Jeff Cirillo	.15
47	Joe Mays	.15
48	Todd Walker	.15
49	Vladimir Guerrero	.75
50	Michael Barrett	.15
51	Rickey Henderson	.25
52	Mike Piazza	1.50
53	Robin Ventura	.25
54	John Olerud	.25
55	Edgardo Alfonzo	.15
56	Derek Jeter	2.00
57	Orlando Hernandez	.15
58	Tino Martinez	.25
59	Bernie Williams	.50
60	Roger Clemens	1.50
61	Eric Chavez	.25
62	Ben Grieve	.15
63	Jason Giambi	1.00
64	Scott Rolen	.50
65	Bobby Abreu	.25
66	Curt Schilling	.40
67	Mike Lieberthal	.15
68	Warren Morris	.15
69	Brian Giles	.25
70	Eric Owens	.15
71	Tony Gwynn	1.00
72	Reggie Sanders	.15
73	Barry Bonds	2.00
74	J.T. Snow	.15
75	Jeff Kent	.25
76	Ken Griffey Jr.	1.50
77	Alex Rodriguez	2.00
78	Edgar Martinez	.15
79	Jay Buhner	.15
80	Mark McGwire	2.00
81	J.D. Drew	.25
82	Eric Davis	.15
83	Fernando Tatis	.15
84	Wade Boggs	.50
85	Fred McGriff	.25
86	Juan Gonzalez	.75
87	Ivan Rodriguez	.50
88	Rafael Palmeiro	.50
89	Shawn Green	.40
90	Carlos Delgado	.60
91	Pat Burrell (Diamond Debut)	1.00
92	Eric Munson (Diamond Debut)	.50
93	Jorge Toca (Diamond Debut)	.50
94	Rick Ankiel (Diamond Debut)	.50
95	Tony Armas Jr. (Diamond Debut)	.75
96	Byung-Hyun Kim (Diamond Debut)	.75
97	Alfonso Soriano (Diamond Debut)	3.00
98	Mark Quinn (Diamond Debut)	.50
99	Ryan Rupe (Diamond Debut)	.50
100	Adam Kennedy (Diamond Debut)	.50
101	Jeff Weaver (Diamond Debut)	.75
102	Ramon Ortiz (Diamond Debut)	.75
103	Eugene Kingsale (Diamond Debut)	.50
104	Josh Beckett (Diamond Debut)	1.00
105	Eric Gagne (Diamond Debut)	1.00
106	Peter Bergeron (Diamond Debut)	.50
107	Erubiel Durazo (Diamond Debut)	.75
108	Chad Meyers (Diamond Debut)	.50
109	Kip Wells (Diamond Debut)	.50
110	Chad Harville (Diamond Debut)	.50
111	Matt Riley (Diamond Debut)	.50
112	Ben Petrick (Diamond Debut)	.50
113	Ed Yarnall (Diamond Debut)	.50
114	Calvin Murray (Diamond Debut)	.50
115	Vernon Wells (Diamond Debut)	1.00
116	A.J. Burnett (Diamond Debut)	.75
117	Jacque Jones (Diamond Debut)	.75
118	Francisco Cordero (Diamond Debut)	.50
119	Tomokazu Ohka RC (Diamond Debut)	1.50
120	Julio Ramirez (Diamond Debut)	.50

Final Cut

Stars (1-90):	5-10X
Diamond Debuts:	2-4X
Production 100 Sets	

(See 2000 UD Black Diamond for checklist and base card values.)

Reciprocal Cut

Stars (1-90):	2-5X
Diamond Debuts:	1-1.5X
1-90 inserted 1:7	
Diamond Debuts inserted 1:12	

(See 2000 UD Black Diamond for checklist and base card values.)

A Piece of History Single

	NM/M
Common Player:	8.00

Inserted 1:179

AB	Albert Belle	8.00
BB	Barry Bonds	40.00
JC	Jose Canseco	10.00
DE	Darin Erstad	8.00
JR	Ken Griffey Jr.	25.00
VG	Vladimir Guerrero	15.00
TG	Tony Gwynn	20.00
TH	Todd Helton	10.00
DJ	Derek Jeter	40.00
AJ	Andruw Jones	10.00
CJ	Chipper Jones	20.00
TL	Travis Lee	8.00
RM	Raul Mondesi	8.00
MP	Mike Piazza	25.00
CAL	Cal Ripken Jr.	50.00
AR	Alex Rodriguez	25.00
IR	Ivan Rodriguez	10.00
SR	Scott Rolen	10.00
MV	Mo Vaughn	8.00

A Piece of History Double

NM/M

Common Player: 10.00
Inserted 1:1079

AB	Albert Belle	10.00
BB	Barry Bonds	75.00
JC	Jose Canseco	20.00
DE	Darin Erstad	15.00
JR	Ken Griffey Jr.	50.00
VG	Vladimir Guerrero	30.00
TG	Tony Gwynn	40.00
TH	Todd Helton	15.00
DJ	Derek Jeter	75.00
AJ	Andruw Jones	15.00
CJ	Chipper Jones	40.00
TL	Travis Lee	10.00
RM	Raul Mondesi	10.00
MP	Mike Piazza	50.00
CAL	Cal Ripken Jr.	80.00
AR	Alex Rodriguez	50.00
IR	Ivan Rodriguez	15.00
SR	Scott Rolen	15.00
MV	Mo Vaughn	10.00

Barrage

NM/M

Complete Set (10): 15.00
Common Player: 1.00
Inserted 1:29

1	Mark McGwire	3.00
2	Ken Griffey Jr.	2.00
3	Sammy Sosa	2.50
4	Jeff Bagwell	1.00
5	Juan Gonzalez	1.00
6	Alex Rodriguez	3.00
7	Manny Ramirez	1.00
8	Ivan Rodriguez	1.00
9	Chipper Jones	2.00
10	Mike Piazza	2.00

Constant Threat

NM/M

Complete Set (10): 20.00
Common Player: 1.00
Inserted 1:29

1	Ken Griffey Jr.	2.00
2	Vladimir Guerrero	1.00
3	Alex Rodriguez	3.00
4	Sammy Sosa	2.50
5	Juan Gonzalez	1.00
6	Derek Jeter	3.00
7	Nomar Garciaparra	3.00
8	Barry Bonds	4.00
9	Chipper Jones	2.00
10	Mike Piazza	2.00

Diamonation

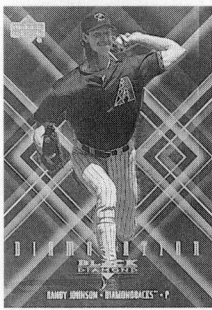

NM/M

Complete Set (10): 6.00
Common Player: .50
Inserted 1:4

1	Ken Griffey Jr.	1.00
2	Randy Johnson	1.00
3	Mark McGwire	1.50
4	Manny Ramirez	.75
5	Scott Rolen	.75
6	Bernie Williams	.75
7	Roger Clemens	1.50
8	Mo Vaughn	.50
9	Frank Thomas	.75
10	Sean Casey	.50

Diamond Gallery

NM/M

Complete Set (10): 20.00
Common Player: 1.50
Inserted 1:14

1	Derek Jeter	3.00
2	Alex Rodriguez	3.00
3	Nomar Garciaparra	3.00
4	Cal Ripken Jr.	4.00
5	Sammy Sosa	2.50
6	Tony Gwynn	1.50
7	Mark McGwire	3.00
8	Roger Clemens	2.50
9	Greg Maddux	2.00
10	Pedro Martinez	1.50

Diamonds in the Rough

NM/M

Complete Set (10): 8.00
Common Player: .75
Inserted 1:9

1	Pat Burrell	2.00
2	Eric Munson	.75
3	Alfonso Soriano	3.00
4	Ruben Mateo	.75
5	A.J. Burnett	1.00
6	Ben Davis	.75
7	Lance Berkman	1.50
8	Ed Yarnall	.75
9	Rick Ankiel	1.00
10	Ryan Bradley	.75

DiamondMight

NM/M

Complete Set (10): 15.00
Common Player: 1.00
Inserted 1:14

1	Ken Griffey Jr.	2.00

2	Mark McGwire	3.00
3	Sammy Sosa	2.50
4	Manny Ramirez	1.00
5	Jeff Bagwell	1.00
6	Frank Thomas	2.00
7	Mike Piazza	2.00
8	Juan Gonzalez	1.00
9	Barry Bonds	4.00
10	Alex Rodriguez	3.00

500 Club Piece of History

NM/M

Reggie Jackson	165.00
Reggie Jackson/Auto./44	500.00

2000 Upper Deck Black Diamond Rookie Edition

NM/M

Complete Set (154):	200.00
Common Player:	.15
Common Rookie Gem (91-120):	4.00
Production 1,000	
Rookie Jersey Gems (121-136):	
Inserted 1:24	
USA Authentics (137-154):	
Inserted 1:96	
Golds (1-90):	2-4X
Gold Gems (91-120):	1X
Gold Jerseys (121-136):	1-2X
Pack (6):	
Box (24):	40.00

1	Troy Glaus	.75
2	Mo Vaughn	.40
3	Darin Erstad	.40
4	Jason Giambi	.40
5	Tim Hudson	.25
6	Ben Grieve	.25
7	Eric Chavez	.25
8	Tony Batista	.15
9	Carlos Delgado	.60
10	David Wells	.15
11	Greg Vaughn	.15
12	Fred McGriff	.25
13	Manny Ramirez	.75
14	Roberto Alomar	.60
15	Jim Thome	.40
16	Alex Rodriguez	2.50
17	Edgar Martinez	.15
18	John Olerud	.20
19	Albert Belle	.40
20	Mike Mussina	.40
21	Cal Ripken Jr.	2.50
22	Ivan Rodriguez	.40
23	Rafael Palmeiro	.40
24	Pedro J. Martinez	.75
25	Nomar Garciaparra	2.00
26	Carl Everett	.15
27	Jermaine Dye	.15
28	Mike Sweeney	.15
29	Juan Gonzalez	.75
30	Bobby Higginson	.15
31	Dean Palmer	.15
32	Jacque Jones	.15
33	Eric Milton	.15
34	Matt Lawton	.15
35	Magglio Ordonez	.25
36	Paul Konerko	.15
37	Frank Thomas	1.00
38	Ray Durham	.15
39	Roger Clemens	1.00
40	Derek Jeter	2.50
41	Bernie Williams	.50
42	Jose Canseco	.40
43	Craig Biggio	.25
44	Richard Hidalgo	.15
45	Jeff Bagwell	.75
46	Greg Maddux	1.50
47	Chipper Jones	1.50
48	Rafael Furcal	.25
49	Andruw Jones	.50
50	Geoff Jenkins	.25
51	Jeromy Burnitz	.15
52	Mark McGwire	3.00
53	Rick Ankiel	.50
54	Jim Edmonds	.25
55	Kerry Wood	.25
56	Sammy Sosa	2.00
57	Matt Williams	.25
58	Randy Johnson	.75
59	Steve Finley	.15
60	Curt Schilling	.15
61	Kevin Brown	.15
62	Gary Sheffield	.30
63	Shawn Green	.30
64	Jose Vidro	.15
65	Vladimir Guerrero	1.00
66	Jeff Kent	.15
67	Barry Bonds	1.00
68	Ryan Dempster	.15
69	Cliff Floyd	.15
70	Preston Wilson	.15
71	Mike Piazza	2.00
72	Al Leiter	.15
73	Edgardo Alfonzo	.25
74	Derek Bell	.15
75	Ryan Klesko	.15
76	Tony Gwynn	1.00
77	Bobby Abreu	.15
78	Pat Burrell	.50
79	Scott Rolen	.50
80	Mike Lieberthal	.15
81	Jason Kendall	.15
82	Brian Giles	.25
83	Ken Griffey Jr.	2.00
84	Pokey Reese	.15
85	Dmitri Young	.15
86	Sean Casey	.15
87	Jeff Cirillo	.15
88	Todd Helton	.75
89	Jeffrey Hammonds	.15
90	Larry Walker	.30
91	Barry Zito RC	15.00
92	Keith Ginter RC	6.00
93	Dane Sardinha RC	4.00
94	Kenny Kelly RC	4.00
95	Ryan Kohlmeier RC	4.00
96	Leo Estrella RC	4.00
97	Danys Baez RC	4.00
98	Paul Rigdon RC	4.00
99	Mike Lamb RC	4.00
100	Aaron McNeal RC	4.00
101	Juan Pierre RC	6.00
102	Rico Washington RC	4.00
103	Luis Matos RC	8.00
104	Adam Bernero RC	4.00
105	Wascar Serrano RC	4.00
106	Chris Richard RC	4.00
107	Justin Miller RC	4.00
108	Julio Zuleta RC	4.00
109	Alex Cabrera RC	4.00
110	Gene Stechschulte RC	4.00
111	Tony Mota RC	4.00
112	Tomokazu Ohka RC	4.00
113	Geraldo Guzman RC	4.00
114	Scott Downs RC	4.00
115	Timoniel Perez RC	4.00
116	Chad Durbin RC	4.00
117	Sun-Woo Kim RC	4.00
118	Tomas de la Rosa RC	4.00
119	Javier Cardona RC	4.00
120	Kazuhiro Sasaki RC	6.00
121	Brad Cresse RC (Rookie Jersey Gems)	5.00
122	Matt Wheatland RC (Rookie Jersey Gems)	5.00
123	Joe Torres RC (Rookie Jersey Gems)	5.00
124	Dave Krynzel RC (Rookie Jersey Gems)	5.00
125	Ben Diggins RC (Rookie Jersey Gems)	5.00
126	Sean Burnett RC (Rookie Jersey Gems)	8.00
127	David Espinosa RC (Rookie Jersey Gems)	5.00
128	Scott Heard RC (Rookie Jersey Gems)	5.00
129	Daylan Holt RC (Rookie Jersey Gems)	5.00
130	Koyie Hill RC (Rookie Jersey Gems)	5.00
131	Mark Buehrle RC (Rookie Jersey Gems)	15.00
132	Xavier Nady RC (Rookie Jersey Gems)	8.00
133	Mike Tonis RC (Rookie Jersey Gems)	5.00
134	Matt Ginter RC (Rookie Jersey Gems)	5.00

135	Lorenzo Barcelo **RC** (Rookie Jersey Gems)	5.00
136	Cory Vance **RC** (Rookie Jersey Gems)	5.00
137	Sean Burroughs (USA Authentics)	8.00
138	Todd Williams (USA Authentics)	5.00
139	Brad Wilkerson **RC** (USA Authentics)	5.00
140	Ben Sheets **RC** (USA Authentics)	20.00
141	Kurt Ainsworth **RC** (USA Authentics)	8.00
142	Anthony Sanders (USA Authentics)	5.00
143	Ryan Franklin (USA Authentics)	5.00
144	Shane Heams **RC** (USA Authentics)	5.00
145	Roy Oswalt **RC** (USA Authentics)	20.00
146	Jon Rauch **RC** (USA Authentics)	5.00
147	Brent Abernathy **RC** (USA Authentics)	5.00
148	Ernie Young (USA Authentics)	5.00
149	Chris George (USA Authentics)	5.00
150	Gookie Dawkins (USA Authentics)	5.00
151	Adam Everett (USA Authentics)	5.00
152	John Cotton **RC** (USA Authentics)	5.00
153	Pat Borders (USA Authentics)	5.00
154	Doug Mientkiewicz (USA Authentics)	5.00

Authentics

	NM/M
Jeter Authentic Pinstripes	
APJ Derek Jeter/Jsy/1,000	35.00
APB Derek Jeter/Bat/1,000	35.00
APC Derek Jeter/Cap/200	70.00
APG Derek Jeter/Glv/200	80.00

Combos

NM/M

Random game-used inserts.
25 produced of each combo bat.
100 produced of combo jersey.

	NM/M
JDM Derek Jeter, Joe DiMaggio, Mickey Mantle/Bat	925.00
JWO Derek Jeter, Bernie Williams, Paul O'Neill/Jersey	150.00

tion

	NM/M
Complete Set (9):	10.00
Common Player:	.50
Inserted 1:12	
1 Pedro J. Martinez	1.00
2 Derek Jeter	2.50
3 Jason Giambi	1.00
4 Todd Helton	.75
5 Nomar Garciaparra	2.50
6 Randy Johnson	1.00
7 Jeff Bagwell	.75
8 Cal Ripken Jr.	3.00
9 Ivan Rodriguez	.50

Gallery

	NM/M
Complete Set (6):	10.00
Common Player:	1.00
Inserted 1:20	
1 Sammy Sosa	2.00
2 Barry Bonds	3.00
3 Vladimir Guerrero	1.00
4 Cal Ripken Jr.	3.00
5 Mike Piazza	1.50
6 Mark McGwire	2.00

Might

	NM/M
Complete Set (9):	10.00
Common Player:	.50
Inserted 1:12	
1 Mark McGwire	2.50
2 Mike Piazza	1.50
3 Frank Thomas	.75
4 Ken Griffey Jr.	1.50
5 Sammy Sosa	2.00
6 Alex Rodriguez	2.50
7 Carlos Delgado	.50
8 Vladimir Guerrero	1.00
9 Barry Bonds	3.00

Skills

	NM/M
Complete Set (6):	8.00
Common Player:	.75
Inserted 1:20	
1 Alex Rodriguez	2.50
2 Chipper Jones	1.50
3 Ken Griffey Jr.	1.50
4 Pedro J. Martinez	1.00
5 Ivan Rodriguez	.75
6 Derek Jeter	2.50

2000 Upper Deck Gold Reserve

	NM/M
Complete Set (300):	75.00
Common Player:	.15
Common 268-297:	3.00
Production 2,500 Sets	
Pack (10):	2.00
Box (24):	40.00
1 Mo Vaughn	.20
2 Darin Erstad	.25
3 Garret Anderson	.25
4 Troy Glaus	.50
5 Troy Percival	.15
6 Kent Bottenfield	.15
7 Orlando Palmeiro	.15
8 Tim Salmon	.25
9 Jason Giambi	.75
10 Eric Chavez	.25
11 Matt Stairs	.15
12 Miguel Tejada	.40
13 Tim Hudson	.25
14 John Jaha	.15
15 Ben Grieve	.15
16 Kevin Appier	.15
17 David Wells	.15
18 Jose Cruz Jr.	.15
19 Homer Bush	.15
20 Shannon Stewart	.15
21 Carlos Delgado	.50
22 Roy Halladay	.25
23 Tony Batista	.15
24 Raul Mondesi	.25
25 Fred McGriff	.25
26 Jose Canseco	.40
27 Roberto Hernandez	.15
28 Vinny Castilla	.15
29 Gerald Williams	.15
30 Ryan Rupe	.15
31 Greg Vaughn	.15
32 Miguel Cairo	.15
33 Roberto Alomar	.40
34 Jim Thome	.50
35 Bartolo Colon	.15
36 Omar Vizquel	.25
37 Manny Ramirez	.50
38 Chuck Finley	.15
39 Travis Fryman	.25
40 Kenny Lofton	.25
41 Richie Sexson	.40
42 Charles Nagy	.15
43 John Halama	.15
44 David Bell	.15
45 Jay Buhner	.15
46 Edgar Martinez	.15
47 Alex Rodriguez	1.50
48 Fred Garcia	.15
49 Aaron Sele	.15
50 Jamie Moyer	.15
51 Mike Cameron	.15
52 Albert Belle	.20
53 Jerry Hairston Jr.	.15
54 Sidney Ponson	.15
55 Cal Ripken Jr.	2.00
56 Mike Mussina	.40
57 B.J. Surhoff	.15
58 Brady Anderson	.15
59 Mike Bordick	.15
60 Ivan Rodriguez	.40
61 Rusty Greer	.15
62 Rafael Palmeiro	.40
63 John Wetteland	.15
64 Ruben Mateo	.15
65 Gabe Kapler	.15
66 David Segui	.15
67 Justin Thompson	.15
68 Rick Helling	.15
69 Jose Offerman	.15
70 Trot Nixon	.15
71 Pedro Martinez	.75
72 Jason Varitek	.15
73 Troy O'Leary	.15
74 Nomar Garciaparra	1.50
75 Carl Everett	.15
76 Wilton Veras	.15
77 Tim Wakefield	.15
78 Ramon Martinez	.15
79 Johnny Damon	.25
80 Mike Sweeney	.15
81 Rey Sanchez	.15
82 Carlos Beltran	.25
83 Carlos Febles	.15
84 Jermaine Dye	.15
85 Joe Randa	.15
86 Jose Rosado	.15
87 Jeff Suppan	.15
88 Juan Encarnacion	.15
89 Damion Easley	.15
90 Brad Ausmus	.15
91 Todd Jones	.15
92 Juan Gonzalez	.50
93 Bobby Higginson	.15
94 Tony Clark	.15
95 Brian Moehler	.15
96 Dean Palmer	.15
97 Joe Mays	.15
98 Eric Milton	.15
99 Corey Koskie	.15
100 Ron Coomer	.15
101 Brad Radke	.15
102 Todd Walker	.15
103 Butch Huskey	.15
104 Jacque Jones	.15
105 Frank Thomas	.50
106 Mike Sirotka	.15
107 Carlos Lee	.15
108 Ray Durham	.15
109 Bob Howry	.15
110 Magglio Ordonez	.25
111 Paul Konerko	.15
112 Chris Singleton	.15
113 James Baldwin	.15
114 Derek Jeter	2.00
115 Tino Martinez	.25
116 Orlando Hernandez	.25
117 Chuck Knoblauch	.15
118 Bernie Williams	.50
119 David Cone	.25
120 Paul O'Neill	.25
121 Roger Clemens	1.25
122 Mariano Rivera	.25
123 Ricky Ledee	.15
124 Richard Hidalgo	.25
125 Jeff Bagwell	.50
126 Jose Lima	.15
127 Billy Wagner	.15
128 Shane Reynolds	.15
129 Moises Alou	.25
130 Craig Biggio	.25
131 Roger Cedeno	.15
132 Octavio Dotel	.15
133 Greg Maddux	1.00
134 Brian Jordan	.15
135 Kevin Millwood	.25
136 Javy Lopez	.25
137 Bruce Chen	.15
138 Chipper Jones	1.00
139 Tom Glavine	.40
140 Andruw Jones	.40
141 Andres Galarraga	.25
142 Reggie Sanders	.15
143 Geoff Jenkins	.25
144 Jeromy Burnitz	.15
145 Ron Belliard	.15
146 Mark Loretta	.15
147 Steve Woodard	.15
148 Marquis Grissom	.15
149 Bob Wickman	.15
150 Mark McGwire	1.50
151 Fernando Tatis	.15
152 Edgar Renteria	.15
153 J.D. Drew	.20
154 Ray Lankford	.15
155 Fernando Vina	.15
156 Pat Hentgen	.15
157 Jim Edmonds	.15
158 Mark Grace	.25
159 Kerry Wood	.40
160 Eric Young	.15
161 Ismael Valdes	.15
162 Sammy Sosa	1.25
163 Henry Rodriguez	.15
164 Kyle Farnsworth	.15
165 Glenallen Hill	.15
166 Jon Lieber	.15
167 Luis Gonzalez	.25
168 Tony Womack	.15
169 Omar Daal	.15
170 Randy Johnson	.75
171 Erubiel Durazo	.15
172 Jay Bell	.15
173 Steve Finley	.15
174 Travis Lee	.15
175 Matt Williams	.15
176 Matt Mantei	.15
177 Jeff Bagwell	.25
178 Kevin Beltre	.25
179 Chan Ho Park	.25
180 Mark Grudzielanek	.15
181 Jeff Shaw	.15
182 Shawn Green	.25
183 Gary Sheffield	.40
184 Todd Hundley	.15
185 Eric Karros	.15
186 Kevin Elster	.15
187 Vladimir Guerrero	.75
188 Michael Barrett	.15
189 Chris Widger	.15
190 Ugueth Urbina	.15
191 Dustin Hermanson	.15
192 Rondell White	.15
193 Jose Vidro	.15
194 Hideki Irabu	.15
195 Lee Stevens	.15
196 Livan Hernandez	.15
197 Ellis Burks	.15
198 J.T. Snow	.15
199 Jeff Kent	.25
200 Robb Nen	.15
201 Marvin Benard	.15
202 Barry Bonds	1.50
203 Russ Ortiz	.15
204 Rich Aurilia	.15
205 Joe Nathan	.15
206 Preston Wilson	.25
207 Cliff Floyd	.15
208 Mike Lowell	.15
209 Ryan Dempster	.15
210 Luis Castillo	.15
211 Alex Fernandez	.15
212 Mark Kotsay	.15
213 Brant Brown	.15

214	Edgardo Alfonzo	.15
215	Robin Ventura	.25
216	Rickey Henderson	.25
217	Mike Hampton	.15
218	Mike Piazza	1.00
219	Al Leiter	.15
220	Derek Bell	.15
221	Armando Benitez	.15
222	Rey Ordonez	.15
223	Todd Zeile	.15
224	Tony Gwynn	.75
225	Eric Owens	.15
226	Damian Jackson	.15
227	Trevor Hoffman	.15
228	Ben Davis	.15
229	Sterling Hitchcock	.15
230	Ruben Rivera	.15
231	Ryan Klesko	.15
232	Phil Nevin	.15
233	Mike Lieberthal	.15
234	Bobby Abreu	.25
235	Doug Glanville	.15
236	Rico Brogna	.15
237	Scott Rolen	.50
238	Andy Ashby	.15
239	Robert Person	.15
240	Curt Schilling	.25
241	Mike Jackson	.15
242	Warren Morris	.15
243	Kris Benson	.15
244	Kevin Young	.15
245	Brian Giles	.25
246	Jason Schmidt	.15
247	Jason Kendall	.25
248	Todd Ritchie	.15
249	Wil Cordero	.15
250	Aramis Ramirez	.15
251	Sean Casey	.25
252	Barry Larkin	.25
253	Pokey Reese	.15
254	Scott Williamson	.15
255	Aaron Boone	.25
256	Dante Bichette	.15
257	Ken Griffey Jr.	1.00
258	Denny Neagle	.15
259	Dmitri Young	.15
260	Todd Helton	.50
261	Larry Walker	.25
262	Pedro Astacio	.15
263	Neifi Perez	.15
264	Jeff Cirillo	.15
265	Jeffrey Hammonds	.15
266	Tom Goodwin	.15
267	Rolando Arrojo	.15
268	Rick Ankiel (Fantastic Finds)	3.00
269	Pat Burrell (Fantastic Finds)	4.00
270	Eric Munson (Fantastic Finds)	3.00
271	Rafael Furcal (Fantastic Finds)	3.00
272	Brad Penny (Fantastic Finds)	3.00
273	Adam Kennedy (Fantastic Finds)	3.00
274	Mike Lamb RC (Fantastic Finds)	3.00
275	Matt Riley (Fantastic Finds)	3.00
276	Eric Gagne (Fantastic Finds)	5.00
277	Kazuhiro Sasaki RC (Fantastic Finds)	3.00
278	Julio Lugo (Fantastic Finds)	3.00
279	Kip Wells (Fantastic Finds)	3.00
280	Danys Baez RC (Fantastic Finds)	3.00
281	Josh Beckett (Fantastic Finds)	4.00
282	Alfonso Soriano (Fantastic Finds)	4.00
283	Vernon Wells (Fantastic Finds)	4.00
284	Nick Johnson (Fantastic Finds)	3.00
285	Ramon Ortiz (Fantastic Finds)	3.00
286	Peter Bergeron (Fantastic Finds)	3.00
287	Wascar Serrano RC (Fantastic Finds)	3.00
288	Josh Paul (Fantastic Finds)	3.00
289	Mark Quinn (Fantastic Finds)	3.00
290	Jason Marquis (Fantastic Finds)	3.00
291	Rob Bell (Fantastic Finds)	3.00
292	Pablo Ozuna (Fantastic Finds)	3.00
293	Milton Bradley (Fantastic Finds)	3.00
294	Roosevelt Brown (Fantastic Finds)	3.00
295	Terrence Long (Fantastic Finds)	3.00
296	Chad Durbin RC (Fantastic Finds)	3.00
297	Matt LeCroy (Fantastic Finds)	3.00
298	Ken Griffey Jr. (Checklist)	.50
299	Mark McGwire (Checklist)	.75
300	Derek Jeter (Checklist)	1.00

Game-Used Ball

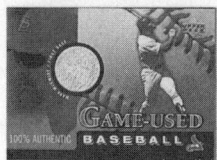

		NM/M
Common Player:		10.00
Inserted 1:480		
JB	Jeff Bagwell	25.00
BB	Barry Bonds	70.00
SC	Sean Casey	10.00
RC	Roger Clemens	35.00
NG	Nomar Garciaparra	40.00
SG	Shawn Green	10.00
KG	Ken Griffey Jr.	30.00
TG	Tony Gwynn	25.00
DJ	Derek Jeter	60.00
AJ	Andruw Jones	15.00
CJ	Chipper Jones	30.00
GM	Greg Maddux	30.00
MM	Mark McGwire	60.00
MP	Mike Piazza	30.00
MR	Manny Ramirez	15.00
IR	Ivan Rodriguez	15.00
SR	Scott Rolen	10.00
GS	Gary Sheffield	10.00
SS	Sammy Sosa	30.00
BW	Bernie Williams	10.00

Setting the Standard

		NM/M
Complete Set (15):		25.00
Common Player:		.50
Inserted 1:11		
1	Tony Gwynn	1.50
2	Manny Ramirez	1.00
3	Derek Jeter	3.00
4	Cal Ripken Jr.	4.00
5	Mo Vaughn	.50
6	Jose Canseco	.75
7	Barry Bonds	2.00
8	Nomar Garciaparra	3.00
9	Juan Gonzalez	1.00
10	Mark McGwire	3.00
11	Alex Rodriguez	3.00
12	Jeff Bagwell	1.00
13	Ken Griffey Jr.	2.00
14	Frank Thomas	1.00
15	Sammy Sosa	2.50

Solid Gold Gallery

		NM/M
Complete Set (12):		20.00
Common Player:		1.00
Inserted 1:13		
1	Ken Griffey Jr.	2.00
2	Alex Rodriguez	3.00

3	Mike Piazza	2.00
4	Sammy Sosa	2.50
5	Derek Jeter	3.00
6	Jeff Bagwell	1.00
7	Mark McGwire	3.00
8	Cal Ripken Jr.	4.00
9	Pedro Martinez	1.50
10	Chipper Jones	2.00
11	Ivan Rodriguez	1.00
12	Vladimir Guerrero	1.00

UD Authentics

		NM/M
Inserted 1:480		
CB	Carlos Beltran	40.00
JC	Jose Canseco	35.00
SG	Shawn Green	20.00
TG	Tony Gwynn	30.00
CJ	Chipper Jones	60.00
MR	Manny Ramirez	25.00
CR	Cal Ripken Jr.	100.00
AR	Alex Rodriguez	80.00
IR	Ivan Rodriguez	20.00

UD Authentics Gold

Values Undetermined
No Pricing

3,000 Hit Club

		NM/M
AK-B	Al Kaline/Bat/400	20.00
AK-BS	Al Kaline/Bat/Auto./6	

24-Karat Gems

		NM/M
Complete Set (15):		12.00
Common Player:		.50
Inserted 1:7		
1	Pedro Martinez	1.50
2	Scott Rolen	1.00
3	Jason Giambi	1.50
4	Jeromy Burnitz	.50
5	Rafael Palmeiro	1.00
6	Rick Ankiel	.50
7	Carlos Beltran	.75
8	Derek Jeter	3.00
9	Jason Kendall	.50
10	Carlos Delgado	1.00
11	Chipper Jones	2.00
12	Alex Rodriguez	3.00
13	Randy Johnson	1.50
14	Tony Gwynn	1.50
15	Shawn Green	.75

2000 Upper Deck Hitter's Club

		NM/M
Complete Set (90):		20.00
Common Player:		.15
Pack (5):		1.50
Wax Box (24):		25.00
1	Mo Vaughn	.20
2	Troy Glaus	.40
3	Jeff Bagwell	.50
4	Craig Biggio	.25
5	Jason Giambi	.75
6	Eric Chavez	.25
7	Carlos Delgado	.50

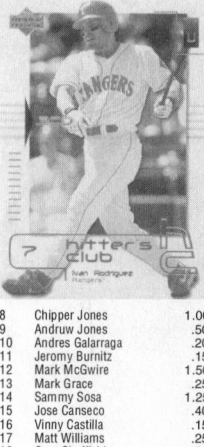

8	Chipper Jones	1.00
9	Andruw Jones	.50
10	Andres Galarraga	.20
11	Jeromy Burnitz	.15
12	Mark McGwire	1.50
13	Mark Grace	.25
14	Sammy Sosa	1.25
15	Jose Canseco	.40
16	Vinny Castilla	.15
17	Matt Williams	.25
18	Gary Sheffield	.25
19	Shawn Green	.25
20	Vladimir Guerrero	.50
21	Barry Bonds	1.50
22	Manny Ramirez	.50
23	Roberto Alomar	.40
24	Jim Thome	.50
25	Ken Griffey Jr.	1.00
26	Alex Rodriguez	1.50
27	Edgar Martinez	.15
28	Preston Wilson	.25
29	Mike Piazza	1.00
30	Robin Ventura	.25
31	Albert Belle	.20
32	Cal Ripken Jr.	2.00
33	Tony Gwynn	.75
34	Scott Rolen	.50
35	Bob Abreu	.25
36	Brian Giles	.25
37	Ivan Rodriguez	.40
38	Rafael Palmeiro	.40
39	Nomar Garciaparra	1.50
40	Sean Casey	.20
41	Larry Walker	.25
42	Todd Helton	.50
43	Carlos Beltran	.25
44	Dean Palmer	.15
45	Juan Gonzalez	.50
46	Corey Koskie	.15
47	Frank Thomas	.50
48	Magglio Ordonez	.25
49	Derek Jeter	2.00
50	Bernie Williams	.40
51	Paul Waner (Why 3k?)	.25
52	Honus Wagner (Why 3k?)	.50
53	Tris Speaker (Why 3k?)	.25
54	Nap Lajoie (Why 3k?)	.25
55	Eddie Collins (Why 3k?)	.25
56	Roberto Clemente (Why 3k?)	1.00
57	Ty Cobb (Why 3k?)	1.50
58	Cap Anson (Why 3k?)	.50
59	Robin Yount (Why 3k?)	.50
60	Carl Yastrzemski (Why 3k?)	.50
61	Dave Winfield (Why 3k?)	.25
62	Stan Musial (Why 3k?)	1.00
63	Eddie Murray (Why 3k?)	.40
64	Paul Molitor (Why 3k?)	.50
65	Willie Mays (Why 3k?)	1.50
66	Al Kaline (Why 3k?)	.50
67	Tony Gwynn (Why 3k?)	.75
68	Rod Carew (Why 3k?)	.40
69	Lou Brock (Why 3k?)	.25
70	George Brett (Why 3k?)	1.00
71	Wade Boggs (Why 3k?)	.25
72	Hank Aaron (Why 3k?)	1.50
73	Jorge Luis Toca (Hitting the Show)	.15
74	J.D. Drew (Hitting the Show)	.15
75	Pat Burrell (Hitting the Show)	.25
76	Vernon Wells (Hitting the Show)	.25
77	Julio Ramirez (Hitting the Show)	.15
78	Gabe Kapler (Hitting the Show)	.25
79	Erubiel Durazo (Hitting the Show)	.15
80	Lance Berkman (Hitting the Show)	.25
81	Peter Bergeron (Hitting the Show)	.15
82	Alfonso Soriano (Hitting the Show)	.75
83	Jacque Jones (Hitting the Show)	.15
84	Ben Petrick (Hitting the Show)	.15
85	Jerry Hairston Jr. (Hitting the Show)	.15
86	Kevin Witt (Hitting the Show)	.15

87	Dermal Brown (Hitting the Show)	.15
88	Chad Hermansen (Hitting the Show)	.15
89	Ruben Mateo (Hitting the Show)	.15
90	Ken Griffey Jr. Checklist	.50

Accolades

		NM/M
Complete Set (10):		12.00
Common Player:		.75
Inserted 1:11		
1	Robin Yount	1.00
2	Tony Gwynn	1.00
3	Sammy Sosa	2.00
4	Mike Piazza	1.50
5	Cal Ripken Jr.	3.00
6	Mark McGwire	2.50
7	Barry Bonds	2.50
8	Wade Boggs	.75
9	Ken Griffey Jr.	1.50
10	Willie Mays	2.00

Autographs

		NM/M
Common Player:		15.00
Inserted 1:215		
HA	Hank Aaron #44	275.00
WB	Wade Boggs #12	30.00
GB	George Brett #5	80.00
Lou	Lou Brock #20	15.00
Rod	Rod Carew #29	15.00
TG	Tony Gwynn #19	40.00
AI	Al Kaline #6	30.00
WM	Willie Mays #24	150.00
PM	Paul Molitor #4	30.00
EM	Eddie Murray #33	30.00
Man	Stan Musial #6	75.00
Cal	Cal Ripken Jr. #8	150.00
DW	Dave Winfield #31	20.00
Yaz	Carl Yastrzemski #7	60.00
RY	Robin Yount #19	40.00

Epic Performances

		NM/M
Complete Set (10):		12.00
Common Player:		1.00
Inserted 1:3		
1	Mark McGwire	2.50
3	Sammy Sosa	2.00
4	Ken Griffey Jr.	1.50
5	Carl Yastrzemski	1.00
6	Tony Gwynn	1.00
7	Nomar Garciaparra	2.50
8	Cal Ripken Jr.	3.00
9	George Brett	1.50
10	Hank Aaron	2.00
11	Wade Boggs	1.00

Eternals

		NM/M
Complete Set (10):		20.00
Common Player:		1.00
Inserted 1:23		
1	Cal Ripken Jr.	4.00
2	Mark McGwire	3.00
3	Ken Griffey Jr.	2.00
4	Nomar Garciaparra	3.00
5	Tony Gwynn	1.50
6	Derek Jeter	3.00
7	Jose Canseco	1.00
8	Mike Piazza	2.00
9	Alex Rodriguez	3.00
10	Barry Bonds	4.00

Generations of Excellence

		NM/M
Complete Set (10):		15.00
Common Card:		1.00
Inserted 1:6		
1	Cal Ripken Jr., Eddie Murray	3.00
2	Vladimir Guerrero, Roberto Clemente	2.00
3	George Brett, Robin Yount	2.00
4	Barry Bonds, Willie Mays	3.00
5	Chipper Jones, Hank Aaron	2.00
6	Mark McGwire, Sammy Sosa	2.00
7	Tony Gwynn, Wade Boggs	1.00
8	Rickey Henderson, Lou Brock	1.00
9	Derek Jeter, Nomar Garciaparra	3.00
10	Alex Rodriguez, Ken Griffey Jr.	2.50

On Target

		NM/M
Complete Set (10):		12.00
Common Player:		.50
Inserted 1:23		
1	Nomar Garciaparra	3.00
2	Sean Casey	.50
3	Alex Rodriguez	3.00
4	Troy Glaus	1.00
5	Ivan Rodriguez	1.00
6	Chipper Jones	2.00
7	Manny Ramirez	1.00
8	Derek Jeter	3.00

9	Vladimir Guerrero	1.00
10	Scott Rolen	1.00

The Hitters' Club

		NM/M
Complete Set (10):		60.00
Common Player:		3.00
1	Rod Carew	5.00
2	Alex Rodriguez	15.00
3	Willie Mays	10.00
4	George Brett	10.00
5	Tony Gwynn	8.00
6	Stan Musial	8.00
7	Frank Thomas	5.00
8	Wade Boggs	3.00
9	Larry Walker	3.00
10	Nomar Garciaparra	15.00

3,000 Hit Club

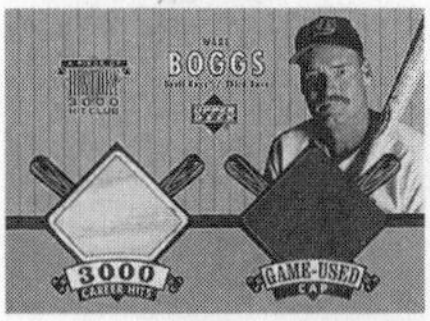

		NM/M
Common Player:		25.00
WB	Wade Boggs/Bat/350	25.00
WB	Wade Boggs/Bat & Cap/50	65.00
TG	Tony Gwynn/Bat/350	25.00
TG	Tony Gwynn/ Bat & Cap/50	100.00
TG	Tony Gwynn AU/19	550.00
GB	Tony Gwynn, Wade Boggs/Bat/99	85.00

2000 Upper Deck HoloGrFX

		NM/M
Complete Set (90):		20.00
Common Player:		.15
Pack (4):		1.50
Wax Box (32):		25.00
1	Mo Vaughn	.20
2	Troy Glaus	.50
3	Daryle Ward	.15
4	Jeff Bagwell	.50
5	Craig Biggio	.25
6	Jose Lima	.15
7	Jason Giambi	.75
8	Eric Chavez	.25
9	Tim Hudson	.25
10	Raul Mondesi	.25
11	Carlos Delgado	.50
12	David Wells	.15
13	Chipper Jones	1.00
14	Greg Maddux	1.00
15	Andruw Jones	.50
16	Brian Jordan	.15
17	Jeromy Burnitz	.15
18	Ron Belliard	.15
19	Mark McGwire	1.50
20	Fernando Tatis	.15
21	J.D. Drew	.25
22	Sammy Sosa	1.00
23	Mark Grace	.40
24	Greg Vaughn	.15
25	Jose Canseco	.40
26	Vinny Castilla	.15
27	Fred McGriff	.25
28	Matt Williams	.25
29	Randy Johnson	.75
30	Erubiel Durazo	.15
31	Shawn Green	.25
32	Gary Sheffield	.40
33	Kevin Brown	.25
34	Vladimir Guerrero	.50
35	Michael Barrett	.15
36	Russ Ortiz	.15
37	Barry Bonds	1.50
38	Jeff Kent	.25
39	Kenny Lofton	.25
40	Manny Ramirez	.50
41	Roberto Alomar	.40
42	Richie Sexson	.25
43	Edgar Martinez	.25
44	Alex Rodriguez	1.50
45	Fred Garcia	.15
46	Preston Wilson	.15
47	Alex Gonzalez	.15
48	Mike Hampton	.15
49	Mike Piazza	1.00
50	Robin Ventura	.25
51	Edgardo Alfonzo	.15
52	Albert Belle	.15
53	Cal Ripken Jr.	2.00
54	B.J. Surhoff	.15
55	Tony Gwynn	.75
56	Trevor Hoffman	.15
57	Mike Lieberthal	.15
58	Scott Rolen	.50
59	Bob Abreu	.25
60	Curt Schilling	.40
61	Jason Kendall	.25
62	Brian Giles	.25
63	Kris Benson	.15
64	Rafael Palmeiro	.40
65	Ivan Rodriguez	.50
66	Gabe Kapler	.40
67	Nomar Garciaparra	1.50
68	Pedro Martinez	.75
69	Troy O'Leary	.15
70	Barry Larkin	.25
71	Dante Bichette	.15
72	Sean Casey	.20
73	Ken Griffey Jr.	1.00
74	Jeff Cirillo	.15
75	Todd Helton	.50
76	Larry Walker	.25
77	Carlos Beltran	.25
78	Jermaine Dye	.15
79	Juan Gonzalez	.50
80	Juan Encarnacion	.15
81	Dean Palmer	.15
82	Corey Koskie	.15
83	Eric Milton	.15
84	Frank Thomas	.50
85	Magglio Ordonez	.25
86	Carlos Lee	.15
87	Derek Jeter	2.00
88	Tino Martinez	.25
89	Bernie Williams	.50
90	Roger Clemens	1.50

A Piece of the Series

		NM/M
Common Player:		5.00
Inserted 1:215		
1	Derek Jeter	40.00
2	Chipper Jones	20.00
3	Roger Clemens	30.00
4	Greg Maddux	30.00
5	Bernie Williams	10.00
6	Andruw Jones	10.00
7	Tino Martinez	8.00
8	Brian Jordan	5.00
9	Mariano Rivera	8.00
11	Paul O'Neill	8.00
12	Tom Glavine	10.00

A Piece of Series Autograph

		NM/M
Common Player:		40.00
Production 25 Sets		
PSA1	Derek Jeter	300.00
PSA2	Chipper Jones	125.00
PSA3	Roger Clemens	220.00
PSA4	Greg Maddux	220.00
PSA6	Andruw Jones	85.00
PSA7	Tino Martinez	65.00
PSA8	Brian Jordan	40.00
PSA11	Paul O'Neill	75.00
PSA12	Tom Glavine	100.00

Bomb Squad

		NM/M
Complete Set (6):		15.00
Common Player:		2.00
Inserted 1:34		
1	Ken Griffey Jr.	2.00
2	Mark McGwire	3.00
3	Chipper Jones	2.00
4	Alex Rodriguez	3.00
5	Sammy Sosa	2.50
6	Barry Bonds	4.00

Future Fame

		NM/M
Complete Set (6):		10.00
Common Player:		2.00
Inserted 1:34		
1	Cal Ripken Jr.	4.00
2	Mark McGwire	3.00
3	Greg Maddux	2.00
4	Tony Gwynn	1.50
5	Ken Griffey Jr.	2.00
6	Roger Clemens	2.50

Longball Legacy

		NM/M
Complete Set (15):		15.00
Common Player:		.50
Inserted 1:6		
1	Mike Piazza	2.00
2	Ivan Rodriguez	.75
3	Jeff Bagwell	1.00
4	Alex Rodriguez	3.00
5	Jose Canseco	.75
6	Mark McGwire	3.00
7	Scott Rolen	.75
8	Carlos Delgado	.75
9	Mo Vaughn	.50
10	Manny Ramirez	1.00
11	Matt Williams	.50
12	Sammy Sosa	2.50
13	Ken Griffey Jr.	2.00
14	Nomar Garciaparra	3.00
15	Larry Walker	.50

Stars of the System

		NM/M
Complete Set (10):		8.00
Common Player:		.75
Inserted 1:8		
1	Rick Ankiel	.75
2	Alfonso Soriano	2.00
3	Vernon Wells	1.00
4	Ben Petrick	.75
5	Francisco Cordero	.75
6	Matt Riley	.75
7	A.J. Burnett	1.00
8	Pat Burrell	1.50
9	Ed Yarnall	.75
10	Dermal Brown	.75

StarView

		NM/M
Complete Set (8):		15.00
Common Player:		2.00
Inserted 1:11		
1	Ken Griffey Jr.	2.00
2	Nomar Garciaparra	3.00
3	Chipper Jones	2.00
4	Mark McGwire	3.00
5	Sammy Sosa	2.50
6	Derek Jeter	4.00
7	Mike Piazza	2.00
8	Alex Rodriguez	3.00

3,000 Hit Club

		NM/M
Common Card:		20.00
RY	Robin Yount/Bat/350	20.00
RYJ	Robin Yount/Jsy/350	20.00
GB	George Brett/Bat/350	35.00
GBJ	George Brett/Jsy/350	35.00
BY	George Brett,	
	Robin Yount/Bat/99	120.00
BYJ	George Brett,	
	Robin Yount/Jersey/99	120.00

2000 Upper Deck Legends

		NM/M
Complete Set (135):		80.00
Common Player:		.15
Common Y2K:		.75
Inserted 1:9		
Common 20th Century Legend		1.00
Inserted 1:5		
Pack (7):		5.00
Box (24):		90.00
1	Darin Erstad	.25
2	Troy Glaus	.75
3	Mo Vaughn	.20
4	Craig Biggio	.25
5	Jeff Bagwell	.75
6	Reggie Jackson	1.00
7	Tim Hudson	.25
8	Jason Giambi	1.00
9	Hank Aaron	2.00
10	Greg Maddux	1.50
11	Chipper Jones	1.50
12	Andres Galarraga	.25
13	Robin Yount	.50
14	Jeromy Burnitz	.15
15	Paul Molitor	.50
16	David Wells	.15
17	Carlos Delgado	.75
18	Ernie Banks	.75
19	Sammy Sosa	2.00
20	Kerry Wood	.40
21	Stan Musial	.75
22	Bob Gibson	.50
23	Mark McGwire	2.00
24	Fernando Tatis	.15
25	Randy Johnson	1.00
26	Matt Williams	.40
27	Jackie Robinson	2.00
28	Sandy Koufax	1.50
29	Shawn Green	.40
30	Kevin Brown	.25
31	Gary Sheffield	.40
32	Greg Vaughn	.15
33	Jose Canseco	.50
34	Gary Carter	.15
35	Vladimir Guerrero	.75
36	Willie Mays	2.00
37	Barry Bonds	2.00
38	Jeff Kent	.25
39	Bob Feller	.40
40	Roberto Alomar	.50
41	Jim Thome	.75
42	Manny Ramirez	.75
43	Alex Rodriguez	2.00
44	Preston Wilson	.15
45	Tom Seaver	.75
46	Robin Ventura	.15
47	Mike Piazza	1.50
48	Mike Hampton	.15
49	Brooks Robinson	.75
50	Frank Robinson	.75
51	Cal Ripken Jr.	2.50
52	Albert Belle	.20
53	Eddie Murray	.40
54	Tony Gwynn	1.00
55	Roberto Clemente	1.50
56	Willie Stargell	.25
57	Brian Giles	.25
58	Jason Kendall	.25
59	Mike Schmidt	1.00
60	Bob Abreu	.25
61	Scott Rolen	.50
62	Curt Schilling	.40
63	Johnny Bench	1.00
64	Sean Casey	.15
65	Barry Larkin	.25
66	Ken Griffey Jr.	1.50
67	George Brett	1.50
68	Carlos Beltran	.15
69	Nolan Ryan	3.00
70	Ivan Rodriguez	.75
71	Rafael Palmeiro	.40
72	Larry Walker	.25
73	Todd Helton	.75
74	Jeff Cirillo	.15
75	Carl Everett	.15
76	Nomar Garciaparra	2.00
77	Pedro Martinez	1.00
78	Harmon Killebrew	.50
79	Corey Koskie	.15
80	Ty Cobb	2.00
81	Dean Palmer	.15
82	Juan Gonzalez	.75
83	Carlton Fisk	.15
84	Frank Thomas	.75
85	Magglio Ordonez	.25
86	Lou Gehrig	2.00
87	Babe Ruth	3.00
88	Derek Jeter	2.50
89	Roger Clemens	1.50
90	Bernie Williams	.50
91	Rick Ankiel (Generation Y2K)	.75
92	Kip Wells (Generation Y2K)	.75
93	Pat Burrell (Generation Y2K)	1.50
94	Mark Quinn (Generation Y2K)	.75
95	Ruben Mateo	
	(Generation Y2K)	.75
96	Adam Kennedy	
	(Generation Y2K)	.75
97	Brad Penny (Generation Y2K)	.75
98	Kazuhiro Sasaki RC	
	(Generation Y2K)	2.00
99	Peter Bergeron	
	(Generation Y2K)	.75
100	Rafael Furcal	
	(Generation Y2K)	1.00
101	Eric Munson	
	(Generation Y2K)	.75
102	Nick Johnson	
	(Generation Y2K)	1.00
103	Rob Bell (Generation Y2K)	.75
104	Vernon Wells	
	(Generation Y2K)	1.00
105	Ben Petrick (Generation Y2K)	.75
106	Babe Ruth	
	(20th Century Legends)	8.00
107	Mark McGwire	
	(20th Century Legends)	6.00
108	Nolan Ryan	
	(20th Century Legends)	8.00
109	Hank Aaron	
	(20th Century Legends)	5.00
110	Barry Bonds	
	(20th Century Legends)	6.00
111	Nomar Garciaparra	
	(20th Century Legends)	5.00
112	Roger Clemens	
	(20th Century Legends)	5.00
113	Johnny Bench	
	(20th Century Legends)	2.50
114	Alex Rodriguez	
	(20th Century Legends)	6.00
115	Cal Ripken Jr.	
	(20th Century Legends)	8.00
116	Willie Mays	
	(20th Century Legends)	6.00
117	Mike Piazza	
	(20th Century Legends)	4.00
118	Reggie Jackson	
	(20th Century Legends)	2.00
119	Tony Gwynn	
	(20th Century Legends)	3.00
120	Cy Young (20th Century Legends)	
		2.00
121	George Brett	
	(20th Century Legends)	4.00
122	Greg Maddux	
	(20th Century Legends)	4.00
123	Yogi Berra	
	(20th Century Legends)	2.00
124	Sammy Sosa	
	(20th Century Legends)	5.00
125	Randy Johnson	
	(20th Century Legends)	2.50
126	Bob Gibson	
	(20th Century Legends)	2.00
127	Lou Gehrig	
	(20th Century Legends)	6.00
128	Ken Griffey Jr.	
	(20th Century Legends)	4.00
129	Derek Jeter	
	(20th Century Legends)	6.00
130	Mike Schmidt	
	(20th Century Legends)	3.00
131	Pedro Martinez	
	(20th Century Legends)	2.50
132	Jackie Robinson	
	(20th Century Legends)	5.00
133	Jose Canseco	
	(20th Century Legends)	1.00
134	Ty Cobb	
	(20th Century Legends)	5.00
135	Stan Musial	
	(20th Century Legends)	3.00

Commemorative Collection

Stars (1-90):	4-8X
Y2K:	1-2X
20th Century Legends:	2-3X
Production 100 Sets	
(See 2000 Upper Deck Legends for	
checklist and base card values.)	

Eternal Glory

		NM/M
Complete Set (7):		15.00
Common Player:		2.00
Inserted 1:24		
1	Nolan Ryan	4.00
2	Ken Griffey Jr.	2.00
4	Sammy Sosa	2.50
5	Derek Jeter	4.00
6	Willie Mays	3.00
7	Roger Clemens	3.00

Defining Moments

		NM/M
Complete Set (10):		20.00
Common Player:		1.00
Inserted 1:12		
1	Reggie Jackson	1.50
2	Hank Aaron	3.00
3	Babe Ruth	4.00
4	Cal Ripken Jr.	4.00
5	Carlton Fisk	1.00
6	Ken Griffey Jr.	2.00
7	Nolan Ryan	4.00

8	Roger Clemens	2.50
9	Willie Mays	3.00
10	Mark McGwire	3.00

Legendary Jerseys

		NM/M
Common Player:		8.00
Inserted 1:48		
HA	Hank Aaron	40.00
JB	Jeff Bagwell	10.00
JB	Johnny Bench	20.00
WB	Wade Boggs	10.00
BaB	Barry Bonds	40.00
BoB	Bobby Bonds	8.00
GB	George Brett	30.00
LB	Lou Brock	8.00
JC	Jose Canseco	10.00
RC	Roger Clemens	30.00
DC	Dave Concepcion	8.00
DD	Don Drysdale	25.00
RF	Rollie Fingers	8.00
LG	Lou Gehrig/Pants	250.00
BG	Bob Gibson/Pants	20.00
KG	Ken Griffey Jr.	35.00
TG	Tony Gwynn	20.00
RJ	Reggie Jackson	10.00
DJ	Derek Jeter	40.00
RaJ	Randy Johnson	20.00
CJ	Chipper Jones	20.00
SK	Sandy Koufax	250.00
SK	Sandy Koufax/Auto./32	1,200
GM	Greg Maddux	30.00
MM	Mickey Mantle	150.00
RM	Roger Maris/Pants	60.00
EM	Eddie Mathews	20.00
WM	Willie Mays/SP/29	675.00
BM	Bill Mazeroski	8.00
WMc	Willie McCovey	10.00
TM	Thurman Munson	30.00
DM	Dale Murphy	10.00
SM	Stan Musial/SP/28	650.00
JP	Jim Palmer	8.00
GP	Gaylord Perry	8.00
MR	Manny Ramirez	10.00
CR	Cal Ripken Jr.	40.00
BR	Brooks Robinson	20.00
FR	Frank Robinson	10.00
AR	Alex Rodriguez	35.00
NR	Nolan Ryan	40.00
MS	Mike Schmidt	25.00
TS	Tom Seaver	20.00
OS	Ozzie Smith	20.00
WS	Willie Stargell	8.00
FT	Frank Thomas	10.00
JT	Joe Torre	8.00
EW	Earl Weaver	8.00
MW	Matt Williams	8.00
MW	Maury Wills	8.00
DW	Dave Winfield	10.00

Legendary Signatures

		NM/M
Common Player:		8.00
Inserted 1:23		
Golds:		1-2X
Production 50 Sets		
HA	Hank Aaron SP/94	300.00
JB	Johnny Bench	30.00
BB	Bobby Bonds	8.00
LB	Lou Brock	8.00
GB	George Brett	60.00
JC	Jose Canseco	20.00
GC	Gary Carter	10.00
SC	Sean Casey	8.00
RC	Roger Clemens	80.00
DC	Dave Concepcion	8.00
AD	Andre Dawson	10.00
KG	Ken Griffey Jr.	85.00

VG	Vladimir Guerrero	30.00
TG	Tony Gwynn	40.00
RJ	Reggie Jackson	20.00
DJ	Derek Jeter/SP/61	400.00
RaJ	Randy Johnson	50.00
CJ	Chipper Jones	50.00
HK	Harmon Killebrew	25.00
FL	Fred Lynn	8.00
DM	Dale Murphy	15.00
SM	Stan Musial	50.00
PN	Phil Niekro	8.00
JP	Jim Palmer	10.00
MP	Mike Piazza	120.00
MR	Manny Ramirez/SP/141	60.00
CR	Cal Ripken Jr.	120.00
AR	Alex Rodriguez	85.00
IR	Ivan Rodriguez	25.00
NR	Nolan Ryan	85.00
MS	Mike Schmidt	50.00
TS	Tom Seaver	30.00
OS	Ozzie Smith	40.00
WS	Willie Stargell	60.00
FT	Frank Thomas	30.00
AT	Alan Trammell	10.00
BW	Matt Williams	8.00

Ones for the Ages

		NM/M
Complete Set (7):		15.00
Inserted 1:24		
01	Ty Cobb	2.50
02	Cal Ripken Jr.	4.00
03	Babe Ruth	4.00
04	Jackie Robinson	2.50
05	Mark McGwire	3.00
06	Alex Rodriguez	3.00
07	Mike Piazza	4.00

Reflections in Time

		NM/M
Complete Set (10):		25.00
Common Player:		2.00
Inserted 1:12		
1	Ken Griffey Jr., Hank Aaron	3.00
2	Sammy Sosa, Roberto Clemente	3.00
3	Roger Clemens, Nolan Ryan	4.00
4	Ivan Rodriguez, Johnny Bench	2.00
5	Alex Rodriguez, Ernie Banks	3.00
6	Tony Gwynn, Stan Musial	3.00
7	Barry Bonds, Willie Mays	4.00
8	Cal Ripken Jr., Lou Gehrig	4.00
9	Chipper Jones, Mike Schmidt	2.50
10	Mark McGwire, Babe Ruth	4.00

UD Millennium Team

		NM/M
Complete Set (10):		15.00
Common Player:		1.50
Inserted 1:4		
1	Mark McGwire	2.00
2	Jackie Robinson	2.00
3	Mike Schmidt	1.50
4	Cal Ripken Jr.	3.00
5	Babe Ruth	3.00
6	Willie Mays	2.00
7	Johnny Bench	1.50
8	Nolan Ryan	3.00
10	Ken Griffey Jr.	1.50

3,000 Hit Club

		NM/M
CY	Carl Yastrzemski/Bat/350	30.00
CY	Carl Yastrzemski/Jsy/350	30.00
CY	Carl Yastrzemski/Bat/Jsy/100	80.00

2000 Upper Deck MVP

		NM/M
Complete Set (220):		20.00
Common Player:		.10
Pack (10):		1.25
Wax Box (28):		25.00
1	Garret Anderson	.25
2	Mo Vaughn	.15
3	Tim Salmon	.20
4	Ramon Ortiz	.10
5	Darin Erstad	.25
6	Troy Glaus	.50
7	Troy Percival	.10
8	Jeff Bagwell	.50
9	Ken Caminiti	.10
10	Daryle Ward	.10
11	Craig Biggio	.25
12	Jose Lima	.10
13	Moises Alou	.20
14	Octavio Dotel	.10
15	Ben Grieve	.20
16	Jason Giambi	.50
17	Tim Hudson	.20
18	Eric Chavez	.20
19	Matt Stairs	.10
20	Miguel Tejada	.25
21	John Jaha	.10
22	Chipper Jones	1.00

23	Kevin Millwood	.20
24	Brian Jordan	.10
25	Andruw Jones	.25
26	Andres Galarraga	.20
27	Greg Maddux	1.00
28	Reggie Sanders	.10
29	Javy Lopez	.20
30	Jeromy Burnitz	.10
31	Kevin Barker	.10
32	Jose Hernandez	.10
33	Ron Belliard	.10
34	Henry Blanco	.10
35	Marquis Grissom	.10
36	Geoff Jenkins	.10
37	Carlos Delgado	.50
38	Raul Mondesi	.20
39	Roy Halladay	.20
40	Tony Batista	.10
41	David Wells	.10
42	Shannon Stewart	.10
43	Vernon Wells	.20
44	Sammy Sosa	1.00
45	Ismael Valdes	.10
46	Joe Girardi	.10
47	Mark Grace	.20
48	Henry Rodriguez	.10
49	Kerry Wood	.25
50	Eric Young	.10
51	Mark McGwire	2.00
52	Daryle Kile	.10
53	Fernando Vina	.10
54	Ray Lankford	.10
55	J.D. Drew	.20
56	Fernando Tatis	.10
57	Rick Ankiel	.10
58	Matt Williams	.20
59	Erubiel Durazo	.15
60	Tony Womack	.10
61	Jay Bell	.10
62	Randy Johnson	.75
63	Steve Finley	.10
64	Matt Mantei	.10
65	Luis Gonzalez	.20
66	Gary Sheffield	.25
67	Eric Gagne	.10
68	Adrian Beltre	.20
69	Mark Grudzielanek	.10
70	Kevin Brown	.10
71	Chan Ho Park	.10
72	Shawn Green	.40
73	Vinny Castilla	.15
74	Fred McGriff	.25
75	Wilson Alvarez	.10
76	Greg Vaughn	.10
77	Gerald Williams	.10
78	Ryan Rupe	.10
79	Jose Canseco	.25
80	Vladimir Guerrero	.50
81	Dustin Hermanson	.10
82	Michael Barrett	.10
83	Rondell White	.20
84	Tony Armas Jr.	.10
85	Wilton Guerrero	.10
86	Jose Vidro	.10
87	Barry Bonds	1.50
88	Russ Ortiz	.10
89	Ellis Burks	.10
90	Jeff Kent	.20
91	Russ Davis	.10
92	J.T. Snow	.10
93	Roberto Alomar	.40
94	Manny Ramirez	.50
95	Chuck Finley	.10
96	Kenny Lofton	.20
97	Jim Thome	.50
98	Bartolo Colon	.20
99	Omar Vizquel	.20
100	Richie Sexson	.25
101	Mike Cameron	.10
102	Brett Tomko	.10
103	Edgar Martinez	.20
104	Alex Rodriguez	1.50
105	John Olerud	.20
106	Fred Garcia	.10
107	Kazuhiro Sasaki RC	1.00
108	Preston Wilson	.10
109	Luis Castillo	.10
110	A.J. Burnett	.10
111	Mike Lowell	.10
112	Cliff Floyd	.10
113	Brad Penny	.10
114	Alex Gonzalez	.10
115	Mike Piazza	1.00
116	Derek Bell	.10
117	Edgardo Alfonzo	.10
118	Rickey Henderson	.20
119	Todd Zeile	.10
120	Mike Hampton	.10
121	Al Leiter	.20
122	Robin Ventura	.20
123	Cal Ripken Jr.	1.50
124	Mike Mussina	.40
125	B.J. Surhoff	.10
126	Jerry Hairston Jr.	.10
127	Brady Anderson	.10
128	Albert Belle	.20
129	Sidney Ponson	.10
130	Tony Gwynn	.75
131	Ryan Klesko	.10
132	Sterling Hitchcock	.10
133	Eric Owens	.10
134	Trevor Hoffman	.10
135	Al Martin	.10
136	Bret Boone	.25
137	Brian Giles	.25

138	Chad Hermansen	.10
139	Kevin Young	.10
140	Kris Benson	.10
141	Warren Morris	.10
142	Jason Kendall	.20
143	Wil Cordero	.10
144	Scott Rolen	.50
145	Curt Schilling	.40
146	Doug Glanville	.10
147	Mike Lieberthal	.10
148	Mike Jackson	.10
149	Rico Brogna	.10
150	Andy Ashby	.10
151	Bob Abreu	.20
152	Sean Casey	.20
153	Pete Harnisch	.10
154	Dante Bichette	.10
155	Pokey Reese	.10
156	Aaron Boone	.20
157	Ken Griffey Jr.	1.00
158	Barry Larkin	.25
159	Scott Williamson	.10
160	Carlos Beltran	.20
161	Jermaine Dye	.10
162	Jose Rosado	.10
163	Joe Randa	.10
164	Johnny Damon	.20
165	Mike Sweeney	.10
166	Mark Quinn	.10
167	Ivan Rodriguez	.40
168	Rusty Greer	.10
169	Ruben Mateo	.10
170	Doug Davis	.10
171	Gabe Kapler	.10
172	Justin Thompson	.10
173	Rafael Palmeiro	.40
174	Larry Walker	.20
175	Neifi Perez	.10
176	Rolando Arrojo	.10
177	Jeffrey Hammonds	.10
178	Todd Helton	.50
179	Pedro Astacio	.10
180	Jeff Cirillo	.10
181	Pedro Martinez	.75
182	Carl Everett	.10
183	Troy O'Leary	.10
184	Nomar Garciaparra	1.25
185	Jose Offerman	.10
186	Bret Saberhagen	.10
187	Trot Nixon	.10
188	Jason Varitek	.10
189	Todd Walker	.10
190	Eric Milton	.10
191	Chad Allen	.10
192	Jacque Jones	.10
193	Brad Radke	.10
194	Corey Koskie	.10
195	Joe Mays	.10
196	Juan Gonzalez	.50
197	Jeff Weaver	.10
198	Juan Encarnacion	.10
199	Deivi Cruz	.10
200	Damion Easley	.10
201	Tony Clark	.10
202	Dean Palmer	.10
203	Frank Thomas	.50
204	Carlos Lee	.10
205	Mike Sirotka	.10
206	Kip Wells	.10
207	Magglio Ordonez	.20
208	Paul Konerko	.20
209	Chris Singleton	.10
210	Derek Jeter	1.50
211	Tino Martinez	.25
212	Mariano Rivera	.20
213	Roger Clemens	.75
214	Nick Johnson	.25
215	Paul O'Neill	.20
216	Bernie Williams	.40
217	David Cone	.20
218	Ken Griffey Jr. Checklist	.50
219	Sammy Sosa Checklist	.50
220	Mark McGwire Checklist	.75

Silver

Stars:	1-2X
Inserted 1:2	

Gold

Stars:	10-20X
Production 50 Sets	

2000 Upper Deck
MVP All-Star Game

		NM/M
Complete Set (30):		25.00
Common Player:		.25
AS1	Mo Vaughn	.25
AS2	Jeff Bagwell	.75
AS3	Jason Giambi	.75
AS4	Chipper Jones	1.50
AS5	Greg Maddux	1.00
AS6	Tony Batista	.25
AS7	Sammy Sosa	2.00
AS8	Mark McGwire	2.50
AS9	Randy Johnson	.75
AS10	Shawn Green	.50
AS11	Greg Vaughn	.25
AS12	Vladimir Guerrero	.75
AS13	Barry Bonds	2.50
AS14	Manny Ramirez	.75
AS15	Alex Rodriguez	2.50
AS16	Preston Wilson	.25
AS17	Mike Piazza	1.50
AS18	Cal Ripken Jr.	3.00
AS19	Tony Gwynn	1.00
AS20	Scott Rolen	.75
AS21	Ken Griffey Jr.	1.50
AS22	Carlos Beltran	.25
AS23	Ivan Rodriguez	.60
AS24	Larry Walker	.25
AS25	Nomar Garciaparra	2.00
AS26	Pedro Martinez	.75
AS27	Juan Gonzalez	.75
AS28	Frank Thomas	.75
AS29	Derek Jeter	2.50
AS30	Bernie Williams	.50

Drawing Power

		NM/M
Complete Set (7):		12.00
Common Player:		1.00
Inserted 1:28		
1	Mark McGwire	3.00
2	Ken Griffey Jr.	2.00
3	Mike Piazza	2.00
4	Chipper Jones	2.00
5	Nomar Garciaparra	3.00
6	Sammy Sosa	2.50
7	Jose Canseco	1.00

Game Used Souvenirs

		NM/M
Common Glove:		8.00
Inserted 1:130		
RA	Roberto Alomar	15.00
JB	Jeff Bagwell	20.00
AB	Albert Belle	8.00
BB	Barry Bonds	65.00
JC	Jose Canseco	15.00
WC	Will Clark	20.00
AF	Alex Fernandez	8.00
JG	Jason Giambi	15.00
TGl	Troy Glaus	15.00

AG	Alex Gonzalez	8.00
BG	Ben Grieve	8.00
KG	Ken Griffey Jr.	40.00
VG	Vladimir Guerrero	15.00
TG	Tony Gwynn	30.00
AJ	Andruw Jones	15.00
CJ	Chipper Jones	30.00
KL	Kenny Lofton	8.00
RM	Raul Mondesi	8.00
PO	Paul O'Neill	10.00
RP	Rafael Palmeiro	15.00
MR	Manny Ramirez	15.00
CR	Cal Ripken Jr.	65.00
AR	Alex Rodriguez	40.00
IR	Ivan Rodriguez	15.00
NR	Nolan Ryan	65.00
TS	Tim Salmon	8.00
LW	Larry Walker	8.00
BW	Bernie Williams	15.00
MW	Matt Williams	8.00

Game Used Souvenirs - Bats

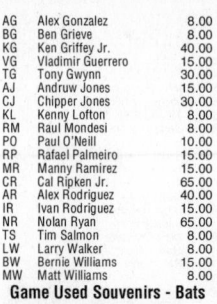

		NM/M
Common Bat:		8.00
Inserted 1:130		
BB	Barry Bonds	40.00
JC	Jose Canseco	8.00
KG	Ken Griffey Jr.	20.00
VG	Vladimir Guerrero	10.00
TG	Tony Gwynn	15.00
CJ	Chipper Jones	15.00
MR	Manny Ramirez	10.00
AR	Alex Rodriguez	20.00
IR	Ivan Rodriguez	8.00
BW	Bernie Williams	10.00

Pure Grit

		NM/M
Complete Set (10):		10.00
Common Player:		.50
Inserted 1:6		
1	Derek Jeter	2.00
2	Kevin Brown	.50
3	Craig Biggio	.50
4	Ivan Rodriguez	.75
5	Scott Rolen	.75
6	Carlos Beltran	.50
7	Ken Griffey Jr.	1.50
8	Cal Ripken Jr.	2.50
9	Nomar Garciaparra	2.00
10	Randy Johnson	1.00

Prolifics

	NM/M
Complete Set (7):	10.00

Common Player:		.50
Inserted 1:28		
1	Manny Ramirez	1.00
2	Vladimir Guerrero	1.00
3	Derek Jeter	3.00
4	Pedro Martinez	1.50
5	Shawn Green	.50
6	Alex Rodriguez	3.00
7	Cal Ripken Jr.	4.00

ProSign

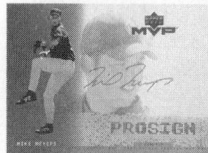

		NM/M
Common Player:		5.00
Inserted 1:216 R		
RA	Rick Ankiel	10.00
MB	Michael Barrett	5.00
RB	Rob Bell	5.00
CB	Carlos Beltran	20.00
LB	Lance Berkman	25.00
RB	Rico Brogna	5.00
SC	Sean Casey	8.00
DD	Doug Davis	8.00
ED	Erubiel Durazo	8.00
RF	Robert Fick	8.00
NG	Nomar Garciaparra	65.00
AG	Alex Gonzalez	8.00
KG	Ken Griffey Jr.	60.00
TG	Tony Gwynn	40.00
TH	Tim Hudson	15.00
DJ	Derek Jeter	80.00
CJ	Chipper Jones	50.00
MM	Mike Meyers	5.00
EM	Eric Milton	8.00
JM	Jim Morris	8.00
WM	Warren Morris	5.00
TN	Trot Nixon	8.00
BP	Ben Petrick	5.00
AP	Adam Piatt	5.00
MP	Mike Piazza	60.00
MQ	Mark Quinn	5.00
MR	Manny Ramirez	25.00
RR	Rob Ramsay	5.00
MRe	Mike Redmond	5.00
MRi	Mariano Rivera	15.00
AR	Alex Rodriguez	65.00
MS	Mike Sweeney	8.00
BT	Bubba Trammell	5.00
JV	Jose Vidro	8.00
DW	Daryle Ward	5.00
KW	Kip Wells	8.00
SW	Scott Williamson	5.00
PW	Preston Wilson	8.00
KW	Kevin Witt	5.00
TW	Tony Womack	5.00
EY	Ed Yarnall	5.00
JZ	Jeff Zimmerman	5.00

Scout's Choice

		NM/M
Complete Set (10):		8.00
Common Player:		.50
Inserted 1:14		
1	Rick Ankiel	.50
2	Vernon Wells	1.00
3	Pat Burrell	1.50
4	Travis Dawkins	.50
5	Eric Munson	.50
6	Nick Johnson	1.00
7	Dermal Brown	.50
8	Alfonso Soriano	2.00
9	Ben Petrick	.50
10	Adam Everett	.50

Second Season Standouts

		NM/M
Complete Set (10):		6.00
Common Player:		.25
Inserted 1:6		

1	Pedro Martinez	1.00
2	Mariano Rivera	.40
3	Orlando Hernandez	.25
4	Ken Caminiti	.25
5	Bernie Williams	.50
6	Jim Thome	.75
7	Nomar Garciaparra	2.00
8	Edgardo Alfonzo	.25
9	Derek Jeter	2.50
10	Kevin Millwood	.40

Super

Stars: 15-30X
Production 25 Sets

3,000 Hit Club

		NM/M
Common Player:		
SM	Stan Musial/Jsy/350	30.00
SM	Stan Musial/Bat/350	30.00
SM	Stan Musial/Jsy/Bat/100	80.00

2000 Upper Deck Ovation

	NM/M
Complete Set (90):	65.00
Common Player:	.25
Common World Prem. (61-80):	1.00
Inserted 1:3	
Common Super. Spot (81-90):	1.50
Inserted 1:6	
Pack (5):	2.00

Wax Box (20):		30.00
1	Mo Vaughn	.25
2	Troy Glaus	.75
3	Jeff Bagwell	.75
4	Craig Biggio	.40
5	Mike Hampton	.25
6	Jason Giambi	.75
7	Tim Hudson	.40
8	Chipper Jones	1.50
9	Greg Maddux	1.50
10	Kevin Millwood	.40
11	Brian Jordan	.25
12	Jeromy Burnitz	.25
13	David Wells	.25
14	Carlos Delgado	.75
15	Sammy Sosa	2.50
16	Mark McGwire	3.00
17	Matt Williams	.25
18	Randy Johnson	.75
19	Erubiel Durazo	.40
20	Kevin Brown	.40
21	Shawn Green	.75
22	Gary Sheffield	.50
23	Jose Canseco	.50
24	Vladimir Guerrero	1.00
25	Barry Bonds	3.00
26	Manny Ramirez	.75
27	Roberto Alomar	.75
28	Richie Sexson	.40
29	Jim Thome	.75
30	Alex Rodriguez	2.50
31	Ken Griffey Jr.	1.50
32	Preston Wilson	.25
33	Mike Piazza	1.50
34	Al Leiter	.25
35	Robin Ventura	.25
36	Cal Ripken Jr.	3.00
37	Albert Belle	.25
38	Tony Gwynn	1.00
39	Brian Giles	.40
40	Jason Kendall	.40
41	Scott Rolen	.75
42	Bob Abreu	.40
43	Ken Griffey Jr.	1.50
44	Sean Casey	.25
45	Carlos Beltran	.40
46	Gabe Kapler	.25
47	Ivan Rodriguez	.75
48	Rafael Palmeiro	.50
49	Larry Walker	.40
50	Nomar Garciaparra	2.00
51	Pedro J. Martinez	1.00
52	Eric Milton	.25
53	Juan Gonzalez	.75
54	Tony Clark	.25
55	Frank Thomas	.75
56	Magglio Ordonez	.40
57	Roger Clemens	1.50
58	Derek Jeter	2.50
59	Bernie Williams	.50
60	Orlando Hernandez	.40
61	Rick Ankiel (World Premiere)	1.00
62	Josh Beckett (World Premiere)	1.50
63	Vernon Wells (World Premiere)	1.50
64	Alfonso Soriano (World Premiere)	3.00
65	Pat Burrell (World Premiere)	2.00
66	Eric Munson (World Premiere)	1.00
67	Chad Hutchinson (World Premiere)	1.00
68	Eric Gagne (World Premiere)	1.00
69	Peter Bergeron (World Premiere)	1.00
70	Ryan Anderson (Supposed to have been withdrawn, all known cards have embossed UD racing mark.)	300.00
71	A.J. Burnett (World Premiere)	1.00
72	Jorge Luis Toca (World Premiere)	1.00
73	Matt Riley (World Premiere)	1.00
74	Chad Hermansen (World Premiere)	1.00
75	Doug Davis (World Premiere)	1.00
76	Jim Morris (World Premiere)	1.00
77	Ben Petrick (World Premiere)	1.00
78	Mark Quinn (World Premiere)	1.00
79	Ed Yarnall (World Premiere)	1.00
80	Ramon Ortiz (World Premiere)	1.00
81	Ken Griffey Jr. (Superstar Spotlight)	3.00
82	Mark McGwire (Superstar Spotlight)	5.00
83	Derek Jeter (Superstar Spotlight)	5.00
84	Jeff Bagwell (Superstar Spotlight)	1.50
85	Nomar Garciaparra (Superstar Spotlight)	5.00
86	Sammy Sosa (Superstar Spotlight)	4.00
87	Mike Piazza (Superstar Spotlight)	3.00
88	Alex Rodriguez (Superstar Spotlight)	5.00

89	Cal Ripken Jr. (Superstar Spotlight)	6.00
90	Pedro Martinez (Superstar Spotlight)	2.00

Standing Ovation

Stars (1-60):	8-15X
World Prem. (61-80):	2-3X
Super. Spot. (81-90):	3-5X
Production 50 Sets	

(See 2000 UD Ovation for checklist and base card values.)

A Piece of History

	NM/M
Common Player:	5.00
Production 400 Sets	
JB	Jeff Bagwell	10.00
CB	Carlos Beltran	10.00
SC	Sean Casey	5.00
KG	Ken Griffey Jr.	25.00
DJ	Derek Jeter	35.00
TG	Tony Gwynn	15.00
AJ	Andruw Jones	10.00
CJ	Chipper Jones	20.00
RP	Rafael Palmeiro	10.00
MP	Mike Piazza	20.00
MR	Manny Ramirez	10.00
CR	Cal Ripken Jr.	35.00
AR	Alex Rodriguez	25.00
SR	Scott Rolen	15.00
SS	Sammy Sosa	25.00
FT	Frank Thomas	10.00

Center Stage

	NM/M
Complete Set (10):	20.00
Common Player:	1.00
Inserted 1:9	
Gold:	2X
Inserted 1:39	
Rainbow:	3-4X
Inserted 1:99	
1	Jeff Bagwell	1.00
2	Ken Griffey Jr.	2.00
3	Nomar Garciaparra	3.00
4	Mike Piazza	2.00
5	Mark McGwire	3.00
6	Alex Rodriguez	3.00
7	Cal Ripken Jr.	4.00
8	Derek Jeter	3.00
9	Chipper Jones	2.00
10	Sammy Sosa	2.50

Curtain Calls

		NM/M
Complete Set (20):		15.00
Common Player:		.50
Inserted 1:3		
1	David Cone	.50
2	Mark McGwire	2.00
3	Sammy Sosa	2.00
4	Eric Milton	.50
5	Bernie Williams	.75
6	Tony Gwynn	1.00
7	Nomar Garciaparra	2.00
8	Manny Ramirez	1.00
9	Wade Boggs	.50
10	Randy Johnson	1.00
11	Cal Ripken Jr.	3.00
12	Pedro J. Martinez	1.00
13	Alex Rodriguez	2.00
14	Fernando Tatis	.50
15	Vladimir Guerrero	1.00
16	Robin Ventura	.50
17	Larry Walker	.50
18	Carlos Beltran	.50
19	Jose Canseco	.75
20	Ken Griffey Jr.	1.50

Diamond Futures

		NM/M
Complete Set (10):		8.00
Common Player:		.50
Inserted 1:6		
1	J.D. Drew	.75
2	Alfonso Soriano	2.50
3	Preston Wilson	1.00
4	Erubiel Durazo	.75
5	Rick Ankiel	.50
6	Octavio Dotel	.50
7	A.J. Burnett	.50
8	Carlos Beltran	.75
9	Vernon Wells	1.00
10	Troy Glaus	2.00

Lead Performers

		NM/M
Complete Set (10):		20.00
Common Player:		1.00
Inserted 1:19		
1	Mark McGwire	3.00
2	Derek Jeter	3.00
3	Vladimir Guerrero	1.00
4	Mike Piazza	2.00
5	Cal Ripken Jr.	4.00
6	Sammy Sosa	2.50
7	Jeff Bagwell	1.00
8	Nomar Garciaparra	3.00
9	Chipper Jones	2.00
10	Ken Griffey Jr.	2.00

Superstar Theatre

		NM/M
Complete Set (20):		20.00
Common Player:		.50
Inserted 1:19		
1	Ivan Rodriguez	1.00
2	Brian Giles	.50
3	Bernie Williams	1.00
4	Greg Maddux	2.00
5	Frank Thomas	1.00
6	Sean Casey	.50
7	Mo Vaughn	.50
8	Carlos Delgado	1.00
9	Tony Gwynn	1.50
10	Pedro Martinez	1.50
11	Scott Rolen	1.00
12	Mark McGwire	3.00
13	Manny Ramirez	1.00
14	Rafael Palmeiro	.75
15	Jose Canseco	.75
16	Randy Johnson	1.50
17	Gary Sheffield	.75
18	Larry Walker	.50
19	Barry Bonds	4.00
20	Roger Clemens	3.00

Super Signatures

		NM/M
Common Card:		
KG	Ken Griffey/Gold/50	180.00
KG	Ken Griffey/Silver/100	100.00
MP	Mike Piazza/Gold/50	180.00
MP	Mike Piazza/Silver/100	150.00

3,000 Hit Club

		NM/M
1	Willie Mays/Jsy/350	40.00
2	Willie Mays/Bat/300	40.00
3	Willie Mays/Jsy/Bat/50	180.00
4	Willie Mays/Jsy/Bat/Auto./24	675.00

2000 Upper Deck Pros and Prospects

		NM/M
Complete Set (132):		300.00
Common Player (1-90):		.15
Common (91-120):		5.00
Common (121-132):		4.00
Production 1,350 Sets		
Production 1,000 Sets		
Pack (5):		2.50
Box (24):		40.00
1	Darin Erstad	.40
2	Troy Glaus	.75
3	Mo Vaughn	.20
4	Jason Giambi	.75
5	Tim Hudson	.25
6	Ben Grieve	.15
7	Eric Chavez	.25
8	Shannon Stewart	.15
9	Raul Mondesi	.25

10	Carlos Delgado	.75
11	Jose Canseco	.40
12	Fred McGriff	.25
13	Greg Vaughn	.15
14	Manny Ramirez	.75
15	Roberto Alomar	.50
16	Jim Thome	.75
17	Alex Rodriguez	2.50
18	Fred Garcia	.15
19	John Olerud	.25
20	Cal Ripken Jr.	2.50
21	Albert Belle	.20
22	Mike Mussina	.40
23	Ivan Rodriguez	.50
24	Rafael Palmeiro	.50
25	Ruben Mateo	.15
26	Gabe Kapler	.15
27	Pedro Martinez	1.00
28	Nomar Garciaparra	2.00
29	Carl Everett	.15
30	Carlos Beltran	.25
31	Jermaine Dye	.15
32	Johnny Damon	.25
33	Juan Gonzalez	.75
34	Juan Encarnacion	.15
35	Dean Palmer	.15
36	Jacque Jones	.15
37	Matt Lawton	.15
38	Frank Thomas	.75
39	Paul Konerko	.15
40	Magglio Ordonez	.25
41	Derek Jeter	2.00
42	Bernie Williams	.50
43	Mariano Rivera	.25
44	Roger Clemens	1.50
45	Jeff Bagwell	.75
46	Craig Biggio	.25
47	Richard Hidalgo	.25
48	Chipper Jones	1.50
49	Andres Galarraga	.50
50	Andruw Jones	.50
51	Greg Maddux	1.50
52	Jeromy Burnitz	.15
53	Geoff Jenkins	.25
54	Mark McGwire	2.00
55	Jim Edmonds	.25
56	Fernando Tatis	.15
57	J.D. Drew	.15
58	Sammy Sosa	2.00
59	Kerry Wood	.50
60	Randy Johnson	.75
61	Matt Williams	.25
62	Erubiel Durazo	.15
63	Shawn Green	.25
64	Kevin Brown	.25
65	Gary Sheffield	.25
66	Adrian Beltre	.25
67	Vladimir Guerrero	.75
68	Jose Vidro	.15
69	Barry Bonds	2.00
70	Jeff Kent	.25
71	Preston Wilson	.15
72	Ryan Dempster	.15
73	Mike Lowell	.15
74	Mike Piazza	1.50
75	Robin Ventura	.25
76	Edgardo Alfonzo	.15
77	Derek Bell	.15
78	Tony Gwynn	1.00
79	Matt Clement	.15
80	Scott Rolen	.75
81	Bobby Abreu	.25
82	Curt Schilling	.40
83	Brian Giles	.25
84	Jason Kendall	.25
85	Kris Benson	.15
86	Ken Griffey Jr.	1.50
87	Sean Casey	.25
88	Pokey Reese	.15
89	Larry Walker	.75
90	Todd Helton	.75
91	Rick Ankiel (Prospective Superstars)	5.00
92	Milton Bradley (Prospective Superstars)	5.00
93	Vernon Wells (Prospective Superstars)	6.00
94	Rafael Furcal (Prospective Superstars)	6.00

95	Kazuhiro Sasaki RC (Prospective Superstars)	8.00
96	Joe Torres RC (Prospective Superstars)	5.00
97	Adam Kennedy (Prospective Superstars)	5.00
98	Adam Piatt (Prospective Superstars)	5.00
99	Matt Wheatland RC (Prospective Superstars)	5.00
100	Alex Cabrera RC (Prospective Superstars)	5.00
101	Barry Zito RC (Prospective Superstars)	25.00
102	Mike Lamb RC (Prospective Superstars)	5.00
103	Scott Heard RC (Prospective Superstars)	5.00
104	Danys Baez RC (Prospective Superstars)	8.00
105	Matt Riley (Prospective Superstars)	5.00
106	Mark Mulder (Prospective Superstars)	6.00
107	Wilfredo Rodriguez RC (Prospective Superstars)	5.00
108	Luis Matos RC (Prospective Superstars)	10.00
109	Alfonso Soriano (Prospective Superstars)	8.00
110	Pat Burrell (Prospective Superstars)	6.00
111	Mike Tonis RC (Prospective Superstars)	5.00
112	Aaron McNeal RC (Prospective Superstars)	5.00
113	Dave Krynzel RC (Prospective Superstars)	8.00
114	Josh Beckett (Prospective Superstars)	5.00
115	Sean Burnett RC (Prospective Superstars)	5.00
116	Eric Munson (Prospective Superstars)	5.00
117	Scott Downs RC (Prospective Superstars)	5.00
118	Brian Tollberg RC (Prospective Superstars)	5.00
119	Nick Johnson (Prospective Superstars)	5.00
120	Leo Estrella RC (Prospective Superstars)	5.00
121	Ken Griffey Jr. (Pro Fame)	8.00
122	Frank Thomas (Pro Fame)	4.00
123	Cal Ripken Jr. (Pro Fame)	15.00
124	Ivan Rodriguez (Pro Fame)	4.00
125	Derek Jeter (Pro Fame)	12.00
126	Mark McGwire (Pro Fame)	12.00
127	Pedro Martinez (Pro Fame)	5.00
128	Chipper Jones (Pro Fame)	8.00
129	Sammy Sosa (Pro Fame)	10.00
130	Alex Rodriguez (Pro Fame)	10.00
131	Vladimir Guerrero (Pro Fame)	4.00
132	Jeff Bagwell (Pro Fame)	4.00

Future Forces

		NM/M
Complete Set (10):		5.00
Common Player:		.50
Inserted 1:6		
1	Pat Burrell	2.00
2	Brad Penny	.50
3	Rick Ankiel	.50
4	Adam Kennedy	.50
5	Eric Munson	.50
6	Rafael Furcal	.75
7	Mark Mulder	.75
8	Vernon Wells	.75
9	Matt Riley	.50
10	Nick Johnson	.75

ProMotion

		NM/M
Complete Set (10):		15.00
Common Player:		.75
Inserted 1:6		
1	Derek Jeter	3.00

2	Mike Piazza	1.50
3	Mark McGwire	2.50
4	Ivan Rodriguez	.75
5	Kerry Wood	.75
6	Nomar Garciaparra	2.00
7	Sammy Sosa	2.00
8	Alex Rodriguez	2.50
9	Ken Griffey Jr.	1.50
10	Vladimir Guerrero	1.00

Rare Breed

		NM/M
Complete Set (12):		15.00
Common Player:		.50
Inserted 1:12		
1	Mark McGwire	3.00
2	Frank Thomas	1.00
3	Mike Piazza	2.00
4	Barry Bonds	4.00
5	Manny Ramirez	1.00
6	Ken Griffey Jr.	2.00
7	Nomar Garciaparra	3.00
8	Randy Johnson	1.50
9	Vladimir Guerrero	1.00
10	Jeff Bagwell	1.00
11	Rick Ankiel	.50
12	Alex Rodriguez	3.00

Signed Game-Worn Jerseys

		NM/M
Common Player:		25.00
Inserted 1:96		
BB	Barry Bonds	200.00
JC	Jose Canseco	40.00
JD	J.D. Drew	25.00
TG	Tom Glavine	40.00
LG	Luis Gonzalez	25.00
KG	Ken Griffey Jr.	100.00
TG	Tony Gwynn	50.00
DJ	Derek Jeter/SP	350.00
RJ	Randy Johnson	80.00
CJ	Chipper Jones	50.00
KL	Kenny Lofton	25.00

CR	Cal Ripken Jr.	140.00
AR	Alex Rodriguez	120.00
IR	Ivan Rodriguez	40.00
SR	Scott Rolen	50.00
GS	Gary Sheffield	40.00
FT	Frank Thomas	40.00
MV	Mo Vaughn	25.00
RV	Robin Ventura	25.00
MW	Matt Williams	25.00
PW	Preston Wilson	25.00

The Best in the Bigs

NM/M

Complete Set (10): 15.00
Common Player: 1.00
Inserted 1:12

1	Sammy Sosa	2.50
2	Tony Gwynn	1.50
3	Pedro Martinez	1.50
4	Mark McGwire	3.00
5	Chipper Jones	2.00
6	Derek Jeter	3.00
7	Ken Griffey Jr.	2.00
8	Cal Ripken Jr.	4.00
9	Greg Maddux	2.00
10	Ivan Rodriguez	1.00

3,000 Hit Club

NM/M

Lou Brock/Bat/350	20.00
Lou Brock/Jsy/350	20.00
Lou Brock/Bat/Jsy/100	40.00
Rod Carew/Bat/350	20.00
Rod Carew/Jsy/350	20.00
Rod Carew/Bat/Jsy/100	40.00

2000 Upper Deck Rookie Update

NM/M

Common Player: .25
Common Rookie: 5.00
Pack (4): 4.50
Box (15): 50.00

SP Authentic Update
(136-164) Production 1,700

136	Barry Zito RC	
	(Future Watch)	25.00
137	Aaron McNeal RC	
	(Future Watch)	5.00
138	Teofilo Perez (Future Watch)	5.00
139	Sun-Woo Kim RC	
	(Future Watch)	5.00
140	Xavier Nady RC	
	(Future Watch)	15.00
141	Matt Wheatland RC	
	(Future Watch)	5.00
142	Brent Abernathy RC	
	(Future Watch)	5.00
143	Cory Vance RC	
	(Future Watch)	5.00
144	Scott Heard RC	
	(Future Watch)	5.00
145	Mike Meyers RC	

146	Ben Diggins RC	
	(Future Watch)	5.00
147	Luis Matos RC	
	(Future Watch)	5.00
148	Ben Sheets RC	
	(Future Watch)	15.00
149	Kurt Ainsworth RC	
	(Future Watch)	5.00
150	Dave Krynzel RC	
	(Future Watch)	5.00
151	Alex Cabrera RC	
	(Future Watch)	5.00
152	Mike Tonis RC	
	(Future Watch)	5.00
153	Dane Sardinha RC	
	(Future Watch)	5.00
154	Keith Ginter RC	
	(Future Watch)	5.00
155	David Espinosa RC	
	(Future Watch)	5.00
156	Joe Torres RC	
	(Future Watch)	5.00
157	Daylan Holt RC	
	(Future Watch)	5.00
158	Koyie Hill RC	
	(Future Watch)	5.00
159	Brad Wilkerson RC	
	(Future Watch)	8.00
160	Juan Pierre RC	
	(Future Watch)	10.00
161	Matt Ginter RC	
	(Future Watch)	5.00
162	Dane Artman RC	
	(Future Watch)	5.00
163	Jon Rauch RC	
	(Future Watch)	5.00
164	Sean Burnett RC	
	(Future Watch)	5.00
166	Darin Erstad	.50
167	Ben Grieve	.25
168	David Wells	.25
169	Fred McGriff	.40
170	Bob Wickman	.25
171	Al Martin	.25
172	Melvin Mora	.25
173	Ricky Ledee	.25
174	Dante Bichette	.25
175	Mike Sweeney	.25
176	Bobby Higginson	.25
177	Matt Lawton	.25
178	Charles Johnson	.25
179	David Justice	.50
180	Richard Hidalgo	.40
181	B.J. Surhoff	.25
182	Richie Sexson	.50
183	Jim Edmonds	.25
184	Rondell White	.25
185	Curt Schilling	.50
186	Tom Goodwin	.25
187	Jose Vidro	.25
188	Ellis Burks	.25
189	Henry Rodriguez	.25
190	Mike Bordick	.25
191	Eric Owens	.25
192	Travis Lee	.25
193	Kevin Young	.25
194	Aaron Boone	.40
195	Todd Hollandsworth	.25

SPx Update
(121-135, 182-196) 1,600
(136-151) Production 1,500
Common Autograph 10.00

121	Brad Wilkerson RC	15.00
122	Roy Oswalt RC	100.00
123	Wascar Serrano RC	5.00
124	Sean Burnett RC	10.00
125	Alex Cabrera RC	5.00
126	Timoniel Perez RC	5.00
127	Juan Pierre RC	15.00
128	Daylan Holt RC	5.00
129	Tomokazu Ohka RC	5.00
130	Kazuhiro Sasaki RC	10.00
131	Kurt Ainsworth RC	10.00
132	Brent Abernathy RC	5.00
133	Danys Baez RC	5.00
134	Brad Cresse RC	5.00
135	Ryan Franklin	5.00
136	Mike Lamb RC	10.00
137	David Espinosa RC	5.00
138	Matt Wheatland RC	5.00
139	Xavier Nady RC	50.00
140	Scott Heard RC	5.00
141	Pascual Coco RC	5.00
142	Justin Miller RC	5.00
143	Dave Krynzel RC	5.00
144	Dane Sardinha RC	5.00
145	Ben Sheets RC	40.00
146	Leo Estrella RC	10.00
147	Ben Diggins RC	10.00
148	Barry Zito RC	40.00
149	Joe Torres RC	10.00
150	Mike Meyers RC	10.00
151	Kris Wilson RC	10.00
152	Darin Erstad	.50
153	Richard Hidalgo	.40
154	Eric Chavez	.50
155	B.J. Surhoff	.25
156	Richie Sexson	.75
157	Raul Mondesi	.50
158	Rondell White	.50
159	Jim Edmonds	.75
160	Curt Schilling	.75
161	Tom Goodwin	.25

162	Fred McGriff	.50
163	Jose Vidro	.25
164	Ellis Burks	.25
165	David Segui	.25
166	Aaron Sele	.25
167	Henry Rodriguez	.25
168	Mike Bordick	.25
169	Mike Mussina	1.00
170	Ryan Klesko	.25
171	Kevin Young	.25
172	Travis Lee	.25
173	Aaron Boone	.50
174	Jermaine Dye	.25
175	Ricky Ledee	.25
176	Jeffrey Hammonds	.25
177	Carl Everett	.25
178	Matt Lawton	.25
179	Bobby Higginson	.25
180	Charles Johnson	.25
181	David Justice	.75
182	Joey Nation RC	4.00
183	Rico Washington RC	4.00
184	Luis Matos RC	10.00
185	Chris Wakeland RC	4.00
186	Sun-Woo Kim RC	4.00
187	Keith Ginter RC	5.00
188	Geraldo Guzman RC	4.00
189	Jay Spurgeon RC	4.00
190	Jace Brewer RC	4.00
191	Juan Guzman RC	4.00
192	Ross Gload RC	4.00
193	Paxton Crawford RC	4.00
194	Ryan Kohlmeier RC	4.00
195	Julio Zuleta RC	4.00
196	Matt Ginter RC	4.00

UD Pros & Prospects Update
(133-162) Production 1,600

133	Dane Artman RC	5.00
134	Juan Pierre RC	8.00
135	Jace Brewer RC	5.00
136	Sun-Woo Kim RC	6.00
137	Jon Rauch RC	6.00
138	Juan Guzman RC	5.00
139	Daylan Holt RC	5.00
140	Rico Washington RC	5.00
141	Ben Diggins RC	8.00
142	Mike Meyers RC	5.00
143	Chris Wakeland RC	5.00
144	Cory Vance RC	5.00
145	Keith Ginter RC	5.00
146	Koyie Hill RC	8.00
147	Julio Zuleta RC	5.00
148	Geraldo Guzman RC	5.00
149	Jay Spurgeon RC	5.00
150	Ross Gload RC	5.00
151	Ben Sheets RC	15.00
152	Josh Kalinowski RC	6.00
153	Kurt Ainsworth RC	5.00
154	Paxton Crawford RC	8.00
155	Xavier Nady RC	8.00
156	Brad Wilkerson RC	10.00
157	Kris Wilson RC	5.00
158	Paul Rigdon RC	5.00
159	Ryan Kohlmeier RC	5.00
160	Dane Sardinha RC	5.00
161	Javier Cardona RC	5.00
162	Brad Cresse RC	5.00
163	Ron Gant	.25
164	Mark Mulder	.50
165	David Wells	.25
166	Jason Tyner	.25
167	David Segui	.25
168	Al Martin	.25
169	Melvin Mora	.25
170	Ricky Ledee	.25
171	Rolando Arrojo	.25
172	Mike Sweeney	.25
173	Bobby Higginson	.25
174	Eric Milton	.25
175	Charles Johnson	.25
176	David Justice	.50
177	Moises Alou	.50
178	Andy Ashby	.25
179	Richie Sexson	.75
180	Will Clark	.75
181	Rondell White	.40
182	Curt Schilling	.75
183	Tom Goodwin	.25
184	Lee Stevens	.25
185	Ellis Burks	.25
186	Henry Rodriguez	.25
187	Mike Bordick	.25
188	Ryan Klesko	.50
189	Travis Lee	.25
190	Kevin Young	.25
191	Barry Larkin	.75
192	Jeff Cirillo	.25

Winning Materials

NM/M

Common Card: 10.00
Inserted 1:15

NG-PM	Nomar Garciaparra, Pedro Martinez	40.00
DJ-AR	Derek Jeter, Alex Rodriguez	40.00
DJ-NG	Derek Jeter, Nomar Garciaparra	40.00
MM-KG	Mark McGwire, Ken Griffey Jr.	40.00
MM-SS	Mark McGwire, Sammy Sosa	40.00
MM-RA	Mark McGwire, Rick Ankiel	30.00
KG-SS	Ken Griffey Jr., Sammy Sosa	25.00
RC-PM	Roger Clemens, Pedro Martinez	30.00
CR-TG	Cal Ripken Jr., Tony Gwynn	40.00
JC-BB	Jose Canseco, Barry Bonds	30.00
FT-MO	Frank Thomas, Magglio Ordonez	10.00
JB-CB	Jeff Bagwell, Craig Biggio	10.00
MP-RV	Mike Piazza, Robin Ventura	25.00
IR-RP	Ivan Rodriguez, Rafael Palmeiro	10.00
J-G-R	Derek Jeter, Nomar Garciaparra, Alex Rodriguez	75.00
G-S-R	Ken Griffey Jr., Sammy Sosa, Alex Rodriguez	40.00

Winning Materials Gold

NM/M

	Common Player:	5.00
JC	John Cotton	5.00
BS	Ben Sheets	15.00
SB	Sean Burroughs	8.00
MN	Mike Neill	5.00
DM	Doug Mientkiewicz	8.00
EY	Ernie Young	5.00
GD	Travis Dawkins, Mike Kinkade	5.00
BS	Sean Burroughs, Ben Sheets	15.00
AE	Brent Abernathy, Adam Everett	5.00
EY	Brad Wilkerson, Ernie Young	8.00

2000 Upper Deck Ultimate Victory

NM/M

Complete Set (120): 200.00
Common Player: .15
Common Ultimate Rookie (91-120): 4.00
Varying Production Levels
Pack (5): 1.50
Box (24): 25.00

1	Mo Vaughn	.20
2	Darin Erstad	.40
3	Troy Glaus	.75
4	Adam Kennedy	.15
5	Jason Giambi	.75
6	Ben Grieve	.15
7	Terrence Long	.25
8	Tim Hudson	.25
9	David Wells	.15
10	Carlos Delgado	.75
11	Shannon Stewart	.15
12	Greg Vaughn	.15
13	Gerald Williams	.15
14	Manny Ramirez	.75
15	Roberto Alomar	.60
16	Jim Thome	.75
17	Edgar Martinez	.25
18	Alex Rodriguez	2.50
19	Matt Riley	.15
20	Cal Ripken Jr.	2.50
21	Mike Mussina	.75
22	Albert Belle	.20
23	Ivan Rodriguez	.75
24	Rafael Palmeiro	.50
25	Nomar Garciaparra	2.00
26	Pedro Martinez	1.00
27	Carl Everett	.15
28	Tomokazu Ohka RC	.40
29	Jermaine Dye	.15
30	Johnny Damon	.25
31	Dean Palmer	.15

32	Juan Gonzalez	.75
33	Eric Milton	.15
34	Matt Lawton	.15
35	Frank Thomas	.75
36	Paul Konerko	.15
37	Magglio Ordonez	.25
38	Jon Garland	.15
39	Derek Jeter	2.50
40	Roger Clemens	1.50
41	Bernie Williams	.50
42	Nick Johnson	.15
43	Julio Lugo	.15
44	Jeff Bagwell	.75
45	Richard Hidalgo	.15
46	Chipper Jones	1.50
47	Greg Maddux	1.50
48	Andruw Jones	.50
49	Andres Galarraga	.25
50	Rafael Furcal	.25
51	Jeromy Burnitz	.15
52	Geoff Jenkins	.25
53	Mark McGwire	2.00
54	Jim Edmonds	.25
55	Rick Ankiel	.25
56	Sammy Sosa	2.00
57	Julio Zuleta **RC**	.25
58	Kerry Wood	.40
59	Randy Johnson	.75
60	Matt Williams	.25
61	Steve Finley	.15
62	Gary Sheffield	.40
63	Kevin Brown	.25
64	Shawn Green	.25
65	Milton Bradley	.15
66	Vladimir Guerrero	.75
67	Jose Vidro	.15
68	Barry Bonds	2.00
69	Jeff Kent	.25
70	Preston Wilson	.15
71	Mike Lowell	.15
72	Mike Piazza	2.00
73	Robin Ventura	.25
74	Edgardo Alfonzo	.15
75	Jay Payton	.15
76	Tony Gwynn	1.00
77	Adam Eaton	.15
78	Phil Nevin	.15
79	Scott Rolen	.75
80	Bob Abreu	.25
81	Pat Burrell	.50
82	Brian Giles	.25
83	Jason Kendall	.15
84	Kris Benson	.15
85	Gookie Dawkins	.15
86	Ken Griffey Jr.	1.50
87	Barry Larkin	.40
88	Larry Walker	.25
89	Todd Helton	.75
90	Ben Petrick	.15
91	Alex Cabrera 3,500 **RC**	
	(Ultimate Rookie 2000)	4.00
92	Matt Wheatland 1,000 **RC**	
	(Ultimate Rookie 2000)	4.00
93	Joe Torres 1,000 **RC**	
	(Ultimate Rookie 2000)	4.00
94	Xavier Nady 1,000 **RC**	
	(Ultimate Rookie 2000)	12.00
95	Kenny Kelly 3,500 **RC**	
	(Ultimate Rookie 2000)	4.00
96	Matt Ginter 3,500 **RC**	
	(Ultimate Rookie 2000)	4.00
97	Ben Diggins 1,000 **RC**	
	(Ultimate Rookie 2000)	8.00
98	Danys Baez 3,500 **RC**	
	(Ultimate Rookie 2000)	6.00
99	Daylan Holt 2,500 **RC**	
	(Ultimate Rookie 2000)	4.00
100	Kazuhiro Sasaki 3,500 **RC**	
	(Ultimate Rookie 2000)	5.00
101	Dane Artman 2,500 **RC**	
	(Ultimate Rookie 2000)	4.00
102	Mike Tonis 1,000 **RC**	
	(Ultimate Rookie 2000)	4.00
103	Timoniel Perez 2,500 **RC**	
	(Ultimate Rookie 2000)	4.00
104	Barry Zito 2,500 **RC**	
	(Ultimate Rookie 2000)	20.00
105	Koyie Hill 2,500 **RC**	
	(Ultimate Rookie 2000)	4.00
106	Brad Wilkerson 2,500 **RC**	
	(Ultimate Rookie 2000)	8.00
107	Juan Pierre 3,500 **RC**	
	(Ultimate Rookie 2000)	8.00
108	Aaron McNeal 3,500 **RC**	
	(Ultimate Rookie 2000)	4.00
109	Jay Spurgeon 3,500 **RC**	
	(Ultimate Rookie 2000)	4.00
110	Sean Burnett 1,000 **RC**	
	(Ultimate Rookie 2000)	8.00
111	Luis Matos 3,500 **RC**	
	(Ultimate Rookie 2000)	8.00
112	Dave Krynzel 1,000 **RC**	
	(Ultimate Rookie 2000)	6.00
113	Scott Heard 1,000 **RC**	
	(Ultimate Rookie 2000)	4.00
114	Ben Sheets 2,500 **RC**	
	(Ultimate Rookie 2000)	15.00
115	Dane Sardinha 1,000 **RC**	
	(Ultimate Rookie 2000)	4.00
116	David Espinosa 1,000 **RC**	
	(Ultimate Rookie 2000)	4.00

117	Leo Estrella 3,500 **RC**	
	(Ultimate Rookie 2000)	4.00
118	Kurt Ainsworth 2,500 **RC**	
	(Ultimate Rookie 2000)	4.00
119	Jon Rauch 2,500 **RC**	
	(Ultimate Rookie 2000)	4.00
120	Ryan Franklin 2,500	
	(Ultimate Rookie 2000)	4.00

Collection

Parallel 25 Stars:	20-40X
Rookies (91-120):	2-4X
Production 25 Sets	
Parallel 100 Stars:	4-8X
Rookies (91-120):	1-2X
Production 100 Sets	
Parallel 250 Stars:	2-4X
Rookies (91-120):	1-2X
Production 250 Sets	

Diamond Dignitaries

NM/M

Complete Set (10):		20.00
Common Player:		1.00
Inserted 1:23		
1	Ken Griffey Jr.	2.00
2	Nomar Garciaparra	3.00
3	Chipper Jones	2.00
4	Ivan Rodriguez	1.00
5	Mark McGwire	3.00
6	Cal Ripken Jr.	4.00
7	Vladimir Guerrero	1.00
8	Alex Rodriguez	3.00
9	Sammy Sosa	2.50
10	Derek Jeter	3.00

HOF Game Jersey

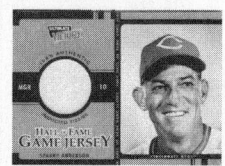

NM/M

Common Card:		8.00
SA	Sparky Anderson	8.00
CF	Carlton Fisk	10.00
TP	Tony Perez	8.00

HOF Game Jersey Combo

NM/M

UV-C	Sparky Anderson, Carlton Fisk, Tony Perez	40.00

Lasting Impressions

NM/M

Complete Set (10):		15.00
Common Player:		1.00
Inserted 1:11		
1	Barry Bonds	3.00
2	Mike Piazza	2.00
3	Manny Ramirez	1.00
4	Pedro J. Martinez	1.50
5	Mark McGwire	2.00
6	Ken Griffey Jr.	2.00
7	Ivan Rodriguez	1.00
8	Jeff Bagwell	1.00
9	Randy Johnson	1.50
10	Alex Rodriguez	3.00

Starstruck

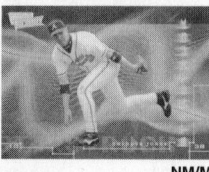

NM/M

Complete Set (10):		20.00
Common Player:		1.00
Inserted 1:11		
1	Alex Rodriguez	3.00
2	Frank Thomas	1.00
3	Derek Jeter	3.00
4	Mark McGwire	3.00
5	Nomar Garciaparra	3.00
6	Chipper Jones	2.00
7	Cal Ripken Jr.	4.00
8	Sammy Sosa	2.00
9	Vladimir Guerrero	1.00
10	Ken Griffey Jr.	2.00

2000 Upper Deck Victory

NM/M

Complete Set (440):		20.00
Complete Factory Set (466):		25.00
Common Player:		.10
Common Griffey (391-440):		.50
Common USA (441-466):		.40
Pack (12):		1.00
Wax Box (36):		25.00
1	Mo Vaughn	.15
2	Garret Anderson	.20
3	Tim Salmon	.20
4	Troy Percival	.10
5	Orlando Palmeiro	.10
6	Darin Erstad	.20
7	Ramon Ortiz	.10
8	Ben Molina	.10
9	Troy Glaus	.40
10	Jim Edmonds	.20
11	Mo Vaughn, Troy Percival	.15
12	Craig Biggio	.25
13	Roger Cedeno	.10
14	Shane Reynolds	.10
15	Jeff Bagwell	.50
16	Octavio Dotel	.10
17	Moises Alou	.20
18	Jose Lima	.10
19	Ken Caminiti	.15
20	Richard Hidalgo	.10
21	Billy Wagner	.10
22	Lance Berkman	.20
23	Jeff Bagwell, Jose Lima	.25
24	Jason Giambi	.50
25	Randy Velarde	.10
26	Miguel Tejada	.25
27	Matt Stairs	.10
28	A.J. Hinch	.10
29	Olmedo Saenz	.10
30	Ben Grieve	.20
31	Ryan Christenson	.10
32	Eric Chavez	.20
33	Tim Hudson	.20
34	John Jaha	.10
35	Jason Giambi, Matt Stairs	.25
36	Raul Mondesi	.20
37	Tony Batista	.10
38	David Wells	.10
39	Homer Bush	.10
40	Carlos Delgado	.40
41	Billy Koch	.10
42	Darrin Fletcher	.10
43	Tony Fernandez	.10
44	Shannon Stewart	.10
45	Roy Halladay	.20
46	Chris Carpenter	.10
47	Carlos Delgado, David Wells	.20
48	Chipper Jones	1.00
49	Greg Maddux	1.00
50	Andruw Jones	.40
51	Andres Galarraga	.20
52	Tom Glavine	.20

53	Brian Jordan	.10
54	John Smoltz	.15
55	John Rocker	.10
56	Javy Lopez	.15
57	Eddie Perez	.10
58	Kevin Millwood	.20
59	Chipper Jones, Greg Maddux	.50
60	Jeromy Burnitz	.10
61	Steve Woodard	.10
62	Ron Belliard	.10
63	Geoff Jenkins	.20
64	Bob Wickman	.10
65	Marquis Grissom	.10
66	Henry Blanco	.10
67	Mark Loretta	.10
68	Alex Ochoa	.10
69	Marquis Grissom, Jeromy Burnitz	.10
70	Mark McGwire	1.50
71	Edgar Renteria	.10
72	Dave Veres	.10
73	Eli Marrero	.10
74	Fernando Tatis	.10
75	J.D. Drew	.20
76	Ray Lankford	.10
77	Daryle Kile	.10
78	Kent Bottenfield	.10
79	Joe McEwing	.10
80	Mark McGwire, Ray Lankford	.75
81	Sammy Sosa	1.25
82	Jose Nieves	.10
83	Jon Lieber	.10
84	Henry Rodriguez	.10
85	Mark Grace	.20
86	Eric Young	.10
87	Kerry Wood	.25
88	Ismael Valdes	.10
89	Glenallen Hill	.10
90	Sammy Sosa, Mark Grace	.60
91	Greg Vaughn	.10
92	Fred McGriff	.20
93	Ryan Rupe	.10
94	Bubba Trammell	.10
95	Miguel Cairo	.10
96	Roberto Hernandez	.10
97	Jose Canseco	.40
98	Wilson Alvarez	.10
99	John Flaherty	.10
100	Vinny Castilla	.15
101	Jose Canseco, Roberto Hernandez	.25
102	Randy Johnson	.50
103	Matt Williams	.15
104	Matt Mantei	.10
105	Steve Finley	.10
106	Luis Gonzalez	.20
107	Travis Lee	.10
108	Omar Daal	.10
109	Jay Bell	.10
110	Erubiel Durazo	.10
111	Tony Womack	.10
112	Todd Stottlemyre	.10
113	Randy Johnson, Matt Williams	.25
114	Gary Sheffield	.25
115	Adrian Beltre	.10
116	Kevin Brown	.20
117	Todd Hundley	.10
118	Eric Karros	.10
119	Shawn Green	.40
120	Chan Ho Park	.10
121	Mark Grudzielanek	.10
122	Todd Hollandsworth	.10
123	Jeff Shaw	.10
124	Darren Dreifort	.10
125	Gary Sheffield, Kevin Brown	.15
126	Vladimir Guerrero	.50
127	Michael Barrett	.10
128	Dustin Hermanson	.10
129	Jose Vidro	.10
130	Chris Widger	.10
131	Mike Thurman	.10
132	Wilton Guerrero	.10
133	Brad Fullmer	.10
134	Rondell White	.20
135	Ugueth Urbina	.10
136	Vladimir Guerrero, Rondell White	.40
137	Barry Bonds	1.50
138	Russ Ortiz	.10
139	J.T. Snow	.10
140	Joe Nathan	.10
141	Rich Aurilia	.10
142	Jeff Kent	.20
143	Armando Rios	.10
144	Ellis Burks	.10
145	Robb Nen	.10
146	Marvin Benard	.10
147	Barry Bonds, Russ Ortiz	.75
148	Manny Ramirez	.50
149	Bartolo Colon	.10
150	Kenny Lofton	.20
151	Sandy Alomar Jr.	.10
152	Travis Fryman	.15
153	Omar Vizquel	.10
154	Roberto Alomar	.40
155	Richie Sexson	.25
156	David Justice	.20
157	Jim Thome	.50
158	Manny Ramirez, Roberto Alomar	.25
159	Ken Griffey Jr.	1.00
160	Edgar Martinez	.15
161	Fred Garcia	.10
162	Alex Rodriguez	1.50

163 John Halama .10
164 Russ Davis .10
165 David Bell .10
166 Gil Meche .10
167 Jamie Moyer .10
168 John Olerud .20
169 Ken Griffey Jr., Fred Garcia .50
170 Preston Wilson .20
171 Antonio Alfonseca .10
172 A.J. Burnett .10
173 Luis Castillo .10
174 Mike Lowell .10
175 Alex Fernandez .10
176 Mike Redmond .10
177 Alex Gonzalez .10
178 Vladimir Nunez .10
179 Mark Kotsay .10
180 Preston Wilson, Luis Castillo .10
181 Mike Piazza 1.00
182 Darryl Hamilton .10
183 Al Leiter .20
184 Robin Ventura .20
185 Rickey Henderson .20
186 Rey Ordonez .10
187 Edgardo Alfonzo .10
188 Derek Bell .10
189 Mike Hampton .10
190 Armando Benitez .10
191 Mike Piazza, Rickey Henderson .50
192 Cal Ripken Jr. 1.50
193 B.J. Surhoff .10
194 Mike Mussina .40
195 Albert Belle .15
196 Jerry Hairston Jr. .10
197 Will Clark .20
198 Sidney Ponson .10
199 Brady Anderson .10
200 Scott Erickson .10
201 Ryan Minor .10
202 Cal Ripken Jr., Albert Belle .75
203 Tony Gwynn .75
204 Bret Boone .20
205 Ryan Klesko .10
206 Ben Davis .10
207 Matt Clement .10
208 Eric Owens .10
209 Trevor Hoffman .10
210 Sterling Hitchcock .10
211 Phil Nevin .10
212 Tony Gwynn, Trevor Hoffman .40
213 Scott Rolen .50
214 Bob Abreu .20
215 Curt Schilling .25
216 Rico Brogna .10
217 Robert Person .10
218 Doug Glanville .10
219 Mike Lieberthal .10
220 Andy Ashby .10
221 Randy Wolf .10
222 Bob Abreu, Curt Schilling .20
223 Brian Giles .20
224 Jason Kendall .20
225 Kris Benson .10
226 Warren Morris .10
227 Kevin Young .10
228 Al Martin .10
229 Wil Cordero .10
230 Bruce Aven .10
231 Todd Ritchie .10
232 Jason Kendall, Brian Giles .10
233 Ivan Rodriguez .50
234 Rusty Greer .10
235 Ruben Mateo .10
236 Justin Thompson .10
237 Rafael Palmeiro .25
238 Chad Curtis .10
239 Royce Clayton .10
240 Gabe Kapler .10
241 Jeff Zimmerman .10
242 John Wetteland .10
243 Ivan Rodriguez, Rafael Palmeiro .25
244 Nomar Garciaparra 1.25
245 Pedro Martinez .75
246 Jose Offerman .10
247 Jason Varitek .10
248 Troy O'Leary .10
249 John Valentin .10
250 Trot Nixon .10
251 Carl Everett .10
252 Wilton Veras .10
253 Bret Saberhagen .10
254 Nomar Garciaparra, Pedro J. Martinez .60
255 Sean Casey .10
256 Barry Larkin .25
257 Pokey Reese .10
258 Pete Harnisch .10
259 Aaron Boone .20
260 Dante Bichette .10
261 Scott Williamson .10
262 Steve Parris .10
263 Dmitri Young .10
264 Mike Cameron .10
265 Sean Casey, Scott Williamson .10
266 Larry Walker .25
267 Rolando Arrojo .10
268 Pedro Astacio .10
269 Todd Helton .50
270 Jeff Cirillo .10
271 Neifi Perez .10
272 Brian Bohanon .10
273 Jeffrey Hammonds .10
274 Tom Goodwin .10
275 Larry Walker, Todd Helton .25
276 Carlos Beltran .15
277 Jermaine Dye .10
278 Mike Sweeney .10
279 Joe Randa .10
280 Jose Rosado .10
281 Carlos Febles .10
282 Jeff Suppan .10
283 Johnny Damon .20
284 Jeremy Giambi .10
285 Mike Sweeney, Carlos Beltran .10
286 Tony Clark .10
287 Damion Easley .10
288 Jeff Weaver .10
289 Dean Palmer .10
290 Juan Gonzalez .50
291 Juan Encarnacion .10
292 Todd Jones .10
293 Karim Garcia .10
294 Deivi Cruz .10
295 Dean Palmer, Juan Encarnacion .10
296 Corey Koskie .10
297 Brad Radke .10
298 Doug Mientkiewicz .10
299 Ron Coomer .10
300 Joe Mays .10
301 Eric Milton .10
302 Jacque Jones .10
303 Chad Allen .10
304 Cristian Guzman .10
305 Jason Ryan .10
306 Todd Walker .10
307 Corey Koskie, Eric Milton .10
308 Frank Thomas .50
309 Paul Konerko .10
310 Mike Sirotka .10
311 Jim Parque .10
312 Magglio Ordonez .25
313 Bob Howry .10
314 Carlos Lee .10
315 Ray Durham .10
316 Chris Singleton .10
317 Brook Fordyce .10
318 Frank Thomas, Magglio Ordonez .25
319 Derek Jeter 1.50
320 Roger Clemens 1.00
321 Paul O'Neill .20
322 Bernie Williams .40
323 Mariano Rivera .20
324 Tino Martinez .20
325 David Cone .20
326 Chuck Knoblauch .10
327 Darryl Strawberry .20
328 Orlando Hernandez .10
329 Ricky Ledee .10
330 Derek Jeter, Bernie Williams .75
331 Pat Burrell (Rookie 2000) .50
332 Alfonso Soriano (Rookie 2000) .75
333 Josh Beckett (Rookie 2000) .25
334 Matt Riley (Rookie 2000) .15
335 Brian Cooper (Rookie 2000) .10
336 Eric Munson (Rookie 2000) .20
337 Vernon Wells (Rookie 2000) .25
338 Juan Pena (Rookie 2000) .10
339 Mark DeRosa (Rookie 2000) .10
340 Kip Wells (Rookie 2000) .10
341 Roosevelt Brown (Rookie 2000) .10
342 Jason LaRue (Rookie 2000) .10
343 Ben Petrick (Rookie 2000) .10
344 Mark Quinn (Rookie 2000) .10
345 Julio Ramirez (Rookie 2000) .10
346 Rod Barajas (Rookie 2000) .10
347 Robert Fick (Rookie 2000) .10
348 David Newhan (Rookie 2000) .10
349 Eric Gagne (Rookie 2000) .15
350 Jorge Toca (Rookie 2000) .10
351 Mitch Meluskey (Rookie 2000) .10
352 Ed Yarnall (Rookie 2000) .10
353 Chad Hermansen (Rookie 2000) .10
354 Peter Bergeron (Rookie 2000) .10
355 Dermal Brown (Rookie 2000) .10
356 Adam Kennedy (Rookie 2000) .10
357 Kevin Barker (Rookie 2000) .10
358 Francisco Cordero (Rookie 2000) .10
359 Travis Dawkins (Rookie 2000) .10
360 Jeff Williams (Rookie 2000) .10
361 Chad Hutchinson (Rookie 2000) .10
362 D'Angelo Jimenez (Rookie 2000) .10
363 Derrick Gibson (Rookie 2000) .10
364 Calvin Murray (Rookie 2000) .10
365 Doug Davis (Rookie 2000) .10
366 Rob Ramsay **RC** (Rookie 2000) .20
367 Mark Redman (Rookie 2000) .10
368 Rick Ankiel (Rookie 2000) .10
369 Domingo Guzman (Rookie 2000) .10
370 Eugene Kingsale (Rookie 2000) .10
371 Nomar Garciaparra (Big Play Makers) .75
372 Ken Griffey Jr. (Big Play Makers) .50
373 Randy Johnson (Big Play Makers) .25
374 Jeff Bagwell (Big Play Makers) .25
375 Ivan Rodriguez (Big Play Makers) .25
376 Derek Jeter (Big Play Makers) .75
377 Carlos Beltran (Big Play Makers) .10
378 Vladimir Guerrero (Big Play Makers) .40
379 Sammy Sosa (Big Play Makers) .60
380 Barry Bonds (Big Play Makers) .75
381 Pedro Martinez (Big Play Makers) .40
382 Chipper Jones (Big Play Makers) .50
383 Mo Vaughn (Big Play Makers) .10
384 Mike Piazza (Big Play Makers) .50
385 Alex Rodriguez (Big Play Makers) .75
386 Manny Ramirez (Big Play Makers) .25
387 Mark McGwire (Big Play Makers) .75
388 Tony Gwynn (Big Play Makers) .40
389 Sean Casey (Big Play Makers) .10
390 Cal Ripken Jr. (Big Play Makers) .75
391-440 Ken Griffey Jr. .40
441 Tommy Lasorda .50
442 Sean Burroughs .75
443 Rick Krivda .40
444 Ben Sheets **RC** 1.50
445 Pat Borders .40
446 Brent Abernathy **RC** .75
447 Tim Young .40
448 Adam Everett .50
449 Anthony Sanders .40
450 Ernie Young .40
451 Brad Wilkerson **RC** 1.50
452 Kurt Ainsworth 1.00
453 Ryan Franklin .40
454 Todd Williams .40
455 Jon Rauch **RC** .50
456 Roy Oswalt **RC** 5.00
457 Shane Heams .50
458 Chris George .50
459 Bobby Seay .40
460 Mike Kinkade .40
461 Marcus Jensen .40
462 Travis Dawkins .50
463 Doug Mientkiewicz .40
464 John Cotton .40
465 Mike Neill .40
466 Team Photo USA 2.50

2000 Upper Deck Yankees Legends

NM/M

Complete Set (90): 20.00
Common Player: .15
Pack (5): 6.00
Box (24): 100.00

1 Babe Ruth 2.00
2 Mickey Mantle 2.00
3 Lou Gehrig 2.00
4 Joe DiMaggio 2.00
5 Yogi Berra .75
6 Don Mattingly 1.00
7 Reggie Jackson .75
8 Dave Winfield .40
9 Bill Skowron .15
10 Willie Randolph .15
11 Phil Rizzuto .50
12 Tony Kubek .15
13 Thurman Munson 1.00
14 Roger Maris 1.00
15 Billy Martin .40
16 Elston Howard .15
17 Graig Nettles .15
18 Whitey Ford .50
19 Earl Combes .15
20 Tony Lazzeri .15
21 Bob Meusel .15
22 Joe Gordon .15
23 Jerry Coleman .15
24 Joe Torre .50
25 Bucky Dent .15
26 Don Larsen .40
27 Bobby Richardson .15
28 Ron Guidry .15
29 Bobby Murcer .15
30 Tommy Henrich .15
31 Hank Bauer .15
32 Joe Pepitone .15
33 Clete Boyer .15
34 Chris Chambliss .15
35 Tommy John .15
36 Goose Gossage .15
37 Red Ruffing .15
38 Charlie Keller .15
39 Billy Gardner .15
40 Hector Lopez .15
41 Cliff Johnson .15
42 Oscar Gamble .15
43 Allie Reynolds .15
44 Mickey Rivers .15
45 Bill Dickey .40
46 Dave Righetti .15
47 Mel Stottlemyre .15
48 Waite Hoyt .15
49 Lefty Gomez .15
50 Wade Boggs .50
51 Billy Martin (Magic Numbers) .25
52 Babe Ruth (Magic Numbers) 1.00
53 Lou Gehrig (Magic Numbers) 1.00
54 Joe DiMaggio (Magic Numbers) 1.00
55 Mickey Mantle (Magic Numbers) 1.00
56 Yogi Berra (Magic Numbers) .40
57 Bill Dickey (Magic Numbers) .25
58 Roger Maris (Magic Numbers) .50
59 Phil Rizzuto (Magic Numbers) .25
60 Thurman Munson (Magic Numbers) .50
61 Whitey Ford (Magic Numbers) .25
62 Don Mattingly (Magic Numbers) .50
63 Elston Howard (Magic Numbers) .15
64 Casey Stengel (Magic Numbers) .15
65 Reggie Jackson (Magic Numbers) .50
66 Babe Ruth/1923) (The Championship Years) 1.00
67 Lou Gehrig/1927 (The Championship Years) 1.00
68 Tony Lazzeri/1928 (The Championship Years) .15
69 Babe Ruth/1932 (The Championship Years) 1.00
70 Lou Gehrig/1936 (The Championship Years) 1.00
71 Lefty Gomez/1937 (The Championship Years) .15
72 Bill Dickey/1938 (The Championship Years) .25
73 Tommy Henrich/1939 (The Championship Years) .15
74 Joe DiMaggio/1941 (The Championship Years) 1.00
75 Spud Chandler/1943 (The Championship Years) .15
76 Tommy Henrich/1947 (The Championship Years) .15
77 Phil Rizzuto/1949 (The Championship Years) .25
78 Whitey Ford/1950 (The Championship Years) .25
79 Yogi Berra/1951 (The Championship Years) .40
80 Casey Stengel/1952 (The Championship Years) .15
81 Billy Martin/1953 (The Championship Years) .25
82 Don Larsen/1956 (The Championship Years) .25
83 Elston Howard/1958 (The Championship Years) .15
84 Roger Maris/1961 (The Championship Years) .50
85 Mickey Mantle/1962 (The Championship Years) 1.00
86 Reggie Jackson/1977 (The Championship Years) .50
87 Bucky Dent/1978 (The Championship Years) .15
88 Wade Boggs/1996 (The Championship Years) .25
89 Joe Torre/1998 (The Championship Years) .25
90 Joe Torre/1999 (The Championship Years) .25

DiMaggio Memorabilia

		NM/M
YLB-JD	Joe DiMaggio/Bat	125.00
YLG-JD	Joe DiMaggio/ Gold Bat/56	200.00
YLC-JD	Joe DiMaggio/ Bat, Cut Sig./5	650.00

Legendary Pinstripes

		NM/M
Common Player:		20.00
Inserted 1:144		
BD	Bucky Dent	20.00
WF	Whitey Ford	50.00
LG	Lou Gehrig	300.00
GG	Goose Gossage	20.00
RG	Ron Guidry	20.00
TH	Tommy Henrich	20.00
EH	Elston Howard	20.00
RJ	Reggie Jackson	40.00
HL	Hector Lopez	20.00
MM	Mickey Mantle	250.00
RM	Roger Maris	75.00
BM	Billy Martin	40.00
DM	Don Mattingly	60.00
TM	Thurman Munson	75.00
JP	Joe Pepitone	20.00
AR	Allie Reynolds	20.00
BR	Bobby Richardson	20.00
PR	Phil Rizzuto	40.00
DW	Dave Winfield	40.00

Auto. Legend. Pinstripe

		NM/M
Common Player:		30.00
BD	Bucky Dent	30.00
WF	Whitey Ford	60.00
GG	Goose Gossage	30.00
RG	Ron Guidry	35.00
TH	Tommy Henrich	30.00
GM	Gil MacDougald	30.00
DM	Don Mattingly	150.00
JP	Joe Pepitone	30.00
PR	Phil Rizzuto	60.00
DW	Dave Winfield	35.00

Legendary Lumber

		NM/M
Common Player:		5.00
Inserted 1:23		
HB	Hank Bauer	8.00
YB	Yogi Berra	20.00
PB	Paul Blair	5.00
CB	Clete Boyer	5.00
CC	Chris Chambliss	8.00

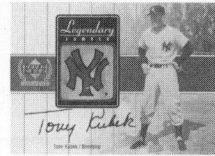

JC	Joe Collins	5.00
BD	Bucky Dent	8.00
JD	Joe DiMaggio	140.00
OG	Oscar Gamble	5.00
BG	Billy Gardner	5.00
TH	Tommy Henrich	5.00
RH	Ralph Houk	8.00
EH	Elston Howard	8.00
RJ	Reggie Jackson	20.00
TJ	Tommy John	8.00
CJ	Cliff Johnson	5.00
CK	Charlie Keller	5.00
TK	Tony Kubek	8.00
HL	Hector Lopez	5.00
MM	Mickey Mantle	165.00
BM	Roger Maris	70.00
DM	Don Mattingly	45.00
TM	Thurman Munson	35.00
BM	Bobby Murcer	8.00
GN	Graig Nettles	10.00
JP	Joe Pepitone	6.00
WR	Willie Randolph	6.00
MR	Mickey Rivers	5.00
BR	Babe Ruth	185.00
MS	Moose Skowron	6.00
DW	Dave Winfield	15.00

Leg. Lumber/Sign. Cut

		NM/M
MM-LC	Mickey Mantle/7	4,000

Monument Park

		NM/M
Complete Set (6):		20.00
Common Player:		1.50
Inserted 1:23		3.00
1	Lou Gehrig	6.00
2	Babe Ruth	6.00
3	Mickey Mantle	6.00
4	Joe DiMaggio	6.00
5	Thurman Munson	3.00
6	Elston Howard	1.50

Murderer's Row

		NM/M
Complete Set (10):		17.50
Common Player:		1.50
Inserted 1:11		
1	Tony Lazzeri	1.50
2	Babe Ruth	6.00
3	Bob Meusel	1.50
4	Lou Gehrig	6.00
5	Joe Dugan	1.50
6	Bill Dickey	1.50
7	Waite Hoyt	1.50
8	Red Ruffing	1.50
9	Earl Combes	1.50
10	Lefty Gomez	1.50

Pride of the Pinstripes

		NM/M
Complete Set (6):		17.50
Common Player:		2.50
Inserted 1:23		
1	Babe Ruth	6.00
2	Mickey Mantle	6.00
3	Joe DiMaggio	5.00
4	Lou Gehrig	5.00
5	Reggie Jackson	2.50
6	Yogi Berra	2.50

The Golden Years

		NM/M
Complete Set (10):		20.00
Common Player:		1.50
Inserted 1:11		
1	Joe DiMaggio	6.00
2	Phil Rizzuto	2.50
3	Yogi Berra	3.00
4	Billy Martin	2.50
5	Whitey Ford	2.50
6	Roger Maris	5.00
7	Mickey Mantle	7.50
8	Elston Howard	1.50
9	Tommy Henrich	1.50
10	Joe Gordon	1.50

The New Dynasty

		NM/M
Complete Set (10):		15.00
Common Player:		1.50
Inserted 1:11		
1	Reggie Jackson	3.50
2	Graig Nettles	1.50
3	Don Mattingly	6.50
4	Goose Gossage	1.50
5	Dave Winfield	3.00
6	Chris Chambliss	1.50
7	Thurman Munson	4.00
8	Willie Randolph	1.50
9	Ron Guidry	2.50
10	Bucky Dent	2.50

2000 UD Ionix

		NM/M
Complete Set (90):		50.00
Common Player:		.15
Common Futuristic:		1.00
Inserted 1:4		
Reciprocal (1-60):		1.5-2X
Reciprocal (61-90):		1-1.5X
Inserted 1:4		
Future Recip. 1:11		
Pack (4):		2.00
Wax Box (24):		35.00
1	Mo Vaughn	.20
2	Troy Glaus	.75
3	Jeff Bagwell	.75
4	Craig Biggio	.40

5	Jose Lima	.15
6	Jason Giambi	1.00
7	Tim Hudson	.40
8	Shawn Green	.50
9	Carlos Delgado	.75
10	Chipper Jones	1.50
11	Andruw Jones	.75
12	Greg Maddux	1.50
13	Jeromy Burnitz	.15
14	Mark McGwire	2.00
15	J.D. Drew	.25
16	Sammy Sosa	2.00
17	Jose Canseco	.50
18	Fred McGriff	.40
19	Randy Johnson	.75
20	Matt Williams	.25
21	Kevin Brown	.40
22	Gary Sheffield	.40
23	Vladimir Guerrero	.75
24	Barry Bonds	2.50
25	Jim Thome	.75
26	Manny Ramirez	.75
27	Roberto Alomar	.50
28	Kenny Lofton	.25
29	Ken Griffey Jr.	1.50
30	Alex Rodriguez	2.50
31	Alex Gonzalez	.15
32	Preston Wilson	.15
33	Mike Piazza	1.50
34	Robin Ventura	.25
35	Cal Ripken Jr.	2.50
36	Albert Belle	.20
37	Tony Gwynn	1.00
38	Scott Rolen	.75
39	Curt Schilling	.50
40	Brian Giles	.25
41	Juan Gonzalez	.75
42	Ivan Rodriguez	.75
43	Rafael Palmeiro	.60
44	Pedro J. Martinez	1.00
45	Nomar Garciaparra	2.00
46	Sean Casey	.25
47	Aaron Boone	.25
48	Barry Larkin	.40
49	Larry Walker	.25
50	Vinny Castilla	.20
51	Carlos Beltran	.25
52	Gabe Kapler	.15
53	Dean Palmer	.15
54	Eric Milton	.15
55	Corey Koskie	.15
56	Frank Thomas	.75
57	Magglio Ordonez	.40
58	Roger Clemens	2.00
59	Bernie Williams	.75
60	Derek Jeter	2.50
61	Josh Beckett (Futuristics)	1.50
62	Eric Munson (Futuristics)	1.00
63	Rick Ankiel (Futuristics)	1.00
64	Matt Riley (Futuristics)	1.00
65	Robert Ramsay (Futuristics)	1.00
66	Vernon Wells (Futuristics)	2.00
67	Eric Gagne (Futuristics)	1.50
68	Robert Fick (Futuristics)	1.50
69	Mark Quinn (Futuristics)	1.00
70	Kip Wells (Futuristics)	1.00
71	Peter Bergeron (Futuristics)	1.00
72	Ed Yarnall (Futuristics)	1.00
73	Jorge Luis Toca (Futuristics)	1.00
74	Alfonso Soriano (Futuristics)	4.00
75	Calvin Murray (Futuristics)	1.00
76	Ramon Ortiz (Futuristics)	1.50
77	Chad Meyers (Futuristics)	1.00
78	Jason LaRue (Futuristics)	1.00
79	Pat Burrell (Futuristics)	2.00
80	Chad Hermansen (Futuristics)	1.00
81	Lance Berkman (Futuristics)	1.50
82	Erubiel Durazo (Futuristics)	1.50
83	Juan Pena (Futuristics)	1.00
84	Adam Kennedy (Futuristics)	1.00
85	Ben Petrick (Futuristics)	1.00
86	Kevin Barker (Futuristics)	1.00
87	Bruce Chen (Futuristics)	1.00
88	Jerry Hairston Jr. (Futuristics)	1.00
89	A.J. Burnett (Futuristics)	1.00
90	Gary Matthews Jr. (Futuristics)	1.00

Atomic

		NM/M
Complete Set (15):		25.00
Common Player:		1.00
Inserted 1:8		
1	Pedro J. Martinez	1.50
2	Mark McGwire	3.00
3	Ken Griffey Jr.	2.00
4	Jeff Bagwell	1.00
5	Greg Maddux	2.00
6	Derek Jeter	3.00
7	Cal Ripken Jr.	4.00
8	Manny Ramirez	1.00
9	Randy Johnson	1.50
10	Nomar Garciaparra	3.00
11	Tony Gwynn	1.50
12	Bernie Williams	1.00
13	Mike Piazza	2.00
14	Roger Clemens	3.00
15	Alex Rodriguez	3.00

Awesome Powers

		NM/M
Complete Set (15):		50.00
Common Player:		1.00
Inserted 1:23		
1	Ken Griffey Jr.	4.00
2	Mike Piazza	4.00
3	Carlos Delgado	2.00
4	Mark McGwire	6.00
5	Chipper Jones	4.00
6	Scott Rolen	2.00
7	Cal Ripken Jr.	8.00
8	Alex Rodriguez	6.00
9	Larry Walker	1.00
10	Sammy Sosa	5.00
11	Barry Bonds	6.00
12	Nomar Garciaparra	6.00
13	Jose Canseco	1.50
14	Manny Ramirez	2.00
15	Jeff Bagwell	2.00

BIOrhythm

		NM/M
Complete Set (15):		25.00
Common Player:		.50
Inserted 1:11		
1	Randy Johnson	1.50
2	Derek Jeter	3.00
3	Sammy Sosa	2.50
4	Jose Lima	.50
5	Chipper Jones	2.00
6	Barry Bonds	4.00
7	Ken Griffey Jr.	2.00

8	Nomar Garciaparra	3.00
9	Frank Thomas	1.00
10	Pedro Martinez	1.50
11	Larry Walker	.50
12	Greg Maddux	2.00
13	Alex Rodriguez	3.00
14	Mark McGwire	3.00
15	Cal Ripken Jr.	4.00

Pyrotechnics

		NM/M
Complete Set (15):		125.00
Common Player:		5.00
Inserted 1:72		
1	Roger Clemens	12.00
2	Chipper Jones	10.00
3	Alex Rodriguez	15.00
4	Jeff Bagwell	5.00
5	Mark McGwire	15.00
6	Pedro Martinez	6.00
7	Manny Ramirez	5.00
8	Cal Ripken Jr.	20.00
9	Mike Piazza	10.00
10	Derek Jeter	15.00
11	Ken Griffey Jr.	10.00
12	Frank Thomas	5.00
13	Sammy Sosa	12.00
14	Nomar Garciaparra	15.00
15	Greg Maddux	10.00

Shockwave

		NM/M
Complete Set (15):		15.00
Common Player:		.50
Inserted 1:4		
1	Mark McGwire	2.00
2	Sammy Sosa	2.00
3	Manny Ramirez	1.00
4	Ken Griffey Jr.	1.50
5	Vladimir Guerrero	1.00
6	Barry Bonds	2.50
7	Albert Belle	.50
8	Ivan Rodriguez	1.00
9	Chipper Jones	1.50
10	Mo Vaughn	.50
11	Jose Canseco	.75
12	Jeff Bagwell	1.00
13	Matt Williams	.50
14	Alex Rodriguez	2.50
15	Carlos Delgado	.75

UD Authentics

		NM/M
Common Player:		10.00
Inserted 1:144		

CBE	Carlos Beltran	30.00
AB	Adrian Beltre	15.00
PB	Pat Burrell	15.00
JC	Jose Canseco	25.00
SC	Sean Casey	15.00
BD	Ben Davis	10.00
SG	Shawn Green	20.00
JR	Ken Griffey Jr.	100.00
VG	Vladimir Guerrero	30.00
DJ	Derek Jeter	100.00
GK	Gabe Kapler	10.00
PM	Pedro Martinez	
RM	Ruben Mateo	10.00
RB	Joe McEwing	10.00
MR	Manny Ramirez	35.00
SR	Scott Rolen	30.00
MW	Matt Williams	15.00

Warp Zone

		NM/M
Complete Set (15):		250.00
Common Player:		8.00
Inserted 1:288		
1	Cal Ripken Jr.	30.00
2	Barry Bonds	30.00
3	Ken Griffey Jr.	20.00
4	Nomar Garciaparra	25.00
5	Chipper Jones	20.00
6	Ivan Rodriguez	8.00
7	Greg Maddux	20.00
8	Derek Jeter	25.00
9	Mike Piazza	20.00
10	Sammy Sosa	20.00
11	Roger Clemens	20.00
12	Alex Rodriguez	25.00
13	Vladimir Guerrero	10.00
14	Pedro Martinez	10.00
15	Mark McGwire	25.00

3,000 Hit Club

		NM/M
RC1	Roberto Clemente/	
	Bat/350	125.00

2001 Upper Deck

		NM/M
Complete Set (450):		125.00
Complete Series 1 (270):		25.00
Complete Series 2 (180):		100.00
Common Player:		.15
Series 1 Pack (10):		2.00
Series 1 Box (24):		35.00
Series 2 Pack (10):		6.00
Series 2 Box (24):		120.00

1	Jeff DaVanon (Star Rookie)	.25
2	Aubrey Huff (Star Rookie)	.25
3	Pascual Coco (Star Rookie)	.25
4	Barry Zito (Star Rookie)	.75
5	Augie Ojeda (Star Rookie)	.25
6	Chris Richard (Star Rookie)	.25
7	Josh Phelps (Star Rookie)	.25
8	Kevin Nicholson (Star Rookie)	.25
9	Juan Guzman (Star Rookie)	.25
10	Brandon Kolb (Star Rookie)	.25
11	Johan Santana (Star Rookie)	4.00
12	Josh Kalinowski (Star Rookie)	.25
13	Tike Redman (Star Rookie)	.25
14	Ivanon Coffie (Star Rookie)	.25
15	Chad Durbin (Star Rookie)	.25
16	Derrick Turnbow (Star Rookie)	.25
17	Scott Downs (Star Rookie)	.25
18	Jason Grilli (Star Rookie)	.25
19	Mark Buehrle (Star Rookie)	.25
20	Paxton Crawford (Star Rookie)	.25
21	Bronson Arroyo (Star Rookie)	.25
22	Tomas de la Rosa (Star Rookie)	.25
23	Paul Rigdon (Star Rookie)	.25
24	Rob Ramsay (Star Rookie)	.25
25	Damian Rolls (Star Rookie)	.25
26	Jason Conti (Star Rookie)	.25
27	John Parrish (Star Rookie)	.25
28	Geraldo Guzman (Star Rookie)	.25
29	Tony Mota (Star Rookie)	.25
30	Luis Rivas (Star Rookie)	.25
31	Brian Tollberg (Star Rookie)	.25
32	Adam Bernero (Star Rookie)	.25
33	Michael Cuddyer (Star Rookie)	.25
34	Josue Espada (Star Rookie)	.25
35	Joe Lawrence (Star Rookie)	.25
36	Chad Moeller (Star Rookie)	.25
37	Nick Bierbrodt (Star Rookie)	.25
38	Dewayne Wise (Star Rookie)	.25
39	Javier Cardona (Star Rookie)	.25
40	Hiram Bocachica (Star Rookie)	.25
41	Giuseppe Chiaramonte (Star Rookie)	.25
42	Alex Cabrera (Star Rookie)	.25
43	Jimmy Rollins (Star Rookie)	1.00
44	Pat Flury RC (Star Rookie)	.25
45	Leo Estrella (Star Rookie)	.25
46	Darin Erstad	.40
47	Seth Etherton	.15
48	Troy Glaus	.40
49	Brian Cooper	.15
50	Tim Salmon	.25
51	Adam Kennedy	.15
52	Bengie Molina	.15
53	Jason Giambi	.50
54	Miguel Tejada	.40
55	Tim Hudson	.25
56	Eric Chavez	.25
57	Terrence Long	.15
58	Jason Isringhausen	.15
59	Ramon Hernandez	.15
60	Raul Mondesi	.25
61	David Wells	.15
62	Shannon Stewart	.15
63	Tony Batista	.15
64	Brad Fullmer	.15
65	Chris Carpenter	.15
66	Homer Bush	.15
67	Gerald Williams	.15
68	Miguel Cairo	.15
69	Ryan Rupe	.15
70	Greg Vaughn	.15
71	John Flaherty	.15
72	Dan Wheeler	.15
73	Fred McGriff	.25
74	Roberto Alomar	.40
75	Bartolo Colon	.25
76	Kenny Lofton	.25
77	David Segui	.15
78	Omar Vizquel	.25
79	Russ Branyan	.15
80	Chuck Finley	.15
81	Manny Ramirez	.50
82	Alex Rodriguez	1.50
83	John Halama	.15
84	Mike Cameron	.15
85	David Bell	.15
86	Jay Buhner	.15
87	Aaron Sele	.15
88	Rickey Henderson	.40
89	Brook Fordyce	.15
90	Cal Ripken Jr.	2.00
91	Mike Mussina	.40
92	Delino DeShields	.15
93	Melvin Mora	.15
94	Sidney Ponson	.15
95	Brady Anderson	.15
96	Ivan Rodriguez	.50
97	Ricky Ledee	.15
98	Rick Helling	.15
99	Ruben Mateo	.15
100	Luis Alicea	.15
101	John Wetteland	.15
102	Mike Lamb	.15
103	Carl Everett	.15
104	Troy O'Leary	.15
105	Wilton Veras	.15
106	Pedro Martinez	.75
107	Rolando Arrojo	.15
108	Scott Hatteberg	.15

109 Jason Varitek .15
110 Jose Offerman .15
111 Carlos Beltran .50
112 Johnny Damon .50
113 Mark Quinn .15
114 Rey Sanchez .15
115 Mac Suzuki .15
116 Jermaine Dye .15
117 Chris Fussell .15
118 Jeff Weaver .15
119 Dean Palmer .15
120 Robert Fick .15
121 Brian Moehler .15
122 Damion Easley .15
123 Juan Encarnacion .15
124 Tony Clark .15
125 Cristian Guzman .15
126 Matt LeCroy .15
127 Eric Milton .15
128 Jay Canizaro .15
129 David Ortiz .75
130 Brad Radke .15
131 Jacque Jones .15
132 Magglio Ordonez .40
133 Carlos Lee .25
134 Mike Sirotka .15
135 Ray Durham .15
136 Paul Konerko .25
137 Charles Johnson .15
138 James Baldwin .15
139 Jeff Abbott .15
140 Roger Clemens 1.50
141 Derek Jeter 2.00
142 David Justice .25
143 Ramiro Mendoza .15
144 Chuck Knoblauch .15
145 Orlando Hernandez .25
146 Alfonso Soriano .75
147 Jeff Bagwell .50
148 Julio Lugo .15
149 Mitch Meluskey .15
150 Jose Lima .15
151 Richard Hidalgo .15
152 Moises Alou .25
153 Scott Elarton .15
154 Andruw Jones .40
155 Quilvio Veras .15
156 Greg Maddux 1.00
157 Brian Jordan .15
158 Andres Galarraga .20
159 Kevin Millwood .25
160 Rafael Furcal .40
161 Jeromy Burnitz .15
162 Jimmy Haynes .15
163 Mark Loretta .15
164 Ron Belliard .15
165 Richie Sexson .40
166 Kevin Barker .15
167 Jeff D'Amico .15
168 Rick Ankiel .50
169 Mark McGwire 1.50
170 J.D. Drew .25
171 Eli Marrero .15
172 Darryl Kile .15
173 Edgar Renteria .15
174 Will Clark .40
175 Eric Young .15
176 Mark Grace .40
177 Jon Lieber .15
178 Damon Buford .15
179 Kerry Wood .40
180 Rondell White .15
181 Joe Girardi .15
182 Curt Schilling .40
183 Randy Johnson .75
184 Steve Finley .15
185 Kelly Stinnett .15
186 Jay Bell .15
187 Matt Mantei .15
188 Luis Gonzalez .25
189 Shawn Green .25
190 Todd Hundley .15
191 Chan Ho Park .15
192 Adrian Beltre .40
193 Mark Grudzielanek .15
194 Gary Sheffield .40
195 Tom Goodwin .15
196 Lee Stevens .15
197 Javier Vazquez .15
198 Milton Bradley .15
199 Vladimir Guerrero .75
200 Carl Pavano .15
201 Orlando Cabrera .15
202 Tony Armas Jr. .15
203 Jeff Kent .25
204 Calvin Murray .15
205 Ellis Burks .15
206 Barry Bonds 2.00
207 Russ Ortiz .15
208 Marvin Benard .15
209 Joe Nathan .15
210 Preston Wilson .15
211 Cliff Floyd .15
212 Mike Lowell .25
213 Ryan Dempster .15
214 Brad Penny .15
215 Mike Redmond .15
216 Luis Castillo .15
217 Derek Bell .15
218 Mike Hampton .25
219 Todd Zeile .15
220 Robin Ventura .25
221 Mike Piazza 1.00
222 Al Leiter .25
223 Edgardo Alfonzo .15
224 Mike Bordick .15
225 Phil Nevin .15
226 Ryan Klesko .25
227 Adam Eaton .15
228 Eric Owens .15
229 Tony Gwynn .75
230 Matt Clement .15
231 Wiki Gonzalez .15
232 Robert Person .15
233 Doug Glanville .15
234 Scott Rolen .50
235 Mike Lieberthal .15
236 Randy Wolf .15
237 Bobby Abreu .40
238 Pat Burrell .40
239 Bruce Chen .15
240 Kevin Young .15
241 Todd Ritchie .15
242 Adrian Brown .15
243 Chad Hermansen .15
244 Warren Morris .15
245 Kris Benson .15
246 Jason Kendall .25
247 Pokey Reese .15
248 Rob Bell .15
249 Ken Griffey Jr. 1.00
250 Sean Casey .15
251 Aaron Boone .15
252 Pete Harnisch .15
253 Barry Larkin .40
254 Dmitri Young .15
255 Todd Hollandsworth .15
256 Pedro Astacio .15
257 Todd Helton .50
258 Terry Shumpert .15
259 Neifi Perez .15
260 Jeffrey Hammonds .15
261 Ben Petrick .15
262 Mark McGwire .75
263 Derek Jeter 1.00
264 Sammy Sosa .75
265 Cal Ripken Jr. 1.00
266 Pedro J. Martinez .40
267 Barry Bonds 1.00
268 Fred McGriff .20
269 Randy Johnson .40
270 Darin Erstad .25
271 Ichiro Suzuki **RC** (Star Rookie) 10.00
272 Wilson Betemit **RC** (Star Rookie) .50
273 Corey Patterson (Star Rookie) .25
274 Sean Douglass **RC** (Star Rookie) .25
275 Mike Penney **RC** (Star Rookie) .25
276 Nate Teut **RC** (Star Rookie) .25
277 Ricardo Rodriguez **RC** (Star Rookie) .25
278 Brandon Duckworth **RC** (Star Rookie) .50
279 Rafael Soriano **RC** (Star Rookie) .75
280 Juan Diaz **RC** (Star Rookie) .25
281 Horacio Ramirez **RC** (Star Rookie) .50
282 Tsuyoshi Shinjo **RC** (Star Rookie) .50
283 Keith Ginter (Star Rookie) .25
284 Esix Snead **RC** (Star Rookie) .25
285 Erick Almonte **RC** (Star Rookie) .25
286 Travis Hafner **RC** (Star Rookie) 2.00
287 Jason Smith **RC** (Star Rookie) .25
288 Jackson Melian **RC** (Star Rookie) .25
289 Tyler Walker **RC** (Star Rookie) .25
290 Jason Standridge (Star Rookie) .25
291 Juan Uribe **RC** (Star Rookie) .50
292 Adrian Hernandez **RC** (Star Rookie) .25
293 Jason Michaels **RC** (Star Rookie) .25
294 Jason Hart (Star Rookie) .15
295 Albert Pujols **RC** (Star Rookie) 40.00
296 Morgan Ensberg **RC** (Star Rookie) 1.50
297 Brandon Inge (Star Rookie) .25
298 Jesus Colome (Star Rookie) .25
299 Kyle Kessel **RC** (Star Rookie) .25
300 Timo Perez (Star Rookie) .25
301 Mo Vaughn .20
302 Ismael Valdes .15
303 Glenallen Hill .15
304 Garret Anderson .40
305 Johnny Damon .50
306 Jose Ortiz .15
307 Mark Mulder .25
308 Adam Piatt .15
309 Gil Heredia .15
310 Mike Sirotka .15
311 Carlos Delgado .50
312 Alex Gonzalez .15
313 Jose Cruz Jr. .15
314 Darrin Fletcher .15
315 Ben Grieve .15
316 Vinny Castilla .15
317 Wilson Alvarez .15
318 Brent Abernathy .15
319 Ellis Burks .15
320 Jim Thome .75
321 Juan Gonzalez .50
322 Ed Taubensee .15
323 Travis Fryman .15
324 John Olerud .25
325 Edgar Martinez .25
326 Fred Garcia .15
327 Bret Boone .25
328 Kazuhiro Sasaki .15
329 Albert Belle .15
330 Mike Bordick .15
331 David Segui .15
332 Pat Hentgen .15
333 Alex Rodriguez 1.50
334 Andres Galarraga .25
335 Gabe Kapler .15
336 Ken Caminiti .15
337 Rafael Palmeiro .50
338 Manny Ramirez .50
339 David Cone .15
340 Nomar Garciaparra .75
341 Trot Nixon .15
342 Derek Lowe .15
343 Roberto Hernandez .15
344 Mike Sweeney .15
345 Carlos Febles .15
346 Jeff Suppan .15
347 Roger Cedeno .15
348 Bobby Higginson .15
349 Deivi Cruz .15
350 Mitch Meluskey .15
351 Matt Lawton .15
352 Mark Redman .15
353 Jay Canizaro .15
354 Corey Koskie .15
355 Matt Kinney .15
356 Frank Thomas .50
357 Sandy Alomar Jr. .15
358 David Wells .15
359 Jim Parque .15
360 Chris Singleton .15
361 Tino Martinez .25
362 Paul O'Neill .25
363 Mike Mussina .40
364 Bernie Williams .50
365 Andy Pettitte .40
366 Mariano Rivera .40
367 Brad Ausmus .15
368 Craig Biggio .40
369 Lance Berkman .50
370 Shane Reynolds .15
371 Chipper Jones 1.00
372 Tom Glavine .40
373 B.J. Surhoff .15
374 John Smoltz .40
375 Rico Brogna .15
376 Geoff Jenkins .25
377 Jose Hernandez .15
378 Tyler Houston .15
379 Henry Blanco .15
380 Jeffrey Hammonds .15
381 Jim Edmonds .25
382 Fernando Vina .15
383 Andy Benes .15
384 Ray Lankford .15
385 Dustin Hermanson .15
386 Todd Hundley .15
387 Sammy Sosa 1.00
388 Tom Gordon .15
389 Bill Mueller .15
390 Ron Coomer .15
391 Matt Stairs .15
392 Mark Grace .40
393 Matt Williams .25
394 Todd Stottlemyre .15
395 Tony Womack .15
396 Erubiel Durazo .15
397 Reggie Sanders .15
398 Andy Ashby .15
399 Eric Karros .15
400 Kevin Brown .25
401 Darren Dreifort .15
402 Fernando Tatis .15
403 Jose Vidro .15
404 Peter Bergeron .15
405 Geoff Blum .15
406 J.T. Snow .15
407 Livan Hernandez .15
408 Robb Nen .15
409 Bobby Estalella .15
410 Rich Aurilia .15
411 Eric Davis .15
412 Charles Johnson .15
413 Alex Gonzalez .15
414 A.J. Burnett .15
415 Antonio Alfonseca .15
416 Derrek Lee .50
417 Jay Payton .15
418 Kevin Appier .15
419 Steve Trachsel .15
420 Rey Ordonez .15
421 Darryl Hamilton .15
422 Ben Davis .15
423 Damian Jackson .15
424 Mark Kotsay .15
425 Trevor Hoffman .15
426 Travis Lee .15
427 Omar Daal .15
428 Paul Byrd .15
429 Reggie Taylor .15
430 Brian Giles .25
431 Derek Bell .15
432 Francisco Cordova .15
433 Pat Meares .15
434 Scott Williamson .15
435 Jason LaRue .15
436 Michael Tucker .15
437 Wilton Guerrero .15
438 Mike Hampton .15
439 Ron Gant .15
440 Jeff Cirillo .15
441 Denny Neagle .15
442 Larry Walker .40
443 Juan Pierre .15
444 Todd Walker .15
445 Jason Giambi .40
446 Jeff Kent .25
447 Mariano Rivera .40
448 Edgar Martinez .15
449 Troy Glaus .25
450 Alex Rodriguez .75

Exclusives

Silver Stars: 8-15X
Production 100 Sets
Gold Stars: 15-30X
Production 25 Sets

All-Star Heroes Base Cards

NM/M

Quantity produced listed
DJ Derek Jeter/2000 20.00
MP Mike Piazza/1996 10.00

All-Star Heroes Jersey Cards

NM/M

Common Player: 10.00
RC Roger Clemens/1986 20.00
JD Joe DiMaggio/36 300.00
TG Tony Gwynn/1994 10.00
RJ Randy Johnson/1993 10.00
ASH-MM Mickey Mantle/54 400.00
ASH-SS Sammy Sosa - 2000 20.00

All-Star Heroes Bat Cards

NM/M

Common Player: 10.00
RoC Roberto Clemente/1961 75.00
KG Ken Griffey Jr./1992 20.00
TP Tony Perez/1967 10.00
CR Cal Ripken Jr./1991 40.00
AR Alex Rodriguez/1998 20.00
BR Babe Ruth/1933 175.00

All-Star Salute

NM/M

Common Player: 10.00
Inserted 1:288
HA Hank Aaron/Bat 40.00
HA Hank Aaron/Jsy 40.00
LA Luis Aparicio/Jsy 10.00
JB Johnny Bench/Bat 20.00
JB Johnny Bench/Jsy 20.00
LB Lou Brock/Bat 15.00
RC Roberto Clemente/Jsy 100.00
RJ Reggie Jackson/Jsy 20.00
TM Thurman Munson/Jsy 35.00
BR Brooks Robinson/Bat 20.00
FR Frank Robinson/Jsy 15.00
TS Tom Seaver/Jsy 20.00

Big League Beat

NM/M

Complete Set (20): 15.00
Common Player: .50
Inserted 1:3
1 Barry Bonds 2.00
2 Nomar Garciaparra .75
3 Mark McGwire 1.50
4 Roger Clemens 1.25
5 Chipper Jones 1.00
6 Jeff Bagwell .50
7 Sammy Sosa 1.00

8	Cal Ripken Jr.	2.00
9	Randy Johnson	.75
10	Carlos Delgado	.50
11	Manny Ramirez	.50
12	Derek Jeter	2.00
13	Tony Gwynn	.75
14	Pedro J. Martinez	.75
15	Jose Canseco	.50
16	Frank Thomas	.75
17	Alex Rodriguez	1.50
18	Bernie Williams	.50
19	Greg Maddux	1.00
20	Rafael Palmeiro	.50

Big League Challenge Jerseys

		NM/M
Common Player:		5.00
Inserted 1:288		
BB	Barry Bonds	40.00
JC	Jose Canseco	8.00
JE	Jim Edmonds	8.00
TF	Steve Finley	5.00
TG	Troy Glaus	8.00
TH	Todd Helton	10.00
RH	Richard Hidalgo	5.00
RP	Rafael Palmeiro	10.00
MP	Mike Piazza	20.00
GS	Gary Sheffield	8.00
FT	Frank Thomas	10.00

Classic Midsummer Moments

		NM/M
Complete Set (20):		25.00
Common Player:		.50
Inserted 1:12		
CM1	Joe DiMaggio/1936	3.00
CM2	Joe DiMaggio/1951	3.00
CM3	Mickey Mantle/1952	4.00
CM4	Mickey Mantle/1968	4.00
CM5	Roger Clemens/1986	2.50
CM6	Mark McGwire/1987	2.50
CM7	Cal Ripken Jr./1991	3.00
CM8	Ken Griffey Jr./1992	1.50
CM9	Randy Johnson/1993	1.00
CM10	Tony Gwynn/1994	1.00
CM11	Fred McGriff/1994	.75
CM12	Hideo Nomo/1995	.75
CM13	Jeff Conine/1995	.50
CM14	Mike Piazza/1996	1.50
CM15	Sandy Alomar Jr./1997	.50
CM16	Alex Rodriguez/1998	2.50
CM17	Roberto Alomar/1998	.75
CM18	Pedro Martinez/1999	1.50
CM19	Andres Galarraga/2000	.50
CM20	Derek Jeter/2000	2.50

E-Card

		NM/M
Complete Set (6):		10.00
Common Player:		1.00
Inserted 1:24		
1	Andruw Jones	1.00
2	Alex Rodriguez	3.00
3	Frank Thomas	1.50
4	Todd Helton	1.50
5	Troy Glaus	1.00
6	Barry Bonds	4.00

Evolve Jersey

		NM/M
Common Player:		10.00
BB	Barry Bonds	30.00
TG	Troy Glaus	8.00
TH	Todd Helton	10.00
AJ	Andruw Jones	10.00
AR	Alex Rodriguez	25.00
SS	Sammy Sosa	15.00
IS	Ichiro Suzuki	50.00
FT	Frank Thomas	15.00

Evolve Signature

		NM/M
Common Player:		35.00
BB	Barry Bonds	150.00
TG	Troy Glaus	30.00
TH	Todd Helton	30.00
AJ	Andruw Jones	25.00
AR	Alex Rodriguez	100.00
SS	Sammy Sosa	80.00
IS	Ichiro Suzuki	250.00
FT	Frank Thomas	40.00

Jersey Autograph

		NM/M
Common Player:		50.00
BB	Barry Bonds	150.00
TG	Troy Glaus	40.00
TH	Todd Helton	40.00
AJ	Andruw Jones	25.00
AR	Alex Rodriguez	120.00
SS	Sammy Sosa	100.00
IS	Ichiro Suzuki	300.00
FT	Frank Thomas	75.00

Game Jersey

	NM/M
Common Player:	8.00
Inserted 1:288	

KG	Ken Griffey Jr.	30.00
TG	Tony Gwynn	20.00
TH	Todd Helton	12.00
TiH	Tim Hudson	10.00
DJ	Derek Jeter	50.00
AJ	Andruw Jones	8.00
SK	Sandy Koufax	100.00
PO	Paul O'Neill	10.00
MR	Manny Ramirez	10.00
CR	Cal Ripken Jr.	60.00
AR	Alex Rodriguez	40.00
IR	Ivan Rodriguez	10.00
NRa	Nolan Ryan	65.00
NRr	Nolan Ryan	65.00
FT	Fernando Tatis	8.00
RV	Robin Ventura	8.00
BW	Bernie Williams	10.00
MW	Matt Williams	8.00

Game Jersey Autograph

		NM/M
Print Runs Listed		
KG	Ken Griffey/30	150.00
RA	Rick Ankiel/66	40.00
SK	Sandy Koufax/32	900.00
NRa	Nolan Ryan/Mets/30	150.00
NRr	Nolan Ryan/Angels/30	150.00

Game Jersey Auto. Series 2

		NM/M
Common Player:		30.00
Inserted 1:288 H		
JB	Johnny Bench	50.00
BB	Barry Bonds	150.00
JC	Jose Canseco	30.00
RC	Roger Clemens	100.00
TG	Troy Glaus	30.00
KG	Ken Griffey Jr.	100.00
AJ	Andruw Jones	30.00
CJ	Chipper Jones	50.00
CR	Cal Ripken Jr./SP	200.00
AR	Alex Rodriguez	100.00
IR	Ivan Rodriguez/SP	75.00
NR	Nolan Ryan	150.00
GS	Gary Sheffield	30.00
SS	Sammy Sosa/SP	100.00

Game Jersey Hobby Autograph

		NM/M
Common Player:		15.00
Inserted 1:288		
RA	Rick Ankiel	40.00
JB	Jeff Bagwell	40.00
BB	Barry Bonds	150.00
JC	Jose Canseco	40.00
SC	Sean Casey	20.00
JD	J.D. Drew	30.00
JG	Jason Giambi	30.00
SG	Shawn Green	20.00
KG	Ken Griffey Jr.	100.00
MH	Mike Hampton	20.00
RJ	Randy Johnson	75.00
JL	Javy Lopez	20.00
GM	Greg Maddux	125.00
RP	Rafael Palmeiro	40.00
AR	Alex Rodriguez	125.00
NRm	Nolan Ryan	125.00
NRa	Nolan Ryan	125.00
FT	Frank Thomas	50.00

Game Jersey Combo

	NM/M
Production 50 Sets	
BB-KG	Barry Bonds, Ken Griffey Jr.	100.00

IR-RP	Ivan Rodriguez, Rafael Palmeiro	25.00
DJ-AR	Derek Jeter, Alex Rodriguez	100.00
MM-KG	Mickey Mantle, Ken Griffey Jr.	250.00
TG-CR	Tony Gwynn, Cal Ripken Jr.	100.00
NR-AR	Nolan Ryan/ Astros/Rangers	100.00
NR-MA	Nolan Ryan/Mets/Astros	100.00
RJ-GM	Randy Johnson, Greg Maddux	50.00
VG-MR	Vladimir Guerrero, Manny Ramirez	40.00
BB-JC	Barry Bonds, Jose Canseco	80.00
FT-JB	Frank Thomas, Jeff Bagwell	40.00
AJ-KG	Andruw Jones, Ken Griffey Jr.	60.00

Game Jersey Combo Autograph

Production 10 Sets
Values Undetermined
No Pricing

Game Jersey Patch

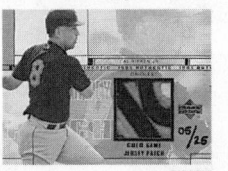

		NM/M
Common Player:		40.00
Production 25 Sets		
RA	Rick Ankiel	40.00
JB	Jeff Bagwell	50.00
BB	Barry Bonds	125.00
JC	Jose Canseco	50.00
JG	Jason Giambi	50.00
KG	Ken Griffey Jr.	75.00
TG	Tony Gwynn	75.00
DJ	Derek Jeter	125.00
RP	Rafael Palmeiro	50.00
CR	Cal Ripken Jr.	150.00
AR	Alex Rodriguez	100.00
IR	Ivan Rodriguez	50.00
NRa	Nolan Ryan	150.00
NRr	Nolan Ryan	150.00
FT	Frank Thomas	60.00

Game Jersey Patch Gold

		NM/M
Production 25 Sets		
BB	Barry Bonds	100.00
JC	Jose Canseco	40.00
JG	Jason Giambi	50.00
KG	Ken Griffey Jr.	120.00
TG	Tony Gwynn	60.00
DJ	Derek Jeter	150.00
CR	Cal Ripken Jr.	150.00
NRa	Nolan Ryan	150.00
NRr	Nolan Ryan	150.00
FT	Frank Thomas	75.00

Game Jersey Patch Autograph

		NM/M
Print Runs Listed		
RA	Rick Ankiel /66	75.00
KG	Ken Griffey Jr./30	400.00

Game-Used Ball

		NM/M
Common Player:		10.00
Production 100 Sets		
RA	Rick Ankiel	15.00
JB	Jeff Bagwell	15.00
BB	Barry Bonds	40.00
JG	Jason Giambi	15.00
SG	Shawn Green	10.00

KG	Ken Griffey Jr.	30.00
ToG	Tony Gwynn	25.00
DJ	Derek Jeter	50.00
RJ	Randy Johnson	25.00
AJ	Andruw Jones	10.00
MM	Mark McGwire	75.00
AR	Alex Rodriguez	40.00
IR	Ivan Rodriguez	10.00
SS	Sammy Sosa	25.00

Game-Used Ball Series 2

		NM/M
Common Player:		5.00
Inserted 1:288		
JB	Jeff Bagwell	10.00
BB	Barry Bonds	30.00
RC	Roger Clemens	20.00
NG	Nomar Garciaparra	10.00
KG	Ken Griffey Jr.	20.00
VG	Vladimir Guerrero	10.00
DJ	Derek Jeter	30.00
AJ	Andruw Jones	8.00
CJ	Chipper Jones	15.00
JK	Jeff Kent	5.00
MM	Mark McGwire	40.00
MP	Mike Piazza	20.00
CR	Cal Ripken Jr.	25.00
MR	Mariano Rivera	8.00
AR	Alex Rodriguez	20.00
GS	Gary Sheffield	8.00
SS	Sammy Sosa	20.00
BW	Bernie Williams	10.00

Game-Used Ball Autographs

		NM/M
Production 25 Sets		
RA	Rick Ankiel	40.00
JB	Jeff Bagwell	60.00
BB	Barry Bonds	150.00
JG	Jason Giambi	75.00
KG	Ken Griffey Jr.	90.00
SG	Shawn Green	60.00
TH	Todd Helton	60.00
RJ	Randy Johnson	90.00
AR	Alex Rodriguez	80.00

Home Run Derby Heroes

		NM/M
Complete Set (10):		25.00
Common Player:		1.00
Inserted 1:36		
HD1	Mark McGwire/1999	5.00
HD2	Sammy Sosa/2000	3.00
HD3	Frank Thomas/1996	2.00
HD4	Cal Ripken Jr./1991	5.00
HD5	Tino Martinez/1997	1.00
HD6	Ken Griffey Jr./1999	3.00
HD7	Barry Bonds/1996	5.00
HD8	Albert Belle/1995	1.00
HD9	Mark McGwire/1992	5.00
HD10	Juan Gonzalez/1993	2.00

Home Run Explosion

		NM/M
Complete Set (15):		20.00
Common Player:		.50
Inserted 1:12		
1	Mark McGwire	3.00
2	Chipper Jones	2.00
3	Jeff Bagwell	1.00
4	Carlos Delgado	1.00
5	Barry Bonds	4.00
6	Troy Glaus	1.00
7	Sammy Sosa	2.50
8	Alex Rodriguez	3.00
9	Mike Piazza	2.00
10	Vladimir Guerrero	1.50
11	Ken Griffey Jr.	2.00
12	Frank Thomas	1.00
13	Ivan Rodriguez	1.00
14	Jason Giambi	1.00
15	Carl Everett	.50

Midseason Superstar Summit

		NM/M
Complete Set (15):		25.00
Common Player:		.75
Inserted 1:24		
MS1	Derek Jeter	5.00
MS2	Sammy Sosa	3.00
MS3	Jeff Bagwell	1.50
MS4	Tony Gwynn	1.50
MS5	Alex Rodriguez	4.00
MS6	Greg Maddux	2.50
MS7	Jason Giambi	1.50
MS8	Mark McGwire	4.00
MS9	Barry Bonds	5.00
MS10	Ken Griffey Jr.	3.00
MS11	Carlos Delgado	1.50
MS12	Troy Glaus	1.00
MS13	Todd Helton	1.50
MS14	Manny Ramirez	1.50
MS15	Jeff Kent	.75

Most Wanted

		NM/M
Complete Set (15):		20.00
Common Player:		.75
Inserted 1:14 Series 1		
MW1	Mark McGwire	2.50
MW2	Cal Ripken Jr.	3.00
MW3	Ivan Rodriguez	.75
MW4	Pedro Martinez	1.00
MW5	Sammy Sosa	2.00
MW6	Tony Gwynn	1.00
MW7	Vladimir Guerrero	1.00
MW8	Derek Jeter	3.00
MW9	Mike Piazza	1.50
MW10	Chipper Jones	1.50
MW11	Alex Rodriguez	2.50
MW12	Barry Bonds	3.00
MW13	Jeff Bagwell	.75
MW14	Frank Thomas	.75
MW15	Nomar Garciaparra	2.00

Rookie Roundup

		NM/M
Complete Set (10):		5.00
Common Player:		.50
Inserted 1:6		
1	Rick Ankiel	1.00
2	Adam Kennedy	.50
3	Mike Lamb	.50
4	Adam Eaton	.50
5	Rafael Furcal	1.00
6	Pat Burrell	1.50
7	Adam Piatt	.50
8	Eric Munson	.50
9	Brad Penny	.50
10	Mark Mulder	.75

Subway Series Jersey Cards

		NM/M
Common Player:		5.00
Inserted 1:144		
SS-EA	Edgardo Alfonzo	5.00
SS-RC	Roger Clemens	40.00
SS-JF	John Franco	5.00
SS-OH	Orlando Hernandez	8.00
SS-AL	Al Leiter	5.00
SS-PO	Paul O'Neill	10.00
SS-JP	Jay Payton	5.00
SS-TP	Timo Perez	5.00
SS-AP	Andy Pettitte	15.00
SS-BW	Bernie Williams	15.00

The Franchise

		NM/M
Complete Set (10):		25.00
Common Player:		1.50
Inserted 1:36		
F1	Frank Thomas	1.50
F2	Mark McGwire	5.00
F3	Ken Griffey Jr.	3.00
F4	Manny Ramirez	1.50
F5	Alex Rodriguez	5.00
F6	Greg Maddux	3.00
F7	Sammy Sosa	4.00
F8	Derek Jeter	6.00
F9	Mike Piazza	3.00
F10	Vladimir Guerrero	2.00

The People's Choice

		NM/M
Complete Set (15):		35.00
Common Player:		1.50
Inserted 1:24		
PC1	Alex Rodriguez	5.00
PC2	Ken Griffey Jr.	3.00
PC3	Mark McGwire	5.00
PC4	Todd Helton	1.50
PC5	Manny Ramirez	1.50
PC6	Mike Piazza	3.00
PC7	Vladimir Guerrero	2.00
PC8	Randy Johnson	2.00
PC9	Cal Ripken Jr.	6.00
PC10	Andruw Jones	1.50
PC11	Sammy Sosa	4.00
PC12	Derek Jeter	6.00
PC13	Pedro Martinez	2.00
PC14	Frank Thomas	1.50
PC15	Nomar Garciaparra	4.00

Superstar Summit

		NM/M
Complete Set (15):		25.00
Common Player:		1.00
Inserted 1:12		
1	Derek Jeter	4.00
2	Randy Johnson	1.50
3	Barry Bonds	4.00
4	Frank Thomas	1.00
5	Cal Ripken Jr.	4.00
6	Pedro J. Martinez	1.50
7	Ivan Rodriguez	1.00
8	Mike Piazza	2.00
9	Mark McGwire	3.00
10	Manny Ramirez	1.00
11	Ken Griffey Jr.	2.00
12	Sammy Sosa	2.50
13	Alex Rodriguez	3.00
14	Chipper Jones	2.00
15	Nomar Garciaparra	2.50

UD's Most Wanted

		NM/M
Complete Set (15):		25.00
Common Player:		1.00
Inserted 1:14		
1	Mark McGwire	3.00
2	Cal Ripken Jr.	4.00
3	Ivan Rodriguez	1.00
4	Pedro J. Martinez	1.50
5	Sammy Sosa	2.50
6	Tony Gwynn	1.50
7	Vladimir Guerrero	1.50
8	Derek Jeter	4.00
9	Mike Piazza	2.00
10	Chipper Jones	2.00
11	Alex Rodriguez	3.00
12	Barry Bonds	4.00
13	Jeff Bagwell	1.00
14	Frank Thomas	1.00
15	Nomar Garciaparra	3.00

UD Game-Worn Patch

		NM/M
Common Player:		60.00
P-JB	Johnny Bench	120.00
P-BB	Barry Bonds	150.00
P-KG	Ken Griffey Jr.	100.00
P-CJ	Chipper Jones	60.00
P-CR	Cal Ripken Jr.	150.00
P-AR	Alex Rodriguez	125.00
P-IR	Ivan Rodriguez	60.00
P-NR	Nolan Ryan	150.00
P-SS	Sammy Sosa	100.00

2001 Upper Deck Decade

Al Kaline
Outfield

		NM/M
Complete Set (180):		25.00
Common Player:		.15
Pack (5):		1.50
Box (24):		30.00
1	Nolan Ryan	3.00
2	Don Baylor	.15
3	Bobby Grich	.15
4	Reggie Jackson	.50
5	Jim "Catfish" Hunter	.25
6	Gene Tenace	.15
7	Rollie Fingers	.25
8	Sal Bando	.15
9	Bert Campaneris	.15
10	John Mayberry	.15
11	Rico Carty	.15
12	Gaylord Perry	.25
13	Andre Thornton	.15
14	Buddy Bell	.15
15	Dennis Eckersley	.25
16	Ruppert Jones	.15
17	Brooks Robinson	.75
18	Tommy Davis	.15
19	Eddie Murray	.25
20	Boog Powell	.15
21	Al Oliver	.15
22	Jeff Burroughs	.15
23	Mike Hargrove	.15
24	Dwight Evans	.15
25	Fred Lynn	.15
26	Rico Petrocelli	.15
27	Carlton Fisk	.50
28	Luis Aparicio	.15
29	Amos Otis	.15
30	Hal McRae	.15
31	Jason Thompson	.15
32	Al Kaline	.75
33	Jim Perry	.15
34	Bert Blyleven	.15
35	Harmon Killebrew	1.00
36	Wilbur Wood	.15
37	Jim Kaat	.15
38	Ron Guidry	.15
39	Thurman Munson	1.00
40	Graig Nettles	.15
41	Bobby Murcer	.15
42	Chris Chambliss	.15
43	Roy White	.15
44	J.R. Richard	.15
45	Jose Cruz	.15
46	Hank Aaron	2.00
47	Phil Niekro	.15
48	Bob Horner	.15
49	Darryl Evans	.15
50	Gorman Thomas	.15
51	Don Money	.15
52	Robin Yount	.75
53	Joe Torre	.25
54	Tim McCarver	.15
55	Lou Brock	.40
56	Keith Hernandez	.15
57	Bill Madlock	.15
58	Ron Santo	.15
59	Billy Williams	.15
60	Ferguson Jenkins	.25
61	Steve Garvey	.15
62	Bill Russell	.15
63	Maury Wills	.25
64	Ron Cey	.15
65	Manny Mota	.15
66	Ron Fairly	.15
67	Steve Rogers	.15
68	Gary Carter	.15
69	Andre Dawson	.25
70	Bobby Bonds	.25
71	Jack Clark	.15
72	Willie McCovey	.15
73	Tom Seaver	1.00
74	Bud Harrelson	.15
75	Dave Kingman	.15
76	Jerry Koosman	.15
77	Jon Matlack	.15
78	Randy Jones	.15
79	Ozzie Smith	1.00
80	Garry Maddox	.15
81	Mike Schmidt	1.00
82	Greg Luzinski	.15
83	Tug McGraw	.15
84	Willie Stargell	.75
85	Dave Parker	.15
86	Roberto Clemente	2.00
87	Johnny Bench	1.50
88	Joe Morgan	.40
89	George Foster	.15
90	Ken Griffey Sr.	.15
91	Carlton Fisk 1972 (1970s Rookie Flashbacks)	.50
92	Andre Dawson 1977 (1970s Rookie Flashbacks)	.25
93	Fred Lynn 1975 (1970s Rookie Flashbacks)	.15
94	Eddie Murray 1977 (1970s Rookie Flashbacks)	.25
95	Bob Horner 1978 (1970s Rookie Flashbacks)	.15
96	Jon Matlack 1972 (1970s Rookie Flashbacks)	.15
97	Mike Hargrove 1974 (1970s Rookie Flashbacks)	.15
98	Robin Yount 1974 (1970s Rookie Flashbacks)	.50
99	Mike Schmidt 1972 (1970s Rookie Flashbacks)	.50
100	Gary Carter 1974 (1970s Rookie Flashbacks)	.15
101	Ozzie Smith 1978 (1970s Rookie Flashbacks)	.50
102	Paul Molitor 1978 (1970s Rookie Flashbacks)	.50
103	Dennis Eckersley 1975 (1970s Rookie Flashbacks)	.25
104	Dale Murphy 1976 (1970s Rookie Flashbacks)	.15
105	Bert Blyleven 1970 (1970s Rookie Flashbacks)	.15
106	Thurman Munson 1970 (1970s Rookie Flashbacks)	.75
107	Dave Parker 1973 (1970s Rookie Flashbacks)	.15
108	Jack Clark 1975 (1970s Rookie Flashbacks)	.15
109	Keith Hernandez 1974 (1970s Rookie Flashbacks)	.15
110	Ron Cey 1971 (1970s Rookie Flashbacks)	.15
111	Billy Williams 1970 (Decade Dateline)	.15
112	Tom Seaver 1970 (Decade Dateline)	.75
113	Reggie Jackson 1971 (Decade Dateline)	.75
114	Barry Bonds 1971 (Decade Dateline)	.15
115	Willie Stargell 1971 (Decade Dateline)	.40
116	Harmon Killebrew 1971 (Decade Dateline)	.50
117	Roberto Clemente 1972 (Decade Dateline)	1.00
118	Wilbur Wood 1972 (Decade Dateline)	.15
119	Billy Williams 1972 (Decade Dateline)	.15
120	Nolan Ryan 1973 (Decade Dateline)	1.50
121	Ron Blomberg 1973 (Decade Dateline)	.15
122	Hank Aaron 1974 (Decade Dateline)	1.00
123	Lou Brock 1974 (Decade Dateline)	.25
124	Al Kaline 1974 (Decade Dateline)	.40
125	Brooks Robinson 1975 (Decade Dateline)	.40
126	Bill Madlock 1975 (Decade Dateline)	.15
127	Rennie Stennett 1975 (Decade Dateline)	.15
128	Carlton Fisk 1975 (Decade Dateline)	.40
129	Chris Chambliss 1976 (Decade Dateline)	.15
130	Ruppert Jones 1977 (Decade Dateline)	.15
131	Ron Fairly 1977 (Decade Dateline)	.15
132	George Foster 1977 (Decade Dateline)	.15
133	Reggie Jackson 1977 (Decade Dateline)	.75
134	Ron Guidry 1978 (Decade Dateline)	.15
135	Gaylord Perry 1978 (Decade Dateline)	.15
136	Bucky Dent 1978 (Decade Dateline)	.15
137	Dave Kingman 1979 (Decade Dateline)	.15
138	Lou Brock 1979 (Decade Dateline)	.15
139	Thurman Munson 1979 (Decade Dateline)	.75
140	Willie Stargell 1979 (Decade Dateline)	.40
141	Johnny Bench 1970 NL MVP (1970s Award Winners)	.75
142	Boog Powell 1970 AL MVP (1970s Award Winners)	.15
143	Jim Perry 1970 AL CY (1970s Award Winners)	.15
144	Joe Torre 1971 NL MVP (1970s Award Winners)	.15
145	Chris Chambliss 1971 AL ROY (1970s Award Winners)	.15
146	Ferguson Jenkins 1971 NL CY (1970s Award Winners)	.15
147	Carlton Fisk 1972 AL ROY (1970s Award Winners)	.40
148	Gaylord Perry 1972 AL CY (1970s Award Winners)	.15
149	Johnny Bench 1972 NL MVP (1970s Award Winners)	.75
150	Reggie Jackson 1973 AL MVP (1970s Award Winners)	.75
151	Tom Seaver 1973 NL CY (1970s Award Winners)	.75
152	Thurman Munson 1973 AL GG (1970s Award Winners)	.75
153	Steve Garvey 1974 NL MVP (1970s Award Winners)	.15
154	Jim "Catfish" Hunter 1974 AL CY (1970s Award Winners)	.15
155	Mike Hargrove 1974 AL ROY (1970s Award Winners)	.15
156	Joe Morgan 1975 NL MVP (1970s Award Winners)	.15
157	Fred Lynn 1975 AL MVP & ROY (1970s Award Winners)	.15
158	Tom Seaver 1975 NL CY (1970s Award Winners)	.75
159	Thurman Munson 1976 AL MVP (1970s Award Winners)	.75
160	Randy Jones 1976 NL CY (1970s Award Winners)	.15
161	Joe Morgan 1976 NL ROY (1970s Award Winners)	.15
162	George Foster 1977 NL MVP (1970s Award Winners)	.15
163	Eddie Murray 1977 AL ROY (1970s Award Winners)	.25
164	Andre Dawson 1977 NL ROY (1970s Award Winners)	.25
165	Gaylord Perry 1978 NL CY (1970s Award Winners)	.15
166	Ron Guidry 1978 AL CY (1970s Award Winners)	.15
167	Dave Parker 1978 NL MVP (1970s Award Winners)	.15
168	Don Baylor 1979 AL MVP (1970s Award Winners)	.15
169	Bruce Sutter 1979 NL CY (1970s Award Winners)	.30
170	Willie Stargell 1979 NL co-MVP (1970s Award Winners)	.40
171	Brooks Robinson 1970 (1970s World Series Highlights)	.50
172	Roberto Clemente 1971 (1970s World Series Highlights)	1.00
173	Gene Tenace 1972 (1970s World Series Highlights)	.15
174	Reggie Jackson 1973 (1970s World Series Highlights)	.75
175	Rollie Fingers 1974 (1970s World Series Highlights)	.15
176	Carlton Fisk 1975 (1970s World Series Highlights)	.40
177	Johnny Bench 1976 (1970s World Series Highlights)	.75
178	Reggie Jackson 1977 (1970s World Series Highlights)	.75
179	Bucky Dent 1978 (1970s World Series Highlights)	.15
180	Willie Stargell 1979 (1970s World Series Highlights)	.40

Bellbottomed Bashers

		NM/M
Complete Set (10):		12.00
Common Player:		1.00
Inserted 1:14		
BB1	Reggie Jackson	2.00
BB2	Gorman Thomas	1.00
BB3	Willie McCovey	1.50
BB4	Willie Stargell	1.50
BB5	Mike Schmidt	3.00
BB6	George Foster	1.00
BB7	Johnny Bench	2.50
BB8	Dave Kingman	1.00
BB9	Graig Nettles	1.00
BB10	Steve Garvey	1.00

Decade Dynasties

		NM/M
Complete Set (10):		15.00
Common Player:		1.00
Inserted 1:14		
D1	Boog Powell	1.00
D2	Johnny Bench	3.00
D3	Willie Stargell	1.50
D4	Jim "Catfish" Hunter	1.00
D5	Steve Garvey	1.00
D6	Carlton Fisk	2.00
D7	Mike Schmidt	4.00
D8	Hal McRae	1.00
D9	Tom Seaver	3.00
D10	Reggie Jackson	2.50

Game-Used Bat

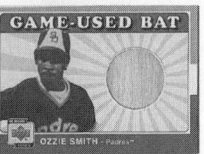

OZZIE SMITH - Padres*

		NM/M
Common Player:		5.00
Inserted 1:24 H		
HA	Hank Aaron	40.00
DB	Don Baylor	5.00
BB	Bobby Bonds	5.00
GC	Gary Carter	8.00
JaC	Jack Clark	5.00
RC	Roberto Clemente/243	100.00
DC	Dave Concepcion	5.00
JoC	Jose Cruz	5.00
TD	Tommy Davis	5.00
AD	Andre Dawson	8.00
DaE	Darryl Evans	5.00
DwE	Dwight Evans	5.00
CF	Carlton Fisk	10.00
GF	George Foster	5.00
SG	Steve Garvey	5.00
BG	Bobby Grich	5.00
KG	Ken Griffey Sr.	5.00
BH	Bud Harrelson/290	5.00
KH	Keith Hernandez/243	20.00
RH	Ron Hunt	5.00
ReJ	Reggie Jackson	15.00
RaJ	Randy Jones	5.00
GL	Greg Luzinski	5.00
FL	Fred Lynn	5.00
GM	Garry Maddox	5.00
BiM	Bill Madlock	5.00
TiM	Tim McCarver	5.00
TuM	Tug McGraw/97	25.00
HM	Hal McRae	5.00
RM	Rick Monday	5.00
WM	Willie Montanez	5.00
JM	Joe Morgan	5.00
BoM	Bobby Murcer	20.00
EM	Eddie Murray	10.00
GN	Graig Nettles/219	15.00
AO	Al Oliver	5.00
DP	Dave Parker	5.00
BP	Boog Powell	5.00
WR	Willie Randolph	5.00
BR	Bill Russell	5.00
NR	Nolan Ryan	50.00
RS	Ron Santo	5.00
ToS	Tom Seaver/121	20.00
OS	Ozzie Smith	15.00
RW	Roy White	5.00
MW	Maury Wills	5.00
DW	Dave Winfield	8.00

Game-Used Bat Combo

	NM/M
Common Card:	20.00

Inserted 1:336
NYY	Reggie Jackson, Graig Nettles, Chris Chambliss, Roy White	40.00
LA	Steve Garvey, Ron Cey, Bill Russell, Rick Monday	25.00
NYM	Tom Seaver, Bud Harrelson, Ron Hunt, Tug McGraw	50.00
CIN	Johnny Bench, George Foster, Ken Griffey Sr., Joe Morgan	50.00
ROY	Andre Dawson, Fred Lynn, Carlton Fisk, Eddie Murray	40.00
MVPN	Johnny Bench, Steve Garvey, Willie Stargell, George Foster	50.00
BAT	Keith Hernandez, Bill Madlock, Fred Lynn, Dave Parker	20.00
GGA	Carlton Fisk, Graig Nettles, Bobby Grich, Fred Lynn	25.00
GGN	Johnny Bench, Roberto Clemente, Dave Concepcion, Garry Maddox	100.00
WS72	Reggie Jackson, Bert Campaneris, Dave Concepcion, Johnny Bench/97	80.00
WS73	Reggie Jackson, Bert Campaneris, Tom Seaver, Bud Harrelson	40.00
WS74	Reggie Jackson, Bert Campaneris, Steve Garvey, Ron Cey	40.00
WS75	Carlton Fisk, Fred Lynn, George Foster, Joe Morgan	40.00
WS76	Chris Chambliss, Graig Nettles, Johnny Bench, Ken Griffey Sr./97	80.00
WS77	Reggie Jackson, Graig Nettles, Steve Garvey, Ron Cey	40.00
WS78	Graig Nettles, Chris Chambliss, Bill Russell, Ron Cey/238	50.00
ASMV	Bill Madlock, Joe Morgan, Steve Garvey, Dave Parker	40.00
RY	Chris Chambliss, Reggie Jackson, Roy White, Hal McRae/238	40.00
RD	George Foster, Joe Morgan, Ron Cey, Bill Russell	25.00

Game-Used Jersey

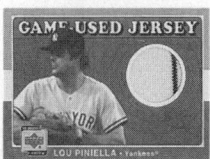

		NM/M
Common Player:		8.00

Inserted 1:168
HA	Hank Aaron	40.00
LA	Luis Aparicio	8.00
JB	Johnny Bench	15.00
RC	Roberto Clemente	100.00
WD	Willie Davis	8.00
RF	Rollie Fingers	8.00
CF	Carlton Fisk	10.00
RG	Ron Guidry	8.00
BH	Burt Hooton	8.00
CH	Jim "Catfish" Hunter	10.00
RJ	Reggie Jackson	15.00
JKa	Jim Kaat	8.00
JKo	Jerry Koosman	8.00
BM	Bill Madlock	8.00
JM	Jon Matlack	8.00
TM	Tug McGraw	8.00
BM	Bobby Murcer	15.00
JP	Jim Perry	8.00
LP	Lou Piniella	10.00
WR	Willie Randolph	8.00
NR	Nolan Ryan/50	75.00
TS	Tom Seaver	20.00
WS	Willie Stargell	8.00
MW	Maury Wills	8.00

Game-Used Jersey Autograph

		NM/M
Common Autograph:		20.00

Inserted 1:168 H
HA	Hank Aaron/97	250.00
LA	Luis Aparicio	30.00
SB	Sal Bando	20.00
JB	Johnny Bench	70.00
RF	Rollie Fingers	25.00
CF	Carlton Fisk/243	40.00
KG	Ken Griffey Sr.	20.00
RG	Ron Guidry	30.00
BH	Burt Hooton	20.00
RJ	Reggie Jackson/291	65.00

JKa	Jim Kaat	25.00
JKo	Jerry Koosman	20.00
BM	Bill Madlock	20.00
TM	Tug McGraw	20.00
BM	Bobby Murcer	50.00
RP	Rico Petrocelli	25.00
NR	Nolan Ryan/291	125.00
MW	Maury Wills	20.00

The Arms Race

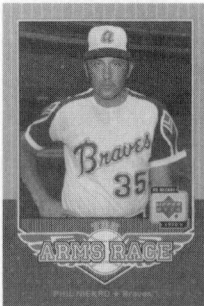

		NM/M
Complete Set (10):		10.00
Common Player:		.50

Inserted 1:14
AR1	Nolan Ryan	4.00
AR2	Ferguson Jenkins	1.00
AR3	Jim "Catfish" Hunter	1.00
AR4	Tom Seaver	2.00
AR5	Randy Jones	.50
AR6	J.R. Richard	.50
AR7	Rollie Fingers	1.00
AR8	Gaylord Perry	.75
AR9	Ron Guidry	.75
AR10	Phil Niekro	.75

70s Disco Era Dandies

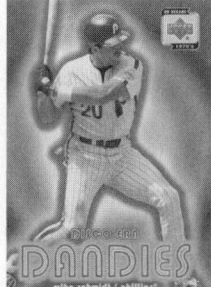

		NM/M
Complete Set (6):		5.00
Common Player:		.50

Inserted 1:23
DE1	Mike Schmidt	2.00
DE2	Johnny Bench	1.00
DE3	Lou Brock	.50
DE4	Reggie Jackson	2.00
DE5	Willie Stargell	.50
DE6	Tom Seaver	1.00

70s Super Powers

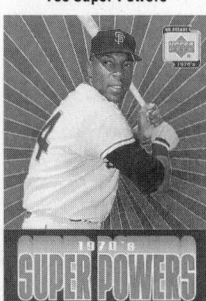

		NM/M
Complete Set (6):		12.00
Common Player:		1.50

Inserted 1:24
SP1	Reggie Jackson	3.00

SP2	Joe Morgan	1.50
SP3	Willie Stargell	2.00
SP4	Willie McCovey	1.50
SP5	Mike Schmidt	4.00
SP6	Nolan Ryan	5.00

2001 Upper Deck Evolution

		NM/M
Complete Set (120):		125.00
Common Player:		.15
Common SP (91-120):		3.00
Production 2,250		
Pack (5):		2.00
Box (24):		40.00
1	Darin Erstad	.25
2	Troy Glaus	.50
3	Jason Giambi	.50
4	Tim Hudson	.40
5	Jermaine Dye	.15
6	Barry Zito	.40
7	Carlos Delgado	.50
8	Shannon Stewart	.15
9	Jose Cruz Jr.	.15
10	Greg Vaughn	.15
11	Juan Gonzalez	.50
12	Roberto Alomar	.50
13	Omar Vizquel	.25
14	Jim Thome	.50
15	Edgar Martinez	.25
16	John Olerud	.25
17	Kazuhiro Sasaki	.15
18	Cal Ripken Jr.	2.00
19	Alex Rodriguez	1.50
20	Ivan Rodriguez	.50
21	Rafael Palmeiro	.50
22	Pedro Martinez	.75
23	Nomar Garciaparra	.75
24	Manny Ramirez	.50
25	Carl Everett	.15
26	Mark Quinn	.15
27	Mike Sweeney	.25
28	Neifi Perez	.15
29	Tony Clark	.15
30	Eric Milton	.15
31	Doug Mientkiewicz	.15
32	Corey Koskie	.15
33	Frank Thomas	.50
34	David Wells	.15
35	Magglio Ordonez	.40
36	Derek Jeter	2.00
37	Mike Mussina	.40
38	Bernie Williams	.50
39	Roger Clemens	1.50
40	David Justice	.25
41	Jeff Bagwell	.50
42	Richard Hidalgo	.25
43	Wade Miller	.15
44	Chipper Jones	1.00
45	Greg Maddux	1.50
46	Andruw Jones	.50
47	Rafael Furcal	.40
48	Geoff Jenkins	.25
49	Jeromy Burnitz	.15
50	Ben Sheets	.25
51	Richie Sexson	.40
52	Mark McGwire	1.50
53	Jim Edmonds	.40
54	Darryl Kile	.15
55	J.D. Drew	.25
56	Sammy Sosa	1.00
57	Kerry Wood	.50
58	Randy Johnson	.75
59	Luis Gonzalez	.25
60	Matt Williams	.25
61	Kevin Brown	.25
62	Gary Sheffield	.40
63	Shawn Green	.40
64	Chan Ho Park	.15
65	Vladimir Guerrero	.75
66	Jose Vidro	.15
67	Fernando Tatis	.15
68	Barry Bonds	2.00
69	Jeff Kent	.25
70	Russ Ortiz	.15
71	Preston Wilson	.15
72	Ryan Dempster	.15
73	Charles Johnson	.15
74	Mike Piazza	1.00
75	Edgardo Alfonzo	.15
76	Robin Ventura	.25
77	Jay Payton	.15

78	Tony Gwynn	.75
79	Phil Nevin	.15
80	Pat Burrell	.40
81	Scott Rolen	.50
82	Bob Abreu	.40
83	Brian Giles	.25
84	Jason Kendall	.25
85	Ken Griffey Jr.	1.00
86	Barry Larkin	.40
87	Sean Casey	.25
88	Todd Helton	.50
89	Larry Walker	.25
90	Mike Hampton	.15
91	Ichiro Suzuki RC	20.00
92	Albert Pujols RC	40.00
93	Wilson Betemit RC	3.00
94	Jay Gibbons RC	3.00
95	Juan Uribe RC	4.00
96	Morgan Ensberg RC	3.00
97	Christian Parker RC	3.00
98	Tsuyoshi Shinjo RC	3.00
99	Jack Wilson RC	4.00
100	Donaldo Mendez RC	3.00
101	Ryan Freel RC	4.00
102	Juan Diaz RC	3.00
103	Horacio Ramirez RC	3.00
104	Ricardo Rodriguez RC	3.00
105	Erick Almonte RC	3.00
106	Josh Towers RC	3.00
107	Adrian Hernandez RC	3.00
108	Brandon Duckworth RC	3.00
109	Travis Hafner RC	8.00
110	Martin Vargas RC	3.00
111	Kris Keller RC	3.00
112	Brian Lawrence RC	3.00
113	Esix Snead RC	3.00
114	Wilken Ruan RC	3.00
115	Jose Mieses RC	3.00
116	Johnny Estrada RC	4.00
117	Elpidio Guzman RC	3.00
118	Sean Douglass RC	3.00
119	Billy Sylvester RC	3.00
120	Bret Prinz RC	3.00

UD Classics

		NM/M
Complete Set (15):		15.00
Common Player:		.50

Prices for unscratched cards.
Winners Evolve Into Game Jersey.
Inserted 1:4
EC1	Ken Griffey Jr.	3.00
EC2	Gary Sheffield	.75
EC3	Randy Johnson	1.50
EC4	Sammy Sosa	3.00
EC5	Carlos Delgado	1.00
EC6	Ichiro Suzuki	3.00
EC7	Andruw Jones	1.00
EC8	Chipper Jones	2.00
EC9	Kazuhiro Sasaki	.50
EC10	Shawn Green	.75
EC11	Alex Rodriguez	3.00
EC12	Brian Giles	.75
EC13	J.D. Drew	.50
EC14	Pat Burrell	1.00
EC15	Ivan Rodriguez	1.00

Autographed Bat/Jersey

		NM/M
Common Player:		25.00
RB	Russell Branyan	25.00
PB	Pat Burrell	40.00
CD	Carlos Delgado	40.00
JD	J.D. Drew	25.00
JaG	Jason Giambi	50.00
SG	Shawn Green	40.00
KG	Ken Griffey Jr.	100.00
AJ	Andruw Jones	40.00
CJ	Chipper Jones	75.00

JK	Jason Kendall	25.00
CR	Cal Ripken Jr.	150.00
AR	Alex Rodriguez	150.00
GS	Gary Sheffield	50.00
SS	Sammy Sosa	100.00
IS	Ichiro Suzuki	300.00

Game-Used Bat Cards

NM/M

Common Player: 5.00
Winners Evolve Into Bat/Jsy Auto.
Inserted 1:120

RB	Russell Branyan	5.00
PB	Pat Burrell	8.00
CD	Carlos Delgado	8.00
JD	J.D. Drew	5.00
JaG	Jason Giambi	8.00
KG	Ken Griffey Jr.	20.00
AJ	Andruw Jones	8.00
JK	Jason Kendall	5.00
AR	Alex Rodriguez	15.00
GS	Gary Sheffield	6.00

Game-Used Jersey Cards

NM/M

Common Player: 5.00
Inserted 1:120

RB	Russell Branyan	5.00
PB	Pat Burrell	8.00
JD	J.D. Drew	5.00
JaG	Jason Giambi	10.00
BG	Brian Giles	6.00
TG	Troy Glaus	8.00
SG	Shawn Green	6.00
KG	Ken Griffey Jr.	20.00
AJ	Andruw Jones	8.00
CJ	Chipper Jones	10.00
JK	Jason Kendall	5.00
CR	Cal Ripken Jr.	30.00
AR	Alex Rodriguez	15.00
GS	Gary Sheffield	8.00
SS	Sammy Sosa	15.00

Ichiro Suzuki All-Star Game

NM/M

Random Inserts

51B	Ichiro Suzuki/Bronze	8.00
51S	Ichiro Suzuki/Silver/2001	20.00
51G	Ichiro Suzuki/Gold/51	120.00

2001 Upper Deck Gold Glove

NM/M

Common Player: .25
Common SP (91-129): 4.00
Production 1,000

Common SP (130-135):		8.00
Production 500		
Pack (4):		8.00
Box (20):		140.00
1	Troy Glaus	.50
2	Darin Erstad	.50
3	Jason Giambi	.75
4	Tim Hudson	.50
5	Jermaine Dye	.25
6	Raul Mondesi	.25
7	Carlos Delgado	.50
8	Shannon Stewart	.25
9	Greg Vaughn	.25
10	Aubrey Huff	.25
11	Juan Gonzalez	.50
12	Roberto Alomar	1.00
13	Omar Vizquel	.25
14	Jim Thome	1.00
15	John Olerud	.50
16	Edgar Martinez	.50
17	Kazuhiro Sasaki	.25
18	Aaron Sele	.25
19	Cal Ripken Jr.	4.00
20	Chris Richard	.25
21	Ivan Rodriguez	.75
22	Rafael Palmeiro	.75
23	Alex Rodriguez	3.00
24	Pedro Martinez	1.50
25	Nomar Garciaparra	1.00
26	Manny Ramirez	1.00
27	Neifi Perez	.25
28	Mike Sweeney	.25
29	Bobby Higginson	.25
30	Dean Palmer	.25
31	Tony Clark	.25
32	Doug Mientkiewicz	.25
33	Brad Radke	.25
34	Joe Mays	.25
35	Frank Thomas	1.00
36	Magglio Ordonez	.50
37	Carlos Lee	.40
38	Bernie Williams	.75
39	Mike Mussina	.75
40	Derek Jeter	4.00
41	Roger Clemens	2.50
42	Craig Biggio	.40
43	Jeff Bagwell	.75
44	Lance Berkman	.50
45	Andruw Jones	.50
46	Greg Maddux	2.00
47	Chipper Jones	2.00
48	Geoff Jenkins	.40
49	Ben Sheets	.25
50	Jeromy Burnitz	.25
51	Jim Edmonds	.50
52	Mark McGwire	2.00
53	Mike Matheny	.25
54	J.D. Drew	.50
55	Sammy Sosa	1.00
56	Kerry Wood	.50
57	Fred McGriff	.40
58	Randy Johnson	1.50
59	Steve Finley	.25
60	Mark Grace	.50
61	Matt Williams	.40
62	Luis Gonzalez	.40
63	Shawn Green	.40
64	Kevin Brown	.40
65	Gary Sheffield	.50
66	Vladimir Guerrero	1.00
67	Tony Armas Jr.	.25
68	Barry Bonds	4.00
69	J.T. Snow	.25
70	Jeff Kent	.40
71	Charles Johnson	.25
72	Preston Wilson	.25
73	Cliff Floyd	.25
74	Robin Ventura	.25
75	Mike Piazza	2.00
76	Edgardo Alfonzo	.25
77	Tony Gwynn	1.50
78	Ryan Klesko	.50
79	Scott Rolen	1.00
80	Mike Lieberthal	.25
81	Pat Burrell	.50
82	Jason Kendall	.25
83	Brian Giles	.50
84	Ken Griffey Jr.	2.50
85	Barry Larkin	.50
86	Pokey Reese	.25
87	Larry Walker	.40
88	Mike Hampton	.25
89	Juan Pierre	.25
90	Todd Helton	1.00
91	Mike Penney RC	4.00
92	Wilkin Ruan RC	4.00
93	Greg Miller RC	4.00
94	Johnny Estrada RC	6.00
95	Tsuyoshi Shinjo RC	4.00
96	Josh Towers RC	4.00
97	Horacio Ramirez RC	4.00
98	Ryan Freel RC	6.00
99	Morgan Ensberg RC	4.00
100	Adrian Hernandez RC	4.00
101	Juan Uribe RC	4.00
102	Jose Mieses RC	4.00
103	Jack Wilson RC	6.00
104	Cesar Crespo RC	4.00
105	Bud Smith RC	4.00
106	Erick Almonte RC	4.00
107	Elpidio Guzman RC	4.00
108	Brandon Duckworth RC	4.00
109	Juan Diaz RC	4.00
110	Kris Keller RC	4.00
111	Jason Michaels RC	4.00
112	Bret Prinz RC	4.00
113	Henry Mateo RC	4.00
114	Ricardo Rodriguez RC	4.00
115	Travis Hafner RC	10.00
116	Nate Teut RC	4.00
117	Alexis Gomez RC	4.00
118	Billy Sylvester RC	4.00
119	Adam Pettyjohn RC	4.00
120	Josh Fogg RC	4.00
121	Juan Cruz RC	4.00
122	Carlos Valderrama RC	4.00
123	Jay Gibbons RC	4.00
124	Donaldo Mendez RC	4.00
125	William Ortega RC	4.00
126	Sean Douglass RC	4.00
127	Christian Parker RC	4.00
128	Grant Balfour RC	4.00
129	Joe Kennedy RC	4.00
130	Albert Pujols RC	120.00
131	Wilson Betemit RC	10.00
132	Mark Teixeira RC	25.00
133	Mark Prior RC	10.00
134	Dewon Brazelton RC	4.00
135	Ichiro Suzuki RC	40.00

Limited

Stars (1-90):	4-8X
Rookies (91-135):	.75-1.5X
Production 100 Sets	

(See 2001 Upper Deck Gold Glove for checklist and base card values.)

Finite

Stars (1-90):	15-25X
Rookies (91-135):	3-5X
Production 25 Sets	

(See 2001 Upper Deck Gold Glove for checklist and base card values.)

Batting Gloves

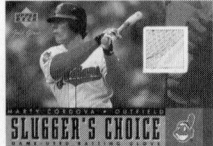

NM/M

Common Player: 5.00
Inserted 1:20

BA	Bobby Abreu	8.00
BA	Brady Anderson	5.00
TB	Tony Batista	5.00
BB	Barry Bonds	30.00
MC	Marty Cordova	5.00
JC	Jose Cruz	5.00
RF	Rafael Furcal	8.00
AG	Andres Galarraga	5.00
JG	Juan Gonzalez	8.00
KGR	Ken Griffey Jr./Reds	20.00
KGM	Ken Griffey Jr.	20.00
CJ	Chipper Jones	10.00
EM	Edgar Martinez	8.00

PO	Paul O'Neill	8.00
RP	Rafael Palmeiro	10.00
NP	Neifi Perez	5.00
MR	Manny Ramirez	5.00
ARR	Alex Rodriguez/Rangers	20.00
ARM	Alex Rodriguez/M's	20.00
HR	Henry Rodriguez	5.00
IR	Ivan Rodriguez	8.00
GS	Gary Sheffield	8.00
SS	Sammy Sosa	10.00
FT	Fernando Tatis	5.00
MT	Miguel Tejada	5.00

Fielder's Gloves

NM/M

Common Player: 6.00
Inserted 1:60

GA	Garret Anderson/100	15.00
CB	Craig Biggio	15.00
JBi	Johnny Blanchard	10.00
BB	Barry Bonds	50.00
KC	Ken Caminiti	10.00
RCa	Roy Campanella	125.00
GC	Gary Carter	10.00
RCe	Roger Cedeno	10.00
JD	Johnny Damon	20.00
LD	Leon Day/100	150.00
OD	Octavio Dotel	6.00
JE	Jim Edmonds	15.00
DE	Dock Ellis	6.00
AF	Alex Fernandez	6.00
CF	Cliff Floyd	10.00
NF	Nellie Fox	40.00
RF	Rafael Furcal	6.00
AG	Alex Gonzalez	6.00
BG	Ben Grieve	6.00
KG	Ken Griffey Jr.	30.00
MG	Marquis Grissom	8.00
LG	Lefty Grove	100.00
THe	Todd Helton	20.00
OH	Orlando Hernandez	8.00
THo	Todd Hollandsworth	8.00
HI	Hideki Irabu	8.00
JI	Jason Isringhausen	10.00
RJ	Reggie Jackson	20.00
CJ	Chipper Jones	25.00
JKa	Jim Kaat	10.00
JKe	Jason Kendall	10.00
RK	Ryan Klesko	8.00
HK	Harvey Kuenn	20.00
CL	Carlos Lee	10.00
KL	Kenny Lofton	10.00
JL	Javy Lopez	10.00
GL	Greg Luzinski	10.00
EM	Edgar Martinez	15.00
PM	Pedro Martinez	25.00
JO	John Olerud	10.00
PO	Paul O'Neill	15.00
RP	Rafael Palmeiro	15.00
CP	Chan Ho Park	10.00
MP	Mike Piazza	30.00
MR	Manny Ramirez	25.00
FR	Frank Robinson	25.00
AR	Alex Rodriguez	30.00
IR	Ivan Rodriguez	15.00
TS	Tim Salmon	8.00
AS	Aaron Sele	8.00
GS	Gary Sheffield	15.00
OS	Ozzie Smith	40.00
SS	Sammy Sosa	25.00
I	Ichiro Suzuki	250.00
FT	Frank Thomas	20.00
OV	Omar Vizquel	15.00
DW	Dave Winfield	20.00
MY	Masato Yoshii	10.00

Fielder's Gloves Autograph

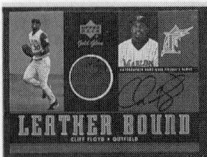

NM/M

Inserted 1:240

JD	Johnny Damon	50.00
CF	Cliff Floyd	25.00
RF	Rafael Furcal	25.00
RP	Ken Griffey Jr./49	150.00
RJ	Reggie Jackson/68	60.00
JK	Jim Kaat	20.00
JK	Jason Kendall	20.00
RK	Ryan Klesko	20.00
KL	Kenny Lofton	20.00
JL	Javy Lopez	20.00
GL	Greg Luzinski	20.00

EM	Edgar Martinez	50.00
JO	John Olerud	25.00
PO	Paul O'Neill	50.00
FR	Frank Robinson	50.00
IR	Ivan Rodriguez	60.00
OS	Ozzie Smith	85.00
FT	Frank Thomas	60.00
DW	Dave Winfield	50.00

Game-Used Ball

		NM/M
Common Player:		5.00
Inserted 1:20		
GC	Ken Griffey Jr., Sean Casey	20.00
RR	Alex Rodriguez,	
	Ivan Rodriguez	20.00
SW	Sammy Sosa,	
	Rondell White	15.00
MP	Mark McGwire,	
	Albert Pujols	75.00
RE	Manny Ramirez,	
	Carl Everett	15.00
GE	Troy Glaus, Darin Erstad	8.00
GT	Jason Giambi,	
	Miguel Tejada	10.00
IO	Ichiro Suzuki, John Olerud	40.00
RP	Ivan Rodriguez,	
	Rafael Palmeiro	10.00
GV	Vladimir Guerrero,	
	Jose Vidro	10.00
PS	Mike Piazza,	
	Tsuyoshi Shinjo	20.00
JJ	Chipper Jones,	
	Andruw Jones	15.00
RB	Scott Rolen, Pat Burrell	10.00
WF	Preston Wilson, Cliff Floyd	5.00
JF	Andruw Jones,	
	Rafael Furcal	10.00
BB	Jeff Bagwell,	
	Lance Berkman	15.00
PE	Albert Pujols, Jim Edmonds	35.00
JB	Geoff Jenkins,	
	Jeromy Burnitz	5.00
KG	Jason Kendall, Brian Giles	5.00
BK	Barry Bonds, Jeff Kent	25.00
NK	Phil Nevin, Ryan Klesko	5.00
SG	Gary Sheffield, Shawn Green	8.00
GG	Luis Gonzalez, Mark Grace	10.00
HW	Todd Helton, Larry Walker	10.00
WP	Larry Walker, Juan Pierre	5.00
AG	Roberto Alomar,	
	Juan Gonzalez	10.00
VM	Greg Vaughn, Fred McGriff	5.00
RB	Cal Ripken Jr., Tony Batista	30.00
DM	Carlos Delgado,	
	Raul Mondesi	8.00
MG	Doug Mientkiewicz,	
	Cristian Guzman	5.00
TO	Frank Thomas,	
	Magglio Ordonez	5.00
HC	Bobby Higginson, Tony Clark	5.00
SB	Mike Sweeney,	
	Carlos Beltran	5.00
MO	Edgar Martinez, John Olerud	8.00
EA	Darin Erstad,	
	Garret Anderson	8.00
TC	Miguel Tejada, Eric Chavez	8.00
PR	Rafael Palmeiro,	
	Alex Rodriguez	20.00
BA	Pat Burrell, Bobby Abreu	5.00
FJ	Cliff Floyd, Charles Johnson	5.00
VP	Robin Ventura, Mike Piazza	15.00
WS	Kerry Wood, Sammy Sosa	20.00
DP	J.D. Drew, Albert Pujols	40.00
BH	Lance Berkman,	
	Richard Hidalgo	8.00
BS	Jeromy Burnitz,	
	Richie Sexson	5.00
LG	Barry Larkin, Ken Griffey Jr.	20.00
GR	Brian Giles, Aramis Ramirez	5.00
JG	Randy Johnson,	
	Luis Gonzalez	15.00
GB	Shawn Green, Adrian Beltre	8.00
KA	Jeff Kent, Rich Aurilia	5.00
GK	Tony Gwynn, Ryan Klesko	15.00
MJ	Greg Maddux,	
	Chipper Jones	20.00
HH	Mike Hampton,	
	Todd Helton	10.00
SV	Tsuyoshi Shinjo,	
	Robin Ventura	5.00
GJ	Cristian Guzman,	
	Jacque Jones	5.00
CJ	Roger Clemens,	
	Derek Jeter	125.00

Jerseys

	NM/M
Common Player:	5.00
Inserted 1:20	

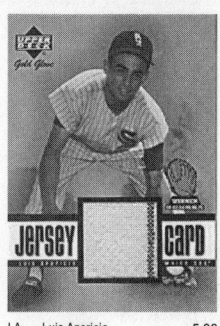

LA	Luis Aparicio	5.00
JB	Jeff Bagwell	8.00
BB	Barry Bonds	25.00
GC	Gary Carter	5.00
CC	Cesar Cedeno	5.00
DE	Darin Erstad	6.00
CF	Carlton Fisk	8.00
MG	Mark Grace	8.00
SG	Shawn Green	5.00
KG	Ken Griffey Jr.	20.00
RG	Ron Guidry	5.00
AJ	Andruw Jones	8.00
JK	Jim Kaat	5.00
GM	Greg Maddux	15.00
MM	Mickey Mantle	150.00
RM	Roger Maris	75.00
DM	Don Mattingly	30.00
TM	Thurman Munson	60.00
MM	Mike Mussina	10.00
RP	Rafael Palmeiro	10.00
BR	Bobby Richardson	8.00
CR	Cal Ripken Jr.	35.00
IR	Ivan Rodriguez	10.00
OS	Ozzie Smith	15.00
IS	Ichiro Suzuki	65.00
OV	Omar Vizquel	8.00
BW	Bernie Williams	8.00

2001 Upper Deck Hall of Famers

		NM/M
Complete Set (90):		25.00
Common Player:		.15
Hobby Pack (5):		4.00
Box (24):		80.00
1	Reggie Jackson	.75
2	Hank Aaron	1.50
3	Eddie Mathews	.75
4	Warren Spahn	.40
5	Robin Yount	.40
6	Lou Brock	.25
7	Dizzy Dean	.15
8	Bob Gibson	.40
9	Stan Musial	.75
10	Enos Slaughter	.15
11	Rogers Hornsby	.40
12	Ernie Banks	.50
13	Ferguson Jenkins	.15
14	Roy Campanella	.75
15	Pee Wee Reese	.15
16	Jackie Robinson	1.50
17	Juan Marichal	.15
18	Christy Mathewson	.15
19	Willie Mays	1.50
20	Hoyt Wilhelm	.15
21	Buck Leonard	.15
22	Bob Feller	.40
23	Cy Young	.40
24	Satchel Paige	.40
25	Tom Seaver	.50
26	Brooks Robinson	.40
27	Mike Schmidt	.75
28	Roberto Clemente	1.50
29	Ralph Kiner	.15
30	Willie Stargell	.50
31	Honus Wagner	.75
32	Josh Gibson	.40

33	Nolan Ryan	1.50
34	Carlton Fisk	.15
35	Jimmie Foxx	.75
36	Johnny Bench	.75
37	Joe Morgan	.40
38	George Brett	.75
39	Walter Johnson	.40
40	Cool Papa Bell	.15
41	Ty Cobb	1.00
42	Al Kaline	.15
43	Harmon Killebrew	.15
44	Luis Aparicio	.15
45	Yogi Berra	.75
46	Joe DiMaggio	1.50
47	Whitey Ford	.25
48	Lou Gehrig	2.00
49	Mickey Mantle	2.00
50	Babe Ruth	2.00
51	Josh Gibson (Origins of the Game)	.15
52	Honus Wagner (Origins of the Game)	.20
53	Hoyt Wilhelm (Origins of the Game)	.15
54	Cy Young (Origins of the Game)	.20
55	Walter Johnson (Origins of the Game)	.20
56	Satchel Paige (Origins of the Game)	.25
57	Rogers Hornsby (Origins of the Game)	.20
58	Christy Mathewson (Origins of the Game)	.15
59	Tris Speaker (Origins of the Game)	.20
60	Nap Lajoie (Origins of the Game)	.15
61	Mickey Mantle (The National Pastime)	1.00
62	Jackie Robinson (The National Pastime)	.75
63	Nolan Ryan (The National Pastime)	.75
64	Josh Gibson (The National Pastime)	.20
65	Yogi Berra (The National Pastime)	.40
66	Brooks Robinson (The National Pastime)	.20
67	Stan Musial (The National Pastime)	.40
68	Mike Schmidt (The National Pastime)	.40
69	Joe DiMaggio (The National Pastime)	1.00
70	Ernie Banks (The National Pastime)	.25
71	Willie Stargell (The National Pastime)	.25
72	Johnny Bench (The National Pastime)	.40
73	Willie Mays (The National Pastime)	.75
74	Satchel Paige (The National Pastime)	.25
75	Bob Gibson (The National Pastime)	.20
76	Harmon Killebrew (The National Pastime)	.15
77	Al Kaline (The National Pastime)	.15
78	Carlton Fisk (The National Pastime)	.15
79	Tom Seaver (The National Pastime)	.25
80	Reggie Jackson (The National Pastime)	.40
81	Bob Gibson (The Hall of Records)	.20
82	Nolan Ryan (The Hall of Records)	.75
83	Walter Johnson (The Hall of Records)	.20
84	Stan Musial (The Hall of Records)	.40
85	Josh Gibson (The Hall of Records)	.20
86	Cy Young (The Hall of Records)	.20
87	Joe DiMaggio (The Hall of Records)	1.00
88	Hoyt Wilhelm (The Hall of Records)	.15
89	Lou Brock (The Hall of Records)	.15
90	Mickey Mantle (The Hall of Records)	1.00

Hall of Fame Gallery

		NM/M
Complete Set (15):		25.00
Common Player:		1.00
Inserted 1:6		
1	Reggie Jackson	1.50
2	Tom Seaver	1.50
3	Bob Gibson	1.50
4	Jackie Robinson	3.00
5	Joe DiMaggio	3.00
6	Ernie Banks	1.50
7	Mickey Mantle	4.00

8	Willie Mays	3.00
9	Cy Young	1.50
10	Nolan Ryan	4.00
11	Johnny Bench	1.50
12	Yogi Berra	1.50
13	Satchel Paige	1.00
14	George Brett	2.00
15	Stan Musial	2.00

The Endless Summer

		NM/M
Complete Set (11):		15.00
Common Player:		1.00
Inserted 1:8		
1	Mickey Mantle	4.00
2	Yogi Berra	1.00
3	Mike Schmidt	2.50
4	Jackie Robinson	2.50
5	Johnny Bench	1.50
6	Tom Seaver	1.50
7	Ernie Banks	1.50
8	Harmon Killebrew	1.00
9	Joe DiMaggio	3.00
10	Willie Mays	3.00
11	Brooks Robinson	1.00

20th Century Showcase

		NM/M
Complete Set (11):		15.00
Common Player:		1.00
Inserted 1:8		
1	Cy Young	1.00
2	Joe DiMaggio	3.00
3	Harmon Killebrew	1.00
4	Stan Musial	2.00
5	Mickey Mantle	4.00
6	Satchel Paige	1.00
7	Nolan Ryan	4.00
8	Bob Gibson	1.50
9	Ernie Banks	1.50
10	Mike Schmidt	2.00
11	Willie Mays	3.00

The Class of '36

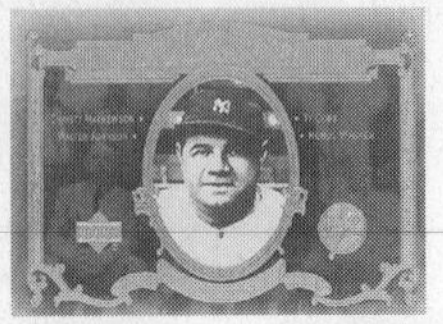

		NM/M
Complete Set (5):		8.00
Common Player:		1.50
Inserted 1:17		
1	Ty Cobb	2.00
2	Babe Ruth	5.00
3	Christy Mathewson	1.50
4	Walter Johnson	1.50
5	Honus Wagner	1.50

Coop. Coll. Game Bat

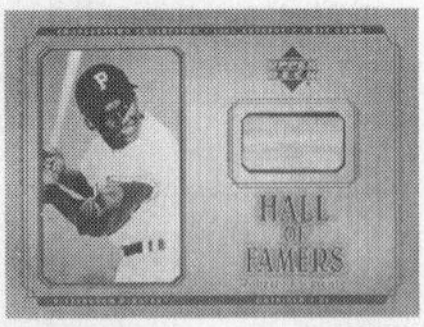

		NM/M
Common Player:		5.00
Inserted 1:24		
HA	Hank Aaron	30.00
LA	Luis Aparicio	5.00
EB	Ernie Banks	15.00
JB	Johnny Bench	15.00
YB	Yogi Berra	10.00
JBo	Jim Bottomley	5.00
GB	George Brett	20.00
RC	Roy Campanella	30.00
OC	Orlando Cepeda	5.00
RC	Roberto Clemente/SP/409	120.00
JD	Joe DiMaggio	100.00
CF	Carlton Fisk	10.00
RF	Rollie Fingers	5.00
JF	Jimmie Foxx	50.00
HG	Hank Greenberg	40.00
RH	Rogers Hornsby	100.00
RJ	Reggie Jackson	15.00
GK	George Kell	5.00
RK	Ralph Kiner	10.00
MM	Mickey Mantle	125.00
WM	Willie Mays	30.00
JM	Johnny Mize	10.00
JMo	Joe Morgan	5.00
MO	Mel Ott	50.00
JP	Jim Palmer/SP/372	50.00
TP	Tony Perez	5.00
BR	Brooks Robinson	10.00
FR	Frank Robinson	10.00
JR	Jackie Robinson/SP/371	175.00
BR	Babe Ruth	200.00
NR	Nolan Ryan	50.00
RS	Red Schoendienst	5.00
ES	Enos Slaughter	5.00
DS	Duke Snider	10.00
WS	Willie Stargell	5.00
BW	Billy Williams	5.00
EW	Early Wynn	5.00
RY	Robin Yount	15.00

Coop. Coll. Game Jersey

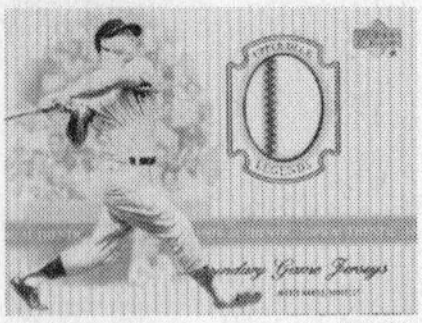

		NM/M
Common Player:		10.00
Inserted 1:168		
LA	Luis Aparicio	10.00
OC	Orlando Cepeda	10.00
RC	Roberto Clemente	100.00
JD	Joe DiMaggio	100.00
DD	Don Drysdale/SP/49	200.00
LG	Lou Gehrig/SP/194	250.00
MM	Mickey Mantle/SP/216	250.00
WM	Willie Mays	80.00
JM	Joe Morgan	10.00
TP	Tony Perez	10.00
PW	Pee Wee Reese	15.00
BR	Brooks Robinson	20.00
FR	Frank Robinson	10.00
NR	Nolan Ryan	30.00
TS	Tom Seaver	15.00
DS	Duke Snider/SP/267	50.00
WS	Willie Stargell	15.00
DSu	Don Sutton	10.00

Coop. Coll. Jersey Auto.

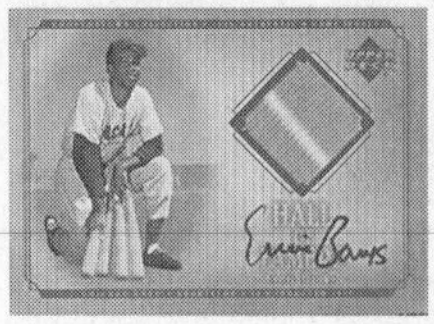

		NM/M
Common Autograph:		40.00
Inserted 1:504		
LA	Luis Aparicio	40.00
OC	Orlando Cepeda	40.00
RJ	Reggie Jackson	75.00
EB	Ernie Banks	90.00
JM	Joe Morgan	40.00
TP	Tony Perez	40.00
GB	George Brett	125.00
BR	Brooks Robinson	80.00
FR	Frank Robinson	60.00
NR	Nolan Ryan	175.00
TS	Tom Seaver	75.00
DS	Duke Snider	65.00
WS	Willie Stargell	75.00
DSu	Don Sutton	40.00

Mantle Pinstripes Excl.

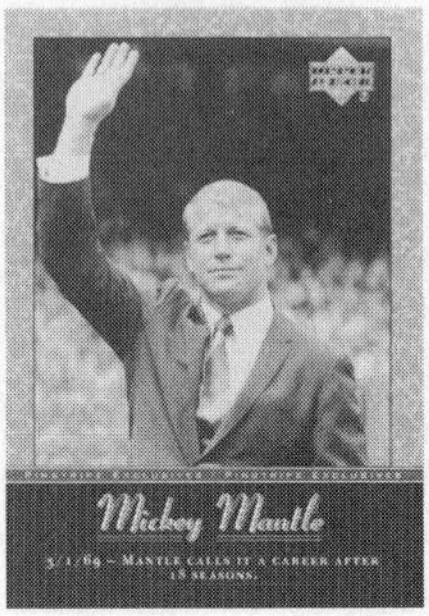

	NM/M
Complete Set (56):	75.00
Common Mantle:	2.00
One Pack/Box	

Mantle Pinstripe Memor.

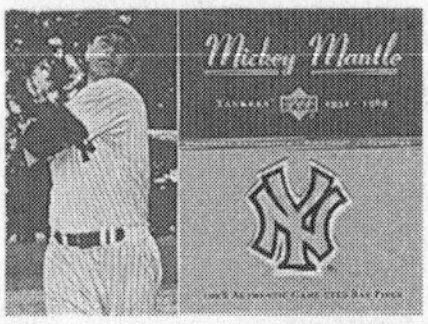

		NM/M
Print Runs Listed		
MMBC	Mickey Mantle/Bat/Cut/7	
MMB	Mickey Mantle/Bat/100	100.00
MMCJ	Mickey Mantle, Joe DiMaggio/Jsy/50	300.00
MMC	Mickey Mantle/Cut/7	
MMJ	Mickey Mantle/Jsy/100	125.00

2001 Upper Deck Legends

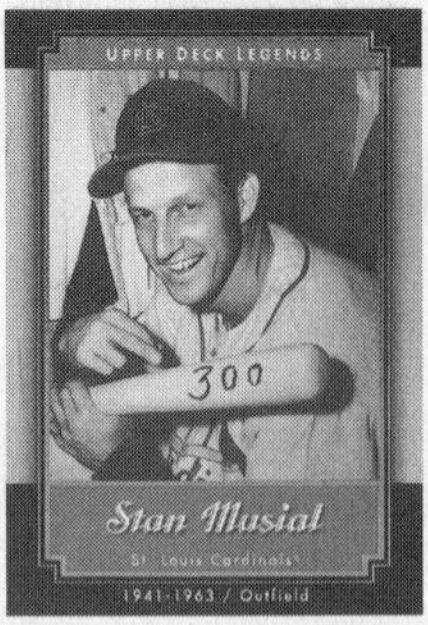

		NM/M
Complete Set (90):		20.00
Common Player:		.20
Pack (5):		4.00
Box (24):		80.00
1	Darin Erstad	.40
2	Troy Glaus	.75
3	Nolan Ryan	3.00
4	Reggie Jackson	.50
5	Jim "Catfish" Hunter	.20
6	Jason Giambi	.50
7	Tim Hudson	.30
8	Miguel Tejada	.30
9	Carlos Delgado	.50
10	Shannon Stewart	.20
11	Greg Vaughn	.20
12	Larry Doby	.20
13	Jim Thome	.40
14	Juan Gonzalez	.75
15	Roberto Alomar	.50
16	Edgar Martinez	.20
17	John Olerud	.40
18	Eddie Murray	.40
19	Cal Ripken Jr.	2.50
20	Alex Rodriguez	2.00
21	Ivan Rodriguez	.75
22	Rafael Palmeiro	.40
23	Jimmie Foxx	.50
24	Cy Young	.50
25	Manny Ramirez	.75
26	Pedro Martinez	1.00
27	Nomar Garciaparra	2.00
28	George Brett	1.00
29	Mike Sweeney	.20
30	Jermaine Dye	.20
31	Ty Cobb	1.50
32	Dean Palmer	.20
33	Harmon Killebrew	.50
34	Matt Lawton	.20
35	Luis Aparicio	.20
36	Frank Thomas	.75
37	Magglio Ordonez	.20
38	David Wells	.20
39	Mickey Mantle	3.00
40	Joe DiMaggio	3.00
41	Roger Maris	.75
42	Babe Ruth	3.00
43	Derek Jeter	2.50
44	Roger Clemens	1.00
45	Bernie Williams	.50
46	Jeff Bagwell	.75
47	Richard Hidalgo	.40
48	Warren Spahn	.40
49	Greg Maddux	1.50
50	Chipper Jones	1.50
51	Andruw Jones	.50
52	Robin Yount	.50
53	Jeromy Burnitz	.20
54	Jeffrey Hammonds	.20
55	Ozzie Smith	.50
56	Stan Musial	1.00
57	Mark McGwire	2.50
58	Jim Edmonds	.30
59	Sammy Sosa	1.50
60	Ernie Banks	.50
61	Kerry Wood	.20
62	Randy Johnson	.75
63	Luis Gonzalez	.40
64	Don Drysdale	.50
65	Jackie Robinson	2.00
66	Gary Sheffield	.20
67	Kevin Brown	.20
68	Vladimir Guerrero	1.00
69	Willie Mays	1.50
70	Mel Ott	.20
71	Jeff Kent	.20
72	Barry Bonds	1.00
73	Preston Wilson	.20
74	Ryan Dempster	.20
75	Tom Seaver	.40
76	Mike Piazza	2.00
77	Robin Ventura	.20
78	Dave Winfield	.40
79	Tony Gwynn	1.00
80	Bob Abreu	.20
81	Scott Rolen	.40
82	Mike Schmidt	.75
83	Roberto Clemente	1.50
84	Brian Giles	.20
85	Ken Griffey Jr.	2.00
86	Frank Robinson	.40
87	Johnny Bench	.75
88	Todd Helton	.75
89	Larry Walker	.40
90	Mike Hampton	.20

Legendary Cuts

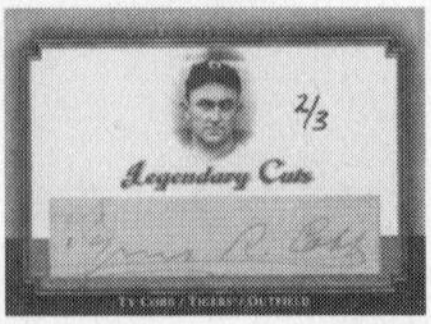

		NM/M
Most not priced due to scarcity.		
C-TC	Ty Cobb/3	3,150
C-BRu	Babe Ruth/7	6,000

Fiorentino Collection

		NM/M
Complete Set (14):		40.00
Common Player:		1.50
Inserted 1:12		

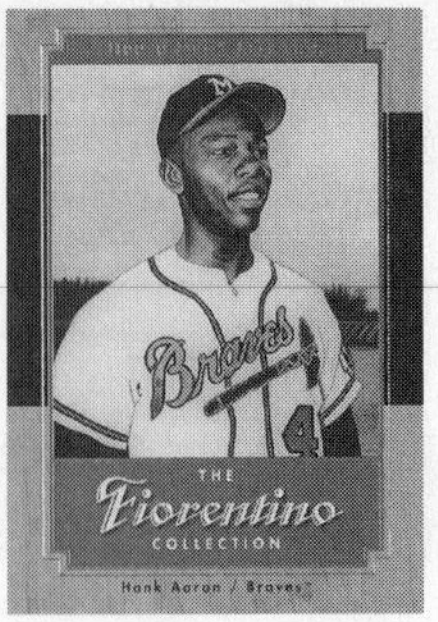

F1	Babe Ruth	6.00
F2	Satchel Paige	1.50
F3	Joe DiMaggio	5.00
F4	Willie Mays	4.00
F5	Ty Cobb	3.00
F6	Nolan Ryan	5.00
F7	Lou Gehrig	5.00
F8	Jackie Robinson	4.00
F9	Hank Aaron	4.00
F10	Roberto Clemente	4.00
F11	Stan Musial	3.00
F12	Johnny Bench	2.00
F13	Honus Wagner	1.50
F14	Reggie Jackson	1.50

Reflections

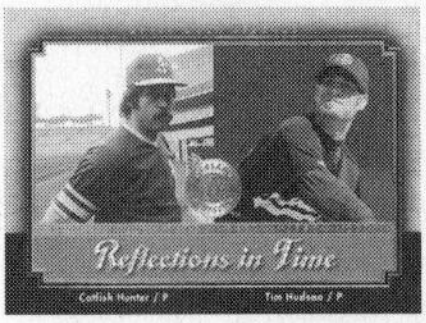

		NM/M
Complete Set (10):		25.00
Common Card:		1.00
Inserted 1:18		
R1	Bernie Williams, Mickey Mantle	6.00
R2	Pedro Martinez, Cy Young	2.00
R3	Barry Bonds, Willie Mays	5.00
R4	Scott Rolen, Mike Schmidt	3.00
R5	Mark McGwire, Stan Musial	4.00
R6	Ken Griffey Jr., Frank Robinson	3.00
R7	Sammy Sosa, Andre Dawson	3.00
R8	Kevin Brown, Don Drysdale	1.50
R9	Jason Giambi, Reggie Jackson	1.50
R10	Tim Hudson, Jim "Catfish" Hunter	1.00

Legendary Game Jerseys

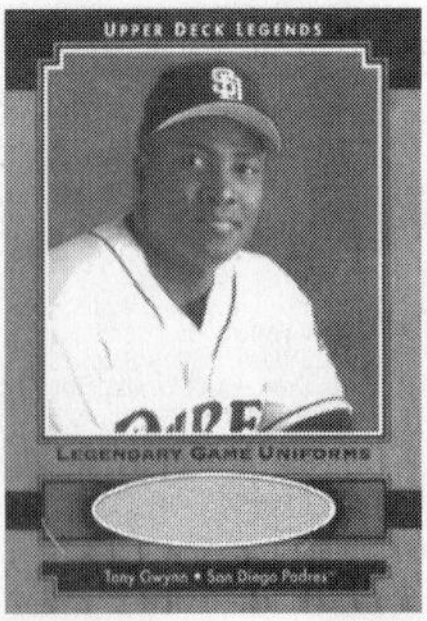

		NM/M
Common Player:		5.00
Inserted 1:24		
HA	Hank Aaron	40.00
JB	Jeff Bagwell	8.00
EB	Ernie Banks	15.00
YB	Yogi Berra	10.00
BB	Barry Bonds	25.00
JC	Jose Canseco	10.00
RCl	Roger Clemens	20.00
RoC	Roberto Clemente/195	170.00
JD	Joe DiMaggio/245	175.00
KG	Ken Griffey Jr.	15.00
TG	Tony Gwynn	10.00
RJa	Reggie Jackson	10.00
RJo	Randy Johnson	10.00
CJ	Chipper Jones	10.00
GM	Greg Maddux	15.00

MM	Mickey Mantle/245	200.00
RM	Roger Maris/343	65.00
PM	Pedro Martinez	10.00
WM	Willie Mays	30.00
SM	Stan Musial/490	30.00
MP	Mike Piazza	20.00
MR	Manny Ramirez	8.00
CR	Cal Ripken Jr.	30.00
AR	Alex Rodriguez	20.00
IR	Ivan Rodriguez	8.00
NR	Nolan Ryan	50.00
KS	Kazuhiro Sasaki	15.00
TS	Tom Seaver	15.00
GS	Gary Sheffield	5.00
OS	Ozzie Smith	15.00
SS	Sammy Sosa	15.00
DW	Dave Winfield	5.00
RY	Robin Yount	12.00

Legendary Jerseys Gold

	NM/M
Common Player:	30.00
Production 25 Sets	
RCI	Roger Clemens	75.00
RoC	Roberto Clemente	180.00
KG	Ken Griffey Jr.	75.00
RJ	Reggie Jackson	40.00
WM	Willie Mays	120.00
AR	Alex Rodriguez	75.00
NR	Nolan Ryan	100.00
SS	Sammy Sosa	75.00
DW	Dave Winfield	30.00

Legendary Jerseys Auto.

	NM/M
Inserted 1:288	
EB	Ernie Banks	75.00
RC	Roger Clemens/211	100.00
KG	Ken Griffey Jr.	80.00
RJ	Reggie Jackson/224	60.00
SM	Stan Musial/266	100.00
AR	Alex Rodriguez	85.00
NR	Nolan Ryan	125.00
TS	Tom Seaver	60.00
OS	Ozzie Smith	60.00
SS	Sammy Sosa/91	175.00

Legendary Jerseys Gold Auto.

No pricing due to scarcity.
Production 25 Sets
No Pricing

Legendary Lumber

	NM/M
Common Player:	5.00
Inserted 1:24	
HA	Hank Aaron	30.00
LA	Luis Aparicio	5.00
EB	Ernie Banks/80	50.00
JB	Johnny Bench	15.00
BB	Barry Bonds	25.00
RCa	Roy Campanella/335	40.00
JC	Jose Canseco	8.00
RCI	Roger Clemens	20.00
RoC	Roberto Clemente/170	120.00
JD	Joe DiMaggio	85.00
JF	Jimmie Foxx/351	50.00

KG	Ken Griffey Jr.	15.00
TG	Tony Gwynn	10.00
RJ	Reggie Jackson	10.00
RJ	Randy Johnson	10.00
AJ	Andruw Jones	8.00
CJ	Chipper Jones	10.00
MM	Mickey Mantle	150.00
RM	Roger Maris	40.00
WM	Willie Mays	30.00
EM	Eddie Murray	8.00
MO	Mel Ott/355	40.00
MP	Mike Piazza	15.00
AP	Albert Pujols	45.00
MR	Manny Ramirez	8.00
FR	Frank Robinson	8.00
CR	Cal Ripken Jr.	40.00
AR	Alex Rodriguez	15.00
IR	Ivan Rodriguez	8.00
GS	Gary Sheffield	5.00
OS	Ozzie Smith	10.00
SS	Sammy Sosa	15.00

Legendary Lumber Gold

	NM/M
Common Player:	25.00
Production 25 Sets	
RC	Roger Clemens	75.00
RC	Roberto Clemente	180.00
KG	Ken Griffey Jr.	75.00
RJ	Reggie Jackson	40.00
WM	Willie Mays	120.00
AR	Alex Rodriguez	75.00
GS	Gary Sheffield	25.00
SS	Sammy Sosa	15.00

Legendary Lumber Auto.

	NM/M
Common Player:	25.00
Inserted 1:288	
LA	Luis Aparicio	25.00
EB	Ernie Banks	65.00
RC	Roger Clemens/227	100.00
KG	Ken Griffey Jr.	80.00
TG	Tony Gwynn	60.00
RJ	Reggie Jackson/211	65.00
EM	Eddie Murray	40.00
AR	Alex Rodriguez	100.00
SS	Sammy Sosa/66	240.00

2001 Upper Deck Legends of New York

	NM/M
Complete Set (200):	40.00
Common Player:	.20
Pack (5):	2.50
Box (24):	50.00
1	Billy Herman	.20
2	Carl Erskine	.20
3	Burleigh Grimes	.20
4	Don Newcombe	.20
5	Gil Hodges	.75
6	Pee Wee Reese	.75
7	Jackie Robinson	2.00
8	Duke Snider	1.00
9	Jim Gilliam	.20
10	Roy Campanella	1.50

DEM BUMS

GIL HODGES POWERS DODGERS TO PENNANT

11	Carl Furillo	.20
12	Casey Stengel	.75
13	Casey Stengel	.40
14	Billy Herman	.20
15	Jackie Robinson	1.00
16	Jackie Robinson	1.00
17	Gil Hodges	.40
18	Carl Furillo	.20
19	Roy Campanella	.50
20	Don Newcombe	.40
21	Duke Snider	.75
22	Casey Stengel	.40
23	Burleigh Grimes	.20
24	Pee Wee Reese	.50
25	Jackie Robinson	1.00
26	Jackie Robinson	1.00
27	Carl Erskine	.20
28	Roy Campanella	.75
29	Duke Snider	.75
30	Rube Marquard	.20
31	Ross Youngs	.20
32	Bobby Thomson	.20
33	Christy Mathewson	1.00
34	Carl Hubbell	.20
35	Hoyt Wilhelm	.20
36	Johnny Mize	.40
37	John McGraw	.20
38	Monte Irvin	.50
39	Travis Jackson	.20
40	Mel Ott	1.00
41	Dusty Rhodes	.20
42	Leo Durocher	.50
43	John McGraw	.20
44	Christy Mathewson	.50
45	The Polo Grounds	.20
46	Travis Jackson	.20
47	Mel Ott	.50
48	Johnny Mize	.20
49	Leo Durocher	.30
50	Bobby Thomson	.20
51	Monte Irvin	.30
52	Bobby Thomson	.20
53	Christy Mathewson	.50
54	Christy Mathewson	.50
55	Christy Mathewson	.50
56	John McGraw	.20
57	John McGraw	.20
58	John McGraw	.20
59	Travis Jackson	.20
60	Mel Ott	.50
61	Mel Ott	.50
62	Carl Hubbell	.20
63	Bobby Thomson	.20
64	Monte Irvin	.20
65	Al Weis	.20
66	Donn Clendenon	.20
67	Ed Kranepool	.20
68	Gary Carter	.20
69	Tommie Agee	.20
70	Jon Matlack	.20
71	Ken Boswell	.20
72	Len Dykstra	.20
73	Nolan Ryan	3.00
74	Ray Sadecki	.20
75	Ron Darling	.20
76	Ron Swoboda	.20
77	Dwight Gooden	.20
78	Tom Seaver	1.00
79	Wayne Garrett	.20
80	Casey Stengel	.50
81	Tom Seaver	.50
82	Tommie Agee	.20
83	Tom Seaver	.50
84	Yogi Berra	.50
85	Yogi Berra	.50
86	Tom Seaver	.50
87	Dwight Gooden	.20
88	Gary Carter	.20
89	Ron Darling	.20
90	Tommie Agee	.20
91	Tom Seaver	.50
92	Gary Carter	.20
93	Len Dykstra	.20
94	Babe Ruth	3.00
95	Bill Dickey	.50
96	Rich "Goose" Gossage	.20
97	Casey Stengel	.50
98	Jim "Catfish" Hunter	.75
99	Charlie Keller	.20
100	Chris Chambliss	.20
101	Don Larsen	.40

102	Dave Winfield	.75
103	Don Mattingly	2.00
104	Elston Howard	.20
105	Frankie Crosetti	.20
106	Hank Bauer	.20
107	Joe DiMaggio	3.00
108	Graig Nettles	.20
109	Lefty Gomez	.20
110	Phil Rizzuto	1.00
111	Lou Gehrig	2.00
112	Lou Piniella	.20
113	Mickey Mantle	3.00
114	Red Rolfe	.20
115	Reggie Jackson	1.00
116	Roger Maris	1.50
117	Ray White	.20
118	Thurman Munson	1.50
119	Tom Tresh	.20
120	Tommy Henrich	.20
121	Waite Hoyt	.20
122	Willie Randolph	.20
123	Whitey Ford	.75
124	Yogi Berra	1.00
125	Babe Ruth	1.50
126	Babe Ruth	1.50
127	Lou Gehrig	1.25
128	Babe Ruth	1.50
129	Joe DiMaggio	1.50
130	Joe DiMaggio	1.50
131	Mickey Mantle	1.50
132	Roger Marris	.75
133	Mickey Mantle	1.50
134	Reggie Jackson	.75
135	Babe Ruth	1.50
136	Babe Ruth	1.50
137	Babe Ruth	1.50
138	Lefty Gomez	.20
139	Lou Gehrig	1.25
140	Lou Gehrig	1.25
141	Joe DiMaggio	1.50
142	Joe DiMaggio	1.50
143	Casey Stengel	.40
144	Mickey Mantle	1.50
145	Yogi Berra	.50
146	Mickey Mantle	1.50
147	Elston Howard	.40
148	Whitey Ford	.50
149	Reggie Jackson	.50
150	Reggie Jackson	.50
151	John McGraw, Babe Ruth	1.00
152	Babe Ruth, John McGraw	1.00
153	Lou Gehrig, Mel Ott	.75
154	Joe DiMaggio, Mel Ott	1.00
155	Joe DiMaggio, Billy Herman	1.00
156	Joe DiMaggio, Jackie Robinson	1.50
157	Mickey Mantle, Bobby Thomson	1.00
158	Yogi Berra, Pee Wee Reese	.75
159	Roy Campanella, Mickey Mantle	1.00
160	Don Larsen, Duke Snider	.50
161	Christy Mathewson	.75
162	Christy Mathewson	.50
163	Rube Marquard	.20
164	Christy Mathewson	.50
165	John McGraw	.20
166	Burleigh Grimes	.20
167	Babe Ruth	1.50
168	Burleigh Grimes	.20
169	Babe Ruth	1.50
170	John McGraw	.40
171	Lou Gehrig	1.25
172	Babe Ruth	1.50
173	Babe Ruth	1.50
174	Carl Hubbell	.20
175	Joe DiMaggio	1.50
176	Lou Gehrig	1.25
177	Leo Durocher	.40
178	Mel Ott	.50
179	Joe DiMaggio	1.50
180	Jackie Robinson	1.00
181	Babe Ruth	1.50
182	Bobby Thomson	.20
183	Joe DiMaggio	1.50
184	Mickey Mantle	1.50
185	Monte Irvin	.20
186	Roy Campanella	.50
187	Duke Snider	.50
188	Dusty Rhodes	.20
189	Yogi Berra	.50
190	Mickey Mantle	1.50
191	Mickey Mantle	1.50
192	Casey Stengel	.40
193	Tom Seaver	.50
194	Mickey Mantle	1.50
195	Tommie Agee	.20
196	Tom Seaver	.50
197	Chris Chambliss	.20
198	Reggie Jackson	.50
199	Reggie Jackson	.50
200	Gary Carter	.20

Bat Cards

	NM/M
Common Player:	5.00
Inserted 1:24	
DODGERS	
JG	Jim Gilliam	10.00
BH	Billy Herman	8.00
DN	Don Newcombe/67	40.00
GIANTS	
BTh	Bobby Thomson	25.00

METS

KB	Ken Boswell	5.00
GC	Gary Carter	15.00
LD	Len Dykstra	5.00
WG	Wayne Garrett	8.00
EK	Ed Kranepool	10.00
JM	J.C. Martin	8.00
NR	Nolan Ryan	40.00
TS	Tom Seaver	20.00
RSw	Ron Swoboda	8.00
AW	Al Weis	5.00

YANKEES

HB	Hank Bauer	10.00
YB	Yogi Berra	15.00
CC	Chris Chambliss/130	15.00
BD	Bill Dickey	15.00
TH	Tommy Henrich	8.00
EH	Elston Howard	10.00
RJ	Reggie Jackson	15.00
CK	Charlie Keller	8.00
MM	Mickey Mantle/134	200.00
RM	Roger Maris/60	85.00
DM	Don Mattingly	30.00
TM	Thurman Munson	20.00
LP	Lou Piniella	8.00
MR	Mickey Rivers	5.00
BR	Babe Ruth/107	250.00
TT	Tom Tresh	10.00
DW	Dave Winfield	10.00

Bat Autographs

NM/M

Common Autograph:

DODGERS

DN	Don Newcombe	30.00

METS

GC	Gary Carter	40.00
DC	Donn Clendenon	30.00
NR	Nolan Ryan/129	200.00
TS	Tom Seaver/89	100.00
RS	Ron Swoboda	

YANKEES

YB	Yogi Berra	75.00
CC	Chris Chambliss	30.00
RJ	Reggie Jackson/123	75.00
DM	Don Mattingly	100.00
MR	Mickey Rivers	25.00
RW	Roy White	25.00

Combination Signatures

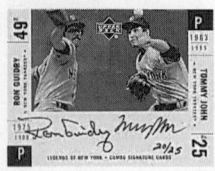

NM/M

Common Card: 75.00

NP	Don Newcombe,	
	Johnny Podres	85.00
WM	Dave Winfield,	
	Don Mattingly	200.00
RS	Nolan Ryan, Tom Seaver	400.00
LB	Don Larsen, Yogi Berra	150.00
GJ	Ron Guidry, Tommy John	60.00
CN	Chris Chambliss,	
	Graig Nettles	60.00
RD	Willie Randolph,	
	Bucky Dent	60.00
RW	Mickey Rivers, Roy White	60.00
WJ	Dave Winfield,	
	Reggie Jackson	150.00

Cut Signatures

NM/M

Most not priced due to scarcity.

LC-JD	Joe DiMaggio (38 Issued)	1,000

Dodgers Game Jersey

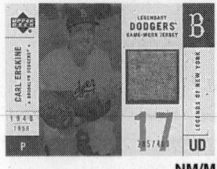

NM/M

Common Player:		5.00
Gold Edition of 400:		1.25X
HB	Hank Behrman	5.00
CD	Chuck Dressen	5.00
CE	Carl Erskine	10.00
SJ	Spider Jurgenson	5.00
JR	Jackie Robinson/126	120.00

Giants Game Jersey

NM/M

Complete Set (1):		
CM	Christy Mathewson/63	350.00

Mets Game Jersey

NM/M

Common Player:		5.00
Gold Edition of 400:		1.25X
RD	Ron Darling	5.00
JM	Jon Matlack	5.00
RS	Ray Sadecki	5.00
TS	Tom Seaver	15.00
CS	Casey Stengel	8.00
JT	Joe Torre	5.00

Yankees Game Jersey

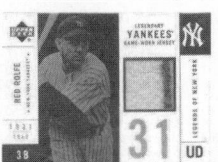

NM/M

Common Player:		5.00
Gold Edition of 400:		1.25X
HB	Hank Bauer	8.00
FC	Frank Crosetti	10.00
TH	Tommy Henrich	10.00
EH	Elston Howard	10.00
CH	Jim "Catfish" Hunter	10.00
DM	Duke Maas	5.00
MM	Mickey Mantle/63	250.00
LM	Lindy McDaniel	5.00
TM	Thurman Munson	30.00
GN	Graig Nettles	10.00
PN	Phil Niekro	10.00
JP	Joe Pepitone	8.00
WR	Willie Randolph	8.00
RR	Red Rolfe	5.00
BT	Bob Turley	8.00
DW	Dave Winfield	15.00

Signed Game Jersey

NM/M

Common Autograph: 15.00

DODGERS

CE	Carl Erskine	50.00
JP	Johnny Podres/193	50.00

METS

GF	George Foster/196	30.00
NR	Nolan Ryan/47	200.00
CS	Craig Swan	30.00

YANKEES

YG	Yogi Berra/73	125.00
BD	Bucky Dent	30.00
RG	Rich Gossage/145	40.00
RG	Ron Guidry	50.00
TJ	Tommy John	30.00
DL	Don Larsen	60.00
HL	Hector Lopez/195	15.00
SL	Sparky Lyle	30.00
DM	Don Mattingly/72	125.00
PN	Phil Niekro/195	40.00
GN	Graig Nettles	30.00
JP	Joe Pepitone	30.00
WR	Willie Randolph	30.00
DR	Dave Righetti	

Ebbets Field Seat

NM/M

Complete Set (1):		
JR	Jackie Robinson	50.00

Ebbets Field G-U Base

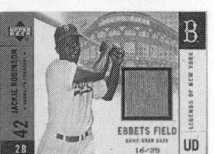

NM/M

Complete Set (1):		
JR	Jackie Robinson/100	50.00
JR	Jackie Robinson/Silver/50	60.00
JR	Jackie Robinson/Gold/25	75.00

Shea Stadium G-U Base

NM/M

Quantity produced listed

TS	Tom Seaver/100	25.00
TS	Tom Seaver/Silver/50	40.00
TS	Tom Seaver/Gold/25	50.00

United We Stand

NM/M

Complete Set (15):		10.00
Common Card:		1.00
Inserted 1:12		
USA1-15	United We Stand	1.00

Yankee Stadium Seat

No Pricing

2001 Upper Deck MVP

NM/M

Complete Set (330): 35.00

Common Player:		.10
Pack (8):		1.50
Box (24):		30.00
1	Mo Vaughn	.10
2	Troy Percival	.10
3	Adam Kennedy	.10
4	Darin Erstad	.25
5	Tim Salmon	.10
6	Bengie Molina	.10
7	Troy Glaus	.40
8	Garret Anderson	.25
9	Ismael Valdes	.10
10	Glenallen Hill	.10
11	Tim Hudson	.25
12	Eric Chavez	.20
13	Johnny Damon	.20
14	Barry Zito	.40
15	Jason Giambi	.40
16	Terrence Long	.10
17	Jason Hart	.10
18	Jose Ortiz	.10
19	Miguel Tejada	.25
20	Jason Isringhausen	.10
21	Adam Piatt	.10
22	Jeremy Giambi	.10
23	Tony Batista	.10
24	Darrin Fletcher	.10
25	Mike Sirotka	.10
26	Carlos Delgado	.40
27	Billy Koch	.10
28	Shannon Stewart	.10
29	Raul Mondesi	.15
30	Brad Fullmer	.10
31	Jose Cruz Jr.	.10
32	Kelvim Escobar	.10
33	Greg Vaughn	.10
34	Aubrey Huff	.10
35	Albie Lopez	.10
36	Gerald Williams	.10
37	Ben Grieve	.10
38	John Flaherty	.10
39	Fred McGriff	.15
40	Ryan Rupe	.10
41	Travis Harper	.10
42	Steve Cox	.10
43	Roberto Alomar	.40
44	Jim Thome	.50
45	Russell Branyan	.10
46	Bartolo Colon	.20
47	Omar Vizquel	.15
48	Travis Fryman	.15
49	Kenny Lofton	.15
50	Chuck Finley	.10
51	Ellis Burks	.10
52	Eddie Taubensee	.10
53	Juan Gonzalez	.40
54	Edgar Martinez	.20
55	Aaron Sele	.10
56	John Olerud	.20
57	Jay Buhner	.10
58	Mike Cameron	.10
59	John Halama	.10
60	Ichiro Suzuki RC	8.00
61	David Bell	.10
62	Freddy Garcia	.10
63	Carlos Guillen	.10
64	Bret Boone	.20
65	Al Martin	.10
66	Cal Ripken Jr.	1.50
67	Delino DeShields	.10
68	Chris Richard	.10
69	Sean Douglass RC	.25
70	Melvin Mora	.10
71	Luis Matos	.10
72	Sidney Ponson	.10
73	Mike Bordick	.10
74	Brady Anderson	.10
75	David Segui	.10
76	Jeff Conine	.10
77	Alex Rodriguez	1.25
78	Gabe Kapler	.10
79	Ivan Rodriguez	.40
80	Rick Helling	.10
81	Kenny Rogers	.10
82	Andres Galarraga	.15
83	Rusty Greer	.10
84	Justin Thompson	.10
85	Ken Caminiti	.10
86	Rafael Palmeiro	.40
87	Ruben Mateo	.10
88	Travis Hafner RC	1.00

89	Manny Ramirez	.40
90	Pedro Martinez	.50
91	Carl Everett	.10
92	Dante Bichette	.10
93	Derek Lowe	.10
94	Jason Varitek	.10
95	Nomar Garciaparra	1.25
96	David Cone	.10
97	Tomokazu Ohka	.10
98	Troy O'Leary	.10
99	Trot Nixon	.10
100	Jermaine Dye	.10
101	Joe Randa	.10
102	Jeff Suppan	.10
103	Roberto Hernandez	.10
104	Mike Sweeney	.10
105	Mac Suzuki	.10
106	Carlos Febles	.10
107	Jose Rosado	.10
108	Mark Quinn	.10
109	Carlos Beltran	.20
110	Dean Palmer	.10
111	Mitch Meluskey	.10
112	Bobby Higginson	.10
113	Brandon Inge	.10
114	Tony Clark	.10
115	Brian Moehler	.10
116	Juan Encarnacion	.10
117	Damion Easley	.10
118	Roger Cedeno	.10
119	Jeff Weaver	.10
120	Matt Lawton	.10
121	Jay Canizaro	.10
122	Eric Milton	.10
123	Corey Koskie	.10
124	Mark Redman	.10
125	Jacque Jones	.10
126	Brad Radke	.10
127	Cristian Guzman	.10
128	Joe Mays	.10
129	Denny Hocking	.10
130	Frank Thomas	.40
131	David Wells	.10
132	Ray Durham	.10
133	Paul Konerko	.10
134	Joe Crede	.10
135	Jim Parque	.10
136	Carlos Lee	.10
137	Magglio Ordonez	.25
138	Sandy Alomar Jr.	.10
139	Chris Singleton	.10
140	Jose Valentin	.10
141	Roger Clemens	1.00
142	Derek Jeter	1.50
143	Orlando Hernandez	.15
144	Tino Martinez	.10
145	Bernie Williams	.40
146	Jorge Posada	.25
147	Mariano Rivera	.20
148	David Justice	.20
149	Paul O'Neill	.15
150	Mike Mussina	.25
151	Christian Parker RC	.10
152	Andy Pettitte	.25
153	Alfonso Soriano	.50
154	Jeff Bagwell	.40
155	Morgan Ensberg RC	.50
156	Daryle Ward	.10
157	Craig Biggio	.20
158	Richard Hidalgo	.10
159	Shane Reynolds	.10
160	Scott Elarton	.10
161	Julio Lugo	.10
162	Moises Alou	.20
163	Lance Berkman	.20
164	Chipper Jones	.75
165	Greg Maddux	1.00
166	Javy Lopez	.15
167	Andruw Jones	.40
168	Rafael Furcal	.25
169	Brian Jordan	.10
170	Wes Helms	.10
171	Tom Glavine	.25
172	B.J. Surhoff	.10
173	John Smoltz	.10
174	Quilvio Veras	.10
175	Rico Brogna	.10
176	Jeromy Burnitz	.10
177	Jeff D'Amico	.10
178	Geoff Jenkins	.20
179	Henry Blanco	.10
180	Mark Loretta	.10
181	Richie Sexson	.25
182	Jimmy Haynes	.10
183	Jeffrey Hammonds	.10
184	Ron Belliard	.10
185	Tyler Houston	.10
186	Mark McGwire	1.00
187	Rick Ankiel	.25
188	Darryl Kile	.10
189	Jim Edmonds	.25
190	Mike Matheny	.10
191	Edgar Renteria	.10
192	Ray Lankford	.10
193	Garrett Stephenson	.10
194	J.D. Drew	.20
195	Fernando Vina	.10
196	Dustin Hermanson	.10
197	Sammy Sosa	1.00
198	Corey Patterson	.25
199	Jon Lieber	.10
200	Kerry Wood	.40
201	Todd Hundley	.10
202	Kevin Tapani	.10
203	Rondell White	.10
204	Eric Young	.10
205	Matt Stairs	.10
206	Bill Mueller	.10
207	Randy Johnson	.50
208	Mark Grace	.25
209	Jay Bell	.10
210	Curt Schilling	.25
211	Erubiel Durazo	.10
212	Luis Gonzalez	.20
213	Steve Finley	.10
214	Matt Williams	.10
215	Reggie Sanders	.10
216	Tony Womack	.10
217	Gary Sheffield	.25
218	Kevin Brown	.15
219	Adrian Beltre	.20
220	Shawn Green	.20
221	Darren Dreifort	.10
222	Chan Ho Park	.10
223	Eric Karros	.15
224	Alex Cora	.10
225	Mark Grudzielanek	.10
226	Andy Ashby	.10
227	Vladimir Guerrero	.75
228	Tony Armas Jr.	.10
229	Fernando Tatis	.10
230	Jose Vidro	.10
231	Javier Vazquez	.10
232	Lee Stevens	.10
233	Milton Bradley	.10
234	Carl Pavano	.10
235	Peter Bergeron	.10
236	Wilton Guerrero	.10
237	Ugueth Urbina	.10
238	Barry Bonds	1.50
239	Livan Hernandez	.15
240	Jeff Kent	.15
241	Pedro Feliz	.10
242	Bobby Estalella	.10
243	J.T. Snow	.10
244	Shawn Estes	.10
245	Robb Nen	.10
246	Rich Aurilia	.10
247	Russ Ortiz	.10
248	Preston Wilson	.10
249	Brad Penny	.10
250	Cliff Floyd	.10
251	A.J. Burnett	.10
252	Mike Lowell	.10
253	Luis Castillo	.10
254	Ryan Dempster	.10
255	Derrek Lee	.10
256	Charles Johnson	.10
257	Pablo Ozuna	.10
258	Antonio Alfonseca	.10
259	Mike Piazza	1.00
260	Robin Ventura	.10
261	Al Leiter	.15
262	Timoniel Perez	.10
263	Edgardo Alfonzo	.10
264	Jay Payton	.10
265	Tsuyoshi Shinjo RC	.75
266	Todd Zeile	.10
267	Armando Benitez	.10
268	Glendon Rusch	.10
269	Rey Ordonez	.10
270	Kevin Appier	.10
271	Tony Gwynn	.50
272	Phil Nevin	.10
273	Mark Kotsay	.10
274	Ryan Klesko	.20
275	Adam Eaton	.10
276	Mike Darr	.10
277	Damian Jackson	.10
278	Woody Williams	.10
279	Chris Gomez	.10
280	Trevor Hoffman	.10
281	Xavier Nady	.15
282	Scott Rolen	.40
283	Bruce Chen	.10
284	Pat Burrell	.30
285	Mike Lieberthal	.10
286	Brandon Duckworth RC	.40
287	Travis Lee	.10
288	Bobby Abreu	.25
289	Jimmy Rollins	.25
290	Robert Person	.10
291	Randy Wolf	.10
292	Jason Kendall	.10
293	Derek Bell	.10
294	Brian Giles	.25
295	Kris Benson	.10
296	John Vander Wal	.10
297	Todd Ritchie	.10
298	Warren Morris	.10
299	Kevin Young	.10
300	Francisco Cordova	.10
301	Aramis Ramirez	.10
302	Ken Griffey Jr.	1.00
303	Pete Harnisch	.10
304	Aaron Boone	.10
305	Sean Casey	.20
306	Jackson Melian RC	.40
307	Rob Bell	.10
308	Barry Larkin	.25
309	Dmitri Young	.10
310	Danny Graves	.10
311	Pokey Reese	.10
312	Leo Estrella	.10
313	Todd Helton	.40
314	Mike Hampton	.15
315	Juan Pierre	.10
316	Brent Mayne	.10
317	Larry Walker	.25
318	Denny Neagle	.10
319	Jeff Cirillo	.10
320	Pedro Astacio	.10
321	Todd Hollandsworth	.10
322	Neifi Perez	.10
323	Ron Gant	.10
324	Todd Walker	.10
325	Alex Rodriguez CL	.50
326	Ken Griffey Jr. CL	.50
327	Mark McGwire CL	.50
328	Pedro Martinez CL	.30
329	Derek Jeter CL	.75
330	Mike Piazza CL	.40

Authentic Griffey

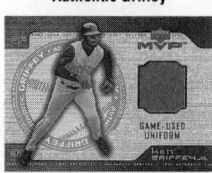

NM/M

Inserted 1:288

AGS	Ken Griffey Jr./Auto.	125.00
AGJ	Ken Griffey Jr./Jsy	15.00
AGC	Ken Griffey Jr./Cap	40.00
AGB	Ken Griffey Jr./Bat	15.00
AGU	Ken Griffey Jr./Uniform	15.00
AGGS	Ken Griffey/Gold Auto./30	250.00
AGGJ	Ken Griffey Jr/Gold Jsy/30	75.00
AGGC	Ken Griffey/Gold Cap/30	75.00
AGGB	Ken Griffey/Gold Bat/30	75.00
CGR	Ken Griffey Jr., Alex Rodriguez/100	35.00
CGS	Ken Griffey Jr., Sammy Sosa/100	35.00
CGT	Ken Griffey Jr., Frank Thomas/100	25.00

Drawing Power

NM/M

Complete Set (10):		10.00
Common Player:		.75
Inserted 1:12		
DP1	Mark McGwire	2.00
DP2	Vladimir Guerrero	1.00
DP3	Manny Ramirez	.75
DP4	Frank Thomas	.75
DP5	Ken Griffey Jr.	1.50
DP6	Alex Rodriguez	2.50
DP7	Mike Piazza	1.50
DP8	Derek Jeter	3.00
DP9	Sammy Sosa	2.00
DP10	Todd Helton	.75

Mantle Pinstripes Exclusive

NM/M

Complete Set (56): 75.00
Common Mantle: 2.00
One Pack/Box

Mantle Pinstripes Excl. Memorabilia

NM/M

Print Runs Listed
MMCJ3 Mickey Mantle, Ken Griffey Jr./50 200.00

Mickey Mantle

MMJ3 Mickey Mantle/Jsy/100 125.00

Souvenirs Batting Gloves

NM/M

Common Player:		8.00
Inserted 1:96 H		20.00
BB	Barry Bonds	40.00
TrG	Troy Glaus	10.00
JG	Juan Gonzalez	10.00
KG	Ken Griffey Jr.	20.00
ToG	Tony Gwynn/200	30.00
CJ	Chipper Jones	15.00
JL	Javy Lopez	8.00
GM	Greg Maddux/95	60.00
EM	Edgar Martinez	8.00
FM	Fred McGriff	8.00
RP	Rafael Palmeiro	15.00
CR	Cal Ripken Jr.	50.00
AR	Alex Rodriguez	20.00
IR	Ivan Rodriguez	10.00
SS	Sammy Sosa	20.00
MT	Miguel Tejada	8.00
FT	Frank Thomas	10.00
MV	Mo Vaughn	8.00

Souvenirs Batting Gloves Autographs

NM/M

Production 25 Sets		
KG	Ken Griffey Jr.	150.00
ToG	Tony Gwynn	80.00
CR	Cal Ripken Jr.	250.00
AR	Alex Rodriguez	150.00
IR	Ivan Rodriguez	80.00
SS	Sammy Sosa	250.00
FT	Frank Thomas	80.00

Souvenirs Two-Player Bat Combo

NM/M

Common Combo:		10.00
Inserted 1:144		
TS	Frank Thomas, Sammy Sosa	25.00
RR	Alex Rodriguez, Ivan Rodriguez	25.00
TG	Jim Thome, Ken Griffey Jr.	25.00
GS	Ken Griffey Jr., Sammy Sosa	30.00
WA	Kerry Wood, Rick Ankiel	10.00
3K	Tony Gwynn, Cal Ripken Jr.	40.00
DV	Carlos Delgado, Jose Vidro	10.00
JJ	Andruw Jones, Chipper Jones	20.00
HR	Jose Canseco, Ken Griffey Jr.	20.00
JF	Chipper Jones, Rafael Furcal	15.00
OW	Paul O'Neill, Bernie Williams	10.00

TO	Frank Thomas, Magglio Ordonez	15.00
RM	Alex Rodriguez, Edgar Martinez	20.00
RP	Ivan Rodriguez, Rafael Palmeiro	15.00

Souvenirs Three Player Bat Combo

No pricing due to scarcity.
Production 25 Sets

Souvenirs Two-Player Bat Autograph

NM/M

Production 25 Sets

RG	Alex Rodriguez, Ken Griffey Jr.	250.00
SG	Sammy Sosa, Ken Griffey Jr.	300.00
RR	Alex Rodriguez, Ivan Rodriguez	200.00
JG	Chipper Jones, Troy Glaus	125.00
TS	Frank Thomas, Sammy Sosa	275.00
GD	Jason Giambi, Carlos Delgado	75.00
3K	Cal Ripken Jr., Tony Gwynn	300.00
TG	Frank Thomas, Jason Giambi	85.00
HH	Todd Helton, Mike Hampton	60.00

Super Tools

NM/M

Complete Set (20):		20.00
Common Player:		.50
Inserted 1:6		
ST1	Ken Griffey Jr.	1.50
ST2	Carlos Delgado	.75
ST3	Alex Rodriguez	2.50
ST4	Troy Glaus	.75
ST5	Jeff Bagwell	.75
ST6	Ichiro Suzuki	3.00
ST7	Derek Jeter	3.00
ST8	Jim Edmonds	.50
ST9	Vladimir Guerrero	1.00
ST10	Jason Giambi	.75
ST11	Todd Helton	.75
ST12	Cal Ripken Jr.	3.00
ST13	Barry Bonds	3.00
ST14	Nomar Garciaparra	2.00
ST15	Randy Johnson	1.00
ST16	Jermaine Dye	.50
ST17	Andruw Jones	.75
ST18	Ivan Rodriguez	.75
ST19	Sammy Sosa	2.00
ST20	Pedro Martinez	1.00

2001 Upper Deck Ovation

NM/M

Complete Set (90):		100.00
Common Player:		.20
Common WP (61-90):		3.00
WP Production 2,000		
Pack (5):		5.00
Box (20):		80.00
1	Troy Glaus	.50
2	Darin Erstad	.40
3	Jason Giambi	.50
4	Tim Hudson	.40
5	Eric Chavez	.30
6	Carlos Delgado	.50
7	David Wells	.20
8	Greg Vaughn	.20

Pedro Martinez • P

9	Omar Vizquel	.20
10	Jim Thome	.50
11	Roberto Alomar	.40
12	John Olerud	.30
13	Edgar Martinez	.20
14	Cal Ripken Jr.	2.00
15	Alex Rodriguez	1.50
16	Ivan Rodriguez	.50
17	Manny Ramirez	.50
18	Nomar Garciaparra	1.50
19	Pedro Martinez	.75
20	Jermaine Dye	.20
21	Juan Gonzalez	.50
22	Matt Lawton	.20
23	Frank Thomas	.50
24	Magglio Ordonez	.40
25	Bernie Williams	.40
26	Derek Jeter	2.00
27	Roger Clemens	1.50
28	Jeff Bagwell	.50
29	Richard Hidalgo	.20
30	Chipper Jones	1.00
31	Greg Maddux	1.00
32	Andruw Jones	.50
33	Jeromy Burnitz	.20
34	Mark McGwire	1.50
35	Jim Edmonds	.40
36	Sammy Sosa	1.50
37	Kerry Wood	.50
38	Randy Johnson	.75
39	Steve Finley	.20
40	Gary Sheffield	.40
41	Kevin Brown	.40
42	Shawn Green	.40
43	Vladimir Guerrero	.75
44	Jose Vidro	.20
45	Barry Bonds	2.00
46	Jeff Kent	.30
47	Preston Wilson	.20
48	Luis Castillo	.20
49	Mike Piazza	1.00
50	Edgardo Alfonzo	.20
51	Tony Gwynn	.75
52	Ryan Klesko	.30
53	Scott Rolen	.50
54	Bob Abreu	.30
55	Jason Kendall	.20
56	Brian Giles	.30
57	Ken Griffey Jr.	1.00
58	Barry Larkin	.40
59	Todd Helton	.50
60	Mike Hampton	.20
61	Corey Patterson (World Premiere)	3.00
62	Timoniel Perez (World Premiere)	3.00
63	Toby Hall (World Premiere)	3.00
64	Brandon Inge (World Premiere)	3.00
65	Joe Crede (World Premiere)	3.00
66	Xavier Nady (World Premiere)	3.00
67	Adam Pettyjohn RC (World Premiere)	3.00
68	Keith Ginter (World Premiere)	3.00
69	Brian Cole (World Premiere)	3.00
70	Tyler Walker RC (World Premiere)	3.00
71	Juan Uribe RC (World Premiere)	5.00
72	Alex Hernandez (World Premiere)	3.00
73	Leo Estrella (World Premiere)	3.00
74	Joey Nation (World Premiere)	3.00
75	Aubrey Huff (World Premiere)	3.00
76	Ichiro Suzuki RC (World Premiere)	75.00
77	Jay Spurgeon (World Premiere)	3.00
78	Sun-Woo Kim (World Premiere)	3.00
79	Pedro Feliz (World Premiere)	3.00
80	Pablo Ozuna (World Premiere)	3.00
81	Hiram Bocachica (World Premiere)	3.00

82	Brad Wilkerson (World Premiere)	3.00
83	Rocky Biddle (World Premiere)	3.00
84	Aaron McNeal (World Premiere)	3.00
85	Adam Bernero (World Premiere)	3.00
86	Danys Baez (World Premiere)	3.00
87	Dee Brown (World Premiere)	3.00
88	Jimmy Rollins (World Premiere)	4.00
89	Jason Hart (World Premiere)	3.00
90	Ross Gload (World Premiere)	3.00

A Piece of History

NM/M

Common Player:		5.00
Inserted 1:40		
RA	Rick Ankiel	6.00
JB	Johnny Bench	15.00
BB	Barry Bonds	30.00
KB	Kevin Brown	5.00
JC	Jose Canseco	8.00
RC	Roger Clemens	15.00
DC	David Cone	5.00
CD	Carlos Delgado	8.00
JD	Joe DiMaggio	100.00
DD	Don Drysdale/SP	25.00
DE	Darin Erstad	5.00
RF	Rollie Fingers/SP	8.00
CF	Carlton Fisk	10.00
RF	Rafael Furcal	5.00
TrG	Troy Glaus	8.00
TG	Tom Glavine	8.00
SG	Shawn Green	5.00
KG	Ken Griffey Jr.	15.00
KGs	Ken Griffey Sr.	5.00
MH	Mike Hampton	5.00
RJ	Randy Johnson	10.00
AJ	Andruw Jones	8.00
CJ	Chipper Jones	10.00
GM	Greg Maddux	15.00
MM	Mickey Mantle	125.00
JP	Jim Palmer	10.00
CR	Cal Ripken Jr.	30.00
BR	Brooks Robinson	15.00
AR	Alex Rodriguez	15.00
IR	Ivan Rodriguez	8.00
NR	Nolan Ryan/SP	120.00
TS	Tom Seaver	10.00
GS	Gary Sheffield	5.00
OS	Ozzie Smith/SP	20.00
SS	Sammy Sosa	15.00
FT	Frank Thomas	8.00
BW	Bernie Williams	8.00
MW	Matt Williams	5.00
EW	Early Wynn	5.00

A Piece of History Autograph

No Pricing
Values Undetermined

Curtain Calls

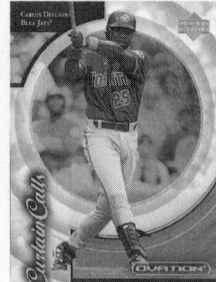

NM/M

Complete Set (10):		10.00
Common Player:		.50
Inserted 1:7		
1	Sammy Sosa	2.00
2	Darin Erstad	.50
3	Barry Bonds	2.50
4	Todd Helton	.75
5	Mike Piazza	1.50
6	Ken Griffey Jr.	1.50
7	Nomar Garciaparra	2.00
8	Carlos Delgado	.75

9	Jason Giambi	.75
10	Alex Rodriguez	2.00

DiMaggio Pinstripes Exclusive

NM/M

Complete Set (56):	60.00
Common DiMaggio:	1.50
One Pack/Box	

DiMaggio Pinstripes Memorabilia

NM/M

Print Runs Listed:		150.00
JDB	Joe DiMaggio/Bat/100	75.00
JDCJ	Joe DiMaggio, Mickey Mantle/Jsy/50	300.00
JDJ	Joe DiMaggio/Jsy/100	100.00

Lead Performers

NM/M

Complete Set (11):		15.00
Common Player:		1.00
Inserted 1:12		
1	Mark McGwire	3.00
2	Derek Jeter	4.00
3	Alex Rodriguez	3.00
4	Frank Thomas	1.00
5	Sammy Sosa	2.50
6	Mike Piazza	2.00
7	Vladimir Guerrero	1.50
8	Pedro Martinez	1.50
9	Carlos Delgado	1.00
10	Ken Griffey Jr.	2.00
11	Jeff Bagwell	1.00

POH Combo Cards

Production 25 Sets
Values Undetermined
No Pricing

Superstar Theatre

NM/M

Complete Set (11):	20.00

	Common Player:	1.00
	Inserted 1:12	
1	Nomar Garciaparra	2.50
2	Ken Griffey Jr.	2.00
3	Frank Thomas	1.00
4	Derek Jeter	4.00
5	Mike Piazza	2.00
6	Sammy Sosa	2.50
7	Barry Bonds	4.00
8	Alex Rodriguez	3.00
9	Todd Helton	1.00
10	Mark McGwire	3.00
11	Jason Giambi	1.00

2001 Upper Deck Prospect Premieres

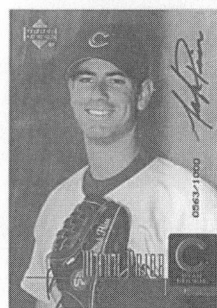

		NM/M
	Complete Set (90):	100.00
	Common Player:	.25
	Common Auto. SP (91-102):	10.00
	Auto. Production 1,000	
	Pack (4):	8.00
	Box (18):	125.00
1	Jeff Mathis RC	.50
2	Jake Woods RC	.25
3	Dallas McPherson RC	.50
4	Steven Shell RC	.25
5	Ryan Budde RC	.25
6	Kirk Saarloos RC	.40
7	Ryan Stegall RC	.25
8	Bobby Crosby RC	1.50
9	J.T. Stotts RC	.25
10	Neal Cotts RC	.50
11	Jeremy Bonderman RC	1.50
12	Brandon League RC	.40
13	Tyrell Godwin RC	.25
14	Gabe Gross RC	.75
15	Chris Neylan RC	.25
16	Michael Rouse RC	.25
17	Macay McBride RC	.25
18	Josh Burrus RC	.25
19	Adam Stern RC	.25
20	Richard Lewis RC	.40
21	Cole Barthel RC	.50
22	Mike Jones RC	.25
23	J.J. Hardy RC	2.00
24	Brad Nelson RC	.75
25	Justin Pope RC	.25
26	Dan Haren RC	2.00
27	Andy Sisco RC	.50
28	Ryan Theriot RC	2.50
29	Ricky Nolasco RC	2.00
30	Jon Switzer RC	.25
31	Justin Wechsler RC	.25
32	Mike Gosling RC	.25
33	Scott Hairston RC	1.00
34	Brian Pilkington RC	.25
35	Kole Strayhorn RC	.25
36	David Taylor RC	.25
37	Donald Levinski RC	.25
38	Mike Hinckley RC	.50
39	Nick Long RC	.25
40	Brad Hennessey RC	.25
41	Noah Lowry RC	.75
42	Josh Cram RC	.25
43	Jesse Foppert RC	.50
44	Julian Benavidez RC	.25

45	Daniel Denham RC	.25
46	Travis Foley RC	.40
47	Mike Conroy RC	.25
48	Jake Dittler RC	.25
49	Rene Rivera RC	.25
50	John Cole RC	.25
51	Lazaro Abreu RC	.25
52	David Wright RC	30.00
53	Aaron Heilman RC	.40
54	Lenny DiNardo RC	.40
55	Alhaji Turay RC	.25
56	Chris Smith RC	.25
57	Rommie Lewis RC	.25
58	Bryan Bass RC	.25
59	David Crouthers RC	.25
60	Josh Barfield RC	.75
61	Jake Peavy RC	4.00
62	Ryan Howard RC	30.00
63	Gavin Floyd RC	1.50
64	Mike Floyd RC	.25
65	Stefan Bailie RC	.25
66	Jon DeVries RC	.25
67	Steve Kelly RC	.25
68	Alan Moye RC	.25
69	Justin Gillman RC	.25
70	Jayson Nix RC	.50
71	John Draper RC	.25
72	Kenny Baugh RC	.25
73	Michael Woods RC	.25
74	Preston Larrison RC	.25
75	Matt Coenen RC	.25
76	Scott Tyler RC	.50
77	Jose Morales RC	.25
78	Corwin Malone RC	.50
79	Dennis Ulacia RC	.40
80	Andy Gonzalez RC	.25
81	Kris Honel RC	.50
82	Wyatt Allen RC	.25
83	Ryan Wing RC	.25
84	Sean Henn RC	.40
85	John-Ford Griffin RC	.50
86	Bronson Sardinha RC	.25
87	Jon Skaggs RC	.25
88	Shelley Duncan RC	.25
89	Jason Arnold RC	.50
90	Aaron Rifkin RC	.50
91	Colt Griffin RC	10.00
92	J.D. Martin RC	10.00
93	Justin Wayne RC	10.00
94	John VanBenschotten RC	15.00
95	Chris Burke RC	10.00
96	Casey Kotchman RC	25.00
97	Michael Garciaparra RC	10.00
98	Jake Gautreau RC	10.00
99	Jerome Williams RC	10.00
100	Greg Nash RC	10.00
101	Joe Borchard RC	10.00
102	Mark Prior RC	30.00

Heroes of Baseball Bat

		NM/M
	Common Player:	4.00
	Inserted 1:18	
DB	Don Baylor	4.00
WB	Wade Boggs	8.00
BB	Bill Buckner	4.00
GC	Gary Carter	8.00
DE	Dwight Evans	4.00
SG	Steve Garvey	4.00
KiG	Kirk Gibson	4.00
KeG	Ken Griffey Sr.	4.00
RJ	Reggie Jackson	10.00
DL	Davey Lopes	4.00
FL	Fred Lynn	4.00
BM	Bill Madlock	4.00
TM	Tim McCarver	4.00
JM	Joe Morgan	4.00
MM	Manny Mota	4.00
EM	Eddie Murray	8.00
AO	Al Oliver	4.00
DP	Dave Parker	4.00
TP	Tony Perez	4.00
KP	Kirby Puckett	15.00
OS	Ozzie Smith	10.00
DW	Dave Winfield	8.00

MJ Grandslam Bat

		NM/M
	Common MJ:	25.00

MJ1-4	Michael Jordan	25.00
MJ5	Michael Jordan (White Sox)	40.00

HOB Bat Autograph

Production 25 Sets
Values Undetermined
No Pricing

HOB Dual Combo Jersey

		NM/M
	Common Duo:	8.00
	Inserted 1:144	
BH	Bryan Bass, J.J. Hardy	10.00
DG	Shelley Duncan,	
	Tyrell Godwin	8.00
GS	Steve Garvey, Reggie Smith	10.00
HB	Aaron Heilman,	
	Jeremy Bonderman	10.00
JJ	Michael Jordan,	
	Michael Jordan	100.00
SG	Jon Switzer, Mike Gosling	8.00
WP	Dave Winfield,	
	Kirby Puckett	20.00

HOB Dual Combo Jersey Auto.

Values Undetermined
No Pricing

HOB Triple Combo Jersey

		NM/M
	Common Card:	
	Inserted 1:144	
BKH	Bobby Crosby,	
	Michael Garciaparra,	
	Bronson Sardinha	15.00
BBC	Chris Burke, Bryan Bass,	
	Bubba Crosby	10.00
GGH	Jake Gautreau, Tyrell Godwin,	
	Aaron Heilman	8.00
GMS	Colt Griffin, J.D. Martin,	
	Jon Switzer	8.00
GKB	Gabe Gross, Casey Kotchman,	
	Kenny Baugh	10.00
JMD	Michael Jordan, Mickey Mantle,	
	Joe DiMaggio	350.00
JPW	Michael Jordan, Kirby Puckett,	
	Dave Winfield	40.00
MMD	Roger Maris, Mickey Mantle,	
	Joe DiMaggio	700.00
VPJ	John VanBenschotten, Mark Prior,	
	Mike Jones	25.00

HOB Triple Combo Jersey Auto.

Values Undetermined
No Pricing

Tribute to 42

		NM/M
	Inserted 1:750	
42-B	Jackie Robinson/Bat	40.00
42-J	Jackie Robinson/Jsy	60.00
42-C	Jackie Robinson/Cut	500.00
42-B	Jackie Robinson/Bat/42	100.00
42-J	Jackie Robinson/Jsy/42	100.00

2001 Upper Deck Pros & Prospects

		NM/M
	Complete Set (141):	
	Common Player:	.15
	Common (91-135):	4.00
	Production 1,250	
	Common (136-141):	8.00
	Production 500	
	Pack (5):	6.00
	Box (24):	120.00
1	Troy Glaus	.50
2	Darin Erstad	.25
3	Tim Hudson	.40
4	Jason Giambi	.50
5	Jermaine Dye	.15
6	Barry Zito	.40
7	Carlos Delgado	.50
8	Shannon Stewart	.15
9	Raul Mondesi	.15
10	Greg Vaughn	.15
11	Ben Grieve	.15
12	Roberto Alomar	.40
13	Juan Gonzalez	.50
14	Jim Thome	.50
15	C.C. Sabathia	.40
16	Edgar Martinez	.25
17	Kazuhiro Sasaki	.15
18	Aaron Sele	.15
19	John Olerud	.25
20	Cal Ripken Jr.	2.00
21	Rafael Palmeiro	.50
22	Ivan Rodriguez	.50
23	Alex Rodriguez	1.50
24	Manny Ramirez	.50
25	Pedro Martinez	.75
26	Carl Everett	.15
27	Nomar Garciaparra	.75
28	Neifi Perez	.15
29	Mike Sweeney	.15
30	Bobby Higginson	.15
31	Tony Clark	.15
32	Doug Mientkiewicz	.15
33	Cristian Guzman	.15
34	Brad Radke	.15
35	Magglio Ordonez	.40
36	Carlos Lee	.25
37	Frank Thomas	.50
38	Roger Clemens	1.50
39	Bernie Williams	.50
40	Derek Jeter	2.00
41	Tino Martinez	.25
42	Wade Miller	.15
43	Jeff Bagwell	.50
44	Lance Berkman	.50
45	Richard Hidalgo	.15
46	Greg Maddux	1.00
47	Andruw Jones	.50
48	Chipper Jones	1.00
49	Rafael Furcal	.40
50	Jeromy Burnitz	.15
51	Geoff Jenkins	.25
52	Ben Sheets	.25
53	Mark McGwire	1.50
54	Jim Edmonds	.40
55	J.D. Drew	.25
56	Fred McGriff	.25
57	Sammy Sosa	1.00
58	Kerry Wood	.50
59	Randy Johnson	.75
60	Luis Gonzalez	.25
61	Curt Schilling	.40
62	Kevin Brown	.25
63	Shawn Green	.25
64	Gary Sheffield	.40
65	Vladimir Guerrero	.75
66	Jose Vidro	.15
67	Barry Bonds	2.00
68	Jeff Kent	.40
69	Rich Aurilia	.15
70	Preston Wilson	.15
71	Charles Johnson	.15
72	Cliff Floyd	.15
73	Mike Piazza	1.00
74	Al Leiter	.25
75	Matt Lawton	.15
76	Tony Gwynn	.75
77	Ryan Klesko	.25
78	Phil Nevin	.15
79	Scott Rolen	.50

80	Pat Burrell	.40
81	Jimmy Rollins	.75
82	Jason Kendall	.25
83	Brian Giles	.25
84	Aramis Ramirez	.50
85	Ken Griffey Jr.	1.00
86	Barry Larkin	.40
87	Sean Casey	.25
88	Larry Walker	.25
89	Todd Helton	.50
90	Mike Hampton	.15
91	Juan Cruz RC	4.00
92	Brian Lawrence RC	4.00
93	Brandon Lyon RC	4.00
94	Adrian Hernandez RC	4.00
95	Jose Mieses RC	4.00
96	Juan Uribe RC	4.00
97	Morgan Ensberg RC	4.00
98	Wilson Betemit RC	8.00
99	Ryan Freel RC	6.00
100	Jack Wilson RC	6.00
101	Cesar Crespo RC	4.00
102	Bret Prinz RC	4.00
103	Horacio Ramirez RC	4.00
104	Elpidio Guzman RC	4.00
105	Josh Towers RC	4.00
106	Brandon Duckworth RC	4.00
107	Esix Snead RC	4.00
108	Billy Sylvester RC	4.00
109	Alexis Gomez RC	4.00
110	Johnny Estrada RC	4.00
111	Joe Kennedy RC	4.00
112	Travis Hafner RC	20.00
113	Martin Vargas RC	4.00
114	Jay Gibbons RC	4.00
115	Andres Torres RC	4.00
116	Sean Douglass RC	4.00
117	Juan Diaz RC	4.00
118	Greg Miller RC	4.00
119	Carlos Valderrama RC	4.00
120	William Ortega RC	4.00
121	Josh Fogg RC	4.00
122	Wilken Ruan RC	4.00
123	Kris Keller RC	4.00
124	Erick Almonte RC	4.00
125	Ricardo Rodriguez RC	4.00
126	Grant Balfour RC	4.00
127	Nick Maness RC	4.00
128	Jeremy Owens RC	4.00
129	Doug Nickle RC	4.00
130	Bert Snow RC	4.00
131	Jason Smith RC	4.00
132	Henry Mateo RC	4.00
133	Mike Penney RC	4.00
134	Bud Smith RC	4.00
135	Junior Spivey RC	4.00
136	Ichiro Suzuki RC	75.00
137	Albert Pujols RC	180.00
138	Mark Teixeira RC	100.00
139	Dewon Brazelton RC	8.00
140	Mark Prior RC	20.00
141	Tsuyoshi Shinjo RC	8.00

Bats

NM/M

Common Card: 4.00
Inserted 1:24
Golds: 3-5X
Production 25 Sets

WI	Bernie Williams, Ichiro Suzuki	35.00
RG	Manny Ramirez, Juan Gonzalez	8.00
RP	Ivan Rodriguez, Mike Piazza	15.00
BT	Jeff Bagwell, Frank Thomas	8.00
GBo	Ken Griffey Jr., Barry Bonds	35.00
SG	Sammy Sosa, Luis Gonzalez	15.00
KA	Jeff Kent, Roberto Alomar	4.00
RF	Alex Rodriguez, Rafael Furcal	15.00
PT	Rafael Palmeiro, Jim Thome	10.00
JP	Chipper Jones, Albert Pujols	40.00
GBu	Shawn Green, Jeromy Burnitz	4.00
JL	Andruw Jones, Kenny Lofton	6.00
MJ	Greg Maddux, Randy Johnson	15.00

Ichiro World Tour

NM/M

Complete Set (15): 25.00
Common Ichiro: 2.00
Inserted 1:12
WT1-15 Ichiro Suzuki 2.00

Legends Bats

NM/M

Common Card: 15.00

Inserted 1:216
Gold: 3-5X
Production 25 Sets

RF	Manny Ramirez, Carlton Fisk	15.00
BY	Jeromy Burnitz, Robin Yount	15.00
WJ	Bernie Williams, Reggie Jackson	15.00
RG	Cal Ripken Jr., Tony Gwynn	50.00

Specialty Jersey

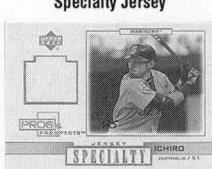

NM/M

Common Player: 4.00
Inserted 1:24
Golds: 3-5X
Production 25 Sets

RA	Roberto Alomar	6.00
BB	Barry Bonds	25.00
JE	Jim Edmonds	4.00
JG	Juan Gonzalez	6.00
SG	Shawn Green	4.00
TG	Tony Gwynn	10.00
RJ	Randy Johnson	10.00
CR	Cal Ripken Jr.	30.00
AR	Alex Rodriguez	15.00
SR	Scott Rolen	8.00
SS	Sammy Sosa	10.00
I	Ichiro	60.00
JT	Jim Thome	8.00
LW	Larry Walker	4.00

Then & Now Jersey

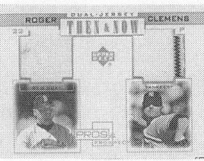

NM/M

Common Player: 4.00
Inserted 1:24
Golds: 3-5X
Production 25 Sets

RA	Rick Ankiel	4.00
BB	Barry Bonds	30.00
KB	Kevin Brown	6.00
RC	Roger Clemens	20.00
JE	Jim Edmonds	6.00
FG	Freddy Garcia	4.00
JGi	Jason Giambi	8.00
JGo	Juan Gonzalez	8.00
KG	Ken Griffey Jr.	20.00
RJ	Randy Johnson	10.00
GM	Greg Maddux	20.00
PM	Pedro Martinez	10.00
XN	Xavier Nady	4.00
PN	Phil Nevin	4.00
MP	Mike Piazza	15.00
MR	Manny Ramirez	8.00
AR	Alex Rodriguez	15.00
CS	Curt Schilling	6.00
GS	Gary Sheffield	6.00
RV	Robin Ventura	4.00

2001 Upper Deck Rookie Update

NM/M

Common Player: .25
Common Rookie:

Pack (4):		15.00
Box (18):		250.00

Sweet Spot

Common SP (121-150): 3.00
Production 1,500

91	Garret Anderson	.50
92	Jermaine Dye	.25
93	Shannon Stewart	.25
94	Ben Grieve	.25
95	Juan Gonzalez	.50
96	Bret Boone	.25
97	Tony Batista	.25
98	Rafael Palmeiro	1.00
99	Carl Everett	.25
100	Mike Sweeney	.25
101	Tony Clark	.25
102	Doug Mientkiewicz	.25
103	Jose Canseco	.50
104	Mike Mussina	.75
105	Lance Berkman	.50
106	Andruw Jones	.50
107	Geoff Jenkins	.40
108	Matt Morris	.25
109	Fred McGriff	.40
110	Luis Gonzalez	.50
111	Kevin Brown	.25
112	Tony Armas Jr.	.25
113	John Vander Wal	.25
114	Cliff Floyd	.25
115	Matt Lawton	.25
116	Phil Nevin	.25
117	Pat Burrell	.50
118	Aramis Ramirez	.50
119	Sean Casey	.40
120	Larry Walker	.40
121	Albert Pujols RC	150.00
122	Johnny Estrada RC	4.00
123	Wilson Betemit RC	3.00
124	Adrian Hernandez RC	3.00
125	Morgan Ensberg RC	3.00
126	Horacio Ramirez RC	3.00
127	Josh Towers RC	3.00
128	Juan Uribe RC	3.00
129	Wilken Ruan RC	3.00
130	Andres Torres RC	3.00
131	Brian Lawrence RC	3.00
132	Ryan Freel RC	6.00
133	Brandon Duckworth RC	3.00
134	Juan Diaz RC	3.00
135	Rafael Soriano RC	4.00
136	Ricardo Rodriguez RC	3.00
137	Bud Smith RC	3.00
138	Mark Teixeira RC	40.00
139	Mark Prior RC	15.00
140	Jackson Melian RC	3.00
141	Dewon Brazelton RC	3.00
142	Greg Miller RC	3.00
143	Billy Sylvester RC	3.00
144	Elpidio Guzman RC	3.00
145	Jack Wilson RC	5.00
146	Jose Mieses RC	3.00
147	Brandon Lyon RC	3.00
148	Tsuyoshi Shinjo RC	3.00
149	Juan Cruz RC	3.00
150	Jay Gibbons RC	3.00

SPx

Common (181-205): 3.00
Production 1,500
Cards (206-210) Autographed

151	Garret Anderson	.50
152	Jermaine Dye	.25
153	Shannon Stewart	.25
154	Toby Hall	.25
155	C.C. Sabathia	.50
156	Bret Boone	.50
157	Tony Batista	.25
158	Gabe Kapler	.25
159	Carl Everett	.25
160	Mike Sweeney	.25
161	Dean Palmer	.25
162	Doug Mientkiewicz	.25
163	Carlos Lee	.50
164	Mike Mussina	.75
165	Lance Berkman	.75
166	Ken Caminiti	.25
167	Ben Sheets	.40
168	Matt Morris	.25
169	Fred McGriff	.40
170	Curt Schilling	.75
171	Paul LoDuca	.25
172	Javier Vazquez	.25
173	Rich Aurilia	.25
174	A.J. Burnett	.40
175	Al Leiter	.40
176	Mark Kotsay	.25
177	Jimmy Rollins	.75
178	Aramis Ramirez	.50
179	Aaron Boone	.25
180	Jeff Cirillo	.25
181	Johnny Estrada RC	5.00
182	Dave Williams RC	3.00
183	Donaldo Mendez RC	3.00
184	Junior Spivey RC	3.00
185	Jay Gibbons RC	3.00
186	Kyle Lohse RC	5.00
187	Willie Harris RC	3.00
188	Juan Cruz RC	3.00
189	Joe Kennedy RC	3.00
190	Duaner Sanchez RC	3.00
191	Jorge Julio RC	3.00
192	Cesar Crespo RC	3.00
193	Casey Fossum RC	3.00
194	Brian Roberts RC	15.00
195	Troy Mattes RC	3.00
196	Rob Mackowiak RC	3.00

197	Tsuyoshi Shinjo RC	3.00
198	Nick Punto RC	3.00
199	Wilmy Caceres RC	3.00
200	Jeremy Affeldt RC	3.00
201	Bret Prinz RC	3.00
202	Delvin James RC	3.00
203	Luis Pineda RC	3.00
204	Matt White RC	3.00
205	Brandon Knight RC	3.00
206	Albert Pujols RC	500.00
207	Mark Teixeira RC	125.00
208	Mark Prior RC	40.00
209	Dewon Brazelton RC	10.00
210	Bud Smith RC	8.00

SP Authentic

Common (211-240): 4.00
Production 1,500

181	Garret Anderson	.50
182	Jermaine Dye	.25
183	Shannon Stewart	.25
184	Ben Grieve	.25
185	Ellis Burks	.25
186	John Olerud	.25
187	Tony Batista	.25
188	Ruben Sierra	.25
189	Carl Everett	.25
190	Neifi Perez	.25
191	Tony Clark	.25
192	Doug Mientkiewicz	.50
193	Carlos Lee	.50
194	Jorge Posada	.50
195	Lance Berkman	.50
196	Ken Caminiti	.25
197	Ben Sheets	.50
198	Matt Morris	.25
199	Fred McGriff	.40
200	Mark Grace	.50
201	Paul LoDuca	.25
202	Tony Armas, Jr.	.25
203	Andres Galarraga	.40
204	Cliff Floyd	.25
205	Matt Lawton	.25
206	Ryan Klesko	.40
207	Jimmy Rollins	.75
208	Aramis Ramirez	.50
209	Aaron Boone	.25
210	Jose Ortiz	.25
211	Mark Prior RC	20.00
212	Mark Teixeira RC	80.00
213	Bud Smith RC	4.00
214	Wilmy Caceres RC	4.00
215	Dave Williams RC	4.00
216	Delvin James RC	4.00
217	Endy Chavez RC	4.00
218	Doug Nickle RC	4.00
219	Bret Prinz RC	4.00
220	Troy Mattes RC	4.00
221	Duaner Sanchez RC	4.00
222	Dewon Brazelton RC	4.00
223	Brian Bowles RC	4.00
224	Donaldo Mendez RC	4.00
225	Jorge Julio RC	4.00
226	Matt White RC	4.00
227	Casey Fossum RC	4.00
228	Mike Rivera RC	4.00
229	Joe Kennedy RC	4.00
230	Kyle Lohse RC	6.00
231	Juan Cruz RC	4.00
232	Jeremy Affeldt RC	4.00
233	Brandon Lyon RC	4.00
234	Brian Roberts RC	15.00
235	Willie Harris RC	4.00
236	Pedro Santana RC	4.00
237	Rafael Soriano RC	6.00
238	Steve Green RC	4.00
239	Junior Spivey RC	4.00
240	Rob Mackowiak RC	4.00

Ichiro ROY

NM/M

Complete Set (51): 35.00
Common Ichiro: 1.00
1-50 Ichiro Suzuki 1.00
51 Ichiro Suzuki Checklist 1.00

Ichiro ROY Game Jersey

NM/M

Numbers 1-12 Production 100 50.00
Numbers 13-17 Production 50 75.00
Numbers 18-19 Production 25 150.00
J-I1-12 Ichiro Suzuki 50.00

J-I13-17 Ichiro Suzuki 75.00
J-I18-19 Ichiro Suzuki 150.00

Ichiro ROY Game-Used Bat

	NM/M
Numbers 1-12 Production 100	50.00
Numbers 13-17 Production 50	75.00
Numbers 18-19 Production 25	150.00
B-I1-12 Ichiro Suzuki	50.00
B-I13-17 Ichiro Suzuki	75.00
B-I18-19 Ichiro Suzuki	150.00

SP Chirography

	NM/M
Common Autograph:	15.00
Production 250	
Silver:	.75-1.5X
Production 100	
Gold:	No Pricing
Production 25 Sets	
LB Lance Berkman/100	25.00
KG Ken Griffey Jr./250	90.00
TG Tony Gwynn/250	30.00
TG Tony Gwynn/100	40.00
MS Doug Mientkiewicz/100	10.00
JP Jorge Posada/250	25.00
JP Jorge Posada/100	30.00
CR Cal Ripken Jr.	100.00
MS Mike Sweeney/100	10.00

SP Chirography - Ichiro

	NM/M
Ichiro (Unnumbered)	300.00
Ichiro Silver/100	500.00

USA Touch of Gold

	NM/M
Common Autograph:	8.00
Production 500 Sets	
BA Brent Abernathy	8.00
KU Kurt Ainsworth	10.00
PB Pat Borders	8.00
SB Sean Burroughs	12.00
JC John Cotton	8.00
TD Gookie Dawkins	8.00
AE Adam Everett	8.00
RF Ryan Franklin	8.00
CG Chris George	8.00
SH Shane Heams	8.00
MJ Marcus Jensen	8.00
MK Mike Kinkade	8.00
RK Rick Krivda	8.00
DM Doug Mientkiewicz	12.00
MN Mike Neill	8.00
RO Roy Oswalt	20.00
JR Jon Rauch	8.00
AS Anthony Sanders	8.00
BSe Bobby Seay	8.00
BSh Ben Sheets	12.00
BW Brad Wilkerson	8.00
TW Todd Williams	8.00
EY Ernie Young	8.00
TY Tim Young	8.00

Materials 2-Player

	NM/M
Common Card:	10.00
Inserted 1:15	
BB-LG Barry Bonds, Luis Gonzalez	25.00
JG-BB Jason Giambi, Barry Bonds	25.00
IR-AR Ivan Rodriguez, Alex Rodriguez	25.00
AP-JE Albert Pujols, Jim Edmonds	35.00
GS-SG Gary Sheffield, Shawn Green	15.00
MP-EA Mike Piazza, Edgardo Alfonzo	20.00
LW-TH Larry Walker, Todd Helton	15.00
MR-JG Manny Ramirez, Juan Gonzalez	15.00
TG-CR Tony Gwynn, Cal Ripken Jr.	40.00
SR-BA Scott Rolen, Bobby Abreu	15.00
JB-CB Jeff Bagwell, Craig Biggio	20.00
KG-SC Ken Griffey Jr., Sean Casey	25.00
EM-JM Eric Milton, Joe Mays	10.00
HN-MY Hideo Nomo, Masato Yoshii	20.00
TS-HN Tsuyoshi Shinjo, Hideo Nomo	15.00
CS-RJ Curt Schilling, Randy Johnson	20.00
AS-KS Aaron Sele, Kazuhiro Sasaki	10.00
PM-RJ Pedro Martinez, Randy Johnson	15.00
BW-MR Bernie Williams, Mariano Rivera	15.00
TG-X2 Tony Gwynn	15.00
CR-X2 Cal Ripken Jr.	40.00
JB-RY Jeromy Burnitz, Robin Yount	15.00
CR-EM Cal Ripken Jr., Eddie Murray	30.00
TG-DW Tony Gwynn, Dave Winfield	15.00
FT-MO Frank Thomas, Magglio Ordonez	15.00
PM-GM Pedro Martinez, Greg Maddux	20.00
BW-RJ Bernie Williams, Reggie Jackson	20.00
SS-EB Sammy Sosa, Ernie Banks	30.00
CP-FV Chan Ho Park, Fernando Valenzuela	10.00

Materials 3-Player Jersey

	NM/M
Common Card:	10.00
Inserted 1:15	
KBA Jeff Kent, Barry Bonds, Rich Aurilia	25.00
JAF Chipper Jones, Andruw Jones, Rafael Furcal	15.00
GZH Jason Giambi, Barry Zito, Tim Hudson	15.00
SKB Gary Sheffield, Eric Karros, Kevin Brown	10.00
SSM Aaron Sele, Ichiro Suzuki, Edgar Martinez	40.00
HDG Todd Helton, Carlos Delgado, Jason Giambi	15.00
VRF Omar Vizquel, Alex Rodriguez, Rafael Furcal	25.00
SYN Kazuhiro Sasaki, Masato Yoshii, Hideo Nomo	20.00
BTD Jeff Bagwell, Frank Thomas, Carlos Delgado	15.00
BGG Barry Bonds, Luis Gonzalez, Ken Griffey Jr.	30.00
RPK Ivan Rodriguez, Mike Piazza, Jason Kendall	20.00
PPV Jay Payton, Mike Piazza, Robin Ventura	15.00
CHN Roger Clemens, Tim Hudson, Hideo Nomo	15.00
PWO Andy Pettitte, Bernie Williams, Paul O'Neill	20.00
TDK Frank Thomas, Ray Durham, Roger Clemens	15.00
SJC Curt Schilling, Randy Johnson, Roger Clemens	20.00
DEA J.D. Drew, Jim Edmonds, Bobby Abreu	15.00
DOP Carlos Delgado, Magglio Ordonez, Albert Pujols	35.00
TGA Jim Thome, Juan Gonzalez, Roberto Alomar	15.00
GWS Luis Gonzalez, Matt Williams, Curt Schilling	20.00
MGJ Greg Maddux, Tom Glavine, Andruw Jones	20.00

2001 Upper Deck Sweet Spot

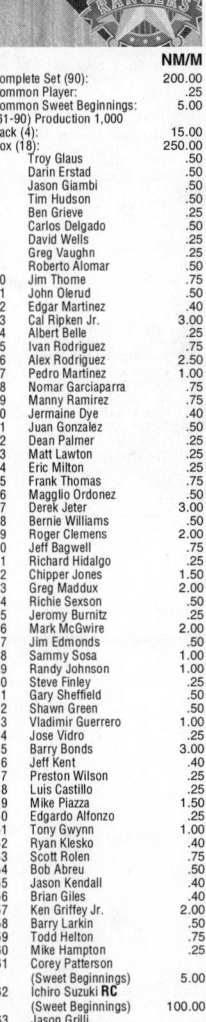

	NM/M
Complete Set (90):	200.00
Common Player:	.25
Common Sweet Beginnings:	5.00
(61-90) Production 1,000	
Pack (4):	15.00
Box (18):	250.00
1 Troy Glaus	.50
2 Darin Erstad	.50
3 Jason Giambi	.50
4 Tim Hudson	.50
5 Ben Grieve	.25
6 Carlos Delgado	.50
7 David Wells	.25
8 Greg Vaughn	.25
9 Roberto Alomar	.50
10 Jim Thome	.75
11 John Olerud	.50
12 Edgar Martinez	.40
13 Cal Ripken Jr.	3.00
14 Albert Belle	.25
15 Ivan Rodriguez	.75
16 Alex Rodriguez	2.50
17 Pedro Martinez	1.00
18 Nomar Garciaparra	.75
19 Manny Ramirez	.75
20 Jermaine Dye	.40
21 Juan Gonzalez	.25
22 Dean Palmer	.25
23 Matt Lawton	.25
24 Eric Milton	.25
25 Frank Thomas	.75
26 Magglio Ordonez	.50
27 Derek Jeter	3.00
28 Bernie Williams	.50
29 Roger Clemens	2.00
30 Jeff Bagwell	.75
31 Richard Hidalgo	.25
32 Chipper Jones	1.50
33 Greg Maddux	2.00
34 Richie Sexson	.50
35 Jeromy Burnitz	.25
36 Mark McGwire	2.00
37 Jim Edmonds	.50
38 Sammy Sosa	1.00
39 Randy Johnson	1.00
40 Steve Finley	.25
41 Gary Sheffield	.50
42 Shawn Green	.50
43 Vladimir Guerrero	1.00
44 Jose Vidro	.25
45 Barry Bonds	3.00
46 Jeff Kent	.40
47 Preston Wilson	.25
48 Luis Castillo	.25
49 Mike Piazza	1.50
50 Edgardo Alfonzo	.25
51 Tony Gwynn	1.00
52 Ryan Klesko	.40
53 Scott Rolen	.75
54 Bob Abreu	.50
55 Jason Kendall	.40
56 Brian Giles	.40
57 Ken Griffey Jr.	2.00
58 Barry Larkin	.50
59 Todd Helton	.75
60 Mike Hampton	.25
61 Corey Patterson (Sweet Beginnings)	5.00
62 Ichiro Suzuki RC (Sweet Beginnings)	100.00
63 Jason Grilli (Sweet Beginnings)	5.00
64 Brian Cole (Sweet Beginnings)	5.00
65 Juan Pierre (Sweet Beginnings)	5.00
66 Matt Ginter (Sweet Beginnings)	5.00

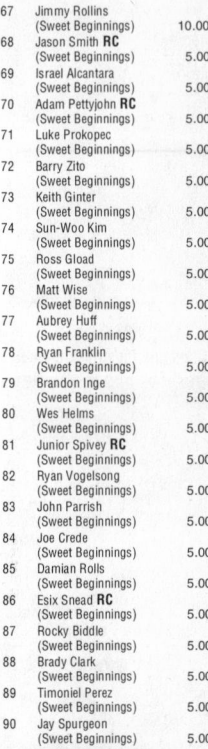

67 Jimmy Rollins (Sweet Beginnings)	10.00
68 Jason Smith RC (Sweet Beginnings)	5.00
69 Israel Alcantara (Sweet Beginnings)	5.00
70 Adam Pettyjohn RC (Sweet Beginnings)	5.00
71 Luke Prokopec (Sweet Beginnings)	5.00
72 Barry Zito (Sweet Beginnings)	5.00
73 Keith Ginter (Sweet Beginnings)	5.00
74 Sun-Woo Kim (Sweet Beginnings)	5.00
75 Ross Gload (Sweet Beginnings)	5.00
76 Matt Wise (Sweet Beginnings)	5.00
77 Aubrey Huff (Sweet Beginnings)	5.00
78 Ryan Franklin (Sweet Beginnings)	5.00
79 Brandon Inge (Sweet Beginnings)	5.00
80 Wes Helms (Sweet Beginnings)	5.00
81 Junior Spivey RC (Sweet Beginnings)	5.00
82 Ryan Vogelsong (Sweet Beginnings)	5.00
83 John Parrish (Sweet Beginnings)	5.00
84 Joe Crede (Sweet Beginnings)	5.00
85 Damian Rolls (Sweet Beginnings)	5.00
86 Esix Snead RC (Sweet Beginnings)	5.00
87 Rocky Biddle (Sweet Beginnings)	5.00
88 Brady Clark (Sweet Beginnings)	5.00
89 Timoniel Perez (Sweet Beginnings)	5.00
90 Jay Spurgeon (Sweet Beginnings)	5.00

Big League Challenge

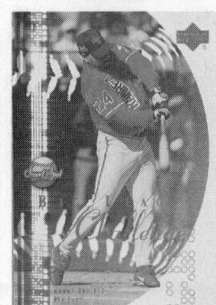

	NM/M
Complete Set (20):	20.00
Common Player:	.50
Inserted 1:6	
1 Mark McGwire	2.50
2 Richard Hidalgo	.50
3 Alex Rodriguez	2.50
4 Shawn Green	.75
5 Frank Thomas	1.00
6 Chipper Jones	1.50
7 Rafael Palmeiro	1.00
8 Troy Glaus	1.00
9 Mike Piazza	1.50
10 Andruw Jones	1.00
11 Todd Helton	1.00
12 Jason Giambi	1.00
13 Sammy Sosa	2.00
14 Carlos Delgado	1.00
15 Barry Bonds	3.00
16 Jose Canseco	.75
17 Jim Edmonds	.75
18 Manny Ramirez	1.00
19 Gary Sheffield	.75
20 Nomar Garciaparra	2.00

DiMaggio Pinstripes Excl.

	NM/M
Complete Set (56):	60.00

Common DiMaggio: 1.50
One Pack/Box

DiMaggio Pinstripes Memor.

Print Runs Listed:		NM/M
JDB	Joe DiMaggio/Bat/100	150.00
JDCJ	Joe DiMaggio,	80.00
	Lou Gehrig/Jsy/50	600.00
JDJ	Joe DiMaggio/Jsy/100	100.00

Game-Used Bat

Common Player:		5.00 NM/M
Inserted 1:18		
HA	Hank Aaron	60.00
RA	Rick Ankiel	6.00
BB	Barry Bonds	25.00
JC	Jose Canseco	8.00
TC	Ty Cobb	175.00
JD	Joe DiMaggio	80.00
KG	Ken Griffey Jr.	15.00
RJ	Reggie Jackson	10.00
AJ	Andruw Jones	10.00
MM	Mickey Mantle	140.00
WM	Willie Mays	75.00
SM	Stan Musial	50.00
CR	Cal Ripken Jr.	40.00
AR	Alex Rodriguez	20.00
IR	Ivan Rodriguez	8.00
NR	Nolan Ryan	65.00
GS	Gary Sheffield	8.00
SS	Sammy Sosa	20.00
FT	Frank Thomas	10.00

Game Jerseys

Common Player:		8.00 NM/M
Inserted 1:18		
BB	Barry Bonds	25.00
JC	Jose Canseco	8.00
RC	Roger Clemens	20.00
RC	Roberto Clemente	125.00
JD	Joe DiMaggio	80.00
KG	Ken Griffey Jr.	20.00
RJ	Randy Johnson	10.00
AJ	Andruw Jones	8.00
CJ	Chipper Jones	15.00
MM	Mickey Mantle	150.00
WM	Willie Mays	100.00
SM	Stan Musial	65.00
CR	Cal Ripken Jr.	40.00
AR	Alex Rodriguez	20.00
IR	Ivan Rodriguez	8.00

NR	Nolan Ryan	65.00
DS	Duke Snider	10.00
SS	Sammy Sosa	15.00
IS	Ichiro Suzuki	100.00
FT	Frank Thomas	10.00

S.S. Game-Used Bases Tier 1

		NM/M
Common Card:		5.00
BH	Barry Bonds, Todd Helton	25.00
MG	Mark McGwire, Ken Griffey Jr.,	60.00
JG	Chipper Jones, Nomar Garciaparra	20.00
GD	Vladimir Guerrero, Carlos Delgado	8.00
ST	Sammy Sosa, Frank Thomas	20.00
SR	Gary Sheffield, Alex Rodriguez	15.00
GR	Tony Gwynn, Ivan Rodriguez	10.00
PJ	Mike Piazza, Derek Jeter	30.00
HG	Jeffrey Hammonds, Troy Glaus	5.00
JGi	Randy Johnson, Jason Giambi	8.00
BD	Jeff Bagwell, Jermaine Dye	8.00
RR	Scott Rolen, Cal Ripken Jr.	25.00
GR	Ken Griffey Jr., Manny Ramirez	15.00
RJ	Alex Rodriguez, Derek Jeter	40.00
MP	Mark McGwire, Timoniel Perez	35.00
CP	Roger Clemens, Mike Piazza	20.00

S.S. Game-Used Bases Tier 2

		NM/M
Common Card:		20.00
Production 50 Sets		
BHK	Barry Bonds, Todd Helton, Jeff Kent	75.00
MGE	Mark McGwire, Ken Griffey Jr., Bobby Edmonds	120.00
JGJ	Chipper Jones, Nomar Garciaparra, Andruw Jones	60.00
GDM	Vladimir Guerrero, Carlos Delgado, Raul Mondesi	20.00
STO	Sammy Sosa, Frank Thomas, Magglio Ordonez	50.00
SRM	Gary Sheffield, Alex Rodriguez, Edgar Martinez	50.00
GRP	Tony Gwynn, Ivan Rodriguez, Rafael Palmeiro	40.00
PJW	Mike Piazza, Derek Jeter, Bernie Williams	75.00
HGH	Jeffrey Hammonds, Troy Glaus, Todd Helton	20.00
JGC	Randy Johnson, Jason Giambi, Eric Chavez	25.00
BDH	Jeff Bagwell, Jermaine Dye, Richard Hidalgo	20.00
RRB	Scott Rolen, Cal Ripken Jr., Albert Belle	75.00
GRT	Ken Griffey Jr., Manny Ramirez, Jim Thome	50.00

Players Party

		NM/M
Complete Set (10):		10.00
Common Player:		.75
Inserted 1:12		
1	Derek Jeter	3.00

2	Randy Johnson	1.00
3	Frank Thomas	1.00
4	Nomar Garciaparra	2.00
5	Ken Griffey Jr.	1.50
6	Carlos Delgado	.75
7	Mike Piazza	1.50
8	Barry Bonds	3.00
9	Sammy Sosa	2.00
10	Pedro Martinez	1.00

2001 Upper Deck Ultimate Collection

		NM/M
Common Player:		1.00
Common SP (91-100):		5.00
Production 1,000		
Common SP (101-110):		5.00
Production 750		
Common (111-120):		15.00
Production 250		
Pack (4):		160.00
Box (4):		575.00
1	Troy Glaus	2.50
2	Darin Erstad	1.50
3	Jason Giambi	3.00
4	Barry Zito	2.00
5	Tim Hudson	2.00
6	Miguel Tejada	1.50
7	Carlos Delgado	2.50
8	Shannon Stewart	1.00
9	Greg Vaughn	1.00
10	Toby Hall	1.00
11	Roberto Alomar	2.00
12	Juan Gonzalez	2.50
13	Jim Thome	3.00
14	Edgar Martinez	1.50
15	Freddy Garcia	1.50
16	Bret Boone	1.50
17	Kazuhiro Sasaki	1.00
18	Cal Ripken Jr.	10.00
19	Tim Raines Jr.	1.00
20	Alex Rodriguez	8.00
21	Ivan Rodriguez	2.50
22	Rafael Palmeiro	2.50
23	Pedro Martinez	3.00
24	Nomar Garciaparra	6.00
25	Manny Ramirez	2.50
26	Hideo Nomo	2.00
27	Mike Sweeney	1.00
28	Carlos Beltran	1.50
29	Tony Clark	1.00
30	Dean Palmer	1.00
31	Doug Mientkiewicz	1.00
32	Cristian Guzman	1.00
33	Corey Koskie	1.00
34	Frank Thomas	3.00
35	Magglio Ordonez	1.50
36	Jose Canseco	2.00
37	Roger Clemens	6.00
38	Derek Jeter	10.00
39	Bernie Williams	2.00
40	Mike Mussina	2.00
41	Tino Martinez	1.00
42	Jeff Bagwell	2.50
43	Lance Berkman	2.00
44	Roy Oswalt	1.50
45	Chipper Jones	5.00
46	Greg Maddux	5.00
47	Andruw Jones	2.50
48	Tom Glavine	2.00
49	Richie Sexson	2.00
50	Jeromy Burnitz	1.00
51	Ben Sheets	1.00
52	Mark McGwire	8.00
53	Matt Morris	1.00
54	Jim Edmonds	2.00
55	J.D. Drew	1.50
56	Sammy Sosa	6.00
57	Fred McGriff	1.00
58	Kerry Wood	2.50
59	Randy Johnson	3.00
60	Luis Gonzalez	2.00
61	Curt Schilling	2.00
62	Shawn Green	1.50
63	Kevin Brown	1.50
64	Gary Sheffield	2.00
65	Vladimir Guerrero	3.00
66	Barry Bonds	10.00
67	Jeff Kent	1.50
68	Rich Aurilia	1.00

69	Cliff Floyd	1.00
70	Charles Johnson	1.00
71	Josh Beckett	2.00
72	Mike Piazza	5.00
73	Edgardo Alfonzo	1.00
74	Robin Ventura	1.00
75	Tony Gwynn	2.50
76	Ryan Klesko	1.50
77	Phil Nevin	1.00
78	Scott Rolen	2.50
79	Bobby Abreu	1.00
80	Jimmy Rollins	1.50
81	Brian Giles	1.50
82	Jason Kendall	1.00
83	Aramis Ramirez	1.00
84	Ken Griffey Jr.	6.00
85	Adam Dunn	2.00
86	Sean Casey	1.50
87	Barry Larkin	2.00
88	Larry Walker	1.50
89	Mike Hampton	1.00
90	Todd Helton	2.50
91	Ken Harvey	5.00
92	William Ortega RC	5.00
93	Juan Diaz RC	5.00
94	Greg Miller RC	5.00
95	Brandon Berger RC	5.00
96	Brandon Lyon RC	5.00
97	Jay Gibbons RC	5.00
98	Rob Mackowiak RC	5.00
99	Erick Almonte RC	5.00
100	Jason Middlebrook RC	5.00
101	Johnny Estrada RC	8.00
102	Juan Uribe RC	8.00
103	Travis Hafner RC	25.00
104	Morgan Ensberg RC	8.00
105	Mike Rivera RC	5.00
106	Josh Towers RC	5.00
107	Adrian Hernandez RC	5.00
108	Rafael Soriano RC	5.00
109	Jackson Melian RC	5.00
110	Wilken Ruan RC	5.00
111	Albert Pujols RC	500.00
112	Tsuyoshi Shinjo RC	15.00
113	Brandon Duckworth RC	15.00
114	Juan Cruz RC	15.00
115	Dewon Brazelton RC	15.00
116	Mark Prior/Auto. RC	50.00
117	Mark Teixeira/Auto. RC	200.00
118	Wilson Betemit/Auto. RC	25.00
119	Bud Smith/Auto. RC	15.00
120	Ichiro Suzuki/Auto. RC	1,800

Game Jersey

		NM/M
Common Player:		10.00
Inserted 1:2		
RA	Roberto Alomar	20.00
JB	Jeff Bagwell	20.00
BB	Barry Bonds	50.00
JC	Jose Canseco	10.00
RC	Roger Clemens	40.00
CD	Carlos Delgado	10.00
DE	Darin Erstad	10.00
JaG	Jason Giambi	20.00
JG	Juan Gonzalez	20.00
LG	Luis Gonzalez	10.00
SG	Shawn Green	10.00
KG	Ken Griffey Jr.	40.00
TG	Tony Gwynn	20.00
TH	Todd Helton	15.00
RJ	Randy Johnson	15.00
AJ	Andruw Jones	10.00
CJ	Chipper Jones	15.00
GM	Greg Maddux	40.00
MO	Magglio Ordonez	10.00
MP	Mike Piazza	30.00
AP	Albert Pujols	75.00
CR	Cal Ripken Jr.	75.00
AR	Alex Rodriguez	40.00
IR	Ivan Rodriguez	15.00
SR	Scott Rolen	15.00
GS	Gary Sheffield	10.00
SS	Sammy Sosa	40.00
FT	Frank Thomas	15.00
LW	Larry Walker	10.00
BW	Bernie Williams	10.00

Ichiro

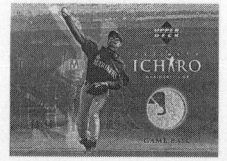

		NM/M
Pricing not available for all Ichiro's.		
B-IA	Ichiro Suzuki/Bat/Away	65.00
B-IH	Ichiro Suzuki/Bat/Home	65.00
B-IS	Ichiro Suzuki/Bat/250	80.00
B-IG	Ichiro Suzuki/Bat/200	90.00
SB-I	Ichiro Suzuki/Bat/ Auto./50	675.00
J-IA	Ichiro Suzuki/Jsy/Away	50.00
J-IH	Ichiro Suzuki/Jsy/Home	50.00
J-IS	Ichiro Suzuki/Jsy/250	75.00
J-IG	Ichiro Suzuki/Jsy/200	85.00
SJ-I	Ichiro Suzuki/Jsy/ Auto./50	675.00
UB-I	Ichiro Suzuki/Base	25.00
UB-IC	Ichiro Suzuki/Base/150	80.00
UB-IS	Ichiro Suzuki/Base/50	100.00
BB-I	Ichiro Suzuki/Ball	60.00
BB-IC	Ichiro Suzuki/Ball/150	85.00
BB-IS	Ichiro Suzuki/Ball/50	100.00
SBB-I	Ichiro Suzuki/Ball/ Auto./25	675.00
C-I	Ichiro Suzuki/Glove/75	180.00
BG-I	Ichiro Suzuki/Bat/ Glove/75	180.00

Magic Numbers

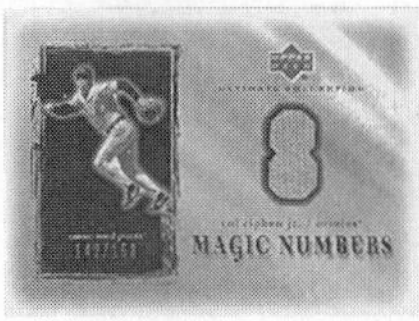

		NM/M
Common Player:		10.00
Production 150		
Coppers #'d to 24 not priced.		
Silvers #'d to 20 not priced.		
Golds #'d to 15 not priced.		
RA	Roberto Alomar	20.00
JB	Jeff Bagwell	20.00
BB	Barry Bonds	50.00
JC	Jose Canseco	15.00
RC	Roger Clemens	50.00
CD	Carlos Delgado	15.00
DE	Darin Erstad	10.00
JaG	Jason Giambi	20.00
JG	Juan Gonzalez	15.00
LG	Luis Gonzalez	10.00
SG	Shawn Green	10.00
KG	Ken Griffey Jr.	40.00
TG	Tony Gwynn	20.00
TH	Todd Helton	15.00
RJ	Randy Johnson	15.00
AJ	Andruw Jones	10.00
CJ	Chipper Jones	15.00
GM	Greg Maddux	40.00
MO	Magglio Ordonez	10.00
MP	Mike Piazza	30.00
AP	Albert Pujols	75.00
CR	Cal Ripken Jr.	90.00
AR	Alex Rodriguez	40.00
IR	Ivan Rodriguez	15.00
SR	Scott Rolen	15.00
GS	Gary Sheffield	10.00
SS	Sammy Sosa	40.00
FT	Frank Thomas	15.00
LW	Larry Walker	10.00
BW	Bernie Williams	10.00

Ultimate Signatures

		NM/M
Common Autograph:		20.00
Inserted 1:4		
Silvers #'d to 24 not priced.		
Golds #'d to 15 not priced.		
RA	Roberto Alomar	40.00
EB	Ernie Banks	50.00
BaB	Barry Bonds	200.00
RC	Roger Clemens	100.00
CD	Carlos Delgado	25.00
CF	Carlton Fisk	40.00
JaG	Jason Giambi	25.00
TGl	Tom Glavine	40.00
LG	Luis Gonzalez	25.00
KG	Ken Griffey Jr.	100.00
TG	Tony Gwynn	60.00
RK	Ryan Klesko	20.00
SK	Sandy Koufax	275.00
EM	Edgar Martinez	30.00
TP	Tony Perez	20.00
KP	Kirby Puckett	50.00
CR	Cal Ripken Jr.	125.00
AR	Alex Rodriguez	80.00
IR	Ivan Rodriguez	50.00
TS	Tom Seaver	40.00
GS	Gary Sheffield	30.00
DS	Duke Snider	35.00
SS	Sammy Sosa	120.00
FT	Frank Thomas	40.00
JT	Jim Thome	50.00
RY	Robin Yount	60.00

2001 Upper Deck Victory

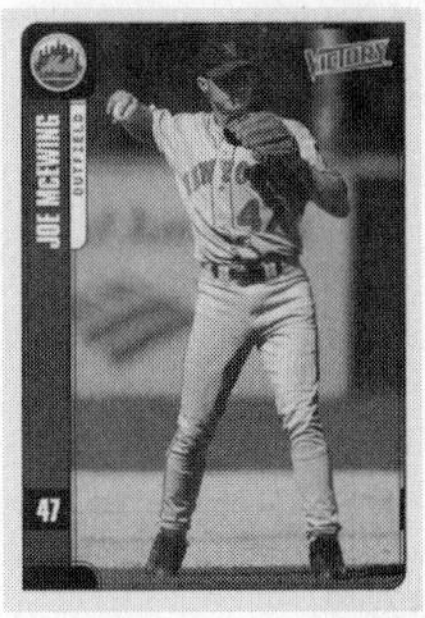

		NM/M
Complete Set (660):		50.00
Common Player:		.15
1	Troy Glaus	.50
2	Scott Spiezio	.15
3	Gary DiSarcina	.15
4	Darin Erstad	.20
5	Tim Salmon	.20
6	Troy Percival	.15
7	Ramon Ortiz	.15
8	Orlando Palmeiro	.15
9	Tim Belcher	.15
10	Mo Vaughn	.15
11	Bengie Molina	.15
12	Benji Gil	.15
13	Scott Schoeneweis	.15
14	Garret Anderson	.15
15	Matt Wise	.15
16	Adam Kennedy	.15
17	Jarrod Washburn	.15
18	Darin Erstad, Troy Percival	.15
19	Jason Giambi	.20
20	Tim Hudson	.20
21	Ramon Hernandez	.15
22	Eric Chavez	.15
23	Gil Heredia	.15
24	Jason Isringhausen	.15
25	Jeremy Giambi	.15
26	Miguel Tejada	.15
27	Barry Zito	.50
28	Terrence Long	.15
29	Ryan Christenson	.15
30	Mark Mulder	.15
31	Olmedo Saenz	.15
32	Adam Piatt	.15
33	Ben Grieve	.20
34	Omar Olivares	.15
35	John Jaha	.15
36	Jason Giambi, Tim Hudson	.15
37	Carlos Delgado	.40
38	Esteban Loaiza	.15
39	Brad Fullmer	.15
40	David Wells	.15
41	Chris Woodward	.15
42	Billy Koch	.15
43	Shannon Stewart	.15
44	Chris Carpenter	.15
45	Steve Parris	.15
46	Darrin Fletcher	.15
47	Joey Hamilton	.15
48	Jose Cruz Jr.	.15
49	Vernon Wells	.15
50	Raul Mondesi	.15
51	Kelvim Escobar	.15
52	Tony Batista	.15
53	Alex Gonzalez	.15
54	Carlos Delgado, David Wells	.20
55	Greg Vaughn	.15
56	Albie Lopez	.15
57	Randy Winn	.15
58	Ryan Rupe	.15
59	Steve Cox	.15
60	Vinny Castilla	.15
61	Jose Guillen	.15
62	Wilson Alvarez	.15
63	Bryan Rekar	.15
64	Gerald Williams	.15
65	Esteban Yan	.15
66	Felix Martinez	.15
67	Fred McGriff	.20
68	John Flaherty	.15
69	Jason Tyner	.15
70	Russ Johnson	.15
71	Roberto Hernandez	.15
72	Greg Vaughn, Albie Lopez	.15
73	Eddie Taubensee	.15
74	Bob Wickman	.15
75	Ellis Burks	.15
76	Kenny Lofton	.20
77	Einar Diaz	.15
78	Travis Fryman	.15
79	Omar Vizquel	.15
80	Jason Bere	.15
81	Bartolo Colon	.15
82	Jim Thome	.20
83	Roberto Alomar	.40
84	Chuck Finley	.15
85	Steve Woodard	.15
86	Russ Branyan	.15
87	Dave Burba	.15
88	Jaret Wright	.15
89	Jacob Cruz	.15
90	Steve Karsay	.15
91	Manny Ramirez, Bartolo Colon	.20
92	Raul Ibanez	.15
93	Freddy Garcia	.15
94	Edgar Martinez	.15
95	Jay Buhner	.15
96	Jamie Moyer	.15
97	John Olerud	.20
98	Aaron Sele	.15
99	Kazuhiro Sasaki	.20
100	Mike Cameron	.15
101	John Halama	.15
102	David Bell	.15
103	Gil Meche	.15
104	Carlos Guillen	.15
105	Mark McLemore	.15
106	Stan Javier	.15
107	Al Martin	.15
108	Dan Wilson	.15
109	Alex Rodriguez, Kazuhiro Sasaki	.50
110	Cal Ripken Jr.	1.50
111	Delino DeShields	.15
112	Sidney Ponson	.15
113	Albert Belle	.15
114	Jose Mercedes	.15
115	Scott Erickson	.15
116	Jerry Hairston Jr.	.15
117	Brook Fordyce	.15
118	Luis Matos	.15
119	Eugene Kingsale	.15
120	Jeff Conine	.15
121	Chris Richard	.15
122	Fernando Lunar	.15
123	John Parrish	.15
124	Brady Anderson	.15
125	Ryan Kohlmeier	.15
126	Melvin Mora	.15
127	Albert Belle, Jose Mercedes	.15
128	Ivan Rodriguez	.50
129	Justin Thompson	.15
130	Kenny Rogers	.15
131	Rafael Palmeiro	.30
132	Rusty Greer	.15
133	Gabe Kapler	.15
134	John Wetteland	.15
135	Mike Lamb	.15
136	Doug Davis	.15
137	Ruben Mateo	.15
138	Alex Rodriguez	1.25
139	Chad Curtis	.15
140	Rick Helling	.15
141	Ryan Glynn	.15
142	Andres Galarraga	.25
143	Ricky Ledee	.15
144	Frank Catalanotto	.15
145	Rafael Palmeiro, Rick Helling	.20
146	Pedro Martinez	.60
147	Wilton Veras	.15
148	Manny Ramirez	.50
149	Rolando Arrojo	.15
150	Nomar Garciaparra	1.00
151	Darren Lewis	.15
152	Troy O'Leary	.15
153	Tomokazu Ohka	.15
154	Carl Everett	.15
155	Jason Varitek	.15
156	Frank Castillo	.15
157	Pete Schourek	.15
158	Jose Offerman	.15
159	Derek Lowe	.15
160	John Valentin	.15
161	Dante Bichette	.15
162	Trot Nixon	.15
163	Nomar Garciaparra, Pedro Martinez	.25
164	Jermaine Dye	.15
165	Dave McCarty	.15
166	Jose Rosado	.15
167	Mike Sweeney	.15
168	Rey Sanchez	.15
169	Jeff Suppan	.15
170	Chad Durbin	.15
171	Carlos Beltran	.15
172	Brian Meadows	.15
173	Todd Dunwoody	.15
174	Johnny Damon	.15
175	Blake Stein	.15
176	Carlos Febles	.15
177	Joe Randa	.15
178	Makoto Suzuki	.15
179	Mark Quinn	.15
180	Gregg Zaun	.15
181	Mike Sweeney, Jeff Suppan	.15
182	Juan Gonzalez	.50
183	Dean Palmer	.15
184	Wendell Magee	.15
185	Todd Jones	.15
186	Bobby Higginson	.15
187	Brian Moehler	.15
188	Juan Encarnacion	.15
189	Tony Clark	.15
190	Rich Becker	.15
191	Roger Cedeno	.15
192	Mitch Meluskey	.15
193	Shane Halter	.15
194	Jeff Weaver	.15
195	Deivi Cruz	.15
196	Damion Easley	.15
197	Robert Fick	.15
198	Matt Anderson	.15
199	Bobby Higginson, Brian Moehler	.15
200	Brad Radke	.15
201	Mark Redman	.15
202	Corey Koskie	.15
203	Matt Lawton	.15
204	Eric Milton	.15
205	Chad Moeller	.15
206	Jacque Jones	.15
207	Matt Kinney	.15
208	Jay Canizaro	.15
209	Torii Hunter	.15
210	Ron Coomer	.15
211	Chad Allen	.15
212	Denny Hocking	.15
213	Cristian Guzman	.15
214	LaTroy Hawkins	.15
215	Joe Mays	.15
216	David Ortiz	.15
217	Matt Lawton, Eric Milton	.15
218	Frank Thomas	.60
219	Jose Valentin	.15
220	Mike Sirotka	.15
221	Kip Wells	.15
222	Magglio Ordonez	.25
223	Herbert Perry	.15
224	James Baldwin	.15
225	Jon Garland	.15
226	Sandy Alomar	.15
227	Chris Singleton	.15
228	Keith Foulke	.15
229	Paul Konerko	.15
230	Jim Parque	.15
231	Greg Norton	.15
232	Carlos Lee	.15
233	Cal Eldred	.15
234	Ray Durham	.15
235	Jeff Abbott	.15
236	Frank Thomas, Mike Sirotka	.20
237	Derek Jeter	1.50
238	Glenallen Hill	.15
239	Roger Clemens	1.00
240	Bernie Williams	.40
241	David Justice	.25
242	Luis Sojo	.15
243	Orlando Hernandez	.20
244	Mike Mussina	.25
245	Jorge Posada	.20
246	Andy Pettitte	.20
247	Paul O'Neill	.20
248	Scott Brosius	.15
249	Alfonso Soriano	.50
250	Mariano Rivera	.20
251	Chuck Knoblauch	.20
252	Ramiro Mendoza	.15
253	Tino Martinez	.15
254	David Cone	.15
255	Derek Jeter, Andy Pettitte	.40
256	Jeff Bagwell	.50
257	Lance Berkman	.15
258	Craig Biggio	.20
259	Scott Elarton	.15
260	Bill Spiers	.15
261	Moises Alou	.15
262	Billy Wagner	.15
263	Shane Reynolds	.15
264	Tony Eusebio	.15
265	Julio Lugo	.15
266	Jose Lima	.15
267	Octavio Dotel	.15
268	Brad Ausmus	.15
269	Daryle Ward	.15
270	Glen Barker	.15
271	Wade Miller	.15
272	Richard Hidalgo	.25
273	Chris Truby	.15
274	Jeff Bagwell, Scott Elarton	.25
275	Greg Maddux	.75
276	Chipper Jones	.75
277	Tom Glavine	.25
278	Brian Jordan	.15
279	Andruw Jones	.40
280	Kevin Millwood	.15
281	Rico Brogna	.15
282	George Lombard	.15
283	Reggie Sanders	.15
284	John Rocker	.15
285	Rafael Furcal	.25
286	John Smoltz	.15
287	Javy Lopez	.15
288	Walt Weiss	.15
289	Quilvio Veras	.15
290	Eddie Perez	.15
291	B.J. Surhoff	.15
292	Chipper Jones, Tom Glavine	.25
293	Jeromy Burnitz	.15
294	Charlie Hayes	.15
295	Jeff D'Amico	.15
296	Jose Hernandez	.15
297	Richie Sexson	.15
298	Tyler Houston	.15
299	Paul Rigdon	.15
300	Jamey Wright	.15
301	Mark Loretta	.15
302	Geoff Jenkins	.20
303	Luis Lopez	.15
304	John Snyder	.15
305	Henry Blanco	.15

306 Curtis Leskanic .15
307 Ron Belliard .15
308 Jimmy Haynes .15
309 Marquis Grissom .15
310 Geoff Jenkins, Jeff D'Amico .15
311 Mark McGwire 1.00
312 Rick Ankiel .20
313 Dave Veres .15
314 Carlos Hernandez .15
315 Jim Edmonds .20
316 Andy Benes .15
317 Garrett Stephenson .15
318 Ray Lankford .15
319 Dustin Hermanson .15
320 Steve Kline .15
321 Mike Matheny .15
322 Edgar Renteria .15
323 J.D. Drew .15
324 Craig Paquette .15
325 Darryl Kile .15
326 Fernando Vina .15
327 Eric Davis .15
328 Placido Polanco .15
329 Jim Edmonds, Darryl Kile .15
330 Sammy Sosa 1.00
331 Rick Aguilera .15
332 Willie Greene .15
333 Kerry Wood .20
334 Todd Hundley .15
335 Rondell White .20
336 Julio Zuleta .15
337 Jon Lieber .15
338 Joe Girardi .15
339 Damon Buford .15
340 Kevin Tapani .15
341 Ricky Gutierrez .15
342 Bill Mueller .15
343 Ruben Quevedo .15
344 Eric Young .15
345 Gary Matthews Jr. .15
346 Daniel Garibay .15
347 Sammy Sosa, Jon Lieber .30
348 Randy Johnson .50
349 Matt Williams .20
350 Kelly Stinnett .15
351 Brian Anderson .15
352 Steve Finley .15
353 Curt Schilling .20
354 Erubiel Durazo .15
355 Todd Stottlemyre .15
356 Mark Grace .20
357 Luis Gonzalez .20
358 Danny Bautista .15
359 Matt Mantei .15
360 Tony Womack .15
361 Armando Reynoso .15
362 Greg Colbrunn .15
363 Jay Bell .15
364 Byung-Hyun Kim .15
365 Luis Gonzalez, Randy Johnson .20
366 Gary Sheffield .20
367 Eric Karros .15
368 Jeff Shaw .15
369 Jim Leyritz .15
370 Kevin Brown .20
371 Alex Cora .15
372 Andy Ashby .15
373 Eric Gagne .15
374 Chan Ho Park .15
375 Shawn Green .20
376 Kevin Elster .15
377 Mark Grudzielanek .15
378 Darren Dreifort .15
379 Dave Hansen .15
380 Bruce Aven .15
381 Adrian Beltre .20
382 Tom Goodwin .15
383 Gary Sheffield, Chan Ho Park .15
384 Vladimir Guerrero .60
385 Ugueth Urbina .15
386 Michael Barrett .15
387 Geoff Blum .15
388 Fernando Tatis .15
389 Carl Pavano .15
390 Jose Vidro .15
391 Orlando Cabrera .15
392 Terry Jones .15
393 Mike Thurman .15
394 Lee Stevens .15
395 Tony Armas Jr. .15
396 Wilton Guerrero .15
397 Peter Bergeron .15
398 Milton Bradley .15
399 Javier Vazquez .15
400 Fernando Seguignol .15
401 Vladimir Guerrero, Dustin Hermanson .25
402 Barry Bonds .60
403 Russ Ortiz .15
404 Calvin Murray .15
405 Armando Rios .15
406 Livan Hernandez .15
407 Jeff Kent .20
408 Bobby Estalella .15
409 Felipe Crespo .15
410 Shawn Estes .15
411 J.T. Snow .15
412 Marvin Benard .15
413 Joe Nathan .15
414 Robb Nen .15
415 Shawon Dunston .15
416 Mark Gardner .15
417 Kirk Rueter .15
418 Rich Aurilia .15
419 Doug Mirabelli .15
420 Russ Davis .15
421 Barry Bonds, Livan Hernandez .30
422 Cliff Floyd .15
423 Luis Castillo .15
424 Antonio Alfonseca .15
425 Preston Wilson .15
426 Ryan Dempster .15
427 Jesus Sanchez .15
428 Derrek Lee .15
429 Brad Penny .15
430 Mark Kotsay .15
431 Alex Fernandez .15
432 Mike Lowell .15
433 Chuck Smith .15
434 Alex Gonzalez .15
435 Dave Berg .15
436 A.J. Burnett .15
437 Charles Johnson .15
438 Reid Cornelius .15
439 Mike Redmond .15
440 Preston Wilson, Ryan Dempster .15
441 Mike Piazza .75
442 Kevin Appier .15
443 Jay Payton .15
444 Steve Trachsel .15
445 Al Leiter .20
446 Joe McEwing .15
447 Armando Benitez .15
448 Edgardo Alfonzo .15
449 Glendon Rusch .15
450 Mike Bordick .15
451 Lenny Harris .15
452 Matt Franco .15
453 Darryl Hamilton .15
454 Bobby J. Jones .15
455 Robin Ventura .15
456 Todd Zeile .15
457 John Franco .15
458 Mike Piazza, Al Leiter .40
459 Tony Gwynn .75
460 John Mabry .15
461 Trevor Hoffman .15
462 Phil Nevin .15
463 Ryan Klesko .15
464 Wiki Gonzalez .15
465 Matt Clement .15
466 Alex Arias .15
467 Woody Williams .15
468 Ruben Rivera .15
469 Sterling Hitchcock .15
470 Ben Davis .15
471 Bubba Trammell .15
472 Jay Witasick .15
473 Eric Owens .15
474 Damian Jackson .15
475 Adam Eaton .15
476 Mike Darr .15
477 Phil Nevin, Trevor Hoffman .15
478 Scott Rolen .25
479 Robert Person .15
480 Mike Lieberthal .15
481 Reggie Taylor .15
482 Paul Byrd .15
483 Bruce Chen .15
484 Pat Burrell .25
485 Kevin Jordan .15
486 Bobby Abreu .15
487 Randy Wolf .15
488 Kevin Sefcik .15
489 Brian Hunter .15
490 Doug Glanville .15
491 Kent Bottenfield .15
492 Travis Lee .15
493 Jeff Brantley .15
494 Omar Daal .15
495 Bobby Abreu, Randy Wolf .15
496 Jason Kendall .15
497 Adrian Brown .15
498 Warren Morris .15
499 Brian Giles .20
500 Jimmy Anderson .15
501 John Vander Wal .15
502 Mike Williams .15
503 Aramis Ramirez .15
504 Pat Meares .15
505 Jason Schmidt .15
506 Todd Ritchie .15
507 Abraham Nunez .15
508 Jose Silva .15
509 Francisco Cordova .15
510 Kevin Young .15
511 Derek Bell .15
512 Kris Benson .15
513 Brian Giles, Jose Silva .15
514 Ken Griffey Jr. 1.00
515 Scott Williamson .15
516 Dmitri Young .15
517 Sean Casey .20
518 Barry Larkin .25
519 Juan Castro .15
520 Danny Graves .15
521 Aaron Boone .15
522 Pokey Reese .15
523 Elmer Dessens .15
524 Michael Tucker .15
525 Benito Santiago .15
526 Pete Harnisch .15
527 Alex Ochoa .15
528 Gookie Dawkins .15
529 Seth Etherton .15
530 Rob Bell .15
531 Ken Griffey Jr., Steve Parris .50
532 Todd Helton .50
533 Jose Jimenez .15
534 Todd Walker .15
535 Ron Gant .15
536 Neifi Perez .15
537 Butch Huskey .15
538 Pedro Astacio .15
539 Juan Pierre .15
540 Jeff Cirillo .15
541 Ben Petrick .15
542 Brian Bohanon .15
543 Larry Walker .25
544 Masato Yoshii .15
545 Denny Neagle .15
546 Brent Mayne .15
547 Mike Hampton .20
548 Todd Hollandsworth .15
549 Brian Rose .15
550 Todd Helton, Pedro Astacio .20
551 Jason Hart .15
552 Joe Crede .15
553 Timoniel Perez .15
554 Brady Clark .15
555 Adam Pettyjohn **RC** .15
556 Jason Grilli .15
557 Paxton Crawford .15
558 Jay Spurgeon .15
559 Hector Ortiz .15
560 Vernon Wells .15
561 Aubrey Huff .15
562 Xavier Nady .25
563 Billy McMillon .15
564 Ichiro Suzuki **RC** 8.00
565 Tomas de la Rosa .15
566 Matt Ginter .15
567 Sun-Woo Kim .15
568 Nick Johnson .15
569 Pablo Ozuna .15
570 Tike Redman .15
571 Brian Cole .15
572 Ross Gload .15
573 Dee Brown .15
574 Tony McKnight .15
575 Allen Levrault .15
576 Lesli Brea .15
577 Adam Bernero .15
578 Tom Davey .15
579 Morgan Burkhart .15
580 Britt Reames .15
581 Dave Coggin .15
582 Trey Moore .15
583 Matt Kinney .15
584 Pedro Feliz .15
585 Brandon Inge .15
586 Alex Hernandez .15
587 Toby Hall .15
588 Grant Roberts .15
589 Brian Sikorski .15
590 Aaron Myette .15
591 Derek Jeter (Big Play Makers) 1.00
592 Ivan Rodriguez (Big Play Makers) .40
593 Alex Rodriguez (Big Play Makers) .75
594 Carlos Delgado (Big Play Makers) .30
595 Mark McGwire (Big Play Makers) .75
596 Troy Glaus (Big Play Makers) .40
597 Sammy Sosa (Big Play Makers) .75
598 Vladimir Guerrero (Big Play Makers) .50
599 Manny Ramirez (Big Play Makers) .40
600 Pedro J. Martinez (Big Play Makers) .50
601 Chipper Jones (Big Play Makers) .75
602 Jason Giambi (Big Play Makers) .20
603 Frank Thomas (Big Play Makers) .50
604 Ken Griffey Jr. (Big Play Makers) .75
605 Nomar Garciaparra (Big Play Makers) .75
606 Randy Johnson (Big Play Makers) .40
607 Mike Piazza (Big Play Makers) .75
608 Barry Bonds (Big Play Makers) .50
609 Todd Helton (Big Play Makers) .40
610 Jeff Bagwell (Big Play Makers) .40
611 Ken Griffey Jr. (Victory's Best) .75
612 Carlos Delgado (Victory's Best) .40
613 Jeff Bagwell (Victory's Best) .40
614 Jason Giambi (Victory's Best) .20
615 Cal Ripken Jr. (Victory's Best) 1.00
616 Brian Giles (Victory's Best) .15
617 Bernie Williams (Victory's Best) .30
618 Greg Maddux (Victory's Best) .75
619 Troy Glaus (Victory's Best) .40
620 Greg Vaughn (Victory's Best) .15
621 Sammy Sosa (Victory's Best) .75
622 Pat Burrell (Victory's Best) .20
623 Ivan Rodriguez (Victory's Best) .40
624 Chipper Jones (Victory's Best) .75
625 Barry Bonds (Victory's Best) .50
626 Roger Clemens (Victory's Best) .50
627 Jim Edmonds (Victory's Best) .15
628 Nomar Garciaparra (Victory's Best) .75
629 Frank Thomas (Victory's Best) .50
630 Mike Piazza (Victory's Best) .75
631 Randy Johnson (Victory's Best) .40
632 Andruw Jones (Victory's Best) .30
633 David Wells (Victory's Best) .15
634 Manny Ramirez (Victory's Best) .40
635 Preston Wilson (Victory's Best) .15
636 Todd Helton (Victory's Best) .40
637 Kerry Wood (Victory's Best) .15
638 Albert Belle (Victory's Best) .15
639 Juan Gonzalez (Victory's Best) .40
640 Vladimir Guerrero (Victory's Best) .50
641 Gary Sheffield (Victory's Best) .15
642 Larry Walker (Victory's Best) .15
643 Maggio Ordonez (Victory's Best) .15
644 Jermaine Dye (Victory's Best) .15
645 Scott Rolen (Victory's Best) .20
646 Tony Gwynn (Victory's Best) .50
647 Shawn Green (Victory's Best) .15
648 Roberto Alomar (Victory's Best) .30
649 Eric Milton (Victory's Best) .15
650 Mark McGwire (Victory's Best) .75
651 Tim Hudson (Victory's Best) .15
652 Jose Canseco (Victory's Best) .20
653 Tom Glavine (Victory's Best) .20
654 Derek Jeter (Victory's Best) 1.00
655 Alex Rodriguez (Victory's Best) .75
656 Darin Erstad (Victory's Best) .15
657 Jason Kendall (Victory's Best) .15
658 Pedro Martinez (Victory's Best) .50
659 Richie Sexson (Victory's Best) .15
660 Rafael Palmeiro (Victory's Best) .20

2001 Upper Deck Vintage

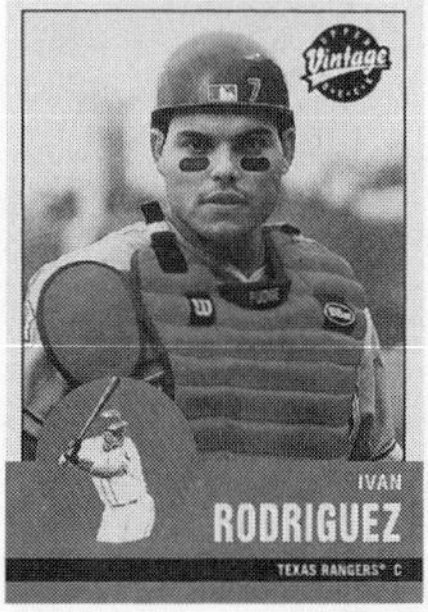

NM/M

Complete Set (400): 30.00
Common Player: .10
Pack (10): 2.00
Box (24): 40.00

1 Darin Erstad .25
2 Seth Etherton .10
3 Troy Glaus .50
4 Bengie Molina .10
5 Mo Vaughn .20
6 Tim Salmon .25
7 Ramon Ortiz .10
8 Adam Kennedy .10
9 Garret Anderson .25
10 Troy Percival .10
11 2000 Angels Lineup .10
12 Jason Giambi .50
13 Tim Hudson .25
14 Adam Piatt .10
15 Miguel Tejada .25
16 Mark Mulder .25
17 Eric Chavez .25
18 Ramon Hernandez .10
19 Terrence Long .10
20 Jason Isringhausen .10
21 Barry Zito .50
22 Ben Grieve .10
23 2000 Athletics Lineup .10
24 David Wells .10
25 Raul Mondesi .20
26 Darrin Fletcher .10
27 Shannon Stewart .10
28 Kelvim Escobar .10
29 Tony Batista .10
30 Carlos Delgado .50
31 Brad Fullmer .10
32 Billy Koch .10
33 Jose Cruz Jr. .10
34 2000 Blue Jays Lineup .10

35 Greg Vaughn .10
36 Roberto Hernandez .10
37 Vinny Castilla .10
38 Gerald Williams .10
39 Aubrey Huff .10
40 Bryan Rekar .10
41 Albie Lopez .10
42 Fred McGriff .25
43 Miguel Cairo .10
44 Ryan Rupe .10
45 2000 Devil Rays Lineup .10
46 Jim Thome .50
47 Roberto Alomar .50
48 Bartolo Colon .25
49 Omar Vizquel .20
50 Travis Fryman .20
51 Manny Ramirez .50
52 Dave Burba .10
53 Chuck Finley .10
54 Russ Branyan .10
55 Kenny Lofton .25
56 2000 Indians Lineup .10
57 Alex Rodriguez 1.50
58 Jay Buhner .10
59 Aaron Sele .10
60 Kazuhiro Sasaki .20
61 Edgar Martinez .20
62 John Halama .10
63 Mike Cameron .10
64 Fred Garcia .10
65 John Olerud .20
66 Jamie Moyer .10
67 Gil Meche .10
68 2000 Mariners Lineup .10
69 Cal Ripken Jr. 2.00
70 Sidney Ponson .10
71 Chris Richard .10
72 Jose Mercedes .10
73 Albert Belle .15
74 Mike Mussina .50
75 Brady Anderson .15
76 Delino DeShields .10
77 Melvin Mora .10
78 Luis Matos .10
79 Brook Fordyce .10
80 2000 Orioles Lineup .10
81 Rafael Palmeiro .50
82 Rick Helling .10
83 Ruben Mateo .10
84 Rusty Greer .10
85 Ivan Rodriguez .50
86 Doug Davis .10
87 Gabe Kapler .15
88 Mike Lamb .10
89 Alex Rodriguez 1.50
90 Kenny Rogers .10
91 2000 Rangers Lineup .10
92 Nomar Garciaparra .50
93 Trot Nixon .10
94 Tomokazu Ohka .10
95 Pedro Martinez .75
96 Dante Bichette .10
97 Jason Varitek .10
98 Rolando Arrojo .10
99 Carl Everett .10
100 Derek Lowe .10
101 Troy O'Leary .10
102 Tim Wakefield .10
103 2000 Red Sox Lineup .10
104 Mike Sweeney .10
105 Carlos Febles .10
106 Joe Randa .10
107 Jeff Suppan .10
108 Mac Suzuki .10
109 Jermaine Dye .10
110 Carlos Beltran .25
111 Mark Quinn .10
112 Johnny Damon .20
113 2000 Royals Lineup .10
114 Tony Clark .10
115 Dean Palmer .10
116 Brian Moehler .10
117 Brad Ausmus .10
118 Juan Gonzalez .50
119 Juan Encarnacion .10
120 Jeff Weaver .10
121 Bobby Higginson .10
122 Todd Jones .10
123 Deivi Cruz .10
124 2000 Tigers Lineup .10
125 Corey Koskie .10
126 Matt Lawton .10
127 Mark Redman .10
128 David Ortiz .10
129 Jay Canizaro .10
130 Eric Milton .10
131 Jacque Jones .10
132 J.C. Romero .10
133 Ron Coomer .10
134 Brad Radke .10
135 2000 Twins Lineup .10
136 Carlos Lee .10
137 Frank Thomas .75
138 Mike Sirotka .10
139 Charles Johnson .10
140 James Baldwin .10
141 Magglio Ordonez .25
142 Jon Garland .10
143 Paul Konerko .10
144 Ray Durham .10
145 Keith Foulke .10
146 Chris Singleton .10
147 2000 White Sox Lineup .10
148 Bernie Williams .50
149 Orlando Hernandez .15
150 David Justice .25
151 Andy Pettitte .25
152 Mariano Rivera .25
153 Derek Jeter 2.00
154 Jorge Posada .25
155 Jose Canseco .50
156 Glenallen Hill .10
157 Paul O'Neill .25
158 Denny Neagle .10
159 Chuck Knoblauch .10
160 Roger Clemens 1.50
161 2000 Yankees Lineup .10
162 Jeff Bagwell .50
163 Moises Alou .20
164 Lance Berkman .40
165 Shane Reynolds .10
166 Ken Caminiti .10
167 Craig Biggio .25
168 Jose Lima .10
169 Octavio Dotel .10
170 Richard Hidalgo .20
171 Scott Elarton .10
172 2000 Astros Lineup .10
173 Rafael Furcal .25
174 Greg Maddux 1.00
175 Quilvio Veras .10
176 Chipper Jones 1.00
177 Andres Galarraga .25
178 Brian Jordan .10
179 Tom Glavine .25
180 Kevin Millwood .25
181 Javier Lopez .25
182 B.J. Surhoff .10
183 Andruw Jones .50
184 Andy Ashby .10
185 2000 Braves Lineup .10
186 Richie Sexson .40
187 Jeff D'Amico .10
188 Ron Belliard .10
189 Jeromy Burnitz .10
190 Jimmy Haynes .10
191 Marquis Grissom .10
192 Jose Hernandez .10
193 Geoff Jenkins .20
194 Jamey Wright .10
195 Mark Loretta .10
196 2000 Brewers Lineup .10
197 Rick Ankiel .25
198 Mark McGwire 1.50
199 Fernando Vina .10
200 David Renteria .10
201 Darryl Kile .10
202 Jim Edmonds .25
203 Ray Lankford .10
204 Garrett Stephenson .10
205 Fernando Tatis .10
206 Will Clark .40
207 J.D. Drew .15
208 2000 Cardinals Lineup .10
209 Mark Grace .25
210 Eric Young .10
211 Sammy Sosa 1.00
212 Jon Lieber .10
213 Joe Girardi .10
214 Kevin Tapani .10
215 Ricky Gutierrez .10
216 Kerry Wood .50
217 Rondell White .20
218 Damon Buford .10
219 2000 Cubs Lineup .10
220 Luis Gonzalez .25
221 Randy Johnson .75
222 Jay Bell .10
223 Erubiel Durazo .10
224 Matt Williams .25
225 Steve Finley .10
226 Curt Schilling .40
227 Todd Stottlemyre .10
228 Tony Womack .10
229 Brian Anderson .10
230 2000 Diamondbacks Lineup .10
231 Gary Sheffield .40
232 Adrian Beltre .25
233 Todd Hundley .10
234 Chan Ho Park .10
235 Shawn Green .25
236 Kevin Brown .25
237 Tom Goodwin .10
238 Mark Grudzielanek .10
239 Ismael Valdes .10
240 Eric Karros .10
241 2000 Dodgers Lineup .10
242 Jose Vidro .10
243 Javier Vazquez .20
244 Orlando Cabrera .10
245 Peter Bergeron .10
246 Vladimir Guerrero .75
247 Dustin Hermanson .10
248 Tony Armas Jr. .10
249 Lee Stevens .10
250 Milton Bradley .10
251 Carl Pavano .10
252 2000 Expos Lineup .10
253 Ellis Burks .10
254 Robb Nen .10
255 J.T. Snow .10
256 Barry Bonds 2.00
257 Shawn Estes .10
258 Jeff Kent .20
259 Kirk Rueter .10
260 Bill Mueller .10
261 Livan Hernandez .10
262 Rich Aurilia .10
263 2000 Giants Lineup .10
264 Ryan Dempster .10
265 Cliff Floyd .10
266 Mike Lowell .10
267 A.J. Burnett .10
268 Preston Wilson .10
269 Luis Castillo .10
270 Henry Rodriguez .10
271 Antonio Alfonseca .10
272 Derek Lee .10
273 Mark Kotsay .10
274 Brad Penny .10
275 2000 Marlins Lineup .10
276 Mike Piazza 1.00
277 Jay Payton .10
278 Al Leiter .15
279 Mike Bordick .10
280 Armando Benitez .10
281 Todd Zeile .10
282 Mike Hampton .20
283 Edgardo Alfonzo .10
284 Derek Bell .10
285 Robin Ventura .20
286 2000 Mets Lineup .10
287 Tony Gwynn .75
288 Trevor Hoffman .10
289 Ryan Klesko .20
290 Phil Nevin .10
291 Matt Clement .10
292 Ben Davis .10
293 Ruben Rivera .10
294 Bret Boone .25
295 Adam Eaton .10
296 Eric Owens .10
297 2000 Padres Lineup .10
298 Bob Abreu .20
299 Mike Lieberthal .10
300 Robert Person .10
301 Scott Rolen .50
302 Randy Wolf .10
303 Bruce Chen .10
304 Travis Lee .10
305 Kent Bottenfield .10
306 Pat Burrell .50
307 Doug Glanville .10
308 2000 Phillies Lineup .10
309 Brian Giles .25
310 Todd Ritchie .10
311 Warren Morris .10
312 John Vander Wal .10
313 Kris Benson .10
314 Jason Kendall .10
315 Kevin Young .10
316 Francisco Cordova .10
317 Jimmy Anderson .10
318 2000 Pirates Lineup .10
319 Ken Griffey Jr. 1.00
320 Pokey Reese .10
321 Chris Stynes .10
322 Barry Larkin .40
323 Steve Parris .10
324 Michael Tucker .10
325 Dmitri Young .10
326 Pete Harnisch .10
327 Adam Graves .10
328 Aaron Boone .10
329 Sean Casey .10
330 2000 Reds Lineup .10
331 Todd Helton .50
332 Pedro Astacio .10
333 Larry Walker .25
334 Ben Petrick .10
335 Brian Bohanon .10
336 Juan Pierre .10
337 Jeffrey Hammonds .10
338 Jeff Cirillo .10
339 Todd Hollandsworth .10
340 2000 Rockies Lineup .10
341 Matt Wise, Keith Luuloa, Derrick Turnbow (Vintage Rookies) .10
342 Jason Hart, Jose Ortiz, Mario Encarnacion (Vintage Rookies) .10
343 Vernon Wells, Pascual Coco, Josh Phelps (Vintage Rookies) .25
344 Travis Harper, Kenny Kelley, Toby Hall (Vintage Rookies) .10
345 Danys Baez, Tim Drew, Martin Vargas **RC** (Vintage Rookies) .10
346 Ichiro Suzuki, Ryan Franklin, Ryan Christianson (Vintage Rookies) 10.00
347 Jay Spurgeon, Lesli Brea, Carlos Casimiro (Vintage Rookies) .10
348 B.J. Waszgis, Brian Sikorski, Joaquin Benoit (Vintage Rookies) .10
349 Sun-Woo Kim, Paxton Crawford, Steve Lomasney (Vintage Rookies) .10
350 Kris Wilson, Orber Moreno, Dee Brown (Vintage Rookies) .10
351 Mark Johnson, Brandon Inge, Adam Bernero (Vintage Rookies) .10
352 Danny Ardoin, Matt Kinney, Jason Ryan (Vintage Rookies) .10
353 Rocky Biddle, Joe Crede, Aaron Myette (Vintage Rookies) .10
354 Nick Johnson, D'Angelo Jimenez, Willi Mo Pena (Vintage Rookies) .10
355 Tony McKnight, Aaron McNeal, Keith Ginter (Vintage Rookies) .10
356 Mark DeRosa, Jason Marquis, Wes Helms (Vintage Rookies) .10
357 Allen Levrault, Horacio Estrada, Santiago Perez (Vintage Rookies) .10
358 Luis Saturria, Gene Stechschulte, Britt Reames (Vintage Rookies) .10
359 Joey Nation, Corey Patterson, Cole Liniak (Vintage Rookies) .25
360 Alex Cabrera, Geraldo Guzman, Nelson Figueroa (Vintage Rookies) .10
361 Hiram Bocachica, Mike Judd, Luke Prokopec (Vintage Rookies) .10
362 Tomas de la Rosa, Yohanny Valera, Talmadge Nunnar (Vintage Rookies) .10
363 Ryan Vogelsong, Juan Melo, Chad Zerbe (Vintage Rookies) .10
364 Jason Grilli, Pablo Ozuna, Ramon Castro (Vintage Rookies) .10
365 Timoniel Perez, Grant Roberts, Brian Cole (Vintage Rookies) .10
366 Tom Davey, Xavier Nady, Dave Maurer (Vintage Rookies) .50
367 Jimmy Rollins, Mark Brownson, Reggie Taylor (Vintage Rookies) .25
368 Alex Hernandez, Adam Hyzdu, Tike Redman (Vintage Rookies) .10
369 Brady Clark, John Riedling, Mike Bell (Vintage Rookies) .10
370 Giovanni Carrara, Josh Kalinowski, Elvis Pena (Vintage Rookies) .10
371 Jim Edmonds (Postseason Scrapbook) .10
372 Edgar Martinez (Postseason Scrapbook) .10
373 Rickey Henderson (Postseason Scrapbook) .10
374 Barry Zito (Postseason Scrapbook) .25
375 Tino Martinez (Postseason Scrapbook) .10
376 J.T. Snow (Postseason Scrapbook) .10
377 Bobby Jones (Postseason Scrapbook) .10
378 Alex Rodriguez (Postseason Scrapbook) 1.00
379 Mike Hampton (Postseason Scrapbook) .10
380 Roger Clemens (Postseason Scrapbook) .50
381 Jay Payton (Postseason Scrapbook) .10
382 John Olerud (Postseason Scrapbook) .10
383 David Justice (Postseason Scrapbook) .25
384 Mike Hampton (Postseason Scrapbook) .10
385 Yankees Celebrate (Postseason Scrapbook) .75
386 Jose Vizcaino (Postseason Scrapbook) .10
387 Roger Clemens (Postseason Scrapbook) .75
388 Todd Zeile (Postseason Scrapbook) .10
389 Derek Jeter (Postseason Scrapbook) 1.25
390 Yankees Celebrate (Postseason Scrapbook) .50
391 Nomar Garciaparra - AL Batting (Big League Leaders) .75
392 Todd Helton - NL Batting (Big League Leaders) .25
393 Troy Glaus - AL HR (Big League Leaders) .25
394 Sammy Sosa - NL HR (Big League Leaders) .50
395 Edgar Martinez - AL RBI (Big League Leaders) .10
396 Todd Helton - NL RBI (Big League Leaders) .25
397 Pedro Martinez - AL ERA (Big League Leaders) .40
398 Kevin Brown - NL ERA (Big League Leaders) .10
399 David Wells, Tim Hudson - AL Wins (Big League Leaders) .10
400 Tom Glavine - NL Wins (Big League Leaders) .10

All-Star Tributes

		NM/M
Complete Set (10):		20.00
Common Player:		1.00
Inserted 1:23		
1	Derek Jeter	4.00
2	Mike Piazza	2.00
3	Carlos Delgado	1.00
4	Pedro Martinez	1.50
5	Vladimir Guerrero	1.50
6	Mark McGwire	3.00
7	Alex Rodriguez	3.00
8	Barry Bonds	4.00
9	Chipper Jones	2.00
10	Sammy Sosa	2.50

Fantasy Outfield Combo Jersey

	NM/M
Production 25 Cards	
FO-CJ Joe DiMaggio, Mickey Mantle,	
Ken Griffey Jr.	1,000

Glory Days

		NM/M
Complete Set (15):		15.00
Common Player:		.50
Inserted 1:15		
1	Jermaine Dye	.50
2	Chipper Jones	2.00
3	Todd Helton	1.00
4	Magglio Ordonez	.75
5	Tony Gwynn	1.50
6	Jim Edmonds	.75
7	Rafael Palmeiro	1.00
8	Barry Bonds	4.00
9	Carl Everett	.50
10	Mike Piazza	2.00
11	Brian Giles	.50
12	Tony Batista	.50
13	Jeff Bagwell	1.00
14	Ken Griffey Jr.	2.00
15	Troy Glaus	1.00

Mantle Pinstripes Exclusive

	NM/M
Complete Set (56):	75.00
Common Mantle:	2.00
One Pack/Box	

Mantle Pinstripes Memorabilia

		NM/M
Print Runs Listed:		
MMB	Mickey Mantle/Bat/100	100.00
MMCJ	Mickey Mantle,	
	Roger Maris/Jsy/50	300.00
MMJ	Mickey Mantle/Jsy/100	125.00

Matinee Idols

		NM/M
Complete Set (20):		10.00
Common Player:		.50
Inserted 1:4		
1	Ken Griffey Jr.	1.00

2	Derek Jeter	2.00
3	Barry Bonds	2.00
4	Chipper Jones	1.00
5	Mike Piazza	1.00
6	Todd Helton	.50
7	Randy Johnson	.75
8	Alex Rodriguez	1.50
9	Sammy Sosa	1.50
10	Cal Ripken Jr.	2.00
11	Nomar Garciaparra	1.50
12	Carlos Delgado	.50
13	Jason Giambi	.50
14	Ivan Rodriguez	.50
15	Vladimir Guerrero	.75
16	Gary Sheffield	.50
17	Frank Thomas	.50
18	Jeff Bagwell	.50
19	Pedro Martinez	.75
20	Mark McGwire	1.50

Retro Rules

		NM/M
Complete Set (15):		20.00
Common Player:		.50
Inserted 1:15		
1	Nomar Garciaparra	3.00
2	Frank Thomas	1.00
3	Jeff Bagwell	1.00
4	Sammy Sosa	2.50
5	Derek Jeter	4.00
6	David Wells	.50
7	Vladimir Guerrero	1.50
8	Jim Thome	1.00
9	Mark McGwire	3.00
10	Todd Helton	1.00
11	Tony Gwynn	1.50
12	Bernie Williams	.75
13	Cal Ripken Jr.	4.00
14	Brian Giles	.75
15	Troy Glaus	1.50

Timeless Teams Bat

	NM/M
Common Player:	8.00
Inserted 1:15	
NYY-JD Joe DiMaggio	150.00
NYY-TH Tommy Henrich	8.00
NYY-CK Charlie Keller	8.00
NYY-BD Bill Dickey	20.00
BK-JR Jackie Robinson	90.00
BK-RC Roy Campanella	50.00
BK-GH Gil Hodges	25.00
BK-DN Don Newcombe	8.00
LA-SG Steve Garvey	8.00
LA-RC Ron Cey	8.00

LA-BR	Bill Russell	8.00
LA-DB	Dusty Baker	8.00
BA-BP	Boog Powell	8.00
BA-BR	Brooks Robinson	25.00
BA-FR	Frank Robinson	20.00
BA-MB	Mark Belanger	8.00
PI-RC	Roberto Clemente	100.00
PI-WS	Willie Stargell	20.00
PI-MS	Manny Sanguillen	8.00
PI-AO	Al Oliver	8.00
OA-RJ	Reggie Jackson	20.00
OA-SB	Sal Bando	8.00
OA-GT	Gene Tenace	8.00
OA-JR	Joe Rudi	8.00
CI2-JB	Johnny Bench	25.00
CI2-TP	Tony Perez	15.00
CI2-JM	Joe Morgan	8.00
CI2-KG	Ken Griffey Sr.	8.00
NYM-NR	Nolan Ryan	40.00
NYM-RS	Ron Swoboda	8.00
NYM-EK	Ed Kranepool	8.00
NYM-TA	Tommie Agee	8.00

Timeless Teams Jersey

		NM/M
Common Player:		15.00
Inserted 1:288		
NYY-MM	Mickey Mantle	160.00
NYY-RM	Roger Maris	50.00
NYY-BR	Bobby Richardson	15.00
CI-DC	Dave Concepcion	15.00
CI-TP	Tony Perez	20.00
CI-KG	Ken Griffey Sr.	15.00
CI-JM	Joe Morgan	20.00

Timeless Teams Combo Bat

		NM/M
Common Card:		75.00
Production 100 Sets		
NYY41	Joe DiMaggio, Tommy Henrich,	
	Bill Dickey,	
	Charlie Keller	200.00
BKN55	Jackie Robinson,	
	Roy Campanella, Gil Hodges,	
	Don Newcombe	175.00
BAL70	Frank Robinson,	
	Brooks Robinson,	
	Mark Belanger,	
	Boog Powell	120.00
LA81	Steve Garvey, Ron Cey,	
	Dusty Baker, Bill Russell 75.00	
PIT71	Roberto Clemente,	
	Willie Stargell, Bill Mazeroski,	
	Al Oliver	200.00
OAK72	Reggie Jackson, Sal Bando,	
	Gene Tenace, Joe Rudi	80.00
CIN75	Johnny Bench, Tony Perez,	
	Joe Morgan,	
	Ken Griffey Sr.	120.00
NYM69	Nolan Ryan, Ron Swoboda,	
	Ed Kranepool,	
	Tommie Agee	200.00

Timeless Teams Combo Jersey

	NM/M
Production 100 Sets	
NYY61	Mickey Mantle, Roger Maris,	
	Bobby Richardson	250.00
CIN75	Dave Concepcion, Tony Perez,	
	Ken Griffey Sr.	120.00

2001 UD Reserve

		NM/M
Complete Set (210):		
Common Player:		.15
Common SP (181-210):		3.00
Production 2,500		
Pack (5):		3.00
Box (24):		60.00
1	Darin Erstad	.25
2	Tim Salmon	.25
3	Bengie Molina	.15
4	Troy Glaus	.50
5	Glenallen Hill	.15
6	Garret Anderson	.25
7	Jason Giambi	.50
8	Johnny Damon	.40
9	Eric Chavez	.25
10	Tim Hudson	.25
11	Miguel Tejada	.40
12	Barry Zito	.25
13	Jose Ortiz	.15
14	Tony Batista	.15
15	Carlos Delgado	.50
16	Shannon Stewart	.15
17	Raul Mondesi	.15
18	Ben Grieve	.15
19	Aubrey Huff	.15
20	Greg Vaughn	.15
21	Fred McGriff	.25
22	Gerald Williams	.15
23	Bartolo Colon	.25
24	Roberto Alomar	.40
25	Jim Thome	.50
26	Omar Vizquel	.25
27	Juan Gonzalez	.50
28	Ellis Burks	.15
29	Edgar Martinez	.25
30	Aaron Sele	.15
31	Jay Buhner	.15
32	Mike Cameron	.15
33	Kazuhiro Sasaki	.15
34	John Olerud	.25
35	Cal Ripken Jr.	2.00
36	Brady Anderson	.15
37	Pat Hentgen	.15
38	Chris Richard	.15
39	Jerry Hairston Jr.	.15
40	Mike Bordick	.15
41	Ivan Rodriguez	.50
42	Rick Helling	.15
43	Rafael Palmeiro	.50
44	Alex Rodriguez	1.50
45	Andres Galarraga	.25
46	Rusty Greer	.15
47	Ruben Mateo	.15
48	Ken Caminiti	.15
49	Nomar Garciaparra	.75
50	Pedro Martinez	.75
51	Manny Ramirez	.50
52	Carl Everett	.15
53	Dante Bichette	.15
54	Hideo Nomo	.40
55	Mike Sweeney	.15
56	Carlos Beltran	.50
57	Jeff Suppan	.15
58	Jermaine Dye	.25
59	Mark Quinn	.15
60	Joe Randa	.15
61	Bobby Higginson	.15
62	Tony Clark	.15
63	Brian Moehler	.15
64	Dean Palmer	.15
65	Brandon Inge	.15
66	Damion Easley	.15
67	Brad Radke	.15
68	Corey Koskie	.15
69	Cristian Guzman	.15
70	Eric Milton	.15
71	Jacque Jones	.15
72	Matt Lawton	.15
73	Frank Thomas	.50
74	David Wells	.15
75	Magglio Ordonez	.40
76	Paul Konerko	.25
77	Sandy Alomar Jr.	.15
78	Ray Durham	.15
79	Roger Clemens	1.50
80	Bernie Williams	.50
81	Derek Jeter	2.00
82	David Justice	.25

83	Paul O'Neill	.25
84	Mike Mussina	.40
85	Jorge Posada	.40
86	Jeff Bagwell	.50
87	Richard Hidalgo	.15
88	Craig Biggio	.25
89	Scott Elarton	.15
90	Moises Alou	.25
91	Greg Maddux	1.00
92	Rafael Furcal	.25
93	Andruw Jones	.50
94	Tom Glavine	.40
95	Chipper Jones	1.00
96	Javy Lopez	.25
97	Richie Sexson	.40
98	Jeromy Burnitz	.15
99	Jeff D'Amico	.15
100	Jeffrey Hammonds	.15
101	Geoff Jenkins	.25
102	Ben Sheets	.25
103	Mark McGwire	1.50
104	Rick Ankiel	.40
105	Darryl Kile	.15
106	Edgar Renteria	.25
107	Jim Edmonds	.25
108	J.D. Drew	.25
109	Sammy Sosa	1.00
110	Corey Patterson	.25
111	Kerry Wood	.50
112	Todd Hundley	.15
113	Rondell White	.15
114	Matt Stairs	.15
115	Randy Johnson	.75
116	Mark Grace	.40
117	Steve Finley	.15
118	Luis Gonzalez	.25
119	Matt Williams	.25
120	Curt Schilling	.40
121	Gary Sheffield	.40
122	Kevin Brown	.25
123	Shawn Green	.25
124	Eric Karros	.15
125	Chan Ho Park	.15
126	Adrian Beltre	.25
127	Vladimir Guerrero	.75
128	Fernando Tatis	.15
129	Lee Stevens	.15
130	Jose Vidro	.15
131	Peter Bergeron	.15
132	Michael Barrett	.15
133	Jeff Kent	.25
134	Russ Ortiz	.15
135	Barry Bonds	2.00
136	J.T. Snow	.15
137	Livan Hernandez	.15
138	Rich Aurilia	.15
139	Preston Wilson	.15
140	Mike Lowell	.25
141	Ryan Dempster	.15
142	Charles Johnson	.15
143	Matt Clement	.15
144	Luis Castillo	.15
145	Mike Piazza	1.00
146	Al Leiter	.15
147	Robin Ventura	.25
148	Jay Payton	.15
149	Todd Zeile	.15
150	Edgardo Alfonzo	.15
151	Tony Gwynn	.75
152	Ryan Klesko	.25
153	Phil Nevin	.15
154	Mark Kotsay	.15
155	Trevor Hoffman	.15
156	Damian Jackson	.15
157	Scott Rolen	.50
158	Mike Lieberthal	.15
159	Bruce Chen	.15
160	Bobby Abreu	.40
161	Pat Burrell	.40
162	Travis Lee	.15
163	Jason Kendall	.15
164	Derek Bell	.15
165	Kris Benson	.15
166	Kevin Young	.15
167	Brian Giles	.25
168	Pat Meares	.15
169	Sean Casey	.25
170	Pokey Reese	.15
171	Pete Harnisch	.15
172	Barry Larkin	.25
173	Ken Griffey Jr.	1.00
174	Dmitri Young	.15
175	Mike Hampton	.15
176	Todd Helton	.50
177	Jeff Cirillo	.15
178	Denny Neagle	.15
179	Larry Walker	.25
180	Todd Hollandsworth	.15
181	Ichiro Suzuki RC	
	(Rookie Reserve)	30.00
182	Wilson Betemit RC	
	(Rookie Reserve)	6.00
183	Adrian Hernandez RC	
	(Rookie Reserve)	3.00
184	Travis Hafner RC	
	(Rookie Reserve)	10.00
185	Sean Douglass RC	
	(Rookie Reserve)	3.00
186	Juan Diaz RC	
	(Rookie Reserve)	3.00
187	Horacio Ramirez RC	
	(Rookie Reserve)	5.00
188	Morgan Ensberg RC	
	(Rookie Reserve)	8.00

189	Brandon Duckworth RC	
	(Rookie Reserve)	3.00
190	Jack Wilson RC	
	(Rookie Reserve)	8.00
191	Erick Almonte RC	
	(Rookie Reserve)	3.00
192	Ricardo Rodriguez RC	
	(Rookie Reserve)	3.00
193	Elpidio Guzman RC	
	(Rookie Reserve)	3.00
194	Juan Uribe RC	
	(Rookie Reserve)	5.00
195	Ryan Freel RC	
	(Rookie Reserve)	6.00
196	Christian Parker RC	
	(Rookie Reserve)	3.00
197	Jackson Melian RC	
	(Rookie Reserve)	3.00
198	Jose Mieses RC	
	(Rookie Reserve)	3.00
199	Andres Torres RC	
	(Rookie Reserve)	3.00
200	Jason Smith RC	
	(Rookie Reserve)	3.00
201	Johnny Estrada RC	
	(Rookie Reserve)	5.00
202	Cesar Crespo RC	
	(Rookie Reserve)	3.00
203	Carlos Valderrama RC	
	(Rookie Reserve)	3.00
204	Albert Pujols RC	
	(Rookie Reserve)	100.00
205	Wilken Ruan RC	
	(Rookie Reserve)	3.00
206	Josh Fogg RC	
	(Rookie Reserve)	4.00
207	Bert Snow RC	
	(Rookie Reserve)	3.00
208	Brian Lawrence RC	
	(Rookie Reserve)	5.00
209	Esix Snead RC	
	(Rookie Reserve)	3.00
210	Tsuyoshi Shinjo RC	
	(Rookie Reserve)	4.00

Big Game Reserve

		NM/M
Complete Set (10):		15.00
Common Player:		1.00
Inserted 1:24		
BG1	Alex Rodriguez	3.00
BG2	Ken Griffey Jr.	2.00
BG3	Mark McGwire	3.00
BG4	Derek Jeter	4.00
BG5	Sammy Sosa	2.50
BG6	Pedro Martinez	1.50
BG7	Jason Giambi	1.00
BG8	Todd Helton	1.00
BG9	Carlos Delgado	1.00
BG10	Mike Piazza	2.00

G-U Reserve Base/Ball Duo

		NM/M
Inserted 1:240		
JR	Derek Jeter, Alex Rodriguez	50.00
JP	Derek Jeter, Mike Piazza	60.00
MP	Mark McGwire, Mike Piazza	100.00
MJ	Mark McGwire, Derek Jeter	100.00
RM	Alex Rodriguez, Mark McGwire	100.00
CR	Roger Clemens, Alex Rodriguez	40.00

ST	Sammy Sosa, Frank Thomas	40.00
GD	Vladimir Guerrero, Carlos Delgado	20.00
BH	Barry Bonds, Todd Helton	35.00
MG	Mark McGwire, Ken Griffey Jr.	40.00
GS	Ken Griffey Jr., Sammy Sosa	20.00
GJ	Ken Griffey Jr., Derek Jeter	35.00
JN	Chipper Jones, Nomar Garciaparra	20.00
NJ	Nomar Garciaparra, Derek Jeter	35.00
GR	Nomar Garciaparra, Alex Rodriguez	30.00

G-U Reserve Base/Ball Trio

		NM/M
Inserted 1:480		
JRG	Derek Jeter, Alex Rodriguez, Nomar Garciaparra	50.00
SGM	Sammy Sosa, Ken Griffey Jr., Mark McGwire	65.00
PRS	Mike Piazza, Alex Rodriguez, Sammy Sosa	40.00
GSG	Ken Griffey Jr., Sammy Sosa, Vladimir Guerrero	30.00
THM	Frank Thomas, Todd Helton, Mark McGwire	45.00
CMJ	Roger Clemens, Pedro Martinez, Derek Jeter	45.00
BSH	Barry Bonds, Gary Sheffield, Todd Helton	40.00
GPJ	Vladimir Guerrero, Mike Piazza, Chipper Jones	30.00
MJR	Mark McGwire, Derek Jeter, Alex Rodriguez	75.00
JGS	Derek Jeter, Ken Griffey Jr., Sammy Sosa	45.00

G-U Reserve Base/Ball Quad

		NM/M
Production 50 Sets		
SGRM	Sammy Sosa, Ken Griffey Jr., Alex Rodriguez, Mark McGwire	175.00
GPJG	Vladimir Guerrero, Mike Piazza, Chipper Jones, Nomar Garciaparra	65.00
THMJ	Frank Thomas, Todd Helton, Mark McGwire, Derek Jeter	90.00
GBJE	Ken Griffey Jr., Barry Bonds, Andruw Jones, Jim Edmonds	75.00
PMJR	Mike Piazza, Mark McGwire, Derek Jeter, Alex Rodriguez	150.00

Jerseys Duo

		NM/M
Common Duo:		15.00
Inserted 1:240		
HG	Tim Hudson, Jason Giambi	25.00
BK	Barry Bonds, Jeff Kent	40.00
JJ	Andruw Jones, Chipper Jones	25.00
GE	Troy Glaus, Darin Erstad	15.00
WO	David Wells, Magglio Ordonez	15.00
WE	Bernie Williams, Jim Edmonds	15.00
DG	Carlos Delgado, Jason Giambi	20.00
GK	Jason Giambi, Jeff Kent	20.00
JW	Randy Johnson, David Wells	25.00
JG	Chipper Jones, Troy Glaus	25.00
SB	Gary Sheffield, Barry Bonds	40.00
HE	Todd Helton, Darin Erstad	15.00
RB	Alex Rodriguez, Tony Batista	25.00
GW	Brian Giles, Bernie Williams	15.00
SG	Sammy Sosa, Troy Glaus	30.00

Jerseys Trio

Common Trio:		25.00
Inserted 1:480		
GHD	Jason Giambi, Todd Helton, Carlos Delgado	30.00
RSS	Alex Rodriguez, Sammy Sosa, Gary Sheffield	50.00
WEJ	Bernie Williams, Jim Edmonds, Andruw Jones	25.00
HJW	Tim Hudson, Randy Johnson, David Wells	30.00
SOD	Sammy Sosa, Magglio Ordonez, Carlos Delgado	40.00
GGR	Jason Giambi, Troy Glaus, Alex Rodriguez	40.00
BWD	Tony Batista, Bernie Williams, Carlos Delgado	25.00
BSH	Barry Bonds, Gary Sheffield, Todd Helton	50.00
WSH	David Wells, Sammy Sosa, Todd Helton	40.00
EKE	Darin Erstad, Jeff Kent, Jim Edmonds	25.00

Jerseys Quad

		NM/M
Common Quad:		25.00
Production 50 Sets		
DRGS	Carlos Delgado, Alex Rodriguez, Troy Glaus, Sammy Sosa	40.00
GWBG	Jason Giambi, Bernie Williams, Barry Bonds, Brian Giles	75.00
HKEJ	Todd Helton, Jeff Kent, Jim Edmonds, Chipper Jones	40.00
HKEJ	Gary Sheffield, Magglio Ordonez, Darin Erstad, Tony Batista	25.00
JRSB	Andruw Jones, Alex Rodriguez, Sammy Sosa, Barry Bonds	100.00

The New Order

		NM/M
Complete Set (10):		15.00
Common Player:		.75
Inserted 1:24		
NO1	Vladimir Guerrero	1.50
NO2	Andruw Jones	1.00
NO3	Corey Patterson	.75
NO4	Derek Jeter	4.00
NO5	Alex Rodriguez	3.00
NO6	Pat Burrell	.75
NO7	Ichiro Suzuki	5.00
NO8	Barry Zito	.75
NO9	Rafael Furcal	.75
NO10	Troy Glaus	1.00

UD Royalty

		NM/M
Complete Set (10):		15.00
Common Player:		1.00
Inserted 1:24		
R1	Ken Griffey Jr.	2.00
R2	Derek Jeter	4.00
R3	Alex Rodriguez	3.00
R4	Sammy Sosa	2.50
R5	Mark McGwire	3.00
R6	Mike Piazza	2.00
R7	Vladimir Guerrero	1.50
R8	Chipper Jones	2.00

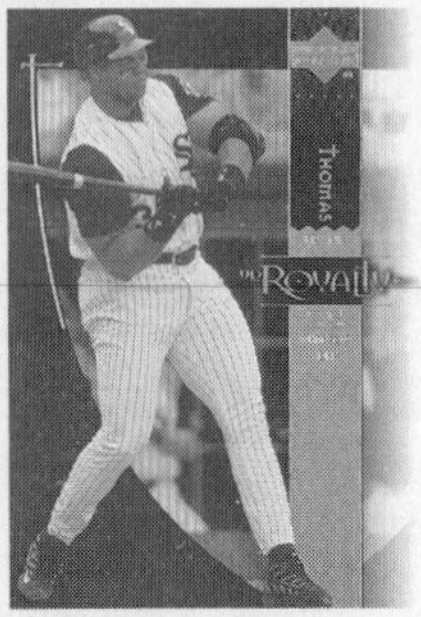

R9 Frank Thomas 1.00
R10 Nomar Garciaparra 3.00

2002 Upper Deck

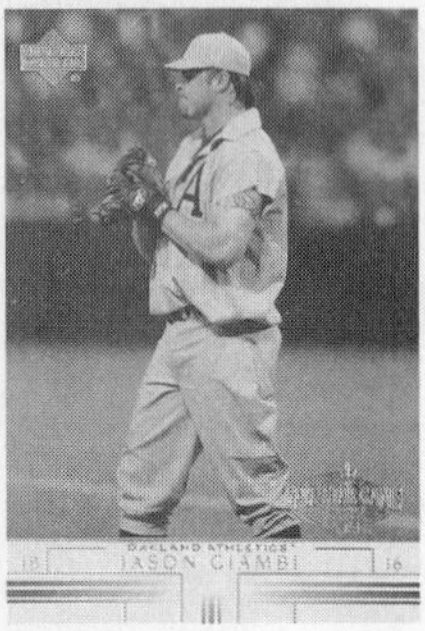

	NM/M
Complete Set (745):	150.00
Complete Series I (500):	100.00
Complete Series II (245):	50.00
Common Player:	.15
Series 1 Hobby Pack (8):	4.00
Series 1 Hobby Box (24):	75.00
Series 2 Hobby Pack (8):	1.25
Series 2 Hobby Box (24):	25.00

1 Mark Prior (Star Rookie) 4.00
2 Mark Teixeira (Star Rookie) 1.50
3 Brian Roberts (Star Rookie) .25
4 Jason Romano (Star Rookie) .25
5 Dennis Stark **RC** (Star Rookie) .50
6 Oscar Salazar (Star Rookie) .50
7 John Patterson (Star Rookie) .25
8 Shane Loux (Star Rookie) .25
9 Marcus Giles (Star Rookie) .40
10 Juan Cruz (Star Rookie) .25
11 Jorge Julio (Star Rookie) .25
12 Adam Dunn (Star Rookie) .50
13 Delvin James (Star Rookie) .25
14 Jeremy Affeldt (Star Rookie) .25
15 Tim Raines Jr. (Star Rookie) .25
16 Luke Hudson (Star Rookie) .25
17 Todd Sears (Star Rookie) .25
18 George Perez (Star Rookie) .25
19 Wilmy Caceres (Star Rookie) .25
20 Abraham Nunez (Star Rookie) .25
21 Mike Amrhein (Star Rookie) .25
22 Carlos Hernandez (Star Rookie) .25
23 Scott Hodges (Star Rookie) .25
24 Brandon Knight (Star Rookie) .25
25 Geoff Goetz (Star Rookie) .25
26 Carlos Garcia (Star Rookie) .25
27 Luis Pineda (Star Rookie) .25
28 Chris Gissell (Star Rookie) .25
29 Jae Weong (Star Rookie) .25
30 Paul Phillips (Star Rookie) .25
31 Cory Aldridge (Star Rookie) .25
32 Aaron Cook **RC** (Star Rookie) .50
33 Rendy Espina (Star Rookie) .25
34 Jason Phillips (Star Rookie) .25
35 Carlos Silva (Star Rookie) .25
36 Ryan Mills (Star Rookie) .25
37 Pedro Santana (Star Rookie) .25
38 John Grabow (Star Rookie) .25
39 Cody Ransom (Star Rookie) .15
40 Orlando Woodlands (Star Rookie) .25
41 Bud Smith (Star Rookie) .25
42 Junior Guerrero (Star Rookie) .25
43 David Brous (Star Rookie) .25
44 Steve Green (Star Rookie) .25
45 Brian Rogers (Star Rookie) .25
46 Juan Figueroa (Star Rookie) .25
47 Nick Punto (Star Rookie) .25
48 Junior Herndon (Star Rookie) .25
49 Justin Kaye (Star Rookie) .25
50 Jason Karnuth (Star Rookie) .25
51 Troy Glaus .40
52 Bengie Molina .15
53 Ramon Ortiz .15
54 Adam Kennedy .15
55 Jarrod Washburn .15
56 Troy Percival .15
57 David Eckstein .15
58 Ben Weber .15
59 Larry Barnes .15
60 Ismael Valdes .15
61 Benji Gil .15
62 Scott Schoeneweis .15
63 Pat Rapp .15
64 Jason Giambi .50
65 Mark Mulder .25
66 Ron Gant .15
67 Johnny Damon .25
68 Adam Piatt .15
69 Jermaine Dye .25
70 Jason Hart .15
71 Eric Chavez .40
72 Jim Mecir .15
73 Barry Zito .40
74 Jason Isringhausen .15
75 Jeremy Giambi .15
76 Olmedo Saenz .15
77 Terrence Long .15
78 Ramon Hernandez .15
79 Chris Carpenter .15
80 Raul Mondesi .15
81 Carlos Delgado .50
82 Billy Koch .15
83 Vernon Wells .25
84 Darrin Fletcher .15
85 Homer Bush .15
86 Pasqual Coco .15
87 Shannon Stewart .15
88 Chris Woodward .15
89 Joe Lawrence .15
90 Esteban Loaiza .15
91 Cesar Izturis .15
92 Kelvim Escobar .15
93 Greg Vaughn .15
94 Brent Abernathy .15
95 Tanyon Sturtze .15
96 Steve Cox .15
97 Aubrey Huff .15
98 Jesus Colome .15
99 Ben Grieve .15
100 Esteban Yan .15
101 Joe Kennedy .15
102 Felix Martinez .15
103 Nick Bierbrodt .15
104 Damian Rolls .15
105 Russ Johnson .15
106 Toby Hall .15
107 Roberto Alomar .40
108 Bartolo Colon .25
109 John Rocker .15
110 Juan Gonzalez .50
111 Einar Diaz .15
112 Chuck Finley .15
113 Kenny Lofton .25
114 Danys Baez .15
115 Travis Fryman .25
116 C.C. Sabathia .25
117 Paul Shuey .15
118 Marty Cordova .15
119 Ellis Burks .15
120 Bob Wickman .15
121 Edgar Martinez .25
122 Freddy Garcia .15
123 Ichiro Suzuki 1.50
124 John Olerud .25
125 Gil Meche .15
126 Dan Wilson .15
127 Aaron Sele .15
128 Kazuhiro Sasaki .15
129 Mark McLemore .15
130 Carlos Guillen .15
131 Al Martin .15
132 David Bell .15
133 Jay Buhner .15
134 Stan Javier .15
135 Tony Batista .15
136 Jason Johnson .15
137 Brook Fordyce .15
138 Mike Kinkade .15
139 Willis Roberts .15
140 David Segui .15
141 Josh Towers .15
142 Jeff Conine .15
143 Chris Richard .15
144 Pat Hentgen .15
145 Melvin Mora .15
146 Jerry Hairston Jr. .15
147 Calvin Maduro .15
148 Brady Anderson .15
149 Alex Rodriguez 1.50
150 Kenny Rogers .15
151 Chad Curtis .15
152 Ricky Ledee .15
153 Rafael Palmeiro .50
154 Rob Bell .15
155 Rick Helling .15
156 Doug Davis .15
157 Mike Lamb .15
158 Gabe Kapler .15
159 Jeff Zimmerman .15
160 Bill Haselman .15
161 Tim Crabtree .15
162 Carlos Pena .15
163 Nomar Garciaparra 1.00
164 Shea Hillenbrand .15
165 Hideo Nomo .40
166 Manny Ramirez .50
167 Jose Offerman .15
168 Scott Hatteberg .15
169 Trot Nixon .25
170 Darren Lewis .15
171 Derek Lowe .25
172 Troy O'Leary .15
173 Tim Wakefield .15
174 Chris Stynes .15
175 John Valentin .15
176 David Cone .15
177 Neifi Perez .15
178 Brent Mayne .15
179 Dan Reichert .15
180 A.J. Hinch .15
181 Chris George .15
182 Mike Sweeney .15
183 Jeff Suppan .15
184 Roberto Hernandez .15
185 Joe Randa .15
186 Paul Byrd .15
187 Luis Ordaz .15
188 Kris Wilson .15
189 Dee Brown .15
190 Tony Clark .15
191 Matt Anderson .15
192 Robert Fick .15
193 Juan Encarnacion .15
194 Dean Palmer .15
195 Victor Santos .15
196 Damion Easley .15
197 Jose Lima .15
198 Deivi Cruz .15
199 Roger Cedeno .15
200 Jose Macias .15
201 Jeff Weaver .15
202 Brandon Inge .15
203 Brian Moehler .15
204 Brad Radke .15
205 Doug Mientkiewicz .15
206 Cristian Guzman .15
207 Corey Koskie .15
208 LaTroy Hawkins .15
209 J.C. Romero .15
210 Chad Allen .15
211 Torii Hunter .25
212 Travis Miller .15
213 Joe Mays .15
214 Todd Jones .15
215 David Ortiz .40
216 Brian Buchanan .15
217 A.J. Pierzynski .15
218 Carlos Lee .15
219 Gary Glover .15
220 Jose Valentin .15
221 Aaron Rowand .15
222 Sandy Alomar Jr. .15
223 Herbert Perry .15
224 Jon Garland .15
225 Mark Buehrle .15
226 Chris Singleton .15
227 Kip Wells .15
228 Ray Durham .15
229 Joe Crede .15
230 Keith Foulke .15
231 Royce Clayton .15
232 Andy Pettitte .40
233 Derek Jeter 2.00
234 Jorge Posada .40
235 Roger Clemens 1.50
236 Paul O'Neill .25
237 Nick Johnson .15
238 Gerald Williams .15
239 Mariano Rivera .25
240 Alfonso Soriano .50
241 Ramiro Mendoza .15
242 Mike Mussina .50
243 Luis Sojo .15
244 Scott Brosius .15
245 David Justice .25
246 Wade Miller .15
247 Brad Ausmus .15
248 Jeff Bagwell .50
249 Daryle Ward .15
250 Shane Reynolds .15
251 Chris Truby .15
252 Billy Wagner .15
253 Craig Biggio .25
254 Moises Alou .25
255 Vinny Castilla .15
256 Tim Redding .15
257 Roy Oswalt .40
258 Julio Lugo .15
259 Chipper Jones .75
260 Greg Maddux 1.00
261 Ken Caminiti .15
262 Kevin Millwood .25
263 Keith Lockhart .15
264 Rey Sanchez .15
265 Jason Marquis .15
266 Brian Jordan .15
267 Steve Karsay .15
268 Wes Helms .15
269 B.J. Surhoff .15
270 Wilson Betemit .15
271 John Smoltz .25
272 Rafael Furcal .25
273 Jeromy Burnitz .15
274 Jimmy Haynes .15
275 Mark Loretta .15
276 Jose Hernandez .15
277 Paul Rigdon .15
278 Alex Sanchez .15
279 Chad Fox .15
280 Devon White .15
281 Tyler Houston .15
282 Ronnie Belliard .15
283 Luis Lopez .15
284 Ben Sheets .40
285 Curtis Leskanic .15
286 Henry Blanco .15
287 Mark McGwire 2.00
288 Edgar Renteria .25
289 Matt Morris .25
290 Gene Stechschulte .15
291 Dustin Hermanson .15
292 Eli Marrero .15
293 Albert Pujols 1.50
294 Luis Saturria .15
295 Bobby Bonilla .15
296 Garrett Stephenson .15
297 Jim Edmonds .40
298 Rick Ankiel .25
299 Placido Polanco .15
300 Dave Veres .15
301 Sammy Sosa 1.50
302 Eric Young .15
303 Kerry Wood .75
304 Jon Lieber .15
305 Joe Girardi .15
306 Fred McGriff .25
307 Jeff Fassero .15
308 Julio Zuleta .15
309 Kevin Tapani .15
310 Rondell White .15
311 Julian Tavarez .15
312 Tom Gordon .15
313 Corey Patterson .25
314 Bill Mueller .15
315 Randy Johnson .75
316 Chad Moeller .15
317 Tony Womack .15
318 Erubiel Durazo .15
319 Luis Gonzalez .25
320 Brian Anderson .15
321 Reggie Sanders .15
322 Greg Colbrunn .15
323 Robert Ellis .15
324 Jack Cust .15
325 Bret Prinz .15
326 Steve Finley .15
327 Byung-Hyun Kim .15
328 Albie Lopez .15
329 Gary Sheffield .40
330 Mark Grudzielanek .15
331 Paul LoDuca .15
332 Tom Goodwin .15
333 Andy Ashby .15
334 Hiram Bocachica .15
335 Dave Hansen .15
336 Kevin Brown .25
337 Marquis Grissom .15
338 Terry Adams .15
339 Chan Ho Park .15
340 Adrian Beltre .25
341 Luke Prokopec .15
342 Jeff Shaw .15
343 Vladimir Guerrero .75
344 Orlando Cabrera .15
345 Tony Armas Jr. .15
346 Michael Barrett .15
347 Geoff Blum .15
348 Ryan Minor .15
349 Peter Bergeron .15
350 Graeme Lloyd .15
351 Jose Vidro .15
352 Javier Vazquez .15
353 Matt Blank .15
354 Masato Yoshii .15
355 Carl Pavano .15
356 Barry Bonds 2.00
357 Shawon Dunston .15
358 Livan Hernandez .15
359 Felix Rodriguez .15
360 Pedro Feliz .15
361 Calvin Murray .15
362 Robb Nen .15
363 Marvin Benard .15
364 Russ Ortiz .15
365 Jason Schmidt .25
366 Rich Aurilia .15
367 John Vander Wal .15
368 Benito Santiago .15
369 Ryan Dempster .15
370 Charles Johnson .15
371 Alex Gonzalez .15
372 Luis Castillo .15
373 Mike Lowell .25
374 Antonio Alfonseca .15
375 A.J. Burnett .15
376 Brad Penny .15
377 Jason Grilli .15
378 Derrek Lee .25
379 Matt Clement .15
380 Eric Owens .15
381 Vladimir Nunez .15
382 Cliff Floyd .15
383 Mike Piazza 1.25
384 Lenny Harris .15
385 Glendon Rusch .15
386 Todd Zeile .15
387 Al Leiter .25
388 Armando Benitez .15
389 Alex Escobar .15
390 Kevin Appier .15
391 Matt Lawton .15
392 Bruce Chen .15
393 John Franco .15
394 Tsuyoshi Shinjo .15
395 Rey Ordonez .15
396 Joe McEwing .15

397 Ryan Klesko .15
398 Brian Lawrence .15
399 Kevin Walker .15
400 Phil Nevin .15
401 Bubba Trammell .15
402 Wiki Gonzalez .15
403 D'Angelo Jimenez .15
404 Rickey Henderson .40
405 Mike Darr .15
406 Trevor Hoffman .15
407 Damian Jackson .15
408 Santiago Perez .15
409 Cesar Crespo .15
410 Robert Person .15
411 Travis Lee .15
412 Scott Rolen .75
413 Turk Wendell .15
414 Randy Wolf .15
415 Kevin Jordan .15
416 Jose Mesa .15
417 Mike Lieberthal .15
418 Bobby Abreu .25
419 Tomas Perez .15
420 Doug Glanville .15
421 Reggie Taylor .15
422 Jimmy Rollins .40
423 Brian Giles .25
424 Rob Mackowiak .15
425 Bronson Arroyo .15
426 Kevin Young .15
427 Jack Wilson .15
428 Adam Brown .15
429 Chad Hermansen .15
430 Jimmy Anderson .15
431 Aramis Ramirez .25
432 Todd Ritchie .15
433 Pat Meares .15
434 Warren Morris .15
435 Derek Bell .15
436 Ken Griffey Jr. 1.00
437 Elmer Dessens .15
438 Ruben Rivera .15
439 Jason LaRue .15
440 Sean Casey .25
441 Pete Harnisch .15
442 Danny Graves .15
443 Aaron Boone .15
444 Dmitri Young .15
445 Brandon Larson .15
446 Pokey Reese .15
447 Todd Walker .15
448 Juan Castro .15
449 Todd Helton .50
450 Ben Petrick .15
451 Juan Pierre .15
452 Jeff Cirillo .15
453 Juan Uribe .15
454 Brian Bohanon .15
455 Terry Shumpert .15
456 Mike Hampton .15
457 Shawn Chacon .15
458 Adam Melhuse .15
459 Greg Norton .15
460 Gabe White .15
461 Ichiro Suzuki (World Stage) 1.50
462 Carlos Delgado (World Stage) .40
463 Manny Ramirez (World Stage) .50
464 Miguel Tejada (World Stage) .25
465 Tsuyoshi Shinjo (World Stage) .15
466 Bernie Williams (World Stage) .40
467 Juan Gonzalez (World Stage) .50
468 Andruw Jones (World Stage) .40
469 Ivan Rodriguez (World Stage) .50
470 Larry Walker (World Stage) .25
471 Hideo Nomo (World Stage) .25
472 Albert Pujols (World Stage) 1.00
473 Pedro Martinez (World Stage) .75
474 Vladimir Guerrero (World Stage) .75
475 Tony Batista (World Stage) .15
476 Kazuhiro Sasaki (World Stage) .15
477 Richard Hidalgo (World Stage) .15
478 Carlos Lee (World Stage) .15
479 Roberto Alomar (World Stage) .40
480 Rafael Palmeiro (World Stage) .50
481 Ken Griffey Jr. (Griffey Gallery) .50
482 Ken Griffey Jr. (Griffey Gallery) .50
483 Ken Griffey Jr. (Griffey Gallery) .50
484 Ken Griffey Jr. (Griffey Gallery) .50
485 Ken Griffey Jr. (Griffey Gallery) .50
486 Ken Griffey Jr. (Griffey Gallery) .50
487 Ken Griffey Jr. (Griffey Gallery) .50
488 Ken Griffey Jr. (Griffey Gallery) .50
489 Ken Griffey Jr. (Griffey Gallery) .50
490 Ken Griffey Jr. (Griffey Gallery) .50
491 Barry Bonds (Season Highlights Checklist) .75
492 Hideo Nomo (Season Highlights Checklist) .15
493 Ichiro Suzuki (Season Highlights Checklist) .50
494 Cal Ripken Jr. (Season Highlights Checklist) .75
495 Tony Gwynn (Season Highlights Checklist) .40
496 Randy Johnson (Season Highlights Checklist) .40
497 A.J. Burnett (Season Highlights Checklist) .15
498 Rickey Henderson (Season Highlights Checklist) .15
499 Albert Pujols (Season Highlights Checklist) .75
500 Luis Gonzalez (Season Highlights Checklist) .25
501 Brandon Puffer **RC** .50
502 Rodrigo Rosario **RC** .50
503 Tom Shearn **RC** .50
504 Reed Johnson **RC** .50
505 Chris Baker **RC** .50
506 John Ennis **RC** .50
507 Luis Martinez **RC** .50
508 So Taguchi **RC** .75
509 Scotty Layfield **RC** .50
510 Francis Beltran **RC** .50
511 Brandon Backe **RC** .50
512 Doug DeVore **RC** .50
513 Jeremy Ward **RC** .50
514 Jose Vaverde **RC** .50
515 P.J. Bevis **RC** .50
516 Victor Alvarez **RC** .50
517 Kazuhisa Ishii **RC** 2.00
518 Jorge Nunez **RC** .50
519 Eric Good **RC** .50
520 Ron Calloway **RC** .50
521 Valentino Pasucci .25
522 Nelson Castro **RC** .50
523 Deivis Santos .25
524 Luis Ugueto **RC** .50
525 Matt Thornton .25
526 Hansel Izquierdo **RC** .75
527 Tyler Yates **RC** .50
528 Mark Corey **RC** .50
529 Jaime Cerda **RC** .50
530 Satoru Komiyama **RC** .50
531 Steve Bechler **RC** .50
532 Ben Howard **RC** .50
533 Anderson Machado **RC** .50
534 Jorge Padilla **RC** .50
535 Eric Junge **RC** .50
536 Adrian Burnside **RC** .50
537 Mike Gonzalez **RC** .50
538 Josh Hancock **RC** .50
539 Colin Young **RC** .50
540 Rene Reyes **RC** .50
541 Cam Esslinger **RC** .50
542 Tim Kalita **RC** .50
543 Kevin Frederick **RC** .50
544 Kyle Kane **RC** .50
545 Edwin Almonte **RC** .50
546 Aaron Sele .15
547 Garret Anderson .40
548 Darin Erstad .25
549 Brad Fullmer .15
550 Kevin Appier .15
551 Tim Salmon .25
552 David Justice .25
553 Billy Koch .15
554 Scott Hatteberg .15
555 Tim Hudson .25
556 Miguel Tejada .25
557 Carlos Pena .15
558 Mike Sirotka .15
559 Jose Cruz Jr. .15
560 Josh Phelps .15
561 Brandon Lyon .15
562 Luke Prokopec .15
563 Felipe Lopez .15
564 Jason Standridge .15
565 Chris Gomez .15
566 John Flaherty .15
567 Jason Tyner .15
568 Bobby Smith .15
569 Wilson Alvarez .15
570 Matt Lawton .15
571 Omar Vizquel .25
572 Jim Thome .75
573 Brady Anderson .15
574 Alex Escobar .15
575 Russell Branyan .15
576 Bret Boone .25
577 Ben Davis .15
578 Mike Cameron .15
579 Jamie Moyer .15
580 Ruben Sierra .15
581 Jeff Cirillo .15
582 Marty Cordova .15
583 Mike Bordick .15
584 Brian Roberts .15
585 Luis Matos .15
586 Geronimo Gil .15
587 Jay Gibbons .15
588 Carl Everett .15
589 Ivan Rodriguez .50
590 Chan Ho Park .15
591 Juan Gonzalez .50
592 Hank Blalock .40
593 Todd Van Poppel .15
594 Pedro J. Martinez .75
595 Jason Varitek .15
596 Tony Clark .15
597 Johnny Damon .25
598 Dustin Hermanson .15
599 John Burkett .15
600 Carlos Beltran .40
601 Mark Quinn .15
602 Chuck Knoblauch .15
603 Michael Tucker .15
604 Carlos Febles .15
605 Jose Rosado .15
606 Dmitri Young .15
607 Bobby Higginson .15
608 Craig Paquette .15
609 Mitch Meluskey .15
610 Wendell Magee .15
611 Mike Rivera .15
612 Jacque Jones .15
613 Luis Rivas .15
614 Eric Milton .15
615 Eddie Guardado .15
616 Matt LeCroy .15
617 Mike Jackson .15
618 Magglio Ordonez .25
619 Frank Thomas .50
620 Rocky Biddle .15
621 Paul Konerko .25
622 Todd Ritchie .15
623 Jon Rauch .15
624 John Vander Wal .15
625 Rondell White .15
626 Jason Giambi .50
627 Robin Ventura .25
628 David Wells .15
629 Bernie Williams .50
630 Lance Berkman .25
631 Richard Hidalgo .15
632 Gregg Zaun .15
633 Jose Vizcaino .15
634 Octavio Dotel .15
635 Morgan Ensberg .15
636 Andruw Jones .50
637 Tom Glavine .40
638 Gary Sheffield .40
639 Vinny Castilla .15
640 Javy Lopez .25
641 Albie Lopez .15
642 Geoff Jenkins .25
643 Jeffrey Hammonds .15
644 Alex Ochoa .15
645 Richie Sexson .40
646 Eric Young .15
647 Glendon Rusch .15
648 Tino Martinez .25
649 Fernando Vina .15
650 J.D. Drew .25
651 Woody Williams .15
652 Darryl Kile .15
653 Jason Isringhausen .15
654 Moises Alou .25
655 Alex Gonzalez .15
656 Delino DeShields .15
657 Todd Hundley .15
658 Chris Stynes .15
659 Jason Bere .15
660 Curt Schilling .40
661 Craig Counsell .15
662 Mark Grace .40
663 Matt Williams .25
664 Jay Bell .15
665 Rick Helling .15
666 Shawn Green .40
667 Eric Karros .15
668 Hideo Nomo .40
669 Omar Daal .15
670 Brian Jordan .15
671 Cesar Izturis .15
672 Fernando Tatis .15
673 Lee Stevens .15
674 Tomokazu Ohka .15
675 Brian Schneider .15
676 Brad Wilkerson .15
677 Bruce Chen .15
678 Tsuyoshi Shinjo .15
679 Jeff Kent .25
680 Kirk Rueter .15
681 J.T. Snow .15
682 David Bell .15
683 Reggie Sanders .15
684 Preston Wilson .15
685 Vic Darensbourg .15
686 Josh Beckett .40
687 Pablo Ozuna .15
688 Mike Redmond .15
689 Scott Strickland .15
690 Mo Vaughn .25
691 Roberto Alomar .50
692 Edgardo Alfonzo .15
693 Shawn Estes .15
694 Roger Cedeno .15
695 Jeromy Burnitz .15
696 Ray Lankford .15
697 Mark Kotsay .15
698 Kevin Jarvis .15
699 Bobby Jones .15
700 Sean Burroughs .15
701 Ramon Vazquez .15
702 Pat Burrell .40
703 Marlon Byrd .15
704 Brandon Duckworth .15
705 Marlon Anderson .15
706 Vicente Padilla .15
707 Kip Wells .15
708 Jason Kendall .15
709 Pokey Reese .15
710 Pat Meares .15
711 Kris Benson .15
712 Armando Rios .15
713 Mike Williams .15
714 Barry Larkin .40
715 Adam Dunn .50
716 Juan Encarnacion .15
717 Scott Williamson .15
718 Wilton Guerrero .15
719 Chris Reitsma .15
720 Larry Walker .25
721 Denny Neagle .15
722 Todd Zeile .15
723 Jose Ortiz .15
724 Jason Jennings .15
725 Tony Eusebio .15
726 Ichiro Suzuki 1.00
727 Barry Bonds 1.50
728 Randy Johnson .50
729 Albert Pujols 1.00
730 Roger Clemens .50
731 Sammy Sosa .50
732 Alex Rodriguez .50
733 Chipper Jones .40
734 Rickey Henderson .25
735 Marioners Team Photo .15
736 Luis Gonzalez .25
737 Derek Jeter 1.50
738 Ichiro Suzuki 1.00
739 Barry Bonds 1.50
740 Curt Schilling .25
741 Shawn Green .25
742 Jason Giambi .50
743 Roberto Alomar .25
744 Larry Walker .15
745 Mark McGwire .75

2001's Greatest Hits

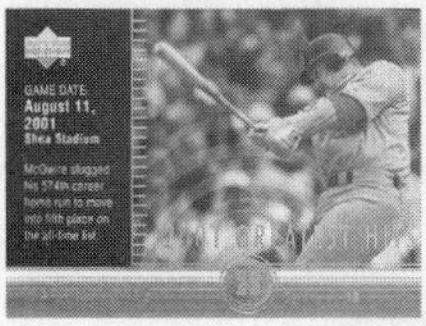

		NM/M
Complete Set (10):		20.00
Common Player:		1.00
Inserted 1:14		
GH1	Barry Bonds	4.00
GH2	Ichiro Suzuki	3.00
GH3	Albert Pujols	3.00
GH4	Mike Piazza	2.50
GH5	Alex Rodriguez	3.00
GH6	Mark McGwire	3.00
GH7	Manny Ramirez	1.00
GH8	Ken Griffey Jr.	2.00
GH9	Sammy Sosa	3.00
GH10	Derek Jeter	4.00

AL Centennial G-U Jerseys Autograph

No Pricing
Production 25 Sets

AL Centennial Bats

		NM/M
Inserted 1:144		
JD	Joe DiMaggio	125.00
MM	Mickey Mantle	150.00
BR	Babe Ruth	150.00

AL Centennial Jerseys

		NM/M
Common Player:		10.00
Inserted 1:144		
PM	Pedro Martinez	10.00
CR	Cal Ripken Jr.	40.00
AR	Alex Rodriguez	15.00
IR	Ivan Rodriguez	10.00
NR	Nolan Ryan	40.00
FT	Frank Thomas	10.00

All-Star Salute Game Jerseys

		NM/M
Common Player:		10.00
Inserted 1:288		
SA	Sparky Anderson	10.00
LB	Lou Boudreau	10.00
DE	Dennis Eckersley	10.00
NF	Nellie Fox	15.00
KG	Ken Griffey Jr.	25.00
AR	Alex Rodriguez	25.00
DS	Don Sutton	10.00
IS	Ichiro Suzuki	40.00

Big Fly Zone

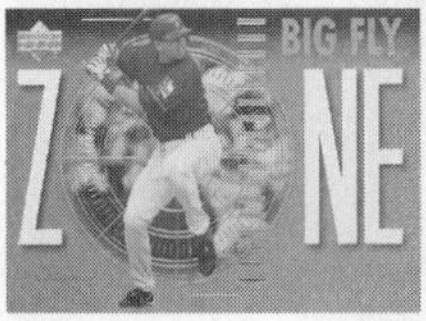

		NM/M
Complete Set (10):		15.00
Common Player:		.50
Inserted 1:14		
Z1	Mark McGwire	4.00
Z2	Ken Griffey Jr.	3.00
Z3	Manny Ramirez	1.00
Z4	Sammy Sosa	3.00
Z5	Todd Helton	1.00
Z6	Barry Bonds	4.00
Z7	Luis Gonzalez	.50
Z8	Alex Rodriguez	4.00
Z9	Carlos Delgado	1.00
Z10	Chipper Jones	1.50

Breakout Performers

		NM/M
Complete Set (10):		10.00

	NM/M
Common Player:	.50
Inserted 1:14	
BP1 Ichiro Suzuki	3.00
BP2 Albert Pujols	4.00
BP3 Doug Mientkiewicz	.50
BP4 Lance Berkman	1.00
BP5 Tsuyoshi Shinjo	.50
BP6 Ben Sheets	1.00
BP7 Jimmy Rollins	.75
BP8 J.D. Drew	.75
BP9 Bret Boone	.50
BP10 Alfonso Soriano	1.00

Championship Caliber

	NM/M
Complete Set (6):	10.00
Common Player:	1.00
Inserted 1:23	
CC1 Derek Jeter	5.00
CC2 Roberto Alomar	1.00
CC3 Chipper Jones	2.00
CC4 Gary Sheffield	1.00
CC5 Roger Clemens	3.00
CC6 Greg Maddux	2.50

Championship Caliber Swatches

	NM/M
Common Player:	8.00
Inserted 1:288	
RA Roberto Alomar/SP	20.00
KB Kevin Brown/SP	10.00
CF Cliff Floyd	10.00
ChJ Charles Johnson	8.00
RJ Randy Johnson	10.00
CJo Chipper Jones/SP	25.00
BL Barry Larkin	10.00
GM Greg Maddux/SP	40.00
TM Tino Martinez	8.00
JO John Olerud	8.00
AP Andy Pettitte	10.00
JP Jorge Posada	10.00
CS Curt Schilling	10.00
BW Bernie Williams	10.00

Chasing History

	NM/M
Complete Set (15):	12.00
Common Player:	.50
Inserted 1:11	
CH1 Sammy Sosa	2.00
CH2 Ken Griffey Jr.	1.50
CH3 Roger Clemens	2.00
CH4 Barry Bonds	3.00
CH5 Rafael Palmeiro	1.00
CH6 Andres Galarraga	.50
CH7 Juan Gonzalez	1.00
CH8 Roberto Alomar	1.00
CH9 Randy Johnson	1.00
CH10 Jeff Bagwell	1.00
CH11 Fred McGriff	.50
CH12 Matt Williams	.50
CH13 Greg Maddux	1.50
CH14 Robb Nen	.50
CH15 Kenny Lofton	.50

Combo Bat

	NM/M
Inserted 1:288	
CB-RG Alex Rodriguez,	
Ken Griffey Jr.	30.00
CB-DM Joe DiMaggio,	
Mickey Mantle	200.00

Combo Jersey

	NM/M
Common Duo:	10.00
Inserted 1:288	
RS Alex Rodriguez,	
Sammy Sosa	30.00
RM Nolan Ryan,	
Pedro Martinez	40.00
RC Nolan Ryan,	
Roger Clemens	50.00
BS Barry Bonds, Sammy Sosa	40.00
HK Shigetoshi Hasegawa,	
Byung-Hun Kim	10.00

Double Game-Worn Gems

	NM/M
Common Card:	8.00
Production 450 Sets	
Golds:	1-2X
Production 100 Sets	
NK Phil Nevin, Ryan Klesko	8.00
VB Omar Vizquel,	
Russell Branyan	10.00
DH Jermaine Dye, Tim Hudson	10.00
TO Frank Thomas,	
Magglio Ordonez	15.00
MI Edgar Martinez,	
Ichiro Suzuki/150	80.00
GS Luis Gonzalez,	
Curt Schilling	15.00
AP Roberto Alomar,	
Mike Piazza	20.00
PL Robert Person,	
Mike Lieberthal	8.00
MM Kevin Millwood,	
Greg Maddux	20.00
KG Jason Kendall, Brian Giles	10.00
DF Carlos Delgado,	
Shannon Stewart	10.00
PN Chan Ho Park, Hideo Nomo	30.00

First Timers Jerseys

	NM/M
Common Player:	8.00
Inserted 1:288	
RB Russell Branyan	8.00
OD Omar Daal	8.00
FG Freddy Garcia	8.00
ML Matt Lawton	8.00
JM Joe Mays	8.00
EM Eric Milton	8.00
CP Corey Patterson	10.00
AP Albert Pujols	50.00
SS Shannon Stewart	8.00

First Timers Jerseys Autograph

No Pricing
Production 25 Sets

Game Jerseys

	NM/M
Common Player:	8.00
Production 350 Sets	
Golds:	.75-1.5X
Production 100	
TB Tony Batista	8.00
AB Adrian Beltre	8.00
JC Jeff Cirillo	8.00
KG Ken Griffey Jr.	20.00
TH Tim Hudson	8.00
MP Mike Piazza	15.00
SR Scott Rolen	15.00
CS Curt Schilling	15.00
SS Sammy Sosa	25.00
FT Frank Thomas	12.00
PW Preston Wilson	8.00

Game Jersey Autograph

	NM/M
Common Player:	20.00
Production 200 Sets	
BB Barry Bonds	200.00
CD Carlos Delgado	25.00
RF Rafael Furcal	20.00
JGi Jason Giambi	35.00
KG Ken Griffey Jr.	125.00
AJ Andruw Jones	35.00
AP Albert Pujols	125.00
CR Cal Ripken Jr.	200.00
NR Nolan Ryan	140.00

GS Gary Sheffield	20.00
IS Ichiro Suzuki	300.00
PW Preston Wilson	20.00

Game-Used Base

	NM/M
Common Player:	5.00
Inserted 1:288	
BB Barry Bonds	20.00
RC Roger Clemens	20.00
CD Carlos Delgado	5.00
JG Jason Giambi	10.00
TG Troy Glaus	8.00
JG Juan Gonzalez	10.00
LG Luis Gonzalez	5.00
SG Shawn Green	5.00
KG Ken Griffey Jr.	15.00
DJ Derek Jeter	25.00
AJ Andruw Jones	8.00
CJ Chipper Jones	10.00
MM Mark McGwire	40.00
MP Mike Piazza	15.00
CR Cal Ripken Jr.	40.00
AR Alex Rodriguez	15.00
IR Ivan Rodriguez	8.00
KS Kazuhiro Sasaki	5.00
SS Sammy Sosa	20.00
IS Ichiro Suzuki	50.00

Game-Used Base Combo

	NM/M
Common Combo:	40.00
Inserted 1:288	
RG Alex Rodriguez,	
Ken Griffey Jr.	40.00
MJ Mark McGwire, Derek Jeter	60.00

Game-Used Base Autograph

No Pricing

Game-Worn Gems

	NM/M
Common Player:	5.00
Inserted 1:48	
Golds:	1-2X
Production 100 Sets	
RA Roberto Alomar	8.00
EC Eric Chavez	6.00
CD Carlos Delgado	8.00
DE Darin Erstad/SP	10.00
FG Freddy Garcia/SP	8.00
TG Tom Glavine	8.00
JG Juan Gonzalez	8.00
LG Luis Gonzalez/SP	10.00
MH Mike Hampton/SP	8.00
CJ Chipper Jones	10.00
JK Jason Kendall	5.00
RK Ryan Klesko/SP	8.00
GM Greg Maddux	15.00
EM Edgar Martinez	8.00
PM Pedro Martinez/SP	15.00
TM Tino Martinez	8.00
JM Joe Mays	5.00
EM Eric Milton	5.00
PN Phil Nevin	5.00
HN Hideo Nomo/SP	30.00
JO John Olerud/SP	8.00
RP Robert Person	5.00
CR Cal Ripken Jr.	40.00
IR Ivan Rodriguez	10.00
SR Scott Rolen	15.00
CS Curt Schilling	10.00
AS Aaron Sele	5.00
GS Gary Sheffield/SP	8.00
FT Frank Thomas	10.00
OV Omar Vizquel/SP	10.00
RY Robin Yount	15.00

Global Swatch Jerseys

	NM/M
Common Player:	5.00
Inserted 1:144	
CD Carlos Delgado	8.00
SH Shigetoshi Hasegawa	5.00
BK Byung-Hun Kim	5.00
HN Hideo Nomo	35.00
CP Chan Ho Park	5.00
MR Manny Ramirez	5.00
KS Kazuhiro Sasaki	5.00
TS Tsuyoshi Shinjo	5.00
IS Ichiro Suzuki	50.00
MY Masato Yoshii	5.00

Global Swatch Jerseys Autograph

No Pricing
Production 25 Sets

McGwire Memorabilia

	NM/M
Common Card:	
AM-J Mark McGwire/Jsy/70	75.00
AM-B Mark McGwire/Bat/70	75.00
MMc Mark McGwire/	
500 HR Club Bat/350	300.00
MM-SS Mark McGwire,	
Sammy Sosa/25	
(Combo Jersey)	200.00
MM-KG Mark McGwire,	
Ken Griffey Jr./25	
(Combo Jersey)	250.00
MM-JG Mark McGwire,	
Jason Giambi/25	
(Combo Jersey)	200.00

Patch Stripes Autograph

No Pricing

Patch Numbers

No Pricing

Return of the Ace

	NM/M
Complete Set (15):	15.00
Common Player:	1.00
Inserted 1:11	
RA1 Randy Johnson	2.00
RA2 Greg Maddux	3.00
RA3 Pedro Martinez	2.00
RA4 Freddy Garcia	1.00
RA5 Matt Morris	1.00
RA6 Mark Mulder	1.00
RA7 Wade Miller	1.00
RA8 Kevin Brown	1.00
RA9 Roger Clemens	4.00
RA10 Jon Lieber	1.00
RA11 C.C. Sabathia	1.00
RA12 Tim Hudson	1.50
RA13 Curt Schilling	2.00
RA14 Al Leiter	1.00
RA15 Mike Mussina	1.50

Sons of Summer Game Jerseys

	NM/M
Common Player:	10.00
Inserted 1:288	
RA Roberto Alomar	10.00
JB Jeff Bagwell	10.00
RC Roger Clemens	15.00
JG Juan Gonzalez	10.00
GM Greg Maddux	15.00
PM Pedro Martinez/SP	15.00
MP Mike Piazza	15.00
AR Alex Rodriguez	15.00

Superstar Summit

	NM/M
Complete Set (6):	15.00
Common Player:	1.50
Inserted 1:23	
SS1 Sammy Sosa	3.00
SS2 Alex Rodriguez	4.00
SS3 Mark McGwire	4.00
SS4 Barry Bonds	4.00
SS5 Mike Piazza	3.00
SS6 Ken Griffey Jr.	2.50

Superstar Summit II

	NM/M
Complete Set (15):	25.00
Common Player:	1.00
Inserted 1:11	
SS1 Alex Rodriguez	4.00
SS2 Jason Giambi	1.00
SS3 Vladimir Guerrero	1.50
SS4 Randy Johnson	1.50
SS5 Chipper Jones	1.50
SS6 Ichiro Suzuki	3.00
SS7 Sammy Sosa	2.50
SS8 Greg Maddux	2.00
SS9 Ken Griffey Jr.	2.50
SS10 Todd Helton	1.00
SS11 Barry Bonds	4.00
SS12 Derek Jeter	4.00
SS13 Mike Piazza	3.00
SS14 Ivan Rodriguez	1.00
SS15 Frank Thomas	1.00

The People's Choice Game Jerseys

	NM/M
Common Player:	5.00
Inserted 1:24	
Golds:	1-2X
Production 100 Sets	
JBa Jeff Bagwell	10.00
EB Ellis Burks/SP	10.00
JBu Jeromy Burnitz	5.00
OD Omar Daal	5.00
CD Carlos Delgado	6.00
RF Rafael Furcal	6.00
AG Andres Galarraga/SP	10.00
BG Brian Giles	5.00
JG Juan Gonzalez	10.00
KG Ken Griffey Jr.	20.00
TG Tony Gwynn	12.00
SH Sterling Hitchcock	5.00
HI Hideki Irabu	5.00
CJ Charles Johnson	5.00
DL Derek Lowe	8.00
GM Greg Maddux	15.00
TM Tino Martinez	10.00
JN Jeff Nelson	5.00
RO Rey Ordonez	5.00
RP Rafael Palmeiro/SP	15.00
RP Robert Person/SP	10.00
AP Andy Pettitte	10.00
MP Mike Piazza	15.00
TR Tim Raines	5.00
MRa Manny Ramirez	10.00
MRi Mariano Rivera	8.00
AR Alex Rodriguez	15.00
TS Tim Salmon	6.00
CS Curt Schilling	10.00
TSh Tsuyoshi Shinjo	5.00
JS J.T. Snow	5.00
SS Sammy Sosa	20.00
MS Mike Stanton	5.00
FT Frank Thomas	10.00
RV Robin Ventura	6.00
OV Omar Vizquel	6.00
DW David Wells	6.00
BW Bernie Williams	8.00
MW Matt Williams/SP	10.00

UD Patch Logo

	NM/M
Common Player:	60.00
Inserted 1:2,500	
Prices for Stripes & Numbers identical.	
BB Barry Bonds	125.00
JG Jason Giambi	60.00
KG Ken Griffey Jr.	100.00
PM Pedro Martinez	80.00
CR Cal Ripken Jr.	150.00
AR Alex Rodriguez	125.00
SS Sammy Sosa	100.00

UD Patch Stripes

No Pricing

UD Patch Numbers

No Pricing

UD-Plus

	NM/M
Common Player:	2.00

ANDRUW JONES

Production 1,125 Sets
1 two-card pack per Series 2 H pack
Comp. Set can be exchanged for Jsy cards.
Redemption deadline 5-16-03.

UD1	Darin Erstad	3.00
UD2	Troy Glaus	3.00
UD3	Tim Hudson	3.00
UD4	Jermaine Dye	2.00
UD5	Barry Zito	2.00
UD6	Carlos Delgado	3.00
UD7	Shannon Stewart	2.00
UD8	Greg Vaughn	2.00
UD9	Jim Thome	5.00
UD10	C.C. Sabathia	2.00
UD11	Ichiro Suzuki	10.00
UD12	Edgar Martinez	2.00
UD13	Bret Boone	2.00
UD14	Freddy Garcia	2.00
UD15	Matt Thornton	2.00
UD16	Jeff Conine	2.00
UD17	Steve Bechler	2.00
UD18	Rafael Palmeiro	4.00
UD19	Juan Gonzalez	4.00
UD20	Alex Rodriguez	10.00
UD21	Ivan Rodriguez	4.00
UD22	Carl Everett	2.00
UD23	Manny Ramirez	4.00
UD24	Nomar Garciaparra	10.00
UD25	Pedro J. Martinez	4.00
UD26	Mike Sweeney	2.00
UD27	Chuck Knoblauch	2.00
UD28	Dmitri Young	2.00
UD29	Bobby Higginson	2.00
UD30	Dean Palmer	2.00
UD31	Doug Mientkiewicz	2.00
UD32	Corey Koskie	2.00
UD33	Brad Radke	2.00
UD34	Cristian Guzman	2.00
UD35	Frank Thomas	4.00
UD36	Magglio Ordonez	3.00
UD37	Carlos Lee	2.00
UD38	Roger Clemens	10.00
UD39	Bernie Williams	3.00
UD40	Derek Jeter	15.00
UD41	Jason Giambi	4.00
UD42	Mike Mussina	3.00
UD43	Jeff Bagwell	4.00
UD44	Lance Berkman	3.00
UD45	Wade Miller	2.00
UD46	Greg Maddux	8.00
UD47	Chipper Jones	5.00
UD48	Andruw Jones	4.00
UD49	Gary Sheffield	3.00
UD50	Richie Sexson	2.00
UD51	Albert Pujols	10.00
UD52	J.D. Drew	3.00
UD53	Matt Morris	2.00
UD54	Jim Edmonds	3.00
UD55	So Taguchi	2.00
UD56	Sammy Sosa	10.00
UD57	Fred McGriff	3.00
UD58	Kerry Wood	5.00
UD59	Moises Alou	3.00
UD60	Randy Johnson	5.00
UD61	Luis Gonzalez	3.00
UD62	Mark Grace	4.00
UD63	Curt Schilling	4.00
UD64	Matt Williams	2.00
UD65	Kevin Brown	2.00
UD66	Brian Jordan	2.00
UD67	Shawn Green	3.00
UD68	Hideo Nomo	3.00
UD69	Kazuhisa Ishii	3.00
UD70	Vladimir Guerrero	4.00
UD71	Jose Vidro	2.00
UD72	Eric Good	2.00
UD73	Barry Bonds	15.00
UD74	Jeff Kent	3.00
UD75	Rich Aurilia	2.00
UD76	Deivis Santos	2.00
UD77	Preston Wilson	2.00
UD78	Cliff Floyd	2.00
UD79	Josh Beckett	4.00
UD80	Hansel Izquierdo	2.00
UD81	Mike Piazza	10.00
UD82	Roberto Alomar	3.00
UD83	Mo Vaughn	3.00
UD84	Jeromy Burnitz	2.00
UD85	Rick Helling	2.00
UD86	Ryan Klesko	2.00
UD87	Bobby Abreu	3.00

UD88	Scott Rolen	5.00
UD89	Jimmy Rollins	2.50
UD90	Jason Kendall	2.00
UD91	Brian Giles	3.00
UD92	Aramis Ramirez	3.00
UD93	Ken Griffey Jr.	10.00
UD94	Sean Casey	2.00
UD95	Barry Larkin	3.00
UD96	Adam Dunn	4.00
UD97	Todd Helton	4.00
UD98	Larry Walker	3.00
UD99	Mike Hampton	2.00
UD100	Rene Reyes	2.00

UD-Plus Memorabila Moments Jerseys

	NM/M
Common DiMaggio (1-5):	125.00
Common Mantle: (1-5):	200.00
MM-JD1-5 Joe DiMaggio	125.00
MM-MM1 Mickey Mantle/25 (Pants)	200.00
MM-MM2-5 Mickey Mantle	200.00

UD-Plus Pinstripe Immortals

No Pricing

UD-Plus Memorabilia

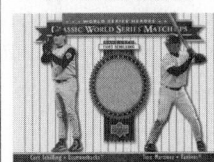

	NM/M
Common Card:	8.00
Inserted 1:24	
MU00 Mike Piazza, Roger Clemens	15.00
MU00a Andy Pettitte, Mike Piazza	15.00
MU00b Al Leiter, Derek Jeter	10.00
MU00d Edgardo Alfonzo, Mariano Rivera	8.00
MU00e John Franco, Derek Jeter	15.00
MU00c Robin Ventura, Roger Clemens	8.00
MU01 Mariano Rivera, Luis Gonzalez	8.00
MU01a Paul O'Neill, Curt Schilling	8.00
MU01b Bernie Williams, Randy Johnson	8.00
MU01c David Justice, Curt Schilling	
MU01d Randy Johnson, Bernie Williams	8.00
MU01e Curt Schilling, Tino Martinez	8.00
MU01f Roger Clemens, Luis Gonzalez	15.00
MU01g Paul O'Neill, Byung-Hyun Kim	10.00
MU01h Luis Gonzalez, Mariano Rivera/97	12.00
MU03 Honus Wagner, Cy Young	100.00
MU09 Ty Cobb, Honus Wagner/SP	125.00
MU30 Jimmie Foxx, Mel Ott/SP	25.00
MU36 Joe DiMaggio, Mel Ott/SP	80.00
MU49 Duke Snider, Joe DiMaggio	25.00
MU53 Jackie Robinson, Billy Martin	25.00
MU55 Mickey Mantle, Jackie Robinson	110.00
MU56 Don Larsen, Duke Snider	25.00
MU56a Don Larsen, Jackie Robinson	20.00
MU57 Eddie Mathews, Yogi Berra	15.00
MU58 Yogi Berra, Eddie Mathews	15.00
MU62 Roger Maris, Juan Marichal	40.00
MU63 Sandy Koufax, Mickey Mantle	100.00
MU66 Don Drysdale, Brooks Robinson/SP	40.00
MU69 Nolan Ryan, Brooks Robinson	50.00

MU72	Joe Morgan, Jim "Catfish" Hunter	8.00
MU72a	Rollie Fingers, Johnny Bench	10.00
MU73	Tom Seaver, "Catfish" Hunter	15.00
MU74	Jim "Catfish" Hunter, Steve Garvey	8.00
MU74a	Davey Lopes, Jim "Catfish" Hunter	8.00
MU76	Ken Griffey Sr., Thurman Munson	12.00
MU76a	Thurman Munson, Johnny Bench	20.00
MU78	Thurman Munson, Steve Garvey	15.00
MU78a	Bill Russell, Thurman Munson	12.00
MU81	Steve Garvey, Dave Winfield	8.00
MU82	Robin Yount, Ozzie Smith	15.00
MU83	Cal Ripken Jr., Joe Morgan	25.00
MU84	Jack Morris, Tony Gwynn	12.00
MU86	Jesse Orosco, Roger Clemens	15.00
MU87	Ozzie Smith, Kirby Puckett	15.00
MU88	Mark McGwire, Kirk Gibson/SP	60.00
MU90	Barry Larkin, Mark McGwire/SP	20.00
MU91	Tom Glavine, Kirby Puckett	15.00
MU93	Joe Carter, Curt Schilling	8.00
MU95	Dennis Martinez, David Justice	8.00
MU96	Andruw Jones, Andy Pettitte	8.00
MU96a	Tim Raines, Tom Glavine	10.00
MU96b	Kenny Rogers, Chipper Jones	8.00
MU95a	Kenny Lofton, John Smoltz	8.00
MU97	Jim Thome, Kevin Brown	10.00
MU98	Tony Gwynn, Bernie Williams	10.00
MU98a	Trevor Hoffman, Bernie Williams/SP	8.00
MU99	Jorge Posada, Greg Maddux	15.00
MU99a	Greg Maddux, Derek Jeter	15.00
MU99b	Paul O'Neill, John Smoltz	8.00
MU99c	Chipper Jones, Mariano Rivera	15.00

Collection Autographs

	NM/M
Inserted 1:336	
WS93 Joe Carter	40.00
WS99 Roger Clemens	100.00
WS74 Rollie Fingers	30.00
WS75 Carlton Fisk	60.00
WS81 Steve Garvey	35.00
WS65 Sandy Koufax	250.00
WS80 Don Larsen	60.00
WS89 Mark McGwire	275.00
WS76 Joe Morgan	40.00
WS91 Kirby Puckett	60.00
WS83 Cal Ripken Jr.	175.00
WS70 Brooks Robinson	80.00
WS69 Nolan Ryan	200.00
WS73 Tom Seaver	60.00
WS55 Duke Snider	75.00
WS82 Ozzie Smith	90.00

Yankees Dynasty Jerseys

	NM/M
Common Combo:	20.00
Inserted 1:288	
PR Andy Pettitte, Mariano Rivera	25.00
BT Wade Boggs, Joe Torre	25.00
CP Roger Clemens, Jorge Posada	50.00
DM Joe DiMaggio, Mickey Mantle	300.00
RK Willie Randolph, Chuck Knoblauch	20.00
BJ Scott Brosius, David Justice	20.00
OM Paul O'Neill, Tino Martinez	25.00
WO Bernie Williams, Paul O'Neill	25.00
WG David Wells, Dwight Gooden	25.00
GC Joe Girardi, David Cone	25.00
KR Chuck Knoblauch, Tim Raines	25.00

Yankees Dynasty Combo Base

	NM/M
Common Combo:	50.00
JW Derek Jeter, Bernie Williams	60.00
CJ Roger Clemens, Derek Jeter	75.00

2001 All-Star HR Derby Jerseys

	NM/M
Common Player:	10.00
Inserted 1:288	
BrB Bret Boone	10.00
JG Jason Giambi	15.00
TH Todd Helton	15.00
AR Alex Rodriguez	20.00
SS Sammy Sosa	25.00

2002 Upper Deck Ballpark Idols

	NM/M
Complete Set (245):	125.00
Common Player:	.15
Common (201-245):	3.00
Production 1,750	
Pack (5):	2.00
Box (24 + Bobber):	50.00
1 Troy Glaus	.40
2 Kevin Appier	.15
3 Darin Erstad	.25
4 Garret Anderson	.25
5 Brad Fullmer	.15
6 Tim Salmon	.25
7 Eric Chavez	.25
8 Tim Hudson	.25
9 David Justice	.25
10 Barry Zito	.25
11 Miguel Tejada	.40
12 Mark Mulder	.40
13 Jermaine Dye	.15
14 Carlos Delgado	.40
15 Jose Cruz Jr.	.15
16 Brandon Lyon	.15
17 Shannon Stewart	.15
18 Eric Hinske	.25
19 Chris Carpenter	.15
20 Greg Vaughn	.15
21 Tanyon Sturtze	.15
22 Jason Tyner	.15
23 Toby Hall	.15
24 Ben Grieve	.15
25 Jim Thome	.75
26 Omar Vizquel	.25
27 Ricky Gutierrez	.15
28 C.C. Sabathia	.15
29 Ellis Burks	.15
30 Matt Lawton	.15
31 Milton Bradley	.15
32 Edgar Martinez	.25
33 Ichiro Suzuki	1.50
34 Bret Boone	.25
35 Freddy Garcia	.15
36 Mike Cameron	.15
37 John Olerud	.25
38 Kazuhiro Sasaki	.15
39 Jeff Cirillo	.15
40 Jeff Conine	.15
41 Marty Cordova	.15
42 Tony Batista	.15
43 Jerry Hairston Jr.	.15
44 Jason Johnson	.15
45 David Segui	.15
46 Alex Rodriguez	2.00
47 Rafael Palmeiro	.50
48 Carl Everett	.25
49 Chan Ho Park	.15
50 Ivan Rodriguez	.50
51 Juan Gonzalez	.50
52 Hank Blalock	.50
53 Manny Ramirez	.50
54 Pedro J. Martinez	.75
55 Tony Clark	.15
56 Nomar Garciaparra	1.25
57 Johnny Damon	.25
58 Trot Nixon	.15
59 Rickey Henderson	.50
60 Mike Sweeney	.15
61 Neifi Perez	.15
62 Joe Randa	.15
63 Carlos Beltran	.25
64 Chuck Knoblauch	.15
65 Michael Tucker	.15
66 Dean Palmer	.15
67 Bobby Higginson	.15
68 Dmitri Young	.15
69 Randall Simon	.15
70 Mitch Meluskey	.15
71 Damion Easley	.15
72 Joe Mays	.15
73 Doug Mientkiewicz	.15
74 Corey Koskie	.15
75 Brad Radke	.15
76 Cristian Guzman	.15
77 Torii Hunter	.25
78 Eric Milton	.15
79 Frank Thomas	.50
80 Paul Konerko	.25
81 Mark Buehrle	.15
82 Magglio Ordonez	.25
83 Carlos Lee	.15
84 Joe Crede	.15
85 Derek Jeter	2.00
86 Bernie Williams	.50
87 Mike Mussina	.50
88 Jorge Posada	.40
89 Roger Clemens	1.50
90 Jason Giambi	.50
91 Alfonso Soriano	.75
92 Rondell White	.15
93 Jeff Bagwell	.50
94 Lance Berkman	.40
95 Roy Oswalt	.25
96 Richard Hidalgo	.15
97 Wade Miller	.15
98 Craig Biggio	.25
99 Greg Maddux	1.00
100 Chipper Jones	.75
101 Gary Sheffield	.25
102 Rafael Furcal	.15
103 Andruw Jones	.50
104 Vinny Castilla	.15
105 Marcus Giles	.15
106 Tom Glavine	.40
107 Richie Sexson	.25
108 Geoff Jenkins	.15
109 Glendon Rusch	.15
110 Eric Young	.15
111 Ben Sheets	.25
112 Alex Sanchez	.15
113 Albert Pujols	1.50
114 J.D. Drew	.25
115 Matt Morris	.25
116 Jim Edmonds	.40
117 Tino Martinez	.25
118 Scott Rolen	.75
119 Edgar Renteria	.25
120 Sammy Sosa	1.50
121 Kerry Wood	.75
122 Moises Alou	.25
123 Jon Lieber	.15
124 Fred McGriff	.25
125 Juan Cruz	.15
126 Alex Gonzalez	.15
127 Corey Patterson	.25
128 Randy Johnson	.75
129 Luis Gonzalez	.25
130 Steve Finley	.15
131 Matt Williams	.15
132 Curt Schilling	.50
133 Mark Grace	.40
134 Craig Counsell	.15
135 Shawn Green	.25
136 Kevin Brown	.25
137 Hideo Nomo	.40
138 Paul LoDuca	.15
139 Brian Jordan	.15
140 Eric Karros	.15
141 Adrian Beltre	.15
142 Vladimir Guerrero	.75
143 Fernando Tatis	.15
144 Javier Vazquez	.15
145 Orlando Cabrera	.15
146 Tony Armas Jr.	.15
147 Jose Vidro	.15
148 Barry Bonds	2.00
149 Rich Aurilia	.15
150 Tsuyoshi Shinjo	.15
151 Jeff Kent	.25
152 Russ Ortiz	.15
153 Jason Schmidt	.15
154 Reggie Sanders	.15
155 Preston Wilson	.15
156 Luis Castillo	.15
157 Charles Johnson	.15
158 Josh Beckett	.40
159 Derek Lee	.25
160 Mike Lowell	.25
161 Mike Piazza	1.00
162 Roberto Alomar	.40
163 Al Leiter	.25
164 Mo Vaughn	.25
165 Jeromy Burnitz	.15
166 Edgardo Alfonzo	.15
167 Roger Cedeno	.15
168 Ryan Klesko	.15
169 Brian Lawrence	.15
170 Sean Burroughs	.15
171 Phil Nevin	.15
172 Ramon Vazquez	.15
173 Mark Kotsay	.15
174 Marlon Anderson	.15
175 Mike Lieberthal	.15
176 Bobby Abreu	.25
177 Pat Burrell	.40
178 Robert Person	.15
179 Brandon Duckworth	.15
180 Jimmy Rollins	.25
181 Brian Giles	.25
182 Pokey Reese	.15
183 Kris Benson	.15
184 Aramis Ramirez	.25
185 Jason Kendall	.15
186 Kip Wells	.15
187 Ken Griffey Jr.	1.00
188 Adam Dunn	.50
189 Barry Larkin	.40
190 Sean Casey	.25
191 Austin Kearns	.25
192 Aaron Boone	.15
193 Todd Helton	.50
194 Juan Pierre	.15
195 Mike Hampton	.15
196 Jose Ortiz	.15
197 Larry Walker	.25
198 Juan Uribe	.15
199 Ichiro Suzuki (Checklist)	.75
200 Jason Giambi (Checklist)	.25
201 Franklyn German RC	3.00
202 Rodrigo Rosario RC	3.00
203 Brandon Puffer RC	3.00
204 Kirk Saarloos	3.00
205 Chris Baker RC	3.00
206 John Ennis RC	3.00
207 Luis Martinez RC	3.00
208 So Taguchi RC	6.00
209 Michael Crudale RC	3.00
210 Francis Beltran RC	3.00
211 Brandon Backe RC	3.00
212 Felix Escalona RC	3.00
213 Jose Valverde RC	4.00
214 Doug DeVore RC	3.00
215 Kazuhisa Ishii RC	6.00
216 Victor Alvarez RC	3.00
217 Ron Calloway RC	3.00
218 Eric Good RC	3.00
219 Jorge Nunez	3.00
220 Deivis Santos	3.00
221 Nelson Castro RC	3.00
222 Matt Thornton	3.00
223 Jason Simontacchi RC	3.00
224 Hansel Izquierdo RC	3.00
225 Tyler Yates RC	4.00
226 Jaime Cerda RC	3.00
227 Satoru Komiyama RC	3.00
228 Steve Bechler RC	3.00
229 Ben Howard RC	3.00
230 Todd Donovan RC	3.00
231 Jorge Padilla RC	3.00
232 Eric Junge RC	3.00
233 Anderson Machado RC	3.00
234 Adrian Burnside RC	3.00
235 Mike Gonzalez RC	3.00
236 Josh Hancock RC	3.00
237 Anastacio Martinez RC	3.00
238 Chris Booker RC	3.00
239 Rene Reyes RC	3.00
240 Cam Esslinger RC	3.00
241 Oliver Perez RC	8.00
242 Tim Kalita RC	3.00
243 Kevin Frederick RC	3.00
244 Mitch Wylie RC	3.00
245 Edwin Almonte RC	3.00

Bronze

Stars (1-200):	5-10X
SP's (201-245):	.75-1.5X
Production 100 Sets	

Gold

No pricing due to scarcity.
Production 25 Sets

Bobbers

	NM/M
Inserted 1:Box	
Roberto Alomar	10.00
Jeff Bagwell	15.00
Josh Beckett	10.00
Barry Bonds	30.00
Sean Burroughs	8.00
Roger Clemens	20.00
Joe DiMaggio/555/Away	40.00
Joe DiMaggio/361/Home	50.00
Nomar Garciaparra	20.00
Jason Giambi	10.00
Luis Gonzalez	8.00
Ken Griffey Jr.	20.00
Vladimir Guerrero	15.00
Kazuhisa Ishii	10.00
Derek Jeter/SP/Away	40.00
Randy Johnson/D'backs	15.00
Randy Johnson/Expos	15.00
Chipper Jones	15.00
Greg Maddux	20.00
Mickey Mantle/777/Away	40.00
Mickey Mantle/536/Home	60.00
Mark McGwire/Cards	35.00
Mike Piazza/Mets	20.00
Mark Prior	15.00
Albert Pujols	25.00
Alex Rodriguez	20.00
Ivan Rodriguez	10.00
Curt Schilling/D'backs	10.00
Sammy Sosa/Cubs/Away	25.00
Ichiro Suzuki/SP/Away	30.00
Frank Thomas	10.00
Jim Thome	15.00

Bobbers Gold

	NM/M
Amount produced listed	
Joe DiMaggio/56/Away	100.00
Joe DiMaggio/41/Home	125.00
Mickey Mantle/77/Away	140.00
Mickey Mantle/61/Home	125.00

Field Garb Jerseys

	NM/M
Common Player:	4.00
Inserted 1:72	
TB Tony Batista	4.00
BG Brian Giles	4.00
RJ Randy Johnson	10.00
JK Jeff Kent	4.00
TM Tino Martinez	4.00
JO John Olerud	4.00
AR Alex Rodriguez	12.00
IR Ivan Rodriguez	6.00
MS Mike Sweeney	4.00
RV Robin Ventura	4.00
LW Larry Walker	4.00
BZ Barry Zito	6.00

Figure Heads

	NM/M
Complete Set (10):	20.00
Common Player:	1.00
Inserted 1:12	
F1 Ichiro Suzuki	3.00
F2 Sammy Sosa	2.50
F3 Alex Rodriguez	4.00
F4 Jason Giambi	1.00
F5 Barry Bonds	4.00
F6 Chipper Jones	1.50
F7 Mike Piazza	2.00
F8 Derek Jeter	4.00
F9 Nomar Garciaparra	2.50
F10 Ken Griffey Jr.	2.00

Player's Club Jerseys

	NM/M
Common Player:	6.00
Inserted 1:72	
KB Kevin Brown	6.00
DE Darin Erstad	8.00
RF Rafael Furcal	6.00
TH Tim Hudson	8.00
AJ Andruw Jones	8.00
JK Jason Kendall	6.00
MM Mark McGwire/SP	70.00
PN Phil Nevin	6.00
HN Hideo Nomo	20.00
MO Magglio Ordonez	6.00
CS Curt Schilling	8.00
IS Ichiro Suzuki/SP	40.00
JT Jim Thome	12.00

Playmakers 2002

	NM/M
Complete Set (20):	25.00
Common Player:	.75
Inserted 1:6	
P1 Ken Griffey Jr.	2.00
P2 Alex Rodriguez	4.00
P3 Sammy Sosa	2.50
P4 Derek Jeter	4.00
P5 Mike Piazza	2.00
P6 Jason Giambi	1.00
P7 Barry Bonds	4.00
P8 Frank Thomas	1.00
P9 Randy Johnson	1.50
P10 Chipper Jones	1.50
P11 Jeff Bagwell	1.00
P12 Vladimir Guerrero	1.50
P13 Albert Pujols	3.00
P14 Nomar Garciaparra	2.50
P15 Ichiro Suzuki	3.00
P16 Troy Glaus	1.00
P17 Ivan Rodriguez	1.00
P18 Carlos Delgado	.75
P19 Greg Maddux	2.00
P20 Todd Helton	1.00

Uniform Sluggers

	NM/M
Common Player:	5.00
Inserted 1:72	
JB Jeff Bagwell	8.00
JGi Jason Giambi	8.00
JGo Juan Gonzalez	8.00
SG Shawn Green	5.00
KG Ken Griffey Jr./SP	25.00
TH Todd Helton	8.00
CJ Chipper Jones	10.00

MM	Mickey Mantle/SP	100.00
MP	Mike Piazza	15.00
AR	Alex Rodriguez	12.00
BW	Bernie Williams	8.00

2002 Upper Deck Diamond Connection

	NM/M
Complete Set (550):	
Common Player:	.15
Common Rk (91-200): Production 1,500	4.00
Common Jersey (201-270): Production 775	4.00
Common Jersey (271-320): Production 200	5.00
Common Jersey (321-353): Production 150	5.00
Common Jersey (354-368): Production 100	6.00
Common Bat (369-438): Production 775	5.00
Common Bat (439-488): Production 200	5.00
Common Bat (489-521): Production 150	5.00
Common Bat (522-536): Production 100	10.00
Pack (5):	4.00
Box (14):	50.00

1	Troy Glaus	.50
2	Darin Erstad	.40
3	Barry Zito	.40
4	Eric Chavez	.40
5	Tim Hudson	.40
6	Miguel Tejada	.40
7	Carlos Delgado	.40
8	Shannon Stewart	.15
9	Greg Vaughn	.15
10	Jim Thome	.75
11	C.C. Sabathia	.15
12	Ichiro Suzuki	1.50
13	Edgar Martinez	.25
14	Bret Boone	.25
15	Freddy Garcia	.15
16	Jeff Conine	.15
17	Alex Rodriguez	2.00
18	Rafael Palmeiro	.50
19	Ivan Rodriguez	.50
20	Juan Gonzalez	.50
21	Pedro J. Martinez	.75
22	Nomar Garciaparra	1.50
23	Manny Ramirez	.50
24	Carlos Beltran	.25
25	Mike Sweeney	.15
26	Dmitri Young	.15
27	Bobby Higginson	.15
28	Corey Koskie	.15
29	Cristian Guzman	.15
30	Doug Mientkiewicz	.15
31	Torii Hunter	.25
32	Frank Thomas	.50
33	Mark Buehrle	.15
34	Carlos Lee	.15
35	Magglio Ordonez	.40
36	Roger Clemens	1.50
37	Bernie Williams	.50
38	Jason Giambi	.75
39	Derek Jeter	2.00
40	Mike Mussina	.50
41	Jeff Bagwell	.50
42	Richard Hidalgo	.15
43	Lance Berkman	.40
44	Roy Oswalt	.40
45	Chipper Jones	.75
46	Gary Sheffield	.40
47	Andruw Jones	.50
48	Greg Maddux	1.00
49	Geoff Jenkins	.15
50	Ben Sheets	.25
51	Richie Sexson	.40
52	Albert Pujols	1.50
53	Matt Morris	.25
54	J.D. Drew	.40
55	Tino Martinez	.25
56	Sammy Sosa	1.50
57	Kerry Wood	.75
58	Moises Alou	.25
59	Fred McGriff	.25
60	Randy Johnson	.75
61	Luis Gonzalez	.25
62	Curt Schilling	.50
63	Kevin Brown	.25
64	Shawn Green	.40
65	Paul LoDuca	.15
66	Vladimir Guerrero	.75
67	Jose Vidro	.15
68	Barry Bonds	2.00
69	Jeff Kent	.25
70	Rich Aurilia	.15
71	Preston Wilson	.15
72	Josh Beckett	.40
73	Cliff Floyd	.25
74	Mike Piazza	1.00
75	Mo Vaughn	.25
76	Roberto Alomar	.40
77	Jeromy Burnitz	.15
78	Phil Nevin	.15
79	Sean Burroughs	.15
80	Scott Rolen	.75
81	Bobby Abreu	.25
82	Pat Burrell	.40
83	Brian Giles	.40
84	Jason Kendall	.15
85	Ken Griffey Jr.	1.00
86	Adam Dunn	.50
87	Aaron Boone	.15
88	Larry Walker	.25
89	Todd Helton	.50
90	Mike Hampton	.15
91	Brandon Puffer **RC**	4.00
92	Rodrigo Rosario **RC**	4.00
93	Tom Shearn **RC**	4.00
94	Morgan Ensberg	4.00
95	Jason Lane	4.00
96	Franklyn German **RC**	4.00
97	Carlos Pena	4.00
98	Joe Orloski **RC**	4.00
99	Reed Johnson **RC**	6.00
100	Chris Baker **RC**	4.00
101	Corey Thurman **RC**	4.00
102	Gustavo Chacin **RC**	4.00
103	Eric Hinske	4.00
104	John Foster **RC**	4.00
105	John Ennis **RC**	4.00
106	Kevin Gryboski **RC**	4.00
107	Jung Bong	4.00
108	Travis Wilson	4.00
109	Luis Martinez **RC**	4.00
110	Brian Mallette **RC**	4.00
111	Takahito Nomura **RC**	4.00
112	Bill Hall	4.00
113	Jeff Deardorff **RC**	4.00
114	Cristian Guerrero	4.00
115	Scotty Layfield **RC**	4.00
116	Michael Crudale **RC**	4.00
117	So Taguchi **RC**	6.00
118	Jeremy Lambert **RC**	4.00
119	Jimmy Journell	4.00
120	Francis Beltran **RC**	4.00
121	Mark Prior	6.00
122	Ben Christensen	4.00
123	Jorge Sosa **RC**	4.00
124	Brandon Backe **RC**	4.00
125	Steve Kent **RC**	4.00
126	Felix Escalona **RC**	4.00
127	P.J. Bevis **RC**	4.00
128	Jose Valverde **RC**	4.00
129	Doug DeVore **RC**	4.00
130	Jeremy Ward **RC**	4.00
131	Mike Koplove	4.00
132	Luis Terrero	4.00
133	John Patterson	4.00
134	Victor Alvarez **RC**	4.00
135	Kirk Saarloos	4.00
136	Kazuhisa Ishii **RC**	8.00
137	Steve Colyer	4.00
138	Cesar Izturis	4.00
139	Ron Calloway **RC**	4.00
140	Eric Good **RC**	4.00
141	Jorge Nunez **RC**	4.00
142	Ron Chiavacci	4.00
143	Donnie Bridges	4.00
144	Nelson Castro **RC**	4.00
145	Deivis Santos	4.00
146	Kurt Ainsworth	4.00
147	Arturo McDowell	4.00
148	Allan Simpson **RC**	4.00
149	Matt Thornton	4.00
150	Luis Ugueto **RC**	4.00
151	J.J. Putz **RC**	4.00
152	Hansel Izquierdo **RC**	4.00
153	Oliver Perez **RC**	4.00
154	Jaime Cerda **RC**	4.00
155	Mark Corey **RC**	4.00
156	Tyler Yates **RC**	6.00
157	Satoru Komiyama **RC**	4.00
158	Adam Walker **RC**	4.00
159	Steve Bechler **RC**	6.00
160	Erik Bedard	4.00
161	Todd Donovan **RC**	4.00
162	Clifford Bartosh **RC**	4.00
163	Ben Howard **RC**	8.00
164	Andy Shibilo **RC**	4.00
165	Dennis Tankersley	4.00
166	Mike Bynum	4.00
167	Anderson Machado **RC**	4.00
168	Peter Zamora **RC**	5.00
169	Eric Junge **RC**	4.00
170	Elio Serrano **RC**	4.00
171	Jorge Padilla **RC**	4.00
172	Marlon Byrd	4.00
173	Adrian Burnside **RC**	4.00
174	Mike Gonzalez **RC**	4.00
175	J.R. House	4.00
176	Hank Blalock	6.00
177	Travis Hughes **RC**	4.00
178	Mark Teixeira	6.00
179	Josh Hancock **RC**	4.00
180	Anastacio Martinez **RC**	4.00
181	Jorge de la Rosa **RC**	4.00
182	Ben Broussard	4.00
183	Austin Kearns	4.00
184	Corky Miller	4.00
185	Colin Young **RC**	4.00
186	Cam Esslinger **RC**	4.00
187	Rene Reyes **RC**	4.00
188	Aaron Cook **RC**	4.00
189	Alexis Gomez	4.00
190	Nate Field **RC**	4.00
191	Miguel Asencio **RC**	4.00
192	Brandon Berger	4.00
193	Fernando Rodney	4.00
194	Andy Van Hekken	4.00
195	Kevin Frederick **RC**	4.00
196	Todd Sears	4.00
197	Edwin Almonte **RC**	4.00
198	Kyle Kane **RC**	4.00
199	Mitch Wylie **RC**	4.00
200	Mike Porzio	4.00
201	Darin Erstad	6.00
202	Tim Salmon	6.00
203	Jeff Bagwell	10.00
204	Lance Berkman	6.00
205	Eric Chavez	6.00
206	Tim Hudson	6.00
207	Carlos Delgado	6.00
208	Chipper Jones	10.00
209	Gary Sheffield	6.00
210	Greg Maddux	15.00
211	Tom Glavine	6.00
212	Mike Mussina	10.00
213	J.D. Drew	6.00
214	Rick Ankiel	4.00
215	Sammy Sosa	15.00
216	Mike Lieberthal	6.00
217	Fred McGriff	8.00
218	David Wells	4.00
219	Curt Schilling	10.00
220	Luis Gonzalez	6.00
221	Mark Grace	10.00
222	Kevin Brown	4.00
223	Hideo Nomo	20.00
224	Jose Vidro	4.00
225	Jeff Kent	4.00
226	Rich Aurilia	4.00
227	Kenny Lofton	4.00
228	C.C. Sabathia	4.00
229	Edgar Martinez	8.00
230	Freddy Garcia	4.00
231	Cliff Floyd	4.00
232	Preston Wilson	4.00
233	Mike Piazza	10.00
234	Roberto Alomar	8.00
235	Trevor Hoffman	4.00
236	Ryan Klesko	5.00
237	Sean Burroughs	4.00
238	Scott Rolen	10.00
239	Pat Burrell	8.00
240	Edgardo Alfonzo	4.00
241	Brian Giles	8.00
242	Jason Kendall	5.00
243	Alex Rodriguez	15.00
244	Juan Gonzalez	8.00
245	Ivan Rodriguez	8.00
246	Rafael Palmeiro	8.00
247	Ken Griffey Jr.	12.00
248	Adam Dunn	15.00
249	Barry Larkin	5.00
250	Manny Ramirez	10.00
251	Pedro Martinez	10.00
252	Todd Helton	8.00
253	Larry Walker	6.00
254	Randy Johnson	10.00
255	Mike Sweeney	4.00
256	Carlos Beltran	6.00
257	Dmitri Young	4.00
258	Joe Mays	4.00
259	Doug Mientkiewicz	4.00
260	Corey Koskie	4.00
261	Magglio Ordonez	8.00
262	Frank Thomas	8.00
263	Ray Durham	4.00
264	Jason Giambi	10.00
265	Bernie Williams	8.00
266	Roger Clemens	15.00
267	Mariano Rivera	6.00
268	Robin Ventura	6.00
269	Andy Pettitte	10.00
270	Jorge Posada	8.00
271	Mike Piazza	15.00
272	Alex Rodriguez	15.00
273	Ken Griffey Jr.	15.00
274	Jason Giambi	10.00
275	Frank Thomas	8.00
276	Greg Maddux	15.00
277	Sammy Sosa	15.00
278	Roger Clemens	15.00
279	Jeff Bagwell	10.00
280	Todd Helton	8.00
281	Ichiro Suzuki	40.00
282	Randy Johnson	10.00
283	Jim Thome	15.00
284	Ivan Rodriguez	8.00
285	Darin Erstad	6.00
286	Eric Chavez	8.00
287	Barry Zito	10.00
288	Carlos Delgado	8.00
289	Omar Vizquel	6.00
290	Edgar Martinez	8.00
291	Manny Ramirez	10.00
292	Mike Sweeney	6.00
293	Tom Glavine	8.00
294	Joe Mays	6.00
295	Eric Milton	6.00
296	Magglio Ordonez	8.00
297	Bernie Williams	8.00
298	Trevor Hoffman	6.00
299	Andruw Jones	8.00
300	Aubrey Huff	5.00
301	Jim Edmonds	8.00
302	Kerry Wood	10.00
303	Luis Gonzalez	8.00
304	Shawn Green	6.00
305	Jose Vidro	5.00
306	Jeff Kent	5.00
307	Edgardo Alfonzo	5.00
308	Preston Wilson	5.00
309	Roberto Alomar	10.00
310	Jeromy Burnitz	5.00
311	Phil Nevin	5.00
312	Ryan Klesko	5.00
313	Bobby Abreu	6.00
314	Scott Rolen	12.00
315	Kazuhiro Sasaki	5.00
316	Jason Kendall	5.00
317	Sean Casey	5.00
318	Larry Walker	5.00
319	Mike Hampton	5.00
320	Juan Gonzalez	8.00
321	Darin Erstad	8.00
322	Tim Hudson	8.00
323	Carlos Delgado	8.00
324	Greg Vaughn	5.00
325	Jim Thome	15.00
326	Ichiro Suzuki	40.00
327	Rafael Palmeiro	8.00
328	Alex Rodriguez	15.00
329	Juan Gonzalez	8.00
330	Manny Ramirez	10.00
331	Carlos Beltran	6.00
332	Eric Milton	5.00
333	Frank Thomas	8.00
334	Roger Clemens	15.00
335	Jason Giambi	10.00
336	Lance Berkman	8.00
337	Greg Maddux	15.00
338	Chipper Jones	10.00
339	Sean Casey	8.00
340	Jim Edmonds	8.00
341	Kerry Wood	10.00
342	Sammy Sosa	15.00
343	Luis Gonzalez	8.00
344	Shawn Green	6.00
345	Jeff Kent	6.00
346	Preston Wilson	5.00
347	Roberto Alomar	10.00
348	Phil Nevin	5.00
349	Scott Rolen	12.00
350	Mike Sweeney	5.00
351	Ken Griffey Jr.	15.00
352	Todd Helton	8.00
353	Larry Walker	5.00
354	Alex Rodriguez	15.00
355	Pedro J. Martinez	10.00
356	Frank Thomas	10.00
357	Jason Giambi	10.00
358	Bernie Williams	10.00
359	Jeff Bagwell	10.00
360	Chipper Jones	10.00
361	Sammy Sosa	20.00
362	Randy Johnson	10.00
363	Shawn Green	6.00
364	Mike Piazza	15.00
365	Ichiro Suzuki	50.00
366	Ken Griffey Jr.	15.00
367	Larry Walker	8.00
368	Jim Edmonds	8.00
369	Darin Erstad	8.00
370	Tim Salmon	8.00
371	Mark Kotsay	5.00
372	Craig Biggio	8.00
373	Eric Chavez	10.00
374	David Justice	8.00
375	Carlos Delgado	8.00
376	Chipper Jones	15.00
377	Gary Sheffield	6.00
378	Greg Maddux	10.00
379	Eric Karros	5.00
380	Fred McGriff	8.00
381	J.D. Drew	8.00
382	Rick Ankiel	5.00
383	Sammy Sosa	15.00
384	Moises Alou	5.00
385	Ben Grieve	5.00
386	Greg Vaughn	5.00
387	Jay Payton	5.00
388	Luis Gonzalez	6.00
389	Ray Durham	5.00
390	Shawn Green	8.00
391	Hideo Nomo	20.00
392	Jose Vidro	5.00
393	Jeff Kent	5.00
394	Adrian Beltre	5.00
395	Jim Thome	15.00
396	Bobby Abreu	5.00
397	Edgar Martinez	10.00
398	Carl Everett	5.00
399	Luis Castillo	5.00
400	Preston Wilson	5.00
401	Jermaine Dye	8.00
402	Roberto Alomar	8.00
403	Todd Hundley	5.00
404	Ryan Klesko	5.00
405	Phil Nevin	5.00

406 Scott Rolen 10.00
407 Rafael Furcal 5.00
408 Miguel Tejada 8.00
409 Brian Giles 6.00
410 Jason Kendall 5.00
411 Alex Rodriguez 15.00
412 Juan Gonzalez 8.00
413 Ivan Rodriguez 8.00
414 Rafael Palmeiro 5.00
415 Ken Griffey Jr. 15.00
416 Edgardo Alfonzo 5.00
417 Barry Larkin 8.00
418 Manny Ramirez 8.00
419 Pedro J. Martinez 12.00
420 Todd Helton 8.00
421 Larry Walker 8.00
422 Garret Anderson 6.00
423 Mike Sweeney 5.00
424 Carlos Beltran 5.00
425 Javier Lopez 5.00
426 J.T. Snow 5.00
427 Doug Mientkiewicz 5.00
428 John Olerud 5.00
429 Magglio Ordonez 6.00
430 Frank Thomas 10.00
431 Kenny Lofton 5.00
432 Al Leiter 5.00
433 Bernie Williams 8.00
434 Roger Clemens 15.00
435 Tom Glavine 8.00
436 Robin Ventura 5.00
437 Chan Ho Park 5.00
438 Jorge Posada 8.00
439 Charles Johnson 5.00
440 Alex Rodriguez 20.00
441 Ken Griffey Jr. 15.00
442 Mark Kotsay 5.00
443 Frank Thomas 10.00
444 Greg Maddux 20.00
445 Sammy Sosa 10.00
446 Tom Glavine 10.00
447 Chipper Jones 15.00
448 Todd Helton 10.00
449 Jeff Cirillo 5.00
450 Steve Finley 8.00
451 Jim Thome 15.00
452 Ivan Rodriguez 8.00
453 Darin Erstad 8.00
454 Eric Chavez 8.00
455 Miguel Tejada 8.00
456 Carlos Delgado 5.00
457 Omar Vizquel 5.00
458 Edgar Martinez 10.00
459 Johnny Damon 8.00
460 Russell Branyan 5.00
461 Kenny Lofton 5.00
462 Jermaine Dye 5.00
463 Ellis Burks 5.00
464 Magglio Ordonez 8.00
465 Bernie Williams 10.00
466 Tim Salmon 5.00
467 Andruw Jones 8.00
468 Jeffrey Hammonds 5.00
469 Jim Edmonds 10.00
470 Kerry Wood 15.00
471 Luis Gonzalez 8.00
472 Shawn Green 8.00
473 Jose Vidro 5.00
474 Jeff Kent 6.00
475 Javier Lopez 5.00
476 Preston Wilson 5.00
477 Roberto Alomar 10.00
478 Robin Ventura 6.00
479 Phil Nevin 8.00
480 Ryan Klesko 8.00
481 Bobby Abreu 8.00
482 Scott Rolen 10.00
483 Brian Giles 8.00
484 Jason Kendall 5.00
485 Tsuyoshi Shinjo 5.00
486 Larry Walker 5.00
487 Mike Lieberthal 5.00
488 Juan Gonzalez 8.00
489 Darin Erstad 5.00
490 Tom Glavine 10.00
491 Carlos Delgado 6.00
492 Greg Vaughn 5.00
493 Jim Thome 15.00
494 Mark Grace 15.00
495 Rafael Palmeiro 5.00
496 Alex Rodriguez 20.00
497 Juan Gonzalez 10.00
498 Miguel Tejada 8.00
499 Carlos Beltran 5.00
500 Andruw Jones 8.00
501 Frank Thomas 10.00
502 Andres Galarraga 5.00
503 Gary Sheffield 8.00
504 Craig Biggio 8.00
505 Greg Maddux 20.00
506 Chipper Jones 15.00
507 Pat Burrell 10.00
508 Jim Edmonds 8.00
509 Kerry Wood 15.00
510 Sammy Sosa 20.00
511 Luis Gonzalez 8.00
512 Shawn Green 8.00
513 Edgardo Alfonzo 5.00
514 Preston Wilson 5.00
515 Roberto Alomar 10.00
516 Phil Nevin 5.00
517 Scott Rolen 15.00
518 Brian Giles 5.00
519 Jorge Posada 10.00
520 Todd Helton 12.00

521 Larry Walker 8.00
522 Alex Rodriguez 25.00
523 Pedro J. Martinez 20.00
524 Frank Thomas 12.00
525 Jason Giambi 15.00
526 Bernie Williams 10.00
527 J.D. Drew 10.00
528 Chipper Jones 20.00
529 Sammy Sosa 25.00
530 Randy Johnson 15.00
531 Shawn Green 10.00
532 Kevin Brown 10.00
533 Brian Giles 10.00
534 Ken Griffey Jr. 20.00
535 Larry Walker 10.00
536 Jim Edmonds 10.00
537 Sean Casey/Jsy/775 5.00
538 Ichiro Suzuki/Jsy/775 40.00
539 Pat Burrell/Jsy/200 10.00
540 Adam Dunn/Jsy/200 20.00
541 Lance Berkman/Jsy/200 10.00
542 Cliff Floyd/Jsy/150 8.00
543 Roger Clemens/Jsy/100 20.00
544 Kerry Wood/Bat/775 15.00
545 Andruw Jones/Bat/775 8.00
546 Manny Ramirez/Bat/200 10.00
547 Jorge Posada/Bat/200 10.00
548 Fred McGriff/Bat/200 8.00
549 Mike Sweeney/Bat/150 6.00
550 Todd Helton/Bat/100 12.00

Great Connections

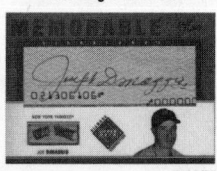

NM/M
Production 50 Sets
GC-GR Jason Giambi, Babe Ruth 350.00
GC-MD Mickey Mantle, Joe DiMaggio 350.00
GC-MR Mark McGwire, Babe Ruth 350.00
GC-MS Mark McGwire, Sammy Sosa 200.00
GC-RR Alex Rodriguez, Nolan Ryan 150.00
GC-IG Ichiro Suzuki, Ken Griffey Jr. 150.00

Mem. Signatures Bat

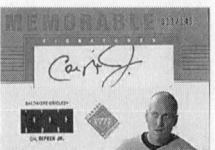

NM/M
Varying quantities produced
JD Joe DiMaggio/20 600.00
JG Jason Giambi/49 60.00
KG Ken Griffey Jr./49 150.00
MMc Mark McGwire/49 300.00
JM Joe Morgan/99 35.00
KP Kirby Puckett/145 75.00
CR Cal Ripken Jr/145 150.00
AR Alex Rodriguez/145 100.00
NR Nolan Ryan/99 150.00
SS Sammy Sosa/99 150.00
IS Ichiro Suzuki/99 250.00

Mem. Signatures Jsy

NM/M
Varying quantities produced

Gold: .75-1X
Production 150
EB Ernie Banks/150 80.00
JD Joe DiMaggio/20 550.00
KG Ken Griffey Jr./49 150.00
SK Sandy Koufax/150 300.00
MMc Mark McGwire/49 300.00
JM Joe Morgan/99 35.00
CR Cal Ripken Jr/145 150.00
AR Alex Rodriguez/145 100.00
NR Nolan Ryan/99 150.00
SS Sammy Sosa/99 200.00
IS Ichiro Suzuki/99 250.00

2002 Upper Deck Honor Roll

NM/M
Complete Set (100): 25.00
Common Player: .15
Pack (5): 2.00
Box (24): 30.00
1 Randy Johnson .50
2 Mike Piazza .75
3 Albert Pujols 1.00
4 Roberto Alomar .25
5 Chipper Jones .50
6 Rich Aurilia .15
7 Barry Bonds 1.00
8 Ken Griffey Jr. .75
9 Sammy Sosa .75
10 Roger Clemens .75
11 Ivan Rodriguez .40
12 Jason Giambi .40
13 Bret Boone .15
14 Troy Glaus .25
15 Alex Rodriguez .75
16 Manny Ramirez .40
17 Bernie Williams .40
18 Ichiro Suzuki .75
19 Matt Thornton .25
20 Chris Baker RC .25
21 Tyler Yates RC .50
22 Jorge Nunez RC .50
23 Rene Reyes RC .50
24 Ben Howard RC .50
25 Ron Calloway RC .40
26 Danny Wright .15
27 Reed Johnson RC .50
28-31 Randy Johnson .25
32-35 Mike Piazza .50
36-39 Albert Pujols .75
40-43 Roberto Alomar .20
44-47 Chipper Jones .50
48-51 Rich Aurilia .15
52-55 Barry Bonds 1.00
56-59 Ken Griffey Jr. .75
60-63 Sammy Sosa .50
64-67 Roger Clemens .75
68-71 Ivan Rodriguez .25
72-75 Jason Giambi .25
76-79 Bret Boone .15
80-83 Troy Glaus .20
84-87 Alex Rodriguez .75
88-91 Manny Ramirez .25
92-95 Bernie Williams .20
96-99 Ichiro Suzuki 1.00
100 Checklist (names.) Original nine players. (Nine team) .25

Silver
Stars: 4-8X
Production 100 Sets

Gold
Gold Stars (1-100): 15-25X
Production 25 Sets

Batting Glove
NM/M
Numbered to 250
BB Bret Boone/89 20.00
JG Jason Giambi 20.00
KG Ken Griffey Jr. 40.00
AR Alex Rodriguez 25.00
IR1 Ivan Rodriguez 20.00
IR2 Ivan Rodriguez 20.00
SS Sammy Sosa 30.00
I Ichiro Suzuki/46 150.00

Game Jersey

NM/M
Common Player: 10.00
Inserted 1:90
Golds: 2-3X
Production 99 Sets
Each player has multiple versions.
BB Bret Boone/SP/45 10.00
RC Roger Clemens 20.00
JG Jason Giambi/SP 15.00
KG Ken Griffey Jr. 25.00
CJ Chipper Jones 15.00
AR Alex Rodriguez 15.00
IR Ivan Rodriguez 10.00
SS Sammy Sosa/SP 25.00
I Ichiro Suzuki/SP 40.00

Game-Used Bat

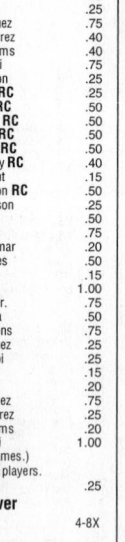
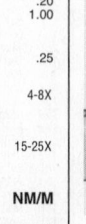

NM/M
Common Player: 10.00
Numbered to 99.
Each player has multiple versions.
BB Bret Boone 10.00
RC Roger Clemens 30.00
JG Jason Giambi 25.00
KG Ken Griffey Jr. 40.00
CJ Chipper Jones 20.00
AR Alex Rodriguez 20.00
IR Ivan Rodriguez 15.00
SS Sammy Sosa 30.00
I Ichiro Suzuki 40.00

Star Swatches Game Jersey

NM/M
Common Player: 10.00
Inserted 1:90
Golds: 2-5X
Production 24
BB Bret Boone/45 10.00
RC Roger Clemens/29 40.00
JG Jason Giambi 10.00

KG	Ken Griffey Jr./SP	25.00
CJ	Chipper Jones	15.00
AR	Alex Rodriguez	15.00
IR	Ivan Rodriguez	10.00
SS	Sammy Sosa	20.00
I	Ichiro Suzuki/SP	40.00

Stitch of Nine Game Jersey

		NM/M
Common Player:		10.00
Inserted 1:90		
Golds:		2-5X
Production 24 Sets		
BB	Bret Boone/45	10.00
RC	Roger Clemens	20.00
JG	Jason Giambi/SP	10.00
KG	Ken Griffey Jr.	15.00
CJ	Chipper Jones	10.00
AR	Alex Rodriguez	15.00
IR	Ivan Rodriguez	10.00
SS	Sammy Sosa	20.00
I	Ichiro Suzuki/85	40.00

Time Capsule Game Jersey

		NM/M
Common Player:		8.00
Inserted 1:90		
Golds:		2-3X
Production 99 Sets		
BB	Bret Boone	8.00
RC	Roger Clemens	20.00
JG	Jason Giambi/52	15.00
CJ	Chipper Jones	10.00
AR	Alex Rodriguez	15.00
IR	Ivan Rodriguez/SP	15.00
SS	Sammy Sosa	20.00
I	Ichiro Suzuki	40.00

2002 Upper Deck MVP

		NM/M
Complete Set (300):		20.00
Common Player:		.10
Pack (8):		1.50
Box (24):		25.00
1	Darin Erstad	.20
2	Ramon Ortiz	.10
3	Garret Anderson	.20
4	Jarrod Washburn	.10
5	Troy Glaus	.20
6	Brendan Donnelly RC	.10
7	Troy Percival	.10
8	Tim Salmon	.15
9	Aaron Sele	.10
10	Brad Fullmer	.10
11	Scott Hatteberg	.10
12	Barry Zito	.20
13	Tim Hudson	.20
14	Miguel Tejada	.25
15	Jermaine Dye	.20
16	Mark Mulder	.20
17	Eric Chavez	.15
18	Terrence Long	.10
19	Carlos Pena	.20
20	David Justice	.20
21	Jeremy Giambi	.10
22	Shannon Stewart	.10
23	Raul Mondesi	.15
24	Chris Carpenter	.10
25	Carlos Delgado	.20
26	Mike Sirotka	.10
27	Reed Johnson RC	.15
28	Darrin Fletcher	.10
29	Jose Cruz Jr.	.10
30	Vernon Wells	.10
31	Tanyon Sturtze	.10
32	Toby Hall	.10
33	Brent Abernathy	.10
34	Ben Grieve	.10
35	Joe Kennedy	.10
36	Dewon Brazelton	.10
37	Aubrey Huff	.10
38	Steve Cox	.10
39	Greg Vaughn	.10
40	Brady Anderson	.10
41	Chuck Finley	.10
42	Jim Thome	.40
43	Russell Branyan	.10
44	C.C. Sabathia	.10
45	Matt Lawton	.10
46	Omar Vizquel	.10
47	Bartolo Colon	.15
48	Alex Escobar	.10
49	Ellis Burks	.10
50	Bret Boone	.10
51	John Olerud	.20
52	Jeff Cirillo	.10
53	Ichiro Suzuki	1.00
54	Kazuhiro Sasaki	.10
55	Freddy Garcia	.10
56	Edgar Martinez	.15
57	Matt Thornton	.10
58	Mike Cameron	.10
59	Carlos Guillen	.10
60	Jeff Conine	.10
61	Tony Batista	.10
62	Jason Johnson	.10
63	Melvin Mora	.10
64	Brian Roberts	.10
65	Josh Towers	.10
66	Steve Bechler RC	.10
67	Jerry Hairston Jr.	.10
68	Chris Richard	.10
69	Alex Rodriguez	1.00
70	Chan Ho Park	.10
71	Ivan Rodriguez	.25
72	Jeff Zimmerman	.10
73	Mark Teixeira	.20
74	Gabe Kapler	.10
75	Frank Catalanotto	.10
76	Rafael Palmeiro	.25
77	Doug Davis	.10
78	Carl Everett	.10
79	Pedro J. Martinez	.40
80	Nomar Garciaparra	.75
81	Tony Clark	.10
82	Trot Nixon	.10
83	Manny Ramirez	.25
84	Josh Hancock RC	.10
85	Johnny Damon	.20
86	Jose Offerman	.10
87	Rich Garces	.10
88	Shea Hillenbrand	.10
89	Carlos Beltran	.20
90	Mike Sweeney	.10
91	Jeff Suppan	.10
92	Joe Randa	.10
93	Chuck Knoblauch	.10
94	Mark Quinn	.10
95	Neifi Perez	.10
96	Carlos Febles	.10
97	Miguel Asencio RC	.10
98	Michael Tucker	.10
99	Dean Palmer	.10
100	Jose Lima	.10
101	Craig Paquette	.10
102	Dmitri Young	.10
103	Bobby Higginson	.10
104	Jeff Weaver	.10
105	Matt Anderson	.10
106	Damion Easley	.10
107	Eric Milton	.10
108	Doug Mientkiewicz	.10
109	Cristian Guzman	.10
110	Brad Radke	.10
111	Torii Hunter	.20
112	Corey Koskie	.10
113	Joe Mays	.10
114	Jacque Jones	.10
115	David Ortiz	.20
116	Kevin Frederick RC	.10
117	Magglio Ordonez	.20
118	Ray Durham	.10
119	Mark Buehrle	.10
120	Jon Garland	.10
121	Paul Konerko	.10
122	Todd Ritchie	.10
123	Frank Thomas	.40
124	Edwin Almonte RC	.10
125	Carlos Lee	.10
126	Kenny Lofton	.15
127	Roger Clemens	.75
128	Derek Jeter	1.00
129	Jorge Posada	.20
130	Bernie Williams	.25
131	Mike Mussina	.25
132	Alfonso Soriano	.40
133	Robin Ventura	.15
134	John Vander Wal	.10
135	Jason Giambi	.25
136	Mariano Rivera	.20
137	Rondell White	.10
138	Jeff Bagwell	.25
139	Wade Miller	.10
140	Richard Hidalgo	.10
141	Julio Lugo	.10
142	Roy Oswalt	.20
143	Rodrigo Rosario RC	.10
144	Lance Berkman	.20
145	Craig Biggio	.10
146	Shane Reynolds	.10
147	John Smoltz	.10
148	Chipper Jones	.40
149	Gary Sheffield	.20
150	Rafael Furcal	.10
151	Greg Maddux	.50
152	Tom Glavine	.20
153	Andruw Jones	.25
154	John Ennis RC	.20
155	Vinny Castilla	.10
156	Marcus Giles	.10
157	Javy Lopez	.10
158	Richie Sexson	.20
159	Geoff Jenkins	.10
160	Jeffrey Hammonds	.10
161	Alex Ochoa	.10
162	Ben Sheets	.20
163	Jose Hernandez	.10
164	Eric Young	.10
165	Luis Montanez	.10
166	Albert Pujols	.75
167	Darryl Kile	.10
168	So Taguchi RC	.50
169	Jim Edmonds	.20
170	Fernando Vina	.10
171	Matt Morris	.10
172	J.D. Drew	.20
173	Bud Smith	.10
174	Edgar Renteria	.20
175	Placido Polanco	.10
176	Tino Martinez	.10
177	Sammy Sosa	.75
178	Moises Alou	.20
179	Kerry Wood	.40
180	Delino DeShields	.10
181	Alex Gonzalez	.10
182	Jon Lieber	.10
183	Fred McGriff	.15
184	Corey Patterson	.15
185	Mark Prior	.50
186	Tom Gordon	.10
187	Francis Beltran RC	.10
188	Randy Johnson	.40
189	Luis Gonzalez	.20
190	Matt Williams	.15
191	Mark Grace	.25
192	Curt Schilling	.25
193	Doug DeVore RC	.20
194	Erubiel Durazo	.10
195	Steve Finley	.15
196	Craig Counsell	.10
197	Shawn Green	.25
198	Kevin Brown	.20
199	Paul LoDuca	.10
200	Brian Jordan	.15
201	Andy Ashby	.10
202	Darren Dreifort	.10
203	Adrian Beltre	.15
204	Victor Alvarez RC	.10
205	Eric Karros	.10
206	Hideo Nomo	.25
207	Vladimir Guerrero	.40
208	Javier Vazquez	.10
209	Michael Barrett	.10
210	Jose Vidro	.10
211	Brad Wilkerson	.10
212	Tony Armas Jr.	.10
213	Eric Good RC	.10
214	Orlando Cabrera	.10
215	Lee Stevens	.10
216	Jeff Kent	.20
217	Rich Aurilia	.10
218	Robb Nen	.10
219	Calvin Murray	.10
220	Russ Ortiz	.10
221	Deivis Santos	.10
222	Marvin Benard	.10
223	Jason Schmidt	.10
224	Reggie Sanders	.10
225	Barry Bonds	1.00
226	Brad Penny	.10
227	Cliff Floyd	.10
228	Mike Lowell	.20
229	Derek Lee	.10
230	Ryan Dempster	.10
231	Josh Beckett	.20
232	Hansel Izquierdo RC	.10
233	Preston Wilson	.10
234	A.J. Burnett	.10
235	Charles Johnson	.10
236	Mike Piazza	.50
237	Al Leiter	.20
238	Jay Payton	.10
239	Roger Cedeno	.10
240	Jeromy Burnitz	.10
241	Roberto Alomar	.20
242	Mo Vaughn	.20
243	Shawn Estes	.10
244	Armando Benitez	.10
245	Tyler Yates RC	.10
246	Phil Nevin	.10
247	D'Angelo Jimenez	.10
248	Ramon Vazquez	.10
249	Bubba Trammell	.10
250	Trevor Hoffman	.10
251	Ben Howard RC	.20
252	Mark Kotsay	.10
253	Ray Lankford	.10
254	Ryan Klesko	.10
255	Scott Rolen	.40
256	Robert Person	.10
257	Jimmy Rollins	.25
258	Pat Burrell	.10
259	Anderson Machado RC	.10
260	Randy Wolf	.10
261	Travis Lee	.10
262	Mike Lieberthal	.10
263	Doug Glanville	.10
264	Bobby Abreu	.10
265	Brian Giles	.15
266	Kris Benson	.10
267	Aramis Ramirez	.10
268	Kevin Young	.10
269	Jack Wilson	.10
270	Mike Williams	.10
271	Jimmy Anderson	.10
272	Jason Kendall	.10
273	Pokey Reese	.10
274	Robert Mackowiak	.10
275	Sean Casey	.20
276	Juan Encarnacion	.10
277	Austin Kearns	.10
278	Danny Graves	.10
279	Ken Griffey Jr.	.50
280	Barry Larkin	.20
281	Todd Walker	.10
282	Elmer Dessens	.10
283	Aaron Boone	.10
284	Adam Dunn	.40
285	Larry Walker	.15
286	Rene Reyes RC	.20
287	Juan Uribe	.10
288	Mike Hampton	.10
289	Todd Helton	.40
290	Juan Pierre	.10
291	Denny Neagle	.10
292	Jose Ortiz	.10
293	Todd Zeile	.10
294	Ben Petrick	.10
295	Ken Griffey Jr. Checklist 1-50	.25
296	Derek Jeter Checklist 51-100	.50
297	Sammy Sosa Checklist 101-150	.30
298	Ichiro Suzuki Checklist 151-200	.50
299	Barry Bonds Checklist 201-250	.50
300	Alex Rodriguez Checklist 251-300	.40

Silver

Stars:	5-10X
Production 100 Sets	

Gold

No Pricing
Production 25 Sets

Ichiro - A Season to Remember

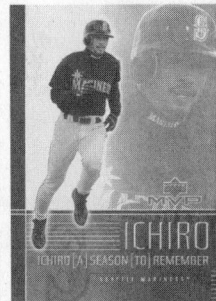

		NM/M
Complete Set (10):		15.00
Ichiro's (1-10):		2.00
Inserted 1:10		
I1-10	Ichiro Suzuki	2.50

- A Season to Remember Jersey

No Pricing

Ichiro - A Season to Remember Bat

No Pricing
Production 25

Souvenirs Jerseys

		NM/M
Common Player:		5.00
Inserted 1:48		
RA	Roberto Alomar	10.00
GA	Garret Anderson	10.00
JB	Jeff Bagwell	10.00
AB	Adrian Beltre	8.00
JB	Jeromy Burnitz	5.00
RC	Roger Clemens	15.00
CD	Carlos Delgado	8.00
DE	Darin Erstad	8.00

RF	Rafael Furcal	8.00
JG	Juan Gonzalez	10.00
THo	Trevor Hoffman	5.00
THu	Tim Hudson	8.00
JK	Jeff Kent	8.00
PK	Paul Konerko/SP	9.00
MK	Mark Kotsay	5.00
KL	Kenny Lofton	8.00
EM	Edgar Martinez	5.00
JP	Jay Payton/SP	10.00
MP	Mike Piazza	15.00
AR	Alex Rodriguez	15.00
IR	Ivan Rodriguez	10.00
SR	Scott Rolen	10.00
TS	Tim Salmon	10.00
FT	Frank Thomas	15.00
JT	Jim Thome/SP	15.00
RV	Robin Ventura	5.00
OV	Omar Vizquel	8.00
PW	Preston Wilson	5.00
TZ	Todd Zeile	5.00

Souvenirs Bat/Jersey Combos

		NM/M
Common Card:		10.00
Inserted 1:144		
Gold:		No Pricing
Production 25 Sets		
EA	Edgardo Alfonso	10.00
RA	Roberto Alomar	15.00
JB	Jeff Bagwell	20.00
AB	Adrian Beltre	15.00
CD	Carlos Delgado	15.00
DE	Darin Erstad	20.00
JG	Jason Giambi	20.00
BG	Brian Giles	15.00
LG	Luis Gonzalez	15.00
SG	Shawn Green	15.00
KG	Ken Griffey Jr.	40.00
TH	Todd Helton	20.00
RJ	Randy Johnson	25.00
CJ	Chipper Jones	20.00
JK	Jeff Kent	15.00
MO	Magglio Ordonez	15.00
RP	Rafael Palmeiro	20.00
MP	Mike Piazza	15.00
AR	Alex Rodriguez	25.00
IR	Ivan Rodriguez	15.00
SR	Scott Rolen	15.00
SS	Sammy Sosa	15.00
JT	Jim Thome	25.00
RV	Robin Ventura	10.00
OV	Omar Vizquel/97	20.00
BW	Bernie Williams/97	15.00
TZ	Todd Zeile	10.00

Souvenirs Bats

		NM/M
Common Player:		8.00
Inserted 1:144		
RA	Roberto Alomar	20.00
CD	Carlos Delgado	8.00
BG	Brian Giles	8.00
LG	Luis Gonzalez	8.00
SG	Shawn Green	8.00
KG	Ken Griffey Jr.	25.00
TH	Todd Helton	15.00
DJ	David Justice	8.00
JK	Jeff Kent	8.00
RK	Ryan Klesko	8.00
GM	Greg Maddux	20.00
EM	Edgar Martinez	10.00
DM	Doug Mientkiewicz	8.00
MO	Magglio Ordonez	8.00
RP	Rafael Palmeiro/97	18.00
MP	Mike Piazza/97	25.00
AR	Alex Rodriguez	15.00
IR	Ivan Rodriguez	10.00
SR	Scott Rolen	10.00
GS	Gary Sheffield	8.00
SS	Sammy Sosa	20.00
MS	Mike Sweeney	8.00
FT	Frank Thomas/97	25.00
JT	Jim Thome	10.00
GV	Greg Vaughn	8.00
LW	Larry Walker	8.00
BW	Bernie Williams	8.00

2002 Upper Deck Piece of History

	NM/M
Complete Set (132):	200.00
Common Player:	.15
Common SP (91-132):	5.00
Production 625	
Pack (5):	2.00
Box (24):	40.00
1 Troy Glaus	.40
2 Darin Erstad	.25
3 Reggie Jackson	.50
4 Miguel Tejada	.40

5	Tim Hudson	.25
6	Jim "Catfish" Hunter	.25
7	Joe Carter	.15
8	Carlos Delgado	.40
9	Greg Vaughn	.15
10	Early Wynn	.15
11	Omar Vizquel	.15
12	Jim Thome	.75
13	Ichiro Suzuki	1.50
14	Edgar Martinez	.25
15	Freddy Garcia	.15
16	Cal Ripken Jr/SP	15.00
17	Jeff Conine	.15
18	Juan Gonzalez	.50
19	Nolan Ryan/SP	15.00
20	Alex Rodriguez/SP	10.00
21	Rafael Palmeiro	.50
22	Ivan Rodriguez	.50
23	Carlton Fisk	.25
24	Wade Boggs	.30
25	Pedro J. Martinez	.75
26	Nomar Garciaparra	1.50
27	Manny Ramirez	.50
28	Mike Sweeney	.15
29	Bobby Higginson	.15
30	Kirby Puckett	.75
31	Doug Mientkiewicz	.15
32	Corey Koskie	.15
33	Joe Mays	.15
34	Frank Thomas	.75
35	Magglio Ordonez	.25
36	Jason Giambi/SP	5.00
37	Derek Jeter/SP	10.00
38	Mickey Mantle/SP	15.00
39	Joe DiMaggio	2.00
40	Roger Maris	1.00
41	Roger Clemens	1.50
42	Bernie Williams	.50
43	Jeff Bagwell	.50
44	Lance Berkman	.25
45	Eddie Mathews	.50
46	Andruw Jones	.40
47	Phil Niekro	.15
48	Gary Sheffield	.25
49	Chipper Jones	.75
50	Greg Maddux	1.00
51	Robin Yount	.25
52	Richie Sexson	.25
53	Jim Edmonds	.25
54	J.D. Drew	.25
55	Albert Pujols	1.50
56	Andre Dawson	.25
57	Billy Williams	.15
58	Ernie Banks	.50
59	Sammy Sosa/SP	10.00
60	Randy Johnson	.75
61	Curt Schilling	.50
62	Luis Gonzalez	.25
63	Kirk Gibson	.15
64	Steve Garvey	.15
65	Sandy Koufax/SP	15.00
66	Shawn Green	.25
67	Hideo Nomo	.25
68	Kevin Brown	.15
69	Vladimir Guerrero	.75
70	Tim Raines	.15
71	Gaylord Perry	.25
72	Mel Ott	.15
73	Willie McCovey	.15
74	Barry Bonds/SP	10.00
75	Jeff Kent	.15
76	Cliff Floyd	.15
77	Dwight Gooden	.15
78	Tom Seaver	.50
79	Mike Piazza	1.00
80	Roberto Alomar	.50
81	Dave Winfield	.25
82	Tony Gwynn	.75
83	Scott Rolen	.75
84	Bill Mazeroski	.15
85	Willie Stargell	.25
86	Brian Giles	.25
87	Ken Griffey Jr./SP	10.00
88	Sean Casey	.25
89	Todd Helton	.50
90	Larry Walker	.25
91	Brendan Donnelly RC	5.00
92	Tom Shearn RC	5.00
93	Brandon Puffer RC	5.00
94	Corey Thurman RC	5.00
95	Reed Johnson RC	8.00
96	Gustavo Chacin RC	5.00
97	Chris Baker RC	5.00
98	John Ennis RC	5.00
99	So Taguchi RC	8.00
100	Michael Crudale RC	5.00
101	Francis Beltran RC	5.00
102	Jose Valverde RC	8.00
103	Doug DeVore RC	5.00
104	Jeremy Ward RC	5.00
105	P.J. Bevis RC	5.00
106	Steve Kent RC	5.00
107	Brandon Backe RC	5.00
108	Jorge Nunez RC	5.00
109	Kazuhisa Ishii RC	10.00
110	Ron Calloway RC	5.00
111	Valentino Pasucci RC	5.00
112	J.J. Putz RC	5.00
113	Matt Thornton RC	5.00
114	Allan Simpson RC	5.00
115	Jaime Cerda RC	5.00
116	Mark Corey RC	5.00
117	Tyler Yates RC	8.00
118	Steve Bechler RC	5.00
119	Ben Howard RC	5.00

120	Clifford Bartosh RC	5.00
121	Todd Donovan RC	5.00
122	Eric Junge RC	5.00
123	Adrian Burnside RC	5.00
124	Andy Pratt RC	5.00
125	Josh Hancock RC	5.00
126	Rene Reyes RC	5.00
127	Cam Esslinger RC	5.00
128	Colin Young RC	5.00
129	Kevin Frederick RC	5.00
130	Kyle Kane RC	5.00
131	Mitch Wylie RC	5.00
132	Danny Wright	5.00

Batting Champs

		NM/M
Complete Set (10):		18.00
Common Player:		1.50
Inserted 1:30		
B1	Tony Gwynn	2.00
B2	Frank Thomas	2.00
B3	Billy Williams	1.50
B4	Edgar Martinez	1.50
B5	Bernie Williams	1.50
B6	Mickey Mantle	6.00
B7	Larry Walker	1.50
B8	Gary Sheffield	1.50
B9	Wade Boggs	1.50
B10	Alex Rodriguez	4.00

Batting Champ Jerseys

		NM/M
Common Player:		5.00
Inserted 1:96		
WB	Wade Boggs	10.00
AG	Andres Galarraga	5.00
TG	Tony Gwynn	15.00
MM	Mickey Mantle/50	200.00
EM	Edgar Martinez	10.00
JO	John Olerud	10.00
PO	Paul O'Neil	10.00
TR	Tim Raines	10.00
AR	Alex Rodriguez	15.00
GS	Gary Sheffield/SP	10.00
FT	Frank Thomas	10.00
LW	Larry Walker/SP	10.00
BeW	Bernie Williams	10.00

Batting Champ Jerseys Auto.

No Pricing

ERA Leaders

		NM/M
Complete Set (10):		18.00
Common Player:		1.00
Inserted 1:30		
E1	Greg Maddux	3.00
E2	Pedro J. Martinez	2.00
E3	Freddy Garcia	1.00
E4	Randy Johnson	2.00
E5	Tom Seaver	1.00
E6	Early Wynn	1.00
E7	Dwight Gooden	1.00
E8	Kevin Brown	1.00
E9	Roger Clemens	1.50
E10	Nolan Ryan	6.00

ERA Leaders Jerseys Autographs

		NM/M
Production 24 Sets		
RC	Roger Clemens	200.00
SK	Sandy Koufax	750.00

ERA Leaders Jerseys

		NM/M
Common Player:		8.00
Inserted 1:96		
KB	Kevin Brown	8.00
RC	Roger Clemens	15.00
FG	Freddy Garcia	8.00
DG	Dwight Gooden	8.00
CH	"Catfish" Hunter/SP	15.00
RJ	Randy Johnson	15.00
SK	Sandy Koufax/SP	100.00
GM	Greg Maddux	15.00
PM	Pedro Martinez	15.00
PN	Phil Niekro	8.00

NR	Nolan Ryan/SP	50.00
TS	Tom Seaver	15.00

Hitting for the Cycle

		NM/M
Complete Set (20):		35.00
Common Player:		1.00
Inserted 1:15		
H1	Alex Rodriguez	4.00
H2	Andre Dawson	1.00
H3	Cal Ripken Jr.	6.00
H4	Carlton Fisk	1.50
H5	Dante Bichette	1.00
H6	Dave Winfield	1.50
H7	Eric Chavez	1.00
H8	Robin Yount	2.00
H9	Jason Kendall	1.00
H10	Jay Buhner	1.00
H11	Jeff Kent	1.00
H12	Joe DiMaggio	6.00
H13	John Olerud	1.00
H14	Kirby Puckett	3.00
H15	Luis Gonzalez	1.50
H16	Mark Grace	1.50
H17	Mickey Mantle	6.00
H18	Miguel Tejada	1.00
H19	Rondell White	1.00
H20	Todd Helton	2.00

Hitting for the Cycle Bats

		NM/M
Inserted 1:576		
DB	Dante Bichette	10.00
JB	Jay Buhner	10.00
EC	Eric Chavez	10.00
AD	Andre Dawson	10.00
CF	Carlton Fisk	25.00
LG	Luis Gonzalez	10.00
MM	Mickey Mantle/50	200.00
CR	Cal Ripken Jr/SP	75.00
AR	Alex Rodriguez	25.00
DW	Dave Winfield	10.00

Hitting for the Cycle Bats Auto.

No Pricing
Production 10 Sets

The MVP Club

		NM/M
Complete Set (14):		30.00
Common Player:		1.00
Inserted 1:22		
M1	Jason Giambi	2.00
M2	Sammy Sosa	3.00
M3	Cal Ripken Jr.	6.00
M4	Robin Yount	2.00
M5	Ken Griffey Jr.	5.00
M6	Kirk Gibson	1.00
M7	Mickey Mantle	6.00
M8	Barry Bonds	3.00
M9	Frank Thomas	2.00
M10	Reggie Jackson	2.00
M11	Jeff Bagwell	2.00
M12	Roger Clemens	3.00
M13	Roger Clemens	1.00
M14	Chipper Jones	3.00

MVP Club Jerseys

		NM/M
Common Player:		8.00
Inserted 1:30		
JB	Jeff Bagwell	10.00
RC	Roger Clemens	15.00
SG	Steve Garvey	8.00
JGi	Jason Giambi	10.00
KGi	Kirk Gibson	10.00
JGo	Juan Gonzalez	10.00

KGr	Ken Griffey Jr.	15.00
RJ	Reggie Jackson	15.00
CJ	Chipper Jones	15.00
JK	Jeff Kent	8.00
BL	Barry Larkin/SP	25.00
MM	Mickey Mantle/50	200.00
RM	Roger Maris/50	100.00
CR	Cal Ripken Jr.	35.00
IR	Ivan Rodriguez	10.00
SS	Sammy Sosa	15.00
FT	Frank Thomas	10.00
RY	Robin Yount/SP	25.00

MVP Club Jerseys Auto.

No Pricing
Production 10 Sets

Tape Measure Heroes

		NM/M
Complete Set (30):		50.00
Common Player:		1.00
Inserted 1:10		
TM1	Joe Carter	1.00
TM2	Cal Ripken Jr.	6.00
TM3	Mike Piazza	4.00
TM4	Shawn Green	1.25
TM5	Mark McGwire	5.00
TM6	Reggie Jackson	1.50
TM7	Mickey Mantle	6.00
TM8	Manny Ramirez	2.00
TM9	Mo Vaughn	1.00
TM10	Jeff Bagwell	2.00
TM11	Sammy Sosa	3.00
TM12	Tony Gwynn	2.00
TM13	Bill Mazeroski	1.00
TM14	Jose Canseco	1.50
TM15	Brian Giles	1.00
TM16	Kirk Gibson	1.00
TM17	Kirby Puckett	3.00
TM18	Wade Boggs	1.50
TM19	Albert Pujols	3.00
TM20	David Justice	1.00
TM21	Steve Garvey	1.00
TM22	Luis Gonzalez	1.50
TM23	Derek Jeter	6.00
TM24	Robin Yount	2.50
TM25	Barry Bonds	5.00
TM26	Alex Rodriguez	4.00
TM27	Willie Stargell	1.50
TM28	Carlton Fisk	1.50
TM29	Carlos Delgado	1.50
TM30	Ken Griffey Jr.	5.00

Tape Measure Heroes Jerseys

		NM/M
Common Player:		5.00
Inserted 1:96		
JB	Jeff Bagwell	12.00
WB	Wade Boggs	15.00
JCa	Jose Canseco	10.00
JoC	Joe Carter	5.00
CD	Carlos Delgado	8.00
CF	Carlton Fisk	10.00
SGa	Steve Garvey	5.00
KGi	Kirk Gibson	8.00
BG	Brian Giles	5.00
SGr	Shawn Green	8.00
KGr	Ken Griffey Jr./90	40.00
MMa	Mickey Mantle/50	200.00
RM	Roger Maris/50	100.00
BM	Bill Mazeroski	10.00
MP	Mike Piazza	15.00
MR	Manny Ramirez	10.00
CR	Cal Ripken Jr.	30.00
AR	Alex Rodriguez	15.00
SS	Sammy Sosa	15.00
WS	Willie Stargell	15.00
RY	Robin Yount/SP	25.00

300 Game Winners

		NM/M
Complete Set (6):		12.00
Common Player:		1.00
Inserted 1:50		
GW1	Nolan Ryan	6.00
GW2	Tom Seaver	3.00
GW3	Cy Young	3.00
GW4	Gaylord Perry	1.00
GW5	Early Wynn	1.00
GW6	Phil Niekro	1.00

300 Game Winners Jerseys

		NM/M
Common Player:		15.00
Inserted 1:576		
PN	Phil Niekro	10.00
GP	Gaylord Perry	10.00
NR	Nolan Ryan/SP	50.00
TS	Tom Seaver/SP	20.00

The 500 Home Run Club

		NM/M
Complete Set (9):		25.00
Common Player:		1.50
Inserted 1:9		
HR1	Harmon Killebrew	3.00
HR2	Jimmie Foxx	3.00
HR3	Reggie Jackson	3.00
HR4	Mickey Mantle	8.00
HR5	Ernie Banks	3.00
HR6	Eddie Mathews	3.00
HR7	Mark McGwire	6.00
HR8	Willie McCovey	1.50
HR9	Mel Ott	3.00

HR Club Jerseys

		NM/M
Inserted 1:336		
HA	Hank Aaron	50.00
EB	Ernie Banks/SP	40.00
JF	Jimmie Foxx	40.00
RJ	Reggie Jackson	25.00
MM	Mickey Mantle/50	200.00
EM	Eddie Mathews	30.00
WM	Willie McCovey	20.00
MO	Mel Ott	40.00

Club Jerseys Auto.

No Pricing
Production 10 Sets

2002 Upper Deck Prospect Premieres

		NM/M
Complete Set (109):		
Common Player (1-60):		.40
Common Jersey (61-85):		5.00
Inserted 1:18		
Common Auto. (86-97):		10.00
Inserted 1:18		
Pack (4):		8.00
Box (18):		120.00
1	Josh Rupe RC	.40
2	Blair Johnson RC	.40
3	Jason Pridie RC	.75
4	Tim Gilhooly RC	.40
5	Kennard Jones RC	.40
6	Darrell Rasner RC	.40
7	Adam Donachie RC	.75
8	Josh Murray RC	.40
9	Brian Dopirak RC	1.00
10	Jason Cooper RC	.50
11	Zach Hammes RC	.40
12	Jon Lester RC	15.00
13	Kevin Jepsen RC	.40
14	Curtis Granderson RC	4.00

15	David Bush RC	.75
16	Joel Guzman RC	.50
17a	Matt Pender RC (Black, photo is Curtis Granderson.)	.40
17b	Matt Pender (White, correct photo.)	2.00
18	Derick Grigsby RC	.40
19	Jeremy Reed RC	3.00
20	Jonathan Broxton RC	1.00
21	Jesse Crain RC	.40
22	Justin Jones RC	1.00
23	Brian Slocum RC	.50
24	Brian McCann RC	5.00
25	Francisco Liriano RC	8.00
26	Fred Lewis RC	1.00
27	Steve Stanley RC	.40
28	Chris Snyder RC	.40
29	Daniel Cevette RC	.40
30	Kiel Fisher RC	.40
31	Brandon Wheeder RC	.40
32	Pat Osborn RC	.40
33	Taber Lee RC	.40
34	Dan Ortmeyer RC	.75
35	Josh Johnson RC	2.00
36	Val Majewski RC	.75
37	Larry Broadway RC	.50
38	Joey Gomes RC	1.00
39	Eric Thomas RC	.40
40	James Loney RC	4.00
41	Charlie Morton RC	.40
42	Mark McLemore RC	.40
43	Matt Craig RC	.40
44	Ryan Rodriguez RC	.40
45	Rich Hill RC	2.00
46	Bob Malek RC	.40
47	Justin Maureau RC	.40
48	Randy Braun RC	.40
49	Brian Grant RC	.50
50	Tyler Davidson RC	.50
51	Travis Hanson RC	.50
52	Kyle Boyer RC	.40
53	James Holcomb RC	.40
54	Ryan Williams RC	.40
55	Ben Crockett RC	.40
56	Adam Greenberg RC	.75
57	John Baker RC	.40
58	Matt Carson RC	.40
59	Jonathan George RC	.40
60	David Jensen RC	.40
61	Nick Swisher RC	15.00
62	Brent Cleven RC	8.00
63	Royce Ring RC	8.00
64	Mike Nixon RC	5.00
65	Ricky Barrett RC	5.00
66	Russ Adams RC	8.00
67	Joe Mauer RC	20.00
68	Jeff Francoeur RC	25.00
69	Joseph Blanton RC	10.00
70	Micah Schilling RC	8.00
71	John McCurdy RC	5.00
72	Sergio Santos RC	5.00
73	Josh Womack RC	5.00
74	Jared Doyle RC	5.00
75	Ben Fritz RC	5.00
76	Greg Miller	5.00
77	Luke Hagerty RC	5.00
78	Matt Whitney RC	5.00
79	Dan Meyer RC	5.00
80	Bill Murphy RC	5.00
81	Zach Segovia RC	5.00
82	Steve Obenchain RC	5.00
83	Matt Clanton RC	5.00
84	Mark Teahen RC	5.00
85	Kyle Pawelczyk RC	5.00
86	Khalil Greene/Auto. RC	25.00
87	Joe Saunders/Auto. RC	20.00
88	Jeremy Hermida/Auto. RC	40.00
89	Drew Meyer/Auto. RC	10.00
90	Jeff Francis/Auto. RC	25.00
91	Scott Moore/Auto. RC	10.00
92	Prince Fielder/Auto. RC	140.00
93	Zack Greinke/Auto. RC	25.00
94	Chris Gruler/Auto. RC	10.00
95	Scott Kazmir/Auto. RC	80.00
96	B.J. Upton/Auto. RC	50.00
97	Clint Everts/Auto. RC	15.00
98	Cal Ripken Jr.	1.00
99	Cal Ripken Jr.	1.00
100-104	Mark McGwire	
105-109	Joe DiMaggio	

Heroes of Baseball Quads

		NM/M
Common Quad:		10.00
Production 85 Sets		
1	Joe DiMaggio, Tony Gwynn	15.00
2	Joe DiMaggio, Tony Gwynn, Cal Ripken Jr.	20.00
3	Joe DiMaggio, Mickey Mantle, Willie Stargell	20.00
4	Tony Gwynn, Ozzie Smith, Willie Stargell	10.00
5	Tony Gwynn, Willie Stargell, Joe DiMaggio, Joe Morgan	15.00
6	Tony Gwynn, Willie Stargell, Cal Ripken Jr., Ozzie Smith	15.00
7	Mickey Mantle, Mark McGwire, Joe Morgan, Tom Seaver	20.00
8	Mickey Mantle, Tom Seaver	20.00
9	Mark McGwire, Joe Morgan	20.00
10	Mark McGwire, Cal Ripken Jr., Tony Gwynn, Joe DiMaggio	25.00
11	Mark McGwire, Tom Seaver, Joe Morgan, Ozzie Smith	15.00
12	Joe Morgan, Tony Gwynn	15.00
13	Joe Morgan, Joe DiMaggio, Mickey Mantle, Cal Ripken Jr.	25.00
14	Joe Morgan, Joe DiMaggio, Willie Stargell, Tony Gwynn	15.00
15	Ozzie Smith, Joe DiMaggio, Ozzie Smith, Willie Stargell	15.00
16	Ozzie Smith, Mark McGwire, Willie Stargell, Tony Gwynn	15.00
17	Ozzie Smith, Tom Seaver, Mark McGwire	15.00
18	Cal Ripken Jr., Mickey Mantle, Joe DiMaggio, Joe Morgan	20.00
19	Cal Ripken Jr., Mark McGwire, Cal Ripken Jr.	20.00
20	Tom Seaver, Joe DiMaggio, Tom Seaver, Joe DiMaggio	15.00
21	Tom Seaver, Joe Morgan, Ozzie Smith, Willie Stargell	10.00
22	Tom Seaver, Cal Ripken Jr., Mark McGwire, Mickey Mantle	20.00
23	Willie Stargell, Ozzie Smith	10.00
24	Willie Stargell, Ozzie Smith, Tom Seaver, Joe Morgan	10.00

Future Gems Quads

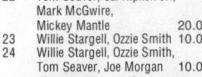

		NM/M
Common Card:		4.00
Inserted 1:Box		
1	David Bush, Matt Craig, Blair Johnson, Brian McCann	4.00
2	Jason Cooper, Jonathan George, Larry Broadway, Joel Guzman	4.00
3	Matt Craig, Josh Murray, Brian McCann, Jason Pridie	4.00
4	Jesse Crain, Brian Grant, Curtis Granderson, Joey Gomes	4.00
5	Tyler Davidson, Val Majewski, Kennard Jones, Daniel Cevette	4.00
6	Joe DiMaggio, Jon Lester, Mac, Mark McLemore	4.00
7	Jonathan George, Jeremy Reed, Adam Donachie, Matt Carson	4.00
8	Jonathan George, Eric Thomas, Joel Guzman, Kiel Fisher	4.00
9	Tim Gilhooly, Brandon Wheeder, Brian Slocum, Brian Dopirak	4.00
10	Brian Grant, Rich Hill, Joey Gomes, Joe DiMaggio	4.00
11	Derick Grigsby, Bob Malek, James Loney, Fred Lewis	4.00
12	Zach Hammes, James Holcomb, Cal Ripken Jr., Kennard Jones	4.00
13	Rich Hill, Mark McGwire, Brian Grant, Matt Carson	4.00
14	James Holcomb, David Jensen, Kennard Jones, Ryan Williams	4.00

15 David Jensen, Francisco Liriano, Ryan Williams, Travis Hanson 4.00
16 Blair Johnson, Jesse Crain, Adam Greenberg, Curtis Granderson 4.00
17 Adam Donachie, Mark McLemore, Jon Lester, Jonathan George 4.00
18 Francisco Liriano, Mark McGwire, Travis Hanson, Taber Lee 4.00
19 Val Majewski, Charlie Morton, Daniel Cevette, Joey Gomes 4.00
20 Bob Malek, Zach Hammes, Fred Lewis, Cal Ripken Jr. 4.00
21 Justin Maureau, Joe DiMaggio, Chris Snyder, Mark McGwire 4.00
22 Mark McGwire, Bob Malek, Joe DiMaggio, Kyle Boyer 4.00
23 Charlie Morton, David Bush, Joey Gomes, Blair Johnson 4.00
24 Josh Murray, Mark McGwire, Jason Pridie, Joe DiMaggio 4.00
25 Matt Pender, Mark McGwire, Mark McLemore, Ryan Rodriguez 4.00
26 Jason Pridie, Josh Murray, Matt Craig, Brian McCann 4.00
27 Jeremy Reed, Blair Johnson, Matt Carson, Adam Greenberg 4.00
28 Cal Ripken Jr., Jason Cooper, Matt Carson, Larry Broadway 4.00
29 Ryan Rodriguez, Eric Thomas, Pat Osborn, Randy Braun 4.00
30 Josh Rupe, Tyler Davidson, John Baker, Kennard Jones 4.00
31 Eric Thomas, Derick Grigsby, Randy Braun, James Loney 4.00
32 Eric Thomas, Matt Pender, Kiel Fisher, Mark McLemore 4.00
33 Brandon Wheeder, Rich Hill, Brian Dopirak, Brian Grant 4.00

Heroes of Baseball

	NM/M
Complete Ripken Set (10):	15.00
Common Ripken:	2.00
Complete Morgan Set (10):	4.00
Common Morgan:	.50
Complete Stargell Set (10):	5.00
Common Stargell:	.50
Complete Seaver Set (10):	10.00
Common Seaver:	1.25
Complete Mantle Set (10):	15.00
Common Mantle:	2.00
Complete DiMaggio Set (10):	12.00
Common DiMaggio:	1.50
Complete Gwynn Set (10):	10.00
Common Gwynn:	1.25
Complete McGwire Set (10):	12.00
Common McGwire:	1.50
Complete Ozzie Smith (10):	8.00
Common Ozzie:	1.00
Sets include Headers	
Inserted 1:1	

2002 Upper Deck Rookie Debut

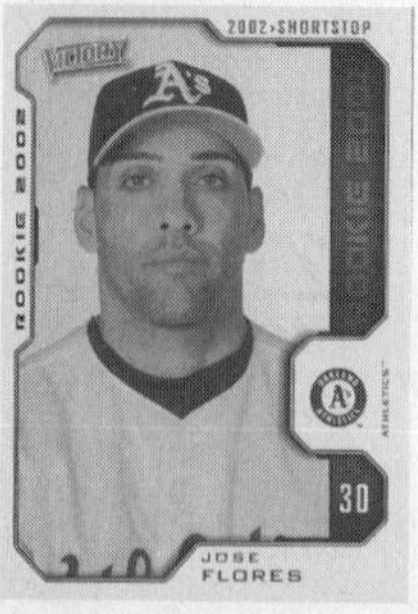

	NM/M
Common Player:	.10
Pack (5):	1.50
Box (24):	30.00

Honor Roll

Common Honor Roll Rk (131-190): .25
Golds (131-190): 5-10X
Production 50
101 Curt Schilling .40
102 Geronimo Gil .10
103 Cliff Floyd .10
104 Derek Lowe .10
105 Hee Seop Choi .10
106 Mark Prior .50
107 Joe Borchard .10
108 Austin Kearns .40
109 Adam Dunn .50
110 Brandon Phillips .10
111 Carlos Pena .10
112 Andy Van Hekken .10
113 Juan Encarnacion .10
114 Lance Berkman .25
115 Torii Hunter .25
116 Bartolo Colon .10
117 Raul Mondesi .20
118 Alfonso Soriano .75
119 Miguel Tejada .40
120 Ray Durham .10
121 Eric Chavez .20
122 Brett Myers .10
123 Marlon Byrd .10
124 Sean Burroughs .10
125 Kenny Lofton .10
126 Scott Rolen .50
127 Carl Crawford .10
128 Josh Phelps .10
129 Eric Hinske .10
130 Orlando Hudson .10
131 Barry Wesson .40
132 Jose Valverde **RC** .25
133 Kevin Gryboski **RC** .25
134 Trey Hodges **RC** .25
135 Howie Clark **RC** .25
136 Josh Hancock **RC** .25
137 Freddy Sanchez **RC** .25
138 Francis Beltran **RC** .10
139 Mike Mahoney .10
140 Brian Tallet .10
141 Jason Davis **RC** .50
142 Carl Sadler **RC** .25
143 Jason Beverlin **RC** .25
144 Josh Bard **RC** .25
145 Aaron Cook **RC** .25
146 Eric Eckenstahler **RC** .25
147 Tim Kalita **RC** .25
148 Franklyn German **RC** .25
149 Hansel Izquierdo **RC** .25
150 Brandon Puffer **RC** .25
151 Rodrigo Rosario **RC** .25
152 Kirk Saarloos .10
153 Jeriome Robertson **RC** .25
154 Jeremy Hill **RC** .25
155 Wes Obermueller **RC** .25
156 Aaron Guiel **RC** .25
157 Kazuhisa Ishii **RC** 1.00
158 David Ross .10
159 Jayson Durocher **RC** .25
160 Luis Martinez **RC** .25
161 Shane Nance **RC** .25
162 Eric Good **RC** .25
163 Jamey Carroll **RC** .25
164 Jaime Cerda **RC** .25
165 Satoru Komiyama **RC** .25
166 Adam Walker **RC** .25
167 Nate Field **RC** .25
168 Cody McKay **RC** .25
169 Jose Flores **RC** .25
170 Eric Junge **RC** .25
171 Jorge Padilla **RC** .25
172 Oliver Perez **RC** 1.00
173 Julius Matos **RC** .25
174 Wilbert Nieves **RC** .25
175 Clay Condrey **RC** .25
176 Mike Crudale **RC** .25
177 Jason Simontacchi **RC** .50
178 So Taguchi **RC** .50
179 Jose Rodriguez .10
180 Jorge Sosa **RC** .25
181 Felix Escalona **RC** .25
182 Lance Carter **RC** .25
183 Travis Hughes .10
184 Reynaldo Garcia **RC** .25
185 Mike Smith .10
186 Corey Thurman **RC** .25
187 Ken Huckaby **RC** .25
188 Reed Johnson **RC** .50
189 Kevin Cash **RC** .25
190 Scott Wiggins **RC** .25

Ovation

Common SP (151-180): 3.00
Production 2,002
Golds (151-180): 2-4X
Production 50
121 Curt Schilling .50
122 Cliff Floyd .15
123 Derek Lowe .15
124 Hee Seop Choi .25
125 Mark Prior .75
126 Joe Borchard .15
127 Austin Kearns .50
128 Adam Dunn .75
129 Jay Payton .15
130 Carlos Pena .15
131 Andy Van Hekken .15
132 Andres Torres .15
133 Ben Diggins .15
134 Torii Hunter .40
135 Bartolo Colon .25
136 Raul Mondesi .25
137 Alfonso Soriano 1.00
138 Miguel Tejada .75
139 Ray Durham .15
140 Eric Chavez .40
141 Marlon Byrd .15
142 Brett Myers .15
143 Sean Burroughs .15
144 Kenny Lofton .15
145 Scott Rolen .75
146 Carl Crawford .15
147 Jayson Werth .15
148 Josh Phelps .15
149 Eric Hinske .15
150 Orlando Hudson .15
151 Jose Valverde **RC** 5.00
152 Trey Hodges **RC** 3.00
153 Joey Dawley 3.00
154 Travis Driskill **RC** 3.00
155 Howie Clark 3.00
156 Jorge De La Rosa **RC** 3.00
157 Freddy Sanchez 3.00
158 Earl Snyder **RC** 5.00
159 Cliff Lee **RC** 10.00
160 Josh Bard **RC** 3.00
161 Aaron Cook **RC** 3.00
162 Franklyn German **RC** 3.00
163 Brandon Puffer **RC** 3.00
164 Kirk Saarloos 3.00
165 Jeriome Robertson **RC** 3.00
166 Miguel Asencio **RC** 3.00
167 Shawn Sedlacek 3.00
168 Jayson Durocher **RC** 3.00
169 Shane Nance **RC** 3.00
170 Jamey Carroll **RC** 8.00
171 Oliver Perez **RC** 8.00
172 Wilbert Nieves 3.00
173 Clay Condrey **RC** 3.00
174 Chris Snelling **RC** 5.00
175 Mike Crudale **RC** 3.00
176 Jason Simontacchi **RC** 3.00
177 Felix Escalona **RC** 3.00
178 Lance Carter **RC** 3.00
179 Scott Wiggins **RC** 3.00
180 Kevin Cash **RC** 3.00

Victory

Common Rk (606-660): .20
551 John Lackey .25
552 Francisco Rodriguez .50
553 Cliff Floyd .10
554 Derek Lowe .10
555 Mark Bellhorn .10
556 Matt Clement .10
557 Hee Seop Choi .25
558 Joe Borchard .10
559 Ryan Dempster .10
560 Russell Branyan .10
561 Brandon Larson .10
562 Coco Crisp .10
563 Karim Garcia .10
564 Brandon Phillips .10
565 Jay Payton .10
566 Gabe Kapler .10
567 Carlos Pena .10
568 George Lombard .10
569 Andy Van Hekken .10
570 Andres Torres .10
571 Justin Wayne .10
572 Juan Encarnacion .10
573 Abraham Nunez .10
574 Peter Munro .10
575 Jason Lane .10
576 Dave Roberts .10
577 Eric Gagne .10
578 Alex Sanchez .10
579 Jim Rushford **RC** .10
580 Ben Diggins .10
581 Eddie Guardado .10
582 Bartolo Colon .20
583 Endy Chavez .10
584 Raul Mondesi .20
585 Jeff Weaver .10
586 Marcus Thames .10
587 Ted Lilly .10
588 Ray Durham .10
589 Jeremy Giambi .10
590 Vicente Padilla .10
591 Brett Myers .10
592 Josh Fogg .10
593 Tony Alvarez .10
594 Jake Peavy .10
595 Dennis Tankersley .10
596 Sean Burroughs .10
597 Kenny Lofton .10
598 Scott Rolen .50
599 Chuck Finley .10
600 Carl Crawford .10
601 Kevin Mench .10
602 Juan Gonzalez .50
603 Jayson Werth .10
604 Eric Hinske .10
605 Josh Phelps .10
606 Jose Valverde **RC** .20
607 John Ennis **RC** .20
608 Trey Hodges **RC** .20
609 Kevin Gryboski **RC** .20
610 Travis Driskill **RC** .20
611 Howie Clark **RC** .20
612 Freddy Sanchez **RC** .20
613 Josh Hancock **RC** .20
614 Jorge De La Rosa **RC** .20
615 Mike Mahoney .10
616 Jason Davis **RC** .20
617 Josh Bard **RC** .20
618 Jason Beverlin **RC** .20
619 Carl Sadler **RC** .20
620 Earl Snyder **RC** .50
621 Aaron Cook **RC** .20
622 Eric Eckenstahler **RC** .20
623 Franklyn German **RC** .20
624 Kirk Saarloos .50
625 Rodrigo Rosario **RC** .20
626 Jeriome Robertson **RC** .20
627 Brandon Puffer **RC** .20
628 Miguel Asencio **RC** .20
629 Aaron Guiel **RC** .30
630 Ryan Bukvich **RC** .20
631 Jeremy Hill **RC** .20
632 Kazuhisa Ishii **RC** .75
633 Jayson Durocher **RC** .20
634 Shane Nance **RC** .20
635 Eric Good **RC** .20
636 Jamey Carroll **RC** .50
637 Jaime Cerda **RC** .20
638 Nate Field **RC** .20
639 Cody McKay **RC** .20
640 Jose Flores **RC** .20
641 Jorge Padilla **RC** .20
642 Anderson Machado **RC** .20
643 Eric Junge **RC** .20
644 Oliver Perez **RC** .75
645 Julius Matos **RC** .20
646 Ben Howard **RC** .20
647 Julio Mateo **RC** .20
648 Matt Thornton .10
649 Chris Snelling **RC** .50
650 Jason Simontacchi **RC** .50
651 So Taguchi **RC** .40
652 Mike Crudale **RC** .20
653 Mike Coolbaugh .10
654 Felix Escalona **RC** .20
655 Jorge Sosa **RC** .20
656 Lance Carter **RC** .20
657 Reynaldo Garcia **RC** .20
658 Kevin Cash **RC** .40
659 Ken Huckaby **RC** .20
660 Scott Wiggins **RC** .20

Climbing the Ladder

No Pricing
Production 25 Sets, Not Priced

Elite Company

No Pricing
Production 25, Not Priced

Making Their Marks

No Pricing
Production 25 Sets, Not Priced

Solid Contact

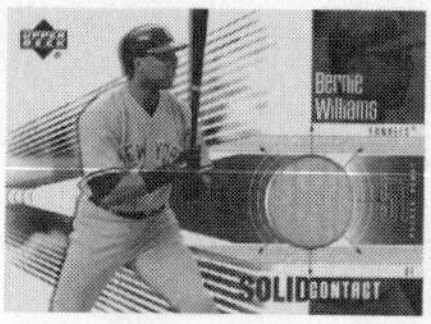

		NM/M
Common Player:		4.00
Inserted 1:24		
BA	Bobby Abreu	4.00
EA	Edgardo Alfonzo	4.00
RA	Roberto Alomar	10.00
MA	Moises Alou	6.00
JC	Jose Cruz Jr.	6.00
CD	Carlos Delgado/SP	8.00
JE	Jim Edmonds	6.00
CE	Carl Everett	4.00
JG	Jason Giambi/50	15.00
BG	Brian Giles	6.00
KG	Ken Griffey Jr.	15.00
TH	Todd Helton	8.00
JK	Jason Kendall	4.00
BL	Barry Larkin	10.00
EM	Edgar Martinez	8.00
FM	Fred McGriff	8.00
DM	Doug Mientkiewicz	6.00
JO	John Olerud	6.00
MO	Magglio Ordonez	6.00
JP	Jorge Posada	10.00
AR	Alex Rodriguez	15.00
IR	Ivan Rodriguez	6.00
GS	Gary Sheffield	6.00
SS	Sammy Sosa	15.00
TA	Fernando Tatis	4.00
FT	Frank Thomas	8.00
JT	Jim Thome	12.00
OV	Omar Vizquel	6.00
BW	Bernie Williams	8.00
MW	Matt Williams	4.00

2002 Upper Deck Rookie Update

	NM/M
Common Player:	.25
Pack (5):	3.00
Box (15):	35.00

SP Authentic

Common SP (201-230): 5.00

Production 1,999

171	Erubiel Durazo	.25
172	Junior Spivey	.25
173	Geronimo Gil	.25
174	Cliff Floyd	.25
175	Brandon Larsen	.25
176	Aaron Boone	.25
177	Shawn Estes	.25
178	Austin Kearns	.75
179	Joe Borchard	.25
180	Russell Branyan	.25
181	Jay Payton	.25
182	Andres Torres	.25
183	Andy Van Hekken	.25
184	Alex Sanchez	.25
185	Endy Chavez	.25
186	Bartolo Colon	.25
187	Raul Mondesi	.40
188	Robin Ventura	.40
189	Mike Mussina	.75
190	Jorge Posada	.75
191	Ted Lilly	.25
192	Ray Durham	.25
193	Brett Myers	.25
194	Marlon Byrd	.25
195	Vicente Padilla	.25
196	Josh Fogg	.25
197	Kenny Lofton	.25
198	Scott Rolen	1.00
199	Jason Lane	.25
200	Josh Phelps	.25
201	Travis Driskill RC	5.00
202	Howie Clark RC	5.00
203	Mike Mahoney	5.00
204	Brian Tallet	5.00
205	Kirk Saarloos	5.00
206	Barry Wesson	5.00
207	Aaron Guiel RC	5.00
208	Shawn Sedlacek	5.00
209	Jose Diaz	5.00
210	Jorge Nunez	5.00
211	Danny Mota	5.00
212	David Ross	5.00
213	Jayson Durocher RC	5.00
214	Shane Nance RC	5.00
215	Wilbert Nieves RC	5.00
216	Freddy Sanchez RC	5.00
217	Alex Pelaez	5.00
218	Jamey Carroll RC	5.00
219	J.J. Trujillo	5.00
220	Kevin Pickford	5.00
221	Clay Condrey RC	5.00
222	Chris Snelling RC	5.00
223	Cliff Lee RC	10.00
224	Jeremy Hill RC	5.00
225	Jose Rodriguez	5.00
226	Lance Carter RC	5.00
227	Ken Huckaby RC	5.00
228	Scott Wiggins RC	5.00
229	Corey Thurman RC	5.00
230	Kevin Cash RC	5.00

SPx
Common SPx Auto.(221-250): 10.00
Production 825

191	Tom Glavine	.75
192	Cliff Floyd	.25
193	Mark Prior	1.50
194	Corey Patterson	.50
195	Paul Konerko	.50
196	Adam Dunn	1.00
197	Joe Borchard	.25
198	Carlos Pena	.25
199	Juan Encarnacion	.25
200	Luis Castillo	.25
201	Torii Hunter	.50
202	Hee Seop Choi	.50
203	Bartolo Colon	.40
204	Raul Mondesi	.40
205	Jeff Weaver	.50
206	Eric Munson	.25
207	Alfonso Soriano	1.00
208	Ray Durham	.25
209	Eric Chavez	.25
210	Brett Myers	.25
211	Jeremy Giambi	.25
212	Vicente Padilla	.25
213	Felipe Lopez	.25
214	Sean Burroughs	.25
215	Kenny Lofton	.25
216	Scott Rolen	1.00
217	Carl Crawford	.25

218	Juan Gonzalez	.75
219	Orlando Hudson	.25
220	Eric Hinske	.25
221	Adam Walker RC	10.00
222	Aaron Cook RC	10.00
223	Cam Esslinger RC	10.00
224	Kirk Saarloos	10.00
225	Jose Diaz	10.00
226	David Ross	10.00
227	Jayson Durocher RC	10.00
228	Brian Mallette	10.00
229	Aaron Guiel RC	10.00
230	Jorge Nunez	10.00
231	Satoru Komiyama RC	15.00
232	Tyler Yates RC	15.00
233	Peter Zamora RC	10.00
234	Mike Gonzalez RC	10.00
235	Oliver Perez RC	20.00
236	Julius Matos RC	10.00
237	Andy Shibilo	10.00
238	Jason Simontacchi RC	10.00
239	Ron Chiavacci	10.00
240	Deivis Santos	10.00
241	Travis Driskill RC	10.00
242	Jorge De La Rosa RC	10.00
243	Anastacio Martinez RC	10.00
244	Earl Snyder RC	10.00
245	Freddy Sanchez RC	10.00
246	Miguel Asencio RC	10.00
247	Juan Brito	10.00
248	Franklyn German RC	10.00
249	Chris Snelling RC	10.00
250	Ken Huckaby RC	10.00

Diamond Connection
Common SP (601-630): 4.00
Production 1,999

571	Erubiel Durazo	.25
572	Geronimo Gil	.25
573	Shea Hillenbrand	.50
574	Cliff Floyd	.25
575	Corey Patterson	.50
576	Joe Borchard	.25
577	Austin Kearns	.75
578	Ryan Dempster	.25
579	Brandon Larsen	.25
580	Luis Castillo	.25
581	Juan Encarnacion	.25
582	Chin-Feng Chen	.25
583	Hideo Nomo	.75
584	Bartolo Colon	.40
585	Raul Mondesi	.40
586	Eric Munson	.25
587	Alfonso Soriano	1.00
588	Ted Lilly	.25
589	Ray Durham	.25
590	Brett Myers	.25
591	Brandon Phillips	.25
592	Kenny Lofton	.25
593	Scott Rolen	1.00
594	Jim Edmonds	.50
595	Carl Crawford	.25
596	Hank Blalock	.50
597	Kevin Mench	.25
598	Josh Phelps	.25
599	Orlando Hudson	.25
600	Eric Hinske	.25
601	Mike Mahoney	5.00
602	Jason Davis RC	8.00
603	Trey Hodges RC	4.00
604	Josh Bard RC	4.00
605	Jeriome Robertson RC	4.00
606	Jose Diaz	4.00
607	Jorge Nunez	4.00
608	Danny Mota	4.00
609	David Ross	4.00
610	Jayson Durocher RC	4.00
611	Freddy Sanchez RC	4.00
612	Julius Matos RC	4.00
613	Wilbert Nieves RC	4.00
614	Brian Kozlowski	4.00
615	Jason Simontacchi RC	4.00
616	Mike Coolbaugh	4.00
617	Travis Driskill RC	4.00
618	Howie Clark RC	4.00
619	Earl Snyder RC	6.00
620	Carl Sadler RC	4.00
621	Jason Beverlin RC	4.00
622	Terry Pearson	4.00
623	Eric Eckenstahler RC	4.00
624	Shawn Sedlacek	4.00
625	Aaron Guiel RC	5.00
626	Ryan Bukvich RC	4.00
627	Julio Mateo RC	4.00
628	Chris Snelling RC	6.00
629	Lance Carter RC	4.00
630	Scott Wiggins RC	4.00

Star Tributes

	NM/M
Common Player:	5.00
Inserted 1:15	
JB Josh Beckett	8.00

LB	Lance Berkman	6.00
RC	Roger Clemens	15.00
CD	Carlos Delgado	5.00
JD	Joe DiMaggio/SP	75.00
AD	Adam Dunn	8.00
JG	Jason Giambi	10.00
TG	Tom Glavine	8.00
LG	Luis Gonzalez/SP	8.00
SG	Shawn Green	8.00
KG	Ken Griffey Jr.	12.00
KI	Kazuhisa Ishii	8.00
RJ	Randy Johnson	10.00
CJ	Chipper Jones	10.00
PM	Pedro J. Martinez	8.00
MM	Mark McGwire/SP	50.00
RP	Rafael Palmeiro	8.00
MPi	Mike Piazza	10.00
MPr	Mark Prior	5.00
AR	Alex Rodriguez	10.00
IR	Ivan Rodriguez	8.00
KS	Kazuhiro Sasaki	5.00
CS	Curt Schilling	8.00
TS	Tsuyoshi Shinjo	5.00
AS	Alfonso Soriano	10.00
SS	Sammy Sosa	12.00
IS	Ichiro Suzuki/19	
MS	Mike Sweeney	5.00
FT	Frank Thomas	8.00

Signed Star Tributes

	NM/M
Production 50 Sets	
Copper & Silver:	No Pricing
Production 5	
Gold:	No Pricing
Production 5	
SS-MM Mark McGwire	350.00

USA Future Watch Swatches

	NM/M
Common Player:	5.00
Inserted 1:15	
Red:	1.5-2X
Production 50	
Copper:	No Pricing
Production 25	
Gold:	No Pricing
Production 5	
AA	Abe Alvarez	5.00
MA	Michael Aubrey	10.00
KB	Kyle Bakker	8.00
CC	Chad Cordero	5.00
SC	Shane Costa	8.00
SF	Sam Fuld	8.00
AH	Aaron Hill	8.00
PH	Philip Humber	8.00
CJ	Conor Jackson	5.00
GJ	Grant Johnson	5.00
MJ	Mark Jurich	5.00
WL	Wes Littleton	8.00
EP	Eric Patterson	5.00
DP	Dustin Pedroia	5.00
LP	Landon Powell	8.00
CQ	Carlos Quentin	10.00
CS	Clint Sammons	5.00
KS	Kyle Sleeth	10.00
HS	Huston Street	5.00
BS	Brad Sullivan	8.00
RW	Rickie Weeks	10.00
BZ	Bob Zimmermann	5.00

2002 Upper Deck Sweet Spot

	NM/M
Complete Set (175):	
Common Player:	.25
Common (91-130):	4.00
Production 1,300	
Common Auto. (131-145):	15.00

	Production 750 or 100	
	Common Game Faces (146-175):	3.00
	Inserted 1:24	
	Parallel (146-175):	1.5X-3X
	Production 100	
	Pack (4):	8.00
	Box (12):	90.00
1	Troy Glaus	.50
2	Darin Erstad	.50
3	Tim Hudson	.50
4	Eric Chavez	.50
5	Barry Zito	.50
6	Miguel Tejada	.50
7	Carlos Delgado	.50
8	Eric Hinske	.25
9	Ben Grieve	.25
10	Jim Thome	1.00
11	C.C. Sabathia	.25
12	Omar Vizquel	.40
13	Ichiro Suzuki	2.00
14	Edgar Martinez	.40
15	Bret Boone	.40
16	Freddy Garcia	.25
17	Tony Batista	.25
18	Geronimo Gil	.25
19	Alex Rodriguez	2.50
20	Rafael Palmeiro	.75
21	Ivan Rodriguez	.75
22	Hank Blalock	.50
23	Juan Gonzalez	.75
24	Nomar Garciaparra	2.00
25	Pedro J. Martinez	1.00
26	Manny Ramirez	1.00
27	Mike Sweeney	.25
28	Carlos Beltran	.50
29	Dmitri Young	.25
30	Torii Hunter	.50
31	Eric Milton	.25
32	Corey Koskie	.25
33	Frank Thomas	.75
34	Mark Buehrle	.25
35	Magglio Ordonez	.50
36	Roger Clemens	2.00
37	Derek Jeter	3.00
38	Jason Giambi	.75
39	Alfonso Soriano	1.00
40	Bernie Williams	.50
41	Jeff Bagwell	.75
42	Roy Oswalt	.50
43	Lance Berkman	.50
44	Greg Maddux	1.50
45	Chipper Jones	1.00
46	Gary Sheffield	.50
47	Andruw Jones	.75
48	Richie Sexson	.50
49	Ben Sheets	.50
50	Albert Pujols	2.00
51	Matt Morris	.40
52	J.D. Drew	.50
53	Sammy Sosa	2.00
54	Kerry Wood	1.00
55	Mark Prior	1.00
56	Moises Alou	.50
57	Corey Patterson	.50
58	Randy Johnson	1.00
59	Luis Gonzalez	.40
60	Curt Schilling	.75
61	Shawn Green	.50
62	Kevin Brown	.40
63	Paul LoDuca	.25
64	Adrian Beltre	.50
65	Vladimir Guerrero	1.00
66	Jose Vidro	.25
67	Javier Vazquez	.25
68	Barry Bonds	3.00
69	Jeff Kent	.40
70	Rich Aurilia	.25
71	Mike Lowell	.40
72	Josh Beckett	.50
73	Brad Penny	.25
74	Roberto Alomar	.50
75	Mike Piazza	1.50
76	Jeromy Burnitz	.25
77	Mo Vaughn	.25
78	Phil Nevin	.25
79	Sean Burroughs	.25
80	Jeremy Giambi	.25
81	Bobby Abreu	.50
82	Jimmy Rollins	.50
83	Pat Burrell	.50
84	Brian Giles	.50
85	Aramis Ramirez	.25
86	Ken Griffey Jr.	1.50
87	Adam Dunn	.75
88	Austin Kearns	.50
89	Todd Helton	.75
90	Larry Walker	.50
91	Earl Snyder RC	6.00
92	Jorge Padilla RC	4.00
93	Felix Escalona RC	4.00
94	John Foster RC	4.00
95	Brandon Puffer RC	4.00
96	Steve Bechler RC	4.00
97	Hansel Izquierdo RC	4.00
98	Chris Baker RC	4.00
99	Jeremy Ward RC	4.00
100	Kevin Frederick RC	4.00
101	Josh Hancock RC	4.00
102	Allan Simpson RC	4.00
103	Mitch Wylie RC	4.00
104	Mark Corey RC	4.00
105	Victor Alvarez RC	4.00
106	Todd Donovan RC	4.00
107	Nelson Castro RC	4.00
108	Chris Booker RC	4.00

109	Corey Thurman RC	4.00
110	Kirk Saarloos RC	4.00
111	Michael Crudale RC	4.00
112	Jason Simontacchi RC	4.00
113	Ron Calloway RC	4.00
114	Brandon Backe RC	4.00
115	Tom Shearn RC	4.00
116	Oliver Perez RC	6.00
117	Kyle Kane RC	4.00
118	Francis Beltran RC	4.00
119	So Taguchi RC	8.00
120	Doug DeVore RC	4.00
121	Juan Brito RC	4.00
122	Clifford Bartosh RC	4.00
123	Eric Junge RC	4.00
124	Joe Orloski RC	4.00
125	Scotty Layfield RC	4.00
126	Jorge Sosa RC	4.00
127	Satoru Komiyama RC	4.00
128	Edwin Almonte RC	4.00
129	Takahito Nomura RC	4.00
130	John Ennis RC	4.00
131	Kazuhisa Ishii/Auto./100	90.00
132	Ben Howard/Auto./100	20.00
133	Aaron Cook/Auto./750	15.00
134	Anderson Machado/Auto./750 RC	15.00
135	Luis Ugueto/Auto./750 RC	15.00
136	Tyler Yates/Auto./750 RC	20.00
137	Rodrigo Rosario/Auto./750 RC	15.00
138	Jaime Cerda/Auto./750 RC	15.00
139	Luis Martinez/Auto./750 RC	15.00
140	Rene Reyes/Auto./750 RC	15.00
141	Eric Good/Auto./750 RC	15.00
142	Matt Thornton/Auto./100	25.00
143	Steve Kent/Auto./750 RC	15.00
144	Jose Valverde/Auto./750 RC	15.00
145	Adrian Burnside/Auto./750 RC	15.00
146	Barry Bonds	15.00
147	Ken Griffey Jr.	10.00
148	Alex Rodriguez	12.00
149	Jason Giambi	4.00
150	Chipper Jones	5.00
151	Nomar Garciaparra	10.00
152	Mike Piazza	5.00
153	Sammy Sosa	10.00
154	Derek Jeter	15.00
155	Jeff Bagwell	4.00
156	Albert Pujols	10.00
157	Ichiro Suzuki	10.00
158	Randy Johnson	5.00
159	Frank Thomas	4.00
160	Greg Maddux	8.00
161	Jim Thome	5.00
162	Scott Rolen	6.00
163	Shawn Green	3.00
164	Vladimir Guerrero	6.00
165	Troy Glaus	3.00
166	Carlos Delgado	4.00
167	Luis Gonzalez	3.00
168	Roger Clemens	10.00
169	Todd Helton	4.00
170	Eric Chavez	3.00
171	Rafael Palmeiro	4.00
172	Pedro J. Martinez	5.00
173	Lance Berkman	3.00
174	Josh Beckett	4.00
175	Sean Burroughs	3.00

Bat Barrels

No Pricing
100 Total Produced

Legendary Signatures

NM/M

Common Autograph: 20.00
Inserted 1:72

LA	Luis Aparicio/485	25.00
RF	Rollie Fingers/866	20.00
SG	Steve Garvey/871	20.00
KH	Keith Hernandez/906	20.00
FJ	Ferguson Jenkins/857	20.00
AK	Al Kaline/835	40.00
SK	Sandy Koufax/485	200.00
FL	Fred Lynn/853	20.00
MM	Mark McGwire/90	275.00
PM	Paul Molitor/852	30.00
GP	Gaylord Perry/921	25.00
BP	Boog Powell/944	20.00
CR	Cal Ripken Jr./194	175.00
BR	Brooks Robinson	35.00
AT	Alan Trammell/843	25.00

Gwire Priority Signing Redem.

NM/M

100 Redemptions Produced
MM Mark McGwire 350.00

Signatures

NM/M

Common Autograph: 20.00
Inserted 1:72

LB	Lance Berkman/291	40.00
HB	Hank Blalock/291	40.00
BB	Barry Bonds/380	200.00
JB	Jeromy Burnitz/291	20.00
SB	Sean Burroughs/291	20.00
RC	Roger Clemens/194	150.00
CD	Carlos Delgado/291	25.00
AD	Adam Dunn/291	40.00
FG	Freddy Garcia/145	25.00
JG	Jason Giambi/291	40.00
BG	Brian Giles/291	25.00
TG	Tom Glavine/291	40.00
LG	Luis Gonzalez/291	20.00
KG	Ken Griffey Jr./291	125.00
AJ	Andruw Jones/291	25.00
RO	Roy Oswalt/291	20.00
MPr	Mark Prior/291	25.00
AR	Alex Rodriguez/291	160.00
SR	Scott Rolen/291	40.00
SS	Sammy Sosa/145	200.00
MS	Mike Sweeney/291	20.00
IS	Ichiro Suzuki/145	400.00
FT	Frank Thomas/291	60.00
JT	Jim Thome/291	50.00
BZ	Barry Zito/291	30.00

Sweet Swatches

Scott Rolen • Phillies

SWEET SPOT SWATCHES

NM/M

Common Player: 5.00
Inserted 1:12

JBa	Jeff Bagwell	8.00
JBe	Josh Beckett	6.00
SB	Sean Burroughs	6.00
EC	Eric Chavez	5.00
JE	Jim Edmonds	8.00
DE	Darin Erstad	6.00
JGi	Jason Giambi	8.00
BG	Brian Giles	5.00
JGo	Juan Gonzalez	6.00
LG	Luis Gonzalez	5.00
SG	Shawn Green	5.00
KG	Ken Griffey Jr.	15.00
KI	Kazuhisa Ishii	10.00
CJ	Chipper Jones	10.00
GM	Greg Maddux	12.00

PM	Pedro J. Martinez	10.00
MP	Mike Piazza	15.00
AR	Alex Rodriguez	15.00
IR	Ivan Rodriguez	8.00
SR	Scott Rolen	8.00
SS	Sammy Sosa	15.00
IS	Ichiro Suzuki	40.00
FT	Frank Thomas	8.00
OV	Omar Vizquel	5.00
BW	Bernie Williams	8.00

USA Jerseys

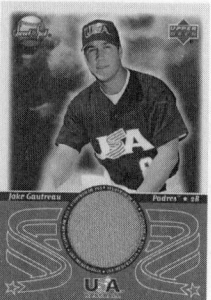

Jake Gautreau ... Padres • SS

NM/M

Common Player: 5.00
Inserted 1:12

BA	Brent Abernathy	5.00
TB	Taggert Bozied	8.00
DB	Dewon Brazelton	5.00
AE	Adam Everett	5.00
DG	Danny Graves	5.00
JG	Jake Gautreau	5.00
JK	Josh Karp	5.00
AK	Adam Kennedy	8.00
JM	Joe Mauer	20.00
DM	Doug Mientkiewicz	6.00
EM	Eric Munson	5.00
XN	Xavier Nady	8.00
RO	Roy Oswalt	5.00
MP	Mark Prior	10.00
JR	Jon Rauch	5.00
MT	Mark Teixeira	8.00
JW	Justin Wayne	5.00

2002 Upper Deck Sweet Spot Classics

NM/M

Complete Set (90):		40.00
Common Player:		.40
Pack (4):		20.00
Box (12):		200.00
1	Mickey Mantle	4.00
2	Joe DiMaggio	3.00
3	Babe Ruth	3.00
4	Ty Cobb	1.50
5	Nolan Ryan	3.00
6	Sandy Koufax	2.00
7	Cy Young	1.00
8	Roberto Clemente	1.00
9	Lefty Grove	.50
10	Lou Gehrig	2.50
11	Walter Johnson	1.00
12	Honus Wagner	1.00
13	Christy Mathewson	.75
14	Jackie Robinson	1.50
15	Joe Morgan	.50
16	Reggie Jackson	.75
17	Eddie Collins	.40
18	Cal Ripken Jr.	3.00
19	Hank Greenberg	.40
20	Harmon Killebrew	.75
21	Johnny Bench	1.00
22	Ernie Banks	1.00
23	Willie McCovey	.40
24	Mel Ott	.40
25	Tom Seaver	1.00
26	Tony Gwynn	.75
27	Dave Winfield	.50

28	Willie Stargell	.40
29	Mark McGwire	2.00
30	Al Kaline	.75
31	Jimmie Foxx	.75
32	Satchel Paige	1.50
33	Eddie Murray	.40
34	Lou Boudreau	.40
35	"Shoeless" Joe Jackson	1.50
36	Luke Appling	.40
37	Ralph Kiner	.40
38	Robin Yount	.75
39	Paul Molitor	.75
40	Juan Marichal	.40
41	Brooks Robinson	.40
42	Wade Boggs	.50
43	Kirby Puckett	1.00
44	Yogi Berra	1.00
45	George Sisler	.40
46	Buck Leonard	.40
47	Billy Williams	.40
48	Duke Snider	.75
49	Don Drysdale	.60
50	Bill Mazeroski	.40
51	Tony Oliva	.40
52	Luis Aparicio	.40
53	Carlton Fisk	.40
54	Kirk Gibson	.40
55	Jim "Catfish" Hunter	.40
56	Joe Carter	.40
57	Gaylord Perry	.40
58	Don Mattingly	2.00
59	Eddie Mathews	1.25
60	Ferguson Jenkins	.40
61	Roy Campanella	1.00
62	Orlando Cepeda	.40
63	Tony Perez	.40
64	Dave Parker	.40
65	Richie Ashburn	.40
66	Andre Dawson	.40
67	Dwight Evans	.40
68	Rollie Fingers	.40
69	Dale Murphy	.40
70	Ron Santo	.40
71	Steve Garvey	.40
72	Monte Irvin	.40
73	Alan Trammell	.40
74	Ryne Sandberg	1.00
75	Gary Carter	.40
76	Fred Lynn	.40
77	Maury Wills	.40
78	Ozzie Smith	1.00
79	Bobby Bonds	.40
80	Mickey Cochrane	.60
81	Dizzy Dean	.40
82	Graig Nettles	.40
83	Keith Hernandez	.40
84	Boog Powell	.40
85	Jack Clark	.40
86	Dave Stewart	.40
87	Tommy Lasorda	.40
88	Dennis Eckersley	.40
89	Ken Griffey Sr.	.40
90	Bucky Dent	.40

Bat Barrels

NM/M

Values undetermined due to scarcity.
No Pricing

Game Jersey

NM/M

Common Player: 5.00
Inserted 1:8

WB	Wade Boggs	12.00
GC	Gary Carter	10.00
JC	Joe Carter	5.00
JD	Joe DiMaggio/53	180.00
RF	Rollie Fingers	5.00
SG	Steve Garvey	5.00
TG	Tony Gwynn	15.00
RJ	Reggie Jackson	15.00
SK	Sandy Koufax/SP	125.00
BM	Bill Madlock	5.00
MM	Mickey Mantle/53	250.00
JMa	Juan Marichal	10.00
DM	Don Mattingly	25.00
PM	Paul Molitor	15.00
EM	Eddie Murray	10.00
GN	Graig Nettles	8.00

DP	Dave Parker	5.00
CR	Cal Ripken Jr.	25.00
NR	Nolan Ryan	40.00
RS	Ryne Sandberg	15.00
TS	Tom Seaver	15.00
OS	Ozzie Smith	15.00
DSn	Duke Snider/53	80.00
WS	Willie Stargell	10.00
DSt	Dave Stewart	5.00
BW	Billy Williams	8.00
RY	Robin Yount	15.00

Game Jersey Gold

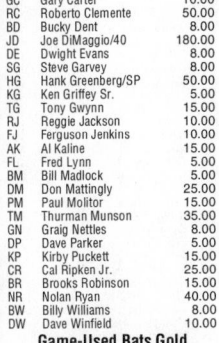

No Pricing
Production 25 Sets

Game-Used Bats

		NM/M
Common Player:		5.00

Inserted 1:8

JB	Johnny Bench	15.00
YB	Yogi Berra	15.00
WB	Wade Boggs	12.00
BBo	Bob Boone	5.00
BBu	Bill Buckner	5.00
GC	Gary Carter	10.00
RC	Roberto Clemente	50.00
BD	Bucky Dent	8.00
JD	Joe DiMaggio/40	180.00
DE	Dwight Evans	8.00
SG	Steve Garvey	50.00
HG	Hank Greenberg/SP	50.00
KG	Ken Griffey Sr.	5.00
TG	Tony Gwynn	15.00
RJ	Reggie Jackson	10.00
FJ	Ferguson Jenkins	10.00
AK	Al Kaline	15.00
FL	Fred Lynn	5.00
BM	Bill Madlock	5.00
DM	Don Mattingly	25.00
PM	Paul Molitor	15.00
TM	Thurman Munson	35.00
GN	Graig Nettles	8.00
DP	Dave Parker	5.00
KP	Kirby Puckett	15.00
CR	Cal Ripken Jr.	25.00
BR	Brooks Robinson	15.00
NR	Nolan Ryan	40.00
BW	Billy Williams	8.00
DW	Dave Winfield	10.00

Game-Used Bats Gold

		NM/M
Common Player:		25.00
JB	Johnny Bench	100.00
YB	Yogi Berra	125.00
WB	Wade Boggs	100.00
BBo	Bob Boone	40.00
BBu	Bill Buckner	35.00
GC	Gary Carter	40.00
RC	Roberto Clemente	250.00
BD	Bucky Dent	250.00
JD	Joe DiMaggio	250.00
DE	Dwight Evans	25.00
SG	Steve Garvey	35.00
HG	Hank Greenberg	125.00
KG	Ken Griffey Sr.	25.00
TG	Tony Gwynn	150.00
RJ	Reggie Jackson	150.00
FJ	Ferguson Jenkins	45.00
AK	Al Kaline	75.00
FL	Fred Lynn	25.00
BM	Bill Madlock	25.00
DM	Don Mattingly	125.00
PM	Paul Molitor	40.00
TM	Thurman Munson	150.00
GN	Graig Nettles	25.00

DP	Dave Parker	25.00
KP	Kirby Puckett	125.00
CR	Cal Ripken Jr.	225.00
BR	Brooks Robinson	75.00
NR	Nolan Ryan	175.00
BW	Billy Williams	45.00
DW	Dave Winfield	45.00

Sweet Spot Signatures

		NM/M
Common Autograph:		20.00

Inserted 1:24

EB	Ernie Banks	60.00
JB	Johnny Bench	60.00
YB	Yogi Berra/100	150.00
AD	Andre Dawson/100	100.00
BD	Bucky Dent	20.00
DeE	Dennis Eckersley	40.00
RF	Rollie Fingers	25.00
CF	Carlton Fisk/100	125.00
SG	Steve Garvey	25.00
KG	Kirk Gibson/SP	50.00
KH	Keith Hernandez	30.00
RJ	Reggie Jackson/SP	100.00
FJ	Ferguson Jenkins	25.00
AK	Al Kaline	40.00
SK	Sandy Koufax/SP	250.00
TL	Tommy Lasorda	35.00
FL	Fred Lynn	25.00
DoM	Don Mattingly	100.00
BM	Bill Mazeroski	40.00
WM	Willie McCovey/SP	75.00
PM	Paul Molitor	40.00
JM	Joe Morgan	25.00
DaM	Dale Murphy	50.00
GP	Gaylord Perry	25.00
BP	Boog Powell	25.00
KP	Kirby Puckett	180.00
CR	Cal Ripken Jr.	180.00
BR	Brooks Robinson	50.00
NR	Nolan Ryan/74	300.00
TS	Tom Seaver	50.00
OS	Ozzie Smith/137	200.00
DaS	Dave Stewart	25.00
AT	Alan Trammell	30.00
DW	Dave Winfield/70	125.00

Sweet Spot Signatures Gold

No Pricing
Production 25 Sets

2002 Upper Deck Ultimate Collection

	NM/M
Complete Set (120):	
Common Player (1-60):	2.00
Production 799	
Common Player (61-110, 114-120):	10.00
Production 550	
Common (111-113):	25.00
Production 330	
Pack (4):	100.00
Box (4):	350.00
1 Troy Glaus	2.50
2 Luis Gonzalez	2.00

3	Curt Schilling	2.50
4	Randy Johnson	4.00
5	Andruw Jones	2.50
6	Greg Maddux	6.00
7	Chipper Jones	5.00
8	Gary Sheffield	2.00
9	Cal Ripken Jr.	12.00
10	Manny Ramirez	3.00
11	Pedro J. Martinez	4.00
12	Nomar Garciaparra	8.00
13	Sammy Sosa	6.00
14	Kerry Wood	4.00
15	Mark Prior	4.00
16	Magglio Ordonez	2.00
17	Frank Thomas	3.00
18	Adam Dunn	3.00
19	Ken Griffey Jr.	8.00
20	Jim Thome	4.00
21	Larry Walker	2.00
22	Todd Helton	3.00
23	Nolan Ryan	12.00
24	Jeff Bagwell	3.00
25	Roy Oswalt	2.00
26	Lance Berkman	2.00
27	Mike Sweeney	2.00
28	Shawn Green	2.00
29	Hideo Nomo	2.00
30	Torii Hunter	2.00
31	Vladimir Guerrero	5.00
32	Tom Seaver	4.00
33	Mike Piazza	8.00
34	Roberto Alomar	2.00
35	Derek Jeter	12.00
36	Alfonso Soriano	5.00
37	Jason Giambi	4.00
38	Roger Clemens	8.00
39	Mike Mussina	2.50
40	Bernie Williams	2.50
41	Joe DiMaggio	10.00
42	Mickey Mantle	15.00
43	Miguel Tejada	3.00
44	Eric Chavez	2.00
45	Barry Zito	2.00
46	Pat Burrell	2.50
47	Jason Kendall	2.00
48	Brian Giles	2.00
49	Barry Bonds	15.00
50	Ichiro Suzuki	8.00
51	Stan Musial	8.00
52	J.D. Drew	2.00
53	Scott Rolen	5.00
54	Albert Pujols	10.00
55	Mark McGwire	10.00
56	Alex Rodriguez	10.00
57	Ivan Rodriguez	3.00
58	Juan Gonzalez	2.00
59	Rafael Palmeiro	3.00
60	Carlos Delgado	2.50
61	Jose Valverde **RC**	10.00
62	Doug DeVore **RC**	10.00
63	John Ennis **RC**	10.00
64	Joey Dawley	10.00
65	Trey Hodges **RC**	10.00
66	Mike Mahoney	10.00
67	Aaron Cook **RC**	10.00
68	Rene Reyes **RC**	10.00
69	Mark Corey	10.00
70	Hansel Izquierdo **RC**	10.00
71	Brandon Puffer **RC**	10.00
72	Jeriome Robertson **RC**	10.00
73	Jose Diaz	10.00
74	David Ross	10.00
75	Jayson Durocher **RC**	10.00
76	Eric Good **RC**	10.00
77	Satoru Komiyama **RC**	10.00
78	Tyler Yates **RC**	10.00
79	Eric Junge **RC**	10.00
80	Anderson Machado **RC**	10.00
81	Adrian Burnside **RC**	10.00
82	Ben Howard **RC**	10.00
83	Clay Condrey **RC**	10.00
84	Nelson Castro **RC**	10.00
85	So Taguchi **RC**	15.00
86	Mike Crudale **RC**	10.00
87	Scotty Layfield **RC**	10.00
88	Steve Bechler **RC**	10.00
89	Travis Driskill **RC**	10.00
90	Howie Clark **RC**	10.00
91	Josh Hancock **RC**	10.00
92	Jorge De La Rosa **RC**	10.00
93	Anastacio Martinez **RC**	10.00
94	Brian Tallet	10.00
95	Carl Sadler **RC**	10.00
96	Cliff Lee **RC**	25.00
97	Josh Bard **RC**	10.00
98	Wes Obermueller **RC**	10.00
99	Juan Brito	10.00
100	Aaron Guiel **RC**	10.00
101	Jeremy Hill **RC**	10.00
102	Kevin Frederick **RC**	10.00
103	Nate Field **RC**	10.00
104	Julio Mateo **RC**	10.00
105	Chris Snelling **RC**	15.00
106	Felix Escalona **RC**	10.00
107	Reynaldo Garcia **RC**	10.00
108	Mike Smith **RC**	10.00
109	Ken Huckaby **RC**	10.00
110	Kevin Cash **RC**	10.00
111	Kazuhisa Ishii/Auto. **RC**	40.00
112	Freddy Sanchez/Auto. **RC**	25.00
113	Jason Simontacchi/ Auto. **RC**	25.00
114	Jorge Padilla/Auto. **RC**	15.00
115	Kirk Saarloos/Auto. **RC**	15.00
116	Rodrigo Rosario/Auto. **RC**	15.00

117	Oliver Perez/Auto. **RC**	25.00
118	Miguel Asencio/Auto. **RC**	15.00
119	Franklyn German/Auto. **RC**	15.00
120	Jaime Cerda/Auto. **RC**	15.00

Double Barrel

Quantity produced listed

DB-RI	Ivan Rodriguez, Alex Rodriguez/5	2,225
DB-RR	Cal Ripken Jr., Alex Rodriguez/9	1,625
DB-TO	Magglio Ordonez, Frank Thomas/4	950.00

Double Patches

		NM/M
Production 100 Sets		
Golds:		.75-1.5X
Production 50 Sets		
DE	J.D. Drew, Jim Edmonds	60.00
GC	Jason Giambi, Roger Clemens	80.00
IG	Ken Griffey Jr., Ichiro Suzuki	125.00
JS	Randy Johnson, Curt Schilling	60.00
MG	Tom Glavine, Greg Maddux	75.00
MS	Sammy Sosa, Mark McGwire	150.00
PA	Mike Piazza, Roberto Alomar	80.00
RG	Alex Rodriguez, Juan Gonzalez	80.00
RM	Manny Ramirez, Pedro J. Martinez	50.00

Jerseys Tier 1

		NM/M
Common Player:		10.00
Production 99 Sets		
Golds:		.75-1.5X
Production 50 Sets		
RC	Roger Clemens	20.00
JD	Joe DiMaggio	100.00
AD	Adam Dunn	15.00
JG	Jason Giambi	15.00
KG	Ken Griffey Jr.	20.00
KI	Kazuhisa Ishii	10.00
RJ	Randy Johnson	10.00
AJ	Andruw Jones	10.00
CJ	Chipper Jones	15.00
MM	Mickey Mantle	125.00
PM	Pedro J. Martinez	15.00
MC	Mark McGwire	60.00
MP	Mike Piazza	15.00
PR	Mark Prior	15.00
MR	Manny Ramirez	10.00
CR	Cal Ripken Jr.	40.00
AR	Alex Rodriguez	25.00
IR	Ivan Rodriguez	15.00
AS	Alfonso Soriano	20.00
SS	Sammy Sosa	25.00
IS	Ichiro Suzuki	45.00

Jerseys Tier 2

	NM/M
Same price as Tier 1.	
Production 99 Sets	
Golds:	1.5-2X
Production 25 Sets	
JF-RC Roger Clemens	20.00
JF-JD Joe DiMaggio	100.00
JF-AD Adam Dunn	15.00
JF-JG Jason Giambi	15.00
JF-KG Ken Griffey Jr.	20.00

JF-KI	Kazuhisa Ishii	10.00
JF-RJ	Randy Johnson	15.00
JF-AJ	Andruw Jones	10.00
JF-CJ	Chipper Jones	15.00
JF-MM	Mickey Mantle	125.00
JF-PM	Pedro J. Martinez	15.00
JF-MC	Mark McGwire	60.00
JF-MP	Mike Piazza	15.00
JF-PR	Mark Prior	20.00
JF-MR	Manny Ramirez	10.00
JF-CR	Cal Ripken Jr.	40.00
JF-AR	Alex Rodriguez	25.00
JF-IR	Ivan Rodriguez	15.00
JF-AS	Alfonso Soriano	20.00
JF-SS	Sammy Sosa	25.00
JF-IS	Ichiro Suzuki	45.00

Jerseys Tier 3
NM/M

Common Player: 8.00
Stars: .4-.6X Tier 1 Price
Production 199 Sets

JP-RC	Roger Clemens	15.00
JP-AD	Adam Dunn	10.00
JP-JG	Jason Giambi	10.00
JP-KG	Ken Griffey Jr.	15.00
JP-KI	Kazuhisa Ishii	8.00
JP-RJ	Randy Johnson	12.00
JP-AJ	Andruw Jones	8.00
JP-CJ	Chipper Jones	12.00
JP-MM	Mickey Mantle	75.00
JP-PM	Pedro J. Martinez	10.00
JP-MC	Mark McGwire	40.00
JP-MP	Mike Piazza	10.00
JP-PR	Mark Prior	10.00
JP-MR	Manny Ramirez	8.00
JP-CR	Cal Ripken Jr.	30.00
JP-AR	Alex Rodriguez	15.00
JP-IR	Ivan Rodriguez	8.00
JP-AS	Alfonso Soriano	12.00
JP-SS	Sammy Sosa	20.00
JP-IS	Ichiro Suzuki	30.00
JP-BW	Bernie Williams	8.00

Jerseys Tier 4
NM/M

Common Player: 8.00
Stars: .4-.6X Tier 1 Price
Production 199 Sets

JR-RC	Roger Clemens	15.00
JR-AD	Adam Dunn	10.00
JR-JG	Jason Giambi	10.00
JR-KG	Ken Griffey Jr.	15.00
JR-KI	Kazuhisa Ishii	8.00
JR-RJ	Randy Johnson	12.00
JR-AJ	Andruw Jones	8.00
JR-CJ	Chipper Jones	12.00
JR-MM	Mickey Mantle	75.00
JR-PM	Pedro J. Martinez	10.00
JR-MC	Mark McGwire	40.00
JR-MP	Mike Piazza	15.00
JR-PR	Mark Prior	10.00
JR-MR	Manny Ramirez	8.00
JR-CR	Cal Ripken Jr.	25.00
JR-AR	Alex Rodriguez	15.00
JR-IR	Ivan Rodriguez	8.00
JR-AS	Alfonso Soriano	15.00
JR-SS	Sammy Sosa	20.00
JR-IS	Ichiro Suzuki	30.00
JR-BW	Bernie Williams	8.00

Gwire Signing Redem.

NM/M

Exchange Card 1:500 Packs:
1-MM Mark McGwire 300.00

Patch
NM/M

Common Player: 25.00
Production 100 Sets

LG	Luis Gonzalez	25.00
SG	Shawn Green	25.00
TH	Todd Helton	40.00
KI	Kazuhisa Ishii	40.00
CJ	Chipper Jones	40.00
MM	Mark McGwire	125.00
MP	Mark Prior	30.00

IR	Ivan Rodriguez	40.00
SS	Sammy Sosa	65.00
IS	Ichiro Suzuki	150.00

Signed Excellence

NM/M

Quantity produced listed
Golds: No Pricing
Production One Set

I1	Ichiro Suzuki/56	375.00
I2	Ichiro Suzuki/51	375.00
I5	Ichiro Suzuki/Batting	250.00
I6	Ichiro Suzuki/Throwing	250.00
MM1	Mark McGwire/70	275.00
MM2	Mark McGwire/65	275.00
MM3	Mark McGwire/49	300.00
MM5	Mark McGwire/Standing	220.00
MM6	Mark McGwire/Waving	220.00
MM7	Mark McGwire/Fielding	220.00
SS1	Sammy Sosa/66	175.00
SS2	Sammy Sosa/64	175.00
SS3	Sammy Sosa/54	175.00
SS5	Sammy Sosa/Running	150.00
SS6	Sammy Sosa/Holding Bat	150.00
SS7	Sammy Sosa/150	150.00

Excellence Gold
No Pricing

Signatures Tier 1

NM/M

Common Autograph: 20.00
Quantity produced listed
Golds: No Pricing
Production 25 Sets

RA1	Roberto Alomar/155	45.00
LB1	Lance Berkman/179	25.00
PB1	Pat Burrell/95	25.00
RC1	Roger Clemens/320	80.00
CD1	Carlos Delgado/95	25.00
JD1	J.D. Drew/220	25.00
AD1	Adam Dunn/125	45.00
JG1	Jason Giambi/295	25.00
BG1	Brian Giles/220	20.00
LG1	Luis Gonzalez/199	20.00
KG1	Ken Griffey Jr./195	100.00
JK1	Jason Kendall/220	20.00
MP1	Mark Prior/160	25.00
CR1	Cal Ripken Jr./75	165.00
AR1	Alex Rodriguez/329	100.00
SR1	Scott Rolen/160	30.00
GS1	Gary Sheffield/95	20.00
JT1	Jim Thome/95	60.00
BZ1	Barry Zito/199	25.00

Signatures Tier 2
NM/M

Quantity produced listed
Golds: No Pricing
Production 10 Sets

JB2	Jeff Bagwell/51	55.00
LB2	Lance Berkman/85	40.00
JG2	Jason Giambi/50	60.00
LG2	Luis Gonzalez/70	25.00
KG2	Ken Griffey Jr./30	150.00
TG2	Tony Gwynn/51	75.00

TH2	Todd Helton/51	60.00
AJ2	Andruw Jones/51	50.00
MP2	Mark Prior/60	50.00
KP2	Kirby Puckett/75	60.00
AR2	Alex Rodriguez/75	100.00
SR2	Scott Rolen/60	50.00
DS2	Duke Snider/51	60.00
FT2	Frank Thomas/51	65.00
KW2	Kerry Wood/51	75.00
BZ2	Barry Zito/70	40.00

2002 Upper Deck Victory

NM/M

Complete Set (550): 40.00
Common Player: .10
Pack (10): 1.00
Box (36): 25.00

1	Troy Glaus	.30
2	Tim Salmon	.20
3	Troy Percival	.10
4	Darin Erstad	.25
5	Adam Kennedy	.10
6	Scott Spiezio	.10
7	Ramon Ortiz	.10
8	Ismael Valdes	.10
9	Jarrod Washburn	.10
10	Garret Anderson	.10
11	David Eckstein	.10
12	Mo Vaughn	.25
13	Benji Gil	.10
14	Bengie Molina	.10
15	Scott Schoeneweis	.10
16	Troy Glaus, Ramon Ortiz	.20
17	David Justice	.25
18	Jermaine Dye	.10
19	Eric Chavez	.25
20	Jeremy Giambi	.10
21	Terrence Long	.10
22	Miguel Tejada	.20
23	Johnny Damon	.10
24	Jason Hart	.10
25	Adam Piatt	.10
26	Billy Koch	.10
27	Ramon Hernandez	.10
28	Eric Byrnes	.10
29	Olmedo Saenz	.10
30	Barry Zito	.20
31	Tim Hudson	.25
32	Mark Mulder	.25
33	Jason Giambi, Mark Mulder	.25
34	Carlos Delgado	.40
35	Shannon Stewart	.10
36	Vernon Wells	.10
37	Homer Bush	.10
38	Brad Fullmer	.10
39	Jose Cruz	.10
40	Felipe Lopez	.10
41	Raul Mondesi	.20
42	Esteban Loaiza	.10
43	Darrin Fletcher	.10
44	Mike Sirotka	.10
45	Luke Prokopec	.10
46	Chris Carpenter	.10
47	Roy Halladay	.10
48	Kelvim Escobar	.10
49	Carlos Delgado, Billy Koch	.20
50	Nick Bierbrodt	.10
51	Greg Vaughn	.10
52	Ben Grieve	.10
53	Damian Rolls	.10
54	Russ Johnson	.10
55	Brent Abernathy	.10
56	Steve Cox	.10
57	Aubrey Huff	.10
58	Randy Winn	.10
59	Jason Tyner	.10
60	Tanyon Sturtze	.10
61	Joe Kennedy	.10
62	Jared Sandberg	.10
63	Esteban Yan	.10
64	Ryan Rupe	.10
65	Toby Hall	.10
66	Greg Vaughn, Tanyon Sturtze	.10
67	Matt Lawton	.10
68	Juan Gonzalez	.40
69	Jim Thome	.25
70	Einar Diaz	.10
71	Ellis Burks	.10
72	Kenny Lofton	.10
73	Omar Vizquel	.10
74	Russell Branyan	.10
75	Brady Anderson	.10
76	John Rocker	.10
77	Travis Fryman	.10
78	Wil Cordero	.10
79	Chuck Finley	.10
80	C.C. Sabathia	.10
81	Bartolo Colon	.10
82	Bob Wickman	.10
83	Roberto Alomar, C.C. Sabathia	.20
84	Ichiro Suzuki	1.50
85	Edgar Martinez	.10
86	Aaron Sele	.10
87	Carlos Guillen	.10
88	Bret Boone	.10
89	John Olerud	.20
90	Jamie Moyer	.10
91	Ben Davis	.10
92	Dan Wilson	.10
93	Jeff Cirillo	.10
94	John Halama	.10
95	Freddy Garcia	.10
96	Kazuhiro Sasaki	.10
97	Mike Cameron	.10
98	Paul Abbott	.10
99	Mark McLemore	.10
100	Ichiro Suzuki, Freddy Garcia	.50
101	Jeff Conine	.10
102	David Segui	.10
103	Marty Cordova	.10
104	Tony Batista	.10
105	Chris Richard	.10
106	Willis Roberts	.10
107	Melvin Mora	.10
108	Mike Bordick	.10
109	Jay Gibbons	.10
110	Mike Kinkade	.10
111	Brian Roberts	.10
112	Jerry Hairston Jr.	.10
113	Jason Johnson	.10
114	Josh Towers	.10
115	Calvin Maduro	.10
116	Sidney Ponson	.10
117	Jeff Conine, Jason Johnson	.10
118	Alex Rodriguez	1.00
119	Ivan Rodriguez	.40
120	Frank Catalanotto	.10
121	Mike Lamb	.10
122	Ruben Sierra	.10
123	Rusty Greer	.10
124	Rafael Palmeiro	.20
125	Gabe Kapler	.15
126	Aaron Myette	.10
127	Kenny Rogers	.10
128	Carl Everett	.10
129	Rick Helling	.10
130	Ricky Ledee	.10
131	Michael Young	.10
132	Doug Davis	.10
133	Jeff Zimmerman	.10
134	Alex Rodriguez, Rick Helling	.40
135	Manny Ramirez	.40
136	Nomar Garciaparra	1.00
137	Jason Varitek	.10
138	Dante Bichette	.10
139	Tony Clark	.10
140	Scott Hatteberg	.10
141	Trot Nixon	.10
142	Hideo Nomo	.25
143	Dustin Hermanson	.10
144	Chris Stynes	.10
145	Jose Offerman	.10
146	Pedro Martinez	.50
147	Shea Hillenbrand	.10
148	Tim Wakefield	.10
149	Troy O'Leary	.10
150	Ugueth Urbina	.10
151	Manny Ramirez, Hideo Nomo	.25
152	Carlos Beltran	.10
153	Dee Brown	.10
154	Mike Sweeney	.10
155	Luis Alicea	.10
156	Raul Ibanez	.10
157	Mark Quinn	.10
158	Joe Randa	.10
159	Roberto Hernandez	.10
160	Neifi Perez	.10
161	Carlos Febles	.10
162	Jeff Suppan	.10
163	Dave McCarty	.10
164	Blake Stein	.10
165	Chad Durbin	.10
166	Paul Byrd	.10
167	Carlos Beltran, Jeff Suppan	.10
168	Craig Paquette	.10
169	Dean Palmer	.10
170	Shane Halter	.10
171	Bobby Higginson	.10
172	Robert Fick	.10
173	Jose Macias	.10
174	Deivi Cruz	.10
175	Damion Easley	.10

176 Brandon Inge .10
177 Mark Redman .10
178 Dmitri Young .10
179 Steve Sparks .10
180 Jeff Weaver .10
181 Victor Santos .10
182 Jose Lima .10
183 Matt Anderson .10
184 Roger Cedeno, Steve Sparks .10
185 Doug Mientkiewicz .10
186 Cristian Guzman .10
187 Torii Hunter .10
188 Matt LeCroy .10
189 Corey Koskie .10
190 Jacque Jones .10
191 Luis Rivas .10
192 David Ortiz .10
193 A.J. Pierzynski .10
194 Brian Buchanan .10
195 Joe Mays .10
196 Brad Radke .10
197 Denny Hocking .10
198 Eric Milton .10
199 LaTroy Hawkins .10
200 Doug Mientkiewicz, Joe Mays .10
201 Magglio Ordonez .20
202 Jose Valentin .10
203 Chris Singleton .10
204 Aaron Rowand .10
205 Paul Konerko .10
206 Carlos Lee .10
207 Ray Durham .10
208 Keith Foulke .10
209 Todd Ritchie .10
210 Royce Clayton .10
211 Jose Canseco .20
212 Frank Thomas .40
213 David Wells .10
214 Mark Buehrle .10
215 Jon Garland .10
216 Magglio Ordonez, Mark Buehrle .15
217 Derek Jeter 1.50
218 Bernie Williams .30
219 Rondell White .10
220 Jorge Posada .20
221 Alfonso Soriano .50
222 Ramiro Mendoza .10
223 Jason Giambi .75
224 John Vander Wal .10
225 Steve Karsay .10
226 Nick Johnson .10
227 Mariano Rivera .20
228 Orlando Hernandez .10
229 Andy Pettitte .20
230 Robin Ventura .10
231 Roger Clemens .60
232 Mike Mussina .40
233 Derek Jeter, Roger Clemens .50
234 Moises Alou .20
235 Lance Berkman .20
236 Craig Biggio .20
237 Octavio Dotel .10
238 Jeff Bagwell .40
239 Richard Hidalgo .10
240 Morgan Ensberg .10
241 Julio Lugo .10
242 Daryle Ward .10
243 Roy Oswalt .20
244 Billy Wagner .10
245 Brad Ausmus .10
246 Jose Vizcaino .10
247 Wade Miller .10
248 Shane Reynolds .10
249 Jeff Bagwell, Wade Miller .20
250 Chipper Jones .75
251 Brian Jordan .10
252 B.J. Surhoff .10
253 Rafael Furcal .10
254 Julio Franco .10
255 Javy Lopez .10
256 John Burkett .10
257 Andruw Jones .20
258 Marcus Giles .10
259 Wes Helms .10
260 Greg Maddux .75
261 John Smoltz .10
262 Tom Glavine .20
263 Vinny Castilla .10
264 Kevin Millwood .10
265 Jason Marquis .10
266 Chipper Jones, Greg Maddux .40
267 Tyler Houston .10
268 Mark Loretta .10
269 Richie Sexson .20
270 Jeromy Burnitz .10
271 Jimmy Haynes .10
272 Geoff Jenkins .20
273 Ron Belliard .10
274 Jose Hernandez .10
275 Jeffrey Hammonds .10
276 Curtis Leskanic .10
277 Devon White .10
278 Ben Sheets .20
279 Henry Blanco .10
280 Jamey Wright .10
281 Allen Levrault .10
282 Jeff D'Amico .10
283 Richie Sexson, Jimmy Haynes .10
284 Albert Pujols .75
285 Jason Isringhausen .10
286 J.D. Drew .25
287 Placido Polanco .10
288 Jim Edmonds .20
289 Fernando Vina .10
290 Edgar Renteria .10
291 Mike Matheny .10
292 Bud Smith .10
293 Mike Defelice .10
294 Woody Williams .10
295 Eli Marrero .10
296 Matt Morris .10
297 Darryl Kile .10
298 Kerry Robinson .10
299 Luis Saturria .10
300 Albert Pujols, Matt Morris .40
301 Sammy Sosa .75
302 Michael Tucker .10
303 Bill Mueller .10
304 Ricky Gutierrez .10
305 Fred McGriff .20
306 Eric Young .10
307 Corey Patterson .10
308 Alex Gonzalez .10
309 Ron Coomer .10
310 Kerry Wood .20
311 Delino DeShields .10
312 Jon Lieber .10
313 Tom Gordon .10
314 Todd Hundley .10
315 Jason Bere .10
316 Kevin Tapani .10
317 Sammy Sosa, Jon Lieber .40
318 Steve Finley .10
319 Luis Gonzalez .25
320 Mark Grace .25
321 Craig Counsell .10
322 Matt Williams .20
323 Tony Womack .10
324 Junior Spivey .10
325 David Dellucci .10
326 Jay Bell .10
327 Curt Schilling .25
328 Randy Johnson .40
329 Danny Bautista .10
330 Miguel Batista .10
331 Erubiel Durazo .10
332 Brian Anderson .10
333 Byung-Hyun Kim .10
334 Luis Gonzalez, Curt Schilling .20
335 Paul LoDuca .10
336 Gary Sheffield .20
337 Shawn Green .25
338 Adrian Beltre .20
339 Darren Dreifort .10
340 Mark Grudzielanek .10
341 Eric Karros .10
342 Cesar Izturis .10
343 Tom Goodwin .10
344 Marquis Grissom .10
345 Kevin Brown .20
346 James Baldwin .10
347 Terry Adams .10
348 Alex Cora .10
349 Andy Ashby .10
350 Chan Ho Park .20
351 Shawn Green, Chan Ho Park .20
352 Jose Vidro .10
353 Vladimir Guerrero .40
354 Orlando Cabrera .10
355 Fernando Tatis .10
356 Michael Barrett .10
357 Lee Stevens .10
358 Geoff Blum .10
359 Brad Wilkerson .10
360 Peter Bergeron .10
361 Javier Vazquez .10
362 Tony Armas Jr. .10
363 Tomokazu Ohka .10
364 Scott Strickland .10
365 Vladimir Guerrero, Javier Vazquez .20
366 Barry Bonds .75
367 Rich Aurilia .10
368 Jeff Kent .10
369 Andres Galarraga .20
370 Desi Relaford .10
371 Shawon Dunston .10
372 Benito Santiago .10
373 Tsuyoshi Shinjo .10
374 Calvin Murray .10
375 Marvin Benard .10
376 J.T. Snow .10
377 Livan Hernandez .10
378 Russ Ortiz .10
379 Robb Nen .10
380 Jason Schmidt .10
381 Barry Bonds, Russ Ortiz .30
382 Cliff Floyd .10
383 Antonio Alfonseca .10
384 Mike Redmond .10
385 Mike Lowell .10
386 Derrek Lee .10
387 Preston Wilson .10
388 Luis Castillo .10
389 Charles Johnson .10
390 Eric Owens .10
391 Alex Gonzalez .10
392 Josh Beckett .10
393 Brad Penny .10
394 Ryan Dempster .10
395 Matt Clement .10
396 A.J. Burnett .10
397 Cliff Floyd, Ryan Dempster .10
398 Mike Piazza 1.00
399 Joe McEwing .10
400 Todd Zeile .10
401 Jay Payton .10
402 Roger Cedeno .10
403 Rey Ordonez .10
404 Edgardo Alfonzo .10
405 Roberto Alomar .30
406 Glendon Rusch .10
407 Timo Perez .10
408 Al Leiter .15
409 Lenny Harris .10
410 Shawn Estes .10
411 Armando Benitez .10
412 Kevin Appier .10
413 Bruce Chen .10
414 Mike Piazza, Al Leiter .40
415 Phil Nevin .10
416 Ryan Klesko .10
417 Mark Kotsay .10
418 Ray Lankford .10
419 Mike Darr .10
420 D'Angelo Jimenez .10
421 Bubba Trammell .10
422 Adam Eaton .10
423 Ramon Vazquez .10
424 Cesar Crespo .10
425 Trevor Hoffman .10
426 Kevin Jarvis .10
427 Wiki Gonzalez .10
428 Damian Jackson .10
429 Brian Lawrence .10
430 Phil Nevin, Trevor Hoffman .10
431 Scott Rolen .25
432 Marlon Anderson .10
433 Bobby Abreu .10
434 Jimmy Rollins .20
435 Doug Glanville .10
436 Travis Lee .10
437 Brandon Duckworth .10
438 Pat Burrell .25
439 Kevin Jordan .10
440 Robert Person .10
441 Johnny Estrada .10
442 Randy Wolf .10
443 Jose Mesa .10
444 Mike Lieberthal .10
445 Bobby Abreu, Robert Person .10
446 Brian Giles .20
447 Jason Kendall .10
448 Aramis Ramirez .10
449 Rob Mackowiak .10
450 Abraham Nunez .10
451 Pat Meares .10
452 Craig Wilson .10
453 Jack Wilson .10
454 Gary Matthews Jr. .10
455 Kevin Young .10
456 Derek Bell .10
457 Kip Wells .10
458 Jimmy Anderson .10
459 Kris Benson .10
460 Brian Giles, Todd Ritchie .10
461 Sean Casey .20
462 Wilton Guerrero .10
463 Jason LaRue .10
464 Juan Encarnacion .10
465 Todd Walker .10
466 Aaron Boone .10
467 Pete Harnisch .10
468 Ken Griffey Jr. 1.00
469 Adam Dunn .40
470 Barry Larkin .20
471 Kelly Stinnett .10
472 Pokey Reese .10
473 Brady Clark .10
474 Scott Williamson .10
475 Danny Graves .10
476 Ken Griffey Jr., Elmer Dessens .10
477 Larry Walker .25
478 Todd Helton .40
479 Juan Pierre .10
480 Juan Uribe .10
481 Mario Encarnacion .10
482 Jose Ortiz .10
483 Todd Hollandsworth .10
484 Alex Ochoa .10
485 Mike Hampton .10
486 Terry Shumpert .10
487 Denny Neagle .10
488 Jose Jimenez .10
489 Jason Jennings .10
490 Todd Helton, Mike Hampton .20
491 Tim Redding .10
492 Mark Teixeira 2.00
493 Alex Cintron .10
494 Tim Raines Jr. .10
495 Juan Cruz .20
496 Joe Crede .10
497 Steve Green .10
498 Mike Rivera .10
499 Mark Prior 1.00
500 Ken Harvey .10
501 Tim Spooneybarger .10
502 Adam Everett .10
503 Jason Standridge .10
504 Nick Neugebauer .10
505 Adam Johnson .10
506 Sean Douglass .10
507 Brandon Berger .10
508 Alex Escobar .10
509 Doug Nickle .10
510 Jason Middlebrook .10
511 Dewon Brazelton .10
512 Yorvit Torrealba .10
513 Henry Mateo .10
514 Dennis Tankersley .10
515 Marlon Byrd .75
516 Andy Barkett .10
517 Orlando Hudson .10
518 Josh Fogg .10
519 Ryan Drese .10
520 Mike MacDougal .10
521 Luis Pineda .10
522 Jack Cust .10
523 Kurt Ainsworth .10
524 Bart Miadich .10
525 Dernell Stenson .10
526 Carlos Zambrano .10
527 Austin Kearns .50
528 Larry Barnes .10
529 Mike Cuddyer .10
530 Carlos Pena .75
531 Derek Jeter 1.00
532 Ken Griffey Jr. .75
533 Manny Ramirez .25
534 Luis Gonzalez .20
535 Sammy Sosa .50
536 Roger Clemens .40
537 Phil Nevin .10
538 Mike Piazza .75
539 Alex Rodriguez .75
540 Jason Giambi .50
541 Randy Johnson .25
542 Albert Pujols .50
543 Jeff Bagwell .25
544 Shawn Green .15
545 Carlos Delgado .15
546 Pedro Martinez .25
547 Todd Helton .25
548 Roberto Alomar .20
549 Barry Bonds .40
550 Ichiro Suzuki 1.00

Gold

Stars: 3-6X
Inserted 1:2

2002 Upper Deck Vintage

NM/M

Complete Set (300): 30.00
Common Player: .10
Pack (10): 2.00
Box (24): 35.00

1 Darin Erstad .20
2 Mo Vaughn .20
3 Ramon Ortiz .10
4 Garret Anderson .25
5 Troy Glaus .40
6 Troy Percival .10
7 Tim Salmon .20
8 Wilmy Caceres, Elpidio Guzman .10
9 2001 Anaheim Angels .10
10 Jason Giambi .50
11 Mark Mulder .25
12 Jermaine Dye .10
13 Miguel Tejada .40
14 Tim Hudson .25
15 Eric Chavez .25
16 Barry Zito .25
17 Oscar Salazar, Juan Pena .10
18 2001 Oakland Athletics .10
19 Carlos Delgado .40
20 Raul Mondesi .15
21 Chris Carpenter .10
22 Jose Cruz Jr. .10
23 Alex Gonzalez .10

24	Brad Fullmer	.10
25	Shannon Stewart	.10
26	Brandon Lyon, Vernon Wells	.10
27	2001 Toronto Blue Jays	.10
28	Greg Vaughn	.10
29	Toby Hall	.10
30	Ben Grieve	.10
31	Aubrey Huff	.10
32	Tanyon Sturtze	.10
33	Brent Abernathy	.10
34	Dewon Brazelton, Delvin James	.10
35	2001 Tampa Bay Devil Rays	.10
36	Roberto Alomar	.40
37	Juan Gonzalez	.50
38	Bartolo Colon	.25
39	C.C. Sabathia	.10
40	Jim Thome	.75
41	Omar Vizquel	.20
42	Russell Branyan	.10
43	Ryan Drese, Roy Smith	.10
44	2001 Cleveland Indians	.10
45	Edgar Martinez	.20
46	Bret Boone	.20
47	Freddy Garcia	.10
48	John Olerud	.25
49	Kazuhiro Sasaki	.10
50	Ichiro Suzuki	1.50
51	Mike Cameron	.10
52	Rafael Soriano, Dennis Stark	.10
53	2001 Seattle Mariners	.10
54	Tony Batista	.10
55	Jeff Conine	.10
56	Jason Johnson	.10
57	Jay Gibbons	.10
58	Chris Richard	.10
59	Josh Towers	.10
60	Jerry Hairston Jr.	.10
61	Sean Douglass, Tim Raines Jr.	.10
62	2001 Baltimore Orioles	.10
63	Alex Rodriguez	1.50
64	Ruben Sierra	.10
65	Ivan Rodriguez	.50
66	Gabe Kapler	.20
67	Rafael Palmeiro	.50
68	Frank Catalanotto	.10
69	Mark Teixeira, Carlos Pena	.40
70	2001 Texas Rangers	.10
71	Nomar Garciaparra	1.00
72	Pedro Martinez	.75
73	Trot Nixon	.10
74	Dante Bichette	.10
75	Manny Ramirez	.50
76	Carl Everett	.10
77	Hideo Nomo	.40
78	Dernell Stenson, Juan Diaz	.10
79	2001 Boston Red Sox	.10
80	Mike Sweeney	.10
81	Carlos Febles	.10
82	Dee Brown	.10
83	Neifi Perez	.10
84	Mark Quinn	.10
85	Carlos Beltran	.25
86	Joe Randa	.10
87	Ken Harvey, Mike MacDougal	.10
88	2001 Kansas City Royals	.10
89	Dean Palmer	.10
90	Jeff Weaver	.10
91	Jose Lima	.10
92	Tony Clark	.10
93	Damion Easley	.10
94	Bobby Higginson	.10
95	Robert Fick	.10
96	Pedro Santana, Mike Rivera	.10
97	2001 Detroit Tigers	.10
98	Doug Mientkiewicz	.10
99	David Ortiz	.25
100	Joe Mays	.10
101	Corey Koskie	.10
102	Eric Milton	.10
103	Cristian Guzman	.10
104	Brad Radke	.10
105	Adam Johnson, Juan Rincon	.10
106	2001 Minnesota Twins	.10
107	Frank Thomas	.50
108	Carlos Lee	.10
109	Mark Buehrle	.10
110	Jose Canseco	.25
111	Magglio Ordonez	.25
112	Jon Garland	.10
113	Ray Durham	.10
114	Joe Crede, Josh Fogg	.10
115	2001 Chicago White Sox	.10
116	Derek Jeter	2.00
117	Roger Clemens	1.50
118	Alfonso Soriano	.75
119	Paul O'Neill	.25
120	Jorge Posada	.25
121	Bernie Williams	.40
122	Mariano Rivera	.25
123	Tino Martinez	.20
124	Mike Mussina	.50
125	Nick Johnson, Erick Almonte	.10
126	2001 New York Yankees	.10
127	Jeff Bagwell	.50
128	Wade Miller	.10
129	Lance Berkman	.25
130	Moises Alou	.25
131	Craig Biggio	.20
132	Roy Oswalt	.20
133	Richard Hidalgo	.15
134	Morgan Ensberg, Tim Redding	.10
135	2001 Houston Astros	.10
136	Greg Maddux	1.00
137	Chipper Jones	.75
138	Brian Jordan	.10
139	Marcus Giles	.10
140	Andruw Jones	.40
141	Tom Glavine	.40
142	Rafael Furcal	.25
143	Wilson Betemit, Horacio Ramirez	.10
144	2001 Atlanta Braves	.10
145	Jeromy Burnitz	.10
146	Ben Sheets	.25
147	Geoff Jenkins	.20
148	Devon White	.10
149	Jimmy Haynes	.10
150	Richie Sexson	.40
151	Jose Hernandez	.10
152	Jose Mieses, Alex Sanchez	.10
153	2001 Milwaukee Brewers	.10
154	Mark McGwire	2.00
155	Albert Pujols	1.50
156	Matt Morris	.20
157	J.D. Drew	.25
158	Jim Edmonds	.25
159	Bud Smith	.10
160	Darryl Kile	.10
161	William Ortega, Luis Saturria	.10
162	2001 St. Louis Cardinals	.10
163	Sammy Sosa	1.00
164	Jon Lieber	.10
165	Eric Young	.10
166	Kerry Wood	.75
167	Fred McGriff	.25
168	Corey Patterson	.25
169	Rondell White	.15
170	Juan Cruz, Mark Prior	1.00
171	2001 Chicago Cubs	.10
172	Luis Gonzalez	.25
173	Randy Johnson	.75
174	Matt Williams	.20
175	Mark Grace	.25
176	Steve Finley	.10
177	Reggie Sanders	.10
178	Curt Schilling	.40
179	Alex Cintron, Jack Cust	.10
180	2001 Arizona Diamondbacks	.10
181	Gary Sheffield	.25
182	Paul LoDuca	.10
183	Chan Ho Park	.10
184	Shawn Green	.25
185	Eric Karros	.15
186	Adrian Beltre	.25
187	Kevin Brown	.25
188	Ricardo Rodriguez, Carlos Garcia	.10
189	2001 Los Angeles Dodgers	.10
190	Vladimir Guerrero	.75
191	Javier Vazquez	.10
192	Jose Vidro	.10
193	Fernando Tatis	.10
194	Orlando Cabrera	.10
195	Lee Stevens	.10
196	Tony Armas Jr.	.10
197	Donnie Bridges, Henry Mateo	.10
198	2001 Montreal Expos	.10
199	Barry Bonds	2.00
200	Rich Aurilia	.10
201	Russ Ortiz	.10
202	Jeff Kent	.20
203	Jason Schmidt	.25
204	John Vander Wal	.10
205	Robb Nen	.10
206	Yorvit Torrealba, Kurt Ainsworth	.10
207	2001 San Francisco Giants	.10
208	Preston Wilson	.10
209	Brad Penny	.10
210	Cliff Floyd	.10
211	Luis Castillo	.10
212	Ryan Dempster	.10
213	Charles Johnson	.10
214	A.J. Burnett	.10
215	Abraham Nunez, Josh Beckett	.20
216	2001 Florida Marlins	.10
217	Mike Piazza	1.00
218	Al Leiter	.20
219	Edgardo Alfonzo	.10
220	Tsuyoshi Shinjo	.10
221	Matt Lawton	.10
222	Robin Ventura	.15
223	Jay Payton	.10
224	Alex Escobar, Jae Weong Seo	.10
225	2001 New York Mets	.10
226	Ryan Klesko	.20
227	D'Angelo Jimenez	.10
228	Trevor Hoffman	.10
229	Phil Nevin	.10
230	Mark Kotsay	.10
231	Brian Lawrence	.10
232	Bubba Trammell	.10
233	Jason Middlebrook, Xavier Nady	.10
234	2001 San Diego Padres	.10
235	Scott Rolen	.75
236	Jimmy Rollins	.25
237	Mike Lieberthal	.10
238	Bobby Abreu	.25
239	Brandon Duckworth	.10
240	Robert Person	.10
241	Pat Burrell	.20
242	Nick Punto, Carlos Silva	.10
243	2001 Philadelphia Phillies	.10
244	Brian Giles	.20
245	Jack Wilson	.10
246	Kris Benson	.10
247	Jason Kendall	.20
248	Aramis Ramirez	.25
249	Todd Ritchie	.10
250	Robert Mackowiak	.10
251	John Grabow, Humberto Cota	.10
252	2001 Pittsburgh Pirates	.10
253	Ken Griffey Jr.	1.00
254	Barry Larkin	.25
255	Sean Casey	.25
256	Aaron Boone	.10
257	Dmitri Young	.10
258	Pokey Reese	.10
259	Adam Dunn	.50
260	David Espinosa, Dane Sardinha	.10
261	2001 Cincinnati Reds	.10
262	Todd Helton	.50
263	Mike Hampton	.20
264	Juan Pierre	.10
265	Larry Walker	.25
266	Juan Uribe	.10
267	Jose Ortiz	.10
268	Jeff Cirillo	.10
269	Jason Jennings, Luke Hudson	.10
270	2001 Colorado Rockies	.10
271	Ichiro Suzuki, Jason Giambi, Roberto Alomar (League Leaders)	.75
272	Larry Walker, Todd Helton, Moises Alou (League Leaders)	.10
273	Alex Rodriguez, Jim Thome, Rafael Palmeiro (League Leaders)	.75
274a	Barry Bonds, Sammy Sosa, Juan Gonzalez (League Leaders)(No player names.))	1.00
274b	Barry Bonds, Sammy Sosa, Juan Gonzalez (League Leaders) (Player names added.)	3.00
275	Roger Clemens, Mark Mulder, Jamie Moyer (League Leaders)	.50
276	Curt Schilling, Matt Morris, Randy Johnson (League Leaders)	.10
277	Freddy Garcia, Mike Mussina, Joe Mays (League Leaders)	.10
278	Randy Johnson, Curt Schilling, John Burkett (League Leaders)	.10
279	Mariano Rivera, Kazuhiro Sasaki, Keith Foulke (League Leaders)	.10
280	Robb Nen, Armando Benitez, Trevor Hoffman (League Leaders)	.10
281	Jason Giambi	.25
282	Jorge Posada	.15
283	Jim Thome	.25
284	Edgar Martinez	.10
285	Andruw Jones	.20
286	Chipper Jones	.50
287	Matt Williams	.15
288	Curt Schilling	.20
289	Derek Jeter	1.00
290	Mike Mussina	.25
291	Bret Boone	.10
292	Alfonso Soriano	.40
293	Randy Johnson	.25
294	Tom Glavine	.20
295	Curt Schilling	.25
296	Randy Johnson	.40
297	Derek Jeter	1.00
298	Tino Martinez	.10
299	Curt Schilling	.20
300	Luis Gonzalez	.20

Day at the Park

		NM/M
Complete Set (6):		15.00
Inserted 1:23		
DP1	Ichiro Suzuki	3.00
DP2	Derek Jeter	5.00
DP3	Alex Rodriguez	4.00
DP4	Mark McGwire	4.00
DP5	Barry Bonds	5.00
DP6	Sammy Sosa	3.00

Night-Gamers

		NM/M
Complete Set (12):		10.00
Common Player:		.50
Inserted 1:11		
NG1	Todd Helton	.75
NG2	Manny Ramirez	.75
NG3	Ivan Rodriguez	.50
NG4	Albert Pujols	2.50
NG5	Greg Maddux	1.50
NG6	Carlos Delgado	.50
NG7	Frank Thomas	.75
NG8	Derek Jeter	3.00

NG9	Troy Glaus	.50
NG10	Jeff Bagwell	.75
NG11	Juan Gonzalez	.75
NG12	Randy Johnson	1.00

Sandlot Stars

		NM/M
Complete Set (12):		15.00
Common Player:		.75
Inserted 1:11		
SS1	Ken Griffey Jr.	1.50
SS2	Derek Jeter	3.00
SS3	Ichiro Suzuki	2.00
SS4	Nomar Garciaparra	2.00
SS5	Sammy Sosa	2.00
SS6	Chipper Jones	1.00
SS7	Jason Giambi	.75
SS8	Alex Rodriguez	2.50
SS9	Mark McGwire	2.50
SS10	Barry Bonds	3.00
SS11	Mike Piazza	2.00
SS12	Vladimir Guerrero	1.00

Special Collection Jerseys

		NM/M
Common Player:		8.00
Inserted 1:144		
StB	Stan Bahnsen	8.00
SaB	Sal Bando	10.00
BC	Bert Campaneris	10.00
AD	Andre Dawson	15.00
RF	Rollie Fingers	15.00
MG	Mark Grace	15.00
MH	Mike Hegan	8.00
CH	"Catfish" Hunter	20.00
RJ	Reggie Jackson	15.00
FJ	Ferguson Jenkins	15.00
PL	Paul Linblad	8.00
JR	Joe Rudi	10.00
RS	Ryne Sandberg	50.00
SS	Sammy Sosa	25.00
BW	Billy Williams	10.00

Timeless Teams Jerseys

		NM/M
Common Player:		10.00
Inserted 1:144		
JB	Johnny Bench	20.00
DE	Dwight Evans	15.00
RF	Rollie Fingers	15.00
CH	"Catfish" Hunter	15.00
RJ	Reggie Jackson	15.00
AJ	Andruw Jones	15.00
CJ	Chipper Jones	15.00
FL	Fred Lynn	15.00
EMa	Edgar Martinez	15.00
WM	Willie McCovey	15.00
EMu	Eddie Murray	15.00
KS	Kazuhiro Sasaki	10.00

Timeless Teams Combos

		NM/M
Inserted 1:288		
NYY00	Roger Clemens, Mariano Rivera, Bernie Williams	40.00

ATL96	Greg Maddux, Chipper Jones, Andruw Jones	40.00
OAK74	Rollie Fingers, Jim "Catfish" Hunter, Reggie Jackson	40.00
HOF36	Ty Cobb, Babe Ruth, Honus Wagner (Pants)	1,500

Timeless Teams Bat

NM/M
Inserted 1:288

SEA	Ichiro Suzuki, Edgar Martinez, John Olerud, Bret Boone	75.00
NYY	Mariano Rivera, Bernie Williams, Paul O'Neill, Jorge Posada	40.00
ATL	Greg Maddux, Chipper Jones, Andruw Jones, Tom Glavine	40.00
CLE	Juan Gonzalez, Jim Thome, Roberto Alomar, Kenny Lofton	30.00
OAK	Jose Canseco, Ricky Henderson, Dave Parker, Don Baylor	30.00
OF	Mickey Mantle, Joe DiMaggio, Reggie Jackson, Babe Ruth	300.00
1B	Willie McCovey, Frank Thomas, Hank Greenberg, Eddie Murray	30.00
OF	Ken Griffey Jr., Barry Bonds, Ricky Henderson, Tony Gwynn	50.00

Vintage Aces Jerseys

NM/M
Common Player: 8.00
Inserted 1:144

JD	John Denny	8.00
TH	Tim Hudson	10.00
FJ	Ferguson Jenkins	10.00
RJ	Randy Johnson	20.00
GM	Greg Maddux	25.00
JM	Juan Marichal	15.00
MMa	Mike Marshall	8.00
PM	Pedro Martinez	20.00
MMu	Mike Mussina	25.00
HN	Hideo Nomo	20.00
NR	Nolan Ryan	100.00
JS	Johnny Sain	20.00
MT	Mike Torrez	8.00

Vintage Signature Combos

NM/M
Production 100 Sets

FB	Carlton Fisk, Johnny Bench	100.00
JM	Reggie Jackson, Willie McCovey	80.00
SD	Ryne Sandberg, Andre Dawson	100.00
BR	Sal Bando, Joe Rudi	40.00
EL	Dwight Evans, Fred Lynn	60.00
AT	Roberto Alomar, Jim Thome	75.00
BB	Yogi Berra, Johnny Bench	100.00
GR	Ken Griffey Jr., Alex Rodriguez	300.00
JO	Edgar Martinez, John Olerud	60.00

2002 Upper Deck World Series Heroes

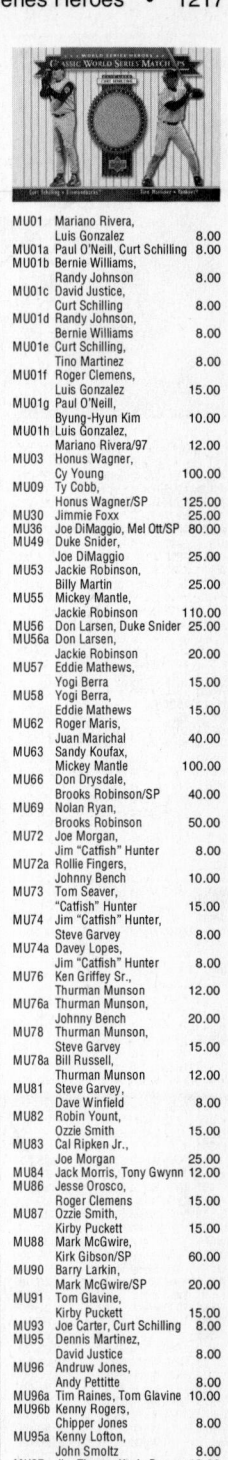

NM/M
Complete Set (180): 20.00
Common Player: .15

Common RC (91-135):		1.50
Common (136-180):		1.00
Inserted 1:10		
Pack (5):		2.00
Box (24):		40.00
1	Jim "Catfish" Hunter	.15
2	Jimmie Foxx	.50
3	Mark McGwire	2.00
4	Rollie Fingers	.25
5	Rickey Henderson	.40
6	Joe Carter	.15
7	John Olerud	.15
8	Roberto Alomar	.50
9	Pat Hentgen	.15
10	Devon White	.15
11	Eddie Mathews	.50
12	Greg Maddux	1.00
13	Chipper Jones	.75
14	Tom Glavine	.25
15	Andruw Jones	.50
16	David Justice	.25
17	Fred McGriff	.15
18	Ryan Klesko	.15
19	John Smoltz	.25
20	Javy Lopez	.25
21	Marquis Grissom	.15
22	Robin Yount	.75
23	Ozzie Smith	.75
24	Frankie Frisch	.15
25	Stan Musial	1.00
26	Randy Johnson	.75
27	Luis Gonzalez	.25
28	Matt Williams	.15
29	Steve Finley	.15
30	Sandy Koufax	1.50
31	Duke Snider	.50
32	Kirk Gibson	.15
33	Steve Garvey	.15
34	Jackie Robinson	1.50
35	Don Drysdale	.50
36	Juan Marichal	.50
37	Mel Ott	.50
38	Orlando Cepeda	.15
39	Jim Thome	.75
40	Manny Ramirez	.50
41	Omar Vizquel	.15
42	Lou Boudreau	.25
43	Gary Sheffield	.25
44	Moises Alou	.25
45	Livan Hernandez	.15
46	Edgar Renteria	.25
47	Al Leiter	.15
48	Tom Seaver	.75
49	Gary Carter	.15
50	Mike Piazza	1.00
51	Nolan Ryan	2.00
52	Robin Ventura	.15
53	Mike Hampton	.15
54	Jesse Orosco	.15
55	Cal Ripken Jr.	2.00
56	Brooks Robinson	.75
57	Tony Gwynn	.75
58	Kevin Brown	.15
59	Curt Schilling	.50
60	Cy Young	.50
61	Honus Wagner	.75
62	Willie Stargell	.40
63	Wade Boggs	.40
64	Carlton Fisk	.40
65	Ken Griffey Sr.	.15
66	Joe Morgan	.25
67	Johnny Bench	1.00
68	Barry Larkin	.40
69	Jose Rijo	.15
70	Ty Cobb	1.50
71	Kirby Puckett	1.00
72	Chuck Knoblauch	.15
73	Harmon Killebrew	.50
74	Mickey Mantle	2.50
75	Joe DiMaggio	2.00
76	Don Larsen	.40
77	Thurman Munson	.75
78	Roger Maris	1.50
79	Phil Rizzuto	.50
80	Babe Ruth	2.50
81	Lou Gehrig	2.00
82	Billy Martin	.40
83	Derek Jeter	2.00
84	Roger Clemens	1.50
85	Tino Martinez	.15
86	Bernie Williams	.50
87	Mariano Rivera	.25
88	Andy Pettitte	.40
89	David Wells	.15
90	Jorge Posada	.40
91	Rodrigo Rosario RC	1.50
92	Brandon Puffer RC	1.50
93	Franklyn German RC	1.50
94	Reed Johnson RC	1.50
95	Chris Baker RC	1.50
96	John Ennis RC	1.50
97	Luis Martinez RC	1.50
98	Takahi Nomura RC	1.50
99	So Taguchi RC	4.00
100	Michael Crudale RC	1.50
101	Francis Beltran RC	1.50
102	Steve Kent RC	1.50
103	Jorge Sosa RC	1.50
104	Felix Escalona RC	1.50
105	Jose Valverde RC	1.50
106	Doug DeVore RC	1.50
107	Kazuhisa Ishii RC	4.00
108	Victor Alvarez RC	1.50
109	Eric Good RC	1.50
110	Jorge Nunez RC	1.50

111	Ron Calloway RC	1.50
112	Nelson Castro RC	1.50
113	Matt Thornton RC	1.50
114	Luis Ugueto RC	1.50
115	Hansel Izquierdo RC	1.50
116	Jaime Cerda RC	1.50
117	Mark Corey RC	1.50
118	Tyler Yates RC	2.50
119	Satoru Komiyama RC	1.50
120	Steve Bechler RC	1.50
121	Ben Howard RC	1.50
122	Anderson Machado RC	1.50
123	Jorge Padilla RC	1.50
124	Eric Junge RC	1.50
125	Adrian Burnside RC	1.50
126	Mike Gonzalez RC	1.50
127	Anastacio Martinez RC	1.50
128	Josh Hancock RC	1.50
129	Rene Reyes RC	1.50
130	Aaron Cook RC	1.50
131	Cam Esslinger RC	1.50
132	Juan Brito RC	1.50
133	Miguel Ascencio RC	1.50
134	Kevin Frederick RC	1.50
135	Edwin Almonte RC	1.50
136	Troy Glaus	1.00
137	Darin Erstad	1.00
138	Jeff Bagwell	1.50
139	Lance Berkman	1.50
140	Tim Hudson	1.25
141	Eric Chavez	1.25
142	Barry Zito	1.50
143	Carlos Delgado	1.00
144	Richie Sexson	1.50
145	Albert Pujols	4.00
146	Sammy Sosa	4.00
147	Kerry Wood	2.00
148	Greg Vaughn	1.00
149	Shawn Green	1.00
150	Vladimir Guerrero	2.50
151	Barry Bonds	6.00
152	C.C. Sabathia	1.00
153	Ichiro Suzuki	5.00
154	Freddy Garcia	1.00
155	Edgar Martinez	1.00
156	Josh Beckett	1.00
157	Cliff Floyd	1.00
158	Mo Vaughn	1.00
159	Jeromy Burnitz	1.00
160	Sean Burroughs	1.00
161	Phil Nevin	1.00
162	Scott Rolen	2.00
163	Brian Giles	1.25
164	Alex Rodriguez	5.00
165	Ivan Rodriguez	1.50
166	Juan Gonzalez	1.25
167	Rafael Palmeiro	1.50
168	Nomar Garciaparra	4.00
169	Pedro J. Martinez	2.00
170	Ken Griffey Jr.	4.00
171	Adam Dunn	1.50
172	Todd Helton	1.50
173	Mike Sweeney	1.00
174	Carlos Beltran	1.00
175	Dmitri Young	1.00
176	Doug Mientkiewicz	1.00
177	Torii Hunter	1.00
178	Frank Thomas	1.50
179	Magglio Ordonez	1.00
180	Jason Giambi	1.50

World Series Heroes Bats

NM/M
Common Player: 15.00
Inserted 1:288

JD	Joe DiMaggio/SP	100.00
MM	Mickey Mantle	125.00
KP	Kirby Puckett	25.00
ES	Enos Slaughter	15.00

World Series Heroes Base

NM/M
Complete Set (1):
DJ Derek Jeter 35.00

World Series Heroes Jerseys

NM/M
Common Player: 10.00
Inserted 1:288

JC	Joe Carter	10.00
CF	Carlton Fisk	15.00
DL	Don Larsen	20.00
BM	Bill Mazeroski	15.00

World Series Heroes Jerseys Autograph

No Pricing
Production 25 Sets

Match-ups Memorabilia

NM/M
Common Card: 8.00
Inserted 1:24

MU00	Mike Piazza, Roger Clemens	15.00
MU00a	Andy Pettitte, Mike Piazza	15.00
MU00b	Al Leiter, Derek Jeter	10.00
MU00d	Edgardo Alfonzo, Mariano Rivera	8.00
MU00e	John Franco, Derek Jeter	10.00
MU00c	Robin Ventura, Roger Clemens	8.00

MU01	Mariano Rivera, Luis Gonzalez	8.00
MU01a	Paul O'Neill, Curt Schilling	8.00
MU01b	Bernie Williams, Randy Johnson	8.00
MU01c	David Justice, Curt Schilling	8.00
MU01d	Randy Johnson, Bernie Williams	8.00
MU01e	Curt Schilling, Tino Martinez	8.00
MU01f	Roger Clemens, Luis Gonzalez	15.00
MU01g	Paul O'Neill, Byung-Hyun Kim	10.00
MU01h	Luis Gonzalez, Mariano Rivera/97	12.00
MU03	Honus Wagner, Cy Young	100.00
MU09	Ty Cobb, Honus Wagner/SP	125.00
MU30	Jimmie Foxx	25.00
MU36	Joe DiMaggio, Mel Ott/SP	80.00
MU49	Duke Snider, Joe DiMaggio	25.00
MU53	Jackie Robinson, Billy Martin	25.00
MU55	Mickey Mantle, Jackie Robinson	110.00
MU56	Don Larsen, Duke Snider	25.00
MU56a	Don Larsen, Jackie Robinson	20.00
MU57	Eddie Mathews, Yogi Berra	15.00
MU58	Yogi Berra, Eddie Mathews	15.00
MU62	Roger Maris, Juan Marichal	40.00
MU63	Sandy Koufax, Mickey Mantle	100.00
MU66	Don Drysdale, Brooks Robinson/SP	40.00
MU69	Nolan Ryan, Brooks Robinson	50.00
MU72	Joe Morgan, Jim "Catfish" Hunter	8.00
MU72a	Rollie Fingers, Johnny Bench	15.00
MU73	Tom Seaver, "Catfish" Hunter	15.00
MU74	Jim "Catfish" Hunter, Steve Garvey	8.00
MU74a	Davey Lopes, Jim "Catfish" Hunter	8.00
MU76	Ken Griffey Sr., Thurman Munson	12.00
MU76a	Thurman Munson, Johnny Bench	20.00
MU78	Thurman Munson, Steve Garvey	15.00
MU78a	Bill Russell, Thurman Munson	12.00
MU81	Steve Garvey, Dave Winfield	8.00
MU82	Robin Yount, Ozzie Smith	15.00
MU83	Cal Ripken Jr., Joe Morgan	25.00
MU84	Jack Morris, Tony Gwynn	12.00
MU86	Jesse Orosco, Roger Clemens	15.00
MU87	Ozzie Smith, Kirby Puckett	15.00
MU88	Mark McGwire, Kirk Gibson/SP	60.00
MU90	Barry Larkin, Mark McGwire/SP	20.00
MU91	Tom Glavine, Kirby Puckett	15.00
MU93	Joe Carter, Curt Schilling	8.00
MU95	Dennis Martinez, David Justice	8.00
MU96	Andruw Jones, Andy Pettitte	15.00
MU96a	Tim Raines, Tom Glavine	10.00
MU96b	Kenny Rogers, Chipper Jones	8.00
MU95a	Kenny Lofton, John Smoltz	8.00
MU97	Jim Thome, Kevin Brown	10.00
MU98	Tony Gwynn, Bernie Williams	10.00
MU98a	Trevor Hoffman, Bernie Williams/SP	8.00
MU99	Jorge Posada, Greg Maddux	15.00
MU99a	Greg Maddux, Derek Jeter	8.00

MU99b Paul O'Neill, John Smoltz 8.00
MU99c Chipper Jones, Mariano Rivera 15.00

Patch Collection

NM/M
Common Patch: 15.00
Inserted 1:Hobby Box

WS03 1903 World Series 25.00
WS05 1905 World Series 25.00
WS06 1906 World Series 20.00
WS07 1907 World Series 20.00
WS08 1908 World Series 25.00
WS09 1909 World Series 20.00
WS10 1910 World Series 20.00
WS11 1911 World Series 20.00
WS12 1912 World Series 30.00
WS13 1913 World Series 20.00
WS14 1914 World Series 25.00
WS15 1915 World Series 20.00
WS16 1916 World Series 20.00
WS17 1917 World Series 20.00
WS18 1918 World Series 30.00
WS19 1919 World Series 20.00
WS20 1920 World Series 20.00
WS21 1921 World Series 15.00
WS22 1922 World Series 20.00
WS23 1923 World Series 20.00
WS24 1924 World Series 25.00
WS25 1925 World Series 25.00
WS26 1926 World Series 25.00
WS27 1927 World Series 30.00
WS28 1928 World Series 20.00
WS29 1929 World Series 20.00
WS30 1930 World Series 20.00
WS31 1931 World Series 25.00
WS32 1932 World Series 30.00
WS33 1933 World Series 20.00
WS34 1934 World Series 20.00
WS35 1935 World Series 20.00
WS36 1936 World Series 20.00
WS37 1937 World Series 20.00
WS38 1938 World Series 25.00
WS39 1939 World Series 20.00
WS40 1940 World Series 20.00
WS41 1941 World Series 20.00
WS42 1942 World Series 20.00
WS43 1943 World Series 20.00
WS44 1944 World Series 30.00
WS45 1945 World Series 25.00
WS46 1946 World Series 25.00
WS47 1947 World Series 25.00
WS48 1948 World Series 30.00
WS49 1949 World Series 25.00
WS50 1950 World Series 25.00
WS51 1951 World Series 25.00
WS52 1952 World Series 20.00
WS53 1953 World Series 25.00
WS54 1954 World Series 15.00
WS55 1955 World Series 25.00
WS56 1956 World Series 25.00
WS57 1957 World Series 25.00
WS58 1958 World Series 20.00
WS59 1959 World Series 20.00
WS60 1960 World Series 20.00
WS61 1961 World Series 35.00
WS62 1962 World Series 20.00
WS63 1963 World Series 20.00
WS64 1964 World Series 20.00
WS65 1965 World Series 20.00
WS66 1966 World Series 20.00
WS67 1967 World Series 20.00
WS68 1968 World Series 20.00
WS69 1969 World Series 35.00
WS70 1970 World Series 20.00
WS71 1971 World Series 20.00
WS72 1972 World Series 20.00
WS73 1973 World Series 20.00
WS74 1974 World Series 30.00
WS75 1975 World Series 30.00
WS76 1976 World Series 30.00
WS77 1977 World Series 20.00
WS78 1978 World Series 20.00
WS79 1979 World Series 20.00
WS80 1980 World Series 20.00
WS81 1981 World Series 20.00
WS82 1982 World Series 25.00
WS83 1983 World Series 20.00
WS84 1984 World Series 20.00
WS85 1985 World Series 20.00
WS86 1986 World Series 20.00

WS87 1987 World Series 20.00
WS88 1988 World Series 20.00
WS89 1989 World Series 20.00
WS90 1990 World Series 20.00
WS91 1991 World Series 20.00
WS92 1992 World Series 20.00
WS93 1993 World Series 20.00
WS95 1995 World Series 20.00
WS96 1996 World Series 20.00
WS97 1997 World Series 20.00
WS98 1998 World Series 15.00
WS99 1999 World Series 20.00
WS01 2001 World Series 20.00

Patch Collection Autographs

NM/M
Inserted 1:336

WS93 Joe Carter 40.00
WS99 Roger Clemens 100.00
WS74 Rollie Fingers 30.00
WS75 Carlton Fisk 60.00
WS81 Steve Garvey 35.00
WS65 Sandy Koufax 250.00
WS56 Don Larsen 60.00
WS89 Mark McGwire 275.00
WS76 Joe Morgan 40.00
WS91 Kirby Puckett 60.00
WS83 Cal Ripken Jr. 175.00
WS70 Brooks Robinson 60.00
WS69 Nolan Ryan 200.00
WS73 Tom Seaver 60.00
WS55 Duke Snider 75.00
WS82 Ozzie Smith 90.00

2002 Upper Deck 40-Man

NM/M
Complete Set (1182): 200.00
Common Player: .15
Silvers: 1-3X
Inserted 1:4
Rainbows: 5-10X
Production 40 Sets
Hobby Pack (10): 1.75
Hobby Box (24): 30.00

1 Darin Erstad .40
2 Kevin Appier .15
3 Scott Schoeneweis .15
4 Bengie Molina .15
5 Troy Glaus .50
6 Adam Kennedy .15
7 Aaron Sele .15
8 Garret Anderson .25
9 Ramon Ortiz .15
10 Dennis Cook .15
11 Scott Spiezio .15
12 Orlando Palmeiro .15
13 Troy Percival .15
14 David Eckstein .15
15 Jarrod Washburn .40
16 Nathan Haynes .15
17 Benji Gil .15
18 Alfredo Amezega .15
19 Ben Weber .15
20 Al Levine .15
21 Brad Fullmer .15
22 Elpidio Guzman .15
23 Tim Salmon .25
24 Jose Nieves .15
25 Shawn Wooten .15
26 Lou Pote .15
27 Mickey Callaway .15
28 Steve Green .15
29 John Lackey .15
30 Mark Lukasiewicz .15
31 Jorge Fabregas .15
32 Jeff Da Vanon .15
33 Elvin Nina .15
34 Donne Wall .15
35 Eric Chavez .50
36 Jermaine Dye .15
37 Scott Hatteberg .15
38 Mark Mulder .50
39 Ramon Hernandez .15
40 Jim Mecir .15
41 Barry Zito .50
42 Greg Myers .15
43 David Justice .50
44 Mike Magnante .15
45 Terrence Long .15
46 Tim Hudson .50
47 Olmedo Saenz .15

48 Billy Koch .15
49 Carlos Pena .50
50 Mike Venafro .15
51 Mark Ellis .15
52 Randy Velarde .15
53 Jeremy Giambi .15
54 Mike Colagelo .15
55 Mike Holtz .15
56 Chad Bradford .15
57 Miguel Tejada .50
58 Mike Fyhrie .15
59 Eric Hiljus .15
60 Juan Pena .15
61 Mario Valdez .15
62 Franklyn German RC .50
63 Carlos Delgado .50
64 Orlando Hudson .15
65 Chris Carpenter .15
66 Kelvim Escobar .15
67 Felipe Lopez .15
68 Brandon Lyon .15
69 Jose Cruz Jr. .15
70 Luke Prokopec .15
71 Darrin Fletcher .15
72 Bob File .15
73 Felix Heredia .15
74 Mike Sirotka .15
75 Shannon Stewart .15
76 Joe Lawrence .15
77 Chris Woodward .15
78 Dan Plesac .15
79 Pedro Borbon .15
80 Roy Halladay .40
81 Raul Mondesi .40
82 Steve Parris .15
83 Homer Bush .15
84 Esteban Loaiza .15
85 Vernon Wells .15
86 Justin Miller .15
87 Scott Eyre .15
88 Dave Berg .15
89 Gustavo Chacin RC .15
90 Joe Orloski RC .40
91 Corey Thurman RC .15
92 Tom Wilson .15
93 Eric Hinske .50
94 Chris Baker RC .40
95 Reed Johnson RC .40
96 Greg Vaughn .15
97 Toby Hall .15
98 Brent Abernathy .15
99 Bobby Smith .15
100 Tanyon Sturtze .15
101 Chris Gomez .15
102 Joe Kennedy .15
103 Ben Grieve .15
104 Aubrey Huff .15
105 Jesus Colome .15
106 Felix Escalona RC .40
107 Paul Wilson .15
108 Ryan Rupe .15
109 Jason Tyner .15
110 Esteban Yan .15
111 Russ Johnson .15
112 Randy Winn .15
113 Wilson Alvarez .15
114 Wilmy Caceres .15
115 Steve Cox .15
116 Dewon Brazelton .15
117 Doug Creek .15
118 Jason Conti .15
119 John Flaherty .15
120 Delvin James .15
121 Steve Kent RC .15
122 Kevin McGlinchy .15
123 Travis Phelps .15
124 Bobby Seay .15
125 Travis Harper .15
126 Victor Zambrano .15
127 Jace Brewer .15
128 Jason Smith .15
129 Ramon Soler .15
130 Brandon Backe RC .50
131 Jorge Sosa RC .25
132 Jim Thome .75
133 Brady Anderson .15
134 C.C. Sabathia .15
135 Einar Diaz .15
136 Ricky Gutierrez .15
137 Danys Baez .15
138 Bob Wickman .15
139 Milton Bradley .15
140 Bartolo Colon .40
141 Joibert Cabrera .15
142 Eddie Taubensee .15
143 Ellis Burks .15
144 Omar Vizquel .40
145 Eddie Perez .15
146 Jaret Wright .15
147 Chuck Finley .15
148 Paul Shuey .15
149 Travis Fryman .15
150 Wil Cordero .15
151 Ricardo Rincon .15
152 Victor Martinez .15
153 Charles Nagy .15
154 Alex Escobar .15
155 Russell Branyan .15
156 Matt Lawton .15
157 Ryan Drese .15
158 Jerrod Riggan .15
159 David Riske .15
160 Jake Westbrook .15
161 Mark Wohlers .15
162 John McDonald .15

163 Ichiro Suzuki 1.50
164 Freddy Garcia .15
165 Edgar Martinez .15
166 Ben Davis .15
167 Shigetoshi Hasegawa .15
168 Carlos Guillen .15
169 Ruben Sierra .15
170 Joel Pineiro .15
171 Norm Charlton .15
172 Bret Boone .15
173 Jamie Moyer .15
174 Jeff Nelson .15
175 Kazuhiro Sasaki .50
176 Jeff Cirillo .15
177 Mark McLemore .15
178 Paul Abbott .15
179 Mike Cameron .15
180 Dan Wilson .15
181 John Olerud .50
182 Arthur Rhodes .15
183 Desi Relaford .15
184 John Halama .15
185 Antonio Perez .15
186 Ryan Anderson .15
187 James Baldwin .15
188 Ryan Franklin .15
189 Justin Kaye .15
190 J.J. Putz RC .40
191 Allan Simpson RC .40
192 Matt Thornton .15
193 Luis Ugueto RC .40
194 Chris Richard .15
195 Sidney Ponson .15
196 Brook Fordyce .15
197 Luis Matos .15
198 Josh Towers .15
199 David Segui .15
200 Chris Brock .15
201 Tony Batista .15
202 Erik Bedard .15
203 Marty Cordova .15
204 Jerry Hairston Jr. .15
205 Jason Johnson .15
206 Buddy Groom .15
207 Mike Bordick .15
208 Melvin Mora .15
209 Calvin Maduro .15
210 Jeff Conine .15
211 Luis Rivera .15
212 Jay Gibbons .15
213 B.J. Ryan .15
214 Sean Douglass .15
215 Rodrigo Lopez .15
216 Rick Bauer .15
217 Scott Erickson .15
218 Jorge Julio .15
219 Willis Roberts .15
220 John Stephens .15
221 Geronimo Gil .15
222 Chris Singleton .15
223 Mike Paradis .15
224 John Parrish .15
225 Steve Bechler RC .50
226 Mike Moriarty RC .15
227 Luis Garcia .15
228 Alex Rodriguez 1.50
229 Mark Teixeira .50
230 Chan Ho Park .15
231 Todd Van Poppel .15
232 Mike Young .15
233 Kenny Rogers .15
234 Rusty Greer .15
235 Rafael Palmeiro .50
236 Francisco Cordero .15
237 John Rocker .15
238 Dave Burba .15
239 Travis Hafner .15
240 Kevin Mench .15
241 Carl Everett .15
242 Ivan Rodriguez .50
243 Jeff Zimmerman .15
244 Juan Gonzalez .50
245 Herbert Perry .15
246 Rob Bell .15
247 Doug Davis .15
248 Frank Catalanotto .15
249 Jay Powell .15
250 Gabe Kapler .15
251 Joaquin Benoit .15
252 Jovanny Cedeno .15
253 Hideki Irabu .15
254 Dan Miceli .15
255 Danny Kolb .15
256 Colby Lewis .15
257 Rich Rodriguez .15
258 Ismael Valdes .15
259 Bill Haselman .15
260 Jason Hart .15
261 Rudy Seanez .15
262 Travis Hughes RC .40
263 Hank Blalock .50
264 Steve Woodard .15
265 Nomar Garciaparra 1.50
266 Pedro J. Martinez .75
267 Frank Castillo .15
268 Johnny Damon .15
269 Doug Mirabelli .15
270 Derek Lowe .40
271 Shea Hillenbrand .50
272 Paxton Crawford .15
273 Tony Clark .15
274 Dustin Hermanson .15
275 Trot Nixon .15
276 John Burkett .15
277 Rich Garces .15

278	Josh Hancock **RC**	.15
279	Michael Coleman	.15
280	Darren Oliver	.15
281	Jason Varitek	.15
282	Jose Offerman	.15
283	Tim Wakefield	.15
284	Rolando Arrojo	.15
285	Rickey Henderson	.50
286	Ugueth Urbina	.15
287	Casey Fossum	.15
288	Manny Ramirez	.50
289	Sun-Woo Kim	.15
290	Juan Diaz	.15
291	Willie Banks	.15
292	Jorge De La Rosa **RC**	.50
293	Juan Pena	.15
294	Jeff Wallace	.15
295	Calvin Pickering	.15
296	Anastacio Martinez **RC**	.40
297	Carlos Baerga	.15
298	Rey Sanchez	.15
299	Mike Sweeney	.15
300	Jeff Suppan	.15
301	Brent Mayne	.15
302	Chad Durbin	.15
303	Dan Reichert	.15
304	Raul Ibanez	.15
305	Joe Randa	.15
306	Chris George	.15
307	Michael Tucker	.15
308	Paul Byrd	.15
309	Kris Wilson	.15
310	Luis Alicea	.15
311	Neifi Perez	.15
312	Brian Shouse	.15
313	Chuck Knoblauch	.15
314	Dave McCarty	.15
315	Blake Stein	.15
316	Alexis Gomez	.15
317	Mark Quinn	.15
318	A.J. Hinch	.15
319	Carlos Febles	.15
320	Roberto Hernandez	.15
321	Brandon Berger	.15
322	Jeff Austin **RC**	.40
323	Corey Bailey	.15
324	Tony Cogan	.15
325	Nate Field **RC**	.40
326	Jason Grimsley	.15
327	Darrell May	.15
328	Donnie Sadler	.15
329	Carlos Beltran	.15
330	Miguel Asencio **RC**	.40
331	Jeff Weaver	.15
332	Bobby Higginson	.15
333	Mike Rivera	.15
334	Matt Anderson	.15
335	Craig Paquette	.15
336	Jose Lima	.15
337	Juan Acevedo	.15
338	Danny Patterson	.15
339	Andres Torres	.15
340	Dean Palmer	.15
341	Randall Simon	.15
342	Craig Monroe	.15
343	Damion Easley	.15
344	Robert Fick	.15
345	Steve Sparks	.15
346	Dmitri Young	.15
347	Nate Cornejo	.15
348	Matt Miller	.15
349	Wendell Magee	.15
350	Shane Halter	.15
351	Brian Moehler	.15
352	Mitch Meluskey	.15
353	Jose Macias	.15
354	Mark Redman	.15
355	Jeff Farnsworth	.15
356	Kris Keller	.15
357	Adam Pettyjohn	.15
358	Fernando Rodney	.15
359	Andy Van Hekken	.15
360	Damian Jackson	.15
361	Jose Paniagua	.15
362	Jacob Cruz	.15
363	Doug Mientkiewicz	.15
364	Torii Hunter	.15
365	Brad Radke	.15
366	Denny Hocking	.15
367	Mike Jackson	.15
368	Eddie Guardado	.15
369	Jacque Jones	.15
370	Joe Mays	.15
371	Matt Kinney	.15
372	Kyle Lohse	.15
373	David Ortiz	.15
374	Luis Rivas	.15
375	Jay Canizaro	.15
376	Dustan Mohr	.15
377	LaTroy Hawkins	.15
378	Warren Morris	.15
379	A.J. Pierzynski	.15
380	Eric Milton	.15
381	Bob Wells	.15
382	Cristian Guzman	.15
383	Brian Buchanan	.15
384	Bobby Kielty	.15
385	Corey Koskie	.15
386	J.C. Romero	.15
387	Jack Cressend	.15
388	Mike Duvall	.15
389	Tony Fiore	.15
390	Tom Prince	.15
391	Todd Sears	.15
392	Kevin Frederick **RC**	.40
393	Frank Thomas	.50
394	Mark Buehrle	.15
395	Jon Garland	.15
396	Jeff Liefer	.15
397	Magglio Ordonez	.50
398	Rocky Biddle	.15
399	Lorenzo Barcelo	.15
400	Ray Durham	.15
401	Bob Howry	.15
402	Aaron Rowand	.15
403	Keith Foulke	.15
404	Paul Konerko	.50
405	Sandy Alomar Jr.	.15
406	Mark Johnson	.15
407	Carlos Lee	.15
408	Jose Valentin	.15
409	Jon Rauch	.15
410	Royce Clayton	.15
411	Kenny Lofton	.40
412	Tony Graffanino	.15
413	Todd Ritchie	.15
414	Antonio Osuna	.15
415	Gary Glover	.15
416	Mike Porzio	.15
417	Danny Wright	.15
418	Kelly Wunsch	.15
419	Miguel Olivo	.15
420	Edwin Almonte **RC**	.15
421	Kyle Kane **RC**	.50
422	Mitch Wylie **RC**	.15
423	Derek Jeter	2.00
424	Jason Giambi	.50
425	Roger Clemens	1.50
426	Enrique Wilson	.15
427	David Wells	.15
428	Mike Mussina	.50
429	Bernie Williams	.50
430	Mike Stanton	.15
431	Sterling Hitchcock	.15
432	Alex Graman	.15
433	Robin Ventura	.50
434	Mariano Rivera	.50
435	Jay Tessmer	.15
436	Andy Pettitte	.50
437	John Vander Wal	.15
438	Adrian Hernandez	.15
439	Alberto Castillo	.15
440	Steve Karsay	.15
441	Alfonso Soriano	.75
442	Rondell White	.15
443	Nick Johnson	.50
444	Jorge Posada	.50
445	Ramiro Mendoza	.15
446	Gerald Williams	.15
447	Orlando Hernandez	.15
448	Randy Choate	.15
449	Randy Keisler	.15
450	Ted Lilly	.15
451	Christian Parker	.15
452	Ron Coomer	.15
453	Marcus Thames	.15
454	Drew Henson	.50
455	Jeff Bagwell	.50
456	Wade Miller	.15
457	Lance Berkman	.50
458	Julio Lugo	.15
459	Roy Oswalt	.40
460	Nelson Cruz	.15
461	Morgan Ensberg	.15
462	Geoff Blum	.15
463	Ryan Jamison **RC**	.50
464	Billy Wagner	.15
465	Dave Mlicki	.15
466	Brad Ausmus	.15
467	Jose Vizcaino	.15
468	Craig Biggio	.50
469	Shane Reynolds	.15
470	Gregg Zaun	.15
471	Octavio Dotel	.15
472	Carlos Hernandez	.15
473	Richard Hidalgo	.15
474	Daryle Ward	.15
475	Orlando Merced	.15
476	John Buck	.15
477	Adam Everett	.15
478	Doug Brocail	.15
479	Brad Lidge	.15
480	Scott Linebrink	.15
481	T.J. Mathews	.15
482	Greg Miller	.15
483	Hipolito Pichardo	.15
484	Brandon Puffer **RC**	.15
485	Ricky Stone	.15
486	Jason Lane	.15
487	Brian L. Hunter	.15
488	Rodrigo Rosario **RC**	.50
489	Tom Shearn **RC**	.50
490	Gary Sheffield	.40
491	Tom Glavine	.40
492	Mike Remlinger	.15
493	Henry Blanco	.15
494	Vinny Castilla	.15
495	Chris Hammond	.15
496	Kevin Millwood	.50
497	Darren Holmes	.15
498	Cory Aldridge	.15
499	Tim Spooneybarger	.15
500	Rafael Furcal	.50
501	Albie Lopez	.15
502	Javy Lopez	.40
503	Greg Maddux	1.00
504	Andruw Jones	.50
505	Steve Torrealba	.15
506	George Lombard	.15
507	B.J. Surhoff	.15
508	Marcus Giles	.15
509	Derrick Lewis	.15
510	Wes Helms	.15
511	John Smoltz	.50
512	Chipper Jones	.75
513	Jason Marquis	.15
514	Mark DeRosa	.15
515	Jung Bong	.15
516	Kevin Gryboski **RC**	.15
517	Damian Moss	.15
518	Horacio Ramirez	.15
519	Scott Sobkowiak	.15
520	Billy Sylvester	.15
521	Nick Green	.15
522	Travis Wilson	.15
523	Ryan Langerhans	.15
524	John Ennis **RC**	.50
525	John Foster **RC**	.15
526	Keith Lockhart	.15
527	Julio Franco	.15
528	Richie Sexson	.50
529	Jeffrey Hammonds	.15
530	Ben Sheets	.50
531	Mike DeJean	.15
532	Mark Loretta	.15
533	Alex Ochoa	.15
534	Jamey Wright	.15
535	Jose Hernandez	.15
536	Glendon Rusch	.15
537	Geoff Jenkins	.50
538	Luis S. Lopez	.15
539	Curtis Leskanic	.15
540	Chad Fox	.15
541	Tyler Houston	.15
542	Nick Neugebauer	.15
543	Matt Stairs	.15
544	Paul Rigdon	.15
545	Bill Hall	.15
546	Luis Vizcaino	.15
547	Lenny Harris	.15
548	Alex Sanchez	.15
549	Raul Casanova	.15
550	Eric Young	.15
551	Jeff Deardorff **RC**	.15
552	Nelson Figueroa	.15
553	Ron Belliard	.15
554	Mike Buddie	.15
555	Jose Cabrera	.15
556	J.M. Gold	.15
557	Ray King	.15
558	Jose Mieses	.15
559	Takahito Nomura **RC**	.50
560	Ruben Quevedo	.15
561	Jackson Melian	.15
562	Cristian Guerrero	.15
563	Paul Bako	.15
564	Luis Martinez **RC**	.50
565	Brian Mallette **RC**	.50
566	Matt Morris	.50
567	Tino Martinez	.40
568	Fernando Vina	.15
569	Gene Stechschulte	.15
570	Andy Benes	.15
571	Placido Polanco	.15
572	Luis Garcia	.15
573	Jim Edmonds	.50
574	Bud Smith	.15
575	Mike Matheny	.15
576	Garrett Stephenson	.15
577	Miguel Cairo	.15
578	Darryl Kile	.15
579	Mike Timlin	.15
580	Rick Ankiel	.50
581	Jason Isringhausen	.15
582	Albert Pujols	1.50
583	Eli Marrero	.15
584	Steve Kline	.15
585	J.D. Drew	.50
586	Mike DiFelice	.15
587	Dave Veres	.15
588	Kerry Robinson	.15
589	Edgar Renteria	.15
590	Woody Williams	.15
591	Chance Caple	.15
592	Michael Crudale **RC**	.15
593	Luther Hackman	.15
594	Josh Pearce	.15
595	Kevin Joseph	.15
596	Jimmy Journell	.15
597	Jeremy Lambert **RC**	.40
598	Mike Matthews	.15
599	Les Walrond	.15
600	Keith McDonald	.15
601	William Ortega	.15
602	Scotty Layfield **RC**	.50
603	So Taguchi **RC**	1.00
604	Eduardo Perez	.15
605	Sammy Sosa	1.50
606	Kerry Wood	.75
607	Kyle Farnsworth	.15
608	Alex Gonzalez	.15
609	Tom Gordon	.15
610	Carlos Zambrano	.15
611	Roosevelt Brown	.15
612	Bill Mueller	.15
613	Mark Prior	1.50
614	Darren Lewis	.15
615	Joe Girardi	.15
616	Fred McGriff	.50
617	Jon Lieber	.15
618	Robert Machado	.15
619	Corey Patterson	.50
620	Joe Borowski	.15
621	Todd Hundley	.15
622	Jason Bere	.15
623	Moises Alou	.40
624	Jeff Fassero	.15
625	Jesus Sanchez	.15
626	Chris Stynes	.15
627	Delino DeShields	.15
628	Augie Ojeda	.15
629	Juan Cruz	.15
630	Ben Christensen	.15
631	Mike Meyers	.15
632	Will Ohman	.15
633	Steve Smyth	.15
634	Mark Bellhorn	.15
635	Nate Frese	.15
636	David Kelton	.15
637	Francis Beltran **RC**	.40
638	Antonio Alfonseca	.15
639	Donovan Osborne	.15
640	Shawn Sonnier	.15
641	Matt Clement	.15
642	Luis Gonzalez	.25
643	Brian Anderson	.15
644	Randy Johnson	.75
645	Mark Grace	.50
646	Danny Bautista	.15
647	Junior Spivey	.15
648	Jay Bell	.15
649	Miguel Batista	.15
650	Tony Womack	.15
651	Byung-Hyun Kim	.15
652	Steve Finley	.40
653	Rick Helling	.15
654	Curt Schilling	.50
655	Erubiel Durazo	.15
656	Chris Donnels	.15
657	Greg Colbrunn	.15
658	Mike Morgan	.15
659	Jose Guillen	.15
660	Matt Williams	.50
661	Craig Counsell	.15
662	Greg Swindell	.15
663	Rod Barajas	.15
664	David Dellucci	.15
665	Todd Stottlemyre	.15
666	P.J. Bevis **RC**	.15
667	Mike Koplove	.15
668	Mike Myers	.15
669	John Patterson	.15
670	Bret Prinz	.15
671	Jeremy Ward **RC**	.50
672	Danny Klassen	.15
673	Luis Terrero	.15
674	Jose Valverde **RC**	.50
675	Doug DeVore **RC**	.50
676	Quinton McCracken	.15
677	Paul LoDuca	.15
678	Mark Grudzielanek	.15
679	Kevin Brown	.50
680	Paul Quantrill	.15
681	Shawn Green	.50
682	Hideo Nomo	.50
683	Eric Gagne	.15
684	Giovanni Carrara	.15
685	Marquis Grissom	.15
686	Hiram Bocachica	.15
687	Guillermo Mota	.15
688	Alex Cora	.15
689	Odalis Perez	.15
690	Brian Jordan	.15
691	Andy Ashby	.15
692	Eric Karros	.40
693	Chad Krueter	.15
694	Dave Roberts	.15
695	Omar Daal	.15
696	Dave Hansen	.15
697	Adrian Beltre	.50
698	Terry Mulholland	.15
699	Cesar Izturis	.15
700	Steve Colyer	.15
701	Carlos Garcia	.15
702	Ricardo Rodriguez	.15
703	Darren Dreifort	.15
704	Jeff Reboulet	.15
705	Victor Alvarez **RC**	.50
706	Kazuhisa Ishii **RC**	2.00
707	Jose Vidro	.15
708	Henry Mateo	.15
709	Tony Armas Jr.	.15
710	Carl Pavano	.15
711	Peter Bergeron	.15
712	Bruce Chen	.15
713	Orlando Cabrera	.15
714	Britt Reames	.15
715	Masato Yoshii	.15
716	Fernando Tatis	.15
717	Graeme Lloyd	.15
718	Scott Stewart	.15
719	Lou Collier	.15
720	Michael Barrett	.15
721	Vladimir Guerrero	.75
722	Troy Mattes	.15
723	Brian Schneider	.15
724	Lee Stevens	.15
725	Javier Vazquez	.15
726	Brad Wilkerson	.15
727	Zach Day	.15
728	Ed Vosberg	.15
729	Tomokazu Ohka	.15
730	Mike Mordecai	.15
731	Donnie Bridges	.15
732	Ron Chiavacci	.15
733	T.J. Tucker	.15
734	Scott Hodges	.15
735	Valentino Pascucci	.15
736	Andres Galarraga	.15
737	Scott Downs	.15

738 Eric Good **RC** .15
739 Ron Calloway **RC** .50
740 Jorge Nunez **RC** .15
741 Henry Rodriguez .15
742 Jeff Kent .15
743 Russ Ortiz .15
744 Felix Rodriguez .15
745 Benito Santiago .15
746 Tsuyoshi Shinjo .50
747 Tim Worrell .15
748 Marvin Benard .15
749 Kurt Ainsworth .15
750 Edwards Guzman .15
751 J.T. Snow .15
752 Jason Christiansen .15
753 Robb Nen .15
754 Barry Bonds 2.00
755 Shawon Dunston .15
756 Chad Zerbe .15
757 Ramon E. Martinez .15
758 Calvin Murray .15
759 Pedro Feliz .15
760 Jason Schmidt .15
761 Damon Minor .15
762 Reggie Sanders .15
763 Rich Aurilia .15
764 Kirk Rueter .15
765 David Bell .15
766 Yorvit Torrealba .15
767 Livan Hernandez .15
768 Felix Diaz .15
769 Aaron Fultz .15
770 Ryan Jensen .15
771 Arturo McDowell .15
772 Carlos Valderrama .15
773 Nelson Castro **RC** .50
774 Jay Witasick .15
775 Deivis Santos .15
776 Josh Beckett .15
777 Charles Johnson .15
778 Derrek Lee .15
779 A.J. Burnett .15
780 Vic Darensbourg .15
781 Cliff Floyd .50
782 Jose Cueto .15
783 Nate Teut .15
784 Alex Gonzalez .15
785 Brad Penny .15
786 Kevin Olsen .15
787 Mike Lowell .15
788 Mike Redmond .15
789 Braden Looper .15
790 Eric Owens .15
791 Andy Fox .15
792 Vladimir Nunez .15
793 Luis Castillo .15
794 Ryan Dempster .15
795 Armando Almanza .15
796 Preston Wilson .15
797 Pablo Ozuna .15
798 Gary Knotts .15
799 Ramon Castro .15
800 Benito Baez .15
801 Michael Tejera .15
802 Claudio Vargas .15
803 Chip Ambres .15
804 Hansel Izquierdo **RC** .50
805 Tim Raines .15
806 Marty Malloy .15
807 Julian Tavarez .15
808 Roberto Alomar .50
809 Al Leiter .50
810 Jeromy Burnitz .15
811 John Franco .15
812 Edgardo Alfonzo .15
813 Mike Piazza 1.00
814 Shawn Estes .15
815 Joe McEwing .15
816 David Weathers .15
817 Pedro Astacio .15
818 Timoniel Perez .15
819 Grant Roberts .15
820 Rey Ordonez .15
821 Steve Trachsel .15
822 Roger Cedeno .15
823 Mark Johnson .15
824 Armando Benitez .15
825 Vance Wilson .15
826 Jay Payton .15
827 Mo Vaughn .50
828 Scott Strickland .15
829 Mark Guthrie .15
830 Jeff D'Amico .15
831 Mark Corey **RC** .50
832 Kane Davis .15
833 Jae Weong Seo .15
834 Pat Strange .15
835 Adam Walker **RC** .15
836 Tyler Walker .15
837 Gary Matthews Jr. .15
838 Jaime Cerda **RC** .25
839 Satoru Komiyama **RC** .50
840 Tyler Yates **RC** .50
841 John Valentin .15
842 Ryan Klesko .40
843 Wiki Gonzalez .15
844 Trevor Hoffman .15
845 Sean Burroughs .40
846 Alan Embree .15
847 Dennis Tankersley .15
848 D'Angelo Jimenez .15
849 Kevin Jarvis .15
850 Mark Kotsay .15
851 Phil Nevin .25
852 Jeremy Fikac .15
853 Brett Tomko .15
854 Brian Lawrence .15
855 Steve Reed .15
856 Bubba Trammell .15
857 Tom Davey .15
858 Ramon Vazquez .15
859 Tom Lampkin .15
860 Bobby Jones .15
861 Ray Lankford .15
862 Mark Sweeney .15
863 Adam Eaton .15
864 Trenidad Hubbard .15
865 Jason Boyd .15
866 Javier Cardona .15
867 Clifford Bartosh **RC** .50
868 Mike Bynum .15
869 Eric Cyr **RC** .50
870 Jose Nunez .15
871 Ron Gant .15
872 Deivi Cruz .15
873 Ben Howard **RC** .50
874 Todd Donovan **RC** .25
875 Andy Shibilo **RC** .15
876 Scott Rolen .75
877 Jose Mesa .15
878 Rheal Cormier .15
879 Travis Lee .15
880 Mike Lieberthal .15
881 Brandon Duckworth .15
882 David Coggin .15
883 Bobby Abreu .50
884 Turk Wendell .15
885 Marlon Byrd .15
886 Jason Michaels .15
887 Robert Person .15
888 Tomas Perez .15
889 Jimmy Rollins .50
890 Vicente Padilla .15
891 Pat Burrell .50
892 Dave Hollins .15
893 Randy Wolf .15
894 Jose Santiago .15
895 Doug Glanville .15
896 Cliff Politte .15
897 Marlon Anderson .15
898 Ricky Bottalico .15
899 Terry Adams .15
900 Brad Baisley .15
901 Hector Mercado .15
902 Elio Serrano **RC** .50
903 Todd Pratt .15
904 Peter Zamora **RC** .50
905 Nick Punto .15
906 Ricky Ledee .15
907 Eric Junge **RC** .15
908 Anderson Machado **RC** .50
909 Jorge Padilla **RC** .50
910 John Mabry .15
911 Brian Giles .50
912 Jason Kendall .40
913 Jack Wilson .15
914 Kris Benson .15
915 Aramis Ramirez .15
916 Mike Fetters .15
917 Adrian Brown .15
918 Pokey Reese .15
919 Dave Williams .15
920 Mike Benjamin .15
921 Kip Wells .15
922 Mike Williams .15
923 Pat Meares .15
924 Ron Villone .15
925 Armando Rios .15
926 Jimmy Anderson .15
927 Robert Mackowiak .15
928 Kevin Young .15
929 Brian Boehringer .15
930 Joe Beimel .15
931 Chad Hermansen .15
932 Scott Sauerbeck .15
933 Josh Fogg .15
934 Mike Gonzalez **RC** .15
935 Mike Lincoln .15
936 Sean Lowe .15
937 Matt Guerrier .15
938 Ryan Vogelsong .15
939 J.R. House .15
940 Craig Wilson .15
941 Tony Alvarez .15
942 J.J. Davis .15
943 Abraham Nunez .15
944 Adrian Burnside **RC** .50
945 Ken Griffey Jr. 1.00
946 Jimmy Haynes .15
947 Juan Castro .15
948 Jose Rijo .15
949 Corky Miller .15
950 Elmer Dessens .15
951 Aaron Boone .15
952 Juan Encarnacion .15
953 Chris Reitsma .15
954 Wilton Guerrero .15
955 Danny Graves .15
956 Jim Brower .15
957 Barry Larkin .50
958 Todd Walker .15
959 Gabe White .15
960 Adam Dunn .50
961 Jason LaRue .15
962 Reggie Taylor .15
963 Sean Casey .40
964 Scott Williamson .15
965 Austin Kearns .50
966 Kelly Stinnett .15
967 Jose Acevedo .15
968 Gookie Dawkins .15
969 Brady Clark .15
970 Scott Sullivan .15
971 Ricardo Aramboles .15
972 Lance Davis .15
973 Seth Etherton .15
974 Luke Hudson .15
975 Joey Hamilton .15
976 Luis Pineda .15
977 John Riedling .15
978 Jose Silva .15
979 Dane Sardinha .15
980 Ben Broussard .15
981 David Espinosa .15
982 Ruben Mateo .15
983 Larry Walker .50
984 Juan Uribe .15
985 Mike Hampton .15
986 Aaron Cook **RC** .15
987 Jose Ortiz .15
988 Todd Jones .15
989 Todd Helton .50
990 Shawn Chacon .15
991 Jason Jennings .15
992 Todd Zeile .15
993 Ben Petrick .15
994 Denny Neagle .15
995 Jose Jimenez .15
996 Juan Pierre .15
997 Todd Hollandsworth .15
998 Kent Mercker .15
999 Greg Norton .15
1000 Terry Shumpert .15
1001 Mark Little .15
1002 Gary Bennett .15
1003 Dennys Reyes .15
1004 Justin Speier .15
1005 John Thomson .15
1006 Rick White .15
1007 Colin Young **RC** .40
1008 Cam Esslinger **RC** .50
1009 Rene Reyes **RC** .50
1010 Mike James .15
1011 Morgan Ensberg .15
1012 Adam Everett .15
1013 Rodrigo Rosario .15
1014 Carlos Pena .15
1015 Eric Hinske .50
1016 Orlando Hudson .15
1017 Reed Johnson .15
1018 Jung Bong .15
1019 Bill Hall .15
1020 Mark Prior 1.50
1021 Francis Beltran .15
1022 David Kelton .15
1023 Felix Escalona .15
1024 Jorge Sosa .15
1025 Dewon Brazelton .15
1026 Jose Valverde .15
1027 Luis Terrero .15
1028 Kazuhisa Ishii 1.00
1029 Cesar Izturis .15
1030 Ryan Jensen .15
1031 Matt Thornton .15
1032 Hansel Izquierdo .15
1033 Jaime Cerda .15
1034 Erik Bedard .15
1035 Sean Burroughs .15
1036 Ben Howard .15
1037 Ramon Vazquez .15
1038 Marlon Byrd .15
1039 Josh Fogg .15
1040 Hank Blalock .50
1041 Mark Teixeira .50
1042 Kevin Mench .15
1043 Dane Sardinha .15
1044 Austin Kearns .50
1045 Anastacio Martinez .15
1046 Eric Munson .15
1047 Jon Rauch .15
1048 Nick Johnson .50
1049 Alex Graman .15
1050 Drew Henson .50
1051 Darin Erstad .50
1052 Garret Anderson .15
1053 Craig Biggio .50
1054 Lance Berkman .50
1055 Jeff Bagwell .50
1056 Shannon Stewart .15
1057 Chipper Jones .75
1058 J.D. Drew .50
1059 Moises Alou .15
1060 Mark Grace .50
1061 Jose Vidro Expos .15
1062 Vladimir Guerrero .75
1063 Matt Lawton .15
1064 Ichiro Suzuki 1.50
1065 Edgar Martinez .15
1066 John Olerud .50
1067 Jeff Cirillo .15
1068 Mike Lowell .15
1069 Mike Piazza 1.00
1070 Roberto Alomar .50
1071 Bobby Abreu .15
1072 Jason Kendall .15
1073 Brian Giles .50
1074 Rafael Palmeiro .50
1075 Ivan Rodriguez .50
1076 Alex Rodriguez 1.50
1077 Juan Gonzalez .50
1078 Nomar Garciaparra 1.50
1079 Manny Ramirez .50
1080 Sean Casey .25
1081 Barry Larkin .25
1082 Larry Walker .40
1083 Carlos Beltran .15
1084 Corey Koskie .15
1085 Magglio Ordonez .25
1086 Frank Thomas .50
1087 Kenny Lofton .25
1088 Derek Jeter 2.00
1089 Bernie Williams .50
1090 Jason Giambi .50
1091 Troy Glaus .50
1092 Jeff Bagwell .50
1093 Lance Berkman .50
1094 David Justice .25
1095 Eric Chavez .25
1096 Carlos Delgado .40
1097 Gary Sheffield .40
1098 Chipper Jones .75
1099 Andruw Jones .50
1100 Richie Sexson .40
1101 Albert Pujols 1.50
1102 Sammy Sosa 1.50
1103 Fred McGriff .40
1104 Greg Vaughn .15
1105 Matt Williams .25
1106 Luis Gonzalez .40
1107 Shawn Green .40
1108 Andres Galarraga .15
1109 Vladimir Guerrero .75
1110 Barry Bonds 2.00
1111 Rich Aurilia .15
1112 Ellis Burks .15
1113 Jim Thome .50
1114 Bret Boone .15
1115 Cliff Floyd .15
1116 Mike Piazza 1.00
1117 Jeromy Burnitz .15
1118 Phil Nevin .15
1119 Brian Giles .50
1120 Rafael Palmeiro .50
1121 Juan Gonzalez .50
1122 Alex Rodriguez 1.50
1123 Manny Ramirez .50
1124 Ken Griffey Jr. 1.00
1125 Larry Walker .40
1126 Todd Helton .50
1127 Mike Sweeney .15
1128 Frank Thomas .50
1129 Paul Konerko .40
1130 Jason Giambi .50
1131 Aaron Sele .15
1132 Roy Oswalt .40
1133 Wade Miller .15
1134 Tim Hudson .40
1135 Barry Zito .40
1136 Mark Mulder .25
1137 Greg Maddux 1.00
1138 Tom Glavine .40
1139 Ben Sheets .40
1140 Darryl Kile .15
1141 Matt Morris .15
1142 Kerry Wood .40
1143 Jon Lieber .15
1144 Juan Cruz .15
1145 Randy Johnson .75
1146 Curt Schilling .50
1147 Kevin Brown .15
1148 Javier Vazquez .15
1149 Russ Ortiz .15
1150 C.C. Sabathia .15
1151 Bartolo Colon .15
1152 Freddy Garcia .15
1153 Jamie Moyer .15
1154 Josh Beckett .50
1155 Brad Penny .15
1156 Al Leiter .40
1157 Brandon Duckworth .15
1158 Robert Person .15
1159 Kris Benson .15
1160 Chan Ho Park .15
1161 Pedro J. Martinez .75
1162 Mike Hampton .15
1163 Jeff Weaver .15
1164 Joe Mays .15
1165 Brad Radke .15
1166 Eric Milton .15
1167 Roger Clemens 1.00
1168 Mike Mussina .50
1169 Andy Pettitte .50
1170 David Wells .15
1171 Ken Griffey Jr. 1.00
1172 Ichiro Suzuki 1.00
1173 Jason Giambi .50
1174 Alex Rodriguez 1.00
1175 Sammy Sosa .75
1176 Nomar Garciaparra 1.00
1177 Barry Bonds 1.00
1178 Mike Piazza .75
1179 Derek Jeter 1.50
1180 Randy Johnson .40
1181 Jeff Bagwell .40
1182 Albert Pujols 1.00

Gargantuan Gear

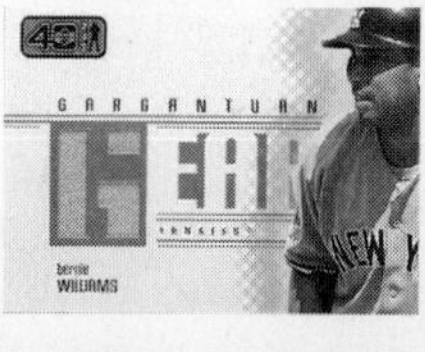

		NM/M
Common Player:		3.00
Gold:		2X
Production 100 Sets		
G-JB	James Baldwin	3.00
G-BC	Bruce Chen	3.00
G-JD	Jermaine Dye/SP	5.00
G-JG	Juan Gonzalez	6.00
G-BG	Ben Grieve	3.00
G-KG	Ken Griffey Jr.	10.00
G-TH	Tim Hudson	6.00
G-AJ	Andruw Jones	6.00
G-JK	Jeff Kent	3.00
G-ML	Mike Lieberthal	3.00
G-TM	Tino Martinez	3.00
G-JO	John Olerud	3.00
G-MO	Magglio Ordonez	5.00
G-MP	Mike Piazza	15.00
G-JP	Jorge Posada	8.00
G-AP	Andy Pettitte	6.00
G-BR	Brad Radke	3.00
G-AR	Alex Rodriguez	10.00
G-SR	Scott Rolen	10.00
G-CS	Curt Schilling	8.00
G-AS	Aaron Sele	3.00
G-IS	Ichiro Suzuki/SP	30.00
G-BW	Bernie Williams	8.00
G-DY	Dmitri Young	3.00
G-TZ	Todd Zeile	3.00

Looming Large Jerseys

		NM/M
Common Player:		8.00
Production 250 Sets		
Gold:		2X
Production 40 Sets		
LBa	Jeff Bagwell	10.00
LB	Lance Berkman	10.00
JBu	John Burkett	8.00
SC	Sean Casey	10.00
TC	Tony Clark	8.00
RC	Roger Clemens	20.00
JC	Jeff Cirillo	8.00
JD	J.D. Drew	10.00
CE	Carl Everett	8.00
CF	Chuck Finley	8.00
TF	Travis Fryman	8.00
JGi	Jason Giambi	10.00
BG	Brian Giles	10.00
TG	Tom Glavine	10.00
JGo	Juan Gonzalez	10.00
KG	Ken Griffey Jr.	20.00
TH	Todd Helton	15.00
RJ	Randy Johnson	15.00
DK	Darryl Kile	8.00
AL	Al Leiter	8.00
ML	Mike Lieberthal	8.00
KL	Kenny Lofton	8.00
GM	Greg Maddux	15.00
EM	Edgar Martinez	10.00
FM	Fred McGriff	10.00
MO	Magglio Ordonez	8.00
HN	Hideo Nomo	50.00
RP	Rafael Palmeiro	10.00
JP	Jorge Posada	10.00
SR	Shane Reynolds	8.00
AR	Alex Rodriguez	15.00
JR	Jimmy Rollins	8.00
KS	Kazuhiro Sasaki	8.00
CS	Curt Schilling	10.00
JS	J.T. Snow	8.00
SS	Sammy Sosa	20.00
FT	Frank Thomas	10.00
IV	Ismael Valdes	8.00
RV	Randy Velarde	8.00
RV	Ron Villone	8.00
BZ	Barry Zito	10.00

Lumber Yard

		NM/M
Common Player:		10.00
Inserted 1:168		
LY1	Chipper Jones	15.00
LY2	Joe DiMaggio	40.00
LY3	Albert Pujols	20.00
LY4	Mark McGwire	30.00
LY5	Sammy Sosa	15.00
LY6	Vladimir Guerrero	15.00
LY7	Barry Bonds	25.00
LY8	Mickey Mantle	50.00
LY9	Mike Piazza	15.00
LY10	Alex Rodriguez	15.00
LY11	Nomar Garciaparra	15.00
LY12	Ken Griffey Jr.	20.00
LY13	Frank Thomas	10.00
LY14	Jason Giambi	15.00
LY15	Derek Jeter	25.00
LY16	Luis Gonzalez	10.00
LY17	Jeff Bagwell	10.00
LY18	Todd Helton	10.00

Mark McGwire Flashbacks

		NM/M
Complete Set (40):		120.00
Common McGwire:		4.00
Inserted 1:24		
MM1-40	Mark McGwire	4.00

Super Swatches

		NM/M
Common Player:		5.00
Production 250 Sets		
Gold:		1-2X
Production 40 Sets		
EA	Edgardo Alfonzo	5.00
RA	Rich Aurilia	5.00
JB	Jeff Bagwell	15.00
SC	Sean Casey	8.00
CD	Carlos Delgado	8.00
RD	Ray Durham	5.00
DE	Darin Erstad	8.00
JG	Juan Gonzalez	8.00
MG	Mark Grace	8.00
SG	Shawn Green	8.00
KG	Ken Griffey Jr.	20.00
TG	Tony Gwynn	15.00
MH	Mike Hampton	5.00
TH	Trevor Hoffman	5.00
CJ	Chipper Jones	10.00
DJ	David Justice	8.00
KL	Kenny Lofton	5.00
JM	Joe Mays	5.00
EM	Eric Milton	5.00
MM	Matt Morris	5.00
HN	Hideo Nomo	50.00
JP	Jorge Posada	10.00
MR	Manny Ramirez	12.00
MR	Mariano Rivera	10.00
AR	Alex Rodriguez	15.00
IR	Ivan Rodriguez	10.00
KS	Kazuhiro Sasaki	5.00
CS	Curt Schilling	10.00
BS	Ben Sheets	8.00
SS	Sammy Sosa	20.00
IS	Ichiro Suzuki	40.00
MS	Mike Sweeney	5.00
FT	Frank Thomas	10.00
GV	Greg Vaughn	5.00
JV	Jose Vidro	5.00
DW	David Wells	5.00
MY	Masato Yoshii	5.00

2002 UD Authentics

Kazuhisa Ishii

		NM/M
Complete Set (200):		50.00
Common Player:		.25
Reversed Negatives:		1-2.5X
Inserted 1:9		
Pack (5):		2.50
Box (18):		35.00
1	Brad Fullmer	.25
2	Garret Anderson	.40
3	Darin Erstad	.40
4	Jarrod Washburn	.25
5	Troy Glaus	.50
6	Barry Zito	.40
7	David Justice	.40
8	Eric Chavez	.40
9	Tim Hudson	.40
10	Miguel Tejada	.40
11	Jermaine Dye	.25
12	Mark Mulder	.40
13	Carlos Delgado	.50
14	Jose Cruz Jr.	.25
16	Shannon Stewart	.25
17	Raul Mondesi	.25
18	Tanyon Sturtze	.25
19	Toby Hall	.25
20	Greg Vaughn	.25
21	Aubrey Huff	.25
22	Ben Grieve	.25
23	Brent Abernathy	.25
24	Jim Thome	.75
25	C.C. Sabathia	.25
26	Matt Lawton	.25
27	Omar Vizquel	.25
28	Ellis Burks	.25
29	Russ Branyan	.25
30	Bartolo Colon	.40
31	Ichiro Suzuki	1.50
32	John Olerud	.40
33	Freddy Garcia	.25
34	Mike Cameron	.25
35	Jeff Cirillo	.25
36	Kazuhiro Sasaki	.25
37	Edgar Martinez	.40
38	Bret Boone	.25
39	Jeff Conine	.25
40	Melvin Mora	.25
41	Jason Johnson	.25
42	Chris Richard	.25
43	Tony Batista	.25
44	Ivan Rodriguez	.50
45	Gabe Kapler	.25
46	Rafael Palmeiro	.50
47	Alex Rodriguez	1.50
48	Juan Gonzalez	.50
49	Carl Everett	.25
50	Nomar Garciaparra	1.50
51	Trot Nixon	.25
52	Manny Ramirez	.50
53	Pedro J. Martinez	.75
54	Johnny Damon	.40
55	Shea Hillenbrand	.25
56	Mike Sweeney	.25
57	Mark Quinn	.25
58	Joe Randa	.25
59	Carlos Beltran	.40
60	Chuck Knoblauch	.25
61	Robert Fick	.25
62	Jeff Weaver	.25
63	Bobby Higginson	.25
64	Dean Palmer	.25
65	Dmitri Young	.25
66	Corey Koskie	.25
67	Doug Mientkiewicz	.25
68	Joe Mays	.25
69	Torii Hunter	.40
70	Cristian Guzman	.25
71	Jacque Jones	.25
72	Magglio Ordonez	.40
73	Paul Konerko	.25
74	Carlos Lee	.25
75	Mark Buehrle	.25
76	Jose Canseco	.50
77	Frank Thomas	.50
78	Roger Clemens	1.50
79	Derek Jeter	2.00
80	Jason Giambi	.50
81	Rondell White	.25
82	Bernie Williams	.50
83	Jorge Posada	.50
84	Mike Mussina	.50
85	Alfonso Soriano	.75
86	Wade Miller	.25
87	Jeff Bagwell	.50
88	Craig Biggio	.40
89	Roy Oswalt	.40
90	Lance Berkman	.40
91	Daryle Ward	.25
92	Chipper Jones	.75
93	Greg Maddux	1.00
94	Marcus Giles	.25
95	Gary Sheffield	.50
96	Tom Glavine	.50
97	Andruw Jones	.50
98	Rafael Furcal	.25
99	Richie Sexson	.40
100	Ben Sheets	.40
101	Jose Hernandez	.25
102	Geoff Jenkins	.40
103	Jeffrey Hammonds	.25
104	Edgar Renteria	.40
105	Matt Morris	.40
106	Tino Martinez	.25
107	Jim Edmonds	.40
108	Albert Pujols	1.50
109	J.D. Drew	.40
110	Fernando Vina	.25
111	Darryl Kile	.25
112	Sammy Sosa	1.50
113	Fred McGriff	.40
114	Kerry Wood	.75
115	Moises Alou	.40
116	Jon Lieber	.25
117	Mark Grace	.50
118	Randy Johnson	.75
119	Curt Schilling	.50
120	Luis Gonzalez	.40
121	Steve Finley	.25
122	Matt Williams	.40
123	Shawn Green	.40
124	Kevin Brown	.40
125	Adrian Beltre	.40
126	Paul LoDuca	.25
127	Hideo Nomo	.50
128	Brian Jordan	.25
129	Vladimir Guerrero	.75
130	Javier Vazquez	.25
131	Jose Vidro	.25
132	Orlando Cabrera	.25
133	Jeff Kent	.25
134	Rich Aurilia	.25
135	Russ Ortiz	.25
136	Barry Bonds	2.00
137	Preston Wilson	.25
138	Ryan Dempster	.25
139	Cliff Floyd	.25
140	Josh Beckett	.40
141	Mike Lowell	.40
142	Mike Piazza	1.00
143	Roberto Alomar	.50
144	Al Leiter	.40
145	Edgardo Alfonzo	.25
146	Roger Cedeno	.25
147	Jeromy Burnitz	.25
148	Phil Nevin	.25
149	Mark Kotsay	.25
150	Ryan Klesko	.25
151	Trevor Hoffman	.25
152	Bobby Abreu	.40
153	Scott Rolen	.75
154	Jimmy Rollins	.40
155	Robert Person	.25
156	Pat Burrell	.40
157	Randy Wolf	.25
158	Brian Giles	.40
159	Aramis Ramirez	.50
160	Kris Benson	.25
161	Jason Kendall	.25
162	Ken Griffey Jr.	1.00
163	Sean Casey	.40
164	Adam Dunn	.50
165	Barry Larkin	.50
166	Todd Helton	.50
167	Mike Hampton	.25
168	Larry Walker	.40
169	Juan Pierre	.25
170	Juan Uribe	.25
171	So Taguchi **RC**	2.00
172	Brendan Donnelly **RC**	.75
173	Chris Baker **RC**	.50
174	John Ennis **RC**	.75
175	Francis Beltran **RC**	.75
176	Danny Wright	.50
177	Brandon Backe **RC**	.75
178	Mark Corey **RC**	.75
179	Kazuhisa Ishii **RC**	3.00
180	Ron Calloway **RC**	.50
181	Kevin Frederick **RC**	.75
182	Jaime Cerda **RC**	.75
183	Doug DeVore **RC**	.50
184	Brandon Puffer **RC**	.75
185	Andy Pratt **RC**	.50
186	Adrian Burnside **RC**	.50
187	Josh Hancock **RC**	.75
188	Jorge Nunez **RC**	.50
189	Tyler Yates **RC**	1.00
190	Kyle Kane **RC**	.75
191	Jose Valverde **RC**	1.00
192	Matt Thornton	.50
193	Ben Howard **RC**	.50
194	Reed Johnson **RC**	1.50
195	Rene Reyes **RC**	.50
196	Jeremy Ward **RC**	.50
197	Steve Bechler **RC**	.50
198	Cam Esslinger **RC**	.50
199	Michael Crudale **RC**	.50
200	Todd Donovan **RC**	.50

Retro UD Jerseys

		NM/M
Common Player:		5.00
Inserted 1:16		
Golds:		1-2X
Production 275 Sets		
Reverse Neg.:		1-2X
Production 350 Sets		
JB	Jeff Bagwell	15.00
KB	Kevin Brown	8.00
EC	Eric Chavez	5.00
RC	Roger Clemens/SP	25.00
CD	Carlos Delgado	8.00
JD	J.D. Drew	10.00
JE	Jim Edmonds	8.00
DE	Darin Erstad	5.00
RF	Rafael Furcal	5.00
JG	Jason Giambi	10.00
TG	Tom Glavine	10.00
LG	Luis Gonzalez	5.00
KG	Ken Griffey Jr.	20.00
TH	Todd Helton	12.00
RJ	Randy Johnson	12.00
AJ	Andruw Jones	8.00
CJ	Chipper Jones	15.00
GM	Greg Maddux	15.00
MP	Mike Piazza	15.00
MR	Manny Ramirez	10.00
AR	Alex Rodriguez	15.00
IR	Ivan Rodriguez	10.00
SS	Sammy Sosa/SP	20.00
MS	Mike Sweeney	5.00
FT	Frank Thomas	10.00
BW	Bernie Williams	10.00
BZ	Barry Zito	8.00

Retro UD Star Rookie Jerseys

		NM/M
Common Player:		5.00
Inserted 1:16		
Golds:		1-2X
Production 275 Sets		
CB	Craig Biggio	8.00
PB	Pat Burrell	8.00
BG	Brian Giles	5.00
JG	Juan Gonzalez	8.00
LG	Luis Gonzalez	8.00
SG	Shawn Green	8.00
KG	Ken Griffey Jr.	20.00
RJ	Randy Johnson	10.00
CJ	Chipper Jones	10.00
DJ	David Justice	5.00
RK	Ryan Klesko	5.00
KL	Kenny Lofton	5.00
PM	Pedro J. Martinez	15.00
HN	Hideo Nomo	15.00
JO	John Olerud	5.00
MO	Magglio Ordonez	8.00
RP	Robert Person	5.00
AP	Albert Pujols	20.00
MR	Manny Ramirez/SP	15.00
AR	Alex Rodriguez	20.00

IR	Ivan Rodriguez	10.00
KS	Kazuhiro Sasaki	5.00
GS	Gary Sheffield	8.00
SS	Sammy Sosa/SP	20.00
I	Ichiro Suzuki	40.00
JT	Jim Thome	12.00
LW	Larry Walker	5.00

Reverse Negative Retro UD Jerseys

No Pricing

Signed UD Heroes of Baseball

		NM/M
Random Inserts:		
G	Ken Griffey Jr./185	125.00
R	Alex Rodriguez/185	90.00
I	Ichiro Suzuki/125	400.00

Signed Retro UD Star Rookie Jerseys

		NM/M
Production 40 Sets		
KG	Ken Griffey Jr.	100.00
AR	Alex Rodriguez	150.00
JT	Jim Thome	75.00

Stars of '89 Jerseys

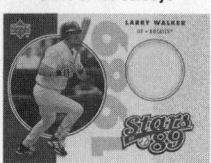

		NM/M
Common Player:		5.00
Inserted 1:16		
RA	Roberto Alomar	8.00
KB	Kevin Brown	8.00
EB	Ellis Burks	5.00
JC	Jose Canseco	8.00
RC	Roger Clemens	15.00
DC	David Cone	5.00
AG	Andres Galarraga	5.00
TG	Tom Glavine	10.00
JG	Juan Gonzalez	10.00
MG	Mark Grace	8.00
KG	Ken Griffey Jr.	20.00
RH	Rickey Henderson	10.00
RJ	Randy Johnson	10.00
DJ	David Justice	5.00
BL	Barry Larkin/SP	15.00
AL	Al Leiter	5.00
GM	Greg Maddux	15.00
EM	Edgar Martinez	8.00
FM	Fred McGriff	5.00
JO	John Olerud	5.00
PO	Paul O'Neill	8.00
RP	Rafael Palmeiro	8.00
CS	Curt Schilling	8.00
GS	Gary Sheffield	8.00
SS	Sammy Sosa	15.00
RV	Robin Ventura	5.00
LW	Larry Walker	5.00
MW	Matt Williams	5.00

UD Heroes of Baseball

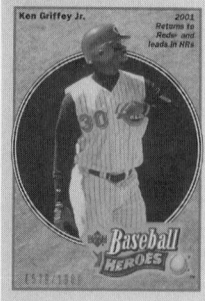

	NM/M
Complete Set (30):	150.00
Ichiro:	8.00
Griffey Jr.:	6.00

	Alex Rodriguez:	8.00
	Production 1,989 Sets	
HB-I1-10	Ichiro Suzuki	8.00
HB-G1-10	Ken Griffey Jr.	6.00
HB-R1-10	Alex Rodriguez	8.00

1989 Flashbacks

		NM/M
Complete Set (12):		30.00
Common Player:		1.50
Production 4,225 Sets		
F1	Ken Griffey Jr.	8.00
F2	Gary Sheffield	1.50
F3	Randy Johnson	3.00
F4	Roger Clemens	4.00
F5	Greg Maddux	5.00
F6	Mark Grace	2.00
F7	Barry Bonds	5.00
F8	Roberto Alomar	2.00
F9	Sammy Sosa	5.00
F10	Rafael Palmeiro	2.00
F11	Edgar Martinez	1.50
F12	Jose Canseco	2.00

2003 Upper Deck

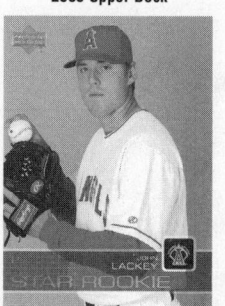

		NM/M
Complete Set (540):		75.00
Common Player:		.15
Common RC (466-529):		.50
Series 1 or 2 Pack (8):		2.50
Series 1 or 2 Box (24):		45.00
1	John Lackey	.15
2	Alex Cintron	.15
3	Jose Leon	.15
4	Bobby Hill	.15
5	Brandon Larson	.15
6	Raul Gonzalez	.15
7	Ben Broussard	.15
8	Earl Snyder	.15
9	Ramon Santiago	.15
10	Jason Lane	.15
11	Keith Ginter	.15
12	Kirk Saarloos	.15
13	Juan Brito	.15
14	Runelvys Hernandez	.15
15	Shawn Sedlacek	.15
16	Jayson Durocher	.15
17	Kevin Frederick	.15
18	Zach Day	.15
20	Marcus Thames	.15
21	Esteban German	.15
22	Brett Myers	.15
23	Oliver Perez	.25
24	Dennis Tankersley	.15
25	Julius Matos	.15
26	Jake Peavy	.15
27	Eric Cyr	.15
28	Mike Crudale	.15
29	Josh Pearce	.15
30	Carl Crawford	.15
31	Tim Salmon	.25
32	Troy Glaus	.50
33	Adam Kennedy	.15
34	David Eckstein	.15
35	Bengie Molina	.15
36	Jarrod Washburn	.15
37	Ramon Ortiz	.15
38	Eric Chavez	.40
39	Miguel Tejada	.50
40	Adam Piatt	.15
41	Jermaine Dye	.15
42	Olmedo Saenz	.15
43	Tim Hudson	.25
44	Barry Zito	.25
45	Billy Koch	.15
46	Shannon Stewart	.15
47	Kelvim Escobar	.15
48	Jose Cruz Jr.	.15
49	Vernon Wells	.15
50	Roy Halladay	.15
51	Esteban Loaiza	.15
52	Eric Hinske	.15
53	Steve Cox	.15
54	Brent Abernathy	.15
55	Ben Grieve	.15
56	Aubrey Huff	.15
57	Jared Sandberg	.15
58	Paul Wilson	.15
59	Tanyon Sturtze	.15
60	Jim Thome	.60
61	Omar Vizquel	.25
62	C.C. Sabathia	.15
63	Chris Magruder	.15
64	Ricky Gutierrez	.15
65	Einar Diaz	.15
66	Danys Baez	.15
67	Ichiro Suzuki	2.00
68	Ruben Sierra	.15
69	Carlos Guillen	.15
70	Mark McLemore	.15
71	Dan Wilson	.15
72	Jamie Moyer	.15
73	Joel Pineiro	.15
74	Edgar Martinez	.25
75	Tony Batista	.15
76	Jay Gibbons	.15
77	Chris Singleton	.15
78	Melvin Mora	.15
79	Geronimo Gil	.15
80	Rodrigo Lopez	.15
81	Jorge Julio	.15
82	Rafael Palmeiro	.50
83	Juan Gonzalez	.50
84	Mike Young	.15
85	Hideki Irabu	.15
86	Chan Ho Park	.15
87	Kevin Mench	.15
88	Doug Davis	.15
89	Pedro Martinez	.75
90	Shea Hillenbrand	.15
91	Derek Lowe	.15
92	Jason Varitek	.25
93	Tony Clark	.15
94	John Burkett	.15
95	Frank Castillo	.15
96	Nomar Garciaparra	2.00
97	Rickey Henderson	.40
98	Mike Sweeney	.15
99	Carlos Febles	.15
100	Mark Quinn	.15
101	Raul Ibanez	.15
102	A.J. Hinch	.15
103	Paul Byrd	.15
104	Chuck Knoblauch	.15
105	Dmitri Young	.15
106	Randall Simon	.15
107	Brandon Inge	.15
108	Damion Easley	.15
109	Carlos Pena	.15
110	George Lombard	.15
111	Juan Acevedo	.15
112	Torii Hunter	.25
113	Doug Mientkiewicz	.15
114	David Ortiz	.50
115	Eric Milton	.15
116	Eddie Guardado	.15
117	Cristian Guzman	.15
118	Corey Koskie	.15
119	Magglio Ordonez	.25
120	Mark Buehrle	.15
121	Todd Ritchie	.15
122	Jose Valentin	.15
123	Paul Konerko	.25
124	Carlos Lee	.15
125	Jon Garland	.15
126	Jason Giambi	.40
127	Derek Jeter	2.00
128	Roger Clemens	1.50
129	Raul Mondesi	.15
130	Jorge Posada	.25
131	Rondell White	.15
132	Robin Ventura	.25
133	Mike Mussina	.25
134	Jeff Bagwell	.50
135	Craig Biggio	.25
136	Morgan Ensberg	.15
137	Richard Hidalgo	.15
138	Brad Ausmus	.15
139	Roy Oswalt	.25
140	Carlos Hernandez	.15
141	Shane Reynolds	.15
142	Gary Sheffield	.25
143	Andruw Jones	.50
144	Tom Glavine	.40
145	Rafael Furcal	.25
146	Javy Lopez	.25
147	Vinny Castilla	.15
148	Marcus Giles	.15
149	Kevin Millwood	.15
150	Jason Marquis	.15
151	Ruben Quevedo	.15
152	Ben Sheets	.15
153	Geoff Jenkins	.15
154	Jose Hernandez	.15
155	Glendon Rusch	.15
156	Jeffrey Hammonds	.15
157	Alex Sanchez	.15
158	Jim Edmonds	.25
159	Tino Martinez	.25
160	Albert Pujols	1.50
161	Eli Marrero	.15
162	Woody Williams	.15
163	Fernando Vina	.15
164	Jason Isringhausen	.15
165	Jason Simontacchi	.15
166	Kerry Robinson	.15
167	Sammy Sosa	1.25
168	Juan Cruz	.15
169	Fred McGriff	.25
170	Antonio Alfonseca	.15
171	Jon Lieber	.15
172	Mark Prior	.50
173	Moises Alou	.25
174	Matt Clement	.15
175	Mark Bellhorn	.15
176	Randy Johnson	.75
177	Luis Gonzalez	.25
178	Tony Womack	.15
179	Mark Grace	.30
180	Junior Spivey	.15
181	Byung-Hyun Kim	.15
182	Danny Bautista	.15
183	Brian Anderson	.15
184	Shawn Green	.25
185	Brian Jordan	.15
186	Eric Karros	.15
187	Andy Ashby	.15
188	Cesar Izturis	.15
189	Dave Roberts	.15
190	Eric Gagne	.40
191	Kazuhisa Ishii	.15
192	Adrian Beltre	.25
193	Vladimir Guerrero	.75
194	Tony Armas Jr.	.15
195	Bartolo Colon	.15
196	Troy O'Leary	.15
197	Tomokazu Ohka	.15
198	Brad Wilkerson	.15
199	Orlando Cabrera	.15
200	Barry Bonds	2.00
201	David Bell	.15
202	Tsuyoshi Shinjo	.15
203	Benito Santiago	.15
204	Livan Hernandez	.15
205	Jason Schmidt	.40
206	Kirk Rueter	.15
207	Ramon E. Martinez	.15
208	Mike Lowell	.25
209	Luis Castillo	.15
210	Derrek Lee	.25
211	Andy Fox	.15
212	Eric Owens	.15
213	Charles Johnson	.15
214	Brad Penny	.15
215	A.J. Burnett	.15
216	Edgardo Alfonzo	.15
217	Roberto Alomar	.50
218	Rey Ordonez	.15
219	Al Leiter	.15
220	Roger Cedeno	.15
221	Timoniel Perez	.15
222	Jeromy Burnitz	.15
223	Pedro Astacio	.15
224	Joe McEwing	.15
225	Ryan Klesko	.15
226	Ramon Vazquez	.15
227	Mark Kotsay	.15
228	Bubba Trammell	.15
229	Wiki Gonzalez	.15
230	Trevor Hoffman	.15
231	Ron Gant	.15
232	Bobby Abreu	.25
233	Marlon Anderson	.15
234	Jeremy Giambi	.15
235	Jimmy Rollins	.25
236	Mike Lieberthal	.15
237	Vicente Padilla	.15
238	Randy Wolf	.15
239	Pokey Reese	.15
240	Brian Giles	.25
241	Jack Wilson	.15
242	Mike Williams	.15
243	Kip Wells	.15
244	Robert Mackowiak	.15
245	Craig Wilson	.15
246	Adam Dunn	.60
247	Sean Casey	.25
248	Todd Walker	.15
249	Corky Miller	.15
250	Ryan Dempster	.15
251	Reggie Taylor	.15
252	Aaron Boone	.15
253	Larry Walker	.30
254	Jose Ortiz	.15
255	Todd Zeile	.15
256	Bobby Estalella	.15
257	Juan Pierre	.15
258	Terry Shumpert	.15
259	Mike Hampton	.15
260	Denny Stark	.15
261	Shawn Green	.25
262	Derek Lowe	.15
263	Barry Bonds	1.00
264	Mike Cameron	.15
265	Luis Castillo	.15
266	Vladimir Guerrero	.40
267	Jason Giambi	.25
268	Eric Gagne	.25
269	Magglio Ordonez	.20
270	Jim Thome	.40
271	Garret Anderson	.40
272	Tony Percival	.15
273	Brad Fullmer	.15
274	Scott Spezio	.15
275	Darin Erstad	.40
276	Francisco Rodriguez	.15
277	Kevin Appier	.15
278	Shawn Wooten	.15

279	Eric Owens	.15
280	Scott Hatteberg	.15
281	Terrence Long	.15
282	Mark Mulder	.25
283	Ramon Hernandez	.15
284	Ted Lilly	.15
285	Erubiel Durazo	.15
286	Mark Ellis	.15
287	Carlos Delgado	.50
288	Orlando Hudson	.15
289	Chris Woodward	.15
290	Mark Hendrickson	.15
291	Josh Phelps	.15
292	Ken Huckaby	.15
293	Justin Miller	.15
294	Travis Lee	.15
295	Jorge Sosa	.15
296	Joe Kennedy	.15
297	Carl Crawford	.15
298	Toby Hall	.15
299	Rey Ordonez	.15
300	Brandon Phillips	.15
301	Matt Lawton	.15
302	Ellis Burks	.15
303	Bill Selby	.15
304	Travis Hafner	.15
305	Milton Bradley	.15
306	Karim Garcia	.15
307	Cliff Lee	.25
308	Jeff Cirillo	.15
309	John Olerud	.25
310	Kazuhiro Sasaki	.15
311	Freddy Garcia	.15
312	Bret Boone	.25
313	Mike Cameron	.15
314	Ben Davis	.15
315	Randy Winn	.15
316	Gary Matthews Jr.	.15
317	Jeff Conine	.15
318	Sidney Ponson	.15
319	Jerry Hairston	.15
320	David Segui	.15
321	Scott Erickson	.15
322	Marty Cordova	.15
323	Hank Blalock	.50
324	Herbert Perry	.15
325	Alex Rodriguez	2.00
326	Carl Everett	.15
327	Einar Diaz	.15
328	Ugueth Urbina	.15
329	Mark Teixeira	.40
330	Manny Ramirez	.75
331	Johnny Damon	.50
332	Trot Nixon	.15
333	Tim Wakefield	.15
334	Casey Fossum	.15
335	Todd Walker	.15
336	Jeremy Giambi	.15
337	Bill Mueller	.15
338	Ramiro Mendoza	.15
339	Carlos Beltran	.50
340	Jason Grimsley	.15
341	Brent Mayne	.15
342	Angel Berroa	.15
343	Albie Lopez	.15
344	Michael Tucker	.15
345	Bobby Higginson	.15
346	Shane Halter	.15
347	Jeremy Bonderman	2.00
348	Eric Munson	.15
349	Andy Van Hekken	.15
350	Matt Anderson	.15
351	Jacque Jones	.15
352	A.J. Pierzynski	.15
353	Joe Mays	.15
354	Brad Radke	.15
355	Dustan Mohr	.15
356	Bobby Kielty	.15
357	Michael Cuddyer	.15
358	Luis Rivas	.15
359	Frank Thomas	.75
360	Joe Borchard	.15
361	D'Angelo Jimenez	.15
362	Bartolo Colon	.25
363	Joe Crede	.15
364	Miguel Olivo	.15
365	Billy Koch	.15
366	Bernie Williams	.50
367	Nick Johnson	.15
368	Andy Pettitte	.40
369	Mariano Rivera	.25
370	Alfonso Soriano	.75
371	David Wells	.15
372	Drew Henson	.15
373	Juan Rivera	.15
374	Steve Karsay	.15
375	Jeff Kent	.25
376	Lance Berkman	.50
377	Octavio Dotel	.15
378	Julio Lugo	.15
379	Jason Lane	.15
380	Wade Miller	.15
381	Billy Wagner	.15
382	Brad Ausmus	.15
383	Mike Hampton	.15
384	Chipper Jones	.75
385	John Smoltz	.25
386	Greg Maddux	1.25
387	Javy Lopez	.25
388	Robert Fick	.15
389	Mark DeRosa	.15
390	Russ Ortiz	.15
391	Julio Franco	.15
392	Richie Sexson	.50
393	Eric Young	.15
394	Robert Machado	.15
395	Mike DeJean	.15
396	Todd Ritchie	.15
397	Royce Clayton	.15
398	Nick Neugebauer	.15
399	J.D. Drew	.25
400	Edgar Renteria	.25
401	Scott Rolen	.75
402	Matt Morris	.25
403	Garrett Stephenson	.15
404	Eduardo Perez	.15
405	Mike Matheny	.15
406	Miguel Cairo	.15
407	Brett Tomko	.15
408	Bobby Hill	.15
409	Troy O'Leary	.15
410	Corey Patterson	.40
411	Kerry Wood	.75
412	Eric Karros	.15
413	Hee Seop Choi	.15
414	Alex Gonzalez	.15
415	Matt Clement	.15
416	Mark Grudzielanek	.15
417	Curt Schilling	.50
418	Steve Finley	.15
419	Craig Counsell	.15
420	Matt Williams	.15
421	Quinton McCracken	.15
422	Chad Moeller	.15
423	Lyle Overbay	.15
424	Miguel Batista	.15
425	Paul LoDuca	.15
426	Kevin Brown	.25
427	Hideo Nomo	.40
428	Fred McGriff	.25
429	Joe Thurston	.15
430	Odalis Perez	.15
431	Darren Dreifort	.15
432	Todd Hundley	.15
433	Dave Roberts	.15
434	Jose Vidro	.15
435	Javier Vazquez	.15
436	Michael Barrett	.15
437	Fernando Tatis	.15
438	Peter Bergeron	.15
439	Endy Chavez	.15
440	Orlando Hernandez	.15
441	Marvin Bernard	.15
442	Rich Aurilia	.15
443	Pedro Feliz	.15
444	Robb Nen	.15
445	Ray Durham	.15
446	Marquis Grissom	.15
447	Damian Moss	.15
448	Edgardo Alfonzo	.15
449	Juan Pierre	.15
450	Braden Looper	.15
451	Alex Gonzalez	.15
452	Justin Wayne	.15
453	Josh Beckett	.25
454	Juan Encarnacion	.15
455	Ivan Rodriguez	.50
456	Todd Hollandsworth	.15
457	Cliff Floyd	.15
458	Rey Sanchez	.15
459	Mike Piazza	1.50
460	Mo Vaughn	.15
461	Armando Benitez	.15
462	Tsuyoshi Shinjo	.15
463	Tom Glavine	.40
464	David Cone	.15
465	Phil Nevin	.15
466	Sean Burroughs	.15
467	Jake Peavy	.15
468	Brian Lawrence	.15
469	Mark Loretta	.15
470	Dennis Tankersley	.15
471	Jesse Orosco	.15
472	Jim Thome	.75
473	Kevin Millwood	.40
474	David Bell	.15
475	Pat Burrell	.40
476	Brandon Duckworth	.15
477	Jose Mesa	.15
478	Marlon Byrd	.15
479	Reggie Sanders	.15
480	Jason Kendall	.25
481	Aramis Ramirez	.40
482	Kris Benson	.15
483	Matt Stairs	.15
484	Kevin Young	.15
485	Kenny Lofton	.25
486	Austin Kearns	.40
487	Barry Larkin	.25
488	Jason LaRue	.15
489	Ken Griffey Jr.	1.25
490	Danny Graves	.15
491	Russell Branyan	.15
492	Reggie Taylor	.15
493	Jimmy Haynes	.15
494	Charles Johnson	.15
495	Todd Helton	.75
496	Juan Uribe	.15
497	Preston Wilson	.15
498	Chris Stynes	.15
499	Jason Jennings	.15
500	Jay Payton	.15
501	Hideki Matsui **RC**	5.00
502	Jose Contreras **RC**	2.00
503	Brandon Webb **RC**	3.00
504	Robby Hammock **RC**	.50
505	Matt Kata **RC**	.50
506	Tim Olson **RC**	.50
507	Michael Hessman **RC**	.50
508	Jon Leicester **RC**	.50
509	Todd Wellemeyer **RC**	.50
510	David Sanders **RC**	.50
511	Josh Stewart **RC**	.50
512	Luis Ayala **RC**	.50
513	Clint Barmes **RC**	2.00
514	Josh Willingham **RC**	.50
515	Alejandro Machado **RC**	.50
516	Felix Sanchez **RC**	.50
517	Willie Eyre **RC**	.50
518	Brent Hoard **RC**	.50
519	Lew Ford **RC**	1.50
520	Terrmel Sledge **RC**	.50
521	Jeremy Griffiths	.15
522	Phil Seibel **RC**	.50
523	Craig Brazell **RC**	.50
524	Prentice Redman **RC**	.50
525	Jeff Duncan **RC**	.50
526	Shane Bazzell **RC**	.75
527	Bernie Castro **RC**	.50
528	Rett Johnson **RC**	.50
529	Bobby Madritsch **RC**	3.00
530	Rocco Baldelli	.40
531	Alex Rodriguez	1.00
532	Eric Chavez	.25
533	Miguel Tejada	.25
534	Ichiro Suzuki	.75
535	Sammy Sosa	.75
536	Barry Zito	.25
537	Darin Erstad	.25
538	Alfonso Soriano	.50
539	Troy Glaus	.25
540	Nomar Garciaparra	.75

Gold

Gold (541-600): 2-3X
One gold set per hobby case.

AL All-Star Swatch

		NM/M
Common Player:		5.00
Inserted 1:144 Retail		
MC	Mike Cameron	5.00
RD	Ray Durham	5.00
CE	Carl Everett	5.00
CF	Chuck Finley	5.00
TF	Travis Fryman	6.00
JG	Juan Gonzalez	8.00
JM	Joe Mays	5.00
MO	Magglio Ordonez	8.00
AP	Andy Pettitte	8.00
JP	Jorge Posada	8.00
MR	Mariano Rivera	10.00
AS	Aaron Sele	5.00
MS	Mike Sweeney	5.00

Big League Breakdown

		NM/M
Complete Set (15):		20.00
Common Player:		.50
Inserted 1:8		
BL1	Troy Glaus	.75
BL2	Miguel Tejada	.75
BL3	Chipper Jones	1.50
BL4	Torii Hunter	.50
BL5	Nomar Garciaparra	3.00
BL6	Sammy Sosa	2.50
BL7	Todd Helton	1.00
BL8	Lance Berkman	.75
BL9	Shawn Green	.50
BL10	Vladimir Guerrero	1.50
BL11	Jason Giambi	.50
BL12	Derek Jeter	4.00
BL13	Barry Bonds	4.00
BL14	Ichiro Suzuki	3.00
BL15	Alex Rodriguez	4.00

Game Swatches Hobby

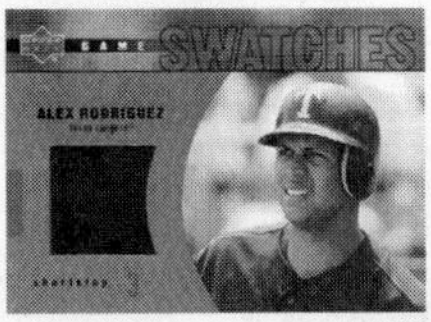

		NM/M
Common Player:		5.00
Inserted 1:72		
SB	Sean Burroughs/SP	8.00
CD	Carlos Delgado/SP	8.00
GM	Greg Maddux	15.00
MM	Mike Mussina	10.00
MO	Magglio Ordonez	5.00
CP	Carlos Pena	5.00
MP	Mike Piazza/SP	15.00
AR	Alex Rodriguez	15.00
CC	C.C. Sabathia	5.00
CS	Curt Schilling/100	10.00
SS	Sammy Sosa	15.00
BW	Bernie Williams	10.00

Game Swatches Retail

		NM/M
Common Player:		5.00
Inserted 1:72		
RC	Roger Clemens	15.00
JD	J.D. Drew	5.00
AD	Adam Dunn	8.00
JE	Jim Edmonds	8.00
DE	Darin Erstad	8.00
JG	Jason Giambi	8.00
KG	Ken Griffey Jr.	12.00
TH	Tim Hudson	6.00
RJ	Randy Johnson	8.00
JK	Jeff Kent	5.00
EM	Edgar Martinez	6.00
IR	Ivan Rodriguez	6.00
FT	Frank Thomas	8.00

Game Jersey Autograph

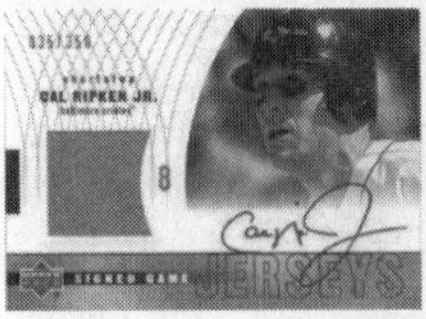

		NM/M
Golds:		1.5-2X
Production 25 or 75		
RC	Roger Clemens/350	100.00
JG	Jason Giambi/350	40.00
KG	Ken Griffey Jr./350	110.00
MM	Mark McGwire/150	350.00
CR	Cal Ripken Jr/350	140.00
AR	Alex Rodriguez/350	120.00
SS	Sammy Sosa/150	140.00

Leading Swatches

		NM/M
Common Player:		4.00
Inserted 1:24		
Golds:		1-2X
Production 100 Sets		
BA	Bobby Abreu	6.00
GA	Garret Anderson	6.00
JB	Jeff Bagwell	6.00
JB1	Jeff Bagwell	6.00
TB	Tony Batista	4.00
AB	Adrian Beltre	6.00
LB	Lance Berkman	4.00
PB	Pat Burrell	6.00
PB1	Pat Burrell	6.00
EC	Eric Chavez	6.00
RC	Roger Clemens	10.00
RC1	Roger Clemens	10.00
CD	Carlos Delgado	6.00
JD	J.D. Drew	4.00
AD	Adam Dunn	8.00
AD1	Adam Dunn	8.00
JE	Jim Edmonds	4.00
JG	Jason Giambi	6.00
JG1	Jason Giambi	6.00
BG	Brian Giles	4.00
TG	Troy Glaus	4.00
GO	Juan Gonzalez	6.00
LG	Luis Gonzalez	4.00
SG	Shawn Green	4.00
SG1	Shawn Green	4.00
KG	Ken Griffey Jr.	12.00
KG1	Ken Griffey Jr.	12.00
VG	Vladimir Guerrero	8.00
THe	Todd Helton	6.00
THu	Tim Hudson	4.00
TH1	Tim Hudson	4.00
KI	Kazuhisa Ishii	4.00
RJ	Randy Johnson	8.00
RJ1	Randy Johnson	8.00
AJ	Andruw Jones	6.00
AJ1	Andruw Jones	6.00
CJ	Chipper Jones	8.00
KE	Jason Kendall	4.00
JL	Javy Lopez	4.00
GM	Greg Maddux	10.00
GM1	Greg Maddux	10.00
PM	Pedro J. Martinez	8.00
HM	Hideki Matsui	40.00
HM1	Hideki Matsui	50.00
HN	Hideo Nomo	8.00
RO	Roy Oswalt	4.00
RO1	Roy Oswalt	4.00
RP	Rafael Palmeiro	6.00
RP1	Rafael Palmeiro	6.00
CP	Corey Patterson	6.00
JP	Jay Payton	4.00
TP	Troy Percival	4.00
AP	Andy Pettitte	6.00
MP	Mike Piazza	10.00
MP1	Mike Piazza	10.00
MR	Manny Ramirez	8.00
AR	Alex Rodriguez	10.00
AR1	Alex Rodriguez	10.00
IR	Ivan Rodriguez	6.00
SR	Scott Rolen	8.00
KS	Kazuhiro Sasaki	4.00
CS	Curt Schilling	8.00
AS	Aaron Sele	4.00

JS	J.T. Snow	4.00
AS	Alfonso Soriano	8.00
AS1	Alfonso Soriano	8.00
SS	Sammy Sosa	12.00
SS1	Sammy Sosa	12.00
MS	Mike Stanton	4.00
IS	Ichiro Suzuki	25.00
IS1	Ichiro Suzuki	25.00
MS	Mike Sweeney	4.00
MT	Miguel Tejada	6.00
MT1	Miguel Tejada	6.00
JT	Jim Thome	8.00
JT1	Jim Thome	8.00
OV	Omar Vizquel	4.00
LW	Larry Walker	4.00
BW	Bernie Williams	6.00
BW1	Bernie Williams	6.00
KW	Kerry Wood	8.00
BZ	Barry Zito	6.00

Lineup Time Jerseys

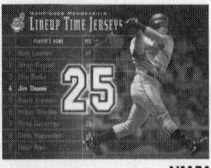

		NM/M
Common Player:		6.00
Inserted 1:96		
RC	Roger Clemens/SP	20.00
CD	Carlos Delgado	8.00
JD	J.D. Drew	6.00
SG	Shawn Green	8.00
TH	Todd Helton	8.00
RJ	Randy Johnson/SP	15.00
GM	Greg Maddux	10.00
IS	Ichiro Suzuki	40.00
JT	Jim Thome	10.00
BW	Bernie Williams	8.00

Magical Performances

		NM/M
Common Player:		8.00
Inserted 1:96		
Golds:		1-2X
Production 50 Sets		
MP1	Hideki Matsui	20.00
MP2	Ken Griffey Jr.	15.00
MP3	Ichiro Suzuki	15.00
MP4	Ken Griffey Jr.	15.00
MP5	Hideo Nomo	8.00
MP6	Mickey Mantle	40.00
MP7	Ken Griffey Jr.	15.00
MP8	Barry Bonds	20.00
MP9	Mickey Mantle	40.00
MP10	Tom Seaver	8.00
MP11	Mike Piazza	15.00
MP12	Roger Clemens	12.00
MP13	Nolan Ryan	30.00
MP14	Nomar Garciaparra	15.00
MP15	Ernie Banks	15.00
MP16	Stan Musial	25.00
MP17	Mickey Mantle	40.00
MP18	Nolan Ryan	30.00
MP19	Nolan Ryan	30.00
MP20	Mickey Mantle	40.00
MP21	Ichiro Suzuki	15.00
MP22	Nolan Ryan	30.00
MP23	Tom Seaver	8.00
MP24	Ken Griffey Jr.	15.00
MP25	Hideo Nomo	8.00
MP26	Ken Griffey Jr.	15.00
MP27	Mark McGwire	30.00
MP28	Barry Bonds	20.00
MP29	Alex Rodriguez	20.00
MP30	Nolan Ryan	30.00
MP31	Mark McGwire	30.00
MP32	Nolan Ryan	30.00
MP33	Sammy Sosa	15.00
MP34	Ichiro Suzuki	15.00
MP35	Barry Bonds	20.00
MP36	Derek Jeter	20.00
MP37	Roger Clemens	15.00
MP38	Jason Giambi	8.00
MP39	Mickey Mantle	40.00
MP40	Ted Williams	40.00
MP41	Ted Williams	40.00
MP42	Ted Williams	40.00

Mark of Greatness

		NM/M
400 Total cards produced		
MoG	Mark McGwire	350.00
MoG	Mark McGwire/Silver/70	400.00

Masters with the Leather

		NM/M
Complete Set (12):		20.00
Common Player:		.75
Inserted 1:12		
L1	Darin Erstad	.75
L2	Andruw Jones	1.50
L3	Greg Maddux	3.00
L4	Nomar Garciaparra	3.00
L5	Torii Hunter	1.00
L6	Roberto Alomar	1.00
L7	Derek Jeter	5.00
L8	Eric Chavez	1.00
L9	Ichiro Suzuki	3.00
L10	Jim Edmonds	1.00
L11	Scott Rolen	1.50
L12	Alex Rodriguez	4.00

Mid-Summer Stars

		NM/M
Common Player:		5.00
Inserted 1:72		
RC	Roger Clemens	12.00
CD	Carlos Delgado	8.00
JE	Jim Edmonds	8.00
DE	Darin Erstad	8.00
FG	Freddy Garcia	5.00
TG	Tom Glavine	8.00
JG	Juan Gonzalez	8.00
SG	Shawn Green/SP	8.00
RJ	Randy Johnson	10.00
AJ	Andruw Jones	6.00
EM	Edgar Martinez	10.00
HN	Hideo Nomo	20.00
MP	Mike Piazza	15.00
MR	Manny Ramirez	8.00
AR	Alex Rodriguez	15.00
KS	Kazuhiro Sasaki	8.00
CS	Curt Schilling	10.00
SS	Sammy Sosa	15.00
IS	Ichiro Suzuki/SP	40.00
FT	Frank Thomas	8.00
RV	Robin Ventura	8.00
DW	David Wells	5.00
BZ	Barry Zito	8.00

National Pride

		NM/M
Common Player:		3.00
Inserted 1:24		
AA	Abe Alvarez	3.00
MA	Michael Aubrey	15.00
KB	Kyle Bakker	3.00
SB	Sean Burroughs	5.00
CC	Chad Cordero	3.00
SC	Shane Costa	5.00
RF	Robert Fick	3.00
SF	Sam Fuld	5.00
AH	Aaron Hill	8.00
BH	Bobby Hill	3.00
BH1	Bobby Hill	3.00
AJ	A.J. Hinch	3.00
PH	Philip Humber	5.00
CJ	Conor Jackson	5.00
JJe	Jason Jennings	3.00
GJ	Grant Johnson	5.00
JJ	Jacque Jones	8.00
JJ1	Jacque Jones	8.00
MJ	Mark Jurich	3.00
AK	Austin Kearns	12.00
AK1	Austin Kearns	12.00
WL	Wes Littleton	3.00
EM	Eric Milton	5.00
EM1	Eric Milton	5.00
RO	Roy Oswalt	6.00
RO1	Roy Oswalt	6.00
EP	Eric Patterson	3.00
DP	Dustin Pedroia	5.00
LP	Landon Powell	5.00
MP	Mark Prior	15.00
MP1	Mark Prior	15.00
CQ	Carlos Quentin	3.00
KSa	Kirk Saarloos	3.00
KSa1	Kirk Saarloos	3.00
CS	Clint Sammons	5.00
KSl	Kyle Sleeth	5.00
HS	Huston Street	5.00
BS	Brad Sullivan	3.00
BS1	Brad Sullivan	3.00
RW	Rickie Weeks	10.00
RW1	Rickie Weeks	10.00
BZ	Bob Zimmermann	3.00

NL All-Star Swatch

		NM/M
Common Player:		5.00
Inserted 1:72		
SC	Sean Casey	5.00
CF	Cliff Floyd	5.00
TGl	Tom Glavine	8.00
TGw	Tony Gwynn	12.00
MH	Mike Hampton	5.00
TH	Trevor Hoffman	5.00
RK	Ryan Klesko	5.00
AL	Al Leiter	5.00
FM	Fred McGriff	5.00
MM	Matt Morris	8.00
CS	Curt Schilling	8.00
JV	Jose Vidro	5.00

Patch Logo

		NM/M
Quantity produced listed		
JB	Jeff Bagwell/41	60.00
KG	Ken Griffey Jr./50	100.00
TH	Todd Helton/41	50.00
KI	Kazuhisa Ishii/54	40.00
RJ	Randy Johnson/50	75.00
CJ	Chipper Jones/52	80.00
GM	Greg Maddux/50	100.00
MP	Mike Piazza/61	120.00
SS	Sammy Sosa/60	100.00
FT	Frank Thomas/52	60.00
BW	Bernie Williams/42	40.00

Patch Number

		NM/M
Quantity produced listed		
JG	Jason Giambi/68	40.00
KG	Ken Griffey Jr./97	70.00
KI	Kazuhisa Ishii/63	40.00
RJ	Randy Johnson/90	75.00
MG	Mark McGwire/60	180.00
AR	Alex Rodriguez/56	90.00
SS	Sammy Sosa/100	80.00
FT	Frank Thomas/91	60.00
BW	Bernie Williams/66	50.00

Patch Stripes

		NM/M
Quantity produced listed		
JB	Jeff Bagwell/73	60.00
JG	Jason Giambi/66	40.00
KG	Ken Griffey Jr./63	75.00
KI	Kazuhisa Ishii/58	40.00
RJ	Randy Johnson/58	65.00
CJ	Chipper Jones/58	60.00
MG	Mark McGwire/63	180.00
AR	Alex Rodriguez/63	80.00
SS	Sammy Sosa/63	100.00
IS	Ichiro Suzuki/63	180.00
FT	Frank Thomas/58	80.00
BW	Bernie Williams/58	50.00

Piece of the Action

		NM/M
Common Player:		5.00
Inserted 1:288		
Cards are not serial numbered.		
Print runs provided by Upper Deck.		
BA	Bobby Abreu/125	5.00
GA	Garret Anderson/150	5.00
AB	Adrian Beltre/100	10.00
BB	Barry Bonds/175	30.00
KB	Kevin Brown/100	5.00
PB	Pat Burrell/150	8.00
DE	Darin Erstad/125	5.00
FG	Freddy Garcia/100	5.00
BG	Brian Giles/100	5.00
TG	Troy Glaus/150	6.00
JG	Juan Gonzalez/100	5.00
LG	Luis Gonzalez/100	5.00
SG	Shawn Green/175	5.00
VG	Vladimir Guerrero/50	15.00
THe	Todd Helton/100	10.00
THo	Trevor Hoffman/150	5.00
DJ	Derek Jeter/65	40.00
RJ	Randy Johnson/100	10.00
CJ	Chipper Jones/62	15.00
JK	Jason Kendall/100	5.00
KE	Jeff Kent/150	5.00
RK	Ryan Klesko/75	6.00
EM	Edgar Martinez/125	5.00
PM	Pedro Martinez/150	10.00
PN	Phil Nevin/75	5.00
HN	Hideo Nomo/100	20.00
RP	Rafael Palmeiro/150	10.00
Ara	Aramis Ramirez/100	8.00
MP	Mike Piazza/150	15.00
ARo	Alex Rodriguez/100	15.00
KS	Kazuhiro Sasaki/100	5.00
CS	Curt Schilling/100	10.00
RS	Richie Sexson/160	8.00
GS	Gary Sheffield/100	5.00
SS	Sammy Sosa/85	20.00
FT	Frank Thomas/150	5.00
JT	Jim Thome/125	10.00
JV	Jose Vidro/100	5.00
LW	Larry Walker/150	5.00
BW	Bernie Williams/125	6.00

2003 Upper Deck Roger Clemens 300 Wins

		NM/M
Complete Set (6):		15.00
Common Card:		3.00
1	Roger Clemens (1999 post-season wins)	3.00
2	Roger Clemens (2000 post-season wins)	3.00
3	Roger Clemens (Sixth Cy Young)	3.00
4	Roger Clemens (4,000 Ks)	3.00
5	Roger Clemens (300th win)	3.00
--	Header Card	3.00

Slammin' Sammy Tribute Jersey

		NM/M
384 Total produced		
SST	Sammy Sosa	175.00
SST	Sammy Sosa/Gold/25	290.00
SST	Sammy Sosa/Silver/66	240.00

Star-Spangled Swatches

		NM/M
Common Player:		4.00
Inserted 1:72		
MA	Michael Aubrey	8.00
KB	Kyle Bakker	4.00
CC	Chad Cordero	4.00
SC	Shane Costa	6.00
AH	Aaron Hill	4.00
PH	Philip Humber	6.00
CJ	Conor Jackson	8.00
GJ	Grant Johnson	4.00
EP	Eric Patterson	8.00
DP	Dustin Pedroia	10.00
LP	Landon Powell	6.00
CQ	Carlos Quentin	8.00
KS	Kyle Sleeth	6.00
HS	Huston Street	10.00
BS	Brad Sullivan	4.00
RW	Rickie Weeks	10.00

Superstar Slam Jerseys

		NM/M
Common Player:		4.00
Inserted 1:48		
JB	Jeff Bagwell	8.00
JG	Jason Giambi	6.00
JGo	Juan Gonzalez	6.00
LG	Luis Gonzalez	4.00
KG	Ken Griffey Jr.	15.00
CJ	Chipper Jones	10.00
MP	Mike Piazza	10.00
AR	Alex Rodriguez	15.00
SS	Sammy Sosa	15.00
FT	Frank Thomas	8.00

The Chase for 755

		NM/M
Complete Set (15):		15.00
Common Player:		.75
Inserted 1:8		
C1	Troy Glaus	.75
C2	Andruw Jones	1.00

C3	Manny Ramirez	1.25
C4	Sammy Sosa	2.50
C5	Ken Griffey Jr.	3.00
C6	Adam Dunn	1.25
C7	Todd Helton	1.00
C8	Lance Berkman	.75
C9	Jeff Bagwell	1.00
C10	Shawn Green	.75
C11	Vladimir Guerrero	1.50
C12	Barry Bonds	4.00
C13	Alex Rodriguez	3.00
C14	Juan Gonzalez	.75
C15	Carlos Delgado	.75

Triple Game Jersey

	NM/M
Quantity produced listed	
Golds:	1.5-2X
Production 50, 25 or 10	
ARZ Randy Johnson, Curt Schilling, Luis Gonzalez/150	40.00
CIN Ken Griffey Jr., Sean Casey, Adam Dunn/150	40.00
HOU Jeff Bagwell, Lance Berkman, Craig Biggio/150	40.00
TEX Rafael Palmeiro, Alex Rodriguez, Juan Gonzalez/150	40.00
ATL Chipper Jones, Greg Maddux, Gary Sheffield/75	65.00
CHC Sammy Sosa, Moises Alou, Kerry Wood/75	50.00
NYM Mike Piazza, Roberto Alomar, Mo Vaughn/75	40.00
SEA Ichiro Suzuki, Freddy Garcia, Bret Boone/75	80.00

Superior Sluggers

	NM/M
Complete Set (18):	30.00
Common Player:	1.00
Inserted 1:8	
S1 Troy Glaus	1.00
S2 Chipper Jones	1.50
S3 Manny Ramirez	1.50
S4 Ken Griffey Jr.	2.50
S5 Jim Thome	1.50
S6 Todd Helton	1.00
S7 Lance Berkman	1.00
S8 Derek Jeter	4.00
S9 Vladimir Guerrero	1.50
S10 Mike Piazza	3.00
S11 Hideki Matsui	3.00
S12 Barry Bonds	4.00
S13 Mickey Mantle	5.00
S14 Alex Rodriguez	3.00
S15 Ted Williams	3.00
S16 Carlos Delgado	1.00
S17 Frank Thomas	1.00
S18 Adam Dunn	1.50

Super Patch Logos

Common Player:
Inserted 1:7,500
No Pricing

Super Patch Numbers

Common Player:
Inserted 1:7,500
No Pricing

Super Patch Stripes

Common Player:
Inserted 1:7,500
No Pricing

500 HR Club

	NM/M
Production 350 Cards	
SS Sammy Sosa/350	150.00
SS Sammy Sosa Auto./21	2,300

2003 UD Authentics

	NM/M
Complete Set (130):	
Common Player:	.25
Common Rk Hype (101-130):	4.00
Production 999	
Pack (4):	10.00
Box (10 + Framed Auto.):	170.00
1 Pee Wee Reese	.25
2 Richie Ashburn	.25
3 Derek Jeter	2.50
4 Alex Rodriguez	2.00
5 Jose Vidro	.25
6 Miguel Tejada	.50
7 Nomar Garciaparra	2.00
8 Pat Burrell	.50
9 Albert Pujols	2.00
10 Jeff Bagwell	.75
11 Stan Musial	1.00
12 Mickey Mantle	3.00
13 J.D. Drew	.25
14 Ivan Rodriguez	.75
15 Joe Morgan	.25
16 Ted Williams	2.00
17 Travis Hafner	.25
18 Chipper Jones	1.50
19 Hideo Nomo	.50
20 Gary Sheffield	.50
21 Jacque Jones	.25
22 Alfonso Soriano	1.50
23 Roberto Alomar	.50
24 Jeff Kent	.40
25 Omar Vizquel	.40
26 Ernie Banks	1.00
27 Shawn Green	.50
28 Tim Hudson	.50
29 Jim Edmonds	.50
30 Brandon Larson	.25
31 Doug Mientkiewicz	.25
32 Darin Erstad	.50
33 Bobby Hill	.25
34 Todd Helton	.75
35 Kazuhisa Ishii	.25
36 Lance Berkman	.50
37 Eric Hinske	.25
38 Jason Kendall	.25
39 Bob Feller	.50
40 Luis Gonzalez	.40
41 Sammy Sosa	2.00
42 Mike Piazza	1.50
43 Roger Clemens	2.00
44 Jose Cruz Jr.	.25
45 Mark Prior	1.50
46 Mark Teixeira	.40
47 Phil Nevin	.25
48 Lyle Overbay	.25
49 Manny Ramirez	.75
50 Brian Giles	.40
51 Preston Wilson	.25
52 Jermaine Dye	.25
53 Troy Glaus	.50
54 Frank Thomas	.75
55 Jim Thome	.75
56 Barry Bonds	2.50
57 Carlos Delgado	.75
58 Jason Giambi	1.00
59 Joe Mays	.25
60 Andruw Jones	.75
61 Billy Williams	.25
62 Vladimir Guerrero	.75
63 Scott Rolen	.75
64 Juan Marichal	.25
65 Austin Kearns	.50
66 Kerry Wood	.75
67 Bret Boone	.25
68 Shea Hillenbrand	.25
69 Mike Sweeney	.25
70 Rocco Baldelli	.25
71 Ken Griffey Jr.	1.50
72 Cliff Floyd	.25
73 Greg Maddux	1.50
74 Mike Hampton	.25
75 Larry Walker	.40
76 Nolan Ryan	3.00
77 Rollie Fingers	.25
78 Mike Mussina	.75
79 Matt Morris	.25
80 Robin Roberts	.25
81 Barry Zito	.50
82 Curt Schilling	.50
83 Ken Harvey	.25
84 Troy Percival	.25
85 Tom Seaver	1.00
86 Mariano Rivera	.40
87 Raul Mondesi	.25
88 Adam Dunn	.50
89 Roy Oswalt	.25
90 Pedro J. Martinez	1.00
91 Andy Pettitte	.50
92 Tom Glavine	.50
93 Torii Hunter	.50
94 Joe Thurston	.25
95 Runelvys Hernandez	.25
96 Randy Johnson	1.00
97 Bernie Williams	.75
98 Ichiro Suzuki	1.50
99 C.C. Sabathia	.25
100 Bobby Abreu	.40
101 Jose Contreras RC	6.00
102 Hideki Matsui RC	15.00
103 Chris Capuano RC	6.00
104 Willie Eyre RC	4.00
105 Lew Ford RC	6.00
106 Shane Bazzell RC	4.00
107 Guillermo Quiroz RC	6.00
108 Fernando Cabrera RC	4.00
109 Francisco Cruceta RC	4.00
110 Jhonny Peralta RC	4.00
111 Bobby Madritsch RC	8.00
112 Diegomar Markwell RC	4.00
113 Matt Bruback RC	4.00
114 Matt Kata RC	6.00
115 Rob Hammock RC	4.00
116 Brandon Webb RC	12.00
117 Jon Leicester RC	4.00
118 Josh Willingham RC	6.00
119 Prentice Redman RC	4.00
120 Jeff Duncan RC	4.00
121 Craig Brazell RC	6.00
122 Jeremy Griffiths RC	4.00
123 Phil Seibel RC	4.00
124 Luis Ayala RC	4.00
125 Miguel Ojeda RC	6.00
126 Jeremy Wedel RC	4.00
127 Josh Hall RC	6.00
128 Oscar Villarreal RC	4.00
129 Clint Barmes RC	8.00
130 Nook Logan RC	4.00

Threads of Time

	NM/M
Common Player:	4.00
Production 350, unless noted.	
Golds:	1-2X
Production 50, 25 or 10	
No Pricing for #'d to 25 or less.	
JB Johnny Bench	10.00
GC Gary Carter	4.00
RC Roger Clemens	15.00
TC Ty Cobb	100.00
DD Don Drysdale	15.00
DE Dennis Eckersley	4.00
RF Rollie Fingers	4.00
LG Lou Gehrig/250	140.00
JG Jason Giambi/250	6.00
JU Juan Gonzalez	5.00
KG Ken Griffey Jr./250	12.00
VG Vladimir Guerrero	6.00
RJ Randy Johnson	8.00
CJ Chipper Jones	8.00
HK Harmon Killebrew	12.00
GM Greg Maddux	8.00
MM Mickey Mantle/250	100.00
RM Roger Maris	40.00
PM Pedro J. Martinez	8.00
DM Don Mattingly	20.00
HN Hideo Nomo	8.00
AP Andy Pettitte	6.00
MP Mike Piazza	10.00
AP Albert Pujols	20.00
CR Cal Ripken Jr.	25.00
FR Frank Robinson	8.00
AR Alex Rodriguez	12.00
IR Ivan Rodriguez	5.00
NR Nolan Ryan	30.00
RS Ryne Sandberg	12.00
TS Tom Seaver	8.00
OS Ozzie Smith	10.00
SS Sammy Sosa/250	12.00
IS Ichiro Suzuki/250	30.00
FT Frank Thomas	6.00
JT Jim Thome	8.00
HW Honus Wagner	75.00
TW Ted Williams/250	65.00
MW Maury Wills	4.00
DW Dave Winfield/250	6.00

Star Quality

	NM/M
Common Player:	4.00
Production 350 unless noted.	
Golds:	1-2X
Production 50, 25 or 10	
No Pricing for #'d to 25 or less.	
RA Roberto Alomar	6.00
JB Jeff Bagwell	8.00
JO Josh Beckett	4.00
LB Lance Berkman	5.00
RC Roger Clemens	15.00
RC1 Roger Clemens	15.00
CD Carlos Delgado	5.00
JD J.D. Drew	4.00
AD Adam Dunn	6.00
JG Jason Giambi	5.00
TR Troy Glaus	5.00
TG Tom Glavine	4.00
SG Shawn Green	4.00
KG Ken Griffey Jr./250	12.00
VG Vladimir Guerrero	6.00
TH Todd Helton	6.00
EH Eric Hinske	4.00
CJ Chipper Jones	8.00
AK Austin Kearns	4.00
JK Jeff Kent	4.00
MM Mickey Mantle/250	100.00
HM Hideki Matsui/250	25.00
PM Paul Molitor/250	15.00
MU Mike Mussina	6.00
HN Hideo Nomo	4.00
RO Roy Oswalt	4.00
RP Rafael Palmeiro	6.00
MP Mark Prior	10.00
AP Albert Pujols	20.00
AP1 Albert Pujols	20.00
CR Cal Ripken Jr./250	25.00
NR Nolan Ryan/130	50.00
TS Tom Seaver	8.00
GS Gary Sheffield	4.00
AS Alfonso Soriano	10.00
SS Sammy Sosa/250	12.00
CS Casey Stengel	15.00
JT Jim Thome	8.00
BW Bernie Williams	8.00
TW Ted Williams/250	65.00
KW Kerry Wood	8.00

Framed Autograph

	NM/M
Common Framed Autograph:	40.00
Inserted 1:Box	
Lance Berkman/150	50.00
Lance Berkman/50	70.00
Hank Blalock/325	45.00
Hank Blalock/300	45.00
Hank Blalock/200	45.00
Hank Blalock/175	45.00
Pat Burrell/330	40.00
Pat Burrell/240	40.00
Pat Burrell/150	40.00
Gary Carter/225	50.00
Gary Carter/75	60.00
Jose Contreras/350	50.00
Jose Contreras/120	50.00
Carlton Fisk/250	50.00
Carlton Fisk/125	75.00
Carlton Fisk/70	80.00
Nomar Garciaparra/250	100.00
Nomar Garciaparra/150	120.00
Nomar Garciaparra/75	120.00
Jason Giambi/350	40.00
Jason Giambi/300	40.00
Jason Giambi/200	40.00
Jason Giambi/150	40.00
Jason Giambi/75	40.00
Bob Gibson/200	60.00
Bob Gibson/50	120.00
Bob Gibson/45	120.00
Troy Glaus/350	40.00
Troy Glaus/200	40.00
Troy Glaus/100	50.00
Tom Glavine/275	50.00
Tom Glavine/150	50.00
Tom Glavine/47	75.00
Ken Griffey Jr/325	90.00
Ken Griffey Jr./200	90.00
Ken Griffey Jr/75	100.00
Ken Griffey Jr./30	120.00
Vladimir Guerrero/150	60.00
Vladimir Guerrero/27	125.00
Drew Henson/350	40.00
Drew Henson/300	40.00
Drew Henson/250	40.00
Drew Henson/100	40.00
Chipper Jones/350	75.00
Chipper Jones/200	75.00
Chipper Jones/100	90.00
Austin Kearns/325	40.00
Austin Kearns/300	40.00
Austin Kearns/200	40.00
Austin Kearns/175	40.00
Austin Kearns/28	80.00
Hideki Matsui/75	300.00
Hideki Matsui/55	300.00
Mark Prior/325	60.00
Mark Prior/250	60.00
Mark Prior/175	60.00
Mark Prior/100	60.00
Cal Ripken Jr/125	175.00
Cal Ripken Jr./50	200.00
Phil Rizzuto/350	60.00
Phil Rizzuto/200	60.00
Phil Rizzuto/100	75.00
Scott Rolen/300	50.00
Scott Rolen/100	65.00
Scott Rolen/27	120.00
Nolan Ryan/150	125.00
Nolan Ryan/100	180.00
Nolan Ryan/50	200.00
Nolan Ryan/34	240.00
Tom Seaver/100	75.00
Tom Seaver/50	100.00
Tom Seaver/41	100.00
Ozzie Smith/150	85.00
Ozzie Smith/50	120.00
Duke Snider/150	100.00
Duke Snider/50	100.00
Ichiro Suzuki/75	300.00
Ichiro Suzuki/51	350.00
Mark Teixeira/325	60.00
Mark Teixeira/200	60.00
Mark Teixeira/175	60.00
Mark Teixeira/150	60.00

Cut Signatures

No Pricing

Rookie Hype Gold

Cards (101-130): 1-2X
Production 50

2003 Upper Deck Classic Portraits

	NM/M
Complete Set (232):	
Common Player:	.15
Common SP (101-145):	2.00
Inserted 1:4	
Common SP (145-190):	3.00
Production 2,003	
Common Royalty (191-232):	2.00
Production 1,200	
Pack (5):	3.00
Box (18 + Bust):	75.00
1 Ken Griffey Jr.	1.50
2 Randy Johnson	1.00
3 Rafael Furcal	.25
4 Omar Vizquel	.25
5 Shawn Green	.40
6 Roy Oswalt	.40
7 Hideo Nomo	.40
8 Jason Giambi	.40
9 Barry Bonds	2.50
10 Mike Piazza	1.50
11 Ichiro Suzuki	2.00
12 Carlos Delgado	.40
13 Preston Wilson	.15
14 Lance Berkman	.25
15 Magglio Ordonez	.25
16 Kerry Wood	.25
17 Ivan Rodriguez	.75
18 Chipper Jones	1.00
19 Adam Dunn	.75
20 C.C. Sabathia	.15
21 Mike MacDougal	.15
22 Torii Hunter	.40
23 Jim Thome	.75
24 Hank Blalock	.75
25 Johnny Damon	.50
26 Troy Glaus	.40
27 Manny Ramirez	.75
28 Mark Prior	1.00
29 Brent Mayne	.15
30 Derek Jeter	2.50
31 Tim Hudson	.40
32 Mike Cameron	.15
33 Mark Teixeira	.40
34 Shannon Stewart	.15
35 Tim Salmon	.25
36 Luis Gonzalez	.25
37 Jason Johnson	.15
38 Shea Hillenbrand	.15
39 Bartolo Colon	.25
40 Austin Kearns	.40
41 Vladimir Guerrero	1.00
42 Tom Glavine	.40
43 Andres Galarraga	.25
44 Kazuhiro Sasaki	.15
45 Juan Gonzalez	.75
46 Vernon Wells	.25
47 Jeff Bagwell	.75
48 Mike Sweeney	.15
49 Carlos Beltran	.50
50 Dave Roberts	.15
51 Todd Helton	.75
52 Carlos Pena	.15
53 Darin Erstad	.15
54 Gary Sheffield	.40
55 Lyle Overbay	.15
56 Sammy Sosa	1.50
57 Mike Mussina	.50
58 Matt Morris	.25
59 Roberto Alomar	.25
60 Larry Walker	.25
61 Jacque Jones	.15
62 Josh Beckett	.40
63 Richie Sexson	.50
64 Derek Lowe	.15
65 Pedro J. Martinez	1.00
66 Moises Alou	.25
67 Craig Biggio	.25
68 Curt Schilling	.25
69 Jesse Foppert	.15
70 Nomar Garciaparra	1.50
71 Barry Zito	.40
72 Alfonso Soriano	.75
73 Miguel Tejada	.50

74 Rafael Palmeiro	.50
75 Albert Pujols	2.00
76 Mariano Rivera	.25
77 Bobby Abreu	.25
78 Alex Rodriguez	2.00
79 Andruw Jones	.50
80 Frank Thomas	.75
81 Greg Maddux	1.50
82 Jim Edmonds	.40
83 Bernie Williams	.50
84 Roger Clemens	2.00
85 Eric Chavez	.25
86 Scott Rolen	1.00
87 Jorge Posada	.50
88 Bret Boone	.25
89 Ben Sheets	.25
90 John Olerud	.15
91 J.D. Drew	.25
92 Aaron Boone	.15
93 Corey Koskie	.15
94 Sean Casey	.25
95 Jose Cruz Jr.	.15
96 Pat Burrell	.40
97 Jose Guillen	.15
98 Mark Mulder	.25
99 Garret Anderson	.25
100 Kazuhisa Ishii	.15
101 Dave Matranga RC	2.00
102 Colin Porter RC	2.00
103 Jason Gilfillan RC	2.00
104 Carlos Mendez RC	2.00
105 Jason Shiell RC	2.00
106 Kevin Tolar RC	2.00
107 Terrmel Sledge RC	3.00
108 Craig Brazell RC	4.00
109 Bernie Castro RC	2.00
110 Tim Olson RC	3.00
111 Kevin Ohme RC	2.00
112 Pedro Liriano RC	2.00
113 Joe Borowski RC	2.00
114 Edgar Gonzalez RC	3.00
115 Joe Thurston RC	2.00
116 Bobby Hill RC	2.00
117 Michel Hernandez RC	2.00
118 Arnie Munoz RC	.15
119 David Sanders RC	2.00
120 Willie Eyre RC	3.00
121 Brent Hoard RC	2.00
122 Lew Ford RC	4.00
123 Beau Kemp RC	2.00
124 Jonathan Pridie RC	2.00
125 Mike Ryan RC	4.00
126 Richard Fischer RC	2.00
127 Luis Ayala RC	2.00
128 Mike Neu RC	2.00
129 Joe Valentine RC	2.00
130 Nate Bland RC	2.00
131 Shane Bazzell RC	2.00
132 Jason Roach RC	2.00
133 Diegomar Markwell RC	2.00
134 Francisco Rosario RC	2.00
135 Guillermo Quiroz RC	4.00
136 Jerome Williams RC	2.00
137 Fernando Cabrera RC	2.00
138 Francisco Cruceta RC	2.00
139 Jhonny Peralta RC	4.00
140 Rett Johnson RC	2.00
141 Aaron Looper RC	2.00
142 Bobby Madritsch RC	6.00
143 Dan Haren RC	3.00
144 Jose Castillo RC	2.00
145 Chris Waters RC	3.00
146 Hideki Matsui RC	10.00
147 Jose Contreras RC	4.00
148 Felix Sanchez RC	3.00
149 Jon Leicester RC	3.00
150 Todd Wellemeyer RC	3.00
151 Matt Bruback RC	3.00
152 Chris Capuano RC	5.00
153 Oscar Villarreal RC	3.00
154 Matt Kata RC	3.00
155 Robby Hammock RC	3.00
156 Gerald Laird RC	3.00
157 Brandon Webb RC	8.00
158 Tommy Whiteman RC	3.00
159 Andrew Brown RC	3.00
160 Alfredo Gonzalez RC	3.00
161 Carlos Rivera RC	3.00
162 Rick Roberts RC	3.00
163 Dontrelle Willis RC	15.00
164 Josh Willingham RC	4.00
165 Prentice Redman RC	3.00
166 Jeff Duncan RC	4.00
167 Jose Reyes RC	3.00
168 Jeremy Griffiths RC	3.00
169 Phil Seibel RC	3.00
170 Heath Bell RC	3.00
171 Anthony Ferrari RC	3.00
172 Mike Nicolas RC	3.00
173 Cory Stewart RC	3.00
174 Miguel Ojeda RC	5.00
175 Rickie Weeks RC	8.00
176 Delmon Young RC	10.00
177 Tommy Phelps RC	3.00
178 Josh Hall RC	4.00
179 Ryan Cameron RC	3.00
180 Garrett Atkins RC	3.00
181 Clint Barmes RC	6.00
182 Michael Hessman RC	3.00
183 Chin-Hui Tsao RC	3.00
184 Rocco Baldelli RC	3.00
185 Bo Hart RC	3.00
186 Wilfredo Ledezma RC	3.00
187 Miguel Cabrera RC	5.00
188 Ian Ferguson RC	3.00

189 Micheal Nakamura RC	3.00
190 Alejandro Machado RC	3.00
191 Mickey Mantle	12.00
192 Ted Williams	10.00
193 Mark Prior	6.00
194 Stan Musial	6.00
195 Phil Rizzuto	3.00
196 Nolan Ryan	12.00
197 Tom Seaver	4.00
198 Robin Yount	5.00
199 Yogi Berra	3.00
200 Ernie Banks	8.00
201 Willie McCovey	3.00
202 Ralph Kiner	3.00
203 Ken Griffey Jr.	4.00
204 Sammy Sosa	5.00
205 Derek Jeter	8.00
206 Nomar Garciaparra	6.00
207 Alex Rodriguez	8.00
208 Ichiro Suzuki	4.00
209 Mike Piazza	4.00
210 Jackie Robinson	6.00
211 Roberto Clemente	8.00
212 Babe Ruth	12.00
213 Duke Snider	3.00
214 Greg Maddux	3.00
215 Juan Marichal	3.00
216 Joe Morgan	2.00
217 Rollie Fingers	2.00
218 Warren Spahn	4.00
219 Pee Wee Reese	2.00
220 Troy Glaus	2.00
221 Jason Giambi	2.00
222 Roger Clemens	6.00
223 Pedro J. Martinez	3.00
224 Chipper Jones	4.00
225 Randy Johnson	3.00
226 Jim Thome	3.00
227 Barry Bonds	8.00
228 Hideo Nomo	2.00
229 Whitey Ford	3.00
230 Bob Gibson	4.00
231 Alfonso Soriano	4.00
232 Richie Ashburn	3.00

Gold

No pricing due to scarcity.
Production 25 Sets

Bronze Bust

	NM/M
Common Player:	
YB Yogi Berra	25.00
RC Roberto Clemente	60.00
NG Nomar Garciaparra	40.00
JG Jason Giambi	25.00
BG Bob Gibson	25.00
KG Ken Griffey Jr./300	40.00
MM Mickey Mantle	70.00
HM Hideki Matsui	30.00
SM Stan Musial	40.00
BRS Babe Ruth/Sox/300	60.00
BRY Babe Ruth/Yanks	60.00
NRA Nolan Ryan/Astros	50.00
NRA Nolan Ryan/Astros/300	50.00
NRM Nolan Ryan/Mets	50.00
TSM Tom Seaver/Mets	25.00
TSR Tom Seaver/Reds/300	25.00
TSR Tom Seaver/Reds	25.00
DS Duke Snider	25.00
SS Sammy Sosa/300	40.00
IS Ichiro Suzuki/300	40.00
TW Ted Williams	50.00

Bronze Bust Autograph

	NM/M
Some not priced due to scarcity.	
YB Yogi Berra	100.00
NG Nomar Garciaparra/106	125.00
BG Bob Gibson	60.00
KG Ken Griffey Jr.	100.00
HM Hideki Matsui	250.00
SM Stan Musial/62	120.00
DS Duke Snider	90.00
IS Ichiro Suzuki/62	275.00

Bust Signature

	NM/M
Complete Set (17):	
Common Player:	
NG Nomar Garciaparra	80.00
HM Hideki Matsui	180.00

Stitches Jersey

	NM/M
Common Player:	4.00
Production 299 Sets	
Golds:	No Pricing
Production 25 Sets	
JB Jeff Bagwell	6.00
RB Rocco Baldelli	4.00
HB Hank Blalock	6.00
HC Hee Seop Choi	4.00
RC Roger Clemens	15.00
JD J.D. Drew	4.00
AD Adam Dunn	8.00
JE Jim Edmonds	6.00
RF Rafael Furcal	4.00
JG Jason Giambi	6.00
TG Troy Glaus	6.00
SG Shawn Green	4.00
KG Ken Griffey Jr.	10.00
VG Vladimir Guerrero	8.00
TH Torii Hunter	6.00
RJ Randy Johnson	8.00
AJ Andruw Jones	6.00
CJ Chipper Jones	8.00
JK Jeff Kent	4.00
ML Mike Lowell	4.00
GM Greg Maddux	10.00
PM Pedro J. Martinez	8.00
HM Hideki Matsui	40.00
MM Matt Morris	6.00
HN Hideo Nomo	8.00
MO Magglio Ordonez	4.00
RO Roy Oswalt	4.00
CP Corey Patterson	6.00
AP Andy Pettitte	6.00
MI Mike Piazza	8.00
MP Mark Prior	8.00
AL Albert Pujols	15.00
AR Alex Rodriguez	10.00
IR Ivan Rodriguez	6.00
CS Curt Schilling	8.00
GS Gary Sheffield	6.00
AS Alfonso Soriano	8.00
SS Sammy Sosa	15.00
IS Ichiro Suzuki	25.00
JT Jim Thome	8.00
DW Dontrelle Willis	8.00
KW Kerry Wood	8.00

Stitches Patch

	NM/M
Common Player:	15.00
Production 99 Sets	
Golds:	No Pricing
Production 10 Sets	
JB Jeff Bagwell	25.00
RB Rocco Baldelli	15.00
HB Hank Blalock	25.00
HC Hee Seop Choi	15.00
RC Roger Clemens	40.00
JD J.D. Drew	15.00
AD Adam Dunn	15.00
JE Jim Edmonds	20.00
RF Rafael Furcal	15.00
JG Jason Giambi	15.00
TG Troy Glaus	15.00
SG Shawn Green	15.00
KG Ken Griffey Jr.	50.00
VG Vladimir Guerrero	25.00
TH Torii Hunter	15.00

RJ	Randy Johnson	30.00
AJ	Andruw Jones	15.00
CJ	Chipper Jones	25.00
JK	Jeff Kent	15.00
ML	Mike Lowell	15.00
GM	Greg Maddux	35.00
PM	Pedro J. Martinez	25.00
HM	Hideki Matsui	85.00
MM	Matt Morris	15.00
HN	Hideo Nomo	40.00
MO	Magglio Ordonez	15.00
RO	Roy Oswalt	15.00
CP	Corey Patterson	20.00
AP	Andy Pettitte	20.00
MI	Mike Piazza	40.00
MP	Mark Prior	15.00
AL	Albert Pujols	40.00
AR	Alex Rodriguez	50.00
IR	Ivan Rodriguez	20.00
CS	Curt Schilling	20.00
GS	Gary Sheffield	15.00
AS	Alfonso Soriano	20.00
SS	Sammy Sosa	35.00
IS	Ichiro Suzuki	120.00
JT	Jim Thome	20.00
DW	Dontrelle Willis	20.00
KW	Kerry Wood	25.00

Marble Bust

		NM/M
Common Player:		
YB	Yogi Berra/125	40.00
YB	Yogi Berra/250	25.00
RC	Roberto Clemente/250	70.00
NG	Nomar Garciaparra/250	40.00
JG	Jason Giambi	25.00
BG	Bob Gibson/125	30.00
BG	Bob Gibson/250	25.00
KG	Ken Griffey Jr./250	40.00
MM	Mickey Mantle/80	80.00
MM	Mickey Mantle/125	80.00
HM	Hideki Matsui/250	60.00
SM	Stan Musial/250	50.00
BRS	Babe Ruth/Sox/250	60.00
BRY	Babe Ruth/Yanks/125	75.00
BRY	Babe Ruth/Yanks/250	65.00
NRA	Nolan Ryan/Astros/125	60.00
NRA	Nolan Ryan/Astros/250	50.00
NRM	Nolan Ryan/Mets/125	60.00
NRM	Nolan Ryan/Mets/250	50.00
TSM	Tom Seaver/Mets/125	40.00
TSM	Tom Seaver/Mets/250	30.00
TSR	Tom Seaver/Reds/125	40.00
TSR	Tom Seaver/Reds/250	30.00
DS	Duke Snider/100	40.00
DS	Duke Snider/250	40.00
SS	Sammy Sosa/250	40.00
IS	Ichiro Suzuki/250	50.00
TW	Ted Williams/125	65.00
TW	Ted Williams/250	50.00

Marble Autograph

No pricing due to scarcity.

Pewter Bust

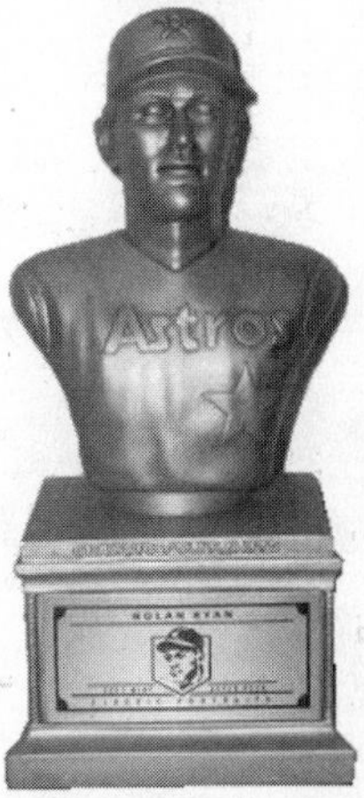

		NM/M
Common Player:		
YB	Yogi Berra/75	40.00
YB	Yogi Berra/100	40.00
RC	Roberto Clemente/100	100.00
NG	Nomar Garciaparra/100	60.00
JG	Jason Giambi/100	40.00
BG	Bob Gibson/75	40.00
BG	Bob Gibson/100	40.00
KG	Ken Griffey Jr./100	70.00
MM	Mickey Mantle/75	125.00
MM	Mickey Mantle/100	125.00
HM	Hideki Matsui/100	50.00
SM	Stan Musial/100	60.00
BRS	Babe Ruth/Sox/100	80.00
BRY	Babe Ruth/Yanks/75	90.00
BRY	Babe Ruth/Yanks/100	90.00
NRA	Nolan Ryan/Astros/75	80.00
NRA	Nolan Ryan/Astros/100	80.00
NRM	Nolan Ryan/Mets/75	80.00
NRM	Nolan Ryan/Mets/100	80.00
TSM	Tom Seaver/Mets/75	40.00
TSM	Tom Seaver/Mets/100	40.00
TSR	Tom Seaver/Reds/100	40.00
TSR	Tom Seaver/Reds/75	40.00
DS	Duke Snider/75	40.00
DS	Duke Snider/100	40.00
SS	Sammy Sosa/100	60.00
IS	Ichiro Suzuki/100	65.00
TW	Ted Williams/75	100.00
TW	Ted Williams/100	100.00

Pewter Autograph Bust

No pricing due to scarcity.

Signs of Success

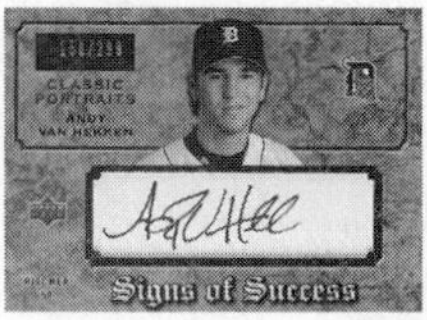

		NM/M
Common Player:		6.00
MI	Milton Bradley/220	10.00
DB	Dewon Brazelton/299	6.00
JB	John Buck/98	8.00
MB	Mark Buehrle/220	10.00
BR	Brandon Claussen/121	6.00
BC	Brad Cresse/121	10.00
JD	Johnny Damon/297	30.00
BD	Ben Diggins/299	6.00
AG	Alex Graman/215	10.00
KG	Ken Griffey Jr./299	90.00
TG	Tony Gwynn/49	80.00
DH	Drew Henson/246	15.00
BH	Ben Howard/299	6.00
HI	Hansel Izquierdo/299	8.00
JJ	Jimmy Journell/98	8.00
DK	David Kelton/102	8.00
KL	Kenny Lofton/296	15.00
CM	Corwin Malone/103	8.00
BP	Brandon Phillips/131	10.00
SR	Scott Rolen/100	20.00
CC	C.C. Sabathia/106	20.00
MT	Mark Teixeira/280	25.00
TH	Matt Thornton/298	6.00
AH	Andy Van Hekken/299	8.00
JU	Justin Wayne/299	8.00
JW	Jayson Werth/299	8.00
JE	Jerome Williams/103	15.00

2003 Upper Deck Finite

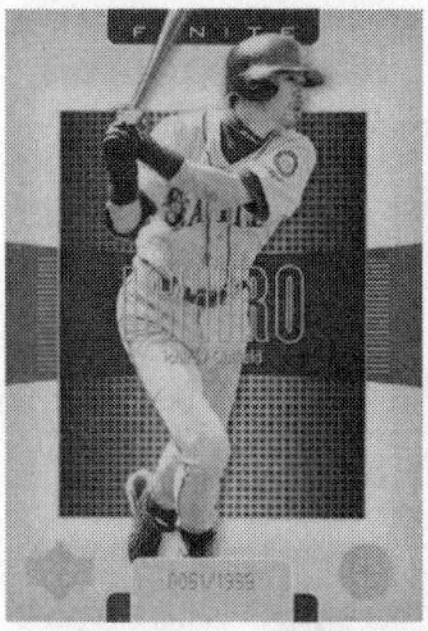

		NM/M
Complete Set (380):		
Common Player (1-100):		1.00
Production 1,999		
Common (101-150):		1.00
Production 1,599		
Common (151-180):		2.00
Production 499		
Common (181-200):		2.50
Production 299		
Common (201-300):		1.50
Production 1,299		
Common (301-330):		3.00
Production 599		
Common (331-360):		3.00
Production 299		
Common (361-380):		5.00
Production 150		
Pack (3):		9.00
Box (10):		80.00
1	Darin Erstad	1.00
2	Garret Anderson	1.50
3	Tim Salmon	1.00
4	Troy Glaus	1.50
5	Luis Gonzalez	1.00
6	Randy Johnson	2.00
7	Curt Schilling	1.50
8	Andruw Jones	1.50
9	Gary Sheffield	1.50
10	Rafael Furcal	1.00
11	Greg Maddux	3.00
12	Chipper Jones	2.50
13	Tony Batista	1.00
14	Jay Gibbons	1.00
15	Johnny Damon	1.00
16	Derek Lowe	1.00
17	Nomar Garciaparra	3.00
18	Pedro J. Martinez	2.00
19	Manny Ramirez	1.50
20	Mark Prior	2.00
21	Kerry Wood	1.50
22	Corey Patterson	1.00
23	Sammy Sosa	3.00
24	Moises Alou	1.00
25	Maggilo Ordonez	1.00
26	Frank Thomas	1.50
27	Paul Konerko	1.00
28	Bartolo Colon	1.00
29	Adam Dunn	1.00
30	Austin Kearns	1.00
31	Aaron Boone	1.00
32	Ken Griffey Jr.	2.50
33	Omar Vizquel	1.00
34	C.C. Sabathia	1.00
35	Brandon Phillips	1.00
36	Larry Walker	1.00
37	Preston Wilson	1.00
38	Todd Helton	1.50
39	Eric Munson	1.00
40	Ivan Rodriguez	1.50
41	Josh Beckett	1.50
42	Roy Oswalt	1.00
43	Craig Biggio	1.00
44	Jeff Bagwell	1.50
45	Dontrelle Willis	1.00
46	Carlos Beltran	1.00
47	Brent Mayne	1.00
48	Hideo Nomo	1.00
49	Rickey Henderson	1.00
50	Adrian Beltre	1.00
51	Miguel Cabrera	2.00
52	Kazuhisa Ishii	1.00
53	Richie Sexson	1.00
54	Torii Hunter	1.00
55	Jacque Jones	1.00
56	A.J. Pierzynski	1.00
57	Jose Vidro	1.00
58	Vladimir Guerrero	2.00
59	Tom Glavine	1.00
60	Jose Reyes	1.00
61	Mike Piazza	2.50
62	Jorge Posada	1.50
63	Mike Mussina	1.50
64	Robin Ventura	1.00
65	Mariano Rivera	1.00
66	Roger Clemens	3.00
67	Jason Giambi	2.00
68	Bernie Williams	1.50
69	Alfonso Soriano	2.00
70	Derek Jeter	5.00
71	Miguel Tejada	1.50
72	Eric Chavez	1.00
73	Tim Hudson	1.00
74	Barry Zito	1.50
75	Pat Burrell	1.00
76	Jim Thome	2.00
77	Bobby Abreu	1.00
78	Brian Giles	1.00
79	Reggie Sanders	1.00
80	Ryan Klesko	1.00
81	Edgardo Alfonzo	1.00
82	Rich Aurilia	1.00
83	Barry Bonds	5.00
84	Mike Cameron	1.00
85	Kazuhiro Sasaki	1.00
86	Bret Boone	1.00
87	Ichiro Suzuki	3.00
88	J.D. Drew	1.00
89	Jim Edmonds	1.00
90	Scott Rolen	2.00
91	Matt Morris	1.00
92	Tino Martinez	1.00
93	Albert Pujols	3.00
94	Rocco Baldelli	1.00
95	Hank Blalock	1.50
96	Alex Rodriguez	3.00
97	Rafael Palmeiro	1.50
98	Eric Hinske	1.00
99	Orlando Hudson	1.00
100	Carlos Delgado	1.50
101	Albert Pujols	3.00
102	Alex Rodriguez	3.00
103	Alfonso Soriano	2.00
104	Andruw Jones	1.50
105	Barry Zito	1.50
106	Bernie Williams	1.50
107	Carlos Delgado	1.50
108	Chipper Jones	2.50
109	Curt Schilling	1.50
110	Doug Mientkiewicz	1.00
111	Frank Thomas	1.50
112	Garret Anderson	1.50
113	Gary Sheffield	1.50
114	Greg Maddux	3.00
115	Hank Blalock	1.00
116	Hideki Matsui	4.00
117	Hideo Nomo	1.00
118	Ichiro Suzuki	3.00
119	Ivan Rodriguez	1.50
120	Jason Giambi	2.00
121	Jeff Bagwell	1.50
122	Jeff Kent	1.00
123	Jerome Williams	1.00
124	Jeromy Burnitz	1.00
125	Jim Thome	2.00
126	Jose Cruz Jr.	1.00
127	Ken Griffey Jr.	2.50
128	Kerry Wood	1.50
129	Lance Berkman	1.00
130	Luis Gonzalez	1.00
131	Manny Ramirez	1.50
132	Mark Prior	2.00
133	Miguel Cabrera	2.00
134	Miguel Tejada	1.50
135	Mike Piazza	2.50
136	Pat Burrell	1.00
137	Pedro J. Martinez	2.00
138	Rafael Furcal	1.00
139	Randy Johnson	2.00
140	Rich Harden	1.00
141	Rickey Henderson	1.50
142	Roberto Alomar	1.50
143	Roger Clemens	3.00
144	Sammy Sosa	3.00
145	Shawn Green	1.00
146	Todd Helton	1.50
147	Tom Glavine	1.00
148	Torii Hunter	1.00
149	Troy Glaus	1.00
150	Vladimir Guerrero	2.00
151	Adam Dunn	2.00
152	Albert Pujols	6.00
153	Alex Rodriguez	6.00
154	Alfonso Soriano	3.00
155	Andruw Jones	2.50
156	Barry Bonds	8.00
157	Carlos Delgado	2.50
158	Chipper Jones	3.00
159	Derek Jeter	8.00
160	Gary Sheffield	2.50
161	Hank Blalock	2.50
162	Hideki Matsui	6.00
163	Ichiro Suzuki	4.00
164	J.D. Drew	2.00
165	Jason Giambi	3.00
166	Jeff Bagwell	3.00
167	Jeff Kent	2.00
168	Jim Edmonds	2.00
169	Jim Thome	3.00
170	Ken Griffey Jr.	5.00
171	Luis Gonzalez	2.00
172	Magglio Ordonez	2.00
173	Manny Ramirez	2.50
174	Mike Lowell	2.00
175	Mike Piazza	4.00
176	Nomar Garciaparra	6.00
177	Rafael Palmeiro	2.50
178	Shawn Green	2.00
179	Troy Glaus	2.00
180	Vladimir Guerrero	3.00
181	Albert Pujols	8.00
182	Alex Rodriguez	8.00
183	Alfonso Soriano	4.00
184	Bernie Williams	2.50
185	Chipper Jones	4.00
186	Derek Jeter	10.00
187	Hideki Matsui	8.00
188	Ichiro Suzuki	6.00
189	Jim Thome	3.00
190	Joe DiMaggio	8.00
191	Ken Griffey Jr.	6.00
192	Mickey Mantle	12.00
193	Mike Piazza	5.00
194	Pedro J. Martinez	4.00
195	Randy Johnson	4.00
196	Roger Clemens	6.00
197	Sammy Sosa	6.00
198	Ted Williams	8.00
199	Troy Glaus	2.50
200	Vladimir Guerrero	3.00
201	Aaron Looper **RC**	2.00
202	Alejandro Machado	1.50
203	Alfredo Gonzalez **RC**	2.00
204	Andrew Brown **RC**	2.00
205	Anthony Ferrari	1.50
206	Aquilino Lopez **RC**	2.00
207	Beau Kemp **RC**	2.00
208	Bernie Castro	1.50
209	Bobby Madritsch **RC**	8.00
210	Brandon Villafuerte	1.50
211	Brent Hoard **RC**	2.00
212	Brian Stokes	1.50
213	Carlos Mendez	1.50
214	Chris Capuano **RC**	4.00
215	Chris Waters	1.50
216	Clint Barmes **RC**	5.00
217	Colin Porter **RC**	1.50
218	Cory Stewart	1.50
219	Craig Brazell **RC**	3.00
220	D.J. Carrasco **RC**	1.50
221	Daniel Cabrera **RC**	1.50
222	Dave Matranga **RC**	2.00
223	David Sanders	1.50
224	Diegomar Markwell	1.50
225	Edgar Gonzalez **RC**	2.00
226	Felix Sanchez	1.50
227	Fernando Cabrera **RC**	2.00
228	Francisco Cruceta **RC**	2.00
229	Francisco Rosario **RC**	2.00
230	Garrett Atkins	1.50
231	Gerald Laird	1.50
232	Guillermo Quiroz **RC**	4.00
233	Heath Bell **RC**	2.00
234	Delmon Young **RC**	10.00
235	Jason Shiell **RC**	2.00
236	Jeremy Bonderman	10.00
237	Jeremy Griffiths	1.50

238	Jeremy Guthrie	1.50
239	Jeremy Wedel **RC**	2.00
240	Carlos Rivera	1.50
241	Joe Valentine	1.50
242	Jon Leicester	1.50
243	Jonathan Pridie	1.50
244	Jorge Cordova	1.50
245	Jose Castillo	1.50
246	Josh Hall **RC**	2.00
247	Josh Stewart **RC**	1.50
248	Josh Willingham **RC**	3.00
249	Julio Manon **RC**	1.50
250	Kevin Correia **RC**	1.50
251	Kevin Ohme **RC**	2.00
252	Kevin Tolar	1.50
253	Luis De Los Santos	1.50
254	Jermaine Clark	1.50
255	Mark Malaska **RC**	2.00
256	Juan Dominguez	1.50
257	Michael Hessman **RC**	1.50
258	Micheal Nakamura **RC**	2.00
259	Miguel Ojeda **RC**	1.50
260	Mike Gallo	1.50
261	Edwin Jackson **RC**	6.00
262	Mike Ryan **RC**	1.50
263	Nate Bland **RC**	1.50
264	Nate Robertson	3.00
265	Nook Logan **RC**	2.00
266	Phil Seibel **RC**	1.50
267	Prentice Redman **RC**	2.00
268	Rafael Betancourt	1.50
269	Rett Johnson **RC**	2.00
270	Richard Fischer	1.50
271	Rick Roberts **RC**	2.00
272	Roger Deago	1.50
273	Ryan Cameron **RC**	1.50
274	Shane Bazzell	2.00
275	Erasmo Ramirez	1.50
276	Termel Sledge **RC**	2.00
277	Tim Olson **RC**	3.00
278	Tommy Phelps	1.50
279	Tommy Whiteman	1.50
280	Willie Eyre **RC**	2.00
281	Alex Prieto **RC**	2.00
282	Michel Hernandez **RC**	1.50
283	Greg Jones **RC**	1.50
284	Victor Martinez	1.50
285	Tom Gregorio **RC**	2.00
286	Marcus Thames	1.50
287	Jorge DePaula **RC**	1.50
288	Aaron Miles **RC**	3.00
289	Reynaldo Garcia	1.50
290	Brian Sweeney **RC**	1.50
291	Pete LaForest **RC**	2.00
292	Pete Zoccolilo **RC**	1.50
293	Danny Garcia **RC**	1.50
294	Jonny Gomes	1.50
295	Rosman Garcia **RC**	1.50
296	Mike Edwards	1.50
297	Marlon Byrd	1.50
298	Khalil Greene	4.00
299	Jose Valverde	1.50
300	Drew Henson	1.50
301	Chris Bootcheck	3.00
302	Matt Belisle	3.00
303	Kevin Gregg	3.00
304	Bobby Jenks	3.00
305	Jason Young	3.00
306	Laynce Nix	3.00
307	Robb Quinlan	3.00
308	Chase Utley	3.00
309	Humberto Quintero **RC**	4.00
310	Tim Raines Jr.	3.00
311	Stephen Smitherman	3.00
312	Jason Anderson	3.00
313	Joe Dawley	3.00
314	Chad Cordero **RC**	3.00
315	Victor Alvarez	3.00
316	Jimmy Gobble	3.00
317	Jared Fernandez	3.00
318	Eric Bruntlett	3.00
319	Neal Cotts	3.00
320	Ryan Madson	3.00
321	Rocco Baldelli	3.00
322	Graham Koonce **RC**	3.00
323	Bobby Crosby	3.00
324	Mike Wood	3.00
325	Jesse Garcia	3.00
326	Noah Lowry	6.00
327	Edwin Almonte	3.00
328	Justin Morneau	3.00
329	Steve Colyer	3.00
330	Vinnie Chulk	3.00
331	Brian Schmack	3.00
332	Stephen Randolph **RC**	3.00
333	Pedro Feliciano	3.00
334	Koyie Hill	3.00
335	Geoff Geary **RC**	3.00
336	Jon Switzer	3.00
337	Xavier Nady	3.00
338	Rich Harden	4.00
339	Dontrelle Willis	4.00
340	Angel Berroa	3.00
341	Jerome Williams	3.00
342	Brandon Claussen	3.00
343	Kurt Ainsworth	3.00
344	Horacio Ramirez	3.00
345	Hee Seop Choi	3.00
346	Billy Traber	3.00
347	Brandon Phillips	3.00
348	Jody Gerut	3.00
349	Mark Teixeira	4.00
350	Javier Lopez	3.00
351	Miguel Cabrera	5.00
352	Brad Lidge	3.00
353	Mike MacDougal	3.00
354	Ken Harvey	3.00
355	Chien-Ming Wang **RC**	40.00
356	Aaron Heilman	3.00
357	Jason Phillips	3.00
358	Jason Bay	3.00
359	Arnie Munoz	3.00
360	Ian Ferguson **RC**	3.00
361	Ryan Wagner **RC**	8.00
362	Rickie Weeks **RC**	15.00
363	Chad Gaudin **RC**	8.00
364	Jason Gilfillan **RC**	5.00
365	Jason Roach	5.00
366	Jhonny Peralta	6.00
367	Mike Neu **RC**	5.00
368	Jose Contreras **RC**	10.00
369	Wilfredo Ledezma **RC**	5.00
370	Lew Ford **RC**	8.00
371	Luis Ayala **RC**	5.00
372	Bo Hart **RC**	5.00
373	Brandon Webb **RC**	20.00
374	Dan Haren	15.00
375	Hideki Matsui **RC**	50.00
376	Jeff Duncan **RC**	8.00
377	Matt Kata **RC**	5.00
378	Oscar Villarreal **RC**	5.00
379	Rob Hammock **RC**	5.00
380	Todd Wellemeyer **RC**	5.00

Game Face (193-217):

Common Rookie: 5.00
Production 299

193	Aaron Looper **RC**	5.00
194	Alex Prieto **RC**	5.00
195	Bo Hart **RC**	5.00
196	Chad Gaudin **RC**	8.00
197	Colin Porter **RC**	5.00
198	D.J. Carrasco **RC**	5.00
199	Dan Haren	10.00
200	Delmon Young **RC**	20.00
201	Dontrelle Willis	5.00
202	Jon Switzer	5.00
203	Edwin Jackson **RC**	8.00
204	Fernando Cabrera **RC**	5.00
205	Garrett Atkins	8.00
206	Jeremy Bonderman	12.00
207	Kevin Ohme **RC**	5.00
208	Khalil Greene	10.00
209	Luis Ayala **RC**	5.00
210	Matt Kata **RC**	5.00
211	Noah Lowry	10.00
212	Rich Harden	5.00
213	Rickie Weeks **RC**	10.00
214	Rosman Garcia **RC**	5.00
215	Ryan Wagner **RC**	5.00
216	Tom Gregorio **RC**	5.00
217	Wilfredo Ledezma **RC**	5.00

SP Authentic (190-239):

Common SP Authentic Rookie: 4.00
Production 699

190	Aaron Looper	4.00
191	Alex Prieto	4.00
192	Alfredo Gonzalez **RC**	4.00
193	Andrew Brown **RC**	4.00
194	Anthony Ferrari	4.00
195	Aquilino Lopez **RC**	4.00
196	Beau Kemp **RC**	4.00
197	Bo Hart **RC**	4.00
198	Chad Gaudin **RC**	10.00
199	Colin Porter **RC**	4.00
200	D.J. Carrasco **RC**	4.00
201	Dan Haren	20.00
202	Danny Garcia **RC**	4.00
203	Jon Switzer	4.00
204	Edwin Jackson **RC**	4.00
205	Fernando Cabrera **RC**	4.00
206	Garrett Atkins	6.00
207	Gerald Laird	4.00
208	Greg Jones **RC**	4.00
209	Ian Ferguson **RC**	4.00
210	Jason Roach	4.00
211	Jason Shiell **RC**	4.00
212	Jeremy Bonderman	15.00
213	Jeremy Wedel **RC**	4.00
214	Jhonny Peralta	4.00
215	Delmon Young **RC**	25.00
216	Jorge DePaula **RC**	4.00
217	Josh Hall **RC**	4.00
218	Julio Manon **RC**	4.00
219	Kevin Correia **RC**	4.00
220	Kevin Ohme **RC**	4.00
221	Kevin Tolar	4.00
222	Luis Ayala **RC**	4.00
223	Luis De Los Santos	4.00
224	Chad Cordero **RC**	4.00
225	Mark Malaska **RC**	4.00
226	Khalil Greene	10.00
227	Micheal Nakamura **RC**	4.00
228	Michel Hernandez **RC**	4.00
229	Miguel Ojeda **RC**	4.00
230	Mike Neu **RC**	4.00
231	Nate Bland **RC**	4.00
232	Pete LaForest **RC**	4.00
233	Rickie Weeks **RC**	15.00
234	Rosman Garcia **RC**	4.00
235	Ryan Wagner **RC**	4.00
236	Lance Niekro	4.00
237	Tom Gregorio **RC**	4.00
238	Tommy Phelps	4.00
239	Wilfredo Ledezma **RC**	4.00

SPX (179-193, 381-387):

179	Chad Gaudin/150 **RC**	15.00
180	Chris Capuano/150 **RC**	15.00
181	Danny Garcia/150 **RC**	8.00
182	Delmon Young/150 **RC**	40.00
183	Edwin Jackson/150 **RC**	20.00
184	Greg Jones/150 **RC**	8.00
185	Jeremy Bonderman/150	25.00
186	Jorge DePaula/150 **RC**	8.00
187	Khalil Greene/150	25.00
188	Chad Cordero/150 **RC**	8.00
189	Miguel Cabrera/150	10.00
190	Rich Harden/150	10.00
191	Rickie Weeks/150 **RC**	25.00
192	Rosman Garcia/150 **RC**	8.00
193	Tom Gregorio/150 **RC**	8.00
381	Andrew Brown/Jsy/Auto./355 **RC**	15.00
382	Delmon Young/Jsy/Auto./355 **RC**	300.00
383	Colin Porter/Jsy/Auto./355 **RC**	15.00
385	Rickie Weeks/Jsy/Auto./355 **RC**	60.00
386	Dave Matranga/Jsy/Auto./355 **RC**	15.00
387	Bo Hart/Jsy/Auto./355 **RC**	15.00

UD Authentics (131-140):

Common Authentics: 5.00
Production 150

131	Dan Haren	10.00
132	Delmon Young **RC**	20.00
133	Dontrelle Willis	6.00
134	Edwin Jackson **RC**	5.00
135	Jeremy Bonderman	15.00
136	Khalil Greene	10.00
137	Rich Harden	5.00
138	Rickie Weeks **RC**	15.00
139	Rosman Garcia **RC**	5.00
140	Ryan Wagner **RC**	5.00

Gold

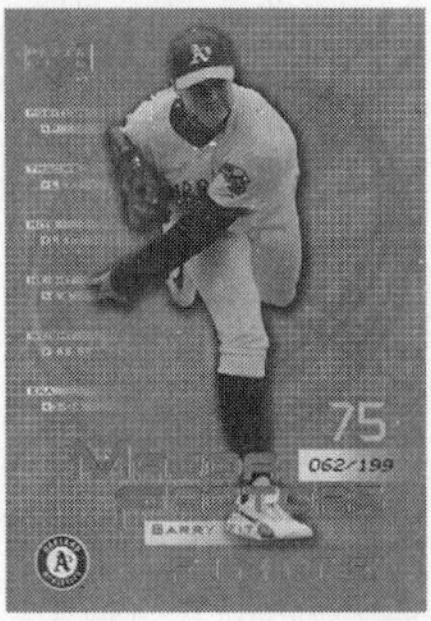

NM/M

Gold (1-150): 1-2X
Gold (151-180): 1X
Production 199
Gold (181-200): 1-2X
Production 99

Elements Jersey

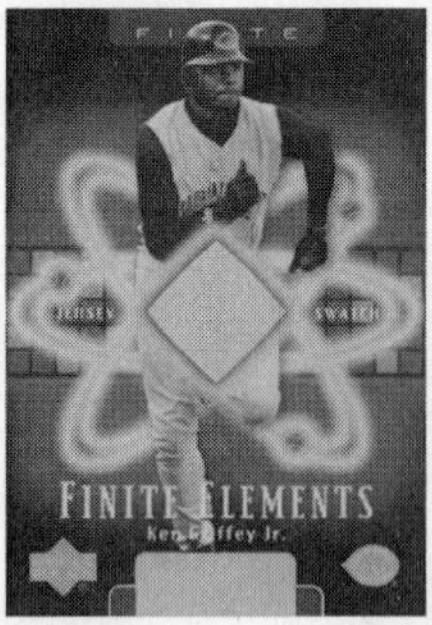

		NM/M
	Common Player:	4.00
JB	Jeff Bagwell	8.00
RB	Rocco Baldelli	6.00
HB	Hank Blalock	6.00
HC	Hee Seop Choi	4.00
JD	J.D. Drew	4.00
AD	Adam Dunn	6.00
JE	Jim Edmonds	5.00
SG	Shawn Green	5.00
KG	Ken Griffey Jr./SP	15.00
TH	Torii Hunter	6.00
CJ	Chipper Jones	6.00
JK	Jeff Kent	4.00
ML	Mike Lowell	4.00
GM	Greg Maddux	8.00
HM	Hideki Matsui	25.00
MM	Matt Morris	5.00
RO	Roy Oswalt	5.00
CP	Corey Patterson	5.00
AP	Andy Pettitte	6.00
MI	Mike Piazza	8.00
MP	Mark Prior	10.00
AL	Albert Pujols	15.00
AR	Alex Rodriguez	10.00
AS	Alfonso Soriano	6.00
IS	Ichiro Suzuki	15.00
JT	Jim Thome	10.00
RW	Rickie Weeks/SP	10.00
DW	Dontrelle Willis	6.00
KW	Kerry Wood	8.00
DY	Delmon Young/SP	15.00

Elements Patch

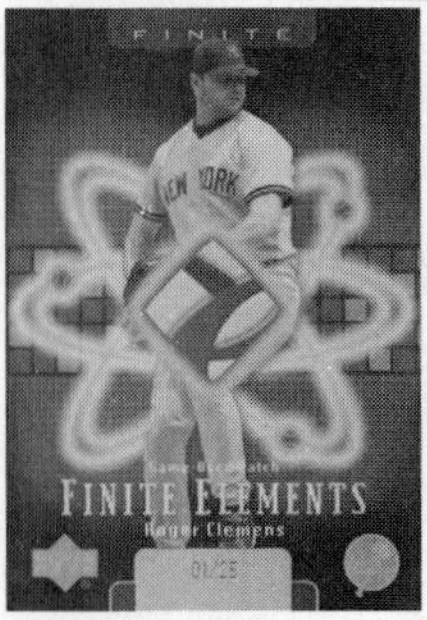

No pricing due to scarcity.
Production 25 Sets
Patch Gold: No Pricing
Production 10 Sets

First Class Jersey

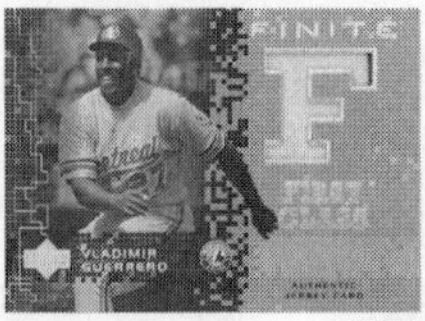

		NM/M
	Common Player:	4.00
RC	Roger Clemens	10.00
JD	Joe DiMaggio/SP	80.00
TG	Troy Glaus	5.00
LG	Luis Gonzalez	4.00
KG	Ken Griffey Jr.	12.00
VG	Vladimir Guerrero	8.00
RJ	Randy Johnson	8.00
CJ	Chipper Jones	6.00
MM	Mickey Mantle/SP	100.00
PM	Pedro J. Martinez	8.00
HM	Hideki Matsui	25.00
MP	Mike Piazza	8.00
AP	Albert Pujols	20.00
AR	Alex Rodriguez	10.00
AS	Alfonso Soriano	6.00
SS	Sammy Sosa	10.00
IS	Ichiro Suzuki	15.00
JT	Jim Thome	10.00
BW	Bernie Williams	6.00
TW	Ted Williams/SP	75.00

Signatures

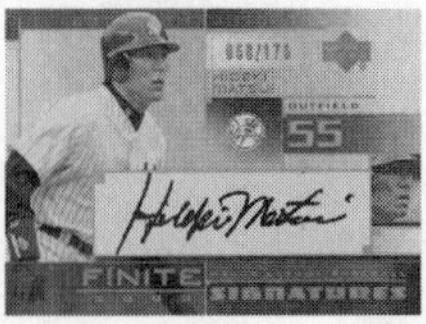

		NM/M
	Common Auto:	6.00
	Varying quantities produced	
EA	Erick Almonte/355	6.00
SZ	Shane Bazzell/250	6.00
MC	Miguel Cabrera/100	50.00
RC	Roger Clemens/50	150.00
WE	Willie Eyre/200	6.00
NG	Nomar Garciaparra/50	80.00
RK	Rob Hammock/200	6.00
RN	Rich Harden/150	25.00
BH	Bo Hart/150	8.00
HM	Hideki Matsui/99	250.00
MP	Mark Prior/75	40.00
JR	Jose Reyes/100	40.00
SR	Scott Rolen/100	40.00
CS	C.C. Sabathia/50	20.00
DS	David Sanders/150	6.00
PS	Phil Seibel/200	6.00
IS	Ichiro Suzuki/25	350.00
MT	Mark Teixeira/200	25.00
BW	Brandon Webb/150	35.00
JW	Jerome Williams/150	15.00
DW	Dontrelle Willis/50	40.00
DY	Delmon Young/50	60.00

Stars and Stripes

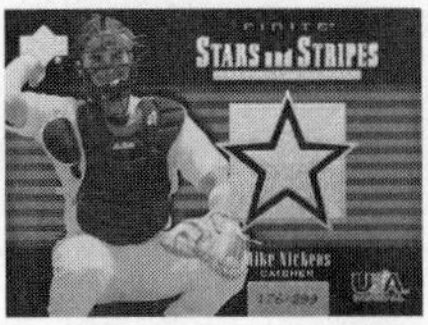

		NM/M
Common Player:		2.00
Production 299 Sets		
USA-1	Justin Orenduff	2.00
USA-2	Micah Owings	2.00
USA-3	Steven Register	2.00
USA-4	Huston Street	6.00
USA-5	Justin Verlander	8.00
USA-6	Jered Weaver	8.00
USA-7	Matt Campbell	4.00
USA-8	Stephen Head	2.00
USA-9	Mark Romanczuk	2.00
USA-10	Jeff Clement	10.00
USA-11	Mike Nickeas	2.00
USA-12	Tyler Greene	2.00
USA-13	Paul Janish	2.00
USA-14	Jeff Larish	2.00
USA-15	Eric Patterson	2.00
USA-16	Dustin Pedroia	6.00
USA-17	Michael Griffin	2.00
USA-18	Brent Lillibridge	2.00
USA-19	Danny Putnam	5.00
USA-20	Seth Smith	5.00

Stars and Stripes Jersey

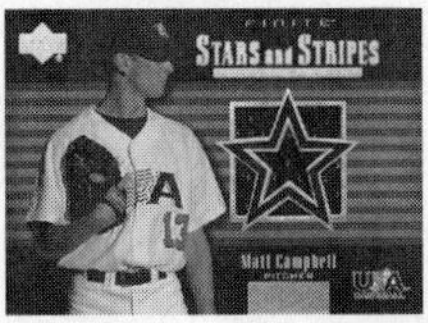

		NM/M
Common Player:		4.00
J1	Justin Orenduff	4.00
J2	Micah Owings	4.00
J3	Steven Register	4.00
J4	Huston Street	8.00
J5	Justin Verlander	8.00
J6	Jered Weaver	8.00
J7	Matt Campbell	6.00
J8	Stephen Head	4.00
J9	Mark Romanczuk	4.00
J10	Jeff Clement	10.00
J11	Mike Nickeas	4.00
J12	Tyler Greene	4.00
J13	Paul Janish	4.00
J14	Jeff Larish	4.00
J15	Eric Patterson	4.00
J16	Dustin Pedroia	8.00
J17	Michael Griffin	4.00
J18	Brent Lillibridge	4.00
J19	Danny Putnam	6.00
J20	Seth Smith	6.00

SPX Jersey Autograph

		NM/M
Production 355		
DW	Dontrelle Willis	40.00
KG	Khalil Greene	60.00
RH	Rich Harden	35.00

2003 Upper Deck First Pitch

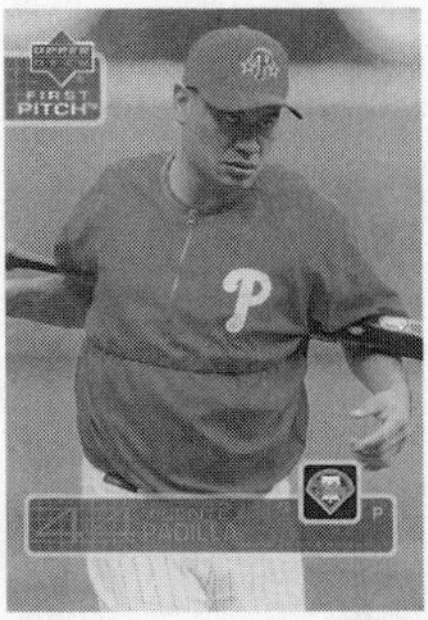

		NM/M
Complete Set (300):		50.00
Common Player:		.10
Common SP (271-300):		1.00
Inserted 1:4		
Pack (5):		1.00
Box (36):		25.00
1	John Lackey	.10
2	Alex Cintron	.10
3	Jose Leon	.10
4	Bobby Hill	.10
5	Brandon Larson	.10
6	Raul Gonzalez	.10
7	Ben Broussard	.10
8	Earl Snyder	.10
9	Ramon Santiago	.10
10	Jason Lane	.10
11	Rob Hammock **RC**	.50
12	Kirk Saarloos	.10
13	Juan Brito	.10
14	Runelvys Hernandez	.10
15	Shawn Sedlacek	.10
16	Jayson Durocher	.10
17	Kevin Frederick	.10
18	Zach Day	.10
19	Marco Scutaro	.10
20	Marcus Thames	.10
21	Esteban German	.10
22	Brett Myers	.10
23	Oliver Perez	.10
24	Dennis Tankersley	.10
25	Julius Matos	.10
26	Jake Peavy	.10
27	Eric Cyr	.10
28	Mike Crudale	.10
29	Josh Pearce	.10
30	Carl Crawford	.10
31	Tim Salmon	.25
32	Troy Glaus	.50
33	Adam Kennedy	.10
34	David Eckstein	.10
35	Bengie Molina	.10
36	Jarrod Washburn	.10
37	Ramon Ortiz	.10
38	Eric Chavez	.25
39	Miguel Tejada	.25
40	Adam Piatt	.10
41	Jermaine Dye	.10
42	Olmedo Saenz	.10
43	Tim Hudson	.20
44	Barry Zito	.25
45	Billy Koch	.10
46	Shannon Stewart	.10
47	Kelvim Escobar	.10
48	Jose Cruz Jr.	.10
49	Vernon Wells	.10
50	Roy Halladay	.10
51	Esteban Loaiza	.10
52	Eric Hinske	.10
53	Steve Cox	.10
54	Brent Abernathy	.10
55	Ben Grieve	.10
56	Aubrey Huff	.10
57	Jared Sandberg	.10
58	Paul Wilson	.10
59	Tanyon Sturtze	.10
60	Jim Thome	.50
61	Omar Vizquel	.20
62	C.C. Sabathia	.10
63	Chris Magruder	.10
64	Ricky Gutierrez	.10
65	Einar Diaz	.10
66	Danys Baez	.10
67	Ichiro Suzuki	.75
68	Ruben Sierra	.10
69	Carlos Guillen	.10
70	Mark McLemore	.10
71	Dan Wilson	.10
72	Jamie Moyer	.10
73	Joel Pineiro	.10
74	Edgar Martinez	.10
75	Tony Batista	.10
76	Jay Gibbons	.10
77	Chris Singleton	.10
78	Melvin Mora	.10
79	Geronimo Gil	.10
80	Rodrigo Lopez	.10
81	Jorge Julio	.10
82	Rafael Palmeiro	.40
83	Juan Gonzalez	.40
84	Mike Young	.10
85	Hideki Irabu	.10
86	Chan Ho Park	.10
87	Kevin Mench	.10
88	Doug Davis	.10
89	Pedro J. Martinez	.75
90	Shea Hillenbrand	.10
91	Derek Lowe	.10
92	Jason Varitek	.10
93	Tony Clark	.10
94	John Burkett	.10
95	Frank Castillo	.10
96	Nomar Garciaparra	1.00
97	Rickey Henderson	.25
98	Mike Sweeney	.10
99	Carlos Febles	.10
100	Mark Quinn	.10
101	Raul Ibanez	.10
102	A.J. Hinch	.10
103	Paul Byrd	.10
104	Chuck Knoblauch	.10
105	Dmitri Young	.10
106	Randall Simon	.10
107	Brandon Inge	.10
108	Damion Easley	.10
109	Carlos Pena	.10
110	George Lombard	.10
111	Juan Acevedo	.10
112	Torii Hunter	.25
113	Doug Mientkiewicz	.10
114	David Ortiz	.10
115	Eric Milton	.10
116	Eddie Guardado	.10
117	Cristian Guzman	.10
118	Corey Koskie	.10
119	Magglio Ordonez	.25
120	Mark Buehrle	.10
121	Todd Ritchie	.10
122	Jose Valentin	.10
123	Paul Konerko	.10
124	Carlos Lee	.10
125	Jon Garland	.10
126	Jason Giambi	.75
127	Derek Jeter	1.50
128	Roger Clemens	1.00
129	Raul Mondesi	.25
130	Jorge Posada	.25
131	Rondell White	.10
132	Robin Ventura	.20
133	Mike Mussina	.40
134	Jeff Bagwell	.50
135	Craig Biggio	.20
136	Morgan Ensberg	.10
137	Richard Hidalgo	.10
138	Brad Ausmus	.10
139	Roy Oswalt	.20
140	Carlos Hernandez	.10
141	Shane Reynolds	.10
142	Gary Sheffield	.25
143	Andruw Jones	.25
144	Tom Glavine	.25
145	Rafael Furcal	.20
146	Javy Lopez	.10
147	Vinny Castilla	.10
148	Marcus Giles	.10
149	Kevin Millwood	.20
150	Jason Marquis	.10
151	Ruben Quevedo	.10
152	Ben Sheets	.10
153	Geoff Jenkins	.10
154	Jose Hernandez	.10
155	Glendon Rusch	.10
156	Jeffrey Hammonds	.10
157	Alex Sanchez	.10
158	Jim Edmonds	.25
159	Tino Martinez	.10
160	Albert Pujols	.75
161	Eli Marrero	.10
162	Woody Williams	.10
163	Fernando Vina	.10
164	Jason Isringhausen	.10
165	Jason Simontacchi	.10
166	Kerry Robinson	.10
167	Sammy Sosa	.75
168	Juan Cruz	.10
169	Fred McGriff	.20
170	Antonio Alfonseca	.10
171	Jon Lieber	.10
172	Mark Prior	.50
173	Moises Alou	.20
174	Matt Clement	.10
175	Mark Bellhorn	.10
176	Randy Johnson	.50
177	Luis Gonzalez	.20
178	Tony Womack	.10
179	Mark Grace	.25
180	Junior Spivey	.10
181	Byung-Hyun Kim	.10
182	Danny Bautista	.10
183	Brian Anderson	.10
184	Shawn Green	.25
185	Brian Jordan	.10
186	Eric Karros	.10
187	Andy Ashby	.10
188	Cesar Izturis	.10
189	Dave Roberts	.10
190	Eric Gagne	.10
191	Kazuhisa Ishii	.10
192	Adrian Beltre	.10
193	Vladimir Guerrero	.50
194	Tony Armas Jr.	.10
195	Bartolo Colon	.10
196	Troy O'Leary	.10
197	Tomokazu Ohka	.10
198	Brad Wilkerson	.10
199	Orlando Cabrera	.10
200	Barry Bonds	1.50
201	David Bell	.10
202	Tsuyoshi Shinjo	.10
203	Benito Santiago	.10
204	Livan Hernandez	.10
205	Jason Schmidt	.10
206	Kirk Rueter	.10
207	Ramon E. Martinez	.10
208	Mike Lowell	.10
209	Luis Castillo	.10
210	Derek Lee	.10
211	Andy Fox	.10
212	Eric Owens	.10
213	Charles Johnson	.10
214	Brad Penny	.10
215	A.J. Burnett	.10
216	Edgardo Alfonzo	.10
217	Roberto Alomar	.40
218	Rey Ordonez	.10
219	Al Leiter	.10
220	Roger Cedeno	.10
221	Timoniel Perez	.10
222	Jeromy Burnitz	.10
223	Pedro Astacio	.10
224	Joe McEwing	.10
225	Ryan Klesko	.20
226	Ramon Vazquez	.10
227	Mark Kotsay	.10
228	Bubba Trammell	.10
229	Wiki Gonzalez	.10
230	Trevor Hoffman	.10
231	Ron Gant	.10
232	Bobby Abreu	.20
233	Marlon Anderson	.10
234	Jeremy Giambi	.10
235	Jimmy Rollins	.20
236	Mike Lieberthal	.10
237	Vicente Padilla	.10
238	Randy Wolf	.10
239	Pokey Reese	.10
240	Brian Giles	.25
241	Jack Wilson	.10
242	Mike Williams	.10
243	Kip Wells	.10
244	Robert Mackowiak	.10
245	Craig Wilson	.10
246	Adam Dunn	.50
247	Sean Casey	.10
248	Todd Walker	.10
249	Corky Miller	.10
250	Ryan Dempster	.10
251	Reggie Taylor	.10
252	Aaron Boone	.10
253	Larry Walker	.10
254	Jose Ortiz	.10
255	Todd Zeile	.10
256	Bobby Estalella	.10
257	Juan Pierre	.10
258	Terry Shumpert	.10
259	Mike Hampton	.10
260	Denny Stark	.10
261	Shawn Green	.20
262	Derek Lowe	.10
263	Barry Bonds	.50
264	Mike Cameron	.10
265	Luis Castillo	.10
266	Vladimir Guerrero	.40
267	Jason Giambi	.40
268	Eric Gagne	.10
269	Magglio Ordonez	.20
270	Jim Thome	.25
271	Hideki Matsui **RC**	20.00
272	Jose Contreras **RC**	4.00
273	Robert Madritsch	1.00
274	Shane Bazzell **RC**	1.50
275	Felix Sanchez **RC**	2.00
276	Todd Wellemeyer **RC**	2.00
277	Lew Ford **RC**	2.00
278	Jeremy Griffiths	1.00
279	Oscar Villarreal **RC**	1.00
280	Brandon Webb **RC**	4.00
281	Delvis Lantigua	3.00
282	Josh Willingham **RC**	1.00
283	Mike Nicolas **RC**	1.00
284	Mike Hampton	1.00
285	Jim Thome	2.00
286	Bartolo Colon	1.00
287	Orlando Hernandez	1.00
288	Jeremy Giambi	1.00
289	Jeff Kent	1.50
290	Tom Glavine	1.50
291	Cliff Floyd	1.00
292	Tsuyoshi Shinjo	1.00
293	Jose Cruz Jr.	1.00
294	Edgardo Alfonzo	1.00
295	Andres Galarraga	1.00
296	Troy O'Leary	1.00
297	Eric Karros	1.00
298	Ivan Rodriguez	1.50
299	Fred McGriff	1.50
300	Preston Wilson	1.00

Signature Stars

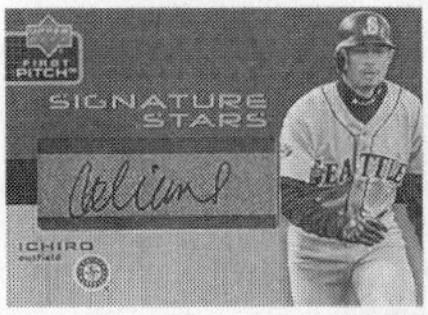

		NM/M
Print runs listed:		
NM	Nomar Garciaparra/100	100.00
JG	Jason Giambi/100	30.00
KG	Ken Griffey Jr./100	75.00
KGS	Ken Griffey Sr./800	6.00
SS	Sammy Sosa/50	175.00
IS	Ichiro Suzuki/50	375.00

2003 Upper Deck Game Face

		NM/M
Complete Set (192):		
Common Player:		.25
Common Base SP:		1.00
Inserted 1:4		
Common SP (121-150):		2.00
Inserted 1:8		
Common SP (151-192):		3.00
Inserted 1:16		
Pack (4):		4.00
Box (24):		75.00
1	Darin Erstad	.50
2	Garret Anderson	.50
3	Tim Salmon	.50
4	Jarrod Washburn	.25
5	Troy Glaus/SP	1.50
6	Luis Gonzalez	.50
7	Junior Spivey	.25
8	Randy Johnson/SP	2.00
9	Curt Schilling/SP	1.50
10	Andruw Jones	.75

Game Face Gear

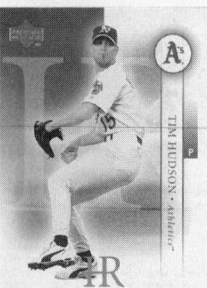

2003 Upper Deck Honor Roll

11	Gary Sheffield	.50
12	Rafael Furcal	.25
13	Greg Maddux/SP	3.00
14	Chipper Jones/SP	3.00
15	Tony Batista	.25
16	Rodrigo Lopez	.25
17	Jay Gibbons	.25
18	Shea Hillenbrand	.25
19	Johnny Damon	.25
20	Derek Lowe	.25
21	Nomar Garciaparra	2.50
22	Pedro J. Martinez/SP	2.00
23	Manny Ramirez/SP	1.50
24	Mark Prior	.50
25	Kerry Wood	.75
26	Corey Patterson	.25
27	Sammy Sosa	2.00
28	Magglio Ordonez	.50
29	Frank Thomas	1.00
30	Paul Konerko	.25
31	Adam Dunn	1.00
32	Austin Kearns	1.00
33	Aaron Boone	.25
34	Ken Griffey Jr./SP	3.00
35	Omar Vizquel	.40
36	C.C. Sabathia	.25
37	Karim Garcia/SP	1.00
38	Larry Walker	.40
39	Preston Wilson	.25
40	Jay Payton	.25
41	Todd Helton/SP	1.50
42	Carlos Pena	.25
43	Eric Munson	.25
44	Mike Lowell	.25
45	Josh Beckett	.25
46	A.J. Burnett	.25
47	Roy Oswalt	.50
48	Craig Biggio	.50
49	Jeff Bagwell/SP	1.50
50	Lance Berkman/SP	1.25
51	Mike Sweeney	.25
52	Carlos Beltran	.25
53	Hideo Nomo	.75
54	Odalis Perez	.25
55	Adrian Beltre	.25
56	Shawn Green/SP	1.00
57	Kazuhisa Ishii/SP	1.00
58	Ben Sheets	.50
59	Richie Sexson	.50
60	Torii Hunter	.50
61	Jacque Jones	.25
62	Eric Milton	.25
63	Corey Koskie	.25
64	A.J. Pierzynski	.25
65	Jose Vidro	.25
66	Bartolo Colon	.25
67	Vladimir Guerrero/SP	1.50
68	Tom Glavine	.50
69	Mike Piazza/SP	3.00
70	Roberto Alomar/SP	1.50
71	Jorge Posada	.25
72	Mike Mussina	.75
73	Robin Ventura	.25
74	Raul Mondesi	.25
75	Roger Clemens/SP	3.00
76	Jason Giambi/SP	2.00
77	Bernie Williams/SP	1.50
78	Alfonso Soriano/SP	2.00
79	Derek Jeter/SP	6.00
80	Miguel Tejada	.75
81	Eric Chavez	.50
82	Tim Hudson	.50
83	Barry Zito	.50
84	Mark Mulder	1.00
85	Pat Burrell	.50
86	Jim Thome	1.00
87	Bobby Abreu	.50
88	Brian Giles	.50
89	Jason Kendall	.40
90	Aramis Ramirez	.25
91	Ryan Klesko	.25
92	Phil Nevin	.25
93	Sean Burroughs	.25
94	J.T. Snow	.25
95	Rich Aurilia	.25
96	Benito Santiago	.25
97	Barry Bonds/SP	6.00
98	Edgar Martinez	.25
99	John Olerud	.50
100	Bret Boone	.25
101	Ichiro Suzuki/SP	3.00
102	J.D. Drew	.50
103	Jim Edmonds	.50
104	Scott Rolen	1.00
105	Matt Morris	.50
106	Tino Martinez	.25
107	Albert Pujols/SP	2.00
108	Aubrey Huff	.25
109	Carl Crawford	.25
110	Rafael Palmeiro	.75
111	Hank Blalock	.50
112	Alex Rodriguez/SP	5.00
113	Kevin Mench/SP	1.00
114	Juan Gonzalez/SP	1.50
115	Shannon Stewart	.25
116	Vernon Wells	.25
117	Josh Phelps	.25
118	Eric Hinske	.25
119	Orlando Hudson	.25
120	Carlos Delgado/SP	1.00
121	David Sanders RC	2.00
122	Rob Hammock RC	2.00
123	Rett Johnson RC	2.00
124	Mike Nicolas RC	2.00
125	Terrmel Sledge RC	3.00
126	Ryan Cameron RC	4.00
127	Prentice Redman RC	2.00
128	Clint Barmes RC	6.00
129	Brent Hoard RC	2.00
130	Willie Eyre RC	2.00
131	Phil Seibel RC	2.00
132	Chris Capuano RC	5.00
133	Bobby Madritsch RC	8.00
134	Shane Bazzell RC	2.00
135	Jeremy Griffiths	3.00
136	Jon Leicester RC	3.00
137	Brandon Webb RC	6.00
138	Todd Wellemeyer RC	2.00
139	Jose Contreras RC	5.00
140	Felix Sanchez RC	2.00
141	Arnie Munoz RC	2.00
142	Delvis Lantigua RC	2.00
143	Francisco Cruceta RC	2.00
144	Josh Willingham RC	3.00
145	Oscar Villarreal RC	2.00
146	Ian Ferguson RC	2.00
147	Pedro Liriano	2.00
148	Lew Ford RC	5.00
149	Jeff Duncan RC	2.00
150	Richard Fischer RC	2.00
151	Troy Glaus	3.00
152	Randy Johnson	5.00
153	Hideki Matsui RC	15.00
154	Chipper Jones	8.00
155	Nomar Garciaparra	10.00
156	Pedro J. Martinez	5.00
157	Ted Williams	15.00
158	Sammy Sosa	8.00
159	Ken Griffey Jr.	8.00
160	Vladimir Guerrero	5.00
161	Mike Piazza	8.00
162	Mickey Mantle	30.00
163	Alfonso Soriano	6.00
164	Derek Jeter	15.00
165	Roger Clemens	8.00
166	Jason Giambi	4.00
167	Barry Bonds	15.00
168	Ichiro Suzuki	8.00
169	Albert Pujols	8.00
170	Mark McGwire	15.00
171	Alex Rodriguez	10.00
172	Ken Griffey Jr., Roy Oswalt	6.00
173	Barry Zito, Troy Glaus	3.00
174	Tim Hudson, Ichiro Suzuki	8.00
175	Alex Rodriguez, Mark Mulder	10.00
176	Tom Glavine, Vladimir Guerrero	4.00
177	Mike Piazza, Greg Maddux	6.00
178	Mark McGwire, Sammy Sosa	10.00
179	Lance Berkman, Mark Prior	4.00
180	Albert Pujols, Kerry Wood	6.00
181	Randy Johnson, Jeff Bagwell	4.00
182	Derek Jeter, Curt Schilling	10.00
183	Barry Bonds, Hideo Nomo	10.00
184	Todd Helton, Kazuhisa Ishii	4.00
185	Freddy Garcia, Eric Chavez	3.00
186	Al Leiter, Chipper Jones	4.00
187	Ted Williams, Nomar Garciaparra	10.00
188	Pedro J. Martinez, Hideki Matsui	15.00
189	Derek Lowe, Bernie Williams	3.00
190	Roger Clemens, Mike Piazza	10.00
191	Mike Mussina, Manny Ramirez	4.00
192	Jason Giambi, Mickey Mantle	20.00

Autograph

		NM/M
Common Player:		
Inserted 1:576		
Golds:		Not Priced
Production 25		
LB	Lance Berkman/SP	50.00
JG	Jason Giambi	40.00
KG	Ken Griffey Jr.	125.00
TH	Todd Helton/SP	45.00
HM	Hideki Matsui/SP	250.00
MM	Mark McGwire/SP	350.00
MP	Mark Prior/SP	40.00
SS	Sammy Sosa	120.00
IS	Ichiro Suzuki/SP	300.00
BZ	Barry Zito	40.00

Gear

		NM/M
Common Player:		4.00
Inserted 1:8		
Patches:		3-5X
Production 100 Sets		
BA	Bobby Abreu	4.00
EA	Edgardo Alfonzo	4.00
JB	Jeff Bagwell	8.00
CB	Carlos Beltran	6.00
LB	Lance Berkman	6.00
AB	Aaron Boone/SP	8.00
PB	Pat Burrell	6.00
EC	Eric Chavez	4.00
RC	Roger Clemens	15.00
CD	Carlos Delgado	4.00
DR	J.D. Drew	4.00
DR2	J.D. Drew	4.00
AD	Adam Dunn	8.00
JE	Jim Edmonds	4.00
DE	Darin Erstad	4.00
DE2	Darin Erstad	4.00
JG	Jason Giambi	6.00
BG	Brian Giles	4.00
TG	Tom Glavine	6.00
GO	Juan Gonzalez	6.00
LG	Luis Gonzalez	4.00
LG2	Luis Gonzalez	4.00
SG	Shawn Green	4.00
KG	Ken Griffey Jr./SP	
TH	Todd Helton/SP	8.00
TI	Tim Hudson	4.00
HU	Torii Hunter	4.00
KI	Kazuhisa Ishii	4.00
RJ	Randy Johnson	8.00
AJ	Andruw Jones	6.00
CJ	Chipper Jones	4.00
JJ	Jacque Jones	4.00
AK	Austin Kearns	4.00
JK	Jason Kendall	4.00
KE	Jeff Kent	6.00
RK	Ryan Klesko	4.00
ML	Mike Lowell	4.00
GM	Greg Maddux	10.00
GM2	Greg Maddux	10.00
EM	Edgar Martinez	6.00
PM	Pedro J. Martinez	8.00
MM	Mike Mussina	8.00
HN	Hideo Nomo	8.00
MO	Magglio Ordonez	4.00
RO	Roy Oswalt	4.00
RP	Rafael Palmeiro	8.00
MiP	Mike Piazza	10.00
JP	Jorge Posada	8.00
MaP	Mark Prior	8.00
MR	Manny Ramirez	8.00
AR	Alex Rodriguez	10.00
AR2	Alex Rodriguez	10.00
IR	Ivan Rodriguez	8.00
SR	Scott Rolen	8.00
CS	Curt Schilling	8.00
RS	Richie Sexson	6.00
AS	Alfonso Soriano	8.00
SS	Sammy Sosa	10.00
IS	Ichiro Suzuki/SP	50.00
MS	Mike Sweeney	4.00
MT	Miguel Tejada	6.00
FT	Frank Thomas	8.00
JT	Jim Thome	8.00
JV	Jose Vidro	4.00
OV	Omar Vizquel	4.00
LW	Larry Walker	4.00
BW	Bernie Williams	6.00
PW	Preston Wilson	4.00
KW	Kerry Wood	8.00
BZ	Barry Zito	4.00
BZ2	Barry Zito	4.00

Patch

Game Face Patch

No Pricing
Production 100 Sets

2003 Upper Deck Honor Roll

		NM/M
Complete Set (161):		
Common Player:		.20
Common Even # SP (2-60):		1.00
Inserted 1:6		
Common SP (131-161):		3.00
Production 2,500		
Pack (5):		1.50
Box (24):		30.00
1	Derek Jeter	2.00
2	Derek Jeter/SP	5.00
3	Alex Rodriguez	1.50
4	Alex Rodriguez/SP	5.00
5	Roger Clemens	1.50
6	Roger Clemens/SP	4.00
7	Mike Piazza	1.00
8	Mike Piazza/SP	3.00
9	Jeff Bagwell	.50
10	Jeff Bagwell/SP	1.50
11	Vladimir Guerrero	.75
12	Vladimir Guerrero/SP	2.00
13	Ken Griffey Jr.	1.00
14	Ken Griffey Jr./SP	3.00
15	Greg Maddux	1.00
16	Greg Maddux/SP	3.00
17	Chipper Jones	.75
18	Chipper Jones/SP	2.00
19	Randy Johnson	.75
20	Randy Johnson/SP	2.00
21	Miguel Tejada	.50
22	Miguel Tejada/SP	1.50
23	Nomar Garciaparra	1.50
24	Nomar Garciaparra/SP	4.00
25	Ichiro Suzuki	1.50
26	Ichiro Suzuki/SP	4.00
27	Sammy Sosa	1.00
28	Sammy Sosa/SP	3.00
29	Albert Pujols	2.00
30	Albert Pujols/SP	5.00
31	Alfonso Soriano	.75
32	Alfonso Soriano/SP	2.00
33	Barry Bonds	2.00
34	Barry Bonds	6.00
35	Jeff Kent	.30
36	Jeff Kent/SP	1.00
37	Jim Thome	1.00
38	Jim Thome/SP	1.50
39	Pedro J. Martinez	.75
40	Pedro J. Martinez/SP	2.00
41	Todd Helton	1.00
42	Todd Helton/SP	1.50
43	Troy Glaus	.50
44	Troy Glaus/SP	1.50
45	Mark Prior	.75
46	Mark Prior/SP	2.00
47	Tom Glavine	.40
48	Tom Glavine/SP	1.00
49	Pat Burrell	.40
50	Pat Burrell/SP	1.00
51	Barry Zito	.40
52	Barry Zito/SP	1.00
53	Bernie Williams	.50
54	Bernie Williams/SP	1.50
55	Curt Schilling	.50
56	Curt Schilling/SP	1.50
57	Darin Erstad	.30
58	Darin Erstad/SP	1.00
59	Carlos Delgado	.50
60	Carlos Delgado/SP	1.50
61	Gary Sheffield	.40
62	Gary Sheffield	.40
63	Frank Thomas	.50
64	Frank Thomas	.50
65	Lance Berkman	.40
66	Lance Berkman	.40
67	Shawn Green	.40
68	Shawn Green	.40
69	Hideo Nomo	.40
70	Hideo Nomo	.40
71	Torii Hunter	.40
72	Torii Hunter	.40
73	Roberto Alomar	.50
74	Roberto Alomar	.50
75	Andruw Jones	.50
76	Andruw Jones	.50
77	Scott Rolen	.75
78	Scott Rolen	.75
79	Eric Chavez	.40
80	Eric Chavez	.40

81	Rafael Palmeiro	.50
82	Rafael Palmeiro	.50
83	Bobby Abreu	.20
84	Bobby Abreu	.20
85	Craig Biggio	.20
86	Craig Biggio	.20
87	Rafael Furcal	.20
88	Rafael Furcal	.20
89	Jose Vidro	.20
90	Jose Vidro	.20
91	Luis Gonzalez	.20
92	Luis Gonzalez	.20
93	Roy Oswalt	.20
94	Roy Oswalt	.20
95	Cliff Floyd	.20
96	Cliff Floyd	.20
97	Larry Walker	.20
98	Larry Walker	.20
99	Jim Edmonds	.30
100	Jim Edmonds	.30
101	Adam Dunn	.40
102	Adam Dunn	.40
103	J.D. Drew	.20
104	J.D. Drew	.20
105	Josh Beckett	.20
106	Josh Beckett	.20
107	Brian Giles	.20
108	Brian Giles	.20
109	Magglio Ordonez	.40
110	Magglio Ordonez	.40
111	Edgardo Alfonzo	.20
112	Edgardo Alfonzo	.20
113	Bartolo Colon	.20
114	Bartolo Colon	.20
115	Roy Halladay	.20
116	Roy Halladay	.20
117	Joe Thurston	.20
118	Joe Thurston	.20
119	Brandon Phillips	.20
120	Brandon Phillips	.20
121	Kazuhisa Ishii	.20
122	Kazuhisa Ishii	.20
123	Mike Mussina	.40
124	Mike Mussina	.40
125	Tim Hudson	.40
126	Tim Hudson	.40
127	Mariano Rivera	.20
128	Mariano Rivera	.20
129	Travis Hafner	.20
130	Travis Hafner	.20
131	Hideki Matsui **RC**	20.00
132	Jose Contreras **RC**	5.00
133	Jason Anderson	3.00
134	Willie Eyre **RC**	3.00
135	Shane Bazzell **RC**	3.00
136	Guillermo Quiroz **RC**	5.00
137	Francisco Cruceta **RC**	3.00
138	Jhonny Peralta	4.00
139	Aaron Looper **RC**	3.00
140	Bobby Madritsch **RC**	6.00
141	Michael Hessman **RC**	3.00
142	Todd Wellemeyer **RC**	3.00
143	Matt Bruback **RC**	3.00
144	Chris Capuano **RC**	5.00
145	Oscar Villarreal **RC**	3.00
146	Prentice Redman **RC**	3.00
147	Jeff Duncan **RC**	5.00
148	Phil Seibel **RC**	3.00
149	Arnaldo Munoz	3.00
150	David Sanders **RC**	3.00
151	Rick Roberts **RC**	3.00
152	Termel Sledge **RC**	4.00
153	Franklin Perez	3.00
154	Jeremy Wedel **RC**	3.00
155	Ian Ferguson **RC**	3.00
156	Josh Hall **RC**	4.00
157	Rocco Baldelli	3.00
158	Alejandro Machado **RC**	3.00
159	Jorge Cordova **RC**	3.00
160	Wilfredo Ledezma **RC**	3.00
161	Luis Ayala **RC**	3.00

Gold

Production 25 Sets
No pricing due to scarcity.

Silver

Even # SP's (2-60):	1-2X
Non-SP's (1-130):	4-8X
SP's (132-161):	.5-1X

Production 150 Sets

Dean's List

NM/M

Common Player:		4.00
Inserted 1:24		
RC	Roger Clemens	10.00
RC1	Roger Clemens	10.00
JG1	Jason Giambi	4.00
JG1	Jason Giambi	4.00
TG	Troy Glaus	4.00
TG1	Troy Glaus	4.00
NG	Shawn Green	4.00
NG1	Shawn Green	4.00
VG	Vladimir Guerrero	6.00
VG	Vladimir Guerrero	6.00
KG	Ken Griffey Jr.	10.00
KG1	Ken Griffey Jr.	10.00
CJ	Chipper Jones	8.00
CJ1	Chipper Jones	8.00
HM	Hideki Matsui	20.00
HM1	Hideki Matsui	20.00
HN	Hideo Nomo	10.00
HN1	Hideo Nomo	10.00
MP	Mike Piazza	10.00
MP1	Mike Piazza	10.00
MA	Mark Prior	8.00
MA1	Mark Prior	8.00
AP	Albert Pujols	15.00
AP1	Albert Pujols	15.00
AR	Alex Rodriguez	10.00
AR1	Alex Rodriguez	10.00
SS	Sammy Sosa	10.00
IS	Ichiro Suzuki	20.00
IS1	Ichiro Suzuki	20.00

Grade A Batting Gloves

NM/M

Most not priced due to scarcity.
Inserted 1:960

RA	Roberto Alomar/65	20.00
CD	Carlos Delgado/65	15.00
TG	Troy Glaus/60	15.00
JG	Juan Gonzalez/65	15.00
RM	Raul Mondesi/65	10.00
RP	Rafael Palmeiro/65	20.00
MR	Manny Ramirez/69	20.00
AR	Alex Rodriguez/67	25.00
IR	Ivan Rodriguez/70	20.00
MT	Miguel Tejada/70	10.00
FT	Frank Thomas/70	20.00

Leather of Distinction

NM/M

Most not priced due to scarcity.
Inserted 1:960

KG	Ken Griffey Jr./70	30.00
RP	Rafael Palmeiro/70	20.00
MP	Mike Piazza/50	40.00
MR	Manny Ramirez/70	20.00
AR	Alex Rodriguez/70	25.00
IR	Ivan Rodriguez/69	20.00
TS	Tim Salmon/70	10.00
GS	Gary Sheffield/70	10.00
FT	Frank Thomas/70	20.00
OV	Omar Vizquel/65	10.00

2003 Upper Deck MVP

NM/M

Complete Set (220):		20.00
Complete Factory Set (330):		30.00
Common Player:		.10
Pack (8):		1.50
Box (24):		25.00
1	Troy Glaus	.40
2	Darin Erstad	.25
3	Jarrod Washburn	.10
4	Francisco Rodriguez	.10
5	Garret Anderson	.20
6	Tim Salmon	.20
7	Adam Kennedy	.10
8	Randy Johnson	.50
9	Luis Gonzalez	.20
10	Curt Schilling	.50
11	Junior Spivey	.10
12	Craig Counsell	.10
13	Mark Grace	.25
14	Steve Finley	.10
15	Javy Lopez	.10
16	Rafael Furcal	.10
17	John Smoltz	.15
18	Greg Maddux	.75
19	Chipper Jones	.50
20	Gary Sheffield	.20
21	Andruw Jones	.20
22	Tony Batista	.10
23	Geronimo Gil	.10
24	Jay Gibbons	.10
25	Rodrigo Lopez	.10
26	Chris Singleton	.10
27	Melvin Mora	.10
28	Jeff Conine	.10
29	Nomar Garciaparra	1.00
30	Pedro J. Martinez	.50
31	Manny Ramirez	.50
32	Shea Hillenbrand	.10
33	Johnny Damon	.40
34	Jason Varitek	.25
35	Derek Lowe	.10
36	Trot Nixon	.10
37	Sammy Sosa	.75
38	Kerry Wood	.50
39	Mark Prior	.50
40	Moises Alou	.20
41	Corey Patterson	.25
42	Hee Seop Choi	.10
43	Mark Bellhorn	.10
44	Frank Thomas	.40
45	Mark Buehrle	.20
46	Magglio Ordonez	.20
47	Carlos Lee	.20
48	Paul Konerko	.20
49	Joe Borchard	.10
50	Joe Crede	.10
51	Ken Griffey Jr.	.75
52	Adam Dunn	.40
53	Austin Kearns	.40
54	Aaron Boone	.10
55	Sean Casey	.10
56	Danny Graves	.10
57	Russell Branyan	.10
58	Matt Lawton	.10
59	C.C. Sabathia	.10
60	Omar Vizquel	.20
61	Brandon Phillips	.10
62	Karim Garcia	.10
63	Ellis Burks	.10
64	Cliff Lee	.10
65	Todd Helton	.40
66	Larry Walker	.20
67	Jay Payton	.10
68	Brent Butler	.10
69	Juan Uribe	.10
70	Jason Jennings	.10
71	Denny Stark	.10
72	Dmitri Young	.10
73	Carlos Pena	.10
74	Andres Torres	.10
75	Andy Van Hekken	.10
76	George Lombard	.10
77	Eric Munson	.10
78	Bobby Higginson	.10
79	Luis Castillo	.10
80	A.J. Burnett	.10
81	Juan Encarnacion	.10
82	Ivan Rodriguez	.40
83	Mike Lowell	.10
84	Josh Beckett	.25
85	Brad Penny	.10
86	Craig Biggio	.25
87	Jeff Kent	.20
88	Morgan Ensberg	.10
89	Daryle Ward	.10
90	Jeff Bagwell	.40
91	Roy Oswalt	.20
92	Lance Berkman	.25
93	Mike Sweeney	.10
94	Carlos Beltran	.40
95	Raul Ibanez	.10
96	Carlos Febles	.10
97	Joe Randa	.10
98	Shawn Green	.25
99	Kevin Brown	.15
100	Paul LoDuca	.10
101	Adrian Beltre	.25
102	Eric Gagne	.20
103	Kazuhisa Ishii	.10
104	Odalis Perez	.10
105	Brian Jordan	.10
106	Geoff Jenkins	.10
107	Richie Sexson	.25
108	Ben Sheets	.20
109	Alex Sanchez	.10
110	Eric Young	.10
111	Jose Hernandez	.10
112	Torii Hunter	.25
113	Eric Milton	.10
114	Corey Koskie	.10
115	Doug Mientkiewicz	.10
116	A.J. Pierzynski	.10
117	Jacque Jones	.10
118	Cristian Guzman	.10
119	Bartolo Colon	.10
120	Brad Wilkerson	.10
121	Michael Barrett	.10
122	Vladimir Guerrero	.50
123	Jose Vidro	.10
124	Javier Vazquez	.10
125	Endy Chavez	.10
126	Roberto Alomar	.25
127	Mike Piazza	1.00
128	Jeromy Burnitz	.10
129	Mo Vaughn	.15
130	Tom Glavine	.25
131	Al Leiter	.15
132	Armando Benitez	.10
133	Timoniel Perez	.10
134	Roger Clemens	1.00
135	Derek Jeter	1.50
136	Jason Giambi	.25
137	Alfonso Soriano	.50
138	Bernie Williams	.25
139	Mike Mussina	.25
140	Jorge Posada	.20
141	Hideki Matsui **RC**	4.00
142	Robin Ventura	.10
143	David Wells	.10
144	Nick Johnson	.10
145	Tim Hudson	.20
146	Eric Chavez	.20
147	Barry Zito	.25
148	Miguel Tejada	.40
149	Jermaine Dye	.10
150	Mark Mulder	.20
151	Terrence Long	.10
152	Scott Hatteberg	.10
153	Marlon Byrd	.10
154	Jim Thome	.40
155	Marlon Anderson	.10
156	Vicente Padilla	.10
157	Bobby Abreu	.20
158	Jimmy Rollins	.25
159	Pat Burrell	.40
160	Brian Giles	.20
161	Aramis Ramirez	.20
162	Jason Kendall	.20
163	Josh Fogg	.10
164	Kip Wells	.10
165	Pokey Reese	.10
166	Kris Benson	.10
167	Ryan Klesko	.20
168	Brian Lawrence	.10
169	Mark Kotsay	.10
170	Jake Peavy	.20
171	Phil Nevin	.10
172	Sean Burroughs	.10
173	Trevor Hoffman	.10
174	Jason Schmidt	.20
175	Kirk Rueter	.10
176	Barry Bonds	1.50
177	Pedro Feliz	.10
178	Rich Aurilia	.10
179	Benito Santiago	.10
180	J.T. Snow	.10
181	Robb Nen	.10
182	Ichiro Suzuki	1.00
183	Edgar Martinez	.10
184	Bret Boone	.10
185	Freddy Garcia	.10
186	John Olerud	.20
187	Mike Cameron	.10
188	Joel Pineiro	.10
189	Albert Pujols	1.25
190	Matt Morris	.20
191	J.D. Drew	.20
192	Scott Rolen	.50
193	Tino Martinez	.20
194	Jim Edmonds	.20
195	Edgar Renteria	.20
196	Fernando Vina	.10
197	Jason Isringhausen	.10
198	Ben Grieve	.10
199	Carl Crawford	.10
200	Dewon Brazelton	.10
201	Aubrey Huff	.10
202	Jared Sandberg	.10
203	Steve Cox	.10
204	Carl Everett	.10
205	Kevin Mench	.10
206	Alex Rodriguez	1.00
207	Rafael Palmeiro	.40
208	Michael Young	.10
209	Hank Blalock	.40
210	Juan Gonzalez	.25
211	Carlos Delgado	.20
212	Eric Hinske	.20
213	Josh Phelps	.10
214	Mark Hendrickson	.10
215	Roy Halladay	.10
216	Orlando Hudson	.10
217	Shannon Stewart	.10
218	Vernon Wells	.10
219	Ichiro Suzuki	.40
220	Jason Giambi	.25
221	Scott Spiezio	.10
222	Rich Fischer	.10
223	Bengie Molina	.10
224	David Eckstein	.10
225	Brandon Webb **RC**	2.00
226	Oscar Villarreal	.10
227	Rob Hammock **RC**	.40
228	Matt Kata **RC**	.40
229	Lyle Overbay	.10
230	Chris Capuano **RC**	.50
231	Horacio Ramirez	.10
232	Shane Reynolds	.10
233	Russ Ortiz	.10
234	Mike Hampton	.10
235	Mike Hessman	.10
236	Byung-Hyun Kim	.10
237	Freddy Sanchez	.10
238	Jason Shiell	.10
239	Ryan Cameron	.10
240	Todd Wellemeyer **RC**	.40
241	Joe Borowski	.10
242	Alex Gonzalez	.10
243	Jon Leicester	.10
244	David Sanders	.10
245	Roberto Alomar	.25
246	Barry Larkin	.25
247	Jhonny Peralta	.10

248	Zach Sorensen	.10
249	Jason Davis	.10
250	Coco Crisp	.10
251	Greg Vaughn	.10
252	Preston Wilson	.10
253	Denny Neagle	.10
254	Clint Barmes RC	1.00
255	Jeremy Bonderman	1.00
256	Wilfredo Ledezma RC	.10
257	Dontrelle Willis	.25
258	Alex Gonzalez	.10
259	Tommy Phelps	.10
260	Kirk Saarloos	.10
261	Colin Porter RC	.10
262	Nate Bland	.10
263	Jason Gilfillan	.10
264	Mike MacDougal	.10
265	Ken Harvey	.10
266	Brent Mayne	.10
267	Miguel Cabrera	.40
268	Hideo Nomo	.25
269	Dave Roberts	.10
270	Fred McGriff	.20
271	Joe Thurston	.10
272	Royce Clayton	.10
273	Micheal Nakamura	.10
274	Brad Radke	.10
275	Joe Mays	.10
276	Lew Ford RC	1.00
277	Michael Cuddyer	.10
278	Luis Ayala	.10
279	Julio Manon	.10
280	Anthony Ferrari	.10
281	Livan Hernandez	.10
282	Jae Weong Seo	.10
283	Jose Reyes	.40
284	Tony Clark	.10
285	Ty Wigginton	.10
286	Cliff Floyd	.10
287	Jeremy Griffiths	.10
288	Jason Roach	.10
289	Jeff Duncan	.10
290	Phil Seibel	.10
291	Prentice Redman RC	.25
292	Jose Contreras RC	1.00
293	Ruben Sierra	.10
294	Andy Pettitte	.25
295	Aaron Boone	.10
296	Mariano Rivera	.20
297	Michel Hernandez	.10
298	Mike Neu	.10
299	Erubiel Durazo	.10
300	Billy McMillon	.10
301	Rich Harden	.10
302	David Bell	.10
303	Kevin Millwood	.20
304	Mike Lieberthal	.10
305	Jeremy Wedel	.10
306	Kenny Lofton	.10
307	Reggie Sanders	.10
308	Randall Simon	.10
309	Xavier Nady	.10
310	Rod Beck	.10
311	Miguel Ojeda	.10
312	Mark Loretta	.10
313	Edgardo Alfonzo	.10
314	Andres Galarraga	.10
315	Jose Cruz Jr.	.10
316	Jesse Foppert	.10
317	Kurt Ainsworth	.10
318	Dan Wilson	.10
319	Ben Davis	.10
320	Rocco Baldelli	.25
321	Al Martin	.10
322	Runelvys Hernandez	.10
323	Dan Haren	.50
324	Bo Hart RC	.25
325	Einar Diaz	.10
326	Mike Lamb	.10
327	Aquilino Lopez	.10
328	Reed Johnson	.10
329	Diegomar Markwell	.10
330	Hideki Matsui	.75

Gold

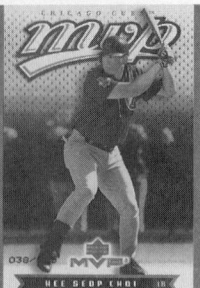

Stars (1-220): 6-12X
Production 150 Sets
Black Stars: 10-20X
Production 50 Sets
Silver Stars: 1-2X
Inserted 1:2

Base-to-Base

		NM/M
Inserted 1:488		
CP	Roger Clemens, Mike Piazza	25.00
IG	Ichiro Suzuki, Ken Griffey Jr.	40.00
IJ	Ichiro Suzuki, Derek Jeter	45.00
JW	Derek Jeter, Bernie Williams	25.00
MB	Mark McGwire, Barry Bonds	60.00
RJ	Alex Rodriguez, Derek Jeter	40.00

Covering the Bases

		NM/M
Common Player:		4.00
Inserted 1:125		
BB	Barry Bonds	15.00
CD	Carlos Delgado	4.00
JD	J.D. Drew	4.00
DE	Darin Erstad	6.00
TG	Troy Glaus	6.00
LG	Luis Gonzalez	6.00
SG	Shawn Green	6.00
DJ	Derek Jeter	15.00
MP	Mike Piazza	12.00
AR	Alex Rodriguez	12.00
IR	Ivan Rodriguez	4.00
IS	Ichiro Suzuki	15.00
MT	Miguel Tejada	4.00
FT	Frank Thomas	8.00
JT	Jim Thome	10.00

Covering the Plate Bat

		NM/M
Common Player:		6.00
Inserted 1:160		
RA	Roberto Alomar	15.00
RF	Rafael Furcal	8.00
VG	Vladimir Guerrero	8.00
FM	Fred McGriff	6.00
MM	Mark McGwire	60.00
JT	Jim Thome	12.00

Dual Aces

		NM/M
Common Card:		8.00
Inserted 1:488		
BS	Kevin Brown, Curt Schilling	10.00
CJ	Roger Clemens, Randy Johnson	20.00
CL	Roger Clemens, Al Leiter	15.00
ML	Matt Morris, Al Leiter	8.00
SJ	Curt Schilling, Randy Johnson	12.00
SM	Curt Schilling, Andy Pettitte	10.00

Express Delivery

		NM/M
Complete Set (15):		10.00
Common Player:		.50
Inserted 1:12		
ED1	Randy Johnson	2.00
ED2	Curt Schilling	1.00
ED3	Pedro J. Martinez	2.00
ED4	Kerry Wood	1.00
ED5	Mark Prior	1.50
ED6	A.J. Burnett	.50
ED7	Josh Beckett	.50
ED8	Roy Oswalt	.75
ED9	Hideo Nomo	.75
ED10	Ben Sheets	.50
ED11	Bartolo Colon	.50
ED12	Roger Clemens	2.50
ED13	Mike Mussina	.75
ED14	Tim Hudson	.75
ED15	Matt Morris	.50

MVP Celebration

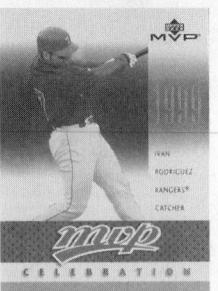

		NM/M
Common Player:		1.50
#'d to yr. MVP was won		
MVP1	Yogi Berra	4.00
MVP2	Mickey Mantle	15.00
MVP3	Mickey Mantle	15.00
MVP4	Mickey Mantle	15.00
MVP5	Roger Clemens	5.00
MVP6	Rickey Henderson	4.00
MVP7	Frank Thomas	4.00
MVP8	Mo Vaughn	1.50
MVP9	Juan Gonzalez	3.00
MVP10	Ken Griffey Jr.	6.00
MVP11	Juan Gonzalez	3.00
MVP12	Ivan Rodriguez	2.00
MVP13	Jason Giambi	4.00
MVP14	Ichiro Suzuki	6.00
MVP15	Miguel Tejada	2.00
MVP16	Barry Bonds	8.00
MVP17	Barry Bonds	8.00
MVP18	Barry Bonds	8.00
MVP19	Jeff Bagwell	4.00
MVP20	Barry Larkin	1.50
MVP21	Larry Walker	1.50
MVP22	Sammy Sosa	6.00
MVP23	Chipper Jones	5.00
MVP24	Jeff Kent	1.50
MVP25	Barry Bonds	8.00
MVP26	Barry Bonds	8.00
MVP27	Ken Griffey Sr.	1.50
MVP28	Roger Clemens	5.00
MVP29	Ken Griffey Jr.	6.00
MVP30	Fred McGriff	1.50
MVP31	Jeff Conine	1.50
MVP32	Mike Piazza	6.00
MVP33	Sandy Alomar Jr.	1.50
MVP34	Roberto Alomar	2.50
MVP35	Pedro J. Martinez	4.00
MVP36	Derek Jeter	8.00
MVP37	Rickey Henderson	4.00
MVP38	Roberto Alomar	2.50
MVP39	Bernie Williams	3.00
MVP40	Marquis Grissom	1.50
MVP41	David Wells	1.50
MVP42	Orlando Hernandez	1.50
MVP43	David Justice	1.50
MVP44	Andy Pettitte	2.00
MVP45	Adam Kennedy	1.50
MVP46	John Smoltz	1.50
MVP47	Curt Schilling	2.00
MVP48	Javy Lopez	1.50
MVP49	Livan Hernandez	1.50
MVP50	Sterling Hitchcock	1.50
MVP51	Mike Hampton	1.50
MVP52	Craig Counsell	1.50
MVP53	Benito Santiago	1.50
MVP54	Tom Glavine	2.00
MVP55	Livan Hernandez	1.50
MVP56	Mariano Rivera	2.50
MVP57	Derek Jeter	8.00
MVP58	Randy Johnson	4.00
MVP59	Curt Schilling	2.50
MVP60	Troy Glaus	4.00
MVP61	Yogi Berra	4.00
MVP62	Yogi Berra	4.00
MVP63	Mickey Mantle	15.00
MVP64	Mickey Mantle	15.00
MVP65	Ken Griffey Sr.	1.50
MVP66	Rickey Henderson	4.00
MVP67	Roberto Alomar	2.50
MVP68	Bernie Williams	3.00
MVP69	Livan Hernandez	1.50
MVP70	Sammy Sosa	6.00
MVP71	Sterling Hitchcock	1.50
MVP72	David Wells	1.50
MVP73	Mariano Rivera	1.50
MVP74	Chipper Jones	5.00
MVP75	Ivan Rodriguez	2.00
MVP76	Derek Jeter	8.00
MVP77	Jason Giambi	4.00
MVP78	Jeff Kent	1.50
MVP79	Mike Hampton	1.50
MVP80	Randy Johnson	4.00
MVP81	Curt Schilling	2.50
MVP82	Barry Bonds	8.00
MVP83	Ichiro Suzuki	6.00
MVP84	Ichiro Suzuki	6.00
MVP85	Adam Kennedy	1.50
MVP86	Benito Santiago	1.50
MVP87	Troy Glaus	3.00
MVP88	Troy Glaus	3.00
MVP89	Miguel Tejada	2.00
MVP90	Barry Bonds	8.00

Prosign

Production 25 Sets
No Pricing

Pro View

		NM/M
Complete Set (45):		65.00
Common Player:		.75
Inserted 2:Box		
Golds:		2-3X
PV1	Troy Glaus	1.50
PV2	Darin Erstad	1.00
PV3	Randy Johnson	2.00
PV4	Curt Schilling	1.50
PV5	Luis Gonzalez	.75
PV6	Chipper Jones	2.00
PV7	Andruw Jones	1.00
PV8	Greg Maddux	3.00
PV9	Pedro J. Martinez	2.00
PV10	Manny Ramirez	2.00
PV11	Sammy Sosa	3.00
PV12	Mark Prior	1.50
PV13	Magglio Ordonez	1.00
PV14	Frank Thomas	1.50
PV15	Ken Griffey Jr.	3.00
PV16	Adam Dunn	1.50
PV17	Jim Thome	1.50
PV18	Todd Helton	1.50
PV19	Jeff Bagwell	1.50
PV20	Lance Berkman	1.00
PV21	Shawn Green	.75
PV22	Hideo Nomo	1.00
PV23	Vladimir Guerrero	2.00
PV24	Roberto Alomar	1.00
PV25	Mike Piazza	4.00
PV26	Jason Giambi	1.00
PV27	Roger Clemens	3.00
PV28	Alfonso Soriano	2.00
PV29	Derek Jeter	6.00
PV30	Miguel Tejada	1.50
PV31	Eric Chavez	.75
PV32	Barry Zito	1.00
PV33	Pat Burrell	1.50
PV34	Brian Giles	.75
PV35	Barry Bonds	6.00
PV36	Ichiro Suzuki	4.00
PV37	Albert Pujols	5.00
PV38	Scott Rolen	1.50
PV39	J.D. Drew	.75
PV40	Mark McGwire	5.00
PV41	Alex Rodriguez	5.00
PV42	Rafael Palmeiro	1.00
PV43	Juan Gonzalez	1.00
PV44	Eric Hinske	.75
PV45	Carlos Delgado	.75

SportsNut Fantasy

		NM/M
Complete Set (90):		45.00
Common Player:		.40
Inserted 1:3		
Prices for unscratched cards.		
SN1	Troy Glaus	1.00
SN2	Darin Erstad	.50
SN3	Luis Gonzalez	.50
SN4	Andruw Jones	.50
SN5	Chipper Jones	2.00
SN6	Gary Sheffield	.50
SN7	Jay Gibbons	.40
SN8	Manny Ramirez	1.00
SN9	Shea Hillenbrand	.40
SN10	Johnny Damon	.40
SN11	Nomar Garciaparra	2.50
SN12	Sammy Sosa	3.00

SN13 Magglio Ordonez .75
SN14 Frank Thomas .75
SN15 Ken Griffey Jr. 1.50
SN16 Adam Dunn 1.00
SN17 Matt Lawton .40
SN18 Larry Walker .40
SN19 Todd Helton .75
SN20 Carlos Pena .40
SN21 Mike Lowell .40
SN22 Jeff Bagwell 1.00
SN23 Lance Berkman .75
SN24 Mike Sweeney .50
SN25 Carlos Beltran .40
SN26 Shawn Green .75
SN27 Richie Sexson .50
SN28 Torii Hunter .40
SN29 Jacque Jones .40
SN30 Vladimir Guerrero 1.50
SN31 Jose Vidro .40
SN32 Roberto Alomar .50
SN33 Mike Piazza 2.00
SN34 Alfonso Soriano 1.50
SN35 Derek Jeter 3.00
SN36 Jason Giambi 2.00
SN37 Bernie Williams .75
SN38 Eric Chavez .75
SN39 Miguel Tejada .75
SN40 Jim Thome 1.00
SN41 Pat Burrell 1.00
SN42 Bobby Abreu .50
SN43 Brian Giles .50
SN44 Jason Kendall .40
SN45 Ryan Klesko .40
SN46 Phil Nevin .40
SN47 Barry Bonds 4.00
SN48 Rich Aurilia .40
SN49 Ichiro Suzuki 2.00
SN50 Bret Boone .40
SN51 J.D. Drew .40
SN52 Jim Edmonds .75
SN53 Albert Pujols 1.50
SN54 Scott Rolen 1.00
SN55 Ben Grieve .40
SN56 Alex Rodriguez 3.00
SN57 Rafael Palmeiro .75
SN58 Juan Gonzalez .50
SN59 Carlos Delgado .40
SN60 Josh Phelps .40
SN61 Jarrod Washburn .40
SN62 Randy Johnson 1.00
SN63 Curt Schilling .75
SN64 Greg Maddux 1.50
SN65 Mike Hampton .40
SN66 Rodrigo Lopez .40
SN67 Pedro J. Martinez 1.50
SN68 Derek Lowe .40
SN69 Mark Prior 1.00
SN70 Kerry Wood .75
SN71 Mark Buehrle .40
SN72 Roy Oswalt .50
SN73 Wade Miller .40
SN74 Odalis Perez .40
SN75 Hideo Nomo .50
SN76 Ben Sheets .40
SN77 Eric Milton .40
SN78 Bartolo Colon .40
SN79 Tom Glavine .40
SN80 Al Leiter .40
SN81 Roger Clemens 2.00
SN82 Mike Mussina .75
SN83 Tim Hudson .75
SN84 Barry Zito .75
SN85 Mark Mulder .50
SN86 Vicente Padilla .40
SN87 Jason Schmidt .40
SN88 Freddy Garcia .40
SN89 Matt Morris .40
SN90 Roy Halladay .40

Talk of the Town

NM/M

Complete Set (15): 20.00
Common Player: .75
Inserted 1:12
TT1 Hideki Matsui 3.00
TT2 Chipper Jones 1.00
TT3 Manny Ramirez 1.50
TT4 Sammy Sosa 2.00
TT5 Ken Griffey Jr. 2.00
TT6 Lance Berkman .75
TT7 Shawn Green .75
TT8 Vladimir Guerrero 1.50
TT9 Mike Piazza 2.50
TT10 Jason Giambi .75
TT11 Alfonso Soriano 1.50
TT12 Ichiro Suzuki 2.50
TT13 Albert Pujols 3.00
TT14 Alex Rodriguez 3.00
TT15 Eric Hinske .75

Three Bagger

NM/M

Inserted 1:488
BMP Barry Bonds, Mark McGwire, Mike Piazza 80.00
GIB Ken Griffey Jr., Ichiro Suzuki, Barry Bonds 60.00
GTD Troy Glaus, Frank Thomas, Carlos Delgado 10.00
IBJ Ichiro Suzuki, Barry Bonds, Derek Jeter 80.00
JWP Derek Jeter, Bernie Williams, Jorge Posada 35.00
SCB Curt Schilling, Roger Clemens, Kevin Brown 20.00

Total Bases

NM/M

Production 150 Sets
BB Barry Bonds 20.00
RC Roger Clemens 20.00
TG Troy Glaus 8.00
KG Ken Griffey Jr. 15.00
DJ Derek Jeter 20.00
MM Mark McGwire 25.00
MP Mike Piazza 15.00
AR Alex Rodriguez 15.00
IS Ichiro Suzuki 30.00

2003 Upper Deck Patch Collection

NM/M

Complete Set (161):
Common Player: .25
Common SP Patch (121-161): 4.00
All-Star & HOF Patches (121-150):
Inserted 1:40
Rookie Patches (151-161):
Inserted 1:20
Pack (5): 4.75
Box (20): 80.00
1 Darin Erstad .40
2 Troy Glaus .75
3 Robby Hammock **RC** .25
4 Luis Gonzalez .50
5 Randy Johnson/SP 3.00
6 Curt Schilling/SP 2.50
7 Oscar Villarreal **RC** .25
8 Gary Sheffield .50
9 Mike Hampton .25
10 Greg Maddux 1.50
11 Chipper Jones 1.50
12 Tony Batista .25
13 Rodrigo Lopez .25
14 Jay Gibbons .25
15 Shea Hillenbrand .25
16 Johnny Damon .25
17 Derek Lowe .25
18 Nomar Garciaparra 2.00
19 Pedro J. Martinez 1.00
20 Manny Ramirez .75
21 Mark Prior .75
22 Kerry Wood .50
23 Corey Patterson .25
24 Sammy Sosa 1.50
25 Troy O'Leary .25
26 Frank Thomas .75
27 Magglio Ordonez .40
28 Bartolo Colon .25
29 Austin Kearns .75
30 Aaron Boone .25
31 Ken Griffey Jr. 1.50
32 Adam Dunn .75
33 C.C. Sabathia .25
34 Karim Garcia .25
35 Larry Walker .40
36 Preston Wilson .40
37 Jason Jennings .25
38 Todd Helton .75
39 Carlos Pena .25
40 Eric Munson .25
41 Ivan Rodriguez .50
42 Josh Beckett .25
43 A.J. Burnett .25
44 Roy Oswalt .25
45 Craig Biggio .40
46 Jeff Bagwell .75
47 Lance Berkman .50
48 Jeff Kent .40
49 Carlos Beltran .25
50 Mike Sweeney .25
51 Hideo Nomo .50
52 Adrian Beltre .25
53 Shawn Green .50
54 Kazuhisa Ishii .25
55 Ben Sheets .25
56 Richie Sexson .50
57 Torii Hunter .50
58 Doug Mientkiewicz .25
59 Eric Milton .25
60 Corey Koskie .25
61 Joe Mays .25
62 Jose Vidro .25
63 Vladimir Guerrero .75
64 Luis Ayala **RC** .25
65 Cliff Floyd .25
66 Tom Glavine .50
67 Mike Piazza 2.00
68 Roberto Alomar .50
69 Al Leiter .25
70 Mike Mussina .50
71 Mariano Rivera .40
72 Drew Henson .25
73 Roger Clemens 1.50
74 Jason Giambi 1.00
75 Bernie Williams .50
76 Alfonso Soriano 1.50
77 Derek Jeter 3.00
78 Miguel Tejada .50
79 Jermaine Dye .25
80 Tim Hudson .50
81 Barry Zito .50
82 Mark Mulder .40
83 Pat Burrell .50
84 Jim Thome .75
85 Bobby Abreu .40
86 Kevin Millwood .40
87 Jason Kendall .40
88 Brian Giles .40
89 Phil Nevin .25
90 Sean Burroughs .25
91 Oliver Perez .25
92 Jose Cruz Jr. .25
93 Rich Aurilia .25
94 Edgardo Alfonzo .25
95 Barry Bonds 3.00
96 J.T. Snow .25
97 Mike Cameron .25
98 John Olerud .50
99 Bret Boone .25
100 Ichiro Suzuki 1.50
101 J.D. Drew .40
102 Jim Edmonds .50
103 Scott Rolen .75
104 Matt Morris .40
105 Tino Martinez .40
106 Albert Pujols 1.50
107 Rocco Baldelli .25
108 Carl Crawford .25
109 Mark Teixeira .50
110 Rafael Palmeiro .50
111 Hank Blalock .50
112 Alex Rodriguez 2.50
113 Kevin Mench .25
114 Juan Gonzalez .75
115 Shannon Stewart .25
116 Vernon Wells .40
117 Josh Phelps .25
118 Eric Hinske .25
119 Orlando Hudson .25
120 Carlos Delgado .50
121 Alex Rodriguez 10.00
122 Nomar Garciaparra 10.00
123 Miguel Tejada 4.00
124 Jim Thome 8.00
125 Alfonso Soriano 6.00
126 Vladimir Guerrero 6.00
127 Derek Jeter 15.00
128 Mike Piazza 8.00
129 Ichiro Suzuki 12.00
130 Pedro J. Martinez 8.00
131 Luis Gonzalez 4.00
132 Adam Dunn 6.00
133 Shawn Green 4.00
134 Barry Zito 4.00
135 Torii Hunter 5.00
136 Ted Williams 20.00
137 Mickey Mantle 25.00
138 Ernie Banks 10.00
139 Yogi Berra 8.00
140 Rollie Fingers 4.00
141 Jim "Catfish" Hunter 4.00
142 Juan Marichal 8.00
143 Eddie Mathews 10.00
144 Willie McCovey 10.00
145 Joe Morgan 5.00
146 Stan Musial 12.00
147 Pee Wee Reese 10.00
148 Phil Rizzuto 6.00
149 Nolan Ryan 20.00
150 Tom Seaver 8.00
151 Hideki Matsui **RC** 15.00
152 Jose Contreras **RC** 5.00
153 Lew Ford **RC** 5.00
154 Jeremy Griffiths 4.00
155 Guillermo Quiroz **RC** 4.00
156 Ryan Cameron **RC** 4.00
157 Jon Leicester **RC** 4.00
158 Josh Willingham **RC** 4.00
159 Shane Bazzell **RC** 4.00
160 Willie Eyre **RC** 4.00
161 Prentice Redman **RC** 4.00

All-Star Game History Patches

NM/M

Common Patch: 8.00
Inserted 2:Box
1 1933 All-Star Game 12.00
2 1934 All-Star Game 15.00
3 1935 All-Star Game 15.00
4 1936 All-Star Game 10.00
5 1937 All-Star Game 10.00
6 1938 All-Star Game 10.00
7 1939 All-Star Game 15.00
8 1940 All-Star Game 15.00
9 1941 All-Star Game 10.00
10 1942 All-Star Game 15.00
11 1943 All-Star Game 12.00
12 1944 All-Star Game 12.00
13 1946 All-Star Game 15.00
14 1947 All-Star Game 15.00
15 1948 All-Star Game 15.00
16 1949 All-Star Game 15.00
17 1950 All-Star Game 12.00
18 1951 All-Star Game 12.00
19 1952 All-Star Game 15.00
20 1953 All-Star Game 12.00
21 1954 All-Star Game 12.00
22 1955 All-Star Game 10.00
23 1956 All-Star Game 12.00
24 1957 All-Star Game 15.00
25 1958 All-Star Game 12.00
26 1959 All-Star Game 15.00
27 1959 All-Star Game 15.00
28 1960 All-Star Game 10.00
29 1960 All-Star Game 15.00
30 1961 All-Star Game 10.00
31 1961 All-Star Game 15.00
32 1962 All-Star Game 8.00
33 1962 All-Star Game 12.00
34 1963 All-Star Game 10.00
35 1964 All-Star Game 15.00
36 1965 All-Star Game 10.00
37 1966 All-Star Game 15.00
38 1967 All-Star Game 12.00
39 1968 All-Star Game 8.00
40 1969 All-Star Game 10.00
41 1970 All-Star Game 15.00
42 1971 All-Star Game 10.00
43 1972 All-Star Game 10.00
44 1973 All-Star Game 10.00
45 1974 All-Star Game 10.00
46 1975 All-Star Game 10.00
47 1976 All-Star Game 15.00
48 1977 All-Star Game 12.00
49 1978 All-Star Game 10.00
50 1979 All-Star Game 8.00
51 1980 All-Star Game 8.00
52 1981 All-Star Game 10.00
53 1982 All-Star Game 8.00
54 1983 All-Star Game 10.00
55 1984 All-Star Game 10.00
56 1985 All-Star Game 10.00
57 1986 All-Star Game 10.00
58 1987 All-Star Game 8.00
59 1988 All-Star Game 10.00
60 1989 All-Star Game 8.00
61 1990 All-Star Game 15.00
62 1991 All-Star Game 8.00
63 1992 All-Star Game 8.00
64 1993 All-Star Game 10.00
65 1994 All-Star Game 15.00
66 1995 All-Star Game 8.00
67 1996 All-Star Game 12.00
68 1997 All-Star Game 10.00
69 1998 All-Star Game 8.00
70 1999 All-Star Game 15.00
71 2000 All-Star Game 10.00
72 2001 All-Star Game 10.00
73 2002 All-Star Game 12.00

MVPs Patches

NM/M

Common Player: 5.00
Inserted 1:20
1 Derek Jeter 15.00
2 Randy Johnson 8.00

3	Curt Schilling	6.00
4	Troy Glaus	5.00
5	Ted Williams	15.00
6	Ted Williams	15.00
7	Mickey Mantle	20.00
8	Mickey Mantle	20.00
9	Phil Rizzuto	5.00
10	Roger Clemens	10.00
11	Ken Griffey Jr.	10.00
12	Jason Giambi	5.00
13	Ichiro Suzuki	15.00
14	Roger Clemens	10.00
15	Yogi Berra	6.00
16	Sammy Sosa	10.00
17	Derek Jeter	15.00
18	Mike Piazza	10.00
19	Barry Bonds	15.00
20	Stan Musial	12.00
21	Joe Morgan	5.00

Signature Patches

JUAN MARICHAL 27

		NM/M
Common Autograph:		25.00
Inserted 1:320		
JB	Jeff Bagwell	50.00
LB	Lance Berkman	50.00
RC	Roger Clemens	160.00
AD	Adam Dunn	60.00
FG	Freddy Garcia	30.00
JG	Jason Giambi	40.00
LG	Luis Gonzalez	40.00
KG	Ken Griffey Jr.	100.00
DH	Drew Henson	40.00
EH	Eric Hinske	25.00
TP	Troy Percival	25.00
SR	Scott Rolen	50.00
CS	Curt Schilling	50.00
GS	Gary Sheffield	50.00
IS	Ichiro Suzuki	300.00
MT	Miguel Tejada	50.00
BZ	Barry Zito	40.00

2003 Upper Deck Play Ball

ROBIN YOUNT

		NM/M
Complete Set (104):		
Common Player:		.25
Common Summer of '41 (74-88):		4.00
Inserted 1:24		
Common Ted Williams (89-103):		10.00
Inserted 1:24		
Pack (5):		2.50
Box (24):		40.00
1	Troy Glaus	.40
2	Darin Erstad	.25
3	Randy Johnson	.75
4	Luis Gonzalez	.40
5	Curt Schilling	.75
6	Tom Glavine	.40
7	Chipper Jones	.75
8	Greg Maddux	1.00
9	Andruw Jones	.40
10	Pedro J. Martinez	.75
11	Manny Ramirez	.75
12	Nomar Garciaparra	1.00
13	Billy Williams	.25
14	Sammy Sosa	1.00
15	Kerry Wood	.75

16	Mark Prior	.75
17	Ernie Banks	1.00
18	Frank Thomas	.75
19	Joe Morgan	.25
20	Ken Griffey Jr.	1.25
21	Adam Dunn	.50
22	Jim Thome	.75
23	Todd Helton	.50
24	Larry Walker	.40
25	Lance Berkman	.40
26	Roy Oswalt	.40
27	Jeff Bagwell	.50
28	Nolan Ryan	2.00
29	Mike Sweeney	.25
30	Shawn Green	.40
31	Hideo Nomo	.40
32	Kazuhisa Ishii	.25
33	Richie Sexson	.40
34	Robin Yount	.75
35	Harmon Killebrew	.75
36	Torii Hunter	.50
37	Vladimir Guerrero	.75
38	Roberto Alomar	.50
39	Mike Piazza	1.00
40	Tom Seaver	.75
41	Phil Rizzuto	.50
42	Yogi Berra	.75
43	Mike Mussina	.50
44	Roger Clemens	1.50
45	Derek Jeter	2.00
46	Jason Giambi	.25
47	Bernie Williams	.50
48	Alfonso Soriano	.25
49	Jim "Catfish" Hunter	.25
50	Barry Zito	.40
51	Eric Chavez	.40
52	Tim Hudson	.40
53	Rollie Fingers	.25
54	Miguel Tejada	.50
55	Pat Burrell	.40
56	Brian Giles	.40
57	Willie Stargell	.50
58	Phil Nevin	.25
59	Orlando Cepeda	.25
60	Barry Bonds	2.00
61	Jeff Kent	.40
62	Willie McCovey	.25
63	Ichiro Suzuki	1.50
64	Stan Musial	1.50
65	Albert Pujols	2.00
66	J.D. Drew	.40
67	Scott Rolen	.75
68	Mark McGwire	1.00
69	Alex Rodriguez	1.00
70	Juan Gonzalez	.40
71	Ivan Rodriguez	.50
72	Rafael Palmeiro	.50
73	Carlos Delgado	.40
74	Ted Williams	15.00
75	Hank Greenberg	6.00
76	Joe DiMaggio	15.00
77	Lefty Gomez	6.00
78	Tommy Henrich	4.00
79	Pee Wee Reese	5.00
80	Mel Ott	6.00
81	Carl Hubbell	6.00
82	Jimmie Foxx	8.00
83	Joe Cronin	4.00
84	Charlie Gehringer	5.00
85	Frank Hayes	4.00
86	Babe Dahlgren	4.00
87	Dolph Camilli	4.00
88	Johnny Vander Meer	4.00
89-103	Ted Williams	10.00
104	Hideki Matsui RC	5.00

Red Back

		NM/M
Stars (1-73):		1.5-2X
SP's (74-103):		1-1.5X
Matsui Red #104:		10.00
Inserted 1:2		

BuyBacks
No Pricing

Game-Used Memorabilia
Tier 1

SAMMY SOSA

	NM/M
Common Player:	5.00
Inserted 1:82	

Golds:		Not Priced
Production 25 Sets		
RC1	Roger Clemens	20.00
CD1	Carlos Delgado	5.00
DR1	J.D. Drew	5.00
AD1	Adam Dunn	10.00
JG1	Jason Giambi	5.00
LG1	Luis Gonzalez	5.00
KG1	Ken Griffey Jr.	15.00
TH1	Tommy Henrich	5.00
KI1	Kazuhisa Ishii	5.00
CJ1	Chipper Jones	10.00
MM1	Mark McGwire	50.00
RP1	Rafael Palmeiro	8.00
MP1	Mike Piazza	10.00
PR1	Mark Prior	8.00
IR1	Ivan Rodriguez	8.00
CS1	Curt Schilling	8.00
AS1	Alfonso Soriano	8.00
SS1	Sammy Sosa	10.00
IS1	Ichiro Suzuki	30.00
MS1	Mike Sweeney	5.00
BW1	Bernie Williams	5.00

Game-Used Memorabilia
Tier 2

		NM/M
Common Player:		5.00
Production 150 Sets		
JB2	Jeff Bagwell	10.00
LB2	Lance Berkman	5.00
JD2	Joe DiMaggio	100.00
DE2	Darin Erstad	5.00
JG2	Jason Giambi	5.00
SG2	Shawn Green	5.00
KG2	Ken Griffey Jr.	15.00
RJ2	Randy Johnson	10.00
AJ2	Andruw Jones	8.00
CJ2	Chipper Jones	10.00
GM2	Greg Maddux	15.00
PM2	Pedro J. Martinez	10.00
MM2	Mark McGwire	60.00
MP2	Mike Piazza	10.00
MR2	Manny Ramirez	10.00
AR2	Alex Rodriguez	10.00
CS2	Curt Schilling	10.00
SS2	Sammy Sosa	15.00
IS2	Ichiro Suzuki	50.00
JT2	Jim Thome	10.00
KW2	Kerry Wood	10.00

Game-Used Memorabilia
Auto.

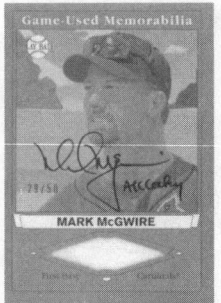

MARK McGWIRE

		NM/M
Production 50 except A-Rod.		
JB2	Jeff Bagwell	75.00
LB2	Lance Berkman	75.00
JG2	Jason Giambi	50.00
KG2	Ken Griffey Jr.	125.00
AJ2	Andruw Jones	50.00
MM2	Mark McGwire	350.00
AR2	Alex Rodriguez/285	100.00
CS2	Curt Schilling	75.00
SS2	Sammy Sosa	180.00
IS2	Ichiro Suzuki	375.00
JT2	Jim Thome	75.00
KW2	Kerry Wood	75.00

Mini

RICHIE SEXSON

		NM/M
		40.00
Complete Set (73):		40.00
Common Player:		.50
Inserted 1:2		
1	Troy Glaus	.50
2	Darin Erstad	.50
3	Randy Johnson	1.00
4	Luis Gonzalez	.50
5	Curt Schilling	.75
6	Tom Glavine	.50
7	Chipper Jones	1.00
8	Greg Maddux	1.50
9	Andruw Jones	.75
10	Pedro J. Martinez	1.00
11	Manny Ramirez	1.00
12	Nomar Garciaparra	2.00
13	Billy Williams	.50
14	Sammy Sosa	2.00
15	Kerry Wood	1.00
16	Mark Prior	1.00
17	Ernie Banks	1.50
18	Frank Thomas	1.00
19	Joe Morgan	.50
20	Ken Griffey Jr.	2.00
21	Adam Dunn	1.00
22	Jim Thome	1.00
23	Todd Helton	.75
24	Larry Walker	.50
25	Lance Berkman	.75
26	Roy Oswalt	.50
27	Jeff Bagwell	1.00
28	Nolan Ryan	3.00
29	Mike Sweeney	.50
30	Shawn Green	.50
31	Hideo Nomo	.75
32	Kazuhisa Ishii	.50
33	Richie Sexson	.50
34	Robin Yount	1.00
35	Harmon Killebrew	1.00
36	Torii Hunter	.75
37	Vladimir Guerrero	1.00
38	Roberto Alomar	.75
39	Mike Piazza	2.00
40	Tom Seaver	1.00
41	Phil Rizzuto	.75
42	Yogi Berra	1.50
43	Mike Mussina	.75
44	Roger Clemens	2.00
45	Derek Jeter	3.00
46	Jason Giambi	.50
47	Bernie Williams	.75
48	Alfonso Soriano	1.00
49	Jim "Catfish" Hunter	.50
50	Barry Zito	.50
51	Eric Chavez	.50
52	Tim Hudson	.50
53	Rollie Fingers	.50
54	Miguel Tejada	1.00
55	Pat Burrell	.50
56	Brian Giles	.50
57	Willie Stargell	.75
58	Phil Nevin	.50
59	Orlando Cepeda	.50
60	Barry Bonds	3.00
61	Jeff Kent	.50
62	Willie McCovey	.50
63	Ichiro Suzuki	2.50
64	Stan Musial	2.00
65	Albert Pujols	3.00
66	J.D. Drew	.50
67	Scott Rolen	1.00
68	Mark McGwire	2.00
69	Alex Rodriguez	2.50
70	Juan Gonzalez	1.00
71	Ivan Rodriguez	1.00
72	Rafael Palmeiro	.75
73	Carlos Delgado	.50

Original Artwork Redemption

89 Total Redemption Cards
No Pricing

Reprint Series Original 1941

		NM/M
Complete Set (25):		15.00
Common Player:		.75
Inserted 1:2		
R1	Ted Williams	2.50
R2	Hank Greenberg	.75
R3	Joe DiMaggio	2.50
R4	Lefty Gomez	.75
R5	Tommy Henrich	.75
R6	Pee Wee Reese	.75
R7	Mel Ott	1.00
R8	Carl Hubbell	.75
R9	Jimmie Foxx	1.00
R10	Joe Cronin	.75
R11	Charley Gehringer	.75
R12	Frank Hayes	.75
R13	Babe Dahlgren	.75
R14	Dolph Camilli	.75
R15	Johnny Vander Meer	.75
R16	Bucky Walters	.75
R17	Red Ruffing	.75
R18	Charlie Keller	.75
R19	Bob Johnson	.75
R20	Emil "Dutch" Leonard	.75
R21	Barney McCosky	.75
R22	Soupy Campbell	.75
R23	Roy Weatherly	.75
R24	Bobby Doerr	.75
R25	Bill Dickey	.75

Yankee Clipper: 1941 Streak

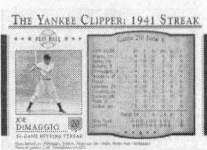

	NM/M
Complete Set (56):	250.00
Common DiMaggio (1-41):	5.00
Inserted 1:12	
Common DiMaggio (42-56):	8.00
Inserted 1:24	
S-1-41 Joe DiMaggio	5.00
S-42-56 Joe DiMaggio	8.00

2003 Upper Deck Prospect Premieres

	NM/M
Complete Set (90):	30.00
Common Player:	.25
Pack (4):	7.00
Box (18):	100.00
1 Bryan Opdyke RC	.25
2 Gabriel Sosa RC	.25
3 Tila Reynolds RC	.25
4 Aaron Hill RC	1.00
5 Aaron Marsden RC	.25
6 Abe Alvarez RC	.75
7 Adam Jones RC	3.00
8 Adam Miller RC	2.50
9 Andre Ethier RC	3.00
10 Tony Gwynn Jr. RC	.75
11 Brad Snyder RC	1.00
12 Brad Sullivan RC	.75
13 Brian Anderson RC	1.50
14 Brian Buscher RC	.25
15 Brian Snyder RC	.75
16 Carlos Quentin RC	3.00
17 Chad Billingsley RC	3.00
18 Fraser Dizard RC	.50
19 Chris Durbin RC	.50
20 Chris Ray RC	.50
21 Conor Jackson RC	2.00
22 Kory Casto RC	.50
23 Craig Whitaker RC	.75
24 Daniel Moore RC	.25
25 Daric Barton RC	2.00
26 Darin Downs RC	.75
27 David Murphy RC	3.00
28 Dustin Majewski RC	.50
29 Edgardo Baez RC	.25
30 Jake Fox RC	.75
31 Jake Stevens RC	.50
32 Jamie D'Antona RC	1.00
33 James Houser RC	.50
34 Jarrod Saltalamacchia RC	2.00
35 Jason Hirsh RC	2.00
36 Javi Herrera RC	1.00
37 Jeff Allison RC	.75
38 John Hudgins RC	.50
39 Jo Jo Reyes RC	.50
40 Justin James RC	.50
41 Kurt Isenberg RC	.50
42 Kyle Boyer RC	.75
43 Lastings Milledge RC	5.00
44 Luis Atilano RC	.50
45 Matt Murton RC	1.50
46 Matt Moses RC	1.00
47 Matt Harrison RC	.50
48 Michael Bourn RC	.50
49 Miguel Vega RC	.50
50 Mitch Maier RC	1.00
51 Omar Quintanilla RC	.50
52 Ryan Sweeney RC	1.50
53 Scott Baker RC	.75
54 Sean Rodriguez RC	.75
55 Steve Lerud RC	.25
56 Thomas Pauly RC	.25
57 Tom Gorzelanny RC	.25
58 Tim Moss RC	.25
59 Robbie Wooley RC	.50
60 Trey Webb RC	.25
61 Wes Littleton RC	.50
62 Beau Vaughan RC	.25
63 Willy Jo Ronda RC	.50
64 Chris Lubanski RC	1.50
65 Ian Stewart RC	4.00
66 John Danks RC	3.00
67 Kyle Sleeth RC	1.00
68 Michael Aubrey RC	1.50
69 Kevin Kouzmanoff RC	3.00
70 Ryan Harvey RC	1.50
71 Tim Stauffer RC	1.00
72 Tony Richie RC	.25
73 Brandon Wood RC	8.00
74 David Aardsma RC	.75
75 David Shinskie RC	.50
76 Dennis Dove RC	.25
77 Eric Sultemeier RC	.25
78 Jay Sborz RC	.25
79 Jimmy Barthmaier RC	.50
80 Josh Whitesell RC	.25
81 Josh Anderson RC	.25
82 Kenny Lewis RC	.25
83 Mateo Miramontes RC	.50
84 Nicholas Markakis RC	4.00
85 Paul Bacot RC	.50
86 Peter Stonard RC	.25
87 Reggie Willits RC	3.00
88 Shane Costa RC	.50
89 Billy Sadler RC	.25
90 Delmon Young RC	8.00

Star Rookie Jersey

	NM/M
Common Player:	4.00
Inserted 1:18	
P72 Tony Richie	4.00
P73 Brandon Wood	15.00
P74 David Aardsma	5.00
P75 David Shinskie	4.00
P76 Dennis Dove	6.00
P77 Eric Sultemeier	4.00
P78 Jay Sborz	4.00
P79 Jimmy Barthmaier	4.00
P80 Josh Whitesell	4.00
P81 Josh Anderson	8.00
P82 Kenny Lewis	8.00
P83 Mateo Miramontes	8.00
P84 Nicholas Markakis	25.00
P85 Paul Bacot	4.00
P86 Peter Stonard	4.00
P87 Reggie Willits	30.00
P88 Shane Costa	4.00
P89 Billy Sadler	4.00
P91 Kyle Sleeth	8.00
P92 Ian Stewart	25.00
P93 Fraser Dizard	6.00
P94 Abe Alvarez	6.00
P95 Adam Jones	15.00
P96 Brian Anderson	8.00
P97 Chris Durbin	8.00
P98 Craig Whitaker	8.00
P99 Jake Fox	4.00
P100 Kurt Isenberg	4.00
P101 Luis Atilano	4.00
P102 Miguel Vega	4.00
P103 Mitch Maier	8.00
P104 Ryan Sweeney	10.00
P105 Scott Baker	4.00
P106 Sean Rodriguez	8.00
P108 Trey Webb	4.00
P109 Willy Jo Ronda	6.00
P110 John Danks	8.00
P111 Michael Aubrey	10.00
P112 Lastings Milledge	30.00
P113 Chris Lubanski	10.00

Star Rookie Signature

	NM/M
Common Autograph:	5.00
Inserted 1:9	
P1 Bryan Opdyke	10.00
P2 Gabriel Sosa	8.00
P3 Tila Reynolds	5.00
P4 Aaron Hill	15.00
P5 Aaron Marsden	10.00
P6 Abe Alvarez	15.00
P7 Adam Jones	90.00
P8 Adam Miller	50.00
P9 Andre Ethier	50.00
P10 Tony Gwynn Jr.	20.00
P11 Brad Snyder	25.00
P12 Brad Sullivan	15.00
P13 Brian Anderson	20.00
P14 Brian Buscher	8.00
P15 Brian Snyder	10.00
P16 Carlos Quentin	60.00
P17 Chad Billingsley	40.00
P19 Chris Durbin	10.00
P20 Chris Ray	8.00
P21 Conor Jackson	40.00
P22 Kory Casto	8.00
P23 Craig Whitaker	10.00
P24 Daniel Moore	10.00
P25 Daric Barton	50.00
P26 Darin Downs	15.00
P27 David Murphy	35.00
P29 Edgardo Baez	12.00
P30 Jake Fox	15.00
P31 Jake Stevens	25.00
P32 Jamie D'Antona	15.00
P33 James Houser	15.00
P34 Jarrod Saltalamacchia	60.00
P35 Jason Hirsh	30.00
P36 Javi Herrera	10.00
P37 Jeff Allison	25.00
P38 John Hudgins	10.00
P39 Jo Jo Reyes	10.00
P40 Justin James	10.00
P41 Kurt Isenberg	10.00
P42 Kyle Boyer	12.00
P43 Lastings Milledge	50.00
P44 Luis Atilano	8.00
P45 Matt Murton	25.00
P46 Matt Moses	35.00
P48 Michael Maier	15.00
P49 Miguel Vega	15.00
P50 Mitch Maier	25.00
P51 Omar Quintanilla	15.00
P52 Ryan Sweeney	40.00
P53 Scott Baker	15.00
P55 Steve Lerud	15.00
P56 Thomas Pauly	10.00
P57 Tom Gorzelanny	30.00
P58 Tim Moss	10.00
P59 Trey Webb	10.00
P60 Wes Littleton	10.00
P61 Beau Vaughan	10.00
P62 Willy Jo Ronda	10.00
P63 Chris Lubanski	25.00
P64 Ian Stewart	85.00
P65 John Danks	40.00
P66 Michael Aubrey	40.00
P67 Ryan Harvey	20.00
P70 Tim Stauffer	30.00

2003 Upper Deck Sweet Spot

	NM/M
Complete Set (232):	
Common Player:	.25
Common SP:	1.00
Inserted 1:4	
Common SP (131-190):	3.00
Production 2,003	
Common SP (191-232):	4.00
Production 1,430 unless noted.	
Pack (4):	9.00
Box (12):	90.00
1 Darin Erstad	.50
2 Garret Anderson	.50
3 Tim Salmon	.50
4 Troy Glaus	.75
5 Luis Gonzalez	.50
6 Randy Johnson	1.00
7 Curt Schilling	.50
8 Lyle Overbay	.25
9 Andruw Jones/SP	2.00
10 Gary Sheffield/SP	1.50
11 Rafael Furcal/SP	1.00
12 Greg Maddux/SP	4.00
13 Chipper Jones/SP	4.00
14 Tony Batista	.25
15 Rodrigo Lopez	.25
16 Jay Gibbons	.25
17 Jason Johnson	.25
18 Byung-Hyun Kim/SP	1.00
19 Johnny Damon/SP	2.50
20 Derek Lowe/SP	1.00
21 Nomar Garciaparra/SP	5.00
22 Pedro Martinez/SP	3.00
23 Manny Ramirez/SP	2.50
24 Mark Prior	1.00
25 Kerry Wood	1.00
26 Corey Patterson	.50
27 Sammy Sosa	2.00
28 Moises Alou	.40
29 Magglio Ordonez	.40
30 Frank Thomas	.75
31 Paul Konerko	.25
32 Roberto Alomar	.50
33 Adam Dunn	.75
34 Austin Kearns	.50
35 Ryan Wagner RC	.25
36 Ken Griffey Jr.	1.50
37 Sean Casey	.25
38 Omar Vizquel	.40
39 C.C. Sabathia	.25
40 Jason Davis	.25
41 Travis Hafner	.25
42 Brandon Phillips	.25
43 Larry Walker	.40
44 Preston Wilson	.25
45 Jay Payton	.25
46 Todd Helton	.75
47 Carlos Pena	.25
48 Eric Munson	.25
49 Ivan Rodriguez	.75
50 Josh Beckett	.50
51 Alex Gonzalez	.25
52 Roy Oswalt	.40
53 Craig Biggio	.40
54 Jeff Bagwell	.75
55 Lance Berkman	.50
56 Mike Sweeney	.25
57 Carlos Beltran	.75
58 Brent Mayne	.25
59 Mike MacDougal	.25
60 Hideo Nomo	.50
61 Dave Roberts	.25
62 Adrian Beltre	.50
63 Shawn Green	.50
64 Kazuhisa Ishii	.25
65 Rickey Henderson	.50
66 Richie Sexson	.50
67 Torii Hunter	.50
68 Jacque Jones	.25
69 Joe Mays	.25
70 Corey Koskie	.25
71 A.J. Pierzynski	.25
72 Jose Vidro	.25
73 Vladimir Guerrero	.75
74 Tom Glavine	.50
75 Mike Piazza	1.50
76 Jose Reyes	.50
77 Jae Weong Seo	.25
78 Jorge Posada/SP	2.00
79 Mike Mussina/SP	2.00
80 Robin Ventura/SP	1.00
81 Mariano Rivera/SP	1.50
82 Roger Clemens/SP	6.00
83 Jason Giambi/SP	1.50
84 Bernie Williams/SP	2.00
85 Alfonso Soriano/SP	3.00
86 Derek Jeter	2.50
87 Miguel Tejada	.75
88 Eric Chavez	.50
89 Tim Hudson	.50
90 Barry Zito	.50
91 Mark Mulder	.50
92 Erubiel Durazo	.25
93 Pat Burrell	.50
94 Jim Thome	.75
95 Bobby Abreu	.50
96 Brian Giles	.40
97 Reggie Sanders	.25
98 Jose Hernandez	.25
99 Ryan Klesko	.25
100 Sean Burroughs	.25
101 Edgardo Alfonzo/SP	1.00
102 Rich Aurilia/SP	1.00
103 Jose Cruz Jr./SP	1.00
104 Barry Bonds/SP	6.00
105 Andres Galarraga/SP	1.00
106 Mike Cameron	.25
107 Kazuhiro Sasaki	.25
108 Bret Boone	.40
109 Ichiro Suzuki	2.00
110 John Olerud	.40
111 J.D. Drew/SP	1.50
112 Jim Edmonds/SP	2.00
113 Scott Rolen/SP	3.00
114 Matt Morris/SP	1.00
115 Tino Martinez/SP	1.00

116	Albert Pujols/SP	6.00
117	Jared Sandberg	.25
118	Carl Crawford	.25
119	Rafael Palmeiro	.50
120	Hank Blalock	.50
121	Alex Rodriguez	2.50
122	Kevin Mench	.25
123	Juan Gonzalez	.75
124	Mark Teixeira	.50
125	Shannon Stewart	.25
126	Vernon Wells	.50
127	Josh Phelps	.25
128	Eric Hinske	.25
129	Orlando Hudson	.25
130	Carlos Delgado	.75
131	Jason Shiell RC	3.00
132	Kevin Tolar RC	3.00
133	Nate Bland RC	3.00
134	Brent Hoard RC	3.00
135	Jonathan Pridie RC	3.00
136	Mike Ryan RC	4.00
137	Francisco Rosario RC	3.00
138	Runelvys Hernandez	3.00
139	Guillermo Quiroz RC	4.00
140	Chin-Hui Tsao	3.00
141	Rett Johnson RC	3.00
142	Colin Porter RC	3.00
143	Jose Castillo	3.00
144	Chris Waters RC	3.00
145	Jeremy Guthrie	3.00
146	Pedro Liriano	3.00
147	Joe Borowski	3.00
148	Felix Sanchez RC	3.00
149	Todd Wellemeyer RC	3.00
150	Gerald Laird	3.00
151	Brandon Webb RC	10.00
152	Tommy Whiteman RC	3.00
153	Carlos Rivera	3.00
154	Rick Roberts RC	3.00
155	Termmel Sledge RC	3.00
156	Jeff Duncan RC	3.00
157	Craig Brazell RC	3.00
158	Bernie Castro RC	3.00
159	Cory Stewart RC	3.00
160	Brandon Villafuerte RC	3.00
161	Tommy Phelps	3.00
162	Josh Hall RC	3.00
163	Ryan Cameron RC	3.00
164	Garrett Atkins	3.00
165	Brian Stokes RC	3.00
166	Rafael Betancourt RC	3.00
167	Jaime Cerda	3.00
168	Danny Carrasco RC	3.00
169	Ian Ferguson RC	3.00
170	Jorge Cordova RC	3.00
171	Eric Munson	3.00
172	Nook Logan RC	3.00
173	Jeremy Bonderman	10.00
174	Kyle Snyder	3.00
175	Rich Harden	4.00
176	Kevin Ohme RC	3.00
177	Roger Deago RC	3.00
178	Marlon Byrd	3.00
179	Dontrelle Willis	5.00
180	Bobby Hill	3.00
181	Jesse Foppert	3.00
182	Andrew Good	3.00
183	Chase Utley	3.00
184	Bo Hart RC	3.00
185	Dan Haren	4.00
186	Tim Olson RC	3.00
187	Joe Thurston	3.00
188	Jason Anderson	3.00
189	Jason Gilfillan RC	3.00
190	Rickie Weeks RC	10.00
191	Hideki Matsui/500 RC	25.00
192	Jose Contreras RC	8.00
193	Willie Eyre RC	4.00
194	Matt Bruback RC	4.00
195	Heath Bell RC	4.00
196	Lew Ford RC	4.00
197	Jeremy Griffiths	5.00
198	Oscar Villarreal/500 RC	5.00
199	Francisco Cruceta RC	5.00
200	Fernando Cabrera RC	5.00
201	Jhonny Peralta	4.00
202	Shane Bazzell RC	4.00
203	Bobby Madritsch/500 RC	15.00
204	Phil Seibel RC	4.00
205	Josh Willingham RC	6.00
206	Robby Hammock/500 RC	5.00
207	Alejandro Machado RC	5.00
208	David Sanders RC	4.00
209	Mike Neu/500 RC	5.00
210	Andrew Brown RC	4.00
211	Nathan Robertson RC	6.00
212	Miguel Ojeda RC	4.00
213	Beau Kemp RC	4.00
214	Aaron Looper RC	4.00
215	Alfredo Gonzalez RC	4.00
216	Richard Fischer/500 RC	5.00
217	Jeremy Wedel RC	6.00
218	Prentice Redman RC	4.00
219	Michel Hernandez RC	6.00
220	Rocco Baldelli/500	5.00
221	Luis Ayala RC	5.00
222	Arnie Munoz RC	4.00
223	Wilfredo Ledezma RC	4.00
224	Chris Capuano RC	8.00
225	Aquilino Lopez RC	4.00
226	Joe Valentine/500 RC	5.00
227	Matt Kata/1,200 RC	5.00
228	Diegomar Markwell/1,200 RC	4.00
229	Clint Barmes/1,200 RC	15.00
230		
231	Mike Nicolas/500 RC	5.00
232	Jon Leicester/1,200 RC	5.00

Autographs Black Ink

NM/M

Common Player:
Red & Blue Ink variations exist.
Reds not priced due to scarcity.

Mirror Parallel:		No Pricing
Production 25		
HB	Hank Blalock	25.00
HB	Hank Blalock/Blue/40	40.00
PB	Pat Burrell	30.00
PB	Pat Burrell/Blue/40	40.00
RC	Roger Clemens/73	125.00
RC	Roger Clemens/Blue/40	150.00
JC	Jose Contreras	40.00
JC	Jose Contreras/Blue/40	50.00
AD	Adam Dunn	30.00
AD	Adam Dunn/Blue/40	50.00
NG	Nomar Garciaparra	40.00
NG	Nomar Garciaparra/Blue/40	50.00
JG	Jason Giambi	20.00
JG	Jason Giambi/Blue/40	30.00
TR	Troy Glaus	25.00
TR	Troy Glaus/Blue/40	40.00
GL	Tom Glavine	30.00
GL	Tom Glavine/Blue/40	50.00
KG	Ken Griffey Jr.	75.00
KG	Ken Griffey Jr./Blue/40	100.00
KGs	Ken Griffey Sr.	15.00
KGs	Ken Griffey Sr./Blue/40	20.00
VG	Vladimir Guerrero	50.00
VG	Vladimir Guerrero/Blue/40	65.00
TG	Tony Gwynn	40.00
HA	Travis Hafner	15.00
HA	Travis Hafner/Blue/40	25.00
BH	Bo Hart	10.00
BH	Bo Hart/Blue/40	15.00
TH	Todd Helton/45	40.00
TH	Todd Helton/Blue/40	75.00
DH	Drew Henson	25.00
DH	Drew Henson/Blue/40	40.00
KI	Kazuhisa Ishii	20.00
KI	Kazuhisa Ishii/Blue/40	40.00
AK	Austin Kearns	20.00
AK	Austin Kearns/Blue/40	25.00
HM	Hideki Matsui	300.00
HM	Hideki Matsui/Blue/40	375.00
RO	Roy Oswalt	25.00
RO	Roy Oswalt/Blue/40	35.00
LO	Lyle Overbay	15.00
LO	Lyle Overbay/Blue/40	20.00
BP	Brandon Phillips	15.00
BP	Brandon Phillips/Blue/40	20.00
MP	Mark Prior	25.00
MP	Mark Prior/Blue/40	40.00
JR	Jose Reyes	40.00
JR	Jose Reyes/Blue/40	60.00
CR	Cal Ripken Jr.	165.00
CR	Cal Ripken Jr./Blue/40	220.00
NR	Nolan Ryan	120.00
NR	Nolan Ryan/Blue/40	165.00
TS	Tim Salmon	25.00
TS	Tim Salmon/Blue/40	30.00
CS	Curt Schilling	40.00
CS	Curt Schilling/Blue/40	75.00
GS	Gary Sheffield	30.00
GS	Gary Sheffield/Blue/40	40.00
SS	Sammy Sosa/Blue/40	120.00
IS	Ichiro Suzuki/Blue/40	400.00
IS	Ichiro Suzuki/Red/35	400.00
MT	Mark Teixeira	40.00
MT	Mark Teixeira/Blue/40	60.00
JT	Jim Thome	40.00
JT	Jim Thome/Blue/40	60.00
BW	Brandon Webb	50.00
BW	Brandon Webb/Blue/40	65.00
RW	Rickie Weeks	40.00
JW	Jerome Williams	15.00
JW	Jerome Williams/Blue/40	20.00
DW	Dontrelle Willis	25.00
DW	Dontrelle Willis/Blue/40	40.00

Barrel Autographs

NM/M

Quantity produced listed		
HB	Hank Blalock/420	35.00
PB	Pat Burrell/345	35.00
RC	Roger Clemens/49	150.00
AD	Adam Dunn/345	40.00
TR	Troy Glaus/345	40.00
TG	Tom Glavine/345	45.00
KG	Ken Griffey Jr./295	125.00
HM	Hideki Matsui/124	400.00
CR	Cal Ripken Jr./149	180.00
NR	Nolan Ryan/445	150.00
JT	Jim Thome/345	65.00

Game-Used Barrel

NM/M

Quantity produced listed
No Pricing due to scarcity.

KW-BB	Kerry Wood/2 (2/04 Auction)	1,000

Game-Used Patch

Production 25 or 10
No pricing due to scarcity.

Patch

NM/M

Common Player:		4.00
Inserted 1:6		
Logo Patch Parallel:		1-2X
Production 75 Sets		
JB1	Jeff Bagwell	6.00
LB1	Lance Berkman	5.00
BB1	Barry Bonds	15.00
PB1	Pat Burrell	5.00
RC1	Roger Clemens	12.00
CD1	Carlos Delgado	4.00
AD1	Adam Dunn	5.00
JE1	Jim Edmonds	4.00
DE1	Darin Erstad	4.00
NG1	Nomar Garciaparra	10.00
JG1	Jason Giambi	5.00
TG1	Troy Glaus	5.00
TO1	Tom Glavine	5.00
LG1	Luis Gonzalez	5.00
SG1	Shawn Green	5.00
KG1	Ken Griffey Jr.	8.00
VG1	Vladimir Guerrero	5.00
TH1	Torii Hunter	5.00
KI1	Kazuhisa Ishii	4.00
DJ1	Derek Jeter	15.00
RJ1	Randy Johnson	5.00
AJ1	Andruw Jones	5.00
CJ1	Chipper Jones	10.00
JK1	Jeff Kent	5.00
GM1	Greg Maddux	10.00
PM1	Pedro J. Martinez	6.00
HN1	Hideo Nomo	5.00
MO1	Magglio Ordonez	5.00
CP1	Corey Patterson	6.00
MP1	Mike Piazza	10.00
MA1	Mark Prior	8.00
AP1	Albert Pujols	15.00
AR1	Alex Rodriguez	10.00
CS1	Curt Schilling	6.00
GS1	Gary Sheffield	6.00
AS1	Alfonso Soriano	8.00
SS1	Sammy Sosa	10.00
IS1	Ichiro Suzuki	10.00
MT1	Miguel Tejada	5.00
JT1	Jim Thome	6.00
BW1	Bernie Williams	5.00
BZ1	Barry Zito	4.00

Swatches

NM/M

Common Player:		4.00
Inserted 1:24		
Tier 2:		1-2X
Production 75		
RA	Roberto Alomar	4.00
PB	Pat Burrell	6.00
RC	Roger Clemens	10.00
NM	Nomar Garciaparra	15.00
NG1	Nomar Garciaparra	4.00
JG	Jason Giambi	8.00
TG	Troy Glaus	4.00
TG1	Troy Glaus	5.00
TO	Tom Glavine	4.00
LG	Luis Gonzalez	4.00
KG	Ken Griffey Jr.	10.00
VG	Vladimir Guerrero	6.00
TH	Torii Hunter	5.00
RJ	Randy Johnson	6.00
AJ	Andruw Jones	5.00
CJ	Chipper Jones	8.00
AK	Austin Kearns	6.00
GM	Greg Maddux	10.00
MM	Mickey Mantle	120.00
HM	Hideki Matsui	45.00
HM1	Hideki Matsui	4.00
RO	Roy Oswalt	4.00
RO1	Roy Oswalt	4.00
MP	Mike Piazza	10.00
MA	Mark Prior	3.00
AP	Albert Pujols	15.00
AR	Alex Rodriguez	10.00
CS	Curt Schilling	5.00
GS	Gary Sheffield	4.00
AS	Alfonso Soriano	10.00
AS1	Alfonso Soriano	4.00
SS	Sammy Sosa	12.00
IS	Ichiro Suzuki	20.00
MT	Miguel Tejada	4.00
FT	Frank Thomas	6.00
JT	Jim Thome	8.00
BW	Bernie Williams	4.00
TW	Ted Williams	60.00
BZ	Barry Zito	4.00

2003 Upper Deck Sweet Spot Classic

NM/M

Complete Set (150):		
Common Player:		.40
Common Ted Williams (91-120):		5.00
Production 1,941		
Common Yankee Heritage		
(121-150):		2.00
Production 1,500		
Pack (4):		12.00
Box (12):		120.00
1	Al Hrabosky	.40
2	Al Lopez	.40
3	Andre Dawson	.75
4	Bill Buckner	.40
5	Billy Williams	.50
6	Bob Feller	.75
7	Bob Lemon	.40
8	Bobby Doerr	.40
9	Cecil Cooper	.40
10	Cal Ripken Jr.	2.50
11	Carlton Fisk	.60
12	Jim "Catfish" Hunter	.40
13	Chris Chambliss	.40
14	Dale Murphy	.75
15	Gaylord Perry	.40
16	Dave Kingman	.40
17	Dave Parker	.40

18	Dave Stewart	.40
19	David Cone	.40
20	Dennis Eckersley	.60
21	Don Baylor	.40
22	Don Sutton	.40
23	Duke Snider	1.00
24	Dwight Evans	.40
25	Dwight Gooden	.40
26	Earl Weaver	.40
27	Early Wynn	.40
28	Eddie Mathews	1.50
29	Enos Slaughter	.40
30	Ernie Banks	1.50
31	Fred Lynn	.40
32	Fred Stanley	.40
33	Gary Carter	.75
34	George Foster	.40
35	Hal Newhouser	.40
36	George Kell	.40
37	Harmon Killebrew	1.50
38	Hoyt Wilhelm	.40
39	Jack Morris	.40
40	Jim Bunning	.40
41	Jim Gilliam	.40
42	Jim Leyritz	.40
43	Jimmy Key	.40
44	Joe Carter	.40
45	Joe Morgan	.40
46	John Montefusco	.40
47	Johnny Bench	2.00
48	Johnny Podres	.40
49	Jose Canseco	.75
50	Juan Marichal	.40
51	Keith Hernandez	.40
52	Ken Griffey Sr.	.40
53	Kirby Puckett	1.50
54	Kirk Gibson	.40
55	Larry Doby	.40
56	Lee May	.40
57	Lee Mazzilli	.40
58	Lou Boudreau	.40
59	Mark McGwire	3.00
60	Maury Wills	.40
61	Mike Pagliarulo	.40
62	Monte Irvin	.75
63	Nolan Ryan	3.00
64	Orlando Cepeda	.40
65	Ozzie Smith	1.50
66	Paul O'Neill	.40
67	Pee Wee Reese	.40
68	Phil Niekro	.40
69	Ralph Kiner	.40
70	Red Schoendienst	.40
71	Richie Ashburn	.40
72	Rick Ferrell	.40
73	Robin Roberts	.40
74	Robin Yount	1.50
75	Hideki Matsui/1,999 **RC**	20.00
75	Hideki Matsui/Red/500	25.00
75	Hideki Matsui/Blue/250	30.00
75	Hideki Matsui/Silver/25	200.00
76	Rollie Fingers	.40
77	Ron Cey	.40
78	Tom Seaver	1.00
79	Sparky Anderson	.40
80	Stan Musial	2.00
81	Steve Garvey	.40
82	Ted Williams	3.00
83	Tommy Lasorda	.40
84	Tony Gwynn	1.00
85	Tony Perez	.40
86	Vida Blue	.40
87	Warren Spahn	.75
88	Bob Gibson	1.00
89	Willie McCovey	.40
90	Willie Stargell	.75
91-120	Ted Williams	5.00
121	Babe Ruth	8.00
122	Bucky Dent	2.00
123	Casey Stengel	3.00
124	Dave Righetti	2.00
125	Dave Winfield	3.00
126	Dick Tidrow	2.00
127	Dock Ellis	2.00
128	Don Mattingly	8.00
129	Hank Bauer	2.00
130	Jim Bouton	2.00
131	Jim Kaat	2.00
132	Joe DiMaggio	6.00
133	Joe Torre	3.00
134	Lou Piniella	2.00
135	Mel Stottlemyre	2.00
136	Mickey Mantle	15.00
137	Mickey Rivers	2.00
138	Phil Rizzuto	4.00
139	Ralph Branca	2.00
140	Ralph Houk	2.00
141	Roger Maris	6.00
142	Ron Guidry	2.00
143	Ruben Amaro Jr.	2.00
144	Sparky Lyle	2.00
145	Thurman Munson	5.00
146	Tommy Henrich	2.00
147	Tommy John	2.00
148	Tony Kubek	2.00
149	Whitey Ford	4.00
150	Yogi Berra	4.00

Game Jersey

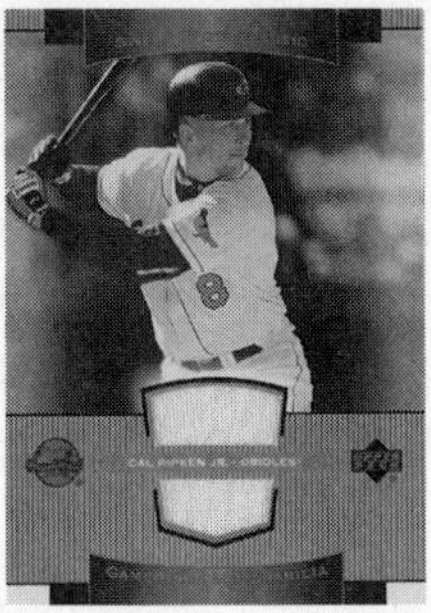

		NM/M
Common Player:		5.00
Inserted 1:16		
EB	Ernie Banks	15.00
JB	Johnny Bench	15.00
JC	Jose Canseco	6.00
GC	Gary Carter	6.00
RC	Ron Cey	5.00
CC	Cecil Cooper	6.00
AD	Andre Dawson	6.00
RF	Rollie Fingers	5.00
CF	Carlton Fisk	8.00
GF	George Foster	5.00
SG	Steve Garvey	5.00
JG	Jim Gilliam	6.00
TG	Tony Gwynn	8.00
HK	Harmon Killebrew	12.00
FL	Fred Lynn	5.00
LM	Lee May	5.00
MM	Mark McGwire	30.00
JM	Joe Morgan	6.00
DM	Dale Murphy	10.00
SM	Stan Musial	25.00
DP	Dave Parker	5.00
JP	Johnny Podres	5.00
KP	Kirby Puckett	12.00
CR	Cal Ripken Jr.	20.00
NR	Nolan Ryan	30.00
OS	Ozzie Smith	10.00
DS	Duke Snider	12.00
WS	Willie Stargell/SP	15.00
TW	Ted Williams/SP	100.00
RY	Robin Yount	10.00

Greats Autograph

		NM/M
Common Autograph:		
Blue, Black and Red ink variations exist		
Listings without notations are blue ink.		
EB	Ernie Banks/Black/73	80.00
DB	Don Baylor	25.00
DB	Don Baylor/Black/50	35.00
JB	Johnny Bench/Black/73	100.00
BB	Bill Buckner	20.00
BB	Bill Buckner/Black/85	25.00
GC	Gary Carter/Black/173	40.00
JC	Joe Carter/Black/173	35.00
OC	Orlando Cepeda	20.00
OC	Orlando Cepeda/Black/34	35.00
AD	Andre Dawson	20.00
AD	Andre Dawson/Black/75	30.00
DEc	Dennis Eckersley	25.00
DE	Dwight Evans	20.00
DE	Dwight Evans/Black/100	30.00
RF	Rollie Fingers/Black/73	30.00
RF	Rollie Fingers/Red/25	90.00
CF	Carlton Fisk	50.00
GF	George Foster/Black/173	35.00
SG	Steve Garvey/Black/174	30.00
GI	Kirk Gibson/Black/173	30.00
KG	Ken Griffey Sr.	20.00
KG	Ken Griffey Sr./Black/100	25.00
TG	Tony Gwynn	45.00
TG	Tony Gwynn/Black/101	60.00
KH	Keith Hernandez/Black/173	40.00
KH	Keith Hernandez/Red/25	110.00
AH	Al Hrabosky	25.00
AH	Al Hrabosky/Black/100	35.00
HK	Harmon Killebrew/Black/73	80.00
MM	Mark McGwire/Black/73	425.00
JoM	Joe Morgan/Black/169	40.00
JMo	Jack Morris/Black/123	40.00
DM	Dale Murphy	30.00
PN	Phil Niekro/Black/173	30.00
PN	Phil Niekro/Red/25	75.00
DP	Dave Parker/Black/113	30.00
TP	Tony Perez/Black/51	65.00
JP	Johnny Podres/Black/173	30.00
JP	Johnny Podres/Red/25	80.00
KP	Kirby Puckett	45.00
KP	Kirby Puckett/Black/174	60.00
CR	Cal Ripken Jr.	150.00
CR	Cal Ripken Jr/Black/38	250.00
RR	Robin Roberts/Black/173	40.00
TS	Tom Seaver/Black/74	80.00
TS	Tom Seaver/Red/25	135.00
SN	Duke Snider	40.00
SN	Duke Snider/Black/100	50.00
DSt	Dave Stewart	15.00
DSu	Don Sutton/Black/123	30.00
AT	Alan Trammell/Black/173	35.00
BW	Billy Williams/Black/173	35.00
TW	Ted Williams/9	3,650
MW	Maury Wills/Black/173	30.00
RY	Robin Yount/Black/73	100.00
RY	Robin Yount/Red/25	200.00

Patch Logo

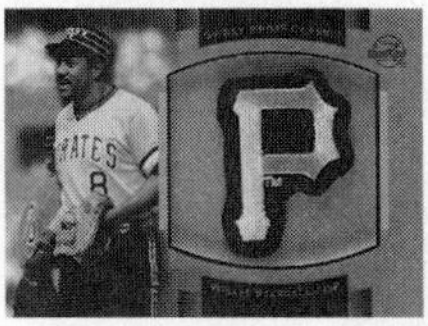

		NM/M
Common Player:		5.00
Note: Some are actual game-used patches.		
EB1	Ernie Banks	12.00
JB1	Johnny Bench	12.00
JB2	Johnny Bench/150	50.00
JB3	Johnny Bench/150	35.00
YB1	Yogi Berra	12.00
YB2	Yogi Berra/350	25.00
YB3	Yogi Berra/150	35.00
JD1	Joe DiMaggio	20.00
JD2	Joe DiMaggio/50	85.00
JD3	Joe DiMaggio/350	30.00
JD4	Joe DiMaggio/150	40.00
CF1	Carlton Fisk	8.00
CF2	Carlton Fisk/150	10.00
GF1	George Foster/350	10.00
GF2	George Foster	5.00
SG1	Steve Garvey	5.00
SG2	Steve Garvey/350	10.00
SG3	Steve Garvey/150	30.00
SG4	Steve Garvey/50	25.00
SG5	Steve Garvey/50	25.00
KG1	Kirk Gibson	5.00
KG2	Kirk Gibson/350	12.00
TG1	Tony Gwynn	8.00
TG2	Tony Gwynn/150	50.00
TG3	Tony Gwynn/350	25.00
CH1	Catfish Hunter/350	10.00
CH2	Catfish Hunter	5.00
CH4	Catfish Hunter/50	30.00
FL1	Fred Lynn	5.00
FL2	Fred Lynn/350	10.00
FL3	Fred Lynn/150	15.00
FL4	Fred Lynn/50	20.00
MM1	Mickey Mantle	35.00
MM2	Mickey Mantle/150	85.00
MM3	Mickey Mantle/150	85.00
MM4	Mickey Mantle/150	75.00
RM1	Roger Maris	15.00
RM2	Roger Maris/350	25.00
RM3	Roger Maris/150	40.00
RM4	Roger Maris/50	60.00
HM1	Hideki Matsui	25.00
MC1	Mark McGwire	20.00
MC2	Mark McGwire/350	50.00
JM1	Joe Morgan	6.00
JM2	Joe Morgan/350	8.00
JM3	Joe Morgan/150	15.00
JM4	Joe Morgan/150	30.00
JM5	Joe Morgan/100	15.00
KP1	Kirby Puckett	10.00
KP2	Kirby Puckett/40	100.00
CR1	Cal Ripken Jr.	25.00
CR2	Cal Ripken Jr/75	100.00
CR3	Cal Ripken Jr./150	50.00
BR1	Babe Ruth/350	40.00
BR2	Babe Ruth	30.00
BR3	Babe Ruth/150	50.00
NR1	Nolan Ryan	25.00
NR2	Nolan Ryan/350	40.00
NR3	Nolan Ryan/150	50.00
NR4	Nolan Ryan/105	100.00
OS1	Ozzie Smith	10.00
OS2	Ozzie Smith/350	20.00
OS3	Ozzie Smith/150	60.00
OS4	Ozzie Smith/100	40.00
OS5	Ozzie Smith/100	35.00
DS1	Duke Snider	8.00
DS2	Duke Snider/150	25.00
DS3	Duke Snider/350	15.00
DS5	Duke Snider/150	20.00
DS6	Duke Snider/150	20.00
WS1	Willie Stargell	5.00
WS2	Willie Stargell/137	50.00
WS3	Willie Stargell/150	25.00
WS4	Willie Stargell/50	40.00
BW1	Billy Williams	6.00
TW1	Ted Williams	20.00
TW2	Ted Williams/350	40.00
RY1	Robin Yount	8.00
RY2	Robin Yount/150	40.00
RY3	Robin Yount/350	20.00

Pinstripes

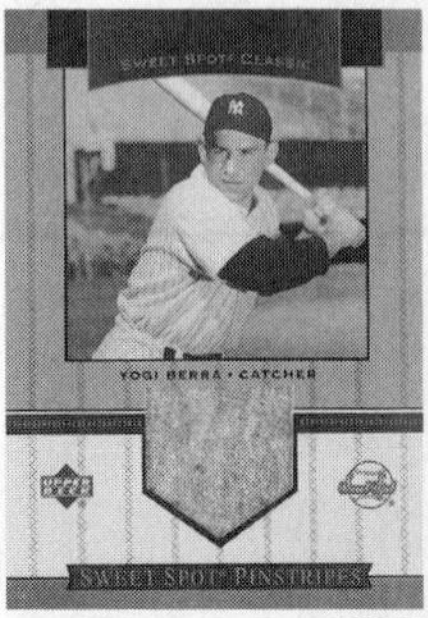

		NM/M
Common Player:		5.00
Inserted 1:40		
YB	Yogi Berra	15.00
JB	Jim Bouton	5.00
DE	Bucky Dent	8.00
JD	Joe DiMaggio	100.00
DG	Dwight Gooden	5.00
MM	Mickey Mantle	140.00
DM	Don Mattingly	25.00
TM	Thurman Munson	30.00
DR	Dave Righetti	5.00
PR	Phil Rizzuto	15.00
BR	Babe Ruth	250.00
CS	Casey Stengel	12.00

Yankee Greats Auto.

		NM/M
Common Autograph:		
RA	Ruben Amaro Sr.	25.00
RA	Ruben Amaro Sr./Black/100	30.00
RA	Ruben Amaro Sr./Red/25	60.00
HB	Hank Bauer	30.00
HB	Hank Bauer/Black/75	40.00
YB	Yogi Berra/Black/73	100.00
JB	Jim Bouton	25.00
JB	Jim Bouton/Black/100	30.00
RB	Ralph Branca	25.00
RB	Ralph Branca/Black/100	30.00
JC	Jose Canseco/Black/73	90.00
JC	Jose Canseco/Red/25	150.00
CC	Chris Chambliss	30.00
CC	Chris Chambliss/Black/101	35.00
CC	Chris Chambliss/Red/25	75.00
DC	David Cone/Black/74	75.00
DC	David Cone/Red/25	110.00
BD	Bucky Dent	20.00
JD	Joe DiMaggio/5	2,325
DE	Dock Ellis/Black/174	25.00
DE	Dock Ellis/Red/25	65.00
DG	Dwight Gooden/Black/74	70.00
GU	Ron Guidry	35.00
GU	Ron Guidry/Black/100	45.00
TH	Tommy Henrich	35.00
TH	Tommy Henrich/Black/100	40.00
TH	Tommy Henrich/Red/25	125.00
RH	Ralph Houk	25.00
RH	Ralph Houk/Black/100	30.00
TJ	Tommy John	30.00
TJ	Tommy John/Black/100	35.00
JKa	Jim Kaat	20.00
JKa	Jim Kaat/Black/25	25.00
JKe	Jimmy Key	40.00
JKe	Jimmy Key/Black/100	50.00
DK	Dave Kingman	25.00
DK	Dave Kingman/Black/100	30.00
TK	Tony Kubek/Black/123	15.00
JL	Jim Leyritz	25.00
JL	Jim Leyritz/Black/100	35.00
JL	Jim Leyritz/Red/25	65.00
SL	Sparky Lyle	30.00
SL	Sparky Lyle/Black/100	40.00
MM	Mickey Mantle/Blue/7	2,850
DM	Don Mattingly/Black/74	100.00
DM	Don Mattingly/Red/25	340.00
LM	Lee Mazzilli	30.00
JM	John Montefusco	20.00
JM	John Montefusco/Black/100	25.00
JM	John Montefusco/Red/25	50.00
PO	Paul O'Neill	50.00
PO	Paul O'Neill/Black/100	65.00
PO	Paul O'Neill/Red/25	100.00
MP	Mike Pagliarulo	20.00
MP	Mike Pagliarulo/Black/99	25.00
MP	Mike Pagliarulo/Red/25	60.00
LP	Lou Piniella	40.00
LP	Lou Piniella/Black/100	45.00
DR	Dave Righetti/Black/173	40.00
DR	Dave Righetti/Red/25	85.00
MR	Mickey Rivers/Black/73	40.00
PR	Phil Rizzuto/Black/173	55.00
FS	Fred Stanley	25.00
FS	Fred Stanley/Black/101	25.00
MS	Mel Stottlemyre/Black/73	85.00
DT	Dick Tidrow	20.00
DT	Dick Tidrow/Black/101	25.00
DT	Dick Tidrow/Red/25	70.00

JT Joe Torre/Black/73 60.00
JT Joe Torre/Red/25 140.00
DW Dave Winfield/Black/25 165.00

2003 Upper Deck Ultimate Collection

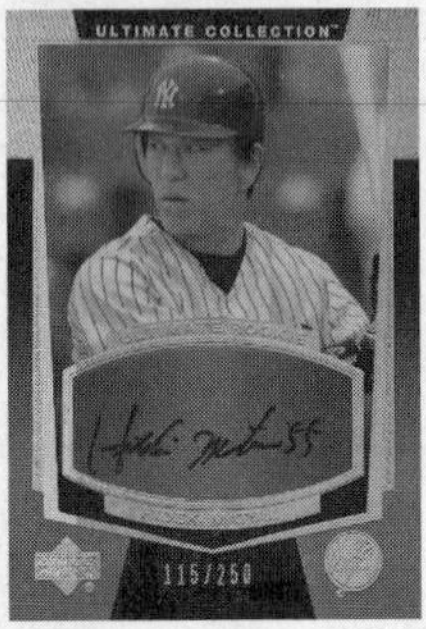

NM/M
Complete Set (181):
Common Player (1-84): 2.00
Production 850
Common (85-117): 3.00
Production 625
Common (118-140): 3.00
Production 399
Common (141-158): 4.00
Production 250
Common (159-168): 6.00
Production 100
Common (169-174): 25.00
Common (175-180): 10.00
169-180 Production 250
Pack (4): 90.00
Box (4): 300.00
1 Ichiro Suzuki 8.00
2 Ken Griffey Jr. 6.00
3 Sammy Sosa 6.00
4 Jason Giambi 2.00
5 Mike Piazza 5.00
6 Derek Jeter 10.00
7 Randy Johnson 4.00
8 Barry Bonds 10.00
9 Carlos Delgado 3.00
10 Mark Prior 3.00
11 Vladimir Guerrero 4.00
12 Alfonso Soriano 4.00
13 Jim Thome 4.00
14 Pedro J. Martinez 4.00
15 Nomar Garciaparra 5.00
16 Chipper Jones 4.00
17 Rocco Baldelli 2.00
18 Dontrelle Willis 2.00
19 Garret Anderson 2.00
20 Jeff Bagwell 2.00
21 Jim Edmonds 2.50
22 Rickey Henderson 3.00
23 Torii Hunter 2.50
24 Tom Glavine 2.50
25 Hideo Nomo 2.50
26 Luis Gonzalez 2.50
27 Alex Rodriguez 8.00
28 Albert Pujols 10.00
29 Manny Ramirez 4.00
30 Rafael Palmeiro 3.00
31 Bernie Williams 3.00
32 Curt Schilling 3.00
33 Roger Clemens 8.00
34 Andruw Jones 2.00
35 J.D. Drew 2.00
36 Kerry Wood 3.00
37 Scott Rolen 3.00
38 Darin Erstad 2.00
39 Joe DiMaggio 8.00
40 Magglio Ordonez 2.00
41 Todd Helton 3.00
42 Barry Zito 2.00
43 Mickey Mantle 10.00
44 Miguel Tejada 3.00
45 Troy Glaus 2.00
46 Kazuhisa Ishii 2.00
47 Adam Dunn 3.00
48 Ted Williams 8.00
49 Mike Mussina 3.00
50 Ivan Rodriguez 3.00
51 Jacque Jones 2.00
52 Stan Musial 6.00
53 Mariano Rivera 2.50
54 Larry Walker 2.50
55 Aaron Boone 2.00
56 Hank Blalock 2.50
57 Rich Harden 2.00
58 Lance Berkman 2.00
59 Eric Chavez 2.00
60 Carlos Beltran 3.00
61 Roy Oswalt 2.00
62 Moises Alou 2.00
63 Nolan Ryan 10.00
64 Jeff Kent 2.00
65 Roberto Alomar 2.00
66 Runelvys Hernandez 2.00
67 Roy Halladay 3.00
68 Tim Hudson 2.50
69 Tom Seaver 4.00
70 Edgardo Alfonzo 2.00
71 Andy Pettitte 2.00
72 Preston Wilson 2.00
73 Frank Thomas 3.00
74 Jerome Williams 2.00
75 Shawn Green 2.50
76 David Wells 2.00
77 John Smoltz 2.00
78 Jorge Posada 3.00
79 Marlon Byrd 2.00
80 Austin Kearns 2.00
81 Bret Boone 2.00
82 Rafael Furcal 2.50
83 Jay Gibbons 2.00
84 Shane Reynolds 2.00
85 Nate Bland **RC** 3.00
86 Willie Eyre **RC** 3.00
87 Jeremy Guthrie 3.00
88 Jeremy Wedel **RC** 3.00
89 Jhonny Peralta 6.00
90 Luis Ayala **RC** 3.00
91 Michael Hessman **RC** 3.00
92 Micheal Nakamura **RC** 3.00
93 Nook Logan **RC** 3.00
94 Rett Johnson **RC** 5.00
95 Josh Hall **RC** 4.00
96 Julio Manon **RC** 3.00
97 Heath Bell **RC** 3.00
98 Ian Ferguson **RC** 3.00
99 Jason Gilfillan **RC** 3.00
100 Jason Roach 3.00
101 Jason Shiell **RC** 3.00
102 Termel Sledge **RC** 5.00
103 Phil Seibel **RC** 3.00
104 Jeff Duncan **RC** 6.00
105 Mike Neu **RC** 3.00
106 Colin Porter **RC** 3.00
107 Dave Matranga **RC** 3.00
108 Aaron Looper **RC** 3.00
109 Jeremy Bonderman 15.00
110 Miguel Ojeda **RC** 3.00
111 Chad Cordero **RC** 3.00
112 Shane Bazell **RC** 4.00
113 Tim Olson **RC** 5.00
114 Michel Hernandez **RC** 3.00
115 Chien-Ming Wang **RC** 50.00
116 Josh Stewart **RC** 3.00
117 Clint Barmes **RC** 10.00
118 Craig Brazell **RC** 5.00
119 Josh Willingham **RC** 8.00
120 Brent Hoard **RC** 3.00
121 Francisco Rosario **RC** 3.00
122 Rick Roberts **RC** 3.00
123 Geoff Geary **RC** 3.00
124 Edgar Gonzalez **RC** 3.00
125 Kevin Correia **RC** 3.00
126 Ryan Cameron **RC** 3.00
127 Beau Kemp **RC** 3.00
128 Tommy Phelps 3.00
129 Mark Malaska **RC** 3.00
130 Kevin Ohme **RC** 3.00
131 Humberto Quintero **RC** 3.00
132 Aquilino Lopez **RC** 3.00
133 Andrew Brown **RC** 3.00
134 Wilfredo Ledezma **RC** 3.00
135 Luis De Los Santos 3.00
136 Garrett Atkins 3.00
137 Fernando Cabrera **RC** 3.00
138 D.J. Carrasco **RC** 3.00
139 Alfredo Gonzalez **RC** 3.00
140 Alex Prieto **RC** 3.00
141 Matt Kata **RC** 5.00
142 Chris Capuano **RC** 15.00
143 Bobby Madritsch **RC** 15.00
144 Greg Jones **RC** 4.00
145 Pete Zoccolillo **RC** 4.00
146 Chad Gaudin **RC** 10.00
147 Rosman Garcia **RC** 4.00
148 Gerald Laird 4.00
149 Danny Garcia **RC** 4.00
150 Stephen Randolph **RC** 4.00
151 Pete LaForest **RC** 8.00
152 Brian Sweeney **RC** 4.00
153 Aaron Miles **RC** 4.00
154 Jorge DePaula **RC** 4.00
155 Graham Koonce **RC** 10.00
156 Tom Gregorio **RC** 4.00
157 Javier Lopez 4.00
158 Oscar Villarreal **RC** 4.00
159 Prentice Redman **RC** 6.00
160 Francisco Cruceta **RC** 6.00
161 Guillermo Quiroz **RC** 15.00
162 Jeremy Griffiths 10.00
163 Lew Ford **RC** 15.00
164 Rob Hammock **RC** 10.00
165 Todd Wellemeyer **RC** 10.00
166 Ryan Wagner **RC** 10.00
167 Edwin Jackson **RC** 20.00
168 Dan Haren 20.00
169 Hideki Matsui/Auto. **RC** 275.00
170 Jose Contreras/Auto. 30.00
171 Delmon Young/Auto. **RC** 150.00
172 Rickie Weeks/Auto. **RC** 50.00
173 Brandon Webb/Auto. **RC** 160.00
174 Bo Hart/Auto. **RC** 10.00
175 Rocco Baldelli/Auto. 20.00
176 Jose Reyes/Auto. 30.00
177 Dontrelle Willis/Auto. 25.00
178 Bobby Hill/Auto. 10.00
179 Jae Weong Seo/Auto. 20.00
180 Jesse Foppert/Auto. 20.00
CL Checklist 2.00

Gold

Stars (1-184): 1.5-3X
(85-117): 1-2X
Production 50
(118-140): 1-2X
Production 35
(141-158): 1-2X
Production 25
(159-168): No Pricing
Production 10
(169-180): No Pricing
Production 25

Buybacks

NM/M
Production 1-75
Hank Blalock/35 40.00
Hank Blalock 03 40M/25 40.00
Hank Blalock 03 GF/25 40.00
Hank Blalock 03 Patch/25 40.00
Hank Blalock 03 SPA/20 40.00
Hank Blalock 03 SPA/25 40.00
Hank Blalock 03 VIN/25 40.00
Luis Gonzalez
03 40M HR/25 40.00
Luis Gonzalez 03 SPA/25 40.00
Luis Gonzalez 03 VIN/25 40.00
Ken Griffey Jr. 02-3 SUP/75 80.00
Ken Griffey Jr.
02-3 SUP Spok/50 80.00
Ken Griffey Jr. 03 40M/50 80.00
Ken Griffey Jr. 03 40M/50 80.00
Ken Griffey Jr. 03 40M/50 80.00
Ken Griffey Jr. 03 40M/50 80.00
Ken Griffey Jr.
03 40M T40/50 80.00
Ken Griffey Jr. 03 GF/50 80.00
Ken Griffey Jr. 03 HON/50 80.00
Ken Griffey Jr.
03 HON SP/30 100.00
Ken Griffey Jr. 03 Patch/75 80.00
Ken Griffey Jr. 03 PB/75 80.00
Ken Griffey Jr. 03 SPA/50 80.00
Ken Griffey Jr. 03 SPA/75 80.00
Ken Griffey Jr. 03 SPx/75 80.00
Ken Griffey Jr. 03 SWS/75 80.00
Ken Griffey Jr. 03 UDA/75 80.00
Ken Griffey Jr. 03 VIN/50 80.00
Torii Hunter 03 Patch/25 40.00
Torii Hunter 03 PB/50 30.00
Torii Hunter 03 VIN/25 40.00
Austin Kearns 03 40M/33 30.00
Hideki Matsui 03 40M/20 250.00
Hideki Matsui
03 40M Flag/20 250.00
Hideki Matsui 03 GF/18 250.00
Hideki Matsui 03 PB/17 250.00
Hideki Matsui 03 UD/25 250.00
Hideki Matsui 03 VIN/25 250.00
Stan Musial 02 SPLC/30 75.00
Stan Musial 02 WSH/25 75.00
Stan Musial 03 PB/50 60.00
Stan Musial 03 SWSC/37 75.00
Stan Musial 03 VIN/50 60.00
Sammy Sosa
02-3 SUP/25 120.00
Sammy Sosa 03 PB/25 120.00
Sammy Sosa 03 SPA/25 120.00
Sammy Sosa 03 VIN/25 120.00
Mark Teixeira 03 40M/50 40.00
Mark Teixeira 03 Patch/50 40.00
Mark Teixeira
03 SPA RA/25 50.00
Mark Teixeira 03 SWS/23 50.00
Mark Teixeira 03 VIN/25 50.00

Double Barrel

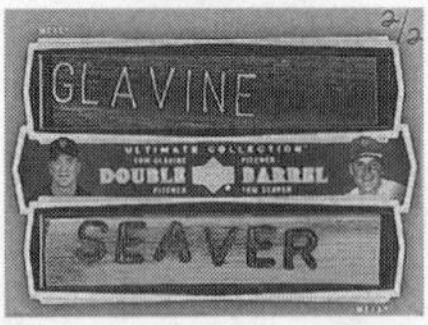

NM/M
No pricing due to scarcity.
DB-AE Darin Erstad, Garret Anderson/3
(3/04 Auction) 645.00
DB-GS Tom Seaver, Tom Glavine/2
(3/04 Auction) 700.00

Dual Jersey

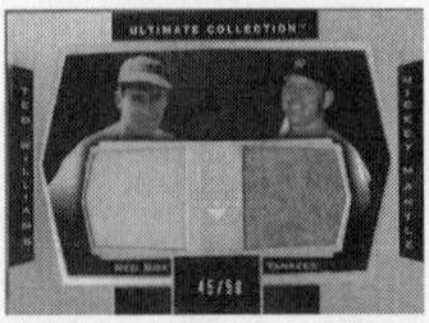

NM/M
Common Duo: 10.00
Production 50 Sets
Gold: 1-1.25X
Production 25 Sets
AH Alfonso Soriano,
Hideki Matsui 40.00
AI Albert Pujols, Ichiro Suzuki 50.00
BK Jeff Kent, Jeff Bagwell 15.00
CA Chipper Jones,
Andruw Jones 15.00
CJ Carlos Delgado,
Jason Giambi 15.00
DE Jim Edmonds, J.D. Drew 10.00
DG Carlos Delgado,
Vladimir Guerrero 15.00
DM Mickey Mantle,
Joe DiMaggio 250.00
DP Carlos Delgado,
Rafael Palmeiro 15.00
DW Joe DiMaggio,
Ted Williams 150.00
GB Shawn Green, Kevin Brown 10.00
GD Adam Dunn, Ken Griffey Jr. 25.00
GE Darin Erstad, Troy Glaus 10.00
GP Rafael Palmeiro,
Ken Griffey Jr. 25.00
GR Alex Rodriguez,
Nomar Garciaparra 25.00
GS Vladimir Guerrero,
Sammy Sosa 25.00
HJ Torii Hunter, Jacque Jones 10.00
HZ Roy Halladay, Barry Zito 10.00
IG Ken Griffey Jr.,
Ichiro Suzuki 50.00
IN Ichiro Suzuki, Hideo Nomo 50.00
IS Sammy Sosa, Ichiro Suzuki 45.00
JF Andruw Jones,
Rafael Furcal 15.00
JM Mike Piazza, Jorge Posada 20.00
MC Greg Maddux,
Roger Clemens 30.00
MW Ted Williams,
Mickey Mantle 250.00
NI Hideo Nomo,
Kazuhisa Ishii 30.00
NM Hideki Matsui, Hideo Nomo 60.00
PC Roger Clemens,
Pedro J. Martinez 25.00
PM Mike Mussina,
Andy Pettitte 15.00
PS Sammy Sosa, Mark Prior 30.00
RM Pedro J. Martinez,
Manny Ramirez 15.00
RP Rafael Palmeiro,
Alex Rodriguez 20.00
SA Albert Pujols, Scott Rolen 40.00
SB Alfonso Soriano,
Bernie Williams 15.00
SJ Randy Johnson,
Curt Schilling 20.00
SM Greg Maddux, John Smoltz 25.00
TB Mark Teixeira, Hank Blalock 15.00
TH Todd Helton, Jim Thome 15.00
TR Alex Rodriguez,
Miguel Tejada 20.00
WL Mike Lowell,
Dontrelle Willis 15.00
YW Delmon Young,
Rickie Weeks 35.00

Dual Patch

NM/M
Common Duo: 20.00
Production 99 unless noted.
Gold: .75-1.25X
Production 35
AI Ichiro Suzuki,
Albert Pujols 100.00
AM Andy Pettitte,
Mike Mussina 25.00
BK Jeff Bagwell, Jeff Kent 25.00
CA Andruw Jones,
Chipper Jones 30.00
CV Carlos Delgado,
Vladimir Guerrero 35.00
DE Jim Edmonds, J.D. Drew 25.00
DG Carlos Delgado,
Jason Giambi 25.00
DP Carlos Delgado,
Rafael Palmeiro/35 40.00
GB Shawn Green, Kevin Brown 20.00
GD Adam Dunn, Ken Griffey Jr. 45.00
GE Darin Erstad, Troy Glaus 30.00
GP Ken Griffey Jr.,
Rafael Palmeiro/35 50.00
GR Alex Rodriguez,
Nomar Garciaparra 75.00
GS Vladimir Guerrero,
Sammy Sosa 40.00
HJ Torii Hunter,
Jacque Jones/83 20.00

HZ	Roy Halladay, Barry Zito	35.00
IG	Ken Griffey Jr.,	
	Ichiro Suzuki	90.00
IN	Ichiro Suzuki,	
	Hideo Nomo	140.00
IS	Sammy Sosa, Ichiro Suzuki	90.00
JF	Rafael Furcal,	
	Andruw Jones	25.00
JG	John Smoltz, Greg Maddux	40.00
MC	Greg Maddux,	
	Roger Clemens/75	60.00
NI	Hideo Nomo,	
	Kazuhisa Ishii/63	65.00
NM	Hideki Matsui,	
	Hideo Nomo/35	180.00
PM	Mike Piazza,	
	Jorge Posada/73	35.00
PR	Roger Clemens,	
	Pedro Martinez/35	60.00
PS	Sammy Sosa, Mark Prior	90.00
RM	Pedro J. Martinez,	
	Manny Ramirez	40.00
RP	Rafael Palmeiro,	
	Alex Rodriguez/35	40.00
SA	Albert Pujols, Scott Rolen	75.00
SJ	Randy Johnson,	
	Curt Schilling	40.00
SM	Alfonso Soriano,	
	Hideki Matsui	80.00
TB	Mark Teixeira, Hank Blalock	40.00
TH	Jim Thome, Todd Helton	35.00
TR	Alex Rodriguez,	
	Miguel Tejada	50.00
WL	Mike Lowell,	
	Dontrelle Willis/85	35.00
YW	Delmon Young,	
	Rickie Weeks/28	75.00

Game Jersey Tier 1

		NM/M
Common Player:		8.00
Production 99 Sets		
Copper:		No Pricing
Production 10 Sets		
Gold:		.75-2X
No pricing production of 20 or less.		
RB	Rocco Baldelli	8.00
PB	Pat Burrell	8.00
RC	Roger Clemens	20.00
CD	Carlos Delgado	10.00
AD	Adam Dunn	10.00
JE	Jim Edmonds	8.00
RF	Rafael Furcal	8.00
JG	Jason Giambi	10.00
TR	Troy Glaus	10.00
TG	Tom Glavine	10.00
SG	Shawn Green	8.00
KG	Ken Griffey Jr.	20.00
VG	Vladimir Guerrero	10.00
TH	Torii Hunter	8.00
KI	Kazuhisa Ishii	8.00
RJ	Randy Johnson	12.00
AJ	Andruw Jones	10.00
CJ	Chipper Jones	15.00
GM	Greg Maddux	15.00
HM	Hideki Matsui	50.00
MM	Mike Mussina	8.00
HN	Hideo Nomo	15.00
MI	Mike Piazza	15.00
MP	Mark Prior	15.00
AP	Albert Pujols	25.00
MR	Manny Ramirez	12.00
JR	Jose Reyes	30.00
AR	Alex Rodriguez	15.00
CS	Curt Schilling	10.00
GS	Gary Sheffield	8.00
AS	Alfonso Soriano	10.00
SS	Sammy Sosa	25.00
IS	Ichiro Suzuki	50.00
MT	Miguel Tejada	10.00
FT	Frank Thomas	15.00
JT	Jim Thome	10.00
RW	Rickie Weeks	15.00
BW	Bernie Williams	10.00
DW	Dontrelle Willis	10.00
KW	Kerry Wood	10.00
DY	Delmon Young	15.00
BZ	Barry Zito	8.00

Game Jersey Tier 2

Tier 2: 1X Tier 1 Price
Production 75 Sets

Game Used Patch

	NM/M
Common Player:	15.00
Production 99 Sets	
Copper:	1-1.5X
Production 35 Sets	
Gold:	1-1.5X
Production 25 Sets	

RB	Rocco Baldelli	20.00
PB	Pat Burrell	20.00
RC	Roger Clemens	50.00
CD	Carlos Delgado	15.00
AD	Adam Dunn	20.00
JE	Jim Edmonds	20.00
RF	Rafael Furcal	15.00
JG	Jason Giambi	20.00
TR	Troy Glaus	25.00
TG	Tom Glavine	25.00
SG	Shawn Green	15.00
KG	Ken Griffey Jr.	45.00
VG	Vladimir Guerrero	30.00
RH	Roy Halladay	20.00
TH	Torii Hunter	20.00
KI	Kazuhisa Ishii	20.00
RJ	Randy Johnson	25.00
AJ	Andruw Jones	25.00
CJ	Chipper Jones	30.00
GM	Greg Maddux	40.00
HM	Hideki Matsui	85.00
MM	Mike Mussina	25.00
HN	Hideo Nomo	40.00
MI	Mike Piazza	35.00
MP	Mark Prior	30.00
AP	Albert Pujols	50.00
MR	Manny Ramirez	30.00
JR	Jose Reyes	30.00
AR	Alex Rodriguez	25.00
CS	Curt Schilling	25.00
AS	Alfonso Soriano/42	25.00
SS	Sammy Sosa	35.00
IS	Ichiro Suzuki	75.00
MT	Miguel Tejada	25.00
FT	Frank Thomas	25.00
JT	Jim Thome	30.00
RW	Rickie Weeks	25.00
BW	Bernie Williams	20.00
DW	Dontrelle Willis	30.00
KW	Kerry Wood	40.00
DY	Delmon Young	35.00
BZ	Barry Zito	20.00

2003 Upper Deck Victory

	NM/M
Complete Set (200):	40.00
Common Player (1-100):	.10
Common (101-200):	.40
Cards (101-128):	Inserted 1:4
(129-168):	1:5
(169-188):	1:10
(189-200):	1:20
Pack (6):	.75
Box (36):	20.00

1	Troy Glaus	.40
2	Garret Anderson	.20
3	Tim Salmon	.20
4	Darin Erstad	.20
5	Luis Gonzalez	.20
6	Curt Schilling	.25
7	Randy Johnson	.50
8	Junior Spivey	.10
9	Andruw Jones	.25
10	Greg Maddux	.75
11	Chipper Jones	.75
12	Gary Sheffield	.20
13	John Smoltz	.25
14	Geronimo Gil	.10
15	Tony Batista	.10
16	Trot Nixon	.10
17	Manny Ramirez	.40
18	Pedro J. Martinez	.50
19	Nomar Garciaparra	.50
20	Derek Lowe	.10
21	Shea Hillenbrand	.10
22	Sammy Sosa	.75
23	Kerry Wood	.40
24	Mark Prior	.40
25	Magglio Ordonez	.20
26	Frank Thomas	.40
27	Mark Buehrle	.10
28	Paul Konerko	.10
29	Adam Dunn	.40
30	Ken Griffey Jr.	.75
31	Austin Kearns	.25
32	Matt Lawton	.10
33	Larry Walker	.20
34	Todd Helton	.25
35	Jeff Bagwell	.20
36	Roy Oswalt	.20
37	Lance Berkman	.25
38	Mike Sweeney	.10
39	Carlos Beltran	.10
40	Kazuhisa Ishii	.10
41	Shawn Green	.20
42	Hideo Nomo	.20
43	Adrian Beltre	.20
44	Richie Sexson	.25
45	Ben Sheets	.20
46	Torii Hunter	.25
47	Jacque Jones	.10
48	Corey Koskie	.10
49	Vladimir Guerrero	.50
50	Jose Vidro	.10
51	Mo Vaughn	.20
52	Mike Piazza	1.00
53	Roberto Alomar	.25
54	Derek Jeter	1.50
55	Alfonso Soriano	.75
56	Jason Giambi	.75
57	Roger Clemens	.75
58	Mike Mussina	.25
59	Bernie Williams	.25
60	Jorge Posada	.20
61	Nick Johnson	.10
62	Hideki Matsui RC	4.00
63	Eric Chavez	.20
64	Barry Zito	.20
65	Miguel Tejada	.20
66	Tim Hudson	.20
67	Pat Burrell	.40
68	Bobby Abreu	.20
69	Jimmy Rollins	.20
70	Brett Myers	.10
71	Jim Thome	.40
72	Jason Kendall	.20
73	Brian Giles	.20
74	Aramis Ramirez	.10
75	Sean Burroughs	.10
76	Ryan Klesko	.20
77	Phil Nevin	.10
78	Barry Bonds	1.50
79	J.T. Snow	.10
80	Rich Aurilia	.10
81	Ichiro Suzuki	1.00
82	Edgar Martinez	.10
83	Freddy Garcia	.10
84	Jim Edmonds	.20
85	J.D. Drew	.10
86	Scott Rolen	.20
87	Albert Pujols	.50
88	Mark McGwire	1.25
89	Matt Morris	.20
90	Ben Grieve	.10
91	Carl Crawford	.10
92	Alex Rodriguez	1.25
93	Carl Everett	.10
94	Juan Gonzalez	.25
95	Rafael Palmeiro	.20
96	Hank Blalock	.20
97	Carlos Delgado	.20
98	Josh Phelps	.10
99	Eric Hinske	.10
100	Shannon Stewart	.10
101	Albert Pujols	1.00
102	Alex Rodriguez	2.50
103	Alfonso Soriano	1.00
104	Barry Bonds	3.00
105	Bernie Williams	.50
106	Brian Giles	.50
107	Chipper Jones	.75
108	Darin Erstad	.50
109	Derek Jeter	3.00
110	Eric Chavez	.50
111	Miguel Tejada	.50
112	Ichiro Suzuki	1.50
113	Rafael Palmeiro	.40
114	Jason Giambi	1.50
115	Jeff Bagwell	.75
116	Jim Thome	.75
117	Ken Griffey Jr.	1.50
118	Lance Berkman	.50
119	Luis Gonzalez	.40
120	Manny Ramirez	.75
121	Mike Piazza	2.00
122	J.D. Drew	.40
123	Sammy Sosa	1.50
124	Scott Rolen	.75
125	Shawn Green	.50
126	Todd Helton	.50
127	Troy Glaus	.75
128	Vladimir Guerrero	1.00
129	Albert Pujols	1.00
130	Brian Giles	.50
131	Carlos Delgado	.50
132	Curt Schilling	.50
133	Derek Jeter	3.00
134	Frank Thomas	.75
135	Greg Maddux	1.50
136	Jeff Bagwell	.75
137	Jim Thome	.75
138	Jorge Posada	.50
139	Kazuhisa Ishii	.40
140	Larry Walker	.40
141	Luis Gonzalez	.40
142	Miguel Tejada	.50
143	Pat Burrell	.75
144	Pedro J. Martinez	1.00
145	Rafael Palmeiro	.50
146	Roger Clemens	1.50
147	Tim Hudson	.50
148	Troy Glaus	.75
149	Alfonso Soriano	1.00
150	Andruw Jones	.50
151	Barry Zito	.50
152	Darin Erstad	.50
153	Eric Chavez	.50
154	Alex Rodriguez	2.50
155	J.D. Drew	.40
156	Jason Giambi	1.50
157	Jason Kendall	.40
158	Ken Griffey Jr.	1.50
159	Lance Berkman	.50
160	Mike Mussina	.50
161	Mike Piazza	2.00
162	Nomar Garciaparra	2.00
163	Randy Johnson	1.00
164	Roberto Alomar	.50
165	Scott Rolen	.75
166	Shawn Green	.50
167	Torii Hunter	.50
168	Vladimir Guerrero	1.00
169	Alex Rodriguez	2.50
170	Andruw Jones	.50
171	Bernie Williams	.50
172	Ichiro Suzuki	1.50
173	Miguel Tejada	.50
174	Nomar Garciaparra	2.00
175	Pedro J. Martinez	1.00
176	Randy Johnson	1.00
177	Todd Helton	1.00
178	Vladimir Guerrero	1.00
179	Barry Bonds	3.00
180	Carlos Delgado	.50
181	Chipper Jones	1.50
182	Frank Thomas	.75
183	Lance Berkman	.50
184	Larry Walker	.40
185	Manny Ramirez	.75
186	Mike Piazza	2.00
187	Sammy Sosa	1.50
188	Shawn Green	.50
189	Chipper Jones	1.50
190	Curt Schilling	.50
191	Derek Jeter	3.00
192	Ken Griffey Jr.	1.50
193	Sammy Sosa	1.50
194	Vladimir Guerrero	1.00
195	Alex Rodriguez	2.50
196	Barry Bonds	3.00
197	Greg Maddux	1.50
198	Ichiro Suzuki	1.50
199	Jason Giambi	1.50
200	Mike Piazza	2.00

Parallels

Tier 1 Green:	1-2X
Inserted 1:1	
Tier 2 Orange:	2-4X
Inserted 1:8	
Tier 3 Blue:	3-6X
Production 650	
Tier 4 Purple:	10-25X
Production 50 Sets	
Tier 5 Red:	No Pricing
Production 25 Sets	

2003 Upper Deck Vintage

	NM/M
Complete Set (280):	
Common Player:	.15
Common SP (223-232):	1.50
Inserted 1:7	
Common SP (233-247):	
Inserted 1:5	
Common 3D SP (248-277):	6.00
Inserted 1:48	
Pack (8):	2.00
Box (24):	45.00

1	Troy Glaus	.25
2	Darin Erstad	.25
3	Garret Anderson	.25
4	Jarrod Washburn	.15
5	Nolan Ryan	2.00
6	Tim Salmon	.25
7	Troy Percival	.15
8	Alex Ochoa/SP	.25
9	Daryle Ward	.15
10	Jeff Bagwell	.50
11	Roy Oswalt	.25
12	Lance Berkman	.40
13	Craig Biggio	.25
14	Richard Hidalgo	.15
15	Tim Hudson	.25
16	Eric Chavez	.25
17	Barry Zito	.25
18	Miguel Tejada	.50

19 Mark Mulder .25
20 Rollie Fingers .15
21 Jim "Catfish" Hunter .25
22 Jermaine Dye .15
23 Ray Durham/SP 4.00
24 Carlos Delgado .25
25 Eric Hinske .15
26 Josh Phelps .15
27 Shannon Stewart .15
28 Vernon Wells .15
29 John Smoltz .25
30 Greg Maddux 1.00
31 Chipper Jones .75
32 Gary Sheffield .25
33 Andruw Jones .40
34 Tom Glavine .25
35 Rafael Furcal .15
36 Phil Niekro .15
37 Eddie Mathews .50
38 Robin Yount .75
39 Richie Sexson .25
40 Ben Sheets .15
41 Geoff Jenkins .15
42 Alex Sanchez .15
43 Jason Isringhausen .15
44 Albert Pujols 1.50
45 Matt Morris .15
46 J.D. Drew .25
47 Jim Edmonds .25
48 Stan Musial 1.00
49 Red Schoendienst .15
50 Edgar Renteria .25
51 Mark McGwire/SP 10.00
52 Scott Rolen/SP 5.00
53 Mark Bellhorn .15
54 Kerry Wood .50
55 Mark Prior .50
56 Moises Alou .25
57 Corey Patterson .25
58 Ernie Banks .75
59 Hee Seop Choi .15
60 Billy Williams .15
61 Sammy Sosa/SP 8.00
62 Ben Grieve .15
63 Jared Sandberg .15
64 Carl Crawford .15
65 Randy Johnson .75
66 Luis Gonzalez .25
67 Steve Finley .15
68 Junior Spivey .15
69 Erubiel Durazo .15
70 Curt Schilling/SP 8.00
71 Al Lopez .15
72 Pee Wee Reese .15
73 Eric Gagne .25
74 Shawn Green .25
75 Kevin Brown .15
76 Paul LoDuca .15
77 Adrian Beltre .25
78 Hideo Nomo .40
79 Eric Karros .15
80 Odalis Perez .15
81 Kazuhisa Ishii/SP 5.00
82 Tommy Lasorda .15
83 Fernando Tatis .15
84 Vladimir Guerrero .75
85 Jose Vidro .15
86 Javier Vazquez .15
87 Brad Wilkerson .15
88 Bartolo Colon/SP 4.00
89 Monte Irvin .15
90 Robb Nen .15
91 Reggie Sanders .15
92 Jeff Kent .25
93 Rich Aurilia .15
94 Orlando Cepeda .15
95 Juan Marichal .25
96 Willie McCovey .25
97 David Bell .15
98 Barry Bonds/SP 10.00
99 Kenny Lofton/SP 4.00
100 Jim Thome .50
101 C.C. Sabathia .15
102 Omar Vizquel .25
103 Lou Boudreau .15
104 Larry Doby .25
105 Bob Lemon .15
106 John Olerud .25
107 Edgar Martinez .15
108 Bret Boone .15
109 Freddy Garcia .15
110 Mike Cameron .15
111 Kazuhiro Sasaki .15
112 Ichiro Suzuki/SP 8.00
113 Mike Lowell .15
114 Josh Beckett .25
115 A.J. Burnett .15
116 Juan Pierre .15
117 Derrek Lee .25
118 Luis Castillo .15
119 Juan Encarnacion/SP 4.00
120 Roberto Alomar .40
121 Edgardo Alfonzo .15
122 Jeromy Burnitz .15
123 Mo Vaughn .25
124 Tom Seaver .50
125 Al Leiter .15
126 Mike Piazza/SP 8.00
127 Tony Batista .15
128 Geronimo Gil .15
129 Chris Singleton .15
130 Rodrigo Lopez .15
131 Jay Gibbons .15
132 Melvin Mora .15
133 Earl Weaver .15
134 Trevor Hoffman .15
135 Phil Nevin .15
136 Sean Burroughs .15
137 Ryan Klesko .15
138 Mark Kotsay .15
139 Mike Lieberthal .15
140 Bobby Abreu .25
141 Jimmy Rollins .25
142 Pat Burrell .40
143 Vicente Padilla .15
144 Richie Ashburn .15
145 Jeremy Giambi/SP 4.00
146 Josh Fogg .15
147 Brian Giles .25
148 Aramis Ramirez .25
149 Jason Kendall .15
150 Ralph Kiner .15
151 Willie Stargell .25
152 Kevin Mench .15
153 Rafael Palmeiro .25
154 Ivan Rodriguez .40
155 Hank Blalock .25
156 Juan Gonzalez .40
157 Carl Everett .15
158 Alex Rodriguez/SP 10.00
159 Nomar Garciaparra 1.25
160 Derek Lowe .15
161 Manny Ramirez .50
162 Shea Hillenbrand .25
163 Bobby Doerr .15
164 Johnny Damon .40
165 Jason Varitek .25
166 Pedro Martinez/SP 8.00
167 Cliff Floyd/SP 4.00
168 Ken Griffey Jr. 1.25
169 Adam Dunn .50
170 Austin Kearns .25
171 Aaron Boone .15
172 Joe Morgan .25
173 Sean Casey .15
174 Todd Walker .15
175 Ryan Dempster/SP 4.00
176 Shawn Estes/SP 4.00
177 Gabe Kapler/SP 4.00
178 Jason Jennings .15
179 Todd Helton .40
180 Larry Walker .25
181 Preston Wilson .15
182 Jay Payton/SP 4.00
183 Mike Sweeney .15
184 Carlos Beltran .50
185 Paul Byrd .15
186 Raul Ibanez .15
187 Rick Ferrell .15
188 Early Wynn .15
189 Dmitri Young .15
190 Jim Bunning .15
191 George Kell .15
192 Hal Newhouser .15
193 Bobby Higginson .15
194 Carlos Pena/SP 4.00
195 Sparky Anderson .15
196 Torii Hunter .25
197 Eric Milton .15
198 Corey Koskie .15
199 Jacque Jones .15
200 Harmon Killebrew .50
201 Doug Mientkiewicz .15
202 Frank Thomas .50
203 Mark Buehrle .15
204 Magglio Ordonez .25
205 Paul Konerko .25
206 Joe Borchard .15
207 Hoyt Wilhelm .15
208 Carlos Lee .15
209 Roger Clemens 1.50
210 Nick Johnson .15
211 Jason Giambi .25
212 Alfonso Soriano .75
213 Bernie Williams .40
214 Robin Ventura .15
215 Jorge Posada .25
216 Mike Mussina .40
217 Yogi Berra .75
218 Phil Rizzuto .40
219 Mariano Rivera .25
220 Derek Jeter/SP 12.00
221 Jeff Weaver/SP 4.00
222 Raul Mondesi/SP 4.00
223 Freddy Sanchez, Josh Hancock 2.00
224 Joe Borchard, Miguel Olivo 2.00
225 Brandon Phillips, Josh Bard 1.50
226 Andy Van Hekken, Andres Torres 1.50
227 Jason Lane, Jeriome Robertson 1.50
228 Chin-Feng Chen, Joe Thurston 1.50
229 Endy Chavez, Jamey Carroll 1.50
230 Drew Henson, Alex Graman 2.50
231 Dewon Brazelton, Lance Carter 1.50
232 Jayson Werth, Kevin Cash 1.50
233 Randy Johnson, Curt Schilling, Barry Zito 1.00
234 Pedro J. Martinez, Randy Johnson, Derek Lowe 1.00
235 Randy Johnson, Curt Schilling, Pedro J. Martinez 1.00
236 John Smoltz, Eric Gagne, Mike Williams .50
237 Randy Johnson, Bartolo Colon, A.J. Burnett 1.00
238 Alfonso Soriano, Ichiro Suzuki, Vladimir Guerrero 1.50
239 Alex Rodriguez, Jim Thome, Sammy Sosa 2.00
240 Barry Bonds, Manny Ramirez, Mike Sweeney 2.00
241 Alfonso Soriano, Alex Rodriguez, Derek Jeter 2.00
242 Alex Rodriguez, Magglio Ordonez, Miguel Tejada 2.00
243 Luis Castillo, Juan Pierre, Dave Roberts .50
244 Nomar Garciaparra, Garret Anderson, Alfonso Soriano 1.00
245 Johnny Damon, Jimmy Rollins, Kenny Lofton .50
246 Barry Bonds, Jim Thome, Manny Ramirez 2.00
247 Barry Bonds, Brian Giles, Manny Ramirez 2.00
248 Troy Glaus 10.00
249 Luis Gonzalez 6.00
250 Chipper Jones 15.00
251 Nomar Garciaparra 15.00
252 Manny Ramirez 10.00
253 Sammy Sosa 15.00
254 Frank Thomas 10.00
255 Maggio Ordonez 6.00
256 Adam Dunn 10.00
257 Ken Griffey Jr. 15.00
258 Jim Thome 10.00
259 Todd Helton 8.00
260 Larry Walker 6.00
261 Lance Berkman 6.00
262 Jeff Bagwell 10.00
263 Mike Sweeney 6.00
264 Shawn Green 6.00
265 Vladimir Guerrero 12.00
266 Mike Piazza 15.00
267 Jason Giambi 15.00
268 Pat Burrell 20.00
269 Barry Bonds 15.00
270 Mark McGwire 20.00
271 Alex Rodriguez 15.00
272 Carlos Delgado 6.00
273 Richie Sexson 6.00
274 Andruw Jones 8.00
275 Derek Jeter 20.00
276 Juan Gonzalez 8.00
277 Albert Pujols 12.00
278 Jason Giambi/CL .75
279 Sammy Sosa/CL .75
280 Ichiro Suzuki/CL .75

All Caps

NM/M
Common Player: 8.00
Production 250 Sets
JB Jeff Bagwell 15.00
LB Lance Berkman 8.00
DE Darin Erstad 8.00
RF Rafael Furcal 8.00
JG Juan Gonzalez 10.00
LG Luis Gonzalez 8.00
TG Tony Gwynn 25.00
TH Tim Hudson 10.00
GM Greg Maddux 30.00
RP Rafael Palmeiro 10.00
CP Chan Ho Park 8.00
MP Mike Piazza 35.00
KS Kazuhiro Sasaki 8.00
MV Mo Vaughn 8.00
RV Robin Ventura 8.00

Capping the Action

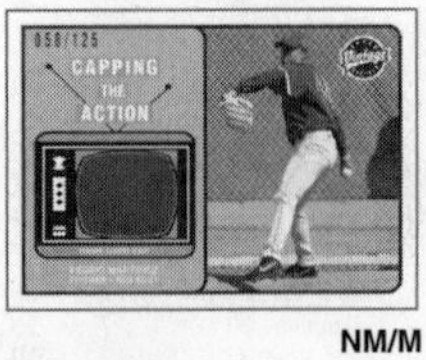

NM/M
Common Player: 10.00
Quantity produced listed
RA Roberto Alomar/101 20.00
CD Carlos Delgado/91 10.00
JG Juan Gonzalez/99 20.00
SG Shawn Green/125 20.00
KG Ken Griffey Jr./102 40.00
TH Todd Helton/99 20.00
PM Pedro Martinez/125 25.00
MM Mike Mussina/109 40.00
HM Hideo Nomo/117 45.00
RP Rafael Palmeiro/125 20.00
AR Alex Rodriguez/110 25.00
IR Ivan Rodriguez/125 15.00
SR Scott Rolen/109 25.00
AS Alfonso Soriano/109 20.00
SS Sammy Sosa/125 40.00

Crackin the Lumber

NM/M
Production 25
Golds: No Pricing
Production 5
JG Jason Giambi 25.00
IS Ichiro Suzuki 125.00

Crowning Glory

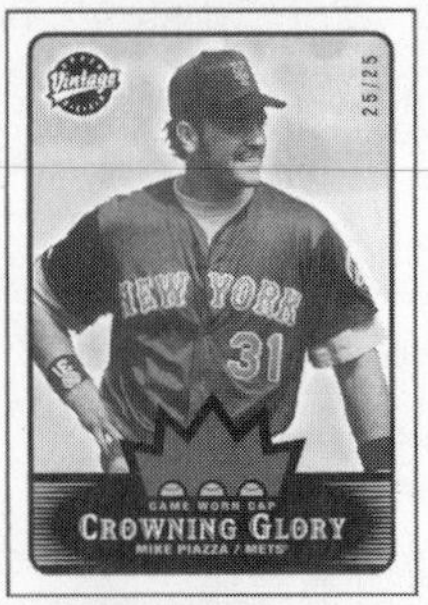

No pricing due to scarcity.
Production 25 Sets

Dropping the Hammer

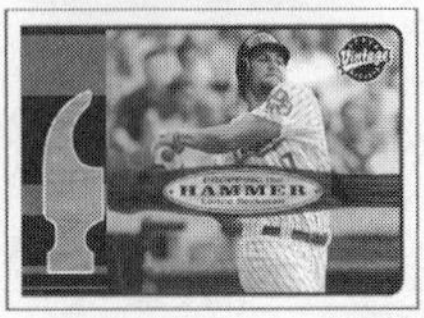

NM/M
Common Player: 6.00
Inserted 1:130
Golds: 1.5-2X
Production 100 Sets
BA Bobby Abreu 8.00
RA Roberto Alomar 10.00
LB Lance Berkman 8.00
RF Rafael Furcal 6.00
JG Jason Giambi 6.00
SG Shawn Green 6.00
KG Ken Griffey Jr. 15.00
TH Todd Helton 8.00
AJ Andruw Jones 8.00
DJ David Justice 8.00
KL Kenny Lofton 6.00
FM Fred McGriff 8.00
MO Magglio Ordonez 6.00
RP Rafael Palmeiro 8.00
MP Mike Piazza 15.00
AR Alex Rodriguez 15.00
SS Sammy Sosa 20.00
TA Fernando Tatis 6.00
MT Miguel Tejada 8.00
FT Frank Thomas 10.00
JT Jim Thome 10.00
RV Robin Ventura 6.00
OV Omar Vizquel 6.00
LW Larry Walker 8.00
PW Preston Wilson 6.00

Men with Hats

NM/M
Common Player: 8.00
Inserted 1:285
VC Vinny Castilla 8.00
EC Eric Chavez 10.00
JD Johnny Damon 15.00
AD Adam Dunn 15.00
JG Jason Giambi 8.00
TH Todd Helton 10.00
HU Tim Hudson 10.00
AJ Andruw Jones 10.00
JK Jason Kendall 8.00
KL Kenny Lofton 8.00
AR Alex Rodriguez 20.00
MT Miguel Tejada 12.00
FT Frank Thomas 12.00
TW Todd Walker 8.00
BW Bernie Williams 10.00

Slugfest

NM/M
Common Player: 8.00
Production 200 Sets
Golds: 1.5-2.5X
Production 50 Sets
CD Carlos Delgado 8.00
SG Shawn Green 8.00
AJ Andruw Jones 8.00
RP Rafael Palmeiro 8.00
MP Mike Piazza 20.00
AR Alex Rodriguez 15.00
FT Frank Thomas 10.00
JT Jim Thome 10.00
LW Larry Walker 8.00
BW Bernie Williams 10.00

Timeless Teams Bat

NM/M
Common Card: 20.00

Production 175 Sets

BLAR	Pat Burrell, Mike Lieberthal, Bobby Abreu, Jimmy Rollins	25.00
CTDJ	Eric Chavez, Miguel Tejada, Jermaine Dye, David Justice	25.00
DEMR	J.D. Drew, Jim Edmonds, Tino Martinez, Scott Rolen	40.00
DGCL	Adam Dunn, Ken Griffey Jr., Sean Casey, Barry Larkin	40.00
GNBL	Shawn Green, Hideo Nomo, Adrian Beltre, Paul LoDuca	40.00
GPMS	Jason Giambi, Jorge Posada, Raul Mondesi, Alfonso Soriano	30.00
GWVS	Jason Giambi, Bernie Williams, Robin Ventura, Alfonso Soriano	40.00
HWPZ	Todd Helton, Larry Walker, Juan Pierre, Todd Zeile	25.00
IMBC	Ichiro Suzuki, Edgar Martinez, Bret Boone, Mike Cameron	90.00
JGSW	Randy Johnson, Luis Gonzalez, Curt Schilling, Matt Williams	40.00
JJSF	Chipper Jones, Andruw Jones, Gary Sheffield, Rafael Furcal	40.00
KNKB	Ryan Klesko, Phil Nevin, Mark Kotsay, Sean Burroughs	20.00
MGLJ	Greg Maddux, Tom Glavine, Javy Lopez, Chipper Jones	40.00
OTLK	Magglio Ordonez, Frank Thomas, Carlos Lee, Paul Konerko	30.00
PVAA	Mike Piazza, Mo Vaughn, Roberto Alomar, Edgardo Alfonzo	40.00
RGRP	Alex Rodriguez, Juan Gonzalez, Ivan Rodriguez, Rafael Palmeiro	40.00
RMHN	Manny Ramirez, Pedro J. Martinez, Shea Hillenbrand, Trot Nixon	30.00
SMAP	Sammy Sosa, Fred McGriff, Moises Alou, Corey Patterson	40.00

UD Giants

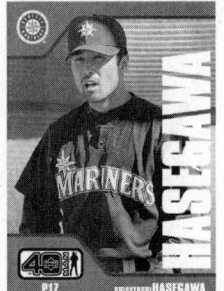

		NM/M
Complete Set (42):		45.00
Common Player:		.75
Inserted 1:Box		
RA	Roberto Alomar	1.00
JB	Jeff Bagwell	1.00
LB	Lance Berkman	1.00
BB	Barry Bonds	4.00
PB	Pat Burrell	1.00
RC	Roger Clemens	4.00
CD	Carlos Delgado	.75
JD	J.D. Drew	.75
AD	Adam Dunn	1.50
NG	Nomar Garciaparra	3.00
JG	Jason Giambi	.75
BG	Brian Giles	.75
GO	Juan Gonzalez	1.00
LG	Luis Gonzalez	.75
SG	Shawn Green	.75
KG	Ken Griffey Jr.	3.00
VG	Vladimir Guerrero	1.50
TH	Todd Helton	1.00
KI	Kazuhisa Ishii	.75
RJ	Randy Johnson	1.50
AJ	Andruw Jones	1.00
CJ	Chipper Jones	2.50
GM	Greg Maddux	2.50
PM	Pedro J. Martinez	1.50
MM	Mike Mussina	1.00
HN	Hideo Nomo	1.00
MO	Magglio Ordonez	.75
RP	Rafael Palmeiro	1.00

MP	Mike Piazza	3.00
PR	Mark Prior	1.00
AP	Albert Pujols	4.00
MR	Manny Ramirez	1.50
AR	Alex Rodriguez	4.00
IR	Ivan Rodriguez	1.50
SR	Scott Rolen	1.50
CS	Curt Schilling	1.50
SS	Sammy Sosa	2.50
IS	Ichiro Suzuki	3.00
FT	Frank Thomas	1.00
JT	Jim Thome	1.50
BW	Bernie Williams	1.00
KW	Kerry Wood	1.50

Vintage Hitmen

		NM/M
Production 150 Sets		
Golds:		No Pricing
Production 10 Sets		
JG	Jason Giambi	10.00
KG	Ken Griffey Jr.	30.00
MM	Mark McGwire	60.00
IS	Ichiro Suzuki	60.00

Vintage Hitmen Double Signed

		NM/M
Production 75		
Gold:		No Pricing
Production 5		
MS	Mark McGwire, Sammy Sosa	600.00

2003 Upper Deck 40-Man

		NM/M
Complete Set (990):		200.00
Common Player:		.25
Common Rk (877-960):		.40
Pack (10):		2.00
Box (24):		35.00
1	Troy Glaus	.50
2	Darin Erstad	.40
3	Garret Anderson	.50
4	Aaron Sele	.25
5	Adam Kennedy	.25
6	Scott Spiezio	.25
7	Troy Percival	.25
8	David Eckstein	.25
9	Ramon Ortiz	.25
10	Bengie Molina	.25
11	Tim Salmon	.50
12	John Lackey	.25
13	Brad Fullmer	.25
14	Jarrod Washburn	.25
15	Shawn Wooten	.25
16	Kevin Appier	.25
17	Ben Weber	.25
18	Eric Owens	.25
19	Matt Wise	.25
20	Francisco Rodriguez	.25
21	Scot Shields	.25
22	Jose Molina	.25
23	Scott Schoeneweis	.25
24	Derrick Turnbow	.25
25	Benji Gil	.25
26	Julio Ramirez	.25
27	Mickey Callaway	.25
28	Barry Zito	.50
29	Tim Hudson	.40
30	Mark Mulder	.40
31	Eric Chavez	.25
32	Miguel Tejada	.50
33	Terrence Long	.25
34	Jermaine Dye	.25
35	Erubiel Durazo	.25
36	Scott Hatteberg	.25
37	Chris Singleton	.25
38	Keith Foulke	.25
39	John Halama	.25
40	Mark Ellis	.25
41	Ted Lilly	.25
42	Jim Mecir	.25
43	Adam Piatt	.25
44	Freddie Bynum	.25
45	Adam Morrissey	.25
46	Jeremy Fikac	.25
47	Ricardo Rincon	.25
48	Ramon Hernandez	.25
49	Mark Bowie	.25
50	Chad Bradford	.25
51	Eric Byrnes	.25

52	Ron Gant	.25
53	Jose Flores	.25
54	Mark Johnson	.25
55	Carlos Delgado	.75
56	Orlando Hudson	.25
57	Kelvim Escobar	.25
58	Eric Hinske	.25
59	Doug Creek	.25
60	Josh Phelps	.25
61	Shannon Stewart	.25
62	Roy Halladay	.40
63	Vernon Wells	.40
64	Mark Henrickson	.25
65	Mike Bordick	.25
66	Jayson Werth	.25
67	Chris Woodward	.25
68	Ken Huckaby	.25
69	Frank Catalanotto	.25
70	Jason Kershner	.25
71	Greg Myers	.25
72	Tanyon Sturtze	.25
73	Trever Miller	.25
74	Pete Walker	.25
75	Alexis Rios	.25
76	Tom Wilson	.25
77	Dave Berg	.25
78	Doug Linton	.25
79	Cliff Politte	.25
80	Damion Easley	.25
81	Toby Hall	.25
82	George Lombard	.25
83	Ben Grieve	.25
84	Aubrey Huff	.25
85	Jesus Colome	.25
86	Dewon Brazelton	.25
87	Rey Ordonez	.25
88	Al Martin	.25
89	Carl Crawford	.25
90	Travis Lee	.25
91	Marlon Anderson	.25
92	Javier Valentin	.25
93	Joe Kennedy	.25
94	Jorge Sosa	.25
95	Travis Harper	.25
96	Bobby Seay	.25
97	Seth McClung	.25
98	Delvin James	.25
99	Victor Zambrano	.25
100	Terry Shumpert	.25
101	Josh Hamilton	.50
102	Jared Sandberg	.25
103	Steve Parris	.25
104	C.C. Sabathia	.25
105	Omar Vizquel	.40
106	Milton Bradley	.25
107	Ellis Burks	.25
108	Danys Baez	.25
109	Jason Davis	.25
110	Terry Mulholland	.25
111	Matt Lawton	.25
112	Alex Escobar	.25
113	Mark Wohlers	.25
114	Josh Bard	.25
115	Bill Selby	.25
116	Brandon Phillips	.25
117	Jason Bere	.25
118	Casey Blake	.25
119	Travis Hafner	.25
120	Brian Anderson	.25
121	David Riske	.25
122	Karim Garcia	.25
123	Ricardo Rodriguez	.25
124	Carl Sadler	.25
125	Jose Santiago	.25
126	Tim Laker	.25
127	John McDonald	.25
128	Jake Westbrook	.25
129	Ichiro Suzuki	1.00
130	Freddy Garcia	.25
131	Edgar Martinez	.40
132	Ben Davis	.25
133	Shigetoshi Hasegawa	.25
134	Carlos Guillen	.25
135	Randy Winn	.25
136	John Mabry	.25
137	Matt Thornton	.25
138	Bret Boone	.40
139	Jamie Moyer	.25
140	Giovanni Carrara	.25
141	Kazuhiro Sasaki	.25
142	Jeff Cirillo	.25
143	Mark McLemore	.25
144	Pat Borders	.25
145	Mike Cameron	.25
146	Dan Wilson	.25
147	John Olerud	.40
148	Arthur Rhodes	.25
149	Rafael Soriano	.25
150	Greg Colbrunn	.25
151	Ryan Franklin	.25
152	Joel Pineiro	.25
153	Jeff Nelson	.25
154	Jerry Hairston	.25
155	Rick Helling	.25
156	Gary Matthews Jr.	.25
157	Jeff Conine	.25
158	Sidney Ponson	.25
159	Tony Batista	.25
160	Jay Gibbons	.25
161	Marty Cordova	.25
162	Geronimo Gil	.25
163	Deivi Cruz	.25
164	B.J. Ryan	.25
165	Jason Johnson	.25
166	Buddy Groom	.25

167	Pat Hentgen	.25
168	Omar Daal	.25
169	Willis Roberts	.25
170	Scott Erickson	.25
171	David Segui	.25
172	Brook Fordyce	.25
173	Rodrigo Lopez	.25
174	Jose Leon	.25
175	Jose Morban	.25
176	Melvin Mora	.25
177	B.J. Surhoff	.25
178	Jorge Julio	.25
179	Alex Rodriguez	2.00
180	Mark Teixeira	.40
181	Chan Ho Park	.25
182	Todd Van Poppel	.25
183	Todd Greene	.25
184	Ismael Valdes	.25
185	Rusty Greer	.25
186	Rafael Palmeiro	.50
187	Francisco Cordero	.25
188	Einar Diaz	.25
189	Doug Glanville	.25
190	Michael Young	.25
191	Kevin Mench	.25
192	Carl Everett	.25
193	Herbert Perry	.25
194	Jeff Zimmerman	.25
195	Juan Gonzalez	.50
196	Ugueth Urbina	.25
197	Jermaine Clark	.25
198	John Thomson	.25
199	Hank Blalock	.50
200	Jay Powell	.25
201	Mike Lamb	.25
202	Aaron Fultz	.25
203	Esteban Yan	.25
204	Nomar Garciaparra	2.00
205	Pedro J. Martinez	.75
206	John Burkett	.25
207	Johnny Damon	.40
208	Doug Mirabelli	.25
209	Derek Lowe	.25
210	Shea Hillenbrand	.25
211	Brandon Lyon	.25
212	Trot Nixon	.25
213	Jason Varitek	.25
214	Tim Wakefield	.25
215	Manny Ramirez	.75
216	Todd Walker	.25
217	Jeremy Giambi	.25
218	Ramiro Mendoza	.25
219	Bill Mueller	.25
220	David Ortiz	.25
221	Mike Timlin	.25
222	Alan Embree	.25
223	Bob Howry	.25
224	Chad Fox	.25
225	Damian Jackson	.25
226	Casey Fossum	.25
227	Steve Woodard	.25
228	Freddy Sanchez	.25
229	Mike Sweeney	.25
230	Desi Relaford	.25
231	Brent Mayne	.25
232	Angel Berroa	.25
233	Albie Lopez	.25
234	Raul Ibanez	.25
235	Joe Randa	.25
236	Chris George	.25
237	Michael Tucker	.25
238	Mendy Lopez	.25
239	Kris Wilson	.25
240	Jason Grimsley	.25
241	Carlos Febles	.25
242	Runelvys Hernandez	.25
243	Mike MacDougal	.25
244	Carlos Beltran	.40
245	Brandon Berger	.25
246	Darrell May	.25
247	Miguel Asencio	.25
248	Ryan Bukvich	.25
249	Dee Brown	.25
250	Jeremy Hill	.25
251	Jeremy Affeldt	.25
252	Ken Harvey	.25
253	Bobby Higginson	.25
254	Matt Anderson	.25
255	Dmitri Young	.25
256	Gene Kingsdale	.25
257	Craig Paquette	.25
258	Adam Bernero	.25
259	Andres Torres	.25
260	Carlos Pena	.25
261	Dean Palmer	.25
262	Eric Munson	.25
263	Omar Infante	.25
264	Shane Halter	.25
265	Jeremy Bonderman	2.00
266	Steve Sparks	.25
267	Gary Knotts	.25
268	Mike Maroth	.25
269	Nate Cornejo	.25
270	Matt Roney	.25
271	Franklyn German	.25
272	Matt Walbeck	.25
273	Brandon Inge	.25
274	Hiram Bocachica	.25
275	Chris Spurling	.25
276	Craig Monroe	.25
277	Ramon Santiago	.25
278	Doug Mientkiewicz	.25
279	Torii Hunter	.50
280	Brad Radke	.25
281	Denny Hocking	.25

282	Tom Prince	.25
283	Eddie Guardado	.25
284	Jacque Jones	.25
285	Joe Mays	.25
286	Mike Fetters	.25
287	LaTroy Hawkins	.25
288	A.J. Pierzynski	.25
289	Eric Milton	.25
290	Cristian Guzman	.25
291	Bobby Kielty	.25
292	Corey Koskie	.25
293	J.C. Romero	.25
294	Mike Cuddyer	.25
295	Luis Rivas	.25
296	Matt LeCroy	.25
297	Tony Fiore	.25
298	Dustan Mohr	.25
299	Chris Gomez	.25
300	Johan Santana	.25
301	Kyle Lohse	.25
302	Frank Thomas	.75
303	Mark Buehrle	.25
304	Jon Garland	.25
305	Magglio Ordonez	.50
306	Paul Konerko	.25
307	Sandy Alomar Jr.	.25
308	Carlos Lee	.25
309	Jon Rauch	.25
310	Esteban Loaiza	.25
311	Gary Glover	.25
312	Kelly Wunsch	.25
313	Tony Graffanino	.25
314	Aaron Rowand	.25
315	Armando Rios	.25
316	Jose Valentin	.25
317	D'Angelo Jimenez	.25
318	Joe Crede	.25
319	Miguel Olivo	.25
320	Rick White	.25
321	Billy Koch	.25
322	Tom Gordon	.25
323	Bartolo Colon	.40
324	Josh Paul	.25
325	Joe Borchard	.25
326	Damaso Marte	.25
327	Derek Jeter	2.00
328	Jason Giambi	.75
329	Roger Clemens	2.00
330	Enrique Wilson	.25
331	Dave Wells	.25
332	Mike Mussina	.50
333	Bernie Williams	.50
334	Todd Zeile	.25
335	Sterling Hitchcock	.25
336	Juan Acevedo	.25
337	Robin Ventura	.25
338	Mariano Rivera	.40
339	John Flaherty	.25
340	Andy Pettitte	.50
341	Antonio Osuna	.25
342	Erick Almonte	.25
343	Chris Hammond	.25
344	Steve Karsay	.25
345	Alfonso Soriano	1.00
346	Bubba Trammell	.25
347	Nick Johnson	.25
348	Jorge Posada	.50
349	Jeff Weaver	.25
350	Raul Mondesi	.25
351	Randy Choate	.25
352	Drew Henson	.25
353	Jeff Bagwell	.75
354	Wade Miller	.25
355	Lance Berkman	.40
356	Julio Lugo	.25
357	Roy Oswalt	.40
358	Bruce Chen	.25
359	Morgan Ensberg	.25
360	Geoff Blum	.25
361	Brian Moehler	.25
362	Billy Wagner	.40
363	Peter Munro	.25
364	Brad Ausmus	.25
365	Jose Vizcaino	.25
366	Craig Biggio	.40
367	Tim Redding	.25
368	Gregg Zaun	.25
369	Octavio Dotel	.25
370	Carlos Hernandez	.25
371	Richard Hidalgo	.25
372	Jeriome Robertson	.25
373	Orlando Merced	.25
374	John Buck	.25
375	Adam Everett	.25
376	Raul Chavez	.25
377	Brad Lidge	.25
378	Jeff Kent	.40
379	Scott Linebrink	.25
380	Greg Miller	.25
381	Kirk Saarloos	.25
382	Brandon Puffer	.25
383	Ricky Stone	.25
384	Jason Lane	.25
385	Brian L. Hunter	.25
386	Rodrigo Rosario	.25
387	Horacio Ramirez	.25
388	Gary Sheffield	.50
389	Mike Hampton	.25
390	Robert Fick	.25
391	Henry Blanco	.25
392	Vinny Castilla	.25
393	Joe Dawley	.25
394	Jung Bong	.25
395	Rafael Furcal	.40
396	Javy Lopez	.40
397	Greg Maddux	1.25
398	Andruw Jones	.50
399	John Smoltz	.40
400	Chipper Jones	1.00
401	Mark DeRosa	.25
402	Shane Reynolds	.25
403	Kevin Gryboski	.25
404	Russ Ortiz	.25
405	Roberto Hernandez	.25
406	Ray King	.25
407	Matt Franco	.25
408	Marcus Giles	.25
409	Trey Hodges	.25
410	Darren Holmes	.25
411	Julio Franco	.25
412	Darren Bragg	.25
413	Richie Sexson	.50
414	Jeffrey Hammonds	.25
415	Ben Sheets	.25
416	Mike DeJean	.25
417	Royce Clayton	.25
418	Wes Helms	.25
419	Valerio de los Santos	.25
420	Brady Clark	.25
421	Glendon Rusch	.25
422	Geoff Jenkins	.40
423	John Foster	.25
424	Curtis Leskanic	.25
425	Todd Ritchie	.25
426	Enrique Cruz	.25
427	Wayne Franklin	.25
428	Matt Ford	.25
429	Matt Kinney	.25
430	Scott Podsednik	2.00
431	Luis Vizcaino	.25
432	Shane Nance	.25
433	Alex Sanchez	.25
434	John Vander Wal	.25
435	Eric Young	.25
436	Eddie Perez	.25
437	Jason Conti	.25
438	Matt Morris	.25
439	Tino Martinez	.25
440	Fernando Vina	.25
441	Kiko Calero	.25
442	Cal Eldred	.25
443	Jimmy Journell	.25
444	Jim Edmonds	.40
445	Jeff Fassero	.25
446	Mike Matheny	.25
447	Garrett Stephenson	.25
448	Brett Tomko	.25
449	So Taguchi	.25
450	Eduardo Perez	.25
451	Lance Painter	.25
452	Jason Isringhausen	.25
453	Albert Pujols	2.00
454	Eli Marrero	.25
455	Jason Simontacchi	.25
456	J.D. Drew	.25
457	Scott Rolen	.75
458	Orlando Palmeiro	.25
459	Dustin Hermanson	.25
460	Edgar Renteria	.25
461	Woody Williams	.25
462	Chris Carpenter	.25
463	Sammy Sosa	1.50
464	Kerry Wood	.75
465	Kyle Farnsworth	.25
466	Alex Gonzalez	.25
467	Eric Karros	.25
468	Troy O'Leary	.25
469	Mark Grudzielanek	.25
470	Alan Benes	.25
471	Mark Prior	1.50
472	Paul Bako	.25
473	Shawn Estes	.25
474	Matt Clement	.25
475	Ramon Martinez	.25
476	Tom Goodwin	.25
477	Corey Patterson	.25
478	Moises Alou	.40
479	Juan Cruz	.25
480	Bobby Hill	.25
481	Mark Bellhorn	.25
482	Mark Guthrie	.25
483	Mike Remlinger	.25
484	Lenny Harris	.25
485	Antonio Alfonseca	.25
486	Dave Veres	.25
487	Hee Seop Choi	.25
488	Luis Gonzalez	.40
489	Lyle Overbay	.25
490	Randy Johnson	.75
491	Mark Grace	.50
492	Danny Bautista	.25
493	Junior Spivey	.25
494	Matt Williams	.25
495	Miguel Batista	.25
496	Tony Womack	.25
497	Byung-Hyun Kim	.25
498	Steve Finley	.25
499	Craig Counsell	.25
500	Curt Schilling	.50
501	Elmer Dessens	.25
502	Rod Barajas	.25
503	David Dellucci	.25
504	Mike Koplove	.25
505	Mike Myers	.25
506	Matt Mantei	.25
507	Stephen Randolph **RC**	.40
508	Chad Moeller	.25
509	Carlos Baerga	.25
510	Andrew Good	.25
511	Quinton McCracken	.25
512	Jason Romano	.25
513	Jolbert Cabrera	.25
514	Darren Dreifort	.25
515	Kevin Brown	.40
516	Paul Quantrill	.25
517	Shawn Green	.40
518	Hideo Nomo	.40
519	Eric Gagne	.25
520	Troy Brohawn	.25
521	Kazuhisa Ishii	.25
522	Guillermo Mota	.25
523	Alex Cora	.25
524	Odalis Perez	.25
525	Brian Jordan	.25
526	Andy Ashby	.25
527	Fred McGriff	.40
528	Adrian Beltre	.40
529	Daryle Ward	.25
530	Todd Hundley	.25
531	David Ross	.25
532	Paul Shuey	.25
533	Paul LoDuca	.25
534	Dave Roberts	.25
535	Mike Kinkade	.25
536	Cesar Izturis	.25
537	Ron Coomer	.25
538	Jose Vidro	.25
539	Henry Mateo	.25
540	Tony Armas Jr.	.25
541	Joey Eischen	.25
542	Orlando Cabrera	.25
543	Jose Macias	.25
544	Fernando Tatis	.25
545	Jeff Liefer	.25
546	Michael Barrett	.25
547	Vladimir Guerrero	.75
548	Javier Vazquez	.25
549	Brad Wilkerson	.25
550	Zach Day	.25
551	Tomokazu Ohka	.25
552	Livan Hernandez	.25
553	Endy Chavez	.25
554	Dan Smith	.25
555	Scott Stewart	.25
556	T.J. Tucker	.25
557	Jamey Carroll	.25
558	Ron Calloway	.25
559	Brian Schneider	.25
560	Orlando Hernandez	.25
561	Wil Cordero	.25
562	Rocky Biddle	.25
563	Edgardo Alfonzo	.25
564	Andres Galarraga	.25
565	Felix Rodriguez	.25
566	Benito Santiago	.25
567	Jose Cruz	.25
568	Tim Worrell	.25
569	Marvin Benard	.25
570	Kurt Ainsworth	.25
571	Jim Brower	.25
572	J.T. Snow	.25
573	Scott Eyre	.25
574	Robb Nen	.25
575	Barry Bonds	2.50
576	Ray Durham	.25
577	Marquis Grissom	.25
578	Pedro Feliz	.25
579	Jason Schmidt	.25
580	Rich Aurilia	.25
581	Kirk Rueter	.25
582	Chad Zerbe	.25
583	Damian Moss	.25
584	Neifi Perez	.25
585	Joe Nathan	.25
586	Ruben Rivera	.25
587	Yorvit Torrealba	.25
588	Josh Beckett	.50
589	Todd Hollandsworth	.25
590	Derrek Lee	.25
591	A.J. Burnett	.25
592	Juan Pierre	.25
593	Mark Redman	.25
594	Blaine Neal	.25
595	Mike Mordecai	.25
596	Alex Gonzalez	.25
597	Brad Penny	.25
598	Tim Spooneybarger	.25
599	Mike Lowell	.25
600	Mike Redmond	.25
601	Braden Looper	.25
602	Ivan Rodriguez	.50
603	Andy Fox	.25
604	Vladimir Nunez	.25
605	Luis Castillo	.25
606	Juan Encarnacion	.25
607	Armando Almanza	.25
608	Gerald Williams	.25
609	Carl Pavano	.25
610	Michael Tejera	.25
611	Ramon Castro	.25
612	Brian Banks	.25
613	Roberto Alomar	.50
614	Al Leiter	.25
615	Jeromy Burnitz	.25
616	John Franco	.25
617	Tom Glavine	.40
618	Mike Piazza	1.00
619	Cliff Floyd	.25
620	Joe McEwing	.25
621	David Weathers	.25
622	Pedro Astacio	.25
623	Timoniel Perez	.25
624	Jason Phillips	.25
625	Ty Wigginton	.25
626	Steve Trachsel	.25
627	Roger Cedeno	.25
628	Tsuyoshi Shinjo	.25
629	Armando Benitez	.25
630	Vance Wilson	.25
631	Mike Stanton	.25
632	Mo Vaughn	.25
633	Scott Strickland	.25
634	Rey Sanchez	.25
635	Jay Bell	.25
636	David Cone	.25
637	Jae Weong So	.25
638	Ryan Klesko	.40
639	Wiki Gonzalez	.25
640	Trevor Hoffman	.25
641	Sean Burroughs	.25
642	Mike Bynum	.25
643	Clay Condrey	.25
644	Gary Bennett	.25
645	Kevin Jarvis	.25
646	Mark Kotsay	.25
647	Phil Nevin	.25
648	Dave Hansen	.25
649	Keith Lockhart	.25
650	Brian Lawrence	.25
651	Jay Witasick	.25
652	Rondell White	.25
653	Jaret Wright	.25
654	Luther Hackman	.25
655	Jake Peavy	.25
656	Brian Buchanan	.25
657	Mark Loretta	.25
658	Oliver Perez	.25
659	Adam Eaton	.25
660	Xavier Nady	.25
661	Jesse Orosco	.25
662	Ramon Vazquez	.25
663	Jim Thome	.75
664	Jose Mesa	.25
665	Rheal Cormier	.25
666	David Bell	.25
667	Mike Lieberthal	.25
668	Brandon Duckworth	.25
669	David Coggin	.25
670	Bobby Abreu	.40
671	Turk Wendell	.25
672	Marlon Byrd	.25
673	Jason Michaels	.25
674	Kevin Millwood	.40
675	Tomas Perez	.25
676	Jimmy Rollins	.50
677	Vicente Padilla	.25
678	Pat Burrell	.50
679	Tyler Houston	.25
680	Hector Mercado	.25
681	Carlos Silva	.25
682	Nick Punto	.25
683	Ricky Ledee	.25
684	Randy Wolf	.25
685	Todd Pratt	.25
686	Placido Polanco	.25
687	Chase Utley	1.00
688	Brian Giles	.25
689	Jason Kendall	.40
690	Matt Stairs	.25
691	Kris Benson	.25
692	Julian Tavarez	.25
693	Reggie Sanders	.25
694	Jeff D'Amico	.25
695	Pokey Reese	.25
696	Kenny Lofton	.25
697	Mike Williams	.25
698	David Williams	.25
699	Kevin Young	.25
700	Brian Boehringer	.25
701	Scott Sauerbeck	.25
702	Josh Fogg	.25
703	Joe Beimel	.25
704	Dennys Reyes	.25
705	Jeff Suppan	.25
706	Solomon Torres	.25
707	Kip Wells	.25
708	Craig Wilson	.25
709	Jack Wilson	.25
710	Robert Mackowiak	.25
711	Abraham Nunez	.25
712	Randall Simon	.25
713	Josias Manzanillo	.25
714	Ken Griffey Jr.	1.00
715	Jimmy Haynes	.25
716	Felipe Lopez	.25
717	Jimmy Anderson	.25
718	Ryan Dempster	.25
719	Russell Branyan	.25
720	Aaron Boone	.25
721	Luke Prokopec	.25
722	Felix Heredia	.25
723	Scott Sullivan	.25
724	Danny Graves	.25
725	Kent Mercker	.25
726	Barry Larkin	.40
727	Jason LaRue	.25
728	Gabe White	.25
729	Adam Dunn	.50
730	Brandon Larson	.25
731	Reggie Taylor	.25
732	Sean Casey	.25
733	Scott Williamson	.25
734	Austin Kearns	.50
735	Kelly Stinnett	.25
736	Ruben Mateo	.25
737	Wily Mo Pena	.25
738	Larry Walker	.40
439	Juan Uribe	.25
740	Denny Neagle	.25
741	Darren Oliver	.25

742 Charles Johnson .25
743 Todd Jones .25
744 Todd Helton .75
745 Shawn Chacon .25
746 Jason Jennings .25
747 Preston Wilson .25
748 Chris Richard .25
749 Chris Stynes .25
750 Jose Jimenez .25
751 Gabe Kapler .25
752 Jay Payton .25
753 Aaron Cook .25
754 Greg Norton .25
755 Scott Elarton .25
756 Brian Fuentes .25
757 Jose Hernandez .25
758 Nelson Cruz .25
759 Justin Speier .25
760 Javier Lopez .40
761 Garret Anderson .40
762 Tony Batista .25
763 Mark Buehrle .25
764 Johnny Damon .40
765 Freddy Garcia .25
766 Nomar Garciaparra .75
767 Jason Giambi .50
768 Roy Halladay .25
769 Shea Hillenbrand .25
770 Torii Hunter .40
771 Derek Jeter 1.00
772 Paul Konerko .25
773 Derek Lowe .25
774 Pedro J. Martinez .50
775 A.J. Pierzynski .25
776 Jorge Posada .40
777 Manny Ramirez .40
778 Mariano Rivera .25
779 Alex Rodriguez 1.00
780 Kazuhiro Sasaki .25
781 Alfonso Soriano .50
782 Ichiro Suzuki .50
783 Mike Sweeney .25
784 Miguel Tejada .40
785 Ugueth Urbina .25
786 Robin Ventura .25
787 Omar Vizquel .25
788 Randy Winn .25
789 Barry Zito .40
790 Lance Berkman .25
791 Barry Bonds 1.00
792 Adam Dunn .40
793 Tom Glavine .25
794 Luis Gonzalez .25
795 Shawn Green .25
796 Vladimir Guerrero .40
797 Todd Helton .40
798 Trevor Hoffman .25
799 Randy Johnson .50
800 Andruw Jones .40
801 Byung-Hyun Kim .25
802 Mike Lowell .25
803 Eric Gagne .25
804 Matt Morris .25
805 Robb Nen .25
806 Vicente Padilla .25
807 Odalis Perez .25
808 Mike Piazza .50
809 Mike Remlinger .25
810 Scott Rolen .40
811 Jimmy Rollins .50
812 Benito Santiago .25
813 Curt Schilling .40
814 Richie Sexson .40
815 John Smoltz .25
816 Sammy Sosa .75
817 Junior Spivey .25
818 Jose Vidro .25
819 Mike Williams .25
820 Luis Castillo .25
821 Jason Giambi .40
822 Luis Gonzalez .25
823 Sammy Sosa .75
824 Ken Griffey Jr. .75
825 Ken Griffey Jr. .75
826 Tino Martinez .25
827 Barry Bonds 1.00
828 Frank Thomas .40
829 Ken Griffey Jr. .75
830 Barry Bonds 1.00
831 Tim Salmon .25
832 Troy Glaus .25
833 Robb Nen .25
834 Jeff Kent .25
835 Scott Spiezio .25
836 Darin Erstad .25
837 Randy Johnson .50
838 Chipper Jones .50
839 Greg Maddux .75
840 Nomar Garciaparra .75
841 Manny Ramirez .40
842 Pedro J. Martinez .50
843 Sammy Sosa .75
844 Ken Griffey Jr. .75
845 Jim Thome .40
846 Vladimir Guerrero .50
847 Mike Piazza .50
848 Derek Jeter 1.00
849 Jason Giambi .40
850 Roger Clemens 1.00
851 Alfonso Soriano .50
852 Hideki Matsui 4.00
853 Barry Bonds 1.00
854 Ichiro Suzuki .50
855 Albert Pujols .75
856 Alex Rodriguez .75
857 Darin Erstad .25
858 Troy Glaus .25
859 Curt Schilling .25
860 Luis Gonzalez .25
861 Tom Glavine .25
862 Andruw Jones .40
863 Gary Sheffield .25
864 Frank Thomas .40
865 Mark Prior 1.00
866 Ivan Rodriguez .40
867 Jeff Bagwell .40
868 Lance Berkman .25
869 Shawn Green .25
870 Hideo Nomo .40
871 Torii Hunter .25
872 Bernie Williams .25
873 Barry Zito .25
874 Pat Burrell .25
875 Carlos Delgado .25
876 Miguel Tejada .25
877 Hideki Matsui **RC** 4.00
878 Jose Contreras **RC** 2.00
879 Jason Anderson .40
880 Jason Shiell **RC** .40
881 Kevin Tolar **RC** .40
882 Michel Hernandez **RC** .40
883 Arnie Munoz **RC** .40
884 David Sanders **RC** .40
885 Willie Eyre **RC** .40
886 Brent Hoard **RC** .40
887 Lew Ford **RC** 2.00
888 Beau Kemp **RC** .75
889 Jonathan Pridie **RC** .40
890 Mike Ryan **RC** .40
891 Richard Fischer **RC** .40
892 Luis Ayala **RC** .40
893 Mike Neu **RC** .40
894 Joe Valentine **RC** .40
895 Nate Bland **RC** .40
896 Shane Bazzell **RC** .75
897 Aquilino Lopez **RC** .40
898 Diegomar Markwell **RC** .40
899 Francisco Rosario **RC** .40
900 Guillermo Quiroz **RC** .75
901 Luis De Los Santos .40
902 Fernando Cabrera **RC** .40
903 Francisco Cruceta **RC** .40
904 Jhonny Peralta .50
905 Rett Johnson **RC** .50
906 Aaron Looper **RC** .40
907 Bobby Madritsch **RC** .40
908 Luis Matos .40
909 Jose Castillo .25
910 Chris Waters **RC** .40
911 Jeremy Guthrie .25
912 Pedro Liriano .25
913 Joe Borowski .25
914 Felix Sanchez **RC** .40
915 Jon Leicester **RC** .40
916 Todd Wellemeyer **RC** .75
917 Matt Bruback **RC** .25
918 Chris Capuano **RC** 1.50
919 Oscar Villarreal **RC** .25
920 Matt Kata **RC** .75
921 Robby Hammock **RC** .75
922 Gerald Laird .25
923 Brandon Webb **RC** 5.00
924 Tommy Whiteman **RC** .40
925 Andrew Brown **RC** .40
926 Alfredo Gonzalez **RC** .40
927 Carlos Rivera .25
928 Rick Roberts **RC** .40
929 Termel Sledge **RC** .40
930 Josh Willingham **RC** .40
931 Prentice Redman **RC** .50
932 Jeff Duncan **RC** 1.50
933 Craig Brazell **RC** 1.00
934 Jeremy Griffiths .25
935 Phil Seibel **RC** .40
936 Heath Bell **RC** .40
937 Bernie Castro **RC** .40
938 Mike Nicolas **RC** .40
939 Cory Stewart **RC** .40
940 Shane Victorino **RC** .40
941 Brandon Villafuerte **RC** .40
942 Jeremy Wedel **RC** .40
943 Tommy Phelps .25
944 Josh Hall **RC** .75
945 Ryan Cameron **RC** .40
946 Garrett Atkins .25
947 Clint Barmes **RC** .75
948 Michael Hessman **RC** .40
949 Brian Stokes **RC** .40
950 Rocco Baldelli 1.00
951 Hector Luna .25
952 Jaime Cerda .25
953 D.J. Carrasco **RC** .40
954 Ian Ferguson **RC** .40
955 Tim Olson **RC** .75
956 Alejandro Machado **RC** .40
957 Jorge Cordova **RC** .40
958 Wilfredo Ledezma **RC** .40
959 Nathan Robertson **RC** .40
960 Nook Logan **RC** .40
961 Anaheim Angels .25
962 Baltimore Orioles .25
963 Boston Red Sox .25
964 Chicago White Sox .25
965 Cleveland Indians .25
966 Detroit Tigers .25
967 Kansas City Royals .25
968 Minnesota Twins .25
969 New York Yankees .25
970 Oakland Athletics .25
971 Seattle Mariners .25
972 Tampa Bay Devil Rays .25
973 Texas Rangers .25
974 Toronto Blue Jays .25
975 Arizona Diamondbacks .25
976 Atlanta Braves .25
977 Chicago Cubs .25
978 Cincinnati Reds .25
979 Colorado Rockies .25
980 Florida Marlins .25
981 Houston Astros .25
982 Los Angeles Dodgers .25
983 Milwaukee Brewers .25
984 Montreal Expos .25
985 New York Mets .25
986 Philadelphia Phillies .25
987 Pittsburgh Pirates .25
988 San Diego Padres .25
989 San Francisco Giants .25
990 St. Louis Cardinals .25

Rainbow

Stars (1-990): 10-20X
Rookies: 4-8X
Production 40 Sets

Red, White & Blue

Stars (1-990): 1-3X
Rookies: 1-2X
#'s 1-752 Inserted 1:6
#'s 877-960 1:36

Endorsements

NM/M

Inserted 1:500
Some not priced due to scarcity.
RA Rick Ankiel 20.00
DB Dewon Brazelton/50 15.00
BD Ben Diggins 15.00
AG Alex Graman/50 15.00
KGS Ken Griffey Sr. 15.00
HI Hansel Izquierdo/50 15.00
JL Jon Lieber 15.00
CM Corwin Malone/50 15.00
TO Tomokazu Ohka 20.00

Vintage Update

NM/M

Complete Set (61): 15.00
Common Player: .40
Inserted 1:Pack
281 Tom Glavine 1.00
282 Josh Stewart .40
283 Aquilino Lopez .40
284 Horacio Ramirez .40
285 Brandon Phillips .40
286 Kirk Saarloos .40
287 Runelvys Hernandez .40
288 Hideki Matsui 5.00
289 Jeremy Bonderman 3.00
290 Russ Ortiz .40
291 Ken Harvey .40
292 Edgardo Alfonzo .40
293 Oscar Villarreal .40
294 Marlon Byrd .40
295 Josh Bard .40
296 David Cone .40
297 Mike Neu .40
298 Cliff Floyd .40
299 Travis Lee .40
300 Jeff Kent .50
301 Ron Calloway .40
302 Bartolo Colon .40
303 Jose Contreras 1.50
304 Mark Teixeira 1.00
305 Ivan Rodriguez 1.00
306 Jim Thome 1.00
307 Shane Reynolds .40
308 Luis Ayala .40
309 Lyle Overbay .40
310 Travis Hafner .40
311 Wilfredo Ledezma .40
312 Rocco Baldelli 1.50
313 Jason Anderson .40
314 Kenny Lofton .75
315 Brandon Larson .40
316 Ty Wigginton .40
317 Fred McGriff .40
318 Antonio Osuna .40
319 Corey Patterson .40
320 Erubiel Durazo .40
321 Mike MacDougal .40
322 Sammy Sosa 2.00
323 Mike Hampton .40
324 Ramiro Mendoza .40
325 Kevin Millwood .75
326 Dave Roberts .40
327 Todd Zeile .40
328 Reggie Sanders .40
329 Billy Koch .40
330 Mike Stanton .40
331 Orlando Hernandez .40
332 Tony Clark .40
333 Chris Hammond .40
334 Michael Cuddyer .40
335 Sandy Alomar .40
336 Jose Cruz Jr. .40
337 Omar Daal .40
338 Robert Fick .40
339 Daryle Ward .40
340 David Bell .40
341 Checklist .40

2003 UD Yankees Signature Series

NM/M

Complete Set (90): 65.00
Common Player: .50
Pack (3): 17.00
Box (10): 140.00
1 Al Downing .50
2 Allen Gettel .50
3 Art Ditmar .50
4 Babe Ruth 6.00
5 Bill Virdon .50
6 Billy Martin 2.00
7 Bob Cerv .50
8 Bob Turley .50
9 Bobby Cox .75
10 Bobby Richardson 1.00
11 Bobby Shantz .50
12 Bucky Dent .75
13 Bud Metheny .50
14 Casey Stengel 2.00
15 Charlie Hayes .50
16 Charlie Silvera .50
17 Chris Chambliss .50
18 Danny Cater .50
19 Dave Kingman .75
20 Dave Righetti .75
21 Dave Winfield 2.00
22 David Cone .75
23 Dick Tidrow .50
24 Doc Medich .50
25 Dock Ellis .50
26 Don Gullett .50
27 Don Mattingly 5.00
28 Dwight Gooden .75
29 Eddie Robinson .50
30 Felipe Alou .50
31 Fred Sanford .50
32 Fred Stanley .50
33 Gene Michael .50
34 Hank Bauer .50
35 Hector Lopez .50
36 Horace Clarke .50
37 Jake Gibbs .50
38 Jerry Coleman .50
39 Jerry Lumpe .50
40 Jim Bouton .50
41 Jim Kaat 1.00
42 Jim Mason .50
43 Jimmy Key .50
44 Joe DiMaggio 5.00
45 Joe Torre 1.00
46 John Montefusco .50
47 Johnny Blanchard .50
48 Johnny Callison .50
49 Lew Burdette .50
50 Johnny Kucks .50
51 Steve Balboni .50
52 Ken Singleton .50
53 Lee Mazzilli .50
54 Lou Gehrig 5.00
55 Lou Piniella 1.00
56 Luis Tiant .50
57 Marius Russo .50
58 Mel Stottlemyre .75
59 Mickey Mantle 6.00
60 Mike Pagliarulo .50
61 Mike Torrez .50
62 Miller Huggins .50
63 Norm Siebern .50
64 Paul O'Neill .75
65 Phil Niekro .50
66 Phil Rizzuto 3.00
67 Ralph Branca .50
68 Ralph Houk .50
69 Ralph Terry .50
70 Randy Gumpert .50
71 Roger Maris 5.00
72 Ron Blomberg .50
73 Ron Guidry 1.00
74 Ruben Amaro .50
75 Ryne Duren .50
76 Sam McDowell .50
77 Sparky Lyle .50
78 Thurman Munson 3.00
79 Tom Sturdivant .50
80 Tom Tresh .50
81 Tommy Byrne .50
82 Tommy Henrich .50
83 Tommy John .75

84	Tony Kubek	.75
85	Tony Lazzeri	.50
86	Virgil Trucks	.50
87	Wade Boggs	1.00
88	Whitey Ford	3.00
89	Willie Randolph	.75
90	Yogi Berra	3.00

Monumental Cuts

NM/M

30 total cards produced:

MC-JD	Joe DiMaggio/4	
MC-LG	Lou Gehrig/1	
	(6/03 Auction)	17,600
MC-MH	Miller Huggins/2	
MC-TL	Tony Lazzeri/2	
MC-MM	Mickey Mantle/1	
	(1/04 Auction)	10,000
MC-RM	Roger Maris/6	
MC-BM	Billy Martin/9	825.00
MC-TM	Thurman Munson/1	
	(3/04 Auction)	2,605
MC-BR	Babe Ruth/1	
	(4/04 Auction)	12,600
MC-CS	Casey Stengel/3	

Pinstripe Excell. Dual

NM/M

Common Dual Autograph: 20.00
Production 125 Sets

AA	Felipe Alou, Ruben Amaro	50.00
BA	Hank Bauer, Felipe Alou	50.00
BP	Wade Boggs, Mike Pagliarulo	60.00
BT	Jim Bouton, Ralph Terry	50.00
CK	Chris Chambliss, Dave Kingman	60.00
DC	Bucky Dent, Chris Chambliss	50.00
DR	Bucky Dent, Willie Randolph	80.00
DS	Ryne Duren, Tom Sturdivant	35.00
FB	Whitey Ford, Yogi Berra	150.00
GB	Jake Gibbs, Johnny Blanchard	40.00
GM	Ron Guidry, John Montefusco	80.00
GR	Ron Guidry, Willie Randolph	80.00
JK	Tommy John, Jim Kaat	60.00
LG	Sparky Lyle, Ron Guidry	75.00
LM	Jerry Lumpe, Jim Mason	25.00
MC	John Montefusco, Chris Chambliss	60.00
MK	Gene Michael, Tony Kubek	60.00
ML	Sam McDowell, Sparky Lyle	60.00
MR	Don Mattingly, Dave Righetti	150.00
NT	Phil Niekro, Luis Tiant	50.00
RB	Bobby Richardson, Hank Bauer	75.00
RC	Bobby Richardson, Jerry Coleman	50.00
SC	Ken Singleton, Jerry Coleman	
ST	Tom Sturdivant, Bob Turley	40.00
TK	Luis Tiant, Jim Kaat	50.00
TM	Mike Torrez, Lee Mazzilli	50.00
BRi	Hank Bauer, Phil Rizzuto	75.00
BRu	Tommy Byrne, Marius Russo	30.00

Pride of New York Auto.

NM/M

Common Autograph: 8.00
Inserted 1:1

JA	Jason Alexander/SP	600.00
FA	Felipe Alou	15.00
RA	Ruben Amaro	8.00
SB	Steve Balboni	8.00
HB	Hank Bauer	10.00
YB	Yogi Berra	85.00
BL	Johnny Blanchard	15.00
RBI	Ron Blomberg	10.00
WB	Wade Boggs	40.00
JB	Jim Bouton	10.00
RBr	Ralph Branca	8.00
LB	Lew Burdette	10.00
TB	Tommy Byrne	10.00
CAS	Johnny Callison	8.00
CAL	Brian Cashman/SP	250.00
DC	Danny Cater	8.00
CE	Bob Cerv	8.00
CC	Chris Chambliss	12.00
HC	Horace Clarke	10.00
JC	Jerry Coleman	10.00
CO	David Cone	25.00
CX	Bobby Cox	12.00
DE	Bucky Dent	12.00
DI	Art Ditmar	10.00
AD	Al Downing	10.00
BD	Brian Doyle	8.00
RD	Ryne Duren	10.00
EL	Dock Ellis	10.00
WF	Whitey Ford	50.00
AG	Allen Gettel	8.00
JG	Jake Gibbs	8.00
GO	Dwight Gooden	15.00
JO	John Goodman	300.00
RaG	Ron Guidry	15.00
DG	Don Gullett	8.00
RoG	Randy Gumpert	8.00
CH	Charlie Hayes	10.00
TH	Tommy Henrich	30.00
RH	Ralph Houk	12.00
TJ	Tommy John	10.00
JK	Jim Kaat	15.00
KE	Jimmy Key	15.00
DK	Dave Kingman	15.00
TK	Tony Kubek	25.00
KU	Johnny Kucks	10.00
HL	Hector Lopez	10.00
JL	Jerry Lumpe	8.00
SL	Sparky Lyle	10.00
JM	Jim Mason	8.00
MA	Don Mattingly	80.00
LM	Lee Mazzilli	10.00
SM	Sam McDowell	8.00
DM	Doc Medich	10.00
GM	Gene Michael	10.00
MO	John Montefusco	8.00
PN	Phil Niekro	15.00
PO	Paul O'Neill/SP	25.00
MP	Mike Pagliarulo	8.00
LP	Lou Piniella/SP	20.00
WR	Willie Randolph/SP	15.00
HR	Hal Reniff	10.00
BR	Bobby Richardson	15.00
DR	Dave Righetti	15.00
PR	Phil Rizzuto	40.00
ER	Eddie Robinson	8.00
MR	Marius Russo	10.00
FS	Fred Sanford	8.00
BS	Bobby Shantz	10.00
NS	Norm Siebern	8.00
CS	Charlie Silvera	10.00
KS	Ken Singleton	10.00
ST	Fred Stanley	8.00
MS	Mel Stottlemyre	15.00
TS	Tom Sturdivant	8.00
RT	Ralph Terry	10.00
LT	Luis Tiant	10.00
DT	Dick Tidrow	10.00
JT	Joe Torre	35.00
MT	Mike Torrez	8.00
TT	Tom Tresh	15.00
VT	Virgil Trucks	10.00
BT	Bob Turley	12.00
BV	Bill Virdon	8.00
DW	Dave Winfield/SP	75.00
JW	Jim Wynn	8.00
DZ	Don Zimmer	40.00

Yankees Forever Triple

NM/M

Common Triple Auto.:
Production 50 Sets

ALB	Felipe Alou, Hector Lopez, Hank Bauer	120.00
AOM	Felipe Alou, Paul O'Neill, Lee Mazzilli	150.00
BSB	Yogi Berra, Bobby Shantz, Hank Bauer	200.00
DFB	Al Downing, Whitey Ford, Yogi Berra	240.00
DRC	Bucky Dent, Willie Randolph, Chris Chambliss	125.00
EMG	Dock Ellis, Doc Medich, Don Gullett	125.00
FKB	Whitey Ford, Johnny Kucks, Jim Bouton	150.00
GCK	Dwight Gooden, David Cone, Jimmy Key	150.00
GRJ	Ron Guidry, Dave Righetti, Tommy John	150.00
HMC	Ralph Houk, Gene Michael, Bobby Cox	150.00
HRB	Tommy Henrich, Phil Rizzuto, Ralph Branca	150.00
JKL	Tommy John, Jim Kaat, Sparky Lyle	120.00
KCC	Dave Kingman, Chris Chambliss, Danny Cater	120.00
KGT	Jim Kaat, Don Gullett, Mike Torrez	120.00
KJB	Jim Kaat, Tommy John, Jim Bouton	120.00
MTT	John Montefusco, Mike Torrez, Dick Tidrow	120.00
OBK	Paul O'Neill, Wade Boggs, Jimmy Key	175.00
PTV	Lou Piniella, Joe Torre, Bill Virdon	150.00
RBC	Phil Rizzuto, Yogi Berra, Jerry Coleman	220.00
RKD	Phil Rizzuto, Tony Kubek, Bucky Dent	150.00
RRC	Bobby Richardson, Willie Randolph, Jerry Coleman	150.00
RSB	Marius Russo, Tom Sturdivant, Tommy Byrne	120.00
SSB	Fred Stanley, Charlie Silvera, Johnny Blanchard	120.00
STE	Mel Stottlemyre, Luis Tiant, Dock Ellis	120.00
TCO	Joe Torre, David Cone, Paul O'Neill	175.00
TLN	Luis Tiant, Sparky Lyle, Phil Niekro	120.00
TMT	Luis Tiant, Sam McDowell, Ralph Terry	120.00
WHM	Dave Winfield, Tommy Henrich, Lee Mazzilli	160.00
WMG	Dave Winfield, Don Mattingly, Ron Guidry	300.00
WPC	Dave Winfield, Lou Piniella, Chris Chambliss	100.00

2003 Upper Deck Yankees 100th Anniversary

NM/M

Complete Set (30):		15.00
Common Player:		.50
1	Babe Ruth	2.00
2	Tony Lazzeri	.50
3	Lou Gehrig	1.50
4	Lou Gehrig	1.50
5	Red Rolfe	.50
6	Lou Gehrig	1.50
7	Bill Dickey	.50
8	Joe DiMaggio	1.50
9	Charlie Keller	.50
10	Frank Crosetti	.50
11	Phil Rizzuto	.50
12	Joe DiMaggio	1.50
13	Joe DiMaggio	1.50
14	Phil Rizzuto	.50
15	Mickey Mantle	2.00
16	Yogi Berra	.75
17	Yogi Berra	.75
18	Mickey Mantle	2.00
19	Whitey Ford	.50
20	Mickey Mantle	2.00
21	Thurman Munson	.75
22	Thurman Munson	.75
23	Bernie Williams	.50
24	Jorge Posada	.50
25	Mariano Rivera	.50
26	Derek Jeter	1.50
27	Hideki Matsui	1.00
28	Hideki Matsui	1.00
29	Roger Clemens	1.50
30	Yankee Stadium	.50

2004 Upper Deck

NM/M

Complete Set (540):		75.00
Common Player:		.15
Hobby Pack (8):		2.00
Hobby Box (24):		40.00
1	Dontrelle Willis	.40
2	Edgar Gonzalez	.15
3	Jose Reyes	.50
4	Jae Weong Seo	.15
5	Miguel Cabrera	.25
6	Jesse Foppert	.15
7	Mike Neu	.15
8	Micheal Nakamura	.15
9	Luis Ayala	.15
10	Jared Sandberg	.15
11	Jhonny Peralta	.15
12	Wilfredo Ledezma	.15
13	Jason Roach	.15
14	Kirk Saarloos	.15
15	Cliff Lee	.15
16	Bobby Hill	.15
17	Lyle Overbay	.15
18	Josh Hall	.15
19	Joe Thurston	.15
20	Matt Kata	.15
21	Jeremy Bonderman	.15
22	Julio Manon	.15
23	Rodrigo Rosario	.15
24	Robby Hammock	.15
25	David Sanders	.15
26	Miguel Ojeda	.15
27	Mark Teixeira	.25
28	Franklyn German	.15
29	Ken Harvey	.15
30	Xavier Nady	.15
31	Tim Salmon	.25
32	Troy Glaus	.40
33	Adam Kennedy	.15
34	David Eckstein	.15
35	Bengie Molina	.15
36	Jarrod Washburn	.15
37	Ramon Ortiz	.15
38	Eric Chavez	.15
39	Miguel Tejada	.25
40	Chris Singleton	.15
41	Jermaine Dye	.15
42	John Halama	.15
43	Tim Hudson	.40
44	Barry Zito	.40
45	Ted Lilly	.15
46	Bobby Kielty	.15
47	Kelvim Escobar	.15
48	Josh Phelps	.15
49	Vernon Wells	.15
50	Roy Halladay	.25
51	Orlando Hudson	.15
52	Eric Hinske	.15
53	Brandon Backe	.15
54	Dewon Brazelton	.15
55	Ben Grieve	.15
56	Aubrey Huff	.15
57	Toby Hall	.15
58	Rocco Baldelli	.40
59	Al Martin	.15
60	Brandon Phillips	.15
61	Omar Vizquel	.25
62	C.C. Sabathia	.15
63	Milton Bradley	.15
64	Ricky Gutierrez	.15
65	Matt Lawton	.15
66	Danys Baez	.15
67	Ichiro Suzuki	1.00
68	Randy Winn	.15
69	Carlos Guillen	.15
70	Mark McLemore	.15
71	Dan Wilson	.15
72	Jamie Moyer	.15
73	Joel Pineiro	.15
74	Edgar Martinez	.25
75	Tony Batista	.15
76	Jay Gibbons	.15
77	Jeff Conine	.15
78	Melvin Mora	.15
79	Geronimo Gil	.15
80	Rodrigo Lopez	.15
81	Jorge Julio	.15
82	Rafael Palmeiro	.50
83	Juan Gonzalez	.40
84	Mike Young	.15
85	Alex Rodriguez	1.50
86	Einar Diaz	.15
87	Kevin Mench	.15
88	Hank Blalock	.40
89	Pedro J. Martinez	.75
90	Byung-Hyun Kim	.15
91	Derek Lowe	.25
92	Jason Varitek	.15
93	Manny Ramirez	.50
94	John Burkett	.15
95	Todd Walker	.15
96	Nomar Garciaparra	1.50
97	Trot Nixon	.15
98	Mike Sweeney	.15
99	Carlos Febles	.15
100	Mike MacDougal	.15
101	Raul Ibanez	.15
102	Jason Grimsley	.15
103	Chris George	.15
104	Brent Mayne	.15
105	Dmitri Young	.15
106	Eric Munson	.15
107	A.J. Hinch	.15
108	Andres Torres	.15
109	Bobby Higginson	.15
110	Shane Halter	.15
111	Matt Walbeck	.15
112	Torii Hunter	.40
113	Doug Mientkiewicz	.15
114	Lew Ford	.15
115	Eric Milton	.15
116	Eddie Guardado	.15
117	Cristian Guzman	.15
118	Corey Koskie	.15
119	Magglio Ordonez	.40
120	Mark Buehrle	.15
121	Billy Koch	.15

122	Jose Valentin	.15
123	Paul Konerko	.15
124	Carlos Lee	.15
125	Jon Garland	.15
126	Jason Giambi	.75
127	Derek Jeter	1.50
128	Roger Clemens	1.50
129	Andy Pettitte	.40
130	Jorge Posada	.40
131	David Wells	.15
132	Hideki Matsui	1.50
133	Mike Mussina	.50
134	Jeff Bagwell	.50
135	Craig Biggio	.25
136	Morgan Ensberg	.15
137	Richard Hidalgo	.15
138	Brad Ausmus	.15
139	Roy Oswalt	.25
140	Billy Wagner	.25
141	Octavio Dotel	.15
142	Gary Sheffield	.40
143	Andruw Jones	.40
144	John Smoltz	.25
145	Rafael Furcal	.25
146	Javy Lopez	.25
147	Shane Reynolds	.15
148	Horacio Ramirez	.15
149	Mike Hampton	.15
150	Jung Bong	.15
151	Ruben Quevedo	.15
152	Ben Sheets	.15
153	Geoff Jenkins	.25
154	Royce Clayton	.15
155	Glendon Rusch	.15
156	John Vander Wal	.15
157	Scott Podsednik	.40
158	Jim Edmonds	.40
159	Tino Martinez	.15
160	Albert Pujols	1.50
161	Matt Morris	.15
162	Woody Williams	.15
163	Edgar Renteria	.15
164	Jason Isringhausen	.15
165	Jason Simontacchi	.15
166	Kerry Robinson	.15
167	Sammy Sosa	1.25
168	Joe Borowski	.15
169	Tony Womack	.15
170	Antonio Alfonseca	.15
171	Corey Patterson	.15
172	Mark Prior	1.00
173	Moises Alou	.25
174	Matt Clement	.15
175	Randall Simon	.15
176	Randy Johnson	.75
177	Luis Gonzalez	.25
178	Craig Counsell	.15
179	Miguel Batista	.15
180	Steve Finley	.15
181	Brandon Webb	.15
182	Danny Bautista	.15
183	Oscar Villarreal	.15
184	Shawn Green	.25
185	Brian Jordan	.15
186	Fred McGriff	.25
187	Andy Ashby	.15
188	Rickey Henderson	.50
189	Dave Roberts	.15
190	Eric Gagne	.15
191	Kazuhisa Ishii	.15
192	Adrian Beltre	.15
193	Vladimir Guerrero	.75
194	Livan Hernandez	.15
195	Ron Calloway	.15
196	Sun-Woo Kim	.15
197	Wil Cordero	.15
198	Brad Wilkerson	.15
199	Orlando Cabrera	.15
200	Barry Bonds	2.00
201	Ray Durham	.15
202	Andres Galarraga	.15
203	Benito Santiago	.15
204	Jose Cruz Jr.	.15
205	Jason Schmidt	.15
206	Kirk Rueter	.15
207	Felix Rodriguez	.15
208	Mike Lowell	.15
209	Luis Castillo	.15
210	Derrek Lee	.25
211	Andy Fox	.15
212	Tommy Phelps	.15
213	Todd Hollandsworth	.15
214	Brad Penny	.15
215	Juan Pierre	.15
216	Mike Piazza	1.00
217	Jae Weong Seo	.15
218	Ty Wigginton	.15
219	Al Leiter	.15
220	Roger Cedeno	.15
221	Timoniel Perez	.15
222	Aaron Heilman	.15
223	Pedro Astacio	.15
224	Joe McEwing	.15
225	Ryan Klesko	.15
226	Brian Giles	.25
227	Mark Kotsay	.15
228	Brian Lawrence	.15
229	Rod Beck	.15
230	Trevor Hoffman	.15
231	Sean Burroughs	.15
232	Bobby Abreu	.25
233	Jim Thome	.50
234	David Bell	.15
235	Jimmy Rollins	.25
236	Mike Lieberthal	.15
237	Vicente Padilla	.15
238	Randy Wolf	.15
239	Reggie Sanders	.15
240	Jason Kendall	.15
241	Jack Wilson	.15
242	Jose Hernandez	.15
243	Kip Wells	.15
244	Carlos Rivera	.15
245	Craig Wilson	.15
246	Adam Dunn	.40
247	Sean Casey	.15
248	Danny Graves	.15
249	Ryan Dempster	.15
250	Barry Larkin	.40
251	Reggie Taylor	.15
252	Wily Mo Pena	.15
253	Larry Walker	.25
254	Mark Sweeney	.15
255	Preston Wilson	.15
256	Jason Jennings	.15
257	Charles Johnson	.15
258	Jay Payton	.15
259	Chris Stynes	.15
260	Juan Uribe	.15
261	Hideki Matsui	1.00
262	Barry Bonds	1.00
263	Dontrelle Willis	.25
264	Kevin Millwood	.15
265	Billy Wagner	.15
266	Rocco Baldelli	.25
267	Roger Clemens	.75
268	Rafael Palmeiro	.25
269	Miguel Cabrera	.25
270	Jose Contreras	.15
271	Aaron Sele	.15
272	Bartolo Colon	.25
273	Darin Erstad	.25
274	Francisco Rodriguez	.15
275	Garret Anderson	.40
276	Jose Guillen	.15
277	Troy Percival	.15
278	Alex Cintron	.15
279	Casey Fossum	.15
280	Elmer Dessens	.15
281	Jose Valverde	.15
282	Matt Mantei	.15
283	Richie Sexson	.40
284	Roberto Alomar	.40
285	Shea Hillenbrand	.15
286	Chipper Jones	.75
287	Greg Maddux	1.00
288	J.D. Drew	.25
289	Marcus Giles	.15
290	Mike Hessman	.15
291	John Thomson	.15
292	Russ Ortiz	.15
293	Adam Loewen	.15
294	Jack Cust	.15
295	Jerry Hairston	.15
296	Kurt Ainsworth	.15
297	Luis Matos	.15
298	Marty Cordova	.15
299	Sidney Ponson	.15
300	Bill Mueller	.15
301	Curt Schilling	.50
302	David Ortiz	.50
303	Johnny Damon	.25
304	Keith Foulke	.15
305	Pokey Reese	.15
306	Scott Williamson	.15
307	Tim Wakefield	.15
308	Alex Gonzalez	.15
309	Aramis Ramirez	.40
310	Carlos Zambrano	.40
311	Juan Cruz	.15
312	Kerry Wood	.75
313	Kyle Farnsworth	.15
314	Aaron Rowand	.15
315	Esteban Loaiza	.15
316	Frank Thomas	.50
317	Joe Borchard	.15
318	Joe Crede	.15
319	Miguel Olivo	.15
320	Willie Harris	.15
321	Aaron Harang	.15
322	Austin Kearns	.25
323	Brandon Claussen	.15
324	Brandon Larson	.15
325	Ryan Freel	.15
326	Ken Griffey Jr.	1.00
327	Ryan Wagner	.15
328	Alex Escobar	.15
329	Coco Crisp	.15
330	David Riske	.15
331	Jody Gerut	.15
332	Josh Bard	.15
333	Travis Hafner	.25
334	Chin-Hui Tsao	.15
335	Denny Stark	.15
336	Jeromy Burnitz	.15
337	Shawn Chacon	.15
338	Todd Helton	.50
339	Vinny Castilla	.15
340	Alex Sanchez	.15
341	Carlos Pena	.15
342	Fernando Vina	.15
343	Jason Johnson	.15
344	Matt Anderson	.15
345	Mike Maroth	.15
346	Rondell White	.15
347	A.J. Burnett	.15
348	Alex Gonzalez	.15
349	Armando Benitez	.15
350	Carl Pavano	.15
351	Hee Seop Choi	.15
352	Ivan Rodriguez	.50
353	Josh Beckett	.50
354	Josh Willingham	.15
355	Adam Everett	.15
356	Brandon Duckworth	.15
357	Jason Lane	.15
358	Jeff Kent	.25
359	Jeriome Robertson	.15
360	Lance Berkman	.25
361	Wade Miller	.15
362	Aaron Guiel	.15
363	Angel Berroa	.15
364	Carlos Beltran	.50
365	David DeJesus	.15
366	Desi Relaford	.15
367	Joe Randa	.15
368	Runelvys Hernandez	.15
369	Edwin Jackson	.15
370	Hideo Nomo	.40
371	Jeff Weaver	.15
372	Juan Encarnacion	.15
373	Odalis Perez	.15
374	Paul LoDuca	.15
375	Robin Ventura	.15
376	Bill Hall	.15
377	Chad Moeller	.15
378	Chris Capuano	.15
379	Junior Spivey	.15
380	Rickie Weeks	.25
381	Wes Helms	.15
382	Brad Radke	.15
383	Jacque Jones	.15
384	Joe Mays	.15
385	Joe Nathan	.15
386	Johan Santana	.15
387	Nick Punto	.15
388	Shannon Stewart	.15
389	Carl Everett	.15
390	Claudio Vargas	.15
391	Jose Vidro	.15
392	Nick Johnson	.15
393	Rocky Biddle	.15
394	Tony Armas	.15
395	Braden Looper	.15
396	Cliff Floyd	.15
397	Jason Phillips	.15
398	Mike Cameron	.15
399	Tom Glavine	.40
400	Kenny Lofton	.25
401	Alfonso Soriano	.50
402	Bernie Williams	.40
403	Javier Vazquez	.15
404	Jon Lieber	.15
405	Jose Contreras	.15
406	Kevin Brown	.25
407	Mariano Rivera	.25
408	Arthur Rhodes	.15
409	Eric Byrnes	.15
410	Erubiel Durazo	.15
411	Graham Koonce	.15
412	Marco Scutaro	.15
413	Mark Mulder	.15
414	Mark Redman	.15
415	Rich Harden	.15
416	Brett Myers	.15
417	Chase Utley	.40
418	Kevin Millwood	.25
419	Marlon Byrd	.15
420	Pat Burrell	.25
421	Placido Polanco	.15
422	Tim Worrell	.15
423	Jason Bay	.15
424	Josh Fogg	.15
425	Kris Benson	.15
426	Mike Gonzalez	.15
427	Oliver Perez	.15
428	Tike Redman	.15
429	Adam Eaton	.15
430	Ismael Valdez	.15
431	Jake Peavy	.15
432	Khalil Greene	.15
433	Mark Loretta	.15
434	Phil Nevin	.15
435	Ramon Hernandez	.15
436	A.J. Pierzynski	.15
437	Edgardo Alfonzo	.15
438	J.T. Snow	.15
439	Jerome Williams	.15
440	Marquis Grissom	.15
441	Robb Nen	.15
442	Bret Boone	.25
443	Freddy Garcia	.15
444	Gil Meche	.15
445	John Olerud	.25
446	Rich Aurilia	.15
447	Shigetoshi Hasegawa	.15
448	Bo Hart	.15
449	Dan Haren	.15
450	Jason Marquis	.15
451	Marlon Anderson	.15
452	Scott Rolen	.75
453	So Taguchi	.15
454	Carl Crawford	.15
455	Delmon Young	.25
456	Geoff Blum	.15
457	Jesus Colome	.15
458	Jonny Gomes	.15
459	Lance Carter	.15
460	Robert Fick	.15
461	Chan Ho Park	.15
462	Francisco Cordero	.15
463	Jeff Nelson	.15
464	Jeff Zimmerman	.15
465	Kenny Rogers	.15
466	Aquilino Lopez	.15
467	Carlos Delgado	.50
468	Frank Catalanotto	.15
469	Reed Johnson	.15
470	Pat Hentgen	.15
471	Curt Schilling	.25
472	Gary Sheffield	.25
473	Javier Vazquez	.15
474	Kazuo Matsui	1.00
475	Kevin Brown	.25
476	Rafael Palmeiro	.25
477	Richie Sexson	.25
478	Roger Clemens	.75
479	Vladimir Guerrero	.50
480	Alex Rodriguez	1.00
481	Jake Woods	.25
482	Tim Bittner	.25
483	Brandon Medders	.50
484	Casey Daigle	.25
485	Jerry Gil	.25
486	Mike Gosling	.25
487	Jose Capellan	1.00
488	Onil Joseph	.25
489	Roman Colon	.25
490	David Crouthers	.25
491	Eddy Rodriguez	.25
492	Franklyn Gracesqui	.50
493	Jamie Brown	.25
494	Jerome Gamble	.25
495	Tim Hamulack	.25
496	Carlos Vasquez	.25
497	Renyel Pinto	.50
498	Ronny Cedeno	.25
499	Enemencio Pacheco	.25
500	Ryan Meaux	.25
501	Ryan Wing	.25
502	Shingo Takatsu	1.00
503	William Bergolla	.25
504	Ivan Ochoa	.25
505	Mariano Gomez	.25
506	Justin Hampson	.25
507	Justin Huisman	.25
508	Scott Dohmann	.25
509	Donnie Kelly	.50
510	Chris Aguila	.25
511	Lincoln Holdzkom **RC**	.25
512	Freddy Guzman	.25
513	Hector Gimenez	.25
514	Jorge Vasquez	.25
515	Jason Frasor	.25
516	Chris Saenz	.50
517	Dennis Sarfate	.25
518	Colby Miller	.25
519	Jason Bartlett	.25
520	Chad Bentz	.25
521	Josh Labandeira	.25
522	Shawn Hill	.25
523	Kazuo Matsui **RC**	3.00
524	Carlos Hines	.25
525	Michael Vento	2.00
526	Scott Proctor	.50
527	Sean Henn	.50
528	David Aardsma	.25
529	Ian Snell	.50
530	Mike Johnson	.25
531	Akinori Otsuka	.75
532	Rusty Tucker	.25
533	Justin Knoedler	.25
534	Merkin Valdez	1.00
535	Greg Dobbs	.25
536	Justin Leone	.25
537	Shawn Camp	.25
538	Edwin Moreno	.25
539	Angel Chavez	.25
540	Jesse Harper	.25
Reflections Update Set (50):		30.00
341	Shingo Takatsu	3.00
342	Franklyn Gracesqui	.75
343	Angel Chavez	.75
344	Jorge Sequea	.75
345	David Aardsma	.75
346	Ramon Ramirez **RC**	.75
347	Lino Urdaneta	.75
348	Orlando Rodriguez	.75
349	Jason Szuminski	.75
350	Luis Gonzalez	.75
351	John Gall	1.00
352	Kevin Cave	.75
353	Chris Oxspring	.75
354	Freddy Guzman	.75
355	Jeff Bennett	.75
356	Jorge Vasquez	.75
357	Merkin Valdez	2.00
358	Tim Hamulack	.75
359	Hector Gimenez	.75
360	Jerry Gil	.75
361	Ryan Wing	.75
362	Shawn Hill	.75
363	Jason Bartlett	.75
364	Renyel Pinto	.75
365	Carlos Vasquez	.75
366	Mike Vento	1.50
367	Casey Daigle	.75
368	Chad Bentz	1.00
369	Chris Saenz	.75
370	Shawn Camp	.75
371	Carlos Hines	.75
372	Edwin Moreno	.75
373	Mike Wuertz	.75
374	Aarom Baldiris **RC**	1.50
375	Ronny Cedeno	.75
376	Akinori Otsuka	1.50
377	Jose Capellan	2.00
378	Justin Germano	.75
379	Justin Knoedler	.75
380	Mariano Gomez	.75

#	Player	Price
381	Fernando Nieve	1.50
382	Scott Proctor	.75
383	Roman Colon	.75
384	Onil Joseph	.75
385	Eddy Rodriguez	.75
386	Enemencio Pacheco	.75
387	William Bergolla	.75
388	Ivan Ochoa	.75
389	Rusty Tucker	.75
390	Roberto Novoa	.75

SPGU Patch Edition Update
Set (50): 85.00

#	Player	Price
121	Richie Sexson	3.00
122	Javier Vazquez	2.00
123	Alex Rodriguez	8.00
124	Javy Lopez	3.00
125	Miguel Tejada	3.00
126	Bartolo Colon	2.00
127	Ivan Rodriguez	4.00
128	Rafael Palmeiro	3.00
129	Kevin Brown	3.00
130	Gary Sheffield	3.00
131	Greg Maddux	5.00
132	Curt Schilling	4.00
133	Roger Clemens	8.00
134	Alfonso Soriano	3.00
135	Vladimir Guerrero	4.00
136	Carlos Vasquez	2.00
137	Roman Colon	2.00
138	William Bergolla	2.00
139	Jason Bartlett	2.00
140	Casey Daigle	2.00
141	Ryan Wing	2.00
142	Chris Saenz	2.00
143	Edwin Moreno	2.00
144	Shawn Hill	2.00
145	Eddy Rodriguez	2.00
146	Justin Knoedler	2.00
147	Renyel Pinto	2.00
148	Kevin Cave	2.00
149	Carlos Hines	2.00
150	Merkin Valdez RC	4.00
151	Tim Hamulack RC	2.00
152	Hector Gimenez RC	2.00
153	Mike Vento RC	5.00
154	Scott Proctor RC	3.00
155	Rusty Tucker RC	2.00
156	Akinori Otsuka RC	4.00
157	Ronny Cedeno RC	2.00
158	Jose Capellan RC	6.00
159	Justin Germano	2.00
160	Shingo Takatsu RC	5.00
161	Fernando Nieve	2.00
162	Mike Wuertz	2.00
163	Jerry Gil	2.00
164	Jorge Vasquez	2.00
165	Chad Bentz	4.00
166	Luis Gonzalez	2.00
167	Ivan Ochoa	2.00
168	Onil Joseph	2.00
169	Enemencio Pacheco	2.00
170	Kazuo Matsui RC	8.00

Play Ball Update Set (50): 20.00

#	Player	Price
183	Kazuo Matsui RC	3.00
184	Jerry Gil	.50
185	Jose Capellan RC	2.00
186	Tim Hamulack	.50
187	Renyel Pinto	.50
188	Carlos Vasquez	.50
189	Enemencio Pacheco	.50
190	Ronny Cedeno	.50
191	Mariano Gomez	.50
192	Carlos Hines	.50
193	Michael Vento	.50
194	David Aardsma	.50
195	Hector Gimenez	.50
196	Fernando Nieve	.50
197	Chris Saenz	.50
198	Shawn Hill	.50
199	Angel Chavez	.50
200	Scott Proctor	.50
201	William Bergolla	.50
202	Justin Germano	.50
203	Onil Joseph	.50
204	Rusty Tucker	.50
205	Justin Knoedler	.50
206	Casey Daigle	.50
207	Edwin Moreno	.50
208	Chad Bentz	.50
209	Ryan Wing	.50
210	Shawn Camp	.50
211	Eddy Rodriguez	.50
212	Roman Colon	.50
213	Jason Bartlett	.50
214	Jorge Vasquez	.50
215	Ivan Ochoa	.50
216	Akinori Otsuka	.50
217	Merkin Valdez RC	2.00
218	Shingo Takatsu RC	2.00
219	Chris Oxspring	.50
220	Kevin Cave	.50
221	Ramon Ramirez	.50
222	Orlando Rodriguez	.50
223	Lino Urdaneta	.50
224	Franklyn Gracesqui	.50
225	Mike Wuertz	.50
226	Jorge Sequea	.50
227	Luis Gonzalez	.50
228	Jason Szuminski	.50
229	John Gall	.50
230	Freddy Guzman	.50
231	Jeff Bennett	.50
232	Roberto Novoa	.50

Vintage Update Set (50): 10.00

#	Player	Price
451	Alex Rodriguez	1.50
452	Javy Lopez	.40
453	Alfonso Soriano	.50
454	Vladimir Guerrero	.50
455	Rafael Palmeiro	.50
456	Gary Sheffield	.50
457	Curt Schilling	.50
458	Miguel Tejada	.50
459	Kevin Brown	.40
460	Richie Sexson	.50
461	Roger Clemens	1.50
462	Javier Vazquez	.25
463	Bartolo Colon	.25
464	Ivan Rodriguez	.50
465	Greg Maddux	1.00
466	Jamie Brown	.25
467	David Crouthers	.25
468	Jason Frasor	.25
469	Greg Dobbs	.25
470	Jesse Harper	.25
471	Nick Regilio RC	.25
472	Ryan Wing	.25
473	Akinori Otsuka RC	1.00
474	Shingo Takatsu RC	1.50
475	Kazuo Matsui RC	3.00
476	Michael Vento RC	1.00
477	Mike Gosling	.25
478	Justin Huisman	.25
479	Justin Hampson	.25
480	Dennis Sarfate	.25
481	Ian Snell RC	1.50
482	Tim Bausher RC	.25
483	Donnie Kelly	.25
484	Jerome Gamble	.25
485	Mike Rouse	.50
486	Merkin Valdez RC	.75
487	Lincoln Holdzkom RC	.25
488	Justin Leone RC	.25
489	Sean Henn	.25
490	Brandon Medders RC	.25
491	Mike Johnston RC	.25
492	Tim Bittner	.25
493	Mike Wuertz	.25
494	Chad Bentz	.50
495	Ryan Meaux RC	.25
496	Chris Aguila RC	.25
497	Jake Woods RC	.25
498	Scott Dohmann RC	.25
499	Colby Miller	.25
500	Josh Labandeira	.25

2004 Upper Deck Glossy

NM/M
Complete Factory Set (590): 85.00
Glossy: 1-2X
Issued only in factory sets.

Authentic Stars Jersey

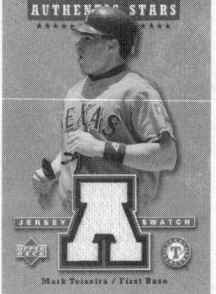

NM/M
Common Player: 4.00
Inserted 1:48
Golds: 1-2X
Production 100 Sets

BA	Bobby Abreu	6.00
RO	Roberto Alomar	6.00
JB	Jeff Bagwell	6.00
RB	Rocco Baldelli	10.00
JH	Josh Beckett	5.00
HB	Hank Blalock	5.00
EC	Eric Chavez	4.00
RC	Roger Clemens	15.00
CD	Carlos Delgado	5.00
JD	J.D. Drew	4.00
DE	Darin Erstad	4.00
JG	Jason Giambi	8.00
TG	Troy Glaus	5.00
TL	Tom Glavine	6.00
VG	Vladimir Guerrero	8.00
SG	Shawn Green	5.00
KG	Ken Griffey Jr.	15.00
TH	Todd Helton	8.00
TO	Torii Hunter	6.00
RJ	Randy Johnson	8.00
AJ	Andruw Jones	8.00
CJ	Chipper Jones	8.00
JK	Jeff Kent	4.00
GM	Greg Maddux	10.00
PM	Pedro J. Martinez	8.00
TM	Tino Martinez	4.00
HM	Hideki Matsui	35.00
PN	Phil Nevin	4.00
MI	Mike Piazza	10.00
MP	Mark Prior	10.00
AP	Albert Pujols	15.00
AR	Alex Rodriguez	12.00
IR	Ivan Rodriguez	8.00
CS	Curt Schilling	5.00
AS	Alfonso Soriano	10.00
SS	Sammy Sosa	12.00
IS	Ichiro Suzuki	30.00
MT	Mark Teixeira	8.00
FT	Frank Thomas	8.00
LW	Larry Walker	4.00
BW	Bernie Williams	6.00
BZ	Barry Zito	6.00

Awesome Honors

NM/M
Complete Set (10): 15.00

#	Player	Price
1	Albert Pujols	5.00
2	Alex Rodriguez	5.00
3	Angel Berroa	5.00
4	Dontrelle Willis	1.00
5	Eric Gagne	1.50
6	Garret Anderson	1.00
7	Ivan Rodriguez	1.50
8	Josh Beckett	1.50
9	Mariano Rivera	1.00
10	Roy Halladay	.75

Awesome Honors Jersey

NM/M
Golds: 1.5-2X
Production 165

GA	Garret Anderson	5.00
JB	Josh Beckett	6.00
BB	Bret Boone	5.00
MC	Mike Cameron	4.00
LC	Luis Castillo	4.00
EC	Eric Chavez	5.00
JE	Jim Edmonds	6.00
EG	Eric Gagne	12.00
EG1	Eric Gagne	12.00
JG	Jason Giambi	8.00
VG	Vladimir Guerrero	8.00
RH	Roy Halladay	5.00
MH	Mike Hampton	4.00
TH	Todd Helton	6.00
HU	Torii Hunter	6.00
AJ	Andruw Jones	6.00
DL	Derrek Lee	5.00
EM	Edgar Martinez	5.00
BM	Bengie Molina	4.00
JM	Jamie Moyer	4.00
MU	Mike Mussina	8.00
JO	John Olerud	5.00
MO	Maggio Ordonez	5.00
AP	Albert Pujols	10.00
AP2	Albert Pujols	10.00
MR	Mariano Rivera	5.00
AR	Alex Rodriguez	10.00
AR3	Alex Rodriguez	10.00
IR	Ivan Rodriguez	8.00
SR	Scott Rolen	8.00
JS	John Smoltz	5.00
AS	Alfonso Soriano	8.00
IS	Ichiro Suzuki	20.00
JT	Jim Thome	8.00
DW	Dontrelle Willis	6.00

Famous Quotes

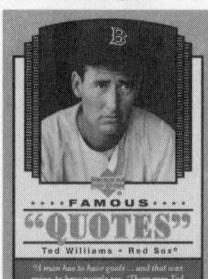

NM/M
Complete Set (20): 30.00

#	Player	Price
Q-1	Al Lopez	.75
Q-2	Bob Feller	1.00
Q-3	Bob Gibson	1.50
Q-4	Brooks Robinson	1.50
Q-5	Cal Ripken Jr.	5.00
Q-6	Carl Yastrzemski	2.00
Q-7	Earl Weaver	.75
Q-8	Eddie Mathews	2.00
Q-9	Ernie Banks	2.00
Q-10	Greg Maddux	3.00
Q-11	Joe DiMaggio	4.00
Q-12	Mickey Mantle	6.00
Q-13	Nolan Ryan	6.00
Q-14	Stan Musial	4.00
Q-15	Ted Williams	3.00
Q-16	Tom Seaver	2.00
Q-17	Tommy Lasorda	.75
Q-18	Warren Spahn	2.00
Q-19	Whitey Ford	1.50
Q-20	Yogi Berra	2.00

First Pitch

NM/M
Common Player: 5.00
Inserted 1:72

SP7	LeBron James	20.00
SP8	Mr. Hockey	10.00
SP10	Ernie Banks	10.00
SP11	General Tommy Franks	5.00
SP12	Ben Affleck	10.00
SP13	Halle Berry	10.00
SP14	George H.W. Bush	5.00
SP15	George W. Bush	5.00

Game Winners

NM/M
Common Player: 5.00
Golds: 1-1.5X
Production 50 Sets

GW-BA	Bobby Abreu	8.00
GW-JB	Jeff Bagwell	8.00
GW-HB	Hank Blalock	8.00
GW-MC	Miguel Cabrera	8.00
GW-JE	Jim Edmonds	5.00
GW-DE	Darin Erstad	5.00
GW-RF	Rafael Furcal (Gold parallel only.)	5.00
GW-JG	Jason Giambi	5.00
GW-TG	Troy Glaus	5.00
GW-AG	Alex Gonzalez	5.00
GW-SG	Shawn Green	5.00
GW-KG	Ken Griffey Jr.	5.00
GW-VG	Vladimir Guerrero	10.00
GW-TH	Todd Helton	5.00
GW-RH	Ramon Hernandez	5.00
GW-HU	Torii Hunter	5.00
GW-DJ	Derek Jeter	25.00
GW-AJ	Andruw Jones	8.00
GW-CJ	Chipper Jones	8.00
GW-RK	Ryan Klesko	5.00
GW-ML	Mike Lowell	5.00
GW-HM	Hideki Matsui	25.00
GW-TN	Trot Nixon (Gold parallel only.)	10.00
GW-MO	Maggio Ordonez	5.00
GW-CP	Corey Patterson	5.00
GW-MP	Mike Piazza	10.00
GW-JP	Jorge Posada	8.00
GW-AP	Albert Pujols	15.00
GW-IR	Ivan Rodriguez	8.00
GW-SR	Scott Rolen	10.00
GW-GS	Gary Sheffield	5.00
GW-AS	Alfonso Soriano	5.00
GW-MT	Mark Teixeira	5.00
GW-TE	Miguel Tejada	5.00
GW-JT	Jim Thome	10.00
GW-BW	Bernie Williams	8.00

Going Deep Bat

NM/M
Common Player: 6.00
Inserted 1:288
Some not priced yet due to scarcity.
Golds: 1-2X
Production 50 Sets

BA	Bobby Abreu/SP/110	6.00
RO	Roberto Alomar	6.00
SC	Sandy Alomar Jr./SP/95	6.00

GA	Garret Anderson	8.00
RA	Rich Aurilia/SP/102	6.00
JB	Jeff Bagwell/SP/92	10.00
RB	Rocco Baldelli/SP/89	15.00
CB	Craig Biggio/SP/89	6.00
JE	Jim Edmonds/SP	8.00
DE	Darin Erstad	6.00
RF	Rafael Furcal/SP	6.00
TG	Troy Glaus/SP/113	8.00
SG	Shawn Green/SP/100	8.00
KG	Ken Griffey Jr./SP	30.00
RH	Rickey Henderson/SP/77	10.00
TH	Torii Hunter/SP/115	8.00
CJ	Chipper Jones/SP/69	15.00
JL	Javy Lopez/SP/77	8.00
HM	Hideki Matsui/SP/70	45.00
DM	Doug Mientkiewicz/SP/123	6.00
HN	Hideo Nomo	15.00
MO	Magglio Ordonez	6.00
PO	Jay Payton/SP/100	6.00
MP	Mike Piazza	15.00
JP	Jorge Posada	8.00
AP	Albert Pujols	20.00
SR	Scott Rolen/SP/77	10.00
CS	Curt Schilling/SP/57	10.00
AS	Alfonso Soriano/SP/53	10.00
JT	Jim Thome	6.00
OV	Omar Vizquel/SP/115	6.00
BW	Bernie Williams/SP/56	8.00
KW	Kerry Wood/SP/108	10.00

Headliners Jersey

		NM/M
Common Player:		4.00
Inserted 1:48		
Golds:		1-2X
Production 100 Sets		
TB	Tony Batista	4.00
JB	Josh Beckett	8.00
LB	Lance Berkman	4.00
MB	Mark Buehrle	4.00
LC	Luis Castillo	4.00
JD	Joe DiMaggio/SP/153	90.00
AD	Adam Dunn	6.00
JE	Jim Edmonds	6.00
RF	Robert Fick	4.00
TG	Tom Glavine	6.00
LG	Luis Gonzalez	4.00
SG	Shawn Green	4.00
KG	Ken Griffey Jr.	15.00
VG	Vladimir Guerrero/SP/153	10.00
RH	Roy Halladay	4.00
JH	Jose Hernandez	4.00
TH	Trevor Hoffman	4.00
BK	Byung-Hyun Kim	4.00
RK	Ryan Klesko	4.00
PK	Paul Konerko	4.00
ML	Mike Lowell	4.00
GM	Greg Maddux	12.00
MM	Mickey Mantle/SP/97	125.00
PM	Pedro J. Martinez	8.00
HM	Hideki Matsui	35.00
MY	Matt Morris	4.00
MU	Mike Mussina	8.00
MO	Magglio Ordonez	4.00
RO	Roy Oswalt	4.00
MR	Manny Ramirez	6.00
MA	Mariano Rivera	6.00
JR	Jimmy Rollins	6.00
BS	Benito Santiago	4.00
CS	Curt Schilling	6.00
JS	Junior Spivey	4.00
IS	Ichiro Suzuki/SP/153	30.00
MS	Mike Sweeney	4.00
MT	Miguel Tejada	6.00
JT	Jim Thome	8.00
JV	Jose Vidro	4.00
TW	Ted Williams/SP/153	75.00

Magical Performances

		NM/M
Common Player:		6.00
Inserted 1:96		
Golds:		1-1.5X
Production 50 Sets		
MP1	Mickey Mantle	35.00
MP2	Mickey Mantle	35.00
MP3	Joe DiMaggio	25.00
MP4	Joe DiMaggio	25.00
MP5	Derek Jeter	25.00
MP6	Derek Jeter	25.00
MP7	Roger Clemens	20.00
MP8	Roger Clemens	20.00
MP9	Alfonso Soriano	10.00
MP10	Andy Pettitte	8.00
MP11	Hideki Matsui	30.00
MP12	Mike Mussina	10.00
MP13	Jorge Posada	10.00
MP14	Jason Giambi	10.00
MP15	David Wells	6.00
MP16	Mariano Rivera	10.00
MP17	Yogi Berra	15.00
MP18	Phil Rizzuto	10.00
MP19	Whitey Ford	10.00
MP20	Jose Contreras	8.00
MP21	Jim "Catfish" Hunter	6.00
MP22	Mickey Mantle	35.00
MP23	Mickey Mantle	35.00
MP24	Joe DiMaggio	25.00
MP25	Joe DiMaggio	25.00
MP26	Derek Jeter	25.00
MP27	Derek Jeter	25.00
MP28	Roger Clemens	20.00
MP29	Roger Clemens	20.00
MP30	Alfonso Soriano	10.00
MP31	Andy Pettitte	8.00
MP32	Hideki Matsui	30.00
MP33	Mike Mussina	10.00
MP34	Jorge Posada	10.00
MP35	Jason Giambi	10.00
MP36	David Wells	6.00
MP37	Mariano Rivera	10.00
MP38	Yogi Berra	15.00
MP39	Phil Rizzuto	10.00
MP40	Whitey Ford	10.00
MP41	Jose Contreras	10.00
MP42	Jim "Catfish" Hunter	6.00

Matsui Chronicles

	NM/M
Complete Set (60):	35.00
Common Matsui:	1.00
HM1-60 Hideki Matsui	1.00

National Pride

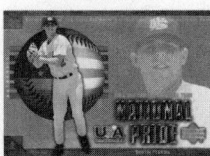

		NM/M
Complete Set (20):		25.00
Common Player:		1.00
Inserted 1:6		
USA1	Justin Orenduff	1.00
USA2	Micah Owings	2.00
USA3	Steven Register	2.00
USA4	Huston Street	1.00
USA5	Justin Verlander	2.00
USA6	Jered Weaver	4.00
USA7	Matt Campbell	1.00
USA8	Stephen Head	1.00
USA9	Mark Romanczuk	1.00
USA10	Jeff Clement	6.00
USA11	Mike Nickeas	2.00
USA12	Tyler Greene	1.00
USA13	Paul Janish	2.00
USA14	Jeff Larish	1.00
USA15	Eric Patterson	1.00
USA16	Dustin Pedroia	1.00
USA17	Michael Griffin	1.00
USA18	Brent Lillibridge	1.00
USA19	Danny Putnam	1.00
USA20	Seth Smith	1.00

National Pride Pants

		NM/M
CB	Chris Burke	9.00
JC	Jesse Crain	4.00
DU	Justin Duchscherer	6.00
GK	Graham Koonce	6.00
JL	Justin Leone	8.00

RM	Ryan Madson	6.00
JM	Joe Mauer	15.00
HR	Horacio Ramirez	8.00
RR	Royce Ring	6.00
ER	Eddie Rodriguez	5.00
MR	Mike Rouse	8.00
GS	Grady Sizemore	10.00
JS	Jason Stanford	6.00
JB	John Van Benschoten	8.00

National Pride Jersey

		NM/M
Common Player:		4.00
Inserted 1:24		
USA1	Justin Orenduff	4.00
USA2	Micah Owings	4.00
USA3	Steven Register	4.00
USA4	Huston Street	4.00
USA5	Justin Verlander	10.00
USA6	Jered Weaver	6.00
USA7	Matt Campbell	8.00
USA8	Stephen Head	4.00
USA9	Mark Romanczuk	4.00
USA10	Jeff Clement	15.00
USA11	Mike Nickeas	4.00
USA12	Tyler Greene	4.00
USA13	Paul Janish	4.00
USA14	Jeff Larish	6.00
USA15	Eric Patterson	4.00
USA16	Dustin Pedroia	10.00
USA17	Michael Griffin	4.00
USA18	Brent Lillibridge	6.00
USA19	Danny Putnam	4.00
USA20	Seth Smith	6.00
USA21	Justin Orenduff	4.00
USA22	Micah Owings	4.00
USA23	Steven Register	4.00
USA24	Huston Street	4.00
USA25	Justin Verlander	10.00
USA26	Jered Weaver	6.00
USA27	Matt Campbell	8.00
USA28	Stephen Head	4.00
USA29	Mark Romanczuk	4.00
USA30	Jeff Clement	15.00
USA31	Mike Nickeas	4.00
USA32	Tyler Greene	4.00
USA33	Paul Janish	4.00
USA34	Jeff Larish	6.00
USA35	Eric Patterson	4.00
USA36	Dustin Pedroia	10.00
USA37	Michael Griffin	4.00
USA38	Brent Lillibridge	6.00
USA39	Danny Putnam	4.00
USA40	Seth Smith	6.00
USA41	Delmon Young	25.00
USA42	Rickie Weeks	10.00
Series 2		
TB	Thad Bosley	4.00
BB	Brian Bruney	6.00
CB	Chris Burke	9.00
JC	Jesse Crain	8.00
DU	Justin Duchscherer	6.00
JD	J.D. Durbin	4.00
JG	John Grabow	6.00
GG	Gabe Gross	4.00
JH	J.J. Hardy	6.00
GK	Graham Koonce	6.00
GL	Gerald Laird	6.00
ML	Mike Lamb	4.00
JL	Justin Leone	8.00
JM	Joe Mauer	15.00
HR	Horacio Ramirez	8.00
JR	Jeremy Reed	10.00
RR	Royce Ring	6.00
ER	Eddie Rodriguez	5.00
MR	Mike Rouse	8.00
GS	Grady Sizemore	10.00
JS	Jason Stanford	6.00
JB	John Van Benschoten	6.00
TW	Todd Williams	4.00
EY	Ernie Young	4.00

Peak Performers

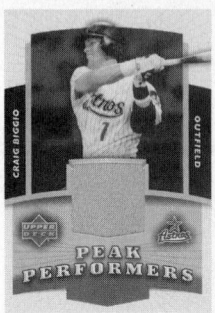

	NM/M
Golds:	1.5X-2X
Production 165	
PP-JB	Jeff Bagwell	8.00
PP-BE	Josh Beckett	6.00
PP-LB	Lance Berkman	5.00
PP-CB	Craig Biggio	5.00
PP-HB	Hank Blalock	8.00
PP-PB	Pat Burrell	6.00
PP-LC	Luis Castillo	4.00
PP-CD	Carlos Delgado	6.00
PP-RF	Rafael Furcal	4.00
PP-EG	Eric Gagne	12.00
PP-SG	Shawn Green	5.00
PP-KG	Ken Griffey Jr.	15.00
PP-VG	Vladimir Guerrero	8.00
PP-TH	Todd Helton	8.00
PP-PL	Paul LoDuca	4.00
PP-PM	Pedro J. Martinez	8.00

PP-HM	Hideki Matsui	25.00
PP-MM	Mike Mussina	8.00
PP-HN	Hideo Nomo	8.00
PP-MO	Magglio Ordonez	5.00
PP-RP	Rafael Palmeiro	8.00
PP-PE	Andy Pettitte	6.00
PP-BP	Brandon Phillips	4.00
PP-MP	Mark Prior	10.00
PP-AP	Albert Pujols	10.00
PP-JR	Jose Reyes	5.00
PP-IR	Ivan Rodriguez	8.00
PP-SR	Scott Rolen	6.00
PP-SA	C.C. Sabathia	4.00
PP-CS	Curt Schilling	8.00
PP-AS	Alfonso Soriano	8.00
PP-IS	Ichiro Suzuki	20.00
PP-MT	Miguel Tejada	8.00
PP-FT	Frank Thomas	8.00
PP-JT	Jim Thome	8.00
PP-DV	Omar Vizquel	4.00
PP-VW	Vernon Wells	4.00
PP-KW	Kerry Wood	10.00

Signature Stars Black Ink

	NM/M
Some not priced due to lack of info.	
Inserted 1:288	
RA	Rich Aurilia/479	8.00
AG	Andres Galarraga/248	10.00
NG	Nomar Garciaparra/69	75.00
VG	Vladimir Guerrero/68	40.00
RH	Rich Harden/163	8.00
AH	Aaron Heilman/49	15.00
TH	Torii Hunter/374	10.00
KI	Kazuhisa Ishii/58	15.00
BK	Billy Koch/429	8.00
HM	Hideki Matsui/25	325.00
MU	Mike Mussina/68	50.00
MO	Magglio Ordonez/377	20.00
JRa	Joe Randa/271	10.00
CR	Cal Ripken Jr./69	200.00
DR	Dave Roberts/278	8.00
NR	Nolan Ryan/69	120.00
Series 2		
BB	Bret Boone/43	15.00
DB	Dewon Brazelton/96	5.00
JC	Jose Canseco/160	25.00
EC	Eric Chavez/60	15.00
EG	Eric Gagne/160	20.00
KG	Ken Griffey Jr./450	90.00
RH	Rich Harden/65	15.00
DR	Dave Roberts/450	5.00
NR	Nolan Ryan/95	100.00
DS	Darryl Strawberry/160	10.00
MT	Mark Teixeira/200	25.00
JV	Javier Vazquez/60	15.00
BW	Brandon Webb/60	15.00
RW	Rickie Weeks/65	15.00
DW	Dontrelle Willis/160	15.00

Signature Stars Blue Ink

	NM/M
No Pricing	
Production 25 Sets	
Matsui #'d to 324.	
HM	Hideki Matsui/324	180.00

Signature Stars Red Ink

No Pricing	
Production 10 Sets	

Signature Stars Gold Ink

Gold Ink:	1-2X Black Ink
Production 99 Sets	

Super Patches Logos

No pricing due to scarcity.
Inserted 1:7,500

Super Patches Numbers

No pricing due to scarcity.
Inserted 1:7,500

Super Patches Stripes

No pricing due to scarcity.
Inserted 1:7,500

Super Sluggers

	NM/M
Complete Set (30):	15.00
Common Player:	.50
Inserted 1:1 Retail	

SL-1	Albert Pujols	2.00
SL-2	Alex Rodriguez	2.00
SL-3	Alfonso Soriano	.75
SL-4	Andruw Jones	.75
SL-5	Bret Boone	.50
SL-6	Carlos Delgado	.50
SL-7	Edgar Renteria	.50
SL-8	Eric Chavez	.50
SL-9	Frank Thomas	.75
SL-10	Garret Anderson	.50
SL-11	Gary Sheffield	.50
SL-12	Jason Giambi	.75
SL-13	Javy Lopez	.50
SL-14	Jeff Bagwell	.75
SL-15	Jim Edmonds	.50
SL-16	Jim Thome	1.00
SL-17	Jorge Posada	.50
SL-18	Lance Berkman	.50
SL-19	Magglio Ordonez	.50
SL-20	Manny Ramirez	.75
SL-21	Mike Lowell	.50
SL-22	Nomar Garciaparra	1.50
SL-23	Preston Wilson	.50
SL-24	Rafael Palmeiro	.75
SL-25	Richie Sexson	.50
SL-26	Sammy Sosa	2.00
SL-27	Shawn Green	.50
SL-28	Todd Helton	.75
SL-29	Vernon Wells	.50
SL-30	Vladimir Guerrero	1.00

500 HR Club

		NM/M
Production 350		
RP	Rafael Palmeiro	180.00

Twenty-Five Salute

		NM/M
Common Player:		6.00
Inserted 1:12		
S1	Barry Bonds	3.00
S2	Troy Glaus	.75
S3	Andruw Jones	.75
S4	Jay Gibbons	.75
S5	Jeremy Giambi	.75
S6	Jason Giambi	1.00
S7	Jim Thome	1.00
S8	Rafael Palmeiro	1.00
S9	Carlos Delgado	1.00
S10	Dmitri Young	.75

2003 Update

		NM/M
Complete Set (60):		18.00
Common Player:		.15
One set per hobby box.		
541	Bo Hart	1.50
542	Dan Haren	.50
543	Ryan Wagner	1.00
544	Rich Harden	.50
545	Dontrelle Willis	.75
546	Jerome Williams	.25
547	Bobby Crosby	1.00
548	Greg Jones	.25
549	Todd Linden	.25
550	Byung-Hyun Kim	.25
551	Rickie Weeks	4.00
552	Jason Roach	.25
553	Oscar Villarreal	.25
554	Justin Duchscherer	.15
555	Chris Capuano	.25
556	Josh Hall	.50
557	Luis Matos	.15
558	Miguel Ojeda	.15
559	Kevin Ohme	.15
560	Julio Manon	.15
561	Kevin Correia	.15
562	Delmon Young	5.00

563	Aaron Boone	.15
564	Aaron Looper	.15
565	Mike Neu	.15
566	Aquilino Lopez	.15
567	Jhonny Peralta	.15
568	Duaner Sanchez	.15
569	Stephen Randolph	.15
570	Nate Bland	.15
571	Chin-Hui Tsao	.15
572	Michel Hernandez	.15
573	Rocco Baldelli	1.00
574	Robb Quinlan	.15
575	Aaron Heilman	.15
576	Jae Weong Seo	.15
577	Joe Borowski	.15
578	Chris Bootcheck	.15
579	Michael Ryan	.15
580	Mark Malaska	.15
581	Jose Guillen	.15
582	Josh Towers	.15
583	Tom Gregorio	.15
584	Edwin Jackson	.15
585	Jason Anderson	.15
586	Jose Reyes	.50
587	Miguel Cabrera	1.00
588	Nate Bump	.15
589	Jeromy Burnitz	.15
590	David Ross	.15
591	Chase Utley	.40
592	Brandon Webb	1.00
593	Masao Kida	.15
594	Jimmy Journell	.15
595	Eric Young	.15
596	Tony Womack	.15
597	Amaury Telemaco	.15
598	Rickey Henderson	.50
599	Esteban Loaiza	.15
600	Sidney Ponson	.15

SPGU Patch Edition Update

Patch

		NM/M
Production 20 unless noted.		
BA	Bobby Abreu	40.00
GA	Garret Anderson	40.00
RB	Rocco Baldelli	30.00
LB	Lance Berkman	40.00
HB	Hank Blalock	40.00
BB	Bret Boone	30.00
BC	Bartolo Colon	25.00
JE	Jim Edmonds	35.00
EG	Eric Gagne	75.00
TG	Troy Glaus	35.00
VG	Vladimir Guerrero	50.00
TH	Torii Hunter	25.00
JJ	Jacque Jones	25.00
AK	Austin Kearns	30.00
JK	Jeff Kent	25.00
RK	Ryan Klesko	25.00
EM	Edgar Martinez	50.00
KM	Kevin Millwood	30.00
MM	Mark Mulder	40.00
HN	Hideo Nomo	40.00
RO	Roy Oswalt	35.00
CP	Corey Patterson	30.00
JR	Jose Reyes	30.00
RS	Richie Sexson	40.00
MS	Mike Sweeney	25.00
BW	Brandon Webb	25.00
VW	Vernon Wells/21	25.00
KW	Kerry Wood	25.00

2004 Upper Deck Diamond Collection

		NM/M
Complete Set (120):		70.00
Common Player:		.15
Common (91-120):		2.00
Inserted 1:6		
Pack (6):		2.00
Box (24):		40.00
1	Garret Anderson	.25
2	Darin Erstad	.25
3	Troy Glaus	.40
4	Curt Schilling	.50
5	Brandon Webb	.15
6	Randy Johnson	.75
7	Andruw Jones	.25
8	Chipper Jones	.75
9	Gary Sheffield	.40

10	Jay Gibbons	.25
11	Miguel Tejada	.40
12	Tony Batista	.15
13	Nomar Garciaparra	1.25
14	Manny Ramirez	.50
15	Pedro J. Martinez	.75
16	Mark Prior	1.00
17	Kerry Wood	.75
18	Sammy Sosa	1.25
19	Bartolo Colon	.25
20	Magglio Ordonez	.25
21	Frank Thomas	.50
22	Adam Dunn	.40
23	Austin Kearns	.25
24	Ken Griffey Jr.	1.00
25	Brandon Phillips	.15
26	Milton Bradley	.15
27	Jody Gerut	.15
28	Todd Helton	.50
29	Larry Walker	.25
30	Preston Wilson	.15
31	Jeremy Bonderman	.15
32	Carlos Pena	.15
33	Dmitri Young	.15
34	Dontrelle Willis	.40
35	Miguel Cabrera	.50
36	Mike Lowell	.25
37	Jeff Bagwell	.50
38	Roy Oswalt	.25
39	Lance Berkman	.25
40	Carlos Beltran	.40
41	Mike Sweeney	.15
42	Rondell White	.15
43	Hideo Nomo	.40
44	Kevin Brown	.25
45	Shawn Green	.25
46	Ben Sheets	.25
47	Geoff Jenkins	.15
48	Richie Sexson	.40
49	Jacque Jones	.15
50	Johan Santana	.15
51	Torii Hunter	.25
52	Javier Vazquez	.25
53	Jose Vidro	.15
54	Vladimir Guerrero	.75
55	Cliff Floyd	.15
56	Mike Piazza	1.00
57	Jose Reyes	.50
58	Derek Jeter	2.00
59	Jason Giambi	.50
60	Alfonso Soriano	.50
61	Eric Chavez	.25
62	Barry Zito	.25
63	Tim Hudson	.25
64	Bobby Abreu	.25
65	Jim Thome	.75
66	Kevin Millwood	.25
67	Roger Clemens	1.50
68	Jason Kendall	.15
69	Reggie Sanders	.15
70	Phil Nevin	.15
71	Ryan Klesko	.25
72	Brian Giles	.25
73	A.J. Pierzynski	.15
74	Jason Schmidt	.25
75	Sidney Ponson	.15
76	Edgar Martinez	.25
77	Ichiro Suzuki	1.00
78	Bret Boone	.25
79	Albert Pujols	1.50
80	Scott Rolen	.75
81	Jim Edmonds	.25
82	Aubrey Huff	.15
83	Delmon Young	.40
84	Rocco Baldelli	.40
85	Alex Rodriguez	1.50
86	Mark Teixeira	.50
87	Rafael Palmeiro	.50
88	Carlos Delgado	.25
89	Vernon Wells	.25
90	Roy Halladay	.25
91	Brandon Medders RC	2.00
92	Colby Miller RC	2.00
93	David Crouthers	2.00
94	Dennis Sarfate RC	3.00
95	Donald Kelly RC	2.00
96	Alec Zumwalt RC	2.00
97	Frank Brooks RC	2.00
98	Greg Dobbs RC	2.00
99	Ian Snell RC	3.00
100	Jake Woods	2.00
101	Jamie Brown RC	2.00
102	Jason Frasor RC	2.00
103	Jerome Gamble RC	2.00
104	Jesse Harper RC	2.00
105	Josh Labandeira RC	2.00
106	Justin Hampson RC	2.00
107	Justin Huisman RC	2.00
108	Justin Leone RC	2.00
109	Chris Aguila RC	2.00
110	Lincoln Holdzkom RC	2.00
111	Mike Bumatay RC	2.00
112	Mike Gosling RC	2.00
113	Mike Johnston RC	2.00
114	Mike Rouse	2.00
115	Nick Regilio RC	2.00
116	Ryan Meaux RC	2.00
117	Scott Dohmann RC	2.00
118	Sean Henn	2.00
119	Tim Bausher RC	2.00
120	Tim Bittner RC	2.00

Gold Honors

	NM/M
Gold (1-90):	5-10X
Gold (91-120):	1-2X
Production 50 Sets	

Silver Honors

Silver (1-90):	2-4X
Silver (91-120):	.75-1X
1-90 inserted 1:6	
91-120 inserted 1:48	

Class of 2004 Autograph

		NM/M
Quantity produced listed		
MC	Miguel Cabrera/50	40.00
KG	Ken Griffey Jr./100	75.00
VG	Vladimir Guerrero/100	40.00
RH	Rich Harden/100	15.00
HM	Hideki Matsui/100	250.00
MP	Mark Prior/100	40.00
JR	Jose Reyes/100	30.00
DW	Dontrelle Willis/100	40.00
BZ	Barry Zito/100	25.00

Dean's List Jersey

		NM/M
Common Player:		4.00
Inserted 1:72		
BA	Jeff Bagwell	8.00
HB	Hank Blalock	8.00
JG	Jason Giambi	6.00
GL	Troy Glaus	6.00
LG	Luis Gonzalez	4.00
SG	Shawn Green	4.00
KG	Ken Griffey Jr.	10.00
VG	Vladimir Guerrero	8.00
GM	Greg Maddux	10.00
HM	Hideki Matsui	20.00
HN	Hideo Nomo	8.00
PI	Mike Piazza	8.00
MP	Mark Prior	8.00
AP	Albert Pujols	15.00
AR	Alex Rodriguez	10.00
AS	Alfonso Soriano	8.00
SS	Sammy Sosa	10.00
IS	Ichiro Suzuki	20.00
JT	Jim Thome	8.00
DW	Dontrelle Willis	6.00

Future Gems Jersey

		NM/M
Common Player:		4.00
Inserted 1:72		
BA	Josh Bard	4.00
JB	Josh Beckett	8.00
SB	Sean Burroughs	6.00
MC	Mike Cameron	4.00
AE	Adam Eaton	4.00
WE	Willie Eyre	4.00
LF	Lew Ford	4.00
GU	Jeremy Guthrie	4.00
TH	Travis Hafner	6.00
RH	Roy Halladay	4.00
AH	Aaron Heilman	4.00
IS	Kazuhisa Ishii	4.00
JJ	Jason Jennings	4.00
KA	Matt Kata	4.00
MK	Mark Kotsay	4.00
JL	Jon Leicester	4.00
EM	Eric Milton	4.00
JR	Jose Reyes	8.00
RR	Rick Roberts	4.00
PS	Phil Seibel	4.00
BS	Ben Sheets	6.00
MT	Mark Teixeira	6.00
TW	Todd Wellemeyer	6.00
WI	Josh Willingham	4.00

Pick the All Star MVP

		NM/M
Common Player:		.50
Inserted 1:1		
BA	Bobby Abreu	.50

GA	Garret Anderson	.50
JB	Jeff Bagwell	.50
BE	Josh Beckett	.50
CB	Carlos Beltran	.50
HB	Hank Blalock	.50
BO	Bret Boone	.50
OC	Orlando Cabrera	.50
EC	Eric Chavez	.50
BC	Bartolo Colon	.50
JD	Johnny Damon	.50
CD	Carlos Delgado	.50
AD	Adam Dunn	.50
JE	Jim Edmonds	.50
RF	Rafael Furcal	.50
NG	Nomar Garciaparra	1.50
JG	Jason Giambi	.75
MG	Marcus Giles	.50
TG	Troy Glaus	.50
SG	Shawn Green	.50
KG	Ken Griffey Jr.	1.00
VG	Vladimir Guerrero	.75
RH	Roy Halladay	.50
TH	Todd Helton	.75
HU	Tim Hudson	.50
TH	Torii Hunter	.50
DJ	Derek Jeter	2.50
RJ	Randy Johnson	.75
AJ	Andruw Jones	.50
CJ	Chipper Jones	.75
JJ	Jacque Jones	.50
AK	Austin Kearns	.50
JK	Jeff Kent	.50
JL	Javy Lopez	.50
ML	Mike Lowell	.50
PM	Pedro J. Martinez	.75
HM	Hideki Matsui	1.50
MM	Mark Mulder	.50
MU	Mike Mussina	.75
MO	Magglio Ordonez	.50
RP	Rafael Palmeiro	.75
PI	Mike Piazza	1.00
JP	Jorge Posada	.50
MP	Mark Prior	1.00
AP	Albert Pujols	2.00
MR	Manny Ramirez	.75
ER	Edgar Renteria	.50
AR	Alex Rodriguez	2.00
IR	Ivan Rodriguez	.75
SR	Scott Rolen	.75
JS	Curt Schilling	.75
JS	Jason Schmidt	.50
RS	Richie Sexson	.50
GS	Gary Sheffield	.50
AS	Alfonso Soriano	.75
SS	Sammy Sosa	1.50
IS	Ichiro Suzuki	1.50
MS	Mike Sweeney	.50
MT	Mark Teixeira	.50
TE	Miguel Tejada	.50
FT	Frank Thomas	.75
JT	Jim Thome	.75
JV	Jason Varitek	.50
VI	Jose Vidro	.50
VW	Vernon Wells	.50
DW	Dontrelle Willis	.50
PW	Preston Wilson	.50
KW	Kerry Wood	1.00
BZ	Barry Zito	.50

2004 UD Diamond Collection
Pro Sigs

	NM/M
Complete Set (1-240):	
Common Player (1-90):	.15
Common SP (91-150):	2.00
Inserted 1:6	
Common Auto. (151-240):	5.00
Inserted 1:24	
Pack (6):	2.00
Box (24):	40.00
1	Alfonso Soriano	.50
2	Josh Beckett	.50
3	Kerry Wood	.75
4	Brandon Webb	.15
5	Shannon Stewart	.15
6	Larry Walker	.25
7	Tim Hudson	.25
8	Carlos Lee	.25
9	Austin Kearns	.25
10	Vernon Wells	.25

11	Jeff Bagwell	.50
12	Hideo Nomo	.40
13	Jerome Williams	.15
14	Kevin Brown	.25
15	Jose Vidro	.15
16	Rocco Baldelli	.25
17	Frank Thomas	.50
18	Albert Pujols	1.50
19	Bartolo Colon	.25
20	C.C. Sabathia	.15
21	Andruw Jones	.50
22	Reggie Sanders	.15
23	Carlos Beltran	.40
24	Curt Schilling	.50
25	Miguel Tejada	.40
26	Barry Zito	.25
27	Pedro Martinez	.75
28	Sean Burroughs	.15
29	Sammy Sosa	1.50
30	Eric Chavez	.25
31	Roy Halladay	.25
32	Todd Helton	.50
33	Mark Prior	1.00
34	Mike Mussina	.50
35	Alex Rodriguez	2.00
36	Ivan Rodriguez	.50
37	Mike Piazza	1.00
38	Angel Berroa	.15
39	Orlando Cabrera	.25
40	Jim Thome	.75
41	Brian Giles	.25
42	Ichiro Suzuki	1.00
43	Edgar Renteria	.25
44	Eric Gagne	.25
45	Gary Sheffield	.40
46	Torii Hunter	.25
47	Roger Clemens	1.50
48	Scott Rolen	.75
49	Johan Santana	.25
50	Jacque Jones	.15
51	Hank Blalock	.40
52	Rafael Palmeiro	.50
53	Dmitri Young	.15
54	Ryan Klesko	.25
55	Mark Teixeira	.25
56	Nomar Garciaparra	1.50
57	Jose Reyes	.25
58	Vladimir Guerrero	.75
59	Mike Sweeney	.15
60	Jorge Posada	.40
61	Derek Jeter	2.00
62	Milton Bradley	.15
63	Bobby Abreu	.25
64	Greg Maddux	1.00
65	Adam Dunn	.25
66	Troy Glaus	.40
67	Luis Gonzalez	.25
68	Shawn Green	.25
69	Bret Boone	.25
70	Mark Mulder	.25
71	Lance Berkman	.40
72	Preston Wilson	.15
73	Phil Nevin	.15
74	Chipper Jones	.75
75	Garret Anderson	.40
76	Jason Giambi	.75
77	Magglio Ordonez	.25
78	Jeff Kent	.25
79	Richie Sexson	.40
80	Mike Lowell	.25
81	Ben Sheets	.25
82	Randy Johnson	.75
83	Dontrelle Willis	.25
84	Javier Vazquez	.25
85	Geoff Jenkins	.25
86	Manny Ramirez	.75
87	Jim Edmonds	.40
88	Roy Oswalt	.25
89	Edgar Martinez	.25
90	Carlos Delgado	.40
91	Chris Saenz RC	5.00
92	Justin Leone RC	2.00
93	Shawn Hill RC	4.00
94	Chad Bentz RC	4.00
95	Jesse Harper RC	2.00
96	David Crouthers	2.00
97	Justin Germano RC	2.00
98	Tim Bausher RC	2.00
99	Greg Dobbs RC	5.00
100	Enemencio Pacheco RC	8.00
101	Dennis Sarfate RC	2.00
102	Edwin Moreno RC	2.00
103	Colby Miller RC	2.00
104	Mike Rouse	2.00
105	Fernando Nieve RC	2.00
106	Tim Hamulack RC	6.00
107	Jason Frasor RC	2.00
108	Jose Capellan RC	5.00
109	Jamie Brown RC	3.00
110	Mariano Gomez RC	2.00
111	Mike Vento	8.00
112	Josh Labandeira RC	3.00
113	Mike Gosling	2.00
114	Shingo Takatsu RC	8.00
115	Justin Hampson RC	2.00
116	Tim Bittner RC	2.00
117	Jerry Gil RC	2.00
118	Carlos Vasquez RC	5.00
119	Lincoln Holdzkom RC	2.00
120	Mike Johnston RC	4.00
121	William Bergolla RC	2.00
122	Luis Gonzalez	2.00
123	Ivan Ochoa RC	2.00
124	Roman Colon RC	2.00
125	Renyel Pinto RC	6.00

126	Donnie Kelly RC	4.00
127	Chris Oxspring RC	2.00
128	Sean Henn	5.00
129	Ryan Meaux RC	2.00
130	Shawn Camp RC	2.00
131	Brandon Medders RC	2.00
132	Rusty Tucker RC	2.00
133	Kazuo Matsui RC	10.00
134	Jorge Sequea RC	2.00
135	Hector Gimenez RC	4.00
136	Casey Daigle RC	2.00
137	Ian Snell RC	3.00
138	Scott Dohmann RC	2.00
139	Ronny Cedeno RC	2.00
140	Jorge Vasquez RC	4.00
141	David Aardsma	4.00
142	Carlos Hines RC	2.00
143	Scott Proctor RC	3.00
144	Jerome Gamble RC	5.00
145	Jason Bartlett RC	6.00
146	Akinori Otsuka RC	8.00
147	Merkin Valdez RC	2.00
148	Jake Woods	4.00
149	Chris Aguila RC	2.00
150	John Gall RC	2.00
151	Aaron Miles	10.00
152	Aquilino Lopez	10.00
153	Bill Hall	10.00
154	Billy Traber	15.00
155	Brad Lidge	12.00
156	Brady Clark	5.00
157	Brandon Duckworth	8.00
158	Brett Tomko	6.00
159	Brian Fuentes	6.00
160	Brooks Kieschnick	8.00
161	Carlos Rivera	6.00
162	Chad Cordero	6.00
163	Chad Tracy	10.00
164	Claudio Vargas	5.00
165	D.J. Carrasco	5.00
166	Damian Rolls	6.00
167	David Sanders	5.00
168	Derrick Turnbow	5.00
170	Desi Relaford	5.00
171	Doug Davis	8.00
172	Dustan Mohr	6.00
173	Frank Catalanotto	8.00
176	Franklyn German	5.00
177	Ron Belliard	5.00
178	Geoff Geary	15.00
179	Greg Colbrunn	5.00
180	Henry Mateo	5.00
181	Brent Mayne	5.00
182	Horacio Ramirez	15.00
183	J.C. Romero	5.00
184	J.J. Putz	8.00
185	Ferdin Tejeda	5.00
186	Jaime Cerda	5.00
187	Jason Michaels	10.00
188	Jason Simontacchi	8.00
189	Jay Witasick	5.00
190	Joe Valentine	8.00
191	Joey Eischen	5.00
192	Johnny Estrada	8.00
193	Jon Garland	5.00
194	Jon Switzer	5.00
195	Jorge Julio	5.00
196	Jorge Sosa	8.00
197	Jose Castillo	5.00
198	Jose Macias	8.00
199	Josh Bard	5.00
200	Juan Cruz	5.00
201	Juan Rivera	5.00
202	Ken Griffey Jr.	150.00
203	Kevin Hooper	5.00
204	Kiko Calero RC	15.00
205	Chad Gaudin	5.00
206	Luis Rivas	5.00
207	Mark Corey	8.00
208	Matt Ford	8.00
209	Matt Herges	5.00
210	Miguel Cairo	15.00
211	Fernando Cabrera	5.00
212	Mike MacDougal	5.00
213	Mike Neu	8.00
214	Lew Ford	15.00
215	Mike Wood	8.00
216	Nate Robertson	5.00
217	Nick Punto	5.00
218	Oscar Villarreal	5.00
219	Ramon Vazquez	10.00
220	Randall Simon	5.00
221	Ricky Stone	5.00
222	Ryan Drese	5.00
223	Ryan Ludwick	8.00
225	Scot Shields	5.00
229	Steve Colyer	5.00
230	Tony Armas	5.00
231	Robby Hammock	5.00
232	Travis Hafner	8.00
233	Victor Martinez	8.00
234	Wilfredo Ledezma	5.00
235	Willie Bloomquist	5.00
236	Yorvit Torrealba	8.00

Gold
Gold (1-90):		3-6X
Overall odds for parallel 1:6.		

Silver (1-90):	2-3X
Overall odds for parallel 1:6.	

Blue Ink Autograph
No Pricing
Production 25 Sets

Red Signature
No Pricing
Production 10 Sets

Hall of Famers
No Pricing

2004 Upper Deck Etchings

	NM/M
Complete Set (150):	
Common Player:	.15
Common SP (91-120):	4.00
Production 2,004	
Common SP Black Auto. (121-150):	8.00
Production 700	
Blue Auto. (121-150):	.75-1.5X
Production 200	
Red Auto. (121-150):	No Pricing
Production 25	
Pack (5):	12.00
Box (12):	120.00
1	Albert Pujols	1.50
2	Torii Hunter	.40
3	Jim Edmonds	.40
4	Alex Rodriguez	1.50
5	Rafael Palmeiro	.50
6	Ken Griffey Jr.	1.00
7	Adam Dunn	.50
8	Andruw Jones	.50
9	Carlos Lee	.15
10	Mike Piazza	1.00
11	Jeff Bagwell	.50
12	Hideki Matsui	1.50
13	Gary Sheffield	.40
14	Edgar Renteria	.40
15	Shawn Green	.25
16	Kerry Wood	.75
17	Ivan Rodriguez	.50
18	Josh Beckett	.40
19	Scott Rolen	.75
20	Brian Giles	.25
21	Derek Lee	.25
22	Mike Lowell	.25
23	Mike Mussina	.40
24	Sammy Sosa	1.50
25	Brandon Webb	.15
26	Jacque Jones	.15
27	Randy Johnson	1.00
28	Luis Gonzalez	.25
29	Eric Chavez	.25
30	Carlos Delgado	.40
31	Phil Nevin	.15
32	Ichiro Suzuki	1.50
33	Roy Oswalt	.25
34	Tim Hudson	.25
35	Juan Gonzalez	.50
36	Frank Thomas	.50
37	Mark Mulder	.40
38	Mark Teixeira	.40

39	Miguel Tejada	.40
40	Jeff Kent	.25
41	Andy Pettitte	.25
42	Barry Zito	.40
43	Roy Halladay	.25
44	Rocco Baldelli	.25
45	Derek Jeter	2.00
46	Corey Patterson	.40
47	Javy Lopez	.40
48	A.J. Burnett	.15
49	Chipper Jones	.75
50	Curt Schilling	.50
51	Todd Helton	.50
52	Pedro J. Martinez	.75
53	Hideo Nomo	.40
54	Jose Reyes	.50
55	Vernon Wells	.15
56	Geoff Jenkins	.15
57	Troy Glaus	.25
58	Greg Maddux	1.00
59	Jason Schmidt	.40
60	Preston Wilson	.15
61	Miguel Cabrera	.75
62	Hank Blalock	.50
63	Rafael Furcal	.15
64	Vladimir Guerrero	.75
65	Lance Berkman	.15
66	Javier Vazquez	.15
67	Bret Boone	.15
68	Mark Prior	1.00
69	Magglio Ordonez	.15
70	Dontrelle Willis	.25
71	Richie Sexson	.25
72	Alfonso Soriano	.75
73	Edwin Jackson	.15
74	Jose Vidro	.15
75	Jason Giambi	.50
76	Kevin Brown	.25
77	Orlando Cabrera	.15
78	Nomar Garciaparra	1.00
79	Bobby Abreu	.25
80	Manny Ramirez	.50
81	J.D. Drew	.15
82	Roger Clemens	1.50
83	Pat Burrell	.15
84	Ryan Klesko	.15
85	Garret Anderson	.40
86	Johan Santana	.15
87	Kevin Millwood	.25
88	Austin Kearns	.25
89	Jim Thome	.75
90	Carlos Beltran	.40
91	Kazuo Matsui **RC**	15.00
92	Jamie Brown **RC**	4.00
93	Brandon Medders **RC**	4.00
94	Carlos Vasquez **RC**	4.00
95	Chris Aguila **RC**	4.00
96	David Aardsma	4.00
97	Justin Leone **RC**	4.00
98	Mike Johnston **RC**	4.00
99	Tim Bittner **RC**	4.00
100	Mike Rouse	4.00
101	Dennis Sarfate **RC**	4.00
102	Jason Frasor **RC**	4.00
103	Jorge Vasquez **RC**	4.00
104	Mike Gosling	4.00
105	Jake Woods	4.00
106	Akinori Otsuka **RC**	8.00
107	Lincoln Holdzkom **RC**	4.00
108	Jesse Harper **RC**	4.00
109	Edwin Moreno **RC**	4.00
110	Shingo Takatsu **RC**	6.00
111	Ryan Meaux **RC**	4.00
112	Donnie Kelly **RC**	4.00
113	Jerome Gamble **RC**	4.00
114	Josh Labandeira **RC**	4.00
115	Ian Snell **RC**	8.00
116	Mike Wuertz **RC**	4.00
117	Greg Dobbs **RC**	4.00
118	Sean Henn	4.00
119	David Crouthers	4.00
120	Hector Gimenez **RC**	4.00
121	Renyel Pinto **RC**	10.00
122	Tim Hamulack **RC**	8.00
123	Chris Saenz **RC**	8.00
124	Carlos Hines **RC**	8.00
125	Justin Knoedler **RC**	10.00
126	Onil Joseph **RC**	10.00
127	Ryan Wing	8.00
128	Scott Proctor **RC**	10.00
129	Rusty Tucker **RC**	8.00
130	Fernando Nieve **RC**	8.00
131	Chad Bentz **RC**	10.00
132	Jerry Gil **RC**	8.00
133	Mariano Gomez **RC**	10.00
134	Justin Germano **RC**	10.00
135	Jason Bartlett **RC**	10.00
136	Ronald Belisario **RC**	8.00
137	Enemencio Pacheco	8.00
138	Justin Hampson **RC**	8.00
139	Michael Vento	8.00
140	Merkin Valdez **RC**	10.00
141	Casey Daigle **RC**	8.00
142	Eddy Rodriguez	8.00
143	William Bergolla **RC**	15.00
144	Jose Capellan **RC**	8.00
145	Ronny Cedeno **RC**	8.00
146	Franklyn Gracesqui **RC**	8.00
147	Roman Colon **RC**	10.00
148	Roberto Novoa **RC**	8.00
149	Ivan Ochoa **RC**	10.00
150	Shawn Hill **RC**	8.00

Combo Etchings

NM/M

Production 5-115

Gold Foil: .75-1.5X
Production 1-50
Silver Foil: .75-1X
Production 4-50
No Pricing 15 or less.

JB	Josh Beckett/25	60.00
MC	Miguel Cabrera/23	50.00
KG	Ken Griffey Jr./100	90.00
KG1	Ken Griffey Jr./90	90.00
KG2	Ken Griffey Jr./90	90.00
VG	Vladimir Guerrero/60	65.00
DJ1	Derek Jeter/25	200.00
MR	Manny Ramirez/60	65.00
MR1	Manny Ramirez/60	65.00
CR	Cal Ripken Jr./15	250.00
CR1	Cal Ripken Jr./15	250.00
AR	Alex Rodriguez/15	200.00
AR1	Alex Rodriguez/15	200.00
AR2	Alex Rodriguez/115	150.00
KW	Kerry Wood/20	65.00
KW1	Kerry Wood/20	65.00
KW2	Kerry Wood/30	50.00

Dual Etchings

NM/M

Production 150 Sets

RJ	Alex Rodriguez, Derek Jeter	60.00
WP	Kerry Wood, Mark Prior	25.00
RP	Jose Reyes, Mike Piazza	30.00
PG	Albert Pujols, Vladimir Guerrero	30.00
MM	Hideki Matsui, Kazuo Matsui	40.00
MW	Mickey Mantle, Ted Williams	180.00

Etched in Time Black Ink

NM/M

Quantity produced listed
Common Autograph: 6.00

AA	Alfredo Amezaga/375	6.00
SA	Sparky Anderson/375	15.00
TA	Tony Armas/325	6.00
BA	Dusty Baker/150	15.00
JB	Jason Bay/375	15.00
BE	Carlos Beltran/150	30.00
AB	Angel Berroa/1,325	6.00
HB	Hank Blalock/375	15.00
GB	Geoff Blum/375	6.00
BB	Bert Blyleven/375	8.00
CB	Chris Bootcheck/375	8.00
DB	Dewon Brazelton/375	8.00
MB	Marlon Byrd/1,025	8.00
EB	Eric Byrnes/Redemp.	8.00
MC	Miguel Cabrera/1,025	15.00
CA	Chris Capuano/375	8.00
EC	Eric Chavez/375	15.00
AC	Alex Cintron/375	8.00
WC	Will Clark/150	20.00
CL	Brandon Claussen/375	8.00
CC	Chad Cordero/375	6.00
BC	Bobby Crosby/1,325	10.00
AD	Andre Dawson/375	10.00
BD	Brandon Duckworth/375	8.00
ME	Morgan Ensberg/1,325	8.00
DE	Dwight Evans/375	15.00
AE	Adam Everett/325	6.00
WE	Willie Eyre/375	6.00
KF	Kyle Farnsworth/1,325	8.00
PF	Pedro Feliz/325	8.00
RF	Rollie Fingers/375	10.00
JF	Josh Fogg/325	8.00
LF	Lew Ford/375	10.00
NG	Nomar Garciaparra/100	50.00
CG	Chad Gaudin/375	6.00
BG	Brian Giles/375	10.00
MG	Marcus Giles/325	10.00
GO	Jonny Gomes/325	6.00
AG	Adrian Gonzalez/325	8.00
DG	Dwight Gooden/375	10.00
KG	Ken Griffey Jr./1,625	60.00
GR	Ken Griffey Sr./375	8.00
TG	Tony Gwynn/150	40.00
SH	Scott Hairston/375	8.00
RH	Rob Hammock/325	8.00
AH	Aaron Harang/375	12.00
HA	Rich Harden/325	10.00
HE	Ramon Hernandez/325	8.00
RI	Raul Ibanez/325	8.00
EJ	Edwin Jackson/325	8.00
DJ	Derek Jeter	100.00
JJ	Jacque Jones/375	10.00
KA	Al Kaline/375	25.00
MK	Matt Kata/325	8.00
AK	Adam Kennedy/375	6.00
BK	Bobby Kielty/1,325	6.00
HK	Harmon Killebrew/Redemp.	35.00
DK	Dave Kingman/375	8.00
GK	Graham Koonce/375	8.00
LA	Adam LaRoche/1,325	8.00
CS	Carlos Lee/325	10.00
LE	Cliff Lee/1,325	8.00
TL	Ted Lilly/325	8.00
AL	Adam Loewen/375	6.00
ML	Mike Lowell/375	10.00
LM	Luis Matos/325	8.00
DM	Don Mattingly/150	50.00
MA	Joe Mauer/375	25.00
JM	Justin Miller/325	8.00
MO	Jack Morris/375	10.00
MM	Mark Mulder/375	10.00
MU	Dale Murphy/375	20.00
MN	Mike Neu/325	6.00
LN	Laynce Nix/Redemp.	10.00
RO	Roy Oswalt/375	12.00
LO	Lyle Overbay/1,325	8.00
PA	Jim Palmer/375	15.00
CP	Corey Patterson/375	10.00
BP	Brad Penny/375	8.00
JP	Jason Phillips/375	8.00
PO	Boog Powell/375	15.00
MP	Mark Prior/150	30.00
JR	Jose Reyes/325	25.00
JI	Jim Rice/375	10.00
CR	Cal Ripken Jr./100	120.00
BR	Brooks Robinson/375	25.00
RS	Ryne Sandberg/150	50.00
SO	Ron Santo/375	25.00
SS	Steve Sax/375	10.00
MS	Mike Scioscia/375	10.00
BS	Ben Sheets/375	15.00
TS	Terrmel Sledge/325	6.00
DS	Darryl Strawberry/150	15.00
MT	Mark Teixeira/325	20.00
LT	Luis Tiant/375	10.00
AT	Alan Trammell/375	15.00
CU	Chase Utley/375	25.00
RW	Ryan Wagner/1,325	8.00
WK	Rickie Weeks/Redemp.	15.00
JW	Jerome Williams/1,325	8.00
WI	Josh Willingham/1,325	6.00
RA	Randy Winn/375	8.00
KW	Kerry Wood/150	15.00
DY	Delmon Young/375	20.00
MY	Michael Young/1,325	15.00
CZ	Carlos Zambrano/375	25.00

Etched in Time Blue Ink

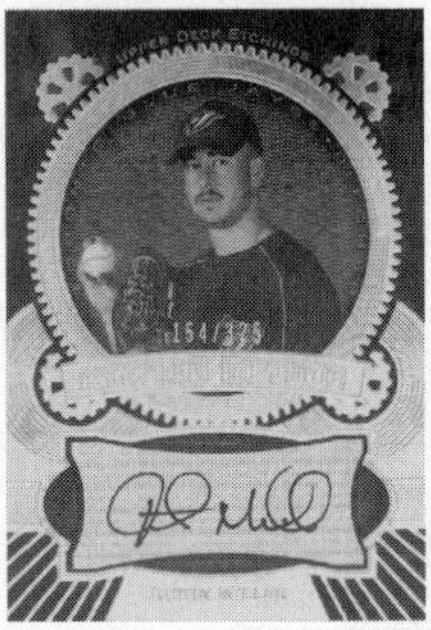

NM/M

Quantity produced listed
Common Autograph: 6.00

AA	Alfredo Amezaga/100	8.00
SA	Sparky Anderson/250	15.00
TA	Tony Armas/150	6.00
JB	Jason Bay/250	15.00
AB	Angel Berroa/150	8.00
HB	Hank Blalock/250	15.00
GB	Geoff Blum/250	6.00
BB	Bert Blyleven/250	8.00
CB	Chris Bootcheck/100	8.00
DB	Dewon Brazelton/250	8.00
MB	Marlon Byrd/150	8.00
EB	Eric Byrnes/Redemp.	8.00
MC	Miguel Cabrera/150	25.00
CA	Chris Capuano/100	8.00
EC	Eric Chavez/250	15.00
AC	Alex Cintron/100	10.00
WC	Will Clark/50	20.00
CL	Brandon Claussen/100	8.00
CC	Chad Cordero/100	6.00
BC	Bobby Crosby/150	10.00
AD	Andre Dawson/250	10.00
BD	Brandon Duckworth/100	8.00
ME	Morgan Ensberg/150	8.00
DE	Dwight Evans/250	15.00
AE	Adam Everett/150	8.00
WE	Willie Eyre/100	8.00
KF	Kyle Farnsworth/150	8.00
PF	Pedro Feliz/150	8.00
RF	Rollie Fingers/250	10.00
JF	Josh Fogg/150	8.00
LF	Lew Ford/200	10.00
NG	Nomar Garciaparra/50	85.00
CG	Chad Gaudin/100	6.00
BG	Brian Giles/250	10.00
MG	Marcus Giles/150	10.00
GO	Jonny Gomes/150	6.00
AG	Adrian Gonzalez/150	6.00
DG	Dwight Gooden/250	10.00
KG	Ken Griffey Jr./150	75.00
GR	Ken Griffey Sr./250	8.00
VG	Vladimir Guerrero/50	50.00
TG	Tony Gwynn/50	50.00
SH	Scott Hairston/100	8.00
RH	Rob Hammock/150	8.00
AH	Aaron Harang/100	15.00
HA	Rich Harden/150	10.00
HE	Ramon Hernandez/150	8.00
RI	Raul Ibanez/150	8.00
EJ	Edwin Jackson/100	8.00
DJ	Derek Jeter/50	120.00
JJ	Jacque Jones/250	10.00
KA	Al Kaline/250	25.00
MK	Matt Kata/150	8.00
AK	Adam Kennedy/100	8.00
BK	Bobby Kielty/150	8.00
DK	Dave Kingman/250	8.00
GK	Graham Koonce/250	8.00
LA	Adam LaRoche/150	10.00
LE	Cliff Lee/150	10.00
TL	Ted Lilly/150	8.00
ML	Mike Lowell/250	10.00
LM	Luis Matos/150	8.00
DM	Don Mattingly/50	60.00
MA	Joe Mauer/250	25.00
JM	Justin Miller/150	8.00
MO	Jack Morris/250	10.00
MM	Mark Mulder/250	10.00
MU	Dale Murphy/250	25.00
RO	Roy Oswalt/250	15.00
LO	Lyle Overbay/150	10.00
PA	Jim Palmer/250	15.00
CP	Corey Patterson/250	15.00
BP	Brad Penny/100	8.00
JP	Jason Phillips/250	8.00
LP	Lou Piniella/50	15.00
PO	Boog Powell/250	15.00
MP	Mark Prior/50	20.00
JR	Jose Reyes/150	30.00
JI	Jim Rice/250	10.00
CR	Cal Ripken Jr./50	150.00
BR	Brooks Robinson/250	25.00
RS	Ryne Sandberg/50	60.00
SO	Ron Santo/250	25.00
SS	Steve Sax/250	10.00
MS	Mike Scioscia/250	10.00
BS	Ben Sheets/250	15.00
TS	Terrmel Sledge/150	6.00
MT	Mark Teixeira/150	25.00
LT	Luis Tiant/250	10.00
AT	Alan Trammell/250	15.00
CU	Chase Utley/100	25.00
RW	Ryan Wagner/150	10.00
JW	Jerome Williams/150	10.00
WI	Josh Willingham/150	6.00
RA	Randy Winn/100	10.00
KW	Kerry Wood/50	20.00
DY	Delmon Young/250	20.00
MY	Michael Young/150	15.00
CZ	Carlos Zambrano/250	25.00

Etched in Time Red Ink

No Pricing
Production 25 Sets

Game Bat Blue

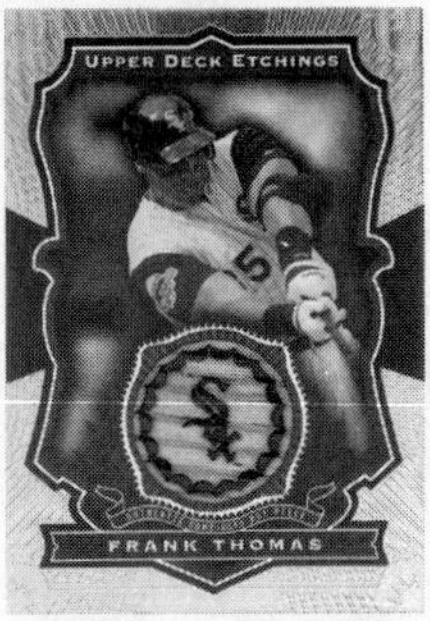

NM/M

Common Player:
Purple: 1X
Production 250
Red: 1X
Production 150
Green: 1-2X
Production 50

BA	Bobby Abreu	6.00
RA	Roberto Alomar	6.00
GA	Garret Anderson	6.00
CB	Carlos Beltran	6.00
AB	Adrian Beltre	6.00
LB	Lance Berkman	4.00
HB	Hank Blalock	6.00
BB	Bret Boone	4.00
SC	Sean Casey	4.00
EC	Eric Chavez	6.00
JC	Jose Cruz Jr.	4.00
CD	Carlos Delgado	6.00
JD	J.D. Drew	4.00
AD	Adam Dunn	8.00
JE	Jim Edmonds	6.00
CF	Cliff Floyd	4.00
RF	Rafael Furcal	4.00
NG	Nomar Garciaparra	10.00
JG	Jason Giambi	6.00
BG	Brian Giles	4.00
TG	Troy Glaus	6.00
LG	Luis Gonzalez	4.00
SG	Shawn Green	6.00
KG	Ken Griffey Jr.	12.00
VG	Vladimir Guerrero	10.00
TH	Todd Helton	8.00
HU	Torii Hunter	6.00
GJ	Geoff Jenkins	4.00
DJ	Derek Jeter	20.00
RJ	Randy Johnson	8.00
AJ	Andruw Jones	8.00
CJ	Chipper Jones	8.00

JL Javy Lopez 6.00
ML Mike Lowell 6.00
KM Kazuo Matsui 10.00
MO Magglio Ordonez 4.00
RP Rafael Palmeiro 8.00
JP Jay Payton 4.00
PI Mike Piazza 10.00
AP Albert Pujols 15.00
MR Manny Ramirez 8.00
JR Jose Reyes 6.00
AR Alex Rodriguez 15.00
IR Ivan Rodriguez 8.00
SR Scott Rolen 15.00
TS Tim Salmon 6.00
CS Curt Schilling 6.00
GS Gary Sheffield 6.00
AS Alfonso Soriano 8.00
SS Sammy Sosa 10.00
IS Ichiro Suzuki 15.00
MT Mark Teixeira 6.00
TE Miguel Tejada 6.00
FT Frank Thomas 8.00
JT Jim Thome 8.00
OV Omar Vizquel 4.00
LW Larry Walker 4.00
VW Vernon Wells 4.00
BW Bernie Williams 8.00
KW Kerry Wood 8.00

Master Etchings

No Pricing
Production One Set

Star Etchings

NM/M

Quantity produced listed
BA Bobby Abreu/50 20.00
GA Garret Anderson/50 15.00
JB Josh Beckett/50 25.00
CB Carlos Beltran/50 40.00
HB Hank Blalock/50 15.00
BB Bret Boone/50 10.00
MC Miguel Cabrera/50 30.00
EC Eric Chavez/50 15.00
JD J.D. Drew/50 15.00
AD Adam Dunn/50 25.00
NG Nomar Garciaparra/15 60.00
KG Ken Griffey Jr./50 85.00
KG1 Ken Griffey Jr./50 85.00
VG Vladimir Guerrero/15 80.00
RH Roy Halladay/50 15.00
TH Tim Hudson/50 25.00
GJ Geoff Jenkins/50 10.00
DL Derrek Lee/50 25.00
JL Javy Lopez/50 10.00
ML Mike Lowell/50 15.00
MU Mark Mulder/50 15.00
MO Magglio Ordonez/50 15.00
RO Roy Oswalt/50 25.00
PR Mark Prior/50 25.00
JS Jason Schmidt/50 15.00
MT Mark Teixeira/50 30.00
TE Miguel Tejada/50 25.00
BW Brandon Webb/50 15.00
VW Vernon Wells/50 15.00
DW Dontrelle Willis/50 15.00
KW Kerry Wood/50 20.00

Triple Etchings

NM/M

Production 50 Sets
RJM Alex Rodriguez, Derek Jeter, Hideki Matsui 125.00
PER Albert Pujols, Jim Edmonds, Scott Rolen 90.00
SRG Curt Schilling, Manny Ramirez, Nomar Garciaparra 40.00
SBT Alfonso Soriano, Hank Blalock, Mark Teixeira 40.00
WPS Kerry Wood, Mark Prior, Sammy Sosa 50.00
DMW Joe DiMaggio, Mickey Mantle, Ted Williams 400.00

2004 Upper Deck First Pitch

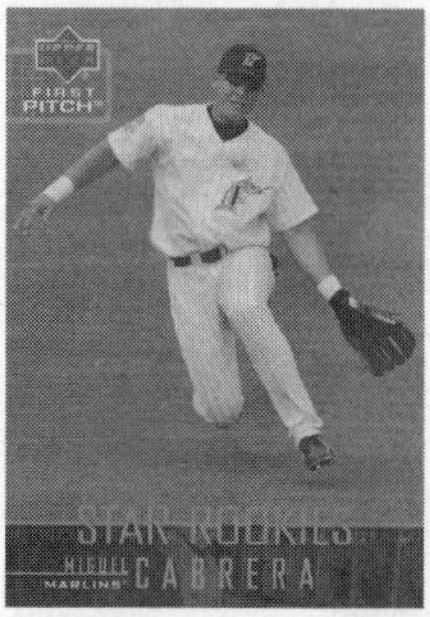

NM/M

Complete Set (300): 40.00
Common Player: .10
Common SP (271-300): 1.00
Inserted 1:4
Pack (5): 1.00
Box (36): 25.00
1 Dontrelle Willis .50
2 Edgar Gonzalez .25
3 Jose Reyes .50
4 Jae Weong Seo .25
5 Miguel Cabrera .75
6 Jesse Foppert .25
7 Mike Neu .25
8 Micheal Nakamura .25
9 Luis Ayala .25
10 Jared Sandberg .25
11 Jhonny Peralta .25
12 Wilfredo Ledezma .25
13 Jason Roach .25
14 Kirk Saarloos .25
15 Cliff Lee .25
16 Bobby Hill .25
17 Lyle Overbay .25
18 Josh Hall .25
19 Joe Thurston .25
20 Matt Kata .25
21 Jeremy Bonderman .25
22 Julio Manon .25
23 Rodrigo Rosario .25
24 Robby Hammock .25
25 David Sanders .25
26 Miguel Ojeda .25
27 Mark Teixeira .50
28 Franklyn German .25
29 Ken Harvey .25
30 Xavier Nady .25
31 Tim Salmon .25
32 Troy Glaus .25
33 Adam Kennedy .10
34 David Eckstein .10
35 Bengie Molina .10
36 Jarrod Washburn .10
37 Ramon Ortiz .10
38 Eric Chavez .25
39 Miguel Tejada .25
40 Chris Singleton .10
41 Jermaine Dye .10
42 John Halama .10
43 Tim Hudson .25
44 Barry Zito .25
45 Ted Lilly .10
46 Bobby Kielty .10
47 Kelvim Escobar .10
48 Josh Phelps .10
49 Vernon Wells .20
50 Roy Halladay .20
51 Orlando Hudson .10
52 Eric Hinske .10
53 Brandon Backe .10
54 Dewon Brazelton .10
55 Ben Grieve .10
56 Aubrey Huff .10
57 Toby Hall .10
58 Rocco Baldelli .50
59 Al Martin .10
60 Brandon Phillips .10
61 Omar Vizquel .10
62 C.C. Sabathia .10
63 Milton Bradley .10
64 Ricky Gutierrez .10
65 Matt Lawton .10
66 Danys Baez .10
67 Ichiro Suzuki 1.00
68 Randy Winn .10
69 Carlos Guillen .10
70 Mark McLemore .10
71 Dan Wilson .10
72 Jamie Moyer .10
73 Joel Pineiro .10
74 Edgar Martinez .20
75 Tony Batista .10
76 Jay Gibbons .10
77 Jeff Conine .10
78 Melvin Mora .10
79 Geronimo Gil .10
80 Rodrigo Lopez .10
81 Jorge Julio .10
82 Rafael Palmeiro .40
83 Juan Gonzalez .40
84 Mike Young .10
85 Alex Rodriguez 1.00
86 Einar Diaz .10
87 Kevin Mench .10
88 Hank Blalock .25
89 Pedro J. Martinez .50
90 Byung-Hyun Kim .10
91 Derek Lowe .20
92 Jason Varitek .10
93 Manny Ramirez .40
94 John Burkett .10
95 Todd Walker .10
96 Nomar Garciaparra 1.00
97 Trot Nixon .10
98 Mike Sweeney .10
99 Carlos Febles .10
100 Mike MacDougal .10
101 Raul Ibanez .10
102 Jason Grimsley .10
103 Chris George .10
104 Brent Mayne .10
105 Dmitri Young .10
106 Eric Munson .10
107 A.J. Hinch .10
108 Andres Torres .10
109 Bobby Higginson .10
110 Shane Halter .10
111 Matt Walbeck .10
112 Torii Hunter .25
113 Doug Mientkiewicz .10
114 Lew Ford .10
115 Eric Milton .10
116 Eddie Guardado .10
117 Cristian Guzman .10
118 Corey Koskie .10
119 Magglio Ordonez .25
120 Mark Buehrle .10
121 Billy Koch .10
122 Jose Valentin .10
123 Paul Konerko .10
124 Carlos Lee .10
125 Jon Garland .10
126 Jason Giambi .50
127 Derek Jeter 1.50
128 Roger Clemens 1.00
129 Andy Pettitte .25
130 Jorge Posada .25
131 David Wells .10
132 Hideki Matsui 1.25
133 Mike Mussina .40
134 Jeff Bagwell .40
135 Craig Biggio .20
136 Morgan Ensberg .10
137 Richard Hidalgo .10
138 Brad Ausmus .10
139 Roy Oswalt .25
140 Billy Wagner .20
141 Octavio Dotel .10
142 Gary Sheffield .25
143 Andruw Jones .40
144 John Smoltz .20
145 Rafael Furcal .20
146 Javy Lopez .25
147 Shane Reynolds .10
148 Horacio Ramirez .10
149 Mike Hampton .10
150 Jung Bong .10
151 Ruben Quevedo .10
152 Ben Sheets .20
153 Geoff Jenkins .20
154 Royce Clayton .10
155 Glendon Rusch .10
156 John Vander Wal .10
157 Scott Podsednik .25
158 Jim Edmonds .25
159 Tino Martinez .20
160 Albert Pujols 1.00
161 Matt Morris .10
162 Woody Williams .10
163 Edgar Renteria .10
164 Jason Isringhausen .10
165 Jason Simontacchi .10
166 Kerry Robinson .10
167 Sammy Sosa 1.00
168 Joe Borowski .10
169 Tony Womack .10
170 Antonio Alfonseca .10
171 Corey Patterson .10
172 Mark Prior .75
173 Moises Alou .20
174 Matt Clement .10
175 Randall Simon .10
176 Randy Johnson .50
177 Luis Gonzalez .20
178 Craig Counsell .10
179 Miguel Batista .10
180 Steve Finley .10
181 Brandon Webb .10
182 Danny Bautista .10
183 Oscar Villarreal .10
184 Shawn Green .25
185 Brian Jordan .10
186 Fred McGriff .20
187 Andy Ashby .10
188 Rickey Henderson .25
189 Dave Roberts .10
190 Eric Gagne .20
191 Kazuhisa Ishii .10
192 Adrian Beltre .10
193 Vladimir Guerrero .50
194 Livan Hernandez .10
195 Ron Calloway .10
196 Sun-Woo Kim .10
197 Wil Cordero .10
198 Brad Wilkerson .10
199 Orlando Cabrera .10
200 Sidney Ponson .10
201 Ray Durham .10
202 Andres Galarraga .10
203 Benito Santiago .10
204 Jose Cruz Jr. .10
205 Jason Schmidt .10
206 Kirk Rueter .10
207 Felix Rodriguez .10
208 Mike Lowell .10
209 Luis Castillo .10
210 Derrek Lee .10
211 Andy Fox .10
212 Tommy Phelps .10
213 Todd Hollandsworth .10
214 Brad Penny .10
215 Juan Pierre .10
216 Mike Piazza .75
217 Jae Weong Seo .10
218 Ty Wigginton .10
219 Al Leiter .10
220 Roger Cedeno .10
221 Timoniel Perez .10
222 Aaron Heilman .10
223 Pedro Astacio .10
224 Joe McEwing .10
225 Ryan Klesko .20
226 Brian Giles .20
227 Mark Kotsay .10
228 Brian Lawrence .10
229 Rod Beck .10
230 Trevor Hoffman .10
231 Sean Burroughs .10
232 Bobby Abreu .20
233 Jim Thome .50
234 David Bell .10
235 Jimmy Rollins .20
236 Mike Lieberthal .10
237 Vicente Padilla .10
238 Randy Wolf .10
239 Reggie Sanders .10
240 Jason Kendall .10
241 Jack Wilson .10
242 Jose Hernandez .10
243 Kip Wells .10
244 Carlos Rivera .10
245 Craig Wilson .10
246 Adam Dunn .25
247 Sean Casey .10
248 Danny Graves .10
249 Ryan Dempster .10
250 Barry Larkin .25
251 Reggie Taylor .10
252 Wily Mo Pena .10
253 Larry Walker .20
254 Mark Sweeney .10
255 Preston Wilson .10
256 Jason Jennings .10
257 Charles Johnson .10
258 Jay Payton .10
259 Chris Stynes .10
260 Juan Uribe .10
261 Hideki Matsui/CL .50
262 Josh Beckett/CL .20
263 Dontrelle Willis/CL .20
264 Kevin Millwood/CL .20
265 Billy Wagner/CL .10
266 Rocco Baldelli/CL .25
267 Roger Clemens/CL .50
268 Rafael Palmeiro/CL .20
269 Miguel Cabrera/CL .25
270 Jose Contreras/CL .10
271 Rickie Weeks 3.00
272 Delmon Young 4.00
273 Chien-Ming Wang 1.00
274 Rich Harden 1.00
275 Edwin Jackson 1.50
276 Dan Haren 1.00
277 Todd Wellemeyer 1.00
278 Prentice Redman 1.00
279 Ryan Wagner 1.50
280 Aaron Looper 1.00
281 Rick Roberts 1.00
282 Josh Willingham 1.00
283 David Crouthers 1.00
284 Chris Capuano 1.00
285 Mike Gosling 1.00
286 Brian Sweeney 1.00
287 Donald Kelly **RC** 1.00
288 Ryan Meaux **RC** 1.50
289 Colin Porter 1.00
290 Jerome Gamble **RC** 1.50
291 Colby Miller **RC** 1.50
292 Ian Ferguson 1.00
293 Tim Bittner **RC** 1.00
294 Jason Frasor **RC** 1.00
295 Brandon Medders **RC** 1.00
296 Mike Johnston **RC** 1.00
297 Tim Bausher **RC** 1.00
298 Justin Leone **RC** 1.00
299 Sean Henn 1.00
300 Michel Hernandez 1.00

First and Foremost

NM/M

Complete Set (14): 40.00
Common Player: 3.00
Inserted 1:Blaster Box
EB Ernie Banks 5.00
GH George H.W. Bush 5.00
GW George W. Bush 5.00
JC Jose Contreras 3.00
WF Whitey Ford 4.00
RH Rich Harden 3.00
DH Dan Haren 3.00
HR Horacio Ramirez 3.00
MS Mike Schmidt 5.00
LT Luis Tiant 3.00
RW Ryan Wagner 3.00
BW Brandon Webb 3.00
JW Jerome Williams 3.00
DW Dontrelle Willis 3.00

2004 Upper Deck Play Ball

NM/M

Complete Set (183):
Common Player: .15
Common SP (133-162): 3.00
Production 2,004
Common Classic Combo (163-183): 2.00
Production 1,999
Pack (5): 3.00
Box (24): 65.00
1 Hideo Nomo .25
2 Curt Schilling .50
3 Barry Zito .40
4 Nomar Garciaparra 1.50
5 Yogi Berra .50
6 Randy Johnson .75
7 Jason Giambi .75
8 Sammy Sosa 1.25
9 David Ortiz .40
10 Derek Jeter 2.00
11 Warren Spahn .50
12 Mark Prior 1.00
13 Roger Clemens 1.50

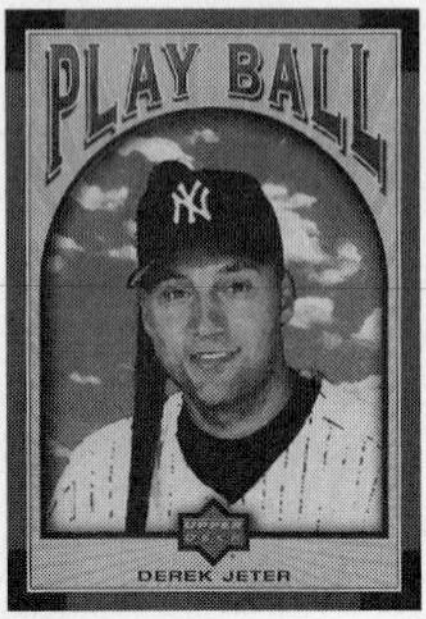

14	Mike Piazza	1.00
15	Nolan Ryan	2.00
16	Joe DiMaggio	1.50
17	Alfonso Soriano	.75
18	Brandon Webb	.25
19	Shawn Green	.25
20	Bob Feller	.25
21	Mike Schmidt	.75
22	Mark Teixeira	.25
23	Pedro J. Martinez	.75
24	Vladimir Guerrero	.75
25	Rafael Furcal	.25
26	Derrek Lee	.25
27	Carlos Delgado	.50
28	Mickey Mantle	3.00
29	Dontrelle Willis	.25
30	Ted Williams	1.50
31	Vernon Wells	.25
32	Alex Rodriguez	1.50
33	Brooks Robinson	.50
34	Tom Seaver	.50
35	Ernie Banks	.50
36	Bob Gibson	.50
37	Jim Thome	.75
38	Mike Mussina	.50
39	Eric Chavez	.25
40	Roy Halladay	.25
41	Eric Gagne	.40
42	Jose Reyes	.40
43	Jeff Bagwell	.50
44	Rich Harden	.15
45	Jeff Kent	.25
46	Lance Berkman	.25
47	Adam Dunn	.40
48	Richie Sexson	.40
49	Andruw Jones	.50
50	Ichiro Suzuki	1.25
51	Edgar Renteria	.25
52	Rocco Baldelli	.25
53	Jim Edmonds	.25
54	Magglio Ordonez	.25
55	Austin Kearns	.25
56	Garret Anderson	.40
57	Manny Ramirez	.50
58	Roy Oswalt	.25
59	Gary Sheffield	.40
60	Mark Mulder	.25
61	Ben Sheets	.25
62	Scott Rolen	.75
63	Greg Maddux	1.00
64	Jose Contreras	.15
65	Miguel Cabrera	.50
66	Hank Blalock	.40
67	Miguel Tejada	.40
68	Albert Pujols	1.50
69	Hideki Matsui	1.50
70	Mike Lowell	.25
71	Tim Hudson	.25
72	Bret Boone	.25
73	Ivan Rodriguez	.50
74	Josh Beckett	.50
75	Todd Helton	.50
76	Brian Giles	.25
77	Orlando Cabrera	.15
78	Carlos Beltran	.40
79	Jason Schmidt	.25
80	Kerry Wood	.75
81	Preston Wilson	.15
82	Troy Glaus	.40
83	Kevin Brown	.25
84	Rafael Palmeiro	.50
85	Chipper Jones	1.00
86	Reggie Sanders	.15
87	Cliff Floyd	.15
88	Corey Patterson	.25
89	Kevin Millwood	.25
90	Aaron Boone	.15
91	Darin Erstad	.25
92	Richard Hidalgo	.15
93	Dmitri Young	.15
94	Jeremy Bonderman	.15
95	Larry Walker	.25
96	Edgar Martinez	.25
97	Jerome Williams	.15
98	Luis Gonzalez	.25
99	Roberto Alomar	.40
100	Jerry Hairston Jr.	.15
101	Luis Matos	.15
102	Andy Pettitte	.40
103	Frank Thomas	.50
104	Rondell White	.25
105	Jody Gerut	.15
106	Bartolo Colon	.25
107	Johnny Damon	.25
108	Ryan Klesko	.25
109	Geoff Jenkins	.25
110	Jorge Posada	.40
111	Melvin Mora	.15
112	Bernie Williams	.40
113	Shannon Stewart	.15
114	Bobby Abreu	.25
115	Jose Guillen	.25
116	Brandon Phillips	.15
117	Jose Vidro	.15
118	Mike Sweeney	.15
119	Jacque Jones	.15
120	Josh Phelps	.15
121	Milton Bradley	.15
122	Torii Hunter	.25
123	Carl Crawford	.15
124	Javier Vazquez	.25
125	Juan Gonzalez	.50
126	Travis Hafner	.15
127	Ken Griffey Jr.	1.00
128	Phil Nevin	.15
129	Trot Nixon	.15
130	Carlos Lee	.15
131	Javy Lopez	.25
132	Jay Gibbons	.15
133	Brandon Medders **RC**	3.00
134	Colby Miller **RC**	3.00
135	David Crouthers	3.00
136	Dennis Sarfate **RC**	5.00
137	Donald Kelly **RC**	3.00
138	Frank Brooks **RC**	5.00
139	Chris Aguila **RC**	3.00
140	Greg Dobbs **RC**	3.00
141	Ian Snell **RC**	5.00
142	Jake Woods	3.00
143	Jamie Brown **RC**	3.00
144	Jason Frasor **RC**	4.00
145	Jerome Gamble **RC**	4.00
146	Jesse Harper **RC**	5.00
147	Josh Labandeira **RC**	4.00
148	Justin Hampson **RC**	4.00
149	Justin Huisman **RC**	4.00
150	Justin Leone **RC**	5.00
151	Lincoln Holdzkom **RC**	3.00
152	Mike Bumatay **RC**	5.00
153	Mike Gosling	5.00
154	Mike Johnston **RC**	3.00
155	Mike Rouse	3.00
156	Nick Regilio **RC**	3.00
157	Ryan Meaux **RC**	3.00
158	Scott Dohmann **RC**	3.00
159	Sean Henn	6.00
160	Tim Bausher **RC**	3.00
161	Tim Bittner **RC**	3.00
162	Alec Zumwalt **RC**	3.00
163	Aaron Boone, Bret Boone, Geoff Jenkins, Mark Prior, Barry Zito	3.00
164	Albert Pujols, Edgar Renteria, Alex Rodriguez	5.00
165	Alfonso Soriano, Sammy Sosa	4.00
166	Bobby Abreu, Jim Thome	2.00
167	Bret Boone, John Olerud, Ichiro Suzuki	4.00
168	Derek Jeter, Alfonso Soriano	6.00
169	Eric Chavez, Miguel Tejada	2.00
170	Garret Anderson, Jim Edmonds, Troy Glaus	2.00
171	Hank Blalock, Alex Rodriguez	5.00
172	Alex Rodriguez, Mark Teixeira, Michael Young, Rafael Palmeiro	5.00
173	Ivan Rodriguez, Dontrelle Willis	2.00
174	Jason Giambi, Derek Jeter	6.00
175	Joe DiMaggio, Mickey Mantle	8.00
176	Joe DiMaggio, Mickey Mantle, Ted Williams	8.00
177	Joe DiMaggio, Ted Williams	6.00
178	Nomar Garciaparra, Alfonso Soriano	4.00
179	Nomar Garciaparra, Jason Giambi	4.00
180	Paul LoDuca, Hideo Nomo	2.00
181	Rafael Palmeiro, Alex Rodriguez, Michael Young	4.00
182	Ralph Kiner, Ted Williams	5.00
183	Aaron Boone, Derek Jeter	6.00

Blue

Blue (1-132): 2-3X
Inserted 1:6

Green

No Pricing
Production 15 Sets

Purple

No Pricing
Production One Set

Die-Cut

Die-Cut (1-132): 3-6X
Production 175

Apparel Collection

NM/M

Common Player: 4.00

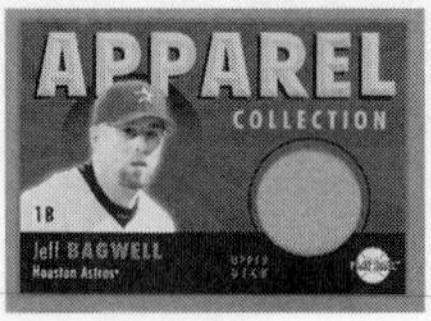

Inserted 1:24

JB	Jeff Bagwell	6.00
RB	Rocco Baldelli	8.00
BE	Josh Beckett	6.00
LB	Lance Berkman	4.00
CD	Carlos Delgado	5.00
JD	Joe DiMaggio/SP/150	75.00
AD	Adam Dunn	6.00
RF	Rafael Furcal	5.00
JG	Jason Giambi	6.00
TG	Troy Glaus	6.00
KG	Ken Griffey Jr.	15.00
HA	Roy Halladay	5.00
RH	Rich Harden/SP	8.00
BH	Bo Hart	4.00
TH	Torii Hunter	4.00
DJ	Derek Jeter	15.00
RJ	Randy Johnson	8.00
CJ	Chipper Jones	8.00
ML	Mike Lowell	5.00
MM	Mickey Mantle/SP/150	100.00
PM	Pedro J. Martinez	8.00
HM	Hideki Matsui	20.00
MU	Mike Mussina	6.00
HN	Hideo Nomo	6.00
RO	Roy Oswalt	4.00
RP	Rafael Palmeiro	6.00
PI	Mike Piazza	10.00
JP	Jorge Posada	8.00
MP	Mark Prior	8.00
AP	Albert Pujols	10.00
MR	Manny Ramirez	6.00
AR	Alex Rodriguez	8.00
CS	Curt Schilling	6.00
AS	Alfonso Soriano	6.00
SS	Sammy Sosa	10.00
IS	Ichiro Suzuki	15.00
JT	Jim Thome	8.00
BW	Bernie Williams	5.00
TW	Ted Williams/SP/150	70.00
DW	Dontrelle Willis	5.00
KW	Kerry Wood	8.00
BZ	Barry Zito	5.00

Artist's Touch

NM/M

Common Player: 4.00
Production 250
Parallel: 1-2X
Production 50

RB	Rocco Baldelli	8.00
JB	Josh Beckett	8.00
LB	Lance Berkman	5.00
CD	Carlos Delgado	6.00
RF	Rafael Furcal	5.00
JG	Jason Giambi	8.00
TG	Troy Glaus	6.00
KG	Ken Griffey Jr.	15.00
HA	Roy Halladay	5.00
BH	Bo Hart	4.00
TH	Torii Hunter	5.00
DJ	Derek Jeter	15.00
RJ	Randy Johnson	8.00
CJ	Chipper Jones	8.00
PM	Pedro J. Martinez	8.00
HM	Hideki Matsui	20.00
MM	Mike Mussina	8.00
HN	Hideo Nomo	8.00
RO	Roy Oswalt	4.00
RP	Rafael Palmeiro	8.00
PI	Mike Piazza	10.00
JP	Jorge Posada	8.00
MP	Mark Prior	10.00
AP	Albert Pujols	10.00
MR	Manny Ramirez/50	10.00
AR	Alex Rodriguez	10.00
AS	Alfonso Soriano	15.00
SS	Sammy Sosa	15.00
IS	Ichiro Suzuki	20.00
JT	Jim Thome	10.00
BW	Bernie Williams	6.00
DW	Dontrelle Willis	5.00
KW	Kerry Wood	8.00
BZ	Barry Zito	6.00

Home Run Heroics

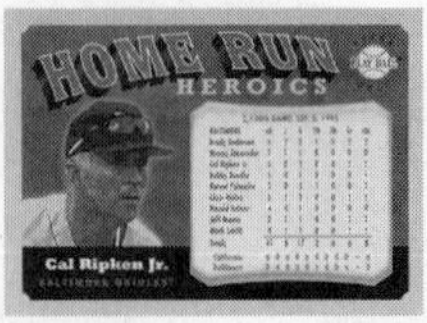

NM/M

Common Player: 2.00
Inserted 1:24

EB	Ernie Banks	4.00
HB	Hank Blalock	3.00
AB	Aaron Boone	2.00
MC	Miguel Cabrera	4.00
CD	Carlos Delgado	3.00
JD	Joe DiMaggio	8.00
JD1	Joe DiMaggio	8.00
JG	Jason Giambi	3.00
SG	Shawn Green	2.00
KG	Ken Griffey Jr.	6.00
KG1	Ken Griffey Jr.	6.00
RH	Rickey Henderson	2.00
RJ	Randy Johnson	3.00
HK	Harmon Killebrew	4.00
MM	Mickey Mantle	15.00
MM1	Mickey Mantle	15.00
MM2	Mickey Mantle	15.00
EM	Eddie Mathews	4.00
HM	Hideki Matsui	6.00
HM1	Hideki Matsui	6.00
WM	Willie McCovey	2.00
BM	Bill Mueller	2.00
SM	Stan Musial	5.00
RP	Rafael Palmeiro	3.00
CR	Cal Ripken Jr.	10.00
CR1	Cal Ripken Jr.	10.00
AR	Alex Rodriguez	6.00
AR1	Alex Rodriguez	6.00
FR	Frank Robinson	3.00
MS	Mike Schmidt	5.00
RS	Red Schoendienst	2.00
AS	Alfonso Soriano	4.00
SS	Sammy Sosa	6.00
SS1	Sammy Sosa	6.00
SS2	Sammy Sosa	6.00
SS3	Sammy Sosa	6.00
TW	Ted Williams	10.00
TW1	Ted Williams	10.00
TW2	Ted Williams	10.00
TW3	Ted Williams	10.00

Rookie Signature Portfolio

NM/M

Common Player: 5.00
Inserted 1:30

CA	Chris Aguila	6.00
TB	Tim Bausher	8.00
BI	Tim Bittner	8.00
FB	Frank Brooks	8.00
JB	Jamie Brown	5.00
MB	Mike Bumatay	8.00
DC	David Crouthers	8.00
GD	Greg Dobbs	6.00
SD	Scott Dohmann	8.00
JF	Jason Frasor	8.00
JG	Jerome Gamble	8.00
MG	Mike Gosling	8.00
HA	Justin Hampson	6.00
JH	Jesse Harper	8.00
SH	Sean Henn	15.00
LH	Lincoln Holdzkom	5.00
HU	Justin Huisman	5.00
MJ	Mike Johnston	10.00
DK	Donald Kelly	5.00
JL	Josh Labandeira	8.00
LE	Justin Leone	10.00
RM	Ryan Meaux	5.00
BM	Brandon Medders	5.00
CM	Colby Miller	5.00
NR	Nick Regilio	5.00
MR	Mike Rouse	6.00
DS	Dennis Sarfate	8.00
IS	Ian Snell	20.00
JW	Jake Woods	5.00
AZ	Alec Zumwalt	8.00

Signature Portfolio

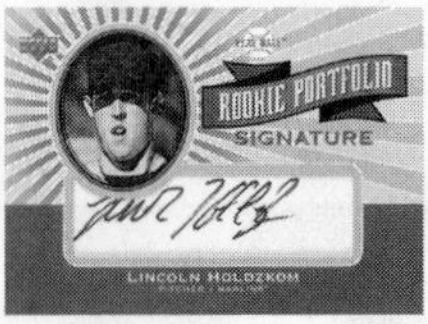

NM/M

Production 100
Parallel: No Pricing
Production 25 or 10

KG	Ken Griffey Jr.	100.00
HM	Hideki Matsui	250.00
CR	Cal Ripken Jr.	120.00
TS	Tom Seaver	40.00
CY	Carl Yastrzemski	50.00
BZ	Barry Zito	30.00

Tools of the Stars

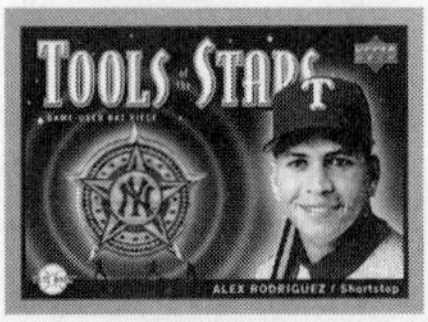

		NM/M
Common Player:		6.00
Inserted 1:48		
Level 1 Parallel:		1-1.5X
Production 250		
Level 2 Parallel:		No Pricing
Production 25		
JB	Josh Beckett	6.00
CD	Carlos Delgado	6.00
KG	Ken Griffey Jr./SP	15.00
DJ	Derek Jeter	15.00
CJ	Chipper Jones	8.00
HM	Hideki Matsui	15.00
HN	Hideo Nomo	6.00
PI	Mike Piazza	10.00
AP	Albert Pujols	15.00
AR	Alex Rodriguez	10.00
AS	Alfonso Soriano	6.00
IS	Ichiro Suzuki	15.00
JT	Jim Thome	8.00
KW	Kerry Wood	8.00

2004 Upper Deck Power Up

KEN GRIFFEY JR. - OF 19

		NM/M
Complete Set (100):		20.00
Common Player:		.15
Pack (9):		1.50
Box (24):		25.00
1	Austin Kearns	.25
2	Rafael Furcal	.25
3	Larry Walker	.25
4	Jeremy Bonderman	.15
5	Scott Rolen	.50
6	Nomar Garciaparra	1.00
7	Jody Gerut	.15
8	Troy Glaus	.25
9	Roy Halladay	.25
10	Barry Zito	.40
11	Gary Sheffield	.40
12	Ichiro Suzuki	1.00
13	Juan Gonzalez	.25
14	Jim Edmonds	.25
15	Hank Blalock	.40
16	Roy Oswalt	.15
17	Magglio Ordonez	.25
18	Garret Anderson	.40
19	Mark Teixeira	.25
20	Mike Sweeney	.15
21	Reggie Sanders	.15
22	Rafael Palmeiro	.40
23	Orlando Cabrera	.15
24	Edgar Renteria	.25
25	Ryan Klesko	.25
26	Torii Hunter	.25
27	Bret Boone	.25
28	Roberto Alomar	.25
29	Frank Thomas	.50
30	Chipper Jones	.50
31	Eric Chavez	.25
32	Miguel Tejada	.40
33	Carlos Beltran	.40
34	Geoff Jenkins	.25
35	Hideki Matsui	1.00
36	Jason Kendall	.15
37	Adam Dunn	.40
38	Jay Gibbons	.15
39	Ivan Rodriguez	.50
40	Sidney Ponson	.15
41	Albert Pujols	1.00
42	Bartolo Colon	.25
43	Lance Berkman	.25
44	Brandon Webb	.15
45	Shannon Stewart	.15
46	Josh Beckett	.25
47	Jason Schmidt	.25
48	Luis Gonzalez	.25
49	Jacque Jones	.15
50	Andruw Jones	.40
51	Todd Helton	.50
52	Javier Vazquez	.25
53	Alfonso Soriano	.50
54	Manny Ramirez	.50
55	Bobby Abreu	.25
56	Rocco Baldelli	.25
57	Kerry Wood	.50
58	Derek Jeter	1.50
59	Phil Nevin	.15
60	Jeff Bagwell	.40
61	Sammy Sosa	1.00
62	Tom Glavine	.25
63	Miguel Cabrera	.50
64	Shawn Green	.25
65	Mark Prior	1.00
66	Jose Reyes	.25
67	Curt Schilling	.40
68	Hideo Nomo	.25
69	Mike Lowell	.25
70	Randy Johnson	.50
71	Edgar Martinez	.25
72	Dontrelle Willis	.25
73	Milton Bradley	.15
74	Preston Wilson	.15
75	Mike Piazza	.75
76	Mike Mussina	.40
77	Darin Erstad	.25
78	Greg Maddux	.75
79	Tim Hudson	.25
80	Kevin Millwood	.25
81	Dmitri Young	.15
82	Ben Sheets	.25
83	Alex Rodriguez	1.00
84	Johan Santana	.15
85	Jeff Kent	.25
86	Pedro Martinez	.50
87	Carlos Delgado	.40
88	Jim Thome	.50
89	Aubrey Huff	.15
90	Ken Griffey Jr.	1.00
91	Kevin Brown	.25
92	Tony Batista	.15
93	Richie Sexson	.15
94	Cliff Floyd	.15
95	Jose Vidro	.15
96	Brian Giles	.25
97	Jorge Posada	.40
98	Vernon Wells	.25
99	Vladimir Guerrero	.50
100	Jason Giambi	.50

Mega Rare
No Pricing
Inserted 1:240

Super Rare
Stars:	5-10X
Inserted 1:96	

Rare
Stars:	3-4X
Inserted 1:6	

Ultra Rare
Stars:	4-6X
Inserted 1:24	

Shining Through

DONTRELLE WILLIS - P 50

		NM/M
1	Hideo Nomo	.25
2	Mark Prior	1.00
3	Scott Rolen	.75
4	Luis Gonzalez	.25
5	Miguel Tejada	.40
6	Richie Sexson	.40
7	Jim Edmonds	.40
8	Carlos Beltran	.40
9	Manny Ramirez	.50
10	Torii Hunter	.40
11	Garret Anderson	.40
12	Eric Chavez	.40
13	Juan Gonzalez	.40
14	Albert Pujols	1.50
15	Tim Hudson	.40
16	Roy Halladay	.40
17	Roy Oswalt	.25
18	Andruw Jones	.50
19	Gary Sheffield	.40
20	Magglio Ordonez	.40
21	Jason Giambi	.75
22	Brian Giles	.40
23	Barry Zito	.40
24	Todd Helton	.50
25	Randy Johnson	.75
26	Pedro Martinez	.75
27	Vernon Wells	.25
28	Lance Berkman	.40
29	Mike Mussina	.50
30	Carlos Delgado	.40
31	Ivan Rodriguez	.50
32	Kevin Brown	.40
33	Kerry Wood	.75
34	Mark Teixeira	.50
35	Hideki Matsui	1.50
36	Troy Glaus	.40
37	Mike Piazza	1.00
38	Nomar Garciaparra	1.50
39	Vladimir Guerrero	.75
40	Derek Jeter	2.00
41	Jason Schmidt	.40
42	Alex Rodriguez/Yanks	1.50
43	Jeff Bagwell	.50
44	Shawn Green	.40
45	Sammy Sosa	1.50
46	Josh Beckett	.75
47	Bret Boone	.40
48	Ichiro Suzuki	1.00
49	Jeff Kent	.40
50	Rafael Palmeiro	.50
51	Curt Schilling	.50
52	Greg Maddux	1.00
53	Mike Lowell	.40
54	Dontrelle Willis	.40
55	Alfonso Soriano	.50
56	Preston Wilson	.40
57	Jorge Posada	.50
58	Frank Thomas	.50
59	Jim Thome	.75
60	Ken Griffey Jr.	1.00
61	Rocco Baldelli	.40
62	Jose Vidro	.25
63	Austin Kearns	.25
64	Cliff Floyd	.25
65	Phil Nevin	.25
66	Darin Erstad	.25
67	Johan Santana	.25
68	Chipper Jones	.75
69	Brandon Webb	.25
70	Hank Blalock	.40
71	Adam Dunn	.40
72	Javier Vazquez	.25
73	Jacque Jones	.25
74	Bobby Abreu	.40
75	Edgar Renteria	.40
76	Roger Clemens	1.50
77	Rafael Furcal	.40
78	Mike Sweeney	.25
79	Geoff Jenkins	.25
80	Orlando Cabrera	.25
81	Ben Sheets	.25
82	Shannon Stewart	.25
83	Ryan Klesko	.40
84	Edgar Martinez	.40
85	Kevin Millwood	.40
86	Bartolo Colon	.40
87	Larry Walker	.40
88	Tom Glavine	.40
89	Miguel Cabrera	.75
90	Jose Reyes	.40

Stickers

POWER UP YOUR POINTS!
SCRATCH OFF

		NM/M
1	Hideo Nomo	.50
2	Mark Prior	2.00
3	Scott Rolen	1.50
4	Luis Gonzalez	.50
5	Miguel Tejada	.75
6	Richie Sexson	.75
7	Jim Edmonds	.75
8	Carlos Beltran	.75
9	Manny Ramirez	1.00
10	Torii Hunter	.75
11	Garret Anderson	.75
12	Eric Chavez	.75
13	Juan Gonzalez	.75
14	Albert Pujols	3.00
15	Tim Hudson	.75
16	Roy Halladay	.75
17	Roy Oswalt	.50
18	Andruw Jones	1.00
19	Gary Sheffield	.75
20	Magglio Ordonez	.75
21	Jason Giambi	1.50
22	Brian Giles	.75
23	Barry Zito	.75
24	Todd Helton	1.00
25	Randy Johnson	1.50
26	Pedro Martinez	1.50
27	Vernon Wells	.50
28	Lance Berkman	.75
29	Mike Mussina	.75
30	Carlos Delgado	.75
31	Ivan Rodriguez	1.00
32	Kevin Brown	.75
33	Kerry Wood	1.50
34	Mark Teixeira	.75
35	Hideki Matsui	2.50
36	Troy Glaus	.75
37	Mike Piazza	2.00
38	Nomar Garciaparra	3.00
39	Vladimir Guerrero	1.50
40	Derek Jeter	4.00
41	Jason Schmidt	.50
42	Alex Rodriguez	3.00
43	Jeff Bagwell	1.00
44	Shawn Green	.75
45	Sammy Sosa	2.50
46	Josh Beckett	1.00
47	Bret Boone	.50
48	Ichiro Suzuki	2.00
49	Jeff Kent	.75
50	Rafael Palmeiro	1.00
51	Curt Schilling	1.00
52	Greg Maddux	2.00
53	Mike Lowell	.75
54	Dontrelle Willis	.75
55	Alfonso Soriano	1.00
56	Preston Wilson	.50
57	Jorge Posada	.75
58	Frank Thomas	1.00
59	Jim Thome	1.50
60	Ken Griffey Jr.	2.00
61	Rocco Baldelli	.75
62	Jose Vidro	.50
63	Austin Kearns	.50
64	Phil Nevin	.50
65	Darin Erstad	.50
66	Johan Santana	.50
67	Chipper Jones	1.50
68	Brandon Webb	.50
69	Hank Blalock	.75
70	Adam Dunn	.75
71	Javier Vazquez	.75
72	Jacque Jones	.50
73	Bobby Abreu	.75
74	Edgar Renteria	.75
75	Rafael Furcal	.75
76	Mike Sweeney	.50
77	Geoff Jenkins	.50
78	Shannon Stewart	.50
79	Ryan Klesko	.75
80	Edgar Martinez	.75
81	Kevin Millwood	.75
82	Bartolo Colon	.75
83	Tom Glavine	.75
84	Miguel Cabrera	1.50
85	Jose Reyes	.75
86	Padres/Astros/A's/ Angels/Cubs/D-Rays	.50
87	Pirates/M's/Expos/ Twins/Reds/Phils	.50
88	Royals/O's/W.Sox/ Dodgers/Marlins/Yanks	.50
89	Giants/Mets/Cards/ Indians/Braves/Rangers	.50
90	Tigers/R.Sox/Rockies/ D-Backs/Brewers/Jay	.50

2004 Upper Deck Reflections

		NM/M
Complete Set (340):		
Common (1-100):		.50
Common SP (101-130):		4.00
Production 1,250		
Common Jersey (131-214):		4.00
Common Jersey (215-298):		4.00
Production 100 (215-298):		
Common Auto. (299-340):		15.00
Production 35		
Pack (4):		8.00
Box (8):		50.00
1	Adam Dunn	1.00
2	Albert Pujols	3.00
3	Alex Rodriguez	3.00
4	Alfonso Soriano	1.00
5	Andruw Jones	1.00
6	Austin Kearns	.50
7	Rafael Furcal	.50
8	Barry Zito	.75
9	Bartolo Colon	.50
10	Ben Sheets	.50
11	Bernie Williams	.75
12	Bobby Abreu	.50
13	Brandon Webb	.50
14	Bret Boone	.50
15	Brian Giles	.50

No.	Player	Price
16	Carlos Beltran	.50
17	Carlos Delgado	.75
18	Carlos Lee	.50
19	Chipper Jones	1.50
20	Corey Patterson	.50
21	Curt Schilling	.75
22	Delmon Young	.50
23	Derek Jeter	4.00
24	Dmitri Young	.50
25	Dontrelle Willis	.50
26	Edgar Martinez	.50
27	Edgar Renteria	.50
28	Eric Chavez	.50
29	Eric Gagne	.75
30	Frank Thomas	1.50
31	Garret Anderson	.50
32	Gary Sheffield	.50
33	Geoff Jenkins	.50
34	Greg Maddux	2.00
35	Hank Blalock	.75
36	Hideki Matsui	3.00
37	Hideo Nomo	.75
38	Ichiro Suzuki	2.50
39	Ivan Rodriguez	1.00
40	Jacque Jones	.50
41	Jason Giambi	1.50
42	Jason Schmidt	.75
43	Javy Lopez	.75
44	Jay Gibbons	.50
45	Jeff Bagwell	1.00
46	Jeff Kent	.50
47	Jeremy Bonderman	.50
48	Jim Edmonds	.75
49	Jim Thome	1.50
50	Johnny Damon	.50
51	Jorge Posada	.75
52	Jose Contreras	.50
53	Jose Reyes	.75
54	Jose Vidro	.50
55	Josh Beckett	1.00
56	Juan Gonzalez	1.00
57	Ken Griffey Jr.	2.50
58	Kerry Wood	1.50
59	Kevin Brown	.50
60	Kevin Millwood	.50
61	Lance Berkman	.50
62	Larry Walker	.50
63	Luis Gonzalez	.50
64	Magglio Ordonez	.50
65	Manny Ramirez	1.00
66	Mark Mulder	.50
67	Mark Prior	2.00
68	Mark Teixeira	.50
69	Miguel Cabrera	1.50
70	Miguel Tejada	.75
71	Mike Lowell	.75
72	Mike Mussina	.75
73	Mike Piazza	2.00
74	Mike Sweeney	.50
75	Milton Bradley	.50
76	Nomar Garciaparra	2.00
77	Orlando Cabrera	.50
78	Pedro Martinez	1.50
79	Phil Nevin	.50
80	Preston Wilson	.50
81	Rafael Palmeiro	1.00
82	Randy Johnson	1.50
83	Rich Harden	.50
84	Richie Sexson	.75
85	Rickie Weeks	.50
86	Rocco Baldelli	.75
87	Roy Halladay	.75
88	Roy Oswalt	.75
89	Ryan Klesko	.50
90	Sammy Sosa	2.50
91	Scott Rolen	1.50
92	Shannon Stewart	.50
93	Shawn Green	.50
94	Tim Hudson	.75
95	Todd Helton	1.00
96	Torii Hunter	.75
97	Trot Nixon	.50
98	Troy Glaus	.75
99	Vernon Wells	.50
100	Vladimir Guerrero	1.50
101	Brandon Medders RC	4.00
102	Colby Miller RC	4.00
103	David Crouthers RC	4.00
104	Dennis Sarfate RC	4.00
105	Donnie Kelly RC	4.00
106	Alec Zumwalt RC	4.00
107	Chris Aguila RC	4.00
108	Greg Dobbs RC	4.00
109	Ian Snell RC	8.00
110	Jake Woods RC	4.00
111	Jamie Brown RC	4.00
112	Jason Frasor RC	4.00
113	Jerome Gamble RC	4.00
114	Jesse Harper RC	4.00
115	Josh Labandeira RC	5.00
116	Justin Hampson RC	4.00
117	Justin Huisman RC	4.00
118	Justin Leone RC	4.00
119	Kazuo Matsui RC	15.00
120	Lincoln Holdzkom RC	4.00
121	Mike Bumatay RC	4.00
122	Mike Gosling RC	4.00
123	Mike Johnston RC	4.00
124	Mike Rouse RC	4.00
125	Nick Regilio RC	4.00
126	Ryan Meaux RC	4.00
127	Scott Dohmann RC	4.00
128	Sean Henn RC	6.00
129	Tim Bausher RC	4.00
130	Tim Bittner RC	4.00
131	Adam Dunn	6.00
132	Andruw Jones	4.00
133	Austin Kearns	4.00
134	Bartolo Colon	4.00
135	Ben Sheets	5.00
136	Bernie Williams	4.00
137	Bobby Abreu	4.00
138	Brian Giles	4.00
139	Carlos Lee	4.00
140	Chipper Jones	8.00
141	Corey Patterson	4.00
142	Darin Erstad	4.00
143	Edgar Martinez	4.00
144	Vladimir Guerrero	8.00
145	Eric Gagne	4.00
146	Frank Thomas	8.00
147	Garret Anderson	4.00
148	Roger Clemens	12.00
149	Greg Maddux	8.00
150	Jacque Jones	4.00
151	Randy Johnson	8.00
152	Javy Lopez	4.00
153	Mike Piazza	8.00
154	Albert Pujols	15.00
155	Jim Edmonds	4.00
156	Jim Milton	4.00
157	Jorge Posada	6.00
158	J.D. Drew	4.00
159	Jose Vidro	4.00
160	Kevin Millwood	4.00
161	Larry Walker	4.00
162	Luis Gonzalez	4.00
163	Mike Sweeney	4.00
164	Kerry Wood	4.00
165	Mike Cameron	4.00
166	Phil Nevin	4.00
167	Rocco Baldelli	4.00
168	Ryan Klesko	4.00
169	Shannon Stewart	4.00
170	Torii Hunter	6.00
171	Trot Nixon	4.00
172	Vernon Wells	4.00
173	Alfonso Soriano	6.00
174	Andruw Jones	6.00
175	Barry Zito	4.00
176	Brandon Webb	4.00
177	Bret Boone	4.00
178	Scott Rolen	6.00
179	Carlos Delgado	6.00
180	Curt Schilling	8.00
181	Dontrelle Willis	8.00
182	Eric Chavez	4.00
183	Frank Thomas	8.00
184	Gary Sheffield	6.00
185	Greg Maddux	8.00
186	Hank Blalock	4.00
187	Hideki Matsui	15.00
188	Hideo Nomo	8.00
189	Ichiro Suzuki	15.00
190	Ivan Rodriguez	6.00
191	Jason Giambi	6.00
192	Rafael Furcal	4.00
193	Jeff Bagwell	8.00
194	Jeff Kent	4.00
195	Jim Thome	6.00
196	Jose Reyes	8.00
197	Josh Beckett	6.00
198	Juan Gonzalez	4.00
199	Ken Griffey Jr.	15.00
200	Kevin Brown	4.00
201	Lance Berkman	6.00
202	Magglio Ordonez	5.00
203	Mark Mulder	4.00
204	Mark Teixeira	6.00
205	Miguel Tejada	6.00
206	Mike Mussina	6.00
207	Preston Wilson	4.00
208	Rafael Palmeiro	6.00
209	Alex Rodriguez	15.00
210	Richie Sexson	4.00
211	Roy Halladay	4.00
212	Roy Oswalt	5.00
213	Tim Hudson	5.00
214	Troy Glaus	4.00
215	Adam Dunn	8.00
216	Austin Kearns	4.00
217	Bartolo Colon	4.00
218	Ben Sheets	5.00
219	Bernie Williams	4.00
220	Bobby Abreu	5.00
221	Bret Boone	4.00
222	Todd Helton	8.00
223	Chipper Jones	8.00
224	Corey Patterson	4.00
225	Darin Erstad	4.00
226	Dontrelle Willis	4.00
227	Edgar Martinez	4.00
228	Eric Gagne	4.00
229	Garret Anderson	4.00
230	Roger Clemens	20.00
231	Hank Blalock	4.00
232	Jacque Jones	4.00
233	Jeff Bagwell	8.00
234	Jeff Kent	4.00
235	Jeremy Bonderman	4.00
236	Jim Edmonds	4.00
237	Jorge Posada	8.00
238	J.D. Drew	4.00
239	Jose Reyes	10.00
240	Jose Vidro	4.00
241	Kevin Millwood	4.00
242	Luis Gonzalez	4.00
243	Mike Sweeney	4.00
244	Jason Giambi	6.00
245	Manny Ramirez	8.00
246	Phil Nevin	4.00
247	Preston Wilson	4.00
248	Alex Rodriguez	20.00
249	Richie Sexson	4.00
250	Rocco Baldelli	4.00
251	Ryan Klesko	4.00
252	Sammy Sosa	8.00
253	Torii Hunter	4.00
254	Mike Lowell	6.00
255	Troy Glaus	4.00
256	Vernon Wells	6.00
257	Albert Pujols	20.00
258	Alex Rodriguez	20.00
259	Alfonso Soriano	8.00
260	Roger Clemens	20.00
261	Barry Zito	4.00
262	Brandon Webb	6.00
263	Carlos Delgado	6.00
264	Curt Schilling	8.00
265	Derek Jeter	25.00
266	Eric Chavez	6.00
267	Gary Sheffield	8.00
268	Hideki Matsui	25.00
269	Hideo Nomo	10.00
270	Ichiro Suzuki	25.00
271	Ivan Rodriguez	8.00
272	Jason Giambi	6.00
273	Jim Thome	8.00
274	Josh Beckett	10.00
275	Juan Gonzalez	8.00
276	Ken Griffey Jr.	20.00
277	Kerry Wood	4.00
278	Kevin Brown	4.00
279	Lance Berkman	6.00
280	Magglio Ordonez	8.00
281	Manny Ramirez	8.00
282	Mark Mulder	4.00
283	Mark Prior	6.00
284	Mark Teixeira	6.00
285	Miguel Tejada	8.00
286	Mike Mussina	8.00
287	Mike Piazza	10.00
288	Pedro Martinez	10.00
289	Rafael Palmeiro	8.00
290	Randy Johnson	10.00
291	Roy Halladay	6.00
292	Roy Oswalt	6.00
293	Sammy Sosa	10.00
294	Scott Rolen	8.00
295	Shawn Green	6.00
296	Tim Hudson	6.00
297	Todd Helton	6.00
298	Vladimir Guerrero	10.00
299	Bret Boone	10.00
300	Alex Rodriguez	200.00
301	Dontrelle Willis	30.00
302	Barry Larkin	30.00
303	Barry Zito	25.00
304	Eric Chavez	20.00
305	Bernie Williams	85.00
306	Brandon Webb	20.00
307	Cal Ripken Jr.	175.00
308	Carl Yastrzemski	65.00
309	Carlos Delgado	25.00
310	Shawn Green	25.00
311	Eric Gagne	15.00
312	Frank Thomas	40.00
313	Carlos Lee	20.00
314	Garret Anderson	20.00
315	Hideki Matsui	300.00
316	Jim Edmonds	40.00
317	Jeff Bagwell	40.00
318	Luis Gonzalez	20.00
319	Mike Mussina	40.00
320	John Smoltz	60.00
321	Jose Reyes	40.00
322	Josh Beckett	50.00
323	Juan Gonzalez	25.00
324	Ken Griffey Jr.	140.00
325	Rich Harden	20.00
326	Pat Burrell	25.00
327	Mark Teixeira	40.00
328	Roy Oswalt	30.00
329	Miguel Tejada	40.00
330	Mike Hampton	15.00
331	Mike Piazza	175.00
332	Nolan Ryan	120.00
333	Orlando Hernandez	25.00
334	Paul Lo Duca	25.00
335	Roberto Alomar	40.00
336	Rocco Baldelli	20.00
337	Trevor Hoffman	25.00
338	Tom Glavine	50.00
339	Tom Seaver	60.00
340	Mark Prior	25.00

Blue

Blue (1-100):	2-4X
Production 250	
Blue (215-256):	1-2X
Production 15	

Red

Red (1-100):	4-6X
Production 50	
Red Jersey (131-214):	1.5-2X
Production 50	
Red Jersey (215-256):	1-1.5X
Production 50	

Gold

Gold (1-100):	5-10X
Production 15	
Gold Auto. (101-130):	2X
Production 250	
Gold Auto. Parallel (101-130):	2X
Production 125	
Gold Jersey (131-172):	1.5-3X
Production 15	
Gold Jersey (257-298):	No Pricing
Production 5	
Gold Jsy Auto. (299-340):	1X
Production 5	

Black

Black (1-100):	No Pricing
Production One Set	
Black Auto. (101-130):	No Pricing
Production One Set	
Black Jersey (173-214):	No Pricing
Production One Set	
Black Jersey (257-298):	No Pricing
Production One Set	
Black Jsy Auto. (299-340):	No Pricing
Production One Set	

2004 Upper Deck R Class

	NM/M
Complete Set (180):	50.00
Common Player:	.10

Pack (6):		2.50
Box (24):		50.00
1	Adam Dunn	.50
2	Jose Vidro	.10
3	Vladimir Guerrero	.75
4	Hideo Nomo	.25
5	Eric Chavez	.25
6	Carlos Delgado	.40
7	Javy Lopez	.25
8	Javier Vazquez	.25
9	Miguel Cabrera	.50
10	Manny Ramirez	.50
11	Scott Rolen	.25
12	Rafael Furcal	.10
13	Jim Thome	.75
14	Edgar Renteria	.25
15	Jason Kendall	.10
16	Alfonso Soriano	.75
17	Troy Glaus	.40
18	Vernon Wells	.10
19	Todd Helton	.50
20	Mark Mulder	.25
21	Albert Pujols	2.00
22	Andy Pettitte	.25
23	Kevin Millwood	.10
24	Bret Boone	.10
25	Ken Griffey Jr.	1.00
26	Kevin Brown	.20
27	J.D. Drew	.25
28	Corey Patterson	.40
29	Jason Giambi	.40
30	Jason Schmidt	.25
31	Jose Reyes	.25
32	Torii Hunter	.25
33	Brian Giles	.25
34	Garret Anderson	.25
35	Mark Teixeira	.40
36	Sammy Sosa	1.50
37	Rocco Baldelli	.50
38	Jeff Bagwell	.50
39	Rafael Palmeiro	.50
40	Derrek Lee	.25
41	Randy Johnson	.75
42	Roger Clemens	1.50
43	Austin Kearns	.25
44	Dontrelle Willis	.10
45	Lance Berkman	.25
46	Juan Gonzalez	.40
47	Ichiro Suzuki	1.50
48	Pat Burrell	.25
49	Miguel Tejada	.40
50	Mike Piazza	1.00
51	Mark Prior	.75
52	C.C. Sabathia	.10
53	Jacque Jones	.10
54	Carlos Beltran	.75
55	Mike Mussina	.40
56	Mike Lowell	.25
57	Phil Nevin	.10
58	Andruw Jones	.40
59	Barry Zito	.25
60	Magglio Ordonez	.25
61	Carlos Lee	.20
62	Nomar Garciaparra	1.00
63	Kerry Wood	.75
64	Luis Gonzalez	.20
65	Derek Jeter	2.00
66	Preston Wilson	.10
67	Greg Maddux	1.00
68	Pedro J. Martinez	.75
69	Richie Sexson	.25
70	Hank Blalock	.50
71	Chipper Jones	.75
72	Ivan Rodriguez	.50
73	Roy Halladay	.25
74	Tim Hudson	.25
75	Ryan Klesko	.25
76	Hideki Matsui	1.50
77	Josh Beckett	.40
78	Brandon Webb	.10
79	Alex Rodriguez	2.00
80	Jim Edmonds	.40
81	Jeff Kent	.10
82	Bobby Abreu	.25
83	Curt Schilling	.75
84	Roy Oswalt	.25
85	Orlando Cabrera	.75
86	Johan Santana	.25
87	Geoff Jenkins	.10
88	Gary Sheffield	.40
89	Shawn Green	.25
90	Frank Thomas	.50
91	Tim Hamulack RC	.25
92	Shingo Takatsu RC	.50
93	Justin Huisman	.25
94	Sean Henn	.25
95	Jamie Brown	.25
96	Dennis Sarfate RC	.25
97	Lincoln Holdzkom RC	.25
98	Roman Colon RC	.25
99	Scott Dohmann RC	.25
100	Ivan Ochoa	.25
101	Akinori Otsuka RC	.50
102	Fernando Nieve RC	.25
103	Mike Johnston RC	.25
104	Mariano Gomez RC	.25
105	Justin Leone RC	.25
106	Evan Rust RC	.25
107	Mike Rouse	.25
108	Ian Snell RC	.50
109	Jason Bartlett	.25
110	Ryan Wing	.25
111	Nick Regilio RC	.25
112	Merkin Valdez RC	.50
113	Josh Labandeira RC	.25

114	David Aardsma	.75
115	Justin Knoedler RC	.25
116	Shawn Hill RC	.25
117	Casey Daigle RC	.25
118	Donnie Kelly RC	.25
119	Justin Germano RC	.25
120	Eddy Rodriguez	.25
121	Onil Joseph RC	.25
122	Mike Wuertz	.50
123	Roberto Novoa RC	.25
124	Jerome Gamble RC	.50
125	Justin Hampson RC	.25
126	Ronald Belisario RC	.25
127	Tim Bausher RC	.25
128	Chris Saenz RC	.25
129	Hector Gimenez RC	.25
130	Ronny Cedeno RC	.25
131	Jason Frasor RC	.25
132	Kazuo Matsui RC	2.00
133	Mike Gosling	.25
134	Jerry Gil RC	.25
135	Orlando Rodriguez RC	.25
136	Jorge Vasquez RC	.50
137	Chris Aguila RC	.25
138	Tim Bittner RC	.25
139	Jake Woods	.25
140	Enemencio Pacheco	.25
141	David Crouthers	.25
142	Jose Capellan RC	1.00
143	Chad Bentz RC	.25
144	Michael Vento	.75
145	Scott Proctor RC	.50
146	Edwin Moreno RC	.25
147	Brandon Medders RC	.25
148	Renyel Pinto RC	.25
149	Rusty Tucker RC	.25
150	Ryan Meaux RC	.25
151	William Bergolla	.25
152	Angel Chavez	.25
153	Colby Miller RC	.25
154	John Gall RC	.25
155	Carlos Hines RC	.25
156	Carlos Vasquez RC	.50
157	Justin Lehr RC	.25
158	Kevin Cave RC	.25
159	Jeff Bennett RC	.25
160	Greg Dobbs RC	.25
161	Jorge Sequea RC	.25
162	Chris Oxspring RC	.25
163	Franklyn Gracesgui RC	.25
164	Shawn Camp RC	.25
165	Lino Urdaneta	.25
166	Luis Gonzalez	.25
167	Ramon Ramirez RC	.50
168	Freddy Guzman RC	.25
169	Chris Shelton RC	1.50
170	Andres Blanco	.25
171	Aarom Baldiris RC	.25
172	Kazuhito Tadano RC	.50
173	Brian Dallimore RC	.25
174	Eduardo Villacis	.25
175	Frank Francisco RC	.25
176	Edwin Jackson	.50
177	Bobby Crosby	.50
178	Joe Mauer	.50
179	Rickie Weeks	.50
180	Delmon Young	.50

First Class Black Ink Auto

		NM/M
Inserted 1:2,880		
SA	Sandy Alomar	20.00
PB	Pat Burrell	30.00
MC	Miguel Cabrera	40.00
CD	Carlos Delgado	30.00
EG	Eric Gagne	50.00
KG	Ken Griffey Jr.	80.00
TH	Trevor Hoffman	30.00
BL	Barry Larkin	40.00
PL	Paul LoDuca	30.00
EM	Edgar Martinez	40.00
MP	Mark Prior	40.00
HR	Horacio Ramirez	20.00
DW	Dontrelle Willis	30.00

First Class Blue Ink Auto.

No Pricing
Production Three Sets

Jersey

		NM/M
Common Player:		4.00
Inserted 1:12		
RA	Roberto Alomar	6.00
BA	Jeff Bagwell	8.00
RB	Rocco Baldelli	4.00
JB	Josh Beckett	8.00
HB	Hank Blalock	8.00
BB	Bret Boone	4.00
KB	Kevin Brown	4.00
EC	Eric Chavez	4.00
RC	Roger Clemens	12.00
CD	Carlos Delgado	4.00
JG	Jason Giambi	6.00
GL	Troy Glaus	4.00
TG	Tom Glavine	6.00
KG	Ken Griffey Jr.	12.00
VG	Vladimir Guerrero	8.00
TH	Todd Helton	8.00
HU	Torii Hunter	4.00
DJ	Derek Jeter	15.00
RJ	Randy Johnson	6.00
AJ	Andruw Jones	6.00
CJ	Chipper Jones	8.00
EM	Edgar Martinez	4.00

PM	Pedro J. Martinez	8.00
HM	Hideki Matsui	20.00
KM	Kazuo Matsui	10.00
HN	Hideo Nomo	8.00
PI	Mike Piazza	10.00
MP	Mark Prior	6.00
AP	Albert Pujols	15.00
MR	Manny Ramirez	8.00
RI	Mariano Rivera	8.00
IR	Ivan Rodriguez	8.00
SR	Scott Rolen	8.00
CS	Curt Schilling	8.00
GS	Gary Sheffield	6.00
AS	Alfonso Soriano	8.00
SS	Sammy Sosa	10.00
IS	Ichiro Suzuki	25.00
MT	Miguel Tejada	6.00
BW	Bernie Williams	6.00
DW	Dontrelle Willis	4.00
KW	Kerry Wood	8.00

Taking Over!

		NM/M
Common Player:		3.00
1-20 production 650		
21-30 production 150		
TO-1	Richie Sexson, Lyle Overbay	3.00
TO-2	Jason Phillips, Mike Piazza	6.00
TO-3	Barry Larkin, William Bergolla	4.00
TO-4	Jason Dubois, Moises Alou	3.00
TO-5	Nook Logan, Alex Sanchez	3.00
TO-6	Robb Nen, Merkin Valdez	4.00
TO-7	Troy Percival, Francisco Rodriguez	3.00
TO-8	Carlos Beltran, David DeJesus	4.00
TO-9	Alex Rodriguez, Michael Young	6.00
TO-10	Alexis Rios, Vernon Wells	3.00
TO-11	Matt Lawton, Grady Sizemore	3.00
TO-12	Danny Graves, Ryan Wagner	3.00
TO-13	Miguel Cabrera, Jeff Conine	4.00
TO-14	Josh Willingham, Ramon Castro	3.00
TO-15	Junior Spivey, Rickie Weeks	3.00
TO-16	Guillermo Quiroz, Greg Myers	3.00
TO-17	Scott Hatteberg, Graham Koonce	3.00
TO-18	Rene Reyes, Larry Walker	4.00
TO-19	Khalil Greene, Ramon Vazquez	4.00
TO-20	Billy Wagner, Octavio Dotel	3.00
TO-21	Joe Mauer, A.J. Pierzynski	8.00
TO-22	Javier Vazquez, Roger Clemens	10.00
TO-23	Curt Schilling, Brandon Webb	3.00
TO-24	Delmon Young, Cirilo Cruz Jr.	8.00
TO-25	Vladimir Guerrero, Tim Salmon	8.00
TO-26	Gary Sheffield, J.D. Drew	3.00
TO-27	Miguel Tejada, Bobby Crosby	8.00
TO-28	Edwin Jackson, Kevin Brown	3.00
TO-29	Kazuo Matsui, Jose Reyes	10.00
TO-30	Wily Mo Pena, Ken Griffey Jr.	10.00

2004 Upper Deck Rivals: Yankees vs Red Sox

		NM/M
Complete Sealed Set (32):		25.00
Common Player (1-30):		.50
1	Alex Rodriguez	2.00
2	Bobby Doerr	.75
3	Don Mattingly	1.50
4	Dwight Evans	.50
5	Fred Lynn	.50
6	Jason Giambi	.50
7	Jim Rice	.50
8	Lou Gehrig	2.00
9	Luis Tiant	.50
10	Manny Ramirez	1.00

11	Mike Mussina	.75
12	Pedro Martinez	1.00
13	Phil Rizzuto	.75
14	Whitey Ford	.75
15	Yogi Berra	1.00
16	Tim Wakefield	.50
17	Billy Martin	.75
18	Mike Torrez, Bucky Dent	.50
19	Nomar Garciaparra, Derek Jeter	2.00
20	Gary Sheffield, Curt Schilling	1.00
21	Joe DiMaggio, Dick Newsome	1.50
22	Joe DiMaggio, Lefty Grove	1.50
23	Joe DiMaggio, Ted Williams	1.50
24	Jorge Posada, Jason Varitek	.50
25	Mickey Mantle, Carl Yastrzemski	2.00
26	Tracy Stallard, Roger Maris	1.00
27	Carlton Fisk, Thurman Munson	1.00
28	Babe Ruth	2.00
29	Roger Clemens	1.50
30	Wade Boggs	.50

Commemorativ

		NM/M
Complete Set (5):		10.00
One oversized card per set.		
	Babe Ruth	4.00
	Ted Williams	3.00
	Derek Jeter	3.00
	Nomar Garciaparra	2.00
	Mickey Mantle	5.00

"What If"

		NM/M
Common Player:		4.00
Production 2,150 Sets		
1	Aaron Boone	4.00
2	Alex Rodriguez	10.00
3	Babe Ruth	10.00
4	Babe Ruth	10.00
5	Billy Martin	4.00
6	Bucky Dent	4.00
7	Carl Yastrzemski	8.00
8	Carlton Fisk	5.00
9	Derek Jeter	10.00
10	Hideki Matsui	8.00
11	Joe DiMaggio	8.00
12	Joe Torre	4.00
13	Mickey Mantle	15.00
14	Pedro Martinez	6.00
15	Pee Wee Reese	4.00
16	Roger Clemens	8.00
17	Roger Maris	8.00
18	Ted Williams	8.00
19	Ted Williams	8.00
20	Carl Yastrzemski	8.00

What If Auto.

No Pricing

2004 Upper Deck Sweet Spot

		NM/M
Complete Set (262):		
Common Player:		.25
Common (91-170):		3.00
Production 799		
Common SP (171-230):		1.50
Production 399		
Common SP (231-250):		1.50
Production 299		
Common SP (251-260):		3.00
Production 199		
Pack (12):		10.00
Box (12):		100.00
1	Albert Pujols	3.00
2	Alex Rodriguez	3.00
3	Alfonso Soriano	1.00

4 Andruw Jones .50
5 Andy Pettitte .50
6 Aubrey Huff .25
7 Austin Kearns .50
8 Barry Zito .50
9 Bobby Abreu .50
10 Brandon Webb .25
11 Bret Boone .25
12 Brian Giles .25
13 C.C. Sabathia .25
14 Carlos Beltran 1.00
15 Carlos Delgado .50
16 Chipper Jones 1.00
17 Cliff Floyd .25
18 Curt Schilling 1.00
19 Delmon Young .50
20 Derek Jeter 3.00
21 Dontrelle Willis .25
22 Edgar Martinez .50
23 Edgar Renteria .50
24 Eric Chavez .50
25 Eric Gagne .50
26 Frank Thomas .75
27 Garret Anderson .50
28 Gary Sheffield .75
29 Geoff Jenkins .25
30 Greg Maddux 1.50
31 Hank Blalock .75
32 Hideo Nomo .50
33 Ichiro Suzuki 2.00
34 Ivan Rodriguez .75
35 Jacque Jones .25
36 Jason Giambi .50
37 Jason Schmidt .50
38 Javier Vazquez .25
39 Javy Lopez .50
40 Jeff Bagwell .75
41 Jim Edmonds .50
42 Jim Thome .75
43 Joe Mauer .50
44 John Smoltz .50
45 Jose Cruz Jr. .25
46 Jose Reyes .50
47 Jose Vidro .25
48 Josh Beckett .50
49 Ken Griffey Jr. 1.50
50 Kerry Wood 1.00
51 Kevin Brown .25
52 Larry Walker .50
53 Magglio Ordonez .25
54 Manny Ramirez .75
55 Mark Mulder .50
56 Mark Prior 1.00
57 Mark Teixeira .50
58 Miguel Cabrera 1.00
59 Miguel Tejada .50
60 Mike Lowell .40
61 Mike Mussina .75
62 Mike Piazza 1.50
63 Nomar Garciaparra 1.50
64 Orlando Cabrera .40
65 Pat Burrell .25
66 Pedro J. Martinez 1.00
67 Phil Nevin .25
68 Preston Wilson .25
69 Rafael Furcal .25
70 Rafael Palmeiro .75
71 Randy Johnson 1.00
72 Craig Wilson .25
73 Rich Harden .25
74 Richie Sexson .50
75 Rickie Weeks .50
76 Rocco Baldelli .50
77 Roger Clemens 2.50
78 Roy Halladay .25
79 Roy Oswalt .50
80 Ryan Klesko .25
81 Sammy Sosa 2.00
82 Scott Podsednik .25
83 Scott Rolen 1.00
84 Shawn Green .40
85 Tim Hudson .40
86 Todd Helton .75
87 Torii Hunter .40
88 Troy Glaus .25
89 Vernon Wells .25
90 Vladimir Guerrero 1.00
91 Aarom Baldiris **RC** 3.00
92 Akinori Otsuka **RC** 8.00
93 Andres Blanco **RC** 5.00
94 Angel Chavez **RC** 3.00
95 Brian Dallimore **RC** 8.00
96 Carlos Hines **RC** 5.00
97 Carlos Vasquez **RC** 5.00
98 Casey Daigle **RC** 3.00
99 Chad Bentz **RC** 3.00
100 Chris Aguila **RC** 3.00
101 Chris Oxspring **RC** 5.00
102 Chris Saenz **RC** 3.00
103 Chris Shelton **RC** 10.00
104 Colby Miller **RC** 5.00
105 David Crouthers 3.00
106 David Aardsma **RC** 5.00
107 Dennis Sarfate **RC** 3.00
108 Donnie Kelly **RC** 3.00
109 Eddy Rodriguez **RC** 3.00
110 Eduardo Villacis **RC** 3.00
111 Edwin Moreno **RC** 5.00
112 Enemencio Pacheco **RC** 5.00
113 Fernando Nieve **RC** 3.00
114 Franklyn Gracesqui **RC** 3.00
115 Freddy Guzman **RC** 3.00
116 Greg Dobbs **RC** 3.00
117 Hector Gimenez **RC** 3.00
118 Ian Snell **RC** 5.00
119 Ivan Ochoa **RC** 5.00
120 Jake Woods 5.00
121 Jamie Brown **RC** 5.00
122 Jason Bartlett **RC** 3.00
123 Jason Frasor **RC** 3.00
124 Jeff Bennett **RC** 3.00
125 Jerome Gamble **RC** 5.00
126 Jerry Gil **RC** 3.00
127 Brandon Medders **RC** 3.00
128 Ryan Meaux **RC** 3.00
129 John Gall **RC** 3.00
130 Jorge Sequea **RC** 3.00
131 Jorge Vasquez **RC** 5.00
132 Jose Capellan **RC** 8.00
133 Josh Labandeira **RC** 3.00
134 Justin Germano **RC** 8.00
135 Justin Hampson **RC** 5.00
136 Justin Huisman **RC** 5.00
137 Justin Knoedler **RC** 5.00
138 Justin Leone **RC** 5.00
139 Kazuhito Tadano **RC** 5.00
140 Kazuo Matsui **RC** 10.00
141 Kevin Cave **RC** 5.00
142 Lincoln Holdzkom **RC** 3.00
143 Lino Urdaneta **RC** 3.00
144 Luis A. Gonzalez **RC** 5.00
145 Mariano Gomez **RC** 5.00
146 Merkin Valdez **RC** 5.00
147 Michael Vento **RC** 8.00
148 Mike Wuertz **RC** 5.00
149 Mike Gosling 5.00
150 Mike Johnston **RC** 3.00
151 Mike Rouse 5.00
152 Nick Regilio **RC** 5.00
153 Onil Joseph **RC** 3.00
154 Orlando Rodriguez **RC** 5.00
155 Ramon Ramirez **RC** 5.00
156 Renyel Pinto **RC** 5.00
157 Roberto Novoa **RC** 5.00
158 Roman Colon **RC** 3.00
159 Ronald Belisario **RC** 5.00
160 Ronny Cedeno **RC** 8.00
161 Rusty Tucker **RC** 5.00
162 Ryan Wing 3.00
163 Scott Dohmann **RC** 3.00
164 Scott Proctor **RC** 5.00
165 Sean Henn 5.00
166 Shawn Camp **RC** 5.00
167 Shawn Hill **RC** 3.00
168 Shingo Takatsu **RC** 8.00
169 Tim Hamulack **RC** 3.00
170 William Bergolla **RC** 3.00
171 Adam Dunn 2.00
172 Albert Pujols 8.00
173 Alex Rodriguez 8.00
174 Alfonso Soriano 3.00
175 Andruw Jones 2.00
176 Bret Boone 1.50
177 Brian Giles 1.50
178 Carlos Delgado 2.00
179 Derrek Lee 2.00
180 Eric Chavez 1.50
181 Frank Thomas 2.00
182 Garret Anderson 1.50
183 Gary Sheffield 2.00
184 Hank Blalock 2.00
185 Jason Giambi 1.50
186 Javy Lopez 1.50
187 Jeff Bagwell 2.00
188 Jim Edmonds 2.00
189 Jim Thome 2.00
190 Ken Griffey Jr. 4.00
191 Lance Berkman 1.50
192 Magglio Ordonez 1.50
193 Manny Ramirez 3.00
194 Mike Lowell 1.50
195 Mike Piazza 5.00
196 Preston Wilson 1.50
197 Rafael Palmeiro 2.00
198 Richie Sexson 1.50
199 Sammy Sosa 5.00
200 Scott Rolen 4.00
201 Shawn Green 1.50
202 Todd Helton 2.00
203 Troy Glaus 1.50
204 Vernon Wells 1.50
205 Vladimir Guerrero 3.00
206 Garret Anderson, Vladimir Guerrero 3.00
207 Luis Gonzalez, Richie Sexson 2.00
208 Andruw Jones, Chipper Jones 3.00
209 Javy Lopez, Miguel Tejada 2.00
210 Manny Ramirez, David Ortiz 5.00
211 Derrek Lee, Sammy Sosa 5.00
212 Frank Thomas, Magglio Ordonez 2.00
213 Austin Kearns, Ken Griffey Jr. 4.00
214 Preston Wilson, Todd Helton 2.00
215 Delmon Young, Ivan Rodriguez 2.00
216 Miguel Cabrera, Mike Lowell 3.00
217 Jeff Bagwell, Lance Berkman 2.00
218 Lyle Overbay, Geoff Jenkins 1.50
219 Adrian Beltre, Shawn Green 2.00
220 Jacque Jones, Torii Hunter 1.50
221 Jose Vidro, N. Johnson 1.50
222 Kazuo Matsui, Mike Piazza 5.00
223 Alex Rodriguez, Jason Giambi 6.00
224 Eric Chavez, Jermaine Dye 1.50
225 Jim Thome, Pat Burrell 2.50
226 Brian Giles, Phil Nevin 1.50
227 Bret Boone, Ichiro Suzuki 6.00
228 Albert Pujols, Scott Rolen 8.00
229 Hank Blalock, Mark Teixeira 3.00
230 Carlos Delgado, Vernon Wells 2.00
231 Albert Pujols 8.00
232 Alex Rodriguez 8.00
233 Chipper Jones 3.00
234 Craig Biggio 1.50
235 Curt Schilling 2.00
236 Derek Jeter 8.00
237 Ivan Rodriguez 2.00
238 Jeff Bagwell 2.00
239 Jim Edmonds 2.00
240 Jim Thome 2.00
241 Josh Beckett 2.00
242 Kerry Wood 3.00
243 Kevin Brown 1.50
244 Mark Prior 2.00
245 Miguel Tejada 2.00
246 Mike Mussina 2.00
247 Nomar Garciaparra 4.00
248 Pedro J. Martinez 3.00
249 Randy Johnson 3.00
250 Roger Clemens 6.00
251 Alex Rodriguez, Derek Jeter 12.00
252 Alfonso Soriano, Hank Blalock 4.00
253 Bobby Abreu, Pat Burrell 3.00
254 Edgar Renteria, Scott Rolen 4.00
255 Garret Anderson, Vladimir Guerrero 4.00
256 Jeff Bagwell, Jeff Kent 3.00
257 Jose Reyes, Kazuo Matsui 4.00
258 K. Greene, S. Burroughs 4.00
259 Marcus Giles, Rafael Furcal 3.00
260 Manny Ramirez, Johnny Damon 6.00
261 Tim Bausher **RC** 3.00
262 Tim Bittner **RC** 5.00

Wood

Stars (1-90): 3-6X
SP's (91-262): .75-1.5X
Production 99 Sets

Limited

No Pricing
Production 10 Sets

Printing Plates

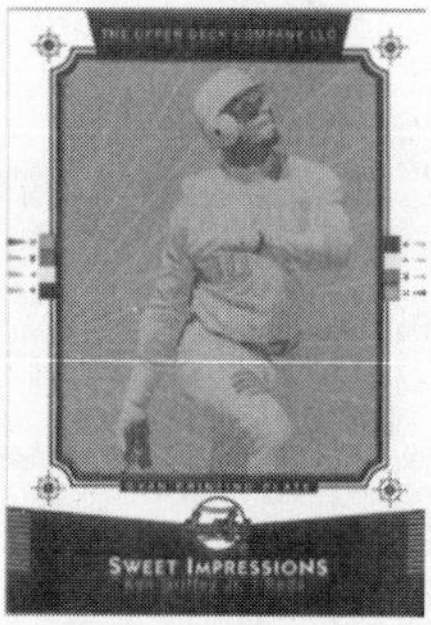

One of each color (black, cyan, magenta and yellow) issued for front and back.
(No values due to scarcity.)

Diamond Champs Jersey

NM/M

Common Player: 5.00
Production 150 Sets
GA Garret Anderson 5.00
JB Josh Beckett 8.00
RC Roger Clemens 12.00
EG Eric Gagne 8.00
KG Ken Griffey Jr. 12.00
RH Roy Halladay 5.00
DJ Derek Jeter 20.00
RJ Randy Johnson 10.00
CJ Chipper Jones 8.00
GM Greg Maddux 10.00
PM Pedro J. Martinez 8.00
PE Andy Pettitte 5.00
MP Mike Piazza 10.00
AP Albert Pujols 20.00
AR Alex Rodriguez/Yanks 15.00
IR Ivan Rodriguez 8.00
CS Curt Schilling 8.00
IS Ichiro Suzuki 30.00
MT Miguel Tejada 6.00
BZ Barry Zito 5.00

Home Run Heroes Jersey

NM/M

Common Player: 5.00
Production 199 Sets
GA Garret Anderson 5.00
JB Jeff Bagwell 8.00
CB Carlos Beltran 8.00
AB Adrian Beltre 8.00
LB Lance Berkman 5.00
HB Hank Blalock 8.00
BB Bret Boone 5.00
PB Pat Burrell 5.00
MC Miguel Cabrera 10.00
EC Eric Chavez 5.00
CD Carlos Delgado 5.00
JD J.D. Drew 5.00
AD Adam Dunn 8.00
JE Jim Edmonds 8.00
JG Jason Giambi 5.00
BG Brian Giles 5.00
TG Troy Glaus 5.00
LG Luis Gonzalez 5.00
SG Shawn Green 5.00
KG Ken Griffey Jr./Bat Up 12.00
KG1 Ken Griffey Jr./Swing 12.00
VG Vladimir Guerrero 10.00
HA Travis Hafner 5.00
TH Todd Helton 8.00
DJ Derek Jeter 20.00
AJ Andruw Jones 6.00
CJ Chipper Jones 8.00
JK Jeff Kent 5.00
DL Derrek Lee 5.00
ML Mike Lowell 5.00
HM Hideki Matsui 25.00
JM Joe Mauer 8.00
FM Fred McGriff 5.00
MO Magglio Ordonez 5.00
DO David Ortiz 15.00
RP Rafael Palmeiro 8.00
MP Mike Piazza 10.00
JP Jorge Posada 5.00
AP Albert Pujols 20.00
MR Manny Ramirez 8.00
AR Alex Rodriguez/Yanks/Bat Up 15.00
AR1 Alex Rodriguez/Yanks/Swing 15.00
IR Ivan Rodriguez 8.00
SR Scott Rolen 10.00
RS Richie Sexson 5.00
GS Gary Sheffield 8.00
AS Alfonso Soriano 8.00
SS Sammy Sosa 12.00
MT Mark Teixeira 6.00
TE Miguel Tejada 6.00
FT Frank Thomas 8.00
JT Jim Thome 10.00
VW Vernon Wells 5.00
BW Bernie Williams 8.00
PW Preston Wilson 5.00

Marquee Attractions Jersey

NM/M

Common Player: 5.00
Production 199 Sets
HB Hank Blalock 8.00
MC Miguel Cabrera 10.00
EC Eric Chavez 5.00
RC Roger Clemens 12.00
CD Carlos Delgado 5.00
EG Eric Gagne 8.00
BG Brian Giles 5.00
KG Ken Griffey Jr. 12.00
VG Vladimir Guerrero 10.00
TH Todd Helton 8.00
HU Torii Hunter 5.00
DJ Derek Jeter 20.00
RJ Randy Johnson 10.00
AJ Andruw Jones 5.00
PI Mike Piazza 10.00
MP Mark Prior 8.00
AP Albert Pujols 20.00
AR Alex Rodriguez 15.00
IR Ivan Rodriguez 8.00
CS Curt Schilling 10.00
JS Jason Schmidt 8.00
BS Ben Sheets 8.00
IS Ichiro Suzuki 30.00
MS Mike Sweeney 5.00
MT Miguel Tejada 8.00
FT Frank Thomas 8.00
JT Jim Thome 10.00

Signatures

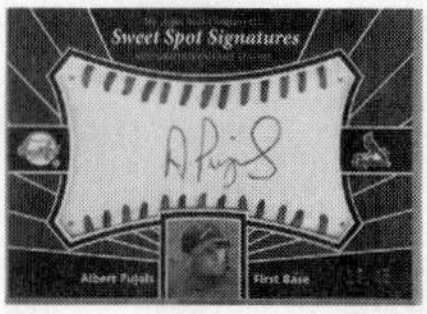

NM/M

Common Player: 10.00
Black Stitch: No Pricing
Production One Set
GA Garret Anderson 20.00
RB Rocco Baldelli 20.00
BE Josh Beckett 40.00
CB Carlos Beltran 25.00
AB Angel Berroa 10.00
HB Hank Blalock 15.00
BB Bret Boone 10.00
PB Pat Burrell 15.00
SB Sean Burroughs 10.00
MC Miguel Cabrera 40.00
EC Eric Chavez 20.00
WC Will Clark 25.00

RC	Roger Clemens	150.00
JD	J.D. Drew	15.00
AD	Adam Dunn	20.00
NG	Nomar Garciaparra	50.00
BG	Brian Giles	10.00
MG	Marcus Giles	10.00
GL	Tom Glavine	40.00
JG	Juan Gonzalez	20.00
LG	Luis Gonzalez	15.00
KG	Ken Griffey Jr.	75.00
VG	Vladimir Guerrero	50.00
TG	Tony Gwynn	40.00
HA	Roy Halladay	20.00
RH	Rich Harden	15.00
TH	Todd Helton	40.00
HI	Richard Hidalgo	10.00
HO	Trevor Hoffman	20.00
TI	Tim Hudson	20.00
HU	Torii Hunter	20.00
GJ	Geoff Jenkins	10.00
DJ	Derek Jeter	160.00
JJ	Jacque Jones	10.00
AK	Austin Kearns	15.00
RK	Ryan Klesko	10.00
CL	Carlos Lee	15.00
DL	Derrek Lee	20.00
ML	Mike Lieberthal	10.00
EL	Esteban Loaiza	10.00
LO	Mike Lowell	20.00
MA	Mike Marshall/SP/34	40.00
EM	Edgar Martinez	50.00
DM	Don Mattingly	60.00
JM	Joe Mauer	25.00
MU	Mark Mulder	20.00
MM	Mike Mussina	40.00
RO	Roy Oswalt	20.00
CP	Corey Patterson	15.00
OP	Odalis Perez	10.00
PI	Mike Piazza	150.00
SP	Scott Podsednik	15.00
MP	Mark Prior	20.00
AP	Albert Pujols	220.00
MR	Manny Ramirez	60.00
JR	Jose Reyes	40.00
CR	Cal Ripken Jr.	180.00
IR	Ivan Rodriguez	50.00
SR	Scott Rolen	30.00
NR	Nolan Ryan	150.00
RS	Ryne Sandberg	75.00
SA	Johan Santana	40.00
JS	Jason Schmidt	15.00
TS	Tom Seaver	50.00
BS	Ben Sheets	20.00
GS	Gary Sheffield	35.00
SM	John Smoltz	50.00
IS	Ichiro Suzuki	250.00
MT	Mark Teixeira	25.00
TE	Miguel Tejada	25.00
FT	Frank Thomas	50.00
JV	Javier Vazquez	15.00
WA	Billy Wagner	15.00
BW	Brandon Webb	15.00
WE	Rickie Weeks	15.00
VW	Vernon Wells/30	25.00
DW	Dontrelle Willis	20.00
RW	Randy Wolf	15.00
KW	Kerry Wood	20.00
DY	Delmon Young	20.00
CZ	Carlos Zambrano	40.00

Signatures Red-Blue Stitch

NM/M

Quantity produced listed

GA	Garret Anderson/45	25.00
RB	Rocco Baldelli/35	25.00
BE	Josh Beckett/45	40.00
CB	Carlos Beltran/45	40.00
AB	Angel Berroa/45	20.00
HB	Hank Blalock/45	25.00
BB	Bret Boone/45	20.00
PB	Pat Burrell/35	25.00
SB	Sean Burroughs/45	15.00
MC	Miguel Cabrera/45	40.00
EC	Eric Chavez/45	25.00
WC	Will Clark/45	25.00
RC	Roger Clemens/30	175.00
JD	J.D. Drew/40	25.00
AD	Adam Dunn/45	25.00
NG	Nomar Garciaparra/45	60.00
BG	Brian Giles/45	15.00
MG	Marcus Giles/45	20.00
GL	Tom Glavine/45	60.00
JG	Juan Gonzalez/45	25.00
LG	Luis Gonzalez/45	25.00
KG	Ken Griffey Jr./44	100.00
VG	Vladimir Guerrero/45	75.00
TG	Tony Gwynn/45	60.00
HA	Roy Halladay/35	25.00
RH	Rich Harden/45	25.00
TH	Todd Helton/45	50.00
HI	Richard Hidalgo/45	15.00
HO	Trevor Hoffman/45	25.00
TI	Tim Hudson/45	25.00
HU	Torii Hunter/45	25.00
EJ	Edwin Jackson/45	15.00
GJ	Geoff Jenkins/45	15.00
DJ	Derek Jeter/35	275.00
JJ	Jacque Jones/45	20.00
AK	Austin Kearns/45	25.00
RK	Ryan Klesko/45	15.00
CL	Carlos Lee/45	20.00
DL	Derrek Lee/45	35.00
ML	Mike Lieberthal/45	25.00
EL	Esteban Loaiza/45	15.00
LO	Mike Lowell/35	30.00
EM	Edgar Martinez/30	50.00
DM	Don Mattingly/45	85.00
JM	Joe Mauer/45	35.00
MU	Mark Mulder/45	20.00
RO	Roy Oswalt/45	25.00
CP	Corey Patterson/45	25.00
OP	Odalis Perez/45	20.00
SP	Scott Podsednik/45	20.00
MP	Mark Prior/45	25.00
AP	Albert Pujols/45	250.00
MR	Manny Ramirez/40	80.00
JR	Jose Reyes/45	50.00
CR	Cal Ripken Jr./35	250.00
IR	Ivan Rodriguez/45	50.00
NR	Nolan Ryan/40	170.00
RS	Ryne Sandberg/40	80.00
SA	Johan Santana/45	65.00
JS	Jason Schmidt/45	25.00
TS	Tom Seaver/35	75.00
BS	Ben Sheets/55	25.00
GS	Gary Sheffield/45	50.00
SM	John Smoltz/40	80.00
IS	Ichiro Suzuki/25	500.00
MT	Mark Teixeira/45	40.00
TE	Miguel Tejada/25	50.00
FT	Frank Thomas/25	75.00
JV	Javier Vazquez/45	20.00
WA	Billy Wagner/45	20.00
BW	Brandon Webb/45	20.00
WE	Rickie Weeks/45	20.00
VW	Vernon Wells/29	25.00
DW	Dontrelle Willis/45	25.00
RW	Randy Wolf/45	20.00
KW	Kerry Wood/45	25.00
DY	Delmon Young/45	25.00
CZ	Carlos Zambrano/30	50.00

Signatures Barrel

NM/M

Cards not serial numbered, quantity produced provided by Upper Deck.

GA	Garret Anderson/74	20.00
RB	Rocco Baldelli/19	25.00
BE	Josh Beckett/65	50.00
CB	Carlos Beltran/55	40.00
AB	Angel Berroa/64	15.00
HB	Hank Blalock/74	25.00
BB	Bret Boone/64	15.00
SB	Sean Burroughs/64	15.00
MC	Miguel Cabrera/64	40.00
EC	Eric Chavez/74	25.00
AD	Adam Dunn/74	30.00
NG	Nomar Garciaparra/38	75.00
BG	Brian Giles/64	15.00
MG	Marcus Giles/64	15.00
GL	Tom Glavine/64	50.00
KG	Ken Griffey Jr./64	125.00
VG	Vladimir Guerrero/38	60.00
HA	Roy Halladay/64	30.00
RH	Rich Harden/64	20.00
TH	Todd Helton/38	60.00
HI	Richard Hidalgo/64	15.00
HO	Trevor Hoffman/68	25.00
TI	Tim Hudson/64	30.00
HU	Torii Hunter/64	30.00
EJ	Edwin Jackson/64 Exch	15.00
GJ	Geoff Jenkins/64	15.00
DJ	Derek Jeter/53	275.00
JJ	Jacque Jones/64	15.00
AK	Austin Kearns/64	20.00
RK	Ryan Klesko/64	15.00
CL	Carlos Lee/64	25.00
DL	Derrek Lee/64	50.00
ML	Mike Lieberthal/64	15.00
EL	Esteban Loaiza/64	15.00
LO	Mike Lowell/64	30.00
EM	Edgar Martinez/64	40.00
DM	Don Mattingly/38	125.00
JM	Joe Mauer/72	50.00
MU	Mark Mulder/64	20.00
MM	Mike Mussina/64	50.00
RO	Roy Oswalt/64	40.00
CP	Corey Patterson/74 Exch	25.00
OP	Odalis Perez/64	15.00
PI	Mike Piazza/38	150.00
SP	Scott Podsednik/64	25.00
MP	Mark Prior/64	25.00
AP	Albert Pujols/64	250.00
MR	Manny Ramirez/63	75.00
JR	Jose Reyes/49	50.00
CR	Cal Ripken Jr./38	220.00
AR	Alex Rodriguez/28	300.00
IR	Ivan Rodriguez/64	50.00
NR	Nolan Ryan/38	180.00
SA	Johan Santana/64	60.00
JS	Jason Schmidt/64	25.00
TS	Tom Seaver/38	75.00
BS	Ben Sheets/64	25.00
GS	Gary Sheffield/38	60.00
IS	Ichiro Suzuki/64	500.00
MT	Mark Teixeira/64	50.00
TE	Miguel Tejada/64	50.00
JV	Javier Vazquez/64	20.00
WA	Billy Wagner/64	20.00
BW	Brandon Webb/64	30.00
WE	Rickie Weeks/64	20.00
VW	Vernon Wells/33	20.00
DW	Dontrelle Willis/64	25.00
RW	Randy Wolf/64	15.00
KW	Kerry Wood/64	25.00
DY	Delmon Young/74	40.00
CZ	Carlos Zambrano/38	40.00

Signatures Dual

No Pricing
Production 10 Sets

Signatures Glove

NM/M

Production 5-25

GA	Garret Anderson/25	40.00
RB	Rocco Baldelli/25	40.00
BE	Josh Beckett/25	75.00
CB	Carlos Beltran/25	50.00
AB	Angel Berroa/25	25.00
HB	Hank Blalock/25	40.00
BB	Bret Boone/25	25.00
PB	Pat Burrell/15	40.00
SB	Sean Burroughs/25	25.00
MC	Miguel Cabrera/25	100.00
EC	Eric Chavez/25	50.00
WC	Will Clark/25	100.00
AD	Adam Dunn/25	60.00
NG	Nomar Garciaparra/25	100.00
BG	Brian Giles/25	35.00
MG	Marcus Giles/25	30.00
GL	Tom Glavine/25	65.00
JG	Juan Gonzalez/25	50.00
LG	Luis Gonzalez/25	40.00
KG	Ken Griffey Jr./25	200.00
VG	Vladimir Guerrero/25	100.00
TG	Tony Gwynn/25	100.00
HA	Roy Halladay/24	50.00
RH	Rich Harden/25	40.00
TH	Todd Helton/25	80.00
HI	Richard Hidalgo/15	25.00
HO	Trevor Hoffman/15	50.00
TI	Tim Hudson/25	65.00
HU	Torii Hunter/25	40.00
EJ	Edwin Jackson/25	20.00
GJ	Geoff Jenkins/25	30.00
JJ	Jacque Jones/25	20.00
AK	Austin Kearns/25	40.00
CL	Carlos Lee/25	50.00
DL	Derrek Lee/25	60.00
ML	Mike Lieberthal/25	30.00
EL	Esteban Loaiza/25	30.00
MA	Mike Marshall/25	50.00
EM	Edgar Martinez/25	75.00
DM	Don Mattingly/25	180.00
JM	Joe Mauer/25	50.00
MU	Mark Mulder/25	40.00
MM	Mike Mussina/25	75.00
RO	Roy Oswalt/25	65.00
CP	Corey Patterson/25	40.00
SP	Scott Podsednik/25	40.00
MP	Mark Prior/25	50.00
AP	Albert Pujols/25	300.00
MR	Manny Ramirez/25	120.00
JR	Jose Reyes/25	75.00
CR	Cal Ripken Jr./25	275.00
IR	Ivan Rodriguez/25	75.00
NR	Nolan Ryan/25	250.00
RS	Ryne Sandberg/20	125.00
SA	Johan Santana/25	75.00
JS	Jason Schmidt/25	40.00
BS	Ben Sheets/25	50.00
GS	Gary Sheffield/20	75.00
MT	Mark Teixeira/25	75.00
TE	Miguel Tejada/25	60.00
JV	Javier Vazquez/25	40.00
WA	Billy Wagner/25	40.00
BW	Brandon Webb/25	40.00
WE	Rickie Weeks/25	25.00
DW	Dontrelle Willis/25	50.00
KW	Kerry Wood/25	50.00
DY	Delmon Young/25	40.00

Signatures Historical Ball

No Pricing
Production One Set

Sweet Impressions Plates

No Pricing
Production One Set

Sweet Sticks

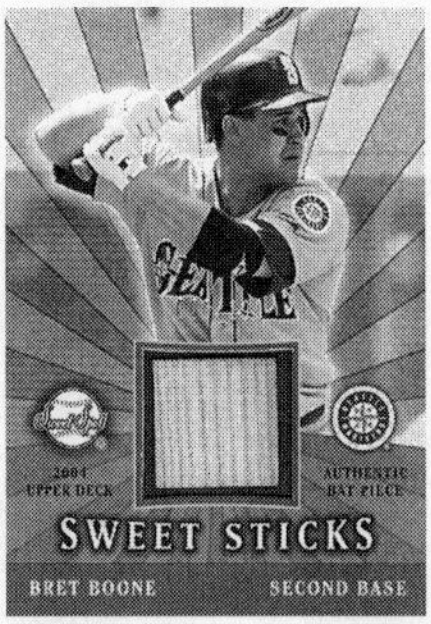

NM/M

Common Player: 4.00
Production 199 Sets

BA	Bobby Abreu	6.00
MA	Moises Alou	6.00
GA	Garret Anderson	4.00
JB	Jeff Bagwell	8.00
BE	Carlos Beltran	8.00
AB	Adrian Beltre	4.00
LB	Lance Berkman	4.00
CB	Craig Biggio	4.00
HB	Hank Blalock	8.00
BB	Bret Boone	4.00
PB	Pat Burrell	4.00
MC	Miguel Cabrera	8.00
EC	Eric Chavez	6.00
RC	Roger Clemens	15.00
CD	Carlos Delgado	6.00
JD	J.D. Drew	6.00
AD	Adam Dunn	8.00
JE	Jim Edmonds	6.00
RF	Rafael Furcal	4.00
NG	Nomar Garciaparra	12.00
JG	Jason Giambi	6.00
BG	Brian Giles	4.00
MG	Marcus Giles	4.00
TG	Troy Glaus	4.00
GL	Tom Glavine	6.00
LG	Luis Gonzalez	4.00
SG	Shawn Green	4.00
KG	Ken Griffey Jr.	15.00
VG	Vladimir Guerrero	8.00
TH	Todd Helton	8.00
DJ	Derek Jeter	25.00
RJ	Randy Johnson	8.00
CJ	Chipper Jones	10.00
AJ	Andruw Jones	6.00
JK	Jeff Kent	4.00
DL	Derrek Lee	4.00
ML	Mike Lowell	4.00
GM	Greg Maddux	10.00
HM	Hideki Matsui	35.00
KM	Kazuo Matsui	15.00
MO	Maggio Ordonez	4.00
RP	Rafael Palmeiro	8.00
MP	Mike Piazza	10.00
PR	Mark Prior	6.00
AP	Albert Pujols	20.00
MR	Manny Ramirez	8.00
ER	Edgar Renteria	6.00
JR	Jose Reyes	6.00
CR	Cal Ripken Jr.	30.00
AR	Alex Rodriguez	15.00
IR	Ivan Rodriguez	8.00
SR	Scott Rolen	10.00
CS	Curt Schilling	6.00
RS	Richie Sexson	6.00
GS	Gary Sheffield	8.00
AS	Alfonso Soriano	8.00
SS	Sammy Sosa	10.00
IS	Ichiro Suzuki	40.00
MT	Mark Teixeira	6.00
TE	Miguel Tejada	6.00
FT	Frank Thomas	8.00
JT	Jim Thome	8.00
LW	Larry Walker	6.00
TW	Ted Williams	60.00
PW	Preston Wilson	4.00

Sweet Sticks Dual

NM/M

Common Duo: 10.00
Production 100 Sets

BT	Hank Blalock, Mark Teixeira	10.00
CL	Miguel Cabrera, Mike Lowell	10.00
JC	Randy Johnson, Roger Clemens	25.00
JG	Derek Jeter, Nomar Garciaparra	25.00
JM	Jose Reyes, Kazuo Matsui	25.00
MM	Hideki Matsui, Kazuo Matsui	40.00
PR	Albert Pujols, Scott Rolen	40.00
RG	Manny Ramirez, Nomar Garciaparra	15.00
RJ	Alex Rodriguez, Derek Jeter	50.00
RP	Ivan Rodriguez, Mike Piazza	15.00
TB	Jim Thome, Pat Burrell	20.00
WP	Kerry Wood, Mark Prior	12.00

Sweet Sticks Triple

NM/M

Production 50 Sets

GPS	Ken Griffey Jr., Rafael Palmeiro, Sammy Sosa	40.00
JJD	Andruw Jones, Chipper Jones, J.D. Drew	25.00
JSG	Derek Jeter, Ichiro Suzuki, Ken Griffey Jr.	120.00
MWP	Greg Maddux, Kerry Wood, Mark Prior	35.00
RJG	Alex Rodriguez, Derek Jeter, Jason Giambi	65.00

Sweet Sticks Quad

NM/M

Production 25 Sets

PRSG	Albert Pujols, Alex Rodriguez, Ichiro Suzuki, Ken Griffey Jr.	125.00
RGDM	Babe Ruth, Lou Gehrig, Joe DiMaggio, Mickey Mantle	1,200

Sweet Threads

NM/M

Common Player: 4.00
Patch: 1.5-2.5X
Production 85 Sets

JB	Jeff Bagwell	8.00
CB	Carlos Beltran	8.00
LB	Lance Berkman	4.00

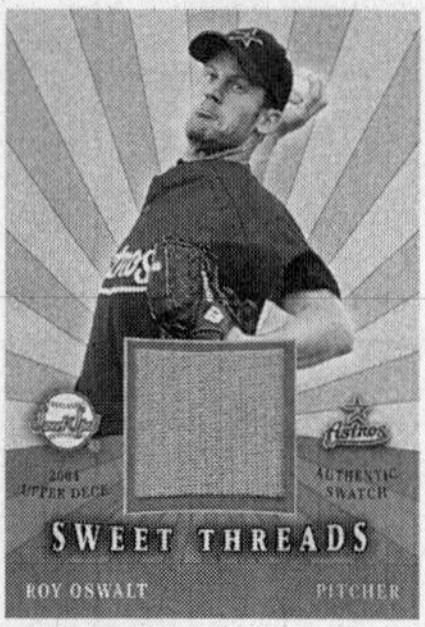

HB Hank Blalock 8.00
BB Bret Boone 4.00
MC Miguel Cabrera 8.00
EC Eric Chavez 4.00
BC Bartolo Colon 4.00
CD Carlos Delgado 4.00
JG Jason Giambi 6.00
BG Brian Giles 4.00
TG Troy Glaus 4.00
SG Shawn Green 4.00
VG Vladimir Guerrero 8.00
RH Rich Harden 4.00
HE Todd Helton 8.00
TH Tim Hudson 4.00
ML Mike Lowell 4.00
EM Edgar Martinez 4.00
KM Kazuo Matsui/SP 15.00
JM Joe Mauer 8.00
MM Mark Mulder 4.00
HN Hideo Nomo 8.00
MO Magglio Ordonez 4.00
RO Roy Oswalt 4.00
MP Mark Prior 6.00
MR Manny Ramirez 8.00
JR Jose Reyes 4.00
SS Sammy Sosa 10.00
JS Jason Schmidt 6.00
RS Richie Sexson 4.00
GS Gary Sheffield 6.00
AS Alfonso Soriano 8.00
MT Mark Teixeira 6.00
FT Frank Thomas 8.00
JT Jim Thome 8.00
RW Rickie Weeks 4.00
VW Vernon Wells 4.00
DW Dontrelle Willis 4.00
PW Preston Wilson 4.00
KW Kerry Wood 8.00
DY Delmon Young 8.00

Sweet Threads Dual

NM/M

Common Duo: 5.00
Production 150 Sets
Patch: 1.5-2X
Production 60 Sets
BP Angel Berroa, Scott Podsednik 4.00
BT Hank Blalock, Mark Teixeira 10.00
CK Curt Schilling, Kevin Brown 10.00
CS Roger Clemens, Sammy Sosa 20.00
DT Carlos Delgado, Jim Thome 8.00
GH Eric Gagne, Roy Halladay 8.00
HG Tim Hudson, Vladimir Guerrero 10.00
JC Randy Johnson, Roger Clemens 25.00
JH Andruw Jones, Torii Hunter 8.00
JJ Andruw Jones, Chipper Jones 10.00
MM Hideki Matsui, Kazuo Matsui 50.00
MP Joe Mauer, Mark Prior 10.00
PC Andy Pettitte, Roger Clemens 20.00
PP Jorge Posada, Mike Piazza 15.00
PS Albert Pujols, Ichiro Suzuki 50.00
PW Albert Pujols, Kerry Wood 15.00
RJ Alex Rodriguez, Derek Jeter 50.00
RM Jose Reyes, Kazuo Matsui 15.00
SB Alfonso Soriano, Bret Boone 8.00
SM Gary Sheffield, Pedro J. Martinez 12.00
WP Kerry Wood, Mark Prior 10.00
YW Delmon Young, Rickie Weeks 8.00

Sweet Threads Triple

NM/M

Common Trio: 10.00
Production 99 Sets
Triple Patch: 2X
No pricing 15 or less.
AGG Garret Anderson, Troy Glaus, Vladimir Guerrero 20.00
BKE Jeff Bagwell, Jeff Kent, Morgan Ensberg 15.00

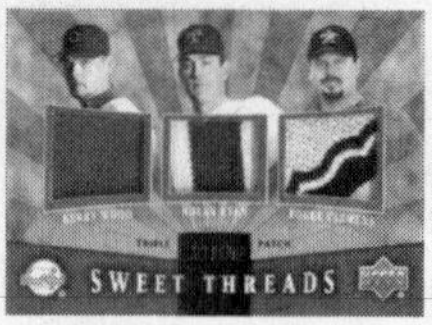

BLR Adrian Beltre, Mike Lowell, Scott Rolen 20.00
BMS Bret Boone, Edgar Martinez, Ichiro Suzuki 50.00
BWC Josh Beckett, Kerry Wood, Roger Clemens 30.00
CMM Bobby Crosby, Joe Mauer, Kazuo Matsui 30.00
DHW Carlos Delgado, Roy Halladay, Vernon Wells 15.00
DKG Adam Dunn, Austin Kearns, Ken Griffey Jr. 20.00
DMJ Joe DiMaggio, Mickey Mantle, Derek Jeter 220.00
DMW Joe DiMaggio, Mickey Mantle, Ted Williams 250.00
DRN Johnny Damon, Manny Ramirez, Trot Nixon 40.00
FRP Keith Foulke, Mariano Rivera, Troy Percival 25.00
GPS Ken Griffey Jr., Rafael Palmeiro, Sammy Sosa 35.00
JJD Andruw Jones, Chipper Jones, J.D. Drew 20.00
JTG Derek Jeter, Miguel Tejada, Nomar Garciaparra 40.00
JWH Edwin Jackson, Jerome Williams, Rich Harden 10.00
KVG Jeff Kent, Jose Vidro, Marcus Giles 10.00
LTO Carlos Lee, Frank Thomas, Magglio Ordonez 20.00
LTP Javy Lopez, Miguel Tejada, Rafael Palmeiro 20.00
MCF Kazuo Matsui, Miguel Cabrera, Rafael Furcal 20.00
MMH Mike Mussina, Pedro J. Martinez, Tim Hudson 25.00
MSH Joe Mauer, Johan Santana, Torii Hunter 35.00
MWP Greg Maddux, Kerry Wood, Mark Prior 25.00
PAS Corey Patterson, Moises Alou, Sammy Sosa 30.00
PCO Andy Pettitte, Roger Clemens, Roy Oswalt 25.00
PRR Albert Pujols, Edgar Renteria, Scott Rolen 40.00
PTH Albert Pujols, Jim Thome, Todd Helton 30.00
RCB Alex Rodriguez, Eric Chavez, Hank Blalock 30.00
RGJ Alex Rodriguez, Ken Griffey Jr., Randy Johnson 35.00
RGW Jose Reyes, Khalil Greene, Rickie Weeks 25.00
RJG Alex Rodriguez, Derek Jeter, Jason Giambi 60.00
RMP Jose Reyes, Kazuo Matsui, Mike Piazza 25.00
SBK Alfonso Soriano, Bret Boone, Jeff Kent 20.00
SBP Jason Schmidt, Josh Beckett, Mark Prior 15.00
SBT Alfonso Soriano, Hank Blalock, Mark Teixeira 20.00
SLM Curt Schilling, Derek Lowe, Pedro J. Martinez 40.00
VBM Javier Vazquez, Kevin Brown, Mike Mussina 20.00
WBP Brandon Webb, Josh Beckett, Mark Prior 15.00
WGS Billy Wagner, Eric Gagne, John Smoltz 20.00
WRC Kerry Wood, Nolan Ryan, Roger Clemens 60.00
YCW Delmon Young, Miguel Cabrera, Rickie Weeks 15.00
ZMH Barry Zito, Mark Mulder, Tim Hudson 10.00

Sweet Threads Quad

NM/M

Common Quad: 20.00
Production 99 Sets
Quad Patch: No Pricing
Production 1-15
BADH Carlos Beltran, Garret Anderson, Johnny Damon, Torii Hunter 30.00
BBGS Angel Berroa, Carlos Beltran, Alex Gonzalez, Mike Sweeney 20.00
BPJC Josh Beckett, Mark Prior, Randy Johnson, Roger Clemens 30.00
BWRC Josh Beckett, Kerry Wood, Nolan Ryan, Roger Clemens 50.00
CAGG Bartolo Colon, Garret Anderson, Troy Glaus, Vladimir Guerrero 25.00
DHHW Carlos Delgado, Eric Hinske, Roy Halladay, Vernon Wells 20.00
DOGP Carlos Delgado, David Ortiz, Jason Giambi, Rafael Palmeiro 25.00
GNKB Brian Giles, Phil Nevin, Ryan Klesko, Sean Burroughs 25.00
GNLG Eric Gagne, Hideo Nomo, Paul LoDuca, Shawn Green 30.00
JBGB Chipper Jones, Lance Berkman, Luis Gonzalez, Pat Burrell 25.00
JEGW Andruw Jones, Jim Edmonds, Ken Griffey Jr., Preston Wilson 35.00
JJDF Andruw Jones, Chipper Jones, J.D. Drew, Rafael Furcal 25.00
JMSH Jacque Jones, Joe Mauer, Shannon Stewart, Torii Hunter 35.00
JRMT Derek Jeter, Edgar Renteria, Kazuo Matsui, Miguel Tejada 40.00
KGCS Austin Kearns, Brian Giles, Miguel Cabrera, Sammy Sosa 25.00
LMRS Carlos Lee, Hideki Matsui, Manny Ramirez, Shannon Stewart 75.00
LTOK Carlos Lee, Frank Thomas, Magglio Ordonez, Paul Konerko 25.00
LTPP Javy Lopez, Miguel Tejada, Raffy, Sidney Ponson 25.00
MMMH Mark Mulder, Mike Mussina, Pedro J. Martinez, Roy Halladay 25.00
MTTS Edgar Martinez, Jim Thome, Mark Teixeira, Mike Sweeney 20.00
NSGH Phil Nevin, Richie Sexson, Shawn Green, Todd Helton 20.00
PBBC Andy Pettitte, Craig Biggio, Jeff Bagwell, Roger Clemens 40.00
PLBT Albert Pujols, Lee, Jeff Bagwell, Jim Thome 40.00
PRER Albert Pujols, Edgar Renteria, Jim Edmonds, Scott Rolen 70.00
PWPS Corey Patterson, Kerry Wood, Mark Prior, Sammy Sosa 40.00
RCBG Alex Rodriguez, Eric Chavez, Hank Blalock, Troy Glaus 30.00
RJDM Alex Rodriguez, Derek Jeter, Joe DiMaggio, Mickey Mantle 275.00
RLPM Ivan Rodriguez, Javy Lopez, Jorge Posada, Joe Mauer 40.00
RMPG Jose Reyes, Kazuo Matsui, Mike Piazza, Tom Glavine 30.00
SBKV Alfonso Soriano, Bret Boone, Jeff Kent, Jose Vidro 20.00
SBMM Curt Schilling, Kevin Brown, Mike Mussina, Pedro J. Martinez 40.00
SDRM Curt Schilling, Johnny Damon, Manny Ramirez, Pedro J. Martinez 60.00
SSOG Gary Sheffield, Ichiro Suzuki, Magglio Ordonez, Vladimir Guerrero 50.00
VCBM Javier Vazquez, Jose Contreras, Kevin Brown, Mike Mussina 25.00
WATM Billy Wagner, Bobby Abreu, Jim Thome, Kevin Millwood 30.00
WBCL Dontrelle Willis, Josh Beckett, Miguel Cabrera, Mike Lowell 20.00
WGJS Brandon Webb, Luis Gonzalez, Randy Johnson, Richie Sexson 25.00
ZMHH Barry Zito, Mark Mulder, Rich Harden, Tim Hudson 35.00

2004 Upper Deck Sweet Spot Classic

NM/M

Complete Set (161):
Common Player (1-90): .40
Common (91-161): 2.00
Production 1,910-1,999
Pack (4): 15.00
Box (12): 150.00
1 Al Kaline 1.00
2 Andre Dawson .40
3 Bert Blyleven .40
4 Bill Dickey .40
5 Bill Mazeroski .40
6 Billy Martin .40
7 Bob Feller .50
8 Bob Gibson 1.00

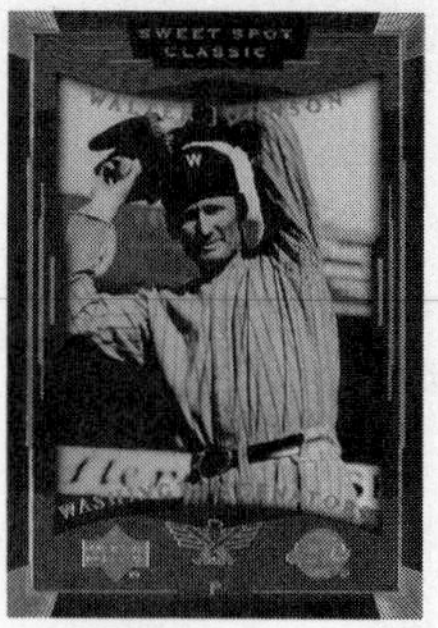

9 Bob Lemon .40
10 George Kell .40
11 Bobby Doerr .40
12 Brooks Robinson 1.00
13 Cal Ripken Jr. 4.00
14 Carl Hubbell .40
15 Carl Yastrzemski 1.50
16 Charlie Keller .40
17 Chuck Dressen .40
18 Cy Young 1.00
19 Dave Winfield .75
20 Dizzy Dean .75
21 Don Drysdale .75
22 Don Larsen .75
23 Don Mattingly 2.50
24 Don Newcombe .40
25 Duke Snider .75
26 Early Wynn .40
27 Eddie Mathews 1.00
28 Elston Howard .40
29 Frank Robinson .75
30 Gary Carter .40
31 Gil Hodges .40
32 Gil McDougald .40
33 Hank Greenberg .75
34 Harmon Killebrew 1.50
35 Harry Caray .40
36 Honus Wagner 1.00
37 Hoyt Wilhelm .40
38 Jackie Robinson 2.00
39 Jim Bunning .40
40 Jim Palmer .75
41 Jimmie Foxx 1.00
42 Jimmy Wynn .40
43 Joe DiMaggio 3.00
44 Joe Torre .40
45 Johnny Mize .40
46 Juan Marichal .75
47 Larry Doby .40
48 Lefty Gomez .40
49 Lefty Grove .40
50 Leo Durocher .40
51 Lou Boudreau .40
52 Lou Brock .50
53 Lou Gehrig 3.00
54 Luis Aparicio .40
55 Maury Wills .40
56 Mel Allen .40
57 Mel Ott .40
58 Mickey Cochrane .40
59 Mickey Mantle 4.00
60 Mike Schmidt 2.00
61 Monte Irvin .40
62 Nolan Ryan 4.00
63 Pee Wee Reese .40
64 Phil Rizzuto .50
65 Ralph Kiner .40
66 Richie Ashburn .40
67 Rick Ferrell .40
68 Roberto Clemente 2.50
69 Robin Roberts .40
70 Robin Yount 1.00
71 Rogers Hornsby .75
72 Rollie Fingers .40
73 Roy Campanella .75
74 Ryne Sandberg 1.50
75 Tony Gwynn 1.00
76 Satchel Paige .75
77 Shoeless Joe Jackson 2.00
78 Stan Musial 2.00
79 Ted Williams 3.00
80 Thurman Munson .75
81 Tom Seaver 1.50
82 Tommy Henrich .40
83 Tony Perez .40
84 Tris Speaker .40
85 Vida Blue .40
86 Wade Boggs .50
87 Walter Johnson .75
88 Warren Spahn 1.00
89 Whitey Ford .75
90 Willie McCovey .40
91 Andre Dawson 2.50
92 Andre Dawson 2.50
93 Ernie Banks 4.00
94 Bob Lemon 2.00
95 Cal Ripken Jr. 8.00
96 Cal Ripken Jr. 8.00
97 Carl Yastrzemski 3.00
98 Carlton Fisk 2.50
99 Cy Young 4.00

100 Don Larsen 2.50
101 Don Newcombe 2.00
102 Don Newcombe 2.00
103 Dwight Evans 2.00
104 Elston Howard 2.50
105 Frank Robinson 3.00
106 Frank Robinson 3.00
107 Frank Robinson 3.00
108 Gil McDougald 2.00
109 Hank Greenberg 4.00
110 Harmon Killebrew 4.00
111 Hoyt Wilhelm 2.00
112 Hoyt Wilhelm 2.00
113 Jackie Robinson 5.00
114 Jackie Robinson 5.00
115 Jackie Robinson 5.00
116 Jackie Robinson 5.00
117 Jim Bunning 2.00
118 Joe DiMaggio 6.00
119 Joe Morgan 2.00
120 Johnny Mize 2.50
121 Johnny Mize 2.50
122 Juan Marichal 3.00
123 Ken Griffey Sr. 2.00
124 Larry Doby 2.50
125 Lefty Gomez 2.00
126 Lou Boudreau 2.00
127 Lou Gehrig 6.00
128 Lou Gehrig 6.00
129 Mark McGwire 6.00
130 Mark McGwire 6.00
131 Maury Wills 2.00
132 Mel Ott 3.00
133 Mike Schmidt 5.00
134 Nolan Ryan 8.00
135 Nolan Ryan 8.00
136 Pee Wee Reese 2.00
137 Nolan Ryan 8.00
138 Richie Ashburn 2.50
139 Roberto Clemente 8.00
140 Roberto Clemente 8.00
141 Robin Roberts 2.00
142 Robin Yount 3.00
143 Roger Clemens 2.00
144 Rollie Fingers 2.00
145 Rollie Fingers 2.00
146 Roy Campanella 3.00
147 Ryne Sandberg 4.00
149 Satchel Paige 4.00
150 Stan Musial 5.00
151 Stan Musial 5.00
152 Stan Musial 5.00
153 Ted Williams 6.00
154 Ted Williams 6.00
155 Tom Seaver 3.00
156 Tom Seaver 3.00
157 Wade Boggs 2.50
158 Warren Spahn 3.00
159 Warren Spahn 3.00
160 Joe DiMaggio 6.00
161 Yogi Berra 4.00

Game Used Patch

NM/M

Some not priced due to scarcity.
Holofoil: No Pricing
Production 10
BB Bert Blyleven/113 25.00
WB Wade Boggs/90 30.00
AD Andre Dawson/100 20.00
TG Tony Gwynn/100 35.00
CK Charlie Keller/55 30.00
ML Mickey Lolich/115 15.00
DM Don Mattingly/176 40.00
GM Gil McDougald/31 25.00
TM Thurman Munson/100 30.00
FR Frank Robinson/50 30.00
NR Nolan Ryan/96 65.00
TS Tom Seaver/94 30.00
MW Maury Wills/78 25.00
CY Carl Yastrzemski/20 65.00
RY Robin Yount/100 30.00

Jersey

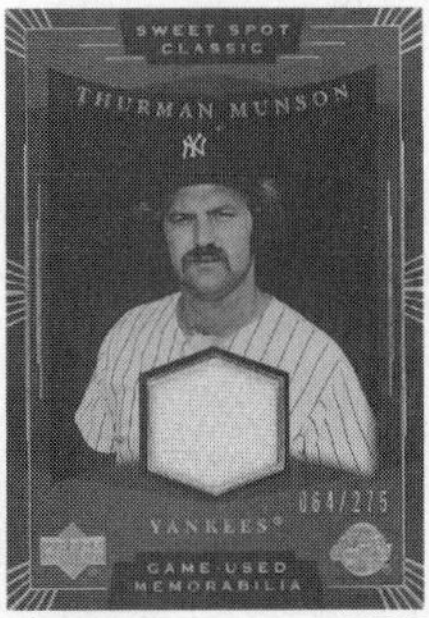

NM/M

Common Player: 5.00
Production 275 Sets
Holofoils: 1.5-2X
Production 50
SA Sparky Anderson 6.00
SB Sal Bando 5.00
RB Ron Blomberg 5.00
BB Bert Blyleven 5.00
WB Wade Boggs 8.00
WB1 Wade Boggs 8.00
JB Jim Bunning 5.00
GC Gary Carter 6.00
RC Roberto Clemente 65.00
AD Andre Dawson 5.00
AD1 Andre Dawson 5.00
JD Joe DiMaggio 70.00
CD Chuck Dressen 5.00
KG Ken Griffey Sr. 5.00
TG Tony Gwynn 10.00
EH Elston Howard 8.00
CK Charlie Keller 15.00
ML Mickey Lolich 6.00
MM Mickey Mantle 125.00
JM Juan Marichal 8.00
RM Roger Maris 45.00
BM Billy Martin 8.00
EM Eddie Mathews 10.00
DM Don Mattingly 20.00
GM Gil McDougald 8.00
JO Johnny Mize 10.00
TM Thurman Munson 20.00
SM Stan Musial 25.00
JP Jim Palmer 8.00
CR Cal Ripken Jr. 20.00
PR Phil Rizzuto 15.00
FR Frank Robinson 8.00
JR Jackie Robinson 40.00
NR Nolan Ryan 25.00
TS Tom Seaver 15.00
OS Ozzie Smith 10.00
JT Joe Torre 8.00
TW Ted Williams 70.00
MW Maury Wills 5.00
CY Carl Yastrzemski 15.00
RY Robin Yount 10.00

Logo Patch

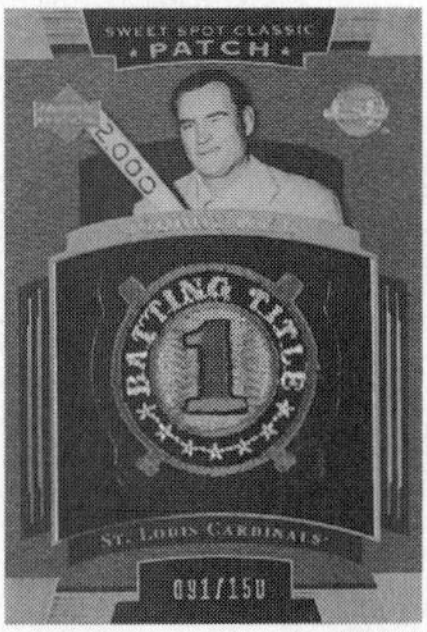

NM/M

Common Level 1: 5.00
Production 300
Level 2: 1X
Production 230
Level 3: 1X
Production 200
Level 4: 1-1.5X
Production 150
Level 5: 1-1.5X
Production 125
Level 6: 1-2X
Production 75
Level 7: 1.5-2.5X
Production 50
Level 8: No Pricing
Production 25
AL Mel Allen 5.00
LA Luis Aparicio 5.00
RA Richie Ashburn 6.00
WB Wade Boggs 8.00
LB Lou Boudreau 5.00
BR Lou Brock 8.00
JB Jim Bunning 5.00
CA Roy Campanella 8.00
GC Gary Carter 5.00
HC Harry Caray 10.00
RC Roberto Clemente 25.00
TC Ty Cobb 12.00
CO Mickey Cochrane 5.00
AD Andre Dawson 8.00
DD Dizzy Dean 8.00
BD Bill Dickey 5.00
JD Joe DiMaggio 15.00
LD Larry Doby 6.00
DO Bobby Doerr 6.00
DR Don Drysdale 6.00
DU Leo Durocher 5.00
BF Bob Feller 8.00
RF Rick Ferrell 5.00
FI Rollie Fingers 6.00
WF Whitey Ford 6.00
JF Jimmie Foxx 8.00
FF Frankie Frisch 5.00
GE Lou Gehrig 15.00
CG Charlie Gehringer 8.00
BG Bob Gibson 8.00
LG Lefty Gomez 5.00
HG Hank Greenberg 10.00
GR Lefty Grove 6.00
TH Tommy Henrich 5.00
GH Gil Hodges 8.00
RH Rogers Hornsby 8.00
CH Carl Hubbell 5.00
IR Monte Irvin 5.00
JJ Shoeless Joe Jackson 20.00
FJ Ferguson Jenkins 6.00
WJ Walter Johnson 8.00
AK Al Kaline 15.00
HK Harmon Killebrew 15.00
RK Ralph Kiner 8.00
DL Don Larsen 6.00
TL Tommy Lasorda 5.00
BL Bob Lemon 5.00
ML Mickey Lolich 5.00
MI Mickey Mantle 40.00
MA Juan Marichal 6.00
BM Billy Martin 8.00
EM Eddie Mathews 8.00
CM Christy Mathewson 10.00
DM Don Mattingly 20.00
WM Willie McCovey 8.00
JM Johnny Mize 6.00
TM Thurman Munson 10.00
SM Stan Musial 10.00
DN Don Newcombe 5.00
MO Mel Ott 6.00
SP Satchel Paige 10.00
JP Jim Palmer 8.00
TP Tony Perez 5.00
GP Gaylord Perry 5.00
PR Pee Wee Reese 6.00
CR Cal Ripken Jr. 30.00
RI Phil Rizzuto 8.00
RR Robin Roberts 6.00
RO Brooks Robinson 12.00
FR Frank Robinson 8.00
JR Jackie Robinson 12.00
RU Babe Ruth 20.00
NR Nolan Ryan 25.00
RS Ryne Sandberg 20.00
MS Mike Schmidt 15.00
TS Tom Seaver 10.00
SK Bill "Moose" Skowron 5.00
ES Enos Slaughter 5.00
DS Duke Snider 8.00
WS Warren Spahn 10.00
TR Tris Speaker 8.00
JT Joe Torre 5.00
HW Honus Wagner 10.00
WI Hoyt Wilhelm 5.00
TW Ted Williams 20.00
MW Maury Wills 5.00
DW Dave Winfield 6.00
EW Early Wynn 5.00
YA Carl Yastrzemski 12.00
CY Cy Young 10.00

Signature Black Ink

NM/M

Common Autograph: 15.00
2 Preacher Roe/225 25.00
4 Bob Feller/65 45.00
5 Bob Gibson/50 50.00
6 Harry Kalas/100 45.00
7 Bobby Doerr/100 25.00
8 Cal Ripken Jr./50 165.00
9 Carl Yastrzemski/35 110.00
10 Carlton Fisk/100 45.00
11 Chuck Tanner/150 15.00
12 Cito Gaston/150 15.00
13 Danny Ozark/150 15.00
14 Dave Winfield/80 50.00
15 Davey Johnson/175 15.00
16 Ernie Harwell/100 50.00
17 Dick Williams/150 15.00
18 Don Mattingly/40 100.00
19 Don Newcombe/40 35.00
20 Duke Snider/35 60.00
21 Steve Carlton/150 35.00
22 Felipe Alou/175 20.00
23 Frank Robinson/65 40.00
24 Gary Carter/100 35.00
25 Gene Mauch/225 15.00
26 George Bamberger/225 15.00
28 Gus Suhr/100 30.00
30 Harmon Killebrew/50 70.00
31 Jack McKeon/225 20.00
32 Jim Bunning/100 25.00
33 Jimmy Piersall/212 20.00
35 Johnny Bench/50 75.00
36 Juan Marichal/50 40.00
37 Lou Brock/50 50.00
38 George Kell/40 50.00
39 Maury Wills/40 30.00
41 Mike Schmidt/40 100.00
42 Nolan Ryan/50 135.00
43 Ozzie Smith/65 75.00
44 Eddie Mayo/140 15.00
45 Phil Rizzuto/50 50.00
46 Ralph Kiner/40 45.00
47 Lonny Frey/114 15.00
48 Bill Mazeroski/50 40.00
49 Robin Roberts/40 40.00
50 Robin Yount/40 75.00
52 Roger Craig/175 15.00
55 Tony Perez/40 70.00
56 Sparky Anderson/175 20.00
57 Stan Musial/40 100.00
58 Ted Radcliffe/225 25.00
60 Tom Seaver/25 70.00
61 Tony Gwynn/65 75.00
62 Tony LaRussa/275 15.00
63 Tony Oliva/150 20.00
64 Tony Pena/150 15.00
66 Whitey Ford/45 65.00
67 Yogi Berra/65 75.00

Signature Blue Ink

NM/M

Common Autograph: 15.00
Some not priced due to scarcity.
2 Preacher Roe/150 25.00
4 Bob Feller/50 45.00
5 Bob Gibson/25 60.00
6 Harry Kalas/50 50.00
7 Bobby Doerr/50 30.00
8 Cal Ripken Jr./25 200.00
10 Carlton Fisk/50 50.00
11 Chuck Tanner/125 15.00
12 Cito Gaston/125 15.00
13 Danny Ozark/125 15.00
14 Dave Winfield/35 60.00
15 Davey Johnson/150 15.00
16 Ernie Harwell/50 50.00
17 Dick Williams/125 15.00
21 Steve Carlton/100 35.00
22 Felipe Alou/150 20.00
23 Frank Robinson/50 40.00
24 Gary Carter/75 35.00
25 Gene Mauch/150 15.00
26 George Bamberger/150 15.00
28 Gus Suhr/85 30.00
31 Jack McKeon/150 25.00
32 Jim Bunning/65 60.00
33 Jimmy Piersall/150 25.00
35 Johnny Bench/20 90.00
38 George Kell/25 50.00
39 Maury Wills/25 40.00
41 Mike Schmidt/25 80.00
42 Nolan Ryan/25 175.00
43 Ozzie Smith/25 75.00
44 Eddie Mayo/50 20.00
45 Phil Rizzuto/25 60.00
47 Lonny Frey/75 15.00
48 Bill Mazeroski/25 40.00
49 Robin Roberts/25 40.00
50 Robin Yount/25 75.00
52 Roger Craig/150 15.00
56 Sparky Anderson/150 25.00
57 Stan Musial/25 120.00
58 Ted Radcliffe/100 50.00
62 Tony LaRussa/145 15.00
63 Tony Oliva/125 25.00
64 Tony Pena/115 15.00
67 Yogi Berra/50 70.00

Signature Holofoil

NM/M

Many not priced due to scarcity.
SSA-4 Bob Feller/25 70.00
SSA-5 Bob Gibson/25 60.00
SSA-11 Chuck Tanner/100 15.00
SSA-12 Cito Gaston/100 15.00
SSA-13 Danny Ozark/100 15.00
SSA-15 Davey Johnson/50 20.00
SSA-17 Dick Williams/100 15.00
SSA-22 Felipe Alou/50 30.00
SSA-24 Gary Carter/50 45.00
SSA-45 Phil Rizzuto/25 60.00
SSA-49 Robin Roberts/25 40.00
SSA-50 Robin Yount/25 75.00
SSA-52 Roger Craig/50 20.00
SSA-56 Sparky Anderson/50 30.00
SSA-57 Stan Musial/25 120.00
SSA-62 Tony LaRussa/50 20.00
SSA-63 Tony Oliva/100 25.00
SSA-64 Tony Pena/100 15.00

Signature Red Ink

NM/M

Many not priced due to scarcity.
SSA-14Dave Winfield/25 65.00
SSA-25Gene Mauch/25 25.00
SSA-26George Bamberger/25 30.00

Wood Barrel Auto.

NM/M

Varying quantities produced
Some not priced due to scarcity.
HB Harold Baines/200 35.00
JB Johnny Bench/50 120.00
WB Wade Boggs/200 60.00
SM Stan Musial/25 185.00
CR Cal Ripken Jr./25 300.00
NR Nolan Ryan/25 200.00
RS Ron Santo/203 45.00
TS Tom Seaver/25 140.00
BW Billy Williams/200 35.00

2004 Upper Deck Ultimate Collection

NM/M

Complete Set (222):
Common Player (1-126): 2.00
Production 675
Common (127-168): 4.00
Production 525
Common (169-194): 6.00
Production 299
Common (195-209, 222) 8.00
Production 199
Common (210-221): 15.00
Production 75
Pack (4): 80.00
Box (4): 275.00
1 Al Kaline 4.00
2 Billy Williams 2.00
3 Bob Feller 2.00

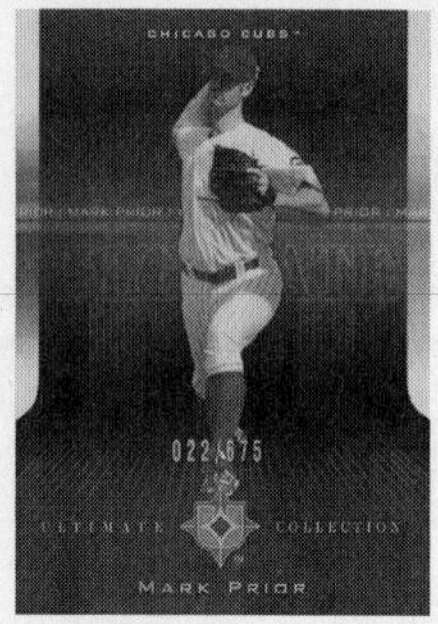

4	Bob Gibson	4.00
5	Bob Lemon	2.00
6	Bobby Doerr	2.00
7	Brooks Robinson	3.00
8	Cal Ripken Jr.	10.00
9	Jim "Catfish" Hunter	2.00
10	Eddie Mathews	4.00
11	Enos Slaughter	2.00
12	Ernie Banks	4.00
13	Fergie Jenkins	2.00
14	Gaylord Perry	2.00
15	Harmon Killebrew	4.00
16	Jim Bunning	2.00
17	Joe DiMaggio	6.00
18	Joe Morgan	2.00
19	Juan Marichal	2.00
20	Lou Brock	2.00
21	Luis Aparicio	2.00
22	Mickey Mantle	12.00
23	Mike Schmidt	6.00
24	Monte Irvin	2.00
25	Nolan Ryan	8.00
26	Pee Wee Reese	2.00
27	Phil Niekro	2.00
28	Phil Rizzuto	3.00
29	Ralph Kiner	3.00
30	Richie Ashburn	2.00
31	Robin Roberts	3.00
32	Robin Yount	5.00
33	Rod Carew	2.00
34	Rollie Fingers	2.00
35	Stan Musial	6.00
36	Ted Williams	8.00
37	Tom Seaver	4.00
38	Warren Spahn	4.00
39	Whitey Ford	3.00
40	Willie McCovey	3.00
41	Willie Stargell	3.00
42	Yogi Berra	4.00
43	Adrian Beltre	2.00
44	Albert Pujols	8.00
45	Alex Rodriguez	6.00
46	Alfonso Soriano	3.00
47	Andruw Jones	2.00
48	Andy Pettitte	2.00
49	Aubrey Huff	2.00
50	Barry Larkin	2.00
51	Ben Sheets	2.00
52	Bernie Williams	2.00
53	Bobby Abreu	2.00
54	Brad Penny	2.00
55	Bret Boone	2.00
56	Brian Giles	2.00
57	Carlos Beltran	3.00
58	Carlos Delgado	2.00
59	Carlos Guillen	2.00
60	Carlos Lee	2.00
61	Carlos Zambrano	2.00
62	Chipper Jones	4.00
63	Craig Biggio	2.00
64	Craig Wilson	2.00
65	Curt Schilling	4.00
66	David Ortiz	4.00
67	Derek Jeter	10.00
68	Eric Chavez	2.00
69	Eric Gagne	3.00
70	Frank Thomas	3.00
71	Garret Anderson	2.00
72	Gary Sheffield	3.00
73	Greg Maddux	5.00
74	Hank Blalock	3.00
75	Hideki Matsui	6.00
76	Ichiro Suzuki	6.00
77	Ivan Rodriguez	3.00
78	J.D. Drew	2.00
79	Jake Peavy	2.00
80	Jason Schmidt	2.00
81	Jeff Bagwell	3.00
82	Jeff Kent	2.00
83	Jim Thome	4.00
84	Joe Mauer	2.00
85	Johan Santana	3.00
86	Jose Reyes	3.00
87	Jose Vidro	2.00
88	Ken Griffey Jr.	5.00
89	Kerry Wood	4.00
90	Larry Walker	2.00
91	Luis Gonzalez	2.00
92	Lyle Overbay	2.00
93	Magglio Ordonez	2.00
94	Manny Ramirez	4.00
95	Mark Mulder	2.00
96	Mark Prior	3.00
97	Mark Teixeira	2.00
98	Melvin Mora	2.00
99	Michael Young	2.00
100	Miguel Cabrera	4.00
101	Miguel Tejada	3.00
102	Mike Lowell	2.00
103	Mike Piazza	6.00
104	Mike Sweeney	2.00
105	Nomar Garciaparra	6.00
106	Oliver Perez	2.00
107	Pedro J. Martinez	4.00
108	Preston Wilson	2.00
109	Rafael Palmeiro	4.00
110	Randy Johnson	4.00
111	Roger Clemens	10.00
112	Roy Halladay	2.00
113	Roy Oswalt	2.00
114	Sammy Sosa	6.00
115	Scott Podsednik	2.00
116	Scott Rolen	4.00
117	Shawn Green	2.00
118	Tim Hudson	2.00
119	Todd Helton	3.00
120	Tom Glavine	3.00
121	Torii Hunter	2.00
122	Travis Hafner	2.00
123	Troy Glaus	2.00
124	Vernon Wells	2.00
125	Victor Martinez	2.00
126	Vladimir Guerrero	4.00
127	Aarom Baldiris **RC**	8.00
128	Alfredo Simon **RC**	4.00
129	Andres Blanco **RC**	4.00
130	Jeff Bajenaru **RC**	4.00
131	Bartolome Fortunato **RC**	4.00
132	Brandon Medders **RC**	4.00
133	Brian Dallimore **RC**	4.00
134	Carlos Hines **RC**	4.00
135	Carlos Vasquez **RC**	8.00
136	Casey Daigle **RC**	4.00
137	Chad Bentz **RC**	4.00
138	Chris Aguila **RC**	4.00
139	Chris Saenz **RC**	4.00
140	Chris Shelton **RC**	10.00
141	Colby Miller **RC**	4.00
142	David Crouthers	4.00
143	David Aardsma **RC**	4.00
144	Dennis Sarfate **RC**	4.00
145	Donnie Kelly **RC**	4.00
146	Eddy Rodriguez **RC**	8.00
147	Eduardo Villacis **RC**	4.00
148	Edwardo Sierra **RC**	6.00
149	Edwin Moreno **RC**	6.00
150	Kyle Denney **RC**	4.00
151	Evan Rust **RC**	4.00
152	Fernando Nieve **RC**	4.00
153	Frank Francisco **RC**	4.00
154	Franklyn Gracesqui **RC**	4.00
155	Freddy Guzman **RC**	4.00
156	Greg Dobbs **RC**	4.00
157	Hector Gimenez **RC**	4.00
158	Jason Alfaro **RC**	4.00
159	Jake Woods **RC**	4.00
160	Andy Green **RC**	4.00
161	Jason Bartlett **RC**	8.00
162	Jason Frasor **RC**	4.00
163	Jeff Bennett **RC**	4.00
164	Jerome Gamble **RC**	4.00
165	Jerry Gil **RC**	4.00
166	Joe Hietpas **RC**	4.00
167	Jorge Sequea **RC**	4.00
168	Jorge Vasquez **RC**	6.00
169	Josh Labandeira **RC**	6.00
170	Justin Germano **RC**	6.00
171	Justin Hampson **RC**	6.00
172	Chris Young **RC**	30.00
173	Justin Knoedler **RC**	6.00
174	Justin Lehr **RC**	6.00
175	Justin Leone **RC**	10.00
176	Kazuhito Tadano **RC**	8.00
177	Kevin Cave **RC**	6.00
178	Lincoln Holdzkom **RC**	6.00
179	Mike Rose **RC**	6.00
180	Luis Gonzalez **RC**	6.00
181	Mariano Gomez **RC**	6.00
182	Rene Rivera **RC**	6.00
183	Mike Wuertz **RC**	8.00
184	Mike Gosling	6.00
185	Mike Johnston **RC**	6.00
186	Mike Rouse	6.00
187	Nick Regilio **RC**	6.00
188	Onil Joseph **RC**	6.00
189	Orlando Rodriguez **RC**	6.00
190	Phil Stockman **RC**	6.00
191	Renyel Pinto **RC**	10.00
192	Roberto Novoa **RC**	12.00
193	Roman Colon **RC**	6.00
194	Ronald Belisario **RC**	6.00
195	Ronny Cedeno **RC**	8.00
196	Ryan Meaux **RC**	8.00
197	Ryan Wing	8.00
198	Scott Dohmann **RC**	8.00
199	Joey Gathright **RC**	10.00
200	Shawn Camp **RC**	8.00
201	Shawn Hill **RC**	8.00
202	Steve Andrade **RC**	8.00
203	Tim Bausher **RC**	8.00
204	Tim Bittner **RC**	8.00
205	Brad Halsey **RC**	10.00
206	William Bergolla **RC**	8.00
207	Kameron Loe **RC**	8.00
208	Jesse Crain **RC**	10.00
209	Scott Kazmir	25.00
210	Akinori Otsuka/Auto. **RC**	60.00
211	Chris Oxspring/Auto. **RC**	15.00
212	Ian Snell/Auto. **RC**	30.00
213	John Gall/Auto. **RC**	20.00
214	Jose Capellan/Auto. **RC**	20.00
215	Yadier Molina/Auto. **RC**	40.00
216	Merkin Valdez/Auto. **RC**	25.00
217	Ramon Ramirez/Auto. **RC**	15.00
218	Rusty Tucker/Auto. **RC**	20.00
219	Scott Proctor/Auto. **RC**	25.00
220	Sean Henn/Auto.	15.00
221	Shingo Takatsu/Auto. **RC**	75.00
222	Kazuo Matsui **RC**	30.00

Gold

Gold (1-194): 1-2X
Production 50
Gold (195-222): No Pricing
Production 25
Gold 210-221 Production 15

Platinum

Platinum (1-126): No Pricing
Production 10
Platinum (210-221): No Pricing
Production One

Rainbow

Rainbows: No Pricing
Production One Set

Achievement Material

NM/M

Common Player:

EB	Ernie Banks/58	25.00
JB	Johnny Bench/68	15.00
YB	Yogi Berra/51	20.00
GB	George Brett/80	25.00
CA	Roy Campanella/51	25.00
RO	Rod Carew/77	15.00
SC	Steve Carlton/72	10.00
OC	Orlando Cepeda/58	10.00
CL	Roger Clemens/86	25.00
RC	Roberto Clemente/66	100.00
JD	Joe DiMaggio/39	100.00
DD	Don Drysdale/62	15.00
BG	Bob Gibson/68	15.00
KG	Ken Griffey Jr./97	25.00
DJ	Derek Jeter/96	40.00
RJ	Randy Johnson/99	15.00
HK	Harmon Killebrew/69	15.00
GM	Greg Maddux/92	20.00
MA	Mickey Mantle/56	200.00
RM	Roger Maris/61	80.00
PM	Pedro J. Martinez/99	15.00
DM	Don Mattingly/85	20.00
MC	Willie McCovey/59	15.00
TM	Thurman Munson/70	15.00
EM	Eddie Murray/77	15.00
JP	Jim Palmer/73	10.00
MP	Mike Piazza/93	20.00
CR	Cal Ripken Jr./82	50.00
BR	Brooks Robinson/64	15.00
FR	Frank Robinson/66	10.00
JR	Jackie Robinson/47	65.00
RS	Ryne Sandberg/84	40.00
MS	Mike Schmidt/80	25.00
TS	Tom Seaver/69	15.00
SS	Sammy Sosa/98	20.00
TW	Ted Williams/42	100.00
CY	Carl Yastrzemski/67	25.00
RY	Robin Yount/82	25.00

All-Stars Signatures

NM/M

Most not priced.

RC	Rod Carew/18	40.00
SM	Stan Musial/24	75.00
BR	Brooks Robinson/15	60.00
CY	Carl Yastrzemski/18	80.00

Bat Barrel Signatures

No Pricing
Production 1-5

Stat Patch

NM/M

Quantity produced listed
5+ Color Patch: 1.5X

JB	Jeff Bagwell/47	25.00
CB	Carlos Beltran/29	35.00
CB1	Carlos Beltran/41	30.00
BE	Johnny Bench/45	50.00
HB	Hank Blalock/29	20.00
GB	George Brett/20	80.00
GB1	George Brett/30	75.00
WC	Will Clark/35	50.00
CL1	Roger Clemens/24	50.00
DD	Don Drysdale/25	50.00
EG	Eric Gagne/55	25.00
VG	Vladimir Guerrero/44	25.00
VG1	Vladimir Guerrero/40	25.00
TG	Tony Gwynn/56	40.00
TG1	Tony Gwynn/25	50.00
DJ	Derek Jeter/32	60.00
DJ1	Derek Jeter/24	60.00
RJ	Randy Johnson/20	40.00
CJ	Chipper Jones/45	25.00
HK	Harmon Killebrew/49	50.00
GM1	Greg Maddux/20	40.00
GM2	Greg Maddux/17	40.00
JM	Juan Marichal/26	30.00
MA	Pedro Martinez/23	35.00
HM	Hideki Matsui/31	120.00
DM	Don Mattingly/35	75.00
PM	Paul Molitor/39	40.00
TM	Thurman Munson/20	75.00
PN	Phil Niekro/23	30.00
PN1	Phil Niekro/23	30.00
RP	Rafael Palmeiro/47	25.00
JP1	Jim Palmer/23	30.00
PI	Mike Piazza/40	40.00
AP	Albert Pujols/43	60.00
AP1	Albert Pujols/51	50.00
MR	Manny Ramirez/45	25.00
JR1	Jim Rice/46	25.00
CR	Cal Ripken Jr./34	100.00
CR1	Cal Ripken Jr./47	75.00
IR	Ivan Rodriguez/35	30.00
IR1	Ivan Rodriguez/25	30.00
SR	Scott Rolen/31	35.00
RS	Ryne Sandberg/40	65.00
RS1	Ryne Sandberg/19	100.00
MS	Mike Schmidt/48	65.00
TS	Tom Seaver/25	50.00
JS	John Smoltz/24	30.00
JS1	John Smoltz/55	25.00
AS	Alfonso Soriano/39	20.00
AS1	Alfonso Soriano/43	20.00
SS1	Sammy Sosa/66	30.00
WS	Willie Stargell/48	50.00
IS	Ichiro Suzuki/56	120.00
MT	Miguel Tejada/34	25.00
JT	Jim Thome/52	25.00
CY	Carl Yastrzemski/44	50.00
RY	Robin Yount/49	50.00
DW	Dave Winfield/37	25.00

Dual Game Patch

NM/M

Production 25 Sets

BB	Carlos Beltran, Jeff Bagwell	40.00
BC	Josh Beckett, Miguel Cabrera	40.00
BG	Lou Brock, Tony Gwynn	75.00
BS	Mike Schmidt, George Brett	100.00
BT	Hank Blalock, Mark Teixeira	40.00
CG	Rod Carew, Tony Gwynn	50.00
CP	Mike Piazza, Gary Carter	50.00
CR	Eric Chavez, Scott Rolen	50.00
FB	Johnny Bench, Carlton Fisk	50.00
FR	Nolan Ryan, Bob Feller	100.00
GC	Will Clark, Mark Grace	40.00
GG	Ken Griffey Sr., Ken Griffey Jr.	75.00
GM	Stan Musial, Bob Gibson	60.00
GS	Mark Grace, Ryne Sandberg	100.00
HF	Rollie Fingers, Jim "Catfish" Hunter	30.00
JC	Roger Clemens, Randy Johnson	75.00
JJ	Chipper Jones, Andruw Jones	40.00
JM	Derek Jeter, Hideki Matsui	125.00
KC	Rod Carew, Harmon Killebrew	60.00
KM	Willie McCovey, Harmon Killebrew	50.00
KS	Sammy Sosa, Ken Griffey Jr.	75.00
LS	Fred Lynn, Ichiro Suzuki	100.00
MG	Greg Maddux, Tom Glavine	50.00
MJ	Chipper Jones, Eddie Mathews	75.00
MM	Kazuo Matsui, Hideki Matsui	120.00
MY	Robin Yount, Paul Molitor	60.00
PC	Will Clark, Rafael Palmeiro	40.00
PR	Scott Rolen, Albert Pujols	100.00
RC	Nolan Ryan, Roger Clemens	100.00
RM	Cal Ripken Jr., Eddie Murray	150.00
RP	Cal Ripken Jr., Jim Palmer	125.00
RR	Jackie Robinson, Pee Wee Reese	150.00
RS	Nolan Ryan, Tom Seaver	100.00
RT	Cal Ripken Jr., Miguel Tejada	75.00
SB	Jim Bunning, Mike Schmidt	75.00
SM	Pedro J. Martinez, Curt Schilling	60.00
ST	Mike Schmidt, Jim Thome	75.00
WM	Don Mattingly, Dave Winfield	75.00
WP	Mark Prior, Kerry Wood	50.00
WS	Billy Williams, Sammy Sosa	60.00
YR	Carl Yastrzemski, Jim Rice	75.00

Dual Legendary Materials

NM/M

Common Player:
Production 50 Sets

BM	Willie McCovey, Ernie Banks	40.00
BR	Roger Maris, Babe Ruth	300.00
CB	Yogi Berra, Roy Campanella	35.00
CM	Roberto Clemente, Thurman Munson	100.00
CS	Duke Snider, Roy Campanella	40.00
DM	Mickey Mantle, Joe DiMaggio	200.00

DW Joe DiMaggio, Ted Williams 150.00
FD Don Drysdale, Bob Feller 25.00
MB Yogi Berra, Thurman Munson 50.00
MC Mickey Mantle, Roberto Clemente 180.00
MM Mickey Mantle, Roger Maris 220.00
MW Mickey Mantle, Ted Williams 200.00
RB Ernie Banks, Jackie Robinson 75.00
RC Jackie Robinson, Roy Campanella 75.00
RD Joe DiMaggio, Babe Ruth 275.00
RM Babe Ruth, Mickey Mantle 400.00
RP Jackie Robinson, Satchel Paige 100.00
RW Roberto Clemente, Willie McCovey 100.00
WM Eddie Mathews, Ted Williams 125.00

Dual Materials

NM/M

Common Player:
Production 60 Sets
BC Brooks Robinson, Cal Ripken Jr. 50.00
BM Yogi Berra, Thurman Munson 40.00
BP Johnny Bench, Mike Piazza 25.00
BS Mike Schmidt, George Brett 40.00
CK Harmon Killebrew, Rod Carew 30.00
CM Willie McCovey, Will Clark 30.00
ER Ryne Sandberg, Ernie Banks 60.00
GS Sammy Sosa, Ken Griffey Jr. 40.00
JC Randy Johnson, Roger Clemens 40.00
JM Derek Jeter, Don Mattingly 60.00
MB Johnny Bench, Thurman Munson 40.00
MC Don Mattingly, Will Clark 40.00
MP Mark Prior, Joe Mauer 25.00
MR Bill Mazeroski, Jackie Robinson 60.00
MT Kazuo Matsui, Shingo Takatsu 30.00
MY Robin Yount, Paul Molitor 40.00
PR Manny Ramirez, Albert Pujols 50.00
RC Nolan Ryan, Roger Clemens 60.00
RP Mike Piazza, Ivan Rodriguez 20.00
RR Brooks Robinson, Frank Robinson 25.00
RT Thurman Munson, Roy Campanella 30.00
SG Ken Griffey Jr., Ichiro Suzuki 60.00
SP Mark Prior, Ben Sheets 10.00
SR Duke Snider, Pee Wee Reese 30.00
SS Sammy Sosa, Ryne Sandberg 50.00
TS Jim Thome, Mike Schmidt 35.00
WM Don Mattingly, Dave Winfield 40.00
WP Mark Prior, Kerry Wood 20.00
WR Kerry Wood, Nolan Ryan 50.00
YR Manny Ramirez, Carl Yastrzemski 35.00

Dual Materials Signature

NM/M

Production 25 Sets
AB Luis Aparicio, Ernie Banks 100.00
BB Wade Boggs, Hank Blalock 80.00
BC Brooks Robinson, Cal Ripken Jr. 250.00
BF Carlton Fisk, Johnny Bench 100.00
BG Carlos Beltran, Ken Griffey Jr. 150.00
BJ Derek Jeter, Yogi Berra 200.00
BM Brian Giles, Marcus Giles 35.00
BP Johnny Bench, Mike Piazza 160.00
BR Jim Bunning, Robin Roberts 40.00
BT Hank Blalock, Mark Teixeira 60.00
CB Hank Blalock, Eric Chavez 50.00
CC Steve Carlton, Roger Clemens 150.00
CJ Roger Clemens, Randy Johnson 300.00
CK Harmon Killebrew, Rod Carew 80.00
CL Miguel Cabrera, Mike Lowell 75.00
CM Miguel Cabrera, Carlos Beltran 125.00
DD Derek Jeter, Don Mattingly 300.00
DG Gaylord Perry, Don Sutton 50.00
DJ Jim Rice, Dave Parker 80.00
DS Ryne Sandberg, Andre Dawson 125.00
DW Andre Dawson, Billy Williams 50.00
ER Ryne Sandberg, Ernie Banks 160.00
FC Bob Feller, Rocky Colavito 75.00
FR Bob Feller, Nolan Ryan 180.00
GB Brooks Robinson, George Brett 140.00
GC Ron Guidry, Steve Carlton 50.00
GG Ken Griffey Sr., Ken Griffey Jr. 150.00
GM Mike Schmidt, George Brett 150.00
GP Rafael Palmeiro, Ken Griffey Jr. 150.00
GR Greg Maddux, Roger Clemens 300.00
GS John Smoltz, Eric Gagne 75.00
IV Ivan Rodriguez, Victor Martinez 65.00
JB Ernie Banks, Fergie Jenkins 100.00
JC Randy Johnson, Steve Carlton 125.00
JD Johnny Podres, Don Sutton 50.00
JG Randy Johnson, Ken Griffey Jr. 200.00
JM Chipper Jones, Dale Murphy 150.00
JP Jim Palmer, Fergie Jenkins 50.00
JR Cal Ripken Jr., Derek Jeter 500.00
KG Ken Griffey Jr., Harmon Killebrew 150.00
KN Kerry Wood, Nolan Ryan 175.00
KT Scott Kazmir, Shingo Takatsu 75.00
LB Yogi Berra, Don Larsen 180.00
MB Johnny Bench, Joe Morgan 80.00
MC Don Mattingly, Will Clark 125.00
MH Mark Mulder, Tim Hudson 50.00
MP Mark Prior, Joe Mauer 80.00
MS Bill Mazeroski, Ryne Sandberg 150.00
MW Will Clark, Mark Grace 75.00
MY Robin Yount, Paul Molitor 150.00
NR Roger Clemens, Nolan Ryan 300.00
OR Manny Ramirez, David Ortiz 200.00
OS Stan Musial, Ozzie Smith 150.00
PC Will Clark, Rafael Palmeiro 100.00
PN Phil Niekro, Gaylord Perry 50.00
PS Johnny Podres, Duke Snider 60.00
RB Rod Carew, Bill Mazeroski 75.00
RC Eric Chavez, Brooks Robinson 60.00
RM Eddie Murray, Cal Ripken Jr. 275.00
RP Brooks Robinson, Jim Palmer 65.00
RR Brooks Robinson, Frank Robinson 75.00
RS Robin Roberts, Steve Carlton 60.00
RT Miguel Tejada, Cal Ripken Jr. 200.00
SC Mike Schmidt, Steve Carlton 150.00
SF Ben Sheets, Bob Feller 50.00
SG Eric Gagne, Bruce Sutter 75.00
SO Ben Sheets, Roy Oswalt 50.00
SP Mark Prior, Ben Sheets 80.00
SR Brooks Robinson, Mike Schmidt 150.00
SS Tom Seaver, Ben Sheets 75.00
TB Tony Gwynn, Brian Giles 75.00
TC Mark Teixeira, Miguel Cabrera 75.00
WM Dave Winfield, Don Mattingly 150.00
WO Orlando Cepeda, Willie McCovey 75.00
WP Mark Prior, Kerry Wood 75.00
WW Will Clark, Willie McCovey 75.00
YR Carl Yastrzemski, Manny Ramirez 160.00

Game Materials

NM/M

Common Player: 8.00
Production 99 Sets
EB Ernie Banks 15.00
JB Johnny Bench 10.00
WB Wade Boggs 8.00
GB George Brett 20.00
LB Lou Brock 8.00
RC Rod Carew 8.00
SC Steve Carlton 8.00
WC Will Clark 8.00
CL Roger Clemens 20.00
TC Ty Cobb 100.00
DD Don Drysdale 8.00
BF Bob Feller 8.00
CF Carlton Fisk 10.00
BG Bob Gibson 10.00
KG Ken Griffey Jr. 20.00
TG Tony Gwynn 10.00
DJ Derek Jeter 30.00
RJ Randy Johnson 15.00
AK Al Kaline 15.00
HK Harmon Killebrew 10.00
MA Juan Marichal 8.00
RM Roger Maris 50.00
ED Eddie Mathews 15.00
DM Don Mattingly 25.00
BM Bill Mazeroski 8.00
WM Willie McCovey 8.00
PM Paul Molitor 10.00
TM Thurman Munson 15.00
EM Eddie Murray 15.00
SM Stan Musial 25.00
JP Jim Palmer 8.00
PI Mike Piazza 15.00
MP Mark Prior 10.00
AP Albert Pujols 25.00
CR Cal Ripken Jr. 40.00
BR Brooks Robinson 10.00
FR Frank Robinson 8.00
JR Jackie Robinson 40.00
RS Ryne Sandberg 25.00
MS Mike Schmidt 15.00
TS Tom Seaver 10.00
OS Ozzie Smith 15.00
DS Duke Snider 10.00
WS Warren Spahn 15.00
WSt Willie Stargell 8.00
IS Ichiro Suzuki 60.00
DW Dave Winfield 8.00
KW Kerry Wood 10.00
CY Carl Yastrzemski 20.00
RY Robin Yount 20.00

Game Patch

NM/M

Common Player:
Production 75 unless noted.
5 Color +: 1.5X
BA Jeff Bagwell 25.00
BE Josh Beckett 15.00
CB Carlos Beltran 25.00
JB Johnny Bench 50.00
YB Yogi Berra 50.00
HB Hank Blalock 15.00
WB Wade Boggs 20.00
GB George Brett 50.00
LB Lou Brock 40.00
BU Jim Bunning/66 30.00
CA Miguel Cabrera 30.00
RC Rod Carew 30.00
RO Rod Carew 30.00
GC Gary Carter 30.00
EC Eric Chavez 15.00
WC Will Clark 30.00
WC1 Will Clark 30.00
RC Roger Clemens 40.00
RB Roberto Clemente 200.00
CO1 Rocky Colavito 80.00
JD Joe DiMaggio 180.00
BF Bob Feller 40.00
NF Nellie Fox/55 125.00
GL Troy Glaus 20.00
KG Ken Griffey Jr. 50.00
VG Vladimir Guerrero 30.00
RG Ron Guidry 30.00
TG Tony Gwynn 30.00
TH Todd Helton 25.00
CH Jim "Catfish" Hunter 30.00
DJ Derek Jeter 40.00
RJ Randy Johnson 25.00
RJ1 Randy Johnson 25.00
CJ Chipper Jones 25.00
HK Harmon Killebrew 40.00
GM Greg Maddux 35.00
GM1 Greg Maddux 35.00
MA Juan Marichal 25.00
PE Pedro J. Martinez 25.00
HM Hideki Matsui/44 100.00
KM Kazuo Matsui 50.00
DM Don Mattingly 40.00
JM Joe Mauer 30.00
BM Bill Mazeroski/55 60.00
WM Willie McCovey 35.00
PM Paul Molitor 30.00
MO Joe Morgan 20.00
TM Thurman Munson 40.00
MU Eddie Murray 40.00
SM Stan Musial 75.00
RP Rafael Palmeiro 25.00
JP Jim Palmer 25.00
PI Mike Piazza 30.00
PO Johnny Podres 30.00
MP Mark Prior 20.00
AP Albert Pujols 50.00
MR Manny Ramirez 25.00
CR Cal Ripken Jr. 60.00
BR Brooks Robinson 40.00
IR Ivan Rodriguez 25.00
SR Scott Rolen 25.00
NR Nolan Ryan/51 50.00
NR1 Nolan Ryan 50.00
NR2 Nolan Ryan 50.00
RS Ryne Sandberg 50.00
CS Curt Schilling 25.00
MS Mike Schmidt 40.00
TS Tom Seaver 20.00
BS Ben Sheets 25.00
GS Gary Sheffield 20.00
OS Ozzie Smith 40.00
AS Alfonso Soriano 25.00
SS Sammy Sosa 35.00
SP Warren Spahn/62 60.00
WS Willie Stargell 30.00
IS Ichiro Suzuki 120.00
MT Mark Teixeira 15.00
TE Miguel Tejada 25.00
JT Jim Thome 35.00
BW Bernie Williams 20.00
WI Billy Williams 20.00
DW Dave Winfield 35.00
KW Kerry Wood 25.00
CY Carl Yastrzemski 50.00
RY Robin Yount 40.00

Gold Glove Sign. Materials

No Pricing
Production 1-16

Game Patch Signatures

NM/M

Common Player:
Production 30 Sets
EB Ernie Banks 75.00
CB Carlos Beltran 65.00
JB Johnny Bench 65.00
HB Hank Blalock 50.00
WB Wade Boggs 65.00
GB George Brett 100.00
MC Miguel Cabrera 65.00
RC Rod Carew 50.00
EC Eric Chavez 40.00
WC Will Clark 60.00
AD Andre Dawson 40.00
BG Bob Gibson 50.00
KG Ken Griffey Jr. 125.00
TG Tony Gwynn 65.00
DJ Derek Jeter 200.00
RJ Randy Johnson 125.00
AK Al Kaline 75.00
HK Harmon Killebrew 75.00
GM Greg Maddux 150.00
MA Juan Marichal 50.00
DM Don Mattingly 100.00
JM Joe Mauer 60.00
WM Willie McCovey 50.00
PM Paul Molitor 60.00
MU Mark Mulder 40.00
EM Eddie Murray 80.00
SM Stan Musial 120.00
RO Roy Oswalt 50.00
JP Jim Palmer 50.00
PI Mike Piazza 125.00
MP Mark Prior 60.00
JR Jim Rice 50.00
CR Cal Ripken Jr. 200.00
BR Brooks Robinson 60.00
FR Frank Robinson 50.00
NR Nolan Ryan 150.00
RS Ryne Sandberg 150.00
MS Mike Schmidt 125.00
SC Red Schoendienst 40.00
TS Tom Seaver 75.00
BS Ben Sheets 50.00
OS Ozzie Smith 75.00
MT Mark Teixeira 50.00
KW Kerry Wood 75.00
CY Carl Yastrzemski 100.00
RY Robin Yount 80.00

Legendary Materials

NM/M

Common Player: 10.00
Production 50 Sets
EB Ernie Banks 20.00
YB Yogi Berra 20.00
CA Roy Campanella 15.00
RC Roberto Clemente 100.00
TC Ty Cobb 100.00
JD Joe DiMaggio 100.00
DD Don Drysdale 15.00
BF Bob Feller 10.00
MM Mickey Mantle 200.00
RM Roger Maris 60.00
EM Eddie Mathews 20.00
WM Willie McCovey 15.00
TM Thurman Munson 25.00
SM Stan Musial 40.00
SP Satchel Paige 50.00
JR Jackie Robinson 60.00
BR Babe Ruth 250.00
DS Duke Snider 15.00
TW Ted Williams 80.00

Logo Patch Signatures

No Pricing
Production One Set

Game Jersey Signatures

NM/M

Quantity produced listed
EB Ernie Banks/19 85.00
GB George Brett/21 100.00
TG Tony Gwynn/20 70.00
HK Harmon Killebrew/21 75.00
CR Cal Ripken Jr./21 200.00
BR Brooks Robinson/23 50.00
MS Mike Schmidt/18 100.00
CY Carl Yastrzemski/23 85.00
RY Robin Yount/20 85.00

Materials Signatures

NM/M

Production 50 Sets
BA Bobby Abreu 25.00
JE Jeff Bagwell 50.00
EB Ernie Banks 75.00
BE Josh Beckett 25.00
CB Carlos Beltran 60.00
JB Johnny Bench 60.00
HB Hank Blalock 30.00

WB	Wade Boggs	50.00
WB1	Wade Boggs	50.00
GB	George Brett	80.00
LB	Lou Brock	40.00
LB1	Lou Brock	40.00
BU	Jim Bunning	30.00
CA	Miguel Cabrera	40.00
RC	Rod Carew	40.00
RC1	Rod Carew	40.00
SC	Steve Carlton	35.00
SC1	Steve Carlton	35.00
GC	Gary Carter	30.00
GC1	Gary Carter	30.00
JC	Joe Carter	30.00
OC	Orlando Cepeda	35.00
OC1	Orlando Cepeda	35.00
EC	Eric Chavez	30.00
WC	Will Clark	40.00
WC1	Will Clark	40.00
WC2	Will Clark	40.00
WC3	Will Clark	40.00
CL	Roger Clemens	125.00
CL1	Roger Clemens	125.00
CL2	Roger Clemens	125.00
CO	Rocky Colavito	75.00
CO1	Rocky Colavito	75.00
AD	Andre Dawson	30.00
AD1	Andre Dawson	30.00
DE	Dennis Eckersley	30.00
DE1	Dennis Eckersley	30.00
BF	Bob Feller	30.00
RF	Rollie Fingers	30.00
RF1	Rollie Fingers	30.00
CF	Carlton Fisk	40.00
CF1	Carlton Fisk	40.00
EG	Eric Gagne	50.00
NG	Nomar Garciaparra	125.00
NG1	Nomar Garciaparra	125.00
BG	Bob Gibson	40.00
MG	Mark Grace	40.00
KG	Ken Griffey Jr.	100.00
KG1	Ken Griffey Jr.	100.00
VG	Vladimir Guerrero	65.00
RG	Ron Guidry	40.00
TG	Tony Gwynn	50.00
HE	Todd Helton	40.00
TH	Tim Hudson	30.00
FJ	Fergie Jenkins	30.00
DJ	Derek Jeter	150.00
RJ	Randy Johnson	100.00
RJ1	Randy Johnson	100.00
CJ	Chipper Jones	50.00
AK	Al Kaline	50.00
HK	Harmon Killebrew	60.00
DL	Don Larsen	50.00
ML	Mike Lowell	20.00
GM	Greg Maddux	100.00
GM1	Greg Maddux	100.00
JU	Juan Marichal	30.00
DO	Don Mattingly	80.00
JM	Joe Mauer	40.00
JM1	Joe Mauer	40.00
BM	Bill Mazeroski	40.00
MC	Willie McCovey	40.00
PM	Paul Molitor	50.00
PM1	Paul Molitor	50.00
PM2	Paul Molitor	50.00
MO	Joe Morgan	30.00
MU	Mark Mulder	30.00
DM	Dale Murphy	40.00
EM	Eddie Murray	80.00
EM1	Eddie Murray	80.00
RO	Roy Oswalt	25.00
RP	Rafael Palmeiro	50.00
JP	Jim Palmer	30.00
TP	Tony Perez	30.00
GP	Gaylord Perry	25.00
GP1	Gaylord Perry	25.00
PI	Mike Piazza	100.00
PI1	Mike Piazza	100.00
PO	Johnny Podres	30.00
MP	Mark Prior	60.00
MP1	Mark Prior	60.00
MR	Manny Ramirez	75.00
JR	Jim Rice	30.00
CR	Cal Ripken Jr.	180.00
RR	Robin Roberts	30.00
BR	Brooks Robinson	40.00
FR	Frank Robinson	35.00
FR1	Frank Robinson	35.00
IR	Ivan Rodriguez	50.00
SR	Scott Rolen	50.00
NR	Nolan Ryan	120.00
NR1	Nolan Ryan	120.00
NR2	Nolan Ryan	120.00
NR3	Nolan Ryan	120.00
SA	Ryne Sandberg	100.00
MS	Mike Schmidt	75.00
RS	Red Schoendienst	30.00
TS	Tom Seaver	50.00
TS1	Tom Seaver	50.00
BS	Ben Sheets	30.00
BS1	Ben Sheets	30.00
OS	Ozzie Smith	60.00
JS	John Smoltz	50.00
SN	Duke Snider	40.00
SN1	Duke Snider	40.00
AS	Alfonso Soriano	40.00
DS	Don Sutton	30.00
MT	Mark Teixeira	40.00
TE	Miguel Tejada	40.00
TE1	Miguel Tejada/34	40.00
FT	Frank Thomas	60.00
RW	Rickie Weeks	30.00
RW1	Rickie Weeks	30.00
BW	Billy Williams	30.00
DW	Dave Winfield	40.00
DW1	Dave Winfield	40.00
KW	Kerry Wood	50.00
CY	Carl Yastrzemski	75.00
DY	Delmon Young	30.00
DY1	Delmon Young	30.00
RY	Robin Yount	60.00

Quadruple Materials

No Pricing
Production 15 Sets

Super Patch

No Pricing
Production 4-20

Signatures

		NM/M
Common Player:		20.00
Production 25 unless noted.		
Gold:		1-1.5X
Production 10-25		
No pricing 20 or less.		
Platinum:		No Pricing
Production One Set		
LA1	Luis Aparicio	20.00
BE	Johnny Bench	50.00
YB	Yogi Berra	50.00
WB	Wade Boggs	50.00
MC1	Miguel Cabrera	50.00
CW	Rod Carew	40.00
CA1	Steve Carlton	30.00
CL	Roger Clemens	125.00
BF1	Bob Feller	35.00
RF1	Rollie Fingers	25.00
WF	Whitey Ford	50.00
NG	Nomar Garciaparra	100.00
GI	Bob Gibson	40.00
VG	Vladimir Guerrero	50.00
RJ	Randy Johnson	100.00
AK1	Al Kaline	50.00
HK1	Harmon Killebrew	60.00
RK1	Ralph Kiner	40.00
GM	Greg Maddux	80.00
WI	Willie McCovey	40.00
MO	Joe Morgan	25.00
EM	Eddie Murray	75.00
MU	Stan Musial	75.00
JP1	Jim Palmer	30.00
PI	Mike Piazza	100.00
MP	Mark Prior	40.00
KP	Kirby Puckett	65.00
CR	Cal Ripken Jr.	160.00
RR1	Robin Roberts	30.00
BR1	Brooks Robinson	50.00
NR	Nolan Ryan/6	
RY	Ryne Sandberg	75.00
MS	Mike Schmidt	
TS	Tom Seaver	50.00
OS	Ozzie Smith	60.00
SN	Duke Snider	40.00
DW	Dave Winfield	35.00
CY	Carl Yastrzemski	75.00

Signatures Tier B

		NM/M
Common Player:		
BA	Bobby Abreu/25	30.00
LA	Luis Aparicio/25	25.00
CB	Carlos Beltran/25	50.00
BI	Craig Biggio/25	40.00
HB	Hank Blalock/25	35.00
BL	Bert Blyleven/99	20.00
JB	Jim Bunning/99	20.00
MC	Miguel Cabrera/99	30.00
SC	Sean Casey/99	20.00
OC	Orlando Cepeda/25	25.00
EC	Eric Chavez/25	30.00
WC	Will Clark/25	40.00
RC	Rocky Colavito/99	50.00
DC	David Cone/99	20.00
CC	Carl Crawford/99	10.00
AD	Andre Dawson/25	25.00
BD	Bobby Doerr/99	25.00
DE	Dennis Eckersley/25	35.00
BF	Bob Feller/25	30.00
RF	Rollie Fingers/25	25.00
GF	George Foster/25	20.00
EG	Eric Gagne/25	50.00
BG	Brian Giles/99	10.00
MG	Marcus Giles/99	10.00
DG	Dwight Gooden/99	20.00
GG	Rich "Goose" Gossage/99	10.00
GR	Mark Grace/99	30.00
KG	Ken Griffey Sr./69	15.00
RG	Ron Guidry/25	40.00
TH	Travis Hafner/99	20.00
KH	Keith Hernandez/99	15.00
FH	Frank Howard/99	15.00
MI	Monte Irvin/25	25.00
JK	Jim Kaat/99	20.00
AK	Al Kaline/25	60.00
GK	George Kell/99	20.00
HK	Harmon Killebrew/25	60.00
RK	Ralph Kiner/25	40.00
ML	Mike Lowell/99	10.00
SL	Sparky Lyle/99	10.00
FL	Fred Lynn/25	20.00
VM	Victor Martinez/99	20.00
JM	Joe Mauer/99	25.00
BM	Bill Mazeroski/25	50.00
MM	Mark Mulder/99	20.00
DM	Dale Murphy/99	30.00
GN	Graig Nettles/99	15.00
DN	Don Newcombe/25	25.00
RO	Roy Oswalt/99	20.00
AO	Akinori Otsuka/99	40.00
JP	Jim Palmer/99	20.00
DP	Dave Parker/25	25.00
CP	Corey Patterson/99	20.00
TP	Tony Perez/25	35.00
GP	Gaylord Perry/25	20.00
PO	Johnny Podres/99	25.00
RR	Robin Roberts/25	30.00
BR	Brooks Robinson/25	50.00
AR	Al Rosen/99	20.00
SA	Ron Santo/99	25.00
JS	Jason Schmidt/99	25.00
RS	Red Schoendienst/25	30.00
BS	Ben Sheets/99	25.00
SM	John Smoltz/25	50.00
SU	Bruce Sutter/99	25.00
ST	Shingo Takatsu/99	40.00
MT	Mark Teixeira/25	40.00
LT	Luis Tiant/99	10.00
RW	Rickie Weeks/99	20.00
BW	Billy Williams/25	30.00
MW	Maury Wills/25	20.00
DY	Delmon Young/99	20.00

Signatures Duals

		NM/M
Production 25 Sets		
BB	Wade Boggs, Hank Blalock	80.00
BC	Miguel Cabrera, Carlos Beltran	120.00
BG	Carlos Beltran, Ken Griffey Jr.	175.00
BR	Jim Bunning, Robin Roberts	75.00
BS	George Brett, Mike Schmidt	150.00
BT	Hank Blalock, Mark Teixeira	70.00
CB	Hank Blalock, Eric Chavez	50.00
CJ	Roger Clemens, Randy Johnson	300.00
CL	Mike Lowell, Miguel Cabrera	50.00
CR	Eric Chavez, Brooks Robinson	65.00
DW	Billy Williams, Andre Dawson	40.00
EF	Rollie Fingers, Dennis Eckersley	50.00
FR	Bob Feller, Nolan Ryan	160.00
GC	Will Clark, Mark Grace	65.00
GG	Marcus Giles, Brian Giles	40.00
GK	Ken Griffey Jr., Harmon Killebrew	150.00
GS	John Smoltz, Eric Gagne	85.00
IC	Monte Irvin, Orlando Cepeda	50.00
JC	Steve Carlton, Randy Johnson	125.00
JM	Derek Jeter, Don Mattingly	300.00
JP	Jim Palmer, Fergie Jenkins	50.00
JT	Fergie Jenkins, Luis Tiant	50.00
KG	Ken Griffey Sr., Ken Griffey Jr.	175.00
KK	Al Kaline, Harmon Killebrew	80.00
MC	Don Mattingly, Will Clark	125.00
MH	Mark Mulder, Tim Hudson	40.00
MP	Joe Mauer, Mark Prior	60.00
NR	Roger Clemens, Nolan Ryan	400.00
NS	Don Sutton, Don Newcombe	40.00
PC	Rafael Palmeiro, Will Clark	120.00
PN	Phil Niekro, Gaylord Perry	40.00
PR	Jim Rice, Dave Parker	60.00
PS	Ben Sheets, Mark Prior	60.00
RC	Steve Carlton, Robin Roberts	40.00
RJ	Derek Jeter, Cal Ripken Jr.	500.00
RP	Brooks Robinson, Jim Palmer	75.00
SF	Ben Sheets, Bob Feller	40.00
SG	Eric Gagne, Bruce Sutter	60.00
SO	Ben Sheets, Roy Oswalt	40.00
SP	Don Sutton, Gaylord Perry	40.00
TC	Mark Teixeira, Miguel Cabrera	80.00
VM	Miguel Cabrera, Vladimir Guerrero	100.00
WS	Billy Williams, Ron Santo	60.00

Signatures Triple

No Pricing
Production 20 Sets

Signatures Quadruple

No Pricing
Production 10 Sets

Signatures Six

No Pricing
Production Five Sets

Signatures Eight

No Pricing
Production One Set

Signature Numbers Patch

		NM/M
Quantity produced listed		
WB	Wade Boggs/26	65.00
LB	Lou Brock/20	50.00
MC	Miguel Cabrera/24	60.00
BF	Bob Feller/19	50.00
EG	Eric Gagne/38	50.00
KG	Ken Griffey Jr./30	120.00
VG	Vladimir Guerrero/27	80.00
DM	Don Mattingly/23	100.00
WM	Willie McCovey/44	60.00
RO	Roy Oswalt/44	30.00
PI	Mike Piazza/31	120.00
MP	Mark Prior/22	60.00
RS	Ryne Sandberg/23	125.00
MS	Mike Schmidt/20	100.00
MT	Mark Teixeira/23	40.00
BW	Billy Williams/26	40.00
DW	Dave Winfield/31	50.00
RY	Robin Yount/19	100.00

2004 Upper Deck USA

		NM/M
Complete Factory Set (204):		50.00
Complete Set (200):		25.00
Common Player:		.15
1	Jim Abbott	.25
2	Brent Abernathy	.15
3	Kurt Ainsworth	.15
4	Abe Alvarez	.15
5	Matt Anderson	.15
6	Jeff Austin	.15
7	Justin Wayne	.15
8	Scott Bankhead	.15
9	Josh Bard	.15
10	Michael Barrett	.15
11	Mark Bellhorn	.25
12	Buddy Bell	.15
13	Andy Benes	.25
14	Kris Benson	.25
15	Peter Bergeron	.15
16	Rocky Biddle	.15
17	Casey Blake	.15
18	Willie Bloomquist	.25
19	Jeremy Bonderman	.25
20	Jeff Weaver	.25
21	Joe Borchard	.15
22	Rickie Weeks	.50
23	Rob Bowen	.15
24	Milton Bradley	.25
25	Dan Wheeler	.15
26	Ben Broussard	.15
27	Brian Bruney	.15
28	Mark Budzinski	.15
29	Kirk Bullinger	.15
30	Chris Burke	.25
31	Sean Burnett	.15
32	Jeromy Burnitz	.25
33	Pat Burrell	.50
34	Sean Burroughs	.50
35	Paul Byrd	.25
36	Chris Capuano	.25
37	Scott Cassidy	.15
38	Will Clark	.75
39	Chad Cordero	.15
40	Carl Crawford	.25
41	Bobby Crosby	.75
42	Brad Wilkerson	.15
43	Michael Cuddyer	.25
44	Ben Davis	.15
45	Gookie Dawkins	.15
46	Rod Dedeaux	.15
47	R.A. Dickey	.15
48	Ben Diggins	.15
49	Lenny DiNardo	.15
50	Ryan Drese	.15
51	Tim Drew	.15
52	Todd Williams	.15
53	Justin Duchscherer	.15
54	J.D. Durbin	.15
55	Scott Elarton	.15
56	Adam Everett	.15
57	Dan Wilson	.15
58	Steve Finley	.25
59	Casey Fossum	.15
60	Terry Francona	.15
61	Ryan Franklin	.15
62	Ryan Freel	.15
63	John Van Benschoten	.15
64	Nomar Garciaparra	1.00
65	Chris George	.15
66	Jody Gerut	.15
67	Jason Giambi	.40
68	Matt Ginter	.15
69	Troy Glaus	.50
70	Tom Goodwin	.15
71	Mike Gosling	.15
72	Danny Graves	.15
73	Shawn Green	.50
74	Khalil Greene	.75
75	Todd Greene	.15
76	Seth Greisinger	.15
77	Gabe Gross	.15
78	Jeffrey Hammonds	.25
79	Aaron Heilman	.15
80	Paul Wilson	.15
81	Todd Helton	.75
82	Dustin Hermanson	.15
83	Bobby Hill	.15
84	Koyie Hill	.15
85	A.J. Hinch	.15
86	Matt Holliday	.50
87	Ted Wood	.15
88	Ken Huckaby	.15
89	Orlando Hudson	.15
90	Ernie Young	.15
91	Jason Jennings	.25
92	Charles Johnson	.25
93	Jacque Jones	.15

94	Matt Kata	.15
95	Austin Kearns	.25
96	Adam Kennedy	.25
97	Brooks Kieschnick	.25
98	Jesse Crain	.15
99	Scott Kazmir	1.50
100	Billy Koch	.25
101	Paul Konerko	.25
102	Graham Koonce	.15
103	Casey Kotchman	.50
104	Chris Snyder	.15
105	Nick Swisher	.50
106	Gerald Laird	.15
107	Barry Larkin	.50
108	Mike Lamb	.15
109	Tommy Lasorda	.25
110	Matt LeCroy	.15
111	Travis Lee	.25
112	Justin Leone	.15
113	John Vander Wal	.15
114	Braden Looper	.15
115	Shane Loux	.15
116	Ryan Ludwick	1.00
117	Jason Varitek	.40
118	Ryan Madson	.15
119	Dave Magadan	.15
120	Tino Martinez	.25
121	Joe Mauer	.50
122	David McCarty	.15
123	Robin Ventura	.25
124	Jack McDowell	.25
125	Todd Walker	.25
126	Mark McGwire	1.50
127	Gil Meche	.15
128	Doug Mientkiewicz	.25
129	Matt Morris	.25
130	Warren Morris	.15
131	Mark Mulder	.50
132	Calvin Murray	.15
133	Eric Munson	.25
134	Mike Mussina	.50
135	Xavier Nady	.15
136	Shane Nance	.15
137	Mike Neill	.15
138	Augie Ojeda	.15
139	John Olerud	.25
140	Gregg Olson	.15
141	Roy Oswalt	.50
142	Jim Parque	.15
143	John Patterson	.15
144	Brad Penny	.15
145	Jay Powell	.15
146	Mark Prior	.75
147	Horacio Ramirez	.15
148	Jon Rauch	.15
149	Jeremy Reed	.25
150	Bob Watson	.15
151	Matt Riley	.15
152	Brian Roberts	.15
153	Dave Roberts	.15
154	Frank Robinson	.15
155	J.C. Romero	.15
156	David Ross	.15
157	Cory Vance	.15
158	Kirk Saarloos	.15
159	Anthony Sanders	.15
160	Dane Sardinha	.15
161	Bobby Seay	.15
162	Phil Seibel	.15
163	Aaron Sele	.15
164	Ben Sheets	.50
165	Paul Shuey	.15
166	Grady Sizemore	.50
167	Reggie Smith	.15
168	John Smoltz	.50
169	Zach Sorensen	.15
170	Scott Spezio	.25
171	Ed Sprague	.15
172	Jason Stanford	.15
173	Dave Stewart	.15
174	Scott Stewart	.15
175	B.J. Surhoff	.15
176	Bill Swift	.15
177	Mike Tonis	.15
178	Jason Tyner	.15
179	Michael Tucker	.15
180	B.J. Upton	.75
181	Eric Valent	.15
182	Ron Villone	.15
183	2000: Team USA Shocks Cuba	.15
184	1984: Abbott halts Japan	.15
185	1996: Berman's Boys Take Third	.15
186	1984: Team USA Takes Second	.15
187	2000: Home Run Heroics	.15
188	1999: Neill's Hit Boosts Team USA	.15
189	1996: High Five for Team USA	.15
190	1992: Garciaparra Makes the Roster	.50
191	2003: USA Rolls to Record	.15
192	1995: Juniors Are Golden In Boston	.15
193	1999: The Streak Goes On	.15
194	1998: Perfect Finish in St. Louis	.15
195	1999: McGwire's Number Retired	1.00
196	2000: Filled with Firsts	.15
197	Red, White and Blue Cardinal	.15
198	2000: Quick Start for Neill	.15
199	1999: Jensen Goes Deep vs. Cuba	.15
200	2000: Mauer on the Mark	.25

Team USA Jersey

		NM/M
Common Player:		4.00
Inserted 1:Factory Set		
KA	Kurt Ainsworth	4.00
BB	Brian Bruney	4.00
CB	Chris Burke	4.00
SB	Sean Burroughs	4.00
JD	Justin Duchscherer	4.00
AE	Adam Everett	4.00
JG	Jason Giambi	6.00
GG	Gabe Gross	4.00
DH	Dustin Hermanson	4.00
MH	Matt Holliday	15.00
GK	Graham Koonce	4.00
GL	Gerald Laird	4.00
JL	Justin Leone	6.00
JM	Joe Mauer	10.00
DM	Doug Mientkiewicz	6.00
EM	Eric Munson	8.00
XN	Xavier Nady	4.00
RO	Roy Oswalt	6.00
MP	Mark Prior	8.00
HR	Horacio Ramirez	4.00
JR	Jon Rauch	4.00
RE	Jeremy Reed	5.00
FR	Frank Robinson	8.00
MR	Mike Rouse	4.00
BS	Ben Sheets	8.00
GS	Grady Sizemore	10.00
DS	Dave Stewart	6.00
JV	John Van Benschoten	4.00
JW	Jeff Weaver	4.00
BW	Brad Wilkerson	4.00

Team USA Signature Black Ink

		NM/M
Common Autograph:		5.00
Signatures Inserted 3:Factory Set		
ABB	Jim Abbott/180	20.00
ABE	Brent Abernathy/360	5.00
AIN	Kurt Ainsworth/360	8.00
ALV	Abe Alvarez/360	10.00
AND	Matt Anderson/360	5.00
AUS	Jeff Austin/360	5.00
BANK	Scott Bankhead/360	5.00
BARD	Josh Bard/350	5.00
BARR	Michael Barrett/360	10.00
BELL	Buddy Bell/81	25.00
BEN	Andy Benes/350	10.00
BENS	Kris Benson/180	15.00
BERG	Peter Bergeron/360	5.00
BLA	Casey Blake/180	10.00
BLO	Willie Bloomquist/175	15.00
BON	Jeremy Bonderman/150	10.00
BOR	Joe Borchard/350	10.00
BRAD	Milton Bradley/360	15.00
BRO	Ben Broussard/210	5.00
BRU	Brian Bruney/160	5.00
BUD	Mark Budzinski/360	5.00
BULL	Kirk Bullinger/360	5.00
BURK	Chris Burke/350	8.00
BU	Sean Burnett/180	5.00
BURN	Jeromy Burnitz/360	15.00
BUR	Pat Burrell/360	15.00
BURR	Sean Burroughs/360	10.00
BYRD	Paul Byrd/360	10.00
CAP	Chris Capuano/150	8.00
CASS	Scott Cassidy/360	5.00
CLA	Will Clark/60	75.00
COR	Chad Cordero/360	5.00
CR	Jesse Crain/180	10.00
CRA	Carl Crawford/60	35.00
CUD	Michael Cuddyer/370	8.00
DAV	Ben Davis/344	5.00
DED	Rod Dedeaux/29	40.00
DIC	R.A. Dickey/180	5.00
DIG	Ben Diggins/180	8.00
DIN	Lenny DiNardo/150	5.00
DRE	Ryan Drese/180	8.00
DREW	Tim Drew/360	5.00
DUCH	Justin Duchscherer/210	10.00
DUR	J.D. Durbin/180	5.00
ELAR	Scott Elarton/180	8.00
EVER	Adam Everett/360	8.00
FIN	Steve Finley/360	10.00
FOSS	Casey Fossum/320	8.00
FRAN	Terry Francona/150	40.00
FRA	Ryan Franklin/360	5.00
FRE	Ryan Freel/360	5.00
GEO	Chris George/360	5.00
GER	Jody Gerut/350	5.00
GIAM	Jason Giambi/60	50.00
GIN	Matt Ginter/179	8.00
GLA	Troy Glaus/120	35.00
GOS	Mike Gosling/150	8.00
DRA	Danny Graves/360	8.00
GR	Shawn Green/150	40.00
GRE	Khalil Greene/180	40.00
GREE	Todd Greene/120	10.00
GREI	Seth Greisinger/360	5.00
GRO	Gabe Gross/150	5.00
HAM	Jeffrey Hammonds/150	10.00
HEIL	Aaron Heilman/350	5.00
HELT	Todd Helton/71	50.00
HERM	Dustin Hermanson/150	10.00
HI	Bobby Hill/360	5.00
HILL	Koyie Hill/150	5.00
HIN	A.J. Hinch/360	5.00
HUCK	Ken Huckaby/360	5.00
HUD	Orlando Hudson/360	10.00
JENN	Jason Jennings/350	8.00
JON	Jacque Jones/150	10.00
KATA	Matt Kata/350	8.00
KAZ	Scott Kazmir/360	30.00
KENN	Adam Kennedy/150	8.00
KIES	Brooks Kieschnick/360	8.00
KOCH	Billy Koch/71	20.00
KON	Paul Konerko/179	15.00
KOO	Graham Koonce/360	8.00
KOTC	Casey Kotchman/150	20.00
LAMB	Mike Lamb/360	5.00
LAR	Barry Larkin/60	75.00
LEC	Matt LeCroy/360	5.00
LEE	Travis Lee/360	8.00
LEO	Justin Leone/150	10.00
LOO	Braden Looper/360	5.00
LOUX	Shane Loux/360	5.00
MAD	Ryan Madson/360	8.00
MAG	Dave Magadan/360	8.00
MART	Tino Martinez/360	20.00
MAU	Joe Mauer/360	35.00
MCC	David McCarty/360	10.00
MCDO	Jack McDowell/60	20.00
MEC	Gil Meche/360	5.00
MIE	Doug Mientkiewicz/300	10.00
MOR	Matt Morris/150	10.00
MORR	Warren Morris/360	5.00
MUL	Mark Mulder/180	10.00
MUN	Eric Munson/510	8.00
MURR	Calvin Murray/360	5.00
MUSS	Mike Mussina/60	50.00
NADY	Xavier Nady/360	5.00
NAN	Shane Nance/150	5.00
NEI	Mike Neill/360	5.00
OJE	Augie Ojeda/360	5.00
OLE	John Olerud/360	20.00
OLS	Gregg Olson/180	5.00
OSW	Roy Oswalt/350	15.00
PARQ	Jim Parque/360	5.00
PATT	John Patterson/210	5.00
PEN	Brad Penny/360	8.00
POW	Jay Powell/180	5.00
PRI	Mark Prior/350	40.00
RAM	Horacio Ramirez/150	10.00
RAU	Jon Rauch/359	5.00
REED	Jeremy Reed/180	10.00
RIL	Matt Riley/60	15.00
ROB	Brian Roberts/60	20.00
ROBE	Dave Roberts/360	10.00
ROM	J.C. Romero/360	5.00
ROSS	David Ross/360	5.00
SAAR	Kirk Saarloos/360	5.00
SAND	Anthony Sanders/360	5.00
SAR	Dane Sardinha/360	5.00
SEAY	Bobby Seay/360	5.00
SEI	Phil Seibel/150	8.00
SELE	Aaron Sele/360	10.00
SHE	Ben Sheets/143	25.00
SHU	Paul Shuey/360	5.00
SIZE	Grady Sizemore/160	35.00
SMI	Reggie Smith/360	10.00
SMO	John Smoltz/360	35.00
SNY	Chris Snyder/360	5.00
SPI	Scott Spiezio/360	10.00
SPR	Ed Sprague/360	10.00
STE	Dave Stewart/180	15.00
STEW	Scott Stewart/360	5.00
SUR	B.J. Surhoff/60	30.00
SWIF	Bill Swift/360	5.00
SWI	Nick Swisher/360	5.00
TON	Mike Tonis/350	5.00
TUCK	Michael Tucker/150	10.00
TYN	Jason Tyner/360	8.00
VAL	Eric Valent/360	8.00
VANB	John Van Benschoten/180	10.00
VAN	Cory Vance/360	5.00
VAND	John Vander Wal/360	10.00
VAR	Jason Varitek/360	40.00
VENT	Robin Ventura/360	15.00
VILL	Ron Villone/359	5.00
WALK	Todd Walker/60	20.00
WAT	Bob Watson/150	8.00
WAY	Justin Wayne/150	8.00
WEA	Jeff Weaver/360	10.00
WEEK	Rickie Weeks/360	15.00
WHEE	Dan Wheeler/360	5.00
WILL	Todd Williams/360	5.00
WI	Dan Wilson/360	10.00
WIL	Paul Wilson/360	5.00
WOOD	Ted Wood/330	5.00
YOUN	Ernie Young/350	8.00

Team USA Signature Blue Ink

		NM/M
Common Autograph:		8.00
ABB	Jim Abbott/60	30.00
ABE	Brent Abernathy/120	8.00
AIN	Kurt Ainsworth/120	8.00
ALV	Abe Alvarez/120	10.00
AND	Matt Anderson/110	8.00
AUS	Jeff Austin/120	8.00
BANK	Scott Bankhead/120	8.00
BARD	Josh Bard/100	8.00
BARR	Michael Barrett/120	8.00
BELL	Buddy Bell/29	25.00
BEN	Andy Benes/100	10.00
BENS	Kris Benson/60	25.00
BERG	Peter Bergeron/120	8.00
BLA	Casey Blake/60	20.00
BLO	Willie Bloomquist/51	20.00
BON	Jeremy Bonderman/90	10.00
BOR	Joe Borchard/100	8.00
BOW	Rob Bowen/510	8.00
BRAD	Milton Bradley/120	15.00
BRO	Ben Broussard/150	8.00
BRU	Brian Bruney/60	10.00
BUD	Mark Budzinski/120	8.00
BULL	Kirk Bullinger/120	8.00
BURK	Chris Burke/110	8.00
BU	Sean Burnett/60	10.00
BURN	Jeromy Burnitz/120	15.00
BUR	Pat Burrell/80	15.00
BURR	Sean Burroughs/142	8.00
BYRD	Paul Byrd/120	8.00
CAP	Chris Capuano/90	8.00
CASS	Scott Cassidy/120	8.00
CLA	Will Clark/30	80.00
COR	Chad Cordero/120	8.00
CR	Jesse Crain/60	15.00
CUD	Michael Cuddyer/89	8.00
DAV	Ben Davis/100	8.00
DED	Rod Dedeaux/25	30.00
DIC	R.A. Dickey/60	10.00
DIG	Ben Diggins/30	15.00
DIN	Lenny DiNardo/60	10.00
DRE	Ryan Drese/60	10.00
DREW	Tim Drew/120	8.00
DUCH	Justin Duchscherer/110	10.00
DUR	J.D. Durbin/60	10.00
ELAR	Scott Elarton/60	10.00
EVER	Adam Everett/120	8.00
FIN	Steve Finley/120	15.00
FOSS	Casey Fossum/100	8.00
FRAN	Terry Francona/40	40.00
FRA	Ryan Franklin/120	8.00
FRE	Ryan Freel/110	8.00
GAR	Nomar Garciaparra/60	75.00
GEO	Chris George/120	8.00
GER	Jody Gerut/100	8.00
GIAM	Jason Giambi/30	50.00
GIN	Matt Ginter/42	10.00
GLA	Troy Glaus/60	30.00
GOS	Mike Gosling/60	10.00
DRA	Danny Graves/120	8.00
GR	Shawn Green/90	30.00
GRE	Khalil Greene/60	50.00
GREE	Todd Greene/60	10.00
GREI	Seth Greisinger/120	8.00
GRO	Gabe Gross/90	8.00
HAM	Jeffrey Hammonds/90	10.00
HEIL	Aaron Heilman/100	8.00
HELT	Todd Helton/20	65.00
HERM	Dustin Hermanson/90	10.00
HI	Bobby Hill/120	8.00
HILL	Koyie Hill/90	8.00
HIN	A.J. Hinch/120	8.00
HUCK	Ken Huckaby/120	8.00
HUD	Orlando Hudson/110	15.00
JENN	Jason Jennings/100	8.00
JON	Jacque Jones/60	20.00
KATA	Matt Kata/100	8.00
KAZ	Scott Kazmir/110	35.00
KEAR	Austin Kearns/110	20.00
KENN	Adam Kennedy/90	8.00
KIES	Brooks Kieschnick/120	8.00
KOCH	Billy Koch/18	25.00
KON	Paul Konerko/52	20.00
KOO	Graham Koonce/120	8.00
KOTC	Casey Kotchman/60	30.00
LAMB	Mike Lamb/120	8.00
LAR	Barry Larkin/20	80.00
LAS	Tommy Lasorda/30	60.00
LEC	Matt LeCroy/120	8.00
LEE	Travis Lee/120	8.00
LEO	Justin Leone/60	15.00
LOO	Braden Looper/120	8.00
LOUX	Shane Loux/110	8.00
LUD	Ryan Ludwick/450	15.00
MAD	Ryan Madson/110	8.00
MAG	Dave Magadan/120	8.00
MART	Tino Martinez/120	20.00
MAU	Joe Mauer/120	35.00
MCC	David McCarty/120	10.00
MCDO	Jack McDowell/30	20.00
MEC	Gil Meche/120	8.00
MIE	Doug Mientkiewicz/120	10.00
MOR	Matt Morris/90	15.00
MORR	Warren Morris/120	8.00
MUL	Mark Mulder/110	15.00
MURR	Calvin Murray/120	8.00
MUSS	Mike Mussina/30	50.00
NADY	Xavier Nady/120	8.00
NAN	Shane Nance/60	10.00
NEI	Mike Neill/110	8.00
OJE	Augie Ojeda/119	8.00
OLE	John Olerud/120	20.00
OLS	Gregg Olson/60	10.00
OSW	Roy Oswalt/100	15.00
PARQ	Jim Parque/120	8.00
PATT	John Patterson/120	8.00
PEN	Brad Penny/110	8.00
POW	Jay Powell/60	10.00
PRI	Mark Prior/108	40.00
RAM	Horacio Ramirez/90	8.00
RAU	Jon Rauch/100	8.00
REED	Jeremy Reed/45	20.00
ROBE	Dave Roberts/120	10.00
ROBI	Frank Robinson/30	90.00
ROM	J.C. Romero/120	8.00
ROSS	David Ross/120	8.00
SAAR	Kirk Saarloos/120	8.00
SAND	Anthony Sanders/120	8.00
SAR	Dane Sardinha/110	8.00
SEAY	Bobby Seay/120	8.00
SEI	Phil Seibel/90	8.00
SELE	Aaron Sele/120	10.00
SHU	Paul Shuey/120	8.00
SIZE	Grady Sizemore/60	35.00
SMI	Reggie Smith/120	10.00
SMO	John Smoltz/120	40.00
SNY	Chris Snyder/120	8.00
SOR	Zach Sorensen/450	8.00
SPI	Scott Spiezio/120	8.00

SPR	Ed Sprague/120	8.00
STAN	Jason Stanford/450	8.00
STE	Dave Stewart/90	10.00
STEW	Scott Stewart/119	8.00
SWIF	Bill Swift/120	8.00
SWI	Nick Swisher/110	20.00
TON	Mike Tonis/100	8.00
TUCK	Michael Tucker/90	10.00
TYN	Jason Tyner/120	8.00
UPT	B.J. Upton/120	30.00
VAL	Eric Valent/120	8.00
VANB	John Van Benschoten/60	20.00
VAN	Cory Vance/120	8.00
VAND	John Vander Wal/120	8.00
VAR	Jason Varitek/100	40.00
VENT	Robin Ventura/120	15.00
VILL	Ron Villone/120	8.00
WAT	Bob Watson/60	10.00
WAY	Justin Wayne/60	10.00
WEA	Jeff Weaver/120	8.00
WEEK	Rickie Weeks/120	15.00
WHEE	Dan Wheeler/120	8.00
WILL	Todd Williams/90	8.00
WI	Dan Wilson/120	10.00
WIL	Paul Wilson/110	8.00
WOOD	Ted Wood/120	8.00
YOUN	Ernie Young/130	10.00

Team USA Signature Red Ink

NM/M

Common Autograph: 10.00
Some not priced due to scarcity.

ABE	Brent Abernathy/20	15.00
AIN	Kurt Ainsworth/20	15.00
AND	Matt Anderson/30	15.00
AUS	Jeff Austin/20	15.00
BARD	Josh Bard/50	10.00
BARR	Michael Barrett/20	20.00
BEN	Andy Benes/50	15.00
BLO	Willie Bloomquist/25	25.00
BOR	Joe Borchard/50	10.00
BRAD	Milton Bradley/20	25.00
BRO	Ben Broussard/40	15.00
BRU	Brian Bruney/30	15.00
BURK	Chris Burke/50	10.00
BURN	Jeromy Burnitz/20	25.00
BUR	Pat Burrell/29	25.00
BYRD	Paul Byrd/20	20.00
CRO	Bobby Crosby/60	50.00
CUD	Michael Cuddyer/40	10.00
DAV	Ben Davis/50	10.00
DIN	Lenny DiNardo/40	10.00
EVER	Adam Everett/20	15.00
FIN	Steve Finley/20	25.00
FOSS	Casey Fossum/42	10.00
FRE	Ryan Freel/30	15.00
GAR	Nomar Garciaparra/30	125.00
GER	Jody Gerut/50	10.00
GLA	Troy Glaus/20	60.00
GOS	Mike Gosling/40	10.00
HEIL	Aaron Heilman/50	10.00
HIN	A.J. Hinch/20	15.00
HUD	Orlando Hudson/30	25.00
JENN	Jason Jennings/50	15.00
JON	Jacque Jones/40	20.00
KATA	Matt Kata/50	15.00
KAZ	Scott Kazmir/30	75.00
KEAR	Austin Kearns/30	35.00
KON	Paul Konerko/23	25.00
KOO	Graham Koonce/20	15.00
KOTC	Casey Kotchman/40	35.00
LEC	Matt LeCroy/20	15.00
LEE	Travis Lee/20	15.00
LEO	Justin Leone/40	20.00
LOUX	Shane Loux/30	15.00
LUD	Ryan Ludwick/50	20.00
MAD	Ryan Madson/30	15.00
MART	Tino Martinez/20	40.00
MAU	Joe Mauer/20	65.00
MCC	David McCarty/20	25.00
MIE	Doug Mientkiewicz/20	25.00
NADY	Xavier Nady/20	15.00
NAN	Shane Nance/40	10.00
NEI	Mike Neill/30	15.00
OSW	Roy Oswalt/50	20.00
PARQ	Jim Parque/20	15.00
PATT	John Patterson/20	15.00
PEN	Brad Penny/30	15.00
PRI	Mark Prior/48	60.00
RAU	Jon Rauch/53	10.00
REED	Jeremy Reed/25	25.00
ROM	J.C. Romero/20	15.00
SAR	Dane Sardinha/30	15.00
SIZE	Grady Sizemore/30	40.00
SMO	John Smoltz/20	65.00
SOR	Zach Sorensen/50	10.00
SPR	Ed Sprague/20	15.00
STAN	Jason Stanford/50	10.00
STE	Dave Stewart/30	25.00
SWI	Nick Swisher/30	40.00
TON	Mike Tonis/50	10.00
UPT	B.J. Upton/20	40.00
VAR	Jason Varitek/30	70.00
VENT	Robin Ventura/20	25.00
WAT	Bob Watson/30	15.00
WAY	Justin Wayne/40	10.00
WEA	Jeff Weaver/20	25.00
WEEK	Rickie Weeks/20	20.00
WILL	Todd Williams/50	10.00
WIL	Paul Wilson/30	15.00
WOOD	Ted Wood/30	15.00
YOUN	Ernie Young/50	10.00

Team USA Signature Green Ink

NM/M

No Pricing
Production 1-3

2004 Upper Deck Vintage

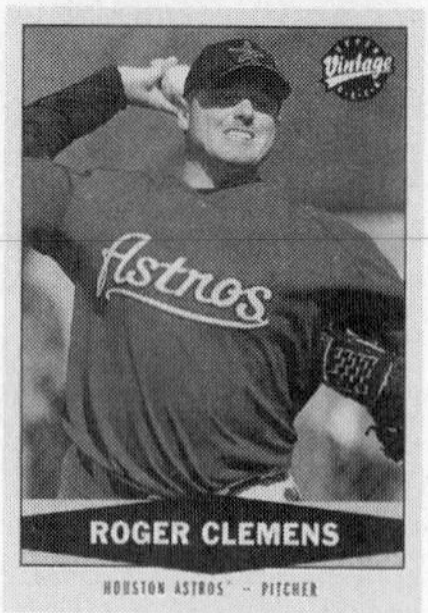
Astros
ROGER CLEMENS
HOUSTON ASTROS - PITCHER

NM/M

Complete Set (450):	
Common Player:	.15
Common SP (301-315):	.50
Inserted 1:5	
Common SP (316-325):	.40
Inserted 1:7	
Common SP (326-350):	.40
Inserted 1:5	
Common 3D SP (351-440):	2.00
Inserted 1:12	
Old Judge (441-450) found in bonus packs	
Pack (8):	2.50
Box (24 + 1 Bonus Pack):	50.00

1	Albert Pujols	1.50
2	Carlos Delgado	.50
3	Todd Helton	.50
4	Nomar Garciaparra	1.50
5	Vladimir Guerrero	.75
6	Alfonso Soriano	.75
7	Alex Rodriguez	1.50
8	Jason Giambi	.75
9	Derek Jeter	2.00
10	Pedro J. Martinez	.75
11	Ivan Rodriguez	.50
12	Mark Prior	1.00
13	Marquis Grissom	.15
14	Barry Zito	.25
15	Alex Cintron	.15
16	Wade Miller	.15
17	Eric Chavez	.25
18	Matt Clement	.15
19	Orlando Cabrera	.15
20	Odalis Perez	.15
21	Lance Berkman	.25
22	Keith Foulke	.15
23	Shawn Green	.25
24	Byung-Hyun Kim	.15
25	Geoff Jenkins	.25
26	Torii Hunter	.40
27	Richard Hidalgo	.15
28	Edgar Martinez	.25
29	Placido Polanco	.15
30	Brad Lidge	.15
31	Alex Escobar	.15
32	Garret Anderson	.25
33	Larry Walker	.25
34	Ken Griffey Jr.	1.00
35	Junior Spivey	.15
36	Carlos Beltran	.25
37	Bartolo Colon	.25
38	Ichiro Suzuki	1.00
39	Ramon Ortiz	.15
40	Roy Oswalt	.25
41	Mike Piazza	1.00
42	Benito Santiago	.15
43	Mike Mussina	.50
44	Jeff Kent	.25
45	Curt Schilling	.50
46	Adam Dunn	.40
47	Mike Sweeney	.15
48	Chipper Jones	1.00
49	Frank Thomas	.50
50	Kerry Wood	.50
51	Rod Beck	.15
52	Brian Giles	.25
53	Hank Blalock	.25
54	Andruw Jones	.50
55	Dmitri Young	.15
56	Juan Pierre	.15
57	Jacque Jones	.15
58	Phil Nevin	.15
59	Rocco Baldelli	.25
60	Greg Maddux	1.00
61	Eric Gagne	.15
62	Tim Hudson	.25
63	Brian Lawrence	.15
64	Sammy Sosa	1.00
65	Corey Koskie	.15
66	Bobby Abreu	.25
67	Preston Wilson	.15
68	Jay Gibbons	.15
69	Dontrelle Willis	.25
70	Richie Sexson	.40
71	Kevin Millwood	.25
72	Randy Johnson	.75
73	Jack Cust	.15
74	Randy Wolf	.15
75	Johan Santana	.15
76	Magglio Ordonez	.25
77	Sean Casey	.15
78	Billy Wagner	.25
79	Javier Vazquez	.15
80	Jorge Posada	.40
81	Jason Schmidt	.15
82	Bret Boone	.25
83	Jeff Bagwell	.50
84	Rickie Weeks	.25
85	Troy Percival	.15
86	Jose Vidro	.15
87	Freddy Garcia	.15
88	Manny Ramirez	.50
89	John Smoltz	.25
90	Moises Alou	.25
91	Ugueth Urbina	.15
92	Bobby Hill	.15
93	Marcus Giles	.15
94	Aramis Ramirez	.25
95	Brad Wilkerson	.15
96	Ray Durham	.15
97	David Wells	.15
98	Paul LoDuca	.15
99	Danny Graves	.15
100	Jason Kendall	.25
101	Carlos Lee	.25
102	Rafael Furcal	.25
103	Mike Lowell	.15
104	Kevin Brown	.25
105	Vicente Padilla	.15
106	Miguel Tejada	.40
107	Bernie Williams	.40
108	Octavio Dotel	.15
109	Steve Finley	.15
110	Lyle Overbay	.15
111	Delmon Young	.25
112	Bo Hart	.15
113	Jason Lane	.15
114	Matt Roney	.15
115	Brian Roberts	.15
116	Tom Glavine	.25
117	Rich Aurilia	.15
118	Adam Kennedy	.15
119	Hee Seop Choi	.15
120	Trot Nixon	.15
121	Gary Sheffield	.40
122	Jay Payton	.15
123	Brad Penny	.15
124	Garrett Atkins	.15
125	Aubrey Huff	.15
126	Juan Gonzalez	.40
127	Jason Jennings	.15
128	Luis Gonzalez	.25
129	Vinny Castilla	.15
130	Esteban Loaiza	.15
131	Erubiel Durazo	.15
132	Eric Hinske	.15
133	Scott Rolen	.75
134	Craig Biggio	.25
135	Tim Wakefield	.15
136	Darin Erstad	.25
137	Denny Stark	.15
138	Ben Sheets	.25
139	Hideo Nomo	.40
140	Derrek Lee	.25
141	Matt Mantei	.15
142	Reggie Sanders	.15
143	Jose Guillen	.15
144	Joe Mays	.15
145	Jimmy Rollins	.25
146	Juan Encarnacion	.15
147	Joe Crede	.15
148	Aaron Guiel	.15
149	Mark Mulder	.25
150	Travis Lee	.15
151	Josh Phelps	.15
152	Michael Young	.15
153	Paul Konerko	.15
154	John Lackey	.15
155	Damian Moss	.15
156	Javy Lopez	.25
157	Joe Borowski	.15
158	Jose Cruz Jr.	.15
159	Ramon Hernandez	.15
160	Raul Ibanez	.15
161	Adrian Beltre	.15
162	Bobby Higginson	.15
163	Jorge Julio	.15
164	Miguel Batista	.15
165	Luis Castillo	.15
166	Aaron Harang	.15
167	Ken Harvey	.15
168	Rocky Biddle	.15
169	Mariano Rivera	.25
170	Matt Morris	.15
171	Laynce Nix	.15
172	Mike Maroth	.15
173	Francisco Rodriguez	.15
174	Livan Hernandez	.15
175	Aaron Heilman	.15
176	Nick Johnson	.15
177	Woody Williams	.15
178	Joe Kennedy	.15
179	Jesse Foppert	.15
180	Ryan Franklin	.15
181	Endy Chavez	.15
182	Chin-Hui Tsao	.15
183	Todd Walker	.15
184	Edgardo Alfonzo	.15
185	Edgar Renteria	.15
186	Matt LeCroy	.15
187	Carl Everett	.15
188	Jeff Conine	.15
189	Jason Varitek	.15
190	Russ Ortiz	.15
191	Melvin Mora	.15
192	Mark Buehrle	.15
193	Bill Mueller	.15
194	Miguel Cabrera	.25
195	Carlos Zambrano	.15
196	Jose Valverde	.15
197	Danys Baez	.15
198	Mike MacDougal	.15
199	Zach Day	.15
200	Roy Halladay	.25
201	Jerome Williams	.15
202	Josh Fogg	.15
203	Mark Kotsay	.15
204	Pat Burrell	.40
205	A.J. Pierzynski	.15
206	Fred McGriff	.25
207	Brandon Larson	.15
208	Robb Quinlan	.15
209	David Ortiz	.15
210	A.J. Burnett	.15
211	John Vander Wal	.15
212	Jim Thome	.75
213	Matt Kata	.15
214	Kip Wells	.15
215	Scott Podsednik	.40
216	Rickey Henderson	.25
217	Travis Hafner	.15
218	Tony Batista	.15
219	Robert Fick	.15
220	Derek Lowe	.25
221	Ryan Klesko	.25
222	Joe Beimel	.15
223	Doug Mientkiewicz	.15
224	Angel Berroa	.15
225	Adam Eaton	.15
226	C.C. Sabathia	.15
227	Wilfredo Ledezma	.15
228	Jason Johnson	.15
229	Ryan Wagner	.15
230	Al Leiter	.15
231	Joel Pineiro	.15
232	Jason Isringhausen	.15
233	John Olerud	.25
234	Ron Calloway	.15
235	Jose Reyes	.40
236	J.D. Drew	.15
237	Jared Sandberg	.15
238	Gil Meche	.15
239	Jose Contreras	.15
240	Eric Milton	.15
241	Jason L. Phillips	.15
242	Luis Ayala	.15
243	Bobby Kielty	.15
244	Jose Lima	.15
245	Brooks Kieschnick	.15
246	Xavier Nady	.15
247	Dan Haren	.15
248	Victor Zambrano	.15
249	Kelvim Escobar	.15
250	Oliver Perez	.15
251	Jamie Moyer	.15
252	Orlando Hudson	.15
253	Danny Kolb	.15
254	Jake Peavy	.15
255	Kris Benson	.15
256	Roger Clemens	1.50
257	Jim Edmonds	.40
258	Rafael Palmeiro	.50
259	Jae Weong Seo	.15
260	Chase Utley	.40
261	Rich Harden	.15
262	Mark Teixeira	.25
263	Johnny Damon	.25
264	Luis Matos	.15
265	Shigetoshi Hasegawa	.15
266	Alfredo Amezaga	.15
267	Tim Worrell	.15
268	Kazuhisa Ishii	.15
269	Miguel Ojeda	.15
270	Kazuhiro Sasaki	.15
271	Hideki Matsui	2.00
272	Troy Glaus	.40
273	Michael Tucker	.15
274	Lew Ford	.15
275	Brian Jordan	.15
276	David Eckstein	.15
277	Robby Hammock	.15
278	Corey Patterson	.25
279	Wes Helms	.15
280	Jermaine Dye	.15
281	Cliff Floyd	.15
282	Dustan Mohr	.15
283	Kevin Mench	.15
284	Ellis Burks	.15
285	Jerry Hairston Jr.	.15
286	Tim Salmon	.25
287	Omar Vizquel	.25
288	Andy Pettitte	.40
289	Guillermo Mota	.15
290	Tino Martinez	.15
291	Lance Carter	.15
292	Francisco Cordero	.15
293	Robb Nen	.15
294	Mike Cameron	.15
295	Jhonny Peralta	.15
296	Braden Looper	.15
297	Jarrod Washburn	.15
298	Mark Prior	.50
299	Alfonso Soriano	.25
300	Rocco Baldelli	.25
301	Pedro J. Martinez	1.50
302	Mark Prior	2.00
303	Barry Zito	.75
304	Roger Clemens	2.50
305	Randy Johnson	1.50

306	Roy Halladay	.50
307	Hideo Nomo	.75
308	Roy Oswalt	.50
309	Kerry Wood	1.00
310	Dontrelle Willis	.75
311	Mark Mulder	.50
312	Brandon Webb	.50
313	Mike Mussina	.75
314	Curt Schilling	.75
315	Tim Hudson	.75
316	Dontrelle Willis	.75
317	Juan Pierre	.40
318	Hideki Matsui	4.00
319	Andy Pettitte	.75
320	Mike Mussina	.75
321	Roger Clemens	2.50
322	Alex Gonzalez	.40
323	Brad Penny	.40
324	Ivan Rodriguez	.75
325	Josh Beckett	1.00
326	Aaron Boone	.40
327	Jeff Suppan	.40
328	Shea Hillenbrand	.40
329	Jeromy Burnitz	.40
330	Sidney Ponson	.40
331	Rondell White	.50
332	Shannon Stewart	.40
333	Armando Benitez	.40
334	Roberto Alomar	1.00
335	Raul Mondesi	.50
336	Morgan Ensberg	.40
337	Milton Bradley	.40
338	Brandon Webb	.50
339	Marlon Byrd	.40
340	Carlos Pena	.40
341	Brandon Phillips	.40
342	Josh Beckett	1.00
343	Eric Munson	.40
344	Brett Myers	.40
345	Austin Kearns	1.00
346	Jody Gerut	.40
347	Vernon Wells	.50
348	Jeff Duncan	.40
349	Sean Burroughs	.40
350	Jeremy Bonderman	.40
351	Hideki Matsui	15.00
352	Jason Giambi	8.00
353	Alfonso Soriano	6.00
354	Derek Jeter	15.00
355	Aaron Boone	3.00
356	Jorge Posada	5.00
357	Bernie Williams	5.00
358	Manny Ramirez	5.00
359	Nomar Garciaparra	12.00
360	Johnny Damon	3.00
361	Jason Varitek	2.50
362	Carlos Delgado	5.00
363	Vernon Wells	4.00
364	Jay Gibbons	4.00
365	Tony Batista	4.00
366	Rocco Baldelli	5.00
367	Aubrey Huff	4.00
368	Carlos Beltran	4.00
369	Mike Sweeney	3.00
370	Magglio Ordonez	4.00
371	Frank Thomas	6.00
372	Carlos Lee	2.00
373	Roberto Alomar	4.00
374	Jacque Jones	2.00
375	Torii Hunter	4.00
376	Milton Bradley	2.00
377	Travis Hafner	2.00
378	Jody Gerut	2.00
379	Dmitri Young	2.00
380	Carlos Pena	2.00
381	Ichiro Suzuki	10.00
382	Bret Boone	3.00
383	Edgar Martinez	3.00
384	Eric Chavez	3.00
385	Miguel Tejada	3.00
386	Erubiel Durazo	2.00
387	Jose Guillen	2.00
388	Garret Anderson	3.00
389	Troy Glaus	4.00
390	Alex Rodriguez	10.00
391	Rafael Palmeiro	5.00
392	Hank Blalock	4.00
393	Mark Teixeira	4.00
394	Gary Sheffield	4.00
395	Andruw Jones	5.00
396	Chipper Jones	8.00
397	Javy Lopez	3.00
398	Marcus Giles	2.00
399	Rafael Furcal	3.00
400	Jim Thome	5.00
401	Bobby Abreu	3.00
402	Pat Burrell	4.00
403	Mike Lowell	3.00
404	Ivan Rodriguez	5.00
405	Derrek Lee	3.00
406	Miguel Cabrera	8.00
407	Vladimir Guerrero	6.00
408	Orlando Cabrera	2.00
409	Jose Vidro	2.00
410	Mike Piazza	8.00
411	Cliff Floyd	3.00
412	Albert Pujols	15.00
413	Scott Rolen	6.00
414	Jim Edmonds	4.00
415	Edgar Renteria	3.00
416	Lance Berkman	3.00
417	Jeff Bagwell	5.00
418	Jeff Kent	3.00
419	Richard Hidalgo	2.00
420	Morgan Ensberg	2.00

421	Sammy Sosa	10.00
422	Moises Alou	3.00
423	Ken Griffey Jr.	10.00
424	Adam Dunn	4.00
425	Austin Kearns	4.00
426	Richie Sexson	4.00
427	Geoff Jenkins	3.00
428	Brian Giles	3.00
429	Reggie Sanders	2.00
430	Rich Aurilia	2.00
431	Jose Cruz Jr.	2.00
432	Shawn Green	3.00
433	Jeromy Burnitz	2.00
434	Luis Gonzalez	3.00
435	Todd Helton	5.00
436	Preston Wilson	2.00
437	Larry Walker	3.00
438	Ryan Klesko	3.00
439	Phil Nevin	2.00
440	Sean Burroughs	2.00
441	Sammy Sosa	3.00
442	Albert Pujols	4.00
443	Magglio Ordonez	.50
444	Vladimir Guerrero	1.50
445	Todd Helton	1.00
446	Jason Giambi	1.50
447	Ichiro Suzuki	3.00
448	Alex Rodriguez	3.00
449	Carlos Delgado	.75
450	Manny Ramirez	1.00

Black & White

Cards (1-300):	1-2X
Inserted 1:6	
SP's (301-325):	1-2X
Inserted 1:24	
SP's (326-350):	1-2X
Inserted 1:20	
B/W Color Variations:	6-10X
Inserted 1:48	

Old Judge

HIDEKI MATSUI, OF
NEW YORK "YANKEES"
THE UPPER DECK COMPANY, LLC

		NM/M
Complete Set (20):		15.00
Common Player:		.40
Inserted 3:bonus pack.		
Blue Back:		1-2X
Inserted 1:4 bonus packs.		
Red Back:		2-3X
Inserted 1:12 bonus packs.		
11	Randy Johnson	1.50
12	Pedro J. Martinez	1.50
13	Mark Prior	2.00
14	Barry Zito	.50
15	Roy Oswalt	.40
16	Roy Halladay	.50
17	Curt Schilling	.75
18	Mike Mussina	.75
19	Kevin Brown	.40
20	Roger Clemens	2.50
21	Eric Gagne	.50
22	Mariano Rivera	.75
23	Mike Piazza	2.00
24	Jorge Posada	.75
25	Jeff Kent	.50
26	Alfonso Soriano	1.00
27	Scott Rolen	1.00
28	Eric Chavez	.50
29	Edgar Renteria	.40
30	Hideki Matsui	4.00

Stellar Signatures

		NM/M
Inserted 1:600		
HM	Hideki Matsui	300.00
MP	Mike Piazza	150.00
AR	Alex Rodriguez	100.00
TS	Tom Seaver	50.00
IS	Ichiro Suzuki	200.00
CY	C. Yastrzemski/125	75.00
BZ	Barry Zito	40.00

Stellar Stat Men

		NM/M
Common Player:		4.00
Inserted 1:24		
1	Jose Reyes	6.00
2	Bo Hart	8.00
3	Hideki Matsui	30.00
4	Dontrelle Willis	6.00
5	Rocco Baldelli	6.00

6	Ichiro Suzuki	20.00
7	Mike Lowell	6.00
8	Derek Jeter	20.00
9	Ken Griffey Jr.	15.00
10	Sammy Sosa	12.00
11	Kerry Wood	10.00
12	Chipper Jones	6.00
13	Alfonso Soriano	8.00
14	Khalil Greene	6.00
16	Jim Thome	8.00
16	Rafael Furcal	5.00
17	Andrew Brown	4.00
18	Mark Prior	10.00
19	Barry Zito	6.00
20	Al Leiter	4.00
21	Carlos Delgado	6.00
22	Pedro J. Martinez	8.00
23	Alex Rodriguez	10.00
24	Lance Berkman	5.00
25	Jeff Bagwell	6.00
26	Bernie Williams	8.00
27	Hideo Nomo	8.00
28	Randy Johnson	8.00
29	Curt Schilling	8.00
30	Mike Piazza	10.00
31	Albert Pujols	12.00
32	Joe DiMaggio	100.00
33	Ted Williams	60.00
34	Mickey Mantle	100.00
35	Mike Mussina	8.00
36	Rich Harden	5.00
37	Roy Oswalt	4.00
38	Torii Hunter	8.00
39	Jorge Posada	6.00
40	Troy Glaus	6.00
41	Manny Ramirez	6.00
42	Roy Halladay	5.00

Timeless Teams

		NM/M
Common Quad:		15.00
Inserted 1:400		
Production 175 Sets		
1	Derek Jeter, Jason Giambi, Alfonso Soriano, Hideki Matsui	90.00
2	Randy Johnson, Luis Gonzalez, Steve Finley, Curt Schilling	20.00
4	Johnny Damon, Manny Ramirez, Nomar Garciaparra, Trot Nixon	35.00
5	Alex Rodriguez, Rafael Palmeiro, Mark Teixeira, Hank Blalock	35.00
6	Roberto Alomar, Frank Thomas, Magglio Ordonez, Carl Everett	20.00
7	Shannon Stewart, Torii Hunter, Jacque Jones, Doug Mientkiewicz	15.00
8	Jim Edmonds, Scott Rolen, J.D. Drew, Albert Pujols	40.00
9	Bret Boone, John Olerud, Mike Cameron, Ichiro Suzuki	45.00
10	Jeff Bagwell, Craig Biggio, Jeff Kent, Lance Berkman	20.00
11	Tim Salmon, Garret Anderson, Darin Erstad, Troy Glaus	15.00
12	Bernie Williams, Alfonso Soriano, Jorge Posada, Hideki Matsui	85.00
13	Carlos Beltran, Michael Tucker, Mike Sweeney, Brent Mayne	15.00
14	Jim Thome, Mike Lieberthal, Bobby Abreu, Marlon Byrd	30.00
15	Ivan Rodriguez, Juan Encarnacion, Mike Lowell, Miguel Cabrera	25.00
16	Sammy Sosa, Kerry Wood, Moises Alou, Corey Patterson	50.00
17	Andres Galarraga, Edgardo Alfonzo, Jose Cruz Jr., Rich Aurilia	15.00
18	Derek Jeter, Bernie Williams, Alfonso Soriano, Hideki Matsui	90.00

2004 Upper Deck Yankees Classics

		NM/M
Complete Set (90):		20.00
Common Player:		.25
Pack (5):		6.00
Box (24):		120.00
1	Bill "Moose" Skowron	.50
2	Bob Cerv	.25
3	Bobby Murcer	.50

Yankees Classics

1B LOU GEHRIG

4	Bobby Richardson	.25
5	Brian Doyle	.25
6	Bucky Dent	.25
7	Chris Chambliss	.25
8	Clete Boyer	.25
9	Dave Kingman	.25
10	Dave Righetti	.25
11	Dave Winfield	.50
12	David Cone	.25
13	Red Ruffing	.25
14	Dock Ellis	.25
15	Don Baylor	.25
16	Don Larsen	.75
17	Don Mattingly	1.50
18	Dwight Gooden	.40
19	Ed Figueroa	.25
20	Joe Torre	.50
21	Darryl Strawberry	.40
22	Horace Clarke	.25
23	Gaylord Perry	.25
24	Phil Linz	.25
25	Gil McDougald	.25
26	Rich "Goose" Gossage	.25
27	Graig Nettles	.25
28	Hank Bauer	.25
29	Jack Clark	.25
30	Don Gullett	.25
31	Jim Abbott	.25
32	Jim Bouton	.25
33	Jim Kaat	.40
34	Jim Leyritz	.25
35	Jim Wynn	.25
36	Jimmy Key	.25
37	Joe Niekro	.25
38	Joe Pepitone	.25
39	John Wetteland	.25
40	Ken Griffey Sr.	.25
41	Felipe Alou	.25
42	Kevin Maas	.25
43	Lindy McDaniel	.25
44	Lou Piniella	.50
45	Luis Tiant	.25
46	Mel Stottlemyre	.25
47	Mickey Rivers	.25
48	Oscar Gamble	.25
49	Pat Dobson	.25
50	Paul O'Neill	.50
51	Phil Niekro	.25
52	Phil Rizzuto	.75
53	Doc Medich	.25
54	Rick Cerone	.25
55	Ron Blomberg	.25
56	Ron Guidry	.50
57	Roy White	.25
58	Rudy May	.25
59	Sam McDowell	.25
60	Sparky Lyle	.25
61	Steve Balboni	.25
62	Steve Sax	.25
63	Jerry Coleman	.25
64	Tom Tresh	.25
65	Tommy John	.25
66	Tony Kubek	.50
67	Wade Boggs	.50
68	Whitey Ford	.75
69	Willie Randolph	.25
70	Yogi Berra	1.00
71	Babe Ruth	3.00
72	Bill Dickey	.50
73	Billy Martin	.50
74	Bob Meusel	.25
75	Casey Stengel	.50
76	Elston Howard	.25
77	Jim "Catfish" Hunter	.50
78	Joe DiMaggio	2.00
79	Lefty Gomez	.50
80	Lou Gehrig	2.00
81	Mickey Mantle	3.00
82	Miller Huggins	.25
83	Roger Maris	1.50
84	Thurman Munson	.75
85	Tony Lazzeri	.50
86	Yankee Stadium	.75
87	Times Square	.50
88	Central Park	.50
89	Empire State Building	.50
90	Statue of Liberty	.50

Bronze

Bronze:	4-8X
Production 99 Sets	

Gold

Gold:	8-15X
Production 30 Sets	

Silver

Silver:	No Pricing

Scripts Single Auto

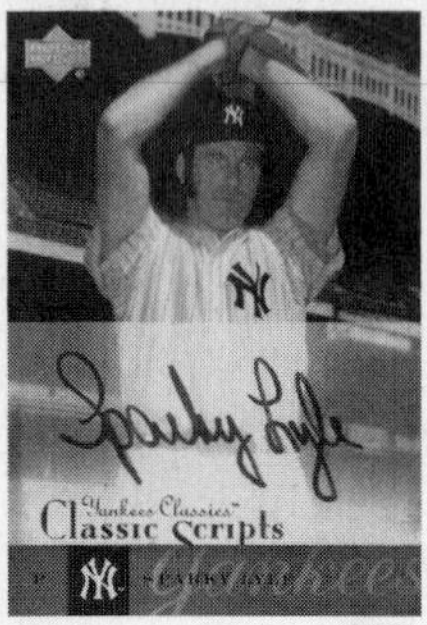

		NM/M
Common Autograph:		10.00
Inserted 1:8		
AU-1	Bill "Moose" Skowron	15.00
AU-2	Bob Cerv	10.00
AU-3	Bobby Murcer/SP	60.00
AU-4	Bobby Richardson	15.00
AU-5	Brian Doyle	10.00
AU-6	Bucky Dent	10.00
AU-7	Chris Chambliss	12.00
AU-8	Clete Boyer	15.00
AU-9	Dave Kingman	10.00
AU-10	Dave Righetti	10.00
AU-11	Dave Winfield/SP	60.00
AU-12	David Cone	10.00
AU-14	Dock Ellis	10.00
AU-15	Don Baylor/SP	25.00
AU-16	Don Larsen/SP	40.00
AU-17	Don Mattingly/SP	85.00
AU-18	Dwight Gooden	15.00
AU-19	Ed Figueroa	10.00
AU-20	Joe Torre/SP	125.00
AU-21	Darryl Strawberry	20.00
AU-23	Gaylord Perry	20.00
AU-24	Phil Linz	10.00
AU-25	Gil McDougald	15.00
AU-26	Rich "Goose" Gossage	20.00
AU-27	Graig Nettles	15.00
AU-28	Hank Bauer	15.00
AU-29	Jack Clark	15.00
AU-31	Jim Abbott	15.00
AU-32	Jim Bouton	15.00
AU-33	Jim Kaat	15.00
AU-34	Jim Leyritz/SP	25.00
AU-35	Jim Wynn	10.00
AU-36	Jimmy Key	10.00
AU-37	Joe Niekro	10.00
AU-38	Joe Pepitone	15.00
AU-39	John Wetteland/SP	20.00
AU-40	Ken Griffey Sr.	12.00
AU-42	Kevin Maas	10.00
AU-43	Lindy McDaniel	10.00
AU-44	Lou Piniella/SP	35.00
AU-45	Luis Tiant	20.00
AU-46	Mel Stottlemyre	15.00
AU-47	Mickey Rivers	15.00
AU-48	Oscar Gamble	15.00
AU-49	Pat Dobson	15.00
AU-50	Paul O'Neill/SP	40.00
AU-51	Phil Niekro	15.00
AU-52	Phil Rizzuto/SP	75.00
AU-53	Doc Medich	10.00
AU-54	Rick Cerone	15.00
AU-55	Ron Blomberg	10.00
AU-56	Ron Guidry	25.00
AU-57	Roy White	12.00
AU-58	Rudy May	10.00
AU-59	Sam McDowell	10.00
AU-60	Sparky Lyle	12.00
AU-61	Steve Balboni	10.00
AU-62	Steve Sax	10.00
AU-63	Jerry Coleman	15.00
AU-64	Tom Tresh	15.00
AU-65	Tommy John	15.00
AU-66	Tony Kubek/SP	400.00
AU-67	Wade Boggs/SP	60.00
AU-68	Whitey Ford/SP	60.00
AU-69	Willie Randolph/SP	25.00
AU-70	Yogi Berra/SP	75.00

Scripts Dual Auto.

		NM/M
Production 100 Sets		
SC	Bill "Moose" Skowron, Bob Cerv	50.00
MP	Bobby Murcer, Lou Piniella	65.00
CB	Chris Chambliss, Ron Blomberg	50.00
BN	Clete Boyer, Graig Nettles	50.00
RC	Dave Righetti, Rick Cerone	60.00
ED	Dock Ellis, Pat Dobson	70.00
BG	Don Baylor, Ken Griffey Sr.	65.00

MW	Don Mattingly, Dave Winfield	150.00
FG	Ed Figueroa, Ron Guidry	60.00
MB	Bobby Murcer, Hank Bauer	75.00
GL	Rich "Goose" Gossage, Sparky Lyle	50.00
NB	Graig Nettles, Wade Boggs	80.00
KJ	Jim Kaat, Tommy John	60.00
KA	Jimmy Key, Jim Abbott	50.00
PS	Joe Pepitone, Bill "Moose" Skowron	50.00
MM	Kevin Maas, Don Mattingly	100.00
RW	Mickey Rivers, Roy White	50.00
OL	Paul O'Neil, Jim Leyritz	75.00
RM	Phil Rizzuto, Gil McDougald	100.00
GK	Ron Guidry, Jim Kaat	
SD	Steve Sax, Brian Doyle	40.00
KR	Tony Kubek, Bobby Richardson	100.00
FL	Whitey Ford, Don Larsen	125.00
BL	Yogi Berra, Don Larsen	150.00
BH	Yogi Berra, Joe Torre	100.00
BF	Yogi Berra, Whitey Ford	150.00
WM	Bobby Murcer, Roy White	75.00
DN	Bucky Dent, Graig Nettles	50.00
CN	Chris Chambliss, Graig Nettles	50.00
CL	David Cone, Don Larsen	100.00
MC	Don Mattingly, Jack Clark	85.00
BM	Don Mattingly, Wade Boggs	150.00
SG	Darryl Strawberry, Dwight Gooden	75.00
CG	David Cone, Dwight Gooden	70.00

Scripts Triple Auto.

No Pricing
Production 20 Sets

Scripts Quad Auto.

No Pricing
Production 10 Sets

Classic Cuts

No Pricing
Production One Set

Mitchell & Ness Pennant

		NM/M
Inserted 1:Box		
Cards:		.3X
P2	1927 World Series/96	25.00
P3	1928 World Series/96	25.00
P4	1932 World Series/96	25.00
P6	1937 World Series/96	25.00
P8	1939 World Series/96	25.00
P10	1943 World Series/97	25.00
P11	1947 World Series/97	25.00
P13	1950 World Series/97	25.00
P15	1952 World Series/97	25.00
P17	1956 World Series/97	25.00
P18	1958 World Series/97	25.00
P23	1996 World Series/99	25.00
P24	1998 World Series/99	25.00
P25	1999 World Series/99	25.00
P26	2000 World Series/100	25.00
MM57	Mickey Mantle/ 1957 MVP/97	30.00
MM62	Mickey Mantle/ 1962 MVP/98	30.00

Mitchell & Ness Pennant Card

		NM/M
Inserted 1:Box		
P2	1927 World Series/1927	5.00
P3	1928 World Series/1,928	5.00
P4	1932 World Series/1,932	5.00
P5	1936 World Series/36	10.00
P6	1937 World Series/1,937	5.00
P7	1938 World Series/38	10.00
P8	1939 World Series/1,939	5.00
P9	1941 World Series/41	10.00
P10	1943 World Series/1,943	5.00
P11	1947 World Series/1,947	5.00
P12	1949 World Series/49	10.00
P13	1950 World Series/1,950	5.00
P14	1951 World Series/51	10.00
P15	1952 World Series/1,952	5.00
P16	1953 World Series/53	10.00
P17	1956 World Series/1,956	5.00
P18	1958 World Series/1,958	5.00
P19	1961 World Series/61	10.00
P20	1962 World Series/62	10.00
P21	1977 World Series/77	8.00
P22	1978 World Series/78	8.00
P23	1996 World Series/1,996	5.00
P24	1998 World Series/1,998	5.00
P25	1999 World Series/1,999	5.00
P26	2000 World Series/2,000	5.00
MM57	Mickey Mantle/ 1957 MVP/1,957	8.00
MM62	Mickey Mantle/ 1962 MVP/1,962	8.00

Mitchell & Ness Jersey Redemption

		NM/M
Inserted 1:384		
Production 40-99		
MNJ1	Babe Ruth/40	350.00
MNJ2	Bill Dickey/75	120.00
MNJ3	Billy Martin/99	150.00
MNJ4	Bobby Murcer/99	100.00
MNJ5	Bucky Dent/92	100.00
MNJ6	Casey Stengel/65	120.00
MNJ7	"Catfish" Hunter/92	120.00
MNJ8	Chris Chambliss/99	80.00
MNJ9	Don Larsen/75	120.00
MNJ10	Don Mattingly/92	150.00
MNJ11	Elston Howard/88	100.00
MNJ12	Rich "Goose" Gossage/92	100.00
MNJ13	Graig Nettles/99	100.00
MNJ14	Joe DiMaggio/55	200.00
MNJ15	Lefty Gomez/81	120.00
MNJ16	Lou Gehrig/40	200.00
MNJ17	Lou Piniella/92	120.00
MNJ18	Mickey Mantle/50	275.00
MNJ19	Bill "Moose" Skowron/85	125.00
MNJ20	Phil Rizzuto/40	150.00
MNJ21	Roy White/50	100.00
MNJ22	Roger Maris/92	200.00
MNJ23	Ron Guidry/99	100.00
MNJ24	Sparky Lyle/99	100.00
MNJ25	Thurman Munson/91	200.00
MNJ26	Tony Kubek/75	150.00
MNJ27	Tony Lazzeri/79	120.00
MNJ28	Whitey Ford/43	180.00
MNJ29	Willie Randolph/92	100.00
MNJ30	Yogi Berra/50	200.00

2004 UD Legends Timeless Teams

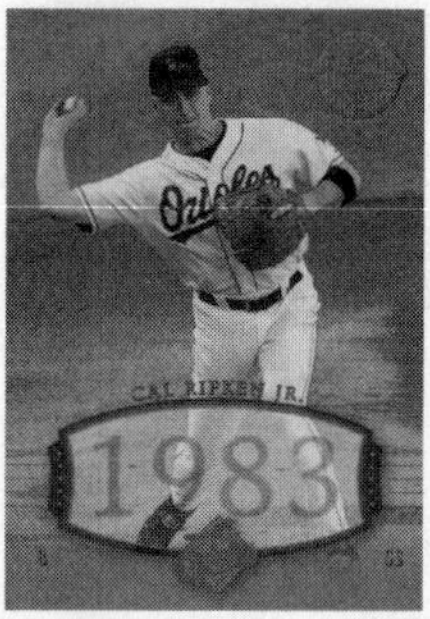

		NM/M
Complete Set (300):		40.00
Common Player:		.15
Pack (5):		5.00
Box (18):		75.00
1	Bob Gibson	.50
2	Lou Brock	.50
3	Ray Washburn	.15
4	Tim McCarver	.15
5	Harmon Killebrew	1.00
6	Jim Kaat	.25
7	Jim Perry	.15
8	Jim "Mudcat" Grant	.15
9	Boog Powell	.15
10	Brooks Robinson	.50
11	Frank Robinson	.50
12	Jim Palmer	.25
13	Carl Yastrzemski	1.00
14	Jim Lonborg	.15
15	George Scott	.15
16	Sparky Lyle	.15
17	Rico Petrocelli	.15
18	Bob Gibson	.50
19	Julian Javier	.15
20	Lou Brock	.50
21	Orlando Cepeda	.15
22	Ray Washburn	.15
23	Steve Carlton	.50
24	Tim McCarver	.15
25	Al Kaline	.50
26	Bill Freehan	.15
27	Denny McLain	.15
28	Dick McAuliffe	.15
29	Jim Northrup	.15
30	John Hiller	.15
31	Mickey Lolich	.15
32	Mickey Stanley	.15
33	Willie Horton	.15
34	Bob Gibson	.50
35	Julian Javier	.15
36	Lou Brock	.50
37	Orlando Cepeda	.25
38	Steve Carlton	.50
39	Boog Powell	.15
40	Brooks Robinson	.50
41	Davey Johnson	.15
42	Merv Rettenmund	.15
43	Eddie Watt	.15
44	Frank Robinson	.50
45	Jim Palmer	.25
46	Mike Cuellar	.15
47	Paul Blair	.15
48	Pete Richert	.15
49	Ellie Hendricks	.15
50	Billy Williams	.25
51	Randy Hundley	.15
52	Ernie Banks	1.00
53	Fergie Jenkins	.25
54	Jim Hickman	.15
55	Ken Holtzman	.15
56	Ron Santo	.25
57	Ed Kranepool	.15
58	Jerry Koosman	.15
59	Nolan Ryan	2.00
60	Tom Seaver	.50
61	Boog Powell	.15
62	Brooks Robinson	.50
63	Davey Johnson	.15
64	Merv Rettenmund	.15
65	Eddie Watt	.15
66	Frank Robinson	.50
67	Jim Palmer	.25
68	Mike Cuellar	.15
69	Paul Blair	.15
70	Pete Richert	.15
71	Ellie Hendricks	.15
72	Al Kaline	.50
73	Bill Freehan	.15
74	Dick McAuliffe	.15
75	Jim Northrup	.15
76	John Hiller	.15
77	Mickey Lolich	.15
78	Mickey Stanley	.15
79	Willie Horton	.15
80	Bert Campaneris	.15
81	Blue Moon Odom	.15
82	Sal Bando	.15
83	Joe Rudi	.15
84	Ken Holtzman	.15
85	Bill North	.15
86	Blue Moon Odom	.15
87	Gene Tenace	.15
88	Manny Trillo	.15
89	Dick Green	.15
90	Rollie Fingers	.25
91	Sal Bando	.15
92	Vida Blue	.15
93	Bill Buckner	.15
94	Davey Lopes	.15
95	Don Sutton	.25
96	Al Downing	.15
97	Ron Cey	.15
98	Steve Garvey	.15
99	Tommy John	.15
100	Bert Campaneris	.15
101	Bill North	.15
102	Joe Rudi	.15
103	Sal Bando	.15
104	Vida Blue	.15
105	Carl Yastrzemski	.75
106	Carlton Fisk	.25
107	Cecil Cooper	.15
108	Dwight Evans	.15
109	Fred Lynn	.15
110	Jim Rice	.25
111	Luis Tiant	.15
112	Rick Burleson	.15
113	Rico Petrocelli	.15
114	Pedro Borbon	.15
115	Dave Concepcion	.15
116	Don Gullett	.15
117	George Foster	.15
118	Joe Morgan	.25
119	Johnny Bench	.50
120	Rawly Eastwick	.15
121	Sparky Anderson	.15
122	Tony Perez	.25
123	Billy Williams	.25
124	Gene Tenace	.15
125	Jim Perry	.15
126	Vida Blue	.15
127	Pedro Borbon	.15
128	Dave Concepcion	.15
129	Don Gullett	.15
130	George Foster	.15
131	Joe Morgan	.25
132	Johnny Bench	.50
133	Ken Griffey Sr.	.15
134	Rawly Eastwick	.15
135	Tony Perez	.25
136	Bill Russell	.15
137	Burt Hooton	.15
138	Davey Lopes	.15
139	Don Sutton	.25
140	Dusty Baker	.15
141	Steve Yeager	.15
142	Ron Cey	.15
143	Steve Garvey	.15

144 Tommy John .15
145 Bucky Dent .15
146 Chris Chambliss .15
147 Ed Figueroa .15
148 Graig Nettles .15
149 Lou Piniella .25
150 Roy White .15
151 Don Gullett .15
152 Sparky Lyle .15
153 Brian Doyle .15
154 Bucky Dent .15
155 Chris Chambliss .15
156 Ed Figueroa .15
157 Graig Nettles .15
158 Lou Piniella .25
159 Roy White .15
160 Rich "Goose" Gossage .15
161 Sparky Lyle .15
162 Bobby Grich .15
163 Brian Downing .15
164 Dan Ford .15
165 Nolan Ryan 2.00
166 Dave Concepcion .15
167 George Foster .15
168 Johnny Bench .50
169 Ray Knight .15
170 Tom Seaver .50
171 Bert Blyleven .15
172 Bill Madlock .15
173 Dave Parker .25
174 Phil Garner .15
175 Bill Russell .15
176 Steve Yeager .15
177 Don Sutton .25
178 Dusty Baker .25
179 Jerry Reuss .15
180 Mickey Hatcher .15
181 Pedro Guerrero .15
182 Ron Cey .15
183 Steve Garvey .15
184 Rudy May .15
185 Brian Doyle .15
186 Bucky Dent .15
187 Jim Kaat .15
188 Lou Piniella .15
189 Luis Tiant .15
190 Tommy John .15
191 Bake McBride .15
192 Bob Boone .15
193 Dickie Noles .15
194 Manny Trillo .15
195 Mike Schmidt 1.00
196 Sparky Lyle .15
197 Steve Carlton .50
198 Steve Yeager .15
199 Burt Hooton .15
200 Dusty Baker .15
201 Jerry Reuss .15
202 Mike Scioscia .15
203 Pedro Guerrero .15
204 Ron Cey .15
205 Steve Garvey .15
206 Alejandro Pena .15
207 Steve Sax .15
208 Cecil Cooper .15
209 Gorman Thomas .15
210 Paul Molitor .50
211 Robin Yount 1.00
212 Rollie Fingers .25
213 Don Money .15
214 Rudy May .15
215 Bucky Dent .15
216 Dave Winfield .50
217 Lou Piniella .25
218 Rich "Goose" Gossage .15
219 Tommy John .15
220 Cecil Cooper .15
221 Gorman Thomas .15
222 Paul Molitor .50
223 Robin Yount 1.00
224 Don Money .15
225 Cal Ripken Jr. 2.00
226 Dan Ford .15
227 Jim Palmer .25
228 John Shelby .15
229 Alan Trammell .25
230 Chet Lemon .15
231 Howard Johnson .15
232 Jack Morris .15
233 Kirk Gibson .25
234 Lou Whitaker .15
235 Sparky Anderson .15
236 Dave Winfield .50
237 Don Mattingly 1.00
238 Ken Griffey Sr. .15
239 Phil Niekro .15
240 Yogi Berra .75
241 Bill Buckner .15
242 Bruce Hurst .15
243 Dave Henderson .15
244 Dwight Evans .15
245 Jim Rice .15
246 Tom Seaver .50
247 Wade Boggs .50
248 Bob Boone .15
249 Bobby Grich .15
250 Brian Downing .15
251 Don Sutton .25
252 Terry Forster .15
253 Rick Burleson .15
254 Wally Joyner .15
255 Darryl Strawberry .15
256 Dwight Gooden .15
257 Gary Carter .15
258 Jesse Orosco .15
259 Keith Hernandez .15
260 Lenny Dykstra .15
261 Mookie Wilson .15
262 Ray Knight .15
263 Wally Backman .15
264 Sid Fernandez .15
265 Alan Trammell .25
266 Dan Petry .15
267 Chet Lemon .15
268 Sparky Anderson .15
269 Jack Morris .15
270 Kirk Gibson .15
271 Lou Whitaker .15
272 Bert Blyleven .15
273 Kent Hrbek .15
274 Kirby Puckett .75
275 Alejandro Pena .15
276 Jesse Orosco .15
277 John Shelby .15
278 Kirk Gibson .15
279 Mickey Hatcher .15
280 Mike Scioscia .15
281 Steve Sax .15
282 Darryl Strawberry .15
283 Dwight Gooden .15
284 Gary Carter .15
285 Howard Johnson .15
286 Keith Hernandez .15
287 Lenny Dykstra .15
288 Mookie Wilson .15
289 Wally Backman .15
290 Sid Fernandez .15
291 Jack Morris .15
292 Kent Hrbek .15
293 Kirby Puckett .75
294 Dave Winfield .50
295 Jack Morris .15
296 Joe Carter .15
297 Don Mattingly 1.00
298 Paul O'Neill .15
299 Jack McDowell .15
300 Wade Boggs .50

Gold

No Pricing
Production Five Sets

Autographs

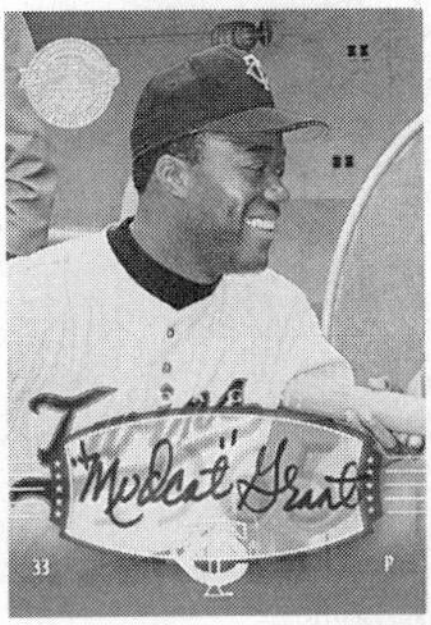

NM/M

Common Autograph: 10.00
Golds: No Pricing
Production Five Sets
Platinum: No Pricing
Production One Set
2 Lou Brock MM/SP/75 20.00
3 Ray Washburn 10.00
4 Tim McCarver 15.00
5 Harmon Killebrew 40.00
6 Jim Kaat 10.00
7 Jim Perry 12.00
9 Boog Powell 10.00
10 Brooks Robinson 35.00
12 Jim Palmer/SP/50 20.00
13 Carl Yastrzemski/SP/25 80.00
14 Jim Lonborg 10.00
15 George Scott 10.00
16 Sparky Lyle 10.00
17 Rico Petrocelli 10.00
18 Bob Gibson/SP/35 40.00
19 Julian Javier 10.00
20 Lou Brock/SP/60 20.00
21 Orlando Cepeda/SP/50 20.00
22 Ray Washburn 10.00
24 Tim McCarver 12.00
25 Al Kaline 25.00
26 Bill Freehan 10.00
27 Denny McLain 20.00
28 Dick McAuliffe 10.00
29 Jim Northrup 15.00
30 John Hiller 10.00
31 Mickey Lolich 15.00
32 Mickey Stanley 10.00
33 Willie Horton 10.00
35 Julian Javier 10.00
36 Lou Brock/SP/50 20.00
38 Steve Carlton/SP/35 30.00
39 Boog Powell 10.00
40 Brooks Robinson/SP/100 40.00
41 Davey Johnson 10.00
42 Merv Rettenmund 10.00
43 Eddie Watt 10.00
46 Mike Cuellar 10.00
47 Paul Blair 10.00
48 Pete Richert 10.00
49 Ellie Hendricks 10.00
50 Billy Williams/SP/75 25.00
51 Randy Hundley 10.00
53 Fergie Jenkins 15.00
54 Jim Hickman 20.00
55 Ken Holtzman 15.00
56 Ron Santo 25.00
57 Ed Kranepool 10.00
58 Jerry Koosman 15.00
59 Nolan Ryan/SP/50 175.00
60 Tom Seaver/SP/50 50.00
61 Boog Powell 12.00
62 Brooks Robinson/SP/35 50.00
63 Davey Johnson 10.00
64 Merv Rettenmund 10.00
65 Eddie Watt 10.00
66 Frank Robinson/SP/50 30.00
67 Jim Palmer/SP/75 20.00
68 Mike Cuellar 12.00
69 Paul Blair 10.00
70 Pete Richert 10.00
71 Ellie Hendricks 10.00
72 Al Kaline 25.00
73 Bill Freehan 10.00
74 Dick McAuliffe 15.00
75 Jim Northrup 15.00
76 John Hiller 10.00
77 Mickey Lolich 15.00
78 Mickey Stanley 10.00
79 Willie Horton 12.00
80 Bert Campaneris 10.00
81 Blue Moon Odom 15.00
82 Sal Bando/Exch. 10.00
83 Joe Rudi 10.00
84 Ken Holtzman 10.00
85 Bill North 10.00
86 Blue Moon Odom 15.00
87 Gene Tenace 10.00
88 Manny Trillo 15.00
89 Dick Green 10.00
90 Rollie Fingers 15.00
91 Sal Bando 10.00
92 Vida Blue 15.00
93 Bill Buckner 15.00
94 Davey Lopes 10.00
95 Don Sutton 15.00
96 Al Downing MM 10.00
100 Bert Campaneris 10.00
101 Bill North 10.00
102 Joe Rudi 10.00
103 Sal Bando 10.00
104 Vida Blue SP/100 15.00
105 Carl Yastrzemski SP/50 60.00
106 Carlton Fisk SP/100 30.00
107 Cecil Cooper SP/75 15.00
108 Dwight Evans SP/75 10.00
109 Fred Lynn 10.00
110 Jim Rice SP/100/Exch. 20.00
111 Luis Tiant/Exch. 10.00
112 Rick Burleson 10.00
113 Rico Petrocelli 10.00
114 Pedro Borbon 10.00
115 Dave Concepcion/Exch. 10.00
116 Don Gullett 15.00
117 George Foster/SP/50 15.00
119 Johnny Bench/SP/85 50.00
120 Rawly Eastwick 10.00
121 Sparky Anderson 10.00
122 Tony Perez 30.00
123 Billy Williams SP/50 20.00
124 Gene Tenace 10.00
125 Jim Perry 10.00
126 Vida Blue SP/75 20.00
127 Pedro Borbon 10.00
128 Dave Concepcion/Exch. 10.00
129 Don Gullett 15.00
133 Ken Griffey Sr. 10.00
134 Rawly Eastwick 10.00
135 Tony Perez 30.00
136 Bill Russell 10.00
137 Burt Hooton 10.00
138 Davey Lopes 10.00
139 Don Sutton 15.00
140 Dusty Baker/Exch. 15.00
141 Steve Yeager/SP/75/Exch. 10.00
144 Tommy John/SP/35 15.00
145 Bucky Dent/SP/75 15.00
146 Chris Chambliss 15.00
147 Ed Figueroa 10.00
148 Graig Nettles 15.00
150 Roy White 10.00
151 Don Gullett 15.00
152 Sparky Lyle 10.00
153 Brian Doyle 10.00
155 Chris Chambliss 15.00
156 Ed Figueroa 10.00
157 Graig Nettles 15.00
159 Roy White 10.00
160 Rich "Goose" Gossage 15.00
161 Sparky Lyle 10.00
162 Bobby Grich 10.00
163 Brian Downing 10.00
164 Dan Ford 10.00
166 Dave Concepcion/
SP/75/Exch. 10.00
169 Ray Knight 10.00
171 Bert Blyleven 15.00
172 Bill Madlock 10.00
173 Dave Parker 12.00
174 Phil Garner 10.00
175 Bill Russell 10.00
176 Steve Yeager 10.00
177 Don Sutton/SP/50 20.00
178 Dusty Baker 15.00
179 Jerry Reuss 10.00
180 Mickey Hatcher 10.00
181 Pedro Guerrero 10.00
182 Ron Cey/SP/50 15.00
183 Steve Garvey/SP/50 15.00
184 Rudy May 10.00
185 Brian Doyle 10.00
186 Bucky Dent/SP/60 15.00
187 Jim Kaat 10.00
188 Lou Piniella/SP/50 15.00
189 Luis Tiant 10.00
190 Tommy John/SP/50 15.00
191 Bake McBride 15.00
192 Bob Boone 10.00
193 Dickie Noles 10.00
194 Manny Trillo 15.00
195 Mike Schmidt/SP/50 75.00
196 Sparky Lyle 10.00
197 Steve Carlton/SP/50 20.00
198 Steve Yeager 10.00
199 Burt Hooton 10.00
200 Dusty Baker/Exch. 15.00
201 Jerry Reuss 10.00
202 Mike Scioscia 10.00
203 Pedro Guerrero 10.00
204 Ron Cey/SP/75 10.00
205 Steve Garvey SP/75 15.00
206 Alejandro Pena 10.00
207 Steve Sax/SP/100 10.00
208 Cecil Cooper/SP/85 15.00
209 Gorman Thomas/Exch. 10.00
212 Rollie Fingers 15.00
213 Don Money 10.00
214 Rudy May 10.00
216 Dave Winfield/SP/50 30.00
217 Lou Piniella/SP/75 15.00
218 Rich "Goose" Gossage 15.00
219 Tommy John/SP/75 10.00
220 Cecil Cooper 15.00
221 Gorman Thomas/Exch. 10.00
222 Paul Molitor/SP/50 45.00
223 Robin Yount/SP/50 75.00
224 Don Money 10.00
225 Cal Ripken Jr./SP/50 180.00
226 Dan Ford 10.00
228 John Shelby 10.00
229 Alan Trammell 15.00
230 Chet Lemon 10.00
231 Howard Johnson 15.00
232 Jack Morris/SP/35 15.00
233 Kirk Gibson 15.00
234 Lou Whitaker/SP/100 15.00
235 Sparky Anderson 10.00
237 Don Mattingly/SP/50 60.00
238 Ken Griffey Sr. 10.00
239 Phil Niekro 15.00
240 Yogi Berra/SP/47 50.00
241 Bill Buckner 15.00
242 Bruce Hurst 15.00
243 Dave Henderson 10.00
245 Jim Rice/SP/75/Exch. 20.00
247 Wade Boggs/SP/50 30.00
248 Bob Boone 10.00
249 Bobby Grich 10.00
250 Brian Downing 10.00
251 Don Sutton/SP/75 15.00
252 Terry Forster 10.00
253 Rick Burleson 10.00
254 Wally Joyner 15.00
255 Darryl Strawberry 15.00
256 Dwight Gooden 15.00
257 Gary Carter/SP/75 20.00
258 Jesse Orosco 10.00
259 Keith Hernandez 15.00
260 Lenny Dykstra 10.00
261 Mookie Wilson 10.00
262 Ray Knight 10.00
263 Wally Backman 10.00
264 Sid Fernandez/Exch. 10.00
265 Alan Trammell 15.00
266 Dan Petry 10.00
267 Chet Lemon 10.00
268 Sparky Anderson 10.00
270 Kirk Gibson 15.00
271 Lou Whitaker/SP/50 20.00
272 Bert Blyleven 10.00
273 Kent Hrbek 15.00
275 Alejandro Pena 10.00
276 Jesse Orosco 10.00
277 John Shelby 10.00
278 Kirk Gibson/SP/50 20.00
279 Mickey Hatcher 10.00
280 Mike Scioscia 10.00
281 Steve Sax 10.00
282 Darryl Strawberry 15.00
283 Dwight Gooden 15.00
284 Gary Carter/SP/50 20.00
285 Howard Johnson 10.00
286 Keith Hernandez 15.00
287 Lenny Dykstra 10.00
288 Mookie Wilson 10.00
289 Wally Backman 10.00
290 Sid Fernandez/Exch. 10.00
291 Jack Morris/SP/50 15.00
292 Kent Hrbek 15.00
293 Kirby Puckett/SP/50 50.00
294 Dave Winfield/SP/35 35.00
295 Jack Morris/SP/75 15.00
298 Paul O'Neill 40.00
299 Jack McDowell 10.00
300 Wade Boggs SP/75 25.00

Legendary Sign. Dual

NM/M

Quantity produced listed

BC	Lou Brock, Orlando Cepeda/75	40.00
BJ	Lou Brock, Julian Javier/150	25.00
BM	Wade Boggs, Don Mattingly/50	140.00
BO	Vida Blue, Blue Moon Odom/150	25.00
BW	Ernie Banks, Billy Williams/25	100.00
CB	Steve Carlton, Bret Boone/150	50.00
CG	Ron Cey, Steve Garvey/150	40.00
CH	Gary Carter, Keith Hernandez/150	30.00
CM	Dave Concepcion, Joe Morgan/75 Exch	35.00
DD	Bucky Dent, Brian Doyle/150	25.00
FR	Fred Lynn, Jim Rice/150	40.00
GA	Kirk Gibson, Sparky Anderson/50	40.00
GB	Bob Gibson, Lou Brock/50	75.00
GC	Dwight Gooden, Gary Carter/150	30.00
GL	Rich "Goose" Gossage, Sparky Lyle/150 Exch	25.00
HJ	Ken Holtzman, Fergie Jenkins/150	40.00
HK	Keith Hernandez, Ray Knight/150	30.00
JH	Fergie Jenkins, Randy Hundley/150	40.00
JS	Tommy John, Don Sutton/150	25.00
KH	Al Kaline, Willie Horton/150	40.00
KK	Harmon Killebrew, Jim Kaat/150	50.00
LM	Mickey Lolich, Denny McLain/75	60.00
MB	Joe Morgan, Johnny Bench/25	80.00
MF	Denny McLain, Bill Freehan/150	40.00
NC	Graig Nettles, Chris Chambliss/150	30.00
OM	Paul O'Neill, Don Mattingly/150	140.00
PC	Jim Palmer, Mike Cuellar/150	30.00
PF	Tony Perez, George Foster/150	40.00
PH	Kirby Puckett, Kent Hrbek/50	65.00
PN	Lou Piniella, Graig Nettles/150	30.00
PR	Jim Palmer, Merv Rettenmund/150	35.00
RL	Bill Russell, Davey Lopes/150	30.00
RR	Brooks Robinson, Frank Robinson/50	70.00
RS	Nolan Ryan, Tom Seaver/25	250.00
SD	Steve Garvey, Davey Lopes/150	25.00
SG	Darryl Strawberry, Dwight Gooden/150	40.00
SY	Don Sutton, Steve Yeager/150	30.00
TF	Luis Tiant, Carlton Fisk/50	45.00
TM	Gorman Thomas, Paul Molitor/150 Exch	35.00
WB	Mookie Wilson, Bill Buckner/150	30.00
WT	Lou Whitaker, Alan Trammell/75	75.00
YM	Robin Yount, Paul Molitor/150	120.00
YP	Carl Yastrzemski, Rico Petrocelli/50	75.00

Legendary Sign. Triple

NM/M

Quantity produced listed

BCM	Johnny Bench, Dave Concepcion, Joe Morgan/25 Exch	100.00
BOM	Wade Boggs, Paul O'Neill, Don Mattingly/150	150.00
BRB	Sal Bando, Joe Rudi, Vida Blue/75	50.00
BSW	Ernie Banks, Ron Santo, Billy Williams/25	140.00
CDK	Gary Carter, Lenny Dykstra, Ray Knight/50	75.00
CND	Chris Chambliss, Graig Nettles, Bucky Dent/50	50.00
ERL	Dwight Evans, Jim Rice, Fred Lynn/50	125.00
GBC	Steve Garvey, Dusty Baker, Ron Cey/50	75.00
GBM	Bob Gibson, Lou Brock, Tim McCarver/100	100.00
GDR	Bobby Grich, Al Downing, Nolan Ryan/25	175.00
GHS	Kirk Gibson, Mickey Hatcher, Mike Scioscia/75	85.00
GMP	Phil Garner, Bill Madlock, Dave Parker/75	75.00
HHS	Jim Hickman, Ken Holtzman, Ron Santo/75	60.00
HSJ	Burt Hooton, Don Sutton, Tommy John/50	50.00
JHH	Fergie Jenkins, Randy Hundley, Ken Holtzman/75	50.00
KKP	Harmon Killebrew, Jim Kaat, Jim Perry/50	65.00
KPG	Jim Kaat, Jim Perry, Jim "Mudcat" Grant/75 Exch	40.00
KSR	Jerry Koosman, Tom Seaver, Nolan Ryan/25	250.00
MHP	Jack Morris, Kent Hrbek, Kirby Puckett/50	100.00
MLF	Denny McLain, Mickey Lolich, Bill Freehan/50	60.00
NKH	Jim Northrup, Al Kaline, Willie Horton/75	65.00
PBH	Kirby Puckett, Bert Blyleven, Kent Hrbek/50	90.00
PCR	Jim Palmer, Mike Cuellar, Pete Richert/75	45.00
PPW	Jim Palmer, Boog Powell, Earl Weaver/75	60.00
RPR	Frank Robinson, Boog Powell, Brooks Robinson/50	80.00
RWP	Cal Ripken Jr., Earl Weaver, Jim Palmer/25	250.00
SCB	Mike Schmidt, Steve Carlton, Bob Boone/50	125.00
SGS	Steve Sax, Pedro Guerrero, Mike Scioscia/75	
TWA	Alan Trammell, Lou Whitaker, Sparky Anderson/50	75.00
YCT	Robin Yount, Cecil Cooper, Gorman Thomas/50 Exch	120.00
YFT	Carl Yastrzemski, Carlton Fisk, Luis Tiant/25	140.00
YMT	Robin Yount, Paul Molitor, Gorman Thomas/75 Exch	140.00

Legendary Combo Signs.

No Pricing

Legendary Combo Cuts

No Pricing

Team Terrific GU Team Logo

NM/M

Quantity produced listed

BO	Baltimore Orioles/85	60.00
BR	Boston Red Sox/85	50.00
CR	Cincinnati Reds/85	75.00
LD	Los Angeles Dodgers/85	50.00
MB	Milwaukee Brewers/100	30.00
NM	New York Mets/85	30.00
OA	Oakland A's/100	30.00
SC	St. Louis Cardinals/100	50.00

Team Terrific GU League

No Pricing

Production 15 Sets

Team Terrific GU Stats

No Pricing

Production 1-5

Team Terrific GU Hat Logo

NM/M

Quantity produced listed

BO	Baltimore Orioles/50	90.00
BR	Boston Red Sox/50	80.00
CR	Cincinnati Reds/50	80.00
LD	Los Angeles Dodgers/50	60.00
MB	Milwaukee Brewers/82	40.00
NM	New York Mets/50	40.00
OA	Oakland A's/50	40.00
SC	St. Louis Cardinals/50	75.00

Team Terrific GU Brand Logo

NM/M

Quantity produced listed

BO	Baltimore Orioles/35	90.00
BR	Boston Red Sox/35	80.00
CR	Cincinnati Reds/35	80.00
LD	Los Angeles Dodgers/35	60.00
MB	Milwaukee Brewers/41	90.00
NM	New York Mets/35	40.00
OA	Oakland A's/39	40.00
SC	St. Louis Cardinals/35	75.00

2005 Upper Deck

NM/M

Complete Set (500):		75.00
Common Player:		.15
Common (211-250):		.50
Hobby Pack (8):		3.00
Hobby Box (24):		65.00
1	Casey Kotchman	.15
2	Chone Figgins	.15
3	David Eckstein	.15
4	Jarrod Washburn	.15
5	Robb Quinlan	.15
6	Troy Glaus	.25
7	Vladimir Guerrero	.75
8	Brandon Webb	.15
9	Danny Bautista	.15
10	Luis Gonzalez	.15
11	Matt Kata	.15
12	Randy Johnson	.75
13	Robby Hammock	.15
14	Shea Hillenbrand	.15
15	Adam LaRoche	.15
16	Andruw Jones	.25
17	Horacio Ramirez	.15
18	John Smoltz	.25
19	Johnny Estrada	.15
20	Mike Hampton	.15
21	Rafael Furcal	.15
22	Brian Roberts	.15
23	Javy Lopez	.25
24	Jay Gibbons	.15
25	Jorge Julio	.15
26	Melvin Mora	.15
27	Miguel Tejada	.25
28	Rafael Palmeiro	.50
29	Derek Lowe	.15
30	Jason Varitek	.25
31	Kevin Youkilis	.15
32	Manny Ramirez	.75
33	Curt Schilling	.75
34	Pedro Martinez	.75
35	Trot Nixon	.15
36	Corey Patterson	.25
37	Derrek Lee	.25
38	LaTroy Hawkins	.15
39	Mark Prior	.75
40	Matt Clement	.15
41	Moises Alou	.25
42	Sammy Sosa	1.50
43	Aaron Rowand	.15
44	Carlos Lee	.15
45	Jose Valentin	.15
46	Juan Uribe	.15
47	Magglio Ordonez	.25
48	Mark Buehrle	.15
49	Paul Konerko	.25
50	Adam Dunn	.50
51	Barry Larkin	.25
52	D'Angelo Jimenez	.15
53	Danny Graves	.15
54	Paul Wilson	.15
55	Sean Casey	.25
56	Wily Mo Pena	.15
57	Ben Broussard	.15
58	C.C. Sabathia	.25
59	Casey Blake	.15
60	Cliff Lee	.15
61	Matt Lawton	.15
62	Omar Vizquel	.15
63	Victor Martinez	.25
64	Charles Johnson	.15
65	Joe Kennedy	.15
66	Jeromy Burnitz	.15
67	Matt Holliday	.50
68	Preston Wilson	.15
69	Royce Clayton	.15
70	Shawn Estes	.15
71	Bobby Higginson	.15
72	Brandon Inge	.15
73	Carlos Guillen	.15
74	Dmitri Young	.15
75	Eric Munson	.15
76	Jeremy Bonderman	.15
77	Ugueth Urbina	.15
78	Josh Beckett	.40
79	Dontrelle Willis	.25
80	Jeff Conine	.15
81	Juan Pierre	.15
82	Luis Castillo	.15
83	Miguel Cabrera	.75
84	Mike Lowell	.25
85	Andy Pettitte	.25
86	Brad Lidge	.15
87	Carlos Beltran	.50
88	Craig Biggio	.50
89	Jeff Bagwell	.50
90	Roger Clemens	1.50
91	Roy Oswalt	.25
92	Benito Santiago	.15
93	Jeremy Affeldt	.15
94	Juan Gonzalez	.25
95	Ken Harvey	.15
96	Mike MacDougal	.15
97	Mike Sweeney	.15
98	Zack Greinke	.15
99	Adrian Beltre	.15
100	Alex Cora	.15
101	Cesar Izturis	.15
102	Eric Gagne	.40
103	Kazuhisa Ishii	.15
104	Milton Bradley	.15
105	Shawn Green	.25
106	Danny Kolb	.15
107	Ben Sheets	.25
108	Brooks Kieschnick	.15
109	Craig Counsell	.15
110	Geoff Jenkins	.15
111	Lyle Overbay	.15
112	Scott Podsednik	.15
113	Corey Koskie	.15
114	Johan Santana	.40
115	Joe Mauer	.25
116	Justin Morneau	.25
117	Lew Ford	.15
118	Matt LeCroy	.15
119	Torii Hunter	.25
120	Brad Wilkerson	.15
121	Chad Cordero	.15
122	Livan Hernandez	.15
123	Jose Vidro	.15
124	Termel Sledge	.15
125	Tony Batista	.15
126	Zach Day	.15
127	Al Leiter	.25
128	Jae Weong Seo	.15
129	Jose Reyes	.40
130	Kazuo Matsui	.15
131	Mike Piazza	1.00
132	Todd Zeile	.15
133	Cliff Floyd	.15
134	Alex Rodriguez	2.00
135	Derek Jeter	2.00
136	Gary Sheffield	.40
137	Hideki Matsui	1.50
138	Jason Giambi	.25
139	Jorge Posada	.25
140	Mike Mussina	.40
141	Barry Zito	.25
142	Bobby Crosby	.25
143	Octavio Dotel	.15
144	Eric Chavez	.25
145	Jermaine Dye	.15
146	Mark Kotsay	.15
147	Tim Hudson	.25
148	Billy Wagner	.15
149	Bobby Abreu	.25
150	David Bell	.15
151	Jim Thome	.50
152	Jimmy Rollins	.25
153	Mike Lieberthal	.15
154	Randy Wolf	.15
155	Craig Wilson	.15
156	Daryle Ward	.15
157	Jack Wilson	.15
158	Jason Kendall	.15
159	Kip Wells	.15
160	Oliver Perez	.15
161	Robert Mackowiak	.15
162	Brian Giles	.15
163	Brian Lawrence	.15
164	David Wells	.15
165	Jay Payton	.15
166	Ryan Klesko	.15
167	Sean Burroughs	.15
168	Trevor Hoffman	.15
169	Brett Tomko	.15
170	J.T. Snow	.15
171	Jason Schmidt	.25
172	Kirk Rueter	.15
173	A.J. Pierzynski	.15
174	Pedro Feliz	.15
175	Ray Durham	.15
176	Eddie Guardado	.15
177	Edgar Martinez	.15
178	Ichiro Suzuki	1.50
179	Jamie Moyer	.15
180	Joel Pineiro	.15
181	Randy Winn	.15
182	Raul Ibanez	.15
183	Albert Pujols	2.00
184	Edgar Renteria	.25
185	Jason Isringhausen	.15
186	Jim Edmonds	.40
187	Matt Morris	.15
188	Reggie Sanders	.15
189	Tony Womack	.15
190	Aubrey Huff	.15
191	Danys Baez	.15
192	Carl Crawford	.15
193	Jose Cruz Jr.	.15
194	Rocco Baldelli	.15
195	Tino Martinez	.15
196	Dewon Brazelton	.15
197	Alfonso Soriano	.75
198	Brad Fullmer	.15
199	Gerald Laird	.15
200	Hank Blalock	.50
201	Laynce Nix	.15
202	Mark Teixeira	.25
203	Mike Young	.15
204	Alexis Rios	.15
205	Eric Hinske	.15
206	Miguel Batista	.15
207	Orlando Hudson	.15
208	Roy Halladay	.15
209	Ted Lilly	.15
210	Vernon Wells	.15
211	Aarom Baldiris	.50
212	B.J. Upton	1.00
213	Dallas McPherson	.50
214	Brian Dallimore	.50
215	Chris Oxspring	.50
216	Chris Shelton	.50

CARLOS BELTRAN
ASTROS
OF

#	Player	Price
217	David Wright	1.50
218	Edwardo Sierra	.50
219	Fernando Nieve	.50
220	Frank Francisco	.50
221	Jeff Bennett	.50
222	Justin Lehr	.50
223	John Gall	.50
224	Jorge Sequea	.50
225	Justin Germano	.50
226	Kazuhito Tadano	.50
227	Kevin Cave	.50
228	Joe Blanton	.50
229	Luis Gonzalez	.50
230	Mike Wuertz	.50
231	Mike Rouse	.50
232	Nick Regilio	.50
233	Orlando Rodriguez	.50
234	Phil Stockman	.50
235	Ramon Ramirez	.50
236	Roberto Novoa	.50
237	Dioner Navarro	.50
238	Tim Bausher	.50
239	Logan Kensing	.50
240	Andy Green	.50
241	Brad Halsey	.50
242	Charles Thomas	.50
243	George Sherrill	.50
244	Jesse Crain	.50
245	Jimmy Serrano	.50
246	Joe Horgan	.50
247	Chris Young RC	1.50
248	Joey Gathright	.50
249	Gavin Floyd	.50
250	Ryan Howard	1.00
251	Lance Cormier	.15
252	Matt Treanor	.15
253	Jeff Francis	.15
254	Nick Swisher	.15
255	Travis Atchison	.15
256	Travis Blackley	.15
257	Travis Smith	.15
258	Yadier Molina	.15
259	Jeff Keppinger	.15
260	Scott Kazmir	1.00
261	Garret Anderson, Vladimir Guerrero	.40
262	Luis Gonzalez, Randy Johnson	.40
263	Andruw Jones, Chipper Jones	.40
264	Miguel Tejada, Rafael Palmeiro	.40
265	Curt Schilling, Manny Ramirez	.50
266	Mark Prior, Sammy Sosa	.75
267	Frank Thomas, Magglio Ordonez	.25
268	Barry Larkin, Ken Griffey Jr.	.75
269	C.C. Sabathia, Victor Martinez	.15
270	Jeromy Burnitz, Todd Helton	.25
271	Dmitri Young, Ivan Rodriguez	.40
272	Josh Beckett, Miguel Cabrera	.25
273	Jeff Bagwell, Roger Clemens	.75
274	Ken Harvey, Mike Sweeney	.15
275	Adrian Beltre, Eric Gagne	.25
276	Ben Sheets, Geoff Jenkins	.15
277	Joe Mauer, Torii Hunter	.15
278	Jose Vidro, Livan Hernandez	.15
279	Kazuo Matsui, Mike Piazza	.50
280	Alex Rodriguez, Derek Jeter	1.00
281	Eric Chavez, Tim Hudson	.15
282	Bobby Abreu, Jim Thome	.40
283	Craig Wilson, Jason Kendall	.15
284	Brian Giles, Phil Nevin	.15
285	A.J. Pierzynski, Jason Schmidt	.15
286	Bret Boone, Ichiro Suzuki	.75
287	Albert Pujols, Scott Rolen	.75
288	Aubrey Huff, Tino Martinez	.15
289	Hank Blalock, Mark Teixeira	.15
290	Carlos Delgado, Roy Halladay	.15
291	Vladimir Guerrero	.40
292	Curt Schilling	.40
293	Mark Prior	.40
294	Josh Beckett	.15
295	Roger Clemens	.75
296	Derek Jeter	.75
297	Eric Chavez	.15
298	Jim Thome	.25
299	Albert Pujols	.75
300	Hank Blalock	.25
301	Bartolo Colon	.15
302	Darin Erstad	.15
303	Garret Anderson	.25
304	Orlando Cabrera	.15
305	Steve Finley	.15
306	Javier Vazquez	.15
307	Russ Ortiz	.15
308	Chipper Jones	.75
309	Marcus Giles	.15
310	Raul Mondesi	.15
311	B.J. Ryan	.15
312	Luis Matos	.15
313	Sidney Ponson	.15
314	Bill Mueller	.15
315	David Ortiz	.75
316	Johnny Damon	.75
317	Keith Foulke	.15
318	Mark Bellhorn	.15
319	Wade Miller	.15
320	Aramis Ramirez	.40
321	Carlos Zambrano	.25
322	Greg Maddux	1.25
323	Kerry Wood	.50
324	Nomar Garciaparra	1.00
325	Todd Walker	.15
326	Frank Thomas	.50
327	Freddy Garcia	.15
328	Joe Crede	.15
329	Jose Contreras	.15
330	Orlando Hernandez	.15
331	Shingo Takatsu	.15
332	Austin Kearns	.15
333	Eric Milton	.15
334	Ken Griffey Jr.	1.00
335	Aaron Boone	.15
336	David Riske	.15
337	Jake Westbrook	.15
338	Kevin Millwood	.15
339	Travis Hafner	.15
340	Aaron Miles	.15
341	Jeff Baker	.15
342	Todd Helton	.50
343	Garrett Atkins	.15
344	Carlos Pena	.15
345	Ivan Rodriguez	.50
346	Rondell White	.15
347	Troy Percival	.15
348	A.J. Burnett	.25
349	Carlos Delgado	.40
350	Guillermo Mota	.15
351	Paul LoDuca	.15
352	Jason Lane	.15
353	Lance Berkman	.25
354	Angel Berroa	.15
355	David DeJesus	.15
356	Ruben Gotay	.15
357	Jose Lima	.15
358	Brad Penny	.15
359	J.D. Drew	.25
360	Jayson Werth	.15
361	Jeff Kent	.25
362	Odalis Perez	.15
363	Brady Clark	.15
364	Junior Spivey	.15
365	Rickie Weeks	.15
366	Jacque Jones	.15
367	Joe Nathan	.15
368	Nick Punto	.15
369	Shannon Stewart	.15
370	Doug Mientkiewicz	.15
371	Kris Benson	.15
372	Tom Glavine	.25
373	Victor Zambrano	.15
374	Bernie Williams	.40
375	Carl Pavano	.15
376	Jaret Wright	.15
377	Kevin Brown	.25
378	Mariano Rivera	.25
379	Dan Haren	.15
380	Eric Byrnes	.15
381	Erubiel Durazo	.15
382	Rich Harden	.25
383	Brett Myers	.15
384	Chase Utley	.25
385	Marlon Byrd	.15
386	Pat Burrell	.25
387	Placido Polanco	.15
388	Freddy Sanchez	.15
389	Jason Bay	.25
390	Josh Fogg	.15
391	Adam Eaton	.15
392	Jake Peavy	.40
393	Khalil Greene	.40
394	Mark Loretta	.15
395	Phil Nevin	.15
396	Ramon Hernandez	.15
397	Woody Williams	.15
398	Armando Benitez	.15
399	Edgardo Alfonzo	.15
400	Marquis Grissom	.15
401	Mike Matheny	.15
402	Richie Sexson	.40
403	Bret Boone	.15
404	Gil Meche	.15
405	Chris Carpenter	.40
406	Jeff Suppan	.15
407	Larry Walker	.25
408	Mark Grudzielanek	.15
409	Mark Mulder	.25
410	Scott Rolen	.15
411	Josh Phelps	.15
412	Jonny Gomes	.15
413	Francisco Cordero	.15
414	Kenny Rogers	.15
415	Richard Hidalgo	.15
416	David Bush	.15
417	Frank Catalanotto	.15
418	Gabe Gross	.15
419	Guillermo Quiroz	.15
420	Reed Johnson	.15
421	Cristian Guzman	.15
422	Esteban Loaiza	.15
423	Jose Guillen	.25
424	Nick Johnson	.15
425	Vinny Castilla	.15
426	Peter Orr RC	.50
427	Tadahito Iguchi RC	4.00
428	Jeff Baker	.15
429	Marcos Carvajal RC	.50
430	Justin Verlander RC	3.00
431	Luke Scott RC	1.00
432	Willy Taveras	.15
433	Ambiorix Burgos RC	.15
434	Andy Sisco	.15
435	Denny Bautista	.15
436	Mark Teahen	.15
437	Ervin Santana	.15
438	Dennis Houlton RC	.50
439	Philip Humber RC	1.00
440	Steve Schmoll RC	.50
441	J.J. Hardy	.50
442	Ambiorix Concepcion RC	.50
443	Dae-Sung Koo RC	.50
444	Andy Phillips	.15
445	Dan Meyer	.15
446	Huston Street	.15
447	Keiichi Yabu RC	.50
448	Jeff Niemann RC	1.00
449	Jeremy Reed	.15
450	Tony Blanco	.15
451	Albert Pujols	.75
452	Alex Rodriguez	.75
453	Curt Schilling	.40
454	Derek Jeter	.75
455	Greg Maddux	.50
456	Ichiro Suzuki	.50
457	Ivan Rodriguez	.25
458	Jeff Bagwell	.25
459	Jim Thome	.25
460	Ken Griffey Jr.	.50
461	Manny Ramirez	.40
462	Mike Mussina	.25
463	Mike Piazza	.40
464	Pedro Martinez	.40
465	Rafael Palmeiro	.25
466	Randy Johnson	.40
467	Roger Clemens	.75
468	Sammy Sosa	.50
469	Todd Helton	.25
470	Vladimir Guerrero	.40
471	Vladimir Guerrero	.25
472	Shawn Green	.15
473	John Smoltz	.15
474	Miguel Tejada	.25
475	Curt Schilling	.25
476	Mark Prior	.40
477	Frank Thomas	.25
478	Ken Griffey Jr.	.50
479	C.C. Sabathia	.15
480	Todd Helton	.25
481	Ivan Rodriguez	.25
482	Miguel Cabrera	.40
483	Roger Clemens	.50
484	Mike Sweeney	.15
485	Eric Gagne	.15
486	Ben Sheets	.15
487	Johan Santana	.25
488	Mike Piazza	.40
489	Derek Jeter	.50
490	Eric Chavez	.15
491	Jim Thome	.25
492	Craig Wilson	.15
493	Jake Peavy	.15
494	Jason Schmidt	.15
495	Ichiro Suzuki	.50
496	Albert Pujols	.50
497	Carl Crawford	.15
498	Mark Teixeira	.25
499	Vernon Wells	.15
500	Jose Vidro	.15

Blue

Stars (301-500): 4-6X
Production 150 Sets
Exclusive to Series 2.

Gold

Stars (301-500): 4-8X
Production 99 Sets
Exclusive to Series 2.

Emerald

Stars (301-500): 10-20X
Production 25 Sets
Exclusive to Series 2.

Platinum

No Pricing
Production Five Sets
Exclusive to Series 2.

Retro

Retro: 2-3X
One retro box per hobby case.

Plates

No Pricing
Production one set per color.

American Flag

No Pricing
Production 15 Sets

Diamond Images - Wingfield Collection

	NM/M
Complete Set (20):	45.00
Common Player:	2.00
	Inserted 1:9
DI-1 Eddie Mathews	3.00
DI-2 Ernie Banks	4.00
DI-3 Joe DiMaggio	6.00
DI-4 Mickey Mantle	8.00
DI-5 Pee Wee Reese	2.00
DI-6 Phil Rizzuto	2.00
DI-7 Stan Musial	4.00
DI-8 Ted Williams	6.00
DI-9 Bob Feller	2.00
DI-10 Whitey Ford	2.00
DI-11 Willie Stargell	2.00
DI-12 Yogi Berra	2.00
DI-13 Roy Campanella	2.00
DI-14 Franklin D. Roosevelt	2.00
DI-15 Harry S. Truman	2.00
DI-16 Dwight D. Eisenhower	2.00
DI-17 John F. Kennedy	2.00
DI-18 Lyndon B. Johnson	2.00
DI-19 Richard Nixon	2.00
DI-20 Thurman Munson	3.00

Game Jersey

	NM/M
Common Jersey:	5.00
	Inserted 1:8
JB Jeff Bagwell/SP	8.00
CB Carlos Beltran/SP	8.00
AB Adrian Beltre	5.00
LB Lance Berkman	5.00
HB Hank Blalock	5.00
MC Miguel Cabrera	8.00
EC Eric Chavez	5.00
EG Eric Gagne	5.00
TG Troy Glaus	5.00
KG Ken Griffey Jr./SP	15.00
VG Vladimir Guerrero	8.00
HE Todd Helton	5.00
TH Tim Hudson	5.00
HU Torii Hunter	5.00
DJ Derek Jeter	25.00
RJ Randy Johnson/SP	10.00
CJ Chipper Jones	8.00
JK Jeff Kent	5.00
GM Greg Maddux/SP	10.00
PM Pedro Martinez	8.00
MM Mark Mulder	5.00
DO David Ortiz/SP	10.00
PI Mike Piazza	8.00
MP Mark Prior	8.00
AP Albert Pujols	20.00
MR Manny Ramirez/SP	10.00
IR Ivan Rodriguez	8.00
SR Scott Rolen	8.00
JS Johan Santana/SP	10.00
CS Curt Schilling	8.00
SM John Smoltz	5.00
AS Alfonso Soriano	8.00
SS Sammy Sosa	10.00
MT Mark Teixeira/SP	8.00
TE Miguel Tejada	5.00
FT Frank Thomas	8.00
JT Jim Thome/SP	8.00
KW Kerry Wood	8.00
DW David Wright	10.00

Game Patch

	NM/M
	Inserted 1:288
DJ Derek Jeter	75.00
CR Cal Ripken Jr.	75.00

Hall of Fame Plaques

	NM/M
Complete Set (10):	40.00
Common Player:	3.00
	Inserted 1:36
SP-16 Ernie Banks	4.00
SP-17 Yogi Berra	4.00
SP-18 Whitey Ford	3.00
SP-19 Bob Gibson	3.00
SP-20 Willie McCovey	3.00
SP-21 Stan Musial	6.00
SP-22 Nolan Ryan	12.00
SP-23 Mike Schmidt	8.00
SP-24 Tom Seaver	4.00
SP-25 Robin Yount	4.00

Lasting Impressions

No Pricing
Production One Set
One press plate per color.

Marquee Attractions

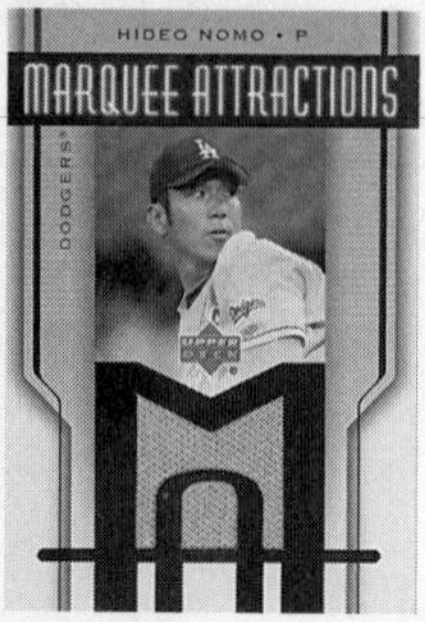

		NM/M
Common Player:		4.00
Inserted 1:12		
GA	Garret Anderson	4.00
JB	Jeff Bagwell	8.00
BE	Josh Beckett	4.00
KB	Kevin Brown	4.00
MC	Miguel Cabrera	8.00
RC	Roger Clemens	15.00
CD	Carlos Delgado	4.00
AD	Adam Dunn	8.00
EG	Eric Gagne	6.00
JG	Jason Giambi	4.00
BG	Brian Giles	4.00
SG	Shawn Green	4.00
KG	Ken Griffey Jr.	12.00
VG	Vladimir Guerrero	8.00
TH	Todd Helton	8.00
HO	Trevor Hoffman	4.00
DJ	Derek Jeter	20.00
RJ	Randy Johnson	10.00
AJ	Andruw Jones	6.00
CJ	Chipper Jones	8.00
GM	Greg Maddux	10.00
PM	Pedro Martinez	10.00
HM	Hideki Matsui	30.00
KM	Kazuo Matsui	8.00
JM	Joe Mauer	8.00
HN	Hideo Nomo	10.00
RO	Roy Oswalt	4.00
PE	Andy Pettitte	6.00
PI	Mike Piazza	10.00
MP	Mark Prior	6.00
AP	Albert Pujols	15.00
IR	Ivan Rodriguez	8.00
CS	Curt Schilling	8.00
JS	Jason Schmidt	6.00
SS	Sammy Sosa	12.00
IS	Ichiro Suzuki	25.00
MT	Miguel Tejada	6.00
JT	Jim Thome	8.00
BW	Billy Wagner	4.00
DW	Dontrelle Willis	4.00
PW	Preston Wilson	4.00
KW	Kerry Wood	8.00

Matinee Idols

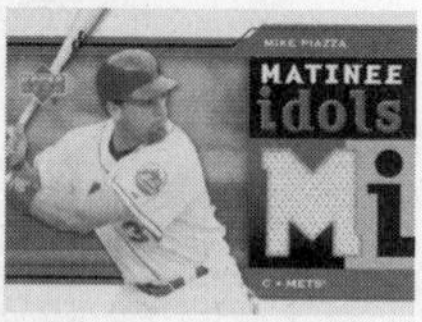

		NM/M
Common Player:		4.00
Inserted 1:12 Hobby		
JB	Jeff Bagwell	8.00
RB	Rocco Baldelli	4.00
BE	Josh Beckett	6.00
HB	Hank Blalock	8.00
BB	Bret Boone/SP	6.00
PB	Pat Burrell	6.00
SB	Sean Burroughs	4.00
EC	Eric Chavez	6.00
RC	Roger Clemens	15.00
CD	Carlos Delgado	4.00
JE	Jim Edmonds	6.00
JG	Jason Giambi	4.00
TG	Troy Glaus	4.00
KG	Ken Griffey Jr.	12.00
VG	Vladimir Guerrero	8.00
RH	Roy Halladay	4.00
TH	Todd Helton	8.00
HU	Torii Hunter	4.00
DJ	Derek Jeter	20.00
RJ	Randy Johnson	8.00
CJ	Chipper Jones	8.00
ML	Mike Lowell	4.00
MM	Mike Mussina	6.00
PI	Mike Piazza	10.00
MP	Mark Prior	6.00
CR	Cal Ripken Jr.	25.00
SR	Scott Rolen	8.00
NR	Nolan Ryan	25.00
CS	Curt Schilling	8.00
TS	Tom Seaver	8.00
GS	Gary Sheffield	6.00
SS	Sammy Sosa	12.00
MT	Mark Teixeira	6.00
JT	Jim Thome	8.00
BW	Billy Wagner	4.00
RW	Rickie Weeks	4.00
VW	Vernon Wells	4.00
DW	Dontrelle Willis	4.00
KW	Kerry Wood	8.00
BZ	Barry Zito	4.00

Milestone Materials

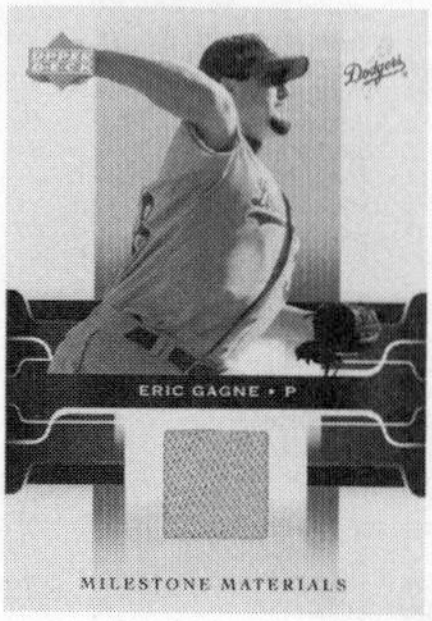

		NM/M
Common Jersey:		5.00
BA	Jeff Bagwell	8.00
JB	Jason Bay	5.00
CB	Carlos Beltran	8.00
BC	Bobby Crosby	5.00
EG	Eric Gagne	5.00
KG	Ken Griffey Jr.	15.00
VG	Vladimir Guerrero	8.00
RJ	Randy Johnson	8.00
GM	Greg Maddux	10.00
DO	David Ortiz	8.00
RP	Rafael Palmeiro	8.00
JP	Jake Peavy	8.00
AP	Albert Pujols	20.00
MR	Manny Ramirez	8.00
JS	Johan Santana	8.00
CS	Curt Schilling	8.00
MT	Mark Teixeira	5.00
TE	Miguel Tejada	8.00
JT	Jim Thome	8.00

Origins

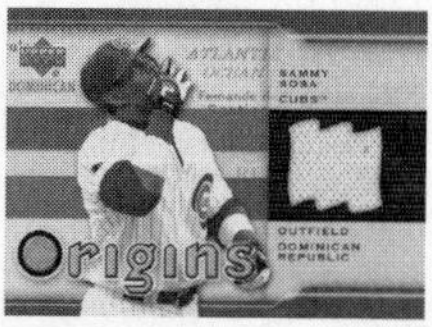

		NM/M
Common Player:		4.00
Inserted 1:12 Hobby		
Inserted 1:24 Retail		
GA	Garret Anderson	4.00
CB	Carlos Beltran	10.00
AB	Adrian Beltre	6.00
LB	Lance Berkman	4.00
MC	Miguel Cabrera	8.00
RF	Rafael Furcal	4.00
EG	Eric Gagne	6.00
BG	Brian Giles	4.00
JG	Juan Gonzalez	8.00
LG	Luis Gonzalez	4.00
VG	Vladimir Guerrero	8.00
TH	Tim Hudson	4.00
AJ	Andruw Jones	6.00
JK	Jeff Kent	4.00
JL	Javy Lopez	4.00
GM	Greg Maddux	10.00
PM	Pedro Martinez	10.00
HM	Hideki Matsui	30.00
KM	Kazuo Matsui	8.00
MM	Mark Mulder	4.00
HN	Hideo Nomo	10.00
MO	Magglio Ordonez	4.00
RP	Rafael Palmeiro	8.00
PE	Jake Peavy	4.00
JP	Jorge Posada	4.00
AP	Albert Pujols	15.00
MR	Manny Ramirez	8.00
JR	Jose Reyes	4.00
IR	Ivan Rodriguez	8.00
JS	Jason Schmidt	4.00
RS	Richie Sexson	4.00
AS	Alfonso Soriano	8.00
SS	Sammy Sosa	12.00
IS	Ichiro Suzuki	25.00
MT	Miguel Tejada	6.00
BU	B.J. Upton	8.00
JV	Javier Vazquez	4.00
PW	Preston Wilson	4.00

Rewind to 1997 Jersey

		NM/M
Common Jersey:		
Inserted 1:288		
JB	Jeff Bagwell	25.00
WC	Will Clark	20.00
KG	Ken Griffey Jr.	40.00
VG	Vladimir Guerrero	25.00
TG	Tony Gwynn	30.00
DJ	Derek Jeter	40.00
RJ	Randy Johnson	25.00
AJ	Andruw Jones	20.00
CJ	Chipper Jones	30.00
GM	Greg Maddux	40.00
PM	Pedro Martinez	25.00
MP	Mike Piazza	30.00
MR	Manny Ramirez	30.00
CR	Cal Ripken Jr.	40.00
IR	Ivan Rodriguez	20.00
SR	Scott Rolen	25.00
CS	Curt Schilling	20.00
JS	John Smoltz	25.00
FT	Frank Thomas	25.00
JT	Jim Thome	25.00

Signature Sensations

No Pricing
Production 15 Sets
Die-Cut: No Pricing
Production 10 Sets

Signature Stars

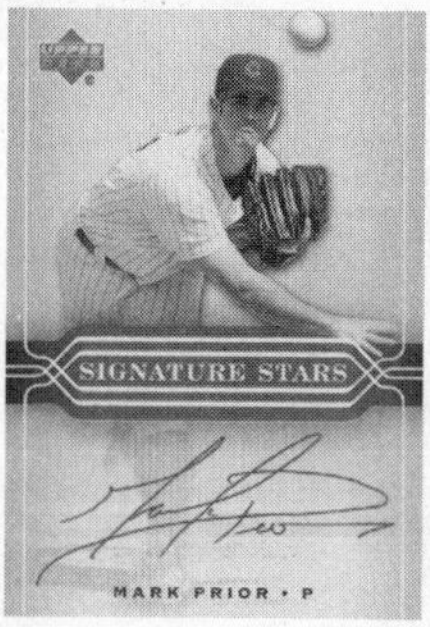

		NM/M
Common Player:		
Inserted 1:288 Hobby		
CB	Carlos Beltran/SP	40.00
HB	Hank Blalock	25.00
MC	Miguel Cabrera	35.00
BC	Bobby Crosby	30.00
LF	Lew Ford	10.00
KG	Ken Griffey Jr.	80.00
JL	Javy Lopez	15.00
JM	Joe Mauer	20.00
OP	Odalis Perez	20.00
CR	Cal Ripken Jr./SP	180.00
BS	Ben Sheets	15.00
DW	Dontrelle Willis	20.00
KW	Kerry Wood	25.00
DY	Delmon Young	20.00
BZ	Barry Zito	

Signature Stars Retail

Inserted 1:480 Retail
No Pricing

Super Patch - Names

No Pricing
Cards are not serial numbered.

Super Patch - Numbers

No Pricing
Cards are not serial numbered.

Super Patch - Logos

No Pricing
Cards are not serial numbered.

World Series Heroes

		NM/M
Complete Set (45):		20.00
Common Player:		.25
Inserted 1:1 Retail		
WS-1	Garret Anderson	.50
WS-2	Troy Glaus	.50
WS-3	Vladimir Guerrero	1.00
WS-4	Andruw Jones	.50
WS-5	Chipper Jones	1.00
WS-6	Curt Schilling	1.00
WS-7	Keith Foulke	.25
WS-8	Manny Ramirez	.75
WS-9	Nomar Garciaparra	1.50
WS-10	Pedro Martinez	1.00
WS-11	Kerry Wood	1.00
WS-12	Mark Prior	1.00
WS-13	Sammy Sosa	2.00
WS-14	Frank Thomas	.75
WS-15	Magglio Ordonez	.25
WS-16	Dontrelle Willis	.25
WS-17	Josh Beckett	.50
WS-18	Miguel Cabrera	.75
WS-19	Jeff Bagwell	.75
WS-20	Lance Berkman	.25
WS-21	Roger Clemens	2.00
WS-22	Eric Gagne	.50
WS-23	Torii Hunter	.50
WS-24	Mike Piazza	1.50
WS-25	Alex Rodriguez	2.00
WS-26	Derek Jeter	2.00
WS-27	Gary Sheffield	.50
WS-28	Hideki Matsui	1.50
WS-29	Jason Giambi	.50
WS-30	Jorge Posada	.50
WS-31	Kevin Brown	.25
WS-32	Mariano Rivera	.50
WS-33	Mike Mussina	.50
WS-34	Eric Chavez	.25
WS-35	Mark Mulder	.25
WS-36	Tim Hudson	.25
WS-37	Billy Wagner	.25
WS-38	Jim Thome	.75
WS-39	Brian Giles	.25
WS-40	Jason Schmidt	.25
WS-41	Albert Pujols	2.00
WS-42	Scott Rolen	.75
WS-43	Alfonso Soriano	.75
WS-44	Hank Blalock	.75
WS-45	Mark Teixeira	.50

4,000-Strikeout Commemorative

	NM/M
Production 4,000	
Steve Carlton, Nolan Ryan, Roger Clemens, Randy Johnson	12.00

4,000 Strikeout Autographs

Production 50 Sets
Quad Signature: No Pricing
Production 10

2004 Update Set

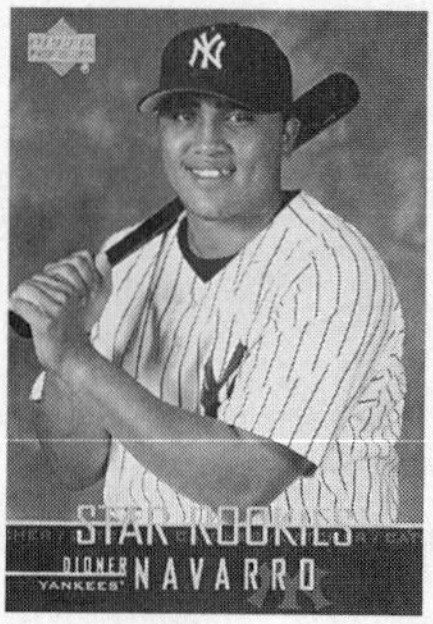

		NM/M
Complete Set (50):		10.00
Common Player:		.15
Inserted 1:Hobby Box		
541	Alex Rodriguez	1.50
542	Roger Clemens	1.50
543	Andy Pettitte	.25
544	Vladimir Guerrero	.75
545	David Wells	.15
546	Derek Lee	.25
547	Carlos Beltran	.50
548	Orlando Cabrera	.25
549	Paul LoDuca	.15
550	Dave Roberts	.15
551	Guillermo Mota	.15
552	Steve Finley	.15
553	Juan Encarnacion	.15
554	Larry Walker	.50
555	Ty Wigginton	.15
556	Doug Mientkiewicz	.15
557	Roberto Alomar	.40
558	B.J. Upton	.50
559	Brad Penny	.15
560	Hee Seop Choi	.15
561	David Wright	1.00
562	Nomar Garciaparra	1.00
563	Felix Rodriguez	.15
564	Victor Zambrano	.15
565	Kris Benson	.15
566	Aarom Baldiris	.15
567	Joey Gathright	.15
568	Charles Thomas	.15
569	Brian Dallimore	.15
570	Chris Oxspring	.15
571	Chris Shelton	.15
572	Dioner Navarro	.25
573	Edwardo Sierra	.15
574	Fernando Nieve	.15
575	Frank Francisco	.15
576	Jeff Bennett	.15
577	Justin Lehr	.15
578	John Gall	.15

579	Jorge Sequea	.15
580	Justin Germano	.15
581	Kazuhito Tadano	.15
582	Kevin Cave	.15
583	Jesse Crain	.15
584	Luis Gonzalez	.15
585	Mike Wuertz	.15
586	Orlando Rodriguez	.15
587	Phil Stockman	.15
588	Ramon Ramirez	.15
589	Roberto Novoa	.15
590	Scott Kazmir	1.50

2004 Update - Awesome Honors

NM/M

Common Player: 8.00
1:12 '04 Update Set
Production 75 Sets

BE	Adrian Beltre	10.00
AB	Angel Berroa	8.00
KB	Kevin Brown	8.00
MC	Miguel Cabrera	15.00
RC	Roger Clemens	20.00
EG	Eric Gagne	12.00
BG	Brian Giles	8.00
DL	Derek Lee	8.00
KM	Kazuo Matsui	20.00
JM	Joe Mauer	10.00
PE	Andy Pettitte	10.00
SP	Scott Podsednik	8.00
AP	Albert Pujols	25.00
IR	Ivan Rodriguez	12.00
SC	Curt Schilling	12.00
RS	Richie Sexson	8.00
GS	Gary Sheffield	8.00
AS	Alfonso Soriano	15.00
VA	Javier Vazquez	8.00

2004 Update - Authentic Stars

NM/M

Common Player: 8.00
1:12 '04 Update Sets
Production 75 Sets

CB	Carlos Beltran	15.00
LB	Lance Berkman	8.00
JE	Jim Edmonds	8.00
RF	Rafael Furcal	8.00
HA	Roy Halladay	8.00
RH	Rich Harden	8.00
HU	Tim Hudson	8.00
DJ	Derek Jeter	35.00
AK	Austin Kearns	8.00
HN	Hideo Nomo	20.00
MO	Magglio Ordonez	8.00
OS	Roy Oswalt	8.00
RP	Rafael Palmeiro	12.00
MR	Manny Ramirez	15.00
JR	Jose Reyes	8.00
SR	Scott Rolen	15.00
TE	Miguel Tejada	8.00
JT	Jim Thome	12.00
WE	Brandon Webb	8.00
VW	Vernon Wells	8.00
PW	Preston Wilson	8.00
KW	Kerry Wood	8.00

2005 UD All-Star Classics

NM/M

Complete Set (100): 25.00
Common Player: .15
Pack (8): 3.00
Box (24): 60.00

1	Albert Pujols	2.00
2	Alex Rodriguez	1.50
3	Alfonso Soriano	.75
4	Barry Zito	.25
5	Bobby Abreu	.40
6	Carlos Beltran	.50
7	Carlos Delgado	.40
8	Chipper Jones	.75
9	Curt Schilling	.75
10	David Ortiz	.75
11	Derek Jeter	2.00
12	Edgar Renteria	.25
13	Eric Gagne	.25
14	Frank Thomas	.50
15	Gary Sheffield	.40
16	Greg Maddux	1.00
17	Hank Blalock	.40
18	Hideki Matsui	1.50
19	Ichiro Suzuki	1.50
20	Ivan Rodriguez	.50
21	Jason Schmidt	.25
22	Jason Varitek	.25
23	Jeff Kent	.25
24	Jim Thome	.75
25	Jorge Posada	.25
26	Ken Griffey Jr.	1.00
27	Kerry Wood	.75
28	Lance Berkman	.25
29	Manny Ramirez	.75
30	Mariano Rivera	.40
31	Mark Mulder	.25
32	Mark Prior	.75
33	Miguel Cabrera	.75
34	Miguel Tejada	.50
35	Mike Piazza	1.00
36	Nomar Garciaparra	1.00
37	Pedro Martinez	.75
38	Randy Johnson	.75
39	Richie Sexson	.25
40	Roger Clemens	2.00
41	Roy Halladay	.25
42	Sammy Sosa	1.50
43	Scott Rolen	.75
44	Sean Casey	.25
45	Tim Hudson	.25
46	Todd Helton	.50
47	Tom Glavine	.40
48	Torii Hunter	.25
49	Troy Glaus	.25
50	Vladimir Guerrero	.75
51	Adrian Beltre	.25
52	Alexis Rios	.15
53	Aubrey Huff	.15
54	Brandon Webb	.25
55	Dallas McPherson	.25
56	David Wright	.75
57	Edwin Jackson	.15
58	Grady Sizemore	.40
59	Tadahito Iguchi RC	3.00
60	Jake Peavy	.40
61	Jake Westbrook	.15
62	Jason Bay	.25
63	Jeff Francis	.15
64	Jeremy Reed	.15
65	Joe Mauer	.40
66	Johan Santana	.50
67	Jose Capellan	.15
68	Jose Reyes	.25
69	Justin Morneau	.40
70	Mark Teixeira	.40
71	Oliver Perez	.25
72	Rich Harden	.25
73	Rickie Weeks	.25
74	Ryan Howard	.25
75	Scott Kazmir	.15
76	Al Kaline	.40
77	Bill Mazeroski	.25
78	Bob Feller	.50
79	Bob Gibson	.50
80	Brooks Robinson	.75
81	Cal Ripken Jr.	3.00
82	Carlton Fisk	.25
83	Eddie Murray	.50
84	Gaylord Perry	.25
85	Harmon Killebrew	.75
86	Jim Palmer	.50
87	Joe DiMaggio	1.50
88	Joe Morgan	.25
89	Johnny Bench	.75
90	Juan Marichal	.25
91	Lou Brock	.25
92	Mike Schmidt	1.00
93	Nolan Ryan	2.00
94	Ozzie Smith	.75
95	Phil Niekro	.25
96	Robin Yount	.50
97	Rollie Fingers	.25
98	Tom Seaver	.50
99	Willie McCovey	.50
100	Yogi Berra	.75

Gold

Stars (1-100) 4-8X
Production 499 Sets

Box Scores

NM/M

Complete Set (20): 50.00
Common Player: 1.50
Inserted 1:24

1	Juan Marichal	2.00
2	Brooks Robinson	3.00
3	Tony Perez	1.50
4	Willie McCovey	2.00
5	Harmon Killebrew	3.00
6	Johnny Bench	3.00
7	Joe Morgan	1.50
8	Lou Brock	1.50
9	Jim Palmer	1.50
10	Mike Schmidt	5.00
11	Ozzie Smith	4.00
12	Roger Clemens	6.00
13	Cal Ripken Jr.	8.00
14	Ken Griffey Jr.	4.00
15	Greg Maddux	4.00
16	Alex Rodriguez	5.00
17	Derek Jeter	6.00
18	Johnny Damon	3.00
19	Garret Anderson	1.50
20	Alfonso Soriano	2.00

Matchups

NM/M

Complete Set (20): 40.00
Common Player: 1.50
Inserted 1:24

1	Hank Blalock	2.00
2	Curt Schilling	3.00
3	Manny Ramirez	3.00
4	Ken Griffey Jr.	4.00
5	Brooks Robinson	3.00
6	Harmon Killebrew	3.00
7	Carl Yastrzemski	4.00
8	Cal Ripken Jr.	8.00
9	Trevor Hoffman	1.50
10	Eric Gagne	2.00
11	Alfonso Soriano	2.00
12	David Ortiz	3.00
13	Andruw Jones	1.50
14	Garret Anderson	1.50
15	Magglio Ordonez	1.50
16	Derek Jeter	6.00
17	Chipper Jones	3.00
18	Roberto Alomar	2.00
19	Mike Piazza	3.00
20	Alex Rodriguez	5.00

Midsummer Classics

NM/M

Complete Set (20): 40.00
Common Player: 1.50
Inserted 1:24

1	Derek Jeter	6.00
2	Pedro Martinez	2.00
3	Mike Piazza	3.00
4	Randy Johnson	2.00
5	Gary Sheffield	2.00
6	Albert Pujols	6.00
7	David Ortiz	3.00
8	Manny Ramirez	3.00
9	Garret Anderson	1.50
10	Todd Helton	1.50
11	Nolan Ryan	2.00
12	Paul Konerko	1.50
13	Alfonso Soriano	2.00
14	Magglio Ordonez	1.50
15	Cal Ripken Jr.	8.00
16	Ken Griffey Jr.	3.00
17	Harmon Killebrew	3.00
18	Mike Schmidt	3.00
19	Frank Thomas	2.00
20	Alex Rodriguez	5.00

Midsummer Swatches

NM/M

Common Player: 4.00
Inserted 1:12
Patches: No Pricing
Production 25 Sets

MA	Moises Alou/Jsy	6.00
JB	Jeff Bagwell/Jsy	6.00
CB	Carlos Beltran/Jsy	8.00
CI	Craig Biggio/Jsy	6.00
BB	Bret Boone/Jsy	4.00
CD	Carlos Delgado/Jsy	6.00
JE	Jim Edmonds/Jsy	6.00
KF	Keith Foulke/Jsy	6.00
RF	Rafael Furcal/Jsy	4.00
EG	Eric Gagne/Jsy	8.00
SG	Shawn Green/Jsy	4.00
KG	Ken Griffey Jr./Jsy	25.00
TH	Todd Helton/Jsy	8.00
TI	Torii Hunter/Jsy	6.00
AJ	Andruw Jones/Pants	6.00
CJ	Chipper Jones/Jsy	8.00
JK	Jeff Kent/Jsy	4.00
RK	Ryan Klesko	4.00
ML	Matt Lawton/Jsy	4.00
PL	Paul LoDuca/Jsy	4.00
JL	Javy Lopez/Jsy	4.00
PM	Pedro Martinez/Jsy	8.00
VM	Victor Martinez/Jsy	4.00
DO	David Ortiz/Pants	8.00
RP	Rafael Palmeiro/Jsy	8.00
MP	Mike Piazza/Jsy	15.00
ER	Edgar Renteria/Jsy	6.00
CR	Cal Ripken Jr./Pants	35.00
CC	C.C. Sabathia/Jsy	4.00
SC	Jason Schmidt/Jsy	4.00
BS	Ben Sheets/Jsy	4.00
GS	Gary Sheffield/Jsy	8.00
JS	John Smoltz/Jsy	10.00
SS	Sammy Sosa/Jsy	10.00
IS	Ichiro Suzuki/Jsy	30.00
MS	Mike Sweeney/Jsy	4.00
MT	Miguel Tejada/Jsy	8.00
FT	Frank Thomas/Jsy	8.00
JT	Jim Thome/Jsy	8.00
OM	Omar Vizquel/Jsy	6.00
WE	David Wells/Jsy	4.00
DW	Dontrelle Willis/Jsy	8.00

MVP's

NM/M

Complete Set (20): 45.00
Common Player: 1.00
Inserted 1:24

1	Alfonso Soriano	2.00
2	Ken Griffey Sr.	4.00
3	Brooks Robinson	3.00
4	Cal Ripken Jr.	8.00
5	Cal Ripken Jr.	8.00
6	Derek Jeter	6.00
7	Carl Yastrzemski	4.00
8	Garret Anderson	1.50
9	Jeff Conine	1.00
10	Joe Morgan	1.50
11	Juan Marichal	2.00
12	Julio Franco	1.00
13	Ken Griffey Jr.	4.00
14	Mike Piazza	3.00
15	Pedro Martinez	3.00
16	Roberto Alomar	2.00
17	Roger Clemens	6.00
18	Sandy Alomar Jr.	1.00
19	Tony Perez	1.50
20	Willie McCovey	2.00

Perennial All-Stars

NM/M

Complete Set (20): 40.00
Common Player: 2.00
Inserted 1:24

1	Albert Pujols	6.00
2	Alex Rodriguez	5.00
3	Alfonso Soriano	2.00

4 Curt Schilling 3.00
5 Derek Jeter 6.00
6 Eric Gagne 2.00
7 Greg Maddux 4.00
8 Ichiro Suzuki 5.00
9 Ivan Rodriguez 2.00
10 Jim Thome 2.00
11 Ken Griffey Jr. 4.00
12 Mariano Rivera 2.00
13 Miguel Tejada 2.00
14 Mike Piazza 3.00
15 Randy Johnson 2.00
16 Roger Clemens 6.00
17 Sammy Sosa 4.00
18 Scott Rolen 3.00
19 Todd Helton 2.00
20 Vladimir Guerrero 2.00

2005 Upper Deck Artifacts

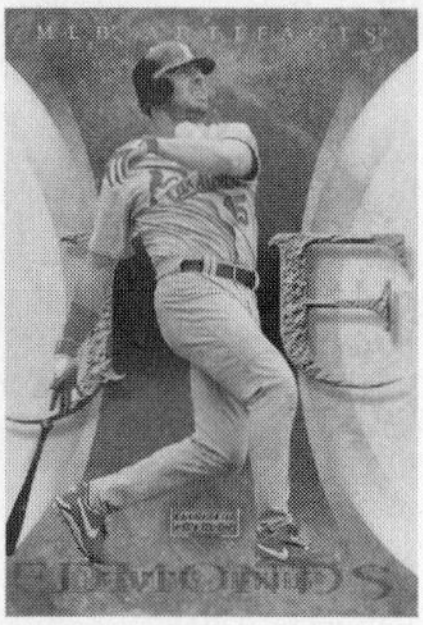

NM/M
Complete Set (200):
Common Player (1-100): .25
Common (101-150): 2.00
Production 1,350
Common (151-200): 2.00
Production 1,999
Pack (4): 10.00
Box (10): 90.00
1 Adam Dunn .75
2 Adrian Beltre .75
3 Albert Pujols 3.00
4 Alex Rodriguez 2.50
5 Alfonso Soriano 1.00
6 Andruw Jones .50
7 Andy Pettitte .50
8 Aramis Ramirez .50
9 Aubrey Huff .25
10 Barry Larkin .50
11 Ben Sheets .50
12 Bernie Williams .50
13 Bobby Abreu .50
14 Brad Penny .25
15 Bret Boone .25
16 Brian Giles .25
17 Carl Crawford .25
18 Carl Pavano .50
19 Carlos Beltran .75
20 Carlos Delgado .75
21 Carlos Guillen .25
22 Carlos Lee .50
23 Carlos Zambrano .50
24 Chipper Jones 1.00
25 Craig Biggio .50
26 Craig Wilson .25
27 Curt Schilling 1.00
28 David Ortiz 1.00
29 Derek Jeter 3.00
30 Eric Chavez .50
31 Eric Gagne .50
32 Frank Thomas .75
33 Garret Anderson .50
34 Gary Sheffield .50
35 Greg Maddux 1.50
36 Hank Blalock .75
37 Hideki Matsui 2.00
38 Ichiro Suzuki 2.50
39 Ivan Rodriguez .75
40 J.D. Drew .50
41 Jake Peavy .50
42 Jason Kendall .25
43 Jason Schmidt .50
44 Jeff Bagwell .75
45 Jeff Kent .50
46 Jim Edmonds .50
47 Jim Thome 1.00
48 Joe Mauer .75
49 Johan Santana .75
50 John Smoltz .50
51 Jose Reyes .50
52 Jose Vidro .25
53 Josh Beckett .50
54 Ken Griffey Jr. 1.50
55 Kerry Wood 1.00
56 Kevin Brown .25
57 Lance Berkman .50
58 Larry Walker .50
59 Livan Hernandez .25
60 Luis Gonzalez .25
61 Lyle Overbay .25
62 Magglio Ordonez .25
63 Manny Ramirez 1.00
64 Mark Mulder .50
65 Mark Prior 1.00
66 Mark Teixeira .50
67 Melvin Mora .25
68 Michael Young .25
69 Miguel Cabrera 1.00
70 Miguel Tejada .75
71 Mike Lowell .25
72 Mike Mussina .50
73 Mike Piazza 1.50
74 Mike Sweeney .25
75 Nomar Garciaparra 2.00
76 Oliver Perez .25
77 Paul Konerko .25
78 Pedro Martinez 1.00
79 Preston Wilson .25
80 Rafael Furcal .25
81 Rafael Palmeiro .75
82 Randy Johnson 1.00
83 Richie Sexson .50
84 Roger Clemens 3.00
85 Roy Halladay .50
86 Roy Oswalt .50
87 Sammy Sosa 2.00
88 Scott Podsednik .25
89 Scott Rolen 1.00
90 Shawn Green .25
91 Steve Finley .25
92 Tim Hudson .50
93 Todd Helton .75
94 Tom Glavine .50
95 Torii Hunter .25
96 Travis Hafner .25
97 Troy Glaus .50
98 Vernon Wells .25
99 Victor Martinez .50
100 Vladimir Guerrero 1.00
101 Aaron Rowand 2.00
102 Adam LaRoche 2.00
103 Adrian Gonzalez 2.00
104 Alexis Rios 2.00
105 Angel Guzman 2.00
106 B.J. Upton 3.00
107 Bobby Crosby 3.00
108 Bobby Madritsch 2.00
109 Brandon Claussen 2.00
110 Bucky Jacobsen 2.00
111 Casey Kotchman 2.00
112 Chad Cordero 2.00
113 Chase Utley 2.00
114 Chris Burke 2.00
115 Dallas McPherson 4.00
116 Daniel Cabrera 2.00
117 David DeJesus 2.00
118 David Wright 6.00
119 Eddy Rodriguez 2.00
120 Edwin Jackson 2.00
121 Gabe Gross 2.00
122 Garrett Atkins 2.00
123 Gavin Floyd 2.00
124 Gerald Laird 2.00
125 Guillermo Quiroz 2.00
126 J.D. Closser 2.00
127 Jason Bay 4.00
128 Jason Dubois 2.00
129 Jason Lane 2.00
130 Jayson Werth 2.00
131 Jeff Francis 2.00
132 Jesse Crain 2.00
133 Joe Blanton 2.00
134 Joe Mauer 4.00
135 Jose Capellan 2.00
136 Kevin Youkilis 2.00
137 Khalil Greene 3.00
138 Laynce Nix 2.00
139 Nick Swisher 2.00
140 Oliver Perez 2.00
141 Rickie Weeks 2.00
142 Robb Quinlan 2.00
143 Roman Colon 2.00
144 Ryan Howard 4.00
145 Ryan Wagner 2.00
146 Scott Kazmir 4.00
147 Scott Proctor 2.00
148 Wily Mo Pena 2.00
149 Yhency Brazoban 2.00
150 Zack Greinke 2.00
151 Al Kaline 5.00
152 Babe Ruth 8.00
153 Billy Williams 2.00
154 Bob Feller 3.00
155 Bob Gibson 4.00
156 Bob Lemon 2.00
157 Bobby Doerr 2.00
158 Brooks Robinson 4.00
159 Cal Ripken Jr. 10.00
160 Christy Mathewson 4.00
161 Cy Young 5.00
162 Dizzy Dean 5.00
163 Don Drysdale 2.00
164 Eddie Mathews 4.00
165 Enos Slaughter 2.00
166 Ernie Banks 5.00
167 Fergie Jenkins 2.00
168 George Sisler 2.00
169 Harmon Killebrew 4.00
170 Honus Wagner 5.00
171 Jackie Robinson 5.00
172 Jimmie Foxx 4.00
173 Joe DiMaggio 6.00
174 Joe Morgan 2.00
175 Juan Marichal 2.00
176 Lou Brock 2.00
177 Lou Gehrig 6.00
178 Luis Aparicio 2.00
179 Mel Ott 4.00
180 Mickey Cochrane 2.00
181 Mickey Mantle 10.00
182 Mike Schmidt 6.00
183 Nolan Ryan 8.00
184 Pee Wee Reese 2.00
185 Phil Rizzuto 2.00
186 Ralph Kiner 2.00
187 Rogers Hornsby 3.00
188 Roy Campanella 3.00
189 Satchel Paige 4.00
190 Stan Musial 5.00
191 Rick Ferrell 2.00
192 Thurman Munson 5.00
193 Tom Seaver 4.00
194 Ty Cobb 6.00
195 Walter Johnson 5.00
196 Warren Spahn 4.00
197 Whitey Ford 4.00
198 Willie McCovey 3.00
199 Willie Stargell 3.00
200 Yogi Berra 4.00

Rainbow Blue

Blue (1-100): 3-5X
Blue (101-200): 1-2X
Production 100 Sets

Rainbow Gold

Gold (1-100): 6-10X
Gold (101-200): 2-3X
Production 25 Sets

Rainbow Platinum

No Pricing
Production One Set

Rainbow Red

Red (1-100): 4-8X
Red (101-200): 1.5-3X
Production 50 Sets

AL/NL Artifacts

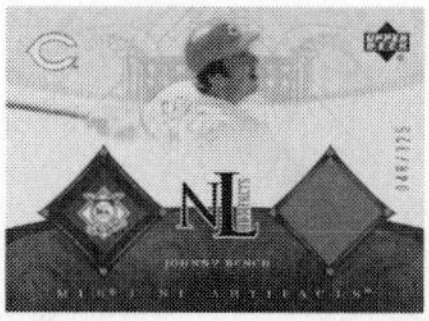

NM/M
Common Player: 4.00
Production 325 unless noted.
Rainbow: .75-1.5X
Production 99 Sets
BA Bobby Abreu/Jsy 6.00
JB Jason Bay/Jsy 6.00
CB Carlos Beltran/Jsy 8.00
AB Adrian Beltre/Jsy 6.00
BE Johnny Bench/Jsy 10.00
YB Yogi Berra/Pants 15.00
HB Hank Blalock/Jsy 8.00
BB Bert Blyleven/Jsy 6.00
WB Wade Boggs/Jsy 8.00
GB George Brett/Jsy 15.00
MC Miguel Cabrera/Jsy 10.00
RCA Rod Carew/Jsy 8.00
CA Steve Carlton/Jsy 6.00
SC Sean Casey/Jsy 4.00
OC Orlando Cepeda/Jsy/185 8.00
EC Eric Chavez/Jsy 4.00
WC Will Clark/Jsy/100 10.00
CN Roger Clemens/Jsy 15.00
BC Bobby Crosby/Jsy 6.00
AD Andre Dawson/Jsy 6.00
BD Bobby Doerr/Bat 6.00
BF Bob Feller/Pants 10.00
EG Eric Gagne/Jsy 8.00
BG Bob Gibson/Pants 10.00
GI Brian Giles/Jsy 4.00
MG Marcus Giles/Jsy 4.00
DG Dwight Gooden/Pants 6.00
MK Mark Grace/Jsy/175 8.00
KG Ken Griffey Jr./Jsy 15.00
GR Ken Griffey Sr./Jsy 4.00
TG Tony Gwynn/Jsy 10.00
TH Travis Hafner/Jsy 4.00
RH Rich Harden/Jsy 8.00
KHN Keith Hernandez/Bat 4.00
KHA Kent Hrbek/Jsy 4.00
AH Aubrey Huff/Jsy 4.00
DJ Derek Jeter/Jsy 20.00
RJ Randy Johnson/Jsy 10.00
JK Jim Kaat/Jsy 6.00
AK Al Kaline/Jsy 10.00
GK George Kell/Bat 6.00
HK Harmon Killebrew/Jsy 10.00
RK Ralph Kiner/Bat 6.00
DK Dave Kingman/Bat 4.00
CK Casey Kotchman/Jsy 4.00
DL Derrek Lee/Jsy 6.00
ML Mike Lowell/Jsy 4.00
SL Sparky Lyle/Pants 4.00
FL Fred Lynn/Bat 4.00
GM Greg Maddux/Jsy/275 12.00
VM Victor Martinez/Jsy 6.00
MA Don Mattingly/Jsy 20.00
JM Joe Mauer/Jsy 10.00
WM Willie McCovey/Jsy 8.00
DMA Dallas McPherson/Jsy 8.00
PM Paul Molitor/Jsy 8.00
MM Mark Mulder/Jsy 6.00
DMN Dale Murphy/Jsy/150 8.00
GN Graig Nettles/Jsy 4.00
PN Phil Niekro/Jsy 4.00
LN Laynce Nix/Jsy 4.00
DO David Ortiz/Jsy 10.00
RO Roy Oswalt/Jsy 4.00
AO Akinori Otsuka/Jsy 4.00
JPA Jim Palmer/Jsy 8.00
CP Corey Patterson/Jsy 6.00
JPN Jake Peavy/Jsy 6.00
BPN Brad Penny/Jsy 4.00
RP Rico Petrocelli/Pants 8.00
SP Scott Podsednik/Jsy 4.00
BPA Boog Powell/Jsy 6.00
MP Mark Prior/Jsy 8.00
AP Albert Pujols/Jsy 25.00
JRN Jose Reyes/Jsy/250 8.00
JRA Jim Rice/Jsy 8.00
CR Cal Ripken Jr./Jsy 25.00
BR Brooks Robinson/Jsy 8.00
FR Frank Robinson/Jsy 8.00
SR Scott Rolen/Jsy 10.00
NR Nolan Ryan/Jsy 25.00
JSA Johan Santana/Jsy 10.00
JSN Jason Schmidt/Jsy 6.00
MS Mike Schmidt/Jsy 15.00
TS Tom Seaver/Jsy 8.00
BS Ben Sheets/Jsy 6.00
SM John Smoltz/Jsy 8.00
SU Bruce Sutter/Jsy 6.00
ST Shingo Takatsu/Jsy 6.00
MT Mark Teixeira/Jsy 8.00
BU B.J. Upton/Jsy 6.00
RW Rickie Weeks/Jsy 6.00
MW Maury Wills/Jsy 6.00
KW Kerry Wood/Jsy 8.00
DW David Wright/Jsy 10.00
CY Carl Yastrzemski/Jsy 15.00
MY Michael Young/Jsy 6.00
RY Robin Yount/Jsy 15.00
CZ Carlos Zambrano/Jsy 6.00

AL/NL Artifacts Signatures

NM/M
Production 30 Sets
Rare Artifacts: No Pricing
Production One Set
BA Bobby Abreu/Jsy/Redemp. 20.00
JB Jason Bay/Jsy 30.00
CB Carlos Beltran/Jsy/Redemp. 25.00
AB Adrian Beltre/Jsy 30.00
BE Johnny Bench/Jsy 65.00
YB Yogi Berra/Pants 60.00
HB Hank Blalock/Jsy 25.00
BB Bert Blyleven/Jsy 30.00
WB Wade Boggs/Jsy 50.00
GB George Brett/Jsy 120.00
MC Miguel Cabrera/Jsy 40.00
RCA Rod Carew/Jsy 40.00
SC Sean Casey/Jsy 30.00
CA Steve Carlton/Jsy 40.00
OC Orlando Cepeda/Jsy 35.00
EC Eric Chavez/Jsy 30.00
WC Will Clark/Jsy 50.00
RCN Roger Clemens/Jsy/Redemp. 100.00
BC Bobby Crosby/Jsy/Redemp. 20.00
AD Andre Dawson/Jsy 30.00
BD Bobby Doerr/Bat 35.00
BF Bob Feller/Pants 40.00
EG Eric Gagne/Jsy/Redemp. 50.00
BG Bob Gibson/Pants 50.00
GI Brian Giles/Jsy 20.00
MG Marcus Giles/Jsy 20.00
DG Dwight Gooden/Pants 30.00
MK Mark Grace/Jsy 50.00
KL Khalil Greene/Jsy 50.00
KG Ken Griffey Jr./Jsy 120.00
GR Ken Griffey Sr./Jsy 25.00
TG Tony Gwynn/Jsy 90.00
TH Travis Hafner/Jsy 20.00
RH Rich Harden/Jsy 40.00
KHN Keith Hernandez/Bat 20.00
KHA Kent Hrbek/Jsy 50.00
AH Aubrey Huff/Jsy 25.00
DJ Derek Jeter/Jsy 200.00
JK Jim Kaat/Jsy 25.00
AK Al Kaline/Jsy 50.00
GK George Kell/Bat 30.00
HK Harmon Killebrew/Jsy 60.00
RK Ralph Kiner/Bat 50.00
DK Dave Kingman/Bat 25.00
CK Casey Kotchman/Jsy 25.00
DL Derrek Lee/Jsy 40.00
ML Mike Lowell/Jsy 20.00
SL Sparky Lyle/Pants 20.00
FL Fred Lynn/Bat 25.00
GM Greg Maddux/Jsy/Redemp. 150.00
VM Victor Martinez/Jsy 30.00
MA Don Mattingly/Jsy 100.00
JM Joe Mauer/Jsy/Redemp. 35.00
BM Bill Mazeroski/Jsy/Redemp. 30.00
WM Willie McCovey/Jsy 50.00
DMA Dallas McPherson/Jsy/Redemp. 30.00
PM Paul Molitor/Jsy 40.00
MM Mark Mulder/Jsy 25.00
DMN Dale Murphy/Jsy 35.00
GN Graig Nettles/Jsy 35.00
PN Phil Niekro/Jsy 25.00
LN Laynce Nix/Jsy 20.00

DO	David Ortiz/Jsy	50.00
RO	Roy Oswalt/Jsy	25.00
AO	Akinori Otsuka/Jsy	40.00
JPA	Jim Palmer/Jsy	40.00
CP	Corey Patterson/Jsy/Redemp.	30.00
JPN	Jake Peavy/Jsy	50.00
BPN	Brad Penny/Jsy	20.00
RP	Rico Petrocelli/Pants	25.00
SP	Scott Podsednik/Jsy	25.00
MP	Mark Prior/Jsy	50.00
AP	Albert Pujols/Jsy/Redemp.	220.00
JRN	Jose Reyes/Jsy/Redemp.	40.00
JRA	Jim Rice/Jsy	40.00
CR	Cal Ripken Jr./Jsy	200.00
BR	Brooks Robinson/Jsy	50.00
FR	Frank Robinson/Jsy	40.00
SR	Scott Rolen/Jsy/Redemp.	75.00
NR	Nolan Ryan/Jsy	125.00
JSA	Johan Santana/Jsy/Redemp.	65.00
JSN	Jason Schmidt/Jsy	50.00
MS	Mike Schmidt/Jsy	60.00
TS	Tom Seaver/Jsy	50.00
BS	Ben Sheets/Jsy/Redemp.	30.00
SM	John Smoltz/Jsy/Redemp.	75.00
SU	Bruce Sutter/Jsy	20.00
ST	Shingo Takatsu/Jsy	50.00
MT	Mark Teixeira/Jsy	45.00
BU	B.J. Upton/Jsy	25.00
RW	Rickie Weeks/Jsy	20.00
MW	Maury Wills/Jsy	25.00
KW	Kerry Wood/Jsy	50.00
DW	David Wright/Jsy	65.00
CY	Carl Yastrzemski/Jsy	85.00
MY	Michael Young/Jsy/Redemp.	25.00
RY	Robin Yount/Jsy	75.00
CZ	Carlos Zambrano/Jsy	35.00

Autofacts

NM/M

Production 15-699
Rainbow: No Pricing
Production One Set

JB	Jason Bay/599	15.00
AB	Adrian Beltre/75 Redemp.	25.00
BE	Johnny Bench/15	75.00
HB	Hank Blalock/25	35.00
GB	George Brett/15	140.00
MI	Miguel Cabrera/25	40.00
OC	Orlando Cepeda/25	35.00
EC	Eric Chavez/25	30.00
RC	Rocky Colavito/75	75.00
BC	Bobby Crosby/350 Redemp.	15.00
AD	Andre Dawson/25	30.00
BF	Bob Feller/25	40.00
SF	Sid Fernandez/599	10.00
LD1	Lenny Dykstra Mets/599	10.00
LD2	Lenny Dykstra Phils/599	10.00
FR	Bill Freehan/599 Redemp.	10.00
GI	Marcus Giles/350	12.00
DG1	Dwight Gooden Mets/350	15.00
DG2	Dwight Gooden Yanks/350	15.00
GR	Khalil Greene/599	25.00
JR	Ken Griffey Jr./699	75.00
KG1	Ken Griffey Sr. Reds/699	10.00
KG2	Ken Griffey Sr. Yanks/699	10.00
TH	Travis Hafner/599	12.00
RH	Rich Harden/599	20.00
KH1	Keith Hernandez Mets/350	15.00
KH2	Keith Hernandez Cards/350	15.00
HO	Ken Holtzman/599	10.00
BH	Burt Hooton/599	8.00
HR	Kent Hrbek/599	15.00
AH	Aubrey Huff/350	8.00
DJ	Derek Jeter/350	150.00
JK1	Jim Kaat Cards/458	15.00
JK2	Jim Kaat Twins/458	15.00
AK	Al Kaline/15	80.00
DK	Dave Kingman/75	25.00
CK	Casey Kotchman/599	10.00
EK	Ed Kranepool	12.00
JL	Jim Lonborg/599	15.00
ML	Mike Lowell/75	15.00
SL1	Sparky Lyle Sox/599	8.00
SL2	Sparky Lyle Yanks/599	8.00
FL	Fred Lynn/25	25.00
VM	Victor Martinez/599	15.00
JM	Joe Mauer/25 Redemp.	30.00
MC	Dallas McPherson/599 Redemp.	20.00
PM	Paul Molitor/15	
DM	Dale Murphy/75	25.00
GN	Graig Nettles/75	25.00
PN1	Phil Niekro Braves/75	20.00
PN2	Phil Niekro Yanks/75	20.00
LN	Laynce Nix/599	10.00
RO	Roy Oswalt/350	15.00
AO	Akinori Otsuka/599	25.00
JP	Jim Palmer/25	35.00
CP	Corey Patterson/75 Redemp.	25.00
JA	Jake Peavy/75	30.00
BP	Brad Penny/599	15.00
OP	Oliver Perez/350	15.00
PE	Jim Perry/599	10.00
RP	Rico Petrocelli/599	15.00
SP	Scott Podsednik/75	15.00
PO	Boog Powell/350	15.00
MP	Mark Prior/15	50.00
CR	Cal Ripken Jr./15	200.00
BR	Brooks Robinson/25	50.00
NR	Nolan Ryan/15	175.00
JS	Johan Santana/350 Redemp.	40.00
BS	Ben Sheets/75 Redemp.	20.00
SU	Bruce Sutter/350	12.00
ST	Shingo Takatsu/599	20.00
MT	Mark Teixeira/25	40.00
LT	Luis Tiant/75	20.00
BU	B.J. Upton/599	15.00
RW	Rickie Weeks/75	15.00
KW	Kerry Wood/15	50.00
DW	David Wright/599	50.00
MY	Michael Young/599 Redemp.	12.00

Dual Artifacts

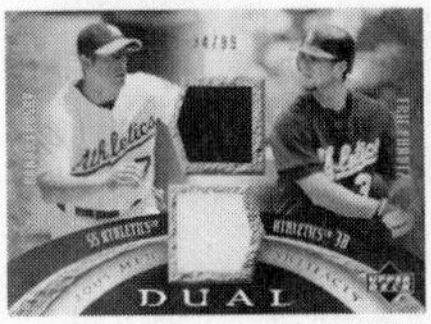

NM/M

Production 99 Sets
Rainbow: 1-2X
Production 25 Sets

AB	Bobby Abreu/Jsy, Carlos Beltran/Jsy	15.00
AD	Adrian Beltre/Jsy, Dallas McPherson/Jsy	15.00
AG	Bobby Abreu/Jsy, Ken Griffey Jr./Jsy	15.00
BB	George Brett/Jsy, Wade Boggs/Jsy	20.00
BC	Adrian Beltre/Jsy, Eric Chavez/Jsy	8.00
BD	Bob Gibson/Pants, Dwight Gooden/Pants	8.00
BE	Bobby Crosby/Jsy, Eric Chavez/Jsy	10.00
BJ	Brooks Robinson/Jsy, Jim Palmer/Jsy	20.00
BK	Jason Bay/Jsy, Ralph Kiner/Bat	10.00
BM	Brian Giles/Jsy, Marcus Giles/Jsy	8.00
BN	Hank Blalock/Jsy, Laynce Nix/Jsy	8.00
BP	Carlos Beltran/Jsy, Corey Patterson/Jsy	12.00
BR	Ernie Banks/Pants, Frank Robinson/Jsy	20.00
BS	Ben Sheets/Jsy, Scott Podsednik/Jsy	8.00
BY	Hank Blalock/Jsy, Michael Young/Jsy	8.00
CB	Jason Bay/Jsy, Bobby Crosby/Jsy	8.00
CC	Miguel Cabrera/Jsy, Orlando Cepeda/Jsy	12.00
CG	Dwight Gooden/Pants, Gary Carter/Jsy	10.00
CH	Sean Casey/Jsy, Travis Hafner/Jsy	8.00
CK	Harmon Killebrew/Jsy, Rod Carew/Jsy	25.00
CL	Miguel Cabrera/Jsy, Mike Lowell/Jsy	10.00
CM	Will Clark/Jsy, Willie McCovey/Jsy/56	25.00
CN	Eric Chavez/Jsy, Graig Nettles/Jsy	8.00
CO	Roger Clemens/Jsy, Roy Oswalt/Jsy	15.00
CR	Bobby Crosby/Jsy, Cal Ripken Jr./Jsy	40.00
DC	Andre Dawson/Jsy, Orlando Cepeda/Jsy	10.00
DK	Bobby Doerr/Bat, George Kell/Bat	10.00
FB	Carlton Fisk/Jsy, Johnny Bench/Jsy	20.00
FW	Bob Feller/Pants, Kerry Wood/Jsy	15.00
GB	Brian Giles/Jsy, Jason Bay/Jsy	8.00
GC	Ken Griffey Jr./Jsy, Sean Casey/Jsy	15.00
GG	Ken Griffey Sr./Jsy, Ken Griffey Jr./Jsy	15.00
GK	Ken Griffey Jr./Jsy, Ralph Kiner/Bat	20.00
GL	Eric Gagne/Jsy, Sparky Lyle/Pants	10.00
GS	Dwight Gooden/Pants, Tom Seaver/Jsy	15.00
HC	Bobby Crosby/Jsy, Rich Harden/Jsy	8.00
HG	Keith Hernandez/Bat, Mark Grace/Jsy	10.00
HH	Aubrey Huff/Jsy, Travis Hafner/Jsy	8.00
HM	Travis Hafner/Jsy, Victor Martinez/Jsy	8.00
HU	Aubrey Huff/Jsy, B.J. Upton/Jsy	10.00
HW	Harmon Killebrew/Jsy, Willie McCovey/Jsy/44	25.00
JG	Derek Jeter/Jsy, Khalil Greene/Jsy	35.00
JJ	Joe Mauer/Jsy, Johan Santana/Jsy	15.00
JR	Jim Rice/Jsy, Rico Petrocelli/Pants	8.00
JW	Derek Jeter/Jsy, Maury Wills/Jsy	35.00
JY	Johnny Bench/Jsy, Yogi Berra/Pants	25.00
KB	Jim Kaat/Jsy, Bert Blyleven/Jsy	10.00
KC	Jim Kaat/Jsy, Steve Carlton/Jsy	10.00
KD	Keith Hernandez/Bat, Don Mattingly/Jsy	20.00
KK	Al Kaline/Jsy, Ralph Kiner/Bat	15.00
KM	Al Kaline/Jsy, Dale Murphy/Jsy	15.00
KN	Jim Kaat/Jsy, Phil Niekro/Jsy	10.00
LC	Derrek Lee/Jsy, Sean Casey/Jsy	10.00
LG	Derrek Lee/Jsy, Mark Grace/Jsy	10.00
LP	Fred Lynn/Bat, Rico Petrocelli/Pants	10.00
LR	Fred Lynn/Bat, Jim Rice/Jsy	10.00
MC	Don Mattingly/Jsy, Will Clark/Jsy	20.00
MD	Bill Mazeroski/Jsy, Bobby Doerr/Bat	10.00
MH	Mark Mulder/Jsy, Rich Harden/Jsy	10.00
MK	Bill Mazeroski/Jsy, Ralph Kiner/Bat	20.00
MM	Joe Mauer/Jsy, Victor Martinez/Jsy	8.00
MS	Dale Murphy/Jsy, Mike Schmidt/Jsy	20.00
MW	Paul Molitor/Jsy, Rickie Weeks/Jsy	15.00
NL	Graig Nettles/Jsy, Sparky Lyle/Pants	15.00
NT	Laynce Nix/Jsy, Mark Teixeira/Jsy	10.00
NY	Laynce Nix/Jsy, Michael Young/Jsy	10.00
OF	David Ortiz/Jsy, Carlton Fisk/Jsy	20.00
OG	Akinori Otsuka/Jsy, Khalil Greene/Jsy	15.00
OP	Akinori Otsuka/Jsy, Jake Peavy/Jsy	15.00
OT	Akinori Otsuka/Jsy, Shingo Takatsu/Jsy	20.00
PD	Andre Dawson/Jsy, Corey Patterson/Jsy	15.00
PG	Brad Penny/Jsy, Eric Gagne/Jsy	10.00
PH	Jake Peavy/Jsy, Rich Harden/Jsy	12.00
PP	Boog Powell/Jsy, Jim Palmer/Jsy	15.00
PR	Boog Powell/Jsy, Brooks Robinson/Jsy	20.00
PS	Brad Penny/Jsy, Jason Schmidt/Jsy	8.00
RB	Ernie Banks/Pants, Cal Ripken Jr./Jsy	40.00
RC	Nolan Ryan/Jsy, Steve Carlton/Jsy	30.00
RJ	Jose Reyes/Jsy, Rickie Weeks/Jsy	10.00
RP	Frank Robinson/Jsy, Boog Powell/Jsy	25.00
RR	Frank Robinson/Jsy, Brooks Robinson/Jsy	25.00
RW	David Wright/Jsy, Scott Rolen/Jsy	15.00
SB	Bert Blyleven/Jsy, Johan Santana/Jsy	15.00
SC	Johan Santana/Jsy, Roger Clemens/Jsy	20.00
SF	Ben Sheets/Jsy, Bob Feller/Pants	15.00
SG	Bruce Sutter/Jsy, Eric Gagne/Jsy	15.00
SM	Jason Schmidt/Jsy, Mark Mulder/Jsy	10.00
SO	Ben Sheets/Jsy, Roy Oswalt/Jsy	10.00
SP	Ben Sheets/Jsy, Brad Penny/Jsy	10.00
TH	Mark Teixeira/Jsy, Travis Hafner/Jsy	10.00
TL	Shingo Takatsu/Jsy, Sparky Lyle/Pants	10.00
TY	Mark Teixeira/Jsy, Michael Young/Jsy	10.00
UJ	B.J. Upton/Jsy, Derek Jeter/Jsy	30.00
WL	David Wright/Jsy, Mike Lowell/Jsy	10.00
WR	David Wright/Jsy, Jose Reyes/Jsy	10.00
YM	Robin Yount/Jsy, Paul Molitor/Jsy	25.00
YP	Carl Yastrzemski/Jsy, Rico Petrocelli/Pants	15.00
ZM	Carlos Zambrano/Jsy, Greg Maddux/Jsy	15.00
ZP	Carlos Zambrano/Jsy, Mark Prior/Jsy	10.00
ZW	Carlos Zambrano/Jsy, Kerry Wood/Jsy	20.00

Dual Artifacts Bat

NM/M

Production 25 Sets

BC	Josh Beckett, Miguel Cabrera	20.00
BW	Josh Beckett, Kerry Wood	20.00
DR	Carlos Delgado, Manny Ramirez	20.00
GC	Ken Griffey Jr., Miguel Cabrera	30.00
GS	Ken Griffey Sr., Ichiro Suzuki	80.00
JP	Derek Jeter, Mike Piazza	50.00
JR	Derek Jeter, Manny Ramirez	50.00
RG	Manny Ramirez, Vladimir Guerrero	20.00
RJ	Cal Ripken Jr., Derek Jeter	100.00
RT	Cal Ripken Jr., Miguel Tejada	60.00
SG	Ichiro Suzuki, Vladimir Guerrero	60.00
WP	Kerry Wood, Mark Prior	25.00

Dual Artifacts Signatures

No Pricing
Production 10 Sets

MLB Apparel

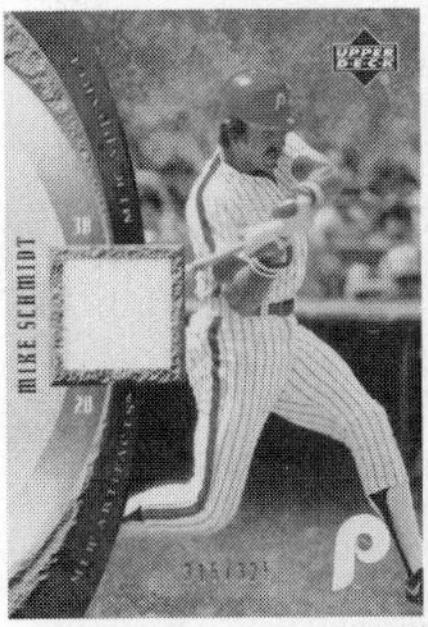

NM/M

Production 325 unless noted.
Rainbow: 1-2X
Production 99 Sets

BA	Bobby Abreu/Jsy	6.00
GA	Garret Anderson/Jsy	6.00
JB	Jason Bay/Jsy	6.00
CB	Carlos Beltran/Jsy	8.00
AB	Adrian Beltre/Jsy	6.00
BE	Johnny Bench/Jsy	10.00
YB	Yogi Berra/Pants	15.00
HB	Hank Blalock/Jsy	8.00
BB	Bert Blyleven/Jsy/150	8.00
WB	Wade Boggs/Jsy	8.00
BO	Bret Boone/Jsy	4.00
GB	George Brett/Jsy	15.00
MI	Miguel Cabrera/Jsy	10.00
RC	Rod Carew/Jsy	8.00
CA	Steve Carlton/Jsy	6.00
GC	Gary Carter/Jsy	8.00
SC	Sean Casey/Jsy	4.00
OC	Orlando Cepeda/Jsy	8.00
EC	Eric Chavez/Jsy	4.00
WC	Will Clark/Jsy/100	10.00
CL	Roger Clemens/Jsy	15.00
BC	Bobby Crosby/Jsy	6.00
AD	Andre Dawson/Jsy	6.00
BF	Bob Feller/Pants	10.00
CF	Carlton Fisk R. Sox/Jsy/175	10.00
CF1	Carlton Fisk W. Sox/Jsy/175	10.00
EG	Eric Gagne/Jsy	8.00
BG	Bob Gibson/Pants	10.00
GI	Brian Giles/Jsy	4.00
GS	Marcus Giles/Jsy	4.00
DG	Dwight Gooden/Pants	6.00
MK	Mark Grace/Jsy/175	8.00
KL	Khalil Greene/Jsy	8.00
KG	Ken Griffey Jr./Jsy	15.00
GR	Ken Griffey Sr./Jsy	4.00
TG	Tony Gwynn/Jsy	10.00
TH	Travis Hafner/Jsy	4.00
RH	Rich Harden/Jsy	8.00
KH	Kent Hrbek/Jsy	4.00
HU	Tim Hudson/Jsy	6.00
AH	Aubrey Huff/Jsy	4.00
TO	Torii Hunter/Jsy	4.00
DJ	Derek Jeter/Jsy	20.00

JJ Jacque Jones/Jsy 4.00
JK Jim Kaat/Jsy 6.00
AK Al Kaline/Jsy 10.00
HK Harmon Killebrew/Jsy 10.00
CK Casey Kotchman/Jsy 4.00
DL Derrek Lee/Jsy 6.00
ML Mike Lowell/Jsy 4.00
SL Sparky Lyle/Pants 4.00
VM Victor Martinez/Jsy 6.00
MA Don Mattingly/Jsy 20.00
JM Joe Mauer/Jsy 10.00
BM Bill Mazeroski/Jsy/100 12.00
WM Willie McCovey/Jsy 8.00
MC Dallas McPherson/Jsy 8.00
PM Paul Molitor/Jsy 8.00
MM Mark Mulder/Jsy 6.00
DM Dale Murphy/Jsy/150 8.00
GN Graig Nettles/Jsy 4.00
PN Phil Niekro/Jsy 4.00
LN Laynce Nix/Jsy 4.00
DO David Ortiz/Jsy 10.00
RO Roy Oswalt/Jsy 4.00
AO Akinori Otsuka/Jsy 4.00
PA Jim Palmer/Jsy 8.00
CP Corey Patterson/Jsy 6.00
JP Jake Peavy/Jsy 6.00
PE Brad Penny/Jsy 4.00
RP Rico Petrocelli/Pants 8.00
SP Scott Podsednik/Jsy 4.00
BP Boog Powell/Jsy 6.00
MP Mark Prior/Jsy 8.00
RE Jose Reyes/Jsy 8.00
JR Jim Rice/Jsy 8.00
CR Cal Ripken Jr./Jsy 25.00
BR Brooks Robinson/Jsy 8.00
FR Frank Robinson/Jsy 8.00
SR Scott Rolen/Jsy 10.00
NR Nolan Ryan/Jsy 25.00
SA Johan Santana/Jsy 10.00
JS Jason Schmidt/Jsy 6.00
MS Mike Schmidt/Jsy 15.00
TS Tom Seaver/Jsy/300 8.00
BS Ben Sheets/Jsy 6.00
SM John Smoltz/Jsy 8.00
SU Bruce Sutter/Jsy 6.00
ST Shingo Takatsu/Jsy 6.00
MT Mark Teixeira/Jsy 8.00
BU B.J. Upton/Jsy 6.00
JV Jose Vidro/Jsy 4.00
RW Rickie Weeks/Jsy 6.00
MW Maury Wills/Jsy 6.00
KW Kerry Wood/Jsy 8.00
DW David Wright/Jsy 10.00
CY Carl Yastrzemski/Jsy 15.00
MY Michael Young/Jsy 6.00
RY Robin Yount/Jsy 15.00
CZ Carlos Zambrano/Jsy 6.00

MLB Apparel Autographs

NM/M

Production 30 Sets
Rare: No Pricing
Production One Set
BA Bobby Abreu/Jsy/Redemp. 25.00
GA Garret Anderson/Jsy 20.00
JB Jason Bay/Jsy 30.00
CB Carlos Beltran/Jsy/Redemp. 25.00
AB Adrian Beltre/Jsy 25.00
BE Johnny Bench/Jsy 65.00
YB Yogi Berra/Pants 60.00
HB Hank Blalock/Jsy 25.00
BB Bert Blyleven/Jsy 30.00
WB Wade Boggs/Jsy 50.00
BO Bret Boone/Jsy 20.00
GB George Brett/Jsy 100.00
MI Miguel Cabrera/Jsy 40.00
RC Rod Carew/Jsy 40.00
CA Steve Carlton/Jsy 30.00
GC Gary Carter/Jsy 30.00
SC Sean Casey/Jsy 30.00
OC Orlando Cepeda/Jsy 35.00
EC Eric Chavez/Jsy/Redemp. 30.00
WC Will Clark/Jsy 50.00
CL Roger Clemens/Jsy/Redemp. 120.00
BC Bobby Crosby/Jsy/Redemp. 20.00
AD Andre Dawson/Jsy 30.00
BF Bob Feller/Pants 40.00
CF Carlton Fisk R. Sox/Jsy 40.00
CF1 Carlton Fisk W. Sox/Jsy 40.00
EG Eric Gagne/Jsy 30.00
BG Bob Gibson/Pants 50.00
GI Brian Giles/Jsy 20.00
GS Marcus Giles/Jsy 20.00
DG Dwight Gooden/Pants 30.00
MK Mark Grace/Jsy 40.00
KL Khalil Greene/Jsy 30.00
KG Ken Griffey Jr./Jsy 120.00
GR Ken Griffey Sr./Jsy 25.00
TG Tony Gwynn/Jsy 80.00
TH Travis Hafner/Jsy 25.00
RH Rich Harden/Jsy 30.00
KH Kent Hrbek/Jsy 50.00
HU Tim Hudson/Jsy 40.00
AH Aubrey Huff/Jsy 25.00
TO Torii Hunter/Jsy 25.00
DJ Derek Jeter/Jsy 200.00
JJ Jacque Jones/Jsy 20.00
JK Jim Kaat/Jsy 25.00
AK Al Kaline/Jsy 50.00
HK Harmon Killebrew/Jsy 60.00
CK Casey Kotchman/Jsy 25.00
DL Derrek Lee/Jsy 40.00
ML Mike Lowell/Jsy 20.00
SL Sparky Lyle/Pants 20.00
VM Victor Martinez/Jsy 25.00
MA Don Mattingly/Jsy 100.00
JM Joe Mauer/Jsy/Redemp. 35.00
BM Bill Mazeroski/Jsy 30.00
WM Willie McCovey/Jsy 50.00
MC Dallas McPherson/Jsy/Redemp. 20.00
PM Paul Molitor/Jsy 40.00
MM Mark Mulder/Jsy 20.00
DM Dale Murphy/Jsy 35.00
GN Graig Nettles/Jsy 35.00
PN Phil Niekro/Jsy 25.00
LN Laynce Nix/Jsy 20.00
DO David Ortiz/Jsy 50.00
RO Roy Oswalt/Jsy 25.00
AO Akinori Otsuka/Jsy 40.00
PA Jim Palmer/Jsy 40.00
CP Corey Patterson/Jsy/Redemp. 30.00
JP Jake Peavy/Jsy 40.00
PE Brad Penny/Jsy 20.00
RP Rico Petrocelli/Pants 25.00
SP Scott Podsednik/Jsy 25.00
BP Boog Powell/Jsy 25.00
MP Mark Prior/Jsy 35.00
RE Jose Reyes/Jsy/Redemp. 40.00
JR Jim Rice/Jsy 30.00
CR Cal Ripken Jr./Jsy 200.00
BR Brooks Robinson/Jsy 50.00
FR Frank Robinson/Jsy 40.00
SR Scott Rolen/Jsy/Redemp. 75.00
NR Nolan Ryan/Jsy 125.00
SA Johan Santana/Jsy/Redemp. 50.00
JS Jason Schmidt/Jsy 30.00
MS Mike Schmidt/Jsy 60.00
TS Tom Seaver/Jsy 50.00
BS Ben Sheets/Jsy/Redemp. 25.00
SM John Smoltz/Jsy/Redemp. 75.00
SU Bruce Sutter/Jsy 20.00
ST Shingo Takatsu/Jsy 25.00
MT Mark Teixeira/Jsy 40.00
BU B.J. Upton/Jsy 25.00
JV Jose Vidro/Jsy 20.00
RW Rickie Weeks/Jsy 25.00
MW Maury Wills/Jsy 25.00
KW Kerry Wood/Jsy 30.00
DW David Wright/Jsy 80.00
CY Carl Yastrzemski/Jsy 85.00
MY Michael Young/Jsy/Redemp. 25.00
RY Robin Yount 75.00
CZ Carlos Zambrano/Jsy 35.00

Patches

NM/M

Production 50 unless noted.
BA Bobby Abreu 15.00
GA Garret Anderson 15.00
JB Jason Bay 20.00
CB Carlos Beltran 20.00
AB Adrian Beltre 20.00
BE Johnny Bench 25.00
HB Hank Blalock 20.00
BB Bert Blyleven 20.00
WB Wade Boggs 20.00
BO Bret Boone 12.00
GB George Brett 40.00
MI Miguel Cabrera 25.00
RC Rod Carew 25.00
CA Steve Carlton/30 25.00
GC Gary Carter 30.00
SC Sean Casey 12.00
EC Eric Chavez 15.00
WC Will Clark/20 50.00
CL Roger Clemens 30.00
BC Bobby Crosby 20.00
AD Andre Dawson 20.00
EG Eric Gagne 20.00
GI Brian Giles 12.00
GS Marcus Giles 12.00
DG Dwight Gooden 20.00
MK Mark Grace 35.00
KL Khalil Greene 25.00
KG Ken Griffey Jr. 40.00
GR Ken Griffey Sr. 12.00
TG Tony Gwynn 25.00
TH Travis Hafner 15.00
RH Rich Harden 20.00
KH Kent Hrbek 35.00
HU Tim Hudson 20.00
AH Aubrey Huff 12.00
TO Torii Hunter 15.00
DJ Derek Jeter 65.00
RJ Randy Johnson 25.00
JJ Jacque Jones 15.00
JK Jim Kaat 20.00
HK Harmon Killebrew 40.00
CK Casey Kotchman 20.00
DL Derrek Lee 15.00
ML Mike Lowell 12.00
GM Greg Maddux 35.00
VM Victor Martinez 15.00
MA Don Mattingly 40.00
JM Joe Mauer 30.00
WM Willie McCovey 25.00
MC Dallas McPherson 20.00
MM Mark Mulder 20.00
DM Dale Murphy 25.00
GN Graig Nettles 20.00
PN Phil Niekro 20.00
LN Laynce Nix 12.00
DO David Ortiz 25.00
RO Roy Oswalt 15.00
AO Akinori Otsuka 25.00
PA Jim Palmer 20.00
CP Corey Patterson 25.00
JP Jake Peavy 20.00
PE Brad Penny 12.00
SP Scott Podsednik 12.00
BP Boog Powell 20.00
MP Mark Prior 20.00
RE Jose Reyes 20.00
CR Cal Ripken Jr. 60.00
BR Brooks Robinson/35 40.00
FR Frank Robinson 20.00
SR Scott Rolen 25.00
NR Nolan Ryan 50.00
SA Johan Santana 25.00
JS Jason Schmidt 25.00
MS Mike Schmidt 30.00
BS Ben Sheets 20.00
SM John Smoltz 30.00
SU Bruce Sutter 15.00
ST Shingo Takatsu 20.00
MT Mark Teixeira 20.00
BU B.J. Upton 20.00
JV Jose Vidro 12.00
RW Rickie Weeks 20.00
MW Maury Wills/20 20.00
KW Kerry Wood 25.00
DW David Wright 35.00
CY Carl Yastrzemski 40.00
MY Michael Young 15.00
RY Robin Yount 30.00
CZ Carlos Zambrano 25.00

Signature Patches

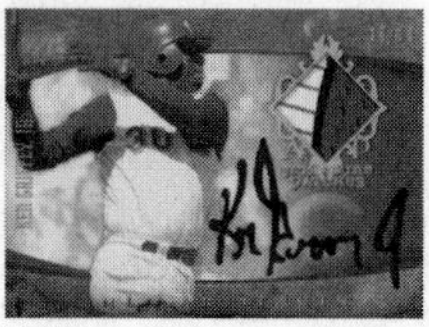

No Pricing
Production 10 unless noted.

2005 Upper Deck Baseball Heroes

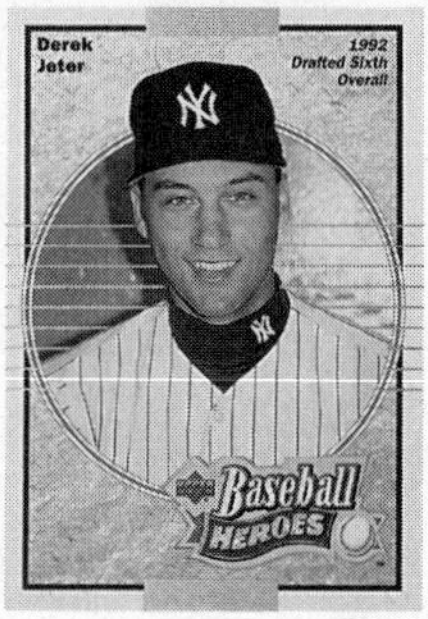

NM/M

Complete Set (200):
Common (1-100): 2.00
Common (101-200): 2.00
Production 575
Tin (8): 50.00
1-5 Bob Feller 3.00
6-10 Brooks Robinson 3.00
11-15 Cal Ripken Jr. 8.00
16-20 Carl Yastrzemski 5.00
21-25 Don Mattingly 6.00
26-30 Tom Seaver 3.00
31-35 Harmon Killebrew 3.00
36-40 Jim Palmer 2.00
41-45 Mike Schmidt 6.00
46-50 Ozzie Smith 4.00
51-55 Paul Molitor 3.00
56-60 Al Kaline 3.00
61-65 Robin Yount 4.00
66-70 Ryne Sandberg 4.00
71-75 Stan Musial 5.00
76-80 Steve Carlton 2.00
81-85 Tony Gwynn 3.00
86-90 Wade Boggs 3.00
91-95 Will Clark 3.00
96-100 Yogi Berra 4.00
101-105 Babe Ruth 8.00
106-110 Roger Maris 6.00
111-115 Don Drysdale 2.00
116-120 Eddie Mathews 4.00
121-125 Honus Wagner 6.00
126-130 Jackie Robinson 5.00
131-135 Jimmie Foxx 5.00
136-140 Joe DiMaggio 6.00
141-145 Johnny Mize 4.00
146-150 Lefty Grove 3.00
151-155 Lou Gehrig 6.00
156-160 Mel Ott 4.00
161-165 Mickey Mantle 12.00
166-170 Roberto Clemente 8.00
171-175 Rogers Hornsby 6.00
176-180 Roy Campanella 3.00
181-185 Satchel Paige 6.00
186-190 Ted Williams 8.00
191-195 Thurman Munson 5.00
196-200 Ty Cobb 5.00

Blue

No Pricing
Production 10 Sets

Emerald

Emerald (1-100): 1-1.5X
Emerald (101-200): 1-1.5X
Production 199 Sets

Gold

No Pricing
Production One Set

Red

Red (1-200): 1-2X
Production 75 Sets

Baseball Heroes Jeter

NM/M

Complete Set (9): 25.00
Common Jeter: 3.00
Inserted 1:6
91-100 Derek Jeter 3.00

Baseball Heroes Jeter Jersey

No Pricing
Production 75 Sets

Baseball Heroes Jeter Signature

No Pricing
Production Two Sets

Memorabilia

No Pricing
Production 10 Sets

Memorabilia Emerald

NM/M

Production 99 Sets
Blue: 1X
Production 99 Sets
Bronze: 1-1.5X
Production 50 Sets
Gold: No Pricing
Production One Set
Red: 1X
Production 99 Sets
Silver: No Pricing
Production 15 Sets
1-5 Bob Feller 10.00
6-10 Brooks Robinson 10.00
11-15 Cal Ripken Jr. 25.00
16-20 Carl Yastrzemski 15.00
21-25 Don Mattingly 20.00
26-30 Tom Seaver 10.00
31-35 Harmon Killebrew 10.00
36-40 Jim Palmer 8.00
41-45 Mike Schmidt 20.00
46-50 Ozzie Smith 20.00
51-55 Paul Molitor 10.00
56-60 Al Kaline 12.00
61-65 Robin Yount 15.00
66-70 Ryne Sandberg 15.00
71-75 Stan Musial 20.00
76-80 Steve Carlton 10.00
81-85 Tony Gwynn 20.00
86-90 Wade Boggs 10.00
91-95 Will Clark 10.00
96-100 Yogi Berra 15.00

Signature Cuts

No Pricing
Production 1-10

Signature Emerald

NM/M

Production 99 Sets
Blue: 1-1.5X
Production 20 Sets
Red: 1X
Production 49 Sets
Gold: No Pricing
Production One Set
Patches: No Pricing
Production Five Sets
1-5 Bob Feller 35.00
6-10 Brooks Robinson 35.00
11-15 Cal Ripken Jr. 125.00
16-20 Carl Yastrzemski 65.00
21-25 Don Mattingly 60.00
26-30 Tom Seaver 50.00
31-35 Harmon Killebrew 40.00
36-40 Jim Palmer 25.00
41-45 Mike Schmidt 50.00
46-50 Ozzie Smith 50.00
51-55 Paul Molitor 30.00
56-60 Al Kaline 40.00
61-65 Robin Yount 40.00
66-70 Ryne Sandberg 50.00
71-75 Stan Musial 75.00
76-80 Steve Carlton 25.00
81-85 Tony Gwynn 40.00
86-90 Wade Boggs 35.00
91-95 Will Clark 30.00
96-100 Yogi Berra 60.00

Signature Memorabilia

No Pricing
Production 15 Sets

2005 Upper Deck Classics

		NM/M
Complete Set (130):		50.00
Common Player:		.15
Common SP (101-130):		1.00
Inserted 1:4		
Pack (8):		3.00
Hobby Box (28):		60.00
1	Al Kaline	.50
2	Al Lopez	.15
3	Allie Reynolds	.15
4	Babe Herman	.15
5	Bill Mazeroski	.15
6	Bill Russell	.15
7	Billy Herman	.15
8	Billy Williams	.25
9	Bob Feller	.50
10	Bob Gibson	.75
11	Bob Lemon	.15
12	Bobby Doerr	.15
13	Boog Powell	.15
14	Ken Hubbs	.15
15	Brooks Robinson	.75
16	Buck Leonard	.15
17	Cal Ripken Jr.	2.00
18	Carl Hubbell	.15
19	Jim "Catfish" Hunter	.25
20	Johnny Hopp	.15
21	Charlie Gehringer	.15
22	Curt Flood	.15
23	Jimmie Foxx	.75
24	Dave McNally	.15
25	Davey Lopes	.15
26	Don Drysdale	.50
27	Don Sutton	.50
28	Earl Weaver	.15
29	Early Wynn	.15
30	Edd Roush	.15
31	Eddie Mathews	.75
32	Enos Slaughter	.15
33	Fergie Jenkins	.50
34	Frank Howard	.15
35	Leon Wagner	.15
36	Frank Crosetti	.15
37	Gaylord Perry	.15
38	George Bell	.15
39	George Kell	.15
40	Graig Nettles	.15
41	Hal Newhouser	.15
42	Harmon Killebrew	.75
43	Harvey Kuenn	.15
44	Howard Johnson	.15
45	Hoyt Wilhelm	.15
46	Jack Clark	.15
47	Jack Morris	.15
48	Jim Bunning	.15
49	Jim Palmer	.50
50	Joe Adcock	.15
51	Joe Carter	.15
52	Casey Stengel	.50
53	Joe Morgan	.50
54	Joe Sewell	.15
55	"Smoky" Joe Wood	.15
56	Johnny Bench	.75
57	Johnny Mize	.15
58	Jose Canseco	.50
59	Juan Marichal	.50
60	Keith Hernandez	.15
61	Ken Griffey Sr.	.15
62	Ken Hrbek	.15
63	Kevin Mitchell	.15
64	Kirk Gibson	.25
65	Larry Doby	.15
66	Lou Boudreau	.15
67	Lou Brock	.50
68	Luis Aparicio	.15
69	Luke Appling	.15
70	Monte Irvin	.50
71	Nellie Fox	.15
72	Norm Cash	.15
73	Orlando Cepeda	.25
74	Pedro Guerrero	.15
75	Pee Wee Reese	.15
76	Phil Niekro	.15
77	Phil Rizzuto	.50
78	Ralph Kiner	.15
79	Ray Dandridge	.15
80	Red Schoendienst	.15
81	Richie Ashburn	.15
82	Rick Ferrell	.15
83	Robin Roberts	.50
84	Rollie Fingers	.15
85	Ron Cey	.15
86	Sparky Anderson	.15
87	Stan Coveleski	.15
88	Ted Kluszewski	.15
89	Ted Lyons	.15
90	Tom Seaver	.50
91	Tommie Agee	.15
92	Tommy Lasorda	.15
93	Tony Perez	.25
94	Vada Pinson	.15
95	Waite Hoyt	.15
96	Warren Spahn	.75
97	Willie McCovey	.50
98	Lyman Bostock	.15
99	Willie Stargell	.50
100	Yogi Berra	.75
101	Andre Dawson	1.00
102	Andy Van Slyke	1.00
103	Bret Saberhagen	1.00
104	Carl Yastrzemski	2.50
105	Carlton Fisk	1.50
106	Dale Murphy	1.50
107	Darryl Strawberry	1.00
108	David Cone	1.00
109	Dennis Eckersley	1.50
110	Don Mattingly	2.50
111	Dwight Gooden	1.00
112	Eddie Murray	1.50
113	Eric Davis	1.00
114	Fred Lynn	1.00
115	George Brett	3.00
116	Jim Rice	1.00
117	John Kruk	1.50
118	Lenny Dykstra	1.00
119	Mickey Mantle	4.00
120	Mike Schmidt	3.00
121	Nolan Ryan	3.00
122	Ozzie Smith	2.00
123	Paul Molitor	2.00
124	Robin Yount	2.00
125	Ryne Sandberg	2.00
126	Steve Carlton	1.50
127	Ted Williams	3.00
128	Tony Gwynn	2.00
129	Wade Boggs	2.00
130	Will Clark	2.00

Gold

Gold (1-100):	2-4X
Gold (101-130):	1-2X
Production 199 Sets	

Platinum

Platinum (1-100):	5-10X
Platinum (101-130):	3-5X
Production 25 Sets	

Silver

Silver (1-100):	2-3X
Silver (101-130):	1-2X
Production 399 Sets	

Classic Counterparts

		NM/M
Common Duo:		2.00
Production 1,999 Sets		
CC	Will Clark, Jack Clark	2.00
CG	David Cone, Dwight Gooden	2.00
DS	Darryl Strawberry, Lenny Dykstra	2.00
GB	Wade Boggs, Tony Gwynn	4.00
GP	Ken Griffey Sr., Tony Perez	2.00
KD	John Kruk, Lenny Dykstra	2.00
KH	John Kruk, Kent Hrbek	2.00
LR	Jim Rice, Fred Lynn	2.00
MC	Kevin Mitchell, Will Clark	2.00
MH	Don Mattingly, Keith Hernandez	6.00
MY	Robin Yount, Paul Molitor	5.00
NC	Ron Cey, Graig Nettles	2.00
PH	Boog Powell, Frank Howard	2.00
RC	Steve Carlton, Nolan Ryan	8.00
RL	Bill Russell, Davey Lopes	2.00
RS	Tom Seaver, Nolan Ryan	8.00
SD	Darryl Strawberry, Eric Davis	2.00
SG	Dwight Gooden, Darryl Strawberry	2.00
SR	Cal Ripken Jr., Mike Schmidt	10.00
VC	Andy Van Slyke, Jack Clark	2.00

Classic Counterparts Materials

		NM/M
CC	Jack Clark, Will Clark	8.00
CG	David Cone, Dwight Gooden	8.00
DS	Darryl Strawberry, Lenny Dykstra	8.00
GB	Wade Boggs, Tony Gwynn	20.00
GP	Ken Griffey Sr., Tony Perez	8.00
KD	John Kruk, Lenny Dykstra	15.00
KH	John Kruk, Kent Hrbek	8.00
LR	Jim Rice, Fred Lynn	8.00
MC	Kevin Mitchell, Will Clark	8.00
MH	Don Mattingly, Keith Hernandez	15.00
MY	Robin Yount, Paul Molitor	15.00
NC	Graig Nettles, Ron Cey	8.00
PH	Boog Powell, Frank Howard	10.00
RC	Steve Carlton, Nolan Ryan	40.00
RL	Bill Russell, Davey Lopes	8.00
RS	Tom Seaver, Nolan Ryan	50.00
SD	Darryl Strawberry, Eric Davis	10.00
SG	Dwight Gooden, Darryl Strawberry	8.00
SR	Cal Ripken Jr., Mike Schmidt	50.00
VC	Andy Van Slyke, Jack Clark	10.00

Classic Counterparts Signature

		NM/M
DS	Darryl Strawberry, Lenny Dykstra	
GP	Ken Griffey Sr., Tony Perez	30.00
KD	John Kruk, Lenny Dykstra	40.00
KH	John Kruk, Kent Hrbek	40.00
LR	Jim Rice, Fred Lynn	40.00
NC	Graig Nettles, Ron Cey	35.00
RL	Bill Russell, Davey Lopes	25.00

Classic Cuts

		NM/M
Quantity produced listed		
FC	Frankie Crosetti/84	100.00
BH	Babe Herman/50	150.00
CH	Carl Hubbell/25	150.00
TL	Ted Lyons/83	120.00

Classic Materials

		NM/M
Common Player:		5.00
WB	Wade Boggs	10.00
GB	George Brett	10.00
CA	Jose Canseco	10.00
JC	Joe Carter	5.00
RC	Ron Cey	5.00
JC	Jack Clark	5.00
WC	Will Clark	8.00
DC	David Cone	8.00
ED	Eric Davis	10.00
AD	Andre Dawson	8.00
AD1	Andre Dawson	8.00
LD	Lenny Dykstra	8.00
DE	Dennis Eckersley	8.00
FI	Carlton Fisk	8.00
GI	Kirk Gibson	5.00
DG	Dwight Gooden	5.00
GG	Rich "Goose" Gossage	5.00
KG	Ken Griffey Jr.	5.00
PG	Pedro Guerrero	5.00
TG	Tony Gwynn	10.00
KH	Keith Hernandez	5.00
FH	Frank Howard	8.00
HR	Kent Hrbek	8.00
DL	Davey Lopes	5.00
FL	Fred Lynn	5.00
MA	Don Mattingly	15.00
PM	Paul Molitor	10.00
PM1	Paul Molitor/SP	10.00
JM	Jack Morris	5.00
DM	Dale Murphy	8.00
GN	Graig Nettles	10.00
BP	Boog Powell/SP	8.00
JR	Jim Rice	5.00
CR	Cal Ripken Jr.	25.00
BR	Bill Russell	5.00
NR	Nolan Ryan	20.00
RS	Ryne Sandberg	15.00
MS	Mike Schmidt	15.00
DS	Darryl Strawberry	10.00
AV	Andy Van Slyke	20.00
CY	Carl Yastrzemski	20.00
RY	Robin Yount	10.00

Classic Moments

		NM/M
Common Player:		2.00
Production 1,999 Sets		

		NM/M
WB	Wade Boggs	4.00
SC	Steve Carlton	2.00
CA	Joe Carter	2.00
JC	Jack Clark	2.00
LD	Lenny Dykstra	2.00
FI	Carlton Fisk	3.00
KG	Kirk Gibson	2.00
TG	Tony Gwynn	4.00
WJ	Wally Joyner	2.00
KM	Kevin Mitchell	2.00
PM	Paul Molitor	4.00
JM	Jack Morris	2.00
GP	Gaylord Perry	2.00
CR	Cal Ripken Jr.	10.00
NR	Nolan Ryan	8.00
BS	Bret Saberhagen	2.00
RS	Ryne Sandberg	5.00
MS	Mike Schmidt	6.00
DS	Don Sutton	2.00
RY	Robin Yount	5.00

Classic Moments Materials

		NM/M
Common Player:		5.00
WB	Wade Boggs	10.00
SC	Steve Carlton	8.00
CA	Joe Carter	5.00
JC	Jack Clark	5.00
LD	Lenny Dykstra	5.00
FI	Carlton Fisk	8.00
KG	Kirk Gibson	5.00
TG	Tony Gwynn	10.00
WJ	Wally Joyner	5.00
KM	Kevin Mitchell	5.00
PM	Paul Molitor	10.00
JM	Jack Morris	5.00
GP	Gaylord Perry	5.00
CR	Cal Ripken Jr.	25.00
NR	Nolan Ryan	20.00
RS	Ryne Sandberg	10.00
MS	Mike Schmidt	15.00
DS	Don Sutton	5.00
RY	Robin Yount	12.00

Classic Moments Signatures

		NM/M
Common Autograph:		10.00
SC	Steve Carlton	20.00
JC	Jack Clark	15.00
LD	Lenny Dykstra	15.00
FI	Carlton Fisk	40.00
KG	Kirk Gibson	25.00
TG	Tony Gwynn	40.00
WJ	Wally Joyner	20.00
KM	Kevin Mitchell	10.00
PM	Paul Molitor	25.00
JM	Jack Morris	20.00
GP	Gaylord Perry	15.00
BS	Bret Saberhagen	15.00
MS	Mike Schmidt	60.00
DS	Don Sutton	15.00
RY	Robin Yount	40.00

Classic Seasons

	NM/M
Common Player:	2.00
Production 1,999 Sets	

BE	George Bell	2.00
JC	Jose Canseco	3.00
CL	Jack Clark	2.00
WC	Will Clark	3.00
DC	David Cone	2.00
ED	Eric Davis	2.00
AD	Andre Dawson	2.00
KG	Kirk Gibson	2.00
DG	Dwight Gooden	2.00
FL	Fred Lynn	2.00
MA	Don Mattingly	6.00
KM	Kevin Mitchell	2.00
DM	Dale Murphy	3.00
JR	Jim Rice	2.00
CR	Cal Ripken Jr.	10.00
NR	Nolan Ryan	8.00
BS	Bret Saberhagen	2.00
RS	Ryne Sandberg	5.00
MS	Mike Schmidt	6.00
CY	Carl Yastrzemski	6.00

Classic Seasons Materials

		NM/M
Common Player:		5.00
BE	George Bell	5.00
JC	Jose Canseco	10.00
CL	Jack Clark	5.00
WC	Will Clark	8.00
DC	David Cone	5.00
ED	Eric Davis SP	8.00
AD	Andre Dawson	5.00
KG	Kirk Gibson	5.00
DG	Dwight Gooden	5.00
FL	Fred Lynn	5.00
MA	Don Mattingly	15.00
KM	Kevin Mitchell	5.00
DM	Dale Murphy	8.00
JR	Jim Rice	5.00
CR	Cal Ripken Jr.	25.00
NR	Nolan Ryan	20.00
RS	Ryne Sandberg	15.00
MS	Mike Schmidt	15.00
CY	Carl Yastrzemski	20.00

Classic Seasons Signatures

		NM/M
Common Auto.:		10.00
BE	George Bell	15.00
JC	Jose Canseco	40.00
CL	Jack Clark	15.00
WC	Will Clark	40.00
DC	David Cone	15.00
ED	Eric Davis	20.00
AD	Andre Dawson	20.00
KG	Kirk Gibson	25.00
DG	Dwight Gooden	12.00
FL	Fred Lynn	15.00
MA	Don Mattingly	60.00
KM	Kevin Mitchell	10.00
DM	Dale Murphy	20.00
BS	Bret Saberhagen	15.00
MS	Mike Schmidt	60.00

League Leaders

		NM/M
Common Player:		2.00
Production 999 Sets		
GB	George Bell	2.00
WB	Wade Boggs	4.00
JC	Jack Clark	2.00
WC	Will Clark	3.00
AD	Andre Dawson	2.00
LD	Lenny Dykstra	2.00
DE	Dennis Eckersley	3.00
DG	Dwight Gooden	2.00
GG	Rich "Goose" Gossage	2.00
PG	Pedro Guerrero	2.00
TG	Tony Gwynn	4.00
KH	Keith Hernandez	2.00
FH	Frank Howard	2.00
HJ	Howard Johnson	2.00
MA	Don Mattingly	8.00
KM	Kevin Mitchell	2.00
PM	Paul Molitor	4.00
DM	Dale Murphy	3.00
JR	Jim Rice	2.00
AV	Andy Van Slyke	2.00

League Leaders Materials

		NM/M
Common Player:		5.00
GB	George Bell	5.00
WB	Wade Boggs	10.00
JC	Jack Clark	5.00
WC	Will Clark	8.00
AD	Andre Dawson	8.00
LD	Lenny Dykstra	5.00
DE	Dennis Eckersley	8.00
DG	Dwight Gooden	5.00
GG	Rich "Goose" Gossage	5.00
PG	Pedro Guerrero	5.00
TG	Tony Gwynn SP	10.00
KH	Keith Hernandez	5.00
FH	Frank Howard	8.00
HJ	Howard Johnson	5.00
MA	Don Mattingly	15.00
KM	Kevin Mitchell	5.00
PM	Paul Molitor	10.00
DM	Dale Murphy	8.00
JR	Jim Rice	8.00
AV	Andy Van Slyke	20.00

League Leaders Signatures

		NM/M
Common Auto.:		10.00
GB	George Bell	10.00
JC	Jack Clark	15.00
WC	Will Clark	40.00
AD	Andre Dawson	20.00
LD	Lenny Dykstra	15.00
DE	Dennis Eckersley	15.00
DG	Dwight Gooden	15.00
GG	Rich "Goose" Gossage	15.00
PG	Pedro Guerrero	10.00
KH	Keith Hernandez	15.00
FH	Frank Howard	15.00
HJ	Howard Johnson	15.00
MA	Don Mattingly	60.00
KM	Kevin Mitchell	10.00
PM	Paul Molitor	25.00
DM	Dale Murphy	20.00
JR	Jim Rice	15.00
AV	Andy Van Slyke	

2005 Upper Deck Classics Pirates All-Stars

		NM/M
Complete Set (7):		20.00
Common Player:		2.00
PP1	Ralph Kiner	4.00
PP2	Bill Mazeroski	5.00
PP3	Roberto Clemente	7.50
PP4	Willie Stargell	4.00
PP5	Tony Pena	2.00
PP6	Andy Van Slyke	2.00
PP7	Jason Bay	2.00

Post Season Performers

		NM/M
Common Player:		2.00
Production 999 Sets		
JO	Jose Canseco	3.00
CA	Joe Carter	2.00
JC	Jack Clark	2.00
WC	Will Clark	3.00
DC	David Cone	2.00
ED	Eric Davis	2.00
LD	Lenny Dykstra	2.00
CF	Carlton Fisk	3.00
DG	Dwight Gooden	2.00
PG	Pedro Guerrero	2.00
KH	Kent Hrbek	2.00
JK	John Kruk	3.00
KM	Kevin Mitchell	2.00
PM	Paul Molitor	4.00
JM	Jack Morris	2.00
CR	Cal Ripken Jr.	10.00
BR	Brooks Robinson	4.00
BS	Bret Saberhagen	2.00
MS	Mike Schmidt	6.00
DS	Darryl Strawberry	2.00

Post Season Performers Mat.

		NM/M
Common Player:		5.00
JO	Jose Canseco	10.00
CA	Joe Carter	5.00
JC	Jack Clark/SP	15.00
WC	Will Clark	8.00
DC	David Cone	8.00
ED	Eric Davis/SP	10.00
LD	Lenny Dykstra/SP	5.00
CF	Carlton Fisk	8.00
DG	Dwight Gooden	5.00
PG	Pedro Guerrero	5.00
KH	Kent Hrbek	8.00
JK	John Kruk/SP	15.00
KM	Kevin Mitchell	5.00
PM	Paul Molitor/SP	10.00
JM	Jack Morris	5.00
CR	Cal Ripken Jr./SP	25.00
BR	Brooks Robinson	5.00
MS	Mike Schmidt	15.00
DS	Darryl Strawberry	5.00

Post Season Performers Sig.

		NM/M
Common Auto.:		10.00
JO	Jose Canseco	40.00
CA	Joe Carter	5.00
JC	Jack Clark	15.00
WC	Will Clark	40.00
DC	David Cone	15.00
ED	Eric Davis	20.00
LD	Lenny Dykstra	15.00
CF	Carlton Fisk	40.00
DG	Dwight Gooden	12.00
PG	Pedro Guerrero	10.00
KH	Kent Hrbek	20.00
JK	John Kruk	30.00
KM	Kevin Mitchell	10.00
PM	Paul Molitor	25.00
JM	Jack Morris	20.00
BR	Brooks Robinson	25.00
BS	Bret Saberhagen	15.00
MS	Mike Schmidt	60.00
SS	Darryl Strawberry	20.00

2005 Upper Deck ESPN

		NM/M
Complete Set (90):		20.00
Common Player:		.15
Pack (9):		3.00
Box (24):		60.00
1	Garret Anderson	.25
2	Troy Glaus	.25
3	Vladimir Guerrero	.75
4	Luis Gonzalez	.25
5	Randy Johnson	.75
6	Andruw Jones	.40
7	Chipper Jones	.75
8	J.D. Drew	.25
9	John Smoltz	.25
10	Miguel Tejada	.50
11	Rafael Palmeiro	.50
12	Curt Schilling	.75
13	David Ortiz	.75
14	Manny Ramirez	.75
15	Pedro J. Martinez	.75
16	Carlos Zambrano	.25
17	Greg Maddux	1.00
18	Kerry Wood	.75
19	Mark Prior	.75
20	Nomar Garciaparra	1.50
21	Sammy Sosa	1.50
22	Carlos Lee	.25
23	Frank Thomas	.50
24	Magglio Ordonez	.25
25	Paul Konerko	.25
26	Adam Dunn	.50
27	Ken Griffey Jr.	1.00
28	Travis Hafner	.15
29	Victor Martinez	.25
30	Todd Helton	.50
31	Ivan Rodriguez	.25
32	Carl Pavano	.15
33	Josh Beckett	.25
34	Miguel Cabrera	.75
35	Mike Lowell	.15
36	Carlos Beltran	.50
37	Craig Biggio	.25
38	Jeff Bagwell	.50
39	Lance Berkman	.25
40	Roger Clemens	2.00
41	Roy Oswalt	.25
42	Mike Sweeney	.15
43	Adrian Beltre	.25
44	Brad Penny	.15
45	Eric Gagne	.40
46	Shawn Green	.15
47	Steve Finley	.15
48	Ben Sheets	.25
49	Scott Podsednik	.15
50	Joe Mauer	.25
51	Johan Santana	.50
52	Torii Hunter	.25
53	Jose Vidro	.15
54	Livan Hernandez	.15
55	Jose Reyes	.25
56	Mike Piazza	1.00
57	Tom Glavine	.25
58	Alex Rodriguez	1.50
59	Bernie Williams	.25
60	Derek Jeter	2.00
61	Gary Sheffield	.50
62	Hideki Matsui	1.50
63	Kevin Brown	.15
64	Mike Mussina	.25
65	Eric Chavez	.25
66	Mark Mulder	.25
67	Tim Hudson	.25
68	Bobby Abreu	.25
69	Jim Thome	.75
70	Craig Wilson	.15
71	Jason Kendall	.15
72	Oliver Perez	.15
73	Brian Giles	.15
74	Jake Peavy	.15
75	Jason Schmidt	.25
76	Bret Boone	.15
77	Ichiro Suzuki	1.50
78	Albert Pujols	2.00
79	Jim Edmonds	.25
80	Larry Walker	.40
81	Scott Rolen	.75
82	Aubrey Huff	.25
83	Carl Crawford	.25
84	Alfonso Soriano	.50
85	Hank Blalock	.50
86	Mark Teixeira	.50
87	Michael Young	.25
88	Carlos Delgado	.40
89	Roy Halladay	.50
90	Vernon Wells	.25

Award Winners

		NM/M
Inserted 1:5		
25th Anniv.:		4X-8X
Production 25 Sets		
AW-1	Gary Sheffield	1.00
AW-2	Greg Maddux	2.00
AW-3	Mike Piazza	2.00
AW-4	Jeff Bagwell	1.00
AW-5	Kenny Rogers	.50
AW-6	Cal Ripken Jr.	4.00
AW-7	Greg Maddux	2.00
AW-8	Hideo Nomo	.75
AW-9	Javier Lopez	.50
AW-10	Jim Edmonds	.75
AW-11	Ken Griffey Jr.	2.00
AW-12	Larry Walker	2.00
AW-13	Nomar Garciaparra	2.50
AW-14	Roger Clemens	4.00
AW-15	David Wells	.50
AW-16	Sammy Sosa	2.50
AW-17	Pedro J. Martinez	1.50
AW-18	Andres Galarraga	.50
AW-19	Derek Jeter	4.00
AW-20	Alfonso Soriano	1.50

Ink
Inserted 1:480
No Pricing

Sports Center Swatches

		NM/M
Common Player:		4.00
Inserted 1:12		
GA	Garret Anderson	4.00
RB	Rocco Baldelli	4.00

CB	Carlos Beltran	8.00
AB	Adrian Beltre	8.00
LB	Lance Berkman	4.00
BI	Craig Biggio	4.00
HB	Hank Blalock	8.00
BB	Bret Boone	4.00
MG	Miguel Cabrera	8.00
EC	Eric Chavez	4.00
BC	Bartolo Colon	4.00
CC	Carl Crawford	4.00
JD	J.D. Drew	4.00
AD	Adam Dunn	8.00
JE	Jim Edmonds	6.00
EG	Eric Gagne	6.00
TG	Troy Glaus	6.00
KG	Ken Griffey Jr.	15.00
TH	Tim Hudson	4.00
AH	Aubrey Huff	4.00
DJ	Derek Jeter	20.00
JK	Jeff Kent	4.00
PK	Paul Konerko	6.00
DL	Derrek Lee	4.00
LO	Derek Lowe	4.00
MM	Mark Mulder	4.00
CP	Corey Patterson	6.00
AP	Albert Pujols	20.00
IR	Ivan Rodriguez	8.00
SA	Johan Santana	8.00
JS	Jason Schmidt	6.00
BS	Ben Sheets	4.00
AS	Alfonso Soriano	8.00
IS	Ichiro Suzuki	25.00
MS	Mike Sweeney	4.00
MT	Mark Teixeira	8.00
JT	Jim Thome	10.00
BU	B.J. Upton	6.00
VW	Vernon Wells	4.00
DW	David Wright/SP	15.00
MY	Mike Young/SP	10.00

Sports Century

		NM/M
Inserted 1:5		
25th Anniv.:		4-8X
Production 25 Sets		
SC-1	Babe Ruth	4.00
SC-2	Jackie Robinson	2.00
SC-4	Ty Cobb	2.00
SC-5	Joe DiMaggio	3.00
SC-6	Lou Gehrig	3.00
SC-7	Mickey Mantle	5.00
SC-8	Walter Johnson	1.00
SC-9	Stan Musial	2.00
SC-10	Satchel Paige	1.00
SC-11	Bob Gibson	1.00
SC-12	Roberto Clemente	3.00
SC-13	Cy Young	1.00
SC-14	Honus Wagner	2.00
SC-15	Rogers Hornsby	1.00

Sports Century Signatures

Inserted 1:480
No Pricing

The Magazine Covers

	NM/M
Inserted 1:5	

25th Anniv.:		4-8X
Production 25 Sets		
MC-1	Roger Clemens	4.00
MC-2	Derek Jeter	4.00
MC-3	Randy Johnson, Pedro J. Martinez	1.50
MC-4	Nomar Garciaparra	2.50
MC-5	Manny Ramirez	1.50
MC-6	Ken Griffey Jr.	2.00
MC-7	Mike Piazza	2.00
MC-8	Ichiro Suzuki	3.00
MC-9	Vladimir Guerrero	1.50
MC-10	Randy Johnson	1.50
MC-11	A.J. Pierzynski, Doug Mientkiewicz, Jacque Jones, Torii Hunter	.50
MC-12	Jason Giambi	.50
MC-13	Jeff Kent	.50
MC-14	Albert Pujols	4.00
MC-15	Kazuo Matsui	.50
MC-16	Miguel Cabrera	1.50
MC-17	Alex Rodriguez	3.00
MC-18	Ivan Rodriguez	1.00
MC-19	Eric Gagne	1.00
MC-20	Jim Edmonds, Albert Pujols, Scott Rolen	.75

This Day in Baseball History

		NM/M
Inserted 1:5		
25th Anniv.:		4-8X
Production 25 Sets		
BH-1	Cal Ripken Jr.	4.00
BH-2	Nolan Ryan	4.00
BH-3	Nolan Ryan	4.00
BH-4	Roger Clemens	4.00
BH-5	Thurman Munson	2.00
BH-6	Mickey Mantle	5.00
BH-7	Ernie Banks	2.00
BH-8	Roy Campanella	1.00
BH-9	Yogi Berra	2.00
BH-10	Mickey Mantle	5.00
BH-11	Jackie Robinson	3.00
BH-12	Joe DiMaggio	3.00
BH-13	Bob Feller	1.00
BH-14	Lou Gehrig	3.00
BH-15	Ty Cobb	2.00
BH-16	Babe Ruth	4.00
BH-17	Walter Johnson	1.00
BH-18	Rogers Hornsby	1.00
BH-19	George Sisler	1.00
BH-20	Cy Young	1.00

Web Gems

	NM/M
Inserted 1:5	

25th Anniv.:		4-8X
Production 25 Sets		
WG-1	Adrian Beltre	.75
WG-2	Alex Rodriguez	3.00
WG-3	Andruw Jones	.75
WG-4	Bernie Williams	.75
WG-5	Bret Boone	.50
WG-6	Cesar Izturis	.50
WG-7	Darin Erstad	.50
WG-8	Derek Jeter	4.00
WG-9	Derek Lee	.75
WG-10	Eric Chavez	.75
WG-11	Greg Maddux	2.00
WG-12	Ichiro Suzuki	3.00
WG-13	Ivan Rodriguez	1.00
WG-14	Jim Edmonds	.75
WG-15	Ken Griffey Jr.	2.00
WG-16	Larry Walker	.75
WG-17	Miguel Tejada	.75
WG-18	Mike Mussina	.75
WG-19	Nomar Garciaparra	2.50
WG-20	Scott Rolen	1.50
WG-21	Steve Finley	.50
WG-22	Todd Helton	1.00
WG-23	Torii Hunter	.50
WG-24	Vernon Wells	.75
WG-25	Vladimir Guerrero	1.50

2005 Upper Deck First Pitch

		NM/M
Complete Set (330):		
Common (1-330):		.10
Common (301-330):		1.00
Inserted 1:4		
Common (321-330):		2.00
Inserted 1:36		
Pack (5):		1.00
Box (36):		30.00
1	Casey Kotchman	.10
2	Chone Figgins	.10
3	David Eckstein	.10
4	Jarrod Washburn	.10
5	Robb Quinlan	.10
6	Troy Glaus	.25
7	Vladimir Guerrero	.50
8	Brandon Webb	.10
9	Danny Bautista	.10
10	Luis Gonzalez	.25
11	Matt Kata	.10
12	Randy Johnson	.50
13	Robby Hammock	.10
14	Shea Hillenbrand	.10
15	Adam LaRoche	.10
16	Andruw Jones	.40
17	Horacio Ramirez	.10
18	John Smoltz	.25
19	Johnny Estrada	.10
20	Mike Hampton	.10
21	Rafael Furcal	.10
22	Brian Roberts	.10
23	Javy Lopez	.25
24	Jay Gibbons	.10
25	Jorge Julio	.10
26	Melvin Mora	.10
27	Miguel Tejada	.40
28	Rafael Palmeiro	.40
29	Derek Lowe	.10
30	Jason Varitek	.25
31	Kevin Youkilis	.10
32	Manny Ramirez	.50
33	Curt Schilling	.50
34	Pedro J. Martinez	.50
35	Trot Nixon	.10
36	Corey Patterson	.25
37	Derek Lee	.25
38	LaTroy Hawkins	.10
39	Mark Prior	.50
40	Matt Clement	.10
41	Moises Alou	.25
42	Sammy Sosa	1.00
43	Aaron Rowand	.10
44	Carlos Lee	.10
45	Jose Valentin	.10
46	Juan Uribe	.10
47	Magglio Ordonez	.10
48	Mark Buehrle	.10
49	Paul Konerko	.10
50	Adam Dunn	.40
51	Barry Larkin	.25
52	D'Angelo Jimenez	.10
53	Danny Graves	.10
54	Paul Wilson	.10
55	Sean Casey	.10
56	Wily Mo Pena	.10
57	Ben Broussard	.10
58	C.C. Sabathia	.10
59	Casey Blake	.10
60	Cliff Lee	.10
61	Matt Lawton	.10
62	Omar Vizquel	.10
63	Victor Martinez	.25
64	Charles Johnson	.10
65	Joe Kennedy	.10
66	Jeromy Burnitz	.10
67	Matt Holliday	.25
68	Preston Wilson	.10
69	Royce Clayton	.10
70	Shawn Estes	.10
71	Bobby Higginson	.10
72	Brandon Inge	.10
73	Carlos Guillen	.10
74	Dmitri Young	.10
75	Eric Munson	.10
76	Jeremy Bonderman	.10
77	Ugueth Urbina	.10
78	Josh Beckett	.25
79	Dontrelle Willis	.25
80	Jeff Conine	.10
81	Juan Pierre	.10
82	Luis Castillo	.10
83	Miguel Cabrera	.50
84	Mike Lowell	.10
85	Andy Pettitte	.25
86	Brad Lidge	.10
87	Carlos Beltran	.40
88	Craig Biggio	.25
89	Jeff Bagwell	.40
90	Roger Clemens	1.50
91	Roy Oswalt	.25
92	Benito Santiago	.10
93	Jeremy Affeldt	.10
94	Juan Gonzalez	.25
95	Ken Harvey	.10
96	Mike MacDougal	.10
97	Mike Sweeney	.10
98	Zack Greinke	.25
99	Adrian Beltre	.25
100	Alex Cora	.10
101	Cesar Izturis	.10
102	Eric Gagne	.25
103	Kazuhisa Ishii	.10
104	Milton Bradley	.10
105	Shawn Green	.25
106	Danny Kolb	.10
107	Ben Sheets	.25
108	Brooks Kieschnick	.10
109	Craig Counsell	.10
110	Geoff Jenkins	.10
111	Lyle Overbay	.10
112	Scott Podsednik	.10
113	Corey Koskie	.10
114	Johan Santana	.50
115	Joe Mauer	.25
116	Justin Morneau	.25
117	Lew Ford	.10
118	Matt LeCroy	.10
119	Torii Hunter	.25
120	Brad Wilkerson	.10
121	Chad Cordero	.10
122	Livan Hernandez	.10
123	Jose Vidro	.10
124	Terrmel Sledge	.10
125	Tony Batista	.10
126	Zach Day	.10
127	Al Leiter	.10
128	Jae Weong Seo	.10
129	Jose Reyes	.25
130	Kazuo Matsui	.10
131	Mike Piazza	.75
132	Todd Zeile	.10
133	Cliff Floyd	.10
134	Alex Rodriguez	1.50
135	Derek Jeter	1.50
136	Gary Sheffield	.40
137	Hideki Matsui	1.00
138	Jason Giambi	.25
139	Jorge Posada	.25
140	Mike Mussina	.25
141	Barry Zito	.25
142	Bobby Crosby	.25
143	Octavio Dotel	.10
144	Eric Chavez	.25
145	Jermaine Dye	.25
146	Mark Kotsay	.10
147	Tim Hudson	.25
148	Billy Wagner	.10
149	Bobby Abreu	.25
150	David Bell	.10
151	Jim Thome	.50
152	Jimmy Rollins	.20
153	Mike Lieberthal	.10
154	Randy Wolf	.10
155	Craig Wilson	.10
156	Daryle Ward	.10
157	Jack Wilson	.10
158	Jason Kendall	.10
159	Kip Wells	.10
160	Oliver Perez	.25
161	Robert Mackowiak	.10
162	Brian Giles	.10
163	Brian Lawrence	.10
164	David Wells	.10
165	Jay Payton	.10
166	Ryan Klesko	.10

167 Sean Burroughs .10
168 Trevor Hoffman .10
169 Brett Tomko .10
170 J.T. Snow .10
171 Jason Schmidt .25
172 Kirk Rueter .10
173 A.J. Pierzynski .10
174 Pedro Feliz .10
175 Ray Durham .10
176 Eddie Guardado .10
177 Edgar Martinez .10
178 Ichiro Suzuki 1.00
179 Jamie Moyer .10
180 Joel Pineiro .10
181 Randy Winn .10
182 Raul Ibanez .10
183 Albert Pujols 1.50
184 Edgar Renteria .25
185 Jason Isringhausen .10
186 Jim Edmonds .25
187 Matt Morris .10
188 Reggie Sanders .10
189 Tony Womack .10
190 Aubrey Huff .10
191 Danys Baez .10
192 Carl Crawford .10
193 Jose Cruz Jr. .10
194 Rocco Baldelli .10
195 Tino Martinez .10
196 Dewon Brazelton .10
197 Alfonso Soriano .50
198 Brad Fullmer .10
199 Gerald Laird .10
200 Hank Blalock .50
201 Laynce Nix .10
202 Mark Teixeira .40
203 Mike Young .25
204 Alexis Rios .10
205 Eric Hinske .10
206 Miguel Batista .10
207 Orlando Hudson .10
208 Roy Halladay .10
209 Ted Lilly .10
210 Vernon Wells .10
211 Aarom Baldiris .10
212 B.J. Upton .25
213 Dallas McPherson .25
214 Brian Dallimore .10
215 Chris Oxspring .10
216 Chris Shelton .10
217 David Wright .75
218 Edwardo Sierra .10
219 Fernando Nieve .10
220 Frank Francisco .10
221 Jeff Bennett .10
222 Justin Lehr .10
223 John Gall .10
224 Jorge Sequea .10
225 Justin Germano .10
226 Kazuhito Tadano .10
227 Kevin Cave .10
228 Joe Blanton .10
229 Luis Gonzalez .10
230 Mike Wuertz .10
231 Mike Rouse .10
232 Nick Regilio .10
233 Orlando Rodriguez .10
235 Ramon Ramirez .10
236 Roberto Novoa .10
237 Dioner Navarro .10
238 Tim Bausher .10
239 Logan Kensing .10
240 Andy Green .10
241 Brad Halsey .10
242 Charles Thomas .10
243 George Sherrill .10
244 Jesse Crain .10
245 Jimmy Serrano .10
246 Joe Horgan .10
247 Chris Young .10
248 Joey Gathright .10
249 Gavin Floyd .10
250 Ryan Howard .50
251 Lance Cormier .10
252 Matt Treanor .10
253 Jeff Francis .10
254 Nick Swisher .10
255 Scott Atchison .10
256 Travis Blackley .10
257 Travis Smith .10
258 Yadier Molina .10
259 Jeff Keppinger .10
260 Scott Kazmir .50
261 Garret Anderson, Vladimir Guerrero .25
262 Luis Gonzalez, Randy Johnson .25
263 Chipper Jones, Andruw Jones .25
264 Miguel Tejada, Rafael Palmeiro .25
265 Manny Ramirez, Curt Schilling .25
266 Mark Prior, Sammy Sosa .50
267 Frank Thomas, Magglio Ordonez .25
268 Barry Larkin, Ken Griffey Jr. .50
269 C.C. Sabathia, Victor Martinez .10
270 Jeromy Burnitz, Todd Helton .25
271 Ivan Rodriguez, Dmitri Young .25
272 Josh Beckett, Miguel Cabrera .25
273 Jeff Bagwell, Roger Clemens .50
274 Mike Sweeney, Ken Harvey .10
275 Eric Gagne, Adrian Beltre .25
276 Ben Sheets, Geoff Jenkins .10
277 Torii Hunter, Joe Mauer .10
278 Jose Vidro, Livan Hernandez .10
279 Mike Piazza, Kazuo Matsui .25
280 Alex Rodriguez, Derek Jeter .75
281 Eric Chavez, Tim Hudson .10
282 Bobby Abreu, Jim Thome .25
283 Jason Kendall, Craig Wilson .10
284 Phil Nevin, Brian Giles .10
285 Jason Schmidt, A.J. Pierzynski .10
286 Bret Boone, Ichiro Suzuki .50
287 Albert Pujols, Scott Rolen .75
288 Aubrey Huff, Tino Martinez .10
289 Hank Blalock, Mark Teixeira .25
290 Roy Halladay, Carlos Delgado .10
291 Vladimir Guerrero .50
292 Curt Schilling .50
293 Mark Prior .50
294 Josh Beckett .25
295 Roger Clemens 1.00
296 Derek Jeter 1.00
297 Eric Chavez .10
298 Jim Thome .50
299 Albert Pujols 1.00
300 Hank Blalock .25
301 Guillermo Quiroz 1.00
302 Jeff Bajenaru 1.00
303 Bartolome Fortunato 1.00
304 Jason Alfaro 1.00
305 Mike Rose 1.00
306 Joe Hietpas 1.00
307 Kyle Denney 1.00
308 Rene Rivera 1.00
309 Kameron Loe 1.00
310 Rickie Weeks 1.50
311 Gustavo Chacin 1.00
312 Chris Burke 1.00
313 Yhency Brazoban 1.00
314 Brandon League 1.00
315 Jose Capellan 1.00
316 Russ Adams 1.00
317 Adrian Gonzalez 1.00
318 Jason Dubois 1.00
319 Abe Alvarez 1.00
320 Eric Crozier 1.00
321 Bengie Molina, Bartolo Colon 2.00
322 C.C. Sabathia, Victor Martinez 2.00
323 Jake Peavy, Ramon Hernandez 2.00
324 A.J. Pierzynski, Jason Schmidt 3.00
325 Joe Mauer, Johan Santana 3.00
326 Mark Prior, Michael Barrett 3.00
327 Jorge Posada, Mike Mussina 3.00
328 Roger Clemens, Brad Ausmus 4.00
329 Roy Halladay, Guillermo Quiroz 2.00
330 Mike Piazza, Tom Glavine 3.00

Fabric

NM/M

Common Player:
Inserted 1:180

JB Jeff Bagwell 8.00
BE Josh Beckett 5.00
BB Bret Boone 5.00
EC Eric Chavez 5.00
JE Jim Edmonds 5.00
EG Eric Gagne 8.00
TG Troy Glaus 5.00
KG Ken Griffey Jr./SP 20.00
TH Torii Hunter 5.00
DJ Derek Jeter 20.00
AJ Andruw Jones 5.00
CJ Chipper Jones 8.00
MM Mark Mulder 5.00
MO Magglio Ordonez 5.00
SR Scott Rolen 8.00
CS Curt Schilling 8.00
GS Gary Sheffield/SP 8.00
AS Alfonso Soriano 8.00
SS Sammy Sosa 10.00
IS Ichiro Suzuki/SP 25.00

Signature Stars

Inserted 1:720
No Pricing

2005 Upper Deck MVP

NM/M

Complete Set (90): 20.00
Common Player: .10
Pack (6): 1.50
Box (24): 30.00

1 Adam Dunn .40
2 Adrian Beltre .40
3 Albert Pujols 1.50
4 Alex Rodriguez 1.50
5 Alfonso Soriano .50
6 Andruw Jones .40
7 Aubrey Huff .10
8 Barry Zito .25
9 Ben Sheets .25
10 Bobby Abreu .25
11 Bobby Crosby .25
12 Bret Boone .10
13 Brian Giles .10
14 Carlos Beltran .40
15 Carlos Delgado .25
16 Carlos Lee .25
17 Chipper Jones .50
18 Craig Biggio .25
19 Curt Schilling .40
20 Dallas McPherson .10
21 David Ortiz .50
22 David Wright .50
23 Derek Jeter 1.50
24 Derek Lowe .10
25 Eric Chavez .25
26 Eric Gagne .25
27 Frank Thomas .40
28 Garret Anderson .25
29 Gary Sheffield .40
30 Greg Maddux 1.00
31 Hank Blalock .25
32 Hideki Matsui 1.00
33 Ichiro Suzuki 1.00
34 Ivan Rodriguez .40
35 J.D. Drew .10
36 Jake Peavy .25
37 Jason Bay .10
38 Jason Giambi .25
39 Jason Schmidt .25
40 Jeff Bagwell .40
41 Jeff Kent .25
42 Jim Edmonds .25
43 Jim Thome .40
44 Joe Mauer .25
45 Johan Santana .50
46 John Smoltz .25
47 Johnny Damon .50
48 Jorge Posada .25
49 Jose Vidro .10
50 Josh Beckett .25
51 Kazuo Matsui .10
52 Ken Griffey Jr. 1.00
53 Kerry Wood .25
54 Khalil Greene .25
55 Lance Berkman .25
56 Livan Hernandez .10
57 Luis Gonzalez .10
58 Magglio Ordonez .10
59 Manny Ramirez .50
60 Mark Mulder .25
61 Mark Prior .50
62 Mark Teixeira .40
63 Miguel Cabrera .50
64 Miguel Tejada .40
65 Mike Mussina .25
66 Mike Piazza 1.00
67 Mike Sweeney .10
68 Moises Alou .25
69 Nomar Garciaparra .75
70 Oliver Perez .10
71 Paul Konerko .25
72 Pedro Martinez .50
73 Rafael Palmeiro .25
74 Randy Johnson .50
75 Richie Sexson .25
76 Roger Clemens 1.50
77 Roy Halladay .25
78 Roy Oswalt .25
79 Sammy Sosa .75
80 Scott Rolen .50
81 Shawn Green .10
82 Steve Finley .10
83 Tim Hudson .25
84 Todd Helton .40
85 Tom Glavine .25
86 Torii Hunter .25
87 Travis Hafner .10
88 Troy Glaus .25
89 Victor Martinez .25
90 Vladimir Guerrero .50

Batter Up!

NM/M

Common Player: .25
Inserted 1:1

BU-1 Al Kaline .50
BU-2 Bill Mazeroski .25
BU-3 Billy Williams .25
BU-4 Bob Feller .50
BU-5 Bob Gibson .50
BU-6 Bob Lemon .25
BU-7 Brooks Robinson .50
BU-8 Carlton Fisk .50
BU-9 Jim "Catfish" Hunter .25
BU-10 Dennis Eckersley .25
BU-11 Eddie Mathews .75
BU-12 Eddie Murray .50
BU-13 Fergie Jenkins .25
BU-14 Gaylord Perry .25
BU-15 Harmon Killebrew .75
BU-16 Jim Bunning .25
BU-17 Jim Palmer .50
BU-18 Joe DiMaggio 1.50
BU-19 Joe Morgan .25
BU-20 Johnny Bench .75
BU-21 Juan Marichal .50
BU-22 Lou Brock .50
BU-23 Luis Aparicio .25
BU-24 Mike Schmidt 1.50
BU-25 Monte Irvin .50
BU-26 Nolan Ryan 2.00
BU-27 Orlando Cepeda .25
BU-28 Ozzie Smith .75
BU-29 Pee Wee Reese .25
BU-30 Phil Niekro .25
BU-31 Phil Rizzuto .50
BU-32 Ralph Kiner .25
BU-33 Richie Ashburn .25
BU-34 Robin Roberts .25
BU-35 Robin Yount .75
BU-36 Rollie Fingers .25
BU-37 Tom Seaver .75
BU-38 Tony Perez .25
BU-39 Warren Spahn .75
BU-40 Willie McCovey .50
BU-41 Willie Stargell .50
BU-42 Yogi Berra .75

All-Star Signatures

No Pricing
Inserted 1:480

Jersey

NM/M

Common Jersey: 4.00
Inserted 1:24

CB Carlos Beltran 6.00
AB Adrian Beltre 4.00
HB Hank Blalock 4.00
SB Sean Burroughs 4.00
MC Miguel Cabrera 6.00
EC Eric Chavez 4.00
EG Eric Gagne 4.00
KG Ken Griffey Jr. 10.00
VG Vladimir Guerrero 6.00
TH Todd Helton 6.00
DJ Derek Jeter 15.00
RJ Randy Johnson 6.00
CJ Chipper Jones 6.00
GM Greg Maddux 8.00
PI Mike Piazza 8.00
MP Mark Prior 6.00
AP Albert Pujols 15.00
MR Manny Ramirez 6.00
IR Ivan Rodriguez 6.00
SR Scott Rolen 6.00
JS Johan Santana 6.00
CS Curt Schilling 6.00
AS Alfonso Soriano 6.00
SS Sammy Sosa 8.00
MT Mark Teixeira 6.00
TE Miguel Tejada 6.00
JT Jim Thome 6.00
KW Kerry Wood 4.00

2005 Upper Deck Portraits

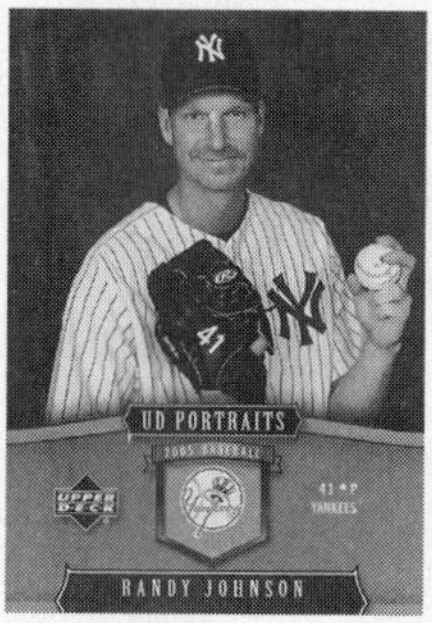

NM/M

Complete Set (100): 25.00
Common Player: .25
Box (7 Cards + 8x10): 100.00

1 Dallas McPherson .25
2 Steve Finley .25
3 Vladimir Guerrero .75
4 Troy Glaus .25
5 Andruw Jones .50
6 Chipper Jones .75
7 John Smoltz .50
8 Marcus Giles .25
9 Tim Hudson .50
10 Cal Ripken Jr. 3.00
11 Miguel Tejada .50
12 Curt Schilling .75
13 David Ortiz .75
14 Edgar Renteria .25
15 Jason Varitek .50
16 Jim Rice .50
17 Johnny Damon .75
18 Matt Clement .25
19 Wade Boggs .75
20 Aramis Ramirez .50
21 Carlos Zambrano .50
22 Corey Patterson .25
23 Fergie Jenkins .25
24 Greg Maddux 1.50
25 Kerry Wood .50
26 Mark Prior .75
27 Nomar Garciaparra .75
28 Ryne Sandberg 1.50
29 Frank Thomas .50
30 Adam Dunn .50
31 Barry Larkin .50
32 Ken Griffey Jr. 1.50
33 Sean Casey .25
34 Travis Hafner .25
35 Victor Martinez .25
36 Todd Helton .50
37 Ivan Rodriguez .50
38 Magglio Ordonez .25
39 Josh Beckett .25
40 Miguel Cabrera .75
41 Mike Lowell .25
42 Craig Biggio .50
43 Jeff Bagwell .50
44 Roger Clemens 2.00
45 Roy Oswalt .25
46 Bo Jackson .50

#	Player	Price
47	Prince Fielder	5.00
48	Eric Gagne	.25
49	J.D. Drew	.25
50	Ben Sheets	.50
51	Robin Yount	.75
52	Jacque Jones	.25
53	Joe Mauer	.50
54	Johan Santana	.75
55	Justin Morneau	.25
56	Torii Hunter	.25
57	Dontrelle Willis	.50
58	David Wright	1.00
59	Gary Carter	.25
60	Jose Reyes	.40
61	Keith Hernandez	.25
62	Mike Piazza	1.00
63	Pedro Martinez	.75
64	Tom Glavine	.50
65	Carl Pavano	.25
66	Derek Jeter	2.00
67	Don Mattingly	1.00
68	Mike Mussina	.50
69	Randy Johnson	.75
70	Bobby Crosby	.25
71	Eric Chavez	.25
72	Rich Harden	.25
73	Bobby Abreu	.50
74	Mike Schmidt	1.00
75	Jason Bay	.25
76	Oliver Perez	.25
77	Brian Giles	.25
78	Jake Peavy	.50
79	Khalil Greene	.25
80	Tony Gwynn	.75
81	Jason Schmidt	.25
82	Will Clark	.50
83	Adrian Beltre	.25
84	Justin Verlander	2.00
85	Albert Pujols	2.00
86	Jim Edmonds	.50
87	Mark Mulder	.50
88	Scott Rolen	.75
89	Aubrey Huff	.25
90	B.J. Upton	.25
91	Carl Crawford	.25
92	Tadahito Iguchi	4.00
93	Scott Kazmir	.25
94	Alfonso Soriano	.75
95	Hank Blalock	.25
96	Mark Teixeira	.50
97	Michael Young	.25
98	Nolan Ryan	2.00
99	Roy Halladay	.50
100	Jose Vidro	.25

Emerald Jersey

NM/M

Common Player: 4.00
Production 99 Sets
Blue: 1-1.5X
Production 25 Sets
Gold: 1-2X
Production 15 Sets

#	Player	Price
1	Dallas McPherson	4.00
2	Steve Finley	4.00
3	Vladimir Guerrero	8.00
4	Troy Glaus	4.00
5	Andruw Jones	8.00
6	Chipper Jones	8.00
7	John Smoltz	6.00
8	Marcus Giles	4.00
9	Tim Hudson	6.00
10	Cal Ripken Jr.	25.00
11	Miguel Tejada	8.00
12	Curt Schilling	8.00
13	David Ortiz	8.00
14	Edgar Renteria	4.00
15	Jason Varitek	8.00
16	Jim Rice	6.00
17	Johnny Damon	8.00
18	Matt Clement	4.00
19	Wade Boggs	8.00
20	Aramis Ramirez	6.00
21	Carlos Zambrano	4.00
22	Corey Patterson	4.00
23	Fergie Jenkins	6.00
24	Greg Maddux	10.00
25	Kerry Wood	6.00
26	Mark Prior	8.00
27	Nomar Garciaparra	12.00
28	Ryne Sandberg	12.00
29	Frank Thomas	6.00
30	Adam Dunn	6.00
31	Barry Larkin	6.00
32	Ken Griffey Jr.	15.00
33	Sean Casey	4.00
34	Travis Hafner	4.00
35	Victor Martinez	4.00
36	Todd Helton	6.00
37	Ivan Rodriguez	6.00
38	Magglio Ordonez	4.00
39	Josh Beckett	4.00
40	Miguel Cabrera	8.00
41	Mike Lowell	4.00
42	Craig Biggio	6.00
43	Jeff Bagwell	8.00
44	Roger Clemens	15.00
45	Roy Oswalt	4.00
46	Bo Jackson	10.00
47	Eric Gagne	6.00
48	J.D. Drew	4.00
49	Ben Sheets	4.00
50	Robin Yount	15.00
51	Jacque Jones	4.00
52	Joe Mauer	6.00
53	Joe Mauer	6.00
54	Johan Santana	6.00
55	Justin Morneau	4.00
56	Torii Hunter	4.00
57	Dontrelle Willis	6.00
58	David Wright	10.00
59	Gary Carter	6.00
60	Jose Reyes	6.00
61	Keith Hernandez	4.00
62	Mike Piazza	8.00
63	Pedro Martinez	8.00
64	Tom Glavine	6.00
65	Carl Pavano	4.00
66	Derek Jeter	15.00
67	Don Mattingly	15.00
68	Mike Mussina	6.00
69	Randy Johnson	8.00
70	Bobby Crosby	4.00
71	Eric Chavez	4.00
72	Rich Harden	4.00
73	Bobby Abreu	6.00
74	Mike Schmidt	10.00
75	Jason Bay	4.00
76	Oliver Perez	4.00
77	Brian Giles	6.00
78	Jake Peavy	6.00
79	Khalil Greene	6.00
80	Tony Gwynn	8.00
81	Jason Schmidt	4.00
82	Will Clark	8.00
83	Adrian Beltre	4.00
84	Will Clark	8.00
85	Albert Pujols	15.00
86	Jim Edmonds	6.00
87	Mark Mulder	6.00
88	Scott Rolen	6.00
89	Aubrey Huff	6.00
90	B.J. Upton	6.00
91	Carl Crawford	4.00
92	Tadahito Iguchi	15.00
93	Scott Kazmir	4.00
94	Alfonso Soriano	6.00
95	Hank Blalock	6.00
96	Mark Teixeira	6.00
97	Michael Young	6.00
98	Nolan Ryan	15.00
99	Roy Halladay	6.00
100	Jose Vidro	4.00

Jersey Auto. Platinum

No Pricing
Production 10 Sets

Scrapbook Materials

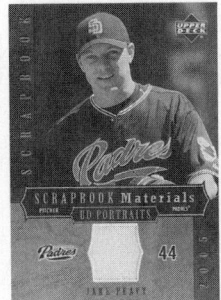

NM/M

Complete Set (59):
Common Player: 4.00

BA	Bobby Abreu	4.00
JB	Jeff Bagwell	6.00
BE	Josh Beckett	4.00
AB	Adrian Beltre	8.00
BI	Craig Biggio	6.00
CA	Miguel Cabrera	8.00
WC	Will Clark	6.00
CL	Matt Clement	4.00
BC	Bobby Crosby	4.00
JE	Jim Edmonds	6.00
SF	Steve Finley	4.00
BG	Brian Giles	6.00
GR	Khalil Greene	6.00
KG	Ken Griffey Jr.	15.00
TG	Tony Gwynn	8.00
RH	Roy Halladay	6.00
TH	Todd Helton	6.00
KH	Keith Hernandez	4.00
HU	Torii Hunter	4.00
BJ	Bo Jackson	10.00
DJ	Derek Jeter	20.00
AJ	Andruw Jones	6.00
CJ	Chipper Jones	8.00
JJ	Jacque Jones	4.00
SK	Scott Kazmir	4.00
BL	Barry Larkin	6.00
ML	Mike Lowell	4.00
VM	Victor Martinez	4.00
MA	Don Mattingly	15.00
JM	Joe Mauer	6.00
MC	Dallas McPherson	4.00
MO	Justin Morneau	4.00
DM	Dale Murphy	6.00
MM	Mike Mussina	6.00
OR	Magglio Ordonez	4.00
DO	David Ortiz	8.00
PA	Corey Patterson	4.00
CP	Carl Pavano	4.00
JP	Jake Peavy	6.00
OP	Oliver Perez	4.00
MP	Mark Prior	6.00
AP	Albert Pujols	15.00
JR	Jim Rice	6.00
CR	Cal Ripken Jr.	20.00
NR	Nolan Ryan	15.00
RS	Ryne Sandberg	10.00
SA	Johan Santana	6.00
JS	Jason Schmidt	4.00
MS	Mike Schmidt	10.00
SM	John Smoltz	6.00
MT	Mark Teixeira	6.00
FT	Frank Thomas	6.00
BU	B.J. Upton	4.00
JV	Jose Vidro	4.00
WI	Dontrelle Willis	6.00
DW	David Wright	10.00
CZ	Carlos Zambrano	6.00

Scrapbook Moments

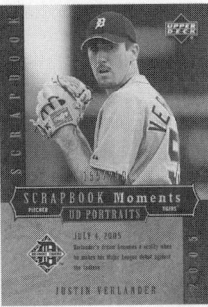

NM/M

Common Player: 1.00
Production 250 Sets

BA	Bobby Abreu	1.50
JB	Jeff Bagwell	1.50
BE	Josh Beckett	1.50
AB	Adrian Beltre	1.50
BI	Craig Biggio	1.50
CA	Miguel Cabrera	2.00
WC	Will Clark	1.50
RC	Roger Clemens	6.00
CL	Matt Clement	1.00
BC	Bobby Crosby	1.50
JE	Jim Edmonds	1.50
PF	Prince Fielder	6.00
SF	Steve Finley	1.00
BG	Brian Giles	1.00
GR	Khalil Greene	1.50
KG	Ken Griffey Jr.	4.00
TG	Tony Gwynn	2.00
RH	Roy Halladay	1.00
TH	Todd Helton	1.50
KH	Keith Hernandez	1.00
HU	Torii Hunter	1.00
BJ	Bo Jackson	2.00
DJ	Derek Jeter	6.00
AJ	Andruw Jones	1.50
CJ	Chipper Jones	2.00
JJ	Jacque Jones	1.00
SK	Scott Kazmir	1.00
BL	Barry Larkin	1.50
ML	Mike Lowell	1.00
VM	Victor Martinez	1.00
MA	Don Mattingly	4.00
JM	Joe Mauer	1.50
MC	Dallas McPherson	1.00
MO	Justin Morneau	1.00
DM	Dale Murphy	2.00
MM	Mike Mussina	1.50
OR	Magglio Ordonez	1.00
DO	David Ortiz	2.00
PA	Corey Patterson	1.00
CP	Carl Pavano	1.00
JP	Jake Peavy	1.50
OP	Oliver Perez	1.00
MP	Mark Prior	2.00
AP	Albert Pujols	6.00
JR	Jim Rice	1.50
CR	Cal Ripken Jr.	8.00
NR	Nolan Ryan	6.00
RS	Ryne Sandberg	4.00
SA	Johan Santana	2.00
JS	Jason Schmidt	1.00
MS	Mike Schmidt	4.00
SM	John Smoltz	1.50
MT	Mark Teixeira	1.50
FT	Frank Thomas	1.50
BU	B.J. Upton	1.00
VE	Justin Verlander	2.00
JV	Jose Vidro	1.50
WI	Dontrelle Willis	1.50
DW	David Wright	3.00
CZ	Carlos Zambrano	1.50

Scrapbook Signatures

No Pricing
Production 20 Sets

Signature Portraits 8x10

NM/M

Common Player:

DB	Dusty Baker/100	25.00
JB	Jason Bay	25.00
HB	Hank Blalock	25.00
WB	Wade Boggs/40	50.00
CA	Miguel Cabrera	40.00
JD	Johnny Damon/99	50.00
GR	Khalil Greene	35.00
VG	Vladimir Guerrero/40	75.00
KH	Keith Hernandez	20.00
DJ	Derek Jeter/150	200.00
SK	Scott Kazmir	25.00
VM	Victor Martinez	25.00
MA	Don Mattingly	65.00
JM	Joe Mauer	30.00
DM	Dale Murphy	30.00
SM	Stan Musial/40	80.00
JN	Jeff Niemann	25.00
RO	Roy Oswalt	30.00
PI	Mike Piazza/35	125.00
MP	Mark Prior/50	40.00
CR	Cal Ripken Jr./50	160.00
BR	Brooks Robinson	50.00
NR	Nolan Ryan/25	140.00
RS	Ryne Sandberg/99	100.00
MS	Mike Schmidt	50.00
BS	Ben Sheets	25.00
OS	Ozzie Smith	50.00
DS	Duke Snider/150	60.00
MT	Mark Teixeira	35.00
BU	B.J. Upton	20.00
VE	Justin Verlander	40.00
DW	David Wright	80.00

Sig. Portraits Cuts 8x10 Card

No Pricing
Production 1-25

Signature Portraits Dual 8x10

NM/M

Production 25-99

BT	Mark Teixeira, Hank Blalock 99	50.00
HS	Rich Harden, Ben Sheets 99	40.00
NV	Justin Verlander, Jeff Niemann 99	50.00
SH	Tim Hudson, John Smoltz 75	75.00
WP	Kerry Wood, Mark Prior 99	85.00
WR	David Wright, Jose Reyes 99	140.00

Sig. Portraits Dual Cuts 8x10

No Pricing
Production 1-2

Signature Portraits Quad 8x10

No Pricing
Production Five Sets

Sign. Portraits Triple 8x10

No Pricing
Production 15 Sets

2005 Upper Deck Pro Sigs

MANNY RAMIREZ

NM/M

Complete Set (132): 25.00
Common Player: .10
Common Rookie (91-132): .25
Inserted 1:1
Pack (6): 2.00
Box (24): 40.00

#	Player	Price
1	Dallas McPherson	.10
2	Garret Anderson	.25
3	Steve Finley	.10
4	Vladimir Guerrero	.50
5	Luis Gonzalez	.10
6	Shawn Green	.10
7	Troy Glaus	.25
8	Andruw Jones	.40
9	Chipper Jones	.50
10	John Smoltz	.25
11	Tim Hudson	.40
12	Miguel Tejada	.40
13	Rafael Palmeiro	.25
14	Sammy Sosa	.75
15	Curt Schilling	.50
16	David Ortiz	.50

17 Johnny Damon .50
18 Manny Ramirez .50
19 Greg Maddux 1.00
20 Kerry Wood .25
21 Mark Prior .50
22 Nomar Garciaparra .50
23 Frank Thomas .40
24 Paul Konerko .25
25 Adam Dunn .40
26 Ken Griffey Jr. 1.00
27 Travis Hafner .10
28 Victor Martinez .10
29 Todd Helton .40
30 Ivan Rodriguez .40
31 Magglio Ordonez .10
32 Carlos Delgado .25
33 Josh Beckett .25
34 Miguel Cabrera .50
35 Craig Biggio .25
36 Jeff Bagwell .40
37 Lance Berkman .25
38 Roger Clemens 1.50
39 Roy Oswalt .25
40 Mike Sweeney .10
41 Derek Lowe .10
42 Eric Gagne .25
43 J.D. Drew .10
44 Jeff Kent .10
45 Ben Sheets .25
46 Carlos Lee .25
47 Joe Mauer .25
48 Johan Santana .50
49 Torii Hunter .25
50 Carlos Beltran .40
51 David Wright 1.00
52 Kazuo Matsui .10
53 Mike Piazza .75
54 Pedro Martinez .50
55 Tom Glavine .25
56 Alex Rodriguez 1.50
57 Derek Jeter 1.50
58 Gary Sheffield .40
59 Hideki Matsui 1.00
60 Jason Giambi .25
61 Jorge Posada .25
62 Mike Mussina .25
63 Randy Johnson .50
64 Barry Zito .25
65 Bobby Crosby .25
66 Eric Chavez .25
67 Bobby Abreu .25
68 Jim Thome .40
69 Jason Bay .25
70 Oliver Perez .10
71 Brian Giles .10
72 Jake Peavy .25
73 Khalil Greene .25
74 Jason Schmidt .10
75 Moises Alou .25
76 Adrian Beltre .25
77 Bret Boone .10
78 Ichiro Suzuki 1.00
79 Richie Sexson .25
80 Albert Pujols 1.50
81 Jim Edmonds .25
82 Mark Mulder .25
83 Scott Rolen .50
84 Aubrey Huff .10
85 Alfonso Soriano .50
86 Hank Blalock .25
87 Mark Teixeira .25
88 Roy Halladay .25
89 Jose Vidro .10
90 Livan Hernandez .10
91 Tony Pena RC .25
92 Luis Hernandez **RC** .25
93 Peter Orr **RC** .25
94 Anibal Sanchez **RC** .75
95 Luis Mendoza **RC** .25
96 Stephen Drew **RC** 6.00
97 Russel Rohlicek **RC** .25
98 Casey Rogowski **RC** .25
99 Pedro Lopez **RC** .25
100 Tadahito Iguchi **RC** 2.00
101 Daylan Childress **RC** .25
102 Juan Morillo **RC** .50
103 Marcos Carvajal **RC** .25
104 Ubaldo Jimenez **RC** .25
105 Justin Verlander **RC** 2.00
106 Chris Resop **RC** .25
107 Yorman Bazardo **RC** .25
108 Jared Gothreaux **RC** .25
109 Luke Scott **RC** 1.00
110 Ambiorix Burgos **RC** .50
111 Prince Fielder 4.00
112 Dennis Houlton **RC** .25
113 Franquelis Osoria **RC** .25
114 Norihiro Nakamura **RC** 1.00
115 Oscar Robles **RC** .25
116 Steve Schmoll **RC** .25
117 Luis Pena **RC** .25
118 David Gassner **RC** .25
119 Ambiorix Concepcion **RC** .50
120 Dae-Sung Koo **RC** .25
121 Matt Lindstrom **RC** .25
122 Colter Bean **RC** .25
123 Keiichi Yabu **RC** .25
124 Philip Humber **RC** 1.00
125 Wladimir Balentien **RC** 1.00
126 Tony Giarratano **RC** .25
127 Shane Costa **RC** .25
128 Jeff Niemann **RC** 1.00
129 Nick Masset **RC** .25
130 Ismael Ramirez **RC** .25
131 John Hattig Jr. **RC** .25
132 Brandon McCarthy **RC** 1.50

Gold

Gold: 2-4X
Production 350 Sets

Silver

Silver: 1-3X
Inserted 1:5

Signature Sensations

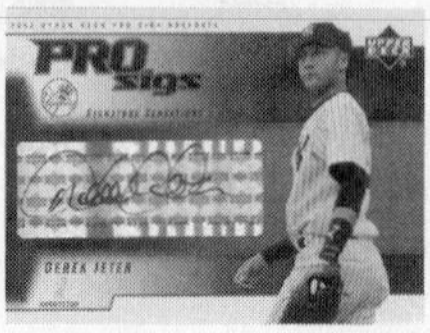

NM/M

Inserted 1:24
Silver: 1-2X
Production 50 Sets
Gold: No Pricing
Production Five Sets

AA Abe Alvarez 10.00
BA Bronson Arroyo 25.00
GA Garrett Atkins 8.00
DB Denny Bautista 5.00
RB Russell Branyan 5.00
MC Miguel Cabrera 35.00
KC Kiko Calero 5.00
CC Chad Cordero 10.00
JC Juan Cruz 5.00
BD Brandon Duckworth 5.00
JE Johnny Estrada 8.00
LF Lew Ford/SP 10.00
TH Travis Hafner 15.00
KH Keith Hernandez/SP 20.00
OH Orlando Hernandez 75.00
OI Omar Infante 5.00
DJ Derek Jeter/SP 150.00
JJ Jorge Julio 5.00
AM Aaron Miles 5.00
YM Yadier Molina 15.00
RN Roberto Novoa 5.00
NP Nick Punto 5.00
HR Horacio Ramirez/SP 10.00
AR Aaron Rowand 25.00
CS Cory Sullivan 8.00
JS Jeff Suppan 10.00
BT Brett Tomko 5.00
MV Merkin Valdez 5.00
DW David Wright 70.00

2005 Upper Deck Pros & Prospects

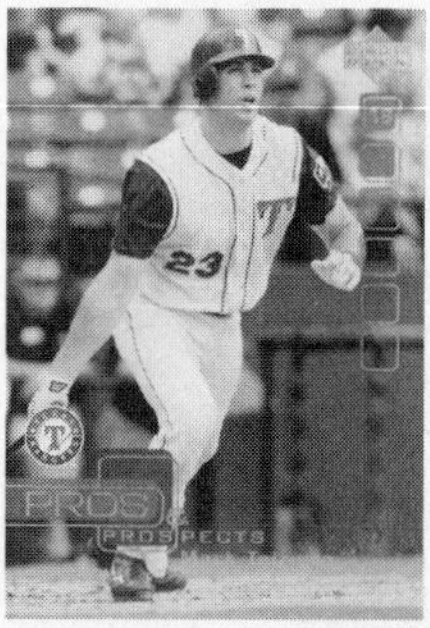

NM/M

Complete Set (200):
Common Player (1-100): .15
Common SP (101-150): 3.00
Production 999
Common SP (151-175): 4.00
Production 499
Common SP (176-200): 5.00
Production 199
Pack (6): 2.75
Box (24): 60.00

1 Adam Dunn .40
2 Aramis Ramirez .40
3 Bobby Abreu .25
4 Mike Lowell .15
5 Josh Beckett .25
6 Derek Jeter 1.50
7 Alex Rodriguez 1.25
8 Andruw Jones .25
9 Brian Giles .15
10 Ivan Rodriguez .40
11 Aubrey Huff .15
12 Jake Peavy .25
13 Hank Blalock .25
14 Curt Schilling .50
15 Carlos Zambrano .40
16 Mike Mussina .40
17 Travis Hafner .15
18 Scott Rolen .50
19 Luis Gonzalez .25
20 Torii Hunter .25
21 Greg Maddux 1.00
22 J.D. Drew .25
23 Kevin Brown .15
24 Carl Pavano .25
25 David Ortiz .50
26 Jose Reyes .40
27 Johan Santana .50
28 Todd Helton .40
29 Jason Kendall .15
30 Pedro Martinez .50
31 Chipper Jones .50
32 Ben Sheets .25
33 Garret Anderson .25
34 Carl Crawford .15
35 Jason Schmidt .25
36 Johnny Damon .50
37 Richie Sexson .25
38 Brad Penny .15
39 Carlos Delgado .40
40 Gary Sheffield .40
41 John Smoltz .25
42 Eric Chavez .25
43 Carlos Guillen .15
44 Jeff Kent .25
45 Miguel Tejada .40
46 Shawn Green .25
47 Vernon Wells .15
48 Albert Pujols 1.50
49 Alfonso Soriano .50
50 Eric Gagne .40
51 Mark Prior .50
52 Rafael Furcal .25
53 Preston Wilson .15
54 Barry Larkin .25
55 Randy Johnson .50
56 Craig Wilson .15
57 Victor Martinez .15
58 Jim Thome .50
59 Paul Konerko .15
60 Jeff Bagwell .40
61 Lyle Overbay .15
62 Miguel Cabrera .50
63 Melvin Mora .15
64 Scott Podsednik .25
65 Mark Mulder .25
66 Mark Teixeira .40
67 Tom Glavine .25
68 Frank Thomas .40
69 Livan Hernandez .15
70 Kazuo Matsui .15
71 Jose Vidro .15
72 Ichiro Suzuki 1.25
73 Roger Clemens 1.50
74 Manny Ramirez .50
75 Michael Young .15
76 Rafael Palmeiro .40
77 Steve Finley .15
78 Andy Pettitte .25
79 Lance Berkman .25
80 Adrian Beltre .25
81 Carlos Lee .25
82 Bret Boone .15
83 Magglio Ordonez .15
84 Sammy Sosa 1.00
85 Tim Hudson .25
86 Vladimir Guerrero .50
87 Carlos Beltran .40
88 Kerry Wood .50
89 Jim Edmonds .25
90 Mike Sweeney .15
91 Nomar Garciaparra 1.00
92 Mike Piazza 1.00
93 Roy Halladay .25
94 Troy Glaus .25
95 Bernie Williams .25
96 Larry Walker .25
97 Craig Biggio .25
98 Roy Oswalt .25
99 Ken Griffey Jr. 1.00
100 Hideki Matsui 1.00
101 Bucky Jacobsen 3.00
102 J.D. Closser 3.00
103 Antonio Perez 3.00
104 Chris Shelton 3.00
105 David Aardsma 3.00
106 Jake Woods 3.00
107 Jung Bong 3.00
108 Kazuhito Tadano 3.00
109 John Van Benschoten 3.00
110 Jesse Foppert 3.00
111 Joe Borchard 3.00
112 Brandon Phillips 3.00
113 J.D. Durbin 3.00
114 Brandon Claussen 3.00
115 Robb Quinlan 3.00
116 Aaron Harang 3.00
117 Chris Burke 3.00
118 Sergio Mitre 3.00
119 David DeJesus 3.00
120 Gustavo Chacin 3.00
121 Xavier Nady 3.00
122 Garrett Atkins 3.00
123 Jimmy Gobble 3.00
124 Yhency Brazoban 3.00
125 David Kelton 3.00
126 Dewon Brazelton 3.00
127 Koyie Hill 3.00
128 Roman Colon 3.00
129 Daniel Cabrera 3.00
130 Chris Bootcheck 3.00
131 Brad Halsey 3.00
132 Bobby Madritsch 3.00
133 Grady Sizemore 3.00
134 Akinori Otsuka 3.00
135 Wilfredo Ledezma 3.00
136 Russ Adams 3.00
137 Joe Crede 3.00
138 Chad Cordero 3.00
139 Willie Harris 3.00
140 Joey Gathright 3.00
141 Logan Kensing 3.00
142 Jon Leicester 3.00
143 Freddy Guzman 3.00
144 Jonny Gomes 3.00
145 Jeff Bajenaru 3.00
146 Andres Blanco 3.00
147 Jhonny Peralta 3.00
148 Jayson Werth 3.00
149 Bill Hall 3.00
150 Jason Davis 3.00
151 Gabe Gross 4.00
152 Abe Alvarez 4.00
153 Josh Willingham 4.00
154 Merkin Valdez 4.00
155 Jeff Niemann **RC** 8.00
156 Yadier Molina 4.00
157 Guillermo Quiroz 4.00
158 Ian Snell 4.00
159 Dan Meyer 4.00
160 Jason Lane 4.00
161 Adrian Gonzalez 4.00
162 Eddy Rodriguez 4.00
163 Jason Dubois 4.00
164 Juan Rincon 4.00
165 Ryan Wagner 4.00
166 Nick Swisher 4.00
167 Chad Tracy 4.00
168 Dioner Navarro 4.00
169 Gerald Laird 4.00
170 Alexis Rios 4.00
171 Aaron Rowand 4.00
172 Adam LaRoche 4.00
173 Kevin Youkilis 4.00
174 Philip Humber **RC** 6.00
175 Chin-Hui Tsao 4.00
176 Jeff Francis 5.00
177 Chase Utley 5.00
178 Gavin Floyd 5.00
179 David Wright 10.00
180 B.J. Upton 5.00
181 Laynce Nix 5.00
182 Joe Mauer 8.00
183 Justin Morneau 5.00
184 Zack Greinke 5.00
185 Jose Capellan 5.00
186 Khalil Greene 5.00
187 Oliver Perez 5.00
188 Joe Blanton 5.00
189 Wily Mo Pena 5.00
190 Dallas McPherson 6.00
191 Edwin Jackson 5.00
192 Casey Kotchman 5.00
193 Jesse Crain 5.00
194 Ryan Howard 6.00
195 Bobby Crosby 5.00
196 Jason Bay 5.00
197 Rickie Weeks 5.00
198 Scott Proctor 5.00
199 Dan Haren 5.00
200 Scott Kazmir 5.00

Gold

Gold (1-100): 4-8X
Production 125
Gold (101-150): 1X
Production 150
Gold (151-175): 1X
Production 99
Gold (176-200): No Pricing
Production 25

Future Fabrics

NM/M

Common Player: 4.00
Gold: 1-2X
Production 75 Sets

MC Miguel Cabrera 8.00
BC Bobby Crosby 6.00
KG Khalil Greene 6.00
RH Rich Harden 4.00
EH Eric Hinske 4.00
JJ Jacque Jones 4.00
KE Austin Kearns 4.00
AK Adam Kennedy 4.00
CK Casey Kotchman 4.00
VM Victor Martinez 4.00
KM Kazuo Matsui 4.00
JM Joe Mauer 8.00
DM Dallas McPherson 6.00
TN Trot Nixon 4.00
SP Sidney Ponson 4.00
JR Jose Reyes 4.00
CS C.C. Sabathia 4.00
SS Shannon Stewart 4.00
BU B.J. Upton 4.00
JW Jayson Werth 4.00
DW David Wright 15.00

Pro Material

NM/M

Common Player: 6.00
Gold: 1-2X
Production 50 Sets

JB Jeff Bagwell 6.00
CB Carlos Beltran 8.00
AB Adrian Beltre 6.00
HB Hank Blalock 6.00
EC Eric Chavez 6.00

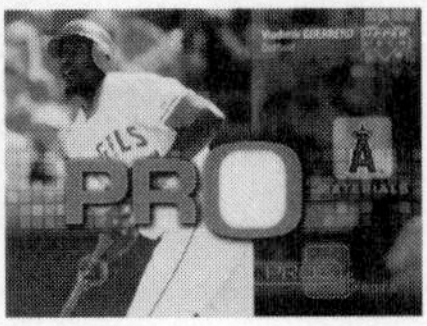

KG	Ken Griffey Jr.	10.00
VG	Vladimir Guerrero	8.00
TH	Todd Helton	8.00
DJ	Derek Jeter	20.00
RJ	Randy Johnson	8.00
CJ	Chipper Jones	8.00
PI	Mike Piazza	8.00
MP	Mark Prior	6.00
AP	Albert Pujols	15.00
MR	Manny Ramirez	8.00
SR	Scott Rolen	8.00
CS	Curt Schilling	8.00
SS	Sammy Sosa	8.00
IS	Ichiro Suzuki	25.00
MT	Miguel Tejada	8.00
JT	Jim Thome	8.00

Signs of Stardom

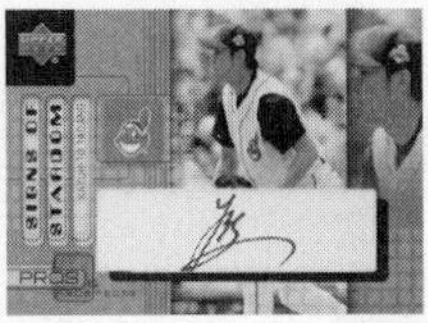

		NM/M
Common Autograph:		8.00
RB	Rocco Baldelli	15.00
JB	Josh Beckett	15.00
AB	Angel Berroa	8.00
HB	Hank Blalock	20.00
SB	Sean Burroughs	8.00
MC	Miguel Cabrera	30.00
CC	Chad Cordero	8.00
BC	Bobby Crosby	15.00
AE	Adam Eaton	12.00
FF	Frank Francisco	8.00
JF	Jason Frasor	8.00
GA	John Gall	8.00
MG	Marcus Giles	15.00
GR	Khalil Greene	25.00
RH	Rich Harden	20.00
MJ	Mike Johnston	8.00
SK	Scott Kazmir	20.00
JK	Jeff Keppinger	8.00
CK	Casey Kotchman	15.00
CL	Cliff Lee	8.00
JL	Justin Leone	8.00
MA	Joe Mauer	25.00
AO	Akinori Otsuka	20.00
LO	Lyle Overbay	10.00
CP	Corey Patterson	15.00
PE	Jake Peavy	30.00
OP	Oliver Perez	15.00
SP	Scott Podsednik	15.00
HR	Horacio Ramirez	8.00
JR	Jose Reyes	30.00
MR	Mike Rouse	8.00
BS	Ben Sheets	15.00
TS	Termel Sledge	10.00
KT	Kazuhito Tadano	20.00
ST	Shingo Takatsu	25.00
MT	Mark Teixeira	30.00
WA	Ryan Wagner	10.00
WE	Brandon Webb	10.00
RW	Rickie Weeks	15.00
JW	Jerome Williams	8.00
DW	Dontrelle Willis	25.00

Stardom Signatures

		NM/M
EB	Ernie Banks/240	50.00
BE	Josh Beckett/50	20.00
BL	Hank Blalock/50	20.00
JG	Jason Giambi/100	15.00
KG	Ken Griffey Jr./198	75.00
AK	Al Kaline/99	50.00
JM	Joe Morgan/194	25.00
KP	Kirby Puckett/156	50.00

2005 Upper Deck Reflections

		NM/M
Complete Set (200):		
Common (1-100):		.50
Common SP (101-150):		1.00
Inserted 1:2		
Common SP (151-200):		2.00
Inserted 1:2		
Pack (4):		8.00
Box (12):		80.00
1	Corey Patterson	.50
2	Curt Schilling	1.00
3	Todd Helton	.75
4	Johnny Damon	1.00
5	Alex Rodriguez	2.50
6	Vladimir Guerrero	1.00

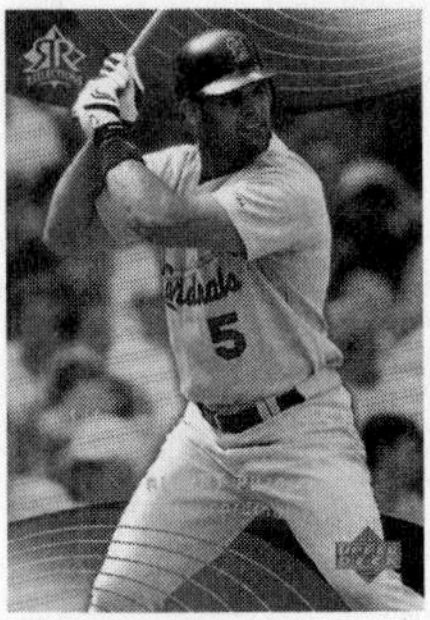

7	John Smoltz	.50
8	Ivan Rodriguez	.75
9	Roy Halladay	.50
10	Carlos Beltran	.75
11	Ichiro Suzuki	2.00
12	Jim Edmonds	.50
13	Andruw Jones	.50
14	Scott Podsednik	.50
15	Troy Glaus	.50
16	Miguel Cabrera	1.00
17	Adrian Beltre	.50
18	Ben Sheets	.50
19	Alfonso Soriano	1.00
20	Brian Giles	.50
21	Carl Crawford	.50
22	Frank Thomas	.75
23	Jeff Kent	.50
24	Eric Gagne	.50
25	Shawn Green	.50
26	Sammy Sosa	2.00
27	Carlos Lee	.50
28	Ken Griffey Jr.	2.00
29	Mike Lowell	.50
30	Magglio Ordonez	.50
31	Aubrey Huff	.50
32	Travis Hafner	.50
33	Albert Pujols	3.00
34	Vernon Wells	.50
35	Roy Oswalt	.50
36	Jose Guillen	.50
37	Jim Thome	.75
38	Bobby Abreu	.50
39	Bret Boone	.50
40	Mark Teixeira	.50
41	Garret Anderson	.50
42	Jose Reyes	.75
43	Bernie Williams	.50
44	Greg Maddux	1.50
45	Gary Sheffield	.50
46	Josh Beckett	.50
47	Chipper Jones	1.00
48	Hank Blalock	.50
49	C.C. Sabathia	.50
50	Manny Ramirez	1.00
51	Pedro Martinez	1.00
52	Michael Young	.50
53	Jacque Jones	.50
54	Marcus Giles	.50
55	Steve Finley	.50
56	Miguel Tejada	.75
57	Mike Sweeney	.50
58	Lance Berkman	.50
59	J.D. Drew	.50
60	Jeromy Burnitz	.50
61	Johan Santana	.75
62	Victor Martinez	.50
63	Carl Pavano	.50
64	Roger Clemens	3.00
65	Richie Sexson	.50
66	Tim Hudson	.50
67	Melvin Mora	.50
68	Angel Berroa	.50
69	Rafael Palmeiro	.75
70	Randy Johnson	1.00
71	Torii Hunter	.50
72	Luis Gonzalez	.50
73	Kazuo Matsui	.50
74	Hideki Matsui	2.00
75	Mark Prior	1.00
76	Jeff Bagwell	.75
77	Eric Chavez	.50
78	Mark Loretta	.50
79	Adam Dunn	.75
80	Kerry Wood	1.00
81	Jose Vidro	.50
82	Jason Schmidt	.50
83	Carlos Delgado	.50
84	Scott Rolen	1.00
85	David Ortiz	1.00
86	Edgar Renteria	.50
87	Nomar Garciaparra	1.50
88	Mike Piazza	1.50
89	Mark Mulder	.50
90	Tom Glavine	.50
91	Paul Konerko	.50
92	Larry Walker	.50
93	Derek Jeter	3.00
94	Jake Peavy	.50
95	Carlos Zambrano	.50
96	Russ Ortiz	.50
97	Barry Zito	.50
98	Austin Kearns	.50
99	Pedro Feliz	.50
100	Rich Harden	.50
101	Adam LaRoche	1.00
102	Brandon Claussen	1.00
103	Gavin Floyd	1.00
104	Daniel Cabrera	1.00
105	Joe Mauer	2.00
106	Khalil Greene	2.00
107	David Wright	3.00
108	Rickie Weeks	2.00
109	Robb Quinlan	1.00
110	Bucky Jacobsen	1.00
111	Ryan Howard	2.00
112	Jeff Francis	1.00
113	Jason Lane	1.00
114	Alexis Rios	1.00
115	Bobby Madritsch	1.00
116	Jesse Crain	1.00
117	Oliver Perez	1.00
118	Garrett Atkins	1.00
119	Casey Kotchman	2.00
120	B.J. Upton	1.00
121	Laynce Nix	1.00
122	Adrian Gonzalez	1.00
123	Joe Blanton	1.00
124	Gabe Gross	1.00
125	Scott Kazmir	2.00
126	Zack Greinke	1.00
127	Edwin Jackson	1.00
128	Jason Bay	1.00
129	J.D. Closser	1.00
130	Jason Dubois	1.00
131	Dallas McPherson	2.00
132	Chad Cordero	1.00
133	Angel Guzman	1.00
134	Jayson Werth	1.00
135	Ryan Wagner	1.00
136	Guillermo Quiroz	1.00
137	Scott Proctor	1.00
138	Chris Burke	1.00
139	Nick Swisher	1.00
140	David DeJesus	1.00
141	Yhency Brazoban	1.00
142	Bobby Crosby	1.00
143	Chase Utley	1.00
144	Wily Mo Pena	1.00
145	Roman Colon	1.00
146	Eddy Rodriguez	1.00
147	Gerald Laird	1.00
148	Jose Capellan	1.00
149	Aaron Rowand	1.00
150	Kevin Youkilis	1.00
151	Bob Feller	2.00
152	Robin Yount	4.00
153	Willie Stargell	2.00
154	Cal Ripken Jr.	8.00
155	Monte Irvin	2.00
156	Nolan Ryan	6.00
157	Bob Lemon	2.00
158	Richie Ashburn	2.00
159	Billy Williams	2.00
160	Luis Aparicio	2.00
161	Phil Niekro	2.00
162	Bobby Doerr	2.00
163	Mike Schmidt	6.00
164	Stan Musial	4.00
165	George Kell	2.00
166	Joe Morgan	2.00
167	Whitey Ford	3.00
168	Rick Ferrell	2.00
169	Jim "Catfish" Hunter	2.00
170	Red Schoendienst	2.00
171	Tom Seaver	4.00
172	Pee Wee Reese	2.00
173	Lou Boudreau	2.00
174	Hal Newhouser	2.00
175	Harmon Killebrew	3.00
176	Jim Bunning	2.00
177	Willie McCovey	3.00
178	Bob Gibson	3.00
179	Juan Marichal	2.00
180	Robin Roberts	2.00
181	Gaylord Perry	2.00
182	Brooks Robinson	4.00
183	Al Lopez	2.00
184	Joe DiMaggio	6.00
185	Al Kaline	3.00
186	Rollie Fingers	2.00
187	Mickey Mantle	10.00
188	Enos Slaughter	2.00
189	Ernie Banks	4.00
190	Eddie Mathews	3.00
191	Tommy Lasorda	2.00
192	Fergie Jenkins	2.00
193	Lou Brock	2.00
194	Larry Doby	2.00
195	Phil Rizzuto	3.00
196	Warren Spahn	4.00
197	Ralph Kiner	2.00
198	Hoyt Wilhelm	2.00
199	Early Wynn	2.00
200	Yogi Berra	4.00

Red

Red (1-100):	2-4X
Red (101-200):	1-2.5X
Production 99 Sets	

Purple

Purple (1-100):	2-4X
Purple (101-200):	1-2.5X
Production 99 Sets	

Blue

Blue (1-100):	2-4X
Blue (101-200):	1-2.5X
Production 75 Sets	

Turquoise

Turquoise (1-100):	3-5X
Turquoise (101-200):	1.5-3X
Production 50 Sets	

Emerald

Emerald (1-100):	4-8X
Emerald (101-200):	3-5X
Production 25 Sets	

Platinum

Platinum (1-200):	No Pricing
Production One Set	

Cut From the Same Cloth

		NM/M
Common Duo:		8.00
Production 225 Sets		
Red:		1-1.5X
Production 99 Sets		
Blue:		1-2X
Production 50 Sets		
Platinum:		No Pricing
Production One Set		
AA	Albert Pujols, Adrian Beltre	20.00
AB	Carlos Beltran, Bobby Abreu	10.00
AG	Garret Anderson, Vladimir Guerrero	10.00
AH	Alfonso Soriano, Hank Blalock	10.00
AJ	Albert Pujols, Jim Thome	20.00
AM	Adrian Beltre, Miguel Cabrera	10.00
AT	Jim Thome, Bobby Abreu	10.00
AW	Albert Pujols, Will Clark	20.00
BB	Jeff Bagwell, Craig Biggio	10.00
BG	Carlos Beltran, Ken Griffey Jr.	15.00
BM	Paul Molitor, George Brett	20.00
BO	Josh Beckett, Roy Oswalt	8.00
BP	Johnny Bench, Mike Piazza	15.00
BR	Adrian Beltre, Scott Rolen	10.00
BS	George Brett, Mike Schmidt	25.00
BT	Mark Teixeira, Hank Blalock	10.00
BW	Hank Blalock, David Wright	15.00
CB	Bobby Crosby, Jason Bay	8.00
CC	Bobby Crosby, Eric Chavez	8.00
CG	Bobby Crosby, Khalil Greene	8.00
CL	Miguel Cabrera, Mike Lowell	10.00
CP	Carl Crawford, Scott Podsednik	8.00
CR	Scott Rolen, Eric Chavez	10.00
CT	Miguel Tejada, Bobby Crosby	10.00
DM	Mike Schmidt, Dale Murphy	15.00
DR	Manny Ramirez, Johnny Damon	15.00
GI	Brian Giles, Marcus Giles	8.00
GS	Sammy Sosa, Ken Griffey Jr.	20.00
GV	Jose Guillen, Jose Vidro	8.00
HH	Tim Hudson, Rich Harden	8.00
HK	Kent Hrbek, Harmon Killebrew	20.00
JD	J.D. Drew, Chipper Jones	10.00
JH	Torii Hunter, Jacque Jones	8.00
JJ	Chipper Jones, Andruw Jones	10.00
JM	Don Mattingly, Derek Jeter	30.00
JR	Randy Johnson, Nolan Ryan	30.00
JS	Steve Carlton, Johan Santana	10.00
JT	Miguel Tejada, Derek Jeter	25.00
KH	Jason Kendall, Tim Hudson	8.00
KM	Dallas McPherson, Casey Kotchman	10.00
MB	Wade Boggs, Don Mattingly	20.00
MC	Don Mattingly, Will Clark	20.00
MH	Mark Mulder, Tim Hudson	8.00
MJ	Dale Murphy, Chipper Jones	15.00
MK	Harmon Killebrew, Justin Morneau	15.00
MM	Kazuo Matsui, Hideki Matsui	30.00
MS	Johan Santana, Joe Mauer	12.00
MW	Dallas McPherson, David Wright	20.00
MY	Robin Yount, Paul Molitor	20.00
OD	Johnny Damon, David Ortiz	15.00
OT	Shingo Takatsu, Akinori Otsuka	15.00
PB	Jim Bunning, Jim Palmer	10.00
PC	Miguel Cabrera, Albert Pujols	20.00
PG	Albert Pujols, Vladimir Guerrero	25.00
PP	Mike Piazza, Jorge Posada	15.00
PR	Albert Pujols, Scott Rolen	25.00
PS	Tom Seaver, Mark Prior	10.00
PT	Mark Teixeira, Albert Pujols	20.00
RJ	Cal Ripken Jr., Derek Jeter	40.00
RM	Ivan Rodriguez, Victor Martinez	8.00
RO	Manny Ramirez, David Ortiz	20.00

RP Ivan Rodriguez, Mike Piazza 15.00
RR Cal Ripken Jr., Brooks Robinson 35.00
RT Miguel Tejada, Cal Ripken Jr. 30.00
RW Scott Rolen, David Wright 15.00
SB Ryne Sandberg, Wade Boggs 25.00
SM Pedro J. Martinez, Curt Schilling 15.00
SO Curt Schilling, David Ortiz 15.00
SP Ben Sheets, Mark Prior 10.00
SR Scott Rolen, Mike Schmidt 15.00
ST Alfonso Soriano, Mark Teixeira 15.00
TC Mark Teixeira, Miguel Cabrera 15.00
TH Todd Helton, Jim Thome 10.00
TP Rafael Palmeiro, Miguel Tejada 10.00
TR Manny Ramirez, Jim Thome 12.00
TS Jim Thome, Mike Schmidt 15.00
UJ Derek Jeter, B.J. Upton 25.00
UK B.J. Upton, Scott Kazmir 8.00
UW B.J. Upton, David Wright 15.00
VJ Jose Vidro, Nick Johnson 8.00
WB Bernie Williams, Carlos Beltran 10.00
WJ Bernie Williams, Derek Jeter 25.00
WM Bernie Williams, Hideki Matsui 30.00
WP Mark Prior, Kerry Wood 10.00
WR Kerry Wood, Nolan Ryan 30.00
YR Manny Ramirez, Carl Yastrzemski 20.00
ZM Mark Mulder, Barry Zito 8.00
BD1 Carlos Beltran, Johnny Damon 10.00
BD2 Johnny Damon, Carlos Beltran 10.00
GG1 Ken Griffey Jr., Ken Griffey Sr. 15.00
GG2 Ken Griffey Sr., Ken Griffey Jr. 15.00

Cut From the Same Cloth Autograph Patch

NM/M
Production 25 Sets
BT Mark Teixeira, Hank Blalock 120.00
DG Ken Griffey Jr., Adam Dunn 240.00
GC Miguel Cabrera, Ken Griffey Jr. 240.00
JR Derek Jeter, Cal Ripken Jr. 500.00
MJ Chipper Jones, Dale Murphy 140.00
PC Albert Pujols, Miguel Cabrera 350.00
RP Mike Piazza, Ivan Rodriguez 140.00
SB Ryne Sandberg, Wade Boggs 160.00
TO Mark Teixeira, David Ortiz 100.00
WB David Wright, Hank Blalock 100.00
WR David Wright, Scott Rolen 100.00

Cut From Same Cloth Patch

NM/M
Production 99 Sets
AM Adrian Beltre, Miguel Cabrera 25.00
BR Adrian Beltre, Scott Rolen 25.00
BS George Brett, Mike Schmidt 40.00
BT Mark Teixeira, Hank Blalock 20.00
CB Jason Bay, Bobby Crosby 20.00
CG Bobby Crosby, Khalil Greene 20.00
CP Gary Carter, Mike Piazza 35.00
CR Eric Chavez, Scott Rolen 25.00
DG Ken Griffey Jr., Adam Dunn 40.00
GC Miguel Cabrera, Ken Griffey Jr. 40.00
GI Brian Giles, Marcus Giles 15.00
JM Derek Jeter, Don Mattingly 60.00
JR Cal Ripken Jr., Derek Jeter 80.00
KM Dallas McPherson, Casey Kotchman 25.00
MJ Chipper Jones, Dale Murphy 30.00
MP Mike Piazza, Joe Mauer 30.00
MW Dallas McPherson, David Wright 30.00
MY Robin Yount, Paul Molitor 40.00
OB Wade Boggs, David Ortiz 30.00
OT Shingo Takatsu, Akinori Otsuka 30.00
PB Albert Pujols, Adrian Beltre 40.00
PC Albert Pujols, Miguel Cabrera 40.00
PR Albert Pujols, Scott Rolen 40.00
RJ Randy Johnson, Nolan Ryan 40.00
RP Ivan Rodriguez, Mike Piazza 30.00
RR Cal Ripken Jr., Brooks Robinson 50.00
RW Nolan Ryan, Kerry Wood 40.00
SB Ryne Sandberg, Wade Boggs 50.00
SP Ben Sheets, Mark Prior 20.00
TC Mark Teixeira, Miguel Cabrera 30.00
TO Mark Teixeira, David Ortiz 25.00
UJ Derek Jeter, B.J. Upton 40.00
UW B.J. Upton, David Wright 25.00
WB David Wright, Hank Blalock 30.00
WP Mark Prior, Kerry Wood 30.00
WR David Wright, Scott Rolen 30.00
YO David Ortiz, Carl Yastrzemski 50.00
GG1 Ken Griffey Sr., Ken Griffey Jr. 40.00
GG2 Ken Griffey Jr., Ken Griffey Sr. 40.00

Dual Signature

NM/M
Red: 1-1.5X
Production 99 Sets
Blue: 1.5-2X
Production 35 Sets
Platinum: No Pricing
Production One Set
ABAR Al Rosen, Adrian Beltre 30.00
ABDM Adrian Beltre, Dallas McPherson 30.00
ABDW David Wright, Adrian Beltre 40.00
ABEC Adrian Beltre, Eric Chavez 30.00
ABJL Adrian Beltre, Justin Leone 30.00
ABSR Adrian Beltre, Scott Rolen 30.00
AHBU Aubrey Huff, B.J. Upton 25.00
AHCC Carl Crawford, Aubrey Huff 25.00
AKDM Al Kaline, Dale Murphy 50.00
AOST Akinori Otsuka, Shingo Takatsu 40.00
ARCC Alexis Rios, Carl Crawford 20.00
ARKG Alexis Rios, Ken Griffey Jr. 65.00
ARTH Al Rosen, Travis Hafner 25.00
BAKY Kevin Youkilis, Bronson Arroyo 50.00
BCCR Bobby Crosby, Cal Ripken Jr. 160.00
BCDJ Derek Jeter, Bobby Crosby 125.00
BCEC Bobby Crosby, Eric Chavez 25.00
BCJB Bobby Crosby, Jason Bay 35.00
BCKG Khalil Greene, Bobby Crosby 35.00
BDWB Bobby Doerr, Wade Boggs 50.00
BGMG Brian Giles, Marcus Giles 25.00
BPFH Frank Howard, Boog Powell 30.00
BRRS Brooks Robinson, Ron Santo 40.00
BSJC Ben Sheets, Jose Capellan 20.00
BSRW Rickie Weeks, Ben Sheets 35.00
BSSK Ben Sheets, Scott Kazmir 20.00
BUDJ B.J. Upton, Derek Jeter 125.00
BURW B.J. Upton, Rickie Weeks 30.00
BUSK B.J. Upton, Scott Kazmir 25.00
BWKG Billy Williams, Ken Griffey Jr. 80.00
CCNJ Nick Johnson, Chad Cordero 25.00
CKDM Casey Kotchman, Dallas McPherson 35.00
CKKH Keith Hernandez, Casey Kotchman 20.00
CKMT Casey Kotchman, Mark Teixeira 35.00
CTDM Charles Thomas, Dale Murphy 30.00
CTJC Charles Thomas, Jose Capellan 15.00
CTRH Charles Thomas, Ryan Howard 50.00
CZJS Johan Santana, Carlos Zambrano 60.00
CZLT Carlos Zambrano, Luis Tiant 20.00
DGDB Dwight Gooden, Dewon Brazelton 20.00
DGJB Jim Bouton, Dwight Gooden 20.00
DGJS Dwight Gooden, Johan Santana 50.00
DJDM Derek Jeter, Don Mattingly 200.00
DJKG Derek Jeter, Khalil Greene 140.00
DKFH Frank Howard, Dave Kingman 25.00
DMDW David Wright, Dallas McPherson 50.00
DMJB Dale Murphy, Jason Bay 40.00
DMJL Justin Leone, Dallas McPherson 20.00
DMKY Dallas McPherson, Kevin Youkilis 20.00
DMMS Dallas McPherson, Mike Schmidt 75.00
DMRH Dallas McPherson, Ryan Howard 50.00
DOKY David Ortiz, Kevin Youkilis 60.00
DWJL Justin Leone, David Wright 40.00
DWKH David Wright, Keith Hernandez 65.00
DWKY David Wright, Kevin Youkilis 40.00
DWMS David Wright, Mike Schmidt 100.00
DWSR David Wright, Scott Rolen 65.00
ECSR Scott Rolen, Eric Chavez 50.00
FHMT Mark Teixeira, Frank Howard 40.00
FHNJ Frank Howard, Nick Johnson 25.00
GPJP Gaylord Perry, Jake Peavy 30.00
ISJC Jose Capellan, Ian Snell 15.00
ISMV Ian Snell, Merkin Valdez 15.00
ISSK Ian Snell, Scott Kazmir 20.00
JBIS Ian Snell, Joe Blanton 20.00
JBJP Jim Bunning, Jim Palmer 30.00
JBMV Merkin Valdez, Joe Blanton 15.00
JBRH Joe Blanton, Rich Harden 20.00
JBSK Scott Kazmir, Joe Blanton 20.00
JCMV Merkin Valdez, Jose Capellan 15.00
JLRH Justin Leone, Ryan Howard 50.00
JPJB Jake Peavy, Joe Blanton 25.00
JPKG Jake Peavy, Khalil Greene 50.00
JPRH Jake Peavy, Rich Harden 40.00
JPSK Jake Peavy, Scott Kazmir 30.00
JRDW Jose Reyes, David Wright 75.00
JSMP Johan Santana, Mark Prior 100.00
JSSC Johan Santana, Steve Carlton 50.00
JSSK Johan Santana, Scott Kazmir 40.00
JVMG Marcus Giles, Jose Vidro 20.00
KGKG Ken Griffey Sr., Ken Griffey Jr. 100.00
KGMC Ken Griffey Jr., Miguel Cabrera 100.00
KYWB Kevin Youkilis, Wade Boggs 50.00
MCRH Ryan Howard, Miguel Cabrera 80.00
MGRW Rickie Weeks, Marcus Giles 35.00
MTHB Hank Blalock, Mark Teixeira 50.00
MTMC Miguel Cabrera, Mark Teixeira 60.00
MTRH Mark Teixeira, Ryan Howard 80.00
MVRH Merkin Valdez, Rich Harden 20.00
PBKG Pat Burrell, Ken Griffey Jr. 85.00
PBMC Pat Burrell, Miguel Cabrera 40.00
RHDO Ryan Howard, David Ortiz 80.00
RHRO Roy Oswalt, Rich Harden 30.00
RHSK Rich Harden, Scott Kazmir 25.00
THVM Victor Martinez, Travis Hafner 20.00
TOKH Kent Hrbek, Tony Oliva 30.00
VMYM Victor Martinez, Yadier Molina 20.00

Fabric Jersey

NM/M
Common Player:
Inserted 1:12
CB Carlos Beltran 8.00
AB Adrian Beltre 6.00
HB Hank Blalock 6.00
WB Wade Boggs/SP 10.00
GB George Brett/SP 15.00
MC Miguel Cabrera 8.00
EC Eric Chavez 4.00
WC Will Clark/SP 10.00
JD Johnny Damon 10.00
KG Ken Griffey Jr. 15.00
VG Vladimir Guerrero 8.00
TH Todd Helton 6.00
DJ Derek Jeter/SP 20.00
RJ Randy Johnson 8.00
CJ Chipper Jones 8.00
GM Greg Maddux 10.00
HM Hideki Matsui 20.00
DM Don Mattingly/SP 20.00
PM Paul Molitor/SP 8.00
DO David Ortiz 8.00
PI Mike Piazza 10.00
MP Mark Prior 6.00
AP Albert Pujols 15.00
MR Manny Ramirez 8.00
CR Cal Ripken Jr./SP 25.00
IR Ivan Rodriguez 8.00
SR Scott Rolen 8.00
NR Nolan Ryan/SP 25.00
JS Johan Santana 8.00
CS Curt Schilling 8.00
MS Mike Schmidt/SP 15.00
AS Alfonso Soriano 8.00
MT Mark Teixeira 6.00
TE Miguel Tejada 8.00
JT Jim Thome 8.00
BW Bernie Williams 6.00
KW Kerry Wood 8.00
DW David Wright 10.00
CY Carl Yastrzemski/SP 25.00
RY Robin Yount/SP 10.00

Reflections Auto. Patch

NM/M
Production 50 Sets
JB Jason Bay 50.00
AB Adrian Beltre 30.00
HB Hank Blalock 40.00
WB Wade Boggs 60.00
PB Pat Burrell 35.00
CA Miguel Cabrera 40.00
EC Eric Chavez 30.00
BC Bobby Crosby 30.00
DG Dwight Gooden 40.00
GR Khalil Greene 50.00
KG Ken Griffey Jr. 125.00
RH Rich Harden 35.00
DJ Derek Jeter 275.00
RJ Randy Johnson 100.00
AJ Andruw Jones 75.00
SK Scott Kazmir 40.00
MA Don Mattingly 125.00
MC Dallas McPherson 30.00
PM Paul Molitor 50.00
DM Dale Murphy 40.00
DO David Ortiz 75.00
RO Roy Oswalt 50.00
JP Jake Peavy 40.00
GP Gaylord Perry 30.00
PI Mike Piazza 120.00
MP Mark Prior 50.00
AP Albert Pujols 300.00
CR Cal Ripken Jr. 225.00
SR Scott Rolen 50.00
NR Nolan Ryan 150.00
JS Johan Santana 50.00
MS Mike Schmidt 100.00
BS Ben Sheets 30.00
ST Shingo Takatsu 40.00
MT Mark Teixeira 50.00
BU B.J. Upton 35.00
DW David Wright 100.00
RY Robin Yount 75.00
CZ Carlos Zambrano 40.00

Fabric Reflections Patch

NM/M
Production 99 Sets
JB Jason Bay 15.00
AB Adrian Beltre 10.00
HB Hank Blalock 15.00
WB Wade Boggs 20.00
GB George Brett 50.00
PB Pat Burrell 15.00
CA Miguel Cabrera 20.00
EC Eric Chavez 10.00
BC Bobby Crosby 10.00
MG Marcus Giles 10.00
DG Dwight Gooden 15.00
GR Khalil Greene 15.00
KG Ken Griffey Jr. 40.00
RH Rich Harden 15.00
DJ Derek Jeter 50.00
RJ Randy Johnson 20.00
AJ Andruw Jones 15.00
SK Scott Kazmir 10.00
MA Don Mattingly 30.00
MC Dallas McPherson 10.00
PM Paul Molitor 20.00
DM Dale Murphy 15.00
DO David Ortiz 20.00
RO Roy Oswalt 10.00
JP Jake Peavy 15.00
GP Gaylord Perry 10.00
PI Mike Piazza 20.00
MP Mark Prior 15.00
AP Albert Pujols 50.00
CR Cal Ripken Jr. 60.00
SR Scott Rolen 20.00
NR Nolan Ryan 40.00
JS Johan Santana 20.00
MS Mike Schmidt 25.00
BS Ben Sheets 15.00
ST Shingo Takatsu 15.00
MT Mark Teixeira 15.00
BU B.J. Upton 10.00
DW David Wright 20.00
RY Robin Yount 30.00
CZ Carlos Zambrano 15.00

Super Swatch

NM/M
Production 50 Sets
Red: 1-1.5X
Production 25 Sets
Blue: No Pricing
Production 10 Sets
BO Bobby Abreu 15.00
RA Roberto Alomar 15.00
MA Moises Alou 10.00
GA Garret Anderson 10.00
BA Jeff Bagwell 15.00
RB Rocco Baldelli 10.00
JB Jason Bay 15.00
BE Josh Beckett 10.00
CB Carlos Beltran 15.00
AB Adrian Beltre 8.00
LB Lance Berkman 10.00
BI Craig Biggio 10.00
HB Hank Blalock 10.00
BB Bret Boone 8.00
KB Kevin Brown 8.00

MC	Miguel Cabrera	15.00
EC	Eric Chavez	10.00
CC	Carl Crawford	10.00
BC	Bobby Crosby	10.00
DA	Johnny Damon	20.00
CD	Carlos Delgado	15.00
JD	J.D. Drew	10.00
AD	Adam Dunn	15.00
JE	Jim Edmonds	15.00
KF	Keith Foulke	10.00
EG	Eric Gagne	10.00
JG	Jason Giambi	10.00
BG	Brian Giles	8.00
MG	Marcus Giles	8.00
TG	Tom Glavine	10.00
LG	Luis Gonzalez	10.00
SG	Shawn Green	10.00
GR	Khalil Greene	12.00
KG	Ken Griffey Jr.	40.00
VG	Vladimir Guerrero	15.00
HA	Roy Halladay	10.00
RH	Rich Harden	10.00
HE	Todd Helton	10.00
HO	Trevor Hoffman	10.00
TH	Tim Hudson	12.00
AH	Aubrey Huff	8.00
HU	Torii Hunter	10.00
DJ	Derek Jeter	40.00
RJ	Randy Johnson	15.00
AJ	Andruw Jones	15.00
CJ	Chipper Jones	15.00
JJ	Jacque Jones	8.00
SK	Scott Kazmir	8.00
JK	Jason Kendall	8.00
ML	Mike Lowell	8.00
GM	Greg Maddux	30.00
PM	Pedro Martinez	15.00
VM	Victor Martinez	8.00
HM	Hideki Matsui	50.00
KM	Kazuo Matsui	15.00
DM	Dallas McPherson	12.00
JM	Justin Morneau	20.00
MM	Mark Mulder	10.00
MU	Mike Mussina	15.00
HN	Hideo Nomo	40.00
MO	Magglio Ordonez	8.00
DO	David Ortiz	15.00
RO	Roy Oswalt	10.00
AO	Akinori Otsuka	15.00
RP	Rafael Palmeiro	10.00
CP	Corey Patterson	10.00
PI	Mike Piazza	20.00
SP	Scott Podsednik	15.00
JP	Jorge Posada	15.00
MP	Mark Prior	15.00
AP	Albert Pujols	40.00
MR	Manny Ramirez	20.00
ER	Edgar Renteria	10.00
JR	Jose Reyes	12.00
IR	Ivan Rodriguez	12.00
SR	Scott Rolen	15.00
CS	C.C. Sabathia	8.00
SA	Johan Santana	15.00
SC	Curt Schilling	15.00
JS	Jason Schmidt	12.00
RS	Richie Sexson	10.00
BS	Ben Sheets	10.00
GS	Gary Sheffield	15.00
AS	Alfonso Soriano	15.00
SS	Sammy Sosa	20.00
MS	Mike Sweeney	8.00
ST	Shingo Takatsu	15.00
MT	Mark Teixeira	15.00
TE	Miguel Tejada	15.00
JT	Jim Thome	15.00
JV	Jose Vidro	8.00
WA	Billy Wagner	10.00
VW	Vernon Wells	8.00
BW	Bernie Williams	15.00
KW	Kerry Wood	15.00
DW	David Wright	25.00
BZ	Barry Zito	10.00

2005 Upper Deck Sweet Spot

	NM/M
Complete Set (90):	20.00
Common Player:	.25
Pack (5):	12.00
Box (12):	120.00
1 Magglio Ordonez	.25
2 Craig Biggio	.50

3	Hank Blalock	.40
4	Nomar Garciaparra	.75
5	Ken Griffey Jr.	1.50
6	Khalil Greene	.40
7	Andruw Jones	.50
8	Ichiro Suzuki	1.50
9	Phillip Humber RC	1.50
10	Vladimir Guerrero	.75
11	Carlos Delgado	.40
12	Jeff Niemann RC	1.50
13	Chipper Jones	.75
14	Jose Vidro	.25
15	Miguel Cabrera	.75
16	Albert Pujols	2.00
17	Tadahito Iguchi RC	2.50
18	Norihiro Nakamura RC	1.50
19	Jeff Bagwell	.50
20	Troy Glaus	.40
21	Scott Rolen	.75
22	Derek Lowe	.25
23	Mark Prior	.75
24	Bobby Abreu	.40
25	David Wright	1.00
26	Barry Zito	.40
27	Livan Hernandez	.25
28	Mark Teixeira	.50
29	Manny Ramirez	.75
30	Paul Konerko	.40
31	Victor Martinez	.25
32	Greg Maddux	1.50
33	Jim Thome	.50
34	Miguel Tejada	.50
35	Ivan Rodriguez	.50
36	Carlos Beltran	.50
37	Steve Finley	.25
38	Torii Hunter	.25
39	Bobby Crosby	.25
40	Jorge Posada	.40
41	Ben Sheets	.40
42	Mike Piazza	1.00
43	Luis Gonzalez	.25
44	Joe Mauer	.50
45	Shawn Green	.25
46	Eric Gagne	.40
47	Kerry Wood	.40
48	Derek Jeter	2.00
49	Josh Beckett	.25
50	Alex Rodriguez	1.50
51	Aubrey Huff	.25
52	Eric Chavez	.40
53	Sammy Sosa	1.00
54	Roger Clemens	2.00
55	Mike Mussina	.50
56	Mike Sweeney	.25
57	Oliver Perez	.25
58	Tim Hudson	.40
59	Justin Verlander RC	2.00
60	Johan Santana	.50
61	Hideki Matsui	1.50
62	Mark Mulder	.40
63	Jake Peavy	.40
64	Adam Dunn	.50
65	Dallas McPherson	.25
66	Jeff Kent	.40
67	Pedro Martinez	.75
68	J.D. Drew	.25
69	Frank Thomas	.50
70	Kazuo Matsui	.25
71	Travis Hafner	.40
72	John Smoltz	.40
73	Jason Schmidt	.25
74	Carlos Lee	.25
75	Todd Helton	.50
76	David Ortiz	.75
77	Roy Oswalt	.40
78	Brian Giles	.25
79	Gary Sheffield	.50
80	Jason Bay	.40
81	Alfonso Soriano	.75
82	Randy Johnson	.75
83	Tom Glavine	.40
84	Richie Sexson	.40
85	Curt Schilling	.75
86	Adrian Beltre	.40
87	Jim Edmonds	.40
88	Roy Halladay	.40
89	Johnny Damon	.75
90	Lance Berkman	.40

Gold
Gold (1-90):	1-2X
Production 599 Sets	

Platinum
Platinum (1-90):	2-4X
Production 99 Sets	

Plutonium
No Pricing	
Production One Set	

Majestic Materials
	NM/M
Common Player:	.25
Gold:	1-1.5X
Production 75 Sets	
Platinum:	No Pricing
Production 10 Sets	
Plutonium:	No Pricing
Production One Set	
Patch:	2-3X
Production 35 Sets	
BA Bobby Abreu	4.00
MA Moises Alou	6.00
JB Jason Bay	4.00
BE Josh Beckett	4.00

LB	Lance Berkman	4.00
CB	Craig Biggio	6.00
BB	Bret Boone	4.00
BC	Bobby Crosby	4.00
CD	Carlos Delgado	4.00
JD	J.D. Drew	4.00
AD	Adam Dunn	6.00
JE	Jim Edmonds	6.00
JG	Jason Giambi	4.00
BG	Brian Giles	4.00
TG	Troy Glaus	4.00
LG	Luis Gonzalez	4.00
SG	Shawn Green	4.00
KG	Khalil Greene	6.00
HA	Travis Hafner	4.00
RH	Roy Halladay	4.00
TH	Tim Hudson	4.00
HU	Torii Hunter	4.00
TI	Tadahito Iguchi	5.00
AJ	Andruw Jones	6.00
SK	Scott Kazmir	4.00
JK	Jeff Kent	4.00
VM	Victor Martinez	4.00
KM	Kazuo Matsui	4.00
JM	Joe Mauer	6.00
DM	Dallas McPherson	4.00
MM	Mark Mulder	6.00
MU	Mike Mussina	6.00
MO	Magglio Ordonez	6.00
RO	Roy Oswalt	4.00
JP	Jake Peavy	4.00
OP	Oliver Perez	4.00
AP	Andy Pettitte	6.00
PO	Jorge Posada	6.00
ER	Edgar Renteria	4.00
JR	Jose Reyes	4.00
JS	Jason Schmidt	6.00
RS	Richie Sexson	6.00
BS	Ben Sheets	4.00
GS	Gary Sheffield	6.00
ST	Shingo Takatsu	4.00
BU	B.J. Upton	4.00
JV	Jose Vidro	4.00
VW	Vernon Wells	4.00
DW	David Wright	10.00
BZ	Barry Zito	4.00

Majestic Materials Dual
	NM/M
Production 25 Sets	
Gold:	No Pricing
Production Five Sets	
Plutonium:	No Pricing
Production One Set	
Patch:	No Pricing
Production Five Sets	
BB Craig Biggio, Jeff Bagwell	15.00
BP Jason Bay, Oliver Perez	10.00
BS Adrian Beltre, Richie Sexson	10.00
BT Hank Blalock, Mark Teixeira	12.00
CC Bobby Crosby, Eric Chavez	10.00
DG Adam Dunn, Ken Griffey Jr.	25.00
DK J.D. Drew, Jeff Kent	10.00
DR Johnny Damon, Manny Ramirez	15.00
GG Shawn Green, Troy Glaus	15.00
GR Eric Gagne, Mariano Rivera	15.00
HM Travis Hafner, Victor Martinez	10.00
JJ Andruw Jones, Chipper Jones	15.00
MC Don Mattingly, Will Clark	25.00
MW Dallas McPherson, David Wright	15.00
PC Albert Pujols, Miguel Cabrera	25.00
PG Jake Peavy, Khalil Greene	12.00
PL Albert Pujols, Derrek Lee	25.00
RM Jose Reyes, Kazuo Matsui	10.00
RO Ivan Rodriguez, Magglio Ordonez	10.00
RT Brian Roberts, Miguel Tejada	15.00
SH John Smoltz, Tim Hudson	15.00
SM Joe Mauer, Johan Santana	15.00
TI Shingo Takatsu, Tadahito Iguchi	20.00
UK B.J. Upton, Scott Kazmir	10.00
WC David Wright, Miguel Cabrera	15.00

Majestic Materials Quad
	NM/M
Production 25 Sets	
Gold:	No Pricing
Production Five Sets	
Plutonium:	No Pricing
Production One Set	
Patch:	No Pricing
Production Five Sets	
JJSH Andruw Jones, Chipper Jones, John Smoltz, Tim Hudson	25.00
JSJP Derek Jeter, Gary Sheffield, Randy Johnson, Jorge Posada	60.00
OVDR David Ortiz, Jason Varitek, Johnny Damon, Manny Ramirez	40.00
PEWR Albert Pujols, Jim Edmonds, Larry Walker, Scott Rolen	50.00
ZMWP Carlos Zambrano, Greg Maddux, Kerry Wood, Mark Prior	30.00

Majestic Materials Triple
	NM/M
Production 25 Sets	
Gold:	No Pricing
Production Five Sets	
Plutonium:	No Pricing
Production One Set	
Patch:	No Pricing
Production Five Sets	
BPO Josh Beckett, Mark Prior, Roy Oswalt	15.00
BSB George Brett, Mike Schmidt, Wade Boggs	30.00
BTH Jeff Bagwell, Jim Thome, Todd Helton	20.00
HRG Torii Hunter, Manny Ramirez, Vladimir Guerrero	20.00
JCG Andruw Jones, Miguel Cabrera, Vladimir Guerrero	15.00
JRT Derek Jeter, Edgar Renteria, Miguel Tejada	25.00
MMP Greg Maddux, Pedro Martinez, Jake Peavy	25.00
MSG Greg Maddux, John Smoltz, Tom Glavine	40.00
OGP David Ortiz, Jason Giambi, Rafael Palmeiro	15.00
PBC Albert Pujols, Carlos Beltran, Miguel Cabrera	40.00
RBW Nolan Ryan, Josh Beckett, Kerry Wood	40.00
RGB Cal Ripken Jr., Tony Gwynn, Wade Boggs	50.00
SSJ Curt Schilling, Johan Santana, Randy Johnson	25.00
VPP Jason Varitek, Jorge Posada, Mike Piazza	25.00
WRG David Wright, Scott Rolen, Troy Glaus	25.00

Signatures Barrel Black Ink
	NM/M
Production 25-50	
JB Jason Bay/50	20.00
HB Hank Blalock/25	25.00
CA Miguel Cabrera/25	70.00
SC Steve Carlton/25	25.00
SE Sean Casey/50	20.00
WC Will Clark/50	25.00
CC Carl Crawford/50	15.00
BC Bobby Crosby/50	30.00
DA Andre Dawson/25	50.00
AD Adam Dunn/25	40.00
GF Gavin Floyd/50	20.00
NG Nomar Garciaparra/25	80.00
MG Marcus Giles/50	15.00
GL Tom Glavine/50	30.00
GR Khalil Greene/50	35.00
KG Ken Griffey Jr./25	85.00
HA Travis Hafner/50	25.00
RH Rich Harden/50	20.00
KH Keith Hernandez/50	20.00
HO Ryan Howard/50	90.00
AH Aubrey Huff/50	15.00
PH Philip Humber/50	25.00
BJ Bo Jackson/25	75.00
DJ Derek Jeter/25	250.00
RJ Randy Johnson/25	125.00
AJ Andruw Jones/25	50.00
SK Scott Kazmir/50	20.00
BL Barry Larkin/25	40.00
MA Don Mattingly/25	85.00
PM Paul Molitor/25	40.00
MO Justin Morneau/50	25.00
MM Mark Mulder/50	25.00
JN Jeff Niemann/50	20.00
RO Roy Oswalt/50	35.00
LO Lyle Overbay/50	15.00
JP Jake Peavy/50	25.00
MP Mark Prior/25	50.00
AP Albert Pujols/25	220.00
AR Aramis Ramirez/50	30.00
CR Cal Ripken Jr./25	180.00
NR Nolan Ryan/25	100.00
RS Ryne Sandberg/25	75.00

MS Mike Schmidt/25 70.00
MT Mark Teixeira/25 40.00
BU B.J. Upton/50 20.00
JV Justin Verlander/50 40.00
DW David Wright/50 100.00
RY Robin Yount/25 90.00
CZ Carlos Zambrano/50 30.00

Signatures Barrel Blue Ink

NM/M
Production 15-30
JB Jason Bay/30 25.00
SE Sean Casey/30 25.00
CC Carl Crawford/30 20.00
BC Bobby Crosby/30 35.00
AD Adam Dunn/15 60.00
GF Gavin Floyd/30 25.00
MG Marcus Giles/30 15.00
GL Tom Glavine/30 40.00
GR Khalil Greene/30 40.00
HA Travis Hafner/30 30.00
RH Rich Harden/30 25.00
KH Keith Hernandez/30 25.00
HO Ryan Howard/30 90.00
AH Aubrey Huff/30 20.00
PH Philip Humber/30 30.00
SK Scott Kazmir/30 20.00
MO Justin Morneau/30 30.00
MM Mark Mulder/30 30.00
JN Jeff Niemann/30 25.00
RO Roy Oswalt/30 40.00
LO Lyle Overbay/30 15.00
CP Corey Patterson/30 20.00
JP Jake Peavy/30 30.00
AP Albert Pujols/15 250.00
AR Aramis Ramirez/30 40.00
BU B.J. Upton/30 25.00
JV Justin Verlander/30 50.00
DW David Wright/30 100.00
CZ Carlos Zambrano/30 35.00

Signatures Barrel Red Ink

No Pricing
Production 5-10

Signatures Glove Blue Ink

No Pricing
Production 5-10
Red Ink: No Pricing
Production 2-5

Sign. Black Stitch Black Ink

No Pricing
Production One Set
Blue Ink: No Pricing
Production One Set
Red Ink: No Pricing
Production One Set

Signatures Dual Barrel

No Pricing
Production 15 Sets

Signatures Dual Glove

No Pricing
Production 10 Sets

Signatures Dual Red Stitch

NM/M
Production 25 Sets
BJ Bobby Crosby, Jason Bay 40.00
CG Bobby Crosby, Khalil Greene 50.00
DC Adam Dunn, Sean Casey 50.00
FH Gavin Floyd, Ryan Howard 120.00
GC Ken Griffey Jr., Miguel Cabrera 120.00
GL Khalil Greene, Mark Loretta 60.00
JC Randy Johnson, Roger Clemens 240.00
JG Andruw Jones, Ken Griffey Jr. 150.00
JM Derek Jeter, Don Mattingly 300.00
LG Barry Larkin, Ken Griffey Jr. 120.00
LR Barry Larkin, Cal Ripken Jr. 160.00
NH Jeff Niemann, Philip Humber 50.00
PB Jason Bay, Oliver Perez 40.00
PC Albert Pujols, Miguel Cabrera 300.00
PO Jake Peavy, Roy Oswalt 75.00
RJ Cal Ripken Jr., Derek Jeter 300.00
SB Ryne Sandberg, Wade Boggs 125.00
SG Nomar Garciaparra, Ryne Sandberg 150.00
SP Ben Sheets, Jake Peavy 50.00
WC David Wright, Miguel Cabrera 120.00
WR David Wright, Jose Reyes 180.00

Signatures Game-Used Ball

No Pricing
Production One Set

Signature Game-Used Barrel

No Pricing
Production 1-10

Signatures Game-Used Glove

No Pricing
Production 9-10

Signatures Glove Black Ink

NM/M
Production 15-30
JB Jason Bay/30 40.00
SE Sean Casey/30 35.00
CC Carl Crawford/30 30.00
BC Bobby Crosby/30 40.00
GF Gavin Floyd/30 30.00
MG Marcus Giles/30 25.00
GL Tom Glavine/30 50.00
GR Khalil Greene/30 50.00
HA Travis Hafner/30 40.00
RH Rich Harden/30 35.00
KH Keith Hernandez/30 30.00
HO Ryan Howard/30 100.00
AH Aubrey Huff/30 25.00
PH Philip Humber/30 40.00
SK Scott Kazmir/30 30.00
MO Justin Morneau/30 40.00
MM Mark Mulder/30 40.00
JN Jeff Niemann/30 30.00
RO Roy Oswalt/30 50.00
LO Lyle Overbay/30 20.00
CP Corey Patterson/30 25.00
JP Jake Peavy/30 40.00
AR Aramis Ramirez/30 50.00
BU B.J. Upton/30 35.00
JV Justin Verlander/30 50.00
DW David Wright/30 100.00
CZ Carlos Zambrano/30 40.00

Sign. Red Stitch Black Ink

NM/M
Production 58-350
JB Jason Bay/350 20.00
HB Hank Blalock/175 20.00
WB Wade Boggs/175 40.00
CA Miguel Cabrera/175 40.00
SC Steve Carlton/58 25.00
SE Sean Casey/350 15.00
WC Will Clark/175 25.00
RC Roger Clemens/175 120.00
CC Carl Crawford/350 15.00
BC Bobby Crosby/350 20.00
DA Andre Dawson/175 20.00
AD Adam Dunn/175 25.00
GF Gavin Floyd/350 15.00
NG Nomar Garciaparra/175 60.00
MG Marcus Giles/350 15.00
GR Khalil Greene/350 20.00
KG Ken Griffey Jr./175 75.00
RH Rich Harden/350 15.00
KH Keith Hernandez/350 15.00
HO Ryan Howard/350 75.00
AH Aubrey Huff/350 15.00
PH Philip Humber/350 15.00
BJ Bo Jackson/175 70.00
DJ Derek Jeter/175 150.00
RJ Randy Johnson/175 75.00
AJ Andruw Jones/175 40.00
SK Scott Kazmir/350 15.00
BL Barry Larkin/175 25.00
EM Edgar Martinez/175 30.00
MA Don Mattingly/175 60.00
PM Paul Molitor/175 25.00
MO Justin Morneau/350 25.00
MM Mark Mulder/350 20.00
JN Jeff Niemann/350 15.00
RO Roy Oswalt/350 25.00
LO Lyle Overbay/350 12.00
JP Jake Peavy/350 20.00
PI Mike Piazza/175 80.00
MP Mark Prior/175 40.00
AP Albert Pujols/175 160.00
AR Aramis Ramirez/350 25.00
RE Jose Reyes/350 35.00
CR Cal Ripken Jr./175 120.00
NR Nolan Ryan/175 80.00
RS Ryne Sandberg/175 65.00
MS Mike Schmidt/175 50.00
MT Mark Teixeira/175 40.00
BU B.J. Upton/350 15.00
JV Justin Verlander/350 35.00
DW David Wright/350 60.00
RY Robin Yount/175 50.00
CZ Carlos Zambrano/350 20.00

Sign. Red Stitch Blue Ink

NM/M
Production 75-135
JB Jason Bay 25.00
HB Hank Blalock/75 20.00
WB Wade Boggs/75 40.00
CA Miguel Cabrera/75 40.00
SE Sean Casey/135 15.00
WC Will Clark/75 25.00
RC Roger Clemens/75 120.00
CC Carl Crawford/135 15.00
BC Bobby Crosby/135 20.00
DA Andre Dawson/75 20.00
AD Adam Dunn/75 30.00
GF Gavin Floyd/135 15.00
NG Nomar Garciaparra/75 65.00
MG Marcus Giles/135 15.00
GL Tom Glavine/135 25.00
GR Khalil Greene/135 25.00
KG Ken Griffey Jr./75 80.00
HA Travis Hafner/135 20.00
RH Rich Harden/135 15.00
KH Keith Hernandez/135 15.00
HO Ryan Howard/135 75.00
AH Aubrey Huff/135 15.00
PH Philip Humber/135 15.00
BJ Bo Jackson/75 75.00
DJ Derek Jeter/75 150.00
RJ Randy Johnson/75 85.00
AJ Andruw Jones/75 40.00
SK Scott Kazmir/135 15.00
BL Barry Larkin/75 30.00
EM Edgar Martinez/75 35.00
MA Don Mattingly/75 70.00
PM Paul Molitor/75 25.00
MO Justin Morneau/135 30.00
MM Mark Mulder/135 25.00
JN Jeff Niemann/135 15.00
RO Roy Oswalt/135 25.00
LO Lyle Overbay/135 12.00
CP Corey Patterson/135 15.00
JP Jake Peavy/135 25.00
PI Mike Piazza/75 80.00
MP Mark Prior/75 50.00
AP Albert Pujols/75 160.00
AR Aramis Ramirez/135 25.00
RE Jose Reyes/135 35.00
CR Cal Ripken Jr./75 120.00
NR Nolan Ryan/75 80.00
RS Ryne Sandberg/75 65.00
MS Mike Schmidt/75 50.00
MT Mark Teixeira/75 40.00
BU B.J. Upton/135 15.00
JV Justin Verlander/135 35.00
DW David Wright/135 60.00
RY Robin Yount/75 50.00
CZ Carlos Zambrano/135 20.00

Sign. Red Stitch Red Ink

NM/M
Production 15-35
JB Jason Bay/35 25.00
SE Sean Casey/35 25.00
CC Carl Crawford/35 20.00
BC Bobby Crosby 35.00
AD Adam Dunn/15 60.00
GF Gavin Floyd/35 25.00
MG Marcus Giles/35 15.00
GL Tom Glavine/35 40.00
GR Khalil Greene/35 40.00
HA Travis Hafner/35 30.00
RH Rich Harden/35 30.00
KH Keith Hernandez/35 25.00
HO Ryan Howard/35 90.00
AH Aubrey Huff/35 20.00
PH Philip Humber/35 30.00
SK Scott Kazmir/35 20.00
MO Justin Morneau/35 30.00
MM Mark Mulder/35 30.00
JN Jeff Niemann/35 25.00
RO Roy Oswalt/35 40.00
LO Lyle Overbay/35 15.00
CP Corey Patterson/35 20.00
JP Jake Peavy/35 30.00
AP Albert Pujols/15 250.00
AR Aramis Ramirez/35 40.00
RE Jose Reyes/35 40.00
BU B.J. Upton/35 25.00
JV Justin Verlander/35 50.00
DW David Wright/35 100.00
CZ Carlos Zambrano/35 35.00

Signature Red-Blue Stitch Black Ink

NM/M
Production 25-50
JB Jason Bay/50 25.00
HB Hank Blalock/25 25.00
WB Wade Boggs/25 50.00
CA Miguel Cabrera/25 65.00
SC Steve Carlton/25 25.00
SE Sean Casey/50 20.00
WC Will Clark/25 35.00
RC Roger Clemens/25 160.00
CC Carl Crawford/50 15.00
BC Bobby Crosby/50 35.00
DA Andre Dawson/25 25.00
AD Adam Dunn/25 40.00
GF Gavin Floyd/50 15.00
NG Nomar Garciaparra/25 65.00
MG Marcus Giles/50 15.00
GR Khalil Greene/50 30.00
KG Ken Griffey Jr./25 120.00
RH Rich Harden/50 20.00
KG Keith Hernandez/50 20.00
HO Ryan Howard/50 85.00
AH Aubrey Huff/50 20.00
PH Philip Humber/50 20.00
BJ Bo Jackson/25 90.00
DJ Derek Jeter/25 250.00
RJ Randy Johnson/25 120.00
AJ Andruw Jones/25 50.00
SK Scott Kazmir/50 20.00
BL Barry Larkin/25 40.00
EM Edgar Martinez/25 40.00
MA Don Mattingly/25 90.00
PM Paul Molitor/25 40.00
MO Justin Morneau/50 25.00
MM Mark Mulder/50 25.00
JN Jeff Niemann/50 20.00
RO Roy Oswalt/50 35.00
JP Jake Peavy/50 25.00
PI Mike Piazza/25 100.00
MP Mark Prior/25 60.00
AP Albert Pujols/25 220.00
CR Cal Ripken Jr./25 165.00
NR Nolan Ryan/25 100.00
RS Ryne Sandberg/25 80.00
JS Johan Santana/25 50.00
MS Mike Schmidt/25 75.00
MT Mark Teixeira/25 50.00
BU B.J. Upton/50 20.00
JV Justin Verlander/50 40.00
DW David Wright/50 120.00
RY Robin Yount/25 65.00
CZ Carlos Zambrano/50 30.00

Signature Red-Blue Stitch Blue Ink

NM/M
Production 15-30
Red Ink: No Pricing
Production 5-10
JB Jason Bay/30 25.00
SE Sean Casey/30 25.00
CC Carl Crawford/30 20.00
BC Bobby Crosby/30 35.00
GF Gavin Floyd/30 25.00
MG Marcus Giles/30 15.00
GL Tom Glavine/30 40.00
GR Khalil Greene/30 40.00
HA Travis Hafner/30 30.00
RH Rich Harden/30 25.00
KH Keith Hernandez/30 25.00
HO Ryan Howard/30 90.00
PH Philip Humber/30 30.00
SK Scott Kazmir/30 20.00
MO Justin Morneau/30 30.00
MM Mark Mulder/30 30.00
JN Jeff Niemann/30 25.00
RO Roy Oswalt/30 40.00
LO Lyle Overbay/30 15.00
JP Jake Peavy/30 30.00
AR Aramis Ramirez/30 40.00
BU B.J. Upton/30 25.00
JV Justin Verlander/30 50.00
DW David Wright/30 120.00
CZ Carlos Zambrano/30 35.00

Sweet Threads

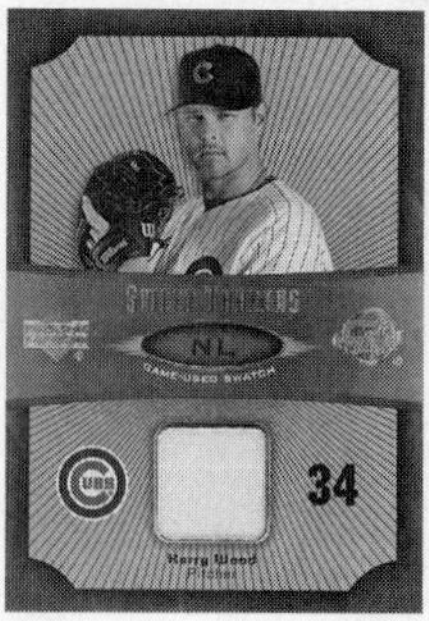

NM/M
Common Player: 4.00
Gold: 1-1.5X
Production 75 Sets
Platinum: No Pricing
Production 10 Sets
Plutonium: No Pricing
Production One Set
Patch: 2-4X
Production 35 Sets
JB Jeff Bagwell 6.00
CB Carlos Beltran 6.00
AB Adrian Beltre 4.00
HB Hank Blalock 4.00
WB Wade Boggs 8.00
GB George Brett 10.00
MC Miguel Cabrera 8.00
EC Eric Chavez 4.00
WC Will Clark 6.00
BC Bartolo Colon 4.00
JD Johnny Damon 6.00
EG Eric Gagne 4.00
TG Tom Glavine 6.00
KG Ken Griffey Jr. 12.00
VG Vladimir Guerrero 8.00
GW Tony Gwynn 8.00
TH Todd Helton 6.00
HO Trevor Hoffman 4.00
BJ Bo Jackson 8.00
DJ Derek Jeter 20.00
RJ Randy Johnson 8.00
CJ Chipper Jones 8.00
CL Carlos Lee 4.00
GM Greg Maddux 10.00
PM Pedro Martinez 8.00
DM Don Mattingly 10.00
DO David Ortiz 8.00
RP Rafael Palmeiro 6.00
PI Mike Piazza 8.00
MP Mark Prior 6.00
AP Albert Pujols 15.00
MR Manny Ramirez 8.00
CR Cal Ripken Jr. 20.00
IR Ivan Rodriguez 6.00
SR Scott Rolen 6.00
NR Nolan Ryan 12.00
RS Ryne Sandberg 8.00
JS Johan Santana 6.00
CS Curt Schilling 6.00
MS Mike Schmidt 10.00
SM John Smoltz 6.00

AS	Alfonso Soriano	6.00
SS	Sammy Sosa	8.00
MT	Mark Teixeira	6.00
TE	Miguel Tejada	6.00
FT	Frank Thomas	6.00
JT	Jim Thome	6.00
JV	Jason Varitek	10.00
BW	Bernie Williams	6.00
KW	Kerry Wood	4.00

Sweet Threads Dual
NM/M

Production 25 Sets
Gold: No Pricing
Production Five Sets
Patch: No Pricing
Production Five Sets
Plutonium: No Pricing
Production One Set

BG	Carlos Beltran, Ken Griffey Jr.	25.00
BM	Carlos Beltran, Pedro Martinez	15.00
DC	Carlos Delgado, Miguel Cabrera	15.00
GC	Ken Griffey Jr., Miguel Cabrera	15.00
GM	Dallas McPherson, Vladimir Guerrero	15.00
JB	Bo Jackson, George Brett	25.00
JJ	Randy Johnson, Derek Jeter	40.00
JM	Derek Jeter, Don Mattingly	50.00
JS	Jim Thome, Mike Schmidt	30.00
MG	Greg Maddux, Tom Glavine	25.00
MJ	Mike Mussina, Randy Johnson	25.00
MP	Greg Maddux, Mark Prior	25.00
OR	David Ortiz, Manny Ramirez	20.00
PO	Andy Pettitte, Roy Oswalt	10.00
PR	Pedro Martinez, Randy Johnson	20.00
PS	Rafael Palmeiro, Sammy Sosa	20.00
PW	David Wright, Mike Piazza	20.00
RJ	Cal Ripken Jr., Derek Jeter	70.00
RP	Albert Pujols, Scott Rolen	30.00
RT	Cal Ripken Jr., Miguel Tejada	40.00
SB	Ryne Sandberg, Wade Boggs	30.00
SJ	Curt Schilling, Randy Johnson	20.00
SV	Curt Schilling, Jason Varitek	20.00
WP	Kerry Wood, Mark Prior	15.00

Sweet Threads Quad
NM/M

Production 25 Sets
Gold: No Pricing
Production Five Sets
Plutonium: No Pricing
Production One Set
Production Five Sets

BMCB	Adrian Beltre, Dallas McPherson, Eric Chavez, Hank Blalock	25.00
BRGG	Carlos Beltran, Manny Ramirez, Ken Griffey Jr., Vladimir Guerrero	40.00
POTH	Albert Pujols, David Ortiz, Jim Thome, Todd Helton	40.00
RBGB	Cal Ripken Jr., Brett George, Tony Gwynn, Wade Boggs	90.00
RVMP	Ivan Rodriguez, Jason Varitek, Joe Mauer, Jorge Posada	30.00

Sweet Threads Triple
NM/M

Production 25 Sets
Gold: No Pricing
Production Five Sets
Plutonium: No Pricing
Production One Set
Patch: No Pricing
Production Five Sets

BBB	Craig Biggio, Jeff Bagwell, Lance Berkman	20.00
BWP	Carlos Beltran, David Wright, Mike Piazza	25.00
GGG	Luis Gonzalez, Shawn Green, Troy Glaus	10.00
JMB	Randy Johnson, Mike Mussina, Kevin Brown	25.00
JWS	Derek Jeter, Bernie Williams, Gary Sheffield	50.00
KGD	Austin Kearns, Ken Griffey Jr., Adam Dunn	30.00
LOP	Brad Lidge, Roy Oswalt, Andy Pettitte	15.00
ODR	David Ortiz, Johnny Damon, Manny Ramirez	25.00
PER	Albert Pujols, Jim Edmonds, Scott Rolen	40.00
PWM	Mark Prior, Kerry Wood, Greg Maddux	30.00
RDN	Manny Ramirez, Johnny Damon, Trot Nixon	30.00
SBT	Alfonso Soriano, Hank Blalock, Mark Teixeira	20.00

SMJ	Curt Schilling, Pedro Martinez, Randy Johnson	25.00
TPS	Miguel Tejada, Rafael Palmeiro, Sammy Sosa	20.00

2005 Upper Deck Sweet Spot Classic

		NM/M
	Complete Set (100):	30.00
	Common Player:	.40
	Pack (4):	12.00
	Box (12):	120.00
1	Al Kaline	1.00
2	Al Rosen	.40
3	Babe Ruth	4.00
4	Bill Mazeroski	.40
5	Billy Williams	.40
6	Bob Feller	.75
7	Bob Gibson	1.00
8	Bobby Doerr	.40
9	Brooks Robinson	1.00
10	Cal Ripken Jr.	4.00
11	Carl Yastrzemski	2.00
12	Carlton Fisk	.40
13	Casey Stengel	.40
14	Christy Mathewson	2.00
15	Cy Young	1.50
16	Dale Murphy	.75
17	Dave Winfield	.75
18	Dennis Eckersley	.40
19	Dizzy Dean	1.00
20	Don Drysdale	.75
21	Don Mattingly	3.00
22	Don Newcombe	.40
23	Don Sutton	.40
24	Duke Snider	.40
25	Dwight Evans	.40
26	Eddie Mathews	1.50
27	Eddie Murray	1.00
28	Enos Slaughter	.40
29	Ernie Banks	2.00
30	Frank Howard	.40
31	Frank Robinson	.75
32	Gary Carter	.40
33	Gaylord Perry	.40
34	George Brett	3.00
35	George Kell	.40
36	George Sisler	.40
37	Larry Doby	.40
38	Harmon Killebrew	1.50
39	Honus Wagner	2.00
40	Jackie Robinson	2.00
41	Jim Bunning	.40
42	Jim Palmer	.75
43	Jim Rice	.40
44	Jimmie Foxx	.40
45	Joe DiMaggio	3.00
46	Joe Morgan	.40
47	Johnny Bench	2.00
48	Johnny Mize	.40
49	Johnny Podres	.40
50	Juan Marichal	.40
51	Keith Hernandez	.40
52	Kirby Puckett	1.00
53	Lefty Grove	.40
54	Lou Brock	.75
55	Lou Gehrig	4.00
56	Luis Aparicio	.40
57	Fergie Jenkins	.40
58	Maury Wills	.40
59	Mel Ott	1.50
60	Mickey Cochrane	1.00
61	Mickey Mantle	4.00
62	Mike Schmidt	3.00
63	Monte Irvin	.75
64	Nolan Ryan	4.00
65	Orlando Cepeda	.40
66	Ozzie Smith	1.50
67	Paul Molitor	1.00
68	Pee Wee Reese	.40
69	Phil Niekro	.40
70	Phil Rizzuto	1.00
71	Ralph Kiner	.40
72	Richie Ashburn	.40
73	Roberto Clemente	4.00
74	Robin Roberts	.40
75	Robin Yount	2.00
76	Rocky Colavito	1.00
77	Rod Carew	.75
78	Rogers Hornsby	1.00
79	Rollie Fingers	.40
80	Roy Campanella	1.00
81	Bob Lemon	.40
82	Red Schoendienst	.40
83	Satchel Paige	2.00
84	Stan Musial	2.50
85	Steve Carlton	.75
86	Ted Williams	3.00
87	Thurman Munson	1.50
88	Tom Seaver	1.00
89	Tony Gwynn	1.50
90	Tony Perez	.40
91	Ty Cobb	2.00
92	Wade Boggs	1.00
93	Walter Johnson	1.00
94	Warren Spahn	1.50
95	Whitey Ford	1.00
96	Will Clark	.75
97	Jim "Catfish" Hunter	.40
98	Willie McCovey	.75
99	Willie Stargell	1.00
100	Yogi Berra	1.50

Gold

Cards (1-100): 4-8X
Production 50 Sets

Silver
Cards (1-100): 2-4X
Production 100 Sets

Classic Materials

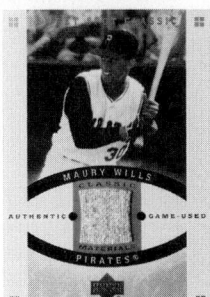

		NM/M
	Common Player:	6.00
BE	Johnny Bench	15.00
YB	Yogi Berra	20.00
WB	Wade Boggs	10.00
GB	George Brett	10.00
GB1	George Brett	10.00
LB	Lou Brock	8.00
JB	Jim Bunning	10.00
CP	Roy Campanella	12.00
CA	Rod Carew	8.00
SC	Steve Carlton	8.00
GC	Gary Carter	6.00
OC	Orlando Cepeda	8.00
WC	Will Clark	10.00
WC1	Will Clark	10.00
RC	Roberto Clemente	60.00
TC	Ty Cobb/SP	100.00
CO	Rocky Colavito	25.00
DC	David Cone	6.00
AD	Andre Dawson	6.00
JD	Joe DiMaggio	80.00
DD	Don Drysdale	10.00
BF	Bob Feller	12.00
CF	Carlton Fisk	8.00
LG	Lou Gehrig/SP	160.00
BG	Bob Gibson	10.00
MG	Mark Grace	8.00
RG	Ron Guidry	8.00
TG	Tony Gwynn	12.00
CH	Jim "Catfish" Hunter	8.00
FJ	Fergie Jenkins	8.00
AK	Al Kaline	10.00
HK	Harmon Killebrew	12.00
MM	Mickey Mantle/SP	120.00
MA	Juan Marichal	8.00
EM	Eddie Mathews	10.00
DM	Don Mattingly	15.00
DM1	Don Mattingly	15.00
BM	Bill Mazeroski	8.00
WI	Willie McCovey	10.00
PM	Paul Molitor	8.00
JM	Joe Morgan	6.00
JM1	Joe Morgan	6.00
TM	Thurman Munson/SP	25.00
MU	Dale Murphy	10.00
ED	Eddie Murray	8.00
ED1	Eddie Murray	8.00
SM	Stan Musial/SP	20.00
PN	Phil Niekro	6.00
SP	Satchel Paige/SP	50.00
JP	Jim Palmer	8.00
TP	Tony Perez	8.00
GP	Gaylord Perry	6.00
RE	Pee Wee Reese/SP	15.00
RI	Jim Rice	8.00
CR	Cal Ripken Jr.	20.00
CR1	Cal Ripken Jr.	20.00
PR	Phil Rizzuto	15.00
RR	Robin Roberts	10.00
RO	Brooks Robinson	10.00
FR	Frank Robinson	8.00
JR	Jackie Robinson	50.00
BR	Babe Ruth/SP	275.00
NR	Nolan Ryan	25.00
NR1	Nolan Ryan	25.00
MS	Mike Schmidt	15.00
MS1	Mike Schmidt	15.00
SD	Red Schoendienst	8.00
TS	Tom Seaver	10.00
OS	Ozzie Smith/SP	15.00
SN	Duke Snider	10.00
WS	Warren Spahn	15.00
DS	Don Sutton	6.00
DS1	Don Sutton	6.00
FV	Fernando Valenzuela	6.00
TW	Ted Williams/SP	75.00
MW	Maury Wills	6.00
MW1	Maury Wills	6.00
DW	Dave Winfield	6.00
DW1	Dave Winfield	6.00
EW	Early Wynn	10.00
CY	Carl Yastrzemski	15.00
RY	Robin Yount	12.00

Dual Signatures
No Pricing
Production 15 Sets

Leather Signatures
No Pricing
Production 25 Sets

Patch
NM/M

Some not priced due to scarcity.

LA	Luis Aparicio/19	150.00
BE	Johnny Bench/32	100.00
WB	Wade Boggs/25	60.00
WB1	Wade Boggs/50	60.00
GB	George Brett/38	80.00
GB1	George Brett/50	80.00
LB	Lou Brock/34	90.00
SC	Steve Carlton/50	60.00
GC	Gary Carter/47	50.00
GC1	Gary Carter/34	50.00
OC	Orlando Cepeda/40	50.00
DC	David Cone/39	50.00
JD	Joe DiMaggio/38	250.00
CF1	Carlton Fisk/50	70.00
RG	Ron Guidry/30	40.00
TG	Tony Gwynn/34	80.00
TG1	Tony Gwynn/30	80.00
FH	Frank Howard/34	85.00
FJ	Fergie Jenkins/34	60.00
WI	Willie McCovey/50	60.00
JM	Joe Morgan/50	60.00
MU	Dale Murphy/34	80.00
ED	Eddie Murray/34	70.00
PN	Phil Niekro/44	50.00
TP	Tony Perez/34	75.00
GP	Gaylord Perry/34	50.00
PO	Johnny Podres/50	60.00
RI	Jim Rice/34	50.00
CR	Cal Ripken Jr./34	150.00
CR1	Cal Ripken Jr./34	150.00
RO	Brooks Robinson/50	85.00
RO1	Brooks Robinson/43	85.00
FR	Frank Robinson/34	80.00
JR	Jackie Robinson/12	250.00
SD	Red Schoendienst/42	60.00
TS	Tom Seaver/50	50.00
TS1	Tom Seaver/34	50.00
OS	Ozzie Smith/34	100.00
ST	Willie Stargell/50	65.00
BS	Bruce Sutter/50	50.00
DS	Don Sutton/34	40.00
DS1	Don Sutton/50	40.00
MW	Maury Wills/34	60.00
MW1	Maury Wills/47	60.00
DW1	Dave Winfield/50	75.00
CY	Carl Yastrzemski/35	100.00
RY	Robin Yount/34	75.00

Sweet Spot Signatures
NM/M

Common Autograph: 20.00
Inserted 1:12
Blue/Red Stitch: 1.5-2X
Production 40 Sets

Black Stitch: No Pricing
Production One Set

LA	Luis Aparicio	25.00
HB	Harold Baines	20.00
EB	Ernie Banks	75.00
BE	Johnny Bench	60.00
YB	Yogi Berra	60.00
WB	Wade Boggs	50.00
GB	George Brett	85.00
JB	Jim Bunning	20.00
JC	Jose Canseco	40.00
CA	Rod Carew	50.00
SC	Steve Carlton	40.00
GC	Gary Carter	25.00
OC	Orlando Cepeda	25.00
WC	Will Clark	30.00
RC	Rocky Colavito/SP	85.00
DC	David Cone	20.00
AD	Andre Dawson	20.00
BD	Bobby Doerr	25.00
DE	Dennis Eckersley	25.00
EV	Dwight Evans	20.00
BF	Bob Feller	40.00
RF	Rollie Fingers	40.00
CF	Carlton Fisk	40.00
WF	Whitey Ford	60.00
BG	Bob Gibson	60.00
MG	Mark Grace	40.00
TG	Tony Gwynn	50.00
EH	Ernie Harwell/SP	40.00
KH	Keith Hernandez	20.00
FH	Frank Howard	25.00
MI	Monte Irvin	25.00
BJ	Bo Jackson	75.00
DJ	David Justice	20.00
KA	Harry Kalas	25.00
AK	Al Kaline	40.00
GK	George Kell	25.00
HK	Harmon Killebrew	50.00
RK	Ralph Kiner/SP	50.00
MA	Juan Marichal	25.00
DM	Don Mattingly	80.00
BM	Bill Mazeroski	40.00
MC	Willie McCovey/SP	60.00
PM	Paul Molitor	40.00
JM	Joe Morgan/SP	35.00
MU	Dale Murphy	25.00
SM	Stan Musial	100.00
DN	Don Newcombe	25.00
PN	Phil Niekro	25.00
JP	Jim Palmer	25.00
TP	Tony Perez	25.00
GP	Gaylord Perry	25.00
PO	Johnny Podres	20.00
KP	Kirby Puckett SP	50.00
JR	Jim Rice	25.00
CR	Cal Ripken Jr.	160.00
PR	Phil Rizzuto	50.00
RR	Robin Roberts	30.00
BR	Brooks Robinson	40.00
FR	Frank Robinson	40.00
AR	Al Rosen	20.00
NR	Nolan Ryan	125.00
RS	Ron Santo	35.00
MS	Mike Schmidt	80.00
RE	Red Schoendienst	30.00
TS	Tom Seaver	60.00
OS	Ozzie Smith	40.00
SN	Duke Snider	40.00
ST	Rusty Staub	20.00
SU	Bruce Sutter	20.00
DS	Don Sutton	20.00
LT	Luis Tiant	20.00
FV	Fernando Valenzuela	30.00
BW	Billy Williams	25.00
MW	Matt Williams	20.00
WI	Maury Wills	20.00
CY	Carl Yastrzemski	100.00
RY	Robin Yount/SP	85.00

Sweet Sticks Signatures
NM/M

Production 35 Sets

LA	Luis Aparicio	50.00
HB	Harold Baines	40.00
EB	Ernie Banks	125.00
BE	Johnny Bench	75.00
YB	Yogi Berra	80.00
WB	Wade Boggs	75.00
GB	George Brett	140.00
JB	Jim Bunning	40.00
JC	Jose Canseco	75.00
CA	Rod Carew	75.00
SC	Steve Carlton	50.00
GC	Gary Carter	40.00
OC	Orlando Cepeda	40.00
WC	Will Clark	65.00
RC	Rocky Colavito	120.00
DC	David Cone	50.00
AD	Andre Dawson	50.00
BD	Bobby Doerr	50.00
DE	Dennis Eckersley	50.00

EV	Dwight Evans	60.00
BF	Bob Feller	75.00
RF	Rollie Fingers	45.00
CF	Carlton Fisk	75.00
WF	Whitey Ford	85.00
BG	Bob Gibson	65.00
MG	Mark Grace	75.00
TG	Tony Gwynn	85.00
EH	Ernie Harwell	50.00
KH	Keith Hernandez	40.00
FH	Frank Howard	50.00
MI	Monte Irvin	50.00
BJ	Bo Jackson	140.00
DJ	David Justice	40.00
AK	Al Kaline	80.00
GK	George Kell	40.00
HK	Harmon Killebrew	80.00
RK	Ralph Kiner	75.00
MA	Juan Marichal	50.00
DM	Don Mattingly	125.00
BM	Bill Mazeroski	90.00
MC	Willie McCovey	85.00
PM	Paul Molitor	60.00
JM	Joe Morgan	50.00
MU	Dale Murphy	50.00
SM	Stan Musial	140.00
DN	Don Newcombe	50.00
PN	Phil Niekro	40.00
JP	Jim Palmer	50.00
TP	Tony Perez	50.00
GP	Gaylord Perry	40.00
PO	Johnny Podres	40.00
KP	Kirby Puckett	100.00
JR	Jim Rice	50.00
CR	Cal Ripken Jr.	240.00
RR	Robin Roberts	50.00
BR	Brooks Robinson	65.00
FR	Frank Robinson	65.00
AR	Al Rosen	50.00
NR	Nolan Ryan	150.00
RS	Ron Santo	65.00
MS	Mike Schmidt	125.00
RE	Red Schoendienst	50.00
TS	Tom Seaver	85.00
OS	Ozzie Smith	90.00
SN	Duke Snider	75.00
ST	Rusty Staub	40.00
SU	Bruce Sutter	30.00
DS	Don Sutton	40.00
LT	Luis Tiant	40.00
BW	Billy Williams	40.00
MW	Matt Williams	50.00
WI	Maury Wills	40.00
CY	Carl Yastrzemski	120.00
RY	Robin Yount	90.00

Wingfield Classic Collection
NM/M

Common Player: 4.00
Inserted 1:Box

1	Al Kaline	4.00
2	Pee Wee Reese	4.00
3	Stan Musial, Ted Williams	6.00
4	Bill Dickey	4.00
5	Frank Robinson	4.00
6	Billy Martin	4.00
7	Casey Stengel, Joe DiMaggio	6.00
8	Bob Feller,	
	Dwight D. Eisenhower	6.00
9	Duke Snider	5.00
10	Carl Yastrzemski	8.00
11	Honus Wagner	6.00
12	Dwight D. Eisenhower,	
	Clark Griffith	4.00
13	Mickey Mantle,	
	Joe DiMaggio	15.00
14	Don Drysdale	4.00
15	Ted Williams	8.00
16	Al Kaline, Mickey Mantle	15.00
17	Ernie Banks	6.00
18	Lou Boudreau	4.00
19	George Sisler,	
	Harmon Killebrew	6.00
20	Gil Hodges	4.00
21	Rogers Hornsby	6.00
22	Luis Aparicio	4.00
23	Jackie Robinson	10.00
24	Joe Morgan	4.00
25	Enos Slaughter	4.00
26	Joe DiMaggio	8.00
27	Mickey Mantle,	
	Ted Kluszewski	15.00
28	John F. Kennedy	6.00
29	Johnny Bench	8.00
30	Juan Marichal	4.00
31	Larry Doby	4.00
32	Don Newcombe,	
	Elston Howard	4.00
33	Harmon Killebrew,	
	Dwight D. Eisenhower	6.00
34	Roger Maris,	
	Mickey Mantle	20.00
35	Mickey Mantle, Stan Musial	15.00
36	Ted Williams, Mickey Mantle,	
	Yogi Berra	15.00
37	Nellie Fox	6.00
38	Richie Ashburn	4.00
39	Roberto Clemente	15.00
40	Stan Musial, Robin Roberts	8.00
41	Tommy Heinrich,	
	Joe DiMaggio	8.00
42	Roy Campanella	6.00
43	Rocky Colavito,	
	Harmon Killebrew	6.00

44	Steve Carlton	4.00
45	Thurman Munson	6.00
46	Luis Aparicio, Ernie Banks	6.00
47	Gil Hodges, Yogi Berra,	
	Dwight D. Eisenhower	6.00
48	Whitey Ford	6.00
49	Mickey Mantle, Yogi Berra,	
	Joe DiMaggio	15.00
50	Yogi Berra	8.00

2005 Upper Deck Trilogy

NM/M

Complete Set (100):	40.00
Common Player:	.50
Pack (5):	20.00
Box (9):	170.00

1	A.J. Burnett	.50
2	Adam Dunn	1.00
3	Adrian Beltre	.50
4	Albert Pujols	4.00
5	Alex Rodriguez	3.00
6	Alfonso Soriano	1.00
7	Andruw Jones	1.00
8	Aramis Ramirez	.50
9	Ben Sheets	.75
10	Bobby Abreu	.75
11	Bobby Crosby	.50
12	Ryan Zimmerman RC	15.00
13	Brian Giles	.50
14	Brian Roberts	.50
15	Carl Crawford	.50
16	Carlos Beltran	1.00
17	Carlos Delgado	.75
18	Carlos Zambrano	.75
19	Chipper Jones	1.00
20	Corey Patterson	.50
21	Craig Biggio	.75
22	Curt Schilling	1.50
23	Dallas McPherson	.50
24	David Ortiz	1.50
25	David Wright	1.50
26	Delmon Young	1.00
27	Derek Jeter	4.00
28	Derrek Lee	1.00
29	Dontrelle Willis	.50
30	Eric Chavez	.50
31	Eric Gagne	.50
32	Francisco Rodriguez	.50
33	Gary Sheffield	1.00
34	Greg Maddux	2.00
35	Hank Blalock	.50
36	Hideki Matsui	2.50
37	Ichiro Suzuki	3.00
38	Ivan Rodriguez	1.00
39	J.D. Drew	.50
40	Jake Peavy	.75
41	Jason Bay	.50
42	Jason Schmidt	.50
43	Jeff Bagwell	1.00
44	Jeff Kent	.50
45	Jeff Niemann RC	2.00
46	Jeremy Bonderman	.50
47	Jim Edmonds	.75
48	Jim Thome	1.00
49	Joe Mauer	.75
50	Johan Santana	1.00
51	John Smoltz	.75
52	Johnny Damon	1.00
53	Jose Reyes	.75
54	Jose Vidro	.50
55	Josh Beckett	.50
56	Justin Morneau	.50
57	Justin Verlander RC	1.00
58	Ken Griffey Jr.	3.00
59	Kendry Morales RC	6.00
60	Kerry Wood	.75
61	Khalil Greene	.75
62	Lance Berkman	.75
63	Luis Gonzalez	.50
64	Manny Ramirez	1.50
65	Mark Buehrle	.75
66	Mark Mulder	.50
67	Mark Prior	1.00
68	Mark Teixeira	1.00
69	Michael Young	.50
70	Miguel Cabrera	1.50
71	Miguel Tejada	1.00
72	Mike Mussina	1.00
73	Mike Piazza	1.50
74	Nomar Garciaparra	1.00
75	Pat Burrell	.50

76	Paul Konerko	.75
77	Pedro Martinez	1.50
78	Philip Humber RC	2.00
79	Prince Fielder	8.00
80	Randy Johnson	1.50
81	Richie Sexson	.75
82	Rickie Weeks	.75
83	Roger Clemens	4.00
84	Roy Halladay	.75
85	Roy Oswalt	.75
86	Sammy Sosa	1.50
87	Scott Kazmir	.50
88	Scott Rolen	1.00
89	Stephen Drew RC	8.00
90	Tadahito Iguchi RC	4.00
91	Tim Hudson	.75
92	Todd Helton	1.00
93	Tom Glavine	.75
94	Torii Hunter	.75
95	Travis Hafner	.75
96	Troy Glaus	.75
97	Vernon Wells	.50
98	Victor Martinez	.50
99	Vladimir Guerrero	1.50
100	Zack Greinke	.50

Generations

No Pricing
Common Player:

Generation Future Lumber Silver

NM/M

Production 100 Sets
Gold: 1X
Production 60 Sets

RC	Robinson Cano	20.00
CA	Jorge Cantu	6.00
GF	Gavin Floyd	4.00
BH	Brad Halsey	4.00
JJ	J.J. Hardy	4.00
RH	Ryan Howard	50.00
LN	Laynce Nix	4.00
JP	Jhonny Peralta	6.00
JR	Jeremy Reed	4.00
AR	Alexis Rios	6.00
RI	Juan Rivera	6.00
JW	Jayson Werth	4.00
YO	Kevin Youkilis	6.00

Generations Future Mat. Silver

NM/M

Common Player: 4.00
Production 120 Sets
Gold: 1X
Production 75 Sets

BA	Bronson Arroyo	6.00
GA	Garrett Atkins	4.00
JE	Jeff Baker	4.00
CL	Clint Barmes	6.00
JB	Jason Bartlett	4.00
BL	Joe Blanton	4.00
DB	Dewon Brazelton	4.00
YB	Yhency Brazoban	4.00
CB	Chris Burke	6.00
DC	Daniel Cabrera	4.00
RC	Robinson Cano	20.00
CA	Jorge Cantu	6.00
GC	Gustavo Chacin	4.00
JD	J.D. Closser	4.00
DD	David DeJesus	4.00
DU	Jason Dubois	4.00
GF	Gavin Floyd	4.00
JF	Jeff Francis	4.00
AG	Adrian Gonzalez	4.00
BH	Brad Halsey	4.00
JJ	J.J. Hardy	4.00
DH	Danny Haren	4.00
AH	Aaron Hill	4.00
HO	Dennis Houlton	4.00
RH	Ryan Howard	20.00
TI	Tadahito Iguchi	15.00
EJ	Edwin Jackson	4.00
DK	Dae-Sung Koo	4.00
KO	Casey Kotchman	4.00
JL	Jason Lane	4.00
DM	Dallas McPherson	6.00
AM	Aaron Miles	4.00
YM	Yadier Molina	4.00
MY	Brett Myers	4.00

XN Xavier Nady 4.00
LN Laynce Nix 4.00
JP Jhonny Peralta 6.00
RQ Robb Quinlan 4.00
JR Jeremy Reed 4.00
AR Alexis Rios 6.00
RI Juan Rivera 4.00
ES Ervin Santana 6.00
SS Steve Schmoll 4.00
LS Luke Scott 4.00
SI Grady Sizemore 10.00
HS Huston Street 10.00
NS Nick Swisher 8.00
WT Willy Taveras 8.00
MT Mark Teahen 4.00
TH Charles Thomas 4.00
CT Chad Tracy 4.00
BJ B.J. Upton 4.00
CU Chase Utley 10.00
WA Ryan Wagner 4.00
RW Rickie Weeks 8.00
JW Jayson Werth 4.00
KY Keiichi Yabu 4.00
YO Kevin Youkilis 6.00

Generations Future Sig. Silver

NM/M

Common Player: 8.00
Production 50-199
Bronze: 1-1.5X
Production 35 Sets
Gold: No Pricing
Production 15 Sets
GA Garrett Atkins/199 10.00
JB Jason Bartlett/199 8.00
BE Colter Bean/199 8.00
BL Joe Blanton/99 10.00
YB Yhency Brazoban/199 10.00
AB Ambiorix Burgos/199 8.00
CB Chris Burke/199 15.00
DC Daniel Cabrera/199 15.00
JO Jose Capellan/199 10.00
JD J.D. Closser/99 10.00
AC Ambiorix Concepcion/199 8.00
DD David DeJesus/99 12.00
SD Stephen Drew/75 100.00
DU Jason Dubois/99 10.00
PF Prince Fielder/75 50.00
GF Gavin Floyd/99 10.00
JF Jeff Francis/99 12.00
AG Adrian Gonzalez/99 15.00
JG Jared Gothreaux/199 8.00
GG Gabe Gross/99 10.00
JJ J.J. Hardy/199 25.00
JH John Hattig Jr./199 10.00
FH Felix Hernandez/60 80.00
HO Dennis Houlton/199 10.00
RH Ryan Howard/99 40.00
PH Philip Humber/75 20.00
TI Tadahito Iguchi/75 150.00
EJ Edwin Jackson/99 8.00
KO Casey Kotchman/99 10.00
JL Jason Lane/99 10.00
ML Matt Lindstrom/199 8.00
PL Pedro Lopez/189 10.00
RM Russell Martin/199 20.00
KM Kendry Morales/199 30.00
JN Jeff Niemann/75 40.00
PO Peter Orr/199 15.00
TP Tony Pena/199 8.00
RQ Robb Quinlan/199 8.00
AR Alexis Rios/99 15.00
CR Casey Rogowski/199 10.00
RR Russel Rohlicek/199 8.00
SS Steve Schmoll/199 8.00
LS Luke Scott/199 10.00
TS Tim Stauffer/199 8.00
NS Nick Swisher/99 15.00
MT Mark Teahen/199 8.00
TH Charles Thomas/199 12.00
BJ B.J. Upton/50 20.00
CU Chase Utley/50 20.00
JV Justin Verlander/75 60.00
RW Rickie Weeks/50 20.00
JW Jayson Werth/99 15.00
KY Keiichi Yabu/199 25.00
YO Kevin Youkilis/99 25.00
DY Delmon Young/50 40.00
RZ Ryan Zimmerman/150 50.00

Generations of Lumber Triple

NM/M

Production 85 Sets 10.00
ARU B.J. Upton, Jimmy Rollins, Luis Aparicio 15.00
BCU Wade Boggs, B.J. Upton, Carl Crawford 15.00
BHH Travis Hafner, Ryan Howard, Harold Baines 15.00
BMY Bill Mueller, Wade Boggs, Kevin Youkilis 15.00
CCC Will Clark, Jack Clark, Orlando Cepeda 12.00
DAR Bobby Abreu, Eric Davis, Alex Rios 10.00
EDY Kevin Youkilis, Dwight Evans, Johnny Damon 20.00
GDP Ken Griffey Jr., Wily Mo Pena, Adam Dunn 25.00
GGC Miguel Cabrera, Ken Griffey Jr., Tony Gwynn 25.00
HDH Ryan Howard, Adam Dunn, Frank Howard 15.00
HOH Frank Howard, Ryan Howard, David Ortiz 20.00
JGU Bo Jackson, Ken Griffey Jr., B.J. Upton 25.00
JHR Alex Rios, Bo Jackson, Torii Hunter 15.00
JSP Bo Jackson, Gary Sheffield, Wily Mo Pena 15.00
KBH Pat Burrell, John Kruk, Ryan Howard 15.00
LJU Barry Larkin, Derek Jeter, B.J. Upton 30.00
LYU B.J. Upton, Barry Larkin, Michael Young 12.00
MDW Jayson Werth, Dale Murphy, Adam Dunn 15.00
MMJ Don Mattingly, Derek Jeter, Bobby Murcer 50.00
MOH Ryan Howard, David Ortiz, Eddie Murray 20.00
NBW Adrian Beltre, David Wright, Graig Nettles 15.00
OAR Bobby Abreu, Tony Oliva, Alex Rios 10.00
PDP Wily Mo Pena, Eric Davis, Tony Perez 10.00
PGP Tony Perez, Ken Griffey Jr., Wily Mo Pena 25.00
RJC Cal Ripken Jr., Derek Jeter, Bobby Crosby 50.00
ROY David Ortiz, Jim Rice, Kevin Youkilis 20.00
RRT Brooks Robinson, Cal Ripken Jr., Miguel Tejada 40.00
SBW Mike Schmidt, Adrian Beltre, David Wright 20.00
SDW Duke Snider, Jayson Werth, J.D. Drew 20.00
SMR Aramis Ramirez, Bill Madlock, Ron Santo 20.00
SSP Ron Santo, Ryne Sandberg, Corey Patterson 35.00

Generations of Materials Triple

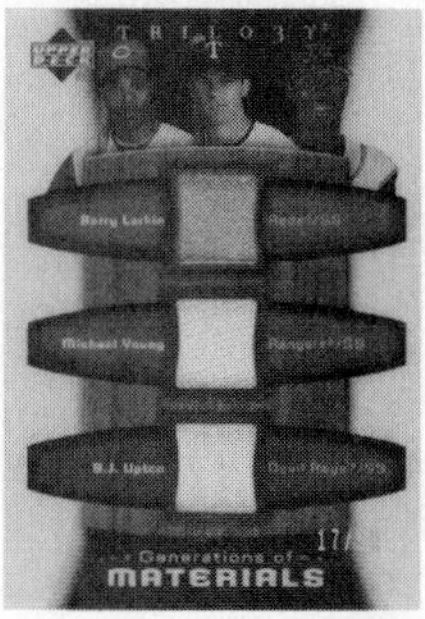

NM/M

Common Trio: 10.00
Production 50 Sets
AAD Aramis Ramirez, Al Rosen, Dallas McPherson 15.00
AFB Luis Aparicio, Rafael Furcal, Jason Bartlett 15.00
API Tadahito Iguchi, Scott Podsednik, Luis Aparicio 25.00
ARU Jimmy Rollins, Luis Aparicio, B.J. Upton 15.00
BCU B.J. Upton, Carl Crawford, Wade Boggs 15.00
BHH Ryan Howard, Harold Baines, Travis Hafner 15.00
BLS Craig Biggio, Jason Lane, Luke Scott 15.00
BMY Kevin Youkilis, Wade Boggs, Bill Mueller 15.00
CCC Will Clark, Jack Clark, Orlando Cepeda 15.00
CCK Sean Casey, Will Clark, Casey Kotchman 15.00
CMG Justin Morneau, Adrian Gonzalez, Will Clark 15.00
CTG Will Clark, Adrian Gonzalez, Mark Teixeira 15.00
DAR Alex Rios, Eric Davis, Bobby Abreu 10.00
DBS Lenny Dykstra, Jason Bay, Nick Swisher 10.00
DGL Jason Lane, Ken Griffey Jr., Andre Dawson 25.00
DHL Lenny Dykstra, Torii Hunter, Jason Lane 10.00
DPD Jason Dubois, Corey Patterson, Andre Dawson 10.00
DPT Lenny Dykstra, Scott Podsednik, Willy Taveras 15.00
EDY Kevin Youkilis, Johnny Damon, Dwight Evans 20.00
GAS Bobby Abreu, Tony Gwynn, Nick Swisher 25.00
GDP Wily Mo Pena, Adam Dunn, Ken Griffey Jr. 25.00
GGC Ken Griffey Jr., Tony Gwynn, Miguel Cabrera 25.00
GMY Kevin Youkilis, Mike Greenwell, Bill Mueller 15.00
GWJ Dwight Gooden, Dontrelle Willis, Edwin Jackson 15.00
HDH Frank Howard, Adam Dunn, Ryan Howard 15.00
HOH Ryan Howard, David Ortiz, Frank Howard 20.00
JGU B.J. Upton, Bo Jackson, Ken Griffey Jr. 25.00
JHR Bo Jackson, Torii Hunter, Alex Rios 20.00
JMK Casey Kotchman, Wally Joyner, Dallas McPherson 10.00
JSP Bo Jackson, Gary Sheffield, Wily Mo Pena 15.00
KBH Pat Burrell, John Kruk, Ryan Howard 15.00
KBU John Kruk, Pat Burrell, Chase Utley 25.00
LJU B.J. Upton, Barry Larkin, Derek Jeter 35.00
LYU Barry Larkin, Michael Young, B.J. Upton 35.00
MBS Nick Swisher, Pat Burrell, Dale Murphy 20.00
MCG Don Mattingly, Sean Casey, Adrian Gonzalez 30.00
MDW Adam Dunn, Jayson Werth, Dale Murphy 20.00
MMJ Don Mattingly, Derek Jeter, Bobby Murcer 60.00
MOH David Ortiz, Ryan Howard, Eddie Murray 20.00
NBW Adrian Beltre, David Wright, Graig Nettles 20.00
OAR Bobby Abreu, Tony Oliva, Alex Rios 10.00
PDP Wily Mo Pena, Eric Davis, Tony Perez 10.00
PGD Tony Perez, Brian Giles, Jason Dubois 10.00
PGP Wily Mo Pena, Ken Griffey Jr., Tony Perez 30.00
RBT Brooks Robinson, Adrian Beltre, Mark Teahen 20.00
RCD Carl Crawford, David DeJesus, Tim Raines 10.00
RJC Derek Jeter, Cal Ripken Jr., Bobby Crosby 50.00
ROY Jim Rice, David Ortiz, Kevin Youkilis 25.00
RRM Brooks Robinson, Cal Ripken Jr., Melvin Mora 50.00
RRT Miguel Tejada, Cal Ripken Jr., Brooks Robinson 50.00
SBM Dallas McPherson, Adrian Beltre, Mike Schmidt 20.00
SBW Mike Schmidt, Adrian Beltre, David Wright 20.00
SDW Duke Snider, Jayson Werth, J.D. Drew 20.00
SGU Ryne Sandberg, Chase Utley, Marcus Giles 35.00
SRU Chase Utley, Mike Schmidt, Jimmy Rollins 40.00
SRW Ryne Sandberg, Brian Roberts, Rickie Weeks 20.00
VGB Jason Bay, Brian Giles, Andy Van Slyke 10.00
VPD Andy Van Slyke, Corey Patterson, David DeJesus 10.00
WBI Tadahito Iguchi, Frank White, Craig Biggio 20.00
WCT Willie Wilson, Willy Taveras, Carl Crawford 15.00

Generations of Signatures

NM/M

Production 35 Sets
AYU B.J. Upton, Luis Aparicio, Michael Young 40.00
BPN Jake Peavy, Jeff Niemann, Jim Bunning 50.00
CTG Will Clark, Mark Teixeira, Adrian Gonzalez 60.00
DBU Chase Utley, Craig Biggio, Bobby Doerr 50.00
DGL Ken Griffey Jr., Andre Dawson, Jason Lane 100.00
DGU Marcus Giles, Chase Utley, Bobby Doerr 50.00
DLB Bobby Doerr, Mark Loretta, Chris Burke 30.00
FPH Rich Harden, Mark Prior, Bob Feller 50.00
GDP Ken Griffey Jr., Adam Dunn, Wily Mo Pena 100.00
HDG Adam Dunn, Frank Howard, Gabe Gross 40.00
JHR Torii Hunter, Bo Jackson, Alex Rios 85.00
JKM Casey Kotchman, Kendry Morales, Wally Joyner 50.00
LJU Barry Larkin, Derek Jeter, B.J. Upton 250.00
MBV Justin Verlander, Jack Morris, Jeremy Bonderman 90.00
MDS Dale Murphy, Nick Swisher, Adam Dunn
MMJ Derek Jeter, Don Mattingly, Bobby Murcer 260.00
NBW David Wright, Graig Nettles, Adrian Beltre 75.00
OHM Tony Oliva, Kent Hrbek, Justin Morneau 50.00
PBF Gaylord Perry, Jeremy Bonderman, Gavin Floyd 35.00
PGP Tony Perez, Ken Griffey Jr., Wily Mo Pena 100.00
PPH Philip Humber, Jim Palmer, Jake Peavy 50.00
PPS Jake Peavy, Tim Stauffer, Gaylord Perry 40.00
RCD Tim Raines, David DeJesus, Carl Crawford 40.00
RCY Miguel Cabrera, Delmon Young, Jim Rice
RJC Bobby Crosby, Cal Ripken Jr., Derek Jeter 400.00
RRM Cal Ripken Jr., Melvin Mora, Brooks Robinson 180.00
RSH Nolan Ryan, John Smoltz, Philip Humber 165.00
SBT Mark Teahen, Adrian Beltre, Ron Santo 50.00
SBW Adrian Beltre, Mike Schmidt, David Wright 100.00
SGH J.J. Hardy, Ozzie Smith, Khalil Greene 70.00
SMR Ron Santo, Bill Madlock, Aramis Ramirez 50.00
SRW Brian Roberts, Ryne Sandberg, Rickie Weeks 75.00
VGB Jason Bay, Brian Giles, Andy Van Slyke 65.00

Generations Past Lumber

NM/M

Common Player: 4.00
Production 115 unless noted.
Gold: 1-1.5X
Production 25-75
LA Luis Aparicio 8.00
HB Harold Baines 4.00
DB Dusty Baker 6.00
JB Johnny Bench 10.00
WB Wade Boggs 8.00
BB Bill Buckner 6.00
CA Rod Carew 8.00
SC Steve Carlton 6.00
GC Gary Carter 6.00
OC Orlando Cepeda 6.00
CY Ron Cey 4.00
JC Jack Clark 4.00
WC Will Clark 8.00
TC Ty Cobb/99 100.00
MC Mickey Cochrane/99 25.00
ED Eric Davis 8.00
AD Andre Dawson 6.00
JD Joe DiMaggio/99 65.00
BD Bobby Doerr 8.00
LD Lenny Dykstra 4.00
DE Dwight Evans 6.00
CF Carlton Fisk 6.00
GF George Foster 4.00
JF Jimmie Foxx/99 50.00
FR Bill Freehan 4.00
LG Lou Gehrig/99 140.00
DG Dwight Gooden 4.00
GR Lefty Grove/99 40.00
TG Tony Gwynn 10.00
KH Keith Hernandez 6.00
RH Rogers Hornsby/99 40.00
FH Frank Howard 6.00
BJ Bo Jackson 10.00
RJ Reggie Jackson 10.00
JO Wally Joyner 4.00
GK George Kell 8.00
JK John Kruk 4.00
BL Barry Larkin 6.00
DL Davey Lopes 4.00
BM Bill Madlock 4.00
MA Don Mattingly 25.00
FM Fred McGriff 6.00
JM Johnny Mize 4.00
TM Thurman Munson 20.00
MU Bobby Murcer 4.00
DM Dale Murphy 8.00
MY Eddie Murray 8.00
SM Stan Musial 20.00
GN Graig Nettles 6.00
TO Tony Oliva 6.00
MO Mel Ott 25.00
TP Tony Perez 6.00
GP Gaylord Perry 6.00
RP Rico Petrocelli 6.00
BP Boog Powell 4.00
TR Tim Raines 4.00
RI Jim Rice 6.00
CR Cal Ripken Jr. 25.00
RO Brooks Robinson 8.00
JR Jackie Robinson 4.00

AR	Al Rosen	10.00
BR	Babe Ruth/99	140.00
NR	Nolan Ryan	25.00
SA	Ryne Sandberg	15.00
RS	Ron Santo	10.00
MS	Mike Schmidt	15.00
SI	George Sisler	20.00
SK	Bill "Moose" Skowron	6.00
OS	Ozzie Smith	20.00
SN	Duke Snider	10.00
DS	Darryl Strawberry	6.00
AT	Alan Trammell	8.00
AV	Andy Van Slyke	8.00
FW	Frank White	4.00
WW	Willie Wilson	4.00
YA	Carl Yastrzemski	25.00

Generation Past Material Silver

NM/M

Common Player: 4.00
Production 99 unless noted.
Gold: 1-1.5X
Production 25 Sets

LA	Luis Aparicio	8.00
HB	Harold Baines	4.00
DB	Dusty Baker	6.00
JB	Johnny Bench	10.00
WB	Wade Boggs	8.00
BU	Jim Bunning	6.00
RC	Roy Campanella	20.00
CA	Rod Carew	8.00
SC	Steve Carlton	6.00
GC	Gary Carter	6.00
OC	Orlando Cepeda	6.00
CY	Ron Cey	4.00
JC	Jack Clark	4.00
WC	Will Clark	8.00
DC	David Cone	4.00
ED	Eric Davis	8.00
AD	Andre Dawson	6.00
DD	Dizzy Dean/75	40.00
JD	Joe DiMaggio/75	85.00
DR	Don Drysdale	10.00
LD	Lenny Dykstra	4.00
BF	Bob Feller	10.00
CF	Carlton Fisk	8.00
LG	Lou Gehrig/75	150.00
DG	Dwight Gooden	4.00
RG	Ron Guidry	8.00
TG	Tony Gwynn	10.00
KH	Keith Hernandez	6.00
RH	Rogers Hornsby/75	65.00
FH	Frank Howard	6.00
HR	Kent Hrbek	8.00
BJ	Bo Jackson	10.00
RJ	Reggie Jackson	10.00
JO	Wally Joyner	6.00
JK	John Kruk	8.00
BL	Barry Larkin	6.00
DL	Davey Lopes	4.00
BM	Bill Madlock	4.00
EM	Eddie Mathews/75	20.00
CM	Christy Mathewson/75	80.00
MA	Don Mattingly	25.00
JM	Johnny Mize	15.00
JA	Jack Morris	4.00
TM	Thurman Munson	20.00
MU	Bobby Murcer	8.00
DM	Dale Murphy	8.00
MY	Eddie Murray	8.00
SM	Stan Musial	20.00
GN	Graig Nettles	6.00
TO	Tony Oliva	6.00
MO	Mel Ott/75	30.00
SP	Satchel Paige/75	50.00
JP	Jim Palmer	6.00
TP	Tony Perez	6.00
GP	Gaylord Perry	6.00
RP	Rico Petrocelli	6.00
BP	Boog Powell	4.00
TR	Tim Raines	4.00
RI	Jim Rice	6.00
CR	Cal Ripken Jr.	25.00
RO	Brooks Robinson	10.00
AR	Al Rosen	10.00
NR	Nolan Ryan	25.00
SA	Ryne Sandberg	15.00
MS	Mike Schmidt	15.00
AV	Andy Van Slyke	8.00
OS	Ozzie Smith	15.00
SN	Duke Snider	10.00
DS	Darryl Strawberry	6.00
FW	Frank White	4.00
WW	Willie Wilson	4.00
YA	Carl Yastrzemski	15.00

Generations Past Auto. Silver

NM/M

Common Player: 10.00
Production 24-99.
Bronze: 1-1.5X
Production 10 or 35.
No pricing for prod. of 10.
Gold: No Pricing
Production 5-15

LA	Luis Aparicio/50	20.00
HB	Harold Baines/199	15.00
DB	Dusty Baker/25	20.00
WB	Wade Boggs/50	35.00
BB	Bill Buckner/50	15.00
BU	Jim Bunning/99	20.00
CA	Rod Carew/25	35.00
SC	Steve Carlton/25	20.00
CY	Ron Cey/199	15.00
JC	Jack Clark/199	10.00
WC	Will Clark/25	40.00
DC	David Cone/99	15.00
ED	Eric Davis/199	15.00
AD	Andre Dawson/99	20.00
BD	Bobby Doerr/199	15.00
LD	Lenny Dykstra/199	15.00
DE	Dwight Evans/50	20.00
BF	Bob Feller/99	25.00
GF	George Foster/199	10.00
FR	Bill Freehan/199	15.00
RG	Ron Guidry/199	15.00
KH	Keith Hernandez/199	15.00
FH	Frank Howard/199	15.00
HR	Kent Hrbek/199	15.00
BJ	Bo Jackson/50	50.00
RJ	Reggie Jackson/25	50.00
JO	Wally Joyner/199	15.00
GK	George Kell/199	15.00
JK	John Kruk/199	20.00
BL	Barry Larkin/99	25.00
DL	Davey Lopes/199	10.00
BM	Bill Madlock/199	10.00
MA	Don Mattingly/25	75.00
FM	Fred McGriff/199	25.00
JA	Jack Morris/199	15.00
MU	Bobby Murcer/199	25.00
DM	Dale Murphy/99	25.00
SM	Stan Musial/25	80.00
GN	Graig Nettles/199	15.00
TO	Tony Oliva/99	15.00
JP	Jim Palmer/50	20.00
TP	Tony Perez/25	30.00
GP	Gaylord Perry/199	15.00
BP	Boog Powell/199	15.00
TR	Tim Raines/199	15.00
RI	Jim Rice/99	15.00
RO	Brooks Robinson/50	30.00
AR	Al Rosen/199	15.00
NR	Nolan Ryan/25	100.00
SA	Ryne Sandberg/50	60.00
RS	Ron Santo/199	30.00
MS	Mike Schmidt/25	60.00
SK	Bill Skowron/199	15.00
OS	Ozzie Smith/25	50.00
DS	Darryl Strawberry/99	15.00
AT	Alan Trammell/50	20.00
AV	Andy Van Slyke/199	20.00
FW	Frank White/199	15.00
WW	Willie Wilson/199	15.00

Generation Present Lumber Silvr

NM/M

Common Player: 4.00
Production 115 Sets
Gold: 1X
Production 75 Sets

BA	Bobby Abreu	4.00
GA	Garret Anderson	4.00
JE	Jeff Bagwell	6.00
CB	Carlos Beltran	6.00
AB	Adrian Beltre	4.00
LB	Lance Berkman	4.00
BI	Craig Biggio	6.00
HB	Hank Blalock	4.00
BO	Jeremy Bonderman	4.00
PB	Pat Burrell	4.00
AJ	A.J. Burnett	4.00
MC	Miguel Cabrera	8.00
SC	Sean Casey	4.00
EC	Eric Chavez	4.00
RC	Roger Clemens	12.00
CC	Carl Crawford	4.00
BC	Bobby Crosby	4.00
DA	Johnny Damon	8.00
CD	Carlos Delgado	4.00
JD	J.D. Drew	4.00
AD	Adam Dunn	6.00
RF	Rafael Furcal	4.00
JG	Jason Giambi	6.00
BG	Brian Giles	4.00
MG	Marcus Giles	4.00
TG	Troy Glaus	4.00
GR	Khalil Greene	6.00
KG1	Ken Griffey Jr.	20.00
KG2	Ken Griffey Jr.	20.00
KG3	Ken Griffey Jr.	20.00
VG	Vladimir Guerrero	8.00
HA	Travis Hafner	4.00
TH	Todd Helton	4.00
AH	Aubrey Huff	6.00
HU	Torii Hunter	4.00
DJ	Derek Jeter	20.00
RJ	Randy Johnson	8.00
JO	Andruw Jones	6.00
CJ	Chipper Jones	8.00
JK	Jeff Kent	4.00
DL	Derrek Lee	8.00
ML	Mark Loretta	4.00
GM	Greg Maddux	15.00
PM	Pedro Martinez	8.00
VM	Victor Martinez	4.00
JM	Joe Mauer	6.00
BM	Bill Mueller	4.00
DO	David Ortiz	8.00
PA	Corey Patterson	4.00
WM	Wily Mo Pena	4.00
PI	Mike Piazza	8.00
SP	Scott Podsednik	4.00
MP	Mark Prior	6.00
AP	Albert Pujols	20.00
AR	Aramis Ramirez	4.00
MR	Manny Ramirez	8.00
RE	Jose Reyes	4.00
BR	Brian Roberts	4.00
IR	Ivan Rodriguez	6.00
SR	Scott Rolen	6.00
JR	Jimmy Rollins	4.00
CS	Curt Schilling	8.00
GS	Gary Sheffield	6.00
SM	John Smoltz	6.00
AS	Alfonso Soriano	6.00
SS	Sammy Sosa	8.00
MT	Mark Teixeira	8.00
TE	Miguel Tejada	6.00
FT	Frank Thomas	6.00
JT	Jim Thome	6.00
JV	Jason Varitek	8.00
VI	Jose Vidro	4.00
BW	Bernie Williams	6.00
WI	Dontrelle Willis	6.00
KW	Kerry Wood	4.00
DW	David Wright	20.00
MY	Michael Young	4.00
CZ	Carlos Zambrano	4.00

Generations Present Materials Silver

NM/M

Common Player: 4.00
Production 99 Sets
Gold: 1-1.5X
Production 25 Sets

BA	Bobby Abreu	4.00
GA	Garret Anderson	4.00
JE	Jeff Bagwell	6.00
JB	Jason Bay	4.00
CB	Carlos Beltran	6.00
AB	Adrian Beltre	4.00
LB	Lance Berkman	4.00
BI	Craig Biggio	6.00
HB	Hank Blalock	4.00
BO	Jeremy Bonderman	4.00
PB	Pat Burrell	4.00
AJ	A.J. Burnett	4.00
MC	Miguel Cabrera	8.00
SC	Sean Casey	4.00
EC	Eric Chavez	4.00
RC	Roger Clemens	12.00
CC	Carl Crawford	4.00
BC	Bobby Crosby	4.00
DA	Johnny Damon	8.00
CD	Carlos Delgado	4.00
JD	J.D. Drew	4.00
AD	Adam Dunn	6.00
RF	Rafael Furcal	4.00
JG	Jason Giambi	6.00
BG	Brian Giles	4.00
MG	Marcus Giles	4.00
TG	Troy Glaus	4.00
GR	Khalil Greene	6.00
ZG	Zack Greinke	4.00
KG1	Ken Griffey Jr.	20.00
KG2	Ken Griffey Jr.	20.00
KG3	Ken Griffey Jr.	20.00
VG	Vladimir Guerrero	8.00
HA	Travis Hafner	4.00
RH	Rich Harden	4.00
TH	Todd Helton	6.00
AH	Aubrey Huff	4.00
HU	Torii Hunter	4.00
DJ	Derek Jeter	20.00
RJ	Randy Johnson	8.00
JO	Andruw Jones	6.00
CJ	Chipper Jones	8.00
SK	Scott Kazmir	4.00
JK	Jeff Kent	4.00
DL	Derrek Lee	8.00
BL	Brad Lidge	4.00
ML	Mark Loretta	4.00
GM	Greg Maddux	15.00
PM	Pedro Martinez	8.00
VM	Victor Martinez	4.00
JM	Joe Mauer	6.00
ME	Melvin Mora	4.00
MO	Justin Morneau	4.00
BM	Bill Mueller	4.00
MM	Mark Mulder	4.00
DO	David Ortiz	8.00
RO	Roy Oswalt	4.00
PA	Corey Patterson	4.00
JP	Jake Peavy	4.00
WM	Wily Mo Pena	4.00
PI	Mike Piazza	8.00
SP	Scott Podsednik	6.00
MP	Mark Prior	6.00
AP	Albert Pujols	20.00
AR	Aramis Ramirez	4.00
MR	Manny Ramirez	8.00
RE	Jose Reyes	4.00
BR	Brian Roberts	4.00
IR	Ivan Rodriguez	6.00
SR	Scott Rolen	6.00
JR	Jimmy Rollins	4.00
JS	Johan Santana	6.00
CS	Curt Schilling	8.00
BS	Ben Sheets	4.00
GS	Gary Sheffield	6.00
SM	John Smoltz	6.00
AS	Alfonso Soriano	6.00
SS	Sammy Sosa	8.00
MT	Mark Teixeira	8.00
TE	Miguel Tejada	6.00
FT	Frank Thomas	6.00
JT	Jim Thome	6.00
JV	Jason Varitek	8.00
VI	Jose Vidro	4.00
BW	Bernie Williams	6.00
WI	Dontrelle Willis	6.00
KW	Kerry Wood	4.00
DW	David Wright	20.00
MY	Michael Young	4.00
CZ	Carlos Zambrano	4.00

Generations Present Signatures

NM/M

Common Player: 10.00
Production 25-199.
Bronze: 1-1.5X
Production 10 or 35.
No pricing for prod. of 10.
Gold: No Pricing
Production 5-15.

GA	Garret Anderson/25	20.00
JB	Jason Bay/199	15.00
BI	Craig Biggio/25	35.00
BO	Jeremy Bonderman/199	15.00
MC	Miguel Cabrera/25	40.00
SC	Sean Casey/50	15.00
CC	Carl Crawford/99	15.00
BC	Bobby Crosby/99	15.00
AD	Adam Dunn/95	25.00
RF	Rafael Furcal/99	15.00
BG	Brian Giles/99	12.00
MG	Marcus Giles/199	10.00
GR	Khalil Greene/135	25.00
ZG	Zack Greinke/199	15.00
KG1	Ken Griffey Jr./199	75.00
KG2	Ken Griffey Jr./199	75.00
KG3	Ken Griffey Jr./199	75.00
HA	Travis Hafner/99	15.00
RH	Rich Harden/199	15.00
AH	Aubrey Huff/199	15.00
HU	Torii Hunter/25	25.00
DJ	Derek Jeter/99	150.00
DL	Derrek Lee/25	40.00
BL	Brad Lidge/99	25.00
ML	Mark Loretta/99	15.00
VM	Victor Martinez/99	15.00
JM	Joe Mauer/25	25.00
ME	Melvin Mora/199	10.00
MO	Justin Morneau/99	20.00
MM	Mark Mulder/99	15.00
DO	David Ortiz/25	50.00
RO	Roy Oswalt/25	30.00
JP	Jake Peavy/99	15.00
WM	Wily Mo Pena/199	15.00
SP	Scott Podsednik/99	20.00
MP	Mark Prior/25	40.00
AR	Aramis Ramirez/99	15.00
BR	Brian Roberts/99	15.00
BS	Ben Sheets/99	15.00
GS	Gary Sheffield/25	35.00
SM	John Smoltz/25	50.00
MT	Mark Teixeira/25	50.00
TE	Miguel Tejada/25	40.00
FT	Frank Thomas/25	50.00
VI	Jose Vidro/99	10.00
WI	Dontrelle Willis/25	30.00
DW	David Wright/135	50.00
MY	Michael Young/199	15.00

Signature Dual Material

NM/M

Common Player: 20.00
Production 75 Sets

HB	Harold Baines	25.00
AB	Adrian Beltre	25.00
BI	Craig Biggio	40.00
WB	Wade Boggs	50.00
MC	Miguel Cabrera	50.00
SC	Sean Casey	25.00
OC	Orlando Cepeda	40.00
CL	Jack Clark	20.00
WC	Will Clark	50.00
CC	Carl Crawford	20.00
BC	Bobby Crosby	30.00
ED	Eric Davis	35.00
AD	Andre Dawson	30.00
DU	Adam Dunn	40.00
LD	Lenny Dykstra	20.00
BG	Brian Giles	20.00
GI	Marcus Giles	20.00
KG	Ken Griffey Jr.	150.00
TG	Tony Gwynn	60.00
TH	Travis Hafner	30.00
FH	Frank Howard	30.00
RH	Ryan Howard	75.00
AH	Aubrey Huff	20.00
HU	Torii Hunter	30.00
DJ	Derek Jeter	300.00
WJ	Wally Joyner	40.00
BL	Barry Larkin	40.00
MA	Bill Madlock	25.00
VM	Victor Martinez	25.00
DM	Don Mattingly	90.00
BM	Bobby Murcer	35.00
GN	Graig Nettles	30.00
TO	Tony Oliva	25.00
DO	David Ortiz	75.00
CP	Corey Patterson	20.00
WP	Wily Mo Pena	25.00
TP	Tony Perez	40.00
SP	Scott Podsednik	50.00
AP	Albert Pujols	250.00
TR	Tim Raines	30.00
RA	Aramis Ramirez	35.00
RE	Jose Reyes	40.00
RI	Jim Rice	35.00

CR	Cal Ripken Jr.	150.00
BR	Brooks Robinson	50.00
RS	Ryne Sandberg	80.00
MS	Mike Schmidt	75.00
MT	Mark Teixeira	60.00
MI	Miguel Tejada	50.00
BU	B.J. Upton	25.00
AV	Andy Van Slyke	30.00
JV	Jose Vidro	20.00
JW	Jayson Werth	20.00
DW	David Wright	80.00
KY	Kevin Youkilis	20.00

2005 Upper Deck Update

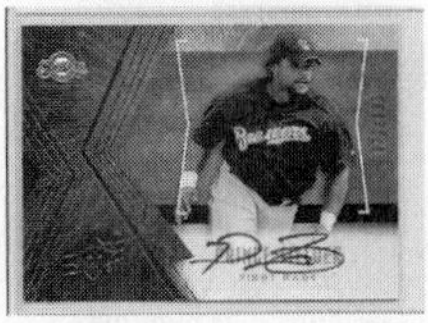

NM/M

Complete Update Set (186):		
Common Player (1-100):		.15
Common Rookie (101-177):		3.00
Production 599		
Common Rk Auto. (178-186):		10.00
Production 75		
Pack (5):		5.00
Box (24):		100.00
1	A.J. Burnett	.15
2	Adam Dunn	.50
3	Adrian Beltre	.25
4	Albert Pujols	2.00
5	Alex Rodriguez	2.00
6	Alfonso Soriano	.50
7	Andruw Jones	.50
8	Aramis Ramirez	.25
9	Barry Zito	.25
10	Bartolo Colon	.25
11	Ben Sheets	.25
12	Bobby Abreu	.25
13	Bobby Crosby	.25
14	Michael Cuddyer	.15
15	Brian Giles	.15
16	Brian Roberts	.15
17	Carl Crawford	.15
18	Carlos Beltran	.50
19	Carlos Delgado	.40
20	Carlos Lee	.15
21	Carlos Zambrano	.25
22	Chase Utley	.25
23	Chipper Jones	.75
24	Chris Carpenter	.25
25	Craig Biggio	.25
26	Curt Schilling	.75
27	David Ortiz	.75
28	David Wright	1.00
29	Derek Jeter	2.00
30	Derrek Lee	.50
31	Dontrelle Willis	.25
32	Eric Chavez	.25
33	Eric Gagne	.25
34	Francisco Rodriguez	.15
35	Gary Sheffield	.40
36	Greg Maddux	1.00
37	Hank Blalock	.25
38	Hideki Matsui	1.50
39	Ichiro Suzuki	1.50
40	Ivan Rodriguez	.50
41	J.D. Drew	.15
42	Jake Peavy	.25
43	Jason Bay	.25
44	Jason Schmidt	.15
45	Jeff Bagwell	.40
46	Jeff Kent	.25
47	Jeremy Bonderman	.15
48	Jim Edmonds	.40
49	Jim Thome	.50
50	Joe Mauer	.25
51	Johan Santana	.50
52	John Smoltz	.25
53	Johnny Damon	.75
54	Jose Reyes	.25
55	Jose Vidro	.15
56	Josh Beckett	.25
57	Justin Morneau	.15
58	Ken Griffey Jr.	1.50
59	Kenny Rogers	.15
60	Kerry Wood	.25
61	Khalil Greene	.25
62	Lance Berkman	.25
63	Livan Hernandez	.15
64	Luis Gonzalez	.15
65	Manny Ramirez	.75
66	Mark Buehrle	.25
67	Mark Mulder	.25
68	Mark Prior	.50
69	Mark Teixeira	.50
70	Michael Young	.25
71	Miguel Cabrera	.75
72	Miguel Tejada	.50
73	Mike Mussina	.40
74	Mike Piazza	.75
75	Moises Alou	.25
76	Morgan Ensberg	.25
77	Nomar Garciaparra	.50
78	Pat Burrell	.25
79	Paul Konerko	.75
80	Pedro Martinez	.75
81	Randy Johnson	.75
82	Rich Harden	.25
83	Richie Sexson	.25
84	Rickie Weeks	.25
85	Robinson Cano	.25
86	Roger Clemens	2.00
87	Roy Halladay	.25
88	Roy Oswalt	.25
89	Sammy Sosa	.75
90	Scott Kazmir	.15
91	Scott Rolen	.75
92	Shawn Green	.25
93	Tim Hudson	.25
94	Todd Helton	.50
95	Tom Glavine	.25
96	Torii Hunter	.25
.25	Travis Hafner	.15
.25	Troy Glaus	.15
99	Vernon Wells	.15
100	Vladimir Guerrero	.75
101	Adam Shabala **RC**	3.00
102	Ambiorix Burgos **RC**	3.00
103	Anibal Sanchez **RC**	5.00
104	Bill McCarthy **RC**	3.00
105	Brandon McCarthy **RC**	5.00
106	Brian Burres **RC**	3.00
107	Carlos Ruiz **RC**	4.00
108	Casey Rogowski **RC**	3.00
109	Chad Orvella **RC**	3.00
110	Chris Resop **RC**	3.00
111	Chris Roberson **RC**	3.00
112	Chris Seddon **RC**	3.00
113	Colter Bean **RC**	3.00
114	Dae-Sung Koo **RC**	3.00
115	David Gassner **RC**	3.00
116	Brian Anderson	3.00
117	D.J. Houlton **RC**	3.00
118	Derek Wathan **RC**	3.00
119	Devon Lowery **RC**	3.00
120	Enrique Gonzalez **RC**	3.00
121	Eude Brito **RC**	3.00
122	Francisco Butto **RC**	3.00
123	Franquelis Osoria **RC**	3.00
124	Garrett Jones **RC**	3.00
125	Geovany Soto **RC**	15.00
126	Hayden Penn **RC**	3.00
127	Ismael Ramirez **RC**	3.00
128	Jared Gothreaux **RC**	3.00
129	Jason Hammel **RC**	3.00
130	Jeff Miller **RC**	3.00
131	Joel Peralta **RC**	3.00
132	John Hattig Jr. **RC**	3.00
133	Jorge Campillo **RC**	5.00
134	Juan Morillo **RC**	3.00
135	Ryan Garko **RC**	6.00
136	Keiichi Yabu **RC**	5.00
137	Luis Hernandez **RC**	5.00
138	Luis Pena **RC**	3.00
139	Luis Rodriguez **RC**	3.00
140	Luke Scott **RC**	5.00
141	Marcos Carvajal **RC**	3.00
142	Mark Woodyard **RC**	3.00
143	Matt Smith **RC**	3.00
144	Matt Lindstrom **RC**	5.00
145	Miguel Negron **RC**	3.00
146	Mike Morse **RC**	3.00
147	Nate McLouth **RC**	5.00
148	Nelson Cruz **RC**	3.00
149	Nick Masset **RC**	3.00
150	Oscar Robles **RC**	3.00
151	Paulino Reynoso **RC**	3.00
152	Pedro Lopez **RC**	3.00
153	Peter Orr **RC**	3.00
154	Randy Messenger **RC**	3.00
155	Randy Williams **RC**	3.00
156	Raul Tablado **RC**	3.00
157	Ronny Paulino **RC**	3.00
158	Russel Rohlicek **RC**	3.00
159	Russell Martin **RC**	12.00
160	Scott Baker **RC**	5.00
161	Scott Munter **RC**	3.00
162	Sean Thompson **RC**	3.00
163	Sean Tracey **RC**	3.00
164	Shane Costa **RC**	3.00
165	Steve Schmoll **RC**	3.00
166	Tony Giarratano **RC**	3.00
167	Tony Pena **RC**	3.00
168	Travis Bowyer **RC**	3.00
169	Ubaldo Jimenez **RC**	3.00
170	Wladimir Balentien **RC**	5.00
171	Yorman Bazardo **RC**	3.00
172	Yuniesky Betancourt **RC**	5.00
173	Chris Denorfia **RC**	3.00
174	Dana Eveland **RC**	5.00
175	Jermaine Van Buren **RC**	3.00
176	Mark McLemore **RC**	3.00
177	Ryan Spilborghs **RC**	3.00
178	Ambiorix Concepcion **RC**	10.00
179	Jeff Niemann **RC**	25.00
180	Justin Verlander **RC**	80.00
181	Kendry Morales **RC**	20.00
182	Philip Humber **RC**	20.00
183	Prince Fielder	125.00
184	Stephen Drew **RC**	75.00
185	Tadahito Iguchi **RC**	50.00
186	Ryan Zimmerman **RC**	80.00
Common Artifacts RC (201-285):		3.00
Production 799		
201	Adam Shabala **RC**	3.00
202	Ambiorix Burgos **RC**	3.00
203	Ambiorix Concepcion **RC**	3.00
204	Anibal Sanchez **RC**	5.00
205	Bill McCarthy **RC**	3.00
206	Brandon McCarthy **RC**	3.00
207	Brian Burres **RC**	3.00
208	Carlos Ruiz **RC**	4.00
209	Casey Rogowski **RC**	3.00
210	Chad Orvella **RC**	3.00
211	Chris Resop **RC**	3.00
212	Chris Roberson **RC**	3.00
213	Chris Seddon **RC**	3.00
214	Colter Bean **RC**	3.00
215	Dae-Sung Koo **RC**	3.00
216	David Gassner **RC**	3.00
217	Brian Anderson	3.00
218	D.J. Houlton **RC**	3.00
219	Derek Wathan **RC**	3.00
220	Devon Lowery **RC**	3.00
221	Enrique Gonzalez **RC**	3.00
222	Eude Brito **RC**	3.00
223	Francisco Butto **RC**	3.00
224	Franquelis Osoria **RC**	3.00
225	Garrett Jones **RC**	3.00
226	Geovany Soto **RC**	10.00
227	Hayden Penn **RC**	3.00
228	Ismael Ramirez **RC**	3.00
229	Jared Gothreaux **RC**	3.00
230	Jason Hammel **RC**	3.00
231	Jeff Miller **RC**	3.00
232	Jeff Niemann **RC**	5.00
233	Joel Peralta **RC**	3.00
234	John Hattig Jr. **RC**	3.00
235	Jorge Campillo **RC**	4.00
236	Juan Morillo **RC**	3.00
237	Justin Verlander **RC**	10.00
238	Ryan Garko **RC**	5.00
239	Keiichi Yabu **RC**	3.00
240	Kendry Morales **RC**	3.00
241	Luis Hernandez **RC**	3.00
242	Luis Pena **RC**	3.00
243	Luis Rodriguez **RC**	3.00
244	Luke Scott **RC**	5.00
245	Marcos Carvajal **RC**	3.00
246	Mark Woodyard **RC**	3.00
247	Matt Smith **RC**	3.00
248	Matt Lindstrom **RC**	3.00
249	Miguel Negron **RC**	3.00
250	Mike Morse **RC**	3.00
251	Nate McLouth **RC**	8.00
252	Nelson Cruz **RC**	3.00
253	Nick Masset **RC**	3.00
254	Oscar Robles **RC**	3.00
255	Paulino Reynoso **RC**	3.00
256	Pedro Lopez **RC**	3.00
257	Peter Orr **RC**	3.00
258	Philip Humber **RC**	3.00
259	Prince Fielder	15.00
260	Randy Messenger **RC**	3.00
261	Randy Williams **RC**	3.00
262	Raul Tablado **RC**	3.00
263	Ronny Paulino **RC**	3.00
264	Russel Rohlicek **RC**	3.00
265	Russell Martin **RC**	8.00
266	Scott Baker **RC**	5.00
267	Scott Munter **RC**	3.00
268	Sean Thompson **RC**	3.00
269	Sean Tracey **RC**	3.00
270	Shane Costa **RC**	3.00
271	Stephen Drew **RC**	10.00
272	Steve Schmoll **RC**	3.00
273	Tadahito Iguchi **RC**	5.00
274	Tony Giarratano **RC**	3.00
275	Tony Pena **RC**	3.00
276	Travis Bowyer **RC**	3.00
277	Ubaldo Jimenez **RC**	4.00
278	Wladimir Balentien **RC**	5.00
279	Yorman Bazardo **RC**	4.00
280	Yuniesky Betancourt	5.00
281	Ryan Zimmerman **RC**	8.00
282	Chris Denorfia **RC**	3.00
283	Dana Eveland **RC**	5.00
284	Jermaine Van Buren **RC**	3.00
285	Mark McLemore **RC**	3.00
Common Reflections RC (201-286):		1.00
201	Adam Shabala **RC**	1.00
202	Ambiorix Burgos **RC**	1.00
203	Ambiorix Concepcion **RC**	1.00
204	Anibal Sanchez **RC**	2.00
205	Bill McCarthy **RC**	1.00
206	Brandon McCarthy **RC**	1.00
207	Brian Burres **RC**	1.00
208	Carlos Ruiz **RC**	1.00
209	Casey Rogowski **RC**	1.00
210	Chad Orvella **RC**	1.00
211	Chris Resop **RC**	1.50
212	Chris Roberson **RC**	1.00
213	Chris Seddon **RC**	1.00
214	Colter Bean **RC**	1.00
215	Dae-Sung Koo **RC**	1.00
216	Yuniesky Betancourt **RC**	2.00
217	David Gassner **RC**	1.00
218	Brian Anderson	1.00
219	Dennis Houlton **RC**	1.00
220	Derek Wathan **RC**	1.00
221	Devon Lowery **RC**	1.00
222	Enrique Gonzalez **RC**	1.00
223	Ryan Zimmerman **RC**	8.00
224	Eude Brito **RC**	1.00
225	Francisco Butto **RC**	1.00
226	Franquelis Osoria **RC**	1.00
227	Garrett Jones **RC**	1.00
228	Geovany Soto **RC**	8.00
229	Hayden Penn **RC**	1.00
230	Ismael Ramirez **RC**	1.00
231	Jared Gothreaux **RC**	1.00
232	Jason Hammel **RC**	1.00
233	Chris Denorfia **RC**	1.00
234	Jeff Miller **RC**	1.00
235	Jeff Niemann **RC**	2.00
236	Dana Eveland **RC**	3.00
237	Joel Peralta **RC**	1.00
238	John Hattig Jr. **RC**	1.00
239	Jorge Campillo **RC**	2.00
240	Juan Morillo **RC**	1.00
241	Justin Verlander **RC**	5.00
242	Ryan Garko **RC**	3.00
243	Keiichi Yabu **RC**	1.00
244	Kendry Morales **RC**	1.50
245	Luis Hernandez **RC**	1.00
246	Jermaine Van Buren **RC**	1.00
247	Luis Pena **RC**	1.00
248	Luis Rodriguez **RC**	1.00
249	Luke Scott **RC**	3.00
250	Marcos Carvajal **RC**	1.00
251	Mark Woodyard **RC**	1.00
252	Matt Smith **RC**	1.00
253	Matt Lindstrom **RC**	1.00
254	Miguel Negron **RC**	1.00
255	Mike Morse **RC**	1.00
256	Nate McLouth **RC**	3.00
257	Nelson Cruz **RC**	1.00
258	Nick Masset **RC**	1.00
259	Mark McLemore **RC**	1.00
260	Oscar Robles **RC**	1.00
261	Paulino Reynoso **RC**	1.00
262	Pedro Lopez **RC**	1.00
263	Peter Orr **RC**	1.00
264	Philip Humber **RC**	2.00
265	Prince Fielder	10.00
266	Randy Messenger **RC**	1.00
267	Randy Williams **RC**	1.00
268	Raul Tablado **RC**	1.00
269	Ronny Paulino **RC**	1.00
270	Russel Rohlicek **RC**	1.00
271	Russell Martin **RC**	5.00
272	Scott Baker **RC**	2.50
273	Scott Munter **RC**	1.00
274	Sean Thompson **RC**	1.00
275	Sean Tracey **RC**	1.00
276	Shane Costa **RC**	1.00
277	Stephen Drew **RC**	5.00
278	Steve Schmoll **RC**	1.00
279	Ryan Spilborghs **RC**	2.00
280	Tadahito Iguchi **RC**	2.00
281	Tony Giarratano **RC**	1.00
282	Tony Pena **RC**	1.00
283	Travis Bowyer **RC**	1.50
284	Ubaldo Jimenez **RC**	1.50
285	Wladimir Balentien **RC**	2.50
286	Yorman Bazardo **RC**	1.00
Common Origins RC (201-286):		.75
201	Adam Shabala **RC**	.75
202	Ambiorix Burgos **RC**	.75
203	Ambiorix Concepcion **RC**	.75
204	Anibal Sanchez **RC**	1.00
205	Bill McCarthy **RC**	.75
206	Brandon McCarthy **RC**	1.00
207	Brian Burres **RC**	.75
208	Carlos Ruiz **RC**	1.00
209	Casey Rogowski **RC**	1.00
210	Chad Orvella **RC**	.75
211	Chris Resop **RC**	1.00
212	Chris Roberson **RC**	1.00
213	Chris Seddon **RC**	.75
214	Colter Bean **RC**	1.00
215	Dae-Sung Koo **RC**	.75
216	Yuniesky Betancourt **RC**	1.50
217	David Gassner **RC**	.75
218	Brian Anderson **RC**	1.00
219	Dennis Houlton **RC**	.75
220	Derek Wathan **RC**	.75
221	Devon Lowery **RC**	.75
222	Enrique Gonzalez **RC**	.75
223	Ryan Zimmerman **RC**	5.00
224	Eude Brito **RC**	.75
225	Francisco Butto **RC**	1.00
226	Franquelis Osoria **RC**	1.00
227	Garrett Jones **RC**	1.00
228	Geovany Soto **RC**	5.00
229	Hayden Penn **RC**	1.00
230	Ismael Ramirez **RC**	1.00
231	Jared Gothreaux **RC**	.75
232	Jason Hammel **RC**	.75
233	Chris Denorfia **RC**	1.00
234	Jeff Miller **RC**	.75
235	Jeff Niemann **RC**	1.50
236	Dana Eveland **RC**	3.00
237	Joel Peralta **RC**	.75
238	John Hattig Jr. **RC**	1.00
239	Jorge Campillo **RC**	1.50
240	Juan Morillo **RC**	1.00
241	Justin Verlander **RC**	5.00
242	Ryan Garko **RC**	2.00
243	Keiichi Yabu **RC**	1.00
244	Kendry Morales **RC**	1.00
245	Luis Hernandez **RC**	.75
246	Jermaine Van Buren **RC**	.75
247	Luis Pena **RC**	.75
248	Luis Rodriguez **RC**	.75
249	Luke Scott **RC**	2.00
250	Marcos Carvajal **RC**	1.00
251	Mark Woodyard **RC**	1.00
252	Matt Smith **RC**	1.00
253	Matt Lindstrom **RC**	1.00
254	Miguel Negron **RC**	1.00
255	Mike Morse **RC**	1.00
256	Nate McLouth **RC**	3.00
257	Nelson Cruz **RC**	1.00
258	Nick Masset **RC**	.75
259	Mark McLemore **RC**	1.00
260	Oscar Robles **RC**	.75
261	Paulino Reynoso **RC**	.75
262	Pedro Lopez **RC**	1.00
263	Peter Orr **RC**	1.00

264 Philip Humber **RC** 1.50
265 Prince Fielder 8.00
266 Randy Messenger **RC** .75
267 Randy Williams **RC** 1.00
268 Raul Tablado **RC** .75
269 Ronny Paulino **RC** 1.00
270 Russel Rohlicek **RC** .75
271 Russell Martin **RC** 5.00
272 Scott Baker **RC** 2.00
273 Ryan Spilborghs **RC** 1.00
274 Scott Munter **RC** .75
275 Sean Thompson **RC** 1.00
276 Sean Tracey **RC** 1.00
277 Shane Costa **RC** 1.00
278 Stephen Drew **RC** 4.00
279 Steve Schmoll **RC** 1.00
280 Tadahito Iguchi **RC** 1.50
281 Tony Giarratano **RC** .75
282 Tony Pena **RC** .75
283 Travis Bowyer **RC** 1.00
284 Ubaldo Jimenez **RC** 1.00
285 Wladimir Balentien **RC** 2.00
286 Yorman Bazardo **RC** 1.00
Common SP Authentic Auto. (101-186): 8.00
Production 185
101 Adam Shabala **RC** 10.00
102 Ambiorix Burgos **RC** 10.00
103 Ambiorix Concepcion **RC** 10.00
104 Anibal Sanchez **RC** 15.00
106 Brandon McCarthy **RC** 15.00
107 Brian Burres **RC** 10.00
108 Carlos Ruiz **RC** 15.00
109 Casey Rogowski **RC** 10.00
110 Chad Orvella **RC** 10.00
111 Chris Resop **RC** 10.00
112 Chris Roberson **RC** 10.00
113 Chris Seddon **RC** 10.00
114 Colter Bean **RC** 10.00
116 David Gassner **RC** 10.00
117 Brian Anderson 15.00
120 Devon Lowery **RC** 10.00
121 Enrique Gonzalez **RC** 10.00
122 Eude Brito **RC** 8.00
123 Francisco Butto **RC** 10.00
124 Franquelis Osoria **RC** 10.00
125 Garrett Jones **RC** 10.00
126 Geovany Soto **RC** 200.00
127 Hayden Penn **RC** 10.00
128 Ismael Ramirez **RC** 8.00
129 Jared Gothreaux **RC** 10.00
130 Jason Hammel **RC** 10.00
131 Jeff Miller **RC** 8.00
132 Jeff Niemann **RC** 25.00
133 Joel Peralta **RC** 10.00
134 John Hattig Jr. **RC** 10.00
135 Jorge Campillo **RC** 15.00
136 Juan Morillo **RC** 10.00
137 Justin Verlander **RC** 150.00
138 Ryan Garko **RC** 40.00
139 Keiichi Yabu **RC** 15.00
140 Kendry Morales **RC** 25.00
141 Luis Hernandez **RC** 10.00
143 Luis Rodriguez **RC** 10.00
144 Luke Scott **RC** 50.00
145 Marcos Carvajal **RC** 10.00
146 Mark Woodyard **RC** 10.00
147 Matt Smith **RC** 8.00
148 Matt Lindstrom **RC** 10.00
149 Miguel Negron **RC** 10.00
150 Mike Morse **RC** 15.00
151 Nate McLouth **RC** 50.00
152 Nelson Cruz **RC** 25.00
153 Nick Masset **RC** 8.00
155 Paulino Reynoso **RC** 10.00
156 Pedro Lopez **RC** 10.00
157 Peter Orr **RC** 10.00
158 Philip Humber **RC** 20.00
159 Prince Fielder 200.00
160 Randy Messenger **RC** 8.00
162 Raul Tablado **RC** 10.00
163 Ronny Paulino **RC** 10.00
164 Russel Rohlicek **RC** 10.00
165 Russell Martin **RC** 125.00
166 Scott Baker **RC** 20.00
167 Scott Munter **RC** 10.00
168 Sean Thompson **RC** 10.00
169 Sean Tracey **RC** 10.00
170 Shane Costa **RC** 10.00
171 Stephen Drew **RC** 80.00
172 Steve Schmoll **RC** 10.00
173 Tadahito Iguchi **RC** 60.00
174 Tony Giarratano **RC** 15.00
175 Tony Pena **RC** 8.00
176 Travis Bowyer **RC** 10.00
177 Ubaldo Jimenez **RC** 20.00
178 Wladimir Balentien **RC** 25.00
179 Yorman Bazardo **RC** 15.00
181 Ryan Zimmerman **RC** 100.00
182 Chris Denorfia **RC** 15.00
184 Jermaine Van Buren **RC** 15.00
185 Mark McLemore **RC** 10.00
Common SPx Auto. (101-179): 8.00
Production 185
101 Adam Shabala **RC** 10.00
102 Ambiorix Burgos **RC** 10.00
103 Ambiorix Concepcion **RC** 10.00
104 Anibal Sanchez **RC** 15.00
106 Brandon McCarthy **RC** 10.00
107 Brian Burres **RC** 10.00
108 Carlos Ruiz **RC** 15.00
109 Casey Rogowski **RC** 10.00
110 Chad Orvella **RC** 10.00
111 Chris Resop **RC** 15.00
112 Chris Roberson **RC** 15.00
113 Chris Seddon **RC** 10.00
114 Colter Bean **RC** 15.00
115 David Gassner **RC** 10.00
116 Brian Anderson **RC** 15.00
118 Devon Lowery **RC** 8.00
119 Enrique Gonzalez **RC** 10.00
120 Eude Brito **RC** 10.00
121 Francisco Butto **RC** 10.00
122 Franquelis Osoria **RC** 10.00
123 Garrett Jones **RC** 10.00
124 Geovany Soto **RC** 150.00
125 Hayden Penn **RC** 15.00
126 Ismael Ramirez **RC** 8.00
127 Jared Gothreaux **RC** 10.00
128 Jason Hammel **RC** 10.00
129 Jeff Miller **RC** 8.00
130 Jeff Niemann **RC** 25.00
131 Joel Peralta **RC** 10.00
132 John Hattig Jr. **RC** 10.00
133 Jorge Campillo **RC** 15.00
134 Juan Morillo **RC** 8.00
135 Justin Verlander **RC** 150.00
136 Ryan Garko **RC** 40.00
137 Kendry Morales **RC** 20.00
138 Luis Hernandez **RC** 10.00
140 Luis Rodriguez **RC** 10.00
141 Mark Woodyard **RC** 10.00
142 Matt Smith **RC** 8.00
143 Matt Lindstrom **RC** 10.00
144 Miguel Negron **RC** 15.00
145 Mike Morse **RC** 20.00
146 Nate McLouth **RC** 40.00
147 Nelson Cruz **RC** 25.00
148 Nick Masset **RC** 8.00
150 Paulino Reynoso **RC** 10.00
151 Pedro Lopez **RC** 10.00
152 Philip Humber **RC** 20.00
153 Prince Fielder 150.00
154 Randy Messenger **RC** 8.00
156 Raul Tablado **RC** 10.00
157 Ronny Paulino **RC** 10.00
158 Russel Rohlicek **RC** 10.00
159 Russell Martin **RC** 125.00
160 Scott Baker **RC** 20.00
161 Scott Munter **RC** 10.00
162 Sean Thompson **RC** 10.00
163 Sean Tracey **RC** 10.00
164 Shane Costa **RC** 10.00
165 Stephen Drew **RC** 75.00
166 Tony Giarratano **RC** 10.00
167 Tony Pena **RC** 8.00
168 Travis Bowyer **RC** 10.00
169 Ubaldo Jimenez **RC** 20.00
170 Wladimir Balentien **RC** 25.00
171 Yorman Bazardo **RC** 10.00
173 Ryan Zimmerman **RC** 80.00
174 Chris Denorfia **RC** 10.00
176 Jermaine Van Buren **RC** 10.00
177 Mark McLemore **RC** 8.00
179 Ryan Speier **RC** 10.00
Common Sweet Spot RC (91-174): .75
91 Adam Shabala **RC** .75
92 Ambiorix Burgos **RC** .75
93 Ambiorix Concepcion **RC** 1.00
94 Anibal Sanchez **RC** 1.00
95 Bill McCarthy **RC** .75
96 Brandon McCarthy **RC** 1.00
97 Brian Burres **RC** .75
98 Carlos Ruiz **RC** 1.00
99 Casey Rogowski **RC** 1.00
100 Chad Orvella **RC** .75
101 Chris Resop **RC** 1.00
102 Chris Roberson **RC** 1.00
103 Chris Seddon **RC** .75
104 Colter Bean **RC** 1.00
105 Dae-Sung Koo **RC** .75
106 Ryan Zimmerman **RC** 5.00
107 David Gassner **RC** .75
108 Brian Anderson 1.00
109 D.J. Houlton **RC** 1.00
110 Derek Wathan **RC** .75
111 Devon Lowery **RC** .75
112 Enrique Gonzalez **RC** .75
113 Chris Denorfia **RC** 1.00
114 Eude Brito **RC** .75
115 Francisco Butto **RC** 1.00
116 Franquelis Osoria **RC** 1.00
117 Garrett Jones **RC** .75
118 Geovany Soto **RC** 5.00
119 Hayden Penn **RC** 1.00
120 Ismael Ramirez **RC** .75
121 Jared Gothreaux **RC** .75
122 Jason Hammel **RC** .75
123 Dana Eveland **RC** 2.00
124 Jeff Miller **RC** .75
125 Jermaine Van Buren **RC** 1.00
126 Joel Peralta **RC** .75
127 John Hattig Jr. **RC** 1.00
128 Jorge Campillo **RC** 1.00
129 Juan Morillo **RC** .75
130 Ryan Garko **RC** 2.00
131 Keiichi Yabu **RC** 1.00
132 Kendry Morales **RC** 1.00
133 Luis Hernandez **RC** .75
134 Mark McLemore **RC** 1.00
135 Luis Pena **RC** .75
136 Luis Rodriguez **RC** .75
137 Luke Scott **RC** 2.00
138 Marcos Carvajal **RC** 1.00
139 Mark Woodyard **RC** 1.00
140 Matt Smith **RC** .75
141 Matt Lindstrom **RC** 1.00
142 Miguel Negron **RC** 1.00
143 Mike Morse **RC** 1.00
144 Nate McLouth **RC** 3.00
145 Nelson Cruz **RC** 1.00
146 Nick Masset **RC** .75
147 Ryan Spilborghs **RC** 1.00
148 Oscar Robles **RC** .75
149 Paulino Reynoso **RC** .75
150 Pedro Lopez **RC** 1.00
151 Peter Orr **RC** .75
152 Prince Fielder 8.00
153 Randy Messenger **RC** .75
154 Randy Williams **RC** 1.00
155 Raul Tablado **RC** .75
156 Ronny Paulino **RC** 1.00
157 Russel Rohlicek **RC** .75
158 Russell Martin **RC** 3.00
159 Scott Baker **RC** 1.50
160 Scott Munter **RC** .75
161 Sean Thompson **RC** 1.00
162 Sean Tracey **RC** 1.00
163 Shane Costa **RC** 1.00
164 Stephen Drew **RC** 4.00
165 Steve Schmoll **RC** .75
166 Ryan Speier **RC** 1.00
167 Tadahito Iguchi **RC** 1.50
168 Tony Giarratano **RC** 1.00
169 Tony Pena **RC** .75
170 Travis Bowyer **RC** .75
171 Ubaldo Jimenez **RC** 1.00
172 Wladimir Balentien **RC** 1.50
173 Yorman Bazardo **RC** .75
174 Yuniesky Betancourt **RC** 1.50
Common Ultimate Signature Ed. (111-193): 8.00
Production 125
111 Adam Shabala **RC** 10.00
112 Anibal Sanchez **RC** 15.00
114 Brandon McCarthy **RC** 15.00
115 Brian Burres **RC** 10.00
116 Carlos Ruiz **RC** 15.00
117 Casey Rogowski **RC** 10.00
118 Chad Orvella **RC** 10.00
119 Chris Resop **RC** 10.00
120 Chris Roberson **RC** 10.00
121 Chris Seddon **RC** 10.00
122 Colter Bean **RC** 15.00
124 David Gassner **RC** 10.00
125 Brian Anderson 15.00
128 Devon Lowery **RC** 10.00
129 Enrique Gonzalez **RC** 10.00
130 Eude Brito **RC** 8.00
131 Francisco Butto **RC** 10.00
132 Franquelis Osoria **RC** 10.00
133 Garrett Jones **RC** 10.00
134 Geovany Soto **RC** 150.00
135 Hayden Penn **RC** 15.00
136 Ismael Ramirez **RC** 8.00
137 Jared Gothreaux **RC** 10.00
138 Jason Hammel **RC** 10.00
139 Jeff Miller **RC** 10.00
140 Jeff Niemann **RC** 25.00
141 Joel Peralta **RC** 10.00
142 John Hattig Jr. **RC** 10.00
143 Jorge Campillo **RC** 15.00
144 Juan Morillo **RC** 10.00
145 Justin Verlander **RC** 125.00
146 Ryan Garko **RC** 40.00
147 Keiichi Yabu **RC** 15.00
148 Kendry Morales **RC** 15.00
149 Luis Hernandez **RC** 10.00
151 Luis Rodriguez **RC** 10.00
152 Luke Scott **RC** 30.00
153 Marcos Carvajal **RC** 10.00
154 Mark Woodyard **RC** 10.00
155 Matt Smith **RC** 10.00
156 Matt Lindstrom **RC** 10.00
157 Miguel Negron **RC** 10.00
158 Mike Morse **RC** 15.00
159 Nate McLouth **RC** 40.00
160 Nelson Cruz **RC** 25.00
161 Nick Masset **RC** 8.00
162 Mark McLemore **RC** 10.00
164 Paulino Reynoso **RC** 10.00
165 Pedro Lopez **RC** 10.00
166 Peter Orr **RC** 10.00
167 Philip Humber **RC** 20.00
168 Prince Fielder 150.00
169 Randy Messenger **RC** 10.00
171 Raul Tablado **RC** 10.00
172 Ronny Paulino **RC** 10.00
173 Russel Rohlicek **RC** 8.00
174 Russell Martin **RC** 65.00
175 Scott Baker **RC** 20.00
176 Scott Munter **RC** 10.00
177 Sean Thompson **RC** 10.00
178 Sean Tracey **RC** 10.00
179 Shane Costa **RC** 10.00
180 Stephen Drew **RC** 60.00
181 Steve Schmoll **RC** 10.00
182 Tadahito Iguchi **RC** 40.00
183 Tony Giarratano **RC** 10.00
184 Tony Pena **RC** 10.00
185 Travis Bowyer **RC** 10.00
186 Ubaldo Jimenez **RC** 20.00
187 Wladimir Balentien **RC** 20.00
188 Yorman Bazardo **RC** 10.00
190 Ryan Zimmerman **RC** 75.00
191 Chris Denorfia **RC** 10.00
192 Ryan Speier **RC** 10.00
193 Jermaine Van Buren **RC** 10.00

Gold

Gold (101-177): 1-1.5X
Production 150
Gold (178-186): No Pricing
Production 10 Sets

Silver

Silver (101-177): 1X
Production 450
Silver (178-186): No Pricing
Production 25 Sets

Platinum

Platinum (101-177): No Pricing
Production 25
Platinum (178-186): No Pricing
Production One Set

Artifacts Blue

Blue (201-285): 1-1.5X
Production 100

Artifacts Gold

Gold (201-285): No Pricing
Production 25 Sets

Artifacts Red

Red (201-285): 1-2X
Production 50

Artifacts Platinum

No Pricing
Production One Set

Reflections Blue

Blue (201-286): 2-4X
Production 75 Sets

Reflections Emerald

Emerald (201-286): 3-6X
Production 25 Sets

Reflections Purple

Purple (201-286): 1.5-3X
Production 99 Sets

Reflections Platinum

No Pricing
Production One Set

Reflections Red

Red (201-286): 1.5-3X
Production 99 Sets

Reflections Turquoise

Turquoise (201-286): 2-4X
Production 50 Sets

Origins Blue

Blue (201-286): 2-4X
Production 50 Sets

Origins Gold

Gold (201-286): No Pricing
Production 20 Sets

Origins Black

No Pricing
Production One Set

Origins Red

Red (201-286): 2-3X
Production 99 Sets

Origins Old Judge

Old Judge (201-286): 1X
Inserted 1:2
Blue: 2-3X
Production 50 Sets
Red: 1-2X
Production 99 Sets
Gold: No Pricing
Production 20 Sets
Black: No Pricing
Production One Set

SP Authentic Gold

Gold (101-186): No Pricing
Production 10

SPx Silver

Silver (101-179): No Pricing
Production 10

Sweet Spot Gold

Gold (91-174): 1.5-2X
Production 399

Sweet Spot Platinum

Platinum (91-174): 2-3X
Production 99

Sweet Spot Plutonium

No Pricing
Production One Set

Ultimate Signature Edition Platinum

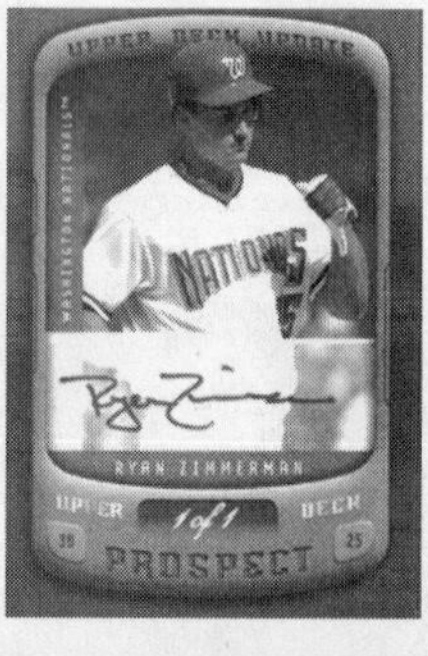

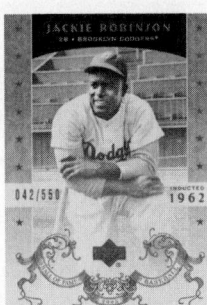

No Pricing
Production One Set

Quad Signatures

No Pricing
Production Five Sets

Draft Generations Triple Signatures

No Pricing
Production 10 Sets

Link to Future Dual Autographs

		NM/M
Common Duo:		15.00
Production 35 Sets		
BR	Wladimir Balentien, Jeremy Reed	15.00
BW	Dontrelle Willis, Yorman Bazardo	20.00
CD	David DeJesus, Shane Costa	15.00
DD	J.D. Drew, Stephen Drew	80.00
DJ	Stephen Drew, Derek Jeter	275.00
FO	Prince Fielder, Lyle Overbay	50.00
FT	Prince Fielder, Mark Teixeira	75.00
FW	Prince Fielder, Rickie Weeks	50.00
GO	Roy Oswalt, Jared Gothreaux	25.00
HF	Luis Hernandez, Rafael Furcal	20.00
HG	Tom Glavine, Philip Humber	50.00
MB	Jason Bay, Nate McLouth	40.00
MK	Casey Kotchman, Kendry Morales	40.00
NK	Scott Kazmir, Jeff Niemann	30.00
NW	Vernon Wells, Miguel Negron	25.00
OB	Yhency Brazoban, Franquelis Osoria	20.00
OG	Peter Orr, Marcus Giles	25.00
PV	Javier Vazquez, Tony Pena	15.00
RH	Roy Halladay, Ismael Ramirez	25.00
SK	Chris Seddon, Scott Kazmir	25.00
SL	Jason Lane, Luke Scott	40.00
VB	Justin Verlander, Jeremy Bonderman	80.00
VC	Roger Clemens, Justin Verlander	140.00
ZC	Ryan Zimmerman, Chad Cordero	60.00

Link to the Past Dual Autographs

		NM/M
Common Duo:		20.00
Production 25 Sets		
BC	Steve Carlton, Eude Brito	30.00
BM	Juan Marichal, Brian Burres	30.00
CS	Darryl Strawberry, Ambiorix Concepcion	25.00
GT	Alan Trammell, Tony Giarratano	30.00
HG	Dwight Gooden, Philip Humber	40.00
HS	Philip Humber, Tom Seaver	50.00
IA	Luis Aparicio, Tadahito Iguchi	125.00
IC	Tadahito Iguchi, Rod Carew	125.00
JH	Kent Hrbek, Garrett Jones	40.00
JJ	Jack Morris, Justin Verlander	75.00
MC	Rod Carew, Kendry Morales	40.00
MJ	Kendry Morales, Wally Joyner	40.00
MV	Andy Van Slyke, Nate McLouth	40.00
NB	Miguel Negron, George Bell	40.00
NR	Nolan Ryan, Jeff Niemann	150.00
PP	Jim Palmer, Hayden Penn	40.00
RD	Lenny Dykstra, Chris Roberson	30.00
TP	Gaylord Perry, Sean Thompson	20.00
VM	Justin Verlander, Denny McLain	75.00

2005 UD Hall of Fame

		NM/M
Complete Set (100):		
Common Player:		3.00
Production 550 Sets		
Tin (4):		125.00
1	Al Kaline	4.00
2	Al Lopez	3.00
3	Bill Mazeroski	3.00
4	Billy Williams	3.00
5	Bob Feller	4.00
6	Bob Gibson	4.00
7	Bob Lemon	3.00
8	Bobby Doerr	3.00
9	Brooks Robinson	5.00
10	Buck Leonard	3.00
11	Carl Yastrzemski	5.00

12	Carlton Fisk	4.00
13	Casey Stengel	4.00
14	Jim "Catfish" Hunter	3.00
15	Dave Winfield	4.00
16	Dennis Eckersley	3.00
17	Dizzy Dean	4.00
18	Don Drysdale	3.00
19	Don Sutton	3.00
20	Duke Snider	4.00
21	Early Wynn	3.00
22	Eddie Mathews	5.00
23	Eddie Murray	4.00
24	Enos Slaughter	3.00
25	Ernie Banks	5.00
26	Fergie Jenkins	3.00
27	Frank Robinson	4.00
28	Gary Carter	3.00
29	Gaylord Perry	3.00
30	George Brett	8.00
31	George Kell	3.00
32	George Sisler	3.00
33	Hal Newhouser	3.00
34	Harmon Killebrew	5.00
35	Hoyt Wilhelm	3.00
36	Jackie Robinson	5.00
37	Jim Bunning	3.00
38	Jim Palmer	5.00
39	Jimmie Foxx	5.00
40	Joe Morgan	3.00
41	Johnny Bench	5.00
42	Johnny Mize	3.00
43	Juan Marichal	3.00
44	Kirby Puckett	4.00
45	Larry Doby	3.00
46	Lefty Grove	3.00
47	Lou Boudreau	3.00
48	Lou Brock	4.00
49	Luis Aparicio	3.00
50	Mel Ott	4.00
51	Mickey Cochrane	4.00
52	Monte Irvin	3.00
53	Orlando Cepeda	3.00
54	Ozzie Smith	5.00
55	Paul Molitor	3.00
56	Pee Wee Reese	4.00
57	Phil Niekro	3.00
58	Phil Rizzuto	3.00
59	Pie Traynor	3.00
60	Ralph Kiner	3.00
61	Red Schoendienst	3.00
62	Richie Ashburn	3.00
63	Rick Ferrell	3.00
64	Robin Roberts	3.00
65	Robin Yount	5.00
66	Rod Carew	3.00
67	Rogers Hornsby	4.00
68	Rollie Fingers	3.00
69	Roy Campanella	4.00
70	Steve Carlton	5.00
71	Tony Perez	3.00
72	Warren Spahn	4.00
73	Whitey Ford	4.00
74	Willie Mays	4.00
75	Willie Stargell	4.00
76	Yogi Berra	5.00
77	Babe Ruth	8.00
78	Honus Wagner	4.00
79	Lou Gehrig	6.00
80	Mickey Mantle	15.00
81	Ty Cobb	6.00
82	Ryne Sandberg	5.00
83	Satchel Paige	5.00
84	Wade Boggs	4.00
85	Reggie Jackson	5.00
86	Babe Ruth	8.00
87	Christy Mathewson	4.00
88	Cy Young	4.00
89	Honus Wagner	5.00
90	Joe DiMaggio	6.00
91	Lou Gehrig	6.00
92	Mickey Mantle	15.00
93	Mike Schmidt	6.00
94	Nolan Ryan	8.00
95	Satchel Paige	5.00
96	Stan Musial	5.00
97	Ted Williams	6.00
98	Tom Seaver	5.00
99	Ty Cobb	6.00
100	Walter Johnson	4.00

Gold

Gold (1-100):		1.5-2X
Production 25 Sets		

Green

Green (1-100):		1X
Production 200 Sets		

Rainbow

No Pricing
Production One Set

Silver

Silver (1-100):		1-1.5X
Production 99 Sets		

Class of Cooperstown

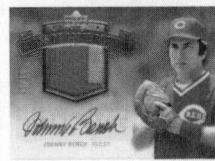

		NM/M
Production 50 Sets		
Gold:		No Pricing
Production Five Sets		
Silver:		No Pricing
Production 15 Sets		
Rainbow:		No Pricing
Production One Set		
LA1	Luis Aparicio	4.00
LA2	Luis Aparicio	4.00
EB1	Ernie Banks	6.00
EB2	Ernie Banks	6.00
BE1	Johnny Bench	6.00
BE2	Johnny Bench	6.00
YB1	Yogi Berra	5.00
YB2	Yogi Berra	5.00
GB1	George Brett	10.00
GB2	George Brett	10.00
GB3	George Brett	10.00
LB1	Lou Brock	4.00
JB1	Jim Bunning	4.00
JB2	Jim Bunning	4.00
RC1	Rod Carew	4.00
RC2	Rod Carew	4.00
SC1	Steve Carlton	4.00
SC2	Steve Carlton	4.00
SC3	Steve Carlton	4.00
SC4	Steve Carlton	4.00
GC1	Gary Carter	4.00
GC2	Gary Carter	4.00
OC1	Orlando Cepeda	4.00
BD1	Bobby Doerr	4.00
BD2	Bobby Doerr	4.00
DE1	Dennis Eckersley	4.00
BF1	Bob Feller	4.00
BF2	Bob Feller	4.00
RF1	Rollie Fingers	4.00
CF1	Carlton Fisk	4.00
CF2	Carlton Fisk	4.00
WF1	Whitey Ford	5.00
WF2	Whitey Ford	5.00
BG1	Bob Gibson	5.00
BG2	Bob Gibson	5.00
MI1	Monte Irvin	4.00
MI2	Monte Irvin	4.00
RJ1	Reggie Jackson	5.00
RJ2	Reggie Jackson	5.00
RJ3	Reggie Jackson	5.00
FJ1	Fergie Jenkins	4.00
AK1	Al Kaline	6.00
AK2	Al Kaline	6.00
AK3	Al Kaline	6.00
GK1	George Kell	4.00
HK1	Harmon Killebrew	6.00
HK2	Harmon Killebrew	6.00
HK3	Harmon Killebrew	6.00
HK4	Harmon Killebrew	6.00
RK1	Ralph Kiner	4.00
RK2	Ralph Kiner	4.00
MA1	Juan Marichal	4.00
MA2	Juan Marichal	4.00
BM1	Bill Mazeroski	4.00
WM1	Willie McCovey	5.00
WM2	Willie McCovey	5.00
PM1	Paul Molitor	5.00
PM2	Paul Molitor	5.00
PM3	Paul Molitor	5.00
JM1	Joe Morgan	4.00
JM2	Joe Morgan	4.00
EM1	Eddie Murray	4.00
SM1	Stan Musial	6.00
SM2	Stan Musial	6.00
PN1	Phil Niekro	4.00
JP1	Jim Palmer	4.00
JP2	Jim Palmer	4.00
TP1	Tony Perez	4.00
GP1	Gaylord Perry	4.00
GP2	Gaylord Perry	4.00
KP1	Kirby Puckett	5.00
RR1	Robin Roberts	4.00
BR1	Brooks Robinson	5.00
BR2	Brooks Robinson	5.00
BR3	Brooks Robinson	5.00
FR1	Frank Robinson	5.00
FR2	Frank Robinson	5.00

NR1	Nolan Ryan	10.00
NR2	Nolan Ryan	10.00
NR3	Nolan Ryan	10.00
NR4	Nolan Ryan	10.00
MS1	Mike Schmidt	6.00
MS2	Mike Schmidt	6.00
MS3	Mike Schmidt	6.00
RS1	Red Schoendienst	4.00
TS1	Tom Seaver	5.00
TS2	Tom Seaver	5.00
OS1	Ozzie Smith	6.00
OS2	Ozzie Smith	6.00
SN1	Duke Snider	5.00
DS1	Don Sutton	4.00
BW1	Billy Williams	4.00
BW2	Billy Williams	4.00
BW3	Billy Williams	4.00
DW1	Dave Winfield	4.00
DW2	Dave Winfield	4.00
CY1	Carl Yastrzemski	6.00
CY2	Carl Yastrzemski	6.00
RY1	Robin Yount	6.00
RY2	Robin Yount	6.00

Class of Cooperstown Autograph

		NM/M
Production 25 Sets		
Gold:		No Pricing
Production Five Sets		
Silver:		No Pricing
Production 15 Sets		
Rainbow:		No Pricing
Material Gold:		No Pricing
Production Five Sets		
Material Silver:		No Pricing
Production 15 Sets		
Patch Gold:		No Pricing
Production Five Sets		
Patch Silver:		No Pricing
Production 10 Sets		
LA1	Luis Aparicio	20.00
LA2	Luis Aparicio	20.00
EB1	Ernie Banks	50.00
EB2	Ernie Banks	50.00
BE1	Johnny Bench	40.00
BE2	Johnny Bench	40.00
YB1	Yogi Berra	60.00
YB2	Yogi Berra	60.00
GB1	George Brett	60.00
GB2	George Brett	60.00
GB3	George Brett	60.00
LB1	Lou Brock	35.00
JB1	Jim Bunning	25.00
JB2	Jim Bunning	25.00
RC1	Rod Carew	30.00
RC2	Rod Carew	30.00
SC1	Steve Carlton	20.00
SC2	Steve Carlton	20.00
SC3	Steve Carlton	20.00
SC4	Steve Carlton	20.00
GC1	Gary Carter	25.00
GC2	Gary Carter	25.00
OC1	Orlando Cepeda	25.00
BD1	Bobby Doerr	15.00
BD2	Bobby Doerr	15.00
DE1	Dennis Eckersley	20.00
BF1	Bob Feller	30.00
BF2	Bob Feller	30.00
RF1	Rollie Fingers	20.00
CF1	Carlton Fisk	30.00
CF2	Carlton Fisk	30.00
WF1	Whitey Ford	50.00
WF2	Whitey Ford	50.00
BG1	Bob Gibson	35.00
BG2	Bob Gibson	35.00
MI1	Monte Irvin	25.00
MI2	Monte Irvin	25.00
RJ1	Reggie Jackson	40.00
RJ2	Reggie Jackson	40.00
RJ3	Reggie Jackson	40.00
FJ1	Fergie Jenkins	20.00
AK1	Al Kaline	40.00
AK2	Al Kaline	40.00
AK3	Al Kaline	40.00
GK1	George Kell	20.00
HK1	Harmon Killebrew	40.00
HK2	Harmon Killebrew	40.00
HK3	Harmon Killebrew	40.00
HK4	Harmon Killebrew	40.00
RK1	Ralph Kiner	40.00
RK2	Ralph Kiner	40.00
MA1	Juan Marichal	25.00
MA2	Juan Marichal	25.00
BM1	Bill Mazeroski	40.00
WM1	Willie McCovey	40.00
WM2	Willie McCovey	40.00
PM1	Paul Molitor	30.00
PM2	Paul Molitor	30.00
PM3	Paul Molitor	30.00
JM1	Joe Morgan	25.00
JM2	Joe Morgan	25.00

EM1 Eddie Murray 50.00
SM1 Stan Musial 60.00
SM2 Stan Musial 60.00
PN1 Phil Niekro 20.00
JP1 Jim Palmer 20.00
JP2 Jim Palmer 20.00
TP1 Tony Perez 20.00
GP1 Gaylord Perry 20.00
GP2 Gaylord Perry 20.00
KP1 Kirby Puckett 40.00
RR1 Robin Roberts 25.00
BR1 Brooks Robinson 30.00
BR2 Brooks Robinson 30.00
BR3 Brooks Robinson 30.00
FR1 Frank Robinson 20.00
FR2 Frank Robinson 20.00
NR1 Nolan Ryan 90.00
NR2 Nolan Ryan 90.00
NR3 Nolan Ryan 90.00
NR4 Nolan Ryan 90.00
MS1 Mike Schmidt 50.00
MS2 Mike Schmidt 50.00
MS3 Mike Schmidt 50.00
RS1 Red Schoendienst 35.00
TS1 Tom Seaver 40.00
TS2 Tom Seaver 40.00
OS1 Ozzie Smith 40.00
OS2 Ozzie Smith 40.00
SN1 Duke Snider 40.00
DS1 Don Sutton 20.00
BW1 Billy Williams 20.00
BW2 Billy Williams 20.00
BW3 Billy Williams 20.00
DW1 Dave Winfield 30.00
DW2 Dave Winfield 30.00
CY1 Carl Yastrzemski 50.00
CY2 Carl Yastrzemski 50.00
RY1 Robin Yount 40.00
RY2 Robin Yount 40.00

Class of Cooperstown Calling

NM/M

Production 50 Sets
Gold: No Pricing
Production Five Sets
Green: .75-1.5X
Production 25 Sets
Silver: No Pricing
Production 15 Sets
Rainbow: No Pricing
Production One Set

LA1 Luis Aparicio 4.00
LA2 Luis Aparicio 4.00
EB1 Ernie Banks 6.00
BE1 Johnny Bench 6.00
YB1 Yogi Berra 5.00
WB1 Wade Boggs 5.00
WB2 Wade Boggs 5.00
WB3 Wade Boggs 5.00
GB1 George Brett 10.00
GB2 George Brett 10.00
LB1 Lou Brock 4.00
LB2 Lou Brock 4.00
JB1 Jim Bunning 4.00
RC1 Rod Carew 4.00
RC2 Rod Carew 4.00
SC1 Steve Carlton 4.00
SC2 Steve Carlton 4.00
GC1 Gary Carter 4.00
GC2 Gary Carter 4.00
GC3 Gary Carter 4.00
OC1 Orlando Cepeda 4.00
OC2 Orlando Cepeda 4.00
BD1 Bobby Doerr 4.00
BD2 Bobby Doerr 4.00
DE1 Dennis Eckersley 4.00
DE2 Dennis Eckersley 4.00
BF1 Bob Feller 4.00
BF2 Bob Feller 4.00
RF1 Rollie Fingers 4.00
RF2 Rollie Fingers 4.00
CF1 Carlton Fisk 4.00
CF2 Carlton Fisk 4.00
WF1 Whitey Ford 5.00
BG1 Bob Gibson 5.00
MI1 Monte Irvin 4.00
RJ1 Reggie Jackson 5.00
RJ2 Reggie Jackson 5.00
RJ3 Reggie Jackson 5.00
FJ1 Fergie Jenkins 4.00
FJ2 Fergie Jenkins 4.00
AK1 Al Kaline 6.00
AK2 Al Kaline 6.00
GK1 George Kell 4.00
HK1 Harmon Killebrew 6.00
HK2 Harmon Killebrew 6.00
RK1 Ralph Kiner 4.00
JM1 Juan Marichal 4.00
BM1 Bill Mazeroski 4.00
WM1 Willie McCovey 5.00
PM1 Paul Molitor 5.00
PM2 Paul Molitor 5.00
PM3 Paul Molitor 5.00
MO1 Joe Morgan 4.00
MO2 Joe Morgan 4.00
EM1 Eddie Murray 4.00
EM2 Eddie Murray 4.00
SM1 Stan Musial 6.00
SM2 Stan Musial 6.00
PN1 Phil Niekro 4.00
PN2 Phil Niekro 4.00
JP1 Jim Palmer 4.00
JP2 Jim Palmer 4.00
TP1 Tony Perez 4.00
TP2 Tony Perez 4.00
GP1 Gaylord Perry 4.00
GP2 Gaylord Perry 4.00
KP1 Kirby Puckett 5.00
KP2 Kirby Puckett 5.00
RR1 Robin Roberts 4.00
BR1 Brooks Robinson 5.00
BR2 Brooks Robinson 5.00
BR3 Brooks Robinson 5.00
FR1 Frank Robinson 5.00
NR1 Nolan Ryan 10.00
NR2 Nolan Ryan 10.00
NR3 Nolan Ryan 10.00
NR4 Nolan Ryan 10.00
SA1 Ryne Sandberg 6.00
SA2 Ryne Sandberg 6.00
SA3 Ryne Sandberg 6.00
MS1 Mike Schmidt 6.00
MS2 Mike Schmidt 6.00
MS3 Mike Schmidt 6.00
RS1 Red Schoendienst 4.00
TS1 Tom Seaver 5.00
OS1 Ozzie Smith 6.00
OS2 Ozzie Smith 6.00
OS3 Ozzie Smith 6.00
SN1 Duke Snider 5.00
DS1 Don Sutton 4.00
DS2 Don Sutton 4.00
DS3 Don Sutton 4.00
BW1 Billy Williams 4.00
BW2 Billy Williams 4.00
DW1 Dave Winfield 4.00
CY1 Carl Yastrzemski 6.00
CY2 Carl Yastrzemski 6.00
RY1 Robin Yount 6.00
RY2 Robin Yount 6.00
RY3 Robin Yount 6.00

Class of Cooperstown Calling Auto.

NM/M

Production 25 Sets
Gold: No Pricing
Production Five Sets
Silver: No Pricing
Production 15 Sets
Rainbow: No Pricing
Production One Set
Material Gold: No Pricing
Production Five Sets
Material Silver: No Pricing
Production 15 Sets
Patch Gold: No Pricing
Production Two Sets
Patch Silver: No Pricing
Production 10 Sets

LA1 Luis Aparicio 20.00
LA2 Luis Aparicio 20.00
EB1 Ernie Banks 50.00
BE1 Johnny Bench 40.00
YB1 Yogi Berra 60.00
WB1 Wade Boggs 35.00
WB2 Wade Boggs 35.00
WB3 Wade Boggs 35.00
GB1 George Brett 60.00
GB2 George Brett 60.00
LB1 Lou Brock 35.00
LB2 Lou Brock 35.00
JB1 Jim Bunning 25.00
RC1 Rod Carew 30.00
RC2 Rod Carew 30.00
SC1 Steve Carlton 20.00
SC2 Steve Carlton 20.00
GC1 Gary Carter 25.00
GC2 Gary Carter 25.00
GC3 Gary Carter 25.00
OC1 Orlando Cepeda 25.00
OC2 Orlando Cepeda 25.00
BD1 Bobby Doerr 15.00
BD2 Bobby Doerr 15.00
DE1 Dennis Eckersley 20.00
DE2 Dennis Eckersley 20.00
BF1 Bob Feller 30.00
BF2 Bob Feller 30.00
RF1 Rollie Fingers 20.00
RF2 Rollie Fingers 20.00
CF1 Carlton Fisk 30.00
CF2 Carlton Fisk 30.00
WF1 Whitey Ford 50.00
BG1 Bob Gibson 35.00
MI1 Monte Irvin 25.00
RJ1 Reggie Jackson 40.00
RJ2 Reggie Jackson 40.00
RJ3 Reggie Jackson 40.00
FJ1 Fergie Jenkins 20.00
FJ2 Fergie Jenkins 20.00
AK1 Al Kaline 40.00
AK2 Al Kaline 40.00
GK1 George Kell 20.00
HK1 Harmon Killebrew 40.00
HK2 Harmon Killebrew 40.00
RK1 Ralph Kiner 40.00
JM1 Juan Marichal 25.00
BM1 Bill Mazeroski 40.00
WM1 Willie McCovey 40.00
PM1 Paul Molitor 30.00
PM2 Paul Molitor 30.00
PM3 Paul Molitor 30.00
MO1 Joe Morgan 25.00
MO2 Joe Morgan 25.00
EM1 Eddie Murray 50.00
EM2 Eddie Murray 50.00
SM1 Stan Musial 60.00
SM2 Stan Musial 60.00
PN1 Phil Niekro 20.00
PN2 Phil Niekro 20.00
JP1 Jim Palmer 20.00
JP2 Jim Palmer 20.00
TP1 Tony Perez 20.00
TP2 Tony Perez 20.00
GP1 Gaylord Perry 20.00
GP2 Gaylord Perry 20.00
KP1 Kirby Puckett 40.00
KP2 Kirby Puckett 40.00
RR1 Robin Roberts 40.00
BR1 Brooks Robinson 30.00
BR2 Brooks Robinson 30.00
BR3 Brooks Robinson 30.00
FR1 Frank Robinson 20.00
NR1 Nolan Ryan 90.00
NR2 Nolan Ryan 90.00
NR3 Nolan Ryan 90.00
NR4 Nolan Ryan 90.00
SA1 Ryne Sandberg 60.00
SA2 Ryne Sandberg 60.00
SA3 Ryne Sandberg 60.00
MS1 Mike Schmidt 50.00
MS2 Mike Schmidt 50.00
MS3 Mike Schmidt 50.00
RS1 Red Schoendienst 35.00
TS1 Tom Seaver 40.00
OS1 Ozzie Smith 40.00
OS2 Ozzie Smith 40.00
OS3 Ozzie Smith 40.00
SN1 Duke Snider 40.00
DS1 Don Sutton 20.00
DS2 Don Sutton 20.00
DS3 Don Sutton 20.00
BW1 Billy Williams 20.00
BW2 Billy Williams 20.00
DW1 Dave Winfield 30.00
CY1 Carl Yastrzemski 50.00
CY2 Carl Yastrzemski 50.00
RY1 Robin Yount 40.00
RY2 Robin Yount 40.00
RY3 Robin Yount 40.00

Cooperstown Cuts

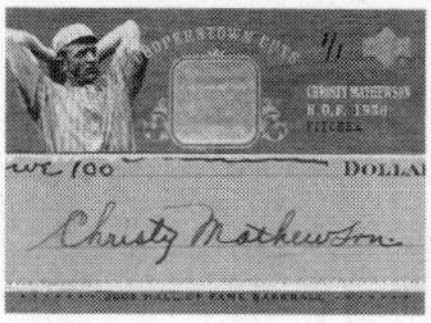

Production 1-20
JM Johnny Mize/20 180.00

Cooperstown Cuts Memorabilia

No Pricing
Production 1-20

Essential Enshrinement

NM/M

Production 50 Sets
Gold: No Pricing
Production Five Sets
Silver: No Pricing
Production 15 Sets
Rainbow: No Pricing
Production One Set

LA1 Luis Aparicio 4.00
EB1 Ernie Banks 6.00
BE1 Johnny Bench 6.00
BE2 Johnny Bench 6.00
YB1 Yogi Berra 5.00
YB2 Yogi Berra 5.00
WB1 Wade Boggs 5.00
WB2 Wade Boggs 5.00
WB3 Wade Boggs 5.00
GB1 George Brett 10.00
GB2 George Brett 10.00
GB3 George Brett 10.00
LB1 Lou Brock 4.00
LB2 Lou Brock 4.00
JB1 Jim Bunning 4.00
RC1 Rod Carew 4.00
RC2 Rod Carew 4.00
SC1 Steve Carlton 4.00
SC2 Steve Carlton 4.00
GC1 Gary Carter 4.00
GC2 Gary Carter 4.00
OC1 Orlando Cepeda 4.00
BD1 Bobby Doerr 4.00
BD2 Bobby Doerr 4.00
DE1 Dennis Eckersley 4.00
BF1 Bob Feller 4.00
BF2 Bob Feller 4.00
RF1 Rollie Fingers 4.00
CF1 Carlton Fisk 4.00
CF2 Carlton Fisk 4.00
WF1 Whitey Ford 5.00
WF2 Whitey Ford 5.00
BG1 Bob Gibson 5.00
BG2 Bob Gibson 5.00
MI1 Monte Irvin 4.00
RJ1 Reggie Jackson 5.00
RJ2 Reggie Jackson 5.00
RJ3 Reggie Jackson 5.00
FJ1 Fergie Jenkins 4.00
FJ2 Fergie Jenkins 4.00
AK1 Al Kaline 6.00
AK2 Al Kaline 6.00
GK1 George Kell 4.00
HK1 Harmon Killebrew 6.00
HK2 Harmon Killebrew 6.00
RK1 Ralph Kiner 4.00
JM1 Juan Marichal 4.00
BM1 Bill Mazeroski 4.00
WM1 Willie McCovey 5.00
PM1 Paul Molitor 5.00
PM2 Paul Molitor 5.00
PM3 Paul Molitor 5.00
MO1 Joe Morgan 4.00
MO2 Joe Morgan 4.00
MO3 Joe Morgan 4.00
EM1 Eddie Murray 4.00
EM2 Eddie Murray 4.00
SM1 Stan Musial 6.00
SM2 Stan Musial 6.00
PN1 Phil Niekro 4.00
PN2 Phil Niekro 4.00
JP1 Jim Palmer 4.00
JP2 Jim Palmer 4.00
TP1 Tony Perez 4.00
GP1 Gaylord Perry 4.00
GP2 Gaylord Perry 4.00
KP1 Kirby Puckett 5.00
KP2 Kirby Puckett 5.00
RR1 Robin Roberts 4.00
BR1 Brooks Robinson 5.00
BR2 Brooks Robinson 5.00
BR3 Brooks Robinson 5.00
FR1 Frank Robinson 5.00
FR2 Frank Robinson 5.00
NR1 Nolan Ryan 10.00
NR2 Nolan Ryan 10.00
NR3 Nolan Ryan 10.00
NR4 Nolan Ryan 10.00
SA1 Ryne Sandberg 6.00
SA2 Ryne Sandberg 6.00
SA3 Ryne Sandberg 6.00
MS1 Mike Schmidt 6.00
MS2 Mike Schmidt 6.00
RS1 Red Schoendienst 4.00
TS1 Tom Seaver 5.00
OS1 Ozzie Smith 6.00
OS2 Ozzie Smith 6.00
SN1 Duke Snider 5.00
SN2 Duke Snider 5.00
DS1 Don Sutton 4.00
DS2 Don Sutton 4.00
BW1 Billy Williams 4.00
BW2 Billy Williams 4.00
DW1 Dave Winfield 4.00
CY1 Carl Yastrzemski 6.00
CY2 Carl Yastrzemski 6.00
CY3 Carl Yastrzemski 6.00
RY1 Robin Yount 6.00
RY2 Robin Yount 6.00
RY3 Robin Yount 6.00

Essential Enshrinement Autograph

NM/M

Production 25 Sets
Gold: No Pricing
Production Five Sets
Silver: No Pricing
Production 15 Sets
Rainbow: No Pricing
Production One Set
Material Gold: No Pricing
Production Five Sets
Material Silver: No Pricing
Production 15 Sets
Patch Gold: No Pricing
Production Five Sets
Patch Silver: No Pricing
Production 10 Sets

LA1 Luis Aparicio 20.00
EB1 Ernie Banks 50.00
BE1 Johnny Bench 40.00
BE2 Johnny Bench 40.00
YB1 Yogi Berra 60.00
YB2 Yogi Berra 60.00
WB1 Wade Boggs 35.00
WB2 Wade Boggs 35.00
WB3 Wade Boggs 35.00
GB1 George Brett 60.00
GB2 George Brett 60.00
GB3 George Brett 60.00
LB1 Lou Brock 35.00
LB2 Lou Brock 35.00
JB1 Jim Bunning 25.00
RC1 Rod Carew 30.00
RC2 Rod Carew 30.00
SC1 Steve Carlton 20.00
SC2 Steve Carlton 20.00
GC1 Gary Carter 25.00
GC2 Gary Carter 25.00
OC1 Orlando Cepeda 25.00
BD1 Bobby Doerr 15.00
BD2 Bobby Doerr 15.00
DE1 Dennis Eckersley 20.00
BF1 Bob Feller 30.00
BF2 Bob Feller 30.00
RF1 Rollie Fingers 20.00
CF1 Carlton Fisk 30.00
CF2 Carlton Fisk 30.00
WF1 Whitey Ford 50.00
WF2 Whitey Ford 50.00
BG1 Bob Gibson 35.00
BG2 Bob Gibson 35.00
MI1 Monte Irvin 25.00
RJ1 Reggie Jackson 40.00
RJ2 Reggie Jackson 40.00

RJ3	Reggie Jackson	40.00
FJ1	Fergie Jenkins	20.00
FJ2	Fergie Jenkins	20.00
AK1	Al Kaline	40.00
AK2	Al Kaline	40.00
GK1	George Kell	20.00
HK1	Harmon Killebrew	40.00
HK2	Harmon Killebrew	40.00
RK1	Ralph Kiner	40.00
JM1	Juan Marichal	25.00
BM1	Bill Mazeroski	40.00
WM1	Willie McCovey	40.00
PM1	Paul Molitor	30.00
PM2	Paul Molitor	30.00
PM3	Paul Molitor	30.00
MO1	Joe Morgan	25.00
MO2	Joe Morgan	25.00
MO3	Joe Morgan	25.00
EM1	Eddie Murray	50.00
EM2	Eddie Murray	50.00
SM1	Stan Musial	60.00
SM2	Stan Musial	60.00
PN1	Phil Niekro	20.00
PN2	Phil Niekro	20.00
JP1	Jim Palmer	20.00
JP2	Jim Palmer	20.00
TP1	Tony Perez	20.00
GP1	Gaylord Perry	20.00
GP2	Gaylord Perry	20.00
KP1	Kirby Puckett	40.00
KP2	Kirby Puckett	40.00
RR1	Robin Roberts	25.00
BR1	Brooks Robinson	30.00
BR2	Brooks Robinson	30.00
BR3	Brooks Robinson	30.00
FR1	Frank Robinson	20.00
FR2	Frank Robinson	20.00
NR1	Nolan Ryan	90.00
NR2	Nolan Ryan	90.00
NR3	Nolan Ryan	90.00
NR4	Nolan Ryan	90.00
SA1	Ryne Sandberg	60.00
SA2	Ryne Sandberg	60.00
SA3	Ryne Sandberg	60.00
MS1	Mike Schmidt	50.00
MS2	Mike Schmidt	50.00
RS1	Red Schoendienst	35.00
TS1	Tom Seaver	40.00
OS1	Ozzie Smith	40.00
OS2	Ozzie Smith	40.00
SN1	Duke Snider	40.00
SN2	Duke Snider	40.00
DS1	Don Sutton	20.00
DS2	Don Sutton	20.00
BW1	Billy Williams	20.00
BW2	Billy Williams	20.00
DW1	Dave Winfield	30.00
CY1	Carl Yastrzemski	50.00
CY2	Carl Yastrzemski	50.00
CY3	Carl Yastrzemski	50.00
RY1	Robin Yount	40.00
RY2	Robin Yount	40.00
RY3	Robin Yount	40.00

Hall of Fame Materials

NM/M

Production 25 Sets
Gold: No Pricing
Production Five Sets
Silver: No Pricing
Production 15 Sets
Rainbow: No Pricing
Production One Set
Green: No Pricing
Production 10 Sets

RC1	Roberto Clemente	120.00
RC2	Roberto Clemente	120.00
RC3	Roberto Clemente	120.00
TC1	Ty Cobb	100.00
TC2	Ty Cobb	100.00
TC3	Ty Cobb	100.00
MC1	Mickey Cochrane	40.00
DD1	Dizzy Dean	80.00
DD2	Dizzy Dean	80.00
JD1	Joe DiMaggio	90.00
JD2	Joe DiMaggio	90.00
JD3	Joe DiMaggio	90.00
JF1	Jimmie Foxx	60.00
JF2	Jimmie Foxx	60.00
LG1	Lou Gehrig	180.00
LG2	Lou Gehrig	180.00
LG3	Lou Gehrig	180.00
RH1	Rogers Hornsby	80.00
MM1	Mickey Mantle	250.00
MM2	Mickey Mantle	250.00
MM3	Mickey Mantle	250.00
JM1	Johnny Mize	30.00
JM2	Johnny Mize	30.00
JM3	Johnny Mize	30.00
MO1	Mel Ott	40.00
MO2	Mel Ott	40.00
SP1	Satchel Paige	50.00
SP2	Satchel Paige	50.00
SP3	Satchel Paige	50.00
JR1	Jackie Robinson	60.00
JR2	Jackie Robinson	60.00
JR3	Jackie Robinson	60.00
BR1	Babe Ruth	250.00
BR2	Babe Ruth	250.00
BR3	Babe Ruth	250.00
GS1	George Sisler	40.00
GS2	George Sisler	40.00
TW1	Ted Williams	85.00
TW2	Ted Williams	85.00
TW3	Ted Williams	85.00

Hall of Fame Seasons

NM/M

Production 50 Sets
Gold: No Pricing
Production Five Sets
Silver: No Pricing
Production 15 Sets
Rainbow: No Pricing
Production One Set

LA1	Luis Aparicio	4.00
EB1	Ernie Banks	6.00
BE1	Johnny Bench	6.00
BE2	Johnny Bench	6.00
YB1	Yogi Berra	5.00
YB2	Yogi Berra	5.00
WB1	Wade Boggs	5.00
WB2	Wade Boggs	5.00
WB3	Wade Boggs	5.00
GB1	George Brett	10.00
GB2	George Brett	10.00
LB1	Lou Brock	4.00
LB2	Lou Brock	4.00
JB1	Jim Bunning	4.00
RC1	Rod Carew	4.00
RC2	Rod Carew	4.00
GC1	Gary Carter	4.00
SC1	Steve Carlton	4.00
SC2	Steve Carlton	4.00
SC3	Steve Carlton	4.00
OC1	Orlando Cepeda	4.00
BD1	Bobby Doerr	4.00
DE1	Dennis Eckersley	4.00
DE2	Dennis Eckersley	4.00
DE3	Dennis Eckersley	4.00
BF1	Bob Feller	4.00
BF2	Bob Feller	4.00
RF1	Rollie Fingers	4.00
CF1	Carlton Fisk	4.00
CF2	Carlton Fisk	4.00
WF1	Whitey Ford	5.00
WF2	Whitey Ford	5.00
BG1	Bob Gibson	5.00
BG2	Bob Gibson	5.00
MI1	Monte Irvin	4.00
RJ1	Reggie Jackson	5.00
RJ2	Reggie Jackson	5.00
RJ3	Reggie Jackson	5.00
FJ1	Fergie Jenkins	4.00
FJ2	Fergie Jenkins	4.00
AK1	Al Kaline	6.00
AK2	Al Kaline	6.00
AK3	Al Kaline	6.00
GK1	George Kell	4.00
HK1	Harmon Killebrew	6.00
HK2	Harmon Killebrew	6.00
HK3	Harmon Killebrew	6.00
RK1	Ralph Kiner	4.00
JM1	Juan Marichal	4.00
BM1	Bill Mazeroski	4.00
WM1	Willie McCovey	5.00
PM1	Paul Molitor	5.00
PM2	Paul Molitor	5.00
PM3	Paul Molitor	5.00
MO1	Joe Morgan	4.00
MO2	Joe Morgan	4.00
EM1	Eddie Murray	4.00
EM2	Eddie Murray	4.00
SM1	Stan Musial	6.00
SM2	Stan Musial	6.00
PN1	Phil Niekro	4.00
PN2	Phil Niekro	4.00
JP1	Jim Palmer	4.00
JP2	Jim Palmer	4.00
JP3	Jim Palmer	4.00
TP1	Tony Perez	4.00
GP1	Gaylord Perry	4.00
GP2	Gaylord Perry	4.00
KP1	Kirby Puckett	5.00
KP2	Kirby Puckett	5.00
RR1	Robin Roberts	4.00
BR1	Brooks Robinson	5.00
BR2	Brooks Robinson	5.00
BR3	Brooks Robinson	5.00
FR1	Frank Robinson	5.00
FR2	Frank Robinson	5.00
NR1	Nolan Ryan	10.00
NR2	Nolan Ryan	10.00
NR3	Nolan Ryan	10.00
NR4	Nolan Ryan	10.00
SA1	Ryne Sandberg	6.00
SA2	Ryne Sandberg	6.00
MS1	Mike Schmidt	6.00
MS2	Mike Schmidt	6.00
MS3	Mike Schmidt	6.00
RS1	Red Schoendienst	4.00
TS1	Tom Seaver	5.00
TS2	Tom Seaver	5.00
OS1	Ozzie Smith	6.00
OS2	Ozzie Smith	6.00
SN1	Duke Snider	5.00
DS1	Don Sutton	4.00
DS2	Don Sutton	4.00
BW1	Billy Williams	4.00
BW2	Billy Williams	4.00
DW1	Dave Winfield	4.00
CY1	Carl Yastrzemski	6.00
CY2	Carl Yastrzemski	6.00
RY1	Robin Yount	6.00
RY2	Robin Yount	6.00

Hall of Fame Seasons Autograph

NM/M

Production 25 Sets
Gold: No Pricing
Production Five Sets
Silver: No Pricing
Production 15 Sets
Rainbow: No Pricing
Production One Set
Material Gold: No Pricing
Production Five Sets
Material Silver: No Pricing
Production 15 Sets
Patch Gold: No Pricing
Production Five Sets
Patch Silver: No Pricing
Production 10 Sets

LA1	Luis Aparicio	20.00
EB1	Ernie Banks	50.00
BE1	Johnny Bench	40.00
BE2	Johnny Bench	40.00
YB1	Yogi Berra	60.00
YB2	Yogi Berra	60.00
WB1	Wade Boggs	35.00
WB2	Wade Boggs	35.00
WB3	Wade Boggs	35.00
GB1	George Brett	60.00
GB2	George Brett	60.00
LB1	Lou Brock	35.00
LB2	Lou Brock	35.00
JB1	Jim Bunning	25.00
RC1	Rod Carew	30.00
RC2	Rod Carew	30.00
GC1	Gary Carter	25.00
SC1	Steve Carlton	20.00
SC2	Steve Carlton	20.00
SC3	Steve Carlton	20.00
OC1	Orlando Cepeda	25.00
BD1	Bobby Doerr	15.00
DE1	Dennis Eckersley	20.00
DE2	Dennis Eckersley	20.00
DE3	Dennis Eckersley	20.00
BF1	Bob Feller	30.00
BF2	Bob Feller	30.00
RF1	Rollie Fingers	20.00
CF1	Carlton Fisk	30.00
CF2	Carlton Fisk	30.00
WF1	Whitey Ford	50.00
WF2	Whitey Ford	50.00
BG1	Bob Gibson	35.00
BG2	Bob Gibson	35.00
MI1	Monte Irvin	25.00
RJ1	Reggie Jackson	40.00
RJ2	Reggie Jackson	40.00
RJ3	Reggie Jackson	40.00
FJ1	Fergie Jenkins	20.00
FJ2	Fergie Jenkins	20.00
AK1	Al Kaline	40.00
AK2	Al Kaline	40.00
AK3	Al Kaline	40.00
GK1	George Kell	20.00
HK1	Harmon Killebrew	40.00
HK2	Harmon Killebrew	40.00
HK3	Harmon Killebrew	40.00
RK1	Ralph Kiner	40.00
JM1	Juan Marichal	25.00
BM1	Bill Mazeroski	40.00
WM1	Willie McCovey	40.00
PM1	Paul Molitor	30.00
PM2	Paul Molitor	30.00
PM3	Paul Molitor	30.00
MO1	Joe Morgan	25.00
MO2	Joe Morgan	25.00
EM1	Eddie Murray	50.00
EM2	Eddie Murray	50.00
SM1	Stan Musial	60.00
SM2	Stan Musial	60.00
PN1	Phil Niekro	20.00
PN2	Phil Niekro	20.00
JP1	Jim Palmer	20.00
JP2	Jim Palmer	20.00
JP3	Jim Palmer	20.00
TP1	Tony Perez	20.00
GP1	Gaylord Perry	20.00
GP2	Gaylord Perry	20.00
KP1	Kirby Puckett	40.00
KP2	Kirby Puckett	40.00
RR1	Robin Roberts	25.00
BR1	Brooks Robinson	30.00
BR2	Brooks Robinson	30.00
BR3	Brooks Robinson	30.00
FR1	Frank Robinson	20.00
FR2	Frank Robinson	20.00
NR1	Nolan Ryan	90.00
NR2	Nolan Ryan	90.00
NR3	Nolan Ryan	90.00
NR4	Nolan Ryan	90.00
SA1	Ryne Sandberg	60.00
SA2	Ryne Sandberg	60.00
MS1	Mike Schmidt	50.00
MS2	Mike Schmidt	50.00
MS3	Mike Schmidt	50.00
RS1	Red Schoendienst	35.00
TS1	Tom Seaver	40.00
TS2	Tom Seaver	40.00
OS1	Ozzie Smith	40.00
OS2	Ozzie Smith	40.00
SN1	Duke Snider	40.00
DS1	Don Sutton	20.00
DS2	Don Sutton	20.00
BW1	Billy Williams	20.00
BW2	Billy Williams	20.00
DW1	Dave Winfield	30.00
CY1	Carl Yastrzemski	50.00
CY2	Carl Yastrzemski	50.00
RY1	Robin Yount	40.00
RY2	Robin Yount	40.00

Hall Worthy

NM/M

Production 50 Sets
Gold: No Pricing
Production Five Sets
Silver: No Pricing
Production 15 Sets
Rainbow: No Pricing
Production One Set

LA1	Luis Aparicio	4.00
EB1	Ernie Banks	6.00
BE1	Johnny Bench	6.00
BE2	Johnny Bench	6.00
YB1	Yogi Berra	5.00
WB1	Wade Boggs	5.00
WB2	Wade Boggs	5.00
WB3	Wade Boggs	5.00
GB1	George Brett	10.00
GB2	George Brett	10.00
GB3	George Brett	10.00
LB1	Lou Brock	4.00
LB2	Lou Brock	4.00
JB1	Jim Bunning	4.00
RC1	Rod Carew	4.00
RC2	Rod Carew	4.00
SC1	Steve Carlton	4.00
SC2	Steve Carlton	4.00
GC1	Gary Carter	4.00
GC2	Gary Carter	4.00
OC1	Orlando Cepeda	4.00
OC2	Orlando Cepeda	4.00
BD1	Bobby Doerr	4.00
DE1	Dennis Eckersley	4.00
DE2	Dennis Eckersley	4.00
DE3	Dennis Eckersley	4.00
DE4	Dennis Eckersley	4.00
BF1	Bob Feller	4.00
BF2	Bob Feller	4.00
RF1	Rollie Fingers	4.00
RF2	Rollie Fingers	4.00
CF1	Carlton Fisk	4.00
CF2	Carlton Fisk	4.00
WF1	Whitey Ford	5.00
BG1	Bob Gibson	5.00
MI1	Monte Irvin	4.00
RJ1	Reggie Jackson	5.00
RJ2	Reggie Jackson	5.00
RJ3	Reggie Jackson	5.00
RJ4	Reggie Jackson	5.00
FJ1	Fergie Jenkins	4.00
FJ2	Fergie Jenkins	4.00
FJ3	Fergie Jenkins	4.00
AK1	Al Kaline	4.00
AK2	Al Kaline	4.00
GK1	George Kell	4.00
HK1	Harmon Killebrew	6.00
HK2	Harmon Killebrew	6.00
RK1	Ralph Kiner	4.00
JM1	Juan Marichal	4.00
BM1	Bill Mazeroski	4.00
WM1	Willie McCovey	5.00
PM1	Paul Molitor	5.00
PM2	Paul Molitor	5.00
MO1	Joe Morgan	4.00
MO2	Joe Morgan	4.00
EM1	Eddie Murray	4.00
EM2	Eddie Murray	4.00
EM3	Eddie Murray	4.00
SM1	Stan Musial	6.00
PN1	Phil Niekro	4.00
PN2	Phil Niekro	4.00
JP1	Jim Palmer	4.00
JP2	Jim Palmer	4.00
TP1	Tony Perez	4.00
TP2	Tony Perez	4.00
GP1	Gaylord Perry	4.00
GP2	Gaylord Perry	4.00
KP1	Kirby Puckett	5.00
RR1	Robin Roberts	4.00
BR1	Brooks Robinson	5.00
BR2	Brooks Robinson	5.00
FR1	Frank Robinson	5.00
FR2	Frank Robinson	5.00
NR1	Nolan Ryan	10.00
NR2	Nolan Ryan	10.00
NR3	Nolan Ryan	10.00
NR4	Nolan Ryan	10.00
SA1	Ryne Sandberg	6.00
SA2	Ryne Sandberg	6.00
SA3	Ryne Sandberg	6.00
MS1	Mike Schmidt	6.00
MS2	Mike Schmidt	6.00
MS3	Mike Schmidt	6.00
RS1	Red Schoendienst	4.00
TS1	Tom Seaver	5.00
TS2	Tom Seaver	5.00
OS1	Ozzie Smith	6.00
OS2	Ozzie Smith	6.00
SN1	Duke Snider	5.00
SN2	Duke Snider	5.00
DS1	Don Sutton	4.00
DS2	Don Sutton	4.00
DS3	Don Sutton	4.00
BW1	Billy Williams	4.00
DW1	Dave Winfield	4.00
CY1	Carl Yastrzemski	6.00
CY2	Carl Yastrzemski	6.00
RY1	Robin Yount	6.00
RY2	Robin Yount	6.00

Hall Worthy Autograph

NM/M

Production 25 Sets
Gold: No Pricing

Production Five Sets
Silver: No Pricing
Production 15 Sets
Rainbow: No Pricing
Production One Set
Material Gold: No Pricing
Production Five Sets
Material Silver: No Pricing
Production 15 Sets
Patch Gold: No Pricing
Production Five Sets
Patch Silver: No Pricing
Production 10 Sets
LA1 Luis Aparicio 20.00
EB1 Ernie Banks 50.00
BE1 Johnny Bench 40.00
BE2 Johnny Bench 40.00
YB1 Yogi Berra 60.00
WB1 Wade Boggs 35.00
WB2 Wade Boggs 35.00
WB3 Wade Boggs 35.00
GB1 George Brett 60.00
GB2 George Brett 60.00
GB3 George Brett 60.00
LB1 Lou Brock 35.00
LB2 Lou Brock 35.00
JB1 Jim Bunning 25.00
RC1 Rod Carew 30.00
RC2 Rod Carew 30.00
SC1 Steve Carlton 20.00
SC2 Steve Carlton 20.00
GC1 Gary Carter 25.00
GC2 Gary Carter 25.00
OC1 Orlando Cepeda 25.00
OC2 Orlando Cepeda 25.00
BD1 Bobby Doerr 15.00
DE1 Dennis Eckersley 20.00
DE2 Dennis Eckersley 20.00
DE3 Dennis Eckersley 20.00
DE4 Dennis Eckersley 20.00
BF1 Bob Feller 30.00
BF2 Bob Feller 30.00
RF1 Rollie Fingers 20.00
RF2 Rollie Fingers 20.00
CF1 Carlton Fisk 30.00
CF2 Carlton Fisk 30.00
WF1 Whitey Ford 50.00
BG1 Bob Gibson 35.00
MI1 Monte Irvin 25.00
RJ1 Reggie Jackson 40.00
RJ2 Reggie Jackson 40.00
RJ3 Reggie Jackson 40.00
RJ4 Reggie Jackson 40.00
FJ1 Fergie Jenkins 20.00
FJ2 Fergie Jenkins 20.00
FJ3 Fergie Jenkins 20.00
AK1 Al Kaline 40.00
AK2 Al Kaline 40.00
GK1 George Kell 20.00
HK1 Harmon Killebrew 40.00
HK2 Harmon Killebrew 40.00
RK1 Ralph Kiner 40.00
JM1 Juan Marichal 25.00
BM1 Bill Mazeroski 40.00
WM1 Willie McCovey 40.00
PM1 Paul Molitor 30.00
PM2 Paul Molitor 30.00
MO1 Joe Morgan 25.00
MO2 Joe Morgan 25.00
EM1 Eddie Murray 50.00
EM2 Eddie Murray 50.00
EM3 Eddie Murray 50.00
SM1 Stan Musial 60.00
PN1 Phil Niekro 20.00
PN2 Phil Niekro 20.00
JP1 Jim Palmer 20.00
JP2 Jim Palmer 20.00
TP1 Tony Perez 20.00
TP2 Tony Perez 20.00
GP1 Gaylord Perry 20.00
GP2 Gaylord Perry 20.00
KP1 Kirby Puckett 40.00
RR1 Robin Roberts 25.00
BR1 Brooks Robinson 30.00
BR2 Brooks Robinson 30.00
FR1 Frank Robinson 20.00
FR2 Frank Robinson 20.00
NR1 Nolan Ryan 90.00
NR2 Nolan Ryan 90.00
NR3 Nolan Ryan 90.00
NR4 Nolan Ryan 90.00
SA1 Ryne Sandberg 60.00
SA2 Ryne Sandberg 60.00
SA3 Ryne Sandberg 60.00
MS1 Mike Schmidt 50.00
MS2 Mike Schmidt 50.00
MS3 Mike Schmidt 50.00
RS1 Red Schoendienst 35.00
TS1 Tom Seaver 40.00
TS2 Tom Seaver 40.00
OS1 Ozzie Smith 40.00
OS2 Ozzie Smith 40.00
SN1 Duke Snider 40.00
SN2 Duke Snider 40.00
DS1 Don Sutton 20.00
DS2 Don Sutton 20.00
DS3 Don Sutton 20.00
BW1 Billy Williams 20.00
DW1 Dave Winfield 30.00
CY1 Carl Yastrzemski 50.00
CY2 Carl Yastrzemski 50.00
RY1 Robin Yount 40.00
RY2 Robin Yount 40.00

Signs of Cooperstown Duals

NM/M

Production 50 Sets
Gold: No Pricing
Production Five Sets
Silver: No Pricing
Production 15 Sets
Rainbow: No Pricing
Production One Set
AB Ernie Banks, Luis Aparicio 6.00
AS Luis Aparicio, Ozzie Smith 8.00
BC Steve Carlton, Jim Bunning 4.00
BF Frank Robinson, Brooks Robinson 5.00
BG George Brett, Brooks Robinson 10.00
BM Lou Brock, Stan Musial 8.00
BR Jim Bunning, Robin Roberts 4.00
BS Ernie Banks, Ryne Sandberg 10.00
CM Orlando Cepeda, Willie McCovey 4.00
CS Tom Seaver, Gary Carter 4.00
DB Wade Boggs, Bobby Doerr 4.00
EF Dennis Eckersley, Rollie Fingers 4.00
FB Johnny Bench, Carlton Fisk 6.00
FC Bob Feller, Steve Carlton 4.00
FP Bob Feller, Gaylord Perry 4.00
GC Bob Gibson, Steve Carlton 5.00
GF Bob Gibson, Whitey Ford 5.00
IM Monte Irvin, Willie McCovey 5.00
JJ Joe Morgan, Johnny Bench 6.00
JM Reggie Jackson, Willie McCovey 5.00
JW Reggie Jackson, Dave Winfield 5.00
JY Yogi Berra, Johnny Bench 6.00
KK Al Kaline, George Kell 6.00
KP Kirby Puckett, Harmon Killebrew 6.00
LO Lou Brock, Ozzie Smith 8.00
MK Bill Mazeroski, Ralph Kiner 5.00
MP Joe Morgan, Tony Perez 4.00
MY Robin Yount, Paul Molitor 6.00
NS Steve Carlton, Nolan Ryan 10.00
PM Gaylord Perry, Juan Marichal 4.00
PN Gaylord Perry, Phil Niekro 4.00
PR Rod Carew, Paul Molitor 5.00
RC Rod Carew, Nolan Ryan 10.00
RP Jim Palmer, Brooks Robinson 5.00
RS Tom Seaver, Nolan Ryan 10.00
RW Ryne Sandberg, Wade Boggs 10.00
SB George Brett, Mike Schmidt 10.00
SC Mike Schmidt, Steve Carlton 10.00
SK Ralph Kiner, Duke Snider 5.00
SM Ozzie Smith, Stan Musial 8.00
SP Gaylord Perry, Don Sutton 4.00
SR Mike Schmidt, Brooks Robinson 10.00
SS Red Schoendienst, Ozzie Smith 8.00
SW Billy Williams, Ryne Sandberg 10.00
WB Billy Williams, Ernie Banks 6.00
WJ Billy Williams, Fergie Jenkins 4.00
WS Ozzie Smith, Dave Winfield 6.00
WY Yogi Berra, Whitey Ford 6.00
YF Carlton Fisk, Carl Yastrzemski 6.00
YJ Reggie Jackson, Carl Yastrzemski 6.00

Signs of Cooperstown Duals Autographs

NM/M

Production 20 Sets
Gold: No Pricing
Production Five Sets
Silver: No Pricing
Production 10 Sets
Rainbow: No Pricing
Production One Set
AB Ernie Banks, Luis Aparicio 80.00
AS Luis Aparicio, Ozzie Smith 60.00
BC Steve Carlton, Jim Bunning 35.00
BF Frank Robinson, Brooks Robinson 60.00
BG George Brett, Brooks Robinson 90.00
BM Lou Brock, Stan Musial 100.00
BR Jim Bunning, Robin Roberts 60.00
BS Ernie Banks, Ryne Sandberg 120.00
CM Orlando Cepeda, Willie McCovey 50.00
CS Tom Seaver, Gary Carter 80.00
DB Wade Boggs, Bobby Doerr 50.00
EF Dennis Eckersley, Rollie Fingers 35.00
FB Johnny Bench, Carlton Fisk 75.00
FC Bob Feller, Steve Carlton 40.00
FP Bob Feller, Gaylord Perry 40.00
GC Bob Gibson, Steve Carlton 60.00
GF Bob Gibson, Whitey Ford 75.00
IM Monte Irvin, Willie McCovey 60.00
JJ Joe Morgan, Johnny Bench 80.00
JM Reggie Jackson, Willie McCovey 100.00
JW Reggie Jackson, Dave Winfield 80.00
JY Yogi Berra, Johnny Bench 150.00
KK Al Kaline, George Kell 85.00
KP Kirby Puckett, Harmon Killebrew 80.00
LO Lou Brock, Ozzie Smith 65.00
MK Bill Mazeroski, Ralph Kiner 75.00
MP Joe Morgan, Tony Perez 50.00
MY Robin Yount, Paul Molitor 85.00
NS Steve Carlton, Nolan Ryan 150.00
PM Gaylord Perry, Juan Marichal 40.00
PN Gaylord Perry, Phil Niekro 40.00
PR Rod Carew, Paul Molitor 50.00
RC Rod Carew, Nolan Ryan 150.00
RP Jim Palmer, Brooks Robinson 50.00
RS Tom Seaver, Nolan Ryan 180.00
RW Ryne Sandberg, Wade Boggs 100.00
SB George Brett, Mike Schmidt 140.00
SC Mike Schmidt, Steve Carlton 85.00
SK Ralph Kiner, Duke Snider 65.00
SM Ozzie Smith, Stan Musial 120.00
SP Gaylord Perry, Don Sutton 40.00
SR Mike Schmidt, Brooks Robinson 75.00
SS Red Schoendienst, Ozzie Smith 65.00
SW Billy Williams, Ryne Sandberg 90.00
WB Billy Williams, Ernie Banks 90.00
WJ Billy Williams, Fergie Jenkins 50.00
WS Ozzie Smith, Dave Winfield 75.00
WY Yogi Berra, Whitey Ford 100.00
YF Carlton Fisk, Carl Yastrzemski 100.00
YJ Reggie Jackson, Carl Yastrzemski 100.00

Signs of Cooperstown Quads

NM/M

Production 50 Sets
Gold: No Pricing
Production Five Sets
Silver: No Pricing
Production 15 Sets
Rainbow: No Pricing
Production One Set
BMYC George Brett, Rod Carew, Robin Yount, Paul Molitor 10.00
BSAY Ernie Banks, Robin Yount, Luis Aparicio, Ozzie Smith 8.00
FCBB Yogi Berra, Johnny Bench, Carlton Fisk, Gary Carter 6.00
FGRC Bob Feller, Bob Gibson, Steve Carlton, Nolan Ryan 10.00
KCPM Tony Perez, Orlando Cepeda, Harmon Killebrew, Willie McCovey 6.00
KYBM Al Kaline, Lou Brock, Carl Yastrzemski, Stan Musial 8.00
MBKM Ernie Banks, Eddie Murray, Harmon Killebrew, Willie McCovey 8.00
MDMC Bill Mazeroski, Rod Carew, Joe Morgan, Bobby Doerr 5.00
MRKS Eddie Murray, Mike Schmidt, Frank Robinson, Harmon Killebrew 10.00
RBKS George Brett, Mike Schmidt, Brooks Robinson, George Kell 10.00
SPNS Tom Seaver, Phil Niekro, Don Sutton, Gaylord Perry 6.00
SPSF Tom Seaver, Jim Palmer, Whitey Ford, Don Sutton 6.00
SRCS Tom Seaver, Steve Carlton, Don Sutton, Nolan Ryan 10.00
WYKM Billy Williams, Ralph Kiner, Carl Yastrzemski, Stan Musial 8.00
YWMM Eddie Murray, Carl Yastrzemski, Stan Musial, Dave Winfield 8.00

Signs of Cooperstown Triple Autographs

NM/M

Production 20 Sets 75.00
Gold: No Pricing
Production Five Sets
Silver: No Pricing
Production 10 Sets
Rainbow: No Pricing
Production One Set
ASY Robin Yount, Luis Aparicio, Ozzie Smith 140.00
BFJ Jim Palmer, Frank Robinson, Brooks Robinson 80.00
BSB George Brett, Mike Schmidt, Wade Boggs 185.00
BSY Ernie Banks, Robin Yount, Ozzie Smith 150.00
CMI Monte Irvin, Orlando Cepeda, Willie McCovey 75.00
DFY Carlton Fisk, Carl Yastrzemski, Bobby Doerr 125.00
DYB Carl Yastrzemski, Wade Boggs, Bobby Doerr 125.00
FRC Bob Feller, Steve Carlton, Nolan Ryan 200.00
GSM Bob Gibson, Ozzie Smith, Stan Musial 185.00
JFB Yogi Berra, Reggie Jackson, Whitey Ford 185.00
JPR Nolan Ryan, Gaylord Perry, Fergie Jenkins 150.00
KPC Rod Carew, Kirby Puckett, Harmon Killebrew 120.00
KSR Ralph Kiner, Duke Snider, Frank Robinson 120.00
MBP Joe Morgan, Tony Perez, Johnny Bench 160.00
MCM Orlando Cepeda, Willie McCovey, Juan Marichal 100.00
MSC Joe Morgan, Rod Carew, Ryne Sandberg 125.00
MYF Robin Yount, Paul Molitor, Rollie Fingers 125.00
PMC Rod Carew, Kirby Puckett, Paul Molitor 100.00
RAP Jim Palmer, Luis Aparicio, Brooks Robinson 80.00
RBC Steve Carlton, Jim Bunning, Robin Roberts 85.00
RBS George Brett, Mike Schmidt, Brooks Robinson 200.00
SRC Mike Schmidt, Steve Carlton, Robin Roberts 150.00
WJB Reggie Jackson, Wade Boggs, Dave Winfield 120.00
WSP Dave Winfield, Ozzie Smith, Gaylord Perry 120.00
YKM Ralph Kiner, Carl Yastrzemski, Stan Musial 140.00

Signs of Cooperstown Triples

NM/M

Production 50 Sets
Gold: No Pricing
Production Five Sets
Silver: No Pricing
Production 15 Sets
Rainbow: No Pricing
Production One Set
ASY Robin Yount, Luis Aparicio, Ozzie Smith 8.00
BFJ Jim Palmer, Frank Robinson, Brooks Robinson 5.00
BSB George Brett, Mike Schmidt, Wade Boggs 10.00
BSY Ernie Banks, Robin Yount, Ozzie Smith 8.00
CMI Monte Irvin, Orlando Cepeda, Willie McCovey 5.00
DFY Carlton Fisk, Carl Yastrzemski, Bobby Doerr 8.00
DYB Carl Yastrzemski, Wade Boggs, Bobby Doerr 8.00
FPE Bob Feller, Dennis Eckersley, Gaylord Perry 4.00
FRC Bob Feller, Steve Carlton, Nolan Ryan 10.00
FSE Dennis Eckersley, Rollie Fingers, Don Sutton 4.00
GCE Bob Gibson, Dennis Eckersley, Steve Carlton 4.00
GSM Bob Gibson, Stan Musial, Ozzie Smith 8.00
JFB Yogi Berra, Reggie Jackson, Whitey Ford 8.00
JPR Nolan Ryan, Gaylord Perry, Fergie Jenkins 10.00
KKB Al Kaline, George Kell, Jim Bunning 6.00
KPC Rod Carew, Kirby Puckett, Harmon Killebrew 6.00
KSR Ralph Kiner, Duke Snider, Frank Robinson 5.00
KWR Al Kaline, Frank Robinson, Dave Winfield 6.00
MBP Johnny Bench, Tony Perez, Joe Morgan 6.00
MCM Orlando Cepeda, Willie McCovey, Juan Marichal 5.00
MMS Joe Morgan, Red Schoendienst, Bill Mazeroski 4.00
MRJ Eddie Murray, Reggie Jackson, Frank Robinson 5.00
MSC Rod Carew, Joe Morgan, Ryne Sandberg 6.00
MYF Robin Yount, Paul Molitor, Rollie Fingers 6.00
PMC Rod Carew, Kirby Puckett, Paul Molitor 6.00
RAP Jim Palmer, Luis Aparicio, Brooks Robinson 5.00
RBC Steve Carlton, Jim Bunning, Robin Roberts 4.00

RBS	George Brett, Mike Schmidt, Brooks Robinson	10.00
RSR	Robin Roberts, Don Sutton, Nolan Ryan	10.00
SRC	Mike Schmidt, Steve Carlton, Robin Roberts	8.00
WBI	Billy Williams, Monte Irvin, Lou Brock	4.00
WBJ	Billy Williams, Ernie Banks, Fergie Jenkins	6.00
WJB	Reggie Jackson, Wade Boggs, Dave Winfield	6.00
WSP	Dave Winfield, Ozzie Smith, Gaylord Perry	6.00
YKM	Ralph Kiner, Carl Yastrzemski, Stan Musial	8.00

Signs of Cooperstown Quads Autographs

No pricing
Production 10 Sets
Gold: No Pricing
Production Five Sets
Rainbow: No Pricing
Production One Set

2005 UD Mini Jersey Collection

NM/M

Complete Set (100):		15.00
Common Player:		.15
Pack (3 + Mini Jersey):		6.00
Box (18):		90.00
1	Garret Anderson	.25
2	Vladimir Guerrero	.75
3	Luis Gonzalez	.15
4	Shawn Green	.25
5	Troy Glaus	.25
6	Andruw Jones	.50
7	Chipper Jones	.75
8	John Smoltz	.40
9	Tim Hudson	.40
10	Miguel Tejada	.50
11	Sammy Sosa	1.00
12	Curt Schilling	.75
13	David Ortiz	.75
14	Johnny Damon	.75
15	Manny Ramirez	.75
16	Greg Maddux	1.00
17	Kerry Wood	.50
18	Mark Prior	.75
19	Nomar Garciaparra	1.00
20	Frank Thomas	.50
21	Adam Dunn	.50
22	Ken Griffey Jr.	1.50
23	Travis Hafner	.25
24	Victor Martinez	.15
25	Todd Helton	.50
26	Ivan Rodriguez	.50
27	Magglio Ordonez	.15
28	Carlos Delgado	.40
29	Miguel Cabrera	.75
30	Jeff Bagwell	.50
31	Lance Berkman	.25
32	Roger Clemens	2.00

33	Roy Oswalt	.25
34	Mike Sweeney	.15
35	Eric Gagne	.15
36	J.D. Drew	.15
37	Ben Sheets	.40
38	Johan Santana	.50
39	Torii Hunter	.15
40	Carlos Beltran	.50
41	Mike Piazza	1.00
42	Pedro Martinez	.75
43	Alex Rodriguez	1.50
44	Derek Jeter	2.00
45	Hideki Matsui	1.50
46	Mike Mussina	.40
47	Randy Johnson	.75
48	Bobby Crosby	.40
49	Eric Chavez	.40
50	Bobby Abreu	.40
51	Jim Thome	.50
52	Jason Bay	.15
53	Oliver Perez	.15
54	Jake Peavy	.40
55	Khalil Greene	.40
56	Jason Schmidt	.15
57	Moises Alou	.40
58	Adrian Beltre	.40
59	Ichiro Suzuki	1.50
60	Albert Pujols	2.00
61	Jim Edmonds	.40
62	Mark Mulder	.40
63	Scott Rolen	.75
64	Aubrey Huff	.15
65	Alfonso Soriano	.50
66	Hank Blalock	.40
67	Mark Teixeira	.50
68	Roy Halladay	.40
69	Jose Vidro	.15
70	Livan Hernandez	.15
71	Atlanta Braves	.15
72	Chicago Cubs	.15
73	Chicago White Sox	.15
74	Cincinnati Reds	.15
75	Cleveland Indians	.15
76	Houston Astros	.15
77	L.A. Angels of Anaheim	.15
78	Los Angeles Dodgers	.15
79	New York Yankees	.15
80	Oakland Athletics	.15
81	Philadelphia Phillies	.15
82	Pittsburgh Pirates	.15
83	San Diego Padres	.15
84	San Francisco Giants	.15
85	Texas Rangers	.15
86	Cal Ripken Jr.	2.00
87	Derek Jeter	2.00
88	Hank Blalock	.40
89	Hideo Nomo	.40
90	Joe DiMaggio	1.00
91	Joe Morgan	.50
92	Ken Griffey Jr.	1.50
93	Larry Doby	.50
94	Pedro J. Martinez	.75
95	Randy Johnson	.75
96	Rick Ferrell	.15
97	Roger Clemens	2.00
98	Stan Musial	1.00
99	Ted Williams	1.50
100	Torii Hunter	.15

Replica Flannel Jerseys

NM/M

Inserted 1:18		
1	Ted Williams	20.00
2	Jackie Robinson	15.00
3	Satchel Paige	15.00
4	Ty Cobb	15.00
5	Babe Ruth	30.00
6	Joe DiMaggio	20.00
7	Lou Gehrig	25.00
8	Mickey Mantle	30.00
9	Roberto Clemente	20.00

Mini Jerseys

NM/M

1	Vladimir Guerrero	5.00
2	Chipper Jones	5.00
3	Curt Schilling	5.00
4	Johnny Damon	5.00
5	Manny Ramirez	5.00
6	Kerry Wood	5.00
7	Nomar Garciaparra	5.00
8	Ken Griffey Jr.	5.00
9	Miguel Cabrera	5.00
10	Roger Clemens	10.00
11	Eric Gagne	5.00
12	Johan Santana	5.00
13	Carlos Beltran	5.00
14	Mike Piazza	5.00
15	Pedro Martinez	5.00
16	Alex Rodriguez	5.00
17	Derek Jeter	15.00
18	Hideki Matsui	8.00
19	Randy Johnson	5.00
20	Jim Thome	5.00
21	Ichiro Suzuki	5.00
22	Albert Pujols	10.00

Mini Jersey Autograph

NM/M

Inserted 1:480		
1	Ken Griffey Jr.	150.00
2	David Wright	50.00
5	Adrian Beltre	50.00

2005 UD Origins

NM/M

Complete Set (200):		
Common Player:		.50
Tin (20):		50.00
1	Jim Edmonds	.75
2	Jason Schmidt	.75
3	J.D. Drew	.75
4	Luis Gonzalez	.50
5	Nomar Garciaparra	2.00
6	Jake Peavy	.75
7	Rafael Furcal	.50
8	Craig Biggio	.75
9	Ken Griffey Jr.	3.00
10	Mike Piazza	2.00
11	Jose Vidro	.50
12	Ivan Rodriguez	1.00
13	Carl Crawford	.50
14	Roger Clemens	4.00
15	Kerry Wood	1.00
16	Vernon Wells	.50
17	Carlos Guillen	.50
18	Tim Hudson	.75
19	Carl Pavano	.50
20	Carlos Beltran	1.00
21	Pedro Martinez	1.50
22	Hideki Matsui	3.00
23	Frank Thomas	1.00
24	Curt Schilling	1.50
25	Manny Ramirez	1.50
26	Alex Rodriguez	4.00
27	Aubrey Huff	.50
28	David Ortiz	1.50
29	Mark Prior	1.00
30	Albert Pujols	4.00
31	Miguel Cabrera	1.50
32	Brad Penny	.50
33	Carlos Delgado	.75
34	Aramis Ramirez	1.00
35	Josh Beckett	.75
36	Rafael Palmeiro	.50
37	Bret Boone	.50
38	Lance Berkman	.75
39	Carlos Zambrano	.75
40	Adam Dunn	1.00
41	Livan Hernandez	.50
42	Mike Mussina	.75
43	Ben Sheets	.75
44	Derek Jeter	4.00
45	Kazuo Matsui	.50
46	Bobby Abreu	.75
47	Jeff Bagwell	1.00
48	Travis Hafner	.50
49	Torii Hunter	.75
50	Kevin Brown	.50
51	Alfonso Soriano	1.50
52	Jim Thome	1.00
53	John Smoltz	.75
54	Mike Sweeney	.50
55	Andy Pettitte	.75
56	Chipper Jones	1.50
57	Randy Johnson	1.50
58	Steve Finley	.50
59	Larry Walker	.75
60	Troy Glaus	.75
61	Greg Maddux	2.50
62	Shawn Green	.50
63	Roy Halladay	.75
64	Jeff Kent	.50
65	Scott Podsednik	.50
66	Miguel Tejada	1.00
67	Lyle Overbay	.50
68	Bernie Williams	.75
69	Todd Helton	1.00
70	Melvin Mora	.50
71	Magglio Ordonez	.50
72	Carlos Lee	.75
73	Roy Oswalt	.75
74	Victor Martinez	.50
75	Scott Rolen	1.50
76	Eric Chavez	.75
77	Paul Konerko	.75
78	Jose Reyes	.75
79	Barry Larkin	.75
80	Johnny Damon	1.00
81	Eric Gagne	.75
82	Andruw Jones	1.00
83	Gary Sheffield	1.00
84	Richie Sexson	.75
85	Sammy Sosa	2.50

86	Mark Teixeira	1.00
87	Vladimir Guerrero	1.50
88	Michael Young	.50
89	Johan Santana	1.00
90	Adrian Beltre	.75
91	Tom Glavine	.75
92	Hank Blalock	.75
93	Preston Wilson	.50
94	Jason Kendall	.50
95	Mike Lowell	.50
96	Craig Wilson	.50
97	Ichiro Suzuki	3.00
98	Mark Mulder	.75
99	Garret Anderson	.75
100	Brian Giles	.50
101	Robin Yount	3.00
102	Ernie Banks	3.00
103	Mike Schmidt	5.00
104	Enos Slaughter	1.00
105	Red Schoendienst	1.00
106	Hoyt Wilhelm	1.00
107	Lou Brock	2.00
108	Rollie Fingers	1.00
109	Gaylord Perry	1.00
110	Bobby Doerr	1.00
111	Larry Doby	1.00
112	Al Lopez	1.00
113	Joe Morgan	1.50
114	Luis Aparicio	1.00
115	Willie McCovey	2.00
116	Bob Lemon	1.00
117	Early Wynn	1.00
118	Bob Feller	2.00
119	Cal Ripken Jr.	8.00
120	George Kell	1.00
121	Juan Marichal	1.50
122	Monte Irvin	1.50
123	Harmon Killebrew	3.00
124	Lou Boudreau	1.00
125	Mickey Mantle	8.00
126	Richie Ashburn	1.00
127	Pee Wee Reese	1.50
128	Whitey Ford	2.00
129	Tom Seaver	2.00
130	Phil Rizzuto	2.00
131	Yogi Berra	3.00
132	Warren Spahn	2.00
133	Billy Williams	1.50
134	Jim Bunning	1.50
135	Ralph Kiner	1.00
136	Ted Williams	6.00
137	Rick Ferrell	1.00
138	Robin Roberts	1.00
139	Brooks Robinson	3.00
140	Hal Newhouser	1.00
141	Jim "Catfish" Hunter	1.00
142	Phil Niekro	1.00
143	Fergie Jenkins	1.00
144	Al Kaline	3.00
145	Stan Musial	4.00
146	Joe DiMaggio	6.00
147	Willie Stargell	2.00
148	Nolan Ryan	6.00
149	Babe Ruth	6.00
150	Bob Gibson	2.00
151	David DeJesus	.50
152	Chris Burke	.50
153	Chad Cordero	.50
154	Kevin Youkilis	.50
155	Bucky Jacobsen	.50
156	B.J. Upton	.50
157	Aaron Rowand	.50
158	Jose Capellan	.50
159	David Wright	2.00
160	Jason Bay	.50
161	Edwin Jackson	.50
162	Scott Kazmir	.50
163	J.D. Closser	.50
164	Chase Utley	1.00
165	Nick Swisher	.50
166	Casey Kotchman	.50
167	Bobby Crosby	.50
168	Zack Greinke	.50
169	Gavin Floyd	.50
170	Jeff Francis	.50
171	Dallas McPherson	.50
172	Gabe Gross	.50
173	Brandon Claussen	.50
174	Wily Mo Pena	.50
175	Robb Quinlan	.50
176	Oliver Perez	.50
177	Guillermo Quiroz	.50
178	Ryan Howard	1.00
179	Gerald Laird	.50
180	Jayson Werth	.50
181	Bobby Madritsch	.50
182	Laynce Nix	.50
183	Eddy Rodriguez	.50
184	Rickie Weeks	1.00
185	Scott Proctor	.50
186	Adam LaRoche	.50
187	Yhency Brazoban	.50
188	Adrian Gonzalez	.50
189	Jason Lane	.50
190	Ryan Wagner	.50
191	Roman Colon	.50
192	Alexis Rios	.50
193	Joe Mauer	1.00
194	Garrett Atkins	.50
195	Daniel Cabrera	.50
196	Khalil Greene	2.00
197	Joe Blanton	.50
198	Jason Dubois	.50
199	Angel Guzman	.50
200	Jesse Crain	.50

Black

No Pricing
Production One Set

Blue

Stars (1-200): 2-4X
Production 50 Sets

Gold

No Pricing
Production 20 Sets

Red

Stars (1-200): 2-3X
Production 99 Sets

Origins Materials Jersey

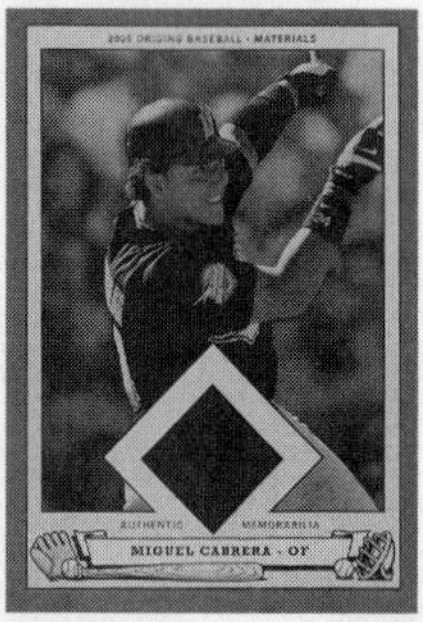

		NM/M
Inserted 2:Tin		
Old Judge:		1X
JB	Jeff Bagwell	8.00
CB	Carlos Beltran	8.00
AB	Adrian Beltre	5.00
LB	Lance Berkman	5.00
HB	Hank Blalock	5.00
MC	Miguel Cabrera	8.00
EC	Eric Chavez	5.00
JD	J.D. Drew	5.00
GL	Troy Glaus	5.00
KG	Ken Griffey Jr.	10.00
VG	Vladimir Guerrero	8.00
TG	Tony Gwynn SP	10.00
HE	Todd Helton	5.00
TH	Tim Hudson	5.00
HU	Torii Hunter	5.00
DJ	Derek Jeter	15.00
RJ	Randy Johnson	8.00
AJ	Andruw Jones	5.00
CJ	Chipper Jones	8.00
GM	Greg Maddux	10.00
HM	Hideki Matsui	15.00
KM	Hideki Matsui	5.00
DO	David Ortiz	8.00
PI	Mike Piazza	8.00
MP	Mark Prior	8.00
AP	Albert Pujols	15.00
MR	Manny Ramirez	8.00
CR	Cal Ripken Jr. SP	25.00
IR	Ivan Rodriguez	8.00
SR	Scott Rolen	8.00
NR	Nolan Ryan SP	30.00
CS	Curt Schilling	8.00
BS	Ben Sheets	5.00
GS	Gary Sheffield	5.00
AS	Alfonso Soriano	8.00
SS	Sammy Sosa	8.00
IS	Ichiro Suzuki	20.00
MT	Mark Teixeira	5.00
TE	Miguel Tejada	8.00
FT	Frank Thomas	8.00
JT	Jim Thome	8.00
KW	Kerry Wood	8.00

Origins Nostalgic Signs

		NM/M
One sign per tin.		
CB	Carlos Beltran	8.00
AB	Adrian Beltre	5.00
HB	Hank Blalock	5.00
MC	Miguel Cabrera	8.00
EC	Eric Chavez	5.00
RC	Roger Clemens	15.00
TC	Ty Cobb	20.00
JD	Joe DiMaggio	20.00
LG	Lou Gehrig	15.00
KG	Ken Griffey Jr.	12.00
VG	Vladimir Guerrero	8.00
TH	Todd Helton	8.00
DJ	Derek Jeter	15.00
RJ	Randy Johnson	8.00
WJ	Walter Johnson	15.00
CJ	Chipper Jones	8.00
PM	Pedro Martinez	8.00
HM	Hideki Matsui	20.00
DO	David Ortiz	8.00
SP	Satchel Paige	12.00
MP	Mike Piazza	10.00
MPR	Mark Prior	8.00
AP	Albert Pujols	20.00
MR	Manny Ramirez	8.00
CR	Cal Ripken Jr.	25.00
JR	Jackie Robinson	12.00
AR	Alex Rodriguez	12.00
IR	Ivan Rodriguez	8.00
SR	Scott Rolen	8.00
BR	Babe Ruth	20.00
NR	Nolan Ryan	20.00
JS	Johan Santana	8.00
CS	Curt Schilling	10.00
AS	Alfonso Soriano	8.00
SS	Sammy Sosa	10.00
IS	Ichiro Suzuki	12.00
MT	Miguel Tejada	8.00
FT	Frank Thomas	8.00
JT	Jim Thome	8.00
HW	Honus Wagner	10.00
TW	Ted Williams	25.00

Origins Old Judge

		NM/M
Common Player:		.50
Blue:		2-3X
Red:		1-2X
Gold:		No Pricing
1	Jake Peavy	1.00
2	Derek Jeter	5.00
3	Adrian Beltre	1.00
4	Hank Blalock	1.00
5	Preston Wilson	.50
6	Randy Johnson	2.00
7	Pedro Martinez	2.00
8	Michael Young	1.00
9	Steve Finley	.50
10	Shawn Green	.75
11	Carlos Beltran	1.50
12	Bernie Williams	1.00
13	Brian Giles	.50
14	Kevin Brown	.50
15	Barry Larkin	1.00
16	Troy Glaus	1.00
17	Bret Boone	.50
18	Jason Kendall	.50
19	Johnny Damon	1.50
20	Josh Beckett	1.00
21	Carl Pavano	.50
22	Chipper Jones	2.00
23	Ivan Rodriguez	1.50
24	Kerry Wood	1.50
25	Ken Griffey Jr.	3.00
26	Greg Maddux	3.00
27	Kazuo Matsui	.50
28	Albert Pujols	5.00
29	Victor Martinez	.50
30	Johan Santana	1.50
31	Bobby Abreu	.75
32	Paul Konerko	.75
33	Gary Sheffield	1.00
34	Jose Vidro	.50
35	Alex Rodriguez	4.00
36	Alfonso Soriano	1.50
37	Mark Teixeira	1.50
38	Nomar Garciaparra	2.50
39	Sammy Sosa	3.00
40	Garret Anderson	1.00
41	Eric Chavez	1.00
42	Magglio Ordonez	.50
43	Larry Walker	1.00
44	Brad Penny	.50
45	Jeff Bagwell	1.50
46	Craig Biggio	.75
47	Torii Hunter	.75
48	Mike Lowell	.50
49	Ben Sheets	1.00
50	Miguel Tejada	1.50
51	Jim Edmonds	1.00
52	Mark Mulder	1.00
53	Curt Schilling	1.50
54	Roger Clemens	5.00
55	Jason Schmidt	.50
56	Rafael Furcal	.50
57	Scott Rolen	2.00
58	Carlos Zambrano	.75
59	Mike Sweeney	.50
60	Vladimir Guerrero	2.00
61	Miguel Cabrera	2.00
62	Lance Berkman	.50
63	Lyle Overbay	.50
64	Livan Hernandez	.50
65	Aramis Ramirez	1.00
66	Ichiro Suzuki	4.00
67	Roy Oswalt	.50
68	Carl Crawford	.50
69	Craig Wilson	.50
70	Carlos Lee	.75
71	J.D. Drew	.50
72	Rafael Palmeiro	1.50
73	Jeff Kent	.50
74	Adam Dunn	1.50
75	Andy Pettitte	1.00
76	Luis Gonzalez	.50
77	Frank Thomas	1.50
78	John Smoltz	1.00
79	Hideki Matsui	3.00
80	Tom Glavine	.50
81	Jose Reyes	.50
82	Jim Thome	1.50
83	Mark Prior	2.00
84	Roy Halladay	.75
85	Carlos Delgado	1.00
86	Melvin Mora	.50
87	David Ortiz	2.00
88	Travis Hafner	.50
89	Carlos Guillen	.50
90	Tim Hudson	.50
91	Vernon Wells	.50
92	Andruw Jones	1.50
93	Mike Mussina	1.00
94	Mike Piazza	3.00
95	Richie Sexson	1.00
96	Aubrey Huff	.50
97	Scott Podsednik	.50
98	Eric Gagne	.50
99	Manny Ramirez	2.00
100	Todd Helton	1.50
101	Joe Morgan	1.00
102	Billy Williams	1.00
103	Pee Wee Reese	1.00
104	Lou Boudreau	1.00
105	Richie Ashburn	1.00
106	Jim Bunning	1.00
107	Hal Newhouser	1.00
108	Rick Ferrell	1.00
109	Ted Williams	5.00
110	Ralph Kiner	1.00
111	Warren Spahn	2.50
112	George Kell	.50
113	Willie Stargell	2.00
114	Jim "Catfish" Hunter	.50
115	Tom Seaver	2.00
116	Cal Ripken Jr.	8.00
117	Al Lopez	.50
118	Ernie Banks	3.00
119	Lou Brock	2.00
120	Robin Yount	3.00
121	Nolan Ryan	6.00
122	Larry Doby	1.00
123	Al Kaline	2.00
124	Willie McCovey	2.00
125	Stan Musial	3.00
126	Phil Niekro	1.00
127	Babe Ruth	6.00
128	Rollie Fingers	1.00
129	Juan Marichal	1.00
130	Early Wynn	1.00
131	Luis Aparicio	1.00
132	Brooks Robinson	3.00
133	Mike Schmidt	5.00
134	Gaylord Perry	1.00
135	Bob Lemon	1.00
136	Monte Irvin	1.50
137	Mickey Mantle	8.00
138	Phil Rizzuto	1.50
139	Robin Roberts	1.50
140	Bobby Doerr	1.00
141	Bob Gibson	2.00
142	Enos Slaughter	1.00
143	Yogi Berra	3.00
144	Whitey Ford	2.00
145	Red Schoendienst	1.00
146	Joe DiMaggio	5.00
147	Harmon Killebrew	2.00
148	Hoyt Wilhelm	1.00
149	Fergie Jenkins	1.00
150	Bob Feller	1.50
151	Scott Proctor	.50
152	Adam LaRoche	.50
153	Ryan Howard	1.00
154	Laynce Nix	.50
155	Garrett Atkins	.50
156	Chris Burke	.50
157	Oliver Perez	.50
158	Wily Mo Pena	.50
159	B.J. Upton	.50
160	Gavin Floyd	.50
161	Jesse Crain	.50
162	Khalil Greene	3.00
163	Eddy Rodriguez	.50
164	Edwin Jackson	.50
165	Scott Kazmir	.50
166	Ryan Wagner	.50
167	Nick Swisher	.50
168	Joe Blanton	.50
169	Alexis Rios	.50
170	Chad Cordero	.50
171	Jason Dubois	.50
172	Chase Utley	1.00
173	David DeJesus	.50
174	Zack Greinke	.50
175	Bobby Crosby	1.00
176	Angel Guzman	.50
177	Adrian Gonzalez	.50
178	Guillermo Quiroz	.50
179	Gerald Laird	.50
180	Rickie Weeks	1.00
181	Jayson Werth	.50
182	Buck Jacobsen	.50
183	J.D. Closser	.50
184	Jason Bay	.50
185	Roman Colon	.50
186	Casey Kotchman	.50
187	Yhency Brazoban	.50
188	Bobby Madritsch	.50
189	Gabe Gross	.50
190	Brandon Claussen	.50
191	Aaron Rowand	.50
192	Jeff Francis	.50
193	David Wright	2.00
194	Jose Capellan	.50
195	Jason Lane	.50
196	Daniel Cabrera	.50
197	Joe Mauer	1.00
198	Kevin Youkilis	.50
199	Dallas McPherson	.50
200	Robb Quinlan	.50

Origins Old Judge Autographs

		NM/M
Common Auto.:		12.00
Bronze:		No Pricing
JB	Jason Bay	15.00
AB	Adrian Beltre	12.00
MC	Miguel Cabrera	25.00
CC	Carl Crawford Exch	12.00
BC	Bobby Crosby Exch	15.00
BD	Bobby Doerr	15.00
BF	Bob Feller	25.00
MG	Marcus Giles Exch	15.00
DG	Dwight Gooden	15.00
GR	Khalil Greene	20.00
KG	Ken Griffey Jr.	75.00
RG	Ron Guidry	15.00
TG	Tony Gwynn	50.00
TH	Travis Hafner	15.00
RH	Rich Harden	15.00
KH	Keith Hernandez	15.00
FH	Frank Howard	20.00
HO	Ryan Howard	75.00
AH	Aubrey Huff	8.00
DJ	Derek Jeter	150.00
SK	Scott Kazmir	20.00
DK	Dave Kingman	15.00
CK	Casey Kotchman	15.00
SL	Sparky Lyle	12.00
VM	Victor Martinez	15.00
MA	Don Mattingly	65.00
DM	Dallas McPherson	12.00
PM	Paul Molitor	40.00
OS	Roy Oswalt	15.00
AO	Akinori Otsuka	15.00
JP	Jim Palmer	15.00
PE	Jake Peavy	25.00
OP	Oliver Perez	10.00
CR	Cal Ripken Jr./25	180.00
BR	Brooks Robinson	30.00
RO	Al Rosen	15.00
JS	Johan Santana Exch	35.00
RS	Ron Santo	25.00
MS	Mike Schmidt	75.00
BS	Ben Sheets	12.00
ST	Shingo Takatsu	15.00
MT	Mark Teixeira	25.00
BU	B.J. Upton	15.00
CU	Chase Utley	25.00
RW	Rickie Weeks	15.00
DW	David Wright	60.00
RY	Robin Yount	50.00
CZ	Carlos Zambrano	20.00

Origins Old Judge Materials Jersey

		NM/M
Common Jersey:		5.00
JB	Jeff Bagwell	8.00
CB	Carlos Beltran	8.00
AB	Adrian Beltre	5.00
LB	Lance Berkman	5.00
HB	Hank Blalock	5.00
MC	Miguel Cabrera	8.00
EC	Eric Chavez	5.00
JD	J.D. Drew	5.00
GL	Troy Glaus	5.00
KG	Ken Griffey Jr.	10.00
VG	Vladimir Guerrero	8.00
TG	Tony Gwynn/SP	10.00
HE	Todd Helton	5.00
TH	Tim Hudson	5.00
HU	Torii Hunter	5.00
DJ	Derek Jeter	15.00
RJ	Randy Johnson	8.00
AJ	Andruw Jones	5.00
CJ	Chipper Jones	8.00
GM	Greg Maddux	10.00
HM	Hideki Matsui	15.00
KM	Kazuo Matsui	5.00
DO	David Ortiz	8.00
PI	Mike Piazza	8.00
MP	Mark Prior	8.00
AP	Albert Pujols	15.00
MR	Manny Ramirez	8.00
CR	Cal Ripken Jr./SP	25.00
SR	Scott Rolen	8.00
NR	Nolan Ryan/SP	30.00
CS	Curt Schilling	8.00
BS	Ben Sheets	5.00
GS	Gary Sheffield	5.00
AS	Alfonso Soriano	8.00
SS	Sammy Sosa	8.00
IS	Ichiro Suzuki	20.00
MT	Mark Teixeira	5.00
TE	Miguel Tejada	8.00
FT	Frank Thomas	8.00
JT	Jim Thome	8.00
KW	Kerry Wood	8.00

Origins Signatures

		NM/M
Common Auto.:		12.00
Bronze:		No Pricing
Production Five Sets		
JB1	Jason Bay	15.00
AB1	Adrian Beltre	12.00
MC1	Miguel Cabrera	25.00
CC1	Carl Crawford/Exch	12.00
BC1	Bobby Crosby/Exch	15.00
BD1	Bobby Doerr	15.00
BF1	Bob Feller	25.00
MG1	Marcus Giles	15.00
DG1	Dwight Gooden	15.00
GR1	Khalil Greene	20.00
KG1	Ken Griffey Jr.	75.00
RG1	Ron Guidry	15.00
TG1	Tony Gwynn	50.00
TH1	Travis Hafner	15.00
RH1	Rich Harden	15.00
KH1	Keith Hernandez	15.00
FH1	Frank Howard	20.00
HO1	Ryan Howard	75.00
AH1	Aubrey Huff	15.00
DJ1	Derek Jeter	150.00
SK1	Scott Kazmir	20.00
DK1	Dave Kingman	15.00
CK1	Casey Kotchman	15.00
SL1	Sparky Lyle	12.00
VM1	Victor Martinez	15.00
MA1	Don Mattingly	65.00
DM1	Dallas McPherson	12.00
PM1	Paul Molitor	40.00
OS1	Roy Oswalt	15.00
AO1	Akinori Otsuka	15.00
JP1	Jim Palmer	15.00
PE1	Jake Peavy	25.00
OP1	Oliver Perez	10.00
CR1	Cal Ripken Jr./25	180.00
BR1	Brooks Robinson	30.00
RO1	Al Rosen	15.00
JS1	Johan Santana Exch	35.00
RS1	Ron Santo	25.00
MS1	Mike Schmidt	75.00
BS1	Ben Sheets	12.00
ST1	Shingo Takatsu	15.00
MT1	Mark Teixeira	25.00
BU1	B.J. Upton	15.00
CU1	Chase Utley	25.00
RW1	Rickie Weeks	15.00
DW1	David Wright	60.00
RY1	Robin Yount	50.00
CZ1	Carlos Zambrano	20.00

Origins Tins

		NM/M
Common Tin:		5.00
TC	Ty Cobb	5.00
DJ	Derek Jeter	10.00
WJ	Walter Johnson	5.00
HW	Honus Wagner	5.00

2005 UD Past Time Pennants

		NM/M
Complete Set (90):		20.00
Common Player:		.20
Pack (5):		4.00
Box (20):		70.00
1	Al Kaline	.50
2	Al Rosen	.20
3	Bert Blyleven	.20
4	Bill Mazeroski	.20
5	Billy Williams	.20
6	Bob Feller	.50
7	Bob Gibson	.75
8	Bob Lemon	.20
9	Bobby Doerr	.40
10	Brooks Robinson	.75
11	Bruce Sutter	.30
12	Bucky Dent	.20
13	Cal Ripken Jr.	2.00
14	Carl Yastrzemski	.75
15	Carlton Fisk	.40
16	Jim "Catfish" Hunter	.20
17	Dale Murphy	.40
18	Dave Parker	.20
19	Don Larsen	.20
20	Don Mattingly	1.00
21	Don Newcombe	.20
22	Duke Snider	.50
23	Early Wynn	.20
24	Eddie Matthews	.75
25	Eddie Murray	.50
26	Enos Slaughter	.20
27	Ernie Banks	.75
28	Fergie Jenkins	.20
29	Frank Howard	.20
30	Frank Robinson	.50
31	Fred Lynn	.20
32	Gary Carter	.20
33	Gaylord Perry	.20
34	George Brett	1.50
35	George Kell	.20
36	Rich "Goose" Gossage	.20
37	Graig Nettles	.20
38	Harmon Killebrew	.75
39	Jack Morris	.20
40	Jim Bunning	.20
41	Felipe Alou	.20
42	Jim Palmer	.40
43	Jim Rice	.20
44	Joe DiMaggio	1.50
45	Joe Morgan	.20
46	Johnny Bench	.75
47	Johnny Podres	.20
48	Juan Marichal	.20
49	Keith Hernandez	.20
50	Kirby Puckett	.75
51	Larry Doby	.20
52	Lou Brock	.40
53	Ozzie Smith	.20
54	Luis Tiant	.20
55	Maury 4illis	.20
56	Mickey Mantle	2.00
57	Mike Schmidt	1.50
58	Monte Irvin	.20
59	Nolan Ryan	1.50
60	Orlando Cepeda	.20
61	Ozzie Smith	.75
62	Paul Molitor	.50
63	Pee Wee Reese	.20
64	Phil Niekro	.20
65	Phil Rizzuto	.50
66	Ralph Kiner	.20
67	Richie Ashburn	.20
68	Rico Petrocelli	.20
69	Robin Roberts	.20
70	Robin Yount	.75
71	Rocky Colavito	.20
72	Rod Carew	.40
73	Rollie Fingers	.20
74	Ron Guidry	.20
75	Ron Santo	.20
76	Tony Gwynn	.75
77	Sparky Lyle	.20
78	Stan Musial	1.00
79	Steve Carlton	.40
80	Rick Ferrell	.20
81	Tom Seaver	.75
82	Tommy John	.20
83	Tony Perez	.20
84	Wade Boggs	.50
85	Warren Spahn	.75
86	Whitey Ford	.40
87	Will Clark	.50
88	Willie McCovey	.50
89	Willie Stargell	.40
90	Yogi Berra	.75

Gold

Gold:		4-8X
Production 50 Sets		

Silver

Gold:		3-5X
Production 100 Sets		

Mitchell & Ness Jersey Redemption

Total Production		
Per Player 36-37		
No Pricing		

Mitchell & Ness Pennants

		NM/M
Common Pennant:		15.00
Inserted 1:Hobby Box		
1903	1903 Boston Americans/100	20.00
1905	1095 New York Giants/100	20.00
1906	1906 Chicago White Sox/100	20.00
1907	1907 Detroit Tigers/100	20.00
1908	1908 Chicago Cubs/105	25.00
1909	1909 Pittsburgh Pirates/125	20.00
1910	1910 Philadelphia A's/125	20.00
1912	1912 Boston Red Sox/125	20.00
1914	1914 Boston Braves/125	20.00
1915	1915 Phildelphia Phillies/125	20.00
1916	1916 Brooklyn Robins/200	20.00
1917	1917 New York/200	20.00
1918	1918 Boston Red Sox/200	20.00
1919	1919 Chicago White Sox/200	20.00
1920	1920 Cleveland Indians/200	15.00
1921	1921 New York Yankees/200	20.00
1922	1922 New York Giants/200	20.00
1924	1924 Washington Senators/200	20.00
1925	1925 Pittsburgh Pirates/200	15.00
1926	1926 Saint Louis Cardinals/200	20.00
1927	1927 New York Yankees/500	25.00
1928	1928 New York Yankees/500	25.00
1929	1929 Chicago Cubs/337	20.00
1930	1930 Philadelphia A's/337	15.00
1931	1931 Saint Louis Cardinals/337	20.00
1932	1932 Chicago Cubs/337	20.00
1934	1934 Detroit Tigers/337	15.00
1935	1935 Chicago Cubs/337	20.00
1936	1936 New York Yankees/337	25.00
1937	1937 New York Giants/337	20.00
1938	1938 New York Yankees/337	25.00
1939	1939 Cincinnati Reds/337	15.00
1940	1940 Cincinnati Reds/337	15.00
1941	1941 Brooklyn Dodgers/337	25.00
1942	1942 Saint Louis Cardinals/337	20.00
1943	1943 New York Yankees/500	25.00
1944	1944 Saint Louis Browns/337	15.00
1945	1945 Chicago Cubs/337	20.00
1946	1946 Boston Red Sox/337	20.00
1947	1947 Brooklyn Dodgers/337	20.00
1948	1948 Boston Braves/337	15.00
1949	1949 New York Yankees/337	25.00
1950	1950 Philadelphia Phillies/337	15.00
1951	1951 New York Giants/337	15.00
1952	1952 Brooklyn Dodgers/500	20.00
1953	1953 New York Yankees/337	25.00
1954	1954 Cleveland Indians/337	15.00
1955	1955 Brooklyn Dodgers/337	20.00
1956	1956 Brooklyn Dodgers/500	25.00
1957	1957 Milwaukee Braves/337	20.00
1958	1958 New York Yankees/500	25.00
1959	1959 Los Angeles Dodgers/337	20.00
1960	1960 Pittsburgh Pirates/337	15.00
1961	1961 Cincinnati Reds/337	15.00
1962	1962 San Francisco Giants/337	20.00
1963	1963 Los Angeles Dodgers/337	20.00
1964	1964 Saint Louis Cardinals/337	20.00
1965	1965 Minnesota Twins/337	15.00
1966	1966 Baltimore Orioles/337	20.00
1967	1967 Boston Red Sox/337	20.00
1968	1968 Detroit Tigers/337	15.00
1969	1969 New York Mets/337	20.00
1970	1970 Baltimore Orioles/337	20.00
1971	1971 Pittsburgh Pirates/337	15.00
1972	1972 Oakland A's/337	20.00
1973	1973 Oakland A's/337	20.00
1974	1974 Los Angeles Dodgers/337	20.00
1977	1977 New York Yankees/337	25.00
1978	1978 Los Angeles Dodgers/337	20.00
1979	1979 Pittsburgh Pirates/337	15.00
1980	1980 Philadelphia Phillies/337	20.00
1981	1981 Los Angeles Dodgers/337	20.00
1982	1982 Milwaukee Brewers/337	20.00
1983	1983 Baltimore Orioles/337	20.00
1984	1984 San Diego Padres/337	15.00
1985	1985 Kansas City Royals/337	15.00
1986	1986 Boston Red Sox/337	25.00
1988	1988 Los Angeles Dodgers/337	20.00
1975B	1975 Boston Red Sox/337	25.00
1975C	1975 Cincinnati Reds/337	20.00

Mitchell & Ness Penn Auto.

		NM/M
Production 86-87		
JB	Johnny Bench/87	80.00
SC	Steve Carlton/87	60.00
RF	Rollie Fingers/87	40.00
CF	Carlton Fisk/87	60.00
SG	Steve Garvey/40	40.00
AK	Al Kaline/87	75.00
PM	Paul Molitor/87	75.00
GN	Graig Nettles/87	50.00
DN	Don Newcombe/87	40.00
BR	Brooks Robinson/87	75.00
TS	Tom Seaver/87	80.00
CY	Carl Yastrzemski/86	80.00

Signatures Bronze

		NM/M
SP's Production 3-25		
FA	Felipe Alou	15.00
RB	Rick Burleson	10.00
DC	David Cone	15.00
LD	Lenny Dykstra	12.00
SF	Sid Fernandez	10.00
BF	Bill Freehan	10.00
DG	Dwight Gooden	15.00
KG	Ken Griffey Sr.	10.00
GU	Don Gullett	8.00
PG	Pedro Guerrero	10.00
HO	Ken Holtzman	10.00
BH	Burt Hooton	10.00
WH	Willie Horton/EXCH	12.00
FH	Frank Howard	15.00
HR	Kent Hrbek	10.00
RH	Randy Hundley	10.00
TJ	Tommy John	15.00
WJ	Wally Joyner	10.00
DK	Dave Kingman	10.00
KN	Ray Knight	10.00
SL	Sparky Lyle	10.00
BM	Bill Madlock	15.00
BO	Bobby Murcer	15.00
RP	Rico Petrocelli	12.00
BP	Boog Powell	25.00
AR	Al Rosen	15.00
SS	Steve Sax	10.00
SC	Mike Scioscia/EXCH	15.00
WI	Mookie Wilson	15.00

Signatures Dual

Production 15-24		
No Pricing		

Signatures Gold

		NM/M
Many not priced		
due to scarcity.		
FA	Felipe Alou	20.00
RB	Rick Burleson	15.00
LD	Lenny Dykstra	20.00
SF	Sid Fernandez	15.00
BF	Bill Freehan	15.00
KG	Ken Griffey Sr.	15.00
PG	Pedro Guerrero	15.00
GU	Don Gullett	10.00
HO	Ken Holtzman	15.00
BH	Burt Hooton	15.00
WH	Willie Horton/Exch.	15.00
HR	Kent Hrbek	20.00
RH	Randy Hundley	15.00
DK	Dave Kingman	15.00
KN	Ray Knight	15.00
SL	Sparky Lyle	15.00
BM	Bill Madlock	15.00
BO	Bobby Murcer	25.00
RP	Rico Petrocelli	15.00

Signatures Silver

		NM/M
FA	Felipe Alou	10.00
LA	Luis Aparicio	20.00
BB	Bert Blyleven	15.00
BR	Lou Brock	30.00
JB	Jim Bunning/Exch.	15.00
RB	Rick Burleson	15.00
ST	Steve Carlton	35.00
GC	Gary Carter	20.00
OC	Orlando Cepeda	20.00
CC	Chris Chambliss	15.00
WC	Will Clark	40.00
RC	Rocky Colavito	65.00
DC	David Cone	15.00
DE	Bucky Dent	12.00
BD	Bobby Doerr	15.00
LD	Lenny Dykstra	15.00
CE	Carl Erskine/Exch.	12.00
EV	Dwight Evans	30.00
FE	Bob Feller	30.00
SF	Sid Fernandez	10.00
RF	Rollie Fingers	20.00
BF	Bill Freehan	15.00
DG	Dwight Gooden	15.00
GG	Rich "Goose" Gossage	15.00
KG	Ken Griffey Sr.	10.00

GU	Don Gullett	8.00
PG	Pedro Guerrero	10.00
KH	Keith Hernandez	15.00
HO	Ken Holtzman	10.00
BH	Burt Hooton	10.00
WH	Willie Horton/Exch.	10.00
FH	Frank Howard	15.00
HR	Kent Hrbek	15.00
RH	Randy Hundley	10.00
MI	Monte Irvin	25.00
FJ	Fergie Jenkins	20.00
TJ	Tommy Jones	15.00
WJ	Wally Joyner	15.00
AK	Al Kaline	50.00
GK	George Kell	15.00
HK	Harmon Killebrew	50.00
RK	Ralph Kiner	40.00
DK	Dave Kingman	10.00
KN	Ray Knight	10.00
DL	Don Larsen/Exch.	30.00
SL	Sparky Lyle	10.00
FL	Fred Lynn	15.00
BM	Bill Madlock	10.00
JU	Juan Marichal/Exch.	20.00
MA	Bill Mazeroski	30.00
PM	Paul Molitor	40.00
MO	Joe Morgan	20.00
JM	Jack Morris	15.00
BO	Bobby Murcer	20.00
MU	Dale Murphy	25.00
GN	Graig Nettles	20.00
DN	Don Newcombe	15.00
JP	Jim Palmer	30.00
DP	Dave Parker	20.00
TP	Tony Perez/Exch.	40.00
GP	Gaylord Perry	15.00
RP	Rico Petrocelli	15.00
PO	Johnny Podres	25.00
BP	Boog Powell	20.00
JR	Jim Rice	20.00
RO	Brooks Robinson	60.00
AR	Al Rosen	15.00
RS	Ron Santo	25.00
SS	Steve Sax	10.00
SC	Mike Scioscia/Exch.	20.00
BS	Bill "Moose" Skowron	15.00
SU	Bruce Sutter	15.00
LT	Luis Tiant	15.00
BW	Billy Williams/Exch.	15.00
MW	Maury Wills	20.00

2005 UD Ultimate Collection

	NM/M
Common (1-100):	1.50
Production 475	
Common (101-237):	3.00
Production 275	
Common (238-242):	50.00
Production 99	
Pack (4):	85.00
Box (4):	300.00

1	A.J. Burnett	1.50
2	Adam Dunn	2.00
3	Adrian Beltre	2.00
4	Albert Pujols	8.00
5	Alex Rodriguez	8.00
6	Alfonso Soriano	3.00
7	Andruw Jones	3.00
8	Andy Pettitte	2.00
9	Aramis Ramirez	2.00
10	Aubrey Huff	1.50
11	Ben Sheets	2.00
12	Bobby Abreu	2.00
13	Bobby Crosby	1.50
14	Chris Carpenter	2.00
15	Brian Giles	1.50
16	Brian Roberts	1.50
17	Carl Crawford	2.00
18	Carlos Beltran	3.00
19	Carlos Delgado	2.00
20	Carlos Zambrano	2.00
21	Chipper Jones	3.00
22	Corey Patterson	1.50
23	Craig Biggio	1.50
24	Curt Schilling	3.00
25	Dallas McPherson	1.50
26	David Ortiz	3.00
27	David Wright	5.00
28	Delmon Young	2.00
29	Derek Jeter	8.00
30	Derrek Lee	3.00
31	Dontrelle Willis	2.00
32	Eric Chavez	2.00
33	Eric Gagne	2.00
34	Francisco Rodriguez	1.50
35	Gary Sheffield	2.00
36	Greg Maddux	5.00
37	Hank Blalock	1.50
38	Hideki Matsui	5.00
39	Ichiro Suzuki	5.00
40	Ivan Rodriguez	3.00
41	J.D. Drew	1.50
42	Jake Peavy	2.00
43	Jason Bay	2.00
44	Jason Schmidt	2.00
45	Jeff Bagwell	2.00
46	Jeff Kent	2.00
47	Jeremy Bonderman	2.00
48	Jim Edmonds	2.00
49	Jim Thome	2.00
50	Joe Mauer	2.00
51	Johan Santana	3.00
52	John Smoltz	2.00
53	Johnny Damon	3.00
54	Jose Reyes	3.00
55	Jose Vidro	1.50
56	Josh Beckett	1.50
57	Justin Morneau	2.00
58	Ken Griffey Jr.	5.00
59	Kerry Wood	2.00
60	Khalil Greene	1.50
61	Lance Berkman	2.00
62	Larry Walker	2.00
63	Luis Gonzalez	1.50
64	Manny Ramirez	3.00
65	Mark Buehrle	2.00
66	Mark Mulder	2.00
67	Mark Prior	3.00
68	Mark Teixeira	3.00
69	Michael Young	2.00
70	Miguel Cabrera	3.00
71	Miguel Tejada	3.00
72	Mike Mussina	2.00
73	Mike Piazza	4.00
74	Moises Alou	2.00
75	Nomar Garciaparra	3.00
76	Oliver Perez	1.50
77	Pat Burrell	2.00
78	Paul Konerko	2.00
79	Pedro Feliz	1.50
80	Pedro Martinez	3.00
81	Randy Johnson	3.00
82	Richie Sexson	2.00
83	Rickie Weeks	2.00
84	Roger Clemens	8.00
85	Roy Halladay	2.00
86	Roy Oswalt	2.00
87	Sammy Sosa	3.00
88	Scott Kazmir	1.50
89	Scott Rolen	3.00
90	Shawn Green	2.00
91	Tim Hudson	2.00
92	Todd Helton	2.00
93	Tom Glavine	2.00
94	Torii Hunter	2.00
95	Travis Hafner	2.00
96	Troy Glaus	2.00
97	Vernon Wells	1.50
98	Victor Martinez	1.50
99	Vladimir Guerrero	3.00
100	Zack Greinke	1.50
101	Al Kaline	4.00
102	Babe Ruth	10.00
103	Bo Jackson	4.00
104	Bob Gibson	5.00
105	Brooks Robinson	5.00
106	Cal Ripken Jr.	12.00
107	Carl Yastrzemski	5.00
108	Carlton Fisk	3.00
109	Jim "Catfish" Hunter	3.00
110	Christy Mathewson	5.00
111	Cy Young	5.00
112	Don Mattingly	6.00
113	Eddie Mathews	5.00
114	Eddie Murray	4.00
115	Gary Carter	3.00
116	Harmon Killebrew	4.00
117	Jim Palmer	3.00
118	Jimmie Foxx	4.00
119	Joe DiMaggio	8.00
120	Johnny Bench	4.00
121	Lefty Grove	3.00
122	Lou Gehrig	8.00
123	Mel Ott	3.00
124	Reggie Jackson	4.00
125	Mike Schmidt	5.00
126	Nolan Ryan	8.00
127	Ozzie Smith	5.00
128	Paul Molitor	4.00
129	Pee Wee Reese	3.00
130	Robin Yount	5.00
131	Ryne Sandberg	6.00
132	Ted Williams	8.00
133	Thurman Munson	4.00
134	Tom Seaver	4.00
135	Tony Gwynn	4.00
136	Wade Boggs	3.00
137	Walter Johnson	4.00
138	Warren Spahn	4.00
139	Will Clark	3.00
140	Willie McCovey	3.00
141	Willie Stargell	4.00
142	Yogi Berra	5.00
143	Ambiorix Burgos **RC**	4.00
144	Ambiorix Concepcion **RC**	4.00
145	Anibal Sanchez **RC**	6.00
146	Bill McCarthy **RC**	4.00
147	Brian Burres **RC**	4.00
148	Carlos Ruiz **RC**	4.00
149	Casey Rogowski **RC**	4.00
150	Chris Resop **RC**	4.00
151	Chris Roberson **RC**	4.00
152	Chris Seddon **RC**	4.00
153	Colter Bean **RC**	4.00
154	Dae-Sung Koo **RC**	4.00
155	Danny Rueckel **RC**	4.00
156	David Gassner **RC**	4.00
157	Ryan Howard	8.00
158	D.J. Houlton **RC**	4.00
159	Derek Wathan **RC**	4.00
160	Devon Lowery **RC**	4.00
161	Enrique Gonzalez **RC**	4.00
162	Erick Threets **RC**	4.00
163	Eude Brito **RC**	4.00
164	Francisco Butto **RC**	4.00
165	Franquelis Osoria **RC**	4.00
166	Garrett Jones **RC**	4.00
167	Geovany Soto **RC**	20.00
168	Ismael Ramirez **RC**	4.00
169	Jared Gothreaux **RC**	4.00
170	Jason Hammel **RC**	4.00
171	Jeff Housman **RC**	4.00
172	Jeff Miller **RC**	4.00
173	Jeff Francoeur	6.00
174	John Hattig Jr. **RC**	4.00
175	Jorge Campillo **RC**	6.00
176	Juan Morillo **RC**	4.00
177	Justin Wechsler **RC**	4.00
178	Keiichi Yabu **RC**	4.00
179	Kendry Morales **RC**	4.00
180	Luis Hernandez **RC**	4.00
181	Luis Mendoza **RC**	4.00
182	Luis Pena **RC**	4.00
183	Luis Rodriguez **RC**	4.00
184	Luke Scott **RC**	10.00
185	Marcos Carvajal **RC**	4.00
186	Mark Woodyard **RC**	4.00
187	Matt Smith **RC**	4.00
188	Matt Lindstrom **RC**	4.00
189	Miguel Negron **RC**	4.00
190	Mike Morse **RC**	4.00
191	Nate McLouth **RC**	10.00
192	Nick Masset **RC**	4.00
193	Paulino Reynoso **RC**	4.00
194	Pedro Lopez **RC**	4.00
195	Peter Orr **RC**	4.00
196	Randy Messenger **RC**	4.00
197	Randy Williams **RC**	4.00
198	Raul Tablado **RC**	4.00
199	Ronny Paulino **RC**	6.00
200	Russel Rohlicek **RC**	4.00
201	Russell Martin **RC**	15.00
202	Scott Baker **RC**	6.00
203	Scott Munter **RC**	4.00
204	Sean Thompson **RC**	4.00
205	Sean Tracey **RC**	4.00
206	Steve Schmoll **RC**	4.00
207	Tony Pena **RC**	4.00
208	Travis Bowyer **RC**	4.00
209	Ubaldo Jimenez **RC**	6.00
210	Wladimir Balentien **RC**	10.00
211	Yorman Bazardo **RC**	4.00
212	Yuniesky Betancourt **RC**	8.00
213	Adam Shabala **RC**	4.00
214	Brandon McCarthy **RC**	6.00
215	Chad Orvella **RC**	4.00
216	Jermaine Van Buren	4.00
217	Anthony Reyes **RC**	6.00
218	Dana Eveland **RC**	10.00
219	Brian Anderson	4.00
220	Hayden Penn **RC**	4.00
221	Chris Denorfia **RC**	4.00
222	Joel Peralta **RC**	4.00
223	Ryan Garko **RC**	10.00
224	Felix Hernandez	10.00
225	Mark McLemore **RC**	4.00
226	Melky Cabrera **RC**	10.00
227	Nelson Cruz **RC**	6.00
228	Norihiro Nakamura	6.00
229	Oscar Robles **RC**	4.00
230	Rick Short **RC**	4.00
231	Ryan Zimmerman **RC**	25.00
232	Ryan Speier **RC**	4.00
233	Ryan Spilborghs **RC**	8.00
234	Shane Costa **RC**	4.00
235	Zach Duke	6.00
236	Tony Giarratano **RC**	4.00
237	Jeff Niemann **RC**	10.00
238	Stephen Drew/Auto. **RC**	180.00
239	Justin Verlander/Auto. **RC**	250.00
240	Prince Fielder/Auto.	400.00
241	Philip Humber/Auto. **RC**	85.00
242	Tadahito Iguchi/Auto. **RC**	100.00

Silver

Silver (101-237): 1X-2X
Production 50 Sets

Baseball Star Signatures

		NM/M
Production 5-25		
JB	Jason Bay/25	25.00
AB	Adrian Beltre/15	25.00
CB	Craig Biggio/15	40.00
HB	Hank Blalock/15	25.00
BO	Jeremy Bonderman/25	25.00
MC	Miguel Cabrera/15	50.00
EC	Eric Chavez/15	25.00
WC	Will Clark/15	40.00
CC	Carl Crawford/25	20.00
CO	Coco Crisp/25	40.00
BC	Bobby Crosby/15	25.00
DA	Andre Dawson/15	25.00
RF	Rafael Furcal/20	25.00
BG	Brian Giles/15	20.00
DG	Dwight Gooden/25	25.00
GR	Khalil Greene/15	40.00
ZG	Zack Greinke/25	15.00
KG	Ken Griffey Jr./25	90.00
TR	Travis Hafner/25	25.00
RH	Rich Harden/25	20.00
KH	Keith Hernandez/15	25.00
TH	Tim Hudson/15	35.00
HU	Torii Hunter/15	25.00
SK	Scott Kazmir/25	25.00
BL	Barry Larkin/15	50.00
JO	Joe Mauer/15	50.00
PM	Paul Molitor/15	30.00
JM	Justin Morneau/25	30.00
MM	Mark Mulder/15	25.00
RO	Roy Oswalt/15	30.00
JP	Jake Peavy/20	30.00
WP	Wily Mo Pena/25	20.00
SP	Scott Podsednik/25	30.00
AR	Aramis Ramirez/20	30.00
JR	Jose Reyes/20	30.00
BR	Brian Roberts/25	20.00
BS	Ben Sheets/15	25.00
SM	John Smoltz/15	75.00
MT	Mark Teixeira/15	40.00
BU	B.J. Upton/25	25.00
JV	Jose Vidro/20	10.00
RW	Rickie Weeks/15	25.00
DW	Dontrelle Willis/15	40.00
WR	David Wright/15	100.00
MY	Michael Young/20	25.00
CZ	Carlos Zambrano/20	30.00

Dual Materials

		NM/M
Production 15 Sets		
Patch:		No Pricing
Production 10 Sets		
AC	Andruw Jones, Chipper Jones	25.00
AE	Adrian Beltre, Eric Chavez	10.00
AH	Adrian Beltre, Hank Blalock	10.00
AJ	Josh Beckett, A.J. Burnett	10.00
AM	Albert Pujols, Miguel Cabrera	40.00
AP	Bobby Abreu, Corey Patterson	10.00
AU	Bobby Abreu, Chase Utley	30.00
BC	Josh Beckett, Miguel Cabrera	20.00
BG	Vladimir Guerrero, Jason Bay	25.00
BH	Adrian Beltre, Felix Hernandez	40.00
BJ	Ben Sheets, Jake Peavy	15.00
BK	Bobby Crosby, Khalil Greene	20.00
BM	Jeremy Bonderman, Matt Cain	40.00
BS	Ryne Sandberg, Wade Boggs	40.00
BT	Mark Teixeira, Hank Blalock	25.00
BY	Michael Young, Hank Blalock	10.00
CB	Bobby Crosby, Jason Bay	10.00
CC	Eric Chavez, Bobby Crosby	10.00
CG	Vladimir Guerrero, Miguel Cabrera	25.00
CJ	Jeff Bagwell, Craig Biggio	25.00
CO	Roger Clemens, Roy Oswalt	40.00
CP	Carl Crawford, Scott Podsednik	20.00
CR	Scott Rolen, Eric Chavez	20.00
CT	Tony Gwynn, Cal Ripken Jr.	80.00
CW	Eric Chavez, David Wright	10.00
DG	Ken Griffey Jr., Adam Dunn	30.00
DJ	David Wright, Jose Reyes	30.00
DP	Adam Dunn, Wily Mo Pena	10.00
DR	Randy Johnson, Derek Jeter	50.00
FW	Rickie Weeks, Prince Fielder	30.00
GC	Ken Griffey Jr., Miguel Cabrera	35.00
GF	Rafael Furcal, Marcus Giles	10.00
GG	Brian Giles, Marcus Giles	10.00
GH	Ken Griffey Jr., Torii Hunter	30.00
GJ	Ken Griffey Jr., Derek Jeter	50.00
GL	Mark Loretta, Khalil Greene	20.00
GP	Ken Griffey Jr., Wily Mo Pena	30.00
GR	Eric Gagne, Francisco Rodriguez	10.00
HC	Felix Hernandez, Matt Cain	60.00
HH	Rich Harden, Danny Haren	10.00
HM	Travis Hafner, Victor Martinez	10.00
HO	Roy Oswalt, Rich Harden	10.00
HS	Ben Sheets, Rich Harden	15.00
JC	Randy Johnson, Roger Clemens	40.00
JF	Johan Santana, Felix Hernandez	35.00
JG	Ken Griffey Jr., Andruw Jones	30.00
JH	Andruw Jones, Torii Hunter	20.00
JJ	Derek Jeter, Reggie Jackson	50.00
JL	Barry Larkin, Derek Jeter	50.00
JO	Johan Santana, Oliver Perez	20.00
JR	Derek Jeter, Jose Reyes	50.00
JV	Victor Martinez, Joe Mauer	10.00
LG	Eric Gagne, Brad Lidge	10.00
LO	Roy Oswalt, Brad Lidge	10.00
LR	Brad Lidge, Francisco Rodriguez	10.00
ME	Johnny Estrada, Joe Mauer	10.00
MG	Greg Maddux, Mark Prior	30.00
MH	Mark Mulder, Tim Hudson	15.00
MJ	Randy Johnson, Pedro Martinez	25.00
MM	Justin Morneau, Joe Mauer	10.00
MP	Mark Prior, Joe Mauer	20.00
MR	Mike Mussina, Randy Johnson	25.00
NR	Randy Johnson, Nolan Ryan	50.00
OF	David Ortiz, Prince Fielder	30.00
PC	Roger Clemens, Mark Prior	40.00

PD Pedro Martinez, Dwight Gooden 20.00
PG Ken Griffey Jr., Albert Pujols 50.00
PH Jake Peavy, Rich Harden 15.00
PJ Derek Jeter, Albert Pujols 60.00
PL Derrek Lee, Albert Pujols 40.00
PM Mike Piazza, Pedro Martinez 25.00
PS Ben Sheets, Mark Prior 20.00
RB Aramis Ramirez, Hank Blalock 10.00
RC Roger Clemens, Nolan Ryan 50.00
RE Eric Chavez, Aramis Ramirez 10.00
RF Rafael Furcal, Jose Reyes 10.00
RG Brian Roberts, Marcus Giles 10.00
RJ Cal Ripken Jr., Derek Jeter 85.00
RL Derrek Lee, Aramis Ramirez 20.00
RP Aaron Rowand, Scott Podsednik 20.00
RR Aaron Rowand, Jeremy Reed 10.00
RS Cal Ripken Jr., Mike Schmidt 75.00
RT Cal Ripken Jr., Miguel Tejada 60.00
RU B.J. Upton, Jose Reyes 10.00
RW Aramis Ramirez, David Wright 30.00
SB Wade Boggs, Mike Schmidt 40.00
SC Roger Clemens, Johan Santana 30.00
SH John Smoltz, Tim Hudson 25.00
SJ Randy Johnson, Curt Schilling 25.00
SM Johan Santana, Joe Mauer 20.00
SO Curt Schilling, David Ortiz 25.00
SP Mark Prior, Johan Santana 20.00
SR Mike Schmidt, Scott Rolen 40.00
TC Mark Teixeira, Miguel Cabrera 20.00
UJ Derek Jeter, B.J. Upton 50.00
WR Scott Rolen, David Wright 35.00
ZH Carlos Zambrano, Rich Harden 10.00
ZO Roy Oswalt, Carlos Zambrano 10.00
ZP Carlos Zambrano, Oliver Perez 10.00

Dual Material Signatures
No Pricing
Production 10 Sets
Patch: No Pricing
Production Five Sets

Dual Signatures
NM/M
Production 25 Sets
RW Aramis Ramirez, David Wright 90.00
RP Aaron Rowand, Scott Podsednik 50.00
BB Jeff Bagwell, Craig Biggio 100.00
BC Adrian Beltre, Eric Chavez 35.00
BH Adrian Beltre, Felix Hernandez 125.00
BJ Bobby Crosby, Jason Bay 35.00
BT Mark Teixeira, Hank Blalock 50.00
BY Michael Young, Hank Blalock 30.00
CC Eric Chavez, Bobby Crosby 30.00
CG Bobby Crosby, Khalil Greene 40.00
CP Carl Crawford, Scott Podsednik 50.00
CT Tony Gwynn, Cal Ripken Jr. 180.00
CY Carl Crawford, Delmon Young 50.00
DG Ken Griffey Jr., Adam Dunn 100.00
DJ Derek Jeter, Jose Reyes 150.00
DK Ken Griffey Jr., Derek Jeter 220.00
DM Mike Schmidt, David Wright 100.00
DP Andre Dawson, Corey Patterson 35.00
FF Gavin Floyd, Jeff Francis 20.00
GC Ken Griffey Jr., Miguel Cabrera 120.00
GH Ken Griffey Jr., Torii Hunter 100.00
GJ Ken Griffey Jr., Andruw Jones 120.00
GL Mark Loretta, Khalil Greene 40.00
GP Ken Griffey Jr., Wily Mo Pena 100.00
GR Eric Gagne, Francisco Rodriguez 50.00
HH Rich Harden, Danny Haren 35.00
HM Travis Hafner, Victor Martinez 40.00
HO Roy Oswalt, Rich Harden 40.00
HS Ben Sheets, Rich Harden 40.00
JB Ben Sheets, Jake Peavy 35.00

JG Derek Jeter, Nomar Garciaparra 180.00
JH Andruw Jones, Torii Hunter 40.00
JJ Andruw Jones, Chipper Jones 120.00
JM Don Mattingly, Derek Jeter 250.00
JV Victor Martinez, Joe Mauer 35.00
KH Scott Kazmir, Felix Hernandez 125.00
LO Roy Oswalt, Brad Lidge 50.00
LR Brad Lidge, Francisco Rodriguez 50.00
MC Don Mattingly, Will Clark 100.00
MG Greg Maddux, Tom Glavine 150.00
MH Travis Hafner, Justin Morneau 35.00
MM Justin Morneau, Joe Mauer 40.00
MP Mark Prior, Joe Mauer 60.00
MT Mark Mulder, Tim Hudson 50.00
NH Philip Humber, Jeff Niemann 50.00
NK Scott Kazmir, Jeff Niemann 40.00
NV Justin Verlander, Jeff Niemann 65.00
PH Jake Peavy, Rich Harden 35.00
PJ Derek Jeter, Albert Pujols 500.00
PP Gaylord Perry, Jake Peavy 30.00
RB Aramis Ramirez, Hank Blalock 30.00
RC Roger Clemens, Nolan Ryan 220.00
RE Eric Chavez, Aramis Ramirez 40.00
RF Rafael Furcal, Jose Reyes 35.00
RJ Cal Ripken Jr., Derek Jeter 300.00
RL Derrek Lee, Aramis Ramirez 60.00
RP Aaron Rowand, Corey Patterson 30.00
RR Aaron Rowand, Jeremy Reed 30.00
RW Ryne Sandberg, Wade Boggs 100.00
SH John Smoltz, Tim Hudson 65.00
SJ Randy Johnson, Curt Schilling 80.00
SO Curt Schilling, David Ortiz 90.00
SP Ben Sheets, Mark Prior 50.00
SW Ben Sheets, Rickie Weeks 30.00
TC Mark Teixeira, Miguel Cabrera 75.00
UJ Derek Jeter, B.J. Upton 140.00
UW Rickie Weeks, B.J. Upton 25.00
WR David Wright, Jose Reyes 100.00
YU B.J. Upton, Delmon Young 50.00
YW Rickie Weeks, Delmon Young 40.00
ZH Carlos Zambrano, Rich Harden 35.00
ZO Roy Oswalt, Carlos Zambrano 35.00

Eight Star Signatures
No Pricing
Production Five Sets

Four Star Signatures
No Pricing
Production 15 Sets

Game Materials
NM/M
Production 25 Sets
Patch: 1X-2X
Production 5-25
No patch pricing 15 or less.
BA Bobby Abreu 10.00
JB Jeff Bagwell 10.00
JA Jason Bay 10.00
BE Josh Beckett 8.00
AB Adrian Beltre 8.00
CB Craig Biggio 10.00
HB Hank Blalock 8.00
BO Jeremy Bonderman 8.00
BU A.J. Burnett 8.00
CA Miguel Cabrera 15.00
MA Matt Cain 25.00
CW Rod Carew 25.00
SC Sean Casey 8.00
EC Eric Chavez 10.00
RC Roger Clemens 25.00
MC Matt Clement 8.00
CR Carl Crawford 8.00
CO Bobby Crosby 8.00
JD J.D. Drew 8.00
AD Adam Dunn 8.00
ES Johnny Estrada 8.00
PF Prince Fielder 30.00
GF Gavin Floyd 8.00
KF Keith Foulke 8.00
JF Jeff Francis 8.00
RF Rafael Furcal 8.00
EG Eric Gagne 10.00
BG Brian Giles 8.00
MG Marcus Giles 8.00
GR Khalil Greene 10.00
ZG Zack Greinke 8.00
KG Ken Griffey Jr. 25.00
VG Vladimir Guerrero 20.00

TR Travis Hafner 10.00
HA Roy Halladay 8.00
RH Rich Harden 8.00
FH Felix Hernandez 25.00
HO Trevor Hoffman 8.00
TH Tim Hudson 10.00
AH Aubrey Huff 8.00
HU Torii Hunter 8.00
TI Tadahito Iguchi 20.00
DJ Derek Jeter 30.00
RJ Randy Johnson 15.00
AJ Andruw Jones 10.00
SK Scott Kazmir 8.00
JK Jeff Kent 8.00
LE Derrek Lee 15.00
BL Brad Lidge 8.00
ML Mark Loretta 8.00
DL Derek Lowe 8.00
GM Greg Maddux 20.00
PM Pedro Martinez 15.00
VM Victor Martinez 8.00
JM Joe Mauer 8.00
MO Justin Morneau 8.00
MM Mark Mulder 8.00
DO David Ortiz 15.00
OS Roy Oswalt 8.00
RP Rafael Palmeiro 10.00
PA Corey Patterson 8.00
CP Carl Pavano 8.00
JP Jake Peavy 10.00
WP Wily Mo Pena 8.00
OP Oliver Perez 8.00
SP Scott Podsednik 10.00
MP Mark Prior 8.00
AP Albert Pujols 30.00
RA Aramis Ramirez 10.00
JR Jeremy Reed 8.00
ER Edgar Renteria 8.00
RE Jose Reyes 10.00
RI Cal Ripken Jr. 50.00
BR Brian Roberts 8.00
FR Francisco Rodriguez 8.00
SR Scott Rolen 12.00
AR Aaron Rowand 8.00
NR Nolan Ryan 30.00
CC C.C. Sabathia 8.00
RS Ryne Sandberg 30.00
SA Johan Santana 15.00
CS Curt Schilling 10.00
MS Mike Schmidt 30.00
BS Ben Sheets 10.00
GS Gary Sheffield 10.00
SM John Smoltz 10.00
MT Mark Teixeira 15.00
TE Miguel Tejada 10.00
BJ B.J. Upton 8.00
CU Chase Utley 15.00
JV Jose Vidro 8.00
TW Tim Wakefield 25.00
RW Rickie Weeks 10.00
JW Jake Westbrook 8.00
DW Dontrelle Willis 10.00
WR David Wright 30.00
MY Michael Young 8.00
CZ Carlos Zambrano 10.00

Material Signatures
NM/M
Production 25 Sets
Patch: No Pricing
Production 10 Sets
JB Jeff Bagwell 75.00
JA Jason Bay 30.00
BE Josh Beckett 35.00
AB Adrian Beltre 20.00
CB Craig Biggio 40.00
HB Hank Blalock 20.00
BO Jeremy Bonderman 20.00
CA Miguel Cabrera 35.00
CW Rod Carew 30.00
MC Matt Clement 25.00
CR Carl Crawford 25.00
BC Bobby Crosby 20.00
JD J.D. Drew 20.00
AD Adam Dunn 25.00
ES Johnny Estrada 15.00
GF Gavin Floyd 15.00
JF Jeff Francis 15.00
RF Rafael Furcal 20.00
EG Eric Gagne 20.00
BG Brian Giles 20.00
GR Khalil Greene 30.00
ZG Zack Greinke 15.00
KG Ken Griffey Jr. 120.00
VG Vladimir Guerrero 50.00
TR Travis Hafner 25.00
HA Roy Halladay 25.00
FH Felix Hernandez 100.00
TH Tim Hudson 35.00
AH Aubrey Huff 15.00
HU Torii Hunter 25.00
TI Tadahito Iguchi 100.00
DJ Derek Jeter 220.00
AJ Andruw Jones 40.00
SK Scott Kazmir 25.00
LA Barry Larkin 40.00
LE Derrek Lee 40.00
BL Brad Lidge 25.00
ML Mark Loretta 20.00
VM Victor Martinez 25.00
JM Joe Mauer 40.00
MO Justin Morneau 30.00
MM Mark Mulder 25.00
DO David Ortiz 50.00
OS Roy Oswalt 25.00

RP Rafael Palmeiro 35.00
JP Jake Peavy 25.00
WP Wily Mo Pena 20.00
SP Scott Podsednik 30.00
MP Mark Prior 40.00
RA Aramis Ramirez 25.00
JR Jeremy Reed 15.00
RE Jose Reyes 35.00
RI Cal Ripken Jr. 180.00
BR Brian Roberts 20.00
FR Francisco Rodriguez 25.00
NR Nolan Ryan 100.00
RS Ryne Sandberg 75.00
MS Mike Schmidt 60.00
BS Ben Sheets 25.00
GS Gary Sheffield 35.00
SM John Smoltz 50.00
MT Mark Teixeira 50.00
TE Miguel Tejada 40.00
BJ B.J. Upton 25.00
CU Chase Utley 40.00
JV Jose Vidro 15.00
TW Tim Wakefield 75.00
RW Rickie Weeks 15.00
JW Jake Westbrook 15.00
DW Dontrelle Willis 35.00
WR David Wright 90.00
MY Michael Young 25.00
CZ Carlos Zambrano 25.00

Hurler Materials
NM/M
Production 20 Sets
Patch: 1X-2X
Production 2-25
No pack pricing 15 or less.
BE Josh Beckett 8.00
JB Joe Blanton 8.00
BO Jeremy Bonderman 8.00
AB A.J. Burnett 8.00
MA Matt Cain 30.00
CA Chris Carpenter 8.00
RC Roger Clemens 25.00
MC Matt Clement 8.00
GF Gavin Floyd 8.00
KF Keith Foulke 8.00
JF Jeff Francis 8.00
EG Eric Gagne 10.00
TG Tom Glavine 8.00
DG Dwight Gooden 8.00
HA Roy Halladay 8.00
RH Rich Harden 10.00
DH Danny Haren 8.00
FH Felix Hernandez 30.00
LH Livan Hernandez 8.00
HO Trevor Hoffman 8.00
TH Tim Hudson 10.00
RJ Randy Johnson 15.00
SK Scott Kazmir 8.00
BL Brad Lidge 8.00
DL Derek Lowe 8.00
GM Greg Maddux 20.00
PM Pedro Martinez 15.00
MM Mark Mulder 10.00
MU Mike Mussina 8.00
BM Brett Myers 8.00
RO Roy Oswalt 10.00
CP Carl Pavano 8.00
JP Jake Peavy 8.00
OP Odalis Perez 8.00
PE Oliver Perez 8.00
GP Gaylord Perry 8.00
MP Mark Prior 15.00
FR Francisco Rodriguez 8.00
NR1 Nolan Ryan 30.00
NR2 Nolan Ryan 8.00
CC C.C. Sabathia 8.00
JS Johan Santana 15.00
BS Ben Sheets 10.00
CS Curt Schilling 15.00
SM John Smoltz 10.00
TW Tim Wakefield 25.00
JW Jake Westbrook 8.00
DW Dontrelle Willis 10.00
KW Kerry Wood 10.00
CZ Carlos Zambrano 10.00

Hurler Material Signatures
NM/M
No Pricing
Production 20 Sets
Patch: No Pricing
Production 10 Sets
BE Josh Beckett 25.00
JB Joe Blanton 15.00
BO Jeremy Bonderman 25.00
CA Chris Carpenter 40.00
MC Matt Clement 25.00
GF Gavin Floyd 15.00
JF Jeff Francis 15.00
EG Eric Gagne 25.00
DG Dwight Gooden 25.00
HA Roy Halladay 25.00
DH Danny Haren 20.00
FH Felix Hernandez 100.00
LH Livan Hernandez 25.00
TH Tim Hudson 35.00
SK Scott Kazmir 25.00
BL Brad Lidge 30.00
MM Mark Mulder 25.00
MU Mike Mussina 50.00
BM Brett Myers 15.00
RO Roy Oswalt 25.00
JP Jake Peavy 25.00
GP Gaylord Perry 25.00

MP Mark Prior 30.00
FR Francisco Rodriguez 25.00
NR1 Nolan Ryan 100.00
NR2 Nolan Ryan 100.00
BS Ben Sheets 25.00
SM John Smoltz 50.00
TW Tim Wakefield 75.00
JW Jake Westbrook 15.00
DW Dontrelle Willis 40.00
KW Kerry Wood 30.00
CZ Carlos Zambrano 25.00

Quad Materials

Production 10 Sets
Patch: No Pricing
Production Five Sets

Signatures

NM/M

Production 10-99
Platinum: No Pricing
Production Five Sets
JE Jeff Bagwell/15 60.00
BA Jason Bay/69 25.00
BE Josh Beckett/35 30.00
AB Adrian Beltre/69 20.00
JB Johnny Bench/15 50.00
CB Craig Biggio 40.00
HB Hank Blalock/69 20.00
WB Wade Boggs/15 50.00
MC Miguel Cabrera/69 40.00
CW Rod Carew/35 30.00
GC Gary Carter/35 30.00
EC Eric Chavez/52 25.00
WC Will Clark/69 35.00
CO Coco Crisp/69 50.00
BC Bobby Crosby/69 25.00
JD J.D. Drew/29 20.00
SD Stephen Drew/69 180.00
AD Adam Dunn/35 25.00
PF Prince Fielder/35 100.00
CF Carlton Fisk/15 40.00
EG Eric Gagne/35 25.00
GR Khalil Greene/69 30.00
ZG Zack Greinke/69 15.00
KG Ken Griffey Jr./69 80.00
GW Tony Gwynn/25 50.00
TR Travis Hafner/69 20.00
HA Roy Halladay/35 25.00
RH Rich Harden/69 20.00
FH Felix Hernandez/69 80.00
TH Tim Hudson/69 30.00
PH Philip Humber/69 15.00
HU Torii Hunter/69 20.00
TI Tadahito Iguchi/69 85.00
BJ Bo Jackson/35 50.00
JO Andruw Jones/35 40.00
SK Scott Kazmir/69 25.00
BL Barry Larkin/69 50.00
VM Victor Martinez/69 20.00
MA Don Mattingly/25 90.00
JM Joe Mauer/69 25.00
PM Paul Molitor/49 30.00
KM Kendry Morales/69 60.00
MM Mark Mulder/69 20.00
MU Mike Mussina/15 50.00
JN Jeff Niemann/69 25.00
DO David Ortiz/35 50.00
RO Roy Oswalt/69 20.00
RP Rafael Palmeiro/25 35.00
JP Jake Peavy/69 25.00
MP Mark Prior/15 35.00
AR Aramis Ramirez/69 25.00
JR Jose Reyes/69 35.00
BR Brian Roberts/35 20.00
RS Ryne Sandberg/15 90.00
MS Mike Schmidt/25 60.00
BS Ben Sheets/69 20.00
GS Gary Sheffield/25 35.00
OS Ozzie Smith/35 50.00
SM John Smoltz/49 50.00
MT Mark Teixeira/99 35.00
BU B.J. Upton/69 20.00
JV Justin Verlander/69 80.00
RW Rickie Weeks/30 20.00
DW Dontrelle Willis/69 35.00
KW Kerry Wood/15 40.00
WR David Wright/69 75.00
MY Michael Young/69 20.00
RY Robin Yount/15 50.00
CZ Carlos Zambrano/69 30.00

Six Star Signatures

No Pricing
Production 10 Sets

Slugger Material

NM/M

Production 20 Sets
Patch: 1X-2X
Production 19-25
BA Bobby Abreu 8.00
JB Jeff Bagwell 10.00
JA Jason Bay 10.00
AB Adrian Beltre 8.00
CB Craig Biggio 10.00
HB Hank Blalock 8.00
MC Miguel Cabrera 15.00
CA Rod Carew 15.00
SC Sean Casey 8.00
EC Eric Chavez 8.00
CC Carl Crawford 10.00
CO Coco Crisp 10.00
BC Bobby Crosby 8.00
JD J.D. Drew 8.00
AD Adam Dunn 10.00
ES Johnny Estrada 8.00
RF Rafael Furcal 8.00
BG Brian Giles 8.00
MG Marcus Giles 8.00
GR Khalil Greene 10.00
KG Ken Griffey Jr. 25.00
VG Vladimir Guerrero 15.00
HA Travis Hafner 10.00
RH Ryan Howard 20.00
AH Aubrey Huff 8.00
TH Torii Hunter 8.00
CJ Derek Jeter 30.00
CJ Chipper Jones 15.00
JK Jeff Kent 8.00
DL Derrek Lee 15.00
ML Mark Loretta 8.00
VM Victor Martinez 8.00
MA Joe Mauer 8.00
JM Justin Morneau 8.00
DO David Ortiz 20.00
RP Rafael Palmeiro 10.00
CP Corey Patterson 8.00
WP Wily Mo Pena 8.00
AP Albert Pujols 30.00
AR Aramis Ramirez 10.00
ER Edgar Renteria 8.00
JR Jose Reyes 10.00
BR Brian Roberts 8.00
SR Scott Rolen 12.00
GS Gary Sheffield 10.00
MT Mark Teixeira 15.00
JV Jose Vidro 8.00
DW David Wright 30.00
MY Michael Young 10.00

Slugger Material Signatures

NM/M

Production 20 Sets
Patch: No Pricing
Production 3-10
JB Jeff Bagwell 75.00
JA Jason Bay 30.00
AB Adrian Beltre 20.00
CB Craig Biggio 40.00
HB Hank Blalock 20.00
MC Miguel Cabrera 40.00
CA Rod Carew 30.00
EC Eric Chavez 25.00
BC Bobby Crosby 20.00
JD J.D. Drew 20.00
AD Adam Dunn 25.00
ES Johnny Estrada 20.00
RF Rafael Furcal 20.00
BG Brian Giles 20.00
GR Khalil Greene 30.00
KG Ken Griffey Jr. 120.00
HA Travis Hafner 25.00
RH Ryan Howard 90.00
AH Aubrey Huff 15.00
TH Torii Hunter 25.00
CJ Derek Jeter 220.00
CJ Chipper Jones 50.00
DL Derrek Lee 40.00
ML Mark Loretta 20.00
VM Victor Martinez 20.00
MA Joe Mauer 30.00
JM Justin Morneau 25.00
DO David Ortiz 50.00
RP Rafael Palmeiro 35.00
WP Wily Mo Pena 20.00
AR Aramis Ramirez 25.00
JR Jose Reyes 25.00
BR Brian Roberts 20.00
GS Gary Sheffield 35.00
MT Mark Teixeira 50.00
JV Jose Vidro 15.00
DW David Wright 90.00
MY Michael Young 25.00

Three Star Signatures

No Pricing
Production 20 Sets

Triple Materials

No Pricing
Production 15 Sets
Patch: No Pricing
Production 10 Sets

Veteran Materials

NM/M

Production 20 Sets
Patch: 1X-2X
Production 7-30
No patch pricing 15 or less.
BA Bobby Abreu 10.00
JB Jeff Bagwell 12.00
BE Josh Beckett 8.00
AB Adrian Beltre 8.00
CB Craig Biggio 10.00
HB Hank Blalock 8.00
CA Rod Carew 15.00
SC Sean Casey 8.00
EC Eric Chavez 10.00
RC Roger Clemens 25.00
MC Matt Clement 8.00
JD J.D. Drew 8.00
AD Adam Dunn 10.00
KF Keith Foulke 8.00
EG Eric Gagne 10.00
BG Brian Giles 8.00
KG Ken Griffey Jr. 25.00
VG Vladimir Guerrero 20.00
RH Roy Halladay 10.00
LH Livan Hernandez 8.00
HO Trevor Hoffman 8.00
TH Tim Hudson 10.00
AH Aubrey Huff 8.00
HU Torii Hunter 8.00
DJ Derek Jeter 30.00
RJ Randy Johnson 15.00
AJ Andruw Jones 12.00
JK Jeff Kent 8.00
LE Derrek Lee 15.00
ML Mark Loretta 8.00
DL Derek Lowe 8.00
GM Greg Maddux 20.00
MM Mark Mulder 8.00
BM Brett Myers 8.00
DO David Ortiz 15.00
RO Roy Oswalt 10.00
OP Odalis Perez 8.00
MP Mark Prior 10.00
AR Aramis Ramirez 10.00
ER Edgar Renteria 8.00
CR Cal Ripken Jr. 50.00
SR Scott Rolen 12.00
NR Nolan Ryan 30.00
CS C.C. Sabathia 8.00
AS Alfonso Soriano 10.00
SM John Smoltz 15.00
MT Miguel Tejada 10.00
JV Jose Vidro 8.00
TW Tim Wakefield 25.00
DW Dontrelle Willis 10.00

Veteran Material Signatures

NM/M

Production 20 Sets
Patch: No Pricing
Production 10 Sets
JB Jeff Bagwell 75.00
BE Josh Beckett 35.00
AB Adrian Beltre 20.00
CB Craig Biggio 40.00
HB Hank Blalock 20.00
CA Rod Carew 35.00
EC Eric Chavez 25.00
MC Matt Clement 25.00
JD J.D. Drew 20.00
AD Adam Dunn 25.00
EG Eric Gagne 25.00
BG Brian Giles 20.00
KG Ken Griffey Jr. 120.00
VG Vladimir Guerrero 50.00
RH Roy Halladay 30.00
LH Livan Hernandez 20.00
TH Tim Hudson 35.00
AH Aubrey Huff 15.00
HU Torii Hunter 25.00
DJ Derek Jeter 220.00
AJ Andruw Jones 40.00
LE Derrek Lee 40.00
ML Mark Loretta 20.00
MM Mark Mulder 25.00
BM Brett Myers 15.00
DO David Ortiz 50.00
RO Roy Oswalt 25.00
MP Mark Prior 40.00
AR Aramis Ramirez 25.00
CR Cal Ripken Jr. 180.00
NR Nolan Ryan 100.00
SM John Smoltz 50.00
MT Miguel Tejada 40.00
JV Jose Vidro 15.00
TW Tim Wakefield 75.00
DW Dontrelle Willis 35.00

Young Star Materials

NM/M

Production 20 Sets
Patch: 1X-2X
Production 6-30
No patch pricing 15 or less.
BA Jason Bay 12.00
JB Joe Blanton 8.00
BO Jeremy Bonderman 8.00
AB A.J. Burnett 8.00
MC Miguel Cabrera 15.00
MA Matt Cain 30.00
CC Carl Crawford 10.00
CO Coco Crisp 10.00
BC Bobby Crosby 8.00
JE Johnny Estrada 8.00
PF Prince Fielder 30.00
GF Gavin Floyd 8.00
JF Jeff Francis 8.00
RF Rafael Furcal 8.00
MG Marcus Giles 8.00
KG Khalil Greene 12.00
ZG Zack Greinke 8.00
TH Travis Hafner 10.00
RH Rich Harden 10.00
DH Danny Haren 8.00
FH Felix Hernandez 35.00
HO Ryan Howard 25.00
TI Tadahito Iguchi 25.00
SK Scott Kazmir 8.00
BL Brad Lidge 8.00
VM Victor Martinez 10.00
JM Joe Mauer 10.00
MO Justin Morneau 8.00
PA Corey Patterson 8.00
CP Carl Pavano 8.00
JP Jake Peavy 10.00
WP Wily Mo Pena 10.00
OP Oliver Perez 8.00
SP Scott Podsednik 10.00
JR Jeremy Reed 8.00
RE Jose Reyes 10.00
BR Brian Roberts 10.00
FR Francisco Rodriguez 10.00
AR Aaron Rowand 8.00
JS Johan Santana 15.00
BS Ben Sheets 10.00
MT Mark Teixeira 15.00
BU B.J. Upton 10.00
CU Chase Utley 25.00
RW Rickie Weeks 10.00
JW Jake Westbrook 8.00
DW David Wright 30.00
MY Michael Young 10.00
CZ Carlos Zambrano 10.00

Young Star Material Sign.

NM/M

Production 20 Sets
Patch: No Pricing
Production 10 Sets
BA Jason Bay 30.00
JB Joe Blanton 20.00
BO Jeremy Bonderman 20.00
MA Matt Cain 125.00
CC Carl Crawford 25.00
BC Bobby Crosby 25.00
JE Johnny Estrada 15.00
GF Gavin Floyd 20.00
JF Jeff Francis 15.00
RF Rafael Furcal 20.00
KG Khalil Greene 35.00
ZG Zack Greinke 15.00
TH Travis Hafner 20.00
DH Danny Haren 15.00
TI Tadahito Iguchi 140.00
SK Scott Kazmir 20.00
BL Brad Lidge 40.00
VM Victor Martinez 25.00
JM Joe Mauer 25.00
JP Jake Peavy 25.00
WP Wily Mo Pena 25.00
SP Scott Podsednik 30.00
JR Jeremy Reed 15.00
RE Jose Reyes 25.00
BR Brian Roberts 25.00
FR Francisco Rodriguez 25.00
AR Aaron Rowand 25.00
BS Ben Sheets 25.00
MT Mark Teixeira 50.00
BU B.J. Upton 20.00
RW Rickie Weeks 15.00
JW Jake Westbrook 15.00
DW David Wright 90.00
MY Michael Young 20.00
CZ Carlos Zambrano 30.00

2005 UD Ultimate Signature Edition

NM/M

Complete Set (110):
Common (1-100): 2.00
Production 825
Common (101-110): 8.00
Production 225
Tin (3): 85.00
1 Al Kaline 4.00
2 Babe Ruth 10.00
3 Billy Williams 2.00

4 Bob Feller 2.00
5 Bob Gibson 3.00
6 Brooks Robinson 3.00
7 Carlton Fisk 2.00
8 Cy Young 3.00
9 Dizzy Dean 3.00
10 Don Drysdale 2.00
11 Eddie Mathews 4.00
12 Enos Slaughter 2.00
13 Ernie Banks 5.00
14 Fergie Jenkins 2.00
15 Eddie Murray 3.00
16 Harmon Killebrew 4.00
17 Honus Wagner 3.00
18 Jackie Robinson 5.00
19 Jimmie Foxx 4.00
20 Joe DiMaggio 6.00
21 Joe Morgan 2.00
22 Juan Marichal 2.00
23 Larry Doby 2.00
24 Jim Palmer 2.00
25 Johnny Bench 4.00
26 Lou Brock 2.00
27 Lou Gehrig 6.00
28 Mel Ott 3.00
29 Mickey Cochrane 2.00
30 Mickey Mantle 12.00
31 Mike Schmidt 5.00
32 Nolan Ryan 8.00
33 Pee Wee Reese 2.00
34 Phil Rizzuto 3.00
35 Ralph Kiner 2.00
36 Robin Yount 3.00
37 Ozzie Smith 4.00
38 Roy Campanella 3.00
39 Satchel Paige 4.00
40 Stan Musial 5.00
41 Ted Williams 8.00
42 Thurman Munson 4.00
43 Tom Seaver 3.00
44 Ty Cobb 4.00
45 Walter Johnson 3.00
46 Warren Spahn 4.00
47 Whitey Ford 3.00
48 Willie McCovey 3.00
49 Willie Stargell 3.00
50 Yogi Berra 4.00
51 Adrian Beltre 8.00
52 Albert Pujols 6.00
53 Alex Rodriguez 3.00
54 Alfonso Soriano 2.00
55 Andruw Jones 2.00
56 B.J. Upton 2.00
57 Ben Sheets 2.00
58 Bret Boone 2.00
59 Brian Giles 2.00
60 Carlos Beltran 3.00
61 Carlos Delgado 2.00
62 Chipper Jones 4.00
63 Curt Schilling 4.00
64 David Ortiz 4.00
65 Derek Jeter 8.00
66 Eric Chavez 2.00
67 Frank Thomas 3.00
68 Gary Sheffield 2.00
69 Greg Maddux 5.00
70 Hank Blalock 2.00
71 Hideki Matsui 6.00
72 Ichiro Suzuki 6.00
73 Ivan Rodriguez 3.00
74 Jason Schmidt 2.00
75 Jeff Bagwell 2.00
76 Jim Thome 3.00
77 Johnny Damon 4.00
78 Jose Vidro 2.00
79 Ken Griffey Jr. 5.00
80 Kerry Wood 3.00
81 Manny Ramirez 4.00
82 Mark Prior 2.00
83 Mark Teixeira 2.00
84 Miguel Cabrera 3.00
85 Miguel Tejada 3.00
86 Mike Mussina 2.00
87 Mike Piazza 4.00
88 Mike Sweeney 2.00
89 Oliver Perez 2.00
90 Pedro Martinez 4.00
91 Rafael Palmeiro 3.00
92 Randy Johnson 4.00
93 Roger Clemens 8.00
94 Sammy Sosa 5.00
95 Scott Rolen 3.00
96 Tim Hudson 2.00
97 Todd Helton 2.00
98 Torii Hunter 2.00
99 Victor Martinez 2.00
100 Vladimir Guerrero 4.00
101 Adrian Gonzalez 8.00
102 Ambiorix Burgos **RC** 25.00
103 Ambiorix Concepcion **RC** 20.00
104 Dan Meyer 15.00
105 Ervin Santana 25.00
106 Gavin Floyd 20.00
107 Joe Blanton 20.00
108 Eric Crozier 10.00
109 Mark Teahen 25.00
110 Ryan Howard 50.00

Platinum

Cards (101-110):
Production One Set

Immortal Inscriptions

NM/M

Production 10-99
Platinum: No Pricing
Production One Set
WB Wade Boggs/75 80.00
JB Jim Bunning/99 60.00
SC Steve Carlton/99 40.00
WC Will Clark/99 60.00
EG Eric Gagne/99 80.00
KG Ken Griffey Jr./99 200.00
TG Tony Gwynn/50 140.00
DM Don Mattingly/75 150.00
TS Tom Seaver/25 90.00
OS Ozzie Smith/75 80.00
FT Frank Thomas/50 100.00

Signature Cuts

Production One Set
No Pricing

Signature Cy Young

NM/M

Production 1-250
CM David Cone, Greg Maddux/35 150.00
EG Eric Gagne, Dennis Eckersley/200 50.00
ES Dennis Eckersley, Bruce Sutter/250 30.00
GF Ron Guidry, Whitey Ford/250 65.00
GM Bob Gibson, Denny McLain/175 40.00
LC Sparky Lyle, Steve Carlton/250 30.00
MS Tom Seaver, Denny McLain 50.00
NF Don Newcombe, Whitey Ford 60.00
PC Gaylord Perry, Steve Carlton/250 40.00
PS Jim Palmer, Tom Seaver/100 75.00

Signature Decades

NM/M

Some not priced due to scarcity.
Platinum: No Pricing
Production One Set
LA Luis Aparicio 20.00
LA1 Luis Aparicio 20.00
CB Carlos Beltran/99 35.00
YB Yogi Berra/25 80.00
WB Wade Boggs/25 65.00
WB1 Wade Boggs/25 65.00
LB Lou Brock/50 35.00
JB Jim Bunning 20.00
MC Miguel Cabrera 30.00
JC Jose Canseco/99 40.00
SC Steve Carlton 20.00
SC1 Steve Carlton 20.00
GC Gary Carter/50 25.00
OC Orlando Cepeda 15.00
WC Will Clark/99 40.00
RC Rocky Colavito 50.00
RC1 Rocky Colavito 50.00
AD Andre Dawson 15.00
BD Bobby Doerr 15.00
DE Dennis Eckersley 25.00
BF Bob Feller 25.00
RF Rollie Fingers 15.00
KG Ken Griffey Jr. 65.00
RG Ron Guidry 25.00
KH Keith Hernandez 10.00
KH1 Keith Hernandez 10.00
MI Monte Irvin 20.00
BJ Bo Jackson/50 60.00
FJ Fergie Jenkins/50 20.00
DJ Derek Jeter/99 160.00
AK Al Kaline/99 30.00
GK George Kell 15.00
HK Harmon Killebrew/99 40.00
RK Ralph Kiner/99 30.00
DL Don Larsen/99 25.00
FL Fred Lynn 15.00
JM Juan Marichal/99 25.00
DM Don Mattingly/25 85.00
BM Bill Mazeroski/99 40.00
PM Paul Molitor/99 25.00
MO Joe Morgan/50 25.00
MU Dale Murphy 25.00
DN Don Newcombe/99 20.00
PN Phil Niekro 20.00
DO David Ortiz 40.00
RO Roy Oswalt 15.00
JP Jim Palmer 20.00
TP Tony Perez 25.00
GP Gaylord Perry 15.00
GP1 Gaylord Perry 15.00
JR Jim Rice 20.00
BR Brooks Robinson 30.00
FR Frank Robinson/25 40.00
AR Al Rosen 15.00
JS Johan Santana 40.00
RS Ron Santo 25.00
BS Ben Sheets 15.00
SU Don Sutton 15.00
MT Mark Teixeira 25.00
LT Luis Tiant 15.00
LT1 Luis Tiant 15.00
BU B.J. Upton 15.00
RW Rickie Weeks 20.00
BW Billy Williams 20.00
MW Maury Wills 15.00
RY Robin Yount/25 70.00

Signature Hits

NM/M

Production 1-125
BM Stan Musial, Lou Brock/35 125.00
MY Robin Yount, Paul Molitor/125 75.00
WG Dave Winfield, Tony Gwynn/35 90.00
YB Wade Boggs, Carl Yastrzemski/35 100.00

Signature HRs

NM/M

Production 1-250
BS Mike Schmidt, Ernie Banks/25 180.00
GM Ken Griffey Jr., Willie McCovey/250 100.00
KM Willie McCovey, Harmon Killebrew/35 75.00
RG Frank Robinson, Ken Griffey Jr./250 85.00

Signature MVPs

NM/M

Production 1-250
BM Don Mattingly, Yogi Berra/175 100.00
BS Ernie Banks, Ryne Sandberg/25 200.00
CM Stan Musial, Orlando Cepeda/100 75.00
DS Ryne Sandberg, Andre Dawson/175 80.00
EF Dennis Eckersley, Rollie Fingers/250 30.00
FC George Foster, Rod Carew/125 40.00
GM Joe Morgan, Ken Griffey Jr./250 75.00
HY Robin Yount, Keith Hernandez/200 50.00
JR Ivan Rodriguez, Chipper Jones/35 125.00
KC Harmon Killebrew, Rod Carew/100 80.00
KM Harmon Killebrew, Willie McCovey/35 80.00
LM Fred Lynn, Joe Morgan/200 30.00
LW Maury Wills, Barry Larkin/250 35.00
MB Joe Morgan, Johnny Bench/100 60.00
MG Denny McLain, Bob Gibson/175 40.00
MY Robin Yount, Dale Murphy/175 60.00
PR Dave Parker, Jim Rice/250 40.00
SF Mike Schmidt, Rollie Fingers/175 60.00
SS Mike Schmidt, Ryne Sandberg/75 140.00
TB Frank Thomas, Jeff Bagwell/50 90.00
YC Orlando Cepeda, Carl Yastrzemski/100 65.00
YS Carl Yastrzemski, Jim Rice/100 75.00

Signature No-Hitters

NM/M

Production 1-250
BG Bob Gibson, Jim Bunning/125 60.00
CL Don Larsen, David Cone/250 40.00
FR Nolan Ryan, Bob Feller/25 150.00
GP Bob Gibson, Jim Palmer/125 50.00

Signature Numbers

NM/M

Production 1-49
Platinum: No Pricing
Production One Set
WB Wade Boggs/26 40.00
MC Miguel Cabrera/24 50.00
JC Jose Canseco/33 50.00
CA Rod Carew/29 35.00
SC Steve Carlton/32 25.00
OC Orlando Cepeda/30 25.00
WC Will Clark/22 60.00
CL Roger Clemens/22 200.00
RF Rollie Fingers/34 20.00
CF Carlton Fisk/27 40.00
EG Eric Gagne/38 40.00
BG Bob Gibson/45 25.00
GL Tom Glavine/47 40.00
KG Ken Griffey Jr./30 125.00
VG Vladimir Guerrero/27 50.00
RG Ron Guidry/49 60.00
TG Tony Gwynn/19 80.00
MI Monte Irvin/20 30.00
FJ Fergie Jenkins/31 20.00
MA Juan Marichal/27 40.00
DM Don Mattingly/23 125.00
WM Willie McCovey/44 40.00
EM Eddie Murray/33 120.00
DO David Ortiz/34 50.00
RO Roy Oswalt/44 25.00
JP Jim Palmer/22 30.00
PI Mike Piazza/31 100.00
MP Mark Prior/22 60.00
KP Kirby Puckett/34 85.00
FR Frank Robinson/20 50.00
SR Scott Rolen/27 40.00
NR Nolan Ryan/34 120.00
TS Tom Seaver/41 75.00
JS John Smoltz/29 60.00
FT Frank Thomas/35 80.00
BW Billy Williams/26 30.00
DW Dave Winfield/31 35.00
KW Kerry Wood/34 40.00
RY Robin Yount/19 75.00

Signature ROYs

NM/M

Production 1-250
CM Willie McCovey, Orlando Cepeda/75 65.00
CS Rod Carew, Tom Seaver/25 100.00
DM Andre Dawson, Eddie Murray/25 70.00
FB Carlton Fisk, Johnny Bench/35 80.00
FL Fred Lynn/125, Carlton Fisk/125 60.00
GR Nomar Garciaparra, Scott Rolen/200 85.00
GS Dwight Gooden, Tom Seaver/100 60.00
JG Derek Jeter, Nomar Garciaparra/75 185.00
RA Frank Robinson, Luis Aparicio/125 50.00
RJ Derek Jeter, Cal Ripken Jr./75 300.00
SG Dwight Gooden, Darryl Strawberry/250 40.00
WD Andre Dawson, Billy Williams/250 30.00

Signature Supremacy

NM/M

Production 15-99
LA Luis Aparicio/50 40.00
JB Jeff Bagwell 75.00
CB Carlos Beltran/50 30.00
BE Johnny Bench/25 60.00
YB Yogi Berra/25 60.00
HB Hank Blalock/50 25.00
WB Wade Boggs/25 60.00
LB Lou Brock/25 40.00
BU Jim Bunning/99 25.00
MC Miguel Cabrera/99 40.00
JC Jose Canseco/25 60.00
CA Rod Carew/25 35.00
SC Steve Carlton/99 25.00
OC Orlando Cepeda/99 20.00
EC Eric Chavez/99 15.00
WC Will Clark/50 40.00
AD Andre Dawson/99 20.00
BD Bobby Doerr/99 20.00
BF Bob Feller/99 25.00
RF Rollie Fingers/99 15.00
CF Carlton Fisk/25 40.00
EG Eric Gagne/50 25.00
KG Ken Griffey Jr./99 80.00
RG Ron Guidry/99 20.00
TH Tim Hudson/50 25.00
MI Monte Irvin/99 20.00
DJ Derek Jeter/50 200.00
AK Al Kaline/50 60.00
GK George Kell/99 25.00
HK Harmon Killebrew/50 40.00
RK Ralph Kiner/25 40.00
JU Juan Marichal/25 50.00
MA Don Mattingly/25 80.00
BM Bill Mazeroski/50 40.00
PM Paul Molitor/50 40.00
JM Joe Morgan/25 30.00
MM Mark Mulder/99 15.00
DM Dale Murphy/99 25.00
MU Stan Musial/25 125.00
DN Don Newcombe/99 20.00
DO David Ortiz/99 40.00
RO Roy Oswalt/99 15.00
JP Jim Palmer/99 25.00
TP Tony Perez/99 25.00
MP Mark Prior/25 60.00
JR Jim Rice/99 15.00
RR Robin Roberts/99 30.00
BR Brooks Robinson/99 30.00
FR Frank Robinson/25 40.00
SR Scott Rolen/25 50.00
AR Al Rosen/99 25.00
SA Ryne Sandberg/25 85.00
JS Johan Santana/99 40.00
RS Ron Santo 25.00
MS Mike Schmidt/25 100.00

TS Tom Seaver/25 50.00
BS Ben Sheets/99 20.00
OS Ozzie Smith/25 50.00
SM John Smoltz/50 50.00
AS Alfonso Soriano/25 40.00
MT Mark Teixeira/99 25.00
FT Frank Thomas/25 80.00
BW Billy Williams/99 25.00
DW Dave Winfield/25 40.00
CY Carl Yastrzemski/25 100.00
RY Robin Yount/25 75.00

Signs of October

NM/M

Production 1-250
BW Mookie Wilson, Bill Buckner/250 40.00
CS John Smoltz, Joe Carter/250 50.00
EG Kirk Gibson, Dennis Eckersley/200 40.00
FM Carlton Fisk, Joe Morgan/100 50.00
GB Bob Gibson, Lou Brock/100 70.00
GG Ron Guidry, Steve Garvey/250 30.00
GL Mickey Lolich, Bob Gibson/100 40.00
JG Derek Jeter, Tony Gwynn/250 185.00
LB Yogi Berra, Don Larsen/250 85.00
MP Jack Morris, Kirby Puckett/100 85.00
PS Ozzie Smith, Kirby Puckett/35 125.00
RR Frank Robinson, Brooks Robinson/250 65.00
SB George Brett, Ozzie Smith 150.00
SY Ozzie Smith, Robin Yount/100 85.00
TG Kirk Gibson, Alan Trammell/250 40.00

2006 Upper Deck

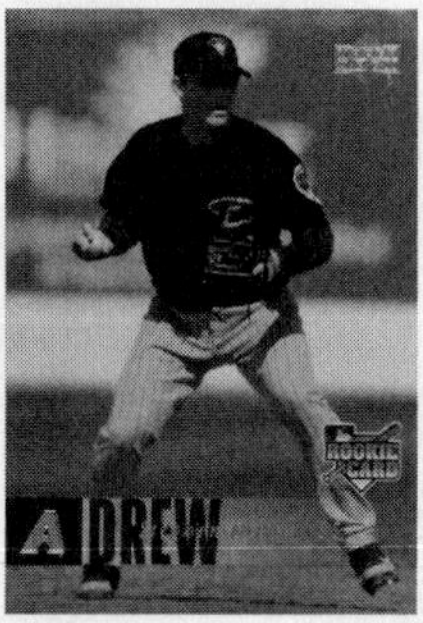

NM/M

Complete Series 1 (500): 150.00
Complete Series 2 (500): 100.00
Complete Update (250):
Common Player: .15
Common Update SP: 4.00
Inserted 1:2 Update
Series 1 Pack (8): 3.00
Series 1 Box (24): 60.00
Series 2 Pack (6): 3.00
Series 2 Box (24): 60.00
Update Pack (8): 3.00
Update Box (24): 60.00

1 Adam Kennedy .15
2 Bartolo Colon .25
3 Bengie Molina .15
4 Casey Kotchman .15
5 Chone Figgins .25
6 Dallas McPherson .15
7 Darin Erstad .25
8 Ervin Santana .25
9 Francisco Rodriguez .15
10 Garret Anderson .25
11 Jarrod Washburn .15
12 John Lackey .25
13 Juan Rivera .15
14 Orlando Cabrera .25
15 Paul Byrd .15
16 Steve Finley .15
17 Vladimir Guerrero .75
18 Alex Cintron .15
19 Brandon Lyon .15
20 Brandon Webb .50
21 Chad Tracy .15
22 Chris Snyder .15
23 Claudio Vargas .15
24 Conor Jackson **(RC)** .50
25 Craig Counsell .15
26 Javier Vazquez .15
27 Jose Valverde .15
28 Luis Gonzalez .15
29 Royce Clayton .15
30 Russ Ortiz .15
31 Shawn Green .15
32 Dustin Nippert **(RC)** .15
33 Tony Clark .15
34 Troy Glaus .25
35 Adam LaRoche .25
36 Andruw Jones .50
37 Craig Hansen **RC** 3.00
38 Chipper Jones .75
39 Horacio Ramirez .15
40 Jeff Francoeur .50
41 John Smoltz .25
42 Joey Devine **RC** .50
43 Johnny Estrada .15
44 Anthony Lerew **(RC)** .15
45 Julio Franco .15
46 Kyle Farnsworth .15
47 Marcus Giles .15
48 Mike Hampton .15
49 Rafael Furcal .25
50 Chuck James **(RC)** .25
51 Tim Hudson .40
52 B.J. Ryan .15
53 Bernie Castro .15
54 Brian Roberts .25
55 Walter Young .15
56 Daniel Cabrera .15
57 Eric Byrnes .25
58 Alejandro Freire **RC** .50
59 Erik Bedard .25
60 Javy Lopez .25
61 Jay Gibbons .15
62 Jorge Julio .15
63 Luis Matos .15
64 Melvin Mora .15
65 Miguel Tejada .40
66 Rafael Palmeiro .25
67 Rodrigo Lopez .15
68 Sammy Sosa .75
69 Alejandro Machado .15
70 Bill Mueller .15
71 Bronson Arroyo .15
72 Curt Schilling .75
73 David Ortiz .75
74 David Wells .15
75 Edgar Renteria .25
76 Ryan Jorgensen **RC** .25
77 Jason Varitek .50
78 Johnny Damon .75
79 Keith Foulke .15
80 Kevin Youkilis .25
81 Manny Ramirez .75
82 Matt Clement .15
83 Hanley Ramirez **(RC)** 1.50
84 Tim Wakefield .15
85 Trot Nixon .15
86 Wade Miller .15
87 Aramis Ramirez .40
88 Carlos Zambrano .40
89 Corey Patterson .15
90 Derrek Lee .50
91 Geovany Soto **(RC)** 1.00
92 Greg Maddux 1.00
93 Jeromy Burnitz .15
94 Jerry Hairston .15
95 Kerry Wood .25
96 Mark Prior .25
97 Matt Murton .15
98 Michael Barrett .15
99 Neifi Perez .15
100 Nomar Garciaparra .50
101 Rich Hill .25
102 Ryan Dempster .15
103 Todd Walker .15
104 A.J. Pierzynski .15
105 Aaron Rowand .25
106 Bobby Jenks .15
107 Carl Everett .15
108 Dustin Hermanson .15
109 Frank Thomas .40
110 Freddy Garcia .15
111 Jermaine Dye .25
112 Joe Crede .15
113 Jon Garland .15
114 Jose Contreras .25
115 Juan Uribe .15
116 Mark Buehrle .25
117 Orlando Hernandez .15
118 Paul Konerko .40
119 Scott Podsednik .15
120 Tadahito Iguchi .25
121 Aaron Harang .25
122 Adam Dunn .50
123 Austin Kearns .25
124 Brandon Claussen .15
125 Chris Denorfia **(RC)** .15
126 Edwin Encarnacion .15
127 Miguel Perez **(RC)** .15
128 Felipe Lopez .15
129 Jason LaRue .15
130 Ken Griffey Jr. 1.50
131 Chris Booker .15
132 Luke Hudson .15
133 Jason Bergmann **RC** .50
134 Ryan Freel .15
135 Sean Casey .15
136 Wily Mo Pena .15
137 Aaron Boone .15
138 Ben Broussard .15
139 Ryan Garko **(RC)** .25
240 C.C. Sabathia .40
141 Casey Blake .15
142 Cliff Lee .15
143 Coco Crisp .15
144 David Riske .15
145 Grady Sizemore .50
146 Jake Westbrook .15
147 Jhonny Peralta .25
148 Josh Bard .15
149 Kevin Millwood .25
150 Ronnie Belliard .15
151 Scott Elarton .15
152 Travis Hafner .40
153 Victor Martinez .25
154 Aaron Cook .15
155 Aaron Miles .15
156 Brad Hawpe .25
157 Mike Esposito .15
158 Chin-Hui Tsao .15
159 Clint Barmes .15
160 Cory Sullivan .15
161 Garrett Atkins .25
162 J.D. Closser .15
163 Jason Jennings .15
164 Jeff Baker .15
165 Jeff Francis .15
166 Luis Gonzalez .15
167 Matt Holliday .50
168 Todd Helton .50
169 Brandon Inge .15
170 Carlos Guillen .40
171 Carlos Pena .40
172 Chris Shelton .15
173 Craig Monroe .15
174 Curtis Granderson .50
175 Dmitri Young .15
176 Ivan Rodriguez .40
177 Jason Johnson .15
178 Jeremy Bonderman .15
179 Magglio Ordonez .25
180 Mark Woodyard **(RC)** .15
181 Nook Logan .15
182 Omar Infante .15
183 Placido Polanco .15
184 Chris Heintz **RC** .50
185 A.J. Burnett .25
186 Alex Gonzalez .15
187 Josh Johnson **(RC)** .15
188 Carlos Delgado .40
189 Dontrelle Willis .25
190 Josh Wilson **(RC)** .15
191 Jason Vargas .15
192 Jeff Conine .15
193 Jeremy Hermida **(RC)** .15
194 Josh Beckett .50
195 Juan Encarnacion .15
196 Juan Pierre .15
197 Luis Castillo .15
198 Miguel Cabrera .75
199 Mike Lowell .40
200 Paul LoDuca .15
201 Todd Jones .15
202 Adam Everett .15
203 Andy Pettitte .50
204 Brad Ausmus .15
205 Brad Lidge .15
206 Brandon Backe .15
207 Charlton Jimerson .15
208 Chris Burke .15
209 Craig Biggio .25
210 Daniel Wheeler .15
211 Jason Lane .15
212 Jeff Bagwell .50
213 Lance Berkman .50
214 Luke Scott .15
215 Morgan Ensberg .25
216 Roger Clemens 2.00
217 Roy Oswalt .25
218 Willy Taveras .15
219 Andres Blanco .15
220 Angel Berroa .15
221 Ruben Gotay .15
222 David DeJesus .15
223 Emil Brown .15
224 J.P. Howell .15
225 Jeremy Affeldt .15
226 Jimmy Gobble .15
227 John Buck .15
228 Jose Lima .15
229 Mark Teahen .15
230 Matt Stairs .15
231 Mike MacDougal .15
232 Mike Sweeney .15
233 Runelvys Hernandez .15
234 Terrence Long .15
235 Zack Greinke .25
236 Ron Flores **RC** .50
237 Brad Penny .15
238 Cesar Izturis .15
239 D.J. Houlton .15
240 Derek Lowe .15
241 Eric Gagne .25
242 Hee Seop Choi .15
243 J.D. Drew .25
244 Jason Phillips .15
245 Jason Repko .15
246 Jayson Werth .15
247 Jeff Kent .25
248 Jeff Weaver .15
249 Milton Bradley .15
250 Odalis Perez .15
251 Hong-Chih Kuo .25
252 Oscar Robles .15
253 Ben Sheets .25
254 Bill Hall .15
255 Brady Clark .15
256 Carlos Lee .25
257 Chris Capuano .15
258 Nelson Cruz **(RC)** .15
259 Derrick Turnbow .15
260 Doug Davis .15
261 Geoff Jenkins .15
262 J.J. Hardy .15
263 Lyle Overbay .15
264 Prince Fielder **(RC)** 1.00
265 Rickie Weeks .25
266 Russell Branyan .15
267 Tomokazu Ohka .15
268 Jonah Bayliss **RC** .75
269 Brad Radke .15
270 Carlos Silva .15
271 Francisco Liriano **(RC)** .50
272 Jacque Jones .15
273 Joe Mauer .25
274 Travis Bower .15
275 Joe Nathan .15
276 Johan Santana .50
277 Justin Morneau .40
278 Kyle Lohse .15
279 Lew Ford .15
280 Matthew LeCroy .15
281 Michael Cuddyer .15
282 Nick Punto .15
283 Scott Baker .15
284 Shannon Stewart .15
285 Torii Hunter .25
286 Braden Looper .15
287 Carlos Beltran .50
288 Cliff Floyd .15
289 David Wright .75
290 Doug Mientkiewicz .15
291 Anderson Hernandez **(RC)** .15
292 Jose Reyes .75
293 Kazuo Matsui .15
294 Kris Benson .15
295 Miguel Cairo .15
296 Mike Cameron .15
297 Robert Andino **RC** .50
298 Mike Piazza .75
299 Pedro Martinez .75
300 Tom Glavine .50
301 Victor Diaz .15
302 Tim Hamulack .15
303 Alex Rodriguez 2.00
304 Bernie Williams .25
305 Carl Pavano .15
306 Chien-Ming Wang .50
307 Derek Jeter 2.00
308 Gary Sheffield .40
309 Hideki Matsui 1.00
310 Jason Giambi .40
311 Jorge Posada .25
312 Kevin Brown .15
313 Mariano Rivera .40
314 Matt Lawton .15
315 Mike Mussina .25
316 Randy Johnson .75
317 Robinson Cano .25
318 Michael Vento .15
319 Tino Martinez .25
320 Tony Womack .15
321 Barry Zito .25
322 Bobby Crosby .15
323 Bobby Kielty .15
324 Dan Johnson .15
325 Danny Haren .40
326 Eric Chavez .25
327 Erubiel Durazo .15
328 Huston Street .25
329 Jason Kendall .15
330 Jay Payton .15
331 Joe Blanton .15
332 Joe Kennedy .15
333 Kirk Saarloos .15
334 Mark Kotsay .15
335 Nick Swisher .25
336 Rich Harden .25
337 Scott Hatteberg .15
338 Billy Wagner .25
339 Bobby Abreu .50
340 Brett Myers .15
341 Chase Utley .75
342 Danny Sandoval **RC** .50
343 David Bell .15
344 Gavin Floyd .15
345 Jim Thome .50
346 Jimmy Rollins .75
347 Jon Lieber .15
348 Kenny Lofton .15
349 Mike Lieberthal .15
350 Pat Burrell .25
351 Randy Wolf .15
352 Ryan Howard .75
353 Vicente Padilla .15
354 Bryan Bullington .15
355 J.J. Furmaniak **(RC)** .15
356 Craig Wilson .15
357 Matt Capps **(RC)** .25
358 Tom Gorzelanny **(RC)** .25
359 Jack Wilson .15
360 Jason Bay .25
361 Jose Mesa .15
362 Josh Fogg .15
363 Kip Wells .15
364 Steve Stemle **RC** .50
365 Oliver Perez .15
366 Robert Mackowiak .15
367 Ronny Paulino **(RC)** .15
368 Tike Redman .15
369 Zach Duke .15
370 Adam Eaton .15
371 Scott Feldman **RC** .50
372 Brian Giles .25
373 Brian Lawrence .15
374 Damian Jackson .15
375 Dave Roberts .15
376 Jake Peavy .50
377 Joe Randa .15
378 Khalil Greene .15

379	Mark Loretta	.25
380	Ramon Hernandez	.15
381	Robert Fick	.15
382	Ryan Klesko	.15
383	Trevor Hoffman	.15
384	Woody Williams	.15
385	Xavier Nady	.15
386	Armando Benitez	.15
387	Brad Hennessey	.15
388	Brian Myrow **RC**	.50
389	Edgardo Alfonzo	.15
390	J.T. Snow	.15
391	Jeremy Accardo **RC**	.15
392	Jason Schmidt	.25
393	Lance Niekro	.15
394	Matt Cain **(RC)**	.25
395	Daniel Ortmeier **(RC)**	.15
396	Moises Alou	.25
397	Doug Clark	.15
398	Omar Vizquel	.15
399	Pedro Feliz	.15
400	Randy Winn	.15
401	Ray Durham	.15
402	Adrian Beltre	.40
403	Eddie Guardado	.15
404	Felix Hernandez	.50
405	Gil Meche	.15
406	Ichiro Suzuki	1.50
407	Jamie Moyer	.15
408	Jeff Nelson	.15
409	Jeremy Reed	.15
410	Joel Pineiro	.15
411	Jaime Bubela **(RC)**	.15
412	Raul Ibanez	.15
413	Richie Sexson	.25
414	Ryan Franklin	.15
415	Willie Bloomquist	.15
416	Yorvit Torrealba	.15
417	Yuniesky Betancourt	.15
418	Jeff Harris **RC**	.25
419	Albert Pujols	2.00
420	Chris Carpenter	.25
421	David Eckstein	.15
422	Jason Isringhausen	.15
423	Jason Marquis	.15
424	Adam Wainwright **(RC)**	.50
425	Jim Edmonds	.25
426	Ryan Theriot **(RC)**	1.00
427	Chris Duncan	.15
428	Mark Grudzielanek	.15
429	Mark Mulder	.25
430	Matt Morris	.25
431	Reggie Sanders	.15
432	Scott Rolen	.50
433	Tyler Johnson **(RC)**	.15
434	Yadier Molina	.15
435	Alex Gonzalez	.15
436	Aubrey Huff	.15
437	Tim Corcoran **RC**	.40
438	Carl Crawford	.25
439	Casey Fossum	.15
440	Danys Baez	.15
441	Edwin Jackson	.15
442	Joey Gathright	.15
443	Jonny Gomes	.25
444	Jorge Cantu	.15
445	Julio Lugo	.15
446	Nick Green	.15
447	Rocco Baldelli	.15
448	Scott Kazmir	.25
449	Seth McClung	.15
450	Toby Hall	.15
451	Travis Lee	.15
452	Craig Breslow **RC**	.25
453	Alfonso Soriano	.50
454	Chris Young	.40
455	David Dellucci	.15
456	Francisco Cordero	.15
457	Gary Matthews	.15
458	Hank Blalock	.25
459	Juan Dominguez	.15
460	Josh Rupe	.15
461	Kenny Rogers	.15
462	Kevin Mench	.15
463	Laynce Nix	.15
464	Mark Teixeira	.50
465	Michael Young	.25
466	Richard Hidalgo	.15
467	Jason Botts **(RC)**	.15
468	Aaron Hill	.15
469	Alex Rios	.40
470	Corey Koskie	.15
471	Chris Demaria **RC**	.50
472	Eric Hinske	.15
473	Frank Catalanotto	.15
474	John-Ford Griffin **(RC)**	.15
475	Gustavo Chacin	.15
476	Josh Towers	.15
477	Miguel Batista	.15
478	Orlando Hudson	.15
479	Reed Johnson	.15
480	Roy Halladay	.40
481	Shaun Marcum **(RC)**	.50
482	Shea Hillenbrand	.15
483	Ted Lilly	.15
484	Vernon Wells	.25
485	Brad Wilkerson	.15
486	Darrell Rasner **(RC)**	.15
487	Chad Cordero	.15
488	Cristian Guzman	.15
489	Esteban Loaiza	.15
490	John Patterson	.15
491	Jose Guillen	.15
492	Jose Vidro	.15
493	Livan Hernandez	.15
494	Marlon Byrd	.15
495	Nick Johnson	.15
496	Preston Wilson	.15
497	Ryan Church	.15
498	Ryan Zimmerman **(RC)**	1.00
499	Tony Armas	.15
500	Vinny Castilla	.15
501	Andy Green	.15
502	Damion Easley	.15
503	Eric Byrnes	.25
504	Jason Grimsley	.15
505	Jeff DaVanon	.15
506	Johnny Estrada	.15
507	Luis Vizcaino	.15
508	Miguel Batista	.15
509	Orlando Hernandez	.15
510	Orlando Hudson	.15
511	Terry Mulholland	.15
512	Chris Reitsma	.15
513	Edgar Renteria	.25
514	John Thomson	.15
515	Jorge Sosa	.15
516	Oscar Villarreal	.15
517	Peter Orr	.15
518	Ryan Langerhans	.15
519	Todd Pratt	.15
520	Wilson Betemit	.15
521	Brian Jordan	.15
522	Lance Cormier	.15
523	Matt Diaz	.15
524	Mike Remlinger	.15
525	Bruce Chen	.15
526	Chris Gomez	.15
527	Chris Ray	.15
528	Corey Patterson	.15
529	David Newhan	.15
530	Ed Rogers **(RC)**	.25
531	John Halama	.15
532	Kris Benson	.15
533	LaTroy Hawkins	.15
534	Raul Chavez	.15
535	Alex Cora	.15
536	Alex Gonzalez	.15
537	Coco Crisp	.15
538	David Riske	.15
539	Doug Mirabelli	.15
540	Josh Beckett	.50
541	J.T. Snow	.15
542	Mike Timlin	.15
543	Julian Tavarez	.15
544	Rudy Seanez	.15
545	Wily Mo Pena	.15
546	Bob Howry	.15
547	Glendon Rusch	.15
548	Henry Blanco	.15
549	Jacque Jones	.15
550	Jerome Williams	.15
551	John Mabry	.15
552	Juan Pierre	.25
553	Scott Eyre	.15
554	Scott Williamson	.15
555	Wade Miller	.15
556	Will Ohman	.15
557	Alex Cintron	.15
558	Robert Mackowiak	.15
559	Brandon McCarthy	.15
560	Chris Widger	.15
561	Cliff Politte	.15
562	Javier Vazquez	.15
563	Jim Thome	.75
564	Matt Thornton	.15
565	Neal Cotts	.15
566	Pablo Ozuna	.15
567	Ross Gload	.15
568	Brandon Phillips	.40
569	Bronson Arroyo	.15
570	Dave Williams	.15
571	David Ross	.15
572	David Weathers	.15
573	Eric Milton	.15
574	Javier Valentin	.15
575	Kent Mercker	.15
576	Matt Belisle	.15
577	Paul Wilson	.15
578	Rich Aurilia	.15
579	Rick White	.15
580	Scott Hatteberg	.15
581	Todd Coffey	.15
582	Bob Wickman	.15
583	Danny Graves	.15
584	Eduardo Perez	.15
585	Guillermo Mota	.15
586	Jason Davis	.15
587	Jason Johnson	.15
588	Jason Michaels	.15
589	Rafael Betancourt	.15
590	Ramon Vazquez	.15
591	Scott Sauerbeck	.15
592	Todd Hollandsworth	.15
593	Brian Fuentes	.15
594	Danny Ardoin	.15
595	David Cortes	.15
596	Eli Marrero	.15
597	Jamey Carroll	.15
598	Jason Smith	.15
599	Josh Fogg	.15
600	Miguel Ojeda	.15
601	Mike DeJean	.15
602	Ray King	.15
603	Omar Quintanilla **(RC)**	.25
604	Zach Day	.15
605	Fernando Rodney	.15
606	Kenny Rogers	.15
607	Mike Maroth	.15
608	Nate Robertson	.15
609	Todd Jones	.15
610	Vance Wilson	.15
611	Bobby Seay	.15
612	Chris Spurling	.15
613	Raul Colon	.15
614	Jason Grilli	.15
615	Marcus Thames	.15
616	Ramon Santiago	.15
617	Alfredo Amezaga	.15
618	Brian Moehler	.15
619	Chris Aguila	.15
620	Franklyn German	.15
621	Joe Borowski	.15
622	Logan Kensing **(RC)**	.25
623	Matt Treanor	.15
624	Miguel Olivo	.15
625	Sergio Mitre	.15
626	Todd Wellemeyer	.25
627	Wes Helms	.15
628	Chad Qualls	.15
629	Eric Bruntlett	.15
630	Mike Gallo	.15
631	Mike Lamb	.15
632	Orlando Palmeiro	.15
633	Russ Springer	.15
634	Dan Wheeler	.15
635	Eric Munson	.15
637	Trever Miller	.15
638	Ambiorix Burgos	.15
639	Andrew Sisco	.15
640	Denny Bautista	.15
641	Doug Mientkiewicz	.15
642	Elmer Dessens	.15
643	Esteban German	.15
644	Joe Nelson **(RC)**	.25
645	Mark Grudzielanek	.15
646	Mark Redman	.15
647	Mike Wood	.15
648	Paul Bako	.15
649	Reggie Sanders	.15
650	Scott Elarton	.15
651	Shane Costa	.15
652	Tony Graffanino	.15
653	Jason Bulger **(RC)**	.25
654	Chris Bootcheck **(RC)**	.25
655	Esteban Yan	.15
656	Hector Carrasco	.15
657	J.C. Romero	.15
658	Jeff Weaver	.15
659	Jose Molina	.15
660	Kelvim Escobar	.15
661	Maicer Izturis	.15
662	Robb Quinlan	.15
663	Scot Shields	.15
664	Tim Salmon	.15
665	Bill Mueller	.15
666	Brett Tomko	.15
667	Dioner Navarro	.15
668	Jae Weong Seo	.15
669	Jose Cruz	.15
670	Kenny Lofton	.15
671	Lance Carter	.15
672	Nomar Garciaparra	.75
673	Olmedo Saenz	.15
674	Rafael Furcal	.40
675	Ramon Martinez	.15
676	Ricky Ledee	.15
677	Sandy Alomar	.15
678	Yhency Brazoban	.15
679	Corey Koskie	.15
680	Dan Kolb	.15
681	Gabe Gross	.15
682	Jeff Cirillo	.15
683	Matt Wise	.15
684	Rick Helling	.15
685	Chad Moeller	.15
686	David Bush	.15
687	Jorge De La Rosa	.15
688	Justin Lehr	.15
689	Jason Bartlett	.15
690	Jesse Crain	.15
691	Juan Rincon	.15
692	Luis Castillo	.15
693	Mike Redmond	.15
694	Rondell White	.15
695	Tony Batista	.15
696	Juan Castro	.15
697	Luis Rodriguez	.15
698	Matt Guerrier	.15
699	Willie Eyre **(RC)**	.25
700	Aaron Heilman	.15
701	Billy Wagner	.25
702	Carlos Delgado	.50
703	Chad Bradford	.15
704	Chris Woodward	.15
705	Darren Oliver	.15
706	Duaner Sanchez	.15
707	Endy Chavez	.15
708	Jorge Julio	.15
709	Jose Valentin	.15
710	Julio Franco	.15
711	Paul LoDuca	.15
712	Ramon Castro	.15
713	Steve Trachsel	.15
714	Victor Zambrano	.15
715	Xavier Nady	.15
716	Andy Phillips	.15
717	Bubba Crosby	.15
718	Jaret Wright	.15
719	Kelly Stinnett	.15
720	Kyle Farnsworth	.15
721	Mike Meyers	.15
722	Octavio Dotel	.15
723	Ron Villone	.15
724	Scott Proctor	.15
725	Shawn Chacon	.15
726	Tanyon Sturtze	.15
727	Adam Melhuse	.15
728	Brad Halsey	.15
729	Esteban Loaiza	.15
730	Frank Thomas	.50
731	Jay Witasick	.15
732	Justin Duchscherer	.15
733	Kiko Calero	.15
734	Marco Scutaro	.15
735	Mark Ellis	.15
736	Milton Bradley	.15
737	Aaron Fultz	.15
738	Aaron Rowand	.25
739	Geoff Geary	.15
740	Arthur Rhodes	.15
741	Chris Coste **RC**	.40
742	Rheal Cormier	.15
743	Ryan Franklin	.15
744	Ryan Madson	.15
745	Sal Fasano	.15
746	Tom Gordon	.15
747	Abraham Nunez	.15
748	David Dellucci	.15
749	Julio Santana	.15
750	Shane Victorino	.25
751	Damaso Marte	.15
752	Freddy Sanchez	.15
753	Humberto Cota	.15
754	Jeromy Burnitz	.15
755	Joe Randa	.15
756	Jose Castillo	.15
757	Mike Gonzalez	.15
758	Ryan Doumit	.15
759	Sean Burnett	.15
760	Sean Casey	.15
761	Ian Snell	.15
762	John Grabow	.15
763	Jose Hernandez	.15
764	Roberto Hernandez	.15
765	Ryan Vogelsong	.15
766	Victor Sanchez	.15
767	Adrian Gonzalez	.25
768	Alan Embree	.15
769	Brian Sweeney **(RC)**	.25
770	Chan Ho Park	.15
771	Clay Hensley	.15
772	Dewon Brazelton	.15
773	Doug Brocail	.15
774	Eric Young	.15
775	Geoff Blum	.15
776	Josh Bard	.15
777	Mark Bellhorn	.15
778	Mike Cameron	.15
779	Mike Piazza	.75
780	Rob Bowen	.15
781	Scott Cassidy	.15
782	Scott Linebrink	.15
783	Shawn Estes	.15
784	Terrmel Sledge	.15
785	Vinny Castilla	.15
786	Jeff Fassero	.15
787	Jose Vizcaino	.15
788	Mark Sweeney	.15
789	Matt Morris	.15
790	Steve Finley	.15
791	Tim Worrell	.15
792	Jamey Wright	.15
793	Jason Ellison	.15
794	Noah Lowry	.15
795	Steve Kline	.15
796	Todd Greene	.15
797	Carl Everett	.15
798	George Sherrill	.15
799	J.J. Putz	.15
800	Jake Woods	.15
801	Jose Lopez	.15
802	Julio Mateo	.15
803	Mike Morse	.15
804	Rafael Soriano	.15
805	Roberto Petagine	.15
806	Aaron Miles	.15
807	Braden Looper	.15
808	Gary Bennett	.15
809	Hector Luna	.15
810	Jeff Suppan	.15
811	John Rodriguez	.15
812	Josh Hancock	.15
813	Juan Encarnacion	.15
814	Larry Bigbie	.15
815	Scott Spiezio	.15
816	Sidney Ponson	.15
817	So Taguchi	.15
818	Brian Meadows	.15
819	Damon Hollins	.15
820	Dan Miceli	.15
821	Doug Waechter	.15
822	Jason Childers	.25
823	Josh Paul	.15
824	Julio Lugo	.15
825	Mark Hendrickson	.15
826	Sean Burroughs	.15
827	Shawn Camp	.15
828	Travis Harper	.15
829	Ty Wigginton	.15
830	Adam Eaton	.15
831	Adrian Brown	.15
832	Akinori Otsuka	.15
833	Antonio Alfonseca	.15
834	Brad Wilkerson	.15
835	D'Angelo Jimenez	.15
836	Gerald Laird	.15
837	Joaquin Benoit	.15
838	Kameron Loe	.15
839	Kevin Millwood	.15

840 Mark DeRosa .15
841 Phil Nevin .15
842 Rod Barajas .15
843 Vicente Padilla .15
844 A.J. Burnett .25
845 Bengie Molina .15
846 Gregg Zaun .15
847 John McDonald .15
848 Lyle Overbay .15
849 Russ Adams .15
850 Troy Glaus .25
851 Vinnie Chulk .15
852 B.J. Ryan .15
853 Justin Speier .15
854 Pete Walker .15
855 Scott Downs .15
856 Scott Schoeneweis .15
857 Alfonso Soriano .75
858 Brian Schneider .15
859 Daryle Ward .15
860 Felix Rodriguez .15
861 Gary Majewski .15
862 Joey Eischen .15
863 Jon Rauch .15
864 Marlon Anderson .15
865 Matthew LeCroy .15
866 Mike Stanton .15
867 Ramon Ortiz .15
868 Robert Fick .15
869 Royce Clayton .15
870 Ryan Drese .15
871 Vladimir Guerrero .50
872 Craig Biggio .25
873 Barry Zito .15
874 Vernon Wells .25
875 Chipper Jones .50
876 Prince Fielder .75
877 Albert Pujols 1.00
878 Greg Maddux .75
879 Carl Crawford .15
880 Brandon Webb .40
881 J.D. Drew .15
882 Jason Schmidt .15
883 Victor Martinez .25
884 Ichiro Suzuki .75
885 Miguel Cabrera .40
886 David Wright .75
887 Alfonso Soriano .40
888 Miguel Tejada .40
889 Khalil Greene .15
890 Ryan Howard 1.00
891 Jason Bay .25
892 Mark Teixeira .25
893 Manny Ramirez .40
894 Ken Griffey Jr. .75
895 Todd Helton .25
896 Angel Berroa .15
897 Ivan Rodriguez .25
898 Johan Santana .25
899 Paul Konerko .25
900 Derek Jeter 1.00
901 Macay McBride **(RC)** .25
902 Tony Pena **(RC)** .25
903 Peter Moylan **RC** .50
904 Aaron Rakers **(RC)** .25
905 Chris Britton **RC** .50
906 Nick Markakis **(RC)** 1.00
907 Sendy Rleal **RC** .50
908 Val Majewski **(RC)** .25
909 Jermaine Van Buren **(RC)** .25
910 Jonathan Papelbon **(RC)** 4.00
911 Angel Pagan **(RC)** .50
912 David Aardsma **(RC)** .25
913 Sean Marshall **(RC)** .25
914 Brian Anderson **(RC)** .25
915 Freddie Bynum **(RC)** .25
916 Fausto Carmona **(RC)** .50
917 Kelly Stoppach **(RC)** .25
918 Choo Freeman **(RC)** .25
919 Ryan Shealy **(RC)** .25
920 Joel Zumaya **(RC)** 2.00
921 Jordan Tata **RC** 1.00
922 Justin Verlander **(RC)** 1.00
923 Carlos Martinez **RC** .50
924 Chris Resop **(RC)** .25
925 Dan Uggla **(RC)** 1.00
926 Eric Reed **(RC)** .25
927 Hanley Ramirez **(RC)** 2.00
928 Yusmeiro Petit **(RC)** .50
929 Josh Willingham **(RC)** .25
930 Mike Jacobs **(RC)** .50
931 Reggie Abercrombie **(RC)** .25
932 Ricky Nolasco **(RC)** .25
933 Scott Olsen **(RC)** .25
934 Fernando Nieve **(RC)** .25
935 Taylor Buchholz **(RC)** .25
936 Cody Ross **(RC)** .25
937 James Loney **(RC)** .75
938 Takashi Saito **RC** 2.00
939 Tim Hamulack **(RC)** .25
940 Chris Demaria **RC** .50
941 Jose Capellan **(RC)** .25
942 David Gassner **(RC)** .25
943 Jason Kubel **(RC)** .25
944 Brian Bannister **(RC)** .25
945 Mike Thompson **RC** .50
946 Cole Hamels **(RC)** 5.00
947 Paul Maholm **(RC)** .25
948 John Van Benschoten **(RC)** .25
949 Nate McLouth **(RC)** .50
950 Ben Johnson **(RC)** .25
951 Josh Barfield **(RC)** .25
952 Travis Ishikawa **(RC)** .25
953 Jack Taschner **(RC)** .25
954 Kenji Johjima **RC** 3.00
955 Skip Schumaker **(RC)** .25
956 Ruddy Lugo **(RC)** .25
957 Jason Hammel **(RC)** .25
958 Chris Roberson **(RC)** .25
959 Fabio Castro **RC** .50
960 Ian Kinsler **(RC)** .50
961 John Koronka **(RC)** .25
962 Brandon Watson **(RC)** .25
963 Jon Lester **(RC)** 5.00
964 Ben Hendrickson **(RC)** .25
965 Martin Prado **(RC)** .25
966 Erick Aybar **(RC)** .50
967 Bobby Livingston **(RC)** .25
968 Ryan Spilborghs **(RC)** .25
969 Tommy Murphy **(RC)** .25
970 Howie Kendrick **(RC)** 3.00
971 Casey Janssen **RC** 1.00
972 Michael O'Connor **RC** .50
973 Conor Jackson **(RC)** .50
974 Jeremy Hermida **(RC)** .50
975 Renyel Pinto **(RC)** .25
976 Prince Fielder **(RC)** 1.50
977 Kevin Frandsen **(RC)** .25
978 Ty Taubenheim **RC** .50
979 Rich Hill **(RC)** .50
980 Jonathan Broxton **(RC)** .50
981 Jamie Shields **RC** .50
982 Carlos Villanueva **RC** .50
983 Boone Logan **RC** 1.00
984 Brian Wilson **RC** .50
985 Andre Ethier **(RC)** 3.00
986 Michael Napoli **RC** 1.50
987 Agustin Montero **(RC)** .25
988 Jack Hannahan **RC** .50
989 Boof Bonser **(RC)** .25
990 Carlos Ruiz **(RC)** .25
991 Jason Botts **(RC)** .25
992 Kendry Morales **(RC)** .50
993 Alay Soler **RC** .75
994 Santiago Ramirez **(RC)** .25
995 Saul Rivera **(RC)** .25
996 Anthony Reyes **(RC)** .25
997 Matthew Kemp **(RC)** 1.00
998 Jae-Kuk Ryu **RC** .50
999 Lastings Milledge **(RC)** 1.00
1000 Jered Weaver **(RC)** 3.00
1001 Stephen Drew **(RC)** 1.00
1002 Carlos Quentin **(RC)** .50
1003 Livan Hernandez .15
1004 Chris Young **(RC)** .50
1005 Alberto Callaspo/SP **(RC)** 6.00
1006 Enrique Gonzalez **(RC)** .25
1007 Tony Pena **(RC)** .25
1008 Bob Melvin .15
1009 Fernando Tatis .15
1010 Willy Aybar **(RC)** .25
1011 Ken Ray **(RC)** .25
1012 Scott Thorman **(RC)** .50
1013 Eric Hinske SP 4.00
1014 Kevin Barry **(RC)** .50
1015 Bobby Cox .15
1016 Phil Stockman **(RC)** .25
1017 Brayan Pena **(RC)** .25
1018 Adam Loewen **(RC)** .25
1019 Brandon Fahey **RC** .50
1020 Jim Hoey **RC** .50
1021 Kurt Birkins SP **RC** 5.00
1022 Jim Johnson **RC** .75
1023 Sam Perlozzo .15
1024 Cory Morris **RC** .50
1025 Hayden Penn **(RC)** .25
1026 Javy Lopez .15
1027 Dustin Pedroia **(RC)** .50
1028 Kason Gabbard **(RC)** .50
1029 David Pauley **(RC)** .25
1030 Kyle Snyder .15
1031 Terry Francona .15
1032 Craig Breslow **RC** .50
1033 Bryan Corey **(RC)** .25
1034 Manny Delcarmen **(RC)** 1.00
1035 Carlos Marmol **RC** .50
1036 Buck Coats **(RC)** .25
1037 Ryan O'Malley/SP **RC** 8.00
1038 Angel Guzman **(RC)** .25
1039 Ronny Cedeno .15
1040 Juan Mateo **RC** .50
1041 Cesar Izturis .15
1042 Les Walrond **(RC)** .50
1043 Geovany Soto **(RC)** .50
1044 Sean Tracey **(RC)** .25
1045 Ozzie Guillen/SP 6.00
1046 Royce Clayton .15
1047 Norris Hopper **RC** .50
1048 Bill Bray **(RC)** .25
1049 Jerry Narron .15
1050 Brendan Harris **(RC)** .25
1051 Brian Shackelford .15
1052 Jeremy Sowers **(RC)** .50
1053 Joe Inglett **RC** 1.50
1054 Brian Slocum **(RC)** .25
1055 Andrew Brown **(RC)** .25
1056 Rafael Perez **RC** .50
1057 Edward Mujica **RC** .50
1058 Andy Marte **(RC)** .25
1059 Shin-Soo Choo **(RC)** .50
1060 Jeremy Guthrie **(RC)** .25
1061 Franklin Gutierrez/SP **(RC)** 6.00
1062 Kazuo Matsui .15
1063 Chris Iannetta **RC** .50
1064 Manny Corpas **RC** .50
1065 Clint Hurdle .15
1066 Ramon Ramirez **(RC)** .25
1067 Sean Casey .15
1068 Zach Miner **(RC)** .25
1069 Brent Clevlen/SP **(RC)** 4.00
1070 Bob Wickman .15
1071 Jim Leyland .15
1072 Alexis Gomez **(RC)** .25
1073 Anibal Sanchez **(RC)** .50
1074 Taylor Tankersley **(RC)** .25
1075 Eric Wedge .15
1076 Jonah Bayliss **RC** .50
1077 Paul Hoover SP **(RC)** 4.00
1078 Eddie Guardado .15
1079 Cody Ross **(RC)** .25
1080 Aubrey Huff .15
1081 Jason Hirsh **(RC)** .25
1082 Brandon League .15
1083 Matt Albers **(RC)** .25
1084 Chris Sampson **RC** 1.50
1085 Phil Garner .15
1086 J.R. House **(RC)** .25
1087 Ryan Shealy **(RC)** .25
1088 Stephen Andrade **(RC)** .25
1089 Bob Keppel **(RC)** .25
1090 Buddy Bell .15
1091 Justin Huber **(RC)** .25
1092 Paul Phillips **(RC)** .25
1093 Greg Jones SP **(RC)** 4.00
1094 Jeff Mathis **(RC)** .50
1095 Dustin Moseley **(RC)** .50
1096 Joe Saunders **(RC)** .50
1097 Reggie Willits **(RC)** .75
1098 Mike Scioscia .15
1099 Greg Maddux 1.50
1100 Wilson Betemit .15
1101 Chad Billingsley/SP **(RC)** 8.00
1102 Russell Martin **(RC)** .75
1103 Grady Little .15
1104 David Bell .15
1105 Kevin Mench .15
1106 Laynce Nix .15
1107 Chris Barnwell **RC** .50
1108 Tony Gwynn Jr. **(RC)** .50
1109 Corey Hart **(RC)** .50
1110 Zach Jackson **(RC)** .25
1111 Francisco Cordero .15
1112 Joe Winklesas **(RC)** .25
1113 Ned Yost .15
1114 Matt Garza **(RC)** .50
1115 Chris Heintz .15
1116 Pat Neshek **RC** 4.00
1117 Josh Rabe SP **RC** 10.00
1118 Mike Rivera .15
1119 Ron Gardenhire .15
1120 Shawn Green .15
1121 Oliver Perez .15
1122 Heath Bell .15
1123 Bartolome Fortunato **(RC)** .25
1124 Anderson Garcia **RC** .75
1125 John Maine SP **(RC)** 8.00
1126 Henry Owens **RC** .50
1127 Mike Pelfrey **RC** 3.00
1128 Royce Ring **(RC)** .25
1129 Willie Randolph .15
1130 Bobby Abreu .50
1131 Craig Wilson .15
1132 T.J. Beam **(RC)** .25
1133 Colter Bean SP **(RC)** 4.00
1134 Melky Cabrera **(RC)** .50
1135 Mitch Jones **(RC)** .50
1136 Jeffrey Karstens **RC** 1.00
1137 Wilbert Nieves **(RC)** .25
1138 Kevin Reese **(RC)** .50
1139 Kevin Thompson **(RC)** .50
1140 Jose Veras **RC** .15
1141 Joe Torre .50
1142 Jeremy Brown **(RC)** .25
1143 Santiago Casilla **(RC)** .25
1144 Shane Komine **RC** 1.00
1145 Mike Rouse **(RC)** .25
1146 Jason Windsor **(RC)** .75
1147 Ken Macha .15
1148 Jamie Moyer .15
1149 Phil Nevin SP 8.00
1150 Eude Brito **(RC)** .50
1151 Fabio Castro .15
1152 Jeff Conine .15
1153 Scott Mathieson **(RC)** .25
1154 Brian Sanches **(RC)** .25
1155 Matt Smith **RC** .50
1156 Joe Thurston **(RC)** .25
1157 Marlon Anderson/SP 4.00
1158 Xavier Nady .15
1159 Shawn Chacon .15
1160 Rajai Davis **(RC)** .25
1161 Yurendell de Caster **(RC)** .50
1162 Marty McLeary **(RC)** .25
1163 Chris Duffy .15
1164 Joshua Sharpless **RC** 1.00
1165 Jim Tracy .15
1166 David Wells .15
1167 Russell Branyan .15
1168 Todd Walker .15
1169 Paul McAnulty **(RC)** .25
1170 Bruce Bochy .15
1171 Shea Hillenbrand .15
1172 Eliezer Alfonzo **RC** .50
1173 Justin Knoedler/SP **(RC)** 4.00
1174 Jonathan Sanchez **(RC)** .50
1175 Travis Smith **(RC)** .25
1176 Cha Sueng Baek .15
1177 T.J. Bohn **(RC)** .25
1178 Emiliano Fruto **RC** .50
1179 Sean Green **RC** .50
1180 Jon Huber **RC** .50
1181 Adam Jones SP **(RC)** 8.00
1182 Mark Lowe **(RC)** .25
1183 Eric O'Flaherty **RC** .50
1184 Preston Wilson .15
1185 Mike Hargrove .15
1186 Jeff Weaver .15
1187 Ronnie Belliard .15
1188 John Gall **(RC)** .25
1189 Josh Kinney/SP **RC** 6.00
1190 Tony LaRussa .15
1191 Scott Dunn **(RC)** .25
1192 B.J. Upton .40
1193 Jon Switzer **(RC)** .25
1194 Benjamin Zobrist **(RC)** .50
1195 Joe Maddon .15
1196 Carlos Lee .40
1197 Matt Stairs .15
1198 Nick Massett **(RC)** .25
1199 Nelson Cruz **(RC)** .50
1200 Francisco Rosario **(RC)** .25
1201 Wes Littleton **(RC)** .25
1202 Drew Meyer **(RC)** .25
1203 John Rheinecker **(RC)** .25
1204 Robinson Tejeda .15
1205 Jeremy Accardo/SP 4.00
1206 Luis Figueroa **RC** .50
1207 John Hattig Jr. **(RC)** .25
1208 Dustin McGowan **(RC)** .25
1209 Ryan Roberts **RC** .50
1210 Davis Romero **(RC)** .25
1211 Ty Taubenheim .15
1212 John Gibbons .15
1213 Shawn Hill/SP **(RC)** 6.00
1214 Brandon Harper **RC** .25
1215 Travis Hughes **(RC)** .25
1216 Chris Schroder **RC** .50
1217 Austin Kearns .15
1218 Felipe Lopez .15
1219 Roy Corcoran **RC** .25
1220 Melvin Dorta **RC** .50
1221 Brandon Webb/SP 6.00
1222 Andruw Jones/SP 4.00
1223 Miguel Tejada/SP 6.00
1224 David Ortiz/SP 8.00
1225 Derrek Lee/SP 6.00
1226 Jim Thome/SP 6.00
1227 Ken Griffey Jr./SP 8.00
1228 Travis Hafner/SP 6.00
1229 Todd Helton/SP 6.00
1230 Magglio Ordonez/SP 4.00
1231 Miguel Cabrera/SP 8.00
1232 Lance Berkman/SP 6.00
1233 Mike Sweeney/SP 4.00
1234 Vladimir Guerrero/SP 8.00
1235 Nomar Garciaparra/SP 4.00
1236 Prince Fielder/SP 8.00
1237 Johan Santana/SP 8.00
1238 Pedro Martinez/SP 6.00
1239 Derek Jeter/SP 10.00
1240 Barry Zito/SP 4.00
1241 Ryan Howard/SP 10.00
1242 Jason Bay/SP 6.00
1243 Trevor Hoffman/SP 4.00
1244 Jason Schmidt/SP 4.00
1245 Ichiro Suzuki/SP 8.00
1246 Albert Pujols/SP 10.00
1247 Carl Crawford/SP 5.00
1248 Mark Teixeira/SP 6.00
1249 Vernon Wells/SP 5.00
1250 Alfonso Soriano/SP 8.00

Blue

Blue: 2-4X
Production 299 Sets

Gold

Gold: 2-4X
Production 299 Sets

Silver Spectrum

No Pricing
Production 25 Sets

Rookie Foil Gold

Gold:	4-8X
Production 99 Sets	
Platinum:	No Pricing
Production 15 Sets	

Rookie Foil Silver

NM/M

Silver:	2X-4X
Production 399 Sets	

Printing Plates

No Pricing
Production one set per color.

All-Time Legends

NM/M

Common Player:		1.00
AT-1	Ty Cobb	3.00
AT-2	Lou Gehrig	4.00
AT-3	Babe Ruth	5.00
AT-4	Jimmie Foxx	3.00
AT-5	Honus Wagner	3.00
AT-6	Lou Brock	2.00
AT-7	Christy Mathewson	2.00
AT-8	Walter Johnson	2.00
AT-9	Mike Schmidt	3.00
AT-10	Al Kaline	2.00
AT-11	Robin Yount	2.00
AT-12	Johnny Bench	2.00
AT-13	Yogi Berra	2.00
AT-14	Rod Carew	1.00
AT-15	Bob Feller	1.00
AT-16	Carlton Fisk	1.00
AT-17	Bob Gibson	2.00
AT-18	Cy Young	2.00
AT-19	Jackie Robinson	3.00
AT-22	Harmon Killebrew	2.00
AT-23	Mickey Cochrane	1.00
AT-24	Eddie Mathews	2.00
AT-25	Bill Mazeroski	1.00
AT-26	Willie McCovey	2.00
AT-27	Eddie Murray	2.00
AT-28	Lefty Grove	1.00
AT-29	Jim Palmer	1.00
AT-30	Pee Wee Reese	1.00
AT-31	Phil Rizzuto	2.00
AT-32	Brooks Robinson	2.00
AT-33	Nolan Ryan	4.00
AT-34	Tom Seaver	2.00
AT-35	Ozzie Smith	2.00
AT-36	Roy Campanella	2.00
AT-37	Thurman Munson	3.00
AT-38	Mel Ott	2.00
AT-39	Satchel Paige	2.00
AT-40	Rogers Hornsby	2.00

All-Upper Deck Team

NM/M

2:Series 1 Fat pack		.75
UD-1	Ken Griffey Jr.	3.00
UD-2	Derek Jeter	4.00
UD-3	Albert Pujols	4.00
UD-4	Alex Rodriguez	4.00
UD-5	Vladimir Guerrero	1.50
UD-6	Roger Clemens	3.00
UD-7	Derrek Lee	1.00
UD-8	David Ortiz	1.50
UD-9	Miguel Cabrera	1.50
UD-10	Bobby Abreu	1.00
UD-11	Mark Teixeira	1.00
UD-12	Johan Santana	1.50
UD-13	Hideki Matsui	2.50
UD-14	Ichiro Suzuki	3.00
UD-15	Andruw Jones	1.00
UD-16	Eric Chavez	.75
UD-17	Roy Oswalt	1.00
UD-18	Curt Schilling	1.50
UD-19	Randy Johnson	1.50
UD-20	Ivan Rodriguez	1.00
UD-21	Chipper Jones	2.00
UD-22	Mark Prior	.75
UD-23	Jason Bay	.75
UD-24	Pedro Martinez	1.50
UD-25	David Wright	3.00
UD-26	Carlos Beltran	1.50
UD-27	Jim Edmonds	.75
UD-28	Chris Carpenter	1.00
UD-29	Roy Halladay	1.00
UD-30	Jake Peavy	1.00
UD-31	Paul Konerko	1.00
UD-32	Travis Hafner	1.00
UD-33	Barry Zito	.75
UD-34	Miguel Tejada	1.00
UD-35	Josh Beckett	1.50
UD-36	Todd Helton	1.00
UD-37	Dontrelle Willis	.75
UD-38	Manny Ramirez	1.50
UD-39	Mariano Rivera	1.00
UD-40	Jeff Kent	.75

Amazing Greats

NM/M

Complete Set:		25.00
Common Player:		.50
BA	Bobby Abreu	.75
JB	Jeff Bagwell	.75
CB	Carlos Beltran	1.00
AB	Adrian Beltre	.50
MC	Miguel Cabrera	1.00
RC	Roger Clemens	3.00
CC	Carl Crawford	.50
JD	Johnny Damon	1.00
JE	Jim Edmonds	.50
RF	Rafael Furcal	.50
EG	Eric Gagne	.50
JG	Jason Giambi	.75
TG	Tom Glavine	.50
KG	Ken Griffey Jr.	2.00
HE	Todd Helton	.75
TH	Tim Hudson	.50
DJ	Derek Jeter	3.00
RJ	Randy Johnson	1.00
AJ	Andruw Jones	1.00
CJ	Chipper Jones	1.00
JJ	Jacque Jones	.50
PK	Paul Konerko	.75
CL	Carlos Lee	.50
JL	Javy Lopez	.50
GM	Greg Maddux	2.00
PM	Pedro Martinez	1.00
DO	David Ortiz	1.00
RO	Roy Oswalt	.50
RP	Rafael Palmeiro	.75
CP	Corey Patterson	.50
MP	Mike Piazza	1.00
PR	Mark Prior	1.00
AP	Albert Pujols	3.00
MR	Manny Ramirez	1.00
JR	Jose Reyes	.75
IR	Ivan Rodriguez	.75
SR	Scott Rolen	1.00
JS	Johan Santana	1.00
CS	Curt Schilling	1.00
GS	Gary Sheffield	.75
SM	John Smoltz	.50
AS	Alfonso Soriano	.75
SS	Sammy Sosa	1.00
MT	Mark Teixeira	.75
TE	Miguel Tejada	.75
FT	Frank Thomas	.75
JT	Jim Thome	.75
DW	Dontrelle Willis	.50
KW	Kerry Wood	.50
WR	David Wright	1.50

Diamond Collection

NM/M

Gold:		1-2X
Production 699 Sets		
AL	Moises Alou	.50
JB	Jeff Bagwell	.75
RB	Rocco Baldelli	.50
OC	Orlando Cabrera	.50
MC	Mike Cameron	.50
EC	Eric Chavez	.50
CO	Jose Contreras	.50
JC	Jesse Crain	.50
BC	Bobby Crosby	.50
JD	Johnny Damon	1.00
AE	Adam Eaton	.50
JE	Jim Edmonds	.50
SF	Steve Finley	.50
FG	Freddy Garcia	.50
GO	Juan Gonzalez	.50
KG	Ken Griffey Jr.	2.00
JG	Jose Guillen	.50
MH	Mike Hampton	.50

Amazing Greats Materials

NM/M

Complete Set:		
Common Player:		
BA	Bobby Abreu	6.00
JB	Jeff Bagwell	6.00
CB	Carlos Beltran	6.00
AB	Adrian Beltre	4.00
MC	Miguel Cabrera	8.00
RC	Roger Clemens	15.00
CC	Carl Crawford	5.00
JD	Johnny Damon	10.00
JE	Jim Edmonds	5.00
RF	Rafael Furcal	4.00
EG	Eric Gagne	4.00
JG	Jason Giambi	5.00
TG	Tom Glavine	6.00
KG	Ken Griffey Jr.	20.00
HE	Todd Helton	6.00
TH	Tim Hudson	4.00
DJ	Derek Jeter	20.00
RJ	Randy Johnson	8.00
AJ	Andruw Jones	8.00
CJ	Chipper Jones	8.00
JJ	Jacque Jones	4.00
PK	Paul Konerko	6.00
CL	Carlos Lee	5.00
JL	Javy Lopez	4.00
GM	Greg Maddux	12.00
PM	Pedro Martinez	8.00
DO	David Ortiz	8.00
RO	Roy Oswalt	6.00
RP	Rafael Palmeiro	6.00
CP	Corey Patterson	4.00
MP	Mike Piazza	10.00
PR	Mark Prior	6.00
AP	Albert Pujols	20.00
MR	Manny Ramirez	8.00
JR	Jose Reyes	8.00
IR	Ivan Rodriguez	6.00
SR	Scott Rolen	5.00
JS	Johan Santana	8.00
CS	Curt Schilling	8.00
GS	Gary Sheffield	6.00
SM	John Smoltz	8.00
AS	Alfonso Soriano	6.00
SS	Sammy Sosa	10.00
MT	Mark Teixeira	8.00
TE	Miguel Tejada	10.00
FT	Frank Thomas	8.00
JT	Jim Thome	8.00
DW	Dontrelle Willis	6.00
KW	Kerry Wood	4.00
WR	David Wright	15.00

AH	Aubrey Huff	.50
EJ	Edwin Jackson	.50
DJ	Derek Jeter	3.00
NJ	Nick Johnson	.50
RJ	Randy Johnson	1.00
JJ	Jacque Jones	.50
SK	Scott Kazmir	.50
KE	Austin Kearns	.50
JK	Jason Kendall	.50
AK	Adam Kennedy	.50
CK	Casey Kotchman	.50
LA	Matt Lawton	.50
ML	Mike Lieberthal	.50
PL	Paul LoDuca	.50
KL	Kenny Lofton	.50
LO	Mike Lowell	.50
GM	Greg Maddux	2.00
MA	Kazuo Matsui	.50
KM	Kevin Millwood	.50
DO	David Ortiz	1.00
AO	Akinori Otsuka	.50
CP	Carl Pavano	.50
JP	Jorge Posada	.50
BR	Brad Radke	.50
IR	Ivan Rodriguez	.75
CC	C.C. Sabathia	.50
CS	Chris Shelton	.50
JS	John Smoltz	.75
SS	Shannon Stewart	.50
JT	Jim Thome	.75
JW	Jayson Werth	.50
PW	Preston Wilson	.50

Diamond Collection Materials

NM/M

Common Player:		4.00
AL	Moises Alou	6.00
JB	Jeff Bagwell	6.00
RB	Rocco Baldelli	4.00
OC	Orlando Cabrera	4.00
MC	Mike Cameron	4.00
EC	Eric Chavez	4.00
CO	Jose Contreras	4.00
JC	Jesse Crain	4.00
BC	Bobby Crosby	4.00
JD	Johnny Damon	10.00
AE	Adam Eaton	4.00
JE	Jim Edmonds	4.00
SF	Steve Finley	4.00
FG	Freddy Garcia	4.00
GO	Juan Gonzalez	4.00
KG	Ken Griffey Jr.	20.00
JG	Jose Guillen	4.00
MH	Mike Hampton	4.00
AH	Aubrey Huff	4.00
EJ	Edwin Jackson	4.00
DJ	Derek Jeter	20.00
NJ	Nick Johnson	4.00
RJ	Randy Johnson	8.00
JJ	Jacque Jones	4.00
SK	Scott Kazmir	4.00
KE	Austin Kearns	4.00
JK	Jason Kendall	4.00
AK	Adam Kennedy	4.00
CK	Casey Kotchman	4.00
LA	Matt Lawton	4.00
ML	Mike Lieberthal	4.00
PL	Paul LoDuca	4.00
KL	Kenny Lofton	4.00
LO	Mike Lowell	4.00
GM	Greg Maddux	12.00
MA	Kazuo Matsui	4.00
KM	Kevin Millwood	4.00
DO	David Ortiz	8.00
AO	Akinori Otsuka	4.00
CP	Carl Pavano	4.00
JP	Jorge Posada	6.00
BR	Brad Radke	4.00
IR	Ivan Rodriguez	6.00
CC	C.C. Sabathia	6.00
CS	Chris Shelton	6.00
JS	John Smoltz	8.00
SS	Shannon Stewart	4.00
JT	Jim Thome	8.00
JW	Jayson Werth	4.00
PW	Preston Wilson	4.00

Diamond Debut

NM/M

Common Player: 1.00
#'s 1-40 found in Series 1 packs
#'s 41-82 found in Series 2 packs
Inserted 1:4 Walmart packs.

Series 2 Common Player:		.50
1	Tadahito Iguchi	1.00
2	Huston Street	.50
3	Norihiro Nakamura	.50
4	Chien-Ming Wang	3.00
5	Pedro Lopez	.50
6	Robinson Cano	2.00
7	Tim Stauffer	.50
8	Ervin Santana	.50
9	Brandon McCarthy	.50
10	Hayden Penn	.50
11	Derek Jeter	5.00
12	Ken Griffey Jr.	3.00
13	Prince Fielder	3.00
14	Edwin Encarnacion	.50
15	Scott Olsen	.50
16	Chris Resop	.50
17	Justin Verlander	2.00
18	Melky Cabrera	.50
19	Jeff Francoeur	1.50
20	Yuniesky Betancourt	.50
21	Conor Jackson	1.00

22	Felix Hernandez	1.50
23	Anthony Reyes	.50
24	John-Ford Griffin	.50
25	Adam Wainwright	1.00
26	Ryan Garko	.50
27	Ryan Zimmerman	3.00
28	Tom Seaver	2.00
29	Johnny Bench	2.00
30	Reggie Jackson	2.00
31	Rod Carew	2.00
32	Nolan Ryan	4.00
33	Richie Ashburn	1.00
34	Yogi Berra	2.50
35	Lou Brock	2.00
36	Carlton Fisk	2.00
37	Joe Morgan	2.00
38	Bob Gibson	2.00
39	Willie McCovey	2.00
40	Harmon Killebrew	2.00
41	Takashi Saito	2.00
42	Kenji Johjima	3.00
43	Joel Zumaya	1.50
44	Dan Uggla	2.00
45	Taylor Buchholz	1.00
46	Josh Barfield	1.00
47	Brian Bannister	1.00
48	Nick Markakis	2.00
49	Carlos Martinez	1.00
50	Macay McBride	1.00
51	Brian Anderson	1.00
52	Freddie Bynum	1.00
53	Kelly Stoppach	1.00
54	Choo Freeman	1.00
55	Ryan Shealy	1.00
56	Chris Resop	1.00
57	Hanley Ramirez	2.50
58	Mike Jacobs	1.00
59	Cody Ross	1.00
60	Jose Capellan	1.00
61	David Gassner	1.00
62	Jason Kubel	1.00
63	Jered Weaver	3.00
64	Paul Maholm	1.00
65	Nate McLouth	1.00
66	Ben Johnson	1.00
67	Jack Taschner	1.00
68	Skip Schumaker	1.00
69	Brandon Watson	1.00
70	David Wright	3.00
71	David Ortiz	2.50
72	Alex Rodriguez	4.00
73	Johan Santana	2.00
74	Greg Maddux	3.00
75	Ichiro Suzuki	3.00
76	Albert Pujols	4.00
77	Hideki Matsui	3.00
78	Vladimir Guerrero	2.00
79	Pedro Martinez	2.00
80	Mike Schmidt	4.00
81	Al Kaline	3.00
82	Robin Yount	3.00

First Class Cuts
No Pricing
Production One Set

First Class Legends

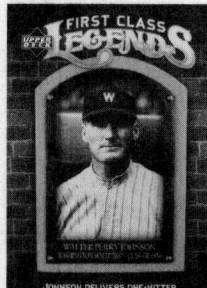

NM/M
Gold: 1-2X
Production 699 Sets
Platinum: 2-3X
Production 99 Sets
Spectrum: No Pricing
Production One Set

1-20	Babe Ruth	3.00
21-40	Ty Cobb	2.00
41-60	Honus Wagner	2.00
61-80	Christy Mathewson	1.00
81-100	Walter Johnson	1.00

Game Jersey
NM/M

Common Player:		4.00
JB	Jeff Bagwell	6.00
MC	Miguel Cabrera	8.00
EC	Eric Chavez	4.00
RC	Roger Clemens	15.00
JD	Johnny Damon	10.00
JE	Jim Edmonds	4.00
RF	Rafael Furcal	6.00
EG	Eric Gagne	4.00

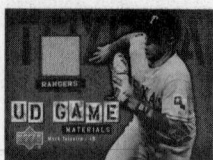

UD GAME MATERIALS

JG	Jason Giambi	6.00
KG	Ken Griffey Jr.	20.00
VG	Vladimir Guerrero	8.00
RH	Roy Halladay	4.00
DJ	Derek Jeter	20.00
RJ	Randy Johnson	8.00
AJ	Andruw Jones	4.00
CJ	Chipper Jones	8.00
JJ	Jacque Jones	4.00
DL	Derrek Lee	8.00
GM	Greg Maddux	12.00
PM	Pedro Martinez	8.00
DO	David Ortiz	8.00
RP	Rafael Palmeiro	8.00
CP	Corey Patterson	4.00
JP	Jake Peavy	8.00
MP	Mike Piazza	8.00
PO	Jorge Posada	6.00
PR	Mark Prior	4.00
AP	Albert Pujols	20.00
MR	Manny Ramirez	8.00
BR	Brian Roberts	6.00
IR	Ivan Rodriguez	6.00
SR	Scott Rolen	8.00
JS	Johan Santana	8.00
CS	Curt Schilling	8.00
SM	John Smoltz	8.00
AS	Alfonso Soriano	8.00
MT	Mark Teixeira	6.00
TE	Miguel Tejada	8.00
FT	Frank Thomas	8.00
JT	Jim Thome	8.00
DW	Dontrelle Willis	4.00
WR	David Wright	15.00

Series 2

BA	Bobby Abreu	6.00
GA	Garrett Atkins	6.00
JB	Josh Beckett	8.00
CB	Carlos Beltran	8.00
AB	Adrian Beltre	4.00
BI	Craig Biggio	8.00
HB	Hank Blalock	4.00
SC	Sean Casey	4.00
JD	Johnny Damon	10.00
CD	Carlos Delgado	8.00
AD	Adam Dunn	8.00
PF	Prince Fielder	15.00
TG	Tom Glavine	6.00
GR	Khalil Greene	4.00
KG	Ken Griffey Jr.	20.00
HA	Travis Hafner	6.00
TH	Todd Helton	6.00
RH	Ryan Howard	20.00
TI	Tadahito Iguchi	4.00
DJ	Derek Jeter	20.00
PK	Paul Konerko	6.00
CL	Carlos Lee	6.00
JL	Javy Lopez	4.00
VM	Victor Martinez	6.00
JM	Joe Mauer	6.00
MM	Mike Mussina	6.00
MO	Magglio Ordonez	6.00
RO	Roy Oswalt	6.00
AP	Andy Pettitte	6.00
MP	Mike Piazza	8.00
JR	Jose Reyes	10.00
GS	Gary Sheffield	6.00
SI	Grady Sizemore	10.00
JV	Jason Varitek	8.00
CW	Chien-Ming Wang	15.00
RW	Rickie Weeks	6.00
KW	Kerry Wood	6.00
MY	Michael Young	4.00
RZ	Ryan Zimmerman	10.00
BZ	Barry Zito	4.00

Game Patch
NM/M
Inserted 1:288

JB	Jeff Bagwell	20.00
MC	Miguel Cabrera	25.00
RC	Roger Clemens	30.00
JD	Johnny Damon	25.00
JE	Jim Edmonds	20.00
RF	Rafael Furcal	15.00
KG	Ken Griffey Jr.	40.00
VG	Vladimir Guerrero	25.00
RH	Roy Halladay	15.00
DJ	Derek Jeter	50.00
RJ	Randy Johnson	25.00
AJ	Andruw Jones	20.00
DL	Derrek Lee	20.00
GM	Greg Maddux	30.00
PM	Pedro Martinez	25.00
RP	Rafael Palmeiro	15.00
JP	Jake Peavy	20.00
MP	Mike Piazza	20.00
PR	Mark Prior	20.00
AP	Albert Pujols	50.00
MR	Manny Ramirez	30.00
BR	Brian Roberts	15.00
SR	Scott Rolen	20.00
JS	Johan Santana	25.00
SM	John Smoltz	25.00
TE	Miguel Tejada	20.00
FT	Frank Thomas	20.00
JT	Jim Thome	20.00
DW	Dontrelle Willis	15.00
WR	David Wright	40.00
Series 2:		No Pricing

Inaugural Images

DANIEL CABRERA / P / TEAM DOMINICAN REPUBLIC

NM/M

Common Player:		.50
II-1	Sung-Heon Hong	.50
II-2	Yulieski Gourriel	.50
II-3	Tsuyoshi Nishioka	1.00
II-4	Miguel Cabrera	1.50
II-5	Yung-Chi Chen	.50
II-6	Omari Romero	.50
II-7	Ken Griffey Jr.	2.00
II-8	Bernie Williams	.75
II-9	Daniel Cabrera	.50
II-10	David Ortiz	1.50
II-11	Alex Rodriguez	3.00
II-12	Frederich Cepeda	.50
II-13	Derek Jeter	3.00
II-14	Jorge Cantu	.50
II-15	Alexi Ramirez	.50
II-16	Yoandy Garlobo	.50
II-17	Koji Uehara	.50
II-18	Nobuhiko Matsunaka	.50
II-19	Tomoya Satozaki	.50
II-20	Seung-Yeop Lee	.50
II-21	Yulieski Gourriel	.50
II-22	Adrian Beltre	.50
II-23	Ken Griffey Jr.	2.00
II-24	Jong Beom Lee	.50
II-25	Ichiro Suzuki	2.00
II-26	Yoandy Garlobo	.50
II-27	Daisuke Matsuzaka	15.00
II-28	Yadel Marti	.50
II-29	Chan Ho Park	.50
II-30	Daisuke Matsuzaka	15.00

INKredible
NM/M
Inserted 1:288

JB	Joe Blanton	10.00
CA	Miguel Cabrera	40.00
CO	Chad Cordero	10.00
JC	Jesse Crain	10.00
CC	Carl Crawford	20.00
NG	Nomar Garciaparra	60.00
KG	Ken Griffey Jr.	120.00
TH	Travis Hafner	20.00
JH	J.J. Hardy	10.00
TI	Tadahito Iguchi/SP 91	50.00
DJ	Derek Jeter	125.00
SK	Scott Kazmir	20.00
CK	Casey Kotchman	10.00
VM	Victor Martinez	20.00
JM	Joe Mauer/SP 91	40.00
MO	Justin Morneau	25.00
BM	Brett Myers/SP 72	15.00
LO	Lyle Overbay/SP 91	15.00
JR	Jeremy Reed	10.00
RE	Jose Reyes/SP 91	40.00
AR	Alexis Rios	20.00
BR	Brian Roberts	20.00
MT	Mark Teixeira	25.00
JV	Justin Verlander/SP 91	40.00
WI	Dontrelle Wilis	15.00
DW	David Wright/SP 91	60.00
KY	Kevin Youkilis	15.00
RZ	Ryan Zimmerman/SP 91	40.00

Player Highlights
NM/M

Common Player:		.50
PH-1	Andruw Jones	1.00
PH-2	Manny Ramirez	1.00
PH-3	Travis Hafner	1.00
PH-4	Johnny Damon	1.00
PH-5	Miguel Cabrera	1.00
PH-6	Chris Carpenter	.75
PH-7	Derek Lee	1.00
PH-8	Jason Bay	.75
PH-9	Jason Varitek	1.00
PH-10	Ryan Howard	2.00
PH-11	Mark Teixeira	.75
PH-12	Carlos Delgado	.75
PH-13	Bartolo Colon	.50

TEJADA EARNS ALL-STAR MVP

PH-14	David Wright	2.00
PH-15	Miguel Tejada	.75
PH-16	Mike Piazza	1.00
PH-17	Paul Konerko	.75
PH-18	Jermaine Dye	.75
PH-19	Ichiro Suzuki	2.00
PH-20	Brad Wilkerson	.50
PH-21	Hideki Matsui	2.00
PH-22	Albert Pujols	3.00
PH-23	Chris Burke	.50
PH-24	Derek Jeter	3.00
PH-25	Brian Roberts	.75
PH-26	David Ortiz	1.50
PH-27	Alex Rodriguez	3.00
PH-28	Ken Griffey Jr.	2.00
PH-29	Prince Fielder	2.00
PH-30	Bobby Abreu	.75
PH-31	Vladimir Guerrero	1.00
PH-32	Tadahito Iguchi	1.00
PH-33	Jose Reyes	1.00
PH-34	Scott Podsednik	.75
PH-35	Gary Sheffield	.75

Run Producers

run producers DEREK JETER

NM/M

Common Player:		.50
RP-1	Ty Cobb	2.00
RP-2	Derrek Lee	1.00
RP-3	Andruw Jones	1.00
RP-4	David Ortiz	1.50
RP-5	Lou Gehrig	3.00
RP-6	Ken Griffey Jr.	2.00
RP-7	Albert Pujols	3.00
RP-8	Derek Jeter	3.00
RP-9	Manny Ramirez	1.00
RP-10	Alex Rodriguez	3.00
RP-11	Gary Sheffield	.75
RP-12	Miguel Cabrera	1.00
RP-13	Hideki Matsui	2.00
RP-14	Vladimir Guerrero	1.00
RP-15	David Wright	2.00
RP-16	Mike Schmidt	2.00
RP-17	Mark Teixeira	.75
RP-18	Babe Ruth	4.00
RP-19	Jimmie Foxx	2.00
RP-20	Honus Wagner	2.00

Signature Sensations
NM/M
Inserted 1:288 Hobby

BA	Bronson Arroyo	15.00
GA	Garrett Atkins	10.00
SB	Scott Baker	15.00
KC	Kiko Calero	5.00
JE	Johnny Estrada	8.00
KG	Ken Griffey Jr.	100.00
TR	Travis Hafner	15.00
BH	Bobby Hill	5.00
JJ	Josh Johnson	15.00
AL	Al Leiter	10.00
AM	Aaron Miles	10.00
YM	Yadier Molina	15.00
NP	Nick Punto	8.00
AR	Aaron Rowand	15.00
CS	Cory Sullivan	10.00
JS	Jeff Suppan	10.00
JV	Joe Valentine	10.00
DY	Delmon Young	20.00

Speed to Burn

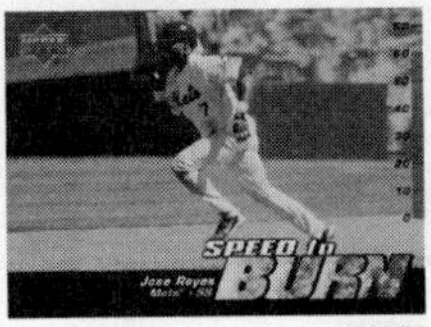

NM/M
Common Player: .50
SB-1 Lou Brock 1.00
SB-3 Alfonso Soriano 1.50
SB-4 Carl Crawford .75
SB-5 Chone Figgins .50
SB-6 Ichiro Suzuki 2.00
SB-7 Jose Reyes 1.00
SB-8 Juan Pierre .50
SB-9 Scott Podsednik .75
SB-11 Alex Rodriguez 3.00
SB-12 David Wright 2.00
SB-14 Bobby Abreu .75
SB-15 Brian Roberts .75

Star Attractions

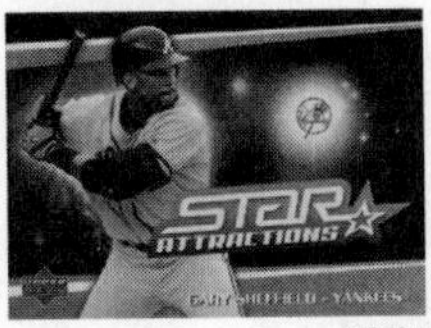

NM/M
Gold: 1X-2X
Production 699 Sets
BA Bobby Abreu .75
GA Garret Anderson .50
JB Josh Beckett .50
CB Carlos Beltran .75
AB Adrian Beltre .50
LB Lance Berkman .50
JC Jose Contreras .50
JD Johnny Damon 1.00
CD Carlos Delgado .75
JE Jim Edmonds .75
EG Eric Gagne .50
JG Jason Giambi .75
SG Shawn Green .50
GR Khalil Greene .50
KG Ken Griffey Jr. 2.00
GU Jose Guillen .50
RH Rich Harden .50
AH Aubrey Huff .50
TH Torii Hunter .50
TI Tadahito Iguchi .50
DJ Derek Jeter 3.00
AJ Andruw Jones 1.00
CJ Chipper Jones 1.00
JJ Jacque Jones .50
CL Carlos Lee .50
DL Derrek Lee 1.00
JL Javy Lopez .50
GM Greg Maddux 2.00
PM Pedro Martinez 1.00
JM Joe Mauer .50
MM Mark Mulder .50
MO Magglio Ordonez .50
DO David Ortiz 1.00
AP Andy Pettitte .75
JP Jorge Posada .75
MP Mark Prior .75
PU Albert Pujols 3.00
MR Manny Ramirez 1.00
JR Jose Reyes .75
CS Curt Schilling 1.00
JS Jason Schmidt .50
GS Gary Sheffield .75
SM John Smoltz .75
AS Alfonso Soriano .75
MT Mark Teixeira .75
FT Frank Thomas .75
DW Dontrelle Willis .50
KW Kerry Wood .50
WR David Wright 1.50
BZ Barry Zito .50

Star Attractions Swatches

NM/M
Common Player: 4.00
BA Bobby Abreu 6.00
GA Garret Anderson 4.00
JB Josh Beckett 6.00
CB Carlos Beltran 6.00
AB Adrian Beltre 4.00
LB Lance Berkman 6.00
JC Jose Contreras 4.00
JD Johnny Damon 10.00
CD Carlos Delgado 6.00
JE Jim Edmonds 4.00
EG Eric Gagne 4.00
JG Jason Giambi 6.00
SG Shawn Green 4.00
GR Khalil Greene 4.00
KG Ken Griffey Jr. 20.00
GU Jose Guillen 4.00
RH Rich Harden 6.00
AH Aubrey Huff 4.00
TH Torii Hunter 4.00
TI Tadahito Iguchi 5.00
DJ Derek Jeter 20.00
AJ Andruw Jones 4.00
CJ Chipper Jones 8.00
JJ Jacque Jones 4.00
CL Carlos Lee 4.00
DL Derrek Lee 8.00
JL Javy Lopez 4.00
GM Greg Maddux 12.00
PM Pedro Martinez 8.00
JM Joe Mauer 4.00
MM Mark Mulder 4.00
MO Magglio Ordonez 4.00
DO David Ortiz 8.00
AP Andy Pettitte 6.00
JP Jorge Posada 6.00
MP Mark Prior 4.00
PU Albert Pujols 20.00
MR Manny Ramirez 8.00
JR Jose Reyes 8.00
CS Curt Schilling 8.00
JS Jason Schmidt 4.00
GS Gary Sheffield 6.00
SM John Smoltz 8.00
AS Alfonso Soriano 6.00
MT Mark Teixeira 8.00
FT Frank Thomas 6.00
DW Dontrelle Willis 4.00
KW Kerry Wood 4.00
WR David Wright 15.00
BZ Barry Zito 4.00

Team Pride

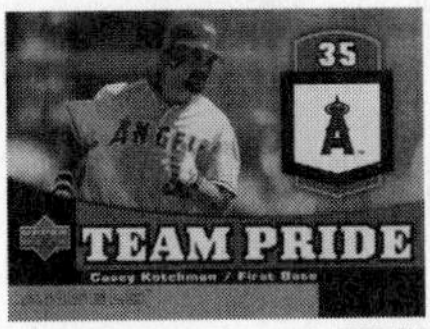

NM/M
Gold: 1X-2X
Production 699 Sets
BA Bobby Abreu .75
GA Garret Anderson .50
JB Jeff Bagwell .75
RB Rocco Baldelli .50
SC Sean Casey .50
LC Luis Castillo .50
EC Eric Chavez .50
JD Johnny Damon 1.00
CD Carlos Delgado .75
JE Jim Edmonds .75
ME Morgan Ensberg .50
KF Keith Foulke .50
EG Eric Gagne .50
LG Luis Gonzalez .50
GR Khalil Greene .50
KG Ken Griffey Jr. 2.00
RH Rich Harden .50
TH Trevor Hoffman .50
AH Aubrey Huff .50
DJ Derek Jeter 3.00
NJ Nick Johnson .50
AJ Andruw Jones 1.00
CJ Chipper Jones 1.00
RK Ryan Klesko .50
CK Casey Kotchman .50
ML Mike Lieberthal .50
LO Mike Lowell .50
GM Greg Maddux 2.00
MA Joe Mauer .50
JM Jamie Moyer .50
DO David Ortiz 1.00
PE Andy Pettitte .75
JP Jorge Posada .50
MP Mark Prior .75
AP Albert Pujols 3.00
JR Jose Reyes .50
IR Ivan Rodriguez .75
CC C.C. Sabathia .50
CS Curt Schilling 1.00
JS John Smoltz .75
MS Mike Sweeney .50
FT Frank Thomas .75
JT Jim Thome .75
VA Jason Varitek .75
JV Jose Vidro .50
BW Bernie Williams .50
DW Dontrelle Willis .50
KW Kerry Wood .50
MY Michael Young .50

Team Pride Materials

NM/M
Common Player: 4.00
BA Bobby Abreu 6.00
GA Garret Anderson 4.00
JB Jeff Bagwell 6.00
RB Rocco Baldelli 4.00
SC Sean Casey 4.00
LC Luis Castillo 4.00
EC Eric Chavez 4.00
JD Johnny Damon 10.00
CD Carlos Delgado 6.00
JE Jim Edmonds 4.00
ME Morgan Ensberg 4.00
KF Keith Foulke 4.00
EG Eric Gagne 4.00
LG Luis Gonzalez 4.00
GR Khalil Greene 4.00
KG Ken Griffey Jr. 20.00
RH Rich Harden 4.00
TH Trevor Hoffman 4.00
AH Aubrey Huff 4.00
DJ Derek Jeter 20.00
NJ Nick Johnson 4.00
AJ Andruw Jones 8.00
CJ Chipper Jones 8.00
RK Ryan Klesko 4.00
CK Casey Kotchman 4.00
ML Mike Lieberthal 4.00
LO Mike Lowell 4.00
GM Greg Maddux 12.00
MA Joe Mauer 4.00
JM Jamie Moyer 4.00
DO David Ortiz 8.00
PE Andy Pettitte 6.00
JP Jorge Posada 6.00
MP Mark Prior 4.00
AP Albert Pujols 20.00
JR Jose Reyes 8.00
IR Ivan Rodriguez 6.00
CC C.C. Sabathia 6.00
CS Curt Schilling 8.00
JS John Smoltz 8.00
MS Mike Sweeney 4.00
FT Frank Thomas 6.00
JT Jim Thome 8.00
VA Jason Varitek 6.00
JV Jose Vidro 4.00
BW Bernie Williams 6.00
DW Dontrelle Willis 4.00
KW Kerry Wood 4.00
MY Michael Young 4.00
BZ Barry Zito 4.00

Update Gold

NM/M
Gold (1001-1250): 4-8X
Gold SP's: .5-1X
Production 99 Sets

Update Inkredible

NM/M
Inserted 1:24 Retail
EA Erick Aybar 10.00
BA Brandon Backe 10.00
CB Colter Bean 10.00
YB Yuniesky Betancourt 10.00
EB Eude Brito 15.00
BB Ben Broussard 10.00
AB Ambiorix Burgos 15.00
GC Gustavo Chacin 8.00
BC Brandon Claussen 10.00
CO Chad Cordero/SP 15.00
CA Carl Crawford 15.00
CC Coco Crisp 15.00
CD Chris Duffy 10.00
JD Jermaine Dye 15.00
GF Gavin Floyd 8.00
RF Ryan Freel 15.00
RG Ryan Garko 15.00
KG Ken Griffey Jr./SP 125.00
AH Aaron Harang 10.00
JH John Hattig Jr. 10.00
MH Matt Holliday 20.00
TI Tadahito Iguchi/SP 30.00
CI Cesar Izturis 5.00
DJ Derek Jeter/SP 200.00
AJ Adam Jones 25.00
JO Jacque Jones 10.00
JJ Jorge Julio/SP 10.00
CK Casey Kotchman 10.00
CL Cliff Lee 10.00
NL Noah Lowry 15.00
BM Brandon McCarthy/SP 15.00
ZM Zach Miner 10.00
YM Yadier Molina 15.00
MM Matt Murton 20.00
LN Leo Nunez 8.00
AP Angel Pagan 10.00
PA John Patterson 5.00
RP Ronny Paulino 15.00
JP Jhonny Peralta 15.00
PE Joel Peralta 8.00
PI Joel Pineiro 8.00
DR Darrell Rasner 10.00
KR Ken Ray 8.00
AR Alex Rios SP 30.00
JR Juan Rivera SP 20.00
BR Brian Roberts 15.00
MR Mike Rouse 10.00
RS Ryan Shealy 15.00
NS Nick Swisher 15.00
MT Mark Teahen 15.00
MV Michael Vento 8.00
BW Brian Wilson 8.00
CW C.J. Wilson 5.00
KY Kevin Youkilis 15.00

Update Star Attractions

NM/M
Inserted 1:2 Retail
Silver: 2-3X
Production 99 Sets
BR Brian Anderson .50
EA Erick Aybar .50
WA Willy Aybar .50
JO Josh Barfield .50
BI Chad Billingsley .75
MC Matt Cain .75
RC Ronny Cedeno .50
SD Stephen Drew 1.50
AE Andre Ethier 1.00
PF Prince Fielder 1.50
TG Tony Gwynn Jr. .50
CH Cole Hamels 1.00
HI Jason Hirsh .50
HU Justin Huber .50
CO Conor Jackson .50
JA Chuck James .50
KJ Kenji Johjima 1.50
JJ Josh Johnson .50
AJ Adam Jones .50
MK Matthew Kemp .50
HK Howie Kendrick 1.00
JK Jason Kubel .50
LE Jon Lester 1.50
FL Francisco Liriano 1.00
AL Adam Loewen .50
NM Nicholas Markakis .75
AM Andy Marte .50
RM Russell Martin .50
MA Jeff Mathis .50
DM Dustin McGowan .50
LM Lastings Milledge 1.00
KM Kendry Morales .50
SO Scott Olsen .50
PA Jonathan Papelbon 1.00
DP Dustin Pedroia .50
PE Mike Pelfrey 1.50
HP Hayden Penn .50
CQ Carlos Quentin .50
HR Hanley Ramirez 1.00
AR Anthony Reyes .50
AN Anibal Sanchez .50
SW Jeremy Sowers .50
DU Dan Uggla .50
JV Justin Verlander 2.00
CY Chris Young .50
AW Adam Wainwright .50
JW Jered Weaver 1.00
RZ Ryan Zimmerman 1.50
JZ Joel Zumaya 1.00

2006 Upper Deck World Baseball Classic

NM/M
Complete Set (50): 20.00
Common Player: .25
1 Derek Jeter 1.50
2 Ken Griffey Jr. 1.00
3 Derrek Lee .50
4 Dontrelle Willis .25
5 Alex Rodriguez 1.50
6 Jeff Francoeur .25
7 Roger Clemens 1.50
8 Johnny Damon .50
9 Chipper Jones .50
10 Mark Teixeira .50
11 Chase Utley .50
12 Jake Peavy .50
13 Michael Collins .25
14 Justin Huber .25
15 Jason Bay .50
16 Jeff Francis .25
17 Justin Morneau .25
18 Guogang Yang .25
19 Wei Wang .25
20 Chia-Hsien Hseih .25
21 Chin-Lung Hu .25
22 Wei-Lun Pan .25
23 Yung-Chi Chen .25
24 Mike Piazza .50
25 Albert Pujols 1.50
26 David Ortiz .50
27 Jose Reyes .50
28 Miguel Tejada .50
29 Ichiro Suzuki 1.00
30 Nobuhiko Matsunaka .25
31 Toshiaki Imae .25
32 Kazuhiro Wada .25
33 Shunsuke Watanabe .25
34 Jung Bong .25
35 Jong Beom Lee .25
36 Seung-Yeop Lee .25
37 Vinny Castilla .25
38 Oliver Perez .50
39 Jorge Cantu .25
40 Andruw Jones .50
41 Carlos Lee .50
42 Carlos Beltran .50
43 Carlos Delgado .50
44 Ivan Rodriguez .50
45 Bernie Williams .50
46 Bobby Abreu .50
47 Miguel Cabrera .50
48 Johan Santana .50
49 Victor Martinez .50
50 Omar Vizquel .25

World Baseball Classic Jersey

NM/M
Inserted 1:24
Patch: No Pricing
Production Eight Sets
JB Jason Bay 10.00
EB Erik Bedard 8.00
CB Carlos Beltran 15.00
MC Miguel Cabrera 15.00
VC Vinny Castilla 4.00
FC Frederich Cepeda 15.00

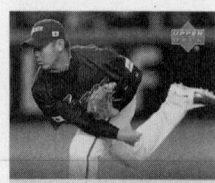

DAISUKE MATSUZAKA

TC	Tai-San Chang	200.00
RC	Roger Clemens	30.00
JD	Johnny Damon	15.00
CD	Carlos Delgado	10.00
ME	Michel Enriquez	20.00
MF	Maikel Folch	20.00
JF	Jeff Francis	4.00
FR	Jeff Francoeur	15.00
FG	Freddy Garcia	4.00
YG	Yulieski Gourriel	25.00
KG	Ken Griffey Jr.	25.00
JG	Jason Grilli	4.00
HS	Chia-Hsien Hseih	100.00
CH	Chin-Lung Hu	75.00
JH	Justin Huber	4.00
AI	Akinori Iwamura	40.00
AJ	Andruw Jones	15.00
MK	Munenori Kawasaki	50.00
PL	Pedro Lazo	20.00
CL	Carlos Lee	8.00
DL	Derrek Lee	10.00
JL	Jong Beom Lee	8.00
WL	Wei-Chu Lin	150.00
GL	Guangbiao Liu	10.00
VM	Victor Martinez	10.00
NM	Nobuhiko Matsunaka	60.00
DM	Daisuke Matsuzaka	180.00
YM	Yunieski Maya	15.00
JM	Justin Morneau	10.00
TN	Tsuyoshi Nishioka	60.00
MO	Michihiro Ogasawara	60.00
DO	David Ortiz	20.00
WP	Wei-Lun Pan	80.00
EP	Eduardo Paret	20.00
JP	Jin Man Park	15.00
OP	Oliver Perez	4.00
PE	Ariel Pestano	20.00
MP	Mike Piazza	25.00
AP	Albert Pujols	30.00
AR	Alex Rodriguez	25.00
IR	Ivan Rodriguez	10.00
JS	Johan Santana	15.00
MS	Min Han Son	10.00
AS	Alfonso Soriano	15.00
IS	Ichiro Suzuki	220.00
HT	Hitoshi Tamura	50.00
MT	Mark Teixeira	10.00
TE	Miguel Tejada	15.00
KU	Koji Uehara	40.00
JV	Jason Varitek	20.00
TW	Tsuyoshi Wada	25.00
WW	Wei Wang	15.00
SW	Shunsuke Watanabe	30.00
GY	Guogang Yang	10.00

2006 Upper Deck Artifacts

Justin Verlander 35

	NM/M
Complete Set (100):	35.00
Common Player:	.25
Pack (4):	8.00
Box (10):	70.00
1	Luis Gonzalez	.50
2	Conor Jackson (RC)	.25
3	Joey Devine RC	1.00
4	Andruw Jones	.50
5	Chipper Jones	1.00
6	John Smoltz	.50

7	Jeff Francoeur	.50
8	Brian Roberts	.25
9	Miguel Tejada	.75
10	Nick Markakis (RC)	.75
11	Curt Schilling	1.00
12	David Ortiz	1.00
13	Johnny Damon	1.00
14	Manny Ramirez	1.00
15	Jonathan Papelbon (RC)	5.00
16	Aramis Ramirez	.50
17	Carlos Zambrano	.50
18	Derrek Lee	.75
19	Greg Maddux	2.00
20	Mark Prior	.50
21	Mark Buehrle	.50
22	Paul Konerko	.50
23	Adam Dunn	.75
24	Ken Griffey Jr.	2.00
25	Travis Hafner	.50
26	Victor Martinez	.50
27	Todd Helton	.75
28	Ivan Rodriguez	.75
29	Jeremy Bonderman	.25
30	Jeremy Hermida (RC)	.50
31	Carlos Delgado	.50
32	Dontrelle Willis	.50
33	Josh Beckett	.75
34	Miguel Cabrera	1.00
35	Craig Biggio	.50
36	Lance Berkman	.50
37	Roger Clemens	3.00
38	Roy Oswalt	.50
39	Josh Willingham (RC)	.25
40	Hanley Ramirez (RC)	2.00
41	Prince Fielder (RC)	2.00
42	Zack Greinke	.25
43	Francisco Rodriguez	.25
44	Vladimir Guerrero	1.00
45	Tim Hamulack (RC)	.25
46	Jeff Kent	.50
47	Ben Sheets	.50
48	Rickie Weeks	.50
49	Francisco Liriano (RC)	2.00
50	Joe Mauer	.75
51	Johan Santana	1.00
52	Justin Morneau	.50
53	Torii Hunter	.50
54	Carlos Beltran	.75
55	David Wright	2.00
56	Jose Reyes	1.00
57	Mike Piazza	1.00
58	Pedro Martinez	1.00
59	Alex Rodriguez	3.00
60	Derek Jeter	3.00
61	Hideki Matsui	2.00
62	Randy Johnson	1.00
63	Justin Verlander (RC)	2.00
64	Bobby Crosby	.25
65	Eric Chavez	.50
66	Brian Anderson (RC)	.25
67	Bobby Abreu	.50
68	Pat Burrell	.50
69	Jason Bay	.50
70	Oliver Perez	.25
71	Chuck James (RC)	.25
72	Brian Giles	.25
73	Jake Peavy	.50
74	Khalil Greene	.25
75	Jason Schmidt	.25
76	Kenji Johjima RC	3.00
77	Jeremy Accardo RC	.50
78	Adrian Beltre	.50
79	Ichiro Suzuki	2.00
80	Jeff Harris RC	.50
81	Felix Hernandez	.75
82	Albert Pujols	3.00
83	Chris Carpenter	.75
84	Jim Edmonds	.50
85	Scott Rolen	.75
86	Mike Jacobs (RC)	.75
87	Carl Crawford	.50
88	Anderson Hernandez (RC)	.25
89	Scott Kazmir	.50
90	Josh Rupe (RC)	.25
91	Scott Feldman RC	.50
92	Alfonso Soriano	.75
93	Hank Blalock	.50
94	Mark Teixeira	.75
95	Michael Young	.50
96	Roy Halladay	.50
97	Vernon Wells	.50
98	Jason Bergmann RC	.50
99	Ryan Zimmerman (RC)	4.00
100	Jose Vidro	.25

AL/NL Artifacts

	NM/M
Common Player:	4.00
Production 325 Sets	
Red:	.75-1.5X
Production 100-250	
Green:	.75-1.5X
Production 150 Sets	
GA	Garrett Atkins	4.00
JB	Jeff Bagwell	8.00
SB	Scott Baker	4.00
RB	Rocco Baldelli	4.00
CL	Clint Barmes	4.00
JA	Jason Bay	6.00
HB	Hank Blalock	4.00
BL	Joe Blanton	4.00
JB	Jeremy Bonderman	4.00
BB	Ben Broussard	4.00
MB	Mark Buehrle	6.00
CB	Chris Burke	4.00

245/325   N. 39

NL ARTIFACTS

MC	Miguel Cabrera	8.00
MA	Matt Cain	6.00
JC	Jorge Cantu	4.00
CA	Chris Capuano	4.00
CC	Chris Carpenter	10.00
GC	Gustavo Chacin	4.00
EC	Eric Chavez	4.00
RC	Ryan Church	4.00
CH	Chad Cordero	4.00
CC	Carl Crawford	6.00
CR	Joe Crede	4.00
CO	Coco Crisp	6.00
ZD	Zachary Duke	4.00
AD	Adam Dunn/250	8.00
JE	Jim Edmonds	4.00
ME	Morgan Ensberg	4.00
PF	Prince Fielder	10.00
JF	Jeff Francoeur	8.00
EG	Eric Gagne	4.00
GA	Jon Garland	4.00
MG	Marcus Giles	4.00
JG	Jonny Gomes	4.00
KG	Ken Griffey Jr.	15.00
VG	Vladimir Guerrero	8.00
TH	Travis Hafner	4.00
BH	Bill Hall/235	6.00
AH	Aaron Harang	4.00
DH	Danny Haren	4.00
TH	Todd Helton	6.00
FH	Felix Hernandez	6.00
RH	Ramon Hernandez	4.00
TR	Trevor Hoffman	4.00
MH	Matt Holliday	8.00
RY	Ryan Howard	15.00
TI	Tadahito Iguchi	4.00
CO	Conor Jackson	4.00
DJ	Derek Jeter	25.00
DA	Dan Johnson	4.00
NJ	Nick Johnson	4.00
RJ	Randy Johnson/235	8.00
CJ	Chipper Jones	8.00
SK	Scott Kazmir	6.00
LE	Carlos Lee	6.00
CL	Cliff Lee	4.00
DL	Derrek Lee	8.00
BL	Brad Lidge	4.00
FL	Felipe Lopez	4.00
ML	Mark Loretta	4.00
NL	Noah Lowry	4.00
PM	Pedro Martinez	8.00
VM	Victor Martinez	6.00
JM	Joe Mauer	10.00
BM	Brian McCann	8.00
BM	Brandon McCarthy	4.00
YM	Yadier Molina	4.00
JU	Justin Morneau	8.00
JN	Joe Nathan	4.00
DO	David Ortiz	10.00
RO	Roy Oswalt	6.00
JP	Jake Peavy	6.00
PE	Jhonny Peralta	4.00
JP	Joel Pineiro	4.00
SP	Scott Podsednik	4.00
MP	Mark Prior	4.00
AP	Albert Pujols/250	20.00
MR	Manny Ramirez	8.00
JR	Jose Reyes	8.00
IR	Ivan Rodriguez	6.00
ES	Ervin Santana	4.00
CS	Chris Shelton	4.00
GS	Grady Sizemore	10.00
JS	John Smoltz/250	8.00
AS	Alfonso Soriano	8.00
HS	Huston Street	4.00
NS	Nick Swisher	4.00
MT	Miguel Tejada	6.00
CU	Chase Utley	10.00
JV	Jason Varitek	8.00
RW	Rickie Weeks	6.00
JW	Jake Westbrook	4.00
DW	Dontrelle Willis	8.00
WR	Jack Wilson/200	4.00
DW	David Wright	20.00
DY	Dmitri Young	4.00
MY	Michael Young	8.00
RZ	Ryan Zimmerman	10.00

Apparel

	NM/M
Common Player:	
Production 325 Sets	

SILVER

Gold:	.75-1.5X
Production 150 Sets	
Silver:	1X
Production 250 Sets	
Rare Apparel:	No Pricing
Production One Set	
AT	Garrett Atkins	6.00
HB	Harold Baines	4.00
SB	Scott Baker	4.00
RB	Rocco Baldelli	4.00
BA	Clint Barmes	4.00
BY	Jason Bay	6.00
YB	Yuniesky Betancourt	4.00
JO	Joe Blanton	4.00
JE	Jeremy Bonderman	4.00
BB	Ben Broussard	4.00
CB	Chris Burke	4.00
MC	Miguel Cabrera	8.00
MA	Matt Cain	6.00
JU	Jorge Cantu	4.00
CS	Chris Capuano	4.00
CH	Chris Carpenter	4.00
GC	Gustavo Chacin	4.00
RC	Ryan Church	4.00
WC	Will Clark	8.00
CD	Chad Cordero	6.00
CA	Carl Crawford	6.00
CO	Coco Crisp	6.00
PF	Prince Fielder	10.00
CF	Carlton Fisk	8.00
GF	Gavin Floyd	4.00
GA	Jon Garland	4.00
SG	Steve Garvey	6.00
MG	Marcus Giles	4.00
JG	Jonny Gomes	4.00
GO	Adrian Gonzalez	6.00
GG	Rich "Goose" Gossage	4.00
KG	Ken Griffey Jr.	15.00
AH	Aaron Harang	4.00
DH	Danny Haren	4.00
JH	Jeremy Hermida	4.00
FH	Felix Hernandez	8.00
RH	Ramon Hernandez	4.00
MH	Matt Holliday	8.00
HO	Ryan Howard	15.00
TI	Tadahito Iguchi	4.00
BO	Bo Jackson	10.00
CJ	Conor Jackson	4.00
DJ	Derek Jeter	25.00
DA	Dan Johnson	4.00
SK	Scott Kazmir	4.00
KE	Jason Kendall	4.00
CK	Casey Kotchman	4.00
JK	John Kruk	4.00
JL	Jason Lane	4.00
DO	Don Larsen	15.00
LE	Carlos Lee	6.00
CL	Cliff Lee	4.00
DL	Derrek Lee	8.00
BL	Brad Lidge	4.00
FL	Felipe Lopez	4.00
ML	Mark Loretta	4.00
NL	Noah Lowry	4.00
BI	Bill Madlock	4.00
JM	Joe Mauer	8.00
BC	Brian McCann	6.00
BM	Brandon McCarthy	4.00
FM	Fred McGriff	6.00
YM	Yadier Molina	4.00
MO	Justin Morneau	6.00
JN	Joe Nathan	4.00
GN	Graig Nettles	4.00
OR	Magglio Ordonez	4.00
RO	Roy Oswalt	6.00
PE	Jake Peavy	6.00
JP	Jhonny Peralta	4.00
GP	Gaylord Perry	6.00
PI	Joel Pineiro	4.00
SP	Scott Podsednik	4.00
BP	Boog Powell	4.00
JY	Jeremy Reed	4.00
HR	Jose Reyes	6.00
CR	Cal Ripken Jr.	20.00
BR	Brian Roberts	6.00
AR	Aaron Rowand	4.00
ES	Ervin Santana	4.00
RS	Ron Santo	15.00
MS	Mike Schmidt	10.00
SH	Chris Shelton	4.00
GS	Grady Sizemore	10.00
HS	Huston Street	4.00
NS	Nick Swisher	4.00
ST	So Taguchi	4.00
CU	Chase Utley	10.00
AV	Andy Van Slyke	4.00
RW	Rickie Weeks	4.00
JW	Jake Westbrook	4.00
DW	Dontrelle Willis	8.00
WR	David Wright	20.00
CY	Carl Yastrzemski	15.00

DY	Dmitri Young	4.00
MY	Michael Young	4.00
RZ	Ryan Zimmerman	10.00

Apparel Autographs

NM/M

Production 30 Sets
Patch Auto.: No Pricing
Production 10 Sets

AT	Garrett Atkins	20.00
HB	Harold Baines	20.00
SB	Scott Baker	15.00
BA	Clint Barmes	15.00
BY	Jason Bay	25.00
YB	Yuniesky Betancourt	25.00
JO	Joe Blanton	15.00
JE	Jeremy Bonderman	20.00
BB	Ben Broussard	15.00
CB	Chris Burke	15.00
MC	Miguel Cabrera	40.00
MA	Matt Cain	40.00
CS	Chris Capuano	15.00
CH	Chris Carpenter	50.00
GC	Gustavo Chacin	15.00
RC	Ryan Church	20.00
WC	Will Clark	40.00
CD	Chad Cordero	15.00
CA	Carl Crawford	25.00
CO	Coco Crisp	40.00
JD	Jermaine Dye	20.00
PF	Prince Fielder	50.00
CF	Carlton Fisk	40.00
SG	Steve Garvey	25.00
MG	Marcus Giles	15.00
JG	Jonny Gomes	15.00
GO	Adrian Gonzalez	20.00
GG	Rich "Goose" Gossage	25.00
KG	Ken Griffey Jr.	100.00
AH	Aaron Harang	15.00
DH	Danny Haren	20.00
JH	Jeremy Hermida	25.00
FH	Felix Hernandez	50.00
RH	Ramon Hernandez	15.00
HO	Ryan Howard/23	85.00
TI	Tadahito Iguchi	50.00
BO	Bo Jackson	100.00
CJ	Conor Jackson	40.00
DJ	Derek Jeter	200.00
DA	Dan Johnson	15.00
SK	Scott Kazmir	40.00
CK	Casey Kotchman	25.00
JK	John Kruk	20.00
DO	Don Larsen	25.00
LE	Carlos Lee	25.00
CL	Cliff Lee	15.00
DL	Derrek Lee	40.00
BL	Brad Lidge	15.00
FL	Felipe Lopez	15.00
NL	Noah Lowry	25.00
BI	Bill Madlock	15.00
JM	Joe Mauer	50.00
BM	Brandon McCarthy	15.00
YM	Yadier Molina	40.00
MO	Justin Morneau	30.00
JN	Joe Nathan	25.00
GN	Graig Nettles	30.00
OR	Magglio Ordonez	35.00
RO	Roy Oswalt	25.00
PE	Jake Peavy	40.00
JP	Jhonny Peralta	15.00
GP	Gaylord Perry	25.00
PI	Joel Pineiro	15.00
SP	Scott Podsednik	30.00
BP	Boog Powell	25.00
JR	Jose Reyes	40.00
CR	Cal Ripken Jr.	180.00
AR	Aaron Rowand	20.00
RS	Ron Santo	75.00
MS	Mike Schmidt	60.00
SH	Chris Shelton	15.00
HS	Huston Street	20.00
NS	Nick Swisher	25.00
CU	Chase Utley	75.00
AV	Andy Van Slyke	25.00
RW	Rickie Weeks	25.00
JW	Jake Westbrook	20.00
DW	Dontrelle Willis	20.00
WR	David Wright	85.00
CY	Carl Yastrzemski	65.00
DY	Dmitri Young	15.00
MY	Michael Young	25.00
RZ	Ryan Zimmerman	40.00

Autofacts

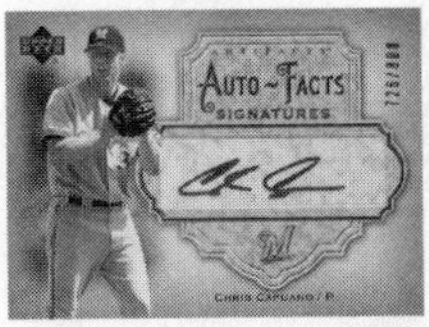

NM/M

Production 5-800

JA	Jeremy Accardo/800	10.00
LA	Luis Aparicio/250	15.00
GA	Garrett Atkins/800	15.00
CB	Clint Barmes/800	10.00
JB	Jason Bay/200	20.00
GB	George Bell/715	10.00
BE	Jason Bergmann/800	10.00
BY	Clete Boyer/485	10.00
MC	Miguel Cabrera/250	30.00
MA	Matt Cain/700	20.00
CP	Jose Capellan/800	10.00
CA	Chris Capuano/800	15.00
CH	Chris Carpenter/51	40.00
JC	Joe Carter/400	15.00
GC	Gustavo Chacin/800	10.00
CC	Chris Chambliss/400	15.00
RC	Ryan Church/800	10.00
CK	Jack Clark/800	10.00
CO	Coco Crisp/600	25.00
ED	Eric Davis/487	15.00
AD	Andre Dawson/300	20.00
CD	Chris Demaria/800	10.00
DA	Chris Denorfia/659	10.00
DE	Joey Devine/150	10.00
JD	Jermaine Dye/652	15.00
LD	Lenny Dykstra/412	15.00
SF	Scott Feldman/800	10.00
PF	Prince Fielder/200	40.00
GF	George Foster/300	10.00
SG	Steve Garvey/300	15.00
MG	Marcus Giles/350	10.00
GO	Jonny Gomes/700	10.00
GG	Rich "Goose" Gossage/300	20.00
KG	Ken Griffey Jr./800	60.00
TH	Travis Hafner/400	15.00
TM	Tim Hamulack/742	10.00
AH	Aaron Harang/800	10.00
DH	Danny Haren/800	15.00
JE	Jeff Harris/800	10.00
FH	Felix Hernandez/300	30.00
KH	Kent Hrbek/239	15.00
TI	Tadahito Iguchi/700	30.00
BO	Bo Jackson/250	50.00
CJ	Conor Jackson/800	15.00
RJ	Reggie Jackson/200	50.00
DJ	Derek Jeter/100	150.00
AJ	Andruw Jones/150	25.00
IK	Ian Kinsler/800	25.00
JK	Jason Kubel/400	10.00
JL	Jason Lane/800	10.00
BL	Barry Larkin/300	35.00
CL	Cliff Lee/600	15.00
DL	Derrek Lee/300	30.00
BI	Bill Madlock/300	15.00
PM	Pedro Martinez/100	60.00
JM	Joe Mauer/400	35.00
AM	Aaron Miles/494	10.00
YM	Yadier Molina/800	15.00
JN	Joe Nathan/800	15.00
GN	Graig Nettles/300	20.00
TO	Tony Oliva/300	15.00
MO	Magglio Ordonez/437	25.00
JP	Jhonny Peralta/700	10.00
TP	Tony Perez/251	25.00
HR	Hanley Ramirez/500	25.00
RE	Chris Resop/800	10.00
JR	Jim Rice/200	20.00
CR	Cal Ripken Jr./100	100.00
BR	Brian Roberts/200	15.00
AR	Aaron Rowand/520	15.00
JS	Johan Santana/150	50.00
CS	Chris Shelton/350	10.00
HS	Huston Street/500	15.00
NS	Nick Swisher/700	15.00
WT	Willy Taveras/500	10.00
CU	Chase Utley/200	50.00
AV	Andy Van Slyke/800	15.00
JV	Justin Verlander/700	40.00
RW	Rickie Weeks/91	25.00
JW	Jake Westbrook/650	10.00
WI	Dontrelle Willis/50	15.00
MW	Maury Wills/150	15.00
DW	David Wright/300	65.00
CY	Chris Young/700	15.00
DY	Dmitri Young/300	10.00
MY	Michael Young/600	20.00
CZ	Carlos Zambrano/200	25.00
RZ	Ryan Zimmerman/800	25.00

Awesome Artifacts

NM/M

Common Player: 10.00
Production 45 unless noted.

BA	Jeff Bagwell	12.00
HB	Harold Baines	10.00
SB	Scott Baker	10.00
RB	Rocco Baldelli	10.00
CB	Clint Barmes	10.00
JB	Jason Bay	12.00
HA	Hank Blalock	10.00
BL	Joe Blanton	10.00
MB	Mark Buehrle	10.00
BU	Chris Burke	10.00
MC	Miguel Cabrera	15.00
CA	Matt Cain	10.00
CH	Chris Carpenter	15.00
GC	Gustavo Chacin	10.00
EC	Eric Chavez	10.00
WC	Will Clark	12.00
CC	Carl Crawford	12.00
DD	Don Drysdale/25	25.00
ZD	Zachary Duke	10.00
AD	Adam Dunn	15.00
JE	Jim Edmonds	12.00
ME	Morgan Ensberg	10.00
PF	Prince Fielder	15.00
CF	Carlton Fisk	15.00
FG	Gavin Floyd	10.00
JF	Jeff Francoeur	20.00
EG	Eric Gagne	10.00
FG	Freddy Garcia/21	10.00
GA	Jon Garland	10.00
SG	Steve Garvey	10.00
JG	Jonny Gomes	10.00
KG	Ken Griffey Jr.	30.00
VG	Vladimir Guerrero	20.00
BH	Bill Hall	10.00
AH	Aaron Harang	10.00
DH	Danny Haren	10.00
TH	Todd Helton	10.00
FH	Felix Hernandez	15.00
TR	Trevor Hoffman	10.00
RH	Rogers Hornsby/25	100.00
RY	Ryan Howard	30.00
BO	Bo Jackson	15.00
CO	Conor Jackson	10.00
DJ	Derek Jeter	40.00
DA	Dan Johnson	10.00
NJ	Nick Johnson	10.00
RA	Randy Johnson	15.00
CJ	Chipper Jones	15.00
JL	Jason Lane	10.00
DL	Don Larsen/25	25.00
CL	Cliff Lee	10.00
DE	Derrek Lee	15.00
NL	Noah Lowry	10.00
PM	Pedro Martinez	15.00
EM	Eddie Mathews	40.00
BR	Brian McCann	15.00
BM	Brandon McCarthy	10.00
JM	Johnny Mize/25	20.00
YM	Yadier Molina	10.00
JU	Justin Morneau	15.00
DO	David Ortiz	25.00
RO	Roy Oswalt	10.00
SP	Satchel Paige	100.00
DP	Dave Parker	10.00
JP	Jake Peavy	10.00
PE	Jhonny Peralta	10.00
GP	Gaylord Perry	10.00
JO	Joel Pineiro	10.00
MP	Mark Prior	10.00
AP	Albert Pujols	40.00
MR	Manny Ramirez	15.00
CR	Cal Ripken Jr.	40.00
IR	Ivan Rodriguez	10.00
AR	Aaron Rowand	10.00
ES	Ervin Santana	10.00
RS	Ron Santo	10.00
JA	Jason Schmidt	10.00
CS	Chris Shelton	10.00
GS	Grady Sizemore	15.00
JS	John Smoltz	15.00
AS	Alfonso Soriano	15.00
HS	Huston Street	10.00
NS	Nick Swisher	10.00
MI	Miguel Tejada	10.00
FT	Frank Thomas	15.00
CU	Chase Utley	25.00
AV	Andy Van Slyke	10.00
JV	Jason Varitek	20.00
RW	Rickie Weeks	10.00
DW	David Wells	10.00
WE	Jake Westbrook	10.00
WI	Dontrelle Willis	12.00
JW	Jack Wilson	10.00
WR	David Wright	30.00
CY	Carl Yastrzemski/25	40.00
RZ	Ryan Zimmerman	15.00

2006 Upper Deck Epic

NM/M

Complete Set (300):
Common Player: 2.00
Production 450 Sets
Pack (3): 35.00
Box (5): 150.00

1	Conor Jackson **(RC)**	4.00
2	Brandon Webb	3.00
3	Craig Counsell	2.00
4	Luis Gonzalez	2.00
5	Miguel Batista	2.00
6	Orlando Hudson	2.00
7	Russ Ortiz	2.00
8	Shawn Green	2.00
9	Andruw Jones	3.00
10	Chipper Jones	5.00
11	Edgar Renteria	3.00
12	Jeff Francoeur	4.00
13	John Smoltz	3.00
14	Marcus Giles	2.00
15	Mike Hampton	2.00
16	Tim Hudson	3.00
17	Erik Bedard	3.00
18	Brian Roberts	2.00
19	Javy Lopez	2.00
20	Jay Gibbons	2.00
21	Jeff Conine	2.00
22	Melvin Mora	2.00
23	Miguel Tejada	4.00
24	Daniel Cabrera	2.00
25	Rodrigo Lopez	2.00
26	Ramon Hernandez	2.00
27	Bronson Arroyo	2.00
28	Curt Schilling	5.00
29	David Ortiz	5.00
30	David Wells	2.00
31	Jason Varitek	4.00
32	Josh Beckett	4.00
33	Kevin Youkilis	3.00
34	Manny Ramirez	5.00
35	Matt Clement	2.00
36	Mike Lowell	3.00
37	Tim Wakefield	2.00
38	Trot Nixon	2.00
39	Aramis Ramirez	3.00
40	Carlos Zambrano	3.00
41	Derrek Lee	4.00
42	Greg Maddux	10.00
43	Juan Pierre	2.00
44	Kerry Wood	3.00
45	Mark Prior	2.00
46	Michael Barrett	2.00
47	Ryan Dempster	2.00
48	Todd Walker	2.00
49	Wade Miller	2.00
50	A.J. Pierzynski	2.00
51	Brian Anderson **(RC)**	2.00
52	Frank Thomas	4.00
53	Javier Vazquez	2.00
54	Jim Thome	4.00
55	Joe Crede	2.00
56	Jon Garland	2.00
57	Juan Uribe	2.00
58	Mark Buehrle	3.00
59	Paul Konerko	3.00
60	Scott Podsednik	2.00
61	Tadahito Iguchi	3.00
62	Aaron Harang	2.00
63	Adam Dunn	4.00
64	Austin Kearns	2.00
65	Edwin Encarnacion	2.00
66	Eric Milton	2.00
67	Felipe Lopez	2.00
68	Jason LaRue	2.00
69	Ken Griffey Jr.	10.00
70	Wily Mo Pena	2.00
71	Aaron Boone	2.00
72	Ben Broussard	2.00
73	C.C. Sabathia	4.00
74	Casey Blake	2.00
75	Cliff Lee	2.00
76	Grady Sizemore	4.00
77	Jake Westbrook	2.00
78	Josh Bard	2.00
79	Travis Hafner	3.00
80	Victor Martinez	3.00
81	Chin-Hui Tsao	2.00
82	Clint Barmes	2.00
83	Garrett Atkins	3.00
84	Josh Wilson **(RC)**	2.00
85	Luis Gonzalez	2.00
86	Matt Holliday	4.00
87	Todd Helton	4.00
88	Brandon Inge	2.00
89	Carlos Guillen	3.00
90	Chris Shelton	2.00
91	Craig Monroe	2.00
92	Dmitri Young	2.00
93	Ivan Rodriguez	3.00
94	Jeremy Bonderman	3.00
95	Magglio Ordonez	3.00
96	Alberto Gonzalez **RC**	2.00
97	Brian Moehler	2.00
98	Dontrelle Willis	2.00
99	Jeremy Hermida **(RC)**	3.00
100	Jason Vargas	2.00
101	Miguel Cabrera	5.00
102	Adam Everett	2.00
103	Andy Pettitte	3.00
104	Brad Ausmus	2.00
105	Brad Lidge	2.00
106	Craig Biggio	3.00
107	Dan Wheeler	2.00
108	Jeff Bagwell	4.00
109	Lance Berkman	3.00
110	Morgan Ensberg	2.00
111	Preston Wilson	2.00
112	Roger Clemens	10.00
113	Roy Oswalt	3.00
114	David Gassner **(RC)**	2.00
115	Angel Berroa	2.00
116	Doug Mientkiewicz	2.00
117	Joe Mays	2.00
118	Mark Grudzielanek	2.00
119	Mike Sweeney	2.00
120	Reggie Sanders	2.00
121	Runelvys Hernandez	2.00
122	Scott Elarton	2.00
123	Brandon Watson **(RC)**	2.00
124	Zack Greinke	2.00
125	Brad Penny	2.00
126	Derek Lowe	2.00
127	Eric Gagne	2.00
128	J.D. Drew	3.00
129	Jayson Werth	2.00
130	Jeff Kent	3.00
131	Nomar Garciaparra	3.00
132	Olmedo Saenz	2.00
133	Rafael Furcal	3.00
134	Ben Sheets	3.00
135	Bill Hall	2.00
136	Carlos Lee	3.00
137	Geoff Jenkins	2.00
138	Prince Fielder **(RC)**	10.00
139	Rickie Weeks	3.00
140	Jose Capellan **(RC)**	2.00
141	Brad Radke	2.00
142	Joe Mauer	4.00
143	Joe Nathan	2.00
144	Johan Santana	5.00
145	Justin Morneau	3.00
146	Kyle Lohse	2.00
147	Lew Ford	2.00
148	Luis Castillo	2.00
149	Matthew LeCroy	2.00
150	Michael Cuddyer	2.00
151	Shannon Stewart	2.00
152	Torii Hunter	3.00
153	Billy Wagner	2.00
154	Carlos Beltran	5.00

155	Carlos Delgado	4.00
156	Cliff Floyd	2.00
157	David Wright	10.00
158	Jose Reyes	8.00
159	Kazuo Matsui	2.00
160	Mike Piazza	6.00
161	Paul LoDuca	2.00
162	Pedro Martinez	5.00
163	Tom Glavine	3.00
164	Victor Diaz	2.00
165	Alex Rodriguez	15.00
166	Bernie Williams	3.00
167	Carl Pavano	2.00
168	Chien-Ming Wang	5.00
169	Derek Jeter	15.00
170	Gary Sheffield	4.00
171	Hideki Matsui	8.00
172	Jason Giambi	3.00
173	Johnny Damon	5.00
174	Jorge Posada	4.00
175	Robinson Cano	5.00
176	Mariano Rivera	4.00
177	Mike Mussina	4.00
178	Randy Johnson	5.00
179	Miguel Cairo	2.00
180	Barry Zito	2.00
181	Bobby Crosby	2.00
182	Bobby Kielty	2.00
183	Eric Chavez	2.00
184	Josh Barfield **(RC)**	2.00
185	Esteban Loaiza	2.00
186	Huston Street	2.00
187	Jason Kendall	2.00
188	Nick Swisher	3.00
189	Aaron Rowand	3.00
190	Bobby Abreu	3.00
191	Chase Utley	5.00
192	Gavin Floyd	2.00
193	Jimmy Rollins	5.00
194	Mike Lieberthal	2.00
195	Pat Burrell	3.00
196	Ryan Howard	8.00
197	Craig Wilson	2.00
198	Jack Wilson	2.00
199	Jason Bay	4.00
200	Joe Randa	2.00
201	Josh Fogg	2.00
202	Kip Wells	2.00
203	Sean Casey	2.00
204	Zachary Duke	2.00
205	Brian Giles	2.00
206	Dave Roberts	2.00
207	Jake Peavy	4.00
208	Khalil Greene	2.00
209	Mike Cameron	2.00
210	Ryan Klesko	2.00
211	Trevor Hoffman	2.00
212	Vinny Castilla	2.00
213	Armando Benitez	2.00
214	Jason Schmidt	2.00
215	Matt Morris	2.00
216	Moises Alou	3.00
217	Omar Vizquel	2.00
218	Ray Durham	2.00
219	Adrian Beltre	3.00
220	Carl Everett	2.00
221	Kenji Johjima **RC**	15.00
222	Felix Hernandez	4.00
223	Ichiro Suzuki	10.00
224	Jamie Moyer	2.00
225	Jeremy Reed	2.00
226	Joel Pineiro	2.00
227	Raul Ibanez	2.00
228	Rickie Sexson	3.00
229	Albert Pujols	15.00
230	Chris Carpenter	5.00
231	David Eckstein	2.00
232	Jason Marquis	2.00
233	Jeff Suppan	2.00
234	Jim Edmonds	4.00
235	Yadier Molina	2.00
236	Mark Mulder	2.00
237	Scott Rolen	5.00
238	Alex Gonzalez	2.00
239	Aubrey Huff	2.00
240	Carl Crawford	3.00
241	Casey Fossum	2.00
242	Joey Gathright	2.00
243	Scott Kazmir	3.00
244	Toby Hall	2.00
245	Travis Lee	2.00
246	Adam Eaton	2.00
247	Francisco Cordero	2.00
248	Hank Blalock	3.00
249	Kevin Mench	2.00
250	Kevin Millwood	2.00
251	Laynce Nix	2.00
252	Mark Teixeira	4.00
253	Michael Young	3.00
254	A.J. Burnett	3.00
255	Alex Rios	3.00
256	B.J. Ryan	2.00
257	Corey Koskie	2.00
258	Josh Towers	2.00
259	Lyle Overbay	2.00
260	Reed Johnson	2.00
261	Roy Halladay	3.00
262	Russ Adams	2.00
263	Troy Glaus	3.00
264	Vernon Wells	3.00
265	Alfonso Soriano	4.00
266	John Patterson	2.00
267	Damian Jackson	2.00
268	Jose Guillen	2.00
269	Jose Vidro	2.00
270	Livan Hernandez	2.00
271	Adam Kennedy	2.00
272	Bartolo Colon	2.00
273	Bengie Molina	2.00
274	Casey Kotchman	2.00
275	Chone Figgins	3.00
276	Matt Cain **(RC)**	5.00
277	Darin Erstad	2.00
278	Edgardo Alfonzo	2.00
279	Francisco Rodriguez	2.00
280	Garret Anderson	2.00
281	Vladimir Guerrero	5.00
282	Chris Denorfia **(RC)**	2.00
283	Joey Devine **RC**	4.00
284	Justin Verlander **(RC)**	10.00
285	Scott Feldman **RC**	5.00
286	Jason Bergmann **RC**	4.00
287	Jeremy Accardo **RC**	4.00
288	Adam Wainwright **(RC)**	8.00
289	Hanley Ramirez **(RC)**	5.00
290	Josh Johnson **(RC)**	3.00
291	Ryan Zimmerman **(RC)**	15.00
292	Anderson Hernandez **(RC)**	4.00
293	Francisco Liriano **(RC)**	15.00
294	Josh Willingham **(RC)**	3.00
295	Hong-Chih Kuo **(RC)**	8.00
296	Steve Stemle **RC**	4.00
297	Jeff Harris **RC**	4.00
298	John Van Benschoten **(RC)**	4.00
299	Jonathan Papelbon **(RC)**	20.00
300	Jason Kubel **(RC)**	4.00

Awesome 8 Materials

Production 1-10
No Pricing

Epic Endorsements

		NM/M
Production 10-45		
JB	Jason Bay/45	30.00
BE	Johnny Bench/10	
CB	Craig Biggio/30	60.00
WB	Wade Boggs/30	75.00
LB	Lou Brock/30	75.00
JI	Jim Bunning/30	30.00
MC1	Miguel Cabrera/30	50.00
MC2	Miguel Cabrera/30	50.00
RC	Rod Carew/30	50.00
SC1	Steve Carlton/27	35.00
SC2	Steve Carlton/27	35.00
EC	Eric Chavez/30	30.00
WC	Will Clark/23	50.00
AD	Adam Dunn/45	40.00
BF1	Bob Feller/45	40.00
BF2	Bob Feller/45	40.00
PF	Prince Fielder/45	50.00
CF	Carlton Fisk/30	50.00
SG	Steve Garvey/45	30.00
BG	Bob Gibson/30	60.00
KG1	Ken Griffey Jr./30	120.00
KG2	Ken Griffey Jr./30	120.00
KG3	Ken Griffey Jr./30	120.00
TG	Tony Gwynn/30	50.00
JH1	Jeremy Hermida/45	30.00
JH2	Jeremy Hermida/45	30.00
FH1	Felix Hernandez/30	50.00
FH2	Felix Hernandez/30	50.00
RH	Ryan Howard/45	100.00
BO	Bo Jackson/30	85.00
DJ1	Derek Jeter/30	180.00
DJ2	Derek Jeter/30	180.00
DJ3	Derek Jeter/30	180.00
AJ	Andruw Jones/30	30.00
LA	Don Larsen/30	40.00
FL	Fred Lynn/45	25.00
BM	Bill Mazeroski/30	60.00
PM1	Paul Molitor/30	40.00
PM2	Paul Molitor/30	40.00
TO	Tony Oliva/45	30.00
DO	David Ortiz/30	85.00
RO1	Roy Oswalt/45	40.00
RO2	Roy Oswalt/45	40.00
JP1	Jim Palmer/30	40.00
JP2	Jim Palmer/30	40.00
JA	Jake Peavy/45	25.00
TP	Tony Perez/45	40.00
AP	Albert Pujols/15	400.00
CR	Cal Ripken Jr./15	280.00
BN	Brian Roberts/45	30.00
BR1	Brooks Robinson/30	75.00
BR2	Brooks Robinson/30	75.00
FR	Frank Robinson/30	40.00
RS1	Ryne Sandberg/23	100.00
CS	Curt Schilling/15	75.00
TS	Tom Seaver/30	60.00
OS	Ozzie Smith/30	75.00
SM	John Smoltz/30	150.00
AS	Alfonso Soriano/30	40.00
DS	Don Sutton/30	30.00
CU	Chase Utley/45	50.00
BW	Billy Williams/45	25.00
DW1	Dontrelle Willis/30	40.00
DW2	Dontrelle Willis/30	40.00
MW	Maury Wills/45	25.00
WR	David Wright/25	100.00
RZ1	Ryan Zimmerman/30	50.00
RZ2	Ryan Zimmerman/30	50.00

Epic Events

		NM/M
Common Player:		2.00
Production 675 Sets		
EE1	Ryan Howard	4.00
EE2	Tadahito Iguchi	2.00
EE3	Paul Konerko	2.00
EE4	Craig Biggio	2.00
EE5	Alex Rodriguez	6.00
EE6	Ichiro Suzuki	5.00
EE7	David Ortiz	4.00
EE8	Miguel Cabrera	3.00
EE9	Dontrelle Willis	2.00
EE10	Mark Teixeira	3.00
EE11	Hideki Matsui	5.00
EE12	Albert Pujols	8.00
EE13	Albert Pujols	8.00
EE14	Greg Maddux	5.00
EE15	Greg Maddux	5.00
EE16	Manny Ramirez	3.00
EE17	Mark Teixeira	3.00
EE18	Alex Rodriguez	6.00
EE19	Manny Ramirez	3.00
EE20	Randy Johnson	3.00
EE21	Jason Varitek	3.00
EE22	Vladimir Guerrero	3.00
EE23	Roger Clemens	8.00
EE24	Manny Ramirez	3.00
EE25	Curt Schilling	3.00
EE26	Johnny Damon	3.00
EE27	David Ortiz	4.00
EE28	David Wright	6.00
EE29	Ichiro Suzuki	5.00
EE30	Ichiro Suzuki	5.00
EE31	Adam Dunn	3.00
EE32	Adrian Beltre	2.00
EE33	Javy Lopez	2.00
EE34	Greg Maddux	5.00
EE35	Randy Johnson	3.00
EE36	Jim Thome	3.00
EE37	Adam Dunn	3.00
EE38	Bobby Abreu	3.00
EE39	Felix Hernandez	3.00
EE40	Greg Maddux	5.00
EE41	Ken Griffey Jr.	6.00
EE42	Randy Johnson	3.00
EE43	Johan Santana	3.00
EE44	Magglio Ordonez	3.00
EE45	Josh Beckett	4.00
EE46	Ivan Rodriguez	3.00
EE47	Alfonso Soriano	3.00
EE48	Eric Gagne	2.00
EE49	Hank Blalock	2.00
EE50	Roger Clemens	8.00
EE51	Derek Jeter	8.00
EE52	Derek Jeter	8.00
EE53	Barry Zito	2.00
EE54	Alex Rodriguez	6.00
EE55	Nomar Garciaparra	3.00
EE56	Torii Hunter	2.00
EE57	Ichiro Suzuki	5.00
EE58	Randy Johnson	3.00
EE59	Ichiro Suzuki	5.00
EE60	Albert Pujols	8.00
EE61	Albert Pujols	8.00
EE62	Ichiro Suzuki	5.00
EE63	Derek Jeter	8.00
EE64	Pedro Martinez	3.00
EE65	Chris Shelton	2.00
EE66	Ivan Rodriguez	3.00
EE67	Chipper Jones	3.00
EE68	Pedro Martinez	3.00
EE69	Ken Griffey Jr.	6.00
EE70	Jeff Bagwell	3.00
EE71	Nomar Garciaparra	3.00
EE72	Mark Prior	3.00
EE73	Kerry Wood	2.00
EE74	Andruw Jones	3.00
EE75	Derek Jeter	8.00
EE76	Cal Ripken Jr.	10.00
EE77	Ken Griffey Jr.	6.00
EE78	Ken Griffey Jr.	6.00
EE79	Mike Piazza	4.00
EE80	Nolan Ryan	6.00
EE81	Greg Maddux	5.00
EE82	Greg Maddux	5.00
EE83	Roger Clemens	8.00
EE84	Ozzie Smith	4.00
EE85	Tom Seaver	4.00
EE86	Thurman Munson	4.00
EE87	Reggie Jackson	3.00
EE88	Johnny Bench	4.00
EE89	Mike Schmidt	4.00
EE90	Carlton Fisk	2.00
EE91	Eddie Mathews	3.00
EE92	Roy Campanella	4.00
EE93	Jackie Robinson	6.00
EE94	Joe DiMaggio	6.00
EE95	Jimmie Foxx	5.00
EE96	Lou Gehrig	10.00
EE97	Babe Ruth	10.00
EE98	Ty Cobb	6.00
EE99	Honus Wagner	5.00
EE100	Cy Young	5.00

Four Barrel

No Pricing
Production One Set

Foursome Fabrics

		NM/M
Production 5-50		
CMBF	Carlton Fisk, Thurman Munson, Johnny Bench, Gary Carter/25	70.00
GRSM	Tom Seaver, Nolan Ryan, Juan Marichal, Bob Gibson/50	60.00
MBSP	Albert Pujols, Lou Brock, Stan Musial, Ozzie Smith/30	100.00
PJGG	Ken Griffey Jr., Derek Jeter, Vladimir Guerrero, Albert Pujols/50	100.00
RCJP	Mark Prior, Nolan Ryan, Roger Clemens, Randy Johnson/50	50.00
WRRJ	Pee Wee Reese, Honus Wagner, Cal Ripken Jr., Derek Jeter/20	300.00
WYBS	Ted Williams, Wade Boggs, Curt Schilling, Carl Yastrzemski/50	85.00

Materials

		NM/M
Production 10-185		
No pricing production 15 or less.		
Orange:		.75-1.5X
Production 5-185		
Red:		.75-1.5X
Production 10-185		
Light Purple:		.75-1.5X
Production 4-185		
Dark Purple:		.75-1.5X
Production 3-185		
Blue:		.75-1.5X
Production 3-99		
Teal:		.75-1.5X
Production 5-99		
Green:		1-1.5X
Production 3-75		
Dark Green:		1-2X
Production 3-50		
Grey:		1-2X
Production 3-40		
Gold:		1-1.25X
Production 1-25		
EB	Ernie Banks/155	15.00
JB1	Johnny Bench/155	10.00
JB2	Johnny Bench/155	10.00
WB1	Wade Boggs/185	10.00
WB2	Wade Boggs/185	10.00
LB1	Lou Brock/48	10.00
LB2	Lou Brock/48	10.00
RC1	Roger Clemens/155	20.00
RC2	Roger Clemens/155	20.00
RC3	Roger Clemens/155	20.00
CL1	Roberto Clemente/50	75.00
JD1	Joe DiMaggio/185	65.00
JD2	Joe DiMaggio/173	65.00
JD3	Joe DiMaggio/99	75.00
CF	Carlton Fisk/169	10.00
CF2	Carlton Fisk/185	10.00
WF	Whitey Ford/155	15.00
LG1	Lou Gehrig/15	165.00
LG2	Lou Gehrig/15	165.00
LG3	Lou Gehrig/15	165.00
BG	Bob Gibson/155	10.00
BG2	Bob Gibson/155	15.00
HG	Hank Greenberg/50	40.00
KG1	Ken Griffey Jr./175	15.00
KG2	Ken Griffey Jr./175	15.00
KG3	Ken Griffey Jr./175	15.00
VG	Vladimir Guerrero/145	8.00
VG2	Vladimir Guerrero/145	8.00
GH	Gil Hodges/39	15.00
RH	Rogers Hornsby/50	75.00
RE1	Reggie Jackson/52	12.00
RE2	Reggie Jackson/52	12.00
RE3	Reggie Jackson/52	12.00
DJ1	Derek Jeter/185	25.00
DJ2	Derek Jeter/185	25.00
DJ3	Derek Jeter/185	25.00
RJ1	Randy Johnson/145	10.00
RJ2	Randy Johnson/145	10.00
HK	Harmon Killebrew/155	15.00
JM	Juan Marichal/155	8.00
ED	Eddie Mathews/75	10.00
DM1	Don Mattingly/185	15.00
DM2	Don Mattingly/185	15.00
WM	Willie McCovey/155	15.00
WM2	Willie McCovey/155	15.00
WM3	Willie McCovey/155	15.00
PM1	Paul Molitor/155	10.00
PM2	Paul Molitor/155	10.00
JO	Joe Morgan/145	8.00
JO2	Joe Morgan/155	8.00
TH1	Thurman Munson/35	30.00
TH2	Thurman Munson/35	30.00
EM1	Eddie Murray/185	8.00
EM2	Eddie Murray/165	8.00
EM3	Eddie Murray/155	8.00
SM1	Stan Musial/50	25.00
SM2	Stan Musial/75	25.00
MP1	Mike Piazza/145	12.00
MP2	Mike Piazza/145	12.00
MA	Mark Prior/185	8.00
MA2	Mark Prior/185	8.00
KP1	Kirby Puckett/155	15.00
KP2	Kirby Puckett/155	15.00
AP1	Albert Pujols/185	20.00
AP2	Albert Pujols/185	20.00
AP3	Albert Pujols/185	20.00
PR1	Pee Wee Reese/145	15.00
PR2	Pee Wee Reese/145	15.00
CR1	Cal Ripken Jr./185	25.00
CR2	Cal Ripken Jr./177	25.00
CR3	Cal Ripken Jr./155	25.00
RO	Brooks Robinson/49	15.00
RO2	Brooks Robinson/99	15.00
FR1	Frank Robinson/130	10.00
FR2	Frank Robinson/130	10.00
BR1	Babe Ruth/15	250.00
BR2	Babe Ruth/15	250.00

NR1	Nolan Ryan/155	20.00
NR2	Nolan Ryan/155	20.00
NR3	Nolan Ryan/155	20.00
RS1	Ryne Sandberg/155	15.00
RS2	Ryne Sandberg/155	15.00
RS3	Ryne Sandberg/155	15.00
MS1	Mike Schmidt/185	15.00
MS2	Mike Schmidt/185	15.00
MS3	Mike Schmidt/185	15.00
TS	Tom Seaver/155	15.00
TS2	Tom Seaver/155	15.00
OS1	Ozzie Smith/155	15.00
OS2	Ozzie Smith/185	15.00
HW	Honus Wagner/16	200.00
TW1	Ted Williams/125	50.00
TW2	Ted Williams/125	50.00
CY1	Carl Yastrzemski/185	15.00
CY2	Carl Yastrzemski/185	15.00
CY3	Carl Yastrzemski/185	15.00
RY1	Robin Yount/155	10.00
RY2	Robin Yount/155	10.00

Materials Signatures

No Pricing
Production Five Sets

Pairings

		NM/M
Production 5-99		
BB	Wade Boggs, Brooks Robinson/99	25.00
BM	Johnny Bench, Joe Morgan/99	20.00
BR	Bob Gibson, Nolan Ryan/99	30.00
BS	Lou Brock, Ozzie Smith/99	30.00
BS2	Wade Boggs, Ryne Sandberg/99	25.00
CJ	Roger Clemens, Randy Johnson/99	25.00
CR	Roger Clemens, Nolan Ryan/99	40.00
DG	Joe DiMaggio, Lou Gehrig/25	220.00
FB	Carlton Fisk, Johnny Bench/99	20.00
FP	Carlton Fisk, Mike Piazza/99	20.00
GB	Bob Gibson, Lou Brock/99	25.00
GC	Hank Greenberg, Ty Cobb/25	150.00
GG	Ken Griffey Jr., Vladimir Guerrero/99	40.00
GP	Ken Griffey Jr., Kirby Puckett/99	35.00
GR	Lou Gehrig, Cal Ripken Jr./45	180.00
JD	Derek Jeter, Joe DiMaggio/99	125.00
JG	Derek Jeter, Ken Griffey Jr./99	75.00
JJ	Reggie Jackson, Derek Jeter/99	40.00
JK	Reggie Jackson, Harmon Killebrew/99	30.00
JM	Derek Jeter, Don Mattingly/99	80.00
JS	Reggie Jackson, Mike Schmidt/99	30.00
KP	Harmon Killebrew, Kirby Puckett/99	30.00
MB	Thurman Munson, Johnny Bench/30	40.00
MM	Juan Marichal, Willie McCovey/99	25.00
MM2	Don Mattingly, Thurman Munson/30	75.00
MR	Eddie Mathews, Brooks Robinson/50	50.00
MS	Eddie Mathews, Mike Schmidt/50	40.00
MY	Paul Molitor, Robin Yount/99	25.00
PH	Albert Pujols, Rogers Hornsby/99	75.00
PM	Albert Pujols, Stan Musial/99	60.00
RJ	Pee Wee Reese, Derek Jeter/99	35.00
RM	Cal Ripken Jr., Eddie Murray/99	40.00
RR2	Brooks Robinson, Frank Robinson/99	25.00
RY	Frank Robinson, Carl Yastrzemski/99	40.00
SB	Ryne Sandberg, Ernie Banks/99	40.00
SM	Ryne Sandberg, Joe Morgan/99	30.00
SR	Tom Seaver, Nolan Ryan/99	40.00
SS	Ryne Sandberg, Ozzie Smith/99	35.00
WC	Honus Wagner, Roberto Clemente/25	225.00
WD	Ted Williams, Joe DiMaggio/45	200.00
WM	Ted Williams, Stan Musial/45	75.00
YW	Carl Yastrzemski, Ted Williams/50	100.00

Swatch

		NM/M
Common Player:		10.00
Production 50 Sets		
JB	Jason Bay	15.00
EC	Eric Chavez	10.00
RC	Roger Clemens	30.00
CF	Carlton Fisk	15.00
KG1	Ken Griffey Jr.	30.00
KG2	Ken Griffey Jr.	30.00
VG	Vladimir Guerrero	15.00
TG	Tony Gwynn	25.00
DJ1	Derek Jeter	50.00
DJ2	Derek Jeter	50.00
RJ	Randy Johnson	20.00
PM	Pedro J. Martinez	15.00
JM	Joe Morgan	10.00
DO	David Ortiz	25.00
RO	Roy Oswalt	10.00
JP	Jake Peavy	10.00
MP	Mark Prior	10.00
AP	Albert Pujols	40.00
MR	Manny Ramirez	15.00
JR	Jose Reyes	15.00
CR	Cal Ripken Jr.	40.00
IR	Ivan Rodriguez	12.00
SR	Scott Rolen	15.00
JS	Johan Santana	10.00
CS	Curt Schilling	15.00
MT	Mark Teixeira	12.00
MI	Miguel Tejada	10.00
DW	Dontrelle Willis	10.00
CY	Carl Yastrzemski	20.00
RZ	Ryan Zimmerman	20.00

Triple Materials

		NM/M
Production 3-99		
BER	Eddie Murray, Brooks Robinson, Johnny Bench/60	35.00
BMR	Brooks Robinson, Wade Boggs, Paul Molitor/99	30.00
BSP	Ryne Sandberg, Ernie Banks, Mark Prior/99	40.00
CDG	Ken Griffey Jr., Ty Cobb, Joe DiMaggio/15	300.00
FJJ	Whitey Ford, Reggie Jackson, Derek Jeter/99	60.00
FMJ	Don Mattingly, Reggie Jackson, Whitey Ford/51	40.00
GJC	Randy Johnson, Roger Clemens, Bob Gibson/99	40.00
GMG	Eddie Murray, Hank Greenberg, Lou Gehrig/25	150.00
GPS	Tom Seaver, Bob Gibson, Mark Prior/99	30.00
GRM	Ken Griffey Jr., Willie McCovey, Frank Robinson/99	40.00
GJK	Vladimir Guerrero, Reggie Jackson, Harmon Killebrew/99	40.00
JKR	Harmon Killebrew, Frank Robinson, Reggie Jackson/99	40.00
JMM	Derek Jeter, Don Mattingly, Thurman Munson/25	125.00
JPG	Albert Pujols, Ken Griffey Jr., Derek Jeter/99	100.00
MBF	Carlton Fisk, Thurman Munson, Johnny Bench/99	40.00
MBG	Johnny Bench, Joe Morgan, Ken Griffey Jr./99	50.00
MBP	Albert Pujols, Lou Brock, Stan Musial/24	90.00
MFM	Carlton Fisk, Eddie Murray, Thurman Munson/99	30.00
MMG	Steve Garvey, Eddie Murray, Don Mattingly/49	40.00
MPS	Tom Seaver, Mike Piazza, Eddie Murray/99	30.00
MSY	Ozzie Smith, Paul Molitor, Robin Yount/49	40.00
RBS	Cal Ripken Jr., Wade Boggs, Mike Schmidt/99	50.00
RCJ	Nolan Ryan, Roger Clemens, Randy Johnson/75	50.00
RJD	Reggie Jackson, Joe DiMaggio, Babe Ruth/99	300.00
RRM	Jackie Robinson, Frank Robinson, Willie McCovey/50	50.00
SMH	Ryne Sandberg, Rogers Hornsby, Joe Morgan/25	80.00
WSR	Honus Wagner, Pee Wee Reese, Ozzie Smith/99	100.00
YRJ	Cal Ripken Jr., Derek Jeter, Robin Yount/99	60.00
YWB	Ted Williams, Wade Boggs, Carl Yastrzemski/25	140.00

2006 Upper Deck First Pitch

		NM/M
Complete Set (220):		35.00
Common Player:		.10
Pack (5):		1.50
Box (36):		40.00
1	Chad Tracy	.10
2	Conor Jackson **(RC)**	.10
3	Craig Counsell	.10
4	Javier Vazquez	.10
5	Luis Gonzalez	.10
6	Shawn Green	.25
7	Troy Glaus	.25
8	Joey Devine **RC**	1.00
9	Andruw Jones	.40
10	Chipper Jones	.50
11	John Smoltz	.25
12	Marcus Giles	.10
13	Jeff Francoeur	.25
14	Tim Hudson	.25
15	Brian Roberts	.10
16	Erik Bedard	.10
17	Javy Lopez	.10
18	Melvin Mora	.10
19	Miguel Tejada	.40
20	Alejandro Freire **RC**	1.00
21	Sammy Sosa	.75
22	Craig Hansen **RC**	3.00
23	Curt Schilling	.50
24	David Ortiz	.50
25	Edgar Renteria	.25
26	Johnny Damon	.50
27	Manny Ramirez	.50
28	Matt Clement	.10
29	Trot Nixon	.10
30	Aramis Ramirez	.25
31	Carlos Zambrano	.25
32	Derrek Lee	.50
33	Greg Maddux	1.00
34	Jeromy Burnitz	.10
35	Kerry Wood	.25
36	Mark Prior	.40
37	Nomar Garciaparra	.50
38	Aaron Rowand	.10
39	Chris Demaria **RC**	.25
40	Jon Garland	.10
41	Mark Buehrle	.25
42	Paul Konerko	.25
43	Scott Podsednik	.25
44	Tadahito Iguchi	.25
45	Adam Dunn	.40
46	Austin Kearns	.10
47	Felipe Lopez	.10
48	Ken Griffey Jr.	1.00
49	Ryan Freel	.10
50	Sean Casey	.10
51	Wily Mo Pena	.10
52	C.C. Sabathia	.10
53	Cliff Lee	.10
54	Coco Crisp	.10
55	Grady Sizemore	.25
56	Jake Westbrook	.10
57	Travis Hafner	.25
58	Victor Martinez	.25
59	Aaron Miles	.10
60	Clint Barmes	.10
61	Garrett Atkins	.10
62	Jeff Baker	.10
63	Jeff Francis	.10
64	Matt Holliday	.25
65	Todd Helton	.40
66	Carlos Guillen	.10
67	Chris Shelton	.10
68	Dmitri Young	.10
69	Ivan Rodriguez	.40
70	Jeremy Bonderman	.10
71	Magglio Ordonez	.25
72	Placido Polanco	.10
73	A.J. Burnett	.10
74	Carlos Delgado	.40
75	Dontrelle Willis	.25
76	Josh Beckett	.25
77	Juan Pierre	.10
78	Ryan Jorgensen **RC**	.50
79	Miguel Cabrera	.10
80	Robert Andino **RC**	.50
81	Andy Pettitte	.25
82	Brad Lidge	.10
83	Craig Biggio	.25
84	Jeff Bagwell	.40
85	Lance Berkman	.25
86	Morgan Ensberg	.25
87	Roger Clemens	1.50
88	Roy Oswalt	.25
89	Angel Berroa	.10
90	David DeJesus	.10
91	Steve Stemle **RC**	1.00
92	Jonah Bayliss **RC**	2.00
93	Mike Sweeney	.10
94	Ryan Theriot **(RC)**	1.00
95	Zack Greinke	.10
96	Brad Penny	.10
97	Cesar Izturis	.10
98	Brian Myrow **RC**	1.00
99	Eric Gagne	.25
100	J.D. Drew	.10
101	Jeff Kent	.25
102	Milton Bradley	.10
103	Odalis Perez	.10
104	Ben Sheets	.25
105	Brady Clark	.10
106	Carlos Lee	.25
107	Geoff Jenkins	.10
108	Lyle Overbay	.10
109	Prince Fielder **(RC)**	.50
110	Rickie Weeks	.25
111	Jacque Jones	.10
112	Joe Mauer	.25
113	Joe Nathan	.10
114	Johan Santana	.50
115	Justin Morneau	.20
116	Chris Heintz **RC**	1.00
117	Torii Hunter	.25
118	Carlos Beltran	.40
119	Cliff Floyd	.10
120	David Wright	.75
121	Jose Reyes	.40
122	Mike Cameron	.10
123	Mike Piazza	.50
124	Pedro Martinez	.50
125	Tom Glavine	.25
126	Alex Rodriguez	1.50
127	Derek Jeter	1.50
128	Gary Sheffield	.40
129	Hideki Matsui	.75
130	Jason Giambi	.25
131	Jorge Posada	.25
132	Mariano Rivera	.25
133	Mike Mussina	.25
134	Randy Johnson	.50
135	Barry Zito	.25
136	Bobby Crosby	.10
137	Danny Haren	.10
138	Eric Chavez	.25
139	Huston Street	.10
140	Ron Flores **RC**	.50
141	Nick Swisher	.10
142	Rich Harden	.25
143	Bobby Abreu	.25
144	Danny Sandoval **RC**	.50
145	Chase Utley	.25
146	Jim Thome	.40
147	Jimmy Rollins	.25
148	Pat Burrell	.25
149	Ryan Howard	.50
150	Craig Wilson	.10
151	Jack Wilson	.10
152	Jason Bay	.25
153	Matt Lawton	.10
154	Oliver Perez	.10
155	Robert Mackowiak	.10
156	Zachary Duke	.10
157	Brian Giles	.25
158	Jake Peavy	.25
159	Craig Breslow **RC**	1.00
160	Khalil Greene	.10
161	Mark Loretta	.10
162	Ryan Klesko	.10
163	Trevor Hoffman	.10
164	J.T. Snow	.10
165	Jason Schmidt	.25
166	Marquis Grissom	.10
167	Moises Alou	.25
168	Omar Vizquel	.10
169	Pedro Feliz	.10
170	Jeremy Accardo **RC**	.50
171	Adrian Beltre	.25
172	Ichiro Suzuki	1.00
173	Felix Hernandez	.50
174	Jeff Harris **RC**	.25
175	Randy Winn	.10
176	Raul Ibanez	.10
177	Richie Sexson	.25
178	Albert Pujols	1.50
179	Chris Carpenter	.25
180	David Eckstein	.10
181	Jim Edmonds	.25
182	Larry Walker	.25
183	Matt Morris	.10
184	Reggie Sanders	.10
185	Scott Rolen	.40
186	Aubrey Huff	.10
187	Jonny Gomes	.10
188	Carl Crawford	.25
189	Tim Corcoran **RC**	1.00
190	Julio Lugo	.10
191	Rocco Baldelli	.10
192	Scott Kazmir	.10
193	Alfonso Soriano	.40
194	Hank Blalock	.25
195	Kenny Rogers	.10
196	Scott Feldman **RC**	1.00
197	Laynce Nix	.10
198	Mark Teixeira	.50
199	Michael Young	.10
200	Aaron Hill	.10
201	Alex Rios	.10
202	Eric Hinske	.10
203	Gustavo Chacin	.10
204	Roy Halladay	.25
205	Shea Hillenbrand	.10
206	Vernon Wells	.25
207	Brad Wilkerson	.10
208	Chad Cordero	.10
209	Jose Guillen	.10
210	Jose Vidro	.10
211	Livan Hernandez	.10
212	Preston Wilson	.10
213	Jason Bergmann **RC**	1.00
214	Bartolo Colon	.25
215	Chone Figgins	.10
216	Darin Erstad	.25
217	Francisco Rodriguez	.10
218	Garret Anderson	.25
219	Steve Finley	.10
220	Vladimir Guerrero	.50

Diamond Stars

		NM/M
Complete Set (35):		30.00
Common Player:		.50
Inserted 1:3		
1	Luis Gonzalez	.50
2	Andruw Jones	1.00
3	John Smoltz	.75
4	Miguel Tejada	1.00
5	Johnny Damon	1.50
6	Manny Ramirez	1.50
7	Derrek Lee	1.50
8	Mark Prior	1.00
9	Mark Buehrle	.50
10	Ken Griffey Jr.	3.00

11 Travis Hafner .75
12 Todd Helton 1.00
13 Ivan Rodriguez .75
14 Miguel Cabrera 1.50
15 Roger Clemens 4.00
16 Mike Sweeney .50
17 Jeff Kent .75
18 Carlos Lee .50
19 Johan Santana 1.50
20 Torii Hunter .50
21 Pedro Martinez 1.50
22 Alex Rodriguez 4.00
23 Derek Jeter 4.00
24 Eric Chavez .75
25 Bobby Abreu .75
26 Jason Bay .75
27 Jake Peavy .75
28 Moises Alou .50
29 Ichiro Suzuki 3.00
30 Albert Pujols 4.00
31 Carl Crawford .75
32 Mark Teixeira 1.50
33 Roy Halladay .50
34 Jose Guillen .50
35 Vladimir Guerrero 1.50

Goin' Deep

NM/M

Complete Set (35): 20.00
Common Player: .50
Inserted 1:3
1 Adam Dunn 1.00
2 Albert Pujols 4.00
3 Alex Rodriguez 4.00
4 Alfonso Soriano 1.00
5 Andruw Jones 1.00
6 Aramis Ramirez .75
7 Bobby Abreu .75
8 Brian Giles .50
9 Carlos Delgado .75
10 Carlos Lee .50
11 Chipper Jones 1.50
12 David Ortiz 1.50
13 David Wright 2.00
14 Derrek Lee 1.00
15 Eric Chavez .50
16 Gary Sheffield .75
17 Hideki Matsui 2.50
18 Jeff Kent .75
19 Jim Edmonds .75
20 Ken Griffey Jr. 3.00
21 Luis Gonzalez .50
22 Manny Ramirez 1.50
23 Mark Teixeira 1.00
24 Miguel Cabrera 1.50
25 Miguel Tejada 1.00
26 Moises Alou .50
27 Pat Burrell .75
28 Paul Konerko .75
29 Rafael Palmeiro .75
30 Richie Sexson .75
31 Todd Helton 1.00
32 Torii Hunter .50
33 Travis Hafner .75
34 Vernon Wells .50
35 Vladimir Guerrero 1.50

Hot Stove Headlines

NM/M

Complete Set (20): 15.00
Common Player: .50
Inserted 1:3
1 Alex Rodriguez 3.00
2 Carlos Beltran .75
3 Carlos Delgado .50
4 Curt Schilling 1.00
5 Derrek Lee .75
6 Greg Maddux 2.00
7 Hideki Matsui 2.00
8 Ichiro Suzuki 2.00
9 Ivan Rodriguez .50
10 Jim Thome .50
11 Johnny Damon 1.00
12 Ken Griffey Jr. 2.00
13 Manny Ramirez 1.00
14 Miguel Tejada .75
15 Nomar Garciaparra .75
16 Pedro Martinez 1.00
17 Randy Johnson 1.00
18 Roger Clemens 3.00
19 Scott Rolen .75
20 Vladimir Guerrero 1.00

Signature Stars

NM/M

Common Player:
DR J.D. Drew 15.00
JE Johnny Estrada 10.00
RH Rich Harden 15.00
PL Paul LoDuca 15.00
VM Victor Martinez 15.00
YM Yadier Molina 10.00
GQ Guillermo Quiroz 10.00
RI Juan Rivera 10.00
IS Ian Snell 15.00
RW Ryan Wagner 10.00

2006 Upper Deck Future Stars

NM/M

Complete Set (159):
Common Player (1-75): .25
Common Autograph (76-159): 5.00
Some SP Auto's not priced yet.
Pack (4): 4.00

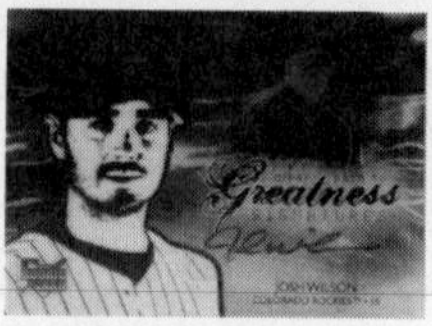

Box (24): 80.00
1 Miguel Tejada .75
2 Brian Roberts .50
3 Brandon Webb .50
4 Luis Gonzalez .25
5 Andruw Jones .50
6 Chipper Jones 1.00
7 John Smoltz .75
8 Curt Schilling 1.00
9 Josh Beckett 1.00
10 David Ortiz 1.00
11 Manny Ramirez 1.00
12 Jim Thome .75
13 Paul Konerko .50
14 Jermaine Dye .25
15 Derrek Lee .75
16 Greg Maddux 2.00
17 Ken Griffey Jr. 2.00
18 Adam Dunn .75
19 Felipe Lopez .25
20 Travis Hafner .50
21 Victor Martinez .50
22 Grady Sizemore .75
23 Todd Helton .75
24 Matt Holliday .75
25 Jeremy Bonderman .25
26 Ivan Rodriguez .75
27 Miguel Cabrera 1.00
28 Dontrelle Willis .25
29 Roger Clemens 2.00
30 Roy Oswalt .50
31 Lance Berkman .75
32 Reggie Sanders .25
33 Vladimir Guerrero 1.00
34 Chone Figgins .50
35 Jeff Kent .25
36 Eric Gagne .25
37 Carlos Lee .50
38 Rickie Weeks .25
39 Johan Santana 1.00
40 Torii Hunter .50
41 Alex Rodriguez 2.00
42 Derek Jeter 2.50
43 Randy Johnson 1.00
44 Hideki Matsui 1.50
45 Johnny Damon 1.00
46 Pedro Martinez 1.00
47 David Wright 2.00
48 Carlos Beltran .75
49 Rich Harden .25
50 Eric Chavez .25
51 Huston Street .25
52 Ryan Howard 2.00
53 Bobby Abreu .75
54 Chase Utley 1.00
55 Jason Bay .75
56 Jake Peavy .75
57 Brian Giles .25
58 Trevor Hoffman .25
59 Jason Schmidt .25
60 Randy Winn .25
61 Kenji Johjima **RC** 2.00
62 Ichiro Suzuki 1.50
63 Felix Hernandez .75
64 Albert Pujols 2.50
65 Chris Carpenter .75
66 Jim Edmonds .25
67 Carl Crawford .50
68 Scott Kazmir .50
69 Jonny Gomes .25
70 Mark Teixeira .75
71 Michael Young .50
72 Vernon Wells .75
73 Roy Halladay .50
74 Nick Johnson .25
75 Alfonso Soriano .75
76 Adam Wainwright **(RC)** 20.00
77 Anderson Hernandez **(RC)** 5.00
78 Andre Ethier/SP **(RC)** 20.00
79 Colter Bean/SP **(RC)** 10.00
80 Ben Johnson **(RC)** 5.00
81 Boof Bonser/SP **(RC)** 15.00
82 Boone Logan **RC** 8.00
83 Brian Anderson **(RC)** 5.00
84 Brian Bannister **(RC)** 8.00
85 Chris Denorfia/SP **(RC)** 8.00
86 Chad Billingsley/SP **(RC)** 25.00
87 Cody Ross **(RC)** 5.00
88 Cole Hamels SP **(RC)** 50.00
89 Conor Jackson **(RC)** 15.00
91 Dave Gassner/SP **(RC)** 8.00
92 Jordan Tata **RC** 10.00
93 Eric Reed **(RC)** 8.00
94 Fausto Carmona **(RC)** 15.00
95 Luis Figueroa/SP **RC** 10.00
96 Francisco Liriano/SP **(RC)** 20.00
97 Freddie Bynum **(RC)** 5.00
98 Hanley Ramirez/SP **(RC)** 35.00
99 Hong-Chih Kuo/SP **(RC)** 50.00
100 Ian Kinsler **(RC)** 25.00
101 Nelson Cruz/SP **(RC)** 10.00
102 Ruddy Lugo **(RC)** 5.00
103 Jason Kubel **(RC)** 10.00
104 Jeff Harris **RC** 5.00
105 Santiago Ramirez **(RC)** 5.00
106 Jered Weaver/SP **(RC)** 40.00
107 Jeremy Accardo/SP **RC** 10.00
108 Jeremy Hermida/SP **(RC)** 10.00
109 Joel Zumaya/SP **(RC)** 25.00
110 Joey Devine 8.00
111 John Koronka **(RC)** 5.00
112 Jonathan Papelbon **(RC)** 40.00
113 Jose Capellan **(RC)** 5.00
114 Josh Johnson **(RC)** 10.00
115 Josh Rupe/SP **(RC)** 10.00
116 Josh Willingham/SP **(RC)** 10.00
117 Josh Wilson **(RC)** 8.00
119 Kelly Shoppach **(RC)** 8.00
120 Kendry Morales **(RC)** 10.00
121 Sean Tracey **(RC)** 8.00
122 Macay McBride **(RC)** 8.00
123 Martin Prado/SP **(RC)** 15.00
124 Matt Cain **(RC)** 20.00
125 Russell Martin **(RC)** 20.00
126 Tim Hamulack/SP **(RC)** 8.00
127 Mike Jacobs **(RC)** 10.00
128 Ben Hendrickson **(RC)** 5.00
129 Jack Taschner **(RC)** 5.00
130 Nate McLouth **(RC)** 15.00
131 Jeremy Sowers/SP **(RC)** 15.00
132 Paul Maholm **(RC)** 5.00
134 Jason Bergmann **RC** 10.00
135 Rich Hill/SP **(RC)** 15.00
137 Scott Dunn **(RC)** 5.00
138 Ryan Zimmerman **(RC)** 40.00
139 Anibal Sanchez **(RC)** 10.00
140 Sean Marshall **(RC)** 10.00
141 Takashi Saito SP **RC** 40.00
142 Taylor Buchholz **(RC)** 10.00
143 Carlos Quentin SP **(RC)** 15.00
144 Matt Garza **(RC)** 15.00
145 Wilbert Nieves **(RC)** 8.00
146 Jamie Shields **RC** 15.00
147 Jon Lester/SP **(RC)** 30.00
149 Aaron Rakers **(RC)** 5.00
150 Bobby Livingston **(RC)** 8.00
151 Brendan Harris **(RC)** 5.00
152 Alay Soler/SP **RC** 8.00
153 Chris Britton **RC** 8.00
154 Howie Kendrick/SP **(RC)** 40.00
155 Jermaine Van Buren **(RC)** 8.00
156 Choo Freeman/SP **(RC)** 8.00
157 Matt Capps **(RC)** 10.00
158 Peter Moylan **RC** 5.00
159 Ty Taubenheim **RC** 8.00

Black

Black (1-75): 8-15X
Production 50 Sets

Blue

Blue (1-75): 4-8X
Production 99 Sets

Gold

Gold (1-75): 15-25X
Production 25 Sets

Green

Green (1-75): 2-4X
Production 499 Sets

Purple

Purple (1-75): 1-2X
Production 1,799 Sets

Red

Red (1-75): 3-5X
Production 299 Sets

Clear Patch to Hist. Triple Sign.

NM/M

BSJ Andruw Jones, Alfonso Soriano, Jason Bay 40.00
CPO Chris Carpenter, Roy Oswalt, Jake Peavy 40.00
CUK Carl Crawford, Scott Kazmir, B.J. Upton 50.00
DRR Jose Reyes, Stephen Drew, Hanley Ramirez 80.00
GEH Andre Ethier, Jeremy Hermida, Tony Gwynn Jr. 40.00
JVW Josh Johnson, Justin Verlander, Jered Weaver 50.00
KTZ Ryan Zimmerman, Howie Kendrick, Troy Tulowitzki 50.00
MKW Kendry Morales, Howie Kendrick, Jered Weaver 50.00
MML Justin Morneau, Joe Mauer, Francisco Liriano 75.00
MOH Travis Hafner, Justin Morneau, Lyle Overbay 40.00
NHP Trevor Hoffman, Joe Nathan, Jonathan Papelbon 60.00
PSO Ben Sheets, Roy Oswalt, Jake Peavy 50.00
PVW Justin Verlander, Jonathan Papelbon, Jered Weaver 100.00
SBH Chad Billingsley, Alay Soler, Cole Hamels 40.00
SHL Francisco Liriano, Jeremy Sowers, Cole Hamels 60.00
TZU Ryan Zimmerman, B.J. Upton, Troy Tulowitzki 50.00
URB Craig Biggio, Brian Roberts, Chase Utley 50.00
VBZ Jeremy Bonderman, Justin Verlander, Joel Zumaya 75.00

Future Stars

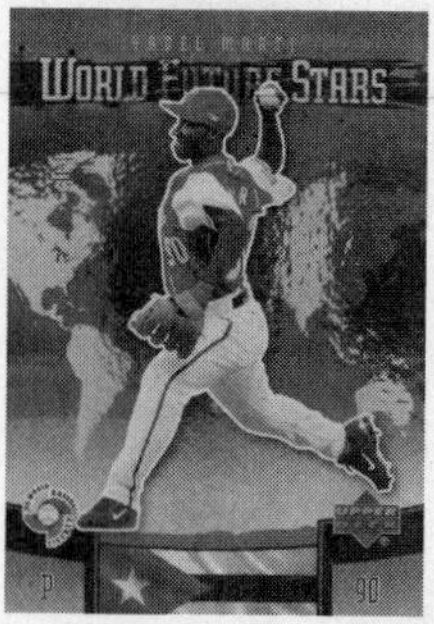

NM/M

Common Player: 1.00
Black: 8-15X
Production 50 Sets
Blue: 4-8X
Production 99 Sets
Gold: 15-25X
Production 25 Sets
Green: 2-4X
Production 499 Sets
Purple: 1-2X
Production 1,799 Sets
Red: 3-5X
Production 299 Sets
1 Adam Loewen 1.00
2 Nan Wang 2.00
3 Yi Feng 1.50
4 Chien-Ming Chang 2.00
5 Yung-Chi Chen 2.00
6 Chin-Lung Hu 1.50
7 Yadel Marti 1.00
8 Frederich Cepeda 1.00
9 Pedro Luis Lazo 1.00
10 Osmany Urrutia 1.00
11 Yoandy Garlobo 1.00
12 Nobuhiko Matsunaka 2.00
13 Daisuke Matsuzaka 5.00
14 Tsuyoshi Nishioka 2.00
15 Tomoya Satozaki 1.00
16 Koji Uehara 1.00
17 Shunsuke Watanabe 2.00
18 Jong Beom Lee 1.00
19 Sidney de Jong 1.00
20 Shairon Martis 1.00
21 Len Pecota 1.00
22 Dicky Gonzalez 1.00
23 Nicholas Dempsey 1.00
24 Jason Kubel 1.00
25 Chase Utley 2.00

Rookie Signatures Red Ink

Red Ink (76-159): 1.5-2X
Production 35 Sets

2006 Upper Deck Ovation

NM/M

Complete Set (126):
Common (1-84): .25
Common SP (85-126): 5.00
Production 999
Pack (5): 3.00
Box (18): 40.00
1 Vladimir Guerrero .75
2 Bartolo Colon .25
3 Chone Figgins .40
4 Lance Berkman .40
5 Roy Oswalt .40
6 Craig Biggio .40
7 Rich Harden .25
8 Eric Chavez .25
9 Huston Street .25
10 Vernon Wells .40
11 Roy Halladay .50
12 Troy Glaus .40
13 Andruw Jones .50
14 Chipper Jones .75
15 John Smoltz .40
16 Carlos Lee .40
17 Rickie Weeks .40
18 J.J. Hardy .25
19 Albert Pujols 2.00
20 Chris Carpenter .50
21 Scott Rolen .50
22 Derrek Lee .50
23 Mark Prior .50
24 Aramis Ramirez .40
25 Carl Crawford .40
26 Scott Kazmir .40
27 Luis Gonzalez .25
28 Brandon Webb .50
29 Chad Tracy .25
30 Jeff Kent .40
31 J.D. Drew .40
32 Jason Schmidt .25

33	Randy Winn	.25
34	Travis Hafner	.50
35	Victor Martinez	.40
36	Grady Sizemore	.40
37	Ichiro Suzuki	1.50
38	Felix Hernandez	.40
39	Adrian Beltre	.40
40	Miguel Cabrera	.75
41	Dontrelle Willis	.25
42	David Wright	1.50
43	Jose Reyes	.75
44	Pedro Martinez	.75
45	Carlos Beltran	.50
46	Alfonso Soriano	.75
47	Livan Hernandez	.25
48	Jose Guillen	.25
49	Miguel Tejada	.50
50	Brian Roberts	.40
51	Melvin Mora	.25
52	Jake Peavy	.40
53	Brian Giles	.25
54	Khalil Greene	.25
55	Bobby Abreu	.40
56	Ryan Howard	1.00
57	Chase Utley	.75
58	Jason Bay	.40
59	Sean Casey	.25
60	Mark Teixeira	.50
61	Michael Young	.40
62	Hank Blalock	.40
63	Manny Ramirez	.75
64	David Ortiz	.75
65	Josh Beckett	.75
66	Jason Varitek	.50
67	Ken Griffey Jr.	1.50
68	Adam Dunn	.50
69	Todd Helton	.50
70	Garrett Atkins	.40
71	Reggie Sanders	.25
72	Mike Sweeney	.25
73	Chris Shelton	.25
74	Ivan Rodriguez	.50
75	Johan Santana	.75
76	Torii Hunter	.40
77	Justin Morneau	.50
78	Jim Thome	.50
79	Paul Konerko	.40
80	Scott Podsednik	.25
81	Derek Jeter	2.00
82	Hideki Matsui	1.50
83	Johnny Damon	.75
84	Alex Rodriguez	2.00
85	Conor Jackson **(RC)**	8.00
86	Joey Devine **RC**	5.00
87	Jonathan Papelbon **(RC)**	15.00
88	Freddie Bynum **(RC)**	5.00
89	Chris Denorfia **(RC)**	5.00
90	Ryan Shealy **(RC)**	5.00
91	Josh Wilson **(RC)**	5.00
92	Brian Anderson **(RC)**	5.00
93	Justin Verlander **(RC)**	15.00
94	Jeremy Hermida **(RC)**	5.00
95	Mike Jacobs **(RC)**	8.00
96	Josh Johnson **(RC)**	5.00
97	Hanley Ramirez **(RC)**	12.00
98	Josh Willingham **(RC)**	8.00
99	Cole Hamels **(RC)**	12.00
100	Hong-Chih Kuo **(RC)**	15.00
101	Cody Ross **(RC)**	5.00
102	Jose Capellan **(RC)**	5.00
103	Prince Fielder **(RC)**	10.00
104	Dave Gassner **(RC)**	5.00
105	Jason Kubel **(RC)**	5.00
106	Francisco Liriano **(RC)**	10.00
107	Anderson Hernandez **(RC)**	5.00
108	Boof Bonser **(RC)**	5.00
109	Jered Weaver **(RC)**	10.00
110	Ben Johnson **(RC)**	5.00
111	Jeff Harris **RC**	5.00
112	Stephen Drew **(RC)**	10.00
113	Matt Cain **(RC)**	8.00
114	Skip Schumaker **(RC)**	5.00
115	Adam Wainwright **(RC)**	8.00
116	Jeremy Sowers **(RC)**	5.00
117	Jason Bergmann **RC**	5.00
118	Chad Billingsley **(RC)**	10.00
119	Ryan Zimmerman **(RC)**	10.00
120	Macay McBride **(RC)**	5.00
121	Aaron Rakers **(RC)**	5.00
122	Alay Soler **RC**	5.00
123	Melky Cabrera **(RC)**	15.00
124	Tim Hamulack **(RC)**	5.00
125	Andre Ethier **(RC)**	10.00
126	Kenji Johjima **RC**	10.00

Gold

Gold (1-84): 4-8X
Production 499 Sets

Gold Autographs

		NM/M
Production 99 Sets		
85	Conor Jackson	25.00
86	Joey Devine	15.00
87	Jonathan Papelbon	75.00
88	Freddie Bynum	10.00
89	Chris Denorfia	10.00
90	Ryan Shealy	10.00
91	Josh Wilson	
92	Brian Anderson	10.00
93	Justin Verlander	50.00
94	Jeremy Hermida	20.00
95	Mike Jacobs	15.00
96	Josh Johnson	10.00
97	Hanley Ramirez	35.00
98	Josh Willingham	15.00
99	Cole Hamels	60.00
101	Cody Ross	20.00
102	Jose Capellan	10.00
104	Dave Gassner	10.00
105	Jason Kubel	15.00
106	Francisco Liriano	35.00
107	Anderson Hernandez	10.00
108	Boof Bonser	15.00
109	Jered Weaver	40.00
110	Ben Johnson	10.00
111	Jeff Harris	10.00
112	Stephen Drew	25.00
113	Matt Cain	25.00
114	Skip Schumaker	15.00
115	Adam Wainwright	25.00
116	Jeremy Sowers	10.00
117	Jason Bergmann	10.00
118	Chad Billingsley	25.00
119	Ryan Zimmerman	50.00
120	Macay McBride	10.00
121	Aaron Rakers	10.00
122	Alay Soler	10.00
123	Melky Cabrera	50.00
124	Tim Hamulack	10.00
125	Andre Ethier	60.00

Apparel

		NM/M
Common Player:		4.00
BA	Jason Bay	8.00
LB	Lance Berkman	8.00
JB	Jeremy Bonderman	8.00
AB	A.J. Burnett	6.00
EC	Eric Chavez	6.00
CC	Carl Crawford	6.00
JE	Jim Edmonds	8.00
PF	Prince Fielder	10.00
CF	Chone Figgins	6.00
JF	Jeff Francoeur	10.00
JG	Jonny Gomes	6.00
KG	Khalil Greene	8.00
GR	Ken Griffey Jr.	20.00
VG	Vladimir Guerrero	8.00
HA	Travis Hafner	8.00
JH	J.J. Hardy	4.00
HE	Todd Helton	8.00
FH	Felix Hernandez	8.00
TH	Trevor Hoffman	8.00
RH	Ryan Howard	20.00
HU	Torii Hunter	6.00
DJ	Derek Jeter	25.00
JK	Jeff Kent	6.00
RK	Ryan Klesko	4.00
CL	Carlos Lee	6.00
VM	Victor Martinez	8.00
JM	Joe Mauer	8.00
TN	Trot Nixon	6.00
DO	David Ortiz	15.00
RO	Roy Oswalt	8.00
AO	Akinori Otsuka	6.00
MP	Mark Prior	6.00
AP	Albert Pujols	25.00
MR	Manny Ramirez	10.00
SR	Scott Rolen	8.00
CS	Chris Shelton	4.00
GS	Grady Sizemore	8.00
HS	Huston Street	6.00
MT	Mark Teixeira	8.00
VW	Vernon Wells	8.00
DW	David Wright	15.00
RZ	Ryan Zimmerman/SP	15.00

Center Stage

		NM/M
Common Player:		1.00
JB	Josh Beckett	3.00
DC	Daniel Cabrera	1.00
CA	Miguel Cabrera	3.00
JC	Jose Contreras	1.00
AC	Aaron Cook	1.00
BC	Bobby Crosby	1.00
MC	Michael Cuddyer	1.00
DD	David DeJesus	1.00
SD	Stephen Drew	2.00
JF	Jason Frasor	1.00
KG	Ken Griffey Jr.	5.00
VG	Vladimir Guerrero	3.00
FH	Felix Hernandez	2.00
RH	Runelvys Hernandez	1.00
DJ	Derek Jeter	8.00
DL	Derrek Lee	2.00
YM	Yadier Molina	1.00
MP	Mark Prior	2.00
AP	Albert Pujols	8.00
FS	Freddy Sanchez	1.00
CS	Chris Shelton	1.00
IS	Ian Snell	1.00
MT	Mark Teixeira	2.00
CW	Chien-Ming Wang	10.00
DW	David Wright	4.00

Center Stage Signatures

No Pricing
Production 25 Sets

Curtain Calls

		NM/M
Common Player:		1.00
DC	Daniel Cabrera	1.00
EC	Eric Chavez	1.00
JC	Jose Contreras	1.00
BC	Bobby Crosby	1.00
DD	David DeJesus	1.00
KG1	Ken Griffey Jr.	4.00
KG2	Ken Griffey Jr.	4.00
RH	Rich Harden	1.00
HE	Runelvys Hernandez	1.00
YM	Yadier Molina	1.00
TO	Tomokazu Ohka	1.00
MP	Mark Prior	2.00
HR	Horacio Ramirez	1.00
FS	Freddy Sanchez	1.00
CS	Chris Shelton	1.00
MT	Miguel Tejada	2.00
CW	Chien-Ming Wang	10.00
JE	Jered Weaver	2.00
JW	Josh Willingham	1.00
MY	Michael Young	1.00

Curtain Calls Signatures

No Pricing
Production 25 Sets

Ovation Nation

		NM/M
Common Player:		2.00
JB	Jason Bay	3.00
DC	Daniel Cabrera	2.00
MC	Miguel Cabrera	4.00
FC	Frederich Cepeda	2.00
YG	Yoandy Garlobo	2.00
KG	Ken Griffey Jr.	8.00
DJ	Derek Jeter	8.00
AJ	Andruw Jones	3.00
SL	Seung-Yeop Lee	4.00
DM	Daisuke Matsuzaka	15.00
NM	Nobuhiko Matsunaka	4.00
AP	Albert Pujols	8.00
JS	Johan Santana	3.00
JA	Jae Weong Seo	2.00
MT	Miguel Tejada	3.00

Ovation Nation Signatures

No Pricing
Production 25 Sets

Spotlight Signatures

		NM/M
Common Autograph:		10.00
JB	Josh Beckett/SP	40.00
DC	Daniel Cabrera	15.00
CA	Miguel Cabrera	25.00
SC	Shawn Camp	8.00
EC	Eric Chavez/SP	15.00
JC	Jose Contreras	15.00
AC	Aaron Cook	6.00
LC	Lance Cormier	8.00
BC	Bobby Crosby	10.00
MC	Michael Cuddyer/SP	15.00
DD	David DeJesus	15.00
JD	Jorge De La Rosa	8.00
JF	Jason Frasor	15.00
FG	Franklyn German	10.00
MG	Mike Gonzalez	10.00
AG	Andy Green	6.00
KG1	Ken Griffey Jr.	75.00
KG2	Ken Griffey Jr.	75.00
HA	Rich Harden/SP	15.00
RH	Runelvys Hernandez	10.00
EJ	Edwin Jackson	10.00
YM	Yadier Molina	15.00
FN	Fernando Nieve	10.00
TO	Tomokazu Ohka	20.00
MP	Mark Prior	20.00
HR	Horacio Ramirez/SP	10.00
DR	David Ross	15.00
KS	Kirk Saarloos	10.00
FS	Freddy Sanchez	20.00
CS1	Chris Shelton	10.00
CS2	Chris Shelton	10.00
TE	Miguel Tejada/SP	20.00
MT	Matt Thornton	10.00
TR	Matt Treanor	10.00
RW	Ryan Wagner	10.00
CW	Chien-Ming Wang	100.00
JW	Josh Willingham/SP	15.00
MW	Mike Wuertz	10.00
MY	Michael Young	15.00

Superstar Theatre

		NM/M
Common Player:		1.00
BA	Jason Bay	2.00
JB	Josh Beckett	1.00
DC	Daniel Cabrera	1.00
MC	Miguel Cabrera	3.00
CC	Chris Carpenter	2.00
JC	Jose Contreras	1.00
BC	Bobby Crosby	1.00
DD	David DeJesus	1.00
KG1	Ken Griffey Jr.	6.00
KG2	Ken Griffey Jr.	6.00
TH	Travis Hafner	2.00
RH	Rich Harden	1.00
DJ	Derek Jeter	8.00
AJ	Andruw Jones	2.00
DL	Derrek Lee	3.00
PM	Pedro Martinez	3.00
HM	Hideki Matsui	4.00
YM	Yadier Molina	1.00
TO	Tomokazu Ohka	1.00
DO	David Ortiz	3.00
MP	Mark Prior	2.00
AP	Albert Pujols	8.00
MR	Manny Ramirez	3.00
AR	Alex Rodriguez	6.00
CS	Chris Shelton	1.00
IS	Ichiro Suzuki	6.00
TE	Mark Teixeira	2.00
MT	Miguel Tejada	2.00
CW	Chien-Ming Wang	10.00
MY	Michael Young	2.00

Superstar Theatre Signatures

No Pricing
Production 25 Sets

2006 Upper Deck Special FX

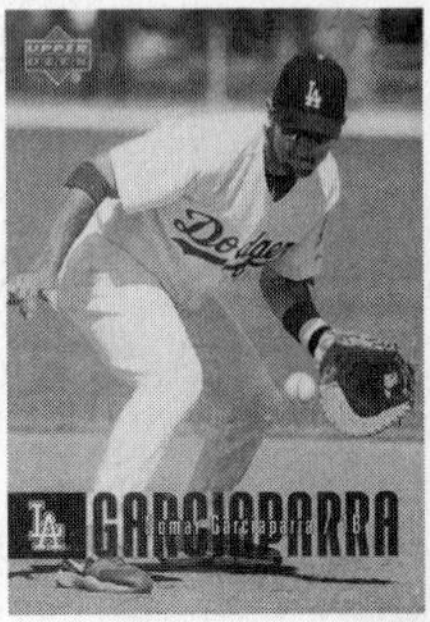

		NM/M
Complete Set (1025):		
Common Player:		.25
Common RC (901-1025):		.50
Pack (4):		5.00
Box (16):		75.00
1	Adam Kennedy	.25
2	Bartolo Colon	.25
3	Bengie Molina	.25
4	Casey Kotchman	.25
5	Chone Figgins	.50
6	Dallas McPherson	.25
7	Darin Erstad	.25
8	Ervin Santana	.50
9	Francisco Rodriguez	.25
10	Garret Anderon	.25
11	Jarrod Washburn	.25
12	John Lackey	.50
13	Juan Rivera	.25
14	Orlando Cabrera	.50
15	Paul Byrd	.25
16	Steve Finley	.25
17	Vladimir Guerrero	1.00
18	Alex Cintron	.25
19	Brandon Lyon	.25
20	Brandon Webb	.75
21	Chad Tracy	.25
22	Chris Snyder	.25
23	Claudio Vargas	.25
24	Conor Jackson	.50
25	Craig Counsell	.25
26	Javier Vazquez	.25
27	Jose Valverde	.25
28	Luis Gonzalez	.25
29	Royce Clayton	.25
30	Russ Ortiz	.25
31	Shawn Green	.25
32	Dustin Nippert	.25
33	Tony Clark	.25
34	Troy Glaus	.50
35	Adam LaRoche	.25
36	Andruw Jones	.50
37	Craig Hansen	.50
38	Chipper Jones	1.00
39	Horacio Ramirez	.25
40	Jeff Francoeur	.75
41	John Smoltz	.75
42	Joey Devine	.25
43	Johnny Estrada	.25
44	Anthony Lerew	.25
45	Julio Franco	.25
46	Kyle Farnsworth	.25
47	Marcus Giles	.25
48	Mike Hampton	.25
49	Rafael Furcal	.50
50	Chuck James	.25
51	Tim Hudson	.50
52	B.J. Ryan	.25
53	Bernie Castro	.25
54	Brian Roberts	.50
55	Walter Young	.25
56	Daniel Cabrera	.25
57	Eric Byrnes	.25
58	Alejandro Freire	.25
59	Erik Bedard	.50
60	Javy Lopez	.25
61	Jay Gibbons	.25
62	Jorge Julio	.25
63	Luis Matos	.25
64	Melvin Mora	.25
65	Miguel Tejada	.75
66	Rafael Palmeiro	.75
67	Rodrigo Lopez	.25
68	Sammy Sosa	.75
69	Alejandro Machado	.25
70	Bill Mueller	.25
71	Bronson Arroyo	.25
72	Curt Schilling	.75
73	David Ortiz	1.00
74	David Wells	.25
75	Edgar Renteria	.25
76	Ryan Jorgensen	.25

77	Jason Varitek	.75
78	Johnny Damon	1.00
79	Keith Foulke	.25
80	Kevin Youkilis	.50
81	Manny Ramirez	1.00
82	Matt Clement	.25
83	Hanley Ramirez	1.00
84	Tim Wakefield	.25
85	Trot Nixon	.25
86	Wade Miller	.25
87	Aramis Ramirez	.50
88	Carlos Zambrano	.50
89	Corey Patterson	.25
90	Derrek Lee	.75
91	Geovany Soto	.50
92	Greg Maddux	2.00
93	Jeromy Burnitz	.25
94	Jerry Hairston Jr.	.25
95	Kerry Wood	.50
96	Mark Prior	.50
97	Matt Murton	.25
98	Michael Barrett	.25
99	Neifi Perez	.25
100	Nomar Garciaparra	.50
101	Rich Hill	.50
102	Ryan Dempster	.25
103	Todd Walker	.25
104	A.J. Pierzynski	.25
105	Aaron Rowand	.50
106	Bobby Jenks	.25
107	Carl Everett	.25
108	Dustin Hermanson	.25
109	Frank Thomas	1.00
110	Freddy Garcia	.25
111	Jermaine Dye	.25
112	Joe Crede	.50
113	Jon Garland	.25
114	Jose Contreras	.25
115	Juan Uribe	.25
116	Mark Buehrle	.25
117	Orlando Hernandez	.25
118	Paul Konerko	.75
119	Scott Podsednik	.25
120	Tadahito Iguchi	.25
121	Aaron Harang	.25
122	Adam Dunn	.75
123	Austin Kearns	.25
124	Brandon Claussen	.25
125	Chris Denorfia	.25
126	Edwin Encarnacion	.25
127	Miguel Perez	.25
128	Felipe Lopez	.25
129	Jason LaRue	.25
130	Ken Griffey Jr.	2.00
131	Chris Booker	.25
132	Luke Hudson	.25
133	Jason Bergmann	.25
134	Ryan Freel	.25
135	Sean Casey	.25
136	Wily Mo Pena	.25
137	Aaron Boone	.25
138	Ben Broussard	.25
139	Ryan Garko	.25
140	C.C. Sabathia	.75
141	Casey Blake	.25
142	Cliff Lee	.25
143	Coco Crisp	.25
144	David Riske	.25
145	Grady Sizemore	.75
146	Jake Westbrook	.25
147	Jhonny Peralta	.25
148	Josh Bard	.25
149	Kevin Millwood	.25
150	Ronnie Belliard	.25
151	Scott Elarton	.25
152	Travis Hafner	.50
153	Victor Martinez	.50
154	Aaron Cook	.25
155	Aaron Miles	.25
156	Brad Hawpe	.25
157	Mike Esposito	.25
158	Chin-Hui Tsao	.25
159	Clint Barmes	.25
160	Cory Sullivan	.25
161	Garrett Atkins	.50
162	J.D. Closser	.25
163	Jason Jennings	.25
164	Jeff Baker	.25
165	Jeff Francis	.25
166	Luis Gonzalez	.25
167	Matt Holliday	.75
168	Todd Helton	.75
169	Brandon Inge	.25
170	Carlos Guillen	.50
171	Carlos Pena	.50
172	Chris Shelton	.25
173	Craig Monroe	.25
174	Curtis Granderson	.75
175	Dmitri Young	.25
176	Ivan Rodriguez	.75
177	Jason Johnson	.25
178	Jeremy Bonderman	.50
179	Magglio Ordonez	.50
180	Mark Woodyard	.25
181	Nook Logan	.25
182	Omar Infante	.25
183	Placido Polanco	.25
184	Chris Heintz	.25
185	A.J. Burnett	.50
186	Alex Gonzalez	.25
187	Josh Johnson	.25
188	Carlos Delgado	.75
189	Dontrelle Willis	.50
190	Josh Wilson	.25
191	Jason Vargas	.25
192	Jeff Conine	.25
193	Jeremy Hermida	.50
194	Josh Beckett	.75
195	Juan Encarnacion	.25
196	Juan Pierre	.25
197	Luis Castillo	.25
198	Miguel Cabrera	1.00
199	Mike Lowell	.50
200	Paul LoDuca	.25
201	Todd Jones	.25
202	Adam Everett	.25
203	Andy Pettitte	.50
204	Brad Ausmus	.25
205	Brad Lidge	.25
206	Brandon Backe	.25
207	Charlton Jimerson	.25
208	Chris Burke	.25
209	Craig Biggio	.50
210	Dan Wheeler	.25
211	Jason Lane	.25
212	Jeff Bagwell	.50
213	Lance Berkman	.75
214	Luke Scott	.25
215	Morgan Ensberg	.25
216	Roger Clemens	2.50
217	Roy Oswalt	.50
218	Willy Taveras	.25
219	Andres Blanco	.25
220	Angel Berroa	.25
221	Ruben Gotay	.25
222	David DeJesus	.25
223	Emil Brown	.25
224	J.P. Howell	.25
225	Jeremy Affeldt	.25
226	Jimmy Gobble	.25
227	John Buck	.25
228	Jose Lima	.25
229	Mark Teahen	.25
230	Matt Stairs	.25
231	Mike MacDougal	.25
232	Mike Sweeney	.25
233	Runelvys Hernandez	.25
234	Terrence Long	.25
235	Zack Greinke	.50
236	Ron Flores	.25
237	Brad Penny	.25
238	Cesar Izturis	.25
239	D.J. Houlton	.25
240	Derek Lowe	.25
241	Eric Gagne	.25
242	Hee Seop Choi	.25
243	J.D. Drew	.50
244	Jason Phillips	.25
245	Jason Repko	.25
246	Jayson Werth	.25
247	Jeff Kent	.50
248	Jeff Weaver	.25
249	Milton Bradley	.25
250	Odalis Perez	.25
251	Hong-Chih Kuo	.25
252	Oscar Robles	.25
253	Ben Sheets	.50
254	Bill Hall	.25
255	Brady Clark	.25
256	Carlos Lee	.50
257	Chris Capuano	.25
258	Nelson Cruz	.25
259	Derrick Turnbow	.25
260	Doug Davis	.25
261	Geoff Jenkins	.25
262	J.J. Hardy	.25
263	Lyle Overbay	.25
264	Prince Fielder	.75
265	Rickie Weeks	.50
266	Russell Branyan	.25
267	Tomokazu Ohka	.25
268	Jonah Bayliss	.25
269	Brad Radke	.25
270	Carlos Silva	.25
271	Francisco Liriano	.50
272	Jacque Jones	.25
273	Joe Mauer	.50
274	Travis Bowyer	.25
275	Joe Nathan	.25
276	Johan Santana	1.00
277	Justin Morneau	.75
278	Kyle Lohse	.25
279	Lew Ford	.25
280	Matthew LeCroy	.25
281	Michael Cuddyer	.25
282	Nick Punto	.25
283	Scott Baker	.25
284	Shannon Stewart	.25
285	Torii Hunter	.50
286	Braden Looper	.25
287	Carlos Beltran	.75
288	Cliff Floyd	.25
289	David Wright	1.50
290	Doug Mientkiewicz	.25
291	Anderson Hernandez	.25
292	Jose Reyes	1.00
293	Kazuo Matsui	.25
294	Kris Benson	.25
295	Miguel Cairo	.25
296	Mike Cameron	.25
297	Robert Andino	.25
298	Mike Piazza	1.00
299	Pedro Martinez	1.00
300	Tom Glavine	.50
301	Victor Diaz	.25
302	Tim Hamulack	.25
303	Alex Rodriguez	2.50
304	Bernie Williams	.50
305	Carl Pavano	.25
306	Chien-Ming Wang	1.00
307	Derek Jeter	2.50
308	Gary Sheffield	.50
309	Hideki Matsui	1.50
310	Jason Giambi	.75
311	Jorge Posada	.50
312	Kevin Brown	.25
313	Mariano Rivera	.50
314	Matt Lawton	.25
315	Mike Mussina	.50
316	Randy Johnson	1.00
317	Robinson Cano	.50
318	Michael Vento	.25
319	Tino Martinez	.25
320	Tony Womack	.25
321	Barry Zito	.50
322	Bobby Crosby	.25
323	Bobby Kielty	.25
324	Dan Johnson	.25
325	Dan Haren	.50
326	Eric Chavez	.50
327	Erubiel Durazo	.25
328	Huston Street	.25
329	Jason Kendall	.25
330	Jay Payton	.25
331	Joe Blanton	.25
332	Joe Kennedy	.25
333	Kirk Saarloos	.25
334	Mark Kotsay	.25
335	Nick Swisher	.50
336	Rich Harden	.25
337	Scott Hatteberg	.25
338	Billy Wagner	.25
339	Bobby Abreu	.50
340	Brett Myers	.25
341	Chase Utley	1.00
342	Danny Sandoval	.25
343	David Bell	.25
344	Gavin Floyd	.25
345	Jim Thome	.75
346	Jimmy Rollins	.75
347	Jon Lieber	.25
348	Kenny Lofton	.25
349	Mike Lieberthal	.25
350	Pat Burrell	.50
351	Randy Wolf	.25
352	Ryan Howard	1.50
353	Vicente Padilla	.25
354	Bryan Bullington	.25
355	J.J. Furmaniak	.25
356	Craig Wilson	.25
357	Matt Capps	.25
358	Tom Gorzelanny	.25
359	Jack Wilson	.25
360	Jason Bay	.50
361	Jose Mesa	.25
362	Josh Fogg	.25
363	Kip Wells	.25
364	Steve Stemle	.25
365	Oliver Perez	.25
366	Robert Mackowiak	.25
367	Ronny Paulino	.25
368	Tike Redman	.25
369	Zach Duke	.25
370	Adam Eaton	.25
371	Scott Feldman	.25
372	Brian Giles	.25
373	Brian Lawrence	.25
374	Damian Jackson	.25
375	Dave Roberts	.25
376	Jake Peavy	.50
377	Joe Randa	.25
378	Khalil Greene	.25
379	Mark Loretta	.25
380	Ramon Hernandez	.25
381	Robert Fick	.25
382	Ryan Klesko	.25
383	Trevor Hoffman	.25
384	Woody Williams	.25
385	Xavier Nady	.25
386	Armando Benitez	.25
387	Brad Hennessey	.25
388	Brian Myrow	.25
389	Edgardo Alfonzo	.25
390	J.T. Snow	.25
391	Jeremy Accardo	.25
392	Jason Schmidt	.50
393	Lance Niekro	.25
394	Matt Cain	.25
395	Daniel Ortmeier	.25
396	Moises Alou	.50
397	Doug Clark	.25
398	Omar Vizquel	.25
399	Pedro Feliz	.25
400	Randy Winn	.25
401	Ray Durham	.25
402	Adrian Beltre	.50
403	Eddie Guardado	.25
404	Felix Hernandez	.50
405	Gil Meche	.25
406	Ichiro Suzuki	1.50
407	Jamie Moyer	.25
408	Jeff Nelson	.25
409	Jeremy Reed	.25
410	Joel Pineiro	.25
411	Jaime Bubela	.25
412	Raul Ibanez	.25
413	Richie Sexson	.50
414	Ryan Franklin	.25
415	Willie Bloomquist	.25
416	Yorvit Torrealba	.25
417	Yuniesky Betancourt	.25
418	Jeff Harris	.25
419	Albert Pujols	2.50
420	Chris Carpenter	.75
421	David Eckstein	.50
422	Jason Isringhausen	.25
423	Jason Marquis	.25
424	Adam Wainwright	.50
425	Jim Edmonds	.50
426	Ryan Theriot	.50
427	Tim Duncan	.25
428	Mark Grudzielanek	.25
429	Mark Mulder	.50
430	Matt Morris	.25
431	Reggie Sanders	.25
432	Scott Rolen	1.00
433	Tyler Johnson	.25
434	Yadier Molina	.25
435	Alex Gonzalez	.25
436	Aubrey Huff	.25
437	Tim Corcoran	.25
438	Carl Crawford	.50
439	Casey Fossum	.25
440	Danys Baez	.25
441	Edwin Jackson	.25
442	Joey Gathright	.25
443	Jonny Gomes	.25
444	Jorge Cantu	.25
445	Julio Lugo	.25
446	Nick Green	.25
447	Rocco Baldelli	.25
448	Scott Kazmir	.50
449	Seth McClung	.25
450	Toby Hall	.25
451	Travis Lee	.25
452	Craig Breslow	.25
453	Alfonso Soriano	1.00
454	Chris Young	.50
455	David Dellucci	.25
456	Francisco Cordero	.25
457	Gary Matthews	.25
458	Hank Blalock	.50
459	Juan Dominguez	.25
460	Josh Rupe	.25
461	Kenny Rogers	.25
462	Kevin Mench	.25
463	Laynce Nix	.25
464	Mark Teixeira	.75
465	Michael Young	.50
466	Richard Hidalgo	.25
467	Jason Botts	.25
468	Aaron Hill	.25
469	Alex Rios	.50
470	Corey Koskie	.25
471	Chris Demaria	.25
472	Eric Hinske	.25
473	Frank Catalanotto	.25
474	John-Ford Griffin	.25
475	Gustavo Chacin	.25
476	Josh Towers	.25
477	Miguel Batista	.25
478	Orlando Hudson	.25
479	Reed Johnson	.25
480	Roy Halladay	.50
481	Shaun Marcum	.25
482	Shea Hillenbrand	.25
483	Ted Lilly	.25
484	Vernon Wells	.50
485	Brad Wilkerson	.25
486	Darrell Rasner	.25
487	Chad Cordero	.25
488	Cristian Guzman	.25
489	Esteban Loaiza	.25
490	John Patterson	.25
491	Jose Guillen	.25
492	Jose Vidro	.25
493	Livan Hernandez	.25
494	Marlon Byrd	.25
495	Nick Johnson	.25
496	Preston Wilson	.25
497	Ryan Church	.25
498	Ryan Zimmerman	.50
499	Tony Armas	.25
500	Vinny Castilla	.25
501	Andy Green	.25
502	Damion Easley	.25
503	Eric Byrnes	.50
504	Jason Grimsley	.25
505	Jeff DaVanon	.25
506	Johnny Estrada	.25
507	Luis Vizcaino	.25
508	Miguel Batista	.25
509	Orlando Hernandez	.25
510	Orlando Hudson	.25
511	Terry Mulholland	.25
512	Chris Reitsma	.25
513	Edgar Renteria	.25
514	John Thomson	.25
515	Jorge Sosa	.25
516	Oscar Villarreal	.25
517	Peter Orr	.25
518	Ryan Langerhans	.25
519	Todd Pratt	.25
520	Wilson Betemit	.25
521	Brian Jordan	.25
522	Lance Cormier	.25
523	Matt Diaz	.25
524	Mike Remlinger	.25
525	Bruce Chen	.25
526	Chris Gomez	.25
527	Chris Ray	.25
528	Corey Patterson	.25
529	David Newhan	.25
530	Ed Rogers	.25
531	John Halama	.25
532	Kris Benson	.25
533	LaTroy Hawkins	.25
534	Raul Chavez	.25
535	Alex Cora	.25
536	Alex Gonzalez	.25

537	Coco Crisp	.25
538	David Riske	.25
539	Doug Mirabelli	.25
540	Josh Beckett	.75
541	J.T. Snow	.25
542	Mike Timlin	.25
543	Julian Tavarez	.25
544	Rudy Seanez	.25
545	Wily Mo Pena	.25
546	Bob Howry	.25
547	Glendon Rusch	.25
548	Henry Blanco	.25
549	Jacque Jones	.25
550	Jerome Williams	.25
551	John Mabry	.25
552	Juan Pierre	.25
553	Scott Eyre	.25
554	Scott Williamson	.25
555	Wade Miller	.25
556	Will Ohman	.25
557	Alex Cintron	.25
558	Robert Mackowiak	.25
559	Brandon McCarthy	.25
560	Chris Widger	.25
561	Cliff Politte	.25
562	Javier Vazquez	.25
563	Jim Thome	.75
564	Matt Thornton	.25
565	Neal Cotts	.25
566	Pablo Ozuna	.25
567	Ross Gload	.25
568	Brandon Phillips	.50
569	Bronson Arroyo	.25
570	Dave Williams	.25
571	David Ross	.25
572	David Weathers	.25
573	Eric Milton	.25
574	Javier Valentin	.25
575	Kent Mercker	.25
576	Matt Belisle	.25
577	Paul Wilson	.25
578	Rich Aurilia	.25
579	Rick White	.25
580	Scott Hatteberg	.25
581	Todd Coffey	.25
582	Bob Wickman	.25
583	Danny Graves	.25
584	Eduardo Perez	.25
585	Guillermo Mota	.25
586	Jason Davis	.25
587	Jason Johnson	.25
588	Jason Michaels	.25
589	Rafael Betancourt	.25
590	Ramon Vazquez	.25
591	Scott Sauerbeck	.25
592	Todd Hollandsworth	.25
593	Brian Fuentes	.25
594	Danny Ardoin	.25
595	David Cortes	.25
596	Eli Marrero	.25
597	Jamey Carroll	.25
598	Jason Smith	.25
599	Josh Fogg	.25
600	Miguel Ojeda	.25
601	Mike DeJean	.25
602	Ray King	.25
603	Omar Quintanilla	.25
604	Zach Day	.25
605	Fernando Rodney	.25
606	Kenny Rogers	.25
607	Mike Maroth	.25
608	Nate Robertson	.25
609	Todd Jones	.25
610	Vance Wilson	.25
611	Bobby Seay	.25
612	Chris Spurling	.25
613	Ramon Colon	.25
614	Jason Grilli	.25
615	Marcus Thames	.25
616	Ramon Santiago	.25
617	Alfredo Amezaga	.25
618	Brian Moehler	.25
619	Chris Aguila	.25
620	Franklyn German	.25
621	Joe Borowski	.25
622	Logan Kensing	.25
623	Matt Treanor	.25
624	Miguel Olivo	.25
625	Sergio Mitre	.25
626	Todd Wellemeyer	.25
627	Wes Helms	.25
628	Chad Qualls	.25
629	Eric Bruntlett	.25
630	Mike Gallo	.25
631	Mike Lamb	.25
632	Orlando Palmeiro	.25
633	Russ Springer	.25
634	Dan Wheeler	.25
635	Eric Munson	.25
636	Preston Wilson	.25
637	Trever Miller	.25
638	Ambiorix Burgos	.25
639	Andrew Sisco	.25
640	Denny Bautista	.25
641	Doug Mientkiewicz	.25
642	Elmer Dessens	.25
643	Esteban German	.25
644	Joe Nelson	.25
645	Mark Grudzielanek	.25
646	Mark Redman	.25
647	Mike Wood	.25
648	Paul Bako	.25
649	Reggie Sanders	.25
650	Scott Elarton	.25
651	Shane Costa	.25
652	Tony Graffanino	.25
653	Jason Bulger	.25
654	Chris Bootcheck	.25
655	Esteban Yan	.25
656	Hector Carrasco	.25
657	J.C. Romero	.25
658	Jeff Weaver	.25
659	Jose Molina	.25
660	Kelvim Escobar	.25
661	Maicer Izturis	.25
662	Robb Quinlan	.25
663	Scot Shields	.25
664	Tim Salmon	.25
665	Bill Mueller	.25
666	Brett Tomko	.25
667	Dioner Navarro	.25
668	Jae Weong Seo	.25
669	Jose Cruz	.25
670	Kenny Lofton	.25
671	Lance Carter	.25
672	Nomar Garciaparra	1.00
673	Olmedo Saenz	.25
674	Rafael Furcal	.25
675	Ramon Martinez	.25
676	Ricky Ledee	.25
677	Sandy Alomar	.25
678	Yhency Brazoban	.25
679	Corey Koskie	.25
680	Danny Kolb	.25
681	Gabe Gross	.25
682	Jeff Cirillo	.25
683	Matt Wise	.25
684	Rick Helling	.25
685	Chad Moeller	.25
686	David Bush	.25
687	Jorge De La Rosa	.25
688	Justin Lehr	.25
689	Jason Bartlett	.25
690	Jesse Crain	.25
691	Juan Rincon	.25
692	Luis Castillo	.25
693	Mike Redmond	.25
694	Rondell White	.25
695	Tony Batista	.25
696	Juan Castro	.25
697	Luis Rodriguez	.25
698	Matt Guerrier	.25
699	Willie Eyre	.25
700	Aaron Heilman	.25
701	Billy Wagner	.25
702	Carlos Delgado	.75
703	Chad Bradford	.25
704	Chris Woodward	.25
705	Darren Oliver	.25
706	Duaner Sanchez	.25
707	Endy Chavez	.25
708	Jorge Julio	.25
709	Jose Valentin	.25
710	Julio Franco	.25
711	Paul LoDuca	.25
712	Ramon Castro	.25
713	Steve Trachsel	.25
714	Victor Zambrano	.25
715	Xavier Nady	.25
716	Andy Phillips	.25
717	Bubba Crosby	.25
718	Jaret Wright	.25
719	Kelly Stinnett	.25
720	Kyle Farnsworth	.25
721	Mike Meyers	.25
722	Octavio Dotel	.25
723	Ron Villone	.25
724	Scott Proctor	.25
725	Shawn Chacon	.25
726	Tanyon Sturtze	.25
727	Adam Melhuse	.25
728	Brad Halsey	.25
729	Esteban Loaiza	.25
730	Frank Thomas	1.00
731	Jay Witasick	.25
732	Justin Duchscherer	.25
733	Kiko Calero	.25
734	Marco Scutaro	.25
735	Mark Ellis	.25
736	Milton Bradley	.25
737	Aaron Fultz	.25
738	Aaron Rowand	.25
739	Geoff Geary	.25
740	Arthur Rhodes	.25
741	Chris Coste	.25
742	Rheal Cormier	.25
743	Ryan Franklin	.25
744	Ryan Madson	.25
745	Sal Fasano	.25
746	Tom Gordon	.25
747	Abraham Nunez	.25
748	David Dellucci	.25
749	Julio Santana	.25
750	Shane Victorino	.25
751	Damaso Marte	.25
752	Freddy Sanchez	.25
753	Humberto Cota	.25
754	Jeromy Burnitz	.25
755	Joe Randa	.25
756	Jose Castillo	.25
757	Mike Gonzalez	.25
758	Ryan Doumit	.25
759	Sean Burnett	.25
760	Sean Casey	.25
761	Ian Snell	.25
762	John Grabow	.25
763	Jose Hernandez	.25
764	Roberto Hernandez	.25
765	Ryan Vogelsong	.25
766	Victor Sanchez	.25
767	Adrian Gonzalez	.25
768	Alan Embree	.25
769	Brian Sweeney	.25
770	Chan Ho Park	.25
771	Clay Hensley	.25
772	Dewon Brazelton	.25
773	Doug Brocail	.25
774	Eric Young	.25
775	Geoff Blum	.25
776	Josh Bard	.25
777	Mark Bellhorn	.25
778	Mike Cameron	.25
779	Mike Piazza	1.00
780	Rob Bowen	.25
781	Scott Cassidy	.25
782	Scott Linebrink	.25
783	Shawn Estes	.25
784	Termel Sledge	.25
785	Vinny Castilla	.25
786	Jeff Fassero	.25
787	Jose Vizcaino	.25
788	Mark Sweeney	.25
789	Matt Morris	.25
790	Steve Finley	.25
791	Tim Worrell	.25
792	Jamey Wright	.25
793	Jason Ellison	.25
794	Noah Lowry	.25
795	Steve Kline	.25
796	Todd Greene	.25
797	Carl Everett	.25
798	George Sherrill	.25
799	J.J. Putz	.25
800	Jake Woods	.25
801	Jose Lopez	.25
802	Julio Mateo	.25
803	Mike Morse	.25
804	Rafael Soriano	.25
805	Roberto Petagine	.25
806	Aaron Miles	.25
807	Braden Looper	.25
808	Gary Bennett	.25
809	Hector Luna	.25
810	Jeff Suppan	.25
811	John Rodriguez	.25
812	Josh Hancock	.25
813	Juan Encarnacion	.25
814	Larry Bigbie	.25
815	Scott Spiezio	.25
816	Sidney Ponson	.25
817	So Taguchi	.25
818	Brian Meadows	.25
819	Damon Hollins	.25
820	Dan Miceli	.25
821	Doug Waechter	.25
822	Jason Childers	.25
823	Josh Paul	.25
824	Julio Lugo	.25
825	Mark Hendrickson	.25
826	Sean Burroughs	.25
827	Shawn Camp	.25
828	Travis Harper	.25
829	Ty Wigginton	.25
830	Adam Eaton	.25
831	Adrian Brown	.25
832	Akinori Otsuka	.25
833	Antonio Alfonseca	.25
834	Brad Wilkerson	.25
835	D'Angelo Jimenez	.25
836	Gerald Laird	.25
837	Joaquin Benoit	.25
838	Kameron Loe	.25
839	Kevin Millwood	.25
840	Mark DeRosa	.25
841	Phil Nevin	.25
842	Rod Barajas	.25
843	Vicente Padilla	.25
844	A.J. Burnett	.25
845	Bengie Molina	.25
846	Gregg Zaun	.25
847	John McDonald	.25
848	Lyle Overbay	.25
849	Russ Adams	.25
850	Troy Glaus	.50
851	Vinnie Chulk	.25
852	B.J. Ryan	.25
853	Justin Speier	.25
854	Pete Walker	.25
855	Scott Downs	.25
856	Scott Schoeneweis	.25
857	Alfonso Soriano	1.00
858	Brian Schneider	.25
859	Daryle Ward	.25
860	Felix Rodriguez	.25
861	Gary Majewski	.25
862	Joey Eischen	.25
863	Jon Rauch	.25
864	Marlon Anderson	.25
865	Matthew LeCroy	.25
866	Mike Stanton	.25
867	Ramon Ortiz	.25
868	Robert Fick	.25
869	Royce Clayton	.25
870	Ryan Drese	.25
871	Vladimir Guerrero	.50
872	Craig Biggio	.25
873	Barry Zito	.25
874	Vernon Wells	.25
875	Chipper Jones	.50
876	Prince Fielder	.50
877	Albert Pujols	1.50
878	Greg Maddux	1.00
879	Carl Crawford	.25
880	Brandon Webb	.25
881	J.D. Drew	.25
882	Jason Schmidt	.25
883	Victor Martinez	.25
884	Ichiro Suzuki	.75
885	Miguel Cabrera	.50
886	David Wright	.75
887	Alfonso Soriano	.50
888	Miguel Tejada	.25
889	Khalil Greene	.25
890	Ryan Howard	1.00
891	Jason Bay	.25
892	Mark Teixeira	.50
893	Manny Ramirez	.75
894	Ken Griffey Jr.	1.00
895	Todd Helton	.50
896	Angel Berroa	.25
897	Ivan Rodriguez	.50
898	Johan Santana	.50
899	Paul Konerko	.50
900	Derek Jeter	1.50
901	Macay McBride **(RC)**	.50
902	Tony Pena **(RC)**	.50
903	Peter Moylan **RC**	.75
904	Aaron Rakers **(RC)**	.50
905	Chris Britton **RC**	.75
906	Nick Markakis **(RC)**	1.00
907	Sendy Rleal **RC**	.50
908	Val Majewski **(RC)**	.50
909	Jermaine Van Buren **(RC)**	.50
910	Jonathan Papelbon **(RC)**	3.00
911	Angel Pagan **(RC)**	.50
912	David Aardsma **(RC)**	.50
913	Sean Marshall **(RC)**	.50
914	Brian Anderson **(RC)**	.50
915	Freddie Bynum **(RC)**	.50
916	Fausto Carmona **(RC)**	.50
917	Kelly Shoppach **(RC)**	.50
918	Choo Freeman **(RC)**	.50
919	Ryan Shealy **(RC)**	.50
920	Joel Zumaya **(RC)**	2.00
921	Jordan Tata **RC**	1.00
922	Justin Verlander **(RC)**	2.00
923	Carlos Martinez **RC**	.50
924	Chris Resop **(RC)**	.50
925	Dan Uggla **(RC)**	2.00
926	Eric Reed **(RC)**	.50
927	Hanley Ramirez **(RC)**	2.50
928	Yusmeiro Petit **(RC)**	.50
929	Josh Willingham **(RC)**	.75
930	Mike Jacobs **(RC)**	1.00
931	Reggie Abercrombie **(RC)**	.50
932	Ricky Nolasco **(RC)**	.50
933	Scott Olsen **(RC)**	.50
934	Fernando Nieve **(RC)**	.50
935	Taylor Buchholz **(RC)**	.50
936	Cody Ross **(RC)**	.50
937	James Loney **(RC)**	.75
938	Takashi Saito **RC**	1.00
939	Tim Hamulack **(RC)**	.50
940	Chris Demaria **RC**	.50
941	Jose Capellan **(RC)**	.50
942	Dave Gassner **(RC)**	.50
943	Jason Kubel **(RC)**	.50
944	Brian Bannister **(RC)**	.50
945	Mike Thompson **RC**	.50
946	Cole Hamels **(RC)**	2.00
947	Paul Maholm **(RC)**	.50
948	John Van Benschoten **(RC)**	.50
949	Nate McLouth **(RC)**	1.00
950	Ben Johnson **(RC)**	.50
951	Josh Barfield **(RC)**	.50
952	Travis Ishikawa **(RC)**	.50
953	Jack Taschner **(RC)**	.50
954	Kenji Johjima **RC**	3.00
955	Skip Schumaker **(RC)**	.50
956	Ruddy Lugo **(RC)**	.50
957	Jason Hammel **(RC)**	.50
958	Chris Roberson **(RC)**	.50
959	Fabio Castro **RC**	.50
960	Ian Kinsler **(RC)**	1.00
961	John Koronka **(RC)**	.50
962	Brandon Watson **(RC)**	.50
963	Jon Lester **(RC)**	4.00
964	Ben Hendrickson **(RC)**	.50
965	Martin Prado **(RC)**	.50
966	Erick Aybar **(RC)**	.50
967	Bobby Livingston **(RC)**	.50
968	Ryan Spilborghs **(RC)**	.50
969	Tommy Murphy **(RC)**	.50
970	Howie Kendrick **(RC)**	1.50
971	Casey Janssen **RC**	.50
972	Michael O'Connor **RC**	.50
973	Conor Jackson **(RC)**	1.00
974	Jeremy Hermida **(RC)**	.50
975	Renyel Pinto **(RC)**	.50
976	Prince Fielder **(RC)**	2.00
977	Kevin Frandsen **(RC)**	.50
978	Ty Taubenheim **RC**	.50
979	Rich Hill **(RC)**	.75
980	Jonathan Broxton **(RC)**	.50
981	Jamie Shields **RC**	1.00
982	Carlos Villanueva **RC**	1.00
983	Boone Logan **RC**	.50
984	Brian Wilson **RC**	.50
985	Andre Ethier **(RC)**	2.00
986	Michael Napoli **RC**	1.00
987	Agustin Montero **(RC)**	.50
988	Jack Hannahan **RC**	.50
989	Boof Bonser **(RC)**	.50
990	Carlos Ruiz **(RC)**	.50
991	Jason Botts **(RC)**	.50
992	Kendry Morales **(RC)**	.50
993	Alay Soler **RC**	.50
994	Santiago Ramirez **(RC)**	.50
995	Saul Rivera **(RC)**	.50
996	Anthony Reyes **(RC)**	.50

997	Matthew Kemp (RC)	1.00
998	Jae-Kuk Ryu RC	1.00
999	Lastings Milledge (RC)	1.00
1000	Jered Weaver (RC)	2.00
1001	Jeremy Sowers (RC)	.50
1002	Chad Billingsley (RC)	1.00
1003	Stephen Drew (RC)	2.00
1004	Tony Gwynn Jr. (RC)	1.00
1005	Melky Cabrera (RC)	1.00
1006	Eliezer Alfonzo RC	.50
1007	Dana Eveland RC	.50
1008	Luis Figueroa RC	.50
1009	Emiliano Fruto RC	.50
1010	Clay Hensley (RC)	.50
1011	Zach Jackson (RC)	.50
1012	Bobby Keppel (RC)	.50
1013	Carlos Marmol RC	1.00
1014	Russell Martin (RC)	1.00
1015	Leo Nunez (RC)	.50
1016	Ken Ray (RC)	.50
1017	Mike Rouse (RC)	.50
1018	Kevin Thompson (RC)	.50
1019	C.J. Wilson (RC)	.50
1020	Steve Andrade (RC)	.50
1021	Ed Rogers (RC)	.50
1022	Joe Nelson (RC)	.50
1023	Omar Quintanilla (RC)	.50
1024	Chris Bootcheck (RC)	.50
1025	Jason Childers RC	.50

Blue

Blue (1-900):	1-1.5X
Blue RC:	1X
Inserted 1:4	

Green

Green (1-900):	2-3X
Green RC:	1-2X
Production 99 Sets	

Purple

Purple (1-900):	2-3X
Purple RC:	1-2X
Production 150 Sets	

Red

Red (1-900):	3-4X
Red RC:	2-3X
Production 50 Sets	

Materials

		NM/M
	Common Player:	5.00
JB	Jason Bay	8.00
LB	Lance Berkman	5.00
MC	Miguel Cabrera	10.00
MA	Matt Cain	10.00
CA	Chris Carpenter	8.00
CC	Carl Crawford	5.00
CR	Coco Crisp	5.00
AD	Adam Dunn	8.00
PF	Prince Fielder	10.00
RF	Rafael Furcal	5.00
JG	Jason Giambi	5.00
TG	Troy Glaus	5.00
KG	Ken Griffey Jr.	15.00
VG	Vladimir Guerrero	8.00
TH	Travis Hafner	8.00
HA	Roy Halladay	8.00
CH	Cole Hamels	15.00
JH	Jeremy Hermida	5.00
FH	Felix Hernandez	10.00
RH	Ryan Howard	20.00
DJ	Derek Jeter	20.00
KJ	Kenji Johjima	15.00
AJ	Andruw Jones	8.00
SK	Scott Kazmir	5.00
IK	Ian Kinsler	8.00
DL	Derrek Lee	10.00
FL	Francisco Liriano	10.00
PM	Pedro Martinez	8.00
VM	Victor Martinez	5.00
JM	Joe Mauer	10.00
LM	Lastings Milledge	10.00
KM	Kendry Morales	5.00
DO	David Ortiz	8.00
JP	Jonathan Papelbon	15.00
AP	Albert Pujols	20.00
HR	Hanley Ramirez	5.00
JR	Jose Reyes	15.00
JS	Johan Santana	10.00
GS	Grady Sizemore	10.00

AS	Alfonso Soriano	8.00
MT	Mark Teixeira	8.00
TE	Miguel Tejada	8.00
JT	Jim Thome	10.00
CU	Chase Utley	15.00
JV	Justin Verlander	15.00
WE	Jered Weaver	10.00
RW	Rickie Weeks	8.00
JW	Josh Willingham	5.00
RZ	Ryan Zimmerman	10.00

Player Highlights

REYES SCORES KEY RUN FOR METS

		NM/M
	Common Player:	.50
1	Andruw Jones	1.00
2	Manny Ramirez	1.00
3	Travis Hafner	.75
4	Johnny Damon	1.00
5	Miguel Cabrera	1.00
6	Chris Carpenter	1.00
7	Derrek Lee	1.00
8	Jason Bay	.75
9	Jason Varitek	1.00
10	Ryan Howard	3.00
11	Mark Teixeira	1.00
12	Carlos Delgado	.75
13	Bartolo Colon	.50
14	David Wright	2.00
15	Miguel Tejada	.75
16	Mike Piazza	1.50
17	Paul Konerko	.75
18	Jermaine Dye	.50
19	Ichiro Suzuki	2.00
20	Brad Wilkerson	.50
21	Hideki Matsui	2.00
22	Albert Pujols	3.00
23	Chris Burke	.50
24	Derek Jeter	3.00
25	Brian Roberts	.50
26	David Ortiz	1.00
27	Alex Rodriguez	2.00
28	Ken Griffey Jr.	2.00
29	Prince Fielder	.75
30	Bobby Abreu	.75
31	Vladimir Guerrero	1.00
32	Tadahito Iguchi	.50
33	Jose Reyes	.75
34	Scott Podsednik	.50
35	Gary Sheffield	.75

Run Producers

run producers
TY COBB

		NM/M
	Common Player:	1.00
1	Ty Cobb	3.00
2	Derrek Lee	1.50
3	Andruw Jones	1.50
4	David Ortiz	1.50
5	Lou Gehrig	4.00
6	Ken Griffey Jr.	4.00
7	Albert Pujols	5.00
8	Derek Jeter	5.00
9	Manny Ramirez	1.50
10	Alex Rodriguez	5.00
11	Gary Sheffield	1.00
12	Miguel Cabrera	1.50
13	Hideki Matsui	3.00
14	Vladimir Guerrero	1.50
15	David Wright	3.00
16	Mike Schmidt	1.50
17	Mark Teixeira	1.00
18	Babe Ruth	5.00
19	Jimmie Foxx	3.00
20	Honus Wagner	3.00

Special Endorsements

	NM/M
Common Player:	5.00
Inserted 1:16	

RA	Reggie Abercrombie	5.00
AC	Jeremy Accardo	5.00
BA	Brian Anderson	5.00
AN	Robert Andino	5.00
BR	Brian Bannister	12.00
JB	Jason Bay	15.00
BW	Craig Breslow	8.00
CB	Chris Britton	5.00
TB	Taylor Buchholz	10.00
FB	Freddie Bynum	8.00
MI	Miguel Cabrera	20.00
MC	Matt Cain	15.00
JC	Jose Capellan/SP	8.00
CM	Matt Capps	5.00
FC	Fausto Carmona	10.00
TC	Tim Corcoran	8.00
DE	Chris Denorfia	8.00
JD	Joey Devine	8.00
AE	Andre Ethier	15.00
EV	Dana Eveland	12.00
RF	Ron Flores	5.00
KF	Kevin Frandsen	5.00
DG	Dave Gassner	8.00
KG	Ken Griffey Jr.	60.00
TH	Travis Hafner	15.00
CH	Cole Hamels	40.00
BH	Brendan Harris	5.00
HA	Jeff Harris	5.00
HG	Keith Hattig	8.00
HE	Jeremy Hermida	15.00
AH	Anderson Hernandez/SP	5.00
JU	Justin Huber	8.00
JA	Conor Jackson	15.00
MJ	Mike Jacobs	10.00
DJ	Derek Jeter	200.00
BJ	Ben Johnson	8.00
JJ	Josh Johnson	8.00
KE	Howie Kendrick	15.00
IK	Ian Kinsler	15.00
KO	John Koronka	8.00
JK	Jason Kubel	8.00
HK	Hong-Chih Kuo	40.00
FL	Francisco Liriano	20.00
BL	Boone Logan	5.00
RL	Ruddy Lugo	5.00
PM	Paul Maholm	8.00
SM	Sean Marshall	10.00
NI	Nick Massett	8.00
MM	Macay McBride	8.00
NM	Nate McLouth	15.00
KM	Kendry Morales	8.00
PE	Peter Moylan	8.00
FN	Fernando Nieve	5.00
WN	Wilbert Nieves	8.00
JP	Jonathan Papelbon	30.00
AA	Aaron Rakers	5.00
HR	Hanley Ramirez	30.00
RE	Chris Resop	5.00
RB	Chris Roberson	8.00
CR	Cody Ross	8.00
RC	Carlos Ruiz	8.00
RU	Josh Rupe	8.00
TS	Takashi Saito	25.00
RS	Ryan Shealy	10.00
JS	James Shields	20.00
KS	Kelly Shoppach	8.00
MS	Matt Smith	8.00
GS	Geovany Soto	35.00
DU	Dan Uggla	20.00
CU	Chase Utley	30.00
JV	John Van Benschoten	5.00
VE	Justin Verlander/SP	30.00
AW	Adam Wainwright	20.00
JW	Jered Weaver	15.00
RW	Rickie Weeks	15.00
WI	Josh Willingham	15.00
DW	Dontrelle Willis	15.00
JO	Josh Wilson	8.00
RZ	Ryan Zimmerman/SP	30.00
JZ	Joel Zumaya	15.00

Star Attractions

STAR ATTRACTIONS

		NM/M
	Common Player:	.50
	Inserted 1:8	
BA	Bobby Abreu	.75
JB	Josh Beckett	.75
CB	Carlos Beltran	1.00
LB	Lance Berkman	.75
JC	Jose Contreras	.50
JD	Johnny Damon	1.50
CD	Carlos Delgado	.75
JE	Jim Edmonds	.75
JG	Jason Giambi	1.00
KG	Ken Griffey Jr.	3.00
RH	Rich Harden	.50
DJ	Derek Jeter	4.00
AJ	Andruw Jones	1.00
CJ	Chipper Jones	1.50
DL	Derrek Lee	1.50
GM	Greg Maddux	3.00
PM	Pedro Martinez	1.50

JM	Joe Mauer	1.00
MO	Magglio Ordonez	.50
DO	David Ortiz	1.50
PU	Albert Pujols	4.00
MR	Manny Ramirez	1.50
JR	Jose Reyes	1.50
CS	Curt Schilling	1.50
JS	Jason Schmidt	.50
SM	John Smoltz	.75
AS	Alfonso Soriano	1.50
MT	Mark Teixeira	1.00
DW	Dontrelle Willis	.50
WR	David Wright	2.50

WBC Counterparts

COUNTERPARTS

		NM/M
	Common Duo:	1.00
	Inserted 1:6	
1	Yulieski Gourriel,	
	Daisuke Matsuzaka	5.00
2	Ken Griffey Jr.,	
	Yoandy Garlobo	3.00
3	Ken Griffey Jr., Ichiro Suzuki	4.00
4	Derek Jeter, Chin-Lung Hu	4.00
5	Frederich Cepeda,	
	Jong Beom Lee	1.00
6	Nobuhiko Matsunaka,	
	Seung-Yeop Lee	2.00
7	Tsuyoshi Nishioka,	
	Guangbiao Liu	1.00
8	Ichiro Suzuki,	
	Osmany Urrutia	2.50
9	Daisuke Matsuzaka,	
	Roger Clemens	8.00
10	Yadel Marti, Chan Ho Park	1.00
11	Koji Uehara, Jae Weong Seo	1.00
12	Shunsuke Watanabe,	
	Bartolo Colon	2.00
13	Daisuke Matsuzaka,	
	Johan Santana	5.00
14	Pedro Luis Lazo,	
	Freddy Garcia	1.00
15	Koji Uehara, Roger Clemens	3.00

2006 Upper Deck Sweet Spot

SIGNATURES

	NM/M
Complete Set (184):	
Common Player:	.25
Common Auto. (101-184):	15.00
Production 45-275	
Pack (5):	10.00
Box (12):	100.00

1	Bartolo Colon	.25
2	Garret Anderson	.25
3	Francisco Rodriguez	.25
4	Dallas McPherson	.25
5	Andy Pettitte	.40
6	Lance Berkman	.50
7	Willy Taveras	.25
8	Bobby Crosby	.25
9	Dan Haren	.50
10	Nick Swisher	.50
11	Vernon Wells	.50
12	Orlando Hudson	.25
13	Roy Halladay	.50
14	Andruw Jones	.75
15	Chipper Jones	.75
16	Jeff Francoeur	.50
17	John Smoltz	.50
18	Carlos Lee	.50
19	Rickie Weeks	.40
20	Bill Hall	.25
21	Jim Edmonds	.40
22	David Eckstein	.25
23	Mark Mulder	.25
24	Aramis Ramirez	.50
25	Greg Maddux	1.50
26	Nomar Garciaparra	.50
27	Carlos Zambrano	.50
28	Scott Kazmir	.40
29	Jorge Cantu	.25
30	Carl Crawford	.50
31	Luis Gonzalez	.25
32	Troy Glaus	.40
33	Shawn Green	.25
34	Jeff Kent	.40
35	Milton Bradley	.25
36	Cesar Izturis	.25
37	Omar Vizquel	.25

38 Moises Alou .50
39 Randy Winn .25
40 Jason Schmidt .40
41 Coco Crisp .25
42 C.C. Sabathia .50
43 Cliff Lee .25
44 Ichiro Suzuki 1.50
45 Richie Sexson .50
46 Jeremy Reed .25
47 Carlos Delgado .50
48 Miguel Cabrera .75
49 Luis Castillo .25
50 Carlos Beltran .50
51 Tom Glavine .50
52 David Wright 1.50
53 Cliff Floyd .25
54 Chad Cordero .25
55 Jose Vidro .25
56 Jose Guillen .25
57 Nick Johnson .25
58 Miguel Tejada .50
59 Melvin Mora .25
60 Javy Lopez .25
61 Khalil Greene .25
62 Brian Giles .25
63 Trevor Hoffman .25
64 Bobby Abreu .50
65 Jimmy Rollins .75
66 Pat Burrell .40
67 Billy Wagner .25
68 Jack Wilson .25
69 Zach Duke .25
70 Craig Wilson .25
71 Mark Teixeira .50
72 Hank Blalock .40
73 David Dellucci .25
74 Manny Ramirez .75
75 Johnny Damon .75
76 Jason Varitek .50
77 Trot Nixon .25
78 Adam Dunn .50
79 Felipe Lopez .25
80 Brandon Claussen .25
81 Sean Casey .25
82 Todd Helton .50
83 Clint Barmes .25
84 Matt Holliday .50
85 Mike Sweeney .25
86 Zack Greinke .25
87 David DeJesus .25
88 Ivan Rodriguez .50
89 Jeremy Bonderman .25
90 Magglio Ordonez .50
91 Torii Hunter .50
92 Joe Nathan .25
93 Michael Cuddyer .25
94 Paul Konerko .50
95 Jermaine Dye .25
96 Jon Garland .25
97 Alex Rodriguez 2.00
98 Hideki Matsui 1.50
99 Jason Giambi .50
100 Mariano Rivera .40
101 Adrian Beltre/99 25.00
102 Matt Cain/275 **(RC)** 30.00
103 Craig Biggio/99 35.00
104 Eric Chavez/99 25.00
105 J.D. Drew/99 25.00
106 Eric Gagne/99 25.00
107 Tim Hudson/99 40.00
108 Tom Glavine/275 40.00
109 David Ortiz/99 85.00
110 Scott Rolen/275 30.00
111 Johan Santana/99 50.00
112 Curt Schilling/96 75.00
113 John Smoltz/99 60.00
114 Alfonso Soriano/99 50.00
115 Kerry Wood/99 30.00
116 Edwin Jackson/99 20.00
117 Felix Hernandez/125 50.00
118 Prince Fielder/99 **(RC)** 60.00
119 Vladimir Guerrero/86 50.00
120 Roger Clemens/99 80.00
121 Albert Pujols/45 250.00
122 Chris Carpenter/99 50.00
123 Derrek Lee/99 40.00
124 Dontrelle Willis/99 25.00
125 Roy Oswalt/99 35.00
126 Ryan Garko/275 **(RC)** 25.00
127 Tadahito Iguchi/275 40.00
128 Mark Loretta/275 25.00
129 Joe Mauer/275 40.00
130 Victor Martinez/275 25.00
131 Wily Mo Pena/275 20.00
132 Oliver Perez/274 10.00
133 Corey Patterson/275 20.00
134 Ben Sheets/275 20.00
135 Michael Young/275 25.00
136 Jonny Gomes/275 20.00
137 Derek Jeter/99 150.00
138 Ken Griffey Jr./275 75.00
139 Ryan Zimmerman/275 **(RC)** 40.00
140 Scott Baker/275 **(RC)** 15.00
141 Huston Street/275 25.00
142 Jason Bay/275 25.00
143 Ryan Howard/275 75.00
145 Travis Hafner/275 25.00
146 Brian Myrow/275 **RC** 20.00
147 Scott Podsednik/275 25.00
148 Brian Roberts/275 25.00
149 Grady Sizemore/135 45.00
150 Chris Demaria/275 **RC** 15.00
151 Jonah Bayliss/275 **RC** 15.00
152 Geovany Soto/275 **(RC)** 50.00
153 Lyle Overbay/275 15.00
154 Joey Devine/275 **RC** 20.00
155 Alejandro Freire/275 **RC** 15.00
156 Conor Jackson/275 **(RC)** 25.00
157 Danny Sandoval/275 **RC** 15.00
158 Chase Utley/275 60.00
159 Jeff Harris/275 **RC** 15.00
160 Ron Flores/275 **RC** 15.00
161 Scott Feldman/275 **RC** 15.00
162 Yadier Molina/275 25.00
163 Tim Corcoran/275 **RC** 15.00
164 Craig Hansen/275 **RC** 25.00
165 Jason Bergmann/275 **RC** 25.00
166 Craig Breslow/275 **RC** 15.00
167 Jhonny Peralta/275 15.00
168 Jeremy Hermida/275 **(RC)** 25.00
169 Scott Kazmir/275 25.00
170 Bobby Crosby/99 15.00
171 Rich Harden/275 15.00
172 Casey Kotchman/275 15.00
173 Tim Hamulack/275 **(RC)** 15.00
174 Justin Morneau/275 30.00
175 Jake Peavy/275 30.00
176 Yuniesky Betancourt/275 25.00
177 Jeremy Accardo/275 **RC** 15.00
178 Jorge Cantu/200 20.00
179 Marlon Byrd/275 15.00
180 Ryan Jorgensen/275 **RC** 15.00
181 Chris Denorfia/275 **(RC)** 15.00
182 Steve Stemle/275 15.00
183 Robert Andino/275 **RC** 15.00
184 Chris Heintz/275 **RC** 15.00

Sign. Bat Barrel Black Ink

NM/M

Production 13-25
107 Tim Hudson/25 50.00
110 Scott Rolen/25 50.00
111 Johan Santana/25 60.00
115 Kerry Wood/25 30.00
117 Felix Hernandez/25 60.00
118 Prince Fielder/25 60.00
119 Vladimir Guerrero/25 75.00
121 Albert Pujols/25 275.00
125 Roy Oswalt/25 40.00
127 Tadahito Iguchi/25 90.00
131 Wily Mo Pena/25 40.00
139 Ryan Zimmerman/25 75.00
143 Ryan Howard/25 90.00
151 Jonah Bayliss/25 30.00
153 Lyle Overbay/25 30.00
154 Joey Devine/25 30.00
160 Ron Flores/25 30.00
167 Jhonny Peralta/25 40.00
174 Justin Morneau/25 50.00
178 Jorge Cantu/25 40.00
182 Steve Stemle/25 25.00

Sign. Bat Barrel Blue Ink

No Pricing
Production Three to Five Sets

Sign. Black Stitch Black Ink

No Pricing
Production One Set
Blue Ink: No Pricing
Production One Set

Sig. Glove Leather Black Ink

No Pricing
Production 5-15
Blue Ink: No Pricing
Production 5-15

Sign. Red Stitch Blue Ink

NM/M

Production 15-150
101 Adrian Beltre/25 35.00
102 Matt Cain/150 40.00
103 Craig Biggio/25 50.00
106 Eric Gagne/25 60.00
107 Tim Hudson/25 40.00
109 David Ortiz/25 120.00
110 Scott Rolen/150 40.00
111 Johan Santana/25 60.00
112 Curt Schilling/25 100.00
113 John Smoltz/25 90.00
116 Edwin Jackson/150 20.00
118 Prince Fielder/25 60.00
119 Vladimir Guerrero/25 80.00
122 Chris Carpenter/25 60.00
123 Derrek Lee/25 50.00
124 Dontrelle Willis/25 40.00
125 Roy Oswalt/25 40.00
126 Ryan Garko/150 25.00
127 Tadahito Iguchi/150 75.00
128 Mark Loretta/114 35.00
129 Joe Mauer/150 40.00
130 Victor Martinez/150 35.00
131 Wily Mo Pena/150 30.00
132 Oliver Perez/135 10.00
133 Corey Patterson/150 30.00
134 Ben Sheets/150 25.00
135 Michael Young/150 30.00
136 Jonny Gomes/150 40.00
137 Derek Jeter/25 200.00
138 Ken Griffey Jr./150 100.00
139 Ryan Zimmerman/150 40.00
140 Scott Baker/150 20.00
141 Huston Street/150 40.00
142 Jason Bay/150 35.00
143 Ryan Howard/150 75.00
144 Mike Piazza/100 100.00
145 Travis Hafner/150 40.00
146 Brian Myrow/150 20.00
147 Scott Podsednik/150 40.00
148 Brian Roberts/150 25.00
149 Grady Sizemore/75 50.00
150 Chris Demaria/150 20.00
151 Jonah Bayliss/150 20.00
152 Geovany Soto/150 40.00
153 Lyle Overbay/150 20.00
154 Joey Devine/150 20.00
155 Alejandro Freire/150 20.00
156 Conor Jackson/150 40.00
157 Danny Sandoval/150 20.00
158 Chase Utley/150 60.00
159 Jeff Harris/150 20.00
160 Ron Flores/150 20.00
161 Scott Feldman/150 20.00
162 Yadier Molina/135 30.00
163 Tim Corcoran/150 20.00
164 Craig Hansen/150 40.00
165 Jason Bergmann/150 20.00
166 Craig Breslow/150 25.00
167 Jhonny Peralta/120 30.00
168 Jeremy Hermida/150 35.00
169 Scott Kazmir/150 35.00
170 Bobby Crosby/25 35.00
171 Rich Harden/150 25.00
172 Casey Kotchman/150 20.00
173 Tim Hamulack/150 20.00
174 Justin Morneau/150 35.00
175 Jake Peavy/150 30.00
176 Yuniesky Betancourt/150 30.00
177 Jeremy Accardo/150 25.00
178 Jorge Cantu/25 40.00
179 Marlon Byrd/40 30.00
180 Ryan Jorgensen/150 20.00
181 Chris Denorfia/150 25.00
182 Steve Stemle/150 15.00
183 Robert Andino/150 25.00
184 Chris Heintz/150 20.00

Signature Red-Blue Stitch Black Ink

NM/M

Production 25-99
101 Adrian Beltre/50 30.00
102 Matt Cain/99 40.00
103 Craig Biggio/50 50.00
105 J.D. Drew/50 30.00
106 Eric Gagne/50 40.00
107 Tim Hudson/50 40.00
108 Tom Glavine/99 50.00
109 David Ortiz/50 85.00
110 Scott Rolen/99 40.00
111 Johan Santana/50 50.00
112 Curt Schilling/45 80.00
113 John Smoltz/50 80.00
114 Alfonso Soriano/50 80.00
115 Kerry Wood/49 30.00
116 Edwin Jackson/50 20.00
117 Felix Hernandez/60 65.00
118 Prince Fielder/50 50.00
119 Vladimir Guerrero/50 50.00
120 Roger Clemens/50 100.00
121 Albert Pujols/25 250.00
122 Chris Carpenter/50 50.00
123 Derrek Lee/50 40.00
124 Dontrelle Willis/50 25.00
125 Roy Oswalt/50 40.00
126 Ryan Garko/99 30.00
127 Tadahito Iguchi/99 50.00
128 Mark Loretta/99 25.00
129 Joe Mauer/99 40.00
130 Victor Martinez/99 30.00
131 Wily Mo Pena/99 25.00
132 Oliver Perez/99 10.00
133 Corey Patterson/99 30.00
134 Ben Sheets/99 25.00
135 Michael Young/99 30.00
136 Jonny Gomes/99 25.00
137 Derek Jeter/50 175.00
138 Ken Griffey Jr./99 100.00
139 Ryan Zimmerman/99 50.00
140 Scott Baker/99 20.00
141 Huston Street/99 25.00
142 Jason Bay/99 35.00
143 Ryan Howard/99 75.00
145 Travis Hafner/99 40.00
146 Brian Myrow/99 20.00
147 Scott Podsednik/99 40.00
148 Brian Roberts/99 25.00
149 Grady Sizemore/50 50.00
150 Chris Demaria/99 20.00
151 Jonah Bayliss/99 20.00
152 Geovany Soto/99 65.00
153 Lyle Overbay/99 20.00
154 Joey Devine/99 20.00
155 Alejandro Freire/99 20.00
156 Conor Jackson/99 40.00
157 Danny Sandoval/99 20.00
158 Chase Utley/99 60.00
159 Jeff Harris/99 20.00
160 Ron Flores/99 20.00
161 Scott Feldman/99 20.00
162 Yadier Molina/99 30.00
163 Tim Corcoran/99 20.00
164 Craig Hansen/99 25.00
165 Jason Bergmann/99 20.00
166 Craig Breslow/99 25.00
167 Jhonny Peralta/90 30.00
168 Jeremy Hermida/99 35.00
169 Scott Kazmir/99 35.00
170 Bobby Crosby/50 25.00
171 Rich Harden/99 25.00
172 Casey Kotchman/99 20.00
173 Tim Hamulack/99 20.00
174 Justin Morneau/99 35.00
175 Jake Peavy/99 30.00
176 Yuniesky Betancourt/99 30.00
177 Jeremy Accardo/99 25.00
178 Jorge Cantu/50 30.00
179 Marlon Byrd/99 25.00
180 Ryan Jorgensen/99 15.00
181 Chris Denorfia/99 25.00
182 Steve Stemle/99 15.00
183 Robert Andino/91 25.00
184 Chris Heintz/99 15.00

Signature Red-Blue Stitch Blue Ink

NM/M

Production 10-50
102 Matt Cain/40 30.00
110 Scott Rolen/50 40.00
116 Edwin Jackson/50 20.00
127 Tadahito Iguchi/50 50.00
128 Mark Loretta/50 30.00
129 Joe Mauer/50 30.00
130 Victor Martinez/50 30.00
131 Wily Mo Pena/50 25.00
132 Oliver Perez/30 15.00
133 Corey Patterson/50 20.00
134 Ben Sheets/50 25.00
136 Jonny Gomes/50 20.00
138 Ken Griffey Jr./50 125.00
139 Ryan Zimmerman/50 50.00
140 Scott Baker/50 20.00
141 Huston Street/50 30.00
142 Jason Bay/50 25.00
143 Ryan Howard/50 75.00
144 Mike Piazza/50 140.00
145 Travis Hafner/50 25.00
146 Brian Myrow/50 20.00
147 Scott Podsednik/50 25.00
148 Brian Roberts/50 25.00
149 Grady Sizemore/25 50.00
150 Chris Demaria/50 15.00
151 Jonah Bayliss/50 15.00
152 Geovany Soto/50 60.00
153 Lyle Overbay/50 15.00
154 Joey Devine/50 20.00
155 Alejandro Freire/50 15.00
156 Conor Jackson/50 40.00
157 Danny Sandoval/50 15.00
158 Chase Utley/50 65.00
159 Jeff Harris/50 15.00
160 Ron Flores/50 15.00
161 Scott Feldman/50 15.00
162 Yadier Molina/30 30.00
163 Tim Corcoran/50 15.00
164 Craig Hansen/50 40.00
165 Jason Bergmann/50 20.00
166 Craig Breslow/50 20.00
167 Jhonny Peralta/50 25.00
168 Jeremy Hermida/50 30.00
170 Bobby Crosby/50 20.00
171 Rich Harden/50 25.00
172 Casey Kotchman/50 20.00
173 Tim Hamulack/50 20.00
174 Justin Morneau/50 30.00
175 Jake Peavy/49 30.00
177 Jeremy Accardo/50 25.00
180 Ryan Jorgensen/50 20.00
181 Chris Denorfia/50 20.00
182 Steve Stemle/50 15.00
183 Robert Andino/50 20.00
184 Chris Heintz/50 20.00

Super Sweet Swatch

NM/M

Production 299 Sets
Gold: 1-2X
Production 75 Sets
Platinum: 1.5-3X
Production 45 Sets
BA Bobby Abreu 8.00
GA Garret Anderson 5.00
AT Garrett Atkins 8.00
JL Jeff Bagwell 10.00
RB Rocco Baldelli 5.00
JB Jason Bay 10.00
BE Josh Beckett 8.00
LB Lance Berkman 10.00
CB Craig Biggio 6.00
HB Hank Blalock 6.00
MI Miguel Cabrera 12.00
MA Matt Cain 10.00
EC Eric Chavez 5.00
BC Brandon Claussen 5.00
MC Matt Clement 5.00
CR Bobby Crosby/136 5.00
CD Carlos Delgado 8.00
ZD Zachary Duke 5.00
AD Adam Dunn 8.00
DY Jermaine Dye 5.00
AE Adam Eaton 5.00
ED Jim Edmonds 8.00
JE Johnny Estrada 5.00
PF Prince Fielder 15.00
FR Jeff Francoeur 10.00
EG Eric Gagne 5.00
FG Freddy Garcia 5.00
JG Jason Giambi 8.00
BG Brian Giles 5.00
MG Marcus Giles 5.00
TG Troy Glaus/160 8.00
GL Tom Glavine 8.00
KG Ken Griffey Jr. 30.00
VG Vladimir Guerrero 10.00
HA Travis Hafner 8.00

HY	Roy Halladay	8.00
TO	Todd Helton/232	10.00
FH	Felix Hernandez	10.00
HE	Ramon Hernandez	5.00
HO	Trevor Hoffman	5.00
RH	Ryan Howard	20.00
TH	Tim Hudson	8.00
HU	Torii Hunter	5.00
DJ	Derek Jeter	30.00
NJ	Nick Johnson	5.00
AJ	Andruw Jones	8.00
CJ	Chipper Jones	10.00
JJ	Jacque Jones	5.00
SK	Scott Kazmir	8.00
RK	Ryan Klesko	5.00
KO	Paul Konerko	8.00
DL	Derrek Lee	10.00
ML	Mark Loretta	5.00
NL	Noah Lowry	5.00
PM	Pedro Martinez	15.00
VM	Victor Martinez	8.00
JM	Joe Mauer	8.00
JU	Justin Morneau	8.00
MM	Mark Mulder	5.00
TN	Trot Nixon	5.00
DO	David Ortiz	12.00
RO	Roy Oswalt	5.00
JA	Jay Payton	5.00
PE	Jake Peavy	8.00
AN	Andy Pettitte	8.00
PI	Mike Piazza	15.00
JP	Jorge Posada	10.00
MP	Mark Prior	5.00
AP	Albert Pujols	30.00
MR	Manny Ramirez	10.00
JR	Jose Reyes	10.00
IR	Ivan Rodriguez/193	10.00
SR	Scott Rolen	8.00
SA	Johan Santana	10.00
CS	Curt Schilling	10.00
JS	Jason Schmidt	5.00
RS	Richie Sexson	5.00
BS	Ben Sheets	5.00
GS	Gary Sheffield	10.00
GR	Grady Sizemore	20.00
JO	John Smoltz	10.00
ST	Huston Street	5.00
MS	Mike Sweeney	5.00
NS	Nick Swisher	8.00
TX	Mark Teixeira	10.00
MT	Miguel Tejada	10.00
FT	Frank Thomas	10.00
JV	Jason Varitek	15.00
RW	Rickie Weeks	8.00
WE	David Wells	5.00
VW	Vernon Wells	5.00
BW	Bernie Williams	8.00
DW	Dontrelle Willis	5.00
JW	Jack Wilson	5.00
KW	Kerry Wood	5.00
MY	Michael Young/221	
RZ	Ryan Zimmerman	10.00
BZ	Barry Zito	5.00

2006 UD Sweet Spot Update

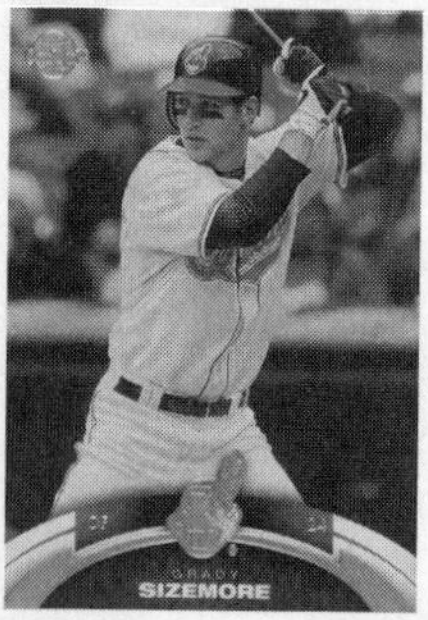

		NM/M
Complete Set (182):		
Common Player (1-100):		.25
Common Auto. (101-184):		10.00
Production 98-499		
Pack (5):		10.00
Box (12):		100.00
1	Luis Gonzalez	.25
2	Chad Tracy	.25
3	Brandon Webb	.50
4	Andruw Jones	.50
5	Chipper Jones	1.00
6	John Smoltz	.50
7	Tim Hudson	.50
8	Miguel Tejada	.50
9	Brian Roberts	.50
10	Ramon Hernandez	.25
11	Curt Schilling	.75
12	David Ortiz	1.00
13	Manny Ramirez	1.00
14	Jason Varitek	1.00
15	Josh Beckett	.75
16	Greg Maddux	2.00
17	Derrek Lee	.75
18	Mark Prior	.50
19	Aramis Ramirez	.50
20	Jim Thome	.75
21	Paul Konerko	.50
22	Scott Podsednik	.25
23	Jose Contreras	.25
24	Ken Griffey Jr.	2.00
25	Adam Dunn	.75
26	Felipe Lopez	.25
27	Travis Hafner	.50
28	Victor Martinez	.50
29	Grady Sizemore	.75
30	Jhonny Peralta	.25
31	Todd Helton	.75
32	Garrett Atkins	.50
33	Clint Barmes	.25
34	Ivan Rodriguez	.75
35	Chris Shelton	.25
36	Jeremy Bonderman	.50
37	Miguel Cabrera	1.00
38	Dontrelle Willis	.50
39	Lance Berkman	.50
40	Morgan Ensberg	.25
41	Roy Oswalt	.50
42	Reggie Sanders	.25
43	Mike Sweeney	.25
44	Vladimir Guerrero	1.00
45	Bartolo Colon	.50
46	Chone Figgins	.50
47	Nomar Garciaparra	.50
48	Jeff Kent	.50
49	J.D. Drew	.50
50	Carlos Lee	.50
51	Ben Sheets	.50
52	Rickie Weeks	.50
53	Johan Santana	1.00
54	Torii Hunter	.50
55	Joe Mauer	.75
56	Pedro Martinez	1.00
57	David Wright	2.00
58	Carlos Beltran	.75
59	Carlos Delgado	.50
60	Jose Reyes	1.00
61	Derek Jeter	3.00
62	Alex Rodriguez	2.50
63	Randy Johnson	1.00
64	Hideki Matsui	2.00
65	Gary Sheffield	.75
66	Rich Harden	.50
67	Eric Chavez	.25
68	Huston Street	.25
69	Bobby Crosby	.25
70	Bobby Abreu	.50
71	Ryan Howard	2.00
72	Chase Utley	1.00
73	Pat Burrell	.50
74	Jason Bay	.50
75	Sean Casey	.25
76	Mike Piazza	1.50
77	Jake Peavy	.50
78	Brian Giles	.25
79	Milton Bradley	.25
80	Omar Vizquel	.25
81	Jason Schmidt	.25
82	Ichiro Suzuki	2.00
83	Felix Hernandez	.50
84	Kenji Johjima	.50
85	Albert Pujols	3.00
86	Chris Carpenter	.75
87	Scott Rolen	1.00
88	Jim Edmonds	.50
89	Carl Crawford	.50
90	Jonny Gomes	.25
91	Scott Kazmir	.50
92	Mark Teixeira	.75
93	Michael Young	.50
94	Phil Nevin	.25
95	Vernon Wells	.50
96	Roy Halladay	.50
97	Troy Glaus	.50
98	Alfonso Soriano	1.00
99	Nick Johnson	.25
100	Jose Vidro	.25
101	Adam Wainwright/100 **(RC)**	40.00
102	Anderson Hernandez/100 **(RC)**	15.00
103	Andre Ethier/150 **(RC)**	30.00
104	Jason Botts/100 **(RC)**	15.00
105	Ben Johnson/400 **(RC)**	10.00
106	Boof Bonser/100 **(RC)**	15.00
107	Boone Logan/200 **RC**	10.00
108	Brian Anderson/200 **(RC)**	10.00
109	Brian Bannister/100 **(RC)**	15.00
110	Chris Denorfia/100 **(RC)**	10.00
111	Agustin Montero/100 **(RC)**	15.00
112	Cody Ross/100 **(RC)**	10.00
113	Cole Hamels/399 **(RC)**	35.00
114	Conor Jackson/400 **(RC)**	10.00
115	Dan Uggla/125 **(RC)**	35.00
116	Dave Gassner/100 **(RC)**	10.00
117	C.J. Wilson/150 **(RC)**	10.00
118	Eric Reed/150 **(RC)**	10.00
119	Fausto Carmona/99 **(RC)**	15.00
120	Fernando Nieve/100 **(RC)**	10.00
121	Francisco Liriano/499 **(RC)**	25.00
122	Freddie Bynum/100 **(RC)**	10.00
123	Hanley Ramirez/100 **(RC)**	40.00
124	Hong-Chih Kuo/100 **(RC)**	125.00
125	Ian Kinsler/100 **(RC)**	50.00
126	Carlos Marmol/100 **RC**	25.00
127	Bobby Keppel/200 **(RC)**	10.00
128	Jason Kubel/100 **(RC)**	15.00
129	Jeff Harris/100 **RC**	10.00
130	Alay Soler/100 **RC**	10.00
131	Jered Weaver/100 **(RC)**	30.00
132	Carlos Quentin/100 **(RC)**	30.00
133	Jeremy Hermida/100 **(RC)**	20.00
134	Joel Zumaya/100 **(RC)**	40.00
135	Joey Devine/100 **RC**	15.00
136	John Koronka/98 **(RC)**	10.00
137	Jonathan Papelbon/399 **(RC)**	40.00
138	Jose Capellan/240 **(RC)**	10.00
139	Josh Johnson/100 **(RC)**	10.00
140	Josh Rupe/100 **(RC)**	10.00
141	Josh Willingham/100 **(RC)**	15.00
143	Justin Verlander/100 **(RC)**	40.00
144	Kelly Shoppach/100 **(RC)**	10.00
145	Kendry Morales/100 **(RC)**	10.00
146	Kevin Thompson/100 **(RC)**	10.00
147	Macay McBride/100 **(RC)**	10.00
148	Martin Prado/100 **(RC)**	10.00
149	Matt Cain/150 **(RC)**	25.00
150	Clay Hensley/100 **(RC)**	10.00
151	Ty Taubenheim/100 **RC**	10.00
152	Mike Jacobs/200 **(RC)**	15.00
153	Saul Rivera/100 **(RC)**	10.00
154	Mike Thompson/100 **RC**	10.00
155	Nate McLouth/100 **(RC)**	20.00
156	Michael Vento/100 **(RC)**	15.00
157	Paul Maholm/200 **(RC)**	10.00
159	Reggie Abercrombie/100 **(RC)**	10.00
160	Mike Rouse/100 **(RC)**	10.00
161	Ken Ray/100 **(RC)**	10.00
162	Ron Flores/100 **RC**	10.00
163	Ryan Zimmerman/100 **(RC)**	40.00
164	Erick Aybar/100 **(RC)**	20.00
165	Sean Marshall/150 **(RC)**	15.00
166	Takashi Saito/100 **RC**	40.00
167	Taylor Buchholz/100 **(RC)**	15.00
168	Matt Murton/100 **(RC)**	25.00
169	Luis Figueroa/100 **RC**	15.00
170	Wilbert Nieves/100 **(RC)**	10.00
171	James Shields/100 **RC**	20.00
172	Jon Lester/399 **(RC)**	40.00
173	Craig Hansen/100 **RC**	25.00
174	Aaron Rakers/100 **(RC)**	10.00
175	Bobby Livingston/100 **(RC)**	10.00
176	Brendan Harris/100 **(RC)**	10.00
177	Zach Jackson/100 **(RC)**	10.00
178	Chris Britton/100 **RC**	10.00
179	Howie Kendrick/399 **(RC)**	25.00
180	Zach Miner/100 **(RC)**	10.00
181	Kevin Frandsen/100 **(RC)**	10.00
182	Matt Capps/100 **(RC)**	10.00
183	Peter Moylan/100 **RC**	10.00
184	Melky Cabrera/100 **(RC)**	50.00

Dual Signatures

		NM/M
Production 1-55		
BN	Taylor Buchholz, Fernando Nieve/55	25.00
CK	Scott Kazmir, Carl Crawford/55	40.00
CU	Carl Crawford, B.J. Upton/45	40.00
CW	Chris Carpenter, Dontrelle Willis/35	40.00
CZ	Miguel Cabrera, Ryan Zimmerman/35	50.00
EG	Andre Ethier, Tony Gwynn Jr./35	40.00
GG	Vladimir Guerrero, Ken Griffey Jr./35	150.00
GT	Ken Griffey Jr., Jim Thome/35	150.00
HD	Dan Uggla, Howie Kendrick/55	40.00
HK	Jeremy Hermida, Jason Kubel/55	30.00
HW	Jeremy Hermida, Josh Willingham/55	30.00
KR	Brian Roberts, Howie Kendrick/35	40.00
KU	B.J. Upton, Scott Kazmir/55	35.00
KW	Scott Kazmir, Dontrelle Willis/35	30.00
LN	Francisco Liriano, Joe Nathan/35	50.00
MM	Joe Mauer, Justin Morneau/35	60.00
MO	Justin Morneau, Lyle Overbay/35	40.00
PO	Jake Peavy, Roy Oswalt/35	40.00
PZ	Jonathan Papelbon, Joel Zumaya/35	90.00
RO	Alex Rios, Lyle Overbay/35	30.00
RR	Jose Reyes, Hanley Ramirez/35	60.00
SN	Huston Street, Joe Nathan/35	30.00
TI	Jim Thome, Tadahito Iguchi/35	100.00
TJ	Jeremy Sowers, Travis Hafner/35	30.00
UD	Stephen Drew, B.J. Upton/35	75.00
UH	Cole Hamels, Chase Utley/35	90.00
UU	Chase Utley, Dan Uggla/35	50.00
UW	Dan Uggla, Josh Willingham/55	30.00
ZU	Ryan Zimmerman, B.J. Upton/35	40.00

Sig. Red/Blue Stitch Red Ink

		NM/M
Production 40-225		
101	Adam Wainwright/50	40.00
103	Andre Ethier/50	40.00
105	Ben Johnson/50	10.00
106	Boof Bonser/50	20.00
107	Boone Logan/50	15.00
108	Brian Anderson/100	10.00
109	Brian Bannister/100	15.00
110	Chris Denorfia/50	10.00
112	Cody Ross/50	10.00
113	Cole Hamels/225	40.00
114	Conor Jackson/100	20.00
115	Dan Uggla/50	40.00
116	Dave Gassner/50	10.00
117	C.J. Wilson/50	10.00
118	Eric Reed/100	10.00
119	Fausto Carmona/50	15.00
120	Fernando Nieve/50	10.00
121	Francisco Liriano/175	30.00
122	Freddie Bynum/100	10.00
123	Hanley Ramirez/50	60.00
124	Hong-Chih Kuo/50	200.00
125	Ian Kinsler/45	60.00
126	Carlos Marmol/50	30.00
127	Bobby Keppel/100	10.00
128	Jason Kubel/50	20.00
130	Alay Soler/50	20.00
131	Jered Weaver/50	40.00
132	Carlos Quentin/50	30.00
133	Jeremy Hermida/50	20.00
134	Joel Zumaya/50	40.00
135	Joey Devine/50	20.00
136	John Koronka/50	10.00
137	Jonathan Papelbon/175	50.00
138	Jose Capellan/50	10.00
139	Josh Johnson/100	20.00
140	Josh Rupe/50	10.00
141	Josh Willingham/50	20.00
143	Justin Verlander/50	50.00
144	Kelly Shoppach/50	15.00
146	Kevin Thompson/50	10.00
147	Macay McBride/50	15.00
150	Clay Hensley/49	10.00
151	Ty Taubenheim/50	20.00
152	Mike Jacobs/100	20.00
153	Saul Rivera/50	15.00
154	Mike Thompson/50	15.00
155	Nate McLouth/50	20.00
156	Michael Vento/50	15.00
159	Reggie Abercrombie/50	15.00
160	Mike Rouse/50	10.00
161	Ken Ray/50	15.00
162	Ron Flores/50	10.00
163	Ryan Zimmerman/50	50.00
164	Erick Aybar/50	20.00
165	Sean Marshall/50	20.00
167	Taylor Buchholz/50	15.00
168	Matt Murton/50	40.00
169	Luis Figueroa/50	20.00
170	Wilbert Nieves/50	20.00
171	James Shields/50	30.00
172	Jon Lester/175	40.00
174	Aaron Rakers/50	10.00
175	Bobby Livingston/50	20.00
176	Brendan Harris/50	10.00
177	Zach Jackson/50	20.00
178	Chris Britton/50	10.00
179	Howie Kendrick/175	30.00
181	Kevin Frandsen/50	10.00
182	Matt Capps/50	10.00
183	Peter Moylan/50	15.00

Signatures Black Stitch/Ink

NM/M

No Pricing
Production One Set

Signatures Barrels Black Ink

		NM/M
Production 34-70		
Blue Ink:		No Pricing
Production 9-20		
Silver Ink:		No Pricing
Production One Set		
101	Adam Wainwright/35	50.00
103	Andre Ethier/35	50.00
105	Ben Johnson/35	20.00
106	Boof Bonser/35	25.00
107	Boone Logan/35	20.00
108	Brian Anderson/35	20.00
109	Brian Bannister/35	25.00
110	Chris Denorfia/35	20.00
112	Cody Ross/35	20.00
113	Cole Hamels/70	50.00
114	Conor Jackson/35	25.00
115	Dan Uggla/35	35.00
116	Dave Gassner/35	20.00
117	C.J. Wilson/35	15.00
118	Eric Reed/35	20.00
119	Fausto Carmona/35	20.00
120	Fernando Nieve/35	15.00
121	Francisco Liriano/70	40.00
122	Freddie Bynum/35	15.00
123	Hanley Ramirez/35	50.00
124	Hong-Chih Kuo/35	200.00
125	Ian Kinsler/35	60.00
126	Carlos Marmol/35	30.00
127	Bobby Keppel/35	15.00
128	Jason Kubel/35	20.00
130	Alay Soler/35	20.00
132	Carlos Quentin/35	30.00
133	Jeremy Hermida/35	25.00

134 Joel Zumaya/35 60.00
135 Joey Devine/35 20.00
136 John Koronka/35 15.00
137 Jonathan Papelbon/70 60.00
138 Jose Capellan/35 20.00
139 Josh Johnson/35 20.00
141 Josh Willingham/35 20.00
143 Justin Verlander/35 50.00
144 Kelly Shoppach/35 20.00
146 Kevin Thompson/35 20.00
147 Macay McBride/35 15.00
149 Matt Cain/35 40.00
150 Clay Hensley/35 20.00
151 Ty Taubenheim/35 20.00
152 Mike Jacobs/35 30.00
153 Saul Rivera/35 15.00
154 Mike Thompson/35 20.00
155 Nate McLouth/35 30.00
156 Michael Vento/35 20.00
157 Paul Maholm/35 20.00
159 Reggie Abercrombie/35 20.00
160 Mike Rouse/35 15.00
161 Ken Ray/35 15.00
162 Ron Flores/35 15.00
163 Ryan Zimmerman/35 50.00
164 Erick Aybar/35 25.00
165 Sean Marshall/35 20.00
167 Taylor Buchholz/35 15.00
168 Matt Murton/35 40.00
169 Luis Figueroa/34 20.00
170 Wilbert Nieves/30 20.00
171 Jamie Shields/35 35.00
172 Jon Lester/70 60.00
174 Aaron Rakers/35 15.00
175 Bobby Livingston/35 15.00
176 Brendan Harris/35 15.00
177 Zach Jackson/35 15.00
178 Chris Britton/35 15.00
179 Howie Kendrick/70 40.00
181 Kevin Frandsen/35 15.00
182 Matt Capps/35 15.00
183 Peter Moylan/35 15.00

Signatures Leather Black Ink

NM/M

Production 20-40
Blue Ink: No Pricing
Production 5-10
Silver Ink: No Pricing
Production One Set
113 Cole Hamels/40 60.00
121 Francisco Liriano/40 60.00
137 Jonathan Papelbon/40 75.00
172 Jon Lester/40 60.00
179 Howie Kendrick/40 50.00

Spokesmen Signatures

No Pricing
Production Five Sets

Sweet Beginnings Swatches

NM/M

Common Player: 5.00
AB Adrian Beltre 5.00
AI Akinori Iwamura 30.00
AJ Andruw Jones 10.00
AP Ariel Pestano 5.00
AR Alex Rios 8.00
AS Alfonso Soriano 10.00
BA Bobby Abreu 5.00
BB Brian Bannister 5.00
BI Chad Billingsley 10.00
BW Bernie Williams 10.00
CA Miguel Cabrera 10.00
CB Carlos Beltran 10.00
CD Carlos Delgado 8.00
CH Chin-Lung Hu 50.00
CJ Conor Jackson 8.00
CL Carlos Lee 5.00
CM Matt Cain 10.00
CU Chris Duncan 10.00
CZ Carlos Zambrano 8.00
DL Derrek Lee 8.00
DO David Ortiz 15.00
EB Erik Bedard 10.00
EP Eduardo Paret 8.00
FA Fausto Carmona 5.00
FC Frederich Cepeda 8.00
FL Francisco Liriano/SP 35.00
GY Guogang Yang 5.00
HA Cole Hamels 15.00
HC Hee Seop Choi 5.00
HT Hitoshi Tamura 30.00
IK Ian Kinsler 10.00
IR Ivan Rodriguez 10.00
IS Ichiro Suzuki 150.00
JB Jason Bay 10.00
JD Johnny Damon 10.00
JF Jeff Francis 5.00
JH Jeremy Hermida 8.00
JL Jong Beom Lee 8.00
JM Justin Morneau 15.00
JP Jin Man Park 8.00
JS Johan Santana 15.00
JV Jason Varitek 20.00
JZ Joel Zumaya 15.00
KE Matthew Kemp 10.00
KG Ken Griffey Jr. 20.00
KJ Kenji Johjima/SP 35.00
KU Koji Uehara 30.00
LO Javy Lopez 8.00
MA Moises Alou 8.00
MC Michael Collins 8.00
ME Michel Enriquez 8.00
MF Maikel Folch 5.00
MJ Mike Jacobs 8.00
MK Munenori Kawasaki 40.00
MN Michael Napoli 8.00
MO Michihiro Ogasawara 30.00
MP Mike Piazza 15.00
MS Min Han Son 10.00
MT Miguel Tejada 8.00
NM Nobuhiko Matsunaka 30.00
NS Naoyuki Shimizu 25.00
OU Osmany Urrutia 10.00
PF Prince Fielder/SP 20.00
PL Pedro Luis Lazo 5.00
PU Albert Pujols 25.00
RO Alex Rodriguez 20.00
SH Jamie Shields 10.00
SW Shunsuke Watanabe 30.00
TN Tsuyoshi Nishioka 30.00
TW Tsuyoshi Wada 30.00
VE Justin Verlander 15.00
VM Victor Martinez 8.00
VO Vicyohandry Odelin 5.00
WI Josh Willingham 8.00
WL Wei-Chu Lin 50.00
YG Yulieski Gourriel 10.00
YM Yuneiski Maya 10.00

Sweet Beginnings Patch

NM/M

Common Player:
AB Adrian Beltre 30.00
AE Andre Ethier 50.00
AJ Andruw Jones 25.00
AP Ariel Pestano 30.00
AS Alfonso Soriano 75.00
BA Bobby Abreu 60.00
BB Brian Bannister 40.00
BI Chad Billingsley 40.00
BW Bernie Williams 80.00
CA Miguel Cabrera 60.00
CB Carlos Beltran 60.00
CD Carlos Delgado 50.00
CJ Conor Jackson 60.00
CL Carlos Lee 40.00
CM Matt Cain 75.00
CU Chris Duncan 50.00
CZ Carlos Zambrano 50.00
DL Derrek Lee 60.00
DO David Ortiz 75.00
DU Dan Uggla 35.00
EB Erik Bedard 40.00
EP Eduardo Paret 30.00
FA Fausto Carmona 40.00
FC Frederich Cepeda 40.00
FL Francisco Liriano 50.00
HA Cole Hamels 50.00
HK Hong-Chih Kuo 200.00
JB Jason Bay 50.00
JD Johnny Damon 50.00
JF Jeff Francis 40.00
JH Jeremy Hermida 40.00
JJ Josh Johnson 40.00
JO Josh Barfield 40.00
JS Johan Santana 80.00
JV Jason Varitek 50.00
JZ Joel Zumaya 50.00
KE Matthew Kemp 50.00
KJ Kenji Johjima 150.00
KU Koji Uehara 200.00
LE Jon Lester 60.00
LO Javy Lopez 50.00
MC Michael Collins 40.00
ME Michel Enriquez 50.00
MF Maikel Folch 40.00
MJ Mike Jacobs 40.00
MK Munenori Kawasaki 250.00
MN Michael Napoli 40.00
MO Michihiro Ogasawara 200.00
MP Mike Piazza 85.00
MS Min Han Son/SP 140.00
NI Nick Markakis 60.00
NM Nobuhiko Matsunaka 75.00
NS Naoyuki Shimizu 120.00
OU Osmany Urrutia 50.00
PA Jonathan Papelbon 85.00
PE Mike Pelfrey 75.00
PL Pedro Luis Lazo 40.00
PU Albert Pujols 150.00
RN Ricky Nolasco 25.00
RZ Ryan Zimmerman 40.00
TW Tsuyoshi Wada 250.00
VE Justin Verlander 60.00
VM Victor Martinez 50.00
VO Vicyohandry Odelin 30.00
WE Jered Weaver 50.00
WI Josh Willingham 40.00
YG Yulieski Gourriel 75.00
YM Yuneiski Maya 35.00
RM Russell Martin 60.00

Veteran Red Stitch Blue Ink

NM/M

Production 30-525
AG Tony Gwynn Jr./425 20.00
AH Aaron Harang/425 20.00
AP Albert Pujols/30 250.00
AZ Aramis Ramirez/225 25.00
BJ B.J. Upton/193 15.00
BR Brian Roberts/300 15.00
CC Carl Crawford/425 15.00
CU Chase Utley/425 60.00
DJ Derek Jeter/75 200.00
DW Dontrelle Willis/125 25.00
HS Huston Street/200 15.00
JB Jason Bay/425 20.00
JM Joe Mauer/57 40.00
JN Joe Nathan/200 20.00
JS Jeremy Sowers/425 15.00
JT Jim Thome/75 50.00
KG Ken Griffey Jr./359 80.00
KG2 Ken Griffey Jr./358 80.00
KY Kevin Youkilis/425 25.00
LO Lyle Overbay/525 15.00
MC Miguel Cabrera/525 25.00
MO Justin Morneau/425 25.00
RC Roger Clemens/30 150.00
SD Stephen Drew/525 25.00
SK Scott Kazmir/522 20.00
SM John Smoltz/507 35.00
SP Scott Podsednik/247 15.00
SS Mark Mulder/300 15.00
TH Travis Hafner/525 25.00
TI Tadahito Iguchi/425 25.00
VM Victor Martinez/71 20.00

Veterans Barrels Black Ink

NM/M

Production 10-35
Blue Ink: No Pricing
Production 1-20
Silver Ink: No Pricing
Production One Set
AG Tony Gwynn Jr./35 30.00
AH Aaron Harang/35 35.00
AZ Aramis Ramirez/35 30.00
BJ B.J. Upton/35 35.00
BR Brian Roberts/35 25.00
CC Carl Crawford/35 30.00
CU Chase Utley/35 75.00
HS Huston Street/35 30.00
JB Jason Bay/35 30.00
JN Joe Nathan/35 30.00
JS Jeremy Sowers/35 35.00
KG Ken Griffey Jr./28 100.00
KG2 Ken Griffey Jr./27 100.00
KY Kevin Youkilis/35 40.00
LO Lyle Overbay/35 25.00
MC Miguel Cabrera/35 50.00
MO Justin Morneau/35 35.00
SD Stephen Drew/35 60.00
SK Scott Kazmir/33 30.00
SM John Smoltz/35 50.00
SO Scott Podsednik/35 25.00
SS Mark Mulder/35 25.00
TH Travis Hafner/35 40.00
TI Tadahito Iguchi/35 60.00
VM Victor Martinez/35 30.00

Veteran Lether Black Ink

NM/M

Production 5-20
Blue Ink: No Pricing
Production 1-5
Silver Ink: No Pricing
Production One Set

2006 UD Exquisite Collection

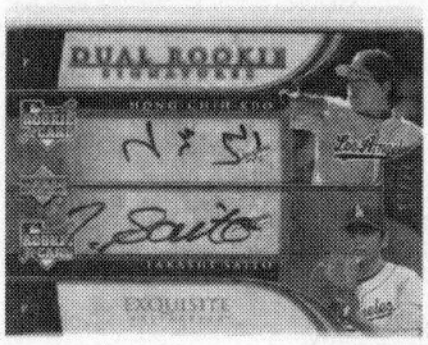

NM/M

Common Auto RC (1-90): 20.00
1-90 Production 55
Autos. 91-100: No Pricing
Production 10
Issued as exchange cards in 06 products
1 Melky Cabrera, Jeremy Hermida 25.00
2 Fausto Carmona, Craig Hansen 25.00
3 Andre Ethier, Jason Kubel 25.00
4 Boof Bonser, Chad Billingsley 30.00
5 Jeremy Sowers, Fausto Carmona 50.00
6 Josh Willingham, Ronny Paulino 25.00
7 Andre Ethier, Takashi Saito 50.00
8 Cole Hamels, James Shields 100.00
9 Carlos Quentin, Chris Denorfia 30.00
10 Jason Hammel, James Shields 30.00
11 Ian Kinsler, Dan Uggla 40.00
12 Matt Cain, Jeremy Accardo 40.00
13 Jeremy Sowers, Paul Maholm 20.00
14 Jeremy Sowers, Cole Hamels 50.00
15 Boof Bonser, Francisco Liriano 40.00
16 Justin Verlander, Joel Zumaya 80.00
17 Stephen Drew, Hanley Ramirez 50.00
18 Alay Soler, Brian Bannister 20.00
19 Boof Bonser, Dave Gassner 20.00
20 Ryan Theriot, Angel Pagan 65.00
21 Jeremy Hermida, Dan Uggla 30.00
23 Fausto Carmona, Cole Hamels 60.00
24 Hong-Chih Kuo, Takashi Saito 90.00
25 Paul Maholm, Sean Marshall 20.00
26 Dan Uggla, Howie Kendrick 50.00
27 Josh Johnson, Yusmeiro Petit 20.00
29 Andre Ethier, Russell Martin 80.00
30 Francisco Liriano, Jered Weaver 50.00
31 Cole Hamels, Zach Jackson 50.00
32 Jonathan Papelbon, Craig Hansen 50.00
34 Chris Denorfia, Jeremy Hermida 25.00
35 Cody Ross, Josh Willingham 25.00
36 Stephen Drew, Jered Weaver 60.00
38 Scott Dunn, James Shields 40.00
39 Kendry Morales, Howie Kendrick 50.00
40 Paul Maholm, Matt Capps 25.00
41 Ian Kinsler, Howie Kendrick 40.00
42 Matt Cain, Alay Soler 40.00
44 Justin Verlander, Jeremy Sowers 50.00
46 Josh Willingham, Hanley Ramirez 50.00
47 Hanley Ramirez, Jeremy Hermida 40.00
48 Josh Willingham, Dan Uggla 30.00
49 Alay Soler, Cole Hamels 50.00
50 Boof Bonser, Jason Kubel 25.00
51 Mike Jacobs, Kendry Morales 25.00
52 Jonathan Papelbon, Takashi Saito 50.00
53 Justin Verlander, Jonathan Papelbon 75.00
54 Andre Ethier, Chad Billingsley 35.00
55 Jeremy Hermida, Tony Gwynn Jr. 40.00
56 Ryan Zimmerman, Stephen Drew 60.00
57 Josh Barfield, Tony Gwynn Jr. 30.00
58 Clay Hensley, Mike Thompson 25.00
59 Josh Johnson, Justin Verlander 50.00
62 Andre Ethier, Tony Gwynn Jr. 40.00
63 Carlos Quentin, Stephen Drew 50.00
64 Conor Jackson, Carlos Quentin 40.00
65 Ryan Zimmerman, Brendan Harris 40.00
66 Russell Martin, Takashi Saito 80.00
67 Josh Willingham, Mike Jacobs 25.00
68 Mike Jacobs, Hanley Ramirez 30.00
71 Craig Hansen, Cole Hamels 50.00
72 Freddie Bynum, Hanley Ramirez 30.00
74 Taylor Buchholz, Fernando Nieve 25.00
75 Josh Johnson, Adam Wainwright 40.00
76 Josh Willingham, Russell Martin 40.00
77 Wilbert Nieves, Russell Martin 30.00
78 Ben Johnson, Mike Thompson 20.00
79 Ben Hendrickson, Zach Jackson 20.00
80 Jonathan Papelbon, Joel Zumaya 50.00
81 Ben Hendrickson, Jose Capellan 20.00
82 Joey Devine, Ken Ray 20.00
84 Russell Martin, Kelly Stoppach 30.00
85 Josh Johnson, Alay Soler 20.00
86 Alay Soler, Craig Hansen 25.00
87 Chad Billingsley, Craig Hansen 30.00
88 Chad Billingsley, Matt Cain 40.00
89 Francisco Liriano, Craig Hansen 40.00
90 Conor Jackson, Mike Jacobs 25.00

Gold

Gold (1-90): .75-1.5X
Production 30 Sets
Gold (91-100): No Pricing
Production Five Sets

Platinum
Production One Set

Cuts
NM/M

Common Auto.:
Production 25-65

AC	Al Campanis/65	100.00
BD	Bill Dickey/65	100.00
BG	Burleigh Grimes/65	120.00
BH	Billy Herman/65	100.00
CG	Charlie Gehringer/65	100.00
CH	Carl Hubbell/65	140.00
DC	Dolph Camilli/65	100.00
EA	Earl Averill/65	120.00
EM	Eddie Mathews/65	150.00
ER	Edd Roush/65	120.00
GE	George Selkirk/65	150.00
GS	George Sisler/65	200.00
HG	Hank Greenberg/65	200.00
JC	Joe Cronin/65	100.00
JM	Johnny Mize/65	120.00
LA	Luke Appling/65	100.00
LB	Lou Boudreau/65	100.00
LG	Lefty Gomez/65	120.00
MC	Max Carey/65	120.00
PW	Pee Wee Reese/65	150.00
RR	Red Ruffing/52	150.00
RS	Ray Schalk/30	250.00
SC	Stan Coveleski/65	80.00
VW	Vic Wertz/65	100.00
WG	Warren Giles/65	100.00
WH	Waite Hoyt/65	100.00
WS	Warren Spahn/65	120.00

Dual Cuts
No Pricing
Production Five Sets

Endorsed Emblems
NM/M

Production 25 Sets

AD	Adam Dunn	50.00
AJ	Andruw Jones	75.00
AR	Alex Rios	50.00
BJ	B.J. Upton	50.00
BR	Brian Roberts	60.00
BS	Ben Sheets	50.00
CB	Craig Biggio	125.00
CU	Chase Utley	60.00
CZ	Carlos Zambrano	75.00
DL	Derrek Lee	100.00
DO	David Ortiz	200.00
FL	Francisco Liriano	80.00
HS	Huston Street	50.00
JM	Joe Mauer	100.00
JO	Jonathan Papelbon	125.00
JP	Jake Peavy	80.00
JR	Jose Reyes	250.00
JS	Jeremy Sowers	50.00
JT	Jim Thome	125.00
JU	Justin Morneau	100.00
JU2	Justin Morneau	100.00
JV	Justin Verlander	100.00
JW	Jered Weaver	60.00
KG	Ken Griffey Jr.	200.00
KG2	Ken Griffey Jr.	200.00
KG3	Ken Griffey Jr.	200.00
KH	Khalil Greene	60.00
MC	Miguel Cabrera	150.00
MG	Marcus Giles	40.00
MH	Matt Holliday	50.00
MT	Mark Teixeira	50.00
MY	Michael Young	50.00
NS	Nick Swisher	60.00
RW	Rickie Weeks	50.00
SD	Stephen Drew	100.00
SM	John Smoltz	140.00
TH	Travis Hafner	100.00
TR	Trevor Hoffman	80.00

Endorsements
NM/M

Production 40 Sets

AP	Albert Pujols	
AS	Alay Soler	25.00
BF	Bob Feller	50.00
BJ	B.J. Upton	40.00
BR	Brooks Robinson	60.00
CC	Chris Carpenter	60.00
CF	Carlton Fisk	60.00
CH	Cole Hamels	75.00
CJ	Chipper Jones	80.00
CR	Cal Ripken Jr.	150.00
DO	David Ortiz	80.00
DW	Dontrelle Willis	40.00
FH	Felix Hernandez	100.00
FL	Francisco Liriano	40.00
FR	Frank Robinson	50.00
GP	Gaylord Perry	40.00
HK	Howie Kendrick	50.00
JB	Johnny Bench	60.00
JM	Joe Mauer	75.00
JO	Jonathan Papelbon	60.00
JP	Jake Peavy	60.00
JR	Jose Reyes	100.00
JS	Jeremy Sowers	20.00
JV	Justin Verlander	60.00
JW	Jered Weaver	40.00
KG	Ken Griffey Jr.	100.00
KG2	Ken Griffey Jr.	100.00
MC	Miguel Cabrera	60.00
MT	Mark Teixeira	40.00
NR	Nolan Ryan	140.00
PM	Paul Molitor	40.00
RC	Roger Clemens	180.00
RJ	Reggie Jackson	75.00
RO	Roy Oswalt	60.00
RS	Ryne Sandberg	75.00
RZ	Ryan Zimmerman	40.00
SD	Stephen Drew	50.00
SK	Scott Kazmir	40.00
SM	Stan Musial	80.00
TH	Travis Hafner	60.00
TI	Tadahito Iguchi	60.00
VG	Vladimir Guerrero	75.00
VM	Victor Martinez	40.00
WC	Will Clark	40.00

Endorsements Dual
No Pricing
Production 20 Sets

Endorsements Triple
No Pricing
Production 15 Sets

Endorsements Quad
No Pricing
Production 10 Sets

Ensemble Dual Patch
No Pricing
Production 25 Sets

Ensemble Triple Patch
No Pricing
Production 15 Sets

Ensemble Quad Patch
No Pricing
Production 10 Sets

Legends Memorabilia
NM/M

Production 15 Sets
Platinum: No Pricing
Production One Set

AK	Al Kaline	40.00
BD	Bill Dickey	60.00
BD2	Bill Dickey	60.00
BM	Bill Mazeroski	50.00
BM2	Bill Mazeroski	50.00
BR	Babe Ruth	900.00
BR2	Babe Ruth	900.00
CF	Carlton Fisk	40.00
CR	Cal Ripken Jr.	100.00
CR2	Cal Ripken Jr.	100.00
CR3	Cal Ripken Jr.	100.00
DM	Don Mattingly	80.00
FR	Frank Robinson	40.00
JB	Johnny Bench	40.00
JB2	Johnny Bench	40.00
JC	Joe Cronin	40.00
JD	Joe DiMaggio	180.00
JD2	Joe DiMaggio	180.00
JF	Jimmie Foxx	250.00
JM	Joe Morgan	30.00
LG	Lou Gehrig	400.00
LG2	Lou Gehrig	400.00
MO	Mel Ott	150.00
MS	Mike Schmidt	40.00
NR	Nolan Ryan	100.00
NR2	Nolan Ryan	100.00
OC	Orlando Cepeda	30.00
RC	Roberto Clemente	225.00
RC2	Roberto Clemente	225.00
RH	Rogers Hornsby	120.00
RH2	Rogers Hornsby	120.00
RJ	Reggie Jackson	40.00
RJ2	Reggie Jackson	40.00
RO	Brooks Robinson	40.00
RS	Ryne Sandberg	60.00
SM	Stan Musial	60.00
TG	Tony Gwynn	50.00
TG2	Tony Gwynn	50.00
TM	Thurman Munson	100.00
TM2	Thurman Munson	100.00
TW	Ted Williams	200.00
WB	Wade Boggs	50.00

Material Cuts
Production Two Sets
No Pricing

Maximum Patch
NM/M

Production 25 Sets

AD	Adam Dunn	75.00
AP	Albert Pujols	250.00
AS	Alfonso Soriano	80.00
CA	Carl Crawford	80.00
CB	Carlos Beltran	100.00
CC	Chris Carpenter	100.00
CD	Carlos Delgado	80.00
CJ	Chipper Jones	120.00
CR	Craig Biggio	80.00
CS	Curt Schilling	75.00
DJ	Derek Jeter	350.00
DO	David Ortiz	125.00
FH	Felix Hernandez	120.00
FL	Francisco Liriano	75.00
FT	Frank Thomas	120.00
JF	Jeff Francoeur	100.00
JG	Jason Giambi	120.00
JM	Justin Morneau	120.00
JO	Jonathan Papelbon	75.00
JP	Jake Peavy	75.00
JR	Jose Reyes	120.00
JS	Johan Santana	80.00
JT	Jim Thome	75.00
JV	Justin Verlander	75.00
JW	Jered Weaver	75.00
KG	Ken Griffey Jr.	140.00
MC	Miguel Cabrera	75.00
MI	Miguel Tejada	75.00
MT	Mark Teixeira	75.00
MY	Michael Young	60.00
PF	Prince Fielder	75.00
PM	Pedro Martinez	100.00
TG	Troy Glaus	60.00
TH	Todd Helton	75.00
TO	Tom Glavine	100.00
TR	Travis Hafner	75.00
VG	Vladimir Guerrero	75.00
VM	Victor Martinez	60.00

Memorabilia
NM/M

Production 45 Sets
Gold: .75-1.5X
Production 25 Sets
Platinum: No Pricing
Production 15 Sets
Mem. 1: No Pricing
Production One Set

AD	Adam Dunn	15.00
AD2	Adam Dunn	15.00
AJ	Andruw Jones	15.00
AJ2	Andruw Jones	15.00
AP	Albert Pujols	50.00
AP2	Albert Pujols	50.00
AR	Alex Rodriguez	50.00
AS	Alfonso Soriano	20.00
AS2	Alfonso Soriano	20.00
BR	Babe Ruth	450.00
BR2	Babe Ruth	450.00
BZ	Barry Zito	15.00
BZ2	Barry Zito	15.00
CB	Carlos Beltran	20.00
CB2	Carlos Beltran	20.00
CF	Carlton Fisk	15.00
CF2	Carlton Fisk	15.00
CJ	Chipper Jones	25.00
CJ2	Chipper Jones	25.00
CR	Cal Ripken Jr.	50.00
CR2	Cal Ripken Jr.	50.00
CR3	Cal Ripken Jr.	50.00
CS	Curt Schilling	15.00
CU	Chase Utley	35.00
CU2	Chase Utley	35.00
CY	Carl Yastrzemski	25.00
CY2	Carl Yastrzemski	25.00
DA	Daisuke Matsuzaka	250.00
DJ	Derek Jeter	60.00
DJ2	Derek Jeter	60.00
DL	Derrek Lee	60.00
DM	Don Mattingly	40.00
DO	David Ortiz	30.00
DO2	David Ortiz	30.00
FL	Francisco Liriano	20.00
FL2	Francisco Liriano	20.00
GM	Greg Maddux	25.00
GM2	Greg Maddux	25.00
HO	Ryan Howard	25.00
HO2	Ryan Howard	25.00
IS	Ichiro Suzuki	200.00
JA	Jason Bay	15.00
JA2	Jason Bay	15.00
JB	Jeff Bagwell	20.00
JB2	Jeff Bagwell	20.00
JD	Joe DiMaggio	200.00
JM	Joe Mauer	25.00
JP	Jake Peavy	20.00
JP2	Jake Peavy	20.00
JS	Johan Santana	20.00
JS2	Johan Santana	20.00
JT	Jim Thome	20.00
JT2	Jim Thome	20.00
JV	Justin Verlander	35.00
JV2	Justin Verlander	35.00
JW	Jered Weaver	15.00
JW2	Jered Weaver	15.00
KG	Ken Griffey Jr.	30.00
KG2	Ken Griffey Jr.	30.00
KG3	Ken Griffey Jr.	30.00
KJ	Kenji Johjima	30.00
KJ2	Kenji Johjima	30.00
MA	Manny Ramirez	20.00
MA2	Manny Ramirez	20.00
MA3	Manny Ramirez	20.00
MC	Miguel Cabrera	20.00
MC2	Miguel Cabrera	20.00
MI	Miguel Tejada	15.00
MI2	Miguel Tejada	15.00
MR	Mariano Rivera	35.00
MR2	Mariano Rivera	35.00
MS	Mike Schmidt	25.00
MS2	Mike Schmidt	25.00
MT	Mark Teixeira	15.00
NR	Nolan Ryan	50.00
NR2	Nolan Ryan	50.00
PE	Pedro Martinez	30.00
PF	Prince Fielder	25.00
PF2	Prince Fielder	25.00
PM	Paul Molitor	20.00
PM2	Paul Molitor	20.00
RC	Roger Clemens	35.00
RC2	Roger Clemens	35.00
RC3	Roger Clemens	35.00
RE	Reggie Jackson	30.00
RE2	Reggie Jackson	30.00
RH	Roy Halladay	15.00
RH2	Roy Halladay	15.00
RJ	Randy Johnson	20.00
RO	Roy Oswalt	15.00
RO2	Roy Oswalt	15.00
RY	Robin Yount	25.00
RY2	Robin Yount	25.00
SM	Stan Musial	40.00
SM2	Stan Musial	40.00
TG	Tony Gwynn	35.00
TH	Travis Hafner	20.00
VG	Vladimir Guerrero	25.00
VG2	Vladimir Guerrero	25.00
WB	Wade Boggs	20.00

Patch
NM/M

Production 25 Sets
Patch 10: No Pricing
Production 10 Sets
Patch 1: No Pricing
Production One Set

AD	Adam Dunn	40.00
AD2	Adam Dunn	40.00
AJ	Andruw Jones	50.00
AJ2	Andruw Jones	50.00
AP	Albert Pujols	150.00
AP2	Albert Pujols	150.00
AS	Alfonso Soriano	60.00
AS2	Alfonso Soriano	60.00
BZ	Barry Zito	40.00
BZ2	Barry Zito	40.00
CB	Carlos Beltran	50.00
CB2	Carlos Beltran	50.00
CF	Carlton Fisk	50.00
CF2	Carlton Fisk	50.00
CJ	Chipper Jones	80.00
CJ2	Chipper Jones	80.00
CR	Cal Ripken Jr.	120.00
CR2	Cal Ripken Jr.	120.00
CR3	Cal Ripken Jr.	120.00
CS	Curt Schilling	60.00
CU	Chase Utley	60.00
CU2	Chase Utley	60.00
DJ	Derek Jeter	150.00
DJ2	Derek Jeter	150.00
DL	Derrek Lee	50.00
DM	Don Mattingly	100.00
DO	David Ortiz	75.00
DO2	David Ortiz	75.00
FL	Francisco Liriano	40.00
FL2	Francisco Liriano	40.00
GM	Greg Maddux	75.00
GM2	Greg Maddux	75.00
HO	Ryan Howard	100.00
HO2	Ryan Howard	100.00
JA	Jason Bay	40.00
JA2	Jason Bay	40.00
JM	Joe Mauer	60.00
JP	Jake Peavy	50.00
JP2	Jake Peavy	50.00
JS	Johan Santana	60.00
JS2	Johan Santana	60.00
JT	Jim Thome	50.00
JT2	Jim Thome	50.00
JV	Justin Verlander	60.00
JV2	Justin Verlander	60.00
JW	Jered Weaver	50.00
JW2	Jered Weaver	50.00
KG	Ken Griffey Jr.	120.00
KG2	Ken Griffey Jr.	120.00
KG3	Ken Griffey Jr.	120.00
KJ	Kenji Johjima	50.00
KJ2	Kenji Johjima	50.00
MA	Manny Ramirez	50.00
MA2	Manny Ramirez	50.00
MA3	Manny Ramirez	50.00
MC	Miguel Cabrera	50.00
MC2	Miguel Cabrera	50.00
MI	Miguel Tejada	40.00
MI2	Miguel Tejada	40.00
MR	Mariano Rivera	60.00
MR2	Mariano Rivera	60.00
MS	Mike Schmidt	40.00
MS2	Mike Schmidt	40.00
MT	Mark Teixeira	40.00
NR	Nolan Ryan	120.00
NR2	Nolan Ryan	120.00
PE	Pedro Martinez	50.00
PF	Prince Fielder	50.00
PF2	Prince Fielder	50.00
PM	Paul Molitor	30.00
PM2	Paul Molitor	30.00
RC	Roger Clemens	75.00
RC2	Roger Clemens	75.00
RC3	Roger Clemens	75.00
RE	Reggie Jackson	50.00
RE2	Reggie Jackson	50.00
RH	Roy Halladay	50.00
RH2	Roy Halladay	50.00
RJ	Randy Johnson	40.00
RO	Roy Oswalt	40.00
RO2	Roy Oswalt	40.00
RY	Robin Yount	75.00
RY2	Robin Yount	75.00
TG	Tony Gwynn	80.00
TH	Travis Hafner	50.00
VG	Vladimir Guerrero	50.00
VG2	Vladimir Guerrero	50.00
WB	Wade Boggs	40.00

Signature Patch
NM/M

Production 30 Sets
Triple: No Pricing
Production One Set
Dual: No Pricing
Production One Set

AB	A.J. Burnett	

AD Adam Dunn 60.00
AJ Andruw Jones 75.00
AR Alex Rios 60.00
BJ B.J. Upton 50.00
BR Brian Roberts 50.00
BS Ben Sheets 40.00
CB Craig Biggio 90.00
CC Chris Carpenter 75.00
CL Carlos Lee 50.00
CU Chase Utley 100.00
CZ Carlos Zambrano 50.00
DJ Derek Jeter 300.00
DL Derrek Lee 100.00
DO David Ortiz 180.00
FH Felix Hernandez 150.00
JP Jake Peavy 60.00
JR Jose Reyes 200.00
JS Jeremy Sowers 40.00
JT Jim Thome 80.00
JU Justin Morneau 75.00
JU2 Justin Morneau 75.00
JV Justin Verlander 150.00
JW Jered Weaver 60.00
KH Khalil Greene 75.00
MC Miguel Cabrera 120.00
MG Marcus Giles 40.00
MH Matt Holliday 75.00
MT Mark Teixeira 50.00
MY Michael Young 50.00
NS Nick Swisher 50.00
RO Roy Oswalt 60.00
RW Rickie Weeks 50.00
SD Stephen Drew 80.00
SK Scott Kazmir 80.00
TH Travis Hafner 100.00
TI Tadahito Iguchi 50.00
VM Victor Martinez 60.00

2006 UD Ultimate Collection

NM/M

Complete Set (290):
Common Player (1-100): 1.50
Common RC Auto. (101-175): 10.00
Production 180 unless noted.
Common (191-290): 2.00
Production 799
Pack (4): 75.00
Box (4): 250.00
1 Babe Ruth 8.00
2 Chad Tracy 1.50
3 Brandon Webb 2.00
4 Andruw Jones 3.00
5 Chipper Jones 4.00
6 John Smoltz 2.00
7 Eddie Mathews 4.00
8 Miguel Tejada 3.00
9 Brian Roberts 2.00
10 Mickey Cochrane 2.00
11 Curt Schilling 3.00
12 David Ortiz 4.00
13 Manny Ramirez 4.00
14 Johnny Bench 4.00
15 Cy Young 3.00
16 Greg Maddux 5.00
17 Derrek Lee 3.00
18 Yogi Berra 4.00
19 Walter Johnson 2.00
20 Jim Thome 3.00
21 Paul Konerko 2.00
22 Lou Gehrig 6.00
23 Jose Contreras 1.50
24 Ken Griffey Jr. 5.00
25 Adam Dunn 3.00
26 Reggie Jackson 3.00
27 Travis Hafner 2.00
28 Victor Martinez 2.00
29 Grady Sizemore 3.00
30 Casey Stengel 3.00
31 Todd Helton 3.00
32 Nolan Ryan 8.00
33 Clint Barmes 1.50
34 Ivan Rodriguez 3.00
35 Chris Shelton 1.50
36 Ty Cobb 5.00
37 Miguel Cabrera 4.00
38 Dontrelle Willis 1.50
39 Lance Berkman 2.00
40 Tom Seaver 4.00
41 Roy Oswalt 2.00
42 Christy Mathewson 3.00
43 Luis Aparicio 1.50
44 Vladimir Guerrero 4.00
45 Bartolo Colon 1.50
46 Roy Campanella 2.00
47 George Sisler 1.50
48 Jeff Kent 1.50
49 J.D. Drew 1.50
50 Carlos Lee 2.00
51 Willie Stargell 3.00
52 Rickie Weeks 1.50
53 Johan Santana 4.00
54 Torii Hunter 2.00
55 Joe Mauer 2.00
56 Pedro Martinez 4.00
57 David Wright 5.00
58 Carlos Beltran 3.00
59 Jimmie Foxx 3.00
60 Jose Reyes 4.00
61 Derek Jeter 8.00
62 Alex Rodriguez 6.00
63 Randy Johnson 4.00
64 Hideki Matsui 5.00
65 Thurman Munson 4.00
66 Rich Harden 1.50
67 Eric Chavez 1.50
68 Don Drysdale 3.00
69 Bobby Crosby 1.50
70 Pee Wee Reese 1.50
71 Ryan Howard 6.00
72 Chase Utley 4.00
73 Jackie Robinson 5.00
74 Jason Bay 3.00
75 Honus Wagner 4.00
76 Lefty Grove 3.00
77 Jake Peavy 3.00
78 Brian Giles 1.50
79 Eddie Murray 3.00
80 Omar Vizquel 1.50
81 Jason Schmidt 2.00
82 Ichiro Suzuki 5.00
83 Felix Hernandez 3.00
84 Kenji Johjima **RC** 5.00
85 Albert Pujols 8.00
86 Chris Carpenter 3.00
87 Brooks Robinson 3.00
88 Dizzy Dean 3.00
89 Carl Crawford 2.00
90 Rogers Hornsby 3.00
91 Scott Kazmir 2.00
92 Mark Teixeira 3.00
93 Michael Young 2.00
94 Johnny Mize 1.50
95 Vernon Wells 3.00
96 Roy Halladay 2.00
97 Mel Ott 1.50
98 Alfonso Soriano 4.00
99 Joe Morgan 3.00
100 Satchel Paige 4.00
101 Adam Wainwright **(RC)** 30.00
102 Anderson Hernandez **(RC)** 10.00
103 Andre Ethier **(RC)** 25.00
104 Ben Johnson **(RC)** 15.00
105 Boof Bonser **(RC)** 15.00
106 Boone Logan **RC** 10.00
107 Brian Anderson **(RC)** 10.00
108 Brian Bannister **(RC)** 25.00
109 Chris Demaria **RC** 10.00
110 Chris Denorfia **(RC)** 10.00
111 Cody Ross **(RC)** 10.00
112 Cole Hamels **(RC)** 50.00
113 Conor Jackson **(RC)** 20.00
114 Dan Uggla **(RC)** 40.00
115 Dave Gassner **(RC)** 10.00
116 Eric Reed **(RC)** 10.00
117 Fausto Carmona **(RC)** 35.00
118 Fernando Nieve **(RC)** 10.00
119 Francisco Liriano **(RC)** 40.00
120 Freddie Bynum **(RC)** 10.00
121 Hanley Ramirez **(RC)** 50.00
122 Hong-Chih Kuo **(RC)** 40.00
123 Ian Kinsler **(RC)** 50.00
124 Jason Hammel **(RC)** 10.00
125 Jason Kubel **(RC)** 10.00
126 Jeff Harris **RC** 10.00
127 Jered Weaver/150 **(RC)** 40.00
128 Jeremy Accardo **(RC)** 10.00
129 Jeremy Hermida **(RC)** 20.00
130 Joel Zumaya **(RC)** 20.00
131 Joey Devine **RC** 10.00
132 John Koronka **(RC)** 15.00
133 John Van Benschoten **(RC)** 10.00
134 Jonathan Papelbon **(RC)** 40.00
135 Jose Capellan **(RC)** 10.00
136 Josh Johnson **(RC)** 10.00
137 Josh Rupe **(RC)** 10.00
138 Josh Willingham **(RC)** 15.00
139 Josh Wilson **(RC)** 10.00
140 Justin Verlander **(RC)** 50.00
141 Kelly Shoppach **(RC)** 10.00
142 Kendry Morales **(RC)** 10.00
143 Macay McBride **(RC)** 10.00
144 Martin Prado **(RC)** 10.00
145 Matt Cain **(RC)** 30.00
146 Mike Jacobs **(RC)** 20.00
147 Mike Thompson **RC** 10.00
148 Nate McLouth **(RC)** 20.00
149 Paul Maholm **(RC)** 10.00
150 Prince Fielder **(RC)** 75.00
151 Reggie Abercrombie **(RC)** 10.00
152 Rich Hill **(RC)** 25.00
153 Ron Flores **RC** 10.00
154 Ruddy Lugo **(RC)** 10.00
155 Ryan Zimmerman **(RC)** 50.00
156 Sean Marshall **(RC)** 15.00
157 Takashi Saito **RC** 30.00
158 Taylor Buchholz **(RC)** 15.00
159 Tony Pena **(RC)** 10.00
160 Wilbert Nieves **(RC)** 10.00
161 Jamie Shields **RC** 20.00
162 Jon Lester **(RC)** 50.00
163 Craig Hansen **RC** 25.00
164 Aaron Rakers **(RC)** 10.00
165 Yusmeiro Petit **(RC)** 10.00
166 Bobby Livingston **(RC)** 10.00
167 Brendan Harris **(RC)** 10.00
169 Carlos Ruiz **(RC)** 10.00
170 Chris Britton **RC** 10.00
171 Howie Kendrick **(RC)** 40.00
172 Jermaine Van Buren 10.00
173 Kevin Frandsen **(RC)** 15.00
174 Matt Capps **(RC)** 10.00
175 Peter Moylan **RC** 10.00
191 Richie Ashburn/799 3.00
192 Lou Brock 4.00
193 Lou Boudreau 2.00
194 Orlando Cepeda 2.00
195 Bobby Doerr 2.00
196 Dennis Eckersley 2.00
197 Bob Feller 3.00
198 Rollie Fingers 2.00
199 Carlton Fisk 4.00
200 Bob Gibson 4.00
201 Jim "Catfish" Hunter 3.00
202 Fergie Jenkins 3.00
203 Al Kaline 5.00
204 Harmon Killebrew 5.00
205 Ralph Kiner 3.00
206 Buck Leonard 3.00
207 Juan Marichal 2.00
208 Bill Mazeroski 4.00
209 Willie McCovey 4.00
210 Jim Palmer 2.00
211 Tony Perez 2.00
212 Gaylord Perry 2.00
213 Phil Rizzuto 4.00
214 Robin Roberts 2.00
215 Mike Schmidt 6.00
216 Enos Slaughter 2.00
217 Ozzie Smith 5.00
218 Billy Williams 2.00
219 Robin Yount 5.00
220 Carlos Quentin **(RC)** 4.00
221 Jeff Francoeur 2.00
222 Brian McCann 2.00
223 Nicholas Markakis **(RC)** 6.00
224 Josh Beckett 2.00
225 Jason Varitek 4.00
226 Mark Prior 4.00
227 Aramis Ramirez 3.00
228 Jermaine Dye 2.00
229 Tadahito Iguchi 2.00
230 Bobby Jenks 2.00
231 C.C. Sabathia 2.00
232 Jeff Francis 2.00
233 Matt Holliday 2.00
234 Magglio Ordonez 2.00
235 Kenny Rogers 2.00
236 Roger Clemens 8.00
237 Andy Pettitte 3.00
238 Craig Biggio 3.00
239 Chone Figgins 2.00
240 John Lackey 2.00
241 Nomar Garciaparra 4.00
242 Prince Fielder **(RC)** 6.00
243 Ben Sheets 3.00
244 Bill Hall 2.00
245 Justin Morneau 4.00
246 Joe Nathan 2.00
247 Carlos Delgado 3.00
248 Shawn Green 2.00
249 Billy Wagner 2.00
250 Jason Giambi 4.00
251 Mike Mussina 4.00
252 Mariano Rivera 4.00
253 Robinson Cano 4.00
254 Bobby Abreu 3.00
255 Huston Street 2.00
256 Frank Thomas 4.00
257 Danny Haren 2.00
258 Jason Kendall 2.00
259 Nick Swisher 3.00
260 Pat Burrell 3.00
261 Tom Gordon 2.00
262 Freddy Sanchez 2.00
263 Trevor Hoffman 2.00
264 Khalil Greene 2.00
265 Adrian Gonzalez 2.00
266 Moises Alou 2.00
267 Matt Morris 2.00
268 Pedro Feliz 2.00
269 Richie Sexson 3.00
270 Hoyt Wilhelm 2.00
271 Adrian Beltre 2.00
272 Jim Edmonds 3.00
273 Scott Rolen 4.00
274 Jason Isringhausen 2.00
275 Jorge Cantu 2.00
276 Hank Blalock 2.00
277 Kevin Millwood 2.00
278 Alex Rios 2.00
279 Troy Glaus 3.00
280 B.J. Ryan 2.00
281 Nick Johnson 2.00
282 Chad Cordero 2.00
283 Austin Kearns 2.00
284 Ricky Nolasco **(RC)** 2.00
285 Travis Ishikawa **(RC)** 2.00
286 Lastings Milledge **(RC)** 4.00
287 James Loney **(RC)** 4.00
288 Red Schoendienst 3.00
289 Warren Spahn 4.00
290 Early Wynn **(RC)** 2.00

Printing Plates

No Pricing
Production one set per color.

Ensemble Materials 3

Production 25 Sets
Patch: No Pricing
Production 20 Sets

Ensemble Materials 4

Production 20 Sets
Patch: No Pricing
Production 15 Sets

Ensemble Signature 3

NM/M

Production 50 Sets
Triple 15: No Pricing
Production 15 Sets
Triple 1 of 1: No Pricing
AHW Josh Willingham, Reggie Abercrombie, Jeremy Hermida 40.00
BBB Jeff Bagwell, Craig Biggio, Lance Berkman 100.00
BBW Taylor Buchholz, Adam Wainwright, Brian Bannister 50.00
BDD George Bell, Eric Davis, Andre Dawson 50.00
BHR Roy Halladay, A.J. Burnett, Alex Rios 40.00
BKM Ralph Kiner, Bill Mazeroski, Jason Bay 85.00
BNO Taylor Buchholz, Roy Oswalt, Fernando Nieve 30.00
BSH A.J. Burnett, Rich Harden, Ben Sheets 40.00
BUK Craig Biggio, Chase Utley, Ian Kinsler 75.00
BWC Matt Cain, Brian Bannister, Adam Wainwright 40.00
BWV Justin Verlander, Boof Bonser, Jered Weaver 85.00
CBP Oliver Perez, Jason Bay, Sean Casey 30.00
CBS Ron Cey, Dusty Baker, Don Sutton 50.00
CBZ Boof Bonser, Joel Zumaya, Matt Cain 50.00
CDV Jack Clark, Eric Davis, Andy Van Slyke 50.00
CHK Jason Kubel, Melky Cabrera, Jeremy Hermida 50.00
CHO Chris Carpenter, Roy Oswalt, Rich Harden 60.00
CKH Rich Harden, Bobby Crosby, Jason Kendall 40.00
CKS Carl Crawford, Scott Kazmir, Jamie Shields 50.00
CLH Cole Hamels, Fausto Carmona, Francisco Liriano 80.00
CMH Victor Martinez, Travis Hafner, Fausto Carmona 60.00
CNS Graig Nettles, Ron Cey, Ron Santo 50.00
CPC Carl Crawford, Coco Crisp, Scott Podsednik 40.00
CSS John Smoltz, Roger Clemens, Curt Schilling 200.00
CWW Josh Willingham, Dontrelle Willis, Miguel Cabrera 50.00
CZC Miguel Cabrera, Eric Chavez, Ryan Zimmerman 60.00
DJH Hanley Ramirez, Derek Jeter, Jose Reyes 200.00
DPA Scott Podsednik, Jermaine Dye, Brian Anderson 40.00
DPI Jermaine Dye, Scott Podsednik, Tadahito Iguchi 60.00
FGC David Cone, Dwight Gooden, Sid Fernandez 75.00
FJM Prince Fielder, Conor Jackson, Kendry Morales 40.00
FWL Rickie Weeks, Prince Fielder, Carlos Lee 40.00
GCN Graig Nettles, Rich "Goose" Gossage, Chris Chambliss 50.00
GCS Bret Saberhagen, Dwight Gooden, David Cone 30.00
GJB Derek Jeter, Ken Griffey Jr., Jason Bay 250.00
GJP Derek Jeter, Albert Pujols, Ken Griffey Jr. 500.00
GLK Dave Gassner, Jason Kubel, Francisco Liriano 50.00
GPN Joe Nathan, Eric Gagne, Jonathan Papelbon 50.00
GRS Alex Rios, Alfonso Soriano, Vladimir Guerrero 90.00
HBS Rich Harden, Nick Swisher, Joe Blanton 50.00
HKP Boog Powell, John Kruk, Kent Hrbek 40.00
HMK Mark Mulder, Scott Kazmir, Cole Hamels 60.00
HNP Jonathan Papelbon, Trevor Hoffman, Joe Nathan 75.00
HOT David Ortiz, Travis Hafner, Mark Teixeira 100.00
HWU Josh Willingham, Jeremy Hermida, Dan Uggla 30.00
IKU Dan Uggla, Ian Kinsler, Tadahito Iguchi 85.00
JCN Melky Cabrera, Wilbert Nieves, Derek Jeter 150.00
JGS Ken Griffey Jr., Andruw Jones, Alfonso Soriano 120.00
JRR Derek Jeter, Jose Reyes, Hanley Ramirez 200.00
JWV Jered Weaver, Justin Verlander, Josh Johnson 75.00
KGJ John Kruk, Mark Grace, Wally Joyner 80.00
KLB Francisco Liriano, Boof Bonser, Jason Kubel 50.00

KUU	Ian Kinsler, Dan Uggla, Chase Utley	65.00
KWM	Josh Willingham, Victor Martinez, Jason Kendall	30.00
LGB	Francisco Liriano, Boof Bonser, Dave Gassner	40.00
LHC	Felix Hernandez, Fausto Carmona, Francisco Liriano	50.00
LPO	Derrek Lee, David Ortiz, Albert Pujols	250.00
MCN	Ron Cey, Graig Nettles, Bill Madlock	50.00
MMK	Jason Kendall, Joe Mauer, Victor Martinez	40.00
MNL	Joe Mauer, Francisco Liriano, Joe Nathan	50.00
MWC	Chris Carpenter, Mark Mulder, Adam Wainwright	75.00
MWP	Josh Willingham, Russell Martin, Ronny Paulino	30.00
NLP	Jonathan Papelbon, Brad Lidge, Joe Nathan	50.00
OBL	Brad Lidge, Roy Oswalt, Taylor Buchholz	40.00
PCL	Oliver Perez, Francisco Liriano, Fausto Carmona	50.00
PHL	Cole Hamels, Francisco Liriano, Oliver Perez	65.00
PSO	Roy Oswalt, Jake Peavy, Ben Sheets	40.00
PVW	Justin Verlander, Jered Weaver, Jonathan Papelbon	90.00
RHW	Jeremy Hermida, Josh Willingham, Cody Ross	30.00
RMM	Victor Martinez, Joe Mauer, Ivan Rodriguez	65.00
RRB	Jose Reyes, Yuniesky Betancourt, Hanley Ramirez	60.00
SGM	Greg Maddux, John Smoltz, Tom Glavine	180.00
SJF	Prince Fielder, Mike Jacobs, Chris Shelton	30.00
SKM	Russell Martin, Takashi Saito, Hong-Chih Kuo	200.00
SWB	Taylor Buchholz, Jamie Shields, Jered Weaver	60.00
TGB	Frank Thomas, Ken Griffey Jr., Jeff Bagwell	150.00
TKY	Michael Young, Mark Teixeira, Ian Kinsler	75.00
UHC	Jeremy Hermida, Dan Uggla, Miguel Cabrera	75.00
URC	Miguel Cabrera, Dan Uggla, Hanley Ramirez	40.00
URW	Hanley Ramirez, Dan Uggla, Josh Willingham	35.00
VBZ	Justin Verlander, Jeremy Bonderman, Joel Zumaya	120.00
VWL	Jered Weaver, Francisco Liriano, Justin Verlander	120.00
WJC	Josh Johnson, Jered Weaver, Matt Cain	70.00
WJO	Scott Olsen, Josh Johnson, Dontrelle Willis	40.00
WSV	Justin Verlander, Jered Weaver, Jamie Shields	65.00
ZBC	Joel Zumaya, Matt Cain, Boof Bonser	60.00
ZHZ	Carlos Zambrano, Felix Hernandez, Joel Zumaya	60.00

Ensemble Signatures 4

No Pricing
Production 25 Sets

Ensemble Signatures 5

No Pricing
Production 15 Sets

Ensemble Signatures 6

No Pricing
Production 10 Sets

Ensemble Signatures 8

Production One Set
No Pricing

Game Materials

		NM/M
Common Player:		8.00
Production 50 Sets		
AB	A.J. Burnett	8.00
AD	Adam Dunn	10.00
AJ	Andruw Jones	12.00
AP	Albert Pujols	30.00
AR	Alex Rios	8.00
AS	Alfonso Soriano	10.00
BA	Brian Bannister	8.00
BG	Brian Giles	8.00
BM	Bill Mazeroski	15.00
BO	Jeremy Bonderman	10.00
BR	Brian Roberts	8.00
CA	Melky Cabrera	15.00
CC	Carl Crawford	10.00
CH	Chris Carpenter	15.00
CJ	Conor Jackson	10.00
CL	Carlos Lee	10.00
CR	Coco Crisp	10.00
CS	Chris Shelton	8.00
CU	Chase Utley	20.00
CZ	Carlos Zambrano	10.00
DJ	Derek Jeter	30.00
DJ2	Derek Jeter	30.00
DL	Derrek Lee	30.00
DU	Dan Uggla	10.00
DW	Dontrelle Willis	10.00
FH	Felix Hernandez	12.00
FL	Francisco Liriano	15.00
GA	Garrett Atkins	8.00
GP	Gaylord Perry	10.00
HA	Cole Hamels	15.00
HB	Hank Blalock	10.00
HC	Craig Hansen	15.00
HO	Trevor Hoffman	10.00
HR	Hanley Ramirez	15.00
HT	Tim Hudson	10.00
HU	Torii Hunter	10.00
HY	Roy Halladay	10.00
IK	Ian Kinsler	10.00
IR	Ivan Rodriguez	10.00
JB	Jason Bay	12.00
JD	Jermaine Dye	10.00
JH	Jeremy Hermida	8.00
JJ	Josh Johnson	8.00
JK	Jason Kendall	8.00
JM	Joe Mauer	10.00
JN	Joe Nathan	10.00
JP	Jake Peavy	10.00
JR	Jose Reyes	15.00
JS	Johan Santana	12.00
JV	Justin Verlander	15.00
JW	Jered Weaver	15.00
JZ	Joel Zumaya	15.00
KG	Ken Griffey Jr.	25.00
KG2	Ken Griffey Jr.	25.00
KH	Khalil Greene	8.00
KJ	Kenji Johjima	20.00
KM	Kendry Morales	8.00
KU	Jason Kubel	8.00
KY	Kevin Youkilis	10.00
LA	Luis Aparicio	10.00
LM	Lastings Milledge	10.00
LY	Fred Lynn	8.00
MA	Matt Cain	15.00
MC	Miguel Cabrera	15.00
MG	Marcus Giles	8.00
MH	Matt Holliday	15.00
ML	Mark Loretta	8.00
MM	Melvin Mora	8.00
MO	Justin Morneau	12.00
MS	Mike Schmidt	20.00
MT	Mark Teixeira	12.00
MU	Mark Mulder	10.00
MY	Michael Young	10.00
NS	Nick Swisher	10.00
PA	Jonathan Papelbon	20.00
PF	Prince Fielder	10.00
PM	Paul Molitor	15.00
RC	Cal Ripken Jr.	40.00
RH	Rich Harden	10.00
RI	Jim Rice	15.00
RO	Roy Oswalt	10.00
RW	Rickie Weeks	10.00
RZ	Ryan Zimmerman	15.00
SK	Scott Kazmir	10.00
SP	Scott Podsednik	10.00
TE	Miguel Tejada	12.00
TG	Tony Gwynn	15.00
TH	Travis Hafner	10.00
TI	Tadahito Iguchi	10.00
TP	Tony Perez	10.00
VM	Victor Martinez	10.00
WC	Will Clark	15.00
WI	Josh Willingham	8.00
YB	Yuniesky Betancourt	8.00

Game Materials Signatures

		NM/M
Production 35 Sets		
AB	A.J. Burnett	25.00
AD	Adam Dunn	25.00
AJ	Andruw Jones	50.00
AP	Albert Pujols	250.00
AR	Alex Rios	25.00
AS	Alfonso Soriano	60.00
BA	Brian Bannister	25.00
BG	Brian Giles	25.00
BM	Bill Mazeroski	40.00
BO	Jeremy Bonderman	50.00
BR	Brian Roberts	25.00
CA	Melky Cabrera	40.00
CC	Carl Crawford	25.00
CH	Chris Carpenter	30.00
CJ	Conor Jackson	35.00
CL	Carlos Lee	25.00
CR	Coco Crisp	30.00
CS	Chris Shelton	25.00
CU	Chase Utley	60.00
CZ	Carlos Zambrano	40.00
DJ	Derek Jeter	250.00
DJ2	Derek Jeter	250.00
DL	Derrek Lee	35.00
DU	Dan Uggla	40.00
DW	Dontrelle Willis	30.00
FH	Felix Hernandez	40.00
FL	Francisco Liriano	50.00
GA	Garrett Atkins	25.00
GP	Gaylord Perry	25.00
HA	Cole Hamels	60.00
HB	Hank Blalock	25.00
HC	Craig Hansen	40.00
HO	Trevor Hoffman	30.00
HR	Hanley Ramirez	60.00
HT	Tim Hudson	30.00
HU	Torii Hunter	25.00
HY	Roy Halladay	25.00
IK	Ian Kinsler	30.00
IR	Ivan Rodriguez	35.00
JB	Jason Bay	30.00
JD	Jermaine Dye	25.00
JH	Jeremy Hermida	25.00
JJ	Josh Johnson	35.00
JK	Jason Kendall	25.00
JM	Joe Mauer	40.00
JN	Joe Nathan	25.00
JP	Jake Peavy	30.00
JR	Jose Reyes	40.00
JS	Johan Santana	50.00
JV	Justin Verlander	60.00
JW	Jered Weaver	40.00
JZ	Joel Zumaya	60.00
KG	Ken Griffey Jr.	120.00
KG2	Ken Griffey Jr.	120.00
KH	Khalil Greene	35.00
KM	Kendry Morales	30.00
KU	Jason Kubel	25.00
KY	Kevin Youkilis	25.00
LA	Luis Aparicio	25.00
LY	Fred Lynn	25.00
MA	Matt Cain	40.00
MC	Miguel Cabrera	50.00
MG	Marcus Giles	25.00
MH	Matt Holliday	30.00
ML	Mark Loretta	25.00
MM	Melvin Mora	25.00
MO	Justin Morneau	40.00
MS	Mike Schmidt	50.00
MU	Mark Mulder	25.00
MY	Michael Young	25.00
NS	Nick Swisher	25.00
PA	Jonathan Papelbon	60.00
PM	Paul Molitor	35.00
RC	Cal Ripken Jr.	150.00
RH	Rich Harden	30.00
RI	Jim Rice	30.00
RO	Roy Oswalt	30.00
RW	Rickie Weeks	25.00
RZ	Ryan Zimmerman	50.00
SK	Scott Kazmir	30.00
SP	Scott Podsednik	25.00
TE	Miguel Tejada	30.00
TG	Tony Gwynn	60.00
TH	Travis Hafner	30.00
TI	Tadahito Iguchi	40.00
TP	Tony Perez	30.00
VM	Victor Martinez	30.00
WC	Will Clark	35.00
WI	Josh Willingham	25.00
YB	Yuniesky Betancourt	25.00

Legendary Materials

		NM/M
Production 5-55		
AR	Al Rosen/55	15.00
BD	Bill Dickey/55	30.00
BD2	Bill Dickey/55	30.00
BG	Bob Gibson/25	20.00
BM	Bill Mazeroski/25	20.00
BO	Bo Jackson/55	20.00
BO2	Bo Jackson/55	20.00
CF	Carlton Fisk/55	10.00
CF2	Carlton Fisk/55	10.00
CW	Rod Carew/55	10.00
CW2	Rod Carew/55	10.00
CY	Carl Yastrzemski/25	20.00
CY2	Carl Yastrzemski/25	20.00
GP	Gaylord Perry/55	10.00
GP2	Gaylord Perry/55	10.00
JB	Johnny Bench/55	20.00
JO	Joe Morgan/55	10.00
JO2	Joe Morgan/55	10.00
JU	Juan Marichal/55	10.00
KI	Kirk Gibson/55	10.00
KP	Kirby Puckett/55	20.00
KP2	Kirby Puckett/55	20.00
MA	Don Mattingly/55	25.00
MA2	Don Mattingly/55	25.00
MW	Maury Wills/41	10.00
NR	Nolan Ryan/55	35.00
NR2	Nolan Ryan/25	40.00
NR3	Nolan Ryan/25	40.00
OS	Ozzie Smith/55	20.00
OS2	Ozzie Smith/55	20.00
PM	Paul Molitor/55	10.00
PM2	Paul Molitor/55	10.00
PN	Phil Niekro/55	10.00
PN2	Phil Niekro/55	10.00
RJ	Reggie Jackson/25	20.00
RJ2	Reggie Jackson/35	15.00
RK	Ralph Kiner/25	20.00
RO	Brooks Robinson/35	15.00
RO2	Brooks Robinson/35	15.00
RS	Ryne Sandberg/35	25.00
RY	Robin Yount/25	15.00
RY2	Robin Yount/25	15.00
SC	Steve Carlton/55	10.00
SC2	Steve Carlton/47	10.00
SU	Don Sutton/55	10.00
SU2	Don Sutton/55	10.00
TG	Tony Gwynn/55	20.00
TG2	Tony Gwynn/55	20.00
TP	Tony Perez/55	15.00
TP2	Tony Perez/55	15.00
WB	Wade Boggs/55	15.00
WB2	Wade Boggs/55	15.00
WC	Will Clark/45	15.00
WC2	Will Clark/45	15.00

Legendary Ensemble Signatures

No Pricing
Production 25 Sets

Maximum Materials

Production 25 Sets
Patch: No Pricing
Production 15 Sets

Numbers Materials

		NM/M
Production 35 Sets		
AB	A.J. Burnett	10.00
AD	Adam Dunn	12.00
AJ	Andruw Jones	15.00
AP	Albert Pujols	40.00
AR	Alex Rios	10.00
AS	Alfonso Soriano	15.00
BA	Brian Bannister	10.00
BG	Brian Giles	10.00
BM	Bill Mazeroski	15.00
BO	Jeremy Bonderman	15.00
BR	Brian Roberts	10.00
CA	Melky Cabrera	15.00
CC	Carl Crawford	10.00
CH	Chris Carpenter	15.00
CJ	Conor Jackson	15.00
CL	Carlos Lee	10.00
CR	Coco Crisp	10.00
CS	Chris Shelton	10.00
CU	Chase Utley	20.00
CZ	Carlos Zambrano	15.00
DJ	Derek Jeter	40.00
DJ2	Derek Jeter	40.00
DL	Derrek Lee	15.00
DU	Dan Uggla	15.00
DW	Dontrelle Willis	15.00
FH	Felix Hernandez	15.00
FL	Francisco Liriano	20.00
GA	Garrett Atkins	10.00
GP	Gaylord Perry	15.00
HA	Cole Hamels	25.00
HB	Hank Blalock	10.00
HC	Craig Hansen	20.00
HO	Trevor Hoffman	10.00
HR	Hanley Ramirez	20.00
HT	Tim Hudson	10.00
HU	Torii Hunter	10.00
HY	Roy Halladay	10.00
IK	Ian Kinsler	10.00
IR	Ivan Rodriguez	15.00
JB	Jason Bay	15.00
JD	Jermaine Dye	10.00
JH	Jeremy Hermida	10.00
JJ	Josh Johnson	12.00
JK	Jason Kendall	10.00
JM	Joe Mauer	15.00
JN	Joe Nathan	10.00
JP	Jake Peavy	10.00
JR	Jose Reyes	20.00
JS	Johan Santana	20.00
JV	Justin Verlander	20.00
JW	Jered Weaver	20.00
JZ	Joel Zumaya	20.00
KG	Ken Griffey Jr.	35.00
KG2	Ken Griffey Jr.	35.00
KH	Khalil Greene	10.00
KJ	Kenji Johjima	30.00
KM	Kendry Morales	10.00
KU	Jason Kubel	10.00
KY	Kevin Youkilis	15.00
LA	Luis Aparicio	10.00
LM	Lastings Milledge	15.00
LY	Fred Lynn	10.00
MA	Matt Cain	15.00
MC	Miguel Cabrera	15.00
MG	Marcus Giles	10.00
MH	Matt Holliday	10.00
ML	Mark Loretta	10.00
MM	Melvin Mora	10.00
MO	Justin Morneau	15.00
MS	Mike Schmidt	25.00
MT	Mark Teixeira	15.00
MU	Mark Mulder	10.00
MY	Michael Young	10.00
NS	Nick Swisher	10.00
PA	Jonathan Papelbon	25.00
PF	Prince Fielder	15.00
PM	Paul Molitor	15.00
RC	Cal Ripken Jr.	75.00
RH	Rich Harden	10.00
RI	Jim Rice	15.00
RO	Roy Oswalt	15.00
RW	Rickie Weeks	10.00
RZ	Ryan Zimmerman	15.00
SK	Scott Kazmir	10.00
SP	Scott Podsednik	10.00
TE	Miguel Tejada	15.00
TG	Tony Gwynn	20.00
TH	Travis Hafner	15.00
TI	Tadahito Iguchi	15.00
TP	Tony Perez	15.00
VM	Victor Martinez	10.00
WC	Will Clark	15.00
WI	Josh Willingham	10.00
YB	Yuniesky Betancourt	10.00

Numbers Patch

		NM/M
Production 35 unless noted.		
AB	A.J. Burnett	20.00
AD	Adam Dunn	25.00
AJ	Andruw Jones	25.00

AP	Albert Pujols	80.00
AR	Alex Rios	20.00
AS	Alfonso Soriano	25.00
BA	Brian Bannister	15.00
BG	Brian Giles	20.00
BO	Jeremy Bonderman	25.00
BR	Brian Roberts	20.00
CC	Carl Crawford	20.00
CH	Chris Carpenter	25.00
CJ	Conor Jackson	20.00
CL	Carlos Lee	20.00
CR	Coco Crisp	20.00
CS	Chris Shelton	15.00
CU	Chase Utley	40.00
CZ	Carlos Zambrano	25.00
DJ	Derek Jeter	65.00
DJ2	Derek Jeter	65.00
DL	Derrek Lee	25.00
DU	Dan Uggla	25.00
DW	Dontrelle Willis	25.00
FH	Felix Hernandez	25.00
FL	Francisco Liriano	30.00
GA	Garrett Atkins	20.00
HA	Cole Hamels	40.00
HB	Hank Blalock	20.00
HO	Trevor Hoffman	20.00
HR	Hanley Ramirez	30.00
HT	Tim Hudson	20.00
HU	Torii Hunter	20.00
HY	Roy Halladay	20.00
IK	Ian Kinsler	20.00
IR	Ivan Rodriguez	25.00
JB	Jason Bay	25.00
JD	Jermaine Dye	20.00
JH	Jeremy Hermida	20.00
JJ	Josh Johnson	20.00
JK	Jason Kendall	20.00
JM	Joe Mauer	40.00
JN	Joe Nathan	20.00
JP	Jake Peavy	20.00
JR	Jose Reyes	40.00
JS	Johan Santana	30.00
JV	Justin Verlander	40.00
JW	Jered Weaver	30.00
JZ	Joel Zumaya	35.00
KG	Ken Griffey Jr.	50.00
KG2	Ken Griffey Jr.	50.00
KH	Khalil Greene	20.00
KJ	Kenji Johjima	50.00
KM	Kendry Morales	20.00
KU	Jason Kubel	20.00
KY	Kevin Youkilis	20.00
LA	Luis Aparicio	20.00
LM	Lastings Milledge	20.00
LY	Fred Lynn	20.00
MA	Matt Cain	30.00
MC	Miguel Cabrera	25.00
MG	Marcus Giles	20.00
MH	Matt Holliday	20.00
ML	Mark Loretta	20.00
MM	Melvin Mora	20.00
MO	Justin Morneau	25.00
MS	Mike Schmidt	50.00
MT	Mark Teixeira	25.00
MU	Mark Mulder	20.00
MY	Michael Young	20.00
NS	Nick Swisher	20.00
PF	Prince Fielder	25.00
PM	Paul Molitor	30.00
RC	Cal Ripken Jr.	100.00
RH	Rich Harden	20.00
RI	Jim Rice	25.00
RO	Roy Oswalt	20.00
RW	Rickie Weeks	20.00
RZ	Ryan Zimmerman	25.00
SK	Scott Kazmir	20.00
SP	Scott Podsednik	20.00
TE	Miguel Tejada	25.00
TG	Tony Gwynn	30.00
TH	Travis Hafner	25.00
TI	Tadahito Iguchi	25.00
VM	Victor Martinez	20.00
WC	Will Clark	25.00
WI	Josh Willingham	20.00
YB	Yuniesky Betancourt	15.00

Signature Patch

No Pricing
Production 10 Sets

Ultimate Patch

NM/M

Production 50 unless noted.
Patch Signature: No Pricing
Production 10 Sets

AB	A.J. Burnett	15.00
AD	Adam Dunn	20.00
AJ	Andruw Jones	20.00
AP	Albert Pujols	60.00
AR	Alex Rios	15.00
AS	Alfonso Soriano	25.00
BA	Brian Bannister	15.00
BG	Brian Giles	15.00
BO	Jeremy Bonderman	25.00
BR	Brian Roberts	15.00
CA	Melky Cabrera	25.00
CC	Carl Crawford	15.00
CH	Chris Carpenter	20.00
CJ	Conor Jackson	15.00
CL	Carlos Lee	15.00
CR	Coco Crisp	20.00
CS	Chris Shelton	15.00
CU	Chase Utley	35.00
CZ	Carlos Zambrano	20.00
DJ	Derek Jeter	50.00
DJ2	Derek Jeter	50.00
DL	Derrek Lee	20.00
DU	Dan Uggla	20.00
DW	Dontrelle Willis	15.00
FH	Felix Hernandez	20.00
FL	Francisco Liriano	25.00
GA	Garrett Atkins	15.00
GP	Gaylord Perry/27	20.00
HA	Cole Hamels	25.00
HB	Hank Blalock	15.00
HO	Trevor Hoffman	15.00
HR	Hanley Ramirez	25.00
HT	Tim Hudson	15.00
HU	Torii Hunter	15.00
HY	Roy Halladay	15.00
IR	Ivan Rodriguez	20.00
JB	Jason Bay	20.00
JD	Jermaine Dye	15.00
JH	Jeremy Hermida	20.00
JJ	Josh Johnson	20.00
JK	Jason Kendall	15.00
JM	Joe Mauer	25.00
JN	Joe Nathan	15.00
JP	Jake Peavy	15.00
JR	Jose Reyes	30.00
JS	Johan Santana	25.00
JV	Justin Verlander	40.00
JW	Jered Weaver	25.00
JZ	Joel Zumaya/47	30.00
KG	Ken Griffey Jr.	50.00
KG2	Ken Griffey Jr.	50.00
KH	Khalil Greene	15.00
KJ	Kenji Johjima	35.00
KM	Kendry Morales	20.00
KU	Jason Kubel	15.00
LA	Luis Aparicio	20.00
LM	Lastings Milledge	30.00
LY	Fred Lynn	15.00
MA	Matt Cain	25.00
MC	Miguel Cabrera	25.00
MG	Marcus Giles	15.00
MH	Matt Holliday	30.00
ML	Mark Loretta/40	15.00
MM	Melvin Mora	15.00
MO	Justin Morneau	30.00
MS	Mike Schmidt	30.00
MT	Mark Teixeira	20.00
MU	Mark Mulder	15.00
MY	Michael Young	20.00
NS	Nick Swisher	20.00
PF	Prince Fielder	20.00
PM	Paul Molitor	20.00
RC	Cal Ripken Jr.	75.00
RH	Rich Harden	20.00
RI	Jim Rice/31	20.00
RO	Roy Oswalt	25.00
RW	Rickie Weeks	20.00
RZ	Ryan Zimmerman	40.00
SK	Scott Kazmir	20.00
SP	Scott Podsednik	15.00
TE	Miguel Tejada	20.00
TG	Tony Gwynn	30.00
TH	Travis Hafner	20.00
TI	Tadahito Iguchi	30.00
VM	Victor Martinez	15.00
WC	Will Clark	20.00
WI	Josh Willingham	15.00
YB	Yuniesky Betancourt	15.00

Tandem Materials

NM/M

Production 25 Sets
Signature: No Pricing
Production 15 Sets
Signature Patch: No Pricing
Production Five Sets
Signature Logo: No Pricing
Production One Set

AA	Alfonso Soriano, Alex Rios	20.00
AH	Garrett Atkins, Matt Holliday	10.00
BH	Felix Hernandez, Yuniesky Betancourt	20.00
BM	Brian Bannister, Lastings Milledge	20.00
BR	Yuniesky Betancourt, Hanley Ramirez	25.00
BV	Justin Verlander, Jeremy Bonderman	40.00
CL	Coco Crisp, Mark Loretta	20.00
CP	Carl Crawford, Scott Podsednik	15.00
CS	Cole Hamels, Scott Kazmir	25.00
CW	Dontrelle Willis, Chris Carpenter	15.00
CZ	Miguel Cabrera, Ryan Zimmerman	20.00
FP	Tony Perez, Prince Fielder	15.00
FW	Prince Fielder, Rickie Weeks	15.00
GP	Ken Griffey Jr., Albert Pujols	50.00
HB	Matt Holliday, Jason Bay	15.00
HF	Prince Fielder, Travis Hafner	15.00
HG	Trevor Hoffman, Brian Giles	10.00
HJ	Andruw Jones, Torii Hunter	15.00
HK	Jeremy Hermida, Jason Kubel	10.00
HM	Travis Hafner, Victor Martinez	10.00
HN	Trevor Hoffman, Joe Nathan	10.00
HO	Roy Oswalt, Rich Harden	15.00
HP	Trevor Hoffman, Jonathan Papelbon	25.00
HR	Hanley Ramirez, Jeremy Hermida	15.00
HW	Jeremy Hermida, Josh Willingham	10.00
ID	Jermaine Dye, Tadahito Iguchi	15.00
JB	Bill Mazeroski, Jason Bay	20.00
JG	Derek Jeter, Ken Griffey Jr.	40.00
JR	Derek Jeter, Cal Ripken Jr.	60.00
KB	Brian Giles, Khalil Greene	10.00
KM	Joe Mauer, Jason Kendall	15.00
KU	Ian Kinsler, Dan Uggla	10.00
KY	Ian Kinsler, Michael Young	10.00
LF	Prince Fielder, Carlos Lee	15.00
MH	Livan Hernandez, Kendry Morales	10.00
MM	Joe Mauer, Victor Martinez	20.00
MP	Tony Perez, Kendry Morales	15.00
MR	Melvin Mora, Brian Roberts	10.00
MW	Rickie Weeks, Paul Molitor	20.00
NJ	Joe Mauer, Joe Nathan	20.00
NM	Joe Mauer, Joe Nathan	15.00
PO	Roy Oswalt, Jake Peavy	15.00
PP	Jake Peavy, Gaylord Perry	15.00
SH	Rich Harden, Nick Swisher	15.00
TY	Michael Young, Mark Teixeira	15.00
VM	Justin Verlander, Jack Morris	20.00
WM	Josh Willingham, Joe Mauer	20.00
YL	Kevin Youkilis, Mark Loretta	15.00
ZJ	Josh Johnson, Joel Zumaya	20.00
ZZ	Joel Zumaya, Carlos Zambrano	20.00

Tandem Patch

NM/M

Production 35 Sets

AA	Alfonso Soriano, Alex Rios	15.00
AH	Garrett Atkins, Matt Holliday	15.00
AJ	Luis Aparicio, Derek Jeter	40.00
BH	Felix Hernandez, Yuniesky Betancourt	20.00
BM	Brian Bannister, Lastings Milledge	15.00
BR	Yuniesky Betancourt, Hanley Ramirez	20.00
BV	Justin Verlander, Jeremy Bonderman	40.00
CH	Melky Cabrera, Jeremy Hermida	20.00
CL	Coco Crisp, Mark Loretta	15.00
CM	Lastings Milledge, Melky Cabrera	25.00
CO	Roy Oswalt, Roger Clemens	50.00
CP	Carl Crawford, Scott Podsednik	15.00
CR	Miguel Cabrera, Hanley Ramirez	20.00
CS	Cole Hamels, Scott Kazmir	50.00
CV	Justin Verlander, Matt Cain	40.00
CW	Dontrelle Willis, Chris Carpenter	30.00
CZ	Miguel Cabrera, Ryan Zimmerman	25.00
DH	Hanley Ramirez, Derek Jeter	60.00
FW	Prince Fielder, Rickie Weeks	25.00
GD	Adam Dunn, Ken Griffey Jr.	40.00
GG	Tony Gwynn, Brian Giles	30.00
GP	Ken Griffey Jr., Albert Pujols	80.00
GR	Ken Griffey Jr., Alex Rios	40.00
GT	Ken Griffey Jr., Frank Thomas	50.00
HB	Matt Holliday, Jason Bay	20.00
HF	Prince Fielder, Travis Hafner	25.00
HG	Trevor Hoffman, Brian Giles	15.00
HJ	Andruw Jones, Torii Hunter	25.00
HK	Jeremy Hermida, Jason Kubel	15.00
HM	Travis Hafner, Victor Martinez	15.00
HN	Trevor Hoffman, Joe Nathan	15.00
HO	Roy Oswalt, Rich Harden	20.00
HP	Trevor Hoffman, Jonathan Papelbon	30.00
HR	Hanley Ramirez, Jeremy Hermida	25.00
HW	Jeremy Hermida, Josh Willingham	15.00
ID	Jermaine Dye, Tadahito Iguchi	25.00
JC	Derek Jeter, Melky Cabrera	65.00
JG	Derek Jeter, Ken Griffey Jr.	80.00
JJ	Derek Jeter, Reggie Jackson	60.00
JK	Kendry Morales, Jered Weaver	30.00
JM	Kenji Johjima, Victor Martinez	30.00
JR	Derek Jeter, Cal Ripken Jr.	100.00
KB	Brian Giles, Khalil Greene	20.00
KC	Scott Kazmir, Carl Crawford	15.00
KM	Joe Mauer, Jason Kendall	25.00
KU	Ian Kinsler, Dan Uggla	20.00
KY	Ian Kinsler, Michael Young	15.00
LC	Fred Lynn, Coco Crisp	20.00
LF	Prince Fielder, Carlos Lee	15.00
LH	Francisco Liriano, Cole Hamels	40.00
MF	Kendry Morales, Prince Fielder	20.00
MH	Livan Hernandez, Kendry Morales	15.00
ML	Francisco Liriano, Joe Mauer	35.00
MM	Joe Mauer, Victor Martinez	25.00
MR	Melvin Mora, Brian Roberts	15.00
MW	Rickie Weeks, Paul Molitor	20.00
NJ	Joe Mauer, Joe Nathan	20.00
NL	Joe Nathan, Francisco Liriano	30.00
NM	Joe Mauer, Joe Nathan	30.00
NP	Joe Nathan, Jonathan Papelbon	30.00
PC	Matt Cain, Gaylord Perry	30.00
PH	Jonathan Papelbon, Craig Hansen	50.00
PO	Roy Oswalt, Jake Peavy	20.00
PP	Jake Peavy, Gaylord Perry	15.00
RC	Coco Crisp, Alex Rios	15.00
RM	Lastings Milledge, Jose Reyes	30.00
RR	Jose Reyes, Hanley Ramirez	40.00
RS	Mike Schmidt, Cal Ripken Jr.	75.00
RU	Hanley Ramirez, Dan Uggla	25.00
RV	Ivan Rodriguez, Justin Verlander	35.00
SH	Rich Harden, Nick Swisher	15.00
SJ	Conor Jackson, Chris Shelton	25.00
SZ	Ryan Zimmerman, Mike Schmidt	30.00
TY	Michael Young, Mark Teixeira	20.00
UK	Chase Utley, Ian Kinsler	40.00
UM	Chase Utley, Joe Morgan	40.00
UR	Brian Roberts, Dan Uggla	15.00
VM	Justin Verlander, Jack Morris	40.00
VZ	Justin Verlander, Joel Zumaya	40.00
WM	Josh Willingham, Joe Mauer	25.00
WR	Hanley Ramirez, Josh Willingham	25.00
WV	Justin Verlander, Jered Weaver	40.00
YL	Kevin Youkilis, Mark Loretta	20.00
ZA	Garrett Atkins, Ryan Zimmerman	30.00
ZC	Ryan Zimmerman, Miguel Cabrera	30.00
ZJ	Josh Johnson, Joel Zumaya	20.00
ZZ	Joel Zumaya, Carlos Zambrano	30.00

Tri-Marks Signatures

No Pricing
Production 15 Sets

2007 Upper Deck

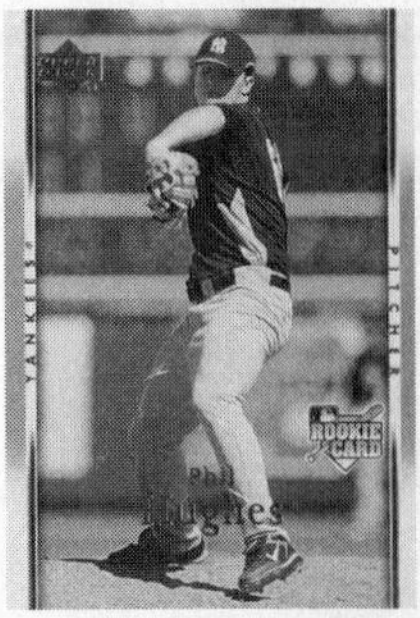

NM/M

Complete Set (1020):		
Common Player:		.15
Rookie Redemption:		75.00
Hobby Pack (15):		5.00
Hobby Box (16):		70.00
1	Doug Slaten **RC**	.50
2	Miguel Montero **(RC)**	.25
3	Brian Burres **(RC)**	.25
4	Devern Hansack **RC**	1.50
5	David Murphy **(RC)**	.25
6	Jose Reyes **RC**	.50
7	Scott Moore **(RC)**	.25
8	Josh Fields **(RC)**	.50

9	Chris Stewart **RC**	.50
10	Jerry Owens **(RC)**	.25
11	Ryan Sweeney **(RC)**	.25
12	Kevin Kouzmanoff **(RC)**	.50
13	Jeff Baker **(RC)**	.25
14	Justin Hampson **(RC)**	.25
15	Jeff Salazar **(RC)**	.25
16	Alvin Colina **RC**	.50
17	Troy Tulowitzki **(RC)**	.50
18	Andrew Miller **RC**	4.00
19	Mike Rabelo **RC**	1.00
20	Jose Diaz **(RC)**	.25
21	Angel Sanchez **RC**	.50
22	Ryan Braun **(RC)**	1.00
23	Delwyn Young **(RC)**	.25
24	Drew Anderson **(RC)**	.25
25	Dennis Sarfate **(RC)**	.25
26	Vinny Rottino **(RC)**	.25
27	Glen Perkins **(RC)**	.25
28	Alexi Casilla **RC**	1.00
29	Philip Humber **(RC)**	.50
30	Andy Cannizaro **RC**	.50
31	Jeremy Brown	.25
32	Sean Henn **(RC)**	.25
33	Brian Rogers	.15
34	Carlos Maldonado **(RC)**	.25
35	Juan Morillo **(RC)**	.25
36	Fred Lewis **(RC)**	.25
37	Patrick Misch **(RC)**	.25
38	Billy Sadler **(RC)**	.25
39	Ryan Feierabend **(RC)**	.25
40	Cesar Jimenez **RC**	.75
41	Oswaldo Navarro **RC**	.50
42	Travis Chick **(RC)**	.25
43	Delmon Young **(RC)**	1.00
44	Shawn Riggans **(RC)**	.25
45	Brian Stokes **(RC)**	.25
46	Juan Salas **(RC)**	.25
47	Joaquin Arias **(RC)**	.25
48	Adam Lind **(RC)**	.50
49	Beltran Perez **(RC)**	.25
50	Brett Campbell **RC**	.50
51	Brian Roberts	.25
52	Miguel Tejada	.50
53	Brandon Fahey	.15
54	Jay Gibbons	.15
55	Corey Patterson	.15
56	Nicholas Markakis	.25
57	Ramon Hernandez	.15
58	Kris Benson	.15
59	Adam Loewen	.15
60	Erik Bedard	.25
61	Chris Ray	.15
62	Chris Britton	.15
63	Daniel Cabrera	.15
64	Sendy Rleal	.15
65	Manny Ramirez	.75
66	David Ortiz	.75
67	Gabe Kapler	.15
68	Alex Cora	.15
69	Dustin Pedroia	.15
70	Trot Nixon	.15
71	Doug Mirabelli	.15
72	Mark Loretta	.15
73	Curt Schilling	.75
74	Jonathan Papelbon	.50
75	Tim Wakefield	.15
76	Jon Lester	.25
77	Craig Hansen	.15
78	Keith Foulke	.15
79	Jermaine Dye	.15
80	Jim Thome	.50
81	Tadahito Iguchi	.15
82	Robert Mackowiak	.15
83	Brian Anderson	.15
84	Juan Uribe	.15
85	A.J. Pierzynski	.15
86	Alex Cintron	.15
87	Jon Garland	.15
88	Jose Contreras	.15
89	Neal Cotts	.15
90	Bobby Jenks	.15
91	Mike MacDougal	.15
92	Javier Vazquez	.15
93	Travis Hafner	.40
94	Jhonny Peralta	.25
95	Ryan Garko	.15
96	Victor Martinez	.25
97	Hector Luna	.15
98	Casey Blake	.15
99	Jason Michaels	.15
100	Shin-Soo Choo	.15
101	C.C. Sabathia	.25
102	Paul Byrd	.15
103	Jeremy Sowers	.15
104	Cliff Lee	.15
105	Rafael Betancourt	.15
106	Francisco Cruceta	.15
107	Sean Casey	.15
108	Brandon Inge	.15
109	Placido Polanco	.15
110	Omar Infante	.15
111	Ivan Rodriguez	.50
112	Magglio Ordonez	.25
113	Craig Monroe	.15
114	Marcus Thames	.15
115	Justin Verlander	.50
116	Todd Jones	.15
117	Kenny Rogers	.15
118	Joel Zumaya	.25
119	Jeremy Bonderman	.50
120	Nate Robertson	.15
121	Mark Teahen	.15
122	Ryan Shealy	.25
123	Mitch Maier **(RC)**	.25
124	Doug Mientkiewicz	.15
125	Mark Grudzielanek	.15
126	Shane Costa	.15
127	John Buck	.15
128	Reggie Sanders	.15
129	Mike Sweeney	.15
130	Mark Redman	.15
131	Todd Wellemeyer	.15
132	Scott Elarton	.15
133	Ambiorix Burgos	.15
134	Joe Nelson	.15
135	Howie Kendrick	.40
136	Chone Figgins	.15
137	Orlando Cabrera	.25
138	Maicer Izturis	.15
139	Jose Molina	.15
140	Vladimir Guerrero	.75
141	Darin Erstad	.15
142	Juan Rivera	.15
143	Jered Weaver	.40
144	John Lackey	.25
145	Joe Saunders	.15
146	Bartolo Colon	.15
147	Scot Shields	.15
148	Francisco Rodriguez	.25
149	Justin Morneau	.50
150	Jason Bartlett	.15
151	Luis Castillo	.15
152	Nick Punto	.15
153	Shannon Stewart	.15
154	Michael Cuddyer	.15
155	Jason Kubel	.15
156	Joe Mauer	.50
157	Francisco Liriano	.25
158	Joe Nathan	.25
159	Dennys Reyes	.15
160	Brad Radke	.15
161	Boof Bonser	.15
162	Juan Rincon	.15
163	Derek Jeter	2.00
164	Jason Giambi	.50
165	Robinson Cano	.50
166	Andy Phillips	.15
167	Bobby Abreu	.40
168	Gary Sheffield	.50
169	Bernie Williams	.40
170	Melky Cabrera	.25
171	Mike Mussina	.50
172	Chien-Ming Wang	.50
173	Mariano Rivera	.50
174	Scott Proctor	.15
175	Jaret Wright	.15
176	Kyle Farnsworth	.15
177	Eric Chavez	.25
178	Bobby Crosby	.15
179	Frank Thomas	.50
180	Dan Johnson	.15
181	Marco Scutaro	.15
182	Nick Swisher	.40
183	Milton Bradley	.25
184	Jay Payton	.15
185	Joe Blanton	.15
186	Barry Zito	.40
187	Rich Harden	.25
188	Esteban Loaiza	.15
189	Huston Street	.25
190	Chad Gaudin	.15
191	Richie Sexson	.40
192	Yuniesky Betancourt	.15
193	Willie Bloomquist	.15
194	Ben Broussard	.15
195	Kenji Johjima	.25
196	Ichiro Suzuki	1.00
197	Raul Ibanez	.15
198	Chris Snelling SP	.15
199	Felix Hernandez	.50
200	Cha Sueng Baek	.15
201	Joel Pineiro	.15
202	Julio Mateo	.15
203	J.J. Putz	.15
204	Rafael Soriano	.15
205	Jorge Cantu	.15
206	B.J. Upton	.25
207	Ty Wigginton	.15
208	Greg Norton	.15
209	Dioner Navarro	.15
210	Carl Crawford	.40
211	Jonny Gomes	.15
212	Damon Hollins	.15
213	Scott Kazmir	.25
214	Casey Fossum	.15
215	Ruddy Lugo	.15
216	James Shields	.15
217	Tyler Walker	.15
218	Shawn Camp	.15
219	Mark Teixeira	.50
220	Hank Blalock	.25
221	Ian Kinsler	.25
222	Jerry Hairston Jr.	.15
223	Gerald Laird	.15
224	Carlos Lee	.40
225	Gary Matthews	.15
226	Mark DeRosa	.15
227	Kip Wells	.15
228	Akinori Otsuka	.15
229	Vicente Padilla	.15
230	John Koronka	.15
231	Kevin Millwood	.25
232	Wes Littleton	.15
233	Troy Glaus	.40
234	Lyle Overbay	.25
235	Aaron Hill	.15
236	John McDonald	.15
237	Bengie Molina	.15
238	Vernon Wells	.25
239	Reed Johnson	.15
240	Frank Catalanotto	.15
241	Roy Halladay	.40
242	B.J. Ryan	.15
243	Gustavo Chacin	.15
244	Scott Downs	.15
245	Casey Janssen	.15
246	Justin Speier	.15
247	Stephen Drew	.40
248	Conor Jackson	.25
249	Orlando Hudson	.15
250	Chad Tracy	.15
251	Johnny Estrada	.15
252	Luis Gonzalez	.15
253	Eric Byrnes	.15
254	Carlos Quentin	.15
255	Brandon Webb	.25
256	Claudio Vargas	.15
257	Juan Cruz	.15
258	Jorge Julio	.15
259	Luis Vizcaino	.15
260	Livan Hernandez	.15
261	Chipper Jones	.75
262	Edgar Renteria	.25
263	Adam LaRoche	.25
264	Willy Aybar	.15
265	Brian McCann	.40
266	Ryan Langerhans	.15
267	Jeff Francoeur	.40
268	Matt Diaz	.15
269	Tim Hudson	.25
270	John Smoltz	.40
271	Oscar Villarreal	.15
272	Horacio Ramirez	.15
273	Bob Wickman	.15
274	Chad Paronto	.15
275	Derrek Lee	.50
276	Ryan Theriot	.15
277	Cesar Izturis	.15
278	Ronny Cedeno	.15
279	Michael Barrett	.25
280	Juan Pierre	.15
281	Jacque Jones	.15
282	Matt Murton	.25
283	Carlos Zambrano	.25
284	Mark Prior	.25
285	Rich Hill	.40
286	Sean Marshall	.15
287	Ryan Dempster	.15
288	Ryan O'Malley	.15
289	Scott Hatteberg	.15
290	Brandon Phillips	.15
291	Edwin Encarnacion	.15
292	Rich Aurilia	.15
293	David Ross	.15
294	Ken Griffey Jr.	1.00
295	Ryan Freel	.15
296	Chris Denorfia	.15
297	Bronson Arroyo	.15
298	Aaron Harang	.15
299	Brandon Claussen	.15
300	Todd Coffey	.15
301	David Weathers	.15
302	Eric Milton	.15
303	Todd Helton	.50
304	Clint Barmes	.15
305	Kazuo Matsui	.15
306	Jamey Carroll	.15
307	Yorvit Torrealba	.15
308	Matt Holliday	.50
309	Choo Freeman	.15
310	Brad Hawpe	.25
311	Jason Jennings	.15
312	Jeff Francis	.25
313	Josh Fogg	.15
314	Aaron Cook	.15
315	Ubaldo Jimenez	.15
316	Manny Corpas	.15
317	Miguel Cabrera	.75
318	Dan Uggla	.15
319	Hanley Ramirez	.50
320	Wes Helms	.15
321	Miguel Olivo	.15
322	Jeremy Hermida	.15
323	Cody Ross	.15
324	Josh Willingham	.15
325	Dontrelle Willis	.25
326	Anibal Sanchez	.15
327	Josh Johnson	.15
328	Jose Garcia	.15
329	Joe Borowski	.15
330	Taylor Tankersley	.15
331	Lance Berkman	.50
332	Craig Biggio	.40
333	Aubrey Huff	.15
334	Adam Everett	.15
335	Brad Ausmus	.15
336	Willy Taveras	.25
337	Luke Scott	.15
338	Chris Burke	.15
339	Roger Clemens	1.50
340	Andy Pettitte	.40
341	Brandon Backe	.15
342	Hector Gimenez	.15
343	Brad Lidge	.15
344	Dan Wheeler	.15
345	Nomar Garciaparra	.75
346	Rafael Furcal	.25
347	Wilson Betemit	.15
348	Julio Lugo	.15
349	Russell Martin	.25
350	Andre Ethier	.25
351	Matthew Kemp	.25
352	Kenny Lofton	.15
353	Brad Penny	.15
354	Derek Lowe	.25
355	Chad Billingsley	.25
356	Greg Maddux	1.00
357	Takashi Saito	.15
358	Jonathan Broxton	.25
359	Prince Fielder	1.00
360	Rickie Weeks	.40
361	Bill Hall	.25
362	J.J. Hardy	.15
363	Jeff Cirillo	.15
364	Tony Gwynn Jr.	.15
365	Corey Hart	.15
366	Laynce Nix	.15
367	Doug Davis	.15
368	Ben Sheets	.40
369	Chris Capuano	.15
370	David Bush	.15
371	Derrick Turnbow	.15
372	Francisco Cordero	.15
373	Jose Reyes	1.00
374	Carlos Delgado	.50
375	Julio Franco	.15
376	Jose Valentin	.15
377	Paul LoDuca	.15
378	Carlos Beltran	.50
379	Shawn Green	.15
380	Lastings Milledge	.25
381	Endy Chavez	.15
382	Pedro Martinez	.75
383	John Maine	.15
384	Orlando Hernandez	.15
385	Steve Trachsel	.15
386	Billy Wagner	.15
387	Ryan Howard	1.50
388	Chase Utley	.75
389	Jimmy Rollins	.50
390	Chris Coste	.15
391	Jeff Conine	.15
392	Aaron Rowand	.15
393	Shane Victorino	.15
394	David Dellucci	.15
395	Cole Hamels	.40
396	Jamie Moyer	.15
397	Ryan Madson	.15
398	Brett Myers	.25
399	Tom Gordon	.15
400	Geoff Geary	.15
401	Freddy Sanchez	.15
402	Xavier Nady	.15
403	Jose Castillo	.15
404	Joe Randa	.15
405	Jason Bay	.40
406	Chris Duffy	.15
407	Jose Bautista	.15
408	Ronny Paulino	.15
409	Ian Snell	.25
410	Zachary Duke	.15
411	Tom Gorzelanny	.15
412	Shane Youman	.15
413	Mike Gonzalez	.15
414	Matt Capps	.15
415	Adrian Gonzalez	.25
416	Josh Barfield	.25
417	Todd Walker	.15
418	Khalil Greene	.15
419	Mike Piazza	.75
420	Dave Roberts	.15
421	Mike Cameron	.15
422	Geoff Blum	.15
423	Jake Peavy	.40
424	Chris Young	.25
425	Woody Williams	.15
426	Clay Hensley	.15
427	Cla Meredith	.15
428	Trevor Hoffman	.15
429	Shea Hillenbrand	.15
430	Pedro Feliz	.15
431	Ray Durham	.15
432	Mark Sweeney	.15
433	Eliezer Alfonzo	.15
434	Moises Alou	.25
435	Steve Finley	.15
436	Todd Linden	.15
437	Jason Schmidt	.25
438	Matt Cain	.25
439	Noah Lowry	.15
440	Brad Hennessey	.15
441	Armando Benitez	.15
442	Jonathan Sanchez	.15
443	Albert Pujols	2.00
444	Ronnie Belliard	.15
445	David Eckstein	.15
446	Aaron Miles	.15
447	Yadier Molina	.15
448	Jim Edmonds	.25
449	Chris Duncan	.15
450	Juan Encarnacion	.15
451	Chris Carpenter	.50
452	Jeff Suppan	.15
453	Jason Marquis	.15
454	Jeff Weaver	.15
455	Jason Isringhausen	.15
456	Braden Looper	.15
457	Ryan Zimmerman	.40
458	Nick Johnson	.15
459	Felipe Lopez	.25
460	Brian Schneider	.15
461	Alfonso Soriano	.75
462	Austin Kearns	.15
463	Ryan Church	.15
464	Alex Escobar	.15
465	Ramon Ortiz	.15
466	Tony Armas	.15
467	Michael O'Connor	.15
468	Chad Cordero	.15

469	Jon Rauch	.15
470	Pedro Astacio	.15
471	Miguel Tejada	.25
472	David Ortiz	.50
473	Jermaine Dye	.25
474	Travis Hafner	.25
475	Maggio Ordonez	.25
476	Mark Teahen	.15
477	Vladimir Guerrero	.50
478	Justin Morneau	.50
479	Derek Jeter	1.00
480	Nick Swisher	.25
481	Ichiro Suzuki	.50
482	Scott Kazmir	.25
483	Mark Teixeira	.25
484	Vernon Wells	.25
485	Brandon Webb	.25
486	Andruw Jones	.40
487	Carlos Zambrano	.25
488	Adam Dunn	.25
489	Matt Holliday	.50
490	Miguel Cabrera	.50
491	Lance Berkman	.25
492	Nomar Garciaparra	.50
493	Prince Fielder	1.00
494	Carlos Beltran	.40
495	Ryan Howard	1.00
496	Jason Bay	.25
497	Adrian Gonzalez	.25
498	Matt Cain	.25
499	Albert Pujols	1.00
500	Ryan Zimmerman	.25
501	Daisuke Matsuzaka/Suit **RC**	30.00
502	Kei Igawa **RC**	5.00
503	Akinori Iwamura **RC**	6.00
521	Randy Johnson	.75
522	Brandon Lyon	.15
523	Robby Hammock	.15
524	Micah Owings **(RC)**	.25
525	Doug Davis	.15
526	Brian Barden **RC**	.50
527	Alberto Callaspo	.15
528	Stephen Drew	.25
529	Chris Young	.25
530	Edgar Gonzalez	.15
531	Brandon Medders	.15
532	Tony Pena	.15
533	Jose Valverde	.15
534	Chris Snyder	.15
535	Tony Clark	.15
536	Scott Hairston	.15
537	Jeff DaVanon	.15
538	Randy Johnson	.40
539	Mark Redman	.15
540	Andruw Jones	.50
541	Rafael Soriano	.15
542	Scott Thorman	.15
543	Chipper Jones	.75
544	Mike Gonzalez	.15
545	Lance Cormier	.15
546	Kyle Davies	.15
547	Mike Hampton	.15
548	Chuck James	.15
549	Macay McBride	.15
550	Tanyon Sturtze	.15
551	Tyler Yates	.15
552	Peter Orr	.15
553	Craig Wilson	.15
554	Chris Woodward	.15
556	Chipper Jones	.40
557	Chad Bradford	.15
558	John Parrish	.15
559	Jeremy Guthrie	.15
560	Steve Trachsel	.15
561	Scott Williamson	.15
562	Jaret Wright	.15
563	Paul Bako	.15
564	Chris Gomez	.15
565	Melvin Mora	.15
566	Freddie Bynum	.15
567	Aubrey Huff	.15
568	Jay Payton	.15
569	Miguel Tejada	.50
570	Kurt Birkins	.15
571	Danys Baez	.15
572	Brian Roberts	.25
573	Josh Beckett	.50
574	Matt Clement	.15
575	Hideki Okajima **RC**	3.00
576	Javier Lopez	.15
577	Joel Pineiro	.15
578	J.C. Romero	.15
579	Kyle Snyder	.15
580	Julian Tavarez	.15
581	Mike Timlin	.15
582	Jason Varitek	.50
583	Mike Lowell	.25
584	Kevin Youkilis	.25
585	Coco Crisp	.15
586	J.D. Drew	.25
587	Eric Hinske	.15
588	Wily Mo Pena	.15
589	Julio Lugo	.15
590	David Ortiz	.75
591	Manny Ramirez	.75
592	Daisuke Matsuzaka	5.00
593	Scott Eyre	.15
594	Angel Guzman	.15
595	Bob Howry	.15
596	Ted Lilly	.15
597	Juan Mateo	.15
598	Wade Miller	.15
599	Carlos Zambrano	.25
600	Will Ohman	.15
601	Mike Wuertz	.15
602	Henry Blanco	.15
603	Aramis Ramirez	.40
604	Cliff Floyd	.15
605	Kerry Wood	.25
606	Alfonso Soriano	.75
607	Daryle Ward	.15
608	Jason Marquis	.15
609	Mark DeRosa	.15
610	Neal Cotts	.15
611	Derrek Lee	.50
612	Aramis Ramirez	.25
613	David Aardsma	.15
614	Mark Buehrle	.25
615	Nick Massett	.15
616	Andrew Sisco	.15
617	Matt Thornton	.15
618	Toby Hall	.15
619	Joe Crede	.15
620	Paul Konerko	.25
621	Darin Erstad	.15
622	Pablo Ozuna	.15
623	Scott Podsednik	.15
624	Jim Thome	.50
625	Jermaine Dye	.15
626	Jim Thome	.25
627	Adam Dunn	.50
628	Bill Bray	.15
629	Alex Gonzalez	.15
630	Josh Hamilton **(RC)**	1.00
631	Matt Belisle	.15
632	Rheal Cormier	.15
633	Kyle Lohse	.15
634	Eric Milton	.15
635	Kirk Saarloos	.15
636	Mike Stanton	.15
637	Javier Valentin	.15
638	Juan Castro	.15
639	Jeff Conine	.15
640	Jon Coutlangus **(RC)**	.50
641	Ken Griffey Jr.	1.50
642	Ken Griffey Jr.	.75
643	Fernando Cabrera	.15
644	Fausto Carmona	.25
645	Jason Davis	.15
646	Aaron Fultz	.15
647	Roberto Hernandez	.15
648	Jake Westbrook	.15
649	Kelly Stoppach	.15
650	Josh Barfield	.25
651	Andy Marte	.15
652	Joe Inglett	.15
653	David Dellucci	.15
654	Joe Borowski	.15
655	Franklin Gutierrez	.15
656	Trot Nixon	.15
657	Grady Sizemore	.50
658	Mike Rouse	.15
659	Travis Hafner	.40
660	Victor Martinez	.40
661	C.C. Sabathia	.40
662	Grady Sizemore	.25
663	Jeremy Affeldt	.15
664	Taylor Buchholz	.15
665	Brian Fuentes	.15
666	LaTroy Hawkins	.15
667	Byung-Hyun Kim	.15
668	Brian Lawrence	.15
669	Rodrigo Lopez	.15
670	Jeff Francis	.15
671	Chris Iannetta	.15
672	Garrett Atkins	.25
673	Todd Helton	.50
674	Steve Finley	.15
675	John Mabry	.15
676	Willy Taveras	.15
677	Jason Hirsh	.15
678	Ramon Ramirez	.15
679	Matt Holliday	.75
680	Todd Helton	.25
681	Roman Colon	.15
682	Chad Durbin	.15
683	Jason Grilli	.15
684	Wilfredo Ledezma	.15
685	Mike Maroth	.15
686	Jose Mesa	.15
687	Justin Verlander	.50
688	Fernando Rodney	.15
689	Vance Wilson	.15
690	Carlos Guillen	.15
691	Neifi Perez	.15
692	Curtis Granderson	.15
693	Gary Sheffield	.50
694	Justin Verlander	.25
695	Kevin Gregg	.15
696	Logan Kensing	.15
697	Randy Messenger	.15
698	Sergio Mitre	.15
699	Ricky Nolasco	.15
700	Scott Olsen	.25
701	Renyel Pinto	.15
702	Matt Treanor	.15
703	Alfredo Amezaga	.15
704	Aaron Boone	.15
705	Mike Jacobs	.15
706	Miguel Cabrera	.75
707	Joe Borchard	.15
708	Jorge Julio	.15
709	Rick Vanden Hurk **RC**	2.00
710	Lee Gardner **(RC)**	.50
711	Matt Lindstrom **(RC)**	.50
712	Henry Owens	.15
713	Hanley Ramirez	.50
714	Alejandro De Aza **RC**	.50
715	Hanley Ramirez	.25
716	Dave Borkowski	.15
717	Jason Jennings	.15
718	Trever Miller	.15
719	Roy Oswalt	.40
720	Wandy Rodriguez	.15
721	Humberto Quintero	.15
722	Morgan Ensberg	.15
723	Mike Lamb	.15
724	Mark Loretta	.15
725	Jason Lane	.15
726	Carlos Lee	.40
727	Orlando Palmeiro	.15
728	Woody Williams	.15
729	Chad Qualls	.15
730	Lance Berkman	.40
731	Rick White	.15
732	Chris Sampson	.15
733	Carlos Lee	.15
734	Jorge De La Rosa	.15
735	Octavio Dotel	.15
736	Jimmy Gobble	.15
737	Zack Greinke	.15
738	Luke Hudson	.15
739	Gil Meche	.15
740	Joel Peralta	.15
741	Odalis Perez	.15
742	David Riske	.15
743	Jason LaRue	.15
744	Tony Pena	.15
745	Esteban German	.15
746	Ross Gload	.15
747	Emil Brown	.15
748	David DeJesus	.15
749	Brandon Duckworth	.15
750	Alex Gordon **RC**	3.00
751	Jered Weaver	.50
752	Vladimir Guerrero	.75
753	Hector Carrasco	.15
754	Kelvim Escobar	.15
755	Darren Oliver	.15
756	Dustin Moseley	.15
757	Ervin Santana	.15
758	Mike Napoli	.15
759	Shea Hillenbrand	.15
760	Casey Kotchman	.15
761	Reggie Willits	.15
762	Robb Quinlan	.15
763	Garret Anderson	.15
764	Gary Mathews	.15
765	Justin Speier	.15
766	Jered Weaver	.25
767	Joe Beimel	.15
768	Yhency Brazoban	.15
769	Elmer Dessens	.15
770	Mark Hendrickson	.15
771	Hong-Chih Kuo	.25
772	Jason Schmidt	.25
773	Brett Tomko	.15
774	Randy Wolf	.15
775	Mike Lieberthal	.15
776	Marlon Anderson	.15
777	Jeff Kent	.25
778	Ramon Martinez	.15
779	Olmedo Saenz	.15
780	Luis Gonzalez	.25
781	Juan Pierre	.25
782	Jason Repko	.15
783	Nomar Garciaparra	.75
784	Wilson Valdez	.15
785	Jason Schmidt	.15
786	Greg Aquino	.15
787	Brian Shouse	.15
788	Jeff Suppan	.15
789	Carlos Villanueva	.15
790	Matt Wise	.15
791	Johnny Estrada	.15
792	Craig Counsell	.15
793	Tony Graffanino	.15
794	Corey Koskie	.15
795	Claudio Vargas	.15
796	Brady Clark	.15
797	Gabe Gross	.15
798	Geoff Jenkins	.15
799	Kevin Mench	.15
800	Bill Hall	.25
801	Sidney Ponson	.15
802	Jesse Crain	.15
803	Matt Guerrier	.15
804	Pat Neshek	.15
805	Ramon Ortiz	.15
806	Johan Santana	.75
807	Carlos Silva	.15
808	Mike Redmond	.15
809	Jeff Cirillo	.15
810	Luis Rodriguez	.15
811	Lew Ford	.15
812	Torii Hunter	.40
813	Jason Tyner	.15
814	Rondell White	.15
815	Justin Morneau	.50
816	Joe Mauer	.40
817	Johan Santana	.40
818	David Newhan	.15
819	Aaron Sele	.15
820	Ambiorix Burgos	.15
821	Pedro Feliciano	.15
822	Tom Glavine	.50
823	Aaron Heilman	.15
824	Guillermo Mota	.15
825	Jose Reyes	1.00
826	Oliver Perez	.15
827	Duaner Sanchez	.15
828	Scott Schoeneweis	.15
829	Ramon Castro	.15
830	Damion Easley	.15
831	David Wright	1.50
832	Moises Alou	.25
833	Carlos Beltran	.50
834	Dave Williams	.15
835	David Wright	.75
836	Brian Bruney	.15
837	Mike Myers	.15
838	Carl Pavano	.15
839	Andy Pettitte	.40
840	Luis Vizcaino	.15
841	Jorge Posada	.40
842	Miguel Cairo	.15
843	Doug Mientkiewicz	.15
844	Derek Jeter	2.00
845	Alex Rodriguez	2.00
846	Johnny Damon	.75
847	Hideki Matsui	1.00
848	Josh Phelps	.15
849	Phil Hughes **(RC)**	4.00
850	Roger Clemens	2.00
851	Jason Giambi	.25
852	Kiko Calero	.15
853	Justin Duchscherer	.15
854	Alan Embree	.15
855	Todd Walker	.15
856	Rich Harden	.15
857	Danny Haren	.40
858	Joe Kennedy	.15
859	Jason Kendall	.15
860	Adam Melhuse	.15
861	Mark Ellis	.15
863	Mark Kotsay	.15
864	Shannon Stewart	.15
865	Mike Piazza	.75
866	Mike Piazza	.40
867	Antonio Alfonseca	.15
868	Carlos Ruiz	.15
869	Adam Eaton	.15
870	Freddy Garcia	.15
871	Jon Lieber	.15
872	Matt Smith	.15
873	Rod Barajas	.15
874	Wes Helms	.15
875	Abraham Nunez	.15
876	Pat Burrell	.25
877	Jayson Werth	.15
878	Greg Dobbs	.15
879	Joseph Bisenius **RC**	.50
880	Michael Bourn **(RC)**	.50
881	Chase Utley	.75
882	Ryan Howard	1.50
883	Chase Utley	.40
884	Tony Armas	.15
885	Shawn Chacon	.15
886	John Grabow	.15
887	Paul Maholm	.15
888	Damaso Marte	.15
889	Salomon Torres	.15
890	Humberto Cota	.15
891	Ryan Doumit	.15
892	Adam LaRoche	.25
893	Jack Wilson	.15
894	Nate McLouth	.15
895	Brad Eldred	.15
896	Jonah Bayliss	.15
897	Juan Perez **RC**	.50
898	Jason Bay	.40
899	Adam LaRoche	.15
900	Doug Brocail	.15
901	Scott Cassidy	.15
902	Scott Linebrink	.15
903	Greg Maddux	1.50
904	Jake Peavy	.40
905	Mike Thompson	.15
906	David Wells	.15
907	Josh Bard	.15
908	Rob Bowen	.15
909	Marcus Giles	.15
910	Russell Branyan	.15
911	Jose Cruz	.15
912	Terrmel Sledge	.15
913	Trevor Hoffman	.25
914	Brian Giles	.25
915	Trevor Hoffman	.25
916	Vinnie Chulk	.15
917	Kevin Correia	.15
918	Tim Lincecum **RC**	25.00
919	Matt Morris	.15
920	Russ Ortiz	.15
921	Barry Zito	.25
922	Bengie Molina	.15
923	Rich Aurilia	.15
924	Omar Vizquel	.25
925	Jason Ellison	.15
926	Ryan Klesko	.15
927	Dave Roberts	.15
928	Randy Winn	.15
929	Barry Zito	.25
930	Miguel Batista	.15
931	Horacio Ramirez	.15
932	Chris Reitsma	.15
933	George Sherrill	.15
934	Jarrod Washburn	.15
935	Jeff Weaver	.15
936	Jake Woods	.15
937	Adrian Beltre	.25
938	Jose Lopez	.15
939	Ichiro Suzuki	1.50
940	Jose Vidro	.15
941	Jose Guillen	.15
942	Sean White **RC**	.50
943	Brandon Morrow **RC**	4.00
944	Felix Hernandez	.50
945	Felix Hernandez	.25
946	Randy Flores	.15
947	Ryan Franklin	.15

No.	Player	Price
948	Kelvin Jimenez RC	.50
949	Tyler Johnson	.15
950	Mark Mulder	.15
951	Anthony Reyes	.15
952	Russ Springer	.15
953	Brad Thompson	.15
954	Adam Wainwright	.15
955	Kip Wells	.15
956	Gary Bennett	.15
957	Adam Kennedy	.15
958	Scott Rolen	.75
959	Scott Spiezio	.15
960	So Taguchi	.15
961	Preston Wilson	.15
962	Skip Schumaker	.15
963	Albert Pujols	2.00
964	Chris Carpenter	.50
965	Chris Carpenter	.25
966	Edwin Jackson	.15
967	Jae-Kuk Ryu	.15
968	Jae Weong Seo	.15
969	Jon Switzer	.15
970	Josh Paul	.15
971	Benjamin Zobrist	.15
972	Rocco Baldelli	.15
973	Scott Kazmir	.25
974	Carl Crawford	.25
975	Delmon Young	.50
976	Bruce Chen	.15
977	Joaquin Benoit	.15
978	Scott Feldman	.15
979	Eric Gagne	.15
980	Kameron Loe	.15
981	Brandon McCarthy	.15
982	Robinson Tejeda	.15
983	C.J. Wilson	.15
984	Mark Teixeira	.50
985	Michael Young	.25
986	Kenny Lofton	.25
987	Brad Wilkerson	.15
988	Nelson Cruz	.15
989	Sammy Sosa	.75
990	Michael Young	.25
991	Vernon Wells	.40
992	Matt Stairs	.15
993	Jeremy Accardo	.15
994	A.J. Burnett	.15
995	Jason Frasor	.15
996	Roy Halladay	.40
997	Shaun Marcum	.15
998	Tomokazu Ohka	.15
999	Josh Towers	.15
1000	Gregg Zaun	.15
1001	Royce Clayton	.15
1002	Jason Smith	.15
1003	Alex Rios	.25
1004	Frank Thomas	.75
1005	Roy Halladay	.25
1006	Jesus Flores RC	.15
1007	Dmitri Young	.15
1008	Ray King	.15
1009	Micah Bowie	.15
1010	Shawn Hill	.15
1011	John Patterson	.15
1012	Levale Speigner RC	.50
1013	Ryan Wagner	.15
1014	Jerome Williams	.15
1015	Ryan Zimmerman	.50
1016	Cristian Guzman	.15
1017	Nook Logan	.15
1018	Chris Snelling	.15
1019	Ronnie Belliard	.15
1020	Nick Johnson	.15

Gold

Gold:	8-15X

Production 75 Sets

Printing Plates

No Pricing
Production one per color.

Cal Ripken Jr. and Tony Gwynn Road to the Hall

No Pricing

2007 Upper Deck Cal Ripken Box Set

	NM/M
Complete Set (45):	35.00
Common Ripken:	1.00
1-45 Cal Ripken Jr.	1.00

Cal Ripken Jr. Chronicles

	NM/M
Common Ripken:	8.00
1-50 Cal Ripken Jr.	8.00

Cal Ripken Jr./ Lou Gehrig Iron Man

	NM/M
Common Ripken/Gehrig:	20.00
Autograph:	No Pricing

Production One

1-50 Cal Ripken Jr., Lou Gehrig	20.00

Cooperstown Calling

		NM/M
Common Player:		1.00
AJ	Andruw Jones	1.50
AP	Albert Pujols	5.00
AR	Alex Rodriguez	5.00
AS	Alfonso Soriano	2.00
BI	Craig Biggio	1.00
BW	Billy Wagner	1.00
CA	Chris Carpenter	1.50
CB	Carlos Beltran	2.00
CC	Carl Crawford	1.00
CD	Carlos Delgado	1.50
CJ	Chipper Jones	2.00
CR	Cal Ripken Jr.	5.00
CS	Curt Schilling	2.00
DJ	Derek Jeter	5.00
DO	David Ortiz	2.00
FT	Frank Thomas	1.50
GM	Greg Maddux	3.00
GS	Gary Sheffield	1.50
HA	Travis Hafner	1.00
HE	Todd Helton	1.50
HO	Ryan Howard	4.00
IR	Ivan Rodriguez	1.50
IS	Ichiro Suzuki	3.00
JD	Johnny Damon	2.00
JG	Jason Giambi	1.50
JK	Jeff Kent	1.00
JM	Justin Morneau	2.00
JS	Johan Santana	2.00
JT	Jim Thome	1.50
KG	Ken Griffey Jr.	4.00
MC	Miguel Cabrera	2.00
MM	Mike Mussina	1.50
MP	Mike Piazza	3.00
MR	Manny Ramirez	2.00
MT	Mark Teixeira	1.50
OV	Omar Vizquel	1.00
PE	Andy Pettitte	1.00
PM	Pedro Martinez	1.00
RH	Roy Halladay	1.00
RI	Mariano Rivera	1.50
RJ	Randy Johnson	2.00
RO	Roy Oswalt	1.50
SI	Grady Sizemore	2.00
SM	John Smoltz	1.50
SR	Scott Rolen	1.50
SS	Sammy Sosa	2.00
TE	Miguel Tejada	1.50
TG	Tom Glavine	1.00
TH	Trevor Hoffman	1.00
VG	Vladimir Guerrero	2.00

Cooperstown Calling Autograph

No Pricing

Game Materials

		NM/M
Common Player:		4.00
Patch:		2-4X
AJ	Andruw Jones	8.00
AP	Albert Pujols	20.00
BE	Josh Beckett	6.00
BR	Brian Roberts	6.00
BS	Ben Sheets	6.00
CA	Chris Carpenter	8.00
CB	Carlos Beltran	10.00
CC	Carl Crawford	6.00
CD	Carlos Delgado	8.00
CL	Carlos Lee	6.00
CP	Corey Patterson	4.00
CS	C.C. Sabathia	6.00
DJ	Derek Jeter	20.00
DO	David Ortiz	10.00
DW	Dontrelle Willis	6.00
EC	Eric Chavez	4.00
FH	Felix Hernandez	8.00
HU	Torii Hunter	6.00
IR	Ivan Rodriguez	8.00
JB	Jason Bay	8.00
JG	Jason Giambi	8.00
JM	Joe Mauer	8.00
JR	Jose Reyes	10.00
JS	Johan Santana	8.00
JU	Juan Uribe	4.00
JV	Justin Verlander	15.00
KG	Ken Griffey Jr.	15.00
MC	Miguel Cabrera	8.00
MH	Matt Holliday	8.00
MM	Melvin Mora	4.00
MO	Justin Morneau	10.00
MR	Manny Ramirez	8.00
MS	Mike Sweeney	4.00
MT	Miguel Tejada	6.00
MU	Mike Mussina	8.00
OR	Magglio Ordonez	4.00
PF	Prince Fielder	10.00
RH	Roy Halladay	6.00
RZ	Ryan Zimmerman	8.00
SR	Scott Rolen	8.00
TH	Tim Hudson	4.00
VM	Victor Martinez	6.00
Series 2:		
AB	A.J. Burnett	4.00
AP	Albert Pujols	20.00
AR	Alex Rios	4.00
BA	Bobby Abreu	5.00
BC	Bartolo Colon	4.00
BJ	Bobby Jenks	4.00
CC	Carl Crawford	5.00
CJ	Chipper Jones	10.00
CS	Curt Schilling	8.00
CU	Chase Utley	10.00
DJ	Derek Jeter	20.00
EB	Erik Bedard	12.00
EN	Juan Encarnacion	4.00
FR	Jeff Francoeur SP	10.00
GS	Gary Sheffield	8.00
HB	Mark Blalock	4.00
HO	Trevor Hoffman	4.00
JD	Johnny Damon	8.00
JE	Jim Edmonds	5.00
JF	Jeff Francis	4.00
JS	John Smoltz	10.00
JT	Jim Thome	8.00
JV	Jose Vidro	4.00
KG	Ken Griffey Jr.	15.00
LB	Lance Berkman	4.00
LG	Luis Gonzalez	4.00
MR	Manny Ramirez	8.00
MT	Mark Teixeira	8.00
RB	Rocco Baldelli	8.00
RJ	Randy Johnson	8.00
RN	Ricky Nolasco	4.00
RO	Roy Oswalt	4.00
RW	Rickie Weeks	4.00
SD	Stephen Drew	4.00
SK	Scott Kazmir	4.00
SR	Scott Rolen	8.00
TG	Tom Glavine	8.00
TH	Todd Helton	8.00
TN	Trot Nixon	4.00
VG	Vladimir Guerrero	8.00
ZD	Zachary Duke	4.00

Ken Griffey Jr. Chronicles

		NM/M
Common Griffey:		5.00
1-50	Ken Griffey Jr.	5.00

Playoff Predictors

		NM/M
Common Predictor:		3.00
1	Arizona Diamondbacks	5.00
2	Atlanta Braves	5.00
3	Baltimore Orioles	3.00
4	Boston Red Sox	25.00
5	Chicago Cubs	5.00
6	Chicago White Sox	5.00
7	Cincinnati Reds	3.00
8	Cleveland Indians	5.00
9	Colorado Rockies	5.00
10	Detroit Tigers	5.00
11	Florida Marlins	3.00
12	Houston Astros	5.00
13	Kansas City Royals	3.00
14	Los Angeles Angels	5.00
15	Los Angeles Dodgers	5.00
16	Milwaukee Brewers	5.00
17	Minnesota Twins	5.00
18	New York Mets	5.00
19	New York Yankees	15.00
20	Oakland Athletics	5.00
21	Philadelphia Phillies	5.00
22	Pittsburgh Pirates	3.00
23	San Diego Padres	5.00
24	San Francisco Giants	5.00
25	Seattle Mariners	5.00
26	St. Louis Cardinals	5.00
27	Tampa Bay Devil Rays	3.00
28	Texas Rangers	5.00
29	Toronto Blue Jays	5.00
30	Washington Nationals	5.00

Rookie of the Year Predictor

		NM/M
Common Player:		3.00
1	Doug Slaten	3.00
2	Miguel Montero	3.00
4	Kory Casto	3.00
5	Jesus Flores	3.00
6	John Danks	3.00
7	Daisuke Matsuzaka	60.00
9	Chris Stewart	3.00
10	Kevin Cameron	3.00
13	Kevin Kouzmanoff	5.00
14	Jeff Baker	3.00
15	Donald Kelly	3.00
16	Troy Tulowitzki	8.00
18	Cesar Jimenez	3.00
20	Jose Garcia	3.00
21	Micah Owings	3.00
22	Josh Hamilton	6.00
24	Jamie Burke	3.00
25	Mike Rabelo	3.00
26	Elijah Dukes	3.00
27	Travis Buck	3.00
28	Kei Igawa	3.00
29	Sean Henn	3.00
32	Michael Bourn	3.00
33	Alex Gordon	20.00
35	Matt Chico	3.00
38	Gustavo Molina	3.00
39	Jared Burton	3.00
40	Jay Marshall	3.00
42	Akinori Iwamura	20.00
43	Delmon Young	8.00
44	Juan Salas	3.00
45	Zack Segovia	3.00
46	Brian Stokes	3.00
47	Joaquin Arias	3.00
48	Hector Gimenez	3.00
49	Ryan Braun	3.00
50	Juan Perez	3.00

Star Power

		NM/M

Inserted 2:1 Fat Packs

AJ	Andruw Jones	1.50
AP	Albert Pujols	5.00
AR	Alex Rodriguez	5.00
BR	Brian Roberts	1.00
BZ	Barry Zito	.75
CA	Chris Carpenter	1.50
CB	Carlos Beltran	1.50
CC	Carl Crawford	1.00
CJ	Chipper Jones	2.00
CS	Curt Schilling	1.50
CU	Chase Utley	1.50
CZ	Carlos Zambrano	1.00
DA	Johnny Damon	1.50
DJ	Derek Jeter	5.00
DO	David Ortiz	2.00
DW	Dontrelle Willis	.75
FS	Freddy Sanchez	.75
FT	Frank Thomas	1.50
HA	Roy Halladay	1.00
HO	Trevor Hoffman	.75
IS	Ichiro Suzuki	3.00
JB	Jason Bay	1.00
JD	Jermaine Dye	.75
JM	Joe Mauer	1.00
JP	Jake Peavy	1.00
JR	Jose Reyes	2.00
JS	Johan Santana	1.50
JT	Jim Thome	1.50
JU	Justin Morneau	1.50
JV	Justin Verlander	1.50
KG	Ken Griffey Jr.	4.00
KR	Kenny Rogers	.75
LB	Lance Berkman	1.00
MA	Matt Cain	1.00
MC	Miguel Cabrera	2.00
MH	Matt Holliday	1.00
MO	Magglio Ordonez	.75
MR	Manny Ramirez	1.50
MT	Mark Teixeira	1.00
MY	Michael Young	1.50
NG	Nomar Garciaparra	1.50
NS	Nick Swisher	.75
PF	Prince Fielder	1.50
RH	Ryan Howard	3.00
RO	Roy Oswalt	1.00
RZ	Ryan Zimmerman	1.00
SM	John Smoltz	1.00
TH	Travis Hafner	1.00
VG	Vladimir Guerrero	1.50
WR	David Wright	2.00

Star Signings

		NM/M
Common Auto.:		5.00
AB	Ambiorix Burgos	8.00
AC	Aaron Cook	5.00
AH	Aubrey Huff/SP	15.00
AR	Alex Rios	20.00
BA	Bobby Abreu	35.00
BL	Joe Blanton	8.00
BO	Jeremy Bonderman	25.00
BR	Brandon Backe	8.00

CJ	Conor Jackson	15.00
CO	Chad Cordero	10.00
CP	Corey Patterson	10.00
CS	Chris Shelton	8.00
CY	Chris Young/SP	20.00
DH	Danny Haren	10.00
DJ	Derek Jeter	150.00
DU	Chris Duffy	10.00
GA	Garrett Atkins	10.00
GC	Gustavo Chacin	8.00
HS	Huston Street	15.00
HU	Torii Hunter	15.00
IS	Ian Snell/SP	15.00
JA	Jeremy Accardo	8.00
JB	Jason Bergmann/SP	8.00
JD	Joey Devine	8.00
JG	Jonny Gomes	8.00
JJ	Jorge Julio	8.00
JK	Jason Kubel	8.00
JM	Justin Morneau	25.00
JN	Joe Nathan	15.00
JS	Jason Bay	15.00
KW	Jake Westbrook	10.00
KF	Keith Foulke	10.00
KG	Ken Griffey Jr.	75.00
KM	Kevin Mench	10.00
KS	Kirk Saarloos	8.00
KY	Kevin Youkilis	20.00
LN	Laynce Nix/SP	8.00
LO	Lyle Overbay	10.00
MH	Matt Holliday	25.00
MK	Mark Kotsay	10.00
MM	Melvin Mora	15.00
NM	Nate McLouth/SP	15.00
RC	Ryan Church	15.00
RG	Ryan Garko	15.00
RI	Juan Rivera/SP	8.00
RJ	Reed Johnson	15.00
RU	Carlos Ruiz	10.00
SC	Sean Casey/SP	10.00
SD	Stephen Drew	20.00
SP	Scott Podsednik/SP	20.00
TI	Tadahito Iguchi	20.00
VE	Justin Verlander	30.00
WM	Wily Mo Pena	15.00
XN	Xavier Nady	15.00
YB	Yuniesky Betancourt	20.00
Common Player:		10.00
AC	Alberto Callaspo	10.00
AG	Alex Gordon	40.00
AI	Akinori Iwamura/SP	30.00
AS	Angel Sanchez	10.00
BA	Jeff Baker	10.00
BB	Brian Burres	10.00
BE	Josh Beckett/SP	40.00
BO	Ben Broussard	10.00
BU	B.J. Upton/SP	40.00
CB	Craig Biggio/SP	40.00
CC	Carl Crawford/SP	20.00
CR	Cal Ripken Jr./SP	125.00
DJ	Derek Jeter	140.00
DY	Delmon Young/SP	20.00
ED	Elijah Dukes	15.00
FH	Felix Hernandez	30.00
IK	Ian Kinsler/SP	15.00
IS	Ian Snell	15.00
JD	J.D. Drew/SP	15.00
KG	Ken Griffey Jr./SP	75.00
KI	Kei Igawa/SP	50.00
NC	Nelson Cruz	10.00
OP	Oliver Perez/SP	15.00
RA	Chris Ray	10.00
SA	Juan Salas	10.00
SH	Sean Henn	10.00
YO	Chris Young	20.00
ZS	Zack Segovia	15.00

Ticket to Stardom

		NM/M
Common Player:		2.00
AG	Alex Gordon	8.00
AI	Akinori Iwamura	4.00
AS	Angel Sanchez	2.00
BN	Jared Burton	2.00
BU	Jamie Burke	2.00
CH	Matt Chico	2.00
CJ	Cesar Jimenez	2.00
CS	Chris Stewart	2.00
DA	John Danks	2.00
DK	Donald Kelly	2.00
DM	Daisuke Matsuzaka	2.00
DS	Doug Slaten	2.00
DY	Delmon Young	4.00
ED	Elijah Dukes	2.00
GM	Gustavo Molina	2.00
HG	Hector Gimenez	2.00
JA	Joaquin Arias	2.00
JB	Jeff Baker	2.00
JF	Jesus Flores	2.00
JG	Jose Garcia	2.00
JH	Josh Hamilton	4.00
JM	Jay Marshall	2.00
JP	Juan Perez	2.00
KC	Kevin Cameron	2.00
KI	Kei Igawa	2.00
KK	Kevin Kouzmanoff	3.00
KO	Kory Casto	2.00
MB	Michael Bourn	2.00
MM	Miguel Montero	2.00
MO	Micah Owings	2.00
MR	Mike Rabelo	2.00
RB	Ryan Braun	2.00
SA	Juan Salas	2.00
SH	Sean Henn	2.00
SO	Joakim Soria	2.00

ST	Brian Stokes	2.00
TB	Travis Buck	2.00
TT	Troy Tulowitzki	4.00
ZS	Zack Segovia	2.00

Ticket to Stardom Autograph

No Pricing

1989 Reprints

Jackie Robinson

		NM/M
Common Player:		1.00
AK	Al Kaline	2.00
BF	Bob Feller	1.00
BR	Babe Ruth	5.00
CA	Rod Carew	1.00
CF	Carlton Fisk	1.00
CM	Christy Mathewson	1.00
CS	Casey Stengel	1.00
CY	Cy Young	1.00
DR	Don Drysdale	1.00
FR	Frank Robinson	1.00
GE	Lou Gehrig	3.00
HW	Honus Wagner	2.00
JB	Johnny Bench	1.50
JF	Jimmie Foxx	2.00
JR	Jackie Robinson	2.00
LG	Lefty Grove	1.00
LJ	LeBron James	3.00
MJ	Michael Jordan	5.00
MO	Mel Ott	1.00
RB	Reggie Bush	2.00
RC	Roy Campanella	1.00
RH	Rogers Hornsby	1.00
RJ	Reggie Jackson	1.50
RO	Brooks Robinson	1.50
SC	Sidney Crosby	4.00
SM	Stan Musial	1.50
SP	Satchel Paige	2.00
TC	Ty Cobb	3.00
TM	Thurman Munson	3.00
WJ	Walter Johnson	2.00

1989 Rookie Reprints

Joakim Soria

		NM/M
Common Player:		1.00
AG	Alex Gordon	3.00
AI	Akinori Iwamura	3.00
AS	Angel Sanchez	1.00
BN	Jared Burton	1.00
BU	Jamie Burke	1.00
CJ	Cesar Jimenez	1.00
CS	Chris Stewart	1.00
DK	Donald Kelly	1.00
DM	Daisuke Matsuzaka	20.00
DY	Delmon Young	2.00
ED	Elijah Dukes	1.00
GM	Gustavo Molina	1.00
HG	Hector Gimenez	1.00
JA	Joaquin Arias	1.00
JB	Jeff Baker	1.00
JD	John Danks	1.00
JF	Jesus Flores	1.00
JG	Jose Garcia	1.00
JH	Josh Hamilton	2.00
JM	Jay Marshall	1.00
JP	Juan Perez	1.00
KC	Kevin Cameron	1.00

KI	Kei Igawa	2.00
KK	Kevin Kouzmanoff	2.00
KO	Kory Casto	1.00
MB	Michael Bourn	1.00
MC	Matt Chico	1.00
MM	Miguel Montero	1.00
MO	Micah Owings	1.00
MR	Mike Rabelo	1.00
RB	Ryan Braun	1.00
SA	Juan Salas	1.00
SH	Sean Henn	1.00
SL	Doug Slaten	1.00
SO	Joakim Soria	1.00
ST	Brian Stokes	1.00
TB	Travis Buck	1.00
TT	Troy Tulowitzki	2.00
ZS	Zack Segovia	1.00

1989 Rookie Reprint Signatures

No Pricing
Production Five Sets

2007 Upper Deck Cal Ripken Box Set

	NM/M
Complete Set (45):	35.00
Common Ripken:	1.00
1-45 Cal Ripken Jr.	1.00

2007 Upper Deck Artifacts

		NM/M
Complete Set (100):		35.00
Common Player:		.25
Pack (4):		10.00
Box (10):		90.00
1	Miguel Tejada	.50
2	David Ortiz	1.00
3	Manny Ramirez	1.00
4	Curt Schilling	.75
5	Jim Thome	.75
6	Paul Konerko	.50
7	Jermaine Dye	.50
8	Travis Hafner	.50
9	Victor Martinez	.50
10	Grady Sizemore	.50
11	Ivan Rodriguez	.75
12	Magglio Ordonez	.50
13	Justin Verlander	.75
14	Mark Teahen	.25
15	Vladimir Guerrero	1.00
16	Jered Weaver	.50
17	Justin Morneau	.50
18	Joe Mauer	.50
19	Torii Hunter	.50
20	Johan Santana	1.00
21	Derek Jeter	3.00
22	Alex Rodriguez	3.00
23	Johnny Damon	.75
24	Huston Street	.25
25	Nick Swisher	.50
26	Ichiro Suzuki	2.00
27	Richie Sexson	.50
28	Carl Crawford	.50
29	Scott Kazmir	.50
30	Michael Young	.50
31	Mark Teixeira	.75
32	Vernon Wells	.50
33	Roy Halladay	.50
34	Brandon Webb	.50
35	Stephen Drew	.50
36	Chipper Jones	1.00
37	Andruw Jones	.75
38	Derrek Lee	.75
39	Aramis Ramirez	.75
40	Ken Griffey Jr.	2.00
41	Adam Dunn	.50
42	Todd Helton	.75
43	Matt Holliday	.50
44	Miguel Cabrera	1.00
45	Hanley Ramirez	.50
46	Dontrelle Willis	.50
47	Lance Berkman	.50
48	Roy Oswalt	.50
49	Craig Biggio	.50
50	Nomar Garciaparra	1.00
51	Derek Lowe	.25
52	Prince Fielder	1.00
53	Rickie Weeks	.25
54	Jose Reyes	2.00

55	David Wright	2.00
56	Carlos Beltran	.75
57	Ryan Howard	2.00
58	Chase Utley	1.00
59	Jimmy Rollins	.75
60	Jason Bay	.50
61	Freddy Sanchez	.25
62	Trevor Hoffman	.50
63	Adrian Gonzalez	.50
64	Omar Vizquel	.25
65	Matt Cain	.50
66	Albert Pujols	3.00
67	Jim Edmonds	.50
68	Chris Carpenter	.75
69	David Eckstein	.25
70	Ryan Zimmerman	.50
71	Alexi Casilla RC	.50
72	Andrew Miller RC	5.00
73	Andy Cannizaro RC	1.00
74	Brian Stokes (RC)	.50
75	Carlos Maldonado (RC)	.50
76	Cesar Jimenez RC	1.00
77	Daisuke Matsuzaka RC	8.00
78	Delmon Young (RC)	1.00
79	Delwyn Young (RC)	.50
80	Fred Lewis (RC)	1.00
81	Glen Perkins (RC)	.50
82	Jeff Baker (RC)	.50
83	Jeff Fiorentino (RC)	.50
84	Jeff Salazar (RC)	.50
85	Jerry Owens (RC)	.50
86	Josh Fields (RC)	.50
87	Juan Perez RC	.50
88	Juan Salas (RC)	.50
89	Justin Hampson (RC)	.50
90	Kevin Kouzmanoff (RC)	.50
91	Michael Bourn (RC)	.50
92	Miguel Montero (RC)	.50
93	Mike Rabelo RC	.50
94	Oswaldo Navarro (RC)	.50
95	Philip Humber (RC)	.50
96	Ryan Braun RC	.50
97	Ryan Sweeney (RC)	.50
98	Sean Henn (RC)	.50
99	Jose Reyes RC	1.00
100	Troy Tulowitzki (RC)	1.00

Antiquity Artifacts

Jermaine Dye

		NM/M
Production 199 Sets		
Patch:		1.5-3X
Production 50 Sets		
AB	Adrian Beltre	6.00
AJ	Andruw Jones	6.00
AL	Adam LaRoche	4.00
AP	Albert Pujols	20.00
AR	Aramis Ramirez	6.00
AT	Garrett Atkins	4.00
BA	Bobby Abreu	6.00
BC	Bartolo Colon	4.00
BE	Carlos Beltran	8.00
BG	Brian Giles	4.00
BO	Jeremy Bonderman	6.00
BR	Brian Roberts	4.00
BU	B.J. Upton	6.00
BW	Billy Wagner	4.00
BZ	Barry Zito	4.00
CA	Miguel Cabrera	8.00
CB	Craig Biggio	6.00
CC	Carl Crawford	6.00
CF	Chone Figgins	4.00
CH	Chris Carpenter	8.00
CJ	Chipper Jones	8.00
CL	Carlos Lee	6.00
CR	Cal Ripken Jr.	25.00
CS	Curt Schilling	8.00
CU	Chase Utley	10.00
DJ	Derek Jeter	20.00
DO	David Ortiz	10.00
DR	J.D. Drew	4.00
DU	Dan Uggla	4.00
DW	Dontrelle Willis	4.00
EC	Eric Chavez	4.00
ED	Jim Edmonds	6.00
FG	Freddy Garcia	4.00
FH	Felix Hernandez	6.00
FL	Francisco Liriano	6.00
FT	Frank Thomas	8.00
GA	Garret Anderson	4.00
GJ	Geoff Jenkins	4.00
GM	Greg Maddux	10.00

GR Ken Griffey Jr. 20.00
GS Grady Sizemore 8.00
HA Rich Harden 4.00
HB Hank Blalock 4.00
HO Trevor Hoffman 6.00
HR Hanley Ramirez 8.00
HS Huston Street 4.00
HU Torii Hunter 6.00
IR Ivan Rodriguez 8.00
JA Jason Bay 6.00
JC Jorge Cantu 4.00
JD Jermaine Dye 4.00
JE Johnny Estrada 4.00
JF Jeff Francoeur 8.00
JG Jason Giambi 6.00
JJ Josh Johnson 4.00
JK Jeff Kent 6.00
JM Joe Mauer 8.00
JP Jake Peavy 8.00
JR Jimmy Rollins 8.00
JS Jason Schmidt 4.00
JT Jim Thome 8.00
JV Justin Verlander 8.00
JZ Joel Zumaya 6.00
KG Khalil Greene 4.00
LB Lance Berkman 6.00
LG Luis Gonzalez 4.00
MO Justin Morneau 8.00
MR Manny Ramirez 8.00
MT Mark Teixeira 6.00
MY Michael Young 6.00
NS Nick Swisher 4.00
OR Magglio Ordonez 4.00
PA Jonathan Papelbon 10.00
PB Pat Burrell 4.00
PE Jhonny Peralta 4.00
PF Prince Fielder 8.00
PK Paul Konerko 6.00
PM Pedro Martinez 8.00
PO Jorge Posada 8.00
RC Roger Clemens 10.00
RE Jose Reyes 10.00
RH Roy Halladay 6.00
RJ Randy Johnson 8.00
RO Roy Oswalt 6.00
RW Rickie Weeks 4.00
RZ Ryan Zimmerman 5.00
SA Johan Santana 8.00
SK Scott Kazmir 4.00
SM John Smoltz 6.00
SR Scott Rolen 6.00
TE Miguel Tejada 6.00
TG Tom Glavine 6.00
TH Todd Helton 8.00
TI Tim Hudson 4.00
VA Jason Varitek 6.00
VG Vladimir Guerrero 8.00
VM Victor Martinez 6.00
VW Vernon Wells 4.00

Apparel

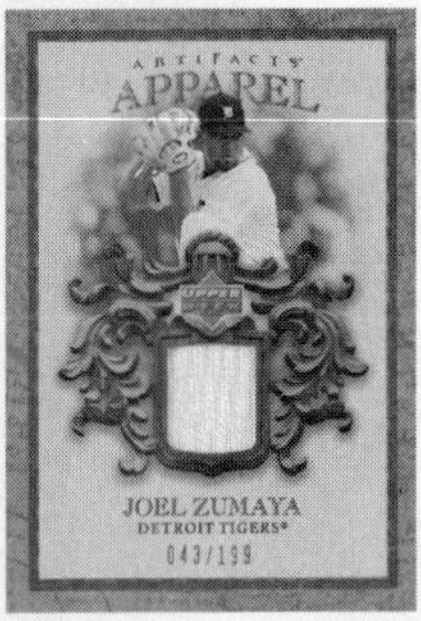

NM/M

Production 199 unless noted.
Rare Apparel: No Pricing
Production One Set
Gold: 1X
Production 130 Sets
AB Adrian Beltre 6.00
AD Adam Dunn 8.00
AJ Andruw Jones/25 10.00
AL Adam LaRoche 6.00
AP Albert Pujols 20.00
AR Aramis Ramirez 10.00
AT Garrett Atkins 6.00
BA Bobby Abreu 6.00
BC Bartolo Colon 4.00
BG Brian Giles 4.00
BI Craig Biggio 6.00
BO Jeremy Bonderman 10.00
BR Brian Roberts 6.00
BU B.J. Upton 8.00
BW Billy Wagner 6.00
BZ Barry Zito 6.00
CB Carlos Beltran 8.00
CC Carl Crawford 6.00
CH Cole Hamels 10.00
CJ Chipper Jones 8.00
CL Carlos Lee 6.00
CR Cal Ripken Jr. 25.00
CS Curt Schilling 8.00
CU Chase Utley 10.00
DJ Derek Jeter 25.00
DO David Ortiz 15.00
DU Dan Uggla 6.00
DW Dontrelle Willis 6.00
DY Jermaine Dye 4.00
EC Eric Chavez 6.00
ES Johnny Estrada 8.00
FG Freddy Garcia 4.00
FH Felix Hernandez 6.00
FL Francisco Liriano 8.00
FT Frank Thomas 8.00
GA Garret Anderson 4.00
GJ Geoff Jenkins 4.00
GM Greg Maddux 10.00
GR Khalil Greene 8.00
GS Grady Sizemore 10.00
HA Roy Halladay 6.00
HB Hank Blalock 4.00
HE Todd Helton 8.00
HO Trevor Hoffman 6.00
HR Hanley Ramirez 8.00
HU Torii Hunter 6.00
IR Ivan Rodriguez 8.00
JB Jason Bay 6.00
JC Jorge Cantu 4.00
JD J.D. Drew 6.00
JE Jim Edmonds 6.00
JF Jeff Francoeur 10.00
JG Jason Giambi 8.00
JJ Josh Johnson 4.00
JK Jeff Kent 6.00
JM Joe Mauer 8.00
JN Joe Nathan 6.00
JO Johnny Damon 8.00
JP Jake Peavy 6.00
JR Jimmy Rollins 10.00
JS Jason Schmidt 4.00
JT Jim Thome 8.00
JV Justin Verlander 10.00
JZ Joel Zumaya 8.00
KG Ken Griffey Jr. 20.00
LB Lance Berkman 6.00
LG Luis Gonzalez 4.00
MC Miguel Cabrera/67 10.00
MO Justin Morneau 8.00
MR Manny Ramirez 8.00
MT Mark Teixeira 8.00
MY Michael Young 8.00
OR Magglio Ordonez 8.00
PA Jonathan Papelbon 15.00
PB Pat Burrell 6.00
PE Jhonny Peralta 6.00
PF Prince Fielder 10.00
PM Pedro Martinez 10.00
PO Jorge Posada 8.00
RC Roger Clemens 15.00
RE Jose Reyes 15.00
RH Rich Harden 4.00
RI Mariano Rivera 10.00
RJ Randy Johnson 8.00
RO Roy Oswalt 6.00
RW Rickie Weeks 8.00
RZ Ryan Zimmerman 10.00
SA Johan Santana 8.00
SK Scott Kazmir/31 6.00
SM John Smoltz 8.00
SR Scott Rolen 8.00
TG Tom Glavine 8.00
TH Tim Hudson 6.00
TR Travis Hafner 6.00
VA Jason Varitek 10.00
VG Vladimir Guerrero/99 8.00
VM Victor Martinez 8.00
VW Vernon Wells 6.00

Apparel Autograph

NM/M

Production 25 unless noted.
AL Adam LaRoche 20.00
AT Garrett Atkins/55 15.00
BI Craig Biggio 40.00
BO Jeremy Bonderman 50.00
BR Brian Roberts 40.00
BU B.J. Upton 25.00
CC Carl Crawford/55 20.00
CH Cole Hamels 40.00
CL Carlos Lee 25.00
CR Cal Ripken Jr. 180.00
CS Curt Schilling 50.00
DO David Ortiz 60.00
DW Dontrelle Willis 20.00
EC Eric Chavez 20.00
ES Johnny Estrada 20.00
FH Felix Hernandez/23 50.00
FT Frank Thomas 75.00
GA Garret Anderson/55 20.00
GR Khalil Greene/55 25.00
HA Roy Halladay 35.00
HR Hanley Ramirez 25.00
JB Jason Bay/55 20.00
JJ Josh Johnson 15.00
JP Jake Peavy 30.00
JT Jim Thome 50.00
JZ Joel Zumaya 25.00
MC Miguel Cabrera 35.00
MO Justin Morneau 40.00
PA Jonathan Papelbon 30.00
PE Jhonny Peralta 20.00
PM Pedro Martinez 80.00
RC Roger Clemens 120.00
RH Rich Harden 20.00
OW Rickie Weeks 15.00
SK Scott Kazmir 25.00
VG Vladimir Guerrero 50.00
VW Victor Martinez 30.00

Autofacts

NM/M

Common Auto.: 10.00
AD Adam Dunn 20.00
AK Austin Kearns 10.00
AL Adam LaRoche 10.00
AM Andrew Miller 25.00
AS Angel Sanchez 10.00
BC Bobby Crosby 10.00
BE Josh Beckett 35.00
BO Jeremy Bonderman/SP 30.00
BT Jason Bartlett 10.00
BU Ambiorix Burgos/SP 10.00
CJ Cesar Jimenez 10.00
CL Carlos Lee/SP 15.00
CR Cal Ripken Jr. 125.00
CY Chris Young 20.00
CZ Carlos Zambrano 30.00
DJ Derek Jeter 140.00
DO David Ortiz/SP 50.00
DW Dontrelle Willis 15.00
DY Delmon Young/SP 15.00
EC Eric Chavez 15.00
GA Garrett Atkins 10.00
HA Rich Harden 15.00
HG Hector Gimenez 10.00
HK Hong-Chih Kuo 25.00
HR Hanley Ramirez 20.00
IK Ian Kinsler 15.00
JA Joaquin Arias 10.00
JB Jason Bay 15.00
JC Jesse Crain 10.00
JE Johnny Estrada 15.00
JG Jonny Gomes 10.00
JJ Josh Johnson 10.00
JW Jered Weaver 15.00
JZ Joel Zumaya/SP 20.00
KE Howie Kendrick 15.00
KG Ken Griffey Jr. 75.00
KM Kendry Morales 10.00
KN Jon Knott 10.00
KW Kerry Wood 15.00
MJ Mike Jacobs 10.00
MM Miguel Montero 10.00
PA Jonathan Papelbon 25.00
PE Jhonny Peralta 15.00
PH Philip Humber 10.00
RA Chris Ray 10.00
RC Roger Clemens 100.00
RH Rich Hill 15.00
RW Rickie Weeks 10.00
SB Scott Baker 10.00
SD Stephen Drew 15.00
SK Scott Kazmir 15.00
SR Scott Rolen/SP 20.00
TI Tadahito Iguchi 20.00
TT Troy Tulowitzki 20.00
UP B.J. Upton 15.00
VE Justin Verlander 20.00
VG Vladimir Guerrero/SP 40.00
VM Victor Martinez 15.00
WI Josh Willingham 10.00
YB Yuniesky Betancourt 15.00
ZG Zack Greinke 10.00
ZS Zack Segovia 10.00

Awesome Artifacts

NM/M

Production 50 Sets
AD Adam Dunn 15.00
AG Adrian Gonzalez 15.00
AP Albert Pujols 40.00
AR Aramis Ramirez 15.00
AS Alfonso Soriano 20.00
BA Bobby Abreu 15.00
BC Bartolo Colon 10.00
BG Brian Giles 10.00
BI Craig Biggio 15.00
BR Brian Roberts 15.00
BW Billy Wagner 15.00
BZ Barry Zito 15.00
CA Carl Crawford 15.00
CB Carlos Beltran 20.00
CC Carl Crawford 15.00
CD Carlos Delgado 15.00
CF Chone Figgins 15.00
CJ Chipper Jones 20.00
CL Carlos Lee 15.00
CR Cal Ripken Jr. 40.00
CS Curt Schilling 15.00
CU Chase Utley 20.00
DJ Derek Jeter 40.00
DO David Ortiz 20.00
DU Dan Uggla 15.00
DW Dontrelle Willis 15.00
EC Eric Chavez 15.00
FG Freddy Garcia 10.00
FH Felix Hernandez 15.00
FL Francisco Liriano 15.00
FT Frank Thomas 20.00
GA Garret Anderson 15.00
GM Greg Maddux 25.00
GR Khalil Greene 15.00
GS Grady Sizemore 20.00
HA Roy Halladay 15.00
HB Hank Blalock 15.00
HE Todd Helton 15.00
HR Hanley Ramirez 20.00
HS Huston Street 15.00
HU Torii Hunter 15.00
IK Ian Kinsler 15.00
IR Ivan Rodriguez 15.00
JA Jason Bay 15.00
JB Jeremy Bonderman 20.00
JC Jorge Cantu 10.00
JD Jermaine Dye 10.00
JE Jim Edmonds 15.00
JF Jeff Francoeur 20.00
JG Jason Giambi 15.00
JH Johnny Damon 20.00
JJ Josh Johnson 10.00
JK Jeff Kent 15.00
JM Joe Mauer 15.00
JO Josh Barfield 15.00
JP Jake Peavy 15.00
JR Jimmy Rollins 15.00
JS Jason Schmidt 15.00
JT Jim Thome 15.00
JV Justin Verlander 20.00
JW Jered Weaver 15.00
JZ Joel Zumaya 15.00
KG Ken Griffey Jr. 30.00
KM Kendry Morales 15.00
MC Miguel Cabrera 20.00
MO Justin Morneau 15.00
MR Manny Ramirez 20.00
MT Mark Teixeira 15.00
MY Michael Young 15.00
OR Magglio Ordonez 15.00
OS Roy Oswalt 15.00
PA Jonathan Papelbon 20.00
PB Pat Burrell 15.00
PE Jhonny Peralta 15.00
PF Prince Fielder 15.00
PO Jorge Posada 20.00
RC Robinson Cano 20.00
RE Jose Reyes 30.00
RF Rafael Furcal 15.00
RH Rich Harden 15.00
RJ Randy Johnson 20.00
RO Roger Clemens 25.00
RW Rickie Weeks 10.00
RZ Ryan Zimmerman 15.00
SK Scott Kazmir 15.00
SM John Smoltz 15.00
SR Scott Rolen 20.00
TG Tom Glavine 20.00
TH Trevor Hoffman 15.00
TI Tim Hudson 15.00
TR Travis Hafner 15.00
VA Jason Varitek 20.00
VG Vladimir Guerrero 15.00
VM Victor Martinez 15.00
VW Vernon Wells 15.00

Bat Knobs

Production One Set
No Pricing

Divisional Artifacts

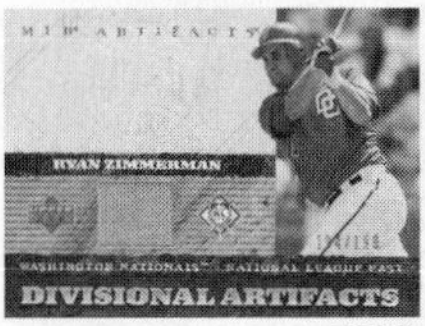

NM/M

Common Player:
Production 199 Sets
Gold: 1X
Production 130 Sets
AA Aaron Rowand 6.00
AD Adam Dunn 6.00
AJ Andruw Jones 8.00
AL Adam LaRoche 6.00
AR Aramis Ramirez 10.00
BA Bobby Abreu 6.00
BC Bartolo Colon 4.00
BE Carlos Beltran 8.00
BG Brian Giles 4.00
BO Jeremy Bonderman 10.00
BR Brian Roberts 6.00
BW Billy Wagner 6.00
BZ Barry Zito 6.00
CA Robinson Cano 10.00
CB Craig Biggio 6.00
CC Carl Crawford 6.00
CD Carlos Delgado/178 8.00
CH Chris Carpenter 8.00
CJ Chipper Jones 8.00
CL Carlos Lee 6.00
CR Cal Ripken Jr. 25.00
CS Curt Schilling 8.00
CU Chase Utley 10.00
DJ Derek Jeter 25.00
DO David Ortiz 15.00
DU Dan Uggla 6.00
DW Dontrelle Willis 6.00
EC Eric Chavez 6.00
FG Freddy Garcia 4.00
FH Felix Hernandez 6.00
FL Francisco Liriano 8.00
FT Frank Thomas 8.00
GA Garret Anderson 4.00
GM Greg Maddux 10.00
GR Ken Griffey Jr. 20.00
GS Grady Sizemore 10.00
HA Rich Harden 4.00
HB Hank Blalock 4.00
HO Trevor Hoffman 6.00
HR Hanley Ramirez 8.00
HU Torii Hunter 6.00

IK	Ian Kinsler	6.00
IR	Ivan Rodriguez	8.00
JA	Jason Bay	6.00
JC	Jorge Cantu	4.00
JD	Jermaine Dye	6.00
JE	Jim Edmonds	6.00
JF	Jeff Francoeur	10.00
JG	Jason Giambi	8.00
JJ	Josh Johnson	4.00
JK	Jeff Kent	6.00
JM	Joe Mauer	8.00
JN	Joe Nathan	6.00
JO	Josh Barfield	4.00
JP	Jake Peavy	6.00
JR	Jimmy Rollins	10.00
JS	Jason Schmidt	4.00
JT	Jim Thome	8.00
JV	Justin Verlander	10.00
JW	Jered Weaver	8.00
JZ	Joel Zumaya	8.00
KG	Khalil Greene	8.00
KM	Kendry Morales	4.00
LB	Lance Berkman	6.00
MC	Miguel Cabrera	8.00
ME	Melky Cabrera	8.00
MO	Justin Morneau	8.00
MR	Manny Ramirez	8.00
MT	Mark Teixeira	8.00
MY	Michael Young	8.00
NS	Nick Swisher	6.00
OR	Magglio Ordonez	8.00
PA	Jonathan Papelbon	15.00
PB	Pat Burrell	6.00
PE	Jhonny Peralta	6.00
PF	Prince Fielder	10.00
PK	Paul Konerko	8.00
PO	Jorge Posada	8.00
RC	Roger Clemens	15.00
RE	Jose Reyes	15.00
RH	Roy Halladay	6.00
RJ	Randy Johnson	8.00
RO	Roy Oswalt	6.00
RW	Rickie Weeks	8.00
RZ	Ryan Zimmerman	10.00
SK	Scott Kazmir	6.00
SM	John Smoltz	8.00
SR	Scott Rolen	8.00
TG	Tom Glavine	8.00
TH	Todd Helton	8.00
TI	Tim Hudson	6.00
TR	Travis Hafner/117	6.00
VA	Jason Varitek	10.00
VG	Vladimir Guerrero	8.00
VM	Victor Martinez	8.00
VW	Vernon Wells	6.00

Divisional Artifacts Auto.

NM/M

Production 25 unless noted.

AD	Adam Dunn	
BO	Jeremy Bonderman	50.00
BR	Brian Roberts	40.00
CB	Craig Biggio	40.00
CC	Carl Crawford/55	20.00
CL	Carlos Lee	25.00
CR	Cal Ripken Jr.	180.00
CS	Curt Schilling	50.00
DO	David Ortiz	60.00
DW	Dontrelle Willis/55	20.00
EC	Eric Chavez	20.00
FH	Felix Hernandez/55	50.00
FT	Frank Thomas	75.00
GA	Garret Anderson/55	20.00
HA	Rich Harden	20.00
HR	Hanley Ramirez/55	25.00
IK	Ian Kinsler	20.00
JA	Jason Bay	20.00
JD	Jermaine Dye	20.00
JJ	Josh Johnson/55	15.00
JM	Joe Mauer	40.00
JP	Jake Peavy	30.00
JT	Jim Thome	50.00
JZ	Joel Zumaya	25.00
KG	Khalil Greene	25.00
KM	Kendry Morales/55	15.00
MC	Miguel Cabrera	35.00
MO	Justin Morneau	40.00
MY	Michael Young	20.00
PA	Jonathan Papelbon	30.00
PE	Jhonny Peralta	20.00
PM	Pedro Martinez	80.00
RC	Roger Clemens	120.00
RH	Roy Halladay	35.00
RW	Rickie Weeks	15.00
SK	Scott Kazmir	25.00
TI	Tim Hudson	30.00
VG	Vladimir Guerrero	50.00
VM	Victor Martinez	30.00

2007 Upper Deck Elements

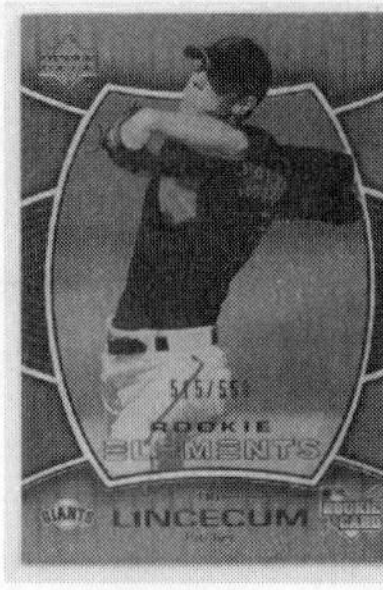

NM/M

Complete Set (252):	.50
Common player (1-126):	.25
Common RC (127-252):	5.00
Production 550	
Pack (3):	7.00
Box (15):	80.00

1	Stephen Drew	.50
2	Andruw Jones	1.00
3	Chipper Jones	1.00
4	Miguel Tejada	.75
5	David Ortiz	1.00
6	Manny Ramirez	1.00
7	Derrek Lee	.75
8	Alfonso Soriano	1.00
9	Jermaine Dye	.50
10	Jim Thome	.75
11	Ken Griffey Jr.	2.00
12	Adam Dunn	.75
13	Travis Hafner	.50
14	Grady Sizemore	1.00
15	Todd Helton	.75
16	Gary Sheffield	.75
17	Miguel Cabrera	1.00
18	Lance Berkman	.50
19	Mark Teahen	.25
20	Vladimir Guerrero	1.00
21	Jered Weaver	.50
22	Rafael Furcal	.50
23	Prince Fielder	1.00
24	Justin Morneau	.75
25	Johan Santana	1.00
26	David Wright	2.00
27	Jose Reyes	2.00
28	Derek Jeter	3.00
29	Alex Rodriguez	3.00
30	Nick Swisher	.50
31	Ryan Howard	2.00
32	Jason Bay	.50
33	Adrian Gonzalez	.50
34	Ray Durham	.25
35	Ichiro Suzuki	2.00
36	Albert Pujols	3.00
37	Scott Rolen	.75
38	Carl Crawford	.50
39	Mark Teixeira	.75
40	Michael Young	.50
41	Vernon Wells	.50
42	Ryan Zimmerman	.50
43	Stephen Drew	.50
44	Andruw Jones	1.00
45	Chipper Jones	1.00
46	Miguel Tejada	.75
47	David Ortiz	1.00
48	Manny Ramirez	1.00
49	Derrek Lee	.75
50	Alfonso Soriano	1.00
51	Jermaine Dye	.50
52	Jim Thome	.75
53	Ken Griffey Jr.	2.00
54	Adam Dunn	.75
55	Travis Hafner	.50
56	Grady Sizemore	1.00
57	Todd Helton	.75
58	Gary Sheffield	.75
59	Miguel Cabrera	1.00
60	Lance Berkman	.50
61	Mark Teahen	.25
62	Vladimir Guerrero	1.00
63	Jered Weaver	.50
64	Rafael Furcal	.50
65	Prince Fielder	1.00
66	Justin Morneau	.75
67	Johan Santana	1.00
68	David Wright	2.00
69	Jose Reyes	2.00
70	Derek Jeter	3.00
71	Alex Rodriguez	3.00
72	Nick Swisher	.50
73	Ryan Howard	2.00
74	Jason Bay	.50
75	Adrian Gonzalez	.50
76	Ray Durham	.25
77	Ichiro Suzuki	2.00
78	Albert Pujols	3.00
79	Scott Rolen	.75
80	Carl Crawford	.50
81	Mark Teixeira	.75
82	Michael Young	.50
83	Vernon Wells	.50
84	Ryan Zimmerman	.50
85	Stephen Drew	.50
86	Andruw Jones	1.00
87	Chipper Jones	1.00
88	Miguel Tejada	.75
89	David Ortiz	1.00
90	Manny Ramirez	1.00
91	Derrek Lee	.75
92	Alfonso Soriano	1.00
93	Jermaine Dye	.50
94	Jim Thome	.75
95	Ken Griffey Jr.	2.00
96	Adam Dunn	.75
97	Travis Hafner	.50
98	Grady Sizemore	1.00
99	Todd Helton	.75
100	Gary Sheffield	.75
101	Miguel Cabrera	1.00
102	Lance Berkman	.50
103	Mark Teahen	.25
104	Vladimir Guerrero	1.00
105	Jered Weaver	.50
106	Rafael Furcal	.50
107	Prince Fielder	1.00
108	Justin Morneau	.75
109	Johan Santana	1.00
110	David Wright	2.00
111	Jose Reyes	2.00
112	Derek Jeter	3.00
113	Alex Rodriguez	3.00
114	Nick Swisher	.50
115	Ryan Howard	2.00
116	Jason Bay	.50
117	Adrian Gonzalez	.50
118	Ray Durham	.25
119	Ichiro Suzuki	2.00
120	Albert Pujols	3.00
121	Scott Rolen	.75
122	Carl Crawford	.50
123	Mark Teixeira	.75
124	Michael Young	.50
125	Vernon Wells	.50
126	Ryan Zimmerman	.50
127	Miguel Montero **(RC)**	5.00
128	Doug Slaten **RC**	5.00
129	Hunter Pence **(RC)**	15.00
130	Brian Burres **(RC)**	5.00
131	Daisuke Matsuzaka **RC**	20.00
132	Hideki Okajima **RC**	8.00
133	Devern Hansack **RC**	5.00
134	Felix Pie **(RC)**	8.00
135	Ryan Sweeney **(RC)**	5.00
136	Chris Stewart **RC**	5.00
137	Jarrod Saltalamacchia **(RC)**	8.00
138	John Danks **(RC)**	10.00
139	Travis Buck **(RC)**	5.00
140	Troy Tulowitzki **(RC)**	8.00
141	Chase Wright **RC**	5.00
142	Matt DeSalvo **(RC)**	5.00
143	Micah Owings **(RC)**	5.00
144	Jeff Baker **(RC)**	5.00
145	Andy LaRoche **(RC)**	8.00
146	Billy Butler **(RC)**	8.00
147	Jose Garcia **RC**	5.00
148	Angel Sanchez **RC**	5.00
149	Alex Gordon **RC**	10.00
150	Glen Perkins **(RC)**	5.00
151	Alexi Casilla **RC**	5.00
152	Joe Smith **RC**	5.00
153	Kei Igawa **RC**	8.00
154	Sean Henn **(RC)**	5.00
155	Phil Hughes **(RC)**	8.00
156	Michael Bourn **(RC)**	8.00
157	Josh Hamilton **(RC)**	10.00
158	Kevin Kouzmanoff **(RC)**	5.00
159	Tim Lincecum **RC**	30.00
160	Brandon Morrow **RC**	10.00
161	Brandon Wood **(RC)**	8.00
162	Akinori Iwamura **RC**	8.00
163	Delmon Young **(RC)**	8.00
164	Juan Salas **(RC)**	5.00
165	Elijah Dukes **RC**	5.00
166	Joaquin Arias **(RC)**	5.00
167	Adam Lind **(RC)**	5.00
168	Matt Chico **(RC)**	5.00
169	Miguel Montero **(RC)**	5.00
170	Doug Slaten **RC**	5.00
171	Hunter Pence **(RC)**	15.00
172	Brian Burres **(RC)**	5.00
173	Daisuke Matsuzaka **RC**	20.00
174	Hideki Okajima **RC**	8.00
175	Devern Hansack **RC**	5.00
176	Felix Pie **(RC)**	8.00
177	Ryan Sweeney **(RC)**	5.00
178	Chris Stewart **RC**	5.00
179	Jarrod Saltalamacchia **(RC)**	8.00
180	John Danks **(RC)**	10.00
181	Travis Buck **(RC)**	5.00
182	Troy Tulowitzki **(RC)**	8.00
183	Chase Wright **RC**	5.00
184	Matt DeSalvo **(RC)**	5.00
185	Micah Owings **(RC)**	5.00
186	Jeff Baker **(RC)**	5.00
187	Andy LaRoche **(RC)**	8.00
188	Billy Butler **(RC)**	8.00
189	Jose Garcia **RC**	5.00
190	Angel Sanchez **RC**	5.00
191	Alex Gordon **RC**	10.00
192	Glen Perkins **(RC)**	5.00
193	Alexi Casilla **RC**	5.00
194	Joe Smith **RC**	5.00
195	Kei Igawa **RC**	8.00
196	Sean Henn **(RC)**	5.00
197	Phil Hughes **(RC)**	8.00
198	Michael Bourn **(RC)**	5.00
199	Josh Hamilton **(RC)**	10.00
200	Kevin Kouzmanoff **(RC)**	5.00
201	Tim Lincecum **RC**	30.00
202	Brandon Morrow **RC**	10.00
203	Brandon Wood **(RC)**	8.00
204	Akinori Iwamura **RC**	8.00
205	Delmon Young **(RC)**	8.00
206	Juan Salas **(RC)**	5.00
207	Elijah Dukes **RC**	8.00
208	Joaquin Arias **(RC)**	5.00
209	Adam Lind **(RC)**	5.00
210	Matt Chico **(RC)**	5.00
211	Miguel Montero **(RC)**	5.00
212	Doug Slaten **RC**	5.00
213	Hunter Pence **(RC)**	15.00
214	Brian Burres **(RC)**	5.00
215	Daisuke Matsuzaka **RC**	20.00
216	Hideki Okajima **RC**	8.00
217	Devern Hansack **RC**	5.00
218	Felix Pie **(RC)**	8.00
219	Ryan Sweeney **(RC)**	5.00
220	Chris Stewart **RC**	5.00
221	Jarrod Saltalamacchia **(RC)**	8.00
222	John Danks **(RC)**	10.00
223	Travis Buck **(RC)**	5.00
224	Troy Tulowitzki **(RC)**	8.00
225	Chase Wright **RC**	8.00
226	Matt DeSalvo **(RC)**	5.00
227	Micah Owings **(RC)**	5.00
228	Jeff Baker **(RC)**	5.00
229	Andy LaRoche **(RC)**	8.00
230	Billy Butler **(RC)**	8.00
231	Jose Garcia **RC**	5.00
232	Angel Sanchez **RC**	5.00
233	Alex Gordon **RC**	10.00
234	Glen Perkins **(RC)**	5.00
235	Alexi Casilla **RC**	8.00
236	Joe Smith **RC**	5.00
237	Kei Igawa **RC**	8.00
238	Sean Henn **(RC)**	5.00
239	Phil Hughes **(RC)**	8.00
240	Michael Bourn **(RC)**	5.00
241	Josh Hamilton **(RC)**	10.00
242	Kevin Kouzmanoff **(RC)**	5.00
243	Tim Lincecum **RC**	30.00
244	Brandon Morrow **RC**	10.00
245	Brandon Wood **(RC)**	8.00
246	Akinori Iwamura **RC**	8.00
247	Delmon Young **(RC)**	8.00
248	Juan Salas **(RC)**	5.00
249	Elijah Dukes **RC**	8.00
250	Joaquin Arias **(RC)**	5.00
251	Adam Lind **(RC)**	5.00
252	Matt Chico **(RC)**	5.00

Printing Plates

Production one set per color.

Clear-Cut Elements

NM/M

Production 350 unless noted.

Gold:	1X
Production 49-199 Sets	
Silver:	1.5X
Production 13-99 Sets	

AH	Aaron Harang	20.00
AK	Austin Kearns/234	15.00
AS	Alfonso Soriano	40.00
BB	Brian Bannister	15.00
BR	Brian Roberts	20.00
CA	Matt Cain	15.00
CC	Chris Carpenter	20.00
CP	Corey Patterson	15.00
CR	Cal Ripken Jr.	100.00
CR	Carl Crawford	20.00
DJ	Derek Jeter	150.00
DW	Dontrelle Willis	15.00
FL	Francisco Liriano	20.00
GR	Ken Griffey Jr.	75.00
HR	Hanley Ramirez	25.00
JB	Jason Bay	20.00
JG	Jonny Gomes	10.00
JH	Jeremy Hermida	15.00
JP	Jake Peavy	20.00
JT	Jim Thome	30.00
JV	Justin Verlander	30.00
JZ	Joel Zumaya	20.00
KG	Khalil Greene	15.00
KW	Kerry Wood	15.00
MC	Miguel Cabrera	30.00
MG	Marcus Giles	10.00
MH	Matt Holliday	20.00
ML	Mark Loretta	10.00
MM	Melvin Mora	10.00
MT	Miguel Tejada	25.00
RH	Rich Harden	10.00
RJ	Reed Johnson	10.00
RZ	Ryan Zimmerman	20.00
SA	Johan Santana	30.00
SK	Scott Kazmir	20.00
SR	Scott Rolen	25.00
TH	Travis Hafner	20.00
VM	Victor Martinez	20.00

Dual Elements

NM/M

Production 50 unless noted.

BB	Craig Biggio	15.00
BB	Lance Berkman	15.00
BM	Josh Beckett	60.00
BM	Daisuke Matsuzaka	60.00
BS	Freddy Sanchez	15.00
BS	Jason Bay	15.00
CA	Carlos Beltran	20.00
CA	Alfonso Soriano	20.00
CB	Carl Crawford	10.00
CB	Rocco Baldelli	10.00
CM	Mark Mulder	15.00
CM	Chris Carpenter	15.00
DB	Carlos Delgado	20.00
DB	Carlos Beltran	20.00
DG	Ken Griffey Jr./29	25.00
DG	Adam Dunn	25.00
DJ	Derek Jeter	40.00
DJ	Johnny Damon	40.00
GG	Brian Giles	10.00
GG	Marcus Giles	10.00
GJ	Ken Griffey Jr.	50.00
GJ	Derek Jeter	50.00
GM	Tom Glavine	25.00

GM	Pedro Martinez	25.00
GS	Vladimir Guerrero	20.00
GS	Alfonso Soriano	20.00
GT	Ken Griffey Jr.	30.00
GT	Frank Thomas	30.00
HB	Roy Halladay	15.00
HB	A.J. Burnett	15.00
HU	Chase Utley	25.00
HU	Cole Hamels	25.00
JJ	Andruw Jones	25.00
JJ	Chipper Jones	25.00
JR	Derek Jeter	50.00
JR	Jose Reyes	50.00
JT	Derek Jeter	30.00
JT	Miguel Tejada	30.00
LP	Jon Lester	30.00
LP	Jonathan Papelbon	30.00
MM	Victor Martinez	15.00
MM	Joe Mauer	15.00
MS	Greg Maddux	30.00
MS	John Smoltz	30.00
MT	Justin Morneau	20.00
MT	Joe Mauer	20.00
OR	Manny Ramirez	30.00
OR	David Ortiz	30.00
PG	Ken Griffey Jr.	50.00
PG	Albert Pujols	50.00
PZ	Jonathan Papelbon	25.00
PZ	Joel Zumaya	25.00
RH	Mariano Rivera	15.00
RH	Trevor Hoffman	15.00
RR	Jose Reyes	30.00
RR	Hanley Ramirez	30.00
RW	Vernon Wells	15.00
RW	Alex Rios	15.00
SB	Curt Schilling	30.00
SB	Josh Beckett	30.00
SH	Travis Hafner	25.00
SH	Grady Sizemore	25.00
SZ	Barry Zito	20.00
SZ	Johan Santana	20.00
TH	Jim Thome	20.00
TH	Travis Hafner	20.00
TK	Jim Thome	20.00
TK	Paul Konerko	20.00
TM	Mark Teixeira	20.00
TM	Justin Morneau	20.00
TR	Miguel Tejada	20.00
TR	Brian Roberts	20.00
TY	Michael Young	20.00
TY	Mark Teixeira	20.00
UU	Chase Utley	20.00
UU	Dan Uggla	20.00
VB	Jeremy Bonderman	20.00
VB	Justin Verlander	20.00
WH	Vernon Wells	15.00
WH	Torii Hunter	15.00
WJ	Randy Johnson	20.00
WJ	Brandon Webb	20.00
WS	Johan Santana	25.00
WS	Brandon Webb	25.00
ZR	Scott Rolen	25.00
ZR	Ryan Zimmerman	20.00

Elemental Autographs

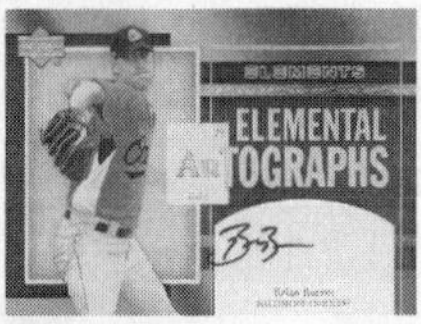

		NM/M
Common Autograph:		8.00
AI	Akinori Iwamura	15.00
AL	Adam LaRoche	15.00
BA	Bronson Arroyo	10.00
BH	Bill Hall	10.00
BL	Joe Blanton	10.00
BN	Brendan Harris	8.00
BO	Jeremy Bonderman	10.00
BR	Jared Burton	20.00
BT	Jason Bartlett	8.00
BU	Brian Burres	8.00
BW	Brandon Wood	15.00
CB	Cha Sueng Baek	8.00
CO	Jon Coutlangus	10.00
CR	Cal Ripken Jr.	100.00
CU	Chase Utley	30.00
CW	Chase Wright	15.00
DB	Denny Bautista	8.00
DC	Daniel Cabrera	8.00
DJ	Derek Jeter	150.00
DU	Dan Uggla	15.00
DW	Dontrelle Willis	15.00
FP	Felix Pie	10.00
GA	Garrett Atkins	10.00
GC	Gustavo Chacin	15.00
GO	Alex Gordon	40.00
GP	Glen Perkins	8.00
HA	Rich Harden	10.00
HE	Sean Henn	8.00
HR	Hanley Ramirez	25.00
IK	Ian Kinsler	15.00
JA	Joaquin Arias	8.00
JB	Jason Bay	15.00
JC	Jesse Crain	8.00
JG	Jonny Gomes	10.00
JH	Josh Hamilton	25.00
JK	Jon Knott	10.00
JO	Josh Willingham	10.00
JP	Jake Peavy	20.00
JV	Justin Verlander	25.00
JW	Jayson Werth	10.00
KE	Howie Kendrick	10.00
KI	Kei Igawa	20.00
KM	Kendry Morales	8.00
KY	Kevin Youkilis	15.00
LA	Andy LaRoche	15.00
LI	Bobby Livingston	10.00
LS	Luke Scott	10.00
PA	Jonathan Papelbon	25.00
PE	Jhonny Peralta	15.00
RC	Roger Clemens	80.00
RH	Rich Hill	15.00
RL	Ruddy Lugo	8.00
RO	Scott Rolen	15.00
RT	Ryan Theriot	20.00
SD	Stephen Drew	20.00
SH	James Shields	15.00
SK	Scott Kazmir	15.00
SM	John Smoltz	25.00
SO	Jeremy Sowers	10.00
SS	Skip Schumaker	10.00
ST	Scott Thorman	8.00
TB	Travis Buck	15.00
TH	Travis Hafner	15.00
TI	Tadahito Iguchi	15.00
VG	Vladimir Guerrero	25.00
VM	Victor Martinez	15.00
WO	Jason Wood	8.00

Elemental Autographs Dual

Production 15 Sets
No Pricing

Elemental Autographs Triple

Production Five Sets
No Pricing

Elemental Autographs Quad

Production One Set
No Pricing

Essential Elements

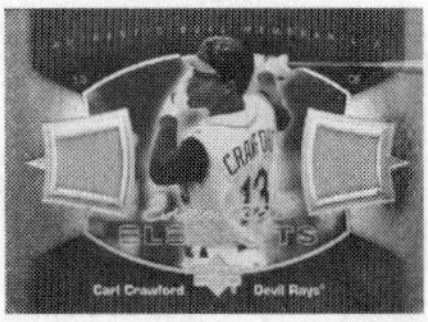

		NM/M
Common Player:		5.00
Patches:		2-4x
AB	Adrian Beltre	5.00
AD	Adam Dunn	8.00
AJ	Andruw Jones	8.00
AP	Andy Pettitte	8.00
AR	Aramis Ramirez	8.00
AS	Alfonso Soriano	8.00
BA	Bobby Abreu	5.00
BC	Bobby Crosby	5.00
BE	Carlos Beltran	8.00
BG	Brian Giles	5.00
BO	Jeremy Bonderman	15.00
BR	Brian Roberts	8.00
BU	B.J. Upton	5.00
BW	Billy Wagner	5.00
BZ	Barry Zito	5.00
CA	Miguel Cabrera	10.00
CB	Craig Biggio	8.00
CC	Carl Crawford	8.00
CH	Cole Hamels	20.00
CJ	Chipper Jones	10.00
CS	Curt Schilling	8.00
CU	Chase Utley	20.00
DA	Johnny Damon	10.00
DM	Daisuke Matsuzaka	60.00
DO	David Ortiz	15.00
DR	J.D. Drew	5.00
DU	Dan Uggla	8.00
DW	Dontrelle Willis	5.00
EC	Eric Chavez	5.00
ED	Jim Edmonds	5.00
FG	Freddy Garcia	5.00
FH	Felix Hernandez	8.00
FL	Francisco Liriano	8.00
FT	Frank Thomas	15.00
GA	Garret Anderson	5.00
GJ	Geoff Jenkins	5.00
GM	Greg Maddux	20.00
GS	Grady Sizemore	20.00
HA	Rich Harden	5.00
HB	Hank Blalock	5.00
HO	Trevor Hoffman	8.00
HS	Huston Street	5.00
HU	Torii Hunter	8.00
IR	Ivan Rodriguez	8.00
JA	Jason Bay	8.00
JB	Josh Beckett	8.00
JC	Jorge Cantu	5.00
JD	Jermaine Dye	8.00
JE	Johnny Estrada	5.00
JF	Jeff Francoeur	15.00
JG	Jason Giambi	8.00
JJ	Josh Johnson	5.00
JK	Jeff Kent	5.00
JM	Joe Mauer	8.00
JP	Jake Peavy	8.00
JR	Jimmy Rollins	8.00
JS	Johan Santana	10.00
JT	Jim Thome	8.00
JV	Justin Verlander	10.00
KG	Khalil Greene	8.00
LB	Lance Berkman	8.00
LG	Luis Gonzalez	5.00
MM	Mike Mussina	10.00
MO	Justin Morneau	10.00
MP	Mike Piazza	20.00
MR	Manny Ramirez	10.00
MT	Mark Teixeira	10.00
MY	Michael Young	8.00
OR	Magglio Ordonez	10.00
PA	Jonathan Papelbon	15.00
PB	Pat Burrell	8.00
PE	Jhonny Peralta	8.00
PO	Jorge Posada	10.00
PU	Albert Pujols	25.00
RE	Jose Reyes	15.00
RH	Roy Halladay	10.00
RI	Mariano Rivera	10.00
RJ	Randy Johnson	15.00
RO	Roy Oswalt	10.00
RW	Rickie Weeks	8.00
RZ	Ryan Zimmerman	10.00
SK	Scott Kazmir	8.00
SM	John Smoltz	10.00
SR	Scott Rolen	10.00
TE	Miguel Tejada	8.00
TH	Todd Helton	10.00
TI	Tim Hudson	10.00
TR	Travis Hafner	8.00
VG	Vladimir Guerrero	10.00
VM	Victor Martinez	8.00

Quad Elements

No Pricing
Production 10 Sets

Triple Elements

Production 25 Sets
No Pricing

2007 Upper Deck First Edition

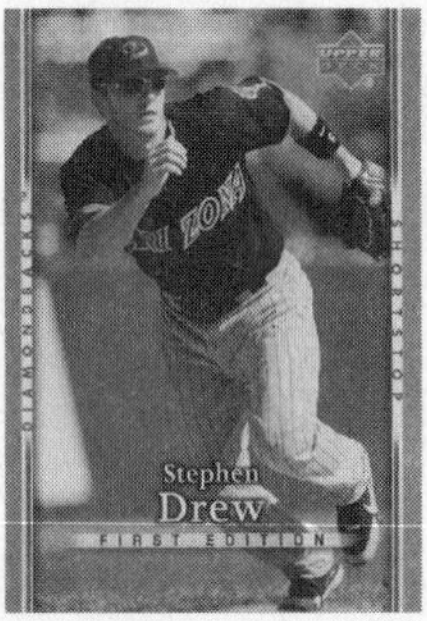

		NM/M
Complete Set (300):		35.00
Common Player:		.10
Pack (10):		1.00
Box (36):		30.00
1	Doug Slaten **RC**	.25
2	Miguel Montero **(RC)**	.25
3	Brian Burres **(RC)**	.25
4	Devern Hansack **RC**	1.00
5	David Murphy **(RC)**	.25
6	Jose Reyes **RC**	.25
7	Scott Moore **(RC)**	.25
8	Josh Fields **(RC)**	.25
9	Chris Stewart **RC**	.25
10	Jerry Owens **(RC)**	.25
11	Ryan Sweeney **(RC)**	.25
12	Kevin Kouzmanoff **(RC)**	.40
13	Jeff Baker **(RC)**	.25
14	Justin Hampson **(RC)**	.25
15	Jeff Salazar **(RC)**	.25
16	Alvin Colina **RC**	.25
17	Troy Tulowitzki **(RC)**	.50
18	Andrew Miller **RC**	3.00
19	Mike Rabelo **RC**	.25
20	Jose Diaz **(RC)**	.25
21	Angel Sanchez **RC**	.25
22	Ryan Braun **(RC)**	.25
23	Delwyn Young **(RC)**	.25
24	Drew Anderson **(RC)**	.25
25	Dennis Sarfate **(RC)**	.25
26	Vinny Rottino **(RC)**	.25
27	Glen Perkins **(RC)**	.25
28	Alexi Casilla **RC**	.25
29	Philip Humber **(RC)**	.25
30	Andy Cannizaro **RC**	.25
31	Jeremy Brown	.10
32	Sean Henn **(RC)**	.25
33	Brian Rogers **(RC)**	.25
34	Carlos Maldonado **(RC)**	.25
35	Juan Morillo **(RC)**	.25
36	Fred Lewis **(RC)**	.25
37	Patrick Misch **(RC)**	.25
38	Billy Sadler **(RC)**	.25
39	Ryan Feierabend **(RC)**	.25
40	Cesar Jimenez **RC**	.25
41	Oswaldo Navarro **RC**	.25
42	Travis Chick **(RC)**	.25
43	Delmon Young **(RC)**	.50
44	Shawn Riggans **(RC)**	.25
45	Brian Stokes **(RC)**	.25
46	Juan Salas **(RC)**	.25
47	Joaquin Arias **(RC)**	.25
48	Adam Lind **(RC)**	.50
49	Beltran Perez **(RC)**	.25
50	Brett Campbell **RC**	.25
51	Miguel Tejada	.40
52	Brandon Fahey	.10
53	Jay Gibbons	.10
54	Nicholas Markakis	.25
55	Kris Benson	.10
56	Erik Bedard	.25
57	Chris Ray	.10
58	Chris Britton	.10
59	Manny Ramirez	.50
60	David Ortiz	.50
61	Alex Cora	.10
62	Trot Nixon	.10
63	Doug Mirabelli	.10
64	Curt Schilling	.50
65	Jonathan Papelbon	.50
66	Craig Hansen	.10
67	Jermaine Dye	.25
68	Jim Thome	.40
69	Robert Mackowiak	.10
70	Brian Anderson	.10
71	A.J. Pierzynski	.10
72	Alex Cintron	.10
73	Jose Contreras	.10
74	Bobby Jenks	.10
75	Mike MacDougal	.10
76	Travis Hafner	.40
77	Ryan Garko	.10
78	Victor Martinez	.25
79	Casey Blake	.10
80	Shin-Soo Choo	.10
81	Paul Byrd	.10
82	Jeremy Sowers	.10
83	Cliff Lee	.10
84	Sean Casey	.10
85	Brandon Inge	.10
86	Omar Infante	.10
87	Magglio Ordonez	.10
88	Marcus Thames	.10
89	Justin Verlander	.50
90	Todd Jones	.10
91	Joel Zumaya	.25
92	Nate Robertson	.10
93	Mark Teahen	.25
94	Ryan Shealy	.10
95	Mark Grudzielanek	.10
96	Shane Costa	.10
97	Reggie Sanders	.10
98	Mark Redman	.10
99	Todd Wellemeyer	.10
100	Ambiorix Burgos	.10
101	Joe Nelson	.10
102	Orlando Cabrera	.25
103	Maicer Izturis	.10
104	Vladimir Guerrero	.50
105	Juan Rivera	.10
106	Jered Weaver	.40
107	Joe Saunders	.10
108	Bartolo Colon	.10
109	Francisco Rodriguez	.25
110	Justin Morneau	.50
111	Luis Castillo	.10
112	Michael Cuddyer	.10
113	Joe Mauer	.40
114	Francisco Liriano	.25
115	Joe Nathan	.25
116	Brad Radke	.10
117	Juan Rincon	.10
118	Derek Jeter	1.50
119	Jason Giambi	.40
120	Bobby Abreu	.40
121	Gary Sheffield	.40
122	Melky Cabrera	.25
123	Chien-Ming Wang	.50
124	Mariano Rivera	.40
125	Jaret Wright	.10
126	Kyle Farnsworth	.10
127	Frank Thomas	.50
128	Dan Johnson	.10
129	Marco Scutaro	.10
130	Jay Payton	.10
131	Joe Blanton	.10
132	Rich Harden	.25
133	Esteban Loaiza	.10
134	Chad Gaudin	.10
135	Yuniesky Betancourt	.10
136	Willie Bloomquist	.10
137	Ichiro Suzuki	1.00
138	Raul Ibanez	.10
139	Chris Snelling	.10
140	Cha Sueng Baek	.10
141	Julio Mateo	.10
142	Rafael Soriano	.10
143	Jorge Cantu	.10
144	B.J. Upton	.10
145	Dioner Navarro	.10
146	Carl Crawford	.40
147	Damon Hollins	.10
148	Casey Fossum	.10
149	Ruddy Lugo	.10
150	Tyler Walker	.10
151	Shawn Camp	.10
152	Ian Kinsler	.25
153	Jerry Hairston Jr.	.10
154	Gerald Laird	.10
155	Mark DeRosa	.10

156	Kip Wells	.10
157	Vicente Padilla	.10
158	John Koronka	.10
159	Wes Littleton	.10
160	Lyle Overbay	.10
161	Aaron Hill	.10
162	John McDonald	.10
163	Vernon Wells	.10
164	Frank Catalanotto	.10
165	Roy Halladay	.25
166	B.J. Ryan	.10
167	Casey Janssen	.10
168	Stephen Drew	.50
169	Conor Jackson	.10
170	Chad Tracy	.10
171	Johnny Estrada	.10
172	Eric Byrnes	.10
173	Carlos Quentin	.10
174	Brandon Webb	.25
175	Jorge Julio	.10
176	Luis Vizcaino	.10
177	Chipper Jones	.50
178	Adam LaRoche	.25
179	Brian McCann	.25
180	Ryan Langerhans	.10
181	Matt Diaz	.10
182	John Smoltz	.25
183	Oscar Villarreal	.10
184	Chad Paronto	.10
185	Derrek Lee	.40
186	Ryan Theriot	.10
187	Ronny Cedeno	.10
188	Juan Pierre	.10
189	Matt Murton	.10
190	Carlos Zambrano	.25
191	Mark Prior	.25
192	Ryan Dempster	.10
193	Ryan O'Malley	.10
194	Brandon Phillips	.10
195	Rich Aurilia	.10
196	Ken Griffey Jr.	1.00
197	Ryan Freel	.10
198	Aaron Harang	.10
199	Brandon Claussen	.10
200	David Weathers	.10
201	Eric Milton	.10
202	Kazuo Matsui	.10
203	Jamey Carroll	.10
204	Matt Holliday	.25
205	Brad Hawpe	.10
206	Jason Jennings	.10
207	Josh Fogg	.10
208	Aaron Cook	.10
209	Miguel Cabrera	.50
210	Dan Uggla	.10
211	Hanley Ramirez	.40
212	Jeremy Hermida	.10
213	Cody Ross	.10
214	Josh Willingham	.10
215	Anibal Sanchez	.10
216	Jose Garcia	.10
217	Taylor Tankersley	.10
218	Lance Berkman	.40
219	Craig Biggio	.25
220	Brad Ausmus	.10
221	Willy Taveras	.10
222	Chris Burke	.10
223	Roger Clemens	1.00
224	Brandon Backe	.10
225	Brad Lidge	.10
226	Dan Wheeler	.10
227	Wilson Betemit	.10
228	Julio Lugo	.10
229	Russell Martin	.25
230	Kenny Lofton	.10
231	Brad Penny	.10
232	Chad Billingsley	.10
233	Greg Maddux	1.00
234	Jonathan Broxton	.10
235	Rickie Weeks	.25
236	Bill Hall	.25
237	Tony Gwynn Jr.	.10
238	Corey Hart	.10
239	Laynce Nix	.10
240	Ben Sheets	.25
241	David Bush	.10
242	Francisco Cordero	.10
243	Jose Reyes	.50
244	Carlos Delgado	.40
245	Paul LoDuca	.10
246	Carlos Beltran	.40
247	Lastings Milledge	.25
248	Pedro Martinez	.50
249	John Maine	.10
250	Steve Trachsel	.10
251	Ryan Howard	1.00
252	Jimmy Rollins	.25
253	Chris Coste	.10
254	Jeff Conine	.10
255	David Dellucci	.10
256	Cole Hamels	.25
257	Ryan Madson	.10
258	Brett Myers	.10
259	Freddy Sanchez	.10
260	Xavier Nady	.10
261	Jose Castillo	.10
262	Jason Bay	.25
263	Jose Bautista	.10
264	Ronny Paulino	.10
265	Zachary Duke	.10
266	Shane Youman	.10
267	Matt Capps	.10
268	Adrian Gonzalez	.25
269	Josh Barfield	.10
270	Mike Piazza	.75

271	Dave Roberts	.10
272	Geoff Blum	.10
273	Chris Young	.10
274	Woody Williams	.10
275	Cla Meredith	.10
276	Trevor Hoffman	.25
277	Ray Durham	.10
278	Mark Sweeney	.10
279	Eliezer Alfonzo	.10
280	Todd Linden	.10
281	Jason Schmidt	.25
282	Noah Lowry	.10
283	Brad Hennessey	.10
284	Jonathan Sanchez	.10
285	Albert Pujols	1.50
286	David Eckstein	.10
287	Jim Edmonds	.25
288	Chris Duncan	.10
289	Juan Encarnacion	.10
290	Jeff Suppan	.10
291	Jeff Weaver	.10
292	Braden Looper	.10
293	Ryan Zimmerman	.25
294	Nick Johnson	.10
295	Alfonso Soriano	.50
296	Austin Kearns	.10
297	Alex Escobar	.10
298	Tony Armas	.10
299	Chad Cordero	.10
300	Jon Rauch	.10

Printing Plates

No Pricing
Production one set per color.

Aces

		NM/M
Common Player:		.50
Inserted 1:6		
BW	Brandon Webb	.50
CC	Chris Carpenter	.75
CS	Curt Schilling	.75
CZ	Carlos Zambrano	.50
DW	Dontrelle Willis	.50
FH	Felix Hernandez	.50
JS	Johan Santana	.75
JV	Justin Verlander	.75
PM	Pedro Martinez	.75
RC	Roger Clemens	2.00
RH	Roy Halladay	.50
SA	C.C. Sabathia	.50
SM	John Smoltz	.50
RJ	Randy Johnson	.75
SK	Scott Kazmir	.50

Foundations

		NM/M
Common Player:		.50
Inserted 1:6		
AL	Adam Lind	1.00
AM	Andrew Miller	3.00
DM	David Murphy	.50
DY	Delmon Young	1.00
FL	Fred Lewis	.50
GP	Glen Perkins	.50
JA	Joaquin Arias	.50
JF	Josh Fields	.50

JO	Jerry Owens	.50
JS	Jeff Salazar	.50
MM	Mitch Maier	.50
MO	Miguel Montero	.50
PH	Philip Humber	.50
RB	Ryan Braun	.50
RS	Ryan Sweeney	.50
SM	Scott Moore	.50
SR	Shawn Riggans	.50
TC	Travis Chick	.50
TT	Troy Tulowitzki	1.00
UJ	Ubaldo Jimenez	.50

Leading Off

		NM/M
Common Player:		.50
Inserted 1:6		
AS	Alfonso Soriano	1.00
BR	Brian Roberts	.50
CF	Chone Figgins	.50
DR	Dave Roberts	.50
FR	Ryan Freel	.50
GS	Grady Sizemore	1.00
HR	Hanley Ramirez	1.00
IS	Ichiro Suzuki	2.00
JD	Johnny Damon	1.00
JP	Juan Pierre	.50
JR	Jose Reyes	2.00
RF	Rafael Furcal	.50
RO	Jimmy Rollins	.75
SP	Scott Podsednik	.50
WT	Willy Taveras	.50

Momentum Swing

		NM/M
Common Player:		.50
Inserted 1:6		
AD	Adam Dunn	.75
AJ	Andruw Jones	1.00
AP	Albert Pujols	2.50
AR	Alex Rodriguez	2.50
AS	Alfonso Soriano	1.00
CB	Carlos Beltran	1.00
CD	Carlos Delgado	.75
DL	Derrek Lee	.75
DO	David Ortiz	1.00
JB	Jason Bay	.75
JD	Jermaine Dye	.50
JG	Jason Giambi	.75
JM	Justin Morneau	.75
JT	Jim Thome	.75
LB	Lance Berkman	.75
MC	Miguel Cabrera	1.00
MT	Mark Teixeira	.75
RH	Ryan Howard	2.00
TH	Travis Hafner	.75
VG	Vladimir Guerrero	1.00

Pennant Chasers

		NM/M
Common Player:		.25
Inserted 1:4		
AR	Aramis Ramirez	.75
CC	Carl Crawford	.75
CG	Carlos Guillen	.25
CJ	Chipper Jones	1.00
CU	Chase Utley	1.00

DA	Johnny Damon	1.00
DU	Dan Uggla	.25
DW	David Wright	1.50
FS	Freddy Sanchez	.25
JM	Joe Mauer	.75
JR	Juan Rivera	.25
KG	Ken Griffey Jr.	2.00
MH	Matt Holliday	.50
MR	Manny Ramirez	1.00
MT	Miguel Tejada	.50
MY	Michael Young	.50
NG	Nomar Garciaparra	.50
NS	Nick Swisher	.25
OH	Orlando Hudson	.25
PF	Prince Fielder	.75
PK	Paul Konerko	.25
RD	Ray Durham	.25
RI	Raul Ibanez	.25
RO	Roy Oswalt	.50
RZ	Ryan Zimmerman	.75
SR	Scott Rolen	.25
TE	Mark Teahen	.25
TH	Trevor Hoffman	.50
VM	Victor Martinez	.50
VW	Vernon Wells	.50

2007 Upper Deck Future Stars

		NM/M
Common Player (1-100):		.25
Common RC Auto. (101-189):		8.00
Pack (4):		4.00
Box (24):		75.00
1	Brandon Webb	.50
2	Conor Jackson	.50
3	Stephen Drew	.40
4	Chipper Jones	.75
5	Andruw Jones	.40
6	Jeff Francoeur	.75
7	John Smoltz	.50
8	Miguel Tejada	.50
9	Nicholas Markakis	.50
10	Brian Roberts	.40
11	David Ortiz	.75
12	Manny Ramirez	.75
13	Josh Beckett	.75
14	Curt Schilling	.75
15	Derrek Lee	.50
16	Aramis Ramirez	.50
17	Carlos Zambrano	.75
18	Alfonso Soriano	.50
19	Jim Thome	.50
20	Paul Konerko	.50
21	Jon Garland	.25
22	Ken Griffey Jr.	1.50
23	Adam Dunn	.50
24	Aaron Harang	.25
25	Travis Hafner	.40
26	Victor Martinez	.50
27	Grady Sizemore	.75
28	C.C. Sabathia	.50
29	Todd Helton	.50
30	Matt Holliday	.50
31	Garrett Atkins	.40
32	Ivan Rodriguez	.50
33	Magglio Ordonez	.40
34	Gary Sheffield	.50
35	Justin Verlander	.50
36	Miguel Cabrera	.75
37	Hanley Ramirez	.75
38	Dontrelle Willis	.25
39	Lance Berkman	.50
40	Roy Oswalt	.50
41	Carlos Lee	.50
42	Gil Meche	.25
43	Emil Brown	.25
44	Mark Teahen	.25
45	Vladimir Guerrero	.75
46	Jered Weaver	.40

47	Howie Kendrick	.25
48	Juan Pierre	.40
49	Nomar Garciaparra	.75
50	Rafael Furcal	.40
51	Jeff Kent	.40
52	Prince Fielder	1.00
53	Ben Sheets	.40
54	Rickie Weeks	.40
55	Justin Morneau	.50
56	Joe Mauer	.50
57	Torii Hunter	.40
58	Johan Santana	.75
59	Jose Reyes	.75
60	David Wright	.75
61	Carlos Delgado	.50
62	Carlos Beltran	.50
63	Derek Jeter	2.00
64	Alex Rodriguez	2.00
65	Johnny Damon	.50
66	Jason Giambi	.50
67	Bobby Abreu	.50
68	Mike Piazza	.75
69	Nick Swisher	.40
70	Eric Chavez	.25
71	Ryan Howard	1.00
72	Chase Utley	.75
73	Jimmy Rollins	.50
74	Jason Bay	.40
75	Freddy Sanchez	.25
76	Zachary Duke	.25
77	Greg Maddux	1.00
78	Adrian Gonzalez	.25
79	Jake Peavy	.40
80	Ray Durham	.25
81	Barry Zito	.25
82	Matt Cain	.25
83	Ichiro Suzuki	1.50
84	Felix Hernandez	.50
85	Richie Sexson	.40
86	Albert Pujols	2.00
87	Scott Rolen	.75
88	Chris Carpenter	.50
89	Chris Duncan	.25
90	Carl Crawford	.40
91	Rocco Baldelli	.25
92	Scott Kazmir	.25
93	Michael Young	.25
94	Mark Teixeira	.50
95	Ian Kinsler	.25
96	Troy Glaus	.40
97	Vernon Wells	.40
98	Roy Halladay	.40
99	Ryan Zimmerman	.50
100	Nick Johnson	.25
101	Zack Segovia **(RC)**	8.00
102	Joaquin Arias **(RC)**	8.00
104	Travis Buck **(RC)**	10.00
105	Mike Schultz **RC**	8.00
107	Sean Henn **(RC)**	8.00
108	Ryan Braun **RC**	10.00
109	Rick Vanden Hurk **RC**	10.00
110	Carlos Gomez SP **RC**	40.00
111	Mike Rabelo **RC**	10.00
112	Felix Pie **(RC)**	15.00
113	Miguel Montero **(RC)**	8.00
114	Michael Bourn **(RC)**	15.00
115	Micah Owings/SP **(RC)**	30.00
116	Matt Lindstrom **(RC)**	8.00
117	Matt Chico **(RC)**	8.00
118	Levale Speigner **RC**	8.00
119	Lee Gardner **(RC)**	8.00
120	Kory Casto **(RC)**	8.00
121	Kevin Kouzmanoff **(RC)**	15.00
122	Kevin Cameron **RC**	8.00
124	Tyler Clippard **(RC)**	15.00
125	Juan Perez **RC**	8.00
126	Josh Hamilton SP **(RC)**	30.00
127	Joseph Bisenius **RC**	8.00
128	Jose Garcia **RC**	8.00
129	Jon Knott **RC**	8.00
130	Jon Coutlangus **(RC)**	8.00
131	John Danks **(RC)**	15.00
132	Joe Smith **RC**	8.00
133	Matt Brown **RC**	8.00
134	Joakim Soria **RC**	20.00
135	Jesus Flores **RC**	8.00
136	Jeff Baker **(RC)**	8.00
137	Jay Marshall **RC**	10.00
138	Jared Burton **RC**	10.00
139	Jamie Vermilyea **RC**	8.00
140	Jamie Burke **(RC)**	8.00
141	Ryan Rowland-Smith **RC**	8.00
142	Connor Robertson **RC**	8.00
143	Hector Gimenez **(RC)**	8.00
144	Gustavo Molina **RC**	8.00
145	Glen Perkins **(RC)**	8.00
146	Joba Chamberlain/SP **RC**	250.00
147	Doug Slaten **RC**	8.00
148	Ryan Braun **(RC)**	60.00
149	Delmon Young/SP **(RC)**	40.00
150	Garrett Jones **(RC)**	8.00
152	Cesar Jimenez **RC**	8.00
153	Brian Stokes **(RC)**	8.00
154	Brian Burres **(RC)**	10.00
155	Brian Barden SP **RC**	15.00
156	Kyle Kendrick **RC**	25.00
157	Andrew Miller **RC**	20.00
158	Alexi Casilla **RC**	10.00
159	Alex Gordon/SP **RC**	60.00
159	A.J. Murray **RC**	8.00
162	Adam Lind **(RC)**	8.00
163	Chase Wright **RC**	10.00
164	Dallas Braden **RC**	8.00
165	Rocky Cherry **RC**	10.00
166	Andy Gonzalez **RC**	8.00
167	Neal Musser **RC**	10.00
168	Mark Reynolds **RC**	20.00
169	Dennis Dove **(RC)**	10.00
170	Justin Hampson **(RC)**	8.00
171	Phil Hughes/SP **(RC)**	50.00
172	Kelvin Jimenez **RC**	8.00
173	Hunter Pence/SP **(RC)**	40.00
174	Brad Salmon **RC**	10.00
175	Ryan Sweeney **(RC)**	10.00
176	Brandon Wood **(RC)**	15.00
177	Billy Butler/SP **(RC)**	30.00
178	Ben Francisco **(RC)**	8.00
180	Yoel Hernandez **RC**	8.00
181	Tim Lincecum/SP **RC**	100.00
182	Danny Putnam **(RC)**	8.00
183	Jarrod Saltalamacchia/ SP **(RC)**	15.00
184	Andy LaRoche/SP **(RC)**	25.00
185	Matt DeSalvo **(RC)**	10.00
186	Fred Lewis **(RC)**	10.00
187	Anthony Lerew **(RC)**	8.00
188	Jesse Litsch **RC**	10.00
189	Daisuke Matsuzaka/ SP **RC**	250.00

Gold

Gold (1-100, 189):	3-6X
Production 99 Sets	

Red

Red (1-100, 189):	2-4X
Production 199 Sets	

All-Star Futures

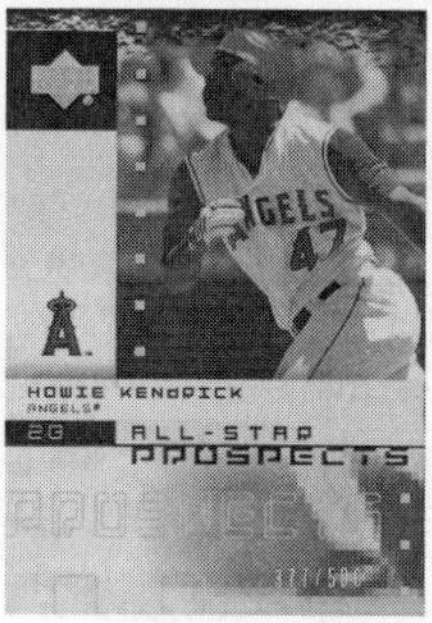

		NM/M
Common Player:		2.00
Production 500 Sets		
AD	Alejandro De Aza	2.00
AG	Alex Gordon	8.00
AI	Akinori Iwamura	3.00
AL	Adam Lind	2.00
AM	Andrew Miller	4.00
BA	Jeff Baker	2.00
BI	Billy Butler	5.00
BM	Brandon Morrow	3.00
BU	B.J. Upton	3.00
BW	Brandon Wood	3.00
CA	Alexi Casilla	2.00
CG	Carlos Gomez	3.00
CW	Chase Wright	2.00
CY	Chris Young	3.00
DM	Daisuke Matsuzaka	15.00
DP	Danny Putnam	2.00
DY	Delmon Young	4.00
FL	Fred Lewis	2.00
FP	Felix Pie	3.00
GP	Glen Perkins	2.00
HA	Josh Hamilton	2.00
HK	Howie Kendrick	3.00
HP	Hunter Pence	8.00
IK	Ian Kinsler	3.00
JA	Joaquin Arias	2.00
JD	John Danks	2.00
JS	Jarrod Saltalamacchia	2.00
JV	Justin Verlander	3.00
KC	Kory Casto	2.00
KI	Kei Igawa	2.00
KK	Kevin Kouzmanoff	2.00
LA	Andy LaRoche	3.00
MA	Matt Chico	3.00
MB	Michael Bourn	2.00
MC	Matt Cain	2.00
MI	Miguel Montero	2.00
ML	Matt Lindstrom	2.00
MO	Micah Owings	2.00
PF	Prince Fielder	3.00
PH	Phil Hughes	6.00
RB	Ryan Braun	10.00
RS	Ryan Sweeney	2.00
RZ	Ryan Zimmerman	4.00
SD	Stephen Drew	3.00
SM	Joe Smith	2.00
SO	Joakim Soria	2.00
TB	Travis Buck	2.00
TL	Tim Lincecum	8.00
TP	Tony Pena	2.00
TT	Troy Tulowitzki	4.00

All-Star Futures Auto.

		NM/M
Common Auto.:		8.00
AG	Alex Gordon/SP	60.00
AI	Akinori Iwamura/SP	15.00
AL	Adam Lind	8.00
AM	Andrew Miller	20.00
BA	Jeff Baker	8.00
BI	Billy Butler	25.00
BU	B.J. Upton	10.00
BW	Brandon Wood	15.00
CA	Alexi Casilla	8.00
CG	Carlos Gomez	20.00
CW	Chase Wright	8.00
CY	Chris Young	15.00
DM	Daisuke Matsuzaka/SP	250.00
DP	Danny Putnam	8.00
DY	Delmon Young/SP	8.00
FL	Fred Lewis	10.00
FP	Felix Pie	15.00
GP	Glen Perkins	8.00
HA	Josh Hamilton	20.00
HK	Howie Kendrick	15.00
HP	Hunter Pence	50.00
IK	Ian Kinsler	15.00
JA	Joaquin Arias	8.00
JD	John Danks	10.00
JS	Jarrod Saltalamacchia	15.00
JV	Justin Verlander/SP	40.00
KC	Kory Casto	8.00
KI	Kei Igawa/SP	15.00
KK	Kevin Kouzmanoff	10.00
LA	Andy LaRoche	15.00
MA	Matt Chico	8.00
MC	Matt Cain	15.00
MI	Miguel Montero	8.00
ML	Matt Lindstrom	8.00
MO	Micah Owings	15.00
PF	Prince Fielder/SP	50.00
PH	Phil Hughes/SP	60.00
RB	Ryan Braun	60.00
RS	Ryan Sweeney	10.00
RZ	Ryan Zimmerman/SP	20.00
SD	Stephen Drew/SP	15.00
SM	Joe Smith	10.00
SO	Joakim Soria	15.00
TB	Travis Buck	10.00
TL	Tim Lincecum	65.00
TP	Tony Pena	8.00
TT	Troy Tulowitzki	25.00

Clear Path to History Triple Autographs

		NM/M
Some not priced due to scarcity.		
CCH	Eric Chavez, Bobby Crosby, Rich Harden	20.00
CWR	Miguel Cabrera, Dontrelle Willis, Hanley Ramirez	60.00
DMY	Chris Young, Stephen Drew, Miguel Montero	30.00
FEG	Luis Gonzalez, Andre Ethier, Rafael Furcal	40.00
GKW	Vladimir Guerrero, Howie Kendrick, Jered Weaver/SP	100.00
GPC	Vladimir Guerrero, Albert Pujols, Miguel Cabrera/SP	200.00
HAT	Garrett Atkins, Matt Holliday, Troy Tulowitzki	100.00
HMS	Travis Hafner, Victor Martinez, Jeremy Sowers	50.00
KUC	Carl Crawford, Scott Kazmir, B.J. Upton	60.00
KUK	Ian Kinsler, Dan Uggla, Howie Kendrick	25.00
MPM	Melvin Mora, Corey Patterson, Nick Markakis	25.00
VZR	Justin Verlander, Ryan Zimmerman, Hanley Ramirez	40.00

Cy Young Futures

		NM/M
Common Player:		2.00
Production 500 Sets		
AL	Anthony Lerew	2.00
AM	Andrew Miller	4.00
BM	Brandon Morrow	3.00
CH	Cole Hamels	4.00
CW	Chase Wright	2.00
DM	Daisuke Matsuzaka	15.00
GP	Glen Perkins	2.00
JD	John Danks	2.00
JG	Jose Garcia	2.00
JL	Jon Lester	4.00
JS	Jeremy Sowers	2.00
JV	Justin Verlander	3.00
JZ	Joel Zumaya	2.00
KI	Kei Igawa	3.00
MA	Matt Chico	2.00
MC	Matt Cain	2.00
MO	Micah Owings	2.00
PH	Phil Hughes	6.00
RV	Rick Vanden Hurk	2.00
SH	Sean Henn	2.00
SK	Scott Kazmir	3.00
SM	Joe Smith	2.00
TC	Tyler Clippard	2.00
TL	Tim Lincecum	8.00
ZS	Zack Segovia	2.00

Cy Young Futures Auto.

		NM/M
Common Auto.:		8.00
AL	Anthony Lerew	8.00

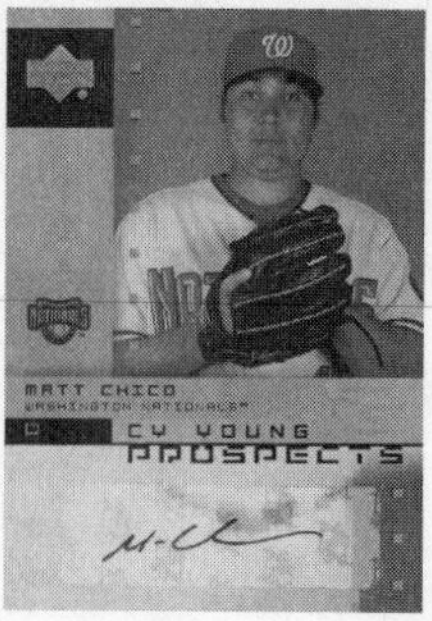

AM	Andrew Miller	20.00
CW	Chase Wright	15.00
DM	Daisuke Matsuzaka/SP	250.00
GP	Glen Perkins	8.00
JD	John Danks	10.00
JG	Jose Garcia	8.00
JZ	Joel Zumaya	15.00
MA	Matt Chico	8.00
MC	Matt Cain	15.00
MO	Micah Owings	15.00
PH	Phil Hughes SP	60.00
RV	Rick Vanden Hurk	10.00
SH	Sean Henn	8.00
SM	Joe Smith	10.00
TC	Tyler Clippard	15.00
TL	Tim Lincecum	60.00
ZS	Zack Segovia	8.00

MVP Futures

		NM/M
Common Player:		2.00
Production 500 Sets		
AD	Alejandro De Aza	2.00
AG	Alex Gordon	8.00
AI	Akinori Iwamura	3.00
AL	Adam Lind	2.00
DM	Daisuke Matsuzaka	15.00
DY	Delmon Young	4.00
FP	Felix Pie	3.00
HP	Hunter Pence	8.00
IK	Ian Kinsler	3.00
JA	Joaquin Arias	2.00
JB	Jeff Baker	2.00
JH	Josh Hamilton	2.00
JS	Jarrod Saltalamacchia	2.00
JV	Justin Verlander	3.00
KI	Kei Igawa	2.00
KK	Kevin Kouzmanoff	2.00
LA	Andy LaRoche	3.00
MB	Michael Bourn	2.00
MM	Miguel Montero	2.00
PF	Prince Fielder	3.00
RB	Ryan Braun	10.00
RS	Ryan Sweeney	2.00
RZ	Ryan Zimmerman	4.00
TB	Travis Buck	2.00
TT	Troy Tulowitzki	4.00

MVP Futures Auto.

		NM/M
Common Auto.:		8.00
AG	Alex Gordon/SP	50.00
AL	Adam Lind	8.00
DM	Daisuke Matsuzaka/SP	250.00
FP	Felix Pie	15.00
HP	Hunter Pence	50.00
IK	Ian Kinsler	15.00
JA	Joaquin Arias	8.00
JB	Jeff Baker	8.00
JH	Josh Hamilton	20.00
JS	Jarrod Saltalamacchia	15.00
KK	Kevin Kouzmanoff	10.00
LA	Andy LaRoche	15.00
MB	Michael Bourn	15.00
MM	Miguel Montero	8.00
PF	Prince Fielder	50.00
RB	Ryan Braun	60.00
RS	Ryan Sweeney	10.00
TB	Travis Buck	10.00

Rookie Dated Debuts

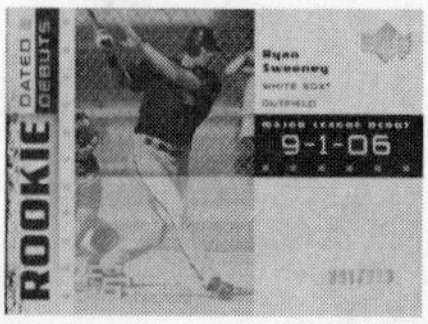

		NM/M
Common Player:		2.00
Production 999 Sets		
Autographs:		No Pricing
Production 10 Sets		
AC	Alexi Casilla	2.00
AD	Alejandro De Aza	2.00

AG	Alex Gordon	5.00
AI	Akinori Iwamura	2.00
AL	Adam Lind	2.00
BA	Jeff Baker	2.00
BB	Brian Barden	2.00
BI	Joseph Bisenius	2.00
BM	Brandon Morrow	2.00
BW	Brandon Wood	2.00
CA	Kory Casto	2.00
CG	Carlos Gomez	3.00
CR	Cal Ripken Jr.	10.00
CW	Chase Wright	2.00
DA	John Danks	2.00
DJ	Derek Jeter	10.00
DM	Daisuke Matsuzaka	10.00
DY	Delmon Young	3.00
ED	Elijah Dukes	2.00
FL	Fred Lewis	2.00
FP	Felix Pie	2.00
GM	Gustavo Molina	2.00
GP	Glen Perkins	2.00
HO	Hideki Okajima	3.00
HP	Hunter Pence	6.00
JA	Joaquin Arias	2.00
JC	Jon Coutlangus	2.00
JF	Jesus Flores	2.00
JH	Josh Hamilton	2.00
JM	Jay Marshall	2.00
JP	Juan Perez	2.00
JS	Joakim Soria	2.00
KC	Kevin Cameron	2.00
KG	Ken Griffey Jr.	8.00
KI	Kei Igawa	2.00
KK	Kevin Kouzmanoff	2.00
LA	Andy LaRoche	3.00
LG	Lee Gardner	2.00
MB	Michael Bourn	2.00
MC	Matt Chico	2.00
MM	Miguel Montero	2.00
MO	Micah Owings	2.00
MR	Mike Rabelo	2.00
PH	Phil Hughes	5.00
RS	Ryan Sweeney	2.00
SA	Jarrod Saltalamacchia	2.00
SM	Joe Smith	2.00
TB	Travis Buck	2.00
TL	Tim Lincecum	5.00
TT	Troy Tulowitzki	4.00

Two for the Bigs

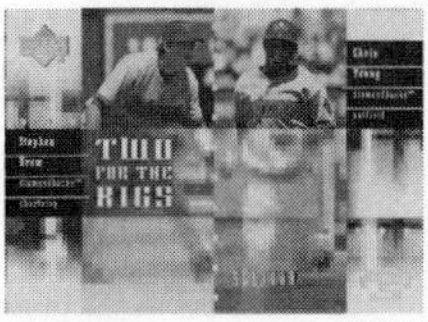
TWO FOR THE BIGS

NM/M

Common Duo: 2.00
Production 999 Sets
Autographs: No Pricing
Production 10 Sets

AS	Joaquin Arias, Chris Stewart	2.00
BB	Michael Bourn, Joseph Bisenius	2.00
BD	Travis Buck, Elijah Dukes	2.00
BG	Ryan Braun, Alex Gordon	8.00
BS	Ryan Braun, Joakim Soria	2.00
BT	Jeff Baker, Troy Tulowitzki	4.00
CF	Kory Casto, Jesus Flores	2.00
CL	Matt Chico, Tim Lincecum	4.00
CP	Alexi Casilla, Glen Perkins	2.00
CS	Matt Chico, Levale Speigner	2.00
DG	Alejandro De Aza, Lee Gardner	2.00
DK	Daisuke Matsuzaka, Kei Igawa	6.00
DM	John Danks, Gustavo Molina	2.00
DT	Stephen Drew, Troy Tulowitzki	4.00
DV	Alejandro De Aza, Rick Vanden Hurk	2.00
DW	Chase Wright, Matt DeSalvo	2.00
DY	Chris Young, Stephen Drew	3.00
GB	Alex Gordon, Billy Butler	5.00
GF	Hector Gimenez, Jesus Flores	2.00
GI	Alex Gordon, Akinori Iwamura	5.00
GL	Alex Gordon, Andy LaRoche	5.00
GM	Alex Gordon, Daisuke Matsuzaka	8.00
GP	Hector Gimenez, Hunter Pence	4.00
HB	Josh Hamilton, Jared Burton	2.00
HD	Josh Hamilton, Alejandro De Aza	2.00
HL	Phil Hughes, Tim Lincecum	8.00
HP	Josh Hamilton, Hunter Pence	4.00
II	Akinori Iwamura, Kei Igawa	3.00
KC	Kevin Kouzmanoff, Kevin Cameron	2.00
LG	Matt Lindstrom, Lee Gardner	2.00
LV	Adam Lind	2.00
MG	Hector Gimenez, Miguel Montero	2.00
MI	Daisuke Matsuzaka, Akinori Iwamura	5.00
MO	Daisuke Matsuzaka, Hideki Okajima	5.00
MR	Gustavo Molina, Mike Rabelo	2.00
MW	Brandon Morrow, Sean White	2.00
OL	Micah Owings, Tim Lincecum	4.00
OM	Micah Owings, Miguel Montero	2.00
PB	Danny Putnam, Travis Buck	2.00
PD	Hunter Pence, Alejandro De Aza	4.00
PH	Josh Hamilton, Felix Pie	2.00
PP	Felix Pie, Hunter Pence	4.00
RS	Mike Rabelo, Chris Stewart	2.00
SM	Jarrod Saltalamacchia, Miguel Montero	2.00
ST	Jarrod Saltalamacchia, Troy Tulowitzki	4.00
SW	Joe Smith, Chase Wright	2.00
TB	Travis Buck, Billy Butler	3.00
WH	Chase Wright, Phil Hughes	4.00
YD	Delmon Young, Elijah Dukes	2.00
YM	Delmon Young, Daisuke Matsuzaka	5.00

2007 Upper Deck Goudey

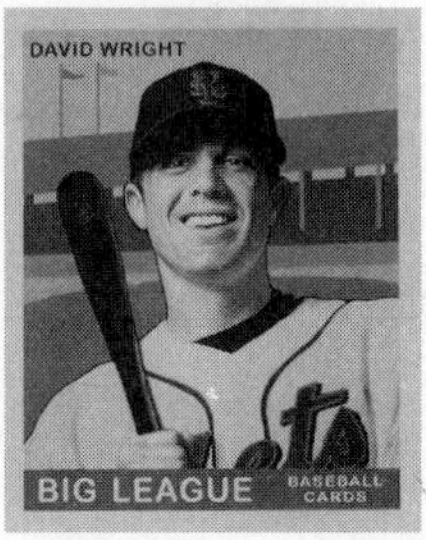
DAVID WRIGHT
BIG LEAGUE
BASEBALL CARDS

NM/M

Complete Set (288):
Common Player (1-200): .15
Common SP (201-240): 1.50
Inserted 1:6
Common Heads Up (241-288): 2.00
Inserted 1:10
Hobby Pack (8): 4.00
Hobby Box (24): 80.00

1	A.J. Burnett	.25
2	Aaron Boone	.15
3	Aaron Rowand	.25
4	Adam Dunn	.50
5	Adrian Beltre	.25
6	Albert Pujols	2.00
7	Ivan Rodriguez	.50
8	Alfonso Soriano	.75
9	Andruw Jones	.50
10	Andy Pettitte	.50
11	Aramis Ramirez	.40
12	B.J. Upton	.25
13	Barry Zito	.25
14	Bartolo Colon	.15
15	Ben Sheets	.25
16	Bobby Abreu	.25
17	Bobby Crosby	.15
18	Brian Giles	.15
19	Brian Roberts	.25
20	C.C. Sabathia	.40
21	Carlos Beltran	.75
22	Carlos Delgado	.50
23	Carlos Lee	.25
24	Carlos Zambrano	.25
25	Chad Cordero	.15
26	Chad Tracy	.15
27	Chipper Jones	.75
28	Craig Biggio	.25
29	Curt Schilling	.50
30	Danny Haren	.25
31	Darin Erstad	.15
32	David Ortiz	.75
33	Billy Wagner	.15
34	Derek Jeter	2.00
35	Derek Lee	.50
36	Dontrelle Willis	.25
37	Edgar Renteria	.25
38	Eric Chavez	.25
39	Felix Hernandez	.25
40	Garret Anderson	.25
41	Garrett Atkins	.25
42	Gary Sheffield	.50
43	Grady Sizemore	.75
44	Greg Maddux	1.50
45	Hank Blalock	.25
46	Hanley Ramirez	.75
47	J.D. Drew	.25
48	Jacque Jones	.15
49	Jake Peavy	.40
50	Jake Westbrook	.15
51	Jason Bay	.25
52	Jason Giambi	.50
53	Jason Schmidt	.25
54	Jason Varitek	.40
55	Troy Tulowitzki	.40
56	Jeff Francoeur	.40
57	Jeff Kent	.25
58	Jeremy Bonderman	.25
59	Jim Edmonds	.25
60	Jim Thome	.50
61	Jimmy Rollins	.50
62	Joe Mauer	.25
63	Johan Santana	.75
64	John Smoltz	.40
65	Johnny Damon	.75
66	Jose Reyes	.75
67	Josh Beckett	.40
68	Justin Morneau	.50
69	Ken Griffey Jr.	1.50
70	Kerry Wood	.15
71	Khalil Greene	.25
72	Lance Berkman	.25
73	Livan Hernandez	.15
74	Manny Ramirez	.75
75	Mark Mulder	.25
76	Chase Utley	.75
77	Mark Teixeira	.50
78	Miguel Tejada	.40
79	Miguel Cabrera	.75
80	Mike Piazza	.75
81	Pat Burrell	.25
82	Paul LoDuca	.15
83	Pedro Martinez	.75
84	Prince Fielder	1.00
85	Rafael Furcal	.25
86	Randy Johnson	.75
87	Richie Sexson	.25
88	Robinson Cano	.75
89	Roy Halladay	.40
90	Roy Oswalt	.40
91	Scott Rolen	.50
92	Tim Hudson	.25
93	Todd Helton	.50
94	Tom Glavine	.50
95	Torii Hunter	.40
96	Travis Hafner	.40
97	Trevor Hoffman	.25
98	Vernon Wells	.40
99	Vladimir Guerrero	.75
100	Zachary Duke	.15
101	Alex Rodriguez	2.00
102	Ryan Howard	1.00
103	Michael Barrett	.15
104	Ichiro Suzuki	1.50
105	Hideki Matsui	1.50
106	Jered Weaver	.40
107	Dan Uggla	.25
108	Ryan Freel	.15
109	Bill Hall	.25
110	Ray Durham	.15
111	Morgan Ensberg	.15
112	Shawn Green	.25
113	Brandon Webb	.40
114	Frank Thomas	.75
115	Corey Patterson	.15
116	Edwin Encarnacion	.15
117	Mike Cameron	.15
118	Matt Holliday	.40
119	Jhonny Peralta	.25
120	Nick Swisher	.25
121	Brad Penny	.15
122	Kenji Johjima	.25
123	Francisco Rodriguez	.15
124	Mark Teahen	.15
125	Jonathan Papelbon	.50
126	Carlos Guillen	.15
127	Freddy Sanchez	.15
128	Chien-Ming Wang	.75
129	Andre Ethier	.15
130	Matt Cain	.25
131	Austin Kearns	.15
132	Ramon Hernandez	.15
133	Chris Carpenter	.40
134	Michael Cuddyer	.15
135	Stephen Drew	.25
136	David Wright	.75
137	David DeJesus	.15
138	Gary Matthews	.15
139	Brandon Phillips	.15
140	Josh Barfield	.15
141	Alex Gordon	1.00
142	Scott Kazmir	.15
143	Luis Gonzalez	.15
144	Mike Sweeney	.15
145	Luis Castillo	.15
146	Huston Street	.15
147	Phil Hughes	1.00
148	Adrian Gonzalez	.25
149	Raul Ibanez	.15
150	Joe Crede	.15
151	Mark Loretta	.15
152	Adam LaRoche	.25
153	Troy Glaus	.40
154	Conor Jackson	.15
155	Michael Young	.25
156	Scott Podsednik	.15
157	David Eckstein	.15
158	Mike Jacobs	.15
159	Nomar Garciaparra	.75
160	Mariano Rivera	.50
161	Pedro Feliz	.15
162	Josh Hamilton	.15
163	Ryan Langerhans	.15
164	Willy Taveras	.15
165	Carl Crawford	.25
166	Melvin Mora	.15
167	Francisco Liriano	.25
168	Orlando Cabrera	.25
169	Chris Duncan	.15
170	Johnny Estrada	.15
171	Ryan Zimmerman	.50
172	Rickie Weeks	.25
173	Paul Konerko	.40
174	Jack Wilson	.15
175	Jorge Posada	.40
176	Maggio Ordonez	.25
177	Nick Johnson	.15
178	Geoff Jenkins	.15
179	Reggie Sanders	.15
180	Moises Alou	.25
181	Glen Perkins	.15
182	Brad Lidge	.15
183	Kevin Kouzmanoff	.15
184	Jorge Cantu	.15
185	Carlos Quentin	.15
186	Rich Harden	.15
187	Jose Vidro	.15
188	Aaron Harang	.15
189	Noah Lowry	.15
190	Jermaine Dye	.25
191	Victor Martinez	.25
192	Chone Figgins	.25
193	Aubrey Huff	.15
194	Jason Isringhausen	.15
195	Brian McCann	.40
196	Juan Pierre	.15
197	Delmon Young	.50
198	Felipe Lopez	.15
199	Brad Hawpe	.15
200	Justin Verlander	.40
201	Mike Schmidt	3.00
202	Nolan Ryan	4.00
203	Cal Ripken Jr.	4.00
204	Harmon Killebrew	3.00
205	Reggie Jackson	2.00
206	Johnny Bench	2.00
207	Carlton Fisk	2.00
208	Yogi Berra	3.00
209	Al Kaline	3.00
210	Alan Trammell	1.50
211	Bill Mazeroski	2.00
212	Bob Gibson	2.00
213	Brooks Robinson	3.00
214	Carl Yastrzemski	3.00
215	Don Mattingly	3.00
216	Fergie Jenkins	1.50
217	Jim Rice	1.50
218	Lou Brock	2.00
219	Rod Carew	2.00
220	Stan Musial	3.00
221	Tom Seaver	3.00
222	Tony Gwynn	3.00
223	Wade Boggs	2.00
224	Alex Rodriguez	4.00
225	David Wright	3.00
226	Ryan Howard	3.00
227	Ichiro Suzuki	3.00
228	Ken Griffey Jr.	3.00
229	Daisuke Matsuzaka	4.00
230	Kei Igawa	1.50
231	Akinori Iwamura	2.00
232	Derek Jeter	4.00
233	Albert Pujols	4.00
234	Greg Maddux	3.00
235	David Ortiz	3.00
236	Manny Ramirez	2.00
237	Johan Santana	2.00
238	Pedro Martinez	2.00
239	Roger Clemens	4.00
240	Vladimir Guerrero	2.00
241	Ken Griffey Jr.	4.00
242	Derek Jeter	5.00
243	Ichiro Suzuki	4.00
244	Cal Ripken Jr.	5.00
245	Daisuke Matsuzaka	5.00
246	Kei Igawa	2.00
247	Joe Mauer	2.00
248	Babe Ruth	5.00
249	Johnny Bench	3.00
250	Reggie Jackson	3.00
251	Carlton Fisk	3.00
252	Albert Pujols	5.00
253	Nolan Ryan	5.00
254	Ryan Howard	4.00
255	Mike Schmidt	4.00
256	Brooks Robinson	4.00
257	Harmon Killebrew	4.00
258	Alex Rodriguez	5.00
259	David Ortiz	4.00
260	David Wright	4.00
261	Al Kaline	4.00
262	Justin Verlander	3.00
263	Chase Utley	4.00
264	Justin Morneau	3.00
265	Ken Griffey Jr.	4.00
266	Derek Jeter	5.00
267	Ichiro Suzuki	4.00
268	Cal Ripken Jr.	5.00
269	Daisuke Matsuzaka	5.00
270	Kei Igawa	2.00
271	Joe Mauer	2.00
272	Babe Ruth	5.00
273	Johnny Bench	3.00
274	Reggie Jackson	3.00
275	Carlton Fisk	3.00
276	Albert Pujols	5.00
277	Nolan Ryan	5.00
278	Ryan Howard	4.00
279	Mike Schmidt	4.00
280	Brooks Robinson	4.00
281	Harmon Killebrew	4.00
282	Alex Rodriguez	5.00
283	David Ortiz	4.00
284	David Wright	4.00
285	Al Kaline	4.00
286	Justin Verlander	3.00
287	Chase Utley	4.00
288	Justin Morneau	3.00

Graphs

		NM/M
	Common Autograph:	5.00
AC	Alberto Callaspo	10.00
AH	Aaron Harang	15.00
AK	Al Kaline/SP	150.00
AM	Andy Marte	8.00
AR	Aaron Rowand	15.00
BA	Brian Anderson	5.00
BB	Brian Bannister	10.00
BE	Johnny Bench/SP	150.00
BO	Boof Bonser	10.00
BU	B.J. Upton	15.00
CC	Carl Crawford	10.00
CF	Carlton Fisk/SP	50.00
CL	Cliff Lee	10.00
CO	Coco Crisp	15.00
CR	Cal Ripken Jr./SP	150.00
CY	Chris Young	15.00
DJ	Derek Jeter	150.00
FH	Felix Hernandez	30.00
GA	Garrett Atkins	10.00
GP	Glen Perkins	5.00
HA	Bill Hall	10.00
HI	Rich Hill	15.00
HR	Hanley Ramirez	25.00
JB	Jason Bay	10.00
JW	Jered Weaver	15.00
JZ	Joel Zumaya	15.00
KG	Ken Griffey Jr./SP	100.00
KJ	Kelly Johnson	15.00
KK	Kevin Kouzmanoff	15.00
LS	Luke Scott	8.00
MO	Justin Morneau	25.00
MS	Mike Schmidt/SP	80.00
RA	Reggie Abercrombie	8.00
RT	Ryan Theriot	25.00
RZ	Ryan Zimmerman	20.00
SA	Anibal Sanchez	5.00
SK	Scott Kazmir	15.00
TB	Taylor Buchholz	8.00
VM	Victor Martinez	15.00
YB	Yogi Berra/SP	75.00

Immortals Memorabilia

Inserted 1:288
No Pricing

Memorabilia

		NM/M
	Common Player:	4.00
1	A.J. Burnett	4.00
2	Aaron Boone SP	
3	Aaron Rowand	4.00
4	Adam Dunn	8.00
5	Adrian Beltre	6.00
6	Albert Pujols	20.00
7	Ivan Rodriguez	8.00
8	Alfonso Soriano	15.00
9	Andruw Jones	6.00
10	Andy Pettitte	8.00
11	Aramis Ramirez	8.00
12	B.J. Upton	6.00
13	Barry Zito	6.00
14	Bartolo Colon SP	
15	Ben Sheets	6.00
16	Bobby Abreu SP	6.00
17	Bobby Crosby	4.00
18	Brian Giles	4.00
19	Brian Roberts	6.00
20	C.C. Sabathia	8.00
21	Carlos Beltran	8.00
22	Carlos Delgado	6.00
23	Carlos Lee	6.00
24	Carlos Zambrano	6.00
26	Chad Tracy	4.00
27	Chipper Jones	8.00
28	Craig Biggio	6.00
29	Curt Schilling	8.00
31	Darin Erstad	4.00
32	David Ortiz	10.00
33	Billy Wagner	6.00
34	Derek Jeter	20.00
35	Derrek Lee	8.00
36	Dontrelle Willis	6.00
37	Edgar Renteria	4.00
38	Eric Chavez	4.00
39	Felix Hernandez	8.00
40	Garret Anderson	4.00
41	Garrett Atkins	4.00
42	Gary Sheffield	8.00
43	Grady Sizemore	8.00
44	Greg Maddux	15.00
45	Hank Blalock	4.00
46	Hanley Ramirez	10.00
47	J.D. Drew	4.00
49	Jake Peavy	6.00
50	Jake Westbrook	4.00
51	Jason Bay	8.00
52	Jason Giambi	6.00
54	Jason Varitek	10.00
56	Jeff Francoeur	10.00
57	Jeff Kent	6.00
58	Jeremy Bonderman	6.00
59	Jim Edmonds	6.00
60	Jim Thome	6.00
61	Jimmy Rollins	8.00
62	Joe Mauer	8.00
63	Johan Santana	8.00
64	John Smoltz	6.00
66	Jose Reyes	20.00
67	Josh Beckett	8.00
68	Justin Morneau	8.00
69	Ken Griffey Jr.	15.00
70	Kerry Wood	6.00
71	Khalil Greene	4.00
72	Lance Berkman	6.00
73	Livan Hernandez	4.00
74	Manny Ramirez	8.00
75	Mark Mulder	4.00
76	Chase Utley	15.00
77	Mark Teixeira	8.00
78	Miguel Tejada	6.00
79	Miguel Cabrera	8.00
80	Mike Piazza	10.00
81	Pat Burrell	6.00
82	Paul LoDuca	4.00
83	Pedro Martinez	8.00
84	Prince Fielder	10.00
85	Rafael Furcal	6.00
86	Randy Johnson	6.00
87	Richie Sexson	6.00
88	Robinson Cano	8.00
89	Roy Halladay	8.00
90	Roy Oswalt	8.00
91	Scott Rolen	6.00
92	Tim Hudson	6.00
93	Todd Helton	8.00
94	Tom Glavine	8.00
95	Torii Hunter	6.00
96	Travis Hafner	6.00
97	Trevor Hoffman	6.00
98	Vernon Wells	6.00
99	Vladimir Guerrero	8.00
100	Zachary Duke	4.00

Sports Royalty

		NM/M
	Common Card:	2.00
AI	Akinori Iwamura	2.00
AP	Albert Pujols	8.00
AS	Alfonso Soriano	3.50
CC	Chris Carpenter	2.00
CR	Cal Ripken Jr.	15.00
DJ	Derek Jeter	8.00
DM	Daisuke Matsuzaka	8.00
DO	David Ortiz	6.00
DS	Dean Smith	3.00
ES	Emmitt Smith	5.00
GH	Gordie Howe	10.00
GM	Greg Maddux	5.00
HI	Martina Hingis	3.00
HR	Hanley Ramirez	3.00
JM	Justin Morneau	3.00
JN	Joe Namath	5.00
JV	Justin Verlander	2.00
JW	John Wooden	2.00
KB	Kobe Bryant	4.00
KD	Kevin Durant	8.00
KG	Ken Griffey Jr.	8.00
KH	Katie Hoff	2.00
KI	Kei Igawa	2.00
LE	Jeanette Lee	2.00
LJ	LeBron James	10.00
LT	LaDainian Tomlinson	6.00
MH	Mia Hamm	5.00
MJ	Michael Jordan	15.00
NR	Nolan Ryan	15.00
PI	Mike Piazza	4.00
PM	Peyton Manning	8.00
RH	Roy Halladay	2.00
RJ	Randy Johnson	3.00
RL	Ryan Lochte	2.00
SA	Johan Santana	3.00
SC	Sidney Crosby	15.00
TH	Trevor Hoffman	2.00
TW	Tiger Woods	20.00
VG	Vladimir Guerrero	3.00

Sports Royalty Auto.

		NM/M
	Common Autograph:	25.00
AI	Akinori Iwamura	25.00
CR	Cal Ripken Jr.	250.00
DJ	Derek Jeter	175.00
DM	Daisuke Matsuzaka	200.00
DO	David Ortiz	75.00
GH	Gordie Howe	100.00
GM	Greg Maddux	160.00
HI	Martina Hingis	100.00
HR	Hanley Ramirez	30.00
JM	Justin Morneau	25.00
JV	Justin Verlander	60.00
JW	John Wooden	125.00
KG	Ken Griffey Jr.	100.00
KH	Katie Hoff	75.00
KI	Kei Igawa	30.00
LE	Jeanette Lee	150.00
LJ	LeBron James	300.00
LT	LaDainian Tomlinson	150.00
MH	Mia Hamm	125.00
RH	Roy Halladay	30.00
RL	Ryan Lochte	65.00
SC	Sidney Crosby	250.00
VG	Vladimir Guerrero	120.00

1933 Goudey Originals

Inserted 2:Case
See 1933 Goudey Pricing

1934-36 Diamond Stars

No Pricing

Production 15 Sets	
Autographs:	No Pricing
Production One Set	

1941 Double Play

No Pricing

Production 15 Sets	
Autographs:	No Pricing
Production One Set	

2007 Upper Deck Premier

		NM/M
	Common Player (1-200):	4.00
	Production 99 Sets	
	Common RC (201-244):	4.00
	Production 199 Sets	
	Box (1):	250.00
1	Roy Campanella	10.00
2	Ty Cobb	12.00
3	Mickey Cochrane	4.00
4	Dizzy Dean	8.00
5	Don Drysdale	6.00
6	Jimmie Foxx	10.00
7	Lou Gehrig	15.00
8	Lefty Grove	4.00
9	Rogers Hornsby	6.00
10	Walter Johnson	10.00
11	Eddie Mathews	4.00
12	Christy Mathewson	10.00
13	Johnny Mize	8.00
14	Thurman Munson	10.00
15	Mel Ott	8.00
16	Satchel Paige	10.00
17	Jackie Robinson	10.00
18	Babe Ruth	20.00
19	George Sisler	4.00
20	Honus Wagner	10.00
21	Cy Young	10.00
22	Luis Aparicio	4.00
23	Johnny Bench	10.00
24	Yogi Berra	10.00
25	Rod Carew	4.00
26	Orlando Cepeda	6.00
27	Bob Feller	8.00
28	Carlton Fisk	8.00
29	Bob Gibson	8.00
30	Jim "Catfish" Hunter	4.00
31	Reggie Jackson	8.00
32	Al Kaline	8.00
33	Harmon Killebrew	8.00
34	Buck Leonard	4.00
35	Juan Marichal	4.00
36	Bill Mazeroski	6.00
37	Willie McCovey	6.00
38	Joe Morgan	6.00
39	Eddie Murray	6.00
40	Jim Palmer	6.00
41	Tony Perez	6.00
42	Pee Wee Reese	4.00
43	Brooks Robinson	8.00
44	Nolan Ryan	20.00
45	Mike Schmidt	10.00
46	Tom Seaver	8.00
47	Enos Slaughter	4.00
48	Willie Stargell	6.00
49	Early Wynn	4.00
50	Robin Yount	8.00
51	Tony Gwynn	8.00
52	Cal Ripken Jr.	20.00
53	Ernie Banks	10.00
54	Wade Boggs	8.00
55	Steve Carlton	8.00
56	Will Clark	4.00
57	Fergie Jenkins	4.00
58	Bo Jackson	10.00
59	Don Mattingly	15.00
60	Stan Musial	8.00
61	Frank Robinson	8.00
62	Ryne Sandberg	8.00
63	Ozzie Smith	10.00
64	Carl Yastrzemski	10.00
65	Dave Winfield	8.00
66	Paul Molitor	8.00
67	Jason Bay	6.00
68	Freddy Sanchez	4.00
69	Josh Beckett	6.00
70	Carlos Beltran	6.00
71	Craig Biggio	6.00
72	Matt Holliday	6.00
73	A.J. Burnett	6.00
74	Miguel Cabrera	8.00
75	Dontrelle Willis	6.00
76	Chris Carpenter	8.00
77	Roger Clemens	15.00
78	Johnny Damon	8.00
79	Jermaine Dye	4.00
80	Jim Thome	8.00
81	Vladimir Guerrero	8.00
82	Travis Hafner	6.00
83	Victor Martinez	8.00
84	Trevor Hoffman	6.00
85	Derek Jeter	20.00
86	Ken Griffey Jr.	15.00
87	Randy Johnson	8.00
88	Andruw Jones	8.00
89	Derrek Lee	8.00
90	Greg Maddux	10.00
91	Magglio Ordonez	4.00
92	David Ortiz	10.00
93	Jake Peavy	6.00
94	Roy Oswalt	6.00
95	Mike Piazza	10.00
96	Jose Reyes	15.00
97	Ivan Rodriguez	8.00
98	Johan Santana	8.00
99	Scott Rolen	8.00
100	Curt Schilling	8.00
101	John Smoltz	6.00
102	Alfonso Soriano	8.00
103	Miguel Tejada	6.00
104	Frank Thomas	8.00
105	Chase Utley	10.00
106	Joe Mauer	8.00
107	Alex Rodriguez	20.00
108	Alex Rios	6.00
109	Justin Verlander	8.00
110	Ryan Howard	15.00
111	Jered Weaver	6.00
112	Francisco Liriano	6.00
113	David Wright	10.00
114	Felix Hernandez	8.00
115	Jeremy Sowers	4.00
116	Cole Hamels	8.00
117	B.J. Upton	6.00
118	Chien-Ming Wang	35.00
119	Justin Morneau	8.00
120	Jonny Gomes	6.00
121	Adrian Gonzalez	8.00
122	Bill Hall	6.00
123	Rich Harden	6.00
124	Rich Hill	4.00
125	Tadahito Iguchi	6.00
126	Scott Kazmir	4.00
127	Howie Kendrick	6.00
128	Dan Uggla	4.00
129	Hanley Ramirez	4.00
130	Josh Willingham	4.00
131	Nicholas Markakis	6.00
132	Grady Sizemore	6.00
133	Ian Kinsler	6.00
134	Jonathan Papelbon	6.00

135 Ryan Zimmerman 8.00
136 Stephen Drew 8.00
137 Adam Wainwright 4.00
138 Joel Zumaya 6.00
139 Prince Fielder 10.00
140 Carl Crawford 6.00
141 Huston Street 4.00
142 Matt Cain 8.00
143 Andre Ethier 6.00
144 Brian McCann 4.00
145 Josh Barfield 4.00
146 Anibal Sanchez 4.00
147 Brian Roberts 6.00
148 Brandon Webb 6.00
149 Chipper Jones 10.00
150 Tim Hudson 4.00
151 Adam LaRoche 4.00
152 Jeff Francoeur 8.00
153 Marcus Giles 4.00
154 Jason Varitek 8.00
155 Coco Crisp 4.00
156 Manny Ramirez 8.00
157 Trot Nixon 4.00
158 Carlos Zambrano 6.00
159 Mark Prior 6.00
160 Aramis Ramirez 6.00
161 Mark Buehrle 4.00
162 Paul Konerko 6.00
163 Adam Dunn 8.00
164 C.C. Sabathia 6.00
165 Todd Helton 8.00
166 Garrett Atkins 4.00
167 Jeremy Bonderman 6.00
168 Curtis Granderson 4.00
169 Sean Casey 4.00
170 Lance Berkman 6.00
171 Brad Lidge 4.00
172 Reggie Sanders 4.00
173 Brad Penny 4.00
174 Nomar Garciaparra 8.00
175 Jeff Kent 4.00
176 Chone Figgins 4.00
177 Ben Sheets 6.00
178 Rickie Weeks 6.00
179 Joe Nathan 4.00
180 Torii Hunter 6.00
181 Carlos Delgado 8.00
182 Tom Glavine 6.00
183 Paul LoDuca 4.00
184 Mariano Rivera 8.00
185 Robinson Cano 8.00
186 Bobby Abreu 6.00
187 Hideki Matsui 10.00
188 Barry Zito 6.00
189 Eric Chavez 4.00
190 Jimmy Rollins 6.00
191 Khalil Greene 4.00
192 Brian Giles 4.00
193 Jason Schmidt 4.00
194 Ichiro Suzuki 30.00
195 David Eckstein 4.00
196 Jim Edmonds 6.00
197 Mark Teixeira 8.00
198 Michael Young 6.00
199 Vernon Wells 6.00
200 Roy Halladay 6.00
201 Delmon Young **(RC)** 8.00
202 Andrew Miller **RC** 20.00
203 Troy Tulowitzki **(RC)** 6.00
204 Jeff Fiorentino **(RC)** 4.00
205 David Murphy **(RC)** 4.00
206 Jeff Baker **(RC)** 4.00
207 Kevin Hooper **(RC)** 4.00
208 Kevin Kouzmanoff **(RC)** 6.00
209 Adam Lind **(RC)** 6.00
210 Mike Rabelo **RC** 6.00
212 Mitch Maier **RC** 4.00
213 Ryan Braun **(RC)** 4.00
214 Vinny Rottino **(RC)** 4.00
215 Drew Anderson **(RC)** 4.00
216 Alexi Casilla **RC** 6.00
217 Glen Perkins **(RC)** 4.00
218 Cesar Jimenez **RC** 4.00
219 Tim Gradoville **RC** 4.00
220 Shane Youman **RC** 4.00
221 Billy Sadler **(RC)** 4.00
222 Patrick Misch **(RC)** 4.00
223 Juan Salas **(RC)** 4.00
224 Beltran Perez **(RC)** 4.00
225 Hector Gimenez **(RC)** 4.00
226 Philip Humber **(RC)** 4.00
227 Eric Stults **RC** 8.00
228 Dennis Sarfate **(RC)** 4.00
229 Andy Cannizaro **RC** 4.00
230 Juan Morillo **(RC)** 6.00
231 Fred Lewis **(RC)** 4.00
232 Ryan Sweeney **(RC)** 4.00
233 Chris Narveson **(RC)** 4.00
234 Michael Bourn **(RC)** 4.00
235 Joaquin Arias **(RC)** 4.00
236 Carlos Maldonado **(RC)** 4.00
237 Alvin Colina **RC** 4.00
238 Jon Knott **(RC)** 4.00
239 Justin Hampson **(RC)** 4.00
240 Jeff Salazar **(RC)** 4.00
241 Josh Fields **(RC)** 4.00
242 Delwyn Young **(RC)** 4.00
243 Daisuke Matsuzaka **RC** 75.00
244 Kei Igawa **RC** 15.00

Bronze

Bronze (201-244): 1X
Production 75 Sets

Printing Plates

Production one set per color.

Gold

Gold (201-244): 1-1.5X
Production 49 Sets

Platinum

Production One Set

Silver

Silver (201-244): 1X
Production 99 Sets

Autograph Parallel

No Pricing
Production 25 Sets

Emerging Stars Dual Auto.

NM/M

Production 50 Sets
Bronze: 1-1.5X
Production 25 Sets
Gold: No Pricing
Production 10 Sets
Platinum: No Pricing
Production One Set
BU Josh Barfield, Dan Uggla 25.00
BV Jeremy Bonderman, Justin Verlander 50.00
CA Carlos Rios, Carl Crawford 30.00
FJ Felix Hernandez, Jered Weaver 50.00
GB Josh Barfield, Adrian Gonzalez 25.00
GC Carl Crawford, Jonny Gomes 25.00
HP Philip Humber, Mike Pelfrey 35.00
HS Huston Street, Rich Harden 30.00
HV Rich Harden, Justin Verlander 40.00
IK Tadahito Iguchi, Ian Kinsler 25.00
KL Francisco Liriano, Scott Kazmir 35.00
KS Scott Kazmir, Jeremy Sowers 25.00
LH Jon Lester, Craig Hansen 40.00
MB Jeremy Brown, Joe Mauer 35.00
MG Justin Morneau, Adrian Gonzalez 40.00
MH Andrew Miller, Cole Hamels 65.00
MZ Andrew Miller, Joel Zumaya 50.00
PH Jonathan Papelbon, Craig Hansen 50.00
PW Jonathan Papelbon, Adam Wainwright 50.00
QD Carlos Quentin, Stephen Drew 30.00
RB Rickie Weeks, Bill Hall 30.00
RD Jose Reyes, Stephen Drew 60.00
RR Hanley Ramirez, Jose Reyes 75.00
RY Alex Rios, Delmon Young 40.00
SH Jeremy Sowers, Cole Hamels 25.00
SJ Anibal Sanchez, Josh Johnson 20.00
SW Adam Wainwright, Huston Street 30.00
TD Stephen Drew, Troy Tulowitzki 30.00
TR Troy Tulowitzki, Hanley Ramirez 30.00
UG Jonny Gomes, B.J. Upton 25.00
UR Dan Uggla, Hanley Ramirez 30.00
UU Chase Utley, Dan Uggla 50.00
VH Felix Hernandez, Justin Verlander 75.00
VM Justin Verlander, Andrew Miller 75.00
WE Josh Willingham, Andre Ethier 25.00
WK Jered Weaver, Howie Kendrick 40.00
WL Jered Weaver, Francisco Liriano 50.00
YT Delmon Young, Troy Tulowitzki 40.00
ZW Joel Zumaya, Adam Wainwright 30.00

Emerging Stars Triple Auto

NM/M

Production 50 Sets
Bronze: 1-1.5X
Production 25 Sets
Gold: No Pricing
Production 10 Sets
Platinum: No Pricing
Production One Set
ELS James Loney, Andre Ethier, Takashi Saito 50.00
HHL Cole Hamels, Rich Hill, Francisco Liriano 75.00
HQE Carlos Quentin, Matt Holliday, Andre Ethier 40.00
KUK Howie Kendrick, Dan Uggla, Ian Kinsler 40.00
LBG Matt Garza, Francisco Liriano, Boof Bonser 50.00
MHL Francisco Liriano, Cole Hamels, Andrew Miller 80.00
MKL Jason Kubel, Francisco Liriano, Justin Morneau 40.00
MSK Scott Kazmir, Jeremy Sowers, Andrew Miller 40.00
MVB Andrew Miller, Justin Verlander, Jeremy Bonderman 100.00
MYE Andre Ethier, Nicholas Markakis, Delmon Young 70.00
PSW Adam Wainwright, Huston Street, Jonathan Papelbon 50.00
QEY Carlos Quentin, Delmon Young, Andre Ethier 40.00
RRD Hanley Ramirez, Stephen Drew, Jose Reyes 75.00
SHK Scott Kazmir, Jeremy Sowers, Cole Hamels 50.00
TDR Troy Tulowitzki, Stephen Drew, Hanley Ramirez 50.00
THA Matt Holliday, Garrett Atkins, Troy Tulowitzki 50.00
UKW Howie Kendrick, Chase Utley, Rickie Weeks 50.00
UUW Rickie Weeks, Chase Utley, Dan Uggla 40.00
UYK B.J. Upton, Scott Kazmir, Delmon Young 50.00
VMZ Justin Verlander, Joel Zumaya, Andrew Miller 80.00
WHV Jered Weaver, Justin Verlander, Felix Hernandez 85.00
WZS Adam Wainwright, Joel Zumaya, Takashi Saito 40.00
YER Alex Rios, Delmon Young, Andre Ethier 40.00

Hallmarks Autographs

NM/M

Production 5-57
Gold: No Pricing
Production 25 Sets
Platinum: No Pricing
Production One Set
LA Luis Aparicio/57 25.00
MS Mike Schmidt/48 40.00
OS Ozzie Smith/57 50.00
PM Paul Molitor/39 25.00
RJ Reggie Jackson/47 50.00
RS Ryne Sandberg/40 60.00
RY Robin Yount/46 40.00
SC Steve Carlton/27 35.00
WF Whitey Ford/25 50.00
WM Willie McCovey/45 30.00

Insignias Autographs

NM/M

Production 50 Sets
Gold: 1-1.5X
Production 25 Sets
Platinum: No Pricing
Production One Set
AK Al Kaline 35.00
AM Andrew Miller 60.00
BU B.J. Upton 25.00
CR Cal Ripken Jr. 100.00
DJ Derek Jeter 150.00
DL Derrek Lee 30.00
DM Don Mattingly 60.00
DY Delmon Young 25.00
EB Ernie Banks 50.00
FH Felix Hernandez 50.00
JM Joe Mauer 40.00
JP Jake Peavy 30.00
JR Jose Reyes 80.00
JT Jim Thome 50.00
JW Jered Weaver 30.00
KG Ken Griffey Jr. 90.00
MO Justin Morneau 30.00
OS Ozzie Smith 50.00
PA Jim Palmer 20.00
TG Tony Gwynn 40.00
TT Troy Tulowitzki 25.00
WC Will Clark 25.00

Noteworthy Autographs

NM/M

Production 1-86 15.00
Gold: No Pricing
Production 25 Sets
Platinum: No Pricing
Production One Set
AD Andre Dawson/50 50.00
AK Al Kaline/50 50.00
AS Alfonso Soriano/35 35.00
BA Jeff Bagwell/75 75.00
BE Josh Beckett/50 40.00
BJ Bo Jackson/35 75.00
BR Brooks Robinson/35 40.00
CB Craig Biggio/65 40.00
CC Chris Carpenter/50 40.00
DB Dusty Baker/25 30.00
DE Dennis Eckersley/75 15.00
DS Don Sutton/50 15.00
FJ Fergie Jenkins/74 15.00
FR Frank Robinson/31 40.00
GS Gary Sheffield/86 30.00
JB Jim Bunning/54 30.00
JC Jack Clark/75 15.00
JM Juan Marichal/65 25.00
JP Jim Palmer/65 20.00
JS Johan Santana/65 50.00
KW Kerry Wood/35 20.00
LA Luis Aparicio/35 15.00
MM Mark Mulder/35 15.00
MO Justin Morneau/50 30.00
MT Miguel Tejada/50 25.00
PE Jake Peavy/55 30.00
PM Paul Molitor/40 25.00
RS Ryne Sandberg/45 50.00
TG Tom Glavine/47 60.00
TH Torii Hunter/26 30.00
WB Wade Boggs/45 25.00
AP Albert Pujols/49 200.00
BF Bob Feller/62 30.00
CF Carlton Fisk/37 40.00
CR Cal Ripken Jr./34 125.00
DJ Derek Jeter/44 150.00
DM Don Mattingly/35 75.00
HR Hanley Ramirez/51 30.00
JB Johnny Bench/45 50.00
JM Joe Mauer/36 40.00
JT Jim Thome/52 40.00
JZ Joel Zumaya/62 15.00
KG Ken Griffey Jr./56 75.00
RY Robin Yount/29 50.00
TG Tony Gwynn/56 40.00

Foursomes

No Pricing
Production 15 Sets

Octographs

No Pricing
Production Five Sets

Pairings

NM/M

Production 25 Sets
AK Andruw Jones, Ken Griffey Jr. 125.00
BD Dave Winfield, Bo Jackson 75.00
BF Johnny Bench, Carlton Fisk 75.00
BJ Yogi Berra, Derek Jeter 250.00
BM Don Mattingly, Wade Boggs 120.00
BU Chase Utley, Craig Biggio 75.00
CG Chris Carpenter, Bob Gibson 50.00
CO Chris Carpenter, Roy Oswalt 60.00
CR Craig Biggio, Ryne Sandberg 100.00
ER Ernie Banks, Ryne Sandberg 150.00
FO Bob Feller, Roy Oswalt 125.00
GF Bob Feller, Bob Gibson 50.00
GR Cal Ripken Jr., Ken Griffey Jr. 250.00
JG Ken Griffey Jr., Derek Jeter 250.00
JW Dave Winfield, Reggie Jackson 75.00
MC Don Mattingly, Will Clark 80.00
MG Tony Gwynn, Stan Musial 125.00
MM Joe Mauer, Victor Martinez 50.00
MR Frank Robinson, Eddie Murray 75.00
OY Carl Yastrzemski, David Ortiz 125.00
PG Albert Pujols, Ken Griffey Jr. 250.00
RG Tony Gwynn, Cal Ripken Jr. 200.00
RJ Cal Ripken Jr., Derek Jeter 250.00
RN Roger Clemens, Nolan Ryan 275.00
RP Ivan Rodriguez, Mike Piazza 75.00
RR Cal Ripken Jr., Brooks Robinson 180.00
SA Luis Aparicio, Ozzie Smith 75.00
SB Brooks Robinson, Scott Rolen 60.00
SG Alfonso Soriano, Vladimir Guerrero 80.00
SM Ryne Sandberg, Joe Morgan 75.00
TM Willie McCovey, Jim Thome 60.00
UM Joe Morgan, Chase Utley
WC Dontrelle Willis, Miguel Cabrera 50.00
YM Paul Molitor, Robin Yount 80.00

Patches Dual

NM/M

Production 75 unless noted.
Platinum: No Pricing
Production 5-10
Masterpiece: No Pricing
Production One Set
Gold: .75-1X
Production 6-58
No pricing prod. 25 or less.
AD Adam Dunn 20.00
AP Albert Pujols 60.00
AS Alfonso Soriano 20.00
BU B.J. Upton 20.00
CH Cole Hamels 25.00
CR Cal Ripken Jr. 50.00
CU Chase Utley 25.00
DJ Derek Jeter 40.00
DJ2 Derek Jeter 40.00
DM Don Mattingly 35.00
ED Jim Edmonds 20.00
FL Francisco Liriano 15.00
GM Greg Maddux 30.00
IR Ivan Rodriguez 20.00
JB Johnny Bench 25.00

JG	Jason Giambi	15.00
JM	Joe Mauer	20.00
JO	Randy Johnson	20.00
JP	Jake Peavy	15.00
JR	Jose Reyes	40.00
JT	Jim Thome	20.00
JT2	Jim Thome	20.00
JV	Justin Verlander/42	25.00
JW	Jered Weaver	20.00
KG	Ken Griffey Jr.	40.00
KG2	Ken Griffey Jr.	40.00
KM	Kendry Morales	15.00
LB	Lance Berkman	15.00
MC	Miguel Cabrera	30.00
MR	Manny Ramirez	25.00
MS	Mike Schmidt	30.00
MT	Mark Teixeira	20.00
NR	Nolan Ryan	50.00
PF	Prince Fielder	30.00
PM	Pedro Martinez	30.00
RJ	Reggie Jackson	25.00
RS	Ryne Sandberg	40.00
RZ	Ryan Zimmerman	25.00
SA	Johan Santana	25.00
TE	Miguel Tejada	20.00
TG	Tony Gwynn	25.00
TO	Tom Glavine	30.00
VG	Vladimir Guerrero	25.00
VG2	Vladimir Guerrero	25.00

Patches Dual Auto.

NM/M

Production 25 Sets

AD	Adam Dunn	40.00
BR	Brooks Robinson	50.00
BU	B.J. Upton	40.00
CH	Cole Hamels	50.00
CR	Cal Ripken Jr.	180.00
DJ	Derek Jeter	200.00
DM	Don Mattingly	140.00
FL	Francisco Liriano	40.00
IR	Ivan Rodriguez	50.00
JB	Johnny Bench	60.00
KM	Kendry Morales	30.00
NR	Nolan Ryan	150.00
RJ	Reggie Jackson	75.00
RS	Ryne Sandberg	75.00

Patches Triple

NM/M

Production 1-99
Gold: .75-1X
Production 1-57
No pricing prod. 25 or less.
Platinum: No Pricing
Production Five Sets
Masterpiece: No Pricing
Production One Set

AJ	Andruw Jones/97	30.00
CC	Chris Carpenter/97	30.00
CD	Carlos Delgado/94	25.00
CJ	Chipper Jones/95	40.00
CL	Carlos Lee/99	20.00
CR	Cal Ripken Jr./82	60.00
CS	Curt Schilling/90	30.00
EM	Eddie Murray/77	30.00
FR	Frank Robinson/56	25.00
FT	Frank Thomas/90	30.00
GM	Greg Maddux/87	40.00
JT	Jim Thome/91	20.00
KG	Ken Griffey Jr./89	50.00
MR	Manny Ramirez/94	30.00
OS	Ozzie Smith/78	50.00
RJ	Randy Johnson/89	30.00
RO	Roy Halladay/99	25.00
TE	Miguel Tejada/98	20.00
TG	Tony Gwynn/82	40.00
TS	Tom Seaver/67	35.00
VG	Vladimir Guerrero/97	30.00
WB	Wade Boggs/82	30.00
JT2	Jim Thome/91	20.00
KG2	Ken Griffey Jr./89	50.00

Patches Triple Auto.

No Pricing
Production 15 Sets

Penmanship Autographs

NM/M

Production 1-98
Masterpiece: No Pricing
Production One Set

AK	Al Kaline/53	30.00
BF	Bob Feller/36	25.00
BJ	Bo Jackson/86	40.00
BR	Brooks Robinson/57	30.00
CB	Craig Biggio/88	50.00
CC	Chris Carpenter/97	40.00
CF	Carlton Fisk/72	25.00
CR	Cal Ripken Jr./82	100.00
CR2	Cal Ripken Jr./82	100.00
CY	Carl Yastrzemski/61	60.00
DJ	Derek Jeter/96	150.00
DJ2	Derek Jeter/96	150.00
DL	Derrek Lee/97	25.00
DM	Don Mattingly/83	50.00
DM2	Don Mattingly/83	50.00
EB	Ernie Banks/54	60.00
GM	Greg Maddux/87	80.00
IR	Ivan Rodriguez/91	40.00
JB	Johnny Bench/68	50.00
JI	Jim Palmer/65	25.00
JS	John Smoltz/88	75.00
JT	Jim Thome/91	40.00
KG	Ken Griffey Jr./89	75.00
KG2	Ken Griffey Jr./89	75.00
LA	Luis Aparicio/56	25.00
MS	Mike Schmidt/73	50.00
NR	Nolan Ryan/68	100.00
OZ	Ozzie Smith/78	50.00
PM	Paul Molitor/78	35.00
PM2	Paul Molitor/78	35.00
RA	Randy Johnson/89	50.00
RC	Roger Clemens/84	100.00
RJ	Reggie Jackson/68	65.00
RS	Ryne Sandberg/82	50.00
RY	Robin Yount/74	40.00
SC	Steve Carlton/67	25.00
SM	Stan Musial/42	60.00
SR	Scott Rolen/97	35.00
TE	Miguel Tejada/98	25.00
TG	Tony Gwynn/82	40.00
TG2	Tony Gwynn	40.00
TP	Tony Perez/65	30.00
VG	Vladimir Guerrero/97	60.00
WB	Wade Boggs/82	35.00
WC	Will Clark/86	25.00
WF	Whitey Ford/50	50.00
WM	Willie McCovey/59	40.00
YB	Yogi Berra/47	50.00

Penmanship Auto. Jersey Number

NM/M

Production 1-58

AM	Andrew Miller/50	60.00
CF	Carlton Fisk/27	40.00
CH	Cole Hamels/35	50.00
CZ	Carlos Zambrano/38	25.00
DL	Derrek Lee/25	35.00
DW	Dontrelle Willis/35	25.00
DY	Delmon Young/35	25.00
FH	Felix Hernandez/34	50.00
FL	Francisco Liriano/47	30.00
GM	Greg Maddux/36	100.00
JG	Jonny Gomes/31	20.00
JP	Jake Peavy/44	40.00
JS	John Smoltz/29	65.00
JV	Justin Verlander/35	50.00
JW	Jered Weaver/56	25.00
JZ	Joel Zumaya/54	30.00
MO	Justin Morneau/33	30.00
NR	Nolan Ryan/34	100.00
NS	Nick Swisher/33	30.00
PA	Jonathan Papelbon/58	50.00
PH	Philip Humber/49	20.00
RA	Randy Johnson/41	60.00
RO	Roy Oswalt/45	25.00
SA	Johan Santana/57	40.00
SC	Steve Carlton/32	25.00
SR	Scott Rolen/27	40.00
VG	Vladimir Guerrero/27	50.00
VM	Victor Martinez/41	25.00
WB	Wade Boggs/26	40.00
WM	Willie McCovey/44	40.00

Preeminence

NM/M

Production 50 Sets
Gold: 1-1.5X
Production 25 Sets
Platinum: No Pricing
Production One Set

AP	Albert Pujols	200.00
BJ	Bo Jackson	60.00
BR	Brooks Robinson	25.00
CC	Chris Carpenter	25.00
CR	Cal Ripken Jr.	120.00
CY	Carl Yastrzemski	50.00
DJ	Derek Jeter	150.00
GM	Greg Maddux	100.00
JB	Johnny Bench	50.00
JM	Joe Mauer	40.00
JT	Jim Thome	40.00
JV	Justin Verlander	50.00
KG	Ken Griffey Jr.	75.00
MS	Mike Schmidt	50.00
NR	Nolan Ryan	90.00
RC	Roger Clemens	100.00
RJ	Reggie Jackson	50.00
RS	Ryne Sandberg	60.00
SM	Stan Musial	60.00
TG	Tony Gwynn	40.00
VG	Vladimir Guerrero	50.00

Rare Patches Dual

NM/M

Production 50 Sets
Gold: 1-1.5X
Production 25 Sets
Platinum: No Pricing
Production 10 Sets
Masterpiece: No Pricing
Production One Set

BM	Joe Mauer, Johnny Bench	40.00
BR	Brian Roberts, Robinson Cano	25.00
BS	Anibal Sanchez, A.J. Burnett	20.00
CP	Jake Peavy, Chris Carpenter	30.00
CW	Miguel Cabrera, Dontrelle Willis	30.00
DB	Carlos Beltran, Carlos Delgado	30.00
DT	Miguel Tejada, Stephen Drew	25.00
ER	Scott Rolen, Jim Edmonds	40.00
FM	Justin Morneau, Prince Fielder	30.00
FW	Prince Fielder, Rickie Weeks	25.00
GP	Albert Pujols, Ken Griffey Jr.	75.00
HR	Trevor Hoffman, Mariano Rivera	40.00
HS	Jeremy Sowers, Cole Hamels	30.00
JG	Ken Griffey Jr., Derek Jeter	75.00
JJ	Andruw Jones, Chipper Jones	40.00
MG	Tom Glavine, Greg Maddux	70.00
MH	Travis Hafner, Victor Martinez	25.00
MJ	Derek Jeter, Don Mattingly	80.00
OT	Jim Thome, David Ortiz	35.00
PO	Roy Oswalt, Jake Peavy	25.00
PS	Curt Schilling, Jonathan Papelbon	50.00
RC	Roger Clemens, Nolan Ryan	80.00
RD	Derek Jeter, Reggie Jackson	50.00
RG	Cal Ripken Jr., Tony Gwynn	75.00
RJ	Roy Halladay, Johan Santana	40.00
RU	Jimmy Rollins, Chase Utley	50.00
SG	Alfonso Soriano, Vladimir Guerrero	40.00
SH	Johan Santana, Felix Hernandez	40.00
SM	Joe Morgan, Ryne Sandberg	50.00
TR	Miguel Tejada, Jose Reyes	40.00
TT	Jim Thome, Frank Thomas	40.00
UC	Carl Crawford, B.J. Upton	40.00
WJ	Josh Johnson, Dontrelle Willis	20.00
WL	Francisco Liriano, Jered Weaver	30.00
YM	Robin Yount, Paul Molitor	40.00
ZU	Ryan Zimmerman, B.J. Upton	30.00

Rare Patches Triple

NM/M

Production 25 Sets
Gold: No Pricing
Production 10 Sets
Platinum: No Pricing
Production Five Sets
Masterpiece: No Pricing
Production One Set

CRM	Nolan Ryan, Greg Maddux, Roger Clemens	125.00
MRM	Ivan Rodriguez, Victor Martinez, Joe Mauer	40.00
POG	Albert Pujols, David Ortiz, Vladimir Guerrero	80.00
RGM	Cal Ripken Jr., Tony Gwynn, Paul Molitor	100.00
SHK	Scott Kazmir, Jeremy Sowers, Cole Hamels	30.00
UWR	Chase Utley, Rickie Weeks, Brian Roberts	30.00
WLV	Francisco Liriano, Justin Verlander, Jered Weaver	50.00

Rare Remnants Quad

No Pricing
Production 25 Sets
Gold: No Pricing
Production 10 Sets
Platinum: No Pricing
Production Five Sets
Masterpiece: No Pricing
Production One Set

Rare Remnants Triple

NM/M

Production 50 Sets
Gold: 1-1.5X
Production 25 Sets
Platinum: No Pricing
Production 10 Sets
Masterpiece: No Pricing
Production One Set

BMP	Tony Perez, Joe Morgan, Johnny Bench	30.00
BZV	Jeremy Bonderman, Justin Verlander, Joel Zumaya	40.00
CBF	Brooks Robinson, Frank Robinson, Cal Ripken Jr.	50.00
CFY	Jimmie Foxx, Joe Cronin, Carl Yastrzemski	60.00
CMK	Ralph Kiner, Bill Mazeroski, Roberto Clemente	100.00
CPR	Chris Carpenter, Albert Pujols, Scott Rolen	40.00
DMP	Jorge Posada, Thurman Munson, Bill Dickey	50.00
DMR	Pedro Martinez, Carlos Delgado, Jose Reyes	40.00
DRB	Jose Reyes, Carlos Delgado, Carlos Beltran	40.00
FBM	Carlton Fisk, Thurman Munson, Johnny Bench	35.00
FGG	Hank Greenberg, Lou Gehrig, Jimmie Foxx	180.00
FMT	Justin Morneau, Mark Teixeira, Prince Fielder	25.00
GGJ	Andruw Jones, Ken Griffey Jr., Vladimir Guerrero	40.00
JCM	Greg Maddux, Randy Johnson, Roger Clemens	40.00
JJR	Derek Jeter, Randy Johnson, Mariano Rivera	50.00
JMM	Thurman Munson, Don Mattingly, Reggie Jackson	75.00
KUC	B.J. Upton, Carl Crawford, Scott Kazmir	25.00
KVJ	Joe Mauer, Victor Martinez, Kenji Johjima	25.00
LMS	Joe Mauer, Francisco Liriano, Johan Santana	25.00
LSH	Francisco Liriano, Jeremy Sowers, Cole Hamels	25.00
OPS	Jake Peavy, Roy Oswalt, Ben Sheets	20.00
OTB	Lance Berkman, David Ortiz, Jim Thome	25.00
PJG	Derek Jeter, Ken Griffey Jr., Albert Pujols	50.00
PMH	Albert Pujols, Stan Musial, Rogers Hornsby	80.00
RCD	Nolan Ryan, Don Drysdale, Roger Clemens	50.00
RDG	Lou Gehrig, Joe DiMaggio, Babe Ruth	475.00
RFS	Bruce Sutter, Rollie Fingers, Mariano Rivera	25.00
RRR	Nolan Ryan	60.00
RWH	Nolan Ryan, Felix Hernandez, Jered Weaver	30.00
RYS	Robin Yount, Cal Ripken Jr., Ozzie Smith	40.00
SGA	Vladimir Guerrero, Bobby Abreu, Alfonso Soriano	25.00
SHM	Joe Morgan, Rogers Hornsby, Ryne Sandberg	50.00
SJZ	Randy Johnson, Barry Zito, Johan Santana	25.00
SRB	Brooks Robinson, Wade Boggs, Mike Schmidt	40.00
TJY	Miguel Tejada, Derek Jeter, Michael Young	30.00
TTH	Mark Teixeira, Jim Thome, Todd Helton	20.00
VWJ	Josh Johnson, Justin Verlander, Jered Weaver	25.00
YBM	Paul Molitor, Wade Boggs, Robin Yount	25.00

Remnants Triple Autograph

No Pricing
Production 25 Sets

Remnants Triple

NM/M

Production 75 Sets
Gold: .75-1.5X
Production 6-60
No pricing prod. 25 or less.
Platinum: No Pricing
Production 10 Sets
Masterpiece: No Pricing
Production One Set

AP	Albert Pujols	30.00
AP2	Albert Pujols	30.00
AS	Alfonso Soriano	15.00
BM	Bill Mazeroski	20.00
BR	Babe Ruth	400.00
CA	Roy Campanella	35.00
CF	Carlton Fisk	15.00
CJ	Chipper Jones	25.00
CL	Roger Clemens	25.00
CR	Cal Ripken Jr.	30.00
CS	Curt Schilling	15.00
CU	Chase Utley	25.00
CY	Carl Yastrzemski	25.00
DJ	Derek Jeter	30.00
DJ2	Derek Jeter	30.00
DM	Don Mattingly	40.00
DO	David Ortiz	25.00
EM	Eddie Mathews	30.00
FR	Frank Robinson	20.00
HO	Rogers Hornsby	80.00
JB	Johnny Bench	20.00
JD	Joe DiMaggio	125.00
JO	Jose Reyes	30.00
JR	Jackie Robinson	75.00
JT	Jim Thome	15.00
KG	Ken Griffey Jr.	25.00
KG2	Ken Griffey Jr.	25.00
MO	Mel Ott	50.00
MR	Manny Ramirez	15.00
MS	Mike Schmidt	25.00
NR	Nolan Ryan	40.00
PM	Paul Molitor	15.00
PR	Pee Wee Reese	25.00
RC	Roberto Clemente	75.00
RJ	Reggie Jackson	30.00
RO	Brooks Robinson	15.00
RS	Ryne Sandberg	25.00
RY	Robin Yount	25.00
SM	Stan Musial	30.00
TG	Tony Gwynn	20.00

TM	Thurman Munson	35.00
VG	Vladimir Guerrero	15.00

Remnants Quad

NM/M

Production 1-96		
Gold:		.75-1.5X
Production 2-57		
No pricing prod. 25 or less.		
Platinum:		No Pricing
Production Five Sets		
Masterpiece:		No Pricing
Production One Set		
AK	Al Kaline/53	35.00
BM	Bill Mazeroski/56	30.00
CL	Roberto Clemente/55	120.00
CR	Cal Ripken Jr./82	50.00
CY	Carl Yastrzemski/61	30.00
DJ	Derek Jeter/96	50.00
DM	Don Mattingly/83	35.00
EM	Eddie Mathews/52	40.00
HK	Harmon Killebrew/55	40.00
JB	Johnny Bench/68	25.00
JD	Joe DiMaggio/36	125.00
JF	Jimmie Foxx/27	100.00
JR	Jackie Robinson/47	100.00
JT	Jim Thome/91	15.00
KG	Ken Griffey Jr./89	30.00
LG	Lou Gehrig/25	400.00
MI	Johnny Mize/36	40.00
MS	Mike Schmidt/73	30.00
NR	Nolan Ryan/68	60.00
RC	Roger Clemens/84	30.00
RJ	Reggie Jackson/68	25.00
RN	Brooks Robinson/57	25.00
RO	Roy Campanella/48	25.00
SM	Stan Musial/42	50.00
TM	Thurman Munson/70	40.00

Remnants Quad Autograph

Production 15 Sets
No Pricing

Six

Production 10 Sets
No Pricing

Stitchings

NM/M

Production 50 Sets		
Stitchings 35:		1X
Production 35 Sets		
1	Babe Ruth	40.00
2	Babe Ruth	40.00
3	Babe Ruth	40.00
4	Ty Cobb	25.00
5	Ty Cobb	25.00
6	Lou Gehrig	30.00
7	Lou Gehrig	30.00
8	Joe DiMaggio	30.00
9	Joe DiMaggio	30.00
12	Roberto Clemente	30.00
13	Roberto Clemente	30.00
14	Jackie Robinson	30.00
15	Jackie Robinson	30.00
16	Cy Young	15.00
17	Cy Young	15.00
18	Nolan Ryan	30.00
19	Nolan Ryan	30.00
20	Reggie Jackson	15.00
21	Reggie Jackson	15.00
22	Ken Griffey Jr.	25.00
23	Ken Griffey Jr.	25.00
24	Derek Jeter	30.00
25	Derek Jeter	30.00
26	Jimmie Foxx	20.00
27	Jimmie Foxx	20.00
28	Rogers Hornsby	25.00
30	Walter Johnson	25.00
31	Walter Johnson	25.00
32	Ernie Banks	25.00
33	Ernie Banks	25.00
34	Christy Mathewson	15.00
35	Johnny Mize	15.00
36	Thurman Munson	25.00
37	Thurman Munson	25.00
38	Mel Ott	15.00
39	Satchel Paige	20.00
40	George Sisler	15.00
41	Casey Stengel	15.00
42	Honus Wagner	25.00
43	Honus Wagner	25.00
44	Roy Campanella	20.00
45	Mickey Cochrane	15.00
46	Dizzy Dean	15.00
47	Don Drysdale	15.00
48	Lefty Grove	15.00
49	Roger Clemens	25.00
50	Roger Clemens	25.00
51	Cal Ripken Jr.	40.00
52	Cal Ripken Jr.	40.00
53	Tony Gwynn	20.00
54	Tony Gwynn	20.00
55	Johnny Bench	20.00
56	Yogi Berra	20.00
57	Carlton Fisk	15.00
58	Joe Morgan	15.00
59	Brooks Robinson	15.00
60	Mike Schmidt	20.00
61	Willie Stargell	20.00
62	Tom Seaver	20.00
63	Ozzie Smith	25.00
64	Albert Pujols	30.00
65	Albert Pujols	30.00
66	Ryan Howard	20.00
67	David Ortiz	20.00
68	Randy Johnson	25.00
69	Greg Maddux	20.00
70	Greg Maddux	20.00
71	Johan Santana	15.00
72	Al Kaline	15.00
73	Ryne Sandberg	20.00
74	Robin Yount	20.00
75	Frank Robinson	15.00
76	Frank Robinson	15.00
78	Stan Musial	30.00
79	Carl Yastrzemski	20.00
80	Don Mattingly	30.00
81	Ichiro Suzuki	30.00
82	Yogi Berra	15.00
83	Carlton Fisk, Johnny Bench	20.00
84	Johnny Bench, Thurman Munson	25.00
85	Babe Ruth, Lou Gehrig	30.00
86	Yogi Berra, Whitey Ford	20.00
87	Yogi Berra, Don Larsen	20.00
88	Dennis Eckersley, Kirk Gibson	15.00
90	Pee Wee Reese, Jackie Robinson	20.00
91	Jackie Robinson, Satchel Paige	25.00
92	Lou Gehrig, Cal Ripken Jr.	30.00
93	George Sisler, Ichiro Suzuki	30.00
94	Steve Carlton, Roger Clemens, Randy Johnson, Nolan Ryan	40.00
95	Dave Concepcion, Tony Perez, Johnny Bench, Joe Morgan	25.00
96	Babe Ruth, Jimmie Foxx, Mel Ott, Eddie Mathews	40.00
97	Roger Clemens, Greg Maddux, Tom Seaver, Nolan Ryan	40.00
98	Roberto Clemente, Tony Gwynn, Stan Musial, Cal Ripken Jr.	40.00
DM	Daisuke Matsuzaka	60.00
KI	Kei Igawa	25.00
MI	Daisuke Matsuzaka, Kei Igawa	50.00

Stitchings Autograph

No Pricing
Production 25 Sets

Stitchings Cuts

Production One Set
No Pricing

Trios Autographs

No Pricing
Production 20 Sets

World Series Ticket

Production One
No Pricing

2007 Upper Deck Spectrum

NM/M

Complete Set (149):		
Common Player (1-100):		.25
Common Auto. (101-149):		8.00
Pack (5):		5.00
Box (20):		80.00
1	Miguel Tejada	.50
2	Brian Roberts	.40
3	Melvin Mora	.25
4	David Ortiz	1.00
5	Manny Ramirez	.75
6	Jason Varitek	.50
7	Curt Schilling	.75
8	Jim Thome	.75
9	Paul Konerko	.40
10	Jermaine Dye	.40
11	Travis Hafner	.40
12	Victor Martinez	.40
13	Grady Sizemore	.50
14	C.C. Sabathia	.50
15	Ivan Rodriguez	.40
16	Magglio Ordonez	.40
17	Carlos Guillen	.40
18	Justin Verlander	.50
19	Shane Costa	.25
20	Emil Brown	.25
21	Mark Teahen	.25
22	Vladimir Guerrero	.75
23	Jered Weaver	.50
24	Juan Rivera	.25
25	Justin Morneau	.75
26	Joe Mauer	.50
27	Torii Hunter	.40
28	Johan Santana	.75
29	Derek Jeter	2.00
30	Alex Rodriguez	2.00
31	Johnny Damon	.75
32	Jason Giambi	.50
33	Frank Thomas	.50
34	Nick Swisher	.40
35	Eric Chavez	.40
36	Ichiro Suzuki	1.50
37	Raul Ibanez	.25
38	Richie Sexson	.40
39	Carl Crawford	.40
40	Rocco Baldelli	.40
41	Scott Kazmir	.40
42	Michael Young	.40
43	Mark Teixeira	.50
44	Carlos Lee	.50
45	Gary Matthews	.25
46	Vernon Wells	.40
47	Roy Halladay	.50
48	Lyle Overbay	.25
49	Brandon Webb	.50
50	Conor Jackson	.25
51	Stephen Drew	.50
52	Chipper Jones	.75
53	Andruw Jones	.50
54	Adam LaRoche	.25
55	John Smoltz	.50
56	Derrek Lee	.50
57	Aramis Ramirez	.50
58	Carlos Zambrano	.50
59	Ken Griffey Jr.	1.50
60	Adam Dunn	.50
61	Aaron Harang	.40
62	Todd Helton	.50
63	Matt Holliday	.50
64	Garrett Atkins	.40
65	Miguel Cabrera	.75
66	Hanley Ramirez	.50
67	Dontrelle Willis	.25
68	Lance Berkman	.50
69	Roy Oswalt	.50
70	Roger Clemens	1.50
71	J.D. Drew	.40
72	Nomar Garciaparra	.75
73	Rafael Furcal	.40
74	Jeff Kent	.40
75	Prince Fielder	1.00
76	Bill Hall	.40
77	Rickie Weeks	.40
78	Jose Reyes	.75
79	David Wright	1.00
80	Carlos Delgado	.50
81	Carlos Beltran	.50
82	Ryan Howard	1.50
83	Chase Utley	.75
84	Jimmy Rollins	.75
85	Jason Bay	.40
86	Freddy Sanchez	.25
87	Zachary Duke	.25
88	Trevor Hoffman	.25
89	Adrian Gonzalez	.25
90	Mike Piazza	.75
91	Ray Durham	.25
92	Omar Vizquel	.25
93	Jason Schmidt	.40
94	Albert Pujols	2.00
95	Scott Rolen	.75
96	Jim Edmonds	.40
97	Chris Carpenter	.50
98	Alfonso Soriano	.75
99	Ryan Zimmerman	.75
100	Nick Johnson	.25
101	Adam Lind (RC)	10.00
102	Alexi Casilla/SP RC	30.00
103	Andrew Miller RC	25.00
104	Andy Cannizaro RC	8.00
105	Angel Sanchez/SP RC	15.00
106	Brian Stokes (RC)	8.00
107	Carlos Maldonado (RC)	8.00
108	Cesar Jimenez RC	8.00
109	Chris Stewart RC	8.00
111	David Murphy (RC)	10.00
112	Delmon Young/SP (RC)	20.00
113	Delwyn Young (RC)	8.00
114	Dennis Sarfate (RC)	8.00
116	Drew Anderson (RC)	8.00
117	Fred Lewis (RC)	10.00
118	Glen Perkins (RC)	8.00
119	Hector Gimenez (RC)	10.00
120	Jeff Baker (RC)	10.00
121	Jeff Fiorentino (RC)	8.00
122	Jeff Salazar (RC)	8.00
123	Joaquin Arias (RC)	8.00
124	Jon Knott (RC)	8.00
125	Juan Morillo RC	8.00
126	Juan Perez RC	8.00
127	Juan Salas (RC)	8.00
129	Justin Hampson (RC)	10.00
131	Kevin Hooper/SP (RC)	25.00
132	Kevin Kouzmanoff (RC)	15.00
133	Michael Bourn (RC)	15.00
134	Miguel Montero (RC)	8.00
135	Mike Rabelo/SP RC	25.00
136	Mitch Maier (RC)	8.00
138	Oswaldo Navarro/SP RC	15.00
139	Patrick Misch (RC)	10.00
140	Philip Humber (RC)	15.00
141	Ryan Braun (RC)	10.00
143	Ryan Sweeney (RC)	8.00
144	Scott Moore (RC)	8.00
145	Sean Henn SP (RC)	10.00
146	Shawn Riggans (RC)	10.00
148	Troy Tulowitzki (RC)	25.00
149	Ubaldo Jimenez (RC)	10.00

Gold

Stars (1-100):		5-10X
Production 99 Sets		

Red

Stars (1-100):		5-10X
Production 99 Sets		

Aligning the Stars

NM/M

Production 99 Sets		
BPO	David Ortiz, Lance Berkman, Albert Pujols	30.00
CJM	Roger Clemens, Greg Maddux, Randy Johnson	30.00
CRR	Scott Rolen, Aramis Ramirez, Miguel Cabrera	25.00
DBF	Lance Berkman, Prince Fielder, Carlos Delgado	15.00
GRS	Manny Ramirez, Gary Sheffield, Ken Griffey Jr.	35.00
HRW	Trevor Hoffman, Mariano Rivera, Billy Wagner	20.00
HTT	Travis Hafner, Frank Thomas, Jim Thome	20.00
JDB	Andruw Jones, Carlos Beltran, Adam Dunn	25.00
JGC	Jason Giambi, Derek Jeter, Robinson Cano	60.00
JTY	Derek Jeter, Miguel Tejada, Michael Young	30.00
LHP	Albert Pujols, Derrek Lee, Todd Helton	30.00
LVP	Francisco Liriano, Justin Verlander, Jonathan Papelbon	30.00
MKT	Mark Teixeira, Justin Morneau, Paul Konerko	20.00
MOW	Pedro Martinez, Roy Oswalt, Dontrelle Willis	20.00
RFR	Jose Reyes, Jimmy Rollins, Rafael Furcal	20.00
RMM	Ivan Rodriguez, Victor Martinez, Joe Mauer	20.00
RSV	Jason Varitek, Curt Schilling, Manny Ramirez	25.00
SBA	Carlos Beltran, Alfonso Soriano, Bobby Abreu	25.00
SCF	Carl Crawford, Grady Sizemore, Chone Figgins	20.00
SHS	Johan Santana, Roy Halladay, C.C. Sabathia	20.00
WGD	Vladimir Guerrero, Vernon Wells, Johnny Damon	20.00

Grand Slamarama

NM/M

Common Player:		10.00
AD	Adam Dunn	15.00
AP	Albert Pujols	50.00
AR	Alex Rodriguez	40.00
BA	Bobby Abreu	15.00
BG	Brian Giles	10.00
CD	Carlos Delgado	20.00
CJ	Chipper Jones	30.00
DA	Johnny Damon	25.00
DO	David Ortiz	30.00
DW	David Wright	40.00
HA	Travis Hafner	15.00
JD	Jermaine Dye	15.00
JM	Justin Morneau	20.00
JT	Jim Thome	25.00
KG	Ken Griffey Jr.	40.00
MR	Manny Ramirez	25.00
NG	Nomar Garciaparra	15.00
RH	Ryan Howard	40.00
RS	Richie Sexson	20.00
VG	Vladimir Guerrero	20.00

Jersey Number

Jersey # (25-57):		5-10X
No pricing production 1-24.		
Cards are #'d to jersey number.		

Ripken Road to the Hall

	NM/M
Common Ripken:	8.00
Production 99 Sets	
Autographs:	No Pricing
Production Five Sets	
CR1-100 Cal Ripken Jr.	8.00

Rookie Retrospectrum

	NM/M
Common Player:	.50
Red:	2-4X
Production 99 Sets	
AE	Andre Ethier	.50
AW	Adam Wainwright	1.00
BA	Josh Barfield	.50
BB	Boof Bonser	.50
BO	Jason Botts	.50
CA	Matt Capps	.50
CB	Chad Billingsley	.50
CD	Chris Demaria	.50
CF	Choo Freeman	.50
CH	Clay Hensley	.50
CQ	Carlos Quentin	.50
DE	Chris Denorfia	.50
DU	Dan Uggla	.50
FC	Fausto Carmona	.50
FL	Francisco Liriano	1.00
HA	Cole Hamels	1.00
HK	Howie Kendrick	1.00
HR	Hanley Ramirez	1.00
JA	Jeremy Accardo	.50
JB	Jason Bergmann	.50
JC	Jose Capellan	.50
JD	Joey Devine	.50
JH	Jeremy Hermida	.50
JK	Jason Kubel	.50
JL	Jon Lester	1.00
JP	Jonathan Papelbon	1.00
JV	Justin Verlander	1.00
JW	Jered Weaver	1.00
JZ	Joel Zumaya	1.00
KM	Kendry Morales	.50
LM	Lastings Milledge	1.00
MA	Nicholas Markakis	1.00
MC	Matt Cain	1.00
ME	Melky Cabrera	.50
MG	Matt Garza	1.00
MJ	Mike Jacobs	.50
MM	Matt Murton	.50
NM	Nate McLouth	.50
PF	Prince Fielder	1.00
RA	Reggie Abercrombie	.50
RG	Ryan Garko	.50
RM	Russell Martin	.50
RP	Ronny Paulino	.50
RS	Ryan Shealy	.50
RZ	Ryan Zimmerman	1.00
SD	Stephen Drew	.50
TB	Taylor Buchholz	.50
TG	Tony Gwynn Jr.	.50
TS	Takashi Saito	.50
WI	Josh Willingham	.50

Retrospectrum Signatures

	NM/M
Production 199 unless noted.	
BB	Boof Bonser	15.00
BO	Jason Botts	10.00
CA	Matt Capps/134	10.00
CD	Chris Demaria	8.00
CF	Choo Freeman	8.00
CH	Clay Hensley	10.00
CQ	Carlos Quentin	25.00
DU	Dan Uggla	15.00
FC	Fausto Carmona/158	10.00
FL	Francisco Liriano	25.00
HA	Cole Hamels/90	35.00
HK	Howie Kendrick	20.00
HR	Hanley Ramirez	25.00
JA	Jeremy Accardo/32	20.00
JC	Jose Capellan	6.00
JD	Joey Devine	8.00
JH	Jeremy Hermida	10.00
JK	Jason Kubel	12.00
JL	Jon Lester	20.00
JP	Jonathan Papelbon	40.00
JW	Jered Weaver/99	40.00
JZ	Joel Zumaya	20.00
KM	Kendry Morales	15.00
MG	Matt Garza	20.00
MJ	Mike Jacobs	20.00
MM	Matt Murton	20.00
RA	Reggie Abercrombie	8.00
RG	Ryan Garko	15.00
RM	Russell Martin	15.00
RS	Ryan Shealy	15.00
RZ	Ryan Zimmerman	30.00
SD	Stephen Drew	25.00
TB	Taylor Buchholz	10.00
TS	Takashi Saito	30.00
WI	Josh Willingham	15.00

Season Retrospectrum

	NM/M
Common Player:	.50
Red:	2-4X
Production 99 Sets	
AH	Aaron Harang	.50
AP	Albert Pujols	4.00
AR	Aramis Ramirez	1.00
AS	Alfonso Soriano	1.50
BA	Bobby Abreu	.50
BH	Bill Hall	.50
BL	Joe Blanton	.50
CA	Miguel Cabrera	1.50
CB	Carlos Beltran	1.00
CC	Chris Carpenter	1.00
CD	Carlos Delgado	1.00
CO	Jose Contreras	.50
CU	Chase Utley	1.50
CW	Chien-Ming Wang	1.50
CY	Chris Young	.50
CZ	Carlos Zambrano	1.00
DJ	Derek Jeter	4.00
DO	David Ortiz	1.50
FS	Freddy Sanchez	.50
FT	Frank Thomas	1.00
GM	Greg Maddux	2.50
GS	Grady Sizemore	1.50
HO	Trevor Hoffman	.50
HR	Hanley Ramirez	1.00
JB	Jason Bay	1.00
JC	Joe Crede	.50
JD	Johnny Damon	1.50
JM	Joe Mauer	1.00
JR	Jose Reyes	1.50
JS	Jeff Suppan	1.50
JT	Jim Thome	1.00
KG	Ken Griffey Jr.	3.00
MC	Michael Cuddyer	.50
MH	Matt Holliday	1.00
ML	Mark Loretta	.50
MO	Justin Morneau	1.50
MY	Michael Young	1.00
NG	Nomar Garciaparra	1.50
OR	Magglio Ordonez	.50
OV	Omar Vizquel	.50
RC	Roger Clemens	3.00
RF	Rafael Furcal	.50
RH	Ryan Howard	3.00
SA	Johan Santana	1.50
SK	Scott Kazmir	1.00
TH	Travis Hafner	1.00
TI	Tadahito Iguchi	.50
VG	Vladimir Guerrero	1.50
VW	Vernon Wells	.50
WT	Willy Taveras	.50

Retrospectrum Signatures

	NM/M
Production 25 unless noted.	
AH	Aaron Harang	
AR	Aramis Ramirez/3	
AS	Alfonso Soriano	75.00
BA	Bobby Abreu	40.00
BH	Bill Hall	20.00
BL	Joe Blanton	15.00
CA	Miguel Cabrera	50.00
CU	Chase Utley	65.00
CZ	Carlos Zambrano	35.00
DJ	Derek Jeter	180.00
DO	David Ortiz	80.00
FT	Frank Thomas	75.00
GM	Greg Maddux	150.00
HO	Trevor Hoffman	30.00
HR	Hanley Ramirez	25.00
JB	Jason Bay	30.00

JM	Joe Mauer	30.00
JR	Jose Reyes	
JT	Jim Thome	
KG	Ken Griffey Jr.	120.00
MH	Matt Holliday	35.00
ML	Mark Loretta	15.00
MO	Justin Morneau	30.00
RC	Roger Clemens	120.00
RF	Rafael Furcal	30.00
SA	Johan Santana	50.00
SK	Scott Kazmir	25.00
TH	Travis Hafner	40.00
TI	Tadahito Iguchi	40.00
VG	Vladimir Guerrero	60.00

Rookie Signatures Gold
Die-cut

	NM/M
Production 50 Sets	
101	Adam Lind	25.00
103	Andrew Miller	60.00
104	Andy Cannizaro	15.00
105	Angel Sanchez	15.00
106	Brian Stokes	15.00
109	Chris Stewart	15.00
111	David Murphy	20.00
112	Delmon Young	40.00
113	Delwyn Young	20.00
114	Dennis Sarfate	15.00
116	Drew Anderson	20.00
117	Fred Lewis	20.00
118	Glen Perkins	15.00
120	Jeff Baker	15.00
121	Jeff Fiorentino	15.00
122	Jeff Salazar	15.00
125	Jon Knott	15.00
128	Juan Morillo	15.00
131	Justin Hampson	15.00
132	Kevin Hooper	40.00
133	Kevin Kouzmanoff	25.00
134	Michael Bourn	25.00
137	Mitch Maier	15.00
139	Patrick Misch	15.00
140	Philip Humber	20.00
141	Ryan Braun	15.00
143	Ryan Sweeney	20.00
144	Scott Moore	15.00
145	Sean Henn	15.00
146	Shawn Riggans	15.00
148	Troy Tulowitzki	35.00
149	Ubaldo Jimenez	15.00

Shining Star Signatures

	NM/M
Production 15-99	
AD	Adam Dunn/99	25.00
AG	Adrian Gonzalez/99	15.00
AP	Albert Pujols/50	180.00
AR	Alex Rios/99	15.00
BH	Bill Hall/99	20.00
CJ	Conor Jackson/54	15.00
CZ	Carlos Zambrano/99	30.00
DJ	Derek Jeter/33	200.00
DL	Derrek Lee/99	30.00
DO	David Ortiz/99	60.00
GA	Garrett Atkins/99	15.00
HR	Hanley Ramirez/99	25.00
JB	Jason Bay/99	15.00
JM	Joe Mauer/99	25.00
JR	Jose Reyes/99	40.00
JS	Johan Santana/99	50.00
KG	Ken Griffey Jr./99	70.00
KY	Kevin Youkilis/99	20.00
MH	Matt Holliday/99	25.00
MO	Justin Morneau/99	25.00
RI	Juan Rivera/99	15.00
TH	Travis Hafner/72	20.00

Signature Patch

	NM/M
Production 6-25	
AG	Adrian Gonzalez/25	40.00
AS	Alfonso Soriano/25	65.00
BA	Bobby Abreu/25	50.00
BJ	B.J. Upton/25	30.00
BS	Ben Sheets/25	35.00
CR	Bobby Crosby/25	25.00
CZ	Carlos Zambrano/25	40.00
DJ	Derek Jeter/25	200.00
DL	Derrek Lee/25	40.00
DO	David Ortiz/25	100.00
DU	Dan Uggla/25	35.00
DW	Dontrelle Willis/25	40.00
GA	Garrett Atkins/25	30.00

Spectrum Swatches

Brian Giles/OF

	NM/M
Production 199 Sets	
Gold:	1X
Production 75 Sets	
Patch:	2-3X

Production 50 Sets

AB	Adrian Beltre	4.00
AG	Adrian Gonzalez	6.00
AH	Aaron Hill	4.00
AK	Austin Kearns	4.00
AP	Albert Pujols	25.00
AR	Aaron Rowand	4.00
AS	Alfonso Soriano	10.00
BA	Bobby Abreu	6.00
BC	Bartolo Colon	4.00
BG	Brian Giles	4.00
BI	Brandon Inge	4.00
BJ	B.J. Upton	6.00
BL	Joe Blanton	4.00
BR	B.J. Ryan	4.00
BS	Ben Sheets	6.00
BW	Billy Wagner	4.00
CA	Jorge Cantu	4.00
CB	Clint Barmes	4.00
CC	Chad Cordero	4.00
CD	Chris Duffy	4.00
CG	Carlos Guillen	4.00
CK	Casey Kotchman	4.00
CO	Coco Crisp	6.00
CR	Bobby Crosby	4.00
CS	C.C. Sabathia	6.00
CU	Chase Utley	15.00
CY	Chris Young	6.00
CZ	Carlos Zambrano	8.00
DA	Johnny Damon	10.00
DC	Daniel Cabrera	6.00
DH	Danny Haren	6.00
DJ	Derek Jeter	25.00
DL	Derrek Lee	8.00
DM	Dallas McPherson	4.00
DO	David Ortiz	15.00
DU	Dan Uggla	6.00
DW	Dontrelle Willis	6.00
ES	Johnny Estrada	6.00
FG	Freddy Garcia	4.00
FL	Francisco Liriano	10.00
FS	Freddy Sanchez	4.00
GA	Garrett Atkins	8.00
GC	Gustavo Chacin	4.00
GR	Curtis Granderson	8.00
GS	Grady Sizemore	10.00
HR	Hanley Ramirez	8.00
HS	Huston Street	6.00
HU	Aubrey Huff	4.00
IS	Ian Snell	4.00
JB	Jeremy Bonderman	10.00
JC	Joe Crede	4.00
JD	J.D. Drew	8.00
JE	Jermaine Dye	6.00
JF	Jeff Francoeur	8.00
JH	J.J. Hardy	6.00
JM	Joe Mauer	10.00
JN	Joe Nathan	6.00
JP	Jake Peavy	8.00
JR	Jose Reyes	15.00
JT	Jim Thome	8.00
JU	Jim Duchscherer	4.00
JW	Jake Westbrook	4.00
KG	Ken Griffey Jr.	25.00
KH	Khalil Greene	6.00
LN	Laynce Nix	4.00
MA	Matt Cain	8.00
MB	Mark Buehrle	6.00
MC	Mike Cameron	4.00
ME	Morgan Ensberg	4.00
MH	Matt Holliday	6.00
MI	Michael Cuddyer	4.00
MM	Melvin Mora	4.00
MO	Justin Morneau	10.00
MT	Miguel Tejada	8.00
NL	Noah Lowry	4.00
NS	Nick Swisher	6.00
OR	Magglio Ordonez	8.00
PA	Jonathan Papelbon	15.00
PE	Jhonny Peralta	6.00
PF	Prince Fielder	10.00
PL	Paul LoDuca	4.00
RA	Aramis Ramirez	8.00
RF	Rafael Furcal	8.00
RH	Rich Harden	8.00
RJ	Reed Johnson	4.00
RO	Brian Roberts	8.00
RQ	Robb Quinlan	4.00
RW	Rickie Weeks	8.00
RZ	Ryan Zimmerman	15.00
SC	Sean Casey	4.00
SK	Scott Kazmir	6.00
TH	Torii Hunter	6.00
TI	Tadahito Iguchi	6.00
TN	Trot Nixon	6.00
VM	Victor Martinez	6.00
WT	Willy Taveras	6.00
YM	Yadier Molina	6.00
ZD	Zachary Duke	6.00
ZG	Zack Greinke	4.00

Super Swatches

	NM/M
Production 50 Sets	
AD	Adam Dunn	10.00
AJ	Andruw Jones	15.00
AP	Albert Pujols	35.00
AR	Aramis Ramirez	10.00
BA	Bobby Abreu	10.00
BE	Josh Beckett	10.00
BU	B.J. Upton	10.00
BZ	Barry Zito	10.00
CB	Carlos Beltran	10.00
CC	Carl Crawford	10.00

CD Carlos Delgado 15.00
CJ Chipper Jones 15.00
CL Roger Clemens 25.00
CS Curt Schilling 15.00
CU Chase Utley 20.00
DA Johnny Damon 15.00
DJ Derek Jeter 35.00
DL Derrek Lee 15.00
DO David Ortiz 25.00
FT Frank Thomas 15.00
GS Gary Sheffield 15.00
HA Travis Hafner 10.00
HR Hanley Ramirez 10.00
JB Jeremy Bonderman 15.00
JD J.D. Drew 10.00
JR Jose Reyes 25.00
JS Johan Santana 15.00
JT Jim Thome 15.00
JV Jason Varitek 15.00
JW Jered Weaver 15.00
KG Ken Griffey Jr. 30.00
KJ Kenji Johjima 15.00
LB Lance Berkman 10.00
MT Miguel Tejada 10.00
PE Andy Pettitte 10.00
PF Prince Fielder 10.00
PK Paul Konerko 10.00
RB Rocco Baldelli 10.00
RC Robinson Cano 20.00
RH Roy Halladay 10.00
RJ Randy Johnson 15.00
RS Richie Sexson 10.00
SR Scott Rolen 15.00
TH Todd Helton 10.00
VE Justin Verlander 15.00
VG Vladimir Guerrero 15.00
VW Vernon Wells 10.00

2007 UD Black

NM/M

Common Jersey Auto. (1-42): 15.00
Production 16-75
Common RC Auto. (43-72): 25.00
Production 99
Pack (1): 80.00
Box (2): 150.00
1 Brandon Webb/75 25.00
2 Tim Hudson/75 30.00
3 Cal Ripken Jr./75 150.00
4 Nicholas Markakis/35 40.00
5 David Ortiz/52 100.00
6 Jonathan Papelbon/75 40.00
7 Coco Crisp/43 30.00
8 Derrek Lee/62 30.00
10 Adam Dunn/75 40.00
11 Ken Griffey Jr./75 80.00
12 Travis Hafner/52 60.00
13 Victor Martinez/75 40.00
14 Garrett Atkins/75 20.00
15 Justin Verlander/75 40.00
16 Jeremy Bonderman/75 25.00
17 Curtis Granderson/75 40.00
18 Hanley Ramirez/75 40.00
19 Dan Uggla/74 15.00
20 Lance Berkman/75 35.00
21 Mark Teahen/75 15.00
22 John Lackey/75 20.00
23 Howie Kendrick/75 30.00
25 Prince Fielder/75 50.00
26 Torii Hunter/75 25.00
27 Justin Morneau/75 40.00
28 John Maine/75 40.00
30 Danny Haren/75 25.00
31 Eric Chavez/64 25.00
32 Cole Hamels/75 30.00
33 Jason Bay/75 25.00
34 Adrian Gonzalez/75 20.00
35 Chris Young/75 30.00
36 Matt Cain/75 30.00
37 Felix Hernandez/75 60.00
38 Chris Duncan/75 30.00
39 B.J. Upton/75 30.00
40 Ian Kinsler/75 40.00
41 Roy Halladay/75 25.00
42 Chad Cordero/72 25.00
43 Adam Lind **(RC)** 25.00
44 Akinori Iwamura **RC** 100.00
45 Alex Gordon **RC** 120.00
46 Andy LaRoche **(RC)** 30.00
47 Billy Butler **(RC)** 50.00
48 David Murphy **(RC)** 30.00
49 Brandon Wood **(RC)** 40.00
50 Carlos Gomez **RC** 60.00
51 Chase Headley **(RC)** 30.00
52 Curtis Thigpen **(RC)** 25.00
53 Joba Chamberlain **RC** 300.00
54 Delmon Young **(RC)** 40.00
55 Felix Pie **(RC)** 40.00
56 Homer Bailey **(RC)** 40.00
57 Hunter Pence **(RC)** 100.00
58 Josh Hamilton **(RC)** 100.00
59 Kei Igawa **RC** 60.00
60 Kevin Slowey **(RC)** 30.00
61 Kurt Suzuki **(RC)** 40.00
62 Mark Reynolds **RC** 50.00
63 Daisuke Matsuzaka **RC** 450.00
64 Justin Upton **RC** 75.00
65 Phil Hughes **(RC)** 75.00
66 Ryan Braun **(RC)** 100.00
67 Ryan Sweeney **(RC)** 25.00
68 Sean Gallagher **(RC)** 25.00
69 Tim Lincecum **RC** 200.00
70 Travis Buck **(RC)** 25.00
71 Troy Tulowitzki **(RC)** 80.00
72 Yovani Gallardo **(RC)** 60.00

Printing Plates

No Pricing
Production one set per color.

Natural Pearl

No Pricing
Production One Set

Gold

No Pricing
Production 10 Sets

Pure White Pack Autographs

Production One Set

August - Auto. Patch

NM/M

Production 25 unless noted.
Gold: No Pricing
Production Five Sets
Pearl: No Pricing
Production One Set
BS Ben Sheets 30.00
BU B.J. Upton 40.00
CC Carl Crawford 40.00
CD Chris Duncan 40.00
CG Curtis Granderson 60.00
CH Cole Hamels 40.00
CO Chad Cordero 30.00
DL Derrek Lee 50.00
DW Dontrelle Willis 30.00
FH Felix Hernandez 80.00
FT Frank Thomas 125.00
GA Garrett Atkins 30.00
GR Khalil Greene 40.00
HR Hanley Ramirez 75.00
JM Justin Morneau 50.00
MH Matt Holliday 60.00
PK Paul Konerko 50.00
RH Roy Halladay 60.00
TH Travis Hafner 75.00
VM Victor Martinez 40.00

Exclusive - Eight Autos

Production Three Sets
Gold: No Pricing
Production Two Sets

Game Day - Box Score Autos

NM/M

Production 50 Sets
Gold: No Pricing
Production 10 Sets
AE Andre Ethier 25.00
AG Adrian Gonzalez 25.00
AH Aaron Harang 20.00
AI Akinori Iwamura 35.00
AL Adam LaRoche 15.00
AM Andrew Miller 30.00
AR Aaron Rowand 20.00
BA Bronson Arroyo 15.00
BB Billy Butler 30.00
BP Brandon Phillips 20.00
BS Ben Sheets 20.00
CC Coco Crisp 20.00
CG Curtis Granderson 40.00
CH Cole Hamels 30.00
DH Danny Haren 20.00
DW Dontrelle Willis 20.00
FC Fausto Carmona 25.00
FL Fred Lewis 15.00
GO Alex Gordon 40.00
JB Joe Blanton 15.00
JM John Maine 20.00
JN Joe Nathan 15.00
JV Justin Verlander 35.00
KG Ken Griffey Jr. 80.00
KI Kei Igawa 30.00
KJ Kelly Johnson 15.00
LI Francisco Liriano 25.00
MC Matt Cain 20.00
MM Melvin Mora 15.00
PH Phil Hughes 60.00
RB Ryan Braun 50.00
RZ Ryan Zimmerman 25.00
TB Travis Buck 15.00
TH Tim Hudson 30.00

Game Day - Lineup Card Autographs

NM/M

Production 50 Sets
Gold: No Pricing
Production 10 Sets
AE Andre Ethier 25.00
AG Alberto Gonzalez 25.00
AH Aaron Harang 20.00
AI Akinori Iwamura 35.00
AL Adam LaRoche 15.00
AM Andre Miller 30.00
AR Aaron Rowand 20.00
BA Bronson Arroyo 15.00
BB Billy Butler 30.00
BP Brandon Phillips 20.00
BS Ben Sheets 20.00
CC Coco Crisp 20.00
CG Curtis Granderson 40.00
CH Cole Hamels 30.00
DH Danny Haren 20.00
20 Dontrelle Willis 20.00
FC Fausto Carmona 25.00
FL Fred Lewis 15.00
GO Alex Gordon 40.00
JB Joe Blanton 15.00
JM John Maine 20.00
JN Joe Nathan 15.00
JV Justin Verlander 35.00
KG Ken Griffey Jr. 80.00
KI Kei Igawa 30.00
KJ Kelly Johnson 15.00
LI Francisco Liriano 25.00
MC Matt Cain 20.00
MM Melvin Mora 15.00
PH Phil Hughes 60.00
RB Ryan Braun 50.00
RZ Ryan Zimmerman 25.00
TB Travis Buck 15.00
TH Tim Hudson 30.00

Game Day - Ticket Autos

NM/M

Production 50 unless noted.
Gold: No Pricing
Production 10 Sets
AE Andre Ethier 25.00
AG Alberto Gonzalez 25.00
AH Aaron Harang 20.00
AI Akinori Iwamura 35.00
AL Adam LaRoche 15.00
AM Andre Miller 30.00
AR Aaron Rowand 20.00
BA Bronson Arroyo 15.00
BB Billy Butler 30.00
BP Brandon Phillips 20.00
BS Ben Sheets 20.00
CC Coco Crisp 20.00
CG Curtis Granderson 40.00
CH Cole Hamels 30.00
DH Danny Haren 20.00
20 Dontrelle Willis 20.00
FC Fausto Carmona 25.00
FL Fred Lewis 15.00
GO Alex Gordon 40.00
JB Joe Blanton 15.00
JN Joe Nathan 15.00
JV Justin Verlander 35.00
KG Ken Griffey Jr./15 80.00
KI Kei Igawa 30.00
KJ Kelly Johnson 15.00
LI Francisco Liriano 25.00
MC Matt Cain 20.00
MM Melvin Mora 15.00
PH Phil Hughes 60.00
RB Ryan Braun 50.00
RZ Ryan Zimmerman 25.00
TB Travis Buck 15.00
TH Tim Hudson 30.00

Illustrious - Dual Autographs

NM/M

Production 25 unless noted.
Gold: No Pricing
Production 15 Sets
BB Joe Blanton, Dallas Braden 20.00
BH Chase Headley, Ryan Braun 50.00
CK Austin Kearns, Chad Cordero 25.00
CL Matt Cain, Tim Lincecum 75.00
GB Alex Gordon, Billy Butler 50.00
GL Adam LaRoche, Tom Gorzelanny 20.00
HB Matt Holliday, Jeff Baker 25.00
HC Aaron Harang, Jon Coutlangus 25.00
HG Rich Hill, Sean Gallagher 25.00
HP Josh Hamilton, Brandon Phillips 20.00
KW Howie Kendrick, Brandon Wood 20.00
LL Adam LaRoche, Andy LaRoche 25.00
MF Victor Martinez, Ben Francisco 20.00
MM Melvin Mora, Nicholas Markakis 40.00
PS Kevin Slowey, Cal Ripken Jr. 25.00
SM John Maine, Ben Sheets 25.00
YI Delmon Young, Akinori Iwamura 35.00

Illustrious - Dual Materials Autographs

NM/M

Production 50 unless noted.
Patch: No Pricing
Production 15 Sets
CI Akinori Iwamura, Eric Chavez 30.00
CK Carl Crawford, Scott Kazmir 30.00
CP Coco Crisp, Jonathan Papelbon 40.00
GB Alex Gordon, Ryan Braun 180.00
GC Coco Crisp, Curtis Granderson 40.00
GY Adrian Gonzalez, Chris Young 25.00
HH Danny Haren, Rich Harden 25.00
HM John Maine, Aaron Harang 25.00
HW Dontrelle Willis, Jeremy Hermida 20.00
LC Matt Cain, Tim Lincecum 75.00
LK John Lackey, Howie Kendrick 30.00
LP Carlos Lee, Hunter Pence 60.00
MM Victor Martinez, Russell Martin 40.00
NH Torii Hunter, Joe Nathan 25.00
NM Melvin Mora, Nicholas Markakis 30.00
RG Brian Giles, Aaron Rowand 25.00
SB Huston Street, Joe Blanton 20.00
UW Josh Willingham, Dan Uggla 20.00
UY B.J. Upton, Delmon Young 30.00
ZB Jeremy Bonderman, Joel Zumaya 30.00

Lustrous - Autographs

NM/M

Production 50 unless noted.
Gold: No Pricing
Production 10 Sets
AG Alex Gordon 40.00
BB Billy Butler 30.00
BU B.J. Upton 20.00
CC Carl Crawford 20.00
CH Cole Hamels 30.00
DL Derrek Lee 25.00
DU Dan Uggla 20.00
DW Dontrelle Willis 20.00
GA Garrett Atkins 20.00
GR Khalil Greene 20.00
HA Josh Hamilton 35.00
HP Hunter Pence 40.00
HR Hanley Ramirez 30.00
HS Huston Street 20.00
IK Ian Kinsler 20.00
JB Jason Bay 25.00
JH Jeremy Hermida 15.00
JL Jon Lester 30.00
JN Joe Nathan 20.00
JV Justin Verlander 40.00
KE Howie Kendrick 20.00
KG Ken Griffey Jr. 80.00
KI Kei Igawa 30.00
MO Justin Morneau 25.00
PA Jonathan Papelbon 35.00
PF Prince Fielder 50.00
PH Phil Hughes 60.00
PK Paul Konerko 30.00
RO Roy Oswalt 30.00
RT Ryan Theriot 25.00
RZ Ryan Zimmerman 25.00
TH Torii Hunter 20.00
JW Vernon Wells 20.00

Lustrous - Materials Autographs

NM/M

Production 32-50
Gold: No Pricing
Production 10 Sets
AD Adam Dunn/35 25.00
AE Andre Ethier/50 20.00
BO Jeremy Bonderman/46 30.00
BU B.J. Upton/48 20.00
CC Carl Crawford/43 20.00
CL Carlos Lee/46 20.00
CR Cal Ripken Jr./50 140.00
DH Danny Haren/50 20.00
DJ Derek Jeter/50 150.00
DL Derrek Lee/46 25.00
DU Dan Uggla/46 20.00
DW Dontrelle Willis/45 20.00
FH Felix Hernandez/32 40.00
GR Khalil Greene/37 20.00
HR Hanley Ramirez/33 30.00
HS Huston Street/32 20.00
IK Ian Kinsler/50 20.00
JB Jason Bay/48 25.00
JH Jeremy Hermida/49 15.00
JM Joe Mauer/50 25.00
JN Joe Nathan/34 20.00
JV Justin Verlander/37 40.00
KE Howie Kendrick/41 20.00
KG Ken Griffey Jr./50 80.00
KM Kendry Morales/50 15.00
MC Matt Cain/50 25.00
MM Melvin Mora/46 15.00
NM Nicholas Markakis/50 30.00
PA Jonathan Papelbon/48 35.00
PF Prince Fielder/49 50.00
RZ Ryan Zimmerman/44 25.00
SD Stephen Drew/45 25.00
TH Torii Hunter/50 20.00
VW Vernon Wells/50 20.00

Bat Barrels - Autographs

NM/M

Production 50 Sets
Gold: No Pricing
Production 10 Sets
AD Adam Dunn 50.00
AE Andre Ethier 25.00
AI Akinori Iwamura 50.00
AL Andy LaRoche 30.00
BO Jeremy Bonderman 30.00
BU B.J. Upton 20.00
CC Carl Crawford 20.00
CL Carlos Lee 25.00
DY Delmon Young 25.00
GA Garrett Atkins 25.00
HK Howie Kendrick 25.00
HR Hanley Ramirez 40.00
HU Torii Hunter 25.00
IK Ian Kinsler 20.00
JB Jason Bay 25.00
JH Josh Hamilton 30.00
JM Joe Mauer 25.00
KG Ken Griffey Jr. 75.00

KJ	Kelly Johnson	20.00
MO	Justin Morneau	35.00
MT	Mark Teixeira	30.00
RB	Ryan Braun	75.00
TH	Travis Hafner	35.00
TT	Troy Tulowitzki	60.00

Pride of a Nation

NM/M

Production 75 Sets
Gold: No Pricing
Production 10 Sets

AH	Aaron Harang	20.00
AR	Aaron Rowand	20.00
BO	Jeremy Bonderman	30.00
BP	Brandon Phillips	30.00
CA	Carl Crawford	25.00
CC	Coco Crisp	25.00
CG	Curtis Granderson	45.00
CL	Carlos Lee	35.00
DH	Danny Haren	25.00
DL	Derrek Lee	30.00
DU	Dan Uggla	25.00
DW	Dontrelle Willis	25.00
EC	Eric Chavez	60.00
FH	Felix Hernandez	75.00
FT	Frank Thomas	60.00
HR	Hanley Ramirez	60.00
JB	Jason Bay	30.00
JL	John Lackey	25.00
JM	John Maine	20.00
LB	Lance Berkman	40.00
MM	Melvin Mora	25.00
MO	Justin Morneau	40.00
PF	Prince Fielder	40.00
RO	Roy Oswalt	50.00
SK	Scott Kazmir	25.00
VM	Victor Martinez	30.00

Prodigious - Materials Autographs

NM/M

Production 50 Sets unless noted.
Gold: No Pricing
Production 10 Sets

AD	Adam Dunn	40.00
AE	Andre Ethier	25.00
AR	Aaron Rowand	20.00
BO	Jeremy Bonderman	30.00
BP	Brandon Phillips	25.00
BU	B.J. Upton	25.00
CC	Coco Crisp	25.00
CD	Chris Duncan	25.00
CH	Cole Hamels	30.00
CL	Cliff Lee	15.00
CR	Carl Crawford	20.00
CY	Chris Young	20.00
DH	Danny Haren	20.00
DU	Dan Uggla	20.00
DW	Dontrelle Willis	20.00
FH	Felix Hernandez	50.00
GA	Garrett Atkins	20.00
HA	Josh Hamilton	30.00
HK	Hong-Chih Kuo	20.00
HR	Hanley Ramirez	40.00
HS	Huston Street	25.00
IK	Ian Kinsler	20.00
JB	Joe Blanton	20.00
JH	Jeremy Hermida	15.00
JL	Jon Lester	25.00
JN	Joe Nathan	20.00
JS	Johan Santana	50.00
JV	Justin Verlander	35.00
JZ	Joel Zumaya	20.00
KE	Howie Kendrick	20.00
KW	Kerry Wood	20.00
MO	Justin Morneau	35.00
MT	Mark Teixeira	30.00
PA	Jonathan Papelbon	40.00
RI	Cal Ripken Jr.	125.00
RW	Rickie Weeks	20.00
SK	Scott Kazmir	25.00
SR	Scott Rolen	25.00
TG	Tom Glavine	50.00
VW	Vernon Wells	25.00

Prodigious Autographs

NM/M

Production 75 unless noted.
Gold: 1-1.5X
Production 25 Sets

AE	Andre Ethier	25.00
AG	Adrian Gonzalez	25.00
AH	Aaron Harang	20.00
AI	Akinori Iwamura	50.00
AR	Aaron Rowand/50	25.00
BB	Billy Butler	25.00
BP	Brandon Phillips/50	25.00
BS	Ben Sheets/50	20.00
BU	B.J. Upton	20.00
CA	Carl Crawford	20.00
CC	Coco Crisp/50	20.00
CG	Curtis Granderson/50	40.00
CH	Cole Hamels/50	30.00
CO	Chad Cordero/50	20.00
CR	Cal Ripken Jr.	150.00
CY	Chris Young/50	25.00
DH	Danny Haren	20.00
DU	Dan Uggla	20.00
DY	Delmon Young	20.00
FP	Felix Pie	25.00
GA	Garrett Atkins	20.00
GO	Alex Gordon	40.00
GP	Glen Perkins	15.00

HB	Homer Bailey	35.00
HK	Howie Kendrick/50	25.00
HP	Hunter Pence	40.00
HS	Huston Street/50	25.00
JB	Jeremy Bonderman	25.00
JE	Johnny Estrada	15.00
JH	Josh Hamilton/50	30.00
JL	John Lackey/50	20.00
JM	John Maine/50	20.00
JP	Jonathan Papelbon	40.00
JS	Joakim Soria	15.00
JV	Justin Verlander/50	35.00
JW	Josh Willingham/50	20.00
KI	Kei Igawa	35.00
KJ	Kelly Johnson/50	20.00
LE	Jon Lester	25.00
MC	Matt Cain	25.00
MH	Matt Holliday	30.00
MM	Melvin Mora/50	15.00
MO	Justin Morneau	35.00
NM	Nicholas Markakis	25.00
NS	Nick Swisher	25.00
PK	Paul Konerko/50	20.00
RB	Ryan Braun	50.00
RH	Rich Harden/50	15.00
RZ	Ryan Zimmerman	30.00
SK	Scott Kazmir	25.00
TH	Tim Hudson	30.00
TL	Tim Lincecum	65.00
VM	Victor Martinez/50	30.00
YG	Yovani Gallardo/50	30.00

Prominent Numbers Autographs

NM/M

Production 1-58
Gold: No Pricing
Production 10 Sets

AH	Aaron Harang/39	25.00
BL	Joe Blanton/55	15.00
CG	Curtis Granderson/28	40.00
CH	Cole Hamels/35	30.00
CY	Chris Young/32	25.00
DY	Delmon Young/26	20.00
FH	Felix Hernandez/34	25.00
GA	Garrett Atkins/27	25.00
HK	Howie Kendrick/47	25.00
JB	Jason Bay/38	20.00
JE	Johnny Estrada/33	15.00
JN	Joe Nathan/36	20.00
JP	Jonathan Papelbon/58	40.00
JV	Justin Verlander/35	40.00
JZ	Joel Zumaya/34	20.00
MA	John Maine/33	25.00
MB	Michael Bourn/45	20.00
RH	Rich Harden/40	25.00

Triptych - Triple Autographs

No Pricing
Production 15 Sets
Gold: No Pricing
Production Five Sets

Triptych - Triple Materials Autographs

NM/M

Production 25 Sets

DU	Dan Uggla	30.00
PF	Prince Fielder	40.00
TH	Torii Hunter	25.00

Upper Echelon - Quad Autographs

No Pricing
Production Five Sets
Gold: No Pricing
Production Three Sets

Upper Echelon - Quad Materials Autographs

Production 2-5
Patch: No Pricing
Production One Set

2007 UD Exquisite Rookie Signatures

NM/M

Common Player (1-100): 4.00

Production 99
Common RC Auto. (101-191): 15.00
Production 125-235

Box (Six Cards):		250.00
1	Ichiro Suzuki	15.00
2	Alex Rodriguez	20.00
3	David Wright	15.00
4	Ryan Howard	15.00
5	Ken Griffey Jr.	15.00
6	Derek Jeter	20.00
7	Vladimir Guerrero	8.00
8	Roger Clemens	10.00
9	Greg Maddux	10.00
10	Johan Santana	8.00
11	Nomar Garciaparra	4.00
12	Carlos Beltran	6.00
13	Carlos Delgado	5.00
14	Manny Ramirez	6.00
15	John Lackey	4.00
16	David Ortiz	8.00
17	Curt Schilling	6.00
18	Cal Ripken Jr.	20.00
19	Albert Pujols	20.00
20	Frank Thomas	5.00
21	Chris Carpenter	4.00
22	Prince Fielder	8.00
23	Justin Morneau	6.00
24	Joe Mauer	5.00
25	Torii Hunter	5.00
26	Jake Peavy	6.00
27	Roy Oswalt	5.00
28	Craig Biggio	4.00
29	Lance Berkman	4.00
30	Carlos Zambrano	4.00
31	Derek Lee	5.00
32	Aramis Ramirez	4.00
33	Noah Lowry	4.00
34	Magglio Ordonez	4.00
35	Ivan Rodriguez	4.00
36	Johnny Damon	5.00
37	Justin Verlander	5.00
38	John Smoltz	5.00
39	Chipper Jones	8.00
40	Jeff Francoeur	5.00
41	Hanley Ramirez	8.00
42	Miguel Cabrera	8.00
43	Josh Beckett	8.00
44	Cole Hamels	6.00
45	Chase Utley	8.00
46	Grady Sizemore	8.00
47	Travis Hafner	5.00
48	Victor Martinez	5.00
49	Russell Martin	5.00
50	Jason Varitek	4.00
51	Hideki Matsui	10.00
52	Carl Crawford	5.00
53	Scott Kazmir	5.00
54	Miguel Tejada	5.00
55	Erik Bedard	5.00
56	Carlos Lee	5.00
57	Sammy Sosa	5.00
58	Mark Teixeira	6.00
59	Michael Young	6.00
60	Jim Thome	6.00
61	Paul Konerko	5.00
62	Jermaine Dye	4.00
63	Mark Teahen	4.00
64	Felix Hernandez	6.00
65	Andruw Jones	5.00
66	Pedro Martinez	6.00
67	Randy Johnson	6.00
68	Ryan Zimmerman	6.00
69	Matt Holliday	8.00
70	Todd Helton	5.00
71	Brian Bannister	4.00
72	Jeremy Bonderman	4.00
73	Adam Dunn	5.00
74	Aaron Harang	4.00
75	Jason Bay	5.00
76	Adam LaRoche	4.00
77	Freddy Sanchez	4.00
78	Dan Uggla	4.00
79	Joe Nathan	4.00
80	Brad Penny	4.00
81	Takashi Saito	4.00
82	Jimmy Rollins	8.00
83	Jose Reyes	10.00
84	Jered Weaver	6.00
85	Chien-Ming Wang	8.00
86	Jonathan Papelbon	10.00
87	Mariano Rivera	6.00
88	Eric Byrnes	5.00
89	Nicholas Markakis	5.00
90	Brian Roberts	4.00
91	Omar Vizquel	5.00
92	Vernon Wells	5.00
93	Danny Haren	5.00
94	Ben Sheets	4.00
95	B.J. Upton	6.00
96	Adrian Gonzalez	5.00
97	J.J. Hardy	5.00
98	Mike Piazza	8.00
99	Roy Halladay	5.00
100	Alfonso Soriano	5.00
101	Sean Henn/Auto./235 (RC)	15.00
102	Sean White/Auto./235 (RC)	15.00
103	Mike Schultz/Auto./235 RC	15.00
104	Michael Bourn/ Auto./235 (RC)	20.00
105	Matt Chico/Auto./235 (RC)	15.00
106	Matt Lindstrom/ Auto./235 (RC)	15.00
107	Connor Robertson/ Auto./235 RC	15.00
108	Jay Marshall/Auto./235 RC	15.00
109	Jared Burton/Auto./235 RC	15.00
110	Juan Perez/Auto./235 RC	15.00
111	Scott Moore/ Auto./235 (RC)	15.00
112	Brad Salmon/Auto./235 RC	15.00
113	Danny Putnam/ Auto./235 (RC)	15.00
114	Kelvin Jimenez/ Auto./235 RC	15.00
115	Dennis Dove/ Auto./235 (RC)	15.00
116	Yoel Hernandez/ Auto./235 RC	20.00
117	Devern Hansack/ Auto./235 (RC)	15.00
118	Mike Rabelo/ Auto./235 (RC)	15.00
119	Miguel Montero/ Auto./235 (RC)	15.00
120	Kevin Cameron/ Auto./235 (RC)	15.00
121	Joseph Bisenius/ Auto./235 RC	15.00
122	Ryan Z. Braun/ Auto./235 RC	60.00
123	Levale Speigner/ Auto./235 RC	15.00
124	Lee Gardner/ Auto./235 (RC)	15.00
125	Ryan Rowland-Smith/ Auto./235 (RC)	15.00
126	Zack Segovia/ Auto./235 (RC)	15.00
127	Rick Vanden Hurk/ Auto./235 RC	15.00
128	Dallas Braden/ Auto./235 RC	15.00
129	Rocky Cherry/ Auto./235 (RC)	15.00
130	Andy Gonzalez/ Auto./235 (RC)	15.00
131	Neal Musser/Auto./235 RC	15.00
132	Garrett Jones/ Auto./235 (RC)	15.00
133	Ben Francisco/ Auto./235 (RC)	15.00
134	Jon Coutlangus/ Auto./235 (RC)	15.00
135	A.J. Murray/Auto./235 RC	15.00
136	Brett Carroll/Auto./235 RC	15.00
137	John Danks/ Auto./235 (RC)	20.00
138	Kyle Kendrick/ Auto./235 (RC)	25.00
139	Joaquin Arias/ Auto./235 (RC)	15.00
140	Matt Brown/Auto./235 RC	15.00
141	Kurt Suzuki/ Auto./150 (RC)	25.00
142	Curtis Thigpen/ Auto./150 (RC)	15.00
143	Jerry Owens/ Auto./150 (RC)	15.00
144	Billy Butler/Auto./150 (RC)	35.00
145	Kei Igawa/Auto./150 RC	40.00
146	Mike Fontenot/ Auto./150 (RC)	15.00
147	Brandon Wood/ Auto./150 (RC)	30.00
148	Alexi Casilla/Auto./150 RC	15.00
149	Jeff Baker/Auto./150 RC	15.00
150	Brian Barden/Auto./150 RC	20.00
151	Chris Stewart/Auto./150 (RC)	15.00
152	Jon Knott/Auto./150 (RC)	15.00
153	Chase Wright/ Auto./150 RC	15.00
154	Chase Headley/ Auto./150 (RC)	30.00
155	Jesse Litsch/Jsy Auto./199 RC	20.00
156	Tyler Clippard/ Auto./150 (RC)	15.00
157	Matt DeSalvo/ Auto./150 (RC)	15.00
158	Kory Casto/ Auto./150 (RC)	15.00
159	Jarrod Saltalamacchia/ Jsy Auto./199 (RC)	25.00
160	Glen Perkins/ Auto./150 (RC)	15.00
161	Ryan Braun/ Jsy Auto./199 (RC)	75.00
162	Justin Upton/ Jsy Auto./199 RC	60.00
163	Tim Lincecum/ Jsy Auto./199 RC	120.00
164	Fred Lewis/Auto./150 (RC)	15.00
165	Alex Gordon/ Jsy Auto./199 RC	60.00
166	Akinori Iwamura/ Jsy Auto./199 RC	30.00
167	Delmon Young/ Jsy Auto./199 RC	40.00
168	Troy Tulowitzki/ Jsy Auto./199 RC	50.00
169	Daisuke Matsuzaka/ Jsy Auto./199 RC	450.00
170	Josh Hamilton/ Jsy Auto./199 (RC)	80.00

171 Kevin Kouzmanoff/ Jsy Auto./199 **(RC)** 25.00
172 Hunter Pence/ Jsy Auto./199 **(RC)** 60.00
173 Felix Pie/ Jsy Auto./199 **(RC)** 30.00
174 Andrew Miller/ Jsy Auto./199 **RC** 40.00
175 Yovani Gallardo/ Jsy Auto./199 **(RC)** 50.00
176 Ryan Sweeney/ Jsy Auto./199 **(RC)** 15.00
177 Josh Fields/ Jsy Auto./199 **(RC)** 30.00
178 Mark Reynolds/ Jsy Auto./199 **RC** 30.00
180 Homer Bailey/ Auto./150 **(RC)** 25.00
182 Joba Chamberlain/ Auto./150 **RC** 375.00
184 Travis Metcalf/ Jsy Auto./125 **RC** 15.00
185 Kevin Slowey/ Jsy Auto./199 **(RC)** 25.00
186 Phil Hughes/ Auto./150 **(RC)** 50.00
187 Micah Owings/ Auto./150 **(RC)** 25.00
188 Joe Smith/Auto./150 **RC** 15.00
189 Joakim Soria/ Jsy Auto./199 **RC** 15.00
190 Adam Lind/ Jsy Auto./199 **(RC)** 20.00
191 Andy LaRoche/ Jsy Auto./199 **(RC)** 25.00
192 Brandon Morrow/ Jsy/175 **RC** 30.00
193 Carlos Gomez/ Jsy Auto./125 **RC** 40.00
194 Yunel Escobar/ Auto./150 **(RC)** 50.00

Gold

Gold (1-100): 1-1.5X
Production 75
Gold RC (101-191): 1-1.5X
Production 25-99

Gold Spectrum Patch

Production One Set

Silver Spectrum

Production One Set

Rookie Team Autographs

NM/M

No Pricing
Production 8 Sets
Silver Spectrum: No Pricing
Production One Set

College Ties Autographs

NM/M

Production 25 unless noted
Gold: No Pricing
Production 2 Sets
Silver Spectrum: No Pricing
Production One Set
CT Bobby Crosby, Troy Tulowitzki 40.00
DE Andre Ethier, Chris Duffy 20.00
EB Andre Ethier, Travis Buck 20.00
GG Jeremy Guthrie, Ryan Garko 25.00
GH Aaron Harang, Tony Gwynn Jr. 20.00
KO Lyle Overbay, Kevin Kouzmanoff 25.00
RS Kurt Suzuki, Aaron Rowand 30.00
TF Ryan Theriot, Mike Fontenot 50.00

Common Ground Signatures

NM/M

Production 25 Sets
Gold: No Pricing
Production 2 Sets
Silver Spectrum: No Pricing
Production One Set
BL Homer Bailey, Tim Lincecum 50.00
BR Ryan Braun, Mark Reynolds 20.00
GB Alex Gordon, Billy Butler 40.00
LB Fred Lewis, Michael Bourn 30.00
MB Jay Marshall, Dallas Braden 30.00
MF Jesus Flores, Gustavo Molina 20.00
PG Felix Pie, Carlos Gomez 40.00
SB Nick Swisher, Travis Buck 30.00

Derek Jeter All Rookie Team

Production 2 Sets
Silver Spectrum: No Pricing
Production One Set

Rookie Team Autographs

NM/M

Production 20 Sets
Copper Spectrum: No Pricing
Production 5 Sets
Silver Spectrum: No Pricing
Production 15 Sets
JB Jeff Baker 15.00
RB Ryan Braun 60.00
TB Travis Buck 20.00
MC Matt Chico 15.00
TC Tyler Clippard 20.00
DA John Danks 30.00
JD J.D. Durbin 15.00
MF Mike Fontenot 20.00
AG Alex Gordon 40.00
JH Josh Hamilton 30.00
HA Justin Hampson 15.00
SH Sean Henn 15.00
AI Akinori Iwamura 30.00
KE Kyle Kendrick 15.00
KK Kevin Kouzmanoff 20.00
FL Fred Lewis 15.00
TL Tim Lincecum 50.00
JL Jesse Litsch 15.00
AL Adam Lind 15.00
AM Andrew Miller 30.00
FP Felix Pie 25.00
MR Mark Reynolds 30.00
SA Juan Salas 20.00
KS Kevin Slowey 25.00
DY Delmon Young 30.00

Common Numbers

NM/M

Production 2-60
Silver: No Pricing
Production 2 Sets
Gold: No Pricing
Production One Set
BB Jeremy Bonderman, Jason Bay/38 25.00
BC Matt Chico, Ryan Z. Braun/47 15.00
CP Manny Corpas, Glen Perkins/60 20.00
FR Josh Fields, Mark Reynolds/27 25.00
GH Philip Humber, Yovani Gallardo/49 30.00
GS Jose Garcia, Kevin Slowey/59 20.00
LT Jim Thome, Derrek Lee/25 40.00
MS Andrew Miller, Joakim Soria/48 25.00
VG Sean Gallagher, Jamie Vermilyea/36 15.00
VT Frank Thomas, Justin Verlander/35 100.00

Draft Choice Autographs

NM/M

Production 20 Sets
Copper: No Pricing
Production One Set
Gold: No Pricing
Production 5 Sets
Silver: No Pricing
Production 15 Sets
AG Alex Gordon 40.00
AM Andrew Miller 30.00
DY Delmon Young 30.00
HB Homer Bailey 25.00
JH Josh Hamilton 30.00
KS Kevin Slowey 25.00
TL Tim Lincecum 50.00

Draft Duals Autographs

NM/M

Production 25 Sets
Gold: No Pricing
Production 2 Sets
Silver: No Pricing
Production One Set
BP Homer Bailey, Glen Perkins 30.00
BS Jeremy Bonderman, Jeremy Sowers
GB Alex Gordon, Ryan Braun 80.00
GT Ryan Theriot, Curtis Granderson 40.00
GY Ken Griffey Jr., Delmon Young 100.00
HS Kevin Slowey, Chase Headley 40.00
MB Hank Blalock, Justin Morneau 30.00
MS Nick Swisher, Nick Markakis 35.00
PG Yovani Gallardo, Hunter Pence 50.00
ZB Ryan Zimmerman, Ryan Braun 50.00
ZG Alex Gordon, Ryan Zimmerman 50.00

Dual Signatures

NM/M

Production 35 Sets
Gold: No Pricing
Production 5-25
Silver: No Pricing
Production 1-10
AC Andrew Miller, Cameron Maybin 60.00
AD Alexi Casilla, Don Kelly 15.00
AJ Aaron Harang, Jeff Keppinger 25.00
AM Joaquin Arias, Travis Metcalf 15.00
BB Ryan Z. Braun, Ryan Braun 60.00
BC Jared Burton, Jon Coutlangus 20.00
BG Jason Bay, Tom Gorzelanny 20.00
BH Ramon Hernandez, Brian Burres 15.00
BI Akinori Iwamura, Ryan Braun 60.00
BJ Johnny Estrada, Bill Hall 20.00
50 Hong-Chih Kuo, Chad Billingsley 50.00
BL Homer Bailey, Tim Lincecum 50.00
BR Brian Barden, Mark Reynolds 15.00
BW Brandon Wood, Billy Butler 30.00
CC Curtis Granderson, Cameron Maybin 50.00
CD Matt Chico, Matt DeSalvo 15.00
CH Phil Hughes, Joba Chamberlain 200.00
CJ Garrett Jones, Alexi Casilla 15.00
CK Cesar Jimenez, Kelvin Jimenez 15.00
CY Carl Crawford, Delmon Young 30.00
DH J.D. Durbin, Yoel Hernandez 15.00
DM Doug Slaten, Mike Schultz 15.00
DO Micah Owings, Stephen Drew 30.00
DW Chase Wright, Matt DeSalvo 15.00
FE Mark Ellis, Mike Fontenot 20.00
FL Carlos Lee, Prince Fielder 40.00
GB Alex Gordon, Ryan Braun 60.00
GC Sean Gallagher, Rocky Cherry 15.00
GG Jose Garcia, Lee Gardner 15.00
GJ Andruw Jones, Vladimir Guerrero 50.00
GK Casey Kotchman, Adrian Gonzalez 25.00
GL Jose Garcia, Matt Lindstrom 15.00
GM Gustavo Molina, Miguel Montero 15.00
GP Felix Pie, Carlos Gomez 35.00
GV Lee Gardner, Rick Vanden Hurk 15.00
HA Aaron Harang, Homer Bailey 25.00
HB Joseph Bisenius, Yoel Hernandez 15.00
HC Sean Henn, Tyler Clippard 20.00
HD Sean Henn, Matt DeSalvo 15.00
HE Ramon Hernandez, Johnny Estrada 15.00
HG Josh Hamilton, Curtis Granderson 50.00
HH Justin Hampson, Chase Headley 25.00
HK Hong-Chih Kuo, Phil Hughes 75.00
HL Phil Hughes, Tim Lincecum 100.00
HM Cole Hamels, Andrew Miller 50.00
HP Homer Bailey, Phil Hughes 50.00
IC Kei Igawa, Tyler Clippard 40.00
IH Kei Igawa, Phil Hughes 50.00
JE Kelly Johnson, Yunel Escobar 50.00
JJ Juan Salas, James Shields 20.00
KB Hank Blalock, Ian Kinsler 25.00
KH Kevin Kouzmanoff, Chase Headley 40.00
KK Casey Kotchman, Howie Kendrick 30.00
KW Howie Kendrick, Brandon Wood 40.00
LA Andy LaRoche, Tony Abreu 25.00
LB Fred Lewis, Michael Bourn 20.00
LE Kelvim Escobar, John Lackey 25.00
LH Jon Lester, Devern Hansack 30.00
LO Roy Oswalt, Tim Lincecum 60.00
LP Carlos Lee, Hunter Pence 60.00
LS Jesse Litsch, Kevin Slowey 15.00
ME Brian McCann, Yunel Escobar 40.00
MH Josh Hamilton, Nick Markakis 40.00
MM Brian McCann, Russell Martin 40.00
MO Micah Owings, Andrew Miller 30.00
MS John Maine, Joe Smith 30.00
NT Nick Swisher, Travis Buck 25.00
OC Micah Owings, Matt Chico 25.00
PH Josh Hamilton, Hunter Pence 50.00
PM Corey Patterson, Nick Markakis 40.00
PO Jerry Owens, Felix Pie 20.00
RB Ryan Braun, Mark Reynolds 50.00
RJ Cal Ripken Jr., Derek Jeter
RM Jay Marshall, Connor Robertson 15.00
RO Micah Owings, Mark Reynolds 30.00
RU Hanley Ramirez, Dan Uggla 30.00
RZ Aramis Ramirez, Carlos Zambrano 50.00
SA Jeremy Accardo, Joakim Soria 15.00
SB Ryan Z. Braun, Joakim Soria 15.00
SG Joe Smith, Carlos Gomez 25.00
SM Kurt Suzuki, Gustavo Molina 15.00
SO Ryan Sweeney, Jerry Owens 15.00
SR Mike Rabelo, Chris Stewart 15.00
SS Joe Smith, Kevin Slowey 20.00
ST Sean Henn, Tyler Clippard 15.00
TB Jeff Baker, Troy Tulowitzki 40.00
TE Ryan Theriot, Yunel Escobar 35.00
TF Ryan Theriot, Mike Fontenot 50.00
TJ Curtis Thigpen, Garrett Jones 15.00
TL Curtis Thigpen, Adam Lind 15.00
TR Travis Hafner, Ryan Garko 35.00
TT Frank Thomas, Jim Thome 100.00
TV Travis Hafner, Victor Martinez 35.00
VL Matt Lindstrom, Rick Vanden Hurk 15.00
VM Justin Verlander, Andrew Miller 50.00
WI Kei Igawa, Chase Wright 40.00
YT Yovani Gallardo, Tim Lincecum 50.00
ZB Ryan Zimmerman, Ryan Braun 50.00
ZG Alex Gordon, Ryan Zimmerman 50.00

Exquisite Endorsements

NM/M

Production 50 Sets
Gold: No Pricing
Production 15 Sets
Silver: No Pricing
Production One Set
AC Alexi Casilla 10.00
AE Andre Ethier 15.00
AL Adam Lind 15.00
BH Brendan Harris 10.00
BO Jeremy Bonderman 20.00
CP Corey Patterson 10.00
DH Danny Haren 10.00
DL Derrek Lee 25.00
DM David Murphy 10.00
DU Dan Uggla 15.00
FL Fred Lewis 10.00
FP Felix Pie 15.00
GP Glen Perkins 10.00
HB Homer Bailey 20.00
HP Hunter Pence 40.00
HR Hanley Ramirez 25.00
JB Jason Bay 15.00
JF Josh Fields 10.00
JL Jon Lester 20.00
JP Jonathan Papelbon 30.00
JS James Shields 15.00
JV Justin Verlander 40.00
KI Kei Igawa 30.00
KS Kevin Slowey 20.00
LG Luis Gonzalez 15.00
MH Matt Holliday 35.00
MO Micah Owings 15.00
NS Nick Swisher 20.00
PF Prince Fielder 40.00
RB Ryan Braun 60.00
RM Russell Martin 30.00
RS Ryan Sweeney 10.00
RT Ryan Theriot 20.00
RZ Ryan Zimmerman 30.00
SM Joe Smith 15.00
TH Travis Hafner 30.00
TL Tim Lincecum 60.00
TT Troy Tulowitzki 40.00
VM Victor Martinez 25.00
YE Yunel Escobar 30.00

Ensemble Triple Autos.

NM/M

Production 35 unless noted
Gold: No Pricing
Production 3 Sets
Silver: No Pricing
Production One Set
BGL Alex Gordon, Andy LaRoche, Ryan Braun 100.00
BLG Fred Lewis, Michael Bourn, Carlos Gomez 30.00
BTY Delmon Young, Troy Tulowitzki, Ryan Braun 120.00
BWL Adam Lind, Brandon Wood, Billy Butler 50.00
CSP Glen Perkins, Joakim Soria, Joba Chamberlain 200.00
FCE Alexi Casilla, Mike Fontenot, Yunel Escobar 50.00
GFC Sean Gallagher, Rocky Cherry, Mike Fontenot 25.00
GIB Alex Gordon, Akinori Iwamura, Ryan Braun 120.00
GJR Ken Griffey Jr., Cal Ripken Jr., Derek Jeter/10

IGR Alex Gordon, Akinori Iwamura, Mark Reynolds 100.00
KHH Justin Hampson, Kevin Kouzmanoff, Chase Headley 40.00
LHB Homer Bailey, Phil Hughes, Tim Lincecum 120.00
LLT Curtis Thigpen, Adam Lind, Jesse Litsch 30.00
MKI Andrew Miller, Kei Igawa, Kyle Kendrick 50.00
PHY Josh Hamilton, Delmon Young, Hunter Pence 75.00
SHG Justin Hampson, Sean Gallagher, Joakim Soria 25.00
SMA David Murphy, Jarrod Saltalamacchia, Joaquin Arias 35.00
UBB Travis Buck, Billy Butler, Justin Upton 50.00

Ensemble Quad Autographs

No Pricing
Production 15 Sets
Gold: No Pricing
Production One Set
Silver: No Pricing
Production 4 Sets

First Signs Autographs

No Pricing
Production 20 Sets
Silver Spectrum: No Pricing
Production 15 Sets
Gold: No Pricing
Production 5 Sets
Silver Ink: No Pricing
Production One Set

Futures Autographs

No Pricing
Production 20 Sets
Gold: No Pricing
Production One Set
Silver: No Pricing
Production 5 Sets

Debut Signatures

NM/M

Production 20 Sets
Silver Spectrum: No Pricing
Production 15 Sets
Gold: No Pricing
Production 5 Sets
Silver Ink: No Pricing
Production One Set
TA Tony Abreu 15.00
JA Joaquin Arias 15.00
HB Homer Bailey 25.00
JE Jeff Baker 15.00
BB Brian Bannister 15.00
BA Brian Barden 20.00
BI Joseph Bisenius 15.00
BO Michael Bourn 20.00
DB Dallas Braden 15.00
RB Ryan Braun 80.00
BR Ryan Z. Braun 15.00
MB Matt Brown 15.00
JB Jared Burton 15.00
BU Billy Butler 30.00
KC Kevin Cameron 15.00
AC Alexi Casilla 15.00
JC Joba Chamberlain 300.00
RC Rocky Cherry 25.00
MC Matt Chico 15.00
TC Tyler Clippard 20.00
CO Jon Coutlangus 15.00
CC Carl Crawford 25.00
DA John Danks 30.00
MD Matt DeSalvo 15.00
DD Dennis Dove 15.00
JD J.D. Durbin 15.00
YE Yunel Escobar 40.00
JF Josh Fields 20.00
MF Mike Fontenot 20.00
BF Ben Francisco 15.00
YG Yovani Gallardo 40.00
JG Jose Garcia 15.00
LG Lee Gardner 15.00
CG Carlos Gomez 30.00
AG Alex Gordon 75.00
TH Travis Hafner 25.00
HA Cole Hamels 30.00
JH Josh Hamilton 30.00
JU Justin Hampson 15.00
DH Devern Hansack 20.00
CH Chase Headley 40.00
HE Sean Henn 20.00
YH Yoel Hernandez 15.00
PH Phil Hughes 80.00
KI Kei Igawa 30.00
AI Akinori Iwamura 35.00
CJ Cesar Jimenez 20.00
GJ Garrett Jones 15.00
DK Don Kelly 15.00
JK Jon Knott 15.00
KK Kevin Kouzmanoff 25.00
FL Fred Lewis 15.00
TL Tim Lincecum 60.00
AL Adam Lind 20.00
ML Matt Lindstrom 15.00
JL Jesse Litsch 15.00
JM Jay Marshall 20.00
VM Victor Martinez 25.00
TM Travis Metcalf 15.00
AM Andrew Miller 30.00
GM Gustavo Molina 15.00
MO Justin Morneau 30.00
NM Neal Musser 15.00
RO Roy Oswalt 25.00
JO Jerry Owens 15.00
OW Micah Owings 25.00
HP Hunter Pence 40.00
GP Glen Perkins 15.00
BP Brandon Phillips 25.00
FP Felix Pie 20.00
DP Danny Putnam 15.00
HR Hanley Ramirez 40.00
MR Mark Reynolds 30.00
RI Shawn Riggans 15.00
CR Connor Robertson 15.00
RR Ryan Rowland-Smith 15.00
JS Juan Salas 15.00
SA Jarrod Saltalamacchia 25.00
BS Brad Salmon 15.00
LS Luke Scott 15.00
SH James Shields 25.00
KS Kevin Slowey 30.00
SM Joe Smith 15.00
SO Joakim Soria 15.00
CS Chris Stewart 15.00
ST Brian Stokes 15.00
SU Kurt Suzuki 15.00
RS Ryan Sweeney 20.00
CT Curtis Thigpen 15.00
TT Troy Tulowitzki 50.00
RV Rick Vanden Hurk 20.00
JV Justin Verlander 40.00
JW Josh Willingham 20.00
BW Brandon Wood 25.00
CW Chase Wright 20.00
DY Delmon Young 30.00
CZ Carlos Zambrano 35.00
RZ Ryan Zimmerman 30.00

Imagery Autographs

NM/M

Production 25 Sets
Gold: No Pricing
Production 10 Sets
Silver: No Pricing
Production One Set
AC Alexi Casilla 15.00
AG Alex Gordon 75.00
AL Adam Lind 20.00
BB Billy Butler 30.00
BH Bill Hall 20.00
BO Michael Bourn 20.00
BR Ryan Z. Braun 15.00
BS Brian Stokes 15.00
CG Chris Gomez 30.00
CH Chase Headley 40.00
CT Curtis Thigpen 15.00
CW Chase Wright 20.00
CZ Carlos Zambrano 35.00
DD Dennis Dove 15.00
DH Devern Hansack 20.00
DM David Murphy 20.00
FL Fred Lewis 15.00
FP Felix Pie 20.00
GJ Garrett Jones 15.00
GM Gustavo Molina 15.00
GP Glen Perkins 15.00
HA Justin Hampson 15.00
HB Homer Bailey 30.00
HP Hunter Pence 40.00
HR Hanley Ramirez 40.00
JB Jason Bay 20.00
JF Josh Fields 20.00
JH Josh Hamilton 30.00
JL Jesse Litsch 15.00
JO Jerry Owens 15.00
JS James Shields 20.00
JU Justin Upton 60.00
JW Josh Willingham 20.00
KE Kyle Kendrick 15.00
KI Kei Igawa 30.00
KK Kevin Kouzmanoff 25.00
KS Kevin Slowey 30.00
LA Andy LaRoche 25.00
MB Matt Brown 15.00
MD Matt DeSalvo 15.00
MF Mike Fontenot 20.00
MH Matt Holliday 40.00
MO Micah Owings 25.00
MR Mark Reynolds 30.00
MT Miguel Tejada
NM Nick Markakis 30.00
RB Ryan Braun 80.00
RC Rocky Cherry 25.00
RM Russell Martin 40.00
RS Ryan Sweeney 20.00
RV Rick Vanden Hurk 20.00
RZ Ryan Zimmerman 30.00
SA Jarrod Saltalamacchia 25.00
SG Sean Gallagher 20.00
SH Sean Henn 20.00
SM Joe Smith 15.00
TA Tony Abreu 15.00
TB Travis Buck 15.00
TC Tyler Clippard 20.00
TH Travis Hafner 25.00
TM Travis Metcalf 15.00
VM Victor Martinez 25.00
YE Yunel Escobar 40.00
YG Yovani Gallardo 40.00
YH Yoel Hernandez 15.00
ZS Zack Segovia 15.00

Phenoms Autographs

NM/M

Production 20 Sets
Gold: No Pricing
Production 15 Sets
Silver Spectrum: No Pricing
Production 15 Sets
Silver Ink: No Pricing
Production One Set
AG Alex Gordon 75.00
AI Akinori Iwamura 35.00
AL Adam Lind 20.00
BB Brian Bannister 15.00
CT Curtis Thigpen 15.00
FL Fred Lewis 15.00
FP Felix Pie 20.00
HB Homer Bailey 30.00
JD John Danks 30.00
JS James Shields 20.00
KK Kevin Kouzmanoff 25.00
KS Kevin Slowey 30.00
MC Matt Chico 15.00
MR Mark Reynolds 30.00
NM Nick Markakis 30.00
PH Phil Hughes 80.00
RB Ryan Braun 80.00
SU Kurt Suzuki 15.00
TL Tim Lincecum 60.00
TT Troy Tulowitzki 50.00

Reflections Autographs

NM/M

Common Dual Auto.:
Production 40 unless noted
Gold: No Pricing
Production 5-20
Silver Ink: No Pricing
Production 5-20
Silver Spectrum: No Pricing
Production 1-10
AB Alex Gordon, Billy Butler 50.00
AC Joaquin Arias, Alexi Casilla 15.00
AH Aaron Harang, Homer Bailey 30.00
AJ Jeremy Sowers, Andrew Miller 25.00
BA Matt Brown, Tony Abreu 20.00
BB Boof Bonser, Brian Bannister 20.00
BD John Danks, Brian Bannister 20.00
BG Alex Gordon, Ryan Braun 75.00
BH Travis Hafner, Josh Barfield 25.00
BJ Jared Burton, Brad Salmon 20.00
BL Fred Lewis, Michael Bourn 25.00
BS Joseph Bisenius, Zack Segovia 15.00
BT Mark Teahen, Brian Bannister 25.00
BV Jeremy Bonderman, Justin Verlander 40.00
BW Brandon Wood, Matt Brown 25.00
CG Carl Crawford, Carlos Gomez 30.00
CH Justin Hampson, Kevin Cameron 15.00
CK Curtis Thigpen, Kurt Suzuki 25.00
CS Joakim Soria, Rocky Cherry 20.00
DC Matt Chico, Matt DeSalvo 15.00
DH J.D. Durbin, Yoel Hernandez 15.00
DO Micah Owings, John Danks 25.00
DS J.D. Durbin, Zack Segovia 20.00
EC Alexi Casilla, Yunel Escobar 15.00
EL Fred Lewis, Andre Ethier 20.00
EP Mark Ellis, Danny Putnam 20.00
FM Josh Fields, Travis Metcalf 15.00
FO David Ortiz, Prince Fielder 40.00
FY Yovani Gallardo, Felix Hernandez 40.00
GA Alexi Casilla, Glen Perkins 15.00
GB Jeremy Guthrie, Brian Burres 20.00
GC Sean Gallagher, Rocky Cherry 20.00
GG Jeremy Guthrie, Tom Gorzelanny 20.00
GK Alex Gordon, Kevin Kouzmanoff 50.00
GL Matt Lindstrom, Lee Gardner 15.00
GM Gustavo Molina, Miguel Montero 15.00
GV Jose Garcia, Rick Vanden Hurk 15.00
HB Homer Bailey, Phil Hughes 50.00
HC Justin Hampson, Jon Coutlangus 15.00
HD Huston Street, Dallas Braden 15.00
HG Rich Hill, Sean Gallagher 25.00
HH Sean Henn, Phil Hughes 50.00
HK Kevin Kouzmanoff, Chase Headley 40.00
HM Cole Hamels, Andrew Miller 50.00
HP Josh Hamilton, Hunter Pence 50.00
HT Homer Bailey, Tim Lincecum 50.00
HW Josh Willingham, Jeremy Hermida 20.00
IM Andrew Miller, Kei Igawa 40.00
JC Chad Billingsley, James Shields 30.00
JD Kelvin Jimenez, Dennis Dove 15.00
JE Kelly Johnson, Yunel Escobar 40.00
JJ Josh Fields, Jerry Owens 30.00
JK Jarrod Saltalamacchia, Kurt Suzuki 25.00
JL Reed Johnson, Adam Lind 15.00
JM John Danks, Matt Chico 15.00
KC Cesar Jimenez, Kelvin Jimenez 25.00
KG Kurt Suzuki, Gustavo Molina 20.00
LA Andy LaRoche, Tony Abreu 25.00
LB Jeff Baker, Adam Lind 15.00
LH Jon Lester, Cole Hamels 60.00
LL Adam Lind, Jesse Litsch 25.00
LO Fred Lewis, Jerry Owens 15.00
MA Mark Ellis, Alexi Casilla 15.00
MB Jay Marshall, Dallas Braden 15.00
MG Jeremy Guthrie, Nick Markakis 40.00
MJ Matt Holliday, Jason Bay 40.00
MK Nick Markakis, Jon Knott 25.00
MM Brian McCann, Russell Martin 40.00
MR Jay Marshall, Connor Robertson 25.00
MS Kurt Suzuki, Russell Martin 30.00
NR Ryan Z. Braun, Neal Musser 20.00
OB Micah Owings, Homer Bailey 20.00
PB Danny Putnam, Travis Buck 15.00
PC Matt Chico, Glen Perkins 15.00
PD Glen Perkins, Matt DeSalvo 15.00
PG Felix Pie, Carlos Gomez 40.00
PO Jerry Owens, Felix Pie 15.00
RB Ryan Braun, Mark Reynolds 60.00
RC Ryan Braun, Chase Headley 60.00
RM Gustavo Molina, Mike Rabelo 15.00
RR Ryan Z. Braun, Ryan Braun 50.00
SB Ryan Z. Braun, Joakim Soria 15.00
SG Ben Sheets, Yovani Gallardo 40.00
SH Justin Hampson, Joe Smith 15.00
SM David Murphy, Jarrod Saltalamacchia 25.00
SP Glen Perkins, Kevin Slowey 25.00
SR Kurt Suzuki, Shawn Riggans 15.00
SS Joe Smith, Kevin Slowey 20.00
ST Sean Henn, Tyler Clippard 15.00
TJ Curtis Thigpen, Garrett Jones 15.00
TR Curtis Thigpen, Shawn Riggans 15.00
TS Mark Teahen, Angel Sanchez 15.00
VG Lee Gardner, Rick Vanden Hurk 15.00
WD John Danks, Chase Wright 25.00
WH Bill Hall, Josh Willingham 20.00
ZY Zack Segovia, Yoel Hernandez 15.00

Retro Rookie Duals

No Pricing
Production 5-15
Gold: No Pricing
Production 2 Sets
Silver: No Pricing
Production One Set

Rookie Biography Autographs

NM/M

Production 20 Sets
Blue: No Pricing
Production One Set
Gold: No Pricing
Production 15 Sets
Silver Spectrum: No Pricing
Production 10 Sets
Silver Ink: No Pricing
Production One Set
AC Alexi Casilla 15.00
AG Alex Gordon 75.00
AI Akinori Iwamura 35.00
AL Adam Lind 20.00
AM Andrew Miller 30.00
AS Anibal Sanchez 15.00
BA Brian Barden 20.00
BB Billy Butler 30.00
BF Ben Francisco 15.00
BH Bill Hall 20.00
BI Joseph Bisenius 15.00
BS Ben Sheets 20.00
BU Jamie Burke 15.00
BW Brandon Wood 25.00
CC Chris Carpenter 25.00
CG Carlos Gomez 30.00
CH Chase Headley 40.00
CJ Cesar Jimenez 20.00
CO Manny Corpas 15.00
CS Chris Stewart 15.00
CT Curtis Thigpen 15.00
CW Chase Wright 20.00

DA	John Danks	30.00
DB	Dallas Braden	15.00
DD	Dennis Dove	15.00
DH	Danny Haren	20.00
DK	Don Kelly	15.00
DL	Derrek Lee	30.00
DS	Doug Slaten	15.00
DY	Delmon Young	30.00
FL	Fred Lewis	15.00
FP	Felix Pie	20.00
FT	Frank Thomas	60.00
GJ	Garrett Jones	15.00
GO	Tom Gorzelanny	25.00
GP	Glen Perkins	15.00
HA	Devern Hansack	20.00
HB	Homer Bailey	25.00
HG	Hector Gimenez	15.00
HP	Hunter Pence	40.00
JA	Joaquin Arias	15.00
JB	Jeff Baker	15.00
JC	Jon Coutlangus	15.00
JD	J.D. Durbin	15.00
JF	Josh Fields	20.00
JG	Jose Garcia	15.00
JH	Justin Hampson	15.00
JK	Jon Knott	15.00
JL	Jesse Litsch	15.00
JM	Jay Marshall	20.00
JO	Jerry Owens	15.00
JS	Jarrod Saltalamacchia	25.00
JT	Jim Thome	40.00
JV	Justin Verlander	40.00
JW	Josh Willingham	20.00
KI	Kei Igawa	30.00
KJ	Kelvin Jimenez	20.00
KK	Kevin Kouzmanoff	15.00
KS	Kevin Slowey	30.00
LA	Andy LaRoche	25.00
LG	Lee Gardner	15.00
LS	Levale Speigner	15.00
MA	Nick Markakis	40.00
MB	Michael Bourn	20.00
MC	Matt Chico	15.00
MD	Matt DeSalvo	15.00
MF	Mike Fontenot	20.00
ML	Matt Lindstrom	15.00
MM	Miguel Montero	15.00
MO	Micah Owings	25.00
MR	Mark Reynolds	30.00
NM	Neal Musser	15.00
PH	Phil Hughes	80.00
RA	Mike Rabelo	15.00
RB	Ryan Braun	80.00
RC	Rocky Cherry	15.00
RO	Connor Robertson	15.00
RR	Ryan Rowland-Smith	15.00
RS	Ryan Sweeney	20.00
RV	Rick Vanden Hurk	20.00
SA	Brad Salmon	15.00
SG	Sean Gallagher	20.00
SH	Sean Henn	15.00
SM	Joe Smith	15.00
SO	Joakim Soria	15.00
SR	Shawn Riggans	15.00
SU	Kurt Suzuki	20.00
SW	Sean White	15.00
TA	Tony Abreu	15.00
TB	Travis Buck	15.00
TC	Tyler Clippard	20.00
TG	Tom Glavine	50.00
TL	Tim Lincecum	60.00
TT	Troy Tulowitzki	50.00
VM	Victor Martinez	25.00
YE	Yunel Escobar	40.00
YH	Yoel Hernandez	15.00
ZS	Zack Segovia	15.00

Rookie Heroes Autographs
NM/M

Production 25 Sets
Gold: 1-1.5X
Production 15 Sets
Silver Spectrum: 1-2X
Production 10 Sets
Silver Ink: No Pricing
Production One Set

AI1-5	Akinori Iwamura	35.00
AM1-5	Andrew Miller	30.00
BB1-5	Billy Butler	25.00
CG1-5	Carlos Gomez	30.00
FL1-5	Fred Lewis	15.00
FP1-5	Felix Pie	20.00
HB1-5	Homer Bailey	20.00
HP1-5	Hunter Pence	20.00
JD1-5	John Danks	20.00
JS1-5	Jarrod Saltalamacchia	25.00
KE1-5	Kyle Kendrick	20.00
KK1-5	Kevin Kouzmanoff	20.00
KS1-5	Kevin Slowey	20.00
MR1-5	Mark Reynolds	20.00
RB1-5	Ryan Braun	60.00
SO1-5	Joakim Soria	15.00
TB1-5	Travis Buck	20.00
TL1-5	Tim Lincecum	50.00
TT1-5	Troy Tulowitzki	50.00
YE1-5	Yunel Escobar	40.00

Signature Materials
NM/M

Production 85 unless noted
Gold: 1-1.5X
Production 15-50
Gold Spectrum: No Pricing
Production One Set
Silver Spectrum: No Pricing

Production 10-25

AD	Adam Dunn	25.00
AG	Adrian Gonzalez	15.00
AH	Aaron Harang	20.00
AR	Aramis Ramirez	25.00
BA	Bronson Arroyo	20.00
BH	Bill Hall	15.00
BL	Joe Blanton	15.00
BO	Jeremy Bonderman	25.00
BR	Brian Roberts	20.00
BS	Ben Sheets	20.00
BU	B.J. Upton	20.00
CC	Carl Crawford	20.00
CH	Cole Hamels	40.00
CL	Carlos Lee	20.00
CR	Cal Ripken Jr.	125.00
CZ	Carlos Zambrano	30.00
DH	Danny Haren	20.00
DL	Derrek Lee	25.00
DU	Dan Uggla	15.00
DW	Dontrelle Willis	20.00
FH	Felix Hernandez	40.00
FT	Frank Thomas	60.00
HA	Travis Hafner	25.00
HK	Howie Kendrick	20.00
HR	Hanley Ramirez	40.00
HS	Huston Street	15.00
IK	Ian Kinsler	20.00
JB	Jason Bay	20.00
JM	John Maine	30.00
JO	Josh Barfield	10.00
JP	Jonathan Papelbon	50.00
JV	Justin Verlander	35.00
JW	Josh Willingham	15.00
LS	Luke Scott	15.00
MC	Matt Cain	15.00
MO	Justin Morneau	25.00
MT	Mark Teixeira	25.00
NM	Nick Markakis	15.00
NS	Nick Swisher	15.00
PF	Prince Fielder	40.00
RH	Rich Harden	15.00
RM	Russell Martin	30.00
RW	Rickie Weeks	25.00
RZ	Ryan Zimmerman	25.00
SD	Stephen Drew	30.00
TH	Torii Hunter	20.00
VM	Victor Martinez	20.00

Future Autographs
No Pricing

Production 20 Sets
Gold: No Pricing
Production 15 Sets
Silver: No Pricing
Production One Set

Griffey All Rookie Team Autos.

Production 3 Sets
Silver: No Pricing
Production One Set

Generation Signatures
NM/M

Production 20 Sets
Gold: No Pricing
Production 15 Sets
Silver: No Pricing
Production One Set

AC	Alexi Casilla	15.00
AG	Alex Gordon	40.00
AM	Andrew Miller	30.00
BB	Brian Bannister	15.00
BF	Ben Francisco	15.00
CH	Chase Headley	40.00
CT	Curtis Thigpen	15.00
DD	Dennis Dove	15.00
DH	Devern Hansack	20.00
DP	Danny Putnam	15.00
FL	Fred Lewis	15.00
FP	Felix Pie	25.00
GP	Glen Perkins	15.00
HB	Homer Bailey	25.00
HP	Hunter Pence	40.00
HR	Hanley Ramirez	15.00
JA	Joaquin Arias	15.00
JD	J.D. Durbin	15.00
JF	Josh Fields	20.00
JH	Justin Hampson	15.00
JS	Joakim Soria	15.00
JV	Justin Verlander	40.00
JW	Josh Willingham	20.00
KI	Kei Igawa	30.00
KK	Kevin Kouzmanoff	25.00
KS	Kevin Slowey	30.00
MF	Mike Fontenot	20.00
MR	Mark Reynolds	30.00
RB	Ryan Braun	80.00
RS	Ryan Sweeney	20.00
RT	Ryan Theriot	20.00
RV	Rick Vanden Hurk	15.00
SG	Sean Gallagher	15.00
SM	Joe Smith	15.00
SU	Kurt Suzuki	15.00
TL	Tim Lincecum	60.00
TT	Troy Tulowitzki	50.00
YE	Yunel Escobar	40.00
YH	Yoel Hernandez	15.00
ZS	Zack Segovia	15.00

2007 UD Masterpieces
NM/M

Complete Set (90): 50.00
Common Player (1-90): .50
Pack (4): 8.00

Box (18):		120.00
1	Babe Ruth	4.00
2	Babe Ruth	4.00
3	Bobby Thomson	.50
4	Bill Mazeroski	1.00
5	Carlton Fisk	1.00
6	Kirk Gibson	1.00
7	Don Larsen	2.00
8	Lou Gehrig	4.00
9	Roger Maris	3.00
10	Cal Ripken Jr.	4.00
11	Bucky Dent	.50
12	Ryan Howard	3.00
13	Brooks Robinson	2.00
14	David Ortiz	3.00
15	Hideki Matsui	3.00
16	Roger Clemens	4.00
17	Sandy Koufax	5.00
18	Reggie Jackson	4.00
19	Ozzie Smith	3.00
20	Ty Cobb	4.00
21	Walter Johnson	2.00
22	Babe Ruth	4.00
23	Roy Campanella	2.00
24	Jackie Robinson	3.00
25	Carl Yastrzemski	3.00
26	Sandy Koufax	5.00
27	Daisuke Matsuzaka RC	8.00
28	Kei Igawa RC	1.00
29	Ken Griffey Jr.	3.00
30	Derek Jeter	4.00
31	David Ortiz	2.00
32	Vladimir Guerrero	2.00
33	Chase Utley	2.00
34	Troy Tulowitzki (RC)	2.00
35	Joe Mauer	1.00
36	Travis Hafner	1.00
37	Miguel Cabrera	2.00
38	Albert Pujols	4.00
39	Frank Thomas	2.00
40	Mike Piazza	2.00
41	Josh Hamilton	.50
42	Cal Ripken Jr., Tony Gwynn	3.00
43	Ichiro Suzuki	3.00
44	Hideki Matsui	3.00
45	Ken Griffey Jr.	3.00
46	Michael Jordan	4.00
47	John F. Kennedy	4.00
48	Randy Johnson	2.00
49	Albert Pujols	4.00
50	Carlos Beltran	1.50
51	Delmon Young (RC)	1.00
52	Johan Santana	2.00
53	Cal Ripken Jr.	3.00
54	Yogi Berra, Jackie Robinson	3.00
55	Cal Ripken Jr.	3.00
56	Hanley Ramirez	2.00
57	Victor Martinez	1.00
58	Cole Hamels	2.00
59	Bobby Doerr	1.00
60	Bruce Sutter	.50
61	Jason Bay	1.00
62	Luis Aparicio	.50
63	Stephen Drew	1.00
64	Jered Weaver	1.00
65	Alex Gordon RC	5.00
66	Howie Kendrick	.50
67	Ryan Zimmerman	1.00
68	Akinori Iwamura RC	1.00
69	Chien-Ming Wang	2.00
70	David Wright	2.00
71	Ryan Howard	3.00
72	Alex Rodriguez	4.00
73	Justin Morneau	1.50
74	Andrew Miller RC	1.00
75	Richard Nixon	1.00
76	Bill Clinton	1.00
77	Phil Hughes (RC)	3.00
78	Tom Glavine	1.00
79	Chipper Jones	2.00
80	Craig Biggio	1.00
81	Chris Chambliss	.50
82	Tim Lincecum RC	5.00
83	Billy Butler (RC)	1.00
84	Andy LaRoche (RC)	1.00
85	1969 New York Mets	2.00
86	2004 Boston Red Sox	2.00
87	Roberto Clemente	3.00
88	Chase Utley	2.00
89	Reggie Jackson	2.00
90	Curt Schilling	2.00

Printing Plates
No Pricing
Production one set per color.

Artist's Proof
Production One Set

Black Linen
Black Linen (1-90): 4-6X
Production 99 Sets

Blue Steel
Blue Steel (1-90): 4-8X
Production 50 Sets

Bronze
Production One Set

Celestial Blue
Production One Set

Deep Blue
Black Linen (1-90): 4-6X
Production 75 Sets

Green Linen
Green (1-90): 2-3X

Hades
Hades (1-90): 4-8X
Production 50 Sets

Ionised
Production One Set

Persian Blue Linen
Production One Set

Pinot Red
Pinot Red (1-90): 4-6X
Production 75 Sets

Red Linen
Production One Set

Rusted
Rusted (1-90): 4-8X
Production 50 Sets

Black
Black (1-90): 4-6X
Production 99 Sets

Urban Gray
Production One Set

Captured on Canvas

NM/M

Common Player: 4.00
Bronze: No Pricing
Forest Green: No Pricing
Production One Set

AB	Adrian Beltre	4.00
AD	Adam Dunn	8.00
AI	Akinori Iwamura	15.00
AJ	Andruw Jones	6.00
AP	Albert Pujols	25.00
BA	Bobby Abreu	6.00
BC	Bobby Crosby	4.00
BE	Carlos Beltran	8.00
BG	Brian Giles	4.00
BL	Brad Lidge	4.00
BO	Jeremy Bonderman	6.00
BR	Brian Roberts	6.00
BS	Ben Sheets	6.00
CA	Chris Carpenter	8.00
CB	Craig Biggio	8.00
CC	Carl Crawford	8.00
CF	Carlton Fisk	8.00
CJ	Chipper Jones	10.00
CL	Carlos Lee	6.00
CR	Coco Crisp	4.00
CS	C.C. Sabathia	6.00
CU	Chase Utley	15.00
CY	Carl Yastrzemski	10.00
DJ	Derek Jeter	25.00
DL	Derrek Lee	8.00
DM	Don Mattingly	20.00
DO	David Ortiz	10.00
DR	J.D. Drew	4.00
DW	Dontrelle Willis	4.00
EB	Erik Bedard	6.00
EC	Eric Chavez	6.00
EG	Eric Gagne	4.00
FH	Felix Hernandez	8.00

FL	Francisco Liriano	6.00
GA	Garrett Atkins	6.00
GL	Tom Glavine	8.00
GR	Khalil Greene	6.00
GS	Grady Sizemore	10.00
HA	Roy Halladay	6.00
HB	Hank Blalock	6.00
HE	Todd Helton	8.00
HR	Hanley Ramirez	10.00
HS	Huston Street	4.00
IR	Ivan Rodriguez	8.00
JA	Jason Bay	6.00
JB	Josh Beckett	8.00
JH	J.J. Hardy	6.00
JK	Jason Kendall	4.00
JM	Joe Mauer	6.00
JN	Joe Nathan	6.00
JP	Jake Peavy	8.00
JR	Jose Reyes	15.00
JS	John Smoltz	8.00
JV	Jason Varitek	8.00
JW	Jered Weaver	6.00
KG	Ken Griffey Jr.	20.00
LB	Lance Berkman	6.00
MA	Daisuke Matsuzaka	50.00
MC	Miguel Cabrera	8.00
MG	Marcus Giles	4.00
MH	Matt Holliday	8.00
MO	Magglio Ordonez	6.00
MR	Mariano Rivera	8.00
MT	Miguel Tejada	8.00
MY	Michael Young	6.00
PA	Jonathan Papelbon	15.00
RA	Manny Ramirez	8.00
RB	Rocco Baldelli	6.00
RC	Roger Clemens	15.00
RH	Rich Harden	4.00
RI	Cal Ripken Jr.	20.00
RJ	Randy Johnson	8.00
RO	Roy Oswalt	8.00
RW	Rickie Weeks	6.00
RZ	Ryan Zimmerman	10.00
SA	Johan Santana	10.00
SC	Curt Schilling	10.00
SH	Gary Sheffield	8.00
SK	Scott Kazmir	6.00
SR	Scott Rolen	8.00
TE	Mark Teixeira	8.00
TG	Tony Gwynn	15.00
TH	Tim Hudson	6.00
TR	Travis Hafner	6.00
VG	Vladimir Guerrero	8.00
VM	Victor Martinez	8.00
WC	Will Clark	8.00

Stroke of Genius Signatures

NM/M

Common Autograph: 10.00
Parallel: No Pricing
Production One Set

AD	Adam Dunn	
AG	Adrian Gonzalez	15.00
AK	Al Kaline	30.00
AL	Andy LaRoche	15.00
BA	Bronson Arroyo	15.00
BB	Billy Butler	25.00
BO	Boof Bonser	10.00
BR	Brooks Robinson	40.00
BS	Ben Sheets	15.00
BU	B.J. Upton	15.00
CD	Chris Duffy	10.00
CF	Chone Figgins	15.00
CH	Cole Hamels	40.00
CQ	Carlos Quentin	15.00
CR	Cal Ripken Jr.	125.00
DH	Danny Haren	15.00
DJ	Derek Jeter	150.00
DO	David Ortiz	50.00
DU	Dan Uggla	10.00
DW	Dontrelle Willis	15.00
EC	Eric Chavez	10.00
GO	Alex Gordon	50.00
GP	Glen Perkins	10.00
HA	Justin Hampson	10.00
HI	Rich Hill	10.00
HK	Howard Kendrick	15.00
HP	Hunter Pence	50.00
HR	Hanley Ramirez	25.00
HS	Huston Street	10.00
HU	Torii Hunter	15.00
IK	Ian Kinsler	15.00
JA	Jason Bay	15.00
JB	Jeff Baker	10.00
JH	Josh Hamilton	25.00
JP	Jonathan Papelbon	35.00
JT	Jim Thome	30.00
JU	Justin Morneau	15.00
JV	Justin Verlander	30.00
JW	Jered Weaver	15.00
JZ	Joel Zumaya	10.00
KE	Austin Kearns	10.00
KG	Ken Griffey Jr.	80.00
KK	Kevin Kouzmanoff	15.00
LE	Cliff Lee	10.00
LI	Adam Lind	10.00
MB	Michael Bourn	15.00
MC	Matt Cain	15.00
MO	Micah Owings	20.00
MS	Mike Schmidt	50.00
PS	Phil Hughes	60.00
RA	Aramis Ramirez	15.00
RC	Roger Clemens	75.00
RH	Rich Harden	10.00
RO	Roy Oswalt	15.00
RZ	Ryan Zimmerman	25.00
SD	Stephen Drew	15.00
SH	Sean Henn	10.00
SK	Scott Kazmir	25.00
SO	Jeremy Sowers	10.00
TI	Tim Hudson	10.00
TL	Tim Lincecum	50.00
TR	Travis Hafner	15.00
TT	Troy Tulowitzki	25.00
VM	Victor Martinez	20.00
XN	Xavier Nady	10.00

5x7 Box Topper

NM/M

Common Player: 5.00
Inserted 1:Box

1	Cal Ripken Jr.	15.00
2	Ken Griffey Jr.	10.00
3	Derek Jeter	15.00
4	Sandy Koufax	15.00
5	Babe Ruth	15.00
6	Lou Gehrig	15.00
7	Travis Hafner	5.00
8	Victor Martinez	5.00
9	Jered Weaver	5.00
10	Phil Hughes	8.00
11	Bobby Doerr	5.00
12	Billy Butler	5.00
13	Andy LaRoche	5.00
14	Josh Hamilton	5.00
15	Reggie Jackson	8.00
16	Hanley Ramirez	8.00
17	Don Larsen	8.00
18	Ken Griffey Jr.	10.00
19	Jason Bay	5.00
20	Daisuke Matsuzaka	15.00

5x7 Box Topper Autograph

NM/M

Inserted 1:Case

1	Cal Ripken Jr.	
2	Ken Griffey Jr.	85.00
3	Derek Jeter	150.00
7	Travis Hafner	35.00
8	Victor Martinez	25.00
9	Jered Weaver	30.00
10	Phil Hughes	60.00
11	Bobby Doerr	50.00
12	Billy Butler	50.00
13	Andy LaRoche	20.00
14	Josh Hamilton	25.00
15	Reggie Jackson	50.00
16	Hanley Ramirez	35.00
17	Don Larsen	65.00
18	Ken Griffey Jr.	85.00
19	Jason Bay	20.00
20	Daisuke Matsuzaka	275.00

2007 UD Sweet Spot

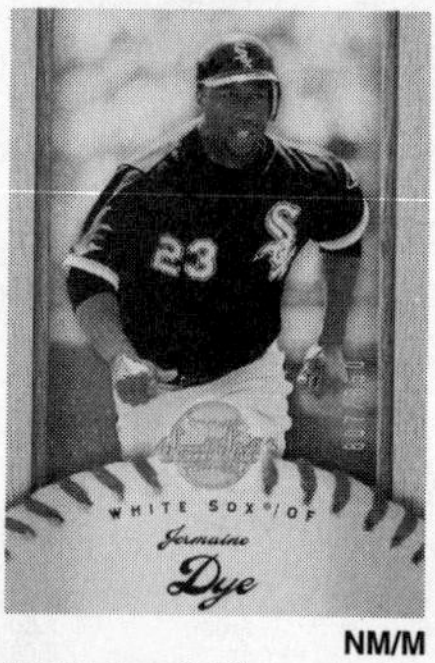

NM/M

Common Player (1-100): 2.00
Production 850
Common RC Auto. (101-142): 8.00
Tin (6): 100.00

1	Adam Dunn	3.00
2	Adrian Beltre	3.00
3	Albert Pujols	10.00
4	Alex Rios	3.00
5	Alex Rodriguez	10.00
6	Alfonso Soriano	4.00
7	Andruw Jones	3.00
8	Aramis Ramirez	3.00
9	B.J. Upton	3.00
10	Barry Zito	2.00
11	Bartolo Colon	2.00
12	Ben Sheets	2.00
13	Bill Hall	2.00
14	Brad Penny	2.00
15	Brandon Webb	3.00
16	C.C. Sabathia	3.00
17	Carl Crawford	2.00
18	Carlos Beltran	3.00
19	Carlos Guillen	2.00
20	Carlos Lee	3.00
21	Chase Utley	5.00
22	Chien-Ming Wang	6.00
23	Chipper Jones	4.00
24	Chris Carpenter	3.00
25	Cole Hamels	4.00
26	Craig Biggio	3.00
27	Curt Schilling	4.00
28	Danny Haren	3.00
29	David Ortiz	5.00
30	David Wright	5.00
31	Delmon Young	2.00
32	Derek Jeter	10.00
33	Derrek Lee	3.00
34	Dontrelle Willis	2.00
35	Felix Hernandez	4.00
36	Frank Thomas	4.00
37	Gil Meche	2.00
38	Grady Sizemore	5.00
39	Greg Maddux	6.00
40	Ian Kinsler	2.00
41	Ichiro Suzuki	6.00
42	Ivan Rodriguez	3.00
43	Jake Peavy	3.00
44	Jason Bay	3.00
45	Jason Varitek	3.00
46	Jeff Kent	3.00
47	Jermaine Dye	2.00
48	Jim Edmonds	2.00
49	Jim Thome	3.00
50	Jimmy Rollins	5.00
51	Joe Mauer	3.00
52	Johan Santana	4.00
53	John Smoltz	3.00
54	Jonathan Papelbon	4.00
55	Jorge Posada	3.00
56	Jose Reyes	4.00
57	Josh Beckett	4.00
58	Justin Morneau	3.00
59	Justin Verlander	3.00
60	Ken Griffey Jr.	8.00
61	Kenji Johjima	2.00
62	Lance Berkman	3.00
63	Magglio Ordonez	3.00
64	Manny Ramirez	4.00
65	Mariano Rivera	3.00
66	Mark Buehrle	2.00
67	Mark Teixeira	3.00
68	Matt Holliday	4.00
69	Matt Morris	2.00
70	Melvin Mora	2.00
71	Michael Young	2.00
72	Miguel Cabrera	4.00
73	Miguel Tejada	3.00
74	Mike Lowell	3.00
75	Mike Mussina	3.00
76	Mike Piazza	4.00
77	Nick Swisher	2.00
78	Orlando Hudson	2.00
79	Paul Konerko	3.00
80	Paul LoDuca	2.00
81	Pedro Martinez	4.00
82	Prince Fielder	4.00
83	Randy Johnson	4.00
84	Rickie Weeks	2.00
85	Roger Clemens	6.00
86	Roy Halladay	3.00
87	Roy Oswalt	3.00
88	Russell Martin	3.00
89	Ryan Howard	6.00
90	Ryan Zimmerman	3.00
91	Sammy Sosa	3.00
92	Scott Rolen	3.00
93	Shawn Green	2.00
94	Todd Helton	3.00
95	Tom Glavine	3.00
96	Torii Hunter	2.00
97	Travis Hafner	3.00
98	Vernon Wells	2.00
99	Victor Martinez	3.00
100	Vladimir Guerrero	4.00
101	Adam Lind **(RC)**	10.00
102	Akinori Iwamura/SP **RC**	25.00
103	Alex Gordon **RC**	60.00
104	Alexi Casilla **RC**	15.00
105	Andy LaRoche **(RC)**	15.00
106	Billy Butler **(RC)**	25.00
107	Ryan Rowland-Smith **RC**	10.00
108	Brandon Wood **(RC)**	15.00
109	Brian Burres **(RC)**	10.00
110	Chase Wright **RC**	15.00
111	Chris Stewart **RC**	10.00
112	Daisuke Matsuzaka/ SP **RC**	300.00
113	Delmon Young/SP **(RC)**	20.00
114	Andrew Sonnanstine **RC**	15.00
115	Andrew Miller **RC**	30.00
116	Fred Lewis **(RC)**	15.00
117	Glen Perkins SP **(RC)**	15.00
118	David Murphy **(RC)**	15.00
119	Hunter Pence **(RC)**	35.00
120	Jarrod Saltalamacchia **(RC)**	20.00
121	Jeff Baker/SP **(RC)**	15.00
122	Jesus Flores/SP **RC**	20.00
123	Joakim Soria/SP **RC**	20.00
124	Joe Smith **RC**	15.00
125	Jon Knott **(RC)**	10.00
126	Josh Hamilton **(RC)**	40.00
127	Justin Hampson **(RC)**	10.00
128	Kei Igawa/SP **RC**	20.00
129	Kevin Cameron **RC**	8.00
130	Matt Chico **(RC)**	8.00
131	Matt DeSalvo **(RC)**	15.00
132	Micah Owings/SP **(RC)**	30.00
133	Michael Bourn **(RC)**	15.00
134	Miguel Montero **(RC)**	10.00
135	Phil Hughes SP **(RC)**	40.00
136	Rick Vanden Hurk **RC**	10.00
138	Tim Lincecum **RC**	100.00
139	Travis Buck **(RC)**	15.00
140	Troy Tulowitzki/SP **(RC)**	30.00
141	Sean Henn **(RC)**	10.00
142	Zack Segovia **(RC)**	10.00
MB	Michael Buysner/SP	20.00

Dual Signatures Red Stitch Blue Ink

No pricing
Production 5-15

Dual Signatures Black Glove Gold Ink

No Pricing
Production 5-10
Silver Ink: No Pricing
Production One Set
Leather Black Ink: No Pricing
Production 5-15

Dual Signatures Gold Stitch Gold Ink

No Pricing
Production 5-10
Silver Ink: No Pricing
Production Five Sets

Signatures Bat Barrel Blue Ink

NM/M

Production 1-99
Silver Ink: 1-1.5X
Production 25 or 15
Gold Ink: No Pricing
Production One Set
Red Ink: No Pricing
Production Five Sets
No pricing production under 25.

AK	Austin Kearns/25	15.00
AL	Adam LaRoche/25	20.00
BB	Boof Bonser/26	20.00
BR	Brian Bruney/99	20.00
CB	Chad Billingsley/58	30.00
CC	Chris Capuano/39	10.00
CL	Cliff Lee/31	20.00
CY	Chris Young/32	20.00
DC	Daniel Cabrera/35	15.00
DR	Darrell Rasner/27	20.00
EA	Erick Aybar/23	20.00
GP	Glen Perkins/60	10.00
HK	Howie Kendrick/47	25.00
JH	Josh Hamilton/33	45.00
JN	Joe Nathan/36	20.00
KS	Kurt Suzuki/99	20.00
LI	Adam Lind/99	15.00
RH	Rich Hill/51	15.00
RM	Russell Martin/55	40.00
SE	Sergio Mitre/99	15.00
AD	Adam Dunn/44	25.00
AM	Andrew Miller/48	35.00
BP	Brandon Phillips/99	20.00
CH	Cole Hamels/35	35.00
CK	Casey Kotchman/99	15.00
FH	Felix Hernandez/34	50.00
FP	Felix Pie/99	20.00
HA	Travis Hafner/48	20.00
JL	Jon Lester/31	40.00
JP	Jonathan Papelbon/58	50.00
JS	Jeremy Sowers/45	20.00
JV	Jason Varitek/33	50.00
PH	Phil Hughes/65	50.00
PK	Paul Konerko/99	25.00
RI	Rich Harden/40	15.00
TG	Tom Glavine/47	40.00
TH	Torii Hunter/48	20.00
TL	Tim Lincecum/55	75.00
VE	Justin Verlander/35	50.00
VM	Victor Martinez/41	30.00

Sign. Black Bat Barrel Silver Ink

Production 10 or 15
Gold Ink: No Pricing
Production One Set
Red Ink: No Pricing
Production Five Sets

Signatures Black Glove Silver Ink

NM/M

Production 10 or 25
Gold Ink: No Pricing
Production Five Sets
Metallic Blue Ink: No Pricing
Production One Set
No pricing prod. under 25.

AG	Adrian Gonzalez/25	25.00
AK	Austin Kearns/25	20.00
AL	Adam LaRoche/25	20.00
BB	Boof Bonser/25	15.00
BR	Brian Bruney/25	20.00
BW	Brandon Wood/25	25.00
CB	Chad Billingsley/25	35.00
CC	Chris Capuano/25	15.00
CJ	Conor Jackson/25	20.00
CL	Cliff Lee/25	20.00
CQ	Carlos Quentin/25	15.00
CY	Chris Young/25	20.00
DC	Daniel Cabrera/25	15.00
DH	Danny Haren/25	35.00
DR	Darrell Rasner/25	15.00
EA	Erick Aybar/25	20.00
GP	Glen Perkins/25	15.00
HP	Hunter Pence/25	75.00
JH	Josh Hamilton/25	50.00
JK	Jason Kubel/25	20.00
JN	Joe Nathan/25	20.00
JW	Josh Willingham/25	20.00
KA	Jeff Karstens/25	15.00

KS Kurt Suzuki/25 20.00
LO Lyle Overbay/25 15.00
MC Matt Cain/25 30.00
RH Rich Hill/25 30.00
RM Russell Martin/25 50.00
SE Sergio Mitre/25 15.00
TB Travis Buck/25 25.00
YG Chris B. Young/25 30.00

Signatures Glove Black Ink

NM/M

Production 25 or 75
Silver Ink: 1-1.5X
Production 25 or 10
Green Ink: No Pricing
Production One Set
No pricing product. under 25.

AG Adrian Gonzalez/75 20.00
AK Austin Kearns/75 15.00
AL Adam LaRoche/75 15.00
BB Boof Bonser/75 15.00
BR Brian Bruney/75 20.00
BW Brandon Wood/75 20.00
CB Chad Billingsley/75 30.00
CC Chris Capuano/75 15.00
CJ Conor Jackson/75 20.00
CL Cliff Lee/75 20.00
CQ Carlos Quentin/75 15.00
CY Chris Young/75 20.00
DC Daniel Cabrera/75 15.00
DH Dan Haren/75 30.00
DR Darrell Rasner/75 15.00
EA Erick Aybar/75 20.00
GP Glen Perkins/75 15.00
HK Howie Kendrick/75 20.00
HP Hunter Pence/75 50.00
JH Josh Hamilton/75 30.00
JK Jason Kubel/75 15.00
JN Joe Nathan/75 20.00
JW Josh Willingham/75 20.00
KA Jeff Karstens/75 15.00
KS Kurt Suzuki/75 20.00
LO Lyle Overbay/75 15.00
MC Matt Cain/75 25.00
RH Rich Hill/75 20.00
RM Russell Martin/75 30.00
SE Sergio Mitre/75 15.00
TB Travis Buck/75 25.00
YG Chris B. Young/75 25.00
AD Adam Dunn/25 30.00
AI Akinori Iwamura/25 40.00
AM Andrew Miller/25 35.00
AX Alex Gordon/25 75.00
BP Brandon Phillips/25 30.00
CA Carl Crawford/25 25.00
CH Cole Hamels/25 40.00
CK Casey Kotchman/25 20.00
DY Delmon Young/25 25.00
FH Felix Hernandez/25 50.00
FP Felix Pie/25 30.00
HA Travis Hafner/25 20.00
HS Huston Street/25 20.00
JL Jon Lester/25 20.00
JP Jonathan Papelbon/25 50.00
JS Jeremy Sowers/25 15.00
JV Jason Varitek/25 60.00
MH Matt Holliday/25 60.00
MM Melvin Mora/25 15.00
PH Phil Hughes/25 60.00
PK Paul Konerko/25 40.00
RC Roger Clemens/25 100.00
RI Rich Harden/25 20.00
RW Rickie Weeks/25 25.00
RZ Ryan Zimmerman/25 30.00
SK Scott Kazmir/25 30.00
TG Tom Glavine/25 50.00
TH Torii Hunter/25 25.00
TL Tim Lincecum/25 100.00
VE Justin Verlander/25 50.00
VM Victor Martinez/25 35.00

Signatures Gold Stitch Gold Ink

NM/M

Production 25 or 99
Red/Blue Stitch Red Ink: No Pricing
Production 5 or 15

AG Adrian Gonzalez/99 20.00
AK Austin Kearns/99 20.00
AL Adam LaRoche/99 20.00
BB Boof Bonser/99 15.00
BR Brian Bruney/99 20.00
BW Brandon Wood/99 20.00
CB Chad Billingsley/99 30.00
CC Chris Capuano/99 15.00
CJ Conor Jackson/99 20.00
CL Cliff Lee/99 20.00
CQ Carlos Quentin/99 15.00
CY Chris Young/99 20.00
DC Daniel Cabrera/99 15.00
DH Danny Haren/99 30.00
DR Darrell Rasner/99 15.00
EA Erick Aybar/99 20.00
GP Glen Perkins/99 15.00
HK Howie Kendrick/99 20.00
HP Hunter Pence/99 65.00
JH Josh Hamilton/99 40.00
JK Jason Kubel/99 20.00
JN Joe Nathan/99 20.00
JW Josh Willingham/99 20.00
KA Jeff Karstens/99 15.00
KS Kurt Suzuki/99 20.00
LI Adam Lind/99 15.00
LO Lyle Overbay/99 15.00

MC Matt Cain/99 25.00
RH Rich Hill/99 25.00
RM Russell Martin/99 30.00
SE Sergio Mitre/99 15.00
TB Travis Buck/99 25.00
YG Chris B. Young/99 25.00
AD Adam Dunn/25 30.00
AI Akinori Iwamura/25 40.00
AM Andrew Miller/25 35.00
AX Alex Gordon/25 75.00
BP Brandon Phillips/25 30.00
CA Carl Crawford/25 25.00
CH Cole Hamels/25 40.00
CK Casey Kotchman/25 20.00
DY Delmon Young/25 50.00
FH Felix Hernandez/25 50.00
FP Felix Pie/25 30.00
HA Travis Hafner/25 20.00
HS Huston Street/25 20.00
JL Jon Lester/25 50.00
JP Jonathan Papelbon/25 50.00
JS Jeremy Sowers/25 15.00
JV Jason Varitek/25 60.00
MH Matt Holliday/25 50.00
MM Melvin Mora/25 15.00
PH Phil Hughes/25 80.00
PK Paul Konerko/25 50.00
RC Roger Clemens/25 100.00
RI Rich Harden/25 20.00
RW Rickie Weeks/25 20.00
RZ Ryan Zimmerman/25 30.00
SK Scott Kazmir/25 30.00
TG Tom Glavine/25 50.00
TH Torii Hunter/25 25.00
TL Tim Lincecum/25 100.00
VE Justin Verlander/25 50.00
VM Victor Martinez/25 35.00

Signatures Red Stitch Blue Ink

NM/M

Common Auto.: 10.00
AG Adrian Gonzalez/350 15.00
AK Austin Kearns/299 10.00
AL Adam LaRoche/350 15.00
BB Boof Bonser/299 10.00
BR Brian Bruney/299 10.00
BW Brandon Wood/350 15.00
CB Chad Billingsley/299 25.00
CC Chris Capuano/299 10.00
CJ Conor Jackson/299 15.00
CL Cliff Lee/299 10.00
CQ Carlos Quentin/299 10.00
CY Chris Young/350 15.00
DC Daniel Cabrera/299 10.00
DH Danny Haren/299 20.00
DR Darrell Rasner/299 10.00
EA Erick Aybar/299 15.00
GP Glen Perkins/350 15.00
HK Howie Kendrick/350 15.00
HP Hunter Pence/350 35.00
JH Josh Hamilton/350 35.00
JK Jason Kubel/299 10.00
JN Joe Nathan/299 15.00
JW Josh Willingham/299 10.00
KA Jeff Karstens/299 10.00
KS Kurt Suzuki/299 15.00
LI Adam Lind/299 10.00
LO Lyle Overbay/299 15.00
MC Matt Cain/299 15.00
RH Rich Hill/299 15.00
RM Russell Martin/299 25.00
SE Sergio Mitre/299 10.00
TB Travis Buck/299 20.00
YG Chris B. Young/299 20.00
AD Adam Dunn/99 20.00
AI Akinori Iwamura/99 35.00
AM Andrew Miller/99 30.00
AX Alex Gordon/99 50.00
BP Brandon Phillips/99 20.00
CA Carl Crawford/99 15.00
CH Cole Hamels/99 30.00
CK Casey Kotchman/99 15.00
DY Delmon Young/99 25.00
FH Felix Hernandez/99 35.00
FP Felix Pie/99 20.00
HA Travis Hafner/99 25.00
HS Huston Street/99 15.00
JL Jon Lester/99 25.00
JP Jonathan Papelbon/99 50.00
JS Jeremy Sowers/99 15.00
JV Jason Varitek/99 50.00
MH Matt Holliday/99 40.00
MM Melvin Mora/99 10.00
PH Phil Hughes/99 60.00
PK Paul Konerko/99 30.00
RC Roger Clemens/99 80.00
RI Rich Harden/99 10.00
RW Rickie Weeks/99 15.00
RZ Ryan Zimmerman/99 20.00
SK Scott Kazmir/99 20.00
TG Tom Glavine/99 40.00
TH Torii Hunter/99 15.00
TL Tim Lincecum/99 60.00
VE Justin Verlander/99 40.00
VM Victor Martinez/99 20.00

Signatures Silver Stitch Silver Ink

NM/M

Production 1-99
No pricing product. under 25
AK Austin Kearns/25 20.00
AL Adam LaRoche/25 25.00
BB Boof Bonser/26 20.00

BR Brian Bruney/99 20.00
CB Chad Billingsley/58 30.00
CC Chris Capuano/39 15.00
CL Cliff Lee/31 20.00
CY Chris Young/32 20.00
DC Daniel Cabrera/35 15.00
DR Darrell Rasner/27 20.00
EA Erick Aybar/32 25.00
GP Glen Perkins/60 15.00
HK Howie Kendrick/47 20.00
JH Josh Hamilton/33 40.00
JN Joe Nathan/36 20.00
KS Kurt Suzuki/29 20.00
AI Adam Lind/99 15.00
RH Rich Hill/51 25.00
RM Russell Martin/55 30.00
SE Sergio Mitre/99 15.00
YG Chris B. Young/24 30.00
AD Adam Dunn/44 25.00
AM Andrew Miller/48 30.00
BP Brandon Phillips/99 20.00
CH Cole Hamels/35 35.00
CK Casey Kotchman/99 15.00
FH Felix Hernandez/34 50.00
FP Felix Pie/99 20.00
HA Travis Hafner/48 25.00
JL Jon Lester/31 40.00
JP Jonathan Papelbon/58 40.00
JS Jeremy Sowers/45 20.00
JV Jason Varitek/33 50.00
PH Phil Hughes/65 50.00
PK Paul Konerko/99 30.00
RI Rich Harden/40 15.00
TG Tom Glavine/47 40.00
TH Torii Hunter/48 20.00
TL Tim Lincecum/55 75.00
VE Justin Verlander/35 50.00
VM Victor Martinez/41 30.00

Sweet Swatch Memorabilia

NM/M

Common Player: 4.00
Patch: 2-4X
Production 25 Sets
AD Adam Dunn 8.00
AJ Andruw Jones 6.00
AP Albert Pujols 15.00
AS Alfonso Soriano 8.00
AT Garrett Atkins 4.00
BA Bobby Abreu 6.00
BE Josh Beckett 10.00
BG Brian Giles 4.00
BI Craig Biggio 6.00
BO Jeremy Bonderman 4.00
BR Brian Roberts 6.00
BU B.J. Upton 6.00
BW Billy Wagner 4.00
CA Chris Carpenter 6.00
CB Carlos Beltran 6.00
CC Carl Crawford 4.00
CH Cole Hamels 8.00
CJ Chipper Jones 8.00
CL Carlos Lee 6.00
CS Curt Schilling 8.00
CU Chase Utley 15.00
DJ Derek Jeter 20.00
DM Daisuke Matsuzaka 30.00
DO David Ortiz 10.00
DW Dontrelle Willis 4.00
EB Erik Bedard 6.00
EC Eric Chavez 4.00
FG Freddy Garcia 4.00
FH Felix Hernandez 8.00
FL Francisco Liriano 6.00
FT Frank Thomas 8.00
GA Garret Anderson 4.00
GM Greg Maddux 8.00
GR Khalil Greene 6.00
GS Grady Sizemore 15.00
HA Roy Halladay 6.00
HB Hank Blalock 4.00
HE Todd Helton 6.00
HO Trevor Hoffman 4.00
HR Hanley Ramirez 8.00
HS Huston Street 4.00
HU Torii Hunter 6.00
IK Ian Kinsler 6.00
IR Ivan Rodriguez 6.00
JB Jason Bay 6.00
JD Jermaine Dye 4.00
JE Jim Edmonds 4.00
JF Jeff Francoeur 8.00
JG Jason Giambi 4.00
JK Jeff Kent 4.00
JM Joe Mauer 6.00
JN Joe Nathan 4.00
JP Jake Peavy 6.00
JR Jimmy Rollins 10.00
JS Jason Schmidt 4.00
JT Jim Thome 8.00
JV Jason Varitek 8.00
JW Jered Weaver 8.00
JZ Joel Zumaya 4.00
KG Ken Griffey Jr. 15.00
KM Kendry Morales 4.00
LB Lance Berkman 6.00
LG Luis Gonzalez 4.00
MC Miguel Cabrera 8.00
MM Mike Mussina 6.00
MO Justin Morneau 8.00
MR Manny Ramirez 8.00
MT Mark Teixeira 6.00
MY Michael Young 6.00
OR Magglio Ordonez 6.00
OS Roy Oswalt 6.00

PA Jonathan Papelbon 10.00
PB Pat Burrell 4.00
PE Jhonny Peralta 4.00
PF Prince Fielder 8.00
PM Pedro Martinez 8.00
PO Jorge Posada 8.00
RC Robinson Cano 10.00
RE Jose Reyes 10.00
RH Rich Harden 4.00
RI Mariano Rivera 8.00
RJ Randy Johnson 8.00
RO Roger Clemens 10.00
RW Rickie Weeks 4.00
RZ Ryan Zimmerman 6.00
SA Johan Santana 8.00
SD Stephen Drew 6.00
SK Scott Kazmir 6.00
SM John Smoltz 6.00
SR Scott Rolen 6.00
TE Miguel Tejada 6.00
TG Tom Glavine 6.00
TH Tim Hudson 4.00
TR Travis Hafner 6.00
VE Justin Verlander 8.00
VG Vladimir Guerrero 8.00
VM Victor Martinez 6.00
VW Vernon Wells 4.00

2007 UD Sweet Spot Classic

NM/M

Common Player: 2.00
Production 575 sets
Tin (5): 100.00
1 Phil Niekro 2.00
2 Fred McGriff 3.00
3 Bob Horner 2.00
4 Earl Weaver 2.00
5 Boog Powell 2.00
6 Eddie Murray 4.00
7 Fred Lynn 2.00
8 Dwight Evans 2.00
9 Jim Rice 3.00
10 Carlton Fisk 4.00
11 Luis Tiant 2.00
12 Robin Yount 4.00
13 Bobby Doerr 3.00
14 Ryne Sandberg 5.00
15 Billy Williams 3.00
16 Andre Dawson 2.00
17 Mark Grace 3.00
18 Ron Santo 3.00
19 Shawon Dunston 2.00
20 Harold Baines 2.00
21 Carlton Fisk 4.00
22 Sparky Anderson 2.00
23 George Foster 2.00
24 Dave Parker 2.00
25 Ken Griffey Jr. 8.00
26 Dave Concepcion 2.00
27 Rafael Palmeiro 3.00
28 Al Rosen 2.00
29 Kirk Gibson 2.00
30 Alan Trammell 3.00
31 Jack Morris 2.00
32 Willie Horton 2.00
33 J.R. Richard 2.00
34 Jose Cruz 2.00
35 Willie Wilson 2.00
36 Willie Wilson 2.00
37 Bo Jackson 8.00
38 Nolan Ryan 8.00
39 Don Baylor 2.00
40 Maury Wills 2.00
41 Tommy John 2.00
42 Ron Cey 2.00
43 Davey Lopes 2.00
44 Tommy Lasorda 2.00
45 Burt Hooton 2.00
46 Reggie Smith 2.00
47 Rollie Fingers 2.00
48 Cecil Cooper 2.00
49 Paul Molitor 4.00
50 Vern Stephens 2.00
51 Tony Oliva 3.00
52 Andres Galarraga 2.00
53 Tim Raines 3.00
54 Dennis Martinez 2.00
55 Lee Mazzilli 2.00
56 Rusty Staub 2.00
57 David Cone 2.00
58 Reggie Jackson 4.00
59 Ron Guidry 2.00

60 Tino Martinez 3.00
61 Don Mattingly 6.00
62 Chris Chambliss 2.00
63 Sparky Lyle 2.00
64 Rich "Goose" Gossage 2.00
65 Dave Righetti 2.00
66 Phil Garner 2.00
67 Bill Madlock 2.00
68 Kent Hrbek 2.00
69 Al Oliver 2.00
70 John Kruk 2.00
71 Greg Luzinski 2.00
72 Dick Allen 2.00
73 Richie Ashburn 3.00
74 Gary Matthews 2.00
76 Mike Schmidt 5.00
77 Waite Hoyt 2.00
78 Bruce Sutter 2.00
79 Roger Maris 6.00
80 Joe Torre 3.00
81 Kevin Mitchell 2.00
82 John Montefusco 2.00
83 Rick Reuschel 2.00
84 Will Clark 3.00
85 Jack Clark 2.00
86 Matt Williams 2.00
87 Steve Garvey 3.00
88 Dave Winfield 3.00
89 Jay Buhner 2.00
90 Edgar Martinez 2.00
91 Carney Lansford 2.00
92 Sal Bando 2.00
93 Dave Stewart 2.00
94 Dennis Eckersley 3.00
95 Jose Canseco 3.00
96 Dennis Eckersley 3.00
97 Roberto Alomar 3.00
98 George Bell 2.00
99 Joe Carter 2.00
100 Frank Howard 2.00
101 Brooks Robinson 4.00
102 Frank Robinson 4.00
103 Jim Palmer 3.00
104 Cal Ripken Jr. 8.00
105 Warren Spahn 4.00
106 Cy Young 4.00
107 Waite Hoyt 2.00
108 Carl Yastrzemski 4.00
109 Johnny Pesky 3.00
110 Wade Boggs 3.00
111 Jackie Robinson 4.00
112 Roy Campanella 4.00
113 Pee Wee Reese 2.00
114 Don Newcombe 2.00
115 Rod Carew 4.00
116 Ernie Banks 4.00
117 Fergie Jenkins 2.00
118 Al Lopez 2.00
119 Luis Aparicio 2.00
120 Toby Harrah 2.00
121 Joe Morgan 3.00
122 Johnny Bench 4.00
123 Tony Perez 3.00
124 Ted Kluszewski 2.00
125 Bob Feller 3.00
126 Bob Lemon 2.00
127 Larry Doby 3.00
128 Lou Boudreau 2.00
129 George Kell 2.00
130 Hal Newhouser 2.00
131 Al Kaline 4.00
132 Ty Cobb 5.00
133 Denny McLain 2.00
134 Buck Leonard 3.00
135 Dean Chance 2.00
136 Don Drysdale 3.00
137 Don Sutton 3.00
138 Eddie Mathews 4.00
139 Paul Molitor 4.00
140 Kirby Puckett 5.00
141 Rod Carew 3.00
142 Harmon Killebrew 4.00
143 Monte Irvin 3.00
144 Mel Ott 3.00
145 Christy Mathewson 4.00
146 Hoyt Wilhelm 2.00
147 Tom Seaver 4.00
148 Joe McCarthy 2.00
149 Joe DiMaggio 5.00
150 Lou Gehrig 6.00
151 Babe Ruth 8.00
152 Casey Stengel 3.00
153 Phil Rizzuto 4.00
154 Thurman Munson 5.00
155 Johnny Mize 2.00
156 Yogi Berra 4.00
157 Roger Maris 5.00
158 Don Larsen 3.00
159 Bill "Moose" Skowron 2.00
160 Lou Piniella 3.00
161 Joe Pepitone 2.00
162 Ray Dandridge 2.00
163 Rollie Fingers 2.00
165 Reggie Jackson 4.00
166 Mickey Cochrane 3.00
167 Jimmie Foxx 4.00
168 Lefty Grove 3.00
169 Gus Zernial 2.00
170 Jim Bunning 2.00
171 Steve Carlton 3.00
172 Robin Roberts 3.00
173 Ralph Kiner 3.00
174 Willie Stargell 4.00
175 Roberto Clemente 6.00
176 Bill Mazeroski 2.00
177 Honus Wagner 5.00
178 Pie Traynor 3.00
179 Elroy Face 2.00
180 Dick Groat 2.00
181 Tony Gwynn 4.00
182 Willie McCovey 3.00
183 Gaylord Perry 2.00
184 Juan Marichal 3.00
185 Orlando Cepeda 3.00
186 Satchel Paige 4.00
187 George Sisler 3.00
188 Rogers Hornsby 4.00
189 Stan Musial 4.00
190 Dizzy Dean 3.00
191 Bob Gibson 4.00
192 Red Schoendienst 2.00
193 Lou Brock 3.00
194 Enos Slaughter 2.00
195 Nolan Ryan 8.00
196 Mickey Vernon 2.00
197 Walter Johnson 4.00
198 Rick Ferrell 2.00
199 Roy Sievers 2.00
200 Judy Johnson 2.00

Classic Memorabilia

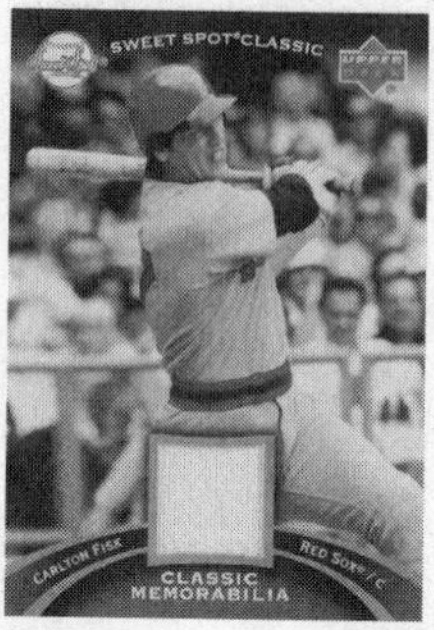

NM/M
Common Player: 5.00
Patch: 2-4X
Production 55 Sets
AD Andre Dawson 8.00
AK Al Kaline 10.00
AO Al Oliver 8.00
BE Johnny Bench 15.00
BJ Bo Jackson 15.00
BM Bill Madlock 5.00
BO Wade Boggs 8.00
BR Babe Ruth/SP 200.00
BS Bruce Sutter 5.00
CL Roberto Clemente 40.00
CM Christy Mathewson/SP 125.00
CR Cal Ripken Jr. 20.00
CS Casey Stengel 10.00
CY Carl Yastrzemski 10.00
DD Dizzy Dean 30.00
DE Dennis Eckersley 5.00
DM Don Mattingly 15.00
DP Dave Parker 5.00
DR Don Drysdale 10.00
DS Don Sutton 5.00
DW Dave Winfield 10.00
ED Eddie Murray 8.00
EM Eddie Mathews 15.00
EV Dwight Evans 5.00
EW Early Wynn 8.00
FG Fred McGriff 5.00
FI Rollie Fingers 5.00
FR Frank Robinson 10.00
GF George Foster 5.00
GG Rich "Goose" Gossage 8.00
GI Kirk Gibson 5.00
GP Gaylord Perry 5.00
GW Tony Gwynn 10.00
HB Harold Baines/SP 8.00
HK Harmon Killebrew/SP 10.00
JB Jim Bunning 8.00
JD Joe DiMaggio 60.00
JI Jim Rice 8.00
JM Jack Morris 5.00
JP Jim Palmer 8.00
JU Juan Marichal 8.00
KG Ken Griffey Jr. 5.00
KH Kent Hrbek 5.00
KP Kirby Puckett 15.00
LA Luis Aparicio 5.00
LB Lou Brock 8.00
LG Lou Gehrig 150.00
MA Don Mattingly 15.00
ME Eddie Murray 8.00
MG Mark Grace 8.00
MO Mel Ott 20.00
MP Paul Molitor 10.00
MR Edgar Martinez 5.00
MS Mike Schmidt 15.00
MW Maury Wills 5.00
NR Nolan Ryan 20.00
PA Dave Parker 5.00
PE Tony Perez 5.00
PM Paul Molitor 10.00
PN Phil Niekro 5.00
PR Pee Wee Reese SP 25.00
RF Rollie Fingers 5.00
RG Ron Guidry 10.00
RH Rogers Hornsby 25.00
RK Ralph Kiner 10.00
RM Roger Maris 30.00
RO Roy Campanella 15.00
RS Ron Santo 10.00
RY Nolan Ryan 20.00
SC Red Schoendienst 8.00
SG Steve Garvey 5.00
ST Steve Carlton 8.00
SU Bruce Sutter 5.00
TG Tony Gwynn 10.00
TM Thurman Munson 20.00
TO Tony Oliva 8.00
TP Tony Perez 5.00
TR Tim Raines 5.00
WB Wade Boggs 8.00
WC Will Clark 5.00
WM Willie McCovey 8.00
WS Willie Stargell 8.00
YO Robin Yount 10.00
CF1 Carlton Fisk 8.00
CF2 Carlton Fisk 8.00
FR1 Frank Robinson 10.00
MI1 Johnny Mize 10.00
MI2 Johnny Mize 10.00
RC1 Rod Carew 8.00
RC2 Rod Carew 8.00
RJ1 Reggie Jackson 10.00
RJ2 Reggie Jackson 10.00
RJ3 Reggie Jackson 10.00

Dual Sig Red Stitch-Blue Ink

NM/M
Production 50 Sets
Black Stitch Red Ink: No Pricing
Production One Set
Gold Stitch Black Ink: No Pricing
Production 15 sets
AG Luis Aparicio, Ozzie Guillen 30.00
BC Cal Ripken Jr., Brooks Robinson 140.00
BF Carlton Fisk, Johnny Bench 75.00
BG Harold Baines, Ozzie Guillen 50.00
BR Robin Roberts, Jim Bunning 60.00
CG Tony Gwynn, Rod Carew 90.00
CO Tony Oliva, Rod Carew 40.00
FE Dennis Eckersley, Rollie Fingers 50.00
FG Elroy Face, Dick Groat 50.00
FM Mike Schmidt, Frank Robinson 80.00
FR Carlton Fisk, Jim Rice 50.00
GR Bob Gibson, J.R. Richard 50.00
GS Steve Garvey, Reggie Smith 30.00
GW Tony Gwynn, Dave Winfield 80.00
HK Al Kaline, Willie Horton 80.00
JS Reggie Smith, Reggie Jackson 50.00
KM Ralph Kiner, Bill Mazeroski 75.00
LT Tim Raines, Lou Brock 40.00
MC Jack Clark, Willie McCovey 75.00
MG Juan Marichal, Bob Gibson 60.00
MK Stan Musial, Al Kaline 125.00
MM Don Mattingly, Tino Martinez 80.00
MR Edgar Martinez, Harold Reynolds 50.00
OH Tony Oliva, Kent Hrbek 40.00
RG Tony Gwynn, Cal Ripken Jr. 160.00
RR Nolan Ryan, J.R. Richard 150.00
RS Cal Ripken Jr., Mike Schmidt 180.00
SB Ron Santo, Ernie Banks 125.00
SC Mike Schmidt, Steve Carlton 80.00
SD Ryne Sandberg, Shawon Dunston 80.00
SF Rollie Fingers, Bruce Sutter 60.00
SS Ron Santo, Ryne Sandberg 125.00
SV Mickey Vernon, Roy Sievers 30.00
WC Cal Ripken Jr., Wade Boggs 125.00
YP Carl Yastrzemski, Johnny Pesky 100.00

Immortal Signatures

No Pricing

Legendary Lettermen

NM/M
Represents total cards produced
LL1 Babe Ruth/100 150.00
LL2 Ty Cobb/100 75.00
LL3 Christy Mathewson/90 50.00
LL4 Jackie Robinson/80 60.00
LL5 Roy Campanella/100 50.00
LL6 Lou Gehrig/90 150.00
LL7 Mel Ott/75 25.00
LL8 Jimmie Foxx/100 50.00
LL9 Satchel Paige/125 40.00
LL10 Don Drysdale/200 30.00
LL11 Rogers Hornsby/175 60.00
LL12 Honus Wagner/150 50.00
LL13 Babe Ruth/105 150.00
LL14 Dizzy Dean/100 50.00
LL15 Ty Cobb/60 75.00
LL16 Walter Johnson/105 50.00
LL17 Walter Johnson/80 50.00
LL18 Cal Ripken Jr./200 100.00
LL19 Sandy Koufax/150 250.00
LL20 Thurman Munson/150 40.00
LL21 Thurman Munson/70 40.00
LL22 Cal Ripken Jr./175 100.00
LL23 Tony Gwynn/125 50.00
LL24 Nolan Ryan/80 50.00
LL25 Nolan Ryan/165 50.00
LL26 Jackie Robinson/70 60.00
LL27 Carlton Fisk/80 40.00
LL28 Carl Yastrzemski/165 60.00
LL29 Johnny Bench/125 50.00
LL30 Ryne Sandberg/200 100.00
LL31 Don Mattingly/135 75.00
LL32 Ernie Banks/165 40.00
LL33 Bill Mazeroski/135 50.00
LL34 Ernie Banks/125 40.00
LL35 Bob Gibson/150 40.00
LL36 Mike Schmidt/175 60.00
LL37 Al Kaline/150 40.00
LL38 Reggie Jackson/175 50.00
LL39 Stan Musial/150 50.00
LL40 Bo Jackson/175 50.00
LL41 Bo Jackson/105 50.00
LL42 Stan Musial/150 50.00

Ripken Immortal Membership

Production One Set
No Pricing

Signatures Black Ink

NM/M
Common Signature: 15.00
Production 175 unless noted.
AG Andres Galarraga 20.00
AK Al Kaline 30.00
AO Al Oliver 15.00
BJ Bo Jackson 50.00
BM Bill Mazeroski 40.00
BO Wade Boggs/75 40.00
BS Bruce Sutter/75 20.00
CF Carlton Fisk/75 35.00
DA Dick Allen 20.00
DL Don Larsen 30.00
DM Don Mattingly/75 60.00
EC Dennis Eckersley 20.00
EM Edgar Martinez 30.00
FM Fred McGriff 25.00
GP Gaylord Perry 20.00
HB Harold Baines 15.00
JB Johnny Bench/75 60.00
JK John Kruk 20.00
MO Jack Morris 20.00
MS Mike Schmidt/75 50.00
NR Nolan Ryan/75 80.00
OG Ozzie Guillen 20.00
RA Roberto Alomar 25.00
RI Jim Rice 20.00
RJ Reggie Jackson/75 60.00
RS Ryne Sandberg/75 60.00
SA Ron Santo 30.00
SM Reggie Smith 20.00
TG Tony Gwynn/75 50.00
TM Tino Martinez 35.00
TP Tony Perez 25.00
TR Tim Raines 20.00
WB Wade Boggs/75 40.00
WD Willie Davis/75 20.00
WM Willie McCovey/75 50.00
YB Yogi Berra/75 80.00
BR Brooks Robinson 30.00
BW Billy Williams 30.00
CL Carney Lansford 20.00
CO Dave Concepcion 25.00
CY Carl Yastrzemski 50.00
DG Dick Groat 30.00
DS Don Sutton 20.00
DW Dave Winfield 25.00
EB Ernie Banks 60.00
EF Elroy Face 20.00
EV Dwight Evans 20.00
FL Fred Lynn 15.00
FR Frank Robinson/35 50.00
GI Bob Gibson 40.00
JI Jim Bunning 20.00
JP Johnny Pesky 30.00
JR Jim Rice 20.00
KG Ken Griffey Sr. 15.00
KO Sandy Koufax 350.00
LA Luis Aparicio 25.00
LB Lou Brock/75 40.00
MA Juan Marichal 25.00
MG Mark Grace 30.00
MU Stan Musial/75 80.00
MV Mickey Vernon 20.00
OS Ozzie Smith/75 60.00
PN Phil Niekro 20.00
RC Rod Carew 30.00
RF Rollie Fingers 20.00
RK Ralph Kiner/75 40.00
RR Robin Roberts 30.00
RY Robin Yount 40.00
SC Steve Carlton 30.00
SD Shawon Dunston 25.00
SG Steve Garvey 25.00
SK Bill "Moose" Skowron 20.00
TH Toby Harrah 15.00
TO Tony Oliva 20.00
WH Willie Horton 20.00

Signatures Blue Ink

NM/M
Common Signature: 20.00
Production 125 unless noted.

AG	Andres Galarraga	20.00
AK	Al Kaline	30.00
AO	Al Oliver	20.00
BJ	Bo Jackson	50.00
BM	Bill Mazeroski	40.00
BO	Wade Boggs/35	50.00
BS	Bruce Sutter/35	25.00
CF	Carlton Fisk/35	40.00
DA	Dick Allen	20.00
DL	Don Larsen	30.00
DM	Don Mattingly/35	60.00
EC	Dennis Eckersley	20.00
EM	Edgar Martinez	30.00
FM	Fred McGriff	30.00
GP	Gaylord Perry	20.00
HB	Harold Baines	20.00
JB	Johnny Bench/35	60.00
JK	John Kruk	20.00
MO	Jack Morris	20.00
MS	Mike Schmidt/35	75.00
NR	Nolan Ryan/35	120.00
OG	Ozzie Guillen	20.00
RA	Roberto Alomar	25.00
RI	Jim Rice	20.00
RJ	Reggie Jackson/35	60.00
RS	Ryne Sandberg/35	60.00
SA	Ron Santo	30.00
SM	Reggie Smith	20.00
TG	Tony Gwynn/35	60.00
TM	Tino Martinez	40.00
TP	Tony Perez	25.00
TR	Tim Raines	20.00
WB	Wade Boggs/35	50.00
WD	Willie Davis/35	20.00
WM	Willie McCovey/35	60.00
YB	Yogi Berra/35	80.00
BR	Brooks Robinson	30.00
BW	Billy Williams	20.00
CL	Carney Lansford	15.00
CO	Dave Concepcion	15.00
CY	Carl Yastrzemski	60.00
DG	Dick Groat	25.00
DS	Don Sutton	20.00
DW	Dave Winfield	25.00
EB	Ernie Banks	60.00
EF	Elroy Face	30.00
EV	Dwight Evans	20.00
FL	Fred Lynn	15.00
FR	Frank Robinson/75	40.00
GI	Bob Gibson	30.00
JI	Jim Bunning	20.00
JP	Johnny Pesky	25.00
JR	Jim Rice	20.00
KG	Ken Griffey Sr.	20.00
KO	Sandy Koufax	300.00
LA	Luis Aparicio	20.00
LB	Lou Brock/35	40.00
MA	Juan Marichal	30.00
MG	Mark Grace	25.00
MU	Stan Musial/35	80.00
MV	Mickey Vernon	20.00
OS	Ozzie Smith/35	60.00
PN	Phil Niekro	15.00
RC	Rod Carew	30.00
RF	Rollie Fingers	20.00
RK	Ralph Kiner/35	40.00
RR	Robin Roberts	20.00
RY	Robin Yount	40.00
SC	Steve Carlton	25.00
SD	Shawon Dunston	25.00
SG	Steve Garvey	20.00
SK	Bill "Moose" Skowron	20.00
TH	Toby Harrah	15.00
TO	Tony Oliva	20.00
WH	Willie Horton	25.00

Signatures Sepia Black Ink

NM/M

Production 16-199
Red Ink: No Pricing
Production 15 Sets

CF	Carlton Fisk/124	30.00
CY	Carl Yastrzemski/124	50.00
DM	Don Mattingly/124	50.00
DS	Duke Snider/30	75.00
JM	Juan Marichal/124	30.00
JR	Jim Rice/85	30.00
MU	Dale Murphy/183	25.00
NR	Nolan Ryan/123	80.00
OS	Ozzie Smith/183	50.00
RS	Ryne Sandberg/199	50.00
TG	Tony Gwynn/199	50.00
TS	Tom Seaver/16	

Signatures Barrel Black Ink

NM/M

Production 50 or 15
Barrel Blue Ink: 1X
Production 25 or 75
No pricing for production 15 or 25.

AG	Andres Galarraga/50	25.00
AK	Al Kaline/50	50.00
AO	Al Oliver/50	30.00
BJ	Bo Jackson/50	60.00
BM	Bill Mazeroski/50	50.00
DL	Don Larsen/50	50.00
EC	Dennis Eckersley/50	30.00
EM	Edgar Martinez/50	40.00
FM	Fred McGriff/50	30.00
GP	Gaylord Perry/50	30.00
HB	Harold Baines/50	25.00
JK	John Kruk/50	30.00
MO	Jack Morris/50	20.00
OG	Ozzie Guillen/50	25.00
RA	Roberto Alomar/50	40.00
RI	Jim Rice/50	30.00
SA	Ron Santo/50	50.00
SM	Reggie Smith/50	25.00
TM	Tino Martinez/50	50.00
TP	Tony Perez/50	30.00
TR	Tim Raines/50	30.00
EV	Dwight Evans/50	20.00
JI	Jim Bunning/50	25.00
KG	Ken Griffey Sr./50	20.00
LA	Luis Aparicio/50	20.00
MA	Juan Marichal/50	30.00
WH	Willie Horton/50	30.00

Signatures Sepia Blue Ink

NM/M

Production 15-199

AK	Al Kaline/199	30.00
BW	Billy Williams/199	20.00
CF	Carlton Fisk/78	30.00
CY	Carl Yastrzemski/90	60.00
DM	Don Mattingly/78	60.00
DS	Duke Snider/199	40.00
EM	Edgar Martinez/74	40.00
JM	Juan Marichal/84	25.00
JR	Jim Rice/75	25.00
LM	Lee Mazzilli/199	15.00
MU	Dale Murphy/75	50.00
NR	Nolan Ryan/80	80.00
OS	Ozzie Smith/75	60.00
RC	Rocky Colavito/199	50.00
TG	Tony Gwynn/199	50.00
WC	Will Clark/199	25.00
WF	Whitey Ford/15	

Sig. Black Barrel Silver Ink

NM/M

Production 3-47
Gold Ink: No Pricing
Production One Set

EC	Dennis Eckersley/43	30.00
FM	Fred McGriff/27	40.00
GP	Gaylord Perry/36	25.00
JK	John Kruk/29	30.00
MO	Jack Morris/47	25.00
TM	Tino Martinez/24	50.00
TP	Tony Perez/24	40.00
TR	Tim Raines/30	40.00
EV	Dwight Evans/24	35.00
KG	Ken Griffey Sr./30	25.00
WH	Willie Horton/23	35.00

Signature Black Leather Silver Ink

NM/M

Production 3-47
Green Ink: No Pricing
Production One Set

BS	Bruce Sutter/42	30.00
CF	Carlton Fisk/27	40.00
EC	Dennis Eckersley/43	30.00
FM	Fred McGriff/27	40.00
GP	Gaylord Perry/36	25.00
JK	John Kruk/29	30.00
MO	Jack Morris/47	25.00
NR	Nolan Ryan/30	140.00
RJ	Reggie Jackson/44	60.00
TM	Tino Martinez/24	50.00
TP	Tony Perez/24	40.00
TR	Tim Raines/30	40.00
WM	Willie McCovey/44	60.00
BW	Billy Williams/26	25.00
DG	Dick Groat/24	50.00
DW	Dave Winfield/31	30.00
EF	Elroy Face/26	30.00
EV	Dwight Evans/24	35.00
GI	Bob Gibson/45	50.00
KG	Ken Griffey Sr./30	25.00
KO	Sandy Koufax/32	350.00
MA	Juan Marichal/27	35.00
PN	Phil Niekro/35	35.00
RC	Rod Carew/29	30.00
RF	Rollie Fingers/34	20.00
RR	Robin Roberts/36	40.00
SC	Steve Carlton/32	30.00
WH	Willie Horton/23	35.00

Sig. Gold Stitch Black Ink

NM/M

Production 25 or 99
Blue Ink: 1-1.5X
Production 15 or 50

AG	Andres Galarraga/99	20.00
AK	Al Kaline/99	40.00
AO	Al Oliver/99	15.00
BJ	Bo Jackson/99	60.00
BM	Bill Mazeroski/99	40.00
BO	Wade Boggs/25	40.00
CF	Carlton Fisk/25	40.00
DA	Dick Allen/99	20.00
DL	Don Larsen/99	30.00
DM	Don Mattingly/25	75.00
EC	Dennis Eckersley/99	30.00
EM	Edgar Martinez/99	40.00
FM	Fred McGriff/99	40.00
GP	Gaylord Perry/99	20.00
HB	Harold Baines/99	20.00
JK	John Kruk/99	25.00
MO	Jack Morris/99	15.00
MS	Mike Schmidt/25	80.00
OG	Ozzie Guillen/99	20.00
RA	Roberto Alomar/99	30.00
RI	Jim Rice/99	20.00
RS	Ryne Sandberg/25	80.00
SA	Ron Santo/99	40.00
SM	Reggie Smith/99	20.00
TG	Tony Gwynn/25	75.00
TM	Tino Martinez/99	30.00
TP	Tony Perez/99	20.00
TR	Tim Raines/99	15.00
WB	Wade Boggs/25	40.00
WD	Willie Davis/25	30.00
WM	Willie McCovey/25	60.00
YB	Yogi Berra/25	80.00
BR	Brooks Robinson/99	35.00
BW	Billy Williams/99	25.00
CL	Carney Lansford/99	20.00
CO	Dave Concepcion/99	25.00
CY	Carl Yastrzemski/99	65.00
DG	Dick Groat/99	30.00
DS	Don Sutton/99	20.00
DW	Dave Winfield/99	30.00
EB	Ernie Banks/99	65.00
EF	Elroy Face/99	25.00
EV	Dwight Evans/99	20.00
FL	Fred Lynn/99	20.00
FR	Frank Robinson/25	40.00
GI	Bob Gibson/99	40.00
JI	Jim Bunning/99	25.00
JP	Johnny Pesky/99	30.00
JR	Jim Rice/99	25.00
KG	Ken Griffey Sr./99	20.00
KO	Sandy Koufax/99	300.00
LA	Luis Aparicio/99	20.00
LB	Lou Brock/25	40.00
MA	Juan Marichal/99	30.00
MG	Mark Grace/99	30.00
MU	Stan Musial/25	100.00
MV	Mickey Vernon/99	25.00
OS	Ozzie Smith/25	75.00
PN	Phil Niekro/99	20.00
RC	Rod Carew/99	35.00
RF	Rollie Fingers/99	20.00
RK	Ralph Kiner/25	60.00
RR	Robin Roberts/99	30.00
RY	Robin Yount/99	40.00
SC	Steve Carlton/99	30.00
SD	Shawon Dunston/99	20.00
SG	Steve Garvey/99	20.00
SK	"Moose" Skowron/99	20.00
TH	Toby Harrah/99	15.00
TO	Tony Oliva/99	20.00
WH	Willie Horton/99	20.00

Signatures Leather Blue Ink

NM/M

Production 75 unless noted.
Gold Ink: 1-1.5X
Production 15 or 50

AG	Andres Galarraga	25.00
AK	Al Kaline	50.00
AO	Al Oliver	25.00
BJ	Bo Jackson	75.00
BM	Bill Mazeroski	50.00
BO	Wade Boggs/25	40.00
CF	Carlton Fisk/25	40.00
DA	Dick Allen	20.00
DL	Don Larsen	40.00
DM	Don Mattingly/25	75.00
EC	Dennis Eckersley	30.00
EM	Edgar Martinez	50.00
FM	Fred McGriff	40.00
GP	Gaylord Perry	20.00
HB	Harold Baines	20.00
JK	John Kruk	20.00
MO	Jack Morris	20.00
MS	Mike Schmidt/25	80.00
OG	Ozzie Guillen	20.00
RA	Roberto Alomar	50.00
RI	Jim Rice	25.00
RS	Ryne Sandberg/25	80.00
SA	Ron Santo	50.00
SM	Reggie Smith	20.00
TG	Tony Gwynn/25	75.00
TM	Tino Martinez	30.00
TP	Tony Perez	30.00
TR	Tim Raines	20.00
WB	Wade Boggs/25	40.00
WD	Willie Davis/25	30.00
WM	Willie McCovey/25	60.00
YB	Yogi Berra/25	80.00
BR	Brooks Robinson/25	60.00
CL	Carney Lansford/25	20.00
CO	Dave Concepcion/25	20.00
CY	Carl Yastrzemski/25	80.00
DG	Dick Groat/25	25.00
DS	Don Sutton/25	20.00
DW	Dave Winfield/25	40.00
EB	Ernie Banks/25	80.00
EF	Elroy Face/25	30.00
EV	Dwight Evans	25.00
FL	Fred Lynn/25	20.00
FR	Frank Robinson/25	50.00
JI	Jim Bunning	25.00
JP	Johnny Pesky/25	35.00
JR	Jim Rice/25	25.00
KG	Ken Griffey Sr.	15.00
KO	Sandy Koufax/25	350.00
LA	Luis Aparicio	30.00
LB	Lou Brock/25	40.00
MA	Juan Marichal	35.00
MG	Mark Grace/25	40.00
MU	Stan Musial/25	100.00
MV	Mickey Vernon/25	30.00
OS	Ozzie Smith/25	80.00
PN	Phil Niekro/25	25.00
RC	Rod Carew/25	50.00
RF	Rollie Fingers/25	30.00
RK	Ralph Kiner/25	50.00
RR	Robin Roberts/25	40.00
RY	Robin Yount/25	60.00
SC	Steve Carlton/25	25.00
SD	Shawon Dunston/25	25.00
SG	Steve Garvey/25	30.00
SK	"Moose" Skowron/25	30.00
TH	Toby Harrah/25	20.00
TO	Tony Oliva/25	30.00
WH	Willie Horton/25	30.00

Sig. Silver Stitch Blue Ink

NM/M

Production 3-47
Black Ink: No Pricing
Production 15 or 25

BS	Bruce Sutter/42	25.00
CF	Carlton Fisk/27	40.00
EC	Dennis Eckersley/43	30.00
FM	Fred McGriff/27	40.00
GP	Gaylord Perry/36	25.00
JK	John Kruk/29	30.00
MO	Jack Morris/47	25.00
NR	Nolan Ryan/30	140.00
RJ	Reggie Jackson/44	60.00
TM	Tino Martinez/24	50.00
TP	Tony Perez/24	40.00
TR	Tim Raines/30	40.00
WB	Wade Boggs/26	50.00
WM	Willie McCovey/44	60.00
BW	Billy Williams/26	25.00
DG	Dick Groat/24	50.00
DW	Dave Winfield/31	40.00
EF	Elroy Face/26	30.00
EV	Dwight Evans/24	35.00
GI	Bob Gibson/45	50.00
KG	Ken Griffey Sr./30	25.00
KO	Sandy Koufax/32	350.00
MA	Juan Marichal/27	40.00
PN	Phil Niekro/35	35.00
RC	Rod Carew/29	40.00
RF	Rollie Fingers/34	20.00
RR	Robin Roberts/36	40.00
SC	Steve Carlton/32	30.00
WH	Willie Horton/23	35.00

2007 UD SP Rookie Edition

NM/M

Complete Set (284):	
Common Player (1-100):	.25
Common RC (101-142):	.50
Common SP (143-234):	1.00
Inserted 1:2	
Common (235-284):	.25
Pack (8):	5.00
Box (14):	65.00

1	Chipper Jones	.75
2	Andruw Jones	.50
3	Jeff Francoeur	.75
4	Stephen Drew	.25
5	Randy Johnson	.75
6	Brandon Webb	.50
7	Alfonso Soriano	.75
8	Derrek Lee	.50
9	Aramis Ramirez	.50
10	Carlos Zambrano	.40
11	Ken Griffey Jr.	1.50
12	Adam Dunn	.50
13	Bronson Arroyo	.25
14	Todd Helton	.50
15	Jeff Francis	.25
16	Matt Holliday	.50
17	Hanley Ramirez	.75
18	Dontrelle Willis	.25
19	Miguel Cabrera	.75
20	Lance Berkman	.40
21	Roy Oswalt	.50
22	Carlos Lee	.50
23	Nomar Garciaparra	.75
24	Jason Schmidt	.25
25	Juan Pierre	.40
26	Rafael Furcal	.40
27	Rickie Weeks	.25
28	Prince Fielder	.75
29	Ben Sheets	.40
30	David Wright	1.00
31	Jose Reyes	.75
32	Pedro Martinez	.75
33	Carlos Beltran	.50
34	Cole Hamels	.50
35	Jimmy Rollins	.50
36	Ryan Howard	1.00
37	Jason Bay	.40
38	Freddy Sanchez	.25
39	Zachary Duke	.25
40	Jake Peavy	.40
41	Greg Maddux	1.50
42	Trevor Hoffman	.25
43	Matt Cain	.25
44	Barry Zito	.25
45	Omar Vizquel	.25
46	Albert Pujols	2.00
47	Chris Carpenter	.50
48	Jim Edmonds	.40
49	Scott Rolen	.50
50	Ryan Zimmerman	.50
51	Felipe Lopez	.25
52	Austin Kearns	.25
53	Miguel Tejada	.50
54	Erik Bedard	.40
55	Chris Ray	.25
56	David Ortiz	.75
57	Curt Schilling	.50
58	Manny Ramirez	.50
59	Jonathan Papelbon	.50
60	Jim Thome	.50
61	Paul Konerko	.40

62 Bobby Jenks .25
63 Grady Sizemore .75
64 Victor Martinez .40
65 C.C. Sabathia .40
66 Ivan Rodriguez .50
67 Justin Verlander .50
68 Joel Zumaya .25
69 Jeremy Bonderman .40
70 Gil Meche .25
71 Mike Sweeney .25
72 Mark Teahen .25
73 Vladimir Guerrero .75
74 Howie Kendrick .25
75 Francisco Rodriguez .25
76 Johan Santana .75
77 Justin Morneau .50
78 Joe Mauer .50
79 Joe Nathan .25
80 Alex Rodriguez 2.00
81 Derek Jeter 2.00
82 Johnny Damon .75
83 Mariano Rivera .50
84 Rich Harden .25
85 Mike Piazza .75
86 Nick Swisher .40
87 Ichiro Suzuki 1.50
88 Felix Hernandez .50
89 Kenji Johjima .40
90 Richie Sexson .40
91 Carl Crawford .40
92 Scott Kazmir .40
93 B.J. Upton .40
94 Michael Young .40
95 Mark Teixeira .50
96 Eric Gagne .25
97 Hank Blalock .25
98 Vernon Wells .40
99 Roy Halladay .40
100 Frank Thomas .75
101 Joaquin Arias **(RC)** .50
102 Jeff Baker **(RC)** .50
103 Brian Barden **RC** .50
104 Michael Bourn **(RC)** .50
105 Kevin Slowey **(RC)** 1.50
106 Chase Wright **RC** 1.00
107 Kory Casto **(RC)** .50
108 Matt Chico **(RC)** .50
109 Matt DeSalvo **(RC)** 1.00
110 Homer Bailey **(RC)** 1.00
111 Ryan Braun **(RC)** 3.00
112 Felix Pie **(RC)** 1.00
113 Jesus Flores **RC** .50
114 Ryan Sweeney **(RC)** .50
115 Ryan Braun **RC** .50
116 Alex Gordon **RC** 1.50
117 Josh Hamilton **(RC)** 1.50
118 Sean Henn **(RC)** .50
119 Kei Igawa **RC** 1.00
120 Akinori Iwamura **RC** 1.50
121 Andy LaRoche **(RC)** 1.50
122 Kevin Kouzmanoff **(RC)** 1.50
123 Matt Lindstrom **(RC)** .50
124 Tim Lincecum **RC** 4.00
125 Daisuke Matsuzaka **RC** 4.00
126 Gustavo Molina **RC** .50
127 Miguel Montero **(RC)** .50
128 Brandon Morrow **RC** 1.50
129 Hideki Okajima **RC** 1.50
130 Adam Lind **(RC)** .50
131 Mike Rabelo **RC** .50
132 Micah Owings **(RC)** .50
133 Brandon Wood **(RC)** .50
134 Alexi Casilla **RC** 1.00
135 Joe Smith **RC** .50
136 Hunter Pence **(RC)** 3.00
137 Glen Perkins **(RC)** .50
138 Chris Stewart **RC** .50
139 Troy Tulowitzki **(RC)** 2.00
140 Billy Butler **(RC)** 1.00
141 Delmon Young **(RC)** 1.00
142 Phil Hughes **(RC)** 2.00
143 Joaquin Arias 1.00
144 Jeff Baker 1.00
145 Brian Barden 1.00
146 Michael Bourn 1.00
147 Kevin Slowey 2.00
148 Chase Wright 2.00
149 Kory Casto 1.00
150 Matt Chico 1.00
151 Shawn Riggans 1.00
152 Juan Salas 1.00
153 Ryan Braun 5.00
154 Felix Pie 1.00
155 Jesus Flores 1.00
156 Ryan Sweeney 1.00
157 Ryan Braun 1.00
158 Alex Gordon 4.00
159 Josh Hamilton 2.00
160 Sean Henn 1.00
161 Kei Igawa 2.00
162 Akinori Iwamura 2.00
163 Andy LaRoche 1.00
164 Kevin Kouzmanoff 1.00
165 Matt Lindstrom 1.00
166 Tim Lincecum 6.00
167 Daisuke Matsuzaka 6.00
168 Gustavo Molina 1.00
169 Miguel Montero 1.00
170 Brandon Morrow 2.00
171 Hideki Okajima 3.00
172 Adam Lind 1.00
173 Mike Rabelo 1.00
174 Micah Owings 1.00
175 Brandon Wood 1.00
176 Alexi Casilla 2.00
177 Joe Smith 1.00
178 Hunter Pence 5.00
179 Glen Perkins 1.00
180 Chris Stewart 1.00
181 Troy Tulowitzki 3.00
182 Billy Butler 2.00
183 Delmon Young 2.00
184 Phil Hughes 3.00
185 Joaquin Arias 1.00
186 Jeff Baker 1.00
187 Mark Reynolds 1.50
188 Joseph Bisenius 1.00
189 Michael Bourn 1.00
190 Zack Segovia 1.00
191 Kevin Slowey 2.00
192 Chase Wright 2.00
193 Rocky Cherry 1.00
194 Danny Putnam 1.50
195 Kory Casto 1.00
196 Matt Chico 1.00
197 John Danks 1.00
198 Homer Bailey 1.50
199 Ryan Braun 5.00
200 Felix Pie 1.00
201 Jesus Flores 1.00
202 Andy Gonzalez 1.00
203 Ryan Sweeney 1.00
204 Jarrod Saltalamacchia 1.50
205 Alex Gordon 4.00
206 Josh Hamilton 2.00
207 Sean Henn 1.00
208 Kei Igawa 2.00
209 Akinori Iwamura 2.00
210 Andy LaRoche 1.00
211 Rick Vanden Hurk 1.00
212 Kevin Kouzmanoff 1.00
213 Matt Lindstrom 1.00
214 Tim Lincecum 6.00
215 Daisuke Matsuzaka 6.00
216 Gustavo Molina 1.00
217 Miguel Montero 1.00
218 Brandon Morrow 2.00
219 Hideki Okajima 3.00
220 Adam Lind 1.00
221 Mike Rabelo 1.00
222 Brian Burres 1.00
223 Micah Owings 1.00
224 Brandon Wood 1.00
225 Alexi Casilla 2.00
226 Joe Smith 1.00
227 Hunter Pence 5.00
228 Glen Perkins 1.00
229 Chris Stewart 1.00
230 Ben Francisco 1.00
231 Troy Tulowitzki 3.00
232 Billy Butler 2.00
233 Delmon Young 2.00
234 Phil Hughes 3.00
235 Joaquin Arias .50
236 Jeff Baker .50
237 Mark Reynolds 1.00
238 Joseph Bisenius .50
239 Michael Bourn .50
240 Zack Segovia .50
241 Travis Buck .50
242 Chase Wright 1.00
243 Rocky Cherry 1.00
244 Danny Putnam .50
245 Kory Casto .50
246 Matt Chico .50
247 John Danks .50
248 Juan Salas .50
249 Ryan Braun 3.00
250 Felix Pie 1.00
251 Jesus Flores .50
252 Andy Gonzalez .50
253 Ryan Sweeney .50
254 Jarrod Saltalamacchia 1.00
255 Alex Gordon 1.50
256 Josh Hamilton 1.50
257 Sean Henn .50
258 Kei Igawa 1.00
259 Akinori Iwamura 1.50
260 Andy LaRoche 1.50
261 Rick Vanden Hurk .50
262 Kevin Kouzmanoff 1.50
263 Matt Lindstrom .50
264 Tim Lincecum 4.00
265 Daisuke Matsuzaka 4.00
266 Gustavo Molina .50
267 Miguel Montero .50
268 Brandon Morrow 1.50
269 Hideki Okajima 1.50
270 Adam Lind .50
271 Mike Rabelo .50
272 Brian Burres .50
273 Micah Owings .50
274 Brandon Wood .50
275 Alexi Casilla 1.00
276 Joe Smith .50
277 Hunter Pence 3.00
278 Glen Perkins .50
279 Chris Stewart .50
280 Ben Francisco .50
281 Troy Tulowitzki 2.00
282 Billy Butler 1.00
283 Delmon Young 1.00
284 Phil Hughes 2.00

Autographs

NM/M

Common Autograph: 8.00
101 Joaquin Arias 8.00
102 Jeff Baker 8.00
103 Brian Barden 8.00
104 Michael Bourn 10.00
105 Kevin Slowey 15.00
106 Chase Wright 15.00
107 Kory Casto 8.00
108 Matt Chico 8.00
109 Matt DeSalvo 10.00
110 Homer Bailey 15.00
111 Ryan Braun 75.00
112 Felix Pie 15.00
113 Jesus Flores 15.00
114 Ryan Sweeney 8.00
115 Ryan Braun 10.00
116 Alex Gordon/SP 50.00
117 Josh Hamilton 50.00
118 Sean Henn 8.00
121 Andy LaRoche 15.00
122 Kevin Kouzmanoff 15.00
123 Matt Lindstrom 8.00
124 Tim Lincecum/SP 100.00
125 Daisuke Matsuzaka/SP 275.00
126 Gustavo Molina 10.00
127 Miguel Montero 8.00
128 Brandon Morrow 20.00
130 Adam Lind 10.00
131 Mike Rabelo 10.00
132 Micah Owings 15.00
133 Brandon Wood 15.00
134 Alexi Casilla 10.00
135 Joe Smith 10.00
136 Hunter Pence/SP 40.00
137 Glen Perkins 8.00
138 Chris Stewart 8.00
139 Troy Tulowitzk/SP 25.00
140 Billy Butler 20.00
141 Delmon Young/SP
142 Phil Hughes/SP 50.00
143 Joaquin Arias 8.00
144 Jeff Baker 8.00
145 Brian Barden 8.00
146 Michael Bourn 10.00
147 Kevin Slowey 15.00
148 Chase Wright 15.00
149 Kory Casto 8.00
150 Matt Chico 8.00
151 Shawn Riggans 8.00
152 Juan Salas 8.00
153 Ryan Braun 75.00
154 Felix Pie 15.00
155 Jesus Flores 15.00
156 Ryan Sweeney 8.00
157 Ryan Braun 10.00
158 Alex Gordon/SP 50.00
159 Josh Hamilton 50.00
160 Sean Henn 8.00
163 Andy LaRoche 15.00
164 Kevin Kouzmanoff 15.00
165 Matt Lindstrom 8.00
166 Tim Lincecum/SP 100.00
167 Daisuke Matsuzaka/SP 275.00
168 Gustavo Molina 15.00
169 Miguel Montero 8.00
170 Brandon Morrow 20.00
172 Adam Lind 10.00
173 Mike Rabelo 10.00
174 Micah Owings 15.00
175 Brandon Wood 15.00
176 Alexi Casilla 10.00
177 Joe Smith 10.00
178 Hunter Pence 40.00
179 Glen Perkins 8.00
180 Chris Stewart 8.00
181 Troy Tulowitzki 25.00
182 Billy Butler 20.00
184 Phil Hughes/SP 50.00
185 Joaquin Arias 8.00
186 Jeff Baker 8.00
188 Joseph Bisenius 8.00
189 Michael Bourn 8.00
190 Zack Segovia 8.00
191 Kevin Slowey 15.00
192 Chase Wright 15.00
193 Rocky Cherry 20.00
194 Danny Putnam 20.00
195 Kory Casto 8.00
196 Matt Chico 8.00
197 John Danks 8.00
198 Homer Bailey 20.00
199 Ryan Braun 75.00
200 Felix Pie 15.00
201 Jesus Flores 15.00
202 Andy Gonzalez 10.00
203 Ryan Sweeney/SP 10.00
204 Jarrod Saltalamacchia 15.00
205 Alex Gordon/SP 50.00
206 Josh Hamilton/SP 50.00
207 Sean Henn 8.00
210 Andy LaRoche 15.00
211 Rick Vanden Hurk 8.00
212 Kevin Kouzmanoff 15.00
213 Matt Lindstrom 8.00
214 Tim Lincecum/SP 100.00
215 Daisuke Matsuzaka/SP 275.00
216 Gustavo Molina 15.00
217 Miguel Montero 8.00
218 Brandon Morrow 20.00
220 Adam Lind 10.00
221 Mike Rabelo 10.00
222 Brian Burres 8.00
223 Micah Owings 15.00
224 Brandon Wood/SP 15.00
225 Alexi Casilla 10.00
226 Joe Smith 10.00
227 Hunter Pence/SP 40.00
228 Glen Perkins 8.00
229 Chris Stewart 8.00
230 Ben Francisco 8.00
231 Troy Tulowitzki/SP 25.00
232 Billy Butler/SP 20.00
234 Phil Hughes/SP 50.00
235 Joaquin Arias 8.00
236 Jeff Baker 8.00
238 Joseph Bisenius 8.00
239 Michael Bourn 10.00
240 Zack Segovia 10.00
242 Chase Wright 15.00
243 Rocky Cherry 20.00
244 Danny Putnam 20.00
245 Kory Casto 8.00
246 Matt Chico 8.00
247 John Danks 8.00
248 Juan Salas 8.00
249 Ryan Braun/SP 75.00
250 Felix Pie 15.00
251 Jesus Flores 15.00
252 Andy Gonzalez 8.00
253 Ryan Sweeney 8.00
254 Jarrod Saltalamacchia/SP 15.00
255 Alex Gordon/SP 50.00
256 Josh Hamilton 50.00
257 Sean Henn 8.00
260 Andy LaRoche 15.00
261 Rick Vanden Hurk 8.00
262 Kevin Kouzmanoff 15.00
263 Matt Lindstrom 8.00
264 Tim Lincecum/SP 100.00
265 Daisuke Matsuzaka/SP 275.00
266 Gustavo Molina 15.00
267 Miguel Montero 8.00
268 Brandon Morrow 20.00
270 Adam Lind 10.00
271 Mike Rabelo 10.00
272 Brian Burres 8.00
273 Micah Owings 15.00
274 Brandon Wood 15.00
275 Alexi Casilla 10.00
276 Joe Smith 10.00
277 Hunter Pence/SP 40.00
278 Glen Perkins 8.00
279 Chris Stewart 8.00
280 Ben Francisco 8.00
281 Troy Tulowitzki/SP 25.00
282 Billy Butler/SP 20.00
284 Phil Hughes/SP 50.00

2007 UD Ultimate Collection

NM/M

Common Player (1-100): 1.50
Production 450
Common RC Auto. (101-141): 10.00
Production 289-299
Pack (4): 75.00
Box (4): 250.00
1 Chipper Jones 4.00
2 Andruw Jones 2.00
3 Tim Hudson 2.00
4 Stephen Drew 2.00
5 Randy Johnson 3.00
6 Brandon Webb 2.00
7 Alfonso Soriano 3.00
8 Derrek Lee 2.00
9 Aramis Ramirez 2.00
10 Carlos Zambrano 2.00
11 Ken Griffey Jr. 6.00
12 Adam Dunn 2.00
13 Ryan Freel 1.50
14 Todd Helton 2.00
15 Garrett Atkins 1.50
16 Matt Holliday 2.00
17 Hanley Ramirez 3.00
18 Dontrelle Willis 1.50
19 Miguel Cabrera 3.00
20 Lance Berkman 2.00
21 Roy Oswalt 2.00
22 Carlos Lee 2.00
23 Nomar Garciaparra 3.00
24 Jason Schmidt 1.50
25 Juan Pierre 1.50
26 Russell Martin 2.00
27 Rickie Weeks 1.50
28 Prince Fielder 3.00
29 Ben Sheets 1.50
30 David Wright 5.00
31 Jose Reyes 4.00
32 Pedro Martinez 3.00
33 Carlos Beltran 2.00
34 Brett Myers 1.50
35 Jimmy Rollins 3.00
36 Ryan Howard 6.00
37 Jason Bay 2.00
38 Freddy Sanchez 1.50
39 Ian Snell 1.50
40 Jake Peavy 2.00
41 Greg Maddux 5.00
42 Brian Giles 1.50
43 Matt Cain 2.00
44 Barry Zito 1.50
45 Ray Durham 1.50
46 Albert Pujols 8.00
47 Chris Carpenter 2.00
48 Chris Duncan 1.50
49 Scott Rolen 2.00
50 Ryan Zimmerman 2.00
51 Chad Cordero 1.50
52 Ryan Church 1.50
53 Miguel Tejada 2.00
54 Erik Bedard 2.00
55 Brian Roberts 1.50
56 David Ortiz 4.00
57 Josh Beckett 3.00
58 Manny Ramirez 3.00

59	Daisuke Matsuzaka **RC**	25.00
60	Jim Thome	2.00
61	Paul Konerko	2.00
62	Jermaine Dye	1.50
63	Grady Sizemore	3.00
64	Victor Martinez	2.00
65	C.C. Sabathia	2.00
66	Ivan Rodriguez	2.00
67	Justin Verlander	2.00
68	Gary Sheffield	2.00
69	Jeremy Bonderman	2.00
70	Gil Meche	1.50
71	Mike Sweeney	1.50
72	Mark Teahen	1.50
73	Vladimir Guerrero	3.00
74	Howie Kendrick	1.50
75	Francisco Rodriguez	1.50
76	Johan Santana	3.00
77	Justin Morneau	2.00
78	Joe Mauer	2.00
79	Michael Cuddyer	1.50
80	Alex Rodriguez	8.00
81	Derek Jeter	8.00
82	Johnny Damon	3.00
83	Roger Clemens	6.00
84	Rich Harden	1.50
85	Mike Piazza	3.00
86	Huston Street	1.50
87	Ichiro Suzuki	6.00
88	Felix Hernandez	2.00
89	Kenji Johjima	1.50
90	Adrian Beltre	1.50
91	Carl Crawford	1.50
92	Scott Kazmir	1.50
93	B.J. Upton	1.50
94	Michael Young	1.50
95	Mark Teixeira	2.00
96	Sammy Sosa	3.00
97	Hank Blalock	1.50
98	Vernon Wells	2.00
99	Roy Halladay	2.00
100	Frank Thomas	3.00
101	Adam Lind **(RC)**	10.00
102	Akinori Iwamura **RC**	30.00
103	Andrew Miller **RC**	40.00
104	Michael Bourn **(RC)**	10.00
105	Kory Casto **(RC)**	10.00
106	Ryan Braun **(RC)**	75.00
107	Sean Gallagher **(RC)**	10.00
108	Billy Butler **(RC)**	30.00
109	Alexi Casilla **RC**	10.00
110	Chris Stewart **RC**	10.00
111	Matt DeSalvo **(RC)**	15.00
112	Chase Headley **(RC)**	15.00
113	Delmon Young **(RC)**	20.00
114	Homer Bailey **(RC)**	20.00
115	Kurt Suzuki **(RC)**	15.00
116	Alex Gordon **RC**	50.00
117	Josh Hamilton **(RC)**	40.00
118	Fred Lewis **(RC)**	10.00
119	Glen Perkins **(RC)**	10.00
120	Hector Gimenez **(RC)**	10.00
121	Phil Hughes **(RC)**	50.00
122	Jeff Baker **(RC)**	10.00
123	Adam LaRoche **(RC)**	15.00
124	Tim Lincecum **RC**	100.00
125	Joaquin Arias **(RC)**	10.00
126	Daisuke Matsuzaka **RC**	300.00
127	Micah Owings **(RC)**	20.00
128	Hunter Pence **(RC)**	40.00
129	Matt Chico **(RC)**	10.00
130	Kei Igawa **RC**	30.00
131	Kevin Kouzmanoff **(RC)**	15.00
132	Miguel Montero **(RC)**	10.00
133	Mike Rabelo **RC**	10.00
134	Felix Pie **(RC)**	20.00
135	Curtis Thigpen **(RC)**	10.00
136	Ryan Braun **RC**	10.00
137	Ryan Sweeney **(RC)**	10.00
138	Brandon Wood **(RC)**	20.00
139	Troy Tulowitzki **(RC)**	40.00
140	Justin Upton **RC**	80.00
141	Joba Chamberlain **RC**	150.00

Collection Jersey Parallel

NM/M

Production 50 Sets
Patch: No Pricing
Production 25 Sets

1	Chipper Jones	10.00
2	Andruw Jones	8.00
3	Tim Hudson	8.00
4	Stephen Drew	8.00
5	Randy Johnson	10.00
6	Brandon Webb	8.00
7	Alfonso Soriano	10.00
8	Derrek Lee	8.00
9	Aramis Ramirez	8.00
10	Carlos Zambrano	10.00
11	Ken Griffey Jr.	15.00
12	Adam Dunn	8.00
13	Ryan Freel	5.00
14	Todd Helton	8.00
15	Garrett Atkins	5.00
16	Matt Holliday	10.00
17	Hanley Ramirez	10.00
18	Dontrelle Willis	5.00
19	Miguel Cabrera	10.00
20	Lance Berkman	8.00
21	Roy Oswalt	8.00
22	Carlos Lee	8.00
24	Jason Schmidt	5.00
25	Juan Pierre	5.00
26	Russell Martin	8.00
27	Rickie Weeks	5.00
28	Prince Fielder	10.00
29	Ben Sheets	8.00
31	Jose Reyes	10.00
32	Pedro 1artinez	10.00
33	Carlos Beltran	10.00
34	Brett Myers	5.00
35	Jimmy Rollins	15.00
37	Jason Bay	8.00
38	Freddy Sanchez	5.00
39	Ian Snell	5.00
40	Jake Peavy	10.00
41	Greg Maddux	15.00
42	Brian Giles	5.00
43	Matt Cain	8.00
44	Barry Zito	8.00
45	Ray Durham	5.00
46	Albert Pujols	20.00
47	Chris Carpenter	8.00
48	Chris Duncan	5.00
49	Scott Rolen	8.00
50	Ryan Zimmerman	8.00
51	Chad Cordero	5.00
52	Ryan Church	5.00
53	Miguel Tejada	8.00
54	Erik Bedard	15.00
55	Brian Roberts	8.00
56	David Ortiz	15.00
57	Josh Beckett	10.00
58	Manny Ramirez	10.00
59	Daisuke Matsuzaka	60.00
60	Jim Thome	8.00
61	Paul Konerko	8.00
62	Jermaine Dye	8.00
63	Grady Sizemore	15.00
64	Victor Martinez	8.00
65	C.C. Sabathia	8.00
66	Ivan Rodriguez	8.00
67	Justin Verlander	10.00
68	Gary Sheffield	8.00
69	Jeremy Bonderman	8.00
70	Gil Meche	5.00
71	Mike Sweeney	5.00
72	Mark Teahen	5.00
73	Vladimir Guerrero	10.00
74	Howie Kendrick	8.00
75	Francisco Rodriguez	5.00
76	Johan Santana	10.00
77	Justin Morneau	8.00
78	Joe Mauer	8.00
79	Michael Cuddyer	5.00
81	Derek Jeter	25.00
83	Roger Clemens	15.00
84	Rich Harden	5.00
85	Mike Piazza	15.00
86	Huston Street	5.00
88	Felix Hernandez	10.00
89	Kenji Johjima	8.00
90	Adrian Beltre	8.00
91	Carl Crawford	8.00
92	Scott Kazmir	8.00
93	B.J. Upton	8.00
94	Michael Young	5.00
95	Mark Teixeira	8.00
97	Hank Blalock	5.00
98	Vernon Wells	5.00
99	Vernon Wells	8.00
100	Frank Thomas	10.00

America's Pastime Signature

NM/M

AD	Adam Dunn	15.00
AE	Andre Ethier	10.00
AG	Adrian Gonzalez	10.00
AJ	A.J. Burnett	10.00
AK	Al Kaline	30.00
AL	Adam LaRoche	10.00
AP	Albert Pujols	150.00
AV	Andy Van Slyke	15.00
BB	Boof Bonser	10.00
BE	Johnny Bench	30.00
BJ	B.J. Upton	15.00
BM	Bill Mazeroski	25.00
CB	Chad Billingsley	15.00
CC	Chad Cordero	10.00
CH	Cole Hamels	30.00
CK	Casey Kotchman	10.00
CQ	Carlos Quentin	10.00
CR	Craig Biggio	50.00
CT	Curtis Thigpen	10.00
CW	Chien-Ming Wang	100.00
CY	Chris Young	10.00
DH	Danny Haren	15.00
DJ	Derek Jeter	125.00
DM	Don Mattingly	50.00
DS	Don Sutton	15.00
DU	Dan Uggla	15.00
DY	Delmon Young	15.00
EB	Ernie Banks	50.00
FH	Felix Hernandez	25.00
FR	Frank Robinson	25.00
GA	Garrett Atkins	10.00
GP	Gaylord Perry	15.00
GR	Khalil Greene	15.00
GW	Tony Gwynn	50.00
HA	Travis Hafner	15.00
HB	Homer Bailey	15.00
HE	Chase Headley	10.00
HO	Howie Kendrick	10.00
HR	Hanley Ramirez	20.00
HS	Huston Street	10.00
HU	Torii Hunter	15.00
IK	Ian Kinsler	15.00
JB	Jason Bay	15.00
JE	Jeremy Bonderman	15.00
JI	Jim Rice	20.00
JL	James Loney	20.00
JM	Jack Morris	10.00
JN	Joe Nathan	20.00
JO	Joe Blanton	10.00
JT	Jim Thome	30.00
JV	Justin Verlander	30.00
JZ	Joel Zumaya	15.00
KI	Kei Igawa	25.00
KJ	Kelly Johnson	10.00
KM	Kendry Morales	10.00
LA	Andy LaRoche	15.00
LE	Jon Lester	20.00
LY	John Lackey	10.00
MA	Daisuke Matsuzaka	250.00
MB	Matt Brown	10.00
MC	Matt Cain	15.00
MH	Matt Holliday	30.00
MM	Melvin Mora	10.00
MS	Mike Schmidt	40.00
MT	Mark Teixeira	20.00
NM	Nicholas Markakis	20.00
NW	Nick Swisher	10.00
OS	Ozzie Smith	50.00
PA	Jim Palmer	15.00
PB	Jonathan Papelbon	30.00
PK	Paul Konerko	15.00
RA	Aramis Ramirez	20.00
RB	Ryan Braun	50.00
RF	Rafael Furcal	15.00
RG	Ryan Garko	10.00
RH	Rich Harden	10.00
RI	Rich Hill	10.00
RT	Ryan Theriot	15.00
RW	Rickie Weeks	10.00
RZ	Ryan Zimmerman	20.00
SD	Stephen Drew	20.00
SG	Sean Gallagher	10.00
SK	Scott Kazmir	15.00
SM	Stan Musial	75.00
SO	Joakim Soria	10.00
TG	Tom Glavine	50.00
TP	Tony Perez	15.00
TR	Tim Raines	10.00
TT	Troy Tulowitzki	40.00
VM	Victor Martinez	15.00
VW	Vernon Wells	15.00
WC	Will Clark	15.00
WI	Josh Willingham	10.00
WM	Willie McCovey	60.00
XN	Xavier Nady	10.00

America's Ultimate Pastime Materials

NM/M

Production 75 unless noted.
Patch: 2X
Production 5-50
No pricing 25 or less.
Gold: No Pricing
Production 25 Sets

AB	Adrian Beltre	8.00
AJ	Andruw Jones	10.00
AP	Andy Pettitte	10.00
AS	Alfonso Soriano	10.00
BA	Bobby Abreu	8.00
BE	Josh Beckett	10.00
BG	Brian Giles	5.00
BJ	Jeff Bagwell	8.00
BR	Brian Roberts	10.00
BS	Ben Sheets	8.00
BW	Brandon Webb	8.00
CA	Chris Carpenter	8.00
CB	Carlos Beltran	10.00
CC	Carl Crawford	5.00
CF	Carlton Fisk	10.00
CJ	Chipper Jones	10.00
CL	Carlos Lee	8.00
CR	Cal Ripken Jr.	25.00
CS	Curt Schilling	10.00
CU	Chase Utley	15.00
DJ	Derek Jeter	25.00
DL	Derrek Lee	10.00
DO	David Ortiz	15.00
DW	Dontrelle Willis	5.00
FH	Felix Hernandez	10.00
FL	Francisco Liriano	10.00
FR	Francisco Rodriguez/64	5.00
GA	Garrett Atkins	5.00
GM	Greg Maddux	15.00
GS	Gary Sheffield	10.00
GW	Tony Gwynn	15.00
HA	Rich Harden	5.00
HB	Hank Blalock	5.00
HR	Hanley Ramirez	10.00
JA	Jason Bay	8.00
JB	Jeremy Bonderman	8.00
JE	Jim Edmonds	8.00
JG	Jason Giambi	8.00
JM	Justin Morneau	10.00
JN	Joe Nathan	8.00
JO	Randy Johnson	10.00
JP	Jonathan Papelbon	10.00
JR	Jim Rice	8.00
JS	Johan Santana	10.00
JT	Jim Thome	10.00
JV	Justin Verlander	10.00
JW	Josh Willingham	5.00
KG	Ken Griffey Jr.	15.00
KP	Kirby Puckett	25.00
KY	Kevin Youkilis	8.00
LB	Lance Berkman	8.00
LO	Lou Brock/25	15.00
MA	Joe Mauer	8.00
MC	Matt Cain	8.00
MH	Matt Holliday	10.00
MI	Miguel Cabrera	10.00
MM	Mike Mussina	10.00
MR	Manny Ramirez	10.00
MS	Mike Schmidt	20.00
MT	Miguel Tejada	10.00
MY	Michael Young	8.00
MZ	Pedro Martinez	10.00
NR	Nolan Ryan	25.00
OR	Magglio Ordonez	8.00
OS	Ozzie Smith	15.00
PE	Jake Peavy	10.00
PF	Prince Fielder	10.00
PM	Paul Molitor	10.00
PU	Albert Pujols	25.00
RB	Rocco Baldelli	5.00
RC	Roger Clemens	15.00
RE	Jose Reyes	15.00
RH	Roy Halladay	8.00
RJ	Reggie Jackson	15.00
RO	Roy Oswalt	8.00
RS	Ryne Sandberg	15.00
RW	Rickie Weeks	8.00
RZ	Ryan Zimmerman	8.00
SC	Steve Carlton	8.00
SE	Richie Sexson	8.00
SI	Grady Sizemore	15.00
SK	Scott Kazmir	8.00
SM	John Smoltz	10.00
TE	Mark Teixeira	10.00
TG	Troy Glaus	8.00
TH	Todd Helton	8.00
TR	Travis Hafner	8.00
VA	Jason Varitek	10.00
VG	Vladimir Guerrero	10.00
VM	Victor Martinez	8.00
WC	Will Clark	8.00
CF2	Carlton Fisk	10.00
GW2	Tony Gwynn	15.00
MR2	Manny Ramirez	10.00
RE2	Jose Reyes	15.00
SI2	Grady Sizemore	15.00
TR2	Travis Hafner	8.00
VG2	Vladimir Guerrero	10.00

The Ultimate Card

Production One Set
No Pricing

Ultimate Iron Man Signature

Production Eight Sets
No Pricing

The Ultimate Logo

Production One Set
No Pricing

The Ultimate Patch

Production 25 unless noted.
No Pricing

The Ultimate Six Signatures

Production 10 Sets
No Pricng

The Ultimate Champions Signatures

Production 4-10
No Pricing

The Ultimate Ensemble Dual Patches

No Pricing
Production 25 Sets

The Ultimate Ensemble Triple Patch

Production 15 Sets
No Pricing

The Ultimate Ensemble Quad Patch

Production 10 Sets
No Pricing

The Ultimate Ensemble Dual Swatch

NM/M

Production 75 sets unless noted.

BD	J.D. Drew, Jason Bay	10.00
BH	Jeremy Bonderman, Rich Harden	10.00
BZ	Wade Boggs, Ryan Zimmerman	10.00
CG	Vladimir Guerrero, Miguel Cabrera	15.00
CJ	Curt Schilling, Josh Beckett	15.00
CR	Roger Clemens, Nolan Ryan	25.00
CW	Matt Cain, Jered Weaver	10.00
FT	Mark Teixeira, Prince Fielder	10.00
GD	Ken Griffey Jr., Adam Dunn	20.00
GM	Tom Glavine, Pedro Martinez	10.00
GP	Tony Gwynn, Jake Peavy	15.00
GR	Tony Gwynn, Cal Ripken Jr.	30.00
HH	Todd Helton, Matt Holliday	10.00
HJ	Felix Hernandez, Kenji Johjima	10.00
HR	J.J. Hardy, Jose Reyes	10.00
HW	Vernon Wells, Roy Halladay	10.00

IK	Paul Konerko, Tadahito Iguchi	10.00
JJ	Andruw Jones, Chipper Jones	10.00
JR	Derek Jeter, Mariano Rivera	25.00
JV	Victor Martinez, Joe Mauer	10.00
KY	Scott Kazmir, Delmon Young	10.00
LS	Derrek Lee, Alfonso Soriano	10.00
MB	Mike Schmidt, Brooks Robinson	25.00
MC	Michael Cuddyer, Justin Morneau	10.00
MM	Justin Morneau, Joe Mauer	10.00
NR	Mariano Rivera, Joe Nathan	10.00
OB	Lance Berkman, Roy Oswalt	10.00
PC	Chris Carpenter, Albert Pujols	20.00
PO	David Ortiz, Albert Pujols	20.00
RB	Ivan Rodriguez, Johnny Bench	15.00
SB	Carlos Beltran, Grady Sizemore	15.00
SC	Alfonso Soriano, Carl Crawford/52	10.00
SL	Johan Santana, Francisco Liriano	10.00
SP	John Smoltz, Jake Peavy	10.00
SR	Cal Ripken Jr., Ryne Sandberg/63	50.00
SW	Johan Santana, Brandon Webb	10.00
TR	Cal Ripken Jr., Miguel Tejada	20.00
WU	Rickie Weeks, Chase Utley	15.00
YR	Michael Young, Jose Reyes	15.00

The Ultimate Ensemble Triple Swatch

NM/M

Production 50 sets

BCG	Troy Glaus, Eric Chavez, Hank Blalock	15.00
CBG	Tony Gwynn, Will Clark, Wade Boggs	20.00
CRS	Nolan Ryan, Don Sutton, Steve Carlton	25.00
CSK	Johan Santana, Scott Kazmir, Steve Carlton	15.00
FHS	Ben Sheets, J.J. Hardy, Prince Fielder	10.00
GRR	Khalil Greene, Jose Reyes, Hanley Ramirez	25.00
HTP	Mike Piazza, Frank Thomas, Travis Hafner	15.00
LPD	Barry Larkin, Tony Perez, Adam Dunn	15.00
LRS	Ozzie Smith, Barry Larkin, Cal Ripken Jr.	25.00
MCS	Roger Clemens, Pedro Martinez, Don Sutton	25.00
MJG	Ken Griffey Jr., Chipper Jones, Joe Mauer	25.00
MMP	Jorge Posada, Victor Martinez, Joe Mauer	15.00
MSB	Curt Schilling, Josh Beckett, Daisuke Matsuzaka	65.00
MSU	Ryne Sandberg, Bill Mazeroski, Chase Utley	25.00
OCZ	Chris Carpenter, Roy Oswalt, Carlos Zambrano	15.00
ODH	Jermaine Dye, Travis Hafner, David Ortiz	15.00
OMT	David Ortiz, Mark Teixeira, Justin Morneau	15.00
OPR	David Ortiz, Albert Pujols, Jose Reyes	25.00
PJL	Andruw Jones, Derrek Lee, Albert Pujols	25.00
RDB	Carlos Delgado, Carlos Beltran, Ivan Rodriguez	15.00
RJG	Ken Griffey Jr., Cal Ripken Jr., Derek Jeter	50.00
RPJ	Kirby Puckett, Jim Rice, Reggie Jackson	60.00
RPS	Manny Ramirez, Alfonso Soriano, Albert Pujols	25.00
RSB	Wade Boggs, Mike Schmidt, Brooks Robinson	40.00
SHS	Roy Halladay, Josh Beckett, Johan Santana	15.00
UWG	Marcus Giles, Rickie Weeks, Chase Utley	20.00
YBO	Wade Boggs, David Ortiz, Carl Yastrzemski	25.00
YJT	Derek Jeter, Miguel Tejada, Michael Young	25.00
YTS	Sammy Sosa, Michael Young, Mark Teixeira	20.00
ZAJ	Chipper Jones, Garrett Atkins, Ryan Zimmerman	15.00

The Ultimate Ensemble Quad Swatch

No Pricing
Production 25 unless noted.

Ultimate Futures Signatures

Production 25 unless noted.
No Pricing

Ultimate Legendary Signatures

Production 25 Sets
No Pricing

Ultimate Numbers Match Signature

NM/M

Production 2-48

AR	Garrett Atkins, Mark Reynolds/27	15.00
BW	Jeremy Bonderman, Chase Wright/38	15.00
BZ	Carlos Zambrano, Jason Bay/38	25.00
FG	Vladimir Guerrero, Carlton Fisk/27	75.00
HH	Travis Hafner, Torii Hunter/48	25.00
HR	Nolan Ryan, Felix Hernandez/34	100.00
HV	Justin Verlander, Cole Hamels/35	50.00
HW	Chien-Ming Wang, Rich Harden/40	180.00
JD	Adam Dunn, Reggie Jackson/44	50.00
WH	Dontrelle Willis, Cole Hamels/35	50.00

Ultimate Numbers Materials

NM/M

Production 1-75
No pricing 25 or less.

AB	A.J. Burnett/34	8.00
AD	Adam Dunn/44	10.00
AJ	Andruw Jones/25	10.00
AN	Andy Pettitte/46	10.00
BA	Bobby Abreu/53	10.00
BE	Adrian Beltre/29	10.00
BZ	Barry Zito/75	8.00
CC	Chris Carpenter/29	10.00
CF	Carlton Fisk/27	10.00
CL	Carlos Lee/45	8.00
CS	Curt Schilling/38	10.00
CU	Chase Utley/26	15.00
DL	Derrek Lee/25	10.00
DO	David Ortiz/34	15.00
DY	Delmon Young/26	10.00
FH	Felix Hernandez/34	10.00
FL	Francisco Liriano/47	10.00
GA	Garrett Atkins/27	8.00
GL	Troy Glaus/25	8.00
GP	Gaylord Perry/36	10.00
HA	Roy Halladay/32	8.00
HF	Travis Hafner/48	8.00
HU	Torii Hunter/48	8.00
JE	Jeremy Bonderman/38	8.00
JH	Josh Hamilton/33	15.00
JS	Johan Santana/57	10.00
JT	Jim Thome/25	10.00
JV	Jason Varitek/33	20.00
MO	Maggio Ordonez/30	8.00
NR	Nolan Ryan/34	40.00
OS	Roy Oswalt/44	10.00
PF	Prince Fielder/28	10.00
RC	Rod Carew/29	10.00
RH	Rich Harden/40	8.00
RJ	Randy Johnson/51	10.00
SA	C.C. Sabathia/52	8.00
SC	Steve Carlton/32	10.00
SR	Scott Rolen/27	10.00
TG	Tom Glavine/47	15.00
TR	Tim Raines/30	8.00
TV	Trevor Hoffman/51	8.00
VG	Vladimir Guerrero/27	10.00
VM	Victor Martinez/41	10.00
WI	Dontrelle Willis/35	8.00
CF2	Carlton Fisk/72	10.00
DL2	Derrek Le/25	10.00
DO2	David Ortiz/25	15.00

Ultimate Star Materials

NM/M

Common Player:	5.00
Patch Autograph:	No Pricing
Production Five Sets	
Autographs:	No Pricing
Production 15 Sets	

AD	Adam Dunn	8.00
AG	Alex Gordon	15.00
AK	Austin Kearns	5.00
AP	Albert Pujols	20.00
BG	Brian Giles	5.00
BI	Craig Biggio	8.00
BO	Jeremy Bonderman	8.00
BS	Ben Sheets	5.00
BU	B.J. Upton	8.00
CA	Chris Carpenter	8.00
CF	Carlton Fisk	8.00
CL	Carlos Lee	8.00
CR	Cal Ripken Jr.	20.00
CY	Carl Yastrzemski	15.00
CZ	Carlos Zambrano	8.00
DH	Danny Haren	8.00
DJ	Derek Jeter	20.00
DL	Derrek Lee	8.00
DM	Don Mattingly	15.00
DO	David Ortiz	15.00
DW	Dontrelle Willis	5.00
EC	Eric Chavez	5.00
FH	Felix Hernandez	8.00
FL	Francisco Liriano	8.00
FR	Francisco Rodriguez	5.00
FT	Frank Thomas	10.00
GA	Garrett Atkins	5.00
GR	Khalil Greene	8.00
GW	Tony Gwynn	10.00
HA	Roy Halladay	8.00
HP	Hunter Pence	15.00
HR	Hanley Ramirez	10.00
HS	Huston Street	5.00
HU	Torii Hunter	10.00
JA	Jason Bay	8.00
JB	Josh Beckett	10.00
JH	Jeremy Hermida	5.00
JL	John Lackey	5.00
JM	Joe Mauer	8.00
JN	Joe Nathan	5.00
JP	Jonathan Papelbon	15.00
JR	Jim Rice	8.00
JS	John Smoltz	8.00
JT	Jim Thome	8.00
JU	Justin Morneau	8.00
KG	Ken Griffey Jr.	15.00
MA	Matt Cain	8.00
MC	Miguel Cabrera	10.00
MH	Matt Holliday	10.00
MS	Mike Schmidt	15.00
MT	Mark Teixeira	8.00
MY	Michael Young	5.00
NM	Nicholas Markakis	8.00
NR	Nolan Ryan	20.00
NS	Nick Swisher	5.00
OR	Roy Oswalt	8.00
OS	Ozzie Smith	15.00
PA	Jim Palmer	8.00
PE	Jake Peavy	8.00
PF	Prince Fielder	8.00
PK	Paul Konerko	8.00
PM	Paul Molitor	8.00
RA	Roberto Alomar	8.00
RC	Roger Clemens	15.00
RF	Rollie Fingers	8.00
RH	Rich Harden	5.00
RJ	Randy Johnson	10.00
RO	Rod Carew	10.00
RW	Rickie Weeks	8.00
RY	Robin Yount	10.00
RZ	Ryan Zimmerman	10.00
SK	Scott Kazmir	8.00
TG	Tom Glavine	10.00
TH	Travis Hafner	8.00
TI	Tim Hudson	8.00
TT	Troy Tulowitzki	15.00
VM	Victor Martinez	8.00
VW	Vernon Wells	5.00
WB	Wade Boggs	10.00
WI	Josh Willingham	5.00
AG2	Alex Gordon	15.00
AK2	Austin Kearns	5.00
CL2	Carlos Lee	8.00
CR2	Cal Ripken Jr.	20.00
DJ2	Derek Jeter	20.00
DW2	Dontrelle Willis	5.00
FH2	Felix Hernandez	8.00
GA2	Garrett Atkins	5.00
JT2	Jim Thome	8.00
JU2	Justin Morneau	8.00
MA2	Matt Cain	8.00
MH2	Matt Holliday	10.00
MT2	Mark Teixeira	8.00
MY2	Michael Young	5.00
PE2	Jake Peavy	8.00
PM2	Paul Molitor	8.00
RZ2	Ryan Zimmerman	10.00
TH2	Travis Hafner	8.00

Ultimate Team Marks

NM/M

Production 60 sets unless noted.

CL	Carlos Lee/57	20.00
CY	Carl Yastrzemski/58	50.00
DJ	Derek Jeter	140.00
DL	Derrek Lee/58	25.00
DO	David Ortiz	65.00
DW	Dontrelle Willis/56	10.00
FH	Felix Hernandez	30.00
JM	Joe Mauer	25.00
MO	Justin Morneau	25.00
MT	Mark Teixeira	15.00
PF	Prince Fielder	40.00
VM	Victor Martinez	15.00
VW	Vernon Wells	10.00

Ultimate Team Materials

NM/M

Production 50 unless noted.	
Patch:	No Pricing
Production 19-25	
Autographs:	No Pricing
Production 1-10	

AD	Adam Dunn	8.00
AK	Austin Kearns	5.00
AN	Garret Anderson	5.00
AP	Albert Pujols	20.00
BE	Josh Beckett	10.00
BG	Brian Giles	5.00
BS	Ben Sheets	8.00
BU	B.J. Upton	8.00
CA	Rod Carew	10.00
CF	Carlton Fisk	8.00
CH	Chris Carpenter	8.00
CL	Carlos Lee	8.00
CR	Bobby Crosby	5.00
CY	Carl Yastrzemski	15.00
DH	Danny Haren	8.00
DJ	Derek Jeter	25.00
DL	Derrek Lee	8.00
DM	Don Mattingly	15.00
DO	David Ortiz	10.00
DW	Dontrelle Willis	5.00
EC	Eric Chavez	5.00
FH	Felix Hernandez	8.00
FJ	Fergie Jenkins	8.00
FL	Francisco Liriano	10.00
FR	Francisco Rodriguez	5.00
FT	Frank Thomas	10.00
GA	Garrett Atkins	5.00
GR	Khalil Greene	8.00
GW	Tony Gwynn	10.00
HA	Rich Harden	5.00
HP	Hunter Pence	15.00
HR	Hanley Ramirez	10.00
HS	Huston Street	5.00
HU	Tim Hudson	8.00
JA	Jason Bay	8.00
JE	Jeremy Bonderman	8.00
JG	Jonny Gomes	5.00
JH	Jeremy Hermida	5.00
JI	Jim Palmer	8.00
JL	John Lackey	5.00
JM	Joe Mauer	8.00
JN	Joe Nathan	5.00
JP	Jake Peavy	8.00
JR	Jim Rice	8.00
JS	John Smoltz	8.00
JT	Jim Thome	8.00
KG	Ken Griffey Jr.	15.00
KM	Kendry Morales	5.00
MA	Daisuke Matsuzaka	60.00
MC	Matt Cain	8.00
MH	Matt Holliday	10.00
MI	Miguel Cabrera	10.00
MO	Justin Morneau	8.00
MS	Mike Schmidt	10.00
MT	Mark Teixeira	8.00
MY	Michael Young	5.00
NM	Nicholas Markakis	10.00
NR	Nolan Ryan	25.00
OS	Ozzie Smith	15.00
PA	Jonathan Papelbon	10.00
PF	Prince Fielder	10.00
PK	Paul Konerko	8.00
PM	Paul Molitor	10.00
PN	Phil Niekro	8.00
RA	Roberto Alomar	8.00
RC	Roger Clemens	15.00
RF	Rollie Fingers	8.00
RH	Roy Halladay	8.00
RI	Cal Ripken Jr.	30.00
RJ	Randy Johnson	10.00
RO	Roy Oswalt	8.00
RS	Ryne Sandberg	15.00
RW	Rickie Weeks	8.00
RY	Robin Yount/25	15.00
RZ	Ryan Zimmerman	8.00
SK	Scott Kazmir	8.00
TG	Tom Glavine	10.00
TH	Torii Hunter	8.00
TR	Travis Hafner	8.00
TT	Troy Tulowitzki	10.00
VM	Victor Martinez	8.00
WI	Josh Willingham	5.00
DW2	Dontrelle Willis	5.00
EC2	Eric Chavez	5.00
GA2	Garrett Atkins	5.00
HS2	Huston Street	5.00
KG2	Ken Griffey Jr.	15.00
MH2	Matt Holliday	10.00
MI2	Miguel Cabrera	10.00
MO2	Justin Morneau	8.00
OS2	Ozzie Smith	15.00
RI2	Cal Ripken Jr.	30.00
RZ2	Ryan Zimmerman	8.00
SK2	Scott Kazmir	8.00
TR2	Travis Hafner	8.00
WI2	Josh Willingham	5.00

Ultimate Write of Passage

NM/M

Production 60 Sets

BH	Jeff Baker/Auto., Matt Holliday	10.00
BR	Ryan Braun/Auto., Scott Rolen	75.00
GR	Alex Gordon/Auto., Alex Rodriguez	50.00
HS	Cole Hamels/Auto., Johan Santana	40.00
IC	Kei Igawa/Auto.	25.00
IR	Akinori Iwamura/Auto., Aramis Ramirez	30.00
KB	Howie Kendrick/Auto., Craig Biggio	10.00
KJ	Kevin Kouzmanoff/Auto., Chipper Jones	10.00
LZ	Tim Lincecum/Auto., Barry Zito	60.00
MS	Andrew Miller/Auto., C.C. Sabathia	25.00
PG	Hunter Pence/Auto., Ken Griffey Jr.	50.00
PK	Glen Perkins/Auto., Scott Kazmir	10.00

QC	Carlos Quentin/Auto., Carl Crawford	10.00
RF	Hanley Ramirez/Auto., Rafael Furcal	25.00
SD	Ryan Sweeney/Auto., Jermaine Dye	10.00
SS	Jeremy Sowers/Auto., C.C. Sabathia	10.00
TD	Curtis Thigpen/Auto., Carlos Delgado	10.00
TJ	Troy Tulowitzki/Auto., Derek Jeter	40.00
UU	B.J. Upton/Auto., Chase Utley	15.00
YG	Delmon Young/Auto., Vladimir Guerrero	15.00

2008 Upper Deck

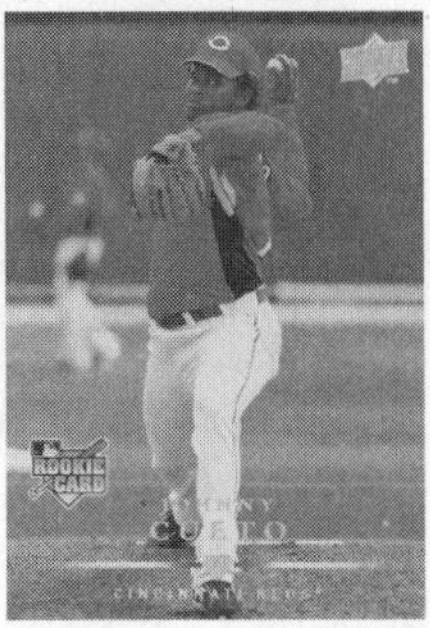

		NM/M
Complete Series 1 Set (400):		50.00
Complete Series 2 Set (399):		40.00
Common Player:		.15
Hobby Pack (20):		5.00
Hobby Box (16):		70.00
1	Joe Saunders	.15
2	Kelvim Escobar	.15
3	Jered Weaver	.25
4	Justin Speier	.15
5	Scot Shields	.15
6	Mike Napoli	.15
7	Orlando Cabrera	.25
8	Casey Kotchman	.15
9	Vladimir Guerrero	.75
10	Garret Anderson	.15
11	Roy Oswalt	.50
12	Wandy Rodriguez	.15
13	Woody Williams	.15
14	Chad Qualls	.15
15	Brian Moehler	.15
16	Mark Loretta	.15
17	Brad Ausmus	.15
18	Ty Wigginton	.15
19	Carlos Lee	.50
20	Hunter Pence	.50
21	Danny Haren	.25
22	Lenny DiNardo	.15
23	Chad Gaudin	.15
24	Huston Street	.15
25	Andrew Brown	.15
26	Mike Piazza	.50
27	Jack Cust	.15
28	Mark Ellis	.15
29	Shannon Stewart	.15
30	Travis Buck	.15
31	Shaun Marcum	.15
32	A.J. Burnett	.25
33	Jesse Litsch	.15
34	Casey Janssen	.15
35	Jeremy Accardo	.15
36	Gregg Zaun	.15
37	Aaron Hill	.15
38	Frank Thomas	.50
39	Matt Stairs	.15
40	Vernon Wells	.25
41	Tim Hudson	.25
42	Chuck James	.15
43	Buddy Carlyle	.15
44	Rafael Soriano	.15
45	Peter Moylan	.15
46	Brian McCann	.25
47	Edgar Renteria	.25
48	Mark Teixeira	.50
49	Willie Harris	.15
50	Andruw Jones	.50
51	Ben Sheets	.25
52	David Bush	.15
53	Yovani Gallardo	.50
54	Francisco Cordero	.15
55	Matt Wise	.15
56	Johnny Estrada	.15
57	Prince Fielder	1.00
58	J.J. Hardy	.15
59	Corey Hart	.25
60	Geoff Jenkins	.15
61	Adam Wainwright	.25
62	Joel Pineiro	.15
63	Brad Thompson	.15
64	Jason Isringhausen	.15
65	Troy Percival	.15
66	Yadier Molina	.15
67	Albert Pujols	2.00
68	David Eckstein	.15
69	Jim Edmonds	.25
70	Rick Ankiel	.25
71	Ted Lilly	.15
72	Rich Hill	.25
73	Jason Marquis	.15
74	Carlos Marmol	.15
75	Ryan Dempster	.15
76	Jason Kendall	.15
77	Aramis Ramirez	.50
78	Ryan Theriot	.15
79	Alfonso Soriano	.50
80	Jacque Jones	.15
81	James Shields	.25
82	Andrew Sonnanstine	.15
83	Scott Dohmann	.15
84	Al Reyes	.15
85	Dioner Navarro	.15
86	B.J. Upton	.50
87	Carlos Pena	.15
88	Brendan Harris	.15
89	Josh Wilson	.15
90	Jonny Gomes	.15
91	Brandon Webb	.25
92	Micah Owings	.15
93	Livan Hernandez	.15
94	Doug Slaten	.15
95	Brandon Lyon	.15
96	Miguel Montero	.15
97	Stephen Drew	.25
98	Mark Reynolds	.15
99	Conor Jackson	.25
100	Chris B. Young	.25
101	Chad Billingsley	.25
102	Derek Lowe	.15
103	Mark Hendrickson	.15
104	Takashi Saito	.15
105	Rudy Seanez	.15
106	Russell Martin	.50
107	Jeff Kent	.25
108	Nomar Garciaparra	.25
109	Matthew Kemp	.50
110	Juan Pierre	.25
111	Matt Cain	.25
112	Barry Zito	.15
113	Kevin Correia	.15
114	Brad Hennessey	.15
115	Jack Taschner	.15
116	Bengie Molina	.15
117	Ryan Klesko	.15
118	Omar Vizquel	.15
119	Dave Roberts	.15
120	Rajai Davis	.15
121	Fausto Carmona	.25
122	Jake Westbrook	.15
123	Cliff Lee	.15
124	Rafael Betancourt	.15
125	Joe Borowski	.15
126	Victor Martinez	.25
127	Travis Hafner	.25
128	Ryan Garko	.25
129	Kenny Lofton	.15
130	Franklin Gutierrez	.15
131	Felix Hernandez	.50
132	Jeff Weaver	.15
133	J.J. Putz	.15
134	Brandon Morrow	.15
135	Sean Green	.15
136	Kenji Johjima	.15
137	Jose Vidro	.15
138	Richie Sexson	.25
139	Ichiro Suzuki	1.50
140	Ben Broussard	.15
141	Sergio Mitre	.15
142	Scott Olsen	.15
143	Rick Vanden Hurk	.15
144	Justin Miller	.15
145	Lee Gardner	.15
146	Miguel Olivo	.15
147	Hanley Ramirez	.75
148	Mike Jacobs	.15
149	Josh Willingham	.15
150	Alfredo Amezaga	.15
151	John Maine	.25
152	Tom Glavine	.50
153	Orlando Hernandez	.15
154	Billy Wagner	.15
155	Aaron Heilman	.15
156	David Wright	1.00
157	Luis Castillo	.15
158	Shawn Green	.15
159	Damion Easley	.15
160	Carlos Delgado	.50
161	Shawn Hill	.15
162	Mike Bacsik	.15
163	John Lannan	.15
164	Chad Cordero	.15
165	Jon Rauch	.15
166	Jesus Flores	.15
167	Dmitri Young	.15
168	Cristian Guzman	.15
169	Austin Kearns	.15
170	Nook Logan	.15
171	Erik Bedard	.25
172	Daniel Cabrera	.15
173	Chris Ray	.15
174	Danys Baez	.15
175	Chad Bradford	.15
176	Ramon Hernandez	.15
177	Miguel Tejada	.50
178	Freddie Bynum	.15
179	Corey Patterson	.15
180	Aubrey Huff	.15
181	Chris Young	.25
182	Greg Maddux	1.50
183	Clay Hensley	.15
184	Kevin Cameron	.15
185	Doug Brocail	.15
186	Josh Bard	.15
187	Kevin Kouzmanoff	.25
188	Geoff Blum	.15
189	Milton Bradley	.15
190	Brian Giles	.15
191	Jamie Moyer	.15
192	Kyle Kendrick	.15
193	Kyle Lohse	.15
194	Antonio Alfonseca	.15
195	Ryan Madson	.15
196	Chris Coste	.15
197	Chase Utley	.75
198	Tadahito Iguchi	.15
199	Aaron Rowand	.15
200	Shane Victorino	.25
201	Paul Maholm	.15
202	Ian Snell	.25
203	Shane Youman	.15
204	Damaso Marte	.15
205	Shawn Chacon	.15
206	Ronny Paulino	.15
207	Jack Wilson	.15
208	Adam LaRoche	.25
209	Ryan Doumit	.15
210	Xavier Nady	.15
211	Kevin Millwood	.15
212	Brandon McCarthy	.15
213	Joaquin Benoit	.15
214	Wes Littleton	.15
215	Mike Wood	.15
216	Gerald Laird	.15
217	Hank Blalock	.25
218	Ian Kinsler	.25
219	Marlon Byrd	.15
220	Brad Wilkerson	.15
221	Tim Wakefield	.15
222	Daisuke Matsuzaka	1.00
223	Julian Tavarez	.15
224	Hideki Okajima	.25
225	Manny Delcarmen	.15
226	Doug Mirabelli	.15
227	Dustin Pedroia	.25
228	Mike Lowell	.15
229	Manny Ramirez	.75
230	Coco Crisp	.15
231	Bronson Arroyo	.15
232	Matt Belisle	.15
233	Jared Burton	.15
234	David Weathers	.15
235	Mike Gosling	.15
236	David Ross	.15
237	Jeff Keppinger	.15
238	Edwin Encarnacion	.25
239	Ken Griffey Jr.	1.50
240	Adam Dunn	.50
241	Jeff Francis	.25
242	Jason Hirsh	.15
243	Josh Fogg	.15
244	Manny Corpas	.15
245	Jeremy Affeldt	.15
246	Yorvit Torrealba	.15
247	Todd Helton	.50
248	Kazuo Matsui	.15
249	Brad Hawpe	.25
250	Willy Taveras	.15
251	Brian Bannister	.15
252	Zack Greinke	.15
253	Kyle Davies	.15
254	David Riske	.15
255	Joel Peralta	.15
256	Joe Buck	.15
257	Mark Grudzielanek	.15
258	Ross Gload	.15
259	Billy Butler	.25
260	David DeJesus	.15
261	Jeremy Bonderman	.25
262	Chad Durbin	.15
263	Andrew Miller	.25
264	Bobby Seay	.15
265	Todd Jones	.15
266	Brandon Inge	.15
267	Sean Casey	.15
268	Placido Polanco	.15
269	Gary Sheffield	.50
270	Magglio Ordonez	.25
271	Matt Garza	.25
272	Boof Bonser	.25
273	Scott Baker	.15
274	Joe Nathan	.15
275	Dennys Reyes	.15
276	Joe Mauer	.50
277	Michael Cuddyer	.15
278	Jason Bartlett	.15
279	Torii Hunter	.50
280	Jason Tyner	.15
281	Mark Buehrle	.15
282	Jon Garland	.15
283	Jose Contreras	.15
284	Matt Thornton	.15
285	Ryan Bukvich	.15
286	Juan Uribe	.15
287	Jim Thome	.50
288	Scott Podsednik	.15
289	Jerry Owens	.15
290	Jermaine Dye	.25
291	Andy Pettitte	.25
292	Phil Hughes	.50
293	Mike Mussina	.25
294	Joba Chamberlain	.50
295	Brian Bruney	.15
296	Jorge Posada	.25
297	Derek Jeter	2.00
298	Jason Giambi	.25
299	Johnny Damon	.50
300	Melky Cabrera	.25
301	Jonathan Albaladejo **RC**	.50
302	Josh Anderson **(RC)**	.25
303	Wladimir Balentien **(RC)**	.25
304	Josh Banks **(RC)**	.25
305	Daric Barton **(RC)**	.25
306	Jerry Blevins **RC**	.50
307	Emilio Bonifacio **RC**	.50
308	Lance Broadway **RC**	.50
309	Clay Buchholz **(RC)**	.50
310	Billy Buckner **(RC)**	.25
311	Jeff Clement **(RC)**	.25
312	Willie Collazo **RC**	.50
313	Ross Detwiler **RC**	.50
314	Sam Fuld **RC**	1.00
315	Harvey Garcia **(RC)**	.25
316	Alberto Gonzalez **(RC)**	.50
317	Ryan Hanigan **RC**	.50
318	Kevin Hart **(RC)**	.50
319	Luke Hochevar **RC**	2.00
320	Chin-Lung Hu **(RC)**	.50
321	Rob Johnson **(RC)**	.25
322	Radhames Liz **RC**	.50
323	Ian Kennedy **RC**	4.00
324	Joe Koshansky **(RC)**	.50
325	Donny Lucy **(RC)**	.25
326	Justin Maxwell **RC**	.50
327	Jonathan Meloan **RC**	.50
328	Luis 1endoza **(RC)**	.25
329	Jose Morales **(RC)**	.25
330	Nyjer Morgan **(RC)**	.50
331	Carlos Muniz **RC**	.50
332	Bill Murphy **(RC)**	.25
333	Josh Newman **RC**	.50
334	Ross Ohlendorf **RC**	1.00
335	Troy Patton **(RC)**	.50
336	Felipe Paulino **RC**	.50
337	Steve Pearce **RC**	2.00
338	Heath Phillips **RC**	.50
339	Justin Ruggiano **RC**	.50
340	Clint Sammons **(RC)**	.50
341	Bronson Sardinha **(RC)**	.50
342	Chris Seddon **(RC)**	.25
343	Seth Smith **(RC)**	.50
344	Mitch Stetter **RC**	.50
345	David Davidson **RC**	.50
346	Rich Thompson **(RC)**	.25
347	J.R. Towles **RC**	2.50
348	Eugenio Velez **RC**	1.00
349	Joey Votto **(RC)**	1.00
350	Bill White **RC**	.50
351	Vladimir Guerrero	.75
352	Lance Berkman	.50
353	Danny Haren	.25
354	Frank Thomas	.50
355	Chipper Jones	.75
356	Prince Fielder	1.00
357	Albert Pujols	2.00
358	Alfonso Soriano	.75
359	B.J. Upton	.50
360	Eric Byrnes	.25
361	Russell Martin	.50
362	Tim Lincecum	.50
363	Grady Sizemore	.50
364	Ichiro Suzuki	1.50
365	Hanley Ramirez	.75
366	David Wright	1.00
367	Ryan Zimmerman	.50
368	Nicholas Markakis	.50
369	Jake Peavy	.50
370	Ryan Howard	1.00
371	Freddy Sanchez	.15
372	Michael Young	.25
373	David Ortiz	.75
374	Ken Griffey Jr.	1.50
375	Matt Holliday	.50
376	Brian Bannister	.15
377	Magglio Ordonez	.25
378	Johan Santana	.75
379	Jim Thome	.50
380	Alex Rodriguez	2.00
381	Alex Rodriguez	2.00
382	Brandon Webb	.50
383	Chone Figgins	.25
384	Clay Buchholz	.50
385	Curtis Granderson	.50
386	Frank Thomas	.50
387	Fred Lewis	.15
388	Garret Anderson	.15
389	J.R. Towles	.25
390	Jake Peavy	.50
391	Jim Thome	.50
392	Jimmy Rollins	.75
393	Johan Santana	.75
394	Justin Verlander	.50
395	Mark Buehrle	.15
396	Matt Holliday	.50
397	Jarrod Saltalamacchia	.15
398	Sammy Sosa	.50
399	Tom Glavine	.50
400	Trevor Hoffman	.15
401	Dan Haren	.25
402	Randy Johnson	.75
403	Chris Burke	.15
404	Orlando Hudson	.15
405	Justin Upton	.25
406	Eric Byrnes	.15
407	Doug Davis	.15
408	Chad Tracy	.15
409	Tom Glavine	.40
410	Kelly Johnson	.15
411	Chipper Jones	.75

412 Matt Diaz .15
413 Jeff Francoeur .25
414 Mark Kotsay .15
415 John Smoltz .40
416 Tyler Yates .15
417 Yunel Escobar .25
418 Mike Hampton .15
419 Luke Scott .15
420 Adam Jones .15
421 Jeremy Guthrie .15
422 Nick Markakis .40
423 Jay Payton .15
424 Brian Roberts .25
425 Melvin Mora .15
426 Adam Loewen .15
427 Luis Hernandez .15
428 Steve Trachsel .15
429 Josh Beckett .50
430 Jon Lester .25
431 Curt Schilling .50
432 Jonathan Papelbon .40
433 Jason Varitek .40
434 David Ortiz .75
435 Jacoby Ellsbury .50
436 Julio Lugo .15
437 Sean Casey .15
438 Kevin Youkilis .25
439 J.D. Drew .15
440 Alex Cora .15
441 Derrek Lee .50
442 Carlos Zambrano .40
443 Sean Marshall .15
444 Matt Murton .15
445 Kerry Wood .25
446 Felix Pie .15
447 Mark DeRosa .15
448 Ronny Cedeno .15
449 Jon Lieber .15
450 Geovany Soto .50
451 Gavin Floyd .15
452 Bobby Jenks .15
453 Scott Linebrink .15
454 Javier Vazquez .15
455 A.J. Pierzynski .15
456 Orlando Cabrera .15
457 Joe Crede .15
458 Josh Fields .15
459 Paul Konerko .25
460 Brian Anderson .15
461 Nick Swisher .25
462 Carlos Quentin .15
463 Homer Bailey .15
464 Francisco Cordero .15
465 Aaron Harang .15
466 Alex Gonzalez .15
467 Brandon Phillips .25
468 Ryan Freel .15
469 Scott Hatteberg .15
470 Juan Castro .15
471 Norris Hopper .15
472 Josh Barfield .15
473 Casey Blake .15
474 Paul Byrd .15
475 Grady Sizemore .50
476 Jason Michaels .15
477 Jhonny Peralta .15
478 Asdrubal Cabrera .15
479 David Dellucci .15
480 C.C. Sabathia .40
481 Andy Marte .15
482 Troy Tulowitzki .40
483 Matt Holliday .40
484 Garrett Atkins .25
485 Aaron Cook .15
486 Brian Fuentes .15
487 Ryan Spilborghs .15
488 Ubaldo Jimenez .15
489 Jayson Nix .15
490 Nate Robertson .15
491 Kenny Rogers .15
492 Justin Verlander .40
493 Dontrelle Willis .15
494 Joel Zumaya .15
495 Ivan Rodriguez .25
496 Miguel Cabrera .75
497 Carlos Guillen .25
498 Edgar Renteria .15
499 Curtis Granderson .50
500 Jacque Jones .15
501 Marcus Thames .15
502 Josh Johnson .15
503 Jeremy Hermida .15
504 Dan Uggla .25
505 Mark Hendrickson .15
506 Luis Gonzalez .15
507 Dallas McPherson .15
508 Cody Ross .15
509 Matt Treanor .15
510 Andrew Miller .25
511 Jorge Cantu .15
512 Kazuo Matsui .15
513 Lance Berkman .50
514 Darin Erstad .15
515 Miguel Tejada .40
516 Jose Valverde .15
517 Geoff Blum .15
518 Reggie Abercrombie .15
519 Brandon Backe .15
520 Michael Bourn .15
521 Gil Meche .15
522 Brett Tomko .15
523 Miguel Olivo .15
524 Shane Costa .15
525 Joey Gathright .15
526 Mark Teahen .15
527 Alex Gordon .40
528 Tony Pena .15
529 Jose Guillen .15
530 Torii Hunter .25
531 Ervin Santana .25
532 Francisco Rodriguez .15
533 Howie Kendrick .15
534 Reggie Willits .15
535 John Lackey .25
536 Gary Matthews .15
537 Jon Garland .15
538 Kendry Morales .15
539 Chone Figgins .25
540 Andruw Jones .25
541 Jason Schmidt .15
542 James Loney .25
543 Andre Ethier .15
544 Rafael Furcal .25
545 Brad Penny .15
546 Hong-Chih Kuo .15
547 Jonathan Broxton .15
548 Esteban Loaiza .15
549 Delwyn Young .15
550 Mike Cameron .15
551 Ryan Braun .75
552 Rickie Weeks .25
553 Bill Hall .15
554 Tony Gwynn .15
555 Eric Gagne .15
556 Jeff Suppan .15
557 Chris Capuano .15
558 Derrick Turnbow .15
559 Jason Kendall .15
560 Livan Hernandez .15
561 Philip Humber .15
562 Francisco Liriano .40
563 Pat Neshek .15
564 Adam Everett .15
565 Brendan Harris .15
566 Justin Morneau .40
567 Craig Monroe .15
568 Carlos Gomez .25
569 Delmon Young .25
570 Mike Lamb .15
571 Oliver Perez .15
572 Jose Reyes .50
573 Moises Alou .25
574 Carlos Beltran .40
575 Endy Chavez .15
576 Ryan Church .15
577 Pedro Martinez .50
578 Johan Santana .50
579 Mike Pelfrey .15
580 Brian Schneider .15
581 Joe Smith .15
582 Matt Wise .15
583 Duaner Sanchez .15
584 Ramon Castro .15
585 Kei Igawa .15
586 Mariano Rivera .40
587 Chien-Ming Wang .50
588 Wilson Betemit .15
589 Robinson Cano .40
590 Alex Rodriguez 2.00
591 Bobby Abreu .40
592 Shelley Duncan .15
593 Hideki Matsui .75
594 Kyle Farnsworth .15
595 Joe Blanton .15
596 Bobby Crosby .15
597 Eric Chavez .15
598 Dan Johnson .15
599 Rich Harden .15
600 Justin Duchscherer .15
601 Kurt Suzuki .15
602 Chris Denorfia .15
603 Emil Brown .15
604 Ryan Howard .75
605 Jimmy Rollins .50
606 Pedro Feliz .15
607 Adam Eaton .15
608 Brad Lidge .15
609 Brett Myers .15
610 Pat Burrell .15
611 So Taguchi .15
612 Geoff Jenkins .15
613 Tom Gordon .15
614 Zach Duke .15
615 Matt Morris .15
616 Tom Gorzelanny .15
617 Jason Bay .25
618 Chris Duffy .15
619 Freddy Sanchez .15
620 Jose Bautista .15
621 Nyjer Morgan .15
622 Matt Capps .15
623 Paul Maholm .15
624 Tadahito Iguchi .15
625 Adrian Gonzalez .25
626 Jim Edmonds .25
627 Jake Peavy .40
628 Khalil Greene .15
629 Trevor Hoffman .15
630 Mark Prior .15
631 Randy Wolf .15
632 Michael Barrett .15
633 Scott Hairston .15
634 Tim Lincecum .40
635 Noah Lowry .15
636 Rich Aurilia .15
637 Aaron Rowand .25
638 Randy Winn .15
639 Daniel Ortmeier .15
640 Ray Durham .15
641 Brian Wilson .15
642 Adrian Beltre .25
643 Jeremy Reed .15
644 Jarrod Washburn .15
645 Yuniesky Betancourt .15
646 Jose Lopez .15
647 Raul Ibanez .15
648 Mike Morse .15
649 Erik Bedard .15
650 Brad Wilkerson .15
651 Chris Carpenter .25
652 Mark Mulder .15
653 Juan Encarnacion .15
654 Skip Schumaker .15
655 Troy Glaus .25
656 Anthony Reyes .15
657 Cesar Izturis .15
658 Adam Kennedy .15
659 Chris Duncan .15
660 Matt Clement .15
661 Scott Kazmir .25
662 Troy Percival .15
663 Akinori Iwamura .15
664 Carl Crawford .40
665 Cliff Floyd .15
666 Jason Bartlett .15
667 Rocco Baldelli .15
668 Matt Garza .25
669 Edwin Jackson .15
670 Vicente Padilla .15
671 Josh Hamilton .50
672 Jason Botts .15
673 Milton Bradley .15
674 Michael Young .15
675 Eddie Guardado .15
676 David Murphy .15
677 Ramon Vazquez .15
678 Ben Broussard .15
679 C.J. Wilson .15
680 Jason Jennings .15
681 Gustavo Chacin .15
682 B.J. Ryan .15
683 David Eckstein .15
684 Alex Rios .25
685 John McDonald .15
686 Rod Barajas .15
687 Lyle Overbay .15
688 Scott Rolen .40
689 Reed Johnson .15
690 Marco Scutaro .15
691 Lastings Milledge .15
692 Johnny Estrada .15
693 Paul LoDuca .15
694 Ryan Zimmerman .15
695 Odalis Perez .15
696 Wily Mo Pena .15
697 Elijah Dukes .15
698 Aaron Boone .15
699 Ronnie Belliard .15
700 Nick Johnson .15
701 Randor Bierd **RC** .50
702 Brian Barton **RC** 1.00
703 Brian Bass **(RC)** .15
704 Brian Bocock **RC** .50
705 Gregor Blanco **(RC)** .15
706 Callix Crabbe **(RC)** .15
707 Johnny Cueto **RC** 1.00
708 Kosuke Fukudome **RC** 6.00
708 Kosuke Fukudome Japanese SP 65.00
709 Scott Kazmir .25
710 Steve Holm **RC** .50
711 Fernando Hernandez **RC** .50
712 Elliot Johnson **(RC)** .15
713 Masahide Kobayashi **RC** 1.00
714 Hiroki Kuroda **RC** 1.00
715 Blake DeWitt **(RC)** .50
716 Kyle McClellan **RC** .50
717 Evan Meek **RC** .50
718 Denard Span **(RC)** .15
719 Darren O'Day **RC** .50
720 Alexei Ramirez **RC** 6.00
721 Alex Romero **(RC)** .15
722 Clete Thomas **RC** .50
723 Matt Tolbert **RC** .50
724 Ramon Troncoso **RC** .50
725 Matt Tupman **RC** .50
726 Rico Washington **(RC)** .15
727 Randy Wells **RC** .50
728 Wesley Wright **RC** .50
729 Yasuhiko Yabuta **RC** 1.00
730 Alex Rodriguez 1.00
731 Andruw Jones .15
732 C.C. Sabathia .25
733 Carlos Beltran .25
734 David Wright .25
735 Derrek Lee .25
736 Dustin Pedroia .25
737 Grady Sizemore .25
738 Greg Maddux .50
739 Ichiro Suzuki .50
740 Ivan Rodriguez .15
741 Jake Peavy .25
742 Jimmy Rollins .25
743 Johan Santana .25
744 Josh Beckett .25
745 Kevin Youkilis .25
746 Matt Holliday .25
747 Mike Lowell .15
748 Ryan Braun .50
749 Torii Hunter .15
750 Alex Rodriguez 1.00
751 Torii Hunter .15
752 Miguel Tejada .25
753 Huston Street .15
754 Scott Rolen .25
755 Tom Glavine .25
756 Ryan Braun .50
757 Troy Glaus .15
758 Carlos Zambrano .25
759 Carl Crawford .15
760 Dan Haren .15
761 Andruw Jones .15
762 Barry Zito .15
763 Victor Martinez .15
764 Erik Bedard .15
765 Josh Willingham .15
766 Johan Santana .25
767 Dmitri Young .15
768 Brian Roberts .15
769 Jim Edmonds .15
770 Jimmy Rollins .25
771 Jason Bay .15
772 Josh Hamilton .25
773 Josh Beckett .25
774 Aaron Harang .15
775 Troy Tulowitzki .15
776 Jose Guillen .15
777 Miguel Cabrera .25
778 Joe Mauer .15
779 Nick Swisher .15
780 Derek Jeter 1.00
781 Brandon Webb .25
782 Brian Roberts .15
783 C.C. Sabathia .25
784 Carl Crawford .15
785 Curtis Granderson .25
786 David Ortiz .25
787 Ichiro Suzuki .50
788 Jake Peavy .25
789 Jimmy Rollins .40
790 Joe Borowski .15
791 Johan Santana .40
792 John Lackey .25
793 Jose Reyes .40
794 Jose Valverde .15
795 Josh Beckett .25
796 Juan Pierre .15
797 Magglio Ordonez .15
798 Matt Holliday .25
799 Prince Fielder .40

Gold

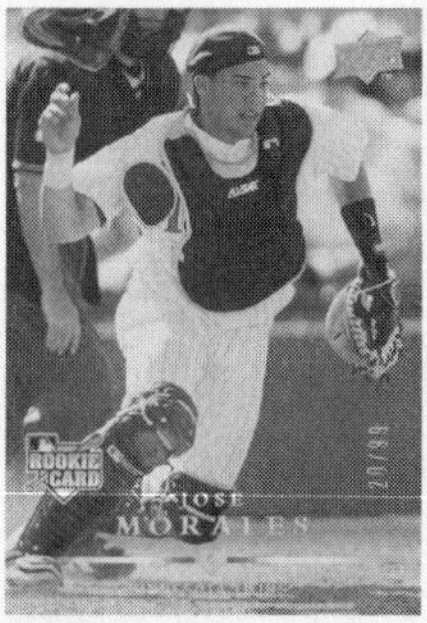

Gold: 4-8X
Production 99 Sets

All Rookie Team Signatures

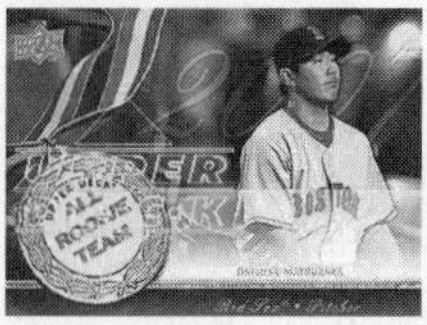

		NM/M
Common Auto.:		10.00
AI	Akinori Iwamura	30.00
AL	Adam Lind	10.00
AM	Andrew Miller	25.00
BB	Billy Butler	15.00
BU	Brian Burres	10.00
DM	Daisuke Matsuzaka	300.00
HA	Justin Hampson	10.00
KC	Kevin Cameron	10.00
KK	Kyle Kendrick	20.00
MB	Michael Bourn	10.00
MF	Mike Fontenot	15.00
MO	Micah Owings	15.00
RB	Ryan Braun	40.00
SO	Joakim Soria	10.00

Autographs

		NM/M
Common Auto.:		8.00
CD	Chris Duffy	8.00
CS	Curt Schilling	25.00
JP	Joel Peralta	8.00
JS	Jorge Sosa	15.00
JV	John Van Benschoten	8.00
LS	Luke Scott	8.00
RH	Ramon Hernandez	15.00
SA	Kirk Saarloos	10.00

SF	Scott Feldman	10.00
SH	James Shields	10.00
SR	Saul Rivera	10.00
SS	Skip Schumaker	15.00
ZG	Zack Greinke	10.00

Derek Jeter Chronicles
		NM/M
Common Jeter:		10.00
1-20	Derek Jeter	10.00

Derek Jeter OPC Reprints
		NM/M
Common Jeter:		8.00
1-15	Derek Jeter	8.00

Diamond Collection
		NM/M
Complete Set (20):		10.00
Common Player:		.50
1	Adam LaRoche	.50
2	Brian McCann	1.00
3	Bronson Arroyo	.50
4	Chad Billingsley	1.00
5	Chin-Lung Hu	1.00
6	Felix Pie	.50
7	Garrett Atkins	1.00
8	Homer Bailey	.50
9	Ian Kennedy	.50
10	James Shields	1.00
11	Jarrod Saltalamacchia	.50
12	Manny Corpas	.50
13	Mark Ellis	.50
14	Micah Owings	.50
15	Nick Swisher	1.00
16	Rich Hill	.50
17	Russell Martin	1.50
18	Ryan Theriot	1.00
19	Steve Pearce	1.00
20	Victor Martinez	1.00

Diamond Collection Autographs
No Pricing
Production Five Sets

Game Jersey

		NM/M
Common Jersey:		4.00
Patch:		2-4X
BR	Brian Roberts	6.00
CB	Carlos Beltran	10.00
CC	Coco Crisp	4.00
CG	Carlos Guillen	6.00
DC	Daniel Cabrera	4.00
DJ	Derek Jeter	20.00
DO	David Ortiz	10.00
DW	Dontrelle Willis	4.00
EG	Eric Gagne	4.00
GC	Gustavo Chacin	4.00
GJ	Geoff Jenkins	4.00
JB	Jason Bay	6.00
JD	Justin Duchscherer	4.00
JP	Jake Peavy	8.00
JS	Jeremy Sowers	4.00
JV	Jason Varitek	10.00
KM	Kazuo Matsui	6.00
ME	Morgan Ensberg	4.00
MM	Melvin Mora	4.00
MS	Mike Sweeney	4.00
MY	Michael Young	6.00
PA	Jonathan Papelbon	15.00
RH	Roy Halladay	6.00
TS	Takashi Saito	6.00
Series 2		
AP	Albert Pujols	20.00
BB	Boof Bonser	4.00
BM	Brandon McCarthy	4.00
BP	Brandon Phillips	6.00
BU	B.J. Upton	6.00
BZ	Barry Zito	4.00
CA	Matt Cain	6.00
CB	Chris Burke	4.00
CC	Chris Carpenter	6.00
CD	Chris Duncan	4.00
CJ	Conor Jackson	4.00
CL	Cliff Lee	4.00
CQ	Carlos Quentin	6.00
CU	Michael Cuddyer	4.00
DJ	Derek Jeter	20.00

DL	Derrek Lee	8.00
DO	David Ortiz	10.00
DW	David Wells	4.00
EC	Eric Chavez	4.00
ES	Ervin Santana	4.00
FH	Felix Hernandez	6.00
FL	Francisco Liriano	6.00
FR	Francisco Rodriguez	6.00
FS	Freddy Sanchez	4.00
GA	Garrett Atkins	6.00
GL	Troy Glaus	4.00
GM	Gil Meche	4.00
GO	Jonny Gomes	4.00
HR	Hanley Ramirez	8.00
IR	Ivan Rodriguez	6.00
JB	Jeremy Bonderman	4.00
JD	Jermaine Dye	4.00
JG	Jason Giambi	6.00
JH	Jeremy Hermida	4.00
JJ	Josh Johnson	4.00
JL	James Loney	6.00
JP	Jonathan Papelbon	10.00
JR	Jeremy Reed	4.00
JS	Jason Schmidt	4.00
JV	Justin Verlander	6.00
JW	Jered Weaver	6.00
KG	Khalil Greene	4.00
KJ	Kenji Johjima	4.00
KW	Kerry Wood	4.00
MC	Miguel Cabrera	8.00
ME	Melky Cabrera	4.00
MG	Marcus Giles	4.00
MJ	Mike Jacobs	4.00
MN	Mike Napoli	4.00
MP	Mark Prior	4.00
MY	Brett Myers	4.00
OL	Scott Olsen	4.00
PE	Mike Pelfrey	4.00
PF	Prince Fielder	8.00
PK	Paul Konerko	6.00
RC	Ryan Church	4.00
RD	Ray Durham	4.00
RF	Ryan Freel	4.00
RJ	Reed Johnson	4.00
RO	Robb Quinlan	4.00
RW	Rickie Weeks	4.00
RZ	Ryan Zimmerman	8.00
SK	Scott Kazmir	6.00
SO	Jeremy Sowers	4.00
TG	Tom Glavine	8.00
VW	Vernon Wells	4.00
WI	Dontrelle Willis	4.00
YM	Yadier Molina	4.00
ZD	Zach Duke	4.00

Hit Brigade
		NM/M
Complete Set (15):		25.00
Common Player:		1.00
1	Albert Pujols	5.00
2	Alex Rodriguez	5.00
3	David Ortiz	2.50
4	David Wright	3.00
5	Derek Jeter	5.00
6	Derrek Lee	2.00
7	Freddy Sanchez	1.00
8	Hanley Ramirez	3.00
9	Ichiro Suzuki	3.00
10	Joe Mauer	1.00
11	Magglio Ordonez	1.00
12	Matt Holliday	1.50
13	Miguel Cabrera	2.00
14	Todd Helton	1.50
15	Vladimir Guerrero	2.00

Hot Commodities
		NM/M
Common Player:		.75
1	Miguel Tejada	.75
2	Daisuke Matsuzaka	3.00
3	David Ortiz	1.50
4	Manny Ramirez	1.00
5	Alex Rodriguez	3.00
6	Derek Jeter	3.00
7	Carl Crawford	.50
8	Alex Rios	.50
9	Jim Thome	.50
10	Grady Sizemore	1.00
11	Travis Hafner	1.00
12	Victor Martinez	1.00
13	Justin Verlander	1.00
14	Magglio Ordonez	.50
15	Gary Sheffield	.75
16	Alex Gordon	.75
17	Justin Morneau	.75
18	Johan Santana	1.00
19	Vladimir Guerrero	1.00
20	Danny Haren	.50
21	Ichiro Suzuki	2.00
22	Mark Teixeira	1.00
23	Chipper Jones	1.00
24	John Smoltz	.50
25	Miguel Cabrera	1.00
26	Hanley Ramirez	1.00
27	Jose Reyes	1.00
28	David Wright	2.00
29	Carlos Beltran	1.00
30	Ryan Howard	2.00
31	Chase Utley	1.00
32	Ryan Zimmerman	1.00
33	Aramis Ramirez	.75
34	Derek Lee	.75
35	Alfonso Soriano	1.00
36	Ken Griffey Jr.	2.00
37	Adam Dunn	1.00

38	Carlos Lee	.75
39	Lance Berkman	.75
40	Prince Fielder	1.50
41	Ryan Braun	1.50
42	Jason Bay	.50
43	Albert Pujols	3.00
44	Brandon Webb	.75
45	Matt Holliday	.75
46	Brad Penny	.50
47	Russell Martin	.75
48	Trevor Hoffman	.50
49	Jake Peavy	.75
50	Tim Lincecum	1.00

Inkredible

INKREDIBLE
JAMES SHIELDS · RAYS

		NM/M
Common Auto.:		10.00
AL	Adam Lind	10.00
CP	Corey Patterson	10.00
CR	Cody Ross	10.00
DL	Derrek Lee	25.00
EA	Erick Aybar	10.00
JB	Josh Barfield	10.00
JH	Jason Hammel	10.00
JS	James Shields	15.00
LS	Luke Scott	10.00
MJ	Mike Jacobs	10.00
RC	Ryan Church	15.00
RL	Ruddy Lugo	10.00
RS	Ryan Shealy	10.00
SO	Jorge Sosa	15.00
TB	Taylor Buchholz	10.00

Milestone Memorabilia
		NM/M
Common Player:		8.00
GS	Gary Sheffield	10.00
KG	Ken Griffey Jr.	25.00
TG	Tom Glavine	15.00
TH	Trevor Hoffman	8.00

Mr. November
		NM/M
Common Jeter:		10.00
1-15	Derek Jeter	10.00

Presidential Predictors

Barack Obama
PRESIDENTIAL PREDICTORS

		NM/M
Common Predictor:		4.00
1	Rudolph Giuliani	8.00
2	John Edwards	8.00
3	John McCain	10.00
4	Barack Obama	10.00
5	Mitt Romney	4.00
6	Fred Thompson	4.00
7	Al Gore	4.00
8	Hillary Clinton	4.00
9	Wild Card	4.00

Presidential Running Mate Predictors
		NM/M
Common Predictor:		4.00
PP10	John McCain, Barack Obama	4.00
PP11	John McCain, Barack Obama	4.00

PP12	John McCain, Barack Obama	4.00
PP13	John McCain, Barack Obama	4.00
PP14	John McCain, Barack Obama	4.00
PP7B	Barack Obama, Hillary Clinton	4.00
PP7H	Barack Obama, Hillary Clinton	4.00
PP10A	John McCain, Hillary Clinton	4.00
PP11A	John McCain, Hillary Clinton	4.00
PP12A	John McCain, Hillary Clinton	4.00
PP13A	John McCain, Hillary Clinton	4.00
PP14A	John McCain, Hillary Clinton	4.00

Season Highlights Signatures
		NM/M
Common Auto.:		10.00
BB	Brian Bannister	15.00
BF	Ben Francisco	10.00
CS	Curt Schilling	30.00
FL	Fred Lewis	10.00
FT	Frank Thomas	100.00
JS	Jarrod Saltalamacchia	15.00
JW	Josh Willingham	8.00
KK	Kevin Kouzmanoff	10.00
MO	Micah Owings	15.00
MR	Mark Reynolds	8.00
MT	Miguel Tejada	20.00
PF	Prince Fielder	40.00
RS	Ryan Spilborghs	10.00

Signature Sensations
		NM/M
Common Auto.:		8.00
AM	Aaron Miles	20.00
BH	Brendan Harris	8.00
CB	Cha Seung Baek	15.00
DL	Derrek Lee	25.00
JP	Joel Peralta	8.00
JS	James Shields	10.00
JV	John Van Benschoten	8.00
LS	Luke Scott	10.00
MC	Matt Cain	15.00
RA	Reggie Abercrombie	10.00
SM	Sean Marshall	15.00

Star Attractions
		NM/M
Complete Set (10):		25.00
Common Player:		1.00
1	B.J. Upton	3.00
2	Carl Crawford	3.00
3	Chris Young	3.00
4	John Maine	2.00
5	Jonathan Papelbon	4.00
6	Nick Markakis	5.00
7	Prince Fielder	5.00
8	Takashi Saito	1.00
9	Tom Gorzelanny	1.00
10	Troy Tulowitzki	3.00

Star Attractions Autographs
No Pricing
Production Five Sets

Star Quest
		NM/M
Common Player:		.75
Blue:		1X
Rainbow:		2-3X
Red:		3-4X
1	Ichiro Suzuki	3.00
2	Ryan Braun	2.00
3	Prince Fielder	2.00
4	Ken Griffey Jr.	3.00
5	Vladimir Guerrero	1.50
6	Travis Hafner	.75
7	Matt Holliday	1.00
8	Ryan Howard	2.50
9	Derek Jeter	4.00
10	Chipper Jones	1.50
11	Carlos Lee	.75
12	Justin Morneau	1.00

13	Magglio Ordonez	1.00
14	David Ortiz	2.00
15	Jake Peavy	1.00
16	Albert Pujols	4.00
17	Hanley Ramirez	1.50
18	Manny Ramirez	1.50
19	Jose Reyes	2.00
20	Alex Rodriguez	4.00
21	Johan Santana	1.50
22	Grady Sizemore	1.50
23	Alfonso Soriano	1.50
24	Mark Teixeira	1.00
25	Frank Thomas	1.00
26	Jim Thome	1.00
27	Chase Utley	1.50
28	Brandon Webb	1.00
29	David Wright	2.50
30	Michael Young	.75

Series 2:

31	Adam Dunn	1.00
32	Albert Pujols	4.00
33	Alex Rodriguez	4.00
34	B.J. Upton	1.00
35	C.C. Sabathia	1.00
36	Carlos Beltran	1.00
37	Carlos Pena	1.00
38	Cole Hamels	1.50
39	Curtis Granderson	1.50
40	Daisuke Matsuzaka	2.00
41	David Ortiz	2.00
42	Derek Jeter	4.00
43	Derrek Lee	1.50
44	Eric Byrnes	.75
45	Felix Hernandez	1.50
46	Ichiro Suzuki	2.50
47	Jeff Francoeur	1.00
48	Jimmy Rollins	1.50
49	Joe Mauer	1.00
50	John Smoltz	1.00
51	Ken Griffey Jr.	3.00
52	Lance Berkman	1.00
53	Miguel Cabrera	1.50
54	Paul Konerko	1.00
55	Pedro Martinez	1.00
56	Randy Johnson	1.50
57	Russell Martin	1.00
58	Troy Tulowitzki	1.00
59	Vernon Wells	1.00
60	Vladimir Guerrero	1.50

Superstar
NM/M
Common Player: 1.00
Retail Jumbo Exclusive
Cards have bronze foil.
Autograph: No Pricing
Production Five Sets

9	Vladimir Guerrero	2.00
48	Mark Teixeira	2.00
57	Prince Fielder	3.00
67	Albert Pujols	4.00
139	Ichiro Suzuki	3.00
147	Hanley Ramirez	2.00
156	David Wright	3.00
239	Ken Griffey Jr.	3.00
270	Magglio Ordonez	1.00
297	Derek Jeter	4.00

Superstar Scrapbook
NM/M
Complete Set (10): 20.00
Common Player: 1.50

1	Albert Pujols	4.00
2	Alex Rodriguez	4.00
3	Chase Utley	2.00
4	Chipper Jones	2.00
5	David Ortiz	2.00
6	Derek Jeter	4.00
7	Ichiro Suzuki	2.00
8	Johan Santana	1.50
9	Jose Reyes	1.50
10	Ken Griffey Jr.	3.00
11	Manny Ramirez	1.50
12	Prince Fielder	1.50
13	Randy Johnson	1.50
14	Ryan Howard	2.00
15	Vladimir Guerrero	1.50

The House that Ruth Built
NM/M
Complete Set (25): 50.00
Common Ruth: 3.00
1-25 Babe Ruth 3.00

USA National Team
NM/M
Complete Set (25): 25.00
Common Player: 1.00

1	Brett Hunter	1.00
2	Brian Matusz	1.50
3	Brett Wallace	2.00
4	Cody Satterwhite	1.00
5	Dan Espinosa	1.00
6	Eric Surkamp	1.00
7	Jordan Danks	1.50
8	Jeremy Hamilton	1.00
9	Joe Kelly	1.00
10	Jordy Mercer	1.00
11	Josh Romanski	1.00
12	Justin Smoak	2.50
13	Jacob Thompson	1.50
14	Logan Forsythe	1.50
15	Lance Lynn	1.00
16	Mike Minor	1.00

17	Pedro Alvarez	2.50
18	Petey Paramore	1.00
19	Ryan Berry	1.50
20	Ryan Flaherty	1.00
21	Roger Kieschnick	1.00
22	Seth Frankoff	1.00
23	Scott Gorgen	1.00
24	Tommy Medica	1.00
25	Tyson Ross	1.00

USA National Team Autographs

NM/M
Common Auto.: 8.00

BH	Brett Hunter/297	8.00
BM	Brian Matusz/264	10.00
BW	Brett Wallace/183	25.00
CS	Cody Satterwhite/375	15.00
DE	Dan Espinosa/285	10.00
JD	Jordan Danks/311	10.00
JH	Jeremy Hamilton/375	8.00
JK	Joe Kelly/457	8.00
JM	Jordy Mercer/375	8.00
JR	Josh Romanski/375	8.00
JS	Justin Smoak/345	20.00
JT	Jacob Thompson/267	8.00
LF	Logan Forsythe/201	15.00
LL	Lance Lynn/425	10.00
MM	Mike Minor/375	10.00
PA	Pedro Alvarez/205	20.00
PP	Petey Paramore/237	10.00
RB	Ryan Berry/375	10.00
RF	Ryan Flaherty/244	10.00
RK	Roger Kieschnick/272	10.00
TM	Tommy Medica/487	8.00
TR	Tyson Ross/500	8.00

USA National Team Blue Autographs
NM/M
Common Auto.: 8.00

BH	Brett Hunter/129	10.00
BM	Brian Matusz/75	10.00
BW	Brett Wallace/75	25.00
CS	Cody Satterwhite/131	20.00
DE	Dan Espinosa/75	15.00
ES	Eric Surkamp/117	8.00
JD	Jordan Danks/75	15.00
JH	Jeremy Hamilton/204	8.00
JK	Joe Kelly/125	8.00
JM	Jordy Mercer/175	10.00
JR	Josh Romanski/175	8.00
JS	Justin Smoak/60	25.00
JT	Jacob Thompson/105	10.00
LF	Logan Forsythe/75	15.00
MM	Mike Minor/175	10.00
PA	Pedro Alvarez/75	25.00
PP	Petey Paramore/175	10.00
RB	Ryan Berry/175	10.00
RF	Ryan Flaherty/75	15.00
RK	Roger Kieschnick/113	10.00
SF	Seth Frankoff/175	8.00
SG	Scott Gorgen/175	10.00
TM	Tommy Medica/175	10.00
TR	Tyson Ross/75	10.00

USA National Team Red Autographs
NM/M
Common Auto.: 8.00
Green Autos: No Pricing
Production 10 Sets

BH	Brett Hunter/50	10.00
BM	Brian Matusz/50	25.00
BW	Brett Wallace/50	25.00
CS	Cody Satterwhite/50	20.00
DE	Dan Espinosa/50	15.00
ES	Eric Surkamp/50	10.00
JD	Jordan Danks/50	15.00
JH	Jeremy Hamilton/50	10.00
JK	Joe Kelly/50	10.00
JM	Jordy Mercer/50	10.00
JR	Josh Romanski/50	10.00
JS	Justin Smoak/50	25.00
JT	Jacob Thompson/30	15.00
LF	Logan Forsythe/50	15.00
LL	Lance Lynn/50	15.00
MM	Mike Minor/50	15.00
PA	Pedro Alvarez/50	25.00
PP	Petey Paramore/50	15.00
RB	Ryan Berry/50	10.00
RF	Ryan Flaherty/50	15.00
RK	Roger Kieschnick/50	10.00
SF	Seth Frankoff/50	10.00
SG	Scott Gorgen/50	10.00
TM	Tommy Medica/50	10.00
TR	Tyson Ross/50	10.00

USA National Team Jerseys

NM/M
Common Jersey: 4.00
Patch: 1.5-2X
Production 99 Sets

BH	Brett Hunter	4.00
BM	Brian Matusz	6.00
BW	Brett Wallace	10.00
CS	Cody Satterwhite	6.00
DE	Dan Espinosa	4.00
ES	Eric Surkamp	4.00
JD	Jordan Danks	4.00
JH	Jeremy Hamilton	4.00
JK	Joe Kelly	4.00
JM	Jordy Mercer	4.00
JR	Josh Romanski	4.00
JS	Justin Smoak	4.00
JT	Jacob Thompson	4.00
LF	Logan Forsythe	6.00
LL	Lance Lynn	4.00
MM	Mike Minor	4.00
PA	Pedro Alvarez	8.00
PP	Petey Paramore	4.00
RB	Ryan Berry	4.00
RF	Ryan Flaherty	4.00
RK	Roger Kieschnick	4.00
SF	Seth Frankoff	4.00
SG	Scott Gorgen	4.00
TM	Tommy Medica	4.00
TR	Tyson Ross	4.00

USA National Team Jersey Black Autographs
NM/M
Common Jersey Auto.: 10.00
Patch Autos: 1.5X
Production 99 Sets

BH	Brett Hunter/99	15.00
BM	Brian Matusz/181	20.00
BW	Brett Wallace/199	25.00
CS	Cody Satterwhite/273	20.00
DE	Dan Espinosa/193	15.00
JD	Jordan Danks/99	15.00
JH	Jeremy Hamilton/271	10.00
JK	Joe Kelly/300	10.00
JM	Jordy Mercer/287	10.00
JR	Josh Romanski/311	10.00
JS	Justin Smoak/199	30.00
JT	Jacob Thompson/199	10.00
LF	Logan Forsythe/199	15.00
LL	Lance Lynn/149	15.00
MM	Mike Minor/359	15.00
PA	Pedro Alvarez/275	25.00
PP	Petey Paramore/199	15.00
RB	Ryan Berry/284	15.00
RF	Ryan Flaherty/149	10.00
RK	Roger Kieschnick/199	15.00
TM	Tommy Medica/400	10.00
TR	Tyson Ross/400	10.00

USA National Team Jersey Blue Autographs
NM/M
Common Blue Jsy Auto.: 8.00
Jersey Red Autos: 1-1.5X
Production 50 Sets
Jersey Green Autos: No Pricing
Production 10 Sets

BH	Brett Hunter/150	15.00
BM	Brian Matusz/100	25.00
BW	Brett Wallace/75	30.00
CS	Cody Satterwhite/200	20.00
DE	Dan Espinosa/200	15.00
ES	Eric Surkamp/200	10.00
JD	Jordan Danks/200	15.00
JH	Jeremy Hamilton/200	10.00
JK	Joe Kelly/187	10.00
JM	Jordy Mercer/136	10.00
JR	Josh Romanski/123	10.00
JS	Justin Smoak/75	30.00

JT	Jacob Thompson/174	10.00
LF	Logan Forsythe/75	15.00
MM	Mike Minor/132	15.00
PA	Pedro Alvarez/89	30.00
PP	Petey Paramore/108	15.00
RB	Ryan Berry/192	10.00
RF	Ryan Flaherty/75	15.00
RK	Roger Kieschnick/99	15.00
SF	Seth Frankoff/69	10.00
SG	Scott Gorgen/247	10.00
TM	Tommy Medica/134	10.00
TR	Tyson Ross/292	10.00

USA Junior National Team

NM/M
Complete Set (20): 15.00
Common USA Junior: 4.00

1	Eric Hosmer	2.00
2	Garrison Lassiter	1.00
3	Harold Martinez	1.00
4	J.P. Ramirez	1.00
5	Jeff Malm	1.00
6	Jordan Swagerty	1.00
7	Kyle Buchanan	1.00
8	Kyle Skipworth	1.00
9	L.J. Hoes	1.50
10	Matt Purke	1.00
11	Mychal Givens	1.00
12	Nick Maronde	1.00
13	Riccio Torrez	1.00
14	Rob Grossman	1.00
15	Ryan Weber	1.00
16	T.J. House	1.00
17	Tim Melville	1.00
18	Tyler Hibbs	1.00
19	Tyler Stovall	1.50
20	Tyler Wilson	1.00

USA Junior National Team Autographs
NM/M
Common Auto.: 8.00

EH	Eric Hosmer/238	20.00
GL	Garrison Lassiter/375	15.00
HI	Tyler Hibbs/375	10.00
HM	Harold Martinez/237	8.00
JM	Jeff Malm/375	10.00
JR	J.P. Ramirez/239	8.00
JS	Jordan Swagerty/350	8.00
KB	Kyle Buchanan/375	8.00
KS	Kyle Skipworth/177	15.00
LH	L.J. Hoes/158	8.00
MG	Mychal Givens/209	8.00
MP	Matt Purke/375	8.00
NM	Nick Maronde/166	10.00
RG	Rob Grossman/155	10.00
RT	Riccio Torrez/500	8.00
RW	Ryan Weber/375	10.00
TH	T.J. House/147	8.00
TM	Tim Melville/133	8.00
TS	Tyler Stovall/375	10.00
TW	Tyler Wilson/75	8.00

USA Junior National Team Blue Autographs
NM/M
Common Auto.: 8.00

EH	Eric Hosmer/75	25.00
GL	Garrison Lassiter/175	15.00
HI	Tyler Hibbs/400	15.00
HM	Harold Martinez/275	10.00
JM	Jeff Malm/175	10.00
JR	J.P. Ramirez/90	15.00
JS	Jordan Swagerty/195	10.00
KB	Kyle Buchanan/175	10.00
KS	Kyle Skipworth/200	15.00
LH	L.J. Hoes/300	8.00
MG	Mychal Givens/309	8.00
MP	Matt Purke/390	8.00
NM	Nick Maronde/100	10.00
RG	Rob Grossman/175	10.00
RT	Riccio Torrez/400	8.00
RW	Ryan Weber/392	10.00
TH	T.J. House/75	10.00
TM	Tim Melville/330	8.00
TS	Tyler Stovall/186	10.00
TW	Tyler Wilson/75	8.00

USA Junior National Team Red Autographs

		NM/M
Production 50 unless noted.		8.00
Green Autos:		No Pricing
Production 10 Sets		
EH	Eric Hosmer	25.00
GL	Garrison Lassiter	15.00
HI	Tyler Hibbs/90	10.00
HM	Harold Martinez	10.00
JM	Jeff Malm	10.00
JR	J.P. Ramirez	15.00
JS	Jordan Swagerty	10.00
KB	Kyle Buchanan	10.00
KS	Kyle Skipworth	15.00
LH	L.J. Hoes	10.00
MG	Mychal Givens	10.00
MP	Matt Purke	15.00
NM	Nick Maronde/75	10.00
RG	Rob Grossman	10.00
RT	Riccio Torrez/150	10.00
RW	Ryan Weber/85	10.00
TH	T.J. House	10.00
TM	Tim Melville	10.00
TS	Tyler Stovall	10.00
TW	Tyler Wilson	10.00

USA Junior National Team Jerseys

		NM/M
Common Jersey:		4.00
Patch:		1.5-2X
Production 99 Sets		
EH	Eric Hosmer	10.00
GL	Garrison Lassiter	6.00
HI	Tyler Hibbs	4.00
HM	Harold Martinez	4.00
JM	Jeff Malm	4.00
JR	J.P. Ramirez	6.00
JS	Jordan Swagerty	4.00
KB	Kyle Buchanan	4.00
KS	Kyle Skipworth	6.00
LH	L.J. Hoes	4.00
MG	Mychal Givens	4.00
MP	Matt Purke	4.00
NM	Nick Maronde	4.00
RG	Rob Grossman	4.00
RT	Riccio Torrez	4.00
RW	Ryan Weber	4.00
TH	T.J. House	4.00
TM	Tim Melville	4.00
TS	Tyler Stovall	4.00
TW	Tyler Wilson	4.00

USA Junior Nat. Team Jersey Black Autographs

		NM/M
Common Jersey Auto.:		8.00
Patch Autos:		1-1.5X
Production 99 Sets		
EH	Eric Hosmer/100	30.00
GL	Garrison Lassiter/226	20.00
HI	Tyler Hibbs/222	10.00
HM	Harold Martinez/99	10.00
JM	Jeff Malm/258	10.00
JR	J.P. Ramirez/99	15.00
JS	Jordan Swagerty/199	10.00
KB	Kyle Buchanan/205	10.00
KS	Kyle Skipworth/99	20.00
LH	L.J. Hoes/150	10.00
MG	Mychal Givens/99	15.00
MP	Matt Purke/209	10.00
NM	Nick Maronde/99	10.00
RG	Rob Grossman/150	10.00
RT	Riccio Torrez/400	10.00
RW	Ryan Weber/222	10.00
TH	T.J. House/149	10.00
TM	Tim Melville/175	10.00
TS	Tyler Stovall/199	10.00
TW	Tyler Wilson/199	8.00

USA Junior Nat. Team Jersey Blue Autographs

		NM/M
Common Jersey Auto.:		8.00
Jersey Red Autos:		1-1.25X
Production 25-150		
Jersey Green Autos:		No Pricing
Production 10 Sets		
EH	Eric Hosmer/121	30.00
GL	Garrison Lassiter/172	20.00
HI	Tyler Hibbs/392	10.00
HM	Harold Martinez/375	10.00
JM	Jeff Malm/107	10.00
JR	J.P. Ramirez/200	15.00
JS	Jordan Swagerty/173	10.00
KB	Kyle Buchanan/131	10.00
KS	Kyle Skipworth/300	20.00
LH	L.J. Hoes/340	10.00
MG	Mychal Givens/300	15.00
MP	Matt Purke/390	10.00
NM	Nick Maronde/50	15.00
RG	Rob Grossman/100	10.00
RT	Riccio Torrez/400	10.00
RW	Ryan Weber/400	10.00
TH	T.J. House/75	10.00
TM	Tim Melville/350	10.00
TS	Tyler Stovall/125	10.00
TW	Tyler Wilson/235	8.00

USA National Team Highlights

USA rallies to pick up victory against Japan

		NM/M
Complete Set (5):		5.00
1	Game 1	1.00
2	Game 2	1.00
3	Game 3	1.00
4	Game 4	1.00
5	Game 5	1.00

1969 O Pee Chee reprints

		NM/M
Common Player:		.25
AG	Alex Gordon	.50
AP	Albert Pujols	2.00
AR	Alex Rodriguez	2.00
BP	Brad Penny	.25
BR	Babe Ruth	2.00
BU	B.J. Upton	.50
BW	Brandon Webb	.50
CD	Chris Duncan	.25
CJ	Chipper Jones	1.00
CL	Carlos Lee	.50
CP	Carlos Pena	.50
CU	Chase Utley	.75
CY	Chris Young	.25
DH	Danny Haren	.25
DJ	Derek Jeter	2.00
DL	Derrek Lee	.50
DM	Daisuke Matsuzaka	1.00
DO	David Ortiz	1.00
DW	David Wright	1.00
EB	Erik Bedard	.50
ER	Edgar Renteria	.25
GS	Gary Sheffield	.50
HP	Hunter Pence	.50
HR	Hanley Ramirez	.75
IS	Ichiro Suzuki	1.50
JB	Jason Bay	.25
JJ	J.J. Putz	.25
JM	Justin Morneau	.50
JP	Jake Peavy	.50
JR	Jose Reyes	.75
JS	Johan Santana	.75
JT	Jim Thome	.75
JW	Jered Weaver	.50
KG	Ken Griffey Jr.	1.50
MC	Miguel Cabrera	.75
MH	Matt Holliday	.50
MO	Magglio Ordonez	.50
MR	Manny Ramirez	.75
MT	Mark Teixeira	.50
NL	Noah Lowry	.25
PF	Prince Fielder	1.00
PH	Brandon Phillips	.50
RA	Aramis Ramirez	.50
RB	Ryan Braun	1.00
RH	Ryan Howard	1.00
RM	Russell Martin	.50
RZ	Ryan Zimmerman	.50
TH	Todd Helton	.50
VG	Vladimir Guerrero	.75
VW	Vernon Wells	.25

1997 UD Jersey

		NM/M
Common Jersey:		4.00

B.J. Ryan

Patch:		2-4X
AP	Albert Pujols	15.00
BC	Bobby Crosby	4.00
BG	Brian Giles	4.00
BR	B.J. Ryan	4.00
BS	Ben Sheets	6.00
CS	Curt Schilling	8.00
DL	Derek Lowe	4.00
DO	David Ortiz	10.00
GJ	Geoff Jenkins	4.00
HK	Hong-Chih Kuo	6.00
IR	Ivan Rodriguez	6.00
JB	Joe Blanton	4.00
JC	Joe Crede	4.00
JJ	Josh Johnson	4.00
JS	James Shields	6.00
JW	Jake Westbrook	4.00
LM	Lastings Milledge	6.00
MC	Miguel Cabrera	8.00
MO	Magglio Ordonez	6.00
NM	Nicholas Markakis	6.00
PE	Andy Pettitte	6.00
RB	Rocco Baldelli	4.00
TH	Todd Helton	6.00
VM	Victor Martinez	6.00
XN	Xavier Nady	4.00
Series 2:		
CH	Cole Hamels	10.00
DO	David Ortiz	10.00
DU	Dan Uggla	8.00
JM	Justin Morneau	8.00
JP	Jonathan Papelbon	10.00
JV	Justin Verlander	8.00
JZ	Joel Zumaya	6.00
PF	Prince Fielder	10.00
PO	Jorge Posada	8.00
VG	Vladimir Guerrero	10.00

1998 UD Jersey

		NM/M
Common Jersey:		4.00
Patch:		2-4X
BH	Bill Hall	4.00
BS	Ben Sheets	6.00
CF	Chone Figgins	4.00
CZ	Carlos Zambrano	6.00
EG	Eric Gagne	4.00
FC	Fausto Carmona	6.00
FH	Felix Hernandez	8.00
GS	Grady Sizemore	8.00
HB	Hank Blalock	6.00
IS	Ian Snell	6.00
JE	Johnny Estrada	4.00
JJ	Jacque Jones	4.00
JK	Jason Kendall	4.00
JS	Johan Santana	8.00
KM	Kevin Millwood	4.00
MB	Mark Buehrle	4.00
MG	Marcus Giles	4.00
NM	Nicholas Markakis	6.00
PK	Paul Konerko	6.00
VM	Victor Martinez	8.00
Series 2:		
AJ	Andruw Jones	4.00
CD	Chris Duncan	4.00
DJ	Derek Jeter	20.00
DL	Derrek Lee	10.00
GM	Greg Maddux	15.00
RM	Russell Martin	10.00
RO	Roy Oswalt	6.00
TH	Travis Hafner	6.00
VG	Vladimir Guerrero	10.00
VM	Victor Martinez	8.00

1999 UD Jersey

		NM/M
Common Jersey:		4.00
Patch:		2-4X

BR	Brian Roberts	6.00
CD	Chris Duffy	4.00
CJ	Chipper Jones	10.00
CS	C.C. Sabathia	8.00
DL	Derrek Lee	8.00
DW	David Wells	4.00
EB	Erik Bedard	8.00
FS	Freddy Sanchez	4.00
JB	Jason Bay	6.00
JD	Johnny Damon	4.00
JG	Jeremy Guthrie	4.00
JH	J.J. Hardy	4.00
JK	Jason Kubel	4.00
JP	Jorge Posada	6.00
KJ	Kenji Johjima	4.00
KM	Kendry Morales	4.00
MT	Mark Teixeira	8.00
RW	Rickie Weeks	6.00
TE	Miguel Tejada	6.00
TH	Travis Hafner	6.00
Series 2:		
BU	B.J. Upton	8.00
BW	Brandon Webb	8.00
CA	Matt Cain	6.00
DO	David Ortiz	10.00
HR	Hanley Ramirez	10.00
JM	Joe Mauer	6.00
KG	Khalil Greene	4.00
MC	Miguel Cabrera	10.00
NM	Nick Markakis	10.00
TH	Torii Hunter	8.00

500 Home Run Club Bat

		NM/M
FT	Frank Thomas	80.00
JT	Jim Thome	50.00

2008 Upper Deck Goudey

		NM/M
Common Player (1-200):		.15
Common SP (201-230):		3.00
Common President (231-250):		.50
Common 36 Goudey B&W (251-270):		1.00
Common Sports Royalty (271-330):		3.00
Pack (8):		5.00
Box (18):		75.00
1	Eric Byrnes	.15
2	Randy Johnson	.75
3	Brandon Webb	.40
4	Dan Haren	.25
5	Chris Young	.15
6	Max Scherzer RC	1.50
7	Mark Teixeira	.50
8	John Smoltz	.40
9	Jeff Francoeur	.25
10	Phil Niekro	.25
11	Chipper Jones	.75
12	Kelly Johnson	.25
13	Tom Glavine	.40
14	Yunel Escobar	.25
15	Erik Bedard	.25
16	Melvin Mora	.15
17	Brian Roberts	.25
18	Eddie Murray	.50
19	Jim Palmer	.50
20	Jeremy Guthrie	.15
21	Nick Markakis	.40
22	David Ortiz	.75
23	Manny Ramirez	.75
24	Josh Beckett	.40
25	Dustin Pedroia	.40
26	Bobby Doerr	.40
27	Clay Buchholz (RC)	.50
28	Daisuke Matsuzaka	.75
29	Jonathan Papelbon	.40
30	Kevin Youkilis	.40
31	Pee Wee Reese	.50
32	Billy Williams	.15
33	Alfonso Soriano	.75
34	Derrek Lee	.50
35	Rich Hill	.25
36	Kosuke Fukudome RC	5.00
37	Aramis Ramirez	.50
38	Carlos Zambrano	.50
39	Ted Lilly	.25
40	Mark Buehrle	.15
41	Orlando Cabrera	.15
42	Paul Konerko	.25
43	Jermaine Dye	.25

44 Jim Thome .40
45 Nick Swisher .25
46 Sparky Anderson .25
47 Johnny Bench .75
48 Joe Morgan .50
49 Tony Perez .40
50 Adam Dunn .50
51 Aaron Harang .25
52 Brandon Phillips .25
53 Edwin Encarnacion .15
54 Ken Griffey Jr. 1.50
55 Larry Doby .50
56 Bob Feller .50
57 C.C. Sabathia .50
58 Travis Hafner .25
59 Grady Sizemore .75
60 Fausto Carmona .15
61 Victor Martinez .25
62 Brad Hawpe .15
63 Todd Helton .50
64 Garrett Atkins .25
65 Troy Tulowitzki .25
66 Matt Holliday .50
67 Jeff Francis .15
68 Justin Verlander .40
69 Curtis Granderson .40
70 Miguel Cabrera .50
71 Gary Sheffield .40
72 Magglio Ordonez .25
73 Jack Morris .15
74 Andrew Miller .25
75 Clayton Kershaw **RC** 1.50
76 Dan Uggla .25
77 Hanley Ramirez .50
78 Jeremy Hermida .15
79 Josh Willingham .15
80 Lance Berkman .40
81 Roy Oswalt .25
82 Miguel Tejada .40
83 Hunter Pence .40
84 Carlos Lee .40
85 J.R. Towles **RC** .50
86 Brian Bannister .15
87 Luke Hochevar **RC** .75
88 Billy Butler .15
89 Alex Gordon .40
90 Kelvim Escobar .15
91 John Lackey .25
92 Chone Figgins .25
93 Jered Weaver .15
94 Torii Hunter .40
95 Vladimir Guerrero .75
96 Brad Penny .15
97 James Loney .25
98 Andruw Jones .15
99 Chad Billingsley .25
100 Chin-Lung Hu **(RC)** .15
101 Russell Martin .40
102 Eddie Mathews .75
103 Warren Spahn .50
104 Prince Fielder .50
105 Ryan Braun .75
106 J.J. Hardy .15
107 Ben Sheets .25
108 Corey Hart .25
109 Yovani Gallardo .15
110 Joe Mauer .25
111 Delmon Young .25
112 Johan Santana .50
113 Glen Perkins .15
114 Justin Morneau .40
115 Carlos Beltran .50
116 Jose Reyes .75
117 David Wright .75
118 Pedro Martinez .50
119 Tom Seaver .50
120 Billy Wagner .15
121 John Maine .25
122 Alex Rodriguez 2.00
123 Chien-Ming Wang .50
124 Hideki Matsui .75
125 Jorge Posada .50
126 Mariano Rivera .50
127 Phil Rizzuto .50
128 Bucky Dent .25
129 Derek Jeter 2.00
130 Graig Nettles .25
131 Ian Kennedy **RC** .50
132 Don Larsen .40
133 Joe Blanton .15
134 Mark Ellis .15
135 Dennis Eckersley .25
136 Rollie Fingers .15
137 "Catfish" Hunter .25
138 Daric Barton .15
139 Jack Cust .15
140 Ryan Howard .75
141 Jimmy Rollins .50
142 Chase Utley .50
143 Shane Victorino .25
144 Cole Hamels .40
145 Richie Ashburn .25
146 Jason Bay .25
147 Freddy Sanchez .15
148 Adam LaRoche .15
149 Jack Wilson .15
150 Ralph Kiner .25
151 Bill Mazeroski .25
152 Tom Gorzelanny .15
153 Jay Bruce **(RC)** 2.00
154 Jake Peavy .40
155 Chris Young .40
156 Trevor Hoffman .15
157 Khalil Greene .15
158 Adrian Gonzalez .40
159 Tim Lincecum .40
160 Matt Cain .25
161 Aaron Rowand .25
162 Orlando Cepeda .25
163 Juan Marichal .25
164 Noah Lowry .15
165 Ichiro Suzuki 1.50
166 Felix Hernandez .40
167 J.J. Putz .15
168 Jose Vidro .15
169 Raul Ibanez .15
170 Wladimir Balentien .15
171 Albert Pujols 2.00
172 Scott Rolen .25
173 Lou Brock .40
174 Chris Duncan .15
175 Vince Coleman .25
176 B.J. Upton .25
177 Carl Crawford .25
178 Carlos Pena .25
179 Scott Kazmir .25
180 Akinori Iwamura .15
181 James Shields .25
182 Michael Young .25
183 Jarrod Saltalamacchia .15
184 Hank Blalock .15
185 Ian Kinsler .25
186 Josh Hamilton .50
187 Marlon Byrd .15
188 David Murphy .15
189 Vernon Wells .25
190 Roy Halladay .25
191 Frank Thomas .50
192 Alex Rios .25
193 Troy Glaus .25
194 David Eckstein .15
195 Ryan Zimmerman .40
196 Dmitri Young .15
197 Austin Kearns .15
198 Chad Cordero .15
199 Ryan Church .15
200 Evan Longoria **RC** 3.00
201 Brooks Robinson 4.00
202 Cal Ripken Jr. 10.00
203 Frank Robinson 4.00
204 Carl Yastrzemski 5.00
205 Carlton Fisk 4.00
206 Fred Lynn 3.00
207 Wade Boggs 4.00
208 Nolan Ryan 10.00
209 Ernie Banks 6.00
210 Ryne Sandberg 6.00
211 Al Kaline 5.00
212 Bo Jackson 5.00
213 Paul Molitor 4.00
214 Robin Yount 5.00
215 Harmon Killebrew 5.00
216 Rod Carew 4.00
217 Bobby Thomson 3.00
218 Gaylord Perry 3.00
219 Dave Winfield 4.00
220 Don Mattingly 6.00
221 Reggie Jackson 5.00
222 Roger Clemens 8.00
223 Whitey Ford 5.00
224 Mike Schmidt 6.00
225 Steve Carlton 4.00
226 Tony Gwynn 5.00
227 Willie McCovey 4.00
228 Bob Gibson 5.00
229 Ozzie Smith 5.00
230 Stan Musial 6.00
231 George Washington 3.00
232 Thomas Jefferson 2.00
233 James Madison 1.00
234 James Monroe 1.00
235 Andrew Jackson .50
236 John Tyler .50
237 Abraham Lincoln 3.00
238 Ulysses S. Grant 2.00
239 Grover Cleveland .50
240 Theodore Roosevelt 1.00
241 Calvin Coolidge .50
242 John Adams 2.00
243 Martin Van Buren .50
244 William McKinley .50
245 Woodrow Wilson .50
246 James K. Polk .50
247 Rutherford B. Hayes .50
248 William Taft .50
249 Andrew Johnson .50
250 James Buchanon .50
251 Albert Pujols 3.00
252 Alex Rodriguez 3.00
253 Alfonso Soriano 1.00
254 C.C. Sabathia 1.00
255 Chase Utley 1.50
256 David Ortiz 1.50
257 David Wright 1.50
258 Derek Jeter 3.00
259 Hanley Ramirez 1.50
260 Ichiro Suzuki 2.00
261 Jake Peavy 1.00
262 Johan Santana 1.00
263 Jose Reyes 1.50
264 Ken Griffey Jr. 2.50
265 Magglio Ordonez 1.00
266 Matt Holliday 1.00
267 Prince Fielder 1.00
268 Ryan Braun 1.50
269 Ryan Howard 1.50
270 Vladimir Guerrero 1.00
271 Carl Yastrzemski 4.00
272 Albert Pujols 10.00
273 Amy Van Dyken 3.00
274 Tom Seaver 5.00
275 Brett Favre 10.00
276 Bruce Jenner 3.00
277 Bill Russell 3.00
278 Barry Sanders 8.00
279 Cynthia Cooper 3.00
280 Mike Schmidt 6.00
281 Chipper Jones 5.00
282 Cal Ripken Jr. 10.00
283 Cael Sanderson 3.00
284 Dan Gable 3.00
285 Derek Jeter 10.00
286 Andre Dawson 3.00
287 Dan O'Brien 3.00
288 Julius Erving 5.00
289 Emmitt Smith 8.00
290 Janet Evans 3.00
291 Chase Utley 5.00
292 Gary Hall Jr. 3.00
293 Gordie Howe 5.00
294 Josh Beckett 4.00
295 John Elway 6.00
296 Julie Foudy 3.00
297 Jackie Joyner-Kersee 3.00
298 Jack Nicklaus 10.00
299 Magic Johnson 6.00
300 Michael Jordan 10.00
301 Bo Jackson 6.00
302 Tom Brady 10.00
303 Wade Boggs 5.00
304 Dan Marino 10.00
305 Dave Winfield 4.00
306 Jenny Thompson 3.00
307 Kobe Bryant 8.00
308 Kevin Durant 6.00
309 Ken Griffey Jr. 8.00
310 Kerri Strug 4.00
311 Kerri Walsh 3.00
312 Larry Bird 15.00
313 LeBron James 10.00
314 Matt Biondi 4.00
315 Mark Messier 6.00
316 Michael Johnson 5.00
317 Misty May-Treanor 5.00
318 Bob Gibson 6.00
319 Nolan Ryan 15.00
320 Ozzie Smith 8.00
321 Prince Fielder 5.00
322 Rulon Gardner 3.00
323 Reggie Jackson 6.00
324 Ernie Banks 10.00
325 Sidney Crosby 15.00
326 Sanya Richards 3.00
327 Terry Bradshaw 10.00
328 Tony Gwynn 6.00
329 Stan Musial 10.00
330 Tiger Woods 60.00

Mini Black Back

Black Back (1-200): 8-12X
Mini Black Back (201-230): 2-3X
Presidents (231-250): 5-10X
B & W (251-270): 4-8X
Sports Royalty (271-330): 2-4X
Production 34 Sets

Mini Blue Back

Blue Back (1-200): 3-4X
Mini Blue Back (201-230): 1-1.5X
Presidents (231-250): 2-3X
B & W (251-270): 2-3X
Sports Royalty (271-330): 1-1.5X

Mini Green Back

Green Back (1-200): 4-6X
Mini Green Back (201-230): 1.5-2X
Presidents (231-250): 4-6X
B & W (251-270): 3-4X
Sports Royalty (271-330): 1.5-2X
Production 88 Sets

Mini Taupe Back

No Pricing
Production Eight Sets

Mini Red Back

Red Back (1-200): 3-4X
Mini Red Back (201-230): 1-1.5X
Presidents (231-250): 2-3X
B & W (251-270): 2-3X
Sports Royalty (271-330): 1-1.5X

Berk Ross Hit Parade of Champion

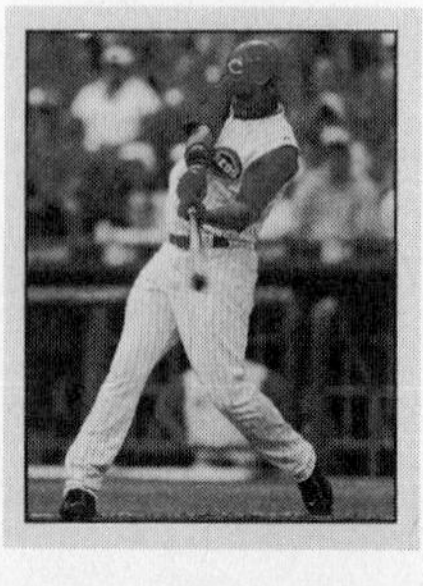

NM/M
Complete Set (30): 35.00
Common Player: 1.00
1 Albert Pujols 2.00
2 Don Mattingly 1.00
3 Ben Roethlisberger 1.00
4 Bill Russell 1.50
5 Bobby Orr 1.50
6 Cal Ripken Jr. 2.00
7 Carl Yastrzemski 1.00
8 Derek Jeter 2.00
9 Emmitt Smith 1.50
10 Gordie Howe 1.50
11 Joe Montana 2.00
12 Joe Namath 1.00
13 Ken Griffey Jr. 1.50
14 Kobe Bryant 2.00
15 LaDainian Tomlinson 1.50
16 Larry Bird 1.50
17 LeBron James 2.00
18 Magic Johnson 1.50
19 Mario Lemieux 1.50
20 Yogi Berra 1.00
21 Michael Jordan 2.00
22 Nolan Ryan 2.00
23 Patrick Roy 1.50
24 Peyton Manning 1.50
25 Reggie Jackson 1.00
26 Roger Clemens 1.50
27 Roger Staubach 1.00
28 Manny Ramirez 1.00
29 Tom Brady 2.00
30 Wayne Gretzky 2.00

Graphs

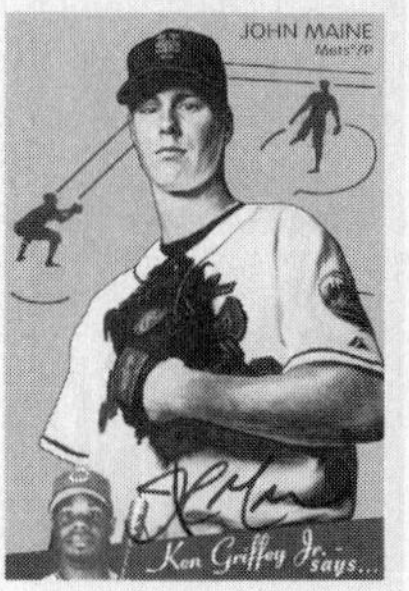

NM/M
Common Auto.: 8.00
SP production less than 100.
AH Aaron Harang 15.00
BB Billy Buckner 8.00
BD Bucky Dent 15.00
BP Brandon Phillips 15.00
BR Brooks Robinson 40.00
BT Bobby Thomson 30.00
BU Taylor Buchholz 8.00
BW Billy Wagner 20.00
CH Corey Hart 20.00
CJ Chipper Jones/SP 120.00
CL Carlos Lee 20.00
DB Daric Barton 8.00
DE David Eckstein 15.00
DL Derrek Lee 30.00
EE Edwin Encarnacion 15.00
FC Fausto Carmona 15.00
FL Fred Lynn/SP 30.00
GN Graig Nettles 15.00
GO Tom Gorzelanny 10.00
GP Glen Perkins 8.00
HU Chin-Lung Hu/SP 35.00
JB Johnny Bench/SP 60.00
JC Jack Cust 8.00
JF Jeff Francis/SP 10.00
JG Jeremy Guthrie 15.00
JH Jeremy Hermida 10.00
JO John Maine 10.00
JP Jonathan Papelbon 25.00
JT J.R. Towles 10.00
JW Josh Willingham 10.00
KJ Kelly Johnson 10.00
KY Kevin Youkilis/SP 40.00
LA Don Larsen/SP 40.00
MA Don Mattingly/SP 75.00
MB Marlon Byrd 8.00
MO Jack Morris 15.00
MS Mike Schmidt/SP 80.00
MU David Murphy 15.00
NL Noah Lowry 10.00
NM Nick Markakis 35.00
NS Nick Swisher 10.00
PM Paul Molitor 40.00
RM Russell Martin/SP 40.00
SP Steve Pearce 10.00
TG Tom Glavine/SP 50.00
VC Vince Coleman 20.00
YG Yovani Gallardo/SP 15.00

Memorabilia

NM/M
Common Player: 4.00
AD Adam Dunn 8.00

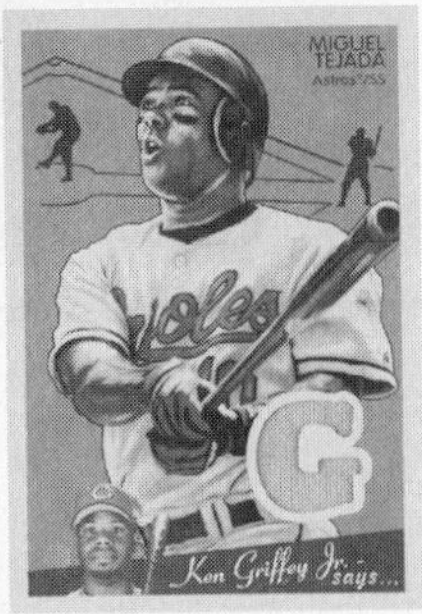

AG Adrian Gonzalez 4.00
AH Aaron Harang 4.00
AI Akinori Iwamura 4.00
AJ Andruw Jones 4.00
AP Albert Pujols 15.00
AR Aaron Rowand 4.00
AS Alfonso Soriano 8.00
BB Billy Butler 4.00
BD Bucky Dent 8.00
BE Josh Beckett 8.00
BR Brian Roberts 4.00
BU B.J. Upton 6.00
BW Brandon Webb 6.00
CC Carl Crawford 6.00
CH Cole Hamels 10.00
CJ Chipper Jones 10.00
CL Carlos Lee 6.00
CR Cal Ripken Jr. 15.00
CU Chase Utley 10.00
CY Chris Young 4.00
CZ Carlos Zambrano 6.00
DJ Derek Jeter 20.00
DL Derrek Lee 6.00
DM Daisuke Matsuzaka 15.00
DO David Ortiz 8.00
DU Dan Uggla 4.00
DY Delmon Young 4.00
FH Felix Hernandez 8.00
FS Freddy Sanchez 4.00
GA Garrett Atkins 4.00
GR Khalil Greene 4.00
GS Gary Sheffield 6.00
HO Trevor Hoffman 4.00
HP Hunter Pence 8.00
HR Hanley Ramirez 8.00
HU "Catfish" Hunter 8.00
JB Jason Bay 6.00
JD Jermaine Dye 4.00
JF Jeff Francoeur 6.00
JH Josh Hamilton 10.00
JM Joe Mauer 6.00
JP Jake Peavy 6.00
JR Jimmy Rollins 10.00
JS Johan Santana
JV Justin Verlander 8.00
JW Jered Weaver 4.00
KG Ken Griffey Jr. 15.00
KY Kevin Youkilis 10.00
LB Lance Berkman 6.00
MA John Maine 6.00
MB Mark Buehrle 4.00
MC Matt Cain 6.00
MH Matt Holliday 8.00
MI Miguel Cabrera 8.00
MO Justin Morneau 6.00
MR Manny Ramirez 8.00
MT Mark Teixeira 6.00
NM Nick Markakis 10.00
OR Magglio Ordonez 6.00
PA Jonathan Papelbon 8.00
PF Prince Fielder 8.00
PM Pedro Martinez 8.00
PO Jorge Posada 8.00
RA Aramis Ramirez 6.00
RE Jose Reyes 8.00
RH Roy Halladay 6.00
RI Mariano Rivera 10.00
RJ Randy Johnson 8.00
RM Russell Martin 8.00
RO Roy Oswalt 6.00
RZ Ryan Zimmerman 8.00
SI Grady Sizemore 10.00
SM John Smoltz 8.00
TE Miguel Tejada 6.00
TH Travis Hafner 4.00
VG Vladimir Guerrero 6.00
VM Victor Martinez 6.00
VW Vernon Wells 4.00
WI Jack Wilson 4.00
WS Warren Spahn 20.00
YG Yovani Gallardo 6.00

Sports Royalty Autographs

NM/M

SP Production less than 50.
AV Amy Van Dyken 35.00
CC Cynthia Cooper 20.00
CS Cael Sanderson 35.00
DO Dan O'Brien 25.00
ER Julius Erving/SP 140.00
EV Janet Evans 35.00
FO Julie Foudy 35.00
GH Gary Hall Jr. 30.00
JE Bruce Jenner 50.00
JJ Jackie Joyner-Kersee 35.00
JT Jenny Thompson 30.00
KG Ken Griffey Jr./SP 120.00
KW Kerri Walsh 50.00
LB Larry Bird/SP 140.00
MA Misty May-Treanor 60.00
MB Matt Biondi 30.00
OS Ozzie Smith/SP 80.00
PD Phil Dalhausser 25.00
RG Rulon Gardner 30.00
RJ Reggie Jackson/SP 150.00
SR Sanya Richards 25.00
TR Todd Rogers 30.00

2008 Upper Deck Heroes

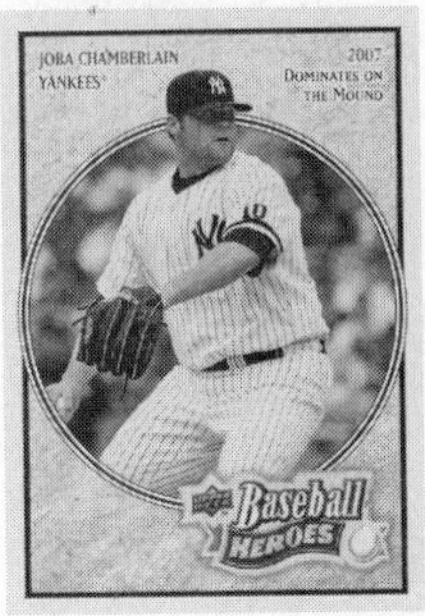

NM/M

Common Player (1-200):
Pack (8): 5.00
Box (24): 100.00
1 Brandon Webb .40
2 Dan Haren .40
3 Chris B. Young .25
4 Justin Upton .25
5 Randy Johnson .75
6 Chipper Jones .75
7 John Smoltz .40
8 Tom Glavine .50
9 Mark Teixeira .40
10 Brian McCann .40
11 Jeff Francoeur .25
12 Josh Hamilton .75
13 Tim Hudson .25
14 Nick Markakis .40
15 Brian Roberts .25
16 Cal Ripken Jr. 2.00
17 John Maine .25
18 Frank Robinson .50
19 Mike Lowell .25
20 Jason Varitek .40
21 David Ortiz .75
22 Manny Ramirez .75
23 Jonathan Papelbon .40
24 Jacoby Ellsbury .40
25 Kevin Youkilis .40
26 Curt Schilling .40
27 Josh Beckett .50
28 Daisuke Matsuzaka .75
29 Clay Buchholz .40
30 Dustin Pedroia .50
31 Ryan Theriot .25
32 Carlton Fisk .40
33 Carl Yastrzemski .75
34 Wade Boggs .40
35 Nolan Ryan 1.50
36 Alfonso Soriano .50
37 Kosuke Fukudome 3.00
38 Derrek Lee .50
39 Carlos Zambrano .40
40 Aramis Ramirez .40
41 Ernie Banks .50
42 Jim Thome .40
43 Jermaine Dye .40
44 Paul Konerko .25
45 Nick Swisher .25
46 Corey Hart .40
47 Ken Griffey Jr. 1.50
48 Adam Dunn .40
49 Aaron Harang .25
50 Johnny Bench .50
51 Grady Sizemore .50
52 Victor Martinez .40
53 C.C. Sabathia .40
54 Travis Hafner .25
55 Jeff Francis .25
56 Matt Holliday .40
57 Troy Tulowitzki .40
58 Garrett Atkins .40
59 Todd Helton .50
60 Curtis Granderson .50
61 Dontrelle Willis .25
62 Magglio Ordonez .40
63 Gary Sheffield .40
64 Miguel Cabrera .75
65 Justin Verlander .50
66 Ivan Rodriguez .40
67 Al Kaline .50
68 Hanley Ramirez .75
69 Edinson Volquez .50
70 Dan Uggla .40
71 Andrew Miller .25
72 Josh Willingham .25
73 J.R. Towles .25
74 Lance Berkman .50
75 Carlos Lee .40
76 Roy Oswalt .40
77 Hunter Pence .40
78 Luke Hochevar .50
79 Alex Gordon .40
80 Matt Cain .40
81 Bo Jackson .50
82 Vladimir Guerrero .50
83 Torii Hunter .40
84 Howie Kendrick .25
85 John Lackey .40
86 Chone Figgins .40
87 Andruw Jones .40
88 Brad Penny .25
89 James Loney .40
90 Matt Kemp .40
91 Nomar Garciaparra .40
92 Jon Lester .40
93 Chin-Lung Hu .75
94 Chad Billingsley .40
95 Kelly Johnson .25
96 Prince Fielder .50
97 Ryan Braun .75
98 Ben Sheets .40
99 Robin Yount .50
100 Justin Morneau .40
101 Joe Mauer .40
102 Delmon Young .25
103 Rod Carew .50
104 Carlos Beltran .50
105 Jose Reyes .75
106 Pedro Martinez .50
107 David Wright 1.00
108 Johan Santana .75
109 Billy Wagner .25
110 Carlos Delgado .40
111 Mariano Rivera .50
112 Chien-Ming Wang .75
113 Phil Hughes .40
114 Derek Jeter 2.00
115 Alex Rodriguez 2.00
116 Robinson Cano .40
117 Jorge Posada .40
118 Hideki Matsui .75
119 Joba Chamberlain .75
120 Ian Kennedy .40
121 Yogi Berra .50
122 Reggie Jackson .50
123 Roger Clemens 1.50
124 Ozzie Smith .75
125 Don Mattingly 1.00
126 Dave Winfield .50
127 Joe DiMaggio 1.50
128 Eric Chavez .25
129 Bill Hall .25
130 Rich Harden .25
131 Andre Ethier .25
132 Daric Barton .25
133 Ryan Howard .75
134 Jimmy Rollins .75
135 Chase Utley .75
136 Cole Hamels .50
137 Pat Burrell .40
138 Mike Schmidt .75
139 Steve Carlton .40
140 Freddy Sanchez .25
141 Joe Blanton .25
142 Felix Pie .25
143 Roberto Clemente 2.00
144 Jake Peavy .40
145 Greg Maddux 1.50
146 Tom Gorzelanny .25
147 Tony Gwynn .75
148 Barry Zito .25
149 Tim Lincecum .50
150 Rich Hill .25
151 Omar Vizquel .25
152 Ichiro Suzuki 1.50
153 Felix Hernandez .40
154 Kenji Johjima .25
155 Erik Bedard .25
156 Albert Pujols 2.00
157 Troy Glaus .40
158 Chris Carpenter .40
159 Chris Duncan .25
160 Mark Mulder .25
161 Scott Rolen .40
162 Stan Musial .75
163 Bob Gibson .50
164 B.J. Upton .40
165 Carl Crawford .40
166 Scott Kazmir .40
167 Michael Young .40
168 Luke Scott .25
169 Roy Halladay .40
170 Vernon Wells .25
171 Kevin Kouzmanoff .25
172 Frank Thomas .50
173 Ryan Zimmerman .40
174 Lastings Milledge .25
175 Ian Kinsler .50
176 Wade Boggs, Don Mattingly 2.00
177 Carlton Fisk, Carl Yastrzemski 1.00
178 Stan Musial, Albert Pujols 3.00
179 Derek Jeter, Jose Reyes 3.00
180 Cal Ripken Jr., Tony Gwynn 3.00
181 Prince Fielder, Eddie Murray 2.00
182 Kosuke Fukudome, Ichiro Suzuki 2.00
183 Steve Carlton, Johan Santana 1.00
184 Jake Peavy, Bob Gibson 1.00
185 Johnny Bench, Ivan Rodriguez 1.50
186 Vladimir Guerrero, Manny Ramirez 3.00
187 Wade Boggs, Carlton Fisk, Carl Yastrzemski 2.00
188 Alex Rodriguez, Derek Jeter, Robinson Cano 4.00
189 Ryan Braun, Miguel Cabrera, Chipper Jones 3.00
190 Don Mattingly, Dave Winfield, Reggie Jackson 2.00
191 Jimmy Rollins, Ryan Howard, Chase Utley 3.00
192 Joe Mauer, Troy Tulowitzki, Hanley Ramirez 2.00
193 Randy Johnson, Nolan Ryan, Greg Maddux 4.00
194 Brandon Webb, Justin Verlander, Felix Hernandez 2.00
195 Mike Schmidt, Ernie Banks, Frank Robinson 3.00

Beige Patch

No pricing
Production 5-10

Beige

Beige (1-200): 1.5-2X
Production 200 Sets

Black

Black (1-200): 1.5-2X
Production 250 Sets

Red

Red (1-200): 2-4X
Production 75 Sets

Charcoal

Charcoal (1-200): 1-1.5X

Emerald

Emerald (1-200): 1.5-2X
Production 300 Sets

Light Blue

Light Blue (1-200): 4-8X
Production 25 Sets

Navy Blue

Navy Blue (1-200): 2-4X
Production 100 Sets

Purple

No pricing
Production 10 Sets

Green

Green (1-200): 2-4X
Production 50 Sets

Charcoal Jersey Patch Autographs

NM/M

Production 4-50
1 Brandon Webb/25 40.00
10 Brian McCann/25 25.00
11 Jeff Francoeur/25 40.00
17 John Maine/50 20.00
23 Jonathan Papelbon/25 35.00
25 Kevin Youkilis/25 75.00
44 Paul Konerko/25 40.00
46 Corey Hart/50 30.00
47 Ken Griffey Jr./25 180.00
49 Aaron Harang/50 15.00
52 Victor Martinez/25 30.00
54 Travis Hafner/25 20.00
55 Jeff Francis/25 15.00
68 Hanley Ramirez/25 25.00
69 Edinson Volquez/50 30.00
72 Josh Willingham/25 15.00
75 Carlos Lee/25 25.00
90 Matt Kemp/25 25.00
94 Chad Billingsley/50 35.00
95 Kelly Johnson/50 20.00
96 Prince Fielder/25 35.00
136 Cole Hamels/25 50.00
141 Joe Blanton/50 10.00
142 Felix Pie/50 15.00
146 Tom Gorzelanny/50 15.00
150 Rich Hill/50 10.00
164 B.J. Upton/25 25.00
171 Kevin Kouzmanoff/25 15.00
175 Ian Kinsler/50 30.00

Charcoal Autograph

NM/M

Production 11-150
12 Josh Hamilton/150 40.00
14 Nick Markakis 20.00
17 John Maine/150 10.00
29 Clay Buchholz/95 20.00
31 Ryan Theriot/150 25.00
45 Nick Swisher/150 15.00
46 Corey Hart/150 20.00
47 Ken Griffey Jr./73 100.00
49 Aaron Harang/150 10.00
69 Edinson Volquez/150 20.00
73 J.R. Towles/150 10.00
80 Matt Cain/150 15.00
86 Chone Figgins/150 15.00
90 Matt Kemp/150 15.00

93	Chin-Lung Hu/150	15.00
94	Chad Billingsley/150	15.00
95	Kelly Johnson/150	8.00
120	Ian Kennedy/95	15.00
131	Andre Ethier/150	15.00
132	Daric Barton/150	10.00
141	Joe Blanton/144	8.00
142	Felix Pie/150	10.00
146	Tom Gorzelanny/150	8.00
150	Rich Hill/100	10.00
168	Luke Scott/148	15.00
171	Kevin Kouzmanoff/150	10.00
175	Ian Kinsler/150	15.00

Beige Autograph

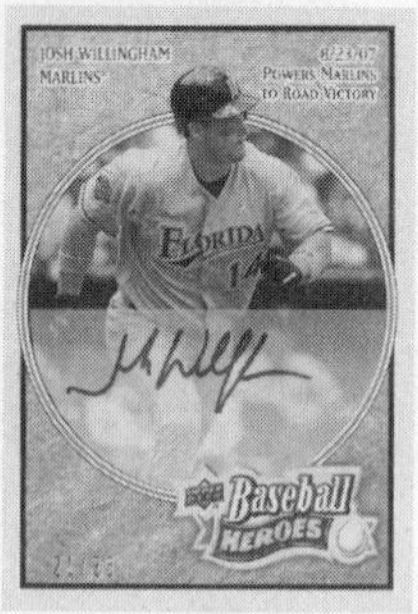

		NM/M
Production 10-25		
10	Brian McCann/25	25.00
17	John Maine/25	15.00
23	Jonathan Papelbon/25	30.00
31	Ryan Theriot/25	30.00
45	Nick Swisher/25	15.00
46	Corey Hart/25	30.00
49	Aaron Harang/25	10.00
68	Hanley Ramirez/25	25.00
69	Edinson Volquez/25	25.00
72	Josh Willingham/25	10.00
73	J.R. Towles/25	15.00
78	Luke Hochevar/25	20.00
86	Chone Figgins/25	15.00
90	Matt Kemp/25	25.00
93	Chin-Lung Hu/25	60.00
94	Chad Billingsley/25	30.00
95	Kelly Johnson/25	15.00
96	Prince Fielder/15	
114	Derek Jeter/15	
120	Ian Kennedy/15	
132	Daric Barton/15	
138	Mike Schmidt/15	
141	Joe Blanton/25	10.00
142	Felix Pie/25	10.00
146	Tom Gorzelanny/25	15.00
150	Rich Hill/25	15.00
168	Luke Scott/25	15.00
171	Kevin Kouzmanoff/25	10.00
175	Ian Kinsler/25	25.00

Black Autograph

		NM/M
Production 25-50		
3	Chris Young/25	20.00
10	Brian McCann/50	20.00
12	Josh Hamilton/50	50.00
17	John Maine/50	20.00
29	Clay Buchholz/35	20.00
31	Ryan Theriot/50	30.00
45	Nick Swisher/50	15.00
46	Corey Hart/50	20.00
49	Aaron Harang/50	15.00
68	Hanley Ramirez/25	25.00
69	Edinson Volquez/50	25.00
71	Andrew Miller/35	25.00
72	Josh Willingham/50	8.00
73	J.R. Towles/50	10.00
78	Luke Hochevar/50	15.00
80	Matt Cain/50	20.00
84	Howie Kendrick/25	15.00
85	John Lackey/25	20.00
86	Chone Figgins/50	20.00
87	Andruw Jones/25	15.00
90	Matt Kemp/50	25.00
93	Chin-Lung Hu/50	25.00
94	Chad Billingsley/50	30.00
95	Kelly Johnson/50	15.00
120	Ian Kennedy/35	15.00
132	Daric Barton/50	10.00
141	Joe Blanton/50	10.00
142	Felix Pie/50	10.00
146	Tom Gorzelanny/50	8.00
150	Rich Hill/50	10.00
168	Luke Scott/50	15.00
171	Kevin Kouzmanoff/50	15.00
175	Ian Kinsler/50	20.00

Emerald Jersey Autographs

No Pricing
Production 5 Sets

Light Blue Jersey Autographs

		NM/M
Production 15-75		
14	Nick Markakis/75	25.00
25	Kevin Youkilis/50	50.00
46	Corey Hart/75	25.00
47	Ken Griffey Jr./50	100.00
49	Aaron Harang/75	10.00
55	Jeff Francis/50	15.00
58	Garrett Atkins/35	15.00
69	Edinson Volquez/75	25.00
90	Matt Kemp/75	25.00
92	Jon Lester/50	40.00
93	Chin-Lung Hu/75	25.00
114	Derek Jeter/35	150.00
138	Mike Schmidt/35	40.00
141	Joe Blanton/75	10.00
142	Felix Pie/75	10.00
146	Tom Gorzelanny/75	10.00
175	Ian Kinsler/75	25.00

Navy Blue Auto

		NM/M
Production 35-100		
Navy Blue Jsy Auto:		No pricing
Production 1-10		
12	Josh Hamilton/100	40.00
17	John Maine/100	15.00
29	Clay Buchholz/55	20.00
31	Ryan Theriot/100	25.00
45	Nick Swisher/100	15.00
46	Corey Hart/100	25.00
47	Ken Griffey Jr./35	125.00
49	Aaron Harang/100	15.00
69	Edinson Volquez/100	25.00
71	Andrew Miller/35	20.00
72	Josh Willingham/100	10.00
73	J.R. Towles/100	10.00
80	Matt Cain/100	20.00
85	John Lackey/65	25.00
90	Matt Kemp/100	20.00
93	Chin-Lung Hu/100	25.00
94	Chad Billingsley/100	20.00
95	Kelly Johnson/100	15.00
120	Ian Kennedy/55	15.00
131	Andre Ethier/100	30.00
132	Daric Barton/50	10.00
141	Joe Blanton/100	8.00
142	Felix Pie/100	10.00
146	Tom Gorzelanny/100	8.00
150	Rich Hill/50	10.00
168	Luke Scott/100	15.00
171	Kevin Kouzmanoff/100	10.00
175	Ian Kinsler/100	20.00

Purple Autographs

No Pricing
Production 5 Sets

Red Autographs

No Pricing
Production 10 Sets

Red Jersey Autographs

		NM/M
Production 3-50		
3	Chris Young/25	20.00
11	Jeff Francoeur/25	30.00
17	John Maine/50	15.00
25	Kevin Youkilis/25	25.00
34	Wade Boggs/25	30.00
35	Nolan Ryan/25	100.00
44	Paul Konerko/25	30.00
46	Corey Hart/50	20.00
47	Ken Griffey Jr./25	100.00
49	Aaron Harang/50	10.00
52	Victor Martinez/25	15.00
54	Travis Hafner/25	10.00
55	Jeff Francis/25	10.00
58	Garrett Atkins/25	15.00
69	Edinson Volquez/50	20.00
80	Matt Cain/50	20.00
81	Bo Jackson/25	75.00
90	Matt Kemp/50	25.00
92	Jon Lester/35	30.00
93	Chin-Lung Hu/50	40.00
94	Chad Billingsley/50	30.00
95	Kelly Johnson/50	15.00
96	Prince Fielder/25	40.00
99	Robin Yount/25	40.00
103	Rod Carew/25	40.00
113	Phil Hughes/25	30.00
114	Derek Jeter/25	125.00
125	Don Mattingly/25	60.00
136	Cole Hamels/25	40.00
138	Mike Schmidt/25	40.00
139	Steve Carlton/25	30.00
141	Joe Blanton/50	10.00
142	Felix Pie/50	15.00
146	Tom Gorzelanny/50	15.00
150	Rich Hill/50	15.00
153	Felix Hernandez/25	40.00
163	Bob Gibson/25	40.00
164	B.J. Upton/25	25.00
169	Roy Halladay/25	25.00
175	Ian Kinsler/50	25.00

Black Jersey

		NM/M
Common player:		4.00
Production 125 sets		
Light Blue Jersey:		.75-1X
Production 200 sets		
Navy Blue Jsy:		1-1.5X
Production 50 sets		
Emerald Jsy:		1.5-2X
Production 25 sets		
Charcoal Jsy:		.5-1X

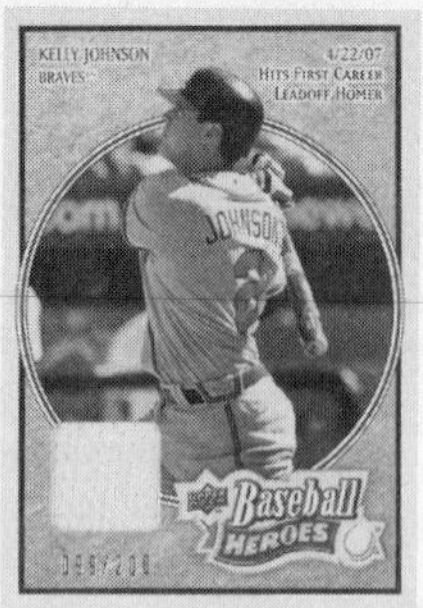

Light Blue Patch:		No pricing
Production 25 sets		
Red Jersey:		No pricing
Production 100 sets		
Purple Patch:		No pricing
Production 5 sets		
1	Brandon Webb	8.00
3	Chris Young	6.00
4	Justin Upton	8.00
5	Randy Johnson	8.00
6	Chipper Jones	15.00
7	John Smoltz	8.00
9	Mark Teixeira	6.00
10	Brian McCann	6.00
11	Jeff Francoeur	6.00
13	Tim Hudson	6.00
14	Nick Markakis	10.00
15	Brian Roberts	4.00
16	Cal Ripken Jr.	25.00
17	John Maine	4.00
18	Frank Robinson	8.00
19	Mike Lowell	6.00
20	Jason Varitek	8.00
21	David Ortiz	15.00
22	Manny Ramirez	8.00
23	Jonathan Papelbon	8.00
24	Jacoby Ellsbury	15.00
25	Kevin Youkilis	10.00
26	Curt Schilling	6.00
27	Josh Beckett	6.00
28	Daisuke Matsuzaka	15.00
29	Clay Buchholz	8.00
33	Carl Yastrzemski	10.00
34	Wade Boggs	8.00
35	Nolan Ryan	20.00
36	Alfonso Soriano	8.00
37	Kosuke Fukudome	25.00
38	Derrek Lee	6.00
39	Carlos Zambrano	6.00
40	Aramis Ramirez	6.00
41	Ernie Banks	15.00
42	Jim Thome	8.00
43	Jermaine Dye	6.00
44	Paul Konerko	6.00
46	Corey Hart	8.00
47	Ken Griffey Jr.	15.00
48	Adam Dunn	6.00
49	Aaron Harang	4.00
50	Johnny Bench	15.00
51	Grady Sizemore	10.00
52	Victor Martinez	6.00
53	C.C. Sabathia	6.00
54	Travis Hafner	4.00
55	Jeff Francis	4.00
56	Matt Holliday	8.00
57	Troy Tulowitzki	6.00
58	Garrett Atkins	6.00
59	Todd Helton	6.00
60	Curtis Granderson	8.00
62	Magglio Ordonez	6.00
65	Justin Verlander	6.00
66	Ivan Rodriguez	6.00
68	Hanley Ramirez	8.00
69	Edinson Volquez	8.00
70	Dan Uggla	6.00
71	Andrew Miller	6.00
72	Josh Willingham	4.00
74	Lance Berkman	6.00
75	Carlos Lee	6.00
76	Roy Oswalt	6.00
77	Hunter Pence	6.00
79	Alex Gordon	8.00
80	Matt Cain	6.00
81	Bo Jackson	10.00
82	Vladimir Guerrero	8.00
84	Howie Kendrick	6.00
85	John Lackey	6.00
86	Chone Figgins	6.00
88	Brad Penny	4.00
89	James Loney	6.00
90	Matt Kemp	8.00
92	Jon Lester	8.00
93	Chin-Lung Hu	8.00
94	Chad Billingsley	8.00
95	Kelly Johnson	4.00
96	Prince Fielder	8.00
97	Ryan Braun	10.00
98	Ben Sheets	4.00
99	Robin Yount	10.00
100	Justin Morneau	6.00
101	Joe Mauer	6.00
103	Rod Carew	8.00
104	Carlos Beltran	6.00
106	Pedro Martinez	6.00
109	Billy Wagner	4.00
110	Carlos Delgado	6.00
111	Mariano Rivera	8.00
112	Chien-Ming Wang	10.00
113	Phil Hughes	6.00
114	Derek Jeter	20.00
115	Alex Rodriguez	20.00
116	Robinson Cano	6.00
117	Jorge Posada	8.00
120	Ian Kennedy	6.00
121	Yogi Berra	10.00
123	Roger Clemens	10.00
124	Ozzie Smith	10.00
125	Don Mattingly	10.00
126	Dave Winfield	8.00
127	Joe DiMaggio	50.00
128	Eric Chavez	4.00
129	Bill Hall	4.00
130	Rich Harden	4.00
131	Andre Ethier	4.00
134	Jimmy Rollins	8.00
135	Chase Utley	8.00
136	Cole Hamels	8.00
137	Pat Burrell	6.00
138	Mike Schmidt	10.00
139	Steve Carlton	6.00
140	Freddy Sanchez	4.00
141	Joe Blanton	4.00
142	Felix Pie	4.00
143	Roberto Clemente	50.00
144	Jake Peavy	6.00
145	Greg Maddux	10.00
146	Tom Gorzelanny	4.00
147	Tony Gwynn	10.00
148	Barry Zito	4.00
149	Tim Lincecum	8.00
150	Rich Hill	4.00
151	Omar Vizquel	4.00
153	Felix Hernandez	6.00
154	Kenji Johjima	4.00
156	Albert Pujols	15.00
158	Chris Carpenter	6.00
159	Chris Duncan	4.00
160	Mark Mulder	4.00
161	Scott Rolen	4.00
163	Bob Gibson	8.00
164	B.J. Upton	6.00
165	Carl Crawford	6.00
166	Scott Kazmir	6.00
167	Michael Young	4.00
169	Roy Halladay	6.00
170	Vernon Wells	4.00
171	Kevin Kouzmanoff	4.00
173	Ryan Zimmerman	6.00
175	Ian Kinsler	6.00
188	Alex Rodriguez, Derek Jeter, Robinson Cano	40.00
190	Don Mattingly, Dave Winfield, Reggie Jackson	30.00
192	Joe Mauer, Hanley Ramirez, Troy Tulowitzki	15.00
193	Randy Johnson, Nolan Ryan, Greg Maddux	35.00
194	Brandon Webb, Justin Verlander, Felix Hernandez	15.00
195	Mike Schmidt, Ernie Banks, Frank Robinson	25.00

2008 Upper Deck X

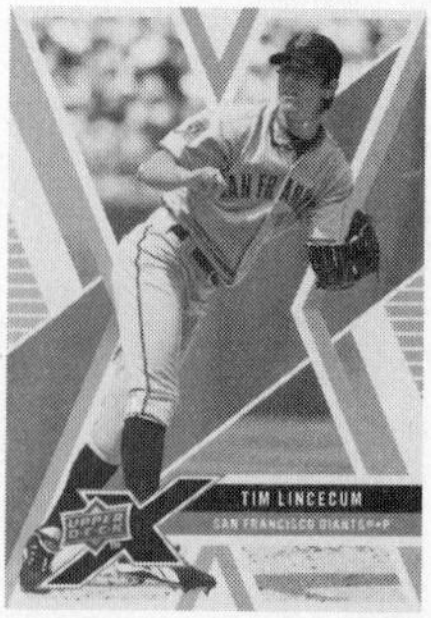

		NM/M
Complete Set (100):		30.00
Common player (1-100):		.25
Pack (8):		3.00
Box (20):		55.00
1	Randy Johnson	.75
2	Conor Jackson	.25
3	Brandon Webb	.50
4	Justin Upton	.25
5	Dan Haren	.40
6	John Smoltz	.50
7	Chipper Jones	.75
8	Mark Teixeira	.50
9	Brian Roberts	.25
10	Nick Markakis	.40
11	Daisuke Matsuzaka	1.00
12	David Ortiz	.75
13	Manny Ramirez	.75

14 Jonathan Papelbon .50
15 Josh Beckett .50
16 Clay Buchholz **(RC)** 1.00
17 Carlos Zambrano .40
18 Derrek Lee .50
19 Aramis Ramirez .50
20 Kerry Wood .25
21 Alfonso Soriano .75
22 Kosuke Fukudome **RC** 3.00
23 Geovany Soto .50
24 Paul Konerko .40
25 Jermaine Dye .40
26 Carlos Quentin .40
27 Jim Thome .50
28 Ken Griffey Jr. 1.50
29 Adam Dunn .50
30 Brandon Phillips .40
31 Edinson Volquez .25
32 Victor Martinez .25
33 Travis Hafner .25
34 C.C. Sabathia .50
35 Grady Sizemore .75
36 Garrett Atkins .40
37 Matt Holliday .50
38 Troy Tulowitzki .40
39 Justin Verlander .40
40 Miguel Cabrera .50
41 Gary Sheffield .50
42 Magglio Ordonez .40
43 Hanley Ramirez .75
44 Jeremy Hermida .25
45 Carlos Lee .40
46 Lance Berkman .40
47 Roy Oswalt .40
48 Alex Gordon .25
49 Zack Greinke .25
50 Howie Kendrick .25
51 Torii Hunter .40
52 Vladimir Guerrero .75
53 Matt Kemp .40
54 Russell Martin .40
55 Rafael Furcal .40
56 Ryan Braun .75
57 Prince Fielder .50
58 Corey Hart .25
59 Justin Morneau .50
60 Joe Mauer .50
61 Jose Reyes .75
62 David Wright 1.00
63 Carlos Beltran .50
64 Johan Santana .75
65 Pedro Martinez .50
66 Ian Kennedy **RC** 1.00
67 Hideki Matsui .75
68 Alex Rodriguez 2.00
69 Chien-Ming Wang .75
70 Derek Jeter 2.00
71 Robinson Cano .50
72 Eric Chavez .25
73 Frank Thomas .75
74 Cole Hamels .50
75 Jimmy Rollins .75
76 Ryan Howard .75
77 Chase Utley .75
78 Nate McLouth .25
79 Jason Bay .40
80 Adrian Gonzalez .40
81 Khalil Greene .25
82 Jake Peavy .50
83 Greg Maddux 1.50
84 Trevor Hoffman .25
85 Aaron Rowand .25
86 Tim Lincecum .75
87 Ichiro Suzuki 1.50
88 Felix Hernandez .50
89 Erik Bedard .25
90 Rick Ankiel .25
91 Albert Pujols 2.00
92 B.J. Upton .40
93 Carl Crawford .40
94 Evan Longoria **RC** 5.00
95 Josh Hamilton .75
96 Michael Young .25
97 Vernon Wells .40
98 Alex Rios .40
99 Ryan Zimmerman .25
100 Lastings Milledge .25

Die-Cut

Die-Cut (1-100): 1-2X
Inserted 1:pack

Die-Cut Gold

Die-Cut Gold (1-100): 3-5X

Printing Plates

No pricing
Production one set per color.

Memorabilia

NM/M

Common player: 4.00
AA Aaron Harang 4.00
AB Adrian Beltre 4.00
AE Andre Ethier 4.00
AG Adrian Gonzalez 6.00
AH Aubrey Huff 4.00
AK Austin Kearns 4.00
AR Alex Rodriguez 20.00
BB Boof Bonser 4.00
BG Brian Giles 4.00
BH Bill Hall 4.00
BJ Brandon Jones 4.00
BM Brian McCann 4.00
BO Jeremy Bonderman 4.00
BP Brad Penny 4.00
BR Brian Roberts 4.00
BU A.J. Burnett 4.00
CA Melky Cabrera 4.00
CC Chris Carpenter 4.00
CD Carlos Delgado 6.00
CH Craig Hansen 4.00
CJ Conor Jackson 4.00
CL Carlos Lee 6.00
CR Joe Crede 4.00
CS Curt Schilling 6.00
CZ Carlos Zambrano 6.00
DL Derrek Lee 6.00
DO David Ortiz 10.00
DR J.D. Drew 4.00
DU Dan Uggla 4.00
DY Jermaine Dye 6.00
EG Eric Gagne 4.00
FR Francisco Rodriguez 4.00
FS Freddy Sanchez 4.00
GA Garrett Atkins 4.00
GJ Geoff Jenkins 4.00
GL Troy Glaus 4.00
GM Greg Maddux 15.00
GS Grady Sizemore 15.00
HA Travis Hafner 4.00
HP Hunter Pence 6.00
HR Hanley Ramirez 10.00
HS Huston Street 4.00
HU Torii Hunter 6.00
IK Ian Kinsler 8.00
IR Ivan Rodriguez 6.00
JB Josh Barfield 4.00
JD Johnny Damon 6.00
JE Johnny Estrada 4.00
JF Jeff Francoeur 4.00
JG Jeremy Guthrie 4.00
JH J.J. Hardy 6.00
JK Jeff Kent 6.00
JM Joe Mauer 6.00
JO Josh Hamilton 15.00
JP Jhonny Peralta 4.00
JR Jeremy Reed 4.00
JS James Shields 6.00
JV Jason Varitek 8.00
JW Jered Weaver 4.00
KE Kelly Johnson 4.00
KJ Kenji Johjima 4.00
KM Kazuo Matsui 4.00
KU Jason Kubel 4.00
KW Kerry Wood 4.00
KY Kevin Youkilis 8.00
LG Luis Gonzalez 4.00
LM Lastings Milledge 4.00
MA John Maine 4.00
MC Matt Cain 4.00
MG Matt Garza 4.00
MI Kevin Millwood 4.00
MK Kendry Morales 4.00
MO Justin Morneau 6.00
MP Mark Prior 4.00
MR Mariano Rivera 8.00
NS Nick Swisher 4.00
PA Jonathan Papelbon 8.00
PE Jake Peavy 6.00
PF Prince Fielder 8.00
PI Juan Pierre 4.00
PO Jorge Posada 8.00
RA Aramis Ramirez 6.00
RF Rafael Furcal 6.00
RH Rich Hill 4.00
RM Russell Martin 6.00
RZ Ryan Zimmerman 4.00
SA Johan Santana 8.00
SC Sean Casey 4.00
SP Scott Podsednik 4.00
TG Tom Gorzelanny 4.00
TH Tim Hudson 4.00
TL Tim Lincecum 8.00
TS Takashi Saito 4.00
TT Troy Tulowitzki 6.00
TW Tim Wakefield 4.00
UP B.J. Upton 6.00
VE Justin Verlander 6.00

Signatures

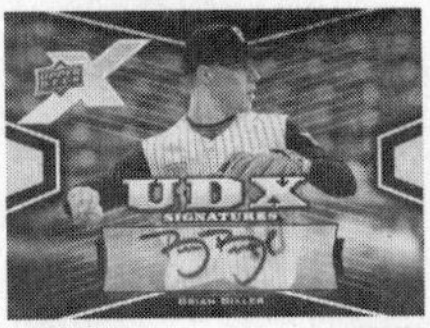

NM/M

Common Auto: 8.00
Inserted 1:10 Hobby
BB Brian Bass 15.00
BI Brian Bixler 10.00
CA Jesse Carlson 10.00
CB Clay Buchholz 25.00
CC Callix Crabbe 8.00
CH Chin-Lung Hu
CM Colt Morton 8.00
CT Clete Thomas 15.00
DJ Derek Jeter 150.00
EL Evan Longoria 75.00
EM Evan Meek 8.00
FC Frank Catalanotto 8.00
JA Jonathan Albaladejo 12.00
JC Johnny Cueto 40.00
JK Jeff Keppinger 10.00
JN Josh Newman 8.00
JT J.R. Towles 10.00
KG Ken Griffey Jr. 80.00
KH Kevin Hart 15.00
LM Luis Mendoza 8.00
MB Marlon Byrd 10.00
RO Ross Ohlendorf 10.00
RT Rich Thompson 10.00
SH Steve Holm 10.00
TI Clay Timpner 8.00
TR Ramon Troncoso 8.00
WB Wladimir Balentien 15.00

UDxponential X

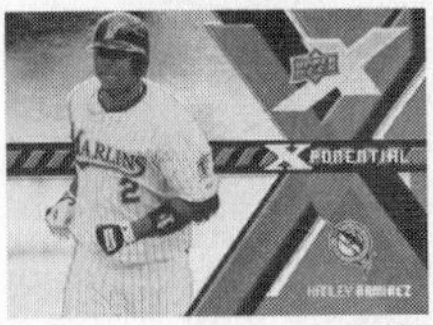

NM/M

Common player: .50
Inserted 1:2
X2: 1X
Inserted 1:3
X3: 1.5-2X
Inserted 1:9
X4: 2-4X
Inserted 1:18
AD Adam Dunn 1.00
AG Adrian Gonzalez 1.00
AJ Andruw Jones .50
AL Alex Rodriguez 3.00
AP Albert Pujols 3.00
AR Aramis Ramirez 1.00
AS Alfonso Soriano 1.00
BA Bobby Abreu 1.00
BP Brandon Phillips .75
BR Brian Roberts .75
BU B.J. Upton .75
BW Brandon Webb 1.00
CB Carlos Beltran 1.00
CC Carl Crawford .75
CG Curtis Granderson 1.00
CH Corey Hart .75
CJ Conor Jackson .50
CL Carlos Lee 1.00
CP Carlos Pena .75
CS C.C. Sabathia 1.50
CU Chase Utley 1.50
CW Chien-Ming Wang 2.00
CY Chris Young .75
CZ Carlos Zambrano .75
DJ Derek Jeter 3.00
DL Derrek Lee 1.00
DM Daisuke Matsuzaka 2.00
DO David Ortiz 1.50
DW Dontrelle Willis .50
EB Erik Bedard .50
FH Felix Hernandez 1.00
FT Frank Thomas 1.00
GA Garrett Atkins .50
GM Greg Maddux 2.50
GR Khalil Greene .50
GS Grady Sizemore 1.50
GU Carlos Guillen .50
HE Todd Helton .75
HM Hideki Matsui 1.50
HO Trevor Hoffman .50
HR Hanley Ramirez 1.50
HU Torii Hunter .75
IR Ivan Rodriguez .75
IS Ichiro Suzuki 2.00
JA Jason Bay .75
JB Josh Beckett 1.00
JC Joba Chamberlain 2.50
JF Jeff Francoeur .50
JH Josh Hamilton 1.50
JI Jimmy Rollins 1.00
JK Jeff Kent .50
JM Justin Morneau 1.00
JO Chipper Jones 2.00
JP Jonathan Papelbon 1.00
JR Jose Reyes 1.50
JS John Smoltz 1.00
JT Jim Thome 1.00
JV Jason Varitek .75
KG Ken Griffey Jr. 2.50
LB Lance Berkman 1.00
MA Joe Mauer .75
MC Miguel Cabrera 1.00
MH Matt Holliday 1.00
MO Magglio Ordonez .75
MR Manny Ramirez 1.00
MT Mark Teixeira 1.00
NM Nick Markakis 1.00
NS Nick Swisher .50
PB Pat Burrell .50
PE Jake Peavy 1.00
PF Prince Fielder 1.00
PK Paul Konerko .50
PM Pedro Martinez 1.00
RA Rick Ankiel 1.00
RB Ryan Braun 1.50
RH Ryan Howard 2.00
RI Mariano Rivera .75
RJ Randy Johnson 1.00
RM Russell Martin 1.00
RO Roy Oswalt .75
RW Rickie Weeks .50
RZ Ryan Zimmerman .50
SA Johan Santana 1.50
SH Gary Sheffield .75
TE Miguel Tejada .50
TH Travis Hafner .50
TT Troy Tulowitzki .50
VG Vladimir Guerrero 1.00
VM Victor Martinez .50
WR David Wright 1.50

2008 Upper Deck Yankee Stadium Box Set

NM/M

Complete Set (100): 25.00

2008 UD A Piece of History

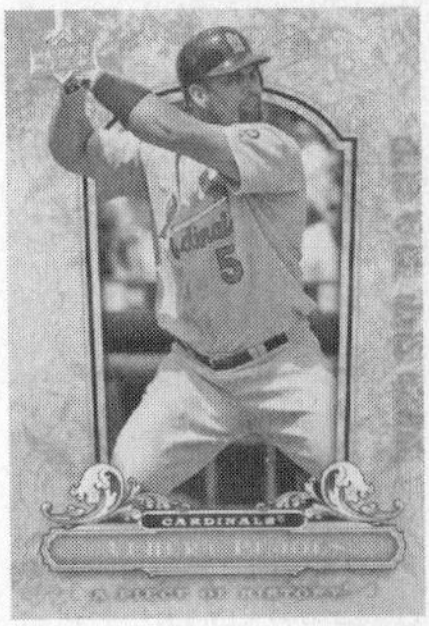

NM/M

Common Player (1-100): .25
Common RC (101-150):
Common Historical Moments (151-200):
Pack (8): 5.00
Box (16): 75.00
1 Brandon Webb .40
2 Dan Haren .40
3 Justin Upton .40
4 Chris B. Young .40
5 Mark Teixeira .50
6 Jeff Francoeur .40
7 John Smoltz .50
8 Tom Glavine .50
9 Brian McCann .40
10 Chipper Jones 1.00
11 Erik Bedard .25
12 Nick Markakis .40
13 Josh Beckett .50
14 David Ortiz .75
15 Manny Ramirez .75
16 Dustin Pedroia .40
17 Grady Sizemore .50
18 Jonathan Papelbon .50
19 Daisuke Matsuzaka 1.00
20 Curt Schilling .50
21 Alfonso Soriano .50
22 Aramis Ramirez .40
23 Carlos Zambrano .40
24 Nick Swisher .25
25 Jim Thome .40
26 Ken Griffey Jr. 1.50
27 Adam Dunn .50
28 Aaron Harang .25
29 Matt Holliday .50
30 Troy Tulowitzki .40
31 Todd Helton .50
32 Magglio Ordonez .40
33 Justin Verlander .50
34 Miguel Cabrera .75
35 Gary Sheffield .40
36 Ivan Rodriguez .50
37 Dontrelle Willis .25
38 Hanley Ramirez .75
39 Andrew Miller .25
40 Lance Berkman .50
41 Roy Oswalt .40
42 Carlos Lee .40
43 Hunter Pence .40
44 Alex Gordon .40
45 Mark Teahen .25
46 Torii Hunter .40
47 Vladimir Guerrero .75
48 Victor Martinez .25
49 Andruw Jones .40
50 James Loney .25
51 Russell Martin .40
52 Jeff Kent .25
53 Ryan Braun .75
54 Prince Fielder .75
55 Joe Mauer .25
56 Justin Morneau .40
57 Delmon Young .25
58 Jose Reyes .75
59 David Wright .75
60 Carlos Beltran .50
61 Johan Santana .50
62 Pedro Martinez .50
63 Alex Rodriguez 2.00
64 Derek Jeter 2.00
65 Hideki Matsui 1.00

66 Robinson Cano .40
67 Joba Chamberlain 2.00
68 Phil Hughes .40
69 Mariano Rivera .50
70 Rich Harden .25
71 Joe Blanton .25
72 Cole Hamels .50
73 Ryan Howard .75
74 Jimmy Rollins .75
75 Chase Utley .75
76 Jason Bay .40
77 Freddy Sanchez .25
78 Jake Peavy .40
79 Greg Maddux 1.50
80 Trevor Hoffman .25
81 Barry Zito .25
82 Tim Lincecum .40
83 Travis Hafner .40
84 C.C. Sabathia .50
85 Felix Hernandez .50
86 Ichiro Suzuki 1.50
87 Troy Glaus .40
88 Albert Pujols 2.00
89 Chris Carpenter .25
90 Scott Kazmir .40
91 Carl Crawford .25
92 B.J. Upton .25
93 Michael Young .25
94 Josh Hamilton .50
95 Vernon Wells .40
96 Alex Rios .40
97 Scott Rolen .40
98 Frank Thomas .50
99 Chad Cordero .25
100 Ryan Zimmerman .40
101 Emilio Bonifacio **RC** .50
102 Bill Murphy **(RC)** .50
103 Billy Buckner **(RC)** .50
104 Brandon Jones **RC** 1.00
105 Clint Sammons **(RC)** .50
106 Clay Buchholz **(RC)** 3.00
107 Kevin Hart **(RC)** .50
108 Lance Broadway **RC** .50
109 Donny Lucy **(RC)** .50
110 Heath Phillips **RC** .50
111 Ryan Hanigan **RC** .50
112 Joey Votto **(RC)** 2.00
113 Joe Koshansky **(RC)** .50
114 Josh Newman **RC** .50
115 Seth Smith **(RC)** .50
116 Harvey Garcia **(RC)** .50
117 Chris Seddon **(RC)** .50
118 Josh Anderson **(RC)** .50
119 Troy Patton **(RC)** .50
120 Felipe Paulino **RC** .50
121 J.R. Towles **RC** 1.00
122 Luke Hochevar **RC** 2.00
123 Chin-Lung Hu **(RC)** 1.00
124 Jonathan Meloan **RC** .50
125 Sam Fuld **RC** 1.00
126 Mitch Stetter **RC** .50
127 Jose Morales **(RC)** .50
128 Carlos Muniz **RC** .50
129 Alberto Gonzalez **(RC)** .50
130 Ian Kennedy **RC** 1.00
131 Ross Ohlendorf **RC** .50
132 Jonathan Albaladejo **RC** 1.00
133 Daric Barton **(RC)** 1.00
134 Jerry Blevins **RC** .50
135 David Davidson **RC** .50
136 Nyjer Morgan **(RC)** 1.00
137 Steve Pearce **RC** 2.00
138 Colt Morton **RC** .50
139 Eugenio Velez **RC** .50
140 Erick Threets **(RC)** .50
141 Bronson Sardinha **(RC)** .50
142 Wladimir Balentien **(RC)** .50
143 Jeff Clement **(RC)** .50
144 Rob Johnson **(RC)** .50
145 Jeff Ridgway **RC** .50
146 Justin Ruggiano **RC** .50
147 Luis Mendoza **(RC)** .50
148 Bill White **RC** .50
149 Ross Detwiler **RC** 1.50
150 Justin Maxwell **RC** .50
151 Fall of Berlin Wall .50
152 Wright Bros. 1st Flight .50
153 Signing of Dec. of Independence .50
154 Columbus Discovers America .50
155 First Space Shuttle launch .50
156 Hawaii becomes 50th state .50
157 Statue of Liberty given to U.S. .50
158 Gettysburg Address .50
159 Completion of Transcontinental Railroad .50
160 Opening of Panama Canal .50
161 U.S. enters World War I .50
162 Treaty of Versailes .50
163 Television invented .50
164 Geneva Summit .50
165 Woodstock .50
166 Invention of Cotton Gin .50
167 Eiffel Tower .50
168 Suez Canal opens .50
169 New York City Subway opens .50
170 Polio Vaccine invented .50
171 Bell X-1 Breaks Sound Barrier .50
172 USS Enterprise Aircraft Carrier launched .50
173 Hubble Telescope launches .50
174 N.A.T.O. created .50
175 Sputnik launched by Russia .50
176 U.S.S.R. Crumbles .50
177 Boston Tea Party .50
178 Paul Revere's Ride .50
179 Civil Rights Act Passes .50
180 Hindenburg blows up .50
181 Franklin discovers electricity .50
182 Creation of the Internet .50
183 1st World's Fair - 1851 London .50
184 Pope John Paul II .50
185 1st Heart Transplant .50
186 California Gold Rush .50
187 Creation of the personal computer .50
188 Louisiana Purchase .50
189 1st Dictionary published .50
190 Steam Engine invented .50
191 History of Nobel Prize .50
192 Liberty Bell .50
193 International Space Station .50
194 Human Genome Project .50
195 The Supreme Court .50
196 Lewis and Clark .50
197 Battle of the Alamo .50
198 The creation of baseball .50
199 Juan Ponce De Leon .50
200 Jamestown - 1607 .50

Silver

Silver (1-100): 2-3X
Silver RC (101-150): 1-2X
Silver (151-200): 2-3X

Red

Red (1-100): 2-4X
Red RC (101-150): 1-2X
Red (151-200): 2-4X
Production 149 Sets

Gold

Gold (1-100): 3-5X
Gold RC (101-150): 2-3X
Gold (151-200): 3-5X
Production 75 Sets

Blue

Blue (1-100): 4-8X
Blue RC (101-150): 3-4X
Blue (151-200): 4-8X
Production 25 Sets

A Piece of Hollywood Memor.

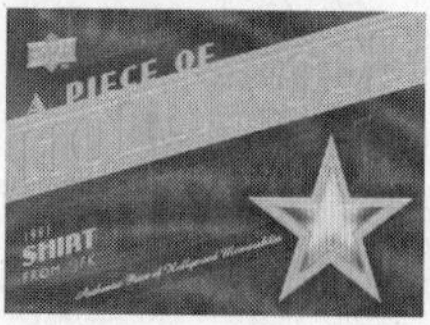

NM/M

Common Memorabilia: 10.00
1 Amanda Bynes/Costume 10.00
2 Mel Gibson/Shirt 10.00
3 Brad Pitt/Shirt 20.00
4 George Clooney/Jacket 15.00
5 Denzell Washington/Jacket 10.00
6 Jamie Foxx/Shirt 10.00
7 Kevin Costner/Shirt 10.00
8 Jack Nicholson/Shirt 15.00
9 Mike Myers/Pants 15.00
10 Dana Carvey/Jsy 15.00
11 Phillip Seymour Hoffman/Sweater 10.00
12 Jim Carrey/Shirt 10.00
13 Scarlett Johanson/T-Shirt 25.00
14 Demi Moore/Jacket 15.00
15 Christopher Reeves/Cape 30.00
16 Mel Gibson Shoe/SP 30.00
17 Denzell Washington/Hat/SP 25.00
18 Jim Carrey/Pants 10.00
19 George Clooney/Pants 15.00
20 Scarlett Johanson/Undershirt/SP 30.00
21 Phillip Seymour Hoffman/Jkt 10.00
22 Denzell Washington/Pants 10.00
23 Mel Gibson/Pants 10.00
24 Woody Harrelson/Jkt 10.00
25 Robin Williams/Shirt 15.00
26 Jennifer Garner/Pajamas 15.00
27 Tom Cruise/Shirt 25.00

Box Score Memories

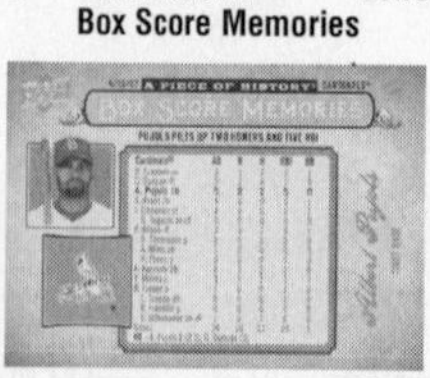

NM/M

Common Player: 2.00
Production 699 Sets
Blue: 2X
Production 75 Sets
Copper: 2X
Production 99 Sets
Red: 1.5-2X
Production 149 Sets
Silver: No Pricing
Production 25 Sets
1 Chris B. Young 2.00
2 Stephen Drew 2.00
3 Chipper Jones 5.00
4 Mark Teixeira 3.00
5 Jeff Francoeur 2.00
6 David Ortiz 3.00
7 Dustin Pedroia 3.00
8 Manny Ramirez 3.00
9 Mike Lowell 3.00
10 Alfonso Soriano 3.00
11 Aramis Ramirez 2.00
12 Jim Thome 2.00
13 Ken Griffey Jr. 6.00
14 Adam Dunn 2.00
15 Grady Sizemore 3.00
16 Travis Hafner 2.00
17 Victor Martinez 2.00
18 Matt Holliday 3.00
19 Todd Helton 2.00
20 Troy Tulowitzki 2.00
21 Ivan Rodriguez 2.00
22 Miguel Cabrera 3.00
23 Magglio Ordonez 2.00
24 Hanley Ramirez 3.00
25 Hunter Pence 2.00
26 Lance Berkman 3.00
27 Carlos Lee 2.00
28 Alex Gordon 3.00
29 Vladimir Guerrero 3.00
30 Andruw Jones 2.00
31 Jeff Kent 2.00
32 Ryan Braun 4.00
33 Prince Fielder 3.00
34 Joe Mauer 2.00
35 Justin Morneau 2.00
36 David Wright 4.00
37 Carlos Beltran 3.00
38 Jose Reyes 4.00
39 Derek Jeter 8.00
40 Alex Rodriguez 8.00
41 Hideki Matsui 4.00
42 Bobby Abreu 2.00
43 Chase Utley 4.00
44 Ryan Howard 4.00
45 Jimmy Rollins 4.00
46 Jason Bay 2.00
47 Khalil Greene 2.00
48 Ichiro Suzuki 4.00
49 Albert Pujols 8.00
50 Frank Thomas 3.00

Box Score Memorabilia Jersey Autographs Blue

NM/M

Production 10-99
1 Chris B. Young/99 25.00
5 Jeff Francoeur/99 25.00
11 Aramis Ramirez/99 30.00
16 Travis Hafner/50 20.00
17 Victor Martinez/99 25.00
20 Troy Tulowitzki/99 25.00
24 Hanley Ramirez/50 40.00
27 Carlos Lee/99 30.00
46 Jason Bay/99 20.00

Box Score Mem. Jersey Red

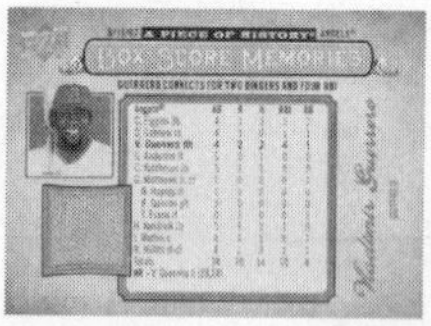

NM/M

Common Jersey: 4.00
Gold: 1.5-2X
Production 75 Sets
Blue: No Pricing
Production 25 Sets
Patch: No Pricing
Production 25 Sets
Jersey Button: No Pricing
Production Five Sets
1 Chris B. Young 6.00
2 Stephen Drew 6.00
3 Chipper Jones 10.00
4 Mark Teixeira 6.00
5 Jeff Francoeur 6.00
6 David Ortiz 10.00
7 Dustin Pedroia 8.00
8 Manny Ramirez 8.00
10 Alfonso Soriano 8.00
11 Aramis Ramirez 6.00
12 Jim Thome 6.00
16 Travis Hafner 4.00
17 Victor Martinez 4.00
18 Matt Holliday 6.00
19 Todd Helton 8.00
20 Troy Tulowitzki 6.00
21 Ivan Rodriguez 4.00
23 Magglio Ordonez 4.00
24 Hanley Ramirez 8.00
25 Hunter Pence 6.00
26 Lance Berkman 8.00
27 Carlos 1ee 6.00
28 Alex Gordon 6.00
29 Vladimir Guerrero 8.00
31 Jeff Kent 4.00
33 Prince Fielder 8.00
34 Joe Mauer 6.00
35 Justin Morneau 6.00
37 Carlos Beltran 8.00
38 Jose Reyes 8.00
39 Derek Jeter 20.00
42 Bobby Abreu 6.00
45 Jimmy Rollins 8.00
46 Jason Bay 4.00
47 Khalil Greene 4.00
49 Albert Pujols 20.00
50 Frank Thomas 8.00

Cut From The Same Cloth

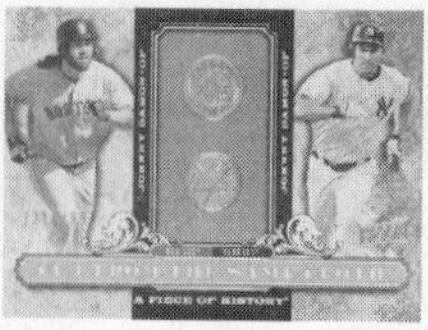

NM/M

Common Duo: 2.00
Silver: 1-2X
Production 149 Sets
Red: 1-2X
Production 99 Sets
Pewter: 1-2X
Production 75 Sets
Blue: 2-3X
Production 25 Sets
BB Jeremy Bonderman, Joe Blanton 2.00
BP A.J. Burnett, Jake Peavy 3.00
BR Carlos Beltran, Jose Reyes 4.00
BS Mark Buehrle, Johan Santana 3.00
BV Mark Buehrle, Justin Verlander 2.00
BZ Ryan Zimmerman, Ryan Braun 3.00
CB Carlos Beltran 3.00
CH Trevor Hoffman, Chad Cordero 2.00
CS Curt Schilling 3.00
DD Johnny Damon 3.00
FT Frank Thomas 3.00
GD Ken Griffey Jr., Adam Dunn 5.00
GM Greg Maddux 5.00
GO Magglio Ordonez, Curtis Granderson 3.00
GT Ken Griffey Jr., Frank Thomas 5.00
HH Todd Helton, Matt Holliday 3.00
HJ Andruw Jones, Matt Holliday 3.00
HL Francisco Liriano, Cole Hamels 3.00
HM Greg Maddux, Tim Hudson 5.00
HP Dan Haren, Jake Peavy 3.00
HS John Smoltz, Tim Hudson 3.00
HY Michael Young, J.J. Hardy 2.00
HZ Carlos Zambrano, Felix Hernandez 3.00
JB Josh Beckett 3.00
JD Jason Varitek, Daisuke Matsuzaka 5.00
JH Andruw Jones, Torii Hunter 2.00
JS Randy Johnson, Johan Santana 3.00
JT Jim Thome 3.00
JY Derek Jeter, Michael Young 8.00
JZ Chipper Jones, Ryan Zimmerman 4.00
KS Johan Santana, Scott Kazmir 3.00
LF Derrek Lee, Prince Fielder 4.00
MA Joe Mauer, Russell Martin 3.00
MJ Mariano Rivera, Jonathan Papelbon 3.00
MK Justin Morneau, Jason Kubel 2.00
MM Victor Martinez, Joe Mauer 2.00
MS Curt Schilling, Daisuke Matsuzaka 4.00
OF David Ortiz, Prince Fielder 4.00
OG Carlos Guillen, Magglio Ordonez 2.00
OP David Ortiz, Albert Pujols 8.00
OR Manny Ramirez, David Ortiz 4.00
OV Jason Varitek, David Ortiz 4.00
PG Vladimir Guerrero, Albert Pujols 8.00
PH Roy Halladay, Jake Peavy 3.00
PM Pedro Martinez 3.00
PO Roy Oswalt, Jake Peavy 3.00
PS Curt Schilling, Jonathan Papelbon 3.00
PV Jason Varitek, Jorge Posada 3.00
RJ Randy Johnson 3.00
RL Derrek Lee, Aramis Ramirez 3.00
RP B.J. Ryan, Jonathan Papelbon 3.00
RR Jose Reyes, Hanley Ramirez 4.00

RU Jimmy Rollins, Chase Utley 4.00
SH Travis Hafner, Grady Sizemore 3.00
SL Johan Santana, Francisco Liriano 3.00
SM Pedro Martinez, Curt Schilling 3.00
TR Tim Hudson, Roy Halladay 2.00
UU Chase Utley, Dan Uggla 3.00
VR Manny Ramirez, Jason Varitek 3.00
WS Dontrelle Willis, C.C. Sabathia 2.00

Cut From the Same Cloth Jersey

NM/M

Common Dual Jersey: 6.00
BB Jeremy Bonderman, Joe Blanton 6.00
BP A.J. Burnett, Jake Peavy 8.00
BR Carlos Beltran, Jose Reyes 10.00
BS Mark Buehrle, Johan Santana 8.00
BV Mark Buehrle, Justin Verlander 6.00
BZ Ryan Zimmerman, Ryan Braun 15.00
CB Carlos Beltran 10.00
CH Trevor Hoffman, Chad Cordero 6.00
CS Curt Schilling 8.00
DD Johnny Damon 10.00
FT Frank Thomas 10.00
GM Greg Maddux 15.00
GO Magglio Ordonez, Curtis Granderson 8.00
HH Todd Helton, Matt Holliday 10.00
HJ Andruw Jones, Matt Holliday 8.00
HL Francisco Liriano, Cole Hamels 8.00
HM Greg Maddux, Tim Hudson 15.00
HP Dan Haren, Jake Peavy 8.00
HS John Smoltz, Tim Hudson 10.00
HY Michael Young, J.J. Hardy 6.00
HZ Carlos Zambrano, Felix Hernandez 10.00
JB Josh Beckett 10.00
JD Jason Varitek, Daisuke Matsuzaka 20.00
JH Andruw Jones, Torii Hunter 6.00
JS Randy Johnson, Johan Santana 10.00
JT Jim Thome 6.00
JY Derek Jeter, Michael Young 25.00
JZ Chipper Jones, Ryan Zimmerman 10.00
LF Derrek Lee, Prince Fielder 10.00
MA Joe Mauer, Russell Martin 8.00
MJ Mariano Rivera, Jonathan Papelbon 10.00
MK Justin Morneau, Jason Kubel 6.00
MM Victor Martinez, Joe Mauer 6.00
MS Curt Schilling, Daisuke Matsuzaka 20.00
OF David Ortiz, Prince Fielder 10.00
OG Carlos Guillen, Magglio Ordonez 6.00
OP David Ortiz, Albert Pujols 20.00
OR Manny Ramirez, David Ortiz 15.00
OV Jason Varitek, David Ortiz 15.00
PG Vladimir Guerrero, Albert Pujols 15.00
PH Roy Halladay, Jake Peavy 6.00
PM Pedro Martinez 8.00
PO Roy Oswalt, Jake Peavy 6.00
PS Curt Schilling, Jonathan Papelbon 8.00
PV Jason Varitek, Jorge Posada 10.00
RJ Randy Johnson 8.00
RL Derrek Lee, Aramis Ramirez 10.00
RP B.J. Ryan, Jonathan Papelbon 8.00
RR Jose Reyes, Hanley Ramirez 10.00
RU Jimmy Rollins, Chase Utley 15.00
SH Travis Hafner, Grady Sizemore 8.00
SL Johan Santana, Francisco Liriano 8.00
SM Pedro Martinez, Curt Schilling 8.00
TR Tim Hudson, Roy Halladay 6.00
UU Chase Utley, Dan Uggla 8.00
VR Manny Ramirez, Jason Varitek 15.00
WS Dontrelle Willis, C.C. Sabathia 6.00

Franchise History

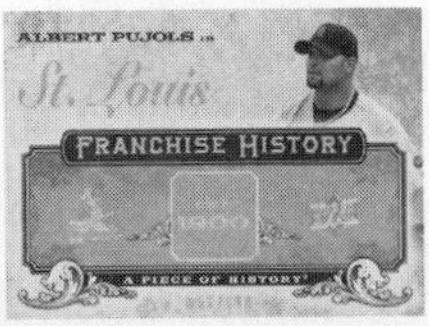

NM/M

Common Player: 1.50
Red: 1-2X
Production 149 Sets
Copper: 1-2X
Production 99 Sets
Blue: 1-2X
Production 75 Sets
Silver: 2-3X
Production 25 Sets
1 Justin Upton 2.00
2 Randy Johnson 3.00
3 Mark Teixeira 2.00
4 John Smoltz 2.00
5 Chipper Jones 4.00
6 Jonathan Papelbon 3.00
7 Manny Ramirez 3.00
8 Daisuke Matsuzaka 5.00
9 Josh Beckett 2.00
10 David Ortiz 3.00
11 Alfonso Soriano 3.00
12 Jim Thome 2.00
13 Adam Dunn 2.00
14 Ken Griffey Jr. 5.00
15 C.C. Sabathia 2.00
16 Grady Sizemore 2.00
17 Travis Hafner 1.50
18 Matt Holliday 2.00
19 Troy Tulowitzki 1.50
20 Magglio Ordonez 1.50
21 Ivan Rodriguez 1.50
22 Miguel Cabrera 3.00
23 Hanley Ramirez 3.00
24 Hunter Pence 2.00
25 Lance Berkman 2.00
26 Vladimir Guerrero 3.00
27 Andruw Jones 1.50
28 Prince Fielder 2.00
29 Ryan Braun 3.00
30 Joe Mauer 1.50
31 Carlos Beltran 2.00
32 Pedro Martinez 2.00
33 Johan Santana 2.00
34 Jose Reyes 3.00
35 David Wright 4.00
36 Joba Chamberlain 6.00
37 Hideki Matsui 4.00
38 Alex Rodriguez 8.00
39 Derek Jeter 8.00
40 Jimmy Rollins 3.00
41 Ryan Howard 4.00
42 Chase Utley 3.00
43 Greg Maddux 5.00
44 Jake Peavy 2.00
45 Trevor Hoffman 1.50
46 Ichiro Suzuki 5.00
47 Felix Hernandez 2.00
48 Albert Pujols 8.00
49 Frank Thomas 3.00
50 Vernon Wells 1.50

Franchise History Jersey Autographs

NM/M

Production 5-99
6 Jonathan Papelbon/99 25.00
17 Travis Hafner/50 20.00
19 Troy Tulowitzki/50 25.00
23 Hanley Ramirez/50 35.00
47 Felix Hernandez/75 30.00

Franchise History Red Jersey

NM/M

Common Jersey: 4.00
Gold Jersey: 1-1.5X
Production 49 Sets
Blue Jersey: 1.5-2X
Production 25 Sets
Patch: No Pricing 1-2X
Production 25 Sets
Jersey Button: No Pricing
Production Five Sets
1 Justin Upton 6.00
2 Randy Johnson 6.00
3 Mark Teixeira 6.00
4 John Smoltz 8.00
5 Chipper Jones 8.00
6 Jonathan Papelbon 6.00
7 Manny Ramirez 8.00
8 Daisuke Matsuzaka 15.00
9 Josh Beckett 6.00
10 David Ortiz 8.00
11 Alfonso Soriano 8.00
12 Jim Thome 6.00
13 Adam Dunn 6.00
14 Ken Griffey Jr. 15.00
15 C.C. Sabathia 6.00
16 Grady Sizemore 8.00
17 Travis Hafner 4.00
18 Matt Holliday 6.00
19 Troy Tulowitzki 4.00
20 Magglio Ordonez 4.00
21 Ivan Rodriguez 6.00
22 Miguel Cabrera 8.00
23 Hanley Ramirez 8.00
24 Hunter Pence 6.00
25 Lance Berkman 6.00
26 Vladimir Guerrero 8.00
27 Andruw Jones 4.00
28 Prince Fielder 8.00
29 Ryan Braun 10.00
30 Joe Mauer 6.00
31 Carlos Beltran 6.00
32 Pedro Martinez 6.00
33 Johan Santana 6.00
34 Jose Reyes 8.00
36 Joba Chamberlain 15.00
38 Alex Rodriguez 15.00
39 Derek Jeter 15.00
40 Jimmy Rollins 8.00
42 Chase Utley 8.00
43 Greg Maddux 10.00
44 Jake Peavy 6.00
45 Trevor Hoffman 4.00
47 Felix Hernandez 6.00
48 Albert Pujols 15.00
49 Frank Thomas 8.00
50 Vernon Wells 4.00

Franchise Members 3

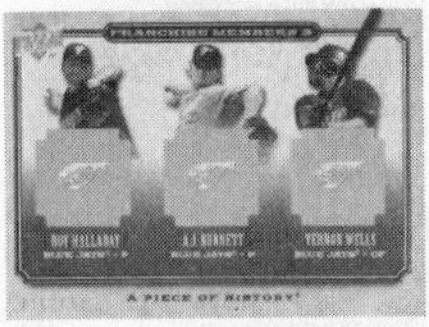

NM/M

Common Trio: 2.00
Production 799 Sets
Silver: 1-2X
Production 149 Sets
Red: 1-2X
Production 99 Sets
Pewter: 1-2X
Production 75 Sets
Blue: 2-3X
Production 25 Sets
1 Tom Glavine, John Smoltz, Tim Hudson 2.00
2 Curt Schilling, Josh Beckett, Daisuke Matsuzaka 4.00
3 Manny Ramirez, Jason Varitek, David Ortiz 4.00
4 Ken Griffey Jr., Frank Thomas, Jim Thome 5.00
5 Travis Hafner, Victor Martinez, Grady Sizemore 2.00
6 Carlos Lee, Matt Holliday, Jason Bay 2.00
7 Carlos Guillen, Magglio Ordonez, Miguel Cabrera 2.00
8 Dan Haren, Roy Oswalt, Jake Peavy 2.00
9 Vladimir Guerrero, Casey Kotchman, Jered Weaver 2.00
10 Joe Mauer, Brian McCann, Russell Martin 2.00
11 Prince Fielder, J.J. Hardy, Ryan Braun 3.00
12 Joe Nathan, Justin Morneau, Joe Mauer 2.00
13 Pedro Martinez, Billy Wagner, Johan Santana 3.00
14 Derek Jeter, Jose Reyes, Hanley Ramirez 6.00
15 Derek Jeter, Jason Giambi, Robinson Cano 6.00
16 Greg Maddux, Trevor Hoffman, Jake Peavy 4.00
17 Rich Harden, Justin Verlander, Felix Hernandez 2.00
18 Randy Johnson, Chris Carpenter, Cole Hamels 2.00
19 Troy Glaus, Albert Pujols, Chris Duncan 5.00
20 Vernon Wells, Roy Halladay, A.J. Burnett 2.00

Franchise Members 3 Jersey

NM/M

Production 99 Sets
1 Tom Glavine, John Smoltz, Tim Hudson 20.00
2 Curt Schilling, Josh Beckett, Daisuke Matsuzaka 30.00
3 Manny Ramirez, Jason Varitek, David Ortiz 20.00
5 Travis Hafner, Victor Martinez, Grady Sizemore 10.00
6 Carlos Lee, Matt Holliday, Jason Bay 10.00
7 Carlos Guillen, Magglio Ordonez, Miguel Cabrera 10.00
8 Dan Haren, Roy Oswalt, Jake Peavy 10.00
9 Vladimir Guerrero, Casey Kotchman, Jered Weaver 10.00
10 Joe Mauer, Brian McCann, Russell Martin 10.00
11 Prince Fielder, J.J. Hardy, Ryan Braun 15.00
12 Joe Nathan, Justin Morneau, Joe Mauer 10.00
13 Pedro Martinez, Billy Wagner, Johan Santana 15.00
14 Derek Jeter, Jose Reyes, Hanley Ramirez 25.00
15 Derek Jeter, Jason Giambi, Robinson Cano 25.00
16 Greg Maddux, Trevor Hoffman, Jake Peavy 15.00
17 Rich Harden, Justin Verlander, Felix Hernandez 10.00
18 Randy Johnson, Chris Carpenter, Cole Hamels 10.00
19 Troy Glaus, Albert Pujols, Chris Duncan 15.00
20 Vernon Wells, Roy Halladay, A.J. Burnett 10.00

Franchise Members 4

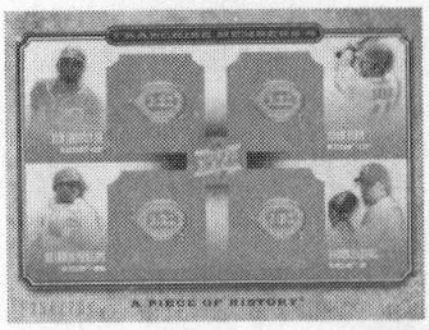

NM/M

Common Quad: 2.00
Production 799 Sets
Silver: 1-2X
Production 149 Sets
Red: 1-2X
Production 99 Sets
Pewter: 1-2X
Production 75 Sets
Blue: 2-3X
Production 25 Sets
1 Derek Jeter, Jason Giambi, Johnny Damon, Jorge Posada 5.00
2 Curt Schilling, Josh Beckett, Jonathan Papelbon, Daisuke Matsuzaka 5.00
3 Carlos Delgado, Carlos Beltran, Johan Santana, Jose Reyes 4.00
4 Chipper Jones, Mark Teixeira, Brian McCann, Jeff Francoeur 3.00
5 Rickie Weeks, Prince Fielder, J.J. Hardy, Ryan Braun 3.00
6 Ken Griffey Jr., Adam Dunn, Brandon Phillips, Aaron Harang 4.00
7 Jeremy Bonderman, Dontrelle Willis, Justin Verlander, Joel Zumaya 2.00
8 Frank Thomas, Jim Thome, Gary Sheffield, David Ortiz 3.00
9 Greg Maddux, Mark Prior, Jake Peavy, Chris Young 4.00
10 Randy Johnson, Dan Haren, Conor Jackson, Brandon Webb 3.00
11 Eric Chavez, Bobby Crosby, Huston Street, Rich Harden 2.00
12 Adrian Beltre, Erik Bedard, Felix Hernandez, Kenji Johjima 2.00
13 Garret Anderson, Vladimir Guerrero, Torii Hunter, Chone Figgins 3.00
14 Derek Jeter, Rafael Furcal, Jose Reyes, Jhonny Peralta 5.00
15 Ken Griffey Jr., Andruw Jones, Carlos Beltran, Jim Edmonds 4.00
16 Ivan Rodriguez, Jason Varitek, Jorge Posada, Joe Mauer 3.00
17 Josh Willingham, Hanley Ramirez, Jeremy Hermida, Dan Uggla 3.00
18 Johan Santana, Francisco Liriano, C.C. Sabathia, Cole Hamels 3.00
19 Derrek Lee, Lance Berkman, Conor Jackson, Prince Fielder 3.00
20 Andruw Jones, Jeff Kent, Rafael Furcal, Matt Kemp 2.00

Franchise Members 4 Jersey

NM/M

Production 99 Sets
1 Derek Jeter, Jason Giambi, Johnny Damon, Jorge Posada 40.00
2 Curt Schilling, Josh Beckett, Jonathan Papelbon, Daisuke Matsuzaka 40.00
3 Carlos Delgado, Carlos Beltran, Johan Santana, Jose Reyes 20.00
4 Chipper Jones, Mark Teixeira, Brian McCann, Jeff Francoeur 20.00
5 Rickie Weeks, Prince Fielder, J.J. Hardy, Ryan Braun 15.00
7 Jeremy Bonderman, Dontrelle Willis, Justin Verlander, Joel Zumaya 15.00

8	Frank Thomas, Jim Thome, Gary Sheffield, David Ortiz	15.00
9	Greg Maddux, Mark Prior, Jake Peavy, Chris Young	20.00
10	Randy Johnson, Dan Haren, Conor Jackson, Brandon Webb	20.00
11	Eric Chavez, Bobby Crosby, Huston Street, Rich Harden	10.00
12	Adrian Beltre, Erik Bedard, Felix Hernandez, Kenji Johjima	15.00
13	Garret Anderson, Vladimir Guerrero, Torii Hunter, Chone Figgins	15.00
14	Derek Jeter, Rafael Furcal, Jose Reyes, Jhonny Peralta	25.00
16	Ivan Rodriguez, Jason Varitek, Jorge Posada, Joe Mauer	20.00
18	Johan Santana, Francisco Liriano, C.C. Sabathia, Cole Hamels	15.00
19	Derrek Lee, Lance Berkman, Conor Jackson, Prince Fielder	15.00
20	Andruw Jones, Jeff Kent, Rafael Furcal, Matt Kemp	10.00

Hair Cuts

Production One Set
No Pricing

Rookie Autographs

	NM/M
Production 50-499	
Blue Autos:	1-1.5X
Production 15-50	
Gold Autos:	1-1.5X
Production 25-75	
Red Autos:	1-1.5X
Production 25-99	
Silver:	1.5-2X
Production 10-25	

No pricing production 20 or less.

101	Emilio Bonifacio/499	10.00
102	Bill Murphy/499	8.00
103	Billy Buckner/149	8.00
104	Brandon Jones/499	8.00
105	Clint Sammons/499	8.00
106	Clay Buchholz/499	25.00
107	Kevin Hart/499	10.00
108	Lance Broadway/499	8.00
111	Ryan Hanigan/499	10.00
112	Joey Votto/50	20.00
113	Joe Koshansky/499	8.00
114	Josh Newman/499	10.00
115	Seth Smith/499	10.00
116	Harvey Garcia/499	8.00
117	Chris Seddon/499	8.00
118	Josh Anderson/499	8.00
119	Troy Patton/499	15.00
120	Felipe Paulino/499	8.00
121	J.R. Towles/499	10.00
123	Chin-Lung Hu/99	20.00
124	Jonathan Meloan/99	8.00
127	Jose Morales/499	8.00
129	Alberto Gonzalez/499	8.00
130	Ian Kennedy/199	15.00
131	Ross Ohlendorf/499	10.00
132	Jonathan Albaladejo/499	8.00
133	Daric Barton/99	10.00
134	Jerry Blevins/499	8.00
135	David Davidson/499	8.00
136	Nyjer Morgan/449	8.00
137	Steve Pearce/499	15.00
138	Colt Morton/499	10.00
139	Eugenio Velez/499	10.00
141	Bronson Sardinha/499	10.00
142	Wladimir Balentien/199	8.00
144	Rob Johnson/499	8.00
146	Justin Ruggiano/499	10.00
147	Luis Mendoza/499	10.00
148	Bill White/499	8.00
149	Ross Detwiler/499	10.00
150	Justin Maxwell/498	15.00

Stadium Scenes

	NM/M
Common Player:	2.00
Production 699 Sets	
Red:	1-2X
Production 149 Sets	
Copper:	1-2X
Production 99 Sets	
Blue:	1-2X
Production 75 Sets	
Silver:	2-3X
Production 25 Sets	

1	Randy Johnson	3.00
2	Justin Upton	2.00
3	Mark Teixeira	2.00
4	Chipper Jones	4.00
5	John Smoltz	3.00
6	David Ortiz	3.00
7	Josh Beckett	3.00
8	Daisuke Matsuzaka	5.00
9	Manny Ramirez	3.00
10	Jonathan Papelbon	3.00
11	Alfonso Soriano	3.00
12	Kerry Wood	2.00
13	Derrek Lee	3.00
14	Jim Thome	3.00
15	Ken Griffey Jr.	5.00
16	Adam Dunn	2.00
17	Grady Sizemore	3.00
18	Travis Hafner	2.00
19	Victor Martinez	2.00
20	C.C. Sabathia	3.00
21	Miguel Cabrera	3.00
22	Justin Verlander	2.00
23	Ivan Rodriguez	2.00
24	Magglio Ordonez	3.00
25	Lance Berkman	3.00
26	Roy Oswalt	2.00
27	Vladimir Guerrero	3.00
28	Andruw Jones	2.00
29	Rickie Weeks	2.00
30	Ryan Braun	4.00
31	Prince Fielder	3.00
32	Joe Mauer	2.00
33	Pedro Martinez	3.00
34	Jose Reyes	4.00
35	David Wright	5.00
36	Johan Santana	4.00
37	Derek Jeter	8.00
38	Alex Rodriguez	8.00
39	Hideki Matsui	5.00
40	Joba Chamberlain	6.00
41	Cole Hamels	3.00
42	Chase Utley	4.00
43	Ryan Howard	4.00
44	Jimmy Rollins	3.00
45	Jake Peavy	2.00
46	Greg Maddux	5.00
47	Felix Hernandez	2.00
48	Ichiro Suzuki	5.00
49	Albert Pujols	8.00
50	Frank Thomas	4.00

Stadium Scenes Jersey Autographs

	NM/M
Production 10-99	

4	Chipper Jones/25	70.00
10	Jonathan Papelbon/99	30.00
12	Kerry Wood/99	20.00
13	Derrek Lee/25	30.00
16	Adam Dunn/25	30.00
18	Travis Hafner/50	20.00
19	Victor Martinez/99	20.00
29	Rickie Weeks/50	20.00
47	Felix Hernandez/75	30.00

Stadium Scenes Red Jersey

	NM/M
Common Jersey:	4.00
Gold Jersey:	1X
Production 99 Sets	
Blue Jersey:	1-1.5X
Production 25 Sets	
Patch:	2-3X
Production 25 Sets	
Jersey Button:	No Pricing
Production 25 Sets	

1	Randy Johnson	6.00
2	Justin Upton	6.00
3	Mark Teixeira	6.00
4	Chipper Jones	8.00
5	John Smoltz	8.00
6	David Ortiz	8.00
7	Josh Beckett	8.00
8	Daisuke Matsuzaka	15.00
9	Manny Ramirez	8.00
10	Jonathan Papelbon	8.00
11	Alfonso Soriano	8.00
12	Kerry Wood	4.00
13	Derrek Lee	4.00
14	Jim Thome	4.00
15	Ken Griffey Jr.	12.00
16	Adam Dunn	4.00
18	Travis Hafner	4.00
19	Victor Martinez	4.00
20	C.C. Sabathia	4.00
21	Miguel Cabrera	6.00
22	Justin Verlander	6.00
23	Ivan Rodriguez	6.00
24	Magglio Ordonez	6.00
25	Lance Berkman	6.00
26	Roy Oswalt	4.00
27	Vladimir Guerrero	8.00
28	Andruw Jones	4.00
29	Rickie Weeks	4.00
30	Ryan Braun	8.00
31	Prince Fielder	8.00
32	Joe Mauer	4.00
33	Pedro Martinez	6.00
34	Jose Reyes	8.00
36	Johan Santana	6.00
37	Derek Jeter	15.00
38	Alex Rodriguez	15.00
40	Joba Chamberlain	15.00
41	Cole Hamels	6.00
42	Chase Utley	8.00
44	Jimmy Rollins	6.00
45	Jake Peavy	6.00
46	Greg Maddux	10.00
47	Felix Hernandez	8.00
49	Albert Pujols	15.00
50	Frank Thomas	8.00

Timeless Moments

	NM/M
Common Player:	2.00
Production 699 Sets	
Red:	1-2X
Production 149 Sets	
Copper:	1-2X
Production 99 Sets	
Blue:	1-2X
Production 75 Sets	
Silver:	1-2.5X
Production 25 Sets	

1	Randy Johnson	3.00
2	Dan Haren	2.00
3	John Smoltz	3.00
4	Chipper Jones	4.00
5	Mark Teixeira	2.00
6	David Ortiz	3.00
7	Dustin Pedroia	3.00
8	Josh Beckett	3.00
9	Curt Schilling	3.00
10	Daisuke Matsuzaka	5.00
11	Alfonso Soriano	3.00
12	Carlos Zambrano	3.00
13	Jim Thome	3.00
14	Ken Griffey Jr.	5.00
15	Adam Dunn	2.00
16	Grady Sizemore	3.00
17	C.C. Sabathia	3.00
18	Troy Tulowitzki	2.00
19	Matt Holliday	3.00
20	Justin Verlander	2.00
21	Ivan Rodriguez	2.00
22	Hanley Ramirez	3.00
23	Alex Gordon	3.00
24	Vladimir Guerrero	3.00
25	Jeff Kent	2.00
26	Nomar Garciaparra	2.00
27	Prince Fielder	3.00
28	Joe Mauer	3.00
29	Justin Morneau	2.00
30	Jose Reyes	4.00
31	David Wright	4.00
32	Pedro Martinez	3.00
33	Johan Santana	3.00
34	Joba Chamberlain	5.00
35	Derek Jeter	8.00
36	Alex Rodriguez	8.00
37	Hideki Matsui	5.00
38	Ryan Howard	4.00
39	Chase Utley	4.00
40	Jimmy Rollins	3.00
41	Cole Hamels	3.00
42	Jake Peavy	3.00
43	Greg Maddux	5.00
44	Phil Hughes	2.00
45	Felix Hernandez	2.00
46	Ichiro Suzuki	5.00
47	Albert Pujols	8.00
48	Chris Carpenter	2.00
49	Frank Thomas	3.00
50	Vernon Wells	4.00

Timeless Moments Jersey

	NM/M
Common Jersey:	4.00
Gold Jersey:	1-1.5X
Production 75 Sets	
Blue Jersey:	1-2X
Production 25 Sets	
Jersey Button:	No Pricing
Production Five Sets	
Patch:	2-3X
Production 25 Sets	

1	Randy Johnson	6.00
2	Dan Haren	4.00

3	John Smoltz	8.00
5	Mark Teixeira	6.00
6	David Ortiz	8.00
7	Dustin Pedroia	8.00
8	Josh Beckett	6.00
9	Curt Schilling	6.00
10	Daisuke Matsuzaka	15.00
11	Alfonso Soriano	8.00
12	Carlos Zambrano	6.00
13	Jim Thome	4.00
17	C.C. Sabathia	4.00
18	Troy Tulowitzki	4.00
19	Matt Holliday	6.00
20	Justin Verlander	6.00
21	Ivan Rodriguez	6.00
22	Hanley Ramirez	8.00
23	Alex Gordon	8.00
24	Vladimir Guerrero	8.00
25	Jeff Kent	4.00
27	Prince Fielder	8.00
28	Joe Mauer	4.00
29	Justin Morneau	6.00
30	Jose Reyes	8.00
32	Pedro Martinez	6.00
33	Johan Santana	6.00
34	Joba Chamberlain	20.00
35	Derek Jeter	15.00
36	Alex Rodriguez	15.00
39	Chase Utley	6.00
40	Jimmy Rollins	6.00
41	Cole Hamels	6.00
42	Jake Peavy	6.00
43	Greg Maddux	10.00
44	Phil Hughes	6.00
45	Felix Hernandez	6.00
47	Albert Pujols	15.00
48	Chris Carpenter	4.00
49	Frank Thomas	8.00
50	Vernon Wells	6.00

Timeless Moments Jersey Autographs

	NM/M
Production 5-75	

2	Dan Haren/50	20.00
4	Chipper Jones/25	70.00
18	Troy Tulowitzki/50	20.00
19	Matt Holliday/25	25.00
22	Hanley Ramirez/50	35.00
23	Alex Gordon/25	35.00
34	Joba Chamberlain/50	180.00
44	Phil Hughes/50	25.00
45	Felix Hernandez/75	30.00

2008 UD Ballpark Collection

	NM/M
Common Player (1-100):	1.00
Common RC Auto (101-150):	8.00
Common Dual Jsy (151-200):	8.00
Common Quad Jsy (201-250):	10.00
Common 6X memorabilia (251-295):	15.00
Common 8x memor. (296-340):	15.00
Pack (5):	50.00
Box (4):	180.00

1	Brandon Webb	2.00

2	Dan Haren	1.50
3	Chris B. Young	1.50
4	Randy Johnson	3.00
5	Mark Teixeira	2.00
6	John Smoltz	2.00
7	Tom Glavine	2.00
8	Brian McCann	1.50
9	Chipper Jones	5.00
10	Nick Markakis	2.00
11	Brian Roberts	1.50
12	Josh Beckett	2.50
13	David Ortiz	4.00
14	Manny Ramirez	3.00
15	Dustin Pedroia	3.00
16	Jonathan Papelbon	2.00
17	Daisuke Matsuzaka	5.00
18	Alfonso Soriano	2.00
19	Aramis Ramirez	2.00
20	Carlos Zambrano	2.00
21	Nick Swisher	1.00
22	Jim Thome	2.00
23	Ken Griffey Jr.	6.00
24	Adam Dunn	2.00
25	Grady Sizemore	2.50
26	Victor Martinez	2.00
27	Travis Hafner	1.50
28	C.C. Sabathia	2.50
29	Garrett Atkins	1.50
30	Matt Holliday	2.00
31	Troy Tulowitzki	1.50
32	Magglio Ordonez	1.50
33	Justin Verlander	2.00
34	Miguel Cabrera	3.00
35	Gary Sheffield	2.00
36	Ivan Rodriguez	2.00
37	Dontrelle Willis	1.00
38	Curtis Granderson	2.50
39	Hanley Ramirez	3.00
40	Dan Uggla	1.50
41	Lance Berkman	2.00
42	Roy Oswalt	2.00
43	Carlos Lee	2.00
44	Hunter Pence	2.00
45	Alex Gordon	2.00
46	Jose Guillen	1.00
47	Torii Hunter	1.50
48	Vladimir Guerrero	3.00
49	Andruw Jones	1.00
50	Matt Kemp	2.50
51	Russell Martin	2.00
52	Jeff Kent	1.50
53	Ryan Braun	4.00
54	Prince Fielder	3.00
55	Delmon Young	1.00
56	Joe Mauer	2.00
57	Justin Morneau	2.00
58	Jose Reyes	4.00
59	David Wright	5.00
60	Carlos Beltran	2.50
61	Johan Santana	3.00
62	Pedro Martinez	2.50
63	Alex Rodriguez	6.00
64	Derek Jeter	8.00
65	Hideki Matsui	3.00
66	Robinson Cano	2.00
67	Joba Chamberlain	5.00
68	Phil Hughes	3.00
69	Mariano Rivera	2.50
70	Eric Chavez	1.00
71	Bobby Crosby	1.00
72	Cole Hamels	2.50
73	Ryan Howard	3.00
74	Jimmy Rollins	2.50
75	Chase Utley	3.00
76	Jason Bay	1.50
77	Freddy Sanchez	1.00
78	Jake Peavy	2.00
79	Greg Maddux	5.00
80	Trevor Hoffman	1.00
81	Kosuke Fukudome **RC**	8.00
82	Barry Zito	1.00
83	Tim Lincecum	3.00
84	Erik Bedard	1.00
85	Felix Hernandez	2.00
86	Ichiro Suzuki	5.00
87	Troy Glaus	1.50
88	Albert Pujols	8.00
89	Chris Carpenter	1.50
90	Scott Kazmir	1.50
91	Carl Crawford	1.50
92	Michael Young	1.50
93	Hank Blalock	1.50
94	Roy Halladay	2.00
95	Vernon Wells	1.00
96	Alex Rios	2.00
97	Scott Rolen	2.00
98	Frank Thomas	3.00
99	Lastings Milledge	1.00
100	Ryan Zimmerman	2.00
101	Bobby Wilson/Auto. **RC**	15.00
102	Alex Romero/Auto. **(RC)**	8.00
104	Brandon Boggs/Auto. **(RC)**	10.00
105	Brian Barton/Auto. **RC**	15.00
106	Brian Bass/Auto. **(RC)**	10.00
107	Brian Bixler **(RC)**	8.00
108	Brian Bocock/Auto. **RC**	8.00
109	Burke Badenhop/Auto. **RC**	8.00
110	Callix Crabbe/Auto. **(RC)**	8.00
111	Clayton Kershaw/Auto. **RC**	35.00
112	Chin-Lung Hu/Auto. **(RC)**	25.00
113	Clay Buchholz/Auto. **(RC)**	20.00
114	Eider Torres/Auto. **(RC)**	10.00
115	Clete Thomas/Auto. **RC**	12.00
116	Colt Morton/Auto. **RC**	8.00
117	Daric Barton/Auto. **(RC)**	8.00

118	Cory Wade/Auto. **(RC)**	12.00
119	Elliot Johnson/Auto. **(RC)**	8.00
120	Emmanuel Burriss **RC**	
121	Evan Longoria/Auto. **RC**	75.00
122	Evan Meek/Auto. **RC**	10.00
123	German Duran/Auto. **RC**	8.00
124	Fernando Hernandez/ Auto. **RC**	8.00
125	Greg Smith/Auto. **RC**	8.00
126	Jay Bruce/Auto. **(RC)**	40.00
127	Wladimir Balentien/ Auto. **(RC)**	10.00
128	Hernan Iribarren/Auto. **(RC)**	8.00
129	Jed Lowrie/Auto. **(RC)**	40.00
130	Ian Kennedy/Auto. **RC**	15.00
131	Jeff Clement/Auto. **(RC)**	15.00
132	Jesse Carlson/Auto. **RC**	15.00
133	Jonathan Herrera/Auto. **RC**	8.00
134	Johnny Cueto/Auto. **RC**	20.00
135	Jonathan Albaladejo/ Auto. **RC**	10.00
136	Josh Newman/Auto. **RC**	8.00
137	Kevin Hart/Auto. **(RC)**	8.00
138	Justin Masterson/Auto. **RC**	30.00
140	Luis Mendoza/Auto. **(RC)**	8.00
141	Matt Tupman/Auto. **RC**	15.00
142	Max Scherzer/Auto. **RC**	25.00
143	Nick Blackburn/Auto. **RC**	20.00
144	Nick Adenhart/Auto. **(RC)**	12.00
145	Ramon Troncoso/ Auto. **(RC)**	10.00
146	Paul Janish/Auto. **(RC)**	10.00
147	Randor Bierd/Auto. **RC**	15.00
148	Robinzon Diaz/Auto. **(RC)**	10.00
149	Steve Holm/Auto **RC**	10.00
150	Wesley Wright/Auto. **RC**	10.00
151	David Ortiz, Jason Giambi	10.00
152	Jonathan Papelbon, Mariano Rivera	15.00
153	Johan Santana, Nolan Ryan	15.00
154	Jorge Posada, Mike Mussina	10.00
155	Jonathan Papelbon, Jason Varitek	10.00
156	Howie Kendrick, Dan Uggla	8.00
157	Kenji Johjima, Jason Varitek	10.00
158	Roy Oswalt, Carlos Lee	8.00
159	Albert Pujols, Derrek Lee	15.00
160	Albert Pujols, Ozzie Smith	20.00
161	Carlos Zambrano, Alfonso Soriano	10.00
162	Trevor Hoffman, Tony Gwynn	10.00
163	Cole Hamels, Johan Santana	10.00
164	Kendry Morales, David Ortiz	10.00
165	Curt Schilling, Randy Johnson	10.00
166	B.J. Upton, Curtis Granderson	10.00
167	Chase Utley, Ryne Sandberg	15.00
168	Nick Markakis, Melvin Mora	10.00
169	Prince Fielder, Conor Jackson	10.00
170	Ben Sheets, Roy Halladay	8.00
171	Kerry Wood, Mark Mulder	8.00
172	Andruw Jones, Ken Griffey Jr.	15.00
173	Troy Tulowitzki, J.J. Hardy	8.00
174	Tim Lincecum, Matt Cain	10.00
175	Orlando Cabrera, Derek Jeter	15.00
176	Prince Fielder, Albert Pujols	15.00
177	Roy Halladay, Frank Thomas	10.00
178	Josh Beckett, Jason Varitek	10.00
179	Miguel Cabrera, Mike Schmidt	12.00
180	Chris Duncan, Albert Pujols	15.00
181	C.C. Sabathia, Dontrelle Willis	10.00
182	Matt Holliday, Manny Ramirez	10.00
183	Zack Greinke, Roy Halladay	8.00
184	Nick Markakis, Vladimir Guerrero	10.00
185	Ben Sheets, Roy Halladay	8.00
186	Albert Pujols, Vladimir Guerrero	15.00
187	Manny Ramirez, Johnny Damon	10.00
188	Johan Santana, Chris Carpenter	10.00
189	Ken Griffey Jr., Frank Thomas	15.00
191	Jonathan Papelbon, Curt Schilling	10.00
192	Derek Jeter, Cal Ripken Jr.	25.00
193	Jason Varitek, Wade Boggs	10.00
194	Alfonso Soriano, Derrek Lee	10.00
196	Kenji Johjima, Hong-Chih Kuo	10.00
197	Alfonso Soriano, Kerry Wood	10.00
198	Albert Pujols, Carlos Delgado	15.00
199	Derek Jeter, Don Mattingly	25.00
200	Johnny Damon, Derek Jeter	15.00

201	Matt Kemp, Prince Fielder, Ben Sheets, James Loney	10.00
202	Kevin Youkilis, Jason Giambi, David Ortiz, Derek Jeter	20.00
203	Troy Tulowitzki, Cal Ripken Jr., Derek Jeter, Khalil Greene	25.00
204	Robin Yount, Prince Fielder, Rickie Weeks, J.J. Hardy	15.00
205	Howie Kendrick, Casey Kotchman, Vladimir Guerrero, Chone Figgins	10.00
206	Kenji Johjima, Jorge Posada, Jason Varitek, Ivan Rodriguez	10.00
207	Joe Nathan, Trevor Hoffman, Mariano Rivera, Eric Gagne	10.00
208	Brandon Inge, Carlos Guillen, Gary Sheffield, Ivan Rodriguez	10.00
209	Scott Kazmir, Randy Johnson, Francisco Liriano, Johan Santana	10.00
210	John Maine, Pedro Martinez, Billy Wagner, Johan Santana	15.00
211	Prince Fielder, Albert Pujols, Derrek Lee, Conor Jackson	15.00
212	Jered Weaver, Justin Verlander, Josh Beckett, Zack Greinke	10.00
213	Chris Young, Trevor Hoffman, Jake Peavy, Greg Maddux	15.00
214	Nolan Ryan, John Smoltz, Mike Mussina, Roy Halladay	
215	Khalil Greene, Tony Gwynn, Trevor Hoffman, Greg Maddux	15.00
216	Aaron Harang, Carlos Zambrano, Alfonso Soriano, Ken Griffey Jr.	15.00
217	Roy Halladay, Mike Mussina, John Smoltz, Greg Maddux	15.00
218	Manny Ramirez, Frank Thomas, Jim Thome, Ken Griffey Jr.	20.00
220	Albert Pujols, Manny Ramirez, Vladimir Guerrero, Johnny Damon	20.00
221	Jason Bay, Derrek Lee, Alfonso Soriano, Ken Griffey Jr.	15.00
222	Pat Burrell, Geoff Jenkins, Cole Hamels, Brad Lidge	10.00
223	Alfonso Soriano, Derek Jeter, Derrek Lee, Jason Giambi	20.00
224	Takashi Saito, Tadahito Iguchi, Akinori Iwamura, Kenji Johjima	10.00
225	Cole Hamels, C.C. Sabathia, Randy Johnson, Scott Kazmir	15.00
226	Albert Pujols, Rick Ankiel, Chris Carpenter, Ozzie Smith	25.00
227	Albert Pujols, David Ortiz, Mike Schmidt, Ken Griffey Jr.	25.00
228	Curtis Granderson, Rickie Weeks, Derek Jeter, Rafael Furcal	15.00
229	David Ortiz, Wade Boggs, Jason Varitek, Manny Ramirez	15.00
230	Jake Peavy, Khalil Greene, Derek Jeter, Andy Pettitte	15.00
231	David Ortiz, Manny Ramirez, Don Mattingly, Derek Jeter	25.00
232	Johan Santana, Carlos Delgado, Chipper Jones, John Smoltz	15.00
233	Brian Roberts, Melvin Mora, Jason Giambi, Derek Jeter	15.00
234	Chris Duncan, Albert Pujols, Aramis Ramirez, Derrek Lee	15.00
235	Prince Fielder, Ben Sheets, Albert Pujols, Mark Mulder	15.00
236	Ken Griffey Jr., Derek Jeter, Albert Pujols, David Ortiz	
237	Albert Pujols, Vladimir Guerrero, Manny Ramirez, Pat Burrell	15.00
238	Justin Verlander, Ivan Rodriguez, Derek Jeter, Andy Pettitte	15.00
239	Kenji Johjima, Jorge Posada, Jason Varitek, Ivan Rodriguez	10.00
240	Dan Uggla, Chase Utley, Rickie Weeks, Brian Roberts	12.00
241	Albert Pujols, Magglio Ordonez, Ivan Rodriguez, Mark Mulder	15.00
242	Nick Markakis, David Ortiz, Prince Fielder, Ken Griffey Jr.	15.00
243	Dan Uggla, Derek Jeter, Brian Roberts, Michael Young	15.00
244	David Ortiz, Vladimir Guerrero, Magglio Ordonez, Manny Ramirez	15.00

245	Chad Billingsley, James Loney, Randy Johnson, Conor Jackson	10.00
246	Josh Willingham, Magglio Ordonez, Manny Ramirez, Pat Burrell	10.00
247	Chien-Ming Wang, Mariano Rivera, Derek Jeter, Jason Giambi	25.00
248	Dan Uggla, B.J. Upton, Carl Crawford, Hanley Ramirez	12.00
249	Prince Fielder, Ken Griffey Jr., Albert Pujols, Derrek Lee	20.00
251	Cole Hamels, Jake Peavy, Dan Haren, Ben Sheets, Chris Carpenter, Randy Johnson	15.00
252	Nick Markakis, Rocco Baldelli, Mark Teahen, Curtis Granderson, Manny Ramirez, Vladimir Guerrero	15.00
253	Scott Kazmir, Francisco Liriano, Mark Mulder, Barry Zito, Johan Santana, Randy Johnson	15.00
255	Howie Kendrick, John Lackey, Vladimir Guerrero, Victor Martinez, C.C. Sabathia, Travis Hafner	15.00
256	Adam LaRoche, Prince Fielder, Adrian Gonzalez, Carlos Delgado, Derrek Lee, Albert Pujols	20.00
257	Josh Willingham, Tony Gwynn, Jason Bay, Matt Holliday, Carlos Lee, Ken Griffey Jr.	25.00
260	Moises Alou, Johan Santana, Carlos Delgado, Jason Giambi, Andy Pettitte, Derek Jeter	30.00
261	Frank Thomas, Jason Giambi, David Ortiz, Aubrey Huff, Casey Kotchman, Rod Carew	15.00
262	Jered Weaver, Howie Kendrick, Scott Kazmir, Khalil Greene, Zack Greinke, Rickie Weeks	15.00
263	Roy Halladay, Tom Glavine, Randy Johnson, John Smoltz, Andy Pettitte, Mike Mussina	20.00
265	Chris Duncan, Mark Mulder, Albert Pujols, Aramis Ramirez, Kerry Wood, Derrek Lee	25.00
266	Jered Weaver, Howie Kendrick, Vladimir Guerrero, Takashi Saito, Rafael Furcal, Andruw Jones	15.00
267	Prince Fielder, Ben Sheets, Kerry Wood, Derrek Lee, Mark Mulder, Albert Pujols	20.00
268	Albert Pujols, David Ortiz, Vladimir Guerrero, Manny Ramirez, Derek Jeter, Ken Griffey Jr.	40.00
269	Moises Alou, Dan Uggla, Josh Willingham, Chipper Jones, Mark Teixeira, Carlos Delgado	15.00
270	Frank Thomas, Manny Ramirez, Vladimir Guerrero, Carlos Lee, Mike Schmidt, Albert Pujols	25.00
271	Kenji Johjima, Brian McCann, Joe Mauer, Jason Varitek, Jorge Posada, Ivan Rodriguez	15.00
272	Nick Markakis, Delmon Young, Josh Willingham, Pat Burrell, Magglio Ordonez, Manny Ramirez	15.00
273	Roy Oswalt, Josh Hamilton, Michael Young, Kevin Millwood, Mark Loretta, Miguel Tejada	15.00
274	Moises Alou, Cole Hamels, Pat Burrell, Cole Hamels, Carlos Delgado, Johan Santana	20.00
275	Akinori Iwamura, Dan Uggla, Chris Burke, Chase Utley, Rickie Weeks, Aaron Hill	15.00
276	Chad Tracy, Dan Haren, Randy Johnson, Aramis Ramirez, Derrek Lee, Kerry Wood	25.00
277	Chris Duncan, Mark Mulder, Albert Pujols, Brandon Inge, Magglio Ordonez, Ivan Rodriguez	20.00
278	Nick Markakis, David Ortiz, Geoff Jenkins, Prince Fielder, Ken Griffey Jr., Garret Anderson	20.00
279	Derek Jeter, Michael Young, Troy Tulowitzki, Brian Roberts, Dan Uggla, Aaron Hill	
280	Kendry Morales, Aramis Ramirez, David Ortiz, Magglio Ordonez, Vladimir Guerrero, Manny Ramirez	15.00

281 Kenji Johjima, Eric Chavez,
Melvin Mora, Miguel Cabrera,
Jorge Posada,
Jason Varitek 15.00
282 Delmon Young, Mark Teahen,
Grady Sizemore, Jason Bay,
Mike Cameron,
Ken Griffey Jr. 15.00
284 Joel Zumaya, Dontrelle Willis,
Magglio Ordonez, Josh Beckett,
Jonathan Papelbon,
David Ortiz 15.00
285 Delmon Young, Francisco Liriano,
Justin Morneau, Rickie Weeks,
Mike Cameron,
Prince Fielder 15.00
286 Carl Crawford, Scott Kazmir,
Akinori Iwamura, Luis Gonzalez,
Dan Uggla, Josh Johnson 15.00
287 Chris Duncan, J.D. Drew,
Xavier Nady, Josh Hamilton,
Rick Ankiel, Nick Markakis 15.00
288 Troy Tulowitzki, Aaron Rowand,
Matt Cain, Jeff Francis,
Chris Young, Jake Peavy 15.00
290 Chien-Ming Wang, Don Mattingly,
Jorge Posada, Mariano Rivera,
Jason Giambi, Derek Jeter 40.00
291 Jonathan Papelbon, Wade Boggs,
J.D. Drew, Josh Beckett,
Jason Varitek,
Manny Ramirez 25.00
292 Troy Tulowitzki, Chad Billingsley,
Rafael Furcal, Jeff Francis,
Conor Jackson, Dan Haren 15.00
294 Dontrelle Willis, Miguel Cabrera,
Magglio Ordonez, Carlos Guillen,
Ivan Rodriguez,
Gary Sheffield 20.00
295 Jered Weaver, Casey Kotchman,
Chone Figgins, John Lackey,
Garret Anderson,
Vladimir Guerrero 15.00
297 Jonathan Papelbon,
Mariano Rivera, Jorge Posada,
Jason Giambi, Derek Jeter,
David Ortiz, Jason Varitek,
Manny Ramirez 40.00
298 Howie Kendrick, Grady Sizemore,
Victor Martinez, C.C. Sabathia,
Travis Hafner, John Lackey,
Vladimir Guerrero,
Kendry Morales 20.00
299 Adam LaRoche, Adrian Gonzalez,
Carlos Delgado, Mark Teixeira,
Derrek Lee, Prince Fielder,
Lance Berkman,
Albert Pujols 25.00
300 Chris Duncan, Mike Cameron,
Carlos Beltran, Ken Griffey Jr.,
Josh Willingham, Carlos Lee,
Matt Holliday, Jason Bay 20.00
301 Cole Hamels, Pat Burrell,
Chipper Jones, John Smoltz,
Josh Willingham, Josh Johnson,
Carlos Delgado,
Johan Santana 20.00
302 Ozzie Smith, Derek Jeter,
Khalil Greene, Stephen Drew,
Brian Roberts, Dan Uggla,
Mark Loretta, Rickie Weeks 25.00
303 Moises Alou, Johnny Damon,
Jason Giambi, Derek Jeter,
Andy Pettitte, Carlos Delgado,
Jose Reyes, Johan Santana 30.00
304 Justin Morneau, Jim Thome,
Aubrey Huff, Richie Sexson,
Frank Thomas, Jason Giambi,
Casey Kotchman,
David Ortiz 30.00
306 Chris Duncan, Prince Fielder,
Alfonso Soriano, Lance Berkman,
Derrek Lee, Carlos Lee,
Albert Pujols,
Ken Griffey Jr. 30.00
307 Randy Johnson, John Smoltz,
Tom Glavine, Pedro Martinez,
Mike Mussina, John Lackey,
Andy Pettitte, Roy Halladay 25.00
308 Brian Roberts, Melvin Mora,
Nick Markakis, Aubrey Huff,
Johnny Damon, Derek Jeter,
Jason Giambi,
Jorge Posada 25.00
311 Tom Gorzelanny, Xavier Nady,
Ben Sheets, Prince Fielder,
Kerry Wood, Albert Pujols,
Mark Mulder, Derrek Lee 25.00
312 Mark Teixeira, Vladimir Guerrero,
David Ortiz, Ken Griffey Jr.,
Albert Pujols, Derek Jeter,
Cal Ripken Jr.,
Manny Ramirez 40.00

314 Albert Pujols, Manny Ramirez,
Aramis Ramirez, Carlos Lee,
Frank Thomas, Jason Giambi,
Pat Burrell,
Vladimir Guerrero 30.00
317 Moises Alou, Delmon Young,
Josh Willingham, Pat Burrell,
Rocco Baldelli, Nick Markakis,
Magglio Ordonez,
Manny Ramirez 15.00
318 Hank Blalock, Mark Loretta,
Miguel Tejada, Roy Oswalt,
Carlos Lee, Josh Hamilton,
Kevin Millwood,
Michael Young 20.00
319 Moises Alou, Johan Santana,
Carlos Delgado, Brad Lidge,
Pat Burrell, Cole Hamels,
Chase Utley, Billy Wagner 25.00
320 Dan Uggla, Chris Burke,
Aaron Hill, Mark Loretta,
Brian Roberts, Rickie Weeks,
Robinson Cano,
Chase Utley 20.00
321 Stephen Drew, Aramis Ramirez,
Derrek Lee, Alfonso Soriano,
Kerry Wood, Chris Burke,
Chad Tracy,
Randy Johnson 20.00
322 Chris Duncan, Chris Carpenter,
Albert Pujols, Ivan Rodriguez,
Brandon Inge, Joel Zumaya,
Magglio Ordonez,
Mark Mulder 25.00
323 Troy Tulowitzki, Garrett Atkins,
Jeff Francis, Matt Holliday,
Jason Varitek, Jonathan Papelbon,
Manny Ramirez,
David Ortiz 20.00
324 Nick Markakis, Garret Anderson,
David Ortiz, Chad Tracy,
Geoff Jenkins, Prince Fielder,
Ken Griffey Jr., Eric Chavez 40.00
325 Lance Berkman, Casey Kotchman,
Aubrey Huff, Justin Morneau,
Carlos Delgado, Jason Giambi,
Kevin Youkilis,
James Loney 20.00
326 Michael Young, Chase Utley,
Troy Tulowitzki, Akinori Iwamura,
Aaron Hill, Khalil Greene,
Dan Uggla, Derek Jeter 20.00
327 Johan Santana, Magglio Ordonez,
Vladimir Guerrero, David Ortiz,
Aramis Ramirez, Kendry Morales,
Ivan Rodriguez,
Manny Ramirez 20.00
329 Ken Griffey Jr., Mike Cameron,
Chris Duncan, Jason Bay,
Magglio Ordonez,
Grady Sizemore, Delmon Young,
Mark Teahen 30.00
330 James Loney, Adam LaRoche,
Mark Teixeira, Aaron Boone,
Casey Kotchman, Kevin Youkilis,
Jason Giambi, Aubrey Huff 20.00
331 Miguel Cabrera, Magglio Ordonez,
Dontrelle Willis, Joel Zumaya,
Manny Ramirez, David Ortiz,
Jonathan Papelbon,
Josh Beckett 20.00
333 Carl Crawford, Scott Kazmir,
Rocco Baldelli, B.J. Upton,
Hanley Ramirez, Josh Johnson,
Josh Willingham,
Dan Uggla 15.00
334 Pat Burrell, Nick Markakis,
Josh Willingham, Xavier Nady,
J.D. Drew, Chris Duncan,
Rick Ankiel, Josh Hamilton 20.00
335 Jake Peavy, Chris Young,
Jeff Francis, Troy Tulowitzki,
Randy Johnson, Chad Tracy,
Matt Cain, Tim Lincecum 20.00
336 Derek Jeter, Mike Mussina,
Mariano Rivera, Chien-Ming Wang,
Andy Pettitte, Jason Giambi,
Don Mattingly, Jorge Posada 50.00
337 David Ortiz, Manny Ramirez,
Jonathan Papelbon, Josh Beckett,
J.D. Drew, Jason Varitek,
Kevin Youkilis,
Wade Boggs 25.00
338 Ken Griffey Jr., Aaron Harang,
Derrek Lee, Carlos Zambrano,
Prince Fielder, Ben Sheets,
Albert Pujols, Mark Mulder 25.00
339 Aaron Harang, Dan Haren,
Roy Oswalt, Chad Billingsley,
Josh Johnson, Zack Greinke,
A.J. Burnett, Jered Weaver 15.00

Jersey Autographs

	NM/M
Common player:	8.00

Some not priced due to scarcity.
1 Aaron Harang 10.00

2	Kevin Saito	30.00
3	Troy Tulowitzki	20.00
4	Adam LaRoche	15.00
5	Adrian Gonzalez	15.00
7	Andre Ethier	20.00
8	Joe Mauer	35.00
9	Justin Upton	25.00
10	Aramis Ramirez	30.00
11	Scott Baker	15.00
12	B.J. Upton	25.00
13	Bill Hall	8.00
14	Billy Wagner	50.00
15	Brandon Phillips	20.00
16	Brandon Webb	25.00
18	Brian McCann	20.00
19	Brian Roberts	15.00
20	Bronson Arroyo	20.00
21	Tim Lincecum	70.00
22	Mark Reynolds	15.00
23	Chad Billingsley	20.00
24	Chad Cordero	8.00
25	Chone Figgins	15.00
27	Chris B. Young	15.00
28	Tom Gorzelanny	8.00
29	Corey Hart	20.00
30	Dan Uggla	15.00
32	Derek Jeter	125.00
33	Edinson Volquez	25.00
38	Xavier Nady	15.00
39	Felix Pie	15.00
42	Garrett Atkins	10.00
43	Ken Griffey Jr.	70.00
44	Derek Jeter	125.00
45	Hanley Ramirez	25.00
46	Hong-Chih Kuo	40.00
47	Ian Kinsler	20.00
49	Derek Lowe	15.00
50	Alfonso Soriano	40.00
51	Jeff Baker	8.00
52	Jeff Francis	10.00
53	Jeff Francoeur	20.00
54	Jered Weaver	10.00
55	Ben Sheets	20.00
56	Jeremy Guthrie	20.00
57	Jeremy Hermida	15.00
60	Joakim Soria	15.00
61	Joe Blanton	10.00
62	Joe Nathan	20.00
64	Chien-Ming Wang	100.00
65	Chris Young	8.00
66	Jon Lester	20.00
67	Jonathan Papelbon	8.00
68	Cole Hamels	50.00
69	Josh Johnson	15.00
70	Josh Willingham	10.00
71	Kelly Johnson	10.00
72	Ken Griffey Jr.	70.00
73	Kevin Kouzmanoff	10.00
74	Kevin Youkilis	30.00
75	Derrek Lee	25.00
76	James Shields	25.00
77	Jason Bay	15.00
78	Jason Varitek	35.00
81	Mark Teahen	10.00
83	Matt Cain	15.00
84	John Lackey	15.00
85	Matt Kemp	25.00
86	John Maine	10.00
88	Melvin Mora	10.00
91	Kerry Wood	25.00
92	Nick Markakis	25.00
93	Lance Berkman	20.00
94	Noah Lowry	10.00
95	Rickie Weeks	15.00
96	Prince Fielder	30.00
97	Roy Halladay	12.00
98	Tim Hudson	15.00
99	Grady Sizemore	40.00
100	Ryan Braun	

Jersey Buttons

	NM/M
Production 5-25	8.00
Laundry Tags:	No pricing
Production 2-15	
MLB Logos:	No pricing
Production 1-5	

6	Albert Pujols/25	125.00
32	Derek Jeter/25	100.00
44	Derek Jeter/25	100.00
55	Ben Sheets/25	25.00
68	Cole Hamels/25	50.00
77	Jason Bay/25	30.00
78	Jason Varitek/25	50.00
83	Matt Cain/20	30.00
97	Roy Halladay/25	35.00

Swatch Memorabilia Auto.

No pricing due to scarcity.

Moments in Time Dual Cut Signatures

No Pricing

2008 UD Masterpieces

	NM/M
Complete Set (120):	75.00
Common player (1-90):	.50
Common SP (91-120):	1.00
Inserted 1:2	
Pack (6):	7.00
Box (12):	70.00

1	Brandon Webb	.75
2	Justin Upton	1.00
3	Randy Johnson	1.00

4	Chipper Jones	1.50
5	Max Scherzer RC	1.50
6	Mark Teixeira	.75
7	Evan Longoria RC	8.00
8	Jim Palmer	.75
9	Brooks Robinson	1.00
10	Nick Markakis	.75
11	Carl Yastrzemski	1.50
12	Wade Boggs	.75
13	Curt Schilling	.75
14	Daisuke Matsuzaka	1.50
15	David Ortiz	1.00
16	Jonathan Papelbon	.75
17	Manny Ramirez	1.00
18	Alfonso Soriano	1.00
19	Ryne Sandberg	2.50
20	Carlos Zambrano	.75
21	Derrek Lee	.75
22	Kosuke Fukudome RC	4.00
23	Jim Thome	.75
24	Adam Dunn	.75
25	Joe Morgan	1.00
26	Grady Sizemore	1.00
27	Victor Martinez	.50
28	Travis Hafner	.50
29	Troy Tulowitzki	.75
30	Matt Holliday	.75
31	Todd Helton	.75
32	Justin Verlander	1.00
33	Asdrubal Cabrera	.50
34	Gary Sheffield	.75
35	Magglio Ordonez	.75
36	Miguel Cabrera	1.00
37	Hanley Ramirez	1.00
38	Lance Berkman	.75
39	Roy Oswalt	.75
40	Alex Gordon	.75
41	Vladimir Guerrero	1.00
42	Andruw Jones	.50
43	Chin-Lung Hu (RC)	1.00
44	James Loney	.75
45	Hunter Pence	.75
46	Robin Yount	1.50
47	Prince Fielder	1.00
48	Ryan Braun	1.50
49	Harmon Killebrew	1.50
50	Joe Mauer	.75
51	Justin Morneau	.75
52	Ken Griffey Jr.	2.00
53	Carlos Beltran	.75
54	David Wright	2.00
55	Johan Santana	1.00
56	Jose Reyes	.75
57	Pedro Martinez	.75
58	Ian Kennedy RC	2.00
59	Jay Bruce (RC)	3.00
60	Whitey Ford	.75
61	Mariano Rivera	.75
62	Alex Rodriguez	2.50
63	Hideki Matsui	1.00
64	Joba Chamberlain	2.00
65	Jorge Posada	.75
66	Robinson Cano	.75
67	Eric Chavez	.50
68	Rich Harden	.50
69	Chase Utley	1.00
70	Jimmy Rollins	.75
71	Ryan Howard	2.50
72	Bill Mazeroski	.50
73	Freddy Sanchez	.50
74	Luke Hochevar RC	2.00
75	Tony Gwynn	1.00
76	Greg Maddux	1.50
77	Jake Peavy	.75
78	Barry Zito	.50
79	Russell Martin	.75
80	Tim Lincecum	1.00
81	Ichiro Suzuki	1.50
82	Felix Hernandez	.75
83	Ozzie Smith	1.50
84	Jason Varitek	.50
85	Chris Carpenter	.50
86	Carl Crawford	.50
87	Michael Young	.50
88	Frank Thomas	1.00
89	Roy Halladay	.75
90	Ryan Zimmerman	.75
91	Eddie Murray	2.00
92	Cal Ripken Jr.	8.00
93	Frank Robinson	1.50
94	Ryne Sandberg	4.00

95 Warren Spahn 1.50
96 Ernie Banks 2.50
97 Carlton Fisk 1.00
98 Johnny Bench 2.50
99 Ken Griffey Jr. 5.00
100 Al Kaline 2.00
101 Cal Ripken Jr. 8.00
102 Nolan Ryan 8.00
103 Jack Morris 1.00
104 Rod Carew 1.50
105 Tom Seaver 1.50
106 Don Mattingly 4.00
107 Lou Brock 1.50
108 Joe DiMaggio 5.00
109 Derek Jeter 6.00
110 Yogi Berra 2.50
111 Reggie Jackson 1.50
112 Mike Schmidt 2.00
113 Steve Carlton 1.00
114 Willie Stargell 2.00
115 Roberto Clemente 5.00
116 Albert Pujols 5.00
117 Stan Musial 2.50
118 Bob Gibson 1.50
119 Dave Winfield 1.50
120 Joe Carter 1.00

Framed Black

Black (1-90): 1-2X
Black SP (91-120): 1X

Framed Blue 125

Blue (1-90): 2-4X
Blue RC's (1-90): 1-2X
Blue SP (91-120): 1-2X
Production 125 Sets
Framed Blue 5: No Pricing
Production 5 Sets

Framed Blue 50

Blue (1-90): 3-5X
Blue RC's (1-90): 2-3X
Blue SP (91-120): 2-3X
Production 50 Sets

Framed Brown

Brown (1-90): 2-4X
Brown RC's (1-90): 1-2X
Brown SP (91-120): 1-2X
Production 100 Sets

Framed Gold

No Pricing
Production 10 Sets

Framed Green

NM/M
Green (1-90): 2-5X
Green RC's (1-90): 1-2X
Green SP (91-120): 1-2X
Production 75 sets

Framed Red

Red (1-90): 2-3X
Red RC (1-90): 1-1.5X
Black SP (91-120): 1-1.5X
Inserted 1:12
Red 1: No Pricing
Production One Set

Framed Silver

No Pricing
Production 25 Sets

Captured on Canvas

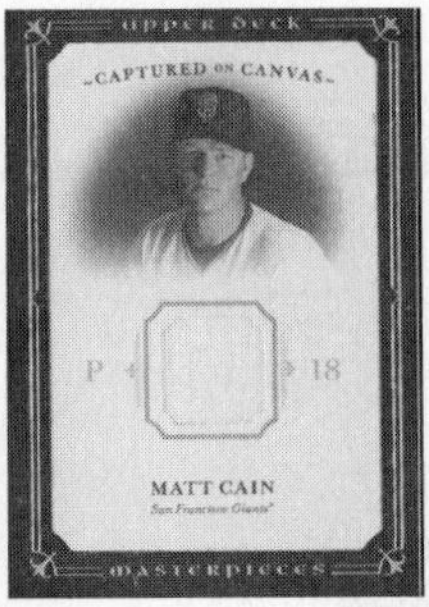

NM/M
Common player: 4.00
Patch: No pricing
Production 5-25
AJ Andruw Jones 4.00
AP Albert Pujols 15.00
AR Alex Rodriguez 20.00
BE Carlos Beltran 8.00
BH Bill Hall 4.00
BM Brian McCann 4.00
BP Brandon Phillips 4.00
BR Brian Roberts 4.00
BS Ben Sheets 4.00
BU B.J. Upton 6.00
CA Matt Cain 6.00
CB Chad Billingsley 6.00
CC Chris Carpenter 6.00
CD Chris Duncan 4.00
CF Carlton Fisk 8.00
CH Cole Hamels 10.00
CJ Chipper Jones 8.00
CL Carlos Lee 6.00
CR Cal Ripken Jr. 40.00
CS C.C. Sabathia 8.00
CW Rod Carew 10.00
CZ Carlos Zambrano 6.00
DJ Derek Jeter 20.00
DL Derrek Lee 8.00
DM Don Mattingly 10.00
DO David Ortiz 8.00
DU Dan Uggla 6.00
DW Dontrelle Willis 4.00
EB Erik Bedard 4.00
EC Eric Chavez 4.00
EM Eddie Murray 8.00
FH Felix Hernandez 8.00
FR Francisco Rodriguez 8.00
FS Freddy Sanchez 4.00
FT Frank Thomas 8.00
GA Garrett Atkins 4.00
GL Tom Glavine 8.00
GM Greg Maddux 10.00
GR Ken Griffey Jr. 15.00
GS Gary Sheffield 8.00
HK Howie Kendrick 4.00
HR Hanley Ramirez 10.00
HU Torii Hunter 6.00
IR Ivan Rodriguez 6.00
JB Josh Beckett 8.00
JE Derek Jeter 20.00
JF Jeff Francoeur 6.00
JL John Lackey 6.00
JM Joe Mauer 8.00
JO Kelly Johnson 4.00
JP Jake Peavy 6.00
JR Jose Reyes 10.00
JS Johan Santana 8.00
JT Jim Thome 8.00
JV Jason Varitek 8.00
JW Jered Weaver 6.00
KG Khalil Greene 4.00
KJ Kenji Johjima 6.00
KY Kevin Youkilis 8.00
LB Lance Berkman 6.00
MC Miguel Cabrera 8.00
MM Mark Mulder 4.00
MO Justin Morneau 8.00
MT Mark Teixeira 6.00
MY Michael Young 6.00
NM Nick Markakis 8.00
NR Nolan Ryan 30.00
PA Jonathan Papelbon 8.00
PF Prince Fielder 8.00
PM Pedro Martinez 6.00
PO Jorge Posada 8.00
RA Aramis Ramirez 8.00
RB Ryan Braun 20.00
RH Rich Harden 6.00
RJ Randy Johnson 8.00
RO Roy Oswalt 6.00
RY Nolan Ryan 30.00
RZ Ryan Zimmerman 6.00
SC Curt Schilling 8.00
TG Tony Gwynn 10.00
TH Travis Hafner 4.00
VE Justin Verlander 6.00
VG Vladimir Guerrero 8.00
VM Victor Martinez 4.00
VW Vernon Wells 6.00
WI Josh Willingham 4.00

Captured on Canvas Jersey Autographs

NM/M
Common Jersey Auto.: 10.00
Patch Auto: No Pricing
Production 5-25
BH Bill Hall 10.00
BM Brian McCann 20.00
BP Brandon Phillips 20.00
BU B.J. Upton 30.00
CA Matt Cain 15.00
CB Chad Billingsley 20.00
CH Cole Hamels 75.00
CJ Chipper Jones 75.00
CL Carlos Lee 25.00
CR Cal Ripken Jr. 150.00
DJ Derek Jeter 140.00
DL Derrek Lee 25.00
DU Dan Uggla 15.00
GR Ken Griffey Jr. 100.00
HR Hanley Ramirez 25.00
JB Josh Beckett 25.00
JE Derek Jeter 140.00
JF Jeff Francoeur 20.00
JO Kelly Johnson 10.00
KY Kevin Youkilis 35.00
LB Lance Berkman 20.00
PA Jonathan Papelbon 35.00
RA Aramis Ramirez 25.00
TG Tony Gwynn 60.00
WI Josh Willingham 10.00
FH Felix Hernandez 20.00
RZ Ryan Zimmerman 15.00
RH Rich Harden 10.00
MC Miguel Cabrera 25.00

Captured on Canvas Patch Autographs

Production 5-25
No Pricing

Stroke of Genius Signatures

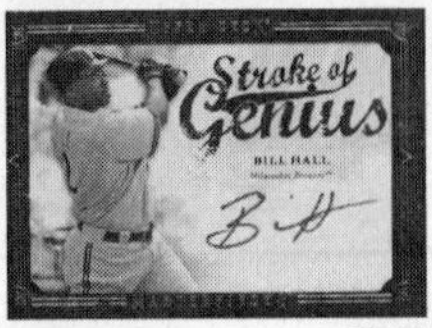

NM/M
Common Auto.: 8.00
AE Andre Ethier 15.00
AG Adrian Gonzalez 10.00
AL Adam LaRoche 8.00
AR Aramis Ramirez 20.00
BC Clay Buchholz 20.00
BH Bill Hall 8.00
BM Brian McCann 20.00
BP Brandon Phillips 15.00
BS Bill "Moose" Skowron 15.00
BU B.J. Upton 25.00
CB Chad Billingsley 20.00
CF Chone Figgins 12.00
CH Cole Hamels 50.00
CR Cal Ripken Jr. 150.00
CY Chris B. Young 15.00
DB Daric Barton 10.00
DC Daniel Cabrera 8.00
EE Edwin Encarnacion 8.00
EL Evan Longoria 125.00
EV Edinson Volquez 25.00
FC Fausto Carmona 10.00
GF Gavin Floyd 15.00
GJ Geoff Jenkins 15.00
GN Graig Nettles 20.00
GP Glen Perkins 10.00
HR Hanley Ramirez 25.00
HU Chin-Lung Hu 40.00
IA Ian Kinsler 15.00
JA James Loney 15.00
JB Joe Blanton 10.00
JC Jack Cust 12.00
JG Jeremy Guthrie 20.00
JK John Kruk 15.00
JN Joe Nathan 15.00
JO Josh Hamilton 40.00
JT J.R. Towles 15.00
JW Josh Willingham 10.00
KG Ken Griffey Jr. 75.00
KJ Kelly Johnson 10.00
KY Kevin Youkilis 25.00
LE Jon Lester 30.00
LH Luke Hochevar 15.00
MA John Maine 10.00
MC Matt Cain 12.00
MK Matt Kemp 20.00
MS Max Scherzer 25.00
NA Nick Adenhart 20.00
NB Nick Blackburn 20.00
NL Noah Lowry 10.00
NS Nick Swisher 10.00
OS Ozzie Smith 80.00
PK Paul Konerko 15.00
RH Rich Hill 8.00
RM Russell Martin 40.00
TG Tom Gorzelanny 8.00
WB Wladimir Balentien 12.00
XN Xavier Nady 15.00
YG Yovani Gallardo 15.00

2008 UD Premier

NM/M
Common Player (1-200): 4.00
Production 99
Common RC Auto. (201-242): 8.00
Production 99-299
Box (Seven Cards): 225.00
1 Chipper Jones 8.00
2 Andruw Jones 5.00
3 John Smoltz 5.00
4 Mark Teixeira 6.00
5 Edgar Renteria 4.00
6 Jeff Francoeur 5.00
7 Tim Hudson 5.00
8 Miguel Cabrera 6.00
9 Hanley Ramirez 6.00
10 Dan Uggla 4.00
11 Dontrelle Willis 4.00
12 Josh Willingham 4.00
13 Pedro Martinez 6.00
14 Carlos Delgado 5.00
15 Carlos Beltran 5.00
16 David Wright 10.00
17 Tom Glavine 5.00
18 Jose Reyes 10.00
19 Paul LoDuca 4.00
20 John Maine 5.00
21 Chase Utley 10.00
22 Cole Hamels 5.00
23 Jimmy Rollins 8.00
24 Shane Victorino 4.00
25 Ryan Howard 10.00
26 Pat Burrell 5.00
27 Aaron Rowand 4.00
28 Ryan Zimmerman 5.00
29 Ryan Church 4.00
30 Matt Chico 4.00
31 Dmitri Young 4.00
32 Derrek Lee 6.00
33 Aramis Ramirez 5.00
34 Carlos Zambrano 5.00
35 Rich Hill 4.00
36 Alfonso Soriano 6.00
37 Kerry Wood 5.00
38 Ted Lilly 4.00
39 Ryan Theriot 4.00
40 Ken Griffey Jr. 15.00
41 Adam Dunn 5.00
42 Homer Bailey 4.00
43 Aaron Harang 4.00
44 Brandon Phillips 5.00
45 Josh Hamilton 5.00
46 Lance Berkman 5.00
47 Carlos Lee 5.00
48 Hunter Pence 5.00
49 Mark Loretta 4.00
50 Roy Oswalt 5.00
51 Prince Fielder 10.00
52 Ryan Braun 8.00
53 J.J. Hardy 4.00
54 Ben Sheets 5.00
55 Rickie Weeks 5.00
56 Corey Hart 5.00
57 Johnny Estrada 4.00
58 Jason Bay 4.00
59 Freddy Sanchez 4.00
60 Adam LaRoche 4.00
61 Ian Snell 4.00
62 Xavier Nady 4.00
63 Tom Gorzelanny 4.00
64 Scott Rolen 5.00
65 Albert Pujols 20.00
66 Jim Edmonds 4.00
67 Chris Duncan 4.00
68 Adam Wainwright 5.00
69 Brandon Webb 5.00
70 Orlando Hudson 4.00
71 Chris B. Young 5.00
72 Stephen Drew 5.00
73 Matt Holliday 6.00
74 Jeff Francis 4.00
75 Brad Hawpe 4.00
76 Todd Helton 5.00
77 Troy Tulowitzki 6.00
78 Russell Martin 5.00
79 Nomar Garciaparra 5.00
80 James Loney 5.00
81 Andre Ethier 4.00
82 Brad Penny 4.00
83 Rafael Furcal 5.00
84 Jeff Kent 5.00
85 Greg Maddux 10.00
86 Chris Young 5.00
87 Khalil Greene 4.00
88 Trevor Hoffman 4.00
89 Adrian Gonzalez 5.00
90 Jake Peavy 6.00
91 Noah Lowry 4.00
92 Omar Vizquel 4.00
93 Tim Lincecum 6.00
94 Matt Cain 5.00
95 Randy Winn 4.00
96 Miguel Tejada 5.00
97 Brian Roberts 5.00
98 Nicholas Markakis 5.00
99 Erik Bedard 5.00
100 Melvin Mora 4.00
101 David Ortiz 8.00
102 Manny Ramirez 6.00
103 Josh Beckett 6.00
104 Jonathan Papelbon 6.00
105 Curt Schilling 6.00
106 Daisuke Matsuzaka 10.00
107 Jason Varitek 4.00
108 Kevin Youkilis 4.00
109 Derek Jeter 20.00
110 Hideki Matsui 10.00
111 Alex Rodriguez 20.00
112 Johnny Damon 6.00
113 Robinson Cano 6.00
114 Jorge Posada 5.00
115 Mariano Rivera 5.00
116 Roger Clemens 12.00
117 Chien-Ming Wang 15.00
118 Carl Crawford 5.00
119 Delmon Young 5.00
120 B.J. Upton 5.00
121 Akinori Iwamura 5.00
122 Scott Kazmir 5.00
123 Alex Rios 5.00
124 Frank Thomas 8.00
125 Roy Halladay 5.00
126 Vernon Wells 5.00
127 Troy Glaus 5.00
128 Jeremy Accardo 4.00
129 A.J. Burnett 4.00
130 Paul Konerko 5.00
131 Jim Thome 5.00
132 Jermaine Dye 4.00
133 Mark Buehrle 4.00
134 Javier Vazquez 4.00
135 Grady Sizemore 5.00
136 Travis Hafner 5.00
137 Victor Martinez 5.00
138 C.C. Sabathia 5.00
139 Ryan Garko 4.00
140 Fausto Carmona 4.00
141 Justin Verlander 6.00
142 Jeremy Bonderman 4.00
143 Magglio Ordonez 5.00
144 Gary Sheffield 5.00
145 Carlos Guillen 5.00
146 Ivan Rodriguez 5.00
147 Curtis Granderson 5.00

148 Alex Gordon 8.00
149 Mark Teahen 4.00
150 Brian Bannister 4.00
151 Billy Butler 4.00
152 Johan Santana 8.00
153 Torii Hunter 5.00
154 Joe Mauer 5.00
155 Justin Morneau 5.00
156 Vladimir Guerrero 6.00
157 Chone Figgins 5.00
158 Jered Weaver 5.00
159 Kelvim Escobar 4.00
160 John Lackey 4.00
161 Danny Haren 5.00
162 Mike Piazza 6.00
163 Nick Swisher 5.00
164 Eric Chavez 4.00
165 Huston Street 4.00
166 Joe Blanton 4.00
167 Kenji Johjima 5.00
168 J.J. Putz 4.00
169 Felix Hernandez 6.00
170 Jose Guillen 4.00
171 Adrian Beltre 5.00
172 Ichiro Suzuki 15.00
173 Marlon Byrd 4.00
174 Hank Blalock 4.00
175 Michael Young 4.00
176 Ian Kinsler 5.00
177 Sammy Sosa 5.00
178 Kevin Millwood 4.00
179 Luis Aparicio 5.00
180 Johnny Bench 8.00
181 Yogi Berra 8.00
182 Lou Brock 8.00
183 Jim Bunning 5.00
184 Rod Carew 6.00
185 Orlando Cepeda 5.00
186 Bobby Doerr 5.00
187 Bob Feller 5.00
188 Dennis Eckersley 5.00
189 Carlton Fisk 5.00
190 Monte Irvin 5.00
191 Rollie Fingers 5.00
192 Al Kaline 8.00
193 Nolan Ryan 20.00
194 Mike Schmidt 10.00
195 Ryne Sandberg 10.00
196 Robin Yount 10.00
197 Brooks Robinson 8.00
198 Bill Mazeroski 5.00
199 Reggie Jackson 8.00
200 Babe Ruth 15.00
201 Ian Kennedy **RC** 25.00
202 Jonathan Albaladejo **RC** 10.00
203 Josh Anderson **(RC)** 8.00
204 Wladimir Balentien **(RC)** 10.00
205 Daric Barton **(RC)** 10.00
206 Jerry Blevins **RC** 10.00
207 Emilio Bonifacio **RC** 10.00
208 Lance Broadway **RC** 10.00
209 Clay Buchholz **(RC)** 35.00
210 Billy Buckner **(RC)** 10.00
212 Ross Detwiler **RC** 10.00
213 Harvey Garcia **(RC)** 10.00
214 Alberto Gonzalez **(RC)** 35.00
215 Ryan Hanigan **RC** 15.00
216 Kevin Hart **(RC)** 15.00
217 Luke Hochevar **RC** 30.00
218 Chin-Lung Hu **(RC)** 35.00
219 Rob Johnson **(RC)** 8.00
220 Brandon Jones **RC** 15.00
221 Joe Koshansky **(RC)** 10.00
222 Donny Lucy **(RC)** 8.00
223 Justin Maxwell **RC** 20.00
224 Jonathan Meloan **RC** 10.00
225 Luis Mendoza **(RC)** 8.00
226 Jose Morales **(RC)** 8.00
227 Nyjer Morgan **(RC)** 15.00
228 Bill Murphy **(RC)** 10.00
229 Josh Newman **RC** 15.00
230 Ross Ohlendorf **RC** 20.00
231 Troy Patton **(RC)** 15.00
232 Felipe Paulino **RC** 15.00
233 Steve Pearce **RC** 15.00
235 Clint Sammons **(RC)** 10.00
236 Bronson Sardinha **RC** 8.00
237 Chris Seddon **(RC)** 15.00
238 Seth Smith **(RC)** 10.00
239 J.R. Towles **RC** 20.00
240 Eugenio Velez **RC** 30.00
241 Joey Votto **(RC)** 20.00
242 Bill White **RC** 8.00

Gold

Gold (1-200): No Pricing
Production 5-15
Gold RC: 1-1.5X
Production 25-99
No RC pricing prod. 20 or less.

AKA Signatures

NM/M

Common Auto.:
Parallel: No Pricing
Production 1-5
AG Andres Galarraga 10.00
BM Bill Mazeroski/25 25.00
DJ Derek Jeter/25 150.00
DM Don Mattingly/25 60.00
FH Felix Hernandez/25 40.00
JB Jeremy Bonderman/25 25.00
JL John Lackey/25 20.00
JZ Joel Zumaya/25 20.00
KG Ken Griffey Jr./25 120.00
RJ Reggie Jackson/25 40.00
RS Ryne Sandberg/25 60.00
RZ Ryan Zimmerman/25 30.00
TH Travis Hafner/25 25.00
VG Vladimir Guerrero/25 50.00
WM Willie McCovey/25 40.00

Base Set Autograph Parallel

NM/M

Production 25 unless noted.
1 Chipper Jones 65.00
2 Andruw Jones 25.00
4 Mark Teixeira 40.00
8 Miguel Cabrera 35.00
12 Josh Willingham 15.00
13 Pedro Martinez 50.00
15 Carlos Beltran 30.00
17 Tom Glavine 40.00
20 John Maine 25.00
22 Cole Hamels 40.00
27 Aaron Rowand 20.00
28 Ryan Zimmerman 35.00
32 Derrek Lee 25.00
34 Carlos Zambrano 30.00
37 Kerry Wood 25.00
39 Ryan Theriot 25.00
40 Ken Griffey Jr. 100.00
41 Adam Dunn 30.00
42 Homer Bailey 20.00
47 Carlos Lee 20.00
48 Hunter Pence 35.00
50 Roy Oswalt 20.00
51 Prince Fielder 40.00
52 Ryan Braun 50.00
54 Ben Sheets 25.00
58 Jason Bay 20.00
60 Adam LaRoche 15.00
64 Scott Rolen 30.00
68 Adam Wainwright 40.00
69 Brandon Webb 25.00
71 Chris B. Young 35.00
72 Stephen Drew 15.00
73 Matt Holliday 25.00
74 Jeff Francis 20.00
77 Troy Tulowitzki 30.00
81 Andre Ethier 20.00
83 Rafael Furcal 25.00
87 Khalil Greene 25.00
90 Jake Peavy 25.00
94 Matt Cain 25.00
97 Brian Roberts 20.00
98 Nick Markakis 35.00
103 Josh Beckett 50.00
107 Jason Varitek 40.00
108 Kevin Youkilis 35.00
116 Roger Clemens 70.00
118 Carl Crawford 20.00
119 Delmon Young 25.00
120 B.J. Upton 25.00
121 Akinori Iwamura 25.00
124 Frank Thomas 60.00
125 Roy Halladay 30.00
126 Vernon Wells 20.00
131 Jim Thome 40.00
136 Travis Hafner 25.00
140 Fausto Carmona 25.00
141 Justin Verlander 30.00
142 Jeremy Bonderman 25.00
146 Ivan Rodriguez 35.00
147 Curtis Granderson 40.00
151 Billy Butler 30.00
152 Johan Santana 35.00
153 Torii Hunter 20.00
154 Joe Mauer 30.00
157 Chone Figgins 25.00
158 Jered Weaver 20.00
161 Danny Haren 20.00
163 Nick Swisher 20.00
165 Huston Street 20.00
179 Luis Aparicio 25.00
180 Johnny Bench 40.00
181 Yogi Berra 65.00
182 Lou Brock 35.00
184 Rod Carew 30.00
192 Al Kaline 40.00
194 Mike Schmidt 50.00
195 Ryne Sandberg 60.00
197 Brooks Robinson 50.00
198 Bill Mazeroski 40.00
199 Reggie Jackson 40.00

Bat Barrels

Production 1-6
No Pricing

Combos Memorabilia

NM/M

Common Duo: 15.00
Parallel 1: 1-1.5X
Production 25 Sets
Parallel 2: No Pricing
Production Five Sets
BF Prince Fielder, Ryan Braun/50 20.00
BY Robin Yount, Ryan Braun/50 25.00
CZ Ryan Zimmerman, Miguel Cabrera/50 15.00
FO David Ortiz, Prince Fielder/150 20.00
FV Carlton Fisk, Jason Varitek/50 15.00
GC Rod Carew, Tony Gwynn/50 25.00
GD Ken Griffey Jr., Adam Dunn/50 25.00
GJ Ken Griffey Jr., Derek Jeter/50 30.00
GM Pedro Martinez, Tom Glavine/50 20.00
GR Manny Ramirez, Vladimir Guerrero/50 20.00
HH Todd Helton, Matt Holliday/50 15.00
JH Andruw Jones, Torii Hunter/50 15.00
JR Cal Ripken Jr., Derek Jeter/50 35.00
LR Phil Rizzuto, Tony Lazzeri/50 50.00
MJ Thurman Munson, Reggie Jackson/50 35.00
MM Joe Mauer, Victor Martinez/50 15.00
MU Joe Morgan, Chase Utley/50 20.00
MY Stan Musial, Carl Yastrzemski/50 35.00
OH David Ortiz, Travis Hafner/50 20.00
OK Al Kaline, Magglio Ordonez/50 35.00
OR Manny Ramirez, David Ortiz/50 25.00
OY David Ortiz, Kevin Youkilis/50 20.00
PB Hunter Pence, Ryan Braun/50 20.00
PM Stan Musial, Albert Pujols/50 40.00
PO Albert Pujols, David Ortiz/50 25.00
PY Jake Peavy, Chris Young/50 15.00
RB Carlos Beltran, Jose Reyes/50 15.00
RC Jackie Robinson, Roy Campanella/50 50.00
RG Ken Griffey Jr., Cal Ripken Jr./50 40.00
RJ Derek Jeter, Hanley Ramirez/50 30.00
SC Johan Santana, Roger Clemens/50 20.00
SH Travis Hafner, Grady Sizemore/50 20.00
SM John Smoltz, Greg Maddux/50 20.00
TG Ken Griffey Jr., Frank Thomas/50 30.00
UH Chase Utley, Cole Hamels/50 30.00
VM Jason Varitek, Victor Martinez/50 15.00
VR Nolan Ryan, Justin Verlander/50 40.00
WH Chien-Ming Wang, Phil Hughes/50 30.00

Combos Patch

NM/M

Common Dual Patch: 20.00
Parallel 1: 1-1.5X
Production 25 Sets
Parallel 2: No Pricing
Production 10 Sets
BD Danny Haren, Ben Sheets/50 20.00
BP Johnny Bench, Albert Pujols/50 50.00
BR Cal Ripken Jr., Ryan Braun/50 75.00
BS Erik Bedard, C.C. Sabathia/50 20.00
BZ Jeremy Bonderman, Carlos Zambrano/50 20.00
CR Manny Ramirez, Miguel Cabrera/50 30.00
CV Carlton Fisk, Vladimir Guerrero/50 25.00
FG Jeff Francoeur, Alex Gordon/50 40.00
FM Joe Mauer, Jeff Francoeur/50 35.00
GR Ken Griffey Jr., Cal Ripken Jr./50 60.00
GY Tony Gwynn, Robin Yount/50 40.00
HG Alex Gordon, J.J. Hardy/50 30.00
HH Todd Helton, Matt Holliday/50 40.00
HM Andrew Miller, Cole Hamels/50 20.00
HR Felix Hernandez, Nolan Ryan/50 60.00
HW Cole Hamels, Dontrelle Willis/50 25.00
JD Adam Dunn, Reggie Jackson/50 30.00
JH Andruw Jones, Torii Hunter/50 20.00
JJ Joe Mauer, Jose Reyes/50 30.00
LC Noah Lowry, Matt Cain/50 20.00
LK Paul Konerko, Derrek Lee/50 30.00
LT Lance Berkman, Todd Helton/50 25.00
MB Jason Bay, Nicholas Markakis/50 30.00
MM Russell Martin, Gil Meche/50 20.00
OR Manny Ramirez, David Ortiz/50 40.00
PO Roy Oswalt, Jake Peavy/50 25.00
PR Tony Perez, Manny Ramirez/50 25.00
RI Brian Roberts, Akinori Iwamura/50 25.00
RJ James Loney, Russell Martin/50 25.00
RM Brian McCann, Aramis Ramirez/50 25.00
RO Manny Ramirez, Magglio Ordonez/50 25.00
RT Troy Tulowitzki, Hanley Ramirez/50 30.00
SB Curt Schilling, Jeremy Bonderman/50 20.00
SH Johan Santana, Cole Hamels/50 25.00
SJ C.C. Sabathia, Randy Johnson/50 25.00
TH Frank Thomas, Travis Hafner/50 40.00
TK Ken Griffey Jr., Torii Hunter/50 40.00
TT Travis Hafner, Torii Hunter/50 20.00
UU Dan Uggla, Chase Utley/50 20.00
UY Delmon Young, Chase Utley/50 25.00
VH Cole Hamels, Justin Verlander/50 30.00
VR Nolan Ryan, Justin Verlander/50 50.00
WJ Vernon Wells, Chipper Jones/50 25.00
YH J.J. Hardy, Robin Yount/50 30.00
ZJ Chipper Jones, Ryan Zimmerman/50 25.00
ZR Ryan Zimmerman, Jimmy Rollins/50 25.00

Emerging Stars Dual Autograph

NM/M

Common Dual Auto.: 20.00
Parallel: No Pricing
Production 1 or 15
BG Alex Gordon, Billy Butler/35 50.00
BH Corey Hart, Ryan Braun/35 80.00
BM Chad Billingsley, Jonathan Meloan/35 25.00
BP Jonathan Papelbon, Clay Buchholz/35 75.00
BV Homer Bailey, Joey Votto/35 30.00
BW Billy Butler, Brandon Wood/35 30.00
CL Noah Lowry, Matt Cain/35 30.00
CT Travis Buck, Corey Hart/35 25.00
FB Josh Fields, Lance Broadway/35 20.00
FO Jocko Fields, Jerry Owens/35 20.00
GH Alex Gordon, Luke Hochevar/35 50.00
GL Fred Lewis, Curtis Granderson/35 20.00
HB Homer Bailey, Phil Hughes/35 50.00
HK Cole Hamels, Scott Kazmir/35 40.00
HL James Loney, Chin-Lung Hu/35 40.00
HS Danny Haren, Huston Street/35 25.00
HV Josh Hamilton, Joey Votto/35 30.00
HW Rickie Weeks, Corey Hart/35 50.00
KB Kevin Kouzmanoff, Brandon Wood/35 20.00
KH Phil Hughes, Ian Kennedy/35 60.00
KU Howie Kendrick, Dan Uggla/35 25.00
KW Howie Kendrick, Jered Weaver/35 35.00
LE James Loney, Andre Ethier/35 25.00
LL James Loney, Andy LaRoche/35 35.00
MB John Maine, Chad Billingsley/35 25.00
MC John Maine, Matt Cain/35 25.00
ME Brian McCann, Yunel Escobar/35 40.00
MH Nicholas Markakis, Jeremy Hermida/35 30.00
ML James Loney, Russell Martin/35 40.00
MM Brian McCann, Russell Martin/35 30.00

MP Steve Pearce,
Nicholas Markakis/35 35.00
MS Jarrod Saltalamacchia,
Brian McCann/35 25.00
MT J.R. Towles,
Russell Martin/35 25.00
NJ Josh Hamilton,
Nicholas Markakis/35 35.00
PL Jon Lester,
Jonathan Papelbon/35 40.00
PZ Jonathan Papelbon,
Joel Zumaya/35 25.00
TA Garrett Atkins,
Troy Tulowitzki/35 30.00
TG Troy Tulowitzki,
Alex Gordon/35 60.00
UR Hanley Ramirez,
Dan Uggla/35 40.00
UY Delmon Young,
B.J. Upton/35 30.00
VH Danny Haren,
Justin Verlander/35 30.00

Emerging Stars Quad

No Pricing
Production 10 Sets
Parallel: No Pricing
Production 1 or 5

Emerging Stars Trio

NM/M

Common Trio Auto.: 30.00
Parallel: No Pricing
Production 1 or 5
BPW Hunter Pence, Billy Butler,
Brandon Wood/25 40.00
CBM John Maine, Matt Cain,
Chad Billingsley/25 30.00
GSB Kevin Slowey, Scott Baker,
Matt Garza/25 35.00
HBP Josh Hamilton, Travis Buck,
Felix Pie/25 30.00
HHG Tom Gorzelanny, Rich Hill,
Cole Hamels/25 40.00
KBH Clay Buchholz, Luke Hochevar,
Ian Kennedy/25 75.00
LEM James Loney, Andre Ethier,
Russell Martin/25 40.00
MHG John Maine, Phil Hughes,
Matt Garza/25 50.00
MHH Josh Hamilton,
Nicholas Markakis,
Jeremy Hermida/25 30.00
TAB Garrett Atkins, Jeff Baker,
Troy Tulowitzki/25 30.00
VBP Joey Votto, Steve Pearce,
Daric Barton/25
VPW Jonathan Papelbon,
Jered Weaver,
Justin Verlander/25 60.00

Foursome Memorabilia

NM/M

Common Quad: 25.00
Paralell: No Pricing
Production 4 or 15
BHFS Ben Sheets, Prince Fielder,
Corey Hart, Ryan Braun/25 40.00
BYGM Wade Boggs, Carl Yastrzemski,
Eddie Murray,
Tony Gwynn/25 40.00
CGBR Cal Ripken Jr., Wade Boggs,
Tony Gwynn, Rod Carew/25 60.00
CKMC Stan Musial, Rod Carew,
Roberto Clemente,
Al Kaline/25 75.00
DRMB Carlos Delgado, Carlos Beltran,
Pedro Martinez,
Jose Reyes/25 25.00
GBMP Ken Griffey Jr., Tony Perez,
Joe Morgan,
Johnny Bench/25 50.00
GTPJ Ken Griffey Jr., Albert Pujols,
Chipper Jones,
Frank Thomas/25 50.00
HHAT Todd Helton, Garrett Atkins,
Matt Holliday,
Troy Tulowitzki/25 35.00
CSCU Carl Crawford, B.J. Upton,
James Shields,
Akinori Iwamura/25 25.00
LRSZ Derrek Lee, Aramis Ramirez,
Alfonso Soriano,
Carlos Zambrano/25 50.00
MGCG Bob Gibson, Tom Glavine,
Greg Maddux,
Steve Carlton/25 40.00
MYRW Cal Ripken Jr., Dave Winfield,
Robin Yount,
Paul Molitor/25 80.00
PCPM Jim Palmer, Pedro Martinez,
Roger Clemens,
Gaylord Perry/25 40.00
SSRY Cal Ripken Jr., Robin Yount,
Ryne Sandberg,
Mike Schmidt/25 100.00
VHBS Josh Beckett, Danny Haren,
C.C. Sabathia,
Justin Verlander/25 30.00
WSGM Tom Glavine, John Smoltz,
Greg Maddux,
Brandon Webb/25 50.00

Legendary Remnants Triple

NM/M

Production 10-50
Parallel: No Pricing
Production 1-25
Die-Cut: No Pricing
Production 5-25
BR Babe Ruth/15
RC Roy Campanella/50 40.00
JD Joe DiMaggio/50 90.00
JR Jackie Robinson/50 60.00
LG Lou Gehrig/50 180.00
MO Mel Ott/50 75.00
RC Roberto Clemente/50 60.00
RM Roger Maris/50 40.00
WS Willie Stargell/50 30.00

Legendary Remnants Quad

Production 10-20
Parallel: No Pricing
Production 1-13

Logo Patch

Production One Set

Memorabilia Triple Autographs

No Pricing
Production 5 or 20

Memorabilia Triple

NM/M

Common Player: 15.00
Parallel: No Pricing
Production Three Sets
AG Alex Gordon/25 30.00
AI Akinori Iwamura/25 15.00
AP Albert Pujols/75 25.00
BE Johnny Bench/50 30.00
BM Bill Mazeroski/25 25.00
CA Rod Carew/25 20.00
CJ Chipper Jones/25 25.00
DJ Derek Jeter/75 30.00
DM Daisuke Matsuzaka/75 25.00
DO David Ortiz/50 15.00
GM Greg Maddux/50 25.00
GS Grady Sizemore/25 20.00
IR Ivan Rodriguez/25 15.00
JD Joe DiMaggio/75 100.00
JP Jonathan Papelbon/25 20.00
KG Ken Griffey Jr./50 25.00
MA Don Mattingly/50 20.00
MR Manny Ramirez/25 20.00
MS Mike Schmidt/50 15.00
NR Nolan Ryan/75 25.00
OS Ozzie Smith/75 25.00
PF Prince Fielder/25 20.00
PM Paul Molitor/25 15.00
RC Roger Clemens/25 20.00
RJ Reggie Jackson/75 15.00
SM Stan Musial/75 30.00
TS Tom Seaver/75 25.00
VG Vladimir Guerrero/25 20.00
WB Wade Boggs/50 10.00
WS Warren Spahn/75 25.00
AP2 Albert Pujols/75 20.00

Memorabilia Quad

NM/M

Common Player: 10.00
Auto Parallel: No Pricing
Production 10 Sets
Parallel: No Pricing
Production Four Sets
AS Alfonso Soriano/40 20.00
CC Chris Carpenter/40 15.00
CH Cole Hamels/40 15.00
CL Roger Clemens/40 20.00
CS Curt Schilling/40 15.00
CU Chase Utley/40 25.00
CW Chien-Ming Wang/40 40.00
CY Carl Yastrzemski/40 25.00
DJ Derek Jeter/40 35.00
DL Derrek Lee/40 15.00
DM Don Mattingly/40 25.00
DO David Ortiz/40 20.00
DP Dave Parker/40 15.00
DW Dontrelle Willis/40 10.00
EM Eddie Mathews/40 35.00
HP Hunter Pence/40 20.00
JM Joe Mauer/40 15.00
JR Jackie Robinson/40 75.00
JS Johan Santana/40 20.00
JV Justin Verlander/40 20.00
MA Russell Martin/40 20.00
MO Justin Morneau/40 15.00
MS Mike Schmidt/40 20.00
MT Mark Teixeira/40 20.00
NM Nicholas Markakis/40 25.00
NR Nolan Ryan/40 35.00
OR Magglio Ordonez/40 15.00
PF Prince Fielder/40 20.00
PH Phil Hughes/40 25.00
PW Pee Wee Reese/40 25.00
RB Ryan Braun/40 30.00
RC Roberto Clemente/40 100.00
RE Jose Reyes/40 25.00
RM Roger Maris/40 60.00
RY Robin Yount/40 30.00
SM Stan Musial/40 40.00
TP Tony Perez/40 25.00
VG Vladimir Guerrero/40 20.00
VM Victor Martinez/40 20.00
DO2 David Ortiz/40 20.00

Milestones

NM/M

Common Auto.: 25.00
Parallel: No Pricing
Production 1 or 5
AJ Andruw Jones/25 25.00
AR Aramis Ramirez/25 25.00
CG Curtis Granderson/25 40.00
FT Frank Thomas/25 65.00
IR Ivan Rodriguez/25 40.00
JT Jim Thome/25 50.00
KG Ken Griffey Jr./25 125.00
LB Lance Berkman/25 20.00
MT Miguel Tejada/25 25.00
PM Pedro Martinez/25 65.00
RB Ryan Braun/25 50.00
TG Tom Glavine/25 75.00
VG Vladimir Guerrero/25 50.00

Octographs

Production One Set
No Pricing

Patches

NM/M

Common Player: 10.00
Auto Parallel: No Pricing
Production 15 Sets
Die-Cut Parallel: 1.5X
Production 10-33
Parallel 1: 1.5X
Production 1-56
Parallel 2: 1X
Production 50 Sets
No pricing prod. 15 or less.
AI Akinori Iwamura/75 20.00
AJ Andruw Jones/75 10.00
AL Adam LaRoche/75 15.00
BR Brian Roberts/75 20.00
CB Carlos Beltran/75 15.00
CJ Chipper Jones/75 30.00
CR Cal Ripken Jr./75 50.00
CU Chase Utley/75 30.00
CW Chien-Ming Wang/75 50.00
DM Daisuke Matsuzaka/75 50.00
DO David Ortiz/75 40.00
DW Dontrelle Willis/75 15.00
EB Erik Bedard/75 20.00
FT Frank Thomas/75 35.00
GS Grady Sizemore/75 30.00
HA Travis Hafner/75 15.00
HK Hong-Chih Kuo/75 30.00
HP Hunter Pence/75 20.00
HR Hanley Ramirez/75 25.00
HU Torii Hunter/75 20.00
IR Ivan Rodriguez/75 20.00
JB Jeremy Bonderman/75 15.00
JF Jeff Francoeur/75 35.00
JM Justin Morneau/75 20.00
JP Jake Peavy/75 20.00
JR Jose Reyes/75 30.00
JS Johan Santana/75 20.00
JV Jason Varitek/75 20.00
MA Don Mattingly/75 35.00
MC Miguel Cabrera/75 30.00
MO Magglio Ordonez/75 15.00
NM Nicholas Markakis/75 25.00
NR Nolan Ryan/75 50.00
RB Ryan Braun/75 30.00
RJ Randy Johnson/75 25.00
RO Roy Oswalt/75 20.00
RW Rickie Weeks/75 20.00
RZ Ryan Zimmerman/75 15.00
SM Stan Musial/75 40.00
TG Tony Gwynn/75 30.00
TH Todd Helton/75 20.00
TL Tim Lincecum/75 20.00
TS Takashi Saito/75 20.00
VE Justin Verlander/75 20.00
WB Wade Boggs/75 25.00

Penmanship

NM/M

Common Auto.: 10.00
Parallel: No Pricing
Production 1-5
AK Al Kaline/50 30.00
BB Billy Butler/50 25.00
BE Johnny Bench/50 40.00
BF Bob Feller/20 30.00
BL Joe Blanton/50 10.00
BT Bobby Thomson/50 30.00
CB Chad Billingsley/50 15.00
CC Carl Crawford/50 20.00
CF Carlton Fisk/50 25.00
CH Cole Hamels/50 30.00
CJ Chipper Jones/50 75.00
CR Cal Ripken Jr./50 100.00
CW Chien-Ming Wang/50 140.00
FC Fausto Carmona/50 20.00
FH Felix Hernandez/50 30.00
FT Frank Thomas/50 60.00
GP Gaylord Perry/45 15.00
HK Howie Kendrick/50 15.00
HP Hunter Pence/50 25.00
IK Ian Kennedy/50 40.00
IR Ivan Rodriguez/50 40.00
JB Jeremy Bonderman/50 20.00
JL John Lackey/50 20.00
JM John Maine/50 20.00
JP Jim Palmer/50 20.00
JV Justin Verlander/50 35.00
JW Josh Willingham/50 10.00
KW Kerry Wood/50 20.00
LA Luis Aparicio/40 20.00
MS Mike Schmidt/50 40.00
NM Nicholas Markakis/50 30.00
NR Nolan Ryan/50 80.00
PA Jonathan Papelbon/50 30.00
RB Ryan Braun/50 40.00
RC Rod Carew/50 30.00
RH Ramon Hernandez/50 10.00
RM Russell Martin/50 30.00
RZ Ryan Zimmerman/50 20.00
TH Travis Hafner/50 15.00
TT Troy Tulowitzki/50 30.00
VM Victor Martinez/50 20.00

Playoff Premiere

No Pricing
Parallel: No Pricing
Production 1 or 5

Premier Pairings

NM/M

Common Dual Auto.: 20.00
BA Bronson Arroyo,
Homer Bailey/25 25.00
BG Alex Gordon,
Ryan Braun/25 65.00
BH Danny Haren,
Josh Beckett/25 50.00
BP Hunter Pence,
Ryan Braun/25 60.00
BZ Jeremy Bonderman,
Joel Zumaya/25 25.00
CH Steve Carlton,
Cole Hamels/25 60.00
CR Miguel Cabrera,
Hanley Ramirez/25 50.00
DT Don Mattingly,
Tino Martinez/25 120.00
FC Jeff Francis,
Manny Corpas/25 25.00
GM Ken Griffey Jr.,
Edgar Martinez/25 150.00
GO David Ortiz,
Vladimir Guerrero/25 75.00
HB Homer Bailey,
Phil Hughes/25 50.00
HM Cole Hamels,
Andrew Miller/25 30.00
JM Jason Bay,
Matt Holliday/25 30.00
KH Cole Hamels,
Scott Kazmir/25 35.00
LE James Loney,
Andre Ethier/25 35.00
LL Carlos Lee, Derrek Lee/25 40.00
LW John Lackey,
Jered Weaver/25 40.00
MB Jeremy Bonderman,
Andrew Miller/25 20.00
MH Andrew Miller, Rich Hill/25 25.00
ML James Loney,
Russell Martin/25 40.00
OM Roy Oswalt,
John Maine/25 25.00
PB Hunter Pence,
Jason Bay/25 30.00
PC Gaylord Perry,
Fausto Carmona/25 40.00
PL Jon Lester,
Jonathan Papelbon/25 60.00
RH Cal Ripken Jr.,
Chin-Lung Hu/25 180.00
RM Edgar Martinez,
Harold Reynolds/25 50.00
RS Cal Ripken Jr.,
Ryne Sandberg/25 200.00
RU Hanley Ramirez,
Dan Uggla/25 35.00
RV Russell Martin,
Victor Martinez/25 30.00
SR Ryne Sandberg,
Aramis Ramirez/25 80.00
TA Garrett Atkins,
Troy Tulowitzki/25 30.00
TR Miguel Tejada,
Brian Roberts/25 30.00
TT Frank Thomas,
Jim Thome/25 80.00
TV Travis Hafner,
Victor Martinez/25 25.00
UK Dan Uggla,
Howie Kendrick/25 20.00
ZB Ryan Zimmerman,
Ryan Braun/25 40.00

Premier Teams 3

NM/M

Common Trio: 20.00
Production 25 or 50
Parallels: 1-1.5X
Production 3-33
No pricing prod. 15 or less.
BFS Ben Sheets, Prince Fielder,
Ryan Braun/50 25.00
BHG Yovani Gallardo, J.J. Hardy,
Ryan Braun/25 30.00
BJH Adrian Beltre, Felix Hernandez,
Kenji Johjima/25 20.00

BMP Tony Perez, Joe Morgan, Johnny Bench/50 40.00
CMW Mike Mussina, Roger Clemens, Chien-Ming Wang/50 40.00
CPB Roberto Clemente, Dave Parker, Jason Bay/50 50.00
CRJ Roger Clemens, Derek Jeter, Mariano Rivera/50 40.00
CRR Jackie Robinson, Pee Wee Reese, Roy Campanella/50 60.00
CSM Michael Cuddyer, Johan Santana, Joe Mauer/20 15.00
DBR Carlos Delgado, Carlos Beltran, Jose Reyes/25 20.00
GBS Mike Sweeney, Alex Gordon, Billy Butler/25 20.00
GDH Ken Griffey Jr., Josh Hamilton, Adam Dunn/50 30.00
GFW Vladimir Guerrero, Chone Figgins, Jered Weaver/25 20.00
IUK Scott Kazmir, B.J. Upton, Akinori Iwamura/25 20.00
JJF Andruw Jones, Chipper Jones, Jeff Francoeur/50 30.00
JWD Randy Johnson, Brandon Webb, Stephen Drew/50 20.00
KBS Hong-Chih Kuo, Chad Billingsley, Takashi Saito/25 20.00
LME James Loney, Andre Ethier, Russell Martin/25 30.00
LRS Derrek Lee, Aramis Ramirez, Alfonso Soriano/25 30.00
LVZ Barry Zito, Omar Vizquel, Tim Lincecum/25 20.00
MJJ Don Mattingly, Derek Jeter, Reggie Jackson/50 50.00
MPB Stan Musial, Lou Brock, Albert Pujols/50 50.00
MSB Curt Schilling, Josh Beckett, Daisuke Matsuzaka/50 30.00
MSM Justin Morneau, Johan Mantana, Joe Mauer/25 20.00
OBY Wade Boggs, David Ortiz, Kevin Youkilis/50 25.00
ORS Gary Sheffield, Ivan Rodriguez, Magglio Ordonez/25 20.00
ORY Manny Ramirez, David Ortiz, Kevin Youkilis/25 25.00
PCR Chris Carpenter, Scott Rolen, Albert Pujols/50 30.00
PMH Greg Maddux, Trevor Hoffman, Jake Peavy/50 20.00
POB Lance Berkman, Roy Oswalt, Hunter Pence/25 20.00
RGD Babe Ruth, Joe DiMaggio, Lou Gehrig/20 450.00
RWU Dontrelle Willis, Hanley Ramirez, Dan Uggla/25 20.00
SBW Ryne Sandberg, Ernie Banks, Billy Williams/50 30.00
SCH Eric Chavez, Danny Haren, Nick Swisher/25 20.00
SMF John Smoltz, Brian McCann, Jeff Francoeur/25 40.00
SMH Travis Hafner, Victor Martinez, Grady Sizemore/25 20.00
TDK Jim Thome, Paul Konerko, Jermaine Dye/25 25.00
UHR Jimmy Rollins, Chase Utley, Cole Hamels/25 30.00
USH Mike Schmidt, Chase Utley, Cole Hamels/50 35.00
VBZ Jeremy Bonderman, Justin Verlander, Joel Zumaya/25 25.00
WHT Frank Thomas, Vernon Wells, Roy Halladay/25 20.00
YPH Trevor Hoffman, Jake Peavy, Chris Young/25 25.00

Quads Patch

No Pricing
Production 20 or less.
Parallel: No Pricing
Production 1-10

Quartet

No Pricing
Production 15 Sets

Remnants Quad

NM/M

Common Player: 10.00
Production 50 Sets
Auto Parallel: No Pricing
Production 15 Sets
Parallel 1: 1X
Production 25 Sets
Parallel 2: No Pricing
Production 10 Sets
Parallel 3: 1-1.5X
Production 2-77
No pricing prod. 15 or less.
AD Adam Dunn 15.00
BE Carlos Beltran 15.00
BR Brooks Robinson 20.00
BS Ben Sheets 10.00
CF Carlton Fisk 15.00
CH Cole Hamels 20.00
CL Roger Clemens 20.00
CR Cal Ripken Jr. 40.00
CS Curt Schilling 15.00
CW Chien-Ming Wang 30.00
DJ Derek Jeter 40.00
DL Derrek Lee 15.00
DM Don Mattingly 30.00
DO David Ortiz 15.00
FH Felix Hernandez 15.00
HK Hong-Chih Kuo 15.00
HR Hanley Ramirez 20.00
JB Johnny Bench 20.00
JH J.J. Hardy 10.00
JP Jake Peavy 15.00
JR Jim Rice 10.00
JS John Smoltz 15.00
KG Ken Griffey Jr. 25.00
MH Matt Holliday 15.00
NR Nolan Ryan 35.00
PF Prince Fielder 20.00
PR Phil Rizzuto 25.00
RC Rod Carew 15.00
RE Jose Reyes 20.00
RJ Reggie Jackson 20.00
RS Ryne Sandberg 25.00
RZ Ryan Zimmerman 15.00
SM Stan Musial 35.00
TG Tony Gwynn 20.00
TM Thurman Munson 35.00
TR Tim Raines 10.00
TS Tom Seaver 20.00
VG Vladimir Guerrero 15.00
WB Wade Boggs 15.00
NR2 Nolan Ryan 35.00

Remnants Triple Auto

NM/M

Production 5-25
AH Aaron Hill/25
AJ Andruw Jones/25 30.00
AP Albert Pujols/5
CA Chris Carpenter/25 40.00
CC Carl Crawford/25 25.00
CF Carlton Fisk/25 50.00
CJ Chipper Jones/25 80.00
CS Curt Schilling/25 50.00
CY Carl Yastrzemski/25 60.00
DJ Derek Jeter/25 150.00
DL Derrek Lee/25 50.00
DM Daisuke Matsuzaka/25 400.00
FH Felix Hernandez/25 60.00
HA Travis Hafner/25 30.00
JM Joe Mauer/25 40.00
KG Ken Griffey Jr./25 120.00
MA Don Mattingly/25 100.00
MC Miguel Cabrera/25 40.00
MS Mike Schmidt/25 60.00
MT Mark Teixeira/25 30.00
NR Nolan Ryan/25 80.00
PA Jonathan Papelbon/25 60.00
PF Prince Fielder/25 40.00
RH Roy Halladay/25 40.00
RJ Reggie Jackson/25 50.00
RY Robin Yount/25 60.00
TR Tim Raines/25 50.00
WB Wade Boggs/25 40.00

Remnants Triple

NM/M

Common Player: 10.00
Parallel: 1X
Production 25-75
Parallel 2: No Pricing
Production 1-25
AJ Andruw Jones/25 10.00
AP Albert Pujols/75 25.00
CF Carlton Fisk/25 15.00
CY Carl Yastrzemski/50 20.00
DJ Derek Jeter/75 30.00
DM Daisuke Matsuzaka/75 25.00
DO David Ortiz/50 15.00
HK Hong-Chih Kuo/25 15.00
JB Josh Beckett/25 20.00
KG Ken Griffey Jr./50 25.00
MA Don Mattingly/25 25.00
MR Manny Ramirez/25 15.00
MS Mike Schmidt/50 15.00
NR Nolan Ryan/75 25.00
PA Jonathan Papelbon/25 20.00
PO Jorge Posada/25 10.00
RJ Reggie Jackson/75 15.00
RY Robin Yount/50 15.00
VG Vladimir Guerrero/25 15.00
WB Wade Boggs/50 15.00

Remnants 5

NM/M

Production 10-25
Parallel: No Pricing
Production 1 or 10
CH Cole Hamels/25 25.00
CJ Chipper Jones/25 40.00
CU Chase Utley/25 35.00
CY Carl Yastrzemski/25 50.00
DJ Derek Jeter/25 60.00
DM Daisuke Matsuzaka/25 50.00
DO David Ortiz/25 30.00
FH Felix Hernandez/25 30.00
GS Grady Sizemore/25 30.00
HK Howie Kendrick/25 20.00
HO Rogers Hornsby/25 140.00
JB Johnny Bench/25 40.00
JM Joe Mauer/25 25.00
JP Jake Peavy/25 20.00
JR Jimmy Rollins/25 40.00
JT Jim Thome/25 25.00
KG Ken Griffey Jr./25 50.00
LB Lou Brock/25 35.00
MA Don Mattingly/25 50.00
MC Miguel Cabrera/25 35.00
MS Mike Schmidt/25 50.00
NR Nolan Ryan/25 60.00
PA Jonathan Papelbon/25 30.00
PO Jorge Posada/25 25.00
PW Pee Wee Reese/25 30.00
RC Roger Clemens/25 40.00
RM Roger Maris/25 65.00
RY Robin Yount/25 50.00
SC Steve Carlton/25 30.00
SM Stan Musial/25 50.00
TG Tony Gwynn/25 35.00
TH Torii Hunter/25 25.00
WB Wade Boggs/25 25.00
CU2 Chase Utley/25 35.00
DJ2 Derek Jeter/25 60.00
DJ3 Derek Jeter/25 60.00
DO2 David Ortiz/25 30.00

Signature Premier

NM/M

Common Auto.: 10.00
AE Andre Ethier/45 15.00
AG Adrian Gonzalez/45 15.00
AI Akinori Iwamura/45 25.00
AM Andrew Miller/45 15.00
AR Aramis Ramirez/45 25.00
BB Billy Buckner/45 10.00
BE Johnny Bench/45 35.00
BH Bill Hall/25 20.00
BI Chad Billingsley/45 15.00
BJ B.J. Upton/45 20.00
BM Brian McCann/45 25.00
BO Jeremy Bonderman/45 15.00
BS Bronson Sardinha/45 10.00
BU Billy Butler/45 25.00
CA Matt Cain/45 20.00
CB Clay Buchholz/45 35.00
CC Chris Carpenter/45 25.00
CF Carlton Fisk/45 35.00
CR Cal Ripken Jr./45 125.00
DH Danny Haren/45 15.00
DL Derrek Lee/45 30.00
DM Don Mattingly/45 50.00
DU Dan Uggla/25 15.00
EB Ernie Banks/37 50.00
EM Edgar Martinez/45 30.00
FC Fausto Carmona/45 25.00
FP Felix Pie/25 15.00
GA Garret Anderson/45 15.00
GO Alex Gordon/45 40.00
GP Gaylord Perry/45 15.00
HK Howie Kendrick/45 15.00
HR Harold Reynolds/45 15.00
HU Chin-Lung Hu/45 40.00
JB Jim Bunning/45 25.00
JL John Lackey/45 20.00
JM John Maine/45 25.00
JP Jim Palmer/45 20.00
JT J.R. Towles/45 20.00
JV Joey Votto/45 25.00
JW Josh Willingham/45 10.00
JZ Joel Zumaya/45 10.00
KE Ian Kennedy/45 40.00
KI Ian Kinsler/45 20.00
KY Kevin Youkilis/45 30.00
LA Luis Aparicio/45 20.00
LE Jon Lester/45 25.00
LH Luke Hochevar/45 20.00
MS Mike Schmidt/45 40.00
MT Miguel Tejada/45 20.00
MU Stan Musial/45 70.00
NL Noah Lowry/45 10.00
NM Nick Markakis/45 30.00
NR Nolan Ryan/45 80.00
NS Nick Swisher/45 15.00
OH Ross Ohlendorf/45 20.00
OW Micah Owings/45 20.00
PF Prince Fielder/45 30.00
PH Phil Hughes/45 40.00
PM Pedro Martinez/45 50.00
RB Ryan Braun/45 40.00
RC Rod Carew/45 25.00
RD Ross Detwiler/45 10.00
RH Rich Hill/45 20.00
RI Jim Rice/20 25.00
RJ Reggie Jackson/45 40.00
RO Roger Clemens/45 60.00
RS Ron Santo/25 60.00
RT Ryan Theriot/45 30.00
RY Ryne Sandberg/45 50.00
SA Jarrod Saltalamacchia/45 15.00
SC Steve Carlton/25 30.00
SD Stephen Drew/45 20.00
SK Scott Kazmir/45 20.00
TB Travis Buck/45 15.00
TG Tony Gwynn/45 40.00
TH Travis Hafner/45 20.00
TP Tony Perez/45 25.00
WB Wladimir Balentien/45 10.00
WF Whitey Ford/45 50.00
YF Yunel Escobar/45 25.00

Significant Six

No Pricing
Production 10 Sets

Significant Stars

NM/M

Production 20 unless noted.
BR Johnny Bench, Ivan Rodriguez 100.00
BW Josh Beckett, Chien-Ming Wang 200.00
CB Jack Cust, Joe Blanton
CG Steve Carlton, Tom Glavine 50.00
FD Adam Dunn, Prince Fielder 40.00
GJ Ken Griffey Jr., Reggie Jackson 150.00
HC Felix Hernandez, Fausto Carmona 60.00
JW Derek Jeter, Chien-Ming Wang 300.00
MH Travis Hafner, Victor Martinez 30.00
MM Victor Martinez, Russell Martin 35.00
RF Rafael Furcal, Hanley Ramirez/15 30.00
RG Cal Ripken Jr., Tony Gwynn 160.00
SC Miguel Cabrera, Mike Schmidt 60.00
SM Russell Martin, Takashi Saito 40.00
SP Jonathan Papelbon, Takashi Saito 40.00
TF Mark Teixeira, Prince Fielder 40.00
TR Miguel Tejada, Hanley Ramirez 35.00
WH Dontrelle Willis, Cole Hamels 30.00
YM Stan Musial, Carl Yastrzemski 80.00

Stitchings

NM/M

Common Player: 15.00
Production 75 Sets
Parallel 1: 1-1.5X
Production 25 Sets
Parallels 2 & 3: No Pricing
Production 1-20:
Variation: 1X
Production 50 Sets
Auto. Parallel: No Pricing
Production 25 Sets
AG Alex Gordon 20.00
AK Al Kaline 30.00
AP Albert Pujols 25.00
AR Alex Rodriguez 30.00
AS Alfonso Soriano 20.00
BD Bobby Doerr 20.00
BE Johnny Bench 20.00
BF Bob Feller 35.00
BG Bob Gibson 20.00
BM Bill Mazeroski 20.00
BR Babe Ruth 40.00
CA Miguel Cabrera 20.00
CB Craig Biggio 15.00
CF Carlton Fisk 15.00
CJ Chipper Jones 20.00
CR Cal Ripken Jr. 40.00
CS Rod Carew, Tom Seaver 20.00
CU Chase Utley 25.00
CW Chien-Ming Wang 30.00
CY Carl Yastrzemski 20.00
DJ Derek Jeter 30.00
DL Derrek Lee 20.00
DM Daisuke Matsuzaka 25.00
DY Delmon Young 15.00
EM Eddie Murray 20.00
FA Nellie Fox, Luis Aparicio 20.00
FH Felix Hernandez 20.00
FJ Fergie Jenkins 20.00
FT Frank Thomas 25.00
GR Babe Ruth, Lou Gehrig 30.00
GS Grady Sizemore 15.00
GW Tony Gwynn 20.00
HA Travis Hafner 15.00
HP Hunter Pence 15.00
HR Hanley Ramirez 20.00
HU Torii Hunter 15.00
JB Jason Bay 15.00
JD Joe DiMaggio 25.00
JE Jim Edmonds 15.00
JH Josh Hamilton 20.00
JM Joe Mauer 15.00
JO Jonathan Papelbon 20.00
JP Jake Peavy 15.00
JR Jackie Robinson, Roy Campanella 20.00
JS Johan Santana 20.00
JU Justin Morneau 15.00
JV Justin Verlander 20.00
JZ Joel Zumaya 15.00
KG Ken Griffey Jr. 25.00
KW Kerry Wood 15.00
LA Luis Aparicio 15.00
LB Lou Brock 15.00
LI Tim Lincecum 20.00
MA Juan Marichal 20.00
MC Brian McCann 15.00
MH Matt Holliday 20.00
MI Monte Irvin 20.00
MJ Derek Jeter, Hideki Matsui 30.00
MO Joe Morgan 20.00
MP Mike Piazza 20.00
MR Manny Ramirez 20.00
MS Mike Schmidt 20.00
NR Nolan Ryan 30.00
OC Orlando Cepeda 15.00
OM Daisuke Matsuzaka, Hideki Okajima 25.00

OR	Manny Ramirez, David Ortiz	20.00
PA	Jim Palmer	15.00
PF	Prince Fielder	20.00
PH	Phil Hughes	20.00
PN	Phil Niekro	15.00
RA	Richie Ashburn	20.00
RB	Ryan Braun	20.00
RC	Rod Carew	20.00
RF	Rollie Fingers	15.00
RH	Roy Halladay	15.00
RI	Mariano Rivera	25.00
RJ	Reggie Jackson	15.00
RK	Ralph Kiner	15.00
RM	Russell Martin	15.00
RO	Brooks Robinson	20.00
RS	Ryne Sandberg	20.00
RY	Ryan Howard	20.00
RZ	Ryan Zimmerman	15.00
SJ	Kenji Johjima	15.00
SJ	Ichiro Suzuki	20.00
SS	Sammy Sosa	20.00
SV	Shane Victorino	15.00
TG	Tom Glavine	20.00
TH	Trevor Hoffman	15.00
TL	Tommy Lasorda	20.00
TS	Tom Seaver	15.00
TT	Troy Tulowitzki	15.00
TW	Ted Williams	
VG	Vladimir Guerrero	15.00
VM	Victor Martinez	15.00
WM	Willie McCovey	20.00
FT2	Frank Thomas	20.00
KG2	Ken Griffey Jr.	25.00
KG3	Ken Griffey Jr.	25.00
MH2	Matt Holliday	15.00

Stitchings Cut Signature

Production One Set
No Pricing

Swatches

NM/M

Common Player: 10.00
Production 50 Sets
Die-Cut: 1.5X
Production 20 Sets
Auto. Parallel: No Pricing
Production 3-10
Parallels: 1-1.5X
Production 1-55
No pricing prod. 15 or less.

AP	Albert Pujols	25.00
AR	Aramis Ramirez	
AS	Alfonso Soriano	20.00
BR	Brian Roberts	15.00
BS	Ben Sheets	15.00
CD	Carlos Delgado	10.00
CH	Cole Hamels	15.00
CS	C.C. Sabathia	15.00
CY	Carl Yastrzemski	20.00
CZ	Carlos Zambrano	15.00
DH	Danny Haren	10.00
DL	Derrek Lee	15.00
EM	Eddie Murray	15.00
FH	Felix Hernandez	20.00
FS	Freddy Sanchez	10.00
GM	Greg Maddux	25.00
GP	Gaylord Perry	20.00
GS	Grady Sizemore	20.00
HK	Howie Kendrick	15.00
JB	Jason Bay	15.00
JM	Joe Mauer	15.00
JS	John Smoltz	15.00
JT	Jim Thome	15.00
KG	Ken Griffey Jr.	25.00
KI	Harmon Killebrew	20.00
KW	Kerry Wood	15.00
LB	Lance Berkman	15.00
MO	Joe Morgan	15.00
MR	Manny Ramirez	20.00
MS	Mike Schmidt	25.00
MT	Miguel Tejada	15.00
NM	Nick Markakis	20.00
NS	Nick Swisher	15.00
OR	Magglio Ordonez	15.00
PM	Pedro Martinez	20.00
RS	Ryne Sandberg	30.00
RY	Robin Yount	30.00
SC	Curt Schilling	15.00
TG	Tom Glavine	20.00
TH	Trevor Hoffman	15.00
VG	Vladimir Guerrero	20.00
VM	Victor Martinez	
VW	Vernon Wells	15.00

The Premier Card

No Pricing
Production 3 Sets

Trios

NM/M

Production 20 Sets

BGZ	Ben Gordon, Ryan Braun, Ryan Zimmerman	100.00
BHP	Hunter Pence, Matt Holliday, Jason Bay	50.00
BTP	Troy Tulowitzki, Hunter Pence, Ryan Braun	100.00
FBH	Bill Hall, Prince Fielder, Ryan Braun	120.00
GJG	Ken Griffey Jr., Derek Jeter, Vladimir Guerrero	300.00
HAF	Jeff Francis, Garrett Atkins, Matt Holliday	40.00
HMC	Travis Hafner, Victor Martinez, Fausto Carmona	75.00
HOB	Homer Bailey, Phil Hughes, Micah Owings	75.00
JCC	Carl Crawford, Andruw Jones, Coco Crisp	40.00
LWF	John Lackey, Chone Figgins, Jered Weaver	65.00
PNZ	Joe Nathan, Jonathan Papelbon, Joel Zumaya	40.00
TRH	Miguel Tejada, Chin-Lung Hu, Hanley Ramirez	70.00
TTH	Frank Thomas, Travis Hafner, Jim Thome	100.00

Trios Memorabilia

NM/M

Common Trio: 15.00
Production 50 unless noted.
Parallels: 1-1.5X
Production 3-33
No pricing prod. 15 or less.

BFB	Johnny Bench, Carlton Fisk, Yogi Berra	35.00
BPG	Ken Griffey Jr., Albert Pujols, Jason Bay	30.00
BRD	Carlos Delgado, Carlos Beltran, Jose Reyes	20.00
BZJ	Chipper Jones, Ryan Zimmerman, Ryan Braun	20.00
CMM	Michael Cuddyer, Justin Morneau, Joe Mauer	15.00
DOF	Adam Dunn, David Ortiz, Prince Fielder	25.00
GTP	Ken Griffey Jr., Albert Pujols, Frank Thomas	35.00
GWK	Vladimir Guerrero, Howie Kendrick, Jered Weaver	15.00
HAT	Garrett Atkins, Matt Holliday, Troy Tulowitzki	20.00
HMS	Travis Hafner, Victor Martinez, Grady Sizemore	15.00
HSS	Danny Haren, Huston Street, Nick Swisher	15.00
JFS	Chipper Jones, John Smoltz, Jeff Francoeur	35.00
JTR	Troy Tulowitzki, Derek Jeter, Hanley Ramirez	25.00
JWP	Andy Pettitte, Derek Jeter, Chien-Ming Wang	40.00
LRS	Derrek Lee, Aramis Ramirez, Alfonso Soriano	25.00
MCG	Tom Glavine, Roger Clemens, Greg Maddux	25.00
MMS	Justin Morneau, Johan Santana, Joe Mauer	20.00
ORY	Manny Ramirez, David Ortiz, Kevin Youkilis	25.00
OVB	Magglio Ordonez, Jeremy Bonderman, Justin Verlander	20.00
PBO	Lance Berkman, Roy Oswalt, Hunter Pence	20.00
PLM	Albert Pujols, Justin Morneau, Derrek Lee	25.00
RCS	Jose Reyes, Grady Sizemore, Carl Crawford	20.00
RDM	Babe Ruth, Joe DiMaggio, Roger Maris/25	350.00
ROF	Jimmie Foxx, Babe Ruth, Mel Ott	
RPV	Manny Ramirez, Jason Varitek, Jonathan Papelbon	25.00
RSB	Wade Boggs, Brooks Robinson, Mike Schmidt	30.00
SRB	Cal Ripken Jr., Wade Boggs, Mike Schmidt	40.00
SWB	Ryne Sandberg, Ernie Banks, Billy Williams	30.00
TOT	David Ortiz, Frank Thomas, Jim Thome	25.00
TWH	Frank Thomas, Vernon Wells, Roy Halladay	20.00
UHR	Jimmy Rollins, Chase Utley, Cole Hamels	25.00
URU	Brian Roberts, Chase Utley, Dan Uggla	15.00
YMC	Stan Musial, Carl Yastrzemski, Rod Carew	30.00

Trios Patch

NM/M

Common Trio: 30.00
Production 30 Sets
Parallels: No Pricing
Production 1-15

AER	Rick Ankiel, Jim Edmonds, Scott Rolen	35.00
BNS	Xavier Nady, Freddy Sanchez, Jason Bay	30.00
BPG	Jason Bay, Albert Pujols, Ken Griffey Jr.	60.00
CRS	Manny Ramirez, Grady Sizemore, Miguel Cabrera	40.00
DZV	Barry Zito, Omar Vizquel, Ray Durham	30.00
GKW	Vladimir Guerrero, Howie Kendrick, Jered Weaver	40.00
JCZ	Chipper Jones, Eric Chavez, Ryan Zimmerman	50.00
JJF	Andruw Jones, Chipper Jones, Jeff Francoeur	60.00
JTR	Troy Tulowitzki, Derek Jeter, Hanley Ramirez	70.00
LMS	James Loney, Russell Martin, Takashi Saito	40.00
LRS	Derrek Lee, Aramis Ramirez, Alfonso Soriano	40.00
MMM	Joe Mauer, Russell Martin, Victor Martinez	30.00
MMR	Brian McCann, Russell Martin, Ivan Rodriguez	30.00
MWM	Pedro Martinez, Billy Wagner, John Maine	40.00
ORY	Manny Ramirez, David Ortiz, Kevin Youkilis	60.00
PRB	Manny Ramirez, Josh Beckett, Jonathan Papelbon	50.00
SCM	Tom Seaver, Greg Maddux, Steve Carlton	40.00
SHC	Eric Chavez, Danny Haren, Nick Swisher	30.00
SZB	Curt Schilling, Carlos Zambrano, Jeremy Bonderman	40.00
TKB	Jim Thome, Paul Konerko, Mark Buehrle	40.00
UHR	Jimmy Rollins, Chase Utley, Cole Hamels	40.00
UUK	Jeff Kent, Chase Utley, Dan Uggla	30.00

2008 UD Spectrum

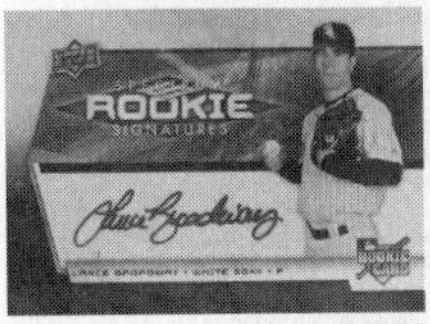

NM/M

Common Player (1-100): .25
Common RC Auto. (101-145): 8.00
Hobby Pack (5): 7.00
Hobby Box (20): 125.00

1	Chris Young	.50
2	Brandon Webb	.50
3	Eric Byrnes	.40
4	John Smoltz	.50
5	Chipper Jones	.75
6	Jeff Francoeur	.50
7	Mark Teixeira	.50
8	Brian Roberts	.40
9	Erik Bedard	.25
10	Miguel Tejada	.50
11	Nicholas Markakis	.50
12	David Ortiz	.75
13	Daisuke Matsuzaka	1.50
14	Manny Ramirez	.75
15	Jonathan Papelbon	.50
16	Josh Beckett	.50
17	Alfonso Soriano	.50
18	Carlos Zambrano	.40
19	Derrek Lee	.50
20	Aramis Ramirez	.40
21	Paul Konerko	.40
22	Jermaine Dye	.25
23	Jim Thome	.50
24	Ken Griffey Jr.	1.50
25	Brandon Phillips	.40
26	Adam Dunn	.50
27	Grady Sizemore	.75
28	Fausto Carmona	.40
29	Victor Martinez	.40
30	Travis Hafner	.40
31	Matt Holliday	.50
32	Troy Tulowitzki	.50
33	Todd Helton	.50
34	Magglio Ordonez	.40
35	Justin Verlander	.50
36	Gary Sheffield	.50
37	Miguel Cabrera	.75
38	Hanley Ramirez	.75
39	Dan Uggla	.25
40	Carlos Lee	.40
41	Roy Oswalt	.40
42	Lance Berkman	.40
43	Hunter Pence	.50
44	Alex Gordon	.50
45	David DeJesus	.25
46	Vladimir Guerrero	.75
47	Kelvim Escobar	.25
48	Chone Figgins	.40
49	Brad Penny	.25
50	Takashi Saito	.25
51	Russell Martin	.40
52	Prince Fielder	1.00
53	Ryan Braun	1.00
54	J.J. Hardy	.25
55	Johan Santana	.75
56	Justin Morneau	.40
57	Torii Hunter	.40
58	Joe Mauer	.40
59	Carlos Beltran	.50
60	David Wright	1.00
61	Carlos Delgado	.40
62	Jose Reyes	1.00
63	Derek Jeter	2.00
64	Alex Rodriguez	2.00
65	Robinson Cano	.50
66	Hideki Matsui	1.00
67	Mariano Rivera	.50
68	Danny Haren	.40
69	Nick Swisher	.40
70	Eric Chavez	.25
71	Jimmy Rollins	.50
72	Ryan Howard	.75
73	Cole Hamels	.50
74	Chase Utley	.75
75	Freddy Sanchez	.25
76	Jason Bay	.40
77	Ian Snell	.25
78	Greg Maddux	1.00
79	Jake Peavy	.40
80	Chris Young	.40
81	Barry Zito	.25
82	Tim Lincecum	.50
83	Omar Vizquel	.25
84	Felix Hernandez	.50
85	Ichiro Suzuki	1.50
86	Richie Sexson	.40
87	Albert Pujols	2.00
88	Scott Rolen	.50
89	Chris Carpenter	.40
90	Delmon Young	.40
91	Carl Crawford	.40
92	B.J. Upton	.40
93	Michael Young	.25
94	Hank Blalock	.25
95	Sammy Sosa	.50
96	Roy Halladay	.40
97	Alex Rios	.40
98	Vernon Wells	.25
99	Ryan Zimmerman	.40
100	Dmitri Young	.25
101	Alberto Gonzalez/Auto. **(RC)**	25.00
102	Bill Murphy/Auto. **(RC)**	10.00
103	Bill White/Auto. **RC**	8.00
104	Billy Buckner/Auto. **(RC)**	8.00
105	Brandon Jones/Auto. **RC**	10.00
106	Bronson Sardinha/Auto. **(RC)**	8.00
107	Chin-Lung Hu/Auto. **(RC)**	25.00
108	Chris Seddon/Auto. **(RC)**	8.00
109	Clay Buchholz/Auto. **(RC)**	30.00
110	Clint Sammons/Auto. **(RC)**	8.00
111	Daric Barton/Auto. **(RC)**	15.00
112	David Davidson/Auto. **RC**	10.00
113	Donny Lucy/Auto. **(RC)**	8.00
114	Emilio Bonifacio/Auto. **RC**	8.00
115	Eugenio Velez/Auto. **RC**	15.00
117	Harvey Garcia/Auto. **(RC)**	8.00
118	Ian Kennedy/Auto. **RC**	30.00
119	J.R. Towles/Auto. **RC**	15.00
121	Jerry Blevins/Auto. **RC**	10.00
122	Joe Koshansky/Auto. **(RC)**	10.00
123	Joey Votto/Auto. **(RC)**	20.00
124	Jonathan Albaladejo/Auto. **RC**	10.00
125	Jonathan Meloan/Auto. **RC**	10.00
126	Jose Morales/Auto. **(RC)**	10.00
127	Josh Anderson/Auto. **(RC)**	10.00
128	Josh Newman/Auto. **RC**	8.00
129	Justin Maxwell/Auto. **RC**	15.00
130	Justin Ruggiano/Auto. **RC**	8.00
131	Kevin Hart/Auto. **(RC)**	15.00
132	Lance Broadway/Auto. **RC**	10.00
133	Luis Mendoza/Auto. **(RC)**	10.00
134	Luke Hochevar/Auto. **RC**	20.00
135	Nyjer Morgan/Auto. **(RC)**	8.00
136	Rob Johnson/Auto. **(RC)**	8.00
137	Ross Detwiler/Auto. **RC**	15.00
138	Ross Ohlendorf/Auto. **RC**	15.00
139	Ryan Hanigan/Auto. **RC**	10.00
140	Seth Smith/Auto. **(RC)**	8.00
141	Steve Pearce/Auto. **RC**	15.00
142	Troy Patton/Auto. **(RC)**	15.00
143	Wladimir Balentien/Auto. **(RC)**	10.00
144	Colt Morton/Auto. **RC**	10.00
145	Carlos Muniz/Auto. **RC**	

Blue

Blue (1-100): 10-15X
Production 25 Sets

Gold

No Pricing
Production One Set

Green

Green (1-100): 3-6X
Production 199 Sets

Orange

Orange (1-100): 2-3X
Production 399 Sets

Red

Red (1-100): 4-8X
Production 99 Sets

RC Autos Die-Cut

No Pricing
Production 10 Sets

Buyback Signatures

NM/M

Production 2-50

JR1	Jose Reyes/70	40.00
KG1	Ken Griffey Jr./50	100.00
KG2	Ken Griffey Jr./50	100.00

KG3	Ken Griffey Jr./49	100.00
KG4	Ken Griffey Jr./50	100.00
KG5	Ken Griffey Jr./49	100.00
KG6	Ken Griffey Jr./50	100.00
KG7	Ken Griffey Jr./50	100.00
KG8	Ken Griffey Jr./50	100.00
KG9	Ken Griffey Jr./49	100.00
RA3	Roberto Alomar/50	25.00
RA4	Roberto Alomar/25	25.00
RA5	Roberto Alomar/30	25.00
RA6	Roberto Alomar/50	25.00

Derek Jeter Retrospectrum

	NM/M
Common Jeter (1-100):	5.00
Red:	2X
Production 99 Sets	
Autos:	No Pricing
Production Two Sets	

Retrospectrum Swatches

	NM/M
Common Player:	4.00
Production 99 Sets	
Parallel:	1-1.5X
Production 45 Sets	
Patch:	1.5-2X
Production 25 Sets	
AK	Adam Kennedy	4.00
AP	Albert Pujols	15.00
DJ	Derek Jeter	20.00
JE	Johnny Estrada	4.00
KM	Kevin Millwood	4.00
LH	Livan Hernandez	4.00
RK	Ryan Klesko	4.00
AB	Aaron Boone	4.00
AG	Adrian Gonzalez	6.00
AH	Aubrey Huff	4.00
AR	A.J. Burnett	4.00
AK	Austin Kearns	4.00
AL	Adam LaRoche	4.00
AP	Andy Pettitte	6.00
AR	Aaron Rowand	4.00
AS	Alfonso Soriano	8.00
BA	Bobby Abreu	6.00
BC	Bartolo Colon	4.00
BE	Adrian Beltre	6.00
BG	Brian Giles	4.00
BZ	Barry Zito	4.00
CA	Sean Casey	4.00
CC	Coco Crisp	4.00
CD	Carlos Delgado	6.00
CL	Carlos Lee	6.00
CY	Chris Young	4.00
DW	David Wells	4.00
EG	Eric Gagne	4.00
ER	Edgar Renteria	4.00
FG	Freddy Garcia	4.00
FT	Frank Thomas	8.00
GM	Greg Maddux	10.00
GS	Gary Sheffield	6.00
IR	Ivan Rodriguez	6.00
JB	Josh Barfield	4.00
JD	J.D. Drew	4.00
JJ	Jacque Jones	4.00
JO	Josh Beckett	8.00
JS	Jason Schmidt	4.00
JT	Jim Thome	6.00
LG	Luis Gonzalez	4.00
MA	Moises Alou	6.00
ME	Morgan Ensberg	4.00
MG	Marcus Giles	4.00
ML	Mark Loretta	4.00
MP	Mike Piazza	10.00
MT	Mark Teixeira	8.00
OV	Omar Vizquel	4.00
RF	Rafael Furcal	4.00
RJ	Randy Johnson	8.00
SS	Shannon Stewart	4.00
TI	Tadahito Iguchi	4.00
WT	Willy Taveras	4.00

Spectrum of Stars Signatures

	NM/M
Common Auto.:	8.00
Die-cuts:	1.5X
Production 25 Sets	
AP	A.J. Pero	8.00
BP	Butch Patrick	30.00
CM	Christopher McDonald	25.00
DA	Taylor Dayne	35.00

STEVEN SWEET
Musician

DD	Don Dokken	15.00
EM	Erin Moran	25.00
EO	Eddie Ojeda	8.00
ER	Eric Roberts	20.00
ET	Erik Turner	8.00
FS	Frank Stallone	15.00
HW	Henry Winkler	60.00
JA	Joey Allen	10.00
JD	Jerry Dixon	10.00
JF	Jay Jay French	8.00
JG	Joe Gannascoli	30.00
JL	Jani Lane	15.00
KO	Martin Kove	25.00
LH	Larry Hagman	35.00
LT	Larry Thomas	15.00
MA	Miljenko Matijevic	8.00
MB	Michael Biehn	50.00
MK	Margot Kidder	25.00
MM	Mark Mendoza	8.00
PP	Pat Priest	25.00
PS	P.J. Soles	25.00
RF	Robert Funaro	20.00
SB	Sebastian Bach	20.00
SE	Shirley Eaton	15.00
SN	Dee Snider	15.00
SP	Stephen Pearcy	15.00
SS	Steven Sweet	10.00
TB	Tom Bosley	40.00
TR	Mike Tramp	10.00
VN	Vince Neil	20.00

Swatches

JORGE POSADA
NEW YORK YANKEES®

	NM/M
Common Player:	4.00
Production 99 Sets	
Dark Gray:	No Pricing
Production One Set	
Green:	1X
Production 50 Sets	
Green Patch:	No Pricing
Production 15 Sets	
Blue:	No Pricing
Production 15 Sets	
Orange:	1X
Production 75 Sets	
Red:	1-1.5X
Production 35 Sets	
Purple:	1-2X
Production 2-58	
No pricing prod. 20 or less	
AB	A.J. Burnett	4.00
AH	Aaron Harang	4.00
AJ	Andruw Jones	6.00
AP	Albert Pujols	15.00
BB	Boof Bonser	4.00
BC	Bartolo Colon	4.00
BE	Adrian Beltre	4.00
BG	Brian Giles	4.00
BM	Brian McCann	6.00
BS	Ben Sheets	4.00
BU	B.J. Upton	6.00
BW	Billy Wagner	4.00
CA	Chris Carpenter	6.00
CB	Carlos Beltran	8.00
CC	Carl Crawford	8.00
CG	Curtis Granderson	4.00
CH	Cole Hamels	8.00
CJ	Chipper Jones	10.00
CS	Curt Schilling	8.00
CU	Chase Utley	10.00
CZ	Carlos Zambrano	8.00
DH	Danny Haren	6.00
DJ	Derek Jeter	20.00
DL	Derrek Lee	8.00
DM	Daisuke Matsuzaka	20.00
DO	David Ortiz	8.00
DU	Dan Uggla	4.00
DW	Dontrelle Willis	4.00

EC	Eric Chavez	4.00
FH	Felix Hernandez	8.00
FS	Freddy Sanchez	4.00
GA	Garrett Atkins	4.00
GJ	Geoff Jenkins	4.00
GM	Greg Maddux	10.00
GR	Curtis Granderson	10.00
GS	Grady Sizemore	8.00
HA	Travis Hafner	6.00
HB	Hank Blalock	6.00
HO	Trevor Hoffman	4.00
HP	Hunter Pence	8.00
HR	Hanley Ramirez	8.00
HU	Torii Hunter	6.00
IK	Ian Kinsler	6.00
IR	Ivan Rodriguez	6.00
JA	Conor Jackson	6.00
JB	Josh Beckett	8.00
JC	Joba Chamberlain	20.00
JD	Jermaine Dye	4.00
JE	Jim Edmonds	4.00
JF	Jeff Francoeur	8.00
JG	Jason Giambi	6.00
JH	J.J. Hardy	4.00
JK	Jeff Kent	6.00
JM	Joe Mauer	6.00
JP	Jhonny Peralta	4.00
JR	Jose Reyes	10.00
JS	Johan Santana	8.00
JT	Jim Thome	6.00
JV	Jason Varitek	6.00
JW	Jered Weaver	6.00
KG	Ken Griffey Jr.	15.00
KJ	Kenji Johjima	6.00
KY	Kevin Youkilis	6.00
LB	Lance Berkman	6.00
MC	Miguel Cabrera	6.00
MG	Matt Garza	4.00
MH	Matt Holliday	6.00
MO	Justin Morneau	8.00
MP	Mike Piazza	10.00
MR	Manny Ramirez	6.00
MT	Miguel Tejada	6.00
MY	Michael Young	6.00
OR	Magglio Ordonez	6.00
OS	Roy Oswalt	6.00
PA	Jonathan Papelbon	15.00
PE	Jake Peavy	6.00
PF	Prince Fielder	10.00
PI	Juan Pierre	4.00
PM	Pedro Martinez	8.00
PO	Jorge Posada	8.00
RA	Aramis Ramirez	4.00
RB	Ryan Braun	15.00
RC	Robinson Cano	10.00
RF	Rafael Furcal	6.00
RH	Roy Halladay	8.00
RJ	Randy Johnson	8.00
RM	Russell Martin	6.00
RS	Richie Sexson	4.00
RZ	Ryan Zimmerman	6.00
SM	John Smoltz	8.00
SO	Jeremy Sowers	4.00
SR	Scott Rolen	6.00
TH	Tim Hudson	6.00
TW	Tim Wakefield	4.00
VG	Vladimir Guerrero	8.00
VM	Victor Martinez	6.00
VW	Vernon Wells	4.00

Swatches Autographs

	NM/M
Production 30 unless noted.	
AH	Aaron Harang	20.00
AJ	Andruw Jones	25.00
BB	Boof Bonser	15.00
BG	Brian Giles	15.00
BS	Ben Sheets	20.00
BU	B.J. Upton	30.00
CC	Carl Crawford	20.00
CH	Cole Hamels	40.00
CJ	Chipper Jones	85.00
DH	Danny Haren	25.00
DL	Derrek Lee	25.00
DM	Daisuke Matsuzaka	250.00
DU	Dan Uggla	15.00
DW	Dontrelle Willis	20.00
EC	Eric Chavez	15.00
FH	Felix Hernandez	40.00
GR	Curtis Granderson	50.00
HA	Travis Hafner	30.00
HP	Hunter Pence	35.00
HR	Hanley Ramirez	40.00
HU	Torii Hunter	30.00
JM	Joe Mauer	40.00
JS	Johan Santana	40.00
JT	Jim Thome	40.00
JV	Jason Varitek	50.00
JW	Jered Weaver	20.00
KG	Ken Griffey Jr./15	100.00
MC	Miguel Cabrera	40.00
MG	Matt Garza	20.00
MH	Matt Holliday	40.00
MT	Miguel Tejada	35.00
OS	Roy Oswalt	25.00
PA	Jonathan Papelbon	50.00
PF	Prince Fielder	40.00
RA	Aramis Ramirez	30.00
RB	Ryan Braun	50.00
RM	Russell Martin	40.00
RZ	Ryan Zimmerman	25.00
SO	Jeremy Sowers	20.00
TH	Tim Hudson	30.00
VG	Vladimir Guerrero	50.00
VM	Victor Martinez	25.00

Three Star Swatches

	NM/M
Common Trio:	10.00
Production 75 Sets	
GDH	Ken Griffey Jr., Adam Dunn, Aaron Harang	20.00
HBK	Erik Bedard, Scott Kazmir, Cole Hamels	10.00
JCC	Derek Jeter, Robinson Cano, Joba Chamberlain	50.00
JPG	Ken Griffey Jr., Derek Jeter, Albert Pujols	40.00
KHS	Freddy Sanchez, Aaron Hill, Ian Kinsler	10.00
MGS	Greg Maddux, Tom Glavine, John Smoltz	30.00
MJS	Randy Johnson, Pedro Martinez, Curt Schilling	20.00
MRM	Ivan Rodriguez, Victor Martinez, Joe Mauer	15.00
OBP	Lance Berkman, Roy Oswalt, Hunter Pence	20.00
OVS	Gary Sheffield, Magglio Ordonez, Justin Verlander	15.00
PER	Jim Edmonds, Scott Rolen, Albert Pujols	20.00
PSB	Josh Beckett, Johan Santana, Jake Peavy	20.00
RBM	Carlos Beltran, Pedro Martinez, Jose Reyes	20.00
RUH	Jimmy Rollins, Chase Utley, Cole Hamels	25.00
SBH	Carlos Beltran, Torii Hunter, Grady Sizemore	15.00
SCG	Vladimir Guerrero, Alfonso Soriano, Miguel Cabrera	20.00
SJT	Chipper Jones, John Smoltz, Mark Teixeira	15.00
SMH	Travis Hafner, Victor Martinez, Grady Sizemore	15.00
SMM	Justin Morneau, Johan Santana, Joe Mauer	20.00
ZSL	Derrek Lee, Alfonso Soriano, Carlos Zambrano	15.00

Four Star Swatches

No Pricing
Production 15 Sets

Dual Swatches

	NM/M
Common Duo:	10.00
Production 99 Sets	
AP	Pat Burrell, Aaron Rowand	10.00
BM	Josh Beckett, Daisuke Matsuzaka	30.00
BP	Hunter Pence, Ryan Braun	25.00
CL	Noah Lowry, Matt Cain	10.00
CT	Tim Wakefield, Curt Schilling	15.00
CW	Miguel Cabrera, Dontrelle Willis	10.00
CY	Carl Crawford, Delmon Young	10.00
DC	Derek Jeter, Joba Chamberlain	80.00
FB	Prince Fielder, Ryan Braun	25.00
FD	Danny Haren, Felix Hernandez	15.00
FK	Jeff Kent, Rafael Furcal	10.00
FM	Brian McCann, Jeff Francoeur	20.00
GC	Bartolo Colon, Vladimir Guerrero	15.00
GD	Ken Griffey Jr., Adam Dunn	20.00
GG	Brian Giles, Adrian Gonzalez	10.00
GM	Greg Maddux, Tom Glavine	30.00
GO	Vladimir Guerrero, Magglio Ordonez	20.00
GP	Jason Giambi, Jorge Posada	15.00
GV	Victor Martinez, Grady Sizemore	15.00
HB	Roy Halladay, A.J. Burnett	10.00
HC	Mike Cameron, Torii Hunter	10.00
HF	Jeff Francoeur, Matt Holliday	15.00
HH	Todd Helton, Matt Holliday	15.00
HJ	Felix Hernandez, Kenji Johjima	10.00
HS	Huston Street, Rich Harden	10.00
JC	Derek Jeter, Robinson Cano	35.00
JF	Andruw Jones, Jeff Francoeur	15.00
JP	Derek Jeter, Albert Pujols	40.00
JR	Derek Jeter, Jose Reyes	40.00
JT	John Smoltz, Tim Hudson	20.00
JW	Randy Johnson, Brandon Webb	20.00
MH	Torii Hunter, Justin Morneau	15.00
ML	Brett Myers, Brad Lidge	10.00
MP	Juan Pierre, Russell Martin	15.00
MR	Ivan Rodriguez, Victor Martinez	15.00
MW	Pedro Martinez, Billy Wagner	20.00

∎B	Lance Berkman,	
	Roy Oswalt	15.00
∎G	Magglio Ordonez,	
	Curtis Granderson	25.00
)P	David Ortiz, Albert Pujols	30.00
)R	Manny Ramirez, David Ortiz	30.00
)E	Jim Edmonds, Albert Pujols	25.00
)J	Justin Morneau,	
	Prince Fielder	20.00
)M	Greg Maddux, Jake Peavy	20.00
)S	Alfonso Soriano,	
	Albert Pujols	30.00
)W	Jake Peavy, Brandon Webb	15.00
)B	Carlos Beltran, Jose Reyes	20.00
)C	Gary Sheffield,	
	Miguel Cabrera	20.00
)F	Rafael Furcal, Jose Reyes	20.00
)H	J.J. Hardy, Hanley Ramirez	15.00
)U	Jimmy Rollins, Jose Reyes	25.00
)U	Hanley Ramirez,	
	Dan Uggla	15.00
)B	Adrian Beltre,	
	Richie Sexson	10.00
)B	Ben Sheets, J.J. Hardy	10.00
)L	Derrek Lee,	
	Alfonso Soriano	15.00
)M	Johan Santana, Joe Mauer	15.00
)W	Johan Santana,	
	Dontrelle Willis	15.00
)D	Jim Thome, Jermaine Dye	15.00
)M	Miguel Tejada,	
	Nick Markakis	15.00
)H	Chase Utley, Cole Hamels	20.00
)B	Jeremy Bonderman,	
	Justin Verlander	25.00
)R	Ivan Rodriguez,	
	Justin Verlander	20.00
)Y	Jason Varitek,	
	Kevin Youkilis	20.00
)R	Vernon Wells, Alex Rios	10.00
)K	Michael Young, Ian Kinsler	10.00
)L	Derrek Lee,	
	Carlos Zambrano	20.00

2008 UD USA

		NM/M
Complete Set (60):		20.00
Sealed Box Set:		75.00
Common USA card (1-60):		.25
7 autos & 2 jsys/ sealed set		
1	Pedro Alvarez	2.00
2	Ryan Berry	.25
3	Jordan Danks	.50
4	Dan Espinosa	.75
5	Ryan Flaherty	1.50
6	Logan Forsythe	1.00
7	Seth Frankoff	.50
8	Scott Gorgen	.50
9	Jeremy Hamilton	.50
10	Brett Hunter	1.00
11	Joe Kelly	.25
12	Roger Kieschnick	.75
13	Lance Lynn	.50
14	Brian Matusz	1.00
15	Tommy Medica	.75
16	Jordy Mercer	.50
17	Mike Minor	.50
18	Petey Paramore	.50
19	Josh Romanski	.25
20	Tyson Ross	.50
21	Cody Satterwhite	.50
22	Justin Smoak	2.00
23	Eric Surkamp	.25
24	Jacob Thompson	.25
25	Brett Wallace	2.00
26	Coaches	.25
27	Team Picture CL	.50
28	Game 1	.25
29	Game 2	.25
30	Game 3	.25
31	Game 4	.25
32	Game 5	.25
33	Kyle Buchanan	.25
34	Mychal Givens	.50
35	Rob Grossman	.25
36	Tyler Hibbs	.50
37	L.J. Hoes	.25
38	Eric Hosmer	1.50
39	T.J. House	.25
40	Garrison Lassiter	.25
41	Jeff Malm	.25
42	Nick Maronde	.25
43	Harold Martinez	.25
44	Tim Melville	.25
45	Matt Purke	.25
46	J.P. Ramirez	.25
47	Kyle Skipworth	1.00
48	Tyler Stovall	.25
49	Jordan Swagerty	.25
50	Riccio Torrez	.25
51	Ryan Weber	.25
52	Tyler Wilson	.25
53	Coaches	.25
54	Team Picture CL	.25
55	Justin Charles, Andrew Aplin,	
	Matt Davidson	.25
56	Robert Refsnyder, Max Stassi,	
	Zach Vincej	.25
57	Colton Cain, Randal Grichuk,	
	Zach Lee	.50
58	A.J. Cole, Nolan Fontana,	
	Nick Franklin	.50

59	Nate Gonzalez, Austin Maddox,	
	Steve Rodriguez	.50
60	Luke Bailey, Richie Shaffer,	
	Jacob Tillotson	.50

Printing Plates
Production one set per color.

Battleground Autographs
Most not priced.

Camo Cloth

		NM/M
Common Player:		3.00
1	Pedro Alvarez	10.00
2	Ryan Berry	8.00
3	Jordan Danks	8.00
4	Dan Espinosa	6.00
5	Ryan Flaherty	6.00
6	Logan Forsythe	5.00
7	Jeremy Hamilton	3.00
8	Brett Hunter	3.00
9	Joe Kelly	3.00
10	Roger Kieschnick	4.00
11	Lance Lynn	4.00
12	Brian Matusz	8.00
13	Tommy Medica	5.00
14	Jordy Mercer	5.00
15	Mike Minor	3.00
16	Petey Paramore	5.00
17	Josh Romanski	3.00
18	Tyson Ross	5.00
19	Cody Satterwhite	4.00
20	Justin Smoak	10.00
21	Jacob Thompson	3.00
22	Brett Wallace	5.00

Japanese National Team Jerseys

		NM/M
Common Jersey:		5.00
Patch:		No Pricing
Production 20 Sets		
1	Sho Aranami	5.00
2	Takeshi Hosoyamada	5.00
3	Takahiro Iwamoto	5.00
4	Tomoyuki Kaida	5.00
5	Mikinori Kato	5.00
6	Testsuya Kokubo	5.00
7	Keijiro Matsumoto	5.00
8	Shirou Mori	5.00
9	Shinya Muramatsu	5.00
10	Ryoji Nakata	5.00
11	Hiroki Nakazawa	5.00
12	Tomohisa Nemoto	8.00
13	Shota Oba	5.00
14	Takashi Ogino	8.00
15	Shota Ohno	8.00
16	Yuki Saitoh	60.00
17	Ryo Sakakibara	8.00
18	Yukinaga Tanaka	5.00
19	Shingo Tatsumi	8.00
20	Hiroki Uemoto	5.00
21	Shota Waizumi	8.00
22	Norihara Yamazaki	5.00

Japanese National Team Autographs

		NM/M
Production 50 Sets		5.00
2	Takeshi Hosoyamada	30.00
4	Tomoyuki Kaida	40.00
10	Ryoji Nakata	15.00
13	Shota Oba	80.00
15	Shota Ohno	40.00

Junior National Team Autographs

		NM/M
Common USA Junior Auto.:		8.00
Autos are "on card."		
82	Kyle Buchanan	8.00
83	Mychal Givens	15.00
84	Rob Grossman	8.00
85	Tyler Hibbs	10.00
86	L.J. Hoes	8.00
87	Eric Hosmer	20.00
88	T.J. House	10.00
89	Garrison Lassiter	8.00
90	Jeff Malm	8.00
91	Nick Maronde	15.00
92	Harold Martinez	10.00
93	Tim Melville	10.00
94	Matt Purke	8.00
95	J.P. Ramirez	10.00
96	Kyle Skipworth	15.00
97	Tyler Stovall	10.00
98	Jordan Swagerty	8.00
99	Riccio Torrez	8.00
100	Ryan Weber	8.00
101	Tyler Wilson	10.00

Junior National Team Black Autographs

		NM/M
Production 249 Sets		
Blue Autos:		1X
Production 150 Sets		
Red:		1-2X
Production 50 Sets		
Green:		No Pricing
Production Two Sets		
1	Kyle Buchanan	8.00

2	Mychal Givens	15.00
3	Rob Grossman	8.00
4	Tyler Hibbs	10.00
5	L.J. Hoes	8.00
6	Eric Hosmer	20.00
7	T.J. House	10.00
8	Garrison Lassiter	8.00
9	Jeff Malm	8.00
10	Nick Maronde	15.00
11	Harold Martinez	10.00
12	Tim Melville	10.00
13	Matt Purke	8.00
14	J.P. Ramirez	8.00
15	Kyle Skipworth	15.00
16	Tyler Stovall	10.00
17	Jordan Swagerty	8.00
18	Riccio Torrez	8.00
19	Ryan Weber	8.00
20	Tyler Wilson	10.00

Junior National Team The Letters
No Pricing
Production 15 Sets

National Team Multi-player Autographs
No Pricing

National Team Team Signed Card
No Pricing

National Team July 4th, 2007 Autographs
No Pricing

National Team Black Autographs

		NM/M
Production 249 Sets		
Blue:		1X
Production 150 Sets		
Red:		1-2X
Production 50 Sets		
Green:		No Pricing
Production Two Sets		
1	Pedro Alvarez	20.00
2	Ryan Berry	8.00
3	Jordan Danks	15.00
4	Dan Espinosa	10.00
5	Ryan Flaherty	8.00
6	Logan Forsythe	8.00
7	Seth Frankoff	10.00
8	Scott Gorgen	8.00
9	Jeremy Hamilton	8.00
10	Brett Hunter	10.00
11	Joe Kelly	10.00
12	Roger Kieschnick	8.00
13	Lance Lynn	8.00
14	Brian Matusz	20.00
15	Tommy Medica	10.00
16	Jordy Mercer	8.00
17	Mike Minor	8.00
18	Petey Paramore	8.00
19	Josh Romanski	8.00
20	Tyson Ross	8.00
21	Cody Satterwhite	8.00
22	Justin Smoak	20.00
23	Jacob Thompson	8.00
24	Brett Wallace	25.00
25	Eric Surkamp	8.00

National Team Signatures Blue Ink

		NM/M
Common Auto.:		8.00
Autos are "on card."		
61	Pedro Alvarez	25.00
62	Ryan Berry	10.00
63	Jordan Danks	15.00
64	Dan Espinosa	8.00
65	Ryan Flaherty	15.00
66	Logan Forsythe	8.00
67	Jeremy Hamilton	8.00
68	Brett Hunter	8.00
69	Joe Kelly	8.00
70	Roger Kieschnick	10.00
71	Brian Matusz	20.00
72	Tommy Medica	10.00
73	Jordy Mercer	15.00
74	Mike Minor	8.00
75	Petey Paramore	8.00
76	Josh Romanski	8.00
77	Tyson Ross	10.00
78	Cody Satterwhite	8.00
79	Justin Smoak	25.00
80	Jacob Thompson	10.00
81	Brett Wallace	25.00

National Team Question & Answer Autographs

		NM/M
All variations are equal value.		8.00
BH	Brett Hunter	8.00
BM	Brian Matusz	20.00
BW	Brett Wallace	25.00
CS	Cody Satterwhite	10.00
DE	Dan Espinosa	8.00
JD	Jordan Danks	15.00
JH	Jeremy Hamilton	8.00
JK	Joe Kelly	10.00

JM	Jordy Mercer	8.00
JR	Josh Romanski	8.00
JS	Justin Smoak	25.00
JT	Jacob Thompson	10.00
LF	Logan Forsythe	8.00
MM	Mike Minor	10.00
PA	Pedro Alvarez	25.00
PP	Petey Paramore	8.00
RB	Ryan Berry	8.00
RF	Ryan Flaherty	8.00
RK	Roger Kieschnick	10.00
TM	Tommy Medica	10.00
TR	Tyson Ross	8.00

Today & Tomorrow Dual Black Autos

		NM/M
Common Dual Auto.:		10.00
Production 295 Sets		
Blue:		1x
Production 150 Sets		
Red:		No Pricing
Production 25 Sets		
Green:		No Pricing
Production Two Sets		
1	Brian Matusz, Tim Melville	15.00
2	Jacob Thompson,	
	Nick Maronde	15.00
3	Brett Hunter, T.J. House	15.00
4	Petey Paramore,	
	Jordan Swagerty	15.00
5	Justin Smoak, Eric Hosmer	30.00
6	Ryan Flaherty,	
	Riccio Torrez	15.00
7	Pedro Alvarez,	
	Harold Martinez	20.00
8	Dan Espinosa,	
	Mychal Givens	15.00
9	Jordan Danks, L.J. Hoes	10.00
10	Roger Kieschnick,	
	Rob Grossman	15.00
11	Logan Forsythe,	
	J.P. Ramirez	15.00
12	Brett Wallace,	
	Kyle Skipworth	25.00

Youth National Team Jersey Autographs

		NM/M
Production 295 Sets		
1	Andrew Aplin	
2	Luke Bailey	
3	Colton Cain	20.00
4	Justin Charles	10.00
5	A.J. Cole	
6	Matt Davidson	20.00
7	Nolan Fontana	10.00
8	Nick Franklin	15.00
9	Nate Gonzalez	15.00
10	Zach Lee	20.00
12	Austin Maddox	15.00
14	Steve Rodriguez	15.00
15	Richie Shaffer	15.00
17	Jacob Tillotson	20.00
18	Zach Vincej	15.00

Z

1995 Zenith

		NM/M
Complete Set (150):		15.00
Common Player:		.10
Pack (6):		1.50
Wax Box (24):		17.50
1	Albert Belle	.10
2	Alex Fernandez	.10
3	Andy Benes	.10
4	Barry Larkin	.10
5	Barry Bonds	2.50
6	Ben McDonald	.10
7	Bernard Gilkey	.10
8	Billy Ashley	.10
9	Bobby Bonilla	.10
10	Bret Saberhagen	.10
11	Brian Jordan	.10
12	Cal Ripken Jr.	2.50

13	Carlos Baerga	.10
14	Carlos Delgado	.35
15	Cecil Fielder	.10
16	Chili Davis	.10
17	Chuck Knoblauch	.10
18	Craig Biggio	.10
19	Danny Tartabull	.10
20	Dante Bichette	.10
21	Darren Daulton	.10
22	Dave Justice	.10
23	Dave Winfield	.75
24	David Cone	.10
25	Dean Palmer	.10
26	Deion Sanders	.20
27	Dennis Eckersley	.65
28	Derek Bell	.10
29	Don Mattingly	1.50
30	Edgar Martinez	.10
31	Eric Karros	.10
32	Erik Hanson	.10
33	Frank Thomas	.75
34	Fred McGriff	.10
35	Gary Sheffield	.45
36	Gary Gaetti	.10
37	Greg Maddux	1.25
38	Gregg Jefferies	.10
39	Ivan Rodriguez	.65
40	Kenny Rogers	.10
41	J.T. Snow	.10
42	Hal Morris	.10
43	Eddie Murray (3,000 hit)	.50
44	Javier Lopez	.10
45	Jay Bell	.10
46	Jeff Conine	.10
47	Jeff Bagwell	.75
48	Hideo Nomo RC	2.00
49	Jeff Kent	.10
50	Jeff King	.10
51	Jim Thome	.65
52	Jimmy Key	.10
53	Joe Carter	.10
54	John Valentin	.10
55	John Olerud	.10
56	Jose Canseco	.45
57	Jose Rijo	.10
58	Jose Offerman	.10
59	Juan Gonzalez	.45
60	Ken Caminiti	.10
61	Ken Griffey Jr.	1.75
62	Kenny Lofton	.10
63	Kevin Appier	.10
64	Kevin Seitzer	.10
65	Kirby Puckett	1.25
66	Kirk Gibson	.10
67	Larry Walker	.10
68	Lenny Dykstra	.10
69	Manny Ramirez	.75
70	Mark Grace	.10
71	Mark McGwire	2.00
72	Marquis Grissom	.10
73	Jim Edmonds	.10
74	Matt Williams	.10
75	Mike Mussina	.45
76	Mike Piazza	1.75
77	Mo Vaughn	.10
78	Moises Alou	.10
79	Ozzie Smith	1.25
80	Paul O'Neill	.10
81	Paul Molitor	.75
82	Rafael Palmeiro	.65
83	Randy Johnson	.75
84	Raul Mondesi	.10
85	Ray Lankford	.10
86	Reggie Sanders	.10
87	Rickey Henderson	.75
88	Rico Brogna	.10
89	Roberto Alomar	.25
90	Robin Ventura	.10
91	Roger Clemens	1.50
92	Ron Gant	.10
93	Rondell White	.10
94	Royce Clayton	.10
95	Ruben Sierra	.10
96	Rusty Greer	.10
97	Ryan Klesko	.10
98	Sammy Sosa	1.25
99	Shawon Dunston	.10
100	Steve Ontiveros	.10
101	Tim Naehring	.10
102	Tim Salmon	.10
103	Tino Martinez	.10
104	Tony Gwynn	1.25
105	Travis Fryman	.10
106	Vinny Castilla	.10
107	Wade Boggs	1.25
108	Wally Joyner	.10
109	Wil Cordero	.10
110	Will Clark	.10
111	Chipper Jones	1.25
112	C.J. Nitkowski	.10
113	Curtis Goodwin	.10
114	Tim Unroe	.10
115	Vaughn Eshelman	.10
116	Marty Cordova	.10
117	Dustin Hermanson	.10
118	Rich Becker	.10
119	Ray Durham	.10
120	Shane Andrews	.10
121	Scott Ruffcorn	.10
122	Mark Grudzielanek RC	.25
123	James Baldwin	.10
124	Carlos Perez RC	.10
125	Julian Tavarez	.10
126	Joe Vitiello	.10
127	Jason Bates	.10

128	Edgardo Alfonzo	.10
129	Juan Acevedo	.10
130	Bill Pulsipher	.10
131	Bob Higginson RC	.25
132	Russ Davis	.10
133	Charles Johnson	.10
134	Derek Jeter	2.50
135	Phil Nevin	.10
136	LaTroy Hawkins	.10
137	Brian Hunter	.10
138	Roberto Petagine	.10
139	Jim Pittsley	.10
140	Garret Anderson	.10
141	Ugueth Urbina	.10
142	Antonio Osuna	.10
143	Michael Tucker	.10
144	Benji Gil	.10
145	Jon Nunnally	.10
146	Alex Rodriguez	2.00
147	Todd Hollandsworth	.10
148	Alex Gonzalez	.10
149	Hideo Nomo RC	2.00
150	Shawn Green	.30
---	Numeric Checklist	.10
---	Chase Program Checklist	.10

All-Star Salute

Kirby Puckett
ALL-STAR GAME VETERAN

		NM/M
Complete Set (18):		16.00
Common Player:		.50
1	Cal Ripken Jr.	3.00
2	Frank Thomas	1.00
3	Mike Piazza	2.00
4	Kirby Puckett	1.50
5	Manny Ramirez	1.00
6	Tony Gwynn	1.50
7	Hideo Nomo	.75
8	Matt Williams	.50
9	Randy Johnson	1.00
10	Raul Mondesi	.50
11	Albert Belle	.50
12	Ivan Rodriguez	1.00
13	Barry Bonds	3.00
14	Carlos Baerga	.50
15	Ken Griffey Jr.	2.00
16	Jeff Conine	.50
17	Frank Thomas	1.00
18	Cal Ripken Jr., Barry Bonds	2.00

Rookie Roll Call

		NM/M
Complete Set (18):		17.50
Common Player:		.60
1	Alex Rodriguez	6.00
2	Derek Jeter	7.50
3	Chipper Jones	5.00
4	Shawn Green	1.50
5	Todd Hollandsworth	.60
6	Bill Pulsipher	.60
7	Hideo Nomo	1.50
8	Ray Durham	.60
9	Curtis Goodwin	.60
10	Brian Hunter	.60
11	Julian Tavarez	.60
12	Marty Cordova	.60
13	Michael Tucker	.60
14	Edgardo Alfonzo	.60

15	LaTroy Hawkins	.60
16	Carlos Perez	.60
17	Charles Johnson	.60
18	Benji Gil	.60

Z-Team

GREG MADDUX P

		NM/M
Complete Set (18):		85.00
Common Player:		2.00
1	Cal Ripken Jr.	15.00
2	Ken Griffey Jr.	10.00
3	Frank Thomas	6.00
4	Matt Williams	2.00
5	Mike Piazza	6.00
6	Barry Bonds	10.00
7	Raul Mondesi	2.00
8	Greg Maddux	7.50
9	Jeff Bagwell	6.00
10	Manny Ramirez	6.00
11	Larry Walker	2.00
12	Tony Gwynn	7.50
13	Will Clark	2.00
14	Albert Belle	2.00
15	Kenny Lofton	2.00
16	Rafael Palmeiro	4.50
17	Don Mattingly	9.00
18	Carlos Baerga	2.00

1996 Zenith

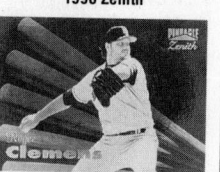

		NM/M
Complete Set (150):		15.00
Common Player:		.10
Common Artist's Proofs:		2.00
Star Artist's Proofs:		12X
Pack (6):		1.50
Wax Box (24):		25.00
1	Ken Griffey Jr.	2.00
2	Ozzie Smith	1.50
3	Greg Maddux	1.50
4	Rondell White	.10
5	Mark McGwire	2.50
6	Jim Thome	.75
7	Ivan Rodriguez	.75
8	Marc Newfield	.10
9	Travis Fryman	.10
10	Fred McGriff	.10
11	Shawn Green	.25
12	Mike Piazza	2.00
13	Dante Bichette	.10
14	Tino Martinez	.10
15	Sterling Hitchcock	.10
16	Ryne Sandberg	1.50
17	Rico Brogna	.10
18	Roberto Alomar	.25
19	Barry Larkin	.10
20	Bernie Williams	.10
21	Gary Sheffield	.50
22	Frank Thomas	1.00
23	Gregg Jefferies	.10
24	Jeff Bagwell	1.00
25	Marty Cordova	.10
26	Jim Edmonds	.10
27	Jay Bell	.10
28	Ben McDonald	.10
29	Barry Bonds	3.00
30	Mo Vaughn	.10
31	Johnny Damon	.35
32	Dante Bichette	.10
33	Ismael Valdes	.10
34	Manny Ramirez	1.00
35	Edgar Martinez	.10
36	Cecil Fielder	.10
37	Ryan Klesko	.10
38	Ray Lankford	.10
39	Tim Salmon	.10
40	Joe Carter	.10
41	Jason Isringhausen	.10
42	Rickey Henderson	1.00

43	Lenny Dykstra	.10
44	Andre Dawson	.25
45	Paul O'Neill	.10
46	Ray Durham	.10
47	Raul Mondesi	.10
48	Jay Buhner	.10
49	Eddie Murray	1.00
50	Henry Rodriguez	.10
51	Hal Morris	.10
52	Mike Mussina	.50
53	Wally Joyner	.10
54	Will Clark	.10
55	Chipper Jones	1.50
56	Brian Jordan	.10
57	Larry Walker	.10
58	Wade Boggs	1.50
59	Melvin Nieves	.10
60	Charles Johnson	.10
61	Juan Gonzalez	.50
62	Carlos Delgado	.35
63	Reggie Sanders	.10
64	Brian Hunter	.10
65	Edgardo Alfonzo	.10
66	Kenny Lofton	.10
67	Paul Molitor	1.00
68	Mike Bordick	.10
69	Garret Anderson	.10
70	Orlando Merced	.10
71	Craig Biggio	.10
72	Chuck Knoblauch	.10
73	Mark Grace	.10
74	Jack McDowell	.10
75	Randy Johnson	1.00
76	Cal Ripken Jr.	3.00
77	Matt Williams	.10
78	Benji Gil	.10
79	Moises Alou	.10
80	Robin Ventura	.10
81	Greg Vaughn	.10
82	Carlos Baerga	.10
83	Roger Clemens	1.75
84	Hideo Nomo	.50
85	Pedro Martinez	1.00
86	John Valentin	.10
87	Andres Galarraga	.10
88	Andy Pettitte	.30
89	Derek Bell	.10
90	Kirby Puckett	1.50
91	Tony Gwynn	1.50
92	Brady Anderson	.10
93	Derek Jeter	3.00
94	Michael Tucker	.10
95	Albert Belle	.10
96	David Cone	.10
97	J.T. Snow	.10
98	Tom Glavine	.35
99	Alex Rodriguez	2.50
100	Sammy Sosa	1.50
101	Karim Garcia	.15
102	Alan Benes	.10
103	Chad Mottola	.10
104	Robin Jennings RC	.10
105	Bob Abreu	.10
106	Tony Clark	.10
107	George Arias	.10
108	Jermaine Dye	.10
109	Jeff Suppan	.10
110	Ralph Milliard RC	.10
111	Ruben Rivera	.10
112	Billy Wagner	.10
113	Jason Kendall	.10
114	Mike Grace RC	.10
115	Edgar Renteria	.10
116	Jason Schmidt	.10
117	Paul Wilson	.10
118	Rey Ordonez	.10
119	Rocky Coppinger RC	.10
120	Wilton Guerrero RC	.10
121	Brooks Kieschnick	.10
122	Raul Casanova	.10
123	Alex Ochoa	.10
124	Chan Ho Park	.10
125	John Wasdin	.10
126	Eric Owens	.10
127	Justin Thompson	.10
128	Chris Snopek	.10
129	Terrell Wade	.10
130	Darin Erstad RC	1.50
131	Albert Belle (Honor Roll)	.10
132	Cal Ripken Jr. (Honor Roll)	1.50
133	Frank Thomas (Honor Roll)	.60
134	Greg Maddux (Honor Roll)	.75
135	Ken Griffey Jr. (Honor Roll)	1.00
136	Mo Vaughn (Honor Roll)	.10
137	Chipper Jones (Honor Roll)	.75
138	Mike Piazza (Honor Roll)	1.00
139	Ryan Klesko (Honor Roll)	.10
140	Hideo Nomo (Honor Roll)	.20
141	Roberto Alomar (Honor Roll)	.10
142	Manny Ramirez (Honor Roll)	.10
143	Gary Sheffield (Honor Roll)	.10
144	Barry Bonds (Honor Roll)	1.50
145	Matt Williams (Honor Roll)	.10
146	Jim Edmonds (Honor Roll)	.10
147	Derek Jeter (Honor Roll)	1.50
148	Sammy Sosa (Honor Roll)	.75
149	Kirby Puckett (Honor Roll)	.75
150	Tony Gwynn (Honor Roll)	.75

1996 Zenith Artist's Proofs

Paul O'Neill

	NM/M
Common Player:	2.00
Stars:	12X

(See 1996 Zenith for checklist and base card values.)

Diamond Club

Mike Piazza

		NM/M
Complete Set (20):		17.50
Common Player:		.45
Diamond Versions:		12X
1	Albert Belle	.45
2	Mo Vaughn	.45
3	Ken Griffey Jr.	1.50
4	Mike Piazza	1.50
5	Cal Ripken Jr.	2.50
6	Jermaine Dye	.45
7	Jeff Bagwell	1.00
8	Frank Thomas	1.00
9	Alex Rodriguez	2.00
10	Ryan Klesko	.45
11	Roberto Alomar	.60
12	Sammy Sosa	1.25
13	Matt Williams	.45
14	Gary Sheffield	.75
15	Ruben Rivera	.45
16	Darin Erstad	.60
17	Randy Johnson	1.00
18	Greg Maddux	1.25
19	Karim Garcia	.60
20	Chipper Jones	1.25

Mozaics

		NM/M
Complete Set (25):		30.00
Common Card:		.45
1	Greg Maddux, Chipper Jones, Ryan Klesko	3.00
2	Juan Gonzalez, Will Clark, Ivan Rodriguez	1.00
3	Frank Thomas, Robin Ventura, Ray Durham	1.00

4	Matt Williams, Barry Bonds, Osvaldo Fernandez	5.00
5	Ken Griffey Jr., Randy Johnson, Alex Rodriguez	4.00
6	Sammy Sosa, Ryne Sandberg, Mark Grace	4.00
7	Jim Edmonds, Tim Salmon, Garret Anderson	.45
8	Cal Ripken Jr., Roberto Alomar, Mike Mussina	5.00
9	Mo Vaughn, Roger Clemens, John Valentin	3.50
10	Barry Larkin, Reggie Sanders, Hal Morris	.45
11	Ray Lankford, Brian Jordan, Ozzie Smith	1.50
12	Dante Bichette, Larry Walker, Andres Galarraga	.45
13	Mike Piazza, Hideo Nomo, Raul Mondesi	4.00
14	Ben McDonald, Greg Vaughn, Kevin Seitzer	.45
15	Joe Carter, Carlos Delgado, Alex Gonzalez	.60
16	Gary Sheffield, Charles Johnson, Jeff Conine	.45
17	Rondell White, Moises Alou, Henry Rodriguez	.45
18	Albert Belle, Manny Ramirez, Carlos Baerga	1.00
19	Kirby Puckett, Paul Molitor, Chuck Knoblauch	1.50
20	Tony Gwynn, Rickey Henderson, Wally Joyner	2.00
21	Mark McGwire, Mike Bordick, Scott Brosius	4.00
22	Paul O'Neill, Bernie Williams, Wade Boggs	1.50
23	Jay Bell, Orlando Merced, Jason Kendall	.45
24	Rico Brogna, Paul Wilson, Jason Isringhausen	.45
25	Jeff Bagwell, Craig Biggio, Derek Bell	1.00

Z-Team

GARY SHEFFIELD

		NM/M
Complete Set (18):		100.00
Common Player:		3.00
1	Ken Griffey Jr.	12.50
2	Albert Belle	3.00
3	Cal Ripken Jr.	20.00
4	Frank Thomas	7.50
5	Greg Maddux	10.00
6	Mo Vaughn	3.00
7	Chipper Jones	10.00
8	Mike Piazza	12.50
9	Ryan Klesko	3.00
10	Hideo Nomo	4.50
11	Roberto Alomar	3.00
12	Manny Ramirez	6.00
13	Gary Sheffield	3.50
14	Barry Bonds	20.00
15	Matt Williams	3.00
16	Jim Edmonds	3.00
17	Kirby Puckett	10.00
18	Sammy Sosa	10.00

1997 Zenith

		NM/M
Complete Set (50):		15.00
Common Player:		.10
Pack (Five Cards, Two 8 x 10)		2.00
Wax Box (12):		25.00
1	Frank Thomas	.75
2	Tony Gwynn	1.00
3	Jeff Bagwell	.75
4	Paul Molitor	.75
5	Roberto Alomar	.20
6	Mike Piazza	1.25
7	Albert Belle	.10
8	Greg Maddux	1.00
9	Barry Larkin	.10
10	Tony Clark	.10
11	Larry Walker	.10
12	Chipper Jones	1.00
13	Juan Gonzalez	.40
14	Barry Bonds	2.00
15	Ivan Rodriguez	.65

16	Sammy Sosa	1.00
17	Derek Jeter	2.00
18	Hideo Nomo	.40
19	Roger Clemens	1.00
20	Ken Griffey Jr.	1.25
21	Andy Pettitte	.25
22	Alex Rodriguez	1.50
23	Tino Martinez	.10
24	Bernie Williams	.10
25	Ken Caminiti	.10
26	John Smoltz	.10
27	Javier Lopez	.10
28	Mark McGwire	1.50
29	Gary Sheffield	.50
30	David Justice	.10
31	Randy Johnson	.75
32	Chuck Knoblauch	.10
33	Mike Mussina	.40
34	Deion Sanders	.20
35	Cal Ripken Jr.	2.00
36	Darin Erstad	.30
37	Kenny Lofton	.10
38	Jay Buhner	.10
39	Brady Anderson	.10
40	Edgar Martinez	.10
41	Mo Vaughn	.10
42	Ryne Sandberg	1.00
43	Andruw Jones	.75
44	Nomar Garciaparra	1.00
45	Hideki Irabu RC	.25
46	Wilton Guerrero	.10
47	Jose Cruz Jr. RC	.45
48	Vladimir Guerrero	.75
49	Scott Rolen	.65
50	Jose Guillen	.10

V-2

		NM/M
Complete Set (8):		45.00
Common Player:		5.00
1	Ken Griffey Jr.	7.50
2	Andruw Jones	5.00
3	Frank Thomas	5.00
4	Mike Piazza	7.50
5	Alex Rodriguez	10.00
6	Cal Ripken Jr.	12.00
7	Derek Jeter	12.00
8	Vladimir Guerrero	5.00

Z-Team

		NM/M
Complete Set (9):		60.00
Common Player:		3.00
1	Ken Griffey Jr.	9.00
2	Larry Walker	3.00

3	Frank Thomas	6.00
4	Alex Rodriguez	10.00
5	Mike Piazza	9.00
6	Cal Ripken Jr.	12.50
7	Derek Jeter	12.50
8	Andruw Jones	6.00
9	Roger Clemens	7.50

8x10 and 8x10 Dufex

		NM/M
Complete Set (24):		20.00
Common Player:		.50
Dufex versions:		1X
Samples:		1X
1	Frank Thomas	1.00
2	Tony Gwynn	1.50
3	Jeff Bagwell	1.00
4	Ken Griffey Jr.	2.00
5	Mike Piazza	2.00
6	Greg Maddux	1.50
7	Ken Caminiti	.50
8	Albert Belle	.50
9	Ivan Rodriguez	.75
10	Sammy Sosa	1.50
11	Mark McGwire	2.50
12	Roger Clemens	1.75
13	Alex Rodriguez	2.50
14	Chipper Jones	1.50
15	Juan Gonzalez	.60
16	Barry Bonds	3.00
17	Derek Jeter	3.00
18	Hideo Nomo	.60
19	Cal Ripken Jr.	3.00
20	Hideki Irabu	.50
21	Andruw Jones	1.00
22	Nomar Garciaparra	1.50
23	Vladimir Guerrero	1.00
24	Scott Rolen	.75

1998 Zenith

CHARLES Johnson

		NM/M
Complete Set (100):		25.00
Common Player:		.10
Silvers:		2X
Inserted 1:7		
Pack (3):		2.50
Wax Box (18):		35.00
1	Larry Walker	.10
2	Ken Griffey Jr.	1.75
3	Cal Ripken Jr.	2.50
4	Sammy Sosa	1.50
5	Andruw Jones	1.00
6	Frank Thomas	1.00
7	Tony Gwynn	1.50
8	Rafael Palmeiro	.75
9	Tim Salmon	.10
10	Randy Johnson	1.00
11	Juan Gonzalez	.50
12	Greg Maddux	1.50
13	Vladimir Guerrero	1.00
14	Mike Piazza	1.75
15	Andres Galarraga	.10
16	Alex Rodriguez	2.00
17	Derek Jeter	2.50
18	Nomar Garciaparra	1.50
19	Ivan Rodriguez	.75
20	Chipper Jones	1.50
21	Barry Larkin	.10
22	Mo Vaughn	.10

23	Albert Belle	.10
24	Scott Rolen	.65
25	Sandy Alomar Jr.	.10
26	Roberto Alomar	.30
27	Andy Pettitte	.30
28	Chuck Knoblauch	.10
29	Jeff Bagwell	1.00
30	Mike Mussina	.30
31	Fred McGriff	.10
32	Roger Clemens	1.50
33	Rusty Greer	.10
34	Edgar Martinez	.10
35	Paul Molitor	1.00
36	Mark Grace	.10
37	Darin Erstad	.30
38	Kenny Lofton	.10
39	Tom Glavine	.35
40	Javier Lopez	.10
41	Will Clark	.10
42	Tino Martinez	.10
43	Raul Mondesi	.10
44	Brady Anderson	.10
45	Chan Ho Park	.10
46	Jason Giambi	.75
47	Manny Ramirez	1.00
48	Jay Buhner	.10
49	Dante Bichette	.10
50	Jose Cruz Jr.	.10
51	Charles Johnson	.10
52	Bernard Gilkey	.10
53	Johnny Damon	.35
54	David Justice	.10
55	Justin Thompson	.10
56	Bobby Higginson	.10
57	Todd Hundley	.10
58	Gary Sheffield	.50
59	Barry Bonds	2.50
60	Mark McGwire	2.00
61	John Smoltz	.10
62	Tony Clark	.10
63	Brian Jordan	.10
64	Jason Kendall	.10
65	Mariano Rivera	.20
66	Pedro Martinez	1.00
67	Jim Thome	.75
68	Neifi Perez	.10
69	Kevin Brown	.10
70	Hideo Nomo	.50
71	Craig Biggio	.10
72	Bernie Williams	.10
73	Jose Guillen	.10
74	Ken Caminiti	.10
75	Livan Hernandez	.10
76	Ray Lankford	.10
77	Jim Edmonds	.10
78	Matt Williams	.10
79	Mark Kotsay	.10
80	Moises Alou	.10
81	Antone Williamson	.10
82	Jaret Wright	.10
83	Jacob Cruz	.10
84	Abraham Nunez	.10
85	Raul Ibanez	.10
86	Miguel Tejada	.10
87	Derek Lee	.50
88	Juan Encarnacion	.10
89	Todd Helton	.75
90	Travis Lee	.10
91	Ben Grieve	.10
92	Ryan McGuire	.10
93	Richard Hidalgo	.10
94	Paul Konerko	.15
95	Shannon Stewart	.10
96	Homer Bush	.10
97	Lou Collier	.10
98	Jeff Abbott	.10
99	Brett Tomko	.10
100	Fernando Tatis	.10

Z-Silver

	NM/M
Common Player:	1.00
Stars/RC's:	2X
Inserted 1:7	
(See 1998 Zenith for checklist and base card values.)	

Z-Gold

	NM/M
Common Player:	3.00
Stars/Rookies:	12X

Production 100 Sets
(See 1998 Zenith for checklist and base card values.)

Epix

	NM/M
Complete Set (24):	95.00
Common (Orange) Card:	1.50
Purples:	1X
Emeralds:	2X
1	Ken Griffey Jr./S	7.50
2	Juan Gonzalez/S	2.50
3	Jeff Bagwell/S	4.50
4	Ivan Rodriguez/S	4.00
5	Nomar Garciaparra/S	6.00
6	Ryne Sandberg/S	6.00
7	Frank Thomas/M	4.50
8	Derek Jeter/M	12.00
9	Tony Gwynn/M	6.00
10	Albert Belle/M	1.50
11	Barry Larkin/M	1.50
12	Barry Larkin/M	1.50
13	Alex Rodriguez/P	9.00
14	Cal Ripken Jr./P	12.00
15	Chipper Jones/P	6.00
16	Roger Clemens/P	6.50
17	Mo Vaughn/P	1.50
18	Mark McGwire/P	9.00
19	Mike Piazza/G	7.50
20	Andruw Jones/G	4.50
21	Greg Maddux/G	6.00
22	Barry Bonds/G	12.00
23	Paul Molitor/G	4.50
24	Eddie Murray/G	4.50

Raising the Bar

	NM/M
Complete Set (15):	25.00
Common Player:	1.25
Inserted 1:25	
1	Ken Griffey Jr.	3.00
2	Frank Thomas	1.50
3	Alex Rodriguez	3.50
4	Tony Gwynn	2.50
5	Mike Piazza	3.00
6	Ivan Rodriguez	1.25
7	Cal Ripken Jr.	4.50
8	Greg Maddux	2.50
9	Hideo Nomo	1.25
10	Mark McGwire	3.50
11	Juan Gonzalez	1.25
12	Andruw Jones	1.50
13	Jeff Bagwell	1.50
14	Chipper Jones	2.50
15	Nomar Garciaparra	2.50

Rookie Thrills

	NM/M
Complete Set (15):	20.00
Common Player:	1.50
Inserted 1:25	
1	Travis Lee	1.50
2	Juan Encarnacion	1.50
3	Derek Lee	1.50
4	Raul Ibanez	1.50
5	Ryan McGuire	1.50
6	Todd Helton	3.00

7	Jacob Cruz	1.50
8	Abraham Nunez	1.50
9	Paul Konerko	2.00
10	Ben Grieve	1.50
11	Jeff Abbott	1.50
12	Richard Hidalgo	1.50
13	Jaret Wright	1.50
14	Lou Collier	1.50
15	Miguel Tejada	2.00

Z-Team

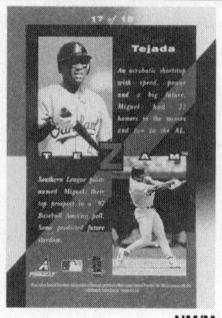

	NM/M
Complete Set (18):	35.00
Common Player:	1.25
Golds:	2X
Inserted 1:175	
1	Frank Thomas	2.50
2	Ken Griffey Jr.	3.50
3	Mike Piazza	3.50
4	Cal Ripken Jr.	6.00
5	Alex Rodriguez	5.00
6	Greg Maddux	3.00
7	Derek Jeter	6.00
8	Chipper Jones	3.00
9	Roger Clemens	3.25
10	Ben Grieve	1.25
11	Derek Lee	1.75
12	Jose Cruz Jr.	1.25
13	Nomar Garciaparra	3.00
14	Travis Lee	1.50
15	Todd Helton	2.00
16	Paul Konerko	1.75
17	Miguel Tejada	1.25
18	Scott Rolen	2.00

5x7

	NM/M
Complete Set (80):	30.00
Common Player:	.25
Impulse Silvers:	1.5X
Inserted 1:7	
1	Nomar Garciaparra	2.00
2	Andres Galarraga	.25
3	Greg Maddux	2.00
4	Frank Thomas	1.00
5	Mark McGwire	3.00
6	Rafael Palmeiro	.75
7	John Smoltz	.25
8	Jeff Bagwell	1.00
9	Andruw Jones	1.00
10	Rusty Greer	.25
11	Paul Molitor	1.00
12	Bernie Williams	.25
13	Kenny Lofton	.25
14	Alex Rodriguez	3.00
15	Derek Jeter	4.00
15s	Derek Jeter ("SAMPLE" overprint on back.)	4.00
16	Scott Rolen	.65
17	Albert Belle	.25
18	Mo Vaughn	.25
19	Chipper Jones	2.00
20	Chuck Knoblauch	.25
21	Mike Piazza	3.00
22	Tony Gwynn	2.00
22s	Tony Gwynn ("SAMPLE" overprint on back.)	2.00

23	Juan Gonzalez	.50
24	Andy Pettitte	.35
25	Tim Salmon	.25
26	Brady Anderson	.25
27	Mike Mussina	.40
28	Edgar Martinez	.25
29	Jose Guillen	.25
30	Hideo Nomo	.50
31	Jim Thome	.65
32	Mark Grace	.25
33	Darin Erstad	.50
34	Bobby Higginson	.25
35	Ivan Rodriguez	.75
36	Todd Hundley	.25
37	Sandy Alomar Jr.	.25
38	Gary Sheffield	.40
39	David Justice	.25
40	Ken Griffey Jr.	2.50
40s	Ken Griffey Jr. ("SAMPLE" overprint on back.)	2.50
41	Vladimir Guerrero	1.00
42	Larry Walker	.25
43	Barry Bonds	4.00
44	Randy Johnson	1.00
45	Roger Clemens	2.25
46	Raul Mondesi	.25
47	Tino Martinez	.25
48	Jason Giambi	.50
49	Matt Williams	.25
50	Cal Ripken Jr.	4.00
51	Barry Larkin	.25
52	Jim Edmonds	.25
53	Ken Caminiti	.25
54	Sammy Sosa	2.00
55	Tony Clark	.25
56	Manny Ramirez	1.00
57	Bernard Gilkey	.25
58	Jose Cruz Jr.	.25
59	Brian Jordan	.25
60	Kevin Brown	.25
61	Craig Biggio	.25
62	Javier Lopez	.25
63	Jay Buhner	.25
64	Roberto Alomar	.40
65	Justin Thompson	.25
66	Todd Helton	.75
67	Travis Lee	.25
68	Paul Konerko	.35
69	Jaret Wright	.25
70	Ben Grieve	.25
71	Juan Encarnacion	.25
72	Ryan McGuire	.25
73	Derek Lee	.60
74	Abraham Nunez	.25
75	Richard Hidalgo	.25
76	Miguel Tejada	.25
77	Jacob Cruz	.25
78	Homer Bush	.25
79	Jeff Abbott	.25
80	Lou Collier	.25
	Checklist	.10

5x7 Impulse Silver

	NM/M
Common Player:	2.00
Stars/RC's:	1.5X
Inserted 1:7	
(See 1998 Zenith 5x7 for checklist and base card values.)	

1998 Zenith 5x7 Impulse Gold

	NM/M
Common Player:	5.00
Stars/RC's:	20X
Inserted 1:7	
(See 1998 Zenith 5x7 for checklist and base card values.)	

Defining Details on CD

The Essential SCD CD

With this CD you'll access straight-forward facts about spotting frauds, authenticating and grading. Coverage includes:

- Top autograph subjects, including Ruth, Cobb, Wagner, Gehrig and many other legends of the game
- Expertise from the leading authenticators, including James Spence, Kevin Keating, Vince Malta, Dave Bushing and Troy Kinunen
- Tips on glove collecting, jersey hunting and bat authenticating

Select the articles you want to read, search by key words, and enlarge the pages by 300% for close-up inspection of cards using this CD.

Format: CD • Item# Z4265 • $12.99

t of Tuff Stuff CD

e No. 1 source for timely and reliable sports card and memorabilia
ng *Tuff Stuff's Sports Collectors Monthly* delivers the details you need
y on top your active collecting market, as well as a whole lot more.

more than 25 years of hobby history there's a lot of great interviews,
ritative authentication tips and collecting advice to gain from this
y leader. This one CD contains the best of Tuff Stuff's article archive
2004 to 2008, including unparalleled feature interviews with today's
ars, and techniques to create the collection of your dreams.

at: CD • Item# Z5809 • $14.99

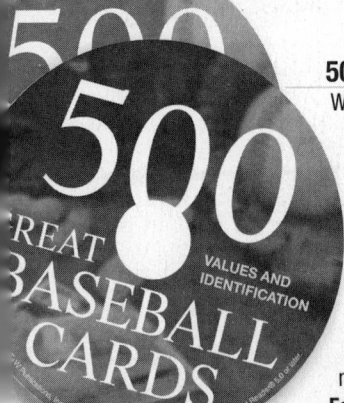

500 Great Baseball Cards CD

Whether you collect by team, era, brand, or any other combination of criteria, there are some cards that are universally sought after or at the very least among the most popular cards of all time. That's what you'll find in this new CD.

Cards are represented in full-color photos, with current collector pricing, and coverage includes:

- Tobacco cards • Pre-war classics • 1950s favorites
- Modern marvels and memorabilia cards

The simple-to-search index and easy-to-enlarge photos of this CD make it a great addition to your library.

Format: CD • Item# Z4966 • $12.99

Order directly from the publisher at **www.krausebooks.com**

Krause Publications, Offer **SBD9**
P.O. Box 5009
Iola, WI 54945-5009
www.krausebooks.com

Call 800-258-0929 M-F 8 a.m. - 5 p.m. to order direct from the publisher, or shop booksellers nationwide and select coin shops.

Please reference offer **SBD9** with all direct-to-publisher orders

---

Get the latest card collecting news at www.tuffstuff.com

Legends of the Game

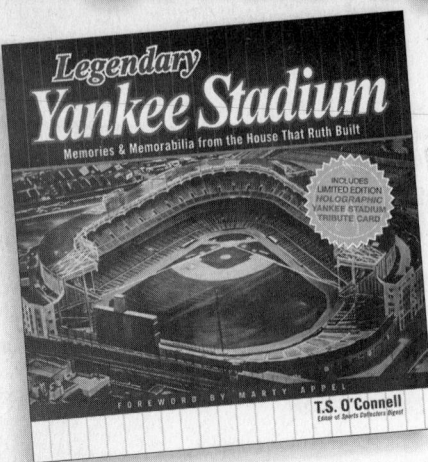
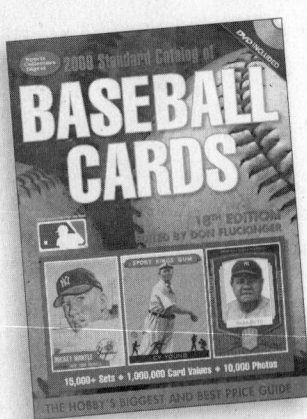